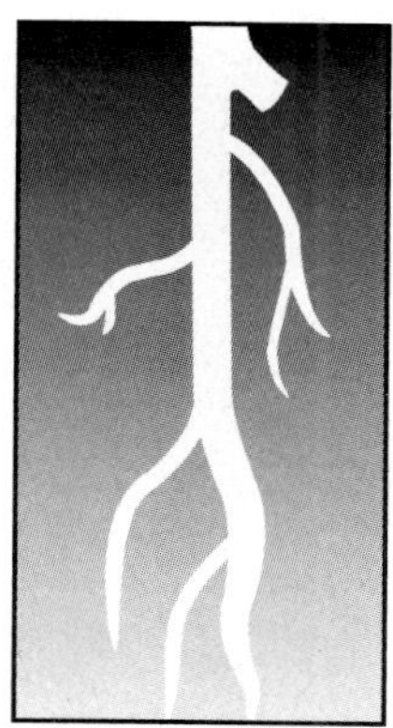

Vascular Surgery

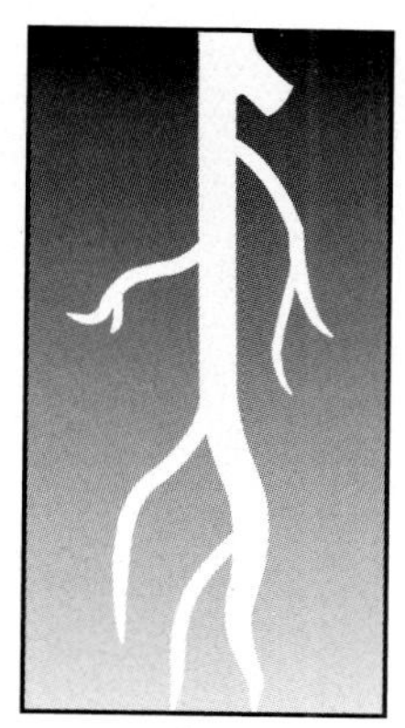

Vascular Surgery

SIXTH EDITION

Robert B. Rutherford, MD, FACS, FRCS (Glasg.)

Emeritus Professor of Surgery
University of Colorado School of Medicine
Denver, Colorado

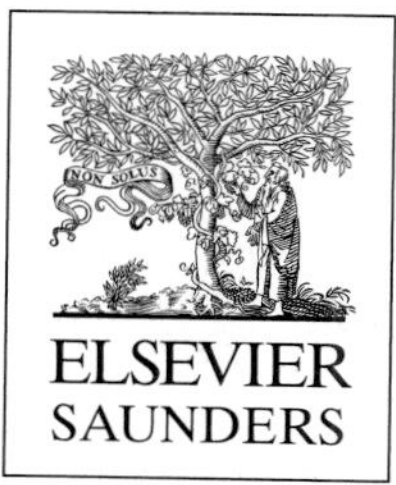

ELSEVIER
SAUNDERS

1600 John F. Kennedy Blvd., Ste 1800
Philadelphia, Pennsylvania 19103

VASCULAR SURGERY ISBN 0-7216-0299-1

Notice

Knowledge and best practice in this field are constantly changing. As new research and experience broaden our knowledge, changes in practice, treatment and drug therapy may become necessary or appropriate. Readers are advised to check the most current information provided (i) on procedures featured or (ii) by the manufacturer of each product to be administered, to verify the recommended dose or formula, the method and duration of administration, and contraindications. It is the responsibility of the practitioner, relying on their own experience and knowledge of the patient, to make diagnoses, to determine dosages and the best treatment for each individual patient, and to take all appropriate safety precautions. To the fullest extent of the law, neither the Publisher nor the Editors assume any liability for any injury and/or damage to persons or property arising out of or related to any use of the material contained in this book.

Library of Congress Cataloging-in-Publication Data

Vascular surgery / [edited by] Robert B. Rutherford.— 6th ed.
p. ; cm.
Includes bibliographical references and index.
ISBN 0-7216-0299-1 (set)
1. Blood-vessels—Surgery. I. Rutherford, Robert B.
[DNLM: 1. Vascular Surgical Procedures. WG 170 V3311 2005]
RD598.5.V37 2005
616.4'13—dc22 2004056630

Publishing Director: Anne Lenehan
Publisher: Natasha Andjelkovic
Developmental Editor: Donna Morrissey
Senior Project Manager: Linda Lewis Grigg
Design Director: Ellen Zanolle
Senior Marketing Manager: Ethel Cathers
Updates Manager: Bob Browne

Printed in the United States of America.

Last digit is the print number: 9 8 7 6 5 4 3 2 1

To vascular surgeons everywhere

who strive for excellence in patient care.

Editors

Associate Editors

Jack L. Cronenwett, MD
Professor of Surgery, Dartmouth Medical School, Hanover.
Chief, Section of Vascular Surgery, Dartmouth-Hitchcock Medical Center, Lebanon, New Hampshire.

Peter Gloviczki, MD
Professor of Surgery, Mayo Clinic College of Medicine.
Chair, Division of Vascular Surgery and Director, Gonda Vascular Center, Mayo Clinic, Rochester, Minnesota.

K. Wayne Johnston, MD, FRCSC
Professor and R. Fraser Elliott Chair in Vascular Surgery, Department of Surgery, University of Toronto, Faculty of Medicine.
Vascular Surgeon, Toronto General Hospital, Toronto, Ontario, Canada.

William C. Krupski, MD*
Formerly Clinical Professor of Surgery, University of California, San Francisco School of Medicine.
Attending Vascular Surgeon, The Kaiser Permanente Medical Group, San Francisco, California.

Kenneth Ouriel, MD, FACS, FACC
Professor of Surgery, Cleveland Clinic Lerner College of Medicine of Case Western Reserve University.
Chairman, Division of Surgery, Cleveland Clinic Foundation, Cleveland, Ohio.

Anton N. Sidawy, MD, MPH
Professor of Surgery, George Washington University School of Medicine.
Chief of Surgery, VA Medical Center, Washington, D.C.

*Deceased.

Assistant Editors

Hugh G. Beebe, MD
Director Emeritus, Jobst Vascular Center, The Toledo Hospital, Toledo, Ohio.

Kimberley J. Hansen, MD, FACS
Professor of Surgery and Head, Section on Vascular Surgery, Division of Surgical Sciences, Wake Forest University School of Medicine, Winston-Salem, North Carolina.

Gregory L. Moneta, MD
Professor of Surgery, Oregon Health and Sciences University School of Medicine.
Chief, Division of Vascular Surgery, Portland, Oregon.

Mark R. Nehler, MD
Associate Professor of Surgery, University of Colorado Health Sciences Center School of Medicine.
Program Director, Surgical Residency Program, University of Colorado Health Sciences Center, Denver, Colorado.

William H. Pearce, MD
Violet R. and Charles A. Baldwin Professor of Vascular Surgery, Northwestern University Feinberg School of Medicine.
Chief, Vascular Surgery Division, Northwestern Memorial Hospital, Chicago, Illinois.

Bruce A. Perler, MD, MBA
Julius H. Jacobson II Professor of Surgery, Johns Hopkins University School of Medicine.
Chief, Division of Vascular Surgery, Johns Hopkins Hospital, Baltimore, Maryland.

John J. Ricotta, MD, FACS
Professor and Chair, Department of Surgery, State University of New York at Stony Brook School of Medicine.
Surgeon in Chief, University Hospital at Stony Brook, Stony Brook, New York.

Russell H. Samson, MD, FACS, RVT
Former Associate Professor of Surgery, Albert Einstein College of Medicine of Yeshiva University, New York, New York.
Staff, Sarasota Memorial Hospital.
President, Mote Vascular Foundation, Inc., Sarasota, Florida.

James M. Seeger, MD
Professor of Surgery, University of Florida College of Medicine.
Chief, Division of Vascular Surgery and Endoscopic Therapy, Shands at University of Florida, Gainesville, Florida.

R. James Valentine, MD
Frank H. Kidd Jr. Distinguished Professor and Vice-Chairman, Department of Surgery, University of Texas Southwestern Medical Center, Dallas, Texas.

Thomas William Wakefield, MD
S. Martin Lindenauer Collegiate Professor of Surgery, University of Michigan Medical School.
Staff Surgeon, Section of Vascular Surgery, Department of Surgery, University of Michigan Hospital and Ann Arbor Veterans Administration Medical Center, Ann Arbor, Michigan.

Fred A. Weaver, MD
Professor of Surgery, University of Southern California Keck School of Medicine.
Chief of Vascular Surgery, University of Southern California Hospital.
Attending Surgeon, Vascular Surgery, Los Angeles County–University of Southern California Medical Center, Los Angeles, California.

Contributors

Ahmed M. Abou-Zamzam, Jr., MD
Associate Professor, Division of Vascular Surgery, Loma Linda University School of Medicine, Loma Linda, California.
Lower Extremity Amputation: Indications, Patient Evaluation, and Level Determination

Ali F. AbuRahma, MD
Professor, Department of Surgery, West Virginia University School of Medicine; Chief, Vascular Section, Robert C. Byrd Health Sciences Center; Co-Director, Vascular Center of Excellence, Charleston Area Medical Center, Charleston, West Virginia.
Causalgia and Post-traumatic Pain Syndromes; Lumbar Sympathectomy: Indications and Technique

Eric D. Adams, MD
Adjunct Assistant Professor of Surgery, Uniformed Services University of the Health Sciences, Bethesda, Maryland; Fellow, Vascular Surgery, Washington Hospital Center and Georgetown University, Washington, D.C.
Nonthrombotic Complications of Arteriovenous Access for Hemodialysis

Samuel S. Ahn, MD
Professor of Surgery, David Geffen School of Medicine at UCLA; Attending Surgeon, UCLA Center for the Health Sciences, Los Angeles, California.
Upper Extremity Sympathectomy

James C. Andrews, MD
Gonda Vascular Center, Mayo Clinic, Rochester, Minnesota.
Surgical Treatment of Superior Vena Cava Syndrome

Enrico Ascher, MD
Professor of Surgery, Division of Vascular Surgery, Maimonides Medical Center, Brooklyn, New York.
Secondary Arterial Reconstructions in the Lower Extremity

Zakaria I. Assi, MD
Diagnostic Radiologist, Department of Interventional Radiology, The Toledo Hospital; Director, Interventional Radiology, Flower Hospital, Toledo, Ohio.
Catheter-Based Interventions for Acute Deep Venous Thrombosis

Juan Ayerdi, MD
Assistant Professor of Surgery, Department of General Surgery, Division of Surgical Sciences, Wake Forest University School of Medicine, Winston-Salem, North Carolina.
Principles of Arteriography; Fundamental Techniques in Endovascular Surgery; Open Surgical Repair of Renovascular Disease

Martin R. Back, MD, FACS
Associate Professor of Surgery, University of South Florida College of Medicine, Tampa, Florida.
Infection in Prosthetic Vascular Grafts

J. Dennis Baker, MD
Professor of Surgery, David Geffen School of Medicine at UCLA; Chief, Vascular Surgery Section, West Los Angeles VA Medical Center, Los Angeles, California.
The Vascular Laboratory

William H. Baker, MD, FACS
Emeritus Professor of Surgery, Loyola University–Chicago Stritch School of Medicine, Maywood, Illinois.
Arteriovenous Fistulae of the Aorta and Its Major Branches

Jeffrey L. Ballard, MD
Clinical Professor of Surgery, University of California, Irvine, School of Medicine; Staff Vascular Surgeon, St. Joseph Hospital of Orange, Orange, California.
Carotid and Vertebral Artery Injuries

Dennis F. Bandyk, MD, FACS
Professor of Surgery, University of South Florida College of Medicine, Tampa, Florida.
Infection in Prosthetic Vascular Grafts

John Bartholomew, MD
Head, Section of Vascular Medicine, Department of Cardiovascular Medicine, Cleveland Clinic, Cleveland, Ohio.
Atheromatous Embolization

Michel A. Bartoli, MD
Fellow, Department of Vascular Surgery, Hospital La Timone, Marseille, France.
Neurogenic Thoracic Outlet Syndrome

Hisham S. Bassiouny, MD
Professor of Surgery, The University of Chicago Pritzker School of Medicine; Attending Surgeon, The University of Chicago Hospitals and Clinics and Louis A. Weiss Memorial Hospital, Chicago, Illinois.
Diagnosis and Treatment of Nonocclusive Mesenteric Ischemia

B. Timothy Baxter, MD
Professor of Surgery, Cell Biology, and Anatomy, University of Nebraska College of Medicine, Omaha, Nebraska.
Arterial Aneurysms: Etiologic Considerations

Hugh G. Beebe, MD
Director Emeritus, Jobst Vascular Center, The Toledo Hospital, Toledo, Ohio.
3D Image Processing

Marshall E. Benjamin, MD
Medical Director, Vascular Laboratory, Maryland Vascular Center, University of Maryland Medical Center, Baltimore, Maryland.
Endovascular Treatment of Renovascular Disease

John J. Bergan, MD, FACS, FRCS Hon. (Eng.)
Professor of Surgery, UCSD School of Medicine, San Diego; Attending Surgeon, Scripps Memorial Hospital, La Jolla, California.
Varicose Veins: Treatment by Intervention Including Sclerotherapy

Ramon Berguer, MD, PhD
Frankel Professor of Vascular Surgery and Professor of Engineering, School of Medicine and Cullen College of Engineering, University of Michigan, Ann Arbor, Michigan; Vascular Surgeon, University of Michigan Health System.
Brachiocephalic Vessel Reconstruction; Vertebrobasilar Ischemia: Indications, Techniques, and Results of Surgical Repair

Joshua W. Bernheim, MD
Vascular Surgery Fellow, New York Presbyterian Hospital, New York.
Renal Artery Imaging and Physiologic Testing

Kerstin Bettermann, MD, PhD
Assistant Professor, Department of Neurology, Wake Forest University School of Medicine; Neurologist, North Carolina Baptist Hospital of Wake Forest University, Winston-Salem, North Carolina.
Diagnostic Evaluation and Medical Management of Patients with Ischemic Cerebrovascular Disease

Rodger L. Bick, MD, PhD, FACP
Clinical Professor of Pathology, University of Texas Southwestern Medical Center; Director, Dallas Thrombosis Hemostasis and Difficult Hematology Clinical Center, Dallas, Texas.
Normal and Abnormal Coagulation

James H. Black III, MD
Assistant Professor of Surgery, Johns Hopkins University School of Medicine; Vascular Surgeon, Division of Vascular and Endovascular Surgery, Johns Hopkins Hospital, Baltimore, Maryland.
Aortic Dissection: Perspectives for the Vascular/Endovascular Surgeon

W. Todd Bohannon, MD
Assistant Professor of Surgery, Texas A & M University Health Science Center; Scott & White Memorial Hospital and Clinic, Temple, Texas.
Venous Transpositions in the Creation of Arteriovenous Access

Thomas C. Bower, MD
Professor of Surgery, Mayo Clinic College of Medicine; Consultant, Division of Vascular Surgery, Mayo Clinic, Rochester, Minnesota.
Evaluation and Management of Malignant Tumors of the Inferior Vena Cava

John G. Brawley, MD
Fellow, Vascular Surgery, University of Texas Southwestern Medical Center, Dallas, Texas.
Traumatic Arteriovenous Fistulae

David C. Brewster, MD
Clinical Professor of Surgery, Harvard Medical School; Vascular Surgeon, Division of Vascular Surgery, Massachusetts General Hospital, Boston, Massachusetts.
Direct Reconstruction for Aortoiliac Occlusive Disease

Patricia E. Burrows, MD
Professor of Radiology, Harvard Medical School; Staff Radiologist, Children's Hospital, Boston, Massachusetts.
Endovascular Treatment of Vascular Anomalies

Ruth L. Bush, MD
Assistant Professor, Division of Vascular Surgery and Endovascular Therapy, Michael E. DeBakey Department of Surgery, Baylor College of Medicine, Houston, Texas.
Complications of Endovascular Procedures; Management of Thrombosed Dialysis Access

Jacob Buth, MD, PhD
Consultant Vascular Surgeon, Department of Surgery, Catharina Hospital, Eindhoven, The Netherlands.
Endovascular Treatment of Aortic Aneurysms

Keith D. Calligaro, MD
Chief, Section of Vascular Surgery, Department of Surgery, Pennsylvania Hospital, Philadelphia, Pennsylvania.
Renal Artery Aneurysms and Arteriovenous Fistulae

Richard P. Cambria, MD
Professor of Surgery, Harvard Medical School; Chief, Division of Vascular and Endovascular Surgery, and Co-Director, Thoracic Aortic Center, Massachusetts General Hospital, Boston, Massachusetts.
Aortic Dissection: Perspectives for the Vascular/Endovascular Surgeon

Teresa L. Carman, MD
Attending, Vascular Medicine, Jobst Vascular Center, The Toledo Hospital, Toledo, Ohio.
Thrombolytic Agents and Their Actions

Jeffrey P. Carpenter, MD
Professor, Department of Surgery; Director, Vascular Laboratory, Hospital of the University of Pennsylvania, Philadelphia, Pennsylvania.
Magnetic Resonance Imaging and Angiography

PATRICK J. CASEY, MD
Vascular Surgery Fellow, Division of Vascular and Endovascular Surgery, Massachusetts General Hospital, Boston, Massachusetts.
Anastomotic Aneurysms

JOAQUIN J. CERVEIRA, MD
Assistant Professor of Surgery and Chief, Endovascular Surgery, Kaiser Permanente Medical Center, Panorama City, California.
The Pathophysiology of Chronic Venous Disorders

JAE-SUNG CHO, MD
Assistant Professor, Department of Surgery, University of Pittsburgh Medical Center, Pittsburgh, Pennsylvania.
Surgical Treatment of Chronic Occlusions of the Iliac Veins and the Inferior Vena Cava

G. PATRICK CLAGETT, MD
Professor, Division of Vascular Surgery, University of Texas Southwestern Medical Center, Dallas, Texas.
Upper Extremity Aneurysms

HARRY CLOFT, MD, PHD
Associate Professor, Radiology, Mayo Medical School; Senior Associate Consultant, Department of Radiology, Mayo Clinic, Rochester, Minnesota.
Carotid Angioplasty and Stenting

RAUL COIMBRA, MD, PHD
Associate Professor, Department of Surgery, Division of Trauma Medicine, University of California, San Diego, School of Medicine; Associate Director of Trauma, Department of Surgery, Division of Trauma, UCSD Medical Center, San Diego, California.
Epidemiology and Natural History of Vascular Trauma

ANTHONY J. COMEROTA, MD, FACS
Clinical Professor of Surgery, University of Michigan Medical School; Director, Jobst Vascular Center, The Toledo Hospital, Toledo, Ohio.
Thrombolytic Agents and Their Actions; Intra-arterial Catheter–Directed Thrombolysis; Catheter-Based Interventions for Acute Deep Venous Thrombosis

JOHN P. CONNORS III, MD
Resident, Department of Plastic and Reconstructive Surgery, Brigham and Women's Hospital, Boston, Massachusetts.
Vascular Tumors and Malformations in Childhood

MICHAEL S. CONTE, MD
Associate Professor of Surgery, Harvard Medical School; Associate Surgeon (Vascular), Brigham and Women's Hospital, Boston, Massachusetts.
Molecular Biology and Gene Therapy in Vascular Disease

JUDITH W. COOK, MD
Fellow, Division of Vascular Surgery, Department of Surgery, University of Washington School of Medicine, Seattle, Washington.
Clinical and Diagnostic Evaluation of the Patient with Deep Venous Thrombosis

MICHAEL J. COSTANZA, MD
Clinical Associate Professor, Division of Vascular Surgery, Department of Surgery, SUNY Upstate Medical Center, Syracuse, New York.
Endovascular Treatment of Renovascular Disease

JACK L. CRONENWETT, MD
Professor of Surgery, Dartmouth Medical School, Hanover; Chief, Section of Vascular Surgery, Dartmouth-Hitchcock Medical Center, Lebanon, New Hampshire.
Overview [Arterial Aneurysms]; Abdominal Aortic and Iliac Aneurysms

JOHN A. CURCI, MD
Assistant Professor of Surgery, Washington University School of Medicine, St. Louis, Missouri.
Arterial Aneurysms: Etiologic Considerations

JACOB CYNAMON, MD
Professor of Clinical Radiology, Albert Einstein College of Medicine of Yeshiva University; Director, Vascular and Interventional Radiology, Montefiore Medical Center, Bronx, New York.
Techniques for Thromboembolectomy of Native Arteries and Bypass Grafts

MICHAEL D. DAKE, MD
Professor of Radiology, Medicine, and Surgery, University of Virginia; Professor and Chairman, Department of Radiology, University of Virginia Health System, Charlottesville, Virginia.
Endovascular Treatment of Vena Caval Occlusions

MICHAEL DALSING, MD
Professor of Surgery, Indiana University School of Medicine; Director of Vascular Surgery, Clarian Health, Indianapolis, Indiana.
The Surgical Treatment of Deep Venous Valvular Incompetence

R. CLEMENT DARLING III, MD
Professor of Surgery, Albany Medical College; Chief, Division of Vascular Surgery, Albany Medical Center Hospital, Albany, New York.
Arterial Thromboembolism

MARK G. DAVIES, MD, PHD
Associate Professor, Department of Vascular and Endovascular Surgery, University of Rochester School of Medicine and Dentistry; Medical Director, Vascular Diagnostic Laboratory, Vascular Biology and Therapeutics Program and Endovascular Therapy Program; Division of Vascular Surgery, Strong Heart and Vascular Center; Attending Physician, Strong Memorial Hospital, Rochester, New York.
Intimal Hyperplasia: Basic Response to Arterial and Vein Graft Injury and Reconstruction

RAJEEV DAYAL, MD
Clinical Instructor in Surgery, Weill Medical College of Cornell University; Fellow, Vascular Surgery, New York–Presbyterian Hospital, New York, New York.
Standardized Reporting Practices

Richard H. Dean, MD
Professor of Surgery, Wake Forest University School of Medicine; President and CEO, Wake Forest University Health Sciences, Winston-Salem, North Carolina.
Atherosclerotic Renovascular Disease and Ischemic Nephropathy

Demetrios Demetriades, MD, PhD, FACS
Professor of Surgery, University of Southern California School of Medicine; Director, Division of Trauma and SICU, Los Angeles County–University of Southern California Medical Center, Los Angeles, California.
Abdominal Vascular Injuries

Ralph G. De Palma, MD, FACS
National Director of Surgery, Department of Veterans Affairs, Medical-Surgical Group; Professor of Surgery, Uniformed Services University of the Health Sciences F. Edward Hébert School of Medicine; Staff Surgeon, Veterans Affairs Medical Center, Washington, D.C.
Atherosclerosis: Plaque Characteristics and Concepts of Evolution; Postoperative Sexual Dysfunction after Aortoiliac Interventions; Vasculogenic Erectile Dysfunction; Superficial Thrombophlebitis: Diagnosis and Management

Tina R. Desai, MD
Assistant Professor of Surgery, The University of Chicago Pritzker School of Medicine; Attending Surgeon, The University of Chicago Hospitals and Clinics, Chicago, Illinois.
Diagnosis and Treatment of Nonocclusive Mesenteric Ischemia; Acute Renovascular Occlusive Events

Larry-Stuart Deutsch, MD, CM, FRCPC, FACR
Chief-of-Service, Vascular and Interventional Radiology Section, Good Samaritan Regional Medical Center and St. Joseph's Hospital and Medical Center, and Chair, Department of Medical Imaging, Clinical Diagnostic Radiology Inc., Phoenix, Arizona.
Anatomy and Angiographic Diagnosis of Extracranial and Intracranial Vascular Disease

Matthew J. Dougherty, MD
Attending Surgeon, Department of Surgery, Pennsylvania Hospital, Philadelphia, Pennsylvania.
Renal Artery Aneurysms and Arteriovenous Fistulae

Walter N. Duran, PhD
Professor of Physiology and Surgery, UMDNJ–New Jersey Medical School, Newark, New Jersey.
The Pathophysiology of Chronic Venous Disorders

Matthew J. Eagleton, MD
Assistant Professor of Surgery, Section of Vascular Surgery, University of Michigan Medical School, Ann Arbor, Michigan.
Perioperative Considerations: Coagulopathy and Hemorrhage

James M. Edwards, MD
Associate Professor, Division of Vascular Surgery, Department of Surgery, Oregon Health and Science University School of Medicine; Chief of Surgery, Portland Veterans Affairs Medical Center, Portland, Oregon.
Upper Extremity Revascularization

Matthew S. Edwards, MD
Assistant Professor of Surgery, Section on Vascular Surgery, Wake Forest University School of Medicine, Winston-Salem, North Carolina.
Endovascular Treatment of Renovascular Disease; Open Surgical Repair of Renovascular Disease

Bo Eklof, MD, PhD
Emeritus Professor of Surgery, University of Hawaii John A. Burns School of Medicine, Honolulu, Hawaii.
Surgical Thrombectomy for Acute Deep Venous Thrombosis

Eric D. Endean, MD, FACS
Gordon L. Hyde Professor of Surgery, Department of Surgery, University of Kentucky College of Medicine; Chief, Division of General and Vascular Surgery, University of Kentucky Chandler Medical Center; Attending Surgeon, Lexington Veterans Affairs Medical Center, Lexington, Kentucky.
Treatment of Acute Intestinal Ischemia Caused by Arterial Occlusions

Mark S. Eskandari, MD
Assistant Professor of Surgery, Division of Vascular Surgery, Northwestern University Feinberg School of Medicine; Attending Surgeon, Division of Vascular Surgery, Northwestern Memorial Hospital, Chicago, Illinois.
Occupational Vascular Problems

Anthony L. Estrera, MD
Assistant Professor, Department of Cardiothoracic and Vascular Surgery, University of Texas at Houston Medical School; Attending, Hermann Memorial City Hospital, Houston, Texas.
Thoracoabdominal Aortic Aneurysms

Jawed Fareed, PhD
Professor, Department of Pathology and Pharmacology; Director, Special Coagulation Laboratory and the Hemostasis and Thrombosis Research Program, Loyola University Medical Center, Maywood, Illinois.
Normal and Abnormal Coagulation

Scott R. Fecteau, MD
Fellow in Training (Vascular Surgery), Albany Medical Center Hospital, Albany, New York.
Arterial Thromboembolism

Mark F. Fillinger, MD
Associate Professor of Surgery, Dartmouth Medical School, Hanover; Faculty (Section of Vascular Surgery), Dartmouth-Hitchcock Medical Center, Lebanon, New Hampshire.
Computed Tomography, CT Angiography, and 3D Reconstruction for the Evaluation of Vascular Disease

Michelle Florian-Kujawski, BS
Department of Pharmacology, Loyola University Medical Center, Maywood, Illinois.
Normal and Abnormal Coagulation

Vivian Gahtan, MD
Chief, Section of Vascular Surgery, Department of Surgery, SUNY Upstate Medical University College of Medicine; Vascular Surgeon, Surgery Service, Syracuse Veterans Affairs Medical Center, Syracuse, New York.
Molecular Biology and Gene Therapy in Vascular Disease

Gail L. Gamble, MD
Assistant Professor of Physical Medicine and Rehabilitation, Mayo Clinic College of Medicine, Rochester, Minnesota.
Nonoperative Management of Chronic Lymphedema

Nicholas J. Gargiulo, MD
Assistant Professor of Surgery, Albert Einstein College of Medicine of Yeshiva University; Attending Surgeon, Weiler Hospital, Bronx, New York.
Techniques for Thromboembolectomy of Native Arteries and Bypass Grafts; Secondary Arterial Reconstructions in the Lower Extremity

Bruce L. Gewertz, MD, FACS
Dallas B. Phemister Professor and Chairman, Department of Surgery, The University of Chicago Pritzker School of Medicine; Attending Surgeon, The University of Chicago Hospitals and Clinics, Chicago, Illinois.
Acute Renovascular Occlusive Events

Joseph Giordano, MD
Professor and Chairman, Department of Surgery, George Washington University School of Medicine; Chief of Surgery, George Washington University Hospital, Washington, D.C.
Embryology of the Vascular System

Mary E. Giswold, MD
Resident, Department of Surgery, Oregon Health and Sciences University School of Medicine, Portland, Oregon.
Nonoperative Treatment of Chronic Venous Insufficiency

Seymour Glagov, MD
Professor Emeritus, Department of Pathology, The University of Chicago Pritzker School of Medicine; Pathologist, University of Chicago Hospitals and Clinics, Chicago, Illinois.
Artery Wall Pathology in Atherosclerosis

Peter Gloviczki, MD
Professor of Surgery, Mayo Clinic College of Medicine; Chair, Division of Vascular Surgery and Director, Gonda Vascular Center, Mayo Clinic, Rochester, Minnesota.
Principles of Venography; Lymphatic Complications of Vascular Surgery; Introduction and General Considerations [The Management of Venous Disorders]; Management of Perforator Vein Incompetence; Surgical Treatment of Chronic Occlusions of the Iliac Veins and the Inferior Vena Cava; Surgical Treatment of Superior Vena Cava Syndrome; Lymphedema: An Overview; Clinical Diagnosis and Evaluation of Lymphedema; Nonoperative Management of Chronic Lymphedema; Surgical Treatment of Chronic Lymphedema and Primary Chylous Disorders

Jerry Goldstone, MD, FACS, FRCS
Professor of Surgery, Case School of Medicine, Case Western Reserve University; Chief, Division of Vascular Surgery, University Hospitals of Cleveland, Cleveland, Ohio.
Aneurysms of the Extracranial Carotid Artery

Michael J. V. Gordon, MD
Director, The Hand Center, Division of Plastic Surgery; Assistant Professor, Department of Surgery, University of Colorado Health Sciences Center, Denver, Colorado.
Upper Extremity Amputation

Richard M. Green, MD
Chairman, Department of Surgery, Lenox Hill Hospital, New York, New York.
Training in Endovascular Surgery; Subclavian-Axillary Vein Thrombosis

Lazar J. Greenfield, MD
Professor of Surgery and Chair Emeritus, Department of Surgery, University of Michigan, Ann Arbor, Michigan.
Vena Caval Interruption Procedures

Howard P. Greisler, MD
Professor of Surgery and Professor of Cell Biology, Neurobiology, and Anatomy, Loyola University Chicago Stritch School of Medicine, Maywood; Attending Surgeon, Loyola University Medical Center, Maywood; Staff Surgeon, Edward Hines Jr. VA Hospital, Hines, Illinois.
Prosthetic Grafts

Navyash Gupta, MD, FACS
Assistant Professor, Department of Surgery, University of Pittsburgh School of Medicine; Attending Surgeon, University of Pittsburgh Hospitals and Clinics, Pittsburgh, Pennsylvania.
Acute Renovascular Occlusive Events

Allen D. Hamdan, MD
Assistant Professor of Surgery, Harvard Medical School; Attending Vascular Surgeon and Director of Clinical Research, Department of Vascular Surgery, Beth Israel Deaconess Medical Center, Boston, Massachusetts.
Management of Foot Ulcers in Diabetes Mellitus

Jaap F. Hamming, MD, PhD
Department of Surgery, Leiden University Medical Center, Leiden, The Netherlands.
Lower Extremity Aneurysms

Kimberley J. Hansen, MD, FACS
Professor of Surgery and Head, Section on Vascular Surgery, Division of Surgical Sciences, Wake Forest University School of Medicine, Winston-Salem, North Carolina.
Renal Complications; Renovascular Disease: An Overview; Atherosclerotic Renovascular Disease and Ischemic Nephropathy; Open Surgical Repair of Renovascular Disease

Linda M. Harris, MD
Assistant Professor of Surgery, University of Buffalo School of Medicine and Biomedical Sciences; Program Director, Vascular Surgery Residency, and Interim Division Chief, Vascular Surgery, Millard Fillmore Hospital, Buffalo, New York.
The Modified Biograft; Endovascular Treatment of Aortic Aneurysms

Peter L. Harris, MD, FRCS
Director, Vascular and Transplant Services, Regional Vascular Unit, Royal Liverpool University Hospital, England, United Kingdom.
Endovascular Treatment of Aortic Aneurysms

Peter K. Henke, MD
Assistant Professor, Section of Vascular Surgery, Department of Surgery, University of Michigan Medical School; Chief, Vascular Surgery, Ann Arbor Veterans Affairs Hospital, Ann Arbor, Michigan.
Vascular Thrombosis Due to Hypercoagulable States; Vena Caval Interruption Procedures

William R. Hiatt, MD
Professor of Medicine, Division of Vascular Medicine, University of Colorado Health Sciences Center School of Medicine, Denver, Colorado.
Atherogenesis and the Medical Management of Atherosclerosis

Kim J. Hodgson, MD
Professor and Chairman, Division of Vascular Surgery, Department of Surgery, Southern Illinois University School of Medicine, Springfield, Illinois.
Principles of Arteriography; Fundamental Techniques in Endovascular Surgery

Debra A. Hoppensteadt, PhD
Assistant Professor, Department of Pathology; Technical Director, Hemostasis and Thrombosis Research Program, Loyola University Medical Center, Maywood, Illinois.
Normal and Abnormal Coagulation

David B. Hoyt, MD, FACS
Professor, Department of Surgery, Division of Trauma, Burns, and Critical Care, University of California, San Diego, School of Medicine; Attending Surgeon, Trauma Center, UCSD Medical Center–Hillcrest, San Diego, California.
Epidemiology and Natural History of Vascular Trauma

Thomas S. Huber, MD, PhD
Associate Professor of Surgery, University of Florida College of Medicine, Gainesville, Florida.
Chronic Mesenteric Ischemia

Joseph Huh, MD
Assistant Professor, Department of Cardiothoracic Surgery, Baylor College of Medicine; Attending Surgeon, Veterans Affairs Medical Center Houston, Houston, Texas.
Thoracic Vascular Trauma

Russell D. Hull, MBBS, MSc
Professor of Medicine, University of Calgary Faculty of Medicine; Director, Thrombosis Research Unit, Foothills Hospital, Calgary, Alberta, Canada.
Prevention and Medical Treatment of Acute Deep Venous Thrombosis

Tam T. Huynh, MD
Assistant Professor, Department of Cardiothoracic and Vascular Surgery, University of Texas at Houston Medical School; Attending, Hermann Memorial City Hospital, Houston, Texas.
Thoracoabdominal Aortic Aneurysms

Erik K. Insko, MD, PhD
Adjunct Assistant Professor of Radiology, University of Pennsylvania School of Medicine; Attending, Hospital of the University of Pennsylvania, Philadelphia, Pennsylvania; Director of Cardiovascular Imaging, Mecklenburg Radiology Associates, Presbyterian Hospital, Charlotte, North Carolina.
Magnetic Resonance Imaging and Angiography

Omer Iqbal, MD
Assistant Professor, Department of Pathology, Hemostasis and Thrombosis Research Program, Loyola University Medical Center, Maywood, Illinois.
Normal and Abnormal Coagulation

Glenn R. Jacobowitz, MD
Associate Professor of Surgery, New York University School of Medicine; Attending Physician, New York University Medical Center, Bellevue Hospital, and New York Harbor VA Medical Center, New York, New York.
Surgical Management of Congenital Vascular Malformations

Walter P. Jeske, PhD
Associate Professor, Departments of Pathology and Thoracic and Cardiovascular Surgery, Hemostasis and Thrombosis Research Laboratories, Loyola University Medical Center, Maywood, Illinois.
Normal and Abnormal Coagulation

Kaj Johansen, MD, PhD
Clinical Professor of Surgery, University of Washington School of Medicine; Director of Surgical Education, Swedish Medical Center, Providence Campus, Seattle, Washington.
Vascular Pain; Compartment Syndrome: Pathophysiology, Recognition, and Management; Portal Hypertension: Surgical Management of Its Complications

K. Wayne Johnston, MD, FRCSC
Professor and R. Fraser Elliott Chair in Vascular Surgery, Department of Surgery, University of Toronto Faculty of Medicine; Vascular Surgeon, Toronto General Hospital, Toronto, Ontario, Canada.
Ischemic Neuropathy; The Chronically Ischemic Leg: An Overview

Peter G. Kalman, MD, FRCSC, FACS
Professor, Departments of Surgery and Radiology, Loyola University Chicago Stritch School of Medicine; Chief, Division of Vascular Surgery, Loyola University Medical Center, Maywood, Illinois.
Profundaplasty: Isolated and Adjunctive Applications

Manju Kalra, MBBS
Assistant Professor of Surgery, Mayo Clinic College of Medicine; Consultant, Division of Vascular Surgery, Mayo Clinic, Rochester, Minnesota.
Management of Perforator Vein Incompetence; Surgical Treatment of Superior Vena Cava Syndrome

Vikram S. Kashyap, MD
Associate Professor of Surgery, Cleveland Clinic Lerner College of Medicine of Case Western Reserve University; Staff, Department of Vascular Surgery, Cleveland Clinic Foundation, Cleveland, Ohio.
Aortoenteric Fistulae

Karthikeshwar Kasirajan, MD, FACS
Assistant Professor of Surgery, Emory University School of Medicine; Attending Surgeon, Emory University Hospital, Atlanta, Georgia.
Acute Limb Ischemia

K. Craig Kent, MD
Professor and Vice Chairman, Department of Surgery, Weill Medical College of Cornell University; Professor of Surgery, Columbia University College of Physicians and Surgeons; Director, Vascular Center, and Chief, Combined Columbia and Cornell Division of Vascular Surgery, New York–Presbyterian Hospital, New York, New York.
Standardized Reporting Practices; Renal Artery Imaging and Physiologic Testing

George E. Kopchok, BS (Biomed.Eng.)
Research Associate, Harbor-UCLA Medical Center, Torrance, California.
Intravascular Ultrasound

Timothy F. Kresowik, MD
Professor of Surgery, University of Iowa Carver College of Medicine; Attending Surgeon, University of Iowa Hospitals and Clinics, Iowa City, Iowa.
Complications Following Carotid Endarterectomy and Perioperative Management

William C. Krupski, MD*
Formerly Clinical Professor of Surgery, University of California, San Francisco, School of Medicine; Attending Vascular Surgeon, The Kaiser Permanente Medical Group, San Francisco, California.
Endarterectomy; Cardiac Complications: Screening and Prevention; Indications, Surgical Technique, and Results for Repair of Extracranial Occlusive Lesions; Uncommon Disorders Affecting the Carotid Arteries

Brajesh K. Lal, MD
Assistant Professor of Surgery; Assistant Professor of Vascular Surgery; Assistant Professor of Pharmacology/Physiology, UMDNJ–New Jersey Medical School, Newark, New Jersey.
The Pathophysiology of Chronic Venous Disorders

Glenn M. LaMuraglia, MD
Associate Professor of Surgery, Harvard Medical School; Attending Surgeon, Division of Vascular and Endovascular Surgery, Massachusetts General Hospital, Boston, Massachusetts.
Anastomotic Aneurysms

W. Anthony Lee, MD
Assistant Professor of Surgery, University of Florida College of Medicine, Gainesville, Florida.
Chronic Mesenteric Ischemia

Lewis J. Levien, MBBCh, PhD, FCSSA
Consultant Vascular Surgeon, Department of Surgery, Milpark Hospital, Johannesburg, South Africa.
Nonatheromatous Causes of Popliteal Artery Disease

Peter H. Lin, MD
Associate Professor, Division of Vascular Surgery and Endovascular Therapy, Michael E. DeBakey Department of Surgery, Baylor College of Medicine, Houston, Texas.
Complications of Endovascular Procedures; Management of Thrombosed Dialysis Access

Thomas F. Lindsay, MD, MDCM, FRCS, FACS
Associate Professor, Division of Vascular Surgery, University of Toronto Faculty of Medicine; Staff Surgeon, Division of Vascular Surgery, Toronto General Hospital, University Health Network, Toronto, Ontario, Canada.
Ruptured Abdominal Aortic Aneurysms

Pamela A. Lipsett, MD, FACS, FCCM
Professor of Surgery, ACCM, and Nursing; Surgical Critical Care Fellowship Director, Johns Hopkins University School of Medicine, Baltimore, Maryland.
Respiratory Complications in Vascular Surgery

Evan C. Lipsitz, MD
Assistant Professor of Surgery, Albert Einstein College of Medicine of Yeshiva University; Attending Surgeon, Montefiore Medical Center, Bronx, New York.
Techniques for Thromboembolectomy of Native Arteries and Bypass Grafts; Secondary Arterial Reconstructions in the Lower Extremity

Jayme E. Locke, MD
Department of Surgery, Johns Hopkins University School of Medicine, Baltimore, Maryland.
Respiratory Complications in Vascular Surgery

*Deceased.

Frank W. LoGerfo, MD
William V. McDermott Professor of Surgery, Harvard Medical School; Chief, Division of Vascular Surgery, Beth Israel Deaconess Medical Center, Boston, Massachusetts.
The Autogenous Vein; Management of Foot Ulcers in Diabetes Mellitus

G. Matthew Longo, MD
Instructor, Department of Surgery, Northwestern University Feinberg School of Medicine; Vascular Surgery Fellow, Northwestern Memorial Hospital, Chicago, Illinois.
Evaluation of Upper Extremity Ischemia

Robert C. Lowell, MD, FACS, RVT
Horizon Vascular Surgery, PC, Gainseville, Georgia.
Lymphatic Complications of Vascular Surgery

Alan B. Lumsden, MD, FACS
Professor and Chief, Division of Vascular Surgery and Endovascular Therapy, Michael E. DeBakey Department of Surgery, Baylor College of Medicine, Houston, Texas.
Complications of Endovascular Procedures; Management of Thrombosed Dialysis Access

M. Ashraf Mansour, MD, FACS
Associate Professor of Surgery, Michigan State University College of Human Medicine, East Lansing; Vascular Surgery Program Director, Grand Rapids Medical Education and Research Center, Grand Rapids, Michigan.
Arteriovenous Fistulae of the Aorta and Its Major Branches

William A. Marston, MD
Associate Professor, Division of Vascular Surgery, University of North Carolina at Chapel Hill School of Medicine, Chapel Hill, North Carolina.
Physiologic Assessment of the Venous System

Jon S. Matsumura, MD
Associate Professor of Surgery, Division of Vascular Surgery, Northwestern University Feinberg School of Medicine; Staff Physician, Division of Vascular Surgery, Northwestern Memorial Hospital, Chicago, Illinois.
Arterial Complications of Thoracic Outlet Compression

Kenneth L. Mattox, MD
Professor and Vice Chair, Department of Surgery, Baylor College of Medicine; Chief of Staff and Chief of Surgery, Ben Taub General Hospital, Houston, Texas.
Thoracic Vascular Trauma

James May, MD, MS, FRACS, FACS
Bosch Professor of Surgery, University of Sydney Faculty of Medicine; Vascular Surgeon, Royal Prince Alfred Hospital, Sydney, New South Wales, Australia.
Basic Techniques of Endovascular Aneurysm Repair

Michael A. McKusick, MD
Assistant Professor of Radiology, Mayo Clinic College of Medicine, Rochester, Minnesota.
Principles of Venography

Robert B. McLafferty, MD
Associate Professor of Surgery, Division of Vascular Surgery, Southern Illinois University School of Medicine; Memorial Medical Center; St. John's Hospital, Springfield, Illinois.
Revascularization versus Amputation

Mark H. Meissner, MD
Associate Professor, Division of Vascular Surgery, University of Washington School of Medicine, Seattle, Washington.
Venous Duplex Scanning; Antithrombotic Therapy; Pathophysiology and Natural History of Acute Deep Venous Thrombosis; Clinical and Diagnostic Evaluation of the Patient with Deep Venous Thrombosis

Robert R. Mendes, MD
Division of Vascular Surgery, University of North Carolina at Chapel Hill School of Medicine, Chapel Hill, North Carolina.
Physiologic Assessment of the Venous System

Louis M. Messina, MD
Professor of Surgery, and Chief, Division of Vascular Surgery, University of California San Francisco; Director, UCSF Heart and Vascular Center, UCSF Medical Center, San Francisco, California.
Endarterectomy; Renal Artery Fibrodysplasia and Renovascular Hypertension

Charles C. Miller III, PhD
Associate Professor, Department of Cardiothoracic and Vascular Surgery, University of Texas at Houston Medical School, Houston, Texas.
Thoracoabdominal Aortic Aneurysms

Joseph L. Mills, Sr., MD
Professor of Surgery, University of Arizona College of Medicine; Chief, Division of Vascular and Endovascular Surgery, University Medical Center, Tucson, Arizona.
Infrainguinal Bypass

Marc E. Mitchell, MD
Assistant Professor of Surgery, University of Pennsylvania School of Medicine; Chief of Surgery, Philadelphia VA Medical Center, Philadelphia, Pennsylvania.
Basic Considerations of the Arterial Wall in Health and Disease

J. Gregory Modrall, MD
Associate Professor, Department of Surgery, University of Texas Southwestern Medical Center at Dallas Southwestern Medical School; Chief, Section of Vascular Surgery, Dallas Veterans Affairs Medical Center, Dallas, Texas.
Traumatic Arteriovenous Fistulae

Gregory L. Moneta, MD
Professor of Surgery, Oregon Health and Sciences University School of Medicine; Chief, Division of Vascular Surgery, OHSU Hospitals and Clinics, Portland, Oregon.
Nonoperative Treatment of Chronic Venous Insufficiency

Samuel R. Money, MD, MBA, FACS
Clinical Associate Professor of Surgery, Tulane University School of Medicine; Chief, Vascular Surgery, Ochsner Clinic Foundation, New Orleans, Louisiana.
Medical Treatment of Intermittent Claudication

Erin Marc Moore, MD
Clinical Instructor in Surgery, University of Kentucky College of Medicine; Staff, Department of Surgery, Section of Vascular Surgery, University of Kentucky Chandler Medical Center and Veterans Affairs Hospital Lexington, Lexington, Kentucky.
Treatment of Acute Intestinal Ischemia Caused by Arterial Occlusions

Wesley S. Moore, MD
Professor of Surgery, Division of Vascular Surgery, David Geffen School of Medicine at UCLA; Vascular Surgeon, Division of Vascular Surgery, UCLA Medical Center, Los Angeles, California.
Fundamental Considerations in Cerebrovascular Disease; Indications, Surgical Technique, and Results for Repair of Extracranial Occlusive Lesions

Mark D. Morasch, MD
Assistant Professor of Surgery, Division of Vascular Surgery, Northwestern University Feinberg School of Medicine; Attending Surgeon, Division of Vascular Surgery, Northwestern Memorial Hospital, Chicago, Illinois.
Brachiocephalic Vessel Reconstruction; Intestinal Ischemia Caused by Venous Thrombosis; Vertebrobasilar Ischemia: Indications, Techniques, and Results of Surgical Repair

John B. Mulliken, MD
Professor of Surgery, Division of Plastic Surgery, Harvard Medical School; Director, Craniofacial Centre, and Co-Director, Vascular Anomalies Center, Children's Hospital Boston, Boston, Massachusetts.
Vascular Tumors and Malformations in Childhood

Peter Neglén, MD, PhD
Vascular Surgeon, River Oaks Hospital, Jackson, Mississippi.
Endovascular Treatment of Chronic Occlusions of the Iliac Veins and the Inferior Vena Cava

Mark R. Nehler, MD
Associate Professor of Surgery, University of Colorado Health Sciences Center School of Medicine; Program Director, Surgical Residency Program, University of Colorado Health Sciences Center, Denver, Colorado.
Selection of Patients for Vascular Interventions; Natural History and nonoperative Treatment of Chronic Lower Extremity Ischemia; Amputation: An Overview; Revascularization versus Amputation

Audra Noel, MD
Assistant Professor of Surgery, Mayo Clinic College of Medicine; Consultant, Division of Vascular Surgery, Mayo Clinic, Rochester, Minnesota.
Surgical Treatment of Chronic Lymphedema and Primary Chylous Disorders

Patrick J. O'Hara, MD
Professor of Surgery, Cleveland Clinic Lerner College of Medicine; Staff, Department of Vascular Surgery, Cleveland Clinic Foundation, Cleveland, Ohio.
Aortoenteric Fistulae

W. Andrew Oldenburg, MD, FACS
Associate Professor of Surgery, Mayo Medical School, Rochester, Minnesota; Head, Section of Vascular Surgery, Mayo Clinic, Jacksonville, Florida.
Primary Tumors of Major Blood Vessels: Diagnosis and Management

Jeffrey W. Olin, DO
Professor of Medicine, Mount Sinai School of Medicine; Director, Vascular Medicine, Zena and Michael A. Wiener Cardiovascular Institute, Mount Sinai Medical Center, New York, New York.
Thromboangiitis Obliterans (Buerger's Disease); Atheromatous Embolization

Kenneth Ouriel, MD, FACS, FACC
Professor of Surgery, Cleveland Clinic Lerner College of Medicine of Case Western Reserve University; Chairman, Division of Surgery, Cleveland Clinic Foundation, Cleveland, Ohio.
Perioperative Considerations: Coagulopathy and Hemorrhage; Training in Endovascular Surgery; Acute Limb Ischemia

Frank T. Padberg, Jr., MD, FACS
Professor of Surgery, Division of Vascular Surgery, UMDNJ–New Jersey Medical School, Newark; Chief, Section of Vascular Surgery, VA New Jersey Health Care System, East Orange, New Jersey.
Classification and Clinical and Diagnostic Evaluation of Patients with Chronic Venous Disorders

Peter J. Pappas, MD
Professor of Surgery, UMDNJ–New Jersey Medical School; Director, Division of Vascular Surgery; Director, General Surgery Residency Program; Director, Vascular Surgery Residency Program, UMDNJ–Newark, New Jersey.
The Pathophysiology of Chronic Venous Disorders

Jeffrey D. Pearce, MD
Research Fellow in Vascular Surgery, Department of General Surgery, Division of Surgical Sciences, Wake Forest University School of Medicine, Winston-Salem, North Carolina.
Renal Complications

William H. Pearce, MD
Violet R. and Charles A. Baldwin Professor of Vascular Surgery, Northwestern University Feinberg School of Medicine; Chief, Vascular Surgery Division, Northwestern Memorial Hospital, Chicago, Illinois.
Overview [Neurovascular Conditions Involving the Upper Extremity]; Evaluation of Upper Extremity Ischemia

Deborah Peate, RVT
Senior Technologist, David B. Pilcher Vascular Diagnostic Laboratory, Division of Vascular Surgery, Fletcher Allen Health Care, Burlington, Vermont.
The Role of Noninvasive Studies in the Diagnosis and Management of Cerebrovascular Disease

Eric K. Peden, MD
Assistant Professor, Division of Vascular Surgery and Endovascular Therapy, Michael E. DeBakey Department of Surgery, Baylor College of Medicine, Houston, Texas.
Complications of Endovascular Procedures; Management of Thrombosed Dialysis Access

Bruce A. Perler, MD, MBA
Julius H. Jacobson II Professor of Surgery, Johns Hopkins University School of Medicine; Chief, Division of Vascular Surgery, Johns Hopkins Hospital, Baltimore, Maryland.
Overview [Complications of Vascular Surgery and Ischemia: Prevention and Management]

Daphne M. Pierre-Paul, MD
Clinical Assistant Instructor, Department of Surgery, Section of Vascular Surgery, SUNY Upstate Medical University College of Medicine, Syracuse, New York.
Molecular Biology and Gene Therapy in Vascular Disease

Graham F. Pineo, MD
Professor of Medicine, University of Calgary Faculty of Medicine; Director, Thrombosis Research Unit, Foothills Hospital, Calgary, Alberta, Canada.
Prevention and Medical Treatment of Acute Deep Venous Thrombosis

Frank B. Pomposelli, Jr., BS, MD
Associate Professor of Surgery, Harvard Medical School; Clinical Chief of Vascular Surgery, Beth Israel Deaconess Medical Center, Boston, Massachusetts.
The Autogenous Vein

Mary C. Proctor, MD
Senior Research Associate, Department of Surgery, University of Michigan School of Medicine, Ann Arbor, Michigan.
Vena Caval Interruption Procedures

William J. Quinones-Baldrich, MD
Professor of Surgery, Division of Vascular Surgery, University of California Los Angeles, Los Angeles, California.
Takayasu's Disease: Nonspecific Aortoarteritis

Joyesh K. Raj, MD
Attending Surgeon, Fairview Hospital, Cleveland Clinic Health System, Westlake, Ohio.
Upper Extremity Amputation

Seshadri Raju, MD
Emeritus Professor of Surgery, University of Mississippi School of Medicine; Honorary Surgeon, University Hospital, Jackson, Mississippi.
Endovascular Treatment of Chronic Occlusions of the Iliac Veins and the Inferior Vena Cava

John E. Rectenwald, MD
Clinical Assistant Professor of Surgery and Radiology, University of Michigan, Department of Surgery, University of Michigan, Ann Arbor, Michigan.
Vena Caval Interruption Procedures

Daniel J. Reddy, MD, FACS
D. Emerick and Eve Szilagyi Chair in Vascular Surgery, Henry Ford Health System, Detroit, Michigan.
Infected Aneurysms

Michael A. Ricci, MD
Roger H. Allbee Professor of Surgery, Division of Vascular Surgery, University of Vermont College of Medicine, Burlington, Vermont.
The Role of Noninvasive Studies in the Diagnosis and Management of Cerebrovascular Disease

John J. Ricotta, MD, FACS
Professor and Chair, Department of Surgery, State University of New York at Stony Brook School of Medicine; Surgeon in Chief, University Hospital at Stony Brook, Stony Brook, New York.
General Strategies: Choice of Procedure and Technique [Open Vascular Surgery: Basic Considerations]; Vascular Conduits: An Overview

David A. Rigberg, MD
Assistant Professor of Surgery, Division of Vascular Surgery, David Geffen School of Medicine at UCLA, Los Angeles, California.
Takayasu's Disease: Nonspecific Aortoarteritis

Thomas S. Riles, MD
George David Stewart Professor and Chair, Department of Surgery, New York University School of Medicine, New York, New York.
Surgical Management of Congenital Vascular Malformations

Kyung M. Ro, MD
Resident, Department of Radiology, UCDavis Medical Center, Sacramento, California.
Upper Extremity Sympathectomy

Sean P. Roddy, MD
Associate Professor of Surgery, Albany Medical College; Attending Vascular Surgeon, Albany Medical Center Hospital, Albany, New York.
Arterial Thromboembolism

Thom Rooke, MD
Krehbiel Professor of Vascular Medicine, Mayo Clinic College of Medicine; Head, Section of Vascular Medicine, Mayo Clinic, Rochester, Minnesota.
Uncommon Arteriopathies; Nonoperative Management of Chronic Lymphedema

Randi Rose, MD
Clinical Instructor, Department of Surgery, Mount Sinai School of Medicine; Staff, Zena and Michael A. Wiener Cardiovascular Institute, Mount Sinai Medical Center, New York, New York.
Atheromatous Embolization

Vincent L. Rowe, MD
Assistant Professor of Surgery, University of Southern California Keck School of Medicine; Attending Surgeon, Los Angeles County–University of Southern California Medical Center, Los Angeles, California.
Vascular Injuries of the Extremities

C. Vaughan Ruckley, MB, ChM, FRCSE
Emeritus Professor of Vascular Surgery, University of Edinburgh; Former Consultant Surgeon, Royal Infirmary, Edinburgh, Lothian, Scotland, United Kingdom.
Lower Extremity Amputation: Technique and Perioperative Care

Robert B. Rutherford, MD, FACS, FRCS (Glasg.)
Emeritus Professor of Surgery, University of Colorado School of Medicine, Denver, Colorado.
Essentials of Clinical Evaluation; Selection of Patients for Vascular Interventions; Essential Considerations in Evaluating the Results of Treatment; Basic Vascular Surgical Techniques; Causalgia and Post-traumatic Pain Syndromes; Lumbar Sympathectomy: Indications and Technique; Overview [Arteriovenous Fistulas, Congenital Vascular Malformations, and Vascular Tumors]; Diagnostic Evaluation of Arteriovenous Fistulas and Vascular Anomalies; Surgical Thombectomy for Acute Deep Venous Thrombosis

Eva M. Rzucidlo, MD
Assistant Professor, Department of Vascular Surgery, Dartmouth Medical School; Vascular Surgeon, Dartmouth Hitchcock Medical Center, Lebanon, New Hampshire.
Arterial Duplex Scanning

Hazim J. Safi, MD
Professor and Chairman, Department of Cardiothoracic and Vascular Surgery, University of Texas at Houston Medical School; Vascular Surgeon, Hermann Memorial City Hospital, Houston, Texas.
Thoracoabdominal Aortic Aneurysms

Russell H. Samson, MD, FACS, RVT
Former Associate Professor of Surgery, Albert Einstein College of Medicine of Yeshiva University, New York, New York; Staff, Sarasota Memorial Hospital; President, Mote Vascular Foundation, Inc., Sarasota, Florida.
Maintaining a Computerized Vascular Registry; Overview: Medical Management in a Vascular Surgery Practice; Hypertension and Patients with Vascular Disorders

Marc L. Schermerhorn, MD
Assistant Professor of Surgery, Harvard Medical School; Chief, Section of Interventional and Endovascular Surgery, Beth Israel Deaconess Medical Center, Boston, Massachusetts.
Abdominal Aortic and Iliac Aneurysms

Alvin Schmaier, MD
Professor of Internal Medicine and Pathology; Course Director, M2 Hematology Sequence, University of Michigan Medical School; Director, Coagulation Laboratory, University of Michigan Hospitals and Health Centers, Ann Arbor, Michigan.
Vascular Thromboses Due to Hypercoagulable States

Darren B. Schneider, MD
Assistant Professor of Surgery and Radiology, University of California San Francisco; Attending Surgeon, Division of Vascular Surgery, UCSF Medical Center, San Francisco, California.
Renal Artery Fibrodysplasia and Renovascular Hypertension

Joseph R. Schneider, MD, PhD
Professor of Surgery, Division of Vascular Surgery, Northwestern University Feinberg School of Medicine, Chicago; Senior Attending, Evanston Northwestern Health Care, Evanston, Illinois.
Extra-anatomic Bypass

Peter A. Schneider, MD
Vascular and Endovascular Surgeon, Division of Vascular Therapy, Hawaii Permanente Medical Group, Honolulu, Hawaii.
Endovascular Surgery in the Management of Chronic Lower Extremity Ischemia; Endovascular and Surgical Management of Extracranial Carotid Fibromuscular Arterial Dysplasia

James M. Seeger, MD
Professor of Surgery, University of Florida College of Medicine; Chief, Division of Vascular Surgery and Endovascular Therapy, Shands at UF, Gainesville, Florida.
Chronic Mesenteric Ischemia

Taqdees Sheikh, MD
Associate Professor, Department of Anesthesiology, Loyola University Health System, Maywood, Illinois.
Normal and Abnormal Coagulation

Roger F. J. Shepherd, MB, BCH
Assistant Professor of Medicine, Mayo College of Medicine; Staff, Gonda Vascular Center, Mayo Clinic, Rochester, Minnesota.
Uncommon Arteriopathies; Raynaud's Syndrome: Vasospastic and Occlusive Arterial Disease Involving the Distal Upper Extremity

Kevin M. Sheridan, MD
Resident (General Surgery), Department of Surgery, Indiana University Hospital; Division of Vascular Surgery, Clarian Health Hospitals, Indianapolis, Indiana.
The Surgical Treatment of Deep Venous Valvular Incompetence

Anton N. Sidawy, MD, MPH
Professor of Surgery, George Washington University School of Medicine; Chief of Surgery, VA Medical Center, Washington, D.C.
Basic Considerations of the Arterial Wall in Health and Disease; Hyperglycemia, Diabetes, and Syndrome X; Strategies of Arteriovenous Dialysis Access; Nonthrombotic Complications of Arteriovenous Access for Hemodialysis

Michael B. Silva, Jr., MD
Professor of Surgery, Texas Tech University Health Sciences Center; Vice-Chairman, Department of Surgery; Chief, Vascular Surgery and Vascular Interventional Radiology, University Medical Center, Lubbock, Texas.
Venous Transpositions in the Creation of Arteriovenous Access

James C. Stanley, MD
Professor and Associate Chair, Department of Surgery, University of Michigan Medical School; Co-Director, University of Michigan Cardiovascular Center, and Head, Section of Vascular Surgery, University Hospital, Ann Arbor, Michigan.
Arterial Fibrodysplasia; Splanchnic Artery Aneurysms; Renal Artery Fibrodysplasia and Renovascular Hypertension

W. Charles Sternbergh III, MD
Clinical Assistant Professor of Surgery, Tulane University School of Medicine; Program Director, Vascular Surgery, Ochsner Clinic Foundation, New Orleans, Louisiana.
Medical Treatment of Intermittent Claudication

Ronald J. Stoney, MD
Professor Emeritus, Division of Vascular Surgery, University of California-San Francisco School of Medicine, San Francisco, California.
Endarterectomy

Eugene Strandness, Jr., MD*
Formerly Professor of Surgery and Chief, Vascular Surgery, University of Washington School of Medicine, Seattle, Washington.
Pathophysiology and Natural History of Acute Deep Venous Thrombosis

Richard J. Strilka, MD, PhD
Division of Vascular Surgery, Department of Surgery, University of Maryland, Baltimore, Maryland.
Endovascular Treatment of Renovascular Disease

Timothy M. Sullivan, MD, FACS
Associate Professor of Surgery, Division of Vascular Surgery, Mayo Clinic, Rochester, Minnesota.
Carotid Angioplasty and Stenting

David S. Sumner, MD
Distinguished Professor of Surgery Emeritus, Department of Surgery, Division of Peripheral Vascular Surgery, Southern Illinois University School of Medicine, Springfield, Illinois.
Vascular Physiology: Essential Hemodynamic Principles; Physiologic Assessment of Peripheral Arterial Occlusive Disease; Evaluation of Upper Extremity Ischemia

Peter R. Taylor, MA, MChir, FRCS
Consultant Vascular and Endovascular Surgeon, Guy's and St. Thomas' NHS Foundation Trust, London, United Kingdom.
Functional Outcome and Natural History of Major Lower Extremity Amputation

Theodore H. Teruya, MD
Clinical Assistant Professor of Surgery, University of Hawaii John A. Burns School of Medicine, Honolulu, Hawaii.
Carotid and Vertebral Artery Injuries

Robert W. Thompson, MD
Professor of Surgery, Radiology, and Cell Biology and Physiology, Washington University School of Medicine; Attending Surgeon, Barnes–Jewish Hospital, St. Louis, Missouri.
Arterial Aneurysms: Etiologic Considerations; Neurogenic Thoracic Outlet Syndrome

Mahmut Tobu, MD
Department of Pathology, Loyola University Medical Center, Maywood, Illinois.
Normal and Abnormal Coagulation

James F. Toole, MD
The Walter C. Teagle Professor of Neurology and Professor of Public Health Sciences, Wake Forest University School of Medicine; Past President of the International Stroke Society and the World Federation of Neurology, Winston-Salem, North Carolina.
Diagnostic Evaluation and Medical Management of Patients with Ischemic Cerebrovascular Disease

J. Jean E. Turley, MD, FRCPC
Associate Professor, Department of Medicine (Neurology), University of Toronto Faculty of Medicine; Staff, St. Michael's Hospital, Toronto, Ontario, Canada.
Ischemic Neuropathy

*Deceased.

Gilbert R. Upchurch, Jr., MD
Associate Professor of Surgery and Leland Ira Doan Research Professor of Vascular Surgery, University of Michigan Medical School, Ann Arbor, Michigan.
Splanchnic Artery Aneurysms

R. James Valentine, MD
Frank H. Kidd Jr. Distinguished Professor and Vice-Chairman, Department of Surgery, University of Texas Southwestern Medical Center, Dallas, Texas.
Anatomy of Commonly Exposed Arteries

J. Hajo van Bockel, MD, PhD
Professor, Department of Surgery, Leiden University Medical Center, Leiden, The Netherlands.
Lower Extremity Aneurysms

Frank J. Veith, MD
Professor and Vice Chairman, Department of Surgery, Albert Einstein College of Medicine of Yeshiva University; William J. von Liebig Chair in Vascular Surgery, Montefiore Medical Center, Bronx, New York.
Techniques for Thromboembolectomy of Native Arteries and Bypass Grafts; Secondary Arterial Reconstructions in the Lower Extremity

Heinz W. Wahner, MD
Professor Emeritus of Radiology, Mayo Clinic, Rochester, Minnesota.
Clinical Diagnosis and Evaluation of Lymphedema

Thomas William Wakefield, MD
S. Martin Lindenauer Collegiate Professor of Surgery, University of Michigan Medical School; Staff Surgeon, Section of Vascular Surgery, Department of Surgery, University of Michigan Hospital and Ann Arbor Veterans Administration Medical Center, Ann Arbor, Michigan.
Arterial Fibrodysplasia; Vascular Thromboses Due to Hypercoagulable States; Vena Caval Interruption Procedures

Matthew J. Wall, Jr., MD
Associate Professor, Michael E. DeBakey Department of Surgery, Baylor College of Medicine; Deputy Chief of Surgery and Chief of Cardiothoracic Surgery, Ben Taub General Hospital, Houston, Texas.
Thoracic Vascular Trauma

Daniel Walsh, MD
Professor of Surgery (Vascular), Dartmouth Medical School, Hanover; Vice-Chair, Department of Surgery, Dartmouth-Hitchcock Medical Center, Lebanon, New Hampshire.
Postoperative Graft Thrombosis: Prevention and Management

MaryAnne Waters, RN, RVT
Instructor in Surgery, Department of Surgery, Division of Vascular Surgery, University of Vermont College of Medicine, Burlington, Vermont.
The Role of Noninvasive Studies in the Diagnosis and Management of Cerebrovascular Disease

James C. Watson, MS, MD
Clinical Instructor in Surgery, University of Washington School of Medicine, Seattle, Washington.
Compartment Syndromes: Pathophysiology, Recognition, and Management

Fred A. Weaver, MD
Professor of Surgery, University of Southern California Keck School of Medicine; Chief of Vascular Surgery, University of Southern California University Hospital; Attending Surgeon, Vascular Surgery, Los Angeles County–University of Southern California Medical Center, Los Angeles, California.
Vascular Injuries of the Extremities

Mitchell R. Weaver, MD
Vascular Surgery Fellow, Henry Ford Health System, Detroit, Michigan.
Infected Aneurysms

Jonathan M. Weiswasser, MD
Assistant Professor of Surgery, George Washington University School of Medicine; Chief, Vascular Surgery, Washington VA Medical Center, Washington, D.C.
Hyperglycemia, Diabetes, and Syndrome X; Strategies of Arteriovenous Dialysis Access

Geoffrey H. White, MD, FRACS
Associate Professor of Surgery, University of Sydney Faculty of Medicine; Head, Department of Vascular Surgery, Royal Prince Alfred Hospital, Sydney, New South Wales, Australia.
Basic Techniques of Endovascular Aneurysm Repair

John V. White, MD
Clinical Professor of Surgery, University of Illinois School of Medicine, Chicago; Chairman, Department of Surgery, Advocate-Lutheran General Hospital, Park Ridge, Illinois.
Proper Outcomes Assessment: Patient-Based and Economic Vascular Interventions; Evaluation of the Patient with Chronic Lower Extremity Ischemia

Rodney A. White, MD
Professor of Surgery, David Geffen School of Medicine at UCLA, Los Angeles; Associate Chair, Department of Surgery, Harbor-UCLA Medical Center, Torrance, California.
Intravascular Ultrasound

David R. Whittaker, MD
Fellow, Section of Vascular Surgery, Dartmouth-Hitchcock Medical Center, Lebanon, New Hampshire.
Computed Tomography, CT Angiography, and 3D Reconstruction for the Evaluation of Vascular Disease

David B. Wilson, MD
Vascular Surgery Fellow, Section of Vascular Surgery, Department of General Surgery, Wake Forest University School of Medicine, Winston-Salem, North Carolina.
Atherosclerotic Renovascular Disease and Ischemic Nephropathy

Gary G. Wind, MD, FACS
Professor of Surgery, Uniformed Services University of the Health Sciences F. Edward Hébert School of Medicine; Staff Surgeon, Bethesda Naval Hospital, Bethesda, Maryland.
Anatomy of Commonly Exposed Arteries

Charles L. Witte, MD*
Former Professor of Surgery, University of Arizona College of Medicine; Former Attending Surgeon, General Surgery/Trauma, University Medical Center, Tucson, Arizona.
Lymph Circulatory Dynamics, Lymphangiogenesis, and Pathophysiology of the Lymphovascular System

Marlys H. Witte, MD
Professor of Surgery; Director, Student Research Programs, University of Arizona College of Medicine; Attending in Surgery (Lymphology), University Medical Center; Secretary-General, International Society of Lymphology, Department of Surgery, University of Arizona, Tucson, Arizona.
Lymph Circulatory Dynamics, Lymphangiogenesis, and Pathophysiology of the Lymphovascular System

Heather Wolford, MD
Chief Resident, Department of Surgery, University of Colorado Health Sciences Center, Denver, Colorado.
Natural History and Nonoperative Treatment of Chronic Lower Extremity Ischemia; Amputation: An Overview; Revascularization versus Amputation

Kenneth R. Woodburn, MD, FRCSG (Gen.)
Honorary Clinical Lecturer, Peninsula Medical School, Devon and Cornwall; Consultant Vascular Surgeon, Royal Cornwall Hospital, Truro, Cornwall, United Kingdom.
Lower Extremity Amputation: Technique and Perioperative Care

Mark C. Wyers, MD
Assistant Professor, Dartmouth Medical School, Hanover; Assistant Professor of Surgery, Vascular, Dartmouth-Hitchcock Medical Center, Lebanon, New Hampshire.
Physiology and Diagnosis of Splanchnic Arterial Occlusion

Chengpei Xu, MD, PhD
Senior Research Scientist, Department of Surgery, Division of Vascular Surgery, Stanford University School of Medicine, Stanford, California.
Artery Wall Pathology in Atherosclerosis

Lian Xue, MD, PhD
Research Assistant Professor, Loyola University Medical Center, Chicago, Illinois.
Prosthetic Grafts

James S. T. Yao, MD, PhD
Magerstadt Professor of Surgery, Division of Vascular Surgery, Northwestern University Feinberg School of Medicine; Attending Surgeon, Division of Vascular Surgery, Northwestern Memorial Hospital, Chicago, Illinois.
Occupational Vascular Problems

Richard A. Yeager, MD
Professor of Surgery, Oregon Health and Sciences University; Vascular Chief, Portland VA Medical Center, Portland, Oregon.
Lower Extremity Amputation: Perioperative Complications

Albert E. Yellin, MD, FACS
Professor of Surgery, Division of Vascular Surgery, University of Southern California Keck School of Medicine; Associate Chief of Staff and Medical Director, Surgical Services, Los Angeles County–University of Southern California Medical Center, Los Angeles, California.
Vascular Injuries of the Extremities

Christopher K. Zarins, MD
Professor of Surgery, Stanford University School of Medicine; Chief, Division of Vascular Surgery, Stanford University Medical Center, Stanford, California.
Artery Wall Pathology in Atherosclerosis

Gerald B. Zelenock, MD
Chair, Department of Surgery, and Chief of Surgical Services, William Beaumont Hospital, Royal Oak, Michigan.
Splanchnic Artery Aneurysms

R. Eugene Zierler, MD
Professor of Surgery, University of Washington School of Medicine; Medical Director, Vascular Diagnostic Service, University of Washington Medical Center, Seattle, Washington.
Vascular Physiology: Essential Hemodynamic Principles; Physiologic Assessment of Peripheral Arterial Occlusive Disease

Robert M. Zwolak, MD, PhD
Professor of Surgery, Dartmouth Medical School; Attending Surgeon, Section of Vascular Surgery, Dartmouth-Hitchcock Medical Center, Lebanon, New Hampshire; Chief, Section of Vascular Surgery, White River Junction Veterans Affairs Medical Center, White River Junction, Vermont.
Arterial Duplex Scanning; Physiology and Diagnosis of Splanchnic Arterial Occlusion

*Deceased.

Preface

Since the publication of the last edition of *Vascular Surgery* 5 years ago, the changes that have occurred in the practice of vascular surgery have been extraordinary, and their impact on this new edition has been major.

The trend of more vascular surgery being done by fewer but better-trained surgeons, those committed to this field as their primary or sole activity, has continued. We will need to train more vascular surgeons to meet the rapidly increasing elderly population, as the "baby boomer" population peak carries on into the "Medicare population," although this may not be as easy to achieve as it once seemed when first predicted by the Stanley and Ernst manpower surveys more than a decade ago. All surgical training programs, vascular surgery included, have encountered a significant decrease in the numbers of applicants and are having difficulty filling the existing fellowships positions, let alone creating more. Length of training has become an issue with applicants, yet this comes at an exciting time when the scope and breadth of vascular surgery is rapidly expanding to the point where additional time to train surgeons in this field is being called for.

The development of stent grafts for endovascular repair of aortic aneurysms opened the doors to new horizons in vascular surgery. Having re-acquired and expanded their angiographic skills and techniques of catheter manipulation under fluoroscopic monitoring, with these procedures vascular surgeons soon embraced many other endovascular procedures. Thus, today's vascular surgeon not only needs experience in the traditional core of our specialty, open vascular reconstructions and repairs (and now how to perform some of them using laparoscopic or mini-incision approaches), but also experience in endovascular aneurysm repair, balloon angioplasty, and stenting of occlusive disease in major arteries (extremity, carotid, and visceral), and an array of other percutaneous procedures. Noninvasive vascular testing (NIT) and vascular imaging, angiography, duplex and computer tomographic (CT) scans, and magnetic resonance imaging and angiography (MRI/MRA) are expanding in versatility and importance in diagnosing vascular disease. Today's vascular surgeon needs expertise not only in interpreting them but also in personally performing some of them (e.g., NITs, duplex scanning, angiography). Traditionally, vascular surgeons have played a major role in the nonoperative management of many vascular conditions (e.g., venous ulcers, deep venous thrombosis [DVT], and claudication). Many also feel a responsibility for risk factor control in their atherosclerotic and venous thromboembolism patients, administering anticoagulant therapy, as indicated.

Clearly, then, training the "complete vascular surgeon" of today is a time-consuming and challenging process. To enable this without lengthening overall surgical training, the Society of Vascular Surgery and the Vascular Surgery Board of the American Board of Surgery have obtained approval to formally pursue different training stratagems. In addition to retaining the current, traditional 5 years of general surgery residency followed by 2 years of vascular surgery fellowship, two shorter plans are proposed: 4 rather than 5 years of general surgery training before vascular surgery fellowship (with a common year devoted largely to vascular surgery) and 3 years of general surgery plus a 3-year vascular surgery fellowship. Should future vascular surgeons be trained in every aspect of managing vascular disease: open surgery, endoluminal techniques, vascular imaging and noninvasive vascular laboratory methods, and vascular medicine, or is a certain degree of specialization within vascular surgery inevitable? Time will tell, but this book continues to be geared toward the "complete" vascular surgeon and, as a result, has undergone major changes with this edition.

This very major change in the makeup of the clinical practice of many if not most vascular surgeons is reflected in the increase in chapters on endovascular surgical procedures in this edition and the fact that vascular surgeons now are the authors, for the most part, of these chapters. Successful endovascular surgery, particularly endovascular AAA repair (EVAR), demands precise imaging, and the applicable vascular imaging techniques have also developed at a rapid rate. This edition's coverage reflects recognition of the importance of modern imaging techniques in vascular surgery.

Arteriovenous hemodialysis access continues to play a major role in the practice of many vascular surgeons, often the most common procedure category in many practices. The DOQI guidelines have had a major impact on the practice of access surgery. The percentage of autogenous accesses will continue to increase; preoperative duplex evaluation has increased vein availability and led to increasing use of vein transposition. Postoperative surveillance is being used increasingly to predict failing access—in time for rescuing interventions. The importance of employing a sound strategy in selecting access site and configuration cannot be overstated; a chapter dedicated to this subject is included. The emergence of thrombolysis and stenting in the management of failing or failed access is also addressed in detail.

In dealing with vascular malformations and tumors, the role of surgery has become even more circumspect, limited, for the most part, to clearly resectable lesions. Attempts at hemodynamic control of unresectable lesions by inflow ligation have been condemned and mostly abandoned, because it cannot achieve control and precludes embolotherapy. Angiography is reserved for cases in which intervention is clearly indicated and imminent. In its place, duplex scan, MRI, and radionuclide AV shunt study provide more appropriate initial evaluation and follow-up. Embolotherapy/sclerotherapy continues to improve in technique, available agents, and "cure rate." Endovascular techniques will provide adequate control and occasional cure for most high-flow lesions and can and should be used more often as an adjunct to enable resection of lesions previously beyond the limits of safe surgical resection. On the other hand, low flow lesions (venous malformations, microfistulous AVMs) can be treated more conservatively, with intervention restricted mainly to localized, superficial "mass lesions" causing symptoms, unacceptable appearance, or significantly interfering with function. This section has been completely revised to reflect these changes.

Carotid endarterectomy (CEA) has survived its challenge from randomized prospective trials versus the best medical therapy, but now has been challenged by carotid artery stenting (CAS). Recent management changes, that is, the use of duplex scanning instead of arteriography as the preoperative imaging method in the majority of patients, same-day admission for surgery, selective avoidance of monitoring in intensive care units, and discharging a sizable portion of patients from the hospital on the day after surgery, although instigated by competitive pressures related to increased managed care, have *not* reduced the safety of carotid endarterectomy while reducing its cost. All of this has improved CEA's chances of withstanding the new challenge of CAS. The popularity of CAS has been spurred by a series of industry-driven trials with carefully selected inclusion and exclusion criteria and participating centers, while still waiting for the results of a prospective, randomized trial, like the current CREST trial.

The management of aneurysms has undergone rapid changes with the availability of EVAR and covered stent grafts elsewhere in the arterial tree. Improving technology may ultimately justify EVAR being applied to older "fit" patients and those with more difficult anatomy using fenestrated or branched endografts. It remains only for the demonstration of a long-term mortality advantage and structural durability. EVAR results are steadily improving, and the results of two recent randomized trials are encouraging in that regard. EVAR will be increasingly applied to ruptured AAAs and thoracic AAs where there is potentially a much greater mortality advantage. Retroperitoneal and mini-incision approaches have increased in popularity, with the aim of decreasing the length of hospital stay and morbidity.

In the area of lower extremity ischemia, a number of trends continue. Bypass for claudication is being more strictly limited. Control of arteriosclerotic risk factors, which has been an appallingly low 30%, needs to become routine. Proximal bypass, both direct and extra-anatomic, has yielded further to PTA/stent, which is now being applied for most TASC C lesions. Prosthetic infrainguinal bypass is being increasingly limited to selected AK fem-pop bypasses, while there has been a further relative increase in crural and pedal artery bypasses with autogenous vein. In those patients with ischemic ulcers or gangrene and renal failure, the results of infrainguinal bypass are known to be poor. It is now becoming apparent that the results of operations for recurrent bypass failure, especially when a single length of adequate vein is not available, are also poor, with higher mortality, recurrent failure, and limb loss rates; this, after many years of advocating bypass over amputation. As a result, there may be a shift away from limb salvage and back to amputation in subgroups like these two, where outcomes are particularly disappointing.

In acute limb ischemia, it is likely that thrombolytic therapy will ultimately prevail over thrombectomy *for restoring patency,* whereas arterial reconstruction will prevail over stenting for correcting most underlying lesions. Angioplasty and stenting will continue to be used for discrete lesions, including anastomotic and valvular stenoses (using newer cutting balloons), but, rather than the previously common practice of persisting with the initial mode of therapy, crossover from percutaneous to open revascularization should become the more common scenario, with vascular surgeons increasingly performing both.

The management of deep venous thrombosis has changed. The use of D-dimer techniques and patient risk profiling will decrease the workload of vascular diagnostic laboratories, inundated by knee-jerk "rule out DVT" requests. Catheter-directed thrombolysis, aided by debulking thrombus using better percutaneous mechanical thrombectomy (PMT) devices, seems likely to supplant anticoagulant therapy for iliofemoral venous thrombosis *in active patients with good longevity outlook,* and primary subclavian venous thrombosis is being increasingly treated—*in young healthy patients with a need for active arm use*—with thrombolysis, stenting, and first rib removal performed during the same hospital admission. Low-molecular-weight heparin has finally pushed unfractionated heparin aside, but the ambulatory outpatient treatment of DVT, which it allows, seems better restricted to more distal DVTs. On the other hand, we can expect a new breed of thrombin inhibitors (e.g., Ximelagatran) to compete strongly with warfarin-like drugs for long-term anticoagulant treatment. Venous thromboembolism is being more aggressively managed, in terms of preventing DVT, not only by antithrombotic therapy in high-risk patients but in IVC filter placement; that is, not only in those in whom anticoagulants are contraindicated, have caused bleeding, or have failed to prevent PE, but also those at high risk of PE, including trauma patients and others. The categorical indications for prophylactic use have grown, and this use has outgrown therapeutic indications. They include major trauma, paralyzed or bed-ridden patients, advanced malignancy/chemotherapy, gastric bypass for morbid obesity, protection during venous interventions, and several other situations. Clearly, the duration of risk differs and needs to be better defined for each category. For those with prophylactic indications, the trend toward greater use of temporary or retrievable filters is likely to continue, particularly in young patients in whom leaving in permanent filters exposes them to unnecessary risks, such as a higher risk of DVT. Further improvements in filter design allowing longer implantation time before safe removal are needed to support this trend.

In the endoluminal management of varicose veins, the original challenger to high ligation and stripping, radiofrequency ablation, is being given a run for its money by endoluminal laser treatment. Increasingly, varicose vein surgery is being displaced to "vein clinics." High ligation may make a comeback if collateral development around the saphenofemoral junction and late recurrence rates prove to be high with the endoluminal techniques. Control of superficial incompetence, by either technique, is being increasingly applied as initial treatment for varicose veins, with subcutaneous perforator interruption (SEPS) being withheld even if perforator incompetence is demonstrated. Thus, SEPS will most likely be limited to treating those with ulceration. Reconstructions for valvular incompetence are likely to become even more limited (i.e., for recurrent ulceration, only after failure of procedures to control superficial and perforator incompetence and a proper trial of compression therapy).

This review is intended to show some of the changes and trends in the 5 years since the last edition of the book. But it has always been a frustration of my colleagues and myself, having worked so hard to produce an up-to-date comprehensive textbook, only to see fast developing areas of it gradually become out of date as the years pass. Well, finally, the need to lament out-of-date passages will have passed for this textbook, for there will be a Web version with this edition, one that will be systematically updated throughout its life, giving subscribers an updated version, with new passages and references identifiably highlighted. Despite that new option, the print version of the Sixth Edition has been greatly revised and reorganized to keep up with the changes alluded to above, and more.

The number of chapters in this edition totals 176, up from 166, but there are more new chapters than the numerical difference would suggest. Some chapters have actually been consolidated, but more than 20 chapters are topically new. There is, as one would expect, a much greater emphasis on endovascular procedures, and, in addition to a heavier endovascular coverage in many chapters dealing with specific vascular disorders, there are 13 chapters devoted entirely or primarily to endovascular interventions, including a new section on basic endovascular techniques. There is also a new section on the medical management of patients with vascular disease, 4 of the 6 chapters of which are entirely new. A new section editor has treated even the seemingly stable subject of amputations to a complete overhaul. In fact, although 4 sections can be identified as being new, there are new section editors for 19 of the 23 sections, which is partly responsible for over 90 chapters being written by new authors or a new primary author. Many other primary authors have enlisted new coauthors in bringing about major revisions. Thus, more than two thirds of the chapters are new or have been extensively revised, and the remainder have been appropriately updated.

I owe my deep appreciation to the associate and assistant editors who have shared the hard work of putting together yet another comprehensive and thoroughly updated edition. With each new edition, we resist the temptation to cut back and make it a more comfortable size, for knowledge is increasing and we believe that there should be one text in this field that endeavors to be almost encyclopedic, one in which the reader can expect essentially every aspect of vascular surgery to be covered. As this work is not meant to be read from cover to cover, there is deliberate repetition in addition to thorough cross-referencing, which saves the reader from having to skip all over to get full coverage of the desired topic.

For those who reserve this book mainly for specific topical reference, yet wish to strengthen their knowledge, there will again be a companion review book, *Review of Vascular Surgery*, coming out with this edition. It contains close to 600 questions, approximately three per each chapter topic. Each question has five possible answers, only one of which is correct, with the correct answer and a point-by-point discussion of all the answers appearing separately. It should serve as an excellent teaching vehicle and study guide, pinpointing topics in which the reader is deficient in knowledge or understanding, and allowing the reader to identify chapters that deserve further study.

The associate and assistant editors join me in thanking each and every author and coauthor of the many chapters. Writing chapters is a difficult and sometimes thankless task, with little reward other than being recognized for one's expertise and the satisfaction of contributing to and perpetuating a textbook that has become, and will continue to be, by their efforts and the efforts of past contributors, a valuable resource in one's chosen field. It is my hope that they all will share my pride in a job well done and that their unselfish efforts will continue to sustain *Vascular Surgery* in the role into which it has grown—that of vascular surgery's leading textbook. We also wish to acknowledge the support of dedicated staff at Elsevier—publishers Natasha Andjelkovic and formerly Richard Lampert, developmental editor Donna Morrissey, senior project manager Linda Grigg, senior book designer Ellen Zanolle, updates manager Bob Browne, and senior marketing manager Ethel Cathers.

In the final words of the last edition's preface I implied that the Fifth Edition might be my last, yet here I am again. Maybe the Sixth Edition will be my last, but at least I am assured that this book will live on and some of the associate and assistant editors will see to it that it goes forth to future editions, with the aid of continual updating via the online version, a process that should pave the way for the next print version.

ROBERT B. RUTHERFORD

Contents

Color Figures appear in the sections in which they are referred to in the text.

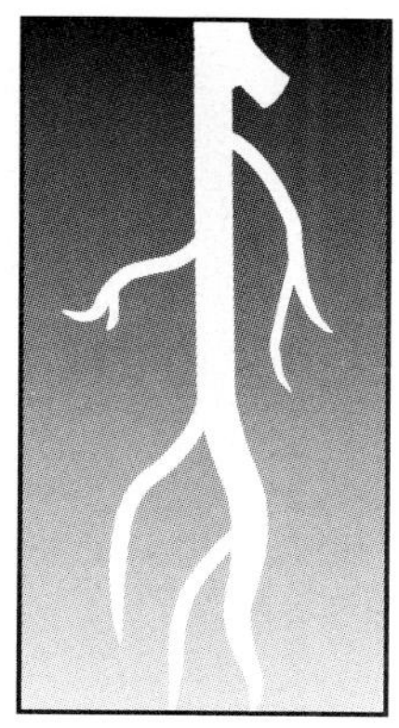

Vascular Surgery

Section I

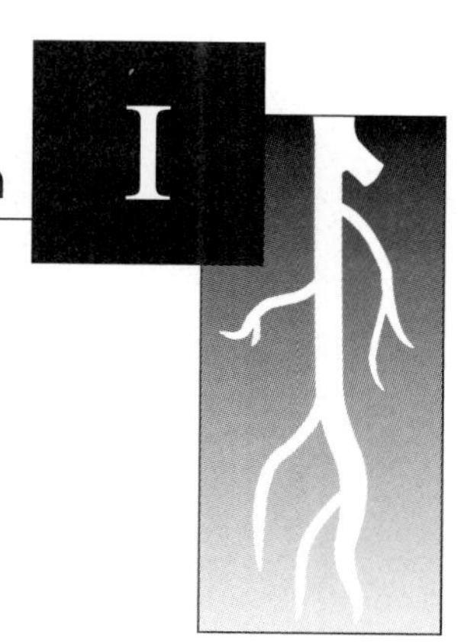

BASIC CONSIDERATIONS FOR CLINICAL PRACTICE

ROBERT B. RUTHERFORD, MD

Chapter 1

Essentials of Clinical Evaluation

ROBERT B. RUTHERFORD, MD

■ BASIC CONSIDERATIONS

The vascular surgeon is usually consulted in order to establish a diagnosis and to recommend or carry out appropriate treatment. This process involves (1) reaching a presumptive diagnosis on clinical grounds; (2) using noninvasive diagnostic measures to either confirm the diagnosis or grade the functional severity of the condition; (3) weighing the degree of disability and natural course of the underlying disease, with best medical treatment, against the risk and success rate of various interventional options; and (4) when necessitated by a likely need to intervene, confirming the diagnosis and the extent and degree of involvement with angiography or some other imaging method that provides sufficiently definitive anatomic information (Fig. 1-1). When percutaneous, catheter-directed interventions are likely options, tentative arrangements should be made to proceed with an appropriate procedure at the time of angiography to avoid duplication of risk, time, and effort.

One can make the final decision only by combining the sociologic, pathologic, anatomic, and physiologic findings in the individual patient. All but the anatomic details of the responsible lesion should be known after the initial consultation, the assessment of risk factors, and hemodynamic studies in the vascular laboratory. At this point or at the time of angiography, the surgeon should be prepared to make a definitive recommendation regarding best therapy. With the growing availability of percutaneous treatments, it is even more important that a basic strategy be worked out before angiography so that a definitive recommendation can be made at that time. Often, if the surgeon makes only a superficial evaluation sufficient to recommend angiography with subsequent review before final recommendation (a common practice in earlier times), others make the decisions about treatment.

Experience and judgment make this important process of patient evaluation and selection of appropriate therapy relatively straightforward in most cases, but there are always some patients in whom the disease process or its management is neither obvious nor definitive. There are few areas in medicine in which the conditions encountered lend themselves so readily to diagnosis solely on the basis of thoughtful history and careful physical examination as do vascular diseases. Specialists in this field are often surprised at their colleagues' difficulties in assessing peripheral vascular problems and, conversely, surprise their colleagues with their clinical acumen.

The majority of vascular problems are caused, in the Western world at least, by one of two basic disease processes: arteriosclerosis or thrombophlebitis. These processes predominantly affect the circulation of the lower extremity rather than of the upper extremity or the viscera; the presenting manifestation is pain, some form of tissue loss (ulceration or gangrene), or a change in appearance or sensation (swelling, discoloration, or temperature change). By applying a systematic, problem-oriented approach to these complaints, clinicians soon find that they can often predict the likely status of the arterial circulation even before examination, recognize the postphlebitic leg at a glance, determine the cause of leg or foot ulcerations from their location and appearance, and predict the cause of leg swelling on the basis of its distribution and associated skin changes.

Unfortunately, there is a tendency—as the clinician becomes adept at this process, is able to turn the anticipated 1-hour consultation with a new patient into a 15-minute interview and spot diagnosis, and can handle a clinic full of patients with chronic but familiar vascular problems in an hour or two—to bypass the systematic approach with increasing frequency and to abbreviate consultation notes

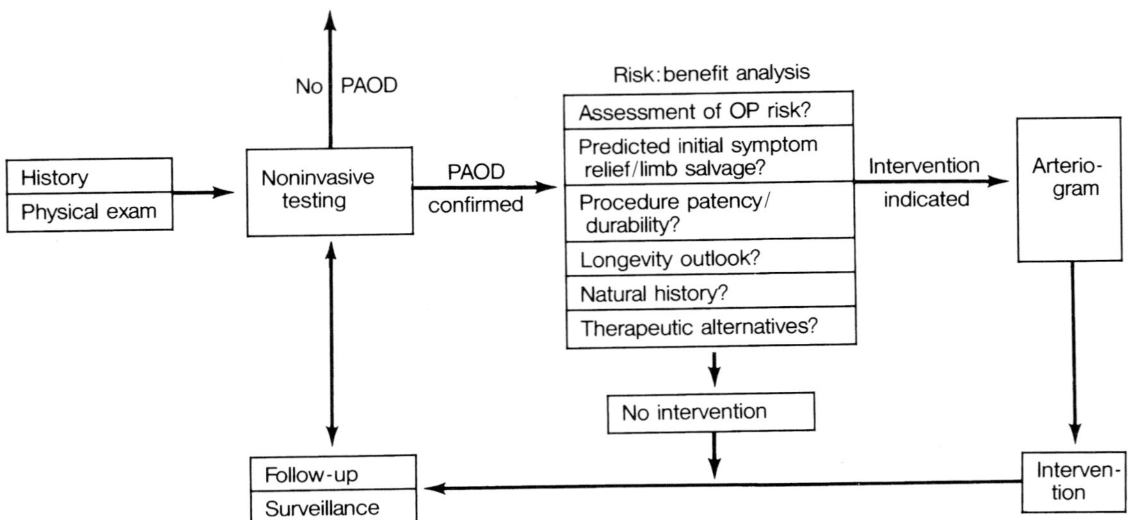

FIGURE 1-1 This algorithm shows the stepwise evaluation and management of patients presenting with peripheral arterial occlusive disease (PAOD). Note the central role played by noninvasive testing and the relegation of arteriography to therapeutic, not diagnostic, indications. OP, operative.

and clinical records. Although this practice is appropriate for many if not most patients in a busy clinic or practice, one must be selective and must apply a systematic approach frequently enough that the skill does not become lost or stinted, along with the ability to transmit this knowledge to others (colleagues, students, house staff) in an organized fashion. It may be useful, therefore, for experienced as well as inexperienced clinicians to have and maintain some formal framework on which their diagnostic skills can be superimposed. A diagnostic checklist or evaluation form, such as the one presented in Figure 1-2, can fill this need. This systematic approach not only avoids embarrassing oversights but also preserves the details of the initial evaluation for later dictation and can function as a temporary record until the transcribed note reaches the files.

Understandably, it is difficult for the experienced clinician to adhere to such a comprehensive approach. He or she usually proceeds in algorithmic fashion, following the branches of a decision tree out to the area of appropriate focus. Algorithmic decision-making texts are available to aid less experienced clinicians in developing these skills.[1] Nevertheless, organized evaluation forms like the one shown in Figure 1-2 can still serve as a guideline for students, house staff, and fellows as they first begin evaluating vascular problems. Auxiliary personnel may fill in parts, and in larger clinic practices, such tabular checklists, particularly if modified for each of the major disease entities or operations encountered, can provide the basis for clinical investigation and computer-based records and a vascular registry (see Chapter 4).

The form shown here is intended only as an example. It is more elaborate than most will need, and physicians should develop their own versions. For most purposes, only the major historical subheadings need to be listed on the form (e.g., location, duration, frequency, course, influencing factors). Further, instead of using tabular forms for pulses, the location of edema, discoloration, or ulceration, one can use and mark an anatomic silhouette, with or without an outline of the arterial tree, to note the pertinent physical findings.

Finally, work forms destined to feed information into a vascular registry must be simpler still, because only essential and unambiguous categorical information should be stored in computers (see Chapter 4). A more complex form can serve both purposes if the items intended for entry into the vascular registry are identified by bold or colored print.

■ HISTORY AND PHYSICAL EXAMINATION

Patients with vascular diseases usually present with key complaints that often can be developed by pointed questioning into a reasonable presumptive diagnosis even before physical examination is performed. The major diagnostic considerations for the various forms of vascular disease are covered later in appropriate sections of this book. The intention in this chapter is to demonstrate, mainly through the use of the lower extremity as an example, the value of knowing which questions to ask and which physical signs to seek. This problem-oriented approach is preferred to simply developing a list of uncorrelated vascular signs and symptoms.

The Painful Extremity

The most common presenting symptom in lower extremity vascular disease is pain. Knowing the pain's character, severity, location, frequency and duration, and temporal pattern, and determining what precipitates or aggravates the pain or makes it subside can allow one to diagnose or rule out arterial and venous diseases with more than 90% certainty *before* the physical examination begins.

PERIPHERAL VASCULAR WORKSHEET

Name ______ **Date** ______

Past History

Allergies______ Operations______
Injuries ______ Major illnesses______
Pregnancies______ Phlebitis ______
Pulmonary embolism ______ Serious infections______
Cardiac: angina______CHF______MI ______
arrhythmia______DOE ______orthopnea______
Respiratory ______
Diabetes ______
Hypertension______
Renal______
Neurological: cerebrovascular ______
peripheral ______
Venereal disease______
Arthritis, collagen vascular______
Other______

Family History

Same condition ______Other vascular______
Diabetes______ Hypertension ______CVA ______ Cardiac______
Clotting abnormalities______

Personal and Social

Alcohol______ Tobacco ______
Education ______ Psychological ______
Occupations______
Travel______
Drug use: past ______
present ______

PERIPHERAL VASCULAR WORKSHEET

Name ______ **Date** ______

I. Complaints:

	Rank	Severity	Descriptive Comments
Pain			
Weakness			
Hot/cold			
Numb/sensitive			
Discoloration			
Swelling			
Ulceration			
Varicose veins			

II. Location: R/L, medial/lateral, dorsal/ventral
Toes ______Foot ______Ankle ______Leg ______Knee ______
Fingers Hand Wrist Forearm Elbow
Thigh ______Hip ______Back ______Other ______
Arm ______Shoulder ______Neck ______
III. Onset: sudden/gradual
IV. Duration: ______ days/weeks/months/years
V. Frequency: ______ times/day/week/month/year
VI. Temporal Pattern: continuous/intermittent/day/night/none
VII. Course: static/better/worse/fluctuates
VIII. Interferes With: sleep/work/exercise/other
IX. Influencing Factors (A-aggravates, R-relieves, O-no effect):
Elevation______Dependency______Exercise ______Rest ______Heat______
Cold ______Weather change______Menses ______Emotions ______Vibration ______
Pressure______Position______
Activity______
Other (including Rx) ______

FIGURE 1-2 Diagnostic checklist for vascular evaluation. B.P., blood pressure; CHF, congestive heart failure; CVA, cerebrovascular accident; DOE, dyspnea on exertion/exercise; Ht., height; L, left; MI, myocardial infarction; R, right; Rx, medications; Wt., weight.

Continued

PERIPHERAL VASCULAR WORKSHEET

Physical Examination

Name ______ **Date** ______
Ht.______ Wt. ______ Pulse______ Temperature______ B.P.______
General ______ Head and neck ______
Heart______
Lungs______ Abdomen ______

Extremities		Upper right	Upper left	Lower right	Lower left
Skin	Warm/cool				
	Atrophied/thickened				
	Cyanosis/mottling				
	Pallor/rubor				
	Capillary filling				
	Hair growth				
	Nails				
Edema	Brawny/pitting/spongy				
	Degree				
	Extent				
	Subcutaneous atrophy				
	fibrosis				
	Ulceration/tissue loss				
	Discoloration/pigmentation				
	Erythema/cellulitis				
	Lymphangitis				
Musculoskeletal	Symmetry/atrophy				
	Hypertrophy				
	Joint enlargement/swelling				
	Range of motion				
	Reflexes				
	Sensory				
	Motor				

PERIPHERAL VASCULAR WORKSHEET

Arterial Survey	Right pulse	Right bruit	Right aneurysm	Left pulse	Left bruit	Left aneurysm
Carotid						
Subclavian						
Brachial						
Radial						
Ulnar						
Abdominal aorta						
Iliac						
Femoral						
Popliteal						
Dorsalis pedis						
Posterior tibial						

Venous Survey **Code:** N = normal; P = prominent, tense; V = varicose; T = thrombosed

	Right	**Left**
Greater saphenous		
Lesser saphenous		
Anterolateral thigh		
Posteromedial thigh		
Anterior tibial		
Posterior arch		
Perforators		
Intracutaneous venules		
Tourniquet test		

Demographic Data
Name______ Date ______ History no. ______
Address______ Occupation ______
Age ______ Sex ______ Nationality/race______
Referring physician ______ Telephone no. ______
Address______

FIGURE 1-2, cont'd Diagnostic checklist for vascular evaluation. B.P., blood pressure; CHF, congestive heart failure; CVA, cerebrovascular accident; DOE, dyspnea on exertion/exercise; Ht., height; L, left; MI, myocardial infarction; R, right; Rx, medications; Wt., weight.

Arterial Causes of Pain

Acute Arterial Occlusion *Acute arterial occlusion* does not always produce the well-known "five Ps," *pain, pallor, pulselessness, paresthesias,* and *paralysis*.

Pain in acute arterial ischemia may be evanescent, cyanosis often replaces pallor, pulses may be difficult to evaluate in persons with preexisting arterial occlusive disease, and early changes in sensation and muscle strength may be easily missed. Early sensory deficits may be subtle. Light touch, two-point discrimination, vibratory perception, and proprioception are usually lost well before appreciation of deep pain and pressure. Similarly, most foot movements are produced by more proximal muscles (e.g., dorsiflexion or plantar flexion of toes is produced by muscles originating just below the knee), where ischemia may be far less profound than in distal muscles. Therefore, to detect early motor weakness, the physician should also test the function of intrinsic muscles of the foot, remembering that in some patients these muscles are not well developed. Capillary filling is usually impaired, the limb segments below the obstruction are noticeably cool, and venous filling may be diminished. These findings and the palpation of pulses should always be compared with findings in the other extremity.

The pain of *acute limb ischemia* (ALI) is variable. In lesser degrees of ischemia, the pain may be absent or evanescent. If their pain is not severe and sustained and if patients do not experience motor or sensory loss, they may not even seek immediate medical help, and the absence of pulses may not be detected until later, when patients present with claudication or are examined for other reasons. Nevertheless, the initial pain of acute arterial occlusion usually is fairly characteristic. It is quite different from the ischemic rest pain of chronic critical ischemia (CCI) (see later). Pain due to ALI is *not* as well localized to the distal forefoot, nor is it clearly affected by gravity. It may share the same compelling intensity as that of CCI but tends to be more diffuse, often extending above the ankle in severer cases. The pain of ALI begins suddenly and reaches a peak rapidly in the case of *arterial embolism,* and patients may describe a sensation of the leg's being "struck" by a severe, shocking pain that renders it weak. If standing at the time, they may be forced to sit down immediately or may even crumple to the ground as the extremity gives way.

With *arterial thrombosis,* the clinical presentation is not usually as dramatic as with embolism, but the patient is usually aware of some sudden change in status; when the severity of ischemia is truly limb-threatening, pain quickly supervenes. The pain may subside in intensity and, depending on the severity of the ischemia that remains after the initial wave of vasospasm has passed and collateral channels are recruited, may either resolve completely or settle into one of the typical pain patterns of chronic ischemia. The persistence of pain, particularly if followed by numbness, weakness, or both, indicates that one is dealing with severe, limb-threatening ALI.

Chronic Arterial Insufficiency *Chronic arterial insufficiency* of the lower extremity causes two very characteristic types of pain: intermittent claudication, and ischemic rest pain.

Claudication, although derived from the Latin word for limp *(claudicatio)*, has by usage come to mean a discomfort or disability associated with exercise. Depending on the level and extent of the arterial occlusive disease, the patient may present with buttock and thigh claudication, calf claudication, or foot claudication, either singly or in contiguous combination. The most common presentation—*calf claudication*—is easily recognized as a "cramping" pain in the calf that can be consistently reproduced by the same level of exercise and that is completely and quickly relieved by rest. This calf cramping pain is not to be confused with that occurring at night in older patients, some of whom may even have pulse deficits or other signs of arterial occlusive disease. Nocturnal muscle cramps have no known vascular basis; rather, they are thought to result from an exaggerated neuromuscular response to stretch. Experienced clinicians can quickly differentiate between these two unrelated causes of leg cramps, one with exercise and the other at rest. They also realize that it is not unusual for older patients to experience no symptoms from superficial femoral artery occlusion, because their sedentary existence protects them from claudication and the occlusive process is gradual enough to allow concomitant development of collateral circulation, so that there is no ischemia at rest.

Pain or discomfort associated with tightness in the calf and precipitated by exercise may result from a *chronic compartment compression syndrome* (see Chapters 74, 155). The patient is often an athlete or a runner with large calf muscles. Muscle swelling, increased compartment pressure, and impaired venous outflow constitute a vicious circle. However, this pain usually comes on after considerable exercise and does not quickly subside with rest.

Patients with arterial occlusive disease of more proximal (aortoiliac) distribution usually suffer from buttock and thigh claudication, although a significant number also complain of calf claudication. Buttock and thigh claudication does not usually produce the severe cramping muscular pain experienced in the calf. The sensation is more of an "aching" discomfort associated with *weakness*. These patients may even deny the existence of pain per se, complaining only that the hip or thigh "gives out" or "tires" after they have walked a certain distance. Patients with *osteoarthritis* of the hip or knee may complain of similar extremity discomfort that is also brought on by exercise; however, important differentiating factors for osteoarthritis are as follows:

1. The amount of exercise causing their symptoms is variable.
2. The pain does not disappear as promptly with rest.
3. The pain varies in severity from day to day, frequently in association with changes in weather conditions or physical activity.

Neurospinal compression, caused by osteophytic narrowing of the lower (lumbar) neurospinal canal, may simulate claudication secondary to aortoiliac occlusive disease. Usually, however, it is more of a numbing weakness that is *also produced by standing* (or anything increasing lumbar lordosis) rather than just ambulation, and it is *not relieved by stopping* unless the patient sits down or leans against a lamp post or tree, with the upper body bent forward, and straightens out the lumbar spine. Further questioning often reveals that this weakness is associated with either numbness or paresthesias, sometimes involving the perineum. Because older patients not infrequently have diminished femoral pulses and proximal bruits, reflecting some degree of aortoiliac occlusive disease, it is not unusual for these other painful conditions to be wrongly ascribed to arterial disease. This is a classic example of the importance of matching symptoms and signs in terms of severity and distribution. It is unusual to have significant hip or buttock pain from iliac artery stenosis without associated thigh claudication. Furthermore, aortic or complete iliac artery occlusion with absence of femoral pulses on at least one side is usually necessary for such proximally distributed symptoms. Finally, bilateral aortoiliac occlusive disease severe enough to produce disabling claudication is nearly always associated with impotence in men. The absence of impotence in a man with bilateral hip or thigh pain suggests that the pain may not be due to aortoiliac occlusive disease unless the occlusive lesions are limited to the external iliac arteries.

Although true claudication is attributable to arterial occlusive disease, venous occlusion can also cause thigh claudication. This venous "claudication" usually results because recanalization has not occurred after iliofemoral venous thrombosis. At rest, collateral vessels allow venous outflow to match arterial inflow without the development of high venous pressures but cannot handle the several-fold increases in arterial inflow associated with exercise. The venous channels in the thigh or leg characteristically become engorged and tense, and it is this high venous pressure—not ischemia—that is the source of the pain, which is often appropriately described as a "bursting" pain or a tight, heavy sensation. Because this venous engorgement is slow to subside, the pain does not abate as quickly as that of claudication due to arterial occlusive disease.

Foot claudication occurring on an ischemic basis is very rare. It may exist independently of calf claudication if the occlusive lesions are diffuse and involve all the infrapopliteal arteries distally, but it is just as commonly associated with more proximal occlusions and calf pain. Foot claudication has a greater relative frequency in thromboangiitis obliterans than in arteriosclerosis obliterans because of the typically more distal distribution of occlusive lesions in the former condition. The patient usually complains of a painful ache, a "drawing" pain or cramp in the forefoot, associated only with walking. Patients usually also complain of a "wooden" sensation or numbness in the same distribution and of a persistently cold foot at night. Frequently, they have visited several podiatrists or have tried a variety of arch supports or "orthopedic" shoes. This rarest form of lower extremity claudication usually occurs only with advanced degrees of arterial insufficiency and, therefore, is commonly associated with ischemic rest pain of the foot. This form of claudication can be confused with arthritic or inflammatory processes involving the foot (e.g., rheumatoid arthritis, plantar fasciitis, or metatarsalgia, the latter two often being seen in those who run daily for exercise). With these other conditions, however, the relationship with exercise and rest is variable and not as precisely precipitated and relieved. Table 1-1 summarizes the differential diagnosis of claudication at these three levels and the conditions that mimic them.

One may encounter cases in which either the clinical diagnosis of arterial claudication is not clear-cut or the symptoms and findings, although compatible with the diagnosis, do not match it in severity. In such cases, noninvasive testing can be extremely helpful (see Chapter 14). For example, the ankle pressure after exercise sufficient to reproduce the pain should fall to the vicinity of 50 mm Hg or less. If not, the patient may have two causes of leg pain, the lesser of which is related to arterial insufficiency.

Ischemic rest pain, as seen in *chronic critical ischemia*, is typically a nocturnal pain of disturbing severity that diffusely involves the foot distal to the tarsal bones, although pain may be sharply localized to the vicinity of an ischemic ulcer or gangrenous toe. The pain may be so severe that it is not relieved even by substantial doses of narcotics. Patients who sleep with the leg in a *horizontal* position are typically awakened by this pain and forced to get up and do something about it. They may sit up and rub or hold the painful foot, get up and pace the floor, or walk to the medicine cabinet to take an analgesic. Any of these responses may relieve the pain fairly promptly, but only through the unwitting recruiting of the help of gravity in improving perfusion to the distal tissues. Although patients may at first wrongly attribute the relief to rubbing the foot, walking, or even an amazingly fast-acting analgesic, they eventually learn to sleep with the foot *dependent*, either dangling it over the side of the bed and resting it on a chair, or sleeping out the night in a lounge chair. This pain pattern is too characteristic to be missed by the careful interrogator, but the unwary may be thrown off by the rubor and apparent prompt capillary filling of the toes observed when seated patients remove their shoes. This "dependent pallor" is matched by "cadaveric pallor" if the leg is elevated (Buerger's signs; see later), but many primary physicians do not go beyond the erroneous initial impression.

Occasionally, patients with arthritic changes in the small bones of the feet (metatarsals, usually) can experience "metatarsalgia" that occurs primarily at night and is relieved by standing. This picture can be seen with either degenerative osteoarthritis or rheumatoid arthritis. Its occurrence is irregular (i.e., it may be present or absent for several days to weeks), thus distinguishing it from ischemic rest pain, which occurs whenever the patient lies down for any length of time.

Venous Causes of Pain

Pain associated with *venous disease* of the lower extremity is not as characteristic as that in the arterial pain syndromes. Fortunately, venous conditions usually are easily recognized from their associated physical findings. The example of pain associated with activity seen in proximal venous obstruction ("venous claudication") has already been mentioned, but most pain from chronic venous insufficiency is a consequence

Table 1-1 Differential Diagnosis of Claudication

CONDITION	LOCATION OF PAIN OR DISCOMFORT	CHARACTERISTIC DISCOMFORT	ONSET RELATIVE TO EXERCISE	EFFECT OF REST	EFFECT OF BODY POSITION	OTHER CHARACTERISTICS
Intermittent claudication of the calf	Calf muscles	Cramping pain	After *same* degree of exercise	Quickly relieved	None	Reproducible
Venous compartment syndrome	Calf muscles	Tight, bursting pain	After *much* exercise (e.g., jogging)	Subsides very slowly	Relief speeded by elevation	Typically, heavily muscled athletes
Venous claudication	Entire leg, but usually worse in thigh and groin	Tight, bursting pain	After walking	Subsides slowly	Relief speeded by elevation	History of iliofemoral deep venous thrombosis, signs of venous congestion, edema
Nerve root compression (e.g., herniated disc)	Radiates down leg, usually posteriorly	Sharp lancinating pain	Soon, if not immediately after onset	Not quickly relieved (also often present at rest)	Relief may be aided by adjustment of back position	History of back problems
Intermittent claudication of the hip, thigh, buttock	Hip, thigh, buttocks	Aching discomfort, weakness	After *same* degree of exercise	Quickly relieved	None	Reproducible
Hip arthritis	Hip, thigh, buttocks	Aching discomfort	After *variable* degree of exercise	*Not* quickly relieved (and may be present at rest)	Patient is more comfortable sitting, with weight taken off legs	*Variable;* may relate to activity level, weather changes
Neurospinal root compression	Hip, thigh, buttocks (follows dermatome)	Weakness more than pain	After walking or standing for same time	Relieved by stopping only if position changed	Relieved by lumbar spine flexion (sitting or stooping forward)	Common history of back problems; provoked by increased intra-abdominal pressure
Intermittent claudication of the foot	Foot, arch	Severe deep pain and numbness	After *same* degree of exercise	Quickly relieved	None	Reproducible
Arthritic, inflammatory processes	Foot, arch	Aching pain	After *variable* degree of exercise	*Not* quickly relieved (and may be present at rest)	May be relieved by not bearing weight	*Variable;* may relate to activity level

of valve reflux in patent veins. Severe pain is not a common complaint of patients with *primary varicose veins*. In fact, one must be suspicious when older patients with varicose veins present because of pain, particularly if the varicosities are of long standing and have not previously been painful. Such patients may be suffering from extremity pain of another, more obscure etiology, although they blame it on the visible varicosities and lead the physician into the same trap. Occasionally, varicose veins produce a "pulling," "pricking," "burning," or "tingling" discomfort that is localized to the varicose veins themselves, unlike the diffuse sensation of fatigue or heaviness that is commonly associated with pain and ache in patients with deep venous insufficiency. Although these symptoms, as with all venous discomfort, are relieved by elevation, the associated tingling and burning sensation often worsens during the initial period of elevation before it subsides.

Venous thrombosis in the lower extremity may cause little or no *acute* pain unless the associated inflammatory reaction is significant, in which case there may also be localized tenderness along the course of the involved vein. Swelling, either early or later in the postphlebitic period, is not uncommonly associated with a moderate aching discomfort and a tight or heavy sensation; severe, "bursting" pain, however, is rare unless the patient is spending too much time in the upright position or still has significant residual obstruction to venous outflow *(venous claudication)*. Although the symptoms associated with venous valvular insufficiency or obstruction (in the absence of associated inflammation) are quite variable, their aggravation by standing and relief by elevation are consistent, and this relationship should always be explored. The presence of significant discomfort after standing for long periods in chronic venous valvular insufficiency or after walking in venous obstruction stands in marked contrast to the relative lack of discomfort associated with lymphedema (see later).

Nonvascular Pain Syndromes

Patients with other forms of extremity pain are often referred to the vascular surgeon through the false presumption that the pain is circulatory in origin. Therefore, the vascular surgeon must be able to recognize the *nonvascular* extremity pain syndromes or at least the common ones associated with nerve or musculoskeletal derangements. As previously pointed out, the pain of *arthritis* or *sciatica* usually is fairly characteristic and is easily distinguishable from that caused by vascular disease. However, two other conditions cause extremity pain that can masquerade as vascular disease because of associated vascular signs. One is a painful *peripheral neuritis* commonly seen in diabetics; because their peripheral pulses may be diminished and they may have rubor and trophic skin changes, the examiner may mistake the problem for arterial insufficiency rather than the early stage of diabetic neuropathy. Later stages of diabetic neuropathy are characteristically painless, and the associated neurologic signs are obvious, but in the early "neuritic" stages, the neurologic signs may be subtle, often no more than a patchy loss of light touch, vibratory sense, and two-point discrimination.

The other misleading type of extremity pain is *reflex sympathetic dystrophy*, or *minor causalgia*. Like the neuritis, the pain this syndrome produces is usually burning in character. *Major causalgia*, associated with incomplete nerve injury, usually is easily recognized; the minor variety, which may follow relatively minor trauma or acute circulatory problems such as venous or arterial thrombosis, must always be kept in mind. Similarly, the residual discomfort in a patient who has undergone back surgery (disc operation, lumbar fusion) is often labeled "arachnoiditis." However, it is actually a form of causalgic pain resulting from the "trauma" of long-standing nerve compression.

Typically, there are associated signs of autonomic imbalance, the "vascular" signs that originally attracted the attention of the referring physician. The causalgic extremity may be warm and dry initially, but it later becomes cool, mottled, or cyanotic. Eventually, trophic changes develop that are not unlike those of advanced arterial insufficiency. The pain is not always classically superficial, burning, and localized to the distribution of a somatic nerve as originally described. If there are reasonable grounds for suspicion after initial evaluation, relief of the pain by a proximal arterial injection of 10 to 15 mg of tolazoline, confirmed later by a paravertebral sympathetic block, establishes the diagnosis (see Chapter 75).

Physical Examination

Physical examination of the painful extremity is usually carried out by a "prejudiced" examiner *if a careful history has been taken*, for the reasons already given, and it is difficult to be systematic when physical findings confirming one's suspicions immediately catch the eye. A complete and thorough initial examination, however, should be carried out. Discovery of a previously undetected diastolic hypertension, carotid bruit, fibrillating heart, or abdominal aortic aneurysm may be the dividend of such thoroughness. Furthermore, documentation of the state of the peripheral pulses may well have future value.

Examination of the abdomen should consist of more than a brief palpation for an occult aneurysm. For example, lower abdominal bruits may provide the only physical clue to aortoiliac occlusive disease in a patient with buttock and thigh claudication, because (1) there may be no signs of chronic ischemia and (2) a femoral pulse may be readily palpated because a hemodynamically significant iliac artery stenosis may produce a pressure gradient of as little as 10 mm Hg at rest.

If such patients (with "critical" stenoses) exercise to the point of claudication, they usually temporarily "lose" the previously palpable pedal pulses because of the marked decrease in vascular resistance that occurs in exercising muscle distal to an obstruction and the increased distribution of flow to muscle beds proximal to the obstruction. This is the basis for the practice of monitoring ankle pressure after a standard treadmill exercise (see Chapter 14).

Another example of claudication with palpable pulses should be kept in mind. If one elicits a good history of claudication in a *young* patient with palpable pedal pulses, one should suspect popliteal entrapment (see Chapter 86) and should recheck the pulses during active plantar flexion or passive dorsiflexion.

Palpating Pulses

Femoral pulses may be difficult to palpate in muscular or obese patients unless the hips are externally rotated and the vessels are palpated over the pubic ramus of the ilium, where they lie 1½ to 2 fingerbreadths lateral to the pubic tubercle and are covered by less fat. Even for the experienced examiner, the *popliteal pulses* are often difficult to palpate—so difficult, in fact, that the knowledgeable vascular surgeon who feels them too easily usually suspects at once the possibility of a popliteal aneurysm. Holding the supine patient's knee partially flexed plus allowing it to fall gently back into the examiner's hand, which is positioned so that the proximal interphalangeal joints hook the tendons while the fingertips sink gently into the middle of the popliteal space, is just as effective a means of palpating popliteal pulses as having the patient turn into the prone position with the knee flexed.

The locations of the *posterior tibial pulse* in the hollow behind the medial malleolus and of the *dorsalis pedis pulse* along the dorsum of the foot between the first and the second metatarsal bones are well known. It is less well appreciated that one or the other of these pedal pulses is not palpable in almost 10% of normal persons. In such cases, the lateral tibial artery, the terminal branch of the peroneal artery, should be sought higher in the foot, just below the ankle and medial to the bony prominence of the fibula. A warm room and a light touch are the best combination for the most accurate detection of pedal pulses. Otherwise, it must be hoped that the examiner's and the patient's pulses are distinctly different in rate.

Finally, it is important to listen for bruits over the course of these major arteries, especially at or above the most proximal pulse that feels weaker than normal. It is surprising how often the telltale bruit of an iliac stenosis is not even auscultated.

Signs of Advanced Ischemia

Severe claudication may be associated with atrophy of the calf muscles, but unless this process is unilateral and produces asymmetry, it may escape detection. Loss of hair growth over the dorsum of the toes and foot is another relatively common sign of arterial insufficiency, and it may be accompanied by thickening of the toenails secondary to slowness of nail growth. More advanced ischemic changes, however, such as atrophy of the skin and its appendages and the subcutaneous tissue, so that the foot becomes shiny, scaly, and "skeletonized," usually do not appear in the absence of ischemic rest pain. Delayed return of the capillary blush after pressure on the pulp of the digit and slow venous filling after the elevated extremity is dropped back into the dependent position are also signs of advanced ischemia.

Buerger's sign (i.e., cadaveric pallor on elevation and rubor on dependency) occurs with very restricted arterial inflow and chronic dilatation of the peripheral vascular bed beyond, particularly the postcapillary venules. The dependent toes may appear so red and may refill so rapidly after pressure application that the uninitiated may mistakenly consider this to be evidence of hyperemia rather than an expression of severe ischemia. Localized pallor or cyanosis associated with poor capillary filling is usually a prelude to ischemic gangrene or ulceration. At this advanced stage of chronic critical ischemia, the foot may be edematous, and the skin tense and shiny, from being continually kept in the dependent position in an attempt to relieve the ischemic pain.

Signs of Venous Insufficiency

As previously stated, lower extremity pain secondary to venous disease is inconstant. In addition, the discomfort caused by venous distention from whatever cause is similar in character, as is its relief by elevation. Therefore, the physical findings associated with these venous problems may be extremely helpful in differentiating between them. For example, *varicose veins* may be the result of superficial venous incompetence—*primary* saphenous incompetence, complete or segmental—or they may be *secondary* to deep venous or perforator incompetence or both, which itself may be primary or secondary, that is, post-thrombotic sequelae. In the untreated state, chronic deep venous insufficiency produces brawny edema, stasis dermatitis, and ulceration. By contrast, the edema associated with primary *uncomplicated* varicose veins is mild and rarely appears early in the day, dermatitis with pigmentation is usually restricted to the skin immediately overlying prominent varicosities, and ulceration does *not* occur in early cases. However it must be understood that primary saphenous incompetence, with time, can lead sequentially to perforator and even deep (usually calf) venous incompetence, so that in late, advanced stages, one might see associated brawny edema, pigmentation, and ulceration, signs clinically indistinguishable from those seen in chronic deep venous insufficiency. Finally, the distribution of the varicosities may provide an additional clue; primary varicose veins typically involve the main saphenous vein and its major branches rather than scattered tributaries, and early on, they do not refill quickly upon standing after a tourniquet has been applied to the upper thigh (positive tourniquet test result).

An acutely thrombosed superficial vein feels like a cord; it is tender and may be surrounded by erythema, skin pigmentation, warmth, swelling, induration, and other localized signs of inflammation. Even acute thrombosis of a deep vein, if associated with a sufficient inflammatory reaction, may result in tenderness along its course. Usually, however, the latter produces a more generalized edema distally. If the deep calf veins are thrombosed, there may be pain on dorsiflexion *(Homans' sign)*, tenderness on anteroposterior but not lateral compression of the calf *(Bancroft's sign)*, and prompt pain in the calf caused by inflation of a sphygmomanometer cuff around it to a pressure of 80 mm Hg *(Löwenberg's sign)*. Unfortunately, these signs are present in less than a third of patients with acute deep venous thrombosis (DVT), and their absence is not to be relied on.

The oft-quoted rates of "one-third false-positive" and "one-third false-negative" for diagnosis of thrombophlebitis or DVT, when made on clinical grounds alone, apply more to a hospital population of patients at bed rest in whom occult thrombosis is more likely to occur and in whom swelling is more likely to be absent. On the other hand, outpatients with this condition usually present *because of* signs or symptoms, and therefore, a higher rate of diagnostic accuracy may be expected in this setting. Nevertheless, this diagnosis can be made confidently on clinical grounds *only* in cases of extensive, major venous thrombosis (e.g., phlegmasia cerulea dolens or phlegmasia alba dolens) or in those whose DVT is associated with a marked inflammatory reaction. Fortunately, examination of the leg veins with a color duplex scanner is 95% accurate in diagnosing DVT (see Chapters 17, 148).

The Swollen Leg

After the painful leg, the swollen leg is the next most common problem on which the vascular surgeon is called to consult. In examining the swollen leg, the consultant should remember another "five Ps":

- Pressure
- Protein
- Permeability
- Paresis
- Pendency

Plasma constituents move into the tissues and return to the vascular space normally during circulation, according to Starling's law. The balance of factors influencing this process is a delicate one, particularly in the lower extremity, where gravity provides an additional complicating factor. The valved venomotor pump mechanism is presumably an evolutionary adaptation to the assumption of the upright position by humans, for if a normal person were to stand motionless long enough, venous pressures at the ankle would stabilize in the range of 80 to 100 mm Hg, and swelling and petechial hemorrhages would appear. With a competent venomotor pump mechanism, however, even modest activity of the calf muscles, such as occurs in intermittently shifting one's weight, reduces this pressure to 20 to 30 mm Hg, and what little swelling accumulates during the day usually disappears overnight, when the body is horizontal. Patients who do not take advantage of this respite (e.g., those who sleep night after night with their feet dependent to relieve ischemic pain) experience chronic swelling, as do patients with peroneal palsy or an arthritic or fused ankle, who cannot activate the venomotor pump.

Increased permeability secondary to inflammation results in swelling if the extremity is not kept elevated. Similarly, swelling is seen in secondary aldosteronism. The lymphatics are the route by which extravasated protein is returned to the central circulation. If the clearance capacity of this system is restricted because it is congenitally hypoplastic, because it is obliterated by episodes of lymphangitis, or because its outflow is obstructed or interrupted by surgery or irradiation, protein-rich lymph will accumulate in the tissues. A similar mechanism, in reverse, applies in hypoproteinemia, and this occasional cause of swelling should be considered in obscure cases.

High venous pressure is the most common cause of extremity swelling. The source of this increased peripheral venous pressure may be (1) a cardiac condition, as in right-sided heart failure or tricuspid valvular disease; (2) *intrinsic* venous obstruction, as in proximal deep venous thrombosis, (3) *extrinsic* venous compression, as of the left iliac vein by the right iliac artery deep venous valvular insufficiency; or, most commonly, (4) widespread venous valvular insufficiency. In the last instance, the increased pressure is a result of the unrelenting and unopposed transmission, in the upright position, of gravitational pressure through incompetent valves of the deep and communicating veins to the superficial tissues. Venous hypertension secondary to arteriovenous fistulae is rarer and seldom causes swelling in the absence of venous obstruction; however, it does cause changes similar to, though more localized than, those generally ascribed to venous "stasis" (discussed later).

Clinically, the differential diagnosis of swelling may be difficult when it is of brief duration; in the chronic state, however, characteristic physical findings appear that greatly simplify matters. When a patient presents with a chronically swollen leg, the experienced examiner may make the correct diagnosis in more than 95% of cases simply by noting the distribution of the swelling, its response to elevation, and the associated discomfort and skin changes. These and other diagnostic considerations pertinent to chronically swollen lower extremities are presented in Table 1-2.

If there are no obvious associated skin changes and the edema "pits" readily on pressure, its cause is usually central or systemic (e.g., heart disease, hypoproteinemia, or secondary aldosteronism). The distribution of this type of swelling, sometimes called *orthostatic edema*, is diffuse, but

Table 1-2 Differential Diagnosis of Chronic Leg Swelling

CLINICAL FEATURE	VENOUS	LYMPHATIC	CARDIAC ORTHOSTATIC	"LIPEDEMA"
Consistency of swelling	Brawny	Spongy	Pitting	Noncompressible (fat)
Relief by elevation	Complete	Mild	Complete	Minimal
Distribution of swelling	Maximal in ankles and legs; feet spared	Diffuse; greatest distally	Diffuse; greatest distally	Maximal in ankles and legs; feet spared
Associated skin changes	Atrophic and pigmented; subcutaneous fibrosis	Hypertrophied, lichenified skin	Shiny, mild pigmentation; no trophic changes	None
Pain	Heavy ache; tight or bursting	None or heavy ache	Little or none	Dull ache; cutaneous sensitivity
Bilaterality	Occasionally, but usually unequal	Occasionally, but usually unequal	Always, but may be unequal	Always

the swelling is greatest peripherally and, to some extent, also involves the foot. The edema associated with lower extremity venous disease, even in the acute stage, does not pit readily. In the chronic stage, it is frankly "brawny" and is associated with characteristic skin changes caused by chronic venous hypertension. The breakdown of extravasated red blood cells causes the characteristic pigmentation and, together with increased fibrin in the interstitial fluid, leads to inflammation ("stasis dermatitis") and ultimately fibrosis (lipodermatofibrosis) in the subcutaneous tissues. Later, the skin becomes atrophic and breaks down with minor trauma. Pigmentation and inflammatory skin changes (stasis dermatitis or eczema) are not predictive of eventual ulceration, but subcutaneous fibrosis (lipodermatofibrosis) and skin atrophy ("atrophie blanche") do correlate with later ulceration.

These components of so-called stasis dermatitis have a "gaiter" distribution (Fig. 1-3), and even in earlier stages, when edema predominates, the feet often are relatively spared compared with the ankles and lower half of the legs. The reason is that this venous hypertension is transmitted to the superficial veins by incompetent perforator veins located in this gaiter area. Eventually, progression of these chronic changes converts the skin and subcutaneous tissues of the lower leg from a diffusely edematous state to a pigmented, atrophic, tightly scarred zone, which, when viewed in contrast to the proximal edema, leads to the descriptive term "inverted-champagne-bottle-leg."

When the vascular surgeon sees a patient with advanced changes of chronic venous insufficiency, it may be impossible, from just looking at the leg, to tell whether these are sequelae of DVT or primary venous valvular incompetence, beginning with varicose veins. A history of DVT or a family history of varicosities is often lacking. A useful approach is to ask which came first. Because it takes considerable time for saphenofemoral venous incompetence to progress downward to involve the perforator and even tibial veins, affected patients will answer that they had the varicose veins for many years before swelling and stasis skin changes developed. Patients with post-thrombotic changes may not know they had DVT but they will remember having normal legs before a particular point in time when there was rather abrupt onset of swelling, with stasis skin changes and secondary varicosities coming some time later.

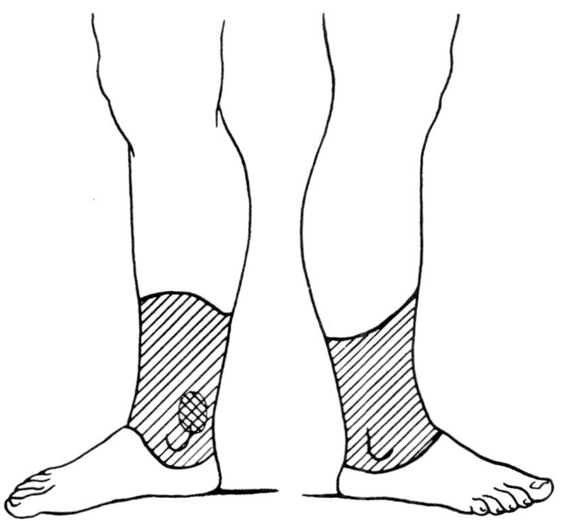

FIGURE 1-3 The "gaiter" distribution of stasis dermatitis and leg ulcers.

The distribution of swelling in *lymphedema* is diffuse, but it is always greater distally, beginning with the toes and moving upward. This swelling is neither pitting nor brawny but firmly "spongy" in character; that is, although it does not significantly resist deformation by pressure, the skin and subcutaneous tissues quickly return to their original position as the pressure is withdrawn. Skin pigmentation and ulceration are rare. If anything, the skin eventually becomes hypertrophic. The end stage of chronic lymphatic insufficiency, *elephantiasis*, with its folds of thickened, lichenified skin hanging over the ankle, is too characteristic to be missed. Infection and inflammation in the depths of these skin folds can, however, lead to pigmentation and open sores, or ulcers. Occasionally, patients with the "post-thrombotic syndrome" whose condition progresses to stasis dermatitis and ulceration early may not have typical scarring and contraction of the subcutaneous tissue but instead have an elephantiasis-like appearance. This confusing variant is caused by invasive infection via the chronically ulcerated skin, which obliterates subcutaneous lymphatics and leads to secondary lymphedema.

Not uncommonly, women present with chronically "swollen" legs that have none of the foregoing characteristics. Although often reluctant to admit it, they usually confess that they have always had "thick" ankles. These patients, and often their female relatives, have a maldistribution of fat, characterized by excessive peripheral deposition in the arms as well as the legs. For unknown reasons, these women are prone to superimposed orthostatic edema and complain of a dull ache and sensitivity of the overlying skin. This swelling, sometimes referred to as *lipedema*, never completely subsides with elevation or diuretics. Furthermore, it is symmetric, with a noticeable sparing of the feet.

Finally, swelling, which always feels greater to the patient than it appears to the examiner, may represent a form of dysesthesia. If patients with swelling also complain of superficial burning discomfort and show signs of autonomic imbalance, a minor form of causalgia or reflex sympathetic dystrophy should be suspected.

The Ulcerated Leg

The third most common problem for which the vascular specialist is likely to be consulted is leg ulcers. There are only three types of chronic ulcers commonly encountered in the lower extremities: (1) ischemic, (2) neurotrophic, and (3) stasis. These forms of ulceration are readily distinguished from one another, as summarized in Table 1-3.

Ischemic ulcers are usually quite painful, and there is likely to be typical ischemic rest pain in the distal forefoot that occurs nocturnally and is relieved by dependency. At first, these ulcers may have irregular edges, but when chronic, they are more likely to be "punched out." They are commonly located distally over the dorsum of the foot or toes but may occasionally be pretibial. The ulcer base usually consists of poorly developed, grayish granulation

Table 1-3 Differential Diagnosis of Common Leg Ulcers

TYPE	USUAL LOCATION	PAIN	BLEEDING WITH MANIPULATION	LESION CHARACTERISTICS	SURROUNDING INFLAMMATION	ASSOCIATED FINDINGS
Ischemic	Distal, on dorsum of foot or toes	Severe, particularly at night; relieved by dependency	Little or none	Irregular edge; poor granulation tissue	Absent	Trophic changes of chronic ischemia; absence of pulses
Stasis	Lower third of leg (gaiter area)	Mild; relieved by elevation	Venous ooze	Shallow, irregular shape; granulating base; rounded edges	Present	Lipodermatofibrosis, pigmentation
Neurotrophic	Under calluses or pressure points (e.g., plantar aspect of first or fifth metatarsophalangeal joint)	None	May be brisk	Punched-out, with deep sinus	Present	Demonstrable neuropathy

tissue. The surrounding skin may be pale or mottled, and the previously described signs of chronic ischemia are invariably present. Notably, the usual signs of inflammation one would expect surrounding such a skin lesion are absent, for it is the lack of enough circulation to provide the necessary inflammatory response for healing that underlies ischemic ulcers. For the same reason, probing or débriding the ulcer causes little bleeding.

Neurotrophic ulcers, however, are completely painless but bleed with manipulation. They are deep and indolent and are often surrounded not only by acute but also by chronic inflammatory reaction and callus. Their location is typically over pressure points or calluses (e.g., the plantar surface of the first or fifth metatarsophalangeal joint, the base of the distal phalanx of the great toe, the dorsum of the interphalangeal joints of toes with flexion contractures, or the callused posterior rim of the heel pad). The patient usually has long-standing diabetes with a neuropathy characterized by patchy hypesthesia and diminution of positional sense, two-point discrimination, and vibratory perception.

The so-called *venous stasis ulcer*, actually due to venous hypertension, is located within the gaiter area (see Fig. 1-3), most commonly near the medial malleolus. It is usually larger than the other types of ulcers and irregular in outline, but also shallower and with a moist granulating base. The ulcer is almost invariably surrounded by a zone containing some of the hallmarks of chronic venous insufficiency—pigmentation and inflammation ("stasis dermatitis"), lipodermatofibrosis, and cutaneous atrophy, as already described.

More than 95% of all chronic leg or foot ulcers fit into one of these three recognizable types. The remainder are difficult to distinguish, except that they are not typical of the other three types. Leg ulcers may also be produced by (1) vasculitis, (2) hypertension, and (3) syphilis. Vasculitis often produces multiple punched-out holes and an inflamed indurated base that, on biopsy, suggests fat necrosis or chronic "panniculitis." Hypertensive ulcers represent focal infarcts and are very painful. They may be located around the malleoli, particularly laterally. Syphilitic ulcers are uncommon today, but in any atypical ulcer, syphilis and other systemic causes of ulceration, such as tuberculosis and chronic ulcerative colitis with pyoderma gangrenosum, should be suspected. Long-standing ulcers that are refractory to treatment may represent underlying osteomyelitis or a secondary malignant lesion.

Finally, most patients with ulcers of one of the specific types just described name trauma as the initiating agent. Occasionally, trauma may actually be the primary causative factor, with the chronicity of the ulcer being related (1) to self-inflicted trauma (i.e., may be factitious); (2) more simply, to the slow healing that is characteristic of the lower third of the leg; or (3) a possibility to be kept in mind, to a degree of arterial insufficiency that would otherwise be subclinical. Uncomplicated traumatic ulcers often heal with nonspecific therapy or with the treatment for venous ulcers, with intermittent elevation and application of a compression bandage such as an Unna boot.

■ SUMMARY

Good vascular consultation is exemplified by the problem-oriented approach to the painful, swollen, or ulcerated leg; by careful interrogation; and by thoughtful examination—all guided by experience and an appropriate index of suspicion. Having completed the initial assessment at the bedside or in the office, the vascular surgeon must next consider the need to proceed further diagnostically, either for the sake of diagnosis itself or to provide further objective information on which to base therapeutic decisions. Whether or not the basic diagnosis is obvious, the location and extent of the vascular disease and the degree of circulatory impairment can often be objectively documented by noninvasive diagnostic methods, such as discussed in Chapter 2, and with the methods described in Section III.

"Angiographic confirmation" is usually obtained *only* if needed for major therapeutic decisions, including the relative feasibility of reconstructive vascular surgery or transluminal balloon angioplasty. The choice between interventional therapy and noninterventional (conservative) treatment (pursued further in Chapter 2) often can and should be made *before* angiographic studies are initiated, and the habitual use of angiography, more common among those less experienced in vascular disease, should be resisted (see Fig. 1-1). The same applies to some of the more expensive imaging techniques, even though their noninvasive nature makes them less objectionable. Simpler noninvasive tests are capable of confirming peripheral arterial occlusive disease and its degree of severity (see Chapter 14).

■ REFERENCE

1. Cronenwett JL, Rutherford RB (eds): Decision Making in Vascular Surgery. Philadelphia, WB Saunders, 2001.

Chapter 2

Selection of Patients for Vascular Interventions

ROBERT B. RUTHERFORD, MD
MARK R. NEHLER, MD

Section I

■ KEY CONSIDERATIONS IN SELECTION OF PATIENTS

The proper selection of patients for interventional treatment, whether it be endovascular or open surgery, is the cornerstone of clinical judgment, equal in importance to technical skill. This is especially true in vascular surgery, in which a significant number of procedures are performed for asymptomatic conditions. The process can be viewed as a risk-benefit analysis that must always be settled in the patient's favor. The key considerations are outlined in Figure 2-1.

One must weigh carefully both the degree of disability and the natural course of the patient's underlying vascular disorder with *optimal medical management* against the risk and projected benefits of the interventions under consideration. However, optimal medical management in the vascular population is problematic. The majority of operative conditions, aortic aneurysms and critical limb ischemia, for example, do not have reasonable nonoperative alternative therapies. The benefits of the various interventional options should be considered in terms of both degree and duration; these will vary from patient to patient for the *same* procedure, but one can estimate them by considering specific variables, such as the morphology of the lesion itself, disease in adjacent vessels or runoff, clinical class, choice of graft, and other factors known to affect outcome and the risk of early or late failure. The risk of any intervention also clearly varies with the patient. Age, gender, co-morbidities, longevity, and, more recently, quality of life and function must be considered as well as the intrinsic risk of the procedure to be performed. Finally, patients and their families commonly come to the vascular specialist with a preconditioned attitude about their treatment. For example, they may have a fear of rupture of an aneurysm regardless of size, may be adamant about undergoing endovascular therapy regardless of the lesion, or may refuse to undergo necessary procedures, such as amputation. Therefore, this decision process must be *individualized,* and predicted outcomes—in terms of such end points as mortality and major morbidity, initial and late patency, and functional improvement—must all be adjusted to apply to a given procedure being performed on a particular patient by a particular surgeon or other interventionist. And patient preferences, once adequately informed, must be taken into account.

Typically, this process begins, as depicted in Figure 2-2, a more elaborate version of Figure 1-1 (also using surgical intervention for peripheral *arterial* occlusive disease as the example), with the initial patient interview and examination, complemented by noninvasive testing when appropriate. This practice often establishes the nature and severity of the vascular problem and determines whether the patient is likely to be a candidate for intervention. Further studies, such as pulmonary function tests, creatinine clearance measurement, and cardiac stress testing, may be required to evaluate risk; *only* after these studies are completed and one is still willing to seriously consider an intervention is an angiogram or some other advanced imaging study (e.g., magnetic resonance angiography, mapping with duplex scanning [duplex ultrasonography]) obtained, to assess the morphologic and anatomic characteristics of the involved vascular segment and, therefore, determine the most appropriate procedure and its technical feasibility. Obtaining an arteriogram at the *end* of the evaluation is like buying a road map—one doesn't need it unless one is going to make the trip! However, the development of percutaneous endovascular approaches to deal with many forms of vascular disease has led to some modification of this traditional approach. In addition, with widespread access to vascular imaging, many patients present to the vascular surgeon with results of detailed anatomic studies already performed elsewhere. Unfortunately, the selection of imaging studies by nonvascular specialists frequently leads to unnecessary use of health-care resources.

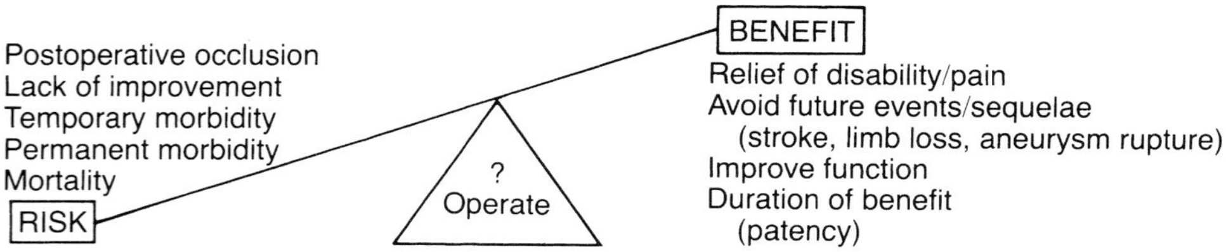

FIGURE 2-1 The risk-benefit analysis that underlies the decision to operate requires accurate assessment of the risks of mortality and morbidity for a given operation, the frequency and consequences of technical and hemodynamic failure (longevity, patency rate), and the likelihood of serious events or sequelae associated with the (medically treated) natural history of the condition.

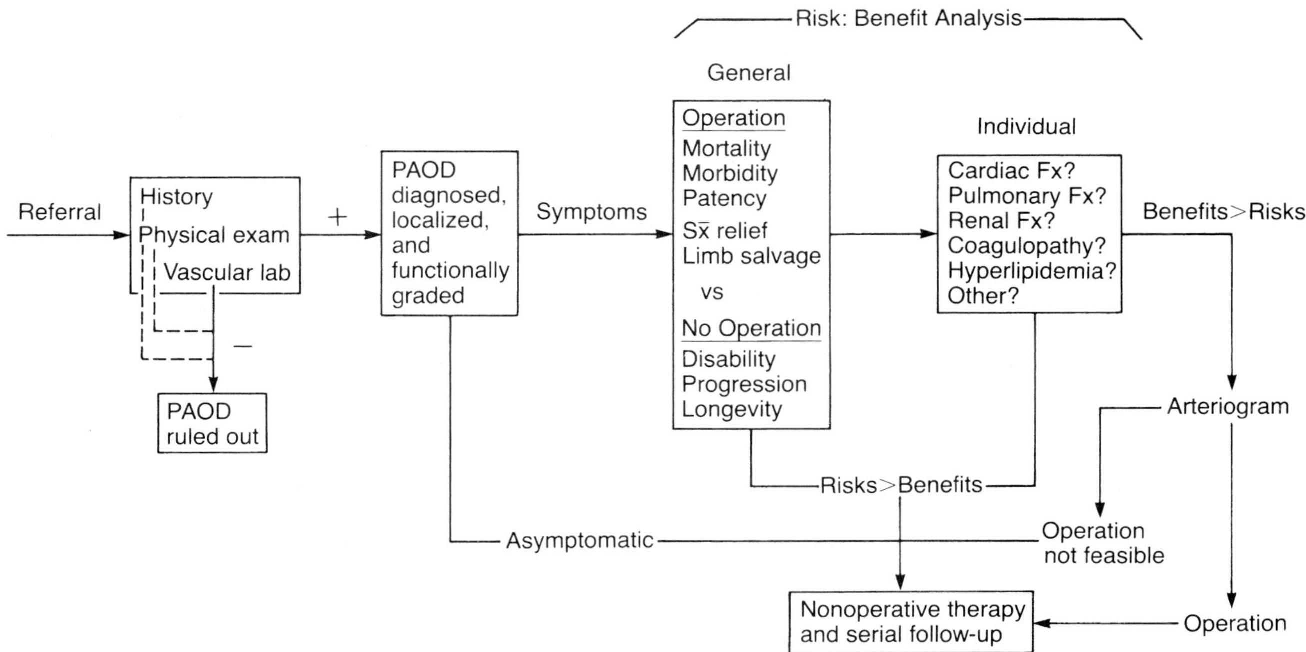

FIGURE 2-2 Stepwise approach to the decision to operate, beginning with initial consultation or outpatient visit and ending, after complete evaluation has confirmed the patient to be a surgical candidate with a reasonable operative risk, with arteriography. Fx, fracture; PAOD, peripheral arterial occlusive disease; Sx, symptom(s).

Historically, angiography has been instrumental in helping one choose among basic treatment options; however, there are certain situations in which, after initial evaluation, one would not recommend an open surgical revascularization but still might recommend balloon angioplasty, with or without stenting, as appropriate, if a discrete lesion favorable for the latter treatment were found during arteriography. Examples of such situations are (1) a significantly disabled claudicant in whom noninvasive imaging suggests inflow disease that is likely to be amenable to angioplasty (e.g., a discrete common iliac stenosis) and patient factors make an open aortic revascularization unwise; and (2) a claudicant with unilateral or bilateral femoropopliteal occlusive lesions, in whom duplex scanning can be used to distinguish between short stenoses and long occlusive lesions. The latter finding may eliminate the need for arteriography because a bypass (particularly bilateral) is not likely to be considered, percutaneous transluminal angioplasty (PTA) and stents would not have durable success, and extraluminal recanalization remains controversial. Conversely, with a short lesion, PTA might be worth considering but would be competing primarily with conservative management (exercise training and possibly pharmacotherapy), not bypass surgery.

Finally, it is important that the preliminary evaluation and investigations be completed before arteriography is performed, because the decision to proceed with balloon angioplasty should be made at the time of arteriography, so that it can be performed during the same session. This practice is in the patient's best interest and reduces costs. Needless to say, it requires all persons involved in the decision to be present at the completion of the arteriogram unless they are willing to abrogate their roles. This approach is a far cry from a previous era, when one could recommend arteriography and review the findings some time later before making therapeutic recommendations.

The value of considering the factors previously mentioned can best be demonstrated by additional examples drawn primarily from cases of chronic arterial and venous insufficiency of the lower extremities.

Degree of Disability

Disability usually constitutes a relative (rather than a mandatory) indication for intervention, in that the degree of disability must be considered against the background of the patient's work and other normal activities. Claudication that arises after walking one block may not interfere significantly with the sedentary lives of many retired persons, but to one who has worked long and hard in anticipation of a retirement filled with golf, hiking, or travel, that same degree of claudication constitutes a serious restriction. Claudication usually interferes significantly with the lives of most working persons and is an accepted indication for intervention when associated risk factors are reasonable and exercise training has been tried. Persistent ischemic rest pain, the next stage of chronic limb ischemia, however, is an utterly disabling symptom that usually cannot be controlled even with strong analgesics or narcotics and usually does not respond to conservative measures. It is, therefore, a widely accepted indication for most patients even for an intervention that involves arterial reconstructive surgery.

Normal daily activities play as major a role in the choice of the appropriate treatment option for chronic venous insufficiency as for claudication. A homemaker, however busy, can usually arrange duties so that the involved leg can be elevated frequently; an automobile assembly line worker, scrub nurse, barber, or shopkeeper may not be able to follow a strict routine of leg elevation (e.g., for 10 minutes out of every 2 hours) in addition to wearing elastic support hose, which is acknowledged to control all but the most severe chronic venous insufficiency. Other jobs allow patients to use lunchtime and morning and afternoon "breaks" for this purpose. One must consider the patients' daily activities and the flexibility allowed by their work before advising such persons to seek other, less suitable employment or recommending one of the procedures designed to combat venous valvular insufficiency or obstruction (see Chapters 155 and 157 to 161).

Similarly, one may be willing to intervene promptly for most patients with primary subclavian-axillary vein thrombosis, for the majority of patients suffered this event because of repetitive use of the involved arm and they will often be significantly disabled because of the ongoing need to use it actively. This is particularly true in high-performance athletes with this condition. In contrast, typically chronically ill and debilitated patients with subclavian-axillary vein thrombosis secondary to indwelling catheters experience little long-term disability, and unless there is a desperate need for angioaccess, they can be treated conservatively (see Chapters 96 and 161).

Clinicians commonly overlook some disabilities. Considerable discussion of the impact of claudication from aortoiliac occlusive disease on a man's work or recreation may take place without the subject of impotence even being broached. Similarly, internists often focus solely on the ability of their drug therapy to control blood pressure in renovascular hypertension without considering the debilitating side effects of multidrug therapy (malaise, asthenia, depression, impotence, cumulative cost, and, in patients with side effects, eventual noncompliance), eschewing both renal PTA and bypass.

Natural Course of Disease

A further dimension in patient selection is the natural course of the underlying condition. The importance of knowing this is exemplified by atherosclerotic occlusive disease involving the lower extremities. Peabody and associates,[5] in the Framingham study, reported that patients with intermittent claudication had little more than a 5% risk of major amputation for gangrene within 5 years of the onset of this symptom if treated expectantly, whereas within the same time frame, 23% had symptoms of coronary insufficiency, 13% suffered cerebrovascular accidents, and 20% died.

From similar experiences, it has been predicted that close to one third of patients undergoing surgery for advanced arteriosclerosis obliterans involving the lower extremity will die of heart disease, stroke, or other consequences of atherosclerosis (ruptured aneurysm, mesenteric ischemia) within 5 years. Even though better medical management and, in some quarters, more aggressive surgical treatment of coronary and carotid occlusive disease may invalidate these statistics to some extent in the future, the severity of atherosclerosis in the coronary and other circulations must still be seriously considered. However, once arteriosclerosis obliterans has progressed to the point of causing ischemic rest pain, ulcers, or gangrene, the likelihood of an eventual major amputation is great if arterial revascularization is not undertaken. Yet the absolute concept of claudication as a benign form to be treated conservatively and of chronic critical ischemia as an immediate threat to limb viability that demands arterial revascularization has been challenged. The ultimate risk of limb loss in the claudicant varies directly with the severity of the occlusive disease and can be stratified according to the level of reduction of the ankle-brachial index (ABI). It is simplistic to say that the risk of limb loss for *all* claudicants is 1% per year on the basis of the Framingham[5] and other epidemiologic studies that used only clinical assessment. The rate of limb loss, *or the threat of it before successful intervention*, is closer to 5% per year, considering all studies in which there is objective hemodynamic confirmation of the diagnosis.[10]

In reviewing the literature, we found the risk of limb loss, or the need for intervention to prevent it, to be 3.7% per year in claudicants in reports based on clinical evaluation and 5.8% per year in patients in whom diagnosis was confirmed objectively by noninvasive diagnostic tests. Furthermore, there was a much higher risk of limb loss, or need for intervention to prevent it (8.5% per year), for claudicants with ABIs in the range between the value associated with rest pain and that associated with the healing of ischemic lesions (0.40 and 0.60, respectively). This has led to the concept of "chronic *subcritical* ischemia."[11] Often, sedentary patients with ABIs in the same range are asymptomatic, do not experience claudication, and do not have ischemic lesions until they are precipitated by some minor local trauma. On the other hand, Taylor and Porter[9] have pointed out that in the patient with chronic critical ischemia, one can succeed in preserving limb viability using general supportive measures alone in up to 25% to 40% of cases, a perspective gained from control groups in randomized prospective trials of prostanoids and other nonoperative forms of therapy.

Of course, the prognosis is not as benign for all claudicants, and not all patients with chronic critical ischemia are doomed to limb loss without successful reconstructive arterial surgery. Furthermore, the longevity outlook for patients with arteriosclerosis obliterans (dominated as it is by associated coronary disease) varies with the severity of the disease and also correlates with the ABI.[12-15] Thus, the temptation to be more aggressive in claudicants with a lower ABI must be tempered by the fact that their risk from coronary disease is relatively higher.

At the other extreme, aggressive attempts to salvage ischemic limbs with bypass surgery in patients in whom repeated previous attempts have failed, who have no adequate vein, or whose outflow arteries are compromised are usually unsuccessful. Such an approach is not preferable to amputation in patients with severe co-morbidities or limited ambulation potential.

The natural history of untreated deep venous thrombosis (DVT) of the lower extremity, as summarized in Table 2-1 from Bauer's classic study,[1] is one of growing frequency of

Table 2-1 Natural History of Untreated Deep Venous Thrombosis of the Lower Extremity

	YEARS AFTER PHLEBITIS		
	5	10	>10
Incidence of stasis dermatitis (%)	45	72	91
Incidence of ulceration (%)	20	52	79

Adapted from Bauer GA: A roentgenological and clinical study of the sequels of thrombosis. Acta Chir Scand Suppl 74:1, 1942.

stasis dermatitis and ulceration with the passage of time. Although later studies suggest that the frequency of these post-thrombotic sequelae is probably less,[4,7] all investigators recognize that large numbers of potentially productive members of Western society are significantly disabled by chronic venous insufficiency after DVT. The indications for operations designed to mitigate these stasis sequelae must not be considered as much in the light of this inevitability, however, as against the established efficacy of nonsurgical treatment, because it has been shown that stasis dermatitis and ulceration can be *completely* controlled in compliant patients with uncomplicated venous valvular insufficiency who follow a strict postphlebitic routine of intermittent leg elevation and use of proper elastic support. This fact underlies the point that one must consider not simply the natural history of the vascular condition in determining the indications for surgical intervention but, rather, the outlook for an affected patient with appropriate nonoperative therapy. The documented effectiveness of exercise therapy in the claudicant (see Chapter 77) and conservative therapy for chronic venous insufficiency (see Chapter 156) are two classic examples of this modified perspective.

The natural history of chronic arterial and venous insufficiency of the lower extremities tends to be a continuum, albeit subject to episodic exacerbations. In vascular surgery for other conditions, one may not uncommonly encounter patients with few or no symptoms, in whom the outlook for serious, even lethal, symptomatic progression is sufficient to warrant prophylactic intervention. Conditions for which the outlook is serious include abdominal aortic aneurysms larger than 5.5 cm in diameter, popliteal aneurysms, splenic aneurysms in women of childbearing age, post-stenotic subclavian aneurysms secondary to cervical rib compression, popliteal artery entrapment, "critical" stenosis of the carotid or mesenteric artery, traumatic arteriovenous fistulae involving central vessels, and large "floating tails" of thrombus after DVT. Because of the element of truth in the adage "It is difficult to make an asymptomatic patient better," the vascular surgeon must be certain of the projections of the threatening natural history of these and similar conditions and of the *relative* safety of the proposed intervention. The latter is particularly pertinent, in this era of endovascular procedures that may offer a significantly lower risk than open reconstructions.

Operative Risk and Success Rate

The risk of morbidity and death after vascular surgery must also be weighed. Even though patients with arteriosclerosis are generally at a higher than average risk for their age, they tolerate operations limited to the extremity, neck, or superficial layers of the trunk relatively well, and vascular procedures confined to these areas carry a relatively small risk if one discounts deaths due to ongoing underlying disease rather than due to new problems precipitated by operation. In patients with limb-threatening ischemia, this risk is no greater than that attending the major amputation that might be required if arterial reconstruction were not undertaken. In fact, statistics gathered from the major series of amputations for "arterial" gangrene suggest that the risk associated with major amputation is greater than that associated with peripheral arterial reconstruction.[2,3] The reason is multifactorial: Patients undergoing amputation frequently have greater co-morbidities than patients undergoing lower extremity bypass. Amputations are commonly undertaken with junior-level anesthesia and surgical staff, house staff, or both. Perioperative monitoring and care are frequently less intensive in patients undergoing major amputation. Thus, although these risks are not truly comparable because the patient populations are not comparable, the risks associated with major amputation should not be taken lightly; they are sufficiently significant that peripheral arterial reconstruction should not be abandoned in favor of amputation simply because of a presumed lesser risk.

These same patients, however, would be exposed to a considerably greater magnitude of surgical stress if arterial reconstruction were performed through the abdominal cavity, as in the case of aortoiliac reconstruction. Even so, mortality rates for those undergoing infrainguinal bypass are *not* significantly less than for those undergoing aortic reconstructions. This is because the former population, often heavily "loaded" with diabetic patients, has proportionately much more visceral atherosclerosis (e.g., coronary, carotid, renal artery involvement). Most patients with chronic limb-threatening ischemia have multilevel occlusive disease, and typically in this situation, one would expect to find superficial femoral artery occlusion in addition to the proximal aortoiliac disease. Parallel experience has also taught us that proximal bypass, performed with a concomitant profundaplasty (thus introducing a full head of systemic arterial pressure into the parallel profunda geniculate collateral bed), obviates the need to deal with the superficial femoral artery occlusion in most cases (i.e., 85% to 90%). Although this greatly reduces the time and extent of the operation required, it does not reduce the major risk that is associated with the transabdominal reconstruction.

Fortunately, this dilemma has been relieved somewhat by the option now provided by the so-called extra-anatomic bypass procedure—the femorofemoral or axillofemoral bypass. Because of these and other "low-risk" alternatives, such as femoral profundaplasty, it is rare today for the vascular surgeon to have to decline to treat a patient with limb-threatening ischemia due in large part to proximal arterial occlusive disease because of the risk of reconstructive arterial surgery itself. However, the patency rates of these low-risk alternatives, such as extra-anatomic bypass, do not compare favorably with those for the direct reconstructive procedures and thus are rarely offered to patients who have "good" surgical risk or experience claudication. Furthermore, these low-risk alternatives often carry paradoxically higher mortality rates than aortoiliac reconstructions in reported comparisons (see Chapter 80). The reason is that these procedures are often reserved for patients with prohibitive surgical risk; when such patients are removed from the ranks of those undergoing direct aortoiliac reconstruction, the mortality statistics improve reciprocally—similar to what is observed in the comparison of perioperative mortality of lower extremity bypass with major amputation (see Chapters 79 and 80).

When one predicts the risk and success of a vascular operation, the common practice of quoting the "bottom line" results of some major reported series may be misleading, for several reasons. First, in general, the surgical literature is biased toward reporting good results. Second, the surgeon in question may be less experienced than the authors of reported surgical series, because most surgical literature comes from a minority of university based or affiliated institutions with large volumes and training programs. Frequently, statewide Medicare surveys do not reproduce the excellent vascular results reported in single series and randomized trials with selected participants.

Third, the particular patient to whom this yardstick is being applied is not likely to exactly fit the profile for the average risk of a particular series. The patient's risk with the same operation depends on the coexistence of other significant systemic disorders, such as hypertension, diabetes, and chronic obstructive pulmonary disease, as well as the extent of arteriosclerotic involvement of the coronary and cerebral arteries. The estimation of operative risk clearly must be individualized.

Fourth, the patient is just as unlikely to have the same severity of occlusive disease reflected in the overall data from reported series. These data reflect a mixture of cases with good runoff and poor runoff; the patient in question is likely to have one or the other. For example, in one report, the overall 5-year patency rate for axillobifemoral bypass performed for occlusive disease was 47%, but for patients with an open superficial femoral artery, this rate was 92%, and for those with poor runoff, 41%.[6]

Finally, it is not uncommon for large series to extend back over a decade or more and, therefore, to fail to accurately reflect more recent technical advances or the subtle but cumulative benefits of experience.

In the 1960s, in what has been referred to as "the golden age of vascular surgery," surgeons were obliged to inform patients of a 5% risk of loss of life and a 10% risk of loss of limb for arterial reconstructive procedures on the lower extremity. Furthermore, in an additional 10% of cases, the procedure would fail either to relieve the patient's symptoms or to salvage the limb. The overall initial success rate (survival without major morbidity and a patent arterial reconstruction with symptomatic relief) was then 75%. Today, these risks have been greatly reduced, and the initial success rate, even with all three adverse risks, is closer to 95%.

Although series that include data from the 1960s and 1970s may not reflect it, most major vascular surgery services can now point to operative mortality rates for *elective* aortic aneurysmectomy, aortobifemoral bypass, femoropopliteal bypass, and carotid endarterectomy—four of the most commonly performed vascular operations—in the range of 1% to 3%. These figures reflect (1) the development of methods of avoiding recognized complications, (2) more sophisticated monitoring techniques for directing intravenous fluid and drug therapy during the perioperative period, and (3) more careful patient selection (e.g., not operating for acute stroke and using extra-anatomic bypass rather than direct aortoiliac reconstruction in high-risk patients). For carotid endarterectomy to be considered preferable to best medical therapy, the risks of mortality and permanent neurologic morbidity must now be less than 5% for symptomatic patients and less than 3% for asymptomatic patients with severe stenosis. Fortunately, most specialized centers now report an overall rate of mortality and permanent neurologic morbidity for carotid endarterectomy of less than 2%.

As mentioned earlier, distal arterial reconstructions, which do not invade a major body cavity or cause much blood loss (e.g., femoropopliteal and femorotibial bypasses), and the "low-risk" alternatives, extra-anatomic bypasses and profundaplasty, actually carry a somewhat higher risk of loss of life *or* limb, in the range of 2% to 5% and 3% to 7%, respectively. This is because the former procedures are performed in patients with more distally distributed atherosclerosis, which in turn is associated with a significantly higher incidence of visceral (coronary and carotid) involvement, and the latter two procedures are offered *only* to poor-risk patients. Furthermore, both are generally reserved for limb salvage situations, in which multisegmental disease and poor runoff are invariably present.

The 25% to 50% 5-year failure rate commonly cited in the past for arterial prosthetic bypass partly reflected a significant incidence of anastomotic aneurysm and occlusion by sloughing pseudointima or intimal hyperplasia. The abandonment of silk sutures and tightly woven Dacron grafts in favor of polypropylene sutures and knitted velour and polytetrafluoroethylene (PTFE) grafts, respectively, and the avoidance of prosthetic grafts in peripheral, small-caliber (<6 mm in diameter) reconstructions in which flexion creases are crossed, runoff is poor, and resting flow rates are slow have contributed to improved results, as have the selective use of antithrombotic drugs and employment of serial graft surveillance protocols. There is no doubt, in the small-caliber, low-flow graft, that saphenous vein grafts (be they in situ, reversed, or translocated in an antegrade orientation after their valves are rendered incompetent) are distinctly superior to any current prosthetic. The rate of failure to use or successfully "harvest" a saphenous vein graft for femoropopliteal bypass used to be reported as between 20% and 40%. Now, with duplex scanning evaluation of prospective veins and the additional use of lesser saphenous or arm veins, this figure is closer to 5% to 10% for primary infrageniculate bypass (see Chapters 47 and 81). Similarly, the frequency of late occlusion of these vein grafts—because of stricture, proliferative or degenerative changes, atheromatous degeneration, intimal fibrosis, or paravalvular stenosis—once noted to be as high as 28%,[8] has decreased now that the causes of damage to the vein during its preparation have been recognized and can be avoided.

Finally, technical developments have allowed in situ bypass to be fully utilized in femorodistal bypass. The suitability of the saphenous vein can be established preoperatively by duplex scanning, and because smaller veins can be used and the aforementioned structural changes are rarer, rates of both vein utilization and patency have been significantly improved. The better results with distal bypass using in situ or reversed saphenous veins, augmented by postoperative surveillance programs (with assisted primary patency rates now approaching those achieved with proximal bypass), are in sharp contrast with those achieved with prosthetic or modified biologic grafts when carried below the knee (<40% for below-knee and <20% for tibial-peroneal [crural] bypass at 5 years). The lack of a small-caliber prosthesis or modified biologic graft that can maintain reasonable patency rates, when anastomosed to the low-flow, high-resistance arteries of the leg, remains the greatest single barrier to successful limb salvage surgery.

The *overall* results in this field do not completely reflect the significant advances that have been made, mainly because more difficult cases (which would have called for primary amputation in the past) are now treated with bypass and because of the inability of most patients who smoke to refrain from tobacco abuse. Nevertheless, the reconstructive procedures, graft choices, and patency rates have changed significantly since the late 1970s. In recommending appropriate therapy, practicing vascular surgeons need to be as aware of this changing outlook as they are of the technical advances that brought it. Similarly, they must be familiar with changes in other modes of therapy, particularly PTA (PTA here being the generic term for balloon angioplasty with or without stenting). The low risk and cost of this procedure compensate for its lesser degree and duration of benefit to make it the initial treatment of choice for discrete stenoses, particularly in the larger, proximal arteries. Now used in anywhere from 25% to 40% of patients requiring intervention, PTA tends to be used more in claudicants with isolated disease and good runoff, whereas bypass surgery still dominates in limb salvage settings. Therefore, PTA is not as much in direct competition with arterial reconstructive surgery as one might think, and in many situations it is complementary and adjunctive (see Chapter 84).

Clearly, it is not possible to predict outcome from past experience; neither should one project outcome on the basis of overall results from others' series. Rather, such reports should serve as a frame of reference on which to project one's own results, for all vascular surgeons should regularly analyze their own experiences (see Chapter 4). Furthermore, adjustment should be made not only for the operation and the operator but also for individual considerations, such as associated risk factors, runoff, and types of graft.

■ DIAGNOSTIC STUDIES

Assessment of Operative Risk

In this chapter, the preoperative evaluation of patients for vascular surgery, including angiography, is deliberately dealt with *after* the discussion of case selection to emphasize the sequence of events and priorities that should be observed in clinical practice. This tentative decision is upheld in most cases, although occasionally, the unexpected discovery of associated disease or discouraging angiographic findings reverses the judgment. Clearly, more is required before surgery than a pertinent history and a physical examination relative to the vascular problem.

The assessment of operative risk is discussed in greater detail in Section X (see Chapters 56 to 58); only the choice of diagnostic studies required to determine operative risk is considered here. Ordinarily, cardiopulmonary and renal functions are carefully evaluated. A complete blood count (CBC), urinalysis, blood urea nitrogen (BUN), creatinine level and blood glucose determinations, electrocardiogram (ECG), and chest x-ray films are almost routinely ordered. (Special studies for each condition are discussed in detail in the chapters dealing with the individual conditions.) Obviously, if the patient's problem is arteriosclerosis, serum cholesterol and triglyceride levels should be determined and serum lipoprotein electrophoresis should be performed; if the disorder is thromboembolic, a coagulation profile should be obtained. Any intercurrent disease should be investigated on its own merits. More extensive preoperative evaluations may be ordered along the lines indicated by history, physical examination, or the results of the previously mentioned routine tests. In patients with known pulmonary problems, abnormal chest x-ray findings, or abnormal blood gas values determined with the patient breathing "room air," formal pulmonary function studies are ordered. In patients with an elevated BUN or creatinine level, hydration and renal protective agents may be given prior to angiography with limited contrast agent, or less toxic agents can be used. In patients with ECG abnormalities, cardiac symptoms, or evidence of such widespread arteriosclerosis that the coronary artery may be involved, radionuclide scanning, Holter monitoring, or both—and, in selected cases, cardiac catheterization and coronary angiography—may be performed to evaluate cardiac perfusion and function.

Noninvasive Studies

Special diagnostic procedures are discussed in detail in the later sections of this book, but the value of selectively employing objective, noninvasive methods of preoperative and postoperative monitoring is worthy of emphasis here. These studies (1) help the surgeon avoid misdiagnoses and to gauge the extent and severity of the vascular disease before angiography; (2) enable one to determine the hemodynamic significance of the lesions visualized by angiography and/or pursue additional images (oblique projections) of areas of interest; and (3) allow angiography to be employed more selectively, potentially limiting the amount of contrast medium used. When the physiologic data and angiographic anatomy are considered together, the surgeon not only can better choose the most appropriate operation but also can better predict the hemodynamic outcome.

Since the superimposition of color-coded velocity information, duplex scanning has been increasingly used to supply anatomic as well as flow information in carotid, venous, and peripheral arterial disease. In most cases, this modality is used selectively to augment the indirect physiologic tests, but in many if not most instances, it can provide all the information necessary for planning arterial surgery (see Chapter 16).

Computed tomography (CT) and magnetic resonance imaging (MRI) are also being used with increasing frequency to evaluate carotid disease, aortic aneurysms, and congenital vascular disease. Now, in many settings, one or more noninvasive physiologic tests or imaging modalities can characterize the lesions so well that preoperative arteriography may be obviated. This situation will become more common as newer, improved forms of vascular imaging become more widely available (see Chapters 14 to 17 and 20 to 22 for details). Additionally, CT and MRI provide readily available means of objectively assessing the initial and continued success of the procedure itself. Noninvasive monitoring of the results of vascular interventions has become an accepted part of overall management.

Furthermore, because newer noninvasive modalities can detect and localize lower extremity occlusive lesions, either singly or in combination, with greater than 95% accuracy, unnecessary "diagnostic" arteriography is eliminated; for all intents and purposes, this latter study is not obtained until the decision has already been made that the patient needs a revascularization procedure and precise anatomic information not supplied by less invasive imaging methods is required before one can determine which is the most appropriate method. The availability of endovascular interventions has caused this position to be modified somewhat, because arteriography is a prelude to these procedures and monitors their technical and anatomic success.

Angiographic Studies

Equally pertinent to this introductory chapter is a discussion of the strategic use of angiography. Arteriographic and phlebographic studies in selected patients provide invaluable information regarding the location and extent of the disease, and occasionally this anatomic information is supplemented by qualitative impressions regarding the rate of blood flow. Now, however, it is often possible to confirm the nature and location of the vascular lesion with reasonable certainty by physical examination, supplemented by some of the newer noninvasive diagnostic methods so that angiography is selectively rather than routinely employed.

Arteriography

Generally, the vascular surgeon obtains an arteriogram to study the condition of the vessels proximal and distal to the lesion rather than the lesion itself. For example, when confronted with superficial femoral artery occlusion, the vascular surgeon wants to ensure that there is no occult iliac artery stenosis proximally, that the profunda femoris artery is widely patent and providing maximal collateral flow, and that the condition of the popliteal and infrapopliteal arteries into which a graft may be placed is suitable. Similarly, if an abdominal aortic aneurysm is large enough to be easily felt or if its calcific outline on a cross-table lateral film or ultrasonography indicates that it is 5 to 6 cm in diameter, there is little reason for aortography before open surgical repair unless significant proximal (e.g., renal or mesenteric artery) or distal (e.g., iliac or femoral artery) occlusive disease is suspected. In fact, because more abdominal aortic aneurysms are lined by intraluminal clot, their internal diameters often appear misleadingly normal on aortograms. Enhanced CT scanning was traditionally the best overall preoperative imaging modality because it reveals most of the associated disease or anomalies that can complicate repair (e.g., inflammatory aneurysms, horseshoe or ectopic kidney, vena caval or renal vein anomalies). Ultrasonography is still the most practical method of screening and monitoring for enlargement. However, the preceding position regarding the relative use of CT scans and aortography in evaluating abdominal aortic aneurysm (AAA) has been greatly modified by the advent of endoluminal-endograft AAA repair (EVAR), for which thin-slice CT scans (often with three-dimensional [3-D] reconstruction) are needed just to screen patients with suitable anatomy for this technique, and aortography via a calibration catheter is usually obtained prior to deployment. Because patients with significant co-morbidities are more likely to undergo EVAR, the majority of patients with AAAs are now undergoing full imaging before surgical treatment.

Now that segmental limb pressures and plethysmographic studies are readily obtainable, arteriograms are ordered not for diagnostic curiosity but for therapeutic intent. Good-quality, multiplanar-view arteriograms are valuable in the detailed evaluation of multisegmental disease. Particularly important in this regard are oblique views of the iliac and proximal profunda femoris arteries and adequate distal visualization of "runoff" vessels.

However if one needs only to establish the most appropriate inflow and outflow vessel for an infrainguinal bypass, color duplex scanning of the arterial tree usually suffices (see Chapter 16). By the same token, when one is treating carotid occlusive or ulcerative lesions, duplex scanning is an adequate preoperative imaging method, and arteriography is obtained only in cases for which duplex scanning is unable to provide the needed information—demonstration of disease in the arch vessels, the ipsilateral upper carotid or siphon, the vertebral arteries, or the intracranial vessels (see Chapters 136 and 137). Finally, in the evaluation of congenital vascular malformations, arteriography and venography are now obtained as only a "prequel" to arterial embolization or, in rare cases, surgical excision, because clinical decisions can almost always be made on the basis of noninvasive tests, primarily duplex scanning or MR angiography (MRA) (see Chapter 110).

Phlebography

Phlebography still suffers from indiscriminate use. It was commonly used during the early 1980s and before to detect DVT, to rule out deep venous insufficiency in candidates for varicose vein stripping, and to localize incompetent perforator vessels in patients with more advanced disease. These evaluations can nearly always be accomplished with duplex scanning, supplemented if needed by physiologic plethysmographic studies (see Chapters 15 and 17).

■ SUMMARY

It is only after confirming the existence, nature, and extent of a vascular lesion, and balancing the disability it causes, or is likely to cause despite proper nonoperative management, against the feasibility, risk, and anticipated success of alternative surgical, endovascular, and nonsurgical forms of therapy, that the vascular surgeon is in a position to advise the patient or the referring physician regarding the need for surgical intervention. The manner in which this evaluation is carried out and the judgment that is applied to this stepwise process are the foundation of a successful practice in vascular surgery.

REFERENCES

1. Bauer GA: A roentgenological and clinical study of the sequels of thrombosis. Acta Chir Scand Suppl 74:1, 1942.
2. DeWeese JA, Blaisdell FW, Foster JH: Optimal resources for vascular surgery. Arch Surg 105:948, 1972.
3. Haeger K: Problems of acute deep venous thrombosis. I: The interpretation of signs and symptoms. Angiology 20:219, 1969.
4. Lindner DJ, Edwards JM, Phinney ES, et al: Long term hemodynamic and clinical sequelae of lower extremity deep vein thrombosis. J Vasc Surg 4:436, 1986.
5. Peabody CN, Kannel WB, McNamara PM: Intermittent claudication: Surgical significance. Arch Surg 109:693, 1974.
6. Rutherford RB, Patt A, Pearce WH: Extra-anatomic bypass: A closer view. J Vasc Surg 6:437, 1987.
7. Strandness DE, Langlois Y, Cramer M, et al: Long term sequelae of acute venous thrombosis. JAMA 250:1289, 1983.
8. Szilagyi DE, Elliot JP, Hageman JH, et al: Biologic fate of autogenous vein implants of arterial substitutes. Surgery 74:731, 1973.
9. Taylor LM Jr, Porter JM: Natural history of chronic lower extremity ischemia. Semin Vasc Surg 4:181, 1991.
10. McDaniel MM, Cronenwett JL: Natural history of claudication. In Porter JM, Taylor LM (eds): Basic Data Underlying Clinical Decision Making in Vascular Surgery. St. Louis, Quality Medical Publishing, 1994, pp 129-133.
11. Rutherford RB, Baker JD, Ernst C, et al: Recommended standards for reports dealing with lower extremity ischemia: Revised version. J Vasc Surg 26:517, 1997.
12. Vogt MT, Cauley JA, Newman AB, et al: Decreased ankle/arm blood pressure index and mortality in elderly women. JAMA 270:465, 1993.
13. McDermott MM, Feinglass J, Slavensky R, Pearce WH: The ankle-brachial index as a predictor of survival in patients with peripheral vascular disease. J Gen Intern Med 9:445, 1994.
14. O'Riordain DS, O'Donnell JA: Realistic expectations for the patient with intermittent claudication. Br J Surg 78:861, 1991.
15. Smith I, Franks PJ, Greenhalgh RM, et al: The influence of smoking cessation and hypertriglyceridaemia on the progression of peripheral arterial disease and the onset of critical ischaemia. Eur J Vasc Endovasc Surg 11:402, 1996.

Chapter 3

Essential Considerations in Evaluating the Results of Treatment

ROBERT B. RUTHERFORD, MD

Evaluating the results of treatment has become an increasingly important consideration for vascular surgeons. In the 5th edition of *Vascular Surgery*, this subject merited a large multi-authored chapter that encompassed patient-based outcomes assessment, standardized reporting practices, and computerized vascular registries. In this edition, each of these components is discussed in detail separately, in Chapters 4 through 6. This chapter focuses only on some basic considerations and pitfalls in the evaluation of the results of treatments, functioning as an overview to tie the three essential components together.

EVALUATING ONE'S OWN RESULTS

It seems axiomatic that vascular surgeons, wherever they practice, should gather, and retain in some readily accessible database, essential information on the procedures they perform and their results, and that this activity should be done in an organized manner that allows the information to be analyzed and summarized, as needed, on an ongoing basis. This is a considerable undertaking, but one that is essential and worth doing well. Fortunately, today's computers allow one to use computerized databases specially designed for this purpose.

The essential considerations in planning and creating a computerized vascular registry are thoroughly discussed in Chapter 4 and so are not reiterated here, but the reasons to commit fully to this practice are worth emphasizing. First, it is important to keep data that define the nature of one's practice in order to determine the characteristics of the patients seen over time, their referral sources, the clinical classification of their vascular disease, the treatments employed, and how successful they were. Practices change with time, and gauging the changes periodically can be valuable in future planning, allowing one to improve one's practice by responding appropriately to recognized trends. Similarly, combining or comparing practices within a group of vascular surgeons in this manner can be extremely helpful.

Further, analyzing the experiences of a group, whether the group is clinic- or hospital-based, can be educational and quite revealing for the group itself. If some aspect of the group's experience is particular noteworthy, documenting it and reporting it to colleagues can be educational for others as well.

Accurate and well-categorized information about one's practice, or the group one practices with, serves as a "profile" for that practice. All of us will be required to develop practice "profiles" in the future, if it is not already being done for us. Many of the profiles developed by third parties may be inaccurate, if not misleading, and do not support valid judgments. The best answer to this problem is a well-kept, accurate practice database.

Linking disease codes and operative codes to the patient information in the database as well as integrating it with key financial data and dated data on hospital stays and outpatient visits can provide the basis for planning appropriate changes in the practice as well as for negotiating contracts with so-called health care providers.

Analyzing one's results *and* comparing them with the results of others can provide additional insights. Are the results superior, equivalent, or inferior to those generally being attained? Differences in outcome may require further investigation. The published literature *should* provide a yardstick against which individual vascular surgical practices and patient outcomes can be measured, and it *should* serve as a common forum for the comparison of the benefits of different therapeutic approaches. However, unless we use universally accepted standards in reporting our outcomes, be they related to pharmacologic, endovascular, or open surgical interventions, the yardstick may not be accurate and the forum (the literature) may not provide sufficient commonality to allow diverse clinical experiences and patient populations to be compared in a valid way. Fortunately, standardized reporting practices have been developed for our specialty over the past couple of decades to allow everyone's results to be reported in the same standardized fashion. These standardized reporting practices are discussed in detail in Chapter 6. Clearly, if one is to analyze one's results and compare them with those in the literature, the data must be entered so that the endpoints of analysis are comparable to those in the literature, that is, compatible with accepted standards. Thus, vascular registries should be set up to conform to these reporting practices and allow the analyzed data to support valid comparisons (see Chapter 4).

Finally, proper assessment of the effectiveness of vascular intervention not only requires evaluation of those markers of successful outcome now generally recognized by vascular surgeons (e.g., categorical clinical improvement, hemodynamic improvement, patency, and freedom from amputation, venous ulceration, stroke, aneurysm-related death and other accepted major adverse events) but also needs to include patient-based assessments of changes in functional status and quality of life. Traditional clinical parameters of success, such as graft patency and limb salvage, continue to be essential for proper evaluation of vascular surgical interventions, but documentation of the effect of the treatment on the patient's functional activity and quality of life deserves comparable interest. Vascular treatments may be performed that successfully reduce risk to life and limb and relieve symptoms yet may have little direct impact on the underlying pathologic process—such is the nature of atherosclerosis and thromboembolism. This drawback does not diminish their benefit, but traditional clinical measures of success and failure represent the physician's perspective and not necessarily the patient's. The benefit of an intervention to the patient lies, ultimately, in better function and an improved quality of life. The latter can, in turn, be related to subtle aspects not taken into account in clinical studies, such as the perceived removal of the threat of an adverse event (rupture of an abdominal aortic aneurysm [AAA]) or relief from surveillance for it (AAA enlargement), so the two are interrelated. Ordinarily, such patient-based outcomes are not essential information in most practice-based databases, but they should be considered in the data collected in a major clinical study of the efficacy of a certain treatment, a study that is intended for publication and to show patient benefit. Ultimately, third party payers, and certainly health care agencies, may be swayed more by quality of life data than by patency and limb salvage rates. These issues are discussed more fully in Chapter 5.

■ EVALUATING RESULTS REPORTED BY OTHERS: UNDERSTANDING THE LITERATURE

It is important for vascular surgeons to be able to evaluate the results published in their specialty's literature as well as the literature of other vascular specialists. Interventional radiologists have adopted many of vascular surgery's reporting standards and have developed some useful ones of their own, but the same cannot be said for other vascular specialists. Understandably, vascular internists or angiologists are unlikely to embrace outcomes that are keyed to patency rates, improvements in ankle-brachial index (ABI), or categorical improvements in clinical status, because many of their treatments can produce improvement without a categorical change in clinical status or an increase in the ABI. For that reason, at least in dealing with peripheral arterial occlusive disease (PAOD), and particularly patients with claudication, these specialists have used other functional measures of improvement, such as initial or absolute claudication distance (ICD, ACD) and improvements in ambulation documented by the WIQ (Walking Improvement Questionnaire). Furthermore, these clinically based results need to be augmented by patient-based outcomes, like quality of life studies. These, and other more comprehensive clinical and patient-based measures of outcome, along with accepted methods of assessing them, are discussed in Chapter 5. Awareness of these measures is essential to the evaluation of current and future literature. Nevertheless, vascular surgeons will naturally continue to focus on the traditional markers of success after vascular interventions, be they endovascular or open procedures, and these markers remain the major focus of this chapter.

The results of therapy for vascular diseases have little meaning if presented in isolation, *no matter how uniform and valid the criteria used for reporting them.* They are intended to be compared with something—the natural (untreated) history, best "medical" therapy, another competitive treatment, the same therapeutic approach carried out in a different manner, or the same treatment carried out by different vascular surgeons. In a comparison of treatment outcomes, it is not always clear whether reported differences are due to the method of treatment or to other intrinsic differences that may or may not be apparent, such as differences between the group of patients treated in regard to severity of disease or lesion, to the prevalence of risk factors (patient severity), or to other factors that could significantly affect outcome, such as differences in operator skill or adjunctive therapy. So the proper comparison of outcomes should go much further than simply comparing "bottom line" results.

Even with the aid of uniform reporting standards based on objective criteria, a number of potential causes of variance and confusion exist in our literature that makes its interpretation difficult at times. There are a number of possible explanations for observed differences in outcome when different surgical procedures or practices are compared, and they deserve consideration in dealing with the literature. Certainly the most obvious reason, and the most commonly offered conclusion, is that a particular procedure, or some other feature of the therapeutic approach being studied, is intrinsically superior. However, other factors may play a significant, if not the major, role in producing the reported differences. The solution to this dilemma lies in identifying these other factors and either avoiding them, when possible (as in a well-designed prospective randomized trial), or uniformly reporting them to allow their potential influence on the results being compared to be gauged objectively.

It is understandable why most practitioners tend to focus on, if not accept outright, the "bottom line" results of studies reported in the literature. With so much to be read, it is easier and more efficient to focus on the abstract, the introduction, and then the results and conclusions rather than reading the entire article. However, at this point, to incorporate the results of this report into his or her fund of knowledge, the reader would do well to ask "Are these results believable?" and "Are they generalizable, that is, are they applicable to my practice?" Equally important is the question "Are the reported results due to the factors to which the authors attribute them in their conclusions?" And the answers to those questions are best found through examination of the Materials and Methods section.

The major confounding factors can be categorized and are listed in Table 3-1 and discussed individually here, along with their potential impact. It will be noted that many of the examples selected to illustrate the effect of these various factors have been taken from the (older) literature on extra-anatomic bypass. The author's reasons for doing this is that the literature on this one controversial area contains excellent examples of many of the different confounding factors and it was this[1] (and the early literature on balloon angioplasty[2]) that first interested the author in the need to develop uniform standardized reporting practices.

Technical Differences

In comparing published outcomes, it is very difficult to determine whether superior surgical skill or judgment of the group of surgeons in one study contributed significantly to better results than those reported by another group. Nevertheless, difference in skill or judgment is a factor that cannot be dismissed. Success rates with procedures vary from institution to institution (and from surgeon to surgeon) to such a degree that the surgical skill of individual surgeons or groups of surgeons (as in the principal investigators in a particular trial) must be conceded to be an important factor, one that can significantly alter outcomes. Even in randomized trials, different specialists may be performing competing procedures (e.g., thrombolysis versus surgery for acute limb ischemia, carotid stenting versus endarterectomy). Their relative skills with the procedure may spell a difference.

The choice of participating centers in randomized clinical trials (RCTs) comparing two treatments may affect the outcome. Their selection in industry-sponsored trials should be scrutinized. Even when the same group, in a single-institution report, performs both procedures, difference in technical skill may create differences, but these differences are difficult to control and assess without inside knowledge. Therefore, in evaluating outcomes, one must consider the source of a reported experience and the experience of the operators with the reported procedure (e.g., their case load or volume over the period covered). Part of the controversy about the claimed superiority of in-situ versus reversed vein graft for femorodistal bypass probably revolves around significant differences in surgical skill, not only between groups practicing either technique but also between the initial and ultimately acquired skills of the same group.[3,4]

Finally, one must consider the learning curve in evaluating any new technique. A good example is the initial trials of endovascular abdominal aortic aneurysm repair (EVAR), for which the technical success rates (in percentage) have shifted from the high 80s to the high 90s. In some trials, there are "run-in periods" during which the skill of the participants in new techniques—such as carotid stenting with embolic protection devices in CREST (Carotid Reconstruction Endarterectomy versus Stenting Trial)—is assessed to ensure good technical results and eliminate the effect of the learning curve on outcomes. Other investigators have imposed strict performance criteria for admission to their trials and have set warning limits on the number of

Table 3-1 Factors Affecting Observed Differences in the Results of Vascular Interventions

Intrinsically superior approach	Technical differences Differences in surgical skill or judgment Differing use of adjunctive and adjuvant therapies Differences in monitoring Differences in study design Independent evaluation of outcome Statistical artifacts and abuses Simple misuse or abuse of statistical testing Artifacts of the life table
Differences in patient populations	Temporal differences When procedure performed Duration of follow-up Selection criteria Patient exclusions Prevalence of disease Severity of disease Lesion severity Extent of disease Associated risk factors including co-morbidities Indications for surgery
Differing criteria for success or failure	Symptomatic relief Technical success, confirmed by imaging study Hemodynamic success Functional improvement Patency (primary, assisted primary, secondary) Survival free of major adverse events Quality of life improvement Cost-effectiveness

adverse events that trigger re-evaluation of a particular participating center. The results of such trials, from carefully selected centers of excellence, may produce good outcomes, but the results may not be generalizable to wider clinical practice. The EVAR trials may or may not be found to exemplify this potentially confounding effect.

The EVAR trials also illustrate the effect of improving technology, as most of the dozen or so endografts have been modified at least once, and often only the results with the current commercially available device are reported, eliminating data for both the learning curve and the first-generation device. This is not to criticize the practice, because it may better reflect the device's true potential, but to note that this practice may be reflected in the results of some devices and not others, producing an unfair comparison. Whether the results of such trials are generalizable, that is, reproducible in the community, requires post-marketing studies, after the devices have been approved for use by the U.S. Food and Drug Administration (FDA), when strict trial inclusion/exclusion criteria are not adhered to. The impetus for these key studies must come from clinical investigators, not industry.

Differences in technical factors that are more easily documented include the use of adjunctive procedures and therapeutic adjuvants that might influence outcome. Examples are the routine use of profundaplasty in association with aortobifemoral bypass performed in the presence of superficial femoral artery occlusion and the routine use of antithrombotic drugs after femorodistal bypass to protect initial patency.[5] Intraoperative monitoring and surveillance programs, such as routine use of imaging studies to ensure technical success and periodic surveillance with duplex scanning (duplex ultrasonography), have been shown to affect rates of patency, if it is expressed as assisted primary patency. Such variations may reflect technologic advances more than philosophical differences in technique, making it important to consider the time span covered by each study, as discussed later.

Differences in Study Design

The primary focus in examining the study protocol in a report is to look for selection bias. Were the cases consecutive, or were they selected in some fashion? Are the selection criteria stated, and are they appropriate for producing a fair comparison? Is this a prospectively randomized comparison or a retrospective comparison of two procedures using a prospective database or registry? Randomized or not, are the groups being compared truly comparable in terms of the (anatomic and patient risk) factors that potentially affect outcomes? Is this demonstrated? Were the compared groups treated over the same period, or was one procedure performed in the first period and the second (new) performed after that? Are the factors that are claimed to affect outcome or to correlate with it properly identified through the use of multivariate and univariate analyses using the Cox hazard regression method? Are the outcome criteria followed over time reported as crude rates or reported using life-table or Kaplan-Meier estimates? These issues are discussed later.

An equally important question is "Who evaluated the outcome?" Ideally, the surgeon or operator who performs the procedure should not be the one to evaluate its outcome for published reports. Ideally, the evaluation should be performed by an independent evaluator using a standardized scheme; this practice was a major feature of the carotid endarterectomy (CEA) trials, in which neurologists did the evaluation. For years neurologists complained that they could not trust the exemplary CEA results reported from centers of excellence. Even though their suspicions about CEA were not borne out by the trials, the principle of independent assessment is correct. In the EVAR trials, core laboratories have been employed to assess the serial images obtained during follow-up. If an outcome can be judged in a blinded fashion, with the judges unaware of the identity of the case, the operator, or the procedure performed, it should be. Blinded evaluation of outcome is usually possible in comparison of diagnostic test accuracies. In industry-sponsored trials, typically device or drug trials, for which by necessity the data from multiple centers must be centrally gathered, company statisticians often analyze the data and produce summarized data analysis for the principal investigators to study. This arrangement represents a clear conflict of interest. Analysis and interpretation of the scientific data from clinical and experimental trials should be the responsibility of the principal investigators, not sponsor-paid personnel. The principal investigators should have access to the raw data and, at the very least, should conduct independent sample analysis—for example, analyzing their own center's data and possibly the data from one or more other centers, and comparing those results with what they have been given by company statisticians. They, not the company, should decide what is to be analyzed and what comparisons are clinically as well as statistically significant. Conflicts of interest are to be expected, and those of the principal investigators (authors) are now usually openly declared in the published report. The company sponsoring a trial has a conflict of interest in the study outcome that is not declared in the publication, however, even though company statisticians may have performed the data analyses. What data analyses were performed *and who performed them* should be clearly stated in the Materials and Methods section of the report. Some of the concerns alluded to in this discussion have been the subject of a number of editorials and position papers.[6-9]

Improper Data Analysis

It is likely that a substantial portion of the medical literature contains errors in the use of statistical methods. This portion has been estimated to range from 40% to 60% according to samples reviewed from American, British, and Canadian medical journals.[10] The more common abuses are multiple comparisons between population stratifications and the reliance on the *t*-test as a universal "test of significance." A critique of statistical techniques is beyond the scope of this chapter; an excellent detailed discussion of statistical methods can be found in *Basic Science of Vascular Disease* by Sidawy and colleagues.[11]

In the past, absolute rates of various outcome parameters (mortality, patency, recurrence, etc.) were stated, followed typically by the statement "—in n = X patients, followed for *up to* Y months/years (mean follow up = Z)." This approach typically overstates the length of follow-up.

Estimates of various outcomes, or freedom from a particular adverse outcome or event, are now more properly performed by Kaplan-Meier or life-table analysis. These methods, now accepted into our specialty's reporting standards (see Chapter 6) deserve elaboration here if the reader is to understand and use them. Although the life-table method was adopted as the method of choice for estimating patency rates in the original reporting standards,[12] the revised standards[13] also recognized the *Kaplan-Meier method*. Both methods require clear criteria for withdrawal and failure. The point of "lost to follow-up" or "dead with patent revascularization" occurs at *the last objective* evaluation.

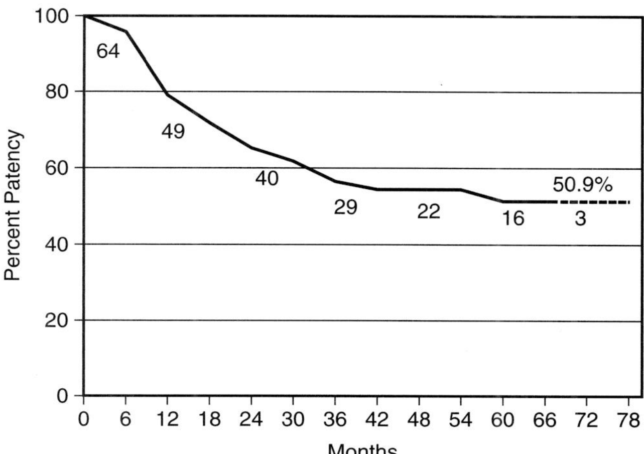

FIGURE 3-1 Patency curve by life-table method. (From Rutherford RB, Baker JD, Ernst C, et al: Recommended standards for reports dealing with lower extremity ischemia: Revised version. J Vasc Surg 26:517, 1997.)

The Life-Table Method

Historically, the methods of the life-table analysis were described in the 1950s[14,15] but gained a wider appreciation in the medical community when they were described by Peto and associates[16,17] in 1976 to 1977 as a means of measuring survival of patients with cancer and the effect of therapeutic intervention on that survival. The life-table analysis method has subsequently been adopted by vascular surgeons, among others, to measure other outcome criteria, especially patency. The life-table method has two characteristic features worth noting. The first is that events on the survival curve (e.g., graft failures) are grouped into intervals. Survival rates are then calculated for each of these intervals and used to generate cumulative patencies that describe the survival curve. The second is the assumption that any withdrawals during an interval occur at the mid-point of the interval. It is this assumption that leads to the characteristic correction to the calculated failure rate in a given interval, as follows:

$$\text{Failure rate} = \frac{\text{Number of failures}}{\text{Number at risk} - \frac{1}{2}\,(\text{Number of withdrawals})}$$

This correction assumes that the individuals who withdraw during an interval contribute to the risk pool for half of the interval. The correction is *equivalent* to increasing the interval failure rate by the number of expected failures in half of the withdrawal group. Inherent in this correction for censored data is the assumption that the failure rate for each interval is constant over that interval.

With this perspective, *the use of the stair-step graphic presentation of the life-table survival curve is, in fact, neither necessary nor appropriate*. The life-table graph (but not the Kaplan-Meier graph) is better represented by straight-line connections between the patency estimates located at the *end* of each interval. The cumulative patency is thus the resulting conditional probability *at the end of the interval* based on the failure rate over the entire interval. In this presentation, the only intervals with level lines are those with no failures. The reader is referred to the original reporting standards for detailed instructions on the calculation of the life-table.[12]

The Kaplan-Meier Method

The Kaplan-Meier survival estimate, which is also called the *product-limit method*, is different from the life-table estimate in that data are *not* grouped into intervals.[18] Events on the survival curve occur only at individual failure points. One can conceptualize the Kaplan-Meier method as a life-table method with intervals that contain a single observation and are very small. Consequently, no corrections are needed for the effect of withdrawals. In contrast to the life-table method, graphic presentation of the Kaplan-Meier survival curve *should* use the stair-step method, because between events on the Kaplan-Meier curve, nothing is really known about the failure rate, and it is assumed to be zero.

The life-table method is a technique that makes calculations easier for large amounts of data,[19] and this may have been the main justification for using it rather than the Kaplan-Meier method, but the power of today's computers would appear to make this distinction moot. Indeed, the life-table method is not valid for numbers less than 30, whereas the Kaplan-Meier method remains appropriate for any data size.[20] Either method is acceptable if used properly and documented.

Figures 3-1 and 3-2 show a life-table plot and a Kaplan-Meier plot based on the same data set. It can be seen that they give equivalent patency estimates. Complete life-table or Kaplan-Meier data, both figures and tables, should be included with each report submitted for publication, even though it may be the choice of the journal editor to print only the graph.

Numbers for the patients at risk at the start of each interval (periodically for the Kaplan-Meier method), or the standard error for each estimate of patency, must be displayed. When the standard error of the patency estimate exceeds 10%, the curve either should not be drawn or should be represented by a dotted line or some other means of indicating lack of reliability of the estimate. Comparisons of patency curves should be performed using the log-rank test of significance.[21*]

*In fairness, I must credit my long-time colleague Darrell N. Jones for many of the preceding insights.

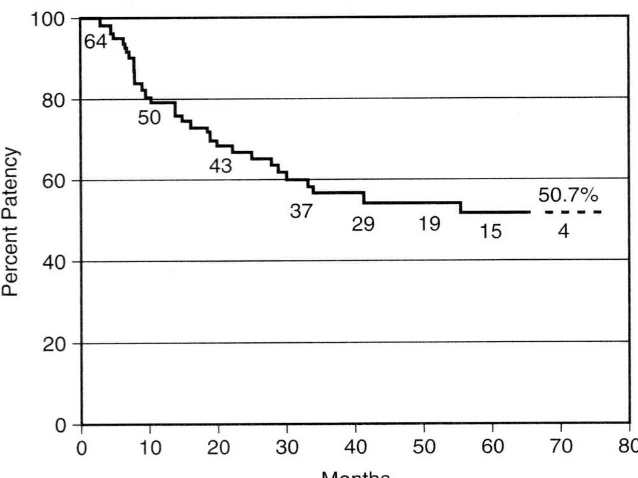

FIGURE 3-2 Kaplan-Meier patency curve. (From Rutherford RB, Baker JD, Ernst C, et al: Recommended standards for reports dealing with lower extremity ischemia: Revised version. J Vasc Surg 26:517, 1997.)

Artifacts

Because it is now common practice to use the life-table method to assess patency, one might assume that two reports employing this method would be comparable. However, a known artifact of this method is the better projected patency rates when a series is "front-loaded" with many recent cases. This practice results in a characteristic leveling off of the declining patency curve near the end, with the telltale final flat plateau representing a relatively small number of grafts remaining patent during the later periods. Patency projections during the first 2 to 3 years of a bypass graft experience made with the life-table method are notoriously misleading.

As DeWeese and Rob[22] have pointed out, the life-table method tends to overestimate the actual patency rate (i.e., that measured at the *end* of a given period). In a classic analysis of "autogenous venous grafts ten years later," they noted that 58% of their femoropopliteal grafts were "patent at the time of death or last follow-up" (once the most common method of projecting patency). The *cumulative* patency of the same grafts using the life-table method was 45% at 10 years, but the *actual* patency of grafts in patients surviving 10 years or more after graft occlusion was only 38%.

Conversely, the effect of the declining population at risk over the duration of the study can result in secondary patency rates that are actually lower than the primary patency rates. This effect results from simply moving an *early* failure, which represents a small percentage of the initial population at risk, to a *later* failure, which represents a larger percentage of the residual population at risk and thus has a larger effect on the cumulative patency rate. This artifact is a direct result of small populations, limited follow-up, and extrapolation of patency rates beyond what the data will support.

As noted previously, the declining numbers of patients at risk over the duration of a study can have detrimental effects on the accuracy of the patency estimates. In addition to the simple loss of numbers of patients, lack of diligent follow-up also biases the data. In some cases, one is more likely to receive bad news than good news; that is, patients are more likely to come back or to be referred when the graft fails and symptoms recur than when they continue to be asymptomatic. Periodic surveillance of bypass grafts with duplex scanning has been demonstrated to detect and, by allowing timely intervention, to prevent impending graft failure.[23] Thus, a reasonable level of follow-up should be required of published reports, and a poorly monitored large series, as indicated by those lost to follow-up in the life-table, may not provide as valid an estimate as a well-monitored small one.

Also not included in the patency calculations of most bypass series are cases in which the procedure was abandoned because of technical difficulties. These cases may constitute a significant number of in-situ or reverse vein bypasses to tibial or peroneal arteries, accounting for as much as 14% of cases in one early experience with the latter bypass.[24] In two reports concerning axillobifemoral bypasses from the same affiliated institutions and by mostly the same investigators, and appearing within 4 months of each other,[25,26] mortality rates of 8% and less than 2% were claimed. The second study covered 10 fewer cases and 1 more year of experience. The apparent explanation for the fourfold difference in mortality rates reported from the same institutions is the elimination of "emergency" operations from consideration in the second report.

The preceding observations are not made to impugn the life-table method or to deny the trends it is used to demonstrate but, rather, to show how it may suggest differences that are more apparent than real and to emphasize that the technique provides an estimate, not an actual measure. For a more explicit critique of the method, see the classic discussion by Underwood and Charlesworth.[27]

Differences in Patient Populations

Temporal differences between groups being compared may lead to misleading conclusions. A frequent error is comparing two sequentially performed treatments, common when a new treatment or technique is adopted and is compared with the previous technique. This approach ignores the benefits of subtle background improvements that in themselves may improve results over time (e.g., better anesthesia, intraoperative monitoring, intensive care, antithrombotic drug use). It is almost akin to using historical controls and is strongly discouraged. For instance, two articles were published within 4 years of each other by Eugene[28] and Ray[29] and their respective colleagues. Although there are other reasons for the twofold differences in patency and mortality rates for both axillo-unifemoral and axillobifemoral bypass (see later), the first series covered a period from 1960 to 1975, and the second series reports on results of operations performed between 1970 and 1979. Thus, there is only a 5-year overlap between the earlier 15-year and the later 9-year experience. Obviously, significant technical advances can emerge during such a time span. In the earlier series, for example, there was a demonstrated effect on patency of improving arterial prostheses, and only 7 of the study's 92 extra-anatomic bypasses used the double velour knitted polyester (Dacron) graft, which is now in widespread use and was used exclusively in the second series.

A more subtle error that can also introduce bias is comparing absolute rates of major endpoints, such as death, recurrence, reoperation, amputation, stroke, or some other major adverse event, between groups with significantly different follow-up durations.[30] Duration of follow-up itself can make significant differences, as suggested in the earlier discussion of life-table estimates. In a report by Ray and colleagues,[29] 84 axillobifemoral grafts with a mean implant time of 30 months were compared with 105 aortobifemoral grafts with a mean implant time of 44 months. Similarly, comparison was made between axillo-unifemoral and axillobifemoral grafts based on "mean implant times" of only 20.4 and 9.4 months, respectively, in a study that covered 9 years! The series with much shorter mean implant times are thus "front-loaded" compared with longer series and have a more rapidly declining population at risk. El Massry and colleagues[31] reported later results (1993) from the same center as Ray and associates (1979).[29] The prosthesis used in the center had *not* changed significantly, although the results continued to improve. On the other hand, Harris and coworkers[4] have reported very significant improvements with axillofemoral bypass grafting, which they credit to the use of a ringed polytetrafluoroethylene (PTFE) prosthesis; yet there are major differences in case selection and, presumably, also in technique and postoperative care between their earlier and later experiences. The reported results with extra-anatomic bypass are referred to again later in the chapter to illustrate other reasons for reported differences in surgical procedures.

Selection Criteria

The patients who were *excluded* from a report are often as important as (if not more important than) the patients *included*. For example, it once was common practice for interventional radiologists to exclude from their projected success rates for transluminal angioplasty patients in whom the procedure was attempted but not successfully completed. Although this technical failure rate is low with proximal balloon dilatations, it is much higher with balloon dilatations of smaller distal vessels (3% versus 17.5%, respectively, in the author's experience).[2] Similarly, some vascular surgeons have *eliminated* from their patency projections any reconstructions that thrombosed during the immediate postoperative period if patency was not restored and have *included* as patent any clotted grafts that were successfully reopened. The latter may represent a significant proportion of cases; for example, the early postoperative thrombosis rate after "difficult" distal bypasses may exceed 20%.[5] Such practices are now prohibited by reporting standards. Most of the early EVAR trials had strict inclusion-exclusion criteria, a selection bias designed to ensure good results with the new devices. The average AAA diameters were 5.5 cm or less, implying that the majority were probably of a size for which the United Kingdom and the U.S. Veterans Administration's ADAM (Aneurysm Detection And Management) small AAA trials concluded that early repair had no advantage over ultrasound surveillance.[30] However, this careful selection also contributed to good outcomes for the open repair "controls" (patients otherwise qualified for surgery whose anatomy was unsuitable for EVAR). This practice has contributed, in part, to the unexpected failure to demonstrate an initial mortality advantage for EVAR, because the mortality rates for open repair averaged close to 1% in the trials of currently approved EVAR devices.

Patient mix is clearly one of the most important contributors to the wide variation in mortality and patency rates between reported series of arterial reconstruction. Possible differences in lesion severity and extent of disease (e.g., runoff) between groups may or may not be taken into consideration. There may be difference in prevalence of the disease, which typically affects assessment of overall accuracy of detection by two competing diagnostic tests; for this reason, test accuracy results are now commonly expressed in terms of sensitivity, specificity, and positive and negative predicting values. Less well appreciated is the impact of differences in co-morbidities in comparison of mortality rates. Anatomic risk factors are important in the evaluation of vascular interventions, EVAR being a good example.

Ultimately, proper comparison of results requires knowing the relative severity of *all* factors known to affect the outcomes being compared. The best surgeons do not necessarily produce the best "bottom line" results. Comparisons that are unadjusted for differences in case severity may be quite unfair. Examples are comparing CEA results of a practice heavily weighted with patients with asymptomatic stenoses and those of a recognized expert to whom high-risk or acutely ill patients are frequently referred and comparing the overall results of an experience of predominantly limb salvage procedures with those of an experience with liberal indications for intervening for claudication. This is the reason that disease severity scores, with standardized grading schemes, are being developed in addition to standardized reporting practices. They have already been developed for chronic venous disease[32] and for abdominal aortic aneurysms, to allow results of open repair and endovascular repair to be better compared, with severity grading available to compare anatomic severity as well as severity of patient risk factors.[33]

Some differences between patient populations may reflect conscious philosophical differences in indications for operation. For example, compared with patients operated on for "limb salvage," that is, with chronic critical ischemia, patients undergoing intervention for the indication of claudication (1) are, as a group, younger; (2) have less coronary, carotid, and visceral artery atherosclerotic involvement; and (3) less commonly have diabetes, multilevel disease, or poor "runoff." These differences are apparent from Table 3-2, which compares two reports of 100 consecutive femoropopliteal vein bypasses each, performed for claudication and for limb salvage by vascular surgeons at the University of Pennsylvania.[34,35] Even within the category of limb salvage, results are better for patients with ischemic rest pain than for those with nonhealing ulcers, and results for both groups, in turn, are better than those for patients with digital gangrene. Furthermore, amputation rates are progressively higher in each of these three categories if the bypass graft fails.[36] Clearly, "limb salvage" rates should be calculated using data only from those patients who were at risk—those with chronic or acute critical ischemia—but it is surprising how often investigators must be reminded of this requirement.

Table 3-2 Comparison of 100 Consecutive Femoropopliteal Bypasses Performed for Claudication and for "Limb Salvage"

RISK FACTORS	CLAUDICATION (%)	LIMB SALVAGE (%)
Risk factors		
Cardiac disease	36	56
Diabetes	22	44
TIA, stroke	5	10
Pulmonary disease	19	29
Outcome		
Operative mortality	0	3
Survival (5-year)	74	60
Limb loss	3	30
Patency (5-year)	69	46

Thus, the indications for surgery, represented in different proportions in different series, can, because of associated differences in severity of disease and risk factors, significantly influence outcome. In the previously cited San Francisco experience with extra-anatomic bypass reported by Eugene and coworkers,[28] only 12% of patients had surgery for claudication. In contrast, in the Seattle series reported by Ray and colleagues,[29] almost two thirds of patients were claudicants. Similarly, in the San Francisco series,[28] axillofemoral bypass graft was limited, for the most part, to extremely poor-risk patients, but in their Boston series, Johnson and associates[26] liberally applied axillobifemoral bypass because they "seldom recommended conventional aortoiliac reconstruction in patients over the age of 65, regardless of risk."

Therefore, the higher mortality and lower patency rates reported by the San Francisco group are not surprising. However, an even greater contribution to these differences in patency rates was made by the criteria used in their estimation (see later). Whenever there are major differences between series in the proportions of patients undergoing surgery for claudication and those undergoing surgery for limb salvage, one should also expect differences in survival and patency. In a comparison of recent and earlier experiences with axillofemoral bypass, in which improved results were attributed to changing to an externally supported prosthesis, the proportion of limb salvage cases also changed from 60% to 24%![37]

Differing Criteria for Success or Failure

In some articles, the patency of an arterial bypass or reconstruction is considered to end with its occlusion. Other reports treat as patent any graft that is still open even if patency has been achieved by thrombectomy, thrombolysis, transluminal angioplasty, local revision, extension, or a new inflow source. More recently, these differences have been designated *primary* patency and *secondary* patency, respectively, and most reports make this distinction clear. However, the confusion caused by not making the distinction was tremendous. For example, the "bottom line" 5-year patency rates quoted in the two contrasting reports on axillobifemoral bypass by Ray and Eugene and their colleagues were 77% and 33%, respectively, but the former is a secondary patency rate and the latter a primary patency rate.[28,29]

Johnson and associates,[26] in comparing axillobifemoral with aortobifemoral bypass, noted essentially identical patency rates (76.4% versus 76.9%), but the former was achieved with a 43% rate of thrombectomy or revision compared with 9% for the latter. It is not possible to tell whether any of the 20 successful thrombectomies in the 56 axillobifemoral grafts reported in the companion series by LoGerfo and associates[25] were multiple procedures performed on the same graft; if they were not (as implied by the term "successful"), the primary 5-year patency rate in this experience from Boston University–affiliated hospitals would be not 76%, but instead would be close to the 33% patency rate reported by Eugene and coworkers[28] from the San Francisco Veterans Hospital.

Why should we argue opposing points of view, which maintain either that a thrombosed graft has clearly failed or that a graft whose patency has been maintained by thrombectomy, balloon dilatations, or revision is open and functioning? Well, one reflects the unmodified natural history of the graft or procedure and the other the ultimate utility that can be achieved by the surgeon's close surveillance and persistent efforts. No surgeon likes to report a low patency rate, lest it be considered a personal reflection on his or her ability. Once it becomes more widely appreciated that primary patency reflects mainly the intrinsic merits of the procedure or graft and that secondary patency is more a reflection of the surgeon's skill and persistence, vascular surgeons will accept the stricter definitions of primary patency and should be content to let the secondary patency rate speak for their efforts. Clearly, however, *both rates should be reported*, as in subsequent articles on extra-anatomic bypass by Ascer[38] and Rutherford[1] and their colleagues, in which the large differences between primary and secondary patency rates are readily apparent.

Finally, reports on arterial reconstructive surgery are often unclear about the manner in which patency was determined. The acceptance of the lack of return of limb-threatening ischemia, of clinical notes such as "palpable pulses" or "patient not bothered by claudication" made by a junior resident, or of other indirect evidence of graft patency is inappropriate. Scientific articles deserve more objective data, and acceptable criteria are recommended later in this discussion.

Some overall clinical measure of success is needed, commonly the combination of continued relief of symptoms or freedom from a major negative endpoint, such as limb loss, venous ulceration, stroke, or AAA rupture. The former measure would apply to the claudicant, and limb salvage to patients with ischemic ulcers and digital gangrene, with both applying to patients with ischemic rest pain. Flanigan and associates[39] reported an 81% 5-year success rate for femorofemoral bypass grafts, considering failure to be (1) graft thrombosis, (2) amputation, or (3) failure to relieve symptoms. This dual requirement of clinical improvement *and* patency is admirable, but it brings out the need for objective patency criteria because both symptomatic relief and credit for avoidance of amputation may be quite subjective, and until recently, patency has not usually been

Table 3-3 Variation in Reported Results for Extra-anatomic Bypass

PROCEDURE	STUDY	OPERATIVE MORTALITY (%)	FIVE-YEAR PATENCY RATE (%)
Axillo-unifemoral	El Massry et al[31]	5	76*
	Ray et al[29]	3	67
	Hepp et al[44]	5	46
	Ascer et al[38]	5	44*
	LoGerfo et al[25]	8	37*
	Chang[45]	NR	33*
	Eugene et al[28]	8	30*
	Rutherford et al[1]	13	19*
Axillobifemoral	El Massry et al[31]	5	79*
	Ray et al[29]	5	77
	Johnson et al[26]	2	76
	Chang[45]	NR	75*
	LoGerfo et al[25]	8	74
	Hepp et al[44]	5	73
	Rutherford et al[1]	11	62*
	Ascer et al[38]	5	50*
	Eugene et al[28]	8	33*

*Primary patency. All others are secondary patency or not defined.
NR, not reported.

confirmed arteriographically or with some other direct imaging technique.

When an aortobifemoral bypass or iliac balloon angioplasty is performed for aortoiliac occlusive disease associated with a significant distal lesion (e.g., superficial femoral artery occlusion), the evaluation of success becomes more difficult (Table 3-3). One may have a significantly higher rate of patency, as reflected by persistent elevation of the thigh-brachial index (TBI), than of symptomatic relief, which correlates better with the ABI. Those investigators who require both symptomatic relief and elevation of the ABI as criteria for success after intervention for aortoiliac occlusive disease, rather than elevation of the TBI, may have contributed to the impression that percutaneous transluminal angioplasty (PTA) for iliac stenoses is not very effective or durable.[40] In contrast are reports in which technical failures are eliminated and an increase in TBI is accepted as the ultimate criterion of continued success regardless of the ABI and the patient's symptoms. Using data from a personal experience with PTA, the author and colleagues found that, depending on the criteria chosen, the projected 3-year success rate for iliac dilations varied between 52% and 86%; similarly, with distal PTA, a rate of success as high as 63% or as low as 27% could be claimed.[2]

In fairness, the same can be said for reported experiences with surgical operations for aortoiliac disease, namely that the patency rates do not reflect the extent of hemodynamic improvement or symptomatic relief attained. In a review of 265 aortobifemoral graft limbs in which the initial patency rate was 97.7% and the late patency rate was 88%, the author and associates found that in spite of excellent patency, 7.3% of grafts failed to bring about improved inflow (a TBI increase < 0.10) because the iliac disease on the better side was not very significant in the first place (a preoperative TBI > 0.95), and 9.4% failed to improve the ABI because of the severity of distal occlusive disease.[41]

In the past, carotid reconstructions have been judged almost exclusively on the basis of continued symptomatic relief; thus, until recently, silent restenosis has not been reported. The vascular laboratory and the use of duplex scanning in particular have changed surgeons' perspective of the progression of disease and restenosis of carotid endarterectomies.[42,43]

Some older examples have been used in the earlier discussion, mainly because they are exemplary of so many of the confounding factors and poor reporting practices discussed that were once very prevalent. They have been gradually reduced, but, on the basis of the author's 6 years as co-editor of the *Journal of Vascular Surgery* and reading of other vascular surgery journals, they certainly have not been completely eliminated. Readers still need to be aware of them, and investigators need to avoid them. From the preceding discussion, however, it should also be apparent that the reader should carry away more than a simple "bottom line" result from each report, such as mortality, patency, or stroke rate.

Fortunately, a number of additional measures of success or failure add to the overall perspective. An excellent example can be seen in assessments of the results of EVAR.[46,47] Freedom from aneurysm-related death may be the best single endpoint, but a more comprehensive measure of success would also be important to report, one that would include technical success with no endoleak or major adverse events (such as procedure mortality, permanently disabling complications, secondary procedures, AAA sac enlargement, or conversion to open repair). By the same token, it is not enough to focus on operative mortality and patency rate after lower extremity arterial construction, because hemodynamic improvement, increased walking distance or relief of claudication, and limb salvage are also important endpoints.

REFERENCES

1. Rutherford RB, Patt A, Pearce WH: Extra-anatomic bypass: A closer view. J Vasc Surg 5:437, 1987.
2. Rutherford RB, Patt A, Kumpe DA: The current role of percutaneous transluminal angioplasty. In Greenhalgh KM, Jamieson CW, Nicolaides AN (eds): Vascular Surgery: Issues in Current Practice. London, Grune & Stratton, 1986, p 229.
3. Veith FJ, Gupta SK, Ascer E, et al: Six-year prospective multicenter randomized comparison of autologous saphenous vein and expanded polytetrafluoroethylene grafts in infrainguinal arterial reconstructions. J Vasc Surg 3:104, 1986.
4. Harris PL, Jones D, How T: A prospective randomized clinical trial to compare in situ and reversed vein grafts for femoro-popliteal bypass. Br J Surg 74:252, 1987.
5. Rutherford RB, Jones DN, Bergentz SE, et al: The efficacy of dextran-40 in preventing early postoperative thrombosis following difficult lower extremity bypass. J Vasc Surg 1:765, 1984.
6. Rennie D: Fair conduct and fair reporting of clinical trials. JAMA 282:766, 1999.
7. Rutherford RB, Johnston KW: Potential problems with industry-supported research. J Vasc Surg 31:1066, 2002.
8. Rutherford RB, Johnston KW: Protecting the rights of investigators in industry-supported clinical research. J Vasc Surg 35:1036, 2002.
9. Polk HC Jr, Bowden TA Jr, Rikkers LF, et al: Scientific data from clinical trials: Investigators' responsibilities and rights. J Vasc Surg 35:1303, 2002.
10. Glantz SA: Primer of Biostatistics. New York, McGraw-Hill, 1981, p 7.

11. Gupta SK, Cadet N, Veith FJ: Statistics for the vascular surgeon. In Sidawy AN, Sumpio BE, Depalma RG (eds): Basic Science of Vascular Disease. Armonk, NY, Futura, 1997, p 621.
12. Suggested standards for reports dealing with lower extremity ischemia. Prepared by the Ad Hoc Committee on Reporting Standards, Society for Vascular Surgery/North American Chapter, International Society for Cardiovascular Surgery [erratum in J Vasc Surg 4:350, 1986]. J Vasc Surg 4:80, 1986.
13. Rutherford RB, Baker JD, Ernst C, et al: Recommended standards for reports dealing with lower extremity ischemia: Revised version. J Vasc Surg 26:517, 1997.
14. Berkson J, Gage RP: Calculation of survival rates for cancer. Mayo Clin Proc 25:270, 1950.
15. Cutler SJ, Ederer F: Maximum utilization of the life table method in analyzing survival. J Chronic Dis 8:699, 1958.
16. Peto R, Pike MC, Armitage P, et al: Design and analysis of randomized trials requiring prolonged observations of each patient. I: Introduction and design. Br J Cancer 34:585, 1976.
17. Peto R, Pike MC, Armitage P, et al: Design and analysis of randomized trials requiring prolonged observations of each patient. II: Analysis and examples. Br J Cancer 35:1, 1977.
18. Kaplan EL, Meier P: Nonparametric estimation from incomplete observations. J Am Stat Assoc 53:457, 1958.
19. Colton T: Statistics in Medicine. Boston, Little, Brown, 1974, p 244.
20. Lee ET: Statistical Methods for Survival Data Analysis. Belmont, CA, Wadsworth, 1980, p 75.
21. Lawless JF: Statistical Models and Methods for Lifetime Data. New York, John Wiley & Sons, 1982.
22. DeWeese JA, Rob CG: Autogenous venous grafts five years later. Am Surg 174:346, 1971.
23. Berkowitz HD, Hobbs CL, Roberts B, et al: Value of routine vascular laboratory studies to identify vein graft stenosis. Surgery 90:971, 1981.
24. Reichle FA, Tyson RR: Bypasses to tibial or popliteal arteries in severely ischemic lower extremities: Comparison of long-term results in 233 patients. Ann Surg 176:315, 1972.
25. LoGerfo FW, Johnson WC, Corson JD, et al: A comparison of the late patency rates of axillobilateral femoral and axillounilateral femoral grafts. Surgery 81:33, 1977.
26. Johnson WC, LoGerfo FW, Vollman RW: Is axillobilateral femoral graft an effective substitute for aortobilateral iliac femoral graft? Ann Surg 186:123, 1976.
27. Underwood CG, Charlesworth D: Uses and abuses of life table analysis in vascular surgery. Br J Surg 71:495, 1984.
28. Eugene J, Goldstone J, Moore WS: Fifteen-year experience with subcutaneous bypass grafts for lower extremity ischemia. Ann Surg 186:177, 1976.
29. Ray LI, O'Connor JB, Davis CC, et al: Axillofemoral bypass: A critical reappraisal of its role in the management of aortoiliac occlusive disease. Am J Surg 138:117, 1979.
30. Arko FR, Filis KA, Hill BB, et al: Morphologic changes and outcome following endovascular abdominal aortic aneurysm repair as a function of aneurysm size [see discussion by A Mansour]. Arch Surg 138:651, 2003.
31. El Massry S, Saad E, Sauvage LR, et al: Axillofemoral bypass using externally supported, knitted Dacron grafts: A follow-up through twelve years. J Vasc Surg 17:107, 1993.
32. Rutherford RB, Padberg FT Jr, Comerota AJ, et al: Venous severity scoring: An adjunct to venous outcome assessment. J Vasc Surg 31:1307, 2000.
33. Chaikof EL, Fillinger MF, Matsumura JS, et al: Identifying and grading factors that modify the outcome of endovascular aortic aneurysm repair. J Vasc Surg 35:1060, 2002.
34. Naji A, Barker CF, Berkowitz HD, et al: Femoropopliteal vein grafts for claudication: Analysis of 100 consecutive cases. Ann Surg 188:79, 1978.
35. Naji A, Jennifer C, McCombs PR, et al: Results of 100 consecutive femoropopliteal vein grafts for limb salvage. Ann Surg 188:162, 1978.
36. Thiele BL, Jones AM, Hobson RW, et al: Standards in noninvasive cerebrovascular testing. J Vasc Surg 15:495, 1992.
37. Harris EJ, Taylor LM, McConnel DB, et al: Clinical results of axillobifemoral bypass using externally supported polytetrafluoroethylene. J Vasc Surg 12:416, 1990.
38. Ascer E, Veith FJ, Gupta SK, et al: Comparison of axillounifemoral and axillobifemoral bypass operations. Surgery 97:169, 1985.
39. Flanigan DP, Pratt DG, Goodreau JJ, et al: Hemodynamic and angiographic guidelines in selection of patients for femoro-femoral bypass. Arch Surg 113:1257, 1978.
40. Johnston KW, Colapinto RF, Baird RJ: Transluminal dilation: An alternative. Arch Surg 117:1604, 1982.
41. Rutherford RB, Jones DN, Martin MS, et al: Serial hemodynamic assessment of aortobifemoral bypass. J Vasc Surg 4:428, 1986.
42. Zeirler RE, Bandyk DF, Thiele BL, et al: Carotid artery stenosis following endarterectomy. Arch Surg 117:1408, 1982.
43. Ouriel K, Green RM: Clinical and technical factors influencing recurrent carotid stenosis and occlusion after endarterectomy. J Vasc Surg 5:702, 1987.
44. Hepp W, deJonge K, Pallua N: Late results following extra-anatomic bypass procedures for chronic aortoiliac occlusive disease. J Cardiovasc Surg 29:181, 1988.
45. Chang JB: Current state of extraanatomic bypasses. Am J Surg 152:202, 1986.
46. Chaikof EL: Capturing an accurate measure of success: Outcomes and endpoints in endovascular aneurysm repair. J Vasc Surg 36: 410, 2002.
47. Chaikof EL, Bernhard VM , Blankensteijn JD, et al: Revised reporting standards for endovascular aortic aneurysm repair. J Vasc Surg 35:1048, 2002.

Chapter

4

Maintaining a Computerized Vascular Registry

RUSSELL SAMSON, MD

■ GENERAL CONSIDERATIONS

A *vascular registry* is a clinical and research tool based on the collected clinical data of patients treated by an individual or group of vascular specialists. In its simplest form it may be a box of index cards upon which are written data such as the patient's name, age, date of surgery, and procedure performed. When these data are analyzed at a later stage, the surgeon can determine patient volume for a given period, average patient age, and most frequently performed procedures. Such a database is referred to as a *flat* database. Flat databases can become extremely complex with thousands of data points recorded, including such variables as risk factors, medications, and surgical techniques (e.g., graft types, suture materials, operative time).

For such complexity, the use of the computer becomes a significant time saver. A computerized database offers many conveniences that will speed up data entry and retrieval and also add the benefit of ensuring uniformity of data collection. For example, entry of a specific procedure into the database can be achieved by clicking on a dropdown menu that lists alphabetically all the many procedures that the vascular specialist may perform. Typing in the first letter of the procedure takes the cursor directly to the relevant group of procedures allowing the user, with a single mouse-click, to insert what may be a very complex procedure. This type of entry procedure also prevents users from entering different phraseology for the same procedure at different times which might, at a later stage, complicate data retrieval. For example, one may refer to a bypass as a "femoropopliteal above-knee bypass" or a "femoral-to-above-knee popliteal bypass"; these two descriptions might be treated as different procedures at data collection, even though they are the same.

Computers offer an added advantage in that they easily allow creation of what are known as *relational databases*, whereby two flat databases can be combined to offer extended information. For example, if one wanted to store follow-up data about a patient's vascular procedure using the flat database of handwritten index cards, one would probably have to use a separate index card with follow-up information for each case. To make sure that the second card was not filed in the wrong place, one would have to (1) enter some salient patient demographic data, such as the patient's name and identity number, on the second card and (2) update the patient's age for the date of the follow-up. If this information were being kept on a relational database, a new screen of information would be set up for the follow-up information, allowing one to tie all the previous information together using one key identifying data point, such as an identity number. The computer program could also automatically update information such as age at follow-up and duration of graft patency whenever new follow-up information was entered.

The major benefit of a computerized database is achieved when one needs to retrieve and analyze data. Sifting through thousands of index cards with hundreds of different data points can be extremely tedious and prone to error. On the other hand, a computerized registry can be "mined" for data, often in an instant, allowing for the production of data output in multiple formats including spreadsheet tables and life-table graphs.

Some concepts must be defined in order for the user to obtain the full potential benefit from a computerized registry. The data points that the user wants to store are entered into *fields*. An example of a field is a label marked "GENDER," where one would choose from appropriate entries "male" or "female." In well-programmed computerized registries, data can be entered into a field by choosing from a list of choices in a dropdown menu or by typing the text or a numeral directly. The former is preferred over the latter technique, because typing errors can lead to mistaken data; for example, the computer program would regard the procedure "aort**o**gram" as being different from "aort**a**gram." The collection of related fields on the screen is referred to as a *form*. An example would be a form to collect patient demographics, such as name, age, sex, address, and insurance carrier. A *query* is a question one asks of the database. A simple example is "What is the average age of all patients?" However, a query could be as complex as "What is the 5-year patency of all infrainguinal prosthetic bypasses in male patients with type 2 diabetes and hypertension?" The resultant life-table graph or table is called a *report*.

■ DESIGN CONSIDERATIONS

Computer software is available to form the basis for these databases. Such software programs are usually called *database management systems*. Examples of database software programs are Microsoft Access (Microsoft Corp., Redmond, CA) and FoxPro (Microsoft Corp., Redmond, CA).

An obvious benefit of establishing one's own registry is that it can be customized specifically to one's own desires and requirements. However, a poorly constructed database will provide erroneous information or will not function at all, not only proving frustrating but also being costly in terms of wasted financial resources and time. Accordingly, before building a personal, customized database, the surgeon must define all the fields that will be required and set up all relevant relationships. It will help to determine the most common queries that will be used, since this information will identify the fields that will be needed. Thus, it should be appreciated that relational databases can become very complex and require careful planning. Poorly designed forms and data input design can prove the aphorism "garbage in, garbage out." Vascular registries can be especially complex if one needs to establish queries for subjects such as assisted and secondary patency life-tables.

Although it may be obvious that the best constructed registry for the most well-intentioned user is useless if the database is not maintained, poor maintenance is an all too common occurrence. It can be traced to design faults as well as human frailty. A common error committed by many designers is to include every data point that they can think of even if it will have little clinical relevance. If a database is too large and complex, too much time and effort are needed to enter all the data, resulting in one's failure to use it on a regular basis.

Registries, including some commercial ones, have been available for many years.[1,2] Varying in expense, capabilities, and ease of use, commercial registries may be difficult to evaluate. It is recommended that the potential user evaluate a working copy of the software *before* acquiring and committing to use it. Certain key functions should be available. The program must be able to let the user define *and add* fields, preferably in a manner that will appear on the monitor screen as a dropdown list, allowing mouse-click selection rather than requiring text entry. This will speed data entry and lessen the possibility of typographical error. Similarly, the program should have an ample selection of predefined reports yet allow the user to add his or her own reports to query the database. Programs that require the software developer, rather than the user, to write the query or generate the report should be avoided unless this process can be achieved in a timely and inexpensive fashion. Because a significant amount of time and energy is required to enter data, it is imperative that the vendor be stable and able to commit to long-term support and to provide upgrades that can be incorporated without re-entry of previous data. The software should also support networking between computers in the same location (office personnel, members of a group practice, research assistants) and, preferably, even in geographically differing locations. Some programs may be web-accessible.

■ RATIONALE FOR COMMITTING TO A REGISTRY

Why should a surgeon invest time or money in a registry? The simple answer is that a registry is a clinical adjunct that may prove to be as important as textbooks and journals. The database not only provides information on one's own practice patterns but, most important, it offers a constantly updated evaluation of one's outcomes. These evaluations can be compared to national or regional norms. On the basis of this information, the surgeon can adjust techniques, modify indications, and, hopefully, improve outcomes over time.[3]

The importance of using government coding for diseases, procedures, and indications as key relationships needs no emphasis. However, these codes do not necessarily reflect patterns of surgical experience. Hospital, insurance, or government agency databases that utilize these codes may not be appropriate for measuring outcome for vascular surgery. For example, hospitals and most insurance companies use a single Current Procedural Terminology (CPT) code for femoropopliteal bypass irrespective of whether the bypass is constructed to the above-knee or below-knee popliteal artery. However, it is well recognized that patency rates for these two variants of infrainguinal bypass grafts differ considerably. Accordingly, patency rates based on such agency data will lack clinical relevance. A well-constructed vascular surgery database should be able to refine data, thus making the registry more valuable. Also, in an age when third parties such as managed care organizations are assessing one's outcomes using these less accurate databases, one's own registry can be used to deal with possible issues raised by third parties. Including fee and cost data will enhance this capability—that is, the ability to adjust fees and bid for contracts. Furthermore, in a litigious age when informed consent has become paramount, one can appropriately inform one's patients about risk based on one's own outcome statistics. Finally, a registry gets more useful as one's practice matures because it provides more relevant data as the database grows. Clearly, the sooner one commits to a computerized registry, the greater the benefit.

■ REGIONAL, SOCIETAL, AND NATIONAL REGISTRIES

By pooling one's data with data from other surgeons, regional and national databases can provide information such as prevalence of disease and practice patterns. The larger numbers that such combined registries offer increases the statistical relevance of data and allows the evaluation of rare diseases or uncommon complications. Several countries have taken the lead in establishing such regional or national vascular registries, including the Swedish and Finnish Vascular Registries[3-5] and the Melbourne Vascular Surgical Association Audit in Australia.[6] The Society for Vascular Surgery (SVS) in the United States, through the Lifeline Foundation, has established a registry focused on aortic endografts. Several attempts have also been made by regional vascular associations to form cooperative registries.[7] Unfortunately, many have failed in their intent because of a lack of enthusiasm from their participants. However, if a relevant regional database is available, one should take its requirements into consideration when defining the fields required for a personal database. This step will facilitate merging or integrating the two databases at a later stage. The joint vascular societies (Society for Vascular Surgery and American Association for Vascular Surgery), under the leadership of Robert Rutherford,[8-17] has defined terms for standardized reporting of procedures and outcomes in most areas of vascular surgery. Adaptation of these terms for fields in one's own database should promote uniformity in reporting (see Chapters 3 and 6).

■ MAINTAINING A REGISTRY

The benefit of a vascular registry is its ability to track outcome over time. Knowledge about what type of procedures we are performing may be interesting and is certainly useful to an extent, but the database will really become a valuable clinical tool only when it provides outcome information, with data on such key outcome parameters as patency, stroke rates, initial and long-term mortality and morbidity, and procedure-specific success rates. Achieving this goal requires a dedication to data entry. Similarly, erroneous or incomplete data will also negate the benefit of the registry. A registry that is not well maintained will ultimately prove valueless.

Tools have been developed by most commercial registries to facilitate data entry. They include printed forms available in the operating room or clinic that can be completed by personnel there, data from which can be entered into the computer database by a different person at a different time and place. Computers can also be strategically placed in the operating room or clinic so that the surgeon can enter the data immediately. Some registries instead use personal digital assistants (PDAs). A benefit of these devices is that fields added on the main program computer are automatically included on the PDA; paper forms must be reprinted every time a new field is added.

No matter which method is used, the surgeon must make a commitment to data entry. Ideally the operating surgeon should enter the data. In a university setting, a qualified resident or fellow may substitute. A research nurse or Physician's Assistant who is well versed in the specialty may also be a suitable data entry person. Assigning data collection to an untrained or uninformed person who has to rely on chart review will lead to input of invalid data. Such persons can, however, be used to transfer data from paper forms into the computer, but data errors can occur even in this process.

The most difficult area for data input occurs with patient follow-up. Often follow-up is done not by the operating surgeon but rather by a resident or nurse. In a busy clinic, time to enter data may be limited. Accordingly, some programs include a vascular laboratory module that links the reporting of the vascular laboratory study to the registry database so that the technologist can update the follow-up at the time of the vascular laboratory study. This measure provides objective data supporting the clinical assessment of success or failure. Losing patients from follow-up also negates the value of long-term data. Accordingly, commercial programs should provide a prompting report that identifies patients who have not been seen for follow-up so that they can be recalled.

■ UTILIZING THE REGISTRY

Data in the registry is useless unless it can be queried for information. One might argue that until data are utilized, information does not exist.[18] Accordingly, it is imperative that extraction of information is easy. Commercial programs should have constructed preprogrammed reports that will answer most clinical questions. Examples would be life-table curves for patency, stroke rate, and mortality. Well-constructed reports should allow the user to define what fields need to be included in the search. For example, one should be able to narrow data in the report to operating surgeon, hospital, graft material, site of distal anastomosis, and any other variable that is required. Frequent use facilitates an understanding of the program and the benefits of the information.

Examples of information that can be gleaned from the registry are:

- *Patients who have not been followed up:* This issue is especially important for patients who have had infrainguinal vein grafts, in whom inadequate follow-up and graft surveillance can lead to graft failure and limb loss. Follow-up is also paramount for aortic endografts, because failure to diagnose endoleak with aneurysm expansion can lead to rupture and death.
- *Comparison of competitive techniques:* This capability becomes important in the evaluation of new procedures such as carotid endarterectomy versus carotid stenting, or lower extremity arterial bypass versus angioplasty.
- *Comparison of equipment or devices*: One may wish to compare different stents or different vascular conduits.
- *Complication rates:* One can calculate rates of complications such as stroke, amputation, renal failure, hematoma, and dissection after angioplasty.
- *Practice management information:* In these times of diminished reimbursement, practice management information may be critical to running a viable practice or department. A registry can provide information such as referral volume and patient demographics. Patient tracking will ensure that patients are not lost from follow-up. Some commercial programs also generate form letters to "lost" patients reminding them of the importance of follow-up care. Marketing opportunities may develop when exemplary results can be documented. Similarly, substandard results should stimulate an improvement in technique that may lead to higher patient volume.

■ THE "TEN COMMANDMENTS" OF COMPUTERIZED REGISTRIES

Following are the "dos and don'ts" for using computer registries in vascular surgery:

1. *Learn the software before entering patient data.* One should be aware of all the features of the software before entering definitive patient data. Accordingly, one *must* read the instruction manual that comes with the package. Many users have "jumped right in" without referring to the manual, only to find that their valuable data are not functional. Most programs will require some basic information to be entered before one can enter the first patient's data. This

information usually consists of names of involved surgeons and assistants, hospitals, and referring physicians and demographic data about the practice. In order to become well versed in the program, one should try entering some test patient data using easily identifiable imaginary patient names, then use the "delete-patient" feature to erase the test data before entering actual patient data.

2. *Always back up the program.* Data entry should be backed up daily. Most software programs have a backup facility. Ideally, a copy of the data should be maintained in a location away from the facility as well. A simple way of doing this is to copy the data to a storage medium such as a compact disc that is kept offsite. There are also data storage areas that can be accessed for a fee through the Internet.
3. *Try to live with the software that you buy, and avoid customization if possible.* When the software company updates the product or brings out a new version, customized features may not be supported. On the other hand, some programs allow the user to add fields to collect data or information that the programmers may not have thought of; for example, a surgeon may want to collect information about patients' cholesterol levels. These are called user-defined fields and will be supported by future upgrades. The ability to add such fields without assistance from programmers is a very valuable benefit offered by such software. However, before adding such a field, one should always consider the goal of seeking this added information and make sure to define in advance the choices that can be entered into the field. If only free-form text can be entered, one should always double-check spelling, because just one letter wrong will prevent that data from being retrieved at a later date.
4. *Keep up with the latest software versions.* Changes in government coding of diseases, procedures, and indications and new research advances are constantly changing the data environment. Out-of-date software can result in useless information.
5. *Get in the habit of entering the data directly into the computer* rather than writing information down and then entering the data later. This practice will prevent transcription errors.
6. *Use the shortcuts that the program may offer.* For example, some programs allow old follow-up information to be copied to a new data form when a patient comes back for a follow-up visit. Then only new data or changes need be entered.
7. *Learn to use the keyboard shortcut keys.* This issue is especially important for users who are not "mouse" proficient.
8. *Proof your entries.* The user should remember the adage "garbage in, garbage out."
9. *Use all the features that the program provides.* Many programs are very sophisticated.
10. *Do not despair when first using these programs.* Their use will become second nature with time.

■ CONCLUSION

In a recent review of the practice patterns of vascular surgeons in Florida, only 13% of respondents knew their 5-year patency data.[19] How then do such surgeons inform their patients about potential outcome and benefits or risks? Is it appropriate to rely solely on other surgeons' data or on vague suppositions about one's own experience? If we do not have outcome data, how can we evaluate changes in technique, graft material, or other variables that may affect our procedures? It is to be hoped that adoption of computerized registries by a majority of surgeons will improve both their own results and vascular surgery as a specialty.

■ REFERENCES

1. Karmody AM, Fitzgerald K, Branagh BS, et al: Development of a computerized registry for large-scale use. J Vasc Surg 1:594, 1984.
2. Plecha FR, Avellone JC, Beven GC, et al: A computerized vascular registry: Experience of the Cleveland Vascular Society. Surgery 886:826, 1979.
3. Bergqvist D, Troeng T, Einarsson E, et al: Vascular surgical audit during a 5-year period. Steering committee on behalf of the Swedish Vascular Registry (Swedvasc). Eur J Vasc Surg 8:472, 1994.
4. Salenius JP, Lepantalo M, Ylonen K, et al: Treatment of peripheral vascular diseases—basic data from the nationwide vascular registry FINNVASC. Ann Chir Gynaecol 82:235, 1993.
5. Vascular surgery in southern Sweden—the first year experience of a vascular registry. Vascular Registry in Southern Sweden (VRISS). Eur J Vasc Surg 3:563, 1989.
6. Beiles CB: Melbourne Vascular Surgical Association audit. Melbourne Vascular Surgical Association Audit Committee. Aust N Z J Surg 73:69, 2003.
7. Taylor SM, Robison JG, Langan EM 3rd, et al: The pitfalls of establishing a statewide vascular registry: The South Carolina experience. Am Surg 65:513, 1999.
8. Rutherford RB, Flanigan DP, Gupta SK, et al: Suggested standards for reports dealing with lower extremity ischemia. J Vasc Surg 4:80, 1986.
9. Rutherford RB, Baker JD, Ernst C: Recommended standards for reports dealing with lower extremity ischemia: Revised version. J Vasc Surg 26:517, 1997.
10. Baker JD, Rutherford RB, Bernstein EF, et al: Suggested standards for reports dealing with cerebrovascular disease. J Vasc Surg 8:721, 1988.
11. Porter JM, Clagett GP, Cranley J, et al: Reporting standards in venous disease. J Vasc Surg 8:172, 1988.
12. Johnston KW, Rutherford RB, Tilson MD, et al: Suggested standards for reporting on arterial aneurysms. J Vasc Surg 13:444, 1991.
13. Thiele BL, Jones AM, Hobson RW, et al: Standards in noninvasive cerebrovascular testing. J Vasc Surg 15:495, 1992.
14. Ahn SS, Rutherford RB, Becker GL, et al: Reporting standards for lower extremity arterial endovascular procedures. J Vasc Surg 17:1103, 1993.
15. Ahn SS, Rutherford RB, Johnston KW, et al: Reporting standards for infrarenal endovascular abdominal aorta aneurysm repair. J Vasc Surg 25:405, 1997.
16. Chaikof EL, Blankensteijn JD, Harris PL, et al: Reporting standards for endovascular aortic aneurysm repair. J Vasc Surg 35:1048, 2002.
17. Rutherford RB, Padberg FT Jr, Comerota AJ: Venous severity scoring: An adjunct to venous outcome assessment. J Vasc Surg 31:1307, 2000.
18. Blois MS: Information and Medicine. Los Angeles, University of California Press, 1980, p 22.
19. Samson RH: Femoropopliteal bypass is not a generic procedure: A survey of the practice patterns of The Florida Vascular Society. Ann Vasc Surg 15:544, 2001.

Chapter

5

Proper Outcomes Assessment:
Patient-Based and Economic Evaluations of Vascular Interventions

JOHN V. WHITE, MD

The evolution of vascular surgery has been rapid, and the development of new diagnostic and therapeutic modalities continues unabated. The goal of these new technologies and techniques is an elevation of the standard of care for patients with vascular disease. Appropriate patient care practice requires that all vascular surgeons continually renew and refine both their cognitive and technical skills to incorporate proven advances. It is essential, therefore, that these new technologies and techniques are carefully and completely assessed prior to their adoption.

Complete assessment of the effectiveness of a vascular intervention requires evaluation of not only the change in the patient's clinical status but also changes in his or her functional status and quality of life. Though clinical parameters of therapeutic success, such as graft patency and limb salvage, are essential for the evaluation of vascular surgical intervention, documentation of an improvement in patient quality of life and personal productivity is equally important. The operative treatments of aneurysms and arterial occlusive disease are performed for the reduction of risk to life and limb and the relief of symptoms but have little direct impact on the underlying pathologic process. The benefit of intervention lies, ultimately, in the improvement of the patient's quality of life. Integrated, complete evaluation of vascular intervention, then, requires the documentation of both clinical and patient-based measures of outcome.

This approach to patient evaluation has been strongly encouraged by the U.S. government. In 1989, Congress created the Agency for Health Care Policy and Research, charging it with the responsibility to conduct research to identify effective health care, develop clinical guidelines based on the findings of effectiveness, and disseminate this information to the public. To evaluate therapeutic effectiveness, the government stresses the "use of outcomes measures that assess factors that affect patients directly (e.g., physical and social functioning and pain), rather than intermediate clinical measures (e.g., laboratory test scores)."[1] The rising costs of health care in the United States mandate that costly interventions that fail to directly increase the well-being and productivity of patients be eliminated. This mandate underscores the need for properly performed patient-based outcomes assessment for vascular interventions. A patient-based outcomes approach, in conjunction with well-defined clinical endpoints, permits the identification of technologies and techniques that raise the standard of care and improve patient well-being. This combined evaluative process is essential because the act of surgery itself creates significant difficulties with clinical research.

■ CLINICAL RESEARCH METHODOLOGIES AND ENDPOINTS

Multiple clinical research methodologies have been constructed to prove the presence or absence of benefit for a given diagnostic or therapeutic modality (Table 5-1). Of these, the prospective, randomized, double-blinded, controlled study has long been considered the optimal method for identifying the risks and benefits of a new therapeutic modality. Investigator bias is minimized through rigorous standardization of the protocol, the randomization process, and the blinding of both investigator and subject to the nature of the treatment. This research methodology has been widely employed for the evaluation of nonsurgical treatments, especially pharmacologic therapy. For pharmacotherapeutics, the experimental drug is specifically created to attack the disease in a consistent and predictable manner.

Table 5-1 Commonly Used Research Methodologies and Risk of Bias

STUDY TYPE	CONTROLS	LIKELIHOOD OF BIAS
Observational studies		
Case report	No	High
Case-control study	Yes	Moderate
Cohort	Yes	Moderate
Experimental studies		
Nonrandomized clinical trial	Yes	Moderate
Randomized, prospective trial	Yes	Low
Secondary (computer-based) studies		
Meta-analysis	Yes	Low
Markov analysis	Yes	Low
Monte Carlo simulation	Yes	Low

From White JV, Barthel G: Evidence-based medicine: Basic concepts, population dynamics, outcomes analysis. In Hallett JW Jr, Mills JL, Earnshaw JJ, Reekers JA (eds): Comprehensive Vascular and Endovascular Surgery. Philadelphia, Mosby, 2004, pp 45-54.

Definitive inclusion and exclusion criteria are established, and the methods of drug administration are standardized to reach target blood levels in all patients. A similar alternative treatment or placebo can be administered to a control group, and comparisons made over time with minimal bias. Ideally, both the investigators and the subjects are unaware of the therapy being administered until the period of data collection has been completed. The specific endpoints of the study are generally directed toward the clinical efficacy of the experimental therapy.

Such methods are frequently not possible when one attempts to demonstrate the benefits of a new surgical procedure.[2] Unlike drug trials, surgical clinical research must accommodate both the underlying disease process and the physiologic changes induced by the surgical intervention. In addition to the pathophysiologic process, numerous additional variables—surgical judgment, surgical skill, unquantified physiologic modifiers, and patient collaboration—can affect clinical outcomes. Patient collaboration may decrease for those assigned to the open surgical category, and patients may withdraw from the study after randomization to push for less invasive therapy even in the absence of demonstrated efficacy of that modality. Assessing the usefulness of randomized, controlled trials to evaluate surgical procedures, Solomon and McLeod[2] noted that 40% of proposed trials would not be possible because of patient preference. The comparison of noninterventional or percutaneous treatments with open surgery often creates an immediate selection bias. Blinding is impossible; few patients would fail to recognize the presence or absence of an incision. Therefore, it is very important to identify outcomes parameters that can clearly identify the risks and benefits to patients of vascular surgical intervention.

Using well-established survey tools, patient-based outcomes parameters provide a clear index for the comparison of different diagnostic or therapeutic modalities. These parameters are relatively free of investigator bias and influence and can provide a strong framework for the assessment of new technologies and techniques. When employed in conjunction with appropriate clinical parameters, patient-based outcomes assessment yields a clear view of the value of a diagnostic or treatment modality.

■ RELATIONSHIP BETWEEN CLINICAL AND PATIENT-BASED OUTCOMES PARAMETERS

There are numerous parameters by which the treatment of vascular disease can be evaluated (Table 5-2). An optimal technical result represents a step toward the achievement of an improved functional status and better quality of life for the patient. The achievement and documentation of an excellent technical outcome are unquestionably important but are not synonymous with improvement in the patient's quality of life. This situation has been documented in several studies evaluating claudicants according to walking distance, ankle-brachial index (ABI), and quality of life. Overall, these comparisons have demonstrated a poor or limited correlation between the clinical parameters and quality of life index. Chetter and colleagues[3] evaluated 235 claudicants with treadmill walking distance, ABI, and the EuroQol generic quality of life survey. A poor correlation was found between the clinical parameters of treadmill walking distance and ABI and the measured quality of life. Similarly, Currie and associates[4] studied 186 patients undergoing treatment for claudication with unsupervised exercise, angioplasty, or surgery. These investigators documented that although angioplasty and surgery improved quality of life scores, the improvement did not correlate with changes in the ABI. This lack of correlation underscores the difference between clinical and patient-based parameters. Both are essential to determine the effect of vascular disease and its treatment.

■ PATIENT-BASED OUTCOMES PARAMETERS

Assessment of the therapeutic risks and benefits associated with treatment of vascular disease requires determination of (1) the manifestations of the condition as reported by both the patient and the physician, (2) the impact of the disease upon the patient's life and level of functioning, and (3) the effect of the treatment and its adverse consequences on the disease and on the patient's life and level of functioning. Physicians most commonly use physical findings and laboratory data to characterize a disease process or condition. This information is essential for appropriate diagnosis and treatment but does not reveal the manner and severity of the symptoms experienced by the patient. Physical examination and laboratory testing cannot measure these patient effects. In broad population studies, a reduction of the ABI to the level of 0.35 indicates limb-threatening ischemia, but an individual patient with such a level of circulatory impairment may not experience rest pain and may have no ulcerations or ischemic gangrene. Conversely, a patient with an ABI of 0.7 and an ambulatory distance of two blocks may be functionally very impaired. Thus, documentation of the patient's manifestations of vascular disease through patient-based reporting improves the physician's understanding of the patient's condition.

Because vascular disease may affect both an end organ, such as the leg, and the overall level of patient function, it is essential that information be collected about the impact of

Table 5-2 Common Parameters for Assessment of Vascular Intervention

Clinical parameters	Physical examination
	Symptomatic measures: Rutherford classification
	Objective anatomic and hemodynamic information:
	  Angiographic information
	  Ankle-brachial indices
	Technical success
	Patency of the treated segment
	Limb salvage
	Procedural morbidity
	Procedural mortality

Patient-based parameters	Disease-specific functional status
	Quality of life/survival
	General health status
	  Functional status
	  Perceived health
	  Psychological well-being
	  Role functioning

vascular disease on both. A patient's level of functioning may be altered not only by the symptoms of vascular disease but also by his or her psychological or emotional response to these physical symptoms. Such responses are unique to individuals and must be directly assessed for each patient. Evidence suggests that physicians are not good reporters of symptoms that cannot be easily observed or measured. This possibility was nicely demonstrated by Pell,[5] who asked 201 claudicants to rate their quality of life before their first visit with a vascular surgeon. After the visit, the surgeon was asked to rate the patient's quality of life on the basis of his or her understanding of the patient's symptoms and examination. The correlation between these two estimates was poor. Only through an understanding of the specific and overall effects of vascular disease on the patient can physicians develop appropriate therapeutic plans.

Both the beneficial and adverse effects of treatment must be recorded in a similar manner. Scientifically sound therapy may not always produce the extent of patient improvement expected by the surgeon. A patent bypass graft and an improved ABI do not ensure an improvement in quality of life for the patient. Schneider and colleagues[6] evaluated the functional status and well-being of 60 patients who had undergone successful aortobifemoral bypass grafting at least 6 months earlier. These investigators found that despite patency of the bypass, physical function, role function, and perceived health were worse, and bodily pain greater, in these patients than in patients without symptomatic arterial occlusive disease. An evaluation of outcomes for patients undergoing distal revascularization for limb-threatening ischemia has documented that limb salvage resulted in greater mobility and independent self-care but also in more patient anxiety and depression.[7] Further analysis of the patients treated with amputation identified a subset of patients, accounting for 22% of the total, who had less mobility but equivalent independent self-care and lifestyle indices compared with patients in whom limb salvage was successful, suggesting that primary amputation may be indicated in some patients. A similar study has documented greater anxieties and less satisfaction among patients requiring repeat vascular surgical interventions than in those undergoing a first procedure.[8] These findings indicate that clinical measures, such as ABI, patency, and limb salvage, effectively assess the physiologic impact of vascular intervention but do not adequately describe overall patient benefit or adverse effect. The benefits of any proposed therapy must outweigh the risks to the patient's overall level of function. Only by documenting all of the benefits and adverse effects of a therapy can a physician evaluate the results of treatment.

Several outcomes parameters have been defined to permit the acquisition of this patient-based information. They are functional status, perceived health, psychological well-being, and role function. Functional status assessment is directed toward the determination of how well the patient can perform tasks commonly required in daily life, such as climbing stairs, walking across a room, reading a newspaper, and holding a pen; these activities are generic in nature and are independent of gender and occupation. Perceived health evaluation attempts to define how healthy a person believes he or she is and those aspects of ill-health that most limit the patient. A patient's perception of his or her health may be adversely affected by disease even after treatment. In a study of 56 patients undergoing successful lower extremity revascularization, Gibbons and colleagues[9] noted that the only independent predictor of improved patient functional status 6 months after surgery was the patient's perception of his or her health status before surgery. Duggan and associates[10] evaluated 17 patients who had successful lower extremity bypass procedures and found that, at a mean of 18 months after surgery, there was a decline in perceived health despite a patent bypass. Psychological well-being assessment identifies how worried, anxious, or depressed a patient is about his or her illnesses and treatment. Perceived health and psychological well-being provide valuable information about the emotional impact of illness and insight into the effects of therapy. Although claudication is not a directly life- or limb-threatening disorder, Khaira and associates[11] documented greater perceived health problems regarding energy, pain, and emotional reactions among claudicants than in a control group without claudication. Evaluation of role functioning is directed toward the assessment of the effect of a patient's illness on his or her ability to work and perform obligatory duties. This dimension provides important information for the choice of treatment for claudication, for example.

■ GENERIC OUTCOMES ASSESSMENT TOOLS

Several survey instruments are available that are capable of assessing these health dimensions (Table 5-3). Each of these instruments has been broadly applied to large patient populations and has demonstrated both reliability and validity, essential properties for the acquisition of meaningful information. *Reliability* refers to the consistency of

Table 5-3 Generic Quality of Life Instruments

INSTRUMENT	SOURCE
Nottingham Health Profile	Bergner M, Bobbitt RA, Carter WB, et al: The sickness impact profile: Development and final revision of a health status measure. Medical Care 19:787-805, 1981.
EuroQol	EuroQol Group: EuroQol—a new facility for the measurement of health-related quality of life. Health Policy 16:199-208, 1990.
Sickness Impact Profile	Hunt SM, McEwen J, McKenna SP (eds): Measuring Health Status. Dover, NH, Croom Helm, 1986.
Medical Outcomes Study Short-Form 36-Item Health Survey (SF-36)	Kaplan RM, Bush JW: Health-related quality of life measurement for evaluation and research and policy analysis. Health Psych 1:61-71, 1982.
Quality of Well-Being Scale	Ware JE, Sherbourne CD: The MOS 36-item short-form health survey SF-36-I: Conceptual framework and item selection. Medical Care 30:473-483, 1992.

Table 5-4 Areas of Assessment on the Medical Outcomes Study Short-Form 36-Item Health Survey (SF-36)

Perception of health
Psychological well-being
Role limitations due to physical health problems
Role limitations due to mental health problems
Physical function
Social relations
Pain
Fatigue

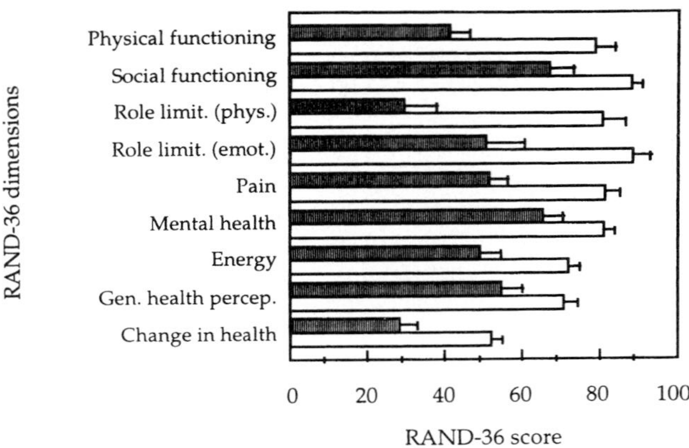

FIGURE 5-1 Impact of claudication on patient quality of life as assessed by the Rand SF-36 health survey, compared with the general population. (From Bosch JL, Hunink MGM: The relationship between descriptive and valuational quality-of-life measures in patients with intermittent claudication. Med Decis Making 116:217-225, 1996.)

measurement of each question within the survey tool. In simplest terms, a reliable question will be answered in the same way by most individuals who have the same overall health condition. *Validity* implies that each question actually measures what is intended and that the answers to similar questions are consistent. In the absence of a change in the patient's condition, answers to specific questions in surveys administered over time should be the same. The most commonly used health assessment tool in the United States is the Medical Outcomes Study Short-Form 36-Item Health Survey, commonly known as SF-36. This instrument is subdivided into an eight-index set of questions (Table 5-4). For each health dimension, the response scores are coded, summed, and converted into a scale from 0 to a high of 100.

As measured by the SF-36, physical function, role function, and pain are significantly affected by peripheral arterial occlusive disease (Fig. 5-1). The eight indices can be used individually or as an overall measure of general health status. Because it is a generic assessment tool, however, the subgroups are not disease specific. Role limitations due to physical health problems, for example, do not specifically identify the effect of claudication on occupation but do manifest the aggregate effect of all co-morbid conditions on the performance of role-related activities.

Generic quality of life instruments have been used to assess the quality of life after vascular intervention for both asymptomatic and symptomatic vascular disease. Perkins and associates[12] used the SF-36 and the York Quality of Life Questionnaire preoperatively and at 1½, 3, and 6 months postoperatively in order to evaluate 59 patients undergoing open infrarenal aortic aneurysm resection. These investigators noted a return to preoperative baseline values by 3 months after surgery and an improvement from baseline at 6 months. This finding is worthy of note in light of the fact that the patients were asymptomatic before surgery. The impact of an aggressive approach to the treatment of ruptured aneurysm has also been evaluated from the patient's perspective through the use of generic quality of life instruments. Joseph and associates[13] used the SF-36 instrument to evaluate 26 patients who survived repair of a ruptured abdominal aortic aneurysm. These researchers reported postoperative quality of life scores equivalent to or above those for age-matched control norms. Korhonen and colleagues[14] also used the SF-36 to evaluate the recovery of 93 patients who had undergone emergency resection of a ruptured abdominal aortic aneurysm 1 to 5 years previously. These investigators noted a prolonged or persistent reduction in the physical functioning domain, but the other domains were within the range of norms for age and sex-adjusted controls 1 to 5 years after surgery. These studies support the aggressive treatment of aortic aneurysms even in the setting of rupture.

Patient-based outcomes can also demonstrate the presence or absence of a lasting quality of life benefit of new technology. Malina and coworkers[15] obtained Nottingham Health Profile scores for 42 patients preoperatively and again at 5, 30, and 90 days after open or endovascular aneurysm repair. The investigators noted that by 3 months after surgery or intervention, the reported health-related quality of life was improved compared with baseline levels. Interestingly, there also was no difference noted in quality of life between those patients who had open procedures and those who had undergone endovascular treatment by this time. The value of this information lies in its suggestion that both the patient with an infrarenal aortic aneurysm and the vascular specialist can proceed with intervention with the belief that they are striving to improve quality of life.

■ DISEASE-SPECIFIC OUTCOMES ASSESSMENT TOOLS

Claudication has been the subject of several survey instruments designed to assess the degree of limitation that this symptom imposes on the patient. One of the most widely used assessment instruments at this time is the Walking Impairment Questionnaire (WIQ). This assessment tool has been designed to elicit information regarding the severity of discomfort experienced while walking, the reason for difficulty walking, walking distance and speed, and stair climbing.[16] In studies of exercise therapy for claudication, the WIQ scores for walking distances and speed have improved in conjunction with increased treadmill walking distances. Regensteiner and associates[17] used the WIQ and the SF-20, a derivative of the SF-36, to evaluate patients with severe claudication before and after participation in a supervised exercise training program and compared the results with those from a non-exercised control group. These investigators noted after 24 weeks that WIQ and SF-20 scores improved commensurate with increased treadmill walking distance. The control group did not show improvement on any testing modality.

OUTCOMES ASSESSMENT OF LOWER EXTREMITY REVASCULARIZATION

Complete evaluation of the effect of treatment of vascular disease requires a multifactorial assessment of the patient, the patient's disease, and the impact of treatment on both. The relationship between various objective clinical parameters, such as ABI and walking distance, and patient-reported outcomes of lower extremity ischemia do not demonstrate a high degree of correlation.[4,6,9,10,18] This is especially true of noninvasive treatments such as exercise therapy.[19] The assessment of benefit to the patient of an intervention may be altered when both clinical and patient-based parameters are used for evaluation. Whyman and colleagues[20] used several clinical and patient-based outcomes parameters to evaluate 30 patients undergoing balloon angioplasty and 32 patients treated with aspirin and exercise for claudication. Measures were ABI, treadmill distance to claudication, and quality of life as reported on the Nottingham Health Profile. These investigators found that at 2 years after treatment, patients treated with angioplasty had fewer occluded arterial segments than controls but treadmill distance to claudication and quality of life were not significantly different. The lack of differences in this and other such studies may arise because quality of life may be significantly affected by co-morbid conditions.[21]

To resolve the confusion in the published literature regarding the benefits of vascular intervention on peripheral arterial occlusive disease, both clinical and patient-based assessments should be reported. Although no formal guidelines have been established, there is now general agreement about the most useful information for the evaluation of the treatment of claudication; recommended parameters are listed in Table 5-5. Similar guidelines can be used for the evaluation of the treatment of critical limb ischemia. The patient-based outcomes information can be obtained by having the patient complete the required questionnaires or by having a nurse administer the forms. The survey tools appear lengthy to some, but the time required for their completion is usually less than that required for the corresponding vascular laboratory testing. A more careful evaluation of the outcomes of treatment of peripheral vascular disease will enable vascular surgeons to better select appropriate forms of intervention for their patients. This integrated approach to critical assessment of the benefit of vascular intervention will confirm not only the technical precision of vascular reconstruction but also the long-term improvement in patient status.

Table 5-5 Recommended Parameters for the Evaluation of Lower Extremity Ischemia*

- Standard clinical parameters
  - Technical success
  - Morbidity
  - Mortality
- Vascular examination
- Ankle-brachial indices
- Patency of treated arterial segment
- Changes in walking distance as measured by a treadmill protocol
- Changes in symptom severity by Rutherford classification
- Walking Impairment Questionnaire scores before and after treatment
- SF-36* quality of life scores before and after treatment

*Medical Outcomes Study Short-Form 36-Item Health Study.

From Dormandy JA, Rutherford RB: Management of peripheral arterial disease (PAD). TransAtlantic Inter-Society Consensus. J Vasc Surg 31:S1-S288, 2000.

ECONOMIC ASSESSMENT OF VASCULAR INTERVENTION

As technology advances and the push for better health care moves forward, there is a growing need to identify the economic effect of beneficial intervention.[22] This is another excellent method for analyzing the impact of vascular therapy. It is especially important because vascular intervention is directed toward improvement in quality of life. Economic evaluations permit the assessment of the cost for the improvement in life quality. Such values can then be used to compare, in a scientifically valid manner, the costs of vascular intervention with the costs of any other interventions that may improve quality of life. There are several acceptable methodologies for the performance of economic evaluation (Table 5-6). The goal of these economic analyses is the determination of the cost to achieve the desired benefit or effect of therapy.

The most commonly employed method for the economic analysis of surgical interventions is a Markov analysis (Table 5-7). This computer-based program tracks the changes in health states of a person after a health care interaction. For example, a patient with severe claudication secondary to inflow occlusion may undergo balloon angioplasty. After a successful angioplasty, the patient's stroke symptoms are significantly reduced and the patient's health state is improved. With time, however, the likelihood of recurrent stenosis and return of symptoms will rise and the patient's health state may be reduced. Re-treatment may be required, with the associated risks of a "redo" intervention or conversion to open surgery. By using ranges of data published in the literature for each possible outcome, a Markov analysis charts the probable changes in health states over time until an endpoint, such as a steady state of perfect health (valued as 1) or death (valued as 0) or amputation, is reached.

The analysis is generally performed on a cohort of hypothetical patients. The status of the hypothetical patient at the onset of the analysis is referred to as the *base-case*. The base-case attempts to define the type of hypothetical patient used in the analysis through demographic descriptors. This identifies the actual patient population to which the outcome of the assessment might apply. For the preceding example, the hypothetical base-case may be a 70-year-old man who smokes and has insulin-requiring diabetes mellitus, controlled hypertension, and an elevated cholesterol value with a prior myocardial infarction and two-block claudication. The Markov analysis describes the outcomes of a large cohort of such patients undergoing treatment for symptoms of claudication. Through identification of the costs associated with each of the health care interactions the patient may experience, a cost-effectiveness analysis can be developed.

Such methodologies have been used to address issues of vascular intervention that would be difficult to study with conventional methodologies, such as a randomized, prospective trial. Investigators have used economic modeling to

Table 5-6 Common Types of Economic Analyses of Diagnostic or Therapeutic Modalities

Cost-benefit	Cost units and benefit units are expressed in monetary terms. The benefit units may be determined by estimating the "willingness" of a payor to pay for a given benefit.
Cost-effectiveness (cost-utility)	A method to compare similar or different therapeutic interventions in which cost units are expressed in monetary terms but effectiveness is expressed in clinical terms, such as dollars per quality-adjusted life-years (QALYs) saved. For example, coronary bypass grafting yields a cost-effectiveness ratio (CER) of $9000/QALY, whereas hemodialysis has a CER of $53,000/QALY.
Cost-minimization	Monetary comparison of health care strategies that yield clinically similar outcomes to determine which is associated with lower costs over the period of observation.

Table 5-7 Economic Analysis: Glossary of Common Terms

Cost-effectiveness analysis	An assessment of the cost of an intervention expressed in clinical units, such as a clinical endpoint of limbs salvaged after distal bypass.
Quality-adjusted life-years	A preference-weighted endpoint that indicates the desired outcome, such as carotid endarterectomy without stroke.
Base-case	The target case for the comparison; for example, a 70-year-old man with carotid artery stenosis of more than 70% who is undergoing an intervention.
Sensitivity analysis	Testing a range of values for variables that are not well defined to determine the impact on outcome.
Cost-effectiveness ratio	The additional lifetime cost of an intervention divided by the quality-adjusted life-years saved.
Monetary unit fixation	The definition for the purpose of the study of the monetary unit used (i.e., dollars, pounds sterling) and the year. In studies conducted over several years, it is necessary to establish a single monetary unit. This is done by noting the base year and calculating all costs in terms of that base year by correcting for inflation in the subsequent years.
Markov analysis	A computer-based analytical tool that identifies the linkage of events using probabilities derived from reports in the literature. Because of the multiple possible outcomes of any vascular intervention and the range of probabilities that each of the outcomes may occur, the likelihood of an event occurrence cannot be directly evaluated with simple calculations. A Markov model will evaluate simultaneously all of the possible outcomes and the probabilities that each will occur for a given group of patients.

ascertain the cost-effectiveness of endovascular aneurysm treatment, to compare the costs of carotid endarterectomy and carotid angioplasty, and to identify the potential benefits of treating small aneurysms. Bosch and associates[23] used a Markov decision model to compare the cost-effectiveness of endovascular and open aneurysm repair on the basis of short-term and long-term outcomes. The hypothetical cohort comprised 70-year-old men with asymptomatic infrarenal aneurysms between 5 and 6 cm in diameter. Costs were fixed to the value of the year 2000 dollar. These researchers calculated an incremental cost-effectiveness ratio (CER) of $9905 per quality-adjusted life-year (QALY) saved, based on an increased survival benefit of endovascular repair with a small increase in lifetime cost compared with open surgery.

Patel and coworkers[24] used similar methodologies to compare endovascular and open surgical aneurysm repair undertaken on a cohort of hypothetical patients who were 70-year-old men with asymptomatic infrarenal aneurysms 5 cm in diameter. The group calculated a CER for endovascular repair of $22,826/QALY. The cost-effectiveness of endovascular repair was diminished as the morbidity and mortality of open repair were reduced. The differences in the CERs calculated in these two studies can be explained by the ranges of probabilities used for each of the possible outcomes in the Markov decision model. Schermerhorn and colleagues[25] evaluated the cost-effectiveness of surgery for small abdominal aortic aneurysms using data generated in the United Kingdom Small Aneurysm Trial. On the basis of Markov modeling, these investigators found that surgery for small aneurysms may be cost effective at $10,800/QALY if the patient was younger than 72 years, the aneurysm was at least 4.5 cm in diameter, and surgical morbidity and mortality were low.

Cronenwett and associates[26] used similar methodology to determine the cost-effectiveness of carotid artery surgery for patients with asymptomatic lesions. With a base-case cohort of patients, 66% male, who were on average 67 years of age with an asymptomatic lesion of at least 60%, these researchers calculated a CER of $8000/QALY. Kuntz and Kent[27] compared the treatment of symptomatic and asymptomatic patients with carotid stenosis. With Markov decision modeling, they calculated a CER of $4100/QALY for symptomatic patients and $52,700/QALY for asymptomatic patients. The CER varied significantly with the assigned perioperative stroke risk for surgery and for medical therapy.

These studies demonstrate that critical issues in vascular surgery can be addressed by advanced computer-based modeling using values of outcomes reported in the literature. In conjunction with patient-based outcomes data, these studies can clearly delineate the impact of vascular diagnostic and therapeutic endeavors on the health and well-being of patients and on the health care system within which they exist. It is only through application of these outcomes parameters and use of them for decision-making and decision analysis that the field of vascular surgery can successfully evolve.

■ REFERENCES

1. US Congress, Office of Technology Assessment: Identifying Health Technologies That Work: Searching for Evidence (OTA-H-608). Washington, DC, US Government Printing Office, September 1994.
2. Solomon MJ, McLeod RS: Should we be performing more randomized controlled trials evaluating surgical operations? Surgery 118:459-467, 1995.
3. Chetter IC, Kester RC, Scott DJ, et al: Correlating clinical indicators of lower-limb ischaemia with quality of life. Cardiovasc Surg 5:361-366, 1997.

4. Currie IC, Lamont PM, Baird RN, Wilson YG: Treatment of intermittent claudication: The impact on quality of life. Eur J Vasc Endovasc Surg 10:356-361, 1995.
5. Pell JP: Impact of intermittent claudication on quality of life. The Scottish Vascular Audit Group. Eur J Vasc Endovasc Surg 9:469-472, 1995.
6. Schneider JR, McHorney CA, Malenka DJ, et al: Functional health and well-being in patients with severe atherosclerotic peripheral vascular occlusive disease. Ann Vasc Surg 7:419-428, 1993.
7. Johnson BF, Evans L, Drury R, et al: Surgery for limb threatening ischemia: A reappraisal of the costs and benefits. Eur J Vasc Endovasc Surg 9:181-188, 1995.
8. Ronayne R: Feelings and attitudes during early convalescence following vascular surgery. J Adv Nurs 10:435-441, 1985.
9. Gibbons GW, Burgess AM, Guadagnoli E, et al: Return of well-being and function after infrainguinal revascularization. J Vasc Surg 21:35-44, 1995.
10. Duggan MM, Woodson J, Scott TE, et al: Functional outcomes in limb salvage vascular surgery. Am J Surg 168:188-191, 1994.
11. Khaira HS, Shearman CP, Hanger R: Quality of life in patients with intermittent claudication. Eur J Vasc Endovasc Surg 12:511-512, 1996.
12. Perkins JM, Magee TR, Hands LJ, et al: Prospective evaluation of quality of life after conventional abdominal aortic aneurysm surgery. Eur J Vasc Endovasc Surg 16:203-207, 1998.
13. Joseph AY, Fisher JB, Toedter LJ, et al: Ruptured abdominal aortic aneurysm and quality of life. Vasc Endovasc Surg 36:65-70, 2002.
14. Korhonen SJ, Kantonen I, Pettila V, et al: Long-term survival and health-related quality of life of patients with ruptured abdominal aortic aneurysm. Eur J Vasc Endovasc Surg 25:350-353, 2003.
15. Malina M, Nilsson M, Brukwall J, et al: Quality of life before and after endovascular and open repair of asymptomatic AAAs: A prospective study. J Endovasc Ther 7:372-379, 2000.
16. Regensteiner JG, Steiner JF, Panzer RJ, Hiatt WR: Evaluation of a walking impairment questionnaire in patients with peripheral arterial disease. J Vasc Med Biol 2:142-152, 1990.
17. Regensteiner JG, Steiner JF, Hiatt WR: Exercise training improves functional status in patients with peripheral arterial disease. J Vasc Surg 23:104-115, 1996.
18. Feinglass J, McCarthy WJ, Slavensky R, et al: Effect of lower extremity blood pressure on physical functioning in patients who have intermittent claudication. J Vasc Surg 24:503-512, 1996.
19. Randomized placebo-controlled, double-blind trial of ketanserin in claudicants: Changes in claudication distance and ankle systolic pressure. PACK Claudication Substudy Investigators. Circulation 80:1544-1548, 1989.
20. Whyman MR, Ruckley CV, Housley E, et al: Is intermittent claudication improved by percutaneous transluminal angioplasty? A randomized controlled trial. J Vasc Surg 26:551-557, 1997.
21. Cook TA, Galland RB: Quality of life changes after angioplasty for claudication: Medium-term results affected by co-morbid conditions. Cardiovasc Surg 5:424-426, 1997.
22. Zierler BK, Gray DT: The principles of cost-effectiveness analysis and their application. J Vasc Surg 37:226-234, 2003.
23. Bosch JL, Kaufman JA, Beinfeld MT, et al: Abdominal aortic aneurysms: Cost-effectiveness of elective endovascular and open surgical repair. Radiology. 225:337-344, 2002.
24. Patel ST, Haser PB, Bush HL, Kent KC: The cost-effectiveness of endovascular repair versus open surgical repair of abdominal aortic aneurysms: A decision analysis model. J Vasc Surg 29:958-972, 1999.
25. Schermerhorn ML, Birkmeyer JD, Gould DA, Cronenwett JL: Cost-effectiveness of surgery for small abdominal aortic aneurysms on the basis of data from the United Kingdom small aneurysm trial. J Vasc Surg 31:217-226, 2000.
26. Cronenwett JL, Birkmeyer JD, Nackman GB, et al: Cost-effectiveness of carotid endarterectomy in asymptomatic patients. J Vasc Surg 25:298-309, 1997.
27. Kuntz KM, Kent KC: Is carotid endarterectomy cost-effective? An analysis of symptomatic and asymptomatic patients. Circulation 94:1194-1198, 1996.

Chapter 6

Standardized Reporting Practices

RAJEEV DAYAL, MD
K. CRAIG KENT, MD

There is a clear need for standardized reporting practices in all areas of medicine, including vascular surgery. The task of surveying the literature to assess the current status of a treatment or intervention is daunting enough, but without standardized reporting practices, there is no sound basis for comparison. Imagine 100 studies of the efficacy of one operation. If the same variables and outcome measures were utilized in all 100 studies, their results are truly comparable, and combining the data through meta-analysis could result in a powerful statement about that procedure. Conversely, if the outcomes and the factors affecting them were gauged differently, not only would it be impossible to reconcile these differences and properly compare the findings but also a meta-analysis would be of questionable value.

Realizing the importance of reporting standards in vascular surgery, an ad hoc committee of the national vascular societies, under the direction first of this book's editor and now of this chapter's senior author (KCK), has developed and promulgated uniform reporting standards for many if not most common vascular procedures, for each of the major disease headings: lower extremity,[1,2] extracranial cerebral[3] and aneurysmal arterial diseases,[4] and venous disease.[5,6] Reporting standards have also been recommended for noninvasive testing of cerebrovascular disease,[7] some of which is procedure oriented (e.g., vena cava filter placement,[8] lower extremity endovascular procedures,[9] hemodialysis access,[10] and AAA endograft repair[11,12]). Disease severity scoring schemes have been introduced for venous disease[13] and aortic aneurysm repair[14] to enable more valid comparisons of reports of different interventions, or of the same intervention performed by different vascular surgeons, with consideration of the different patient populations involved; schemes for operative severity and for carotid and extremity arterial revascularization procedures will also be developed.

In addition, the Society of Cardiovascular and Interventional Radiology (SCVIR) has published reporting standards on the percutaneous treatment of lower extremity arterial disease[15] (based on the original vascular society reporting standards[1]), has jointly reported on vena cava filter placement,[8] and has recommended reporting standards for the treatment of renal artery stenosis,[16] percutaneous interventions for dialysis access,[17] new peripheral arterial revascularization devices,[18] and transluminal treatment of acute limb ischemia.[19]

It is important to distinguish between *reporting standards*, which recommend uniform practices for reporting on the diagnosis and treatment of vascular diseases in scientific journals, and *practice standards*, which recommend standards of vascular surgery care for those diseases. For example, practice standards for the repair of abdominal aortic aneurysms were published in 2003 by an ad hoc committee of the Society for Vascular Surgery.[20] These are in contradistinction to reporting standards, which recommend the variables and outcomes that should be measured by anyone conducting a study of aortic and other aneurysms,[4] and for endoluminal or endograft (endovascular) aortic aneurysm repair (EVAR)[11,12] along with a grading scheme for patient co-morbidities and anatomic variables.[14] On the basis of the last two reporting standards,[12,14] all reports of abdominal aortic aneurysm (AAA) repair should include an evaluation of patient co-morbidities and the main anatomic variables, the methods used for repair should be described in detail, and certain endpoints, such as procedural success, overall success, procedural mortality, and AAA-related mortality, should be documented.

Thus, the goal of reporting standards is to provide a uniform structure that investigators can use when they design and report clinical trials. These reports have several common themes. They define essential terms and make recommendations regarding the following:

- Clinical classification of disease
- Criteria for improvement, deterioration, and failure
- A grading system for risk factors
- Categorization of operations and interventions
- Complications encountered with grades for severity or outcome

Recommendations that are common to all reporting standard documents are summarized in the remainder of this chapter.

RISK FACTORS

Reports that evaluate procedures or interventions may be difficult to interpret when factors that affect outcome are not identified and graded for severity.[21] Such factors are (1) diabetes, (2) tobacco use, (3) hypertension, (4) hyperlipidemia, and (5) the cardiac, renal, or pulmonary status of a patient. These variables should then be analyzed to stratify risk as it relates to procedural outcome. Scoring systems used in other areas of medicine—such as Acute Physiology and Chronic Health Evaluation (APACHE), Pictures of Standard Syndromes and Undiagnosed Malformations (POSSUM), and Trauma and Injury Severity Score (TRISS)—can be cumbersome to use in clinical practice. POSSUM, for example, employs some parameters that are measured intraoperatively, such as blood loss, thereby preventing *preoperative* assessment and prediction of patient risk. Adopting the thesis that a scoring system of pre-intervention risk factors should be simple and practical in its use, developers of the reporting standards have advocated a grading system for risk factors that involves using a four-level scale with the categories 0 (none), 1 (mild), 2 (moderate), and 3 (severe). For example, hypertension is graded as absent, mild, moderate, or severe according to the level of blood pressure, the amount of drug therapy needed to control it, or both. Specific and unambiguous criteria for the various degrees of severity must be created, particularly for critical risk factors.[21] Moreover, there are risk factors that are disease or operation specific, as separately described in the appropriate sections here.

REPORTING DEATH AND COMPLICATIONS

Both early (<30 days) and late (>30 days) mortality rates after revascularization procedures should be reported routinely. The late mortality rates may be included as an additional column in the life-table entitled "cumulative mortality." Late deaths should be categorized as due to the underlying disease (e.g., atherosclerosis), to delayed complications of surgical management, or to unrelated factors.

Complications of intervention are to be reported as well. A complication grading scale similar to the scale used to grade associated risk factors can be employed: 0 (none), 1 (mild), 2 (moderate), and 3 (severe). When possible, complications should be categorized as systemic/remote, local/vascular, and local/nonvascular, and should be assigned a level of severity as previously detailed. Rutherford[22] provides a more detailed description of methods for reporting complications. Recommendations for the reporting of procedure-specific complications are also outlined in this chapter.

DISEASE-SPECIFIC AND PROCEDURE-SPECIFIC REPORTING STANDARDS

Lower Extremity Arterial Disease

Clinical Classification

The outcomes of acute and chronic lower extremity ischemia should not be combined because the results of emergent and elective interventions for the two disease states are influenced by different factors and are not comparable. For chronic ischemia, the proposed clinical categories are listed in Table 6-1. It should be noted that these categories are intended for clinical research, and the classic grades 0 to III are intended for clinical practice.

Table 6-1 Clinical Categories of Chronic Limb Ischemia

GRADE	CATEGORY	CLINICAL DESCRIPTION	OBJECTIVE CRITERIA
0	0	Asymptomatic: no hemodynamically significant occlusive disease	Normal treadmill or stress test result
I	1	Mild claudication	Patient completes treadmill exercise*; AP after exercise > 50 mm Hg but 25 mm Hg less than BP
	2	Moderate claudication	Between categories 1 and 3
	3	Severe claudication	Patient cannot complete treadmill exercise; AP after exercise < 50 mm Hg
II	4	Ischemic rest pain	Resting AP < 40 mm Hg, flat or barely pulsatile ankle or metatarsal PVR; TP < 30 mm Hg
III	5	Minor tissue loss; nonhealing ischemic ulcer, focal gangrene with diffuse pedal ischemia	Resting AP < 60 mm Hg; ankle or metatarsal PVR flat or barely pulsatile; TP < 40 mm Hg
	6	Major tissue loss; extending above TM level; functional foot no longer salvageable	Same as category 5

*Five minutes at 2 miles/hr on a 12% incline.
AP, ankle pressure; BP, brachial pressure; PVR, pulse volume recording; TM, transmetatarsal; TP, toe pressure.

Ischemic rest pain (category 4) indicates diffuse pedal ischemia and is defined as severe pain localized to the forefoot and toes, made worse by elevation, and improved by dependency. It is usually associated with ankle pressures less than 40 mm Hg and toe pressures less than 30 mm Hg, so these levels are used as objective criteria for category 4 designations. *Nonhealing ischemic ulcer* (category 5) indicates that there is inadequate arterial flow to support the *additional* inflammatory response required for healing. Therefore, in the presence of a "nonhealing ischemic ulcer" or gangrene, the higher pressure criteria, 60 mm Hg at the ankle and 40 mm Hg at the toe, are not paradoxical but deliberately used.

Treatments are performed for "limb salvage" if they are performed in patients fitting the clinical and noninvasive criteria of category 4 or 5. Successful limb salvage implies that the patient is left with at most a *minor* amputation, that is, digital amputations no higher than the transmetatarsal level after the intervention. Most higher forefoot and Syme's amputations are considered *major* amputations, and patients with successful amputations at these levels, even though lower than a below-knee amputation, cannot be included in the designation "limb or foot salvage." Similarly, a revascularization procedure that results in a below-knee amputation in the patient in whom an above-knee amputation would have been required is also not considered "limb salvage." Procedures for "blue toe syndrome" or microembolism do not qualify for the designation "limb salvage" unless there is objective (category 5 or 6) evidence of diffuse pedal ischemia or tissue loss and a proximal occlusive lesion that is corrected. These issues are addressed separately in more detail in the criteria for chronic critical ischemia issued by the TransAtlantic Inter-Society Consensus (TASC).[23]

Risk Factors

The standard risk factors discussed previously, such as diabetes and hypertension, should be reported along with the outcomes of revascularization for lower extremity ischemia. In addition, runoff is also thought to contribute to outcome, and a runoff grading system is offered. Further details regarding the current runoff grading scheme may be obtained from the most recent revision of the reporting standards for lower extremity ischemia.[2]

Outcome Criteria

Various outcomes can be measured after treatment, including patency, limb salvage, clinical status, and quality of life. Moreover, early (<30 days) and late (>30 days) outcomes should also be reported. The criterion for defining the various outcomes should be clearly established. Authors of scientific articles should not accept patency rates that are not based on objective findings. "No evidence of occlusion" cannot be equated with "patency" for reporting purposes, nor can "palpable pulses" recorded from a clinic visit, considering the inaccuracy of pulse palpation by relatively inexperienced health care professionals. A bypass graft or otherwise reconstructed arterial segment may be considered patent when any of the following criteria are met:

1. Demonstrated as patent on conventional arteriography or other established imaging technique—e.g., digital subtraction arteriography, duplex ultrasonography (duplex scanning), contrast-enhanced computed tomography (CT) scan, or magnetic resonance imaging (MRI).
2. Maintenance of the achieved improvement in the appropriate segmental pressure index (i.e., no more than 0.10 less than the highest postoperative index).
3. Maintenance of a plethysmographic tracing distal to the reconstruction that is significantly greater in magnitude than the preoperative value (e.g., + 5 mm or + 50% for pulse volume recording). This criterion is the weakest and is acceptable only when segmental limb pressures cannot be accurately measured, as in many diabetic patients. In most such cases, however, direct imaging is preferable.
4. The presence of a palpable pulse or the recording of a biphasic or triphasic Doppler waveform at two points directly over a superficially placed graft.
5. Direct observation of patency at operation or postmortem examination.

Criteria 2 through 4 are less commonly used now with the wide availability of duplex scanning. These criteria, particularly segmental pressure indexes, were routinely used to provide objective proof of patency in the era when serial arteriography was not appropriate. Nevertheless, pressure or plethysmographic deterioration must be given precedence over the simple demonstration of patency by imaging, and the lack of significant stenosis must be ruled out. Scientific reports of patency deserve precise documentation.

It is essential to report separate rates for primary patency, assisted primary patency, and secondary patency for vascular reconstructions. A graft is considered to have *primary patency* if its patency is uninterrupted (i.e., there have been no interval procedures, such as transluminal dilatation and distal extension from the graft). Dilatations or minor revisions performed for anastomotic or graft stenoses, graft dilatations, or other structural defects before occlusion do not constitute exceptions in defining primary patency, because they are intended to prevent eventual graft failure. Because the outcome of such interventions to preserve patency of the "failing" graft is markedly different from the outcome of interventions used to restore patency to a thrombosed graft, an *assisted primary patency* rate may be quoted as long as the pure primary patency rate is also noted. If graft patency is restored after occlusion by thrombectomy or thrombolysis, or if problems with the graft itself or one of its anastomoses require revision or reconstruction, it must be listed under *secondary patency*. However, a reoperation, specifically one that does not preserve flow through most of the original graft and at least one of its anastomoses, is considered a new bypass rather than listed as secondary patency. More detailed descriptions and explanations are provided in the revised version of recommended standards for reports addressing lower extremity ischemia.[2]

Criteria for establishing changes in clinical status have been defined and are summarized in Table 6-2. A combination of clinical assessment and segmental pressure index are used to establish whether the patient's status has improved or deteriorated. For example, status is defined as markedly improved after revascularization (+3) if there are no ischemic symptoms, the foot lesions have completely healed, and the ankle-brachial index (ABI) has "normalized" (>0.90). This scale has been found useful in assigning "continuing success" in follow-up reports on both open and endovascular lower extremity arterial procedures through combination of all cases in the +2 or +3 categories and application of either life-table or Kaplan-Meier analysis methods.

Endovascular Intervention for Lower Extremity Arterial Disease

Early reports of the outcomes of endovascular interventions for lower extremity ischemia were lacking in their use of standard reporting criteria. Some of the issues encountered in these early reports were (1) the exclusion of initial failures from estimates of cumulative success, (2) reporting of only one criterion for success, for example, patency without clinical outcome, (3) the lack of objective, hemodynamic criteria to confirm improvement or patency (e.g., claiming "clinical patency"), (4) absence of a distinction between primary and secondary patency (e.g., including redilatations without listing their number), and (5) not characterizing or stratifying the anatomy of the lesions treated. Most of the reporting standards previously defined for open intervention for lower extremity ischemia apply to endovascular interventions. However, a number of variables are unique to percutaneous treatments, as follows:

- For thrombolysis: agent used, dose and duration of treatment.
- Description of the underlying lesion (e.g., occlusion versus stenosis, length of treated segment, vessel diameter).
- Detailed description of the techniques, including size and length of balloon or stent, method of access, adjunctive measures used to maintain patency (e.g., a covered graft).
- Complications specific to endovascular treatments, including groin hematoma, arterial occlusion, intimal injury/dissection, embolization, arteriovenous fistula, perforation, and/or pseudoaneurysm.

For a more detailed description, the reader should consult Ahn and colleagues[9] and additional documents of the SCVIR.[18,19]

Cerebrovascular Disease

Clinical Classification

With the introduction of new methods of treating cerebrovascular disease (i.e., carotid stenting), the need for standardizing terminology and measurements of outcomes is critical. The use of inconsistent terminology makes comparison of data difficult if not impossible. A scheme for the clinical classification of cerebrovascular disease is summarized in Table 6-3.[3] The CHAT system is based on the

Table 6-2 Scale for Gauging Change in Clinical Status

+3	*Markedly improved*	No ischemic symptoms and any foot lesions completely healed; ABI essentially "normalized" (increased to more than 0.90)
+2	*Moderately improved*	No open foot lesions; still symptomatic but only with exercise and improved by at least one category*; ABI not normalized but increased by more than 0.10
+1	*Minimally improved*	Greater than 0.10 increase in ABI† but no categorical improvement or vice versa (i.e., upward categorical shift without an increase in ABI of more than 0.10
0	*No change*	No categorical shift and less than 0.10 change in ABI
−1	*Mildly worse*	No categorical shift but ABI decreased more than 0.10, or downward categorical shift with ABI decrease less than 0.10
−2	*Moderately worse*	One category worse or unexpected minor amputation
−3	*Markedly worse*	More than one category worse or unexpected major amputations

*Categories refer to clinical classification as shown in Table 6-1.
†In cases in which the ABI cannot be accurately measured, an index based on the toe pressure, or any measurable pressure distal to the site of revascularization, may be substituted.
ABI, ankle-brachial index.

Table 6-3 Clinical Classification Scheme for Cerebrovascular Disease (CHAT)

*C*urrent clinical presentation (<1 yr)	0: *Asymptomatic*
	1: *Brief* stroke (< 24hr):
	a: Carotid-ocular
	b: Carotid-cortical
	c: Vertebrobasilar
	d: Other focal
	e: Diffuse
	2: *Temporary* stroke with full recovery (24 hr to 1 month):
	a, b, c, d, e same as No. 1
	3: *Permanent* stroke (>1 month):
	a, b, c, d, e same as No. 1
	4: *Nonspecific* dysfunction
	5: *Changing* stroke:
	a: Improving
	b: Stable or fluctuating
	c: Deteriorating
Past *h*istory	0: Asymptomatic
	1: *Brief* stroke (<24 hr):
	a: Carotid-ocular
	b: Carotid-cortical
	c: Vertebrobasilar
	d: Other focal
	e: Diffuse
	2: *Temporary* stroke with full recovery (24 hr to 1 month):
	a, b, c, d, e same as No. 1
	3: *Permanent* stroke (>1 month):
	a, b, c, d, e same as No. 1
	4: *Nonspecific* dysfunction
*A*rtery	0: No lesion
	1: Appropriate lesion for symptom
	2: Lesion in other vascular territory only
	3: Combination of 1 & 2
	a: Arteriosclerotic plaque
	c: Cardiogenic (embolic)
	d: Dissection (spontaneous)
	e: Aneurysm
	f: Fibromuscular dysplasia
	r: Arteritis
	t: Trauma
	o: Other
*T*arget organ (brain)	Territory:
	0: No lesion
	1: Appropriate lesion for symptom
	2: Lesion in other vascular territory only
	3: Combination of 1 & 2
	Pathology:
	h: Hemorrhage
	i: Infarct
	l: Lacuna
	m: Arteriovenous malformation
	n: Neoplasm
	o: Other

following categories: clinical status, history, arterial lesion responsible, and target organ (brain or eye). The system includes both current clinical status and past clinical status, and the cutoff between current and past is 1 year.[24,25] The main clinical categories are as follows:

0: Asymptomatic.
1: Brief stroke—full recovery in less than 24 hours (internationally more acceptable than "transient ischemic attack").
2: Temporary stroke—full recovery in 24 hours to 1 month (often called "resolving ischemic neurologic deficit").
3: Permanent stroke—symptoms or signs lasting longer than 1 month.
4: Nonspecific dysfunction—allows identification of cases that do not fit into the precise classifications, a regrettable but necessary concession to the realities of clinical medicine.
5: Changing stroke (formerly stroke-in-evolution)—allows for patients in whom therapeutic intervention is applied before the outcome of the current episode is known. For the changing stroke category, additional coding identifies the nature of the stroke-in-evolution as improving, fluctuating, or deteriorating. After 1 month, a "changing stroke" with residual neurologic signs or symptoms must be reclassified as a "permanent stroke."

Classification of the arterial segment involved consists of the location and pathologic nature of the lesion. Therefore, the artery is classified as follows:

0: No lesion
1: Lesion appropriate for neurologic event
2: Lesion only in another vascular pathway
3: Combination of 1 and 2

The pathologic process is categorized as arteriosclerosis, cardiogenic embolus, dissection, aneurysm, fibromuscular dysplasia, arteritis, trauma, or other.

Classification of the target organ involved comprises the location and pathologic nature of the ischemic lesion. The target organ is classified as follows:

0: No lesion
1: Lesion appropriate for neurologic event
2: Lesion in another vascular territory
3: Combination of 1 and 2

Additional coding can be used to identify the vascular territory involved, such as carotid-ocular, carotid-hemispheric, vertebrobasilar, other focal, or diffuse. The pathologic process is categorized as hemorrhage, infarct, lacunar, arteriovenous malformation (AVM), neoplasm, retinal embolism, or other.

Diagnostic and Clinical Criteria

Strokes may be graded as major or minor, and this distinction may suffice for some reports. However, when additional grading criteria are required, the Neurologic Event Severity Scale should be used (Table 6-4). This scale grades strokes from 1 to 11 depending on the extent of impairment in up to five domains (swallowing, self-care, ambulation, communication, and comprehension).

Contrast angiography is the "gold standard" by which other imaging modalities are judged to image the carotid bifurcation. However, over the past several years, duplex scanning, magnetic resonance angiography (MRA), and spiral CT have emerged as minimally invasive alternatives. Many surgeons now use duplex scanning as the only

Table 6-4 Neurologic Event Severity Scale

SEVERITY GRADE	IMPAIRMENT*	NEUROLOGIC SYMPTOMS	NEUROLOGIC SIGNS
1	None	Present	Absent
2	None	Absent	Present
3	None	Present	Present
4	Minor, in one or more domains	Present	Present
5	Major, in only one domain	NA†	NA
6	Major, in any two domains	NA	NA
7	Major, in any three domains	NA	NA
8	Major, in any four domains	NA	NA
9	Major, in all five domains	NA	NA
10	Reduced level of consciousness	NA	NA
11	Death	NA	NA

*Impairment in the domains of swallowing, self-care, ambulation, speech, and comprehension. If independence is maintained despite the impairment, deficit is classified as minor; if independence is lost, it is classified as major.
†Neurologic signs and symptoms are integrated into the higher grades of impairment.
NA, not applicable.

From the EC/IC Bypass Study Group: The International Cooperative Study of Extracranial/Intracranial Arterial Anastomosis (EC/IC Bypass Study): Methodology and entry characteristics. Stroke 16:397-406, 1985. By permission of the American Heart Association, Inc.

preoperative study. However, before this strategy is adopted, the accuracy of duplex scanning in the laboratory that is performing the study must be proved.

When cerebral angiography is used for imaging, the following definitions regarding degree of stenosis should be used:

- *Normal:* < 20% stenosis
- *Mild:* 20% to 59% stenosis
- *Moderate:* 60% to 79% stenosis
- *Severe:* 80% to 99% stenosis
- *Occluded:* 100% stenosis

A subcategory defining extent of ulceration should be listed as well; categories are as follows:

0: Normal smooth surface
1: Small ulcer, <2 mm deep or 5 mm long
2: Moderate ulcer
3: Large ulcer, >4 mm deep or 10 mm long
4: Complex ulceration irregularity

The techniques used for determining degree of stenosis with duplex scanning are described in detail in Chapter 138.

Reporting Results

With the proliferation of carotid angioplasty and stenting (CAS), it is crucially important that the same standards be applied to endovascular and open techniques.[25] The results of therapeutic intervention for extracranial arteries are best measured according to the occurrence (or absence) of stroke (including transient or temporary cerebrovascular symptoms) in the distribution of the treated artery and the recurrence (or relief) of preoperative symptoms. Post-intervention central neurologic complications should be reported as brief, temporary, or permanent and should be further stratified into major or minor as detailed in the preoperative assessment. These strokes should also be separated into intraprocedural stroke, periprocedural stroke (up to 30 days after procedure), and late postprocedural stroke (>30 days after procedure). A second outcome measure that should be assessed is the residual stenosis that exists after the procedure as well as the degree of restenosis that subsequently develops.[26,27] A greater than 50% lesion is considered to signify recurrent disease or restenosis; it has become increasingly clear, however, that in the absence of symptoms, only restenoses greater than 80% require re-intervention. Thus, measurement of both aspects of recurrent disease is of use.

Venous Disease

Deep Venous Thrombosis

The associated risk factors for venous disease, summarized in Table 6-5, are significantly different from those for other forms of vascular disease. These risk factors are graded according to severity in a grading system similar to those used in other disease states. A composite total score is derived with a maximal score of 28. This composite score allows for the calculation of relative risk for development of deep venous thrombosis (DVT) and enables stratification of studies of DVT prophylaxis and treatment according to calculated risk factor score to ensure that the patient groups being compared are equivalent.[5,6]

The clinical classification is based on extent of thrombus and site of involvement. The relevant segments of the deep venous system are tibial-soleal veins, popliteal vein, common or superficial femoral vein, iliac vein, and vena cava. Superficial sites are the greater saphenous, lesser saphenous, and unnamed cutaneous veins. The following grading system should be applied to the six deep segments and two superficial segments:

0: Patent
1: Nonocclusive thrombus
2: Subsegmental occlusive thrombus
3: Occlusive thrombus throughout the segmental length

When thrombosis is present, it should be described as deep, superficial, or combined, and associated symptoms of pain, erythema, induration, and swelling should be noted.

The methods of detection of DVT should be listed as well, including physiologic tests such as plethysmography and anatomic tests such as contrast phlebography and duplex scanning. Specific details of treatment, such as the use of anticoagulation with heparin sodium or warfarin and the values for activated partial thromboplastin time (aPTT) and International Normalized Ratio (INR) should be noted. Notes on thrombolytic therapy should include the drug, dosage, and route of administration, and those on the results of therapy should include the percentage of patients experiencing total thrombus resolution with preservation of valve function. Valvular competence should be determined

Table 6-5 Associated Risk Factors for Deep Venous Thrombosis (DVT)

RISK FACTOR	SEVERITY SCALE	
Prior deep venous thrombosis	0	None
	1	Suspected
	2	Proven
	3	Multiple suspected
Immobilization	0	None
	1	1-3 days
	2	>3 days
	3	Paraplegia
Anesthesia	0	Local
	1	45 minutes general
	2	>45 minutes general
	3	>3 hr
Age	0	<40 yr
	1	40-70 yr
	2	>70 yr
Malignancy	0	None
	1	Recurrence
	2	Extensive regional tumor
	3	Metastatic
Malignant tissue type	0	Other (see below)
	1	Adenocarcinoma
Cardiac disease	0	New York Heart Association (NYHA) Class 1
	1	NYHA Class 2
	2	NYHA Class 3
	3	NYHA Class 4
Limb trauma	0	None
	1	Soft tissue injury
	2	Fracture of tibia and/or fibula
	3	Fracture of femur
	4	Fracture of hip or pelvis
Thrombotic tendency	0	None suspected
	1	Suspected
	2	Proven treated
	3	Proven untreated
Hormonal therapy?	0	No
	1	Yes
Pregnancy	0	Absent
	1	Present
Obesity	0	Normal to 175% ideal body weight
	1	>175% ideal body weight

Table 6-6 Overall Classification System for Chronic Venous Insufficiency: CEAP

CATEGORY	FINDING	CLASSIFICATION
*C*linical	Asymptomatic	C_0
	Telangiectasias, reticular veins, malleolar flare	C_1
	Varicose veins	C_2
	Edema, no skin changes	C_3
	Skin changes (pigmentation, venous eczema, lipodermatosclerosis	C_4
	Skin changes as above with healed ulcer	C_5
	Skin changes as above with active ulcer	C_6
*E*tiologic	Congenital: present since birth	E_C
	Primary: undetermined cause	E_P
	Secondary: known cause (post-thrombotic, etc.)	E_S
*A*natomic	Superficial veins (A_S)	
	Telangiectasias/reticular veins	A_{S1}
	Greater saphenous vein:	
	Above-knee	A_{S2}
	Below-knee	A_{S3}
	Lesser saphenous vein	A_{S4}
	Nonsaphenous vein	A_{S5}
	Deep veins (A_D)	
	Inferior vena cava	A_{D6}
	Iliac:	
	Common	A_{D7}
	Internal	A_{D8}
	External	A_{D9}
	Pelvic; gonadal, broad ligament	A_{D10}
	Femoral:	
	Common	A_{D11}
	Deep	A_{D12}
	Superficial	A_{D13}
	Popliteal	A_{D14}
	Tibial; anterior, posterior, or peroneal	A_{D15}
	Muscular; gastrointestinal, soleal	A_{D16}
	Perforating veins (A_P)	
	Thigh	A_{P17}
	Calf	A_{P18}
*P*athophysiologic	Reflux	P_R
	Obstruction	P_O
	Reflux and obstruction	$P_{R,O}$

by duplex scanning, and valvular competence and overall patency should be listed in life-table format. Incomplete resolution of thrombus should be regarded as a treatment failure unless major tributaries are cleared of thrombus. Inability to restore valvular competence, unless irrelevant because of location (e.g., vena cava), should be recorded as well.

Chronic Venous Insufficiency

Reports dealing with chronic venous insufficiency (CVI) should classify clinical severity as shown in Table 6-6. This classification system, abbreviated CEAP, utilizes categories for current clinical classification, etiologic classification, anatomic classification, and pathophysiologic classification.[6] The clinical classification ($C_{0\text{-}6}$) uses seven different categories to denote increasing severity from no evidence of disease to skin changes with active ulceration. The etiologic classification utilizes three mutually exclusive categories to denote congenital (E_C), primary (E_P), and secondary (E_S). The anatomic classification is used to denote whether the superficial (A_S), deep (A_D), or perforating (A_P) veins are affected, and these notations may be combined to indicate disease in multiple locations. The pathophysiologic classification is used to denote whether venous reflux (P_R) exists in the superficial, communicating, and deep systems; and to indicate whether a venous outflow obstruction (P_O) exists. Sufficient objective measurements of venous anatomy and hemodynamics should be included in order to document the presence of reflux, obstruction, or both.

A variety of methods are available to document the extent of reflux and venous outflow obstruction. They include measurement of maximal venous outflow (MVO) via plethysmographic techniques to gauge noninvasively the degree of obstruction. Reflux may be measured via Doppler examination coupled with proximal compression, although the use of this method in reports is discouraged because it is a qualitative test. Venous refill time (VRT), which may be obtained invasively via cannulation of foot veins or noninvasively via photoplethysmography, provides a measure of overall reflux. The venous filling index (VFI) is determined via air plethysmography and delivers a quantitative measure of reflux. Duplex scanning with a venous occluding cuff provides the best method of documenting reflux and may be used to identify reflux in perforating veins as well.[28] Regardless of the method used to document the extent of reflux and venous outflow obstruction, the findings should be correlated with the severity of the symptoms and subsequently should be used as an objective measure of success or failure of treatment. To that end, the suggested method of reporting outcomes is summarized in Table 6-7. In addition, reports should contain, at minimum, VRT or ambulatory venous pressure, MVO for venous obstruction, and duplex scanning of valvular competence for reports dealing with procedures that intend to restore competence. The duration of follow-up should be preferably 6 to 12 months, and reports should state whether support stockings were used.

Some measure of disease severity is needed to properly compare the outcomes of the various approaches to treatment of chronic venous insufficiency. The outcomes of two or more different treatments in a clinical trial, or the same treatment in two or more reports from the literature, cannot be compared with confidence unless the relative severity of the venous disease in each treatment group is known. The CEAP system (see Table 6-6) is an excellent classification scheme, but it cannot serve the purpose of venous severity scoring because many of its components are relatively static and others use detailed alphabetical designations. A disease severity scoring scheme must be quantifiable with gradable elements that can change in response to treatment.

The American Venous Forum's committee on venous outcomes assessment has developed a venous severity scoring system based on the best usable elements of the CEAP system.[13] Two scores are proposed and detailed in this document. The first is a Venous Clinical Severity Score, in which nine clinical characteristics of chronic venous disease are graded from 0 to 3 (absent, mild, moderate, severe) with specific criteria to avoid overlap or arbitrary scoring; 0 to 3 points are added for differences in background conservative therapy (compression and elevation) to produce a 30-point-maximum flat scale. The second is a Venous Segmental Disease Score, which combines the Anatomic and Pathophysiologic components of CEAP. Major venous segments are graded according to presence of reflux, obstruction, or both. This score is entirely based on findings of venous imaging, primarily duplex scanning but also phlebography. The scoring scheme weights 11 venous segments for their relative importance when involved with reflux, obstruction, or both, with a maximum score of 10. A third score is simply a modification of the existing CEAP disability score that eliminates reference to work and an 8-hour working day, substituting instead the patient's prior normal activities. These new scoring schemes are intended to complement the current CEAP system.

Arterial Aneurysm

Risk Factors

The identification of preoperative risk factors and patient stratification are critical to the assessment of the outcome of open aortic aneurysm repair. Risk factors should be graded as described previously. The anatomy of the aneurysm and the extent of repair are also important indicators of outcome. For example, the results of pararenal aneurysm repair differ from those of infrarenal AAA repair.

Classification

Arterial aneurysms are defined as focal arterial dilatations with a diameter at least 50% greater than that of the proximal normal arterial segment. Aneurysms may be classified on the basis of several factors, including site, etiology, morphology, and clinicopathologic characteristics. Each of these classifiers may be more appropriate than others, depending on circumstances. For example, etiology is particularly relevant to anastomotic aneurysms but is unknown for arteriosclerotic aneurysms (see also Chapter 29).

Evaluation of Results

Patency is not the most valid measure of long-term success after prosthetic repair of major or central arterial aneurysms. Patient survival and freedom from significant complications are more important factors. Recurrent aneurysm formation should also be included as a major index of long-term success. A more detailed description of reporting standards for AAA repair has been published by Johnston and associates.[4]

Table 6-7 Clinical Outcome for Chronic Venous Insufficiency*

+3	*Asymptomatic*	Improved at least one clinical class. Improvement of VRT and AVP to normal or at least +5 seconds, and −10 torr, respectively
+2	*Moderate improvement*	Continuing mild symptoms with same clinical and VL improvement as in +3
+1	*Mild improvement*	Improvement in either clinical class or VL tests, but not both. Unchanged clinically or by laboratory tests
−1	*Mild worsening*	Worsening of either clinical outcome by one category or VL tests
−2	*Significant worsening*	Both clinical and VL worsening
−3	*Marked worsening*	Same as −2 accompanied by either new or worsening ankle ulceration

*Classification for final clinical outcome.
AVP, ambulatory venous pressure; VL, vascular laboratory; VRT, venous refill time.

Endovascular Aortic Interventions

The development and evaluation of a minimally invasive approach to aortic aneurysm repair has led to a plethora of reports of this technique. Inconsistencies in reporting have made it difficult to compare techniques and devices and to gain a full understanding of the utility of this method of repair. Therefore, in 2002, an ad hoc committee of the Society for Vascular Surgery (SVS) revised and published updated standards for the reporting of outcomes for endovascular aortic aneurysm repair.[12]

Primary outcome criteria for endovascular aneurysm repair should include overall survival, rupture-free survival, and mortality related to primary or secondary interventions. Secondary outcome measures should include aneurysm enlargement and the presence of an endoleak.

Primary technical success is defined on an intent-to-treat basis and requires successful (1) access to the arterial system through a remote site, (2) deployment of the endograft, (3) absence of a type I or III endoleak (Table 6-8), and (4) patency of the graft without evidence of twists, kinks, or obstruction. If an unplanned intervention is required, *assisted primary success* or *secondary technical success* should be used.

Clinical success should be reported on an intent-to-treat basis as well and requires that there be no evidence of (1) a type I or III endoleak, (2) graft infection, (3) thrombosis, (4) aneurysm expansion or rupture, or (5) conversion to open repair. *Primary clinical success* is clinical success without the need for further intervention. *Assisted primary clinical success* is used if an additional endovascular procedure is required, and *secondary clinical success* if an open surgical procedure is necessary. Either life-table or Kaplan-Meier methods should be used to demonstrate primary, assisted primary, or secondary clinical success.

A number of variables contribute to clinical success. Changes in aneurysm diameter, volume, and length should be reported and followed. Generally, a change in aortic diameter of 5mm or a change in aneurysm volume of 5% is considered significant. Similarly, changes in aortic neck and iliac artery diameters and tortuosity may occur. Thus, outcomes measures that should be reported include but are not limited to (1) reduction or enlargement of AAA diameter by 5mm or of AAA volume by 5%, (2) aneurysm resolution, (3) rate of change of aneurysm diameter or volume, (4) prevalence and time of endoleak occurrence (primary, secondary, recurrent), (5) site of endoleak origin (types I to IV), (6) proportion of patients with endoleak and aneurysm expansion, and (7) proportion of patients with endoleak and no aneurysm expansion.

All deaths within 30 days of surgical procedure should be categorized as operative deaths and subcategorized as procedure-related or device-related. Subsequent deaths should be categorized as late deaths, and a relationship to the aneurysm, aneurysm rupture, or a secondary procedure should be noted. Complications should be reported according to the following scoring system:

1: Mild—spontaneous resolution or minimal intervention with no permanent impairment or increased length of stay.
2: Moderate—significant intervention required with minor permanent disability and increased length of stay.
3: Severe—major surgical or medical intervention required, resulting in permanent disability or death.

All complications should be classified as procedure-related or device-related. A more detailed description of these reporting standards was published by Chaikof and colleagues.[12]

Table 6-8 Classification of Endoleak

TYPE	CAUSE OF PERIGRAFT FLOW
I	a: Inadequate seal at proximal end of graft b: Inadequate seal at distal end c: Inadequate seal at iliac occluder
II	Flow from visceral vessel (lumbar, IMA)
III	a: Flow from module disconnection b: Flow from fabric disruption: Minor (<2 mm) Major (≥2 mm)
IV	Flow from porous fabric (<30 days after graft placement)
Endoleak of undefined origin	Flow seen, no source identified

IMA, inferior mesenteric artery.

Renal Artery Stenosis

With the maturation of renal angioplasty and stenting, the number of interventions for patients with asymptomatic and symptomatic renal artery stenosis has grown. Nevertheless, few randomized controlled trials have compared percutaneous renal revascularization with best medical management or surgical reconstruction. To establish criteria for the evaluation of these techniques, a collaborative group consisting of vascular surgeons, interventional radiologists, and cardiologists published guidelines for the reporting of renal artery revascularization.[16]

Clinical Criteria

The indications for renal revascularization should be clearly defined. They are absence of symptoms, hypertension (accelerated hypertension, refractory hypertension, malignant hypertension, or hypertension with intolerance to medication), renal salvage, and recurrent pulmonary edema not attributable to left ventricular dysfunction or unstable angina.

Methodology

Prior to an intervention, the severity of renal artery stenosis (RAS) should be measured, and when appropriate, a functional evaluation should be performed. These measurements can be obtained from duplex scanning, CT angiography (CTA), magnetic resonance angiography (MRA), or radionuclide renal scanning. There is institution-to-institution variability in the accuracy of these techniques. Therefore, the accuracy of the chosen method of renal artery imaging should be demonstrated at the outset of the study. Contrast angiography continues to be the gold standard for the evaluation of RAS. For multicenter trials, images should be made available to a core reference laboratory for review. Percentage stenosis is determined through creation of a ratio between the diameter of the narrowest segment of renal artery and the diameter of a normal segment of artery either proximal or distal to the stenosis. Hemodynamic measurements should be obtained as well.

Technical details regarding the performance of percutaneous transluminal renal angioplasty (PTRA) and stenting—such as balloon size, size and type of stent, procedure time, and contrast type and volume—should be provided. Angioplasty failures and whether stenting is provisional or primary should also be recorded. Technical details about treatment of renovascular disease via open surgical techniques should be provided as well; they include type of procedure, type of graft used, donor artery, and type of anastomoses as well as the need for additional procedures during renal revascularization.

Reporting of Outcomes

Anatomic success for percutaneous reconstruction is defined as a residual narrowing after PTRA or stent placement that is 30% or less. Other outcomes that should be measured are whether or not the lesion has been completely covered and, for ostial lesions, whether the stent is flush with or protruding 2 mm or less into the aortic lumen. Anatomic success after surgical revascularization should be proved by duplex scanning or angiography rather than visual inspection or manual palpation.

The overall success of procedures for renovascular disease should be gauged through assessment of postprocedural survival, or quality of life, or both. Thus, clinical events should be considered the gold standard for evaluating outcome. This evaluation should comprise overall mortality, cardiovascular mortality, and rate of nonfatal cardiovascular events, such as acute myocardial infarction, congestive heart failure, unstable angina, pulmonary edema, and cerebrovascular accident.

The impact of treatment of RAS on hypertension should be graded on the following scale:

- *Cure:* Patient is not taking antihypertensive medications and has a diastolic BP of 90 mm Hg or less and a systolic BP of 140 mm Hg or less.
- *Improvement:* Patient is taking same or reduced amount of medication compared with before treatment and has a diastolic BP 90 mm Hg or less, a systolic BP of 140 mm Hg or less, *or* patient is taking same amount of medication but shows a decrease in diastolic BP of 15 mm Hg.
- *Failure:* Patient shows no change or inability to meet preceding criteria.

The effect of treatment of RAS on renal function should also be determined. Postprocedural creatinine levels should be measured frequently and reported. Although an improvement in glomerular filtration rate (GFR) (or creatinine level) is an obvious sign of success, a decrease in the rate of deterioration in renal function may also substitute as success (although this is difficult to measure). Therefore, determining whether the treatment has had any effect on the rate of deterioration of GFR requires more than 5 data points over a period extending beyond 3 months.

Primary patency, assisted primary patency, and secondary patency outcomes should all be listed. The number and types of procedures required to achieve assisted primary patency and secondary patency and the length of time between procedures should be documented as well.

Arteriovenous Hemodialysis Access

Despite a plethora of reports, it has been difficult to gain a complete understanding of the outcomes of hemodialysis access procedures because of the lack of standardized terminology. This situation is largely related to the heterogeneity of the patients who have been treated and the multitude of different grafts and procedures that can be performed. In an attempt to bring resolution to this problem, Sidawy and coworkers[10] have published reporting standards for hemodialysis access.

A number of preoperative factors are important in the determination of the outcome of a particular access procedure. They have been organized into systemic factors, local limb factors, and miscellaneous factors (Table 6-9). The arterial and venous anatomy clearly affects the outcome of AV access and should therefore be reported in a meaningful way. If this cannot be accomplished by direct clinical examination, noninvasive and invasive testing should be performed. A component-based system has been designed that can be used to describe the anatomic configuration of arteriovenous reconstructions. The components are as follows:

- Conduit (autogenous or nonautogenous)
- Location (body region and arterial/venous sites)
- Configuration (direct and indirect)

The use of this system allows grouping of procedures and, consequently, a more accurate analysis of outcomes. Numerous complications can occur with these procedures, as detailed in Table 6-10; they should be systematically reported. Primary patency, assisted primary patency, and secondary patency categories for AV access should also be included in all reports. Definitions for these terms are similar to those used for other revascularization procedures. The surgical and endovascular techniques that are used to maintain assisted primary and secondary patency should be detailed as well. Lastly, functionality is as important as patency because the access must deliver flow rates of 350 to 400 mL/min in order to allow successful dialysis. A *nonfunctional AV access* is one that cannot be used for hemodialysis regardless of whether it is patent. Life-table analysis and Kaplan-Meier survival curves should be used to display patency.

Endovascular Interventions for Arteriovenous Hemodialysis Access

Percutaneous endoluminal interventions are being used increasingly in the treatment of failing AV access for hemodialysis. Recommendations for reporting of these procedures are as follows.[17] The techniques and methods used to determine the location and extent of the culprit

Table 6-9 Grading of Factors that Affect Outcome of Arteriovenous Hemodialysis

RISK FACTOR	SEVERITY SCALE	
Systemic factors:		
Diabetes	0	None
	1	Adult onset, oral medication
	2	Adult onset, insulin
	3	Juvenile onset
Hypertension	0	None
	1	Controlled with 1 drug
	2	Controlled with 2 drugs
	3	Uncontrolled
Cigarette use	0	None
	1	Quit < 10 yr previously
	2	<1 pack/day
	3	>1 pack/day
HIV	0	None
	1	CD count > 200 cells/mm^3
	2	CD count < 200 cells/mm^3
	3	HIV with current infection
Intravenous drug abuse	0	None
	1	Used in past but not currently
	2	Current use, can have AV access
	3	Current use, cannot have AV access
Limb factors:		
Venous outflow track	0	No stenosis
	1	Stenosis < 50%
	2	Stenosis > 50%
	3	Occluded
Previous procedures same limb	0	None
	1	1
	2	2
	3	3 or more
Miscellaneous factors:		
Timeliness of referral	0	3 month before need
	1	1 month before need
	2	Dialysis imminent
	3	Dialysis immediate
Choice of access location and conduit material	0	Arm, autogenous
	1	Arm, synthetic
	2	Leg, autogenous
	3	Leg, synthetic
Choice of access site	0	Nondominant arm
	1	Dominant arm
	2	Leg
	3	Body wall

AV, arteriovenous; CD, CD4$^+$ lymphocyte; HIV, human immunodeficiency virus.

lesion should be listed. Lesion location, lesion length, and patency of venous runoff should be detailed. The technical details of the chosen percutaneous intervention should be provided. For example, if a balloon angioplasty is performed, the balloon diameter and length, duration of inflation, number of inflations, and balloon pressure should be given. Procedure time, lysis time, lytic agent used, and time to hemostasis should be recorded. Success should be listed as both anatomic and clinical, *clinical success* being defined as resumption of normal dialysis after treatment. Patency should be reported by means of the Kaplan-Meier method as previously described and should include categories for primary, assisted primary, and secondary patency.

Vena Caval Filters

Numerous percutaneous devices that can be used for vena caval interruption are now available. The lack of standardized reporting has made it difficult to compare the outcomes of these various devices. Greenfield and Rutherford[8] have published standards developed through a consensus conference on vena caval filters. Their report includes standards for defining technical success and patency, clinical sequelae, filter stability, and inferior vena cava (IVC) patency.

■ CONCLUSION

Methods of treating vascular disease have changed significantly over the past decade and continue to evolve. Many new and less invasive treatments are now available; however, validation of their efficacy requires rigorous study and comparison with existing techniques. Reporting standards are now available for the majority of vascular interventions. Routine use of these standards will enhance tremendously our ability to evaluate these new techniques.

■ REFERENCES

1. Rutherford RB, Flanigan DP, Gupta SK, et al: Suggested standards for reports dealing with lower extremity ischemia. J Vasc Surg 4:80, 1986.
2. Rutherford RB, Baker JD, Ernst C, et al: Recommended standards for reports dealing with lower extremity ischemia: Revised version. J Vasc Surg 26:517, 1997.
3. Baker JD, Rutherford RB, Bernstein EF, et al: Suggested standards for reports dealing with cerebrovascular disease. J Vasc Surg 8:721, 1988.
4. Johnston KW, Rutherford RB, Tilson MD, et al: Suggested standards for reporting on arterial aneurysms. J Vasc Surg 13:444, 1991.
5. Porter JM, Clagett GP, Cranley J, et al: Reporting standards in venous disease. J Vasc Surg 8:172, 1988.
6. Porter JM, Moneta GL: Reporting standards in venous disease: An update. International Consensus Committee on Chronic Venous Disease. J Vasc Surg 21:635, 1995.
7. Thiele BL, Jones AM, Hobson RW, et al: Standards in noninvasive cerebrovascular testing. J Vasc Surg 15:495, 1992.
8. Greenfield LJ, Rutherford RB: Recommended reporting standards for vena caval filter placement and patient follow-up. J Vasc Interv Radiol 10:1013, 1999.
9. Ahn SS, Rutherford RB, Becker GJ, et al: Reporting standards for lower extremity arterial endovascular procedures. J Vasc Surg 17:1103, 1993.
10. Sidawy AN, Gray R, Besarab A, et al: Recommended standards for reports dealing with arteriovenous hemodialysis accesses. J Vasc Surg 35:603, 2002.
11. Ahn SS, Rutherford RB, Johnston KW, et al: Reporting standards for infrarenal endovascular abdominal aorta aneurysm repair. J Vasc Surg 25:405, 1997.
12. Chaikof EL, Blankensteijn JD, Harris PL, et al: Reporting standards for endovascular aortic aneurysm repair. J Vasc Surg 35:1048, 2002.
13. Rutherford RB, Padberg FT Jr, Comerota AJ, et al: Venous severity scoring: An adjunct to venous outcome assessment. J Vasc Surg 31:1307, 2000.
14. Chaikof EL, Fillinger MF, Matsumura JS, et al: Identifying and grading factors that modify the outcome of endovascular aortic aneurysm repair. J Vasc Surg 35:1060, 2002.
15. Rutherford RB, Becker GJ: Standards for evaluating and reporting the results of surgical and percutaneous therapy for peripheral vascular disease. J Vasc Interv Radiol 2:169, 1991.
16. Rundback JH, Sacks D, Kent KC, et al: Guidelines for the reporting of renal artery revascularization in clinical trials. Circulation 106:1572, 2002.
17. Gray RJ, Sacks D, Martin LG, Trerotola SO: Reporting standards for percutaneous interventions in dialysis access. J Vasc Interv Radiol 15:S433, 2003.

Table 6-10 Grading Severity of Complications of Arteriovenous (AV) Access

	COMPLICATION	SEVERITY SCALE	
Local access complications:			
Bleeding	Early, postoperative; prolonged bleeding from needle puncture	0	None
		1	Resolves without treatment
		2	Medical therapy needed
		3	Intervention needed
Infection	Early/late; site of infection	0	None
		1	Observed
		2	Loss of access
		3	Loss of limb
Noninfectious fluid collections	Hematoma, seroma, lymphocele	0	None
		1	Spontaneous resolution
		2	Aspirated
		3	Loss of access
Anastomotic complications	Hemorrhage, pseudoaneurysm, stenosis	0	None
		1	Observed
		2	Intervention required
		3	Loss of access
Mid-AV access/vein	Aneurysm, dilation, pseudoaneurysm, stenosis	0	None
		1	Observed
		2	Intervention required
		3	Loss of access
Access thrombosis	Early/late; technical cause	0	None
		1	Clot removed
		2	Access revised
		3	Loss of access
AV access malfunction	Insufficient inflow or outflow; unable to puncture	0	None
		1	Not corrected
		2	Revised access
		3	Loss of access
Remote complications:			
Steal syndrome	Normal/abnormal vasculature	0	None
		1	Mild, no treatment
		2	Moderate
		3	Severe, intervention performed
Venous hypertension	Stenosis, central thrombosis, or occlusion	0	None
		1	Mild, no treatment
		2	Moderate
		3	Severe, intervention required
Neuropathy	Systemic/mechanical	0	None
		1	Mild
		2	Moderate
		3	Severe

18. Sacks D, Marinelli DL, Martin LG, et al: Reporting standards for clinical evaluation of new peripheral arterial revascularization devices. J Vasc Interv Radiol 14:S395, 2003.
19. Patel N, Sacks D, Patel RI, et al: SCVIR Reporting standards for the treatment of acute limb ischemia with use of transluminal removal of arterial thrombus. J Vasc Interv Radiol 12:559, 2001.
20. Brewster DC, Cronenwett JL, Hallett JW, et al: Guidelines for the treatment of abdominal aortic aneurysms. J Vasc Surg 37:1106, 2003.
21. Rutherford RB: Presidential Address: Vascular surgery: Comparing outcomes. J Vasc Surg 23:5, 1996.
22. Rutherford RB: Suggested standards for reporting complications in vascular surgery. In Towne JB, Bernhard WM (eds): Complications in Vascular Surgery, 3rd ed. St. Louis, Quality Medical Publishing, 1991, p 1.
23. Dormandy JA, Rutherford RB: Management of peripheral arterial disease (PAD). TASC Working Group. TransAtlantic Inter-Society Consensus (TASC). J Vasc Surg 31:S1, 2000.
24. Rutherford RB: Reporting standards for endovascular surgery: Should existing standards be modified for newer procedures? Semin Vasc Surg 10:197, 1997.
25. Rutherford RB: Comparing outcomes of carotid interventions: The importance of standardized reporting practices. In Branchereau A, Jacobs M (eds): New Trends and Developments in Carotid Artery Disease. Armonk, NY, Futura, 1998, p 1.
26. Zeirler RE, Bandyk DF, Thiele BL, et al: Carotid artery stenosis following endarterectomy. Arch Surg 117:1408, 1982.
27. Ouriel K, Green RM: Clinical and technical factors influencing recurrent carotid stenosis and occlusion after endarterectomy. J Vasc Surg 5:702, 1987.
28. Barnes RW: Noninvasive techniques in chronic venous insufficiency. In Bernstein EF (ed): Noninvasive Diagnostic Techniques in Vascular Disease, 3rd ed. St. Louis, CV Mosby, 1985, p 839.

Section II

BASIC VASCULAR SCIENCE

ANTON N. SIDAWY, MD

Chapter 7

Embryology of the Vascular System

JOSEPH M. GIORDANO, MD

It is difficult to imagine a more complex structure with all its organs and systems than the human body. Yet within 40 weeks, the human body develops almost flawlessly from a small clump of cells that appear after conception. For the first 3 weeks, the embryo receives its nourishment from the yolk sac and through the diffusion of oxygen and nutrients from the maternal circulation. By the end of the third week, a functional vascular system must be present to support the rapidly developing embryo.

■ INITIAL DEVELOPMENT OF THE VASCULAR SYSTEM

The primitive vascular system forms initially from a clump of mesenchymal cells that separate and form channels. These channels eventually unite to form primitive endothelium-lined vessels that become a functioning vascular network by the end of the third week (Fig. 7-1). This system then connects to the developing heart that, although it consists only of two tubes, is still capable of effectively circulating blood.

At the beginning of the fourth week, the cardiovascular system consists of two heart tubes connected to a paired dorsal aorta that extends down the entire length of the embryo. The dorsal aortas each have segmental dorsal, lateral, and ventral branches. At the level of the seventh cervical vertebra, the paired dorsal aortas fuse distally to create the thoracic aorta and abdominal aorta; proximal to the seventh cervical vertebra, however, the paired dorsal aortas persist. As the aortic fusion occurs, the heart tubes fuse to form the heart. Cephalad to the developing heart, the truncus arteriosus and the aortic sac form. Six pairs of arteries, called *aortic arches*, develop from the aortic sac, pass laterally around the developing gut, and connect to the paired dorsal aorta.

During the sixth to eighth week of gestation, the six aortic arches along with the seventh segmental dorsal artery from each dorsal aorta develop into the aortic arch and its major branches. It is interesting that the vascular system of aortic arches present at the beginning of the sixth week of gestation imitates the system found in marine life. Marine animals have a single ventricle. Blood flows from the single ventricular chamber to the aortic sac to the paired aortic arches, which then break up to small capillaries that receive oxygen from the gills. The capillaries re-form to become major vessels again (like the pulmonary veins in the human) that carry the oxygenated blood to the dorsal aorta and the rest of the body.

For the most part, the vascular system in the human is symmetric, with each side of the body a mirror image of the other. One exception to this observation is the aortic arch, which is different on the two sides. The innominate artery, which divides into the right carotid artery and the subclavian artery, is not present on the left side, on which the left carotid and subclavian arteries originating from the aortic arch are found. These differences are directly related to the behavior of the left and right aortic arches as they evolve into the mature thoracic aortic arch in humans. The six pairs of arches (along with the dorsal aorta, truncus arteriosus, and aortic sac) elongate, dilate, regress, and disappear, their configuration changing to become the fully developed aortic arch. The diagrammatic representation of these changes suggests that the aortic arches are all present at the same time, but this is not the case; some arches are developing while others are regressing.

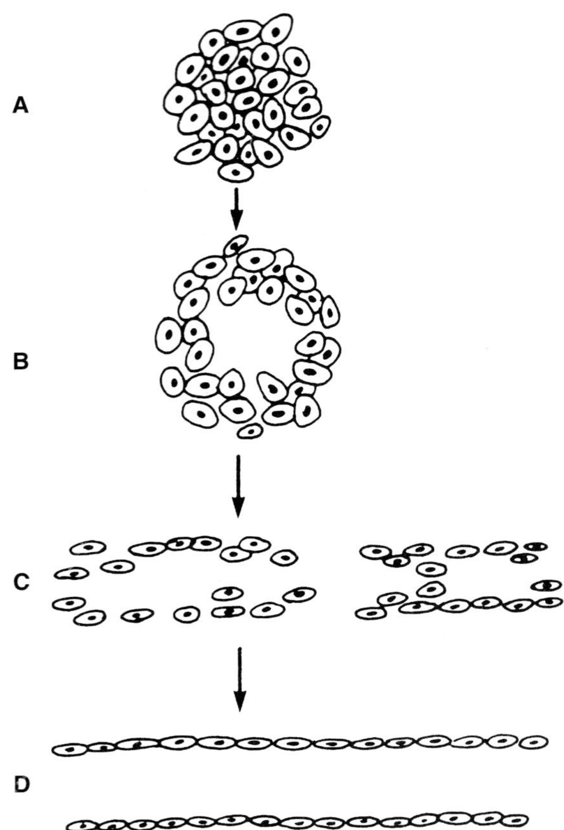

FIGURE 7-1 Initial development of vessels. **A,** Clumps of cells forms. **B,** Cavities develop. **C,** Channels form. **D,** Channels unite to form primitive endothelium-lined vessels.

Aortic Arch

The paired first, second, and fifth aortic arches and the distal section of the right sixth arch disappear (Fig. 7-2A). The dorsal aorta on each side between the third and fourth arches also disappears. Blood to the third aortic arch then flows only to the head and neck (Fig. 7-2B). The third arch becomes the *common carotid artery,* and the dorsal aorta between the first and third arches becomes the *internal carotid arteries*. The right dorsal aorta distal to the seventh intersegmental artery but proximal to the fused thoracic aorta involutes, so that blood entering the right fourth arch flows to the right dorsal aorta and then to the right seventh intersegmental artery. This section eventually becomes the right subclavian and axillary arteries (Fig. 7-2C). The section of the aortic sac connected to the right third and fourth aortic arches elongates, becoming the innominate artery, with the third arch becoming the right common carotid artery and the fourth arch contributing to the right subclavian artery, as noted previously.

The left fourth arch and the left dorsal aorta distal to it dilate and become part of the aortic arch, with the left seventh intersegmental artery becoming the left subclavian and axillary arteries. The proximal parts of both sixth arches become the right and left pulmonary arteries. The distal part of the right sixth arch disappears, but the distal part of the left sixth arch persists as the ductus arteriosus. This ductus connects the left pulmonary artery to the aorta and, in the fetus, shunts blood away from the immature fetal lungs to the aorta (Fig. 7-2D).

Anomalies

In view of the complex events that occur in the development of the aortic arch and its branches, it is not surprising that anomalies occur.[1-5] Parts of the primitive aortic arch that should disappear persist, whereas other parts that should persist disappear.

Patent Ductus Arteriosus Patent ductus arteriosus is the most common vascular anomaly. The ductus arteriosus is formed from the distal part of the left sixth arch. At birth, the ductus constricts, probably as a result of the initial exposure of oxygen-sensitive muscle cells in its wall to blood with high oxygen content. By 1 month, the ductus is normally obliterated to become the ligamentum arteriosum. If the ductus arteriosus does not constrict but remains patent, blood is shunted from the high-pressure thoracic aorta to the low-pressure pulmonary system, eventually causing significant pulmonary hypertension.

Coarctation of the Aorta Aortic coarctation usually occurs at the level of the ligamentum arteriosum. The more common *postductal* type occurs just distal to the ligamentum; the *preductal* type occurs just proximal to the ligamentum.

The etiologic mechanism remains unclear, but the anomaly is thought to result from incorporation of oxygen-sensitive muscle tissue from the ductus arteriosus into the wall of the aorta. Normally, this muscle constricts when exposed to high oxygen tension, closing the ductus arteriosus. If the muscle is also in the wall of the aorta, the aorta constricts at that level. Eventually, chronic changes occur and the constriction becomes permanent.

Double Aortic Arch At times, the right dorsal aorta distal to the right seventh intersegmental artery fails to involute. A double aortic arch forms, with the right limb passing posterior to the esophagus to join the left limb, which passes anterior to the trachea. A vascular ring forms around the esophagus and trachea, sometimes compressing these structures (Fig. 7-3).

Right Aortic Arch Involution of the left dorsal aorta distal to the left seventh segmental artery while the right dorsal aorta persists, opposite to the normal sequence, creates a right aortic arch (Fig. 7-4). The ligamentum arteriosum arises from the distal right sixth arch instead of the distal left sixth arch but still connects to the aorta. If the arch passes to the left side posterior to the esophagus, a vascular ring is formed with the ligamentum arteriosum. If the right aortic arch passes anterior to the esophagus and trachea, a vascular ring is not formed. The right aortic arch with a retroesophageal component may initially be a double aortic arch in which the left dorsal aorta later regresses.

Retroesophageal Right Subclavian Artery The subclavian artery normally forms from the right fourth aortic arch, the right dorsal aorta distal to the right fourth aortic arch, and the seventh intersegmental artery. A retroesophageal right subclavian artery forms because the right aortic arch

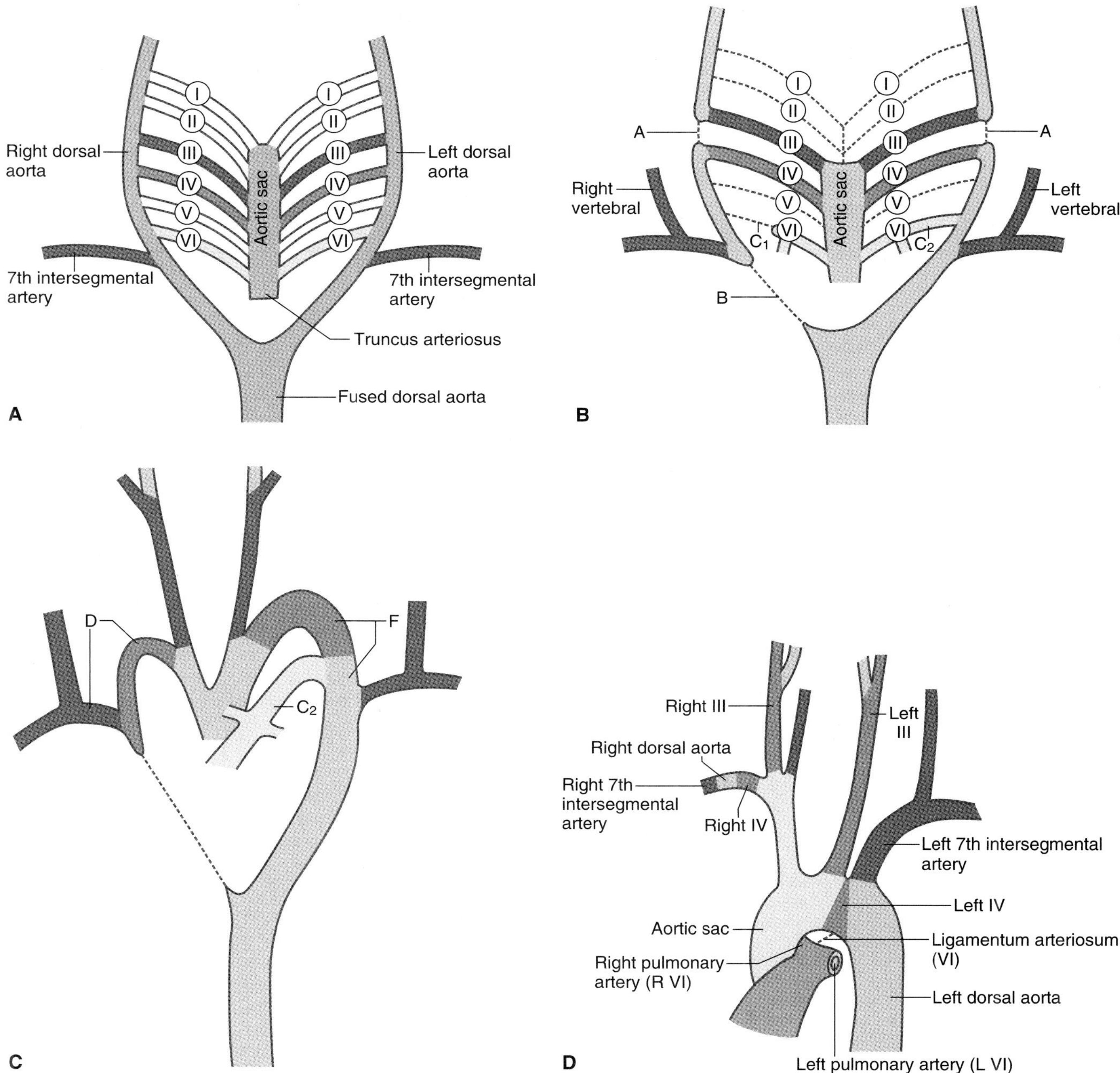

FIGURE 7-2 **A,** The six primitive aortic arches. The first, second, and fifth arches disappear. The paired dorsal aortas fuse at the level of the seventh cervical vertebra to become the thoracic and abdominal aorta. **B,** Differentiation of aortic arches. The dorsal aorta between the third and fourth arches (A) involutes so that blood entering the third arch perfuses the head only. The third arch and its branches become the carotid system. The right dorsal aorta distal to the right seventh intersegmental artery (B) involutes so that blood entering the right fourth arch perfuses the right upper extremity. This system becomes the right subclavian artery. The distal part of the right sixth arch (C_1) involutes, but the distal part of the left sixth arch (C_2) persists, becoming the ductus arteriosus. **C,** Development of aortic arches. The right fourth arch, the dorsal aorta distal to the right fourth arch, and the right seventh intersegmental artery become the right subclavian artery (D). The left fourth arch and the left dorsal aorta distal to it become part of the aortic arch (F). The left seventh intersegmental artery becomes the left subclavian artery. Pulmonary arteries are forming from the sixth arch with the ductus arteriosus (C_2) present. **D,** Segments of the aortic arches that produce the adult aortic arch. The patent ductus arteriosus has become the ligamentum arteriosum.

and the dorsal aorta distal to the right arch abnormally involute (Fig. 7-5). The right dorsal aorta distal to the right intersegmental artery then persists instead of involuting, joining the right seventh intersegmental artery to form the right subclavian artery. As the arch of the aorta enlarges and migrates cranially from the aortic sac, the right subclavian artery in this anomaly also migrates, eventually becoming distal to the left subclavian artery. The right subclavian artery then goes from the aorta, which now is on the left side behind the esophagus, to supply the right arm. Most patients with this entity are asymptomatic, but they may have difficulty swallowing.[2]

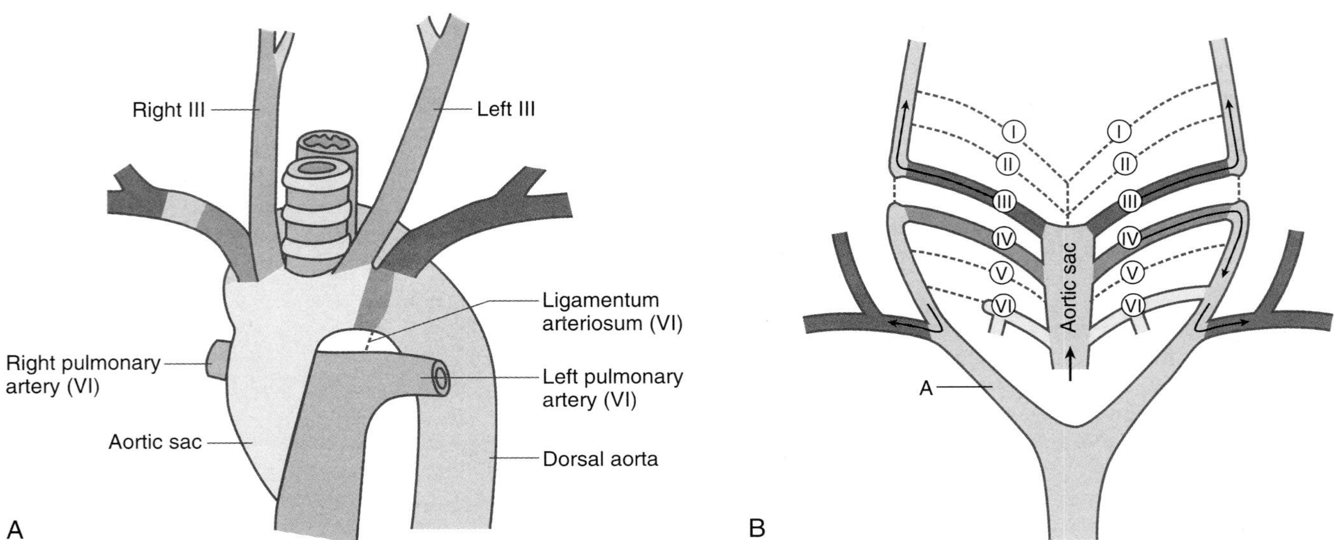

FIGURE 7-3 **A,** Double aortic arch. The aortic arch passes anterior and posterior to the trachea and esophagus, forming a vascular ring. **B,** Double aortic arch. The right dorsal aorta distal to the right seventh intersegmental artery (A), which normally involutes, persists to become part of the double aortic arch.

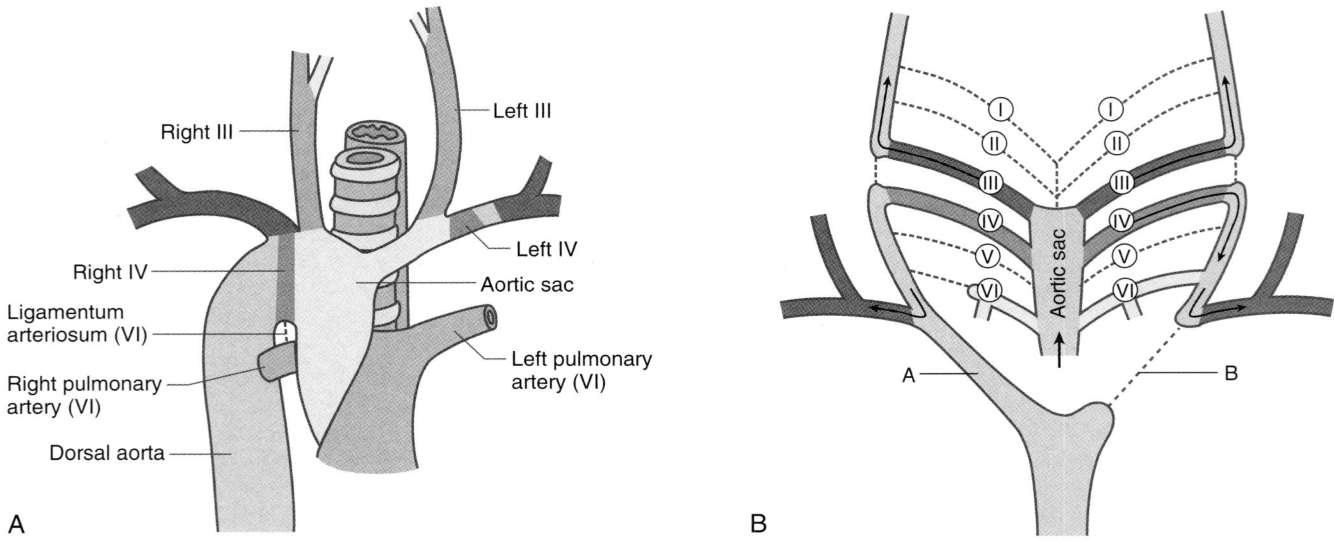

FIGURE 7-4 **A,** The right aortic arch. One of the two types in which the right arch passes anterior to the trachea and esophagus so that no vascular ring is formed. If the right arch passes posterior to the trachea and esophagus, the ligamentum arteriosum and the right arch form a vascular ring. **B,** Right aortic arch. The right dorsal aorta distal to the right seventh intersegmental artery persists (A), but the left dorsal aorta distal to the left seventh intersegmental artery involutes (B), the opposite of the normal occurrence.

Thoracic and Abdominal Aorta

At the third week of gestation, the embryo is developing into a segmental structure throughout its entire length, eventually forming from 36 to 38 segments, or somites. The paired dorsal aorta runs the entire length of the embryo. At each segment, each side of the paired aortas has dorsal, lateral, and ventral branches.

At the fourth week, the paired dorsal aortas at the level of the seventh cervical vertebra fuse to become the thoracic and abdominal aorta. However, the segmental arteries persist, so each segment of fused aorta has two dorsal, ventral, and lateral branches. These branches involute, dilate, and fuse. The dorsal branches become the vertebral arteries in the neck, the intercostal arteries in the chest, and the lumbar arteries in the abdomen. The fifth lumbar dorsal segmental arteries enlarge to become the common iliac arteries. The paired ventral arteries initially become the *vitelline arteries*, which connect to the yolk sac. As the gastrointestinal tract develops, the vitelline arteries become its blood supply; these arteries fuse to become the celiac, superior mesenteric, and the inferior mesenteric arteries. The ventral arteries at the level of the fifth lumbar segment connect to the dorsal

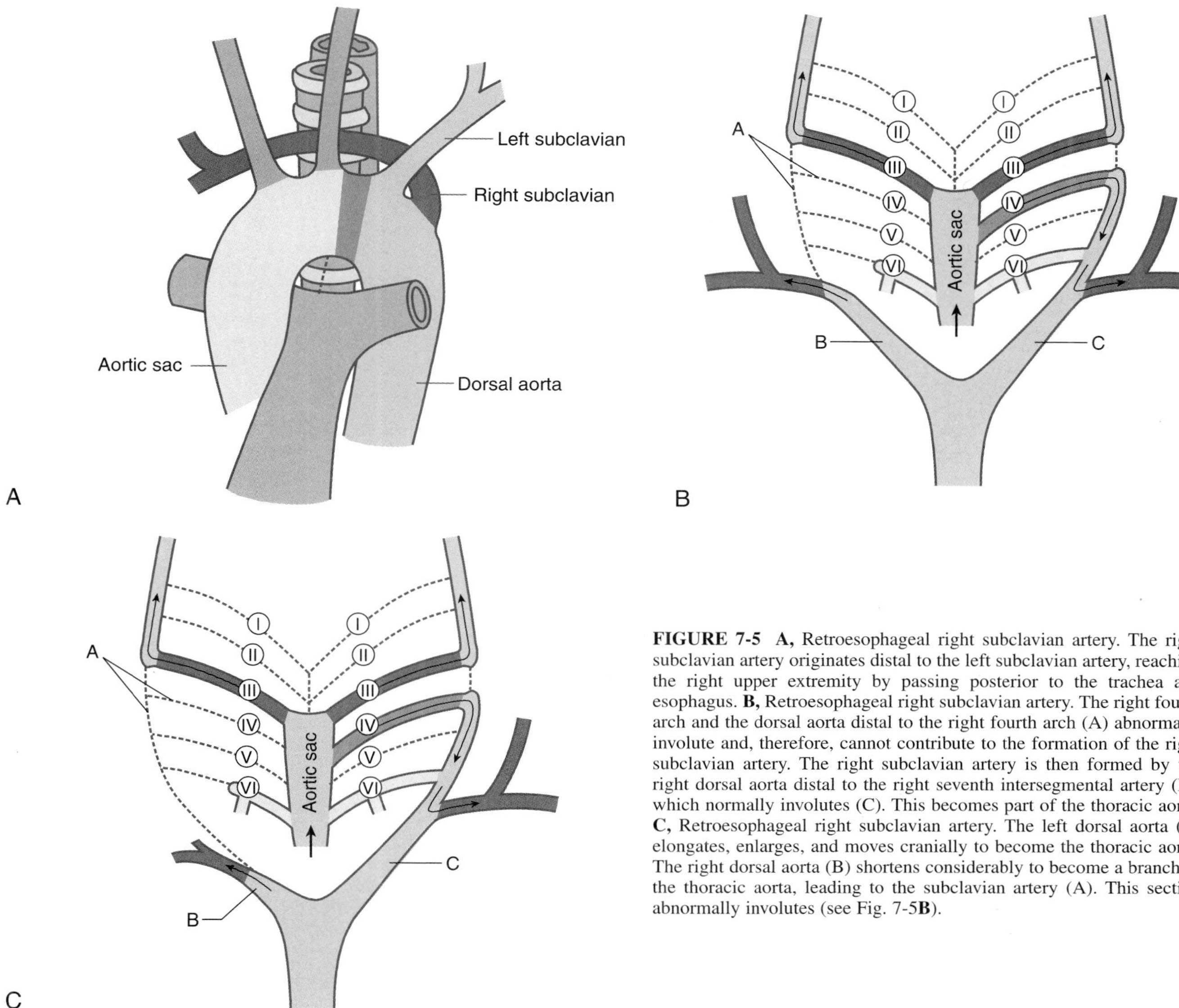

FIGURE 7-5 A, Retroesophageal right subclavian artery. The right subclavian artery originates distal to the left subclavian artery, reaching the right upper extremity by passing posterior to the trachea and esophagus. **B,** Retroesophageal right subclavian artery. The right fourth arch and the dorsal aorta distal to the right fourth arch (A) abnormally involute and, therefore, cannot contribute to the formation of the right subclavian artery. The right subclavian artery is then formed by the right dorsal aorta distal to the right seventh intersegmental artery (B), which normally involutes (C). This becomes part of the thoracic aorta. **C,** Retroesophageal right subclavian artery. The left dorsal aorta (C) elongates, enlarges, and moves cranially to become the thoracic aorta. The right dorsal aorta (B) shortens considerably to become a branch of the thoracic aorta, leading to the subclavian artery (A). This section abnormally involutes (see Fig. 7-5**B**).

segmental arteries to become the internal iliac arteries. The lateral segmental arteries are the blood supply to the primitive urogenital ridge. The pronephros and mesonephros form and then disappear, yielding to the metanephros, which becomes the permanent kidney. At the seventh week, the metanephros ascends. The caudal segmental arteries disappear; the cranial arteries persist initially but then also disappear, leaving only one segmental artery on each side; they become the renal arteries. Not surprisingly, considerable variations in the arterial supply to the kidney exist.[6,7] Only 71% of individuals have single arteries to each kidney. The rest have a variety of combinations of hilar and separate branches to the poles of the kidneys. Fusion of the caudad kidney poles arrests the cranial kidney migration. Segmental arteries persist, providing a separate blood supply to the fused kidney. Similarly, ectopic kidneys frequently have multiple segmental arteries instead of a single renal artery. Therefore, evaluation of either a horseshoe or an ectopic kidney must consider their potential anomalous arterial blood supply.[8]

The Extremities

Each upper and lower extremity begins as an outgrowth of tissue, a limb bud, off the trunk of the embryo. Initially, the limb bud is nourished by a capillary plexus that coalesces to form a single artery as the limb elongates.

In the *upper extremity*, the development of the arterial supply is relatively simple. The developing single artery becomes the axillary artery, the brachial artery, and the anterior interosseous artery. This system unites with the subclavian artery, formed for the most part in the development of the aortic arch by the seventh intersegmental artery. The radial artery and the ulnar artery form later as branches of the brachial artery and replace the anterior interosseous artery as the dominant blood supply of the forearm and hand.

The development of the arterial supply to the *lower extremities* is more complicated than that in the upper extremity (Fig. 7-6). Two systems develop. The *sciatic* system forms initially.[9] The proximal part of the fifth lumbar dorsal segmental artery becomes the common iliac artery. The internal iliac arteries arise from the common iliac arteries.

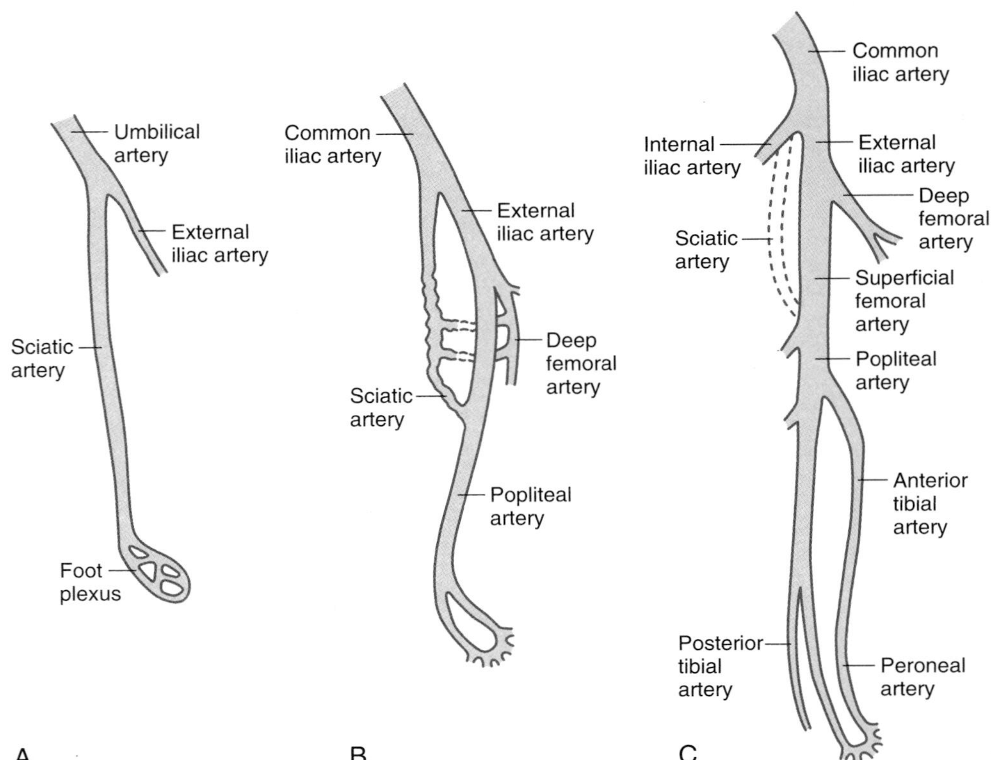

FIGURE 7-6 Arterial supply to the left lower extremity. **A,** Sciatic artery forming as a branch of the umbilical artery initially supplies the entire leg. **B,** The sciatic artery regresses, and the external artery develops into the common femoral artery to supply the thigh. Note that the sciatic artery communicates with the popliteal artery just above the knee. **C,** The sciatic artery disappears, although small portions remain to form the popliteal and peroneal arteries.

The umbilical artery joins the internal iliac artery. The sciatic arteries develop from the internal iliac arteries following the posterior course of the sciatic nerve. In the lower thigh, the sciatic artery joins the iliofemoral system at the popliteal level.

At the sixth week of gestation, the second system of the lower extremity, the *external iliac artery*, develops off the umbilical artery and grows to become the iliofemoral system. The iliofemoral system replaces the sciatic system, which regresses almost completely. In the leg, segments of the sciatic artery persist, forming parts of the popliteal and peroneal arteries. In the pelvis, remnants of the sciatic system form the internal iliac artery and its branches, the inferior and superior gluteal arteries.

The popliteal artery forms from the union of two arteries, (1) the *deep popliteal artery*, which is part of the sciatic system initially supplying blood to the lower leg, and (2) the later-developing *superficial popliteal artery* (Fig. 7-7). The distal section of the deep popliteal artery anterior to the popliteus muscle regresses. The superficial popliteal artery forms posterior to the popliteus muscle and unites with the proximal part of the deep popliteal artery to form the mature popliteal artery.

Lower Extremity Vascular Anomalies

Persistent Sciatic Artery If the femoral system fails to develop, the sciatic artery may persist instead of regressing, supplying blood to the thigh. The incidence of this rare anomaly is 0.05%.[10] The sciatic artery may be complete from its origin off the internal iliac artery to its union with the popliteal artery. It may also be incomplete, so that it connects with the internal iliac or popliteal artery through small collaterals. The anomalous persistent sciatic artery is anatomically next to the sciatic nerve, entering the thigh through the sciatic notch and remaining posterior to the adductor magnus until the insertion of that muscle, where it enters the popliteal fossa to join the popliteal artery.

If the artery is complete, the patient with a persistent sciatic artery may present with a palpable popliteal artery but absence of a femoral pulse. A persistent sciatic artery in the buttocks is superficial and can be traumatized by normal activity, such as sitting. This causes early atherosclerotic changes and, possibly, aneurysm formation in the buttock.[11] The aneurysm may compress the sciatic nerve, causing neurologic symptoms.

Popliteal Entrapment Syndrome The popliteal entrapment syndrome is an anomaly that results from the delayed attachment of the medial head of the gastrocnemius muscle. The gastrocnemius muscle arises from the calcaneus, migrating cephalad until it divides into a lateral head and a medial head.[9,12] The lateral head attaches first to the lateral epicondyle of the femur, and the medial head attaches later to the medial epicondyle. At the time of the attachment of the medial head, the popliteal artery has already formed and is in its normal anatomic location.

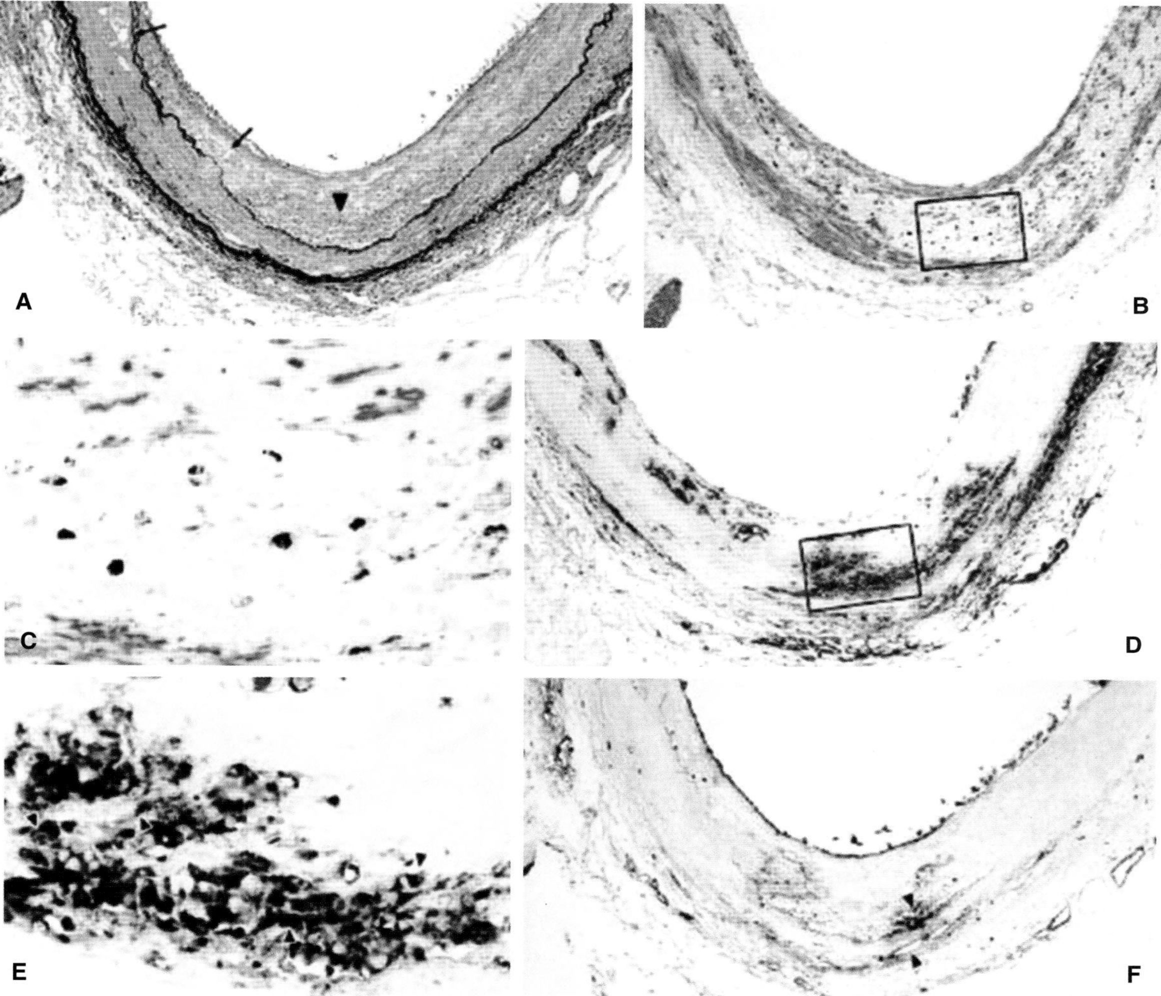

FIGURE 11-2 Photomicrographs of cross-sections from a control iliac artery of an atherosclerotic cynomolgus monkey. Serial sections were stained with Verhoeff–van Gieson stain (**A**) or immunostained (dark red reaction product) with antibodies to SMC (smooth muscle cell) and actin (**B** and **C**), macrophage CD68 (**D** and **E**), or endothelial cell von Willebrand factor (vWF) (**F**). Sections **B** through **F** were also stained with an antibody to BrdU (black nuclear reaction product) to label proliferating cells. **A**, A plaque is shown overlying the media. Calcification (*arrows*) is seen deep in the plaque, and a cellular region in the base of the plaque (*arrowhead*) is composed primarily of macrophages (**D**) covered by more fibrous-appearing tissue containing SMCs (**B**). **C** and **E** are magnified views of the regions outlined in **B** and **D,** respectively. A number of black BrdU-labeled nuclei co-localize to the region of CD68 staining, indicating macrophage proliferation in this region of the uninjured plaque. Staining for vWF (**D**) shows endothelial cells overlying the plaque and in microvessels of the adventitia. Microvessels can also be seen coursing through the media and inner plaque (*small arrowheads*). (**A, B, D,** and **F,** ×100; **C** and **E,** ×400.) (From Geary RL, Williams JK, Golden D, et al: Time course of cellular proliferation, intimal hyperplasia, and remodeling following angioplasty in monkeys with established atherosclerosis: A nonhuman primate model of restenosis. Arterioscler Thromb Vasc Biol 16:34-43, 1996.)

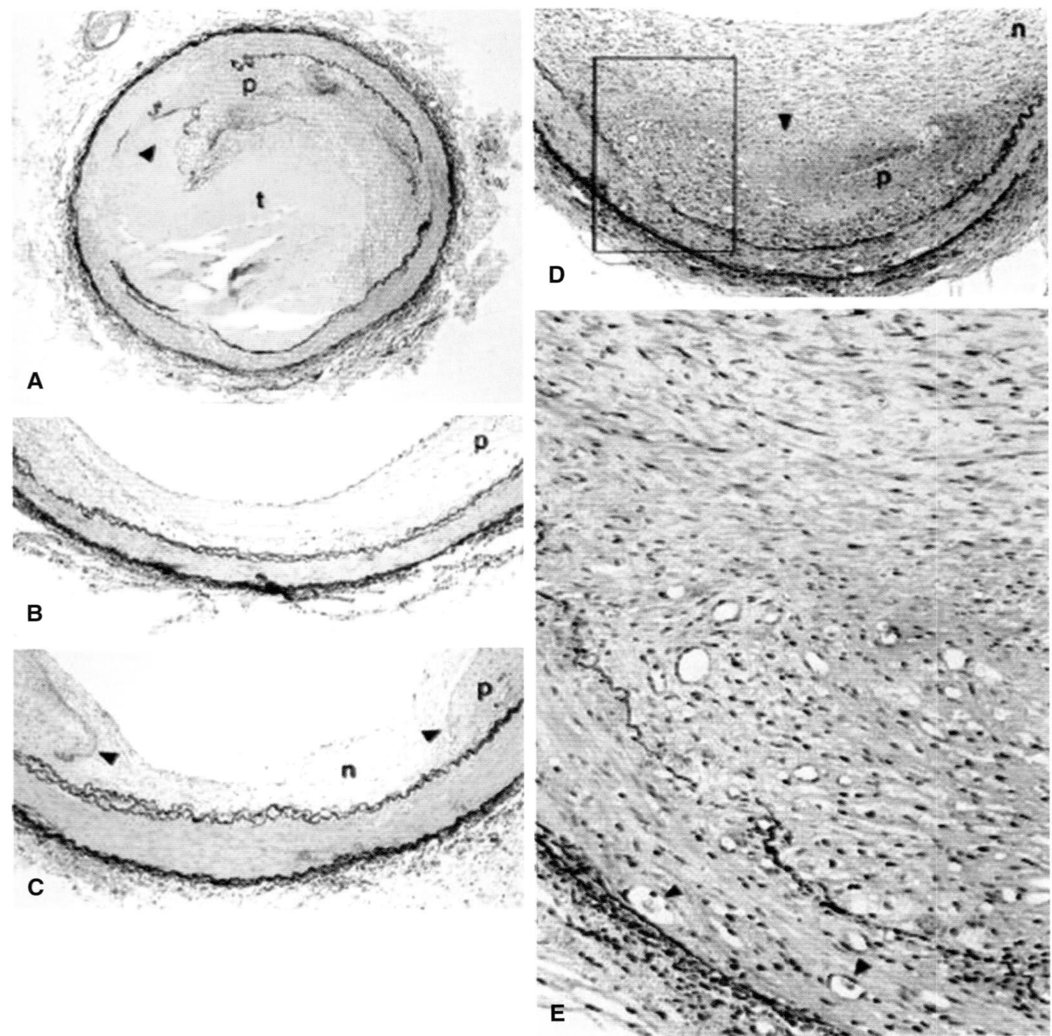

FIGURE 11-3 Photomicrographs of representative cross-sections from injured common iliac arteries of atherosclerotic cynomolgus monkeys. **A,** Angioplasty commonly causes fracture and dissection of preexisting atherosclerotic plaque (*arrowhead*) and, rarely, luminal thrombosis (t). The yellow-staining thrombus (t) can also be seen within the injured media underlying the dissection. **B,** An uninjured iliac artery from another monkey with plaque (p) overlying the media. **C,** The contralateral iliac artery is shown from the same animal as in **B** 14 days after angioplasty. Neointimal ingrowth (n), composed of smooth muscle cells (SMC-actin staining not shown) and extracellular matrix, is seen filling in the site of plaque fracture (*arrowheads*) and has begun to overgrow the primary atherosclerotic plaque (p). **D,** An iliac artery is shown from a third monkey 28 days after angioplasty. A significant accumulation of neointima (n) is seen overlying the primary atherosclerotic plaque (*arrowhead*). The extracellular matrix of the neointima appears homogeneous compared with the underlying plaque, and the pale staining suggests a composition rich in proteoglycans. Microvessels can be seen coursing within the adventitia, media, and primary atheroma but not in the neointima. **E,** A magnified view of the region outlined in **D** shows the plaque microvessels in more detail. Erythrocytes (*arrowheads*) can be seen within the lumina and adjacent to vasa cut in cross-section. (**A,** ×40; **B, C,** and **D,** ×100; **E,** ×400.)

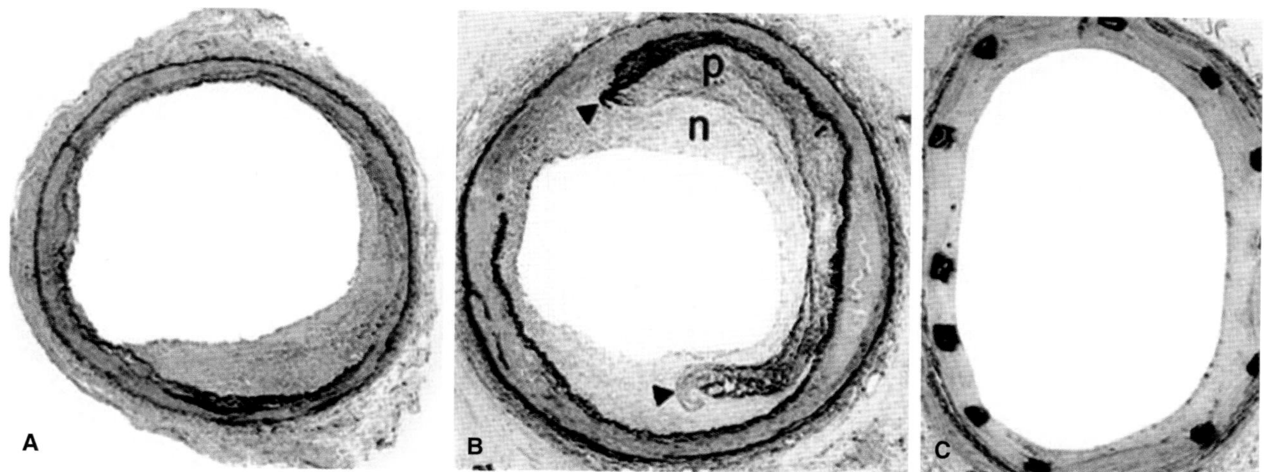

FIGURE 11-6 Photomicrographs of stented vessel. **A,** Atherogenic diet–induced complex intimal lesions shown in uninjured iliac artery. **B,** Contralateral iliac artery was removed 35 days after experimental angioplasty. Angioplasty has fractured the preexisting plaque (p; *arrowheads*) and injured the overlying media, with neointimal ingrowth (n). **C,** Palmaz stents were deployed in the proximal left subclavian artery, and after 35 days, neointimal ingrowth has covered the underlying plaque and stent struts. (Verhoeff–van Gieson stain. **A** and **B**, ×40; **C**, ×100.) (From Deitch JS, Williams JK, Adams MR, et al: Effects of β3-integrin blockade (c7E3) on the response to angioplasty and intra-arterial stenting in atherosclerotic nonhuman primates. Arterioscler Thromb Vasc Biol 18:1730-1737, 1998.)

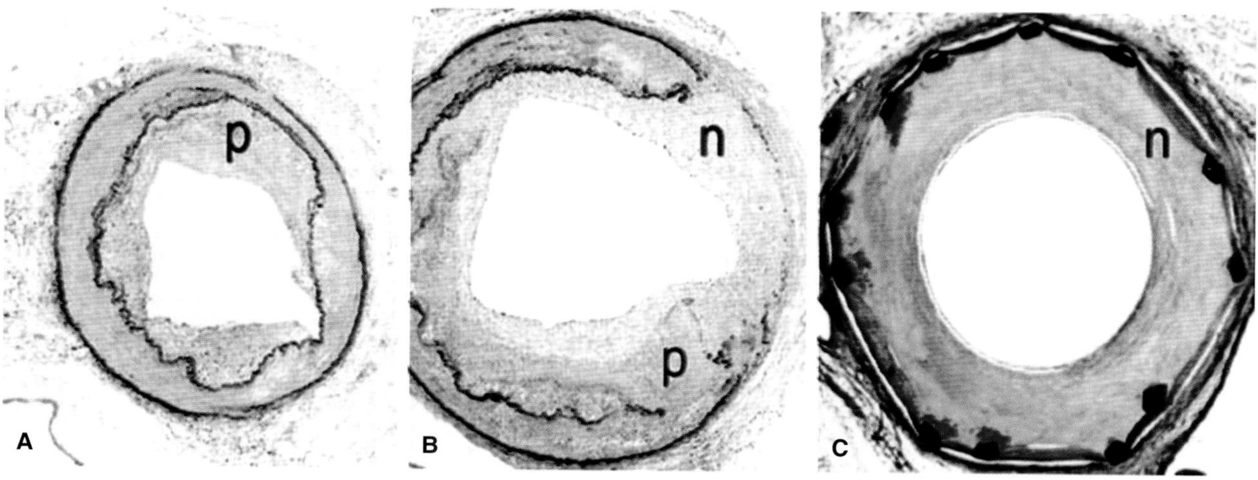

FIGURE 11-7 Photomicrographs of stented vessel. Composite photomicrograph demonstrates a typical response 4 weeks after angioplasty and stenting. **A** and **B** show the uninjured and injured common iliac arteries, respectively, and **C** shows the stented external iliac artery. Animals consumed an atherogenic diet for 2.5 years, thus creating complicated plaques (p). **B** shows fractured plaque (p) and overlying media that have healed with neointimal ingrowth (n). **C** shows a stented external iliac artery with a typical neointimal lesion (n). Vessels were from a single treated animal. (**A** and **B,** Verhoeff–van Gieson stain; **C,** trichrome stain; original magnification, ×40.) (From Cherr GS, Motew SJ, Travis JA, et al: Metalloproteinase inhibition and the response to angioplasty and stenting in atherosclerotic primates. Arterioscler Thromb Vasc Biol 22:161-166, 2002.)

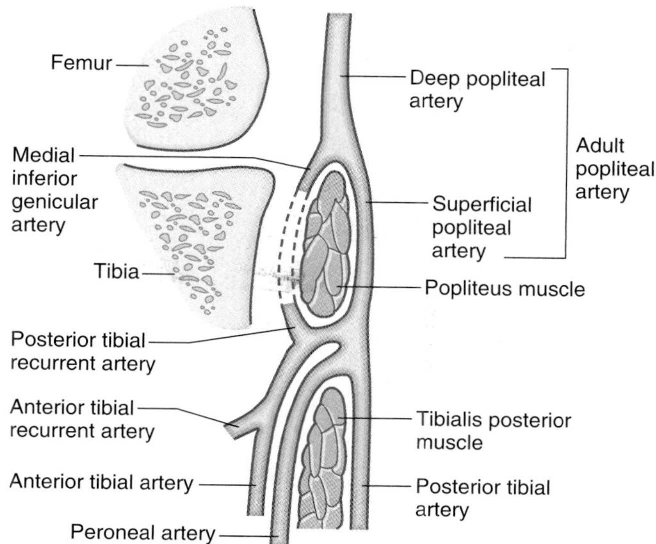

FIGURE 7-7 Embryologic development of the popliteal artery, as modified from Senior (Am J Anat 25:55, 1919[9]). The deep popliteal artery anterior to the popliteus muscle regresses, and the superficial popliteal artery posterior to the popliteus muscle becomes the mature popliteal artery. (From Gibson MHL, Mills JG, Johnson GE, et al: Popliteal entrapment syndrome. Ann Surg 185:341, 1977.)

If the popliteal artery develops late or if the medial head migrates early, the artery is not in its normal location; instead, it is swept medially and impinged against the femur as the medial head attaches to the epicondyle. Actually, no case of compression of the popliteal artery on the lateral epicondyle has been observed, probably because the lateral head attaches early, well before the popliteal artery forms. Clinically, patients with popliteal entrapment syndrome present at an early age. Compression of the artery against the femur by the medial head of the gastrocnemius muscle causes claudication and popliteal artery aneurysm formation.

■ DEVELOPMENT OF THE VENOUS SYSTEM

Like the arterial system, the venous system develops from clumps of cells that form a capillary network. Within 4 weeks of gestation, some of these capillaries enlarge to become the major veins of the embryo. At 4 weeks, three paired venous systems form and drain the yolk sac, the placenta, and the embryo (Fig. 7-8). The vitelline veins drain the yolk sac and intestinal canal, enter the liver, and eventually become the portal vein, the hepatic venous sinusoids, and the hepatic veins. The umbilical vein brings the oxygenated blood from the placenta to the heart. Although the umbilical vein is only a single vein in the umbilical cord, a paired system of umbilical veins develops initially and then regresses; the exception is the portion of the left umbilical vein caudal to the liver, the ductus venosus, which in the mature embryo connects to the right hepatic vein, bringing oxygenated blood from the placenta directly to the heart without traversing the liver.

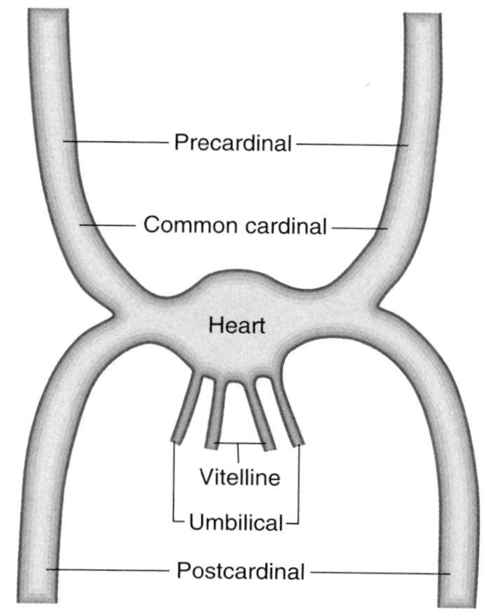

FIGURE 7-8 Venous system of a 4-week-old embryo.

After birth, the ductus venosus atrophies to become the ligamentum teres (round ligament) and the ligamentum venosum of the liver. The paired cardinal veins drain the body of the embryo. The veins cephalad to the heart (the precardinal veins) join the veins caudad to the heart (the postcardinal veins) to form the paired common cardinal veins, which enter the heart. The precardinal veins become the superior vena cava and its major branches; the postcardinal veins below the liver help form the inferior vena cava and its branches.

Superior Vena Cava

The cephalad portions of the paired precardinal systems become the subclavian and jugular veins. At the eighth week of gestation, the left innominate vein develops obliquely, connecting the left precardinal system to the right precardinal system. At the same time, the section of the left precardinal vein caudal to the developing innominate vein and the left postcardinal vein between the liver and the heart atrophies, so that all the blood from the left side of the head and neck enters the heart through the innominate vein and the superior vena cava. The superior vena cava develops from enlargement of the right precardinal and common cardinal vein. The right postcardinal vein above the liver becomes the *azygos system* (Fig. 7-9).

Anomalies

Two anomalies can occur from development of the superior vena cava. Neither anomaly is clinically important, except that it produces unusual shadows on chest radiographs.

A *double superior vena cava* develops from failure of the caudal section of the left precardinal vein to regress.[13] This anomaly may occur with or without development of the innominate vein.

Left-sided superior vena cava occurs if the caudal section of the right precardinal veins regresses but the caudal

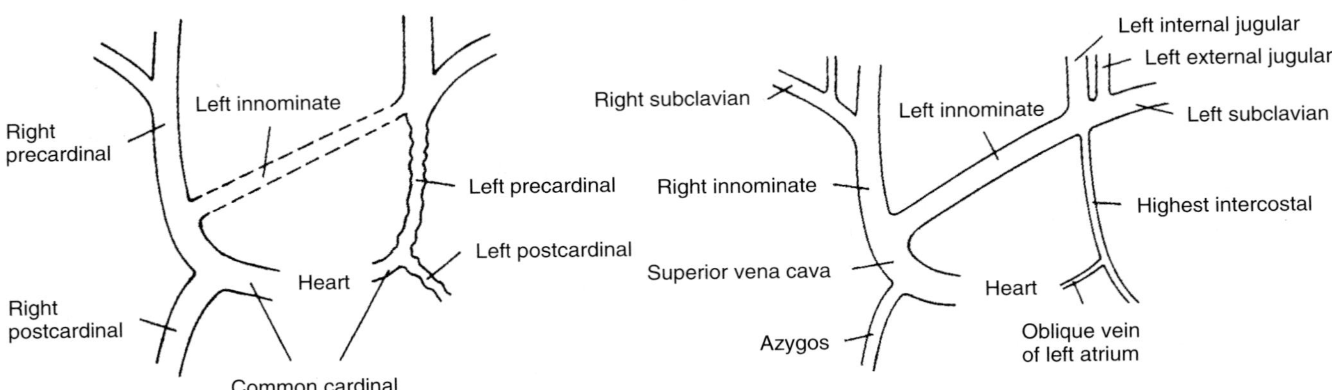

FIGURE 7-9 **A,** Development of the superior vena cava and major branches. **B,** Completed development of the superior vena cava and major branches.

section of the left precardinal vein remains open, the opposite of the normal development.[14] An innominate vein forms but, in this anomaly, connects the right precardinal vein to the left precardinal vein, which is becoming a left-sided superior vena cava.

Inferior Vena Cava

The inferior vena cava and the iliac veins develop from three parallel sets of veins that appear at different times during the sixth to tenth week of gestation (Fig. 7-10A and B). The veins appear to go through various changes, but eventually, parts of each set coalesce to form the inferior vena cava. The postcardinal veins located on the posterior aspect of the fetus appear first. All of this system regresses except the proximal part of the right postcardinal vein above the liver, which becomes the azygos system, and the most distal section, which becomes the iliac veins.

Next, the subcardinal veins located anterior and medial to the postcardinal veins appear. The left subcardinal completely regresses, whereas the right subcardinal vein becomes the suprarenal inferior vena cava. The supracardinal veins located just posterior to the aorta appear last. The left supracardinal vein disappears and the right supracardinal vein becomes the infrarenal section of the inferior vena cava. The suprarenal portions of the supracardinal veins connect to the proximal portion of the postcardinal veins to become the azygos system and the *hemiazygos system*. The junction of the subcardinal and supracardinal systems occurs at the level of the kidney. Small veins form and eventually coalesce to form a large vein anterior and posterior to the aorta at the level of the renal arteries. The posterior vein regresses, but the anterior vein persists to become the left renal vein (Fig. 7-10C and D).

Anomalies

The anomalies of the inferior vena cava and renal veins are as follows.[15-21]

Duplication: Left-Sided Inferior Vena Cava Duplication occurs if the left supracardinal vein fails to regress. Both supracardinal veins persist, joining at the level of the renal arteries and creating a double inferior vena cava. If the left supracardinal vein persists and the right supracardinal vein regresses (the opposite of normal), a left-sided inferior vena cava occurs. The vein crosses to the right side at the level of the renal arteries. It is a mirror image of the normal anatomy. The right adrenal and gonadal veins, instead of emptying into the inferior vena cava as is normal, empty into the right renal vein; likewise, the left adrenal and gonadal veins empty into the inferior vena cava instead of the left renal vein, as is normal.

Renal Vein Anomalies The most common venous anomaly occurs in the left renal vein. Retroaortic left renal vein occurs if the posterior left renal vein persists but the anterior left renal vein regresses; this is the opposite of normal. At times, both anterior and posterior left renal veins persist, forming a circumaortic left renal vein. Both veins join just before entering the inferior vena cava, so that a venous collar is formed.

■ SUMMARY

The arterial and venous systems both begin as clumps of cells that very rapidly develop into mature vascular systems. Anomalies are unusual but interesting. They rarely have a clinical impact. Knowledge of the embryology of the vascular system enables the surgeon to understand the developmental abnormalities. Familiarity with the logic of arterial development enhances our appreciation of the awesome beauty of the human body in general and the vascular system in particular.

■ REFERENCES

1. Arcinegas E, Hakima M, Hertzler JH, et al: Surgical management of congenital vascular rings. J Thorac Cardiovasc Surg 77:721, 1979.
2. Mahoney EB, Manning JA: Congenital abnormalities of the aortic arch. Surgery 55:1, 1964.
3. Richardson JV, Doty DG, Rossi NP, et al: Operation for aortic arch anomalies. Ann Thorac Surg 31:426, 1981.

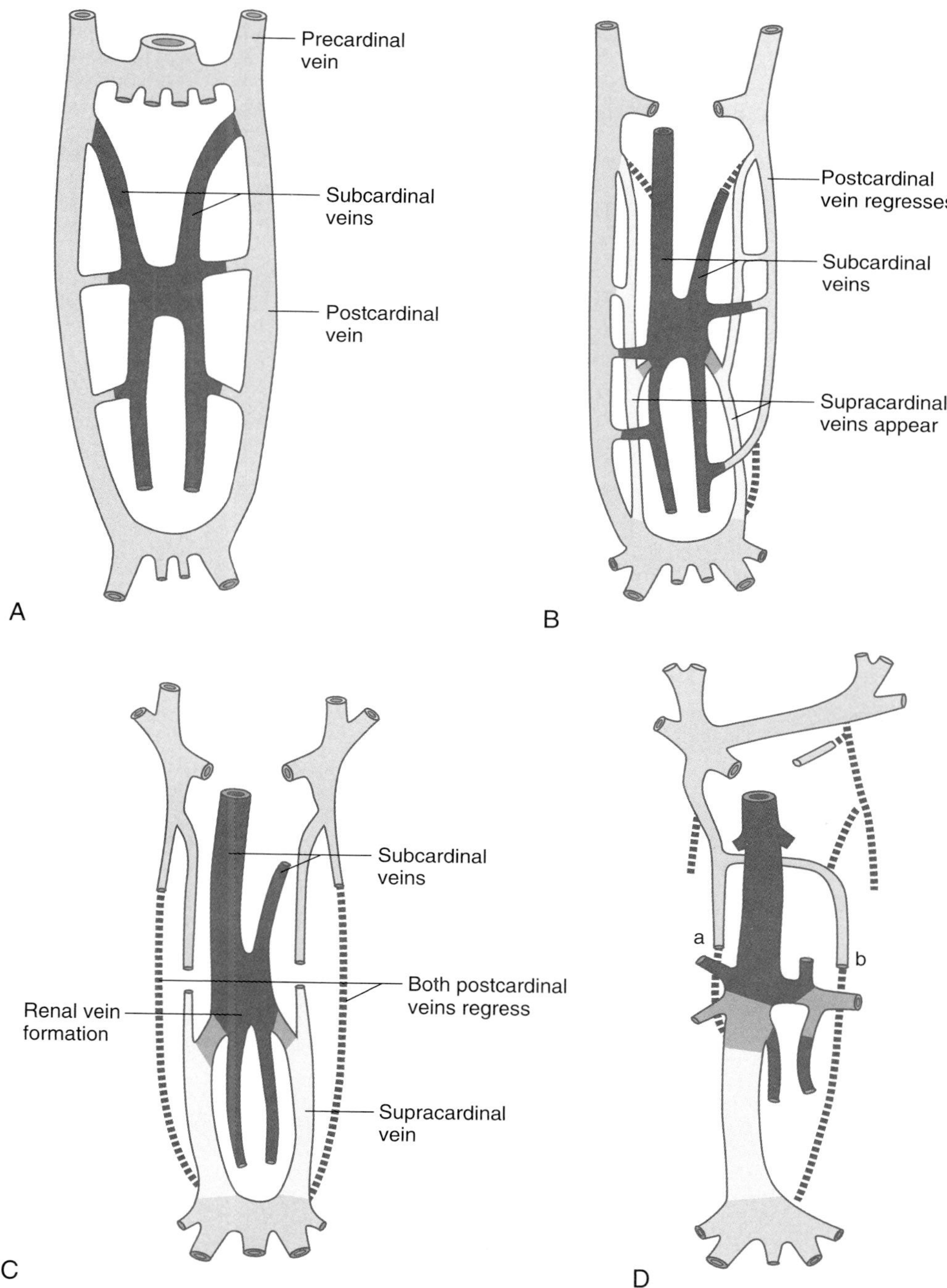

FIGURE 7-10 Development of the inferior vena cava. **A,** At 6 weeks of gestation, postcardinal veins are dominant and the subcardinal system is beginning to appear. **B,** At 7 weeks of gestation, subcardinal veins are dominant, and the supracardinal system begins to appear. Postcardinal veins are beginning to regress. **C,** At 8 weeks of gestation, subcardinal veins form the suprarenal inferior vena cava. Supracardinal veins form the infrarenal inferior vena cava. Postcardinal veins regress. **D,** The adult inferior vena cava. Portions of the postcardinal veins persist to form the azygos system (a) and the hemiazygos system (b). (From Giordano JM, Trout HH III: Anomalies of the inferior vena cava. J Vasc Surg 3:924, 1986.)

4. Binet JP, Langlois J: Aortic arch anomalies in children and infants. J Thorac Cardiovasc Surg 73:248, 1977.
5. Lincoln JCR, Deveall PB, Stark J, et al: Vascular anomalies compressing the esophagus and trachea. Thorax 24:295, 1969.
6. Merklin RJ, Michaels NA: The variant renal and suprarenal blood supply with data on inferior phrenic, urethral, and gonadal arteries. J Int Coll Surg 29:41, 1958.
7. Gray SW, Skandalokis JE: Embryology for Surgeons. Philadelphia, WB Saunders, 1972, p 486.
8. Anson BJ, Richardson GA, Minear WL: Variations in the number and arrangements of the renal vessels. J Urol 36:211, 1936.
9. Senior HD: The development of the arteries of the human lower extremity. Am J Anat 25:55, 1919.
10. Mayschak DT, Flye WM: Treatment of the persistent sciatic artery. Ann Surg 199:69, 1984.
11. McLellan GL, Morettin LB: Persistent sciatic artery: Clinical, surgical, and angiographic aspects. Arch Surg 117:817, 1982.
12. Gibson MHL, Mills JG, Johnson GE, et al: Popliteal entrapment syndrome. Ann Surg 185:341, 1977.
13. Nandy K, Blair CB Jr: Double superior venae cavae with completely paired azygous veins. Anat Rec 151:1, 1965.
14. Winter FS: Persistent left superior vena cava: Survey of world literature and report of thirty additional cases. Angiology 5:90, 1954.
15. Babian RJ, Johnson DE: Major venous anomalies complicating retroperitoneal surgery. South Med J 72:1254, 1979.
16. Chaung VP, Mena CE, Hoskins PA: Congenital anomalies of the left renal vein: Angiographic consideration. Br J Radiol 47:214, 1974.
17. Dardik H, Loop FD, Cox PA, et al: C-pattern inferior vena cava. JAMA 200:248, 1967.
18. Kolbenstvedt A, Kolmannskog F, Lien HH: The anomalous inferior vena cava: Another structure between the aorta and the superior mesenteric artery. Br J Radiol 54:423, 1981.
19. Berner BJ, Darling C, Fredrick PL, et al: Major venous anomalies complicating abdominal aortic surgery. Arch Surg 108:160, 1974.
20. Mayo J, Gray R, St Louis E, et al: Anomalies of the inferior vena cava. Am J Radiol 140:339, 1983.
21. Giordano JM, Trout HH III: Anomalies of the inferior vena cava. J Vasc Surg 3:924, 1986.

Chapter 8

Basic Considerations of the Arterial Wall in Health and Disease

MARC E. MITCHELL, MD
ANTON N. SIDAWY, MD

A thorough knowledge of the cellular components of the arterial wall and atherosclerotic plaque, the role of growth factors in cell cycle control in health and disease, and the role of risk factors in arterial wall injury is of paramount importance to understanding the pathogenesis of atherosclerotic vascular disease. Atherosclerotic arterial disease is the primary condition leading to arterial insufficiency. Complications resulting from advanced atherosclerosis are the most common indication for open vascular reconstructive surgery or endovascular procedures.

Atherosclerosis is a systemic disease affecting the entire arterial tree, but lesions involving the coronary, extracranial cerebral, and lower extremity circulations have the greatest clinical significance for surgeons. The pathogenesis of atherosclerosis involves a complex series of events with the formation of atherosclerotic plaque as the end result. Injury to the arterial endothelial cell, resulting in endothelial cell dysfunction, is the first step in the process. Activated endothelial cells attract platelets, monocytes, and vascular smooth muscle cells (SMCs), which accumulate and proliferate in the arterial wall. These cellular components produce an excessive amount of connective tissue matrix. The ultimate endpoint is the formation of a mature fibrous plaque. Symptoms occur when advanced lesions are complicated by plaque rupture, hemorrhage into the plaque, emboli, or thrombosis.

The response to injury theory of atherosclerosis was first postulated by Ross in 1973,[1] and has become the cornerstone of our current understanding of the pathogenesis of atherosclerosis. The theory states that atherosclerosis is, at least partially, the result of the cellular response to some form of endothelial injury. Over the past 30 years, the theory has been modified and refined, resulting in a characterization of the events involved in the formation of atherosclerotic plaque.[2,3] In many ways, this response to injury is similar to a chronic inflammatory response. The role of inflammation in atherosclerosis has only recently become evident.[3,4]

The process begins with some sort of endothelial cell injury that leads to endothelial dysfunction. This endothelial dysfunction results in changes in endothelial permeability, adhesive characteristics, and responses to various growth and stimulatory factors. Endothelial cells and vascular SMCs interact with monocytes, T lymphocytes, and platelets to form the cellular component of the fibroproliferative response, which ultimately results in the formation of atherosclerotic plaque.

DESCRIPTION AND STAGING OF ATHEROSCLEROTIC LESIONS

Classification

The lesions of atherosclerosis have traditionally been divided into three categories. The *fatty streak*, the earliest stage of atheroma development, is found in children decades before the onset of symptoms. On gross examination, fatty streaks appear as slightly raised yellow discolorations on the intimal surface of the vessel, frequently occurring at branch points. Histologic analysis shows these lesions to consist of lipid-filled macrophages and T lymphocytes.[5,6] These lipid-filled macrophages, also known as "foam cells," accumulate in the intima of the vessel wall.

The intermediate or *fibrofatty lesion*, the next stage of plaque development, consists of layers of macrophages and T lymphocytes alternating with layers of vascular SMCs. The cells are surrounded by a connective tissue matrix of collagen, elastic fibers, and proteoglycans.[7]

The *complicated or fibrous plaque* is the advanced stage of atherosclerosis. At this stage, the plaque projects into the arterial lumen to an extent that impedes blood flow and produces symptoms. These lesions consist of a dense fibrous cap composed of connective tissue and vascular SMCs. When the lesions are examined by electron microscopy, the vascular SMCs are seen to occupy a lacuna-like space surrounded by multiple layers of dense basement membrane collagen.[7] Beneath the fibrous cap is a layer containing vascular SMCs and macrophages along with a core of lipid and necrotic debris. Additional layers of vascular SMCs and connective tissue are present underneath the core. Lesions with thick, dense fibrous caps tend to be stable, whereas those with irregular, thin caps are more likely to develop complications such as plaque rupture, ulceration, and hemorrhage, which can cause acute symptoms.

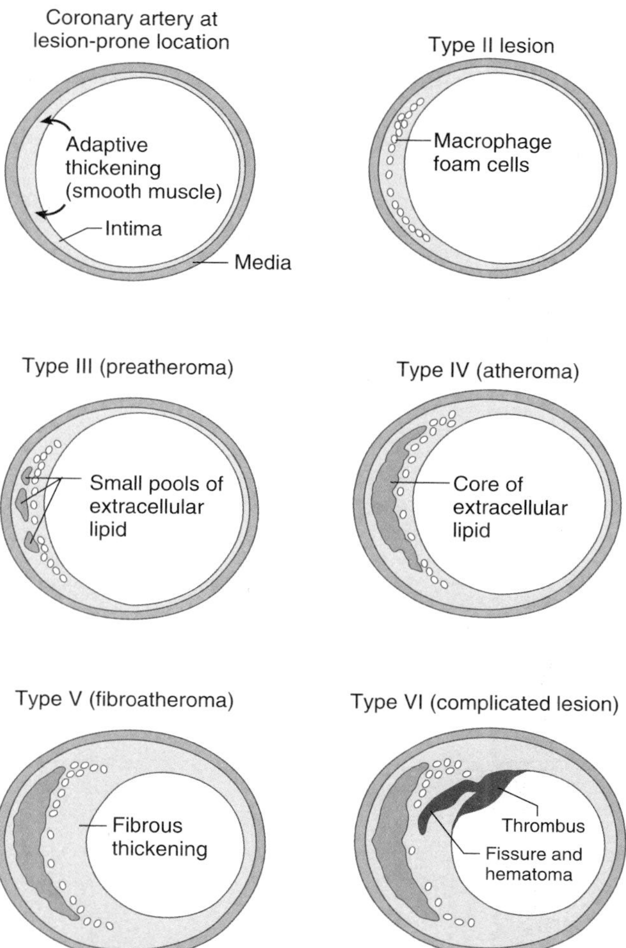

FIGURE 8-1 Cross-sectional drawings of coronary arteries demonstrating the morphology of lesions ranging from adaptive intimal thickening in lesion-prone locations to type VI atherosclerotic lesions. (From Stary HC, Chandler AB, Dinsmore RE, et al: A definition of advanced types of atherosclerotic lesions and a histological classification of atherosclerosis. Circulation 92:1355-1374, 1995.)

Staging

In 1994, the American Heart Association proposed a staging system (Figs. 8-1 and 8-2) for human atherosclerotic lesions based on histologic composition and structure of the plaque.[8,9] Type I and type II lesions are considered early lesions. They are the only lesions found in children but may also occur in adults.

Type I lesions are microscopically characterized by an increase in the number of intimal macrophages and the accumulation of lipid droplets within the macrophages to form foam cells. Type II lesions include fatty streaks and are the first lesions to be visualized grossly. Not all type II lesions are fatty streaks; some lesions meet the microscopic criteria for type II lesions but are still not visible as fatty streaks. Type II lesions consist of layers of foam cells and lipid-containing vascular SMCs. Additionally, higher numbers of macrophages not containing lipids are present within these lesions. T lymphocytes and mast cells are also seen in type II lesions. The turnover of foam cells, vascular SMCs, and endothelial cells is higher than normal in type II lesions. Most of the lipid in type II lesions is intracellular, primarily within foam cells, but some widely dispersed extracellular droplets are present in some lesions.

Type II lesions are further subdivided into those that are progression prone (IIa) and those that are progression resistant (IIb). Type IIa lesions, located in areas of adaptive intimal thickening, contain more foam cells and vascular SMCs than type IIb lesions. Adaptive intimal thickening is the result of mechanical forces on the arterial wall, such as shear stress, and occurs in everyone regardless of lipoprotein levels. Atherosclerosis develops preferentially in areas of adaptive intimal thickening.

Type III lesions are intermediaries between type II lesions and mature atheromas (type IV lesions). They are similar to type II lesions but contain characteristic pools of extracellular lipid droplets dispersed among the layers of vascular SMCs. The lipid within the pool is the same as the extracellular lipid seen in type II lesions. These pools are located beneath the layered macrophages and foam cells, disrupting the coherent layer of vascular SMCs. The presence of these lipid pools signifies the progression of type II lesions to type III lesions.

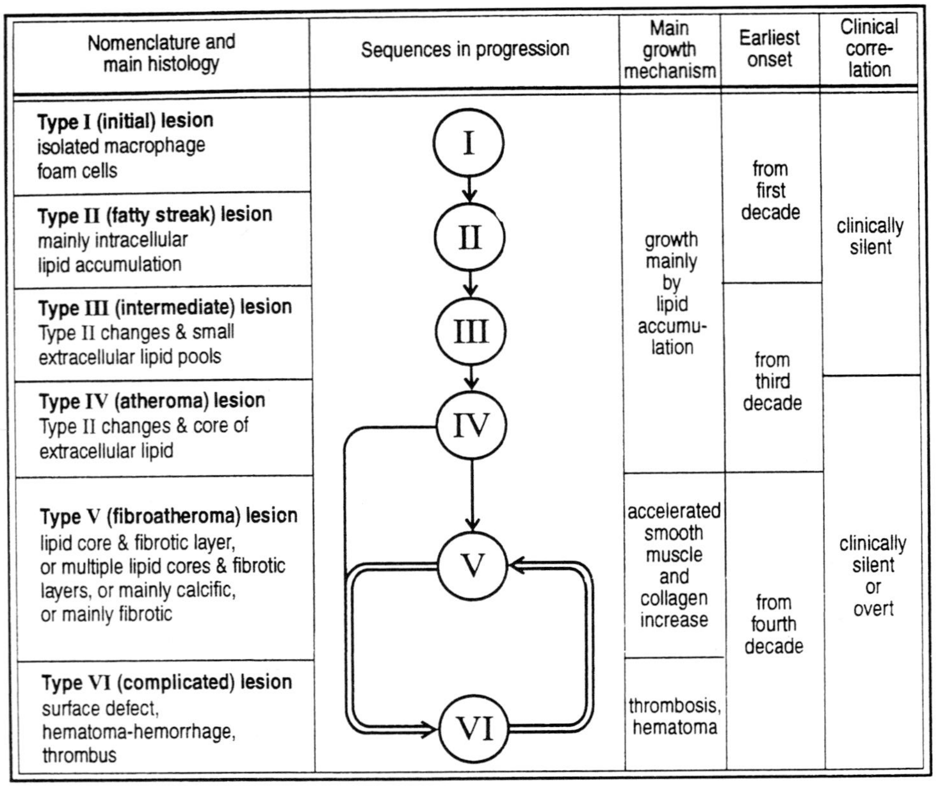

Nomenclature and main histology	Sequences in progression	Main growth mechanism	Earliest onset	Clinical correlation
Type I (initial) lesion isolated macrophage foam cells	I	growth mainly by lipid accumulation	from first decade	clinically silent
Type II (fatty streak) lesion mainly intracellular lipid accumulation	II			
Type III (intermediate) lesion Type II changes & small extracellular lipid pools	III		from third decade	
Type IV (atheroma) lesion Type II changes & core of extracellular lipid	IV			clinically silent or overt
Type V (fibroatheroma) lesion lipid core & fibrotic layer, or multiple lipid cores & fibrotic layers, or mainly calcific, or mainly fibrotic	V	accelerated smooth muscle and collagen increase	from fourth decade	
Type VI (complicated) lesion surface defect, hematoma-hemorrhage, thrombus	VI	thrombosis, hematoma		

FIGURE 8-2 Flow diagram showing the evolution and progression of atherosclerotic lesions. *Roman numerals* indicate the histologic type of lesion, and the direction of the *arrows* indicates the usual sequence in which characteristic morphologic changes occur. The *loop* between types V and VI illustrates how lesions increase in thickness as thrombotic deposits form on their surfaces. (From Stary HC, Chandler AB, Dinsmore RE, et al: A definition of advanced types of atherosclerotic lesions and a histological classification of atherosclerosis. Circulation 92:1355-1374, 1995.)

Types IV, V, and VI are advanced atherosclerotic lesions. Type IV lesions are sometimes called atheromas. They are characterized by a well-defined collection of extracellular lipid within the intima, known as the "lipid core." The lipid core is formed by the confluence of the lipid pools seen in type III lesions. Particles of calcium are sometimes present within the lipid core. The area between the lipid core and the endothelial surface contains macrophages, foam cells, and vascular SMCs, along with scattered T lymphocytes and mast cells. Type IV lesions are frequently eccentric in location and cause a visible thickening of the arterial wall, but they usually do not result in a significant narrowing of the arterial lumen and do not produce symptoms.

Type V lesions are characterized by the formation of prominent new fibrous connective tissue, which forms the fibrous cap. These lesions are subdivided according to the makeup of the connective tissue cap. Type Va lesions consist of a lipid core, similar to that seen in type IV lesions, covered by a thick fibrous layer composed of extracellular connective tissue matrix. In type Vb lesions, the lipid core is calcified. Type Vc lesions do not have a lipid core and contain little if any lipid. Type V lesions generally begin to appear in the fourth decade of life and can cause significant narrowing of the arterial lumen, producing symptoms.

Type VI lesions are also known as complicated lesions. They are responsible for the majority of morbidity and mortality from atherosclerosis. Type VI lesions occur when a type IV or V lesion undergoes disruption of the intimal surface, such as with ulceration of or hemorrhage into a plaque. Type VI lesions may be the source of emboli or may cause arterial thrombosis. These events commonly result in acute ischemia, which may produce life-threatening or limb-threatening symptoms.

■ CELLULAR ELEMENTS

Endothelial cells, macrophages, T lymphocytes, vascular SMCs, and platelets form the cellular component of the atherosclerotic plaque.[6] The interaction of these cells with one another is controlled by the production and release of various chemotactic agents, adhesion molecules, vasoactive agents, growth factors, and cytokines. Once activated, these cells are stimulated to proliferate and produce the connective tissue matrix that forms the fibrous component of the atherosclerotic plaque.

Endothelial Cells

The response to injury hypothesis postulates that endothelial cell dysfunction is the initial event in the cascade leading to the formation of an atherosclerotic plaque, giving the endothelial cell a central role in atherogenesis. The endothelial cell has many normal physiologic functions. Endothelial cells function as a nonadherent surface for platelets and leukocytes. The endothelium is a nonthrombogenic surface and plays a major role in the modulation of the coagulation system. The endothelium functions as a permeability barrier, controlling the flow of fluids and molecules between the plasma and arterial wall. Vascular tone is modulated by the production and release of nitric oxide (NO), prostacyclin (PGI_2), endothelin, and angiotensin II by the endothelium.

Endothelial cells produce and secrete numerous growth factors and cytokines. The oxidation of lipoproteins, such as low-density lipoprotein (LDL), occurs in the endothelium. Abnormalities in one or more of these endothelial functions occur early in atherogenesis.[2,7]

Whereas endothelial dysfunction is characteristically seen early in atherogenesis, endothelial disruption is not. Early atherosclerotic lesions tend to develop in areas where the endothelium is morphologically intact.[2] Even though the endothelium maintains normal structural integrity, abnormalities in the permeability of the endothelium are seen early in atherogenesis. One manifestation of this abnormality in permeability is the transport of lipoproteins through the endothelium. LDL is oxidized by endothelial cells. Oxidized LDL accumulates in the subendothelial space of the intima.[10] Oxidized LDL has several harmful effects, including stimulation of the production of chemotactic agents and growth factors. Additionally, oxidized LDL has an adverse effect on NO metabolism, causing abnormal vasoconstriction and platelet adherence and aggregation.

The formation of adhesive cell-surface glycoproteins by the endothelium, such as intercellular adhesion molecule-1 (ICAM-1), vascular cell adhesion molecule-1 (VCAM-1), and platelet–endothelial cell adhesion molecule (PECAM), is seen early in atherogenesis.[11] These molecules initiate the attachment and adherence of lymphocytes, monocytes, and platelets to the endothelial surface.[12] When activated, the endothelium produces many cytokines and growth factors, including platelet-derived growth factor (PDGF), basic fibroblast growth factor (FGF), transforming growth factor-β (TGF-β), insulin-like growth factor-I (IGF-I), and interleukin-1 (IL-1).[7] These substances attract and stimulate the proliferation of both vascular SMCs and macrophages. Activated endothelial cells produce abnormal amounts of collagen and connective tissue matrix, contributing to the fibrous proliferation seen in atherogenesis.

Macrophages

Macrophages are found in all atherosclerotic lesions but are most prominent in the early stages of the disease. Their normal function is that of a scavenger, presenting antigens to T lymphocytes. The macrophage is the primary inflammatory mediator cell of atherogenesis. Monocytes are attracted by adhesion molecules and by the chemotactic factors produced by endothelial cells. Monocytes migrate to the subendothelial space, becoming macrophages. Early in atherogenesis, these cells take up oxidized LDL and become foam cells. *Foam cells* are simply macrophages filled with lipid; they are characteristically present in early lesions of atherosclerosis. Oxidized LDL causes endothelial cell injury and is one of the main initiators of atherogenesis.

The uptake of oxidized LDL stimulates the production of growth factors and cytokines by the macrophage. This further stimulates endothelial cells to produce adhesion molecules and chemotactic factors, which attract more monocytes in a positive feedback loop. Once activated, macrophages produce a number of growth factors and chemotactic agents. The substances known to be produced by macrophages are as follows[7,13]:

- Monocyte colony-stimulating factor (M-CSF)
- Granulocyte-monocyte CSF (GM-CSF)
- PDGF
- Epidermal growth factor (EGF)
- Basic FGF
- TGF-α
- TGF-β
- Vascular endothelial cell growth factor (VEGF)
- Monocyte chemoattractant protein-1 (MCP-1)

These substances both attract additional monocytes and vascular SMCs and stimulate the proliferation of endothelial cells, monocytes, and vascular SMCs.

T Lymphocytes

T lymphocytes are present in all atherosclerotic lesions in large numbers. Their precise role in atherogenesis has not been fully determined. Although no specific antigens or antibodies have been clearly linked to atherogenesis, autoantibodies to oxidized LDL have been identified in humans. There appears to be a correlation between titers of these antibodies and the progression of atherosclerosis.[14] T lymphocytes are known to adhere to atherosclerotic lesions and produce chemotactic agents and cytokines. Tumor necrosis factor-α (TNF-α), interferon-α (IFN-α), GM-CSF, and IL-2 are produced by activated T lymphocytes.[7] These substances attract and activate both macrophages and vascular SMCs.

The concept that atherogenesis may be an immune response was postulated more than 30 years ago. The involvement of macrophages and T lymphocytes in atherogenesis suggests an immune as well as an inflammatory response. The T lymphocytes found in atherosclerotic lesions are polyclonal, indicating that these cells do not develop in response to a single antigen. Several different subclasses of T lymphocytes have been identified in atherosclerotic plaque, including both CD4 (helper-inducer cells) and CD8 (cytotoxic T cells).[15] There are several indications that the T lymphocytes present in atherosclerotic plaque are activated T cells. High levels of IL-2 receptors are found on the T cells, and high levels of IFN-α have been identified in atherosclerotic plaque. IL-2 receptors are markers suggesting the activation of T lymphocytes, and IFN-α is produced and secreted by activated T lymphocytes.[16]

Accelerated coronary artery atherosclerosis is a unique variant of atherosclerosis that develops and progresses rapidly in transplanted hearts, suggesting an immunologic etiology. The lesions seen in transplanted hearts involve the entire coronary tree and are concentric rather than eccentric in nature. These lesions contain all the cellular elements characteristic of atherosclerosis but have higher numbers of T lymphocytes and macrophages compared with the typical atherosclerotic lesion.[17] The accelerated progression of these lesions in hearts demonstrating chronic rejection indicates that the immune system may have a role in the progression of atherosclerosis.

Activation of the complement system may play a role in both the initiation of atherosclerosis and the acceleration of existing disease. Complement activation may occur by the classical pathway, with the deposition of immune complexes in the arterial wall, or by the binding of specific antibodies to antigens found in vascular tissues. Antibody-independent activation via the alternative pathway may also occur. Cholesterol particles are potent activators of the complement system.[18] Activation of the complement system results in the production of pro-inflammatory molecules and the terminal membrane attack complex (MAC). Pro-inflammatory molecules, such as C5a and C3a, increase vascular permeability, are chemotactic for and activate leukocytes, and cause the expression of adhesion molecules. MAC has been identified in atherosclerotic lesions, particularly fibrous plaque.[19] MAC has been is known to increase the production and secretion of many cytokines, growth factors, and adhesion molecules, including the following:

- Basic FGF
- PDGF
- MCP-1
- P-selectin
- ICAM-1
- TNF-α
- IL-8

Additionally, MAC may stimulate the production of cytokines and growth factors by vascular SMCs and endothelial cells.[18] Complement activation contributes to the stimulation of an inflammatory response, recruitment and activation of leukocytes, and proliferation and activation of vascular SMCs and endothelial cells.

Vascular Smooth Muscle Cells

Vascular SMCs are normally located in the media and are a major component of the arterial wall. Their main function is to maintain vascular tone. As humans age, the intima becomes thicker, and vascular SMCs are found within this layer. The cells tend to accumulate in certain areas, and it is in the intima that atherosclerotic lesions develop. The migration of vascular SMCs to the intima is controlled by the release of various chemotactic agents from endothelial cells, platelets, macrophages, and other vascular SMCs. These cells respond to more than 20 different growth factors.[20] Proliferating vascular SMCs form a significant portion of atherosclerotic plaque and contribute to the narrowing of the vessel lumen by type V lesions.

There are two distinct phenotypes of vascular SMCs.[21] In the contractile state, the cells have more contractile myofilaments in their cytosol and are very responsive to substances that cause vasoconstriction or vasodilatation. When stimulated by various cytokines and growth factors, vascular SMCs are transformed into the synthetic phenotype. In the synthetic state, they have fewer myofilaments but a well-developed rough endoplasmic reticulum and Golgi complex. These cells are geared for the production of large amounts of proteins. In the synthetic state, vascular SMCs express the genes for the production of several growth factors and cytokines as well as extracellular matrix. These substances are chemotactic for other

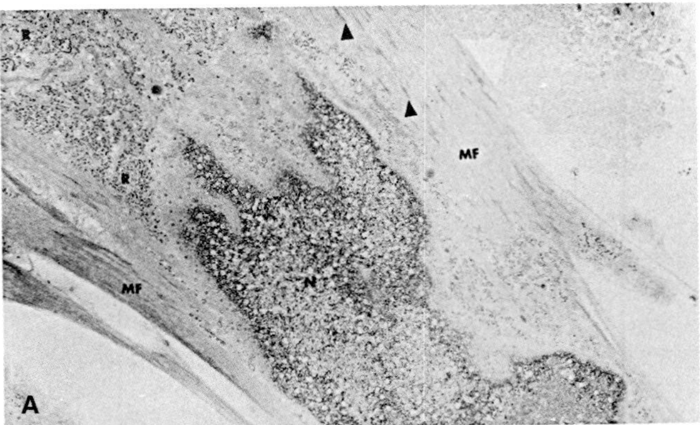

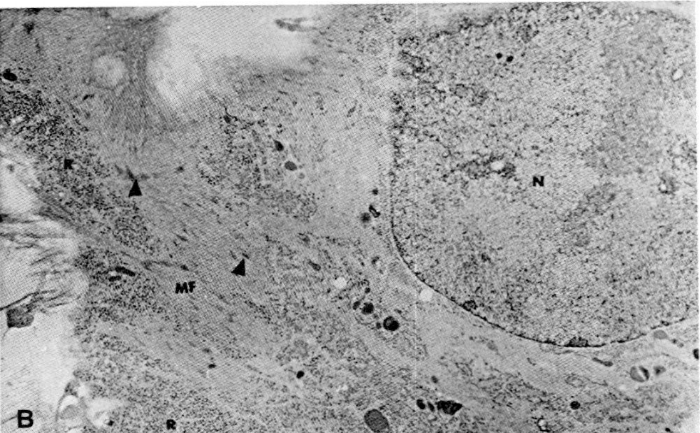

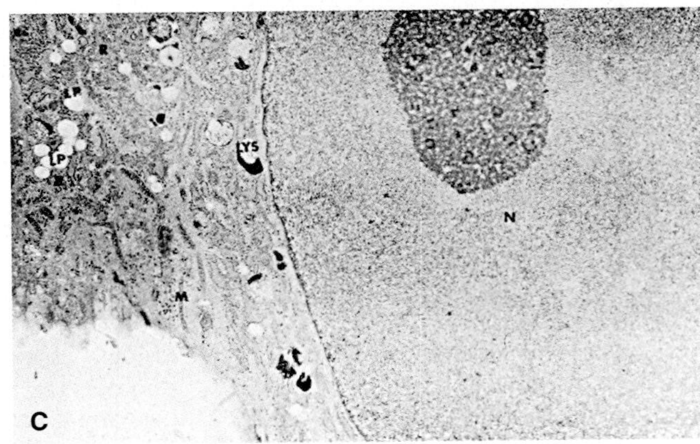

FIGURE 8-3 Composite electron micrograph of cultured tibial vascular smooth muscle cells demonstrating the different phenotypes. **A,** Contractile state (passage 3). Note the extent of microfilaments (MF) throughout the cytoplasm and the highly irregular nuclear shape (N). *Solid arrowheads* denote dense plaques periodicity along MF. **B,** Intermediate state (passage 5). Note the increase in number of ribosomes and polyribosomes. **C,** Synthetic state (passage 7). Microfilaments disappear. LYS, secondary lysosomes; LP, neural lipids. Magnification: **A,** ×1450; **B,** ×3500; **C,** ×5100. (From Jones BA, Aly HM, Forsyth EA, et al: Phenotypic characterization of human smooth muscle cells derived from atherosclerotic tibial and peroneal arteries. J Vasc Surg 24:883-891, 1996.)

vascular SMCs, stimulate cell proliferation, and induce other cells to change from the contractile to the synthetic phenotype. Cultured vascular SMCs demonstrate a rapid change from the contractile to the synthetic state (Fig. 8-3). When stimulated, vascular SMCs in the synthetic state produce excessive amounts of extracellular matrix, which contributes to the volume of the plaque, causing impingement into the lumen of the vessel.

Platelets

The adherence and aggregation of platelets on the endothelial surface occurs relatively early in the development of atherosclerosis. As lesions progress, platelet thrombi become more common, particularly at vessel branch points. Advanced atherosclerotic lesions are susceptible to thrombosis or serve as the nidus for platelet emboli, resulting in severe ischemic complications. Thrombosis is commonly the result of platelet adherence to ulcerated or irregular endothelial surfaces. There is evidence indicating that platelets play a role in stimulating the progression of atherosclerotic lesions. Platelets are known to produce and secrete a number of growth factors and vasoactive substances, including the following[7]:

- PDGF
- TGF-α
- TGF-β
- EGF
- IGF-1
- Thromboxane A_2
- Serotonin
- P-selectin

These substances are important in both recruiting and stimulating the proliferation of leukocytes and vascular SMCs. In animals, platelets have an important role in the progression of atherosclerosis. Rabbits that have been made thrombocytopenic have fewer atherosclerotic lesions than animals with normal platelets.[22] Unlike normal animals, pigs with abnormal von Willebrand factor synthesis are resistant to the development of atherosclerosis when fed a high-cholesterol diet.[23]

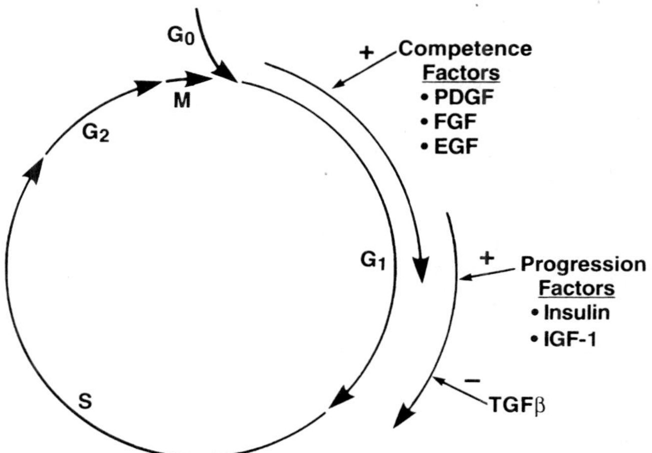

FIGURE 8-4 The cell cycle and the effects that competence factors and progression growth factors have on the cell as it progresses in the G_1 phase of the cycle. The cell must be under the influence of both groups of factors in order to progress to the S phase. In addition, transforming growth factor-β (TGF-β) exerts a negative effect on the cell in the later part of the G_1 phase. IGF-1, insulin-like growth factor-1; EGF, epidermal growth factor; FGF, fibroblast growth factor; PDGF, platelet-derived growth factor. (From Sidawy AN: Peptide growth factors and their role in the proliferative diseases of the vascular system. In Sidawy AN, Sumpio BE, DePalma RG [eds]: The Basic Science of Vascular Disease. Armonk, NY, Futura Publishing, 1997, pp 127-149.)

■ GROWTH FACTORS

Cell differentiation and proliferation are influenced by peptide growth factors.[24] These peptide molecules are important in maintaining the normal development and growth of animal cells; in addition, they play a major role in disease states. The role of growth factors in the development of atherosclerosis and intimal hyperplasia is of great interest to us as physicians caring for patients with peripheral arterial disease. Growth factors such as PDGF, FGF, insulin, IGF-1, TGF-α, and TGF-β play important roles in controlling the progression of cells in the cell cycle.[25] Furthermore, various growth factors have been found to influence the motility of cells, particularly vascular SMCs.[26]

Growth factors are mitogens that exert their effects via receptors located in the cell membrane. The interaction of a growth factor with its specific receptor unleashes a series of chemical reactions within the cell that ultimately lead to the specific action of the growth factor.[25] This action can be one of differentiation,[24] proliferation,[27] or chemotaxis.[26] Greater formation and secretion of growth factors and upregulation of their receptors can be found in disease states such as atherosclerosis and intimal hyperplasia.[28] In injury-induced intimal hyperplasia, local production of growth factors occurs. These growth factors can be secreted by endothelial cells or by vascular SMCs. In addition, macrophages and platelets, which attach themselves to the injured endothelium, also secrete these growth factors.[29] The interaction of these factors with their receptors found on intimal and medial vascular SMCs stimulates the proliferation and migration of these cells through the internal elastic lamina of the arterial wall and their accumulation in the subendothelial layer.[30] The progression of such lesions leads to narrowing or occlusion of the arterial lumen, with resultant ischemia of the organ supplied by the affected artery.

Cell Cycle and Role of Growth Factors

The cell is usually found in a quiescent state called the G_0 phase.[25] To proliferate, the cell goes through multiple phases that culminate in cell division (mitosis) (Fig. 8-4). The cell enters the gap 1 phase (G_1 phase) under the influence of a group of growth factors called competence factors; this group includes PDGF, FGF, and EGF. As the cell progresses in the G_1 phase, it is subject to the influence of another group of growth factors called the progression factors; this group includes insulin and IGF-1. During the G_1 phase, the cell must be under the influence of both groups of factors in order to progress in that phase. If it does not progress, the cell reverts back to the G_0 (quiescent) phase.

If the cell completes the G_1 phase, it enters the S phase, in which deoxyribonucleic acid (DNA) synthesis and chromosome replication take place. After going through the gap 2 phase (G_2 phase), the cell enters the M phase, in which mitosis takes place. Some growth factors can play a negative inhibitory role on the progression of the cell cycle. For

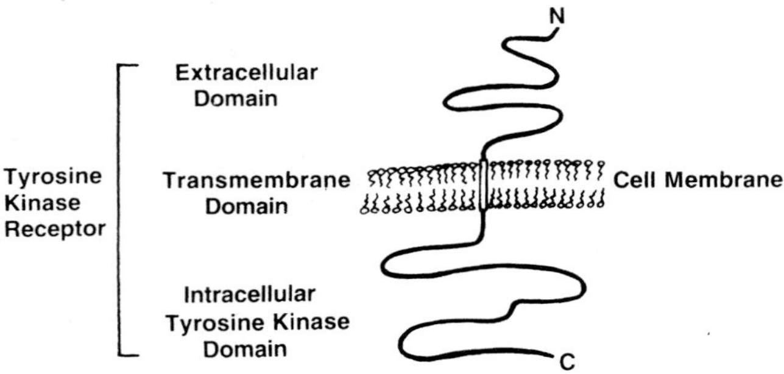

FIGURE 8-5 Depiction of the tyrosine kinase receptor. The N-terminal (N) of the receptor protein molecule is in the extracellular domain, and the C-terminal (C) is located in the intracellular domain. (From Sidawy AN: Peptide growth factors and their role in the proliferative diseases of the vascular system. In Sidawy AN, Sumpio BE, DePalma RG [eds]: The Basic Science of Vascular Disease. Armonk, NY, Futura Publishing, 1997, pp 127-149.)

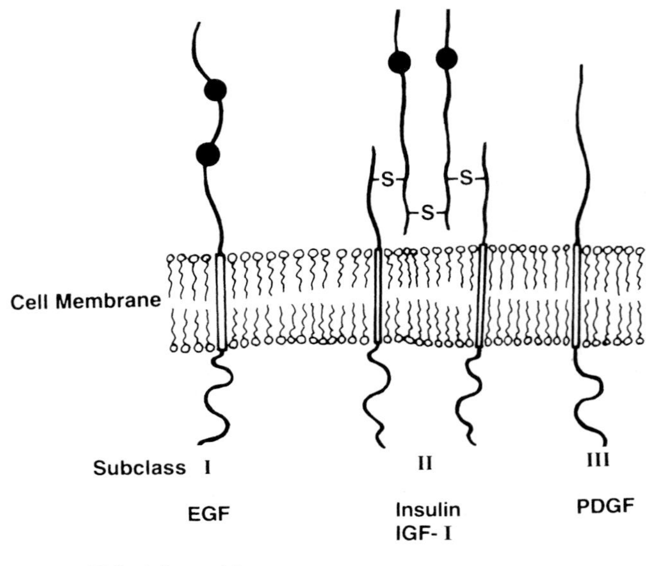

FIGURE 8-6 The three subclasses of the tyrosine kinase receptor. Subclass I is represented by the epidermal growth factor (EGF) receptor containing two cysteine-rich residues in its extracellular domain. Subclass II is represented by the insulin and the insulin-like growth factor-1 (IGF-1) receptors, which are formed of two α and two β subunits. Each α-subunit contains one cysteine-rich residue in its extracellular domain. Subclass III is represented by the platelet-derived growth factor (PDGF) receptor with no cysteine-rich residue in its extracellular domain. (From Sidawy AN: Peptide growth factors and their role in the proliferative diseases of the vascular system. In Sidawy AN, Sumpio BE, DePalma RG [eds]: The Basic Science of Vascular Disease. Armonk, NY, Futura Publishing, 1997, pp 127-149.)

instance, TGF-β has a negative effect on the progression of the cell in the latter part of the cycle.

Although it has been widely held that specific protein synthesis plays an important role in the progression of the cell cycle, protein destruction or proteolysis at specific points of the cell cycle has been discovered to trigger different phases of the cycle.[31]

Growth Factor Receptors and Signal Transduction

In order to exert their effects, growth factors interact with specific receptors located in the cell membrane. These receptors belong to a family of peptide receptors called receptor tyrosine kinases (RTKs). The peptide structure of the receptors is composed of multiple domains. The extracellular domain is found outside the cell. Once a growth factor interacts with the extracellular domain of its receptor, a signal is transmitted along the receptor molecule. The transmembrane domain anchors the receptor to the cell membrane and transmits the signal to the intracellular cytoplasmic domain. The cytoplasmic tyrosine kinase domain or the intracellular domain plays a major role in translating the signal received into specific cellular responses (Fig. 8-5).[32]

Tyrosine kinase receptors are divided into three subclasses according to their molecular structures (the presence or absence of one or more cysteine-rich residues) and the number of subunits of which they are formed.[32] For example, the subclass I family is represented by the EGF receptor, which contains two cysteine-rich residues in its extracellular domain. The IGF-I and insulin receptors, examples of subclass II, are characterized by two α-subunits and two β-subunits. Each of the α-subunits, which forms the extracellular domain of the receptor, contains one cysteine-rich residue. In contrast, the PDGF receptor contains no cysteine-rich residue in its extracellular domain; it is a member of subclass III (Fig. 8-6).[32]

The most important events in the signal transduction take place in the cytoplasm of the cell (Fig. 8-7).[25,33] Triggered by growth factor attachment to the extracellular domain, either dimerization or polymerization of two or more receptor intracellular domains takes place. The intracellular domains become phosphorylated at multiple locations, and they interact on a molecular level. Intracellular protein molecules belonging to various protein families are then recruited and bind to specific sites along the intracellular cytoplasmic domain of the phosphorylated receptor. These proteins carry specific recognition sites that allow a certain family of proteins to bind to a specific area of the receptor. Thus, various cellular signaling pathways are activated. Each pathway controls a specific function of the growth factor.

The recognition sites found on the cellular proteins are called src homology-2 (SH-2) or src homology-3 (SH-3) domains. In addition, the SH-2 and SH-3 phosphorylated sites of the protein serve to bind them to other cellular proteins that belong to the signaling cascade. Various proteins that are involved in these pathways are (1) guanosine triphosphatase–activating protein (GAP), (2) phospholipase-C (PLC), and (3) phosphatidylinositol-3 kinase (PI-3K) binding protein. These cascades of phosphorylation and specific protein binding eventually lead to a specific function of the growth factor; the function may be one of differentiation, proliferation, cell shape change, or motility.[33]

The signaling pathways or cascades rely on the phosphorylation of various proteins for the signal to be transmitted to the nucleus and cause gene activation. One of these pathways is called *Ras pathway*. Once the growth factor attaches to its receptor, the receptor phosphorylates itself. Ras, a protein that attaches to the cytoplasmic aspect of the

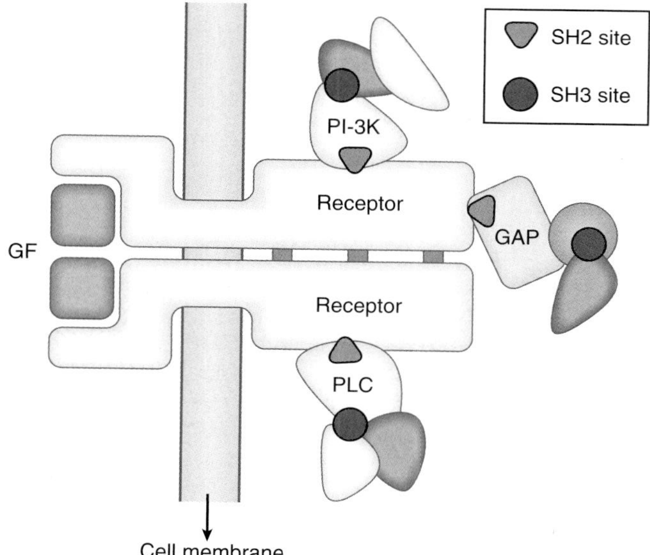

FIGURE 8-7 Once the growth factor (GF) interacts with the extracellular domain of its specific receptor, phosphorylation of the receptor takes place, and the intracellular domains of various receptors interact on the molecular level. This interaction in turn phosphorylates the src homology-2 (SH-2) or src homology-3 (SH-3) domains located on certain cellular proteins that belong to the signaling cascade, leading to recruitment and binding of proteins carrying these recognition sites. Various proteins that are involved in these pathways are guanosine triphosphatase–activating protein (GAP), phospholipase-C (PLC), and phosphatidylinositol-3 kinase (PI-3K) binding protein. These cascades of phosphorylation and specific protein binding eventually lead to a specific function of the growth factor.

cellular membrane, undergoes phosphorylation and activates Raf-1 protein, which in turn phosphorylates mitogen-activated protein kinase (MAPK). MAPK phosphorylates transcription factors inside the nucleus (Myc, jun, etc) that stimulate gene activity.[33]

Jak-STAT pathway is another important signaling pathway.[34,35] Signal transducers and activators of transcription (STATs) are families of protein that have been found to be phosphorylated by Jaks, kinase enzymes activated in response to interaction of a growth factor with its receptor. The two pathways, Ras and Jak-STAT, may intersect on the way to the nucleus to cause gene activation. The specifics of such interaction are still the subject of intense research. It is believed that MAPK from the Ras pathway enhances STAT activity by causing additional phosphorylation.[36]

Platelet-Derived Growth Factor

The discovery of PDGF was reported by Ross and colleagues[27] in 1974; they showed that platelet-rich serum causes vascular SMCs to proliferate. Although called "platelet-derived" because it was first observed in platelet-rich serum, this growth factor has been found in a variety of cells, including vascular SMCs, fibroblasts, and endothelial cells.[37,38]

PDGF has three isoforms (AA, BB, and AB), depending on the molecular composition of its two chains (chain A and chain B).[39] In response to balloon catheter injury, secretion of PDGF by vascular SMCs is increased.[40] In addition, expression of PDGF messenger ribonucleic acid (mRNA) is induced in response to carotid artery injury.[41] The PDGF receptor is formed of two α-subunits and two β-subunits.[42] This receptor has a very high affinity for PDGF.

PDGF is a potent mitogen that causes proliferation and tissue remodeling. It is also a potent vasoconstrictor in a concentration-dependent fashion.[43] Whether it is secreted by platelets, endothelial cells, macrophages, or vascular SMCs themselves, PDGF causes proliferation and multiplication of vascular SMCs. Because the half-life of PDGF is only 2 minutes, it is believed that this growth factor acts near the release site in a paracrine or autocrine fashion.[44] In addition, PDGF plays a role in tissue remodeling. It increases collagen synthesis[45] and stimulates secretion of collagenase by fibroblasts.[46] This effect is important in wound healing and tissue remodeling. Furthermore, PDGF has a chemotactic effect on vascular SMCs and other cells, such as fibroblasts and neutrophils.[47]

Fibroblast Growth Factor

Also in 1974, Gospodarowicz[48] named a material that caused proliferation of fibroblasts in culture fibroblast growth factor. Because that material had a basic isoelectric charge, it was called basic FGF (bFGF). It was not until 1980, when Thomas and associates[49] described an acidic isoelectrically charged FGF, that it was called acidic FGF (aFGF). Many other forms of FGF have been discovered over the years. These growth factors are secreted by a myriad of cells, including fibroblasts, endothelial cells, and vascular SMCs. The same growth factor is given different names, depending on specific characteristics or the tissue of origin. For example, heparin-binding growth factor is an FGF found in the brain.[50] Basic FGF is a more potent growth factor than aFGF; however, this difference depends on target cells.[51]

The FGFs play an important role in extracellular matrix remodeling. Basic FGF is found in an insoluble state in the extracellular matrix and participates in tissue regeneration during repair,[52] including the fibroblast's production of collagen and proteins, the building blocks of the extracellular matrix.[53,54] As an angiogenic factor, FGF promotes the formation of new vessels and other factors important in tissue repair. Basic FGF stimulates the proliferation of endothelial cells and vascular SMCs after catheter-induced arterial injury.[55,56] An antibody to bFGF has been found to inhibit the proliferation of vascular SMCs after injury.[57]

Insulin and Insulin-like Growth Factors

Although insulin is well known for its metabolic effects, it is also a very important growth factor that stimulates the proliferation of animal cells. In this chapter, we concentrate on the growth-promoting effects of insulin. Although IGFs have metabolic effects similar to those of insulin, our main interest here is their mitogenic effects. Both IGF-I and IGF-II have those effects, although IGF-I is more potent. Insulin is secreted by the pancreas; the IGFs are secreted by the liver. Hepatic secretion of the IGFs, which depends on growth hormones, is continuous and steady.[58,59] Once in the circulation, the IGFs travel bound to IGF-binding proteins, which are also secreted by the liver.[58] The IGFs are also secreted at the tissue level. Insulin secretion is not continuous; it is usually produced in reaction to serum glucose levels. In addition, insulin travels freely in the circulation, not bound to protein.

Both insulin and the IGFs exert their effects on animal cells via specific receptors. The receptors for IGF-I and insulin are organized as heterotetramers with two α- and two β-subunits (see Fig. 8-6). The two receptors can be differentiated by their affinity for the growth factor. The insulin receptor has more affinity for insulin than the IGF-I receptor does, whereas the IGF-I receptor has more affinity for IGF-I than for insulin.

The molecular structure of the receptor for IGF-II is different from that of the IGF-I and insulin receptors. The IGF-II receptor has a very large extracellular domain. It is of interest that when insulin exerts its metabolic effects, it does so via the insulin receptor; however, when insulin exerts its mitogenic effect, it does so via the IGF-I receptor.[60] Using monoclonal antibody against the insulin receptor does not alter the proliferative effect of insulin on human tibial arterial SMCs. In contrast, using monoclonal antibody against the IGF-I receptor prevents insulin from exerting its effects on those cells. Furthermore, IGF-II seems to exert its mitogenic effect via the IGF-I receptor as well.[61]

The mitogenic effects of insulin and IGFs are those of proliferation and differentiation of animal cells. These growth factors induce the proliferation of endothelial and vascular SMCs. In addition, balloon de-endothelialization of rat aorta causes an increase in IGF-I mRNA, which has been found to peak at 7 days after injury.[62] Sidawy and associates[28] found that injury-induced intimal hyperplasia in rabbit aorta increases IGF-I receptor binding. IGF-I has been found to induce angiogenesis in rabbit corneal model, and the angiogenic effects of IGF-I and bFGF were evidenced in that model.[63] Avena and colleagues[64] have also reported that the mitogenic effects of insulin and glucose on human arterial SMCs are synergistic. This mimics the conditions in which vascular SMCs are found in non–insulin-dependent diabetic patients, whose serum glucose and insulin levels are found to be elevated.

Epidermal Growth Factor and Transforming Growth Factor-α

The term epidermal growth factor was coined by Cohen[65,66] after studies showing that this factor promoted epidermal growth. The EGF molecule consists of 53 amino acids. TGF-α is an analogue of EGF. They share sequence homology in about half of their molecular structures. In addition, the EGF receptor has a high affinity for TGF-α.[67] The EGF receptor is expressed on most animal cells.

Although the primary target of EGF is epithelial cells, it is a mitogenic factor that stimulates the proliferation and migration of endothelial cells as well. In addition, EGF and TGF-α have been found to induce tube formation by endothelial cells, an important step in angiogenesis.[68] Administration of EGF in the femoral artery of the dog has also shown a vasodilator effect.[69]

Transforming Growth Factor-β

First described in the early 1970s, TGF at that time was called "sarcoma growth factor."[70] Because this factor could cause morphologic changes in animal cells, it was later named transforming growth factor.[71] There are at least five members of the TGF-β family, numbered from 1 to 5. Each member is composed of 112 to 114 amino acids.[72] The TGF-βs exert their effect via specific receptors. There are four TGF-β receptors, varying in molecular weight. The receptors have been found on most animal cells.[73] TGF-βs are found in great concentration in bone, with the bony skeleton acting as a rich pool for these growth factors. TGF-βs are believed to play an important role in the metabolism of bone.[74]

TGF-β1 has an interesting effect on the growth and multiplication of cells. Although it can be a stimulator of cell growth, TGF-β1 can also inhibit cell differentiation and proliferation. The type of action exerted by this growth factor on a cell depends on multiple factors, such as the type of cell and the stage of its differentiation.[75] In addition, TGF-β1 may interfere with the growth and proliferative effects of other growth factors, such as insulin. The effect of insulin on vascular SMCs is one of proliferation; however, TGF-β1 has been found to inhibit the proliferative effect of insulin on these cells.[76] Furthermore, TGF-βs play a role in stimulating synthesis of extracellular matrix protein and its accumulation in bone and other tissues.[77] TGF-βs, especially TGF-β1, interact with multiple growth factors in the proliferation of cells of vascular origin. TGF-β1, as mentioned, inhibits the proliferative effect of insulin in vascular SMCs. It also opposes the proliferative effect of FGF on endothelial cells in culture.[78] This inhibitory effect is not limited to proliferation; TGF-β also inhibits the migratory effect, which is induced by FGF and PDGF.[79]

Vascular Endothelial Growth Factor

VEGF, a peptide growth factor that causes endothelial cell proliferation, has been found to promote the growth of new blood vessels in the myocardium and the peripheral circulation.[80] VEGF is also known as "vascular permeability factor" (VPF) because it was found to cause vascular leakage in guinea pig skin.[81] It has been suggested that this leakage is important in the process of angiogenesis because it forms a fibrin gel medium that acts as a substrate for endothelial cell proliferation.[82] VEGF exerts its effect via two types of receptors, which are localized to the vascular endothelium.[80]

Although FGF had been found to increase the expression of the 165–amino acid isomer of VEGF, it showed no effect on other VEGF isomers ($VEGF_{121}$, $VEGF_{110}$, $VEGF_{189}$, $VEGF_{206}$).[80,83] These isomers differ in their isoelectric charge and in their affinity for heparin. These characteristics affect the bioavailability of various isomers and, in turn, influence their effects.[80] Successful gene transfer of VEGF complementary DNA in Sprague-Dawley rats by means of an adenovirus vector was reported in 1997.[84] Angiogenesis was the result, protecting the animal against acute ischemia produced by ligation of the common iliac artery. Intramuscular injection of naked plasmid DNA encoding for the 165–amino acid VEGF isomer induces formation of new blood vessels in patients with chronic ischemia, leading to limb salvage.[85] Studies have also demonstrated the efficacy of intramyocardial gene therapy with VEGF, a technique that may prove useful for the treatment of ischemic cardiomyopathy.[86,87]

Clinical Implication of Growth Factor Physiology

Therapeutic methods can target any step of the signaling pathway, from the interaction of the growth factor with its specific receptor through every subsequent step involved.[88] We have already mentioned some of the important applications in segments dedicated to individual growth factors; here we describe other, more general methods.

One example that illustrates the efficacy of targeting the signaling pathways is the immunosuppressive drug cyclosporine, which is used to suppress the immune mechanism in organ transplantation.[33] An antibody against FGF has been shown to inhibit the formation of postinjury intimal hyperplasia.[89] Growth factor antagonists can successfully inhibit the binding of the growth factor to its receptor, reversing the process of the disease. Suramin, a drug that serves as an example of this approach, has been found to be effective in the treatment of some kinds of carcinomas.[90] In addition, antibodies against specific growth factor receptors prevent the interaction between a growth factor and its receptor, leading to the inhibition of the growth factor function. SH-2, SH-3, Ras, Raf-1, and MAPK blockers are in the process of being developed to interrupt the signaling pathways and to prevent the progression of disease.[33,88]

■ MECHANISMS OF ENDOTHELIAL CELL INJURY

The well-known risk factors for atherosclerosis have all been implicated as contributors to endothelial injury. It is only recently that the pathogenesis of the injury resulting from these risk factors has been determined. Although the underlying mechanism may vary, the resultant endothelial injury is the common initiating factor in the development of atherosclerosis.

Tobacco

Cigarette smoking is well established as an independent risk factor for the development of atherosclerosis, but the mechanism of smoking-induced atherogenesis is not completely understood. Nearly 5000 chemicals are found in cigarette smoke, the majority of which have yet to be studied. Cigarette smoke has been shown to cause endothelial cell swelling and bleb formation, greater formation of luminal surface projections, subendothelial edema, widening of endothelial junctions, and thickening of the basement membrane.[91-93] Studies with nicotine alone have demonstrated similar effects,[94,95] along with a higher frequency of endothelial cell death and a lower rate of cell replication.[96] This abnormal capability for endothelial cell regeneration results in an impaired ability to repair sites of endothelial cell damage. Thus, cigarette smoke not only is toxic to the endothelial cell, causing injury and death, but also inhibits the ability of the endothelium to repair the injury induced by the cigarette smoke.

In addition to directly injuring the endothelium, smoking can indirectly damage the endothelium, resulting in abnormalities of endothelial function. Smokers have been shown to have abnormal levels of plasma lipoproteins, which return to normal after they cease smoking.[97] Lipoprotein elevations are another initiator of endothelial cell injury. Cigarette smoking is associated with abnormal prostaglandin production, resulting in an imbalance between prostacyclin and thromboxane A_2.[98] The imbalance reduces the antithrombotic potential of the endothelial surface by inducing platelet aggregation and adherence. Smoking inhibits the production of NO, which has adverse effects on vasomotor regulation, SMC proliferation, and platelet and macrophage adhesion.[99] A clinical manifestation of this abnormality in NO metabolism is a reduction in the ability of saphenous vein grafts to dilate in smokers compared with nonsmokers.[100]

Hemodynamic Factors: Hypertension and Shear Forces

Hypertension, another independent risk factor for the development of atherosclerosis, induces morphologic as well as functional changes in the endothelium. Endothelial cells from hypertensive patients are edematous and project farther into the lumen of the vessel than normal.[101] Vessels from hypertensive patients demonstrate vascular SMC proliferation along with thickening of the basement membrane, subendothelial accumulation of fibrin, and increased fibronectin in the extracellular matrix.[102] Levels of growth factors such as TGF-β and PDGF are increased, contributing to vascular SMC proliferation.[103] Endothelium-dependent relaxation is impaired in hypertensive patients via abnormalities of NO metabolism.[104] The effect of an acetylcholine infusion on the release of NO is significantly reduced in hypertensive patients.[101] NO production is decreased both in humans with essential hypertension and in animal models of hypertension.[105,106] Most studies indicate that the endothelial dysfunction seen in hypertensive patients is the result , not the cause, of the elevated blood pressure.[101] It appears that the severity of the endothelial dysfunction associated with hypertension is related to the degree of blood pressure elevation.

Atherosclerosis is seen only in vessels subjected to arterial pressure. Atherosclerosis does not develop in veins but commonly occurs in vein grafts placed into the arterial circulation. Atherosclerotic lesions tend to appear in certain areas, such as branch points and bends in vessels, indicating that hemodynamic forces other than arterial pressure may have an etiologic role in atherogenesis. Shear forces appear to have an effect on the development of atherosclerosis. Certain areas of low shear stress, such as the carotid sinus, have a predilection for the development of atherosclerosis.[13] High shear forces at bifurcations may disrupt the endothelium, contributing to the higher frequency of lesions seen in these areas. Although it appears likely that shear forces have a part in the development of atherosclerosis, the exact role of shear forces in atherogenesis is not fully understood at this time.

Hyperlipidemia

The relationship between elevations of plasma lipoproteins and atherosclerosis has been recognized for many years, but the pathophysiology of lipoprotein-induced endothelial cell injury has only recently been elucidated. It is now known that LDL is taken up by the endothelial cells and converted to the oxidized form of LDL, which plays a significant role in the induction of endothelial cell injury. Oxidized LDL blunts endothelium-dependent relaxation by decreasing the production and release of NO by the endothelial cell, and stimulates the endothelium to produce cytokines and growth factors.[10,13] Additionally, oxidized LDL attracts monocytes and enhances their adhesiveness to the endothelial surface.[12] Subendothelial macrophages ingest oxidized LDL and become foam cells. The role of monocytes and macrophages in the development of atherosclerosis was discussed earlier in this chapter.

Diabetes Mellitus

Diabetes mellitus is another initiator of endothelial cell dysfunction. Avena and colleagues,[107] using brachial artery vasoactivity to evaluate endothelial cell function, found impairment of endothelial-dependent relaxation in patients with occult glucose intolerance as well as overt diabetes. Diabetics also demonstrate blunting of the normal vasorelaxation seen with hyperemia. This abnormality is exacerbated by an oral glucose load, such as during an oral glucose tolerance test.[107] Levels of endothelin and angiotensin-converting enzyme, which cause vasoconstriction, are raised in diabetics and may be responsible for this finding.[108,109]

Several potential mechanisms explain the vascular injury seen in diabetes. Patients with diabetes mellitus type 2 have elevations of both insulin and glucose, which have been shown to be independent stimulants of SMC proliferation (an early step in the development of atherosclerosis). [110] High concentrations of glucose increase the production of endothelial collagen IV and fibronectin as well as the activity of enzymes involved in collagen synthesis.[111] These increases lead to a thickening of the basement membrane and contribute to the excessive production of extracellular matrix seen in atherosclerosis. Additionally, elevated glucose concentrations have been shown to accelerate cell death and impair cell replication in cultured endothelial cells.[112] Like smoking, diabetes not only causes endothelial cell injury but also impairs the ability of the endothelial cell to regenerate and repair the injury. Patients with diabetes commonly have associated diseases such as hypertension and hyperlipidemia, which are also risk factors for the development of atherosclerotic vascular disease. The presence of more than one initiator of endothelial injury may have an additive effect on the severity of the injury and the extent of endothelial cell dysfunction as well as on the rate at which atherosclerosis develops and progresses.

Infection and Atherosclerosis

The role of infection in the development of atherosclerosis has been debated for many years. Evidence implicating both cytomegalovirus (CMV) and *Chlamydia pneumoniae* as etiologic agents for atherosclerosis has emerged. It is known that cardiac transplant recipients with CMV exposure are more likely to develop post-transplantation atherosclerosis than patients without such exposure.[113] CMV infection has been associated with re-stenosis after coronary angioplasty.[114] There is data linking CMV to the development of carotid atherosclerosis. Antigens to CMV have been isolated from carotid plaque, and increased levels of CMV antibody titers are associated with carotid intimal-medial thickening.[115] *C. pneumoniae* organisms have been isolated from atherosclerotic plaque from both carotid and coronary arteries.[116,117]

Although this evidence is suggestive of a link between CMV and *C. pneumoniae* and atherosclerosis, what role, if any, *Chlamydia* organisms play in the initiation or progression of atherosclerosis has not been determined. There is evidence indicating that *C. pneumoniae* may indeed play a role in atherogenesis, but a direct cause-and-effect relationship has not been shown. *C. pneumoniae* has been shown to accelerate the development of atherosclerosis in rabbits fed a high-cholesterol diet. This effect is prevented by treatment with azithromycin.[118] *C. pneumoniae* has been shown to induce endothelial cell dysfunction and vascular SMC proliferation.[119] In vitro studies have demonstrated that *C. pneumoniae* can infect and replicate in vascular SMCs, macrophages, and vascular endothelium.[120,121]

Clinical studies have also demonstrated that treatment with azithromycin improves endothelial dysfunction in *C. pneumoniae*–seropositive patients with coronary artery disease.[122] Treatment with roxithromycin has been shown to improve walking distance in *C. pneumoniae*–seropositive patients with peripheral artery disease.[123] Other studies have shown that treatment with antibiotics effective against *C. pneumoniae* decreases the occurrence of cardiovascular events related to atherosclerosis.[124] Although not furnishing definitive proof of causality, these studies provide strong evidence of an association between *C. pneumoniae* and atherosclerosis. More work needs to be done to definitively establish the relationship between these agents and atherosclerosis.

■ REFERENCES

1. Ross R, Glomset JA: Atherosclerosis and the arterial smooth muscle cell. Science 180:1332-1339, 1973.
2. Ross R: The pathogenesis of atherosclerosis: A perspective for the 1990s. Nature 362:801-809, 1993.
3. Ross R: Mechanism of disease: Atherosclerosis—an inflammatory disease. N Engl J Med 340:115-126, 1999.
4. Biondi-Zoccai GGL, Abbate A, Liuzzo G, et al: Atherothrombosis, inflammation and diabetes. J Am Coll Cardiol 41:1071-1077, 2003.
5. Faggiotto A, Ross R, Harker L: Studies of hypercholesterolemia in the nonhuman primate. I: Changes that lead to fatty streak formation. Atherosclerosis 4:323-340, 1984.
6. Stary HC: Evolution and progression of atherosclerotic lesions in coronary arteries of children and young adults. Atherosclerosis 9(Suppl 1): 19-32, 1989.
7. Ross R: Cell biology of atherosclerosis. Annu Rev Physiol 57:791-804, 1995.
8. Stary HC, Chandler AB, Glagov S, et al.: A definition of intimal, fatty streak, and intermediate lesions of atherosclerosis. Circulation 89:2462-2478, 1994.
9. Stary HC, Chandler AB, Dinsmore RE, et al: A definition of advanced types of atherosclerotic lesions and a histological classification of atherosclerosis. Circulation 92:1355-1374, 1995.
10. Flavahan NA: Atherosclerosis or lipoprotein-induced endothelial dysfunction: Potential mechanisms underlying reduction in EDRF/nitric oxide activity. Circulation 85:1927-1938, 1992.
11. Springer TA: Adhesion receptors of the immune system. Nature 346:425-434, 1990.

12. Berliner JA, Territo MC, Sevanian A, et al: Minimally modified low density lipoprotein stimulates monocyte endothelial interactions. J Clin Invest 85:1260-1266, 1990.
13. Boyle EM, Lille ST, Allaire E, et al: Endothelial cell injury in cardiovascular surgery: Atherosclerosis. Ann Thorac Surg 63:885-894, 1997.
14. Salonen JT, Yla-Harttuala S, Yamamoto R, et al: Autoantibodies against oxidized LDL and progression of carotid atherosclerosis. Lancet 339:883-887, 1992.
15. Libby P, Hansson GK: Involvement of the immune system in human atherogenesis: Current knowledge and unanswered questions. Lab Invest 64:5-15, 1991.
16. Hansson GK, Holm J, Jonasson L, et al: Detection of activated T lymphocytes in human atherosclerotic plaque. Am J Pathol 135: 169-175, 1989.
17. Salomon RN, Hughes CC, Schoen FJ, et al: Human coronary transplantation-associated arteriosclerosis: Evidence for a chronic immune reaction to activated graft endothelial cells. Am J Pathol 138:791-798, 1991.
18. Torzewski J, Bowyer DE, Waltenberger J, et al: Processes in atherosclerosis: Compliment activation. Atherosclerosis 132:131-138, 1997.
19. Rus HG, Niculescu F, Constantinescu E, et al: Immunoelectronmicroscopic localization of the terminal C5b-9 complement complex in human aortic fibrous plaque. Atherosclerosis 61:35-42, 1986.
20. Corson MA, Berk BC: Growth factors and the vessel wall. Heart Dis Stroke 2:166-170, 1993.
21. Jones BA, Aly HM, Forsyth EA, et al: Phenotypic characterization of human smooth muscle cells derived from atherosclerotic tibial and peroneal arteries. J Vasc Surg 24:883-891, 1996.
22. Moore S, Freidman RJ, Singal DP, et al: Inhibition of injury induced thromboatherosclerotic lesions by anti-platelet serum in rabbits. Thromb Haemost 35:70-81, 1976.
23. Fuster V, Bgowie EJW, Lewis JC, et al: Resistance to atherosclerosis in pigs with von Willebrand's disease: Spontaneous and high-cholesterol diet-induced atherosclerosis. J Clin Invest 61:722-730, 1978.
24. Baird A, Bohlen P: Fibroblast growth factors. In Sporn MB, Roberts AB (eds): Peptide Growth Factors and Their Receptors, vol 1. New York, Springer-Verlag, 1990, pp 369-418.
25. Aaronson SA: Growth factors and cancer. Science 254:1146-1153, 1991.
26. Zerwes HG, Risau W: Polarized secretion of a platelet-derived growth factor-like chemotactic factor by endothelial cells in vitro. J Cell Biol 105:2037-2041, 1987.
27. Ross R, Glomset JA, Kariya B, Harker L: A platelet-dependent serum factor that stimulates the proliferation of arterial smooth muscle cells in vitro. Proc Nat Acad Sci U S A 71:1207-1210, 1974.
28. Sidawy AN, Hakim FS, Jones B, et al: Insulin-like growth factor-1 binding in injury-induced intimal hyperplasia of rabbit aorta. J Vasc Surg 23:308-313, 1996.
29. Ross R, Masuda J, Raines EW, et al: Localization of PDGF-B protein in macrophages in all phases of atherogenesis. Science 248:1009-1012, 1990.
30. Ross R: The pathogenesis of atherosclerosis: An update. N Engl J Med 314:488-500, 1986.
31. Baringa M: Research news: A new twist to the cell cycle. Science 269:631-632, 1995.
32. Yarden Y, Ullrich A: Growth factor receptor tyrosine kinase. Annu Rev Biochem 57:443-478, 1988.
33. Brugge JS: New intracellular targets for therapeutic drug design. Science 260, 1993.
34. Schindler C, Shuai K, Prezioso VR, Darnell JE: Interferon-dependent tyrosine phosphorylation of a latent cytoplasmic transcription factor. Science 257:809-813, 1992.
35. Zhong Z, Wen Z, Darnell JE: Stat3: A stat family member activated by tyrosine phosphorylation in response to epidermal growth factor and interleukin. Science 264:95-98, 1994.
36. Baringa M: Two major signaling pathways meet at MAP-kinase. Science 269:1673, 1995.
37. Dicorleto PE, Bowen-Pope DF: Cultured endothelial cells produce a platelet-derived growth factor-like protein. Proc Natl Acad Sci U S A 80:1919-1923, 1983.
38. Seifert RA, Schwartz SM, Bowen-Pope DF: Developmentally regulated production of platelet-derived growth factor-like molecules. Nature 311:669-671, 1984.
39. Hammacher A, Hellman U, Johnsson A, et al: A major part of platelet-derived growth factor purified from human platelets is a heterodimer of one A and one B chain. J Biol Chem 263:493-498, 1988.
40. Walker LN, Bowen-Pope DF, Ross R, Reidy MA: Production of platelet-derived growth factor-like molecules by cultured arterial smooth muscle cells accompanies proliferation after arterial injury. Proc Natl Acad Sci U S A 83:7311-7315, 1986.
41. Majesky MW, Reidy MA, Bowen-Pope DF, et al: PDGF ligand and receptor gene expression during repair of arterial injury. J Cell Biol 111:2149, 1990.
42. Seifert RA, Hart CE, Phillips PE, et al: Two different subunits associate to create iso-form specific platelet-derived growth factor receptors. J Biol Chem 264:8771-8778, 1989.
43. Berk BC, Alexander RW, Brock TA, et al: Vasoconstriction: A new activity of platelet-derived growth factor. Science 232:87-90, 1986.
44. Raines EW, Bowen-Pope DF, Ross R: Platelet-derived growth factor. In Sporn MB, Roberts AB (eds): Peptide Growth Factors and Their Receptors, vol 1. New York, Springer-Verlag, 1990, pp 173-262.
45. Owen AJ, Geyer RP, Antoniades HN: Human platelet-derived growth factor stimulates amino acid transport and protein synthesis by human diploid fibroblasts in plasma-free media. Proc Natl Acad Sci U S A 79:3203-3207, 1982.
46. Bauer EA, Cooper TW, Huang JS, et al: Stimulation of in vitro human skin collagenase expression by platelet-derived growth factor. Proc Natl Acad Sci U S A 82:4132-4136, 1985.
47. Deule TF, Sehior RM, Huang SS, et al: Chemotaxis of monocytes and neutrophils to platelet-derived growth factor. J Clin Invest 69:1046-1049, 1982.
48. Gospodarowicz D: Localization of a fibroblast growth factor and its effect alone and with hydrocortisone on cell growth. Nature 249:123-127, 1974.
49. Thomas KA, Riley MC, Lemmon SK, et al: Brain fibroblast growth factor: Nonidentity with mild and basic protein fragment. J Biol Chem 255:5517-5520, 1980.
50. Lobb RR, Fett JW: Purification of two distinct growth factors from bovine neural tissue by heparin affinity chromatography. Biochemistry 23:6295-6299, 1984.
51. Gospodarowicz D: Biological activities of fibroblast growth factors. Ann N Y Acad Sci 638:1-8, 1991.
52. Saksela O, Moscatelli D, Sommer A, Rifkin DB: Endothelial derived heparan sulfate binds basic fibroblast growth factor and protects it from proteolytic degradation. J Cell Biol 107:743-755, 1988.
53. Chua CC, Barritault D, Geiman DE, Ladda RL: Induction and suppression of type I collagenase in cultured human cells. Col Relat Res 7:277-284, 1987.
54. Davidson JM, Klagsbrun M, Hill KE, et al: Accelerated wound repair, cell proliferation, collagen and accumulation are produced by cartilage-derived growth factor. J Cell Biol 100:1219-1227, 1985.
55. Linder V, Majack RA, Reidy MA: Basic fibroblast growth factor stimulates endothelial regrowth and proliferation in denuded arteries. J Clin Invest 85:2004-2008, 1990.
56. Linder V, Lappi DA, Baird A, et al: Role of basic fibroblast growth factor in vascular lesion formation. Circ Res 68:106-113, 1991.
57. Linder V, Reidy MA: Proliferation of smooth muscle cells after vascular injury is inhibited by an antibody against fibroblast growth factor. Proc Natl Acad Sci U S A 88:3739-3743, 1991.
58. Schwander J, Hauri C, Zapf F, Froesch ER: Synthesis and secretion of insulin like growth factor and its binding protein by the perfused rat liver: Dependence on growth hormone status. Endocrinology 113:297-305, 1983.

59. Froesch ER, Schmid C, Schwander J, Zapf J: Actions of insulin-like growth factors. Annu Rev Physiol 47:443-467, 1985.
60. Avena R, Mitchell ME, Carmody B, et al: Insulin-like growth factor-I receptors mediate infragenicular vascular smooth muscle cell proliferation in response to glucose and insulin not by insulin receptors. Am J Surg 178:156-161, 1999.
61. Nissley SP, Hasckel JF, Sasaki N, et al: Insulin-like growth factor receptors. J Clin Science 3(Suppl):39-51, 1985.
62. Cercek B, Fishbein MC, Forrester JS, et al: Induction of insulin-like growth factor-I messenger RNA in rat aorta after balloon denudation. Circ Res 66:1755-1760, 1990.
63. Grant MB, Mames RN, Fitzgerald C, et al: Insulin-like growth factor-I acts as an angiogenic agent in rabbit cornea and retina: Comparative studies with basic fibroblast growth factor. Diabetologia 36:282-291, 1993.
64. Avena R, Mitchell ME, Neville RF, Sidawy AN: The additive effects of glucose and insulin on the proliferation of infragenicular vascular smooth muscle cells. J Vasc Surg 28:1033-1039, 1998.
65. Cohen S: Isolation and biological effects of epidermal growth-stimulating protein. Natl Cancer Inst Monogr 13-27, 1964.
66. Cohen S: The stimulation of epidermal proliferation by a specific protein (EGF). Dev Biol 12:394-407, 1965.
67. Marquardt H, Hunkapiller MW, Hoot LE, et al: Transforming growth factors produced by retrovirus transformed rodent fibroblasts and human melanoma cells: Amino acid sequence homology with epidermal growth factor. Proc Natl Acad Sci U S A 80:4684-4688, 1983.
68. SatoY, Okamura K, Morimoto A, et al: Indispensable role of tissue-type plasminogen activator in growth factor-dependent tube formation of human microvascular endothelial cells in vitro. Exp Cell Res 204:223-229, 1993.
69. Gan BS, Hollenberg MD, MacCannell KL, et al: Distinct vascular actions of epidermal growth factor-urogastrone and transforming growth factor-α. J Pharmacol Exp Ther 242:331-337, 1987.
70. DeLarco JE, Todaro GJ: Growth factors from murine sarcoma virus-transformed cells. Proc Natl Acad Sci U S A 75:4001-4005, 1978.
71. Roberts AB, Lamb LC, Newton DL, et al: Transforming growth factor: Isolation of polypeptides from viral and chemically transformed cells by acid/ethanol extraction. Proc Natl Acad Sci U S A 77:3493-3498, 1980.
72. Roberts AB, Sporn MB: The transforming growth factors-betas. In Sporn MB, Roberts AB (eds): Handbook of Experimental Pharmacology. New York, Springer-Verlag, 1990, pp 419-472.
73. Massague J, Cheifetz, Boyd FT, Andres JL: TGFβ binding proteoglycans: Recent progress in identifying their functional properties. Ann N Y Acad Sci 593:59-72, 1990.
74. Centrella M, McCarthy TL, Canalis E: Skeletal tissue and transforming growth factor-beta. FASEB J 2:3006-3073, 1988.
75. Sporn MB, Roberts AB, Wakefield LM, deCrombrugghe D: Some recent advances in the chemistry and biology of transforming growth factor-beta. J Cell Biol 105:1039-1045, 1987.
76. Forsyth EA, Aly HM, Najjar SF, et al: Transforming growth factor β I inhibits the proliferative effect of insulin on human infragenicular vascular smooth muscle cells. J Vasc Surg 25:432-436, 1997.
77. Centrella M, McCarthy TL, Canalis E: Transforming growth factor beta is a bifunctional regulator of replication and collagen synthesis in osteoblast-enriched cell cultures from fetal rat bone. J Biol Chem 262:2869-2874, 1987.
78. Baird A, Durkin T: Inhibition of endothelial cell proliferation by type beta transforming growth factor: Interactions with acidic and basic fibroblast growth factors. Biochem Biophys Res Commun 138: 476-482, 1986.
79. Miik S, Ware JA, Kent KC: Transforming growth factor-β inhibits human vascular smooth muscle cell growth and migration. Surgery 114:464-470, 1993.
80. Ferra N, Davis-Smyth T: The biology of vascular endothelial growth factor. Endocr Rev 18:4-25, 1997.
81. Senger DR, Galli SJ, Dorvak AM, et al: Tumor cells secrete a vascular permeability factor that promotes accumulation of ascites fluid. Science 219:983-985, 1983.
82. Dvorak HF, Harvey VS, Estrella P, et al: Fibrin containing gels induce angiogenesis: Implications for tumor stroma generation and wound healing. Lab Invest 57:673-686, 1987.
83. Seghezzi G, Patel S, Ren CJ, et al: Autocrine regulation of blood vessel formation by fibroblast growth factor-2 and vascular endothelial growth factor: A mechanism for tumor angiogenesis. Surg Forum 48:836-837, 1997.
84. Mack CA, Budendender KT, Polce D, et al: Salvage angiogenesis mediated by an adenovirus vector expressing vascular endothelial growth factor protects against acute arterial occlusion: Physiologic evidence of benefit. Surg Forum 48:447-449, 1997.
85. Isner JM, Pieczek A, Schainfeld R, et al: Clinical evidence of angiogenesis after arterial gene transfer of phVEGF165 in patient with ischemic limb. Lancet 348:370-374, 1996.
86. Lee LY, Patel SR, Hackett NR, et al: Focal angiogen therapy using intramyocardial delivery of an adenovirus vector coding of vascular endothelial growth factor 121. Ann Thorac Surg 69:14-23, 2000.
87. Isner JM: Myocardial gene therapy. Nature 415:234-239, 2002.
88. Levitzki A, Gazit A: Tyrosine kinase inhibition: An approach to drug development. Science 267:1782-1788, 1995.
89. Linder V, Reidy MA: Proliferation of smooth muscle cells after vascular injury is inhibited by antibody against fibroblast growth factor. Proc Natl Acad Sci U S A 88:3739-3743, 1995.
90. Gansler T, Vaghmar N, Olson JJ, Graham SD: Suramin inhibits growth factor binding and proliferation of urothelial carcinoma cell cultures. J Urol 148:910-914, 1992.
91. Asmussen I, Kjeldsen K: Intimal ultrastructure of human arteries: Observations on arteries from newborn children of smoking and non-smoking mothers. Circ Res 36:579-589, 1975.
92. Bylock A, Bondjers G, Jansson I, et al: Surface ultrastructure of human arteries with special reference to the effects of smoking. Acta Pathol Microbiol Scand 87A:201-209, 1979.
93. Boutet M, Bazin M, Turcotte H, et al: Effects of cigarette smoke on rat thoracic aorta. Artery 7:56-72, 1980.
94. Booyse FM, Osikowicz G, Quarfoot AJ: Effects of chronic oral consumption of nicotine on the rabbit aortic endothelium. Am J Pathol 102:229-238, 1981.
95. Zimmerman M, McGeachie JK: The effects of nicotine on aortic endothelial cell turnover and ultrastructure. Adv Exp Med Biol 273: 79-88, 1990.
96. Lin SJ, Hong CY, Chang MS, et al: Long-term nicotine exposure increases aortic endothelial cell death and enhances transendothelial macromolecular transport in rats. Arterioscler Thromb 12:1305-1312, 1992.
97. Giordano JM: Cigarette smoking and vascular disease. In Sidawy AN, Sumpio BE, DePalma RG (eds): The Basic Science of Vascular Disease. Armonk, NY, Futura Publishing, 1997, pp 471- 475.
98. Pittilo RM, Mackie JJ, Rowles PM, et al: Effects of cigarette smoking on the ultrastructure of rat thoracic aorta and its ability to produce prostacyclin. Thromb Haemost 48:173-176, 1982.
99. Powell JT, Higman DJ: Smoking, nitric oxide and the endothelium. Br J Surg 81:785-787, 1994.
100. Higman DJ, Greenhalgh RM, Powell JT: Smoking impairs endothelium-dependent relaxation of saphenous vein. Br J Surg 80:1242-1245, 1993.
101. Luscher TF: The endothelium and cardiovascular disease—a complex relation. N Engl J Med 330:1081-1083, 1994.
102. Takasaki I, Chobanian AV, Brecher P: Biosynthesis of fibronectin by rabbit aorta. J Biol Chem 266:17686-17694, 1991.
103. Dzau VJ, Gibbons GH, Cooke JP, et al: Vascular biology and medicine in the 1990s: Scope, concepts, potentials, and perspectives. Circulation 87:705-719, 1993.
104. Panza JA, Quyyumi AA, Brush Jr JE, et al: Abnormal endothelium-dependent vascular relaxation in patients with essential hypertension. N Engl J Med 323:22-27, 1990.
105. Vallance P, Collier J, Moncada S: Effects of endothelium-derived nitric oxide on peripheral arterial tone in man. Lancet 2:997-1000, 1989.

106. Rees D, Ben-Ishay D, Moncada S: Nitric oxide and the regulation of blood pressure in the hypertensive-prone and hypertensive-resistant Sabra rat. Hypertension 28:367-371, 1996.
107. Avena R, Curry KM, Sidawy AN, et al: The effect of occult diabetic status and oral glucose intake on brachial artery vasoactivity in patients with peripheral vascular disease. Cardiovasc Surg 6:584-589, 1998.
108. Takahashi K, Ghatei MA, Lam HC, et al: Elevated plasma endothelin in patients with diabetes mellitus. Diabetologia 33:306-310, 1990.
109. Schernthaner G, Schwarzer C, Kuzmits R, et al: Increased angiotensin converting enzyme activities in diabetes mellitus: Analysis of diabetes type, state of metabolic control and occurrence of diabetic vascular disease. J Clin Pathol 37:307-312, 1984.
110. Avena R, Mitchell ME, Neville RF, et al: The additive effects of glucose and insulin on the proliferation of infragenicular vascular smooth muscle cells. J Vasc Surg 28:1033-1039, 1998.
111. Hseuh WA, Anderson PW: Hypertension, the endothelial cell, and the vascular complications of diabetes mellitus. Hypertension 20:253-263, 1992.
112. Lorenzi M, Cagliero E, Toledo S: Glucose toxicity for human endothelial cells in culture: Delayed replication, disturbed cell cycle, and accelerated cell death. Diabetes 34:621-627, 1985.
113. Grattan MT, Moreno-Cabral CE, Starnes VA, et al: Cytomegalovirus infection is associated with cardiac allograft rejection and atherosclerosis. JAMA 261:3561-3566, 1989.
114. Epstein SE, Speir E, Zhou YF, et al: The role of infection in restenosis and atherosclerosis: Focus on cytomegalovirus. Lancet 348(Suppl): 13-17, 1996.
115. Nieto FJ, Adam E, Sorlie P, et al: Cohort study of cytomegalovirus infection as a risk factor for carotid intimal-medial thickening, a measure of subclinical atherosclerosis. Circulation 94:922-927, 1996.
116. Grayston JT, Kuo CC, Coulson AS, et al: *Chlamydia pneumoniae* (TWAR) in atherosclerosis of the coronary artery. Circulation 92:3397-3400, 1995.
117. Kuo CC, Shor A, Campbell LA, et al: Demonstration of *Chlamydia pneumoniae* in atherosclerotic lesions of coronary arteries. J Infect Dis 167:841-849, 1993.
118. Muhlestein JB, Anderson JL, Hammond EH, et al: Infection with *Chlamydia pneumoniae* accelerates the development of atherosclerosis and treatment with azithromycin prevents it in a rabbit model. Circulation 97:633-636, 1998.
119. Miller SA, Selzman CH, Shames BD, et al: *Chlamydia pneumoniae* activates nuclear kB and activator protein 1 in human vascular smooth muscle and induces cellular proliferation. J Surg Res 90:76-81, 2000.
120. Godzik KL, O'Brien ER, Wang SK, et al: In vitro susceptibility of human vascular wall cells to infection with *Chlamydia pneumoniae.* J Clin Microbiol 33:2411-2414, 1995.
121. Kaukorana-Tolvanen SS, Laitinen K, Saikko P, et al: *Chlamydia pneumoniae* multiplies in human endothelial cells in vitro. Microb Pathog 16:313-319, 1994.
122. Parchure N, Zouridakis EG, Kaski JC: Effect of azithromycin treatment on endothelial function in patients with coronary artery disease and evidence of *Chlamydia pneumoniae* infection. Circulation 105:1298-1303, 2002.
123. Wiesli P, Czerwenka W, Meniconi A, et al: Roxithromycin treatment prevents progression of peripheral arterial occlusive disease in *Chlamydia pneumoniae* seropositive men. Circulation 105:2646-2652, 2002.
124. Meier CR, Derby LE, Jick SS, et al: Antibiotics and risk of subsequent first-time acute myocardial infarction. JAMA 281:427-431, 1999.

Chapter 9

Vascular Physiology: Essential Hemodynamic Principles

DAVID S. SUMNER, MD
R. EUGENE ZIERLER, MD

■ ARTERIAL HEMODYNAMICS

Obstruction, or narrowing of the arterial lumen—whether it is the result of atherosclerosis, fibromuscular dysplasia, thrombi, emboli, dissection, trauma, or external compression—interferes with the efficient transport of blood to the peripheral capillary bed. Within the obstructed vessel, the extent of this interference is related to the degree of narrowing and is determined by strict hemodynamic principles. The actual capillary flow deficit depends not only on the severity of the local obstructive lesion but also on its location and on the ability of the body to compensate by (1) increasing cardiac work, (2) developing collateral channels, and (3) dilating the peripheral arterioles and precapillary sphincters.

The symptoms and signs of obstructive arterial disease reflect the restriction of blood flow to the capillary bed. With mild obstruction, this restriction is evident only when metabolic demands are increased by exercise, trauma, or infection; with more severe disease, however, capillary perfusion is compromised even during the basal state. Consequently, the disease may be relatively asymptomatic, symptomatic only during exercise, or responsible for continued rest pain and eventual tissue loss.

Except for clot formation and occasional dissection, aneurysms seldom produce symptoms of obstruction. The tendency to rupture is determined by both the intraluminal pressure and the diameter of the aneurysm.

The first part of this chapter deals with the hemodynamic alterations produced by arterial obstruction, the effects of shear, the rationale for surgical intervention, the elastic properties of the arterial wall, and the stresses that lead to rupture of aneurysms.

Basic Hemodynamics

The flow of blood in the arterial circulation is governed by the fundamental laws of fluid dynamics. Knowledge of these principles permits a better understanding of the physiologic abnormalities associated with arterial obstruction.*

Fluid Energy

Pressure is often regarded as the force responsible for the motion of blood. Although pressure is the most obvious and most important of the forces involved, other forms of energy also play a role. With more precision, we can state that blood moves from one point to another in the vascular system in response to differences in *total fluid energy.*[19]

Total fluid energy (E) consists of potential energy and kinetic energy. The potential energy component can be broken down into intravascular pressure (P) and gravitational potential energy. P represents the pressure produced by contraction of the heart, the hydrostatic pressure, and the static filling pressure of the resting circulation.[58] Hydrostatic pressure is proportional to the weight of the blood and is given by:

$$P\ (\text{hydrostatic}) = -\rho g h \qquad (9.1)$$

where ρ is the density of blood (about 1.056 gm · cm^{-3}), *g* is the acceleration due to gravity (980 cm · sec^{-2}), and h is the distance in centimeters above a given reference point. In the human body, this reference point is roughly at the level of the right atrium.[18] Obviously, hydrostatic pressure may be quite large in comparison with the dynamic pressure and cannot be neglected. For example, at ankle level in a standing man 5 feet 8 inches tall, this pressure is about 89 mm Hg:

$$-(1.056\ \text{gm} \cdot \text{cm}^{-3})\ (980\ \text{cm} \cdot \text{sec}^{-2})\ (-114\ \text{cm}) = 117{,}976\ \text{dynes} \cdot \text{cm}^{-2} \qquad (9.2)$$

$$117{,}976\ \text{dynes} \cdot \text{cm}^{-2} \div 1333\ \text{dynes} \cdot \text{cm}^{-2}/\text{mm Hg} = 88.5\ \text{mm Hg} \qquad (9.3)$$

In contrast, the static filling pressure is quite low, usually about 7 mm Hg.[63] This pressure is related to the interaction between the elasticity of the vascular walls and the volume of blood contained within.

Gravitational potential energy (+ρgh) is calculated the same way as the hydrostatic pressure but has an opposite sign. It represents the ability of a volume of blood to do work because of its elevation above a given reference point. In many, but not all, circumstances, gravitational potential energy and hydrostatic pressure cancel each other out.

Finally, *kinetic energy* represents the ability of blood to do work because of its motion ($\frac{1}{2}\rho v^2$ [see Eq. 9.4]).

If we put these values together, an expression for total fluid energy per unit volume of blood can be obtained:

$$E = P + \rho g h + \tfrac{1}{2}\rho v^2 \qquad (9.4)$$

where E is in ergs per cubic centimeter and v refers to the velocity (cm · sec^{-1}) of a particle of blood moving steadily in a straight line.

Bernoulli's Principle

When fluid flows steadily (without acceleration or deceleration) from one point in a system to another farther downstream, its total energy content along any given streamline remains constant, provided there are no frictional losses:

$$P_1 + \rho g h_1 + \tfrac{1}{2}\rho v_i^2 = P_2 + \rho g h_2 + \rho v_2^2 \qquad (9.5)$$

This, the one-dimensional *Bernoulli equation,* is derivable from Newton's laws of motion and is a fundamental formula in fluid mechanics.[35]

Bernoulli's equation is instructive, in that it establishes a relationship among kinetic energy, gravitational potential energy, and pressure in a *frictionless* fluid system. Several apparent paradoxes of fluid flow are readily explained by this equation. For example, in Figure 9-1A, fluid with the density of blood enters an inclined tube at a pressure of 100 mm Hg and flows out at a pressure of 178 mm Hg. Thus, fluid moves against the pressure gradient from a point of low pressure to a point where its pressure is high. The total fluid energy remains the same, however, because the gravitational potential energy decreases by an amount exactly equal to the increase in pressure. This situation is analogous to that existing in the arterial tree of a standing person, in whom blood pressure in the arteries at ankle level is greater than blood pressure in the aortic arch.

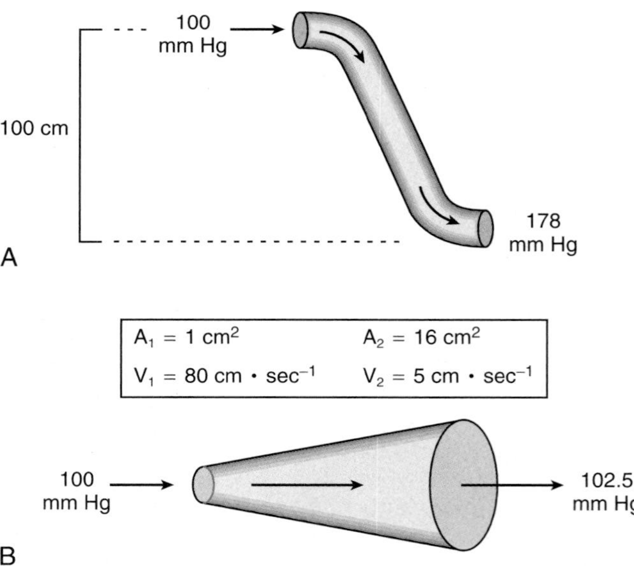

FIGURE 9-1 A, Effect of vertical height on pressure in a frictionless fluid flowing downhill. **B,** Effect of increasing cross-sectional area on pressure in a frictionless fluid system.

*It is interesting that three of the early investigators in the fields of fluid dynamics and elasticity, whose names have been applied to classic laws of hemodynamics, were physicians. They are Daniel Bernoulli (1700-1782) of Switzerland, Thomas Young (1773-1829) of England, and Jean-Leonard-Marie Poiseuille (1799-1869) of France.[69]

In Figure 9-1B, the cross-sectional area of a horizontal tube increases 16 times, resulting in a comparable decrease in fluid velocity. Again, the fluid moves against a pressure gradient, the pressure at the end of the tube being 2.5 mm Hg greater than that at the entrance to the tube. The total fluid energy remains the same, however, because of the decrease in kinetic energy. This phenomenon is seldom manifested in the human circulation because associated energy losses effectively mask the slight rise in pressure.

Intravascular pressure measurements made with catheters are subject to errors owing to the effect of kinetic energy. If the catheter faces the oncoming blood end-on, the pressure recorded will be too high by a factor of $\frac{1}{2}\rho v^2$. On the other hand, if the catheter faces downstream, the recorded pressure will be too low by the same factor. At a velocity of 50 cm $\cdot$ sec^{-1}, these errors would equal about 1.0 mm Hg and would be inconsequential in a high-pressure system such as the aorta. Nevertheless, they could be of importance in low-pressure, high-flow systems such as the vena cava and pulmonary artery.[19,142]

Viscosity and Poiseuille's Law

The conditions required to fulfill the rigid specifications of Bernoulli's relationship are never met in the human vascular tree or in any other real fluid system. Mechanical energy is always "lost" (converted to heat) in the movement of fluid from one point to the next.

Energy losses in the peripheral circulation are related principally to the viscosity of blood and to its inertia. In fluids, *viscosity* may be defined as the friction existing between contiguous layers of fluid. The friction is due to strong intermolecular attractions; under these conditions, the fluid layers tend to resist deformation. The familiar equation known as *Poiseuille's law* describes the viscous losses existing in an idealized situation:

$$P_1 - P_2 = \overline{V} \cdot \frac{8L\eta}{r^2} = Q \cdot \frac{8L\eta}{\pi r^4} \qquad (9.6)$$

where $P_1 - P_2$ represents the drop in potential energy (dynes $\cdot$ cm^{-2}) between two points separated by the distance L (cm); Q is the flow (cm^3 $\cdot$ sec^{-1}); and $\overline{V}$ is the mean flow velocity (cm $\cdot$ sec^{-1}) across a tube with an inside radius r (cm). The coefficient of viscosity, η, is expressed in poise (dynes $\cdot$ sec $\cdot$ cm^{-2}).

Under conditions in which Poiseuille's law is operative, the velocities of each concentric layer of fluid describe a *parabolic profile,* with velocity being highest in the center of the stream and becoming progressively lower toward the inner wall. Blood in contact with the wall is stationary. The ratio of the change in velocity (Δv) to the change in the radius (Δr) between each cylindrical laminar layer is known as the *shear rate* (D); the force required to "shear" the fluid is known as the *shear stress* (τ); and the coefficient of viscosity (η) is the ratio of the shear stress to the shear rate:

$$D = -\frac{\Delta v}{\Delta r} \text{ and } \eta = \frac{\tau}{D} \qquad (9.7)$$

The importance of shear rate and shear stress is discussed later in this chapter.

Because energy losses are inversely proportional to the fourth power of the radius, graphs based on Poiseuille's law are sharply curved (Fig. 9-2). As the diameter of a conduit is reduced, there is little effect on the pressure gradient until a certain degree of narrowing is reached; beyond this point, further reductions in diameter cause the pressure gradient to rise precipitously. Although raising the rate of flow shifts the curves to the left and linearly increases the pressure gradient at any given radius, these effects are much less marked than those due to changes in radius.

Poiseuille's law applies only to steady (nonpulsatile), laminar flow in a straight cylindrical tube with rigid walls. Furthermore, the tube must be long enough to allow a parabolic flow profile to develop.

When fluid passes from a large container into a smaller cylindrical tube, the velocity profile at the entrance is essentially flat (same velocity all across the tube diameter). Just beyond the entrance, friction between the stationary outermost layer and the immediately adjacent concentric layer causes the latter to slow down. This layer, in turn, exerts a drag force on the next layer and so on down the tube until the "boundary layer," where fluid is sheared, extends to the center of the tube. At this point, flow is said to be fully "developed," and the profile is truly parabolic. The "entrance length" (L_x) in centimeters required to develop a parabolic profile depends on the radius of the tube and the *Reynolds number* (Re), which is described later in this chapter:

$$L_x = k\, r\, Re \qquad (9.8)$$

(The constant, k, varies but approximates 0.16 for Reynolds numbers greater than 50.)

All along the entrance length, the velocity profile is "blunt" rather than parabolic. At each branch point in the arterial tree, a certain distance is needed before flow is

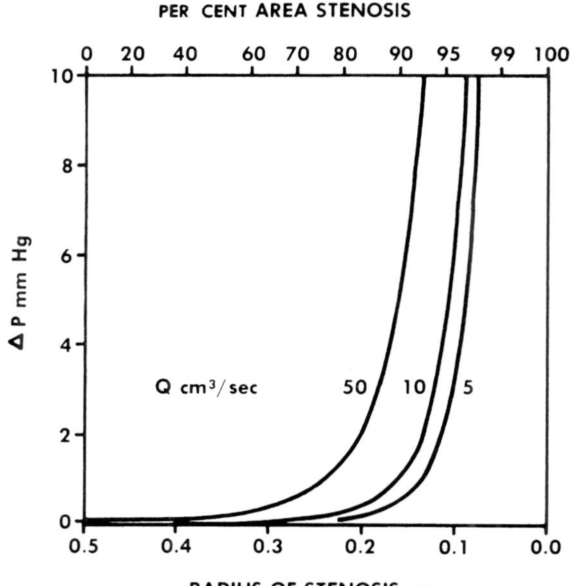

FIGURE 9-2 Curves derived from Poiseuille's law (see Eq. 9.6). The stenotic segment is assumed to be 1.0 cm long. Viscosity is 0.035 poise. ΔP, pressure gradient.

developed. Although velocity profiles in smaller arteries (e.g., radial, mesenteric) may be essentially parabolic, in larger arteries (e.g., iliac, common carotid), the entrance length approaches the length of the artery, and flow profiles remain blunt. Many investigators have shown that the flow profile in the human abdominal aorta is blunted.[134,183]

Entrance effects are, of course, only one of many factors modulating the velocity profile. At branch points or in regions where the vessel curves, the momentum of blood near one wall exceeds that on the other side. As a result, velocity profiles are skewed toward one wall, and complicated helical flow patterns develop.[107,153] Thus, the strict conditions required by Poiseuille's law are seldom, if ever, encountered in the living organism. Furthermore, energy losses are almost never totally viscous, and in many cases, viscous losses are less significant than energy losses related to inertia.

Inertia

Inertial losses depend on the mass or density of the blood, ρ, and on the square of the flow velocity, v:

$$\Delta P = k \tfrac{1}{2} \rho v^2 \qquad (9.9)$$

Because ρ is a constant, the quantity that changes is v. Changes in velocity occur when blood is accelerated or decelerated as in pulsatile flow and when blood passes from a vessel of large lumen (where the velocity is low) to one of small lumen (where the velocity is high), or vice versa. In addition, v is a vector quantity; that is, any change in direction of flow also represents an acceleration.

Flow changes direction whenever the blood vessel forms a curve and at all junctions and branch points. There is also a change in direction when the blood vessel gradually narrows or in pathologic situations in which there is a sudden narrowing and expansion of the flow stream, as in an atherosclerotic stenosis. Moreover, as a result of the expansile nature of the blood vessel wall, velocity vectors must be directed outward during the systolic portion of the pressure wave and inward during the diastolic portion.*

According to the *equation of continuity* (conservation of mass), the product of flow velocity and cross-sectional area (A) is the same at any point along a tube, provided that there are no intervening branches to siphon off the fluid:

$$A_1 v_1 = A_2 v_2 \quad \textit{or} \quad r_1^2 v_1 = r_2^2 v_2 \qquad (9.10)$$

Because kinetic energy losses depend on the square of the velocity (Eq. 9.9) and because the velocity in a stenotic segment is inversely proportional to the square of its radius (Eq. 9.10), kinetic energy losses—like those attributable to viscosity—are inversely proportional to the fourth power of the radius. As illustrated in Figure 9-3, the curves created display little sensitivity to reduction in radius until a certain point is reached, beyond which energy losses increase rapidly. Increasing the velocity of flow has a more marked effect on kinetic energy losses than it does on viscous losses (compare Figs. 9-2 and 9-3). This conclusion follows from the fact that the velocity term is squared in Equation 9.9 but enters Equation 9.6 only in the first power.

Turbulence

Turbulence, with its random velocity vectors, also depletes the total fluid energy stores. The point at which flow changes from laminar to turbulent is best defined in terms of a dimensionless quantity known as the Reynolds number (Re). Re is proportional to the ratio of inertial forces acting on the fluid to the viscous forces:

$$Re = \frac{\rho v d}{\eta} = \frac{vd}{\nu} \qquad (9.11)$$

where d is the diameter of the conduit, η is the viscosity, and ν is the kinematic viscosity (ν = η/ρ). When the Reynolds number exceeds 2000, local disturbances in the laminar flow pattern result in fully developed turbulence. With Re less than 2000, local disturbances are damped out by the viscous forces.

Because Reynolds numbers are well below 2000 in most peripheral blood vessels, turbulence is unlikely to occur under normal circumstances.[173] However, turbulence does appear to develop in the ascending aorta during the peak systolic ejection phase and may persist during deceleration.[151] These turbulent flashes are short-lived. Yet, in spite of the absence of fully developed turbulence, the pattern of blood flow in a large portion of the circulation may be characterized as "disturbed."[5,202] Energy losses calculated with the use of turbulent friction factors may more closely

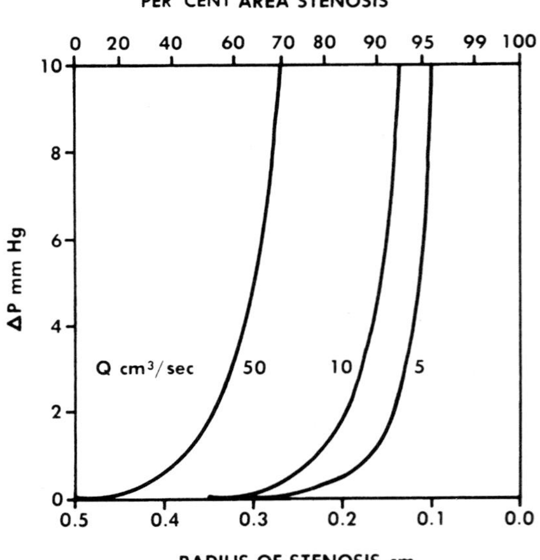

FIGURE 9-3 Effect of increasing stenosis and blood flow on inertial losses at the exit of a stenotic segment that leads into a tube with a radius of 0.5 cm. Curves are based on Equation 9.16. An abrupt exit is assumed. ΔP, pressure gradient.

*Because only flow in the direction of the long axis of the tube is considered in Poiseuille's law, frictional (viscous) energy losses due to molecular interaction involving flow in other directions are neglected in Equation 9.6. Although these losses are difficult to calculate, they are incorporated in a general way in the constant k of Equation 9.9. Thus, *inertial energy loss* is a term of convenience; *all of these losses are ultimately due to viscous effects.*

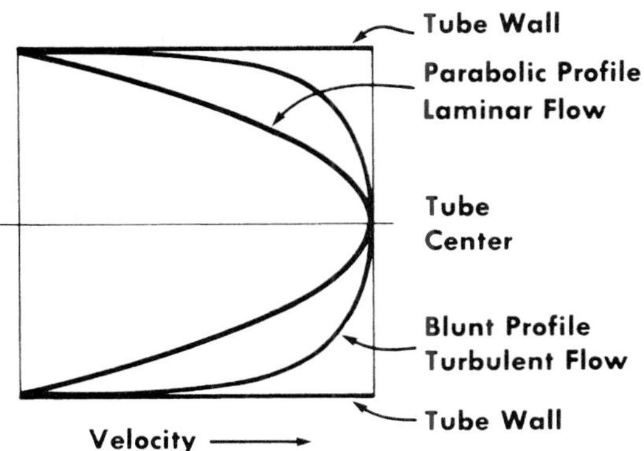

FIGURE 9-4 Velocity profiles of steady laminar flow and turbulent flow. Velocity is zero at the tube wall and reaches its peak value in the center. A blunt profile is also typical of flow within the entrance length of a vessel.

approximate experimental results than losses calculated with Poiseuille's law.[174]

Pulsatile Flow

Applying any of these equations to pulsatile blood flow is very difficult. For example, in *steady flow*, kinetic energy can be estimated from the square of the space-averaged velocity of blood flowing past a given point (see Eq. 9.9). In *pulsatile flow*, a more complicated expression must be employed that integrates the instantaneous product of the mass flux and the square of the velocity. This method predicts kinetic energies that sometimes are 10 times as great as would be suspected on the basis of the average velocity of blood flow.[15,131]

In addition, the shape of the velocity profile must be known before the *spatially averaged velocity* across the lumen of a blood vessel can be used to estimate kinetic energy losses (Fig. 9-4). When the profile is nearly flat, as it is with turbulent flow or when the site of flow measurement is within the entrance length of a blood vessel, k in Equation 9.9 will be 1.06.[35] When the profile is parabolic, k becomes 2.0. With pulsatile flow, a parabolic profile is never really attained (Fig. 9-5).[112] As mentioned previously, in larger blood vessels, such as the aorta, the profile may be quite flat and is often skewed. In smaller arteries, a parabolic profile may be approached, especially during the peak forward phase of the flow pulse.

All of these complexities merely add to the energy losses experienced in the circulation. Thus, for a given level of blood flow, the pressure (energy) drop between any two points in the arterial tree may be several times that predicted by Poiseuille's law (see Eq. 9.6).[6,99,116] Furthermore, the relationship between the pressure gradient and the flow is not linear but defines a curve that is concave to the pressure axis (Fig. 9-6). These nonlinearities are all functions of inertial losses and reflect the effect of the v^2 term. Thus, Poiseuille's law cannot be used to predict pressure-flow relationships in the arterial tree, but it can be used to define the *minimal* energy losses that can be expected under any given flow situation.

Resistance

The concept of hemodynamic resistance is essential for understanding the physiology of arterial occlusive disease. When *hemodynamic resistance* is defined simply as the ratio of the energy drop between two points along a blood vessel ($E_1 - E_2$) to the mean blood flow in the vessel (Q), the

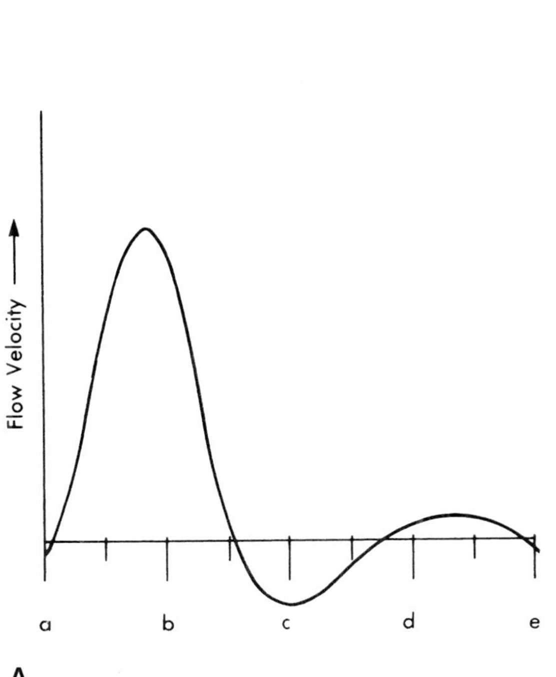

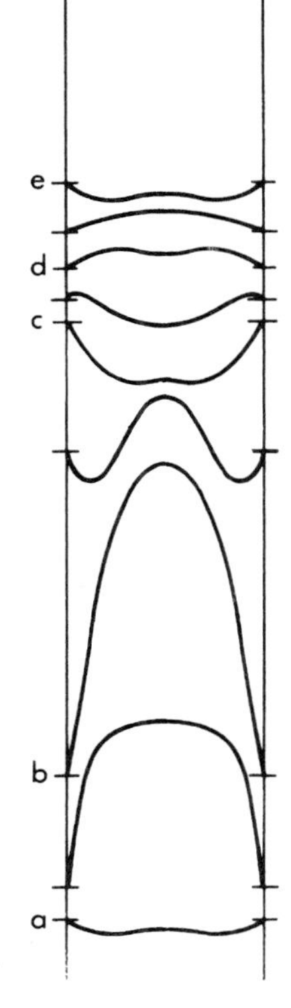

FIGURE 9-5 Velocity profiles (**B**) during various phases of a typical femoral arterial flow pulse (**A**). *Letters* indicate corresponding points in the pulse cycle. In all profiles, the velocity at the wall is zero. At point b, forward flow is nearly maximal and the profile is almost parabolic. At the next point, flow near the wall is reversed but that in the center continues forward. Several profiles, both forward and reverse, are quite blunt. (**A** and **B** adapted from McDonald DA: Blood Flow in Arteries, 2nd ed. Baltimore, Williams & Wilkins, 1974.)

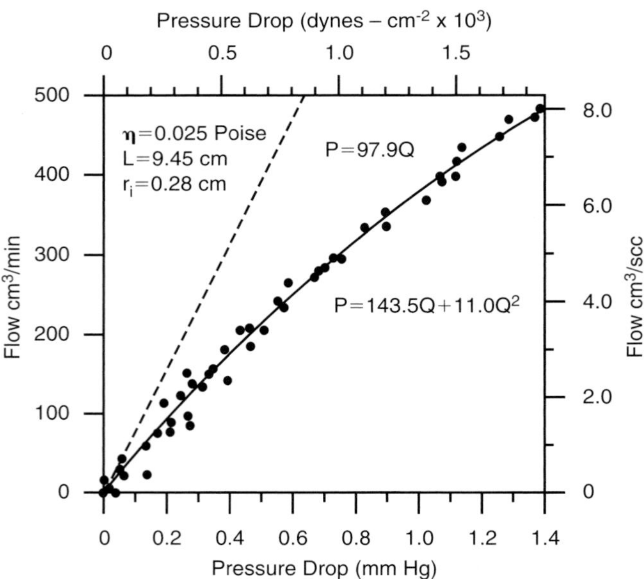

FIGURE 9-6 Pressure drop across a 9.45-cm length of canine femoral artery at varying flow rates. Differential pressure was measured with a specially designed transducer (D. E. Hokanson), and flow, with an electromagnetic flowmeter. Flow rate was varied by constriction of a distally located arteriovenous fistula. The line that fits the experimental data best (*solid line*) has both a linear and a squared term, corresponding to Poiseuille's law plus kinetic energy losses. The pressure-flow curve predicted from Poiseuille's law (*dashed line*) depicts much less energy loss than actually is the case.

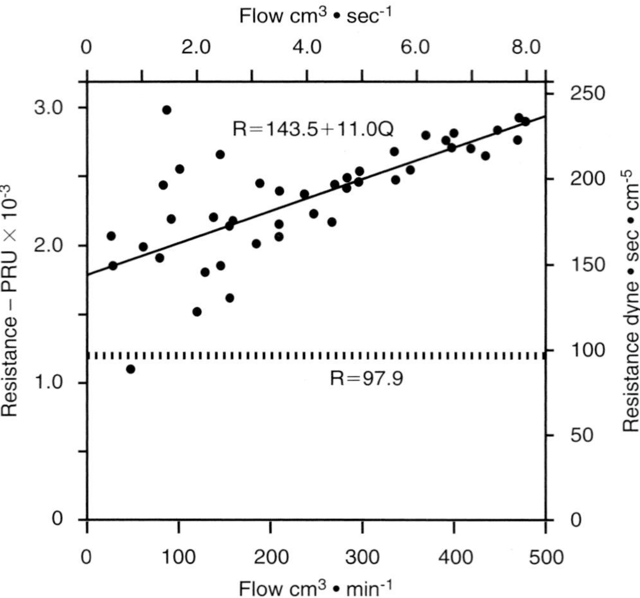

FIGURE 9-7 Resistance derived from pressure-flow curve in Figure 9-6. The constant resistance predicted by Poiseuille's law is depicted by the *dotted line*. Note that the resistance (R) rises with increasing flow. PRU, peripheral resistance unit.

equation for hemodynamic resistance (R) is analogous to Ohm's law in electric circuits:

$$R = \frac{E_1 - E_2}{Q} = \frac{P_1 - P_2}{Q} \qquad (9.12)$$

It is often convenient to drop the kinetic energy term ($\frac{1}{2}\rho v^2$) in Equation 9.4, because it seldom contributes appreciably to the total energy. Also, calculations are simplified if the assumption can be made that the subject is supine. This permits the gravitational terms (ρgh) to cancel. Hence, resistance can be approximated by the ratio of the pressure drop ($P_1 - P_2$) to the flow (Eq. 9.12).

Unlike electric resistance, hemodynamic resistance does not remain constant over a wide range of flows. The minimal possible resistance is given by Poiseuille's law:

$$R_{min} = \frac{8\eta L}{\pi r^4} \qquad (9.13)$$

Because of additional energy losses related to acceleration, disturbed flow, and turbulence (all of which are a function of $\frac{1}{2}\rho v^2$), the resistance of a given vascular segment tends to increase as flow velocity increases, provided that there is no concomitant change in vascular diameter (Fig. 9-7).

For the purposes of studying arterial and venous flow dynamics in complex hemodynamic circuitry, resistances in series can be added to obtain the total value:

$$R_{total} = R_1 + R_2 + \cdots + R_n \qquad (9.14)$$

When resistances are in parallel, the following relationship may be used:

$$\frac{1}{R_{total}} = \frac{1}{R_1} + \frac{1}{R_2} + \cdots + \frac{1}{R_n} \qquad (9.15)$$

The dimensions of hemodynamic resistance are dyne · cm^{-5} · sec. It usually is more convenient, however, to use the *peripheral resistance unit* (PRU), which is millimeters of mercury per milliliter per minute. Thus, 1 PRU is approximately equal to 8×10^4 dyne · cm^{-5} · sec.

Hemodynamics of Arterial Stenosis

Most of the abnormal energy losses in the arterial system result from stenosis or obstruction of the vascular lumen. Because atherosclerosis, the pathologic process in the majority of these lesions, has a predilection for larger arteries, surgical or catheter-based intervention is often possible. Therefore, the study of the hemodynamics of these lesions has a great deal of practical importance.

Energy Losses Associated with Stenoses

In accordance with Poiseuille's law (see Eqs. 9.6 and 9.13), so-called viscous energy losses within the stenotic segment are inversely proportional to the fourth power of its radius and directly proportional to its length (see Fig. 9-2). Thus, the radius of a stenosis is of much more significance than its length.[22,52,83,110] In addition, *inertial losses*, which are related to the square of the velocity of blood flow, are encountered both at the entrance to the stenosis and at its exit.[15,110,173,204] The magnitude of these losses varies greatly with the shapes of the entrance and exit, being much less for a gradual

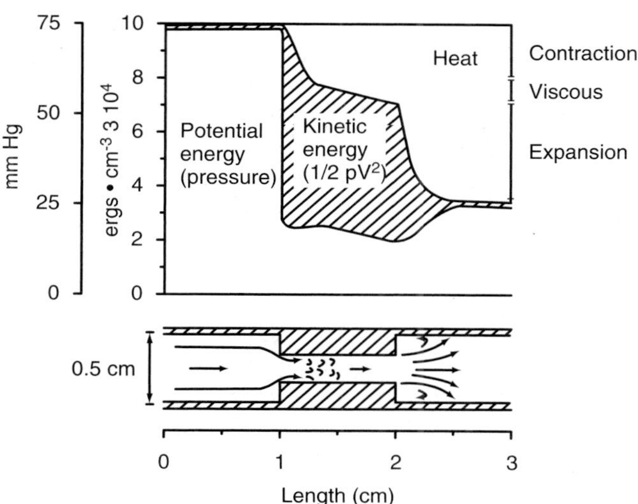

FIGURE 9-8 Diagram illustrating energy losses experienced by blood passing through a stenosis 1 cm long. Flow is assumed to be unidirectional and steady. Very little of the total energy loss is attributable to "viscous" losses. Thus, applications of Poiseuille's law greatly underestimate the pressure drop across an arterial stenosis.

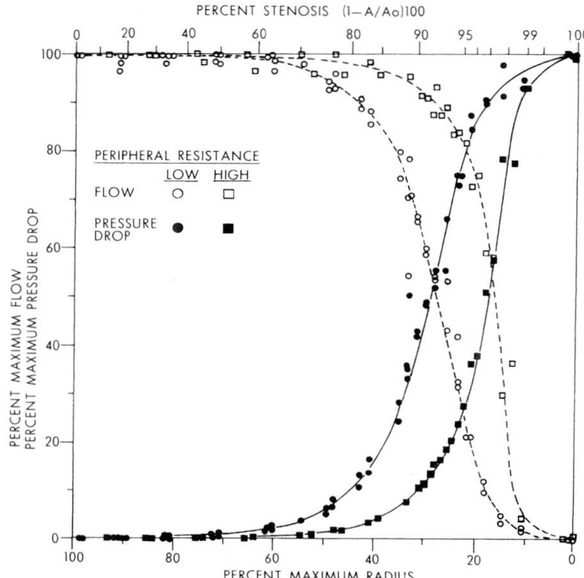

FIGURE 9-9 Relationship of pressure and flow to degree of stenosis in a canine femoral artery. When peripheral resistance is high, the curves are shifted to the right. Percentage change in flow through the stenosis is essentially a mirror image of the percentage of maximal pressure drop across the stenosis.

tapering of the lumen than for an abrupt change. Also, energy losses associated with asymmetric stenoses exceed those associated with axisymmetric stenoses, even when the lumen is compromised to the same extent.[203] Although energy losses at the entrance can be appreciable, they are usually greater at the exit, where much of the excess kinetic energy resulting from the greater fluid velocity within the stenosis may be dissipated in a turbulent jet (see Fig. 9-3):

$$\Delta P = k\frac{\rho}{2}(v_s - v)^2 = k\frac{\rho}{2}v^2\left[\left(\frac{r}{r_s}\right)^2 - 1\right]^2 \quad (9.16)$$

In this expression, ΔP represents the energy lost in expansion, v_s refers to the mean flow velocity within the stenotic segment, and v refers to the velocity in the vessel beyond the stenosis. Similarly, r_s and r indicate the radius of the stenotic lumen and that of the uninvolved distal vessel, respectively. The constant, k, varies from about 1.0 for an abrupt orifice to less than 0.2 for one that expands gradually at a 6-degree angle.[37]

These concepts are illustrated graphically in Figure 9-8. This figure emphasizes the relatively small contribution of *viscous losses* to the total decrease in available fluid energy produced by the stenosis. Even if the obstruction were diaphragm-like (L in Eq. 9.6 approaching zero), the energy losses would still be 85% of those with the 1-cm-long stenosis; in other words, most of the energy losses can be attributed to inertial effects.

Critical Stenosis

How severe does a stenosis have to be to produce a measurable pressure gradient or a decrease in blood flow or both? This is an important question for the clinician who attempts to assess the severity of an arterial obstruction from its angiographic appearance. Experimentally, appreciable changes in pressure and flow do not occur until the cross-sectional area of a vessel has been reduced by more than 75% (usually 80% to 95%).[111,118] Assuming that the obstructing lesion is symmetric, this reduction in cross-sectional area corresponds to at least a 50% reduction in diameter. The degree of narrowing at which pressure and flow begin to be affected has been called the *critical stenosis.*

Energy losses associated with arterial lesions are inversely proportional to the fourth power of the radius of the stenosis (see Eq. 9.6) and to the fourth power of the ratio of the radius of the stenosis to that of the nonstenotic segment (see Eq. 9.16). Because these are exponential functions, graphs relating energy losses across a stenosis to the percentage reduction in cross-sectional area are sharply curved, providing theoretical support for the concept of critical stenosis (Fig. 9-9).[15,22,110,119,204]

Energy losses across stenotic segments also depend on the velocity of blood flow (see Eqs. 9.6 and 9.16). In high-flow (low-resistance) systems, significant drops in pressure and flow occur with less severe narrowing than in low-flow systems.[111,118,181,182] Moreover, the curves are less sharply bent when peripheral resistance is low and flow rates are high (see Fig. 9-9). Consequently, critical stenosis varies with the resistance of the runoff bed. When peripheral resistances are low, as in the carotid, renal, and coronary systems, critical stenosis may be reached with less narrowing of the lumen than in higher-resistance systems, such as the resting lower extremity. Even in the leg, lowering the peripheral resistance sufficiently by exercise or reactive hyperemia may cause a stenosis that is noncritical at rest to become critical.[24,167,169] This fact is well worth emphasizing. It accounts for the common clinical observation that an iliac lesion may severely restrict the patient during exercise even though it causes no symptoms at rest and may not appear particularly significant on arteriography.[117,190]

Precise attempts to relate pressure and flow restriction to percentage stenosis are frustrated by the irregular geometry of the vascular lesions and by the nonlinearities introduced by pulsatile blood flow. Empirical formulas have been devised that fit the experimental data[22]; however, formulas that incorporate known viscous and inertial effects are far more instructive.[15,110,204] Nevertheless, for practical purposes, *none* of the formulas is very helpful. Thus, any lesion that potentially decreases the arterial lumen by about 75% cross-sectional area or 50% diameter must be suspect, and its hemodynamic significance must be determined by objective physiologic tests.

Length of Stenosis and Stenoses in Series

Not infrequently, the surgeon is faced with a series of lesions involving a single unbranched arterial segment. The question arises whether repair of one of the lesions will benefit the patient significantly. This question is particularly pertinent when one of the lesions is in an inaccessible location. Such a problem is presented by a stenosis at the origin of the internal carotid artery combined with a similar stenosis in the carotid siphon.

The length of a stenosis principally affects energy losses related to viscosity. Because length enters Poiseuille's equation (see Eq. 9.6) only in the first power, whereas radius is elevated to the fourth power, the effect of a change in length on viscous losses is far less than that of a change in radius. Doubling the length of a stenosis would merely double the viscous energy losses, but reducing the radius of the vessel lumen by half would increase the losses by a factor of 16. Moreover, the convective acceleration effects at the exit are independent of the length of the stenosis and are related to the fourth power of the ratio of the diameters of the nonstenosed and stenosed portions of the vessel (see Eq. 9.16). Therefore, one would predict that the length of a stenosis is far less important than the lesion's diameter. These predictions are well supported by experimental observations.[17,22,52,110,184]

Because entrance and exit effects contribute a large portion of the resistance offered by a stenosis, doubling the length of a lesion without changing its diameter would not double its resistance (see Fig. 9-8). In contrast, the total resistance of two separate lesions of equal length and diameter is approximately double that of the individual lesion, because entrance and exit effects occur at each of the stenoses.[53,80] Thus, separate stenoses of equal diameter are of more significance than a single stenosis of the same diameter whose length equals the sum of the lengths of the two shorter lesions.

When two stenoses of unequal diameter are in series, the tighter of the two has by far the greater effect on resistance (see Eqs. 9.6 and 9.16). Total resistance is not affected by the sequence of the stenoses; that is, it makes no difference whether the greater occlusion is proximal or distal.[184] Several practical points emerge from these considerations, as follows:

1. The resistances of stenoses in series are roughly additive, although the cumulative effect may be somewhat less than would be anticipated on the basis of the sum of the individual resistances. Therefore, multiple noncritical stenoses may act as a single critical stenosis and may result in arterial insufficiency.[53,80]
2. When two stenotic lesions are of similar caliber, removal of one provides only a modest improvement in blood flow.
3. If the stenoses are of unequal caliber, removal of the less severe lesions results in little increase in blood flow; removal of the more severe stenosis may provide significant improvement.

These principles apply only to unbranched arteries; they do not apply to the situation in which the proximal lesion is in an artery feeding a collateral bed that parallels the distal lesion. Thus, endarterectomy of a stenotic iliac artery is usually beneficial even when the superficial femoral artery is completely occluded. In this case, the profunda femoris artery carries most of the blood to the lower leg, and removal of the proximal iliac obstruction will improve the pressure head at the orifice of the profunda femoris.[45,109,120,168,190]

Circulatory Patterns in Human Limbs

Collateral Circulation and the Peripheral Runoff Bed

Arterial stenoses do not exist in isolation; rather, they are part of a complex hemodynamic circuit.[173,177] As shown in Figure 9-10, this circuit includes the diseased major artery, a parallel system of collateral arteries, and a peripheral runoff bed.

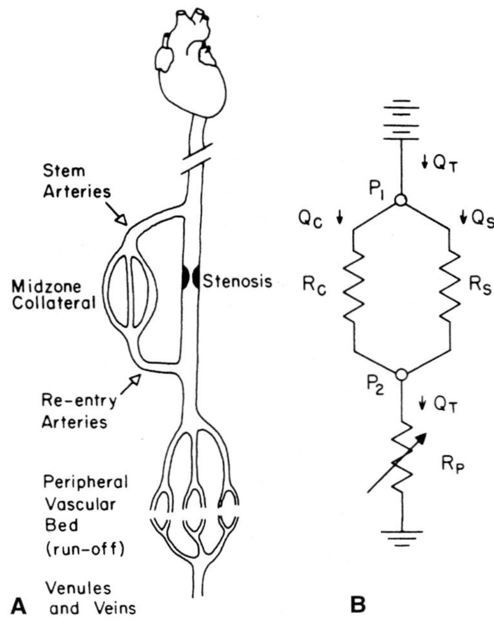

FIGURE 9-10 **A,** The main components of an arterial circuit containing a stenotic major artery. **B,** An electric analogue of this circuit. The battery at the top represents the potential energy source (e.g., the heart); ground potential, at the bottom, indicates the central veins. Q_T is total flow, Q_C is collateral flow, and Q_S is flow through the stenotic artery. Resistances are R_C, collateral; R_S, stenotic artery; and R_P, peripheral "runoff" bed. R_C and R_S are relatively "fixed"; R_P is "variable."

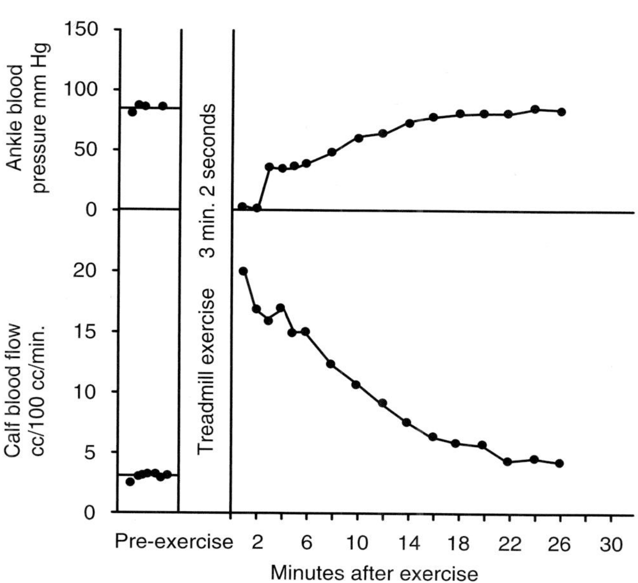

FIGURE 9-15 Ankle blood pressure and calf blood flow before and after exercise in a patient with stenosis of the superficial femoral artery. (From Sumner DS, Strandness DE Jr: The relationship between calf blood flow and ankle blood pressure in patients with intermittent claudication. Surgery 65:763, 1969.)

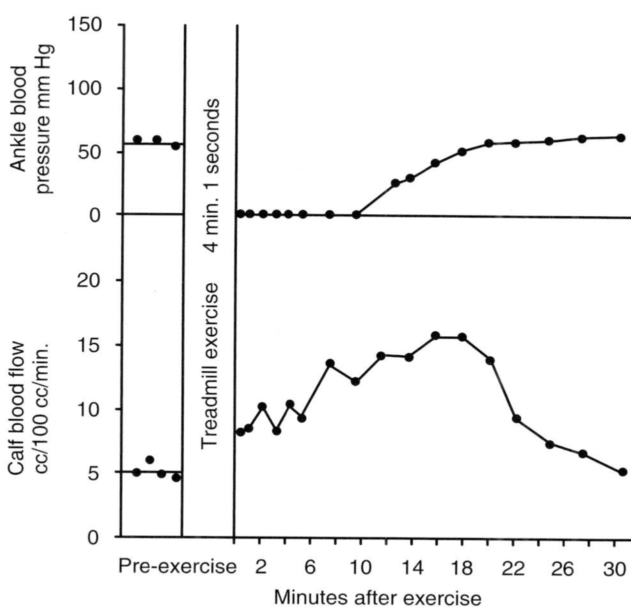

FIGURE 9-16 Ankle blood pressure and calf blood flow before and after exercise in a patient with stenosis of the iliac artery and occlusion of the superficial femoral artery. (From Sumner DS, Strandness DE Jr: The relationship between calf blood flow and ankle blood pressure in patients with intermittent claudication. Surgery 65:763, 1969.)

is normal or nearly normal (see Fig. 9-12).[54,64,97,135,166,176] With further progression of the disease, however, limb blood flow becomes inadequate even when the patient is at rest (see Fig. 9-11).[90] Ischemic rest pain is experienced in the toes and distal portions of the foot, minor trauma may produce painful nonhealing ulcers, and the toes may become gangrenous.[31]

Effect of Reactive Hyperemia and Exercise on Blood Flow

Reactive hyperemia develops in limbs when the circulation is restored after a 5-minute period of ischemia. This response differs significantly in limbs with obstructive arterial disease from that in normal limbs. Peak blood flow not only is lower in obstructed limbs (averaging about 9 to 20 mL/dL/min) but also may be delayed for from 15 seconds to 2 minutes, and the hyperemia is prolonged for several minutes.[64,163,166]

Although blood flow is increased during exercise in limbs with obstructive arterial disease, the increase is far less than that observed in normal limbs undergoing a similar stress (see Fig. 9-12).[55,92,135,194] Flow may even fall below resting levels.[3,92,156,176] After cessation of exercise, the hyperemia is greatly prolonged, subsiding to normal levels in a logarithmic fashion over 4 to 30 minutes (Fig. 9-15). In some limbs with occlusions at two levels (e.g., iliac plus superficial femoral), the peripheral blood flow immediately after exercise may be increased only slightly. Flow then rises for several minutes until a peak level is obtained, before falling gradually to pre-exercise levels (Fig. 9-16). In patients with multilevel occlusions, especially those with rest pain, the flow after exercise may be depressed, peak flow is quite low and very delayed, and the hyperemic state persists for many minutes (Fig. 9-17).[3]

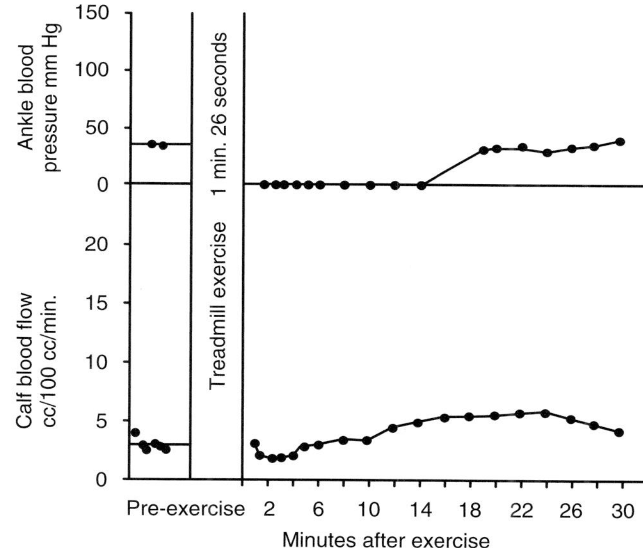

FIGURE 9-17 Ankle blood pressure and calf blood flow before and after exercise in a patient with occlusion of the iliac, common femoral, and superficial femoral arteries. This patient had severe claudication and moderate rest pain. (From Sumner DS, Strandness DE Jr: The relationship between calf blood flow and ankle blood pressure in patients with intermittent claudication. Surgery 65:763, 1969.)

Blood Pressure at Rest and After Exercise Under resting conditions, blood pressure distal to an obstructive arterial lesion is decreased if the lesion is hemodynamically significant at the prevailing level of flow.[103,108,123] Ordinarily, most lesions of surgical significance fall into this category

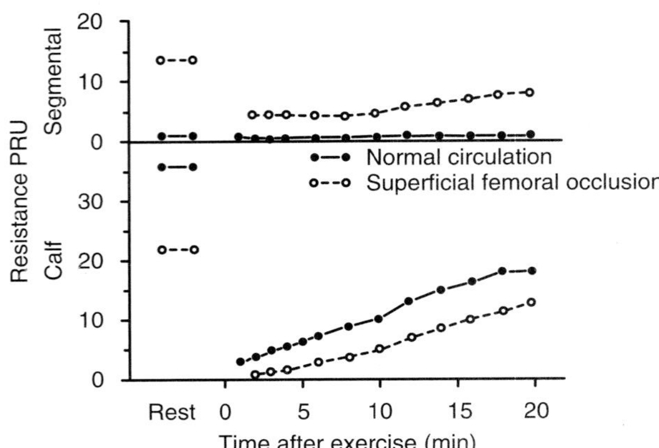

FIGURE 9-18 Segmental (parallel collateral and main channel) resistance and calf (runoff) resistance in normal individuals and in patients with occlusive disease of the superficial femoral artery. Values at rest and after treadmill exercises are shown. PRU, peripheral resistance unit. (Data from Sumner DS, Strandness DE Jr: The effect of exercise on resistance to blood flow in limbs with an occluded superficial femoral artery. Vasc Surg 4:229, 1970.)

(see Fig. 9-14). Measurement of pressures at the ankle by the simple noninvasive techniques described in Chapter 14 provides the clinician with a rapid, accurate, and objective means of assessing the functional severity of the arterial lesion.[23,57,171,176,193,194,199,201]

When blood flow to the extremity is increased during or after exercise, the blood pressure distal to the arterial lesion falls precipitously (see Fig. 9-14). Recovery to pre-exercise levels requires a prolonged period, usually between 10 and 30 minutes (see Figs. 9-15 to 9-17).[96,169,176,194] Even if the stenosis in a limb is not severe enough to produce a decrease in distal pressure at rest, exercise or reactive hyperemia causes a fall in pressure.[24,117,167] Blood pressure begins to recover after peak flows have begun to decline (see Figs. 9-15 to 9-17).[176] These changes account for the disappearance of pedal pulses after exercise in some patients with stenotic lesions.[38,39]

Resistance Changes Accompanying Exercise Figure 9-18 compares resting and postexercise resistances in normal limbs with those in limbs with occlusive disease of the superficial femoral artery. In normal limbs, *segmental resistance* refers to the resistance of the iliac and femoral arteries. In abnormal limbs, segmental resistance primarily reflects the resistance offered by the collateral arteries bypassing the superficial femoral artery occlusion (parallel resistance; see Eq. 9.15). *Calf resistance* represents the runoff resistance imposed by intramuscular arterioles, capillaries, and venules as well as the veins draining the extremity. The major part of this resistance is contributed by the arterioles. In this example, we can approximate the *total vascular resistance* of the limb by adding the segmental and calf resistances (see Eq. 9.14).

Values for the total resistance offered by normal and abnormal limbs at rest are essentially equal; for example, in Figure 9-18, the normal value is 37 PRUs, and the abnormal value is 36 PRUs. Values for distribution of the resistances, however, are markedly different.[50,104,177] Whereas segmental resistance accounts for less than 3% of the total in normal limbs, it makes up about 38% of the total in abnormal limbs. Resting blood flow rates are equal in the two groups of limbs only because peripheral arterioles in the abnormal limbs dilate enough to compensate for the elevated segmental resistance. Thus, calf resistance is much less in abnormal limbs than in normal limbs.

During exercise, intramuscular arterioles become widely dilated, thus markedly reducing calf resistance (see Fig. 9-18). After cessation of exercise, calf resistance gradually recovers toward resting values. Recovery is approximately linearly related to time.[177] In normal limbs, there is little change in segmental (collateral) resistance; in abnormal limbs, segmental resistance may remain unchanged or may drop somewhat.[104,161,177] Nevertheless, the total drop in resistance (segmental plus calf) is less in abnormal than in normal limbs. This explains why blood flow during exercise is greater in normal limbs than in limbs with occlusive arterial disease.

Although segmental resistance may decrease in limbs with arterial obstruction, it actually constitutes a greater percentage of the total resistance than it does at rest. In Figure 9-18, segmental resistance makes up 82% of the total resistance immediately after exercise. During the same period, segmental resistance in normal limbs makes up less than 14% of total limb resistance. The relative increase in segmental resistance in abnormal limbs explains the decrease in ankle blood pressure after walking.[104,176] The following discussion clarifies some of these relationships.

Hemodynamics of Arterial Obstruction Understanding the hemodynamics of intermittent claudication is facilitated by the use of simple models. Figure 9-10 shows a typical vascular circuit containing a stenotic artery. This circuit consists of (1) a proximal fixed (segmental) resistance made up of the stenotic segment and the bypassing collateral vessel and (2) a runoff bed made up of the distal arteries, arterioles, capillaries, and venules as well as the veins that return blood to the heart. As pointed out earlier, the resistance of the runoff bed largely resides in the arterioles and, consequently, is highly variable.

In Figure 9-19, the proximal fixed (segmental) resistance is represented by a compressible tube with a screw-clamp, and the distal runoff resistance is represented by a faucet. The normal situation is depicted in Figure 9-19A and B. Although at rest the resistance of the distal vascular bed is quite high, the proximal resistance is so low that normal flow is maintained (300 mL/min). During exercise, the intramuscular arterioles dilate, reducing the distal runoff resistance to a remarkable extent. Even though blood flow (Q_t) is increased five times, there is little pressure drop across the proximal (segmental) resistance (see also Eq. 9.12):

$$P_2 = P_1 - Q_t R_{seg} \quad (9.17)$$

Now suppose that an obstruction develops in the proximal vasculature, represented by tightening of the screw-clamp (Fig. 9-19C and D). The arterioles within the runoff bed dilate enough to compensate for the increase in proximal resistance. Because of this autoregulatory process, resting blood flow remains within normal limits. However, the resting blood pressure distal to the obstructed segment is lower than normal (60 mm Hg in this example). This is simply a reflection of the higher energy losses that occur across the increased resistance (see Eq. 9.17).

With exercise, the intramuscular arterioles dilate fully (see Fig. 9-19D). Because of the high proximal resistance, the rise in blood flow is inadequate to meet the metabolic demands of the exercising muscle mass, and claudication ensues. In addition, the blood pressure distal to the obstruction experiences a further drop as a result of the increased rate of flow through the high proximal resistance (see also Fig. 9-15).

Finally, an even worse situation is depicted in Figure 9-19E and F. Here, the proximal obstruction is so severe that blood flow at rest is only two-thirds the normal value (200 mL/min) despite complete peripheral vasodilatation; consequently, the patient experiences rest pain. Because no further peripheral dilatation is possible, blood flow does not increase with exercise. Blood pressure distal to the obstruction is more profoundly depressed than in the previous examples, because the increase in proximal (segmental) resistance is proportionally greater than the decrease in blood flow (Eq. 9.17; see also Fig. 9-17).

We can summarize these points as follows:

1. At rest, peripheral blood flow is normal in patients with claudication but is decreased in patients with ischemic rest pain.[54,64,90,135,166,176]
2. During exercise, peripheral blood flow increases in patients with claudication, but the increase is less than that occurring in normal limbs.[65,92,135,156,176,194] In patients with rest pain, exercise may result in no increase in blood flow.[176]
3. At rest, blood pressure distal to the arterial lesion is decreased in patients with claudication and even more so in patients with rest pain.[23,176,194,199] Exercise ordinarily results in a further decrease in peripheral pressure.[24,169,176,194]

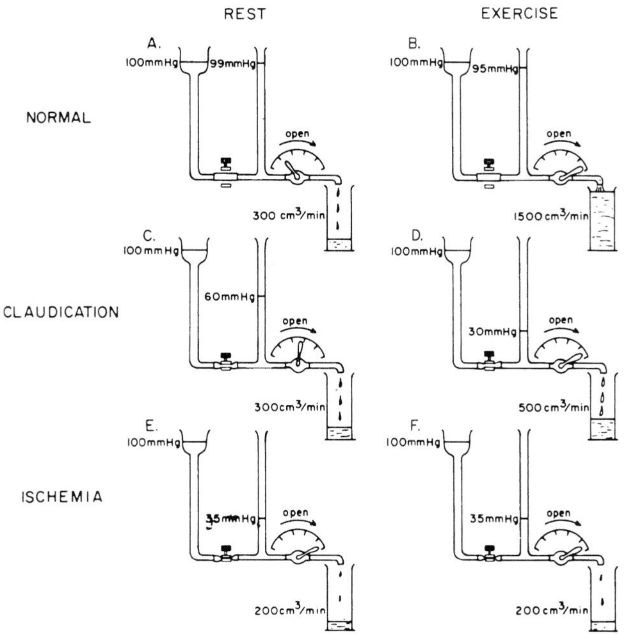

FIGURE 9-19 Hydraulic model of an arterial circuit showing the effect of exercise. See text for details.

Multiple Lesions and the Vascular Steal Phenomenon

Obstructing lesions occupying *one* arterial segment (e.g., iliac or superficial femoral artery) commonly cause claudication but seldom result in ischemia at rest. There are, however, certain exceptions. When the lesion is located far distally in the foot or toe, the involved vessel may be an end artery with no adequate collateral branches. Blockage of such a vessel leads to ischemia. In addition, an acute embolic obstruction to the distal aorta, common femoral artery, or popliteal artery may also obstruct stem or reentry collaterals. In effect, it creates a multilevel occlusion that may be responsible for severe peripheral ischemia.

Multilevel occlusions result when lesions involve two or more major arterial segments. Peripheral blood flow is more severely compromised than in single-level occlusions because blood must traverse two or more high-resistance collateral beds before reaching the periphery. If the lesions are chronic and confined to *two* segments (e.g., common iliac and superficial femoral arteries), collateral development is usually adequate to prevent rest pain or ischemic necrosis; claudication, however, is quite severe. Lesions involving *three* segments (e.g., common iliac, femoral, and popliteal arteries) reduce blood flow markedly and commonly cause rest pain.

Figure 9-20 illustrates the effect of exercise on pressure-flow relationships in limbs with two levels of obstruction. In this example, the more proximal fixed resistance (R_I) represents a lesion within the iliac artery, and the distal fixed resistance (R_{SF}) is in the superficial femoral artery. The variable resistances imposed by the peripheral vascular beds of the thigh and calf are represented by R_T and R_C, respectively. Normal resting blood flow to the calf and thigh is maintained by nearly complete vasodilatation in the calf (R_C open) and by partial vasodilatation in the thigh (R_T partly open) (Fig. 9-20A). Although exercise causes little change in diameter of the calf vessels, which already were nearly maximally dilated (R_C unchanged), the partial dilatation of the thigh vasculature becomes complete, thereby reducing its resistance to a minimal level (R_T open) (Fig. 9-20B). Because the total peripheral resistance is reduced, blood flow through the proximal fixed resistance (R_I) rises, leading to a further drop in pressure P_2 (see Eq. 9.17). Because the series of resistances leading to the calf have not changed ($R_{SF} + R_C$) and because the pressure head (P_2) perfusing the calf drops, blood flow to the calf decreases.

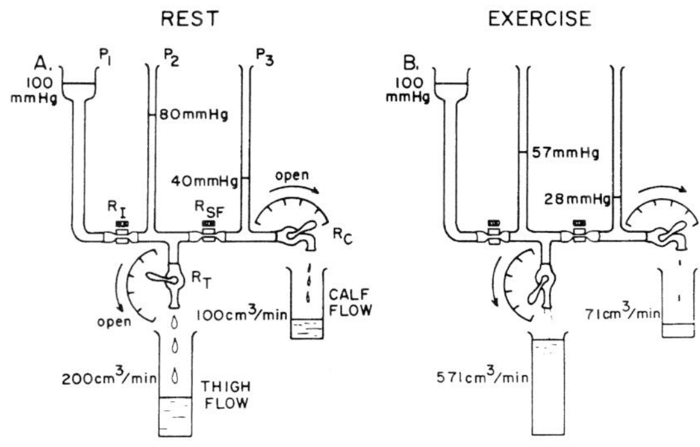

FIGURE 9-20 Hydraulic model illustrating effect of multilevel arterial obstructive disease. See text for details and definitions.

Thus, the effects of exercise are to (1) increase flow to the thigh, (2) reduce flow to the calf, and (3) decrease peripheral blood pressure.[3] Therefore, the proximal vascular bed *steals* blood from the distal. Calf blood flow increases only when thigh blood flow decreases, allowing the distal blood pressure (P_3) to rise (see Fig. 9-16).[3]

In conclusion, exercise or other causes of peripheral vasodilatation have the following effects in limbs with multiple levels of occlusion:

1. Blood flow in the more distal tissues may be normal at rest but may drop to even lower levels during exercise. In fact, the distal tissues may become completely ischemic.[2,38,92,199]
2. Blood pressure below the fixed obstructions is reduced at rest and falls to even lower levels during exercise.[169,176,199]
3. One vascular bed can steal from another only when the artery supplying both beds is functionally obstructed.[48,173,178]

Normal Arterial Flow and Pressure Waves

A portion of the left ventricular stroke volume is stored in the compliant aorta during systole and is then propelled distally by elastic recoil during diastole. When this surge of blood encounters the high resistance imposed by the arterioles, part is transmitted into the capillaries and part is reflected back up the arterial tree (Fig. 9-21).[173,191] The magnitude of the reflected wave relative to that of the incident wave is determined by the peripheral resistance, which is greatest when the recipient vascular bed is constricted and least when the bed is dilated.[143]

As the reflected wave moves up the artery, it subtracts from the forward wave. In normal limbs with a high arteriolar tone, this produces a short period of reversed flow in early diastole. As the reflected wave moves proximally beyond the point of observation, a smaller forward flow wave again appears in late diastole. When the arterioles are dilated (as in exercise) or when the baseline resistance of the recipient bed is low (as in the cerebral or renal circulation), the amplitude of the reflected wave is relatively small and shows up only as a transient downward deflection in the diastolic portion of the flow pulse. In this situation, flow remains antegrade throughout the cardiac cycle; there is no reverse flow component.

Although pressure is also reflected at the periphery, the reflected pressure wave—unlike the flow wave—adds to rather than subtracts from the forward wave, producing a characteristic upward deflection on the downslope of the pressure pulse (see Fig. 9-21). This additive nature of the reflected pressure wave accounts for the amplification of systolic pressure and the decrease in diastolic pressure that is observed as blood moves from the aorta to the peripheral arteries (see Fig. 9-13).

Although, as a first approximation, it is convenient to think of reflections as arising primarily from the high-resistance microvascular bed, reflections actually occur all along the arterial system where the vessel narrows, gives off branches, or bifurcates. The shape of the pulse is also affected by attenuation of the pressure and flow waves as they move antegrade or retrograde along the artery. Consequently, changes in the waveform attributable to

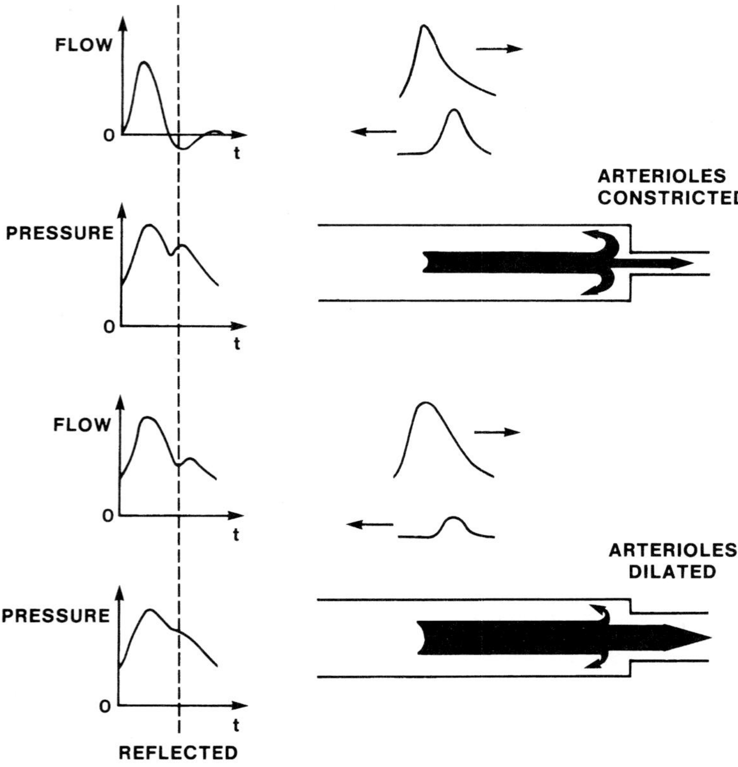

FIGURE 9-21 Effect of reflected waves on the contour of arterial flow and pressure pulses. Reflected waves subtract from forward flow waves but add to pressure waves. Reflection is accentuated by vasoconstriction and attenuated by vasodilatation. t, time. (From Sumner DS: Hemodynamics of abnormal blood flow. In Veith FJ, Hobson RW II, Williams RA, Wilson SE [eds]: Vascular Surgery: Principles and Practice, 2nd ed. New York, McGraw-Hill, 1994.)

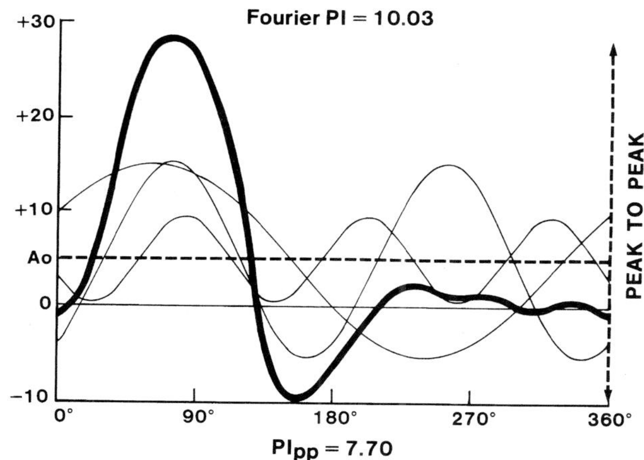

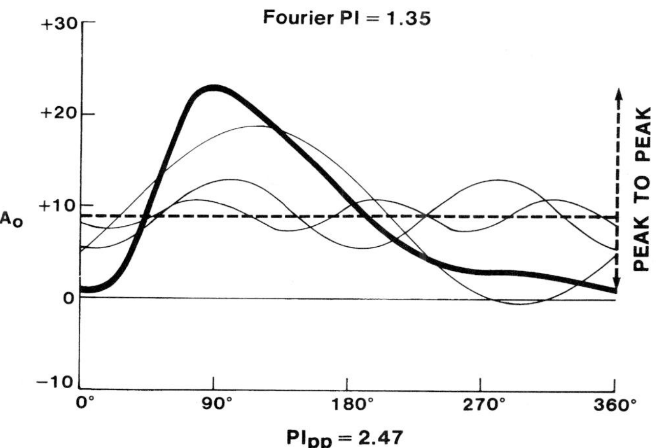

FIGURE 9-22 Fourier analysis of common femoral artery flow waveforms, showing first three harmonics. *Upper panel,* Normal iliac artery. *Lower panel,* Iliac artery obstruction. A_O, mean velocity or amplitude; *vertical arrows* indicate maximum "peak-to-peak" excursion. In comparison with those in the normal pulse, the amplitudes (moduli) of the second and third harmonics in the obstructive pulse are attenuated relative to that of the first harmonic. PI, pulsatility index; PI_{PP}, peak-to-peak pulsatility index.

reflections are more clearly seen in peripheral arteries than they are in the proximal aorta, where the amplitude of the reflected wave is greatly diminished.

Fourier analysis permits arterial pressure and flow pulses to be broken down mathematically into a series of harmonics, each having the configuration of a sine wave (Fig. 9-22).[173] These harmonics are characterized by a modulus (amplitude at peak excursion) and a phase angle, which relates the onset of the sine wave to the beginning of the pulse cycle. The fundamental harmonic has the same frequency as the arterial pulse, the second harmonic has twice the frequency, and so on to the *n*th harmonic. Most of the pulsatile information is contained in the lower-frequency harmonics, allowing the raw waveform to be reduplicated fairly accurately by a summation of the first five to ten harmonics. Because the velocity of the various harmonics depends on their frequency, their relative alignment changes as the pulse wave moves distally along the arterial tree. This is another factor that modifies the overall shape of normal flow and pressure waves.

Effect of Stenoses on Waveforms

As illustrated in Figure 9-23, the compliance of the arterial wall and that of any collateral channels constitute hydraulic capacitors, which, together with the stenosis, create a situation analogous to a low-pass filter. Passage of a pressure or flow pulse through this circuit attenuates the high-frequency harmonics and alters phase relationships, resulting in a damped waveform (see Fig. 9-22).

The arterial pulse pressure distal to a stenosis or occlusion is reduced to a greater extent than the mean pressure.[46,82] This phenomenon is due to energy losses associated with greater velocity flow through high-resistance pathways.[46,82] Usually, no appreciable decrease in pulse pressure occurs until the stenosis reaches a critical value of 75% to 90% reduction in arterial lumen. Complete absence of pulsation requires a stenosis approaching 99%.[39] The absence of palpable peripheral pulses distal to an arterial occlusion or severe stenosis is due to (1) reduction in the arterial pressure pulse and (2) decreased arterial pressure.

In addition to the reduction in pulse pressure, the contour of the pressure pulse is changed radically. The upslope is delayed, the peak becomes more rounded, the wave on the downslope disappears, and the downslope becomes bowed away from the baseline. These changes are reflected in the plethysmographic pulse, thus providing a sensitive indicator of the presence of arterial disease.[29,36,171] Further description of abnormal plethysmographic pulses is found in Chapter 14.

Similar changes are also perceived in the flow pulse distal to an obstructed artery (see Figs. 9-22 and 9-23). In contrast to the normal flow pattern, the wave rises more slowly, has a rounded peak, and declines more gradually toward the baseline during diastole. Almost invariably, the reverse flow component disappears.[8,49,57,60,72,126,172,199,200]

A stenosis, even a relatively minor stenosis, disrupts the normal laminar flow pattern, especially in the region of flow separation just beyond the exit (see Fig. 9-8). Because velocity vectors are no longer parallel, multiple frequencies are detected by the Doppler velocimeter, producing a phenomenon known as "spectral broadening." Because the extent of flow disruption is roughly proportional to the degree of stenosis, this finding has proved useful in the detection and grading of the severity of stenoses in both carotid and peripheral arteries (see Chapters 13 and 16).[71,76,77,145,158] Within the stenosis and in the jet just beyond, velocities are accelerated in accordance with the equation of continuity (see Eq. 9.10). If mean flow velocities above and within the stenoses are known with certainty, the relative degree of narrowing can be measured with precision—at least theoretically. In actual practice, however, degrees of narrowing are estimated from peak systolic velocity thresholds.[210]

Shear Rate at the Arterial Wall

As mentioned earlier, shear rate (D) is the rate at which the velocity of flow changes between concentric laminae of blood (see Eq. 9.7). Although the infinitesimally thin layer of blood in immediate contact with the inner wall of a vessel is static, the contiguous layers are in motion. This creates a shear rate at the wall (D_W) and a corresponding shear stress (τ_W) on the endothelial surface. In terms of mean velocity

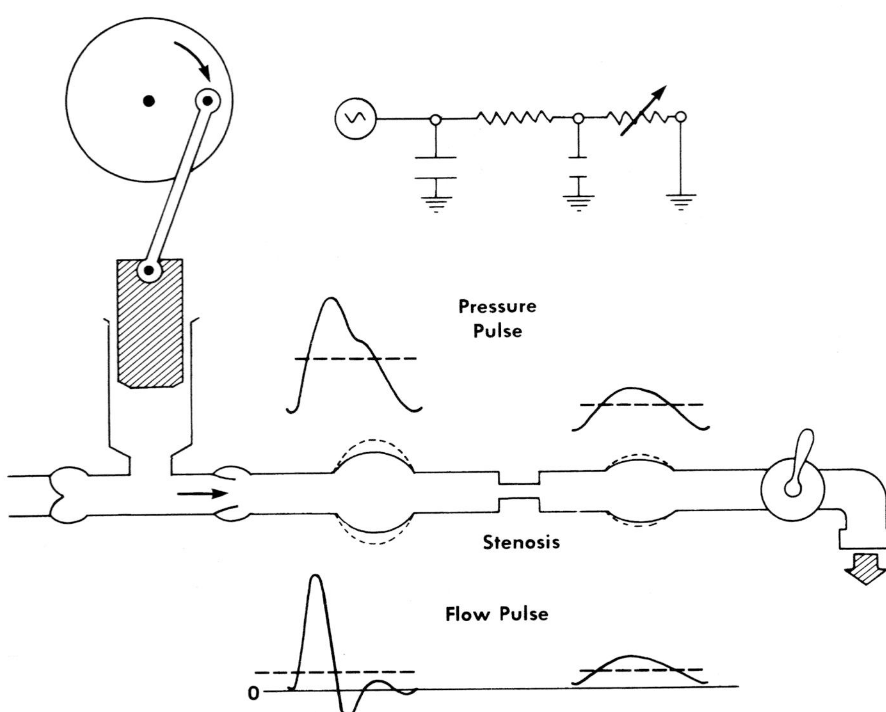

FIGURE 9-23 Effect of a stenosis and compliant vessels on the contour of arterial pressure and flow pulses. Mean pressure (*dashed line* on pressure pulse) is reduced, but mean flow (*dashed line* on flow pulse) is unchanged. Faucet represents the variable resistance of the peripheral vascular bed. This, together with the fixed resistance of the stenosis and the compliance of the major arteries, constitutes a model of input impedance. (From Sumner DS: Correlation of lesion configuration with functional significance. In Bond MG, Insull W Jr, Glagov S [eds]: Clinical Diagnosis of Atherosclerosis: Quantitative Methods of Evaluation. New York, Springer-Verlag, 1983.)

(V) and mean flow (Q) across a vessel in which the flow profile is parabolic, the shear rate and shear stress at the wall are as follows:

$$D_w = 4\frac{V}{R} = 4\frac{Q}{\pi r^3} \quad (9.18)$$

$$\tau_w = 4\eta\frac{V}{r} = 4\eta\frac{Q}{\pi r^3} \quad (9.19)$$

Thus, the shear rate and shear stress at the wall at any instant in the pulse cycle depend on blood viscosity (η) and are directly proportional to the mean velocity of flow and inversely proportional to the inner radius of the vessel. This means that (1) wall shear increases as the mean velocity increases or the radius decreases and (2) shear decreases as the velocity decreases or the radius increases.

Shear rates at the wall are increased when the velocity profile is blunt, reflecting the shorter radial distance from the wall to the cylindrical plug of maximal velocity flow (see Fig. 9-4). When the profile is skewed (as it is at bifurcations and at areas where the vessel curves), shear is greatest near the wall, where the velocity of flow is highest. In these regions, flow may take on a helical pattern, thereby further complicating the pattern of shear.[107] Turbulence not only increases shear stress but also subjects the wall to large oscillatory stresses.[129] At the carotid bulb, shear is greatest near the flow divider and least near the opposite wall, where blood flow may be stagnant or reversed during a large part of the cardiac cycle.[88,121,196] In this area of "flow separation," the direction of shear fluctuates during the pulse cycle, corresponding to the direction of the velocity vectors (Fig. 9-24A).[88] (Flow is said to be "separated" when the boundary of the main body of flow is no longer attached to the vessel wall but is isolated from the wall by a region in which the velocity vectors have a different orientation.) Similarly, in aneurysms, the axial flow stream is separated from flow in the dilated area near the wall, where velocities are low and flow reversal occurs (Fig. 9-24B).[196]

Other regions in which flow separation develops include the lateral walls of the common iliac artery at the aortic bifurcation and just beyond stenoses in atherosclerotic vessels (see Fig. 9-8).[144,155,196] In stenotic arteries, the longitudinal extent of flow separation depends on the velocity of flow and the degree of narrowing.[127]

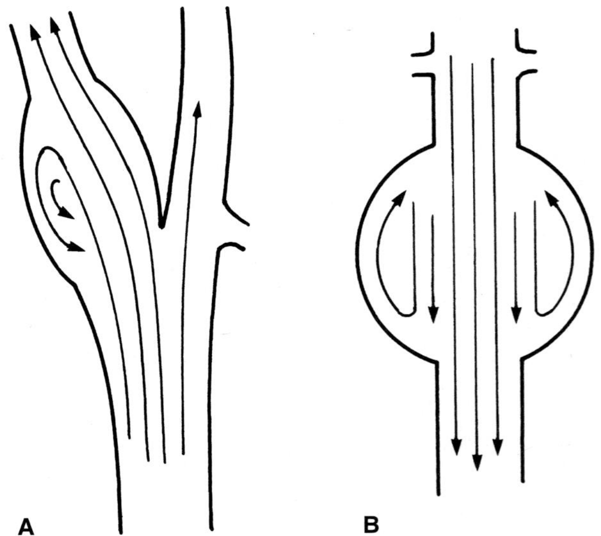

FIGURE 9-24 Diagrammatic representation of flow streamlines in a carotid arterial bifurcation (**A**) and an abdominal aortic aneurysm (**B**). Flow separation and reversal of flow occur in the carotid bulb and in the distended portion of the aneurysm.

The physiologic and pathophysiologic importance of shear rate and shear stress has been recognized only recently. There is evidence that arteries constrict with decreasing shear[89] and dilate with increasing shear.[70,79,115] Teleologically, this feature may be viewed as an effort to "normalize" shear stress.[207] Apparently, the endothelium in some way senses shear, causing the release of endothelium-derived relaxing factor (nitric oxide), which in turn relaxes the smooth muscles of the arterial wall, allowing the vessel to expand.[62] The classic example of this phenomenon is the increased diameter of arteries feeding an arteriovenous fistula.[70,207,218] As mentioned earlier, coronary arteries narrowed by atherosclerotic plaques also tend to dilate, thereby maintaining the lumen at a relatively normal diameter as long as the plaques remain small.[59] This mechanism may be operative in the peripheral circulation as well, where the average diameter of atherosclerotic arteries is usually somewhat larger than that of normal arteries. Post-stenotic dilatation of the axillary artery (frequently observed distal to the site of bony compression in patients with thoracic outlet syndrome) has also been attributed to distorted patterns of shear stress.[129]

Endothelial cells are aligned and are overlapped (like shingles) in the direction of the wall shear stress.[164] In areas where shear is reduced and where the direction of shear oscillates during the pulse cycle, the orientation of these cells is distorted, and the pattern of overlap is disrupted. Atherosclerotic plaques tend to form first and develop most rapidly at sites of decreased shear, possibly because the relative stagnation of blood in these regions prolongs the fluid "residence time," modifying the mass transport of atherogenic substances from the lumen into the wall and fostering the adherence of platelets and macrophages to the endothelial surface.[88,121] The endothelial barrier may in turn be more susceptible to penetration owing to the distorted alignment of the cells and the instability of cellular junctions.[88] This possibility explains the preferential location of plaques in the carotid bulb opposite the flow divider and the frequency with which atherosclerotic plaques form at the bifurcations of the terminal aorta, the common femoral artery, and popliteal artery—all areas in which geometry promotes flow separation and decreased shear rates.[88,155] Once a plaque has formed, further extension may be promoted by the area of stagnant or reversed flow that develops immediately beyond the stenosis (see Fig. 9-8).

Other investigators have observed a positive correlation between shear rate and deposition of platelets and fibrin on damaged endothelial surfaces. They have suggested that increased shear rates may be conducive to arterial thrombosis in certain circumstances.[132]

Treatment of Arterial Insufficiency: Physiologic Aspects

On the basis of the discussion presented earlier in this chapter, it is evident that the elevated fixed resistance imposed by obstructed major arteries and by their associated collaterals is the factor responsible for restricting blood flow to the periphery. It follows that intermittent claudication and other symptoms of peripheral ischemia can be alleviated only by reduction of this fixed resistance. Efforts to reduce the resistance of the peripheral vascular bed are seldom beneficial because this resistance either is automatically adjusted to levels adequate to maintain a normal resting blood flow or already is maximally reduced in limbs with ischemia at rest (see Fig. 9-11); it is also maximally reduced during exercise in patients with intermittent claudication (see Fig. 9-18).[30,66,140,147,221]

Thus, vasodilators may increase the resting blood flow in limbs when resting blood flow is adequate, but they almost never improve flow in an ischemic limb or during exercise.[27,188] In fact, these agents may cause blood to be diverted from areas of relative ischemia to those where disease is less severe.[93]

Many of these same criticisms can be applied to surgical sympathectomy (Fig. 9-25).[33,66,147] Sympathectomy, however, does have the advantage that its effects can be confined to the diseased area. In fact, some relief has been reported in patients with mild rest pain or with superficial ischemic ulcers.[170] Yet even this improvement is difficult to explain, because sympathectomy appears to enhance flow through arteriovenous anastomoses without increasing flow through the nutritive capillary bed.[34,224]

Because no drugs are available that produce appreciable collateral dilatation or cause regression of atherosclerotic plaques, satisfactory reduction of the fixed resistance can be accomplished only by direct surgical or catheter-based interventions; endarterectomy, replacement grafting, bypass grafting, and balloon angioplasty are all effective (see Fig. 9-25). Exercise therapy is the only nonoperative treatment that consistently affords any objective relief.[90,162] Although exercise programs extend maximal walking and claudication distances and appear to decrease the flow debt incurred during muscle activity, there is usually little change in ankle pressure.[51,74] This finding suggests that the benefits are due

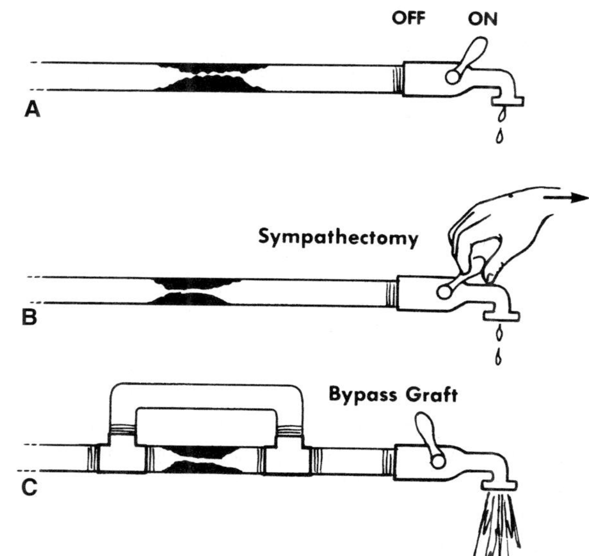

FIGURE 9-25 Hydraulic model contrasting the effects of sympathectomy and bypass grafting on blood flow. **A,** Faucet represents peripheral resistance, which is maximally decreased by exercise. **B,** Resistance cannot be further decreased by sympathectomy. **C,** Bypass graft circumvents the fixed resistance, permitting increased blood flow even with less peripheral vasodilatation. (From Sumner DS: Pathophysiology of arterial occlusive disease. In Hershey FB, Barnes RW, Sumner DS [eds]: Noninvasive Diagnosis of Vascular Disease. Pasadena, CA, Appleton Davies, 1984.)

in large part to metabolic changes rather than to development of collaterals. Although exercise is helpful in patients with claudication, it is applicable only when ischemia is absent at rest, and it cannot match the hemodynamic improvement provided by direct interventions.

Temporary relief of severe ischemia at rest can sometimes be obtained by rendering the patient hypertensive, thereby increasing the pressure head perfusing the obstructed vascular circuit.[90,93] Because of the adverse effects of hypertension, this approach is rarely employed. However, restoring blood pressure to near-normal levels by improving cardiac output in hypotensive patients with pump failure and multilevel arterial disease may reverse acute ischemia of the feet and toes.

Hanging the feet over the edge of the bed or walking a few steps often provides complete or partial relief from ischemic rest pain. The temporary improvement in peripheral perfusion that accompanies dependency can be documented objectively with measurement of transcutaneous oxygen tension, which may be increased severalfold compared with levels measured when the patient is supine.[149] According to Equation 9.1, pressure in the dependent arteries, veins, and capillaries is increased by gravity commensurate with the vertical distance from the foot to the heart. Although there is no increase in the arteriovenous pressure gradient, the increased hydrostatic pressure dilates capillaries and microvascular vessels, thereby reducing their resistance, which in turn augments blood flow. Augmentation of blood flow does not occur in nonischemic limbs, because the venoarterial reflex that serves to constrict arterioles in the dependent position remains functional.

Because the viscosity of blood increases with hematocrit, it is possible to augment blood flow by hemodilution.[43,95,195] The effects, however, are unpredictable, difficult to control, and not applicable on a long-term basis. Pentoxifylline, a drug that decreases plasma fibrinogen and platelet aggregation and increases erythrocyte flexibility, augments walking tolerance somewhat in patients with claudication, but the clinical results are variable.[138]

Arterial Grafts

When the decision to use a graft has been made, the surgeon often has some latitude in the choice of graft material, diameter, and anastomotic configuration (end-to-end, side-to-end, or end-to-side). Because of the importance of radius in determining both viscous and inertial energy losses, the graft selected should be large enough to carry all the flow required at rest without causing an evident pressure drop; it should also be large enough to accommodate any increased flow likely to be required during exercise without an appreciable pressure drop. Any limitation of flow should result from the resistance of the peripheral vascular bed and not from the graft.

Table 9-1 lists the pressure gradients that might be expected across a femoropopliteal graft 40 cm long at several levels of flow. Because these calculations were made with the use of Poiseuille's equation (see Eq. 9.6), they represent minimal values; the actual pressure drops would be several times as great.[148] Clearly, a graft with an inside diameter less than 3 mm would be of marginal value at flow rates normally observed at rest (60 to 150 mL/min) and would be completely unsatisfactory during exercise (300 to 500 mL/min). This theory coincides with the clinical observations of many surgeons.[21,47,128,189]

Blood flow in the common femoral artery averages about 350 mL/min at rest and may increase by a factor of 5 to 10 during exercise. According to Poiseuille's equation, a graft 20 cm long with an inside diameter of 7 mm should be able to carry flows of 3000 mL/min with a pressure drop of only 4.5 mm Hg. Experimentally, the pressure gradient across similar grafts is much higher, approximating 7 to 10 mm Hg at a flow rate of 1200 mL/min.[148,152] At rest, however, a 7-mm graft should result in a pressure gradient of only a few millimeters of mercury. Therefore, under most physiologic conditions, an aortofemoral graft with 7-mm limbs should suffice, restricting flow only during strenuous exercise; 6-mm grafts might begin to show some restriction of flow even with mild to moderate exercise.

Under ideal flow conditions, prosthetic grafts develop a thin layer (0.5 to 1.0 mm) of pseudointima. Thus, after implantation, a 6-mm prosthetic graft might have an internal diameter of 4 to 5 mm, and a 7-mm graft might have a lumen of 5 to 6 mm. For this reason, it seems appropriate, when one performs a femoropopliteal bypass with a prosthetic graft, to select a graft with an original diameter of at least 6 mm. Similarly, the original diameter of an aortofemoral graft limb should be at least 7 mm.

On the other hand, the diameter of the graft must not be too much larger than that of the recipient arteries.[150] It has been shown, both clinically and experimentally, that irregular clots accumulate on the inner walls of grafts of excessive diameter (much as they do in aneurysms) as the flow stream tries to mold itself to the diameter of the recipient vessels. These clots, which are not densely adherent, tend to separate and may be responsible for graft failure. A high flow velocity (high shear) is conducive to the formation of a thin, tightly adherent pseudointima. For a given volume of flow, the wall shear rate (or stress) is inversely proportional to the cube of the radius (see Eqs. 9.18 and 9.19). Therefore, the shear rate at the wall in a 7-mm graft would be 1.5 times that in an 8-mm graft and 2.9 times that in a 10-mm graft. Thus, the diameter of a prosthetic graft should be small enough to ensure a rapid velocity of flow but large enough to avoid restriction of arterial inflow.

Long-term patency of autogenous vein grafts is compromised by intimal hyperplasia, the development of which has also been associated with low shear rates.[14,106,130,198] Low shear rates cause smooth muscle cells to become secretory and enhance platelet adherence;[130] high shear rates foster continued patency and lessen the tendency for the intima to

Table 9-1 Calculated Minimal Pressure Gradients (mm Hg) Across a 40-cm Graft (η = 0.035P)

	DIAMETER (cm)				
FLOW (mL/min)	0.2	0.3	0.4	0.5	0.6
60	27	5.3	1.7	0.7	0.3
100	45	8.8	2.8	1.1	0.6
150	67	13	4.2	1.7	0.8
300	134	27	8.4	3.4	1.7
500	223	44	14	5.8	2.8

become hyperplastic. The protective effect of high shear may be due to suppression of the release of endothelin-1, a peptide found in endothelial cells that acts as a vasoconstrictor and a mitogen for smooth muscle cells.[154]

Studies suggest that diameters of human in situ vein grafts change with time to normalize shear stress.[214] Vein grafts with initially high shear rates tend to dilate, but those with low shear rates tend to contract. The diameters of lower extremity vein grafts appear to increase transiently in response to acute increases in blood flow, a response that may be attributed to the release of nitric oxide from the endothelium in response to increased shear stress.[215] However, nitric oxide activity has been shown to be significantly impaired in vein grafts (especially under low-flow conditions), an alteration that may contribute to intimal hyperplasia.[211,220]

Anastomoses

Because any change in the direction of blood flow increases energy losses due to inertial factors, an end-to-end anastomosis is more hemodynamically efficient than a side-to-end or end-to-side anastomosis.[173] The greater the angle subtended by the graft and host vessels, the greater the energy losses become. Even though energy losses may be increased severalfold by an adverse angle, the increase in pressure drop is only a few millimeters of mercury and is ordinarily of no clinical significance. For example, from the point of view of transmitting blood efficiently, it makes little difference whether the donor anastomosis of a femoral-femoral graft is made with an angle of 135 degrees (requiring flow to reverse itself) or a more hemodynamically satisfactory angle of 45 degrees.[101,105]

Energy losses, however, are only part of the story. Any time a graft leaves or enters a host vessel at an angle, flow disturbances are created, resulting in zones of flow separation, stagnation, turbulence, and distorted velocity vectors (Figs. 9-26 and 9-27).[9,32,101,128] The "floor" of an end-to-side anastomosis (in the recipient vessel opposite the anastomosis), the "toe" of the anastomosis (on the near wall just beyond the suture line), and the "heel" (on the near wall proximal to the junction) appear to be prominent sites of flow separation where shear is low and shear stress fluctuates.[9,128] Low shear and oscillatory shear stresses are conducive to platelet adhesion, intimal hyperplasia, and atherosclerosis, and high shear may result in endothelial damage.[32,101,113,205] The ultimate result is endothelial thickening or thrombus formation that may lead to graft failure.[100] Therefore, the goal, long-term graft patency, is best achieved by construction of an end-to-end anastomosis; when this is not feasible, an anastomosis with an acute angle is recommended.

Computer simulations have shown that large shear stress gradients at the toe and heel of end-to-side distal anastomoses are associated with the development of myointimal hyperplasia and atheroma.[217] Compared with conventional anastomotic configurations, a Taylor patch reduces these gradients somewhat, especially at high flow rates, but a major (50%) reduction in wall shear stress gradients requires an idealized geometry with a smoothly tapered heel and toe, a graft-to-host diameter ratio of 1.6, and an anastomotic angle of 10 to 15 degrees.

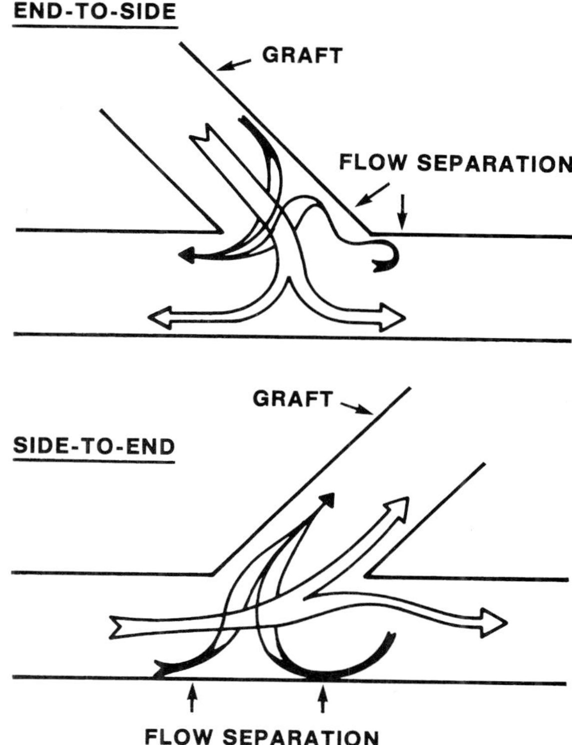

FIGURE 9-26 Flow patterns at end-to-side and side-to-end anastomoses. Near the wall, blood flow may reverse and travel circumferentially to reach the recipient conduit. Areas of flow separation are prone to development of neointimal hyperplasia. (From Sumner DS: Hemodynamics of abnormal blood flow. In Veith FJ, Hobson RW, Russell AW, Wilson SE [eds]: Vascular Surgery: Principles and Practice, 2nd ed. New York, McGraw-Hill, 1994.)

Viscoelasticity of the Arterial Wall

As intraluminal pressure rises during systole, the arterial wall stretches both circumferentially and longitudinally. During diastole, the process is reversed. The magnitude of the stretch is determined by the stiffness of the arterial wall, which in turn is determined by its composition and thickness.

The stiffness of an elastic material can be described by Young's modulus of elasticity (E), which is the ratio of the applied stress (τ) to the resulting strain (ε):

$$E = \tau/\epsilon \tag{9.20}$$

Compliance (C) is the reciprocal of the elastic modulus (1/E). The circumferential stress applied to an arterial wall is a function of the transmural pressure, P (intraluminal pressure minus the extravascular pressure), the inside radius of the artery, r_i, and its wall thickness, δ[137,173]:

$$\tau = P\frac{r_i}{\delta} \tag{9.21}$$

Pressure is in dynes $\cdot$ cm^{-2}, and r_i and d are in centimeters. Circumferential strain, ε, is proportional to the ratio of the change in outside radius, Δr_o, to the original outside radius, r_o:

$$\epsilon = \Delta r_o / r_o \tag{9.22}$$

Therefore, an incremental elastic modulus (E_t) can be obtained by substituting Equations 9.21 and 9.22 in Equation 9.20:

$$E_t = \Delta P \frac{r_o}{\Delta r_o} \cdot \frac{r_i}{\delta} \tag{9.23}$$

Pulse pressure is represented by ΔP. Although this formula allows a first approximation of the stiffness of the materials composing the arterial wall, it does not take into account the variable stress on the different layers (greatest on the inside and least on the outside) and the tendency of the wall thickness to decrease as the radius increases.[173] A more precise formula that incorporates these variables has been devised by Bergel[12]:

$$E = \Delta P \cdot \frac{r_o}{\Delta r_o} \cdot \frac{(1.5)\, r_i^2}{r_o^2 + r_i^2} \tag{9.24}$$

Because it is often difficult to obtain accurate measurements of arterial wall thickness, several purely descriptive formulas are in common use, such as[137]:

$$E_p = \Delta P \frac{r_o}{\Delta r_o} \tag{9.25}$$

Compliance (C) is the reciprocal of E_p:

$$C = \frac{\Delta r_o}{\Delta P \cdot r_o} \tag{9.26}$$

It should be emphasized that Equations 9.25 and 9.26 relate to the behavior of the entire arterial wall, whereas Equations 9.23 and 9.24 describe the stiffness of the materials composing the wall. In other words, two arteries with the same E value (see Eq. 9.24) would have different E_p values if their wall thicknesses were different.

In addition to elasticity, viscosity is also a property of the arterial wall.[13] Viscosity causes the expansion of the artery to lag behind the change in pressure. As a result, the elastic modulus of the arterial wall appears to increase with rising pulse rate. Wall viscosity may also account for some of the energy losses in pulsatile flow, because the storage of energy during systole and its release during diastole may be incomplete owing to the friction encountered in expansion and contraction of the arterial wall.

Two fibrous proteins, *elastin* and *collagen,* determine the mechanical properties of the arterial wall. At *low* transmural pressures (<50 to 75 mm Hg), most of the circumferential distending force is sustained by lamellae composed of elastin, which is highly extensible. At *higher* pressures, the arterial wall stretches and collagen fibers are gradually recruited to bear an increasingly larger portion of the load. Because collagen is about 1000 to 2000 times stiffer than elastin, arteries (and veins) become very stiff at high pressures. Therefore, the typical pressure-diameter curve of arteries has two phases: (1) a low-pressure, compliant part and (2) a high-pressure, stiff part.[40] The elastic modulus of the arterial wall also increases with aging, fibrosis, and calcification—factors that often accompany arteriosclerosis.[122,173,222]

Activation of the smooth muscle within the arterial wall has a complex relationship with the elastic modulus but tends to increase stiffness at a given strain.[42,173] The effect of muscle contraction becomes evident only in the smaller and muscular arteries of the periphery and is most marked in terminal arterioles. In the absence of muscular contraction, all arteries retain a circular cross-section even at zero transmural pressure. Therefore, the phenomenon of "critical closure," in which small arteries appear to collapse (occlude) at low perfusion pressures, can occur only when there is an increase in smooth muscle tone.[7]

Table 9-2 lists some of the stress-strain characteristics of atherosclerotic and normal arteries. Most synthetic grafts are stiffer than the arteries they replace, especially after they have been implanted for some time (Table 9-3). This change is due to ingrowth of fibrous tissue into the interstices of porous grafts and fibrous encapsulation of the grafts.

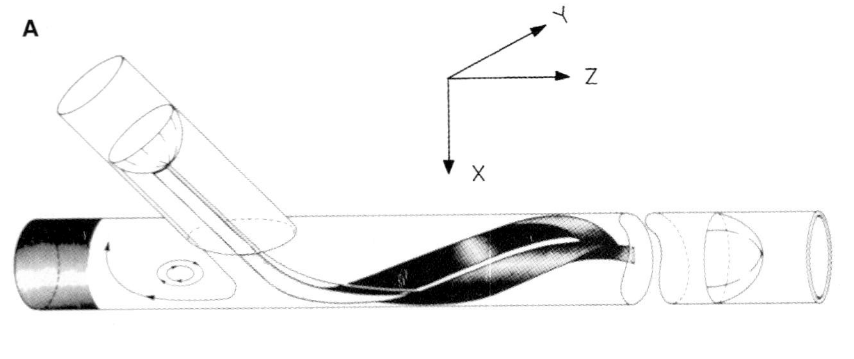

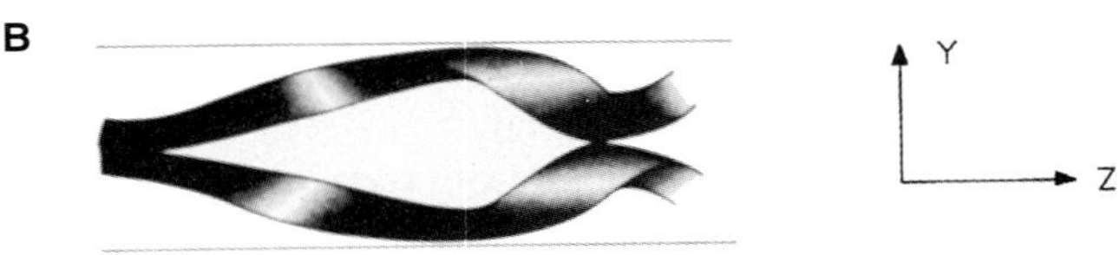

FIGURE 9-27 Flow pattern in a three-dimensional model of an end-to-side anastomosis. Note impingement of high-velocity flow on the "floor" of the anastomosis and the helical pattern that develops beyond the anastomosis. Reversal of flow occurs in the proximal segment of the recipient vessel. **A,** Model tilted toward observer. **B,** Model viewed from above. X, Y, and Z represent coordinates for orientation of the model. (From Ojha M, Ethier CR, Johnston KW, Cobbold RSC: Steady and pulsatile flow fields in an end-to-side arterial anastomosis model. J Vasc Surg 12:747, 1990.)

Table 9-2 Stress-Strain Characteristics of Human Arteries

LOCATION	CHAPTER REFERENCE	REMARKS	ELASTIC MODULUS (E)* (dynes · cm^{-2} · 10^6)	PRESSURE-STRAIN ELASTIC MODULUS† (dynes · cm^{-2} · 10^6)	PERCENT COMPLIANCE (C)‡ NORMALIZED (ΔP = 50 mm Hg)
Infrarenal aorta	173	ASO	26.0 ± 14.5	9.8 ± 3.5	0.8 ± 0.3
Terminal aorta	173	ASO	37.7 ± 17.2	15.1 ± 4.1	0.5 ± 0.2
Common iliac artery	173	ASO	24.7 ± 21.5	14.8 ± 15.8	0.8 ± 0.4
Common femoral artery	122	Age <35 yr	—	2.6 ± 1.3	3.0 ± 1.0
	122	Age 35-60 yr	—	3.9 ± 2.0	2.1 ± 0.9
	122	Age >60 yr	—	6.3 ± 4.8	1.2 ± 0.9
	186	—	—	2.3 ± 0.2	3.0 ± 0.3

*Equation 9.24.
†Equation 9.25.
‡Equation 9.26.
ASO, arteriosclerosis obliterans.

Table 9-3 Stress-Strain Characteristics of Various Arterial Grafts

GRAFT MATERIAL	CHAPTER REFERENCE	MONTHS IMPLANTED	PRESSURE-STRAIN ELASTIC MODULUS* (dynes · cm^{-2} · 10^6)	PERCENT COMPLIANCE (C)† NORMALIZED (ΔP = 50 mm Hg)
Saphenous vein	186	0	3.0 ± 0.6	2.2 ± 0.4
	106	>36	4.9 ± 2.0	1.7 ± 1.0
Umbilical vein	186	0	3.5 ± 0.5	1.9 ± 0.3
Bovine heterograft	186	0	5.1 ± 0.6	1.3 ± 0.2
	67	12	24.2	0.3
Dacron				
Velour	186	0	7.0 ± 1.1	1.0 ± 0.2
Knitted	67	0	17.8	0.4
	67	0	55.5	0.1
Woven	67	0	166.6	0.04
PTFE woven	67	0	148.1	0.05
PTFE	186	0	8.3 ± 1.0	0.8 ± 0.1

*Equation 9.25.
†Equation 9.26.
PTFE, polytetrafluoroethylene.

Palpable Pulses

Motion of the arterial wall is responsible for the palpable pulses that are so important in the physical examination of the patient in whom arterial disease is suspected. Yet, it is apparent from the values in Table 9-2 that a 7-mm femoral artery in a young subject would expand only 0.2 mm under the influence of a 50-mm Hg pulse pressure. Older, stiffer arteries would expand even less. It seems doubtful that the finger could reliably detect this degree of motion. Why, then, are pulses ordinarily so easily felt? When the finger is applied to the skin overlying an artery, the artery is compressed, changing its normally circular cross section into an *ellipse.* It takes much less energy to bend the wall of an elliptically shaped vessel than it does to stretch the wall of a circular vessel.[122] Therefore, when the artery is partially compressed, its expansion in the direction of the compression is greatly augmented. Also, as the artery expands longitudinally, the entire vessel moves toward the skin.

As surgeons, we are accustomed to grading the peripheral pulses on an arbitrary scale (e.g., from 0 to 4+) and to estimating the extent of proximal obstruction on the basis of the magnitude of the pulse. This practice is predicated on the assumption that the strength of the pulse is directly related to the pulse pressure, which should be decreased distal to an obstruction. Stiff, calcified vessels may display little or no pulse, however, even though there is no decrease in pulse pressure. In contrast, relatively good pulses may be palpated despite a proximal arterial obstruction if the arterial wall is compliant, particularly if the systemic pulse pressure is increased.

Although pulse palpation is a valuable tool for the initial evaluation of the patient with suspected arterial disease, both arteriography and noninvasive tests have repeatedly demonstrated its fallibility.

Stresses at Graft-Artery Anastomoses and False Aneurysms

Coupling a stiff graft to a compliant artery places additional stresses on the suture line, which may lead to intimal hyperplasia or the development of a false aneurysm.[1,9,67,114,186,213] With the advent of synthetic sutures, most anastomotic disruptions develop in the arterial wall; the sutures themselves remain intact.[84,125] On the basis of the data in Tables 9-2 and 9-3, the circumference of a young femoral artery measuring 7 mm in diameter would increase 1.32 mm with each 50-mm Hg pressure pulse, whereas the circumference of a woven Dacron graft of the same diameter would increase only 0.02 mm, a disparity of 1.30 mm. As these increases are repeated 100,000 times per day, this small difference would result in fatigue of the arterial wall.

Paasche and colleagues[133] have analyzed the stresses produced at an end-to-end anastomosis by a compliance mismatch. Three components of the stress system were identified: axial, hoop, and shear. Of these, shear, which is greatest at the suture lines, is the most disruptive. Both theoretically and experimentally, stresses can be minimized if the ratio of the diameter of a rigid graft to that of a compliant artery is about 1.4:1.[85,133]

Because the impedance of a stiff graft is greater than that of a compliant artery, pulsatile energy is reflected at the proximal suture line. When a Dacron graft with an E_p of 55×10^6 dynes · cm^{-2} is sutured to an infrarenal aorta with an E_p of 9.8×10^6 dynes · cm^{-2}, about 41% of the incident pulsatile energy is reflected.[173] Because this reflection augments the pressure pulsations proximal to the graft, additional stresses are placed on the suture line,[124] which may contribute to disruption of the proximal anastomosis.

Shear stresses produced by vibrations generated at end-to-side anastomoses may also contribute to the formation of false aneurysms.

Arterial Wall Stress and Rupture of Aortic Aneurysms

An aneurysm ruptures when the tangential stress within its wall exceeds the tensile strength of the wall at any point.

Tangential stress (τ) within the wall of a cylinder is given by Equation 9.21. This equation explains in part why large aneurysms are more likely to rupture than small aneurysms and why rupture is more common in hypertensive patients than in normotensive patients.[16,56]

Note that Equation 9.21 differs from *LaPlace's law,* which usually is stated as follows:

$$T = Pr \tag{9.27}$$

where r is commonly taken as the outside radius (although more properly it should be the inside radius), and T is tension in dynes per centimeter of cylindrical length. LaPlace's law is truly applicable only to very thin-walled structures, such as soap bubbles, and should not be employed to describe stresses in arterial walls.[136]

Because the wall stress in a sphere is half that in a cylinder with the same radius and because the typical configuration of an aneurysm is a cross between a sphere and a cylinder, Equation 9.21 actually overestimates the stress in aneurysm walls.[40] This fact, however, does not change the essential argument—namely, that wall stress is directly proportional to transmural pressure and to the inner radius of the vessel and is inversely proportional to wall thickness.

Figure 9-28 shows a cylinder with an outside diameter of 2 cm and a wall thickness of 0.2 cm. These dimensions are compatible with those found in atherosclerotic terminal aortas.[173,179] The circumferential wall stress within this structure would be 8.0×10^5 dynes · cm^{-2} when the internal pressure is 150 mm Hg. If this tube were distended without the volume of material increasing in the wall, the wall would simultaneously become thinner. In the case illustrated, the tube has been expanded to aneurysmal dimensions, outside diameter 6 cm, and the wall thickness has decreased to 0.06 cm (Fig. 9-28, right-hand panel). Tripling the radius and decreasing the wall thickness cause the circumferential stress in the wall of the expanded cylinder to increase to 98.0×10^5 dynes · cm^{-2}, provided the pressure remains at 150 mm Hg (see Eq. 9.21). Thus, in this highly artificial model, stress per unit area of wall increases by a factor of 12, even though the arterial diameter has enlarged only three times.

Owing to the sluggish flow and low shear stress on the inner wall of aneurysms, layers of clot develop that tend to maintain the diameter of the lumen near that of the normal artery (see Fig. 9-24). This thrombus, by increasing the effective thickness of the arterial wall (δ), may reduce wall stress and afford some protection against rupture (see Eq. 9.21). On the other hand, the clot might simply transmit pressure undiminished to the wall and may therefore have little effect on wall stress. Because thrombi are friable and poorly bonded to the inner surface of the residual wall, they may exert little or no retractive force.[40]

Findings in computer simulations using the finite element method for analyzing mechanical properties of axisymmetric models of abdominal aortic aneurysms suggest that thrombus may reduce wall stress by as much as 50%.[212,216,219] These studies predict that the protective effect is proportional not only to the thickness of the clot relative to the aneurysm diameter but also to the elastic modulus (E_p; see Eq. 9.25) of the clot. In other words, the risk of rupture may be lower in aneurysms lined with stiff, thick clots.

In real life, aneurysms are never truly axisymmetric. As they elongate, they tend to bow forward at the upper end and deviate to the left. Because posterior expansion is limited by the vertebral column, aneurysms are forced to bulge anteriorly. Asymmetry in the anterior-posterior plane has been shown by finite element analysis to increase wall stress even when the diameter remains unchanged.[225] This effect is particularly evident in the posterior wall adjacent to the vertebral column and in the anterior wall, where the direction of curvature gradually changes from concave outward

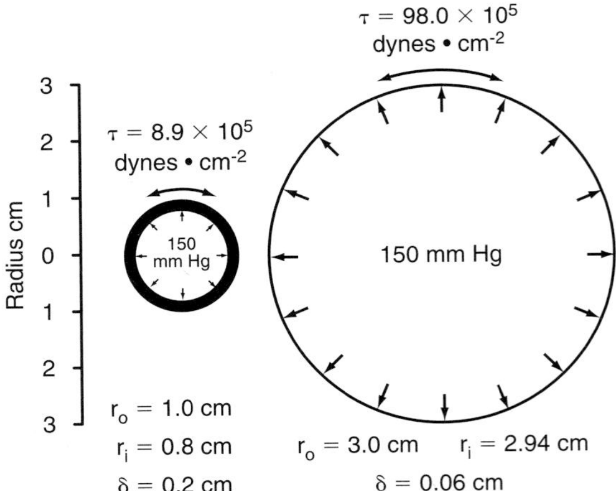

FIGURE 9-28 End-on view of a cylinder 2 cm in diameter before and after expansion to a diameter of 6 cm. Wall area remains the same in the two cases, but wall stress (τ) is greatly increased owing both to the decrease in wall thickness (δ) and to the increase in inside radius (r_i).

to concave inward in the vicinity of the aneurysm–normal artery junction. These points appear to be sites of maximal stress in asymmetric aneurysms.

In normal arteries, most of the wall stress imposed by intraluminal pressure is sustained by elastin. It has been suggested that aneurysm formation may be related to degeneration of elastic lamellae caused by atherosclerosis or the action of endogenous elastases.[41,206,208] Inflammatory cells may also participate in this process, perhaps by serving as a source of elastases.[4] Rupture, however, is prevented by collagen fibers, which are principally responsible for the integrity of the arterial wall.[41] Although the tensile strength of collagen (about 5 to 7×10^7 dynes $\cdot$ cm^{-2}) far exceeds the wall stress developed in the dilated tube shown in Figure 9-28, it must be pointed out that collagen fibers make up only about 25% of the atherosclerotic arterial wall and only 6% to 18% of the aneurysm wall.[175,180] Therefore, one would predict that each collagen fiber sustains a greater load than would be expected if the entire wall were composed of collagen. In addition, the aneurysm wall is weakened by fragmentation and other degenerative changes within the fibrous network. (Collagenase activity may play an important role in this process.[20]) On the basis of these considerations, it is not difficult to imagine how an atherosclerotic artery that has become aneurysmal might rupture. Not only is the wall stress greatly increased but also the collagen fibers are more sparsely distributed, more disorganized, and more fragmented.

■ VENOUS HEMODYNAMICS

Venous physiology is, in many respects, more complex than arterial physiology. Veins differ from arteries in a number of ways; veins (1) have thinner walls, (2) are collapsible, and (3) contain valves that are oriented to ensure unidirectional flow. There are two large venous systems, superficial and deep, which are connected at intervals by "perforating" or "communicating" veins. The *deep veins* run parallel with the arteries of the same name; the *superficial veins* and the *saccular veins* (sinusoids) within the calf muscles have no arterial counterparts.

The deep veins are larger in diameter than their accompanying arteries and in the periphery are usually duplicated. Although veins are seldom completely full and distended, they contain about two thirds of the blood in the body. At corresponding anatomic locations, venous blood pressure is always lower than arterial blood pressure. In veins, the hydrostatic component of the total blood pressure is often proportionately larger than the dynamic component—the opposite of the situation normally prevailing in arteries. Unlike blood flow in arteries, which is pulsatile but relatively constant from one cardiac cycle to the next, blood flow in veins fluctuates with respiration and muscle activity and may cease altogether for brief periods.

Basic Hemodynamics

In order to understand pressure-flow phenomena in veins, it is useful to review the effects of gravity on venous pressure, venous pressure-volume relationships, and the peculiarities associated with flow through collapsible tubes.

Venous Pressure

As discussed in the first part of this chapter, venous pressure is composed of dynamic pressure produced by contraction of the left ventricle, hydrostatic pressure produced by the weight of the column of blood, and static filling pressure related to the elasticity of the vascular wall. Because a large portion of the fluid energy has been dissipated in the arterioles and capillaries, the dynamic component is relatively low, hovering around 15 to 20 mm Hg in the venules and falling to 0 to 6 mm Hg in the right atrium. Consequently, in any position other than horizontal, hydrostatic pressure may greatly exceed dynamic pressure. For practical purposes, we can estimate hydrostatic pressure at any point by measuring the distance from that point to the right atrium (see Eq. 9.1).

For example, in an individual 6 feet tall (ankle-to-atrium distance of 131 cm), venous pressure at the ankle would be increased by 102 mm Hg in the standing position (Fig. 9-29). If the pressure in the ankle veins were 15 mm Hg in a supine position, it would be 15 + 102 = 117 mm Hg in the standing position. The intra-arterial pressure would rise by a similar amount. Static filling pressure is so low (only a few mm Hg) that it can be neglected.

Because of the increased intravenous pressure, dependent veins dilate, allowing blood to accumulate in the veins of the leg. When a typical individual is tilted from a supine to a standing position, about 250 mL of blood is shifted to each leg.[337] This shift might produce syncope were it not for the effect of the muscle pump mechanism that ordinarily is operative in the upright position. Active venous constriction does not occur as a reflex response to orthostasis.[341]

At wrist level in the raised arm of an upright individual, the hydrostatic component would be decreased by about 50 mm Hg. If venous pressure at the wrist were 15 mm Hg in the supine position, the pressure at wrist level might be expected to fall below atmospheric pressure:

$$15 \text{ mm Hg} - 50 \text{ mm Hg} = -35 \text{ mm Hg} \qquad (9.28)$$

Obviously, this is impossible, because the combined effect of the tissue pressure (5 mm Hg) and the atmospheric pressure would collapse the veins. Thus, venous pressure in a portion of the body above the heart cannot fall below tissue pressure (see Fig. 9-29).

Venous Pressure-Volume Relationships

Because veins are collapsible tubes, a great variation in venous capacity is possible with little change in venous pressure—a property that adapts veins to their unique role as the major storage facility for blood.

Transmural pressure is the difference in pressure between the intraluminal pressure acting to expand the vein and the tissue pressure acting from the outside to collapse the vein. When venous transmural pressure is increased from 0 to 15 mm Hg, the volume of the vein may increase by more than 250%.[316] This vast change in volume is due largely to the fact that the cross-section of the venous lumen, which is elliptical at low transmural pressures, becomes circular at higher transmural pressures (Fig. 9-30). Little increase in pressure is required to convert a low-volume

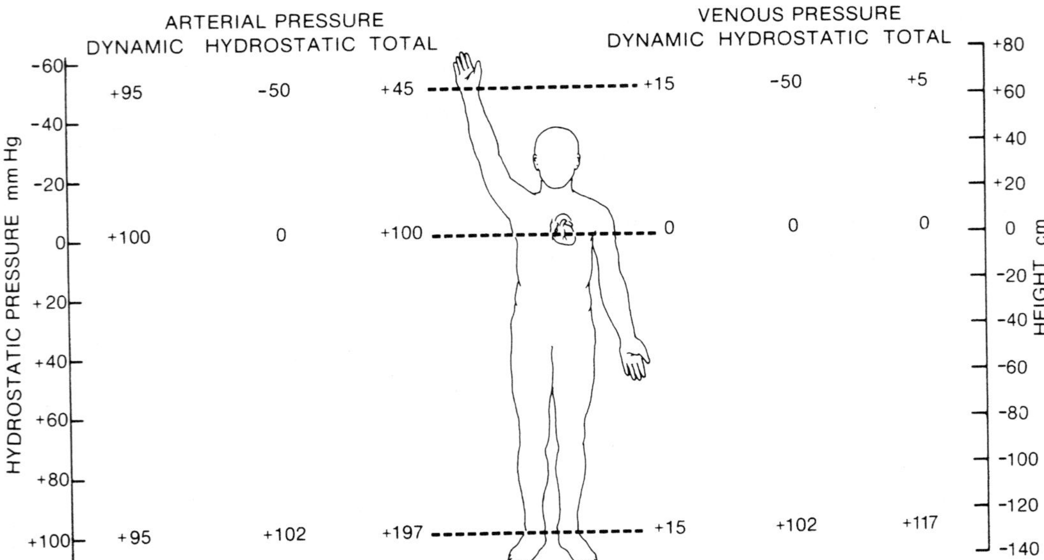

FIGURE 9-29 Effect of standing position on venous and arterial pressures. Zero pressure is at the level of the right atrium. Dynamic pressure represents that produced by the contraction of the left ventricle. If the subject were horizontal, the total intravascular pressure would closely approximate the dynamic pressure because there would be little hydrostatic effect.

elliptical tube into a high-volume circular tube, but much more pressure is required to stretch the venous wall once the circular configuration has been reached. In fact, veins are as stiff as arteries when subjected to arterial pressure (Fig. 9-31).[236,306,316,355]

Venous Blood Flow

Like fluid in all hydraulic systems, blood in the veins is propelled from one point to another by an energy gradient and is impeded by multiple factors that constitute resistance to flow. According to Bernoulli's principle, total fluid energy at any point in the venous system consists of the sum of (1) the hydrostatic pressure, (2) the gravitational potential energy, (3) the kinetic energy, and (4) the dynamic pressure produced by contraction of the left ventricle and the surrounding skeletal muscles (see Eq. 9.4).

Because hydrostatic pressure and gravitational potential energy are equivalent but have opposite signs, they usually cancel each other; therefore, for most purposes, it is sufficient to regard dynamic pressure as the driving force. For example, in the upright individual pictured in Figure 9-29, the energy gradient returning blood from the ankle to the heart is 15 mm Hg (the dynamic pressure gradient), not 117 mm Hg (the sum of the hydrostatic and dynamic pressures at the ankle). The situation is somewhat different in the raised arm. At wrist level, the pressure is only 5 mm Hg (the minimal value necessary to prevent collapse by tissue pressure), but the gradient returning blood to the heart is equivalent to about 50 mm Hg because of the positive gravitational potential energy. Thus, blood in the elevated arm essentially "falls" back to the heart. As explained later, a similar situation prevails in the legs when venous valves are incompetent.

Although veins are commonly considered to be low-resistance conduits, the energy gradient from the venules to the right atrium is equal to that from the left ventricle to the arterioles (≈15 mm Hg). Because veins transport the same amount of blood as arteries and have a potential cross-sectional area three or four times as large, this fact seems

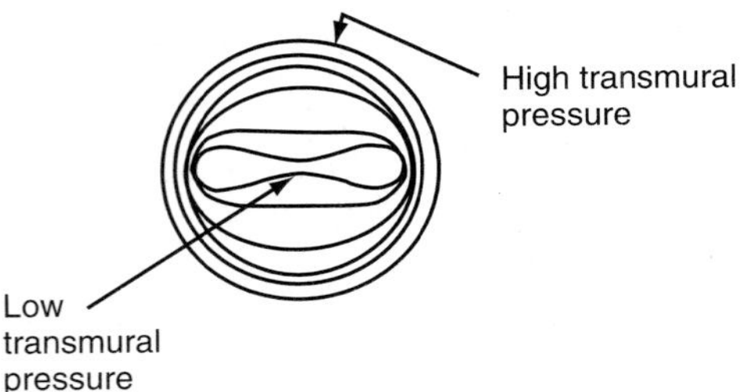

FIGURE 9-30 Cross-section of venous lumen at various transmural pressures. At low pressure, the wall collapses into an elliptical configuration; at higher pressures, it becomes circular. Note that the wall also stretches with rising pressure. (Adapted from Moreno AH, Katz AI, Gold LD, Reddy RV: Mechanics of distention of dog veins and other thin-walled tubular structures. Circ Res 27:1069, 1970. By permission of the American Heart Association, Inc.)

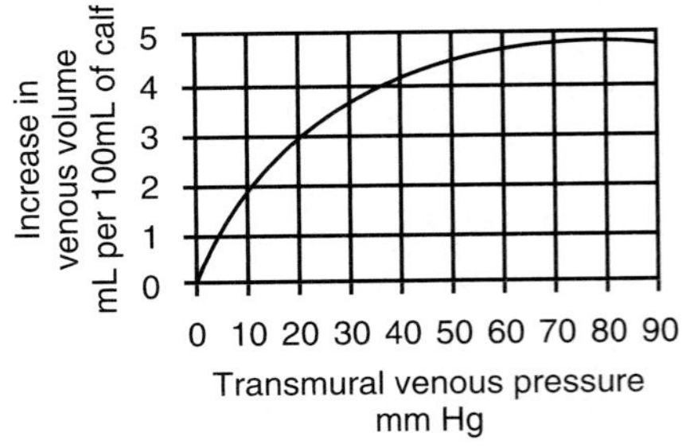

FIGURE 9-31 Relationship of venous volume to transmural pressure. Veins are very compliant at low pressure but are quite stiff at high pressure.

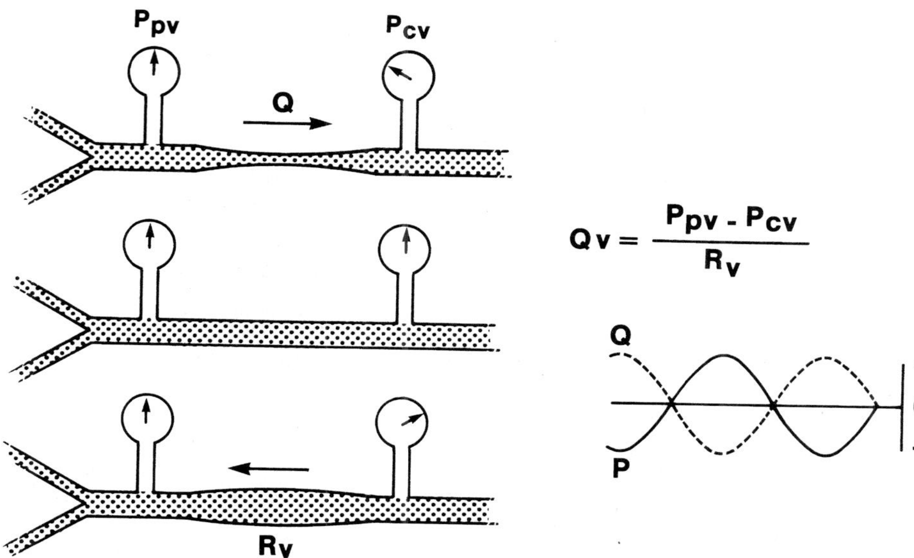

FIGURE 9-32 Relationship of flow (Q_v) in a venous segment to venous resistance (R_v), peripheral venous pressure (P_{pv}), and central venous pressure (P_{cv}). As flow increases, the vein collapses and pressure (P) in the midportion of the venous segment decreases. As flow decreases, the opposite occurs: Pressure increases and the vein expands. Increasing pressure is indicated by a clockwise movement of the arrows on the meters. (From Sumner DS: Applied physiology in venous problems. In Bergan JJ, Yao JST [eds]: Surgery of the Veins. Orlando, Grune & Stratton, 1985, p 3.)

somewhat incongruous. Veins, however, are seldom completely distended. The elliptical cross-section assumed in their usual, partially collapsed state offers far more resistance than that dictated by a circular cross-section. As veins distend, their resistance falls markedly, allowing increases in blood flow to be accommodated with little increase in the energy gradient.

In the arterial system, pressure, vascular volume, and flow usually change in the same direction. In veins, the opposite commonly occurs; venous pressure and venous volume may decrease as flow increases and may increase as flow decreases or reverses (Fig. 9-32). This apparent paradox is explained by the fact that in the resting state, peripheral venous pressure (P_{pv}) tends to remain relatively constant, whereas central venous pressure (P_{cv}) fluctuates. When central venous pressure falls, the pressure gradient across the intervening segment increases and—provided that the venous resistance (R_v) does not change appreciably—flow (Q_v) increases. At the same time, pressure in the venous segment, which must lie somewhere between peripheral and central pressures, falls. Because venous volume is a function of venous pressure, the volume of the segment also falls. In contrast, when central venous pressure rises, pressure and volume increase while flow ceases or reverses. During exercise, however, contraction of the skeletal muscles momentarily raises peripheral pressure, and venous flow, pressure, and volume are augmented simultaneously.

Effect of Cardiac Contraction

The mechanism just described explains how venous flow and pressure are influenced by events occurring in the right side of the heart during the various phases of the cardiac cycle. As shown in Figure 9-33, contraction of the right atrium elevates central venous pressure and causes a transient reversal of venous blood flow. During ventricular systole, the atrium relaxes, venous flow increases, and venous pressure falls. Flow then decreases during diastole until the pressure differential across the tricuspid valve causes the valve to open. At this point, there is again a brief increase in flow, which is followed by a gradual decline to zero.

Although these cardiac cycle–induced flow and pressure pulsations are most easily perceived in the jugular veins, they may be detected with the Doppler flowmeter in the arm veins of resting subjects (Fig. 9-34). Cardiac pulsations are less evident in leg veins, where they tend to be obscured by the large fluctuations in flow produced by respiratory activity. In cases of congestive heart failure, the increased central venous pressure overcomes the respiratory effects, and cardiac pulsations become a prominent feature of the venous flow pattern in the lower extremities.

Flow Through Collapsible Tubes

The collapsible nature of the venous wall is responsible for a peculiar pressure-flow relationship unique to the venous system.[272,283,307,308] These relationships are clarified by the model illustrated in Figure 9-35A. In this figure, the energy (15 cm H_2O) driving blood back to the heart is represented by an elevated fluid reservoir. The collapsible tube passes through a closed container that has a certain pressure, in this case, 5 cm H_2O. The end of the tube, representing the right atrium, is open to the atmosphere at baseline level, giving an outflow pressure of zero.

For the tube to open enough to permit fluid to flow through the system, pressure in the collapsible tube must rise until it slightly exceeds that within the closed container. Thus, flow through the tube depends on the gradient 15 cm H_2O – 5 cm H_2O = 10 cm H_2O rather than on the gradient across the entire length of the tube (15 cm H_2O). It is evident that elevating the driving pressure linearly increases the pressure gradient and, within limits, has the same effect on flow (Fig. 9-35B). On the other hand, changes in outflow pressure have no effect on flow unless the outflow pressure rises above the pressure in the closed container, at which point the collapsible tube remains distended (Fig. 9-35C). Further rises in outflow pressure reduce the pressure gradient (which now depends on the difference between the driving pressure and the outflow pressure). As a result, flow through the system decreases as the outflow pressure rises above the pressure in the closed container. Clearly, raising the pressure within the container, while the driving and

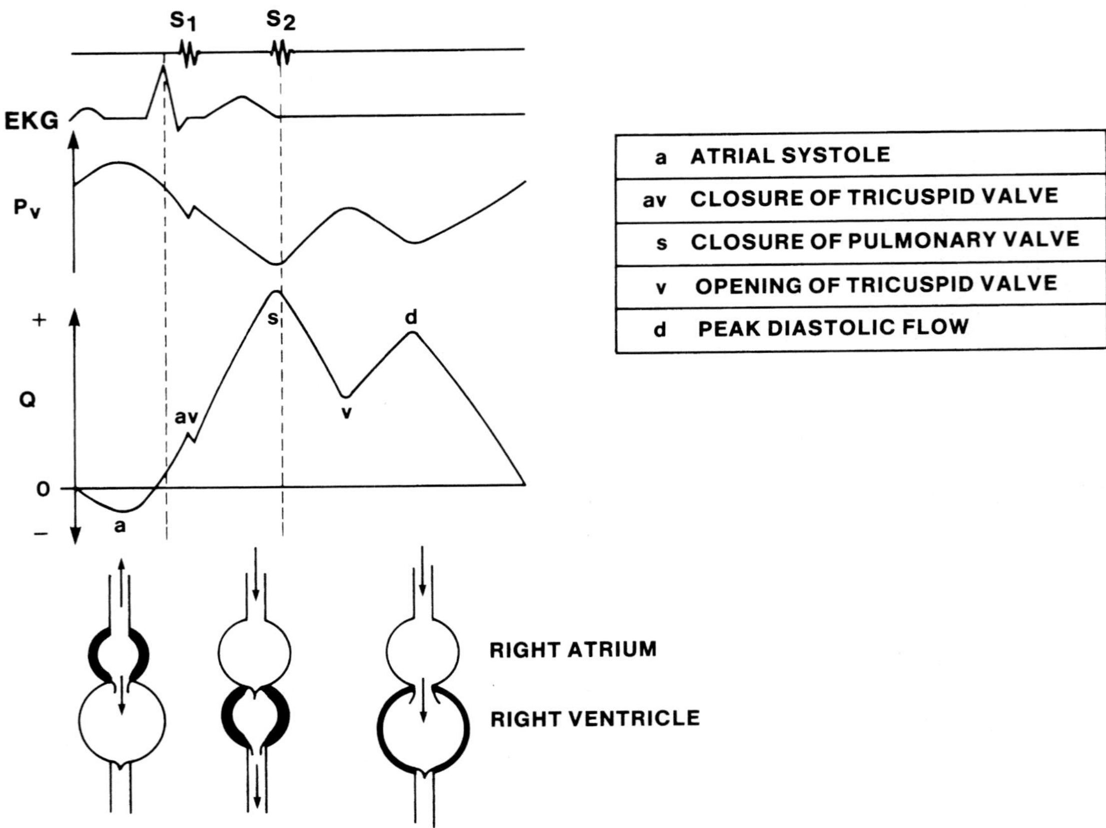

FIGURE 9-33 Effect of cardiac contraction on venous pressure (P_v) and venous blood flow (Q). *Vertical dashed lines* define the period of ventricular systole. First and second heart sounds are indicated by S_1 and S_2, respectively. EKG, electrocardiogram. (From Sumner DS: Applied physiology in venous problems. In Bergan JJ, Yao JST [eds]: Surgery of the Veins. Orlando, Grune & Stratton, 1985, p 3.)

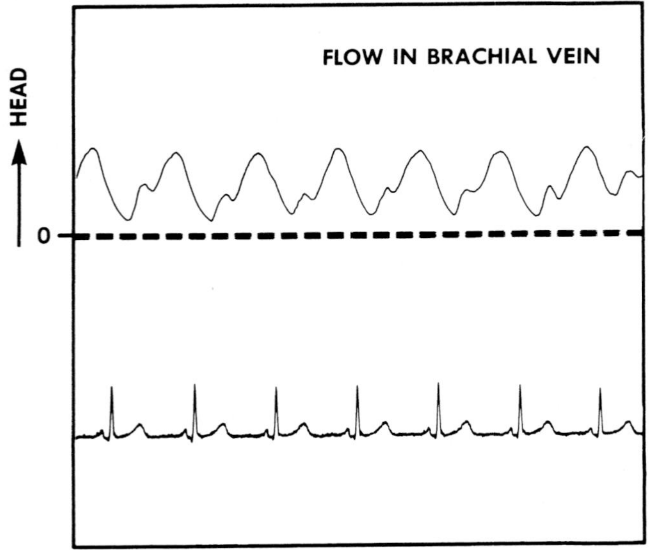

FIGURE 9-34 Doppler recordings of flow in a brachial vein demonstrating pulsations imposed by cardiac contraction. (From Sumner DS: Noninvasive vascular laboratory assessment. In Machleder HI [ed]: Vascular Disorders of the Upper Extremity, 3rd ed. Armonk, NY, Futura, 1998, p 15.)

outflow pressures are maintained at constant levels, decreases flow (Fig. 9-35D).

Effect of Respiration

Respiration has a major effect on patterns of venous flow. In a supine subject, the abdominal cavity corresponds to the "closed container" through which the collapsible inferior vena cava must pass (Fig. 9-36). Thus, the pressure gradient driving blood centrally from the legs is the venous pressure in the legs minus the intra-abdominal pressure. When the subject inspires, the diaphragm descends, thereby increasing intra-abdominal pressure. This has the effect of decreasing the pressure gradient and of reducing blood flow during inspiration. Often the rise in abdominal pressure is sufficient to cause venous outflow from the legs to cease momentarily. During expiration, the diaphragm relaxes, intra-abdominal pressure falls, the inferior vena cava expands, and blood trapped in the leg veins flows cephalad into the abdomen. These patterns are so consistent that they constitute an important indicator of normal venous flow.[356]

When flow from the upper extremities or the head and neck is considered, the high-pressure "closed container" becomes the extrathoracic tissue pressure, and the "outflow" becomes the intrathoracic venous pressure (see Fig. 9-36).

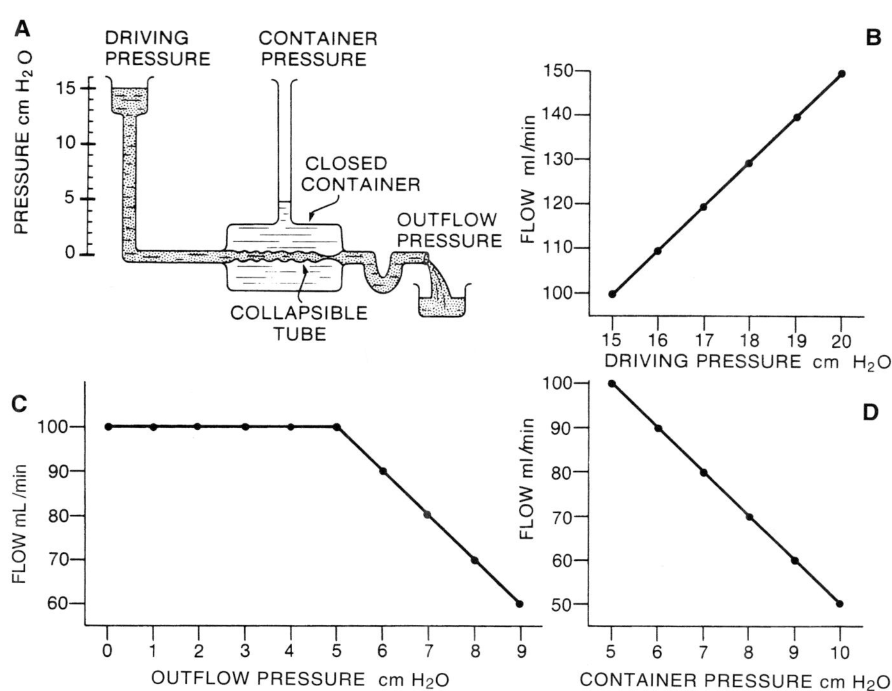

FIGURE 9-35 **A,** Model illustrating "collapsible tube" phenomenon. **B,** Effect of elevating the driving pressure while keeping container pressure and outflow pressure constant. **C,** Effect of elevating outflow pressure while keeping driving pressure and container pressure constant. **D,** Effect of elevating container pressure while keeping driving pressure and outflow pressure constant.

Because the latter ordinarily is lower than the former, respiratory movements have relatively less effect on outflow from the arms and cephalic regions. In general, venous flow *increases* during *inspiration* as the intrathoracic pressure falls and *decreases* during *expiration* as the pressure rises.

As one would predict from the closed container model (see Fig. 9-35), peripheral venous pressures do not reflect the central venous pressure accurately unless the latter is elevated. In cases of congestive heart failure, tricuspid insufficiency, or pulmonary hypertension, central venous pressures rise above tissue pressures and even above abdominal pressures, permitting events on the right side of the heart to be reflected in the peripheral venous flow pattern. As previously discussed, conditions that cause elevated central venous pressure result in a pulsatile flow pattern far distally in the veins of both the upper and the lower extremities.

Venous Function

The primary and most obvious function of the venous system is to return blood to the heart from the capillary beds. In addition, veins play the predominant role in regulating vascular capacity. They also serve as a part of the peripheral pump mechanism, which assists the heart in the transport of blood during exercise. Together with the capillaries, veins contribute to the thermoregulatory system of the body. These vital functions all depend on certain peculiarities of venous anatomy and wall structure and on the presence of venous valves.

Anatomy and Wall Structure

Superficial veins are relatively thick-walled, muscular vessels that lie just under the skin. Among the superficial veins are the greater and lesser saphenous veins of the leg, the cephalic and basilic veins of the arm, and the external jugular veins of the neck. The deep veins are thin-walled and less muscular. They accompany arteries—often as venae comitantes—and bear the same names as the arteries they parallel. The cross-sectional area of these veins is roughly three times that of the adjacent arteries.[257]

Within the skeletal muscles are large, very thin-walled veins sometimes referred to as *sinusoids.* As part of the

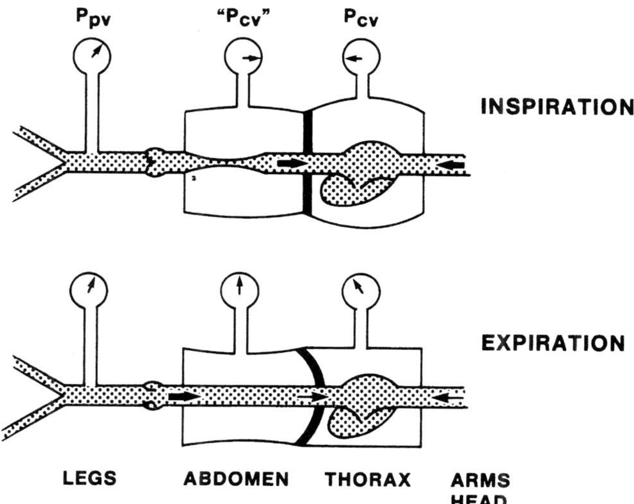

FIGURE 9-36 Effect of respiration on venous blood from the lower extremity, upper abdomen, and brachiocephalic area. Intra-abdominal pressure ("P_{cv}") increases during inspiration and decreases during expiration. P_{cv}, central venous pressure; P_{pv}, peripheral venous pressure. (From Sumner DS: Applied physiology in venous problems. In Bergan JJ, Yao JST [eds]: Surgery of the Veins. Orlando, Grune & Stratton, 1985, p 3.)

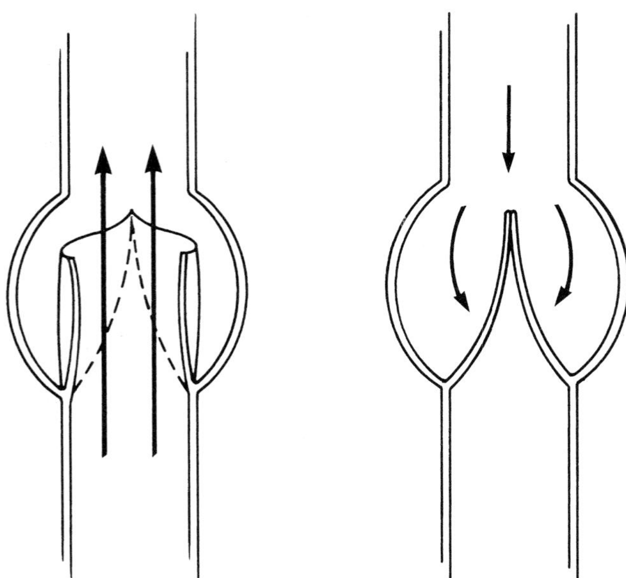

FIGURE 9-37 Representation of a longitudinal section through a venous valve, demonstrating the role of sinuses in facilitating opening and closing of valve cusps. (From Sumner DS: Applied physiology in venous problems. In Bergan JJ, Yao JST [eds]: Surgery of the Veins. Orlando, Grune & Stratton, 1985, p 3.)

"bellows" of the muscle pump mechanism, these vessels serve a particularly important function during exercise. The soleal sinusoids empty into the posterior tibial and peroneal veins, and the gastrocnemius sinusoids usually drain into the popliteal vein.

In addition to the previously described components of the venous system, *perforating veins* connect the deep and superficial systems. Of particular interest to the surgeon are a series of about six medial calf perforators that join the posterior tibial vein to the greater saphenous system through a network of superficial veins known as the "posterior arch vein."[349] Other perforators connect the peroneal vein with superficial tributaries of the saphenous vein. Posteriorly, a series of small perforating veins connects the superficial system with the intramuscular veins; these in turn are united at various levels with the posterior tibial vein. Thus, an indirect connection between the superficial and deep systems is provided via the large intramuscular veins.

Perhaps the most important anatomic feature of veins is the presence of *valves* (Fig. 9-37). Each of these delicate but extremely strong bicuspid structures lies at the base of a segment of vein that is expanded into a sinus. This arrangement permits the valves to open widely without coming into contact with the wall, thus permitting rapid closure when flow begins to reverse (within 0.5 second).[311,366]

There are approximately 9 to 11 valves in the anterior tibial vein, 9 to 19 in the posterior tibial vein, 7 in the peroneal vein, 1 in the popliteal vein, and 3 in the superficial femoral vein. In two thirds of the femoral veins, a valve is present at the upper end within 1 cm of the inguinal ligament. About one quarter of the external iliac veins and one tenth of the internal iliac veins have a valve.[297] The common iliac vein usually has no valves. Superficial veins have fewer valves, approximately 7 to 9 in the greater and lesser saphenous veins.[242,275,303] Valves are present in venules as small as 0.15 mm in diameter.

In all areas of the legs and arms, valve cusps are oriented to direct flow centrally and to prevent reflux. Although the classic teaching is that valves in perforating veins permit blood to flow only from the superficial to the deep venous system, studies have suggested that outward flow occurs in about one fifth of normal limbs under certain conditions.[342] There is also some controversy about the direction of flow in the perforating veins of the foot. Although previous investigators maintained that the foot is unique, in that flow is directed from the deep to the superficial veins,[286,291] studies by Koslow and DeWeese[290] have suggested that the direction is consistent with that in other segments of the leg (i.e., from superficial to deep).

During the course of the day, there may be some deterioration in valve function, even in normal extremities. About one fifth of otherwise normal legs show evidence of venous reflux after 5 or more hours of upright activity, presumably as a result of venous distention, which renders the valves partially incompetent.[243]

Muscle Pump

The return of blood from the legs to the heart against the force of gravity is facilitated by the calf muscle pump mechanism. The muscles of the leg act as the power source, and the veins act as the bellows. Although the superficial veins participate, the deep veins and the intramuscular sinusoids play the major role. The presence of competent valves is necessary to ensure that the pump functions efficiently.

When a person with normal leg veins shifts from a horizontal to a vertical position, blood stored in the abdominal and pelvic veins is prevented from "falling" down the leg (in accordance with the gravitational potential energy gradient) by the rapid closure of functioning valves.[358] Capillary inflow gradually fills the calf veins over 70 to 170 seconds until the hydrostatic pressure and gravitational potential energy levels cancel out.[254,374] From this point on, the dynamic pressure differential again forces blood to flow upward out of the leg. Thus, in the motionless, upright subject, veins simply collect blood from capillaries and transport it passively to the heart, with the energy being supplied totally by left ventricular contraction. Because the venous valves are all open, the column of blood in the veins extends uninterrupted to the right atrium, and the venous pressure at any level equals the sum of the dynamic and hydrostatic pressures (Fig. 9-38A). The volume of blood accumulated depends on the total venous pressure and the compliance of the calf veins.

During exercise, skeletal muscle contraction compresses the intramuscular and surrounding veins, raises venous pressure, and forces blood cephalad toward the heart. Closure of valves below the site of compression prevents retrograde flow (Fig. 9-38B). On relaxation, the pressure gradient reverses; the valves above the site of compression close, precluding reflux, and the veins remain partially collapsed until they are refilled by inflow from the capillaries. Blood in the partially empty veins is now segregated into short compartments a few centimeters long, within which pressure is diminished in accordance with the venous pressure-volume compliance curve (see Figs. 9-31 and 9-38C).[319,332,358]

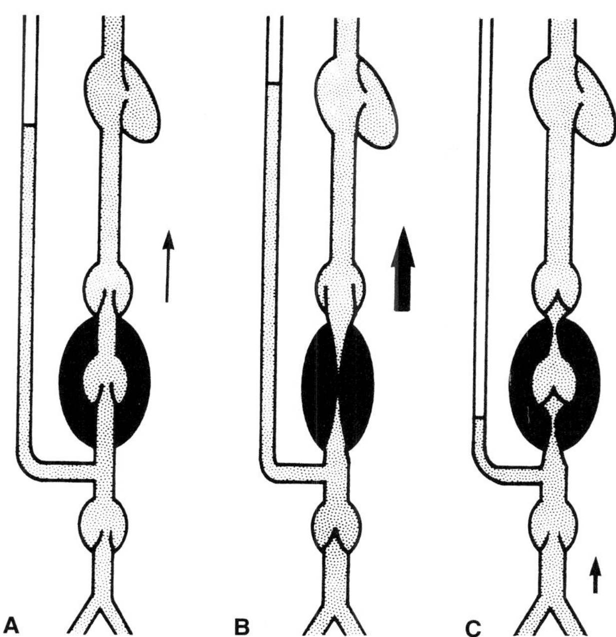

FIGURE 9-38 Operation of the muscle pump. **A,** Resting. **B,** Muscle contraction. **C,** Muscle relaxation. Venous pressure in the distal leg is indicated by the length of the hydrostatic column. (From Sumner DS: Applied physiology in venous disease. In Sakaguchi S [ed]: Advances in Phlebology. London, John Libbey and Company, 1987, p 5.)

(This segregation is seldom visible phlebographically because veins, even at the upper end of each compartment, remain partially filled.) Figure 9-38C presents an exaggerated picture to emphasize the reduction in venous pressure.

After a few strong muscular contractions (as in walking or running), venous pressure at the ankle or foot falls to very low levels in normal limbs, often less than 20 mm Hg (Fig. 9-39).[281,282,328,354,355] The level reached during exercise is commonly referred to as the *ambulatory venous pressure.*

Valves at the top of each segregated compartment remain closed until the venous pressure just below the valve rises to exceed the pressure at the lower end of the compartment immediately above.[358] Thus, the pressure at the lower end of each compartment usually exceeds the length of the hydrostatic column defined by valve closure.[332] With continued venous refilling, the hydrostatic column is re-established all the way to the heart.

The muscle pump mechanism is most highly developed in the calf, where the voluminous soleal and gastrocnemial sinusoids compose the major part of the bellows. Contraction of the calf muscles generates extravascular pressures ranging from 40 to 200 mm Hg.[229,302,303] This produces an equivalent reduction in venous transmural pressure and displaces blood from the compressed venous sinusoids in accordance with the venous volume–transmural pressure compliance curve (see Fig. 9-31).[358] Because of the strong fascial investment of the calf muscles, the intermuscular veins (posterior tibial, anterior tibial, and peroneal) are subjected to similar pressures. Much of the force is also transmitted to the surrounding superficial veins through the connective tissues. Thus, all the veins of the lower leg—both superficial and deep—participate to a greater or lesser extent in the pumping action. All transmit blood centrally with each muscular contraction (Fig. 9-40).[354]

Although pressure in the deep veins exceeds that in the superficial veins during muscle contraction, valves in the perforating veins prevent flow from the deep to the superficial system.[235] (As previously noted, there may be exceptions to this rule.[342]) Valves also prevent the distal displacement of blood toward the foot in the tibial veins. When the muscles relax, the venous sinusoids are refilled by capillary inflow and by flow from the distal deep veins of the leg. Some inflow from superficial to deep veins also occurs, but the magnitude of this flow is less than formerly thought (see Fig. 9-40).[230,354,355]

Studies suggest that the upward flow of blood in the leg may be initiated by compression of the plantar plexus of veins lying between the deep and superficial intrinsic muscles of the foot. This blood is discharged into the deep veins of the calf, thus priming the muscle pump.[290] The events during normal walking are synchronized in the following order[273]:

1. Dorsiflexion of the foot empties the distal calf veins.
2. Weight bearing empties the foot.
3. Plantar flexion empties the proximal calf veins.

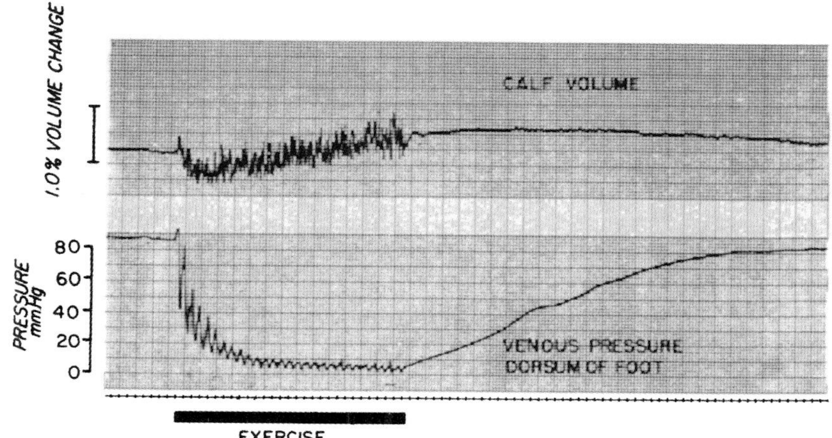

FIGURE 9-39 Effect of exercise on venous pressure at foot level in a subject 5 feet, 8 inches tall. (From Strandness DE Jr, Sumner DS: Hemodynamics for Surgeons. New York, Grune & Stratton, 1975.)

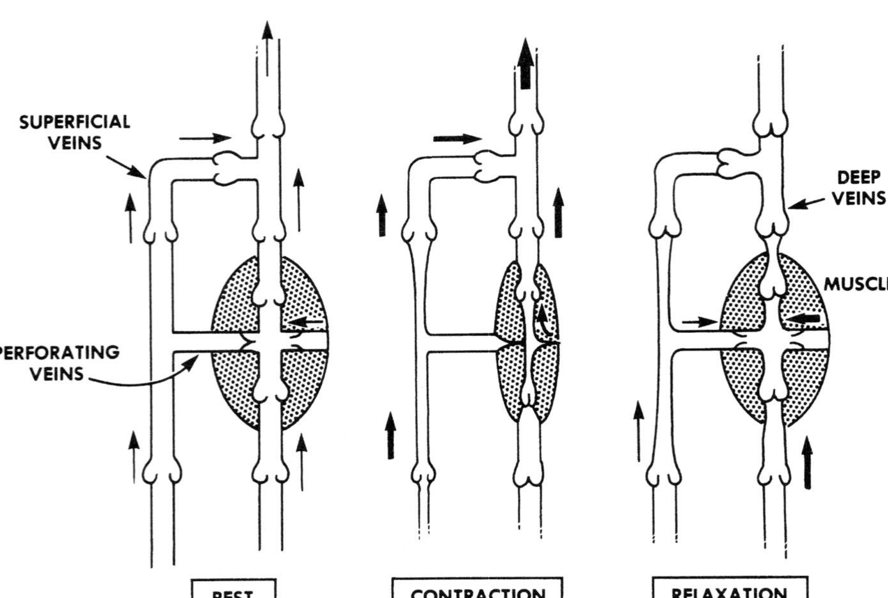

FIGURE 9-40 Dynamics of venous blood flow in response to calf muscle contraction in a normal limb. (From Sumner DS: Venous dynamics—varicosities. Clin Obstet Gynecol 24:743, 1981.)

Effects of Venous Pressure Reduction

Reduction of venous pressure facilitates flow through the capillary bed of exercising muscles in the following manner: total pressure in peripheral arteries equals the sum of hydrostatic pressure and pressure generated by left ventricle.

For example, at the arteriolar end of a calf muscle capillary, the total pressure might be 102 mm Hg (hydrostatic pressure) plus 95 mm Hg (mean dynamic pressure), or 197 mm Hg (see Fig. 9-29). During quiet standing, the venous pressure would be 102 mm Hg (hydrostatic pressure) plus 15 mm Hg (dynamic pressure), or 117 mm Hg. This gives a pressure gradient across the muscle arterioles and capillaries of 197 − 117, or 80 mm Hg. With muscle contraction, however, the venous pressure is reduced to 20 mm Hg or less. Under these circumstances, the pressure gradient rises to 197 − 20, or 177 mm Hg. Together with the reduction in arteriolar resistance that accompanies exercise, this simple method of increasing the pressure gradient affords a remarkably effective way of augmenting muscle perfusion. Indeed, as much as 30% of the energy required to circulate blood during strenuous exercise may be furnished by the muscle pump, which in a sense acts as a "peripheral heart."[354]

Aside from augmenting blood flow to exercising muscles, the muscle pump, by reducing venous pressure, acts to decrease the volume of blood sequestered in dependent parts of the body. By translocating blood from the peripheral to the central veins, the muscle pump also serves to enhance cardiac function, particularly during exercise.

In addition, reduction of venous pressure decreases the rate of edema formation in the dependent parts of the lower extremities. According to the *Starling concept* (Starling equilibrium), most of the fluid escaping from the arteriolar end of a capillary is returned to the circulation at the venular end (Fig. 9-41).[245,295,353,360] Any excess is removed by lymphatics. The forces acting to drive fluid out of the capillary are the capillary pressure, P_c, and the osmotic pressure of the interstitial fluid, π_{IF}. Acting to return fluid to the circulation are the interstitial fluid pressure, P_{IF}, and the osmotic pressure of the blood, π_c. Therefore, the net pressure, P, moving fluid out of the capillary, is:

$$P = P_c + \pi_{IF} - P_{IF} - \pi_c \tag{9.29}$$

As shown in Figure 9-41, the mean capillary pressure of +25 mm Hg is exactly balanced by the sum of the other pressures:*

$$\pi_{IF} - P_{IF} - \pi_c = +5 - 5 - 25 = -25 \text{ mm Hg} \tag{9.30}$$

Thus, in the supine position, there is little or no net pressure gradient across the capillary wall; however, this equilibrium is disturbed in the dependent parts of an upright individual. For example, if the mean capillary pressure, P_c, is assumed to be 25 mm Hg at ankle level in a supine subject, it would rise to about 127 mm Hg (25 + 102) in the standing subject

*The magnitude of the interstitial fluid pressure (P_{IF}) has been the subject of considerable debate.[245,360] Although originally P_{IF} was thought to range between +1 and +5 mm Hg, most current evidence suggests that it is actually subatmospheric, on the order of −2 to −7 mm Hg. Substituting these negative values for P_{IF} in Equation 9.29 gives a value of +13 to +18 for the intravascular pressure at the midpoint of the capillary (P_c). Thus, some of the numbers in Figure 9-41 and in the accompanying text are changed; however, the basic concepts of transcapillary fluid exchange remain the same.

Total tissue pressure is the sum of the interstitial fluid pressure and the "solid tissue pressure" that is exerted by collagen and ground substance. If the structural elements responsible for solid tissue pressure are compressed, the solid tissue pressure is positive. Consequently, total tissue pressure commonly ranges between +1 and +5 mm Hg. It is this total tissue pressure that determines the transmural pressure across the capillaries and veins. Total tissue pressure and interstitial fluid pressure become equal when edema develops.

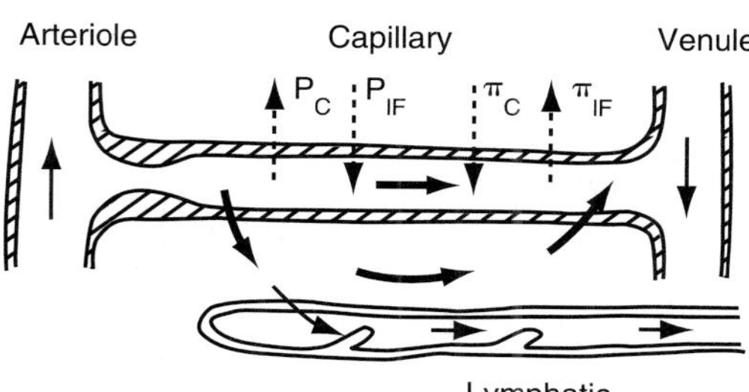

Pressures (mm Hg)

	Arteriolar	Mean capillary	Venular
P_C	35	25	15
P_{IF}	5	5	5
π_C	25	25	25
π_{IF}	5	5	5
P	+10	0	−10

FIGURE 9-41 Fluid exchange in the capillary bed. *Solid arrows* indicate the direction of fluid flow. *Dashed arrows* show the direction of pressure gradients. P, net pressure; P_c, capillary pressure; P_{IF}, interstitial fluid pressure; π_C, osmotic pressure of blood; π_{IF}, osmotic pressure of interstitial fluid. (From Strandness DE Jr, Sumner DS: Hemodynamics for Surgeons. New York, Grune & Stratton, 1975.)

(see Fig. 9-29). This creates a pressure gradient of 127 – 25 = 102 mm Hg across the capillary wall and encourages the outflow of fluid into the interstitial spaces. The escape of fluid continues until interstitial pressure, P_{IF}, rises sufficiently to balance the high intracapillary pressure. (The rate of fluid transfer is controlled by capillary surface area and permeability.[309]) Because the interstitial tissues are remarkably compliant at low interstitial fluid pressures, a great deal of edema fluid must accumulate before a new equilibrium can be established.[276,360]

Fortunately, if venous valvular function is normal, slight to moderate calf muscle activity markedly reduces venous pressure. In turn, mean capillary pressure falls and the rate of edema formation decreases. Together with arteriolar constriction, which occurs in response to standing, this mechanism keeps edema formation to a minimum.

In summary, the muscle pump serves several important functions:

- Assists the heart in circulating blood during exercise
- Increases central blood volume
- Relieves venous congestion in the legs
- Decreases peripheral edema
- Facilitates flow through exercising muscles

Although these are not vital functions, their absence creates significant disability.

Control of Venous Capacity

About two thirds of the blood in the body is contained within the venous system. Even so, the total potential venous volume is far from filled. This means that some veins are always partially or completely collapsed. In a state of partial collapse, great fluctuations in venous volume are possible with little change in transmural pressure. Such flexibility allows the normal venous reservoir to accept transfusions, intravenous fluids, and blood loss over wide ranges without appreciable changes in the central venous pressure. Only when venous pressures are high and veins are filled does excess fluid result in large rises in central venous pressure. Similarly, a nearly empty system may be critically sensitive to sudden blood loss.

Venous capacity is affected not only by fluctuations in transmural pressure but also by the contractile state of the smooth muscle in the venous wall. When transmural pressures are low and veins have collapsed into an elliptical cross-section, venomotor tone has little effect on venous capacity; however, when veins are filled sufficiently to assume a circular cross-section, venomotor tone plays an important role in regulating venous volume.[324]

Unlike arterioles, which are very sensitive to the local chemical environment, venules and veins are controlled almost exclusively by sympathetic adrenergic activity. In addition, unlike the resting tone of arterioles and arteries, which are almost always partially constricted, the resting tone of veins is minimal under comfortable environmental conditions. Veins within skeletal muscles are devoid of sympathetic innervation, and cutaneous veins are primarily thermoregulatory.[305,371] Peripheral veins contract more intensely to sympathetic stimuli than the more centrally located veins.

As a rule, veins constrict in response to stimuli that cause an increase in cardiac output.[347] Simultaneously, there usually is a decrease in total peripheral resistance. Because the systemic resistance to blood flow is largely controlled by arterioles, wall tension in veins must increase in conjunction with a decrease in arteriolar tone. Often this disparity of action is related to the vasodilator effect of the local chemical environment on the arterioles that overpowers the systemic adrenergic activity, but sometimes, adrenergic activity is directly responsible for simultaneous arteriolar constriction and dilatation of the capacitance vessels.[249]

Among the stimuli known to produce venous constriction are pain, emotion, hyperventilation, deep breathing, the Valsalva maneuver, and muscular exercise.[348] The decrease in venous volume that occurs after a deep breath provides a convenient method for assessing the integrity of the sympathetic nerve supply to an extremity. As shown in Chapter 90, Figure 90-7, the volume of a finger or toe, measured plethysmographically, diminishes promptly after a deep breath if the sympathetic nerves are intact.

By reducing the peripheral venous volume, venoconstriction during exercise assists the muscular pump mechanism in transferring blood to the central circulation, where it is required to maintain the higher cardiac output. Moreover, the reduced caliber of the veins serves to accelerate venous return. Although venoconstriction increases the hemodynamic resistance of the veins slightly, this effect is more than offset by the accompanying arteriolar dilatation. The intramuscular sinusoids, which are devoid of sympathetic innervation, do not constrict with exercise.[348] Constriction of these veins would not be beneficial because they constitute the major bellows of the muscle pump.

After hemorrhage, veins constrict both passively, in response to a decreased transmural pressure, and actively, as a result of greater venous tone. With prolonged shock, venoconstriction may give way to dilatation.

Cold causes veins to constrict both directly and as a general reflex response.[367] Although veins do not dilate in response to heat, heat negates the venoconstrictor response to deep breathing, exercise, and other such stimuli. The venous system is particularly important in the regulation of body temperature because superficial veins lie just under the skin, allowing easy transmission of heat from the interior of the body to the skin surface. Within this system, blood flow is slow, giving ample opportunity for the escape of heat. When conservation of heat becomes necessary, the superficial veins constrict, causing venous return to be diverted to the deep veins, which lie in close proximity to the arteries. Not only is the distance to the skin surface increased by this reflex, but the anatomic arrangement of the deep arteries and veins also results in a countercurrent exchange of heat from artery to vein, thus further conserving heat from the interior of the body.

Curiously, venous constriction occurring in response to standing is at best slight and transient and is probably the result of emotional stimuli.[341] Teleologically, leg veins would be expected to constrict in the upright position in order to prevent dependent pooling of blood. Although reflex arteriolar constriction provides some protection against gravitationally induced fluid shifts, the major protection is provided by the muscle pump.

Veins *constrict* in response to epinephrine, norepinephrine, phenylephrine, serotonin, and histamine; they *dilate* in response to phenoxybenzamine, phentolamine, reserpine, guanethidine, nitroglycerin, nitroprusside, barbiturates, and many anesthetic agents. Administration of isoproterenol sometimes appears to cause constriction, but at other times it results in dilatation.

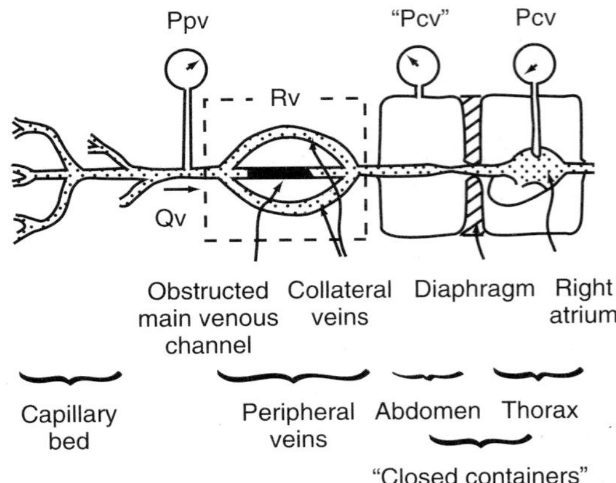

FIGURE 9-42 Major factors involved in venous return from the legs (see text). P_{pv}, peripheral venous pressure; P_{cv}, central venous pressure; "P_{cv}," intra-abdominal pressure; Q_v, venous flow; R_v, peripheral venous resistance.

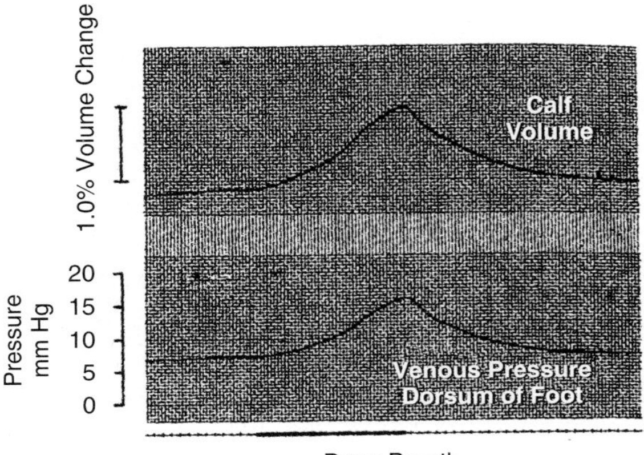

FIGURE 9-43 Effect of a deep breath on the peripheral venous pressure and volume in the lower extremity. The simultaneous increase in pressure and venous volume is caused by a temporary increase in intra-abdominal pressure that interferes with venous outflow from the leg. Volume change was measured with a mercury strain-gauge. (From Strandness DE Jr, Sumner DS: Hemodynamics for Surgeons. New York, Grune & Stratton, 1975.)

Acute Venous Thrombosis

Small nonocclusive venous thrombi produce no recognizable physiologic defects. When venous obstruction becomes sufficiently extensive, however, physiologic aberrations appear. The resulting changes, all related to an elevation in peripheral venous pressure, include venous congestion and edema. Rarely, shock results from leaking of fluid into tissue spaces. In severe cases, the blockage may be so complete that ischemia occurs.

The magnitude of the peripheral venous pressure, P_{pv}, is related to the central venous pressure, P_{cv}; to the blood flow through the part, Q_v; and to the hemodynamic resistance of the intervening veins, R_v (Fig. 9-42):

$$P_{pv} - P_{cv} = Q_v R_v \quad (9.31)$$

or

$$P_{pv} = Q_v R_v + P_{cv}$$

This equation indicates that peripheral venous pressure increases when the central venous pressure rises. Because central venous pressure is usually lower than the intra-abdominal pressure in supine subjects, P_{cv} can be taken to represent the intra-abdominal pressure. This is a manifestation of the *collapsible tube phenomenon,* in which the abdomen acts as a closed container (see Fig. 9-35). As discussed earlier, the inspiratory descent of the diaphragm increases intra-abdominal pressure ("P_{cv}"), decreases blood flow temporarily, and then raises the peripheral pressure, P_{pv}, as blood flow rises to its preinspiratory level (Fig. 9-43). These respiratory fluctuations, so prominent in normal limbs, are partially or completely masked in limbs with deep venous thrombosis (DVT).[356]

Because central venous pressure (P_{cv}) is ordinarily quite low, peripheral venous pressure in limbs with venous obstruction largely depends on the product of the blood flow through the limb and the venous resistance ($Q_v R_v$). Thrombotic venous obstruction raises venous resistance but has little effect on total limb blood flow (unless the obstructive process is very extensive and severe). Because blood flow remains unchanged, peripheral venous pressure is elevated commensurate with the increase in venous resistance (Eq. 9.31). *Thus, most significant increases in peripheral venous pressure are related to an increased hemodynamic resistance of the veins.*

In normal limbs, in which venous resistances are low, transient rises in blood flow have little effect on peripheral venous pressure. However, in post-thrombotic limbs or in limbs with acute venous obstruction, an increase in blood flow may elevate the Q_vR_v product significantly. As discussed later, the increase in venous pressure during exercise is responsible for venous claudication. Increases in peripheral pressure in response to reactive hyperemia are useful in the evaluation of chronic venous obstruction.[330]

Venous resistance depends on:

- Location of the obstructed venous segments
- Length of the obstructions
- Number of veins involved

The immediate effect of an acute venous thrombosis depends on the adequacy of the preexisting collateral channels. A thrombus that blocks large exit or reentry collateral veins elevates the venous resistance more than one that occurs in an isolated venous segment. For example, a thrombus developing in the common femoral vein, where it blocks not only the superficial femoral vein but also reentry of the profunda femoris and saphenous veins (two of the major collaterals from the lower leg), is more devastating than one isolated to the superficial femoral vein.

In limbs with clinically "silent" DVT, there may be no perceptible elevation of venous pressure.[267] Husni and colleagues[284] found the average venous pressure in limbs of supine patients with acute phlebitis, measured at foot level, to be 17 mm Hg. This was roughly 2.5 times that in normal limbs and in limbs with primary varicose veins (Table 9-4). These researchers noted essentially no difference in foot venous pressures between normal subjects and patients with acute phlebitis when they were standing quietly. This observation reflects the overwhelming contribution of the hydrostatic component, which tends to mask the slight pressure differences produced by the increased venous outflow resistance. On ambulation, however, the venous pressure in normal limbs dropped to about 40% of the pre-exercise value but changed little in the limbs with acute phlebitis (see Table 9-4).

DeWeese and Rogoff[263] found that venous pressures at foot level in supine patients ranged from 8 to 18 mm Hg when clots were confined to the popliteal or below-knee veins.[263] Pressures were 20 to 51 mm Hg when the clots were in the superficial femoral vein, and 32 to 83 mm Hg (average, 50 mm Hg) in the limbs with iliofemoral thrombosis. Similar values were reported by Ellwood and Lee.[267]

All veins subjected to increased transmural pressure dilate according to the venous pressure-volume curve and become less compliant (see Fig. 9-31). Superficial veins become more prominent, providing an excellent diagnostic sign of DVT. Sometimes this dilatation can so stretch the venous wall that valves cannot coapt properly, resulting in venous insufficiency. Reflux, however, is seldom an impressive finding in acute phlebitis.[340]

Another clinically important result of increased venous pressure is the concomitant rise in mean capillary pressure. This change upsets the Starling equilibrium (see Eq. 9.29), leading to the formation of edema. Even subclinical venous thrombi may produce minor swelling that can be detected by careful measurements of limb circumference. In fact, unilateral limb swelling is the best clinical sign of acute venous thrombosis.

The extent of swelling is proportional to the elevation in venous pressure. DeWeese and Rogoff[263] found swelling in only 70% of limbs with popliteal or below-knee thrombosis, and in almost all cases the increase in circumference was less than 1 cm at the ankle.[263] However, swelling was present in 86% of patients with femoral vein thrombosis and in all patients with iliofemoral thrombosis. The increase in circumference exceeded 1.0 cm at the ankle, 2.0 cm at the calf, and 3.0 cm at the thigh in limbs with iliofemoral thrombosis.

Edema formation reaches truly massive proportions in phlegmasia cerulea dolens. In this dreaded condition, which is characterized by near-total thrombosis of all the veins in the involved extremity, together with ipsilateral iliac vein occlusion and obstruction of pelvic collateral veins, fluid loss may reach 6 to 10 L within 5 to 10 days.[278] This massive fluid loss reflects the tremendous elevation in venous pressure, which may reach 16 to 17 times normal values within 6 hours.[351] With the rapid formation of edema, tissue pressures attain values of 25 to 48 mm Hg in 1 or 2 days.[247,351]

Shock caused by fluid loss occurs in about one third of patients with phlegmasia cerulea dolens.[246] In addition, a profound circulatory insufficiency develops, characterized by agonizing pain, cyanosis, decreased tissue temperature, absence of pulses, and, often, gangrene. The exact mechanism of this ischemia is uncertain, but it probably involves shock, increased venous outflow resistance, possible narrowing of the resistance vessels in response to the rise in interstitial pressure, and edema (Fig. 9-44).[339,355]

Primary Varicose Veins

Varicosities of the lower limb that develop spontaneously in the absence of DVT or other deep venous abnormalities are referred to as "primary varicose veins." The *greater saphenous vein* and its tributaries are the most frequently involved, followed by the lesser saphenous and pelvic veins.

The etiology remains uncertain. Theories include (1) pressure exerted by incompetent perforating veins,[269] (2) increased venous distensibility,[227,255,265,266,335] (3) greater blood flow through arteriovenous communications,[343,344] and (4) preexisting abnormalities of smooth muscle and endothelial cells in vein walls.[300] Although these factors undoubtedly play a role, much of the evidence seems to favor progressive descending valvular incompetence in response to congenital absence or incompetence of the common femoral and iliac valves.[270,301,304,333] Under these circumstances, the saphenofemoral valve (which lacks

Table 9-4 Venous Pressure at Foot Level

	PRESSURE (mm Hg)*		
	Supine	**Standing**	**Ambulatory**
Control	7 ± 1	90 ± 7	35 ± 9
Varicose veins	7 ± 1	87 ± 5	56 ± 11
Acute phlebitis	17 ± 7	93 ± 4	90 ± 18
Postphlebitic	12 ± 5	90 ± 4	84 ± 16

Adapted from Husni EA, Ximenes JO, Goyette EM: Elastic support of the lower limbs in hospital patients: A critical study. JAMA 214:1456, 1970.

*Values are mean ± standard deviation.

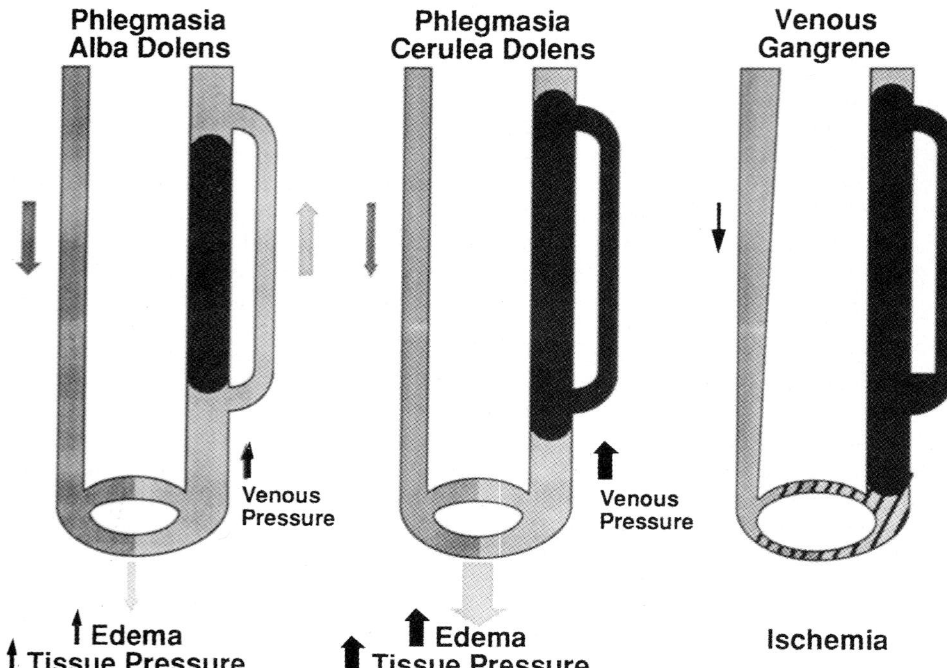

FIGURE 9-44 Pathophysiology of increasing severity of venous obstruction. In each diagram, arterial inflow is shown on the *left* and venous outflow on the *right*. *Black areas* indicate the location and extent of thrombus, which is confined to the major venous channels in phlegmasia alba dolens, involves collateral veins as well in phlegmasia cerulea dolens, and extends to the small veins and capillaries in venous gangrene. *Arrow size* indicates the magnitude of arterial and venous flow, venous and tissue pressure, and edema.

protection not only from hydrostatic pressure but also from episodic pressure increases caused by straining or coughing) becomes incompetent as the vein stretches. Once this valve becomes incompetent, the pressure is transmitted to the next lower valve in the saphenous vein, and so on down the leg. Finally, valves in the *tributary veins* also lose their competence. These subcutaneous veins then elongate, become tortuous, and manifest as typical varicosities.

Regardless of the etiologic mechanism, the essential physiologic defect is venous valvular incompetence. Although valve leaflets appear to be normal, they fail to coapt properly, perhaps because of the abnormally distensible nature of the venous wall.[227,258,266,362] In the typical patient with extensive greater saphenous varicosities, the iliofemoral valves as well as all the valves in the greater saphenous vein, both above and below knee, are either absent or incompetent.[270,304,333] Below the femoral level, the deep venous valves remain competent. Other patterns are common; varicosities may be confined to the above-knee saphenous system or to the below-knee saphenous veins, when the proximal site of venous incompetence is the Hunterian perforator or the popliteal vein. In all cases, there must be a continuous column of blood extending to the right atrium that is uninterrupted by the presence of a competent valve.

When a person with varicose veins shifts from a supine to a standing position, blood "falls" down the involved superficial veins uninhibited by functioning valves. Venous reflux fills the calf veins far more rapidly than capillary inflow can, and typically only 5 to 70 seconds is required.[254] Application of a tourniquet to compress the superficial veins normalizes the filling time, confirming the competency of the deep venous valves.[251] With the person in the supine position or during quiet standing, blood flow in varicose veins is sluggish but is directed in the normal cephalad direction (Figs. 9-45 and 9-46).[355] In addition, the pressure at ankle level is no different from that in limbs without venous incompetence (see Table 9-4).[284] When the upright subject with varicose veins begins to walk or otherwise contract the leg muscles, however, a different picture emerges. In this situation, blood flow reverses (during the relaxation phase), flowing distally and quite rapidly toward the feet (see Figs. 9-45 and 9-46).[244,270] Moreover, the decrease in superficial venous pressure is much less than is normally seen (see Table 9-4).[284,301,329]

In response to calf muscle contraction, deep venous pressure drops markedly as a result of the effect of the muscle pump on the normally valved deep veins. Varicose veins also are partially emptied by the muscle contraction, but because of the lack of valvular protection, pressure within these superficial veins experiences only a moderate fall. Therefore, during calf muscle relaxation, a pressure gradient develops that causes blood to flow from the superficial system into the deep system via the perforating veins.[233] As a result, a "private circulation" or circular movement of blood is established in the exercising leg (see Fig. 9-45).[314] Blood pumped through the deep veins of the calf and thigh reaches the common femoral vein, where a portion reverses direction to flow distally down the functionally valveless saphenous vein. On reaching the lower parts of the leg, this blood returns to the deep system through the perforating veins, thereby completing the parasitic circuit (Fig. 9-47). During exercise, as much as one fifth to one quarter of the total femoral outflow may be involved in this circular motion.[244]

Surprisingly, this circular motion seems to have little effect on exercise tolerance.[232] Coupled with the chronically increased superficial venous pressure, it does contribute to the progressive distention and elongation of the superficial tributaries of the saphenous vein, producing unsightly varicosities.[352] Clinically, the increased pressure probably contributes to the heaviness and tightness of the lower leg

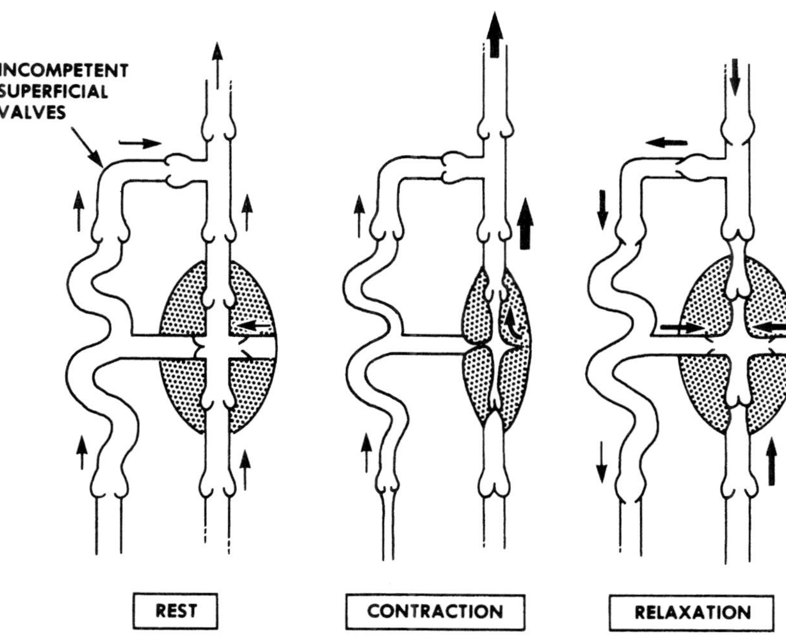

FIGURE 9-45 Primary varicose veins. Dynamics of venous blood flow in response to calf muscle contraction. During relaxation, flow is reversed in the saphenous vein, and circular motion is established through the perforating veins. (From Sumner DS: Venous dynamics—varicosities. Clin Obstet Gynecol 24:743, 1981.)

experienced by some patients with varicose veins. Interstitial tissue pressures have been found to be raised.[327]

Compressing the site of the leak (i.e., the saphenofemoral junction) prevents reflux flow during exercise and permits the muscle pump to reduce venous pressure to near-normal levels (see Fig. 9-47).[301,370] This forms the physiologic basis for high ligation and stripping of varicose veins, the most effective means of treatment.[252] Elastic stockings afford similar protection.[284] The external pressure exerted by the stockings may force the venous valve cusps to come into contact, thereby restoring venous competence.[254]

Chronic Venous Insufficiency

Physiologic abnormalities in limbs of patients with chronic venous insufficiency consist of venous outflow obstruction or valvular incompetence, or both (Fig. 9-48). In the individual case, one or the other of the abnormalities may predominate.

As a rule, the obstruction that follows acute venous thrombosis tends to decrease with time. Some thrombi are completely or partially dissolved by the action of thrombolysins; others become organized and recanalized to a variable extent (see Chapter 147). Of equal importance, however, is the progressive enlargement of collateral venous channels, which carry an increasingly large proportion of the venous outflow. The overall effect of these processes is reduced venous resistance. Venous outflow studies suggest that the average venous resistance in postphlebitic (postthrombotic) limbs is about 1.2 to 1.6 times normal. In contrast, the resistance of postphlebitic limbs is only 0.3 to 0.6 that of limbs with acute thrombosis.[237,239,259,277,340] At rest, with the person in the supine position, these small elevations in venous resistance usually increase the venous pressure by only a few millimeters of mercury at ankle level.[284,320,330] Ordinarily, no pressure elevation can be detected in the quietly standing individual (see Table 9-4).[262,284]

As venous obstruction subsides, venous valvular incompetence increases and is accompanied by progressive hemodynamic deterioration.[289,310,373] Organization of thrombi damages venous valves to a variable extent, leaving them incompetent.[264] The small high-resistance channels of recanalized veins, of course, are valveless. Dilatation of collateral veins and the remaining residual channels often prevents their valves from approximating, thus further aggravating the degree of venous incompetence. Plethysmographic

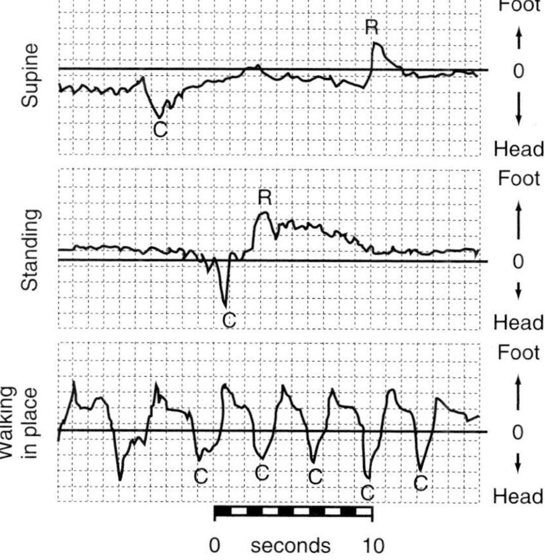

FIGURE 9-46 Blood flow in the greater saphenous vein in a patient with varicose veins. Calf muscle contraction (C) causes blood to flow toward the heart, whereas calf muscle relaxation (R) causes blood to reflux down the leg toward the feet. In the standing position, reflux flow greatly exceeds forward flow. Recordings were made with the Doppler probe pointed cephalad. (From Strandness DE Jr, Sumner DS: Hemodynamics for Surgeons. New York, Grune & Stratton, 1975.)

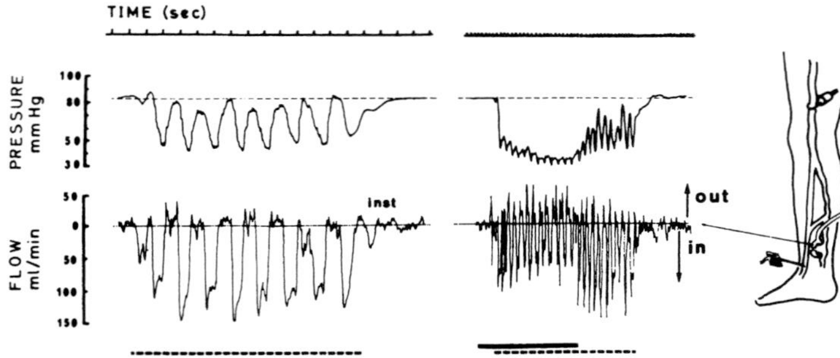

FIGURE 9-47 Flow in an incompetent perforating vein in an erect patient with varicose veins. During walking (*dashed lines*), flow is directed "in," that is, from the superficial to the deep veins. Pressure in the greater saphenous vein is only slightly reduced. Occluding the greater saphenous vein with a "sling" ligature (*solid line*) causes flow in the perforator to seesaw "in" and "out" and causes the saphenous vein pressure to drop in a nearly normal fashion. (From Bjordal RI: Simultaneous pressure and flow recordings in varicose veins of the lower extremity: A hemodynamic study of venous dysfunction. Acta Chir Scand 136:309, 1970.)

studies all show that venous reflux is significantly increased in postphlebitic limbs and that most of the reflux occurs via deep veins rather than via dilated superficial veins.[238,253,340] Postphlebitic calf veins may also become stiffer (less compliant) than normal veins, possibly due to distention or to changes in wall properties.[319]

Approximately two thirds of patients with chronic venous insufficiency have no history of DVT.[279,292,315] There may be no duplex scan or phlebographic evidence of venous thrombosis. Some of these patients may have had an unrecognized thrombotic episode; in others, a predisposition to incompetence may have been present since birth.

In patients with chronic deep venous valvular incompetence, changing from a supine to a standing position fills the calf veins even more rapidly (within 5 to 20 seconds) than it does in patients with primary varicose veins.[254,374] Reflux occurs not only in the deep system but also in any superficial veins that have lost their competence ("secondary varicose veins"). As a rule, application of a tourniquet to prevent reflux in superficial veins does little to prolong venous filling time.[251]

The physiologic aberrations introduced by valvular incompetence and residual obstruction become most evident during exercise (see Fig. 9-48). When calf muscles contract, blood is propelled up the leg in both superficial and deep veins, much as it is in normal limbs. (When valves distal to the site of muscle contraction are incompetent, a small quantity of blood may also be forced retrograde.) The temporary increase in flow exaggerates the effect of even a slight elevation of venous resistance and may actually cause the peripheral venous pressure to rise above resting levels during the phase of active muscle contraction (see Eq. 9.31). If the perforating veins are incompetent (as they often are), blood at high pressure is forced through these veins into the recipient subcutaneous veins. This in turn produces a local increase in capillary pressure.

The overall effect of valvular incompetence and outflow resistance is a reduced quantity of blood ejected with each contraction.[254] Because the volume of blood displaced depends not only on the pressure developed by the calf muscles but also on the compliance of the compressed veins, increased stiffness of the calf veins may play a role in reducing the ejected volume.[319,332]

When the muscles relax between contractions, incompetent valves allow blood to reflux down the leg, rapidly refilling the empty veins. (Reflux flow rates in limbs with stasis changes average 30 mL/sec and may reach 50 mL/sec.[369]) The hydrostatic column is re-established to the heart, and peripheral venous pressure rises rapidly between contractions. As a result, the ability of the calf muscle pump to reduce ambulatory venous pressure is severely impaired (Fig. 9-49).[262,280,284,370] The reduction in ambulatory venous

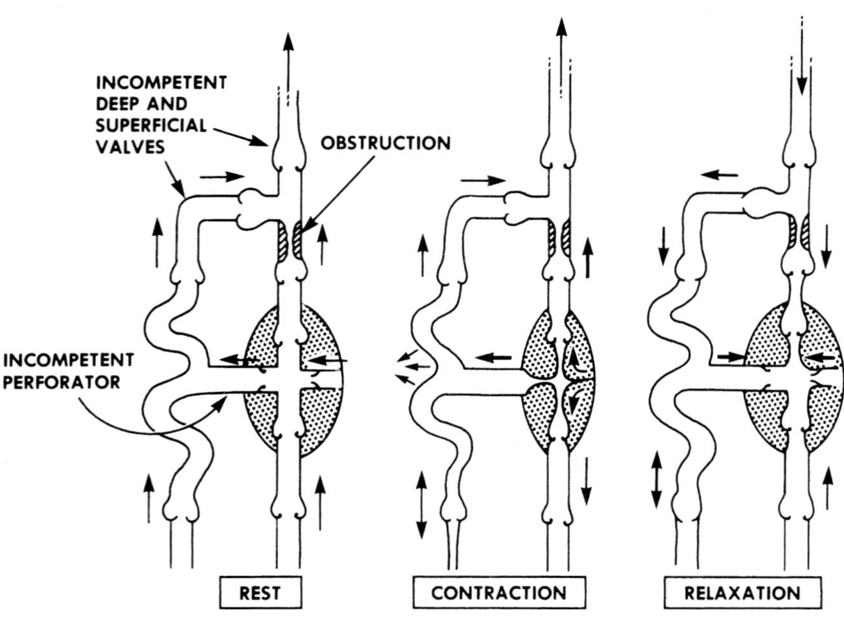

FIGURE 9-48 Chronic venous insufficiency, deep venous incompetence, and secondary varicose veins. Dynamics of venous blood flow in response to calf muscle contraction in a postphlebitic limb with residual deep venous obstruction, incompetent perforating veins, and secondary varicose veins. Note the to-and-fro motion of blood in incompetent perforating veins. (From Sumner DS: Venous dynamics—varicosities. Clin Obstet Gynecol 24:743, 1981.)

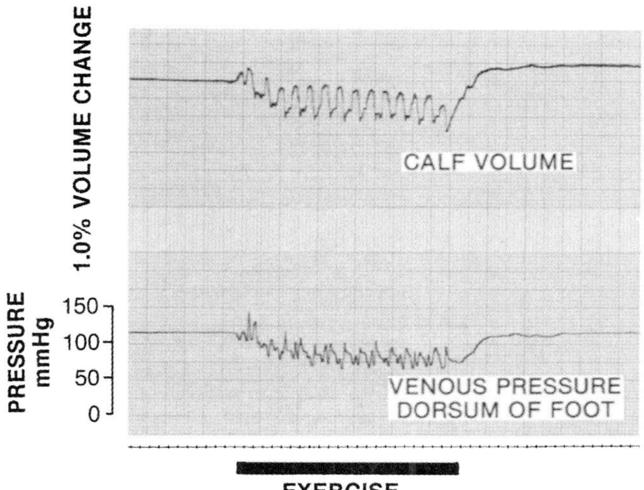

FIGURE 9-49 Effect of exercise on calf volume and venous pressure in a patient with chronic venous insufficiency. (From Strandness DE Jr, Sumner DS: Hemodynamics for Surgeons. New York, Grune & Stratton, 1975.)

pressure tends to be less in limbs with chronic venous insufficiency, in which reflux occurs in both the deep and superficial systems, than it is in limbs with isolated superficial venous incompetence (primary varicose veins), emphasizing the importance of the deep venous valves (see Table 9-4). If, in addition to valvular incompetence, there is a significant element of venous obstruction, there is almost no drop in venous pressure; in some cases, it may even rise.[234,262,280,320] Because ambulatory venous pressure is the parameter that most closely reflects the hemodynamic function of the venous circulation, it is recognized as the "gold standard" for all tests of venous pathophysiology.

Owing to the rapid reflux of blood that occurs in the interval between calf muscle contractions, decreased venous compliance, and (when present) increased outflow resistance, evacuation of the calf veins with exercise is less complete in limbs with chronic venous insufficiency than it is in normal limbs. The dependent veins, therefore, are perpetually in a state of partial congestion. Because the veins that constitute the bellows of the muscle pump are primed with a higher volume of blood, the amplitude of the pressure swing that accompanies each contraction of the calf muscle tends to be exaggerated in proportion to the severity of the postphlebitic process.[280,281] In multilevel disease, the pressure swing may be two or three times that observed in normal limbs.

The efficiency of the venous pump is well demonstrated by radionuclide methods for estimating changes in local blood volume.[338] As shown in Table 9-5, limbs with chronic deep venous insufficiency can pump blood from the calf at only about one-fifth the normal rate. After exercise, the volume reduction is approximately half that achieved in normal limbs. Air plethysmographic studies of limbs with venous valvular incompetence also confirm that a greater amount of blood is left in the calf after exercise (two to four times that remaining in normal limbs).[254] In accordance with the venous pressure-volume compliance curve (see Fig. 9-31), the quantity of blood remaining in the calf after a series of calf contractions, divided by that present at rest in the dependent extremity (residual volume fraction), correlates well with the higher ambulatory venous pressure.[254,373]

Adverse Effects of Venous Hypertension

Patients with proximal deep venous obstruction sometimes complain of a deep "bursting" pain in the leg during exercise. This pain, which has been called *venous claudication,* is explained by the greater venous pressure and congestion that occur in response to the combination of exercise-induced hyperemia and increased outflow resistance.[363] The distal deep veins in these limbs are often radiologically normal, and valvular insufficiency is not a prominent feature.

In most patients with chronic venous insufficiency, symptoms related to valvular incompetence predominate. Clinically, the most significant functional abnormality is the inability of the venous pump mechanism to provide relief from orthostatic venous hypertension. Capillaries in distal parts of legs are chronically exposed to a high pressure when the patient is upright. This leads to persistent edema. Subcutaneous capillaries and venules elongate and dilate.[248,268,271] Blood flow in these dilated and engorged vessels is sluggish compared with blood flow in normal skin.[228] Protein-rich fluid and red blood cells escape into the subcutaneous tissues. As the proteins become organized and the red blood cells disintegrate, the tissues become fibrotic and hyperpigmented, producing a condition known as *lipodermatosclerosis.*[250] Acting on this substrate, trauma (even a mild, often unrecognized injury) may lead to the death of tissue and the development of a chronic ulcer (see Chapter 154).

The frequency with which severe stasis changes and ulcers occur is related to the ambulatory venous pressure. Nicolaides and associates[321,322] showed that the incidence of ulceration in limbs with ambulatory venous pressures exceeding 80 mm Hg is about 80%. In contrast, ulcers seldom develop in limbs with ambulatory venous pressures of less than 30 or 40 mm Hg (Table 9-6). Unless measures are taken to counteract edema formation, 50% of limbs with edema present 1 year after an acute DVT become ulcerated within 10 years.[241]

Stasis changes (induration, dermatitis, hyperpigmentation, and ulceration) are limited to the "gaiter area" of the leg, where hydrostatic pressures are high, and are typically worse on the medial aspect of the ankle just above and posterior to the medial malleolus. This distribution suggests

Table 9-5 Change in Radioactivity of Leg Pumping Against Gravity (45-Degree Dependency)*

	NORMAL	CHRONIC DEEP VENOUS INSUFFICIENCY
Number of legs	21	13
Degree of change (%)	−20.5 (± 6.1)	−10.2 (± 4.8)†
Time required (sec)	0-5.3 (± 2.0)	12.7 (± 7.9)†
Rate of change (%/sec)	−4.6 (± 2.1)	−0.9 (± 0.5)†

From Rutherford JB, Reddy CMK, Walker FG, Wagner HN Jr: A new quantitative method of assessing the functional status of the leg veins. Am J Surg 122:594, 1971.

*Values are mean ± standard deviation.

†Degree of significance of difference from normal: $P < .001$.

Table 9-6 Relationship Between Ambulatory Venous Pressure and the Incidence of Stasis Ulceration

AMBULATORY VENOUS PRESSURE (mm Hg)	INCIDENCE OF ULCERS (%)
≤45	0
45-49	5
50-59	15
60-69	50
70-79	75
≥80	80

Data from Nicolaides AN: Noninvasive assessment of primary and secondary varicose veins. In Bernstein EF (ed): Noninvasive Diagnostic Techniques in Vascular Disease, 2nd ed. St. Louis, CV Mosby, 1982, p 575.

that incompetent perforating veins connecting the deep system to the posterior arch vein play a major role by transmitting pressure impulses to fragile superficial veins, causing localized hypoxia and nutritional deficits.[234,256,268,299,355] The descriptive term *ankle blowout syndrome* was coined to emphasize the importance of incompetent perforating veins to the genesis of venous stasis changes.[256]

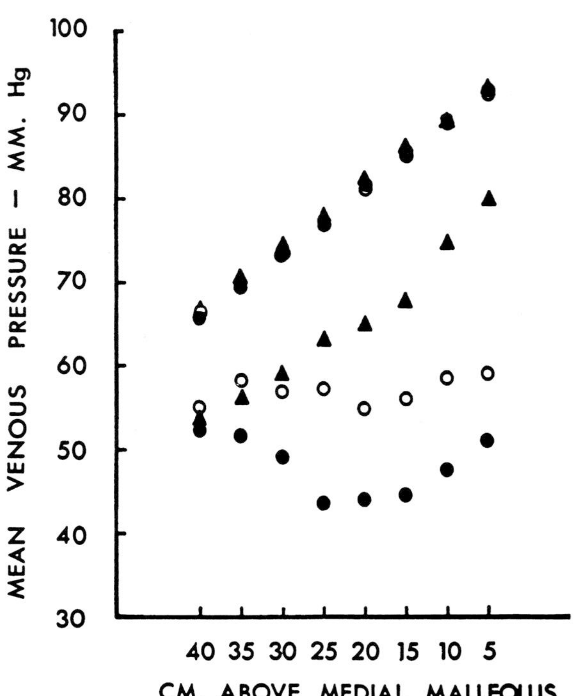

FIGURE 9-50 Pressure in the greater saphenous vein at 5-cm intervals down the leg, starting at the knee (at 40 cm above the medial malleolus) and ending at the ankle (at 5 cm). Symbols indicate normal limbs (*closed circles*), limbs with minimal saphenous varices (*open circles*), and limbs with gross saphenous varices (*triangles*). Pressures at all anatomic levels are superimposed at rest (*upper points*). Ambulatory venous pressures (*lower points*) are identical at the knee but are quite different at the ankle. (From Ludbrook J: Valvular defect in primary varicose veins: Cause or effect? Lancet 2:1289, 1963.)

Distribution of Valvular Incompetence: Relationship to Stasis Changes

The large number of valves in the infrapopliteal veins and the relative paucity of valves above the knee suggest that these structures have evolved to protect against hydrostatic forces imposed by the assumption of an upright posture. Certainly, the distribution of valves coincides with the hydrostatic pressure to which the veins are subjected. The concentration of valves in the lower leg also implies that they are of major importance to the muscle pump mechanism.

Unlike venous pressure at the ankle, pressure in the popliteal veins decreases relatively little with exercise and reaches essentially the same level in limbs with gross saphenous varices, in limbs with minimal varicose veins, and in normal limbs (Fig. 9-50).[233,282,301] This suggests that the presence or absence of valves above the popliteal vein has little effect on ambulatory venous pressure, whereas valves below the knee play a major role in pressure reduction. These and similar observations prompted earlier investigators to speculate that the absence of valves above the knee may be less detrimental to venous function than the absence of valves below the knee.[233,282]

Isolated proximal venous valvular incompetence is a relatively benign condition. About 15% of normal limbs and the majority of limbs with primary saphenous varicosities have incompetent common femoral valves, as shown by Doppler ultrasonography, yet cutaneous manifestations of chronic venous insufficiency are rarely seen.[270,333] Furthermore, reflux to the popliteal level during retrograde phlebography commonly occurs in clinically normal limbs.[361]

Investigators using plethysmographic methods or venous pressure measurements have shown that postexercise peripheral venous refilling times* are more likely to be accelerated and ambulatory venous pressures are more likely to be elevated when popliteal or calf veins are incompetent than when incompetence is confined to the above-knee veins (Table 9-7).[274,293,294,298,326,336,350] Because rapid refilling times (Table 9-8) and elevated ambulatory pressures (see Table 9-6) are correlated with stasis changes, these studies explain why popliteal and distal venous incompetence appears to have a more deleterious clinical effect than does isolated proximal venous incompetence.[274,298,326,350] There is even evidence that incompetence of the deep veins at the ankle may be clinically more important than incompetence of the popliteal or proximal calf veins in determining the stage of chronic venous insufficiency.[336]

Doppler and duplex ultrasonographic studies have been used to study the distribution of venous valvular incompetence in patients with symptoms and signs of chronic venous insufficiency. In limbs with severe stasis changes (ulcers, pigmentation, and induration), combined above-knee and below-knee incompetence is the most common pattern.[231,279,292,315,365] Isolated below-knee incompetence is less frequent, but most reports indicate that it is somewhat more common than isolated proximal vein incompetence. Combined above-knee and below-knee incompetence was present in 45% of the limbs studied by Moore and

*Because venous volume depends on venous pressure (see Fig. 9-31), postexercise plethysmographic tracings are roughly correlated with ambulatory venous pressure, and the times required for the venous volume and the venous pressure to return to baseline levels after cessation of exercise are almost identical.[226,323]

Table 9-7 Postexercise Venous Recovery Time Versus Distribution of Deep Venous Valvular Incompetence

LOCATION OF INCOMPETENT VALVES*	RECOVERY TIME (sec)†	INTERPRETATION
Distal only	16.4 ± 14.0	Abnormal
Distal and proximal	14.1 ± 8.7	Abnormal
Proximal only	43.5 ± 26.8	Normal
No valvular incompetence	42.8 ± 22.4	Normal

Data from Gooley NA, Sumner DS: Relationship of venous reflux to the site of venous valvular incompetence: Implications for venous reconstructive surgery. J Vasc Surg 7:50, 1988.

**Distal* is popliteal and below-knee veins; *proximal* is common and superficial femoral veins.

†Values are mean ± standard deviation.

Table 9-8 Postexercise Venous Recovery Time Versus Clinical Signs in Postphlebitic Limbs

SIGN	RECOVERY TIME (sec)*	LIMBS ABNORMAL (%)
Ulcer, pigmentation	10 ± 7	87
Edema only	26 ± 23	48
None	37 ± 24	27
Varicose veins		
Present	21 ± 19	68
Absent	39 ± 25	21

Data from Gooley NA, Sumner DS: Relationship of venous reflux to the site of venous valvular incompetence: Implications for venous reconstructive surgery. J Vasc Surg 7:50, 1988.

*Values are mean ± standard deviation.

colleagues[315] (Fig. 9-51). An additional 23% had isolated below-knee incompetence, for a total of 68% with below-knee involvement.

In another study, van Bemmelen and coworkers[365] reported that 76% of limbs with ulcers had above-knee and below-knee incompetence; an additional 8% had isolated distal incompetence, for a total of 84% of limbs with below-knee involvement. Thus, in these two studies, more than two thirds of limbs with advanced stasis changes had popliteal or below-knee incompetence, either alone or in conjunction with incompetence of the proximal veins.

In limbs with less severe cutaneous manifestations (edema, venous flares), the distribution differs, in that incompetence isolated to the proximal veins is far more common than incompetence confined to the calf veins. In the study by van Bemmelen and coworkers,[365] 59% of limbs with chronic venous disease but no ulcers had isolated proximal vein incompetence; another 29% had combined proximal and distal incompetence; but only 8% had isolated distal incompetence.[365] This finding suggests that proximal venous incompetence alone is not responsible for the development of ulcers. In contrast, the role of popliteal or below-knee valvular incompetence in the genesis of stasis ulcers is supported by reports that the proportion of limbs

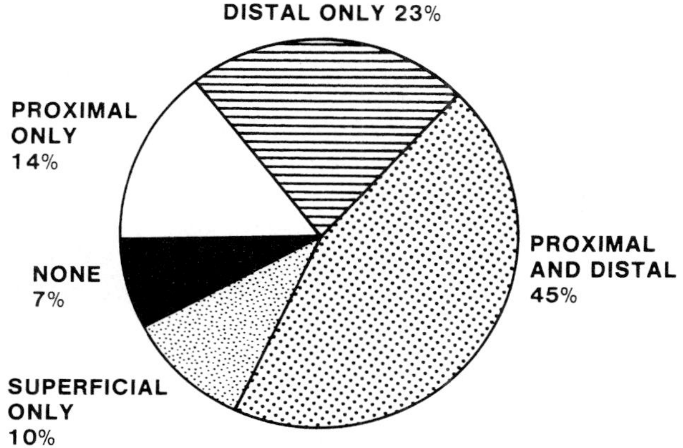

FIGURE 9-51 Distribution of venous valvular incompetence in limbs with stasis ulcers and pigmentation. (From Sumner DS: Pathophysiology of chronic venous insufficiency. Semin Vasc Surg 1:66, 1988.)

with distal incompetence is appreciably higher when ulcers are present (42% to 84%) than when the disease is less severe (3% to 35%).[315,317,318,365]

Although the significance of distal venous incompetence is widely accepted, the relative importance of superficial and deep venous incompetence remains unresolved. Combined superficial and deep venous incompetence, the most common pattern, is found in 20% to 88% of limbs with ulcers or lipodermatosclerosis.[231,368] In the experience of a number of investigators, incompetence confined to the superficial veins is relatively rare in patients with manifestations of chronic venous insufficiency, occurring in only 0 to 10% of cases (see Fig. 9-51).[231,315,318,336,365] Others, however, have found incompetence isolated to the superficial veins in the majority (52% to 70%) of patients with severe stasis changes.[296,346,368] In most cases, when incompetent superficial veins are associated with deep venous insufficiency, they probably represent secondary varicose veins and are unlikely to be directly responsible for the adverse effects of chronic venous insufficiency. This interpretation does not suffice when the only apparent valvular defects are confined to the superficial system. In these cases, superficial venous incompetence must be solely responsible for stasis changes. Nonetheless, patients with massive, long-standing varicose veins are often asymptomatic and have normal skin and soft, pliable subcutaneous tissues in the gaiter area. This observation in itself is a strong argument against the theory that superficial venous incompetence alone is sufficient to cause stasis changes.

Analogous to the situation pertaining in the deep system, incompetence of the below-knee greater saphenous vein and lesser saphenous vein, either alone or in conjunction with incompetence of the above-knee saphenous vein, is more strongly associated with ulceration than is incompetence limited to the proximal superficial veins.[279,292,293,317] In one study, only 4% of limbs with isolated above-knee saphenous vein incompetence underwent skin changes, and none had an ulcer.[294]

Hypothetical Effects of Different Patterns of Venous Incompetence

A mechanism explaining how the location of venous valvular incompetence may affect ambulatory venous pressure is proposed in Figure 9-52.[310] In normal limbs and in limbs

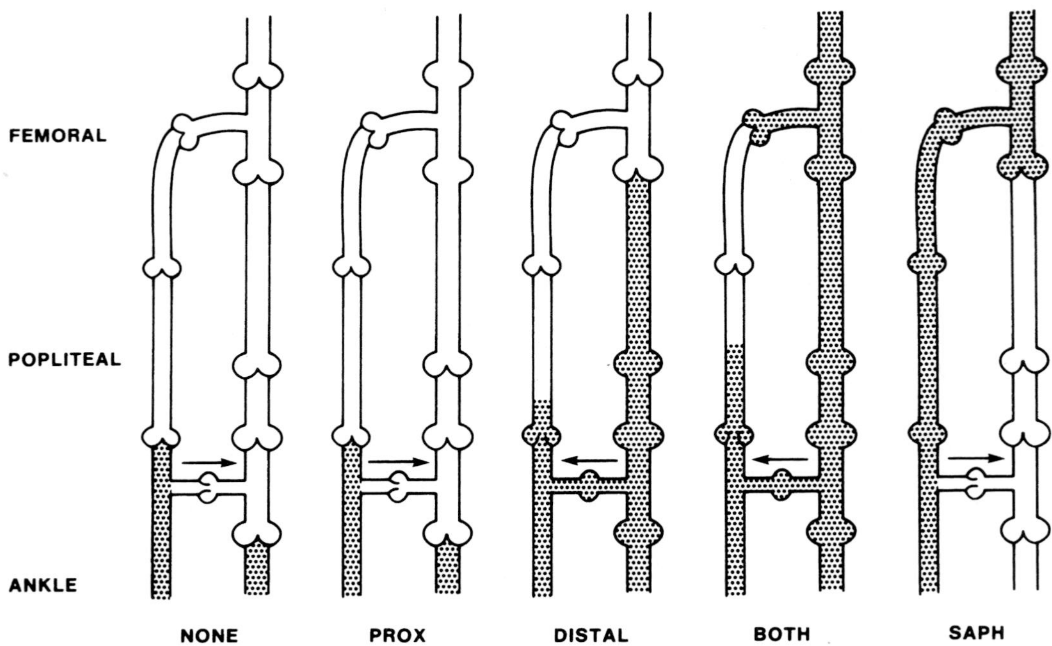

FIGURE 9-52 Comparison of the length of the hydrostatic column of blood measured from the ankle after exercise (*stippled area*) in limbs with no valvular incompetence (NONE), incompetence limited to the proximal deep veins (PROX), incompetence limited to the distal deep veins (DISTAL), incompetence of both proximal and distal deep veins (BOTH), and incompetence limited to the superficial veins (SAPH). In each diagram, saphenous veins are on the *left* and deep veins are on the *right*. *Arrows* indicate the direction of flow in perforating veins. (From Gooley NA, Sumner DS: Relationship of venous reflux to the site of venous valvular incompetence: Implications for venous reconstructive surgery. J Vasc Surg 7:50, 1988.)

with competent distal but incompetent proximal valves, venous pressures at the ankle are low after exercise because the column of blood extends only to the first competent valve, which is located well below the knee.* However, when the proximal valves are competent but the distal valves are incompetent, the postexercise column is relatively long, extending almost the entire length of the leg. Consequently, ambulatory venous pressures are high, and if the perforating veins are also incompetent, the superficial veins are rapidly refilled, even though their valves may remain competent. When both proximal and distal valves are incompetent, the ankle veins are subjected to the weight of an uninterrupted column of blood extending to the heart, there is little reduction in ambulatory venous pressure, and reflux into the superficial system via incompetent perforating veins is accelerated. Although superficial veins in limbs with superficial venous incompetence are rapidly refilled after exercise, external compression or removal of the saphenous veins relieves venous hypertension as long as the deep valves are competent.

*As pointed out earlier, this description is admittedly an oversimplification, because venous pressure in each segregated compartment is determined not only by the length of the hydrostatic column but also by venous compliance and the residual content of blood.[332] Therefore, pressures at the lower end of each compartment may correspond to a hydrostatic column that extends several centimeters above the closed valve located at the proximal end of the compartment. The message, however, is unaltered by the simplification.

Therapeutic Implications

Because venous valvular incompetence is ultimately responsible for stasis changes in the skin and subcutaneous tissues, it seems logical that restoration of normal valve function should correct the pathophysiologic abnormalities and afford the optimal treatment for this disease. Superficial femoral venous valvuloplasty, transposition of a competent segment of vein into the proximal deep venous system, and autotransplantation of valve-containing venous segments into the superficial femoral or popliteal vein are among the ingenious operations that have been devised for this purpose (see Chapter 159). The rationale for all of these procedures is based on the assumption that a single competent valve placed at or above the popliteal level in an otherwise incompetent system will alleviate ambulatory venous hypertension and allow ulcers to heal.

Although clinical results have been encouraging, hemodynamic abnormalities are seldom completely corrected.[260,287,325,331,345,359,372] The models depicted in Figure 9-52 explain this apparent contradiction. When incompetence is confined to the proximal veins and the distal valves remain functional, restoration of proximal venous valvular function is unnecessary. Therefore, valve replacement need be considered only when both proximal and distal veins are incompetent. Although a valve inserted in the proximal superficial femoral vein does interrupt the column of blood to the heart, a long uninterrupted segment of blood remains above the ankle at the cessation of exercise. Ambulatory venous pressure is decreased somewhat but remains high. A popliteal valve replacement would further reduce the length of the hydrostatic column and decrease ambulatory venous pressure but not as efficiently as the multiple competent valves present in normal calf veins, which have the potential of segregating the column of blood into segments only a few centimeters long. Under some circumstances, however, the margin of relief from ambulatory venous hypertension may be sufficient to permit ulcers to heal.

Stripping of incompetent superficial veins would be effective only when the distal deep veins are competent.[252,261,279,312]

Pregnancy

When a woman in the third trimester of pregnancy lies on her back, the enlarged uterus may compress the inferior vena cava and the common iliac veins.[288,357] As a result, venous pressure is increased in the legs, and venous flow patterns become less responsive to respiration.[285,313] Interference with venous return reduces cardiac output, sometimes to the extent that hypotension develops.[364] All these effects are relieved if the patient turns to her side, allowing the uterus to roll away from the pelvic veins.

Early in pregnancy, well before the uterus enlarges significantly, humoral factors cause the veins to become more compliant.[240] Together with the increased venous pressure that occurs later in gestation, these factors cause significant venous distention. Because of these factors, the velocity of blood flow in the leg veins gradually decreases as pregnancy progresses.

Although pregnancy does not cause varicose veins, the increased pressure and venous distensibility exaggerate predisposing factors. Consequently, varicose veins often first appear during pregnancy and become more severe with subsequent pregnancies. In addition, the sluggish venous flow probably contributes to the development of DVT.

Surgical Venous Interruption

Ligation of the femoral vein causes a prompt rise in peripheral venous pressure and a significant decrease in femoral artery flow (Fig. 9-53).[375] Although most of this initial resistance to blood flow can be attributed to an increase in venous outflow resistance, an appreciable portion may be due to reflex constriction of arterioles.[355,376] This information may be pertinent to the treatment of combined trauma to arteries and veins. Collateral development rapidly alleviates much of the venous outflow obstruction, but in the initial period after reconstructive surgery, the patency of the arterial repair may be jeopardized if the accompanying vein is ligated.[334]

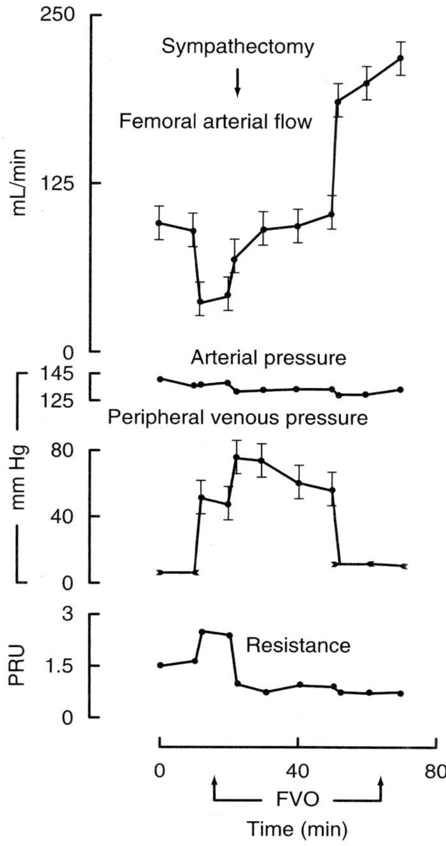

FIGURE 9-53 Effect of femoral vein occlusion (FVO) followed by lumbar sympathectomy on hemodynamics in the canine hindlimb. Peripheral venous pressure was measured from the saphenous vein. Note that occlusion results in a fall in femoral arterial blood flow, a prompt rise in peripheral venous pressure, and a rise in total limb resistance. Sympathectomy increases femoral flow without changing the peripheral venous pressure appreciably, suggesting that the resistance change occurred primarily in the arterioles or venules rather than in the larger venous collaterals. PRU, peripheral resistance unit. (From Wright CB, Sayre JT, Casterline PI, Swan KG: Hemodynamic effects of sympathectomy in canine femoral venous occlusion. Surgery 74:405, 1973.)

■ SELECTED READINGS

Arterial Hemodynamics

Burton AC: Physiology and Biophysics of the Circulation, 2nd ed. Chicago, Year Book Medical, 1972.

Caro CG, Pedley TJ, Schroter RC, Seed WA: The Mechanics of the Circulation. New York, Oxford University Press, 1978.

Conrad MC: Functional Anatomy of the Circulation to the Lower Extremities. Chicago, Year Book Medical, 1971.

Dobrin PB: Mechanical properties of arteries. Physiol Rev 58:397, 1978.

Fung YC: Biomechanics: Circulation, 2nd ed. New York, Springer-Verlag, 1997.

Milnor WR: Hemodynamics, 2nd ed. Baltimore, Williams & Wilkins, 1989.

Nichols WW, O'Rourke MF: McDonald's Blood Flow in Arteries: Theoretical, Experimental, and Clinical Principles, 4th ed. London, Arnold, 1998.

Patel DJ, Vaishnav RN: Basic Hemodynamics and Its Role in Disease Processes. Baltimore, University Park Press, 1980.

Shepherd JT: Physiology of the Circulation in Human Limbs in Health and Disease. Philadelphia, WB Saunders, 1963.

Strandness DE Jr: Peripheral Arterial Disease: A Physiologic Approach. Boston, Little, Brown, 1969.

Strandness DE Jr, Sumner DS: Hemodynamics for Surgeons. New York, Grune & Stratton, 1975.

Venous Hemodynamics

Bergan JJ, Goldman MP (eds): Varicose Veins and Telangiectasias. St. Louis, Quality Medical, 1993.

Bergan JJ, Yao JST: Venous Disorders. Philadelphia, WB Saunders, 1991.

Browse NL, Burnand KG, Thomas ML: Diseases of the Veins: Pathology, Diagnosis and Treatment. London, Edward Arnold, 1988.

Dodd H, Cockett FB: The Pathology and Surgery of the Veins of the Lower Limb, 2nd ed. Edinburgh, Churchill Livingstone, 1976.

Gardner AMN, Fox RH: The Return of Blood to the Heart: Venous Pumps in Health and Disease. London, John Libbey Eurotext, 1989.

Gottlob R, May R: Venous Valves: Morphology, Function, Radiology, Surgery. Vienna, Springer-Verlag, 1986.

Guyton AC, Taylor AE, Granger HJ: Circulatory Physiology. II: Dynamics and Control of the Body Fluids. Philadelphia, WB Saunders, 1975.

Johnson HD, Pflug J: The Swollen Leg: Causes and Treatment. Philadelphia, JB Lippincott, 1975.

Ludbrook J: Aspects of Venous Function in the Lower Limbs. Springfield, Ill, Charles C Thomas, 1966.

Raju S, Villavicencio JL: Surgical Management of Venous Disease. Baltimore, Williams & Wilkins, 1997.

Strandness DE Jr, Sumner DS: Hemodynamics for Surgeons. New York, Grune & Stratton, 1975.

Strandness DE Jr, Thiele BL: Selected Topics in Venous Disorders: Pathophysiology, Diagnosis, and Treatment. Mount Kisco, NY, Futura, 1981.

■ REFERENCES

Arterial Hemodynamics

1. Abbott WM, Bouchier-Hayes DJ: The role of mechanical properties in graft design. In Dardik H (ed): Graft Materials in Vascular Surgery. Miami, Symposia Specialist, 1978, p 59.
2. Allwood MJ: Redistribution of blood flow in limbs with obstruction of a main artery. Clin Sci 22:279, 1962.
3. Angelides NS, Nicolaides AN: Simultaneous isotope clearance from the muscles of the calf and thigh. In Puel P, Boccalon H, Enjalbert A (eds): Hemodynamics of the Limbs: 1. Toulouse, GEPESC, 1979, p 547.
4. Anidjar S, Dobrin PB, Eichorst M, et al: Correlation of inflammatory infiltrate with the enlargement of experimental aortic aneurysms. J Vasc Surg 16:139, 1992.
5. Attinger EO: Flow patterns and vascular geometry. In: Pulsatile Blood Flow. New York, McGraw-Hill, 1964, p 179.
6. Attinger EO, Sugawara H, Navarro A, et al: Pressure flow relations in dog arteries. Circ Res 19:230, 1966.
7. Azuma T, Oka S: Mechanical equilibrium of blood vessel walls. Jpn J Physiol 21:1310, 1971.
8. Baird RN, Bird DR, Clifford PC, et al: Upstream stenosis, its diagnosis by Doppler signals from the femoral artery. Arch Surg 115:1316, 1980.
9. Bassiouny HS, White S, Glagov S, et al: Anastomotic intimal hyperplasia: Mechanical injury or flow-induced? J Vasc Surg 15:708, 1992.
10. Beaconsfield PA: A. Effect of exercise on muscle blood flow in normal and sympathectomized limbs. B. Collateral circulation before and after sympathectomy. Ann Surg 140:786, 1954.
11. Beiser GD, Zelis R, Epstein SE, et al: The role of skin and muscle resistance vessels in reflexes mediated by the baroreceptor system. J Clin Invest 49:225, 1970.
12. Bergel DH: The static elastic properties of the arterial wall. J Physiol 156:445, 1961.
13. Bergel DH: The dynamic elastic properties of the arterial wall. J Physiol 156:458, 1961.
14. Berguer R, Higgins RF, Reddy DJ: Intimal hyperplasia: An experimental study. Arch Surg 115:332, 1980.
15. Berguer R, Hwang NHC: Critical arterial stenosis: A theoretical and experimental solution. Ann Surg 180:39, 1974.
16. Bernstein EF, Fischer JC, Varco RL: Is excision the optimum treatment for all abdominal aortic aneurysms? Surgery 61:83, 1967.
17. Brice JG, Dowsett DJ, Lowe RD: Hemodynamic effects of carotid artery stenosis. Br Med J 2:1363, 1964.
18. Burch GE, Winsor T: The phlebomanometer: A new apparatus for direct measurement of venous pressure in large and small veins. JAMA 123:91, 1943.
19. Burton AC: Physiology and Biophysics of the Circulation, 2nd ed. Chicago, Year Book Medical, 1972.
20. Busuttil RW, Abou-Zamzam AM, Machleder HI: Collagenase activity of the human aorta: Comparison of patients with and without abdominal aortic aneurysms. Arch Surg 115:1373, 1980.
21. Buxton B, Lambert RP, Pitt TTE: The significance of vein wall thickness and diameter in relation to the patency of femoropopliteal saphenous vein bypass grafts. Surgery 87:425, 1980.
22. Byar D, Fiddian RV, Quereau M, et al: The fallacy of applying Poiseuille equation to segmented arterial stenosis. Am Heart J 70:216, 1965.
23. Carter SA: Clinical measurement of systolic pressures in limbs with arterial occlusive disease. JAMA 207:1869, 1969.
24. Carter SA: Response of ankle systolic pressure to leg exercise in mild or questionable arterial disease. N Engl J Med 287:578, 1972.
25. Cobb LA, Smith PH, Lwai S, et al: External iliac vein flow: Its response to exercise and relation to lactate production. J Appl Physiol 26:606, 1969.
26. Coffman JD, Mannick JA: A simple objective test for arteriosclerosis obliterans. N Engl J Med 273:1297, 1965.
27. Coffman JD, Mannick JA: Failure of vasodilator drugs in arteriosclerosis obliterans. Ann Intern Med 76:35, 1972.
28. Conrad MC, Anderson JL III, Garrett JB Jr: Chronic collateral growth after femoral artery occlusion in the dog. J Appl Physiol 31:550, 1971.
29. Conrad MC, Green HD: Hemodynamics of large and small vessels in peripheral vascular disease. Circulation 29:847, 1964.
30. Cousins MJ, Wright CJ: Graft, muscle, skin blood flow after epidural block in vascular surgical procedures. Surg Gynecol Obstet 133:59, 1971.
31. Cranley JJ: Ischemic rest pain. Arch Surg 98:187, 1969.
32. Crawshaw HM, Quist WC, Sarrallach E, et al: Flow disturbance at the distal end-to-side anastomosis: Effect of patency of the proximal outflow segment and angle of anastomosis. Arch Surg 115:1280, 1980.
33. Cronenwett JL, Lindenaur SM: Hemodynamic effects of sympathectomy in ischemic canine hind limbs. Surgery 87:417, 1980.
34. Cronenwett JL, Zelenock GB, Whitehouse WM Jr, et al: The effect of sympathetic innervation on canine muscle and skin blood flow. Arch Surg 118:420, 1983.
35. Daily JW, Harleman DRF: Fluid Dynamics. Reading, Mass, Addison-Wesley, 1966.
36. Darling RC, Raines JK, Brener BJ, et al: Quantitative segmental pulse and volume recorder: A clinical tool. Surgery 72:873, 1973.
37. Daugherty HI, Franzini JB: Steady flow of incompressible fluids in pipes. In: Fluid Mechanics with Engineering Applications, 6th ed. New York, McGraw-Hill, 1965, p 191.
38. DeWeese JA: Pedal pulses disappearing with exercise: A test for intermittent claudication. N Engl J Med 262:1214, 1960.
39. DeWeese JA, Van deBerg L, May AG, et al: Stenoses of arteries of the lower extremity. Arch Surg 89:806, 1964.
40. Dobrin PB: Mechanics of normal and diseased blood vessels. Ann Vasc Surg 2:283, 1988.
41. Dobrin PB, Baker WH, Gley WC: Elastolytic and collagenolytic studies of arteries. Implications for the mechanical properties of aneurysms. Arch Surg 119:405, 1984.

42. Dobrin PB, Rovick AA: Influence of vascular smooth muscle on contractile mechanics and elasticity of arteries. Am J Physiol 217:1644, 1969.
43. Dormandy JA: Significance of hemorrheology in the management of the ischemic limb. World J Surg 7:319, 1983.
44. Dornhorst AC, Sharpey-Schafer EP: Collateral resistance in limbs with arterial obstruction: Spontaneous changes and effects of sympathectomy. Clin Sci 10:371, 1951.
45. Dundas P, Hillestad LK: Profunda revascularization: The early postoperative effect upon calf blood flow. Scand J Thorac Cardiovasc Surg 5:275, 1971.
46. Edholm OG, Howarth S, Sharpey-Schafer EP: Resting blood flow and blood pressure in limbs with arterial obstruction. Clin Sci 10:361, 1951.
47. Edwards WS, Holdefer WF, Mohtashemi M: The importance of proper caliber of lumen in femoral-popliteal artery reconstruction. Surg Gynecol Obstet 122:37, 1966.
48. Ehrenfeld WK, Harris JD, Wylie EJ: Vascular "steal" phenomenon: An experimental study. Am J Surg 116:192, 1968.
49. Evans DH, Barrie WW, Asher MJ, et al: The relationship between ultrasonic pulsatility index and proximal arterial stenosis in a canine model. Circ Res 46:470, 1980.
50. Farrar DJ, Malindzak GS Jr, Johnson G Jr: Large vessel impedance in peripheral atherosclerosis. Circulation 56(Suppl 2):171, 1977.
51. Feinberg RL, Gregory RT, Wheeler JR, et al: The ischemic window: A method for the objective quantitation of the training effect in exercise therapy for intermittent claudication. J Vasc Surg 16:244, 1992.
52. Fiddian RV, Byar D, Edwards EA: Factors affecting flow through a stenosed vessel. Arch Surg 88:105, 1964.
53. Flanigan DP, Tullis JP, Streeter VL, et al: Multiple subcritical arterial stenoses: Effect on poststenotic pressure and flow. Ann Surg 186:663, 1977.
54. Folse JR: Application of the sudden injection dye dilution principle to the study of the femoral circulation. Surg Gynecol Obstet 120:1194, 1965.
55. Folse R: Alterations in femoral blood flow and resistance during rhythmic exercise and sustained muscular contractions in patients with arteriosclerosis. Surg Gynecol Obstet 121:767, 1965.
56. Foster JH, Bolasny BL, Gobbel WG Jr, et al: Comparative study of elective resection and expectant treatment of abdominal aortic aneurysms. Surg Gynecol Obstet 129:1, 1969.
57. Fronek A, Johansen KH, Dilley RB, et al: Non-invasive physiologic tests in the diagnosis and characterization of peripheral arterial occlusive disease. Am J Surg 126:205, 1973.
58. Gauer OH, Thron HL: Postural changes in the circulation. In Hamilton WF, Dow P (eds): Handbook of Physiology, Sect 2: Circulation, Vol III. Washington, DC, American Physiological Society, 1965, p 2409.
59. Glagov S, Weisenberg E, Zarins CK, et al: Compensatory enlargement of human atherosclerotic coronary arteries. N Engl J Med 316:1371, 1987.
60. Gosling RG, Dunbar G, King DH, et al: The quantitative analysis of occlusive peripheral arterial disease by a nonintrusive ultrasonic technique. Angiology 22:52, 1971.
61. Gosling RG, King DH: Continuous wave ultrasound as an alternative and complement to x-rays in vascular examination. In Reneman RS (ed): Cardiovascular Applications of Ultrasound. Amsterdam, North-Holland, 1974, p 266.
62. Griffith TM, Lewis MJ, Newby AC, Henderson AH: Endothelium-derived relaxing factor. J Am Coll Cardiol 12:797, 1988.
63. Guyton AC: Venous return. In Hamilton WF, Dow P (eds): Handbook of Physiology, Sect 2: Circulation, Vol II. Washington, DC, American Physiological Society, 1963, p 1099.
64. Hillestad LK: The peripheral blood flow in intermittent claudication. V: Plethysmographic studies: The significance of the calf blood flow at rest and in response to timed arrest of the circulation. Acta Med Scand 174:23, 1963.
65. Hillestad LK: The peripheral blood flow in intermittent claudication. VI: Plethysmographic studies: The blood flow response to exercise with arrested and free circulation. Acta Med Scand 174:671, 1963.
66. Hoffman DC, Jepson RP: Muscle blood flow and sympathectomy. Surg Gynecol Obstet 127:12, 1968.
67. Hokanson DE, Strandness DE Jr: Stress-strain characteristics of various arterial grafts. Surg Gynecol Obstet 127:57, 1968.
68. Holman E: Problems in the dynamics of blood flow. I: Conditions controlling collateral circulation in the presence of an arteriovenous fistula and following ligation of an artery. Surgery 26:880, 1949.
69. Hopkins RW: Presidential address: Energy, poise, and resilience: Daniel Bernoulli, Thomas Young, J. L. M. Poiseuille, and F. A. Simeone. J Vasc Surg 13:777, 1991.
70. Ingebrigtsen R, Leraand S: Dilatation of a medium-sized artery immediately after local changes of blood pressure and flow as measured by ultrasonic technique. Acta Physiol Scand 79:552, 1970.
71. Jager KA, Phillips DJ, Martin RL, et al: Noninvasive mapping of lower limb arterial lesions. Ultrasound Med Biol 11:515, 1985.
72. James IM, Millar RA, Purves MY: Observations on the extrinsic neural control of cerebral blood flow in the baboon. Circ Res 25:77, 1969.
73. John HT, Warren R: The stimulus to collateral circulation. Surgery 49:14, 1961.
74. Johnson EC, Voyles WF, Atterbom HA, et al: Effects of exercise training on common femoral artery blood flow in patients with intermittent claudication. Circulation 80:III59, 1989.
75. Johnson PC: Review of previous studies and current theories of autoregulation. Circ Res 14:15, 1964.
76. Johnston KW, Maruzzo BC, Cobbold RSC: Errors and artifacts of Doppler flowmeters and their solution. Arch Surg 112:1335, 1977.
77. Johnston KW, Maruzzo BC, Cobbold RSC: Doppler methods for quantitative measurement and localization of peripheral arterial occlusive disease by analysis of the blood velocity waveform. Ultrasound Med Biol 4:209, 1978.
78. Jones RD, Berne RM: Intrinsic regulation of skeletal muscle blood flow. Circ Res 14:126, 1964.
79. Kamiya A, Tagowa T: Adaptive regulation of wall shear stress to flow change in the canine carotid artery. Am J Physiol 239:H14, 1980.
80. Karayannacos PE, Talukder N, Nerem RM, et al: The role of multiple noncritical arterial stenoses in the pathogenesis of ischemia. J Thorac Cardiovasc Surg 73:458, 1977.
81. Keenan RL, Rodbard S: Competition between collateral vessels. Cardiovasc Res 7:670, 1973.
82. Keitzer WF, Fry WJ, Kraft RO, et al: Hemodynamic mechanism for pulse changes seen in occlusive vascular disease. Surgery 57:163, 1965.
83. Kindt GW, Youmans JR: The effect of stricture length on critical arterial stenosis. Surg Gynecol Obstet 128:729, 1969.
84. Kinley CE, Marble AE: Compliance: A continuing problem with vascular grafts. J Cardiovasc Surg 21:163, 1980.
85. Kinley CE, Paasche PE, MacDonald AS, et al: Stress at vascular anastomosis in relation to host artery: Synthetic graft diameter. Surgery 75:28, 1974.
86. Kjellmer I: On the competition between metabolic vasodilatation and neurogenic vasoconstriction in skeletal muscle. Acta Physiol Scand 63:450, 1965.
87. Korner PI: Control of blood flow to special vascular areas: Brain, kidney, muscle, skin, liver and intestine. In Guyton AC, Jones CE (eds): MTP International Review of Science, Physiology: Series 1, Vol 1: Cardiovascular Physiology. London, Butterworths, 1974, pp 123-162.
88. Ku DN, Giddens DP, Zarins CK, Glagov S: Pulsatile flow and atherosclerosis in the human carotid bifurcation: Positive correlation between plaque location and low and oscillating shear stress. Arteriosclerosis 5:293, 1985.
89. Langille BL, O'Donnell F: Reductions in arterial diameter produced by chronic decreases in blood flow are endothelium-dependent. Science 231:405, 1986.
90. Larsen OA, Lassen NA: Medical treatment of occlusive arterial disease of the legs: Walking exercise and medically induced hypertension. Angiologica 6:288, 1969.
91. Lassen NA: Cerebral blood flow and oxygen consumption in man. Physiol Rev 39:183, 1959.

92. Lassen NA, Kampp M: Calf muscle blood flow during walking studied by the ^{133}Xe method in normals and in patients with intermittent claudication. Scand J Clin Lab Invest 17:447, 1965.
93. Lassen NA, Larsen OA, Sørensen AWS, et al: Conservative treatment of gangrene using mineral corticoid-induced moderate hypertension. Lancet 1:606, 1968.
94. Lassen NA, Lindberg IF, Dahn I: Validity of the xenon 133 method for measurement of muscle blood flow evaluated by simultaneous venous occlusion plethysmography: Observations in the calf of normal man and in patients with occlusive vascular disease. Circ Res 16:287, 1965.
95. LeVeen HH, Moon I, Ahmed N, et al: Lowering blood viscosity to overcome vascular resistance. Surg Gynecol Obstet 150:139, 1980.
96. Lewis JD, Papathanaiou C, Yao ST, et al: Simultaneous flow and pressure measurements in intermittent claudication. Br J Surg 59:418, 1972.
97. Lewis P, Psaila JV, Morgan RH, et al: Common femoral artery volume flow in peripheral vascular disease. Br J Surg 77:183, 1990.
98. Lewis T, Pickering GW, Rothschild P: Observations upon muscular pain in intermittent claudication. Heart 15:359, 1931.
99. Ling SC, Atabek HB, Letzing WG, et al: Non-linear analysis of aortic flow in living dogs. Circ Res 33:198, 1973.
100. LoGerfo FW, Quist WC, Nowak MD, et al: Downstream anastomotic hyperplasia: A mechanism of failure of Dacron arterial grafts. Ann Surg 197:479, 1983.
101. LoGerfo FW, Soncrant T, Teel T, et al: Boundary layer separation in models of side-to-end arterial anastomoses. Arch Surg 114:1369, 1979.
102. Longland CJ: The collateral circulation of the limb. Ann R Coll Surg Engl 13:161, 1953.
103. Lorentsen E, Hoel BL, Hol R: Evaluation of the functional importance of atherosclerotic obliterations in the aorto-iliac artery by pressure/flow measurements. Acta Med Scand 191:399, 1972.
104. Ludbrook J: Collateral artery resistance in the human lower limb. J Surg Res 6:423, 1966.
105. Lye CR, Sumner DS, Strandness DE Jr: Hemodynamics of the retrograde cross-pubic anastomosis. Surg Forum 26:298, 1975.
106. Lye CR, Sumner DS, Strandness DE Jr: The transcutaneous measurement of the elastic properties of the human saphenous vein femoropopliteal bypass graft. Surg Gynecol Obstet 141:891, 1975.
107. Malcome AD, Roach MR: Flow disturbances at the apex and lateral angles of a variety of bifurcation models and their role in the development and manifestations of arterial disease. Stroke 10:335, 1979.
108. Mannick JA, Jackson BT: Hemodynamics of arterial surgery in atherosclerotic limbs. I: Direct measurement of blood flow before and after vein grafts. Surgery 59:713, 1966.
109. Martin P, Frawley JE, Barabas AP, et al: On the surgery of atherosclerosis of the profunda femoris artery. Surgery 71:182, 1972.
110. May AG, DeWeese JA, Rob CA: Hemodynamic effects of arterial stenosis. Surgery 53:513, 1963.
111. May AG, Van deBerg L, DeWeese JA, et al: Critical arterial stenosis. Surgery 54:250, 1963.
112. McDonald DA: Blood Flow in Arteries, 2nd ed. Baltimore, Williams & Wilkins, 1974.
113. McMillan DE: Blood flow and the localization of atherosclerotic plaques. Stroke 16:582, 1985.
114. Mehigan DG, Fitzpatrick B, Browne HI, Bouchier-Hayes DJ: Is compliance mismatch the major cause of anastomotic arterial aneurysms? J Cardiovasc Surg 26:147, 1985.
115. Melkumyants AM, Balashov SA, Veselova ES, Khayutin VM: Continuous control of the lumen of feline conduit arteries by blood flow rate. Cardiovasc Res 21:863, 1987.
116. Milnor WR: Pulsatile blood flow. N Engl J Med 287:27, 1972.
117. Moore WS, Hall AD: Unrecognized aortoiliac stenosis: A physiologic approach to the diagnosis. Arch Surg 103:633, 1971.
118. Moore WS, Malone JM: Effect of flow rate and vessel caliber on critical arterial stenosis. J Surg Res 26:1, 1979.
119. Moore WS, Sydorak GR, Newcomb L, et al: Blood pressure gradient to estimate flow changes with progressive arterial stenosis. Surg Forum 24:248, 1973.
120. Morris GC Jr, Edwards W, Cooley DA, et al: Surgical importance of the profunda femoris artery. Arch Surg 82:32, 1961.
121. Motomiya M, Karino T: Flow patterns in the human carotid artery bifurcation. Stroke 15:50, 1984.
122. Mozersky DJ, Sumner DS, Hokanson DE, et al: Transcutaneous measurement of the elastic properties of the human femoral artery. Circulation 46:948, 1972.
123. Mundth ED, Darling RC, Moran JM, et al: Quantitative correlation of distal arterial outflow and patency of femoropopliteal reversed saphenous vein grafts with intraoperative flow and pressure measurements. Surgery 65:197, 1969.
124. Newman DL, Gosling RG, Bowden NLR, et al: Pressure amplitude increase on unmatching the aorto-iliac junction of the dog. Cardiovasc Res 7:6, 1973.
125. Nichols WK, Stanton M, Silver D, et al: Anastomotic aneurysms following lower extremity revascularization. Surgery 88:366, 1980.
126. Nicolaides AN, Gordon-Smith DC, Dayandas J, et al: The value of Doppler blood velocity tracings in the detection of aortoiliac disease in patients with intermittent claudication. Surgery 80:774, 1976.
127. Ojha M, Cobbold RSC, Johnston KW, Hummel RL: Pulsatile flow through constricted tubes: An experimental investigation using photochromic tracer methods. J Fluid Mech 203:173, 1989.
128. Ojha M, Ethier CR, Johnston KW, Cobbold RSC: Steady and pulsatile flow fields in an end-to-side arterial anastomosis model. J Vasc Surg 12:747, 1990.
129. Ojha M, Johnston KW, Cobbold RSC: Evidence of a possible link between poststenotic dilation and wall shear stress. J Vasc Surg 11:127, 1990.
130. Okadone K, Yukizane T, Mii S, Sugimachi K: Ultrastructural evidence of the effects of shear stress variation on intimal thickening in dogs with arterially transplanted autologous grafts. J Cardiovasc Surg 31:719, 1990.
131. O'Rourke MF: Steady and pulsatile energy losses in the systemic circulation under normal conditions and in simulated arterial disease. Cardiovasc Res 1:313, 1967.
132. Ouriel K, Donayre C, Shortell CK, et al: The hemodynamics of thrombus formation in arteries. J Vasc Surg 14:757, 1991.
133. Paasche PE, Kinley CE, Dolan FG, et al: Consideration of suture line stresses in the selection of synthetic grafts for implantation. J Biomech 6:253, 1973.
134. Pedersen EM, Hjortdal JØ, Hjortdal VE, et al: Three-dimensional visualization of velocity profiles in the porcine abdominal aortic trifurcation. J Vasc Surg 15:194, 1992.
135. Pentecost BL: The effect of exercise on the external iliac vein blood flow and local oxygen consumption in normal subjects, and in those with occlusive arterial disease. Clin Sci 27:437, 1964.
136. Peterson LH: Physical factors which influence vascular caliber and blood flow. Circ Res 18/19(Suppl 1):3, 1966.
137. Peterson LH, Jensen RE, Parnell J: Mechanical properties of arteries in vivo. Circ Res 8:622, 1960.
138. Porter JM, Cutler BS, Lee BY, et al: Pentoxifylline efficacy in the treatment of intermittent claudication. Am Heart J 104:66, 1982.
139. Reagan TR, Miller CW, Strandness DE Jr: Transcutaneous measurement of femoral artery flow. J Surg Res 11:477, 1971.
140. Remensnyder JP, Mitchell JH, Sarnoff SJ: Functional sympatholysis during muscular activity. Circ Res 11:370, 1962.
141. Remington JW, Wood EH: Formation of peripheral pulse contour in man. J Appl Physiol 9:433, 1956.
142. Rijsterborgh H, Roelandt J: Doppler assessment of aortic stenosis: Bernoulli revisited. Ultrasound Med Biol 13:241, 1987.
143. Rittenhouse EA, Maxiner W, Burr JW, et al: Directional arterial flow velocity: A sensitive index of changes in peripheral vascular resistance. Surgery 79:359, 1976.
144. Rittgers SE, Shu MCS: Doppler color-flow images from a stenosed arterial model: Interpretation of flow patterns. J Vasc Surg 12:511, 1990.

145. Roederer GO, Langlois YE, Chan AW, et al: Ultrasonic duplex scanning of extracranial carotid arteries: Improved accuracy using new features from the common carotid artery. J Cardiovasc Ultrasonogr 1:373, 1982.
146. Rosenthal SL, Guyton AC: Hemodynamics of collateral vasodilatation following femoral artery occlusion in anesthetized dogs. Circ Res 23:239, 1968.
147. Rutherford RB, Valenta J: Extremity blood flow and distribution: The effects of arterial occlusion, sympathectomy, and exercise. Surgery 69:332, 1971.
148. Sanders RJ, Kempczinski RF, Hammond W, et al: The significance of graft diameter. Surgery 88:856, 1980.
149. Scheffler A, Rieger H: A comparative analysis of transcutaneous oximetry ($tcPO_2$) during oxygen inhalation and leg dependency in severe peripheral arterial occlusive disease. J Vasc Surg 16:218, 1992.
150. Schneider JR, Zwolak RM, Walsh DB, et al: Lack of diameter effect on short-term patency of size-matched Dacron aortofemoral grafts. J Vasc Surg 13:785, 1991.
151. Schultz DL: Pressure and flow in large arteries. In Bergel DH (ed): Cardiovascular Fluid Dynamics, Vol I. New York, Academic Press, 1972, p 287.
152. Schultz RD, Hokanson DE, Strandness DE Jr: Pressure-flow relations of the end-side anastomosis. Surgery 62:319, 1967.
153. Segadal L, Matre K: Blood velocity distribution in the human ascending aorta. Circulation 76:90, 1987.
154. Sharefkin JB, Diamond SL, Eskin SG, et al: Fluid flow decreases preproendothelin mRNA levels and suppresses endothelin-1 peptide release in cultured human endothelial cells. J Vasc Surg 14:1, 1991.
155. Sharp WV, Donovan DL, Teague PC, Mosteller RD: Arterial occlusive disease: A function of vessel bifurcation angle. Surgery 91:680, 1982.
156. Shepherd JT: The blood flow through the calf after exercise in subjects with arteriosclerosis and claudication. Clin Sci 9:49, 1950.
157. Shepherd JT: Physiology of the Circulation in Human Limbs in Health and Disease. Philadelphia, WB Saunders, 1963.
158. Skidmore R, Woodcock JP: Physiological interpretation of Doppler-shift waveforms. I: Theoretical considerations. Ultrasound Med Biol 6:7, 1980.
159. Skidmore R, Woodcock JP: Physiological interpretation of Doppler-shift waveforms. II: Validation of the Laplace transform method for characterization of the common femoral blood-velocity/time waveform. Ultrasound Med Biol 6:219, 1980.
160. Skidmore R, Woodcock JP, Wells PNT, et al: Physiological interpretation of Doppler-shift waveforms. III: Clinical results. Ultrasound Med Biol 6:227, 1980.
161. Skinner JS, Strandness DE Jr: Exercise and intermittent claudication. I: Effect of repetition and intensity of exercise. Circulation 36:15, 1967.
162. Skinner JS, Strandness DE Jr: Exercise and intermittent claudication. II: Effect of physical training. Circulation 36:23, 1967.
163. Snell ES, Eastcott HHG, Hamilton M: Circulation in lower limb before and after reconstruction of obstructed main artery. Lancet 1:242, 1960.
164. Sottiurai VS, Sue SL, Breaux JR, Smith LM: Adaptability of endothelial orientation to blood flow dynamics: A morphologic analysis. Eur J Vasc Surg 3:145, 1989.
165. Stahler C, Strandness DE Jr: Ankle blood pressure response to gradual treadmill exercise. Angiology 18:237, 1967.
166. Strandell T, Wahren J: Circulation in the calf at rest, after arterial occlusion and after exercise in normal subjects and in patients with intermittent claudication. Acta Med Scand 173:99, 1963.
167. Strandness DE Jr: Abnormal exercise response after successful reconstructive arterial surgery. Surgery 59:325, 1966.
168. Strandness DE Jr: Functional results after revascularization of the profunda femoris artery. Am J Surg 119:240, 1970.
169. Strandness DE Jr, Bell JW: An evaluation of the hemodynamic response of the claudicating extremity to exercise. Surg Gynecol Obstet 119:1237, 1964.
170. Strandness DE Jr, Bell JW: Critical evaluation of the results of lumbar sympathectomy. Ann Surg 160:1021, 1964.
171. Strandness DE Jr, Bell JW: Peripheral vascular disease: Diagnosis and objective evaluation using a mercury strain gauge. Ann Surg 161(Suppl):1, 1965.
172. Strandness DE Jr, Schultz RD, Sumner DS, et al: Ultrasonic flow detection: A useful technique in the evaluation of peripheral vascular disease. Am J Surg 113:311, 1967.
173. Strandness DE Jr, Sumner DS: Hemodynamics for Surgeons. New York, Grune & Stratton, 1975.
174. Streeter VC, Keitzer WF, Bohr DF: Pulsatile pressure and flow through distensible vessels. Circ Res 13:3, 1963.
175. Stromberg DD, Weiderhielm CA: Viscoelastic description of a collagenous tissue in simple elongation. J Appl Physiol 26:857, 1969.
176. Sumner DS, Strandness DE Jr: The relationship between calf blood flow and ankle blood pressure in patients with intermittent claudication. Surgery 65:763, 1969.
177. Sumner DS, Strandness DE Jr: The effect of exercise on resistance to blood flow in limbs with an occluded superficial femoral artery. Vasc Surg 4:229, 1970.
178. Sumner DS, Strandness DE Jr: The hemodynamics of the femorofemoral shunt. Surg Gynecol Obstet 134:629, 1972.
179. Sumner DS, Hokanson DE, Strandness DE Jr: Arterial walls before and after endarterectomy, stress-strain characteristics and collagen-elastic content. Arch Surg 99:606, 1969.
180. Sumner DS, Hokanson DE, Strandness DE Jr: Stress-strain characteristics and collagen-elastic content of abdominal aortic aneurysms. Surg Gynecol Obstet 130:459, 1970.
181. Sydorak GR, Moore WS, Newcomb L, et al: Effect of increasing flow rates and arterial caliber on critical arterial stenoses. Surg Forum 23:243, 1972.
182. Van deBerg L, DeWeese JA, Rob CG: The effect of arterial stenosis and sympathectomy on blood flow and the ergogram. Ann Surg 159:623, 1964.
183. Vieli A, Moser U, Maier S, et al: Velocity profiles in the normal human abdominal aorta: A comparison between ultrasound and magnetic resonance data. Ultrasound Biol Med 15:113, 1989.
184. Vonruden WJ, Blaisdell FW, Hall AD, et al: Multiple arterial stenosis: Effect on blood flow. Arch Surg 89:307, 1964.
185. Wahren J, Jorfeldt L: Determinations of leg blood flow during exercise in man: An indicator-dilution technique based on femoral venous dye infusion. Clin Sci Mol Med 45:135, 1973.
186. Walden R, L'Italien GJ, Megerman J, et al: Matched elastic properties and successful arterial grafting. Arch Surg 115:1166, 1980.
187. Walker JR, Guyton AC: Influence of blood oxygen saturation on pressure-flow curve of dog hind leg. Am J Physiol 212:506, 1967.
188. Weissenhofer W, Schenk WG Jr: Hemodynamic response to vasodilation and exercise in "critical" arterial stenosis. Arch Surg 108:712, 1974.
189. Wengerter KR, Veith FJ, Gupta SK, et al: Influence of vein size (diameter) on infrapopliteal reversed vein graft patency. J Vasc Surg 11:525, 1990.
190. Wesolowski SA, Martinez A, Domingo RT, et al: Indications for aortofemoral arterial reconstruction: A study of borderline risk patients. Surgery 60:288, 1966.
191. Westerhof N, Sipkema P, Van Den Bos GC, et al: Forward and backward waves in the arterial system. Cardiovasc Res 6:648, 1972.
192. Winblad JN, Reemtsma K, Vernhet JL, et al: Etiologic mechanisms in the development of collateral circulation. Surgery 45:105, 1959.
193. Winsor T: Influence of arterial disease on the systolic blood pressure gradients of the extremity. Am J Med Sci 220:117, 1950.
194. Wolf EA Jr, Sumner DS, Strandness DE Jr: Correlation between nutritive blood flow and pressure in limbs of patients with intermittent claudication. Surg Forum 23:238, 1972.
195. Wolfe JHN, Waller DG, Chapman MB, et al: The effect of hemodilution upon patients with intermittent claudication. Surg Gynecol Obstet 160:347, 1985.

196. Wong PKC, Johnston KW, Ethier CR, Cobbold RSC: Computer simulation of blood flow patterns in arteries of various geometries. J Vasc Surg 14:658, 1991.
197. Woodcock JP, Gosling RG, Fitzgerald DE: A new non-invasive technique for assessment of superficial femoral artery obstruction. Br J Surg 59:226, 1972.
198. Wyatt MG, Muir RM, Tennant WG, et al: Impedance analysis to identify the at risk femorodistal graft. J Vasc Surg 13:284, 1991.
199. Yao ST: Haemodynamic studies in peripheral arterial disease. Br J Surg 57:761, 1970.
200. Yao ST, Hobbs JT, Irvine WT: Pulse examination by an ultrasonic method. Br Med J 4:555, 1968.
201. Yao ST, Hobbs JT, Irvine WT: Ankle systolic pressure measurements in arterial disease affecting the lower extremities. Br J Surg 56:676, 1969.
202. Yellin EL: Laminar-turbulent transition process in pulsation flow. Circ Res 19:791, 1966.
203. Young DF, Tsai FY: Flow characteristics in models of arterial stenoses. I: Steady flow. J Biomech 6:395, 1973.
204. Young DF, Tsai FY: Flow characteristics of models of arterial stenosis. II: Unsteady flow. J Biomech 6:547, 1973.
205. Zarins CK, Giddens DP, Bharadvaj BK, et al: Carotid bifurcation atherosclerosis: Quantitative correlation of plaque localization with flow velocity profiles and wall shear stress. Circ Res 53:502, 1983.
206. Zarins CK, Xu C, Glagov S: Aneurysmal enlargement of the aorta during regression of experimental atherosclerosis. J Vasc Surg 15:90, 1992.
207. Zarins CK, Zatina MA, Giddens DP, et al: Shear stress regulation of artery lumen diameter in experimental atherogenesis. J Vasc Surg 5:413, 1987.
208. Zarins CK, Glagov S, Vesselinovitch D, Wissler RW: Aneurysm formation in experimental atherosclerosis: Relationship to plaque evolution. J Vasc Surg 12:246, 1990.
209. Zellis R, Mason DT, Braunwald E, et al: Effects of hyperlipoproteinemias and their treatment on the peripheral circulation. J Clin Invest 49:1007, 1970.
210. Zwiebel WJ, Zagzebski JA, Crummy AB, et al: Correlation of peak Doppler frequency with lumen narrowing in carotid stenosis. Stroke 13:386, 1982.
211. Cambria RA, Lowell RC, Gloviczki P, Miller VM: Chronic changes in blood flow alter endothelium-dependent responses in autogenous vein grafts in dogs. J Vasc Surg 20:765, 1994.
212. Di Martino E, Mantero S, Inzoli F, et al: Biomechanics of abdominal aortic aneurysm in the presence of endoluminal thrombus: Experimental characterisation and structural static computational analysis. Eur J Vasc Endovasc Surg 15:290, 1998.
213. Dobrin PB, Mirande R, Kang S, et al: Mechanics of end-to-end artery-to-PTFE graft anastomoses. Ann Vasc Surg 12:317, 1998.
214. Fillinger MF, Cronenwett JL, Besso S, et al: Vein adaptation to the hemodynamic environment of infrainguinal grafts. J Vasc Surg 19:970, 1994.
215. Golledge J, Hicks RCJ, Ellis M, et al: Dilatation of saphenous vein grafts by nitric oxide. Eur J Vasc Endovasc Surg 14:41, 1977.
216. Inzoli F, Boschetti F, Zappa M, et al: Biomechanical factors in abdominal aortic aneurysm rupture. Eur J Vasc Surg 7:667, 1993.
217. Lei M, Archie JP, Kleinstreuer C: Computational design of a bypass graft that minimizes wall shear stress gradients in the region of the distal anastomosis. J Vasc Surg 25:637, 1997.
218. Miller VM, Burnett JC Jr: Modulation of NO and endothelin by chronic increases in blood flow in canine femoral arteries. Am J Physiol 263:H103, 1992.
219. Mower WR, Quiñones WJ, Gambhir SS: Effect of intraluminal thrombus on abdominal aortic aneurysm wall stress. J Vasc Surg 26:602, 1997.
220. Park TC, Harker CT, Edwards JM, et al: Human saphenous vein grafts explanted from the arterial circulation demonstrate altered smooth-muscle and endothelial responses. J Vasc Surg 18:61, 1993.
221. Schwartz LB, Purut CM, Craig DM, et al: Input impedance of revascularized skeletal muscle, renal, and mesenteric vascular beds. Vasc Surg 30:459, 1996.
222. Sonesson B, Hansen F, Stale H, Länne T: Compliance and diameter in the human abdominal aorta: The influence of age and sex. Eur J Vasc Surg 7:690, 1993.
223. Unthank JL, Nixon JC, Dalsing MC: Nitric oxide maintains dilation of immature and mature collateral in the rat hindlimb. J Vasc Res 33:471, 1966.
224. van Dielen FMH, Kurvers HAJM, Dammers R, et al: Effects of surgical sympathectomy on skin blood flow in a rat model of chronic limb ischemia. World J Surg 22:807, 1998.
225. Vorp DA, Raghavan ML, Webster MW: Mechanical wall stress in abdominal aortic aneurysm: Influence of diameter and asymmetry. J Vasc Surg 27:632, 1998.

Venous Hemodynamics

226. Abramowitz HB, Queral LA, Flinn WR, et al: The use of photoplethysmography in the assessment of venous insufficiency: A comparison to venous pressure measurements. Surgery 86:434, 1979.
227. Zoster T, Cronin RFP: Venous distensibility in patients with varicose veins. Can Med Assoc J 4:1293, 1966.
228. Abu-Own AA, Scurr JH, Coleridge Smith PD: Assessment of microangiopathy of the skin in chronic venous insufficiency by laser Doppler fluxmetry. J Vasc Surg 17:429, 1993.
229. Alimi YS, Barthelemy P, Juhan C: Venous pump of the calf: A study of venous and muscular pressures. J Vasc Surg 20:728, 1994.
230. Almén T, Nylander G: Serial phlebography of the normal lower leg during muscular contraction and relaxation. Acta Radiol 57:264, 1962.
231. Araki CT, Back TL, Padberg FT, et al: The significance of calf muscle pump function in venous ulceration. J Vasc Surg 20:872, 1994.
232. Arenander E: Hemodynamic effects of varicose veins and results of radical surgery. Acta Chir Scand 260(Suppl):1, 1960.
233. Arnoldi CC: Venous pressure in patients with valvular incompetence of the veins of the lower limb. Acta Chir Scand 132:628, 1966.
234. Arnoldi CC, Linderholm H: On the pathogenesis of the venous leg ulcer. Acta Chir Scand 134:427, 1968.
235. Arnoldi CC, Linderholm H: Venous blood pressures in the lower limb at rest and during exercise in patients with idiopathic dysfunction of the venous pump of the calf. Acta Chir Scand 135:601, 1969.
236. Attinger EO: Wall properties of veins. IEEE Trans Biomed Eng 16:253, 1969.
237. Barnes RW, Collicott PE, Mozersky DJ, et al: Noninvasive quantitation of maximum venous outflow in acute thrombophlebitis. Surgery 72:971, 1972.
238. Barnes RW, Collicott PE, Mozersky DJ, et al: Noninvasive quantitation of venous reflux in the postphlebitic syndrome. Surg Gynecol Obstet 136:769, 1973.
239. Barnes RW, Collicott PE, Mozersky DJ, et al: Noninvasive quantitation of venous hemodynamics in postphlebitic syndrome. Arch Surg 107:807, 1973.
240. Barwin BN, Roddie IC: Venous distensibility during pregnancy determined by graded venous congestion. Am J Obstet Gynecol 125:921, 1976.
241. Bauer G: A roentgenological and clinical study of the sequels of thrombosis. Acta Chir Scand 86(Suppl 74):1, 1942.
242. Beecher HK, Field ME, Krogh A: The effect of walking on the venous pressure at the ankle. Skand Arch Physiol 73:133, 1936.
243. Bishara RA, Sigel B, Rocco K, et al: Deterioration of venous function in normal lower extremities during daily activity. J Vasc Surg 3:700, 1986.
244. Bjordal RI: Simultaneous pressure and flow recordings in varicose veins of the lower extremity: A hemodynamic study of venous dysfunction. Acta Chir Scand 136:309, 1970.

245. Brace RA: Progress toward resolving the controversy of positive vs. negative interstitial fluid pressure. Circ Res 49:281, 1981.
246. Brockman SK, Vasko JS: Phlegmasia cerulea dolens. Surg Gynecol Obstet 121:1347, 1965.
247. Brockman SK, Vasko JS: The pathologic physiology of phlegmasia cerulea dolens. Surgery 59:997, 1966.
248. Browse NL: The pathogenesis of venous ulceration: A hypothesis. J Vasc Surg 7:468, 1988.
249. Browse NL, Shepherd JT: Differences in response of veins and resistance vessels in limbs to same stimulus. Am J Physiol 211:1241, 1966.
250. Burnand KG, Whimster I, Naidoo A, et al: Pericapillary fibrin in the ulcer-bearing skin of the leg: The cause of lipodermatosclerosis and venous ulcerations. Br Med J 285:1071, 1982.
251. Christopoulos D, Nicolaides AN: Noninvasive diagnosis and quantitation of popliteal reflux in the swollen and ulcerated leg. J Cardiovasc Surg 29:535, 1988.
252. Christopoulos D, Nicolaides AN, Galloway JMD, Wilkinson A: Objective noninvasive evaluation of venous surgical results. J Vasc Surg 8:683, 1988.
253. Christopoulos D, Nicolaides AN, Szendro G: Venous reflux: Quantification and correlation with the clinical severity of chronic venous disease. Br J Surg 75:352, 1988.
254. Christopoulos DG, Nicolaides AN, Szendro G, et al: Air-plethysmography and the effect of elastic compression on venous hemodynamics of the leg. J Vasc Surg 5:148, 1987.
255. Clarke GH, Vasdekis SN, Hobbs JT, Nicolaides AN: Venous wall function in the pathogenesis of varicose veins. Surgery 111:402, 1992.
256. Cockett FB, Jones DEE: The ankle blowout syndrome, a new approach to the varicose ulcer problem. Lancet 1:17, 1953.
257. Conrad MC: Functional Anatomy of the Circulation to the Extremities. Chicago, Year Book Medical, 1971.
258. Cotton LT: Varicose veins, gross anatomy and development. Br J Surg 48:549, 1961.
259. Dahn I, Eiriksson E: Plethysmographic diagnosis of deep venous thrombosis of the leg. Acta Chir Scand 398(Suppl):33, 1968.
260. Dalsing MC, Lalka SG, Unthank JL, et al: Venous valvular insufficiency: Influence of a single venous valve (native and experimental). J Vasc Surg 14:576, 1991.
261. Darke SG, Penfold C: Venous ulceration and saphenous ligation. Eur J Vasc Surg 6:4, 1992.
262. DeCamp PT, Schramel RJ, Roy CJ, et al: Ambulatory venous pressure determinations in postphlebitic and related syndromes. Surgery 29:44, 1951.
263. DeWeese JA, Rogoff SM: Phlebographic patterns of acute deep venous thrombosis of the leg. Surgery 53:99, 1963.
264. Edwards EA, Edwards JE: The effect of thrombophlebitis on the venous valve. Surg Gynecol Obstet 65:310, 1937.
265. Edwards JE, Edwards EA: The saphenous valves in varicose veins. Am Heart J 19:338, 1940.
266. Eiriksson E, Dahn L: Plethysmographic studies of venous distensibility in patients with varicose veins. Acta Chir Scand 398 (Suppl):19, 1968.
267. Ellwood RA, Lee WB: Pedal venous pressure: Correlation with presence and site of deep-venous abnormalities. Radiology 131:73, 1979.
268. Fagrell B: Local microcirculation in chronic venous incompetence and leg ulcers. Vasc Surg 13:217, 1979.
269. Fegan WG, Kline AL: The cause of varicosity in superficial veins of the lower limb. Br J Surg 59:798, 1972.
270. Folse R: The influence of femoral vein dynamics on the development of varicose veins. Surgery 68:974, 1970.
271. Franzeck UK, Bollinger A, Huch R, et al: Transcutaneous oxygen tension and capillary morphologic characteristics and density in patients with chronic venous incompetence. Circulation 70:806, 1984.
272. Fry DL, Thomas LJ, Greenfield JC Jr: Flow in collapsible tubes. In Patel DJ, Vaishnav RN (eds): Basic Hemodynamics and Its Role in Disease Processes. Baltimore, University Park Press, 1980, p 407.
273. Gardner AMN, Fox RH: The Return of Blood to the Heart: Venous Pumps in Health and Disease. London, John Libbey Eurotext, 1989.
274. Gooley NA, Sumner DS: Relationship of venous reflux to the site of venous valvular incompetence: Implications for venous reconstructive surgery. J Vasc Surg 7:50, 1988.
275. Greenfield ADM: The venous system in cardiovascular functions. In Luisada AA (ed): Cardiovascular Functions. New York, McGraw-Hill, 1962.
276. Guyton AC: Interstitial fluid pressure. II: Pressure-volume curves of interstitial space. Circ Res 16:452, 1965.
277. Hallböök T, Göthlin J: Strain gauge plethysmography and phlebography in diagnosis of deep venous thrombosis. Acta Chir Scand 137:37, 1971.
278. Haller JA Jr: Effects of deep femoral thrombophlebitis on the circulation of the lower extremities. Circulation 27:693, 1963.
279. Hanrahan LM, Araki CT, Rodriguez AA, et al: Distribution of valvular incompetence in patients with venous stasis ulceration. J Vasc Surg 13:805, 1991.
280. Hjelmstedt NA: Pressure decrease in the dorsal pedal veins on walking in persons with and without thrombosis. Acta Chir Scand 134:531, 1968.
281. Hjelmstedt NA: The pressure in the veins of the dorsum of the foot in quiet standing and during exercise in limbs without signs of venous disorder. Acta Chir Scand 134:235, 1968.
282. Höjensgard IC, Stürup H: Static and dynamic pressures in superficial and deep veins of the lower extremity in man. Acta Physiol Scand 27:49, 1952.
283. Holt JP: Flow through collapsible tubes and through in situ veins. IEEE Trans Biomed Eng 16:274, 1969.
284. Husni EA, Ximenes JO, Goyette EM: Elastic support of the lower limbs in hospital patients: A critical study. JAMA 214:1456, 1970.
285. Ikard RW, Ueland K, Folse R: Lower limb venous dynamics in pregnant women. Surg Gynecol Obstet 132:483, 1971.
286. Jacobsen BH: The venous drainage of the foot. Surg Gynecol Obstet 131:22, 1970.
287. Johnson ND, Queral LA, Flinn WR, et al: Late objective assessment of venous valve surgery. Arch Surg 116:1461, 1981.
288. Kerr MG, Scott DB, Samuel E: Studies of the inferior vena cava in late pregnancy. Br Med J 1:532, 1964.
289. Killewich LA, Bedford GR, Beach KW, Strandness DE Jr: Spontaneous lysis of deep venous thrombi: Rate and outcome. J Vasc Surg 9:89, 1989.
290. Koslow AR, DeWeese JA: Anatomical and mechanical aspects of a plantar venous plexus. Presented at the Jobst Symposium on Current Issues in Venous Disease, Chicago, 1988.
291. Kuster G, Lofgren CP, Hollinshead WH: Anatomy of the veins of the foot. Surg Gynecol Obstet 127:817, 1968.
292. Labropoulos N, Leon M, Geroulakos G, et al: Venous hemodynamic abnormalities in patients with leg ulceration. Am J Surg 169:572, 1995.
293. Labropoulos N, Leon M, Nicolaides AN, et al: Venous reflux in patients with previous deep venous thrombosis: Correlation with ulceration and other symptoms. J Vasc Surg 20:20, 1994.
294. Labropoulos N, Leon M, Nicolaides AN, et al: Superficial venous insufficiency: Correlation of anatomic extent of reflux with clinical symptoms and signs. J Vasc Surg 20:953, 1994.
295. Landis EM, Pappenheimer JR: Exchange of substances through capillary walls. In Hamilton WF, Dow P (eds): Handbook of Physiology, Vol II. Washington, DC, American Physiological Society, 1963, p 961.
296. Lees TA, Lambert D: Patterns of venous reflux in limbs with skin changes associated with chronic venous insufficiency. Br J Surg 80:725, 1993.
297. LePage PA, Villavicencio JL, Gomez FR, et al: The valvular anatomy of the internal iliac venous system and its clinical implications. J Vasc Surg 14:678, 1991.
298. Lindner DJ, Edwards JM, Phinney ES, et al: Long-term hemodynamic and clinical sequelae of lower extremity deep vein thrombosis. J Vasc Surg 4:436, 1986.

299. Linton RR: Post-thrombotic ulceration of the lower extremity: Its etiology and surgical treatment. Ann Surg 138:415, 1953.
300. Lowell RC, Gloviczki P, Miller VM: In vitro evaluation of endothelial and smooth muscle function of primary varicose veins. J Vasc Surg 16:679, 1992.
301. Ludbrook J: Valvular defect in primary varicose veins, cause or effect? Lancet 2:1289, 1963.
302. Ludbrook J: The musculovenous pumps of the human lower limb. Am Heart J 71:635, 1966.
303. Ludbrook J: Aspects of Venous Function in the Lower Limbs. Springfield, Ill, Charles C Thomas, 1966.
304. Ludbrook J, Beale G: Femoral venous valves in relation to varicose veins. Lancet 1:79, 1962.
305. Ludbrook J, Loughlin J: Regulation of volume in postarteriolar vessels of the lower limb. Am Heart J 67:493, 1964.
306. Lye CR, Sumner DS, Hokanson DE, Strandness DE Jr: The transcutaneous measurement of the elastic properties of the human saphenous vein femoropopliteal bypass graft. Surg Gynecol Obstet 141:891, 1975.
307. Lyon CK, Scott JB, Wang CY: Flow through collapsible tubes at low Reynolds numbers. Circ Res 47:68, 1980.
308. Lyon CK, Scott JB, Anderson DK, Wang CY: Flow through collapsible tubes at high Reynolds numbers. Circ Res 49:988, 1981.
309. Mani R: Venous haemodynamics: A consideration of macro- and microvascular effects. Proc Inst Mech Eng 206:109, 1992.
310. Markel A, Manzo RA, Bergelin RO, Strandness DE Jr: Valvular reflux after deep vein thrombosis: Incidence and time of occurrence. J Vasc Surg 15:377, 1992.
311. Masuda EM, Kistner RL: Prospective comparison of duplex scanning and descending venography in the assessment of venous insufficiency. Am J Surg 164:254, 1992.
312. McEnroe CS, O'Donnell TF Jr, Mackey WC: Correlation of clinical findings with venous hemodynamics in 386 patients with chronic venous insufficiency. Am J Surg 156:148, 1988.
313. McLennan CE: Antecubital and femoral venous pressure in normal and toxemic prégnancy. Am J Obstet Gynecol 45:568, 1943.
314. McPheeters HO, Merkert CE, Lundblad RA: The mechanics of the reverse flow in varicose veins as proved by blood pressure readings. Surg Gynecol Obstet 55:298, 1932.
315. Moore DJ, Himmel PD, Sumner DS: Distribution of venous valvular incompetence in patients with the postphlebitic syndrome. J Vasc Surg 3:49, 1986.
316. Moreno AH, Katz AI, Gold LD, Reddy RV: Mechanics of distention of dog veins and other thin-walled tubular structures. Circ Res 27:1069, 1970.
317. Myers KA, Ziegenbein RW, Zeng GH, Mathews PG: Duplex ultrasonography scanning for chronic venous disease: Patterns of venous reflux. J Vasc Surg 21:605, 1995.
318. Neglén P, Raju S: A rational approach to detection of significant reflux with duplex Doppler scanning and air plethysmography. J Vasc Surg 17:590, 1993.
319. Neglén P, Raju S: Compliance of the normal and post-thrombotic calf. J Cardiovasc Surg 36:225, 1995.
320. Negus D, Cockett FD: Femoral vein pressures in postphlebitic iliac vein obstruction. Br J Surg 54:522, 1967.
321. Nicolaides AN: Noninvasive assessment of primary and secondary varicose veins. In Bernstein EF (ed): Noninvasive Diagnostic Techniques in Vascular Disease, 2nd ed. St. Louis, CV Mosby, 1982, p 575.
322. Nicolaides AN, Hussein MK, Szendro G, et al: The relation of venous ulceration with ambulatory venous pressure measurements. J Vasc Surg 17:414, 1993.
323. Nicolaides AN, Miles C: Photoplethysmography in the assessment of venous insufficiency. J Vasc Surg 5:405, 1987.
324. Öberg B: The relationship between active constriction and passive recoil of the veins at various distending pressures. Acta Physiol Scand 71:233, 1967.
325. O'Donnell TF, Mackey WC, Shephard AD, et al: Clinical, hemodynamic, and anatomic follow-up of direct venous reconstruction. Arch Surg 122:474, 1987.
326. Pearce WH, Ricco J-B, Queral LA, et al: Hemodynamic assessment of venous problems. Surgery 93:715, 1983.
327. Pflug JJ, Zubac DP, Kersten DR, Alexander NDE: The resting interstitial tissue pressure in primary varicose veins. J Vasc Surg 11:411, 1990.
328. Pollack AA, Wood EH: Venous pressure in the saphenous vein at the ankle in man during exercise and changes in posture. J Appl Physiol 1:649, 1949.
329. Pollack AA, Taylor BE, Myers TT, Wood EH: The effect of exercise and body position on the venous pressures at the ankle in patients having venous valvular defects. J Clin Invest 28:559, 1949.
330. Raju S: New approaches in the diagnosis and treatment of venous obstruction. J Vasc Surg 4:42, 1986.
331. Raju S, Fredericks R: Valve reconstruction procedures for nonobstructive venous insufficiency: Rationale, techniques, and results in 107 procedures with two- to eight-year follow-up. J Vasc Surg 71:301, 1988.
332. Raju S, Fredericks R, Lishman P, et al: Observations on the calf pump mechanism: Determinants of postexercise pressure. J Vasc Surg 17:459, 1993.
333. Reagan B, Folse R: Lower limb venous dynamics in normal persons and children of patients with varicose veins. Surg Gynecol Obstet 132:15, 1971.
334. Rich NM, Hobson RW II, Wright CB, Fedde CW: Repair of lower extremity venous trauma: A more aggressive approach required. J Trauma 14:639, 1974.
335. Rose SS, Ahmed A: Some thoughts on the aetiology of varicose veins. J Cardiovasc Surg 27:534, 1986.
336. Rosfors S, Lamke L-O, Nordström E, Bygdeman S: Severity and location of venous valvular insufficiency: The importance of distal valve function. Acta Chir Scand 156:689, 1990.
337. Rushmer RF: Effects of posture. In Cardiovascular Dynamics, 3rd ed. Philadelphia, WB Saunders, 1970, p 192.
338. Rutherford RB, Reddy CMK, Walker FG, Wagner HN Jr: A new quantitative method of assessing the functional status of the leg veins. Am J Surg 122:594, 1971.
339. Saffle JR, Maxwell JG, Warden GD, et al: Measurement of intramuscular pressure in the management of massive venous occlusion. Surgery 89:394, 1981.
340. Sakaguchi S, Ishitobi K, Kameda T: Functional segmental plethysmography with mercury strain gauge. Angiology 23:127, 1972.
341. Samueloff SL, Browse NL, Shepherd JT: Response of capacity vessels in human limbs to head up tilt and suction on lower body. J Appl Physiol 21:47, 1966.
342. Sarin S, Scurr JH, Coleridge Smith PD: Medial calf perforators in venous disease: The significance of outward flow. J Vasc Surg 16:40, 1992.
343. Schalin L: Arteriovenous communications to varicose veins in the lower extremities studied by dynamic angiography. Acta Chir Scand 146:397, 1980.
344. Schalin L: Arteriovenous communications in varicose veins localized by thermography and identified by operative microscopy. Acta Chir Scand 147:409, 1981.
345. Schanzer H, Pierce EC II: A rational approach to surgery of the chronic venous stasis syndrome. Ann Surg 195:25, 1982.
346. Shami SK, Sarin S, Cheatle TR, et al: Venous ulcers and the superficial venous system. J Vasc Surg 17:487, 1993.
347. Shepherd JT: Role of the veins in the circulation. Circulation 33:484, 1966.
348. Shepherd JT: Reflex control of the venous system. In Bergan JJ, Yao JST (eds): Venous Problems. Chicago, Year Book Medical, 1978, p 5.
349. Sherman RS Sr: Varicose veins: Anatomy, reevaluation of Trendelenburg tests, and an operative procedure. Surg Clin North Am 44:1369, 1964.

350. Shull KS, Nicolaides AN, Fernandes é Fernandes J, et al: Significance of popliteal reflux in relation to ambulatory venous pressure and ulceration. Arch Surg 114:1304, 1979.
351. Snyder MA, Adams JT, Schwartz SI: Hemodynamics of phlegmasia cerulea dolens. Surg Gynecol Obstet 125:342, 1967.
352. Somerville JJF, Byrne PJ, Fegan WG: Analysis of flow patterns in venous insufficiency. Br J Surg 61:40, 1974.
353. Starling EH: On the absorption of fluids from the connective tissue spaces. J Physiol 19:312, 1896.
354. Stegall HF: Muscle pumping in the dependent leg. Circ Res 19:180, 1966.
355. Strandness DE Jr, Sumner DS: Hemodynamics for Surgeons. New York, Grune & Stratton, 1975.
356. Sumner DS: Diagnosis of venous thrombosis by Doppler ultrasound. In Bergan JJ, Yao JST (eds): Venous Problems. Chicago, Year Book Medical, 1978, pp 159-185.
357. Sumner DS: Venous dynamics—varicosities. Clin Obstet Gynecol 24:743, 1981.
358. Sumner DS: Hemodynamics of the venous system: Calf pump and valve function. In Raju S, Villavicencio JL (eds): Surgical Management of Venous Disease. Baltimore, Williams & Wilkins, 1997, pp 16-59.
359. Taheri SA, Heffner R, Meenaghan MA, et al: Technique and results of venous valve transplantation. In Bergan JJ, Yao JST (eds): Surgery of the Veins. Orlando, Fla, Grune & Stratton, 1985, p 219.
360. Taylor AE: Capillary fluid filtration, Starling forces and lymph flow. Circ Res 49:557, 1981.
361. Thomas ML, Keeling FP, Ackroyd JS: Descending phlebography: A comparison of three methods and an assessment of the normal range of deep vein reflux. J Cardiovasc Surg 27:27, 1986.
362. Thulesius O: Elastizität und Klappenfunktion peripherer Venen bei primarer Varikosis. Phlebol Proktol 8:97, 1979.
363. Tripolitis AJ, Milligan EB, Bodily KC, Strandness DE Jr: The physiology of venous claudication. Am J Surg 139:447, 1980.
364. Ueland K: Pregnancy and cardiovascular disease. Med Clin North Am 61:17, 1977.
365. van Bemmelen PS, Bedford G, Beach K, Strandness DE Jr: Status of the valves in the superficial and deep venous system in chronic venous disease. Surgery 109:730, 1991.
366. van Bemmelen PS, Bedford G, Beach K, Strandness DE: Quantitative segmental evaluation of venous reflux with duplex ultrasound scanning. J Vasc Surg 10:425, 1989.
367. Vanhoutte PM, Shepherd JT: Thermosensitivity and veins. J Physiol (Paris) 63:449, 1970.
368. van Rij AM, Solomon C, Christie R: Anatomic and physiologic characteristics of venous ulceration. J Vasc Surg 20:759, 1994.
369. Vasdekis SN, Clarke GH, Nicolaides AN: Quantification of venous reflux by means of duplex scanning. J Vasc Surg 10:670, 1989.
370. Warren R, White EA, Belcher CD: Venous pressures in the saphenous system in normal, varicose, and postphlebitic extremities. Surgery 26:435, 1949.
371. Webb-Peploe MM, Shepherd JT: Response of large hindlimb veins of the dog to sympathetic nerve stimulation. Am J Physiol 215:299, 1968.
372. Welch HJ, McLaughlin RL, O'Donnell TF Jr: Femoral vein valvuloplasty: Intraoperative angioscopic evaluation and hemodynamic improvement. J Vasc Surg 16:694, 1992.
373. Welkie JF, Comerota AJ, Katz ML, et al: Hemodynamic deterioration in chronic venous disease. J Vasc Surg 16:733, 1992.
374. Welkie JF, Comerota AJ, Kerr RP, et al: The hemodynamics of venous ulceration. Ann Vasc Surg 6:1, 1992.
375. Wright CB, Swan KG: Hemodynamics of venous occlusion in the canine hindlimb. Surgery 73:141, 1973.
376. Wright CB, Sayre JT, Casterline PI, Swan KG: Hemodynamic effects of sympathectomy in canine femoral venous occlusion. Surgery 74:405, 1973.

Chapter 10

Artery Wall Pathology in Atherosclerosis

CHRISTOPHER K. ZARINS, MD
CHENGPEI XU, MD, PHD
SEYMOUR GLAGOV, MD

Atherosclerosis is the principal pathologic process affecting the large arteries. A degenerative disease, atherosclerosis is characterized by the accumulation of cells, matrix fibers, lipids, and tissue debris in the intima, which may result in narrowing of the lumen and obstruction of blood flow or ulceration, embolization, and thrombosis. Intimal plaque deposition may be accompanied by arterial enlargement and thinning of the underlying artery wall. Such enlargement may compensate for the enlarging intimal plaque and prevent lumen stenosis. It may also, under certain circumstances, lead to aneurysm formation with eventual artery wall rupture. Dissection, arteritis, and other degenerative conditions may also result in similar clinical complications, but they are rare compared with atherosclerosis and are dealt with elsewhere.

This chapter discusses the problem of atherosclerosis as it relates to the functional biomechanical properties of the artery wall. Both normal and pathologic responses of the artery wall are considered, as are differences in the evolution of atherosclerotic lesions. Local differences that may account for the propensity of certain areas to form extensive and complex plaques or aneurysms are also discussed.

■ STRUCTURE AND FUNCTION OF THE ARTERY WALL

Arteries are not simply a passive system of tubes of uniform and fixed composition that distribute blood to organs. Investigation has revealed that the major arteries are intricate biomechanical structures well suited to carry out their metabolic and mechanical functions under a wide range of conditions.[1] Arteries respond to acute hemodynamic alterations by changing caliber, through either constriction or dilatation.[2] Several mechanisms operate to limit hemorrhage in the event of disruptive injury and to restore wall integrity without long-term sequelae.[3] Arteries also adapt to gradual changes in local hemodynamic stresses and to systemic environmental conditions in order to maintain optimal diameter and mechanical characteristics and to ensure continued adequate blood flow.[4] The following brief review of the functional microanatomy of the artery wall indicates the range and limits of artery wall adaptability.

Intima

The intima, the innermost layer of the artery wall, extends from the luminal surface to the internal elastic lamina. The luminal surface is lined by the endothelium, a continuous monolayer of flat, polygonal cells. Between the endothelium and the internal elastic lamina, the intima is normally very narrow, with the endothelium lying directly on the internal elastic lamina and containing only a few scattered leukocytes, smooth muscle cells, and connective tissue fibers. It is in this region that atherosclerotic lesions develop.

Endothelium

The endothelium rests on a basal lamina that provides a continuous, pliable, and compliant substrate. Changes in cell shape and in the extent of junctional overlap among adjacent endothelial cells occur in relation to (1) changes in artery diameter associated with pulsatile wall motion, (2) changes in configuration associated with bending or stretching, and (3) the intimal accumulation of cells and matrix fibers during the development of intimal atherosclerotic plaques.[5] These changes act to prevent the development of discontinuities in the endothelial lining.

The endothelium also has numerous focal attachments to the underlying internal elastic lamina.[6] These relatively tight and rigid junctions contribute to stability by preventing slippage, telescoping, or detachment of endothelial cells and disruption or denudation by elevations in shear stress or by other mechanical forces. The endothelium presents a thromboresistant surface as well as a selective interface for diffusion, convection, and active transport of circulating substances into the underlying artery wall.[7]

Endothelial cells play a critical role in the physiology and pathophysiology of vascular disorders.[8] They respond to hemodynamic stresses and may transduce an atheroprotective force[9] by regulating the ingress, egress, and metabolism of lipoproteins and other agents that may participate in the initiation and progression of intimal plaques.[3,5]

Endothelial Injury

The endothelial surface can be injured or disrupted by various means but regenerates rapidly after focal denudation. The healing response, if extensive, may be accompanied by smooth muscle cell proliferation and migration and intimal thickening.[10,11] A series of reactions set into motion by focal endothelial denudation has been proposed as the initiating event in the pathogenesis of atherosclerosis.

According to this hypothesis, endothelial injury and desquamation may be caused by (1) mechanical forces, such as elevated wall shear stress and hypertension; (2) metabolic intermediates, such as those that characterize hyperlipidemia; (3) immunologic reactions; and (4) increased exposure to vasoactive agents. Such endothelial desquamation would expose subendothelial tissues to the circulation and stimulate platelet deposition, the release of a platelet-derived growth factor, cellular proliferation, and eventual lipid deposition and plaque formation.[12] Focal, repeated disruptive endothelial injuries and responses to those injuries would account for the localized nature of plaque deposition.

There is little evidence, however, to support the belief that endothelial injury or disruption in the form of desquamation, with or without platelet adhesion, occurs in regions of the vascular tree at highest risk for future lesion development.[13] In addition, there is no direct evidence that experimentally induced endothelial damage or removal results in eventual sustained lesion formation,[14] even in the presence of hyperlipidemia. On the contrary, evidence has been advanced that the formation of experimental intimal plaques may require the presence of an endothelial covering.[15,16] Although platelets may play a role in the transition of early plaques to more complex and advanced forms,[17] their effect on plaque initiation remains questionable. Platelet-derived growth factor has been isolated from other cellular elements that participate in plaque formation,[18] and smooth muscle cell proliferation may be an aspect of an overall healing reaction of arteries rather than the underlying primary event in atherosclerosis. Later studies have attempted to define injury in terms of functional alterations that may predispose to the formation of atherosclerotic lesions.[19,20]

Under normal circumstances, the vascular endothelium functions as an antithrombotic surface and contributes to the regulation of vascular tone and artery lumen diameter through the secretion of vasoconstrictors (e.g., angiotensin II) and vasodilators and inhibitors of platelet aggregation (e.g., prostacyclin and endothelium-derived relaxing factor).[21,22] Such factors maintain the smooth muscle cells of the media in a contractile, nonproliferative phenotype with low cholesterol ester content. In response to endothelial cell activation or injury, endothelial cells become increasingly permeable to low-density lipoprotein, have higher replicative rates, develop prothrombotic properties, and express surface glycoproteins that promote the adhesion and ingress of neutrophils, monocytes, and platelets.[23] Endothelial cells and monocytes release cytokines, growth factors, and leukotrienes, inducing prostacyclin production, which further promotes monocyte adhesion and diapedesis. The net effect of cytokine and growth factor production is the

FIGURE 10-1 Transmural organization of the media of large elastic arteries such as the aorta. Groups of smooth muscle cells (C), oriented with their long axes perpendicular to the longitudinal axis of the artery (axis of blood flow), are surrounded by a network of fine type III collagen fibrils within a matrix of basal lamina (M). They are surrounded by a closely associated system of elastic fibers (E) oriented in the same direction as the smooth muscle cells. Wavy bundles or fibers (F) of type I collagen are woven between the adjacent large elastic lamellae and provide much of the tensile strength of the media. Elastin fibers allow for compliance and recoil of the artery during the cardiac cycle. (From Clark JM, Glagov S: Transmural organization of the arterial wall: The lamellar unit revisited. Arteriosclerosis 5:19, 1985.)

stimulation of smooth muscle cell proliferation and migration. As a result of these changes, extracellular lipid as well as foam cells containing cholesterol esters accumulate in the intima.

These observations suggest that humoral mediators, growth factors, and cytokines from altered endothelial cells and from inflammatory cells interacting with other arterial cells are important mediators of macrophage infiltration, smooth muscle cell proliferation, and lipid deposition. Although physical and mechanical endothelial disruption and denudation may not be reactions that initiate or precipitate events in atherosclerotic plaque formation, biologic reactions of the endothelium and artery wall during injury and repair may play important roles in the proliferative and lipid deposition stage of plaque formation.

Media

The media extends from the internal elastic lamina to the adventitia. Although an external elastic lamina demarcates the boundary between the media and adventitia in many vessels, a distinct external elastic lamina may not be present, particularly in vessels with a thick and fibrous adventitial layer. The outer limit of the media can nevertheless be distinguished in nearly all intact arteries, because in contrast to the adventitia, the media consists of closely packed layers of smooth muscle cells in close association with elastin and collagen fibers.

The *smooth muscle cell* layers are composed of groups of similarly oriented cells, each surrounded by a common basal lamina and a closely associated interlacing basketwork of type III collagen fibrils arranged so as to tighten about the cell groups as the media is brought under tension; this configuration tends to hold the groups of cells together and to prevent excessive stretching or slippage. In addition, each cellular subgroup or fascicle is encompassed by a system of similarly oriented *elastic fibers* such that the effective unit of structure is a musculoelastic fascicle. In relation to the curvature of the artery wall, each fascicle is oriented in the direction of the imposed tensile stress. Focal tight attachment sites between smooth muscle cells and elastic fibers are normally abundant.[24]

The aorta and its immediately proximal, larger branches are called *elastic arteries* because of the prominence of their elastic fibers. In such vessels, the elastin fiber systems of the musculoelastic fascicles are thick and closely packed, resulting in an appearance on transverse cross-section of elastin lamellae alternating with smooth muscle layers. Thicker, crimped, type I collagen bundles are woven between adjacent large elastic lamellae.[25] The elastin fibers are relatively extensible and allow for compliance and recoil of the artery wall in relation to pulse propagation during the cardiac cycle. The extensive interconnected transmural arrangement of the elastic fibers of the musculoelastic fascicles tends to ensure uniform distribution of tensile mural stresses and prevent the propagation of flaws that develop in the media with age. The thick, crimped collagen fiber bundles provide much of the tensile strength of the media and, because of their high elastic modulus, limit distention and prevent disruption even at very high blood pressures (Fig. 10-1).[26]

The smaller-caliber *muscular arteries* contain relatively less collagen and elastin and more smooth muscle cells than elastic arteries and can therefore alter their diameter rapidly by constricting or dilating. The musculoelastic fascicles, which are most clearly evident in elastic arteries, are also the structural unit of muscular arteries and, as in elastic arteries, are generally aligned in the direction of the tensile forces. However, because of the preponderance of smooth muscle cells relative to elastin and collagen fibers, they are less prominent and the layering of the media is therefore less distinct (Fig. 10-2).[26]

Medial thickness and the number of musculoelastic layers, or *lamellar units,* are closely related to the lumen radius and to mural tangential tension. Tangential tension on the artery wall is, in general, proportional to the product of pressure and radius (Laplace's law), whereas the actual tensile stress per unit of cross-sectional area is inversely proportional to the wall thickness. The average tension per lamellar unit tends to be constant for homologous vessels in mammals. With increasing species size, mammalian adult aortic radius enlarges, with corresponding increases in medial thickness and in the number of musculoelastic layers, or lamellar units.[27]

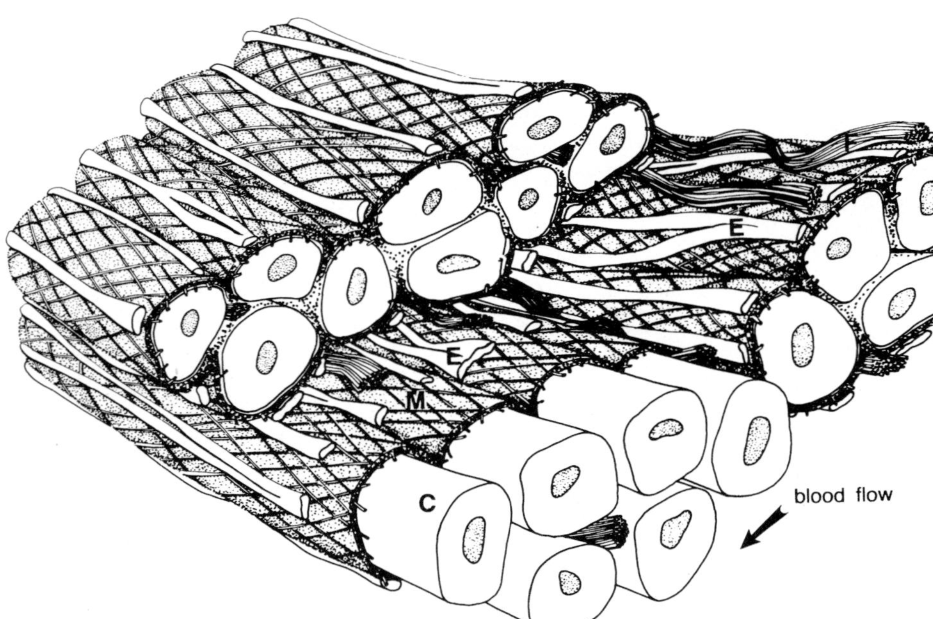

FIGURE 10-2 Transmural organization of a muscular artery. Smooth muscle cells (C) are more numerous and prominent than in elastic arteries (see Fig. 10-1) and are organized in groups oriented with their long axes perpendicular to the long axis of the artery. Contraction or relaxation of smooth muscle cells allows for rapid alterations in lumen diameter. Smooth muscle cells are surrounded by a basal lamina matrix containing a meshwork of type III collagen fibrils (M). Elastin fibers (E) and type I collagen fibers (F) are present but are less prominent than in elastic arteries. (From Clark JM, Glagov S: Transmural organization of the arterial wall: The lamellar unit revisited. Arteriosclerosis 5:19, 1985.)

There are great differences in the media between the thoracic aorta and abdominal aorta (Fig. 10-3). The thoracic aorta is larger in diameter than the abdominal aorta and, accordingly, has a greater number of transmedial lamellar units. The thoracic aorta also contains relatively more elastin and less collagen than the abdominal aorta, allowing greater distensibility and pulse propagation. The abdominal aorta, which contains proportionately more collagen, is stiffer and less compliant than the thoracic segment.[28] Each abdominal aortic lamellar unit is thought to support approximately 3000 dynes/cm circumferential tension, whereas each thoracic lamellar unit supports about 2000 dynes/cm. The outer two thirds of the human thoracic aortic wall is supplied with intramural medial vasa vasorum, whereas the abdominal aorta is largely devoid of medial vasa vasorum. Because intramural vasa vasorum are largely absent from the abdominal aorta, nutrition presumably depends primarily on diffusion from the lumen. Thus, even early intimal plaque deposition may augment the barrier to diffusion, rendering the abdominal aortic media vulnerable to ischemic degeneration and atrophy. Intimal plaque formation would also be expected to increase the diffusion distance across the wall, predisposing to processes that may promote inflammatory cell infiltration, lipid accumulation, and further plaque formation. Extension into the plaque of reactive vasa vasorum may help to clear lipid from the intimal lesion but may also induce further proliferation and plaque enlargement. Conversely, failure of vasa vasorum ingrowth may result in arterial wall atrophy and promote aneurysm formation. Thus, differences in structure and nutrition would appear to be associated with the different vulnerabilities of the thoracic aorta and abdominal aorta to aneurysmal and occlusive diseases.[27]

For muscular arteries, such as the coronary and renal vessels, total tangential tension and the number of transmural layers are also linearly related.[28] In addition, the relative proportions of collagen and elastin differ in muscular and elastic arteries. The media of the proximal aorta and that of the major brachiocephalic elastic arteries contain a larger proportion of elastin and a lower proportion of collagen than the media of the abdominal aorta or of the distal peripheral vessels.[29] The proximal major vessels are therefore more compliant than the abdominal aorta but are also more fragile and prone to tear when sutured.

Medial smooth muscle cells, in addition to synthesizing the collagen and elastin fibers that determine the mechanical properties of the aortic wall, are actively engaged in metabolic processes that contribute to wall tone and may be related to susceptibility to plaque formation.[30] Under conditions of increased pulse pressure, wall motion, and wall tension, such as exist proximal to an aortic coarctation, medial smooth muscle cell metabolism is higher, as is plaque formation.[31] Conversely, when wall motion, pulse pressure, and smooth muscle cell metabolism are decreased, as in areas distal to a severe arterial stenosis, intimal plaque formation is inhibited, despite the continued presence of strong atherogenic stimuli such as marked hyperlipidemia.[32] In vitro studies have revealed that cyclic stretching of smooth muscle cells grown on elastin membranes results in greater biosynthetic activity,[33] and acute arterial injury experiments have revealed that an intact, metabolically active media may be required for intimal plaque formation.[34] The composition and microarchitecture of the media are designed to ensure stability, whereas the metabolic state of the media appears to be an important factor in the pathogenesis of atherosclerotic lesions.

Adventitia

The adventitia is composed of fibrocellular connective tissue and contains a network of vasa vasorum composed of small arteries, arterioles, capillaries, and venous channels as well as nerves that mediate smooth muscle tone and contraction. The adventitia varies in thickness and organization. In some arteries, such as the proximal renal and mesenteric trunks, the adventitia is a layered structure composed of both

Comparison of Human Thoracic and Abdominal Aorta

	Diameter (mm)	Wall thickness (cm)	Lamellar units (LU)		Tension		
			Number	Thickness (mm)	Total (dynes/cm)	Per LU (dynes/cm^2)	Stress (dynes/cm^2)
Thoracic	17	9.5×10^{-2}	56	0.017	117,000	2,095	122×10^4
	Medial vasa in outer 50%						
Abdominal	13	7.3×10^{-2}	28	0.026	89,000	3,180	122×10^4
	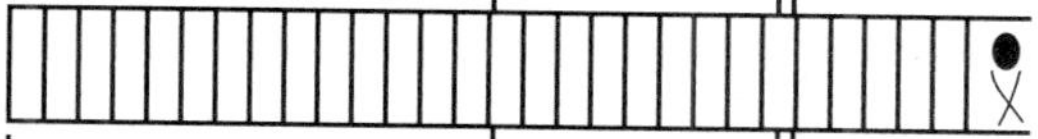 No medial vasa						

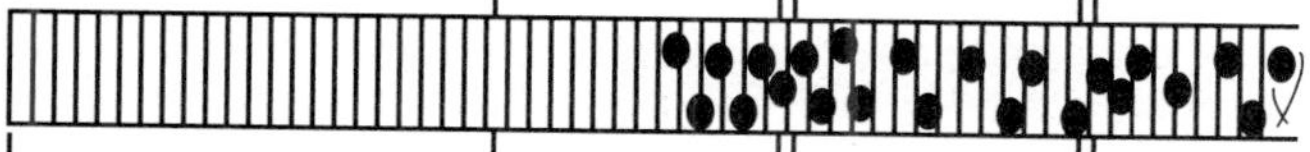

Intima

FIGURE 10-3 Comparison of human thoracic and abdominal aortic segments. The thickness of the media of the abdominal aorta is appropriate for its diameter, but the number of its medial lamellar units is relatively low for the diameter compared with the thoracic aorta. Media total tension of the abdominal aorta is appropriate for its diameter, but tension per lamellar unit is higher than in the thoracic aorta. Furthermore, the abdominal aortic media, only 29 lamellar units thick, is avascular. None of the avascular aortic medias or avascular zones of vascular aortic medias of mammals studied are as thick as the media of the human abdominal aorta. Other mammals' aortas that have comparatively elevated tensions per lamellar unit have more than 29 lamellae and vasa vasorum. LU, lamellar unit. (From Wolinsky H, Glagov S: Comparison of abdominal and thoracic aortic medial structure in mammals: Deviation from the usual pattern in man. Cir Res 25:677, 1969.)

collagen and elastic fibers and may be thicker than the associated media. In the normal aorta, removal of the adventitia has little effect on static pressure-volume relationships.[35] In atherosclerotic arteries, however, increasing intimal plaque thickness may be associated with atrophy of the underlying media.[36] Under these circumstances, a thickened adventitia may contribute to tensile support. The tensile strength and adequacy of the adventitia to provide such support are well demonstrated after carotid or aortoiliac endarterectomy. In these procedures, the entire intima and most or all of the media are usually removed, leaving only the adventitia to provide support, and aneurysmal degeneration after endarterectomy is very rare.

Vasa Vasorum

The inner layers of the aortic media are nourished by diffusion from the lumen. Diffusion of nutrients is apparently sufficient to nourish the inner 0.5 mm of the adult mammalian aortic media, which corresponds to approximately 30 medial fibrocellular lamellar units.[37] When the aorta is thicker than 30 medial lamellar layers, the outer layers of the media are nourished by vasa vasorum that penetrate into the media. Vasa vasorum usually arise from the parent artery at branch junctions and arborize in the adventitia. In thick-walled arteries, mural stresses and deformations may affect vasa vasorum blood flow, and hypertension may impair vasal flow.[38]

Intimal plaque formation increases intimal thickness and may thereby enlarge the diffusion barrier between the lumen and the smooth muscle cells of the media. This increase in wall thickness may be accompanied by an ingrowth of vasa vasorum, and vasa vasorum have been identified in atherosclerotic lesions. Both intraplaque hemorrhage and plaque breakdown or disruption may be potentiated by changes in the vascular supply of the artery wall and plaque.

■ ADAPTIVE RESPONSES OF THE ARTERY WALL

Adaptive responses of arteries and the healing response to arterial injuries serve to maintain the structural and functional integrity of the arterial tree. Normal responses to altered biomechanical and hemodynamic conditions result in compensatory changes in artery wall thickness, lumen diameter, or both, whereas abnormal or pathologic conditions may engender alterations in wall thickness and lumen diameter that proceed to lumen stenosis, aneurysm formation, or obstructive intimal hyperplasia.[1,39,40]

Wall Thickness

Artery wall thickness and composition are closely related to *tangential tension* and strain in the wall. During normal growth and development, arteries adapt to rises in tangential tension by increasing the number of medial lamellar units and through the accumulation of matrix fibers to increase wall thickness.[41]

For example, at birth, the ascending aorta and pulmonary trunk are equal in diameter, in wall thickness, and in the concentration of elastin and collagen. In the immediate postnatal period, however, with expansion of the lungs, pressure in the pulmonary artery falls and pressure in the aorta rises. Volume flow and diameter remain equivalent in the two vessels, but a marked difference in blood pressure develops, resulting in profound alterations in medial growth and development. The high-pressure aortic media becomes thicker with a greater number of medial lamellae.

The differences can be attributed to different rates of collagen and elastin accumulation, which correspond closely to the differences in total tangential tension for the two vessels.[42] At any given interval during early postnatal growth, however, the number of cells is the same for the two vessel segments. Thus, smooth muscle cells of the media are apparently capable of a remarkable range of biosynthetic activity in response to imposed tensile stress.

In adult life, arterial wall thickening also occurs in response to increases in tangential tension, although this thickening occurs not through increases in the number of medial lamellar units but by means of intimal thickening and changes in matrix volume and composition. In patients with hypertension, arterial and arteriolar intimal thickening develops as an adaptive response to the increase in wall tension, and the relative proportion of matrix fiber changes in favor of collagen.[43] Similarly, the performance of a distal arterial bypass increases wall tension by raising pressure as well as by producing a large rise in lumen radius at the anastomotic site. The resulting increase in tangential wall tension can stimulate intimal thickening as an adaptive response to the rise in tension.

Quantitative morphologic studies of human carotid bifurcations have demonstrated greater intimal thickness in association with lumen enlargement with resultant preservation of normal tangential mural tension.[44,45] The factors that differentiate a normal adaptive intimal thickening from an inappropriate intimal hyperplastic response resulting in lumen stenosis at a vascular anastomosis are not well understood. Techniques to precisely measure stresses in the artery wall are now available and may help define the role of mechanical forces in artery wall response.[46,47]

Lumen Diameter

Under normal conditions, adaptive alterations in lumen diameter are determined by *blood flow* in the artery. During embryologic development, arteries with high-volume flow enlarge, and those with low flow become smaller.[48] When parallel flow channels exist, the one with higher flow enlarges and persists, whereas the one with lesser flow atrophies and disappears. Increases in artery lumen diameter also keep pace with changes in flow during extrauterine growth.[49] Arteries exposed to abnormal increases in flow, such as those feeding an arteriovenous fistula, may also enlarge, whereas arteries exposed to abnormal decreases in flow, such as vessels supplying an amputated limb, adapt with a decrease in size.[50]

The mechanism for adjustment of lumen diameter appears to be mediated by wall *shear stress,* which is the effective velocity gradient at the endothelium–blood interface.[4] Because shear stress is inversely related to the cube of the radius, small alterations in radius have a major effect on wall shear stress. In mammals, wall shear stress normally ranges between 10 and 20 dynes/cm^2 at all levels of the arterial tree.[51] In experimentally produced arteriovenous fistulae, the afferent artery has been shown to enlarge just enough to restore shear stress to baseline levels.[52] Wall shear stress thus appears to act as a regulating signal to determine artery size, and this response depends on the presence of an intact endothelial surface.[53-56] The response is mediated by the release of endothelium-derived relaxing factor or nitric oxide (NO).[57,58] Thus, the endothelium functions as a mechanically sensitive signal transduction interface between the blood and the artery wall.[59,60] NO plays an important role in both the acute and chronic increases in vessel caliber that occur in response to greater flow.[61,62] Inhibition of NO synthesis by means of long-term oral administration of the NO synthase inhibitor *N*-omega-nitro-L-arginine-methyl ester (L-NAME) can inhibit flow-induced arterial enlargement.[63,64]

Atherosclerotic arteries are also capable of enlarging in response to increases in blood flow and wall shear stress, but this process may be limited.[65] Atherosclerotic artery enlargement is further discussed later in this chapter. The nature and mechanisms of the artery wall adaptive processes that allow arteries to adjust lumen diameter are currently being actively investigated. Understanding the mechanism and limits of the adaptive process and identifying the consequences for the vessel wall of shear stress that is persistently higher or lower than normal will be of value in clinical efforts to maintain normal lumen caliber.

■ FUNCTIONAL PATHOLOGY OF ATHEROSCLEROSIS

The features that distinguish normal arterial adaptation in response to changing hemodynamic and mechanical conditions from pathologic processes affecting the artery wall are not well defined. Intimal thickening and changes in wall thickness and lumen diameter occur as functions of both age and atherosclerosis. A prominent feature distinguishing atherosclerotic plaques is the presence of lipid in intimal lesions. However, it is unclear whether all lesions containing lipids are necessarily precursors of clinically significant atherosclerotic plaques.

Intimal Thickening

Intimal thickening may represent either an adaptive response, acting to reduce lumen caliber in reaction to conditions of chronically reduced blood flow, or a response designed to augment wall thickness under conditions of chronically increased wall tensile stress.[66,67] Focal intimal thickenings have been observed at or near branch points in the arteries of infants and fetuses and probably represent local remodeling of vessel wall organization related to growth and the associated redistribution of tensile stress.[68] Diffuse fibrocellular intimal thickening can occur as a more generalized phenomenon without a clear relationship to branches or curves and may result in a diffusely thickened intima that is considerably thicker than the media. Lipid accumulation is not a prominent feature in such intimal thickening, and the lumen remains regular and normal or slightly larger than normal in diameter.[69]

There is little direct evidence that diffuse intimal thickening is a precursor of lipid-containing atherosclerotic plaques, but intimal thickening and plaques tend to occur in similar locations and intimal thickening is most evident in vessels that are especially susceptible to atherosclerosis.[70-72] Evidence has also been presented that diffuse forms of intimal thickening do not develop uniformly and that foci of relatively rapid thickening undergo dystrophic changes, which give rise to necrosis and other features characteristic of plaques.[73] The relationship of these findings to usual atherosclerosis remains to be defined.

Fatty Streaks

Fatty streaks are flat yellow focal patches or linear streaks seen on the lumen surface of arteries. They correspond to the accumulation of lipid-laden foam cells in the intima. Fatty streaks are evident in most individuals older than 3 years. They are found with growing frequency between the ages of 8 and 18 years, after which many apparently resolve despite the common presence of matrix materials among the characteristic cells. Fatty streaks may be seen in the arteries of persons of any age and may be noted adjacent to or even superimposed on advanced atherosclerotic plaques. Fatty streaks and atheromata, however, do not have identical patterns of localization, and fatty streaks usually do not compromise the lumen or ulcerate.[74]

In experimental animals, diet-induced lesions resembling fatty streaks occur early, before characteristic atherosclerotic lesions prevail. These lesions are characterized by foam cells under a preserved and intact endothelial surface with no evidence of disruption.[75] There is some evidence that endothelial cells covering experimental fatty streak–type lesions are attenuated and fragile and may predispose to endothelial disruption, platelet adhesion, and possible transformation into a fibrous plaque.[76] Attachment of endothelial projections to underlying basal lamina and elastin, however, remains prominent in early fatty streak lesions. Although morphologic studies have identified transitional features, a firm line of evidence linking fatty streaks to fibrous plaque formation has not yet been established.

Fibrous Plaques

Fibrous plaque is the term used to identify the characteristic and unequivocal atherosclerotic lesion. Such intimal deposits appear in the second decade of life but usually do not become predominant or clinically significant until the fourth decade. Fibrous plaques are usually eccentric, and most are covered by an intact endothelial surface.

Although there is considerable variation in the composition and configuration of plaques, a characteristic architecture prevails for manifest advanced plaques. The immediate subendothelial region usually consists of a compact and well-organized stratified layer of smooth muscle cells and connective tissue fibers known as the *fibrous cap* (Fig. 10-4). This structure may be quite thick and may have architectural features resembling those of the media, including the formation of a subendothelial elastic lamina. The fibrous cap may provide structural support or may function as a barrier to sequester thrombogenic debris in the underlying necrotic core of the plaque from the lumen. Its lumen surface is regular and maintains a concave contour corresponding to the circular or oval cross-sectional lumen contour of the uninvolved vessel wall segment.

The *necrotic core* usually occupies the deeper central regions of the plaque and contains amorphous as well as crystalline and droplet forms of lipid. Cells with morphologic and functional characteristics of smooth muscle cells or macrophages are noted about the necrotic core and at the edges or shoulders of the plaques.[77] Both cell types may contain lipid vacuoles. In addition, calcium salts and myxoid deposits as well as matrix fibers, including collagen, elastin, fine fibrillar material, structures resembling basal lamina, and amorphous ground substance are evident.

Atherosclerotic plaques show evidence of uneven or episodic growth, including dense fibrocellular regions adjacent to organizing thrombus and foci of atheromatous debris. Intermittent ulceration and healing may occur, and there is evidence that thrombi formed on lesions are incorporated into them and resurfaced with a fibrocellular cap and an intact endothelial layer.

Vasa vasorum penetrate from the adventitia or possibly from the lumen to supply the plaque and fibrous cap and serve to organize thrombotic deposits.[78] The *media* underlying an atherosclerotic plaque may become thin and attenuated, with bulging of the plaque toward the adventitia (see Fig. 10-4), but the tissue between the necrotic core and the media is usually densely fibrotic. Support of the artery

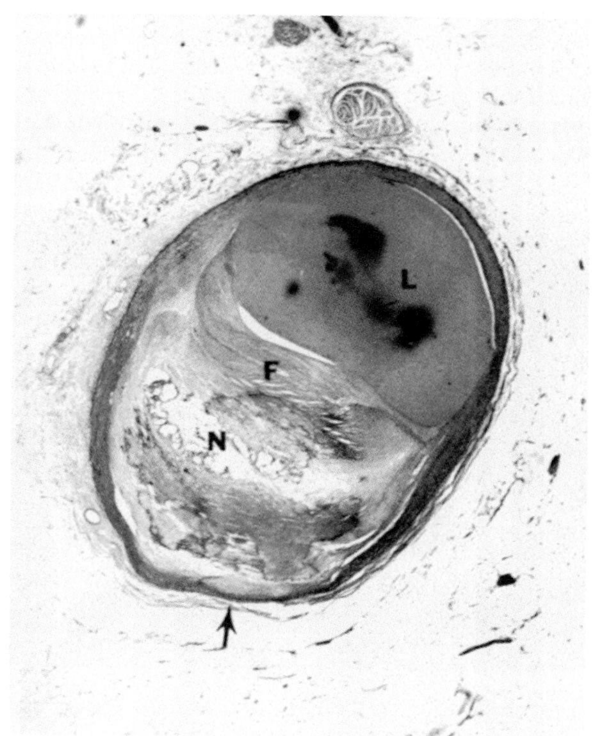

FIGURE 10-4 Cross-section of a human artery with an advanced atherosclerotic plaque. The fibrous cap (F) is a well-organized layer of smooth muscle cells and fibrous tissue that separates the necrotic core (N) of the plaque from the lumen (L). The media beneath the plaque may become thin and atrophic (*arrow*). The lumen contains a gelatin cast used to redistend and maintain lumen contour.

wall may also be taken up by the fibrous cap or a thickened adventitial layer.

Some *advanced lesions,* particularly those associated with aneurysms, may appear to be atrophic and relatively acellular, consisting of dense fibrous tissue, prominent calcific deposits, and only minimal evidence of a necrotic center. *Calcification* is a prominent feature of advanced plaques and may be quite extensive, involving both the superficial and deeper reaches of the plaques. Although there is no consistent relationship between plaque size or complexity and the extent of calcification, calcific deposits are most prominent in plaques in older individuals and in areas such as the abdominal aortic segment and coronary arteries, where plaques form earliest.[79]

Advanced lesions are called fibrocalcific, lipid-rich, fibrocellular, necrotic, myxomatous, and so forth, depending on their morphologic features. The presence of large quantities of lipid, necrotic material, and cells tends to make a lesion *soft* and friable, in contrast to the *hard,* rubbery, or brittle consistency of a mainly fibrocalcific lesion.

Plaque Morphology

The common perception that atherosclerotic plaques bulge into the lumen of arteries reflects the fact that most often, plaques are evaluated with angiography, which reveals the lumen contour in a longitudinal or axial projection. A narrowing of the lumen thus is usually perceived as a protrusion of plaque into the lumen (Fig. 10-5). This perception is supported by the gross observations of vascular surgeons and pathologists, who usually examine the luminal surface of atherosclerotic arteries en face or on cross-section with the arteries collapsed. Without distending intraluminal pressure, the relatively uninvolved sector of the artery wall recoils, and the eccentric plaque is usually thrown up as a protrusion or bulge. Viewed en face in vessels laid open by longitudinal section, the fibrous or complex plaque is seen as an elevation, with either smooth or irregular surface contours (see Fig. 10-5). The purely descriptive term *raised plaque* has been used to contrast this appearance with that of the fatty streak, which usually does not appear to be elevated in such preparations.

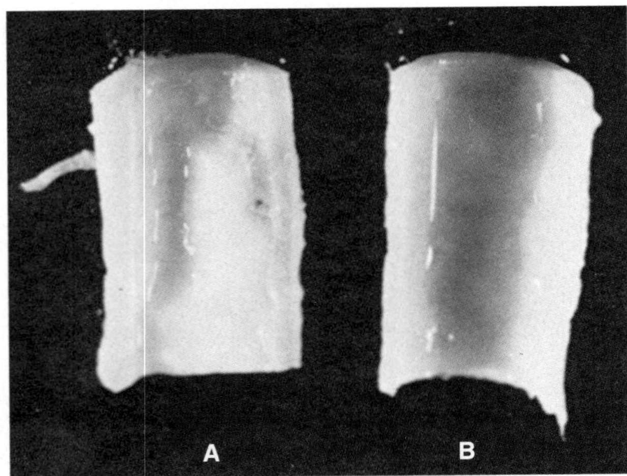

FIGURE 10-5 Effect of vessel collapse on the luminal surface appearance of atherosclerotic plaques. **A,** The artery was fixed while collapsed with no distending intraluminal pressure. Note the apparent bulge of the plaque into the lumen. **B,** The vessel was fixed while distended with an intraluminal pressure of 100 mm Hg. Note that there is no visible protrusion of plaque into the lumen and that the lumen contour is rounded. Both segments are from the same human superficial femoral artery, and multiple histologic sections confirm that the two segments have the same volume of intimal plaque.

Restoration of in vivo configuration can be achieved by redistending the artery during fixation at controlled levels of intraluminal pressure.[80] Under these circumstances, the cross-sectional lumen contour is usually regular and round or oval, even in the presence of very large and extensive atherosclerotic lesions.[81] The usual eccentric atherosclerotic plaque therefore presents a concave luminal contour on transverse section, does not protrude into the lumen, and instead tends to bulge outward from the lumen. Thus, the external cross-sectional contour of an atherosclerotic artery tends to become oval, whereas the lumen tends to remain circular.

Although plaques may appear as focal or segmental projections into the lumen on longitudinal angiographic or ultrasonographic images, cross-sectional views reveal rounded lumen contours. Cross-sectional lumen contours in pressure perfusion–fixed arteries that are irregular or slit-like, with protrusions of the plaque or its contents into the lumen, usually signify that a complication of plaque evolution such as ulceration, hemorrhage, dissection, or thrombosis has occurred. Circumferential, rigid fibrocalcific plaques may retain an in vivo circular lumen configuration, however, even when dilating pressure is absent.

Atherosclerotic Arterial Enlargement

As intimal plaques enlarge, a closely associated enlargement of the affected artery segment tends to limit the stenosing effect of the enlarging intimal plaque (Fig. 10-6). Such enlargement of atherosclerotic arteries has been demonstrated in experimental atherosclerosis[82-86] as well as in human coronary,[65,87-93] carotid,[94-96] and superficial femoral[97,98] arteries and the abdominal aorta.[99,100] Enlargement may proceed by mechanisms suggested by the demonstrated adaptive response to altered flow or through direct effects of the plaque on the artery wall.[101] Focal intimal plaque deposition would tend to reduce lumen diameter, thereby raising local blood flow velocity and wall shear stress and inducing dilatation of the artery to restore baseline shear stress levels. Atrophy of the media underlying the plaque could also result in outward bulging of the artery in the region of the plaque in order to maintain an adequate lumen caliber. Thus, an increase in intimal plaque volume appears to induce an increase in artery size.

In the human left main coronary artery, such enlargement keeps pace with increases in intimal plaque and is effective in preventing lumen stenosis until plaque area occupies, on the average, approximately 40% of the cross-sectional area encompassed by the internal elastic lamina area (i.e., the potential lumen area if a plaque were not present) (Fig. 10-7). Continued plaque enlargement or complication apparently exceeds the ability of the artery to enlarge, and lumen stenosis may then develop.[65,102]

Individual segments of the arterial tree, however, may respond differently to increasing intimal plaque.[103] In the distal left anterior descending coronary artery, arterial

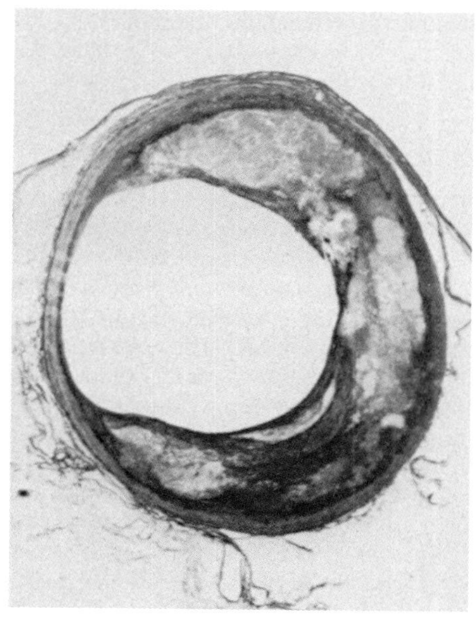

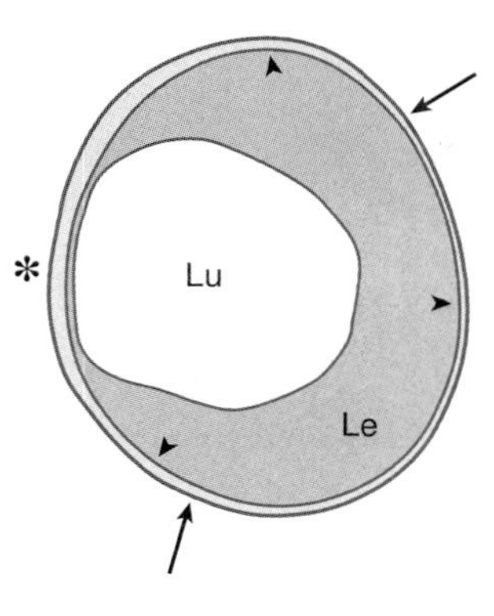

FIGURE 10-6 Cross-section of a human left main coronary artery demonstrating atherosclerotic arterial enlargement. Despite an enlarging lesion (Le) area, the lumen (Lu) area is preserved owing to artery enlargement. The lumen contour remains rounded, but the external artery contour becomes oval because of the eccentric nature of the plaque. When intimal plaque area exceeds 40% of internal elastic lumina area (*arrowheads*), compensatory enlargement apparently fails and stenosis develops. Enlargement may occur by dilatation of the uninvolved artery wall segment (*asterisk*) or atrophy of the media underlying the plaque (*arrows*). (From Glagov S, Weisenberg E, Zarins CK, et al: Compensatory enlargement of human atherosclerotic coronary arteries. Reprinted by permission of The New England Journal of Medicine, 316:1371, 1987.)

enlargement occurs more rapidly than intimal plaque deposition. This may result in a net increase in lumen area rather than lumen stenosis in the most severely diseased arteries.[90] Individual variation has also been demonstrated in the superficial femoral artery[104] as well as in the abdominal aorta.[105,106] Thus, it appears that the development of lumen stenosis, the maintenance of a normal lumen cross-sectional area, or the development of an increase in lumen diameter is determined by the relative rates of plaque growth and artery enlargement.[107] Reduction in artery size can also result in the development of lumen stenosis, and this phenomenon has been demonstrated in vivo with intravascular ultrasound.[108] Further study of this phenomenon of artery enlargement, or reduction in size, particularly in regions associated with great morbidity related to plaque deposition, is needed for a full understanding of the processes involved in the development of atherosclerotic stenoses and aneurysms.

■ LOCALIZATION OF ATHEROSCLEROTIC PLAQUES

Atherosclerosis is a generalized disorder of the arterial tree, and epidemiologic studies have identified a number of clinical risk factors associated with the development and complication of plaques[109]:

- Cigarette smoking
- Elevated serum lipid levels
- Hypertension
- Obesity
- Diabetes mellitus
- Physical inactivity
- Emotional stress
- Genetic predisposition

Some of these factors appear to be more closely associated with atherosclerosis in certain arterial beds than in others. For example, serum levels of cholesterol and low-density lipoprotein are strongly related to coronary heart disease but only moderately related to cerebrovascular or peripheral occlusive disease. Cerebrovascular disease is closely related to hypertension,[110] but cigarette smoking is the principal risk factor for peripheral occlusive disease.[111]

In addition to differences in systemic risk factor associations, variations in local hemodynamic and artery wall properties appear to exert major selective effects on plaque formation.[112,113] Certain regions of each vascular bed are especially prone to plaque formation, whereas others are usually spared.[114] For example, the coronary arteries, carotid bifurcation, infrarenal abdominal aorta, and iliofemoral arteries are particularly susceptible to plaque formation, but

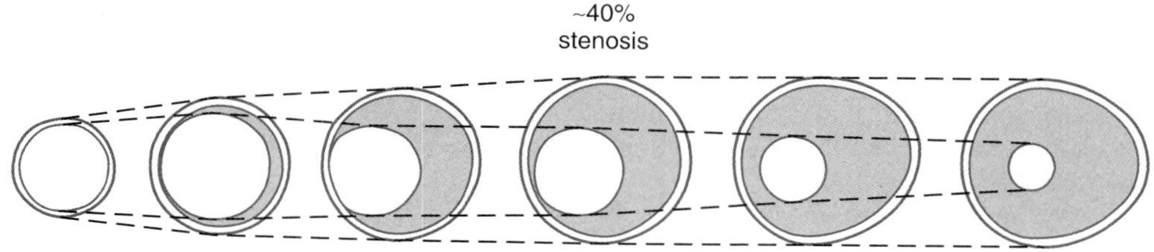

FIGURE 10-7 Possible sequence of changes in atherosclerotic arteries in response to enlarging atherosclerotic plaques. In the early stages of intimal plaque deposition, the lumen remains normal or enlarges slightly (*left*). When intimal plaque enlarges to involve the entire circumference of the vessel and produces more than 40% stenosis, the artery can no longer enlarge at a rate sufficient to prevent narrowing of the lumen. (From Glagov S, Weisenberg E, Zarins CK, et al: Compensatory enlargement of human atherosclerotic coronary arteries. Reprinted by permission of The New England Journal of Medicine, 316:1371, 1987.)

the thoracic aorta and the common carotid, distal internal carotid, renal, mesenteric, and upper extremity arteries are particularly resistant. Such differences have been associated with variations in the distribution of shear and tensile stresses produced by variations in geometry and flow in differing segments of the arterial tree.[1] Although plaques may occur in straight vessels away from branch points, they are usually located at bifurcations or bends, where variations in hemodynamic conditions are especially likely to occur.[115]

Hemodynamic Considerations

The following hemodynamic variables have been proposed to account for the selective distribution of plaques:

- Shear stress
- Flow separation and stasis
- Oscillation of shear stress vectors
- Turbulence
- Hypertension

Several texts have provided detailed, in-depth consideration of the relevant fluid dynamic principles.[1,4]

Wall Shear Stress

Wall shear stress is the tangential drag force produced by blood moving across the endothelial surface. It is a function of the velocity gradient of blood near the endothelial surface. Its magnitude is directly proportional to blood flow and blood viscosity and inversely proportional to the cube of the vessel's radius. Thus, a small change in the radius of a vessel has a large effect on wall shear stress.[116]

High shear stress was implicated in atherogenesis when endothelial desquamation and smooth muscle proliferation were considered to be prime factors in plaque initiation,[12] and experimental studies showed that short-term experimental elevations of shear stress could cause endothelial disruption.[117] Long-term elevations of shear stress were not associated with endothelial injury, however, and regions of relatively high shear stress appeared to be selectively spared from plaque formation.[118]

It is now evident that atherosclerotic plaques localize preferentially in regions of *low shear stress* and not in regions of high shear stress. This fact has been demonstrated in quantitative studies correlating early plaque formation in pressure perfusion–fixed human carotid bifurcations with wall shear stress determinations in analogous geometrically precise flow models (Fig. 10-8).[119] Plaques form where shear stress values are near zero (i.e., at the lateral wall opposite the flow divider), and it has been suggested that a threshold value may exist below which plaque deposition tends to occur.[120] Similar quantitative studies of the human aortic bifurcation have also shown that plaques localize in regions of low rather than high shear stress.[121]

Low shear rates may retard the transport of atherogenic substances away from the wall, resulting in a greater accumulation of lipids.[122] In addition, low shear stress may interfere with endothelial surface turnover of substances essential both to artery wall metabolism and to the maintenance of optimal endothelial metabolic function.[9,123] Low wall shear stress has also been shown to be a factor in the development of intimal hyperplasia.[124]

Flow Separation and Stasis

In especially susceptible areas, such as the outer wall of the carotid bifurcation, where flow velocity is reduced and flow separation occurs, fluid and particles are cleared slowly (Fig. 10-9) and have a *longer residence time*.[4,120,125,126] The vessel wall therefore has a prolonged exposure to atherogenic particles. Time-dependent lipid particle–vessel wall interactions would thus be facilitated and would favor plaque formation. In addition, blood-borne cellular elements that may play a role in atherogenesis would have a greater probability of deposition, adhesion, or diapedesis into the vessel wall in such regions.[127] Flow separation has, for example, been shown to favor deposition of platelets in

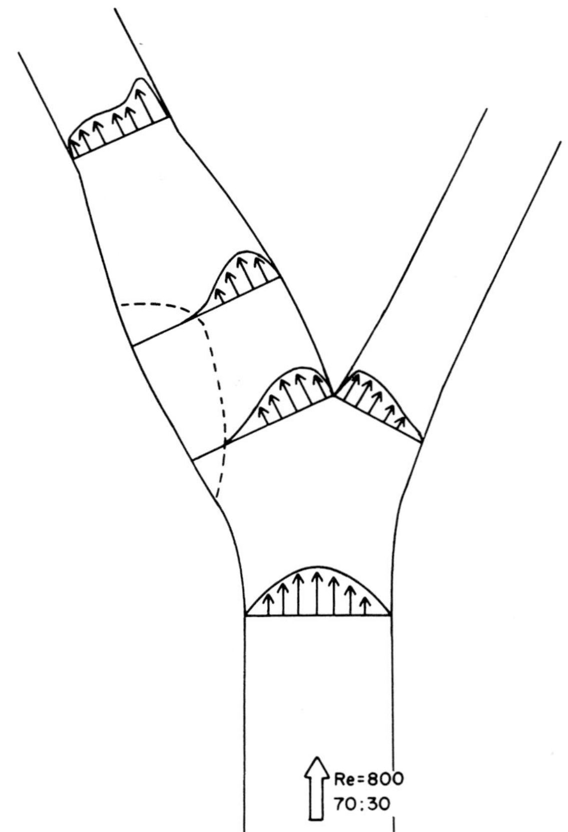

FIGURE 10-8 Axial velocity profiles measured with laser Doppler anemometry in a glass model of carotid bifurcation under conditions of steady flow (Reynolds number, 800; flow division ratio of internal carotid to external carotid, 70:30). The velocity profile is skewed toward the inner wall of the carotid bifurcation, resulting in a steep velocity gradient and high wall shear stress. Along the outer wall of the internal carotid sinus, the velocity profile is flat and there is an area of flow separation with very low flow velocities (*dotted line*) and very low wall shear stress. It is in this region of the human carotid bifurcation that intimal plaques form. (From Zarins CK, Giddens DP, Bharadvaj BK, et al: Carotid bifurcation atherosclerosis: Quantitative correlation of plaque localization with flow velocity profiles and wall shear stress. Circ Res 53:502, 1983.)

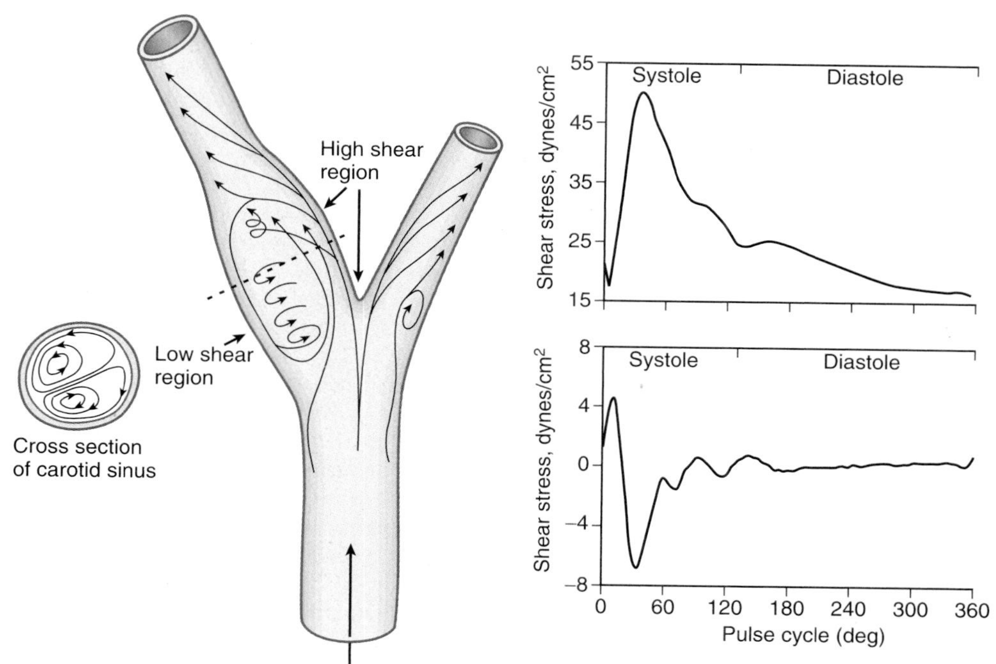

FIGURE 10-9 *Left,* Diagrammatic representation of flow features at the carotid bifurcation. Region of flow separation with formation of secondary vortices is present at the low shear position of the lateral wall of the internal carotid artery, whereas flow remains laminar and mainly unidirectional at high shear flow-divider side. *Right,* Graphs show changes in wall shear stress in course of cardiac cycle for flow-divider region (*upper graph*) and for lateral wall (*lower graph*). At the lateral wall where plaques form, shear stress is low and oscillates in direction. At the flow-divider side, shear stress varies but remains relatively high and unidirectional. Variations are most marked during systole. (From Ku DN, Giddens DP, Zarins CK, et al: Pulsatile flow and atherosclerosis in the human carotid bifurcation: Positive correlation between plaque location and low and oscillating shear stress. Arteriosclerosis 5:293, 1985.)

vitro,[128] which may contribute to plaque induction and complication. Radiographic and ultrasonographic studies confirm the presence of flow separation and stasis in this outer wall region of the carotid bifurcation.[129] Not only do early intimal thickenings and plaques localize in this region; complications, stenoses, and ulcerations also predominate here.

Oscillation of Flow

Blood velocity varies markedly during the course of the cardiac cycle, resulting in a fluctuation in the magnitude of wall shear stress that is a normal feature at the blood-artery interface. Along the inner wall of the carotid bifurcation on the side of the flow divider, blood flow and shear stress vary but the vector is always in the forward direction. Along the outer wall of the carotid bifurcation, opposite the flow divider where intimal plaques form, there is a reversal of axial flow direction during systole and phasic retrograde flow along the wall (see Fig. 10-9). This pattern results in a directional oscillation of the shear stress vector during the cardiac cycle.[120]

Variations in shear stress direction associated with pulsatile flow may favor greater endothelial permeability through direct mechanical effects on cell junctions, whereas relatively high unidirectional shear stresses may not be injurious[130] and may even favor endothelial mechanical integrity.[131] Endothelial cells are normally aligned in the direction of flow[132] in an overlapping arrangement.[133] Cyclic shifts in the relationship between shear stress direction and the orientation of intercellular overlapping borders may disturb the relationships between ingress and egress of particles through junctions. This hypothesis agrees well with reports of (1) increased permeability of cultured, confluent endothelial cells subjected to changes in shear stress[134] and (2) greater permeability to Evans blue dye in relation to differences in endothelial cell orientation,[135] which may be associated with different flow patterns. Oscillatory shear stress has also been shown to influence endothelium and NO synthase expression[136] as well as to stimulate expression of adhesion molecules in cultured human endothelial cells.[137]

Because oscillation of shear stress direction at susceptible sites occurs during systole, the number of such oscillations over time is directly related to the number of systoles (i.e., to heart rate). Heart rate has been implicated as an independent risk factor in coronary atherosclerosis and is discussed further in the section on the coronary arteries. Reduction in heart rate in experimental atherosclerosis has been shown to retard progression of carotid plaques.[83,138]

Turbulence

Turbulence, defined as random, disordered flow, is rarely seen in the normal vascular tree. Turbulent flow has often been implicated as a factor in the pathogenesis of plaque.[139,140] However, in vitro observations and experimental atherosclerosis studies fail to support this concept. In model studies of the carotid bifurcation, a zone of complex secondary and tertiary flow patterns, including counterrotating helical trajectories, is demonstrable in regions of plaque formation, but turbulence does not occur (Fig. 10-10).[141] In vivo pulsed-Doppler ultrasound studies of carotid arteries have confirmed this finding in normal human subjects.[142]

Turbulence may develop in association with stenoses and irregularities of the flow surface caused by atherosclerotic plaques, although the turbulence is located distal to rather than at the lesion. Experimentally produced stenoses show that turbulence is greatest two to four vessel diameters distal to the stenosis in an area in which post-stenotic dilatation commonly develops but diet-induced plaques do not readily occur.[143-145] Thus, turbulence per se has not been shown to be an initiating factor in atherogenesis. Nevertheless, turbulence may play a role in plaque disruption or thrombogenesis. Further investigation is needed to establish these relationships.

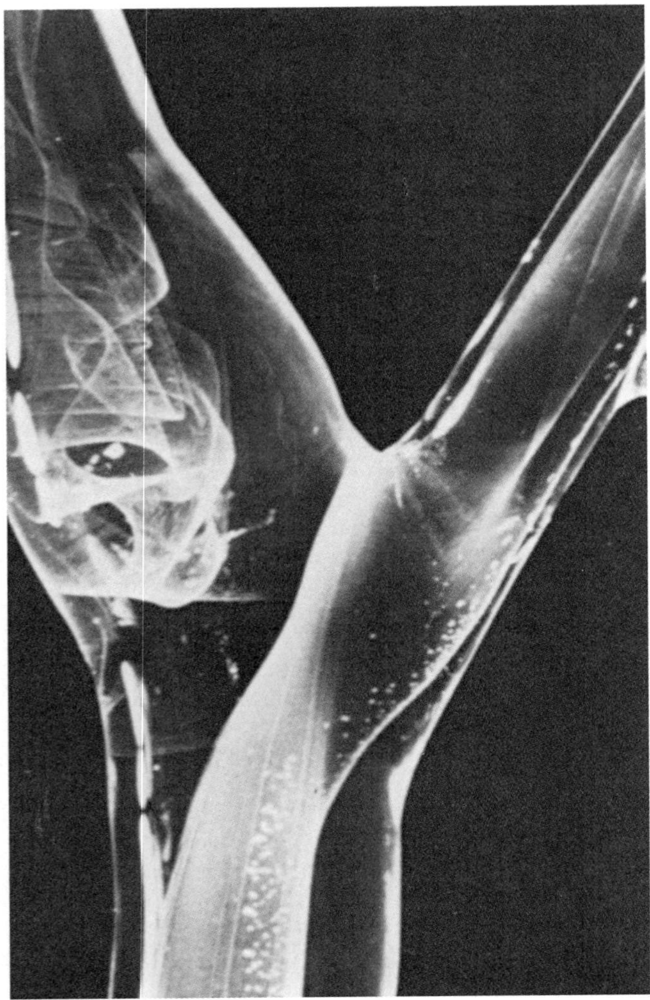

FIGURE 10-10 Hydrogen bubble flow visualization in a glass model of carotid bifurcation. Streamlines are skewed toward the apex of the carotid flow divider, and in the outer wall of the carotid sinus, there is a zone of complex secondary and tertiary flow patterns, including flow reversal and counterrotating helical trajectories. However, no random, disordered flow or turbulence is present.

Hypertension

Hypertension has been identified as an important risk factor in the development of clinical complications of atherosclerosis, such as myocardial infarction and stroke.[146] Postmortem studies have shown that hypertension is associated with increases in both the extent and the severity of atherosclerosis.[114] Elevated blood pressure alone does not induce atherosclerosis in experimental animals. In the presence of hyperlipidemia, however, hypertension enhances plaque formation.[147-150] Yet atherosclerotic plaque does not form despite the presence of hypertension and severe hyperlipidemia when pulse pressure, wall motion, or both are reduced.[151,152]

Experimental hypertension study in aortic coarctation model in rabbit demonstrated that hypertension superimposed with hyperlipidemia resulted in enhanced development of foam cell lesions in the intima of the hypertensive aorta proximal to the coarctation. Furthermore, greater tensile stress induced differential gene expression of collagen types I and III as well as tropoelastin.[153-155]

Although hypertension does enhance experimental plaque formation, it also inhibits plaque regression when cholesterol levels are reduced.[156] Hypertension also enhances progression of coronary artery plaques despite the reduction of hypercholesterolemia.[157] These observations suggest that factors other than blood pressure per se may be of primary importance in plaque pathogenesis. However, hypertension may play an important role in the evolution and clinical complications of atherosclerotic plaques.

Artery Wall Motion

In addition to the role of shear forces in the localization of atherosclerotic lesions, the amplitude of the stretching movements of the arterial wall associated with the excursion in blood pressure during the cardiac cycle may also be implicated in the pathogenesis of atherosclerosis. The relationship between localization of diet-induced lesions and the extent of cyclic arterial wall stretching has been examined, and the data suggest a direct relationship between increased wall motion and plaque deposition. Conversely, reduced cyclic arterial stretching results in sparing from atherosclerosis.[151]

Further evidence for such an interpretation has been obtained in experiments in which cyclic stretching of short segments of aorta was restricted by encirclement, without narrowing, by a surrounding rigid tube.[158,159] The intimal surface in the immobilized segment remained free of atherosclerotic lesions. Pulse pressure and intraluminal flow were presumably unchanged. Other studies have reported similar findings in less than critical constrictions by rigid collars.[160] Clinically, calcification of arteries due to atherosclerosis may diminish wall motion and reduce the rate of subsequent plaque deposition.

Sparing of the artery distal to a stenosis is seen clinically in patients with long-standing chronic occlusions of the abdominal aorta. Whether restoration of arterial wall motion to normal by removal of a proximal obstruction would accelerate the distal atherosclerotic process or enhance intimal hyperplasia at an anastomotic site is unknown. Experimental data suggest that restoration of aortic wall motion to normal after 3 months of stenosis returns the rate of distal lesion formation to control levels but does not accelerate it.[161] Experimental study of aortic stenosis has shown that in contrast to lesion development in the aorta proximal to the stenosis, the intimal lesions in the segment distal to stenotic dilatation were much smaller.[162] Further investigations of the relationships among wall composition, wall compliance, pulse pressure, and plaque localization in both human vessels and experimental models could provide information of practical value with regard to the likely effects on distal segments of the relief of proximal stenosis.

Effects of Exercise

Exercise results in a significant rise in cardiac output and heart rate and a reduction in peripheral resistance. This increase markedly alters the hemodynamic condition in the vascular tree. The adverse hemodynamic conditions that exist in the carotid bifurcation and abdominal aorta under resting flow conditions are transiently eliminated during exercise. Low flow velocity and low wall shear stress are increased, particle residence time is reduced, and oscillatory shear becomes unidirectional. These changes have been studied in model flow systems in the abdominal aorta[163] and at simulated vascular anastomoses.[164] The effects of exercise in the abdominal aorta have been studied with the use of medical imaging and computational flow techniques.

Magnetic resonance imaging (MRI) techniques can be used to quantify blood flow at rest and during exercise conditions.[165,166] As depicted in Figure 10-11 for a representative subject, reverse flow present in the infrarenal aorta under resting conditions is eliminated with light exercise (defined as a 50% increase in resting heart rate). In eight healthy subjects, aged 50 to 70 years, supraceliac blood flow increased from 2.3 ± 0.4 L/min at rest to 6.0 ± 1.4 L/min with exercise ($P < .001$), and infrarenal flow from 0.9 ± 0.3 to 4.9 ± 1.7 L/min ($P < .001$). Wall shear stress increased from 2.0 ± 0.7 to 7.3 ± 2.4 dynes/cm^2 at the supraceliac level ($P < .001$) and from 1.4 ± 0.8 to 16.5 ± 5.1 dynes/cm^2 at the infrarenal level ($P < .001$).

We developed a computer model of the human abdominal aorta to evaluate aortic blood flow quantitatively under rest and graded exercise conditions. Figure 10-11 shows the velocity field in a computer model of the abdominal aorta under simulated resting and exercise conditions at mid-diastole along the midplane of the aorta. It should be noted that under resting conditions, a large vortex develops along the posterior wall of the aorta. This region of flow stasis and long particle residence time disappears with moderate levels of simulated lower limb exercise, such as might be obtained with a brisk walk. We measured wall shear stress and vortex flow patterns and compared the lesion-prone infrarenal aorta with the lesion-resistant suprarenal aorta. At rest, the posterior wall of the infrarenal aorta demonstrated negative, or low, wall shear stress, flow reversal, and vortex flow patterns, whereas the suprarenal aorta showed higher, or positive, shear stress with uniform flow and no vortex formation. Because the suprarenal aorta is less prone to atherosclerotic lesions than the abdominal aorta, we assumed the shear stress at this site, 1.2 dynes/cm^2 under resting conditions, to be the minimum needed to inhibit atherosclerosis. We found that moderate exercise increases infrarenal aortic blood flow and normalizes the shear stress in the lesion-prone infrarenal aorta. An increase of only 2.3 L/min in blood flow to the legs changes the infrarenal blood flow from a complex, recirculating flow to a uniform, unidirectional flow. In addition, under these moderate exercise conditions, the shear stress in the infrarenal aorta exceeds the shear stress in the suprarenal aorta. These data support the growing body of evidence that low levels of exercise have a beneficial effect in limiting atherosclerosis. The duration or frequency of exposure to the higher than resting levels of shear stress necessary to inhibit atherosclerosis is, at present, unknown.[164,167-172]

Susceptible Regions of the Vascular Tree

Carotid Arteries

The carotid bifurcation is particularly prone to plaque formation, with focal plaque deposition occurring principally at the origin of the internal carotid artery, whereas the proximal common carotid artery and the distal internal carotid artery are relatively spared. The geometry of the carotid bifurcation is an important determinant of the hemodynamic conditions that favor plaque formation. The internal carotid sinus has a cross-sectional area twice that of the immediately distal internal carotid segment. This configuration, in combination with the branching angle, results in a large area of flow separation and low and oscillating shear stress along the outer wall of the sinus and a region of laminar flow and high unidirectional shear stress along the inner wall of the sinus.[119,120] The manner in which these differences may determine plaque localization at the outer wall of the sinus has been discussed.

As plaques enlarge at the outer wall, however, the geometric configuration of the lumen is modified so that other flow patterns may develop that favor plaque formation on the side and inner walls. In its most advanced and stenotic form, atherosclerotic disease of the carotid bifurcation may therefore involve the entire circumference of the sinus, including the region of the flow divider, but the plaques are nevertheless largest and most complicated at the outer and side walls of the proximal internal carotid bifurcation.[173] When there is a severe stenosis, the modified hemodynamic conditions that exist at the carotid bifurcation, including the turbulence that may underlie the characteristic bruit, may also compromise integrity of existing carotid plaques and contribute to their tendency to fissure, ulcerate, and form thromboemboli.

Coronary Arteries

Velocity profile and wall shear stress measurements in model human coronary arteries reveal that low wall shear stress, flow separation, and oscillation occur at sites susceptible to plaque localization.[174] These near-wall flow field characteristics are similar to those found in susceptible regions of the carotid bifurcation.

Several special hemodynamic features of the coronary arteries may explain their particular propensity for development of clinically significant plaques. The epicardial coronary

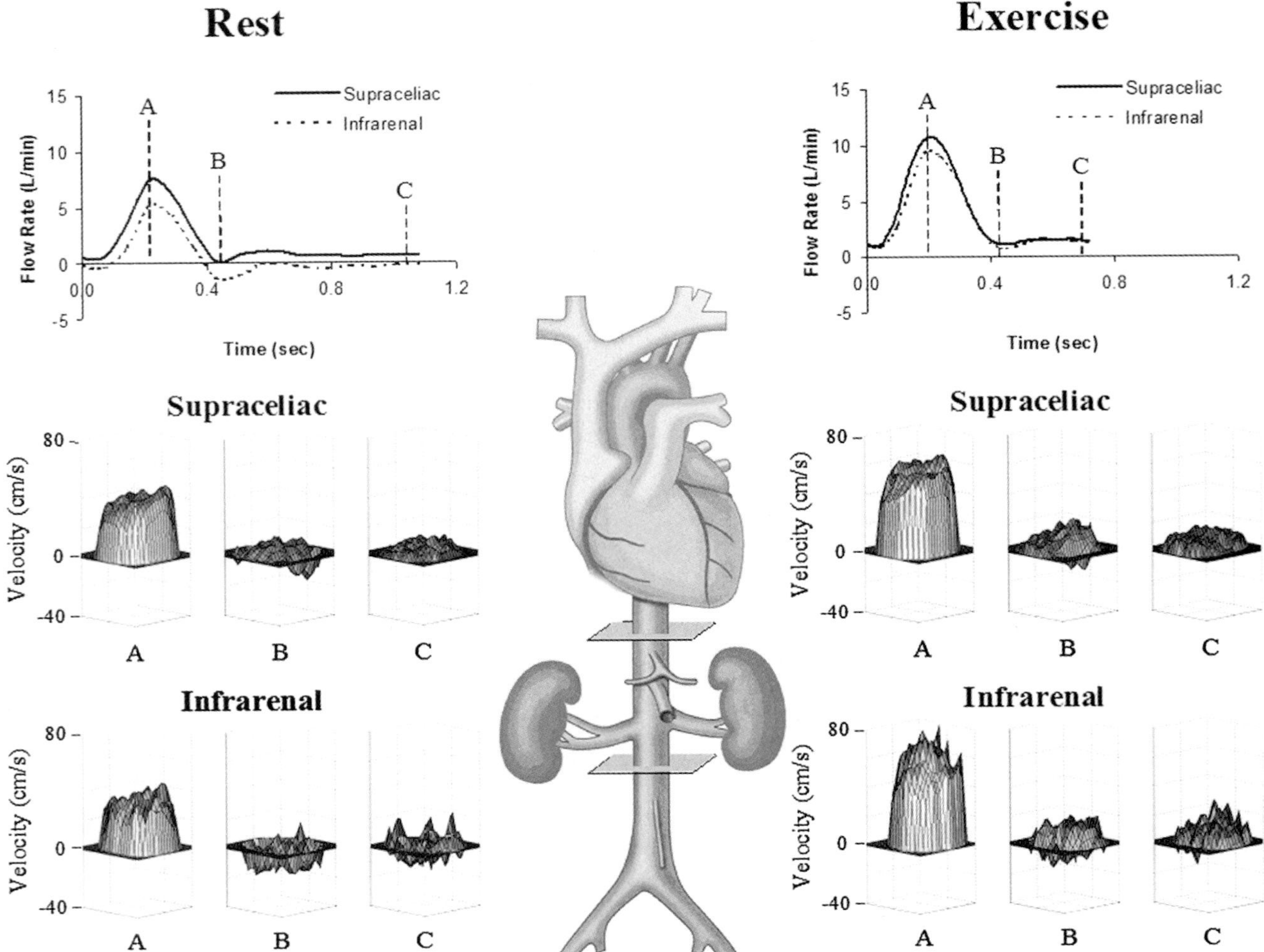

FIGURE 10-11 Schematic diagram of the human aorta with imaging planes at the supraceliac and infrarenal levels and flow data from a representative healthy subject, aged 59, at rest and during cycling exercise. Blood flow rate waveforms (*top*) show significant increases in flow at both the supraceliac and infrarenal levels from rest (*left*) to exercise (*right*) throughout the cardiac cycle. Velocity surface plots are shown for the supraceliac and infrarenal levels of the aorta at rest (*left*) and during exercise (*right*) at peak systole (A), end systole (B), and end diastole (C). Blood velocities increase from rest to exercise for all cardiac phases, and most of the negative blood velocities near the walls of the supraceliac and infrarenal levels at end systole (B) at rest (*left*) become positive during exercise (*right*). (Adapted from Cheng CP, Herfkens RJ, Taylor CA: Abdominal aortic hemodynamics in healthy subjects age 50-70 at rest and during lower limb exercise: In vivo quantification using MRI. Atherosclerosis 168:323, 2003.)

tree has a complex geometric configuration of branchings and curves. Mechanical torsions and flexions of the vessels are evident during the cardiac cycle as the configuration of the cardiac chambers changes. In addition, there are marked variations in flow rate during the cardiac cycle.[175] The coronary arteries experience two different systolic pulses of flow during each cardiac cycle.[176] If oscillation in the direction of the shear stress vector during systole is indeed a major factor in plaque localization,[177] the coronary arteries would be expected to be more vulnerable to plaque formation than other systemic arteries in which only a single systolic pulse is present.

In experimental atherosclerosis, a 20% reduction in mean heart rate resulted in a 50% reduction in diet-induced coronary artery atherosclerotic plaques.[178] Similarly, there was a significant reduction in carotid bifurcation atherosclerosis with drop in heart rate.[83,179] In humans, a number of major prospective clinical studies have found high heart rates in men at rest to be predictors of future clinical coronary heart disease, whereas low heart rates had a protective effect.[180,181] The beneficial effects of exercise on limiting coronary atherosclerosis may result from a reduction in resting heart rate, an intermittent increase in coronary flow and wall shear stress, or a combination of the two.

Abdominal Aorta

Atherosclerotic plaques in humans are found throughout the length of the aorta but are rarely clinically significant in the thoracic segment. In contrast, the infrarenal abdominal aorta is particularly prone to the development of clinically significant lesions, with the formation of obstructive plaques, ulcerations, thrombi, and aneurysmal degeneration. The differences in susceptibility between the thoracic and abdominal portions of the aorta may be related to differences in (1) aortic wall microarchitecture, (2) aortic wall vasa vasorum blood supply, and (3) blood flow patterns and shear stress [28]

The thoracic aorta is larger in diameter than the abdominal aorta and, accordingly, has a greater number of transmedial lamellar units. The thoracic aorta also contains relatively more elastin and less collagen than the abdominal aorta, allowing greater distensibility and pulse propagation. The abdominal aorta, which contains proportionately more collagen, is stiffer and less compliant than the thoracic segment.[27] Each abdominal aortic lamellar unit is thought to support approximately 3000 dynes/cm circumferential tension, whereas each thoracic lamellar unit supports about 2000 dynes/cm. The outer two thirds of the human thoracic aortic wall is supplied with intramural medial vasa vasorum, but the abdominal aorta is largely devoid of medial vasa vasorum. Because intramural vasa vasorum are largely absent from the abdominal aorta, nutrition presumably depends primarily on diffusion from the lumen. Thus, even early intimal plaque deposition may augment the barrier to diffusion, rendering the abdominal aortic media vulnerable to ischemic degeneration and atrophy. Intimal plaque formation would also be expected to increase the diffusion distance across the wall, predisposing to processes that may promote inflammatory cell infiltration, lipid accumulation, and further plaque formation. Extension of reactive vasa vasorum into the plaque may help clear lipid from the intimal lesion but may also induce further proliferation and plaque enlargement. Conversely, failure of vasa vasorum ingrowth may result in arterial wall atrophy and promote aneurysm formation. Thus, differences in structure and nutrition would appear to be associated with the different vulnerabilities of the thoracic aorta and abdominal aorta.[37]

The thoracic aorta is the main conduit carrying blood flow to the viscera and extremities. Much of the cardiac output is delivered to the cerebral and upper extremity vessels as well as to the visceral organs; the renal arteries alone take up to 25% of the cardiac output.[182] Levels of flow in the infrarenal aorta, in contrast, largely depend on the muscular activity of the lower extremities. With mechanized transportation and an increasingly sedentary lifestyle, reduced physical activity may lead to an overall reduction in flow velocity in the abdominal aortic segment. As previously described, Figure 10-11 displays the velocity field in a computer model of the abdominal aorta under simulated resting exercise conditions at mid-diastole along the midplane of the aorta. This region of flow stasis and long particle residence time disappears with moderate levels of simulated lower limb exercise, such as might be obtained with a brisk walk.

The long-term effect of reduced flow velocity may be further accentuated by the tendency of the aorta to enlarge with age. Although the human thoracic aortic media is furnished with intramural vasa vasorum, the abdominal aorta is relatively avascular.[112] Thus, reduced and marked variations in luminal flow rate as well as discrepancies between medial thickness and medial nutrition may combine to enhance the accumulation of atherogenic substances in the abdominal aortic intima.

Conversely, increased flow velocity such as occurs with exercise increases wall shear stress, reduces particle residence time, and eliminates oscillation of shear in the infrarenal aorta.[165,169,183] These factors may be important in plaque formation in the infrarenal aorta and may explain the beneficial effects of exercise in preventing plaque formation.

Superficial Femoral Artery

The arteries of the lower extremities are commonly affected by atherosclerotic plaques, whereas vessels of similar size in the upper extremities are usually spared. In addition to differences in hydrostatic pressure, the arteries of the lower extremities are subjected to more marked variations in flow rate, depending on the level of physical activity. As in the abdominal aorta, a sedentary lifestyle would tend to favor low flow rates and lead to greater plaque deposition in vessels of the lower extremities.

Cigarette smoking and diabetes mellitus are the risk factors most closely associated with atherosclerotic disease of the lower extremities.[184] The manner in which these factors and the special hemodynamic conditions are mutually enhancing in the vessels of the lower extremities remains to be elucidated. The arterial media in the lower extremities may be rendered denser by the greater smooth muscle tone induced by nicotine.[185] Such a change could interfere with transmural transfer of materials entering the intima and favor accumulation of atherogenic materials, as has been suggested by pharmacologic experiments.[186]

Of the arteries of the lower extremity, the superficial femoral artery is the most common site of multiple stenotic lesions, and the profunda femoris tends to be spared. Plaques in the superficial femoral artery have not been shown to occur preferentially at branching sites, but stenotic lesions tend to appear earliest at the adductor hiatus, where the vessel is straight and branches are few. Greater susceptibility to plaque formation because of mechanical trauma caused by the closely associated adductor magnus tendon has been proposed to explain the selective localization of occlusive disease in this area.[187] However, studies have suggested that the adductor canal segment of the superficial femoral artery is not more prone to plaque formation but rather is limited in its ability to dilate or enlarge in response to increasing intimal plaque. Thus, an equivalent volume of intimal plaque results in more stenosis at the adductor canal.[97]

■ EVOLUTION OF ATHEROSCLEROTIC LESIONS

Atherosclerosis is not necessarily a continuous process leading inexorably to arterial stenosis or other clinically significant complications. Plaque formation involves an interaction among systemic risk factors and local conditions in the lumen and artery wall in the context of a living tissue capable of healing and remodeling. The evolution of atherosclerotic lesions therefore involves initiating and sustaining processes as well as adaptive responses and involutional changes. The natural history of atherosclerotic lesions in humans is poorly understood despite the available experimental data on the progression and regression of plaques.

Plaque Initiation

Plaque initiation refers to the earliest detectable biochemical and cellular events leading to or preceding the formation of atherosclerotic lesions. Possible mechanisms of plaque initiation have received a great deal of attention. Research has centered principally on several possibilities, including altered endothelial function or turnover resulting in increased permeability, oxidative alteration of insudated lipids by endothelium, and subsequent ingress of macrophages.[188] Other possibilities are various stimuli to smooth muscle proliferation, including circulating mitogens,[189] and limitations of transmural transfer or egress related to the composition and organization of subendothelial tissues and media.[190] High levels of specific lipoprotein cholesterol fractions have also been implicated.[191] Although each of these possibilities can be related to early lesion development in experimental models and may be related to one or another of the epidemiologically identified risk factors, none has as yet been demonstrated to underlie the mural disturbance that leads to plaque formation. Some or several of these changes may well prove to be significant.

It is not clear, however, that inhibiting the possible initiating injury to the artery wall is of primary importance in the clinical control of atherosclerosis. Later research has focused principally on several possibilities, including (1) altered endothelial function linked to an inflammatory response to injury with leukocyte adhesion and diapedesis and (2) cell proliferation, smooth muscle cell migration, and macrophage foam cell formation with lipid accumulation in both cell types. The lipids accumulated include cholesterol, cholesterol esters, and triglycerides. Greater lipoprotein infiltration coupled with dysregulation of the cholesterol ester cycle activity and cholesterol efflux processes have been proposed to explain the pathobiology of this lipid accumulation process. Moreover, T cells, macrophages, and smooth muscle cells may release specific biologic response modifiers that may participate in the dysregulation of lipid metabolism, thereby enhancing lipid accumulation.[23,30]

It is well recognized that very old people with no clinically manifest atherosclerotic disease during life are found at autopsy to have substantial and advanced atherosclerotic plaques. Longevity and good health in these people were associated not with the prevention of plaque initiation or formation but with (1) the stable nature of the plaque, (2) control of progression, (3) adequate adaptation of the arteries, and (4) prevention of the complications of such lesions.

Plaque Progression

Plaque progression refers to the continuing increase in intimal plaque volume, which may result in narrowing of the lumen and obstruction of blood flow. Progression may be rapid or slow, continuous or episodic. Rates of accretion may also vary with the stage of plaque development, plaque composition, and cell population of the lesion. Some of these factors may be modulated by clinical risk factors, whereas others are related to the changes in circulation and wall composition associated with lesion growth.

At the tissue level, plaque progression involves

1. Cellular migration, proliferation, and differentiation
2. Intracellular and extracellular accumulation of lipids
3. Extracellular matrix accumulation
4. Degeneration and cell necrosis

Progression also implies evolution and differentiation of plaque organization and stratification. In general, these features are designed to maintain an adequate lumen channel for as long as possible. The formation of a fibrous cap, the sequestration of necrotic and degenerative debris, and the persistence of a regular and round luminal cross-section as well as adaptive enlargement of the artery reflect an overall healing process. In the long term, these reactive processes may prove inadequate, but they may also retard or arrest the atherogenic process. If plaque enlargement occurs under these conditions, plaque progression is well tolerated. Lumen diameter and blood flow are maintained even in the presence of advanced and extensive lesions.

Atherosclerotic plaque may lead to either aneurysmal dilatation[105] or occlusion in the abdominal aorta, depending on lesion evolution. Plaque deposition associated with localized dilatation, thinning of the media, and loss of medial elastic lamellae may predispose that segment of aorta to subsequent aneurysm formation. Plaque deposits without medial thinning, without loss of elastic lamellae, and without artery wall dilatation may predispose the aorta, in the event of continuing plaque accumulation, to the development of lumen stenosis (Fig 10-12).[106]

Plaque modeling also includes incorporation and organization of mural thrombi and healing and re-endothelialization of ulcerations, suggesting further means of restoring and preserving optimal conditions for adequate laminar flow. Plaque disruptions that undergo remodeling may leave defects corresponding to healed or restructured walls without the development of clinical symptoms.

One must understand the processes that regulate plaque development, differentiation, and healing in order to comprehend why one plaque progresses unfavorably with stenosis, ulceration, or thrombosis and another progresses without obstruction or complication. It is likely that rates of cell proliferation, lipid deposition, fibrous cap formation, necrosis and healing, calcification, and inflammation vary over time and may differ with location at the same point in time. Such differences probably account for the spectrum of morphologic changes in plaques in a given patient at the same time.

Changes in local hemodynamics that occur during plaque progression may also alter plaque composition and the rate of progression. Increases in shear stress in a developing stenosis may inhibit further plaque formation but may also favor erosion of the fibrous cap and ulceration. Developing stenoses may also alter hemodynamic conditions to enhance distal lesion formation and complication.[192] Severe, hemodynamically significant stenoses, however, enhance plaque formation in the proximal arterial segments[193] and inhibit it in distal segments[156] because of changes in pulse pressure, wall motion, and medial smooth muscle metabolism.[194]

Plaque Regression

Plaque regression refers to a discernible decrease in intimal plaque volume; it may occur through (1) resorption of lipids or extracellular matrix, (2) cell death, and (3) cell migration out of the plaque.

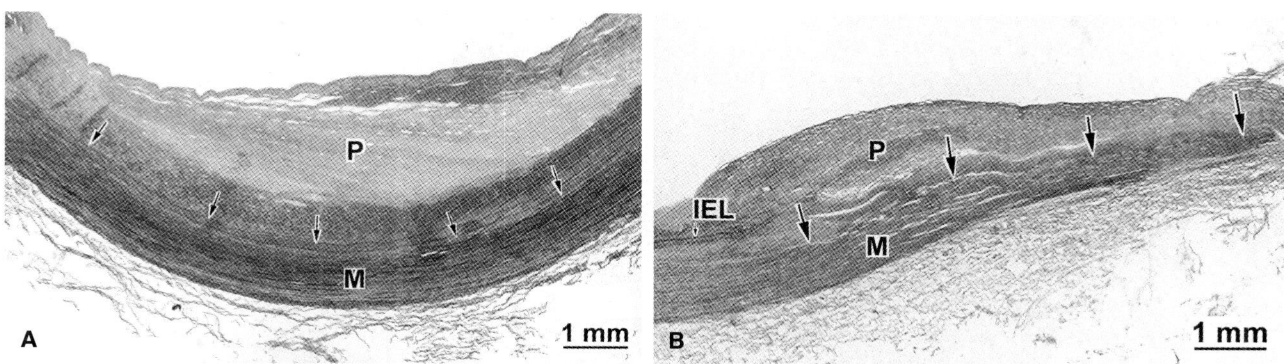

FIGURE 10-12 Evolution of atherosclerotic lesions could lead to different consequences. **A,** Abdominal aorta with well-built-up plaque (P) and relatively normal media (M). The elastic lamellae in the media are stained dark (Weigert–van Gieson staining). *Arrows* indicate the inner margin of the media. The remodeling phenomena are apparent in the bottom part of the intimal plaque with newly formed elastic lamellae. **B,** Abdominal aorta with large plaque (P) and diminishing thickness of the media (M). The internal elastic lamellae (IEL) has mostly disappeared, and the inner part of the media has been eroding (*arrows*). There is little remodeling evidence in the intimal plaque (Weigert–van Gieson staining). (From Xu C, Zarins CK, Glagov S: Aneurysmal and occlusive atherosclerosis of the human abdominal aorta. J Vasc Surg 33:91, 2001.)

Significant reduction in lesion volume has been demonstrated in a number of animal models in which experimental elevations of serum lipids have been markedly reduced by an alteration in diet or administration of lipid-lowering drugs.[195-197] Lesions previously induced by an atherogenic diet respond readily, although not uniformly. Coronary and aortic lesions in monkeys tend to regress, but carotid lesions appear to be resistant.[198] Severe, long-standing lesions in swine are much more resistant to regression than early foam cell lesions.[199] Animal studies usually involve induction and regression periods of several months. Whether human lesions, which may have accumulated over decades, also diminish significantly in volume is as yet unclear.

Local hemodynamic conditions not only exert a profound influence on plaque progression; they also are important in plaque regression. Severe proximal stenosis inhibits plaque formation[193] but also inhibits plaque regression in the distal arterial tree.[156] Hypertension promotes continued experimental plaque progression in the coronary arteries despite the reduction of hypercholesterolemia.[157] Despite both plaque regression elsewhere and the reversal of hypercholesterolemia, experimental plaque formation and complication can continue in the arteries distal to a stenosis, indicating that local hemodynamic factors and metabolic conditions in the artery wall may greatly modify systemic influences on plaque function during both progression and regression.[156]

Plaque Regression Studies in Humans

Apparent regression of atherosclerosis has been documented by serial contrast arteriography in humans. Angiographic regression of atherosclerotic lesions has been demonstrated in humans in coronary[200-202] and peripheral[83] arteries. Each of these trials has demonstrated luminal changes angiographically rather than by direct evidence of plaque regression. It should be noted that each trial to date has demonstrated simultaneous angiographic evidence of lesion progression *and* regression of different lesions during the treatment, indicating the complexity of the process.

Although plaque regression is usually thought of as simply a resorption of plaque material, it may proceed by different mechanisms. A decrease in intimal plaque volume may occur from a change in plaque metabolism, resulting in dissolution of the fibrous cap, ulceration and erosion, and embolization of the necrotic core.

Apparent regression may also take place when the rate of artery wall enlargement exceeds the rate of plaque deposition. Most human plaque regression studies performed to date have used angiography to document lesion regression.[203] However, angiography provides information only on lumen diameter and contour, not on the volume and composition of the atherosclerotic lesion itself. Thus, if intimal plaque deposition and artery wall dilatation keep pace, no change is noted on arteriography despite continued plaque progression. Conversely, if dilatation exceeds plaque deposition, arteriographic demonstration of this change is taken as evidence of regression even if plaque deposition continues.[204] Such a phenomenon occurs at the outset of plaque formation in some vessels and is quite prominent in some locations. Certainty with regard to reduction in lesion volume or regression of atherosclerosis in humans must be based on a direct assessment of the plaque and artery wall as well as of lumen caliber.

Although plaque regression may a priori seem desirable, regression regimens could alter the composition and organization of plaques, especially those with soft, semifluid, or pultaceous contents, leading to plaque ulceration or disruption, release of plaque debris, and thrombosis and embolism. In certain circumstances, particularly with well-organized sclerotic plaques, the plaque may provide mechanical support to the artery wall. This may be especially significant if medial atrophy has occurred underneath the plaque. Plaque dissolution under these circumstances could leave a weakened artery wall and potentiate aneurysm formation. Experimental studies have shown aneurysm formation in monkeys undergoing cholesterol-lowering regression regimens.[205,206]

Further studies of the direct effects of regression regimens on plaques and the artery wall are needed, and plaque regression must be defined in terms of its specific effects on well-established atherosclerotic plaques. An alternative therapeutic goal may be arrest or control of progression, plaque stabilization, and enhancement of artery wall adaptation.

Plaque Complications and Stability

Clinical sequelae of atherosclerotic lesions are usually caused by the complications of plaques. A complication such as plaque disruption or ulceration may result in embolization of plaque materials or the exposure of plaque components to the circulation, thereby causing occlusive or embolizing thrombi. Critical lumen narrowing or the presence of plaque complications at a few critical locations in the vascular tree is the principal determinant of clinical symptoms, rather than plaque size per se.

Susceptibility of plaques to disruption, fracture, or fissuring is likely to be associated with their structure, composition, and consistency.[207] Plaque fracture and disruption are important features in the development of clinical symptoms.[208,209] The various types of plaques are

- Relatively soft and pliable
- Friable or cohesive
- Densely sclerotic
- Calcific and brittle

A plaque may have a well-formed fibrous cap, similar in architecture and thickness to a normal artery wall, which thereby effectively sequesters the plaque and its contents from the lumen. The necrotic interior of other plaques, however, may be separated from the lumen only by a narrow zone of connective tissue or by endothelium alone.[210,211]

Advanced plaques with intact, well-organized fibrous caps would be expected to present smooth and regular lumen surfaces to the blood stream. Abnormal levels of wall shear stress and departures from laminar, unidirectional flow may favor local accumulation, adhesion, and deposition of thrombocytes, monocytes, and fibrin. These hemodynamic disturbances are likely to occur distal to stenoses, at foci of endothelial surface irregularity or extrinsic mechanical trauma, and in regions of softened plaque consistency.[212] Local mechanical stresses resulting from sudden changes in pressure, flow, or pulse rate or from torsion and bending in relation to organ movements may precipitate disruption of friable or brittle plaques. Conversely, changes in vessel configuration associated with plaque progression and stenosis may create conditions favoring the development of hemodynamic shear forces that can cause plaque rupture.[213]

Although vessel segments distal to tight stenoses tend to be spared, degrees of stenosis not tight enough to prevent distal plaque formation may nevertheless engender unstable flow conditions that could modify plaque composition and configuration. In experimental animals, plaques located immediately distal to a region of moderate narrowing have been shown to be more complex in structure and composition than those that occur in the same region in the absence of a proximal stenosis.[192] The likelihood of turbulence is also enhanced as significant stenoses develop and as vessels enlarge and become tortuous with age or when multiple plaques occur in the same vessel in close axial proximity.

Because atherosclerotic plaque deposition is reduced in regions of high flow velocity, it seems likely that increasing flow velocity and shear stress in narrowed areas may induce signaling mechanisms that result in slowing of the atherogenic process. Decreased flow velocity due to distal obstruction, reduced pressure, or greater peripheral resistance may have the opposite effect. Further information is needed about the factors that determine plaque complication or stability in human atherosclerosis.

Assessment of atherosclerotic plaques by imaging techniques is essential for in vivo identification of vulnerable plaques. Several invasive and noninvasive imaging techniques are available. Most techniques identify lumen diameter or stenosis, wall thickness, and plaque volume, and are ineffective in identifying the high-risk plaques that are vulnerable to rupture and thrombosis. In vivo, high-resolution, multiple-contrast MRI holds the best promise for noninvasive imaging of high-risk plaques. The technique allows serial assessment of the progression and regression of atherosclerosis. Application of MRI opens new areas for diagnosis, prevention, and treatment (e.g., lipid-lowering drug regimens) of atherosclerosis in all arterial locations.[214,215]

■ ANEURYSM FORMATION

The association between atherosclerosis and aneurysm formation has long been recognized in humans. The demonstrations of increased proteolytic enzyme activity[216-218] and of a familial tendency for abdominal aortic aneurysm formation[219] have led some investigators to suggest that aneurysm formation is primarily a genetically controlled connective tissue dysfunction with little or no relation to atherosclerosis. However, experimental evidence shows that (1) aneurysms can be induced in animals by high-cholesterol atherogenic diets ingested for prolonged periods and (2) aneurysm formation is associated with destruction of the medial lamellar architecture of the aortic wall.[220,221] Furthermore, aneurysm formation has been noted to be related to plaque regression in both controlled[206] (Fig. 10-13) and uncontrolled[205,222] trials.

Increasing intimal plaque is associated with arterial enlargement and atrophy of the underlying arterial media, as described earlier. Under these circumstances, the atherosclerotic plaque may contribute to the structural support of the artery wall. Significant plaque regression by resorption of lipid and extracellular matrix can reduce plaque volume. Further reduction in plaque volume can occur through erosion of the fibrous cap, elution of the necrotic core, and ulceration of the plaque. The net effect may be a thinned artery wall incapable of supporting the greater mural tension brought about by earlier atherosclerotic arterial enlargement. This increase in wall stress, together with the biologic interaction between metabolic plaque resorption and proteolytic enzyme activity on the arterial wall, can result in progressive arterial dilatation and aneurysm formation. Histologic examination of the aorta in animals with experimentally induced aneurysms and in humans with aneurysms reveals similar atrophic characteristics of atherosclerotic plaque, with loss of the elastin lamellar architecture

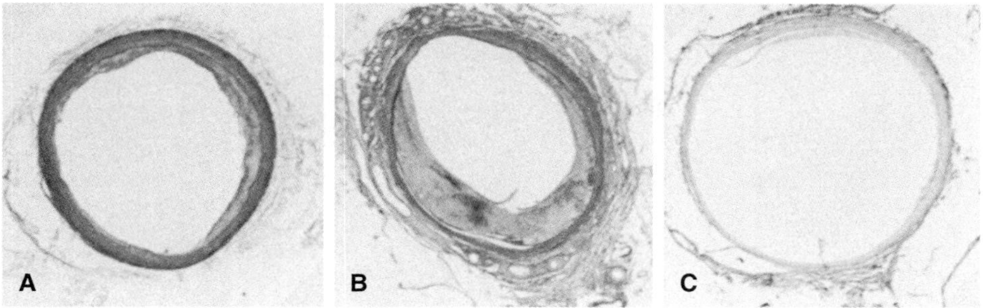

FIGURE 10-13 Aneurysmal enlargement of the abdominal aorta in a controlled trial of regression of experimental atherosclerosis. Transverse sections of the abdominal aorta from three groups of monkeys are shown. In group I (**A**), there was moderate plaque formation after a 6-month diet containing 2% cholesterol and 25% peanut oil. In group II (**B**), plaques were much larger and the media was slightly thinner after 12 months of the atherogenic diet, but the artery size (internal elastic lumina area) did not change significantly. After 6 months of the atherogenic diet, followed by a low-cholesterol regression diet (group III, **C**), plaques were significantly smaller and were absent in some regions. The media was thin, and the artery size (internal elastic lumina area) was increased twofold. (Weigert–van Gieson; original magnification ×10.) (From Zarins CK, Xu C-P, Glagov S: Aneurysmal enlargement of the aorta during regression of experimental atherosclerosis. J Vasc Surg 15:90, 1992.)

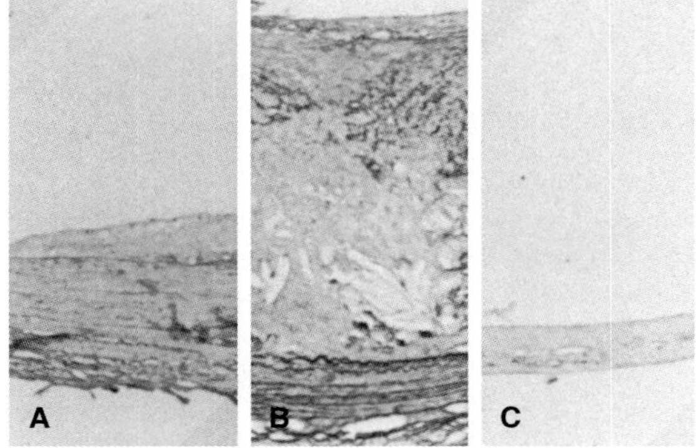

FIGURE 10-14 Histologic changes in the abdominal aorta of the sections shown in Figure 10-13. After 6 months of the atherogenic diet (group I, **A**), a moderate amount of plaque formed, with characteristic foam cell prevalence and little change in the media. After 12 months of the atherogenic diet (group II, **B**), plaques were complex, with the formation of fibrous caps and evidence of necrosis and cholesterol accumulation. The media appeared normal, with clearly stained elastic lamellae and smooth muscle cells. After 6 months of the atherogenic diet and 6 months of the regression diet (group III, **C**), plaques were much smaller and largely fibrotic. The media was thinned, and elastic lamellae were largely inapparent. These histologic changes are similar to those seen in human aneurysms. (Weigert–van Gieson; original magnification ×75.) (From Zarins CK, Xu C-P, Glagov S: Aneurysmal enlargement of the aorta during regression of experimental atherosclerosis. J Vasc Surg 15:90, 1992.)

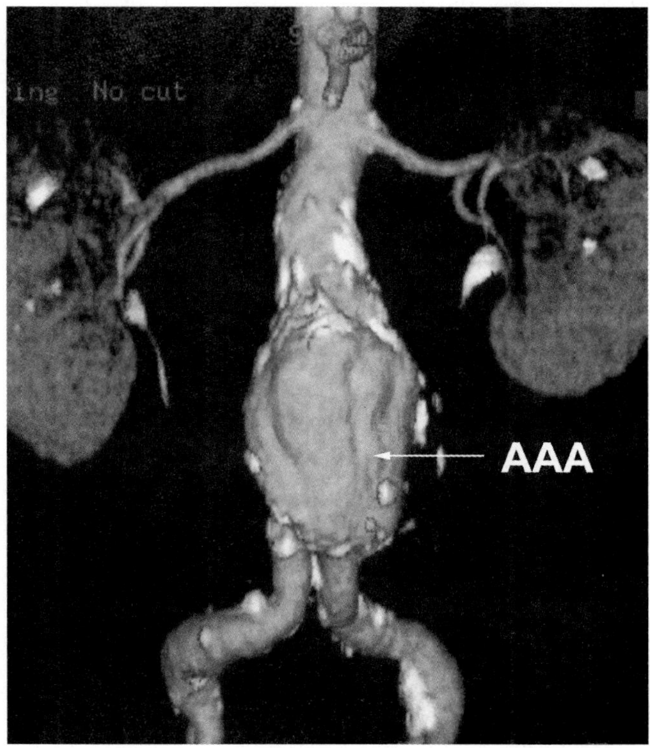

FIGURE 10-15 Three-dimensional imaging of abdominal aortic aneurysm (AAA) by spiral computed tomography (unpublished data).

of the artery wall (Fig. 10-14). Loss of elastin is a prominent feature, along with the loss of collagen and thinning of the aortic wall.

In humans, a strong association exists between atherosclerosis and aneurysm formation, which have common risk factors. Aneurysms form in the same distributions as atherosclerotic plaques, but the greatest vulnerability to aneurysm formation is in the abdominal aorta (Fig. 10-15).[105,106] The abdominal aorta is particularly susceptible to plaque formation and may be particularly vulnerable because of its medial lamellar architecture and limited aortic wall nutrition, as discussed earlier. These considerations suggest that aneurysm formation in the abdominal aorta may complicate the atherosclerotic process under special experimental and human clinical conditions. It appears at a relatively late phase of plaque evolution, when plaque regression and media atrophy predominate, rather than in earlier phases, when cell proliferation, fibrogenesis, and lipid accumulation characterize plaque progression. Figure 10-16 depicts a close relationship between aneurysm formation and atherosclerotic evolution.

The pathogenesis and controlling mechanisms of aneurysm formation are the subject of much investigation. Matrix metalloproteinases (MMPs) and aortic wall degeneration play important roles. Clinical findings and experimental

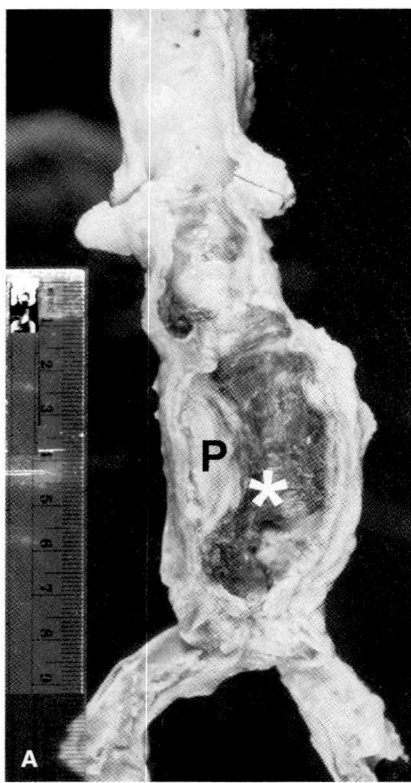

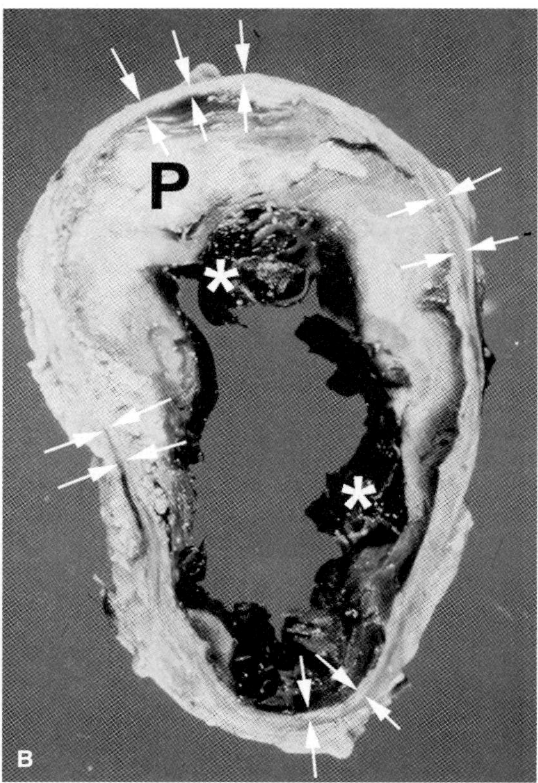

FIGURE 10-16 Human abdominal aortic aneurysm. **A,** A gross specimen of an abdominal aortic aneurysm. The aneurysm is located in the infrarenal segment of the aorta. The longitudinal opening view shows a large atherosclerotic plaque (P) and mural thrombi (*asterisk*). There are also numerous atherosclerotic lesions spreading over the aorta. **B,** A cross-section of an abdominal aortic aneurysm showing large atherosclerotic plaque (P), the reduced media thickness (*arrows*) beneath the plaque, and large amount of mural thrombi (*asterisk*). (From Zarins CK, Xu C: Pathogenesis of aortic aneurysmal disease. In Ballard JL [ed]: Aortic Surgery. Georgetown, TX, Landes Bioscience, 2000, p 1.)

evidence have also shown a relationship between atherosclerotic lesions in the intima in relation to weakening and dilatation of the involved segment of the aorta. As atherosclerotic plaque develops, arterial enlargement may occur. This may compensate for increasing plaque size and may prevent the development of lumen stenosis. We have documented compensatory enlargement in human coronary arteries,[223,224] carotid arteries at the bifurcation,[43] and superficial femoral arteries.[96] This process may also occur as a result of local increase in flow associated with periodic temporary narrowing of the lumen produced by an encroaching intimal plaque. The increase in wall stress may be expected to stimulate endothelial release of NO and/or other factors resulting in smooth muscle relaxation in the media and artery dilatation.[43] Alternatively, the plaque may induce direct proteolytic or involutional changes in the media underlying the plaque, with resulting dilatation. Indeed, the role of MMPs in abdominal aortic aneurysms has been widely demonstrated.[225]

Thinning of the media is a common feature in atherosclerosis and is a constant feature in the formation of abdominal aortic aneurysms. Human aortic aneurysms are characterized by extensive atrophy of the media with almost total loss of normal lamellar architecture. The media is commonly almost totally devoid of the usual elastin layers and is converted into a narrow and calcific fibrous band. The microanatomic features of the abdominal aorta's structure and the susceptibility of this region to atherosclerosis and to the resulting erosive effects on the media give this segment of the aorta special vulnerability to aneurysm formation.

Experimental studies in our laboratory confirm the importance of the destruction of the medial lamellar architecture in the pathogenesis of aneurysms[226] and reveal that diet-induced atherosclerosis may result in the thinning of the media and aneurysm formation.[206] In a controlled trial of cholesterol-lowering therapy in monkeys, we found plaque regression, thinning of the media, and the development of aneurysms in the abdominal aorta.[206] These observations suggest that aneurysm formation is mainly a manifestation of atherosclerotic artery wall degeneration. Thus, observations of the atherosclerotic process in humans and experimental animals suggest possible mechanisms for aneurysm formation related directly to erosion of the artery wall by plaque components. This process may be exacerbated by biomechanical forces acting on the aortic wall.

Plaque enlargement is associated with medial thinning and loss of the medial lamellar architecture. Plaque deposition, medial thinning, and aortic enlargement are maximal at the midpoint of the abdominal aorta and at the bifurcation. There may be different modalities of response of the human aorta to atherosclerotic plaque. Plaque deposition may be accompanied by compensatory enlargement and preservation of normal lumen caliber or may occur without compensatory enlargement and medial thinning, thus leading to the development of lumen stenosis. Plaque formation with erosion and destruction of the underlying medial lamellar architecture may result in excessive dilatation and predisposition to aneurysm formation. Such medial erosion may be promoted by proteolytic enzymes released from components of the atherosclerotic lesion and the associated inflammatory response.

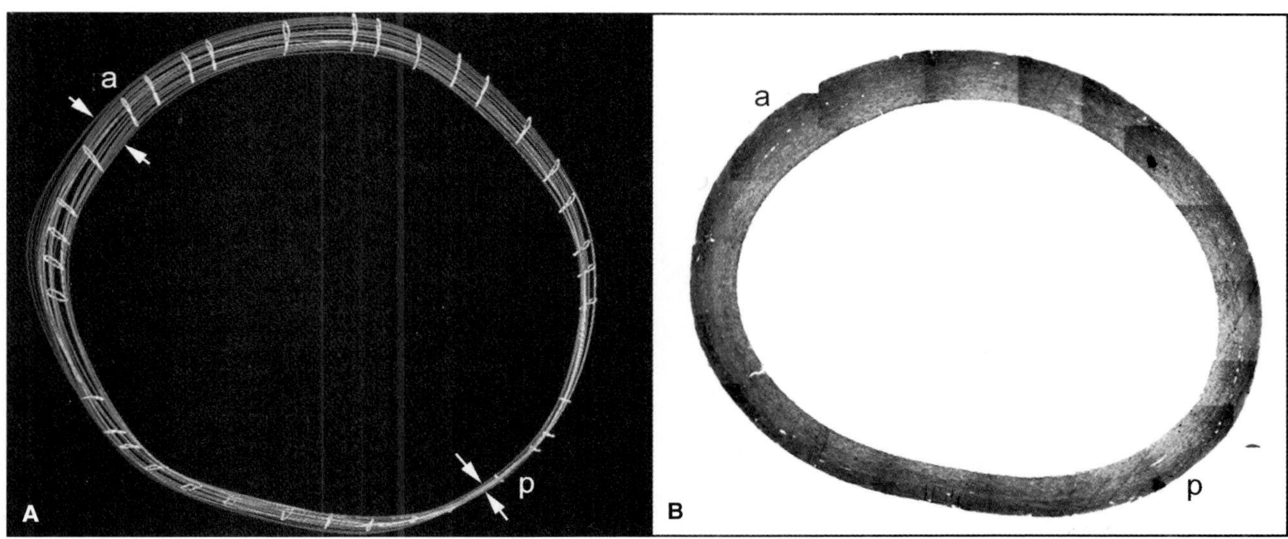

FIGURE 10-17 Variance in aortic wall motion and wall thickness around the circumference of the porcine thoracic aorta. **A** shows the magnitude of wall motion, which was 0.6 ± 0.2 mm at the anterior wall (a) and 0.2 ± 0.1 mm at the posterior wall (p). **B** shows the wall thickness of the same segment. The wall thickness was 2.2 ± 0.3 mm at the anterior wall (a) and 1.6 ± 0.2 at the posterior wall (p). There is a significant correlation between the wall motion and wall thickness ($r = 0.7891$).

In the aorta, it is observed that atherosclerotic disease develops first in the abdominal aorta and is much more common in the abdominal aorta (i.e., below the diaphragm) than in the thoracic aorta (i.e., above the diaphragm). Thoracic aortic plaques are usually less abundant, more discrete, less complicated, and less calcific than abdominal aortic plaques in the same person. Thoracic aortic plaques tend to develop predominantly in relation to intercostal branch ostia, but occlusive or obstructive atherosclerosis is rarely seen. In autopsy studies, Roberts and colleagues[227] noted that the abdominal aorta contained by far the most severe aortic atherosclerosis with the greatest involvement occurring below the celiac artery. Glagov and associates[1] noted that abdominal aortic atherosclerosis was greater than thoracic aortic atherosclerosis in the majority of cases for men and women as well as for normotensive and hypertensive individuals.

Using MRI and histomorphometry, Draney and colleagues[228] found that aortic wall motion and wall thickness vary around the circumference of the porcine thoracic aorta. These variations are significant at the same spatial locations, indicating a direct relationship between wall thickness and wall motion (Fig. 10-17). These differences may play a role in asymmetric localization of pathologic processes in the aorta.

■ SUMMARY

Atherosclerosis is a systemic disorder with localized plaque deposition in selected sites on the arterial tree. Low or oscillatory wall shear stress, or both, and prolonged particle residence time due to flow stasis are the hemodynamic conditions associated with plaque formation. Alterations in local hemodynamic conditions also result in adaptive changes in the artery wall to maintain an adequate lumen caliber for blood flow. The primary adaptive response to enlarging intimal plaque is compensatory artery enlargement. Other responses, such as sequestering the plaque to one side and walling it off with a fibrous cap, can permit long-term clinical stability despite extensive atherosclerotic plaque formation.

Clinical complications of atherosclerosis occur when the normal adaptive and compensatory mechanisms fail and complications such as stenosis, ulceration, embolization, and thrombosis develop. A better understanding is needed of (1) the normal adaptive responses of arteries, (2) the processes and evolution of atherosclerotic lesions, and (3) the means by which plaques can be stabilized to prevent local plaque complications and subsequent clinical consequences.

Acknowledgments This work was supported by the National Heart, Lung, and Blood Institute NHLBI grant HL-15062 and HL-64327 and National Science Foundation NSF grant CME 7921551.

■ REFERENCES

1. Glagov S, Zarins CK, Giddens DP, Ku DN: Hemodynamics and atherosclerosis. Arch Pathol Lab Med 112:1018, 1988.
2. Zarins CK: Adaptive responses of arteries. J Vasc Surg 9:382, 1989.
3. Schwartz S, Heimark R, Majesky M: Developmental mechanisms underlying pathology of arteries. Physiol Rev 70:1177, 1990.
4. Giddens DP, Zarins CK, Glagov S: Response of arteries to near-wall fluid dynamic behavior. Appl Mech Rev 43:S96, 1990.
5. Taylor KE, Glagov S, Zarins CK: Preservation and structural adaptation of endothelium over experimental foam cell lesions. Arteriosclerosis 9:881, 1989.
6. Tsao CH, Glagov S: Basal endothelial attachment: Tenacity at cytoplasmic dense zone in the rabbit aorta. Lab Invest 23:520, 1970.
7. Jaffe EA: Biology of Endothelial Cells. Boston, Martinus Nijhoff, 1984.
8. Cines DB, Pollak ES, Buck CA, et al: Endothelial cells in physiology and in the pathophysiology of vascular disorders. Blood 91:3527, 1998.

9. Traub O, Berk BC: Laminar shear stress: Mechanisms by which endothelial cells transduce an atheroprotective force. Arterioscler Thromb Vasc Biol 18:677, 1998.
10. Boyle EM Jr, Lille ST, Allaire E, et al: Endothelial cell injury in cardiovascular surgery: Atherosclerosis. Ann Thorac Surg 63:885, 1997.
11. Clowes AW, Reidy MA: Prevention of stenosis after vascular reconstruction: Pharmacological control of intimal hyperplasia—-a review. J Vasc Surg 13:885, 1991.
12. Ross R: Atherosclerosis—an inflammatory disease. N Engl J Med 340:115, 1999.
13. Zarins CK, Taylor KE, Bomberger RA, et al: Endothelial integrity at aortic ostial flow dividers. Scanning Electron Microsc 3:249, 1980.
14. Reidy MA, Irvin C, Lindner V: Migration of arterial wall cells: Expression of plasminogen activators and inhibitors in injured rat arteries. Circ Res 78:405, 1996.
15. Doornekamp FN, Borst C, Post MJ: Endothelial cell recoverage and intimal hyperplasia after endothelium removal with or without smooth muscle cell necrosis in the rabbit carotid artery. J Vasc Res 33:146, 1996.
16. Falcone DJ, Hajjar DP, Minick CR: Lipoprotein and albumin accumulation in reendothelialized and deendothelialized aorta. Am J Pathol 114:112, 1984.
17. Faggiotto A, Ross R: Studies of hypercholesterolemia in the nonhuman primate. II: Fatty streak conversion to fibrous plaque. Arteriosclerosis 4:341, 1984.
18. Van Heek M, Schmitt D, Toren P, et al: Cholesteryl hydroperoxy-octadecadienoate from oxidized low density lipoprotein inactivates platelet-derived growth factor. J Biol Chem 273:19405, 1998.
19. Bevilacqua MP, Pober JS, Majeau GR, et al: Interleukin 1 (IL-1) induces biosynthesis and cell surface expression of procoagulant activity in human vascular endothelial cells. J Exp Med 160:618, 1984.
20. Einhorn S, Eldor A, Vladavsky I, et al: Production and characterization of interferon from endothelial cells. J Cell Physiol 122:200, 1985.
21. Whatley R, Zimmerman G, McIntyre T, Prescott S: Lipid metabolism and signal transduction in endothelial cells. Prog Lipid Res 29:45, 1990.
22. Gimbrone MA Jr, Resnick N, Nagel T, et al: Hemodynamics, endothelial gene expression, and atherogenesis. Ann N Y Acad Sci 811:1, 1997.
23. Hajjar DP, Pomerantz KB: Signal transduction in atherosclerosis: Integration of cytokines and the eicosanoid network. FASEB J 6:2933, 1992.
24. Clark JM, Glagov S: Structural integration of the arterial wall. I: Relationships and attachments of medial smooth muscle cells in normally distended and hyperdistended aortas. Lab Invest 40:587, 1979.
25. Gay S, Miller EJ: Collagen in the Physiology and Pathology of Connective Tissue. New York, Gustav Fischer, 1978.
26. Clark JM, Glagov S: Transmural organization of the arterial wall: The lamellar unit revisited. Arteriosclerosis 5:19, 1985.
27. Wolinsky H, Glagov S: A lamellar unit of aortic medial structure and function in mammals. Circ Res 20:99, 1967.
28. Wolinsky H, Glagov S: Comparison of abdominal and thoracic aortic medial structure in mammals: Deviation from the usual pattern in man. Circ Res 25:677, 1969.
29. Fischer GM, Llaurado JG: Collagen and elastin content in canine arteries from functionally different vascular beds. Circ Res 19:3984, 1966.
30. Pomerantz K, Hajjar D: Eicosanoids in regulation of arterial smooth muscle cell phenotype, proliferative capacity, and cholesterol metabolism. Arteriosclerosis 9:413, 1989.
31. Davis HR, Runyon-Hass A, Zarins CK, et al: Interactive arterial effects of hypertension and hyperlipidemia. Fed Proc 43:711, 1984.
32. Lyon RT, Zarins CK, Glagov S: Artery wall motion proximal and distal to stenoses. Fed Proc 44:1136, 1985.
33. Leung DYM, Glagov S, Mathews MB: Cyclic stretching stimulates synthesis of matrix components by arterial smooth muscle cells in vitro. Science 191:475, 1976.
34. Bomberger RA, Zarins CK, Glagov S: Medial injury and hyperlipidemia in development of aneurysms or atherosclerotic plaques. Surg Forum 31:338, 1980.
35. Wolinsky H, Glagov S: Structural basis for the static mechanical properties of the aortic media. Circ Res 14:400, 1964.
36. Crawford T, Levene CI: Medial thinning in atheroma. J Pathol 66:19, 1953.
37. Wolinsky H, Glagov S: Nature of species differences in the medial distribution of aortic vasa vasorum in mammals. Circ Res 20:409, 1967.
38. Heistad DD, Marcus ML, Law EG, et al: Regulation of blood flow to the aortic media in dogs. J Clin Invest 62:133, 1978.
39. Glagov S, Bassiouny HS, Giddens DP, Zarins CK: Pathobiology of plaque modeling and complication. Surg Clin North Am 7:545, 1995.
40. Glagov S: Intimal hyperplasia, vascular modeling and the restenosis problem. Circulation 8:2888, 1994.
41. Wolinsky H, Glagov S: Zonal differences in modeling of the mammalian aortic media during growth. Fed Proc 26:357, 1967.
42. Leung DYM, Glagov S, Mathews MB: Elastin and collagen accumulation in rabbit ascending aorta and pulmonary trunk during postnatal growth: Correlation of cellular synthetic response with medial tension. Circ Res 41:316, 1977.
43. Wolinsky H: Long-term effects of hypertension on the rat aortic wall and their relation to concurrent aging changes. Circ Res 30:301, 1972.
44. Masawa N, Glagov S, Zarins CK: Quantitative morphologic study of intimal thickening at the human carotid bifurcation. I: Axial and circumferential distribution of maximum intimal thickening in asymptomatic uncomplicated plaques. Atherosclerosis 107:137, 1994.
45. Masawa N, Glagov S, Zarins CK: Quantitative morphologic study of intimal thickening at the human carotid bifurcation. II: The compensatory enlargement response and the role of the intima in tensile support. Atherosclerosis 107:147, 1994.
46. Vito RP, Choi HS, Seifferth TA, et al: Measurement of strain in soft biological tissue. In Hanagud S, Kamat M (eds): Developments in Theoretical and Applied Mechanics. Proceedings, Society of Engineering Science, Georgia Institute of Technology, Altanta, 1990.
47. Vito RP, Whang MC, Giddens DP, et al: Stress analysis of the diseased arterial cross-section. ASME Adv Biomed Eng 17:273, 1990.
48. Thoma R: Untersuchungen über die Histogenase and Histomechanik des Gefass Systems. Stuttgart, F Enke, 1893.
49. Mulvihill DA, Harvey SC: The mechanism of the development of collateral circulation. N Engl J Med 104:1032, 1931.
50. Holman E: Problems in the dynamics of blood flow. I: Condition controlling collateral circulation in the presence of an arteriovenous fistula, following the ligation of an artery. Surgery 26:889, 1949.
51. Kamiya A, Togawa T: Adaptive regulation of wall shear stress to flow change in the canine carotid artery. Am J Physiol 239:H14, 1980.
52. Masuda H, Bassiouny HS, Glagov S, Zarins CK: Artery wall restructuring in response to increased flow. Surg Forum 40:285, 1989.
53. Langille BL, O'Donnell F: Reductions in arterial diameter produced by chronic decreases in blood flow are endothelium-dependent. Science 231:405, 1986.
54. Pohl U, Holtz J, Busse R, Bassenge E: Crucial role of endothelium in the vasodilator response to increased flow in vivo. Hypertension 8:37, 1986.
55. Hull SSJ, Kaiser L, Jaffe MD, Sparks HVJ: Endothelium-dependent flow-induced dilatation of canine femoral and saphenous arteries. Blood Vessels 23:183, 1986.
56. Rubanyi GM, Romero CJ, Vanhoutte PM: Flow induced release of endothelium-derived relaxing factor. Am J Physiol 250:H1145, 1986.
57. Furchgott RF: Role of endothelium in responses of vascular smooth muscle. Circ Res 53:557, 1983.
58. Koller S, Sun D, Huang A, Kaley G: Corelease of nitric oxide and prostaglandins mediates flow-dependent dilation of rat gracilis muscle arterioles. Am J Physiol 267:H326, 1994.
59. Davies PF: Flow-mediated endothelial mechanotransduction. Physiol Rev 75:519, 1995.

60. Cooke JP, Rossitch EJ, Andon NA, et al: Flow activates an endothelial potassium channel to release an endogenous nitrovasodilator. J Clin Invest 88:1663, 1991.
61. Holtz J, Fostermann U, Pohl U, et al: Flow-dependent, endothelium-mediated dilatation of epicardial coronary arteries in conscious dogs: Effects of cyclooxygenase inhibition. J Cardiovasc Pharmacol 6:1161, 1984.
62. Miller VM, Burnett JCJ: Modulation of NO and endothelin by chronic increases in blood flow in canine femoral arteries. Am J Physiol 263:H103, 1992.
63. Tronc F, Wassef M, Esposito B, et al: Role of NO in flow-induced remodeling of the rabbit common carotid artery. Arterioscler Thromb Vasc Biol 16:1256, 1996.
64. Guzman RJ, Abe K, Zarins CK: Flow-induced arterial enlargement is uninhibited by suppression of nitric oxide synthase activity in vivo. Surgery 122:273, 1997.
65. Glagov S, Weisenberg E, Zarins CK, et al: Compensatory enlargement of human atherosclerotic coronary arteries. N Engl J Med 316:1371, 1987.
66. Glagov S, Bassiouny HS, Giddens DP, Zarins CK: Intimal thickening: Morphogenesis, functional significance and detection. J Vasc Invest 1:2, 1995.
67. Glagov S, Zarins CK, Masawa N, et al: Mechanical functional role of non-atherosclerotic intimal thickening. Front Med Biol Eng 5:37, 1993.
68. Wilens SL: The nature of diffuse intimal thickening of arteries. Am J Pathol 27:825, 1951.
69. Movat HZ, More TH, Haust MD: The diffuse intimal thickening of the human aorta with aging. Am J Pathol 34:1023, 1958.
70. Tejada C, Strong JP, Montenegro MR, et al: Distribution of coronary and aortic atherosclerosis by geographic location, race and sex. Lab Invest 18:5009, 1968.
71. Gupta V, Nanda NC, Yesilbursa D, et al: Racial differences in thoracic aorta atherosclerosis among ischemic stroke patients. Stroke. 34:408, 2003.
72. Glagov S, Bassiouny H, Masawa N, et al: Induction and composition of intimal thickening and atherosclerosis. In Boccalon H (ed): Vascular Medicine. Paris, Elsevier Science, 1993, p 13.
73. Tracy RE, Kissling GE: Age and fibroplasia as preconditions for atheronecrosis in human coronary arteries. Arch Pathol Lab Med 111:957, 1987.
74. McGill HC Jr, Herderick EE, McMahan CA, et al: Atherosclerosis in youth. Minerva Pediatr 54:437, 2002.
75. Taylor KE, Glagov S, Zarins CK: Preservation and structural adaptation of endothelium over experimental foam cell lesions. Arteriosclerosis 9:881, 1989.
76. Clubb FJ, Cerny JL, Deferrari DA, et al: Development of atherosclerotic plaque with endothelial disruption in Watanabe heritable hyperlipidemic rabbit aortas. Cardiovasc Pathol 10:1, 2001.
77. Stary HC, Chandler AB, Dinsmore RE, et al: A definition of advanced types of atherosclerotic lesions and a histological classification of atherosclerosis: A report from the Committee on Vascular Lesions of the Council on Arteriosclerosis, American Heart Association. Arterioscler Thromb Vasc Biol 15:1512, 1995.
78. Mofidi R, Crotty TB, McCarthy P, et al: Association between plaque instability, angiogenesis and symptomatic carotid occlusive disease. Br J Surg 88:945, 2001.
79. Milker-Zabel S, Zabel A, Manegold C, et al: Calcification in coronary arteries as quantified by CT scans correlated with tobacco consumption in patients with inoperable non-small cell lung cancer treated with three-dimensional radiotherapy. Br J Radiol 76:891, 2003.
80. Glagov S, Eckner FAO, Lev M: Controlled pressure fixation apparatus for hearts. AMA Arch Pathol 76:640, 1963.
81. Zarins CK, Zatina MA, Glagov S: Correlation of postmortem angiography with pathologic anatomy: Quantitation of atherosclerotic lesions. In Bond MG, Insull W Jr, Glagov S, et al (eds): Clinical Diagnosis of Atherosclerosis. New York, Springer-Verlag, 1983, p 283.
82. Bond MG, Adams MR, Bullock BC: Complicating factors in evaluating coronary artery atherosclerosis. Artery 9:21, 1981.
83. Beere PA, Glagov S, Zarins CK: Experimental atherosclerosis at the carotid bifurcation of the cynomolgus monkey. Atherosclerosis Thromb 12:1245, 1992.
84. Armstrong ML, Heistad DD, Marcus MI, et al: Structural and hemodynamic responses of peripheral arteries of macaque monkeys to atherogenic diet. Arteriosclerosis 5:336, 1985.
85. Holvoet P, Theilmeier G, Shivalkar B, et al: LDL hypercholesterolemia is associated with accumulation of oxidized LDL, atherosclerotic plaque growth, and compensatory vessel enlargement in coronary arteries of miniature pigs. Arterioscler Thromb Vasc Biol 18:415, 1998.
86. Clarkson TB, Prichard RW, Morgan TM, et al: Remodeling of coronary arteries in human and nonhuman primates. JAMA 271:289, 1994.
87. Kolodgie FD, Gold HK, Burke AP, et al: Intraplaque hemorrhage and progression of coronary atheroma. N Engl J Med 349:2316, 2003.
88. Ishida S, Hamasaki S, Kamekou M, et al: Advancing age is associated with diminished vascular remodeling and impaired vasodilation in resistance coronary arteries. Coron Artery Dis 14:443, 2003.
89. Britten MB, Zeiher AM, Schachinger V: Effects of cardiovascular risk factors on coronary artery remodeling in patients with mild atherosclerosis. Coron Artery Dis 14:415, 2003.
90. Zarins CK, Weisenberg E, Kolettis G, et al: Differential enlargement of artery segments in response to enlarging atherosclerotic plaques. J Vasc Surg 7:386, 1988.
91. Losordo DW, Rosenfield K, Kaufman J, et al: Focal compensatory enlargement of human arteries in response to progressive atherosclerosis: In vivo documentation using intravascular ultrasound. Circulation 9:2570, 1994.
92. Vavuranakis M, Stefanadis C, Toutouzas K, et al: Impaired compensatory coronary artery enlargement in atherosclerosis contributes to the development of coronary artery stenosis in diabetic patients: An in vivo intravascular ultrasound study. Eur Heart J 18:1090, 1997.
93. Nakamura Y, Takemori H, Shiraishi K, Inoki I, et al: Compensatory enlargement of angiographically normal coronary segments in patients with coronary artery disease: In vivo documentation using intravascular ultrasound. Angiology 47:775, 1996.
94. Masawa N, Glagov S, Bassiouny H, Zarins CK: Intimal thickness normalizes mural tensile stress in regions of increased intimal area and artery size. Arteriosclerosis 8:621a, 1988.
95. Bonithon-Kopp C, Touboul PJ, Berr C, et al: Factors of carotid arterial enlargement in a population aged 59 to 71 years: The EVA study. Stroke 27:654, 1996.
96. Crouse JR, Goldbourt U, Evans G, et al: Risk factors and segment-specific carotid arterial enlargement in the Atherosclerosis Risk in Communities (ARIC) cohort. Stroke 27:69, 1996.
97. Blair JM, Glagov S, Zarins CK: Mechanism of superficial femoral artery adductor canal stenosis. Surg Forum 41:359, 1990.
98. Pasterkamp G, Borst C, Post MJ, et al: Atherosclerotic arterial remodeling in the superficial femoral artery: Individual variation in local compensatory enlargement response. Circulation 93:1818, 1996.
99. Zarins CK, Xu CP, Glagov S: Clinical correlations of atherosclerosis: Aortic disease. In Fuster V (ed): Syndromes of Atherosclerosis: Correlations of Clinical Imaging and Pathology. Armonk, NY, Futura Publishing, 1996, pp 33-42.
100. Zarins CK, Xu CP, Glagov S: Aneurysmal and occlusive atherosclerosis of the human abdominal aorta. J Vasc Surg 18:526, 1993.
101. Zarins CK, Zatina MA, Giddens DP, et al: Shear stress regulation of artery lumen diameter in experimental atherogenesis. J Vasc Surg 5:413, 1987.
102. von Birgelen C, Mintz GS, Bose D, et al: Impact of moderate lesion calcium on mechanisms of coronary stenting as assessed with three-dimensional intravascular ultrasound in vivo. Am J Cardiol 92:5, 2003.

103. Birnbaum Y, Fishbein MC, Luo H, et al: Regional remodeling of atherosclerotic arteries: A major determinant of clinical manifestations of disease. J Am Coll Cardiol 30:1149, 1997.
104. Wong CB: Atherosclerotic arterial remodeling in the superficial femoral artery: Individual variation in local compensatory enlargement response. Circulation 95:279, 1997.
105. Xu C, Zarins CK, Glagov S: Aneurysmal and occlusive atherosclerosis of the human abdominal aorta. J Vasc Surg 33:91, 2001.
106. Zarins CK, Xu C, Glagov S: Atherosclerotic enlargement of the human abdominal aorta. Atherosclerosis 155:157, 2001.
107. Keren G: Compensatory enlargement, remodeling, and restenosis. Adv Exp Med Biol 430:187, 1997.
108. Smits PC, Bos L, Quarles van Ufford MA, et al: Shrinkage of human coronary arteries is an important determinant of de novo atherosclerotic luminal stenosis: An in vivo intravascular ultrasound study. Heart 79:143, 1998.
109. McGill HC Jr, Herderick EE, McMahan CA, et al: Atherosclerosis in youth. Minerva Pediatr 54:437, 2002.
110. Wolfe PA, Kannel WB, Verter J: Epidemiologic appraisal of hypertension and stroke risk. In Guthrie GP Jr, Kotchen TA (eds): Hypertension and the Brain. Mt Kisco, NY, Futura Publishing, 1984, p 221.
111. Greenhalgh RM: Biochemical abnormalities and smoking in arterial ischemia. In Bergan JJ, Yao JST (eds): Gangrene and Severe Ischemia of the Lower Extremities. New York, Grune & Stratton, 1978, p 39.
112. Glagov S: Hemodynamic risk factors: Mechanical stress, mural architecture, medial nutrition and the vulnerability of arteries to atherosclerosis. In Wissler RW, Geer JC (eds): The Pathogenesis of Atherosclerosis. Baltimore, Williams & Wilkins, 1972, p 164.
113. Texon M: The hemodynamic basis of atherosclerosis. Further observations: The linear lesion [erratum in Bull N Y Acad Med 62:1048, 1986]. Bull N Y Acad Med 62:875, 1986.
114. Glagov S, Rowley DA, Kohut R: Atherosclerosis of human aorta and its coronary and renal arteries. Arch Pathol Lab Med 72:558, 1961.
115. Ravensbergen J, Ravensbergen JW, Krijger JK, et al: Localizing role of hemodynamics in atherosclerosis in several human vertebrobasilar junction geometries. Arterioscler Thromb Vasc Biol 18:693, 1998.
116. Stone PH, Coskun AU, Kinlay S, et al: Effect of endothelial shear stress on the progression of coronary artery disease, vascular remodeling, and in-stent restenosis in humans: In vivo 6-month follow-up study. Circulation 108:438, 2003.
117. Fry DL: Arterial intimal-medial permeability and coevolving structural responses to defined shear-stress exposures. Am J Physiol Heart Circ Physiol 283:H2341, 2002.
118. Bassiouny HS, Lieber BB, Giddens DP, et al: Quantitative inverse correlation of wall shear stress with experimental intimal thickening. Surg Forum 39:328, 1988.
119. Zarins CK, Giddens DP, Bharadvaj BK, et al: Carotid bifurcation atherosclerosis: Quantitative correlation of plaque localization with flow velocity profiles and wall shear stress. Circ Res 53:502, 1983.
120. Ku DN, Giddens DP, Zarins CK, et al: Pulsatile flow and atherosclerosis in the human carotid bifurcation: Positive correlation between plaque location and low and oscillating shear stress. Arteriosclerosis 5:293, 1985.
121. Friedman MH, Ding Z: Relation between the structural asymmetry of coronary branch vessels and the angle at their origin. J Biomech 31:273, 1998.
122. Caro CG, Fitz-Gerald JM, Schroter RC: Atheroma and arterial wall shear: Observation, correlation and proposal of a shear dependent mass transfer mechanism for atherogenesis. Proc R Soc Lond 117:109, 1971.
123. Paravicini TM, Gulluyan LM, Dusting GJ, Drummond GR: Increased NADPH oxidase activity, gp91phox expression, and endothelium-dependent vasorelaxation during neointima formation in rabbits. Circ Res 91:54, 2002.
124. Zhuang YJ, Singh TM, Zarins CK, Masuda H: Sequential increases and decreases in blood flow stimulates progressive intimal thickening. Eur J Vasc Endovasc Surg 16:301, 1998.
125. Talukder N, Giddens DP, Vito RP: Quantitative flow visualization studies in a carotid artery bifurcation model. In: 1983 Biomechanics Symposium, Applied Mechanics Division, Vol 56, and Fluids Engineering Division, Vol 1. New York, American Society of Mechanical Engineers, 1983, p 165.
126. Tsao R, Jones SA, Giddens DP, et al: Measurement of particle residence time and particle acceleration in an arterial model by an automatic particle tracking system. Proceedings of the 20th International Congress on High Speed Photography and Photonics, September 21-25, 1992, Victoria, BC, Canada.
127. Gerrity RG, Goss JA, Soby L: Control of monocyte recruitment by chemotactic factor(s) in lesion-prone areas of swine aorta. Arteriosclerosis 5:55, 1985.
128. Parmentier EM, Morton WA, Petschek HE: Platelet aggregate formation in a region of separated blood flow. Phys Fluids 20:2012, 1981.
129. Fox JA, Hugh AE: Static zones in the internal carotid artery: Correlation with boundary layer separation and stasis in model flows. Br J Radiol 43:370, 1976.
130. Fry DL: Mass transport, atherogenesis, and risk. Arteriosclerosis 7:88, 1987.
131. DeKeulenaer GW, Chappell DC, Ishizaka N, et al: Oscillatory and steady laminar shear stress differentially affect human endothelial redox state: Role of a superoxide-producing NADH oxidase. Circ Res 82:1094, 1998.
132. Imberti B, Seliktar D, Nerem RM, Remuzzi A: The response of endothelial cells to fluid shear stress using a co-culture model of the arterial wall. Endothelium 9:11, 2002.
133. Clark JM, Glagov S: Luminal surface of distended arteries by scanning electron microscopy: Eliminating configurational artifacts. Br J Exp Pathol 57:129, 1976.
134. Nagel T, Resnick N, Dewey CF Jr, Gimbrone MA Jr: Vascular endothelial cells respond to spatial gradients in fluid shear stress by enhanced activation of transcription factors. Arterioscler Thromb Vasc Biol 19:1825, 1999.
135. Fry DL, Haupt MW, Pap JM: Effect of endothelial integrity, transmural pressure, and time on the intimal-medial uptake of serum 125I-albumin and 125I-LDL in an in vitro porcine arterial organ-support system. Arterioscler Thromb 12:1313, 1992.
136. Ziegler T, Bouzourene K, Harrison VJ, et al: Influence of oscillatory and unidirectional flow environments on the expression of endothelin and nitric oxide synthase in cultured endothelial cells. Arterioscler Thromb Vasc Biol 18:686, 1998.
137. Chappell DC, Varner SE, Nerem RM, et al: Oscillatory shear stress stimulates adhesion molecule expression in cultured human endothelium. Circ Res 82:532, 1998.
138. Bassiouny HS, Lee DC, Zarins CK, Glagov S: Low diurnal heart rate variability inhibits experimental carotid stenosis. Surg Forum 46:334, 1995.
139. Davies PF, Polacek DC, Shi C, Helmke BP: The convergence of haemodynamics, genomics, and endothelial structure in studies of the focal origin of atherosclerosis. Biorheology 39:299, 2002.
140. Gutstein WH: Vasospasm, vascular injury, and atherogenesis: A perspective. Hum Pathol 30:365, 1999.
141. Bharadvaj BK, Mabon RF, Giddens DP: Steady flow in a model of the human carotid bifurcation. Part II: Laser Doppler anemometer measurements. J Biomech Eng 15:363, 1982.
142. Ku DN, Giddens DP: Pulsatile flow in a model carotid bifurcation. Arteriosclerosis 3:31, 1983.
143. Ku DN, Zarins CK, Giddens DP, et al: Reduced atherogenesis distal to stenosis despite turbulence and hypertension [abstract]. Circulation 74(Suppl II):457, 1986.
144. Khalifa AMA, Giddens DP: Characterization and evolution of post-stenotic flow disturbances. J Biomech 14:279, 1981.
145. Coutard M, Osborne-Pellegrin MJ: Decreased dietary lipid deposition in spontaneous lesions distal to a stenosis in the rat caudal artery. Artery 12:82, 1983.

146. Kannel WB, Schwartz MJ, McNamara PM: Blood pressure and risk of coronary heart disease: The Framingham study. Dis Chest 56:43, 1969.
147. Hollander W, Madoff I, Paddock J, et al: Aggravation of atherosclerosis by hypertension in a subhuman primate model with coarctation of the aorta. Circ Res 38(Suppl 2):63, 1976.
148. McGill HC Jr, Carey KD, McMahan CA, et al: Effects of two forms of hypertension on atherosclerosis in the hyperlipidemic baboon. Arteriosclerosis 5:481, 1985.
149. Folkow BL: Physiological aspects of primary hypertension. Physiol Rev 62:347, 1982.
150. Xu C, Zarins CK, Bassiouny HS, et al: Differential transmural distribution of gene expression for collagen types I and III proximal to aortic coarctation in the rabbit. J Vasc Res 37:170, 2000.
151. Lyon RT, Runyon-Hass A, Davis HR, et al: Protection from atherosclerotic lesion formation by inhibition of artery wall motion. J Vasc Surg 5:59, 1987.
152. Bomberger RA, Zarins CK, Taylor KE, et al: Effect of hypotension on atherogenesis and aortic wall composition. J Surg Res 28:402, 1980.
153. Xu C, Zarins CK, Bassiouny HS, et al: Differential transmural distribution of gene expression for collagen types I and III proximal to aortic coarctation in the rabbit. J Vasc Res 37:170, 2000.
154. Xu C, Zarins CK, Pannaraj PS, et al: Hypercholesterolemia superimposed by experimental hypertension induces differential distribution of collagen types I and III and tropoelastin. Arterioscler Thromb Vasc Biol 20:2566, 2000.
155. Xu C, Zarins CK, Glagov S: Gene expression of tropoelastin is enhanced in the aorta proximal to the coarctation in rabbits. Exp Mol Pathol 72:115, 2002.
156. Zarins CK, Bomberger RA, Taylor KE, et al: Artery stenosis inhibits regression of diet-induced atherosclerosis. Surgery 88:86, 1980.
157. Xu C-P, Glagov S, Zatina MA, Zarins CK: Hypertension sustains plaque progression despite reduction of hypercholesterolemia. Hypertension 18:123, 1991.
158. Tropea BI, Schwarzacher S, Chang A, et al: Reduction of artery wall motion inhibits plaque formation. Surg Forum 47:350, 1996.
159. Tropea BI, Schwarzacher SP, Chang A, et al: Reduction of aortic wall motion inhibits hypertension-mediated experimental atherosclerosis. Arterioscler Thromb Vasc Biol 20:2127, 2000.
160. Suzuki K: Experimental studies on morphogenesis of arteriosclerosis, with special reference to relation between hemodynamic change and developments of cellulofibrous intimal thickening and atherosclerosis. Gunma J Med Sci 16:185, 1967.
161. Lyon RT, Davis HR, Runyon-Hass A, Glagov S: Does relief of critical arterial stenosis accelerate distal atherosclerosis? J Vasc Surg 30:191, 1996.
162. Xu C, Zarins CK, Glagov S: Biphasic response of tropoelastin at the poststenotic dilation segment of the rabbit aorta. J Vasc Surg 36:605, 2002.
163. Ku DN, Glagov S, Moore JE, Zarins CK: Flow patterns in the abdominal aorta under simulated postprandial and exercise conditions: An experimental study. J Vasc Surg 9:309, 1989.
164. Giddens EM, Giddens DP, White SS, et al: Exercise flow conditions eliminate stasis at vascular graft anastomoses. In: Proceedings of the Third Mid-Atlantic Conference in Biofluid Mechanics. New York, New York University Press, 1990, p 255.
165. Taylor C, Cheng C, Espinosa LA, et al: In vivo quantification of blood flow and wall shear stress in the human abdominal aorta during lower limb exercise. Ann Biomed Eng 30:402, 2002.
166. Cheng CP, Herfkens RJ, Taylor CA: Abdominal aortic hemodynamics in healthy subjects age 50-70 at rest and during lower limb exercise: In vivo quantification using MRI. Atherosclerosis 168:323, 2003.
167. Bassiouny HS, Zarins CK, Choi E, et al: Hemodynamic stress and experimental aortoiliac atherosclerosis. J Vasc Surg 19:426, 1994.
168. Taylor CA, Hughes TJR, Zarins CK: Computational investigations in vascular disease. Computers in Physics 10:224, 1996.
169. Schalet BJ, Taylor CA, Harris EJ, et al: Quantitative assessment of human aortic blood flow during exercise. Surg Forum 48:359, 1997.
170. Taylor CA, Hughes TJR, Zarins CK: Finite element modeling of blood flow in arteries. Int Assoc Computational Mechanics "Expressions" 3:4, 1997.
171. Taylor CA, Hughes TJ, Zarins CK: Finite element modeling of three-dimensional pulsatile flow in the abdominal aorta: Relevance to atherosclerosis. Ann Biomed Eng 26:975, 1998.
172. Jones SA, Giddens DP, Loth F, et al: In-vivo measurements of blood flow velocity profiles in canine ilio-femoral anastomotic bypass grafts. J Biomech Eng 119:30, 1997.
173. Bassiouny HS, Davis H, Masawa N, et al: Critical carotid stenoses: Morphologic and biochemical similarity of symptomatic and asymptomatic plaques. J Vasc Surg 9:202, 1989.
174. Tang TD, Giddens DP, Zarins CK, Glagov S: Velocity profile and wall shear measurements in a model human coronary artery. ASME Adv Biomed Eng 17:261, 1990.
175. Klocke FJ, Mates RE, Canty JM, et al: Coronary pressure-flow relationships: Controversial issues and probable implications. Circ Res 56:310, 1985.
176. Granata L, Olsson RA, Huvos A, et al: Coronary inflow and oxygen usage following cardiac sympathetic nerve stimulation in unanesthetized dogs. Circ Res 16:114, 1965.
177. Ku DN, Giddens DP: Pulsatile flow in a model carotid bifurcation. Arteriosclerosis 3:31, 1983.
178. Beere PA, Glagov S, Zarins CK: Retarding effect of lowered heart rate on coronary atherosclerosis. Science 226:180, 1984.
179. Bassiouny HS, Zarins CK, Hovanessian A, Glagov S: Heart rate and experimental carotid atherosclerosis. Surg Forum 48:373, 1992.
180. Dyer AR, Persky V, Stamler J, et al: Heart rate as a prognostic factor for coronary heart disease and mortality: Findings in three Chicago epidemiologic studies. Am J Epidemiol 112:736, 1980.
181. Williams PT, Wood PD, Haskell WL, et al: The effects of running mileage and duration on plasma lipoprotein levels. JAMA 247: 2674, 1982.
182. Guyton AC: Textbook of Medical Physiology, 2nd ed. Philadelphia, WB Saunders, 1961, p 356.
183. Moore JE, Xu CP, Glagov S, et al: Fluid wall shear stress measurements in a model of the human abdominal aorta: Oscillatory behavior and relationship to atherosclerosis. Atherosclerosis 110:225, 1994.
184. Gordon T, Kannel WB: Predisposition to atherosclerosis in the head, heart and legs: The Framingham Study. JAMA 221:661, 1972.
185. Winniford MD, Wheelan KR, Kremers MS, et al: Smoking-induced coronary vasoconstriction in patients with atherosclerotic coronary artery disease: Evidence for adrenergically mediated alterations in coronary artery tone. Circulation 73:662, 1986.
186. Caro CG, Fish PJ, Jay M, et al: Influence of vasoactive agents on arterial hemodynamics: Possible relevance to atherogenesis. Abstr Biorheol 23:197, 1986.
187. Balaji MR, DeWeese JA: Adductor canal outlet syndrome. JAMA 245:167, 1981.
188. Ross R: The pathogenesis of atherosclerosis—-an update. N Engl J Med 314:488, 1986.
189. Benditt EP, Barrett T, McDougall JK: Viruses in the etiology of atherosclerosis. Proc Natl Acad Sci U S A 80:6388, 1983.
190. Transport of material between blood and wall in arteries. Ciba Found Symp 12:127, 1973.
191. Ross R, Harker L: Hyperlipidemia and atherosclerosis. Science 193:1094, 1976.
192. Bomberger RA, Zarins CK, Glagov S: Subcritical arterial stenosis enhances distal atherosclerosis (Resident Research Award). J Surg Res 30:205, 1981.
193. Davis HR, Runyon-Hass A, Zarins CK, et al: Interactive arterial effects of hypertension and hyperlipidemia. Fed Proc 43:711, 1984.
194. Cozzi PJ, Lyon RT, Davis HR, et al: Aortic wall metabolism in relation to susceptibility and resistance to experimental atherosclerosis. J Vasc Surg 7:706, 1988.
195. Malinow MR: Experimental models of atherosclerosis regression. Atherosclerosis 48:105, 1983.

196. Wissler RW, Vesselinovitch D: Combined effects of cholestyramine and probucol on regression of atherosclerosis in rhesus monkey aortas. Appl Pathol 1:89, 1983.
197. Stary HC: Regression of atherosclerosis in primates. Virchows Arch 383:117, 1979.
198. Clarkson TB, Bond MG, Bullock BC, et al: A study of atherosclerosis regression in *Macaca mulatta*. V: Changes in abdominal aorta and carotid and coronary arteries from animals with atherosclerosis induced for 38 months and then regressed for 24 or 48 months at plasma cholesterol concentrations of 300 or 200 mg/dl. Exp Mol Pathol 41:96, 1984.
199. Kunz J: Can atherosclerosis regress? The role of the vascular extracellular matrix and the age-related changes of arteries. Gerontology 48:267, 2002.
200. Blankenhorn DH, Nessim SA, Johnson BL, et al: Beneficial effects of combined colestipol-niacin therapy on coronary atherosclerosis and coronary venous bypass grafts. JAMA 257:3233, 1987.
201. Brown G, Albert JJ, Fisher LD, et al: Regression of coronary artery disease as a result of intensive lipid-lowering therapy in men with high levels of apolipoprotein B. N Engl J Med 323:1290, 1990.
202. Buchwald H, Varco RL, Matts PJ, et al: Effect of partial ileal bypass surgery on mortality and morbidity from coronary heart disease in patients with hypercholesterolemia: Report of the Program on the Surgical Control of the Hyperlipidemias (POSCH). N Engl J Med 323:946, 1990.
203. Barndt R, Blankenhorn DH, Crawford DW, et al: Regression and progression of early femoral atherosclerosis in treated hyperlipoproteinemic patients. Ann Intern Med 86:139, 1977.
204. Zarins CK, Zatina MA, Glagov S: Correlation of postmortem angiography with pathologic anatomy: Quantitation of atherosclerotic lesions. In Bond MG, Insull W Jr, Glagov S, et al (eds): Clinical Diagnosis of Atherosclerosis: Quantitative Methods of Evaluation. New York, Springer-Verlag, 1983, p 283.
205. Zarins CK, Glagov S, Wissler RW, Vesselinovitch D: Aneurysm formation in experimental atherosclerosis: Relationship to plaque evolution. J Vasc Surg 12:246, 1990.
206. Zarins CK, Xu C-P, Glagov S: Aneurysmal enlargement of the aorta during regression of experimental atherosclerosis. J Vasc Surg 15:90, 1992.
207. Glagov S, Bassiouny HS, Sakaguchi Y, et al: Mechanical determinants of plaque modeling, remodeling and disruption. Atherosclerosis 131:S13, 1997.
208. Falk E, Shah P, Fuster V: Coronary plaque disruption. Circulation 92:657, 1995.
209. Fuster V, Badimon L, Badimon IJ, Chesebro JH: The pathogenesis of coronary artery disease and the acute coronary syndromes, parts I and II. N Engl J Med 326:242, 1992.
210. Glagov S, Zarins CK, Giddens DP, et al: Atherosclerosis: What is the nature of the plaque? In Strandness DE Jr, Didisheim P, Clowes AW, et al (eds): Vascular Diseases: Current Research and Clinical Applications. Orlando, Fla, Grune & Stratton, 1987, p 15.
211. Bassiouny HS, Sakaguchi Y, Mikucki SA, et al: Juxtaluminal location of plaque necrosis and neoformation in symptomatic carotid stenosis. J Vasc Surg 26:585, 1997.
212. Felton CV, Crook D, Davies MJ, Oliver MF: Relation of plaque lipid composition and morphology to the stability of human aortic plaques. Arterioscler Thromb Vasc Biol 17:1337, 1997.
213. Gertz SD, Roberts WC: Hemodynamic shear force rupture of coronary arterial atherosclerotic plaques. Am J Cardiol 66:1368, 1990.
214. Fayad ZA, Fuster V: Clinical imaging of the high-risk or vulnerable atherosclerotic plaque. Circ Res 89:305, 2001.
215. Weinberger J, Ramos L, Ambrose JA, Fuster V: Morphologic and dynamic changes of atherosclerotic plaque at the carotid artery bifurction: Sequential imaging by real time B-mode ultrasonography. J Am Coll Cardiol 12:1515, 1988.
216. Campa JS, Greenhalgh RM, Powell JT: Elastin degradation in abdominal aortic aneurysms. Atherosclerosis 65:13, 1987.
217. Dobrin PB, Baker WH, Gley WC: Elastolytic and collagenolytic studies of arteries: Implications for the mechanical properties of aneurysms. Arch Surg 119:405, 1984.
218. Menashi S, Campa JS, Greenhalgh RM, Powell JT: Collagen in abdominal aortic aneurysm: Typing, content and degradation. J Vasc Surg 6:578, 1987.
219. Johansen K, Koepsell T: Familial tendency for abdominal aortic aneurysm. JAMA 256:1934, 1986.
220. Bomberger RA, Zarins CK, Glagov S: Medial injury and hyperlipidemia in development of aneurysms or atherosclerotic plaques. Surg Forum 31:338, 1980.
221. Zatina MA, Zarins CK, Gewertz BL, Glagov S: Role of medial lamellar architecture in the pathogenesis of aortic aneurysms. J Vasc Surg 1:442, 1984.
222. DePalma RG, Koletsky S, Bellon EM, Insull W Jr: Failure of regression of atherosclerosis in dogs with moderated cholesterolemia. Atherosclerosis 27:297, 1977.
223. Glagov S, Weisenberg E, Zarins CK, et al: Compensatory enlargement of human atherosclerotic coronary arteries. N Engl J Med 316:1371, 1987.
224. Zarins CK, Weisenberg E, Kolettis G, et al: Differential enlargement of artery segments in response to enlarging atherosclerotic plaques. J Vasc Surg 7:386, 1988.
225. Thompson RW, Parks WC: Role of matrix metalloproteinases in abdominal aortic aneurysms. Ann N Y Acad Sci 800:157, 1996.
226. Zarins CK, Xu CP, Glagov S: Aneurysmal enlargement of the aorta during regression of experimental atherosclerosis. J Vasc Surg 15:90, 1992.
227. Roberts JC, Moses C, Wilkins RH: Autopsy studies in atherosclerosis. I: Distribution and severity of atherosclerosis in patients dying without morphologic evidence of atherosclerotic catastrophe. Circulation 20:511, 1959.
228. Draney MT, Xu C, Arko FR, et al: In vivo quantitation of aortic wall motion: Relationship to asymmetric wall thickness. J Am Coll Surg 195:S98, 2002.

Chapter

Intimal Hyperplasia:
Basic Response to Arterial and Vein Graft Injury and Reconstruction

MARK G. DAVIES, MD, PHD

Intimal hyperplasia, the universal response of vessels to injury, describes a chronic structural change occurring in denuded arteries, arterialized veins, and prosthetic bypass grafts. Its development can be subdivided chronologically into hyperacute, acute, and chronic stages. Intimal hyperplasia may be further defined as the abnormal migration and proliferation of vascular smooth muscle cells (SMCs) with the associated deposition of extracellular connective tissue matrix, which is then followed by remodeling of this new tissue (Table 11-1). In this respect, the biology of intimal hyperplasia has many of the hallmarks of wound healing. Macroscopically, the chronic lesion appears firm, pale, and homogeneous. The involved area is smooth and uniformly located between the endothelium and the internal elastic lamina of an artery or between the endothelium and the medial SMC layer of a vein graft. The distribution pattern of intimal hyperplastic lesions may be diffuse throughout a vessel, focal at an anastomosis, or focal within the body of the vessel.

The introduction and widespread use of endoluminal therapies (angioplasty and intravascular stenting) and the subsequent reports of high restenosis rates have heightened awareness of the significance of intimal hyperplasia in the current interventional environment. As a result, there has been a greater stimulus to study the biology and pathophysiology of a vessel's response to injury. Because of the particular relevance of intimal hyperplasia to endovascular surgery, techniques of arterial denudation using a balloon catheter have been the most popular experimental models. Systematic classification of arterial intimal injuries has revealed a spectrum of vascular wall injuries from type I (functional alterations without significant morphologic change) to type II (endothelial denudation without intimal and medial damage) to type III (endothelial denudation with intimal and medial damage).[1] Both angioplasty and arterial endarterectomy constitute type III vessel wall injuries, in that both the endothelium and the media of the vessel are damaged. Venous bypass grafts experience a generalized type I and II injury and focal type III lesions at the anastomoses or in areas of injudicious manipulation. The biology of a vessel's response to injury is complex and has many biologic tangents that testify to the therapeutic dilemma which controlling vessel injury poses. Arterial injury and venous injury have many common mechanisms (coagulation, inflammation, cell proliferation, cell migration, proteases and extracellular matrix, and remodeling) but should be considered distinct pathobiologic processes.

Table 11-1 Stages of Intimal Hyperplasia Development

	VESSEL LUMEN	VESSEL WALL
Stage 1: Hyperacute (minutes–hours)	Endothelial cell denudation Platelet aggregation Release of growth promoters	SMC injury Activation of SMCs Proto-oncogene expression Release of growth promoters
Stage 2: Acute (hours–weeks)	Organization of thrombosis Endothelial cell ingrowth Release of growth inhibitors Progenitor cell deposition	Medial SMC replication Medial SMC migration Infiltration of leukocytes Infiltration of adventitial cells Infiltration of progenitor cells Synthesis of growth promoters Synthesis of growth inhibitors
Stage 3: Chronic (weeks–months)	Re-endothelialization Change of luminal dimensions	Intimal SMC replication Intimal SMC synthesis of ECM Remodeling of ECM Synthesis of growth inhibitors Vessel remodeling

ECM, extracellular matrix; SMC, smooth muscle cell.

Section II

■ RESPONSE OF THE ARTERY TO INJURY

Angioplasty is a controlled injury to the vessel wall (Figs. 11-1 through 11-4). Although there is no apparent loss of cells from the media of the vessel wall after balloon injury, studies show that approximately 20% of total wall DNA is lost. Some of this loss is of endothelial origin, but a considerable amount reflects injury to the underlying medial SMCs.[2] In the immediate aftermath of angioplasty, apoptosis can be identified at 1 to 2 hours and appears to disappear by 4 hours.[3] No apoptosis can be identified in the wall after injury at 3 days, but by day 7, 50% of the cells again show signs of apoptosis, and by day 14, the number of apoptotic cells is again markedly decreased.

Proliferation of SMCs within the media, which normally account for less than 1% of cells, raises the proportion to more than 20% within 48 hours after angioplasty.[2,4,5] The fraction of cells proliferating reaches a maximum between 3 and 7 days and occurs as a synchronous wave of entry into the S phase of the medial SMCs.[6,7] This first phase of SMC proliferation appears to be driven by basic fibroblast growth factor (bFGF) released from dead and damaged cells in the vessel wall after balloon injury, and approximately 80% to 90% of this response can be prevented by inhibition with bFGF antibodies. Four weeks after injury, the medial proliferative response returns to baseline levels. Intracoronary irradiation after angioplasty inhibits this first wave of cell proliferation and prevents adventitial proliferation.[8] By day 8 after the injury, SMCs are observed on the luminal side of the internal elastic lamina; they appear to have migrated to the luminal surface through fenestrations in the internal elastic lamina. The number of SMCs in the intima reaches a maximum at 2 weeks after injury, and about 30% of medial SMCs may migrate from the media to the intima. This migration of cells requires the degradation of the cage of matrix surrounding each cell by proteases and the synthesis of new matrix molecules. Migration of the SMCs from the media to the intima across the internal elastic lamina is mediated in part by platelet-derived growth factor (PDGF).[9] Migration of SMCs is unaffected by irradiation and antimitotic drugs. Once within the intima, approximately 50% of the SMCs proliferate (a second phase of mitosis).

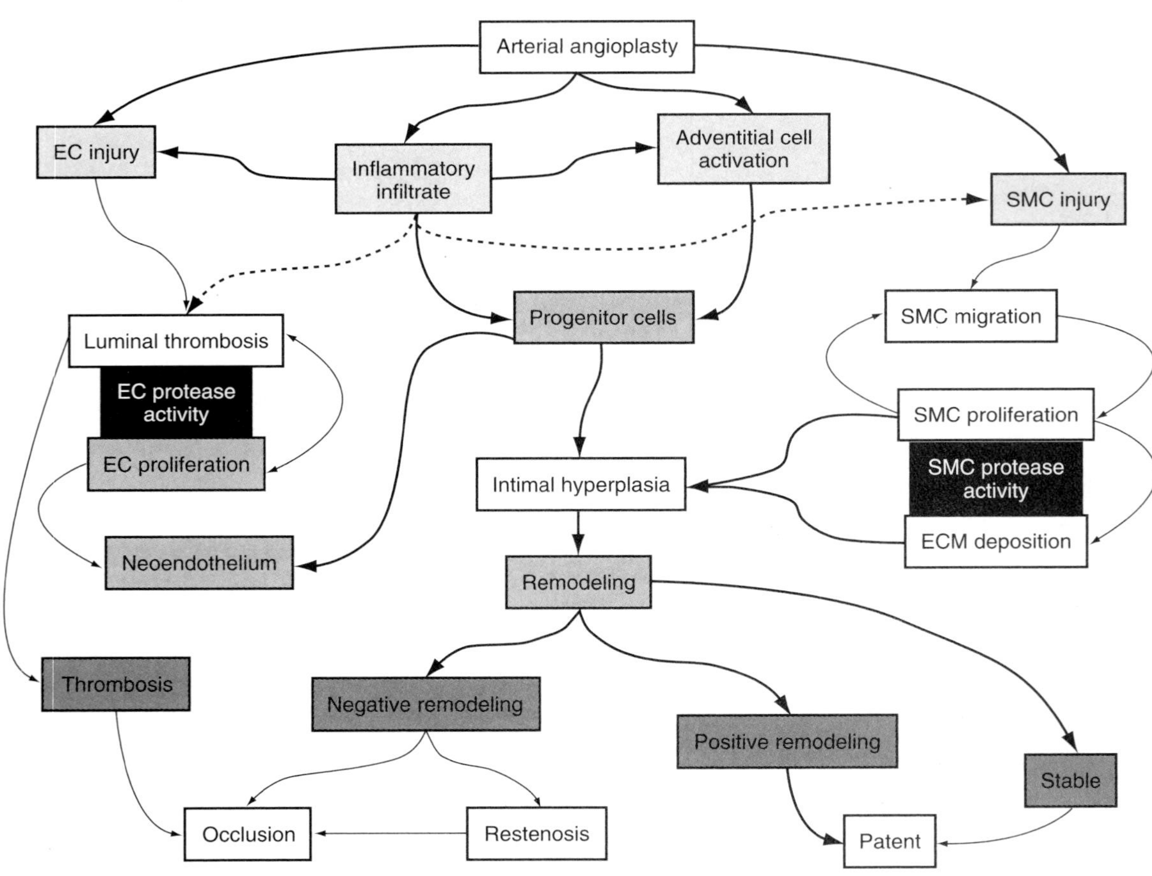

FIGURE 11-1 Pathobiology of the injury response after angioplasty. Flow diagram demonstrating the key elements in the vessel's response to arterial injury. Endothelial cell (EC) injury leads to luminal thrombosis, inflammatory cell infiltration, cellular proliferation, and clearance of the thrombotic material on the surface with development of a neo-endothelium. Injury to smooth muscle cells (SMC) and adventitial cells leads to cell proliferation and migration. Progenitor cells are recruited to the vessel wall. With the migration of proliferation of SMCs and adventitial cells, the appearance of progenitor cells, and the deposition of extracellular matrix (ECM), intimal hyperplasia develops. Over time, this lesion remodels and may either remain stable or demonstrate positive remodeling, with an increase in luminal diameter, or negative remodeling, with a decrease in luminal diameter. These chronic changes in the intimal lesion can lead to continued patency, restenosis, or occlusion.

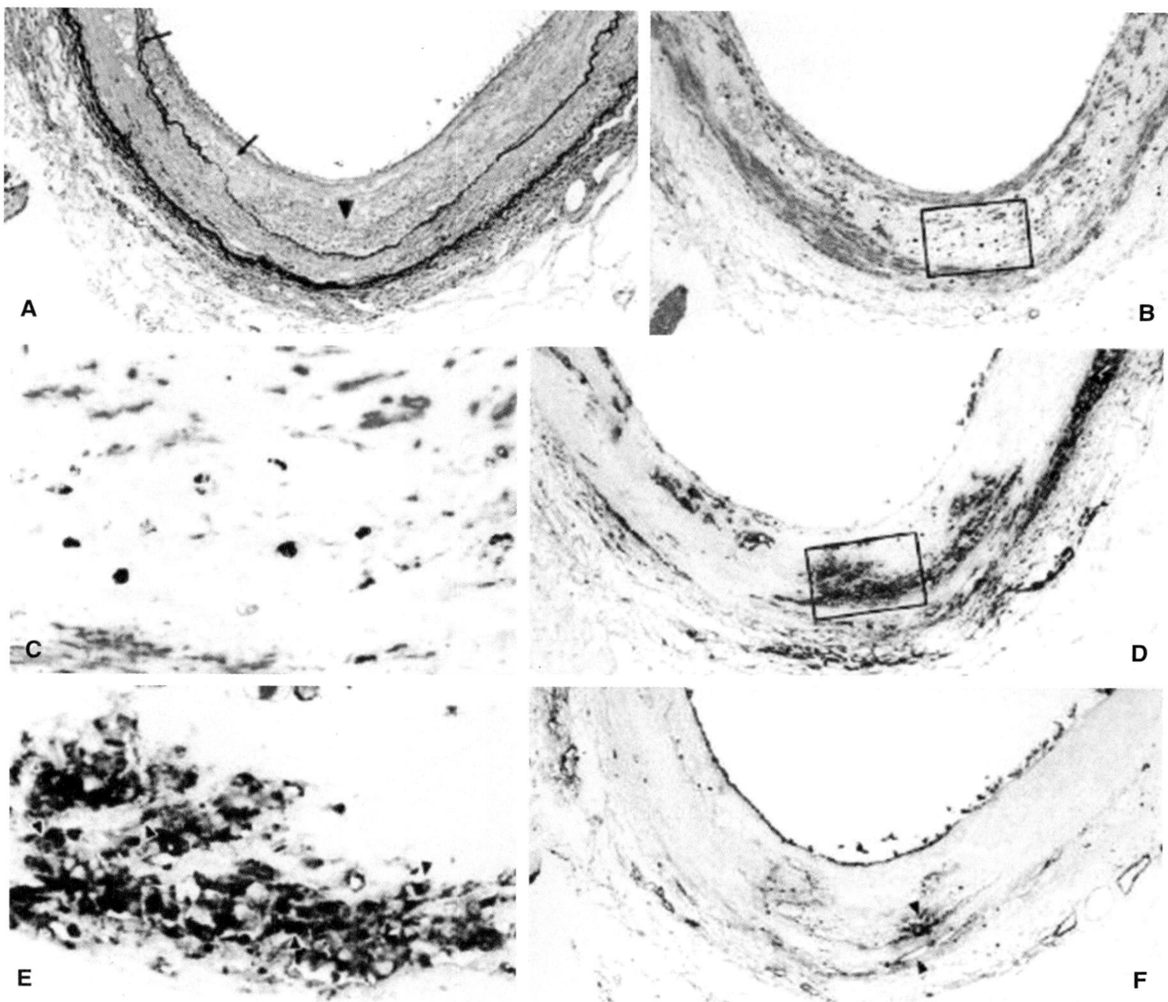

FIGURE 11-2 Photomicrographs of cross-sections from a control iliac artery of an atherosclerotic cynomolgus monkey. Serial sections were stained with Verhoeff–van Gieson stain (**A**) or immunostained (dark red reaction product) with antibodies to SMC (smooth muscle cell) and actin (**B** and **C**), macrophage CD68 (**D** and **E**), or endothelial cell von Willebrand factor (vWF) (**F**). Sections **B** through **F** were also stained with an antibody to BrdU (black nuclear reaction product) to label proliferating cells. **A**, A plaque is shown overlying the media. Calcification (*arrows*) is seen deep in the plaque, and a cellular region in the base of the plaque (*arrowhead*) is composed primarily of macrophages (**D**) covered by more fibrous-appearing tissue containing SMCs (**B**). **C** and **E** are magnified views of the regions outlined in **B** and **D,** respectively. A number of black BrdU-labeled nuclei co-localize to the region of CD68 staining, indicating macrophage proliferation in this region of the uninjured plaque. Staining for vWF (**D**) shows endothelial cells overlying the plaque and in microvessels of the adventitia. Microvessels can also be seen coursing through the media and inner plaque (*small arrowheads*). (See Color Figure in this section.) (**A, B, D,** and **F,** ×100; **C** and **E,** ×400.) (From Geary RL, Williams JK, Golden D, et al: Time course of cellular proliferation, intimal hyperplasia, and remodeling following angioplasty in monkeys with established atherosclerosis: A nonhuman primate model of restenosis. Arterioscler Thromb Vasc Biol 16:34-43, 1996.)

In the intima, a second phase of cellular proliferation is first noted at day 7 and reaches a maximum at 14 days, before returning to baseline by 28 days.[7] It may continue for up to 12 weeks, however, in those areas where re-endothelialization takes longer to complete. This second phase of SMC replication in the intima appears to be mediated by autocrine and paracrine factors and remains poorly understood. It also appears that the thickness of the intimal hyperplasia peaks within 1 month and that its rapid development is due to both cellular elements and the production of proteoglycans.

Associated with the changes in the intima and media are substantial changes in the adventitia, as evidenced by an increased cell proliferation and growth factor synthesis in adventitia relative to the media after angioplasty. In the adventitia, there is a marked infiltrate of cells termed "myofibroblasts" by day 2, which by day 14 can represent up to 50% of cells within the intima.[10,11] The presence of myofibroblasts is common in wound healing and leads to contraction of the wound. A similar phenomenon may occur in the healing vessel. Injured vessels may undergo chronic elastic recoil or negative remodeling, which results in loss of luminal dimensions without a further increase in neointimal area. Retrieved atherectomy material from primary and restenosis lesions has shown that the proportion of cells that can be demonstrated to be proliferating in the restenosis lesion is low[12] but that the migratory activity and collagen synthesis of the human

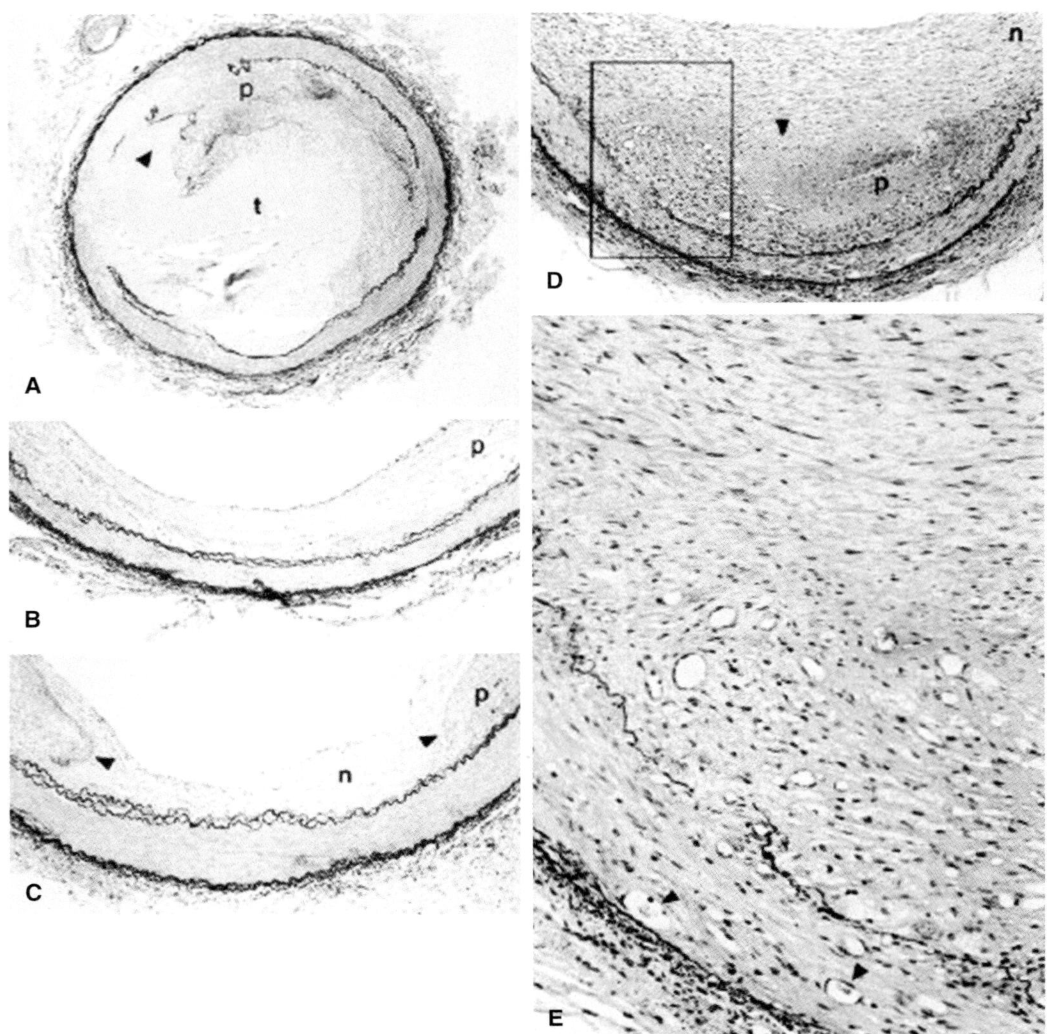

FIGURE 11-3 Photomicrographs of representative cross-sections from injured common iliac arteries of atherosclerotic cynomolgus monkeys. **A,** Angioplasty commonly causes fracture and dissection of preexisting atherosclerotic plaque (*arrowhead*) and, rarely, luminal thrombosis (t). The yellow-staining thrombus (t) can also be seen within the injured media underlying the dissection. **B,** An uninjured iliac artery from another monkey with plaque (p) overlying the media. **C,** The contralateral iliac artery is shown from the same animal as in **B** 14 days after angioplasty. Neointimal ingrowth (n), composed of smooth muscle cells (SMC-actin staining not shown) and extracellular matrix, is seen filling in the site of plaque fracture (*arrowheads*) and has begun to overgrow the primary atherosclerotic plaque (p). **D,** An iliac artery is shown from a third monkey 28 days after angioplasty. A significant accumulation of neointima (n) is seen overlying the primary atherosclerotic plaque (*arrowhead*). The extracellular matrix of the neointima appears homogeneous compared with the underlying plaque, and the pale staining suggests a composition rich in proteoglycans. Microvessels can be seen coursing within the adventitia, media, and primary atheroma but not in the neointima. **E,** A magnified view of the region outlined in **D** shows the plaque microvessels in more detail. Erythrocytes (*arrowheads*) can be seen within the lumina and adjacent to vasa cut in cross-section. (See Color Figure in this section.) (**A,** ×40; **B, C,** and **D,** ×100; **E,** ×400.) (From Geary RL, Williams JK, Golden D, et al: Time course of cellular proliferation, intimal hyperplasia, and remodeling following angioplasty in monkeys with established atherosclerosis: A nonhuman primate model of restenosis. Arterioscler Thromb Vasc Biol 16:34-43, 1996.)

SMCs from the restenosis lesions are greatly elevated, strong support that remodeling is important in the final determination of luminal diameter.[13,14]

The extent of intimal hyperplasia that develops in a vessel depends on the length and depth of the injury.[15] Minimal intimal proliferation occurs when the media is uninjured, but intimal hyperplasia increases in proportion to the depth of the medial injury, indicating that the proliferative response reflects the direct injury to the SMCs.[16,17] In addition, distention of SMCs without significant endothelial cell injury has been shown to result in SMC proliferation. The length of the injury influences the duration of the re-endothelialization process. Re-endothelialization occurs from the margins of the denuded area and possibly from the endothelial cells of the vasa vasorum. The longer there is an incomplete endothelial cell covering, the longer time the SMCs are without the modulating influence of the endothelial cells, and the longer the replication phases of the SMCs will be.[18,19] After deep vessel wall injury, luminal narrowing may depend less on intimal hyperplasia formation and more on vessel wall remodeling.[20] Medial damage is accompanied by a massive adventitial cell proliferation,[21] which in time provides cells capable of contraction and negative remodeling.

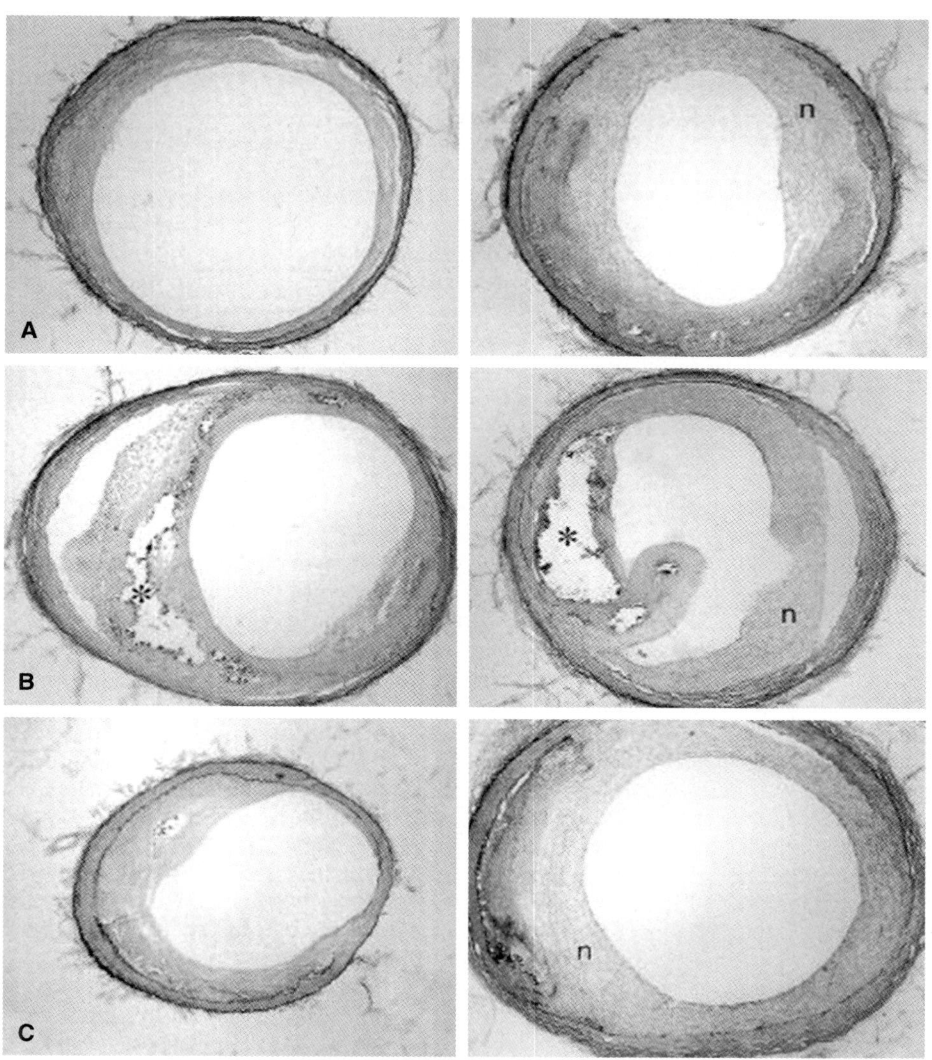

FIGURE 11-4 Photomicrographs of control iliac arteries (*left*) and arteries that have undergone angioplasty (*right*) from three monkeys 28 days after unilateral iliac angioplasty. The lesions depicted are representative of the variation in primary iliac atherosclerosis (*left*) and of the injury response after 28 days (*right*) in this model. In animal **A,** despite fracture of the plaque and media, artery is similar in size to the control artery, and significant neointimal hyperplasia (n) has decreased lumen caliber. In animal **B,** large eccentric plaques with regions of necrosis and calcification (*asterisk*) are present in both arteries. Angioplasty fractured and dissected the plaque, resulting in a complex lumen channel that has been partly filled in with neointima (n). Lumen area is similar. In animal **C,** fracture of the plaque and media led to the formation of a very large neointima (n). Although the EEL appears intact, artery size and lumen caliber have both increased. (×40.) (From Geary RL, Williams JK, Golden D, et al: Time course of cellular proliferation, intimal hyperplasia, and remodeling following angioplasty in monkeys with established atherosclerosis: A nonhuman primate model of restenosis. Arterioscler Thromb Vasc Biol 16:34-43, 1996.)

Coagulation Cascades

The immediate response of the vessel to injury is the hemostatic response. Endothelial denudation exposes the subendothelial matrix and leads to platelet adherence and aggregation. Platelet accumulation occurs in a rapid but time-dependent manner.[22] The subendothelium is totally covered by platelets immediately after denudation, but it appears that approximately 8 to 10 hours after injury, the exposed subendothelium becomes nonreactive to platelets. Platelet levels on the surface decrease over 3 to 7 days. Platelet adhesion requires the interaction of subendothelial collagen with three platelet membrane glycoprotein (GP) receptors (GPIb, GPIc/GPIIa, and GPIa/GPIIa), plasma von Willebrand factor, and fibronectin. The attached platelets release adenosine diphosphate (ADP) and activate the arachidonic acid synthesis pathway to produce thromboxane A_2. Thromboxane A_2 in turn acts as a potent chemoattractant and SMC mitogen and leads to additional platelet recruitment. Once activated, platelets also release PDGF and the constituents of their granules.

Several therapeutic options have been employed to control the early platelet interactions.[23] Temporary inhibition of GPIIb/GPIIIa receptor by a monoclonal antibody can reduce vessel wall–platelet interaction within the first 12 hours in vivo and has also been shown to reduce surface thrombus in vivo.[24,25] This strategy is now common clinical practice. Also, monoclonal antibodies to platelets, which induce thrombocytopenia, reduce but do not prevent the development of intimal hyperplasia.[26] It appears that the SMCs in the thrombocytopenic experimental animals exhibit a normal proliferative response but fail to migrate into the intima.

The current understanding of coagulation is that factor VII must come in contact with tissue factor for the coagulation cascade to proceed.[27] This forms a tissue factor–factor VIIa complex that converts factor X to factor Xa, which in turn leads to the conversion of prothrombin to thrombin. Thrombin cleaves fibrinogen to form insoluble fibrin clot. Formation of fibrin is a stimulus for activation of fibrinolysis. Plasminogen must be converted to plasmin for fibrinolysis to occur. Plasmin degrades cross-linked fibrin, non–cross-linked fibrin, and fibrinogen. The two principal molecules in the procoagulant cascade that have attracted the most attention are tissue factor and α-thrombin.

Tissue factor is present only in the adventitia of the normal vessel. After angioplasty, medial SMCs increase their expression of tissue factor messenger RNA (mRNA), which peaks within 2 hours and returns to baseline within 8 hours; there are suggestions that this may be mediated by PDGF, angiotensin II, and α-thrombin.[28] Tissue factor protein is detectable within the media within 2 hours of injury and is associated with an increase in tissue factor activity that lasts for 72 hours. Other studies have shown that tissue factor can be identified in the SMCs of the neointima and that increased activity and mRNA expression can be noted from 2 to 8 weeks after injury, suggesting that the neointima remains a reservoir of procoagulant activity.[29] Experimental data suggest that tissue factor contributes to development of intimal hyperplasia by both coagulation-dependent and coagulation-independent pathways.[30] The increase in tissue factor protein mediates prolonged procoagulant activity on the luminal surface,[31,32] and overexpression of tissue factor increases thrombus accumulation and promotes re-endothelialization, but enhances neointimal development after injury.[30] Tissue factor pathway inhibitor (TFPI) is the endogenous inhibitor of tissue factor.[33] Its role in the injury response and tissue factor activity is not yet fully defined. Recombinant TFPI (rTFPI) given intravenously for 24 hours inhibits stenosis at 4 weeks in minipigs.[34] In balloon injury and endarterectomy models, rTFPI irrigation reduces both the thrombotic and the intimal hyperplastic responses.[35,36] Gene transfer of TFPI produces the same results as local rTFPI therapy. Specific inhibition of factor V, VIIa, or Xa also reduces intimal hyperplasia.[37-39]

A key enzyme in the cascades below the tissue factor–factor VII–factor X axis is α-thrombin. It can bind specifically to the subendothelial matrix, where it remains active and protected from its circulating inhibitor, antithrombin III, and contributes to platelet activation and fibrin formation.[40] α-Thrombin is a potent mitogen for vascular SMCs, and its effects are mediated through a family of thrombin receptors (protease-activated receptors [PARs] 1 through 4). α-Thrombin is also a chemoattractant that promotes a migratory response of endothelial and SMCs.[41] In the uninjured vessel, thrombin receptors are found in adventitial cells. Gene expression of α-thrombin receptor is stimulated by bFGF, and within 6 hours of vessel wall injury, there is focal expression of α-thrombin receptor in PDGF-synthesizing SMCs. This expression becomes localized throughout the intima within 2 weeks in experimental models.[42] α-Thrombin also upregulates urokinase receptor (uPAR) expression in SMCs. Urokinase and uPAR also promote cell migration. Interestingly, the two isoforms of antithrombin III (α and β), inhibitors of α-thrombin, associate at differing rates to uninjured and injured arterial walls.[43] The use of antithrombins, such as hirudin and desulfatehirudin, has reduced the development of restenosis after experimental angioplasty. Hirudin does not prevent restenosis after angioplasty in humans.[44]

Inflammation

After denudation, there is a robust inflammatory response, with polymorphonuclear neutrophils (PMNs) and monocytes adhering to the subendothelial surface. The precise mechanism by which this response occurs is undetermined. There is a predictable sequential expression of inducible cell surface molecules in both endothelial cells and SMCs after experimental angioplasty.[45,46] Compared with uninjured endothelium, regenerating endothelial cells show high levels of expression of vascular cell adhesion molecule (VCAM) and intercellular adhesion molecule (ICAM); this pattern of expression appears to follow the leading edge of the regenerating endothelium. Regenerated endothelial cells removed from the leading edge continue to express ICAM but not VCAM. Expression of VCAM-1 and monocyte chemoattractant protein-1 (MCP-1) is seen within 4 hours of injury in SMCs. SMCs on the luminal surface continue to express high levels of VCAM-1 and MCP-1 at late time points.[47] ICAM-1 expression is intense at 1 and 2 days within medial SMCs of the wall, and administration of an antibody to ICAM-1 or lymphocyte function–associated antigen-1 (LFA-1) reduces the intimal hyperplastic response.[46] Within 10 days, SMCs show expression for both ICAM and class II major histocompatibility complex (MHC) antigens. However, by 30 days, the expression of adhesion cell molecules in endothelial cells and SMCs returns to the pattern observed in uninjured vessels. In association with this sequential pattern of adhesion molecule expression, the adherence of PMNs and monocytes has been shown to occur in a time-dependent manner.[48-50] PMNs have been shown to accumulate at the site of injury within 1 hour, and the level of PMN adherence becomes significantly higher than in controls at 1 hour and remains elevated at 24 hours and 5 weeks after injury.[48] PMNs can also be observed deep within the arterial wall even after 8 days. Interference with CD18, an important PMN adhesion molecule, does not prevent the development of intimal hyperplasia.[51] In the same model, mononuclear cells adhere to denuded sites from day 1 to day 42, and these cells can also be found deep within the intimal hyperplasia lesion.[49] The peak involvement of the labeled monocytes appears to be from 1 to 7 days, and perioperative inhibition of monocyte chemoattraction by antibodies against MCP-1 decreases experimental intimal hyperplasia.[52] Maximal accumulation of macrophages occurs at day 14 after angioplasty, but maximal SMC proliferative activity occurs by day 7, suggesting that macrophages play only a minor role in the initial induction of SMC proliferation after angioplasty.[45,53,54]

Cell Proliferation

The exact mechanisms whereby SMC proliferation is initiated, controlled, reduced and eventually suppressed are still not fully understood. Growth factors can regulate the proliferation of endothelial cells, the proliferation and migration of SMCs, and the secretion of extracellular matrix throughout the vasculature.

Fibroblast growth factors (FGFs) are a family of heparin-binding growth factors that can be synthesized by both vascular endothelial cells and SMCs.[55,56] The best-characterized of these are basic FGF (bFGF) and acidic FGF (aFGF); bFGF is 30- to 100-fold more potent than aFGF. Basic FGF and aFGF share the same groups of receptors, which are of both high and low affinity; the former are expressed on SMCs after crush injury to blood vessels and concentrate FGF on the cell surface.[55,56] FGF receptors have been shown to be upregulated after balloon injury.[57] The binding of FGF to heparan sulfate within the basement membrane protects and stabilizes FGF in vivo and also allows it to be released from a disrupted matrix after vessel wall injury. Transforming growth factor-β (TGF-β) is a potent inhibitor of both bFGF and aFGF stimulation of endothelial cells, whereas heparin diminishes the affinity of bFGF binding to FGF receptors but enhances the ability of aFGF to stimulate endothelial cell proliferation by 100-fold.[55,56] After arterial denudation, FGF is released from the extracellular matrix at least in part by urokinase and can stimulate proliferation of both endothelium and SMCs. Infusions of bFGF have been shown to increase development of intimal hyperplasia in animal models, and the use of an antibody to bFGF inhibits such development by inhibiting the first phase of cell proliferation.[58,59] Although FGF appears to be important in initiating SMC proliferation, whether it is required for continued proliferation is still unclear.[60,61] In contrast to the effect of bFGF infusion, however, infusions of aFGF can promote vascular repair and decrease intimal hyperplasia in a dose-dependent manner.[62] Insertion of aFGF genes into the arterial wall promotes both angiogenesis and intimal hyperplasia.[63]

The renin-angiotensin system is now recognized as important in the maintenance of cardiovascular homeostasis and the injury response. The components of these local renin-angiotensin systems are located primarily in the endothelial layer, but have also been found in vascular SMCs.[64,65] Angiotensin-converting enzyme (ACE) is a membrane-bound dipeptidyl peptidase that converts angiotensin I to angiotensin II and inactivates bradykinin. The local renin-angiotensin system has been implicated in directing the responses of blood vessels to intimal injury. Local tissue ACE activity can be correlated with the degree of intimal hyperplasia.[66] In this regard, systemic inhibition of ACE has been shown to significantly reduce intimal hyperplasia after balloon catheter injury in the rat carotid injury.[67] This reduction is associated with a dose-dependent inhibition of local tissue ACE activity.[66] However, this response appears to depend on the depth of the injury, and ACE inhibitors do not reduce intimal hyperplasia after deep arterial injury.[68] Angiotensin II can bind to two receptor subtypes, ATR1 and ATR2.[69] ATR1 receptors are found predominantly on SMCs, and ATR2 receptors appear to be mainly on endothelial cells. In uninjured vessels, the ratio of ATR1 receptors to ATR2 receptors is greater. However, after arterial intimal injury, this ratio changes owing to an increase in the number of ATR2 receptors. Angiotensin II is known both to induce SMC hypertrophy and to stimulate cell proliferation, apparently through its interaction with TGF-β, bFGF, and epidermal growth factor receptor (EGFR).[70,71] Evidence also suggests that both ATR1 and ATR2 receptors contribute to the intimal hyperplastic process. Treatment with ATR1 receptor antagonists significantly reduces intimal proliferation after arterial injury.[72,73] Systemic inhibition of ATR2 receptor does not inhibit the intimal proliferative response, but local infusion of an antagonist into the vicinity of a balloon-injured vessel does reduce the extent of intimal hyperplasia formation.[74]

Cell Migration

Another hallmark of remodeling in all tissues is cell migration, which involves the complex regulation of proteases, integrins and extracellular molecules. It can be random (chemokinesis) or directed (chemotaxis—migration toward a soluble protein—and haptotaxis—migration toward an insoluble matrix protein). Cell migration requires the initiation of a cellular program of attachment, detachment, and contraction.[75] More than 1000 molecules signal through G-protein receptors, but little is known about their role in migration. Several distinct events must take place for SMCs to traverse the extracellular matrix of the vessel and enter the intima. A chemotactic gradient must develop, and the cells must have receptors present to sense the chemoattractant. Once the SMC has identified and transduced the chemotactic signal, the cells synthesize, secrete, and activate proteases to allow degradation of the surrounding matrix cage. Once freed from the constraints of this matrix, the cell synthesizes new adhesion, protease, and matrix molecules in order to travel along the chemotactic gradient by a sequence of extension of podia, cell attachment, cell detachment, and cell contraction. Both the receptor tyrosine kinase–linked agonists (PDGF, bFGF, and hepatocyte growth factor) and the G-protein–coupled receptor agonists (vascular endothelial cell growth factor [VEGF], chemokines, lysophosphatidic acid (LPA), thrombin, and urokinase-type plasminogen activator [uPA]) induce cell motility.

PDGF has received most attention as a chemoattractant for vascular SMCs.[76] PDGF consists of four polypeptide chains, A, B, C, and D, which associate into three dimeric isoforms, AA, AB, and BB; the roles of CC and DD are undefined. In addition, there are two separate PDGF receptors (PDGFRs), α and β. Dimerization of the receptors is required for high-affinity ligand binding, such that the α/α receptor binds all three PDGF dimers (AA, AB, and BB), the α/β receptor binds AB and BB, and the β/β receptor binds only PDGF-BB.[77] Upon binding of PDGF to a PDGFR, the receptor dimerizes and activates the receptor tyrosine kinase, which autophosphorylates the receptor. Of the PDGF isoforms, PDGF-BB appears to play the most active role in intimal lesion formation after injury, and use of chimeric antibodies against the β/β receptor inhibits intimal hyperplasia.[78] PDGF-BB is a potent in vitro mitogen and induces a strong migratory response in vascular SMCs.[79,80] Although weaker than PDGF-BB, PDGF-AA is also a potent mitogen for cultured baboon and rat SMCs. However, in a Boyden chamber used to measure cell migration, PDGF-AA inhibits PDGF-BB- and fibronectin-induced migration of SMCs.[79,81] Activation of the PDGFR-α by either PDGF-AA or PDGF-BB (in the presence of an antibody against PDGFR-β) generates an inhibitory signal in baboon SMCs.[81,82] Chimeric antibodies against the α/α receptor do not inhibit intimal hyperplasia.

Shortly after balloon injury, medial SMCs express the mRNA for PDGF A chain; however, by 12 hours after injury, this expression returns to background levels. No expression of the B chain has been observed in the medial SMCs at this time.[83] Thereafter, SMCs of the intima are capable of expressing PDGF B chain, and explants have been shown to be capable of PDGF synthesis in culture.[84]

In-situ hybridization has demonstrated that intimal SMCs continue to express PDGF A chain after the initial period in areas of denudation; it has been noted that the SMCs that are still capable of proliferating at 6 weeks after balloon injury are the cells that continue to express the PDGF A chain.[83] Therefore, SMCs from injured arteries appear to express A and B chain genes for PDGF but to secrete only the A chain of PDGF.[85] However, only the β receptor is upregulated in the SMCs, suggesting that the SMCs may not be capable of responding to the PDGF.[83] Platelets on the luminal surface release mainly the BB isoform, thus providing an agonist for the newly formed SMC PDGF-β receptors.[86] Insertion of the PDGF BB gene, the dominant PDGF isoform, into balloon-injured porcine arteries results in greater development of intimal hyperplasia.[87] Infusion of PDGF BB has been shown to accelerate SMC migration but to have little effect on proliferation.[88] Administration of an anti-PDGF antibody has been demonstrated to inhibit intimal thickening by approximately 40%.[9] Inhibition of PDGFR-β/β with parenteral chimeric antibodies that have been shown to be effective in animal models has failed to limit restenosis in human trials.[78,82,89]

Proteases

Proteases, including plasmin, have been shown to play a role in hemostasis, inflammation, cell migration, cell proliferation and matrix remodeling in many wound healing responses including intimal hyperplasia.[90,91] Plasmin is formed from plasminogen by a series of plasminogen activators: uPA, which activates plasminogen in the fluid phase, and tissue-type PA (tPA), which is most active when bound to fibrin. Plasmin degrades fibrin and is crucial to the removal of thrombus.[92,93] Plasmin also activates matrix metalloproteinases (MMPs). The activity of uPA and tPA is modulated by the serpin proteins, plasminogen activator inhibitors 1 (PAI-1) and 2 (PAI-2).[94] Bindings of uPA to its receptor (uPAR) localize its activity to the membrane. The MMP and plasminogen-plasmin systems are functionally interactive and cooperate in degradation and remodeling of the extracellular matrix.[95]

Elevations of uPA and decreases of PAI-1 levels are predictors for angiographic coronary restenosis.[96] After injury to the rat carotid artery, there is a time-dependent enhanced expression of uPA and tPA and increased plasminogen activator activity on SMCs within the wall compared with the uninjured state.[97] Tranexamic acid, a plasmin inhibitor, inhibits SMC migration after carotid balloon injury.[98] If uPA is placed in a pluronic gel around an injured carotid, there is a significant increase in the earlier development of intimal hyperplasia due to enhanced migration and proliferation of SMCs.[99] Infusion of tPA after arterial injury appears to reduce medial cell proliferation and suppress intimal hyperplasia.[100] This effect may be associated with reduction in mural thrombus burden and earlier recovery of endothelial cell coverage. Expression of PAI-1, the endogenous PAI, is increased sevenfold 3 hours after arterial balloon injury and returns to baseline by 2 days; it then increases again from day 4 to day 7.[101,102] Elevated PAI-1 protein expression (induced by gene therapy) in the rat carotid enhances thrombosis and endothelial cell regeneration and inhibits intimal thickening.[103] Overexpression of uPA or a deficiency of PAI-1 in transgenic mice has been shown to promote neointimal formation in response to transmural electrical injury. A lack of uPA leads to a reduction in neointimal hyperplasia. However, in mice that lack uPAR, neointimal formation is unchanged.[104]

MMPs are classified into three major groups: interstitial collagenases (which degrade type I/III collagen), gelatinases (or type VI collagenases, which degrade gelatin, type IV/V collagen, and elastin) and stromelysins (which degrade many substrates, including laminin, fibronectin, and proteoglycans). MMPs are controlled by tissue inhibitors of matrix metalloproteinases (TIMP-1, -2, -3, and -4). In the normal vessel, MMP-2 is constitutively expressed; activated MMP-2 levels rise 5 days after injury, when SMC migration is identified.[105-107] One of the activators of MMP-2, membrane-type MMP-1 (MT-MMP-1), shows enhanced expression in injured vessels and coincides with increased MMP-2 activity.[108] In contrast, MMP-9 expression increases at 24 hours, and this increase in activity coincides with the onset of cell proliferation.[105-107,109] MMP-1 expression is low in uninjured vessels and is unchanged on day 1 after injury. By day 2, MMP-1 expression is increased deep in the intima and in the adventitia; at 7 days and 14 days, it is enhanced in the intima and media.[110] Similarly, elastolytic enzymes are transiently elevated after balloon angioplasty, with peak levels 1 week after injury.[111]

In association with these changes in MMPs, there are changes in TIMP expression and activity. TIMP-2 mRNA expression rises 24 hours after injury, and both protein expression and activity peak at 3 days; this expression is found in the intima and the media.[101] TIMP-1 expression appears unchanged, but TIMP-3 expression is not detected.[101,112] TIMP-4 is identified within the adventitia after injury, and its expression peaks at 7 days and 14 days after injury.[113] Administration of a metalloproteinase inhibitor can decrease SMC proliferation and migration.[98,105] TIMP-1 and TIMP-2 overexpressions induce similar results.[101,114-116] TIMP-1–deficient mice demonstrate an enhanced response after arterial injury, confirming the role of TIMP-1 in moderating the neointimal response.

Extracellular Matrix

Proteases modulate the extracellular matrix. There is evidence that alterations in the extracellular matrix can induce a phenotypic change in the vascular SMC from a contractile to a synthetic proliferative phenotype. When SMCs are freed from their extracellular matrix and dispersed into monolayer, they undergo frank morphologic changes characteristic of a synthetic phenotype. These cells commence the synthesis and secretion of large amounts of collagen, elastin, and proteoglycans. In vitro, type I collagen promotes modulation of vascular SMCs from a contractile to a synthetic phenotype.[117] Synthesis by the SMCs of these components of the extracellular matrix can be regulated by cytokines and growth factors.[118] Re-integration of cultured SMCs into a three-dimensional network of type I collagen induces a reduction in collagen synthesis and suppression of responses to soluble growth mediators.[119,120] This reduction of collagen synthesis appears to occur at a post-translational level.[121] The inhibitory effects of the collagen matrices on SMC synthesis of extracellular matrix proteins requires contraction of the lattice around the cells and the presence of fibronectin and factor VIII.[119,122,123] Studies also indicate that quiescent SMCs increase their synthesis of proteoglycans when stimulated to divide and that this increase occurs principally during the G_1 phase of the cell cycle.[124,125] Greater proteoglycan synthesis is accompanied by increased synthesis of collagen and thrombospondin by the SMCs.

The activity of several enzymes involved in the synthesis of chondroitin sulfate chains also rises during the proliferative phase of vascular SMCs. Heparan sulfates derived from post-confluent endothelial cells and SMCs inhibit the migration and proliferation of SMCs, and this inhibitory activity depends greatly on the presence of heparanases, which can generate heparan sulfate fragments that in turn act as growth inhibitors.[6,126-128] Furthermore, SMCs possess specific high-affinity receptors for heparin/heparan sulfates. Heparin decreases thrombospondin synthesis, and the decrease in concentrations of thrombospondin in turn reduces DNA synthesis.[129] This process may be to due to the fact that thrombospondin and epidermal growth factor act synergistically to stimulate DNA synthesis. In addition, heparin decreases the number of epidermal growth factor receptors on SMCs thus reducing the ability of the cells to respond to growth stimulation.

With time, the intimal SMCs show a diminished predisposition to replicate and commence to produce large quantities of extracellular matrix. Although the total number and volume of SMCs in the intima remains unchanged after 12 weeks, the fraction of the intima composed of SMCs is smaller. This slow increase in intimal hyperplasia is the result of the synthesis and accumulation of connective tissue components such as collagen and proteoglycans.[130] Specific mRNA for elastin, chondroitin sulfate, and heparan sulfate proteoglycans (perlecan, syndecan, and ryadocan) are induced in the rat model after balloon injury, peak at 2 weeks, and are maintained for at least 4 weeks.[131] Significant increases in collagen, elastin, and proteoglycan synthesis (4 to 10 times control) occur at 1, 2, and 4 weeks, respectively in the rabbit model.[132] This greater synthesis can be correlated with concomitant rises in MMP-2, suggesting that degradation of the newly synthesized collagens occurs within the first week after angioplasty.[133] In the rat carotid artery, the staining response for hyaluron in neointima reaches a maximum 7 days after angioplasty and is associated with proliferating SMCs.[134]

In human restenosis lesions, the staining response for hyaluron is inversely related to collagen I and III staining. Little proteoglycans accumulation occurs over the first 1 to 2 months but dramatically increases from 3 to 6 months after balloon injury and then decreases gradually thereafter in restenosis human coronary atherosclerotic plaque.[135] In atherectomy specimens, zones of collagen and proteoglycan can be identified. The collagen-rich zone contains elongated SMCs packed closely together, and collagen I, elastin, and biglycan predominate in these zones. In contrast, proteoglycan-rich zones contain both elongated and stellate SMCs, which are widely spaced. Versican and biglycan predominate in these areas, but elastin is sparsely identified.[136]

Changes in the extracellular matrix do not occur independent of changes in the SMCs. The cells sense these changes through integrins. Integrins are essential cell surface proteins that allow cells to interact with their environment and, more particularly, with the individual components of the extracellular matrix. They exist as dimers of α and β subunits on the cell surface. No mRNA expression of α_v, β_3, or β_5 integrins is identified in uninjured vessels. A weak pattern of mRNA expression is seen at 2 days, and high expression is seen at 14 days within the intimal hyperplasia but not within the media. This expression is confirmed by immunostaining. There is a decline in these transcripts at 5 weeks.[137] Upregulation of $\alpha_v\beta_3$ integrins by SMCs, endothelial cells, and myofibroblasts peaks at 7 days in the media and adventitia and at 14 days within the neointima[138] and is detected by immunostaining on the luminal edge of the neointima. Inhibition of the RSD moiety of $\alpha_v\beta_3$ integrin inhibits PDGF-induced SMC migration in vitro and reduces experimental intimal hyperplasia in vivo.[139] Although expression of the β_3 integrins increases periluminally after vascular injury, expression of thrombospondin, a β_3 integrin ligand, is upregulated throughout the intima.[140] Osteopontin (OPN) and β_3 integrin mRNA and protein levels correlate temporally and spatially with active endothelial cell proliferation and migration after balloon injury.[141] After angioplasty, osteopontin mRNA expression is induced by 6 hours and peaks at 1 and 3 days. OPN protein is expressed at 6 hours at luminal edge and by 1 day within the media and adventitia. From 3 to 5 days, $\alpha_v\beta_3$ integrin and OPN are downregulated at luminal edge but are still present within the adventitia. Basal $\alpha_v\beta_5$ integrin is very low in the normal vessel; after injury it is rapidly upregulated, and by 3 to 5 days, the expression levels are decreased throughout the arterial wall.[142,143] There is an inverse correlation between the expression of the higher-affinity form of β_1 integrin and the migration and proliferation of SMCs and endothelial cells after arterial injury.[144]

One of the principal cytokines involved in controlling extracellular matrix responses is TGF-β. Transforming growth factor-βs are a family of peptides (a homodimeric β1, a homodimeric β2, and a heterodimeric β1.2). TGF-β exerts bifunctional effects that depend on the context in which the cell encounters the TGF-β signal.[145] In SMCs, TGF-β is a potent inhibitor of migration and proliferation but also induces the production of PDGF. Plasmin has been considered one of the proteolytic enzymes, which can activate latent TGF-β by cleavage of the intact complex. TGF-β, in turn, induces PAI, allowing negative feedback on plasmin production and thus on TGF-β activation.[146] TGF-β can inhibit the migration and proliferation of endothelial and SMCs in vitro. TGF-β is an important factor that regulates extracellular matrix by stimulating production of proteoglycans, collagen, and fibronectin and regulating the receptors for these proteins.[147] TGF-β also reduces the secretion of proteases and increases the formation of protease inhibitors, resulting in the stabilization of the connective tissue matrix.

The transcript for TGF-β1 is seen at 6 hours after injury, and the continued expression of TGF-β1 can be observed in the intimal SMCs for as long as 2 weeks after injury.[148] This period coincides with the expression of both type I and type II receptors.[149] Expression of two TGF-β1–induced extracellular matrix components, fibronectin and versican, is increased in intimal hyperplasia by 2 weeks, and administration of anti–TGF-β1 antibodies nearly completely suppresses this expression.[150] Infusions of TGF-β1 increase intimal SMC proliferation,[151] and the direct transfer of the TGF-β1 gene into an acutely injured vessel wall increases intimal hyperplasia but with a predominant extracellular matrix component and a much reduced cellular component.[152] Anti–TGF-β1 antibodies significantly reduce the development of intimal hyperplasia.[150] However, TGF-β1 is secreted in an inactive form and must be activated, possibly by plasmin. It has also been suggested that the higher level of tPA mRNA noted within 4 days would allow the activation of TGF-β1.

Hemodynamics

Acute distention of a vessel without substantial endothelial cell damage results in a low level of SMC proliferation.[153] Deformation of SMCs leads to activation of protein tyrosine kinases, which may be an additional mechanism whereby SMC proliferation occurs.[154] Furthermore, limited vessel wall injury without associated subintimal dissection or direct media exposure increases transmural fluid flux, thus allowing soluble proliferogenic mediators to gain access to the media of a vessel.[155] Changes in hemodynamic parameters have been shown to affect the arterial structure of both normal and diseased vessels.[156] Clinical studies have suggested that after femoral angioplasty in patients with extensive distal disease, the rate of restenosis is increased. In an experimental study, Hehrlein and coworkers[157] have confirmed that reduced vascular runoff after angioplasty results in greater development of intimal hyperplasia, and Dobrin and colleagues[158] have shown that blood flow (closely associated with shear stress) is best associated with the formation of intimal hyperplasia and that deformation of the vessel wall in a circumferential direction is best associated with medial thickening. Kohler and associates[159,160] have demonstrated correlations between (1) a reduction of intimal thickness, which forms early after angioplasty, and an increase in flow and (2) an increase in intimal hyperplasia and a decrease in flow; these findings suggest a direct effect of flow on SMC function. These researchers did not, however, observe a similar change in mature intimal hyperplastic lesions that had developed under conditions of normal flow and were then subjected to either increased or decreased blood flow conditions.

Systemic Vascular Diseases

The development of intimal hyperplasia in a vessel with an already established atheromatous or hyperplastic lesion has considerable implications for the use of angioplasty as a primary endovascular procedure, because it mirrors the clinical situation. Our understanding of the effects of preexisting vascular diseases on the subsequent development of intimal hyperplasia in the postoperative period is limited. Clinically, hyperlipidemia and diabetes are associated with higher rates of restenosis after percutaneous transluminal coronary angioplasty (PTCA).[161-164] Exposure to cigarette smoke increases the development of experimental intimal hyperplasia twofold.[165] Some studies have shown that cholesterol reduction therapies with lovastatin reduce the development of restenosis,[166,167] but others have suggested that such therapies have no long-term effect on re-stenosis.[168]

The presence of hypercholesterolemia has been shown to result in an increase in intimal hyperplasia development with a rise in SMC proliferation after angioplasty without the presence of significant numbers of macrophages in the initial period after arterial injury.[169-172] There is almost three times more cholesterol ester accumulation in areas of regenerating endothelium than in de-endothelialized areas.[173] In addition, accumulation of low-density lipoprotein (LDL) in the vessel wall after angioplasty occurs via two kinetically and biochemically distinct pathways, in that there is labile LDL accumulation in de-endothelialized areas and persistent accumulation at the edges of these areas.[173] Srinivasan and colleagues[174] have suggested that injury to the arterial wall produces proteoglycan variants with enhanced LDL-binding ability, which may in part explain the differences in LDL binding noted by others.[174] In a hypercholesterolemic miniswine balloon injury model, there is a significant increase in type I collagen mRNA expression and greater collagen deposition in the extracellular matrix. Metalloproteinase activity is markedly decreased. Therefore, the increases in extracellular matrix appear to be due to greater collagen synthesis and reduced degradation.[175] In the normocholesterolemic animal, there is early and high proliferative activity of SMCs after angioplasty; the proliferative response of the atherosclerotic vessel wall is reduced but persists longer.[176] In cholesterol-fed rabbits, a second balloon injury produces the same increases in intimal areas, cell numbers, and cellular proliferation in the intima that are observed after the primary injury.[177]

Diabetes is a predictor for re-stenosis. Tissue from restenosis plaques in diabetic patients is composed primarily of atherosclerotic plaque rather than hypercellular tissue. This finding might suggest that recoil or remodeling may be predominant.[178] The medial response is more pronounced in the diabetic balloon-injured rat carotid.[179]

Intravascular Stents

The biology of in-stent restenosis is different from that seen after balloon angioplasty.[180] A stent is generally used if the result of balloon angioplasty is technically unsatisfactory or if there is arterial occlusion, immediate elastic recoil, dissection, or re-stenosis (Fig. 11-5). The response of a vessel to a stent depends on the stent design, length, and composition, the delivery system, and the deployment technique.[181] In-stent restenosis is classified on the basis of length of restenosis in relation to stented length. Four categories of in-stent restenosis have been defined[182]:

- I: Focal (≤10 mm in length)
- II: Diffuse (>10 mm in length)
- III: Proliferative (>10 mm in length and extending outside the stent)
- IV: Occlusion

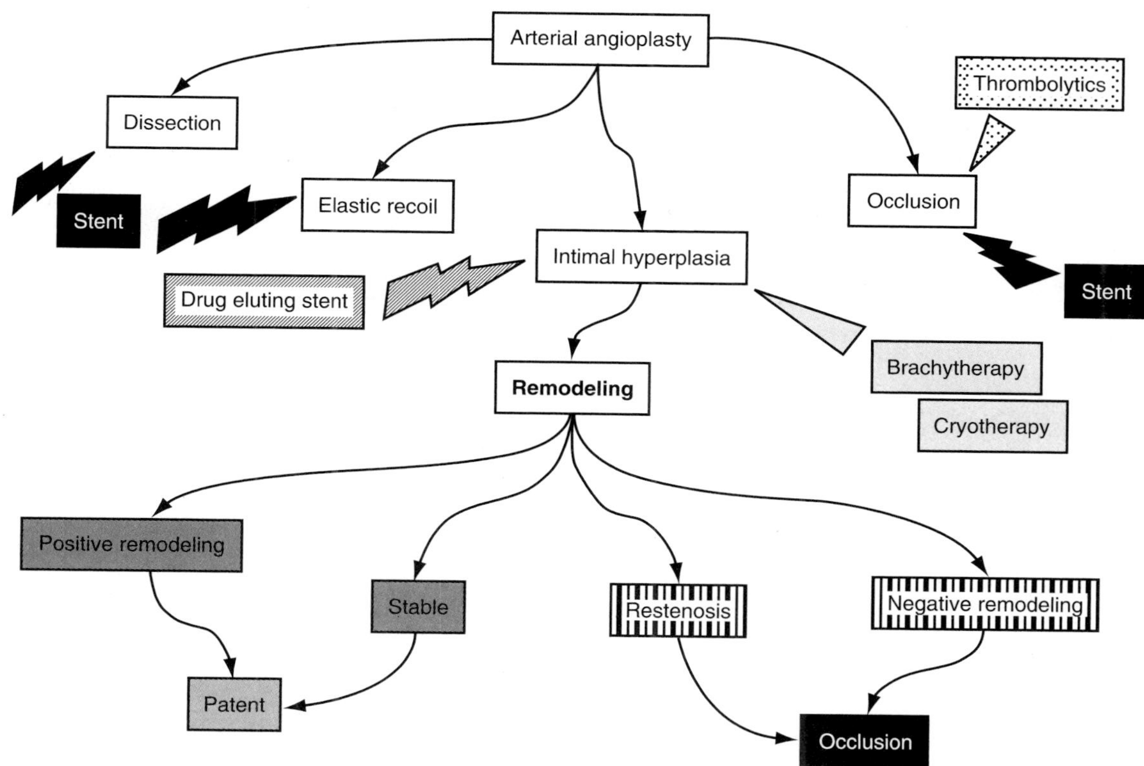

FIGURE 11-5 Consequences and cures of angioplasty. Flow diagram demonstrating the outcomes of a vessel's response to balloon angioplasty and the therapeutic maneuvers to correct the adverse outcomes. If a technical failure occurs after angioplasty because of elastic recoil or dissection, a stent is placed. If there is concern for the development of intimal hyperplasia, brachytherapy or cryotherapy may be applied. Sudden occlusion is corrected with thrombolysis or primary stenting. Remodeling is influenced by placement of stents, drug-eluting stents, brachytherapy, and cryotherapy.

After balloon angioplasty, there is thrombus formation, intimal hyperplasia development, elastic recoil, and negative remodeling. In contrast, after stent placement, elastic recoil and negative remodeling are eliminated,[183] and thrombus formation and then intimal hyperplasia development are the main contributors to in-stent restenosis.[184,185] Patients with diabetes and prior restenosis have a higher rate of in-stent restenosis,[186] and there is a correlation between prolonged in-stent thrombus and hyperglycemia.[187]

Stent placement in a vessel results in both a generalized injury to the length of the vessel exposed and more focal injuries at the areas of strut placement. Intravascular ultrasound has demonstrated that stents do not always completely appose the vessel wall along its entire length, thus resulting in uneven injury along its length.[183] Within 5 seconds after stent placement, the surface of the metal implanted into the vessel is covered by a strongly adherent monolayer of protein. After 1 minute, the surface is covered by fine layers of proteins, predominantly fibrinogen.[188] The holes between the stent wires are filled with thrombus, and the adherence of platelets and leukocytes is enhanced by disturbance of electrostatic equilibrium.[189,190] The basic mechanisms of SMC proliferation and migration after stent placement are the same as those after balloon injury.[191] The intimal hyperplastic process in a stent is more prolonged and robust than in a balloon-injured artery and is proportional to the depth of injury the recipient vessel sustains[192] and the inflammatory response induced;[193] it can often be much more significant at the ends than in the body of the stent (Figs. 11-6 and 11-7). In addition, the adventitial response is prolonged, adventitial giant cell body formation being noted. Stents prevent chronic elastic recoil and cause progressive atrophy of the media.[194]

■ RESPONSE OF VEIN TO INJURY

Saphenous veins demonstrate a spectrum of preexisting pathologic conditions ranging from significantly thickened walls to postphlebitic changes and varicosities at the time of harvest. Histologic analysis shows that 91% of saphenous veins have moderate to severe fibrosis in the vein wall. These changes are not detectable on ultrasound,[195] but poor vein quality can be identified at angioscopy, and veins thus identified have a poor outcome.[196] One study found that 2% to 5% of veins are unusable and up to 12% can be considered "diseased."[197] The patency of "diseased" veins is half that of "nondiseased" controls. The etiology of the venous diseases observed is multifactorial in origin, and at present, without gross morphologic evidence of disease, there is no clear prognostic indicator to identify those veins that should be rejected as grafts.[197,198]

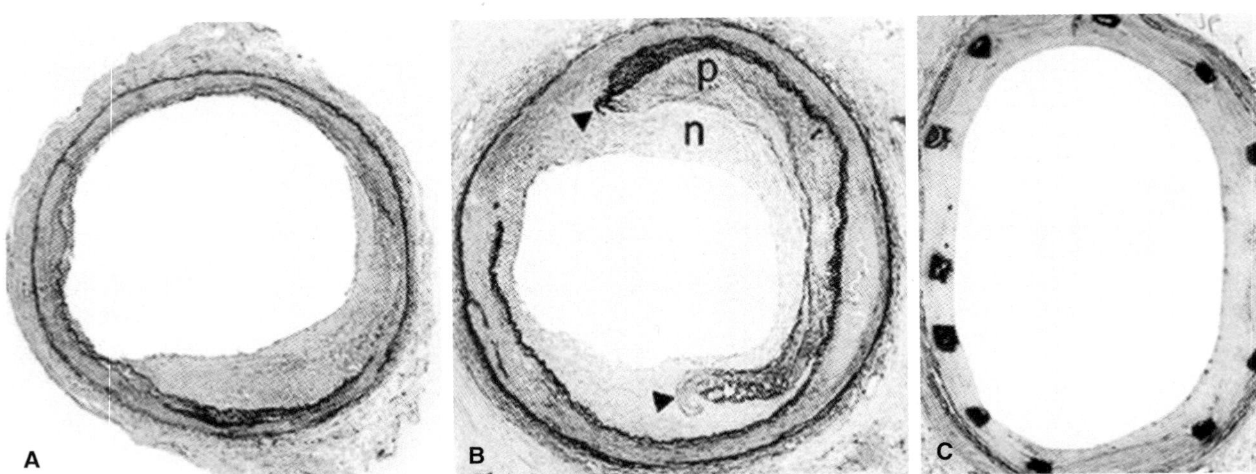

FIGURE 11-6 Photomicrographs of stented vessel. **A,** Atherogenic diet–induced complex intimal lesions shown in uninjured iliac artery. **B,** Contralateral iliac artery was removed 35 days after experimental angioplasty. Angioplasty has fractured the preexisting plaque (p; *arrowheads*) and injured the overlying media, with neointimal ingrowth (n). **C,** Palmaz stents were deployed in the proximal left subclavian artery, and after 35 days, neointimal ingrowth has covered the underlying plaque and stent struts. (Verhoeff–van Gieson stain. **A** and **B**, ×40; **C**, ×100.) (See Color Figure in this section.) (From Deitch JS, Williams JK, Adams MR, et al: Effects of β3-integrin blockade (c7E3) on the response to angioplasty and intra-arterial stenting in atherosclerotic nonhuman primates. Arterioscler Thromb Vasc Biol 18:1730-1737, 1998.)

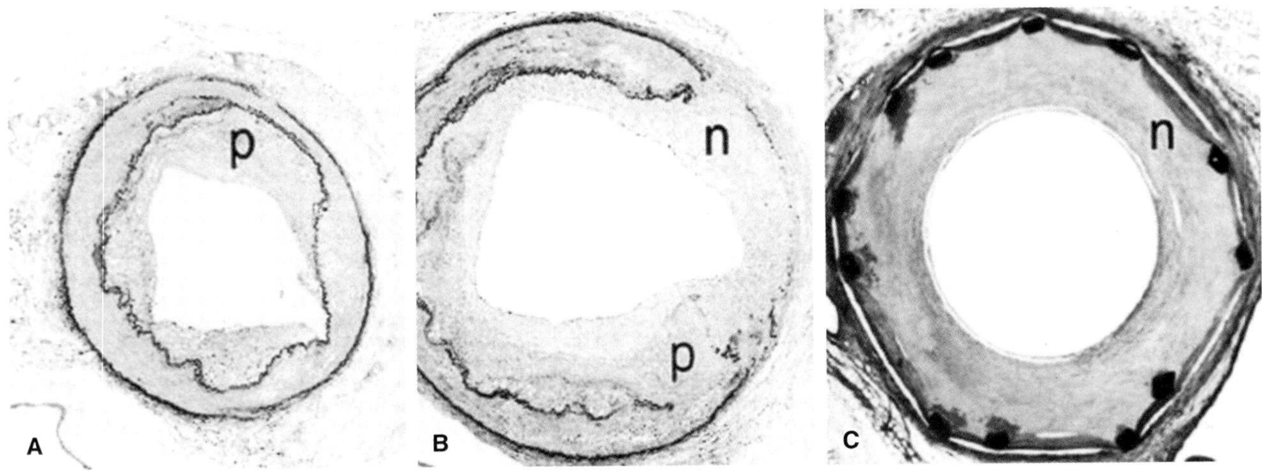

FIGURE 11-7 Photomicrographs of stented vessel. Composite photomicrograph demonstrates a typical response 4 weeks after angioplasty and stenting. **A** and **B** show the uninjured and injured common iliac arteries, respectively, and **C** shows the stented external iliac artery. Animals consumed an atherogenic diet for 2.5 years, thus creating complicated plaques (p). **B** shows fractured plaque (p) and overlying media that have healed with neointimal ingrowth (n). **C** shows a stented external iliac artery with a typical neointimal lesion (n). Vessels were from a single treated animal. (**A** and **B**, Verhoeff–van Gieson stain; **C,** trichrome stain; original magnification, ×40.) (See Color Figure in this section.) (From Cherr GS, Motew SJ, Travis JA, et al: Metalloproteinase inhibition and the response to angioplasty and stenting in atherosclerotic primates. Arterioscler Thromb Vasc Biol 22:161-166, 2002.)

Intimal hyperplasia, the universal response of a vein graft to insertion into the arterial circulation, results from both the migration of SMCs out of the media into the intima and proliferation of these SMCs (Fig. 11-8). Whether the same series of events occurs in a vein graft as in an injured artery remains to be determined. Progenitor cells may play a larger role in the vein graft than in the artery. In experimental models, many endothelial cells of vein grafts appear to be derived from circulating progenitor cells and up to a third to be derived from bone marrow progenitor cells.[199] In general, intimal hyperplasia is a self-limiting process that does not produce luminal compromise and usually becomes quiescent within 2 years of graft insertion. However, in focal areas, the intimal hyperplastic process can proceed to significant stenosis.[200-203] Studies of peripheral vein grafts have documented that the majority of stenotic lesions that develop in a graft are composed of intimal hyperplastic tissue.[202,203] Graft stenoses develop at sites of unrepaired defects or early-appearing conduit abnormalities[204] but not at the sites of valves or tributary ligation.[205]

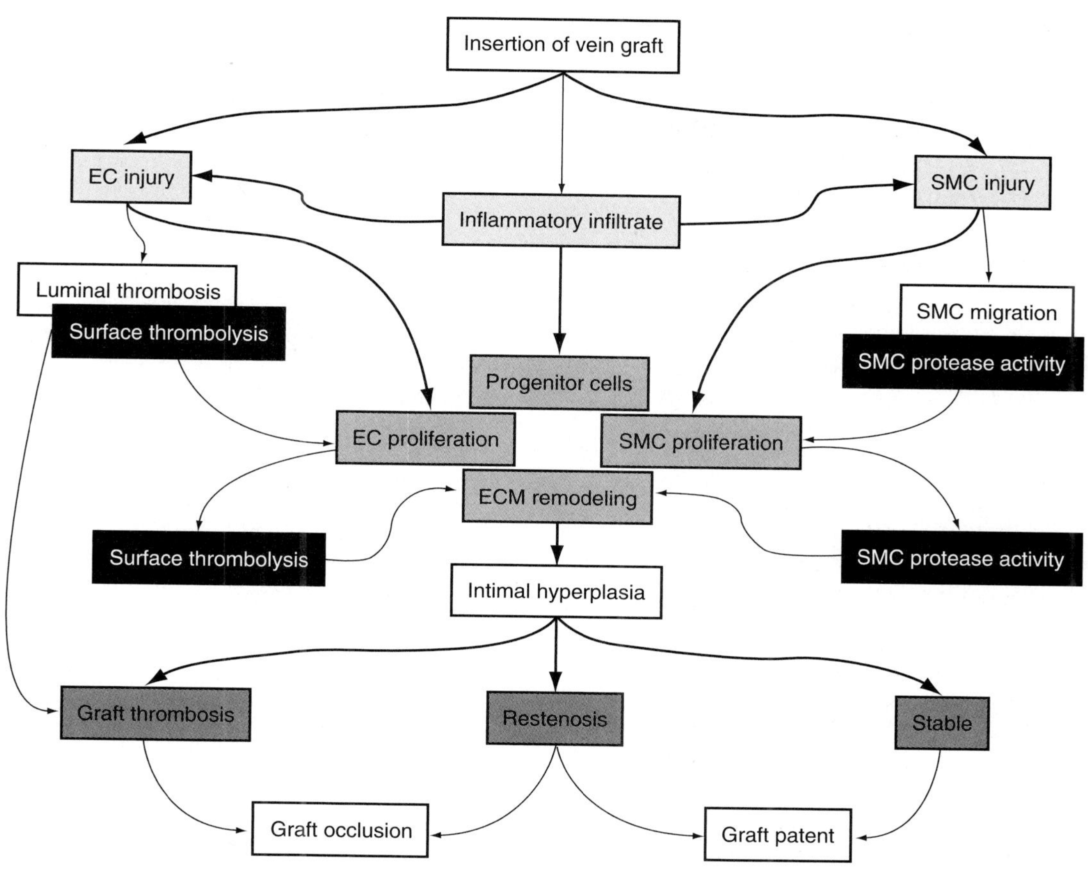

FIGURE 11-8 Pathobiology of the vein graft response after angioplasty. Flow diagram demonstrating the key elements in the vein's response to being inserted into the arterial circulation. Denudation of the endothelium depends on the degree of implantation injury. Endothelial cell (EC) injury leads to luminal thrombosis, inflammatory cell infiltration, cellular proliferation, and clearance of the thrombotic material on the surface with restoration of the endothelium. If this fails to progress adequately, graft thrombosis may occur. Injury to smooth muscle cells (SMCs) leads to cell proliferation and migration. Progenitor cells are recruited to the vessel wall. With proliferation and migration of SMCs, the appearance of progenitor cells, and the deposition of extracellular matrix (ECM), intimal hyperplasia develops to re-establish the tangential stress across the wall. Over time, this lesion remodels and may produce a stenotic lesion due to the bulk of neointima or due to negative remodeling restenosis. This may result in graft occlusion.

Perioperative manipulations of veins before their insertion have been shown to produce significant tissue damage. Such implantation injury leads to endothelial dysfunction, endothelial cell injury, endothelial denudation, and SMC injury, all of which are important factors in the initiation of intimal hyperplasia. It is now recognized that every effort should be made to reduce the implantation injury that a vein graft suffers.[206-209] There appears to be a direct relationship between the morphologic integrity of the vein graft before grafting and its later histopathologic appearance and function.[207,209] Poorly prepared vein grafts develop significantly greater intimal hyperplasia and SMC contractility than carefully prepared vein grafts.[207,209]

Coagulation

Within the first 3 days, there is an accumulation and subsequent clearance of fibrin, platelets, and luminal thrombus from the vein graft's endothelial surface.[210] This simple biologic finding may explain the success of aspirin administration in reducing early vein graft failure rates. For this finding to occur, there is likely a transient increase in procoagulant proteins, a decrease in anticoagulation systems, or a combination of both. Injury to endothelial cells leads to an increase in tissue factor. Tissue factor catalyzes the rate-limiting step of the extrinsic coagulation cascade and serves as the major source of thrombin production in vivo.[211] Channon and colleagues[212] have shown that tissue factor is rapidly upregulated in the vein grafts early after implantation and diminishes with time. Whether TFPI is reduced is not known, but local application of rTFPI has been shown to modulate tissue factor expression, inflammatory infiltration, and intimal hyperplasia development.[213] Concomitant with the increase in tissue factor, thrombomodulin expression decreases, resulting in a 95% reduction in the capacity of the vein grafts to activate protein C; this decrease in thrombomodulin is associated with a rise in bound thrombin activity.[214,215] Restoration of thrombomodulin expression by adenoviral transfer reverses these functional changes.[214] Other studies have shown that grafting of saphenous veins results in the loss of anti-aggregatory potential (decreased nitric oxide and prostaglandin I_2 release and damaged endothelial cells) and diminished local fibrinolytic activity, producing a larger thrombogenic surface. It is notable that two thirds of vein grafts removed during "redo" coronary artery bypass operations show evidence of mural or occlusive thrombus.[216]

Vein Graft Inflammation

Associated with the greater accumulation of thrombus on the graft surface is a significant infiltration of both PMNs and macrophages within the newly implanted vein graft. My colleagues and I[210] found that within 24 hours, numerous PMNs were adherent to endothelium and were also deep within the graft wall. Coincident with this infiltration of PMNs, SMC proliferation was documented to occur maximally at days 1 and 2 in the vein grafts. The number of PMNs on the endothelial surface decreased from day 3 onwards, and by day 5, the vein graft was grossly clear. Vein bypass grafts placed in the venous circulation, however, do not show significant PMN involvement of the vein graft over the same time course,[217] suggesting that the inflammatory response is induced by the change in environment and not simply by the surgical procedure.

To determine whether PMNs are important in the initial phases of vein grafts, we treated animals with vinblastine 6 days and 3 days before surgery, producing a 97% decrease in peripheral PMN numbers. In animals treated with vinblastine, vein grafts harvested at 1 day and 3 days had fewer adherent PMNs on an intact endothelial cell surface and a marked reduction in the transmural inflammatory infiltrate compared with controls. By 28 days, overall mean intimal thickness had decreased by 41% without a change in overall mean medial thickness. Interestingly, such a reduction in PMNs did not have a significant effect on thrombomodulin expression.[215] In several models of vein grafts, there is a prolonged transmural macrophage infiltration.[218] The increase in macrophages can be correlated with increase in interleukin-1β (IL-1B) and MCP-1 expression in the vein graft.[219-223] Depletion of macrophages results in a significant decrease in the development of intimal hyperplasia.[222]

Cell Proliferation and Apoptosis

In experimental vein grafts, SMC proliferation occurs within the first 72 hours and continues for at least 7 days after graft insertion.[224,225] Microscopic development of intimal hyperplasia occurs later, from day 3 to day 5, and increases rapidly between 7 and 14 days.[226,227] Associated with the onset of proliferation are changes in specific membrane G-protein subunit expression in the SMCs with the de novo expression of Gαi and Gαs subunits.[227] In rat vein grafts, an increase in apoptotic cells is detectable by 4 days in the adventitia and luminal surfaces. By 1 to 2 weeks, apoptotic cells are detectable in the intimal hyperplasia. Transmural apoptotic cells are evident by 4 weeks. At 6 weeks, apoptotic cell numbers decrease to baseline.

In rabbit vein grafts, there is an upregulation of uPA mRNA by 20-fold at 2 days and by 18-fold at 1 week, which falls to 5-fold of control vein values from 2 to 8 weeks postoperatively.[228] In one study, baseline expression of tumor necrosis factor-α (TNF-α) was observed in control vein endothelium and subendothelium but not in the media; after 1 week, expression of TNF-α increased in the media (90% of cells), plateauing at 2 weeks, but remained elevated for up to 4 weeks. Peak expression of IL-1β and bFGF occurred by 2 days.[229] IL-1α is expressed early but disappears after 4 weeks. IL-2 receptor mRNA levels fluctuate. PDGF-A mRNA may be found in control vein but is downregulated at 1 hour and absent at 4 hours after grafting. PDGF transcription is upregulated by 1 day with prominent expression from 4 days to 1 week.[220] PDGF-AA expression in the intima parallels the development of intimal hyperplasia, peaking at 2 weeks and then declining,[229] whereas in the media, PDGF-AA expression rises gradually from a low baseline to peak at 1 week.[230] mRNA for PDGF-B is found in porcine vein grafts but not in control veins; in situ hybridization demonstrates PDGF-B in the endothelial and neointima cell layers.[231] In rat vein grafts, PDGF and bFGF production closely precedes intimal hyperplasia formation,[232] and such grafts have been shown to release PDGF and bFGF into the circulation.[233] Basic FGF expression is detectable in the endothelium at 6 hours after implantation, and in the media by day 2, returning to baseline at 1 week. There is a second peak at 2 weeks, with expression returning to baseline at 4 weeks. Release of bFGF by experimental vein graft is five times greater than that by control veins at 4 and 12 weeks, in a pattern that matches the formation of intimal hyperplasia.[234] Arterial grafts produce a smaller quantity of bFGF and PDGF than vein grafts.[232] TGF-β is always expressed, with levels peaking at 4 days to 4 weeks.[219] mRNA for TGF-β1 receptor is evident in vein graft at 1 and 4 hours, with prominent expression from 1 day to 2 weeks. Release of TGF-β from vein grafts is similar to that from control veins for the first 7 days after graft insertion into the arterial circulation. At 7 days after insertion, the release of TGF-β by the graft is doubled, but at 4 and 12 weeks, it is triple that in a control vein.[235] TGF-β gene transfer causes significant rises in intimal hyperplasia as well as increases in SMC content, contraction, and sensitivity to serotonin.[236]

Proteases

There are limited data on the role of proteases in vein grafts. MMPs have been studied in organ cultures of human saphenous veins. There are increases in expression of MMP-9 and MMP-2, which are exacerbated by surgical preparation of the veins.[237-239] Furthermore, expression of MT-MMP-1, an activator of MMPs, is apparently unaffected.[240] However, increases in TIMP-1 and TIMP-2 are greater than those in MMP-9 and MMP-2.[241] Similar results have been seen in rabbit and porcine models of vein interposition grafts.[242-244] Overexpression of TIMPs decreases the development of intimal hyperplasia in organ culture models and in animal models.[245-247] Both uPA and tPA have been detected in the human saphenous veins in culture, and SMC proliferation can be inhibited by inhibition of plasmin activity[248,249]; migration is unaffected. Intimal thickness in these veins is also reduced by plasmin inhibition. A possible mechanism for these responses is the finding that inhibition of plasmin results in a decrease in FGF-2 in the media; blocking FGF-2 produces the same result as plasmin inhibition.[248] Using a perfused transcapillary culture system of SMCs and endothelial cells, Redmond and colleagues[250] demonstrated that uPA expression is significantly elevated in SMCs by increased pulse pressure, and these conditioned SMCs show enhanced migration. This enhanced migration could be inhibited by plasmin inhibitors and uPA antibodies; the findings could not be reproduced in uPA–deficient SMCs.[250] In rabbit vein grafts, there is an upregulation of uPA mRNA by 20-fold at 2 days and by 18-fold at 1 week, which falls to 5-fold the value in control vein 2 to 8 weeks postoperatively.[228]

In a porcine vein graft model, pro-MMP-2 and active MMP-2 were present in veins and were increased 4- to 6-fold at 7 days after insertion of the graft into the arterial circulation. MMP-9 was not detectable in veins but was increased in vein grafts after 2 days, rising further after 7 days (6-fold) and 28 days (15-fold).[244] Expression of MMP-2 and MMP-9 protein was detected in the vessels over the same time course as the activity assays. Immunocytochemical methods showed MMP-2 to be widely distributed but MMP-9 to be concentrated in highly proliferative SMCs at the superficial layers of the neointima.[244] Similar findings have been documented in rabbit vein grafts.[243] Local TIMP-2 gene transfer into vein grafts significantly decreases development of intimal hyperplasia.[251]

In the first week, intimal and medial thickening is associated with an increase in SMC number. Between 1 and 4 weeks, intimal and medial thickening continues without a rise in cell number but with a decrease in cell density.[252] In the intimal hyperplasia of vein grafts, the extracellular matrix consists of type I collagen, heparan sulfate, and chondroitin sulfate with a dedifferentiated SMC phenotype. Between 4 and 39 weeks, a slower increase in intimal and medial thickening continues without a rise in cell number or cell density but with a change in SMC phenotype back to a differentiated phenotype.[252,253] There is a significant increase in transcription of hyaluronic acid synthase-1 and the integrin receptor for hyaluron in vein grafts compared with ungrafted vein grafts.[254]

Hemodynamics

Changes in hemodynamic parameters have been shown to affect the structure of both normal and diseased vessels.[156] Hemodynamic alterations are implicated in the intimal response of vein grafts.[158,255-266] Evidence suggests that deformation of SMCs by arterial hemodynamics can lead to activation of protein tyrosine kinases and thereby initiate SMC proliferation.[154] Vein grafts with lower flows are associated with greater intimal thickening.[259] In one study, 50% reduction in arterial blood flow increased intimal hyperplasia by 60% and medial hypertrophy by 17% in arterial vein grafts after 4 weeks.[267] Similarly, low shear stress is also associated with increased development of intimal hyperplasia in vein grafts.[260,262] Dobrin and associates[158,263] have shown in vein grafts that blood flow (closely associated with shear stress) is best associated with the formation of intimal hyperplasia and that deformation of the vessel wall in a circumferential direction is best associated with medial thickening. Similarly, accelerated intimal thickening develops in vein grafts under low flow conditions (poor distal runoff) and is reversed when these vessels are re-implanted into a system with normal parameters of flow.[264,268] In a poor runoff model, intimal hyperplasia was accelerated at 2 and 4 weeks after implantation. SMC proliferation in the media was equal at 3 to 5 days; however, SMC proliferation was significantly increased at 1 (peak) and 2 weeks in the intima of the grafts with poor runoff compared with controls.[269]

Maximal circumferential tensile stresses in vein graft stenoses are higher than in native coronary artery atherosclerotic stenoses.[270] Several studies have shown that rigid external support of a vein graft reduces intimal hyperplasia and can preserve endothelium-dependent responses in vein grafts.[271-274] In control grafts, Bamberg and colleagues[275] observed initial loss of endothelial cells and SMCs with elastin breakdown, followed by impaired endothelial regeneration and significant graft wall thickening. Elastic tissue was replaced by collagen type I and chondroitin sulfate. In grafts covered with a Vicryl mesh, they found the elastin layers to be "densified, distended, and separated" by a neointimal growth of irregular thickness. Endothelial injury was minimized, but a macrophage reaction was triggered by the mesh.[275] In particular, external stenting of porcine vein grafts decreases cell proliferation and reduces both intimal (71%) and medial response (71%) with an increased luminal area.[276,277] Other studies have suggested a role for higher wall tension in the development of intimal hyperplasia.[261,265] One study has shown that rabbit arterial vein grafts removed from the arterial circulation after 2 weeks and then returned to the venous circulation for 2 weeks demonstrate a significant regression of both intimal and medial thickening in the re-implanted grafts with restoration of endothelium-dependent relaxation to all agonists.[278] Using a similar procedure in a canine model, Fann and colleagues[279] have shown that vein graft intimal hyperplasia is not reduced when a graft implanted for 12 weeks is returned to the venous circulation for 12 weeks and then harvested.[279] However, the medial area regressed significantly in this study, suggesting that circumferential deformation of the vessel wall is the dominant factor in the stimulation of medial thickening and that alterations in flow are responsible for the decreases in intimal hyperplasia. Experimental arterial vein grafts returned to the venous circulation produce PDGF and bFGF equivalent to the control vein at 2 and 8 weeks, a pattern that matches the regression of intimal hyperplasia in the vein grafts.[232,234] Similarly, the release of TGF-β by vein grafts is six times that of the control vein at 2 weeks, and twice that at 8 weeks, after replacement into the arterial circulation; this pattern also matches the regression of intimal hyperplasia.[235]

Systemic Vascular Diseases

With few exceptions, patients who undergo vein bypass grafting have significant arteriopathy and concomitantly have one or more atherogenic risk factors. Hypertension in both human and experimental models does not affect the development of intimal hyperplasia in the short or long term.[280-283] Furthermore, it appears that hypertension is not associated with the later development of vein graft atherosclerosis.[280] In contrast, both experimental and clinical studies have shown an association of hyperlipidemia with the development of intimal hyperplasia-atherosclerosis and with higher vein graft failure rates.[280,284,285] Clinically, diabetes does not appear to significantly affect vein graft patency; experimentally, however, the disorder does increase short-term development of intimal hyperplasia.[280,286] A combination of hypertension and hyperlipidemia appears to have no additive effect on intimal hyperplasia development in vein grafts compared with hyperlipidemia alone. In contrast, however, the combined presence of diabetes and hyperlipidemia has significant additive effects on the formation of intimal hyperplasia in experimental vein grafts. Interestingly, the profile of vasomotor function of vein grafts, in situations in which more than one atherogenic risk factor is present, is attenuated compared with situations in which only one disease state is present, and the observed profiles are very similar to those observed in retrieved human vein grafts.[287]

The intimal hyperplastic lesions of vein grafts retrieved 1 month after aortocoronary bypass in humans have been shown to consist of proliferating SMCs with only scattered macrophages in the subendothelium.[288] Under hyperlipidemic conditions, venous tissue has demonstrated an avidity for the uptake of serum lipid, surpassing that of arterial tissue in the same species.[289,290] Cholesterol concentrations are slightly elevated 1 week after grafting but return to normal 4 weeks after grafting.[291] Intimal hyperplasia of rabbit femoral vein grafts is accelerated in the presence of hypercholesterolemia, and macrophages have been shown to infiltrate the outer layers of intimal hyperplasia. SMC proliferation is higher in the presence of hypercholesterolemia.[268] The mature intimal hyperplastic lesions of these vein grafts are composed predominantly of lipid-laden SMCs, with macrophages in various stages of foam cell formation interspersed between them.[284,285,292] In areas with a valve, there is increased SMC proliferation early and intimal hyperplasia late.[293] Presence of valves in hyperlipidemic vein grafts is associated with augmented and accelerated lesion development.[294]

Macrophages are one of the principal cells involved in the development of atherosclerosis through the oxidation of lipoproteins and the formation of lipid peroxides.[295-297] Oxygen free radicals and lipid peroxides also interfere with the vasomotor function of both endothelial and SMCs.[298-301] Reduction of both cholesterol and LDL is considered useful in slowing and preventing atherogenesis.[302] In experimental vein grafts, reduction in serum cholesterol by 20% in hypercholesterolemic rabbits with either lovastatin therapy or ileal bypass surgery resulted in a significant decrease in total graft cholesterol content.[303] In rabbits, a 74% drop in serum cholesterol concentrations over the first 28 postoperative days is associated with a 26% reduction in graft intimal thickness and the macroscopic absence of atheromatous lesions in the graft wall compared with untreated controls.[304] A reduction of 26% in serum cholesterol in patients at 4 years after aortocoronary bypass surgery, through combined colestipol and niacin therapy for 2 years, reduced the occurrence of stenotic and occlusive lesions in the vein bypass grafts of 16% of the patients, suggesting that reduction of serum cholesterol may improve long-term vein graft patency.[305] In genetically altered atheromatous rabbit vein grafts, there is a marked decrease in superoxide production. Untreated vein grafts show an approximate threefold increase in superoxide production compared with jugular vein and a 50% increase compared with the carotid artery.[306]

With particular regard to peripheral vein graft stenoses, no association has been found with patient age or sex, presenting symptoms, hypertension, diabetes, or the condition of the outflow vessel. The incidence of stenosis appears higher the more distal the insertion.[307] Higher plasma fibrinogen concentrations have been identified as a potent risk factor for vein graft stenosis.[308] Increased homocysteine concentrations are also associated with greater incidence of vein graft stenosis.[309] Antibodies to cardiolipin are associated with failure of infrainguinal vein bypass.[310] Other studies have suggested that platelet dysfunction and lipoprotein(a) may be associated with a higher risk of stenosis development.[311,312] Smoking and plasma concentrations of fibrinogen, lipoprotein(a), and serotonin are associated with the development of postoperative infrainguinal graft stenosis.[307,312,313] Other studies have suggested that there is no association between preoperative serum lipoprotein(a) and homocysteine levels and the frequency of 1 year graft occlusions.[314] Lower serum cholesterol levels are associated with lower rates of vein graft obstruction for up to 7 years,[315] and high patency rates can be achieved in persons with familial hypercholesterolemia by means of aggressive lipid-lowering therapy.[316] The Post Coronary Artery Bypass Graft (CABG) Trial, sponsored by the National Heart, Lung, and Blood Institute (NHLBI), has shown that although saphenous vein graft atherosclerosis worsens with increasing age, lipid-lowering therapy can significantly reduce the probability of saphenous vein graft disease regardless of the time of initiation of lipid-lowering therapy.[317] Gemfibrozil has been shown to retard the progression of coronary atherosclerosis and the formation of bypass graft lesions after CABG in men with a low level of high-density lipoprotein (HDL) cholesterol.[318]

Vein grafts retrieved from patients with angiographic evidence of occlusive disease demonstrate histologic features of atherosclerosis.[281,282,319-322] The earliest these lesions have been seen is 6 months after implantation. Thus, it appears that these late occlusions of vein bypass grafts are due to the development of a rapidly progressive and structurally distinct form of atherosclerosis that has been termed *accelerated atherosclerosis* in order to distinguish it from *spontaneous atherosclerosis*.[201] Accelerated atherosclerosis is morphologically different from spontaneous atherosclerosis in that its lesions appear to be diffuse, to be more concentric, and to have a greater cellularity with varying degrees of lipid accumulation and mononuclear cell infiltration. The syndrome of accelerated atherosclerosis shares many of the pathophysiologic features of intimal hyperplasia; however, the prime mediator of this type of atherosclerosis is likely to be the macrophage. In addition, the endothelium overlying accelerated atherosclerotic lesions expresses the class II MHC antigens, which are not observed in spontaneous atherosclerosis.

■ CONCLUSION

Intimal hyperplasia remains a significant complication of interventional vascular procedures, whether open or percutaneous. Substantial advances in our understanding of vessel wall physiology, biology, pharmacology, and pathology as they relate to the development of intimal hyperplasia have been made in the last two decades. However, we have not, as yet, managed to translate this knowledge into effective therapeutic regimens to allow us to control the progression of this disease. Intimal hyperplasia therefore remains the major short-term obstacle to patent angioplastied vessels and bypass grafts.

REFERENCES

1. Ross R: The pathogenesis of atherosclerosis: An update. N Engl J Med 314:488-500, 1986.
2. Clowes AW, Reidy MA, Clowes MM: Kinetics of cellular proliferation after arterial injury. I: Smooth muscle cell growth in the absence of endothelium. Lab Invest 49:327-333, 1983.
3. Perlman HM, Krasinski L, Walsh K: Evidence for the rapid onset of apoptosis in medial smooth muscle cells after balloon injury. Circulation 95:981-987, 1997.
4. Clowes AW, Schwartz SM: Significance of quiescent smooth muscle cell migration in the injured rat carotid artery. Circ Res 56:139-145, 1985.
5. Hanke H, Strohschneider T, Oberhoff M, et al: Time course of smooth muscle cell proliferation in the intima and media of arteries following experimental angioplasty. Circ Res 67:651-659, 1990.
6. Majesky MW, Schwartz SM, Clowes MM, Clowes AW: Heparin regulates smooth muscle S phase entry in the injured rat carotid artery. Circ Res 61:296-300, 1987.
7. More RS, Rutty G, Underwood MJ, et al: Assessment of myointimal cellular kinetics in a model of angioplasty by means of proliferating cell nuclear antigen expression. Am Heart J 128:681-686, 1994.
8. Waksman R, Rodriquez JC, Robinson KA, et al: Effect of intravascular irradiation on cell proliferation, apoptosis and vascular remodeling after balloon overstretch injury of porcine coronary arteries. Circulation 96:1944-1952, 1997.
9. Ferns GA, Raines EW, Sprugel KH, et al: Inhibition of neointimal smooth muscle accumulation after angioplasty by an antibody to PDGF. Science 253:1129-1132, 1991.
10. Scott NA, Martin F, Simonet L, et al: Contribution of adventitial myofibroblasts to vascular remodeling and lesion formation after experimental angioplasty in pig coronaries [abstract]. FASEB J 9:A845, 1995.
11. Ferrer P, Valentine M, Jenkins-West T, et al: Periadventitial changes in the balloon injured rat carotid artery [abstract]. FASEB J 10:A618, 1996.
12. O'Brien ER, Alpers CE, Stewart DK, et al: Proliferation in primary and restenotic coronary atherectomy tissue: Implications for antiproliferative therapy. Circ Res 73:223-231, 1993.
13. Bauriedel G, Windstetter U, DeMaio SJJ, et al: Migratory activity of human smooth muscle cells cultivated from coronary and peripheral primary and restenotic lesions removed by percutaneous atherectomy. Circulation 85:554-564, 1992.
14. Rekhter MD, Schwartz SM, O'Brien E, et al: Collagen I gene expression in human coronary lesions, primary atherosclerotic versus re-stenosis [abstract]. Circulation 88:I228, 1993.
15. Sarembock IJ, LaVeau PJ, Sigal SL, et al: Influence of inflation pressure and balloon size on the development of intimal hyperplasia after balloon angioplasty: A study in the atherosclerotic rabbit. Circulation 80:1029-1040, 1989.
16. VanErven L, Post MJ, Velema E, Borst C: In the normal rabbit femoral artery increasing arterial wall injury does not lead to increased intimal hyperplasia. J Vasc Res 31:153-162, 1994.
17. Sakamoto H, Nozaki S, Misumi K, et al: Smooth muscle cell proliferation in the arterial intima after stretch injury—relationship between and severity of stretching and intimal hyperplasia in the New Zealand White rabbits. Exp Anim 45:89-93, 1996.
18. Clowes AW, Reidy MA, Clowes MM: Mechanisms of stenosis after arterial injury. Lab Invest 49:208-215, 1983.
19. Clowes AW, Clowes MM, Fingerle J, Reidy MA: Regulation of smooth muscle cell growth in injured artery. J Cardiovasc Pharmacol 14(Suppl 6):S12-S15, 1989.
20. Andersen HR, Maeng M, Thorwest M, Falk E: Remodeling rather than neointimal formation explains luminal narrowing after deep vessel wall injury—insights from a porcine coronary (re)stenosis model. Circulation 93:1716-1724, 1996.
21. Moornekamp FN, Borst C, Post MJ: Endothelial cell recoverage and intimal hyperplasia after endothelium removal with or without smooth muscle cell necrosis in the rabbit carotid artery. J Vasc Res 33:146-155, 1996.
22. Wilentz JR, Sanborn TA, Haudenschild CC, et al: Platelet accumulation in experimental angioplasty: Time course and relation to vascular injury. Circulation 75:635-642, 1987.
23. Kaplan AV, Leung L-K, Leung W-H, et al: Roles of thrombin and platelet membrane glycoprotein IIb/IIIa in platelet-subendothelial deposition after angioplasty in an ex-vivo whole artery model. Circulation 84:1279-1288, 1991.
24. Bates ER, McGillem MJ, Mickelson JK, et al: A monoclonal antibody to the platelet receptor GPIIb/IIIa prevents platelet aggregation and thrombosis in a canine model of coronary angioplasty. Circulation 84:2463-2469, 1991.
25. Bates ER, Walsh DG, Mu D-X, et al: Sustained inhibition of the vessel wall–platelet interaction after deep coronary artery injury by temporary inhibition of the platelet glycoprotein IIb/IIIa receptor. Coron Artery Dis 3:67-76, 1992.
26. Fingerle J, Johnson R, Clowes AW, et al: Role of platelets in smooth muscle cell proliferation and migration after vascular injury in rat carotid artery. Proc Natl Acad Sci U S A 86:8412-8416, 1989.
27. Schmaier AH: Contact activation: A revision. Thromb Haemost 78:101-107, 1997.
28. Marmur JD, Guha A, Nemerson Y, Taubman MB: Arterial smooth muscle expresses tissue factor in response to balloon injury and growth factors [abstract]. Circulation 86(Suppl I):I20, 1992.
29. Hatakeyama K, Asada Y, Marutsuka K, et al: Expression of tissue factor in the rabbit aorta after balloon injury. Atherosclerosis 139:265-271, 1998.
30. Hasentaub D, Lea H, Hart CE, et al: Tissue factor overexpression in rat arterial neointima models thrombosis and progression of advanced atherosclerosis. Circulation 101:2651-2657, 2000.
31. Speidel CM, Eisenberg PR, Ruf W, et al: Tissue factor mediates prolonged procoagulant activity on the luminal surface of balloon injured aortas in rabbits. Circulation 92:3323-3330, 1995.
32. Marmur JD, Rossikhina M, Guha A, et al: Tissue factor is rapidly induced in arterial smooth muscle after balloon injury. J Clin Invest 91:2253-2259, 1993.
33. Kato H: Regulation of functions of vascular wall cells by tissue factor pathway inhibitor. Arterioscler Thromb Vasc Biol 22:539-548, 2002.
34. Oltrona L, Speidel CM, Rechia D, et al: Inhibition of tissue factor mediated coagulation markedly attenuates stenosis after balloon induced arterial injury in minipigs. Circulation 96:646-652, 1997.
35. Khouri RK, Brown DM, Choi ET, et al: Local application of TFPI inhibits intimal hyperplasia induced by arterial interventions. Surg Forum 47:389-391, 1996.
36. Ragni M, Golino P, Scognamiglio A, et al: Endogenous tissue factor pathway inhibitor modulates thrombus formation in an in vivo model of rabbit carotid artery stenosis and endothelial injury. Circulation 102:113-117, 2000.
37. Jang Y, Guzman LA, Lincoff AM, et al: Influence of blockade at specific levels of the coagulation cascade on re-stenosis in a rabbit atherosclerotic femoral artery injury model. Circulation 92:3041-3050, 1995.
38. Ragosta M, Gimple LW, Gertz SD, et al: Specific factor Xa inhibition reduces re-stenosis after balloon angioplasty of atherosclerotic femoral arteries in rabbits. Circulation 89:1262-1271, 1994.

39. Schwartz RS, Holder DJ, Holmes DR, et al: Neointimal thickening after severe coronary injury is limited by short-term administration of factor Xa inhibitor results in a porcine model. Circulation 93:1543-1548, 1996.
40. Bar-Shavit R, Eldor A, Vlodavsky I: Binding of thrombin to subendothelial extracellular matrix: Protection and expression of functional properties. J Clin Invest 84:1096-1104, 1989.
41. Ozazaki H, Majesky MW, Harker LA, Schwartz SM: Regulation of platelet-derived growth factor ligand and receptor gene expression by alpha-thrombin in vascular smooth muscle cells. Circ Res 71:1285-1293, 1992.
42. Wilcox JN, Rodriguez J, Subramanian RR, et al: Characterization of thrombin receptor expression during vascular lesion formation. Circ Res 75:1029-1038, 1994.
43. Witmer MR, Hatton MWC: Antithrombin III-β associates more readily than antithrombin III-α with uninjured and de-endothelialized aortic wall in vitro and in vivo. Arterioscler Thromb 11:530-539, 1991.
44. Serruys PW, Herrman J-P, Simon R, Helvetica I: A comparison of hirudin with heparin in the prevention of re-stenosis after coronary angioplasty. N Engl J Med 333:757-763, 1995.
45. Tanaka H, Sukhova G, Swanson SJ, et al: Sustained activation of vascular cells and leukocytes in the rabbit aorta after balloon injury. Circulation 88:1788-1803, 1993.
46. Yasukawa HI, Imaizumi T, Matsuoka H, et al: Inhibition of intimal hyperplasia after balloon injury by antibodies to ICAM-1 and LFA-1. Circulation 95:1515-1522, 1997.
47. Landry DB, Couper LL, Bryant SR, Lindner V: Activation of the NFκB and IκB system in smooth muscle cells after rat arterial injury: Induction of VCAM-1 and MCP-1. Am J Pathol 151:1085-1095, 1997.
48. Cole EW, Hagen P-O, Mikat E, et al: Association of polymorphonuclear leukocytes with sites of aortic catheter-induced injury in rabbits. Arteriosclerosis 67:229-236, 1987.
49. Lucas JF, Makhoul RG, Cole EW, et al: Mononuclear cells adhere to sites of vascular balloon catheter injury. Curr Surg 43:112-115, 1986.
50. Schwartz RS, Edwards WD, Camrud AR, Holms DRJ: Developmental stages of restenotic neointimal hyperplasia following porcine coronary artery injury: A morphologic review. J Vasc Med Biol 4:70-78, 1993.
51. Kling D, Fingerle J, Harlan JM: Inhibition of leukocyte extravasation with a monoclonal antibody to CD18 during formation of experimental intimal thickening in rabbit carotid arteries. Arterioscler Thromb 12:997-1007, 1992.
52. Guzman LA, Whitlow PL, Beall CJ, Kolattakudy P: Monocyte chemotactic protein antibody inhibits re-stenosis in the rabbit atherosclerotic model [abstract]. Circulation 88:I371, 1993.
53. Kamenz J, Hanke H, Ulmer A, et al: Occurrence of intimal macrophage following experimental balloon angioplasty: Relation to the proliferative response of smooth muscle cells [abstract]. Circulation 86(Suppl I): I847, 1992.
54. Verheyen AK, Vlaminckz EM, Lauwers FM, et al: Identification of macrophages in intimal thickening of rat carotid arteries by cytochemical localization of purine nucleotide phosphorylase. Arteriosclerosis 8:759-767, 1988.
55. Klagsbrun M, Edelman ER: Biological and biochemical properties of fibroblast growth factors. Arteriosclerosis 9:269-278, 1989.
56. Gospodarowicz D, Ferrara N, Schweigerer L, Neufeld G: Structural characterization and biological functions of fibroblast growth factor. Endocr Rev 8:95-114, 1987.
57. Casscells W, Lappi D, Shrivastav S, et al: Regulation of the fibroblast growth factor system in vascular injury [abstract]. Circulation 86(Suppl I):I84, 1992.
58. Lindner V, Majack RA, Reidy MA: Basic fibroblast growth factor stimulates endothelial regrowth and proliferation in denuded arteries. J Clin Invest 85:2004-2008, 1990.
59. Lindner V, Reidy MA: Proliferation of smooth muscle cells after vascular injury is inhibited by an antibody against basic fibroblast growth factor. Proc Natl Acad Sci U S A 88:3739-3743, 1991.
60. Olsen NE, Chao S, Lindner V, Reidy MA: Intimal smooth muscle cell proliferation after balloon catheter injury: The role of basic fibroblast growth factor. Am J Pathol 140:1017-1023, 1992.
61. Lindner V, Reidy MA: Expression of basic fibroblast growth factor and its receptor by smooth muscle cells and endothelium in injured rat arteries: An en face study. Circ Res 73:589-595, 1993.
62. Bjornsson TD, Dryjski M, Tluczek J, et al: Acidic fibroblast growth factor promotes vascular repair. Proc Natl Acad Sci U S A 88:8651-8655, 1991.
63. Nabel EG, Yang ZY, Plautz G, et al: Recombinant fibroblast growth factor-1 promotes intimal hyperplasia and angiogenesis in arteries in vivo. Nature 362:844-846, 1993.
64. Dzau VJ: Evolving concepts of the renin-angiotensin system. Am J Hypertens 1:334S-337S, 1988.
65. Dzau VJ: Implications of local angiotensin production in cardiovascular physiology and pharmacology. Am J Cardiol 59:59A-65A, 1987.
66. Rakugi H, Dzau VJ, Pratt RE: Importance of tissue angiotensin converting enzyme (ACE) in neointimal hyperplasia [abstract]. Circulation 86(Suppl I):I169, 1992.
67. Powell JS, Clozel JP, Muller RKM, et al: Inhibitors of angiotensin converting enzyme prevent myointimal proliferation after vascular injury. Science 245:186-188, 1989.
68. Miyauchi K, Kawai S, Okado R, Yamaguchi H: Limitation of angiotensin converting enzyme (ACE) inhibitor in re-stenosis of deep arterial injury models [abstract]. Circulation 86(Suppl I):I187, 1992.
69. Griendling KK, Murphy TJ, Alexander RW: Molecular biology of the renin angiotensin system. Circulation 87:1816-1828, 1993.
70. Itoh H, Pratt RE, Gibbons G, Dzau VJ: Angiotensin II modulates proliferation of vascular smooth muscle cells (VSMC) via dual autocrine loops of TGF-β and bFGF. Hypertension 18:396, 1991.
71. Daemon M, Lombardi DM, Bosman FT, Schwartz SM: Angiotensin II induces smooth muscle cell proliferation in the normal and injured arterial wall. Circ Res 68:450-456, 1991.
72. Kauffman RF, Bean JS, Zimmerman KM, et al: Losartan, a nonpeptide angiotensin II receptor antagonist inhibits neointima formation following balloon injury to rat carotid arteries. Life Sci 49:223-228, 1991.
73. Bilazarian SD, Currier JW, Kakuta T, et al: Angiotensin II antagonism does not prevent re-stenosis after rabbit iliac angioplasty [abstract]. Circulation 86(Suppl I):I187, 1992.
74. Janiak P, Pillon A, Prost JF, Vilaine JP: Role of angiotensin subtype 2 receptor in neointima formation after vascular injury. Hypertension 20:737-745, 1992.
75. Casscells W: Migration of smooth muscle and endothelial cells. Circulation 86:723-729, 1992.
76. Bornfeldt KE, Raines EW, Graves LM, et al: PDGF: Distinct signal transduction pathways associated with migration versus proliferation. Ann N Y Acad Sci 766:416-430, 1995.
77. Ross R: Platelet-derived growth factor. Lancet i(8648):1179-1182, 1989.
78. Hart CE, Kraiss LW, Vergel S, et al: PDGF beta receptor blockade inhibits intimal hyperplasia in the baboon. Circulation 99:564-569, 1999.
79. Koyama N, Hart CE, Clowes AW: Different functions of the PDGF α and β receptors for the migration and proliferation of cultured baboon smooth muscle cells. Circ Res 75:682-691, 1994.
80. Inui H, Kitami Y, Tani M, et al: Differences in signal transduction between PDGF alpha and beta receptors in vascular smooth muscle cells: PDGF-BB is a potent mitogen but PDGF-AA promotes protein synthesis without activation of DNA synthesis. J Biol Chem 269:30546-30552, 1994.
81. Koyama N, Morisaki N, Saito Y, Yoshida S: Regulatory effects of PDGF-AA homodimer on migration of vascular smooth muscle cells. J Biol Chem 267:22806-22812, 1992.
82. Davies MG, Owens EL, Lea H, et al: Effect of PDGF receptor-α and -β blockade on flow induced neointimal formation in endothelialized baboon vascular grafts. Circ Res 86:779-786, 2000.

83. Majesky MW, Reidy MA, Bowen-Pope DF, et al: PDGF ligand and receptor gene expression during repair of arterial injury. J Cell Biol 111:2149-2158, 1990.
84. Walker LN, Bowen-Pope DF, Ross R, Reidy MA: Production of platelet-derived growth factor-like molecules by cultured arterial smooth muscle cells accompanies proliferation after arterial injury. Proc Natl Acad Sci U S A 83:7311-7315, 1986.
85. Consigny PM, Bilder GE: Expression and release of smooth muscle cell mitogens in the arterial wall after balloon angioplasty. J Vasc Med Biol 4:1-8, 1993.
86. Bowen-Pope DF, Hart CE, Seifert RA: Sera and conditioned media contain different isoforms of platelet-derived growth factors (PDGF) which bind to different classes of PDGF receptors. J Biol Chem 264:2502-2508, 1989.
87. Nabel EG, Yang ZY, Liptay S, et al: Recombinant platelet-derived growth factor B gene expression in porcine arteries induces intimal hyperplasia in vivo. J Clin Invest 91:1822-1829, 1993.
88. Jawien A, Bowen-Pope DF, Lindner V, et al: Platelet-derived growth factor promotes smooth muscle migration and intimal thickening in a rat model of balloon angioplasty. J Clin Invest 89:507-511, 1992.
89. Serruys PW, Heyndrickx GR, Patel J, et al: Effect of an anti-PDGF-β-receptor-blocking antibody on re-stenosis in patients undergoing elective stent placement. Int J Cardiovasc Intervent 5:214-222, 2003.
90. Nagase H, Woessner JF: Matrix metalloproteinases. J Biol Chem 274:21491-21494, 1999.
91. Birkedal-Hansen H: Proteolytic remodeling of extracellular matrix. Curr Opin Cell Biol 7:728-735, 1995.
92. Carmeliet P, Collen D: Development and disease in proteinase-deficient mice: Role of the plasminogen, matrix metalloproteinase and coagulation system. Thromb Res 91:255-285, 1998.
93. Lijnen HR, Collen D: Mechanisms of physiological fibrinolysis. Bailliere's Clin Haematol 8:277-290, 1995.
94. VanLeeuwen RTJ: Extracellular proteolysis and the migrating vascular smooth muscle cell. Fibrinolysis 10:59-74, 1996.
95. Lijnen HR: Molecular interactions between the plasminogen/plasmin and matrix metalloproteinase systems. Fibrinolysis Proteolysis 14:175-181, 2000.
96. Strauss BH, Lau HK, Bowman KA, et al: Plasma urokinase antigen and PAI-1 antigen levels predict angiographic coronary re-stenosis. Circulation 100:1616-1622, 1999.
97. Clowes AW, Reidy MA, Clowes MM, Belin D: Smooth muscle cells express urokinase during mitogenesis and tissue-type plasminogen activator during migration in injured rat carotid. Circ Res 67:61-67, 1990.
98. Bendeck MP, Zempo N, Clowes AW, et al: Smooth muscle cell migration and matrix metalloproteinase expression after arterial injury in the rat. Circ Res 75:539-545, 1994.
99. Plekhanova OS, Parfenova EV, Bibilashvily RS, et al: Urokinase plasminogen activator enhances neointima growth and reduces lumen size in carotid arteries. J Hypertens 18:10065-10069, 2000.
100. Kanamasa K, Otani N, Ishida N, et al: Suppression of cell proliferation by tPA during the early phase after balloon injury minimizes intimal hyperplasia in hypercholesterolemic rabbits. J Cardiovasc Pharmacol 37:155-162, 2001.
101. Hasentaub D, Forough R, Clowes AW: Plasminogen activator inhibitor type I and tissue inhibitor of metalloproteinase-2 increase after arterial injury in rats. Circ Res 80:490-496, 1997.
102. Hamdan AD, Quist WC, Gagne JB, Feener EP: ACE inhibition suppresses PAI-1 expression in the neointima of balloon injured rat aorta. Circulation 93:1073-1078, 1996.
103. Hasentaub D, Lea H, Clowes AW: Local plasminogen activator inhibitor type 1 overexpression in rat carotid artery enhances thrombosis and endothelial regeneration while inhibiting intimal thickening. Arterioscler Thromb Vasc Biol 20:853-859, 2000.
104. Shen GX: Vascular cell-derived fibrinolytic regulators and atherothrombotic vascular disorders. Int J Mol Med 1:399-408, 1998.
105. Zempo N, Kenargy RD, Au YPT, et al: Matrix metalloproteinase of vascular wall cells are increased in balloon injured rat carotid artery. J Vasc Surg 20:209-217, 1994.
106. Southgate KM, Fisher M, Banning A, et al: Upregulation of basement membrane degrading metalloproteinase secretion after balloon injury of pig carotid arteries. Circ Res 79:1177-1187, 1996.
107. Lijnen HR, VanHoef B, Lupu F, et al: Function of the plasminogen/plasmin and MMP systems after vascular injury in mice with targeted inactivation of fibrinolytic genes. Arterioscler Thromb Vasc Biol 18:1035-1045, 1998.
108. Jenkins GM, Crow MT, Bilato C, et al: Increased expression of MT-MMP and preferential localization of matrix metalloproteinase-2 to the neointima of balloon injured rat carotid arteries. Circulation 97:82-90, 1998.
109. Bassiouny HSS, Hong RH, Singh XF, et al: Reduced flow enhances in vivo collagenase IV transcription after arterial injury [abstract]. Circulation 94(Suppl):I349, 1996.
110. DeSmet BJ, VanderHelm Y, Horowitz A, et al: Matrix remodeling in balloon dilated and stented arteries in atherosclerotic Yucatan micropigs: Procollagen alpha1(I), alpha1(III) and MMP1 expression over time [abstract]. Circulation 94(Suppl):I403, 1996.
111. Natarajan MKR, Thompson R, Chisholm KE, et al: Increased elastolytic activity after balloon angioplasty [abstract]. Circulation 94(Suppl):I349, 1996.
112. Webb KE, Henney AM, Anglin S, et al: Expression of MMPs and their inhibitor TIMP-1 in the rat carotid artery after balloon injury. Arterioscler Thromb Vasc Biol 17:1837-1844, 1997.
113. Dollery CM, McEwan JR, Wang M, et al: TIMP-4 is regulated by vascular injury in rats. Circ Res 84:498-504, 1999.
114. Forough R, Koyama N, Hasentaub D, et al: Overexpression of TIMP-1 inhibits vascular smooth muscle cell formation in vitro and in vivo. Circ Res 79:812-820, 1996.
115. Forough R, Lea H, Starcher B, et al: Metalloproteinase blockade by local overexpression of TIMP-1 increases elastin accumulation in rat carotid artery intima. Arterioscler Thromb Vasc Biol 18:803-807, 1998.
116. Furman C, Luo Z, Walsh K, et al: Systemic tissue inhibitor of metalloproteinase-1 gene delivery reduces neointimal hyperplasia in balloon-injured rat carotid artery. FEBS Lett 531:122-126, 2002.
117. Yamamato M, Yamamoto K, Noumura T: Type I collagen promotes modulation of cultured rabbit arterial smooth muscle cells from a contractile to synthetic phenotype. Exp Cell Res 204:121-129, 1993.
118. Amento EP, Ehsani N, Palmer H, Libby P: Cytokines and growth factors positively and negatively regulate interstitial collagen gene expression in human vascular smooth muscle cells. Arterioscler Thromb 11:1223-1230, 1991.
119. Thie M, Schlumberger W, Semich R, et al: Aortic smooth muscle cells in collagen lattice culture: Effects on ultrastructure, proliferation and collagen synthesis. Eur J Cell Biol 55:295-304, 1991.
120. Thie M, Harrach B, Schonhert E, et al: Responsiveness of aortic smooth muscle cells to soluble growth mediators is influenced by cell matrix contact. Arterioscler Thromb 13:994-1003, 1993.
121. Redecker-Beuke B, Thie M, Rauterberg J, Robenek H: Aortic smooth muscle cells in a three dimensional collagen lattice culture: Evidence for post-translational regulation of collagen synthesis. Arterioscler Thromb 13:1572-1579, 1993.
122. Paye M, Nusgens B, Lapiere C: Modulation of cellular biosynthetic activity in the retracting collagen lattice. Eur J Cell Biol 45:44-50, 1987.
123. Gillery P, Leperre A, Coustry F, et al: Different regulation of collagen I gene transcription in three dimensional lattice cultures. FEBS Lett 296:297-299, 1992.
124. Wight TN: Cell biology of arterial proteoglycans. Arteriosclerosis 9:1-20, 1989.
125. Alvani M, Moore S: Glycosaminoglycans composition and biosynthesis in the endothelium-covered neointima and de-endothelialized rabbit aorta. Exp Mol Pathol 42:389-400, 1985.

126. Clowes AW, Karnovsky MJ: Suppression by heparin of smooth muscle cell proliferation in injured arteries. Nature 265:625-627, 1979.
127. Castellot JI, Favreau LV, Karnovsky MJ, Rosenberg RD: Inhibition of vascular smooth muscle cell growth by endothelium cell-derived heparin. J Biol Chem 257:11256-11260, 1982.
128. Majack RA, Clowes AW: Inhibition of vascular smooth muscle cell migration by heparin-like glycosaminoglycans. J Cell Physiol 118:253-256, 1984.
129. Majack RA, Coates-Cook S, Bernstein P: Platelet derived growth factor and heparin-like glycosaminoglycans regulate thrombospondin synthesis and deposition in the matrix by smooth muscle cells. J Cell Biol 105:1059-1070, 1985.
130. Li Z, Alavi M, Wasty F, et al: Collagen biosynthesis by neointimal smooth muscle cells in vitro [abstract]. FASEB J 7:A798, 1993.
131. Nikkari ST, Jarvelainen HT, Wight TN, et al: Smooth muscle cell expression of extracellular matrix genes after arterial injury. Am J Pathol 144:1348-1356, 1994.
132. Strauss BH, Chisholm RJ, Keley FW, et al: Extracellular matrix remodeling after balloon angioplasty injury in a rabbit model of re-stenosis. Circ Res 75:650-658, 1994.
133. Strauss BH, Robinson R, Batchelor WB, et al: In vivo collagen turnover following experimental balloon angioplasty injury and the role of matrix metalloproteinase. Circulation 79:541-550, 1996.
134. Riessen R, Wight TN, Pastore C, et al: Distribution of hyaluron during extracellular matrix remodeling in human restenotic arteries and balloon injured rat carotid arteries. Circulation 93:1141-1147, 1996.
135. Suzuki H, Sunayama S, Kawal S, et al: ECM remodelling in restenotic human coronary atherosclerotic plaque of balloon angioplasty [abstract]. J Am Coll Cardiol 29:421A, 1997.
136. Wight TN, Lara S, Riessen R, et al: Selective deposits of versican in the ECM of restenotic lesions from human peripheral arteries. Am J Pathol 151:963-974, 1997.
137. Graf K, Meehan WP, Chen JZ, et al: Upregulation of αv, β3- and β5-integrin mRNA during neointima formation in rat aorta after balloon injury [abstract]. Circulation 94(Suppl):I41, 1996.
138. Srivatsa SS, Tsao P, Holmes DR, et al: Temporal and spatial variation in αv, β3 integrin expression following deep arterial injury in the porcine coronary re-stenosis model [abstract]. J Am Coll Cardiol 29:153A, 1997.
139. Choi ET, Sun S, Parks W, et al: Early role of collagen type I on smooth muscle cell phenotype change and intimal hyperplasia. Surg Forum 44:349-351, 1993.
140. Stouffer GA, Sajid M, Nakada MT, Runge MS: β3 integrins are upregulated following vascular injury and mediate proliferation of cultured smooth muscle cell [abstract]. J Am Coll Cardiol 29(Suppl A):3A, 1997.
141. Liaw L, Lindner V, Schwartz S, Giachelli C: Osteopontin and beta3 integrin are co-ordinately expressed during endothelial regeneration in rat arteries [abstract]. FASEB J 9:A846, 1995.
142. Corjay MH, Stoltenborg JK, Diamond SM, et al: αvβ3 and αvβ5 integrins and osteopontin are spatially and temporally regulated during early timepoints in a rabbit model of neointima formation [abstract]. Circulation 94(Suppl):I517, 1996.
143. Louden C, Zimmerman D, Wang X, Kerns WD: Expression of osteopontin in PDGF stimulated vascular smooth muscle cells and in rat carotid arteries [abstract]. FASEB J 10:A72, 1996.
144. Koyama N, Seki J, Vergel S, et al: Regulation and function of an activation dependent epitope of the β1 integrin in vascular cells after balloon injury in baboon arteries and in vitro. Am J Pathol 148:749-761, 1996.
145. McCaffrey TA: TGF-β and TGF-β receptors in atherosclerosis. Cytokine Growth Factor Rev 11:103-114, 2000.
146. Reilly CF, McFall RC: Platelet-derived growth factor and transforming growth factor-β regulate plasminogen activator inhibitor-1 synthesis in vascular smooth muscle cells. J Biol Chem 266:9419-9427, 1991.
147. Ignotz RA, Massague J: Transforming growth factor-β stimulates the expression of fibronectin and collagen and their incorporation into the extracellular matrix. J Biol Chem 261:4337-4345, 1986.
148. Majesky MW, Lindner V, Twardzik DR, et al: Production of transforming growth factor β1 during repair of arterial injury. J Clin Invest 88:904-910, 1991.
149. Kanzaki T, Tamura K, Takahashi K, et al: In vivo effect of TGF-β1: Enhanced intimal thickening by administration of TGF-β1 in rabbit arteries injured with a balloon catheter. Arterioscler Thromb 15:1951-1957, 1995.
150. Wolf YG, Rasmussen LM, Ruoslahti E: Antibodies against TGF-B1 suppress intimal hyperplasia in a rat model. J Clin Invest 93:1172-1178, 1994.
151. Reidy MA, Fingerle J, Lindner V: Factors controlling the development of arterial lesions after injury. Circulation 86(Suppl III):43-46, 1992.
152. Nabel EG, Shum L, Pompili VJ, et al: Direct gene transfer of transforming growth factor-β1 in the arterial wall stimulates fibrocellular hyperplasia [abstract]. Proc Natl Acad Sci U S A 90:10759-10763, 1993.
153. Clowes AW, Clowes MM, Fingerle J, Reidy MA: Kinetics of cellular proliferation after arterial injury. V: Role of acute distension in the induction of smooth muscle cell proliferation. Lab Invest 60:360-364, 1989.
154. Yang Z, VonSegesser L, Stulz P, et al: Pulsatile stretch and platelet-derived growth factor (PDGF): Important mechanisms for coronary venous graft disease [abstract]. Circulation 86(Suppl I):I84, 1992.
155. Slepian MJ, Gaballa MA: Vascular wall hydraulic conductivity increases following non dissecting balloon stretch injury [abstract]. Circulation 86(Suppl I):I85, 1992.
156. Glagov S, Zarins CK, Masawa N, et al: Mechanical and functional role of non-atherosclerotic intimal thickening. Front Med Biol Eng 5:37-43, 1993.
157. Hehrlein C, Chuang CH, Tuntelder JR, et al: Effects of vascular runoff on myointimal hyperplasia after mechanical balloon or thermal laser arterial injury in dogs. Circulation 84:884-890, 1991.
158. Dobrin PB, Littooy FN, Endean ED: Mechanical factors predisposing to intimal hyperplasia and medial thickening in autogenous vein grafts. Surgery 105:393-400, 1989.
159. Kohler TR, Kirkman TR, Kraiss LW, et al: Increased blood flow inhibits neointimal hyperplasia in endothelialized vascular grafts. Circ Res 69:1557-1565, 1991.
160. Kohler TR, Jawien A: Flow affects development of intimal hyperplasia after arterial injury in rats. Arterioscler Thromb 12:963-971, 1992.
161. Reis GJ, Kuntz RE, Silverman DI, Pasternak RC: Effects of serum lipid levels on re-stenosis after coronary angioplasty. Am J Cardiol 68:1431-1435, 1991.
162. Rapp JH, Ovarfordt P, Krupski WC, et al: Hypercholesterolemia and early re-stenosis after carotid endarterectomy. Surgery 101:277-282, 1987.
163. Quigley PJ, Hiatky MA, Hinohara T, et al: Repeat percutaneous transluminal coronary angioplasty and predictors of recurrent stenosis. Am J Cardiol 63:409-413, 1989.
164. Carrozza JPJ, Kuntz RE, Fishman RF, Baim DS: Re-stenosis after arterial injury caused by coronary stenting in patients with diabetes mellitus. Ann Intern Med 118:344-349, 1993.
165. Law MM, Gelabert HA, Moore WS, et al: Cigarette smoking increases the development of intimal hyperplasia after vascular injury. J Vasc Surg 23:401-409, 1996.
166. Sahni R, Maniet AR, Voci G, Banka V: Prevention of re-stenosis by lovastatin after successful angioplasty. Am Heart J 121:1600-1608, 1991.
167. Gellman J, Ezekowitz MD, Sarembock IJ, et al: Effect of lovastatin after balloon angioplasty: A study in an atherosclerotic hypercholesterolemic rabbit. J Am Coll Cardiol 17:251-259, 1991.
168. Lovastatin Re-stenosis Trial: Final results [abstract]. Lovastatin Re-stenosis Trial Study Group. Circulation 88:I506, 1993.

169. Weidinger FF, McLenachen JM, Cybulsky MJ, et al: Hypercholesterolemia enhances macrophage recruitment and dysfunction of regenerated endothelium after balloon injury of the rabbit iliac artery. Circulation 84:755-767, 1991.
170. Kisanuki A, Asada Y, Hatakeyama K, et al: Contribution of the endothelium to intimal thickening in normocholesterolemic and hypercholesterolemic rabbits. Arterioscler Thromb 12:1198-1205, 1992.
171. Stevens SL, Hilgarth K, Ryan US, et al: The synergistic effect of hypercholesterolemia and mechanical injury on intimal hyperplasia. Ann Vasc Surg 6:55-61, 1992.
172. Trachtenberg J, Choi E, Sun S, et al: Hypercholesterolemia causes increased smooth muscle cell proliferation following arterial injury [abstract]. In: Association for Academic Surgery (26th Annual Meeting). Montreal, McGill University, 1992, p 57.
173. Chang MY, Lees AM, Lees RS: Time course of ^{125}I labelled LDL accumulation in the healing balloon de-endothelialized rabbit aorta. Arterioscler Thromb 12:1088-1098, 1992.
174. Srinivasan SR, Xu J-H, Vijayagonal P, et al: Injury to the arterial wall produces proteoglycan variants with enhanced low density lipoprotein binding activity. Circulation 86(Suppl 1):I156, 1992.
175. Guarda E, Katwa LC, Campbell SE, et al: Extracellular matrix collagen synthesis and degradation following coronary balloon angioplasty. J Mol Cell Cardiol 28:699-706, 1996.
176. Oberhoff M, Hanke H, Hassenstein S, et al: Difference in the proliferative response of smooth muscle cells in normal and atherosclerotic rabbit carotid arteries after balloon angioplasty [abstract]. Arterioscler Thromb 11:1528A, 1991.
177. Stadius ML, Gown AM, Kernoff R, Schwartz SM: Does sequential balloon injury of an artery lead to a different outcome than a single injury? An experimental study of angioplasty. Coron Artery Dis 7:247-255, 1996.
178. Murcia AM, Fallon JT, Fuster V: Smooth muscle cell proliferation does not account for re-stenosis in diabetic patients [abstract]. Circulation 94(Suppl):I619, 1996.
179. Manciet LH, Copeland JG, Chavez RA, et al: Development of neointimal hyperplasia in balloon injured carotid arteries of normal and streptozocin induced diabetic rats [abstract]. FASEB J 10:A619, 1996.
180. Cwikiel W: Re-stenosis after balloon angioplasty and/or stent insertion—origin and prevention. Acta Radiol 43:442-454, 2002.
181. Lowe HC, Oesterle SN, Khachigan LM: Coronary in stent re-stenosis: Current status and future strategies. J Am Coll Cardiol 39:183-193, 2002.
182. Mehran R, Dangas G, Abizaid A, et al: Angiographic patterns of in stent re-stenosis: Classification and implications for longterm outcome. Circulation 100:1872-1878, 1999.
183. Hoffman R, Mintz GS, Dussaillant RG, et al: Patterns and mechanisms of in stent re-stenosis: A serial intravascular ultrasound study. Circulation 94:1247-1254, 1996.
184. Moreno PR, Palacios IF, Leon MN, et al: Histopathologic comparison of human coronary in stent and post balloon angioplasty restenotic tissue. Am J Cardiol 84:462-466, 1999.
185. Virmani R, Farb A: Pathology of in-stent re-stenosis. Curr Opin Lipidol 10:499-506, 1999.
186. Abizaid A, Kornowski R, Mintz GS, et al: The influence of diabetes mellitus on acute and late outcomes following coronary stent implantation. J Am Coll Cardiol 32:584-589, 1998.
187. Carter AJ, Bailey L, Devries J, Hubbard B: The effects of uncontrolled hyperglycemia on thrombosis and formation of neointima after coronary stent placement in a novel diabetic porcine model of restenosis. Coron Artery Dis 11:473-479, 2000.
188. Baier RE, Dutton RC: Initial events in interaction of blood with a foreign surface. J Biomed Mater Res 3:191, 1969.
189. Emneus H, Stenram U: Metal implants in the human body: A histopathological study. Acta Orthop Scand 36:115-126, 1965.
190. Parsson H, Cwikiel W, Johansson K, et al: Deposition of platelets and neutrophils on porcine iliac arteries and angioplasty and Wallstent placement compared with angioplasty alone. Cardiovasc Intervent Radiol 17:190-196, 1994.
191. Bai H, Masuda J, Sawa Y, et al: Neointima formation after vascular stent implantation: Spatial and chronological distribution of smooth muscle cell proliferation and phenotypic modulation. Arterioscler Thromb 14:1846-1853, 1994.
192. Schwartz RS, Huber KC, Murphy JG, et al: Re-stenosis and the proportional neointimal response to coronary artery injury: Results in a porcine model. J Am Coll Cardiol 19:267-274, 1992.
193. Kornowski R, Hong MK, Fermin OT, et al: In-stent re-stenosis: Contributions of inflammatory responses and arterial injury to neointima hyperplasia. J Am Coll Cardiol 31:224-230, 1998.
194. Sanada JL, Matsui O, Yoshikawa J, Matsuoka T: An experimental study of endovascular stenting with special reference to the effects on the aortic vasa vasorum. Cardiovasc Intervent Radiol 21:45-49, 1998.
195. Giannoukas AD, Labropoulos N, Stavridis G, et al: Pre-bypass quality assessment of the long saphenous vein wall with ultrasound and histology. Eur J Vasc Endovasc Surg 14:37-40, 1997.
196. Wilson YG, Davies AH, Currie IC, et al: Angioscopy for quality control of saphenous vein during bypass grafting. Eur J Vasc Endovasc 11:12-18, 1996.
197. Panetta TF, Marin ML, Veith FJ, et al: Unsuspected pre-existing saphenous vein disease: An unrecognized cause of vein bypass failure. J Vasc Surg 15:102-112, 1992.
198. Varty K, Allen KE, Bell PRF, London NJM: Infrainguinal vein graft stenosis. Br J Surg 80:825-833, 1993.
199. Xu Q, Zhang Z, Davison F, Hu Y: Circulating progenitor cells regenerate endothelium of vein graft atherosclerosis, which is diminished in ApoE-deficient mice. Circ Res 93:e76-e86, 2003.
200. Chervu A, Moore WS: An overview of intimal hyperplasia. Surg Gynecol Obstet 171:433-447, 1990.
201. Ip JH, Fuster V, Badimon L, et al: Syndromes of accelerated atherosclerosis: Role of vascular injury and smooth muscle cell proliferation. J Am Coll Cardiol 15:1667-1687, 1990.
202. Sayers RD, Jones L, Varty K, et al: The histopathology of infrainguinal vein graft stenoses. Eur J Vasc Surg 7:16-20, 1993.
203. Berkowitz HD, Fox AD, Deaton DH: Reversed vein graft stenosis: Early diagnosis and management. J Vasc Surg 15:130-142, 1992.
204. Mills JL, Bandyk DF, Gahtan V, et al: The origin of infrainguinal vein graft stenosis—prospective study based on duplex surveillance. J Vasc Surg 21:16-25, 1995.
205. Moody AP, Edwards PR, Harris PL: The etiology of vein graft strictures: A prospective marker study. Eur J Vasc Surg 6:509-511, 1992.
206. Adcock GD: Vein grafts: Implantation injury. J Vasc Surg 10:587-589, 1989.
207. Quist WC, LoGerfo FW: Prevention of smooth muscle cell phenotypic modulation in vein grafts: A histomorphometric study. J Vasc Surg 16:225-231, 1992.
208. Cavaliari N, Abebe W, Hunter WJ, et al: University of Wisconsin solution prevents intimal proliferation in canine autogenous vein grafts [abstract]. VIIth Annual Meeting of the European Society for Vascular Surgery, Barcelona, Sept 16-19, 1993, p 44.
209. Davies MG, Hagen P-O: Influence of perioperative storage solutions on long term vein graft function and morphology. Ann Vasc Surg 8:150-157, 1994.
210. Davies MG, Klyachkin ML, Dalen H, et al: The integrity of experimental vein graft endothelium: Implications on the etiology of early graft failure. Eur J Vasc Surg 7:156-165, 1993.
211. Carson SD, Bronza JP: The role of tissue factor in the production of thrombin. Blood Coagul Fibrinolysis 4:281-292, 1993.
212. Channon KM, Fulton GJ, Davies MG, et al: Intimal tissue factor protein expression precedes intimal hyperplasia in experimental venous bypass grafts. Arterioscler Thromb Vasc Biol 17:1313-1319, 1997.

213. Huynh TTT, Davies MG, Hagen P-O, et al: Local treatment with tissue factor pathway inhibitor reduces the development of intimal hyperplasia in experimental vein grafts [abstract]. Circulation 96(Suppl):I41, 1997.
214. Kim AY, Walinsky PL, Kolodgie FD, et al: Early loss of thrombomodulin expression impairs vein graft thromboresistance: Implications for vein graft failure. Circ Res 90:205-212, 2002.
215. Sperry JL, Deming CB, Bian C, et al: Wall tension is a potent negative regulator of in vivo thrombomodulin expression. Circ Res 92:41-74, 2003.
216. Solymoss BC, Nadeau P, Millette D, Campeau L: Late thrombosis of saphenous vein coronary bypass graft related to risk factors [abstract]. Circulation 78(Suppl II):140, 1988.
217. Davies MG, Klyachkin ML, Dalen H, et al: The early morphology of veno-venous bypass grafts. Cardiovasc Surg 5:82-91, 1997.
218. Stark VK, Warner TF, Hoch JR: An ultrastructural study of progressive intimal hyperplasia in rat vein grafts. J Vasc Surg 26:94-103, 1997.
219. Hoch JR, Stark VK, Hullett DA, Turnipseed WD: Vein graft intimal hyperplasia—leukocytes and cytokine gene expression. Surgery 116:463-471, 1994.
220. Hoch JR, Stark VK, Turnipseed WD: The temporal relationship between the development of vein graft intimal hyperplasia and growth factor gene expression. J Vasc Surg 22:51-58, 1995.
221. Hoch JR, Stark VK: Apoptosis in vein graft intimal hyperplasia. Surg Forum XLVII:357-360, 1996.
222. Hoch JR, Stark VK, VanRooijen N, et al: Macrophage depletion alters vein graft intimal hyperplasia. Surgery 126:428-437, 1999.
223. Stark VK, Hoch JR, Warner TF, Hullett DA: Monocyte chemotactic protein-1 expression is associated with the development of vein graft intimal hyperplasia. Arterioscler Thromb Vasc Biol 17:1614-1621, 1997.
224. Schwartz LB, Pence JC, Kerns BJ, et al: Kinetics of vein graft cell division and function. Surg Forum 47:362-365, 1991.
225. Zwolak RM, Adams MC, Clowes AW: Kinetics of vein graft hyperplasia: Association with tangential stress. J Vasc Surg 5:126-136, 1987.
226. Angelini GD, Bryan AJ, Williams HMJ, et al: Time course of medial and intimal thickening in pig venous arterial grafts: Relationship to endothelial injury and cholesterol accumulation. J Thorac Cardiovasc Surg 103:1093-1103, 1992.
227. Davies MG, Ramkumar V, Hagen P-O: Temporal expression of G-proteins in intimal hyperplasia. J Surg Res 63:115-122, 1996.
228. Golden MA, Kariko K, David ML, et al: Increased urokinase receptor expression in proliferating vascular smooth muscle cells and in arterialized vein grafts in rabbits. Surg Forum 46:384-386, 1995.
229. Faries PL, Marin ML, Veith FJ, et al: Immunolocalization and temporal distribution of cytokine expression during the development of vein graft intimal hyperplasia in an experimental model. J Vasc Surg 24:463-471, 1996.
230. Faries PL, Gorden RE, Veith FJ, et al: Spatial and temporal distribution of cytokines during the development of vein graft intimal hyperplasia [abstract]. FASEB J 9:A611, 1995.
231. Francis SE, Hunter S, Holt CM, et al: Release of PDGF activity from pig venous arterial grafts. J Thorac Cardiovasc Surg 108:540-548, 1994.
232. Sterpetti AV, Cucina A, Lepidi S, et al: Progression and regression of myointimal hyperplasia in experimental vein grafts depends on PDGF and bFGF production. J Vasc Surg 23:568-575, 1996.
233. Sterpetti AV, Lepidi S, Cucina A, et al: Growth factor production after PTFE and vein arterial grafting—an experimental study. J Vasc Surg 23:453-460, 1996.
234. Lepidi S, Sterpetti AV, Cucina A, et al: bFGF release is dependent on flow conditions in experimental vein grafts. Eur J Vasc Endovasc Surg 10:450-458, 1995.
235. Sterpetti AV, Cucina A, Lepidi S, et al: Formation of myointimal hyperplasia and cytokine production in experimental vein grafts. Surgery 123:461-469, 1998.
236. Brauner RL, Wu L, Bhuta L, McCaffrey S: Structural and vasomotor effects of adenovirus mediated transfer of the TGF-β1 gene in normocholesterolemic and hypercholesterolemic arterialized vein grafts [abstract]. Circulation 94(Suppl):I466, 1996.
237. George SJ, Zaltsman AB, Newby AC: Surgical preparative injury and neointima formation increase MMP-9 expression and MMP-2 activation in human saphenous vein. Cardiovasc Res 33:447-449, 1997.
238. Johnson JL, van Eys GJ, Angelini GD, George SJ: Injury induces dedifferentiation of smooth muscle cells and increased matrix-degrading metalloproteinase activity in human saphenous vein. Arterioscler Thromb Vasc Biol 21:1146-1151, 2001.
239. Meng X, Mavromatis K, Galis ZS: Mechanical stretching of human saphenous vein grafts induces expression and activation of matrix-degrading enzymes associated with vascular tissue injury and repair. Exp Mol Pathol 66:227-237, 1999.
240. Mavromatis K, Fukai T, Tate M, et al: Early effects of arterial hemodynamic conditions on human saphenous veins perfused ex vivo. Arterioscler Thromb Vasc Biol 20:1889-1895, 2000.
241. Kranzhofer A, Baker AH, George SJ, Newby AC: Expression of TIMP-1,-2 and -3 during neointima formation in organ cultures off human saphenous veins. Arterioscler Thromb Vasc Biol 19:255-265, 1999.
242. Crook MF, Newby AC, Smithgate KM: Expression of intercellular adhesion molecules in human saphenous veins: Effects of inflammatory cytokines and neointima formation in culture. Atherosclerosis 150:33-41, 2000.
243. Leville CD, Dassow MS, Seabrook GR, et al: All-trans-retinoic acid decreases vein graft intimal hyperplasia and matrix metalloproteinase activity in vivo. J Surg Res 90:183-190, 2000.
244. Southgate KM, Mehta D, Izzat MB, et al: Increased secretion of basement membrane degrading metalloproteinases in pig saphenous vein into carotid artery interposition grafts. Arterioscler Thromb Vasc Biol 19:1640-1649, 1999.
245. George SJ, Johnson JL, Angelini GD, et al: Adenovirus-mediated gene transfer of human TIMP-1 gene inhibits smooth muscle cell migration and neointimal formation in human saphenous vein. Hum Gene Ther 9:567-577, 1998.
246. George SJ, Baker AH, Angelini GD, Newby AC: Gene transfer of human TIMP-2 inhibits MMP activity and neointimal formation in human saphenous veins. Gene Ther 5:1552-1560, 1998.
247. George SJ, Lloyd CT, Angelini GD, et al: Inhibition of late vein graft neointima formation in human and porcine models by adenovirus-mediated overexpression of TIMP-3. Circulation 101:296-304, 2000.
248. George J, Johnson JL, Smith MA, Jackson CL: Plasmin-mediated fibroblast growth factor-2 mobilization supports smooth muscle cell proliferation in human saphenous vein. J Vasc Res 38:492-501, 2001.
249. Javed Q, Swanson N, Warner EL, et al: Plasminogen activator and plasminogen activator inhibitor gene expression in human saphenous vein organ culture. Exp Mol Pathol 70:146-153, 2001.
250. Redmond EM, Cahill PA, Hirsch M, et al: Effect of pulse pressure on vascular smooth muscle cell migration: The role of urokinase and matrix metalloproteinase. Thromb Haemost 81:293-300, 1999.
251. Hu Y, Baker AH, Zou Y, et al: Local gene transfer of TIMP-2 influences vein graft remodeling in a mouse model. Arterioscler Thromb Vasc Biol 21:1275-1280, 2001.
252. Kohler TR, Kirkman TR, Gordon D, Clowes AW: Mechanism of longterm degeneration of arterialized vein graft. Am J Surg 160:257-261, 1990.
253. Zhang W-D, Bai H-Z, Sawa Y, et al: Association of smooth muscle cell phenotypic modulation with extracellular matrix alterations during neointima formation in rabbit vein grafts. J Vasc Surg 30:169-183, 1999.
254. Dattilo JB, Dattilo MP, Yager DR, Makhoul RG: Hypercholesterolemia alters gene expression of novel components of the ECM in experimental vein grafts. Ann Vasc Surg 12:168-173, 1998.
255. Brody WR, Kosek JG, Angell WV: Changes in vein grafts following aorto-coronary bypass induced by pressure and ischemia. J Thorac Cardiovasc Surg 64:847-854, 1972.

256. Kennedy JH, Wieting DW, Hwang NHC, et al: Hydraulic and morphologic study of fibrous intimal hyperplasia in autogenous saphenous vein bypass grafts. J Thorac Cardiovasc Surg 67:805-813, 1974.
257. Faulkner SL, Fischer RD, Conkle DM, et al: Effect of blood flow rate on subendothelial proliferation in venous autografts used as arterial substitutes [abstract]. Circulation 52(Suppl I):163, 1975.
258. Rittgers SE, Karayannacos PE, Guy JF, et al: Velocity distribution and intimal proliferation in autologous vein grafts in dogs. Circ Res 42:792-801, 1978.
259. Berguer R, Higgins RF, Reddy DJ: Intimal hyperplasia: An experimental study. Arch Surg 115:332-338, 1980.
260. Kamiya A, Togawa T: Adaptive regulation of wall shear stress on intimal thickening of arterially transplanted autogenous veins in dogs. Am J Physiol 239:14-21, 1980.
261. Karayannacos PE, Rittgers SE, Kakos GS, et al: Potential role of velocity and wall tension in vein graft failure. J Cardiovasc Surg 21:171-178, 1980.
262. Morinaga K, Okadome K, Kuroki M, et al: Effect of wall shear stress on intimal thickening of arterially transplanted autologous veins in dogs. J Vasc Surg 2:430-433, 1985.
263. Dobrin PB, Littooy FN, Golan J, et al: Mechanical and histologic changes in canine vein grafts. J Surg Res 14:259-260, 1988.
264. Morinaga K, Eguchi H, Miyazaki T, et al: Development and regression of intimal thickening of arterially transplanted autologous vein grafts in dogs. J Vasc Surg 5:19-30, 1987.
265. Schwartz LB, O'Donohoe MK, Purut CM, et al: Myointimal thickening in experimental vein grafts is dependent on wall tension. J Vasc Surg 15:176-186, 1992.
266. Davies AH, Magee TR, Baird RN, et al: Vein compliance: A preoperative indicator of vein morphology and of veins at risk of vascular graft stenosis. Br J Surg 79:1019-1021, 1992.
267. Galt SW, Zwolak RM, Wagner RJ, Gilbertson JJ: Differential response of arteries and vein grafts to blood flow reduction. J Vasc Surg 17:563-570, 1993.
268. Itoh H, Komori K, Funahashi S, et al: Intimal hyperplasia of experimental autologous vein graft in hyperlipidemic rabbits with poor distal runoff. Atherosclerosis 110:259-270, 1994.
269. Yamamura S, Okadome K, Onohara T, et al: Blood flow and kinetics of smooth muscle cell proliferation in canine autogenous vein grafts: In vivo BrdU incorporation. J Surg Res 56:155-161, 1994.
270. Lee RT, Lorse HM, Fishbein MC: High stress regions in saphenous vein bypass graft atherosclerotic lesions. J Am Coll Cardiol 24:1639-1644, 1994.
271. Karayannacos PE, Geer J, Gast M, et al: Wall strain in arterial vein grafts [abstract]. Clin Res 21:813, 1973.
272. Barra JA, Volant A, Leroy JP, et al: Constrictive perivenous mesh prosthesis for preservation of vein integrity. J Thorac Cardiovasc Surg 92:330-336, 1986.
273. Kohler TR, Kirkman TR, Clowes AW: The effect of rigid external support on vein graft adaptation to the arterial circulation. J Vasc Surg 9:277-285, 1989.
274. Hopson SB, Lust RM, Zeri RS, et al: The effects of wall tension on the development of intimal hyperplasia in vein grafts. XXIst World Congress of the International Society for Cardiovascular Surgery. Lisbon, Sept 9-15, 1993, p 106.
275. Bamberg LS, Moczar M, Lecerf L, Loisance D: External biodegradable supporting conduit protects endothelium in vein graft in arterial interposition. Int J Art Org 20:397-406, 1997.
276. Angelini GD, Izzat MB, Bryan AJ, Newby AC: External stenting reduces early medial and neointimal thickening in a pig model of arteriovenous bypass grafting. J Thorac Cardiovasc Surg 112:79-84, 1996.
277. Violaris AG, Newby AC, Angelini GD: Effects of external stenting on wall thickening in arteriovenous bypass grafts. Ann Thorac Surg 55:667-671, 1993.
278. Davies MG, Klyachkin ML, Dalen H, et al: Regression of intimal hyperplasia with restoration of EDRF-mediated relaxation in experimental vein grafts. Surgery 114:258-271, 1993.
279. Fann JL, Sokoloff MH, Sarris GE, et al: The reversibility of canine vein graft arterialization. Circulation 82(Suppl IV):9-18, 1990.
280. Neitzel GF, Barboriak JJ, Pintar K, Qureshi L: Atherosclerosis in aortocoronary bypass grafts: Morphologic study and risk factor analysis 6 to 12 years after surgery. Arteriosclerosis 6:594-600, 1986.
281. Atkinson JB, Forman MB, Vaughn WK, et al: Morphologic changes in longterm saphenous vein bypass grafts. Chest 88:341-348, 1985.
282. Virami R, Atkinson JB, Forman MB: Aortocoronary saphenous vein bypass grafts. Cardiovasc Clin 18:41-59, 1988.
283. O'Donohoe MK, Radic ZS, Schwartz LB, et al: Systemic hypertension alters vasomotor function in experimental vein grafts. J Vasc Surg 14:30-39, 1991.
284. Landymore RW, Kinley CE, Cameron CA: Intimal hyperplasia in autogenous vein grafts used for arterial bypass: A canine model. Cardiovasc Res 19:589-592, 1985.
285. Klyachkin ML, Davies MG, Svendsen E, et al: Hypercholesterolemia and experimental vein grafts: Accelerated development of intimal hyperplasia and abnormal vasomotor function. J Surg Res 54:451-468, 1993.
286. Rosenblatt MS, Quist WC, Sidawy AN, et al: Results of vein graft reconstruction of the lower extremity in diabetic and non-diabetic patients. Surg Gynecol Obstet 171:331-335, 1990.
287. Davies MG, Hagen P-O: Modeling the pathophysiology of vein graft failure. J Vasc Surg 20:139-140, 1994.
288. Amano J, Suzuki A, Sunamori M, et al: Cytokinetic study of aortocoronary bypass vein grafts in place for less than six months. Am J Cardiol 67:1234-1236, 1991.
289. Fuchs JCA, Hagen P-O, Oldham HNJ, Sabiston DCJ: Lipid composition in venous arterial bypass grafts. Surg Forum 23:139-141, 1972.
290. Scott HWJ, Morgan CV, Bolasny BL, et al: Experimental atherosclerosis in autogenous venous grafts. Arch Surg 101:677, 1970.
291. Angelini GD, Bryan AJ, Hunter S, Newby AC: A surgical technique that preserves human saphenous vein functional integrity. Ann Thorac Surg 53:871-874, 1992.
292. Zwolak RM, Kirkman TR, Clowes AW: Atherosclerosis in rabbit vein grafts. Arteriosclerosis 9:374-379, 1989.
293. Ohki T: [Localized intimal hyperplasia in autologous vein graft: Does presence of the valve induce obliteration?] Nippon Geka Gakkai Zasshi 94:302-310, 1993.
294. Chaux A, Ruan X-M, Fishbein MC, et al: Influence of vein valves on the development of arteriosclerosis in venoarterial grafts in the rabbit. J Thorac Cardiovasc Surg 110:1382-1390, 1995.
295. Lenz M, Hughes H, Raya J, et al: Vascular smooth muscle cell-mediated LDL oxidation: Loss of polyunsaturated fatty acids and formation of specific lipid peroxidation products [abstract]. FASEB J 6:A1323, 1992.
296. Tappel A: Measurement of and protection from in vivo lipid peroxidation. In Pryor W (ed): Free Radicals in Biology. San Diego, Academic Press, 1980, p 1.
297. Piotrowski JJ, Hunter GC, Eskelson CD, et al: Lipid peroxidation: A possible factor in late graft failure of coronary artery bypass grafts. J Vasc Surg 13:652-657, 1991.
298. Beckman JS, Beckman TW, Chen J, et al: Apparent hydroxyl radical production of peroxynitrite: Implications for endothelial injury from nitric oxide and superoxide. Proc Natl Acad Sci U S A 87:1620-1624, 1990.
299. Rubanyi G: Vascular effects of oxygen derived free radicals. Free Radic Biol Med 4:107-120, 1988.
300. Galle J, Bassange E, Busse R: Oxidized low density lipoproteins potentiate vasoconstrictions to various agonists by direct interaction with vascular smooth muscle. Circ Res 66:1287-1293, 1990.
301. Sachinidos A, Mengden T, Locher R, et al: Novel cellular activities for low density lipoproteins in vascular smooth muscle cells. Hypertension 15:704-711, 1990.
302. Fuster V: Progression-regression of atherosclerosis: Molecular, cellular and clinical bases. Circulation 86(Suppl III):1-123, 1992.
303. Menchaca HJ, Morris TJ, Bourdages H, et al: Role of the mechanism of cholesterol reduction on vein graft atherosclerosis. Surg Forum 43:351-352, 1992.

304. Klyachkin ML, Davies MG, Kim JH, et al: Post-operative reduction of high serum cholesterol concentrations and experimental vein bypass grafts: Effect on the development of intimal hyperplasia and abnormal vasomotor function. J Thorac Cardiovasc Surg 107:556-566, 1994.
305. Blankenhorn DH, Nessim SA, Johnson RL, et al: Beneficial effects of combined colestipol-niacin therapy on coronary atherosclerosis and coronary venous bypass grafts. JAMA 257:3233-3240, 1987.
306. Mann MJ, Gibbons GH, Tsao PS, et al: Cell cycle inhibition preserves endothelial function in genetically engineered rabbit vein grafts. J Clin Invest. 99:1295-1301, 1997.
307. Sladen JG, Gilmour JL: Vein graft stenosis: Characteristics and effect of treatment. Am J Surg 141:549-553, 1981.
308. Hicks RCJ, Ellis M, Mirhasseine R, et al: The influence of fibrinogen concentrations on the development of vein graft stenoses. Eur J Vasc Endovasc Surg 9:415-420, 1995.
309. Irvine G, Wilson YG, Currie C, et al: Hyperhomocysteinaemia is a risk factor for vein graft stenosis. Eur J Vasc Endovasc Surg 12:304-309, 1996.
310. Nielsen TG, VonJessen F, Andreasen JJ, et al: Antibodies to cardiolipin increase the risk of failure of infrainguinal vein bypasses. Eur J Vasc Endovasc Surg 14:177-184, 1997.
311. Hoff HF, Beck GJ, Skibinski CJ, et al: Serum Lp(a) level as a predictor of vein graft stenosis after coronary artery bypass surgery in patients. Circulation 77:1238-1244, 1988.
312. Cheshire NJ, Wolfe JH, Barradas M, et al: Smoking and platelet activity predict infrainguinal graft stenosis. Br J Surg 80:520, 1993.
313. Cheshire NJW, Wolfe JHN, Barradas MA, et al: Smoking and plasma fibrinogen, lipoprotein(a) and serotonin are markers for postoperative infrainguinal graft stenosis. Eur J Vasc Endovasc Surg 11:479-486, 1996.
314. Eritsland J, Arnesen H, Seljeflot I, et al: Influence of serum lipoprotein(a) and homocysteine levels on graft patency after coronary artery bypass grafting. Am J Cardiol 74:1099-1102, 1994.
315. Daida H, Yokoi H, Miyano H, et al: Relation of saphenous vein graft obstruction to serum cholesterol levels. J Am Coll Cardiol 25:193-197, 1995.
316. Kawasuji M, Sakakibara N, Takemura H, et al: Coronary artery bypass grafting in familial hypercholesterolemia. J Thorac Cardiovasc Surg 109:364-369, 1995.
317. The effect of aggressive lowering of low-density lipoprotein cholesterol levels and low-dose anticoagulation on obstructive changes in saphenous-vein coronary-artery bypass grafts. The Post Coronary Artery Bypass Graft Trial Investigators. N Engl J Med 336:153-162, 1997.
318. Frick MH, Syvanne M, Nieminen MS: Prevention of the angiographic progression of coronary and vein graft atherosclerosis by gemfibrozil after coronary bypass surgery in men with low levels of HDL cholesterol. Lopid Coronary Angiography Trial (LOCAT) study group. Circulation 96:2137-2143, 1997.
319. Buckley BH, Hutchins GM: Accelerated atherosclerosis: A morphological study of 97 saphenous vein coronary artery bypass grafts. Circulation 50:163-169, 1977.
320. Lorenz RL, Schacky CV, Weber M, et al: Improved aortocoronary bypass patency by low dose aspirin (100 mg): Effects on platelet aggregation and thromboxane formation. Lancet i(8389):1261-1264, 1984.
321. Bourassa MG, Campeau L, Lesperance J, Grondin CM: Changes in grafts and coronary arteries after saphenous vein aortocoronary bypass surgery: Results at repeat angiography. Circulation 65(Suppl II):90-97, 1982.
322. Campeau L, Enjalbert M, Lesperance J, et al: Atherosclerosis and late closure of aortocoronary saphenous vein grafts: Sequential angiographic studies at 2 weeks, 1 year, 5 to 7 years and 10 to 12 years after surgery. Circulation 68(Suppl I):1-7, 1983.

Chapter 12

Molecular Biology and Gene Therapy in Vascular Disease

DAPHNE PIERRE-PAUL, MD
VIVIAN GAHTAN, MD
MICHAEL S. CONTE, MD

In the half century that has passed since the identification of deoxyribonucleic acid (DNA) as the molecular basis of heredity, the entire breadth of medical science and practice has been revolutionized. Advances in genetics and molecular biology, highlighted by the almost incomprehensible accomplishments of the Human Genome Project,[1] have ushered in the era of true "molecular medicine." The use of genetic approaches in animal models of atherosclerosis, intimal hyperplasia, vein grafting, and angiogenesis has broadly advanced the field of vascular biology by defining the role of specific genes in normal cardiovascular function as well as disease. Increasingly, genomic and proteomic approaches are being used to examine the clinical variability in human disease and responses to therapy. Currently, the function of approximately 50% of human genes has been uncovered, and as the role of more genes is discovered, countless targets for treating disease will be unmasked. A broad understanding of the molecular events underlying alterations in cellular function is central to the development of new, more powerful, and more specific approaches to prevent and treat cardiovascular disease. In this chapter we review the basic principles of molecular biology that are requisite for an understanding of this biotechnology revolution and discuss the fundamental precepts of gene-based therapies as they apply to vascular disease. The initiation of cardiovascular gene therapy trials during the last several years has made these topics relevant to all vascular specialists.

■ BASIC PRINCIPLES OF MOLECULAR BIOLOGY

Gene Structure and Basic Concepts of Heredity

Reproduction is the most elementary characteristic of all living things. All offspring inherit the genetic information that determines their structure and function from their parents. Because all cells derive from preexisting cells, the genetic blueprint must be accurately copied before it can be passed on to daughter cells. Molecular biology is the study of how genetic information is transmitted. At the heart of molecular genetics is the central dogma of biologic information flow: from chromosomal DNA, through the intermediate step of ribonucleic acid (RNA), messenger RNA (mRNA), by way of transcription, to protein by way of translation. Proteins are the fundamental building blocks of cells, and their structure, organization, and function largely determine cellular behavior. When one is viewing this process from the global standpoint of information flow within the cell at any moment in time, as opposed to focusing on a single gene, it is useful to use the terms *genome* (total content of chromosomal DNA), *transcriptome* (total population of mRNA species present), and *proteome* (total population and state of cellular proteins).

DNA, the fundamental component of genes, is a long polymer of linked nucleotides, with deoxyribose as their sugar.[2,3] The four nucleic acids that compose DNA are two purines, adenine (A) and guanine (G), and two pyrimidines, cytosine (C) and thymine (T). DNA exists as two complementary strands held together by hydrogen bonds between specific base pairs, forming a double-helix configuration with the sugar-phosphate backbone located on the outside. This base pairing (Watson-Crick) between strands is constant and specific, with A always binding to T and G always binding to C, and this specificity lies at the heart of accurate replication and transmission of the genetic blueprint.

A *gene* is the complete sequence of nucleic acids required for the synthesis of a functional protein. It comprises not only the nucleotides that code for the amino acid sequence of a protein but also the sequences necessary for building specific RNA transcripts. The regions of the gene that encode protein are known as *exons*. In most cases, exons are interrupted by longer noncoding regions called *introns*.[2] Within the exons, each consecutive trinucleotide sequence (known as a *codon*) specifies a unique amino acid (building blocks of proteins), and the sequence of amino acids determines the nature of the protein encoded. The assignment of each unique trinucleotide sequence to an amino acid is known as the *genetic code*. This code, which specifies 20 unique amino acids from a total of 64 trinucleotide combinations, is degenerate primarily in the third nucleotide of each codon; thus, isolated mutations of this position may often not produce a change in amino acid composition. It also includes three specific codons instructing for translation "stop." All eukaryotic proteins begin with the ATG codon, which specifies the amino acid methionine.

In eukaryotes, a portion of the introns is composed of long stretches of nucleotides termed *spacer sequences*.[4] These spacer sequences and the remainder of the noncoding sequences combined represent a majority of the genome in higher organisms. This arrangement explains why the number of genes in a simple organism is more similar to that in a more complex one than would be expected. Many of these noncoding regions, in higher organisms, contain a variety of highly repeated sequences, including *simple-sequence* DNA (5 to 200 nucleotides) and *satellite* DNA (repeated millions of times in a genome). A cluster of genes involved in related functions forms a transcription unit termed an *operon*. Simple operons encode a single protein, whereas complex operons, extremely common in multicellular organisms, contain several different exons that lead to the production of a variety of proteins.

In eukaryotes, genes are arranged into chromosomes in a fashion that is species-specific. The macromolecular organization of chromosomes is complex and involves specific protein molecules called *histones*. The intergenic areas of the chromosome do not code for protein but can influence gene expression by affecting the formation of chromatin. *Chromatin* refers to the combination of substances present in chromosomes.[5] In its most basic form, it comprises DNA and proteins (e.g., histones) around which DNA is wrapped to create structures called *nucleosomes*. *Chaperones* are catalysts that are needed to assemble nucleosomes but do not become a part of the final product. Euchromatin (open chromatin) is necessary for gene expression, whereas heterochromatin (closed chromatin) is transcriptionally silent. Thus the macromolecular structure of chromatin and DNA-protein interactions are critical to the regulation of gene expression.

Genotype is the total set of genes carried by an organism, whereas *phenotype* refers to the structural or functional trait (e.g., eye color) displayed. A major difference between organisms is based on the number of copies of each chromosome they contain. *Haploid* organisms (e.g., bacteria) have a single set of chromosomes, whereas *diploid* organisms have two. Different forms of a gene (normal or variant) are called *alleles*. Diploid organisms, because they have two copies of each gene, may be *homozygous* (carry identical alleles) or *heterozygous* (carry different alleles). The complete set of alleles defines an organism's genotype (or genetic composition); phenotype is often determined by a complex relationship between individual genotype and environmental influences. Phenotypes can be divided into discontinuous and continuous types.[6] In the discontinuous phenotype, a characteristic exists in a population in at least two distinct forms. The genotype is able to create a range of phenotypes based on the above-mentioned interactions, called the *norm of reaction*. In many instances, norms of reactions of different alleles do not overlap, leading to a predictable relationship between genotype and phenotype under almost all conditions. This discovery has enabled geneticists, through the use of *discontinuous variation*, to identify numerous alleles and their function. Mendel exploited this relationship when studying genes controlling flower color in peas. Continuous variation of a characteristic is represented by uninterrupted phenotypes, such as height, weight, and color intensity, in the population. In *continuous variation*, both genetic and environmental influences lead to the differences expressed. In contrast to the discontinuous type, norms of reaction in the continuous type are complex, and the one-to-one relationship between genotype and phenotype does not exist, making the study of these genes more difficult.

In nature DNA may be altered, and even individuals among a given species demonstrate variability in traits. Individuals of a species show significant variability in the exact sequence of their DNA, and common variants in sequence are referred to as *polymorphisms*. *Mutations* are uncommon alterations in the genome that can be passed on from one generation to the next. Understanding what mutations are and how they arise is critical, because many common human diseases are due to mutations of individual genes. Additionally, inheritance patterns for genetic diseases vary according to the nature of the mutations that cause them. Mutations can induce changes in the structure of proteins, depress or completely inhibit their expression, or both. A *recessive mutation* means both alleles must be mutant to express the mutant phenotype, whereas in a *dominant mutation*, only one allele needs to be mutant. Recessive mutations lead to a loss of function of the protein. Alternatively, dominant mutations generally result in a functional gain that increases the activity of a gene product or induces expression at an inappropriate time or location. In some cases, however, dominant mutations may cause a loss of function, when a mutant phenotype results from removal of one allele. These are called *haplo-insufficient* genes.

A *point mutation* is a change in a single base pair in a gene sequence that usually affects the function of an individual gene.[7] This base pair switch can yield one of three mutations: missense, nonsense, or frameshift. A *missense* mutation occurs when one amino acid is substituted for another, whereas a *nonsense* mutation involves replacement of an amino acid codon with a stop codon that terminates translation prematurely. In a *frameshift* mutation, an unrelated amino acid is incorporated into the protein followed by a stop codon. Chromosomal mutations are a second category of mutations. These mutations involve deletion or insertion of several contiguous genes, inversion of genes, or an exchange of large segments of DNA between chromosomes. These abnormalities lead to extensive changes in chromosome structure and influence the function of multiple genes, inducing major phenotypic differences. Mutations can arise spontaneously at a low rate because of chemical instability or as a result of exposure to environmental factors such as ultraviolet light and chemical carcinogens.

Cell replication by mitosis requires accurate replication of the genetic blueprint, and the process of DNA replication in the nucleus of cells is tightly regulated by a family of enzymes involved in the unwinding (*helicase*) and replication by complementary strand synthesis (DNA polymerase) as well as other critical enzymes that perform editing functions as control for accuracy. The regulation of this process is obviously critical for development, growth, and tissue repair, and thus, environmental toxins that affect DNA replication may have profound effects.

Southern Blot

A common technique for the analysis of DNA from cells and tissue is known as Southern blot or Southern hybridization.[8] In this analysis, genomic DNA is harvested and exposed to a restriction enzyme that digests the long stretches of DNA to produce fragments of varying size. The fragments are then separated according to size by electrophoresis on an agarose gel. After separation, the fragments are transferred and irreversibly bound to a solid support (a nitrocellulose microfilter) and hybridized with a specific complementary DNA (cDNA) probe that is radiolabeled. If the probe finds any complementary strands of genomic DNA, it binds to them, and the results are examined by exposing the filter to x rays. This technique can be used to determine the presence of a specific DNA segment (or cloned gene) in the genomic DNA of the tissue of interest.

Gene Expression and Its Regulation

Gene expression is the process by which the genetic information is converted into protein, and it has two components, *transcription* (the transfer of information from DNA to mRNA) and *translation* (assembling of a specific amino acid sequence based on the codon sequence in mRNA).[5] Mechanisms that influence transcription, and its inhibition, are discussed next, followed by a brief discussion on translation and the processing of RNA. Molecular techniques commonly performed to study these processes are listed in Figure 12-1.

Transcription is a tightly regulated process that functions as a primary site of control for the cell. Transcription of a gene requires a coordinated series of molecular events involving DNA-binding proteins and the enzyme RNA polymerase, which synthesizes mRNA as a complementary strand from the DNA template. The assembly and activation of this transcription complex offer numerous steps for control of the process to achieve either increased or decreased expression of a gene at any one point in time.

One important group of proteins involved in gene regulation is transcription factors (TFs).[9] TFs can be divided into categories on the basis of similarities in structure, including common organization in their DNA-binding sites. Three domains constitute these proteins. The DNA-binding domain recognizes a specific DNA sequence, whereas the trans-activating domain activates or suppresses transcription of the gene. The final region is the protein-protein interaction domain, which enables the TF's activity to be modulated by similar proteins. TFs control gene expression by binding to chromosomal DNA at certain promoter or enhancer sites, thereby activating or repressing an adjacent gene.

A *promoter site* is a short DNA sequence, generally upstream from the "start" codon of a gene, that binds regulatory proteins and leads the RNA polymerase enzyme complex to the transcription start site. Promoters must interact with a TF to be functional. The majority of these TF proteins induce initiation, but a few suppress transcription of the target gene. The specific DNA-binding sites for TFs are often short nucleotide sequences that may be present in the promoter regions of several related genes, enabling the

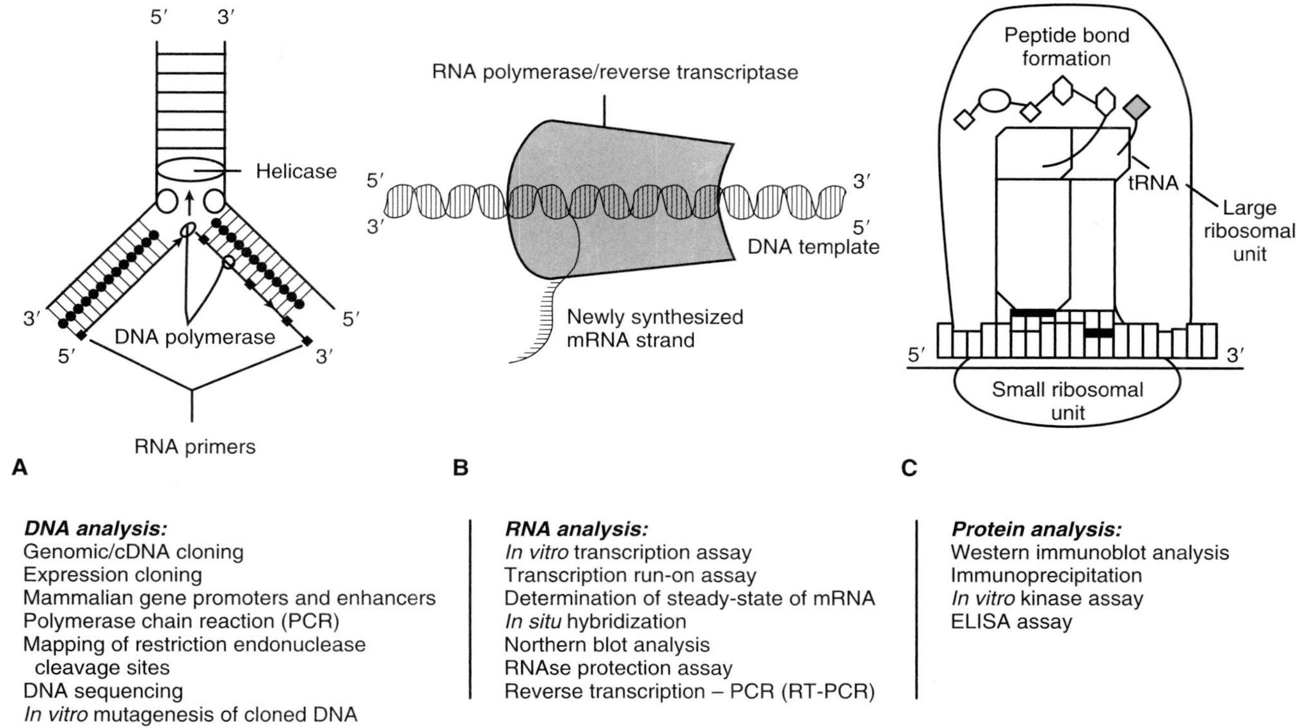

FIGURE 12-1 Flow of biologic information in the cell. **A** and **B**, DNA is transcribed into messenger RNA (mRNA), and mRNA is translated into protein (**C**). For each step, common techniques used to study these processes are listed. cDNA, complementary DNA; ELISA, enzyme-linked immunosorbent assay; tRNA, transfer RNA; TUNEL, terminal deoxyribonucleotidyl transferase (TDT)–mediated deoxyuridine triphosphate (dUTP)–digoxigenin nick-end labeling.

coordinated expression of genes encoding for a family of proteins involved in a specific cellular response. Some of these sequences behave as promoters, enhancers, or repressors for various genes on the chromosome.

Enhancers are DNA sequences that control the efficiency and rate of transcription of those promoters located on the same chromosome as the enhancer. Like promoters, they must bind TFs to function. These sequences may be positioned upstream from (on the 5′ side), downstream from (on the 3′ side), close to, or far from the affected promoter. More than one enhancer may control a given gene, and enhancers can be bound by multiple TFs. Additionally, enhancers can negatively regulate transcription. These negative enhancers are referred to as *silencers*. Another group of proteins involved in negative regulation of genes are repressors. *Repressors* are proteins that adhere to specific DNA sequences and inhibit transcription. This inhibition can be accomplished by preventing other TFs from binding the DNA or by competing with activators that bind certain regulatory sequences. Alternatively, active repressors inhibit transcription through protein-protein interactions mediated by special domains incorporated in their structure.

After transcription, further modification of the resultant mRNA provides additional opportunities for control and heterogeneity. The quantity, size, and cellular localization of mRNA reflect the state of expression of the gene that encodes the RNA. The initial product after transcription is a long heterogeneous nuclear RNA (hnRNA) called *pre-mRNA*. A critical part of gene regulation is designating the sequences in this molecule as either introns or exons, because the final product requires accurate excision of the noncoding regions. The process of RNA splicing, which follows transcription, is mediated by a structure called a *spliceosome*. This complex determines what exons will be created and, therefore, what proteins will be generated. Further modifications, including the addition of a long tail of adenine ribonucleotides (polyadenylation signal), yield the mature mRNA, which translocates to the cytoplasm for translation in subcellular organelles termed *ribosomes*. Although the majority of gene regulation occurs within the context of transcription, regulation can occur at any of these intervening steps, including translation. Two common methods for analyzing the state of RNA molecules within cells or tissue are Northern blot analysis and in-situ hybridization.[8,10]

Northern Blot

Northern blot analysis is a technique used to detect and quantify specific RNA sequences. RNA is a single-stranded molecule that folds back on itself, forming a "secondary structure." Because this configuration is incompatible with electrophoresis, the RNA molecules must be separated by size in the presence of formaldehyde or dimethyl sulfoxide and transferred to a nitrocellulose filter. Once they have been separated and immobilized on the filter, the RNA of interest can then be hybridized to a complementary nucleic acid that has been labeled. Autoradiography is used to detect the labeled probe. The relative amount of signal under different conditions can be compared to assess mRNA abundance.

In-Situ Hybridization

In-situ hybridization allows for the detection, within cells or tissues (in situ), of specific nucleic acid sequences, complementary to labeled probes. It may be used to demonstrate the expression of a specific gene by localizing the mRNA. Specific sense and antisense (complementary) probes are generated and applied to fixed cells or tissues. The sequence-specific binding of these probes may be detected by radiolabeling or by antibody techniques.

Proteins

After translation, the DNA sequence has been converted successfully into a polypeptide chain, and this protein must be localized correctly within the cell and folded in a distinct three-dimensional pattern before it attains its functional state.[11] Many mature proteins are composed of multiple individual polypeptide chains, arranged in a specific macromolecular structure. Localization of proteins to the cytoplasm, membrane, extracellular space (i.e., secreted), or other specific organelles is generally determined by specific amino acid sequences. The final amino acid sequence also specifies the three-dimensional shape of the resultant protein. This change in configuration involves specialized proteins known as chaperones. Although chaperones are required for correct folding of proteins, these proteins do not supply any information that influences this process. They appear to bind to unfolded or partially folded proteins and to stabilize them, thereby preventing incorrect folding or inappropriate aggregation of these structures. After folding, the proteins may undergo further chemical modifications, which greatly expand the total possible number of variants and heterogeneity from a single gene.

Post-translational modifications of proteins are proteolytic changes, glycosylation, and lipid attachment. Proteolytic modifications involve cleavage of polypeptide chains. Such alterations to the structure of proteins are often required before translocation across certain membranes, such as lysosomes, mitochondria, and chloroplasts, or into the plasma membrane. Signal sequences are specific amino-terminus cleavage sites that allow for the processing of premature polypeptides such as prohormones to be cleaved into mature forms by specific cellular enzymes. This cleavage process is important for formation of certain enzymes or hormones from larger precursors. One example is the preproinsulin molecule that undergoes two cleavage procedures before yielding the final product, insulin. *Glycosylation*, or the addition of carbohydrate moieties, is another important type of protein modification. Glycoproteins can be classified as N-linked or O-linked. In the N-linked variety, the carbohydrate group is attached to the nitrogen atom in the side chain of asparagine, whereas in O-linked types, it is added to the oxygen atom in the side chain of serine or threonine. This process facilitates protein folding and directs proteins to the correct intracellular locations and recognition sites for cell-cell interactions. Lastly, polypeptide chains can be modified by way of addition of lipids. Proteins modified in this manner are often intended to anchor in the plasma membrane, which the lipid moiety can facilitate. Intracellular localization signals also aid in post-translational modification of proteins.

The *nuclear envelope*, a complex structure that consists of two phospholipid membranes, separates the contents of the nucleus from the cytoplasm in eukaryotic cells.[12] The envelope acts as a barrier, and the only channels through it are nuclear pore complexes that allow the regulated exchange of molecules. Depending on their size, proteins can pass through this complex by way of one of two mechanisms. Small molecules diffuse through open aqueous channels bidirectionally, whereas macromolecules pass through these regulated channels in only one direction in response to appropriate signals. Proteins intended to function in the nucleus are equipped with specific amino acid sequences, nuclear localization signals, which direct their passage through the nuclear pore complex. The majority of these sequences are short and contain an abundance of basic amino acid residues (lysine and arginine) located near, but not adjacent to, each other. This arrangement means a mutation could involve the stretch of amino acids between sequences of required amino acids without affecting nuclear localization.

Two procedures used commonly for the analysis of proteins in cells and tissues are Western blot analysis and enzyme-linked immunosorbent assay.[8]

Western Blot

Western blot analysis is geared toward identifying the relative abundance of specific proteins. Proteins are harvested by cell disruption and fractionization, then separated by size and charge using electrophoresis through a polyacrylamide gel. The separated proteins are then transferred from the gel to a nitrocellulose filter, which is then probed with protein-specific antibodies. The antibody may then be detected by fluorescent techniques.

Enzyme-Linked Immunosorbent Assay

Enzyme-linked immunosorbent assay (ELISA) allows for the accurate measurement of protein antigens in solution. The antigen is attached to an antibody-enzyme complex and mixed with a chromogenic or fluorogenic substrate. The enzyme complex then proceeds to degrade the substrate; when degradation occurs, a fluorescent product is produced. This assay is based on the premise that the amount of colored fluid produced is proportional to the amount of protein in the sample. The results are quantified by a microplate reader. Figure 12-2 depicts this technique.

Regulation of Cellular Phenotype

The transcriptome, which describes the global state of transcriptional activity of all genes, and the proteome, which describes the total abundance and state of proteins, ultimately define the pattern of cell behavior that determines tissue function. Although all cells in an organism contain the same original genomic information, the structure and

Enzyme-linked Immunosorbent Assay (ELISA):

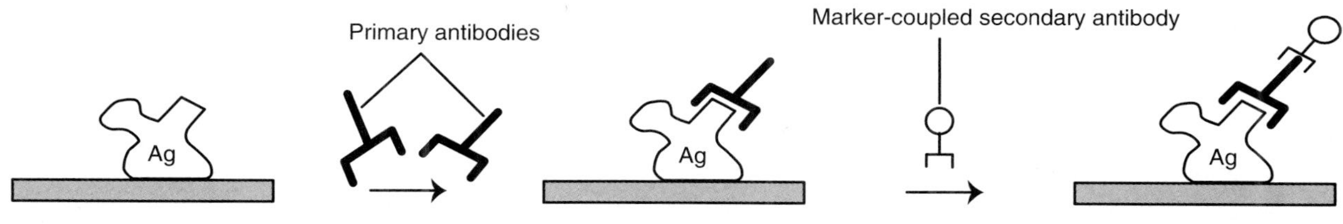

FIGURE 12-2 Quantification of a specific protein by means of enzyme-linked immunosorbent assay (ELISA). This schematic demonstrates exposure of immobilized antigen (Ag) to primary protein-specific antibody and an enzyme-linked secondary antibody. Conversion of a substrate molecule to product by the enzyme is quantified by a colorimetric assay and related to the amount of bound protein.

function of different tissues are based on unique patterns of gene regulation that occur during tissue and organ differentiation. In addition, specific cellular programs, which are coordinated activities of protein interactions and gene regulation, often characterize the response of a specific cell or tissue to a certain stimulus. Some cellular programs, such as the response of endothelial cells to inflammatory stimuli, may be quite specific. Other primordial programs, such as cell replication, may be regulated in a more universal fashion. The central importance of cell growth and survival to numerous pathologic states has led to a great deal of investigation into growth control and the elucidation of the cell cycle.

The *cell cycle* is the series of molecular events by which cells regulate their replication.[5] The four basic phases that compose it are

1. The *gap$_1$ (G_1) phase*, when the majority of protein biosynthesis occurs.
2. The *synthesis (S) phase*, responsible for most of the DNA synthesis and additional S-phase–specific protein synthesis.
3. The *gap$_2$ (G_2) phase*, when proteins necessary for mitosis are synthesized.
4. The *mitosis (M) phase*, during which DNA and protein synthesis are halted, chromosome condensation occurs, and the cell divides.

Quiescent cells that receive signals to divide must pass through the critical G_1 to S checkpoint, which is tightly regulated by a number of cell cycle proteins, including cyclins and cyclin-dependent kinases as well as other proteins that regulate their activity. Diverse environmental and growth factor signals are integrated by the cell and ultimately converge on the activation status of this critical set of proteins to determine passage through the committed step to DNA synthesis. These cell cycle proteins provide opportunities for drug targeting to control cell growth that have been exploited in cancer and cardiovascular disease. It has also been discovered that tissue remodeling in both embryonic development and adult life is also controlled by a specific program for cell suicide. The elucidation of this phenomenon of programmed cell death, termed *apoptosis*, has opened up further avenues for manipulation of growth.

Recombinant DNA Technology and the Manipulation of DNA

In the last quarter of the 20th century, the advent of recombinant DNA technology for the manipulation of genetic material opened the door for a rapid acceleration of the pace of molecular biology discovery. These techniques allow for the manipulation of DNA molecules in vitro by amplification, digestion, splicing, and re-introduction of specific sequences into cells and tissues.[13]

Cloning is a process for creating exact duplicate copies of specific sequences of DNA. To clone a segment of DNA, a vector is needed for amplification, typically in bacterial cells that have been specifically engineered for this purpose (Fig. 12-3). A *vector* is a self-replicating DNA molecule that can transfer a segment of DNA between host cells. An ideal vector is small, making manipulation easy, and has the ability to replicate in a living cell to allow for amplification of the donor fragment. Additionally, the vector should have convenient restriction sites, for insertion of the DNA to be cloned, and there should be easy methods for identifying and recovering the recombinant protein. Vectors may be classified into two categories, viral and nonviral. Choice of vector often depends on the size of the DNA segment that needs to be cloned and the intended goal of the cloned material. A more complete description of vector types can be found in the section on genetic interventions.

A *plasmid* is a small, circular DNA molecule derived from bacteria that is distinct from the chromosome and replicates independently of it. In the circular plasmid form, DNA can be introduced directly into bacterial or mammalian cells through a variety of physical and chemical techniques referred to collectively as *transfection*. Plasmids used routinely as vectors carry genes for drug resistance. These genes are useful because they allow for selection of the drug-resistant transfected cells that contain and express

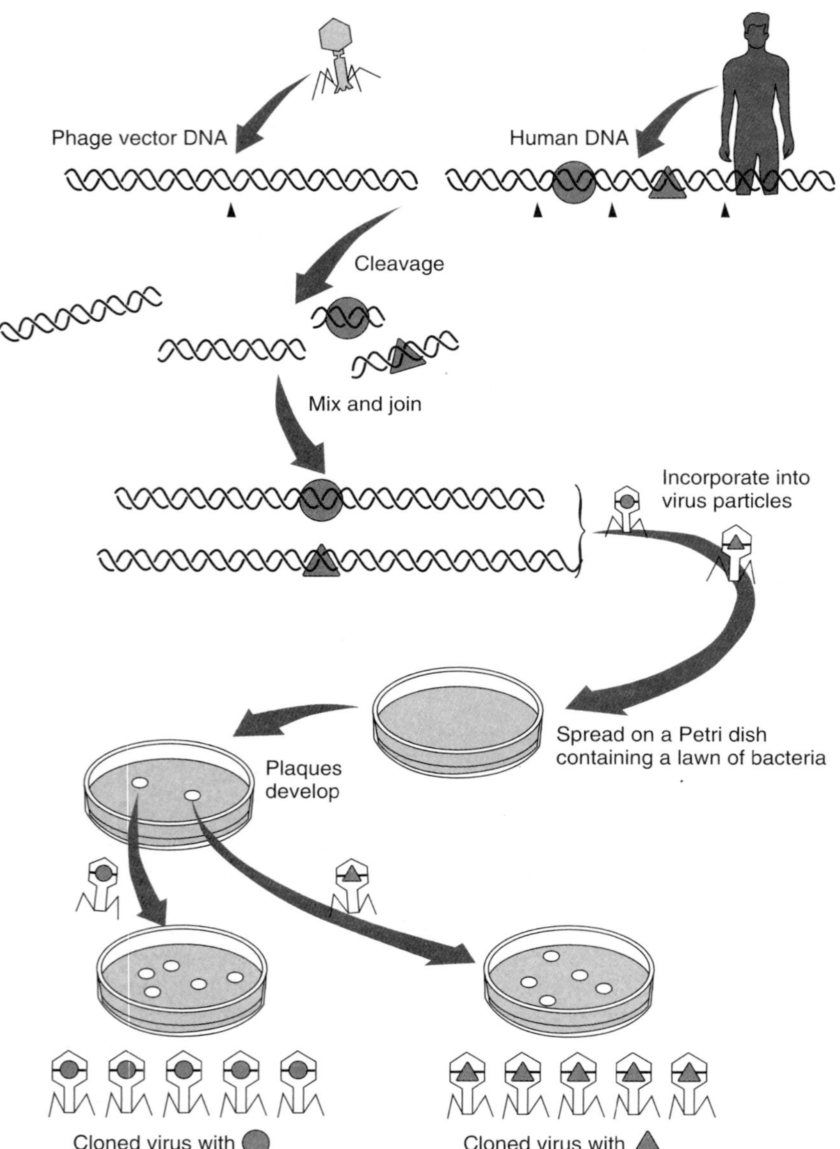

FIGURE 12-3 Cloning of DNA. Processes involved in the cloning of a segment of forming DNA by way of a viral vector are illustrated. (From Berg P, Singer M: Dealing with Genes: The Language of Heredity. New York, WH Freeman, p 93.)

the recombinant vector DNA. Once a copy of the gene segment of interest has been inserted into an appropriate plasmid, it can be amplified on a macro-scale within the transfected bacterial cells, creating larger amounts of DNA for further analyses or manipulations as desired.

Restriction enzymes or *restriction endonucleases* are naturally occurring enzymes that degrade viral DNA when it is introduced into the cell. The discovery of these enzymes, and their subsequent purification, was a critical step in the development of recombinant techniques, because the enzymes allow for exquisitely specific cutting of DNA molecules at specific sites. Some of these enzymes recognize certain base sequences, termed *recognition sites*, and cleave the target DNA precisely at these locations, whereas other restriction enzymes splice DNA in areas farther away from the recognition sites. These enzymes cleave only *cognate* DNA (DNA that contains the proper recognition sites) and do not degrade host DNA. Other enzymes, known as *ligases*, link disparate DNA molecules together. Through the use of restriction enzymes and ligases, unique recombinations of genetic material may be engineered. The recombined fragments may then be ligated into an appropriate plasmid vector and cloned for amplification. Furthermore, specific plasmids and organisms have been engineered for ease of transduction and high-level expression of the introduced genes, yielding large amounts of recombinant protein (e.g., human insulin) for clinical uses.

A special type of cloning exercise involves the amplification of all genes in a given cell type by making a so-called *library*, which is a collection of clones.[13] Choosing the type of library to create, cDNA or genomic, depends on the ultimate goal of the researcher. The technique is commonly employed to identify genes that are uniquely expressed by a specific cell type, for example, endothelial cells. In such cases, total mRNA is harvested from the cells or tissue of interest, converted into cDNA, and digested by restriction enzyme, and then the individual fragments are cloned to form a library. Screening the library to find a specific gene is accomplished through the use of a probe. Clones can also be detected by *functional complementation*, whereby a clone is identified because it confers a missing function on a mutant line of the donor organism. Through these mechanisms, a clone or copy of DNA can be identified and extracted for either further amplification or use in investigational studies.

The development of methods for determining the specific nucleotide sequence in a stretch of DNA was also a critical advance, and one on which the Human Genome Project hinged. DNA sequencing reactions involve DNA synthesis from the template with one or more labeled nucleotides, a universal primer, and base-specific dideoxynucleotides (ddNTPs). ddNTP is different from dNTP (normal state) in that it is missing two hydroxyl groups (at the 3′ and 2′ carbon positions); it cannot form phosphodiester bonds at the 3′ carbon, thereby terminating chain synthesis. When the sequencing reaction is set up, four base-specific reactions occur at once, with the concentration of ddNTP intentionally lower than that of its dNTP analogue. In this way, chain termination occurs randomly at any position, with the targeted base where the ddNTP binds. Because the process usually involves identical DNA molecules, the reactions create a group of varying DNA fragments that are then separated via electrophoresis on a denaturing polyacrylamide gel. The results of the gel are "read" by detecting bands from the bottom of the gel to the top in order from the alternate lanes marked for the nucleotides and recording the sequence in a linear array.

Improvements in sequencing are focused on development of automation with fluorescent labeling. Fluorescent sequencing uses primers and dNTPs combined with fluorophores, so during electrophoresis, the fluorescence signal can be recorded as the DNA passes through a fixed region of the gel. Labeling each of the base-specific reactions with a different fluorophore allows all four to be loaded in a single lane, unlike with traditional sequencing, as well as for simultaneous electronic storage of the information Eliminating the need for sequence interpretation and data entry by hand reduces transcription errors.

Another major development in DNA manipulation was the elucidation of the *polymerase chain reaction (PCR)*, a powerful tool for amplification of DNA.[14] PCR is an in vitro mechanism for synthesizing specific DNA sequences through repetitive cycles of template denaturation, primer annealing, and extension of annealed primers. It hinges on the discovery of unique DNA polymerase enzymes capable of functioning at elevated temperatures. The process involves digestion of DNA into large fractions by restriction enzymes and then heating of the fragments to induce denaturation that yields single strands. Small DNA molecules (oligonucleotides) selected to be complementary to regions upstream and downstream of the region of interest, are then employed as primers for the amplification reaction. The hybridized oligonucleotides become primers for DNA synthesis when deoxynucleotides and DNA polymerase are added to the mixture. After synthesis, the temperature is increased to denature the newly formed copies of the DNA fragment. In this way, at the completion of each cycle, the original DNA template and the product separate and become substrates for subsequent rounds of amplification. With each PCR cycle, the number of sequence copies increases geometrically. In this way, PCR allows for the rapid amplification of minute quantities of original DNA; it has therefore been a critical tool in forensics and other related disciplines.

Transgenic Technology

Incorporation of genes into the germlines of experimental animals is called *transgenic technology*.[15] This technique can result in two categories of mutations: gain-of-function and loss-of-function. Gain-of-function mutations are created by way of injection of a transgene into the zygote, whereas the loss-of-function mutations use embryonic stem cells. DNA inserted in this fashion yields founder animals with random incorporations of the transgene. Individual animals are then bred to give rise to the new phenotype. Unfortunately, resulting organisms may vary uncontrollably, because within individual cell lines there is no control of where the gene is incorporated or how it is expressed or potentially repressed. This variability prompted a search for more controlled ways of altering genes and gave rise to gene targeting.

Gene targeting involves altering a specific gene at its normal locus.[16] Therefore, all progeny of an animal so treated will have the same alteration of their genetic information and, hence, little variation in phenotype. An example is a *gene knockout*, a targeted disruption in a gene.[17] The elements necessary to create a genetic knockout include a targeting vector that contains a selection cassette (e.g., antibiotic resistance) and an endogenous allele.[18] After recombination between these two elements, the selection cassette becomes incorporated into the native allele and renders it modified. The resultant organisms have a different phenotype, and careful examination of this difference can yield information regarding the function of the gene concerned. Gene knockouts have become crucial tools in molecular genetics.

A *gene knockin* involves replacing the mature portion of one gene with that of another.[19] This process, like creation of a knockout, begins with a targeting vector that contains a gene of interest and an endogenous allele. In this case, however, when the gene of interest is incorporated into the genetic material, it is placed under the control of the appropriate promoter and regulatory sequences of the endogenous allele. The result is expression of the gene of interest rather than the endogenous genetic material. Figure 12-4 illustrates how transgenic knockouts and knockins are created.

■ GENETIC INTERVENTIONS: BASIC CONSIDERATIONS

Genetic interventions, broadly defined as therapies designed to influence genetic content or expression in target tissues, may take several forms. In its most common form of usage, the term *gene therapy* implies the delivery of a fully active transcriptional unit (i.e., a gene) to cells of the body to replace or augment the expression of a specific protein in either a local or systemic fashion. The cells that have successfully received the target gene are said to be *transduced*. Although the majority of such approaches would involve the introduction of a normal human gene, exogenous genes (e.g., viral or bacterial) or novel designer constructs may also be exploited for therapeutic benefit. A second broad category consists of approaches that inhibit or regulate endogenous gene expression in cells and tissues. The

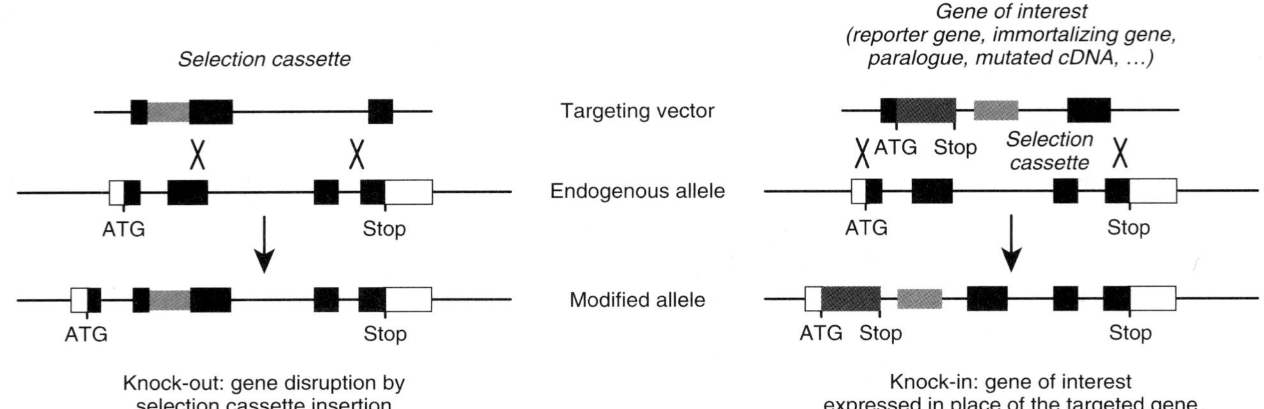

FIGURE 12-4 Transgenic technology: Creation of knockouts and knockins for the study of specific gene influences. Recombination between a target allele and an endogenous allele yields a mutant allele. *Knockouts* involve the insertion of a selection cassette into the endogenous allele, whereas *knockins* incorporate genetic information from the target vector and express this new sequence rather than their endogenous genes. ATG, adenine-thymine-guanine codon; Stop, stop codon. (From Babinet C, Cohen-Tannoudji M: Genome engineering via homologous recombination in mouse embryonic stem (ES) cells: An amazingly versatile tool for the study of mammalian biology. An Acad Bras Cienc 73:365-383, 2001.)

common thread of these strategies is the use of genetic material—specific RNA or DNA sequences—that produce the desired effects in target cells by interacting with the host cell's native gene expression machinery.

Strategies for Gene-Based Therapy

Gene replacement or *augmentation* involves the delivery of a gene that is either missing from a cell, present in a defective form, or simply underexpressed relative to the level of protein product desired by the clinician. In some cases, such as inherited coagulation defects, a relatively low level of gene expression can result in meaningful clinical benefit. In other cases, augmenting the level of an intracellular protein may provide a function only within the individual transduced cell, in which case it may be necessary to successfully transduce a large percentage of target cells to alter tissue function. Genes encoding proteins that are secreted or that participate in downstream signaling pathways can affect other cells in a paracrine or endocrine manner. Such genes are attractive because delivery to a small subpopulation of cells may yield a sufficient therapeutic result. Examples of this category of genes with cardiovascular applications are the nitric oxide synthase (NOS) isoforms (which yield a readily diffusible product, nitric oxide [NO]), plasminogen activators, and other enzymes with extracellular activities.

Introduction of an exogenous (nonhuman) gene is also a potential form of gene therapy. Such approaches might be used to target abnormal tissue for direct, drug, or immune-mediated cytotoxicity. Cytotoxic approaches have been explored in particular for cancer therapy but may also have logical extension for disorders of abnormal vascular cell proliferation, such as intimal hyperplasia. An example is the thymidine kinase (tk) gene of herpes simplex virus, which can be introduced into cells that are then efficiently killed by systemic administration of the drug ganciclovir.[20] Other applications for exogenous genes might involve scenarios whereby transient production of the protein in the target tissue produces a local therapeutic benefit before the transduced cells are eliminated by the host. Potent anticoagulant or fibrinolytic molecules isolated from other species (e.g., hirudin) are potential examples. Finally, normal human genes may be re-engineered to introduce sequences that enable regulation of expression. A unique example is the introduction of a mutation that renders the protein nonfunctional yet capable of competitively inhibiting the function of the normal endogenous protein. Such "dominant-negative" gene constructs constitute one type of loss-of-function approach (see later) that has been applied with success to cell cycle proteins such as the retinoblastoma (Rb) protein.[21]

Another approach to genetic manipulation is *gene inhibition* (Fig. 12-5). A specific gene, or an entire cellular program (e.g., cell cycle), may be inhibited through the use of small nucleic acid molecules—oligonucleotides—that may function to either block the translation of specific mRNAs (e.g. "antisense," ribozyme, or small interfering [si]RNAs) or block the activity of regulatory proteins (transcription factors) that control gene expression. Antisense oligodeoxynucleotides (ODNs) are designed to have a base sequence that is complementary in terms of Watson-Crick binding to a segment of the target gene.[22,23] They are generally 15 to 20 bases in length, conferring specificity to the target mRNA. This binding of ODN to mRNA either results in enzymatic degradation of the mRNA or prevents the translation of RNA into its protein product. The physiologic effects of ODNs may not always be the result of sequence-specific inhibition of target gene expression; several studies have demonstrated a variety of nonspecific but biologically relevant effects of ODN on cells.[24-27] The use of "scrambled-sequence" ODNs (in which the base sequence is mismatched to the target) of similar length is thus an important control for such investigations. A related form of gene blockade involves the use of ribozymes, segments of RNA that can act like enzymes to destroy specific sequences of target mRNA.[28]

A powerful new approach to inhibit specific gene expression based on the intracellular effects of double-stranded

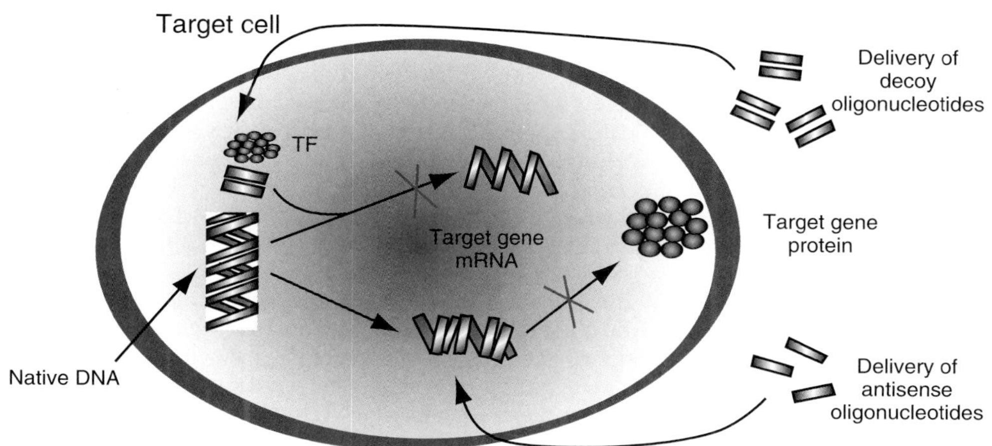

FIGURE 12-5 Cartoon illustrating two therapeutic strategies for gene blockade, antisense oligonucleotides and transcription factor (TF) decoys. The TF decoy oligodeoxynucleotide prevents TF activation of a family of genes that constitute a cellular response to a stimulus such as growth factor signaling. Antisense oligonucleotides bind and inactivate specific messenger RNA (mRNA) species, preventing their translation into protein.

(ds) RNA molecules has now been elucidated.[29] This phenomenon, termed *RNA interference*, is mediated by short (21- to 23-nucleotide) dsRNA constructs known as siRNAs. Intracellular processing of siRNAs culminates in their incorporation into a multiprotein complex (the RNA-induced silencing complex [RISC]), which may then recognize and cleave specific mRNA molecules that have homology to the siRNA. This mechanism yields effective and specific silencing of the targeted gene, usually in a transient fashion. Delivery of siRNAs to cells and tissues may be accomplished in a variety of ways, and there is growing interest in the use of viral vectors (see later) to achieve longer-term suppression of target genes by sustained intracellular production of the siRNA molecules.

Another type of gene inhibition involves the blockade of transcription factors (see Fig. 12-5). As noted previously, TFs regulate gene expression by binding to chromosomal DNA at specific promoter regions, and this binding turns on, or "activates," an adjacent gene. Transcription factor "decoys" are double-stranded ODN designed to mimic the chromosomal binding sites of the target TF. Once delivered to a cell, the decoy ODN binds to the available TF, competitively inhibiting the TF-promoter interaction and thereby preventing the subsequent activation of target genes.[30] TF decoys have now reached the stage of advanced clinical trials in cardiovascular disorders and other diseases.

A major attraction of these gene inhibition strategies is that small synthetic oligonucleotides (typically 1⁄1000 the size of an entire gene) may be delivered far more easily to cells and tissues with high efficiency and do not require specific viral or nonviral vectors. For example, the use of nondistending pressure has been shown to result in the rapid uptake of oligonucleotide by more than 80% of cells within the saphenous vein wall during a 10-minute exposure.[31] Nuclear localization of decoy ODN is thought to be required for target gene inhibition, a requirement that may be an important potential limitation, given that endocytic pathways for ODN uptake may result in sequestration, exocytosis, or degradation.[32]

Cellular Targeting

Genetic manipulation of target tissues can be achieved in one of two ways—ex vivo, employing a cell transplantation strategy, or in vivo, by direct introduction of genetic constructs to cells. In ex-vivo manipulation, the relevant desired cell types (endothelial cells, smooth muscle cells, stem or progenitor cells, myoblasts) are isolated and cultured ex vivo, and the desired genetic modification is performed prior to reintroduction of the cells to the patient. Disadvantages of this approach include the cumbersome inefficiency and potential risks of cell harvesting and culture in vitro as well as the need for subsequent cell engraftment. Conversely, if the cells themselves have potential therapeutic benefit (e.g., endothelial cell seeding of a prosthetic graft, myoblast engraftment in the myocardium for heart failure), this approach may have unique value. Interest in the ex-vivo approach has resurged with the rapid developments in the field of stem cell biology. The apparent plasticity of progenitor cell populations derived from blood, bone marrow, or even differentiated adult tissues has fueled great interest in the use of these cells, with or without genetic modification, for tissue repair.

Direct approaches for in vivo genetic intervention require that the genetic construct be efficiently delivered to the target cell population without inducing undesirable local or systemic effects. Both safety and efficacy are generally improved if the desired recipient cells can be specifically targeted, so that unwanted effects on surrounding cells are avoided. Targeting can be achieved by the use of local delivery approaches (e.g., isolated vessel segments, local application of biodegradable polymer delivery platforms) and by employing specific ligand-receptor binding strategies to enhance the uptake of genetic material by the specific cells of interest.

Pharmacokinetics of Gene Therapy

Pharmacokinetic considerations, including therapeutic dosage, distribution, elimination, and toxicity, are as germane to genetic therapies as they are to conventional pharmacotherapy. In the case of gene delivery strategies, the agent being delivered (i.e., the gene-carrying vector) and the therapeutic protein product are generally not subject to a predictable quantitative relationship, and thus, the process is significantly more complex and unpredictable. The established dosage, toxicity, and temporal expression profile of different vector systems must be carefully tailored into a particular approach, mandating extensive preclinical testing. In the case of gene blockade strategies, it is imperative that the time course of the cellular program being targeted be well characterized, so that the local concentration of the inhibitory molecule is maintained during the critical period. For example, targeting specific genetic programs (e.g., matrix production) after arterialization of the vein graft requires a priori knowledge of the temporal pattern of expression of the endogenous genes involved.

Delivery Systems (Vectors)

Genes are large, double-stranded DNA molecules that are inefficiently taken up by mammalian cells; therefore, a delivery system (vector) is required to achieve meaningful levels of expression in a target tissue. Once the genetic material (transgene) has been delivered into a cell, its expression depends on the cell's normal transcription and translation mechanisms to produce the desired protein product (Fig. 12-6). The form of the delivered genetic material, which may vary according to the type of vector employed, must be converted to a dsDNA template with appropriate regulatory sequences (i.e., promoter, poly-adenylation sites) to be acted upon by the cell's transcription machinery. In the cytoplasm, DNA molecules may be subject to degradation by catalytic enzymes. Generally, transgene expression is transient unless the genetic material crosses the nuclear membrane and becomes integrated into the chromosome. An exception is a special cytoplasmic form of DNA known as an *episome*, which may remain stable and provide long-term expression despite its extra-chromosomal location. If the target cells subsequently undergo rounds of division, however, only integrated transgenes will be passaged on to successive daughter cells. Thus, the durability of transgene expression is strongly linked to the ability of a given vector to achieve chromosomal integration or a stable episomal form.

In the special case of blood vessels, achieving gene transfer to a majority of cells within an artery or vein graft

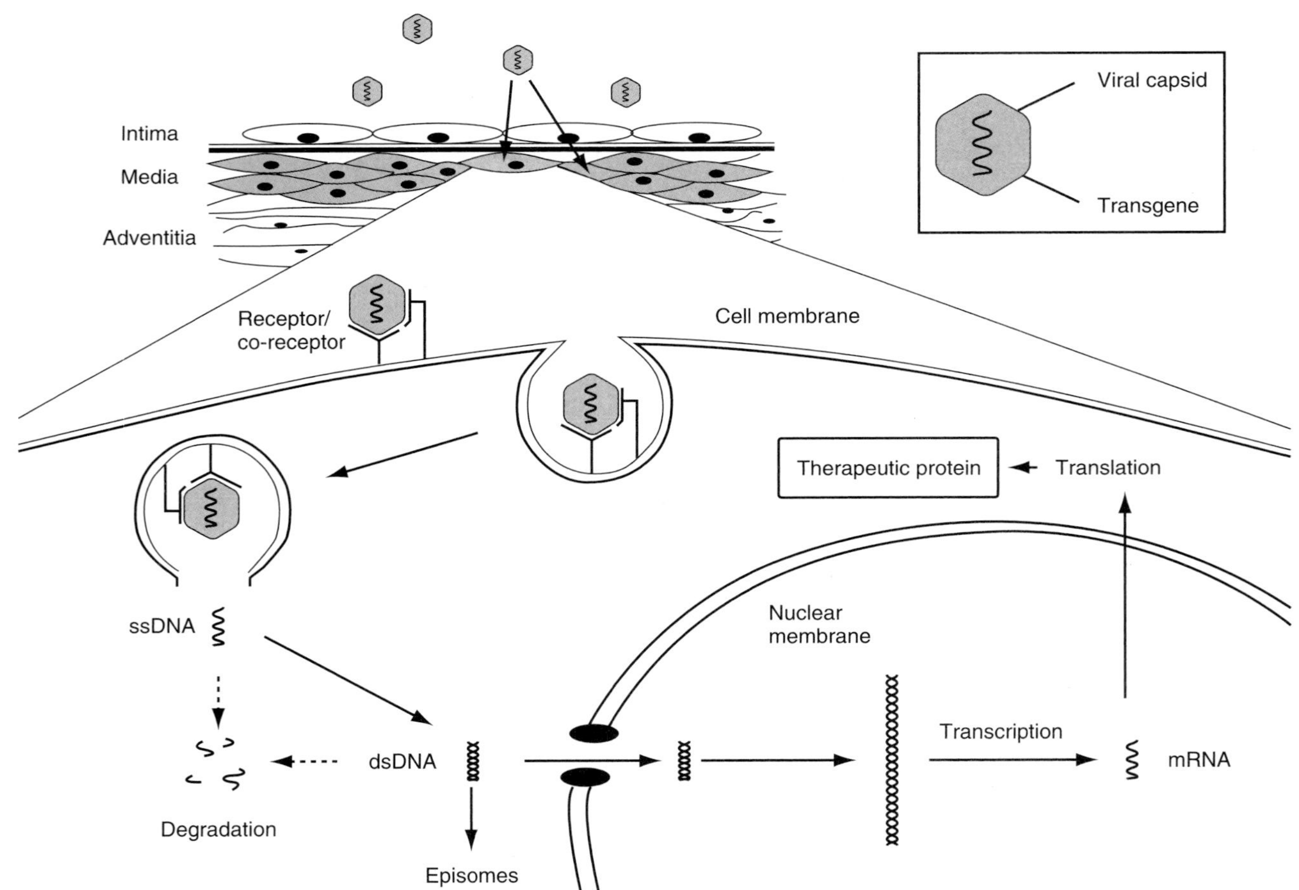

FIGURE 12-6 Gene delivery to a target cell by means of a recombinant viral vector (adeno-associated vector shown for illustration). Engineered viral particle containing the genetic information of interest ("transgene") enters the cell by way of viral receptors that normally mediate virus infection. After processing into a double-stranded DNA (dsDNA) template, the transgene is transcribed and translated into the desired protein product by host cell machinery. mRNA, messenger RNA; ssDNA, single-stranded DNA.

Table 12-1 Characteristics of an Ideal Vector for Vascular Gene Therapy

Safety: elicits minimal host inflammatory response or toxicity
Easily produced, handled, and stored in clinically relevant concentrations
Capable of rapid and efficient delivery of genes to nondividing cells
Confers stable or regulatable levels of gene expression
Flexible to accommodate genes of all sizes

is a significant hurdle, particularly within the temporal constraints of an intraoperative strategy or one that employs temporary flow occlusion. The "ideal vector" for this purpose has yet to be defined but would have the desirable attributes listed in Table 12-1. Safety concerns are paramount; the vector employed should induce little or no host inflammatory response, and its distribution should be ideally restricted to the target tissue of interest. The much publicized, unfortunate death of a patient in a gene therapy trial in 1999 appears to have resulted from a massive inflammatory response after hepatic artery administration of an adenoviral vector.[33] The unique properties of different vectors, as well as the mode of delivery employed, determine the nature and magnitude of the host response, mandating that each approach undergo appropriate preclinical evaluation in suitable animal models.

For clinical applications, a vector must be produced in relevant concentrations with reproducible quality and must be stored and handled easily without loss of potency. For blood vessels, the target cells—endothelial cells (ECs) and smooth muscle cells (SMCs)—are essentially quiescent in the normal state, so the ability of a vector to efficiently transduce nondividing cells is critical. To minimize acute adverse effects on the vessel, the vector and delivery method should preserve endothelial integrity and function. Stable transgene expression, for weeks if not months, may be desirable for many potential molecular targets involved in the generalized vascular injury response. Ideally, the clinician would be able to control the kinetics and magnitude of target gene expression, implying a fully regulatable vector system. Finally, the optimal vector would be flexible to accommodate genes of all sizes without difficulty. Currently available systems involve compromises of all of these aspects to varying degrees, and the success of ongoing efforts in vector technology is critical to realizing the full potential of genetic therapies.

Gene delivery vectors may be divided into two categories, viral and nonviral. For a more complete review of vectors, the reader is referred to a number of excellent treatments of this topic.[34-37] Naturally occurring viruses have evolved elaborate strategies for efficient gene delivery and expression in host cells. The genetic engineering of viruses into therapeutic vectors requires the ability to segregate genetic elements required for new virus production from coding sequences. The recombinant virions thus generated contain the genetic information of interest inserted in place of the native viral sequences, serving as molecular "Trojan horses" (see Fig. 12-6). These re-engineered viruses are defective in that they are unable to replicate in host cells, and therefore cannot propagate in vivo to infect neighboring cells. The ability to generate such recombinants is limited by the innate complexity of a particular virus. The general approach is to delete as much of the native genetic information as possible, given that most of the pathologic consequences of virus infection are due to the expression of these viral genes. The amount of residual viral genes varies for different vector systems and is a major focus of research and development in this field. For most clinically relevant systems, exposure to these agents is well tolerated, and tissue toxicity is minimal.[37] Nonetheless, direct cytotoxicity and host immunologic responses may occur both as a result of viral gene products as well as the viral particle itself.

Nonviral methods of gene delivery have also been a focus of intense development and progress. Naked plasmid DNA, ligand-DNA, and DNA-liposome complexes are all capable of transferring genetic sequences, albeit at relatively low efficiency (high number of particles required per target cell). Conversely, they offer the potential advantages of excluding exogenous (i.e., viral) genetic information, relaxing gene size constraints, having technical simplicity, and inducing less host immune response. Mechanical force (e.g., pressure) may facilitate DNA transfer, although the mechanisms remain unclear.[31] In some cell types (e.g., skeletal muscle) long-term expression has been documented with nonviral transfer. It is notable that smaller molecules such as oligonucleotides, as previously mentioned, are more easily taken up by target tissues in simple solution and may not require vectors to achieve adequate delivery.

Retroviral Vectors

Recombinant retroviral vectors were the first to be developed into clinically usable gene delivery agents.[38] These vectors require active division of the target cell to integrate their genetic material into the chromosome, and thus are best suited to in vitro gene transfer under culture conditions in which target cell division can be manipulated. Such ex vivo approaches have utility for hematopoietic disorders and have also been considered for blood vessels, vascular grafts, and ischemic muscle using a cell seeding approach.[39-43] Given the requirement for target cell proliferation, retroviral vectors are not well suited for direct transfer of genes to intact blood vessels or end organs.

Adenoviral Vectors

Adenoviruses are common causes of non-neoplastic human diseases, particularly in the upper respiratory and digestive tracts. Recombinant adenoviruses have become the most widely used viral vectors for in vivo gene transfer[44] and have been used extensively in experimental cardiovascular systems.[45-48] They have also been employed in clinical trials for a variety of conditions ranging from cystic fibrosis to therapeutic angiogenesis. Adenoviruses can infect nondividing cells effectively and generally do not integrate into the host genome. These vectors can achieve relatively efficient gene transfer to quiescent vascular tissue, but transgene expression is transient in nature. For example, brief (30 minutes) exposure of a vein graft to an adenovirus (Ad) vector typically results in fairly uniform gene delivery to the endothelium and adjacent SMCs on the luminal aspect of the media, with maintenance of high-level gene expression for 1 to 2 weeks.[47,49] Depending on the process being targeted, this time window may or may not be adequate to achieve a therapeutic result.

The host immunologic response to Ad vectors has been a source of considerable concern. Removal of all native viral genes from the vectors has been a difficult task, and most available systems have low-level but detectable expression of remaining viral genes. This feature is likely to be one important cause of cell-mediated immune responses.[50,51] Despite this hypothesis, subsequent generations of Ad vectors with additional deletions of viral genes have not yet demonstrated prolongation of gene expression in blood vessels.[52,53] The possibility for recombination events to yield replication-competent Ad (RCA) has been greatly reduced in current production methods but remains a safety concern that mandates appropriate testing of every batch produced for clinical use.

Inflammatory responses to high concentrations of the viral particle are another important mechanism. In blood vessels, local inflammation and neointima formation have been observed after Ad exposure and appear to be dose-related.[54,55] These potentially undesirable effects on vessels are reduced at lower Ad concentrations ($< 10^{10}$ plaque-forming units/mL)[53] and, importantly, have not mitigated the benefits observed after delivery of therapeutic transgenes in animal models of intimal hyperplasia in both arteries and vein bypass grafts (see later).

Adeno-Associated Virus Vectors

Recombinant adeno-associated virus (AAV) vectors have been under investigation since the early 1980s.[56,57] AAV, a member of the parvovirus family, is nonpathogenic in humans. Wild-type AAV requires both host cell factors and co-infection with other viruses (e.g., adenovirus, herpesvirus) to cause a productive infection. In the absence of such helper viruses, AAV can integrate stably into the host cell DNA. Studies in immunocompetent animals have documented persistent transgene expression in a variety of tissues (muscle, liver, and central nervous system) to beyond 1 year.[58-61] Cardiovascular studies have been limited to date.[49,62-64] AAV vectors are being employed in clinical trials (e.g., muscular dystrophy), and their application is likely to grow.

In vivo, recombinant AAV-mediated gene expression is delayed in onset, with a lag phase of 2 weeks or longer following exposure before appreciable levels are detected in target tissues. These kinetics have been observed in a variety of organs, including blood vessels,[49] constituting an important limitation for any clinical strategy in which high levels of gene expression are desired quickly. An important advantage of the AAV vector, in addition to its long-term persistence, is its lack of immunogenicity. Unlike Ad vectors, AAV vectors contain no viral coding sequences. The major current limitations of AAV for vascular therapy relate to size, transduction efficiency, and production. Limitations of transgene size in AAV vectors to approximately four kilobases is adequate for many relevant genes, but not for larger structural or matrix proteins. Efficiency of transduction with AAV is particularly low in endothelial cells. Production of AAV vectors remains cumbersome, and better methods are required to yield consistent, higher-titer preparations for clinical use. An additional consideration is that soluble heparin is a competitive inhibitor of AAV (serotype 2) infection at clinically relevant concentrations; modifications of the AAV capsid protein may decrease the heparin sensitivity and improve cellular targeting of the vector.[65]

Other Viral Vectors

Lentiviral vectors are under active preclinical investigation for gene therapy. These vectors, based on human immunodeficiency virus type 1 (HIV-1) as well as other, nonhuman lentiviruses, are efficient at integrating into nondividing cells and offer potential long-term expression in target tissues. Experience with these vectors in cardiovascular tissues has been reported in scant fashion thus far.[66,67] Herpes simplex virus type 1 (HSV-1) has been investigated as a vector system primarily in central nervous tissue or in tumor models, with very limited reports of cardiovascular models.[68] Of interest, live attenuated HSV-1 has also been employed as a cytotoxic strategy in both tumors and intimal hyperplasia. In this strategy, tissues infected with HSV-1 are then treated with systemic acyclovir, which eradicates the HSV-1–bearing target cells.[69]

Potential Complications of Therapeutic Gene Transfer

Potential adverse effects associated with gene transfer may be grouped into those associated with the delivery method and those related to the effects of the genetic material itself within target tissues. Viral vectors may induce cellular and humoral host responses that vary according to the dosage and route of administration but tend to be characteristic for the type of virus employed, as described in the preceding paragraphs. Acute toxicity from systemic or local exposure to the foreign viral particles may occur, with total dose and prior exposure history being important individual modifiers. In this context, minimizing systemic exposure is an important parameter of clinical gene therapy protocols. In addition to triggering immune system activation, the viral particles may cause direct inflammatory activation of the target cells themselves (e.g., ECs), inducing a deleterious change in cellular function. Cell-mediated immune responses can be directed against the transduced cells and can trigger secondary cascades of local inflammation. Humoral responses to the therapeutic gene product, particularly if it relates to an exogenous gene, may also occur. Concern regarding the in vivo mutagenic potential of certain vectors that integrate into the chromosome has been validated by the occurrence of leukemias in two patients who had been treated with retroviral transduction of hematopoietic cells for the correction of enzyme deficiencies.[70] Finally, the potential for unwanted effects on germ cells after systemic exposure to these agents is an important safety and ethical concern. Nonviral gene delivery and oligonucleotide-based strategies offer the intrinsic advantage of avoiding viral exposure.

Summary of Current Gene Delivery Systems for Vascular Gene Therapy

At present, Ad vectors are the only agents capable of reproducible, high-efficiency gene delivery to a meaningful percentage of cells in the blood vessel wall within a clinically relevant period of exposure. For delivery of genes to ischemic cardiac or skeletal muscle (i.e., therapeutic angiogenesis), where temporal and bulk flow constraints are far less stringent than in vessels, nonviral delivery approaches (including "naked" plasmid DNA) may provide an adequate solution. In the uniquely controlled, ex vivo setting of vein graft treatment, the risks of dissemination or toxicity from systemic vector exposure appear minimal. An important unknown is the potential proinflammatory effects of Ad in the vessel wall, even at concentrations in the lower effective range. The short window of Ad-mediated gene expression is likely to limit this approach for the targeting of some processes but may be adequate for others. AAV vectors offer important potential advantages, but practical limitations remain significant. Though considerable progress has been made, and clinically usable systems are already available, further development of vector technology is needed to optimize therapeutic gene delivery for the cardiovascular system.

SPECIFIC GENE-BASED THERAPEUTIC APPROACHES IN VASCULAR DISEASE

Disease states based on well-defined single-gene defects are intrinsically attractive targets for genetic therapies. In cardiovascular disease, such disorders are exceedingly rare, but syndromes of abnormal lipid metabolism, blood pressure control, and thrombosis regulation have been identified and considered as possible scenarios for systemic gene correction. However, improved understanding of altered patterns of gene expression in complex diseases such as atherosclerosis, coupled with the predilection for local complications of the disease to occur at specified sites, suggests a much broader potential opportunity for genetic interventions. Atherosclerotic plaque progression or rupture, intimal hyperplasia at sites of angioplasty or bypass grafting, and end-organ ischemia all provide targets for consideration of local genetic therapies to stabilize or reverse the underlying pathophysiology (Table 12-2).

Monogenic Disorders

Familial hypercholesterolemia is a rare disorder characterized by severe, premature coronary atherosclerosis and marked elevations in plasma levels of low-density lipoprotein (LDL) in individuals who are homozygous for dysfunctional mutations in the LDL receptor (LDLR) gene. A gene correction approach based on delivery of the LDLR gene to liver has been under active investigation.[71] Other uncommon monogenic causes of dyslipidemia are mutations in the apolipoprotein B-100 gene and other proteins involved in cholesterol transport.[72] Single-gene defects leading to disorders of coagulation, including bleeding disorders (factor deficiencies) and prothrombotic states (e.g., prothrombin mutations, factor V Leiden mutation) are also candidates for genetic intervention.

Intimal Hyperplasia: Control of the Vascular Injury Response

The cellular response to vascular injury involves a complex interplay between resident cells of the vessel wall (ECs, SMCs, and adventitial cells) and circulating blood elements (platelets, inflammatory cells, progenitor or stem cells) that are recruited to participate in the healing response. Regardless of the mode of vascular injury—lipid accumulation (atherogenesis), mechanical stretch (after angioplasty), prosthetic grafting, or vein arterialization (surgical bypass)—a common paradigm of intimal hyperplasia ensues. This healing process, when excessive, can lead to progressive occlusion of native vessels and failure of all types of vascular reconstructions. The limited long-term patency of interventions in small to medium-sized arteries (i.e., coronary and infrainguinal atherosclerosis) remains a major cause of morbidity and mortality.

The search for therapies to control the vascular injury response has evolved from bench to bedside as basic investigations have illuminated an enlarging array of molecular targets. Although each of these clinical scenarios (angioplasty restenosis, prosthetic and vein graft failure) share certain pathophysiologic features, namely, a component related to intimal hyperplasia, it may be an oversimplification to regard them as a single therapeutic target. Systemic pharmacotherapies, by and large, have yielded minimal results. The definable spatial localization of these processes has engendered great interest in locally delivered therapies, including drugs, biologicals (cells, proteins, peptides), irradiation, and genetic interventions.[73-75]

The cell and molecular biology of intimal hyperplasia have been best characterized in the context of acute arterial injury such as balloon angioplasty (for review, see Chapter 11). However, important parallels to arterial intimal hyperplasia have been documented in animal models of vein and prosthetic graft intimal hyperplasia, particularly with regard to SMC activation, migration, and proliferation. In its most virulent form, intimal hyperplasia produces a flow-restricting lesion at the site of vascular injury. In vein grafts such lesions may occur diffusely throughout the bypass conduit

Table 12-2 Molecular Targets for Genetic Interventions in Vascular Disease

PROCESS	MOLECULAR TARGET(S)	REFERENCES
Thrombosis	Antithrombotics, thrombolytics	79-86
Cell proliferation	Cell cycle genes, NOS, pro-apoptotics	100-110, 114-134
Cell migration/matrix remodeling	TIMPS, plasminogen activators, matrix genes	136-144
Ischemia/reperfusion, inflammation, oxidative stress	Cytoprotectants (NOS, SOD, HO-1)	89-93, 96-98
Angiogenesis	VEGF, FGF, HGF, HIF1-α, angiopoietin	114, 165-170

FGF, fibroblast growth factor; HGF, hepatocyte growth factor; HIF1-α, hypoxia-inducible factor 1-α; HO-1, heme oxygenase-1; NOS, nitric oxide synthase(s); SOD, superoxide dismutase(s); TIMPs, tissue inhibitor(s) of matrix metalloproteinases; VEGF, vascular endothelial growth factor.

or, more commonly, at focal sites near anastomoses or in the body of the graft. In addition to the development of a proliferative neointima, other critical events, including local thrombus generation and active matrix metabolism, simultaneously occur and play important roles in the remodeling vessel. In post-angioplasty arteries, constrictive remodeling ("shrinkage") has been linked to adventitial changes and, in particular, collagen deposition.[76-86] These studies have refocused attention on the role of adventitial cells, particularly myofibroblasts, in neointima formation, matrix synthesis, and perivascular fibrosis. Parallel studies examining the role of the adventitia in vein graft remodeling have suggested similarities.[87-89] The complexity of the vascular healing response yields a broad spectrum of potential molecular targets, with a rationale that improved control (rather than complete abrogation) of the process may be adequate to yield meaningful clinical benefit. A brief consideration of each of these pathophysiologic components ensues.

Cell Proliferation

SMC proliferation is the hallmark of intimal hyperplasia after both arterial injury and vein grafting. A family of cell cycle proteins has been identified as part of the normal feedback control system for cell division, and genetic manipulation of these pathways can induce growth arrest.[90] These critical cell cycle proteins include the retinoblastoma (Rb) protein as well as members of the Cip/Kip family (p21 and p27) and p53. Each of the aforementioned inhibitory proteins has been explored through the use of direct gene transfer to achieve local overexpression in artery or vein graft models.[21,91-95] Conversely, inhibition of genes that promote cell cycle progression, including cyclin-dependent kinases (cdks), proliferating cell nuclear antigen (PCNA), and proto-oncogenes (c-myc, c-myb), through the use of antisense oligonucleotides has also been explored.[96,97] There is some suggestion that inhibition strategies targeting multiple cell cycle genes offer an advantage over single-target approaches. Rabbit vein grafts treated simultaneously with antisense ODN to PCNA and cell division cycle (cdc)-2 kinase demonstrated a more adaptive remodeling response, with marked attenuation of neointima formation and medial hypertrophy, and were less prone to late (6 months) atherosclerotic changes in hypercholesterolemic animals.[98] Remarkably, this cell cycle inhibition was also associated with better endothelial function, as measured by vasomotor responses, adhesion molecule expression, and monocyte binding in comparison with untreated and control ODN-treated grafts.[99]

Further downstream, the transcription factor E2F induces the coordinated expression of a number of critical cell cycle genes leading to progression to mitosis, including PCNA, cdk 1, cdc 2 kinase, c-myc, and c-myb.[90,100] Several of these genes, as noted, have been implicated in intimal hyperplasia by investigations using antisense molecules. E2F function is necessary for normal cell cycle progresion,[101-103] and the antiproliferative activity of Rb appears to depend on its ability to inhibit E2F. A transcription factor decoy approach targeting E2F markedly inhibited intimal hyperplasia in both a rat carotid injury model and a rabbit vein graft model.[100,104-106] A 14–base pair ODN that mimics the consensus binding site for E2F was employed. Rabbit vein grafts demonstrated improvements in neointima formation, wall remodeling, and resistance to plaque formation similar to those seen with the two-target antisense strategy previously described. These preclinical studies formed the basis for proceeding to clinical evaluation of the E2F decoy strategy. A pilot study conducted in patients undergoing lower extremity vein bypass employed ex vivo incubation of the graft with the E2F decoy ODN in a chamber using non-distending pressure (Fig. 12-7).[107] This study demonstrated safety and feasibility for the intraoperative approach and was followed by a phase 2 study in coronary bypass grafting, for which intravascular ultrasound and angiographic follow-up showed promising preliminary results.[108] Currently, a phase 3 program (co-sponsored by Corgentech, Inc., and Bristol-Myers-Squibb, Inc.) for evaluation of the E2F decoy (edifoligide) in both lower extremity and coronary vein grafting is under way, with results expected in early 2005.

A number of growth factors have been hypothesized to play important roles in the development of intimal hyperplasia after arterial injury and in vein grafting. They include platelet-derived growth factor (PDGF), basic fibroblast growth factor (bFGF), insulin-like growth factor (IGF), and angiotensin. Growth factor targeting may be accomplished via an antisense approach,[109,110] via a transcription factor–decoy approach,[111] or by targeting of receptors such as G-proteins,[112,113] which transduce the signals into cellular responses. In general, owing to the multiplicity of mitogens available in the vessel wall after injury, targeted inhibition of an individual growth factor is likely to be intrinsically less efficient than targeting of events further downstream (cell cycle). An alternative growth factor–based strategy is to enhance endothelial recovery using specific endothelial mitogens such as vascular endothelial growth factor (VEGF). Clinical trials have been initiated to examine the utility of this approach in reducing post-angioplasty re-stenosis[114] and distal anastomotic hyperplasia in prosthetic dialysis access grafts.[115]

Secreted or diffusible mediators with antiproliferative properties are particularly attractive because the efficiency limitations of gene transfer are lessened by the potential local effect on neighboring cells ("bystander effect"). The prototype molecule is NO, and indeed, all three of the NOS isoforms (endothelial, neuronal, and inducible) have been investigated for therapeutic gene transfer to arteries and vein grafts.[116-122] Significant inhibition of graft neointima formation has been reported (range 30% to 50%). The antiproliferative effects of NO are complemented by its additional vasculoprotective properties (antimigratory, reduced platelet aggregation and leukocyte adhesion, vasodilatation), making it an extremely attractive target. A current clinical trial is examining the effects of liposome-mediated inducible NOS gene transfer to coronary arteries after angioplasty for the prevention of re-stenosis.[123]

Whereas the strategy of cell cycle inhibition may be viewed as "cytostatic," cytotoxic approaches have also been considered. Delivery of tk, a gene from the herpes simplex virus, followed by administration of the drug ganciclovir leads to death of the tk-expressing cells.[20,124] A similar approach, utilizing the bacterial enzyme cytosine deaminase

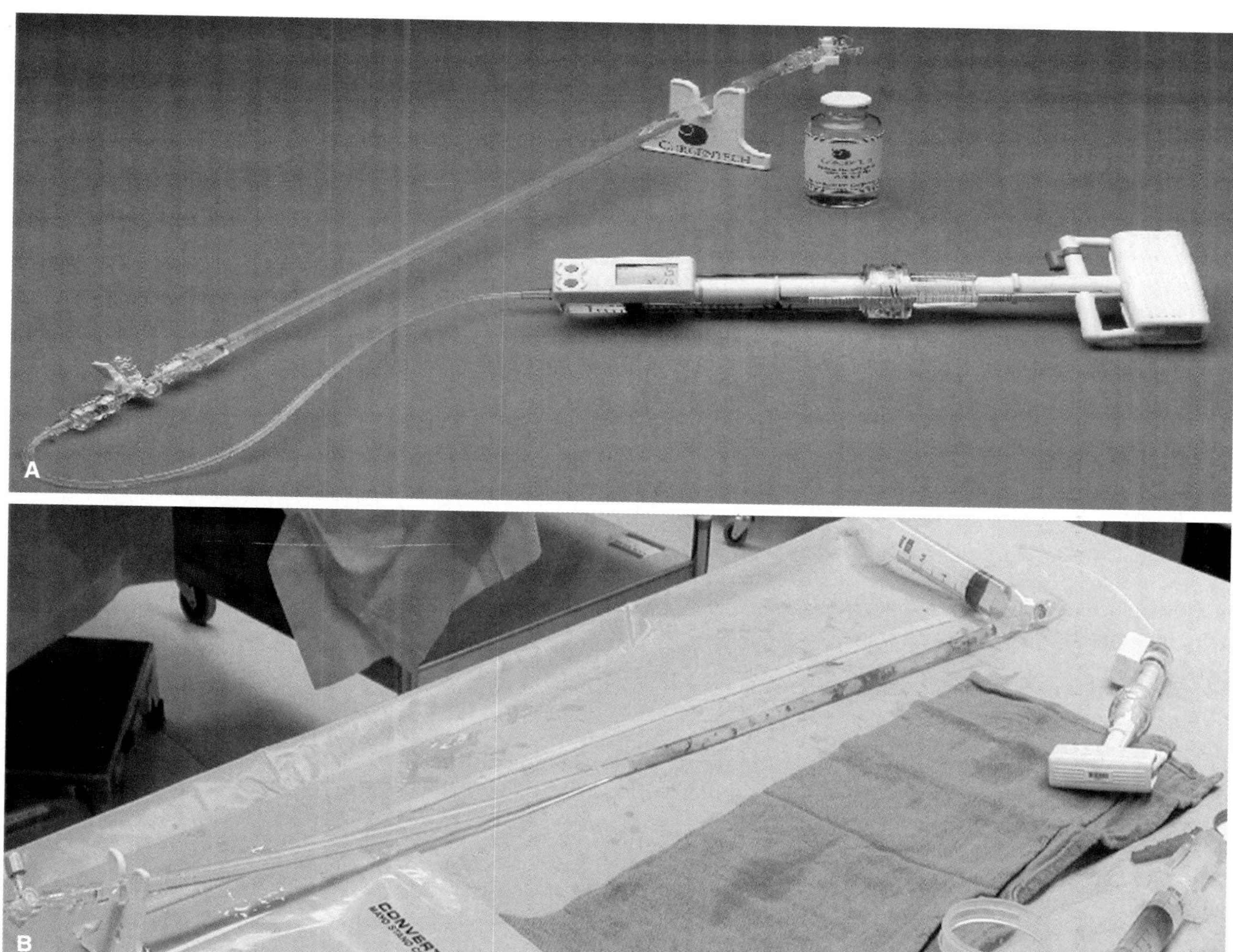

FIGURE 12-7 Ex-vivo treatment of human lower extremity vein grafts with the E2F decoy oligodeoxynucleotide (ODN) (edifoligide). **A,** Photograph of the graft transfection device. **B,** Cannulated vein is placed inside of the chamber and exposed to ODN solution at 6 PSI (0.4 atm), nondistending pressure, for 10 minutes, to achieve delivery of the agent into the graft wall. (**A,** courtesy of Corgentech, Inc, South San Francisco, CA.)

followed by administration of the prodrug 5-fluorocytosine, has been described in a rabbit arterial injury model.[125] Genes involved in regulating the process of apoptosis may also be considered for strategies aimed at promoting cell death and thereby attenuating intimal hyperplasia.[126,127]

It should be noted that in the absence of a means of specific targeting of SMCs within the vessel, each of these antiproliferative strategies carries a potential adverse effect of delaying endothelial healing as well. Similar concerns have been raised by the increase in rate of subacute thrombosis that has been observed in clinical trials of brachytherapy in coronary angioplasty, although the mechanisms remain speculative.[128]

Cell Migration and Matrix Remodeling

Cell migration is a critical element in the pathophysiology of intimal hyperplasia after vascular injury. Migration of SMCs requires active breakdown of the local matrix surrounding the cell, which has been likened to a "cage." The proteolytic enzyme plasmin is involved in this process, which is regulated locally by the balance of plasminogen activators and plasminogen activator inhibitor-1 (PAI-1). Matrix metalloproteinases (MMPs), a family of enzymes capable of degrading vascular extracellular matrix proteins, are expressed by both resident vascular and inflammatory cells recruited to sites of injury. The naturally occurring inhibitors of MMPs are the tissue inhibitors of MMPs (TIMPs), of which several isoforms exist. The balance between matrix-degrading proteins and proteins that inhibit matrix degradation determines the local proteolytic milieu. Matrix accumulation, also a prominent feature of advanced arterial and vein graft lesions, is an important potential therapeutic target. Experimentally, plasmin inhibition,[129,130] transforming growth factor-β inhibition,[131] elastase inhibition,[132] and TIMP overexpression (TIMP-1, 2, and 3 isoforms)[133-137] have been investigated as strategies for reducing neointima formation and improving vessel remodeling.

Thrombosis

The common endpoint for all failed interventions is thrombosis. In a defined subset of high-risk scenarios, such as tibial angioplasty, attempted resurrection of a thrombosed graft by thrombectomy or thrombolysis,[138,139] "redo" distal bypass,[140] and composite grafting with ectopic vein segments,[141] early failure rates are significantly elevated. Damaged or small-diameter conduits, particularly when placed in low-flow environments, may be particularly prone to early thrombosis. Surgical preparative injury is known to result in significant endothelial loss in vein grafts, exposing subendothelial matrix and leading to the adhesion of platelets and proteins such as fibrinogen. Platelet aggregates and mural thrombus may form a nidus for occlusive thrombosis or may play a critical early role in the downstream events leading to intimal hyperplasia. A therapeutic strategy targeting in-situ thrombosis at such sites has obvious relevance.

ECs maintain a nonthrombogenic vascular surface by means of a number of well-characterized natural anticoagulant mechanisms. They include the synthesis of heparan sulfate proteoglycans with anticoagulant activity,[142] the protein C–thrombomodulin (TM) pathway,[143] the hydrolysis of adenosine nucleotides, which promote platelet activation,[144] and a surface-associated fibrinolytic mechanism that results in local production of plasmin. ECs also synthesize prostacyclin and NO, which have potent antiaggregatory effects on platelets. Each of these natural antithrombotic, antiaggregatory, and fibrinolytic pathways has been investigated as a relevant target for gene transfer to injured vascular surfaces or vein bypass grafts.[145-150] Nonhuman antithrombotic genes such as hirudin have also been investigated.[151,152]

Inflammation, Oxidative Stress, and Ischemia-Reperfusion Injury

Local recruitment of inflammatory cells is a critical element of atherosclerosis and intimal hyperplasia in both arteries and veins. Immediately after angioplasty or vein grafting, the vessel wall is targeted by an acute inflammatory response involving recruitment of neutrophils and mononuclear cells. These inflammatory cells provide further amplification of cytokine pathways, promoting local cell activation, migration, and proliferation.[153,154] Oxidative stress in the vessel wall appears to persist, and sustained elevations of superoxide generation have been demonstrated in experimental vein grafts months after implantation.[155] Antioxidant gene therapy might therefore be advantageous in both the acute and subacute stages of the injury response. Other potential anti-inflammatory approaches might include targeting the activated EC or SMC phenotype present in the injured vessel wall with a transcription factor–decoy strategy (e.g., against nuclear factor-κB[156]), soluble adhesion molecules,[157] and other diffusible mediators that decrease leukocyte-EC interactions.[158]

With the possible exception of in-situ grafting, all vein grafts undergo a period of warm ischemia followed by reperfusion. This leads to the local generation of superoxide and other reactive oxygen species (ROS) within the wall, triggering secondary inflammatory cascades as well as direct cytotoxicity to resident endothelial and smooth muscle cells.[155,159] Complement activation, leukocyte recruitment, platelet-fibrin deposition, and endothelial loss are known sequelae of reperfusion injury in end organs. Molecular therapies might be targeted at scavenging the excess of ROS generated locally, or protecting resident cells from their downstream effects. Naturally occurring cytoprotective and antioxidant mechanisms include proteins such as heat shock protein-70 (HSP-70)[160] and scavenging enzymes such as catalase,[161] superoxide dismutase,[162] and heme oxygenase-1.[163,164] These molecules have been examined for their utility in models of arterial injury and cardiac reperfusion, but not to date in vein grafts.

Critical Ischemia: Therapeutic Angiogenesis

The notion of enhancing the development of endogenous collateral vessels to ameliorate the clinical sequelae of chronic ischemia is not new, but advances in the understanding of angiogenesis at the cellular and molecular level have provided new avenues for potential therapeutic manipulation. This scientific field, in large part pioneered by the efforts of a surgeon (Judah Folkman, MD, Children's Hospital of Boston) to understand the mechanisms of tumor neovascularization, has rapidly advanced from bench to bedside during the last decade. However, much is still unknown regarding the precise mechanisms of blood vessel growth in postnatal organisms.

A variety of growth factors and cytokines have been identified as playing critical roles in new vessel formation and maturation.[165,166] VEGF, which has several isoforms, is a potent secreted cytokine that promotes the proliferation, differentiation, and intercellular interactions of endothelial cells. Several receptor tyrosine kinases—including VEGFR1 (Flt), VEGFR2 (Flk), and VEGFR3—have been identified which mediate signaling of the VEGF isoforms. Other growth factors, particularly members of the FGF family[167,168] and hepatocyte growth factor (HGF),[169,170] also have potent angiogenic properties. Other factors, in particular the angiopoietins (Ang-1 and Ang-2), play critical roles in the stabilization and maturation of new vessels through recruitment of pericytes and mesenchymal cells.

The cellular elements involved in angiogenesis have also been under intense investigation, with focus on the role of circulating endothelial precursor cells and other "stem cell" populations that may be mobilized from bone marrow. Several studies in both animal models and humans have demonstrated the existence of a population of circulating endothelial progenitor cells that may be mobilized under certain conditions of stress and may participate in the endothelialization of vascular grafts[171] or the angiogenic responses to ischemia, wound healing, or tumor growth.[172] Major unresolved questions focus on the specific phenotype of precursor cells that are necessary and sufficient for angiogenesis and on the signaling pathways involved in their recruitment and cell-cell interactions. Nonetheless, early clinical studies have been initiated in which endothelial precursor or bone marrow–derived cells have been introduced into ischemic tissues, and this will undoubtedly be an area of active clinical investigation.

Genetic approaches for therapeutic angiogenesis may involve either direct delivery of critical regulatory genes to

Table 12-3 Overview of Phase 1–Phase 2 Clinical Trials Involving Gene Transfer in Cardiovascular Disease

GENE(S)	DISEASE	VECTOR(S)
VEGFs	CAD, PAD, restenosis	Plasmid, adenovirus
FGFs	CAD, PAD	Plasmid, adenovirus
HIF1-α	CAD, PAD	Adenovirus
iNOS	Re-stenosis, arteriovenous graft failure	Plasmid, adenovirus
HGF	CAD, PAD	Adenovirus
Del-1	CAD, PAD	Plasmid
PDGF	Extremity ulcers	Adenovirus

CAD, coronary artery disease; Del-1, developmental endothelial locus-1; FGF, fibroblast growth factor; HGF, hepatocyte growth factor; HIF1-α, hypoxia-inducible factor 1-α; iNOS, inducible nitric oxide synthase; PAD, peripheral arterial disease; PDGF, platelet derived growth factor; VEGF, vascular endothelial growth factor.

From Committee N.R.D.A: NIH RAC Online Database. 2001, Office of Biotechnology Activities. Available at www4.od.nih.gov/oba/rac.

the ischemic tissue or a cell transplantation approach with precursor cells that are genetically modified.[114,173,174] A number of phase 1–phase 2, corporation-sponsored clinical trials have already been undertaken in both the coronary and peripheral circulations (Table 12-3). Both naked DNA and Ad vectors have been employed to deliver VEGFs, FGFs, HGF, and other angiogenic constructs in patients. In general, these studies have largely revealed minimal toxicity and, in some cases, have reported modest improvement in surrogate endpoints such as pain, ulcer healing, and perfusion imaging. This area of investigation remains at a very early stage. Proof of therapeutic efficacy clearly will require randomized, blinded, placebo-controlled studies, and many questions remain about the nature of the induced vessel growth as well as the optimal dosing, mode of delivery, and choice of target gene. Much additional basic, animal, and clinical investigation will be required before definitive phase 3 studies are likely to be conducted.

■ CONCLUSION

Dramatic advances in genetics as well as in cellular and molecular biology have set the stage for a new era of cardiovascular therapeutics. These approaches are based firmly on a better understanding of the molecular mechanisms of complex disease states such as atherosclerosis and intimal hyperplasia. Better characterization of the genetic basis for variable disease phenotypes among patients, made possible by the success of the Human Genome Project, will allow for improved risk stratification and targeting of these novel therapies. Continued basic and translational research, coupled with the conduct of carefully designed clinical trials, will enable the full potential of this biotechnology revolution to improve the health of patients with vascular diseases.

■ REFERENCES

1. Lander ES, et al: Initial sequencing and analysis of the human genome. Nature 409:860-921, 2001.
2. Lodish H, Berk A, Zipursky L: Molecular structure of genes and chromosomes. In: Molecular Cell Biology. New York, WH Freeman, 2000.
3. Gahtan V, Peyman J, Sumpio B: Understanding molecular biology. Semin Vasc Surg 11:125-133, 1998.
4. Cooper G: The organization of cellular genomes. In: The Cell: A Molecular Approach. Sunderland, Mass, Sinauer Associates, 2000.
5. Gahtan V, Olson E, Sumpio B: Molecular biology: A brief overview. J Vasc Surg 35:563-568, 2002.
6. Griffiths A, Gelbart W, Miller J: Genetics and the organism. In: Modern Genetic Analysis. New York, WH Freeman, 1999.
7. Lodish H, Berk A, Zipursky L: Genetic analysis in cell biology. In: Molecular Cell Biology. New York, WH Freeman, 2000.
8. Brent R, et al (eds): Current Protocols in Molecular Biology. New York, John Wiley & Sons, 2003.
9. Gilbert S: The genetic core of development. In: Developmental Biology. Sunderland, Mass, Sinauer Associates, 2000.
10. Bast R, Kufe D, Pollock R: Molecular biology. In: Cancer Medicine. Hamilton, Ont, BC Decker, 2000.
11. Cooper G: Protein synthesis, processing and regulation In: The Cell: A Molecular Approach. Sunderland, Mass, Sinauer Associates, 2000.
12. Cooper G: The nucleus. In: The Cell: A Molecular Approach. Sunderland, Mass, Sinauer Associates, 2000.
13. Griffiths A, Miller J, Suzuki D: Recombinant DNA technology. In: An Introduction to Genetic Analysis. New York, WH Freeman, 2000.
14. Lodish H, Berk A, Zipursky L: Recombinant DNA and genomics. In: Molecular Cell Biology. New York, WH Freeman, 2000.
15. Gordon J, Scangos G, Plotkin D: Genetic transformation of mouse embryos by microinjection of purified DNA. Proc Natl Acad Sci U S A 77:7380-7384, 1980.
16. Moreadith R, Radford N: Gene targeting in embryonic stem cells: The new physiology and metabolism. J Mol Med 75:208-216, 1997.
17. Griffiths A, Gelbart W, Miller J: Applications of recombinant DNA technology. In: Modern Genetic Analysis. New York, WH Freeman, 1999.
18. Babinet C, Cohen-Tannoudji M: Genome engineering via homologous recombination in mouse embryonic stem (ES) cells: An amazingly versatile tool for the study of mammalian biology. An Acad Bras Cienc 73:365-383, 2001.
19. Chang H, Lau A, Matzuk M: Studying TGF-beta superfamily signaling by knockouts and knockins. Mol Cell Endocrinol 180:39-46, 2001.
20. Ohno T, et al: Gene therapy for vascular smooth muscle cell proliferation after arterial injury. Science 265:781-784, 1994.
21. Chang MW, et al: Cytostatic gene therapy for vascular proliferative disorders with a constitutively active form of the retinoblastoma gene product. Science 267:518-522, 1995.
22. Colman A: Antisense strategies in cell and developmental biology. J Cell Sci 97:399-409, 1990.
23. Askari F, McDonnell W: Molecular medicine: Antisense oligonucleotide therapy. N Engl J Med 334:316-318, 1996.
24. Yakubov L: Oligodeoxynucleotides interact with recombinant CD4 at multiple sites. J Biol Chem 268:18818-18823, 1993.
25. Guvakova M, et al: Phosphorothioate oligodeoxynucleotides bind to basic fibroblast growth factor, inhibit its binding to cell surface receptors, and remove it from low affinity binding sites on extracellular matrix. J Biol Chem 270:2620-2627, 1995.
26. Maltese J, et al: Sequence context of antisense RelA/NF-kappa B phosphorothioates determines specificity. Nucleic Acids Res 23:1146-1151, 1995.
27. Stein C: Does antisense exist? Nat Med 1:1119-1121, 1995.
28. Zaug A, Been M, Cech T: The *Tetrahymena* ribozyme acts like an RNA restriction endonuclease. Nature 324:429-433, 1986.
29. Fire A, et al: Potent and specific genetic interference by double-stranded RNA in *Caenorhabditis elegans*. Nature 391:806-811, 1998.
30. Bielinska A, Schivdasani R, Zhang L: Regulation of gene expression with double-stranded phosphothioate oligonucleotides. Science 250:997-1000, 1990.
31. Mann MJ, et al: Pressure-mediated oligonucleotide transfection of rat and human cardiovascular tissues. Proc Natl Acad Sci U S A 96:6411-6416, 1999.
32. Stein C, Cheng Y: Antisense oligonucleotides as therapeutic agents: Is the bullet really magical? Science 261:1004-1012, 1993.

33. Marshall E: Gene therapy death prompts review of adenovirus vector. Science 286:2244-2245, 1999.
34. Friedmann T: Progress toward human gene therapy. Science 244:1275-1281, 1989.
35. Mulligan RC: The basic science of gene therapy. Science 260:926-932, 1993.
36. Crystal RG: Transfer of genes to humans: Early lessons and obstacles to success. Science 270:404-410, 1995.
37. Kay MA, Glorioso JC, Naldini L: Viral vectors for gene therapy: The art of turning infectious agents into vehicles of therapeutics. Nat Med 7:33-40, 2001.
38. Varmus H: Retroviruses. Science 240:1427-1435, 1988.
39. Wilson JM, et al: Implantation of vascular grafts lined with genetically modified endothelial cells. Science 244:1344-1346, 1989.
40. Nabel EG, et al: Recombinant gene expression in vivo within endothelial cells of the arterial wall. Science 244:1342-1344, 1989.
41. Dichek DA: Retroviral vector-mediated gene transfer into endothelial cells. Mol Biol Med 8:257-266, 1991.
42. Conte MS, et al: Efficient repopulation of denuded rabbit arteries with autologous genetically modified endothelial cells. Circulation 89:2161-2169, 1994.
43. Clowes MM, et al: Long-term biological response of injured rat carotid artery seeded with smooth muscle cells expressing retrovirally introduced human genes. J Clin Invest 93:644-651, 1994.
44. Wilson JM: Adenoviruses as gene delivery vehicles. N Engl J Med 334:1185-1187, 1996.
45. Lemarchand P, et al: In vivo gene transfer and expression in normal uninjured blood vessels using replication-deficient recombinant adenovirus vectors. Circ Res 72:1132-1138, 1993.
46. Schneider MD, French BA: The advent of adenovirus: Gene therapy for cardiovascular disease. Circulation 88:1937-1942, 1993.
47. Channon KM, et al: Efficient adenoviral gene transfer to early venous bypass grafts: Comparison with native vessels. Cardiovasc Res 35:505-513, 1997.
48. O'Brien T: Adenoviral vectors and gene transfer to the blood vessel wall [editorial; comment]. Arterioscler Thromb Vasc Biol 20:1414-1416, 2000.
49. Eslami MH, et al: Gene delivery to in situ veins: Differential effects of adenovirus and adeno-associated viral vectors. J Vasc Surg 31:1149-1159, 2000.
50. Yang Y, Ertl HC, Wilson JM: MHC class I-restricted cytotoxic T lymphocytes to viral antigens destroy hepatocytes in mice infected with E1-deleted recombinant adenoviruses. Immunity 1:433-442, 1994.
51. Yang Y, et al: Cellular and humoral immune responses to viral antigens create barriers to lung-directed gene therapy with recombinant adenoviruses. J Virol 69:2004-2015, 1995.
52. Wen S, et al: Inclusion of the E3 region in an adenoviral vector decreases inflammation and neointima formation after arterial gene transfer. Arterioscler Thromb Vasc Biol 21:1777-1782, 2001.
53. Wen S, et al: Second-generation adenoviral vectors do not prevent rapid loss of transgene expression and vector DNA from the arterial wall. Arterioscler Thromb Vasc Biol 20:1452-1458, 2000.
54. Newman KD, et al: Adenovirus-mediated gene transfer into normal rabbit arteries results in prolonged vascular cell activation, inflammation, and neointimal hyperplasia. J Clin Invest 96:2955-2965, 1995.
55. Channon KM, et al: Acute host-mediated endothelial injury after adenoviral gene transfer in normal rabbit arteries: Impact on transgene expression and endothelial function. Circ Res 82:1253-1262, 1998.
56. Muzyczka N: Use of adeno-associated virus as a general transduction vector for mammalian cells. Microbiol Immunol 158:98-129, 1992.
57. Snyder RO: Adeno-associated virus-mediated gene delivery. J Gene Med 1:166-175, 1999.
58. Kaplitt MG, et al: Long-term gene expression and phenotypic correction using adeno-associated virus vectors in the mammalian brain. Nat Genet 8:148-154, 1994.
59. Xiao X, Li J, Samulski RJ: Efficient long-term gene transfer into muscle tissue of immunocompetent mice by adeno-associated virus vector. J Virol 70:8098-8108, 1996.
60. Snyder RO, et al: Efficient and stable adeno-associated virus-mediated transduction in the skeletal muscle of adult immunocompetent mice. Hum Gene Ther 8:1891-1900, 1997.
61. Snyder RO, et al: Correction of hemophilia B in canine and murine models using recombinant adeno-associated viral vectors. Nat Med 5:64-70, 1999.
62. Arnold TE, Gnatenko D, Bahou WF: In vivo gene transfer into rat arterial walls with novel adeno-associated virus vectors. J Vasc Surg 25:347-355, 1997.
63. Lynch CM, et al: Adeno-associated virus vectors for vascular gene delivery. Circ Res 80:497-505, 1997.
64. Richter M, et al: Adeno-associated virus vector transduction of vascular smooth muscle cells in vivo. Physiol Genom 2:117-127, 2000.
65. Girod A, et al: Genetic capsid modifications allow efficient re-targeting of adeno-associated virus type 2. Nat Med 5:1052-1056, 1999.
66. Yang X, et al: Magnetic resonance imaging permits in vivo monitoring of catheter-based vascular gene delivery. Circulation 104:1588-1590, 2001.
67. Yang X, et al: Digital optical imaging of green fluorescent proteins for tracking vascular gene expression: Feasibility study in rabbit and human cell models. Radiology 219:171-175, 2001.
68. Mesri EA, Federoff HJ, Brownlee M: Expression of vascular endothelial growth factor from a defective herpes simplex virus type 1 amplicon vector induces angiogenesis in mice. Circ Res 76:161-167, 1995.
69. Skelly C, et al: Prevention of restenosis by a herpes simplex virus. In: Proceedings for the 56th Annual Session of the Owen H. Wangensteen Surgical Forum 2001 Clinical Congress. New Orleans, American College of Surgeons, 2001.
70. Hacein-Bey-Acina S, et al: A serious adverse event after successful gene therapy for X-linked severe combined immunodeficiency. N Engl J Med 348:255-256, 2003.
71. Koharsky K, et al: In-vivo correction of low density lipoprotein receptor deficiency in Watanabe heritable hyperlipaemic rabbit with recombinant adenoviruses. J Biol Chem 29:13695-13703, 1994.
72. Nabel EG: Genomic medicine: Cardiovascular disease. N Engl J Med 349:60-72, 2003.
73. Clowes AW: Vascular gene therapy in the 21st century. Thromb Haemost 78:605-610, 1997.
74. Kibbe MR, Billiar TR, Tzeng E: Gene therapy for restenosis. Circ Res 86:829-833, 2000.
75. Conte MS, et al: Genetic interventions for vein bypass graft disease: A review. J Vasc Surg 36:1040-1052, 2002.
76. Kakuta T, et al: Differences in compensatory vessel enlargement, not intimal formation, account for restenosis after angioplasty in the hypercholesterolemic rabbit model. Circulation 89:2809-2815, 1994.
77. Gibbons GH, Dzau VJ: The emerging concept of vascular remodeling. N Engl J Med 330:1431-1418, 1994.
78. Scott NA, et al: Identification of a potential role for the adventitia in vascular lesion formation after balloon overstretch injury of porcine coronary arteries. Circulation 93:2178-2187, 1996.
79. Guzman LA, et al: Role of intimal hyperplasia and arterial remodeling after balloon angioplasty: An experimental study in the atherosclerotic rabbit model. Arterioscler Thromb Vasc Biol 16:479-487, 1996.
80. Andersen HR, et al: Remodeling rather than neointimal formation explains luminal narrowing after deep vessel wall injury: Insights from a porcine coronary (re)stenosis model. Circulation 93:1716-1724, 1996.
81. Geary RL, et al: Wound healing: A paradigm for lumen narrowing after arterial reconstruction. J Vasc Surg 27:96-108, 1998.
82. Lafont A, et al: Endothelial dysfunction and collagen accumulation: Two independent factors for restenosis and constrictive remodeling after experimental angioplasty. Circulation 100:1109-1115, 1999.
83. Ishikawa Y, et al: Collagen alteration in vascular remodeling by hemodynamic factors. Virchows Arch 437:138-148, 2000.
84. Pasterkamp G, de Kleijn DP, Borst C: Arterial remodeling in atherosclerosis, restenosis and after alteration of blood flow: Potential mechanisms and clinical implications. Cardiovasc Res 45:843-852, 2000.

85. Turley EA: Extracellular matrix remodeling: Multiple paradigms in vascular disease. Circ Res 88:2-4, 2001.
86. Ward MR, et al: Eplerenone suppresses constrictive remodeling and collagen accumulation after angioplasty in porcine coronary arteries. Circulation 104:467-472, 2001.
87. Shi Y, et al: Remodeling of autologous saphenous vein grafts: The role of perivascular myofibroblasts. Circulation 95:2684-2693, 1997.
88. Kalra M, Miller VM: Early remodeling of saphenous vein grafts: Proliferation, migration and apoptosis of adventitial and medial cells occur simultaneously with changes in graft diameter and blood flow. J Vasc Res 37:576-584, 2000.
89. Wallner K, et al: Arterialization of human vein grafts is associated with tenascin-C expression. J Am Coll Cardiol 34:871-875, 1999.
90. Braun-Dullaeus RC, Mann MJ, Dzau VJ: Cell cycle progression: New therapeutic target for vascular proliferative disease. Circulation 98:82-89, 1998.
91. Chang MW, et al: Adenovirus-mediated over-expression of the cyclin/cyclin-dependent kinase inhibitor, p21 inhibits vascular smooth muscle cell proliferation and neointima formation in the rat carotid artery model of balloon angioplasty. J Clin Invest 96:2260-2268, 1995.
92. Bai H, et al: Inhibition of intimal hyperplasia after vein grafting by in vivo transfer of human senescent cell-derived inhibitor-1 gene. Gene Ther 5:761-769, 1998.
93. Claudio PP, et al: Adenoviral RB2/p130 gene transfer inhibits smooth muscle cell proliferation and prevents restenosis after angioplasty. Circ Res 85:1032-1039, 1999.
94. George SJ, et al: Wild-type p53 gene transfer inhibits neointima formation in human saphenous vein by modulation of smooth muscle cell migration and induction of apoptosis. Gene Ther 8:668-676, 2001.
95. Schwartz LB, et al: Adenoviral-mediated gene transfer of a constitutively active form of the retinoblastoma gene product attenuates neointimal thickening in experimental vein grafts. J Vasc Surg 29:874-883, 1999.
96. Morishita R, et al: Antisense oligonucleotides directed at cell cycle regulatory genes as strategy for restenosis therapy. Trans Assoc Am Physicians 106:54-61, 1993.
97. Fulton GJ, et al: Locally applied antisense oligonucleotide to proliferating cell nuclear antigen inhibits intimal thickening in experimental vein grafts. Ann Vasc Surg 12:412-417, 1998.
98. Mann MJ, et al: Genetic engineering of vein grafts resistant to atherosclerosis. Proc Natl Acad Sci U S A 92:4502-4506, 1995.
99. Mann MJ, et al: Cell cycle inhibition preserves endothelial function in genetically engineered rabbit vein grafts. J Clin Invest 99:1295-1301, 1997.
100. Morishita R, et al: A gene therapy strategy using a transcription factor decoy of the E2F binding site inhibits smooth muscle proliferation in vivo. Proc Natl Acad Sci U S A 92:5855-5859, 1995.
101. Degregori J, Kowalik T, Nevins J: Cellular targets for activation by the E2F1 transcription factor include DNA synthesis- and G1/S-regulatory genes. Mol Cell Biol 15:4215-4224, 1995.
102. Degregori J, et al: Distinct roles for E2F proteins in cell growth control and apoptosis. Proc Natl Acad Sci U S A 94:7245-7250, 1997.
103. Wu C, et al: Expression of dominant negative mutant DP-1 blocks cell cycle progression in G1. Mol Cell Biol 16:3698-3706, 1996.
104. Mann MJ, Kernoff R, Dzau VJ: Vein graft gene therapy using E2F decoy oligonucleotides: Target gene inhibition in human veins and long term resistance to atherosclerosis in rabbits. Surg Forum 48:242-244, 1997.
105. Mann MJ: E2F decoy oligonucleotide for genetic engineering of vascular bypass grafts. Antisense Nucleic Acid Drug Dev 8:171-176, 1998.
106. Ehsan A, et al: Long-term stabilization of vein graft wall architecture and prolonged resistance to experimental atherosclerosis after E2F decoy oligonucleotide gene therapy. J Thorac Cardiovasc Surg 121:714-722, 2001.
107. Mann MJ, et al: Ex-vivo gene therapy of human vascular bypass grafts with E2F decoy: The PREVENT single-centre, randomised, controlled trial. Lancet 354:1493-1498, 1999.
108. Grube E, et al: PREVENT II: Results of E2F decoy treatment of coronary vein bypass grafts [abstract]. In American Heart Association: Late Breaking Clinical Trials. Anaheim, Calif, American Heart Association, 2001.
109. Neschis DG, et al: Antisense basic fibroblast growth factor gene transfer reduces early intimal thickening in a rabbit femoral artery balloon injury model. J Vasc Surg 27:126-134, 1998.
110. Hanna AK, et al: Adenoviral-mediated expression of antisense RNA to basic fibroblast growth factor reduces tangential stress in arterialized vein grafts. J Vasc Surg 31:770-780, 2000.
111. Kume M, et al: Administration of a decoy against the activator protein-1 binding site suppresses neointimal thickening in rabbit balloon-injured arteries. Circulation 105:1226-1232, 2002.
112. Huynh TT, et al: Adenoviral-mediated inhibition of G beta gamma signaling limits the hyperplastic response in experimental vein grafts. Surgery 124:177-186, 1998.
113. Iaccarino G, et al: Targeting Gbg signaling in arterial vascular smooth muscle proliferation: A novel strategy to limit restenosis. Proc Natl Acad Sci U S A 96:3945-3950, 1999.
114. Losordo DP: Phase I trial of VEGF gene transfer to prevent coronary artery restenosis. 2001, NIH RAC on-line database. Available at www4.od.nih.gov/oba/rac.
115. Fuster VP: A Phase IIb, randomized, multicenter, double-blind study of the efficacy and safety of Trinam in stenosis prevention at the graft-vein anastomosis site in dialysis patients. 2001, NIH RAC on-line database. Available at clinicaltrial.htm.
116. Cable DG, et al: Recombinant endothelial nitric oxide synthase-transduced human saphenous veins: Gene therapy to augment nitric oxide production in bypass conduits. Circulation 96(Suppl):II173-II178, 1997.
117. Matsumoto T, et al: Hemagglutinating virus of Japan-liposome-mediated gene transfer of endothelial cell nitric oxide synthase inhibits intimal hyperplasia of canine vein grafts under conditions of poor runoff. J Vasc Surg 27:135-144, 1998.
118. Shears LL 2nd, et al: Efficient inhibition of intimal hyperplasia by adenovirus-mediated inducible nitric oxide synthase gene transfer to rats and pigs in vivo. J Am Coll Surg 187:295-306, 1998.
119. Kibbe MR, et al: Optimization of ex vivo inducible nitric oxide synthase gene transfer to vein grafts. Surgery 126:323-329, 1999.
120. Kalra M, et al: Adventitial versus intimal liposome-mediated ex vivo transfection of canine saphenous vein grafts with endothelial nitric oxide synthase gene. J Vasc Surg 32:1190-1200, 2000.
121. West NE, et al: Nitric oxide synthase (nNOS) gene transfer modifies venous bypass graft remodeling: Effects on vascular smooth muscle cell differentiation and superoxide production. Circulation 104:1526-1532, 2001.
122. Kibbe MR, et al: Adenovirus-mediated gene transfer of human inducible nitric oxide synthase in porcine vein grafts inhibits intimal hyperplasia. J Vasc Surg 34:156-165, 2001.
123. Kuntz RP: Restenosis gene therapy trial: Phase I study. 2000, NIH RAC on-line database.
124. Simari RD, et al: Regulation of cellular proliferation and intimal formation following balloon injury in atherosclerotic rabbit arteries. J Clin Invest 98:225-235, 1996.
125. Fortunato JE, et al: Gene therapy enhances the antiproliferative effect of radiation in intimal hyperplasia. J Surg Res 89:155-162, 2000.
126. Pollman MJ, et al: Inhibition of neointimal cell bcl-x expression induces apoptosis and regression of vascular disease. Nat Med 4:222-227, 1998.
127. Blanc-Brude O, et al: Inhibitor of apoptosis protein survivin regulates vascular injury. Nat Med 8:987-994, 2002.
128. Leon M, et al: Localized intracoronary gamma-radiation therapy to inhibit the recurrence of restenosis after stenting. N Engl J Med, 344:250-256, 2001.
129. Quax PH, et al: Adenoviral expression of a urokinase receptor-targeted protease inhibitor inhibits neointima formation in murine and human blood vessels. Circulation 103:562-569, 2001.

130. Carmeliet P, et al: Inhibitory role of plasminogen activator inhibitor-1 in arterial wound healing and neointima formation: A gene targeting and gene transfer study in mice. Circulation 96:3180-3191, 1997.
131. Yamamoto K, et al: Ribozyme oligonucleotides against transforming growth factor-beta inhibited neointimal formation after vascular injury in rat model: Potential application of ribozyme strategy to treat cardiovascular disease. Circulation 102:1308-1314, 2000.
132. O'Blenes SB, et al: Gene transfer of the serine elastase inhibitor elafin protects against vein graft degeneration. Circulation 102(Suppl 3): III289-III295, 2000.
133. George SJ, et al: Adenovirus-mediated gene transfer of the human TIMP-1 gene inhibits smooth muscle cell migration and neointimal formation in human saphenous vein. Hum Gene Ther 9:867-877, 1998.
134. Fernandez HA, et al: Modulation of matrix metalloproteinase activity in human saphenous vein grafts using adenovirus-mediated gene transfer. Surgery 124:129-136, 1998.
135. George SJ, et al: Gene transfer of tissue inhibitor of metalloproteinase-2 inhibits metalloproteinase activity and neointima formation in human saphenous veins. Gene Ther 5:1552-1560, 1998.
136. George SJ, et al: Inhibition of late vein graft neointima formation in human and porcine models by adenovirus-mediated overexpression of tissue inhibitor of metalloproteinase-3. Circulation 101:296-304, 2000.
137. Hu Y, et al: Local gene transfer of tissue inhibitor of metalloproteinase-2 influences vein graft remodeling in a mouse model. Arterioscler Thromb Vasc Biol 21:1275-1280, 2001.
138. Graor RA, et al: Thrombolysis of peripheral arterial bypass grafts: Surgical thrombectomy compared with thrombolysis. A preliminary report. J Vasc Surg 7:347-355, 1988.
139. Belkin M, et al: Observations on the use of thrombolytic agents for thrombotic occlusion of infrainguinal vein grafts. J Vasc Surg 11:289-296, 1990.
140. Belkin M, et al: Preferred strategies for secondary infrainguinal bypass: Lessons learned from 300 consecutive reoperations. J Vasc Surg 21:282-295, 1995.
141. Chew DK, et al: Autogenous composite vein bypass graft for infrainguinal arterial reconstruction. J Vasc Surg 33:259-265. 2001.
142. Marcum JA, et al: Cloned bovine aortic endothelial cells synthesize anticoagulantly active heparan sulfate proteoglycan. J Biol Chem 261:7507-7517, 1986.
143. Dittman WA, Majerus PW: Structure and function of thrombomodulin: A natural anticoagulant. Blood 75:329-336, 1990.
144. Marcus AJ, et al: Inhibition of platelet function by an aspirin-insensitive endothelial cell ADPase: Thromboregulation by endothelial cells. J Clin Invest 88:1690-1696, 1991.
145. Numaguchi Y, et al: Prostacyclin synthase gene transfer accelerates reendothelialization and inhibits neointimal formation in rat carotid arteries after balloon injury. Arterioscler Thromb Vasc Biol 19:727-733, 1999.
146. Waugh JM, et al: Local overexpression of thrombomodulin for in vivo prevention of arterial thrombosis in a rabbit model. Circ Res 84:84-92, 1999.
147. Waugh JM, et al: Gene therapy to promote thromboresistance: Local overexpression of tissue plasminogen activator to prevent arterial thrombosis in an in vivo rabbit model. Proc Natl Acad Sci U S A 96:1065-1070, 1999.
148. Nishida T, et al: Adenovirus-mediated local expression of human tissue factor pathway inhibitor eliminates shear stress-induced recurrent thrombosis in the injured carotid artery of the rabbit. Circ Res 84:1446-1452, 1999.
149. Zoldhelyi P, et al: Thromboresistance of balloon-injured porcine carotid arteries after local gene transfer of human tissue factor pathway inhibitor. Circulation 101:289-295, 2000.
150. Gangadharan SP, et al: Targeting platelet aggregation: CD39 gene transfer augments nucleoside triphosphate diphosphohydrolase activity in injured rabbit arteries. Surgery 130:296-303, 2001.
151. Rade JJ, et al: Local adenoviral-mediated expression of recombinant hirudin reduces neointima formation after arterial injury. Nat Med 2:293-298, 1996.
152. Bishop GG, et al: Local adenovirus-mediated delivery of hirudin in a rabbit arterial injury model. J Vasc Res 36:343-352; discussion 430-433, 1999.
153. Hoch JR, et al: Vein graft intimal hyperplasia: Leukocytes and cytokine gene expression. Surgery 116:463-471, 1994.
154. Eslami MH, et al: Monocyte adhesion to human vein grafts: A marker for occult intraoperative injury? J Vasc Surg 34:923-929, 2001.
155. West N, et al: Enhanced superoxide production in experimental venous bypass graft intimal hyperplasia: Role of NAD(P)H oxidase. Arterioscler Thromb Vasc Biol 21:189-194, 2001.
156. Morishita R, et al: In vivo transfection of cis element "decoy" against nuclear factor-κB binding site prevents myocardial infarction. Nat Med 3:894-899, 1997.
157. Chen SJ, Wilson JM, Muller DW: Adenovirus-mediated gene transfer of soluble vascular cell adhesion molecule to porcine interposition vein grafts. Circulation 89:1922-1928, 1994.
158. Larson RA, et al: Adenoviral-mediated uteroglobin gene transfer inhibits neointimal hyperplasia after balloon injury in the rat carotid artery. J Vasc Surg 32:1111-1117, 2000.
159. Shi Y, et al: Oxidative stress and lipid retention in vascular grafts: Comparison between venous and arterial conduits. Circulation 103:2408-2413, 2001.
160. Jayakumar J, et al: Gene therapy for myocardial protection: Transfection of donor hearts with heat shock protein 70 gene protects cardiac function against ischemia-reperfusion injury. Circulation 102(Suppl 3):III302-III306, 2000.
161. Erzurum SC, et al: Protection of human endothelial cells from oxidant injury by adenovirus- mediated transfer of the human catalase cDNA. Nucleic Acids Res 21:1607-1612, 1993.
162. Li Q, et al: Gene therapy with extracellular superoxide dismutase protects conscious rabbits against myocardial infarction. Circulation 103:1893-1898, 2001.
163. Yang L, Quan S, Abraham NG: Retrovirus-mediated HO gene transfer into endothelial cells protects against oxidant-induced injury. Am J Physiol 277:L127-L133, 1999.
164. Duckers HJ, et al: Heme oxygenase-1 protects against vascular constriction and proliferation. Nat Med 7:693-698, 2001.
165. Baumgartner I, Isner JM: Gene therapy for peripheral vascular disease [see comments]. Isr Med Assoc J 2:27-32, 2000.
166. Khan T, Selke F, Laham R: Gene therapy progress and prospects: Therapeutic angiogenesis for limb and myocardial ischemia. Gene Ther 10:285-291, 2003.
167. Comerota A, et al: Naked plasmid DNA encoding fibroblast growth factor type I for the treatment of end-stage unreconstructible lower extremity ischemia: Preliminary results of a phase I trial. J Vasc Surg 35:930-936, 2002.
168. Grines C, et al: Angiogenic gene therapy trial in patients with stable angina pectoris. Circulation 105:1291-1297, 2002.
169. Taniyama Y, et al: Therapeutic angiogenesis induced by human hepatocyte growth factor gene in rat diabetic hind limb ischemia model: Molecular mechanisms of delayed angiogenesis in diabetes. Circulation 104:2344-2350, 2001.
170. Taniyama Y, et al: Therapeutic angiogenesis induced by human hepatocyte growth factor gene in rat and rabbit hindlimb ischemia models: Preclinical study for treatment of peripheral arterial disease. Gene Ther 8:181-189, 2001.
171. Shi Q, et al: Evidence for circulating bone marrow-derived endothelial cells. Blood 92:362-367, 1998.
172. Asahara T, et al: Bone marrow origin of endothelial progenitor cells responsible for postnatal vasculogenesis in physiological and pathological neovascularization. Circ Res 85:221-228. 1999.
173. Baumgartner I, et al: Constitutive expression of phVEGF165 after intramuscular gene transfer promotes collateral development in patients with critical limb ischemia. Circulation 97:1114-1123, 1998.
174. Sarkar N, et al: Effects of intramyocardial injection of phVEGF-A165 as sole therapy in patients with refractory coronary artery disease: 12-month follow-up. Angiogenic gene therapy. J Intern Med 250:367-368, 2001.

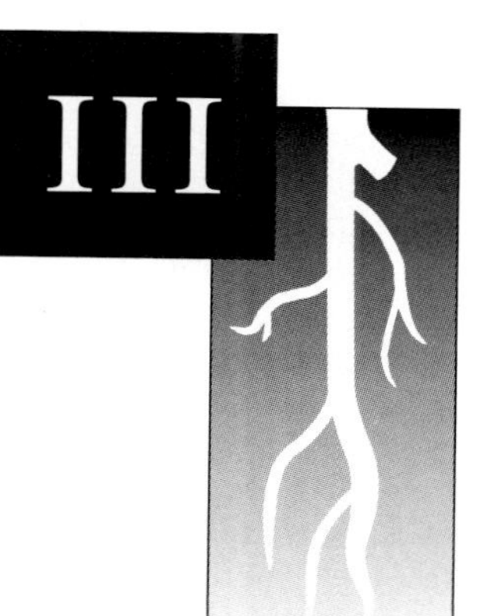

THE VASCULAR DIAGNOSTIC LABORATORY: BASIC TECHNIQUES

GREGORY L. MONETA, MD

Chapter 13

The Vascular Laboratory

J. DENNIS BAKER, MD

■ THE NONINVASIVE TESTS

Like many technical fields in medicine, noninvasive vascular testing had modest origins. The earliest efforts at objective assessment of vascular phenomena date to the days when sympathectomy was the only surgical treatment for vascular insufficiency. Measurement of changes in skin temperature or electrical resistance was used to demonstrate changes in sympathetic activity. The 1940s and 1950s saw the introduction of plethysmographic devices to record pulse pressure waveforms. These early tools were used to measure extremity pressures and to estimate blood flow. Methods included application of a variety of pneumatic and strain gauge sensors. These early devices evolved through the years and in some cases are still used. For example, the Windsor pneumatic plethysmograph was followed by the pulse volume recorder, which continues to be used today. Further applications of pneumatic plethysmography were the Cranley Phleborheograph, Gee's Ocular Pneumoplethysmography (OPG), and, more recently, Air Plethysmography as developed by Nicolaides. Other techniques included recording and analysis of vascular bruits, electrical impedance plethysmography (IPG) (such as described by Wheeler for detection of deep venous thrombosis) and photoplethysmography (PPG).

The application of ultrasound techniques to vascular diagnosis has played a major role in the field. In 1958, Satomura reported using Doppler signal processing for transcutaneous detection of blood flow. His work led to the development of the early nondirectional continuous-wave detectors. The initial application was in the form of a simple ultrasonic stethoscope, with limited qualitative interpretation of signals. Problems with the subjective nature of this assessment led to the measurement of extremity pressures and the recording of analog tracings of the Doppler velocity signals. Technical improvements included the design of directional detectors and later the evolution of processors to measure the frequency characteristics of the Doppler-shifted signals. More than any other device the continuous-wave Doppler velocity detector was responsible for the rapid growth in noninvasive testing in the 1970s.

A parallel development was seen in the ultrasound imaging of blood vessels. Initially, the equipment only provided static, low-resolution images. Technologic improvements provided real-time imaging, analogous to fluoroscopy. The great leap forward came in 1972, when Strandness and his associates developed the duplex scanner, combining both flow and image information in the same examination. By the early 1980s, the duplex scanner became widely used. The initial application was the examination of the carotid artery and its branch vessels. Subsequently, there was expansion into peripheral arterial and venous applications and later, investigation of abdominal visceral vessels. The most important recent development has been color-flow encoding, which has simplified or shortened many of the difficult or tedious examinations. Current researchers are investigating the clinical applications of ultrasound contrast agents and three-dimensional image reconstructions.

■ EVOLUTION OF THE VASCULAR LABORATORY

The initial noninvasive studies were performed in a few hospitals as part of research efforts. The first identifiable vascular laboratory was set up by Linton at the Massachusetts General Hospital in 1946. Because the focus at that time was on sympathetic activity, one can understand why skin temperature and electrical resistance were the measurements performed. During the ensuing decade a few additional pioneer efforts appeared. The growth of arterial reconstruction procedures in the 1960s stimulated interest in clinical investigation by physiologists and vascular surgeons. Publications from research laboratories stimulated the interest in the clinical applicability of the techniques, and by the early 1970s there was increasing use of the tests in decisions about patient management. Where research laboratories existed, they expanded to accommodate the growing demand for clinical testing. In institutions where there had been no research efforts, new facilities were established for the primary purpose of providing routine testing. Another phenomenon was the introduction of noninvasive testing into the office setting. As vascular surgeons became acquainted with different testing modalities, these became firmly incorporated into routine practice. In 1976, a task force of the American Heart Association, the Intersociety Commission for Heart Disease Resources, published a report on testing for peripheral vascular disease.[3] The group concluded that a clinical vascular laboratory was desirable in institutions treating vascular disease (including venous thromboembolism).

The growth in noninvasive testing required training people to carry out the examinations. Much of the work in the original research groups was performed by the doctors who developed the tests. With time, other physicians studied and duplicated the work reported in early publications, but the problem came when clinicians decided to create new testing facilities without going through the learning curve experienced by the researchers. In some cases, interested physicians visited established laboratories for brief periods to learn techniques and pick up practical tips. Lectures and dedicated courses helped to school many in the basics of the new field. There was growth of the complexity of the tests and the time required for examinations, exceeding the time which physicians could dedicate to the studies. Increasingly, technologists were recruited from a variety of backgrounds including nurses, physicians' assistants, catheterization laboratory or operating room technicians, and a variety of research assistants. Special courses were developed to help teach these people the relevant vascular anatomy and physiology as well as the specifics of the different examinations. By the 1980s, almost all vascular laboratory tests in the United States were being done by technologists under the direction of physicians.

Most of the development of the early physiologic tests was carried out by surgeons and other researchers in the field of vascular disease. As technologic improvements made ultrasound imaging a clinical reality, there came increasing interest by radiologists. By the mid 1980s, there was an explosion in noninvasive testing and other specialties became involved including neurology, neurosurgery, cardiology, and urology. Currently, testing is performed in a wide variety of settings ranging from solo practitioners doing the tests themselves in their office to large hospital or clinic departments to far-ranging mobile units. Although there is no accurate count, I estimate that there are at least 10,000 separate facilities performing noninvasive vascular tests in the United States.

The role of the vascular laboratory has undergone major changes when compared with the original research facilities that started the work in this field 5 decades ago. The primary goal of noninvasive testing has always been to refine the clinical assessment of vascular disease by providing objective techniques. In the early days, the testing assisted physicians in their physical assessment and helped select patients for more complete evaluation, usually involving contrast angiography. In the past 15 years, the improvement in the techniques, especially the duplex scan, has resulted in the noninvasive laboratory providing the definitive diagnosis for a number of conditions. In the 1980s, the venous scan became the primary test for acute deep venous thrombosis. More recently, there has been a growing practice of recommending carotid endarterectomy based solely on the ultrasound studies, without subjecting the patient to a routine angiogram. A similar approach is currently being studied in patients requiring lower extremity revascularization. These changes have elevated the importance of the vascular laboratory for patient care.

■ THE QUEST FOR QUALITY

The increasing reliance being placed on the results of the vascular laboratory demands that the studies have high accuracy. Through the years, reports in the literature from major research centers have emphasized the good correlation that can be obtained when noninvasive tests are compared with angiography or with some other reference standard. It is important that every facility strive to achieve similar good results with the routine work. The quality of testing depends on several factors: the physicians, the technologists, and the ongoing evaluation of results.

The Physician

All laboratories need a physician to provide direction and supervision. This director has several roles including establishing the tests to be performed, selection of diagnostic criteria, interpretation of tests, and monitoring of the quality of the work. In 1988, Rutherford addressed the qualifications for a medical director.[6] The most basic is a sound understanding of the clinical principles of vascular disease. Other important areas include (1) knowledge of the principles and the limitations of the equipment, (2) familiarity with the testing procedures, (3) understanding of the diagnostic criteria and (4) experience with the validation of test results. Although other physicians involved with a laboratory may only perform test interpretation, they need similar qualifications.

In the past, vascular surgeons had the clinical knowledge as the result of training and practice and acquired much of the technical background by attending formal courses and reading books and articles on the testing procedures and their interpretation. Other specialists such as radiologists may have had the background in ultrasonography but needed to spend time learning about peripheral vascular disease. In recent years, most vascular surgery fellowships have included the teaching of principles of noninvasive testing together with specific time spent in the laboratory. Residents often interpret large numbers of tests under faculty supervision. These efforts were reinforced in 1996, when the Association of Program Directors in Vascular Surgery published a Core Curriculum for Resident Training in the Vascular Diagnostic Laboratory, thus making this experience a formal part of all approved programs. Noninvasive testing techniques still evolve at a rapid pace, so it is important for all physicians in the field to continue to update their knowledge through reading and attending educational courses

For a number of years, the issue of physician credentialing or certification has been debated. In some centers, there are battles over who should be allowed to run a vascular testing facility or to participate in the interpretation of tests. More often than not, local guidelines for privileging are written which define entry-level knowledge of vascular disease and experience in testing and interpretation. In an effort to establish credibility in noninvasive testing, some physicians have obtained the registered vascular technologist (RVT) credential from the American Registry of Diagnostic Medical Sonographers (ARDMS). Although the examination is not designed to evaluate physician knowledge and skills, passing it at least requires a basic knowledge of ultrasound physics and technology. In 2003, 600 physicians held RVT certificates. The only credential currently designed to identify physician expertise is issued by the American Society of Neuroimaging. The organization has created a written examination, and the certification can be sought by any physician with the requisite education in neuroimaging and prior experience in interpretation of these studies. In response to the interest in having a certifying process that is appropriate for physicians, the ARDMS has announced that it will develop such an examination. Plans call for the process to be available in summer 2005.

The Technologist

The sonographer who performs the examination is likewise a critical element in the laboratory. This is especially true in view of how operator dependent many of the tests are. Knowledge of the relevant anatomy and physiology together with understanding of the common vascular disease processes is essential. In addition, the examiner needs to understand the physical principles and limitations of the techniques being used. Although there was a rapid growth of vascular testing in the 1980s, there remains a paucity of educational opportunities for people interested in entering the field. After more than 2 decades of growth of noninvasive testing, there are only a few associate degree programs and one bachelor level program in the country. Most of the people in the field are still trained by a combination of didactic courses, hands-on instruction, and supervised clinical experience. In 1977, the Society of Noninvasive Vascular Technologists (subsequently to become the Society for Vascular Technology [SVT] and most recently the Society for Vascular Ultrasound [SVU]) was formed.[4,5] One of its goals was to provide relevant courses in the field and to assist members in finding educational opportunities. Unfortunately, there remains great variability in the knowledge and experience of technologists practicing in the field, and some laboratory staff have simply been taught the mechanics of conducting specific examinations.

One of the ways of improving the education of technologists is to define entry level knowledge and experience, so in 1979 the SVT formed a committee to study the issue of voluntary certification.[4,5] The decision was made to work with the ARDMS to develop a certifying process. This organization had existed since 1975 and administered examinations for sonographers covering different areas of ultrasound testing. A new examination was developed and the first RVT credentials were issued in 1983. The basic requirements include 2 years of formal education after high school and 24 months of full-time clinical work in a vascular laboratory. The two-part written examination covers a clinical section and a technical section on vascular physics and instrumentation. Once credentialed, the person is required to accumulate 30 hours of continuing education credits every 3 years to maintain active status. In 2003, there were 12,000 active RVTs. More recently, Cardiovascular Credentialing International, an organization that initially focused primarily on certifying technicians working in invasive and noninvasive cardiac laboratories, extended its process by establishing the credential of registered vascular specialist.

Credentialing was established as a voluntary process, and technologists have participated for a variety of reasons. In some cases, the certificate has led to higher pay scales. Through the years, the number of credentialed workers has been only a fraction of those performing vascular testing. This situation is in the process of changing. A recent phenomenon has been the interest by third-party payers in the quality of the testing and the perception that credentialed technologists represent proof of baseline experience. As of 1998, seven Medicare carriers required that vascular laboratories have credentialed technologists performing the tests or directly supervising all tests as a condition for reimbursement. Additional carriers have announced similar requirements. This trend will likely continue to expand and will be a widespread incentive for technologists to become credentialed.

Quality Control

From the earliest days, the results of noninvasive tests have been validated by comparing with some accepted reference standard, often the contrast angiogram. It was necessary to determine the criteria for separating normal from "abnormal" or for defining different categories or degrees of severity of disease. To a great extent, the acceptance of the vascular laboratory test depended on how well these correlated with other diagnostic procedures. In many cases, the early validation work contributed to improvements through refinements in technique and diagnostic criteria. Once a technique gained acceptance, laboratories would incorporate it, usually buying the same or similar equipment and adopting the published criteria. A common problem arose from the fact that laboratories often modified or combined diagnostic criteria from different sources. Any time that criteria are combined or modified, the effects on accuracy need to be confirmed against a reference standard. Laboratory directors need to be familiar with the methodology for comparing test results to reference standards.[1,7]

A standard assumption is that if one duplicates the equipment and adopts published criteria, the clinical accuracies achieved will be similar to those quoted in the literature. An inherent problem in many noninvasive procedures is that the accuracy is heavily operator dependent. This is particularly true with duplex scanning and transcranial Doppler sonography. A great deal of the accuracy potential depends on the knowledge and experience of the examiner and the care with which each examination is conducted. A separate issue is that similar devices may yield somewhat different objective data. It is the responsibility of each laboratory to determine what its results really are through a formal quality assurance program. Comparing the final interpretation of a study with a "gold standard" is the best way to evaluate the quality of work done.

An important problem is that there are some studies for which we lack a good reference standard. Duplex scanning for the detection of deep venous thrombosis is a good example of this dilemma. Early studies comparing scans with contrast phlebograms showed such good correlation that now the ultrasound study has become the primary diagnostic tool. In most centers there are few, if any, venograms done to permit contemporary comparisons. Several options are currently being assessed to address this problem, including the possibility of using outcome studies to define the accuracy of testing.

Another issue of quality control, especially in the larger facility, is the consistency of testing procedures. The investigators who developed the tests recognized the need to minimize variability and went to great efforts to standardize the test procedures. This is why it is important to have carefully developed written protocols to be followed. There should be a policy in place to evaluate how closely each examiner adheres to the established instructions. Another way to look for potential testing variability is to have two or more people examine the same patient without knowledge of previous findings. This duplicate test process may help identify weaknesses, especially when the routine quality assurance process has identified problems.

Accreditation

Over the past decade, there has been a growing concern about the variable quality of studies performed in vascular laboratories. Surgeons are constantly confronted with the problem of finding major discrepancies between studies done by unknown facilities and the results obtained when the study is repeated. The Intersocietal Commission for the Accreditation of Vascular Laboratories (ICAVL) was established in 1991 with the goal of creating standards and establishing a voluntary review process for the field.[2,8] The commission had wide support from specialty groups involved in vascular testing. The initial sponsors included the American Academy of Neurology, the American College of Radiology, the American Institute of Ultrasound in Medicine, the International Society for Cardiovascular Surgery (North American Chapter), the Society for Vascular Surgery, the Society for Vascular Medicine and Biology, the Society of Diagnostic Medical Sonographers, and the Society of Vascular Technology. The first group of applications was approved in January 1992 and in 2003 1200 laboratories held ICAVL accreditations.

ICAVL took care in writing the standards to be as inclusive as possible. The standards allow applications by everything from large ultrasonography departments in major medical centers to small laboratories in low-population areas. The emphasis of the accreditation review is on the background and experience of the personnel involved and the quality of the work performed. Some of the problems identified in the review of applications include (1) inadequacy of experience, training, or in keeping up to date with appropriate continuing medical education (all personnel are required to have completed 15 hours of courses dedicated to vascular testing every 3 years); (2) lack of formal examination protocols or failure to adhere to these; (3) use of multiple sets of diagnostic criteria for a given test; (4) failure to apply the diagnostic criteria to interpretation of studies; and (5) absence of quality control with comparison studies. The process of preparing the ICAVL application provides the laboratory a thorough self-assessment of all aspects of its organization and function and identifies areas for improvement. Accreditation is provided for 3 years, and the experience has been that laboratories have shown improvement when reviewed for reaccreditation.

The accreditation was set up as a voluntary process, and the number of laboratories that have participated is a testimony to the interest in the ICAVL goals. The accreditation is now being taken to a higher level. Unlike in the past, medical insurance programs are becoming interested in the quality of medical testing for which they are paying. They see ICAVL standards as providing an entry level screen for facilities. Starting in 1998, the Medicare carrier for Virginia required ICAVL accreditation as a condition for payment. Six other carriers have required either accreditation or technologists' certification starting in 1998. Since then, other carriers have been added to the list. In 2003, 23 states required accreditation or certification and carriers in another 13 states recommended such a practice. So even if there is no current requirement for accreditation, directors of vascular laboratories should work toward completing the process both to improve current quality of work and to prepare for future mandates.

Over the past 5 decades we have seen the growth of noninvasive testing into a mature part of the evaluation of vascular disease. Many of the early tests have been phased out, replaced by techniques yielding more detailed and accurate information. The vascular laboratory procedures are not limited to screening tests but often end up providing the definitive diagnosis on which the clinician will act. As a result, all involved with this testing must have a strong commitment to quality of the product. Appropriate training and education of all personnel must be combined with an ongoing quality control program to offer the optimal product to the medical community and their patients.

■ SELECTED READINGS

Baker JD: The vascular laboratory: The past and the future. Am J Surg 164:190, 1992.

Beach KW: 1975-2000: A quarter century of ultrasound technology. Ultrasound Med Biol 18:377, 1992.

Sigel B: A brief history of Doppler ultrasound in the diagnosis of peripheral vascular disease. Ultrasound Med Biol 24:169, 1998.

Yao JST: Presidential address: Precision in vascular surgery. J Vasc Surg 5:535, 1987.

■ REFERENCES

1. Baker JD: Quality assurance in the vascular laboratory. Semin Vasc Surg 7:241, 1994.
2. Baker JD: Accreditation of noninvasive vascular laboratories. In AbuRahma AF, Bergan JJ (eds): Noninvasive Vascular Diagnosis. New York, Springer, 1999, p 11.

3. Bergan JJ, Darling RC, DeWolfe VG, et al: Report of the Intersociety Commission for Heart Disease Resources: Medical instrumentation in peripheral vascular disease. Circulation 54:A1, 1976.
4. Jones AM: Education and certification of the vascular technologist. In Bernstein EF (ed): Vascular Diagnosis. St. Louis, Mosby, 1993, p 28.
5. Jones AM: Training and certification of vascular technologists. In AbuRahma AF, Bergan JJ (eds): Noninvasive Vascular Diagnosis. New York, Springer, 1999, p 3.
6. Rutherford RB: Qualifications of the physician in charge of the vascular diagnostic laboratory. J Vasc Surg 8:732, 1988.
7. Sumner DS: Evaluation of noninvasive testing procedures: Data analysis and interpretation. In Bernstein EF (ed): Vascular Diagnosis. St. Louis, Mosby, 1993, p 39.
8. Thiele BL: Accreditation of vascular laboratories. In Bernstein EF (ed): Vascular Diagnosis. St. Louis, Mosby, 1993, p 36.

Chapter 14

Physiologic Assessment of Peripheral Arterial Occlusive Disease

R. EUGENE ZIERLER, MD
DAVID S. SUMNER, MD

CLINICAL ROLE OF PHYSIOLOGIC TESTING

Interventions for peripheral arterial occlusive disease should be designed to treat a physiologic rather than an anatomic defect. No matter how aesthetically unappealing an arteriosclerotic plaque becomes, it is of no consequence if it does not restrict blood flow. Therefore, the surgeon who evaluates peripheral arterial disease must focus on the physiologic defects that the lesions produce. Although the surgeon gains an appreciation of how these defects limit the patient's activities from the history, the interpretation of symptoms is highly subjective. Beyond an estimate of the physiologic limitations imposed by claudication or the suffering due to ischemic rest pain, the history yields nothing measurable.

The physical examination provides more objectivity, in that pulses can be graded, ulcers measured, gangrenous areas delineated, and pallor, dependent rubor, and skin temperature observed. Even the most skilled surgical diagnostician makes some errors, however, and the nonspecialist physician makes many more.[8,95,106] Thus, the physical examination frequently fails to provide an accurate and objective assessment of the severity of arterial disease.

After the history and physical examination, the next logical step in the evaluation of a patient for arterial occlusive disease is physiologic testing.[14] In general, these tests are designed to answer the following questions:

1. Is significant arterial occlusive disease present?
2. If so, how severe is the physiologic impairment?
3. Where are the responsible lesions located?
4. In multilevel disease, which arterial segments are most severely involved?
5. In limbs with tissue loss, what is the potential for primary healing?

Once these questions are answered, the surgeon is better able to decide whether the deficit is severe enough to warrant more detailed testing, such as arteriography, as a prelude to intervention. There are also a number of clinical problems that are not easily resolved, even with the help of arteriography. For example, patients with pseudoclaudication may be identified by physiologic testing and spared further vascular evaluation.[31,53,82,150] Patients with demonstrable arterial disease may have concomitant orthopedic or neurologic problems. With the help of physiologic testing, the physician can determine the relative magnitude of the deficit caused by each of these conditions and advise the patient accordingly. In limbs with multilevel disease, it is usually possible to identify which of the lesions is most significant, allowing the surgeon to focus on the more critical lesion.[3,16,21,105,115,147,161]

Physiologic tests are helpful in determining whether an ulcer is due to neuropathy, venous stasis, or ischemia and in deciding whether foot pain is primarily neuropathic or ischemic.[68,121] They may also enhance the ability of the surgeon to assess the healing potential of a foot lesion or amputation.[11,20,66,100,159] In cases of suspected vascular trauma, physiologic findings, if negative, may avert an unnecessary vascular exploration or, if positive, may alert the surgeon to the need for immediate operation.[71] Similarly, the recognition and evaluation of suspected iatrogenic vascular injuries, such as those that follow cardiac catheterization or interventional radiologic procedures, are facilitated by physiologic testing.[10] Physiologic tests are uniquely applicable to the diagnosis of intermittent arterial obstructions, such as those arising from entrapment syndromes, and for distinguishing between fixed arterial obstructions and obstructions due to vasospasm. These are but a few of the many areas in which physiologic tests complement the information gleaned from the routine history, physical examination, and anatomic imaging studies.

A comprehensive evaluation of peripheral arterial occlusive disease requires the integration of physiologic, anatomic, and clinical information. This chapter reviews the theory, methods, interpretation, and applications of the various physiologic arterial tests available in the vascular laboratory (see Chapter 13). The use of duplex scanning for assessment of arterial disease is considered in Chapter 16.

■ PRESSURE MEASUREMENT

Measurement of pressure has distinct advantages over measurement of flow for identifying the presence of arterial disease and for assessing its severity. Even though resting flow levels may remain in the normal range, there is almost always a pressure drop across a stenotic lesion that increases resistance to arterial flow.[27,145,155,164,166] Pressure measurements can be made more sensitive by augmentation of blood flow through a stenotic segment. This can be accomplished by exercise, the induction of reactive hyperemia, or the intra-arterial administration of vasodilating drugs. With increased blood flow, pressure drops are greater, and even those that were not noticeable under baseline conditions become evident (see Chapter 9).[9,21,28,138,166]

Ankle Pressure

Of all the noninvasive tests available for evaluating the functional severity of peripheral arterial disease, none is more useful than measurement of systolic blood pressure at the ankle. This test not only provides a simple, reliable means of diagnosing obstructive arterial disease but is also readily applicable to follow-up studies.

Systolic ankle pressure is measured as follows:

1. A pneumatic cuff is placed around the ankle just above the malleolus.
2. A Doppler ultrasound probe is placed over the posterior tibial artery, and the pressure is measured at this site.
3. The Doppler probe is placed over the dorsalis pedis artery, and the pressure is measured at this site.

In normal individuals, the pressure measured at these two sites should differ by no more than 10 mm Hg. A pressure difference greater than 15 mm Hg suggests that there is a proximal occlusion or stenosis in the artery with the lower pressure.[27] The pressure at the site giving the higher value is taken as the ankle pressure.

Occasionally, no audible Doppler flow signal can be obtained over either the posterior tibial or the dorsalis pedis artery. In these cases, a careful search often reveals a peroneal collateral signal anteriorly, near the lateral malleolus. When no Doppler signal can be found, the ankle pressure can often be measured with a plethysmograph placed around the foot or applied to one of the toes.

Normally, the systolic pressure at the ankle exceeds that in the arm by 12 ± 8 to 24 ± 9 mm Hg.[18,28,92] This difference reflects the augmentation of systolic pressure that occurs as the pressure wave travels peripherally (see Chapter 9). Distal to a hemodynamically significant lesion, the ankle pressure is almost always decreased.[18,142,145,146] Usually, a single stenosis that decreases arterial diameter by 50% or more, or multiple mild irregularities of the arterial lumen, reduce the ankle pressure by at least 10 mm Hg.[127] Typical ankle-arm pressure gradients are (1) isolated superficial femoral obstruction, 53 ± 10 mm Hg; (2) isolated aortoiliac obstruction, 61 ± 15 mm Hg; and (3) multilevel obstruction, 91 ± 23 mm Hg.[145]

Ankle-Brachial Index

Because the ankle systolic blood pressure varies with the central aortic pressure, it is convenient to normalize these values by dividing the ankle pressure by the brachial blood pressure.[26,27,162,168] This ratio, which is commonly referred to as the *ankle pressure index* or *ankle-brachial index* (ABI), normally averages about 1.1 when the well-rested subject is lying supine (Table 14-1). Although the ABI in an occasional patient with functionally significant arterial stenosis exceeds 1.0,[1,26,48,112,168] the resting index in most patients with arterial disease is much lower.[1,37,164,167,168] In fact, an ABI less than 1.0 is highly suggestive of functional arterial obstruction[26,27,37,166,167]; only rarely does a normal limb have an index less than 0.92.[58,112]

As shown in Figure 14-1 and Table 14-2, the ABI varies somewhat with the location of the arterial obstruction.[145,164,167] Values tend to be highest when the lesion is confined to the popliteal or below-knee arteries and lowest in limbs with multilevel disease.[90,126,164,168] Carter[27] found that the ABI exceeded 0.50 in 85% of patients with a single level of obstruction but was less than 0.50 in 95% of

Table 14-1 Segmental Pressure Indices in Normal Subjects (Mean ± SD)*

AUTHOR (YEAR)	THIGH	ABOVE KNEE	BELOW KNEE	ANKLE
Carter (1968)[26]	—	1.16 ± 0.05§	—	1.15 ± 0.08‡
Yao (1970, 1973)[166,167]	—	—	—	1.11 ± 0.10
Wolf et al (1972)[164]	—	—	—	1.09 ± 0.08
Fronek et al (1973)[49]	1.34 ± 0.27‖	1.32 ± 0.23‖	1.26 ± 0.24‖	1.08 ± 0.10‡
Cutajar et al (1973)[37]	1.53 ± 0.17†	—	1.17 ± 0.13‡	1.08 ± 0.09‡
Hajjar and Sumner (1976)[58]	1.37 ± 0.20†	1.26 ± 0.11†	1.16 ± 0.10†	1.08 ± 0.08†
Rutherford et al (1979)[126]	1.28 ± 0.17†	1.24 ± 0.17†	1.16 ± 0.17†	1.08 ± 0.17†

*Pressure index equals systolic pressure at site of measurement divided by brachial systolic pressure.
†Cuff 10 × 40 cm.
‡Cuff 12.5 × 30 cm (standard).
§Cuff 15 × 45 cm.
‖Cuff 17 × 50 cm.

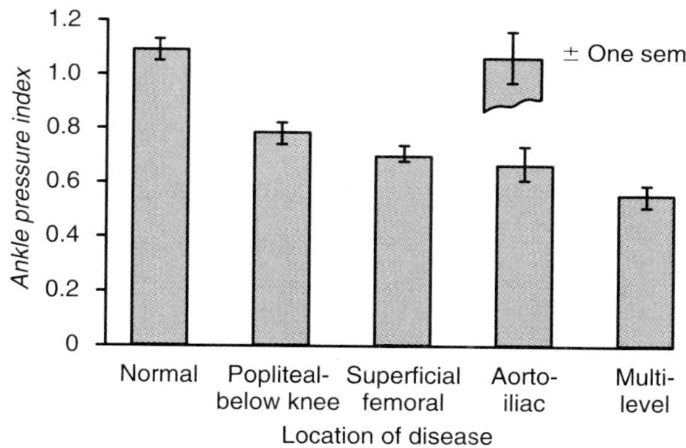

FIGURE 14-1 Resting ankle blood pressure indices (ankle systolic/arm systolic) measured in normal limbs and in limbs with arterial obstruction localized to different anatomic levels. (From Strandness DE Jr, Sumner DS: Hemodynamics for Surgeons. New York, Grune & Stratton, 1975; data from Wolf EA Jr, Sumner DS, Strandness DE Jr: Correlation between nutritive blood flow and pressure in limbs of patients with intermittent claudication. Surg Forum 23:238, 1972.)

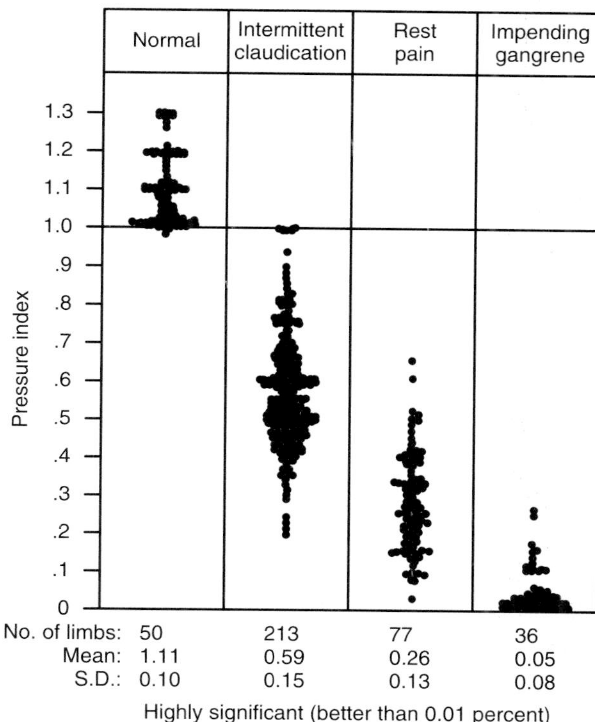

FIGURE 14-2 Relationship of ankle pressure index to functional impairment produced by the occlusive process. (From Yao JST: Hemodynamic studies in peripheral arterial disease. Br J Surg 57:761, 1970.)

those with two or more levels. In addition, the ABI decreases as the functional severity of the disease increases, the lowest values being obtained in limbs with impending gangrene and the highest in limbs with mild claudication (Fig. 14-2).[37,113,118,121,166,167] The ABI also correlates with arteriographic findings.[127,168] Values are lowest when there is complete occlusion and highest when there is minimal atheromatous change (Fig. 14-3).[26,37,153,168] As would be predicted on the basis of hemodynamic principles outlined in Chapter 9, the lengths of the occlusive lesion and of the bypassing collateral vessels are less important than their diameters.[39]

Because the ABI is relatively stable from one examination to the next in the same individual, it is an effective means of following the course of a patient's arterial disease over time. A consistent decrease indicates advancing disease or a failure of arterial reconstruction.[15,101,102,111,148] A spontaneous rise in the ABI is usually attributable to the development of collateral circulation.[131,132] After successful arterial intervention, there is an increase in the ABI.[37,140,147,148,168] If all obstructions have been totally removed or bypassed, the ABI exceeds 1.0; however, if there are residual sites of obstruction, the ABI increases but not to normal levels (Fig. 14-4).[147]

Technical Errors

In general, ankle pressure measurements are easily made and are remarkably free of error. The standard deviation between two measurements repeated within a few minutes is about 5 mm Hg; the deviation increases to approximately 8 to 9 mm Hg between measurements taken a day apart.[108] These figures, however, do not account for variations in the central arterial pressure.

When the ABI rather than the absolute ankle pressure value is considered, the day-to-day results are even more

Table 14-2 Segmental Pressure Indices in Patients with Occlusive Arterial Disease of the Legs (Mean ± SD)*

LOCATION OF OBSTRUCTION	AUTHOR (YEAR)	UPPER THIGH	ABOVE KNEE	BELOW KNEE	ANKLE
Aortoiliac	Fronek et al (1973)[49]	0.72 ± 0.25	0.70 ± 0.24	0.62 ± 0.21	0.57 ± 0.18
	Rutherford et al (1979)[126]	0.81 ± 0.25	0.76 ± 0.25	0.71 ± 0.25	0.68 ± 0.32
	Ramsey et al (1979)[120]	0.81 ± 0.27	0.72 ± 0.25	0.59 ± 0.22	0.54 ± 0.22
Femoropopliteal	Fronek et al (1973)[49]	1.26 ± 0.39	0.92 ± 0.39	0.73 ± 0.30	0.51 ± 0.28
	Rutherford et al (1979)[126]	1.25 ± 0.27	0.86 ± 0.22	0.75 ± 0.18	0.65 ± 0.18
	Ramsey et al (1979)[120]	1.19 ± 0.21	0.87 ± 0.23	0.70 ± 0.18	0.60 ± 0.19
Combined aortoiliac and femoropopliteal	Fronek et al (1973)[49]	0.97 ± 0.34	0.79 ± 0.32	0.61 ± 0.28	0.48 ± 0.31
	Rutherford et al (1979)[126]	0.89 ± 0.17	0.72 ± 0.17	0.58 ± 0.17	0.53 ± 0.28
	Ramsey et al (1979)[120]	0.79 ± 0.21	0.62 ± 0.17	0.49 ± 0.15	0.39 ± 0.15

*Pressure index equals systolic pressure at site of measurement divided by brachial systolic pressure.

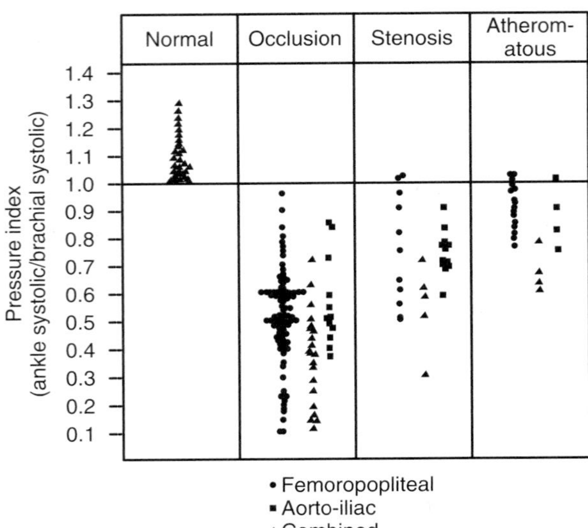

FIGURE 14-3 Relationship of ankle pressure index to the severity of the occlusive process. Note that the index exceeds 1.0 in all normal limbs in this series. (From Yao JST, Hobbs JT, Irvine WT: Ankle systolic pressure measurements in arterial diseases affecting the lower extremities. Br J Surg 56:676, 1969.)

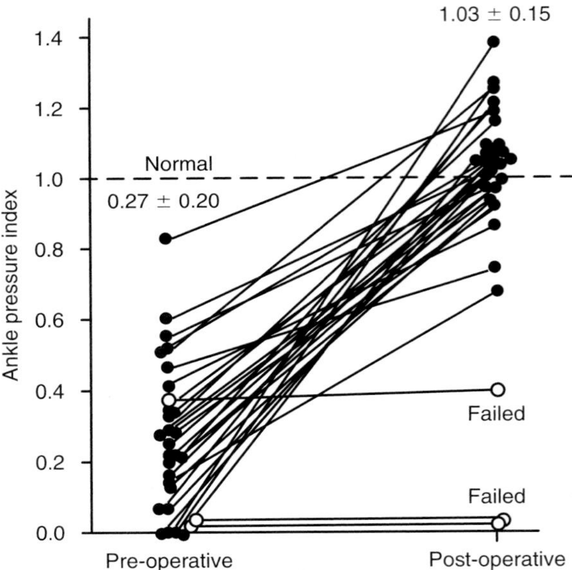

FIGURE 14-4 Results of femorotibial and femoroperoneal grafts. Ankle pressure indices before and after 31 bypass grafts from femoral to tibial, peroneal, or dorsalis pedis arteries. *Open circles* indicate grafts that failed within 30 days. Mean and standard deviations of the patent grafts are indicated. (From Sumner DS, Strandness DE Jr: Hemodynamic studies before and after extended bypass grafts to the tibial and peroneal arteries. Surgery 86:442, 1979.)

consistent. This test is also subject to interobserver and intraobserver variability as well as to nonpathologic biologic variability. A change in the ABI of ± 0.15 or more is highly likely to fall outside the 95% confidence limits of normal variation and therefore implies a significant physiologic change.[6,73]

Medial calcification, which renders the underlying arteries incompressible, is responsible for most of the errors made in measuring ankle pressure with a pneumatic cuff.[48,65,118,139,149] Because patients with diabetes are particularly prone to this problem, ankle pressure measurements in diabetic patients may be 5% or 10% too high.[118] In these cases, it is sometimes possible to estimate the pressure by elevating the foot and noting the vertical distance of the foot from the bed at the point at which the Doppler signal disappears.[52] Multiplying this distance (in centimeters) by 0.735 gives the pressure in millimeters of mercury. Alternatively, the severity of arterial occlusive disease in the lower extremity can be assessed by toe pressure measurements, as discussed later in this chapter.

Inability to distinguish between arterial and venous flow can occur when the arterial flow velocity is decreased and the signal becomes less pulsatile.[1] However, venous signals can be differentiated from arterial signals with a directional Doppler flowmeter. Moreover, venous signals can be augmented by distal compression, but arterial signals either are not affected or diminish. If doubt still remains, a plethysmograph can be used to sense the return of pulsatile arterial flow as the cuff is deflated.

Segmental Pressure

A decrease in the ankle pressure or ABI indicates that arterial occlusive disease is present, but it does not identify the specific segments involved. Further diagnostic information can be obtained by measuring the systolic pressure gradients down the leg.[63,81,139,162] Only rarely do these measurements need to be made when the ankle pressure is normal.[48]

The following four-cuff method is but one of a number of techniques that have been advocated. Pneumatic cuffs 10 cm in width are placed as follows:

- Around the upper thigh at groin level
- Around the thigh just above the knee
- Around the calf just below the knee
- At ankle level

Blood pressure is measured at each level using a Doppler probe on the posterior tibial or dorsalis pedis artery.

Upper Thigh Pressure

In most normal individuals, blood pressures measured with the four-cuff technique at the upper thigh level exceed those measured at the brachial level by 30 to 40 mm Hg.[1,37,63,142] Indices, obtained by dividing the thigh pressure by the brachial pressure, are comparably elevated, averaging around 1.30 to 1.50 (see Table 14-1).

These upper thigh pressures do not accurately reflect the true femoral artery pressure. When measured by invasive techniques, the pressure in the common femoral artery is almost identical to the brachial artery pressure.[114] Furthermore, as indicated by the standard deviations given in Table 14-1, upper thigh pressures are highly variable, even in normal subjects. Because of the disparity between cuff width and thigh diameter, higher pressures are obtained in patients with large thighs, and lower, more accurate pressures are obtained in patients with small thighs.[139]

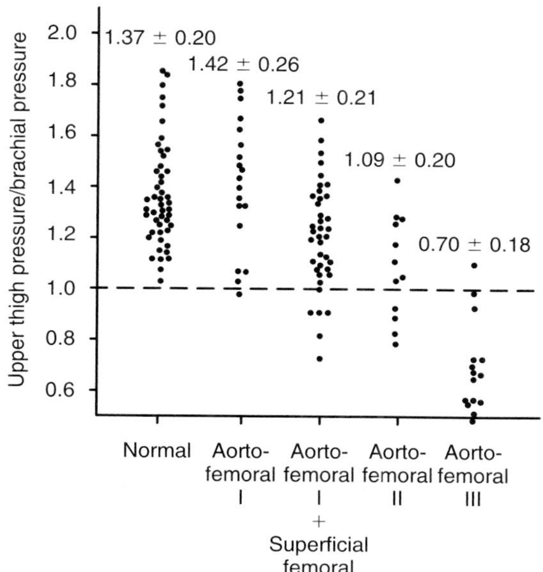

FIGURE 14-5 Identification of aortofemoral obstruction. Upper thigh index in normal limbs and in limbs with arteriosclerotic disease of the aortofemoral segment. Grading of aortofemoral disease is as follows: I, less than 50% diameter stenosis; II, more than 50% diameter stenosis; and III, occlusion. Grades II and III are hemodynamically significant.

An upper thigh pressure equal to or lower than the brachial pressure usually indicates hemodynamically significant aortoiliac disease.[37] When the thigh pressure exceeds arm pressure by less than 15 to 30 mm Hg, iliac disease may be suspected; however, this finding may not indicate iliac disease if the diameter of the thigh is small.[63,126] Comparison of the pressures obtained from the two thighs is of some value in these cases.[49] A 20-mm Hg difference is said to be significant, but some workers have not found this difference to be a reliable indicator.[120]

Thigh pressure indices associated with aortoiliac obstructive disease are shown in Table 14-2 and Figure 14-5. It is apparent from Figure 14-5 that the upper thigh index may be lower than 1.0 in limbs with superficial femoral obstructions, even when there is no hemodynamically significant disease in the aortoiliac segment.[17] This situation is somewhat more likely to occur in the presence of concomitant stenosis of the profunda femoris artery. Although the thigh index seldom exceeds 1.0 in limbs with occlusion of the iliac artery, it is not uncommon to find normal indices in limbs with hemodynamically significant stenoses of the iliac arteries.[17] This finding is most likely when the thighs are large; however, there is another possible explanation. Because compression of the upper thigh by the cuff temporarily restricts arterial inflow, the pressure gradient across the external iliac artery is reduced. Consequently, when a stenosis is confined to this artery, the upper thigh pressure reading may be spuriously high.[48]

If an upper thigh index of 1.0 is taken as the lower limit of normal, the data in Figure 14-5 indicate that there would be no mistakes in the normal control group, but in the patient groups, the sensitivity for detecting hemodynamically significant disease would be only 67% and the specificity for identifying the absence of disease would be 90%.[126] Cutajar and coworkers[37] reported that values exceeding 1.20 are normal, those less than 0.80 suggest occlusion, and those in between usually indicate the presence of aortoiliac occlusive disease. According to these criteria, the data in Figure 14-5 show that only 10% of the studies with indices exceeding 1.20 would be falsely classified as negative results and that only 7% of limbs with indices less than 0.80 would have no hemodynamically significant disease. Between these limits, however, significant disease was found in only 33%. Moreover, 19% of normal control limbs had indices less than 1.20.

Pressure Gradients

The pressure gradient between any two adjacent levels in the normal leg usually is no more than 20 to 30 mm Hg (Table 14-3).[1,139] Gradients greater than 30 mm Hg strongly suggest that a significant degree of arterial obstruction is present in the intervening arterial segment.[1,51,63] When the artery is occluded, the gradient generally exceeds 40 mm Hg.[49,139] Rutherford and associates[126] found that an upper thigh to above-knee gradient of 15 mm Hg best distinguished limbs with superficial femoral artery occlusion from those without. Similar gradients between the above-knee and below-knee levels and between the below-knee and ankle levels were found to have some predictive value related to disease in the popliteal and below-knee segments, respectively.

In addition to measuring "longitudinal" gradients along the leg, it is frequently helpful to compare the pressures in one leg with those at the same level in the other leg. A "horizontal" difference of 20 mm Hg in normotensive patients may be significant, implying greater disease at or above this level in the leg with the lower pressure.[49]

The ratio of the pressures in the leg to those in the arm should exceed 1.0 at all levels (see Tables 14-1 and 14-2).

Table 14-3 Pressure Gradients in Normal Subjects (Mean ± SD)

AUTHOR (YEAR)	ARM–UPPER THIGH	UPPER THIGH–ABOVE KNEE	ABOVE KNEE–BELOW KNEE	BELOW KNEE–ANKLE
Winsor (1950)[162]*	−22	13	11	8
Bell (1973)[13]†	−6 ± 12	2 ± 8	—	—
Hajjar and Sumner (1976)[58]‡	−46 ± 24	13 ± 19	12 ± 4	10 ± 9
Rutherford et al (1979)[126]‡	−35 ± 18	5 ± 12	10 ± 15	11 ± 15

*Cuff 13 cm width.
†Cuff 18 × 60 cm.
‡Cuff 10 × 40 cm.

Table 14-4 Typical Segmental Systolic Arterial Pressures (mm Hg)

		ARTERIAL DISEASE			
LOCATION	**NORMAL**	**Iliac**	**Superficial Femoral**	**Iliac and Superficial Femoral**	**Below Knee**
Arm	120	120	120	120	120
Upper thigh	160	110	160	110	160
Above knee	150	100	100	70	150
Below knee	140	90	90	60	140
Ankle	130	80	80	50	90

Table 14-5 Accuracy of Segmental Pressures for Locating Arterial Obstructive Disease

	DIAGNOSIS BASED ON SEGMENTAL PRESSURE DATA (%)					
ARTERIOGRAPHIC DIAGNOSIS	**Normal**	**Aortoiliac**	**Aortoiliac and Superficial Femoral**	**Superficial Femoral**	**Superficial Femoral and Popliteal**	**Popliteal**
Normal	97.2	1.4	—	—	1.4	—
Disease						
Aortoiliac	12.5	75.0	12.5	—	—	—
Aortoiliac and superficial femoral	6.3	6.3	78.0	3.1	6.3	—
Superficial femoral	15.0	—	10.0	55.0	15.0	5.0
Superficial femoral and popliteal*	8.0	—	4.0	24.0	60.0	4.0
Popliteal*	57.0	—	7.0	—	—	36.0

*Popliteal includes popliteal artery or two or more of the peroneal-tibial arteries.

Modified from Rutherford RB, Lowenstein DH, Klein MF: Combining segmental systolic pressures and plethysmography to diagnose arterial occlusive disease of the legs. Am J Surg 138:211, 1979.

Values lower than this at any level in the leg imply significant obstructive disease in the proximal arteries. Theoretically, by making both longitudinal and horizontal comparisons of the segmental pressures or indices, the examiner should be able to locate the site or sites of arterial obstruction and obtain some idea of their functional significance. Idealized values illustrating this point are shown in Table 14-4.

Isolated disease in the aortoiliac or superficial femoral segments can usually be identified, but in limbs with multilevel disease, identification is frequently less reliable. For example, superficial femoral obstructions may not produce an abnormal gradient in limbs with aortoiliac disease, iliac stenoses may not be recognized in limbs with superficial femoral disease, and below-knee disease is commonly misdiagnosed or overlooked when there is concomitant superficial femoral obstruction (Table 14-5).[63,126]

Indirect blood pressure measurements have been used in patients with extremity trauma to avoid unnecessary arteriography and determine the need for surgical exploration. Lynch and Johansen[94] obtained Doppler cuff pressures in 100 injured limbs of 93 trauma victims who also underwent arteriography. An arterial pressure index (systolic pressure distal to the site of injury divided by brachial systolic pressure in an uninvolved arm) greater than 0.90 was considered normal. Compared with the arteriographic findings, the arterial pressure index had a sensitivity of 87%, specificity of 97%, and overall accuracy of 95% for detecting arterial injuries. When the results of two false-positive arteriograms were excluded, the sensitivity, specificity, and accuracy of the arterial pressure index increased to 95%, 98%, and 97%, respectively. Using an arterial pressure index of less than 0.90 to select trauma patients with possible occult vascular injuries for arteriography was prospectively evaluated in 100 limbs of 96 patients.[71] Among the 17 limbs with a decreased arterial pressure index, arteriograms were abnormal in 16, and 7 underwent arterial repair. For the 83 limbs with a normal arterial pressure index, follow-up evaluation revealed six minor lesions but no major injuries.

Although the arterial pressure index is a simple, rapid, and clinically valuable screening test for arterial injuries, it has several important limitations. This approach cannot be used in cases in which extensive wounds prevent placement of a pneumatic cuff on the injured extremity. In addition, the arterial pressure index does not distinguish between an intrinsic arterial lesion, extrinsic compression, and vasospasm. Finally, distal limb pressure measurement does not detect non–flow-limiting lesions or injuries to nonaxial arteries such as the profunda femoris.

The location and severity of lower extremity arterial lesions can be directly assessed by duplex scanning, as discussed in Chapter 16.

Technical Errors

Cuff width is an important consideration for accurate measurements of limb blood pressure. The use of a cuff that is relatively small compared with the size of the limb results in a falsely high pressure reading, or "cuff artifact." This effect is minimized when the cuff width is at least 50% greater than the diameter of the limb where the pressure is being measured. As noted for upper thigh pressure measurements with the four-cuff technique, the magnitude of the cuff artifact can generally be anticipated.

In an effort to achieve a more accurate assessment of the thigh pressure, some investigators have advocated using a single wide (19-cm) cuff rather than two narrower (10-cm) cuffs.[64] Gray and colleagues[55] compared thigh pressures obtained with a wide cuff and direct measurements of femoral arterial blood pressure in an effort to see how accurately the noninvasive pressure predicted the presence of aortoiliac disease. A thigh-brachial index exceeding 0.90 was generally reliable in ruling out inflow disease, with only 13% false-negative results. The thigh pressure was spuriously low in 59% of the studies, however, implying the presence of aortoiliac disease when in fact there was none. All of these false-positive results occurred in limbs with occlusions of the superficial femoral artery. Thus, it would appear that the wide cuff is less accurate than the narrow cuff for diagnosing aortoiliac stenoses.

Moreover, Heintz and associates[63] have shown that detection of superficial femoral disease by means of the "wide cuff to below-knee pressure gradient" is considerably less accurate than it is with the narrow cuff technique, which allows gradients across both the thigh and the knee to be analyzed. Other workers have reached similar conclusions.[45,125]

Occasionally, the pressure gradient between two adjacent segments of the leg may appear to be reversed. For example, the above-knee pressure may exceed the pressure recorded at the upper thigh or the below-knee pressure may be greater than the pressure recorded at the above-knee level. This reversal of the normal pressure pattern is usually due to local arterial incompressibility or to varying relationships between the size of the cuff and the limb.[1,48] In hypertensive patients, the gradient between any two adjacent levels may be increased. On the other hand, when the cardiac output is low, the pressure drop may be diminished.[162]

Normal blood pressure gradients may be obtained in limbs with arterial obstructions when collateral channels are quite large. These findings do not really constitute errors because the measurements are designed to reveal *functional* rather than *anatomic* obstruction.[139] For example, the pressure gradient from the below-knee level to the ankle is typically normal when either the anterior tibial or the posterior tibial artery is patent.[1,67,93,129,139]

Isolated obstructions of arteries that are not directly responsible for perfusion of the distal leg, such as the internal iliac or profunda femoris artery, cannot be detected by segmental pressure measurements.[1,26] As pointed out earlier in this chapter, occlusions of the profunda femoris artery become evident only if the superficial femoral artery is also occluded. In these cases, the profunda femoris artery constitutes the major collateral channel supplying the lower leg and foot. Therefore, if both of these arteries are obstructed, the upper thigh pressure is abnormally low, even though the aortoiliac segment is completely patent.

Finally, because the ankle is the most distal site of pressure measurement, routine segmental pressures do not detect arterial occlusive lesions distal to the ankle. Lesions involving the plantar or digital arteries, such as vasculitis or microembolism, may be identified by toe pressure measurement or digital plethysmography, as discussed later in the chapter.

Because of the errors inherent in noninvasive assessment of the upper thigh pressure, direct femoral artery pressure measurements, as discussed later, are being used more frequently.[9,21,43,99,157] Direct pressure measurements are also subject to errors; most systems, for example, are underdamped, giving spuriously high systolic pressures.[23] Many vascular laboratories also use segmental plethysmography or Doppler flow signal analysis to supplement segmental pressure studies.[118,126]

Toe Pressure

Toe pressures are measured with a pneumatic cuff of appropriate width (about 1.2 times the diameter of the digit) wrapped around the proximal phalanx, with a flow sensor applied distally.[36,56,91,107] Although mercury strain-gauges work well for this purpose, photoplethysmographs, which are more stable and occupy less space on the tip of the digit, are generally more convenient to use. The systolic blood pressure measured at toe level is usually lower than the brachial or ankle pressure, probably related to measurement techniques. According to Nielsen and associates,[107] pressures in the toes of young normal individuals in the supine position average less than those in the arm. In older subjects, toe pressures are less than arm pressures. Because normal ankle pressure exceeds brachial pressure, normal toe pressures average 24 ± 7 to 41 ± 17 mm Hg less than ankle pressures.[13,30,107] Ankle-toe gradients that exceed 44 mm Hg in young patients or 64 mm Hg in older patients are abnormal.[107] The toe-ankle index, obtained by dividing the toe pressure by the ipsilateral ankle pressure, averages 0.64 ± 0.20 in asymptomatic limbs, 0.52 ± 0.20 in limbs with claudication, and 0.23 ± 0.19 in limbs with ischemic rest pain or ulcers.[121] These findings suggest that obstruction of the pedal or digital arteries plays a major role in causing gangrene or ischemic rest pain.[160]

Figure 14-6 shows the distribution of toe pressures in 296 limbs with arteriosclerosis obliterans.[121] No asymptomatic patient had a toe pressure less than 50 mm Hg, and only 11% of those whose complaints were limited to claudication had toe pressures less than 30 mm Hg. In contrast, 81% of the limbs with ischemic rest pain had toe pressures less than 30 mm Hg, and none had toe pressures exceeding 40 mm Hg. In 81% of the limbs with toe pressures less than 30 mm Hg and in almost all of those with pressures less than 15 mm Hg, there were ischemic symptoms at rest. Patients with rest pain usually have toe pressures less than 20 to 30 mm Hg.[30,68,121,156]

Toe indices (toe pressure divided by brachial pressure) of patients with arteriosclerosis obliterans are listed in Table 14-6 according to the severity of their symptoms. It is noteworthy that there is little difference between the mean values of diabetic and nondiabetic patients. Spuriously high ankle or segmental pressures due to arterial calcification, which are common in diabetic patients, seldom occur at toe level. For this reason, toe indices are reliable indicators of the physiologic severity of arterial occlusive disease and should be used when there is any doubt about the validity of the ankle pressure.[160]

Toe pressures are particularly valuable for demonstrating arterial disease confined to the pedal or digital arteries.[49] In limbs with ischemic ulcers or gangrene, normal ankle

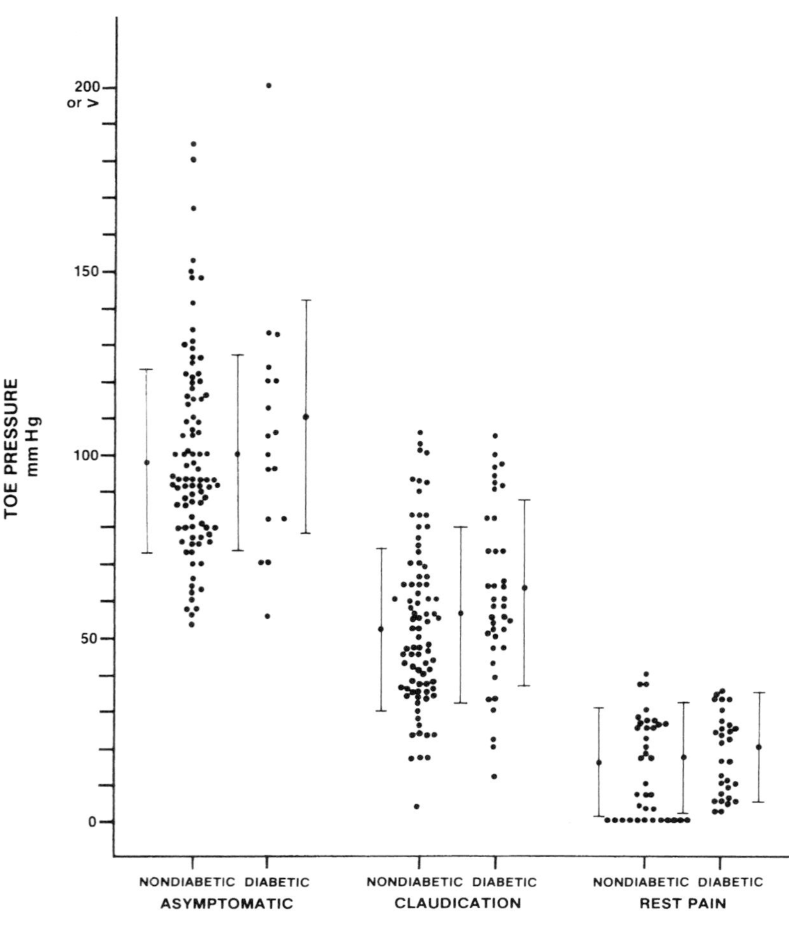

FIGURE 14-6 Toe blood pressures grouped according to symptoms and presence of diabetes in patients with arterial disease. Mean and standard deviations for the nondiabetic and diabetic subgroups and for the two groups combined are indicated by *vertical bars.* (From Ramsey DE, Manke DA, Sumner DS: Toe blood pressure: A valuable adjunct to ankle pressure measurement for assessing peripheral arterial disease. J Cardiovasc Surg 24:43, 1983.)

pressures and normal ankle pressure indices are often associated with toe pressures in the ischemic range (Fig. 14-7).[67,121]

Carter[29] found that foot lesions usually heal if toe pressures exceed 30 mm Hg in nondiabetic patients or 55 mm Hg in diabetic patients. In contrast, Holstein and coworkers[68] found no appreciable difference between the two patient groups. In their study, healing occurred in 91% of the limbs in which toe pressures were greater than 30 mm Hg, in 50% of limbs in which toe pressures were between 20 and 29 mm Hg, and in only 29% of limbs in which toe pressures were less than 20 mm Hg. Bone and Pomajzl[20] noted failure of toe amputations in all patients with toe pressures less than 45 mm Hg and in 25% of patients with toe pressures between 45 and 55 mm Hg; healing occurred in all patients with toe pressures greater than 55 mm Hg. Other investigators have reported uniform healing with toe pressures exceeding 10 to 25 mm Hg.[12,128]

In a study by Ramsey and coworkers,[121] toe pressures proved to be of more prognostic value than ankle pressures (see Fig. 14-7). Ulcers and toe amputations failed to heal in 92% of limbs with an ankle pressure less than 80 mm Hg, but they also failed to heal in 45% of limbs with higher pressures. There were three cases of failure to heal in limbs with ankle pressures of 150 mm Hg; in all three cases, the toe pressures were less than 30 mm Hg. With toe pressures less than 30 mm Hg, the failure rate was 95%, but with toe

Table 14-6 Toe Indices in Patients with Arterial Disease (Mean ± SD)

AUTHOR (YEAR)	NO SYMPTOMS	CLAUDICATION		ISCHEMIA*	
		Nondiabetic	Diabetic	Nondiabetic	Diabetic
Carter and Lezack (1971)[30]	0.91 ± 0.13†	0.43 ± 0.17	0.42 ± 0.16	0.24 ± 0.14	0.19 ± 0.10
Vollrath et al (1980)[160]	0.89 ± 0.16	0.47 ± 0.24	0.60 ± 0.17	0.19 ± 0.15	0.16 ± 0.13‡
Ramsey et al (1983)[121]	0.72 ± 0.19	0.35 ± 0.15	0.38 ± 0.15	0.11 ± 0.10	0.12 ± 0.09

*Ischemic rest pain, ulcers, or gangrene.
†Normal subjects, 52 ± 6 years old; 21 ± 4 years old: 0.86 ± 0.12.
‡Diet-controlled; insulin-dependent: 0.23 ± 0.15.

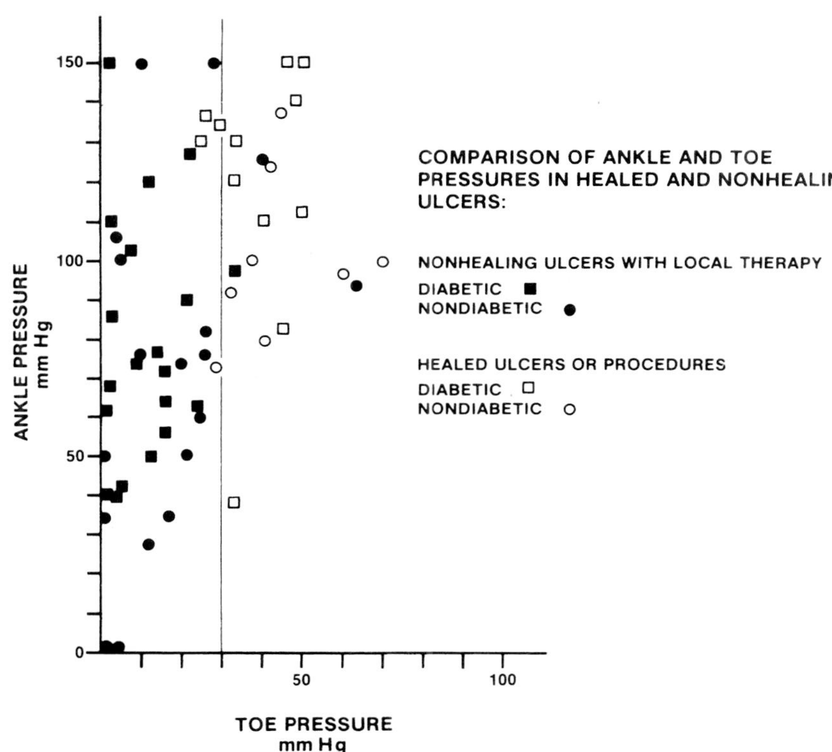

FIGURE 14-7 Comparison of ankle and toe pressures in 58 limbs with healed or nonhealing ischemic ulcers or toe amputations. Note that a toe pressure of 30 mm Hg provides good separation between those limbs that healed and those that did not. (From Ramsey DE, Manke DA, Sumner DS: Toe blood pressure: A valuable adjunct to ankle pressure measurement for assessing peripheral arterial disease. J Cardiovasc Surg 24:43, 1983.)

pressures more than 30 mm Hg, only 14% of the ulcers or amputations did not heal. This experience suggests that toe pressures less than 20 mm Hg almost uniformly predict failure of a toe amputation or ulcer to heal.

Penile Pressure

The penis is supplied by three paired arteries: the dorsal penile, the cavernosal (deep corporal), and the urethral (spongiosal). These arteries are terminal branches of the internal pudendal artery, which originates from the internal iliac artery. The cavernosal artery is most important for erectile function. Obstruction of any of the arteries leading to the corpora cavernosa, including the common iliac artery or terminal aorta, can be responsible for vasculogenic impotence.

Measurement of penile blood pressure is performed with a pneumatic cuff measuring 2.5 cm in width applied to the base of the penis. Return of blood flow when the cuff is deflated can be detected by a mercury strain-gauge plethysmograph, a photoplethysmograph applied to the anterolateral aspect of the shaft, or a Doppler flow probe.[22,83,90] Although some investigators have positioned the probe over the dorsal penile arteries, others have emphasized the importance of detecting flow in the cavernosal artery.[104,116] Because the penile blood supply is paired and obstruction may occasionally be limited to only one side, it has been recommended that pressures be measured on both sides of the penis.[119]

In normal men younger than 40 years, the penile-brachial index (penile pressure divided by brachial systolic pressure) was found by Kempczinski[83] to be 0.99 ± 0.15. Thus, in the absence of any arterial disease, the penile and brachial pressures are roughly equivalent. Older men without symptoms of impotence tend to have lower indices.[83] Penile-brachial indices greater than 0.75 to 0.80 are considered compatible with normal erectile function; an index less than 0.60 is diagnostic of vasculogenic impotence, especially in patients with peripheral vascular disease.[33,50,83,90,104,116] A brachial-penile pressure gradient less than 20 to 40 mm Hg suggests adequate penile blood flow.[22,83,90] Gradients in excess of 60 mm Hg suggest arterial insufficiency.[83]

Knowledge of the penile pressure can be used to guide the vascular surgeon in planning the operative approach to aneurysmal or obstructive lesions of the aorta and iliac arteries.[104] Maintenance of blood flow to the internal iliac artery preserves potency, and restoration of flow to this artery may improve penile pressure and erectile function if more distal arteries are nondiseased.[116]

Stress Testing

Exercise

As noted in Chapter 9, reducing peripheral vascular resistance by walking exercise is an effective physiologic method for stressing the lower extremity circulation. Under such stress, lesions that may not appear to be significant at rest can be evaluated.[28] Exercise testing enables the surgeon to better appreciate the functional disability that the arterial lesions produce.[118] It also permits the surgeon to assess the disability produced by arterial obstruction in relation to the restrictions imposed by orthopedic, neurologic, or cardiopulmonary disease.

However, exercise testing (or other stress testing) is not required for the evaluation of patients with ischemia at rest. Patients with ischemic rest pain, ulcers, or gangrene always have decreased digital artery pressures and usually have low ankle pressures. Moreover, most patients with claudication have decreased ankle pressure at rest, and supplementary stress testing is only occasionally necessary to establish the diagnosis.

Although many different exercise protocols are possible, the following protocol has been widely used[143]:

1. After the patient has rested supine for about 20 minutes, baseline ankle and arm pressures are measured.
2. The patient walks on a treadmill at 2 mph up a 10% grade (a) for 5 minutes or (b) until forced to stop because of claudication or other restrictions. The nature of any symptoms and the time at which they appear are recorded. If leg pain occurs, it is important to note which muscle group is first affected. The final walking time is also recorded.[145,164] However, walking time itself is not a particularly important indicator.[113] The patient's motivation, pain tolerance, and nonvascular symptoms dictate the duration of walking, which tends to correlate poorly with objective hemodynamic measurements.
3. The patient promptly assumes a supine position on the examining table.
4. Ankle and arm pressures are obtained immediately and then every 2 minutes until (a) pre-exercise levels are reached or (b) 10 minutes have elapsed.

A normal individual, regardless of age, is usually able to walk for 5 minutes with little or no drop in ankle pressure.[86,134,136,138,164] Patients with obstructive arterial disease are seldom able to walk for 5 minutes and always experience an immediate drop in ankle pressure (Fig. 14-8).[138,145,164] The magnitude of this drop reflects the extent of the functional disability. Patients with multilevel arterial disease typically walk for a shorter distance and experience a much more extreme drop in ankle pressure.[164,167] Often in such patients, the ankle pressure is unobtainable for several minutes following cessation of exercise.

Brachial systolic pressure increases after exercise, and this increase is usually much more pronounced in patients with arterial disease than in normal subjects. Although an occasional patient with minimal or no symptoms may not demonstrate a distinct decrease in ankle pressure following exercise, the arm-ankle pressure gradient is increased.[152] Arterial disease may be diagnosed when the postexercise arm pressure exceeds the ankle pressure by more than 20 mm Hg. It is rare for arterial reconstruction to be required for claudication in patients with only mild arm-ankle pressure gradients.

The location of arterial lesions also affects the magnitude of the pressure drop and the time required for the pressure to return to baseline levels. Pressure drops following exercise indicate that the obstruction involves arteries supplying the gastrocnemius and soleus muscles. Because a large portion of the blood supply to these muscles is derived from the sural arteries, which have their origin from the popliteal artery, a drop in ankle pressure following walking exercise signifies an obstruction of the popliteal, superficial femoral, or more proximal vessels. When the obstruction is confined to below-knee vessels, walking exercise seldom causes claudication or a significant drop in ankle pressure.[138,139]

In general, the more proximal the occlusive disease, the greater its effect on the ankle pressure response to exercise. For example, an isolated aortoiliac lesion usually has more functional significance than a lesion confined to the superficial femoral artery.[145,167] This phenomenon occurs because the more proximal arteries supply a greater muscle mass than the more distal arteries. Consequently, there is a more severe and prolonged diversion of blood away from the lower leg to the proximal muscle masses.[142,145]

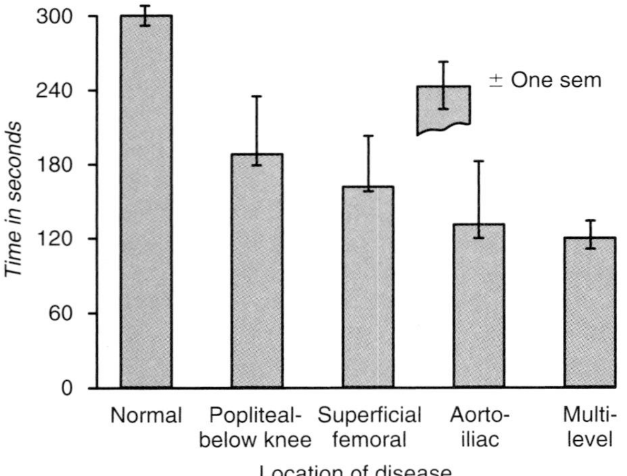

FIGURE 14-8 Treadmill walking times in patients with occlusive arterial disease. Normal subjects almost always can exceed 5 minutes (300 seconds). Treadmill is set at 2 mph, 12% grade. (From Strandness DE Jr, Sumner DS: Hemodynamics for Surgeons. New York, Grune & Stratton, 1975.)

Reactive Hyperemia

Reactive hyperemia, by increasing the rate of blood flow through stenotic arteries or high-resistance collateral vessels, causes a drop in the ankle pressure similar to that observed after exercise (see Chapter 9).[5,69,72,158] For the reactive hyperemia test, a pneumatic cuff placed around the thigh is inflated to more than systolic pressure for 3 to 7 minutes. After release of the compression, ankle pressures are monitored at 15-, 20-, or 30-second intervals for 3 to 6 minutes or until measurements return to precompression levels.

In normal limbs, ankle pressures decrease immediately to about 80% of precompression levels but then rapidly rise, reaching 90% levels within about 30 to 60 seconds. In limbs with obstructive arterial disease, the magnitude of the pressure decrease coincides well with that seen following exercise, but recovery to resting levels is much faster.[5,69] The magnitude of the pressure drop depends on the anatomic extent of the disease process and on the extent of functional impairment.[72,158] Although recovery times are also correlated with the severity of disease (from < 1 minute to > 3 minutes), the correlation is not as good as that between severity of disease and the maximal decrease in ankle pressure.[113]

In some laboratories, reactive hyperemia testing has supplanted treadmill exercise for stress testing.[113] In contrast to the treadmill, this test

1. Is less time consuming
2. Can be performed in the patient's room

3. Uses simple, inexpensive equipment
4. May result in more standardized stress because the duration of cuff compression can be prescribed and walking time cannot be
5. Is less dependent on patient motivation
6. Can be used for patients who cannot walk on the treadmill because of neurologic, cardiac, pulmonary, or orthopedic problems or because of general disability, prior amputation, rest pain, or ischemic ulceration

However, stress testing is not required to diagnose arterial disease in limbs with rest pain, ulcers, or gangrene; disease of that severity is easily detected and evaluated with resting ankle or toe pressures.[113] In patients who cannot walk because of other problems, disease of sufficient severity to threaten the limb is readily detected without stress testing.

Finally, in contrast with reactive hyperemia testing, treadmill exercise duplicates the physiologic stress responsible for claudication and permits neurologic, cardiopulmonary, and orthopedic problems to be evaluated in relation to the leg arterial disease.[69]

Some disadvantages of the reactive hyperemia test[5,69,113] can be listed as follows:

1. It causes mild to moderate discomfort.
2. Thigh compression may be hazardous in limbs with femoropopliteal bypass grafts.
3. Rapid pressure measurements are required to obtain reproducible results.

Ouriel and coworkers[113] found that reactive hyperemia was a less sensitive and less specific indicator than resting ankle pressures or exercise testing. Still, the method has some advantages, and its use may be justified in selected situations in which stress testing is required and treadmill exercise is impossible or impractical.

Direct Measurement of Arterial Pressure

As discussed in Chapter 9, the relationship between arterial pressure, flow, and resistance can be expressed by Poiseuille's law. The degree of narrowing at which pressure and flow begin to decline is called the *critical stenosis*. However, in the intact arterial circulation, autoregulation can maintain normal flow rates distal to a critical stenosis, even when a significant pressure drop is present. Therefore, pressure measurements are more likely than flow measurements to indicate the presence of arterial occlusive disease. Furthermore, measurements of flow rates or peripheral resistance are extremely difficult to perform in the clinical setting.

Direct measurement of arterial pressure in the lower extremity avoids the cuff artifacts and other potential errors associated with noninvasive pressure measurements. Specific approaches include pull-through aortoiliac artery pressures during arteriography, percutaneous measurement of common femoral artery pressures, and intraoperative pressure measurements after arterial exposure. As with the noninvasive methods, direct pressure measurements can be made both in the resting state and following some form of hemodynamic stress. Although a pedal ergometer exercise test has been described for use with percutaneous common femoral artery pressure measurements, a large proportion of patients are unable to perform this test adequately, and it has not been widely used.[133] A simpler technique that does not require strict patient cooperation or any specialized equipment is intra-arterial injection of papaverine to produce peripheral vasodilatation.

Although direct arterial pressure measurements are generally regarded as the reference standard for the physiologic evaluation of peripheral arterial disease, this approach is subject to certain errors that must be recognized. The proper zero level for a particular measurement must be selected, with the relative heights of the patient's heart, the transducer, and the site of measurement taken into account. Underdamping of the needle, transducer, and catheter system is common, especially when air bubbles are present.[23] This tends to augment the pulse pressure and result in excessively high systolic pressure values, although the mean pressure component is less likely to be affected. These problems can be minimized during clinical measurements by (1) the use of stiff tubing with few stopcocks and (2) elimination of fluid leaks and air bubbles.

Percutaneous Pressure Measurement

The direct measurement of arterial pressure is indicated to assess the physiologic severity of aortoiliac disease found on either arteriography or noninvasive testing. Although arteriography is usually adequate to evaluate the significance of infrainguinal arterial disease, it is often not adequate for more proximal arterial lesions.[99] Even biplanar arteriography may not allow an accurate assessment of the aortoiliac system.[44]

Because arteriographic procedures are most commonly performed with the use of a femoral puncture site, direct measurements of arterial pressure during arteriography generally assess the aortic, iliac, and femoral segments. Pull-through pressures taken with the arteriogram catheter indicate the hemodynamic significance of any lesions present in the aortoiliac system. Intra-arterial injection of papaverine can be used as a pharmacologic stress test to assess the pressure gradients during high-flow conditions. Studies of hemodynamically normal patients suggest that a hemodynamically significant lesion in the aortoiliac segment is present when the systolic pressure gradient is more than 10 mm Hg at rest or 20 mm Hg after injection of papaverine hydrochloride (30 mg) into the arteriogram catheter.[151]

Direct measurement of femoral artery pressure is performed by percutaneous puncture of the common femoral artery with a 19-gauge needle attached by rigid fluid-filled tubing to a calibrated pressure transducer. The femoral artery systolic pressure is compared with the brachial artery systolic pressure, and the *femoral-brachial index* (FBI) is calculated. As for the ABI, the brachial artery pressure as measured by Doppler ultrasonography is presumed to represent systemic arterial pressure. A resting FBI greater than or equal to 0.9 is considered normal.[44] Values less than 0.9 indicate the presence of a hemodynamically significant lesion proximal to the common femoral artery.

If the resting FBI is normal, the injection of papaverine can be used to look for less severe lesions that are apparent only at increased flow rates. After direct injection of 30 mg of papaverine hydrochloride through the needle in the common femoral artery, pressures in both the common femoral artery and the brachial artery are monitored. It is particularly important to measure the brachial artery pressure during this test, because papaverine often causes a slight decrease in systemic arterial pressure. The mean decrease in FBI following papaverine injection is 6% for normal subjects, and a decrease of 15% or more indicates a hemodynamically significant lesion.[44] A peak flow increase of 50% or greater is sufficient for a valid test result; reasons for an invalid result include fixed outflow resistance and extravascular injection of papaverine.

Intraoperative Pressure Measurement

The basic principles and techniques for intraoperative pressure measurements are identical to those described for the percutaneous approach. Common femoral artery pressures, taken both before and after papaverine injection, can be used to assess the aortoiliac segment when it is not feasible to obtain these measurements preoperatively. Sequential pressure measurements taken along a native artery or bypass graft can localize areas of hemodynamic abnormality. In this manner, the inflow, graft segment, and distal runoff of an arterial reconstruction can be evaluated, and specific problems identified.

Intraoperative pressure measurements are performed by means of puncture of the exposed artery with a hypodermic needle attached to a length of rigid fluid-filled tubing. A 19-gauge or larger needle provides optimal pressure waveforms, whereas smaller needles are satisfactory for measurement of pressure gradients. The same pressure transducer setup used by the anesthesiologist to monitor radial artery pressure can be used for these measurements. In addition to looking for significant pressure gradients along an arterial reconstruction, one can compare the intraoperative pressures with the systemic pressure, which is typically based on the reading from a radial artery pressure line.

■ DOPPLER ULTRASONOGRAPHY

Although the absolute magnitude of blood flow measured at rest is of little help in the objective assessment of peripheral arterial occlusive disease, the contour of the velocity pulse wave and disturbances of the flow pattern in individual arteries provide a great deal of important information. Before the development of transcutaneous Doppler ultrasonography, this type of information was essentially unavailable. The presence of a bruit on physical examination signifies a flow disturbance of some type; however, bruits (1) are difficult to quantify, (2) do not appear until the arterial lumen is significantly narrowed, (3) disappear when the stenosis is very severe, and (4) are absent when the artery is totally occluded. Moreover, bruits may arise from arteries adjacent to the vessel of interest, causing additional confusion.

Doppler ultrasonography has become an essential part of the noninvasive evaluation of peripheral arterial disease. Ultrasound instruments are not only widely available and easy to use but also provide information instantaneously. Many levels of data analysis are available, ranging from the simple to the extremely complex.

Examination Technique

Doppler recordings should be made in a warm room with the patient resting comfortably in a supine position. For most purposes, a pencil-type probe is preferred. Optimal signals are obtained by placing the probe directly over the vessel to be examined at an angle of 45 to 60 degrees. In the lower limb, the common femoral artery is examined at the groin at or slightly above the inguinal crease to avoid confusion with signals arising from the profunda femoris or the proximal superficial femoral artery. Persson and coworkers[115] have emphasized the importance of accurately locating the common femoral artery by using the line drawn between the anterosuperior iliac spine and the pubic tubercle to determine the site of the inguinal ligament. The inguinal skin crease, especially in obese patients, is often well below the inguinal ligament.

Signals from the superficial femoral artery are best detected with the probe positioned medially on the thigh, in the groove between the quadriceps and adductor muscles. When the patient is supine, flexion of the knee and mild external rotation of the leg provide access to the popliteal artery. Alternatively, the popliteal artery can be examined with the patient prone and the feet supported by a pillow to flex the knee. At the ankle level, the posterior tibial arterial signal is obtained just behind the medial malleolus. The dorsalis pedis artery is consistently located slightly lateral to the extensor hallucis longus tendon a centimeter or so distal to the ankle joint. Finally, the lateral tarsal artery (representing the termination of the peroneal artery) can usually be studied by placing the probe anterior and medial to the lateral malleolus.

Although simple, nondirectional Doppler devices suffice for many clinical applications, such as measurement of the ABI, direction-sensing instruments supply more information and are necessary for any detailed analysis of the Doppler signal. Even in routine surveys of the peripheral arteries, direction sensing is often a valuable adjunct. The choice of frequency depends on the depth of the vessel being examined. Whereas superficial vessels are best studied with a high-frequency probe (10 MHz), the deeper vessels of the leg require the use of lower frequencies (3 to 5 MHz).

Audible Interpretation

The ear serves as the simplest and most readily available interpreter of the output of the Doppler flowmeter. Skilled observers can derive a great deal of information from the audible signal without resorting to recordings or complex methods of analysis. Because good-quality, continuous-wave, nondirectional devices meet most of the requirements for audible interpretation, there is no need for bulky, expensive instrumentation. For many purposes, a handheld Doppler flowmeter is sufficient.

Normal peripheral arterial Doppler signals are biphasic or triphasic,[141] with the following characteristics:

1. The first sound or phase corresponds to the large, high-velocity, forward-flow systolic component of the pulse wave.

2. The second sound or phase is due to the smaller reverse-flow component in early diastole.
3. The third sound or phase is associated with an even smaller, low-velocity, forward-flow component that usually appears in late diastole.

The pitch of the first phase rises rapidly to a peak during systole and then falls abruptly in early diastole. The pitch of the two subsequent phases is always much lower. Finding a clear, crisp, multiphasic signal with a high systolic velocity implies patency of the proximal arteries and almost invariably rules out hemodynamically significant disease.

The characteristics of abnormal Doppler flow signals vary according to whether the probe is positioned proximal to, at, or distal to the site of the occlusive process. Distal to a stenosis or occlusion, flow signals are typically low pitched and monophasic, because the high-frequency components of the pulse wave have been filtered out by passage through the stenosis or high-resistance collateral channels. As long as the velocity of flow exceeds a certain minimal level (determined by the ultrasound transmission frequency and the cutoff frequency of the high-pass filter used to eliminate extraneous signals arising from wall motion), arterial signals are obtained despite the absence of palpable pulses. Absence of a Doppler signal implies either a flow velocity below the threshold level of the instrument or occlusion of the arterial segment being evaluated. In cases of severe arterial obstruction, the Doppler signal may lose much of its characteristic pulsatility and may be difficult to distinguish from an adjacent venous signal. A directional Doppler ultrasonographic evaluation usually resolves this issue.

Signals detected directly over a stenosis or from an artery immediately distal to a stenosis are high-pitched, noisy, and monophasic. These characteristics reflect the increased velocity of flow within the narrowed lumen and the development of disturbed or turbulent flow patterns in the jet of blood emerging from the stenosis.

Signals obtained from a pulsating artery a few centimeters proximal to an occlusion have a characteristic "to-and-fro" or "thumping" quality. This sound is composed of a low-frequency forward-flow wave followed by a relatively large flow wave reflected from the obstruction. In questionable cases, a directional instrument equipped with frequency meters may aid in the interpretation of the audible signal. When the artery is obstructed distal to the probe and there are no intervening branches to provide outflow, the flowmeters indicate (1) no mean forward flow or (2) low-velocity flows of equal magnitude in both the forward and reverse directions.

Waveform Analysis

The main drawback of the simple audible interpretation of the Doppler flowmeter signal is its inherent subjectivity. Waveform analysis not only is objective but also permits more information to be extracted from the Doppler signal. Several methods are available for recording and processing of the Doppler velocity signals. Although the zero-crossing detector output is simple to use, it is often inaccurate and, consequently, is seldom suitable for quantitative work. It does, however, provide a quick method for examining the contour of the waveform, especially in conjunction with segmental pressure measurements. For all quantitative work, spectral analysis of the Doppler signal is the method of choice. In the clinical setting, spectral analysis is most commonly used with the pulsed Doppler component of the duplex scanner (see Chapter 16).

Qualitative Analysis

Simply inspecting the contour of the velocity waveform obtained from a zero-crossing or audiofrequency spectrum analyzer is often of considerable diagnostic value. As illustrated in Figure 14-9A, the normal velocity waveform is triphasic. Velocity increases rapidly in early systole, reaches a peak, and then drops almost equally as rapidly, reversing in early diastole.[79] In late diastole, the velocity tracing again becomes positive before returning to the zero-flow baseline. With increasing peripheral vasoconstriction, the reverse-flow component becomes more exaggerated.[124,142] When peripheral resistance is reduced after exercise, artificially induced reactive hyperemia, or infusion of vasodilating drugs, the reverse-flow component disappears, the baseline rises above the zero-flow level, and the wave assumes a biphasic rather than a triphasic contour.

Atherosclerotic disease in the arteries proximal to the site of the probe initially produces a subtle change in the contour

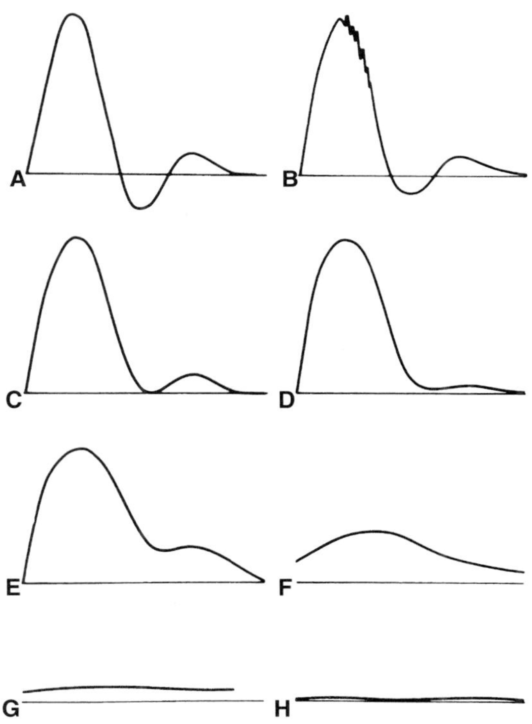

FIGURE 14-9 Different patterns of flow velocity waveforms. **A,** Normal. **B,** Atherosclerotic changes causing turbulence during systolic phase (high frequency). **C** and **D,** Loss of reverse flow due to increasing degree of stenosis. **E-H,** With increasing arterial stenosis, the flow velocity waveform becomes progressively damped. (**A-H,** From Johnston KW, Maruzzo BC, Kassam M, et al: Methods for obtaining, processing, and quantifying Doppler blood velocity waveforms. In Nicolaides AN, Yao JST [eds]: Investigation of Vascular Disorders. New York, Churchill Livingstone, 1981, p 543.)

Table 14-7 Typical Pulsatility Indices (PI_{pp}) and Inverse Damping Factors (DF^{-1})

	LOCATION OF ARTERIAL OBSTRUCTION							
	None		Aortoiliac		Superficial Femoral		Aortoiliac and Superficial Femoral	
RECORDING SITE	PI_{pp}	DF^{-1}	PI_{pp}	DF^{-1}	PI_{pp}	DF^{-1}	PI_{pp}	DF^{-1}
Common femoral	13.0		2.4		6.1		3.1	
Popliteal	16.7	1.3	2.7	1.1	4.4	0.7	2.4	0.8
Dorsalis pedis	17.7	1.1	5.6	2.1	5.6	1.3	3.7	1.5
Posterior tibial	18.0		4.6		4.6		3.1	

Data from Johnston KW, Maruzzo BC, Cobbold RSC: Doppler methods for quantitative measurement and localization of peripheral arterial occlusive disease by analysis of the blood velocity waveform. Ultrasound Med Biol 4:209, 1978.

of the systolic forward-flow wave at the peak or in the early deceleration phase (Fig. 14-9B). With increasing proximal stenosis, the reverse-flow component is damped and then disappears entirely (Fig. 14-9C and D). As the stenosis becomes more severe, progressing to total occlusion, the rate of acceleration of the forward-flow wave decreases, the peak becomes rounded, and the wave becomes continuous and less pulsatile (Fig. 14-9E through H).[142]

Proximal to a stenosis or occlusion, the waveform may have a nearly normal contour, especially when (1) the disease process is located well below the site being evaluated and (2) there are large outflow branches that serve to reduce the peripheral resistance. However, it is not uncommon to find that the contour is modified perceptibly by increased input impedance and that the resulting wave takes on some of the characteristics commonly associated with proximal stenosis.[106a] For example, recordings made from common femoral arteries proximal to superficial femoral artery occlusions often resemble the waveforms in Figure 14-9C and D, even in the absence of any significant iliac stenosis. One must keep this fact in mind when attempting to use the contour of the common femoral waveform to detect inflow disease.

By comparing the contours of the Doppler waveforms obtained from the common femoral, popliteal, and pedal arteries, one can usually identify the presence of hemodynamically significant disease and can often localize the disease to the aortoiliac, superficial femoral, or below-knee segment. The presence of multilevel disease is implied when severely dampened waveforms, such as those shown in Figure 14-9F through H, are recorded from the pedal arteries. Absence of a recordable Doppler signal from any of the pedal arteries indicates severe arterial disease.

Quantitative Analysis

A variety of methods have been proposed for quantitative analysis of Doppler velocity waveforms,[3,4,70,75,130,161] including

- Peak-to-peak pulsatility index
- Laplace transform
- Power frequency spectrum analysis
- Pulse transit time

Few of these techniques, however, have been widely applied in the clinical setting. Many are little better than simple qualitative analysis, despite the aura of accuracy that numbers convey. A major problem is that most such methods derive their information from sites that are remote from the principal lesion, where flow patterns have reverted towards a more normal configuration. For this reason, direct investigation of the artery at the site of the lesion, as accomplished by duplex scanning, is the preferred noninvasive method for evaluating peripheral arterial disease.[87]

One method that has proved to be of some value is the *peak-to-peak pulsatility index* (PI_{pp}), which can be defined as the peak-to-peak frequency difference of the Doppler waveform divided by the mean frequency. In normal lower extremities, the PI_{pp} increases as the recording site moves from proximal to distal portions of the limb, being greatest in the dorsalis pedis and posterior tibial arteries and least in the common femoral artery.[76,77] However, when there is an intervening arterial stenosis or occlusion, the PI_{pp} value obtained below the involved segment tends to decrease (Table 14-7).

To further quantify these changes in PI_{pp} and permit localization of arterial lesions, the use of a damping factor or inverse damping factor has been proposed.[76,89] The *damping factor* (DF) is defined as proximal PI_{pp} divided by distal PI_{pp}; the *inverse damping factor* (DF^{-1}) is defined as distal PI_{pp} divided by proximal PI_{pp}. The DF increases and the DF^{-1} decreases across segments with significant arterial disease.

The common femoral PI_{pp} has been advocated as a method for determining the presence or absence of iliac artery or inflow disease. As shown in Table 14-8, mean values obtained by several investigators agree reasonably well for the various categories of disease severity; however, the standard deviations are large, and data from adjacent categories frequently overlap. When arteriography is used as the "gold standard," the sensitivity of the common femoral PI_{pp} for identifying reductions of the iliac artery greater than 50% of the diameter (hemodynamically significant stenoses) varies from 41% to 100%, depending on the laboratory making the measurements and the value of the index chosen as the dividing point between positive and negative results (Table 14-9). Specificities are equally variable. Similar data are reported when the pressure drop across the aortoiliac segment, a physiologic gold standard, is substituted for the arteriographic image (Table 14-10).

In general, assessment of the hemodynamic status of the iliac artery seems to be more accurate in the absence of concomitant disease in the ipsilateral superficial femoral

Table 14-8 Common Femoral Pulsatility Indices (PI_{pp}) in Limbs with Aortoiliac Occlusive Disease (Mean ± SD)

AUTHOR (YEAR)	SEVERITY OF DIAMETER STENOSIS						
	Normal	Minimal		Less Than 50%	Greater Than or Equal to 50%		Occluded
Johnston et al (1978)[76]	9.6 ± 2.8	8.1 ± 2.8		4.9 ± 1.3	2.3 ± 1.2		1.6 ± 0.7
Baker et al (1984)[7]	8.3 ± 7.9	7.6 ± 5.0		3.9 ± 1.2	2.4 ± 0.8		1.8 ± 1.1
Harris et al (1974)[59]	7.1 ± 1.8		5.7 ± 3.2		2.8 ± 1.1		1.6 ± 0.9
Ward and Martin (1980)[161]	11.1 ± 5.4		4.1 ± 1.8		3.0 ± 1.0		1.9 ± 0.7
Baird et al (1980)[3]	11.8 ± 5.3		7.4 ± 1.6			3.6 ± 1.6	
Aukland and Hurlow (1982)[2]		6.1 ± 2.3			4.3 ± 2.0		1.3 ± 0.6
Hirai and Schoop (1984)[64]	8.0 ± 2.3		6.1 ± 3.0		3.7 ± 1.6		2.0 ± 0.4

Table 14-9 Accuracy of Femoral Pulsatility Indices (PI_{pp}) for Detecting ≥ 50% Diameter Stenoses of the Aortoiliac Arterial Segment

AUTHOR (YEAR)	SUPERFICIAL FEMORAL ARTERY	PI_{pp} CRITERION*	SENSITIVITY, %	SPECIFICITY, %
Flanigan et al (1982)[42]	—	2.5	70	81
Baird et al (1980)[3]	—	3.0	41	55
Baker et al (1984)[7]	—	3.0	76	81
Johnston et al (1984)[75]	—	3.0	95	97
Baird et al (1980)[3]	—	4.0	55	71
Baker et al (1984)[7]	—	4.0	94	66
Campbell et al (1984)[25]	—	4.0	92	75
Junger et al (1984)[78]	Occluded	5.0	90	95
Baker et al (1984)[7]	—	5.5	100	53
Junger et al (1984)[78]	Patent	7.6	78	89

*PI_{pp} below which ≥ 50% stenosis is predicted.

Table 14-10 Accuracy of Femoral Pulsatility Indices (PI_{pp}) for Detecting Hemodynamically Significant Pressure Drops across the Aortoiliac Segment

AUTHOR (YEAR)	CRITICAL PRESSURE DROP, mm Hg	DISTAL ARTERIES	PI_{pp} CRITERION*	SENSITIVITY, %	SPECIFICITY, %
Flanigan et al (1982)[42]	5	—	2.5	62	69
Johnston et al (1983)[74]	10	Patent	5.5	95	100
	10	Occluded	5.3	92	92
Thiele et al (1983)[151]	10	Patent	4.0	95	82
	10	Occluded	4.0	96	45
	20†	Patent	4.0	92	92
	20†	Occluded	4.0	92	51
Bone (1982)[19]	10%‡	—	4.5	94	100

*PI_{pp} below which pressure drop exceeding the critical value is predicted.
†Critical pressure drop during papaverine-induced hyperemia.
‡Critical drop in femoral-brachial index after reactive hyperemia.

artery.[41,122] Distal arterial obstruction tends to lower the femoral pulsatility index in limbs with no stenoses or with low-grade stenoses of the iliac arteries, thereby increasing the number of false-positive results and reducing specificity (see Table 14-10).[7,41,75,122,151,161] However, some investigators maintain that distal arterial obstruction has little effect on accuracy.[2,19,74,75,78]

In theory, simple objective measurements such as the PI_{pp} should be relatively consistent from one laboratory to the next. Since pulsatility indices are independent of heart rate and probe angle, there is no obvious explanation for the observed differences other than biologic variability. It is difficult, therefore, to reconcile the disparate opinions expressed in the literature concerning the value of the PI_{pp} for detecting iliac stenosis.[3,56,75,78,122] Nonetheless, the assumption that a normal femoral pulsatility index (e.g., >4.0) probably rules out significant iliac stenosis is consistent with many reports.[151] An abnormal index, on the other hand, must be interpreted cautiously, particularly in the presence of infrainguinal obstructive disease.[151]

The mean popliteal artery pulsatility index in normal limbs was found by Harris and associates[59] to be 9.3 ± 3.6, with a range of 4 to 20. In limbs with femoropopliteal disease, mean indices for stenoses less than 50% are reported to be 5.9 ± 3.2 and 7.7 ± 1.1; for hemodynamically significant stenoses, they are 4.7 ± 4.0 and 5.9 ± 1.2; and for occlusion, they are reduced to 1.6 ± 0.9 and 2.3 ± 0.2.[2,59] Obviously, there is a great deal of overlap between values for different grades of disease, but it is usually possible to distinguish between occlusion and no stenosis.

Calculation of damping factors may provide somewhat better discrimination. Johnston and coworkers[76] found that a DF^{-1} less than 0.9 indicated superficial femoral occlusion. Aukland and Hurlow reported DF values of 0.8 ± 0.1, 1.3 ± 0.2, and 2.1 ± 0.2 for minimal disease, hemodynamically significant stenosis, and occlusion of the superficial femoral artery, respectively.[2]

Pulsatility indices obtained from the dorsalis pedis or posterior tibial arteries at the ankle are probably of little practical value in the assessment of below-knee arterial disease. According to Aukland and Hurlow,[2] the mean index in limbs with patent popliteal-tibial segments (6.5 ± 1.4) did not differ significantly from that in limbs in which these arteries were occluded (4.1 ± 0.8). Although Harris and associates[59] found a significant difference between the pedal indices in normal limbs (8.3 ± 3.1), and in limbs with below-knee disease, there was no statistically significant difference between any of the angiographic grades (<50% stenosis, 3.1 ± 2.9; >50% stenosis, 1.9 ± 2.4; occlusion, 1.1 ± 0.6).

■ PLETHYSMOGRAPHY

Although direct noninvasive testing by duplex scanning has assumed a more prominent role in recent years, plethysmography remains a valuable noninvasive diagnostic technique. Several types of plethysmographic instruments are available, but they all measure the same physiologic parameter: a volume change. Although the division may be somewhat arbitrary, it is convenient to discuss segmental plethysmography and digital plethysmography separately.

Segmental Plethysmography

Although mercury or indium-gallium strain-gauges are quite sensitive and provide excellent recordings of limb volume changes, the air plethysmograph, owing to its rugged construction and the ease with which it is used, has become the standard instrument for segmental plethysmography. The impedance plethysmograph has been useful for diagnosing deep venous thrombosis, but it has not proved to be a reliable tool for studying peripheral arterial disease.

Much of the original work with the air plethysmograph was done by Raines and colleagues,[38,117] who called their specific instrument the *pulse volume recorder* (PVR), and this term has now become almost synonymous with segmental plethysmography. Their approach has been to apply pneumatic cuffs to the upper thigh, calf, and ankle. Larger cuffs are used around the thigh (bladder = 18 × 36 cm) and smaller cuffs around the other two sites (bladder = 12 × 23 cm). The cuffs are inflated to 65 mm Hg, a pressure that should require about 400 ± 75 cc of air for the thigh cuff and 75 ± 10 cc of air for each of the other two cuffs. Recordings are then made successively from each site. Measurements may be repeated after the patient has exercised on a treadmill.

Pulse Contour

The normal segmental volume pulse contour is characterized by a steep upstroke, a sharp systolic peak, a downslope that bows toward the baseline, and a prominent dicrotic wave approximately in the middle of the downslope (Fig. 14-10).[38]

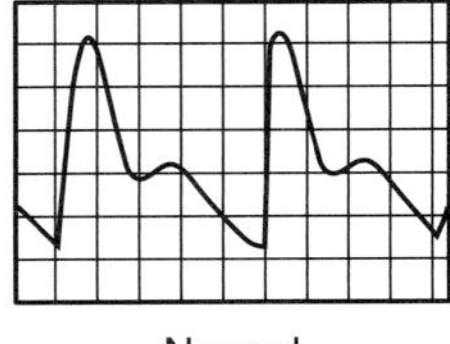

Normal

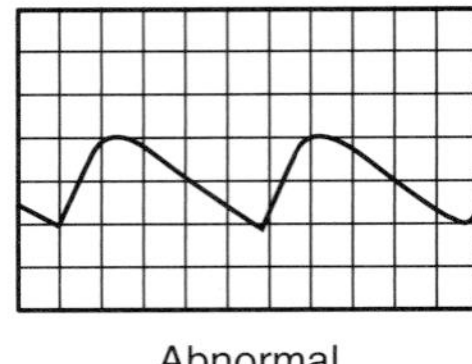

Abnormal

FIGURE 14-10 Normal and abnormal pulse volume contours recorded at ankle level. Normal form shows a prominent dicrotic wave on the downslope. Cuff pressure, 65 mm Hg; cuff volume, 75 cc.

Significant occlusive disease in arterial segments proximal to the recording cuff is virtually excluded by the presence of a dicrotic wave. The absence of a dicrotic wave, however, is of less diagnostic significance. For example, during the hyperemic period following exercise, the dicrotic wave, which represents the reverse-flow phase of the arterial pulse, may disappear.[85]

Distal to an arterial obstruction, the upslope is less steep, the peak becomes delayed and rounded, the downslope bows away from the baseline, and the dicrotic wave disappears (see Fig. 14-10).[38] As the proximal obstruction becomes more severe, the rise and fall times become more nearly equal and the amplitude decreases. A "mildly abnormal" form has been identified, the contour of which lies between normal and distinctly abnormal.[85] This pulse retains the rapid upslope and sharp systolic peak characteristic of the normal form but loses the dicrotic wave. The downslope tends to bow away from the baseline. Arterial occlusions distal to the recording cuff may produce a mildly abnormal waveform in limbs with no proximal disease. Deterioration toward a distinctly abnormal waveform following exercise indicates the presence of significant proximal obstruction.

Pulse Amplitude

According to Darling and associates,[38] the amplitude of the plethysmographic pulse remains highly reproducible in the individual patient provided that constant cuff pressures and volumes are used. Amplitudes, however, vary from patient to patient and are influenced by cardiac stroke volume, blood pressure, blood volume, vasomotor tone, and the size and position of the limb. With progressively severe proximal disease, the pulse amplitude decreases.

Pulses may be classified into five categories that combine amplitude and specific features of the waveform contour (Table 14-11).[118] Category 1 designates a normal pulse contour, and categories 2 through 5 represent waves associated with increasingly severe obstructive disease. Although the actual volume change that occurs during each pulse (maximal segmental volume change per heart beat [DV]) is greater in the thigh than it is in the calf, the chart deflection at calf level normally exceeds that at the thigh by 25% or more (see Table 14-11).[84,126] This so-called augmentation has proved to be an important diagnostic criterion, its absence signifying the presence of superficial femoral artery stenosis.

In normal limbs, pulse amplitude increases after treadmill exercise, reflecting the increased blood flow. Pulse

Table 14-11 Definition of Pulse Volume Recorder Categories

PULSE VOLUME RECORDER CATEGORY	CHART DEFLECTION, mm		DV, mm³		
	Thigh and Ankle	Calf	Ankle	Calf	Thigh
1	>15*	>200*	>160	>213	>715
2	>15†	>20†	>160	>213	>715
3	5–15	5–20	54–160	54–213	240–715
4	<5	<5	<54	<54	<240
5	Flat	Flat	0	0	0

*With reflected wave.
†No reflected wave.
DV, maximal segmental volume change per heart beat.

amplitude at the ankle uniformly diminishes after exercise in limbs with arterial disease, however, owing to the diversion of blood to the proximal musculature.[117]

Analysis of Pulses

Pulse volume recordings are generally reported to be reasonably accurate for detecting and localizing arterial obstructions in the lower extremity. Typical tracings from normal limbs and from those with various combinations of peripheral arterial disease are shown in Figure 14-11.[126] When disease is confined to the aortoiliac segment, pulse contours at all levels are abnormal, but the amplitude of the calf pulse exceeds that of the thigh pulse (a manifestation of the augmentation phenomenon). Although pulse contours

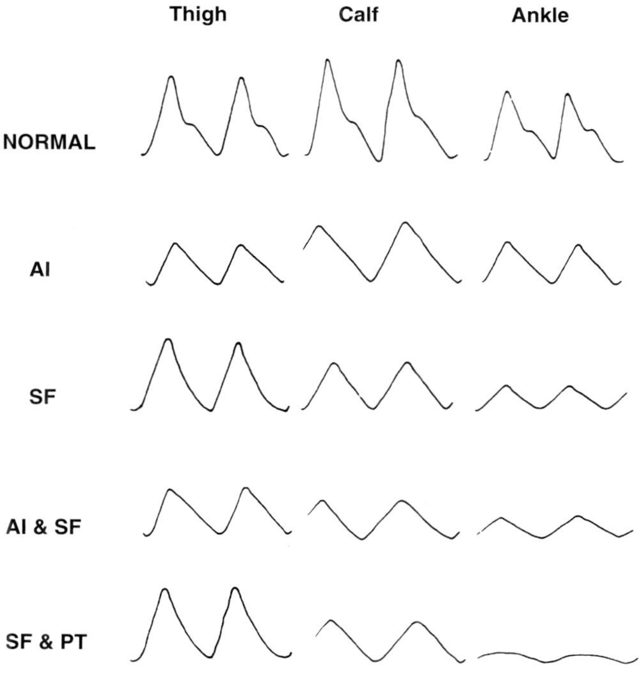

FIGURE 14-11 Pulse volume recorder tracings from normal limbs and from limbs with various combinations of peripheral vascular disease. AI, aortoiliac; SF, superficial femoral; PT, popliteal-tibial. (From Rutherford RB, Lowenstein DH, Klein MF: Combining segmental systolic pressures and plethysmography to diagnose arterial occlusive disease of the legs. Am J Surg 138:216, 1979.)

are also abnormal at all levels when there is combined aortoiliac and superficial femoral arterial disease, the amplitude of the calf pulse is less than that of the thigh pulse. In limbs with isolated superficial femoral arterial obstruction, the thigh pulse is normal but the calf and ankle pulses are abnormal.

The thigh pulse, according to Kempczinski,[84] tends to underestimate the severity of aortoiliac disease. He found, however, that if moderately abnormal waveforms were considered positive, the PVR correctly identified 95% of the significant stenoses in this segment. There were no false-negative results in his series of patients. All false-positive results were obtained in limbs with stenosis of the profunda femoris artery and occlusions of the superficial femoral segment. Limbs with mildly abnormal thigh pulses were subjected to treadmill exercise at 2 mph up a 10% incline. If the contour of the ankle pulse became more abnormal and if its amplitude decreased, significant aortoiliac obstruction was present; if there was no change in the pulse, the abnormal thigh pulse was attributed to superficial femoral artery disease.[84]

The PVR correctly assessed patency of the superficial femoral artery in 97% of the limbs studied by Kempczinski,[84] but pulse changes did not become evident unless the stenosis exceeded a 90% reduction of the diameter. Isolated mid-popliteal occlusions were associated with normal augmentation of the calf pulse. All false-positive results for superficial femoral disease were obtained in limbs with aortoiliac disease, and all false-negative results in limbs with well-developed collateral vessels bypassing short segmental occlusions of the superficial femoral artery.

Reidy and colleagues[123] reported that the PVR was 100% sensitive to the presence of aortoiliac stenoses of more than 50% diameter reduction when disease was isolated to that segment; however, the sensitivity fell to 83% in limbs with concomitant superficial femoral artery occlusions. Although negative predictive values were good for aortoiliac stenoses (87%), positive predictive values were low (64%). Therefore, these researchers considered a positive study result to be of little diagnostic value. Negative and positive predictive values were quite acceptable (85% and 91%, respectively), however, when the PVR was used to detect femoropopliteal disease.[84] On the basis of a similar study, Francfort and coworkers[45] concluded that the PVR was inaccurate for detecting aortoiliac disease but that it was highly sensitive to superficial femoral lesions, even in limbs with proximal disease.

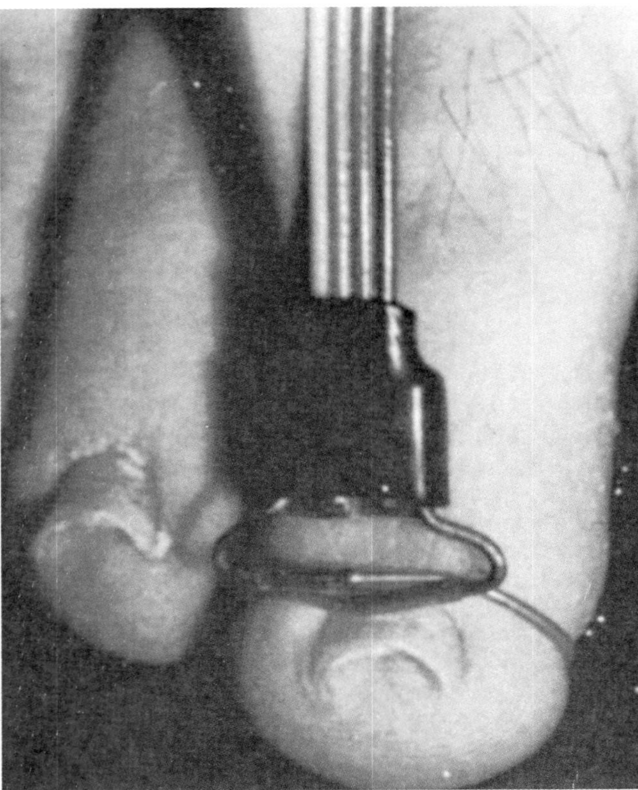

FIGURE 14-12 A mercury strain-gauge applied to the second toe.

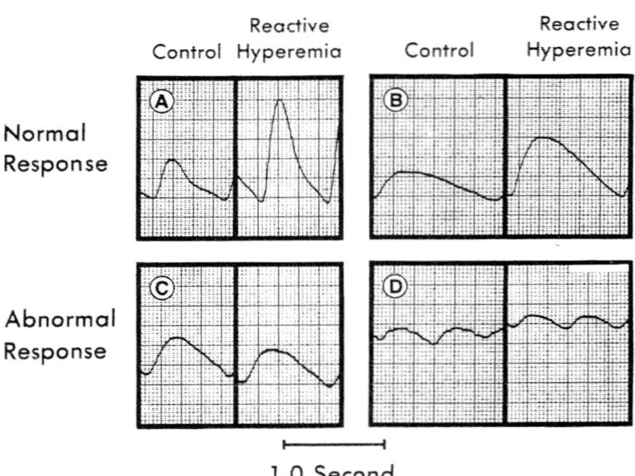

FIGURE 14-13 Reactive hyperemia test: digit pulse, second toe. Digit pulse volume more than doubles in the normal response *(upper panels)*. Little change in pulse volume is evident in abnormal response *(lower panels)*. **A,** Normal circulation (pressure: arm, 130 mm Hg; ankle, 140 mm Hg). **B,** Superficial femoral occlusion (pressure: arm, 100 mm Hg; ankle, 80 mm Hg). **C,** Diabetes for 20 years (pressure: arm, 135 mm Hg; ankle, 135 mm Hg). **D,** Iliac and superficial femoral arterial disease (pressure: arm, 118 mm Hg; ankle, 46 mm Hg). Attenuation of recorder: **A,** ×10; **B-D,** ×20.

Rutherford and associates[126] found that the PVR correctly identified 97% of normal limbs, about 70% of limbs with isolated or combined disease of the aortoiliac and superficial femoral segments, and 100% of limbs with disease confined to the below-knee arteries. When PVR results were considered in conjunction with segmental limb pressures, the accuracy of the combined tests was distinctly better than that of either test alone, ranging between 86% and 100% for all categories of disease. Other investigators have confirmed the complementary roles of the two tests.[45,84] Therefore, the simultaneous use of PVR and segmental limb pressure measurement is generally advocated. Indeed, this approach was originally recommended by Raines and colleagues.[118] PVR findings are especially important in subjects with calcified arteries, in whom the segmental systolic pressure measurements are often unreliable.[112]

Digital Plethysmography

Although digital plethysmography may be regarded as a form of segmental plethysmography, pulses obtained from the tips of the toes or fingers have special diagnostic significance. Because the recordings are taken from the most distal portions of the extremities, they reflect the physiologic status of all proximal arteries, from the aorta to the arterioles. They are sensitive, therefore, not only to mechanical obstruction but also to vasospasm.

Digit pulse volumes may be recorded with specially designed air plethysmographs that use cuffs with bladders measuring 7 × 2 or 9 × 3 cm; however, mercury strain-gauges or photoplethysmographs (PPGs) are usually employed because of their greater sensitivity (Fig. 14-12). Although the photoplethysmograph does not provide quantitative data, it is the most easily used of the three devices and consequently is preferred by many laboratories.

For optimal recordings to be obtained, studies should be conducted in a warm room (≈72° to 75°F) in which relative humidity is maintained at about 40%. To avoid vasospasm, the feet and toes must be warm; this may require immersing the foot in warm water or placing the patient under an electric blanket. At times, it may be necessary to induce postischemic reactive hyperemia, as discussed later.[139]

Pulse Contour

The contour of the digit volume pulse resembles that of the segmental pulses obtained more proximally in the limb (Fig. 14-13).[36,137,139,163,169] Normally, there is a rapid upslope with a sharp peak and a downslope that bows toward the baseline. A dicrotic wave or notch is usually present on the downslope. Distal to an obstruction, the pulse is considerably more rounded, having a slower upslope, a downslope that bows away from the baseline, and no dicrotic wave. In severe cases of arterial obstruction, no pulse may be perceptible.

Finding a normal toe pulse contour is good evidence that all segments from the heart to the digital arteries are free of functionally significant arterial disease. Similarly, finding an obstructive pulse contour indicates the presence of one or more functionally significant areas of obstruction somewhere between the heart and the digital arteries. Thus, digital pulses are especially important in the investigation of ischemia of the toes or forefoot.[144] Pedal or digital artery disease, which may contribute greatly to the ischemic process, may escape detection if the investigation is carried

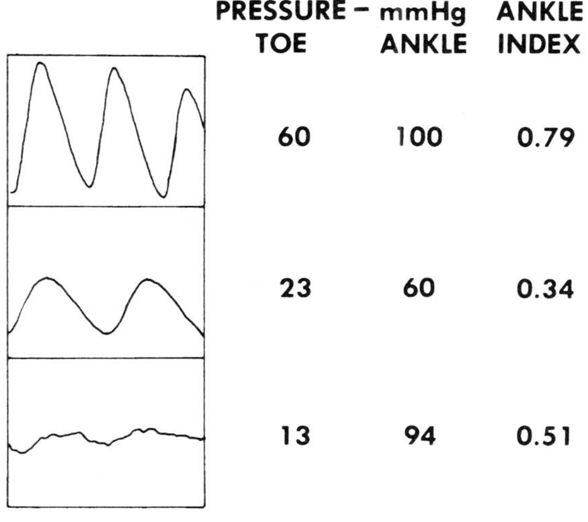

PRESSURE – mmHg
TOE
ANKLE
ANKLE
INDEX
60
100
0.79
23
60
0.34
13
94
0.51

FIGURE 14-14 The configuration of the toe plethysmogram is closely correlated with the toe pressure but is poorly correlated with the ankle pressure or ankle index. *Upper tracing* implies good digital artery perfusion; *middle tracing,* borderline perfusion; *lower tracing,* ischemia. (From Sumner DS: Rational use of noninvasive tests in designing a therapeutic approach to severe arterial disease of the legs. In Puel P, Boccalon H, Enjalbert A [eds]: Hemodynamics of the Limbs, 2nd ed. Toulouse, France, GEPESC, 1981, pp 369-376.)

no further than ankle level. Such errors are easily made in diabetic patients, because the ankle arteries are often incompressible and the disease is more likely to involve pedal vessels. As shown in Figure 14-14, perfusion of the toes may be inadequate even in the presence of a relatively normal ankle pressure.

Although more complex methods for describing digital pulse contours have been proposed (including measurements of slope, pulse width at half maximal excursion, and relative amplitudes at various parts of the curve), these measurements have little physiologic meaning and are unnecessary in clinical work.[14,15]

Reactive Hyperemia

The reactive hyperemia test is valuable as an indicator of the extent of peripheral vascular disease and as a predictor of the efficacy of surgical sympathectomy.[135,139] A pneumatic cuff (1) is placed around the ankle, calf, or thigh, (2) is inflated to above systolic pressure, (3) is kept at that level for 3 to 5 minutes, and (4) is rapidly deflated. The volume of the toe pulse is then monitored over the next several minutes. In normal limbs, the pulse returns almost immediately, attains half its precompression amplitude within a few seconds, and then rapidly reaches a peak volume (Table 14-12).[47,57,144] Maximal excursion is usually more than twice that recorded during the control period (see Fig. 14-13).

The reappearance time of the toe pulse is frequently delayed in legs with arterial occlusive disease, often exceeding 120 seconds in severely involved extremities.[47,57] Because it is difficult to define precisely the time at which the first pulse returns, the time required for the pulse to reach half the precompression volume seems to be a more practical measurement. This value is closely related to the severity of disease and the extent of arterial occlusion (see

Table 14-12 Pulse-Reappearance Time After Release of Arterial Occlusion (sec)

LOCATION OF OCCLUSIVE DISEASE	PULSE-REAPPEARANCE TIME	TIME REQUIRED TO REACH HALF CONTROL VOLUME
No occlusions	0.2 ± 0.1	3.4 ± 0.8
Aortoiliac	7.2 ± 4.0	23.9 ± 6.7
Femoropopliteal	3.7 ± 3.7	26.5 ± 12.7
Popliteal trifurcation	15.2 ± 9.3	23.9 ± 9.4
Multilevel	45.3 ± 5.5	71.2 ± 5.5

Modified from Fronek A, Coel M, Bernstein EF: The pulse-reappearance time: An index of over-all blood flow impairment in the ischemic extremity. Surgery 81:376, 1977.

Table 14-12). Bernstein and colleagues[16] found that the functional results of aortofemoral bypass procedures can be predicted quite well by determining the time required for the pulse to reach half the control volume. Of limbs in which this time was less than 10 seconds, 63% became asymptomatic and 37% were improved. Of limbs in which the time exceeded 90 seconds, however, only 10% became asymptomatic and 50% improved.

The relative increase in pulse volume during reactive hyperemia is an excellent indicator of the functional severity of an arterial obstruction. As discussed in Chapter 9, the peripheral vascular bed is nearly maximally dilated in limbs with severe ischemia, and little further vasodilatation is possible (see Fig. 14-13). Approximately 85% of limbs with obstruction confined to a single segment (e.g., aortoiliac, femoropopliteal, or popliteal trifurcation) display at least a 25% increase in the volume of the toe pulse during reactive hyperemia.[47] In contrast, only about half of the limbs with multilevel disease show a response of this magnitude. Because of preferential flow to the proximal limb, the toe pulse volume in such limbs may remain decreased for a long period after reactive hyperemia and may never exceed the value recorded during the control period.[144]

Experience has shown that surgical sympathectomy is most likely to provide a satisfactory result if the peak reactive hyperemia toe pulse is twice the size of the control pulse. If less dilatation is seen, it is much less likely that sympathectomy would increase peripheral blood flow. Because reactive hyperemia can occur in a fully sympathectomized extremity, the reactive hyperemia test reveals nothing about the integrity of sympathetic innervation; what the test does is to substantiate the ability of the peripheral vessels to dilate in response to a release of vascular tone.

The deep-breath test or one of its modifications is necessary to demonstrate continued function of the sympathetic nervous system.[40] In response to a deep breath, the pulse volume temporarily decreases provided that sympathetic innervation is intact. Absence of this response implies impairment of sympathetic activity and should be considered a contraindication to surgical sympathectomy.

■ TRANSCUTANEOUS OXYGEN TENSION

Unlike the methods previously discussed, which are sensitive to hemodynamic changes, transcutaneous oxygen tension ($tcPo_2$) measurements reflect the metabolic state of the target tissues. Although the technique is susceptible to a host of confounding variables, the potential importance of the information derived is so great that the method deserves close attention.

Measurements may be obtained from almost any area of interest, but common locations for assessment of lower extremity arterial perfusion are the following:

- Dorsum of the foot
- Anteromedial calf about 10 cm below the patella
- Thigh about 10 cm above the patella

The chest in the subclavicular region is often used as a reference site.

In normal limbs, most investigators have observed a modest decrease (5 to 6 mm Hg) in $tcPO_2$ from the more proximal parts of the leg to the foot.[24,34,96] With increasing age, $tcPO_2$ tends to decrease, paralleling a similar decline in arterial PO_2.[34,54,62,103,110] For this reason, Hauser and Shoemaker[62] have advocated dividing the $tcPO_2$ measured in the limb by that measured at the subclavicular region to obtain a regional perfusion index (RPI) that is independent of age, cardiac output, and arterial PO_2. Others maintain that this calculation does not significantly enhance the predictive value of the test.[24,34,103] Values for $tcPO_2$ also depend on the vertical distance between the measurement site and the heart, decreasing when the limb is elevated and increasing when the limb is dependent.[24,46,61,62,96] In addition, there may be some increase in $tcPO_2$ with elevations in venous pressure.[46]

Measured $tcPO_2$ values depend on the following:

- Cutaneous blood flow
- Metabolic activity
- Oxyhemoglobin dissociation
- Oxygen diffusion though the tissues

Changes are not ordinarily perceptible in limbs with mild degrees of arterial disease, because the oxygen supplied far exceeds that required to meet metabolic demands. Under conditions of stress, however, the metabolic demands may use a larger portion of the available oxygen, thereby reducing the measured $tcPO_2$. In cases of severe arterial obstruction, oxygen delivery is often marginal, and the quantity of free oxygen reaching the sensor is reduced, leading to an abnormally low $tcPO_2$ value. Thus, $tcPO_2$ is most sensitive to higher grades of arterial obstruction. Even at low levels of perfusion, $tcPO_2$ values are not linearly related to blood flow.[97] The $tcPO_2$ may fall to zero in areas where cutaneous blood flow is still detectable by other methods.[97] This value does not mean that no oxygen is reaching the tissue but rather implies that all available oxygen is being consumed and none remains for diffusion to the sensor.[23,34,46]

The most appropriate clinical role for $tcPO_2$ measurements is to assist in the assessment of severe ischemia.[154] Because the results are not affected by arterial calcification, this test is particularly valuable for evaluating diabetic vascular disease.[34,46,61,80]

Resting Values

Representative $tcPO_2$ values obtained from resting supine subjects are given in Table 14-13. The tendency for the values to decrease from the more proximal to the more distal parts of the lower limb is minimal in normal limbs but becomes more pronounced with increasing severity of disease. Irrespective of the site of measurement, normal $tcPO_2$ values are approximately 60 mm Hg. Measurements in normal younger subjects are usually about 10 mm Hg higher than those given in Table 14-13, which correspond to the values observed for patients in the age groups most susceptible to atherosclerosis.[34,62,103] In general, a $tcPO_2$ greater than 55 mm Hg may be considered normal at any measurement site regardless of age.[34] The average normal RPI is about 90%.[62]

Peripheral measurements reflect the deleterious effects of increasing obstructive disease more dramatically than more proximal measurements. For example, there is little difference among the thigh $tcPO_2$ values for any of the disease groups listed in Table 14-13. Although statistically significant differences are often demonstrated between the values of normal extremities and extremities with claudication, and between extremities with claudication and those with rest pain, there is enough overlap to prevent individual tests from discriminating accurately among the various disease categories.[34] Many patients with claudication have resting $tcPO_2$ values in the normal range, even at foot level.[24] However, values in limb-threatening ischemia are significantly reduced. At foot level, $tcPO_2$ values are usually less than 20 mm Hg in legs with severe rest pain, ischemic ulcers, or gangrene.[24,34,109] In the series reported by Wyss and coworkers,[165] 46% of nondiabetic limbs with $tcPO_2$ values less than 20 mm Hg required amputation.

Table 14-13 Representative Transcutaneous Oxygen Tension ($tcPO_2$) Values at Rest, Supine Position (mm Hg, Mean ± SD)

	NORMAL*			CLAUDICATION			REST PAIN		
AUTHOR (YEAR)	Foot	Calf	Thigh	Foot	Calf	Thigh	Foot	Calf	Thigh
Clyne et al (1982)[35]	59 ± 4	63 ± 5	64 ± 6	51 ± 10	64 ± 9	67 ± 9	36 ± 16	50 ± 16	55 ± 18
Hauser and Shoemaker (1983)[62]	59 ± 10	56 ± 10	64 ± 7	46 ± 12	49 ± 9	57 ± 9	—	—	—
Cina et al (1984)[34]†	64 ± 4	64 ± 4	—	46 ± 5	55 ± 4	—	17 ± 4	42 ± 6	—
Byrne et al (1984)[24]	60 ± 7	63 ± 8	66 ± 8	56 ± 4 37 ± 12	59 ± 5 48 ± 10	66 ± 7 54 ± 7‡	4 ± 4	29 ± 20	50 ± 14
Kram et al (1985)[89]	47 ± 12	53 ± 15	—	33 ± 14	37 ± 13	—	20 ± 16	29 ± 20	—

*Older subjects.
†Values estimated from published graphs.
‡More severe claudication.

Enhancement Procedures

Recordings of $tcPo_2$ may be made

- After exercise
- Following a period of ischemia
- During oxygen inhalation
- With the legs in a dependent position

These are among the various modifications of the basic measurement procedure that have been advocated to enhance the discriminatory ability of $tcPo_2$ values.

Dependent Position

Franzeck and colleagues[46] observed an average increase of 15 ± 7 mm Hg in the $tcPo_2$ on the dorsum of the foot in normal subjects when they moved from a supine to a sitting position. In the sitting position, the sensor was 54 cm below the heart. With standing, which extended the distance to 84 cm, the $tcPo_2$ rose by an average of 28 ± 14 mm Hg. The increase in $tcPo_2$ that accompanies standing occurs at all levels of the leg but is most evident at foot level, where the hydrostatic pressure is greatest.

In general, this augmentation in $tcPo_2$ is directly proportional to the severity of limb ischemia. Byrne and associates[24] noted an average increase of 20 mm Hg in limbs with rest pain compared with an average increase of 10 mm Hg in normal limbs. On the basis of their data, $tcPo_2$ rises by about 18% in normal limbs; by 22% in limbs with claudication and normal resting $tcPo_2$ values; by 58% in limbs with claudication and abnormal resting $tcPo_2$ values; and by 88% in limbs with rest pain. Oh and associates[109] retrospectively separated severely ischemic extremities into two groups according to the change in $tcPo_2$ that occurred with standing: Group I was defined by a $tcPo_2$ increase of less than 15 mm Hg (average 4 ± 5 mm Hg), and group II, by an increase of more than 15 mm Hg (average 36 ± 11 mm Hg). Despite the fact that both groups had similar supine $tcPo_2$ values (4 ± 5 mm Hg and 6 ± 5 mm Hg, respectively), the manifestations of disease were more severe in group I limbs (61% ulcers or gangrene, 48% rest pain, and 39% claudication) than in group II limbs (29% ulcers or gangrene, 46% rest pain, and 68% claudication).

The increase in oxygen tension that occurs when a patient with an ischemic limb sits or stands may explain how dependency relieves rest pain. As discussed in Chapter 9, elevation of the hydrostatic pressure dilates capillaries and other resistive vessels, thereby permitting more blood to flow at the same arteriovenous pressure gradient. In addition, any muscular activity with the leg dependent may decrease venous pressure and increase the arteriovenous pressure gradient. With the increase in capillary blood flow, more oxygen is delivered to the tissues. In the most severely ischemic extremities, these physiologic compensatory mechanisms are nearly exhausted, and the increase in blood flow is inadequate to provide relief.

Exercise

In limbs with restricted arterial inflow, the dilatation of intramuscular vessels induced by exercise diverts blood away from cutaneous vascular beds, causing $tcPo_2$ to fall. In normal limbs, this "steal" is not evident because arterial inflow is adequate to supply both vascular beds. Therefore, it is not surprising to find that postexercise/pre-exercise ratios of ankle pressures and ankle $tcPo_2$ values are highly correlated ($r = .918$), as demonstrated by the treadmill studies of Matsen and associates.[98]

Byrne and associates[24] observed that $tcPo_2$ values measured on the dorsum of the foot during treadmill exercise remained at about the same level as those obtained during quiet standing; however, during the period following exercise, after the subjects had resumed a supine position, the $tcPo_2$ values fell in all patients with significant arterial obstruction, even in those with normal resting values (Table 14-14). No fall in $tcPo_2$ values was evident in normal subjects. Similar but less marked changes occurred at calf level. These researchers concluded that postexercise $tcPo_2$ measurements accurately distinguished between subjects with intermittent claudication and those who were normal.

Hauser and Shoemaker[62] found that the chest $tcPo_2$ value increased during exercise in patients with claudication, perhaps explaining the failure of limb values to decrease. However, the RPI (limb $tcPo_2$/chest $tcPo_2$) at foot level did decrease during exercise, even in normal extremities. When RPI values obtained during exercise were compared with values obtained when the patient was standing, a decrease of more than 10% at the thigh or more than 15% at the calf was found to be highly specific for intermittent claudication. Normal limbs measured at these levels demonstrated no fall in RPI. After exercise, the RPI at the foot in normal limbs always returned to pre-exercise values within 1 minute. In limbs with claudication, the average time to recover one half of the exercise drop was about 4 minutes.

Table 14-14 Effect of Exercise on Foot Transcutaneous Oxygen Tension ($tcPo_2$) (mm Hg, Mean ± SD)

	$tcPo_2$ VALUES			
TYPE OF OBSTRUCTION	**Supine**	**Standing**	**Exercise**	**Postexercise***
Normal	60 ± 7	71 ± 7	75 ± 9	69 ± 7
Claudication†	56 ± 4	58 ± 8	53 ± 10	33 ± 16
Claudication	37 ± 12	58 ± 12	49 ± 18	23 ± 20
Rest pain	4 ± 4	25 ± 20	26 ± 26	5 ± 7

*Postexercise measurements made with patient supine.
†Claudicators with normal resting $tcPo_2$ values.

Data from Byrne P, Provan JL, Ameli FM, et al: The use of transcutaneous oxygen tension measurements in the diagnosis of peripheral vascular insufficiency. Ann Surg 200:159, 1984.

Table 14-15 Postischemic Transcutaneous Oxygen Tension ($tcPo_2$) Recovery Rate ($T_{1/2}$) (sec)

	NORMAL		CLAUDICATION		REST PAIN	
AUTHOR (YEAR)	**Foot**	**Calf**	**Foot**	**Calf**	**Foot**	**Calf**
Franzeck et al (1982)[46]	87 ± 27	60 ± 15	136 ± 73	131 ± 69	—	—
Cina et al (1984)[34]	49 ± 6	—	114 ± 2	—	—	—
Kram et al (1985)[89]*	66 ± 18	48 ± 18	156 ± 60	126 ± 42	204 ± 78	126 ± 66

*Based on limb-to-chest $tcPo_2$ ratio.

Table 14-16 Laser Doppler Measurements from the Big Toe (Mean ± SD)

	BASELINE VALUES, mV		REACTIVE HYPEREMIA TEST	
	Velocity	**Pulse Amplitude**	**Peak/Baseline Ratio***	**Time to Maximal Velocity, sec**
Normal	197 ± 174	77 ± 63	3.1 ± 0.9	18 ± 7
Ischemic	67 ± 42	5 ± 4	1.7 ± 1.6	150 ± 48

*Ratio of peak postischemic to preischemic velocity.

Data from Karanfilian RG, Lynch TG, Lee BC, et al: The assessment of skin blood flow in peripheral vascular disease by laser Doppler velocimetry. Am Surg 50:641, 1984.

Reactive Hyperemia

In the reactive hyperemia test for $tcPo_2$, inflation of a pneumatic cuff to more than systolic pressure is followed by a rapid decline in the $tcPo_2$ measured more distally on the leg. When the cuff is deflated after a period of ischemia (usually ≈ 4 minutes), the $tcPo_2$ rapidly returns to precompression levels in normal extremities. In limbs with occlusive arterial disease, the rate of recovery is much slower. Recovery rates are usually expressed as the time required for the $tcPo_2$ to return to one half of the precompression value ($T_{1/2}$).

Representative results are shown in Table 14-15. Cina and coworkers[34] reported a range of 43 to 60 seconds in normal limbs and 75 to 150 seconds in limbs with claudication; there were no overlapping values. Kram and associates[88] found that postischemic recovery times based on the RPI were more diagnostic of arterial disease than toe pulse recovery times. Values for $T_{1/2}$ in excess of 84 seconds at the calf and 102 seconds at the foot were considered to indicate disease.[88,89]

Oxygen Inhalation

Inhalation of pure oxygen markedly augments the $tcPo_2$ in normal limbs but has less effect in limbs with severe arterial occlusion. Ohgi and associates[110] reported that pretibial values increased from (1) 70 ± 9 to 365 ± 87 mm Hg in normal legs; (2) 34 ± 33 to 115 ± 109 mm Hg in legs with chronic occlusion; and (3) 23 ± 30 to 96 ± 57 mm Hg in legs with acute occlusion. According to Harward and colleagues,[60] the prediction of amputation healing based on $tcPo_2$ determinations may be enhanced by oxygen inhalation.

■ LASER DOPPLER VELOCIMETRY

A relative index of cutaneous blood flow can be obtained with the laser Doppler velocimeter. The output of this instrument, which is expressed in millivolts (mV), is roughly proportional to the average blood flow in a 1.5-mm^3 volume of skin lying 0.8 to 1.5 mm below the skin surface. According to Karanfilian and associates,[79] tracings from normal skin exhibit the following major characteristics:

1. Pulse waves that coincide with the cardiac cycle
2. Vasomotor waves that occur four to six times per minute
3. A mean blood flow velocity that is represented by the elevation of the tracing above a zero baseline

In the leg, the highest velocities are obtained from the skin of the big toe, followed, in descending order, by velocities from the skin of the plantar surface of the foot, dorsal foot, distal leg, thigh, and proximal leg.

In limbs with peripheral vascular disease, pulse waves are attenuated, mean velocities are decreased, and vasomotor waves may disappear (Table 14-16).[80] The reactive hyperemic response to a period of cuff-induced ischemia is diminished, and the time to reach maximal hyperemia is markedly delayed (see Table 14-16).[80] Karanfilian and associates[80] investigated the ability of laser Doppler studies to predict healing of ulcers or forefoot amputations in a series of ischemic limbs. In limbs in which the mean velocity recorded from the plantar aspect of the foot or big toe exceeded 40 mV and the pulse wave amplitude exceeded 4 mV, 96% of the lesions or amputations healed. In contrast, in limbs in which these criteria were not met, 79% of the lesions or amputations failed to heal. These results were not quite as good as those obtained in the same extremities through the use of $tcPo_2$.

The laser Doppler velocimeter can also be used in conjunction with a pneumatic cuff to estimate skin blood pressure at almost any level of the upper or lower extremities. These measurements are made with the probe (which merely serves as a flow sensor) placed under the pneumatic cuff. Castronuovo and associates[32] obtained cutaneous pressure in normal subjects averaging 47 ± 28 mm Hg in

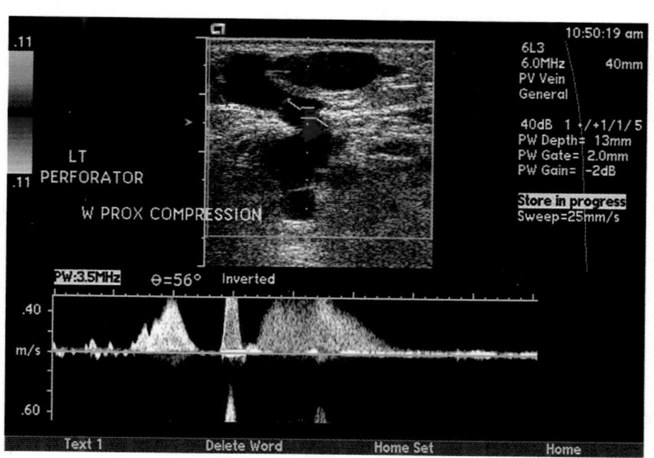

FIGURE 15-2 B-mode imaging of incompetent perforating vein (*upper*) and Doppler waveform identifying reverse flow in the perforator vein (*lower*).

forearms and thighs and 73 ± 28 mm Hg in the plantar skin of the big toe; these pressures are similar to those in precapillary vessels. Much lower values were found in the plantar skin of the toe (17 ± 15 mm Hg) and in the dorsal skin of the foot (10 ± 10 mm Hg) in limbs with rest pain, ulceration, or gangrene.

Although laser Doppler velocimetry is a valid physiologic test, it has not been widely used in vascular laboratories. Results cannot be calibrated in terms of actual blood flow, and much of the information that the test provides can be obtained with more established and commonly available techniques.

■ SUMMARY

Although many different methods for studying the arterial circulation have been discussed in this chapter, not all are indicated in the evaluation or follow-up of every patient.[14] Some tests are not as accurate as others, some are more difficult to perform, and many provide overlapping information or information that is not pertinent to the clinical questions being asked. The best policy is to select those modalities that (1) supply the most relevant information, (2) have been shown to be reliable by critical prospective evaluation, and (3) are known to be economical in terms of both time and cost.

■ REFERENCES

1. Allan JS, Terry HJ: The evaluation of an ultrasonic flow detector for the assessment of peripheral vascular disease. Cardiovasc Res 3:503, 1969.
2. Aukland A, Hurlow RA: Spectral analysis of Doppler ultrasound: Its clinical application in lower limb ischemia. Br J Surg 69:539, 1982.
3. Baird RN, Bird DR, Clifford PC, et al: Upstream stenosis: Its diagnosis by Doppler signals from the femoral artery. Arch Surg 115:1316, 1980.
4. Baker AR, Evans DH, Prytherch DR, et al: Haemodynamic assessment of the femoropopliteal segment: Comparison of pressure and Doppler methods using ROC curve analysis. Br J Surg 73:559, 1986.
5. Baker JD: Post-stress Doppler ankle pressures: A comparison of treadmill exercise with two other methods of induced hyperemia. Arch Surg 113:1171, 1978.
6. Baker JD, Dix D: Variability of Doppler ankle pressures with arterial occlusive disease: An evaluation of ankle index and brachial-ankle gradient. Surgery 89:134, 1981.
7. Baker JD, Machleder HI, Skidmore R: Analysis of femoral artery Doppler signals by Laplace transform damping method. J Vasc Surg 1:520, 1984.
8. Baker WH, String ST, Hayes AC, et al: Diagnosis of peripheral occlusive disease: Comparison of clinical evaluation and noninvasive laboratory. Arch Surg 113:1308, 1978.
9. Barnes RW: Noninvasive methods to evaluate acute vascular problems. In Haimovici H (ed): Vascular Emergencies. New York, Appleton-Century-Crofts, 1982, pp 7-26.
10. Barnes RW, Hafermann MD, Petersen J, et al: Noninvasive assessment of altered limb hemodynamics and complications of arterial catheterization. Radiology 107:505, 1973.
11. Barnes RW, Shanik GD, Slaymaker EF: An index of healing in below-knee amputation: Leg blood pressure by Doppler ultrasound. Surgery 79:13, 1976.
12. Barnes RW, Thornhill B, Nix L, et al: Prediction of amputation wound healing: Roles of Doppler ultrasound and digit photoplethysmography. Arch Surg 116:80, 1981.
13. Bell G: Systolic pressure measurements in occlusive vascular disease to assess run-off preoperatively. Scand J Clin Lab Invest 31(Suppl 128):173, 1973.
14. Bergan JJ, Yao JST: Invited overview: Role of the vascular laboratory. Surgery 88:9, 1980.
15. Berkowitz HD, Hobbs CL, Roberts B, et al: Value of routine vascular laboratory studies to identify vein graft stenosis. Surgery 90:971, 1981.
16. Bernstein EF, Rhodes GA, Stuart SH, et al: Toe pulse-reappearance time in prediction of aortofemoral bypass success. Ann Surg 193:201, 1981.
17. Bernstein EF, Witzel TH, Stotts JS, et al: Thigh pressure artifacts with noninvasive techniques in an experimental model. Surgery 89:319, 1981.
18. Bollinger A, Mahler F, Zehender O: Kombinierte Druck—und Durchflussmessungen in der Beurteilung arterieller Durchblutungsstörungen. Dtsch Med Wochenschr 95:1039, 1970.
19. Bone GE: The relationship between aorto-iliac hemodynamics and femoral pulsatility index. J Surg Res 32:228, 1982.
20. Bone GE, Pomajzl MJ: Toe blood pressure by photoplethysmography: An index of healing in forefoot amputation. Surgery 89:569, 1981.
21. Brener BJ, Raines JK, Darling RC, et al: Measurement of systolic femoral arterial pressure during reactive hyperemia. Circulation 49-50(Suppl II):259, 1974.
22. Britt DB, Kemmerer WT, Robison JR: Penile blood flow determination by mercury strain gauge plethysmography. Invest Urol 8:673, 1971.
23. Bruner JMR, Krenis LJ, Kunsman JM, et al: Comparison of direct and indirect methods of measuring arterial blood pressure. Med Instrum 15:11, 1981.
24. Byrne P, Provan JL, Ameli FM, et al: The use of transcutaneous oxygen tension measurements in the diagnosis of peripheral vascular insufficiency. Ann Surg 200:159, 1984.
25. Campbell WB, Cole SEA, Skidmore R, et al: The clinician and the vascular laboratory in the diagnosis of aorto-iliac stenosis. Br J Surg 71:302, 1984.
26. Carter SA: Indirect systolic pressure and pulse waves in arterial occlusive disease of the lower extremities. Circulation 37:624, 1968.
27. Carter SA: Clinical measurement of systolic pressures in limbs with arterial occlusive disease. JAMA 207:1869, 1969.
28. Carter SA: Response of ankle systolic pressure to leg exercise in mild or questionable arterial disease. N Engl J Med 287:578, 1972.
29. Carter SA: The relationship of distal systolic pressures to healing of skin lesions in limbs with arterial occlusive disease, with special reference to diabetes mellitus. Scand J Clin Lab Invest 31(Suppl 128):239, 1973.
30. Carter SA, Lezack JD: Digital systolic pressures in the lower limb in arterial disease. Circulation 43:905, 1971.
31. Castronuovo JJ, Flanigan DP: Pseudoclaudication of neurospinal origin. Vasc Diagn Ther 5:21, 1984.
32. Castronuovo JJ Jr, Pabst TS, Flanigan DP, et al: Noninvasive determination of skin perfusion pressure using a laser Doppler. J Cardiovasc Surg 28:253, 1987.
33. Chiu RC-J, Lidstone D, Blundell PE: Predictive power of penile/brachial index in diagnosing male sexual impotence. J Vasc Surg 4:251, 1986.
34. Cina C, Katsamouris A, Megerman J, et al: Utility of transcutaneous oxygen tension measurements in peripheral arterial occlusive disease. J Vasc Surg 1:362, 1984.
35. Clyne CAC, Ryan J, Webster JHH, et al: Oxygen tension on the skin of ischemic legs. Am J Surg 143:315, 1982.
36. Conrad MC, Green HD: Hemodynamics of large and small vessels in peripheral vascular disease. Circulation 29:847, 1964.
37. Cutajar CL, Marston A, Newcombe JF: Value of cuff occlusion pressures in assessment of peripheral vascular disease. BMJ 2:392, 1973.
38. Darling RC, Raines JK, Brener BJ, et al: Quantitative segmental pulse volume recorder: A clinical tool. Surgery 72:873, 1972.
39. Delius W, Erikson U: Correlation between angiographic and hemodynamic findings in occlusions of arteries of the extremities. Vasc Surg 3:201, 1969.
40. Delius W, Kellerova E: Reactions of arterial and venous vessels in the human forearm and hand to deep breath or mental strain. Clin Sci 40:271, 1971.

41. Evans DH, Barrie WW, Asher MJ, et al: The relationship between ultrasonic pulsatility index and proximal arterial stenosis in a canine model. Circ Res 46:470, 1980.
42. Flanigan DP, Collins JT, Schwartz JA, et al: Hemodynamic and arteriographic evaluation of femoral pulsatility index. J Surg Res 32:234, 1982.
43. Flanigan DP, Ryan TJ, Williams LR, et al: Aortofemoral or femoropopliteal revascularization? A prospective evaluation of the papaverine test. J Vasc Surg 1:215, 1984.
44. Flanigan DP, Williams LR, Schwartz JA, et al: Hemodynamic evaluation of the aortoiliac system based on pharmacologic vasodilatation. Surgery 93:709, 1983.
45. Francfort JW, Bigelow PS, Davis JT, et al: Noninvasive techniques in the assessment of lower extremity arterial occlusive disease: The advantages of proximal and distal thigh cuffs. Arch Surg 119:1145, 1984.
46. Franzeck UK, Talke P, Bernstein EF, et al: Transcutaneous Po_2 measurements in health and peripheral arterial occlusive disease. Surgery 91:156, 1982.
47. Fronek A, Coel M, Bernstein EF: The pulse-reappearance time: An index of over-all blood flow impairment in the ischemic extremity. Surgery 81:376, 1977.
48. Fronek A, Coel M, Bernstein EF: The importance of combined multisegmental pressure and Doppler flow velocity studies in the diagnosis of peripheral arterial occlusive disease. Surgery 84:840, 1978.
49. Fronek A, Johansen KH, Dilley RB, et al: Noninvasive physiologic tests in the diagnosis and characterization of peripheral arterial occlusive disease. Am J Surg 126:205, 1973.
50. Gaylis H: The assessment of impotence in aorto-iliac disease using penile blood pressure measurements. South Afr J Surg 16:39, 1978.
51. Gibbons GE, Strandness DE Jr, Bell JW: Improvements in design of the mercury strain-gauge plethysmograph. Surg Gynecol Obstet 116:679, 1963.
52. Gilfillan RS, Leeds FH, Spotts RR: The prediction of healing in ischemic lesions of the foot: A comparison of Doppler ultrasound and elevation reactive hyperemia. J Cardiovasc Surg 26:15, 1985.
53. Goodreau JJ, Creasy JK, Flanigan DP, et al: Rational approach to the differentiation of vascular and neurogenic claudication. Surgery 84:749, 1978.
54. Gothgen I, Jacobsen E: Transcutaneous oxygen tension measurement: I. Age variation and reproducibility. Acta Anaesthesiol Scand Suppl 67:66, 1978.
55. Gray B, Kmiecik JC, Spigos DD, et al: Evaluation of Doppler-derived upper thigh pressure in the assessment of aorto-iliac occlusive disease. Bruit 4:29, 1980.
56. Gundersen J: Segmental measurement of systolic blood pressure in the extremities including the thumb and great toe. Acta Chir Scand Suppl 426:1, 1972.
57. Gutierrez IZ, Gage AA, Makuta PA: Toe pulse study in ischemic arterial disease of the legs. Surg Gynecol Obstet 153:889, 1981.
58. Hajjar W, Sumner DS: Segmental pressures in normal subjects 16 to 32 years of age. Unpublished observations, 1976.
59. Harris PL, Taylor LA, Cave FD, et al: The relationship between Doppler ultrasound assessment and angiography in occlusive arterial disease of the lower limbs. Surg Gynecol Obstet 138:911, 1974.
60. Harward TRS, Volny J, Golbranson F, et al: Oxygen inhalation-induced transcutaneous Po_2 changes as a predictor of amputation level. J Vasc Surg 2:220, 1985.
61. Hauser CJ, Klein SR, Mehringer CM, et al: Superiority of transcutaneous oximetry in noninvasive vascular diagnosis in patients with diabetes. Arch Surg 119:690, 1984.
62. Hauser CJ, Shoemaker WC: Use of a transcutaneous Po_2 regional perfusion index to quantify tissue perfusion in peripheral vascular disease. Ann Surg 197:337, 1983.
63. Heintz SE, Bone GE, Slaymaker EE, et al: Value of arterial pressure measurements in the proximal and distal part of the thigh in arterial occlusive disease. Surg Gynecol Obstet 146:337, 1978.
64. Hirai M, Schoop W: Hemodynamic assessment of the iliac disease by proximal thigh pressure and Doppler femoral flow velocity. J Cardiovasc Surg 25:365, 1984.
65. Hobbs JT, Yao ST, Lewis JD, et al: A limitation of the Doppler ultrasound method of measuring ankle systolic pressure. Vasa 3:160, 1974.
66. Holstein P, Dovey H, Lassen NA: Wound healing in above-knee amputations in relation to skin perfusion pressure. Acta Orthop Scand 50:59, 1979.
67. Holstein P, Sager P: Toe blood pressure in peripheral arterial disease. Acta Orthop Scand 44:564, 1973.
68. Holstein P, Noer I, Tønnesen KH, et al: Distal blood pressure in severe arterial insufficiency. Strain-gauge, radioisotopes, and other methods. In Bergan JJ, Yao JST (eds): Gangrene and Severe Ischemia of the Lower Extremities. New York, Grune & Stratton, 1978, pp 95-114.
69. Hummel BW, Hummel BA, Mowbry A, et al: Reactive hyperemia versus treadmill exercise testing in arterial disease. Arch Surg 113:95, 1978.
70. Humphries KN, Hames TK, Smith SWJ, et al: Quantitative assessment of the common femoral to popliteal arterial segment using continuous wave Doppler ultrasound. Ultrasound Med Biol 6:99, 1980.
71. Johansen K, Lynch K, Paun M, et al: Noninvasive vascular tests reliably exclude occult arterial trauma in injured extremities. J Trauma 31:515, 1991.
72. Johnson WC: Doppler ankle pressure and reactive hyperemia in the diagnosis of arterial insufficiency. J Surg Res 18:177, 1975.
73. Johnston KW, Hosang MY, Andrews DF: Reproducibility of noninvasive vascular laboratory measurements of the peripheral circulation. J Vasc Surg 6:147, 1987.
74. Johnston KW, Kassam M, Cobbold RSC: Relationship between Doppler pulsatility index and direct femoral pressure measurements in the diagnosis of aortoiliac occlusive disease. Ultrasound Med Biol 9:271, 1983.
75. Johnston KW, Kassam M, Koers J, et al: Comparative study of four methods for quantifying Doppler ultrasound waveforms from the femoral artery. Ultrasound Med Biol 10:1, 1984.
76. Johnston KW, Maruzzo BC, Cobbold RSC: Doppler methods for quantitative measurement and localization of peripheral arterial occlusive disease by analysis of the blood velocity waveform. Ultrasound Med Biol 4:209, 1978.
77. Johnston KW, Maruzzo BC, Kassam M, et al: Methods for obtaining, processing and quantifying Doppler blood velocity waveforms. In Nicolaides AN, Yao JST (eds): Investigation of Vascular Disorders. London, Churchill Livingstone, 1981, pp 532-558.
78. Junger M, Chapman BLW, Underwood CJ, Charlesworth D: A comparison between two types of waveform analysis in patients with multisegmental arterial disease. Br J Surg 71:345, 1984.
79. Karanfilian RG, Lynch TG, Lee BC, et al: The assessment of skin blood flow in peripheral vascular disease by laser Doppler velocimetry. Am Surg 50:641, 1984.
80. Karanfilian RG, Lynch TG, Zirul VT, et al: The value of laser Doppler velocimetry and transcutaneous oxygen tension determination in predicting healing of ischemic forefoot ulcerations and amputations in diabetic and nondiabetic patients. J Vasc Surg 4:511, 1986.
81. Karpman HL, Winsor T: The plethysmographic peripheral vascular study. J Int Coll Surg 30:425, 1958.
82. Kavanaugh GJ, Svien HJ, Holman CB, et al: "Pseudoclaudication" syndrome produced by compression of the cauda equina. JAMA 206:2477, 1968.
83. Kempczinski RF: Role of the vascular diagnostic laboratory in the evaluation of male impotence. Am J Surg 138:278, 1979.
84. Kempczinski RF: Segmental volume plethysmography in the diagnosis of lower extremity arterial occlusive disease. J Cardiovasc Surg 23:125, 1982.
85. Kempczinski RF: Segmental volume plethysmography: The pulse volume recorder. In Kempczinski RF, Yao JST (eds): Practical Noninvasive Vascular Diagnosis, 2nd ed. Chicago, Year Book, 1987, pp 140-153.
86. King LT, Strandness DE Jr, Bell JW: The hemodynamic response of the lower extremity to exercise. J Surg Res 5:167, 1965.

87. Kohler TR, Nance DR, Cramer MM, et al: Duplex scanning for diagnosis of aortoiliac and femoropopliteal disease: A prospective study. Circulation 76:1074, 1987.
88. Kram HB, Appel PL, White RA, et al: Assessment of peripheral vascular disease by postocclusive transcutaneous oxygen recovery time. J Vasc Surg 1:628, 1984.
89. Kram HB, White RA, Tabrisky J, et al: Transcutaneous oxygen recovery and toe pulse-reappearance time in the assessment of peripheral vascular disease. Circulation 72:1022, 1985.
90. Lane RJ, Appleberg M, Williams WA: A comparison of two techniques for the detection of the vasculogenic component of impotence. Surg Gynecol Obstet 155:230, 1982.
91. Lassen NA, Tuedegaard E, Jeppesen FI, et al: Distal blood pressure measurement in occlusive arterial disease strain gauge compared to xenon-133. Angiology 23:211, 1972.
92. Lorentsen E: Calf blood pressure measurements: The applicability of a plethysmographic method and the result of measurements during reactive hyperemia. Scand J Clin Lab Invest 31:69, 1973.
93. Lorentsen E: The vascular resistance in the arteries of the lower leg in normal subjects and in patients with different degrees of atherosclerotic disease. Scand J Clin Lab Invest 31:147, 1973.
94. Lynch K, Johansen K: Can Doppler pressure measurement replace "exclusion" arteriography in the diagnosis of occult extremity arterial trauma? Ann Surg 241:737, 1991.
95. Marinelli MR, Beach NW, Glass MJ, et al: Noninvasive testing versus clinical evaluation of arterial disease: A prospective study. JAMA 241:2031, 1979.
96. Matsen FA III, Wyss CR, Pedegana LR, et al: Transcutaneous oxygen tension measurement in peripheral vascular disease. Surg Gynecol Obstet 150:525, 1980.
97. Matsen FA III, Wyss CR, Robertson CC, et al: The relationship of transcutaneous Po_2 and laser Doppler measurements in a human model of local arterial insufficiency. Surg Gynecol Obstet 159:418, 1984.
98. Matsen FA III, Wyss CR, Simmons CW, et al: The effect of exercise upon cutaneous oxygen delivery in the extremities of patients with claudication and in a human laboratory model of claudication. Surg Gynecol Obstet 158:522, 1984.
99. Moore WS, Hall AD: Unrecognized aortoiliac stenosis. Arch Surg 103:633, 1971.
100. Moore WS, Henry RE, Malone JM, et al: Prospective use of xenon-133 clearance for amputation level selection. Arch Surg 116:86, 1981.
101. Mozersky DJ, Sumner DS, Strandness DE Jr: Long-term result of reconstructive aortoiliac surgery. Am J Surg 123:503, 1972.
102. Mozersky DJ, Sumner DS, Strandness DE Jr: Disease progression after femoropopliteal surgical procedures. Surg Gynecol Obstet 135:700, 1972.
103. Mustapha NM, Redhead RG, Jain SK, et al: Transcutaneous partial oxygen pressure assessment of the ischemic lower limb. Surg Gynecol Obstet 156:582, 1983.
104. Nath RL, Menzoian JO, Kaplan KH, et al: The multidisciplinary approach to vasculogenic impotence. Surgery 89:124, 1981.
105. Nicholls SC, Kohler TR, Martin RL, et al: Use of hemodynamic parameters in the diagnosis of mesenteric insufficiency. J Vasc Surg 3:507, 1985.
106. Nicolaides AN: Value of noninvasive tests in the investigation of lower limb ischemia. Ann R Coll Surg Engl 60:249, 1978.
106a. Nicolaides AN, Gordon-Smith IC, Dayandas J, et al: The value of Doppler blood velocity tracings in the detection of aortoiliac disease in patients with intermittent claudication. Surgery 80:774, 1976.
107. Nielsen PE, Bell G, Lassen NA: The measurement of digital systolic blood pressure by strain gauge technique. Scand J Clin Lab Invest 29:371, 1972.
108. Nielsen PE, Bell G, Lassen NA: Strain gauge studies of distal blood pressure in normal subjects and in patients with peripheral arterial diseases: Analysis of normal variation and reproducibility and comparison to intraarterial measurements. Scand J Clin Lab Invest 31(Suppl 128):103, 1973.
109. Oh PIT, Provan JL, Amelie FM: The predictability of the success of arterial reconstruction by means of transcutaneous oxygen tension measurements. J Vasc Surg 5:356, 1987.
110. Ohgi S, Ito K, Mori T: Quantitative evaluation of the skin circulation in ischemic legs by transcutaneous measurement of oxygen tension. Angiology 32:833, 1981.
111. O'Mara CS, Flinn WR, Johnson ND, et al: Recognition and surgical management of patent but hemodynamically failed arterial grafts. Ann Surg 193:467, 1981.
112. Osmundson PJ, Chesebro JH, O'Fallon WM, et al: A prospective study of peripheral occlusive arterial disease in diabetes: II. Vascular laboratory assessment. Mayo Clin Proc 56:223, 1981.
113. Ouriel K, McDonnell AE, Metz CE, et al: A critical evaluation of stress testing in the diagnosis of peripheral vascular disease. Surgery 91:686, 1982.
114. Pascarelli EF, Bertrand CA: Comparison of blood pressures in the arms and legs. N Engl J Med 270:693, 1964.
115. Persson AV, Gibbons G, Griffey S: Noninvasive evaluation of the aorto-iliac segment. J Cardiovasc Surg 22:539, 1981.
116. Queral LA, Whitehouse WM Jr, Flinn WR, et al: Pelvic hemodynamics after aorto-iliac reconstruction. Surgery 86:799, 1979.
117. Raines JK: Diagnosis and analysis of arteriosclerosis in the lower limbs from the arterial pressure pulse. Doctoral Thesis, Boston, Massachusetts Institute of Technology, 1972.
118. Raines JK, Darling RG, Buth J, et al: Vascular laboratory criteria for the management of peripheral vascular disease of the lower extremities. Surgery 79:21, 1976.
119. Ramirez C, Box M, Gottesman L: Noninvasive vascular evaluation in male impotence: Technique. Bruit 4:14, 1980.
120. Ramsey DE, Johnson F, Sumner DS: Anatomic validity of segmental pressure measurement. Unpublished observations, 1979.
121. Ramsey DE, Manke DA, Sumner DS: Toe blood pressure: A valuable adjunct to ankle pressure measurement for assessing peripheral arterial disease. J Cardiovasc Surg 24:43, 1983.
122. Reddy DJ, Vincent GS, McPharlin M, et al: Limitations of the femoral pulsatility index with aortoiliac stenosis: An experimental study. J Vasc Surg 4:327, 1986.
123. Reidy NC, Walden R, Abbott WA, et al: Anatomic localization of atherosclerotic lesions by hemodynamic tests. Arch Surg 116:1041, 1981.
124. Rittenhouse EA, Maixner W, Burr JW, et al: Directional arterial flow velocity: A sensitive index of changes in peripheral vascular resistance. Surgery 79:350, 1976.
125. Rutherford RB, Jones DN, Martin MS, et al: Serial hemodynamic assessment of aortofemoral bypass. J Vasc Surg 4:428, 1986.
126. Rutherford RB, Lowenstein DH, Klein MF: Combining segmental systolic pressures and plethysmography to diagnose arterial occlusive disease of the legs. Am J Surg 138:211, 1979.
127. Sanchez SA, Best EB: Correlation of plethysmographic and arteriographic findings in patients with obstructive arterial disease. Angiology 20:684, 1969.
128. Schwartz JA, Schuler JJ, O'Connor RJA, et al: Predictive value of distal perfusion pressure in the healing of amputations of the digit and the forefoot. Surg Gynecol Obstet 154:865, 1982.
129. Siggard-Anderson J, Ulrich J, Engell HC, et al: Blood pressure measurements of the lower limb: Arterial occlusions in the calf determined by plethysmographic blood pressure measurements in the thigh and at the ankle. Angiology 23:350, 1972.
130. Skidmore R, Woodcock JP, Wells PNT, et al: Physiological interpretation of Doppler-shift waveforms: III. Clinical results. Ultrasound Med Biol 6:227, 1980.
131. Skinner JS, Strandness DE Jr: Exercise and intermittent claudication: I. Effect of repetition and intensity of exercise. Circulation 36:15, 1967.
132. Skinner JS, Strandness DE Jr: Exercise and intermittent claudication: II. Effect of physical training. Circulation 36:23, 1967.
133. Sobinsky KR, Williams LR, Gray G, et al: Supine exercise testing in the selection of suprainguinal versus infrainguinal bypass in patients with multisegmental arterial occlusive disease. Am J Surg 152:185, 1986.

134. Stahler C, Strandness DE Jr: Ankle blood pressure response to graded treadmill exercise. Angiology 18:237, 1967.
135. Strandness DE Jr: Long-term value of lumbar sympathectomy. Geriatrics 21:144, 1966.
136. Strandness DE Jr: Abnormal exercise responses after successful reconstructive arterial surgery. Surgery 59:325, 1966.
137. Strandness DE Jr: Peripheral Arterial Disease: A Physiologic Approach. Boston, Little, Brown, 1969.
138. Strandness DE Jr, Bell JW: An evaluation of the hemodynamic response of the claudicating extremity to exercise. Surg Gynecol Obstet 119:1237, 1964.
139. Strandness DE Jr, Bell JW: Peripheral vascular disease: Diagnosis and objective evaluation using a mercury strain gauge. Ann Surg 161(Suppl 4):1, 1965.
140. Strandness DE Jr, Bell JW: Ankle pressure responses after reconstructive arterial surgery. Surgery 59:514, 1966.
141. Strandness DE Jr, Schultz RD, Sumner DS, et al: Ultrasonic flow detection: A useful technic in the evaluation of peripheral vascular disease. Am J Surg 113:311, 1967.
142. Strandness DE Jr, Sumner DS: Hemodynamics for Surgeons. New York, Grune & Stratton, 1975.
143. Strandness DE Jr, Zierler RE: Exercise ankle pressure measurements in arterial disease. In Bernstein EF (ed): Noninvasive Diagnostic Techniques in Vascular Disease, 4th ed. St. Louis, Mosby-Year Book, 1993, p 547.
144. Sumner DS: Rational use of noninvasive tests in designing a therapeutic approach to severe arterial disease of the legs. In Puel P, Boccalon H, Enjalbert A (eds): Hemodynamics of the Limbs, 2nd ed. Toulouse, France, GEPESC, 1981, pp 369-376.
145. Sumner DS, Strandness DE Jr: The relationship between calf blood flow and ankle blood pressure in patients with intermittent claudication. Surgery 65:763, 1969.
146. Sumner DS, Strandness DE Jr: The effect of exercise on resistance to blood flow in limbs with an occluded superficial femoral artery. J Vasc Surg 4:229, 1970.
147. Sumner DS, Strandness DE Jr: Aortoiliac reconstruction in patients with combined iliac and superficial femoral arterial occlusion. Surgery 84:348, 1978.
148. Sumner DS, Strandness DE Jr: Hemodynamic studies before and after extended bypass grafts to the tibial and peroneal arteries. Surgery 86:442, 1979.
149. Taguchi JT, Suwangool P: Pipe-stem brachial arteries: A cause of pseudohypertension. JAMA 228:733, 1974.
150. Tait WF, Charlesworth D, Lemon JG: Atypical claudication. Br J Surg 72:315, 1985.
151. Thiele BL, Bandyk DF, Zierler RE, et al: A systematic approach to the assessment of aortoiliac disease. Arch Surg 118:477, 1983.
152. Thulesius O: Systemic and ankle blood pressure before and after exercise in patients with arterial insufficiency. Angiology 29:374, 1978.
153. Thulesius O, Gjöres JE: Use of Doppler shift detection for determining peripheral arterial blood pressure. Angiology 22:594, 1971.
154. Tønneson KH: Transcutaneous oxygen tension in imminent foot gangrene. Acta Anaesthesiol Scand 68:107, 1978.
155. Tønneson KH, Noer I, Paaske W, et al: Classification of peripheral occlusive arterial diseases based on symptoms, signs, and distal blood pressure measurements. Acta Chir Scand 146:101, 1980.
156. Turnipseed WD, Acker CW: Postoperative surveillance: An effective means of detecting correctable lesions that threaten graft patency. Arch Surg 120:324, 1985.
157. Udoff EJ, Barth KH, Harrington DP, et al: Hemodynamic significance of iliac artery stenosis: Pressure measurements during angiography. Radiology 132:289, 1979.
158. Van De Water JM, Indech CDV, Indech RB, et al: Hyperemic response for diagnosis of arterial insufficiency. Arch Surg 115:851, 1980.
159. Verta MJ Jr, Gross WS, vanBellen B, et al: Forefoot perfusion pressure and minor amputation for gangrene. Surgery 80:729, 1976.
160. Vollrath KD, Salles-Cunha SX, Vincent D, et al: Noninvasive measurement of toe systolic pressures. Bruit 4:27, 1980.
161. Ward AS, Martin TP: Some aspects of ultrasound in the diagnosis and assessment of aortoiliac disease. Am J Surg 140:260, 1980.
162. Winsor T: Influence of arterial disease on the systolic blood pressure gradients of the extremity. Am J Med Sci 220:117, 1950.
163. Winsor T, Sibley AE, Fisher EK, et al: Peripheral pulse contours in arterial occlusive disease. Vasc Dis 5:61, 1968.
164. Wolf EA Jr, Sumner DS, Strandness DE Jr: Correlation between nutritive blood flow and pressure in limbs of patients with intermittent claudication. Surg Forum 23:238, 1972.
165. Wyss CR, Matsen FA III, Simmons CW, et al: Transcutaneous oxygen tension measurements on limbs of diabetic and nondiabetic patients with peripheral vascular disease. Surgery 95:339, 1984.
166. Yao JST: Hemodynamic studies in peripheral arterial disease. Br J Surg 57:761, 1970.
167. Yao JST: New techniques in objective arterial evaluation. Arch Surg 106:600, 1973.
168. Yao JST, Hobbs JT, Irvine WT: Ankle systolic pressure measurements in arterial diseases affecting the lower extremities. Br J Surg 56:676, 1969.
169. Zetterquist S, Bergvall V, Linde B, et al: The validity of some conventional methods for the diagnosis of obliterative arterial disease in the lower limb as evaluated by arteriography. Scand J Clin Lab Invest 28:409, 1971.

Chapter

15

Physiologic Assessment of the Venous System

ROBERT R. MENDES, MD
WILLIAM A. MARSTON, MD

The development of therapies for patients with chronic venous insufficiency (CVI) has been historically hampered by inadequate tools for noninvasive anatomic and hemodynamic evaluation of the venous system. Just as in arterial treatment, it is critical to develop information concerning both the anatomic sites of disease and the hemodynamic significance of these lesions. This chapter focuses on techniques of evaluating the hemodynamic significance of venous insufficiency, including the techniques themselves and the indications for their use.

As duplex ultrasound has gained acceptance in the diagnosis of venous disease, it has become routine to perform extensive scanning of the lower extremity veins identifying the sites of disease. Using various techniques outlined in Chapter 17, the physician can gain extensive knowledge concerning the anatomic sites of disease noninvasively. Rarely is venography required for the diagnosis and treatment of venous disease. Many physicians perform only duplex evaluations and base their decisions on anatomic information alone. However, in the evaluation of peripheral arterial disease, the same physicians would rarely make recommendations without hemodynamic information concerning the significance of those anatomic lesions. A patient with claudication who has an ankle-brachial index (ABI) of 0.8 often is treated different from a patient with an ABI of 0.5, and a patient who complains of typical claudication symptoms but has a normal ABI even with exercise would lead the physician to consider other potential causes of the symptoms. Likewise, prediction of a patient's potential for further limb complications can be made based on the ABI. Also, most surgeons performing endovascular or surgical revascularizations think it is important to gain a hemodynamic measure of the adequacy of revascularization. After an iliac angioplasty, for example, abolition of a pressure gradient is usually documented, as well as a postprocedure ABI. After surgical bypass, a postprocedure ABI is obtained, and significant improvement is expected. If not, the graft is typically evaluated for the reason it did not result in hemodynamic improvement.

In venous disease, several noninvasive techniques are available to evaluate the global hemodynamic function of the venous system. However, none has gained widespread use in the evaluation and management of venous disease. But the same considerations are important in the diagnosis and management of venous disease that exist in arterial disease. Therefore, we believe hemodynamic evaluation in the diagnostic process and the documentation of the hemodynamic results of surgery should be routinely performed. For clinical research on the treatment of venous disease, hemodynamic evaluation should be a mandatory expectation in reporting standards.

■ ANATOMIC EVALUATION OF VENOUS FUNCTION

Duplex Ultrasound

Imaging techniques using ultrasound combined with Doppler interrogation of the venous system have been validated as sensitive methods of diagnosis of deep venous thrombosis (DVT).[1] The standard method of duplex examination for DVT is performed in the supine position with 30 degrees of reverse Trendelenburg (Fig. 15-1) and relies on vein compressibility and Doppler velocity changes in response to augmentation maneuvers for diagnosis.[2] In patients with CVI this technique is useful in detecting the presence or absence of venous obstruction or other changes typical of previous DVT. This information helps determine whether the patient's CVI is due to obstruction, reflux, or both (pathophysiology). However, the assessment of reflux is limited to qualitative information. Valsalva maneuvers or manual compression may be performed with the patient supine to look for reflux in the common femoral vein or saphenous vein, but these are not reproducible quantitative tests of venous reflux.

To fully define the anatomy of venous reflux in patients with CVI using noninvasive techniques, a two-part venous duplex evaluation is required. First, a standard supine examination is performed as outlined above. The presence or absence of previous DVT is noted, and an assessment of outflow obstruction is performed using augmentation distal to the transducer site. In addition to an examination of the deep and superficial systems, the perforator veins are carefully examined for evidence of incompetence (Fig. 15-2). Commencing at the saphenofemoral junction, the deep, superficial, and perforating veins are assessed with Doppler flow patterns and B-mode imaging as described in Chapter 17.[3]

Second, venous reflux in the deep and superficial venous systems is evaluated with the patient in the standing position

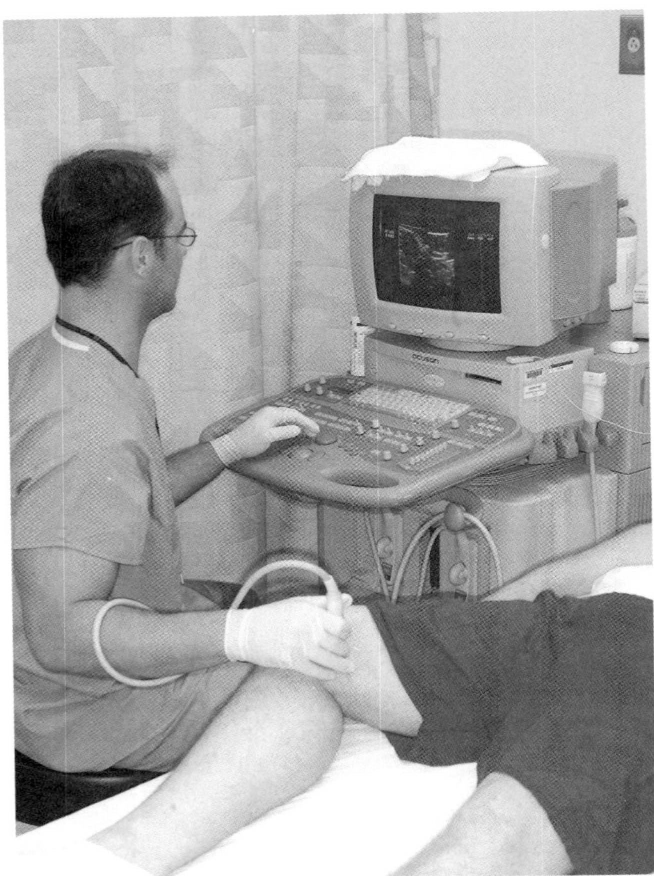

FIGURE 15-1 Position for lower extremity deep venous thrombosis examination.

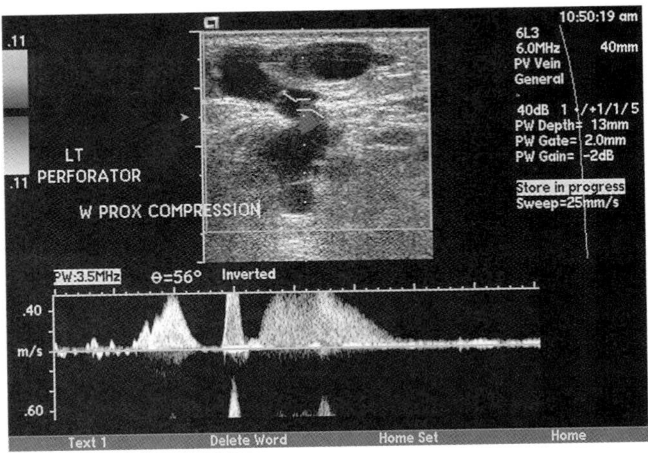

FIGURE 15-2 B-mode imaging of incompetent perforating vein (*upper*) and Doppler waveform identifying reverse flow in the perforator vein (*lower*). (See Color Figure in this section.)

using a rapid inflation/deflation system and duplex ultrasound (Fig. 15-3). This system allows measurement of valve closure times after rapid deflation of the cuff placed distal to the vein segment being interrogated. The technique is fully described in Chapter 17. In studies of normal volunteers and patients with CVI, a normal valve closure time of less than 0.5 seconds has been defined (Fig. 15-4).[4,5] Systematic interrogation of the common femoral, superficial femoral, popliteal, greater saphenous, and lesser saphenous veins is conducted, allowing an anatomic map of venous reflux in the limb to be constructed.

It is difficult to determine the accuracy of venous duplex evaluation for the detection of abnormal reflux, because prior to its development there was no other test that provided accurate determination of the sites of reflux in the lower extremity. Descending phlebography is accurate at detecting proximal reflux or more distal reflux in the presence of proximal reflux. However, if the common femoral and saphenous valves are competent in the groin, little information can be determined concerning the competence of valves in the distal extremity. Though the sensitivity and specificity of standing duplex examination are difficult to determine for abnormal reflux, most authors consider it the "gold standard" in venous reflux evaluation at this time.[4]

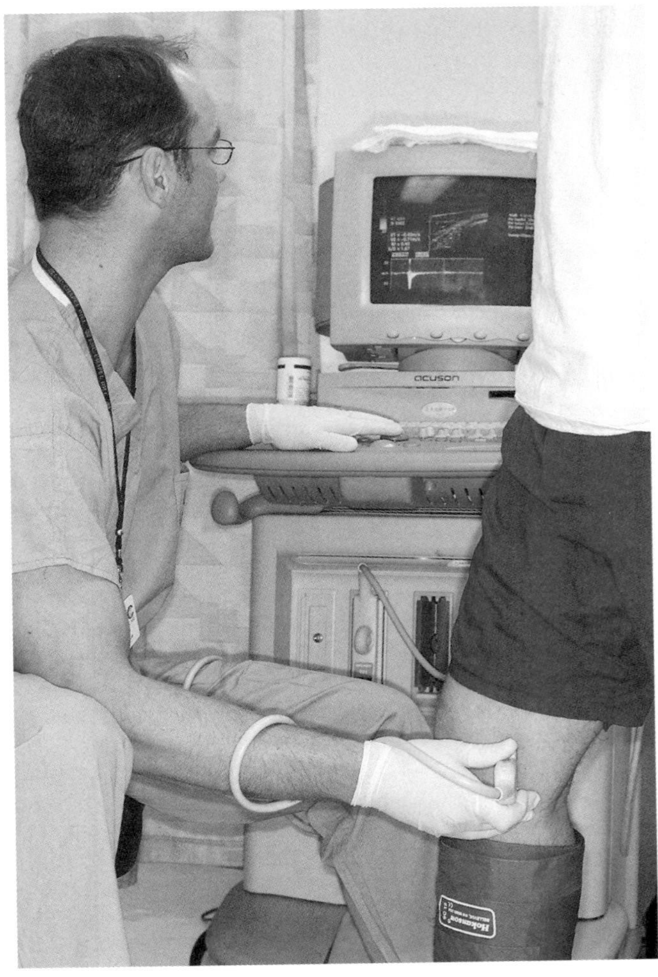

FIGURE 15-3 Position for standard standing reflux examination with a rapid inflation/deflation cuff positioned below the level of vessel interrogation.

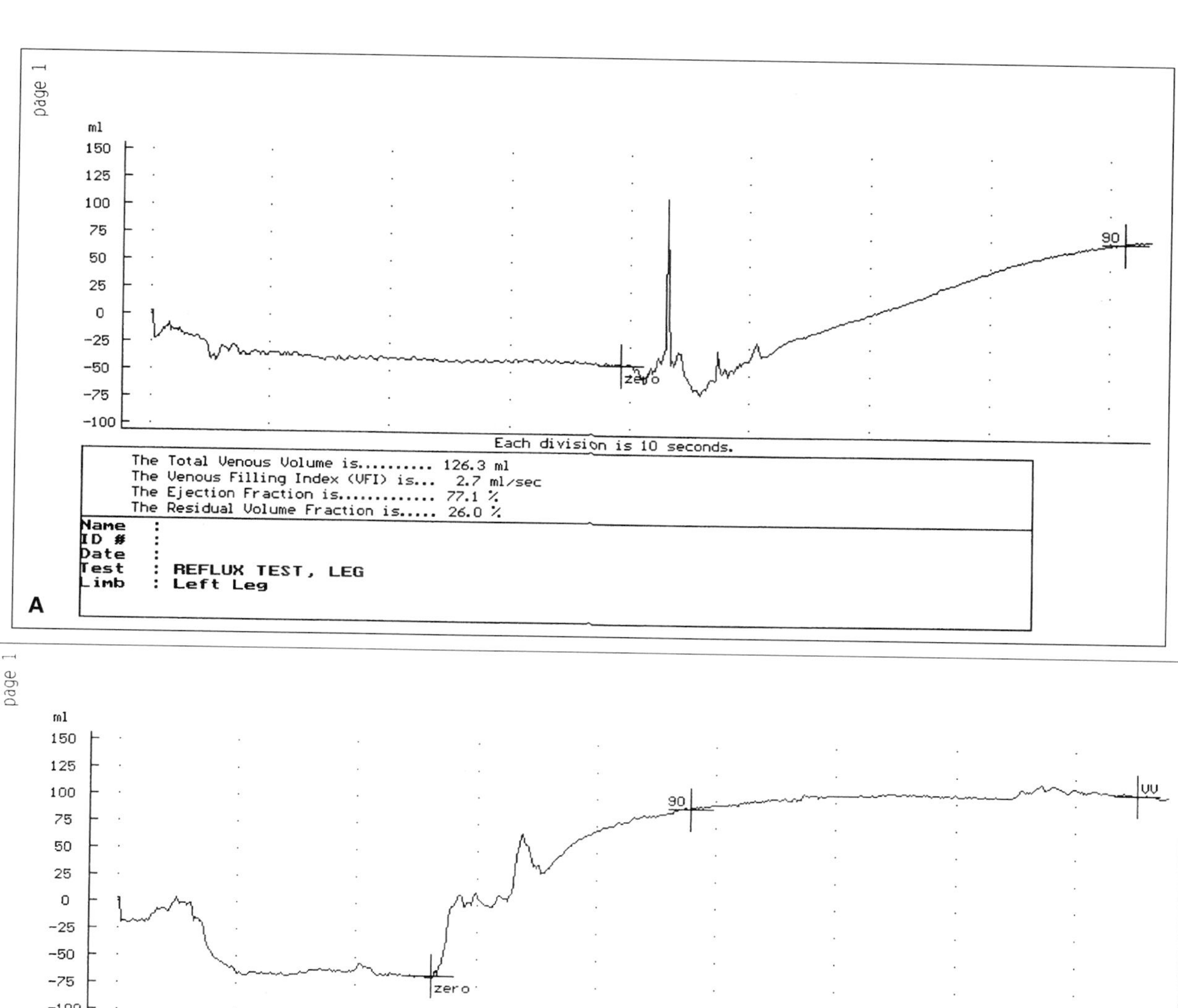

FIGURE 15-4 **A,** Standing reflux tracing with cuff deflation in normal limb. Note minimal reflux time. **B,** Standing reflux tracing with cuff deflation in abnormal limb with venous reflux. Reflux time is prolonged to more than 10 seconds.

Using this information, the clinician can determine the etiology, anatomy, and pathophysiology of CVI for the patient. For example, the patient who has superficial and perforator disease may be differentiated from the patient with superficial and deep reflux, allowing alternate treatment plans to be selected. Although duplex evaluation provides detailed information on the anatomy of venous disease, it cannot define the importance of anatomic abnormalities in the venous function of the limb. Clearly, one patient with gross reflux in the saphenous vein may have no resultant symptoms, whereas another patient may have an active ulcer. The clinical assessment of the severity of CVI is subjective, so the objective measurement of the hemodynamic performance of the lower extremity venous system would greatly improve our ability to evaluate patients and recommend treatment.

HEMODYNAMICS

Ambulatory Venous Pressure

Pollack and Wood[6] first described venous pressure changes in 1949, when they noted that muscle contraction increased the outflow of blood from the lower extremities during exercise, lowering the venous pressure. They also documented the gradual return to a resting venous pressure when the activity ceased. When Arnoldi and associates[7] demonstrated that the venous pressure variations were identical in the superficial and deep venous pathways, it validated the use of a dorsal foot vein for the evaluation of venous hemodynamics.

Venous insufficiency most often results in an elevated venous pressure, or venous hypertension, and may be due to the net result of venous outflow obstruction, valvular incompetence, arteriovenous malformations, or any combination of these conditions. The sum of the hemodynamic factors involved in venous insufficiency can be quantified by the measurement of an ambulatory venous pressure (AVP). The *AVP* is defined as the venous pressure in a dorsal foot vein after the execution of 10 tiptoe maneuvers in a standing position. Many physicians consider the AVP as the gold standard measure of venous hemodynamics.[8]

To measure AVP, a catheter is placed into a dorsal pedal vein and connected to a pressure transducer. The baseline standing pedal venous pressure is recorded. The patient performs 10 tiptoe maneuvers at a rate of one muscle contraction per second to empty the calf veins and then returns to the standing position. The mean pressure recorded at steady state toward the end of tiptoe maneuvers is recorded as the AVP. Refill time is measured as the time required to return to 90% of the baseline venous pressure after cessation of calf muscle contraction. The use of tourniquets to occlude the superficial venous system during the administration of the study may help define the contribution of the superficial and perforator veins to the refill time. In theory, placing a tourniquet on the thigh of the affected limb should occlude reflux occurring in the superficial venous system. If the AVP and refill time correct after tourniquet application, this suggests that the superficial system is the primary source of abnormal function. A lack of correction implicates the deep venous system. However, Payne and colleagues[9] feel that the tourniquet test is unable to reliably distinguish deep from superficial venous incompetence and should not be routinely used to determine the contribution of the individual anatomic components to global hemodynamic dysfunction.

Nicolaides and Zukowski[10] correlated AVP values to the incidence of limb ulceration (Table 15-1) and severity of CVI, showing a progressive incidence of skin ulceration as the mean values of AVP increased. They also reported differences in the AVP based on the anatomic pattern of venous reflux. Patients with deep venous insufficiency had higher AVP than those with superficial insufficiency. Perforator incompetence and outflow obstruction also increased the AVP, with the highest AVP reported in patients with deep valvular incompetence and proximal obstruction. However, overlap can exist between the AVP values of normal limbs and those of varying clinical categories of CVI, as one study identified 20% to 25% of patients with ulcerations to have AVP values within normal limits.[11]

Although AVP is generally perceived to be the gold standard measure of venous function, its direct measurement is an invasive, time-consuming procedure that may be difficult in patients with venous disease, particularly those with active ulcers. Severe edema obscures the pedal veins, making access difficult, and associated dermal changes often result in thickened or inflamed skin on the feet of patients with more advanced CVI. Therefore, in an attempt to circumvent these issues, several techniques to measure venous hemodynamics noninvasively have been developed. They all use a protocol of calf contracture and resting similar to that described for AVP measurement but with a noninvasive technique to estimate the refill rate and AVP in the limb.

Table 15-1 Prevalence of the Sequelae of Venous Disease in Relation to VFI in 134 Limbs with Venous Disease Studied with Air Plethysmography

VFI, mL/sec	SWELLING, %	SKIN CHANGES, %	ULCERATION, %
<3	0	0	0
3-5	12	19	0
5-10	46	61	46
>10	76	76	58

VFI, venous filling index.

From Christopoulos D, Nicolaides AN, Szendro G: Venous reflux: Quantitation and correlation with the clinical severity of chronic venous disease. Br J Surg 75:352, 1988.

Plethysmography

Plethysmography is a noninvasive way of determining blood volume changes in an extremity. This method is based on the hemodynamic principles of venous capacitance and volume displacement. The basic physiologic principles rely on the fact that lower extremity veins are not filled to the maximum capacity when the patient is in the supine position. With positional changes the venous system can accommodate an increased volume before reaching maximal venous capacitance. Patients with normal venous outflow demonstrate rapid emptying of the lower extremity veins with positional changes or with the release of an externally inflated pressure cuff. In the presence of venous outflow obstruction, or venous insufficiency, the baseline venous volume (VV) is elevated. Also, the volume changes in response to positional variations or pressure cuff maneuvers are significantly altered. Several plethysmographic techniques have been described, including strain-gauge plethysmography, impedance plethysmography, photoplethysmography (PPG), and air plethysmography (APG).

Strain-Gauge Plethysmography

The technique of strain-gauge plethysmography employs a Silastic conductor tube connected to a plethysmograph via electrical contacts. As the gauge is stretched by a change in calf circumference, the resistance increases in the conductor and a voltage change is recorded. The strain-gauge is calibrated such that a 1% increase in voltage corresponds to a 1% change in limb volume. The *VV* is defined as the difference between baseline volume and the volume at peak venous capacitance, whereas the maximal venous outflow (MVO) is measured from the steepest portion of the outflow curve.

Strain-gauge plethysmography has primarily been used in the diagnosis of DVT, based on evaluation of the MVO.

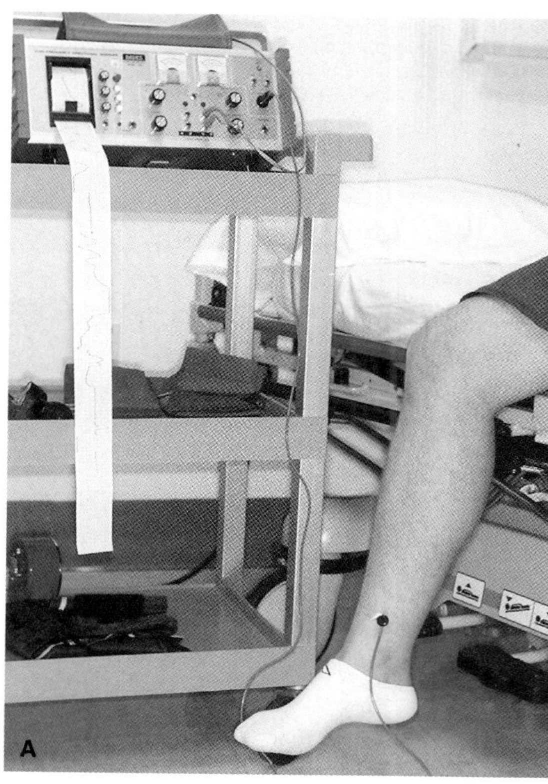

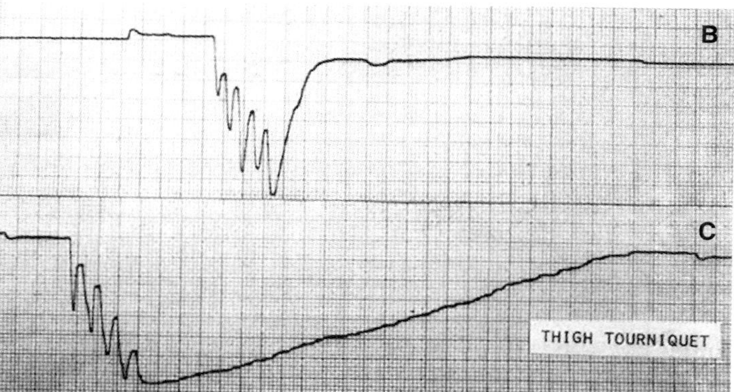

FIGURE 15-5 **A,** Standard position for photoplethysmograph (PPG) examination with the photo transducer located above the medial malleolus. **B,** Tracing of PPG refill time in patient with chronic venous insufficiency. Note rapid refill time indicating abnormal venous function. **C,** Repeat test with thigh tourniquet in place indicating the correction of refill time to normal. This suggests that venous reflux is limited to the superficial system.

Normal values for VVs average 2% to 3% above baseline, whereas limbs with venous outflow pathology would record a VV of less than 2% above baseline. This however, is an unreliable diagnostic criterion, with MVO being a more reliable diagnostic tool.[12,13] Barnes and associates[13] reported the MVO to have a sensitivity of 90% for above-knee DVT, but only 66% for below-knee DVT, whereas the overall specificity was 81%. Rooke and coworkers[14] evaluated patients during exercise using strain-gauge plethysmography by plotting volume against time for each limb, calculating the volume of blood expelled and the time required for veins to refill following exercise. They observed that a shortened postexercise refilling time accurately identified limbs with incompetence, the clinical severity of incompetence was inversely related to refilling time, and the type of exercise performed had little effect on the study results.

Prolonged recumbency, postural changes, muscle wasting, arterial insufficiency, and cardiac failure may alter venous filling and lead to measurement errors with this technique.

Impedance Plethysmography

Impedance plethysmography is a technique that measures the changes in electrical resistance, or the impedance, in the tissues of the extremity in response to volume changes. Two electrodes are placed on the limb to be evaluated, and the voltage change is measured. Ohm's law (voltage = current × resistance) is then applied to calculate the resistance in the limb. Changes in blood volume are inversely related to the calculated impedance.

Sensitivity of this study for diagnosing DVT ranged from 33% to 96%,[15-17] with accuracy improving greatly with symptomatic patients suffering from proximal DVT. Asymptomatic patients and patients with DVT below the knee have significantly lower test sensitivity. The difference can be attributed to nonocclusive thrombi and well-developed collaterals.[18] The inaccuracies of this technique are due to the same issues as strain-gauge plethysmography, since any condition that elevates venous pressure or reduces blood supply can create false-positive results (e.g., postural changes, prolonged recumbency, cardiac failure, arterial insufficiency). For these reasons, given the reliability of duplex ultrasound techniques, both strain-gauge and impedance plethysmography are rarely used to diagnose DVT. Neither modality has been well characterized as a diagnostic technique in the hemodynamic evaluation of CVI.

Photoplethysmography

PPG uses a transducer that emits infrared light from a light-emitting diode into the dermis. The backscattered light is measured by an adjacent photodetector and displayed as a line tracing. The amount of backscattered light varies with the capillary red blood cell volume in the dermis.[19] Using this technology and provocative limb maneuvers similar to those described for AVP measurement, an assessment of the venous system is obtained. A representative PPG tracing is reproduced in Figure 15-5 and illustrates the primary measure obtained, venous refill time (VRT) or recovery time. This represents the time required for the PPG tracing to return to 90% of baseline after cessation of calf contraction.

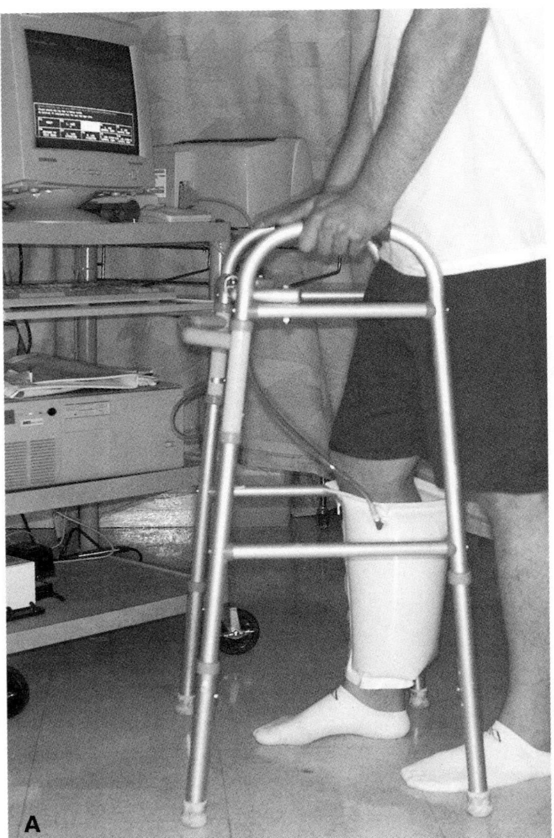

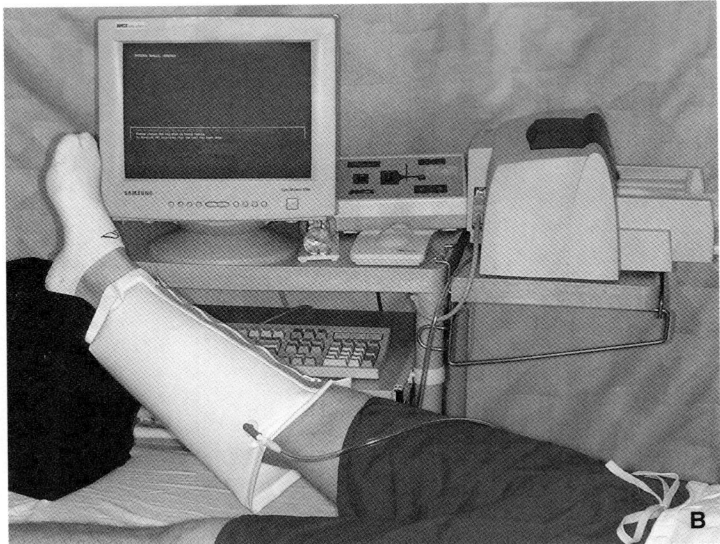

FIGURE 15-6 **A,** Patient demonstrating tiptoe maneuver during air plethysmograph (APG) test protocol. Note the cuff on the lower leg and the use of a walker to allow the limb under examination to remain relaxed. **B,** Calibration of the APG with the patient supine and the leg elevated to minimize venous volume.

Limbs affected with CVI typically have a much shorter VRT than normal limbs. As such, PPG can provide a relatively simple measure of whether venous insufficiency is present. However, the VRT can vary depending on the site of photosensor placement, the small sample area obtained, and the type and amount of exercise performed during the recording.[22] Placement near the site of a varicose vein or perforating vein may affect results, and patient compliance with the maneuvers required can be problematic.

Quantitative measurements are not obtained, so each laboratory should define its own standard for a normal refill time based on the equipment used. PPG measurements have not been proved to be a strong discriminator of the severity of CVI.[20,21] Nicolaides and Miles[20] reported that normal limbs were well identified by a PPG refill time of more than 18 seconds with their protocol. Abnormal limbs with CVI consistently had a refill time of less than 18 seconds. However, in the abnormal group, PPG refill time could not differentiate between degrees of CVI, with similar PPG refill times obtained in patients with AVP measurements ranging from 45 to 100 mm Hg.[20] Therefore, PPG is a poor test for assessing the results of venous corrective surgical procedures.

In summary, PPG is a reasonable measure of the presence or absence of CVI that is best used when no further information concerning the venous hemodynamic situation is desired. However, if information concerning the severity of CVI or an evaluation of the improvement after venous surgery is required, a quantitative test will be more useful.

Air Plethysmography

APG uses a technique to improve on the shortcomings of PPG and other types of plethysmography that have limited sampling areas. It employs a low-pressure air-filled cuff measuring 30 to 40 cm in length that is applied to the lower leg from knee to ankle. The cuff is connected to a plethysmograph that is highly sensitive to volume changes in the cuff, allowing precise quantitative evaluation of volume changes of the entire lower leg from knee to ankle (Fig. 15-6). The patient lies supine initially with the leg elevated and supported at the heel, allowing the cuff to be applied to the lower leg. The cuff is inflated to a pressure of 6 mm Hg to provide snug apposition to the limb without compressing the superficial veins. A baseline volume in the supine position is obtained with the patient resting. The patient then moves to a standing position supported by a walker to remove weight from the tested limb. The volume tracing gradually increases until a plateau is reached. The patient then performs one calf contraction/tiptoe maneuver followed by rest. A subsequent series of 10 tiptoe maneuvers completes the test procedure. The test protocol may be repeated with the use of a thigh tourniquet to isolate the deep venous system from the superficial system.

In Figure 15-7 the data calculated from the tracings obtained are illustrated. The VV is the difference in limb volumes obtained in the resting and standing positions. The venous filling index (VFI) is calculated by measuring 90% of the VV and dividing this volume by the time the

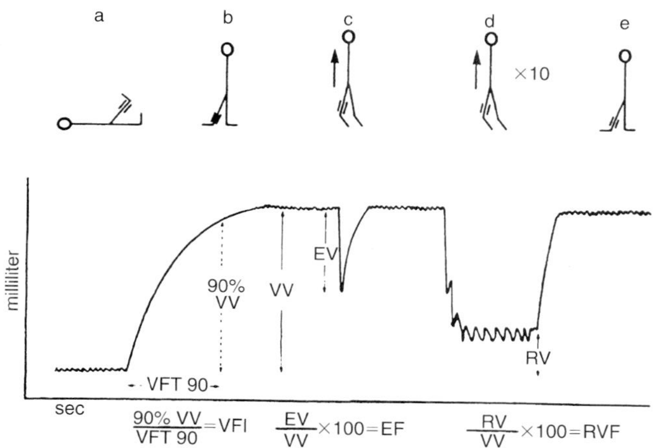

FIGURE 15-7 Air plethysmograph data obtained from tracings. VV, venous volume; VFI, venous filling index; EF, ejection fraction; RVF, residual volume fraction; EV, ejected volume; RV, residual volume; VFT, venous filling time. (From Christopoulos DG, Nicolaides AN, Szendro G, et al: Air plethysmography and the effect of elastic compression on venous hemodynamics of the leg. J Vasc Surg 5:148-159, 1987.)

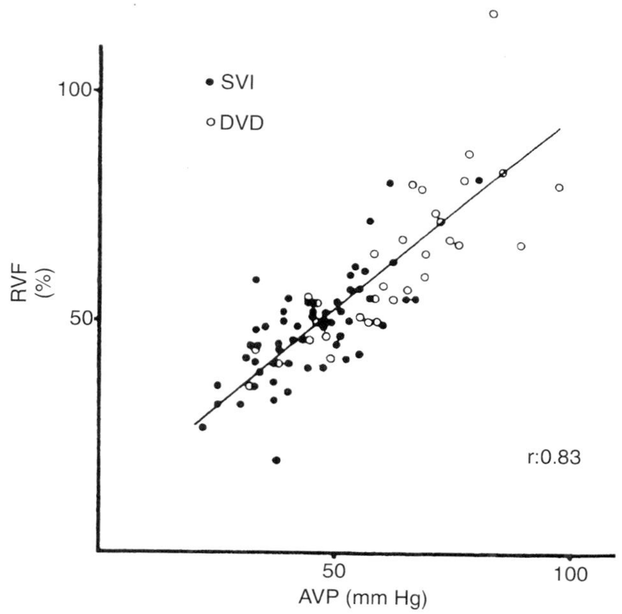

FIGURE 15-8 Correlation of residual volume fraction (RVF) to ambulatory venous pressure (AVP). SVI, superficial venous incompetence; DVD, deep venous disease. (From Nicolaides AN, Sumner DS [eds]: Investigation of Patients with Deep Vein Thrombosis and Chronic Venous Insufficiency. London, UK, Med-Orion, 1991, pp 39-43.)

limb requires to refill to 90% of the VV after moving to the standing position. Expressed in milliliters per second, VFI measures the average filling rate of the dependent leg and is slow in normal limbs. The volume of blood ejected with one tiptoe movement divided by the VV gives the ejection fraction (EF), and the limb volume remaining after 10 tiptoe movements divided by the VV gives the residual volume fraction (RVF).

Limitations of both PPG and APG methodology are seen in patients with limited ability to stand unassisted or perform vigorous tiptoe maneuvers. Also, in patients with advanced CVI, particularly in classes 5 and 6, the ankle joint range of motion is frequently limited, as reported by Back and associates.[23] It is unclear whether some of the changes in EF and RVF seen in these groups are related to intrinsic dysfunction of the calf muscle pump or an inability of the patient to activate the pump due to reduced ankle range of motion. APG is also limited in patients with obesity owing to a maximum cuff size at the ankle. PPG, therefore, may be the only option in patients with larger limbs.

In 1988, Christopoulos and colleagues[24] described the use of APG for evaluation of normal limbs and those affected with CVI. A VFI less than 2 mL/sec was associated with clinically normal limbs, and increasing levels of VFI were associated with more severe symptoms (see Table 15-1). The VFI is believed to provide a reasonable approximation of the global function of the lower extremity venous system and resisting reflux in the standing position. The EF and RVF are measures of the efficacy of the calf muscle to pump blood out of the leg. The RVF was found to correlate closely with AVP throughout the range of AVP measurements (Fig. 15-8), with lower RVF values representing better calf pump function (normal RVF defined as < 35%).[25]

In an evaluation of 186 limbs, Criado and coworkers[26] assessed the ability of APG parameters to predict the clinical severity of CVI. This is important primarily in the objective use of these tests for selection of patients for venous surgery and the monitoring of results and prediction of improvement after surgery. They reported that, of the APG parameters measured, VFI was the best predictor of the clinical severity of CVI: 93% of limbs with a VFI less than 2 mL/sec were clinically class 0, and only 9% of patients with a VFI more than 5 mL/sec were class 0 (see Fig. 15-7). VFI was found to have an 80% sensitivity and 99% positive predictive value for detecting abnormal reflux.[26] Unfortunately, using their methodology, the use of a thigh tourniquet was unreliable in predicting the presence or absence of superficial versus deep venous disease. EF measurements were unable to differentiate between classes of CVI, and RVF measurements, though able to differentiate, were less useful than the VFI.

Further work with APG measurements has demonstrated that the postoperative VFI can predict the long-term symptomatic outcome for patients after venous surgical procedures. In a review of 71 patients undergoing venous surgery, Owens and associates[27] measured APG parameters before and after surgery, then followed the patients for clinical signs and symptoms of recurrence. They reported that 94% of patients in whom the VFI corrected to less than 2 mL/sec after surgery were asymptomatic at a mean follow-up time of 44 months (Fig. 15-9).[27] The VFI was also found to predict recurrence of leg ulcers in patients with CVI. In patients with healed leg ulcers, a VFI of more than 4 mL/sec was associated with an increased risk of recurrence when compared to those with a VFI less than 4 mL/sec. For each milliliter per second greater than 4 mL/sec, the risk of ulcer recurrence increased 17%.[28] Based on this information, APG parameters can be used to assist in the selection of patients at higher risk for recurrent ulceration who may wish to consider venous corrective surgery.

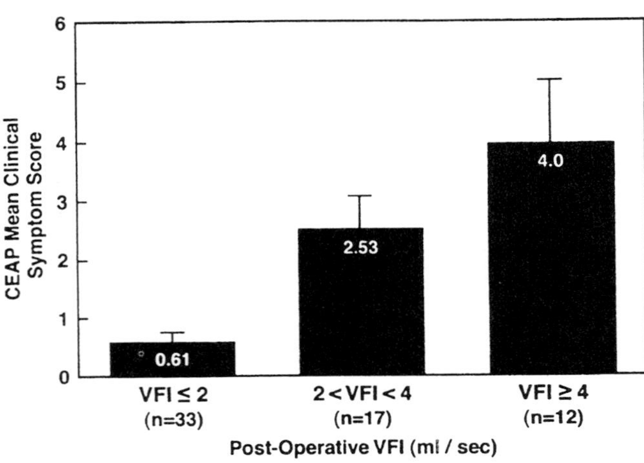

FIGURE 15-9 Correlation of venous filling index (VFI) at early postoperative follow-up to symptom score at late follow-up. Mean values and numbers in each group are shown. CEAP, clinical, etiologic, anatomic-physiologic. (From Owens LV, Farber MA, Young ML: The value of air plethysmography in predicting clinical outcome after surgical treatment of chronic venous insufficiency. J Vasc Surg 32:961-968, 2000.)

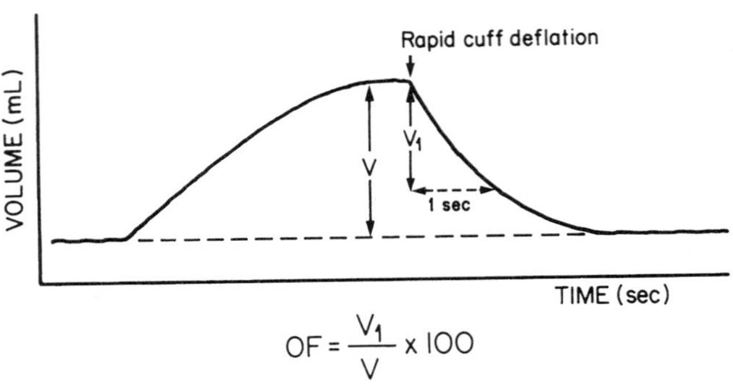

FIGURE 15-10 Typical outflow fraction tracing obtained with air plethysmography. After venous congestion is created with an inflated cuff, rapid deflation allows venous emptying. The outflow fraction (OF) is obtained by dividing the amount of venous volume emptied in 1 second (V_1) by the venous volume (V) and multiplying by 100.

Ibegbuna and colleagues[29] have evaluated the measurement of APG parameters in patients walking on a treadmill. They found that measurements were reproducible and that walking RVF measurements, when compared with tiptoe exercises, may provide a better correlation to AVP in patients who can adequately perform the treadmill test.[29]

Comparison of Air Plethysmography to Photoplethysmography

In summary, APG, by sampling a large portion of the calf area, provides a better measure than PPG of the global venous function of the limb. Bays and coworkers[30] studied the validity of the diagnostic capabilities of the commonly used noninvasive modalities in the evaluation of CVI. They determined that APG accurately separated normal limbs from those with CVI, and the parameters that significantly ($P < 0.05$) differentiated the two groups were VFI, VV, EF, and RVF. PPG refill times had a sensitivity of 100% to identify reflux; however, the specificity was only 60%. Furthermore, the kappa coefficient between duplex and APG was 0.83, whereas between duplex and PPG it was only 0.47, concluding that APG was a better method of evaluating venous reflux than PPG. APG provides a quantitative analysis that appears to be useful in the selection and follow-up of patients undergoing venous reconstructive or ablative surgery.

Measurement of Venous Outflow Obstruction

The rate of venous outflow from the lower extremity is related to the pressure gradient present between the inferior vena cava and the vein of the lower extremity.[31] As such, the outflow rate can be determined from any of the plethysmographic studies, and all use similar techniques. A proximal cuff is placed on the thigh and inflated to 80 mm Hg. VV in the limb is measured until a plateau is reached. The cuff is rapidly deflated, and an outflow curve is recorded as the limb volume decreases (Fig. 15-10). This should be rapid in limbs without proximal outflow obstruction.

Barnes and associates[13] used a standard AVP monitoring device while recording venous outflow with APG. Resistance was then calculated by using the equation

$$\text{Resistance} = \text{pressure/flow (mm Hg/mL/min)}$$

An outflow curve could then be constructed by plotting resistance against pressure for a large number of patients. Nicolaides and Sumner[25] calculated outflow fraction. Dividing the outflow volume at 1 second by the VV gives the outflow fraction (OF). Nicolaides[32] discovered the OF should be higher than 38% in limbs with normal venous outflow, 30% to 38% in patients with partial obstruction, and lower than 30% for limbs with severe obstruction. Nicolaides and Sumner[33] also plotted pressure-resistance curves at various degrees of obstruction and found correlation with the arm-foot pressure gradient classification established by Raju (Fig. 15-11).

Evaluation of Perforating Veins

The normal direction of blood flow in perforating veins is from the superficial to the deep venous system and occurs during muscle relaxation. Perforating veins may have between one and three valves, all located deep to the fascial layer; however, small perforators (<1 mm) commonly have no valves and therefore demonstrate physiologic bidirectional flow.[34-36] Currently, there is no universally accepted definition of an incompetent perforating vein (IPV). Hanrahan and associates[37] used duplex scanning to identify IPVs based solely on vessel size. Still others believe that outward flow after release of distal compression provides accurate identification of IPVs.[35]

The hemodynamic significance of IPVs also remains controversial, as many perforators currently defined as IPVs probably have little clinical importance. Zukowski and colleagues evaluated limbs with IPVs using AVP and reported that 30% of IPVs were hemodynamically insignificant,

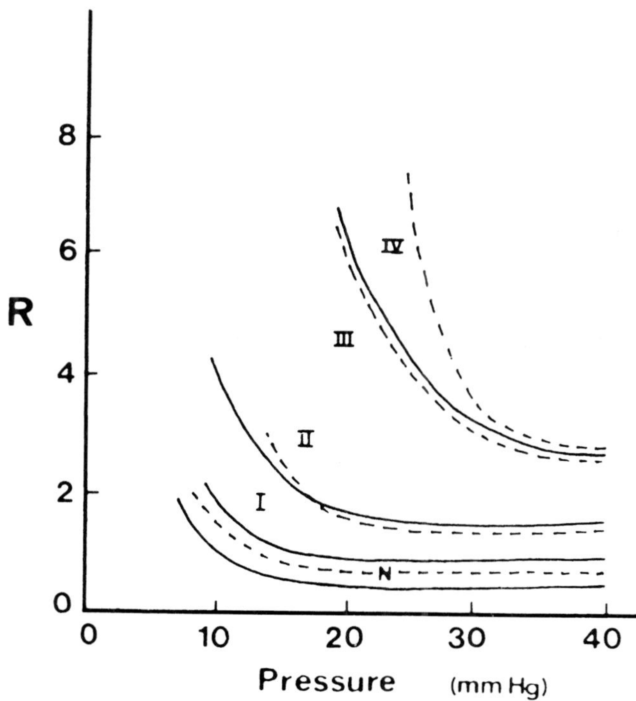

FIGURE 15-11 Relationship between outflow curves and Raju's classification of outflow obstruction (I to IV). More severe forms of outflow obstruction demonstrate a higher resistance (R) at any given venous pressure. A steeper slope is seen in patients with more severe outflow obstruction (grades III and IV). (From Nicolaides AN, Sumner DS [eds]: Investigation of Patients with Deep Vein Thrombosis and Chronic Venous Insufficiency. London, UK, Med-Orion, 1991, pp 39-43.)

35% were moderately significant, and 25% had major hemodynamic significance.[38] The critical question concerns preoperative determination of those IPVs that are of significance and should be treated at the time of initial surgery. Delis and coworkers[39] addressed this issue in an attempt to identify characteristics related to more important IPVs. Using gated-Doppler ultrasonography on real-time B-mode imaging, the amount of VV displaced outward to the superficial venous system in 1 second after compression release was found to correlate well with CEAP (*c*linical, *e*tiologic, *a*natomic-*p*hysiologic) clinical class.

Selective Use of Noninvasive Venous Studies

When considering the need for venous noninvasive testing, several factors must be considered, including the clinical status of the patient, the question(s) being asked in each individual patient, and the ability of the patient to comply with the requested study. Also, for routine clinical use, the technician time required and use of vascular laboratory resources are important issues.

The average time required for an experienced vascular technician to perform duplex ultrasound examination in the supine and standing position and a plethysmographic study is displayed in Table 15-2. Less experienced technicians or those in low-volume laboratories would likely require longer examination times. The frequent use of multiple tests

Table 15-2 Approximate Time Required for Experienced Registered Vascular Technician to Perform Noninvasive Venous Studies

TEST	EXPERIENCED TECHNICIAN TIME (PER LIMB), min
PPG	5-10
APG	15-20
Duplex	
Supine	15-30
Standing	20-40

PPG, photoplethysmograph; APG, air plethysmograph.

results in a large use of vascular technician time, a resource that may be in short supply in some situations. Therefore, studies should be ordered only when the information generated is important to the management of the patient. Some patients are technically poor candidates for study. Morbidly obese patients with suspected venous disease are poor candidates for APG due to cuff size limitations. These patients can generally be studied by PPG, but the results may be less reliable. Duplex examination is more difficult in patients with obesity, but some reflux information can usually be generated, particularly in the lower leg. Patients who have difficulty standing without assistance are occasionally unable to perform proper tiptoe movements, rendering some APG and PPG measurements unreliable. These patients can often have a VFI performed with APG if they can move from a lying to standing position with assistance. In our clinic population we estimate that 25% to 35% of patients with venous leg ulcers are unable to comply with the requirements for a full venous duplex and APG evaluation, including calf muscle exercises.

If the only question asked is whether or not venous disease is present, and no details concerning anatomy or severity of CVI are necessary, PPG is a reasonable choice. It can determine the presence or absence of venous disease and is relatively rapid to perform. But if the primary question concerns the anatomic site of reflux to plan intervention, a supine and standing duplex evaluation should be performed. If the primary question concerns the severity of CVI or whether improvement has occurred after intervention, APG measurements should be performed.

Noninvasive Evaluation Based on the CEAP Clinical Severity Criteria

CEAP Classes 0 (Normal) and 1 (Reticular Veins and Telangiectasias) These patients have no evidence of swelling or limb changes and typically require no further testing prior to treatment of their veins, which usually involves sclerotherapy or other dermal techniques.

CEAP Class 2 (Varicose Veins, No Swelling) This group requires further evaluation only if sclerotherapy or surgical varicose vein removal is under consideration. Duplex reflux examination greatly assists in determining the contribution of greater or lesser saphenous reflux, branch reflux, or other abnormal venous contribution to the development of the varicosities, allowing treatment of these abnormalities when present. This should improve long term results from vein removal or ablative treatment. Plethysmographic studies would likely add little information in this group of patients.

CEAP Classes 3 and 4 (Varicose Veins, Limb Swelling, or Skin Changes) In clinical class 3, symptoms are somewhat subjective and depend primarily on the patient's history. Pain is clearly subjective, and swelling is variable and may not be present at the time of the physician's examination. In clinical class 4, changes are noted on physical examination and are less subjective. In these groups, supine and reflux duplex examination are recommended to determine the sites of reflux, evaluate the deep and perforator systems for reflux or obstruction, and guide the selection of surgical or ablative intervention. PPG or APG can provide evidence of global venous dysfunction, separating class 2 patients with a primarily cosmetic problem, from classes 3 and 4 patients with more significant venous dysfunction. APG is recommended particularly to document the severity of CVI in patients considering intervention and to document improvement and predict long-term outcome after intervention.

CEAP Classes 5 and 6 (Healed or Active Leg Ulcer) Patients in these categories should undergo evaluation with duplex as outlined for classes 3 and 4 patients to determine whether they are candidates for corrective venous surgery to aid in ulcer healing and reduce the risk of ulcer recurrence. Patients with superficial and/or perforator incompetence who do not have deep venous obstruction are good candidates for surgical correction. Patients with deep venous abnormalities may benefit from surgery if they have severe recurrent ulceration. Most should undergo venography prior to surgical reconstruction as outlined by Raju.[40] APG measurements are helpful in predicting patients at high risk for recurrent ulceration and should be performed for patients undergoing venous intervention.

Specific situations in which hemodynamic measurement of venous function are important in clinical management are the following:

- Differentiation of venous symptoms from other causes such as arthritic pain
- Evaluation of the hemodynamic significance of IPVs
- Evaluation of the improvement in venous hemodynamics in a patient with multisystem valvular incompetence after intervention to correct one area of incompetence
- Prediction of long-term outcome after surgical or endoluminal venous procedures

SUMMARY

The goal in diagnosis and management of patients with CVI is to use the history and physical examination, supplemented by noninvasive venous evaluation in the vascular laboratory to provide the information required to optimally manage patients at all levels of disease. This often requires detailed anatomic and hemodynamic testing that cannot be obtained with a handheld Doppler or supine duplex examination. The use of standing duplex evaluation with cuff deflation provides an accurate method of diagnosing the anatomic sites of venous incompetence. Venography is rarely necessary in patient management, unless specific preoperative information is required prior to perforator ligation or deep venous reconstruction. PPG provides gross information about the presence of venous dysfunction, and APG provides a quantitative measure of the severity of CVI. Both the severity of reflux and the calf muscle pump function can be measured and used for predictive and monitoring purposes in the management of surgical and nonsurgical patients with CVI.

REFERENCES

1. Sumner DS, Lambeth A: Reliability of Doppler ultrasound in the diagnosis of acute venous thrombosis both above and below the knee. Am J Surg 138:205, 1979.
2. Salles-Cunha SX, Beebe HG: Direct noninvasive tests (duplex scan) for evaluation of acute venous disease. In Gloviczki P, Yao JST (eds): Handbook of Venous Disorders: Guidelines of the American Venous Forum. London, Chapman & Hall Medical, 1996, pp 112-129.
3. Talbot SR, Liver MA: Techniques of Venous Imaging. Pasadena, CA, Appleton Davies, 1991.
4. Sumner DS: Direct noninvasive tests for the evaluation of chronic venous obstruction and valvular incompetence. In Gloviczki P, Yao JST (eds): Handbook of Venous Disorders: Guidelines of the American Venous Forum. London, Chapman & Hall Medical, 1996, 130-151.
5. Criado E, Daniel PF, Marston WA, et al: Physiologic variations in lower extremity venous valvular function. Ann Vasc Surg 9:102-108, 1995.
6. Pollack AA, Wood EH: Venous pressure in the saphenous vein at the ankle in man during exercise and changes in posture. J Appl Physiol 1:649, 1949.
7. Arnoldi CC, Greitz T, Linderholm H: Variations in the cross-sectional area and pressure in the veins of a normal human leg during rhythmic muscular exercise. Acta Chir Scand 132:507, 1966.
8. Nicolaides AN: Diagnostic evaluation of patients with chronic venous insufficiency. In Rutherford RB (ed): Vascular Surgery, Vol 2, 3rd ed. Philadelphia, WB Saunders,1989, pp 1583-1601.
9. Payne SP, London NJ, Newland CJ, et al: Ambulatory venous pressure: Correlation with skin condition and role in identifying surgically correctable disease. Eur J Vasc Endovasc Surg 11:195, 2000.
10. Nicolaides AN, Zukowski AJ: The value of dynamic venous pressure measurements. World J Surg 10:919, 1986.
11. Raju S, Fredricks R: Hemodynamic basis of stasis ulceration: A hypothesis. J Vasc Surg 13:491, 1991.
12. Hallbook T, Gothlin J: Strain-gauge plethysmography and phlebography in diagnosis of deep venous thrombosis. Acta Chir Scand 137:37, 1971.
13. Barnes RW, Collicott PE, Mozersky DJ, et al: Noninvasive quantitation of maximum venous outflow in acute thrombophlebitis. Surgery 72:971, 1972.
14. Rooke TW, Heser JL, Osmundson PJ: Exercise strain-gauge venous plethysmography: Evaluation of a "new" device for assessing lower limb venous incompetence. Angiology 43:219, 1992.
15. Hall R, Hirsch J, Sackett DL: Impedance plethysmography: The relationship between venous filling and sensitivity and specificity for proximal vein thrombosis. Circulation 53:696, 1978.
16. Wheeler HB: Diagnosis of deep vein thrombosis: Review of clinical evaluation and impedance plethysmography. Am J Surg 150:7, 1985
17. Comerata AJ, Katz ML, Grossi RJ, et al: The comparative value of noninvasive testing for diagnosis and surveillance of deep venous thrombosis. J Vasc Surg 7:40, 1988.
18. Agnelli G, Cosmi B, Radicchia S, et al: Features of thrombi and diagnostic accuracy of impedance plethysmography in symptomatic and asymptomatic deep vein thrombosis. Thromb Haemost 70:266, 1993.

19. Abramowitz HB, Queral LA, Flinn WR, et al: The use of photoplethysmography in the assessment of venous insufficiency: A comparison to venous pressure measurements. Surgery 86:434, 1979.
20. Nicolaides AN, Miles C: Photoplethysmography in the assessment of venous insufficiency. J Vasc Surg 5:405, 1987.
21. Abramowitz HB, Queral LA, Flinn WR, et al: The use of photoplethysmography in the assessment of venous insufficiency: A comparison to venous pressure measurements. Surgery 86:434, 1979.
22. Rosfors S: Venous plethysmography: Relationship between tranducer position and regional distribution of venous insufficiency. J Vasc Surg 11:436, 1990.
23. Back TL, Padberg FT, Araki CT, et al: Limited range of motion is a significant factor in venous ulceration. J Vasc Surg 22:519, 1995.
24. Christopoulos D, Nicolaides AN, Szendro G: Venous reflux: Quantitation and correlation with the clinical severity of chronic venous disease. Br J Surg 75:352, 1988.
25. Nicolaides AN, Sumner DS (eds): Investigation of Patients with Deep Vein Thrombosis and Chronic Venous Insufficiency. London, UK, Med-Orion, 1991, pp 39-43.
26. Criado E, Farber MA, Marston WA, et al: The role of air plethysmography in the diagnosis of chronic venous insufficiency. J Vasc Surg 27:660-670, 1998.
27. Owens LV, Farber MA, Young ML: The value of air plethysmography in predicting clinical outcome after surgical treatment of chronic venous insufficiency. J Vasc Surg 32:961-968, 2000.
28. McDaniel HB, Marston WA, Farber MA, et al: Recurrence of chronic venous ulcers on the basis of clinical, etiologic, anatomic, and pathophysiologic criteria and air plethysmography. J Vasc Surg 35:723, 2002.
29. Ibegbuna V, Aina O, Daskalopoulou SS, Nicolaides AN: Venous haemodynamics during walking in chronic venous disease. Presented at the 13th Annual Meeting of the American Venous Forum, Ft. Myers, FL, February 25, 2001.
30. Bays RA, Healy DA, Atnip RG, et al: Validation of air plethysmography, photoplethysmography, and duplex ultrasonography in the evaluation of severe venous stasis. J Vasc Surg 20:721, 1994.
31. Sumner D: Strain-gauge plethysmography. In Bernstein EF (ed): Noninvasive Diagnostic Techniques in Vascular Disease, 3rd ed. St. Louis, CV Mosby, 1985, p 746.
32. Nicolaides AN: Investigation of chronic venous insufficiency: A consensus statement. Circulation 102:e126-e163, 2000.
33. Raju S: A pressure-based technique for the detection of acute and chronic venous obstruction. Phlebology 3:207, 1988.
34. Criado E, Johnson G: Venous disease. Curr Probl Surg 28:343, 1991.
35. Sarin S, Scurr JH, Coleridge-Smith PD: Medial calf perforators in venous disease: The significance of outward flow. J Vasc Surg 16:154, 1992.
36. Thomson H: The surgical anatomy of superficial and perforating veins of the lower limb. Ann R Coll Surg Engl 61:198, 1979.
37. Hanrahan LM, Araki CT, Rodriguez AA, et al: Distribution of valvular incompetence in patients with venous stasis ulceration. J Vasc Surg 13:805, 1991.
38. Zukowski AJ, Nicolaides AN, Szendro G, et al: Hemodynamic significance of incompetent calf perforating veins. Br J Surg 78:625, 1991.
39. Delis KT, Husmann M, Kalodiki E, et al: In-situ hemodynamics of perforating veins in chronic venous insufficiency. J Vasc Surg 33:773, 2001.
40. Raju S: Surgical treatment of deep venous valvular incompetence. In Rutherford RB (ed): Vascular Surgery, Vol 2, 5th ed. Philadelphia, WB Saunders, 2000, pp 2037-2049.

Chapter 16

Arterial Duplex Scanning

EVA M. RZUCIDLO, MD
ROBERT M. ZWOLAK, MD, PHD

Duplex ultrasound scanning is an integral part of vascular surgery practice. Carotid duplex scan continues to be the standard initial evaluation of patients with extracranial cerebrovascular disease, and many surgeons use duplex as the only preoperative examination before carotid endarterectomy (CEA).[1] Renal and mesenteric duplex scanning are gaining widespread acceptance as screening studies for arterial occlusive disease. Clinicians have come to rely on duplex scanning for postprocedural evaluation of surgical and interventional procedures on the carotid, renal, and mesenteric vessels, and reports now show that duplex information is valuable in predicting a positive clinical response to surgical or interventional treatment in renovascular disease. Aortoiliac and femoropopliteal scanning are gaining widespread use in planning percutaneous intervention. Finally, as experience accrues with endovascular aneurysm surgery, surgeons have found duplex ultrasound scanning to be one means of evaluating the hemodynamic integrity of these reconstructions. Overall, arterial duplex scanning is an increasingly important tool for the vascular surgeon. This chapter provides basic principles, currently accepted diagnostic thresholds, and indications for study.

PRINCIPLES OF ARTERIAL DUPLEX

Current sophisticated duplex scanners provide three types of information: gray-scale B-mode imaging, color-flow imaging, and pulsed-Doppler spectral waveform analysis. Although an increasing amount of information may be gained from review of the B-mode and color-flow images, most duplex algorithms for estimation of arterial stenosis are still based on evaluation of blood flow velocity. The pulsed-Doppler has the ability to sample flow in a small volume of tissue, guided in real time by the B-mode and color-flow images. Velocity values are derived from the Doppler frequency shift of the reflected ultrasound waves, and current scanners automatically convert the frequency shift data to blood flow velocity if the angle between the transmitted ultrasound beam and the blood flow channel can be determined. Duplex provides a remarkably complementary package of anatomic and physiologic information that is unrivaled by other modalities.

Because duplex-derived velocity measurements depend on accurate estimation of the Doppler angle, this modality remains significantly operator dependent. Doppler angle must be maintained at 60 degrees or less to minimize angle correction error. The velocity calculation is a function of the cosine of the angle between the ultrasound beam and the blood flow. At angles greater than 60 degrees, the cosine value changes rapidly; an increasingly greater potential for error accrues with small error in angle. A 2-degree angle measurement error results in a 6% velocity error if a 58-degree angle is incorrectly estimated as a 60-degree angle, but a 17% velocity error results if a 2-degree angle measurement error occurs between 78 degrees and 80 degrees.

To determine the degree of arterial stenosis from duplex data, investigators have drawn correlations between duplex-derived velocities and angiogram stenosis measurements. The implications of this relationship between new technology and the established "gold standard" are manifold. One of the most important has to do with the two-dimensional nature of angiographic images, limiting stenosis measurements to diameter reduction, rather than area reduction. All major duplex publications express results in terms of diameter reduction, although the velocity information obtained by the duplex is ideally suited to the more important parameter of cross-sectional area stenosis. In the clinical setting, this is more than a trivial mathematical relationship because atherosclerotic plaque accumulates in an asymmetric pattern. When duplex and arteriographic stenosis categories disagree, it may be due to inherent limitations of the arteriogram rather than inaccuracy of the duplex.

■ CEREBROVASCULAR DUPLEX

Extracranial Carotid Arteries

Noninvasive evaluation of extracranial cerebrovascular disease was the first widespread application of duplex scanning. The initial diagnostic criteria developed by investigators at the University of Washington are still used by many laboratories (Table 16-1).[2-4] Publication of the North American Symptomatic Carotid Endarterectomy Trial (NASCET) in 1991 and the Asymptomatic Carotid Artery Surgery (ACAS) trial results in 1995 created new challenges for carotid duplex, however.[5,6] First, the NASCET study adopted a technique for interpretation of angiographic stenosis severity not commonly employed before publication of that trial. All duplex criteria published before that date used a different angiographic scale by which to correlate stenosis categories. Second, NASCET and ACAS identified surgical benefit at stenosis thresholds not routinely identified by existing duplex algorithms, and subsequent publications have suggested interpolated criteria to identify these clinically important stenosis levels. These issues are addressed in the following sections.

Carotid Duplex Technique

For routine carotid duplex examination, a 4- to 7-MHz Doppler probe is appropriate.[4] Starting in a transverse plane, B-mode and color-flow are used to identify the common carotid artery (CCA) at the base of the neck, and the carotid is followed distally to the bifurcation. Occasionally the carotid bifurcation may be seen in its entirety as the classic "tuning fork" image (Fig. 16-1). The internal and external carotid artery (ICA, ECA) branches are identified. Although this identification is usually straightforward, the distinction between the ICA and ECA must be absolute in every study. The ICA is usually the posterior branch and reflects a low-resistance (more diastolic flow) Doppler flow signal, whereas the ECA is typically anterior with a high-resistance signal (less diastolic flow). In unusual cases, the relative locations and the Doppler signal characteristics may vary. When the ICA and ECA are severely stenotic, establishing their identity becomes more difficult. Two characteristics can be used to identify the ECA. The first is the presence of branches; the ICA almost never has extracranial branches. The second is the "temporal tap" maneuver. Gently tapping the temporal artery near the zygomatic arch causes a reflected wave that is visible in the ECA Doppler spectrum. Color-flow imaging also may be helpful in situations in which the ICA is tortuous, kinked, or coiled (Fig. 16-2). The

Table 16-1 University of Washington Updated Internal Carotid Stenosis Grading Criteria Based on European Method of Angiographic Stenosis Measurement*

PERCENT DIAMETER REDUCTION	CRITERIA
Normal	PSV <125 cm/sec No visible plaque, smooth arterial walls Boundary layer separation in bulb
1-15	PSV <125 cm/sec Minimal spectral broadening
16-49	PSV <125 cm/sec Marked spectral broadening throughout cardiac cycle, no systolic window
50-79	PSV ≥125 cm/sec EDV <140 cm/sec Marked spectral broadening
80-99	EDV ≥140 cm/sec Poststenotic turbulence
Occlusion	No internal carotid flow signal; flow to zero in common carotid artery

*Criteria based on a pulsed Doppler with a 5-MHz transmitting frequency, a small sample volume relative to the internal carotid artery, and a 60-degree beam-to-vessel angle. Approximate angle-adjusted velocity equivalents are: 4 kHz = 125 cm/sec and 4.5 kHz = 140 cm/sec.
EDV, end-diastolic velocity; PSV, peak systolic velocity.

Data from Primozich JC: Extracranial arterial system. In Strandness DE (ed): Duplex Scanning in Vascular Disorders. Philadelphia, Lippincott Williams & Wilkins, 2002, pp 191-231.

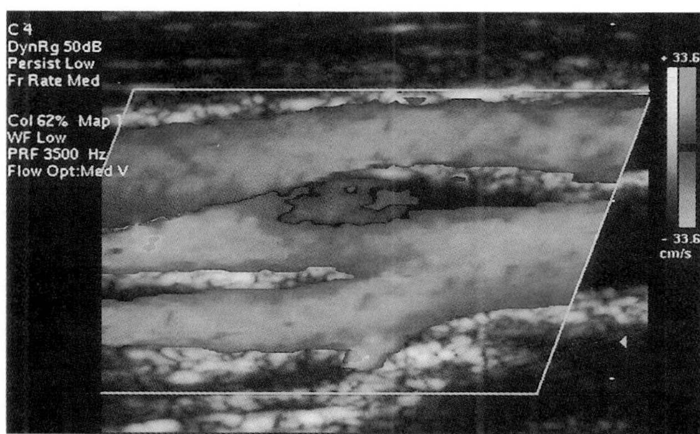

FIGURE 16-1 Color-flow duplex image of normal carotid bifurcation. The superior thyroid branch is visible originating from the external carotid. A small region of color-flow reversal in the carotid bulb is a normal finding in carotid bifurcations entirely free of atherosclerosis.

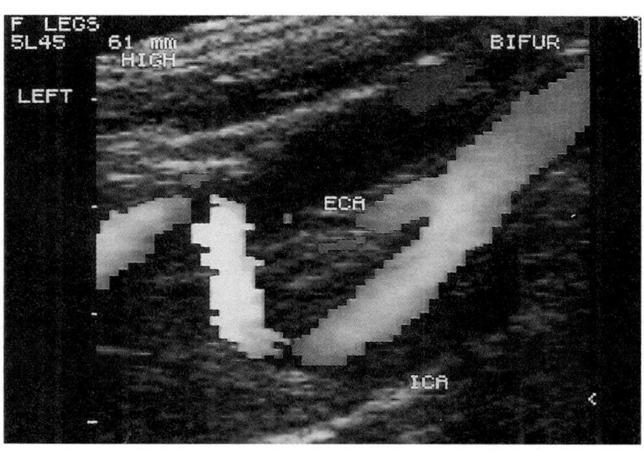

FIGURE 16-2 Color-flow facilitated anatomic definition and Doppler angle correction of a tortuous ICA. Subsequent Doppler sampling through the entire length of the ICA failed to identify significant stenoses.

ICA should be followed as distally as possible. When a preliminary survey of the bifurcation has been completed and an appreciation of the anatomy gained, the examination is repeated in sagittal and transverse imaging planes for collection of Doppler velocity data and representative images.

Doppler signals are recorded from a representative segment of relatively straight, undiseased CCA and from any regions that harbor stenoses. The CCA is examined as far proximally as possible with special attention if turbulence or low velocities suggest a proximal stenosis. The Doppler sample volume is then swept through the bifurcation and the ICA recording spectra in areas showing the highest peak systolic and end-diastolic velocities. Care is taken to maintain a Doppler angle at 60 degrees or less. Color-flow may be used to help identify regions of maximal stenosis for Doppler sampling, but appreciation of plaque characteristics is best done in gray-scale. In a preoperative patient, identification of a relatively normal distal segment of ICA beyond the region of plaque accumulation is an important finding for the surgeon. Likewise, it is helpful for the surgeon to note if an unusually high or low bifurcation is present. In addition, documentation of unusually thick CCA plaque aids the surgeon who hopes to clamp well proximal to a region of significant disease.

Carotid Duplex Interpretation

The carotid duplex study reports angle-corrected velocity data, including peak systolic velocity (PSV) and end-diastolic velocity (EDV) within the tightest portion of an ICA stenosis or representative values if there is no stenosis (Fig. 16-3). PSV in the CCA is also reported in most protocols because several stenosis-grading scales employ the ratio of PSV in the ICA to PSV in the CCA to determine stenosis category. A description of plaque characteristics is included, and careful note is made of unusual anatomy. Use of the NASCET grading scale can result in deceptively low stenosis measurement in situations in which patients have significant thick plaque accumulation in the carotid bulb. For this reason, it is especially important to note bulky plaque because a report of minimal stenosis may mislead one to believe that no atherosclerotic disease is present (Fig. 16-4). Findings suggestive of intrathoracic CCA or innominate occlusive disease or distal ICA or intracranial disease also should be noted.

Accurate estimation of ICA stenosis is crucial. Although a vascular laboratory may adopt a stenosis grading scale published in the peer-reviewed literature, local verification as part of a comprehensive quality assurance program is mandatory. Angiographic and surgical stenosis measurements should be sought for correlation. The importance of verifying duplex-based stenosis estimates cannot be stressed enough.

Development of the various interpretive duplex criteria may be best understood when considered in historical

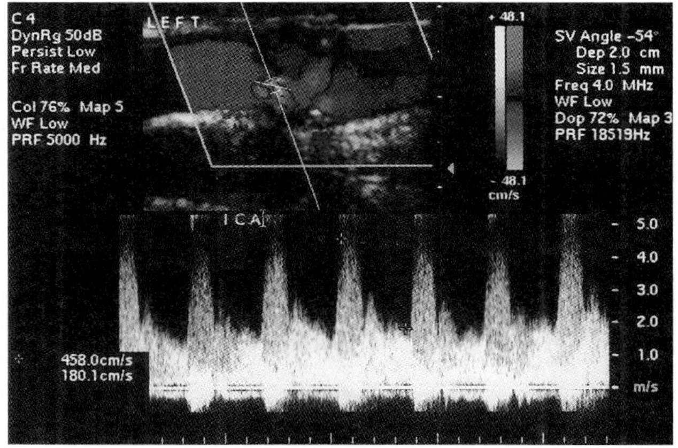

FIGURE 16-3 Identification of carotid stenosis is best performed using angle-corrected Doppler velocity and spectral analysis. In this study, the sample volume is placed in a region of disordered blood flow indicated by the focal color variation in the color-flow inset. Recorded PSV of 458 cm/sec and EDV of 180 cm/sec fall well above thresholds for 70% stenosis on all published grading scales. CCA PSV of 65 cm/sec (not shown) produced calculated ICA/CCA PSV ratio of 7, also indicating greater than 70% stenosis by all published grading scales.

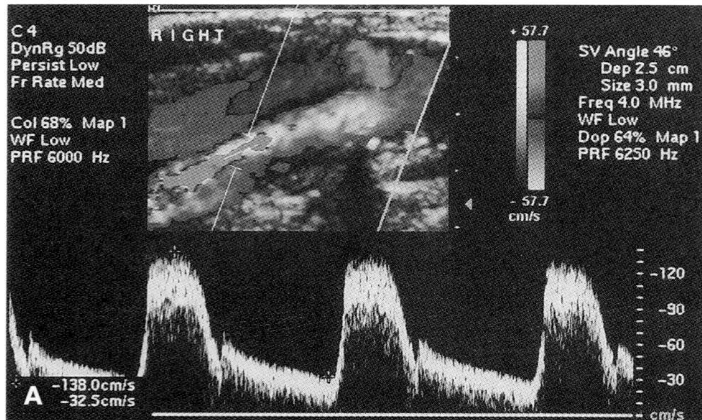

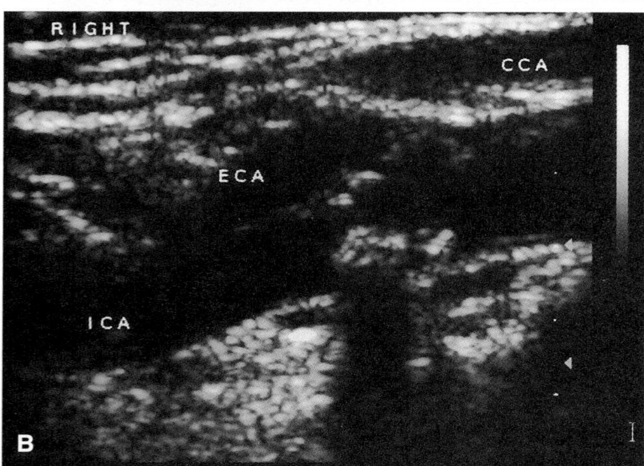

FIGURE 16-4 Examination of the carotid bifurcation with gray-scale B-mode imaging is the best method to evaluate atherosclerotic plaque characteristics. **A,** The Doppler spectral window is clear, and velocities are minimally elevated. Color-flow gain is well adjusted, and by visual interpretation the far wall plaque is unremarkable. **B,** The same carotid bifurcation is examined using magnified B-mode without color flow. A focal, bulky plaque is apparent.

perspective. Contrast arteriography was the obvious gold standard chosen by early investigators to confirm the accuracy of duplex. Duplex studies published before 1990 used what has come to be called the *ECST method* after the European Carotid Surgery Trial.[2,3,7,8] In this technique, the carotid stenosis is calculated by comparing arteriographic measurement of the smallest diameter in the stenosis with an estimate of the normal diameter of the carotid bulb. Because the stenosis is usually in the bulb, the "normal" diameter represents an estimate of how large the bulb was before the plaque developed. The NASCET and ACAS trials introduced a new convention for angiographic measurement of carotid stenosis with a technique that used the diameter of the distal ICA rather than the carotid bulb as the "normal" diameter. The NASCET carotid measurement technique achieves increased measurement reproducibility, but simultaneously introduces an illogical element. Because the normal carotid bulb is substantially larger than the normal distal ICA, a patient may have plaque in the bulb but a residual diameter greater than the distal artery. This situation results in a "negative" stenosis calculation by NASCET, whereas the stenosis may be 50% by ECST. At moderate degrees of stenosis, the difference between ECST and NASCET methods is significant. A 50% stenosis measured by the NASCET formula corresponds roughly to a 70% stenosis by ECST. Carotid stenosis estimations by the early duplex grading schemes systematically overestimate the degree of narrowing compared with angiograms read by the NASCET convention. Most publications since 1990 that provide duplex stenosis grading scales are based on NASCET angiogram measurements.[9-17] The original and still widely used criteria developed at the University of Washington are based on the ECST method of angiogram measurement, however.[4]

The second major issue for carotid duplex related to publication of NASCET and ACAS was the establishment of surgical benefit at degrees of ICA stenosis (50% and 70% for NASCET, 60% for ACAS) that did not correspond to previously determined cut-points in early duplex classification schemes. Many publications ensued, identifying duplex velocity criteria for a 60%[13-15,17,18] and 70% stenosis.[9-12,16-18] All studies used arteriograms measured by the NASCET convention as the gold standard. In general, high levels of diagnostic accuracy were identified in these single-institution reports. The threshold values varied more than would be expected given the uniformly high level of accuracy (Tables 16-2 and 16-3). This variation further illustrates the need for individual laboratory validation studies for accuracy of duplex-identified carotid stenosis.

The second major publication by the NASCET investigators identified surgical benefit for symptomatic patients with 50% or greater stenosis.[19] Duplex studies have also been published identifying velocity thresholds for a 50% stenosis threshold using the NASCET angiogram measurement conventions with recommendations varying from 130 to 150 cm/sec.[11,17,18]

The wide variation in recommended carotid duplex velocity thresholds has resulted in some frustration. In 2003, a multispecialty consensus panel composed of radiologists, neurologists, vascular surgeons, interventional radiologists, and vascular internists tried to resolve this issue by creating a unified reporting standard for carotid duplex.[20] Proposed criteria were based on review of the literature and presentations at the conference. The recommendations included use of gray-scale, color Doppler scanning, and spectral Doppler ultrasound scanning for all carotid artery examinations. Velocity threshold chosen for a 50% stenosis was an ICA PSV equal to or greater than 125 cm/sec with visible plaque in the bifurcation. Recommended velocity threshold for an ICA stenosis greater than 70% was a PSV greater than 230 cm/sec, with visible plaque and luminal narrowing on gray-scale and color images. Near-occlusion would be marked by color Doppler showing an extremely narrow lumen and total occlusion by no detectable lumen on gray-scale ultrasound scans and no flow on color, power, or spectral Doppler scans. The panel recommended use of ICA/CCA PSV ratio and ICA EDV in situations in which it appears that ICA PSV may not represent the extent of stenosis.[20] Table 16-2 identifies the consensus recommendations at the lower end of the NASCET-based ranges; application of these values would generate maximal sensitivity, perhaps at the expense of some specificity.

Carotid artery stenting has emerged as an alternative to CEA for management of carotid stenosis in high-risk

Table 16-2 Carotid Duplex Peak Systolic Velocity Diagnostic Thresholds Based on NASCET Angiogram Measurements*

PERCENT STENOSIS	AUTHOR	VELOCITY THRESHOLD (cm/sec)	INSTRUMENT	ACCURACY (%)
50	Grant et al[20]	125	Consensus panel	
	Faught et al[11]	130	Siemens	97
	AbuRahma et al[17]	140	ATL	93
	Filis et al[18]	150	Acuson	95
60	Carpenter et al[13]	170	Hewlett-Packard	92
	Filis et al[18]	200	Acuson	80-99
	Fillinger et al[15]	240	ATL	91
	Moneta et al[14]	260†	Acuson/ATL	90
70	Faught et al[11]	210	Siemens	93
	Kuntz et al[16]	229	Acuson	87
	Grant et al[20]	230	Consensus panel	
	Huninck et al[9]	230	Acuson	>85
	Filis et al[18]	250	Acuson	80-99
	Neale et al[12]	270	Acuson	88
	Moneta et al[10]	325	Acuson	88
	Kuntz et al[16]	340	ATL	92

*Reported only for reports listing overall accuracy >85%. Presented in order of ascending PSV.
†Moneta et al required addition of EDV >70 cm/sec to reach maximal accuracy of 90%. PSV >260 cm/sec (without additional EDV data) produced highest PSV accuracy of 88%.
ATL, Advanced Technology Laboratories; EDV, end-diastolic velocity; PSV, peak systolic velocity.

Table 16-3 Carotid Duplex Diagnostic Thresholds Using Internal Carotid Artery End-Diastolic Velocity and Angiogram Measurements Performed by NASCET Convention*

PERCENT STENOSIS	AUTHOR	VALUE (cm/sec)	INSTRUMENT	ACCURACY (%)
50	Carpenter et al[13]	40	Hewlett-Packard	86
60	—	—	—	—
70	Kuntz et al[16]	63	Acuson	88
	Faught et al[11]	100†	Siemens	95
	Neale et al[12]	110	Acuson	93
	Moneta et al[10]	130	Acuson	86
	Kuntz et al[16]	131	ATL	89

*Presented in order of ascending EDV.
†Faught also required PSV >130 cm/sec in addition to stated EDV value to reach stated accuracy.
ATL, Advanced Technology Laboratories; EDV, end-diastolic velocity; PSV, peak systolic velocity.

patients. The ultimate value of carotid stenting depends on immediate and long-term results of clinical trials, and carotid duplex is the obvious modality of choice to follow these stented arteries over time. Studies reviewing Doppler velocities within stented carotids are just starting to emerge. Interpretive criteria may differ from criteria of unstented carotid arteries.

Carotid Duplex Caveats, Pitfalls, and Special Issues

Instrument Variation As indicated in Tables 16-2 and 16-3, different authors identified strikingly different threshold velocity values for the same degree of ICA stenosis. This issue is crucial because the randomized trials focus almost exclusively on ICA stenosis in determining which patients should undergo endarterectomy. Commonly obtained velocities may fall above or below surgical thresholds depending on the grading scale used by the interpreting physician (Fig. 16-5). Although ultrasound has always been an operator-dependent technology, several publications document machine-to-machine variation as

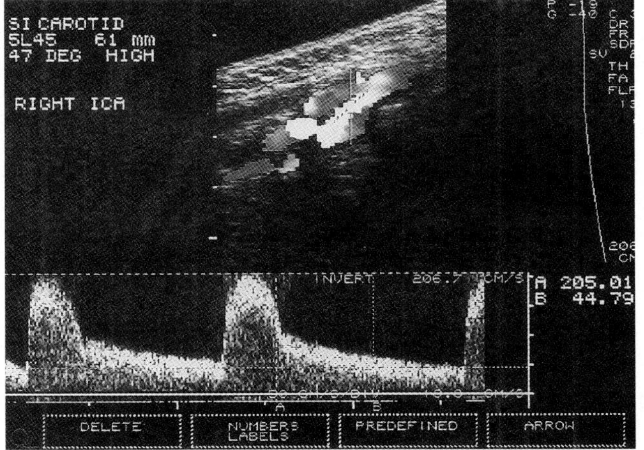

FIGURE 16-5 The Doppler spectrum in this image was obtained at the region of highest velocities. With angle-corrected PSV of 205 cm/sec and EDV of 45 cm/sec, this lesion would be interpreted as greater than 60% stenotic by some published scales,[13] but less than 60% by others.[14,15] The example reinforces the need for local validation of whichever scale is chosen for interpretation.

contributing to this problem.[15,16,21,22] Howard and colleagues[22] studied the individual accuracy results of 63 duplex instruments used in the ACAS trial. They determined the sensitivity of each machine to detect a 60% stenosis at a 90% positive predictive value threshold. Performance varied widely. Only 21% of these instruments achieved what the authors called "excellent" sensitivity of 80% or better. Half of the machines had "marginal" sensitivities of 50% to 80%, whereas 28% could not achieve a 50% sensitivity level. The authors concluded that duplex performance is likely overstated in the literature, but specific devices perform satisfactorily. They emphasized the importance of local standardized series and aggressive quality control if duplex is to be used in the selection of patients for carotid surgery.

Fillinger and associates[15] tested the accuracy of four individual duplex scanners at two Intersocietal Commission for the Accreditation of Vascular Laboratories (ICAVL)-approved vascular laboratories. All four scanners produced criteria resulting in accuracy greater than 90% for detecting a 60% ICA stenosis, but the criteria varied between machines. The log regression equation relating duplex values with angiographic stenosis was statistically different for one of the four scanners. In a similar study, Kuntz and coworkers[16] found markedly different optimal duplex criteria for detection of a 70% ICA stenosis with duplex scanners from two manufacturers. Although duplex can be an extremely accurate means to evaluate carotid stenosis, diagnostic threshold velocities must be verified for each model of scanner and should be confirmed for each individual machine.

True Gold Standard Another perspective regarding the issue of carotid duplex accuracy has been to question the validity of the presumed gold standard measurement of ICA stenosis by contrast angiography. Pan and colleagues[23] hypothesized that the two-dimensional nature of angiography measurement limits its accuracy. These investigators compared duplex velocity measurements, conventional angiography, and magnetic resonance angiography (MRA) for the evaluation of carotid artery stenosis. As a gold standard, they measured excised plaques, calculating stenosis by comparison of the residual lumen with the outer diameter of the specimen. Their stenosis results were analogous to measurement by the ECST technique. They found that duplex ultrasound and MRA correlated more closely to the actual operative specimens than conventional angiogram measurements. Angiography tended to underestimate actual stenosis more often than the other techniques.

In a similar effort, Suwanwela and coworkers[24] used residual ICA lumen diameter from en bloc endarterectomy specimens as their gold standard and arbitrarily defined a residual lumen of 1.5 mm or less as a severe stenosis. In this setting, a PSV greater than 360 cm/sec produced a maximal accuracy of 82% (85% sensitivity and 78% specificity) for identification of a 1.5 mm or less ICA lumen. Combined parameters were identified that resulted in 96% sensitivity but 61% specificity, and another combination had 100% specificity but 72% sensitivity. The concept shown in this study, adjusting diagnostic thresholds depending on whether sensitivity or specificity is to be maximized, is appealing. Without varying far from the point of maximal accuracy, one potentially could apply criteria with higher sensitivity in the clinical setting of a symptomatic patient, a situation in which a false-negative duplex result might have dire natural history consequences. In contrast, higher specificity would be desirable in the clinical setting of an asymptomatic stenosis, in which a more benign natural history demands a lack of false-positive studies that could lead to inappropriate endarterectomies.[25]

Carotid Endarterectomy Based on Duplex In many centers, CEA is performed without contrast arteriography, based on information from duplex ultrasound alone or in combination with MRA. This practice avoids the stroke risk associated with angiography and is supported by a large body of clinical literature.[1,26-43] A smaller number of articles cite the hazards of this approach, focusing on the inevitability of occasional false-positive and false-negative duplex results.[22,44,45] Several studies address specific technical issues to be considered when the duplex examination is the only preoperative imaging study.[43,46]

Stenosis Measurement with Contralateral Internal Carotid Artery Occlusion When one ICA is occluded, brain perfusion is maintained by compensatory flow in the contralateral ICA and the vertebral arteries. The relative contributions of compensatory flow from the vertebral arteries versus the contralateral carotid depend on anatomic integrity of the circle of Willis. Because flow and velocity are linked, it is not surprising that when the remaining patent ICA contributes increased flow, elevated velocities may be found in the absence of stenosis. Several authors observed that velocity-based carotid grading scales may overestimate stenosis when the opposite side is occluded.[47-49] Welch and associates[50] documented a higher incidence of carotid stenosis overestimation in the presence of retrograde vertebral flow. These are important observations for physicians interpreting carotid studies, and appropriate comment should be included in reports when this anatomy is encountered. It remains to be determined whether acceptably accurate duplex stenosis grading scales can be developed for use in the presence of contralateral ICA occlusion or significant vertebral artery disease. A final important clinical note on this topic derives from a report by Abou-Zamzam and colleagues.[51] These authors found that patients with bilateral severe stenosis should be restudied after the first CEA because normalization of flow on one side resulted in reduced carotid velocities on the opposite side. One fifth of their patients slated to undergo bilateral CEA no longer had criteria for a 60% stenosis on the contralateral side after the first CEA.

Intraoperative Carotid Duplex Failure to recognize technical errors during carotid endarterectomy, such as residual flaps, suture line stricture, or plaque dissection, can result in vessel thrombosis or distal embolization. Routine completion angiography was employed in the past to exclude CEA technical errors, but it is now reserved for unusual situations.[52] Subjective completion evaluation with continuous-wave Doppler also has been used for decades, but data to support sensitivity and specificity of this method are lacking. Bandyk and colleagues[53] described the utility of pulsed-wave Doppler velocity and spectrum analysis for evaluation of CEA sites in 1988, and shortly thereafter intraoperative duplex was introduced.[54] Sawchuk and coworkers[54] described intraoperative duplex scanning of the CEA site. They focused on real-time B-mode evaluation and observed that small residual flaps (<3 mm) and minor stenoses identified during completion duplex scans did not seem to result in major postoperative complications. Baker and associates[55] re-explored 3% of 316 CEAs based on intraoperative duplex scanning when large flaps, residual plaques, and severe turbulence were encountered, but they did not intervene on a larger group of minor defects including flaps less than 3 mm. No increase in perioperative complications occurred in the group with minor defects. Baker and associates[55] concluded that routine use of intraoperative completion duplex resulted in more precise performance of the operation as their surgical technique evolved over time based on expectation of the completion duplex. Although Baker and associates encountered a slightly higher incidence of late re-stenosis in the group with minor unrepaired defects, this observation was not made by others.[56] In follow-up studies, Bandyk and colleagues[57,58] continued to emphasize elevated velocities and abnormalities in Doppler velocity spectrum in addition to anatomic defects when deciding whether to reopen CEA sites. They considered a site to be abnormal when spectral broadening plus a PSV greater than 150 cm/sec were encountered, but most of the lesions they actually repaired had velocities greater than 200 cm/sec. Ascher and coworkers[59] showed that excellent clinical outcomes from CEA can be achieved with the help of completion duplex examination.

The technique of intraoperative carotid duplex is straightforward. Linear array probes of 10 MHz transmitting frequencies are typically employed. Several manufacturers market miniature transducers for this purpose. The decision to reopen an endarterectomy site is challenging because the duplex is extremely sensitive. A proportion of minor abnormalities may be left in place without ill effect, as described in the studies. Residual flaps less than 2 mm fit in this category, unless they cause substantial turbulence or high velocities or are found in a small ICA. Intervention is indicated for larger flaps, major turbulence, and high velocities in the CCA or ICA.

Carotid Duplex After Internal Carotid Artery Stenting

Duplex ultrasound scanning is the standard technique to follow patients who have undergone CEA and carotid stenting, but it is unclear whether standard duplex velocity criteria would be accurate after carotid stenting. Three studies report altered velocity profiles after carotid stent placement in the absence of residual or recurrent stenosis.[60-62] These studies noted elevated velocities within nonstenotic carotid stents, causing high false-positive stenosis rates for duplex. Lal and colleagues[62] recommended new higher velocity criteria for determination of in-stent re-stenosis. They suggested that elevated velocities after carotid artery stenting accompany stent-related alterations in compliance and other biomechanical properties of the artery. A reduction in compliance may lead to elevated velocities, unless there is a substantial corresponding increase in diameter. The mechanism, magnitude, and significance of these alterations will be elucidated further as more patients undergo carotid stent placement. If these early findings are confirmed, specific post-stent grading scales will need to be developed.

Brachiocephalic Duplex Evaluation

Occlusive disease of the arch vessels is infrequent, but in patients undergoing evaluation for CEA it is important to know if the artery origin harbors a severe stenosis. Duplex research in this area has not been extensive. Initial reports suggest good sensitivity for identification of severe great vessel stenosis.[63-66] The routine duplex examination does not evaluate arch vessels in detail, however, and in many situations the origins of these vessels cannot be seen. Diagnosis of arch vessel stenosis must be made on indirect cervical duplex findings in the CCA, including a markedly diminished, nonpulsatile, or disorganized waveform; delayed systolic upstroke; post-stenotic spectral broadening; or a low PSV. As detailed subsequently, the finding of a notched or retrograde vertebral artery waveform is an indirect sign of more central subclavian or innominate stenosis.[65] When an arch vessel stenosis is identified directly, generic Doppler criteria, including pre-stenotic, stenotic, and post-stenotic Doppler waveform patterns, and a PSV step-up greater than two times, likely apply.

Vertebral Artery Duplex

Analysis of vertebral artery blood flow is part of the routine extracranial cerebrovascular duplex scan. These vessels can be imaged between the transverse processes of the cervical vertebrae, posterior and slightly medial to the CCA. They usually can be followed centrally to their origins at the subclavian, although this portion of the study is more difficult. Ackerstaff and colleagues[63] and Bendick and Jackson[67] published early reports comparing vertebral duplex with angiography. In Bendick's study, duplex adequately evaluated the vertebral artery in 93% of 900 vessels. There was good correlation with angiographic findings in normal, stenotic, and occluded arteries. Reversed flow in the vertebral artery was readily identifiable by duplex and was a reliable indicator of anatomic subclavian steal. Doppler flow abnormalities were identified in 95% of severely stenotic or occluded vessels, but duplex was insensitive to moderate vertebral artery origin stenosis. The finding of unusually strong flow signals in one vertebral artery was associated with severe contralateral occlusive disease, subclavian steal with reversed contralateral vertebral flow, or severe carotid stenosis.

The findings in these early reports of vertebral duplex have withstood the test of time, but no quantitative grading scales for vertebral stenosis have been generally accepted. In most laboratories, interpretation of vertebral artery duplex includes comments on successful identification of the vessel, patency, flow direction, and a subjective interpretation of the Doppler flow signal. Findings that deserve comment include hyperemic vertebral flow; a damped signal suggesting proximal stenosis; a highly resistive signal suggesting intracranial stenosis or occlusion; or the sequence of pre-stenotic, stenotic, or post-stenotic patterns suggesting a focal stenosis. Publications identify the ability of color-flow imaging to diagnose vertebral artery dissection.[68] Another report suggests that color-flow improves accuracy in the diagnosis of subclavian steal, although determination of vertebral flow direction by pulsed Doppler sampling is usually straightforward.[69] Finally, power Doppler imaging has been suggested as a complementary technique for evaluation of the vertebral artery at the vessel origin, where B-mode, color-flow, and pulsed-Doppler may be difficult.[70]

Transcranial Doppler and Transcranial Duplex

In 1982, Aaslid and coworkers[71] introduced transcranial Doppler (TCD), using a low-frequency (2 MHz) device to penetrate the skull and measure intracranial mean blood flow velocity and direction. The value of TCD in diagnosis of vasospasm after subarachnoid hemorrhage was evident immediately. Instruments employed during the 1980s were "blind" pulsed-Doppler machines without accompanying B-mode or color-flow. Thereafter many duplex manufacturers offered low-frequency transducers that added B-mode imaging and color-flow to the information obtained with TCD. The original pulsed-Doppler and the newer transcranial duplex devices are referred to as TCD, causing some ambiguity, although authorities have now begun to use the term *transcranial imaging* (TCI) to identify the combination color-flow Doppler study. TCD and TCI are complementary. TCI allows more rapid and confident identification of intracranial vessels, and the learning curve is less challenging. Pulsed-Doppler TCD retains an advantage for evaluation through small transtemporal windows.

Transcranial Doppler Indications

Evaluation of cerebral vasospasm remains the dominant and best-established indication for TCD, whereas bubble studies may be used to diagnose a patent foramen ovale, and vasoreactivity can test cerebral blood flow reserve. Intraoperative monitoring during CEA holds interest for vascular surgeons, and the technique continues to undergo a critical appraisal for surgical use in emboli monitoring,[72-74] need for shunt placement,[71,75,76] adequate intraoperative shunt function,[77] and intraoperative carotid thrombosis.[78] Results are not entirely conclusive for most of these indications. In publications regarding identification of shunt requirement, authors reached contradictory conclusions.[71,75,76] Some authors noted the difficulty in maintaining an adequate transtemporal window during surgery, and technical failure on this basis ranges from 15% to 40%.[73,79] Despite limitations and cost of intraoperative TCD monitoring, this technique holds substantial promise. Spencer[80] monitored 500 CEAs with intraoperative TCD. Embolism, hyperperfusion, and hypoperfusion were identified and correlated with cerebrovascular complications. Spencer[80] suggested that routine intraoperative use might reduce perioperative stroke rate. An excellent review of the technique of intraoperative TCD monitoring has been published by Smith.[81]

Another important question is whether TCD should accompany routine extracranial duplex in evaluation of patients with carotid atherosclerosis, but publications have reached different conclusions. Cantelmo and associates[82] and Comerota and colleagues[83] concluded that TCD had no material impact on diagnostic or treatment plans in typical patients with extracranial carotid disease. In contrast, Can and coworkers[84] found that reversed flow in the ipsilateral ophthalmic artery and a 50% side-to-side difference in intracranial ICA velocity were 100% specific markers for identifying a severe ICA stenosis. They concluded that extracranial duplex specificity could be enhanced if TCD were added to the routine examination. Another argument for preoperative TCD involves its ability to predict patients at risk for postoperative hyperperfusion syndrome.[85-87] Several publications associate high postoperative middle cerebral artery (MCA) velocities with onset of hyperperfusion headaches, seizures, and intracranial hemorrhage. The best determinant of an elevated velocity is the patient's own preoperative value, although intraoperative or early postoperative velocities may suffice. Many preoperative studies would need to be done to establish baselines for the few patients who return with symptoms of hyperperfusion. This approach lacks cost-effectiveness. Although investigators assess the value of preoperative TCD in extracranial carotid occlusive disease, practicing surgeons have not embraced it. In a survey of vascular surgeons, only 3% thought preoperative TCD was indicated in the routine evaluation of extracranial atherosclerosis.[1]

Transcranial Duplex Technique

The typical TCD study begins with identification of the transtemporal window.[88] The MCA is identified first with blood flow direction toward the TCD probe. Velocities and sampling depths are recorded at three sites along this artery. The anterior cerebral artery (ACA) ordinarily flows away from the TCD probe and is found deeper than the MCA. The bidirectional MCA/ACA bifurcation signal is a good landmark. The P1 segment of the posterior cerebral artery (PCA) lies slightly posterior to the MCA/ACA complex. P1 flows toward the transducer, whereas P2, the second PCA segment, curves to flow away from the transducer. A transoccipital approach is used to sample the vertebral arteries, which traverse the foramen magnum with flow direction away from the probe. The vertebral arteries are often tortuous, but they eventually converge to form the basilar, which also flows away from the TCD probe under normal circumstances. Mean velocities, sample depth, and flow direction are recorded at each sampling site. Special attention is given to areas of unusual flow velocity or direction.

Transcranial Duplex Interpretation

By convention, TCD blood flow is recorded as mean velocity rather than the angle-corrected PSV used in extracranial carotid duplex. The rationale stems from inability of the blind TCD technique to determine the Doppler angle between the ultrasound beam and the artery, rendering the Doppler velocity equation nonfunctional. Determination of mean velocity assumes an angle of 0 degrees, and this is reasonable for the MCA and ACA. Although angle-corrected normal velocity ranges based on color-flow duplex have been published, most investigators continue to use mean values.[89] Normal mean blood flow velocity in the MCA ranges between 30 and 80 cm/sec, and vasospasm correlates with velocities of 120 cm/sec.[71,90] Comparison of MCA mean velocity with mean velocity in the distal extracranial ICA can help distinguish hyperemia from vasospasm when MCA velocity is elevated.[91]

Interpretation of TCD signals for emboli monitoring during carotid surgery relies on a distinctive chirping or whistling signal that must be distinguished from probe motion artifact.[91-93] Accurate definition of TCD embolic signals has been the subject of a multicenter review.[94]

When TCD is used for identification of patients at risk for post-CEA hyperperfusion syndrome, the diagnostic threshold for concern is a twofold increase in velocity compared with the preoperative examination.[85-87] Comparison with the contralateral MCA also may be useful in these patients.

ABDOMINAL VISCERAL DUPLEX

Renal Artery Duplex

The ability to achieve a surgical or interventional cure for hypertension makes renovascular disease stand out among the vastly greater population of patients with essential hypertension. For several decades, contrast arteriography was the only modality capable of establishing the diagnosis of renal artery stenosis, and the diagnosis was frequently overlooked because physicians were unwilling to order the study. The result of untreated renovascular occlusive disease is progression to renal failure even if other hypertension-related complications are avoided through aggressive blood pressure control.

Norris and colleagues[95] described renal artery duplex scanning in 1984 in a report that combined experimental data with results of an initial human trial. Using low-frequency transducers capable of sampling deep abdominal arteries, they studied parameters that have become standard today, including the ratio of end-diastolic frequency to peak systolic frequency (end-diastolic ratio [EDR]), elevated peak frequency shift, irregular Doppler profile outline, systolic spectral broadening, and a locally increased velocity within the stenosis.

Indications

Renovascular disease in the United States is caused primarily by atherosclerosis and fibromuscular dysplasia. Clinical manifestations include hypertension, ischemic nephropathy, or both. The classic patient with atherosclerotic renovascular disease is older than age 50, has typical atherogenic risk factors, and may have long-standing mild or moderate essential hypertension. Blood pressure suddenly becomes difficult to control, and creatinine levels may begin to increase. The fibromuscular dysplasia patient is younger and almost always female. These patients rarely have preexisting hypertension, and the diagnosis is often made fortuitously or during evaluation for nonspecific symptoms. Renal duplex is an appropriate test in both settings. Clinical decision making depends on the patient's pretest probability of disease and the established accuracy of the laboratory performing the examination.

Renal Duplex Technique

Patients are best examined after an overnight fast to minimize bowel gas interference. A low-frequency (2.25 to 3 MHz) transducer is employed. The examination begins with the patient in supine position. Using an anterior midline approach, a center stream suprarenal aortic velocity is obtained in a long-axis view at a 60-degree Doppler angle. The probe is rotated 90 degrees to obtain a transverse image, and the left renal vein is identified as it crosses anterior to the aorta (Fig. 16-6). This is usually an excellent landmark for the renal artery origins. To achieve a technically complete duplex examination, the arteries should be evaluated along their entire length from the aorta to the renal pelvis (Fig. 16-7). Angle-corrected Doppler velocity spectral waveforms are recorded at the origin, proximal,

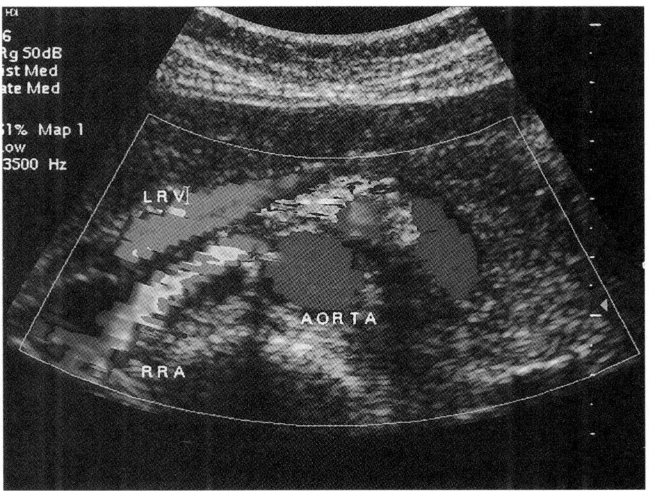

FIGURE 16-6 Transverse view of aorta, right renal artery (RRA), left renal vein (LRV), and origin of left renal artery (unlabeled). This is a typical color-flow landmark enabling the examiner to begin Doppler spectral data collection in the renal arteries.

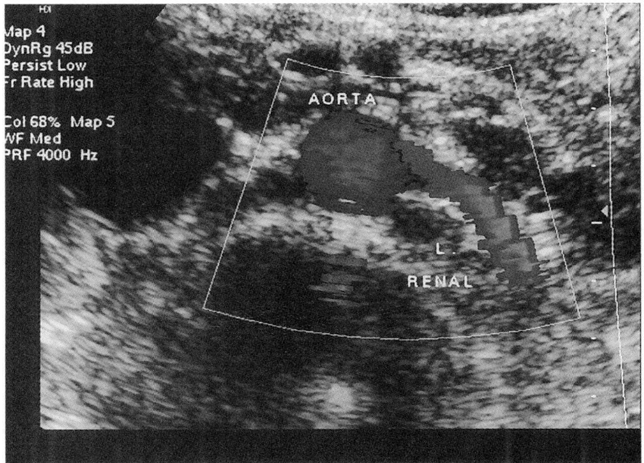

FIGURE 16-7 Color-flow image of left renal artery from aorta to renal pelvis. After location of artery, the entire length is sampled for Doppler velocities and spectra.

mid, and distal locations, with special attention to any focal site where abnormal velocities are found.[96] Patients with atherosclerosis tend to have lesions at or near the renal origins, whereas patients with fibromuscular disease are more likely to have midrenal lesions. If overlying bowel gas prevents visualization, turning the patient into lateral decubitus position allows the renal artery to be identified at the kidney and followed retrograde. Typically a combination of supine and lateral decubitus positions is necessary for thorough evaluation of the entire renal artery. The aorta is searched for accessory renal arteries, and these are examined in detail when identified. Peak systolic velocities and Doppler spectra are recorded, and the ratio of aortic PSV to renal artery PSV is calculated (renal/aortic ratio [RAR]). The kidneys are imaged with the patient in lateral decubitus position using a lateral axillary approach to obtain a coronal and long-axis view. Pole-to-pole length of each kidney is measured with an attempt to maintain a consistent approach for reproducible values.[97] Doppler signals also are obtained from interlobar and arcuate renal arteries. If indirect tests are used to supplement the direct examination (see below), Doppler spectra are obtained from the renal hilum for determination of acceleration time and acceleration index. To determine renal resistive indices (1 − [EDV/maximal systolic velocity] × 100), intrarenal Doppler signals are obtained from segmental arteries. A 0-degree Doppler angle and a sample volume size of about 2 mm are used to record spectral waveforms from representative sites in the renal parenchyma of the upper and lower poles of each kidney. Cortical measurements are easier to obtain and seem to be less variable. An average of the upper and lower pole values is used to determine the renal resistive indices.

Renal Duplex Interpretation and Accuracy

Normal renal arteries have a low-resistance Doppler waveform with PSV less than 180 cm/sec (Fig. 16-8). Kohler and associates[98] introduced the concept of using RAR as a diagnostic criterion for identification of clinically significant renal artery occlusive disease. In a retrospective comparison with angiographic stenosis, a RAR greater than 3.5 corresponded to a 60% or greater diameter-reducing stenosis (Fig. 16-9). Application of this diagnostic threshold resulted in a sensitivity of 91% and a specificity of 95%. Kohler and associates[98] also calculated the EDR as described earlier by Norris and coworkers.[95] They found that EDR was lower in patients with elevated creatinine levels, and their analysis led to the suggestion that a decreased EDR is a marker for renal parenchymal disease.

Taylor and colleagues[99] published a prospective validation of the original University of Washington RAR threshold of 3.5. Overall agreement with angiography was 93%. Duplex scanning identified 38 of 39 arteries with less than 60% stenosis, 11 of 14 arteries with 60% to 99% stenosis, and 4 of 5 totally occluded arteries. This resulted in 84% sensitivity, 97% specificity, and a positive predictive value of 94%, just slightly less accurate than the original retrospective analysis.

Hansen and associates[100] from Bowman Gray published an independent prospective validation in a series of 74 patients. The duplex technique used in this study was thorough with 10 Doppler sampling sites obtained per artery using abdominal and flank approaches. A RAR of 3.5 or greater was used as a threshold indicator of 60% or greater stenosis, as long as a turbulent waveform was also present. An occlusion was diagnosed if the artery was identified by B-mode imaging and no Doppler signal could be obtained. The cohort had a high incidence of disease with 10% of the arteries occluded and more than 25% having a significant stenosis. Twenty kidneys had multiple renal arteries, several of which were stenotic. Duplex was technically inadequate in only 6 of 74 cases, including 4 cases with normal arteries and 2 with stenosis. The remaining studies had a sensitivity of 88%, specificity of 99%, positive predictive value of 98%, and negative predictive value of 92%. Accuracy was influenced by the presence of diseased accessory arteries, but not by concomitant aortoiliac disease or renal insufficiency. Hansen and associates[100] also

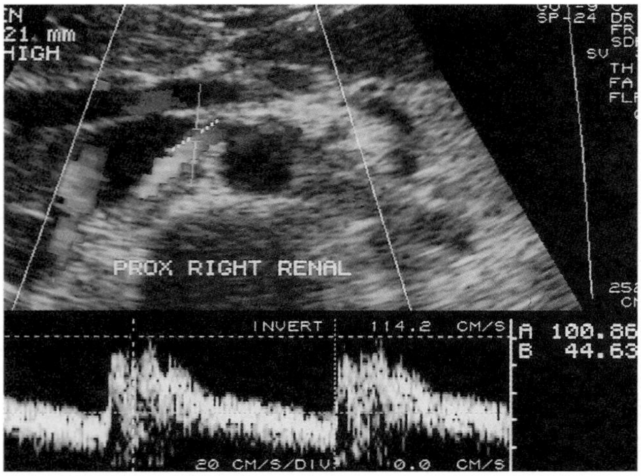

FIGURE 16-8 Normal Doppler spectrum sampled from proximal right renal artery. The waveform has rapid upstroke and high flow throughout diastole. This low-resistance morphology indicates normal low resistance of renal parenchyma.

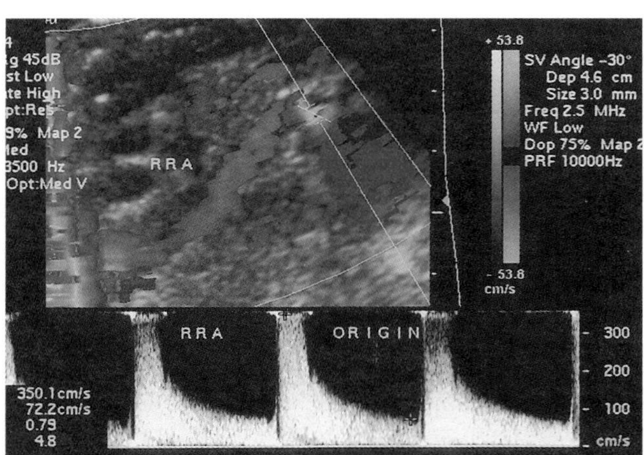

FIGURE 16-9 Abnormal right renal artery with PSV 350 cm/sec. Aortic PSV was 70 cm/sec resulting in RAR of 5. Stenosis subsequently was confirmed by angiogram. This image shows the importance of accurate angle correction in tortuous renal arteries.

examined a PSV of 200 cm/sec or greater as a marker for 60% or greater stenosis. They found that the accuracy of 200 cm/sec equaled that of RAR. Their report emphasized the presence of multiple renal arteries as a major pitfall of renal duplex evaluation. Sensitivity was only 67% in the subset of patients with multiple renal arteries. Similar to other reports, these investigators found that low EDR was statistically associated with elevated serum creatinine. Finally, because negative predictive value was 92%, Hansen and associates[100] concluded that patients with high pretest probability and extreme hypertension should undergo an arteriogram even with a negative renal duplex.

Hoffmann and coworkers[101] tested the accuracy of a PSV 180 cm/sec or greater for identification of any degree of renal artery stenosis. These authors found a 95% sensitivity and 90% specificity for this threshold. They also retested RAR of 3.5 or greater for identification of 60% or greater stenosis, and they found a 92% sensitivity but only a 62% specificity. Based on an amalgamation of the Hoffmann results and the Kohler/Taylor results, the University of Washington group now suggests reporting a renal artery as normal if the PSV is less than 180 cm/sec and the RAR is less than 3.5. With PSV greater than 180 cm/sec but RAR less than 3.5, the algorithm suggests reporting a renal artery stenosis less than 60%. A renal stenosis greater than 60% is reported if the RAR is greater than 3.5, regardless of PSV. A prospective trial of this specific algorithm has not been published.

Olin and colleagues[102] tested an algorithm whereby either a PSV of 200 cm/sec or greater or a RAR of 3.5 or greater indicated the presence of 60% or greater renal artery stenosis. This is perhaps the largest prospective analysis of renal duplex compared with angiography. Their patient cohort was also enriched with renal pathology. Accuracy in this series was excellent with sensitivity 98%, specificity 98%, positive predictive value 99%, and negative predictive value 97%.

Most authors found RAR of greater than 3.5 to be accurate using a variety of instrumentation. Likewise, a PSV of greater than 200 cm/sec was accurate in two large studies. As noted, the Olin algorithm diagnoses a greater than 60% renal artery stenosis if either of these thresholds is identified. As a starting point for laboratories undertaking this examination, either RAR or a combination of PSV and RAR seems reasonable. As noted in the carotid section, however, individual laboratory results are likely to vary. Ongoing quality assessment must be performed with renal duplex to determine if published thresholds retain accuracy in individual laboratories.

Indirect Renal Duplex Methods

Intrarenal sampling has been proposed as a rapid and easy method to determine the presence of a renal artery stenosis without studying the main renal artery directly. Martin and associates[103] suggested that a prolonged hilar acceleration time indicated the presence of a proximal renal artery stenosis. Sampling was done at the interlobar branches within the hilum with a Doppler angle defined as 0 degrees. Time was recorded to the initial or "compliance" peak. An acceleration time greater than 0.100 second indicated a proximal arterial stenosis. This finding has not been widely validated. Handa and coworkers[104] suggested that the slope of frequency change over time, defined as the acceleration index, indicated a proximal renal artery stenosis. The threshold they used was a value less than 3.78 kHz shift/sec. These authors found a sensitivity of 100% and a specificity of 93% for the test. This method has not been validated extensively. Schwerk and colleagues[105] measured the intrarenal resistive index ([PSV − EDV] / PSV × 100) and compared one side with the other. A difference in resistive index of greater than 5% indicated a 50% renal artery stenosis. These authors found a sensitivity of 82% and specificity of 92% with this technique. They pointed out that the method loses accuracy in patients with bilateral stenoses and is not applicable in patients with only one patent renal artery. *Pulsus tardus* and *pulsus parvus* are terms used to describe waveforms with slow and delayed upstrokes. In general, *tardus* and *parvus* describe the intraparenchymal signals found in kidneys beyond a renal artery stenosis. In addition, they have been identified as a sign of thoracoabdominal aortic coarctation in the pediatric age group.[106] Isaacson and Neumyer[97] summarized the indirect methods in more detail. Overall, although the indirect methods require less operator skill and less time to perform, none has undergone a truly rigorous prospective trial. With modern technology and well-trained technologists, there is currently little value for indirect duplex evaluation of renal artery stenosis. Satisfactory direct examination of the renal arteries is almost always possible.

Post–Renal Revascularization Duplex Evaluation

Duplex techniques may be used effectively for evaluation of surgical and percutaneous renal revascularization.[107,108] Parameters used for native renal artery stenosis have been tested and found to have reasonable accuracy. Because renal artery bypass grafts may originate from the infrarenal aorta; the supraceliac aorta; or the splenic, gastroduodenal, hepatic, or iliac arteries, yield from this examination is optimized if the technologist is informed of the inflow source.

Predicting Outcomes of Therapy for Renal Artery Stenosis

Wide application of Doppler ultrasonography in patients with hypertension has led to an increase in the diagnosis of renal artery stenosis. Of patients treated with renal angioplasty, stenting, or surgery, however, 20% to 40% do not experience improvement in blood pressure or renal function. Early reports had limited success in identifying noninvasive tests to predict nonresponders.[109-113] In 1996, Radermacher and coworkers[114] published a retrospective analysis suggesting that duplex-derived intrarenal resistive index (RRI) could identify patients whose clinical outcome would improve after successful renal intervention. Patients with a RRI less than 80 in segmental arteries of both kidneys experienced renal function and blood pressure improvement after correction of renal artery stenosis, whereas patients with RRI greater than 80 did not. The retrospective study was followed by a confirmatory prospective analysis in which correction of renal artery stenosis resulted in blood

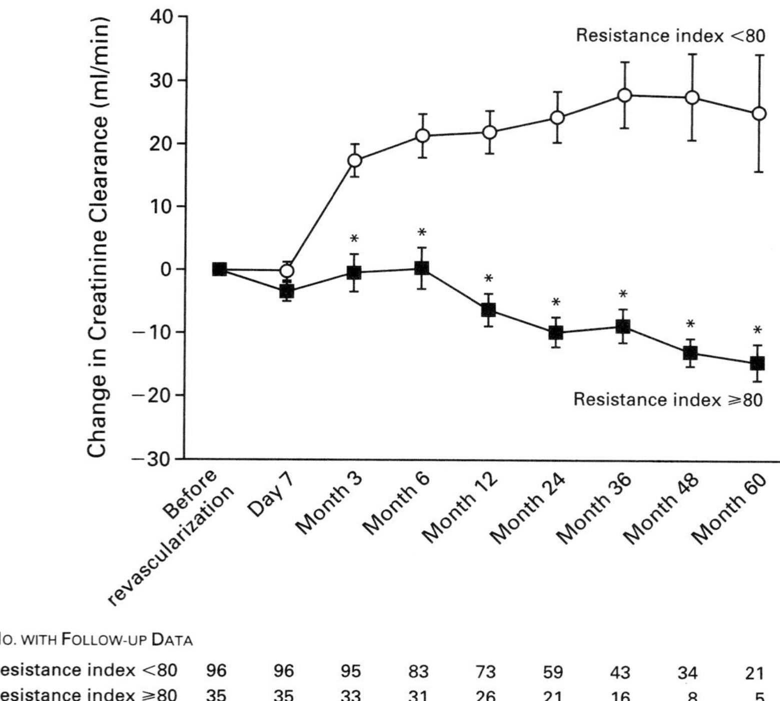

No. with Follow-up Data									
Resistance index <80	96	96	95	83	73	59	43	34	21
Resistance index ≥80	35	35	33	31	26	21	16	8	5

FIGURE 16-10 Mean (± SE) changes in creatinine clearance after the correction of renal artery stenosis, according to the renal resistive index before revascularization. Asterisks indicate a significant difference ($P < .05$) between the two groups.

pressure and renal function improvement in patients with RRI less than 80 (Fig. 16-10).[115] The RRI had a high sensitivity (96%) but a low specificity (53%) for predicting improvement in renal function. For patients with impaired renal function, the overall accuracy of the RRI improved.

Mukherjee and associates[116] also confirmed Radermacher's original observation and added the parameter of EDV as a predictor of outcome after renal stenting. Patients with a RRI greater than 75 and EDV less than 90 had no clinical benefit. Patients with a RRI less than 75 had a reduction in mean blood pressure of 5 ± 5 mm Hg, whereas patients with a RRI greater than 75 had an increase in mean blood pressure of 3 ± 5 mm Hg.

Transplant Evaluation

Original literature regarding transplant evaluation is found in publications by Neumyer and colleagues.[117,118] In brief, the transplant renal artery and vein may be evaluated by duplex ultrasound for patency and the presence of stenosis.[119] Neumyer suggested a transplant artery-to-external iliac artery PSV ratio greater than 3 was a threshold indicating significant stenosis. Increased PSV and spectral broadening within the transplant artery itself may indicate focal stenosis. The ability of duplex ultrasound to distinguish acute rejection from acute tubular necrosis using resistive indices or other measures is controversial.[120] Radermacher and coworkers[121] published convincing evidence that RRI predicts renal allograft survival with a high degree of accuracy. A RRI greater than 80 had a positive predictive value of 88% and negative predictive value of 83% for combined endpoints of decreased creatinine clearance, need for dialysis, or death.

Mesenteric Artery Duplex

Diagnosis of chronic mesenteric ischemia is difficult because the symptoms are nonspecific. Before the mid-1980s, the only means to confirm mesenteric artery stenosis in a patient with clinical suspicion of chronic mesenteric ischemia was contrast angiography. Jager and associates[122] published an early case report of noninvasive diagnosis in 1984. These investigators described an elevated duplex-derived PSV in the superior mesenteric artery (SMA) of a woman with chronic postprandial pain, diarrhea, and a 30-lb weight loss. Angiography confirmed the suspicion of mesenteric occlusive disease. In 1991, two large retrospective comparisons identified duplex flow velocity thresholds that provided accurate identification of severe mesenteric arterial stenosis.[123,124] This duplex examination has been adopted by many laboratories, and several prospective studies confirm accuracy of the velocity thresholds. Similar to renal duplex, the mesenteric examination entails a substantial learning curve. When mastered, however, this is an important and rewarding study.

Indications

Mesenteric duplex is an excellent screening test for patients with symptoms of chronic intestinal ischemia. Although it may be argued that patients with textbook signs and symptoms should proceed directly to diagnostic angiography, duplex is the perfect starting point for patients with less classic presentations. The test is also useful for patients with suspected median arcuate compression syndrome and for postoperative or post-interventional re-evaluation.[108] Finally, duplex may be used for evaluation of portal and hepatic arterial and venous disorders.[125-127]

Mesenteric Duplex Technique

It is important to perform this examination after the patient has fasted at least 6 hours because the SMA waveform changes from a low-flow, high-resistance morphology (Fig. 16-11) to a high-flow, low-resistance form after eating. Examinations generally are performed with the patient supine or in a slight reverse Trendelenburg position. Low-frequency transducers are required; typically Doppler transmitting frequencies range from 2 to 3 MHz, and imaging frequencies range from 2 to 4 MHz. Initial transducer positioning is just below the xiphoid, but a right lateral approach, using the liver as an acoustic window, also offers an excellent view. The celiac artery, common hepatic artery, and SMA are interrogated thoroughly (Fig. 16-12). Doppler waveforms and velocities are recorded with careful attention to angle correction because these vessels may be very tortuous.[128] Attempts are made to identify the splenic, gastroduodenal, and inferior mesenteric arteries. Knowledge of common mesenteric anatomic anomalies is important because prevalence is approximately 20%.[129,130]

Mesenteric Duplex Interpretation and Accuracy

Moneta and colleagues[124] found that a PSV 275 cm/sec or greater or the absence of a flow signal predicted a 70% to 100% SMA stenosis with sensitivity and specificity of 89% and 92%. These authors identified a PSV 200 cm/sec or greater as the most accurate celiac artery threshold with a sensitivity of 75% and specificity of 89%. Bowersox and associates[123] found EDV to be more accurate for diagnosis of SMA stenosis. An EDV 45 cm/sec or greater was the best indicator of a 50% or greater SMA stenosis, with a sensitivity of 100% and specificity of 92%. PSV 300 cm/sec or greater was highly specific but less sensitive for severe SMA stenosis. In this study, no diagnostic velocity threshold was identified for severe celiac stenosis, and it was postulated that the abundant mesenteric collateral circulation might limit the pathophysiologic requirement for high-velocity flow across a narrowed celiac axis. LaBombard and colleagues[131] subsequently identified retrograde flow in the common hepatic artery as a reliable indicator of severe celiac artery stenosis or occlusion.

Moneta and coworkers[132] published a prospective validation of their diagnostic criteria. They confirmed excellent accuracy in the SMA and good accuracy in the celiac artery for the criteria noted earlier. Subsequently, Zwolak and colleagues[130] tested the EDV criteria and confirmed excellent sensitivity and specificity for EDV of 45 cm/sec or greater for identification of a 50% or greater SMA stenosis. Diagnostic accuracy for celiac stenosis was excellent using an EDV of 55 cm/sec or greater or a PSV of 200 cm/sec or greater. Retrograde blood flow direction in the common hepatic artery was 100% predictive of severe celiac stenosis or occlusion.

Perko and coworkers[133] provided independent confirmation of mesenteric duplex accuracy; they compared duplex results with angiographic stenosis in symptomatic patients. Their report emphasized EDV as the more accurate means by which to diagnose significant mesenteric stenosis, but review of their data indicates that PSV and EDV were remarkably accurate (>90%) for this purpose.

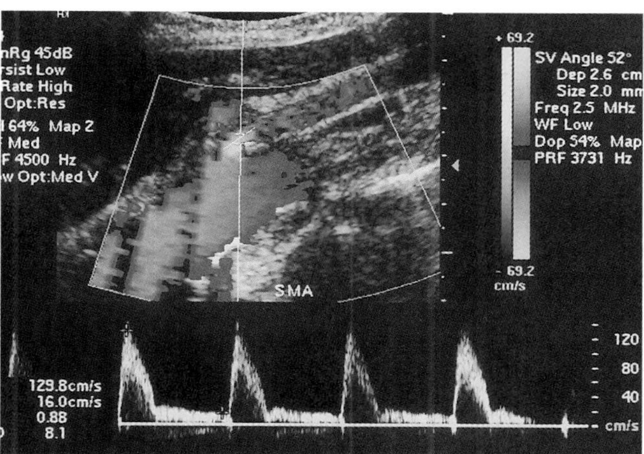

FIGURE 16-11 Normal, fasting, high-resistance waveform in SMA. Angle correction is crucial as the SMA curves sharply beyond its origin from the aorta.

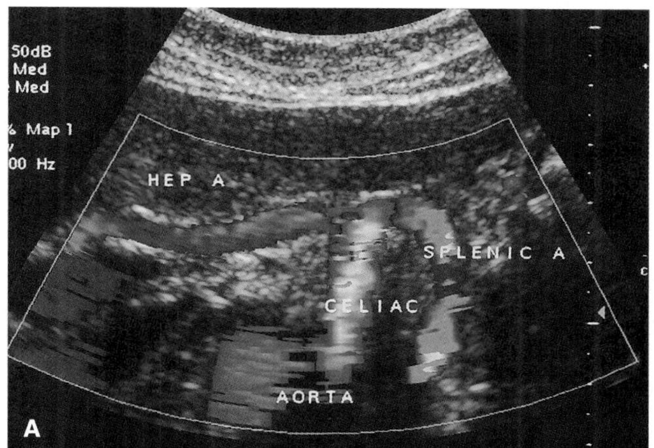

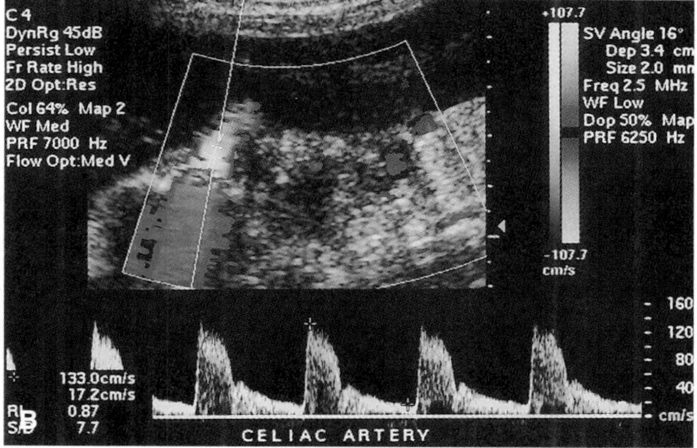

FIGURE 16-12 **A,** Color-flow appearance of celiac axis and bifurcation into splenic and common hepatic artery. **B,** Normal celiac Doppler spectrum shows sharp systolic upstroke and low-resistance flow throughout cardiac cycle.

A final important issue in mesenteric duplex scanning involves identification of anatomic anomalies. These occur in approximately 20% of the population and may substantially affect accurate interpretation of the study. A replaced right hepatic artery arising from the SMA may change the fasting waveform to low-resistance morphology with high end-diastolic flow, and it may increase velocities in the absence of stenosis.[130] With attention to detail, most anomalies can be identified by duplex. Familiarity with these anatomic variants helps prevent study interpretation errors.

Mesenteric duplex is an accurate, noninvasive method to diagnose chronic mesenteric arterial disease. When mastered, the study may be applied with confidence for evaluation of possible chronic mesenteric ischemia and other abdominal vascular disorders. Similar to other arterial duplex examinations, more than one set of diagnostic criteria has been published. For mesenteric duplex, the discrepancy between the published thresholds is not excessive. Individual laboratories must choose one set of criteria and pursue clinical and angiographic correlation.

■ DUPLEX IN LOWER EXTREMITY ARTERIAL DISEASE

Aortoiliac, Femoropopliteal, Tibial, and Pedal Duplex

The potential role of duplex ultrasonography in evaluation and management of lower extremity arterial disease has undergone substantial investigation. Studies published in the 1980s indicated the ability of duplex to identify stenotic lesions from the aorta to the pedal vessels, and several of these described a potential role for duplex to replace arteriography in planning lower extremity revascularization.[134-137] Investigations testing the accuracy of color-flow duplex ultrasonography compared with angiography in patients undergoing lower extremity revascularization reached similar conclusions, calling the accuracy of duplex ultrasonography equal to[138,139] or greater than angiography for prediction of adequate outflow targets.[140]

Indications

Duplex arterial mapping may assist evaluation and treatment of patients with symptomatic lower extremity arterial insufficiency in three ways. First, aortoiliac and femoropopliteal duplex may be used to identify percutaneous intervention targets in patients with intermittent claudication.[136] Patients found to have focal stenoses may be advised regarding potential suitability of percutaneous intervention, whereas patients with long occlusions may be counseled that surgery would likely be required to relieve symptoms. This information may help the patient and physician decide whether to proceed with angiography.[141] In addition, the duplex information helps the interventionist plan an optimal approach for treatment of the target lesion. The second and more encompassing role for duplex lies in its potential as a substitute for angiography in patients requiring aortoiliac or infrainguinal reconstruction. Several small series in the 1990s reached increasingly optimistic results.[137,138,140] Our institution published results confirming duplex ability to predict tibial level bypass and showing similar patency and limb salvage rates for bypass performed by duplex arteriography alone.[139,142] The third potential role for duplex in lower extremity evaluation lies in its potential to find suitable distal revascularization targets when none are visualized by angiography.[143] In these circumstances, performance of duplex arterial mapping requires a skilled technologist and is a relatively labor-intensive effort.

Aortoiliac and Femoropopliteal Duplex Technique

Duplex evaluation of the aorta and iliacs employs low-frequency transducers. Patients are best studied after an overnight fast. Initial positioning is supine, but right and left lateral decubitus positions may help accomplish a complete study. Examination begins below the xiphoid where the aorta is imaged in a sagittal plane. Evaluation is carried to the bifurcation, then each iliac is followed through the pelvis to the groin.[144] A 5- or 7.5-MHz transducer is typically used to study the femoral, popliteal, and tibial vessels. Evaluation of the popliteal and tibial arteries may be performed best with a combination of prone and supine positioning. The tibials are usually studied from the infrageniculate popliteal artery distally, but this portion of the study may be facilitated in patients with advanced disease by starting at the ankle and scanning cephalad. Color-flow is useful for initial vessel identification and subsequent search for stenosis. Doppler velocity sampling is performed in all patent segments. Special attention is paid to areas of stenosis, where images and spectra are recorded within, proximal to, and immediately beyond the narrowed area. Technical adequacy for identification of all vessels exceeds 90% in most reports, although evaluation of the peroneal artery is less successful.[139,145]

Aortoiliac and Femoropopliteal Duplex Interpretation and Accuracy

The most widely recommended criterion for diagnosis of peripheral artery stenosis is a 100% PSV step-up (velocity ratio ≥2) compared with a normal segment of artery proximal to the stenosis. Several investigators determined that this finding correlated closely with a 50% angiographic diameter reduction.[134-136,145] A few studies found best accuracy at velocity ratios of 2.5[146] and 3.[147] Most studies indicate that spectral broadening and loss of a previously present end-systolic reverse flow component also should be present for confident diagnosis of a 50% stenosis. Although many early studies attempted to establish multiple stenosis categories, similar to carotid disease,[135-137] most contemporary publications limit duplex interpretation to (1) patent without significant stenosis, (2) patent with stenosis 50% or greater, or (3) occluded.[138,145,148] Identification of peripheral stenoses by color Doppler imaging without Doppler velocity data has been examined, and the results were predictably poor.[149]

Accuracy data have been compiled using angiography or the determination of best lower extremity bypass target as gold standards. In the aorta and iliac segments, sensitivities from 81% to 91% and specificities from 90% to 99% were determined in blinded comparisons of duplex with angiography.[135,136,141,145,146,148] For identification of femoral and popliteal stenoses, reported accuracy covers a wider range, with sensitivities from 67% to 91% and specificities from 94% to 99%.[135,136,145] Fewer studies compare duplex evaluation of tibial lesions with angiography. Moneta and colleagues[145] evaluated the ability of duplex to determine interruption of patency from tibial origin to ankle. They found sensitivity and specificity of 90% and 93% for anterior and posterior tibial artery stenosis, but lower values (82% and 74%) for the peroneal artery. A study from Dartmouth also noted the shortcomings of duplex arteriography in evaluation of the peroneal artery. Only 5 of 10 peroneal arteries used as bypass graft recipients were selected correctly by duplex, and there was a 20% failure rate of duplex in identification of the peroneal.[139] Sensier and associates[150,151] found substantial agreement between color-flow duplex and arteriography at all arterial levels, but the correspondence was less good for tibial vessels.

Several studies have tested the accuracy of duplex arterial mapping for operative planning before infrainguinal revascularization. Wilson and coworkers[140] performed 44 femorocrural reconstructions for critical ischemia after contrast angiography and duplex mapping. Angiography correctly identified a suitable target artery in 73% of cases but was indeterminate, failed to identify any target, or identified an inferior target in the remainder. Duplex correctly identified a suitable runoff vessel in all patients. The authors concluded that duplex was superior to angiography for preoperative assessment of runoff vessels during this form of reconstruction. Ligush and coworkers[138] performed a similar prospective analysis of 36 patients whose eventual surgical treatment included 34 vascular reconstructions and 4 amputations. Five of the revascularizations were inflow procedures; the remainder were infrainguinal. Duplex allowed correct prediction of surgical treatment in 83% of cases, whereas angiography was correct in 90% (not statistically different). The authors concluded that duplex could be used reliably to predict vascular reconstruction strategies.

The Dartmouth group reported equivalent bypass patency and limb salvage rates when reconstructions based only on duplex mapping were compared with demographically matched historical controls who underwent similar procedures based on contrast arteriography.[142] In addition, this group reported a blinded comparison of preoperative duplex ultrasound scanning and contrast arteriography for planning tibial-level revascularization.[139] Duplex correctly predicted the outflow target in 88% of patients compared with 93% for arteriography.

An important question in duplex analysis of lower extremity arterial disease is the ability of duplex to identify distal stenoses in the presence of multilevel disease. Sensier and coworkers[150] addressed the question directly by comparing the accuracy of duplex with angiography in regions of isolated stenosis and regions where adjacent stenoses were present. They found that duplex assessment was not adversely affected by adjacent stenosis. Ligush and coworkers[138] made a similar observation, although their study was not designed to test this question directly. Despite these optimistic results from several centers, it seems that duplex-based distal bypass graft surgery remains uncommon.

Arterial Bypass Graft Surveillance

Duplex surveillance of infrainguinal arterial bypass grafts has become a pillar of postoperative care after constructions performed with autogenous conduit. Identification of the failing bypass graft is crucial because meaningful long-term graft salvage is often not possible when thrombosis occurs. Clinical symptoms, such as return of ischemic symptoms, and examination findings of weak ankle pulse quality are insensitive markers for significant stenoses within failing grafts. Several studies revealed that only one third of significant graft stenoses could be diagnosed by history and physical examination.[152-154] Early publications argued for and against the benefit of Doppler-derived ankle/arm pressure index to detect failing vein grafts, but at best this index is an insensitive parameter to follow.[155,156]

Early reports suggesting that failing bypass conduits could be identified by duplex were published by Bandyk and Mills and their colleagues.[157,158] Bandyk and colleagues[157] reported that Doppler-derived low peak systolic velocity (<45 cm/sec) and absent diastolic forward flow were predictive of impending graft failure. Mills and colleagues[158] confirmed the predictive utility of a low PSV in a large cohort of reversed vein grafts. Low PSV may be caused by inflow stenosis, sampling beyond a graft stenosis, or even poor runoff. Low PSV also may be normally present in large-caliber grafts. These early bypass sampling techniques have been supplanted in most laboratories by studies that involve scanning the entire graft, searching not only for low velocities, but also for high velocities (with calculation of PSV ratios) and for flow disturbances and loss of the typical Doppler flow pattern.

Arterial Bypass Graft Surveillance Technique

The study is typically performed using transmitting frequencies of 4 to 7.5 MHz. Knowledge of the origin, insertion, and route of the bypass expedites performance of the examination. In situ grafts are usually easy to identify in their subcutaneous route, whereas grafts in anatomic or extra-anatomic tunnels are more challenging. Scanning begins at the inflow artery, crosses the proximal anastomosis, and proceeds distally along the body of the graft to include the distal anastomosis. Color-flow imaging may provide rapid identification of regions with high-velocity or disturbed flow patterns, and Doppler spectral analysis may focus on these areas. To calculate a velocity ratio, a Doppler spectrum must also be recorded proximal to the stenosis in a region of undisturbed flow (Fig. 16-13). Careful angle adjustment is required at the distal anastomosis where the graft may approach the outflow artery at a steep angle. If low PSV (<45 cm/sec) is identified throughout the graft, a search may be undertaken for inflow and outflow disease. As noted, low PSV may be a normal finding in a large-diameter graft, especially basilic vein.

Arterial Graft Surveillance Diagnostic Thresholds and Accuracy

Idu and Mattos and their coworkers published results of graft surveillance protocols similar to that just described.[154,159] Both reports concluded that color-flow duplex surveillance successfully detected graft-threatening stenoses and that

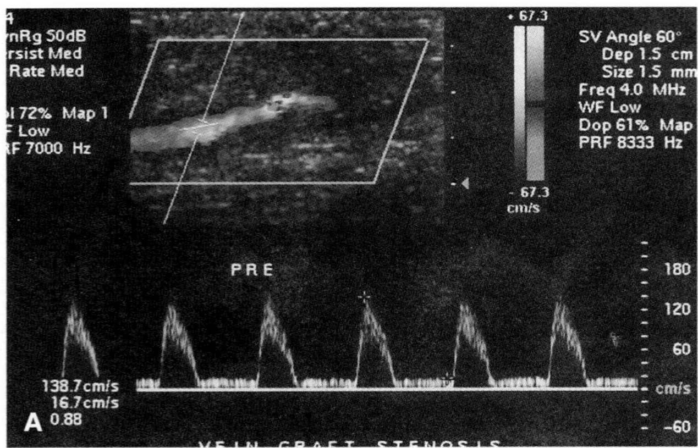

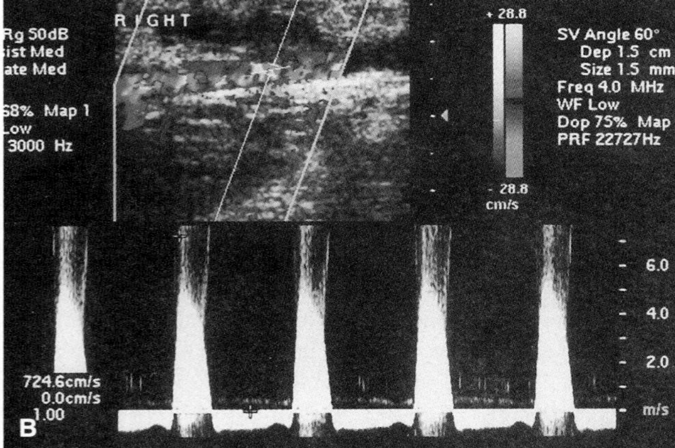

FIGURE 16-13 **A,** Bypass graft Doppler spectrum proximal to stenosis reveals a PSV of 139 cm/sec with a clear systolic window. **B,** Region of bypass stenosis with markedly elevated PSV (725 cm/sec), spectral broadening, and tissue vibration indicated by color pixels outside the flow channel.

elective repair of stenotic lesions within saphenous vein arterial bypass grafts significantly prolonged patency. Although these were not prospective, randomized trials, the studies were thoroughly analyzed. They identified an improvement in assisted primary patency of approximately 20% at 3 to 5 years compared with grafts that were not revised when stenoses were identified or with grafts undergoing only clinical follow-up.

Fillinger and colleagues[160] employed duplex surveillance techniques to evaluate in-situ grafts that remained free of stenosis. These authors found that normally functioning conduits remodel over time such that diameter, volume flow rate, PSV, and shear stress tend to stabilize at uniform values regardless of the initial vein graft diameter. Grafts with small initial diameters enlarged, whereas grafts with large diameters underwent eventual reduction in caliber, such that no significant difference in diameter was present at 1 year postplacement. Of the hemodynamic variables studied, shear stress correlated most strongly with the change in diameter over time. In the absence of focal graft-threatening stenosis, human saphenous vein appears capable of adapting to its hemodynamic environment by modulating diameter to normalize shear stress.

For arterial bypass grafts with developing stenosis, the optimal threshold for intervention is an area of intense investigation. Diagnostic criteria have evolved primarily toward use of the PSV ratio, defined as the highest PSV within a stenosis divided by the PSV within a nonstenotic proximal section of the bypass. Recommended threshold ratios in the literature range from 1.5 to 4, with higher values found in more recent reports.[154,159,161-166] Bandyk's group now recommends intervention based on a combination of PSV ratio greater than 3.4 plus a PSV greater than 300 cm/sec.[164] Likewise, Westerband and coworkers[165] successfully tested a PSV ratio of 3.5 and a PSV greater than 300 cm/sec for identification of graft-threatening stenoses. These latter authors found it additionally important to retain consideration of low-velocity criteria in searching for failing grafts. Although both groups tested some of the highest recommended thresholds in the literature, few bypass grafts failed while under active surveillance, and their graft patency rates were excellent.

The highest velocity ratio threshold (>4) was recommended by Idu and associates.[166] After a prospective analysis, surgical revision without prior angiography was recommended if such a level were encountered. Although still an area undergoing investigation, the current literature supports relative safety in deferring graft revision until a stenosis reaches a velocity ratio of at least 3.4. Similar to all other areas of duplex interpretation, each laboratory should track clinical and angiographic results to determine optimal thresholds for bypass elective revision at their own institution.

Duplex Features of Graft Stenosis That Predict Successful Percutaneous Transluminal Angioplasty

Endovascular treatment for acquired vein graft stenosis is an evolving therapy among open surgical options, which include vein patch angioplasty, interposition grafting, and jump grafting. Gonsalves and associates[167] showed that the selection of candidates for treatment by percutaneous transluminal angioplasty may be based on duplex findings including stenosis severity, lesion length, vein caliber, and time of appearance. Duplex features of the stenosis judged suitable for endovascular treatment include (1) vein diameter greater than 3.5 mm, (2) stenosis length less than 2 cm, (3) appearance time more than 3 months after surgery, and (4) stenosis severity showing PSV of greater than 300 cm/sec with PSV ratio greater than 3.5. In this study, 525 infrainguinal vein bypasses were monitored by duplex, and 118 (22%) underwent revision for stenoses identified by duplex. There were 62 lesions treated by open surgical revision, whereas 56 were treated by percutaneous transluminal angioplasty. Identical 63% stenosis-free patency was identified in the two groups at 2 years' follow-up. An important observation of this study is that lesions appearing in less than 3 months, residual graft stenoses, diffuse stenoses, and focal lesions in small-diameter vein grafts (<3.5 mm) all are poor choices for percutaneous intervention because the failure rate is high (>50% within 3 months).

Ultrasound-Guided Treatment of Pseudoaneurysms

Pseudoaneurysm formation after percutaneous femoral

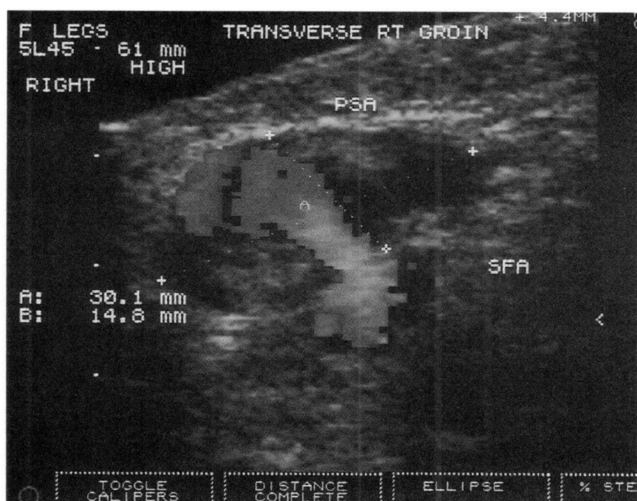

FIGURE 16-14 Pseudoaneurysm (PSA) arising from superficial femoral artery (SFA) just beyond femoral bifurcation. PSA is partially thrombosed. Swirling blood is seen in remainder. Thrombin injection is frequently successful in achieving complete thrombosis.

artery catheterization is a common occurrence in most medical centers (Fig. 16-14). Ultrasound-guided compression was described in 1991, making it perhaps the first therapeutic maneuver in noninvasive vascular technology.[168] Several subsequent series proved the safety of this technique, but efficacy is modest, and the procedure is uncomfortable for patient and provider.[169-172]

Injection of thrombin into the pseudoaneurysm under duplex ultrasound guidance has now replaced compression as treatment for postcatheterization pseudoaneurysms. This technique is safe and effective. It reduces physical effort and time requirements for the technologist and is significantly less uncomfortable for the patient.[173,174] The technique is performed using a 4- to 7-MHz linear-array transducer. A solution of bovine thrombin (1000 U/mL) is prepared fresh by adding 1 mL of sterile normal saline solution to a 1000-U vial of thrombin powder. The solution is loaded into a syringe attached to a long 22- or 25-gauge needle. The ultrasound transducer is positioned directly over the pseudoaneurysm, and the adjacent skin is sterilely prepared. The needle tip is inserted into the center of the aneurysm under ultrasound guidance. This is best visualized without color flow. Color flow is turned on, and 0.5 to 1 mL (500 to 1000 IU) of thrombin solution is injected into the pseudoaneurysm over several seconds. Continuous duplex imaging allows real-time monitoring of pseudoaneurysm thrombosis. Additional thrombin (0.5 to 1 mL) can be injected if complete thrombosis is not obtained with the initial dose.

Kang and associates[174] successfully treated 20 of 21 consecutive postcatheterization pseudoaneurysms; 15 thrombosed immediately after one injection, and 5 required a second thrombin dose. This group subsequently reported expanded indications for ultrasound-guided thrombin injection in 83 patients.[175] This technique is most appropriate for postcatheterization pseudoaneurysms with long thin necks, but it is usually not the right treatment choice for bypass graft anastomotic pseudoaneurysms.

Duplex Surveillance of Abdominal Aortic Stent Grafts
Duplex scanning has become an adjunctive study for postoperative follow-up after endovascular abdominal aortic aneurysm repair.[176,177] Duplex is less expensive than computed tomography (CT), and it delivers no ionizing radiation. Duplex scanning can detect endoleaks, limb stenosis, occlusions, and significant pathologic conditions in the native aorta, visceral vessels, and iliac arteries. Duplex also can follow maximal aneurysm diameter. On the negative side, this examination may be technically difficult in obese patients, and it is operator dependent. The study is best performed after an overnight fast and possibly even a bowel preparation. Technologist experience is essential, as is knowledge of endografts and endoleaks. Knowledge of the patient's specific endograft configuration is also valuable. Finally, the use of intravenous ultrasound contrast agents improves sensitivity and specificity of this examination.

Endoleak surveillance is best performed with sensitive color-flow Doppler scale settings to show low-flow channels. Coronal views with the patient in a decubitus position may improve image quality. Pulsed Doppler spectral waveform sampling of extrastent flow is used to document flow direction. Most branch vessel endoleaks have "to-and-fro" waveforms. Gray-scale images of some endoleaks are characterized by pulsatile echolucencies adjacent to the stent graft. Small, low-flow leaks may be seen as tiny color spots at the stent wall during diastole.

Accuracy of duplex scanning for detection of endoleak is on the order of 80% to 85%, and there is a higher incidence of indeterminate studies compared with CT scanning.[178] Wolf and associates[179] compared CT and duplex over a 30-month postendograft follow-up. Duplex had 81% sensitivity, 95% specificity, 94% positive predictive value, and 90% negative predictive value when CT was used as the gold standard for aneurysm size, presence of endoleak, and graft patency.

To increase the sensitivity of duplex scanning for endoleak, intravenous contrast agents have been used. Not only can endoleak be documented by duplex ultrasonography, but also some centers believe that intrasac flow velocities can predict sealing of type II endoleaks after endovascular aneurysm repair. This predictive ability is important because it is not yet known whether treatment of these branch vessels to eliminate the type II endoleak reduces the subsequent risk of rupture. Arko and coworkers[180] concluded that low-velocity endoleaks (<80 cm/sec) are likely to thrombose without treatment, whereas high-velocity endoleaks (>100 cm/sec) were associated with large branch vessel diameter (>7 mm).

■ SUMMARY

Duplex ultrasound scanning plays a crucial role in current vascular surgery practice. As imaging techniques of ultrasound, CT, and magnetic resonance improve, their relative value and utility for specific vascular disease tasks also will evolve. The availability of rapid and readily interpretable duplex ultrasound imaging to the vascular surgeon for everyday use would seem to ensure its presence for the foreseeable future.

■ REFERENCES

1. Zwolak RM: Expert commentary: Carotid endarterectomy without angiography: Are we ready? Vasc Surg 31:1-9, 1997.
2. Roederer GO, Langlois YE, Chan AW, et al: Ultrasonic duplex scanning of extracranial carotid arteries: Improved accuracy using new features from the common carotid artery. J Cardiovasc Ultrasonography 1:373-380, 1982.
3. Roederer GO, Langlois YE, Jager KA, et al: A simple spectral parameter for accurate classification of severe carotid disease. Bruit 8:174-178, 1984.
4. Primozich JC: Extracranial arterial system. In Strandness DE (ed): Duplex Scanning in Vascular Disorders. Philadelphia, Lippincott Williams & Wilkins, 2002, pp 191-231.
5. North American Symptomatic Carotid Endarterectomy Trial Collaborators: Beneficial effect of carotid endarterectomy in symptomatic patients with high-grade carotid stenosis. N Engl J Med 325:445-453, 1991.
6. Executive Committee for the Asymptomatic Carotid Atherosclerosis Study: Endarterectomy for asymptomatic carotid artery stenosis. JAMA 273:1421-1428, 1995.
7. Barber FE, Baker DW, Strandness DEJ, et al: Duplex scanner II: For simultaneous imaging of artery tissues and flow. 1974 Ultrasonic Symposium Proceedings. IEEE #74 CH0 896-ISU:744-748, 1974.
8. Blackshear WM, Phillips DJ, Chikos PM, et al: Carotid artery velocity patterns in normal and stenotic vessels. Stroke 11:67-71, 1980.
9. Hunink MGM, Polak JF, Barlan MM, O'Leary DH: Detection and quantification of carotid artery stenosis: Efficacy of various Doppler velocity parameters. AJR Am J Roentgenol 160:619-625, 1993.
10. Moneta GL, Edwards JM, Chitwood RW, et al: Correlation of North American Symptomatic Carotid Endarterectomy Trial (NASCET) angiographic definition of 70% to 99% internal carotid artery stenosis with duplex scanning. J Vasc Surg 17:152-159, 1993.
11. Faught WE, Mattos MA, van Bemmelen PS, et al: Color-flow duplex scanning of carotid arteries: New velocity criteria based on receiver operator characteristic analysis for threshold stenoses used in the symptomatic and asymptomatic carotid trials. J Vasc Surg 19:818-828, 1994.
12. Neale ML, Chambers JL, Kelly AT, et al: Reappraisal of duplex criteria to assess significant carotid stenosis with special reference to reports from the North American Symptomatic Carotid Endarterectomy Trial and the European Carotid Surgery Trial. J Vasc Surg 20:642-649, 1994.
13. Carpenter JP, Lexa FJ, Davis JT: Determination of sixty percent or greater carotid artery stenosis by duplex Doppler ultrasonography. J Vasc Surg 22:697-705, 1995.
14. Moneta GL, Edwards JM, Papanicolaou G, et al: Screening for asymptomatic internal carotid artery stenosis: Duplex criteria for discriminating 60% to 99% stenosis. J Vasc Surg 21:989-994, 1995.
15. Fillinger MF, Baker RJ, Zwolak RM, et al: Carotid duplex criteria for a 60% or greater angiographic stenosis: Variation according to equipment. J Vasc Surg 24:856-864, 1996.
16. Kuntz KM, Polak JF, Whittemore AD, et al: Duplex ultrasound criteria for the identification of carotid stenosis should be laboratory specific. Stroke 28:597-602, 1997.
17. AbuRahma AF, Robinson PA, Strickler DL, et al: Proposed new duplex classification for threshold stenoses used in various symptomatic and asymptomatic carotid endarterectomy trials. Ann Vasc Surg 12:349-358, 1998.
18. Filis KA, Arko FR, Johnson BL, et al: Duplex ultrasound criteria for defining the severity of carotid stenosis. Ann Vasc Surg 16:413-421, 2002.
19. Barnett HJ, Taylor DW, Eliasziw M, et al: Benefit of carotid endarterectomy in patients with symptomatic moderate or severe stenosis. North American Symptomatic Carotid Endarterectomy Trial Collaborators. N Engl J Med 339:1415-1425, 1998.
20. Grant EG, Benson CB, Moneta GL, et al: Carotid artery stenosis: Grayscale and Doppler US diagnosis. Society of Radiologists in Ultrasound consensus conference. Radiology 229:340-346, 2003.
21. Daigle RJ, Stavros AT, Lee RM: Overestimation of velocity and frequency values by multielement linear array Dopplers. J Vasc Technol 14:206-212, 1990.
22. Howard G, Baker WH, Chambless LE, et al: An approach for the use of Doppler ultrasound as a screening tool for hemodynamically significant stenosis (despite heterogeneity of Doppler performance). Stroke 26:1951-1957, 1996.
23. Pan XM, Saloner D, Reilly LM, et al: Assessment of carotid artery stenosis by ultrasonography, conventional angiography, and magnetic resonance angiography: Correlation with ex vivo measurement of plaque stenosis. J Vasc Surg 21:82-89, 1995.
24. Suwanwela N, Can U, Furie FL, et al: Carotid Doppler ultrasound criteria for internal carotid artery stenosis based on residual lumen diameter calculated from en bloc carotid endarterectomy specimens. Stroke 27:1965-1969, 1996.
25. Polak JF: Role of duplex US as a screening test for carotid atherosclerotic disease: Benefit without cost? Radiology 197:581-582, 1995.
26. Ricotta JJ, Holen J, Schenk E, et al: Is routine angiography necessary prior to carotid endarterectomy? J Vasc Surg 1:96-102, 1984.
27. Goodson SF, Flanigan DP, Bishara RA, et al: Can carotid duplex scanning supplant arteriography in patients with focal carotid artery symptoms? J Vasc Surg 5:551-557, 1987.
28. Moore WS, Ziomek S, Quinones-Baldrich WJ, et al: Can clinical evaluation and noninvasive testing substitute for arteriography in the evaluation of carotid artery disease? Ann Surg 208:91-94, 1988.
29. Gelabert HA, Moore WS: Carotid endarterectomy without angiography. Surg Clin North Am 70:213-223, 1990.
30. Hill JC, Carbonneau K, Baliga PK, et al: Safe extracranial vascular evaluation and surgery without preoperative arteriography. Ann Vasc Surg 4:34-38, 1990.
31. Dawson DL, Zierler RE, Kohler TR: Role of arteriography in the preoperative evaluation of carotid artery disease. Am J Surg 16:619-624, 1991.
32. Gertler JP, Cambria RP, Kistler JP, et al: Carotid surgery without arteriography: Noninvasive selection of patients. Ann Vasc Surg 5:253-256, 1991.
33. Wagner WH, Treiman RL, Cossman DV, et al: The diminishing role of diagnostic arteriography in carotid artery disease: Duplex scanning as definitive preoperative study. Ann Vasc Surg 5:105-110, 1991.
34. Cartier R, Cartier P, Fontaine A: Carotid endarterectomy without angiography: The reliability of Doppler ultrasonography and duplex scanning in preoperative assessment. Can J Surg 36:411-416, 1993.
35. McKittrick JE, Cisek PL, Pojunas KW, et al: Are both color-flow duplex scanning and cerebral arteriography required prior to carotid endarterectomy? Ann Vasc Surg 7:311-316, 1993.
36. Horn M, Michelini M, Greisler HP, et al: Carotid endarterectomy without arteriography: The preeminent role of the vascular laboratory. Ann Vasc Surg 8:221-224, 1994.
37. Lustgarten JH, Solomon RA, Quest DO, et al: Carotid endarterectomy after noninvasive evaluation by duplex ultrasonography and magnetic resonance angiography. Neurosurgery 34:612-619, 1994.
38. Mattos MA, Hodgson KJ, Faught WE, et al: Carotid endarterectomy without angiography: Is color-flow duplex scanning insufficient? Surgery 116:776-783, 1994.
39. Kent KC, Kuntz KM, Patel MR, et al: Perioperative imaging strategies for carotid endarterectomy. JAMA 274:888-893, 1995.
40. Patel MR, Kuntz KM, Klufas RA, et al: Preoperative assessment of the carotid bifurcation: Can magnetic resonance angiography and duplex ultrasonography replace contrast arteriography? Stroke 26:1753-1758, 1995.
41. Muto PM, Welch HJ, Mackey WC, O'Donnell TF: Evaluation of carotid artery stenosis: Is duplex ultrasonography sufficient? J Vasc Surg 24:17-24, 1996.
42. Shifrin EG, Bornstein NM, Kantarovsky A, et al: Carotid endarterectomy without angiography. Br J Surg 83:1107-1109, 1996.
43. Zaweski JE, Musson AM, Zwolak RM: Carotid endarterectomy without angiography: Guidelines for duplex evaluation. J Vasc Tech 20:151-156, 1996.

44. Geuder JW, Lamarello PJ, Riles TS, et al: Is duplex scanning sufficient evaluation before carotid endarterectomy? J Vasc Surg 9:193-201, 1989.
45. Schwartz SW, Chambless LE, Baker WH, et al: Consistency of Doppler parameters in predicting arteriographically confirmed carotid stenosis. Stroke 28:343-347, 1997.
46. Wain RA, Lyon RT, Veith FJ, et al: Accuracy of duplex ultrasound in evaluating carotid artery anatomy before endarterectomy. J Vasc Surg 27:235-244, 1998.
47. Spadone DP, Barkmeier LD, Hodgson KJ, et al: Contralateral internal carotid artery stenosis or occlusion: Pitfall of correct ipsilateral classification: A study performed with color-flow imaging. J Vasc Surg 11:642-649, 1990.
48. Fujitani RM, Mills JL, Wang LM, Taylor SM: The effect of unilateral internal carotid artery occlusion upon contralateral duplex study: Criteria for accurate interpretation. J Vasc Surg 16:459-468, 1992.
49. Walters GK, Jescovitch AJ, Jones CE: The influence of contralateral carotid stenosis on duplex accuracy: The role of collateral cerebral flow. J Vasc Technol 19:111-114, 1995.
50. Welch HJ, Murphy MC, Raftery KB, Jewell ER: Carotid duplex with contralateral disease: The influence of vertebral artery blood flow. Ann Vasc Surg 14:82-88, 2000.
51. Abou-Zamzam AM Jr, Moneta GL, Edwards JM, et al: Is a single preoperative duplex scan sufficient for planning bilateral carotid endarterectomy? J Vasc Surg 31:282-288, 2000.
52. Westerband A, Mills JL, Berman SS, Hunter GC: The influence of routine completion arteriography on outcome following carotid endarterectomy. Ann Vasc Surg 11:14-19, 1997.
53. Bandyk DF, Kaebnick HW, Adams MB, Towne JB: Turbulence occurring after carotid bifurcation endarterectomy: A harbinger of residual and recurrent carotid stenosis. J Vasc Surg 7:261-274, 1988.
54. Sawchuk AP, Flanigan DP, Machi J, et al: The fate of unrepaired minor technical defects detected by intraoperative ultrasonography during carotid endarterectomy. J Vasc Surg 9:671-676, 1989.
55. Baker WH, Koustas G, Burke K, et al: Intraoperative duplex scanning and late carotid artery stenosis. J Vasc Surg 19:829-833, 1994.
56. Lipski DA, Bergamini TM, Garrison RN, Fulton RL: Intraoperative duplex scanning reduces the incidence of residual stenosis after carotid endarterectomy. J Surg Res 60:317-320, 1996.
57. Bandyk DF, Mills JL, Gahtan V, Esses GE: Intraoperative duplex scanning of arterial reconstructions: Fate of repaired and unrepaired defects. J Vasc Surg 20:426-433, 1994.
58. Johnson BL, Gupta AK, Bandyk DF, et al: Anatomic patterns of carotid endarterectomy healing. Am J Surg 172:188-190, 1996.
59. Ascher E, Markevich N, Kallakuri S, et al: Intraoperative carotid artery duplex scanning in a modern series of 650 consecutive primary endarterectomy procedures. J Vasc Surg 39:416-420, 2004.
60. Robbin ML, Lockhart ME, Weber TM, et al: Carotid artery stents: Early and intermediate follow-up with Doppler US. Radiology 205:749-756, 1997.
61. Ringer AJ, German JW, Guterman LR, Hopkins LN: Follow-up of stented carotid arteries by Doppler ultrasound. Neurosurgery 51:639-643, 2002.
62. Lal BK, Hobson RW 2nd, Goldstein J, et al: Carotid artery stenting: Is there a need to revise ultrasound velocity criteria? J Vasc Surg 39:58-66, 2004.
63. Ackerstaff RGA, Hoeneveld H, Slowikowski JM: Ultrasonic duplex scanning in atherosclerotic disease of the innominate, subclavian, and vertebral arteries: A comparative study with angiography. Ultrasound Med Biol 10:409-418, 1984.
64. Brunholzl C, von Reutern GM: Hemodynamic effects of innominate artery occlusive disease: Evaluation by Doppler ultrasound. Ultrasound Med Biol 15:201-204, 1989.
65. Verlato F, Grego F, Avruscio GP, et al: Diagnosis of high-grade stenosis of innominate artery. Angiology 44:845-851, 1993.
66. Ligush JJ, Criado E, Keagy BA: Innominate artery occlusive disease: Management with central reconstructive techniques. Surgery 121:556-562, 1997.
67. Bendick PJ, Jackson VP: Evaluation of the vertebral arteries with duplex sonography. J Vasc Surg 3:523-530, 1986.
68. Bartels E, Flugel KA: Evaluation of extracranial vertebral artery dissection with duplex color-flow imaging. Stroke 27:290-295, 1996.
69. Kaneko A, Ohno R, Hattori K, et al: Color-coded Doppler imaging of subclavian steal syndrome. Intern Med 37:259-264, 1998.
70. Ries S, Steinke W, Devuyst G, et al: Power Doppler imaging and color Doppler flow imaging for the evaluation of normal and pathological vertebral arteries. J Neuroimaging 8:71-74, 1998.
71. Aaslid R, Markwalder TM, Nornes H: Noninvasive transcranial Doppler ultrasound recording of flow velocity in basal cerebral arteries. J Neurosurg 57:769-774, 1982.
72. Gaunt ME, Martin PJ, Smith JL, et al: Clinical relevance of intraoperative embolization detected by transcranial Doppler ultrasonography during carotid endarterectomy: A prospective study of 100 patients. Br J Surg 81:1435-1439, 1994.
73. Ackerstaff RG, Jansen C, Moll FL, et al: The significance of microemboli detection by means of transcranial Doppler ultrasonography monitoring in carotid endarterectomy. J Vasc Surg 21:963-969, 1995.
74. Lennard N, Smith J, Dumville J, et al: Prevention of postoperative thrombotic stroke after carotid endarterectomy: The role of transcranial Doppler ultrasound. J Vasc Surg 26:579-584, 1997.
75. Arnold M, Sturzenegger M, Schaffler L, Seiler RW: Continuous intraoperative monitoring of middle cerebral artery blood flow velocities and electroencephalography during carotid endarterectomy: A comparison of the two methods to detect cerebral ischemia. Stroke 28:1345-1350, 1997.
76. Cao P, Giordano G, Zannetti S, et al: Transcranial Doppler monitoring during carotid endarterectomy: Is it appropriate for selecting patients in need of a shunt? J Vasc Surg 26:973-980, 1997.
77. Schneider PA, Rossman ME, Torem S, et al: Transcranial Doppler in the management of extracranial cerebrovascular disease: Implications in diagnosis and monitoring. J Vasc Surg 7:223-231, 1988.
78. Gaunt ME, Ratliff DA, Martin PJ, et al: On-table diagnosis of incipient carotid artery thrombosis during carotid endarterectomy by transcranial Doppler scanning. J Vasc Surg 20:104-107, 1994.
79. Bass A, Krupski WC, Schneider PA, et al: Intraoperative transcranial Doppler: Limitations of the method. J Vasc Surg 10:549-553, 1989.
80. Spencer MP: Transcranial Doppler monitoring and causes of stroke from carotid endarterectomy. Stroke 28:685-691, 1997.
81. Smith WB: Transcranial Doppler monitoring for carotid endarterectomy. In Strandness DE Jr (ed): Duplex Scanning in Vascular Surgery. Philadelphia, Lippincott Williams & Wilkins, 2002, pp 244-248.
82. Cantelmo NL, Babikian VL, Johnson WC, et al: Correlation of transcranial Doppler and noninvasive tests with angiography in the evaluation of extracranial carotid disease. J Vasc Surg 11:786-792, 1990.
83. Comerota AJ, Katz ML, Hosking JD, et al: Is transcranial Doppler a worthwhile addition to screening tests for cerebrovascular disease? J Vasc Surg 21:90-97, 1995.
84. Can U, Furie KL, Suwanwela N, et al: Transcranial Doppler ultrasound criteria for hemodynamically significant internal carotid artery stenosis based on residual lumen diameter calculated from en bloc endarterectomy specimens. Stroke 28:1966-1971, 1997.
85. Jorgensen LG, Schroeder TV: Defective cerebrovascular autoregulation after carotid endarterectomy. Eur J Vasc Surg 7:370-379, 1993.
86. Naylor AR, Whyman MR, Wildsmith JAW, et al: Factors influencing the hyperaemic response after carotid endarterectomy. Br J Surg 80:1523-1527, 1993.
87. Jansen C, Sprengers AM, Moll FL, et al: Prediction of intracerebral hemorrhage after carotid endarterectomy by clinical criteria and intraoperative transcranial Doppler monitoring: Results of 233 operations. Eur J Vasc Surg 8:220-225, 1994.
88. Smith WB: Transcranial Doppler: The basic examination. In Strandness DE Jr (ed): Duplex Scanning in Vascular Disorders. Philadelphia, Lippincott Williams & Wilkins, 2002, pp 232-243.
89. Schoning M, Niemann G, Hartig B: Transcranial color duplex sonography of basal cerebral arteries: Reference data of flow velocities from childhood to adulthood. Neuropediatrics 27:249-255, 1996.

90. Newell DW, Winn HR: Transcranial Doppler in cerebral vasospasm. Neurosurg Clin North Am 1:319-328, 1990.
91. Newell DW, Aaslid R: Transcranial Doppler: Clinical and experimental uses. Cerebrovasc Brain Metab Rev 4:122-143, 1992.
92. Spencer MP, Thomas GI, Nicholls SC, Sauvage LR: Detection of middle cerebral artery emboli during carotid endarterectomy using transcranial Doppler ultrasonography. Stroke 21:415-423, 1990.
93. van Zuilen EV, Moll FL, Vermeulen FEE, et al: Detection of cerebral microemboli by means of transcranial Doppler monitoring before and after carotid endarterectomy. Stroke 26:210-213, 1995.
94. Markus HS, Harrison MJ: Microembolic signal detection using ultrasound. Stroke 9:1517-1519, 1995.
95. Norris CS, Pfeiffer JS, Rittgers SE, Barnes RW: Noninvasive evaluation of renal artery stenosis and renovascular resistance. J Vasc Surg 1:192-201, 1984.
96. Cantwell-Gab K: Renal artery evaluation. In Strandness DE Jr (ed): Duplex Scanning in Vascular Disease. Philadelphia, Lippincott Williams & Wilkins, 2002, pp 300-318.
97. Isaacson J, Neumyer MM: Direct and indirect renal arterial duplex and Doppler color flow evaluations. J Vasc Tech 19:309-316, 1995.
98. Kohler TR, Zierler RE, Martin RL, et al: Noninvasive diagnosis of renal artery stenosis by ultrasonic duplex scanning. J Vasc Surg 4:450-456, 1986.
99. Taylor DC, Kettler MD, Moneta GL, et al: Duplex ultrasound scanning in the diagnosis of renal artery stenosis: A prospective evaluation. J Vasc Surg 7:363-369, 1988.
100. Hansen KJ, Tribble RW, Reavis SW, et al: Renal duplex sonography: Evaluation of clinical utility. J Vasc Surg 12:227-236, 1990.
101. Hoffmann U, Edwards JM, Carter S, et al: Role of duplex scanning for the detection of atherosclerotic renal artery disease. Kidney Int 39:1232-1239, 1991.
102. Olin JW, Piedmonte MR, Young JR, et al: The utility of duplex ultrasound scanning of the renal arteries for diagnosing significant renal artery stenosis. Ann Intern Med 122:833-837, 1995.
103. Martin RL, Nanra RS, et al: Renal hilar Doppler analysis in the detection of renal artery stenosis. J Vasc Tech 15:173-180, 1989.
104. Handa N, Fukunaga R, Etani H: Efficacy of echo-Doppler examination for the evaluation of renovascular disease. Ultrasound Med Biol 14:1-5, 1988.
105. Schwerk WB, Restrepo IK, Stellwaag M, et al: Renal artery stenosis: Grading with image-directed Doppler US evaluation of renal resistive index. Radiology 190:785-790, 1994.
106. McLeary MS, Rouse GA: Tardus-parvus Doppler signals in the renal arteries: A sign of pediatric thoracoabdominal aortic coarctations. Am J Radiol 167:521-523, 1996.
107. Eidt JF, Fry RE, Clagett GP, et al: Postoperative follow-up of renal artery reconstruction with duplex ultrasound. J Vasc Surg 8:667-673, 1988.
108. Taylor DC, Houston TM, Anderson C, et al: Follow-up of renal and mesenteric artery revascularization with duplex ultrasonography. Can J Surg 39:17-20, 1996.
109. Grim CE, Luft FC, Yune HJ, et al: Percutaneous transluminal dilatation in the treatment of renal vascular hypertension. Ann Intern Med 95:439-442, 1981.
110. Geyskes GG, Puylaert CBAJ, Oei HY, Mees EJ: Follow up study of 70 patients with renal artery stenosis treated by percutaneous transluminal dilatation. BMJ 287:333-336, 1983.
111. Svetkey LP, Kadir S, Dunnick NR: Similar prevalence of renovascular hypertension in selected blacks and whites. Hypertension 17:678-683, 1991.
112. Mann SJ, Pickering TG, Sos TA, et al: Captopril renography in the diagnosis of renal artery stenosis: Accuracy and limitations. Am J Med 90:30-40, 1991.
113. Fommei E, Ghione S, Hilson AJ: Captopril radionucleotide test in renovascular hypertension: A European multicentre study. Eur J Nucl Med 20:617-623, 1993.
114. Radermacher J, Vitzhum A, Stoess B: Resistive index and improvement of renal function after correction of renal artery stenosis [abstract]. J Am Soc Nephrol 7:1554, 1996.
115. Radermacher J, Chavan A, Bleck J, et al: Use of Doppler ultrasonography to predict the outcome of therapy for renal-artery stenosis. N Engl J Med 344:410-417, 2001.
116. Mukherjee D, Bhatt DL, Robbins M, et al: Renal artery end-diastolic velocity and renal artery resistance index as predictors of outcome after renal stenting. Am J Cardiol 88:1064-1066, 2001.
117. Neumyer MM, Gifford RRM, Thiele BL: Identification of early rejection in renal allografts with duplex ultrasound. J Vasc Tech 12:19-25, 1988.
118. Neumyer MM: Ultrasonographic assessment of renal and pancreatic transplants. J Vasc Tech 19:321-329, 1991.
119. Sorrell K, Blackshear B, Fogle M: Diagnosis of occlusive renal vein thrombosis in renal allografts by duplex ultrasonography. J Vasc Tech 16:119-123, 1992.
120. Frauchiger B, Bock A, Eichlisberger R, et al: The values of different resistive parameters in distinguishing biopsy-proved dysfunction of renal allografts. Nephrol Dial Transplant 10:527-532, 1995.
121. Radermacher J, Mengel M, Ellis S, et al: The renal arterial resistance index and renal allograft survival. N Engl J Med 349:115-124, 2003.
122. Jager KA, Fortner GS, Thiele BL, Strandness DE Jr: Noninvasive diagnosis of intestinal angina. J Clin Ultrasound 12:588-591, 1984.
123. Bowersox JC, Zwolak RM, Walsh DB, et al: Duplex ultrasonography in the diagnosis of celiac and mesenteric artery occlusive disease. J Vasc Surg 14:780-790, 1991.
124. Moneta GL, Yeager RA, Dalman R, et al: Duplex ultrasound criteria for diagnosis of splanchnic artery stenosis or occlusion. J Vasc Surg 14:511-520, 1991.
125. O'Connor SE, LaBombard E, Musson AM, Zwolak RM: Duplex imaging of distal splenorenal shunts. J Vasc Technol 15:28-31, 1991.
126. Grant EG, Melany M: Doppler imaging of the liver. J Vasc Tech 19:277-284, 1995.
127. Sorrell K: The role of color flow duplex ultrasonography in portosystemic shunts. J Vasc Tech 19:285-293, 1995.
128. Rizzo RJ, Sandager G, Astleford P, et al: Mesenteric flow velocity variations as a function of angle of insonation. J Vasc Surg 11:688-694, 1990.
129. Kadir S: Celiac, superior, and inferior mesenteric arteries. In Kadir S (ed): Atlas of Normal and Variant Angiographic Anatomy. Philadelphia, WB Saunders, 1991, pp 297-364.
130. Zwolak RM, Fillinger MF, Walsh DB, et al: Mesenteric and celiac duplex scanning: A validation study. J Vasc Surg 27:1078-1088, 1998.
131. LaBombard FE, Musson A, Bowersox JC, Zwolak RM: Hepatic artery duplex as an adjunct in the evaluation of chronic mesenteric ischemia. J Vasc Tech 16:7-11, 1992.
132. Moneta GL, Lee RW, Yeager RA, et al: Mesenteric duplex scanning: A blinded prospective study. J Vasc Surg 17:79-86, 1993.
133. Perko MJ, Just S, Schroeder TV: Importance of diastolic velocities in the detection of celiac and mesenteric artery disease by duplex ultrasound. J Vasc Surg 26:288-293, 1997.
134. Jager KA, Phillips DJ, Martin RL, et al: Noninvasive mapping of lower limb arterial lesions. Ultrasound Med Biol 11:515-521, 1985.
135. Kohler TR, Nance DR, Cramer MM, et al: Duplex scanning for diagnosis of aortoiliac and femoropopliteal disease: A prospective study. Circulation 76:1074-1080, 1987.
136. Cossman DV, Ellison JE, Wagner WH, et al: Comparison of contrast arteriography to arterial mapping with color-flow duplex imaging in the lower extremities. J Vasc Surg 10:522-529, 1989.
137. Kohler TR, Andros G, Porter JM, et al: Can duplex scanning replace arteriography for lower extremity arterial disease? Ann Vasc Surg 4:280-287, 1990.
138. Ligush J Jr, Reavis SW, Preisser JS, Jansen KJ: Duplex ultrasound scanning defines operative strategies for patients with limb-theatening ischemia. J Vasc Surg 28:482-491, 1998.

139. Grassbaugh JA, Nelson PR, Rzucidlo EM, et al: Blinded comparison of preoperative duplex ultrasound scanning and contrast arteriography for planning revascularization at the level of the tibia. J Vasc Surg 37:1186-1190, 2003.
140. Wilson YG, George JK, Wilkins DC, Ashley S: Duplex assessment of run-off before femorocrural reconstruction. Br J Surg 84:1360-1363, 1997.
141. Currie IC, Jones AJ, Wakeley CJ, et al: Non-invasive aortoiliac assessment. Eur J Vasc Endovasc Surg 9:24-28, 1995.
142. Proia RR, Walsh DB, Nelson PR, et al: Early results of infragenicular revascularization based solely on duplex arteriography. J Vasc Surg 33:1165-1170, 2001.
143. Karacagil S, Lofberg AM, Granbo A, et al: Value of duplex scanning in evaluation of crural and foot arteries in limbs with severe lower limb ischaemia—a prospective comparison with angiography. Eur J Vasc Endovasc Surg 12:300-303, 1996.
144. Cramer MM: Color flow duplex examination of the abdominal aorta: Atherosclerosis, aneurysm, and dissection. J Vasc Tech 19:249-260, 1995.
145. Moneta GL, Yeager RA, Antonovic R, et al: Accuracy of lower extremity arterial duplex mapping. J Vasc Surg 15:275-284, 1992.
146. Legemate DA, Teeuven C, Hoeneveld H, Eikelboom BC: Value of duplex scanning compared with angiography and pressure measurement in the assessment of aortoiliac arterial lesions. Br J Surg 78:1003-1008, 1991.
147. Leng GC, Whyman MR, Donnan PT, et al: Accuracy and reproducibility of duplex ultrasonography in grading femoropopliteal stenoses. J Vasc Surg 17:510-517, 1993.
148. Moneta GL, Yeager RA, Lee RW, Porter JM: Noninvasive localization of arterial occlusive disease: A comparison of segmental Doppler pressures and arterial duplex mapping. J Vasc Surg 17:578-582, 1993.
149. Hatsukami TS, Primozich JF, Zierler RE, et al: Color Doppler imaging of infrainguinal arterial occlusive disease. J Vasc Surg 16:527-533, 1992.
150. Sensier Y, Hartshorne T, Thrush A, et al: The effect of adjacent segment disease on the accuracy of colour duplex scanning for the diagnosis of lower limb arterial disease. Eur J Vasc Endovasc Surg 12:238-242, 1996.
151. Sensier Y, Hartshorne T, Thrush A, et al: A prospective comparison of lower limb colour-coded Duplex scanning with arteriography. Eur J Vasc Endovasc Surg 11:170-175, 1996.
152. Disselhoff B, Bluth J, Jakimowicz J: Early detection of stenosis of femoral-distal grafts: A surveillance study using color-duplex scanning. Eur J Vasc Surg 3:43-48, 1989.
153. Moody P, Gould DA, Harris PL: Vein graft surveillance improves patency in femoropopliteal bypass. Eur J Vasc Surg 4:117-121, 1990.
154. Idu MM, Blankenstein JD, de Gier P, et al: Impact of a color-flow duplex surveillance program on infrainguinal vein graft patency: A five-year experience. J Vasc Surg 17:42-53, 1993.
155. Berkowitz J, Hobbs C, Roberts B, et al: Value of routine vascular laboratory studies to identify vein graft stenoses. Surgery 90:971-979, 1981.
156. Barnes RW, Thompson BW, MacDonald CM, et al: Serial noninvasive studies do not herald postoperative failure of femoropopliteal or femorotibial bypass grafts. Ann Surg 210:486-492, 1989.
157. Bandyk DF, Cato RF, Towne JB: A low flow velocity predicts failure of femoropopliteal and femorotibial bypass grafts. Surgery 98:799-809, 1985.
158. Mills JL, Harris EJ, Taylor LM Jr, et al: The importance of routine surveillance of distal bypass grafts with duplex scanning: A study of 379 reversed vein grafts. J Vasc Surg 12:379-389, 1990.
159. Mattos MA, van Bemmelen PS, Hodgson KJ, et al: Does correction of stenoses identified with color duplex scanning improve infrainguinal graft patency? J Vasc Surg 17:54-66, 1993.
160. Fillinger MF, Cronenwett JL, Besso S, et al: Vein adaptation to the hemodynamic environment of infrainguinal grafts. J Vasc Surg 19:970-979, 1994.
161. Chalmers RT, Hoballah JJ, Kresowik TF, et al: The impact of color duplex surveillance on the outcome of lower limb bypass with segments of arm veins. J Vasc Surg 19:279-288, 1994.
162. Caps MT, Cantwell-Gab K, Bergelin RO, Strandness DE Jr: Vein graft lesions: Time of onset and rate of progression. J Vasc Surg 22:466-475, 1995.
163. Bandyk DF, Johnson BL, Gupta AK, Esses GE: Nature and management of duplex abnormalities encountered during infrainguinal vein bypass grafting. J Vasc Surg 24:430-438, 1996.
164. Gupta AK, Bandyk DF, Cheanvechai D, Johnson BL: Natural history of infrainguinal vein graft stenosis relative to bypass grafting technique. J Vasc Surg 25:211-225, 1997.
165. Westerband A, Mills JL, Kistler S, et al: Prospective validation of threshold criteria for intervention in infrainguinal vein grafts undergoing duplex surveillance. Ann Vasc Surg 11:44-48, 1997.
166. Idu MM, Buth J, Hop WC, et al: Vein graft surveillance: Is graft revision without angiography justified and what criteria should be used? J Vasc Surg 27:399-413, 1998.
167. Gonsalves C, Bandyk DF, Avino A, Johnson BL: Duplex features of vein graft stenosis and the success of percutaneous transluminal angioplasty. J Endovasc Surg 6:66-72, 1999.
168. Fellmeth BD, Roberts AC, Bookstein JJ, et al: Postangiographic femoral artery injuries: Nonsurgical repair with US-guided compression. Radiology 178:671-675, 1991.
169. Schaub F, Theiss W, Heinz M, et al: New aspects in ultrasound-guided compression repair of postcatheterization femoral artery injuries. Circulation 90:1861-1865, 1994.
170. Davies AH, Hayward JK, Irvine CD, et al: Treatment of iatrogenic false aneurysm by compression ultrasonography. Br J Surg 81:1230-1231, 1995.
171. Mooney MJ, Tollefson DFJ, Andersen CA, et al: Duplex-guided compression of iatrogenic femoral pseudoaneurysms. J Am Coll Surg 181:155-159, 1995.
172. Paulson EK, Kliewer MA, Hertzberg BS, et al: Color Doppler sonography of groin complications following femoral artery catheterization. AJR Am J Roentgenol 165:439-444, 1995.
173. Liau C, Ho F, Chen M, Lee Y: Treatment of iatrogenic femoral artery pseudoaneurysm with percutaneous thrombin injection. J Vasc Surg 26:18-23, 1997.
174. Kang SS, Labropoulos N, Mansour A, Baker WH: Percutaneous ultrasound guided thrombin injection: A new method for treating postcatheterization femoral pseudoaneurysms. J Vasc Surg 27:1032-1038, 1998.
175. Kang SS, Labropoulos N, Mansour MA, et al: Expanded indications for ultrasound-guided thrombin injection of pseudoaneurysms. J Vasc Surg 31:289-298, 2000.
176. Heilberger P, Schunn C, Ritter W: Postoperative color flow duplex scanning in aortic endografting. J Endovasc Surg 4:262-271, 1997.
177. Bendick PJ, Bove PG, Long GW, et al: Efficacy of ultrasound scan contrast agents in the noninvasive follow-up of aortic stent grafts. J Vasc Surg 37:381-385, 2003.
178. Sato DT, Goff CD, Gregory RT: Endoleak after aortic stent graft repair: Diagnosis by color duplex ultrasound scan versus computed tomography scan. J Vasc Surg 28:657-663, 1998.
179. Wolf RA, Johnson BL, Hill BB: Duplex ultrasound scanning vs. computed tomographic angiography for postoperative evaluation of endovascular abdominal aortic aneurysm repair. J Vasc Surg 32:1142-1148, 2000.
180. Arko FR, Konstantinos A, Siedel SA, et al: Intrasac flow velocities predict sealing of type II endoleaks after endovascular abdominal aortic aneurysm repair. J Vasc Surg 37:8-15, 2003.

Chapter 17

Venous Duplex Scanning

MARK H. MEISSNER, MD

Section III

Approximately 1 million patients annually undergo investigation for suspected acute deep venous thrombosis (DVT) in North America.[62,133] Accurate diagnosis of DVT is important because improper withholding of anticoagulation is associated with the well-recognized risk of pulmonary embolism, and inappropriate treatment carries the inconvenience, expense, and risks of anticoagulation. Clinical diagnosis of DVT is inaccurate: The classic findings of pain, swelling, and tenderness are equally common in limbs with and without objectively confirmed thrombosis.[8,25,44,61] The diagnosis of DVT requires confirmatory testing, and several diagnostic modalities have been used clinically.

Ascending venography historically has been the "gold standard" for diagnosis for acute DVT.[55] Venography is invasive, is not easily repeatable, may be impossible to perform or interpret in 9% to 14% of patients, and may be associated with interobserver disagreements in 4% to 10% of studies.[31,35,98,128,151] All venous segments are not visualized in 10% to 30% of studies, and the profunda femoris and iliac veins are frequently not seen.[21] In the upper extremity, venography does not show the internal jugular vein and frequently fails to identify venous segments beyond an obstruction.[11,34] The use of contrast agents is associated with occasional allergic reactions and may induce thrombosis in 8% of cases.[18] Impedance plethysmography (IPG), which correlates a reduced rate of venous outflow with proximal thrombosis, was previously the most widely used noninvasive test. Because IPG is insensitive to isolated calf vein and nonocclusive proximal thromboses, however, negative test results require serial follow-up examination. IPG cannot provide precise anatomic localization of an occluding thrombus.

The use of real-time ultrasonography, as described by Talbot in 1982,[136] has overcome many of these limitations and provides an accurate, noninvasive, and portable means of confirming venous thrombosis in the upper and lower extremities. Uniformly high sensitivities of 93% to 97% and specificities of 94% to 99% have been reported for the ultrasound diagnosis of proximal DVT.[14,62,72,155] Accurate localization of thrombus to specific venous segments also has enabled the course of thrombosis to be followed serially, permitting more precise characterization of the natural history of acute DVT. Because anatomic obstruction and valvular reflux can be evaluated with duplex ultrasonography, similar techniques can be used in the diagnosis of acute DVT and the characterization of chronic venous disease.

■ ULTRASOUND APPLICATIONS IN ACUTE DEEP VENOUS THROMBOSIS

Instrumentation

Continuous wave Doppler ultrasound has been used in the diagnosis of acute DVT since the early 1970s.[132] Although acute and chronic venous disease can be diagnosed based on aberrant venous flow, continuous wave Doppler does not allow selective interrogation of vessels within a large sample volume.[70] Real-time B-mode ultrasonography relies on gray-scale imaging and the absence of venous compressibility as the primary diagnostic criteria for acute DVT. Although accurate in the diagnosis of proximal thromboses, compression ultrasonography provides no information regarding venous flow. Real-time gray-scale imaging and Doppler flow are combined in duplex and color-flow instruments. Duplex instruments include a range-gated pulsed Doppler, allowing flow to be characterized at precise anatomic locations defined by the B-mode image, whereas color-flow Doppler superimposes a color map of the Doppler shift on the real-time gray-scale image.[70] Modern equipment for venous applications includes high-resolution B-mode ultrasound with "slow flow" color Doppler ultrasound capable of detecting low venous flow velocities. These technologic advances have made the study less operator dependent and have improved the identification of difficult-to-visualize venous segments. Color-flow Doppler may permit identification of flow in vessels smaller than the limits of gray-scale resolution[157] and is particularly useful in imaging the calf and iliac veins.[92]

Because axial resolution and tissue penetration are inversely related,[70] the highest frequency transducer capable of visualizing the venous segment under study should be used. The iliac veins require a 3- to 3.5-MHz ultrasound probe capable of imaging the depths of the pelvis, whereas a 5- to 7.5-MHz imaging transducer is adequate for the deep veins of the upper and lower extremities. A higher frequency probe (10 MHz) is helpful for imaging the superficial veins of the lower extremity and the upper extremity veins. A pulsed Doppler frequency of 3 MHz is suitable for the iliac veins, and 5 MHz is acceptable for the upper and lower extremity veins. The dynamic range, gray-scale gain, and time gain compensation should be adjusted to minimize intraluminal artifacts, while providing good definition of the venous walls. The color velocity scale and gain should maximize the detection of low venous flow velocities while confining color flow within the sample box to the vessel lumen.

A low wall filter setting facilitates detection of low-flow velocities. As a convention, many laboratories adjust the spectral display to show prograde venous flow below the baseline.

Examination Technique

Although more limited examinations have been proposed,[24,73,115,153] complete examination involves interrogation of the lower extremities from the inferior vena cava to the tibial veins. At each site, venous compressibility and the presence of echogenic thrombus are evaluated on the B-mode image, while the Doppler is used to assess venous flow characteristics. The deep veins are assessed in transverse and longitudinal views. Initial transverse scanning allows identification of the superficial and deep veins in relation to adjacent arterial structures and facilitates recognition of duplicated veins.[104] Gentle pressure on the scan head is required to avoid venous occlusion, particularly in evaluation of the superficial veins. Compression maneuvers, performed in transverse view to avoid lateral displacement of the transducer,[146] are performed every 1 to 2 cm from the inguinal ligament to the calf. Complete coaptation of the venous walls with gentle probe pressure excludes the presence of a thrombus. Moving to a longitudinal view, spectral Doppler signals and color-flow images are obtained from the venous segment being interrogated. Color-flow Doppler may assist in longitudinal tracking and in identifying the luminal encroachment of echolucent thrombus.

To facilitate lower extremity venous filling, the venous duplex examination is performed with the head elevated in 10- to 20-degree reverse Trendelenburg position. The examination is begun in the lower abdomen and pelvis, where Doppler flow evaluation is often possible, even though compressibility may be limited and bowel gas may obscure complete visualization of the inferior vena cava and iliac veins. On crossing the inguinal ligament, the origins of the greater saphenous and profunda femoris veins can be identified in transverse section. The veins of the thigh are examined with the leg slightly flexed and externally rotated to avoid compression of the popliteal vein. The superficial femoral vein is imaged from an anteromedial approach and followed to the distal third of the thigh, where it moves deeply through the adductor canal. The superficial femoral vein is frequently duplicated[104] and requires a critical assessment of the Doppler spectrum and color-flow image at the adductor canal, where it may be incompressible. The popliteal vein is examined most easily with the patient prone or resting on the side opposite that being examined with the hip and knee slightly flexed. The lesser saphenous vein is identified as it courses from the saphenopopliteal junction to a position just above the fascia, whereas the gastrocnemial veins can be observed to penetrate the muscle.

After examination of the distal popliteal vein, the patient is returned to the supine position for examination of the posterior tibial and peroneal veins. The calf veins alternatively may be studied with the patient sitting, a technique that may facilitate venous filling and visualization.[9,32] The paired posterior tibial veins are identified adjacent to the artery between the medial malleolus and the Achilles tendon at the level of the ankle. Moving cephalad, the paired peroneal veins are identified along the medial border of the fibula, although a posterior approach may be necessary in a large calf.[139] In the presence of thrombus, the soleal veins may be distended and readily apparent. Isolated calf vein thrombosis most often involves the peroneal veins followed by the posterior tibial veins; isolated anterior tibial thrombosis is distinctly unusual.[86,87,111,123] Visualization of the posterior tibial and peroneal veins is required to achieve acceptable sensitivity, although routine scanning of the anterior tibial veins may be unnecessary.

Examination of the upper extremity and the thoracic inlet is performed with the patient supine, the neck turned slightly away from the side being examined, and the upper extremity abducted to facilitate access to the axilla. The internal jugular vein is identified in the neck and followed centrally to image the medial subclavian and innominate veins from a supraclavicular approach. The subclavian vein laterally and axillary vein are visualized from an infraclavicular approach. Overlying bone and muscle prevent routine use of compression in evaluating the innominate and the subclavian and axillary veins medially; color-flow Doppler and the venous response to inspiration may be particularly useful in these areas.[41,42] If required, examination proceeds down the medial aspect of the arm, with evaluation of the axillary, paired brachial, basilic, and cephalic veins. The paired radial and ulnar veins are assessed in the forearm.

Diagnostic Criteria for Acute Deep Venous Thrombosis

A complete venous ultrasound evaluation incorporates information from the B-mode image, Doppler spectrum, and color-flow image. Diagnostic criteria for acute DVT include an evaluation of venous compressibility, intraluminal echoes, venous flow characteristics, and luminal color filling (Table 17-1). Venous incompressibility is the most widely used diagnostic criterion for acute DVT. Normal venous walls completely coapt, obliterating the venous lumen, with gentle probe compression (Fig. 17-1). Adjunctive gray-scale findings include the appearance of echogenic thrombi within the vein lumen and dilatation of an acutely thrombosed segment.[48] Acute thrombus is usually less echogenic than older thrombus,[137] however, and may be visible in only 50% to 90% of acute DVTs.[32,64,107]

The Doppler spectrum and color-flow image further support the diagnosis, increase accuracy in regions that are ordinarily difficult to compress, and permit differentiation of occlusive from nonocclusive thrombi. Above the popliteal

Table 17-1 Venous Duplex Ultrasound Criteria for Acute Deep Venous Thrombosis

DIAGNOSTIC CRITERIA	ADJUNCTIVE CRITERIA
Venous incompressibility	Increased venous diameter
Thrombus visualization	<50% diameter increase with Valsalva maneuver
Absent or diminished spontaneous venous flow	Immobile venous valves
Absence of respiratory phasicity	
Absent or incomplete color filling of lumen	

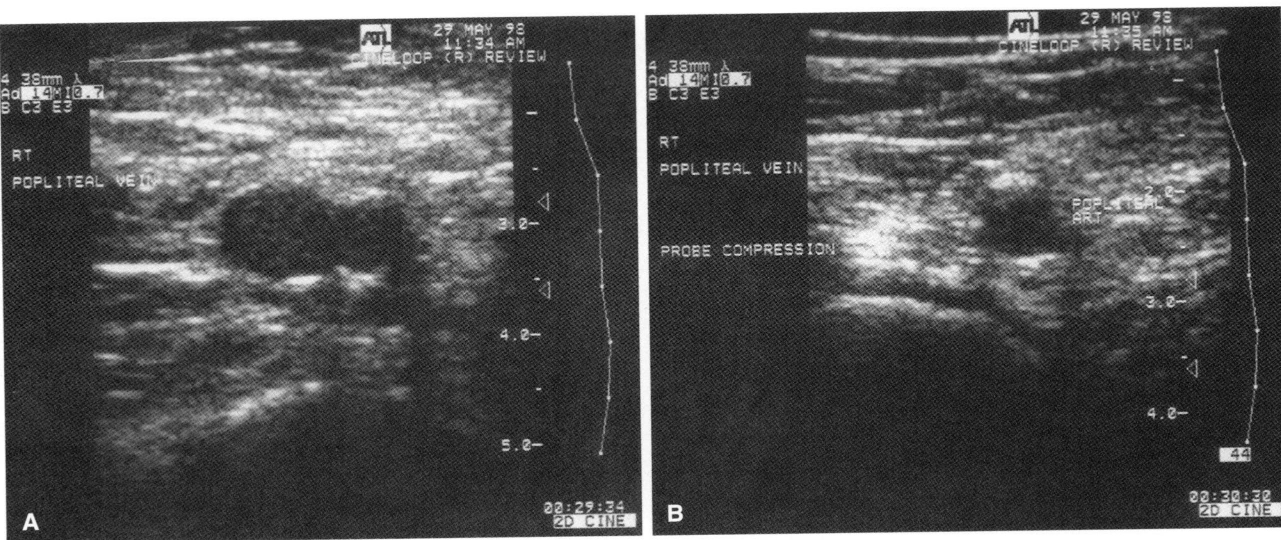

FIGURE 17-1 Compression ultrasonography. **A,** Transverse image of a normal popliteal artery and vein. The normal popliteal vein is larger than the corresponding artery. **B,** With gentle probe compression, the lumen of the normal vein is obliterated, while the popliteal artery remains uncompressed.

vein, normal lower extremity venous flow is spontaneous, varies with respiration, and augments with distal compression or release of proximal compression (Fig. 17-2). Spontaneous flow also should diminish during and augment after a Valsalva maneuver. Although spontaneous flow normally may be absent in the tibioperoneal veins, augmented flow should be present with distal compression of the foot or calf. The absence of flow, either spontaneously or with augmentation, suggests occlusive thrombosis.

Respiratory variation reflects diminished or absent flow with increases in intra-abdominal pressure during the respiratory cycle. Lower extremity venous return diminishes in a supine patient during inspiration. In a supine patient, continuous flow signals in proximal lower extremity veins without respiratory variation, lack of augmentation with release of proximal compression, and continuous flow during a Valsalva maneuver suggest a proximal obstruction, whereas diminished or absent augmentation with distal compression implies an obstruction in the intervening caudal venous segments.[5,134] The observation of cardiac pulsatility in the lower extremity Doppler signal suggests congestive heart failure or another cause of increased central venous pressure.[8] Color-flow Doppler may be particularly helpful in areas where compression is limited by anatomy, edema, obesity, or pain. In the absence of thrombus, the color flow map within the sample box should fill the venous lumen completely (Fig. 17-3).[74] Complete color filling of the lumen may be absent in patent calf veins, however.[9]

Normal upper extremity venous flow shows more cardiac and respiratory variability in the more proximal veins than does lower extremity venous flow, with subclavian flow increasing and diameter decreasing 41% to 78% during rapid inspiration (the sniff maneuver).[34,49] Flow is interrupted or diminished while diameter increases during the Valsalva maneuver. In evaluating the veins of the thoracic inlet, the internal jugular vein is assessed using B-mode criteria similar to criteria for the lower extremity veins. Visualization and compressibility of the subclavian vein are limited by the clavicle, however, and assessment relies on thorough evaluation of indirect flow criteria.[148] Patency of the subclavian vein is confirmed by complete color filling of the lumen, normal respiratory phasicity and cardiac pulsatility of the Doppler signal, and venous collapse with the sniff maneuver. Direct visualization of thrombus, absent or incomplete color filling of the lumen, and an absent diameter response to rapid inspiration suggest thrombosis.[22,41] Although the lung and thoracic cage usually obscure direct visualization, the absence of respiratory phasicity, cardiac pulsatility, and inspiratory venous collapse may also suggest innominate or superior vena cava obstruction.[11,34,54] Such a diagnosis may be supported by the observation of numerous venous collaterals on the color-flow image. These indirect observations cannot distinguish

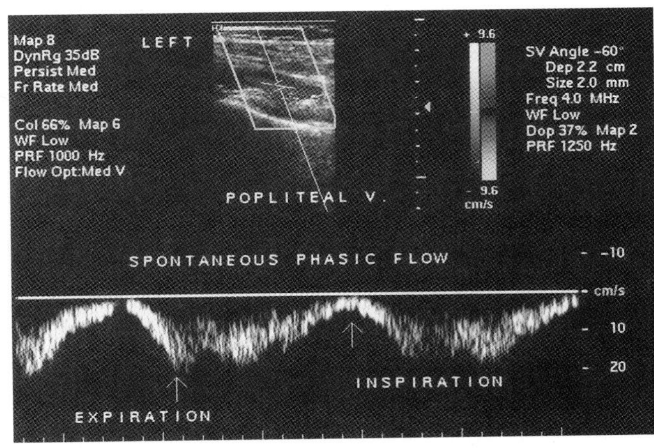

FIGURE 17-2 Doppler spectrum popliteal vein. Antegrade flow in the popliteal vein is displayed below the baseline. Unobstructed venous flow in the proximal veins is spontaneous with respiratory variation. Flow velocity increases with a reduction in intra-abdominal pressure during expiration and is damped or ceases during inspiration.

Table 17-2 Analysis of Venous Duplex Criteria*

CRITERIA	SENSITIVITY (%)	SPECIFICITY (%)	PPV (%)	NPV (%)
Thrombus visualized	50 (34-66)	92 (62-98)	95 (69-100)	37 (14-59)
Incompressibility	79 (66-92)	67 (40-93)	88 (67-95)	50 (18-82)
Absent spontaneous flow	76 (63-90)	100 (88-100)	100 (85-100)	57 (29-85)
Absent phasic flow	92 (79-97)	92 (62-98)	97 (81-99)	79 (41-92)

*Values in parentheses are 95% confidence intervals.
NPV, negative predictive value; PPV, positive predictive value.

From Killewich LA, Bedford GR, Beach KW, Strandness DE: Diagnosis of deep venous thrombosis: A prospective study comparing duplex scanning to contrast venography. Circulation 79:810-814, 1989.

central thrombosis from intrinsic stenosis or extrinsic compression, however.

In contrast to other noninvasive modalities, occlusive and nonocclusive thrombi can be differentiated on the basis of these criteria. Although it does not influence initial treatment, this distinction is important in following the course of a thrombus and defining recurrent thrombotic events. A patent segment is fully compressible, has no pathologic intraluminal echoes, shows complete color filling of the lumen, and has spontaneous flow that varies with respiration and augments with distal compression. A segment with nonocclusive thrombus may have a visible thrombus within the lumen and is not completely compressible, but has flow present either spontaneously or with augmentation. A segment with an occlusive thrombus has similar B-mode characteristics but has no flow present either spontaneously or with augmentation. At the time of presentation, 73% to 94% of thrombi are occlusive.[78]

Although the American Institute of Ultrasound in Medicine recommends evaluation of the real-time image and venous flow signals,[1] use of these diagnostic criteria varies among laboratories. Venous incompressibility is the most widely used criterion and has excellent sensitivity and specificity for the detection of DVT in the common femoral and popliteal veins. It is also among the most objective of these criteria, with interobserver agreement reported to be 100%.[73] Neither venous compressibility nor the other diagnostic elements are equally sensitive in detecting acute venous thrombus at all levels of the venous system. In considering B-mode incompressibility, visualization of thrombus, absence of spontaneous flow, and absence of phasic flow across all venous segments, only the absence of phasic flow has a sensitivity and a specificity greater than 90% (Table 17-2).[64] Venous incompressibility is nonspecific in areas such as the adductor canal, whereas spontaneous flow is insensitive to nonocclusive thrombus. Sensitivity is markedly improved when these criteria are used in combination, with a visible thrombus in the absence of spontaneous flow and the absence of spontaneous, phasic flow having the best overall sensitivity and specificity (Table 17-3).[64] Although instrumentation has improved and color-flow Doppler has become available since this study, these observations caution against using isolated criteria for the diagnosis of DVT and suggest that complete assessment requires integration of the B-mode image and Doppler spectra.

Other thrombus characteristics that may be identified with duplex include the presence of a free-floating thrombus tail. Based on venography, a *free-floating thrombus* has been defined as a greater than 5-cm segment of proximal thrombus surrounded by contrast agent.[95,105] Duplex definitions of a free-floating thrombus have varied, but thrombi can be identified by color imaging when flow is observed completely surrounding a central filling defect. This definition requires that such thrombi be distinguished from thrombus fragmentation occurring during the course of recanalization.[30] It also has been suggested that movement of the unattached segment within the flow stream be included in the definition.[43,145] Free-floating elements have been observed in 6% to 69% of DVTs,[7] and the sensitivity

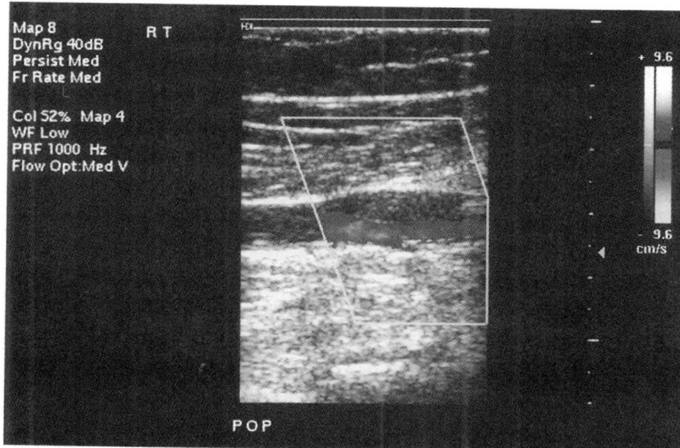

FIGURE 17-3 Partially occlusive popliteal vein thrombosis. Echogenic thrombus encroaches on the color flow Doppler image.

Table 17-3 Sensitivity and Specificity of Combined Diagnostic Variables*

VARIABLES	SENSITIVITY (%)	SPECIFICITY (%)
T + P	95 (82-98)	83 (52-95)
T + F + P	95 (82-98)	83 (52-95)
T + F + P + VC	95 (82-98)	58 (30-86)
F + P	92 (79-97)	92 (62-98)
F + T	87 (76-98)	92 (62-98)
T + F + VC	87 (76-98)	67 (40-93)
F + VC	84 (73-96)	67 (40-93)
T + VC	82 (69-94)	67 (40-93)

*Values in parentheses are 95% confidence limits.
F, absence of spontaneous flow; P, absence of phasic flow with respiration; T, visualization of thrombus; VC, venous incompressibility.

From Killewich LA, Bedford GR, Beach KW, Strandness DE: Diagnosis of deep venous thrombosis: A prospective study comparing duplex scanning to contrast venography. Circulation 79:810-814, 1989.

and specificity of color-flow duplex scanning compared with venography have been reported to be 68% and 86%.[110] Among patients followed with duplex ultrasonography for a mean of 7 days after identification of a free-floating thrombus, 55% showed attachment of the free-floating tail, 24% showed partial or complete resolution of the tail, 9% showed an increase in the size of the free-floating component, and 12% had no change in thrombus characteristics.[7] Some authors have suggested that these nonadherent thrombi are associated with an increased risk of pulmonary embolism and warrant placement of a vena cava filter,[43,105] whereas others have recommended anticoagulation alone[110] or filter placement only for patients failing to show thrombus attachment within 10 days.[17]

In a small venographic series including five free-floating thrombi, the risk of embolism after anticoagulation was significantly higher in patients with free-floating iliofemoral thrombi (60%) than in patients with occlusive thrombi (5.5%).[105] Others have reported, however, that most emboli associated with free-floating thrombi occur before therapy.[7,17,145] Among these patients, most of whom received anticoagulation, only 3% to 10% sustained a pulmonary embolus after institution of treatment. Two prospective series employing routine lung scanning also have reported conflicting results. Monreal and associates[95] found recurrent pulmonary embolism despite anticoagulation in 21% of patients with free-floating iliofemoral thrombosis compared with 5% of patients with adherent thrombus. A more benign prognosis was suggested by Pacouret and colleagues,[110] the incidence of pulmonary embolism after the institution of therapeutic anticoagulation being similar in patients with (3.3%) and without (3.7%) free-floating elements. The clinical relevance of these findings is controversial, and no randomized trials comparing management options have been performed. In addition, such trials are not likely forthcoming in that the incidence of clinically significant pulmonary emboli after initiation of adequate anticoagulation is so low that such a trial powered to detect meaningful endpoints would have to be so large as to preclude feasibility.

Limitations of Venous Ultrasonography

Despite its utility, duplex ultrasonography does have some well-recognized limitations in the diagnosis of acute DVT. Among studies limited to the proximal veins, the results are indeterminate or nondiagnostic in 1% to 6% of patients.[74,138] Technical considerations, such as the presence of bandages, casts, massive obesity, severe swelling, and patient intolerance of compressive maneuvers, may place limits on the performance of the examination. These technical problems and anatomic factors that may limit visualization of the pelvic, superficial femoral, calf, and thoracic inlet veins must be considered when interpreting the results of venous ultrasound studies. Imaging of the inferior vena cava and iliac veins may be precluded by overlying bowel gas, and their deep location often prevents assessment of compressibility. Difficult compressibility similarly may limit evaluation of the superficial femoral vein at the adductor canal. Adequate evaluation of the tibial and peroneal veins may be impeded by large calf size, edema, or operator inexperience. Compression of the medial axillary, subclavian, and innominate veins may be prevented by overlying musculoskeletal structures, whereas acoustic shadowing may prevent visualization of the subclavian vein directly beneath the clavicle. Although occasionally visible with a small footprint transducer in the suprasternal notch, the central innominate vein and superior vena cava often are not routinely able to be imaged with ultrasonography. Interpretation of indirect Doppler evidence also has some limitations because the absence of respiratory phasicity and augmentation may be due to proximal extrinsic compression rather than thrombosis.

Color-flow technology has improved the evaluation of these segments, although assessment of the calf and iliac veins does require more time and technologist experience. Messina and colleagues[92] reported adequate visualization of the common and the external iliac veins in 47% of patients and of the external iliac alone in 79%. Despite being incompressible in most cases, the color-flow and Doppler spectra are frequently sufficient to exclude occlusive thrombus in these segments. The absence of complete iliac obstruction can be inferred by a spontaneous and phasic common femoral Doppler signal in more than 90% of cases. Continuous common femoral vein flow that does not change with a Valsalva maneuver is highly specific for proximal iliac or caval obstruction, although this finding cannot differentiate occlusive DVT from external compression by adenopathy, pelvic masses, or postoperative changes.[5] Spectral flow characteristics also are unable to exclude a nonocclusive proximal thrombus. Using color-flow Doppler with slow-flow capabilities, technically adequate studies of all three paired tibial veins have been reported in 72% to 94% of symptomatic extremities.[86,92]

Recurrent symptoms of pain and edema are common after an episode of acute DVT and are a challenge for most diagnostic tests.[56] Such symptoms may result from persistent obstruction early after an acute event, late manifestations of valvular incompetence, or recurrent DVT. Identification of recurrent thrombosis is particularly important because the risks of pulmonary embolism and more severe post-thrombotic manifestations[89,119] may require a change in treatment. Variable degrees of residual occlusion, partial recanalization, intimal thickening, and collateral formation may mask new intraluminal filling defects on venography and limit the utility of duplex ultrasonography in this setting.[29,78,97]

Despite early recanalization in most patients,[66,90,97,117,143] compression ultrasound studies may remain abnormal in 50% of patients after 6 months and in 27% to 70% of patients after 1 year.[12,78,97,117] Thrombus echogenicity and heterogeneity tend to increase with thrombus age. Marked variation in thrombus echogenicity occurs, however, and this has not proved consistently useful for differentiating acute from chronic thrombus.[97] Despite these limitations, color-flow ultrasonography may be more useful than venography in identifying some characteristics of chronic thrombosis versus recurrent acute DVT (Table 17-4).[15] Acutely thrombosed segments tend to be dilated, whereas the diameter of chronically thrombosed segments is reduced.[48,97,108] A free-floating tail, if present, also tends to suggest an acute thrombus.[134] In contrast, the presence of venous collaterals and multiple flow channels within the lumen is more consistent with chronic thrombosis.

Table 17-4 Ultrasound Characteristics of Acute Versus Chronic Thrombus

DIAGNOSTIC CRITERIA	ACUTE THROMBUS	CHRONIC THROMBUS
Incompressibility	Spongy	Firm
Vein diameter	Dilated	Decreased
Echogenicity	Echolucent	Echogenic
Heterogeneity	Homogeneous	Heterogeneous
Luminal surface	Smooth	Irregular
Collaterals	Absent	Present
Flow channel	Confluent	Multiple
Free-floating tail	May be present	Absent

Several strategies have been proposed to increase the utility of venous ultrasonography in the setting of recurrent symptoms. A baseline venous duplex examination obtained 3 to 6 months after an acute event may be useful in defining recurrent episodes of acute DVT.[12,97,117] Compared with previous examinations, a 2-mm or greater increase in compressed thrombus thickness has been reported to have a sensitivity and specificity of 100% for recurrent proximal venous thrombosis.[117] Demonstration of activated coagulation or new fibrin deposition also may be useful as an adjunct to indeterminate ultrasound findings. Imaging with radioactive iodine (^{125}I)–labeled fibrinogen has previously been useful in this regard,[8,56] although its use is limited by the risk of viral transmission. Strategies incorporating markers of acute intravascular thrombosis, such as D-dimer cross-linked fibrin degradation products, may be a useful alternative,[39] but have not been evaluated in the setting of recurrent DVT.

Extent of Examination

Despite anatomic limitations, the frequency of multisegmental involvement affords duplex ultrasonography a high sensitivity for the diagnosis of acute DVT. The sensitivity of ultrasonography in detecting thrombus within an entire limb is higher than the sensitivity in an individual venous segment. These considerations and the operator experience and time required to perform a complete venous duplex examination have prompted some laboratories to limit examination to the common femoral and popliteal veins in symptomatic patients. Abbreviated studies often include compression in the region of the saphenofemoral junction, including the deep and superficial femoral vein confluences, and the popliteal vein, including the saphenopopliteal junction and tibial vein confluences.[115] Spectral and color-flow Doppler analysis is not routinely performed. Although shorter complete examination times are achievable,[99,133] in direct comparison these abbreviated studies reduced examination time from 18 (unilateral proximal examination) to 57 minutes (bilateral examination including iliac and tibial veins) to 5 to 10 minutes.[113,115,153] Compared with a complete color-flow duplex examination, Poppiti and coworkers[115] reported a sensitivity of 100% and specificity of 98% for limited compression examination of the proximal veins. Other investigators have achieved nearly identical levels of sensitivity and specificity for limited compression studies.[24,73,153]

Despite reports that more than 99% of proximal thrombi involve segments examined by limited compression ultrasonography,[113] other data suggest that this approach may overlook thrombi isolated to the iliac veins in 2% to 5% of cases and to the superficial femoral vein in 5% of patients.[31,38,79,92,127,146] As untreated proximal vein thrombosis is associated with a 20% to 50% risk of recurrent venous thromboembolism,[121] this small percentage cannot be entirely discounted as insignificant. The clinical relevance of thrombosis confined to the calf veins is more controversial. Most early postoperative thrombi begin in the calf veins,[61] whereas clinical series of largely symptomatic patients have reported isolated calf vein thrombosis to account for 12% to 33% of ultrasound-documented thromboses[26,86,88,106] and 9% to 46% of thromboses diagnosed with venography.[21,31,91,119] Although the incidence of major pulmonary embolism and late post-thrombotic symptoms is less than after proximal venous thrombosis, isolated calf vein thrombi may not be clinically insignificant. Concurrent pulmonary embolism has been reported in approximately 10% of patients when clinical suspicion is supplemented by objective tests[88,91,111] and in 33% of patients when routine ventilation-perfusion (V/Q) lung scans have been obtained.[68,96] Approximately one fourth of patients with isolated calf vein thrombosis have persistent symptoms of pain and edema during follow-up.[87,88] More important, approximately 20% of such thrombi propagate proximally[61,71,77,88] with an associated increase in the risk of symptomatic pulmonary embolism. Although management of isolated calf vein thrombosis remains controversial, many authors have concluded that the benefits of treatment exceed the risks and inconvenience of anticoagulation in patients without contraindications.[53,57,121] These considerations would favor routine color-flow evaluation of the calf veins. Restricting studies to the proximal veins requires that calf vein thrombi be considered clinically insignificant and that serial testing be performed to exclude proximal propagation. A single, technically adequate examination including the calf veins could potentially eliminate the need for serial studies in many patients, although the safety of this approach has not been prospectively evaluated in a study large enough to have sufficient endpoints for analysis.

The finding that 32% of venous thrombi may be bilateral has prompted many laboratories to perform bilateral studies on all patients referred for suspected acute DVT.[30,76] Bilateral examination is clearly appropriate for patients with bilateral symptoms, patients undergoing postoperative screening, and patients with suspected pulmonary embolism. A positive venous ultrasound study in an asymptomatic extremity contralateral to a symptomatic extremity without DVT is uncommon. Strothman and associates[133] found a contralateral thrombus in 22% of patients with acute DVT in a unilaterally symptomatic extremity. Thrombi in the asymptomatic extremities were always associated with DVT in the symptomatic extremity, however. Because identification of thrombus in the asymptomatic limb does not change the management, the need for routine bilateral ultrasonography has been questioned.[27,130,133] Other authors have reached the opposite conclusion, finding a thrombus isolated to the contralateral limb in 1% of patients referred for unilateral symptoms and in 5% of patients with

Table 17-5 Duplex Ultrasound for Symptomatic Proximal Deep Venous Thrombosis

AUTHOR	YEAR	METHOD	N (% POSITIVE*)	SENSITIVITY (%)	SPECIFICITY (%)
Cronan et al[28]	1987	Compression	51 (47)	93	100
Appelman et al[2]	1987	Compression	112 (46)	96	97
O'Leary et al[107]	1988	Duplex	50 (48)	92	96
Lensing et al[73]	1989	Compression	220 (30)	100	99
Rose et al[123]	1990	Color Doppler	75 (35)	96	100
Mitchell et al[94]	1991	Duplex	64 (35)	96	85
Cogo et al[24]	1993	Compression	158 (30)	100	100
Aronen et al[4]	1994	Compression	119 (29)	97	100
Lewis et al[74]	1994	Color Doppler	103 (20)	95	99

*Percentage of venograms positive for proximal deep venous thrombosis.

unilateral symptoms and documented thrombosis.[99] A selective approach to the issue has been recommended by some investigators, with bilateral scans limited to patients with bilateral symptoms, pulmonary embolism, and ongoing thrombotic risk factors.[27,104] Such approaches do not consider the potential value, however, of a complete baseline study in the event of future thromboembolic symptoms.[56] In addition, modern imaging equipment allows a well-trained technologist to perform a bilateral examination, including the calf veins, with a minimum of increased total patient time. A reasonable approach is the routine performance of bilateral examinations in patients with unilateral symptoms, unless technical or patient difficulties severely limit the quality of the data to be obtained in the contralateral asymptomatic extremity.

Accuracy of Venous Ultrasonography

The potential morbidity of pulmonary embolism and recurrent thrombosis mandates a high sensitivity for any diagnostic test for DVT, whereas the risks of inappropriate anticoagulation require that specificity also be high. Evaluation of the sensitivity and specificity of venous ultrasound traditionally has been with comparison with venography.[14,72] To eliminate bias, these criteria require that consecutive patients with suspected DVT prospectively undergo ultrasonography and venography with independent, blinded interpretation of the results according to explicitly defined standards.[62,152,155] Although not uniformly conforming to these criteria, more than 60 published studies have evaluated the sensitivity and specificity of ultrasound, with or without spectral Doppler and color-flow imaging, for the detection of DVT.[30] Results indicate that the sensitivity and specificity of venous ultrasound depend on the population studied. The sensitivity for evaluation of symptomatic patients is substantially higher than for surveillance screening of asymptomatic high-risk patients. Even among symptomatic patients, the sensitivity of venous ultrasound depends on the pretest probability of disease. A sensitivity of 91% may be achieved in patients with a high pretest probability of disease, in whom thrombi are presumably larger and more frequently proximal in extent, compared with a sensitivity of only 67% among patients with a low pretest probability.[40,151] Similar factors presumably account for the reduced sensitivity in asymptomatic patients undergoing screening examinations.[53,85]

More than 80% of symptomatic venous thrombi involve the easily interrogated proximal veins,[62] and the sensitivity and specificity for symptomatic proximal venous thrombosis are uniformly high. In reviewing 15 early studies, Becker and colleagues[14] reported a mean sensitivity of 96% and a mean specificity of 99% for the detection of thigh and popliteal thromboses. Among four studies enrolling consecutive patients with blinded interpretation of diagnostic tests, White and colleagues[155] noted a sensitivity of 93%, a specificity of 98%, a positive predictive value of 97%, and a negative predictive value of 93%. In an analysis of 18 studies using a variety of ultrasound techniques, Kearon and coworkers[62] reported a weighted mean sensitivity and specificity of 97% and 94% with mean positive and negative predictive values of 97% and 98% for proximal DVT. The sensitivity and specificity for the detection of proximal DVT in selected studies with prospective enrollment of consecutive patients and blinded interpretation are shown in Table 17-5. The sensitivity and specificity of compression, duplex, and color Doppler ultrasound studies for proximal DVT are similar.[14,74,153]

Because duplex ultrasonography is less sensitive for isolated calf vein thrombosis than for femoropopliteal thrombosis, the sensitivity of ultrasonography within an entire lower extremity is less than for proximal DVT alone. Depending on the incidence of isolated calf vein thrombosis, the sensitivity of proximal venous ultrasonography for detection of DVT within an entire extremity is reduced to 68% to 91%.[4,73,74,94,123] Few studies have systematically evaluated the calf veins beyond their confluence, however, and many of these have employed only B-mode compression or duplex.[62] In contrast to the proximal veins, adequate evaluation of the calf veins is difficult without color imaging. Limited data suggest that normal calf veins are more reliably visualized by color-flow duplex than by venography.[10] In color-flow duplex studies of symptomatic patients, the sensitivity and specificity have varied from 95% and 100% in patients with proximal and distal thromboses[9] to 88% and 96% in patients with isolated calf thrombosis.[156] Edema, calf size, collateral veins, and anatomic inaccessibility may limit visualization of the tibial veins,[86,123] however, and sensitivity in this region highly depends on the technical adequacy of the study. Sensitivity and specificity for calf vein thrombosis may be 95% to 100% for technically adequate studies compared with 30% to 70% for technically limited studies.[123] In laboratories experienced in color-flow Doppler, technically adequate studies of the paired tibial veins have been reported in 100% of normal extremities[9,139] and 60% to 94% of symptomatic limbs.[86,123]

Because ultrasound is noninvasive and easily repeatable, it also has been used to screen asymptomatic patients at high risk for DVT. Populations considered for routine screening have included patients undergoing elective orthopedic[152] and neurosurgical[36] procedures, patients hospitalized in the intensive care unit,[46,52] and high-risk trauma patients.[20] The accuracy of duplex ultrasonography in screening asymptomatic patients is substantially less than for symptomatic patients. This is not surprising because such thrombi are presumably smaller, more often nonocclusive, confined to fewer segments, and more frequently isolated to the calf veins than thrombi that give rise to symptoms.[85] Postoperative swelling and wounds may also limit ultrasound access to all venous segments.

Most screening studies have been performed after elective orthopedic surgical procedures, and this literature has been critically reviewed in a meta-analysis by Wells and associates.[152] Among studies enrolling consecutive patients and using blinded interpretation, the sensitivity and specificity of ultrasound for proximal DVT were 62% and 97%. These results were substantially worse than the sensitivity of 95% and specificity of 100% reported in less methodologically rigorous trials. Other authors have noted similar differences between studies.[72] The clinical relevance of asymptomatic thrombi overlooked by ultrasonography is unknown. It is possible that small, nonocclusive thrombi confined to the calf veins may never cause clinical symptoms. Such thrombi may be analogous to thrombi detected by ^{125}I-labeled fibrinogen, 35% of which spontaneously resolve within 72 hours.[61] Pending prospective studies regarding the outcome of negative examinations in asymptomatic patients, however, the sensitivity and specificity of ultrasound must be regarded as only moderate.[152]

Duplex ultrasonography also has proved to be sensitive for the diagnosis of upper extremity thrombosis. Among 13 patients with effort thrombosis, Grassi and Polak[42] reported no false-negative or false-positive findings with color-flow imaging. Overall sensitivity and specificity of 89% and 100% for axillary-subclavian stenosis or occlusion also have been reported among symptomatic dialysis patients with previous central venous catheterization.[11] In a prospective evaluation of 58 symptomatic patients, Prandoni and colleagues[118] reported sensitivities and specificities of 96% and 93.5% for compression ultrasonography and 100% and 93% for color-flow imaging. Reports of lower sensitivity and specificity have been associated with errors secondary to superior vena cava or central innominate vein thrombosis, inadequate imaging of the subclavian vein, and inability to differentiate extrinsic compression from thrombosis.[69] Venography may be warranted when clinical suspicion or indirect evidence, such as abnormal respiratory variation or prominent venous collaterals, suggests a proximal thrombosis despite an otherwise negative ultrasound examination.

Clinical Utility of Venous Ultrasonography

The high specificity of ultrasonography allows anticoagulation to be instituted without confirmatory venography,[94] whereas the high sensitivity for proximal thrombosis makes it possible to withhold anticoagulation if serial examinations are negative. Three percent to 7% of documented thromboses have an initial study that is negative for proximal thrombosis, however, and if limited to the proximal veins, serial examinations are required.[23,47] Initial diagnostic failure rates may be higher among inpatients and patients with persistent symptoms.[131,138] The incidence of thromboembolism within 6 months of serially negative ultrasound examinations is less than 2%,[47,62] and withholding anticoagulation in symptomatic patients with two negative ultrasound examinations 5 to 7 days apart has proved safe.[19,23]

Venous duplex ultrasonography may also be more cost-effective than other diagnostic strategies.[16] In a cost-effectiveness analysis of several strategies, venous duplex of the proximal veins was associated with an average of 4.53 deaths per 1000 patients at an average cost of $2138 per patient compared with 4.44 deaths and $2437 for routine venography.[51] Addition of a second duplex study 5 to 7 days after a negative study decreased the death rate to 3.79 per 1000, but at a high incremental cost of $390,000 per life saved. Strategies employing venous ultrasonography were more cost-effective than venography as long as the sensitivity and specificity remained greater than 93%.

Alternatives to serial duplex scanning have been proposed, but their cost-effectiveness is unknown. Among these, the combined use of D-dimer measurements and noninvasive studies may eliminate safely the need for serial studies if both are negative.[39] D-dimer may be an effective screening modality for outpatients with a clinically low probability of DVT. The test lacks specificity in an inpatient population. D-dimer frequently is elevated in postsurgical patients, elderly patients, trauma patients, cancer patients, and patients with disorders associated with inflammation. A complete, technically adequate examination including the calf veins also might be more cost-effective if the safety of withholding anticoagulation after a single negative study were known. It is common practice, however, unsupported by data, to regard a single negative and technically adequate duplex examination that includes the calf veins as adequate justification to withhold anticoagulation in a patient with a low probability of venous thromboembolism.

Indications for Venous Ultrasonography

The accuracy, availability, and noninvasive nature of venous duplex ultrasonography have led to its widespread clinical application in a variety of symptomatic and asymptomatic patients. Compared with historical requests for venography, Glover and Bendick[40] noted a sixfold increase in the yearly number of lower extremity venous duplex studies. Criado and Burnham[26] further estimated that approximately 7 venous duplex scans are performed for each DVT diagnosed. Despite the recognized inaccuracy of clinical presentation, concerns about overuse and misuse of limited vascular laboratory resources have forced some consideration of the appropriate indications for venous duplex scanning. Although clinical evaluation cannot confirm or exclude the diagnosis of DVT with absolute accuracy, it can be used to stratify patients into patients with a high or low pretest probability of disease. Based on the presence of thrombotic risk factors, clinical signs and symptoms, and the possibility of alternative diagnoses, high-risk and low-risk groups can be defined with an 85% and 5% prevalence of DVT.[151]

The value of clinical screening before duplex scanning seems to be more clearly defined for symptomatic outpatients than for inpatients. The overall prevalence of acute lower extremity DVT in outpatient vascular laboratory referrals varies from 12% to 25%.[26,40,50,80,99,106] The prevalence of positive outpatient studies increases from 2.1% in patients without swelling or thrombotic risk factors, to 13% in patients with thrombotic risk factors but no swelling, to approximately 50% in patients with acute unilateral swelling.[40] Among outpatients, the negative predictive value of the absence of unilateral swelling or an existing thrombotic risk factor is greater than 97%.[26,40] Chronic unilateral swelling and bilateral swelling are associated with a significant prevalence of chronic findings, although an acute DVT may be found in less than 1%.[40] Other common indications for vascular laboratory referral, such as joint pain or cellulitis in the absence of thrombotic risk factors, are associated with an exceedingly low prevalence of acute DVT.[40] The prevalence of positive studies is higher among inpatient referrals (range 16% to 31%).[26,40,50,106] Bilateral DVT, accounting for 35% of positive inpatient studies,[26] and co-morbid medical problems also are more common in this population. It is more difficult to define the factors that are associated with a negative inpatient study.[106] Among symptomatic inpatients, acute DVT not only has been identified in 55% of patients with the acute onset of unilateral swelling, but also in 20% of patients with bilateral swelling.

Although the absence of acute unilateral limb swelling and recognized risk factors may identify an outpatient population with a low prevalence of positive scan findings, restricting studies to patients meeting these criteria misses 2% to 5% of patients with an acute DVT.[40,151] Ultrasonography also is useful for the identification of chronic DVT in 5% to 10%[37,40,74] and findings such as Baker's cyst, muscle hematoma, popliteal aneurysm, joint effusion, or lymphadenopathy in 5% to 18% of symptomatic outpatients, which may explain their clinical presentation and assist in management.[14,30,131,138,155] The true utility of such clinical criteria may be in selecting studies and maximizing the efficiency of scarce vascular laboratory resources. The positive and negative predictive value of any diagnostic test depends on the probability of disease in a population.[154] High negative predictive value in populations with a low probability of disease and high positive predictive value among populations with a high probability of disease justify management of negative and positive findings in these groups based on noninvasive studies alone. Ultrasound findings that contradict clinical impressions must be regarded with suspicion, however.

Venous duplex ultrasonography also frequently is employed in the evaluation of patients with suspected pulmonary embolism. Although most pulmonary emboli arise from the deep veins of the lower extremities, there are few data to support ultrasound as the initial diagnostic test for suspected pulmonary embolism. Venous duplex is not sufficiently accurate to be used as the sole diagnostic test for pulmonary embolism. Compared with pulmonary angiography, the sensitivity and specificity of lower extremity venous duplex are only 44% and 86%.[65] Such figures are similar to the 38% sensitivity of other noninvasive lower extremity studies (pulse-volume plethysmography and continuous wave Doppler) for the diagnosis of pulmonary embolism.[129] Thrombus associated with a documented pulmonary embolism may have completely embolized or involved segments such as the upper extremity, abdominal, iliac, or profunda veins that were not interrogated. Although a normal duplex scan cannot reliably exclude pulmonary embolism, initial identification of an acute DVT theoretically could avoid further diagnostic evaluation in some patients. Only 9% to 14% of venous duplex studies disclose an acute DVT in this setting, however.[33,37,40,75,84]

Positive duplex scans may be present in 40% of patients with unilateral leg symptoms but only 5% of patients without leg symptoms[33] and 1.6% of patients with neither leg symptoms nor thrombotic risk factors.[40] In contrast, 25% to 35% of pulmonary V/Q scans are either high probability or normal and require no further diagnostic testing unless clinical suspicion is low.[33,84] Most investigators have previously recommended V/Q scanning as the initial diagnostic test for suspected pulmonary embolism,[63] with lower extremity ultrasound reserved for nondiagnostic scintigraphy. Initial V/Q scanning followed by venous duplex for nondiagnostic studies and pulmonary angiography if the ultrasound study is normal are theoretically associated with the lowest morbidity, mortality, and number of patients in whom anticoagulation is inappropriately withheld and are supported by data.[109] Initial venous duplex might be appropriate for patients with concurrent unilateral leg symptoms, although this presentation accounts for less than 10% of patients with suspected pulmonary embolism.[33] Although noninvasive venous testing after a diagnostic (high probability or normal) V/Q scan may be useful as a baseline for future events, this approach changes management in only 4% of patients and has been questioned as a routine measure.[75]

V/Q scanning has been largely replaced in most hospitals with use of computed tomography (CT) for detection of pulmonary emboli. Multidetector CT scans are readily available in most hospitals and are highly accurate for detection of proximal pulmonary emboli. Data are so far limited, but a negative CT scan for pulmonary embolism in patients with respiratory symptoms and suspected pulmonary embolism predicts with high specificity a lack of subsequent detection of pulmonary embolism over the next 30 days. In addition, CT scanning in the setting of suspected pulmonary embolism frequently reveals chest pathology that may be clinically important and is not evident on routine chest radiograph. For patients without contraindications to contrast administration, CT is likely to become the first-line test for patients with suspected pulmonary embolism. The low yield of ultrasound studies of the lower extremity veins in which the indication for the examination is respiratory symptoms combined only with the accuracy of CT for proximal pulmonary emboli strongly suggests a transition from lower extremity ultrasound to chest CT in patients with respiratory symptoms and clinical suspicion for pulmonary embolism.

ULTRASOUND APPLICATIONS IN CHRONIC VENOUS DISEASE

Chronic venous disease may result from primary venous valvular insufficiency or a previous episode of acute DVT and includes a spectrum of clinical problems ranging from telangiectasias and varicose veins to venous ulceration.[116] The hemodynamics underlying the severe manifestations of swelling, hyperpigmentation, and ulceration are similar: Valvular reflux or retrograde flow through damaged or absent valves leads to the development of ambulatory venous hypertension.[67] Residual venous obstruction also plays a role in the post-thrombotic syndrome, a combination of reflux and obstruction being more common than either abnormality alone in patients with skin changes and ulceration.[59,60] Despite the well-characterized hemodynamics, however, clinical manifestations such as pain, swelling, and ulceration are not specific for venous disease. Only two thirds of patients with chronic leg ulcers have objective evidence of venous disease,[125] whereas edema occurring after an episode of DVT may be due to either residual venous obstruction or the development of valvular incompetence and ambulatory venous hypertension. Evaluation of the venous system may be important in establishing an etiology for such nonspecific complaints and in defining the severity and anatomic location of reflux and obstruction, selecting patients for extirpative or reconstructive procedures, assessing hemodynamic improvement after such procedures, and establishing the natural history of chronic venous disease.

Diagnostic Tests for Chronic Venous Disease

The ideal diagnostic test for chronic venous disease should be capable of defining the presence of residual venous obstruction and valvular incompetence, localizing these abnormalities to precise segments of the superficial and deep venous systems, and quantifying the degree of abnormality in a manner that correlates with the clinical severity of disease. The ideal test should provide anatomic and hemodynamic information, for which descending phlebography and ambulatory venous pressure (AVP) measurements are considered the standard reference test. In addition to their invasive nature, however, both of these studies have limitations. Competent proximal valves may prevent venographic assessment of distal reflux, whereas hyperbaric contrast medium may stream past normal valves in the relaxed leg. Evaluation of the greater and lesser saphenous veins also may be limited with this technique.[6] AVP measurements reflect the global hemodynamics within an extremity and show a linear relationship with the prevalence of ulceration.[103,112] AVP cannot localize the hemodynamic aberrations beyond the superficial or deep venous systems, however, and is influenced by reflux and obstruction. Photoplethysmography and air plethysmography are other commonly used noninvasive tests for the evaluation of chronic venous disease, but they have their own specific limitations (see Chapter 15).[13,102,120,142,149,150] All provide only an indirect assessment of global venous hemodynamics, however, without precise characterization of the underlying abnormalities. Because reflux at multiple levels may be required to be hemodynamically significant, these measurements may be insensitive to isolated segmental reflux.[120]

In contrast, duplex ultrasonography has the potential to provide anatomic and physiologic information. Valvular reflux can be identified by Doppler spectral analysis, whereas the B-mode image allows localization of anatomic obstruction and reflux to precise segments of the venous system. Duplex scanning not only provides the anatomic information lacking in global hemodynamic tests, but also avoids the venographic limitations of proximal valve competence and hyperbaric contrast medium, while permitting valve function to be evaluated under conditions that simulate normal calf muscle pump function.[100] Accordingly, it may be the most accurate test for identification of isolated but hemodynamically significant reflux in the distal deep venous segments.[6,124]

Duplex Scanning for Chronic Venous Disease

Duplex scanning is capable of characterizing partial and complete anatomic obstruction and valvular incompetence in the deep, superficial, and perforating veins. The criteria for the diagnosis of obstruction are similar to criteria described for the evaluation of acute DVT. Several methods of assessing valvular incompetence in the deep and superficial venous systems have been proposed, and selection of an appropriate technique requires consideration of the mechanism of valvular closure.

As described by van Bemmelen and associates,[140,141] the lower extremity valve cusps remain open while the patient is resting in the supine position. Valve closure is initiated by reversal of the resting antegrade transvalvular pressure gradient. As the pressure gradient is reversed, there is a short period of retrograde flow, or reflux, until the gradient becomes sufficient to cause valve closure. Valve closure requires not only the cessation of antegrade flow, but also a brief retrograde flow interval of sufficient velocity to coapt the valve cusps (Fig. 17-4). At low velocities, reverse flow may persist even in the presence of competent valves. The determination of valvular incompetence requires that pathologic retrograde flow be shown in response to maneuvers that consistently generate an adequate reverse flow velocity. Because clinically relevant reflux occurs during calf muscle contraction and relaxation in the erect position, these maneuvers should approximate the conditions of upright exercise as closely as possible.

Methods used to elicit reflux with duplex ultrasonography include the Valsalva maneuver, manual proximal compression or distal compression release, and standardized cuff compression proximal to or cuff deflation distal to the venous segment of interest. In addition to the theoretical considerations discussed earlier, the ideal method of eliciting reflux would distinguish clearly competent from incompetent venous segments by providing a short duration of reverse flow in normal subjects and a prolonged duration of reflux in symptomatic patients with incompetent valves. Although all techniques may be performed either supine or standing, the upright position is preferred because the time required for valve closure in normal subjects is greater in the supine position.[3,141] With respect to the individual

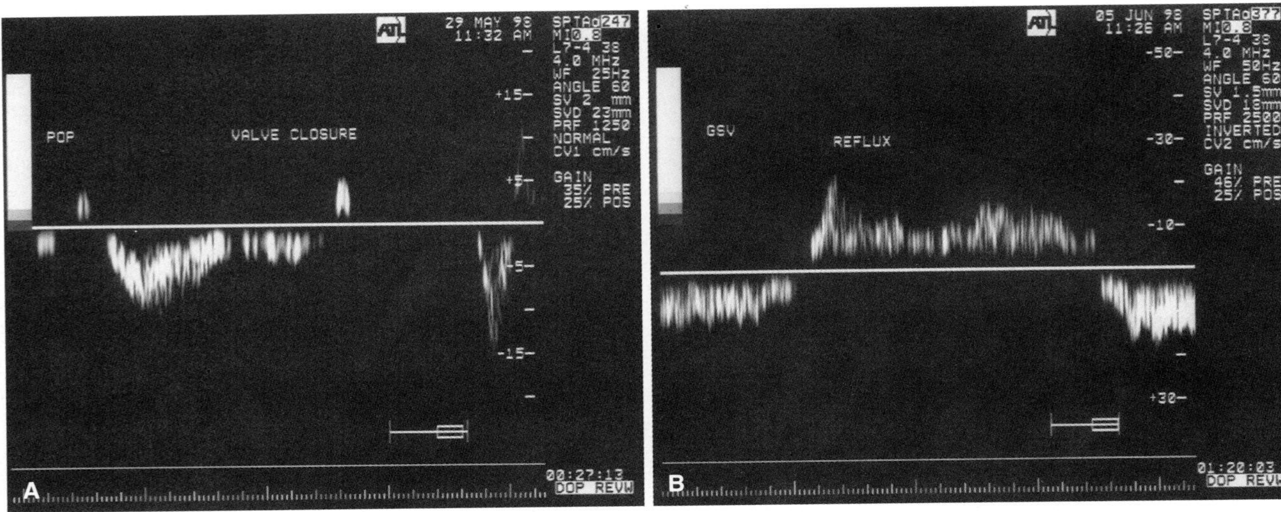

FIGURE 17-4 Duplex detection of valvular reflux. With reversal of normal antegrade flow, there is a brief interval of retrograde flow before valve closure. **A,** In the presence of a competent valve, valve closure appears as a clearly demarcated period of retrograde flow (above the baseline) of less than 0.5 second's duration. **B,** In the presence of valvular incompetence, the duration of reverse flow is prolonged.

maneuvers, acceptable results have been achieved with a Valsalva maneuver,[83] although diminished sensitivity below proximal competent valves and in the distal deep venous segments also has been reported.[6,81,82] The duration of reverse flow across venographically competent valves is also more variable with the Valsalva maneuver.[82] Proximal compression methods are inferior to release of distal compression, producing variable results with a poor separation between normal and diseased limbs.[3,141] Deflation of a cuff distal to the imaged segment in the standing position gives the shortest, most reproducible duration of reverse flow in normal subjects with a sensitivity of 91% and specificity of 100% for the detection of popliteal reflux.[3] Although diligent efforts may produce acceptable results with manual distal compression in the standing position, cuff deflation provides a more consistent and standardized approach.

The accuracy of standing distal cuff deflation has been compared with reflux determination in the supine position using manual limb compression and Valsalva maneuvers.[81,100] Considering standing cuff deflation as the reference standard within individual venous segments, the supine maneuvers are less sensitive than cuff deflation in identifying reflux at all levels (Table 17-6). The Valsalva maneuver is more sensitive in the proximal segments, whereas manual compression is more sensitive in the distal segments. The best sensitivity for the supine maneuvers is achieved when the presence of reflux is defined as a positive result with either limb compression or a Valsalva maneuver. Similarly, when quantified using a multisegment scoring system applied to the entire limb, standing distal cuff deflation provided a sensitivity of 77% and specificity of 85% for the differentiation of clinically mild and severe venous disease compared with 61% and 60% for supine duplex and 50% and 41% for descending phlebography.[100]

Standardized Standing Cuff Deflation

In evaluating reflux using the technique of standing cuff deflation,[100,101,141] the patient stands supported by a frame, with the leg slightly flexed and weight borne by the contralateral extremity. Pneumatic cuffs are placed distal to

Table 17-6 Sensitivity and Specificity of Supine Maneuvers Versus Standing Distal Cuff Deflation for Detecting Venous Reflux

	METHOD (%)					
	Valsalva		Manual Compression		Combined*	
SEGMENT	*Sensitivity*	*Specificity*	*Sensitivity*	*Specificity*	*Sensitivity*	*Specificity*
CFV	75	86	21	98	79	86
GSV	67	100	10	100	67	100
SFV	83	97	50	97	88	93
PPV	49	98	73	88	76	88
PTV	20	99	30	92	30	92

*Combined Valsalva and manual compression maneuvers. Reflux is considered to be present if the result of either individual maneuver is positive.
CFV, common femoral vein; GSV, greater saphenous vein; PPV, popliteal vein; PTV, posterior tibial vein; SFV, superficial femoral vein.

From Markel A, Meissner MH, Manzo RA, et al: A comparison of the cuff deflation method with Valsalva's maneuver and limb compression in detecting venous valvular reflux. Arch Surg 129:701-705, 1994. Copyright 1994 American Medical Association.

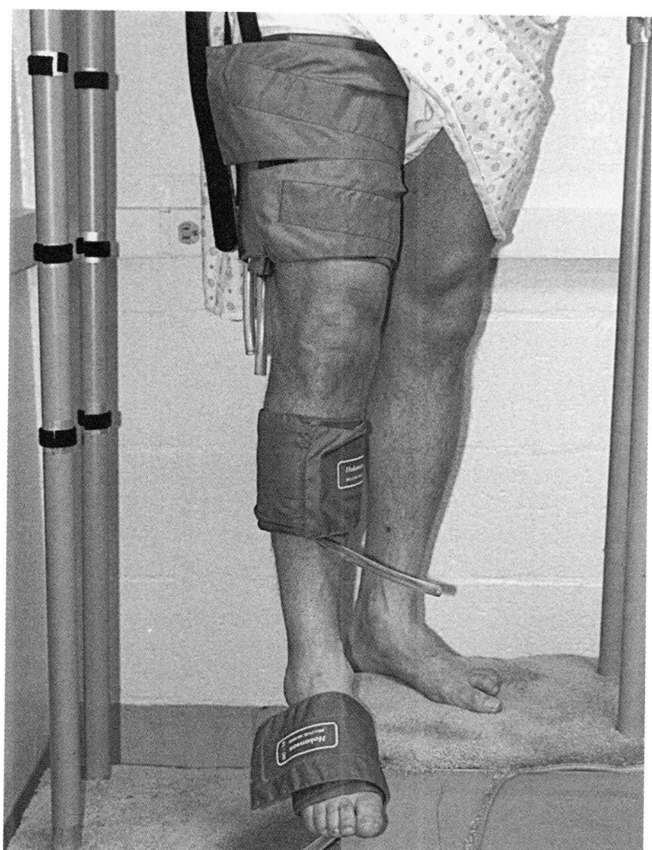

FIGURE 17-5 Reflux determination using standing distal cuff deflation. The patient stands with his weight supported on the contralateral extremity. Inflation pressure is adjusted according to the hydrostatic pressure at the level of the segment being imaged using a 24-cm cuff (Hokanson, Bellevue, Wash) inflated to 80 mm Hg for the thigh, a 12-cm cuff inflated to 100 mm Hg for the calf, and a 7-cm cuff inflated to 120 mm Hg for the foot.

the segment of interest, and inflation pressure is varied according to the hydrostatic pressure at that level. The common femoral, proximal superficial femoral, profunda femoris, and proximal greater saphenous veins are evaluated with a 24-cm thigh cuff inflated to 80 mm Hg; the distal superficial femoral and popliteal veins, with a 12-cm calf cuff inflated to 100 mm Hg; and the posterior tibial veins, using a 7-cm foot cuff inflated to 120 mm Hg (Fig. 17-5). A rapid cuff inflator (Hokanson, Bellevue, Wash) is used to provide inflation over approximately 3 seconds and rapid deflation within 0.3 second. The spectral display is adjusted to show antegrade flow below the baseline and reverse flow, or reflux, above the baseline. Each segment is sequentially imaged in a longitudinal plane at a distance less than 5 cm from the cuff. Doppler signals are recorded as the cuff is inflated until antegrade flow ceases, then as the cuff is rapidly deflated. Within 0.5 second of cuff deflation, 95% of normal valves close (Fig. 17-6),[141] a value that provides complete separation between normal volunteers and subjects with clinical manifestations of chronic venous disease.[3] Although the duration of retrograde flow also can be determined using color-flow Doppler, this may underestimate the duration of reflux compared with spectral measurements.[3]

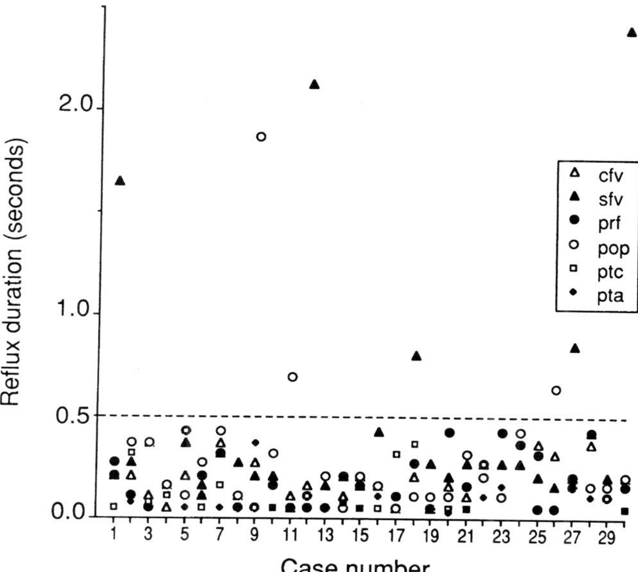

FIGURE 17-6 Duration of reflux in individual venous segments of 30 normal extremities in response to distal cuff deflation in the standing position. The duration of retrograde flow, or reflux, is less than 0.5 second in 95% of venous segments. cfv, common femoral vein; sfv, superficial femoral vein; prf, profunda femoris vein; pop, popliteal vein; ptc, posterior tibial vein, calf; pta, posterior tibial vein, ankle. (From van Bemmelen PS, Bedford G, Beach K, et al: Quantitative segmental evaluation of venous valvular reflux with duplex ultrasound scanning. J Vasc Surg 10:425-431, 1989.)

Standing distal cuff deflation for the detection of reflux does have some disadvantages compared with alternative maneuvers. Although a well-trained technologist can perform the entire study, assigning different technologists to scan and operate the pneumatic cuff inflator facilitates the learning process. The technique also requires additional equipment and a patient capable of standing for approximately 30 minutes. The results of these studies reflect pathologic reflux and its clinical severity better than either supine duplex studies or descending phlebography.[81,100]

Quantitative Applications of Duplex Scanning

Although duplex ultrasonography accurately identifies and localizes segmental venous reflux, the relationship of these findings to global venous hemodynamics is less well defined. Abnormal direct venous pressure measurements are present in only 80% of patients with common femoral or popliteal venous reflux detected by duplex.[135] Theoretically the magnitude of duplex-detected reflux should correlate with the severity of hemodynamic and clinical derangements, and several methods to quantify reflux have been proposed. Neglen and Raju[100,101] have suggested anatomic scoring systems, analogous to systems used for descending phlebography, based on either the axial extent or segmental distribution of reflux. Alternatively, duplex-derived valve closure times may be determined from the duration of reverse flow on the Doppler spectral tracing. Total valve closure times can be calculated as the sum of segmental closure times in the entire extremity or within the superficial and deep venous systems.[122,147] Finally, reflux flow volumes can be calculated from duplex-determined reflux velocities and venous cross-sectional area.[122,144]

Among these, methods of quantifying the anatomic extent of reflux have been more consistent than hemodynamic quantification. Neglen and Raju[100] found the quantitative extent of reflux determined by duplex to reflect better the clinical severity of disease than does standard phlebographic scoring. Quantitative anatomic scores also were correlated with invasive and noninvasive indices of reflux. Other authors[6] similarly have found abnormal foot volumetry results to correlate more closely with the extent of reflux determined by duplex than with that determined by phlebography. Attempts to quantify global venous hemodynamics with duplex have yielded inconsistent results. Segments included in the calculation of total valve closure times have varied among studies, as has the relationship to clinical manifestations and noninvasive measurements of global reflux. No studies have directly correlated duplex-derived valve closure times with AVP.[13] Although a relationship between total valve closure times, air plethysmographic indices of reflux, and the presence of venous ulceration has been noted by some,[147] others have noted a poor correlation with air plethysmography[122] and severe clinical manifestations.[58,122] Valve closure times in individual venous segments are poorly correlated with reflux volume because large volumes may reflux over short intervals, or small volumes may reflux over long intervals.[122] Measurements of peak reflux volume flow may have some utility, however, with peak volume flows greater than 10 mL/sec defining a group with a 66% prevalence of skin changes.[144]

Pending further evaluation of these quantitative duplex methods, there may be no ideal noninvasive study for the evaluation of chronic venous insufficiency. The inherent dichotomy between global assessment of hemodynamics and accurate localization of segmental reflux and obstruction may require a combination of tests in some circumstances. This has been viewed as analogous to lower extremity arterial assessment in which physiologic measurements, such as the ankle-brachial index, and anatomic studies, such as arteriography, provide complementary information.[149] For the present, it may be necessary to combine the unique ability of duplex scanning to assess and localize obstruction and reflux with measurements of hemodynamic severity determined by tests such as air plethysmography.[101] A combination of these studies may obviate the need for invasive tests in all cases but those requiring precise visualization of valvular anatomy in anticipation of venous reconstruction.

Evaluation of Perforator Incompetence

The perforating veins are evaluated in the upright position, scanning along the course of the superficial femoral vein in the mid-thigh and the posterior tibial and posterior arch veins in the calf. One to five perforating veins are usually traceable as they penetrate the fascia between the superficial and deep venous systems.[114] Perforating veins may occur anywhere along the medial calf, most commonly just below the malleolus and 15 to 19 cm and 30 to 34 cm proximally.[93,126] The direction of normal flow and the definition of perforating vein reflux remain controversial.[126] Flow in normal perforating veins is unidirectional and occurs only during distal compression of the foot or calf, whereas incompetent segments are identified by bidirectional flow with reverse flow during the relaxation phase after compression.[93] Duplex identifies more perforating veins than does ascending venography,[45] and compared with surgical findings, has been reported to have a sensitivity of 82% and specificity of 100% for the identification of competent and incompetent perforating veins.[114]

■ SUMMARY

Although duplex ultrasonography has facilitated the investigation of many areas of vascular disease, it has arguably had one of its greatest impacts in the evaluation of acute and chronic venous disease. For the diagnosis of proximal venous thrombosis, sensitivities and specificities approaching 95% have been well documented. Serial compression ultrasonography has largely supplanted contrast venography for the diagnosis of proximal DVT in symptomatic patients, and withholding anticoagulation in patients with negative studies 5 to 7 days apart has been shown to be safe and cost-effective. The use of color-flow Doppler has facilitated DVT diagnosis in areas such as the calf and iliac veins that are difficult to evaluate with compression ultrasonography. Although these advantages may make it theoretically possible to exclude acute DVT on the basis of a single technically adequate and complete color-flow study, the safety of such an approach has not been validated prospectively. Similarly the value of duplex ultrasound in screening high-risk asymptomatic patients for acute DVT will remain unclear until the natural history of patients with overlooked thrombi has been established. Duplex ultrasonography also has become the noninvasive standard for defining valvular incompetence and persistent venous occlusion in chronic venous disease. Erect evaluation using distal cuff deflation allows standardized physiologic assessment of reflux in individual segments. Although global measurements of venous hemodynamics and descending venography will continue to have some role in the evaluation of patients before and after reconstructive procedures, duplex ultrasound is capable of providing precise diagnosis and anatomic localization of the abnormalities underlying chronic venous disease.

■ REFERENCES

1. American Institute of Ultrasound in Medicine: Guidelines for the Performance of Vascular/Doppler Ultrasound Examination. Laurel, Md, American Institute of Ultrasound in Medicine, 1992.
2. Appelman PT, De Jong TE, Lampman LE: Deep venous thrombosis of the leg: US findings. Radiology 163:743, 1987.
3. Araki CT, Back TL, Padberg FT, et al: Refinements in the ultrasonic detection of popliteal vein reflux. J Vasc Surg 18:742, 1993.
4. Aronen RJ, Svedstrom E, Yrjana J, et al: Compression sonography in the diagnosis of deep venous thrombosis of the leg. Ann Med 26:377, 1994.
5. Bach AM, Hahn LE: When the common femoral vein is revealed as flattened on spectral Doppler sonography: Is it a reliable sign for diagnosis of proximal venous obstruction? AJR Am J Roentgenol 168:733, 1997.

6. Baker SR, Burnand KG, Sommerville KM, et al: Comparison of venous reflux assessed by duplex scanning and descending phlebography in chronic venous disease. Lancet 341:400, 1993.
7. Baldridge ED, Martin MA, Welling RE: Clinical significance of free-floating venous thrombi. J Vasc Surg 11:62, 1990.
8. Barnes RW, Wu KK, Hoak JC: Fallibility of the clinical diagnosis of venous thrombosis. JAMA 234:605, 1975.
9. Baxter GM, Duffy P: Calf vein anatomy and flow: Implications for color Doppler imaging. Clin Radiol 46:84, 1992.
10. Baxter GM, Duffy P, Partridge E: Colour flow imaging of calf vein thrombosis. Clin Radiol 46:198, 1992.
11. Baxter GM, Kincaid W, Jeffrey RF, et al: Comparison of colour Doppler ultrasound with venography in the diagnosis of axillary and subclavian vein thrombosis. Br J Radiol 64:777, 1991.
12. Baxter GM, Duffy P, MacKechnie S: Colour Doppler ultrasound of the post-phlebitic limb: Sounding a cautionary note. Clin Radiol 43:301, 1991.
13. Bays RA, Healy DA, Atnip RG, et al: Validation of air plethysmography, photoplethysmography, and duplex ultrasonography in the evaluation of severe venous stasis. J Vasc Surg 30:721, 1994.
14. Becker DM, Philbrick JT, Abbitt PL: Real-time ultrasonography for the diagnosis of lower extremity deep venous thrombosis. Arch Intern Med 149:1731, 1989.
15. Belcaro G: Evaluation of recurrent deep venous thrombosis using color duplex scanning—comparison with contrast venography. Vasa 21:22, 1992.
16. Bendayan P, Boccalon H: Cost-effectiveness of noninvasive tests including duplex scanning for diagnosis of deep venous thrombosis. Vasa 20:348, 1991.
17. Berry RE, George JE, Shaver WA: Free-floating deep venous thrombosis: A retrospective analysis. Ann Surg 211:719, 1990.
18. Bettmann MA, Robbins A, Braun SD, et al: Contrast venography of the leg: Diagnostic efficacy, tolerance, and complication rates with ionic and nonionic contrast media. Radiology 165:113, 1987.
19. Birdwell BG, Raskob GE, Whitsett TL, et al: The clinical validity of normal compression ultrasonography in outpatients suspected of having deep venous thrombosis. Ann Intern Med 128:1, 1998.
20. Brasel KJ, Borgstrom DC, Weigelt JA: Cost-effective prevention of pulmonary embolus in high-risk trauma patients. J Trauma 42:456, 1997.
21. Browse NL, Thomas ML: Source of nonlethal pulmonary emboli. Lancet 1:258, 1974.
22. Burbidge SJ, Finlay DE, Letourneau JG, et al: Effects of central venous catheter placement on upper extremity duplex US findings. J Vasc Interv Radiol 4:399, 1993.
23. Cogo A, Lensing AWA, Koopman MMW, et al: Compression ultrasonography for diagnostic management of patients with clinically suspected deep vein thrombosis: Prospective cohort study. BMJ 316:617, 1998.
24. Cogo A, Lensing AWA, Prandoni P, et al: Comparison of real-time B-mode ultrasonography and Doppler ultrasound with contrast venography in the diagnosis of venous thrombosis in symptomatic outpatients. Thromb Haemost 70:404, 1993.
25. Cranley JJ, Canos AJ, Sull WJ: The diagnosis of deep venous thrombosis: Fallability of clinical symptoms and signs. Arch Surg 111:34, 1976.
26. Criado E, Burnham CB: Predictive value of clinical criteria for the diagnosis of deep vein thrombosis. Surgery 122:578, 1997.
27. Cronan JJ: Deep venous thrombosis: One leg or both legs. Radiology 200:323, 1996.
28. Cronan JJ, Dorfman GS, Scola FH, et al: Deep venous thrombosis: US assessment using vein compression. Radiology 162:191, 1987.
29. Cronan JJ, Leen V: Recurrent deep venous thrombosis: Limitations of US. Radiology 170:739, 1989.
30. Dauzat M, Laroche J-P, Deklunder G, et al: Diagnosis of acute lower limb deep venous thrombosis with ultrasound: Trends and controversies. J Clin Ultrasound 25:343, 1997.
31. de Valois JC, van Schaik CC, Verzibergen F, et al: Contrast venography: From gold standard to "golden backup" in clinically suspected deep vein thrombosis. Eur J Radiol 11:131, 1990.
32. Elias A, Le Corff G, Bouvier JL, et al: Value of real-time B-mode ultrasound imaging in the diagnosis of deep vein thrombosis of the lower limbs. Int Angiol 6:175, 1987.
33. Eze AR, Comerota AJ, Kerr RP, et al: Is venous duplex imaging an appropriate initial screening test for patients with suspected pulmonary embolism? Ann Vasc Surg 10:220, 1996.
34. Falk RL, Smith DF: Thrombosis of upper extremity thoracic inlet veins: Diagnosis with duplex Doppler sonography. AJR Am J Roentgenol 149:677, 1987.
35. Fletcher JP, Kershaw LZ, Barker DS, et al: Ultrasound diagnosis of deep venous thrombosis. Med J Aust 153:453, 1990.
36. Flinn WR, Sandager GP, Cerullo LJ, et al: Duplex venous scanning for the prospective surveillance of perioperative venous thrombosis. Arch Surg 124:901, 1989.
37. Fowl RJ, Strothman GB, Blebea J, et al: Inappropriate use of venous duplex scans: An analysis of indications and results. J Vasc Surg 23:881, 1996.
38. Frederick MG, Hertzberg BS, Kliewer MA, et al: Can the US examination for lower extremity deep venous thrombosis be abbreviated? A prospective study of 755 examinations. Radiology 199:45, 1996.
39. Ginsberg JS, Kearon C, Douketis J, et al: The use of D-dimer testing and impedance plethysmographic examination in patients with clinical indications of deep vein thrombosis. Arch Intern Med 157:1077, 1997.
40. Glover JL, Bendick PJ: Appropriate indications for venous duplex ultrasonic examinations. Surgery 120:725, 1996.
41. Gooding GAW, Hightower DR, Moore EH, et al: Obstruction of the superior vena cava or subclavian veins: Sonographic diagnosis. Radiology 159:663, 1986.
42. Grassi CJ, Polak JF: Axillary and subclavian venous thrombosis: Follow-up evaluation with color flow US and venography. Radiology 175:651, 1990.
43. Greenfield LJ: Free-floating thrombus and pulmonary embolism [letter]. Arch Intern Med 157:2661, 1997.
44. Haeger K: Problems of acute deep venous thrombosis: Part 1. The interpretation of signs and symptoms. Angiology 20:219, 1969.
45. Hanrahan LM, Araki CT, Fisher JB, et al: Evaluation of the perforating veins of the lower extremity using high-resolution duplex imaging. J Cardiovasc Surg 32:87, 1991.
46. Harris LM, Curl GR, Booth FV, et al: Screening for asymptomatic deep vein thrombosis in surgical intensive care patients. J Vasc Surg 26:764, 1997.
47. Heijboer H, Buller HR, Lensing AWA, et al: A comparison of real-time compression ultrasonography with impedance plethysmography for the diagnosis of deep vein thrombosis in symptomatic outpatients. N Engl J Med 329:1365, 1993.
48. Hertzberg BS, Kliewer MA, DeLong DM, et al: Sonographic assessment of lower limb vein diameter: Implications for the diagnosis and characterization of deep venous thrombosis. AJR Am J Roentgenol 168:1253, 1997.
49. Hightower DR, Gooding GA: Sonographic evaluation of the normal respiratory response on subclavian veins to respiratory maneuvers. Invest Radiol 20:517, 1985.
50. Hill S, Holtzman G, Martin D, et al: Selective use of the duplex scan in diagnosis of deep venous thrombosis. Am J Surg 170:201, 1995.
51. Hillner BE, Philbrick JT, Becker DM: Optimal management of suspected lower extremity deep venous thrombosis: An evaluation with cost assessment of 24 management strategies. Arch Intern Med 152:165, 1992.
52. Hirsch DR, Ingenito EP, Goldhaber SZ: Prevalence of deep venous thrombosis among patients in medical intensive care. JAMA 274:335, 1995.
53. Hirsh J, Lensing AWA: Natural history of minimal calf vein deep venous thrombosis. In Bernstein EF (ed): Vascular Diagnosis, 4th ed. St. Louis, Mosby-Year Book, 1993, pp 779-781.

54. Hubsch PJ, Stigbauer RL, Schwaighofer BW, et al: Internal jugular and subclavian vein thrombosis caused by central venous catheters. J Ultrasound Med 7:629, 1988.
55. Hull R, Hirsh J, Sackett DL, et al: Clinical validity of a negative venogram in patients with clinically suspected venous thrombosis. Circulation 64:622, 1981.
56. Hull RD, Carter CJ, Jay RM, et al: The diagnosis of acute, recurrent, deep venous thrombosis: A diagnostic challenge. Circulation 67:901, 1983.
57. Hyers TM, Hull RD, Weg JG: Antithrombotic therapy for venous thromboembolic disease. Chest 108(Suppl):335S, 1995.
58. Iafrati MD, Welch H, O'Donnell TF, et al: Correlation of venous noninvasive tests with the Society for Vascular Surgery/International Society for Cardiovascular Surgery clinical classification for chronic venous insufficiency. J Vasc Surg 19:1001, 1994.
59. Johnson BF, Manzo RA, Bergelin RO, et al: The site of residual abnormalities in the leg veins in long-term follow-up after deep venous thrombosis and their relationship to the development of the post-thrombotic syndrome. Int Angiol 15:14, 1996.
60. Johnson BF, Manzo RA, Bergelin RO, et al: Relationship between changes in the deep venous system and the development of the post-thrombotic syndrome after an acute episode of lower limb deep vein thrombosis: A one- to six-year follow-up. J Vasc Surg 21:307, 1995.
61. Kakkar VV, Flanc C, Howe CT, et al: Natural history of postoperative deep vein thrombosis. Lancet 2:230, 1969.
62. Kearon C, Julian JA, Math M, et al: Noninvasive diagnosis of deep venous thrombosis: McMaster Diagnostic Imaging Practice Guidelines Initiative. Ann Intern Med 128:663, 1998.
63. Kelley MA, Carson JL, Palevsky HI, et al: Diagnosing pulmonary embolism: New facts and strategies. Ann Intern Med 114:300, 1991.
64. Killewich LA, Bedford GR, Beach KW, Strandness DE: Diagnosis of deep venous thrombosis: A prospective study comparing duplex scanning to contrast venography. Circulation 79:810, 1989.
65. Killewich LA, Nunnelee JD, Auer AI: Value of lower extremity venous duplex examination in the diagnosis of pulmonary embolism. J Vasc Surg 17:934, 1993.
66. Killewich LA, Bedford GR, Beach KW, et al: Spontaneous lysis of deep venous thrombi: Rate and outcome. J Vasc Surg 9:89, 1989.
67. Killewich LA, Martin R, Cramer M, et al: An objective assessment of the physiological changes in the postthrombotic syndrome. Arch Surg 120:424, 1985.
68. Kistner RL, Ball JJ, Nordyke RA, et al: Incidence of pulmonary embolism in the course of thrombophlebitis of the lower extremities. Am J Surg 124:169, 1972.
69. Knudson GJ, Wiedmeyer DA, Erickson SJ, et al: Color flow sonographic imaging in the assessment of upper extremity deep venous thrombosis. AJR Am J Roentgenol 154:399, 1990.
70. Kremkau FW: Doppler Ultrasound: Principles and Instrumentation. Philadelphia, WB Saunders, 1990.
71. Lagerstedt CI, Olsson C, Fagher BO, et al: Need for long-term anticoagulant treatment in symptomatic calf vein thrombosis. Lancet 2:515, 1985.
72. Lensing AWA, Davidson BL, Prins MH, et al: Diagnosis of deep vein thrombosis with ultrasound imaging in symptomatic patients and asymptomatic high-risk patients. In Hull R, Raskob G, Pineo G (eds): Venous Thromboembolism: An Evidence-Based Atlas. Armonk, NY: Futura Publishing, 1996, p 115.
73. Lensing AW, Prandoni P, Brandjes D, et al: Detection of deep vein thrombosis by real-time B-mode ultrasonography. N Engl J Med 320:342, 1989.
74. Lewis BD, James EM, Welch TJ, et al: Diagnosis of acute deep venous thrombosis of the lower extremities: Prospective evaluation of color Doppler flow imaging versus venography. Radiology 192:651, 1994.
75. Lipski DA, Shepard AD, McCarthy BD, et al: Noninvasive venous testing in the diagnosis of pulmonary embolism: The impact on decision making. J Vasc Surg 26:757, 1997.
76. Lohr JM, Hasselfeld KA, Byrne MP, et al: Does the asymptomatic limb harbor deep venous thrombosis? Am J Surg 168:184, 1994.
77. Lohr JM, Kerr TM, Lutter KS, et al: Lower extremity calf thrombosis: To treat or not to treat? J Vasc Surg 14:618, 1991.
78. Mantoni M: Deep venous thrombosis: Longitudinal study with duplex US. Radiology 179:271, 1991.
79. Markel A, Manzo RA, Bergelin R, et al: Acute deep vein thrombosis: Diagnosis, localization, and risk factors. J Vasc Med Biol 3:432, 1991.
80. Markel A, Manzo R, Bergelin R, et al: Pattern and distribution of thrombi in acute deep venous thrombosis. Arch Surg 127:305, 1992.
81. Markel A, Meissner MH, Manzo RA, et al: A comparison of the cuff deflation method with Valsalva's maneuver and limb compression in detecting venous valvular reflux. Arch Surg 129:701, 1994.
82. Masuda EM, Kistner RM: Prospective comparison of duplex scanning and descending venography in the assessment of venous insufficiency. Am J Surg 164:254, 1992.
83. Masuda EM, Kistner RL, Eklof B: Prospective study of duplex scanning for venous reflux: Comparison of Valsalva and pneumatic cuff techniques in the reverse Trendelenburg and standing positions. J Vasc Surg 20:711, 1994.
84. Matteson B, Langsfeld M, Schermer C, et al: Role of venous duplex scanning in patients with suspected pulmonary embolism. J Vasc Surg 24:768, 1996.
85. Mattos MA, Londrey GL, Leutz DW, et al: Color-flow duplex scanning for the surveillance and diagnosis of acute deep venous thrombosis. J Vasc Surg 15:366, 1992.
86. Mattos MA, Melendres G, Sumner DS, et al: Prevalence and distribution of calf vein thrombosis in patients with symptomatic deep venous thrombosis: A color flow duplex study. J Vasc Surg 24:738, 1996.
87. McLafferty RB, Moneta GL, Passman MA, et al: Late clinical and hemodynamic sequelae of isolated calf vein thrombosis. J Vasc Surg 27:50, 1998.
88. Meissner MH, Caps MT, Bergelin RO, et al: Early outcome after isolated calf vein thrombosis. J Vasc Surg 26:749, 1997.
89. Meissner MH, Caps MT, Bergelin RO, et al: Propagation, rethrombosis, and new thrombus formation after acute deep venous thrombosis. J Vasc Surg 22:558, 1995.
90. Meissner MH, Manzo RA, Bergelin RO, et al: Deep venous insufficiency: The relationship between lysis and subsequent reflux. J Vasc Surg 18:596, 1993.
91. Menzoian JO, Sequeira JC, Doyle JE, et al: Therapeutic and clinical course of deep venous thrombosis. Am J Surg 146:581, 1983.
92. Messina LM, Sarpa MS, Smith MA, et al: Clinical significance of routine imaging of iliac and calf veins by color flow duplex scanning in patients suspected of having acute lower extremity deep venous thrombosis. Surgery 114:921, 1993.
93. Miller SS, Foote AV: The ultrasonic detection of incompetent perforating veins. Br J Surg 61:653, 1974.
94. Mitchell DC, Grasty MS, Stebbings WS, et al: Comparison of duplex ultrasonography and venography in the diagnosis of deep venous thrombosis. Br J Surg 78:611, 1991.
95. Monreal M, Ruiz J, Salvador R, et al: Recurrent pulmonary embolism: A prospective study. Chest 95:976, 1989.
96. Moreno-Cabral R, Kistner RL, Nordyke RA: Importance of calf vein thrombophlebitis. Surgery 80:735, 1976.
97. Murphy TP, Cronan JJ: Evolution of deep venous thrombosis: A prospective evaluation with US. Radiology 177:543, 1990.
98. Naidich JB, Feinberg AW, Karp-Harman H, et al: Contrast venography: Reassessment of its role. Radiology 168:97, 1988.
99. Naidich JB, Torre JR, Pellerito JS, et al: Suspected deep venous thrombosis: Is US of both legs necessary? Radiology 200:429, 1996.
100. Neglen P, Raju S: A comparison between descending phlebography and duplex Doppler investigation in the evaluation of reflux in chronic venous insufficiency: A challenge to phlebography as the "gold standard." J Vasc Surg 16:687, 1992.
101. Neglen P, Raju S: A rational approach to detection of significant reflux with duplex Doppler scanning and air plethysmography. J Vasc Surg 17:590, 1993.

102. Nicolaides AN, Christopoulos D: Quantification of venous reflux and outflow with air plethysmography. In Bernstein EF (ed): Vascular Diagnosis, 4th ed. St. Louis, Mosby-Year Book, 1993, p 915.
103. Nicolaides AN, Hussein MK, Szendro G, et al: The relationship of venous ulceration with ambulatory venous pressure measurements. J Vasc Surg 17:414, 1993.
104. Nix ML, Troilett RD, Nelson CL, et al: Is bilateral duplex examination necessary for unilateral symptoms of deep venous thrombosis? J Vasc Technol 15:296, 1991.
105. Norris CS, Greenfield LJ, Herrmann JB: Free-floating ileofemoral thrombus: A risk of pulmonary embolism. Arch Surg 120:806, 1985.
106. Nypaver TJ, Shepard AD, Kiell CS, et al: Outpatient duplex scanning for deep vein thrombosis: Parameters predictive of a negative study result. J Vasc Surg 18:821, 1993.
107. O'Leary DH, Kane RA, Chase BM: A prospective study of the efficacy of B-scan sonography in the detection of deep venous thrombosis in the lower extremities. J Clin Ultrasound 16:1, 1988.
108. Ohgi S, Ito K, Tanaka K, et al: Echogenic types of venous thrombi in the common femoral vein by ultrasonic B-mode imaging. Vasc Surg 25:253, 1991.
109. Oudkerk M, van Beek EJR, van Putten WLJ, et al: Cost-effectiveness analysis of various strategies in the diagnostic management of pulmonary embolism. Arch Intern Med 153:947, 1993.
110. Pacouret G, Alison D, Pottier J-M, et al: Free-floating thrombus and embolic risk in patients with angiographically confirmed proximal deep venous thrombosis. Arch Intern Med 157:305, 1997.
111. Passman MA, Moneta GL, Taylor LM, et al: Pulmonary embolism is associated with the combination of isolated calf vein thrombosis and respiratory symptoms. J Vasc Surg 25:39, 1997.
112. Payne SP, London NJ, Newland CJ, et al: Ambulatory venous pressure: Correlation with skin condition and role in identifying surgically correctable disease. Eur J Endovasc Surg 11:195, 1996.
113. Pezullo JA, Perkins AB, Cronan JJ: Symptomatic deep vein thrombosis: Diagnosis with limited compression US. Radiology 198:67, 1996.
114. Pierik EG, Toonder IM, van Urk H, et al: Validation of duplex ultrasonography in detecting competent and incompetent perforating veins in patients with venous ulceration of the lower leg. J Vasc Surg 26:49, 1997.
115. Poppiti R, Papanicolaou G, Perese S: Limited B-mode venous imaging versus complete color flow duplex venous scanning for detection of proximal deep venous thrombosis. J Vasc Surg 22:553, 1995.
116. Porter J, Moneta G: Reporting standards in venous disease: An update. International Consensus Committee on Chronic Venous Disease. J Vasc Surg 21:635, 1995.
117. Prandoni P, Cogo A, Bernardi E, et al: A simple ultrasound approach for detection of recurrent proximal vein thrombosis. Circulation 88 (4 Part 1):1730, 1993.
118. Prandoni P, Polistena P, Bernardi E, et al: Upper extremity deep vein thrombosis: Risk factors, diagnosis, and complications. Arch Intern Med 157:57, 1997.
119. Prandoni P, Villalta S, Polistena P, et al: Symptomatic deep vein thrombosis and the post-thrombotic syndrome. Haematologica 80(2 Suppl):42, 1995.
120. Raju S, Fredericks R: Evaluation of methods for detecting venous reflux: Perspectives in venous insufficiency. Arch Surg 125:1463, 1990.
121. Raskob G: Calf vein thrombosis. In Hull R, Raskob G, Pineo G (eds): Venous Thromboembolism: An Evidence-Based Atlas. Armonk, NY, Futura Publishing, 1996, p 307.
122. Rodriguez AA, Whitehead CM, McLaughlin RL, et al: Duplex-derived valve closure times fail to correlate with reflux flow volumes in patients with chronic venous insufficiency. J Vasc Surg 23:606, 1996.
123. Rose SC, Zwiebel WJ, Nelson BD, et al: Symptomatic lower extremity deep venous thrombosis: Accuracy, limitations, and role of color duplex flow imaging in diagnosis. Radiology 175:639, 1990.
124. Rosfors S, Bygdeman S, Nordstrom E: Assessment of deep venous incompetence: A prospective study comparing duplex scanning with descending phlebography. Angiology 41:463, 1990.
125. Ruckley CV: Does venous reflux matter? Lancet 341:411, 1993.
126. Sarin S, Scurr JH, Coleridge Smith PD: Medial calf perforators in venous diseases: The significance of outward flow. J Vasc Surg 16:40, 1992.
127. Sarpa MS, Messina LM, Smith M, et al: Reliability of venous duplex scanning to image the iliac veins and to diagnose iliac vein thrombosis in patients suspected of having acute deep venous thrombosis. J Vasc Technol 15:299, 1991.
128. Sauerbrei E, Thomson JG, McLachlan MS, et al: Observer variation in lower limb venography. J Can Assoc Radiol 32:28, 1981.
129. Schiff MJ, Feinberg AW, Naidich JB: Noninvasive venous examinations as a screening test for pulmonary embolism. Arch Intern Med 147:505, 1987.
130. Sheiman RG, McArdle CR: Bilateral lower extremity US in the patient with unilateral symptoms of deep venous thrombosis: Assessment of need. Radiology 194:171, 1995.
131. Sluzewski M, Koopman MMW, Schuur KH, et al: Influence of negative ultrasound findings on the management of inpatients and outpatients with suspected deep vein thrombosis. Eur J Radiol 13:174, 1991.
132. Strandness DE, Sumner DS: Ultrasonic velocity detector in the diagnosis of thrombophlebitis. Arch Surg 104:180, 1972.
133. Strothman G, Blebea J, Fowl RJ: Contralateral duplex scanning for deep venous thrombosis is unnecessary in patients with symptoms. J Vasc Surg 22:543, 1995.
134. Sumner DS, Mattos MA: Diagnosis of deep vein thrombosis with real-time color and duplex scanning. In Bernstein EF (ed): Vascular Diagnosis, 4th ed. St. Louis, Mosby-Year Book, 1993, p 785.
135. Szendro G, Nicolaides AN, Zukowski AJ, et al: Duplex scanning in the assessment of deep venous incompetence. J Vasc Surg 4:237, 1986.
136. Talbot SR: Use of real-time imaging in identifying deep venous obstruction: A preliminary report. Bruit 6:41, 1982.
137. Talbot SR: B-mode evaluation of peripheral veins. Semin Ultrasound CT MR 9:295, 1988.
138. Vaccaro JP, Cronan JJ, Dorfman GS: Outcome analysis of patients with normal compression US exams. Radiology 175:645, 1990.
139. van Bemmelen PS, Bedford G, Strandness DE: Visualization of calf veins by color flow imaging. Ultrasound Med Biol 16:15, 1990.
140. van Bemmelen PS, Beach K, Bedford G, et al: The mechanism of venous valve closure—its relationship to the velocity of reverse flow. Arch Surg 125:617, 1990.
141. van Bemmelen PS, Bedford G, Beach K, et al: Quantitative segmental evaluation of venous valvular reflux with duplex ultrasound scanning. J Vasc Surg 10:425, 1989.
142. van Bemmelen PS, van Ramshorst B, Eikelboom BC: Photoplethysmography reexamined: Lack of correlation with duplex scanning. Surgery 112:544, 1992.
143. van Ramshorst B, van Bemmelen PS, Honeveld H, et al: Thrombus regression in deep venous thrombosis: Quantification of spontaneous thrombolysis with duplex scanning. Circulation 86:414, 1992.
144. Vasdekis SN, Clarke GH, Nicolaides AN: Quantification of venous reflux by means of duplex scanning. J Vasc Surg 10:670, 1989.
145. Voet D, Afschrift M: Floating thrombi: Diagnosis and follow-up by duplex ultrasound. Br J Radiol 64:1010, 1991.
146. Vogel P, Laing FC, Jeffrey RB, et al: Deep venous thrombosis of the lower extremity: US evaluation. Radiology 163:747, 1987.
147. Weingarten MS, Czeredarczuk M, Scovell S, et al: A correlation of air plethysmography and color flow-assisted duplex scanning in the quantification of chronic venous insufficiency. J Vasc Surg 24:750, 1996.
148. Weissleder R, Elizondo G, Stark DD: Sonographic diagnosis of subclavian and internal jugular vein thrombosis. J Ultrasound Med 6:577, 1987.

149. Welch HJ, Faliakou EC, McLaughlin RL, et al: Comparison of descending phlebography with quantitative photoplethysmography, air plethysmography, and duplex quantitative valve closure time in assessing deep venous reflux. J Vasc Surg 16:913, 1992.
150. Welkie JF, Comerota AJ, Katz ML, et al: Hemodynamic deterioration in chronic venous disease. J Vasc Surg 16:733, 1992.
151. Wells PS, Hirsh J, Anderson DR, et al: Accuracy of clinical assessment of deep vein thrombosis. Lancet 345:1326, 1995.
152. Wells PS, Lensing AW, Davidson BL, et al: Accuracy of ultrasound for the diagnosis of deep venous thrombosis in asymptomatic patients after orthopedic surgery: A meta-analysis. Ann Intern Med 122:47, 1995.
153. Wester JP, Holtkamp M, Linnebank ER, et al: Noninvasive detection of deep venous thrombosis: Ultrasonography versus duplex scanning. Eur J Vasc Surg 8:357, 1994.
154. Wheeler HB, Hirsh J, Wells P, et al: Diagnostic tests for deep venous thrombosis: Clinical usefulness depends on probability of disease. Arch Intern Med 154:1921, 1994.
155. White RH, McGahan JP, Daschbach MM, et al: Diagnosis of deep vein thrombosis using duplex ultrasound. Ann Intern Med 111:297, 1989.
156. Yucel EK, Fisher JS, Eggin TK, et al: Isolated calf venous thrombosis: Diagnosis with compression US. Radiology 179:443, 1991.
157. Zwiebel WJ: Color-encoded blood flow imaging. Semin Ultrasound CT MR 9:320, 1988.

Section IV

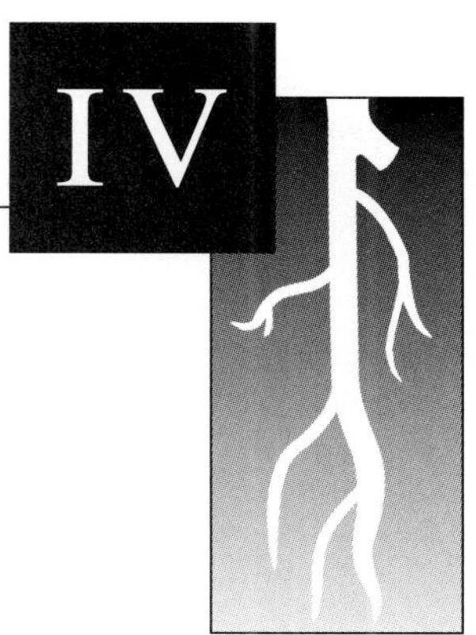

VASCULAR IMAGING: BASIC TECHNIQUES AND APPLICATIONS

HUGH G. BEEBE, MD

Chapter 18

Principles of Arteriography

JUAN AYERDI, MD
KIM J. HODGSON, MD

Noninvasive imaging modalities, such as duplex ultrasonography, computed tomography (CT), arteriography, and magnetic resonance angiography, have gained wide acceptance in recent years because of their high diagnostic accuracy and clinical utility. Nevertheless, arteriography remains the "gold standard" by which all other vascular imaging modalities should be judged because of its superb resolution and minimal artifactual degradation. Since publication of the previous edition of this book, arteriography is being performed by an increasing number of vascular surgeons. Preprocedural, perioperative, and postoperative arteriography studies are an essential part of practically all of the ever-expanding number of endovascular therapeutic procedures that vascular surgeons increasingly are incorporating into their practices. Consequently, it is imperative that vascular surgeons appreciate the techniques involved in performing arteriography and the incumbent complications and sources of error that might mislead the diagnosis and compromise the treatment rendered to patients.

This chapter reviews the general principles applicable to arteriography, including the design of radiologic equipment, operation of radiographic gear, contrast agents, filming procedures, and the related topics of renal protection and radiation safety. Emphasis also is placed on basic methods to improve angiographic imaging. Specific endovascular techniques relevant to angiographic procedures, such as obtaining vascular access, use of catheters and guide wires, and associated interventional procedures, are reviewed elsewhere in this book.

■ BASIC CONCEPTS OF RADIOGRAPHIC IMAGE RECORDING

In its most basic form, the "cut film" radiograph, arteriographic imaging is achieved by performing radiographic exposure of a sheet of x-ray film through an anatomic region positioned between the x-ray source and the film while a relatively radiopaque agent is within the vessel of interest. The disparate radiodensities of the contrast-filled vessel and the surrounding tissues yield an image of the contours and characteristics of the inside of the vessel. Although surgeons routinely perform "single-shot" completion arteriograms to evaluate newly created bypass grafts, comprehensive diagnostic arteriography requires the recording of a series of images obtained while the contrast agent passes through the vessel lumen. To achieve this with cut film requires a mechanism to move a series of x-ray films under the anatomic area of interest as the x-ray exposure is made. Such rapid-sequence film changers can transport 30 individual films at rates of 6 films per second. Viewing the results of the series of angiographic images requires waiting for the films to be developed, which considerably prolongs the angiographic examination, particularly if subsequent interventions are performed and further angiographic re-evaluation is needed. Cut-film angiography requires the patient to be repositioned over the film changer after catheter placement has been effected under the fluoroscopic x-ray source and image intensifier. This additional step adds time, complexity, and potential for catheter dislodgment during or before the examination.

Other methods of recording angiographic images during contrast passage include video radiography, whereby the fluoroscopic images are recorded on videotape for later review, and cineradiography, in which the recording medium is motion picture film. Both of these methods have inferior image resolution compared with cut-film radiography and the newer technique of digital subtraction angiography (DSA) (discussed later) and are generally considered to be inadequate peripheral vascular imaging modalities by today's standards. Cineradiography continues to be the mainstay of coronary angiography archival imaging, however, because the high-speed filming produces the best possible images of the heart and its vessels, which are in constant motion. Review of each coronary contrast injection during the procedure to determine whether adequate visualization occurred typically employs videoradiography because it would be impractical to develop the cine film after each filming run.

Intra-arterial Digital Subtraction Angiography

Advances in computer data processing power have led to the development of DSA, which provides images of comparable quality to conventional film angiography. DSA involves a recording technique whereby the fluoroscopic image is amplified and digitized, allowing for subsequent processing by many means that can enhance visualization of the structures of interest. Perhaps the most powerful of these is the "subtraction" of the radiodensities of the surrounding tissues and vessel wall from the images obtained after contrast material has been introduced into the lumen of the vessel. Typically the computer "subtracts" the pixels of the first image of the series, referred to as the *mask image,* from the subsequent images. As long as there has been no movement between the time the mask image was obtained and contrast material filled the vessel, the result is an image derived solely from the column of contrast within the lumen of the vessel without the image degradation frequently caused by the contrasting radiodensities of the surrounding tissues. Any skeletal or visceral movement that has occurred can degrade the image substantially. Any image of the series can be designated as the mask image, however, frequently allowing the undesirable consequences of movement occurring before the arrival of the contrast agent to be mitigated by selecting a new mask image that had been exposed after the movement occurred, but either before or after the contrast agent was within the vessel of interest (Fig. 18-1A and B). Consequently, when movement is observed during the filming process, filming should be continued until after the contrast agent has cleared the vessel so that these late images also are available to be used as masks to be subtracted from the contrast-enhanced images.

A variety of other postprocessing capabilities are now commonplace on DSA equipment, permitting the trained operator to "clean up" the angiographic images substantially to yield the best possible angiographic visualization. One such capability is the combination of multiple images to show contrast throughout the length of a vessel when any single image alone would have shown only contrast within a limited area (Fig. 18-2). Using another helpful feature, the effect of movement occurring after contrast material has entered the field of view often can be minimized by "pixel shifting" the image, whereby the mask image is slid vertically or horizontally (or both) over the contrast image to "realign" the two, negating the degrading effect of movement (see Fig. 18-1B and C). Subtraction also can be turned off so that the native image with radiographic landmarks is easily visible, a technique that aids in the performance of subsequent selective catheterizations or interventions (see Fig. 18-1D).

The technique called *road mapping* allows an image of the contrast-filled vessel (the "road map") to be displayed on the fluoroscopy monitor while a real-time image of any changing radiodensities, such as the passage of a guide wire, is visualized within the road map. This technique can facilitate the passage of catheters and guide wires through diseased or tortuous vessels, but is sensitive to any movement of the patient that severely degrades the image. At times, fluoroscopic visualization through the road map is suboptimal in resolution. Some radiographic units have a "fade in anatomic background" feature, which allows the density of the road map to be faded in and out to improve fluoroscopic visualization when the road map is not needed, yet maintaining the ability to recall the captured and stored road map later, as long as the table, image intensifier, or patient has not moved in the interim. This technique allows the operator to fade in and out the anatomic background from the stored road-map run, using the road map to see where he or she is when needed without having to endure the sometimes confounding effects of even minor movement throughout the manipulation.

Last, with DSA, image contrast, brightness, edge enhancement, sharpness, and even the color of the contrast agent (image invert) can be modified before storing or printing the image on x-ray film. Laser film printers are essential for high-quality archival image and provide a variety of film formats, from 1 large image to 15 smaller images on a standard 14×17 inch sheet of film. Consequently, with only the most revealing of the images being printed, there is considerable savings in film and storage costs over traditional cut-film angiography. Because the DSA format is digital, a newer and better storage alternative consists of storing the processed images and entire angiographic runs on digital media, such as a computer hard drive or individual CDs or DVDs.

In addition to the myriad of postprocessing capabilities, many other advantages of DSA have resulted in its supplanting cut-film angiography as the standard format in use for peripheral vascular angiographic imaging today. Because "filming" is done using the same x-ray source and image intensifier used for fluoroscopy, there is no need to reposition the patient between catheter placement and image acquisition as required for cut film recording; this significantly expedites the examination, as does the fact that the images obtained can be viewed immediately, without having to wait to develop the films. Any dislodgment of the catheter is immediately apparent and often can be corrected before contrast injection, avoiding unnecessary repetition of filming runs and injection of additional contrast material. Additionally, optical and digital amplifications combined with image subtraction allows for adequate opacification with reduced volume and concentration of contrast, reducing patient discomfort (by way of reduced contrast

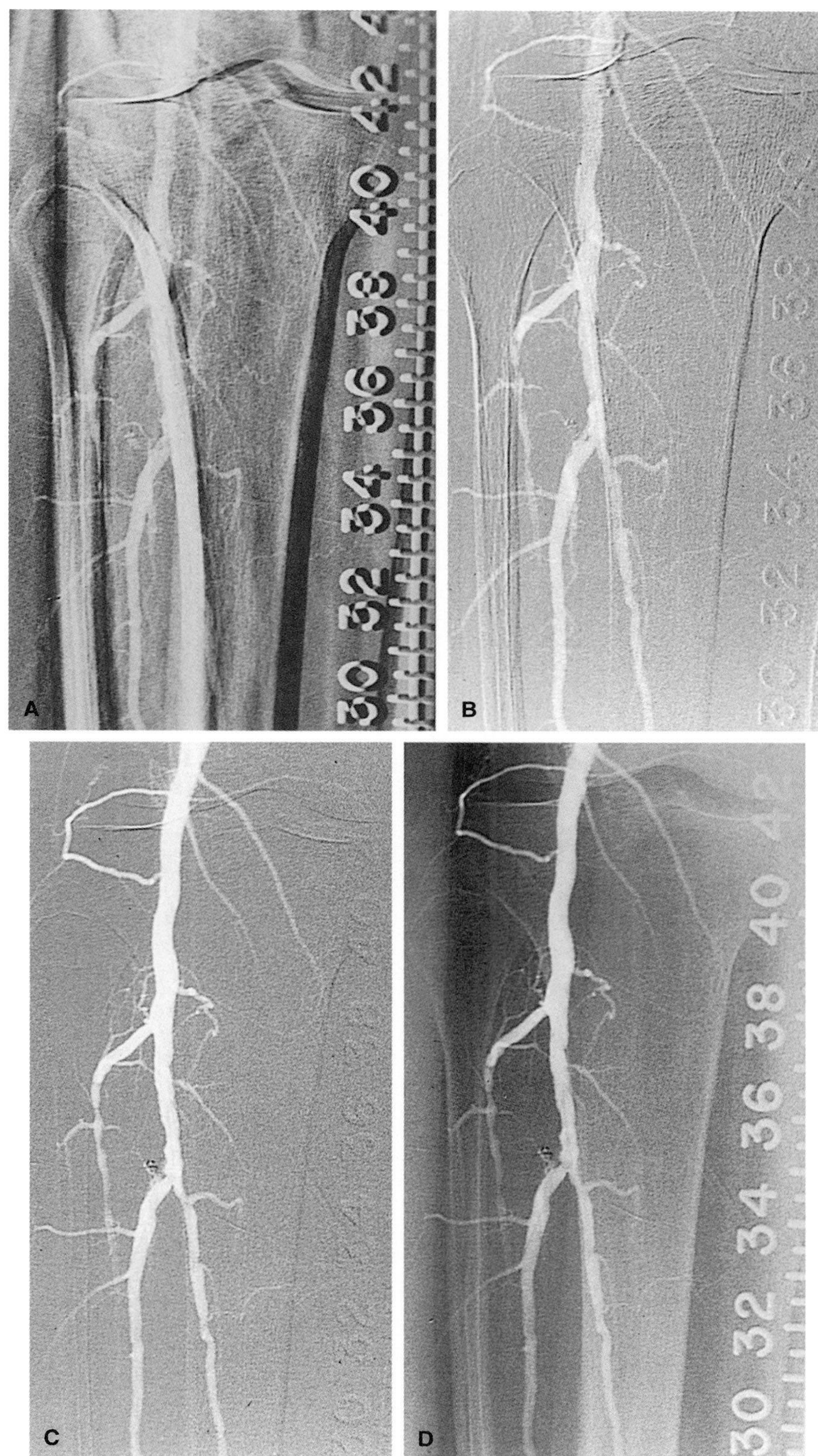

FIGURE 18-1 **A,** Image degradation caused by patient movement, most of which occurred before the arrival of contrast, permitting selection of a new mask image to minimize the effect of the movement. **B,** Image improvement due to new mask image selection, choosing one closer in time to the arrival of the contrast agent. **C,** Further improvement obtained by pixel shifting of the image. **D,** Subtraction can be turned off to reveal anatomic landmarks.

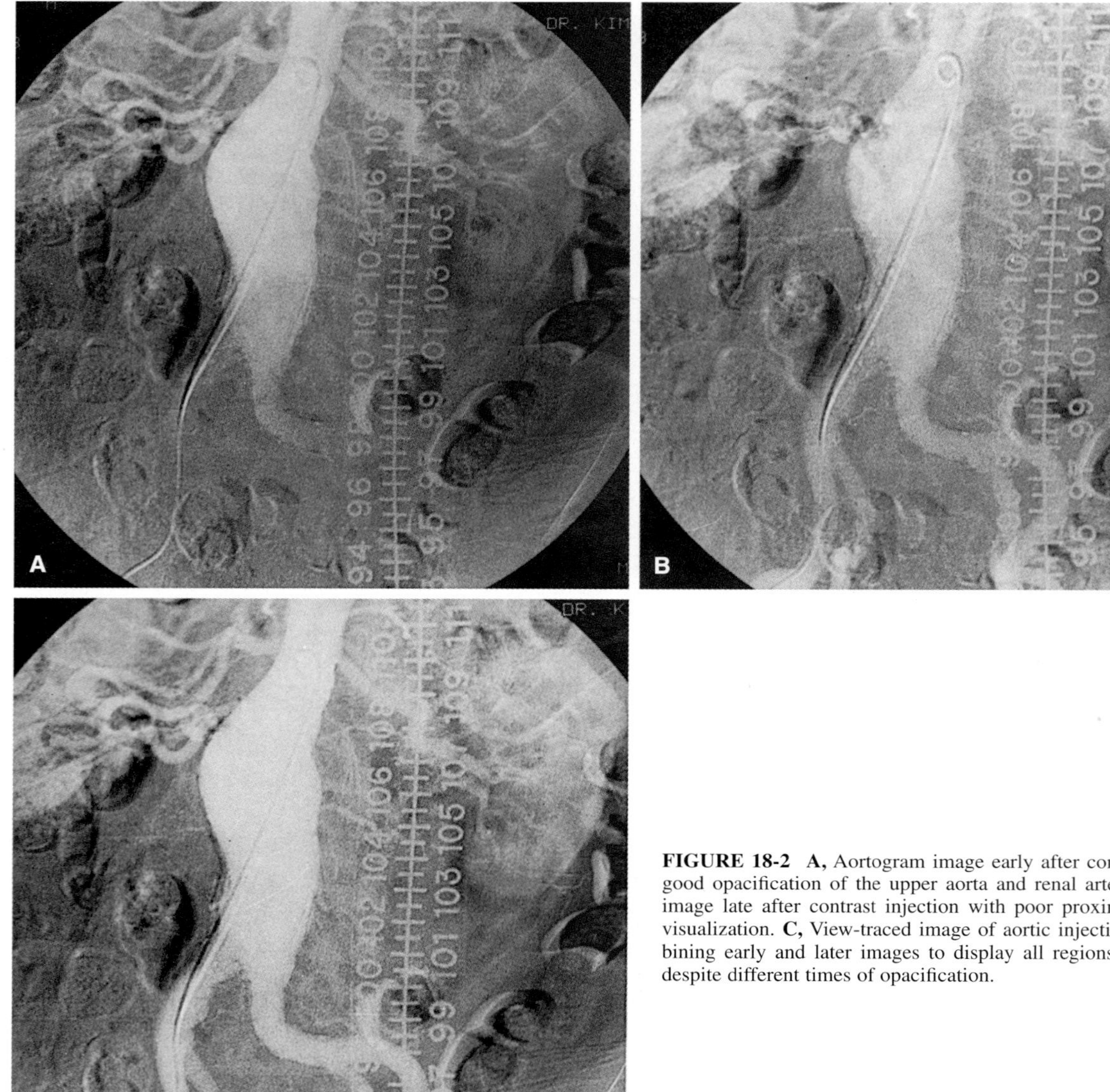

FIGURE 18-2 **A,** Aortogram image early after contrast injection with good opacification of the upper aorta and renal arteries. **B,** Aortogram image late after contrast injection with poor proximal but good distal visualization. **C,** View-traced image of aortic injection created by combining early and later images to display all regions of the vasculature despite different times of opacification.

osmolality) and cost. Although the resolution typically found in currently available DSA units is less than that which can be obtained with cut-film angiography, this is rarely clinically relevant and is more than compensated for by the superior opacification seen with DSA, particularly in small vessels with minimal flow.

A final advantage of DSA is the ability to obtain images with variable levels of magnification, depending on the needs of the examination. A typical DSA suite used for peripheral vascular work includes an image intensifier that can be set to a range of sizes, usually from 17 to 40 cm. Although renal arteries are often evaluated first with a flush aortogram filmed using the 25- or 40-cm setting, subsequent selective catheterization runs are usually performed at magnified views, allowing better visualization of anatomic detail (Fig. 18-3). Similarly, although a unilateral lower extremity runoff series could be obtained with five to seven injections if filming was performed on the 20-cm setting, the same evaluation might only take three or four runs at the 40-cm image intensifier size. With large image intensifiers, most patients can have both of their legs imaged simultaneously, further reducing the number of runs needed to perform the evaluation, although not the amount of contrast material infused.

Intravenous Digital Subtraction Angiography

Although there was initial enthusiasm that DSA could be performed using relatively small volumes of contrast material injected intravenously (IV), eliminating the expense and risk of arterial catheterization and minimizing contrast toxicity, the limitations of this approach soon

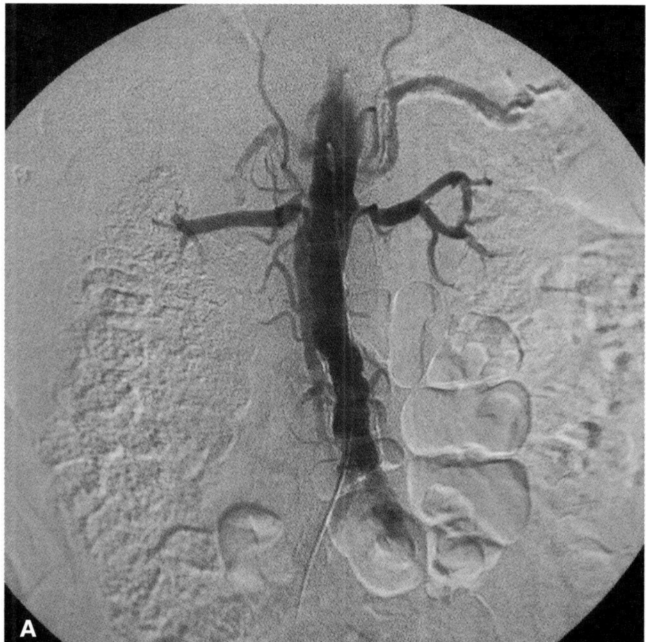

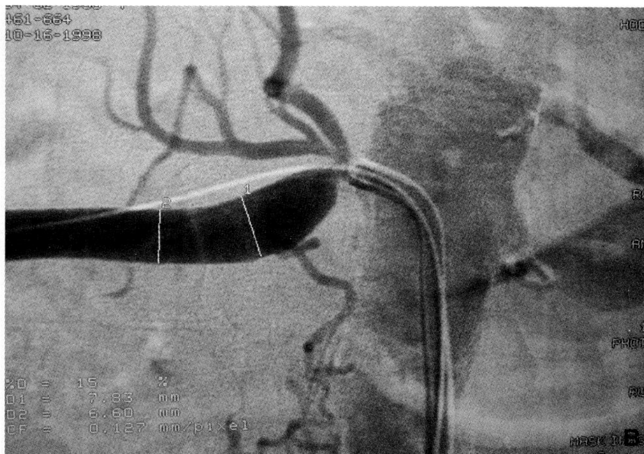

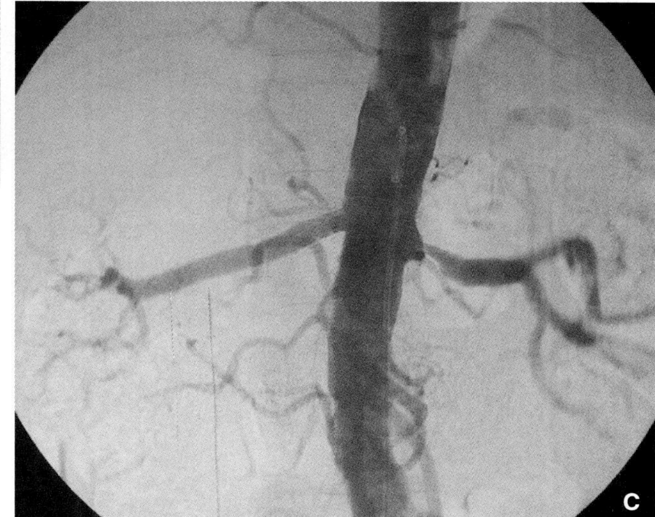

FIGURE 18-3 **A,** Power aortogram with a 40-cm image intensifier shows bilateral renal artery stenosis. **B,** Magnified 20-cm view shows better definition and allows for better wire control to cross the right stenotic lesion. **C,** Completion aortogram after renal dilatation with a 6 × 20 mm balloon expandable stent.

became apparent, and this has largely been abandoned.[1,2] Foremost among the problems is that the contrast agent is usually too dilute by the time it reaches the arterial region of interest to provide adequate resolution. With all of the vessels in the region filling at the same time, overlapping vessels often obscure the vessel of interest and provide a confusing and uninterpretable image. Filming in multiple projections may allow all segments of the artery to be evaluated without overlapping interference, but this requires multiple contrast injections, negating the potential benefit of minimizing the volume of contrast material infused. Conversely, intra-arterial DSA, while maintaining the risks and expense of arterial catheterization, derives the maximal benefit of the digital technique with far superior image quality and can be performed with comparable or even lessened volumes of contrast agent infusion.

Single-Injection Multiple Linear Fields and Rotational Digital Subtraction Angiography

The advent of image intensifiers suitably large to permit simultaneous bilateral lower extremity imaging stimulated interest in the development of a means to allow DSA of the entire length of both legs with one bolus of contrast material delivered into the infrarenal abdominal aorta. The principal obstacle that had to be overcome was the means by which multiple mask images could be obtained for subsequent subtraction from the corresponding contrast-filled images. Two slightly different approaches to this problem have emerged. The first method films in stages, using four to five operator-preset image intensifier positions, or stages, that cover the entire length of the lower extremities, with some overlap of the images. When set up, the run is initiated by the automated procurement of the mask images from each stage as the image intensifier moves to each preset position, starting at the feet and ending in the abdomen. A bolus of contrast material is injected with the camera filming at the uppermost position, typically the lower abdomen. As the contrast bolus begins to fill the femoral arteries, the operator triggers movement of the camera to the exact position where the next mask image was obtained, and filming continues with this new field of view. As contrast nears the distal aspect of each subsequent stage, the camera is moved again, and so on, until the entire area of interest has been covered. Because the mask images were obtained before the contrast run, the progress of contrast through the bed of distribution is viewed in subtraction mode, facilitating visualization and the decision of when to move to the next stage of the series. When the run is completed, images from the various film stages are electronically "seamed" together and can be viewed with or without subtraction of their corresponding masks.

The second approach to long-segment DSA maintains a fixed image intensifier position, moving the table and the patient instead. This technique uses a larger number of smaller incremental movements, referred to as *steps,* than the staged system discussed previously. The steps allow the operator to follow more closely the progress of the bolus of contrast material down the leg. Because the mask images are obtained after the contrast run, however, visualization during filming is in a nonsubtracted format. The rate of movement of the table can be slowed, or even stopped, in areas where contrast opacification is delayed. When the entire area of interest has been covered, the table returns to the beginning position, and the mask run is performed with the table automatically being advanced through the same step sequence that was used during the contrast injection run. Each frame of the mask run is subtracted from its corresponding frame in the contrast run yielding a DSA run of the entire length of the lower extremities. As with the staged format discussed earlier, the images from the filming run may be viewed with or without digital subtraction and may be postprocessed in many of the ways previously discussed to improve on the quality of the raw image.

As with single-field DSA, the principal limitation of both of these multiple-field DSA techniques is the need for the patient to keep absolutely still during the acquisition of the mask and the contrast images. Although the typical single-field filming run lasts for less than 15 seconds, long-segment runs and mask acquisition often last 2 minutes. Patient cooperation is an absolute necessity. Movement and its resulting motion artifact may be reduced by the use of immobilization straps. The use of iso-osmolar contrast agents minimizes patient discomfort and the propensity for leg cramps and movement during the angiographic run. The duration of the imaging run is largely a function of the transit time of the contrast agent and is identical between the two techniques. The mask run is performed more quickly, however, with the staged technique, which may be less prone to motion-related image degradation. The stepped technique allows for finer movements of the subject and often can achieve superior vessel opacification because movement of the field of view can track more closely the progress of the bolus of dye than with the staged technique. In practice, both techniques work reasonably well, and there seems to be little advantage to one over the other.

Bilateral imaging may be compromised with both techniques when more severe disease on one side results in significantly different transit times between the two sides. In such situations, it may not be possible to step or stage the imaging run in such a fashion that adequate contrast opacification is present on both sides simultaneously. This problem can be overcome by performing unilateral filming of each side separately (Fig. 18-4). Additionally, because unilateral filming is typically performed through a selective unilateral catheterization positioned more distally in the arterial tree, there is the added advantage of superior vascular opacification by virtue of injection of the dye closer to the area of interest, resulting in a lessened degree of contrast dilution during transit. Such unilateral examinations can be performed using a single injection of a bolus of contrast material and the multiple-field formats described earlier or with sequential single-field filming and repeated injections of contrast material. Typical contrast injection volumes for single-injection, multiple-field filming range from 80 to 100 mL of full-strength contrast material for bilateral filming and 50 to 60 mL for unilateral filming. For comparison, multiple-injection, single-field lower extremity filming usually employs 10 mL of half-strength contrast material per injection, with complete coverage of the extremity requiring four to six filming runs, depending on the size of the image intensifier. Consequently the contrast usage benefits of single-injection, multiple-field DSA come from being able to image both legs simultaneously through a proximally placed catheter. If that imaging proves infeasible or inadequate, such as in situations in which severe disease prevents adequate visualization, a more distal catheter placement may be necessary to obtain good visualization (Fig. 18-5).

Radiographic equipment capable of generating three-dimensional angiographic images (Fig. 18-6) is now available, although far from commonplace. This technique uses special acquisition programs and a rotating image intensifier allowing angiography with or without DSA. The target region is located at the center, and images are acquired from different angles. The usual rotational angles go from 90 degrees to 213 degrees depending on the C-arm system. These projections are predetermined at different rotational ranges, and the images can be optimized for a three-dimensional arteriographic reconstruction. Rotational angiography is similar to linear multiple-field imaging in that it can be performed with a single contrast injection.

■ EQUIPMENT REQUIREMENTS FOR ANGIOGRAPHIC EVALUATIONS

The requisite equipment to perform an angiographic evaluation depends greatly on the nature, scope, and site of service of the evaluation being undertaken. Although direct exposure, single-shot intraoperative angiography may be adequate for prebypass planning or completion evaluation of bypass grafts or embolectomy procedures, DSA is a practical requirement of almost all other vascular diagnostic or therapeutic procedures. Intraoperative fluoroscopic visualization can substantially aid in the performance of many standard surgical procedures, such as embolectomy, allowing the procedures to be performed more safely, expeditiously, and effectively. Every effort should be made to gain access to equipment and facilities most suitable for the task at hand to achieve the best possible visualization in the most convenient manner under given clinical circumstances. At minimum, access is required to digital subtraction radiographic equipment with instantaneous digital playback. It also is incumbent on the surgeon to become familiar with the features, postprocessing capabilities, and mode of operation of the available equipment so as to ensure that the best possible imaging is achieved.

Currently available DSA equipment can be broadly divided into two categories: fixed (floor or ceiling mounted) units with remote power generators and portable self-contained units. The merits of each of these types of systems are discussed in the next section. Regardless of which type

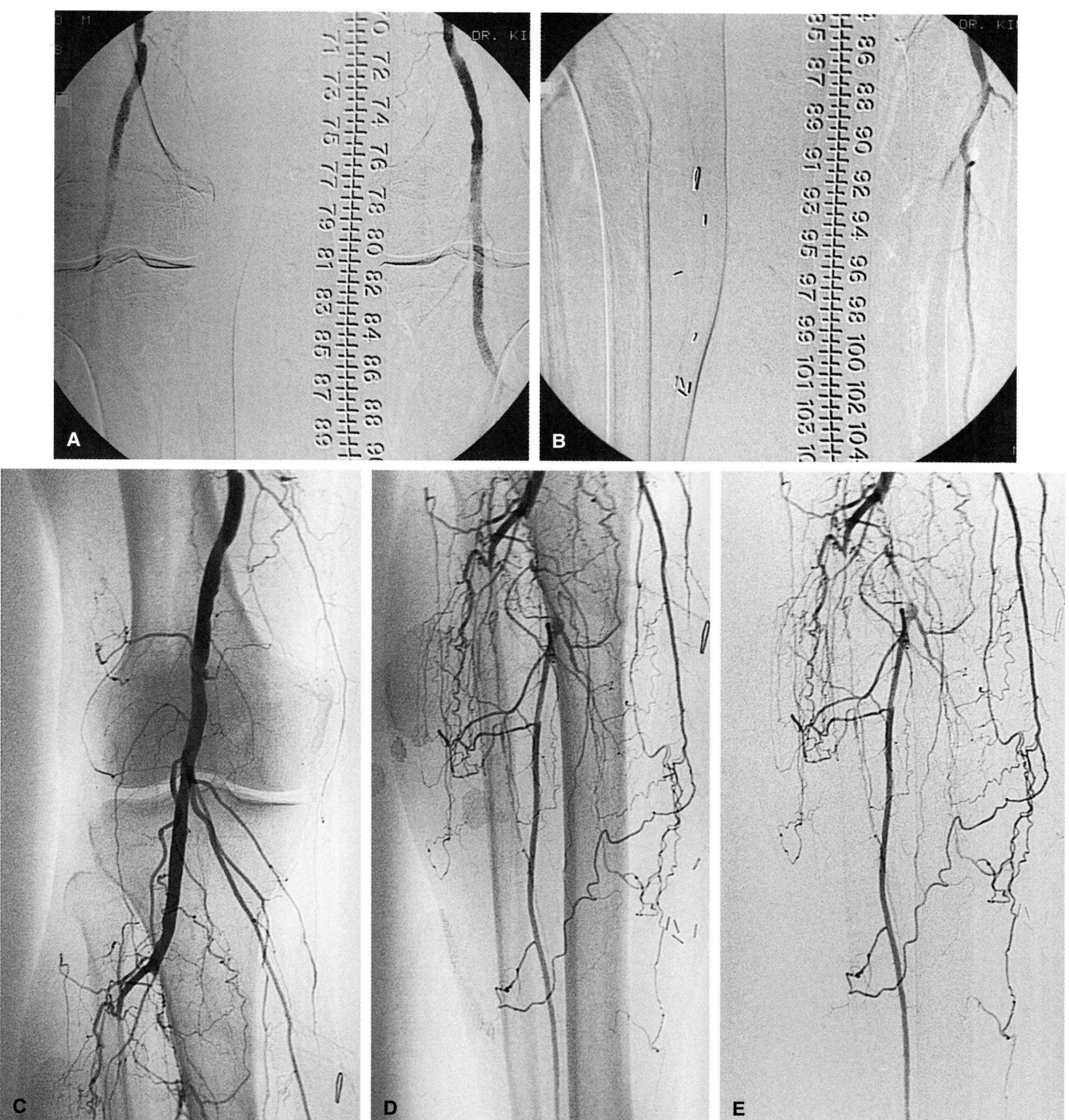

FIGURE 18-4 **A,** Single-injection, multiple-field digital subtraction angiography showing delayed opacification of the right popliteal region compared with that of the left. **B,** Differential opacification becomes a severe impediment to adequate visualization of the trifurcation region on both sides. **C,** Selective catheterization of the external iliac artery with hand injection of contrast material produces the greatest degree of opacification and the greatest detail. Shown here is the popliteal region. **D,** Selective injection of trifurcation region. **E,** Selective injection of trifurcation region with digital subtraction on.

of system is used, however, certain accessory equipment is highly recommended to optimize the utility of the system. Many of the postprocessing and image-enhancing DSA features previously reviewed are now available on portable units, although they are not always standard equipment and are not as convenient to use as the features on fixed units. Nonetheless, these features should all be considered essential to performance of the broad range of endovascular diagnostic and therapeutic procedures. Also commonplace today are dual video monitors, which allow the display of a reference image on one screen, while active fluoroscopy is seen on the other. With intravascular ultrasound (IVUS) playing an increasing role in endovascular interventions, particularly endografting, the ability to display the IVUS image on the fluoroscopy monitor as a "picture in picture" can be a helpful additional feature. Because endovascular

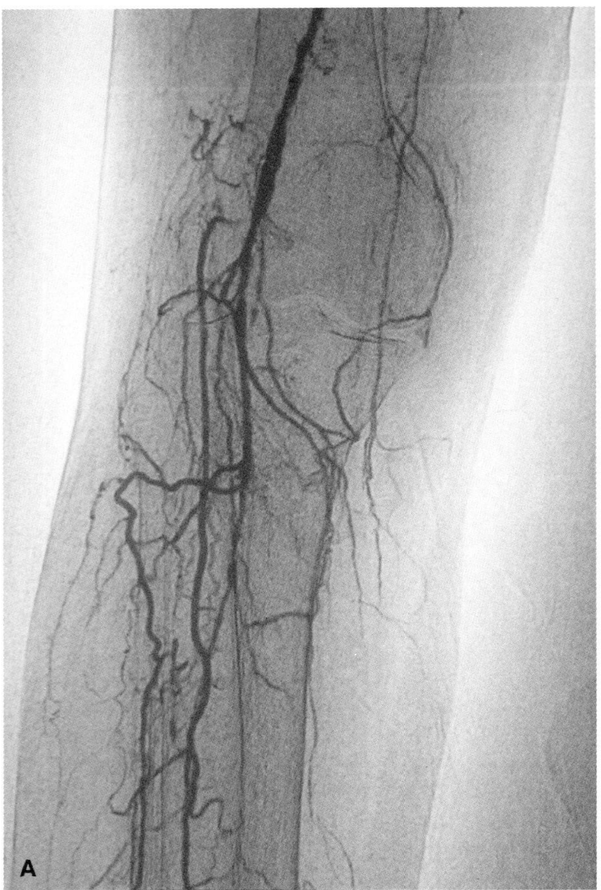

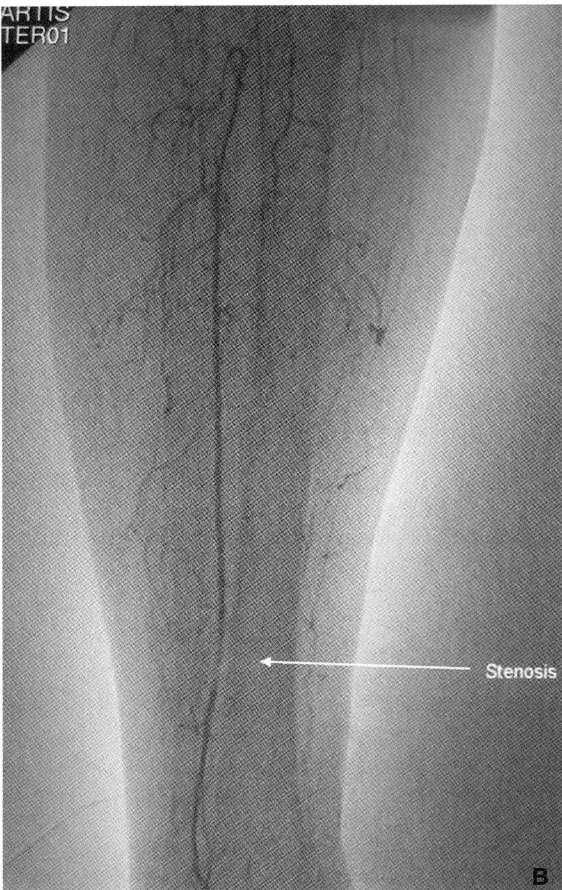

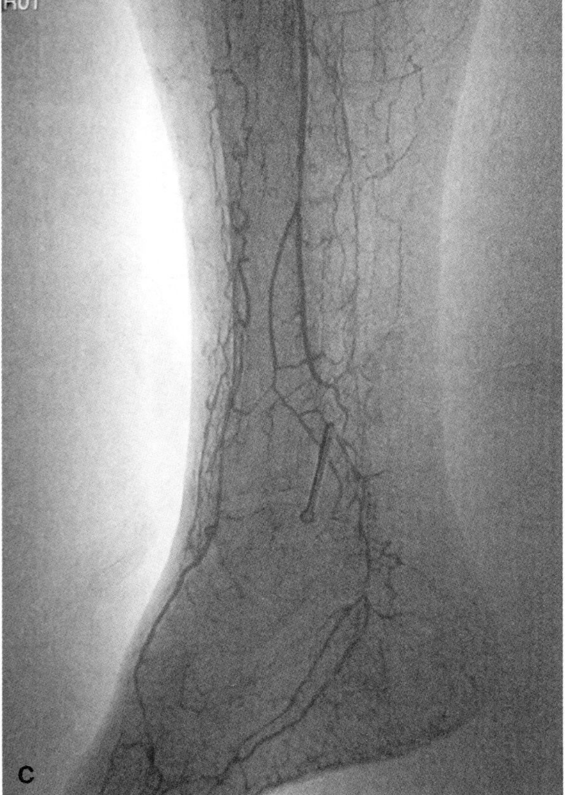

FIGURE 18-5 **A,** Selective injection into the distal superficial femoral or popliteal artery may be required to image the distal runoff. **B,** Imaging the right leg in the right anterior oblique projection opens the interosseous window between the tibia and fibula bones demonstrating single-vessel distal runoff with a mid-stenotic segment. **C,** A lateral right foot projection confirms the peroneal artery as the patent vessel with distal reconstitution of the dorsalis pedis and the posterior tibial arteries via small collaterals.

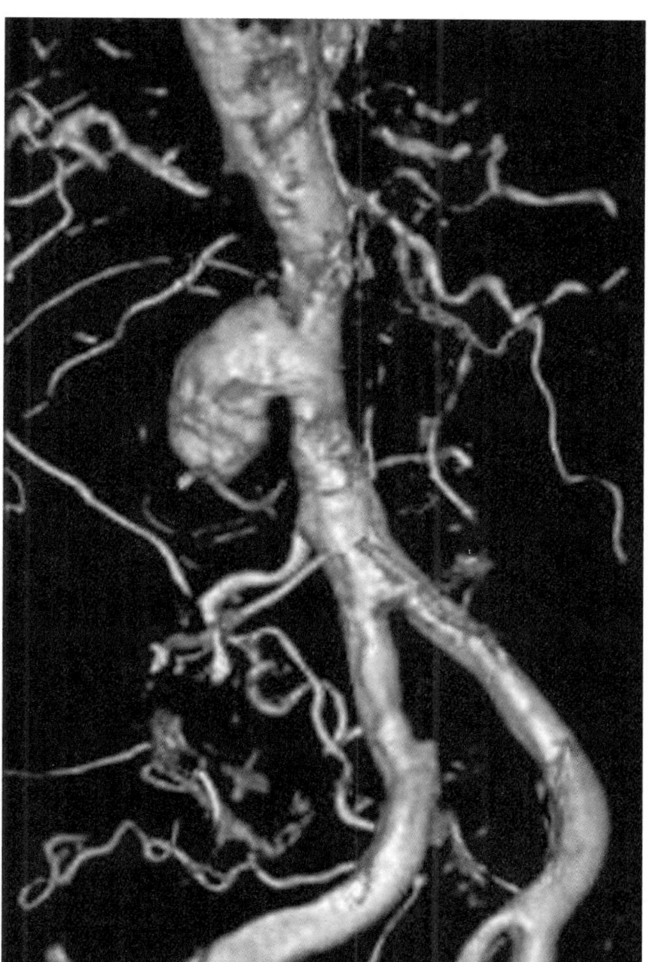

FIGURE 18-6 Rotational three-dimensional arteriogram of the abdominal aorta shows an infrarenal saccular abdominal aortic aneurysm.

interventions usually are performed under local anesthesia with minimal or no anesthesiologist support,[3] routine monitoring equipment, such as electrocardiogram, blood pressure, and pulse oximetry monitoring, is becoming standard.

Although single-injection, multiple-field angiography is a highly convenient feature, it is far from essential, even if full-leg angiography is a commonly performed examination in a surgeon's practice. An image intensifier size of 25 cm would be the minimal practical size to perform full lower extremity angiography with the sequential single-field technique, and a 30- to 40-cm image intensifier would be more beneficial because it would allow the full length of the limb to be filmed with fewer contrast injections and radiographic runs. A pair of x-ray sources (and their corresponding film changers or image intensifiers) positioned at orthogonal angles allows for the simultaneous filming in two different planes during one injection of contrast material; this is termed *biplane angiography*. These systems are expensive and cumbersome and have limited ability to alter the filming angles conveniently.

An often-overlooked piece of radiographic equipment that can have a significant impact on the quality and convenience of radiographic imaging is the fluoroscopy table. In its most basic form, a fluoroscopy table provides adequate support for the patient while allowing x-rays to penetrate without significant distortion. The more open the undercarriage, the more flexibility there is to move the C-arm to different fields of view. The ultimate in an open undercarriage is a fixed position table that is supported only at one end, leaving the other end and the patient on it completely suspended and unobstructed. This type of table permits the x-ray tube to be panned from head to toe without having to be repositioned around table supports. Such tables often are constructed of carbon fiber technology, allowing them to be strong enough to support the patient, yet sufficiently radiolucent to permit good imaging. With this type of table, the patient's position remains stationary while the C-arm is moved to change the field of view—a cumbersome maneuver. It is substantially more convenient for the C-arm to remain relatively stationary and the table to move. This feature allows the angiographer to have much more control over the selected field of view without having to work through an intermediary who moves the C-arm because the table controls are typically on the side of the table and can be operated by the surgeon within the sterile field. Changing the field of view with a mobile table is a much more fluid operation than moving the C-arm assembly to a new position. One limitation of all angiographic tables is the range of positioning options available. Although most can be raised and lowered, and some can be tilted into Trendelenburg or reverse Trendelenburg, few can be rotated side to side or placed in flexion or extension. This is a noteworthy limitation if the table is also to be used for open surgical procedures.

Patient monitoring during angiographic procedures is important to ensure the patient's comfort, cooperation, and safety during the procedure. Real-time electrocardiogram monitoring and automated blood pressure measurements are standard in contemporary endovascular suites. When arterial access has been achieved, it is preferable to monitor blood pressure directly via the angiographic sheath, a capability that also has utility for assessing the hemodynamic significance of occlusive disease and the results of intervention. Although the ability to measure intra-arterial pressures from one source at a time is generally sufficient, it is often helpful to be able to transduce two sources simultaneously, allowing for the comparison of the pressure in a vessel of interest with the pressure in the aorta. Appropriate staffing to attend to the needs of the patient and the angiographer generally includes a radiology technician scrubbed at the table for guide wire and catheter handling support, a second assistant for circulating in the room to provide necessary supplies, and a third assistant for running the radiographic equipment from the control room. A nurse is typically present to monitor the patient and administer any sedation, analgesia, or other medications or fluids requested by the endovascular surgeon.

■ FIXED-MOUNT VERSUS PORTABLE RADIOGRAPHIC EQUIPMENT

Currently available radiographic equipment can generally be divided into two basic categories: fixed-mount units in rooms, typically dedicated to radiographic procedures, and portable C-arm fluoroscopy units with digital capabilities, which can be used in a variety of locations. The advent of endoluminal grafting procedures requiring operative vascular access has created interest in dual-purpose operating rooms with fixed-mount quality angiographic equipment in addition to operating room sterility and supplemental lighting. The goal is to have the imaging quality and convenience of an angiographic suite in a room suitably equipped to perform operative procedures. For the foreseeable future, however, most surgeons will have to choose one aspect or the other as their primary concern and accept the compromises this entails. Because angiography is principally performed as a stand-alone procedure via the percutaneous route of access, the superior imaging environment of the dedicated angiographic suite is the obvious choice, unless a concomitant surgical procedure is anticipated.

The real distinction between these two types of systems lies not in the portability of the x-ray tube and image intensifier component, but rather in that of the power generating units. Fixed units have significantly larger and more powerful generators, which, although they produce superior imaging, exact a price in terms of required space. Despite these drawbacks, such units are able to provide significantly greater power output, which translates into improved imaging and ability to penetrate large and dense objects. Although the focal spot size on portable units usually ranges from 0.3 to 1.4 mm in diameter, the increased power output available with fixed units allows for focal spot sizes of 0.15 mm, which results in substantially improved resolution.

Other differences between these two types of units pertain to the C-arm gantry component, which contains the x-ray source below and the image intensifier above. Fixed-mount units are presently available with image intensifiers 40 cm in diameter, whereas most portable units are 25 cm. With fixed-mount units, there is the ability to vary the distance between the x-ray tube and the image intensifier, an adjustment not available with portable units. This adjustment allows the image intensifier to be placed closer to the patient, which not only improves the image quality, but also enlarges the field of view and minimizes radiation scatter. Another advantageous feature of fixed-mount units is the ability to alter the orientation of the C-arm via electromechanical drives using controls available to the angiographer at tableside within the sterile field. This is a much more fluid and efficient operation than having to unlock and move the C-arm assembly physically, as is typically the case with portable units. The latter situation usually involves working through a radiography technician, removing the surgeon from direct control of the process of field selection.

Although no longer a significant problem with the newer portable fluoroscopy units available today, older units are prone to overheating during fluoroscopy-intensive procedures. Newer equipment has largely overcome this problem through advances in cooling technology and power usage algorithms that switch to pulsed fluoroscopy as the x-ray tube begins to overheat. Although pulsed fluoroscopy may prevent the tube from overheating and shutting down, it does so by reducing the "frame rate" of fluoroscopy, which results in choppy fluoroscopic visualization. For these reasons, these older fluoroscopy units are not well suited to endovascular procedures, but may be acceptable for angiography alone.

As would be expected, the advantages of fixed-mount fluoroscopic units come at a significantly greater price than that of portable units, with the former costing between $750,000 and $1.5 million and the latter costing $150,000 to $200,000. Installation of fixed ceiling-mounted units often requires structural modifications to the room, such as reinforced mounting plates, under-floor electrical conduit, and lead lining in the walls, all of which contribute to the increased cost. Although some surgeons would advocate installing fixed-mount units in the operating room, this may be practical only if operative endovascular volume is high, because use of these rooms for nonangiographic procedures may be encumbered by the radiographic equipment, which can be moved aside only, not removed from the room entirely. Mounted fluoroscopy tables are wider than regular operating tables, are limited in available positions, and do not usually accommodate the self-retaining retractors needed for major open operations. In most circumstances, portable C-arm units remain a more versatile option with regard to operating room use, especially when one considers that they can be moved to other rooms to provide imaging for other procedures when a given case has been completed.

■ CHOOSING THE VENUE—OPERATING ROOM OR ANGIOGRAPHIC SUITE

The choice of working environment should be based entirely on the needs of the patient and the intended procedure, not on the basis of "turf" considerations or interdisciplinary rivalries. Despite significant advances in the image quality available with portable digital fluoroscopy units, angiography performed in a dedicated angiographic facility provides uniformly superior image quality, convenience of acquisition, and most commonly a superior inventory of equipment and trained staff. Lacking a true angiographic operating room, the only reason to consider performing angiography or any other endovascular procedure in the operating room is if the sterile environment present in that venue is necessary for a concomitant procedure. This may include situations in which surgical revascularizations are being performed with the guidance of immediate preprocedure angiography or situations in which these procedures are being assessed at their conclusion by intraoperative angiography.

Although some surgeons would choose to perform inflow dilatations in the operating room concomitant with distal revascularizations, this approach has many disadvantages that render it ill advised, unless access to the lesion being dilated is available only through an operative exposure, which is a rarely encountered situation. Foremost among the disadvantages is the fact that performing the procedure in the operating room generally involves the suboptimal imaging of a portable fluoroscopy unit, complicating the procedure and compromising assessment of the outcome. The hemodynamic and functional success of the intervention cannot be determined before basing a bypass graft off of the intervention, potentially jeopardizing the longevity of the bypass if the intervention is a short-term failure. Additionally, should the intervention be immediately unsuccessful, the patient may have to undergo a much more extensive operative revascularization than had been planned, perhaps even mandating a change in anesthetic, or an inflow and outflow operative revascularization at the same setting. Last, many patients in need of inflow interventions achieve sufficient supplemental perfusion from the angioplasty alone so that they do not need the distal revascularization. For all of these reasons, inflow interventions are best performed in a dedicated angiographic facility before performance of a distal surgical revascularization as long as the lesion can be safely accessed percutaneously or through a minor operative exposure. This sequence allows both procedures to be performed in facilities optimal for each.

In patients with vascular trauma and coexisting life-threatening injuries that mandate prompt surgical treatment, it is often best to perform arteriography in the operating room after the higher priority problems have been addressed. This is relatively simple in cases of extremity vascular trauma because these areas are fairly simple to visualize and usually can be accessed directly at the site of injury or percutaneously proximal to the anticipated vascular defect. Intraoperative angiographic evaluation of central vascular trauma can be more problematic, however, because catheter positioning and quality imaging are more difficult to obtain in this venue. Considering the potential magnitude of the possible problems, the need for power injection, and the importance of superior image quality, such patients are generally best studied with fixed-mount, dedicated angiographic equipment. The angiographic suite usually is better equipped to address issues that can be treated endoluminally, such as with embolization coils or endografts, modes of therapy being used with increasing frequency.

A final scenario in which operative angiography is useful is in the evaluation of patients undergoing thromboembolectomy. Although many surgeons perform simple single-shot radiographs of the distal vasculature after embolectomy, the procedure itself can be greatly facilitated and performed more safely under fluoroscopic guidance (Fig. 18-7). Fluoroscopic visualization during catheter passage can detect deviations in the course of the catheter that might signify passage down a collateral vessel or subintimal dissection, both of which would contraindicate inflation of the balloon. By using half-strength contrast material in the embolectomy balloon, its return passage through the vascular system can be observed, and potentially injurious overdistention can be minimized. Sites of occlusive lesions can be detected, and traction on them can be minimized by observing the deformation of the balloon as it passes through the region. If subsequent angiographic evaluation reveals retained thrombus in the trifurcation vessels, selective catheter passage can be performed, using a leading guide wire if needed, to extract as much thrombus as possible. Last, any significant focal occlusive lesions that are identified and are suitable for endovascular treatment can be dilated subsequently at the same setting. If the lesions are not so suitable to endoluminal therapies, the angiogram at least can delineate the options for open surgical revascularization.

The most appropriate venue in which to perform endovascular procedures that require insertion of devices too large to be achieved percutaneously, such as endoluminal aortic aneurysm grafts, remains a topic of debate. Surgeons generally prefer to direct these procedures to the operating room, which offers the advantage of a seamless conversion to open repair in the event of complications or failure to implant the device successfully. They cite the superior sterile environment present in the operating room as a major deciding factor. Full surgical conversions have been relatively rare, and usually the most that is needed is access to the external iliac artery to repair or bypass insertion-related trauma, exposure that can be readily obtained in an angiographic suite. Graft infections to date have not been a major issue; this is not surprising when one considers that most endoluminal devices are completely enclosed in their delivery systems before release within the body and are not easily contaminated. Consequently, although concerns about sterility persist, the superior imaging environment of a dedicated angiographic suite or a true operating angiographic facility is preferred by most.

■ ANGIOGRAPHIC CONTRAST AGENTS

For intravascular anatomic detail to be apparent under radiographic imaging, an agent with contrasting radiodensity to the surrounding tissues must be present within the vessel at the time of radiographic exposure. Although the contrast agent used for the evaluation is typically of greater radiodensity than the surrounding tissues, intraluminal visualization also can be achieved by injecting an agent that is less radiopaque than the adjacent tissues, such as carbon dioxide (CO_2) gas.

Iodinated Contrast Agents

All currently available angiographic contrast agents achieve their radiopacity by virtue of iodine atoms attached to one or more benzene rings. Conventional angiographic contrast agents are compounds of one fully substituted benzene ring (with three iodine atoms) acting as an anion and a cationic component (sodium, methylglucamine, or a combination of the two). In solution they dissociate, effectively doubling the osmolality of the contrast agent. The osmolality of contrast agents can be reduced by linking two benzene rings with each cation (dimeric formulation), effectively doubling the number of iodine atoms for the same level of osmolality. Another way to lessen the osmolality of contrast agents is to formulate the benzene ring so that it does not dissociate at all—a formulation known as a *non-ionic contrast agent.* Both of these modifications result in agents with osmolalities approximately half of that of conventional contrast agents. Conventional contrast agents range from 1500 to 1700 mOsm at 300 mg/mL of iodine, whereas non-ionic and dimeric compounds range from 580 to 880 mOsm at 300 mg/mL of iodine. Non-ionic dimeric formulations also have been created with osmolalities of about 320 mOsm. Some commonly used contrast agents and their specifications are listed in Table 18-1.

Carbon Dioxide Angiography

Diagnostic CO_2 DSA was introduced by Hawkins[4] in 1982 to visualize the splanchnic and lower extremity circulations. The injection of CO_2 gas transiently displaces blood from the target vessel causing a small difference in densities

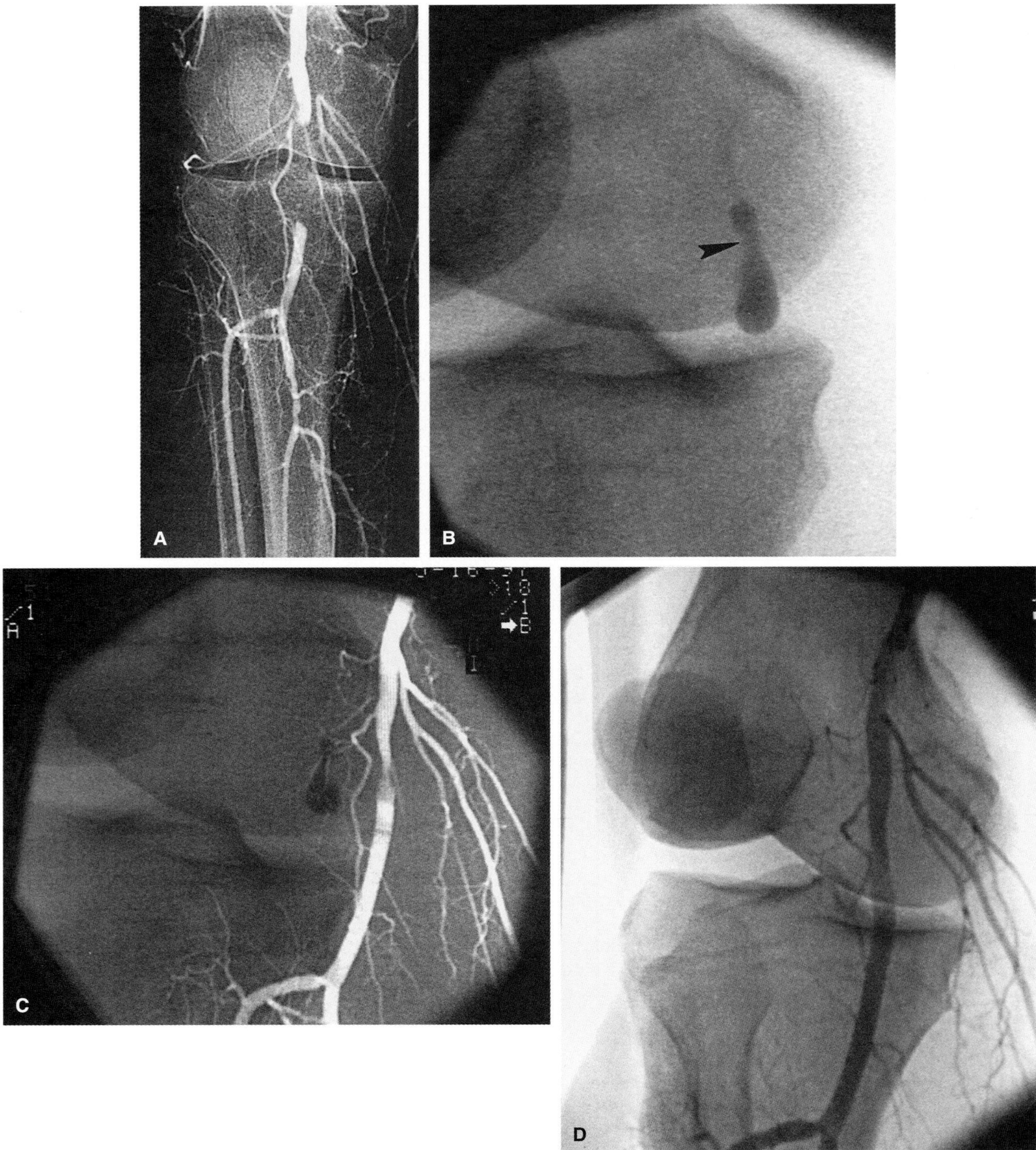

FIGURE 18-7 **A,** Preoperative angiogram reveals abrupt occlusion of the mid-popliteal artery in a patient with acute ischemic symptoms suggestive of embolization. **B,** Deformation of the embolectomy balloon is noted in the popliteal region during extraction of the thrombus suggesting an underlying stenotic lesion. **C,** On-table digital subtraction angiogram after embolectomy reveals the suspected mid-popliteal artery stenosis. **D,** Completion arteriogram after balloon dilatation of the mid-popliteal artery stenosis.

from the surrounding tissues, which is detected using DSA. More recently, with the advent of improvements in imaging techniques and computer software allowing for image enhancement, the applications of CO_2 angiography have expanded to include a wide variety of diagnostic and therapeutic interventions, including imaging of multiple peripheral territories, identification of occult bleeding, peripheral and visceral angioplasty and stenting, placement of inferior vena cava filters, creation of transjugular intrahepatic portosystemic shunts, splenoportography, and aortic

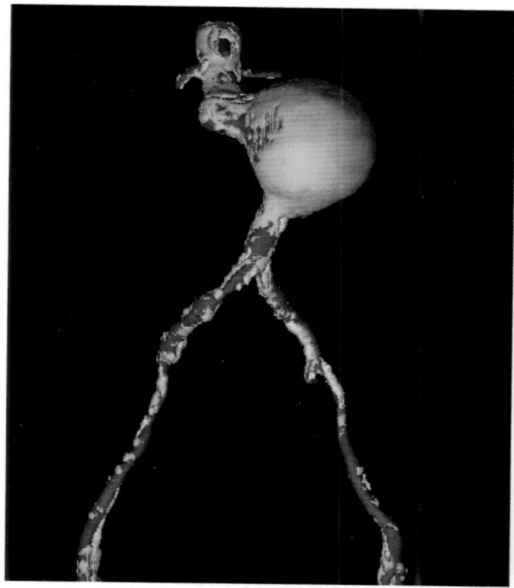

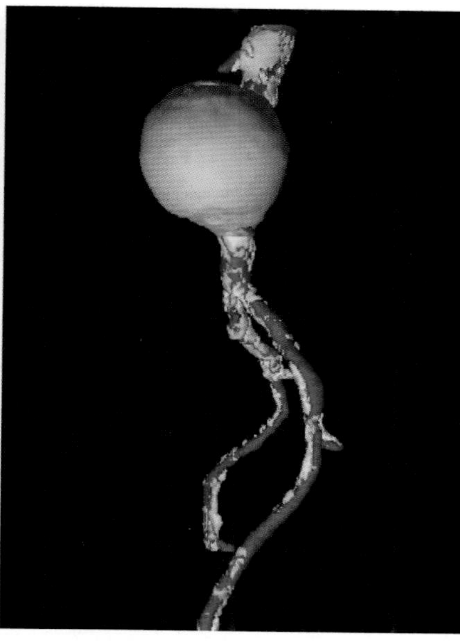

FIGURE 21-10 Multiple-object SSD, anteroposterior *(left)* and left lateral *(right)* views of the same AAA seen in Figures 21-8 and 21-9. Contrast-enhanced blood flow is displayed in red, thrombus and noncalcified plaque are yellow, and calcified plaque is white. In this type of 3D reconstruction, all the components of the aneurysm are seen. Multiple views are helpful, and it is preferable if the display can be rotated and viewed at will on a computer screen. This type of display is most helpful in determining the true extent of an aneurysm because thrombus is clearly visible.

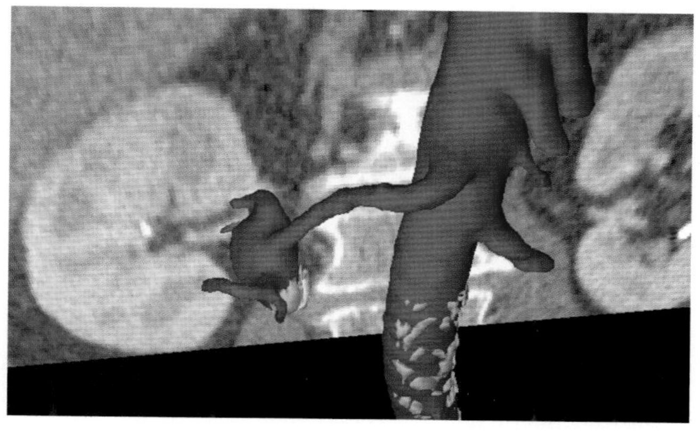

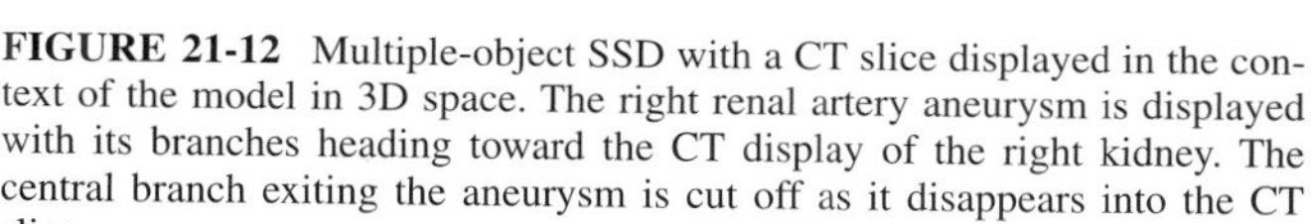

FIGURE 21-12 Multiple-object SSD with a CT slice displayed in the context of the model in 3D space. The right renal artery aneurysm is displayed with its branches heading toward the CT display of the right kidney. The central branch exiting the aneurysm is cut off as it disappears into the CT slice.

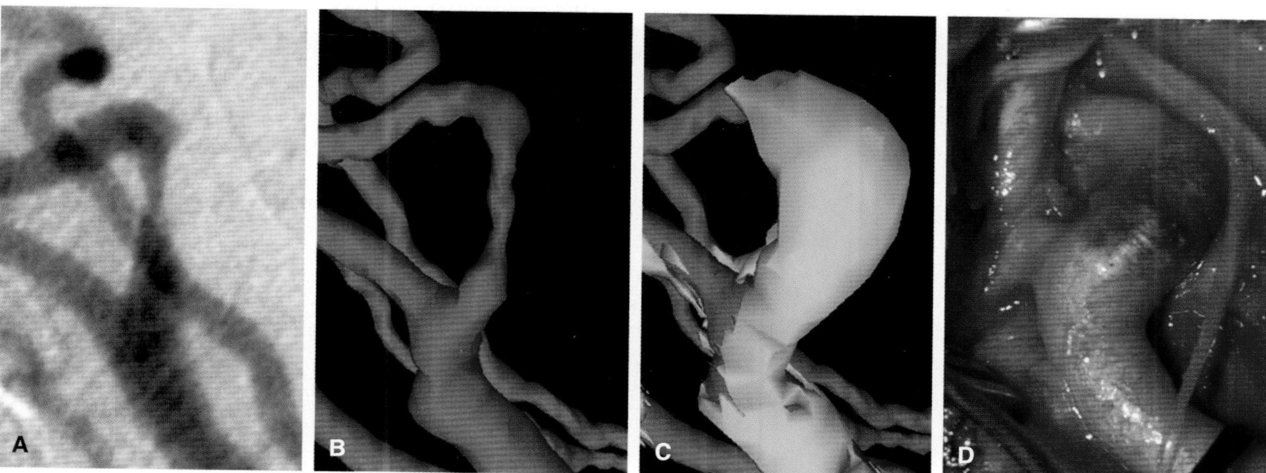

FIGURE 21-19 Demonstration of carotid artery disease. **A,** Angiogram of an internal carotid artery stenosis. **B,** 3D reconstruction of blood flow (red) in the same location. **C,** 3D reconstruction of blood flow and plaque/thrombus (yellow). **D,** Intraoperative photograph of the same location. There is a striking similarity despite rotation of the head and neck in the operative photograph.

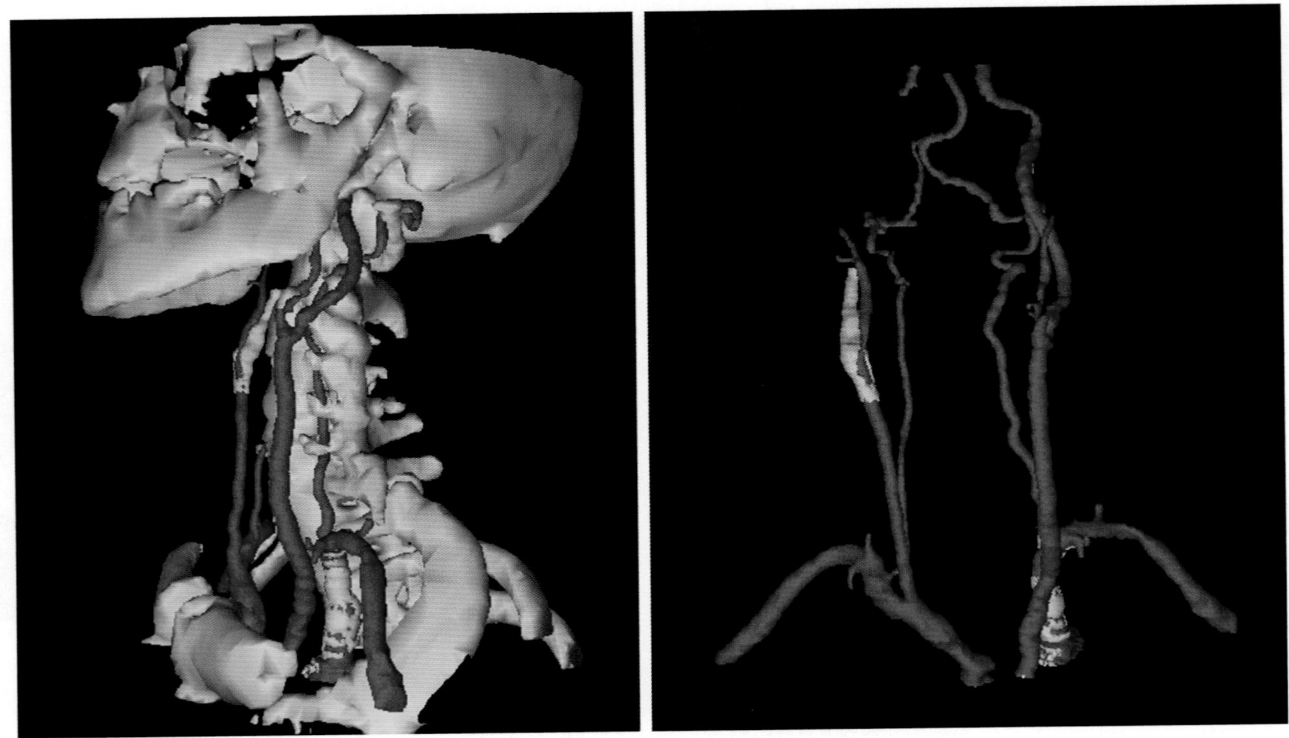

FIGURE 21-20 Multiple-object 3D reconstruction can show the relationship of the extracranial vessels and the bony structures as an aid to surgical planning. Although previously tedious and difficult, such images now are much easier to create with commercially available postprocessing software.

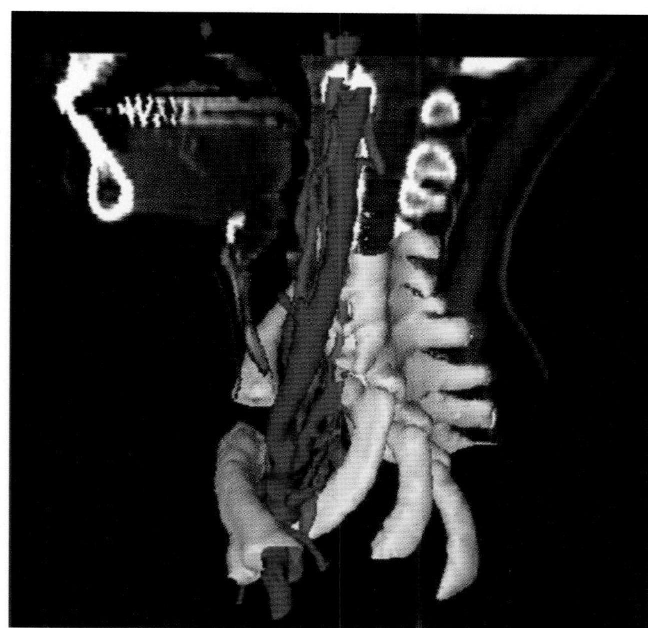

FIGURE 21-22 3D reconstruction of the bony and vascular structures of the thoracic outlet.

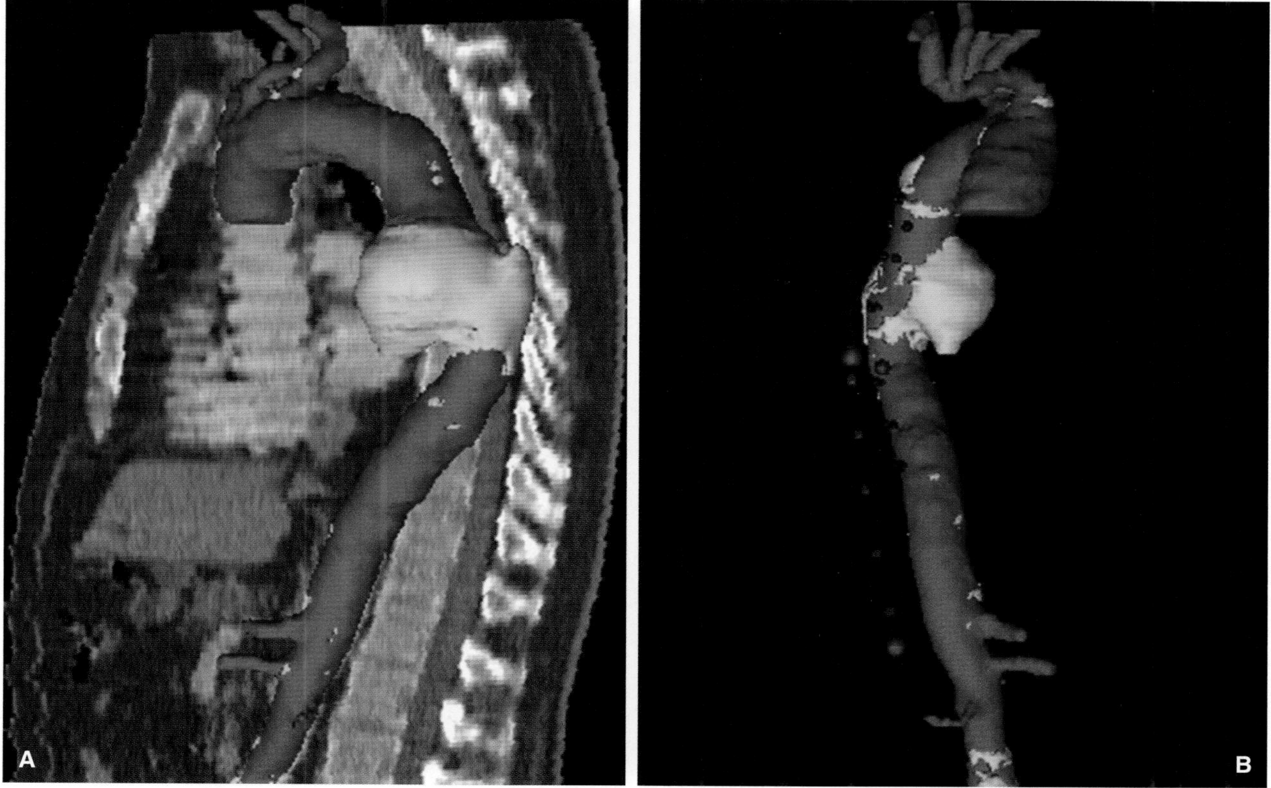

FIGURE 21-25 **A,** Aneurysm of the thoracic aorta shown using 3D reconstruction with simultaneous display of a sagittal CT slice to lend context. Motion artifact is much greater around the heart and proximal ascending aorta. The focal blebs displayed in the model were verified at the time of surgery. **B,** Intercostal arteries are marked on the CT slices and are displayed on the 3D model using interactive software (blue marks). The red marks were placed to denote the top of the 8th thoracic vertebra (T8) and the bottom of the 12th thoracic vertebra. The large intercostal artery near the top of T8 was identified and preserved at the time of operation.

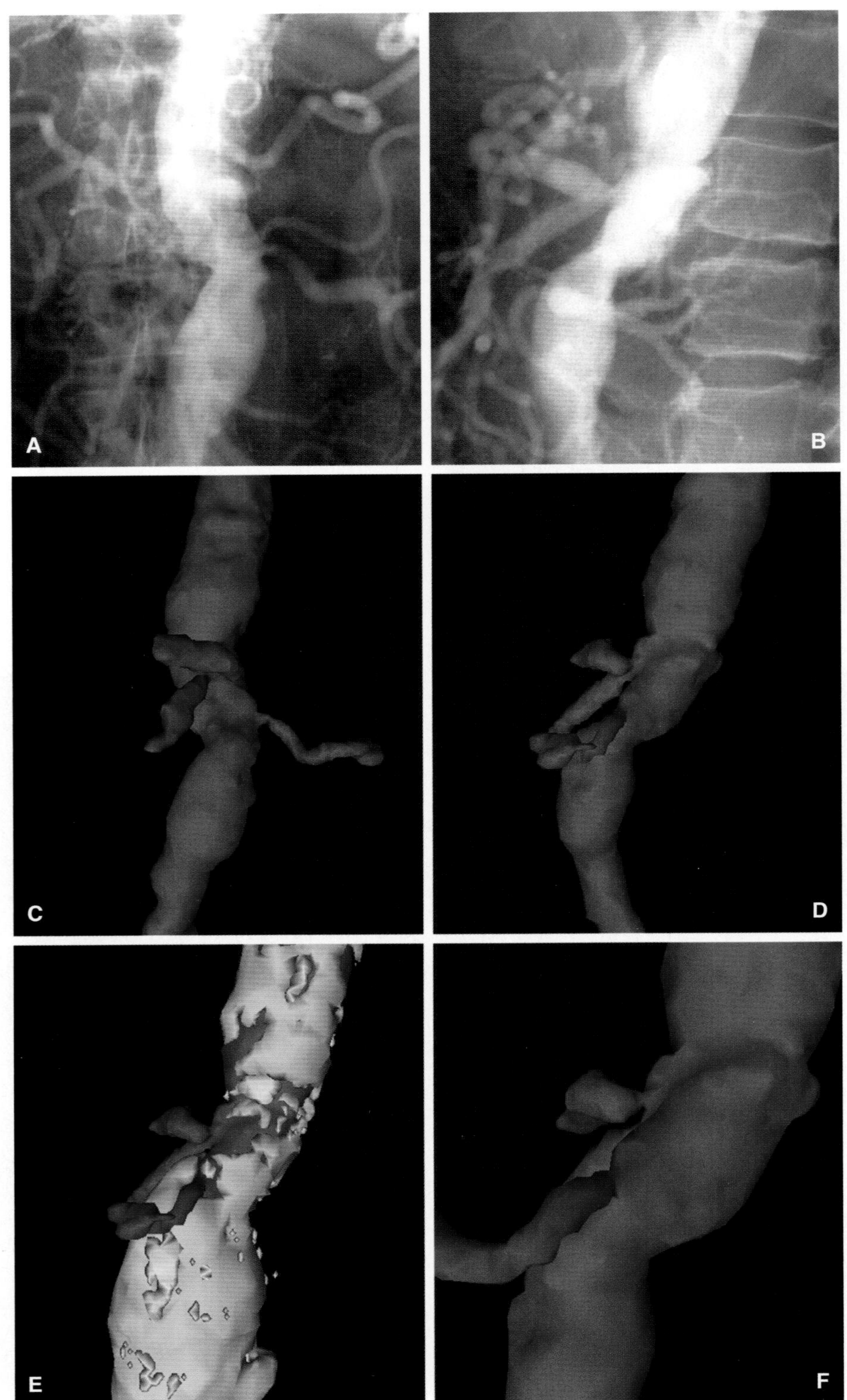

FIGURE 21-27 **A** and **B,** Anteroposterior aortogram **(A)** and lateral aortogram **(B)** of what appears to be an infrarenal AAA. The right renal artery is occluded, and the left renal artery has a mild stenosis. **C** and **D,** Anteroposterior and lateral 3D reconstruction of only the contrast-enhanced blood flow shows the same findings. **E,** Multiobject 3D reconstruction with calcified plaque (white) and thrombus (yellow) made visible shows that the AAA actually involves the suprarenal aorta, including the origin of the superior mesenteric artery. This was confirmed at operation. This view of the reconstruction was useful for determining a good location for the aortic cross-clamp (proximal to the celiac artery) and determining that a beveled anastomosis would be performed along the relatively normal aorta. The left renal artery was reimplanted on an aortic patch after endarterectomy of the plaque at the renal artery origin. **F,** Celiac artery stenosis is shown on a magnified and rotated 3D reconstruction with only blood flow made visible. The lesion was confirmed at operation. The celiac stenosis was missed by angiography because it overlapped the superior mesenteric artery on the lateral view.

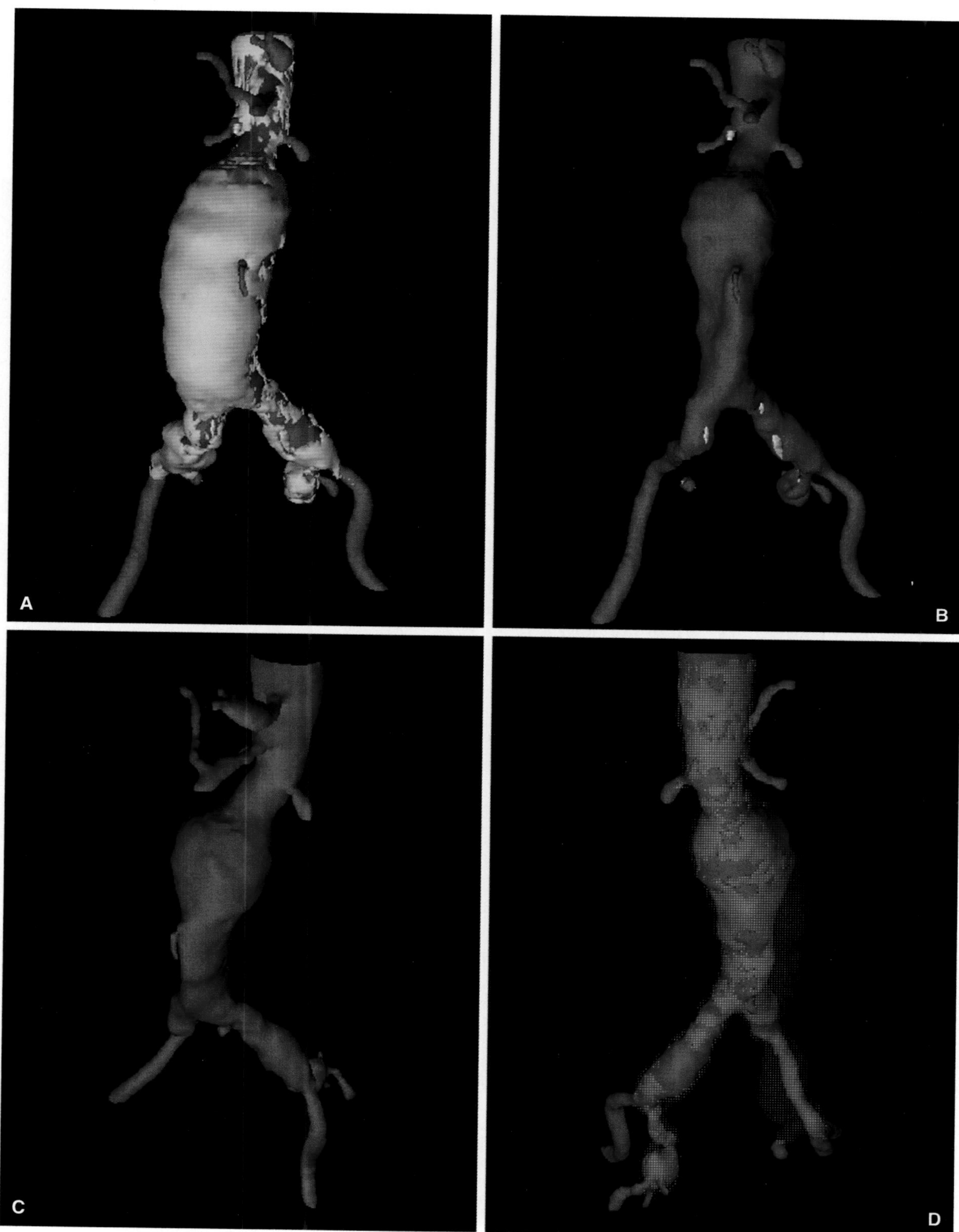

FIGURE 21-32 Several abnormalities on one 3D reconstruction are shown, highlighting the utility of multiple views and a multiple-object display. This study was obtained to evaluate a possible infrarenal AAA and revealed a celiac artery aneurysm, a replaced right hepatic artery arising from the superior mesenteric artery, multiple iliac artery aneurysms, and a right internal iliac artery occlusion. The various abnormalities are best understood by rotating the model and changing the visibility of thrombus, which can be done in real time on a workstation or a personal computer with specialized software. **A,** Anteroposterior view of a multiple-object 3D reconstruction with blood flow (red), thrombus/noncalcified plaque (yellow), and calcified plaque (white) all included in the model. **B,** 3D reconstruction with thrombus made invisible shows the right internal iliac artery occlusion. **C,** Oblique view of the 3D reconstruction shows the celiac artery aneurysm and the replaced right hepatic artery better than other views. **D,** The outflow branches of the left internal iliac artery aneurysm are best seen on a posterior view with thrombus made transparent.

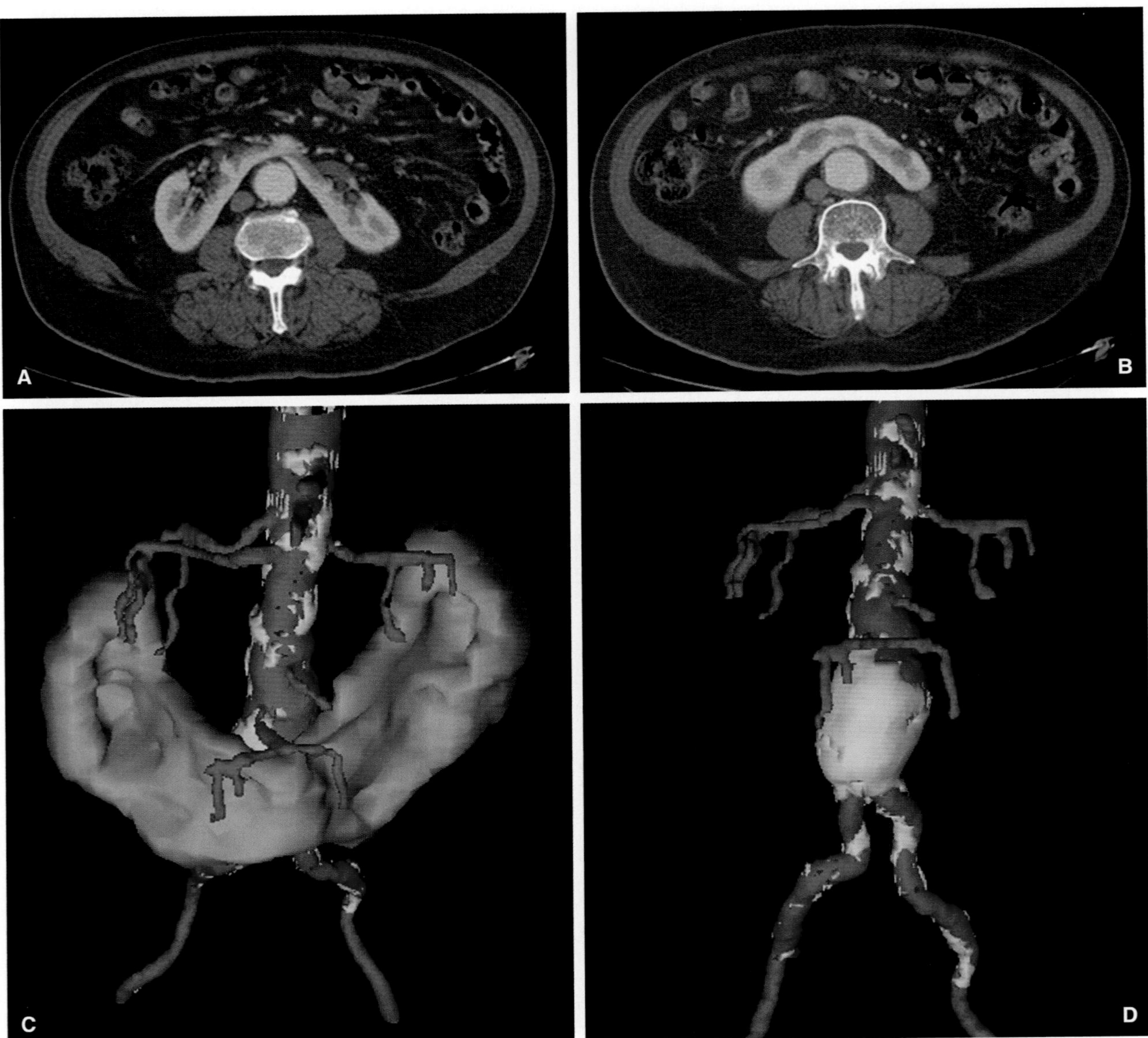

FIGURE 21-33 **A,** Horseshoe kidney on axial CT. **B,** The portion of the horseshoe kidney that crosses the midline is often relatively thin, but in this case the parenchyma does not appear to be attenuated. **C,** 3D reconstruction with the horseshoe kidney and associated complex blood supply clearly visible. The reconstruction is rotated slightly to show a stenosis in the lowest midline renal artery near its origin. A large amount of information is learned rapidly using this technology, as it would be extremely difficult to trace the renal arteries through their course on CT slices. Angiography does not provide a 3D perspective of the renal parenchyma. **D,** Anteroposterior view of the 3D reconstruction with the kidney made invisible, showing a small AAA arising just distal to the lowest renal artery (which is in the midline).

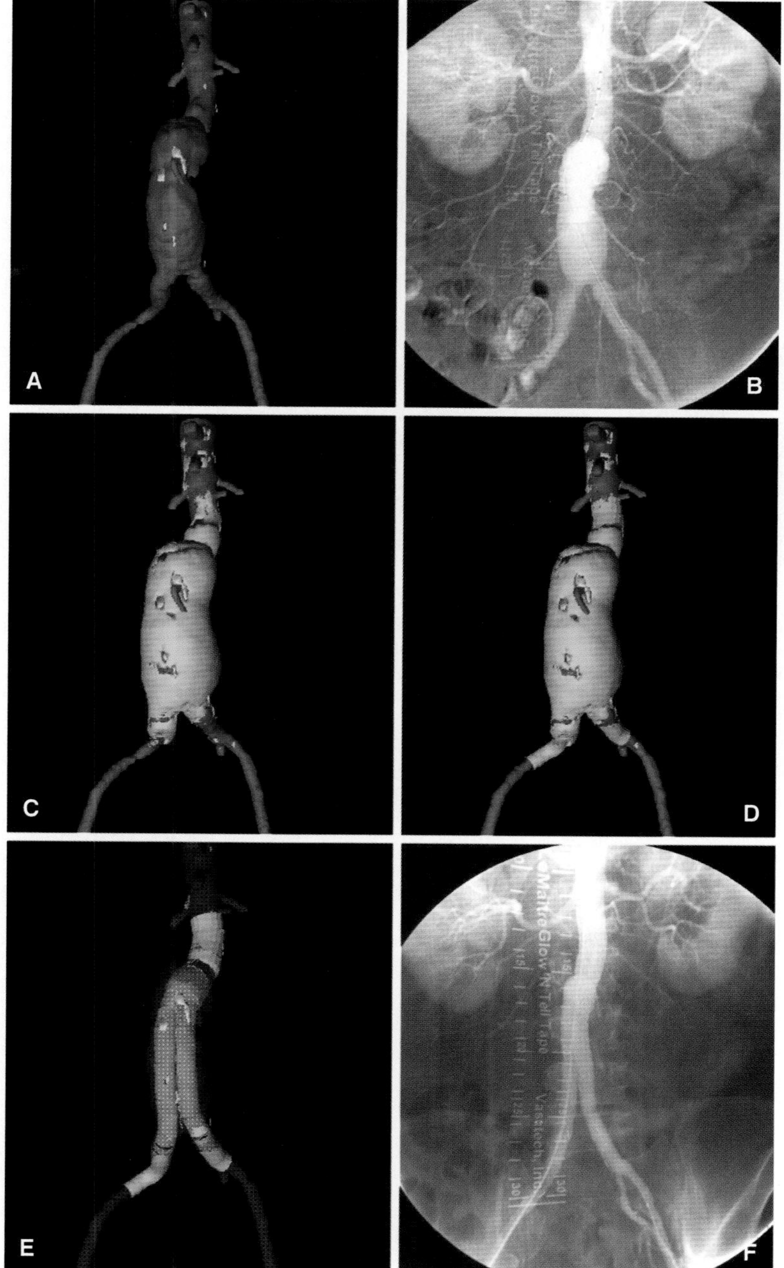

FIGURE 21-37 Use of CT with 3D reconstruction and specialized software in endovascular AAA repair. **A,** Preoperative 3D reconstruction shows contrast-enhanced blood flow (red) and calcified plaque (white). Owing to the accuracy of this technique, preoperative angiograms are not necessary. **B,** Angiogram performed on the operating table at the time of the procedure is necessary to deliver the device even if a preoperative angiogram had been performed. Note the similarity to the 3D reconstruction. **C,** Preoperative 3D reconstruction including thrombus shows the need for CT before endovascular repair. The iliac arteries are aneurysmal proximally, especially on the left. The endograft cannot be implanted into thrombus and must be long enough to achieve a seal in the normal common iliac artery. **D,** Preoperative planning with a "virtual graft," which is displayed in bright yellow. The brighter yellow of the simulated endograft protrudes beyond the red blood flow and the lighter yellow of the thrombus for sufficient lengths proximally and distally so that this 3D reconstruction shows that the proposed graft is appropriately oversized to achieve a seal at the neck of the infrarenal aorta and in the iliac arteries. This view rapidly provides a check to ensure that the proposed endograft is not too small or excessively oversized. It also graphically shows the quality and length of the "seal zone." **E,** Preoperative simulation using the virtual endograft, in this case with thrombus invisible and blood flow made transparent to show better the anticipated course of the proposed endograft. The prediction here is that the endograft will dilate as it exits the aortic neck (consistent with the degree of oversizing) and deviate slightly at the same location because it must follow the aortic lumen. It is anticipated that some deviation and constriction of the limbs will occur at the aortic bifurcation, but this does not appear to be excessive. This same technology and display is used to evaluate graft length along the centerline of the lumen or along a user-defined path. In this case, the length and diameter of the endograft were simulated to coincide with an available graft size. An endograft of this length is anticipated to end just above the left internal iliac artery origin and extend beyond the right iliac artery stenosis if it is deployed appropriately (with the proximal endograft just below the renal arteries). **F,** Completion angiogram at the time of the procedure verifies the accuracy of the preoperative computer simulation. The endograft was deployed just below the renal arteries and ends just above the left internal iliac artery origin. The endograft also extends beyond the right iliac stenosis, which is no longer apparent.

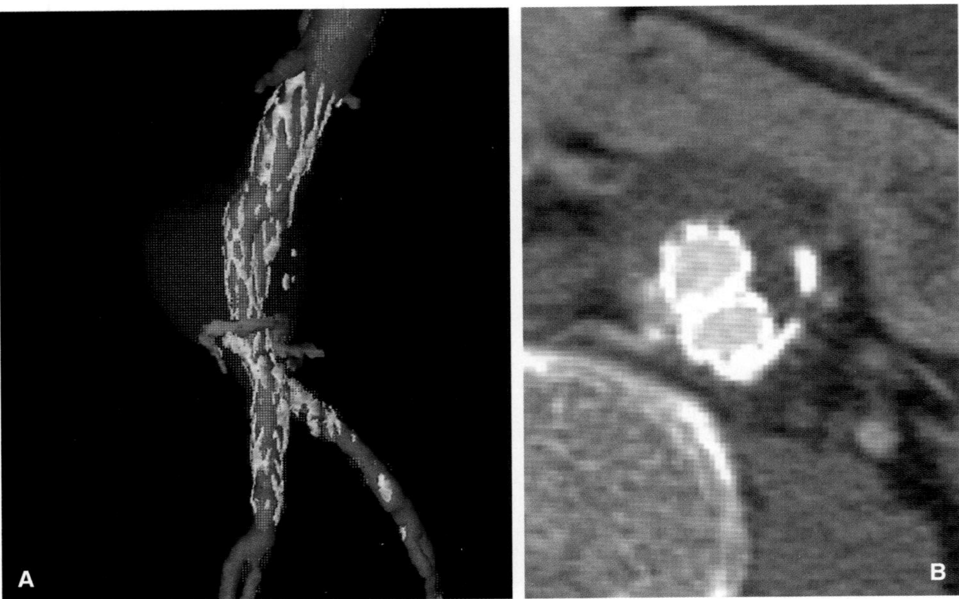

FIGURE 21-39 Perigraft flow (endoleak) after endovascular AAA repair, as displayed on 3D reconstruction **(A)** and axial CT **(B)**. The 3D reconstruction (created from the CT data) is rotated to a posterolateral view. Multiple-object 3D display includes the densities consistent with contrast-enhanced lumen (red), thrombus and noncalcified plaque (yellow, made transparent to display the endoleak), calcified plaque and metallic stent (white), and contrast-enhanced endoleak (magenta). The 3D display shows that the endoleak is associated with a patent lumbar artery and a patent inferior mesenteric artery (IMA). The axial CT cross-section shows the endograft, contrast enhancement outside the lumen of the endograft (endoleak), the patent lumbar connecting to the endoleak, and a contrast-enhanced IMA. From a single axial slice, it is impossible to decipher the connection to the IMA, which could be filling via collateral flow. The 3D reconstruction immediately conveys the relationship of the endoleak to the other structures in a much more intuitive way than scrolling through multiple CT slices.

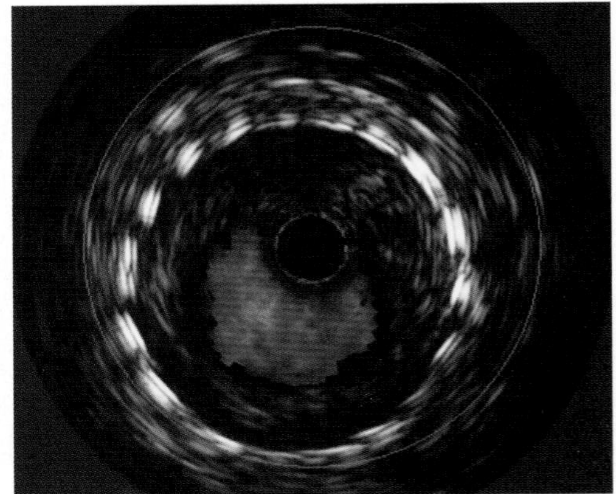

FIGURE 23-3 Color flow IVUS image demonstrating restenosis of a stent at 1 year. Image produced with a Visions PV0.018 FX catheter (Volcano Therapeutics, Rancho Cordova, CA). (Courtesy of EB Diethrich, Arizona Heart Hospital, Phoenix, AZ.)

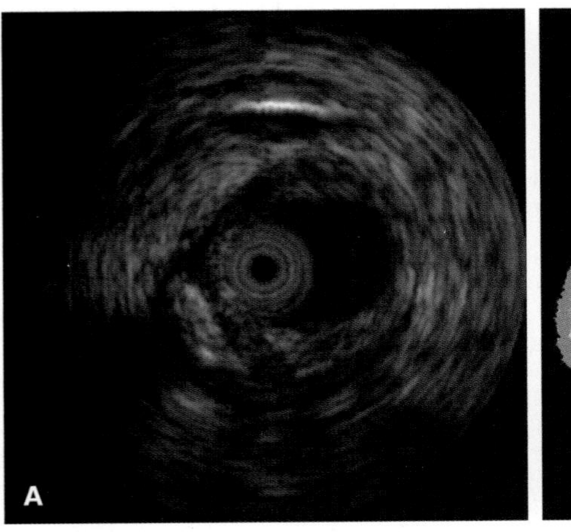

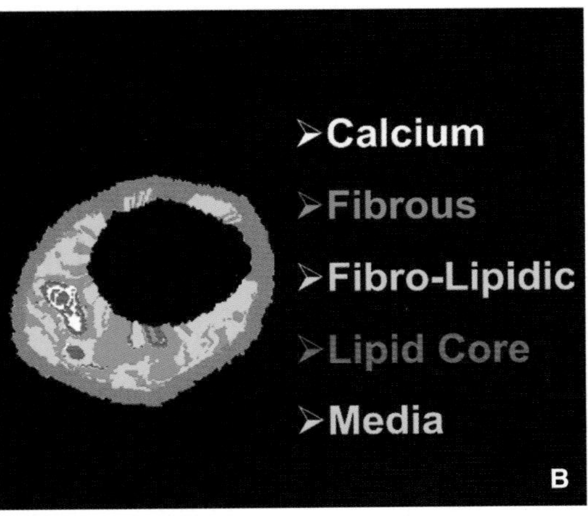

FIGURE 23-17 The frequency shift of the IVUS image can be interpreted as different tissue types, and a color assigned to each type. This approach may enable clinicians to identify troublesome plaque burdens. (Courtesy of Volcano Therapeutics, Rancho Cordova, CA.)

Table 18-1 Characteristics of Commonly Used Contrast Agents

CONTRAST AGENT	MANUFACTURER	STRUCTURE	IODINE CONTENT (mg/mL)	OSMOLALITY (mOsm/kg)	AVERAGE WHOLESALE COST ($/50 mL)
Hexabrix	Mallinckrodt Medical	Ionic dimer	320	600	$53.50
Ioxlian 350	Cook Corporation	Non-ionic	350	695	$50.00
Isovue-200	Bracco Diagnostics	Non-ionic	200	413	$53.75
Isovue-300	Bracco Diagnostics	Non-ionic	300	524	$57.49
Isovue-370	Bracco Diagnostics	Non-ionic	370	796	$62.50
Optiray 160	Mallinckrodt Medical	Non-ionic	160	355	$33.00
Optiray 320	Mallinckrodt Medical	Non-ionic	320	702	$48.00
Omnipaque 140	Amersham Health	Non-ionic	140	322	$38.94
Omnipaque 300	Amersham Health	Non-ionic	300	672	$54.00
Omnipaque 350	Amersham Health	Non-ionic	350	844	$58.81
Renografin-60	Bracco Diagnostics	Ionic	292	1549	$13.35
RenoCal-76	Bracco Diagnostics	Ionic	370	2188	$18.80
Ultravist 150	Abbott Hospitals	Non-ionic	150	774	$32.06
Ultravist 150	Abbott Hospitals	Non-ionic	300	774	$42.75
Visipaque 270	Amersham Health	Non-ionic	270	290	$56.71
Visipaque 320	Amersham Health	Non-ionic	320	290	$61.75

Adapted from Drug Topics Red Book 2003. Montvale, NJ, Thompson, PDR, 2003.

stent grafting.[4-13] This modality is a valuable alternative to iodinated contrast medium in selected cases, primarily owing to the absence of allergic reactions and nephrotoxicity. In addition, owing to its low viscosity, it can be delivered through microcatheters (3F), minimizing the risk of arterial injury. Because it does not mix with blood, CO_2 has no direct effect in osmolarity, minimizing the risk of fluid overload seen with the use of hyperosmolar agents in patients with congestive heart failure. It does not produce the discomfort associated with the administration of hyperosmolar contrast agents, and it is inexpensive.

In general, the image quality achieved with CO_2 is inferior to that obtained with the use of iodinated contrast agents and progressively degrades in the circulation below the inguinal ligament. Nevertheless, in most cases, clinically useful information can be obtained. Because bowel gas interferes with CO_2 angiography to a higher degree than with conventional imaging, it is imperative to take all potential measures to minimize bowel gas. The authors' preference for abdominal aortography is to allow a clear liquid diet the previous day, overnight fasting, and a dose of 80 mg of simethicone 30 minutes before the examination. If there is significant bowel gas artifact, an intravenous bolus of 0.5 mg of glucagon may be given. The commercially available CO_2 delivery system has multiple check valves and a two-way distal stopcock to ensure appropriate administration of CO_2 and prevent an explosive delivery of the gas (AngioDynamics, Glen Falls, NY).[14] The CO_2 setup is connected to a gas tank and primed at least three times to ensure a system that is free of air and liquid (Fig. 18-8). Extreme care should be taken to avoid withdrawal of room air because the nitrogen content is not soluble and can lead to gas embolization. The use of aluminum CO_2 tanks (CMD, Gainesville, Fla) or a microfilter is recommended to prevent contamination of the system with rust formed in the tank.

The DSA image acquisition settings should be changed to subtract radiopaque adjacent structures from the relatively radiolucent CO_2-filled vessel. Because of the normal rapid dissolution of CO_2, no maximal dose recommendations exist, and clinical judgment should be applied on an individual basis. The currently available gas bags (Angioflush III fluid collection bag; AngioDynamics, Glen Falls, NY) accommodate 1500 mL of CO_2; larger volumes should rarely be needed (see Fig. 18-8). The volume of CO_2 infused is usually around 60 to 70 mL for an aortogram and iliac vessels and 30 to 40 mL for the femoral and distal vessels (Table 18-2). Care should be taken to avoid underfilling of a vessel with CO_2, which can lead to overestimation of the degree of stenosis.[15] CO_2 may be injected rapidly by a hand technique or by a designated pump system; the injections should be spaced 3 to 5 minutes apart. For vessels less than 10-mm inner diameter, the recommended flow rates are 20 to 30 mL/sec. For larger arteries, imaging may be improved by intermittent flow with large bubbles.[15] For renal CO_2 angiography, the flank from the kidney to be studied should be elevated above the level of the catheter during imaging, and the patient should be placed back in the supine position

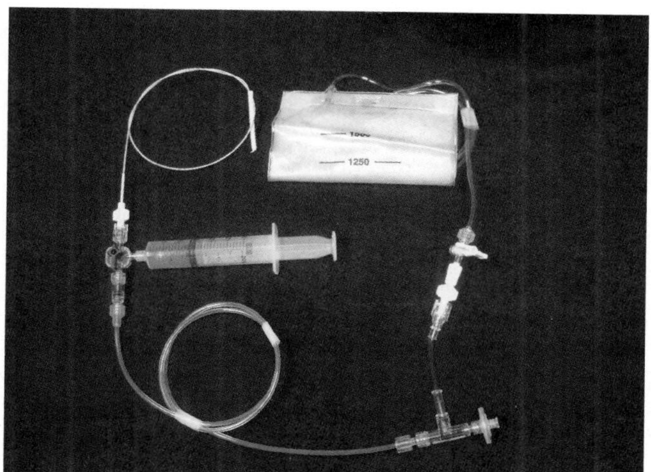

FIGURE 18-8 CO_2 system connected to a diagnostic catheter. The delivery system uses a three-way stopcock; a single check valve with CO_2 delivery port; and a filter port, which is connected to the gas tank for filling the bag (not shown). A 1500-mL bag is attached to the delivery system with low-pressure tubing and a two-way stopcock equipped with gas fitting. A large Luer-Lok syringe (30 to 70 mL) is required for hand insufflation.

Table 18-2 Flow Rates and Volume Infusion Guidelines for Carbon Dioxide Angiography at Various Vascular Regions

LOCATION	SUGGESTED CATHETER POSITION	INJECTION RATE (mL/sec)	TOTAL VOLUME (mL)
Abdominal aorta	At interface of L1-2	40-80	60-100
Iliac and femoral	Distal aorta or iliacs	40	40-80
Popliteal and distal	Proximal to target vessel	40	40-80
Renal and mesenterics	Selective	20-30	30-60
Inferior vena cava	Proximal vena cava	40-60	40-60

rapidly to expedite gas clearance and to minimize the risk of gas trapping. For mesenteric angiography, the supine position is favored. In lower extremity imaging, intra-arterial injection of vasodilators and elevating the extremity or placing the patient in a slight Trendelenburg position may help because it slows the flow rate and the breakup of the gas column as it moves distally. Patient repositioning can be obtained most expeditiously with tiltable x-ray tables.

Complications from CO_2 angiography are extremely rare but potentially serious. Arteriographic CO_2 gas infusion is best avoided above the diaphragm because of the concern of neurotoxicity. Coffey and associates[16] found direct injection of CO_2 in the carotid circulation in albino rats disrupted the blood-brain barrier, resulting in multifocal ischemic infarcts and neurologic deficits. Two other studies injecting CO_2 in the thoracic aorta and in the carotid arteries of dogs and rabbits did not produce any clinical, electroencephalographic, magnetic resonance, or pathologic changes.[7,17] Additional potential risks of CO_2 angiography include gas trapping; embolization to the cerebral, coronary, and splanchnic circulations; and gas contamination.

In one institution experience with more than 1600 arteriograms using CO_2, the only complication attributable to CO_2 was a transient episode of ischemic colitis.[14] This patient had received more than 2000 mL of CO_2 in less than 1 hour and developed trapping of CO_2 gas in a large infrarenal aortic aneurysm, which prevented flow from going into the inferior mesenteric artery. For this reason, repeated injections should not be done when there is the possibility of CO_2 gas trapping. One case of livedo reticularis, rhabdomyolysis, and fatal mesenteric ischemia in a patient who probably had a delayed CO_2 clearance from the mesenteric and peripheral circulation has been described, perhaps affected by congestive heart failure.[18] The authors of this report warned about the use of this technique in patients with congestive heart failure. Other additional cases of mesenteric ischemia have been reported.[19] Occasional reports of patients developing transient hypotension, tachypnea, and tachycardia perhaps secondary to pulmonary embolism or hypercarbia caused by inefficient respiratory excretion of CO_2 have been published.[11,20] This complication may be minimized by spacing out the injections and imaging the heart to rule out an outflow-tract vapor lock. Rare, but serious, complications, such as respiratory arrest and myocardial infarction, also have been described.[10]

Gadolinium Angiography

Options for angiographic evaluation of patients in whom iodinated dye contrast material needs to be minimized and in whom CO_2 angiography is not an option or has provided suboptimal characterization are limited. Small-volume contrast arteriography may be feasible in certain situations; however, in the presence of chronic renal insufficiency, the risk of contrast-related nephropathy with the administration of iodinated contrast material is increased, and even small amounts of iodinated contrast material (30 to 100 mL) may worsen renal function.[9,21,22] Under these circumstances, additional information may be obtained using IVUS or gadolinium arteriography or both. IVUS usually requires larger access sheaths, does not provide direct interventional feedback, and is not widely available.

Gadolinium is a rare earth metal that is extremely toxic in its unbound form. When bound to chelators, however, it is highly stable and has minimal toxicity. Currently, three gadolinium-based contrast agents are approved by the U.S. Food and Drug Administration (FDA) for intravenous use (Table 18-3): gadodiamide (Omniscan; Nycomed Amersham, Princeton, NJ), gadoteridol (ProHance; Bracco Diagnostics, Princeton, NJ), and gadopentetate dimeglumine (Magnevist; Berlex, Princeton, NJ). Omniscan and ProHance are low-ionic, low-osmolar agents; Magnevist is an ionic, high-osmolar contrast preparation. Less injection-related pain with the use of low-ionic, low-osmolar contrast agents may help minimize patient motion.[23] The cost of these agents can be a factor in their use (see Table 18-3), however. Conceivably the same concerns about renal toxicity related to the ionic composition and osmolality of standard contrast agents may apply to the use of gadolinium.[24,25] Gadolinium-enhanced arteriography has been performed successfully in a wide variety of clinical settings, including arteriography of the cerebrovascular, abdominal aorta, renal, mesenteric, and peripheral vascular circulations; for inferior vena cava filter placement; and for evaluation of renovascular disease in patients with unexpected worsening of a preexisting kidney transplant.[8,9,26-30]

The maximal FDA-recommended intravenous doses of gadolinium are 0.3 to 0.4 mmol/kg, which translates into 10 to 50 mL of solution, for a normal–body weight person. The intra-arterial use of gadolinium represents an off-label use of

Table 18-3 Characteristics of Food and Drug Administration–Approved Gadolinium Agents for Intravenous Use

AGENT	MANUFACTURER	OSMOLALITY (mOsm/kg)	AVERAGE WHOLESALE COST ($/10 mL)
Omniscan	Nycomed Amersham	789	$68.24
ProHance	Bracco	630	$77.50
Magnevist	Berlex	1960	$73.03

Adapted from Drug Topics Red Book 2003. Montvale, NJ, Thompson, PDR, 2003.

an FDA-approved medication. Consequently, there is no agreement as to the maximal doses for intra-arterial administration. Complete angiographic evaluations and most interventions usually would require doses of gadolinium that exceed the FDA recommendations for venous use, and even though larger doses have been well tolerated,[26] the amount used should be kept close to the recommendations, using it as an iodinated contrast adjunct, rather than a total substitute. Gadolinium can be administered by a power injection or by hand injection. Owing to dose limitations, however, careful planning is vital. A variable filming program with a frame rate of two to three images per second for 3 seconds and one to two images per second for 5 seconds with a higher kVp, according to the system specifications, may be advantageous.[30,31]

The best clinical arteriographic use of gadolinium is in clinical situations in which the preliminary angiographic planning has been performed with CO_2 arteriography or IVUS, image angulations have been defined, and selective catheterization has been performed. Then the target pathology is confirmed, and therapy is carried out with gadolinium assistance. Exclusive gadolinium arteriograms may be desirable in lieu of CO_2 in patients requiring cerebrovascular or upper extremity imaging or patients with large abdominal aortic aneurysms requiring aortic or mesenteric angiography because of the potentials for cerebral air embolization and mesenteric gas trapping (Fig. 18-9). Intra-arterial gadolinium is easily visualized and provides better opacification than CO_2. Although the overall vessel enhancement with gadolinium is inferior to that of regular iodinated contrast material, this is usually of no practical significance. Spinosa and colleagues[30] found that the image quality from a power aortogram of the abdominal aorta and main renal arteries is comparable using half-strength iodinated contrast material or full-strength gadolinium. There are significant quality differences between these agents, however, regarding opacification of segmental renal branches. This limitation can frequently be overcome with selective infusions (Fig. 18-10).

The most commonly reported adverse events with gadolinium include nausea, headache, and dizziness. Clinically significant changes in vital signs or cardiovascular, neurologic, or liver functions have not been reported.[8,9,26-30,32-34] Allergic reactions to gadolinium have been estimated at only 0.016%.[35] As with other radiographic contrast agents, gadolinium may cause nephrotoxicity by the combined effects of direct cellular toxicity and hyperosmolarity. Gadolinium is thought to be much less toxic to renal tubular cells, however, compared with iodinated agents, despite their similar excretory profiles. Most of the renal complications associated with high doses of gadolinium have been transient, suggesting a nonspecific osmotic response, and all of them have occurred in patients with underlying renal insufficiency. Consequently, when using gadolinium, the same prophylactic measures to prevent contrast-induced nephropathy used with iodinated contrast agents should be applied.

Clinically, renal function with gadolinium usually has been well preserved even at high doses.[8,9,26-30] Only rare cases of renal failure or acute pancreatitis have indirectly been attributed to its arteriographic use.[32,36] In one retrospective review of patients with chronic renal insufficiency, defined by a creatinine clearance of less than 80 mL/min/1.73 m^2, only 3.5% (7 of 195) of patients who received intravenous or intra-arterial doses of gadolinium greater than 0.25 mmol/kg developed acute renal failure.[37] In this series, higher doses of gadolinium were administered during arteriography than during standard magnetic resonance imaging, and patients receiving it intra-arterially were more likely to develop acute renal failure (9.5% versus 1.9%).

■ CONTRAST-RELATED TOXICITY

The toxicity of contrast agents, and specifically iodinated agents, is thought to be principally due to their hyperosmolality. Other factors, such as the side chains on the benzene ring, do exert an influence on the toxicities of these agents, but these differences are fairly minor. Predisposing factors to the development of iodinated contrast agent side effects include advanced or very young age, dehydration, renal disease, history of previous contrast reactions, asthma or bronchospasm, other allergies (e.g., seafood and hay fever), hematologic and metabolic conditions (diabetes, sickle cell anemia, polycythemia, myeloma, and pheochromocytoma), medications (metformin, beta blockers, interleukin-2, aspirin, and nonsteroidal anti-inflammatory drugs), and anxiety.[1,38,39] Adverse events from contrast agents can be considered in two distinct categories: general and organ-specific toxicities.

General Contrast-Related Toxicity

The pathophysiology of acute or delayed side effects from iodinated contrast material has not been well defined and most likely is multifactorial. Most of these reactions are considered to be idiosyncratic (a genetically determined, qualitatively abnormal reaction to a drug related to a metabolic or enzymatic deficiency) or pseudoallergic (an immunologically mediated reaction, which differs from an allergic one in that it lacks immunologic specificity, resulting in nonspecific complement activation and nonspecific histamine release).[40] They are unpredictable; are dose independent; and may involve the liberation of histamine and other humoral mediators, including serotonin, prostaglandins, bradykinin, leukotrienes, adenosine, and endothelin.[40] The most common acute general side effects of contrast injection are nausea, vomiting, and discomfort in the distribution of the vascular bed into which the contrast agent is infused. The discomfort is largely related to the osmolality of the contrast agent, with hyperosmolar agents causing greater discomfort.[23] Below a threshold level of 400 to 500 mOsm, patients usually do not experience any significant discomfort. Nausea and vomiting also are thought to be related to the osmolality of the agent used.[38] For a given osmolality, non-ionic agents tend to produce less nausea and vomiting than ionic agents. Because anxiety and apprehension have been associated with an increased incidence of adverse reactions, efforts should be made to keep patients calm and comfortable. Intravenous analgesics and sedatives, such as midazolam (Versed) (1 to 2 mg IV), nalbuphine (Nubain) (5 to 10 mg IV), fentanyl (25 to 100 μg IV), and morphine (5 to 10 mg), may be administered as needed to achieve the desired degree of patient comfort.

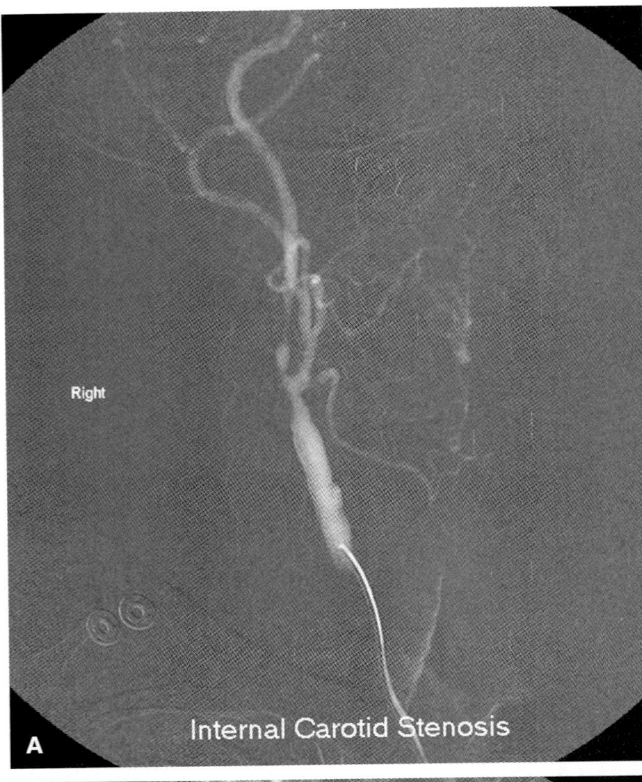

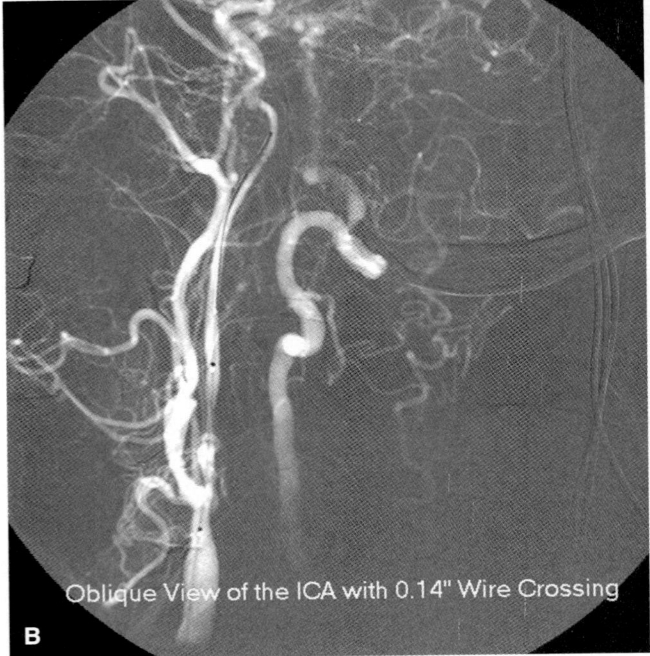

Oblique View of the ICA with 0.14" Wire Crossing
B

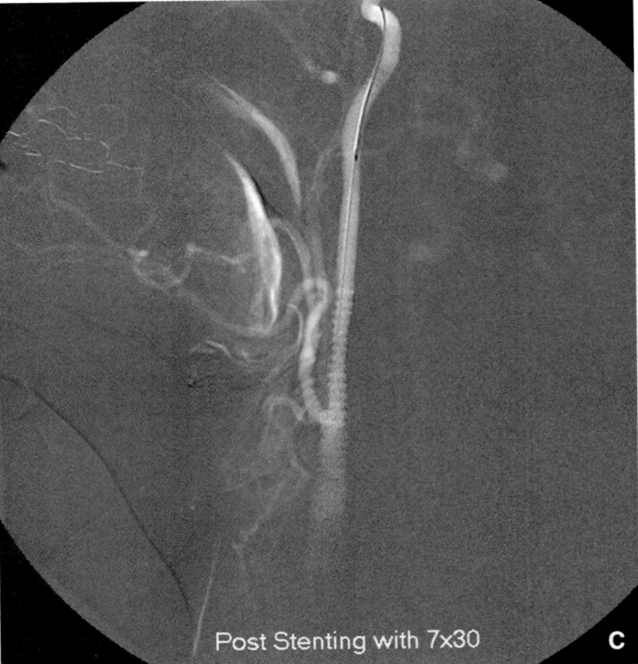

FIGURE 18-9 **A,** Gadolinium selective right carotid angiography confirmed high-grade early restenosis in a patient with significant chronic renal dysfunction. **B,** Predilatation of the right internal carotid artery stenosis with a 4-mL puff hand injection of gadolinium. **C,** Completion gadolinium arteriogram after deployment of a nitinol self-expanding 7 × 30 mm stent.

There are several histamine-related side effects, ranging in severity from minor (e.g., urticaria) to life-threatening (i.e., cardiorespiratory arrest). Laryngeal edema and bronchospasm are generally self-limited but may progress to respiratory distress. Treatment starts with adrenergic inhalers, such as albuterol, and if ineffective, epinephrine (0.5 to 1 mL of 1:10,000 dilution IV or intramuscularly) can be administered. The rare cases of cardiorespiratory collapse must be treated with appropriate hemodynamic and respiratory support with vasopressors and mechanical ventilation. It is important to distinguish histaminic reactions from the more common vagally mediated hypotension because the treatment for these two conditions is vastly different. Vasovagal reactions, which may be related

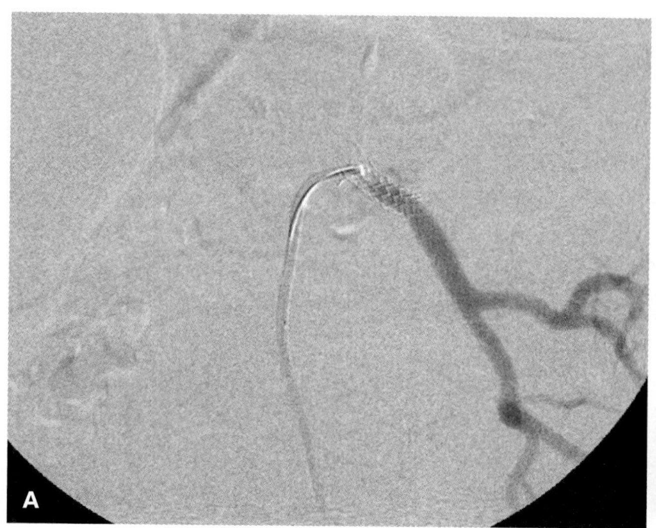

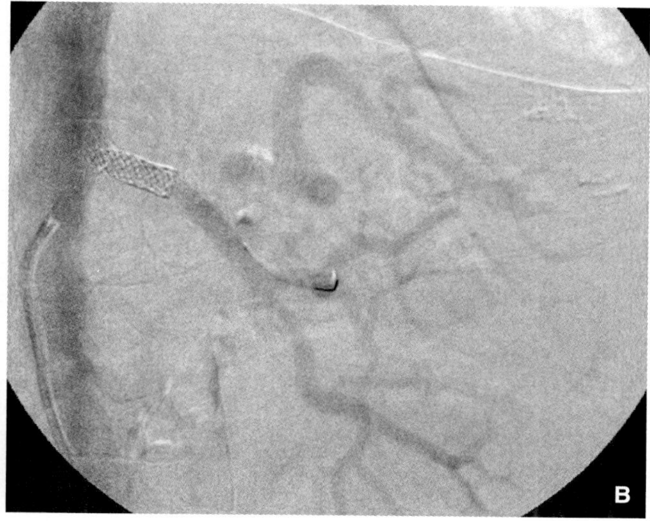

FIGURE 18-10 **A,** Selective gadolinium angiogram of a recurrent ×2 in-stent restenosis of the left renal artery in a patient with flush pulmonary edema. **B,** Completion gadolinium angiogram after angioplasty of the left renal artery stent with a 14 × 15 mm cutting balloon.

to anxiety or catheter placement, are characterized by hypotension accompanied by bradycardia or a lack of tachycardia. These reactions are generally mild and usually require nothing more than close observation and occasionally fluid administration. In the rare cases when such reactions become hemodynamically significant, they can be treated with atropine (0.5 to 1 mg IV). The only situation in which atropine should be given prophylactically is in the setting of carotid angioplasty, in which stimulation of the carotid sinus baroreceptors induces a reflexive parasympathetic discharge, inhibiting the sympathetic tone, resulting in bradycardia and possibly cardiogenic shock.

Late adverse reactions occur 1 hour to 1 week after iodinated contrast exposure and manifest with nausea, vomiting, headache, itching, skin rash, musculoskeletal pain, and fever. Allergy-like skin reactions are well documented and appear with an incidence of approximately 2%. At increased risk are patients with a prior reaction and patients on interleukin-2 treatment. These reactions are probably T-cell mediated and are more common after administration of a non-ionic dimeric contrast agent.[41]

Antihistamines are effective in treating these cutaneous symptoms; however, they have not proved to be effective for prophylaxis. The use of corticosteroids has gained acceptance as an effective prophylaxis for side effects in patients with a prior history of side effects when previously exposed to iodinated contrast material.[42-48] In a study by Lasser and coworkers,[44] two doses of corticosteroid prophylaxis (32 mg of methylprednisolone 12 and 2 hours before contrast administration) offered significant reduction in the incidence of high-osmolality, contrast-related reactions of all types except for skin hives. Administration of steroids only 2 hours before contrast administration did not offer any protective effect. Lasser and coworkers[43] also showed the protective effect of a two-dose oral corticosteroid regimen (methylprednisolone, 32 mg) administered 6 to 24 hours before and again at 2 hours before exposure to low-osmolality, non-ionic contrast media. The adverse event rate decreased from 4.9% in the placebo group to 1.7% in pretreated group.

Greenberger and Patterson[47] considered the effect of prednisolone prophylaxis (50 mg orally, 13, 7, and 1 hours before administration of contrast media) and the use of a single dose of antihistamine (diphenhydramine, 50 mg orally 1 hour before contrast administration) in addition to the use of low-osmolality contrast agents in patients with a previous history of contrast reactions. The risk of an immediate generalized reaction to the contrast agent was reduced from 9.1% when conventional contrast media were used to 0.5% with the low-osmolality media, with the same prophylaxis in both groups. Although the use of non-ionic contrast media does not eliminate these risks entirely, Katayama and associates[49] showed a reduction in all adverse reactions (from 12.6% to 3.1%) and in severe reactions (from 0.22% to 0.04%) in patients receiving intravenous non-ionic, low-osmolality agents compared with patients who received ionic, high-osmolality contrast agents.

Pretesting with an intravenous injection of a small amount of ionic or non-ionic contrast agent has no significant predictive value and offers no clinical benefit.[50] One may consider allergologic testing to confirm the diagnosis, however, and identify the agent responsible in patients who have had a severe anaphylactoid reaction. In one report,[51] the overall risk of having a breakthrough reaction despite the use of a low-osmolality contrast agent and steroid premedication was estimated at 10%. Typically, these breakthrough reactions are of similar severity to the patients' initial reaction, although it may be more severe. Consequently, steroid premedication should be given to patients who are at high risk for reactions, especially patients who have had prior contrast reactions, if there are no contraindications to their use (e.g., diabetes or systemic infections). One should be prepared, however, to treat any breakthrough complications.

Organ-Specific, Contrast-Related Toxicity

Cardiovascular

All contrast agents have the potential to affect cardiac function, by disturbing intracardiac conduction, myocardial function, or coronary artery tone.[52-54] During coronary angiography, there is a passive washout of electrolytes changing the myocardial sodium and calcium balance and cellular calcium control, potentially stimulating arrhythmias.[55] The hemodynamic effect of high-osmolality agents is an increase in stroke volume, cardiac output, and left ventricular work, with a simultaneous decrease in peripheral vascular resistance and heart rate. These changes are temporary and may result in a triphasic arterial blood pressure pattern in which a slight increase is followed by a decrease, then subsequent return to baseline.[55] These effects are markedly attenuated by the use of one of the low-osmolality agents,[56] and they usually are clinically insignificant except perhaps in patients with markedly reduced cardiac function and when injected into or near the heart, as for pulmonary angiography or inferior vena cavography. Additionally, patients with a tight aortic stenosis may be more likely to manifest symptoms by being less able to compensate for the hemodynamic effects of the contrast agent.

Some older contrast agent preparations contained additives capable of binding calcium, leading to sudden decreases in ionized calcium, which could produce electromechanical dissociation, even without a direct cardiac exposure.[53] This is not a major concern in peripheral arteriography with the contrast agents commonly in use today. In a study of non-ionic contrast agents,[54] in which the effects of the iso-osmolar Visipaque and the hyperosmolar Omnipaque were compared in patients with compromised left ventricular function (mean ejection fraction 33.4%), both contrast agents influenced hemodynamics during ventriculography, but Visipaque had significantly less influence on left ventricular end-diastolic pressure than did Omnipaque. These authors suggested that Visipaque may provide benefits in high-risk cardiac patients by allowing a faster return to baseline of left ventricular diastolic pressures.

Pulmonary

There are several possible adverse pulmonary reactions after the intravascular injection of iodinated contrast agents, including bronchospasm, pulmonary arterial hypertension, and pulmonary edema. The pathophysiologic mechanism for these reactions is not yet fully understood but is most likely multifactorial. Increases in airway resistance may be induced by the release of bronchospastic mediators (i.e., histamine, endothelin, 5-hydroxytriptamine, prostaglandins, thromboxane, and bradykinin), vagal reflexes, and direct effects on the bronchi. The effect of iodinated agents on the pulmonary arteries is biphasic, consisting of an initial transient vasorelaxation phase followed by a more sustained vasoconstriction. Finally, pulmonary edema is probably secondary to endothelial injury leading to increased vascular permeability.[55,57]

Hematologic

Although conventional iodinated contrast agents are known to retard coagulation when in contact with blood, there is some evidence that this effect is attenuated with non-ionic contrast agents. Some potential anticoagulant actions of these agents include inhibition of coagulation factors VII, VIII, and X; inhibition of prothrombinase function; inhibition of thrombin by antithrombin III; inhibition of thrombin-to-fibrin binding; and inhibition of the platelet glycoprotein IIb/IIIa receptor.[58-60] Iodinated contrast agents also have shown antifibrinolytic properties.[61] The clinical significance of these actions has not been fully established. Nonetheless, because red blood cell aggregates are known to occur when blood is in contact with any contrast agent,[62,63] it is advisable to minimize contact between the contrast agent and blood. Judicious flushing of catheters with saline after contrast injection and avoidance of blood backup into the sheaths, catheters, and syringes are fundamental measures to minimize this risk. Although controversial, the authors prefer to administer anticoagulation for all endovascular procedures, even short diagnostic ones.

Nephrotoxicity

Many prospective randomized clinical trials have shown that intravascular contrast material is detrimental to renal function.[21,64-70] Despite the advent of low-osmolality, non-ionic contrast agents, the use of DSA, and pretreatment with intravenous hydration, contrast-related nephropathy (CN) continues to represent a major cause of short-term and long-term morbidity in clinical practice.[71-73] The development of CN often leads to prolonged hospital stay, increased hospital cost, end-stage renal dysfunction, and occasionally death.[65,74] As the emphasis on minimally invasive procedures increases with the rapid development of new vascular interventional techniques, the incidence of CN is expected to increase.[75,76]

The pathophysiology of CN has not been clearly defined and remains a topic of extensive review.[40,55,74,77-84] Contrast agents adversely affect renal perfusion by exerting a negative inotropic effect in the heart and by promoting systemic vasodilatation.[55,56] Contrast agents also cause direct tubular toxicity.[40,52,82-84] All contrast agents are cleared from the body by glomerular filtration with no appreciable tubular reabsorption. An osmotic gradient produces diuresis, leading to an increase in intratubular pressure and a decrease in the glomerular filtration rate. Additionally the tubuloglomerular feedback mechanism releases mediators, including angiotensin II, endothelin, and adenosine, causing vasoconstriction of the afferent arterioles, which further impairs glomerular filtration rate. The renal medulla becomes further impaired due to a decrease in the local production of prostaglandins and nitric oxide.[79] Hypo-osmolar contrast agents cause a more brisk diuresis than iso-osmolar ones; this may increase the metabolic demand of the already hypoxic medulla, resulting in acute renal deterioration in patients without the physiologic reserve.[79]

The scope of CN can range from marginal reversible increases in the serum creatinine level to end-stage renal insufficiency requiring lifelong dialysis. Patients at risk for CN include the elderly, patients with chronic renal dysfunction or diabetes mellitus, and especially patients with diabetic nephropathy. Additionally, patients with congestive heart failure, patients with dehydration, and patients requiring larger doses of contrast dye over short periods are at increased risk for CN.[25,70,77,79,82,84] Elderly patients seem to have a higher propensity for CN, which may be related to their underlying co-morbidities.[70] In patients with normal renal function, infusion contrast volumes need not be limited for fear of developing CN, although maintenance of adequate hydration and urine flow rates is generally advisable. In patients with baseline renal dysfunction or hyperosmolar states (e.g., multiple myeloma), contrast administration should be minimized, and adequate hydration and urine flow rates should be monitored carefully.

In the study by Hall and associates,[22] the risk of CN was 2% in patients with normal renal function (<1.2 mg/dL) and increased to 10% in patients with baseline creatinine values of 1.3 to 1.9 mg/dL and to 62% in patients with creatinine values greater than 2 mg/dL. Although diabetes, without renal insufficiency, has not been identified consistently as an independent risk factor for the development of CN,[22,85] the frequent presence of coexisting renal insufficiency in diabetic patients, whether clinically apparent or not, increases the risk. This would explain the extraordinarily high incidence of CN in this population.[21,25,86-88] Manske and colleagues[21] reported an incidence of 50% CN in a group of patients with advanced diabetic nephropathy (mean creatinine 5.9 mg/dL) undergoing coronary angiography, despite the use of low-osmolality agents.[89] A striking 15% of those patients subsequently required dialysis. Azotemic patients with diabetes are at high risk of developing CN even when less than 100 mL of radiocontrast agent is used.[21] The administration of increasing amounts of contrast material predicts the potential risk for CN, but even small-volume contrast arteriography has been associated with CN in certain settings.[9,21,22,70,90]

In the 1980s and 1990s, multiple clinical trials showed that CN represents a significant morbidity in patients with chronic renal insufficiency.[25,64-67,87,91-95] Current evidence suggests that intravenous hydration with normal saline offers the best protection with the fewest adverse effects in the prevention of CN.[65,82,84,93,95-100] Other treatments have been used to prevent CN, including the use of mannitol,[96] furosemide,[64] dopamine,[65] calcium channel blockers,[86] atrial natriuretic factor,[88] magnesium,[66] theophylline,[69,101] and prostaglandin E_1.[89] None of these modalities used alone or in combination has consistently shown superiority to intravenous hydration alone.

Although not routinely used in patients with normal renal function, preprocedural hydration may be in order for patients with preexisting renal dysfunction, as indicated by a baseline creatinine value greater than 1.6 mg/dL. The authors advocate pre-angiographic hydration consisting of liberal oral intake and at least 4 to 6 hours of intravenous fluids before and after the procedure, administered at 1 mL/kg/hr, or, alternatively, a 500-mL bolus within 2 hours before contrast exposure. Outpatient hydration protocols have proved to be effective.[102] Hydration with isotonic saline seems to offer a better protection effect against CN than half-isotonic saline.[95] Patients who go home shortly after their procedures should be encouraged to drink plenty of fluids. Although controversial, the authors selectively administer *N*-acetyl cysteine, an antioxidant, at a dose of 600 mg for 2 days before and after the procedure in patients with elevated baseline creatinine values because of evidence suggesting potential renal function preservation in patients with chronic renal insufficiency exposed to contrast material.[90,103-106] Similar controversy exists with regard to the use of fenoldopam, a selective dopamine agonist with renal vasodilating and natriuretic properties, in preventing CN.[68,107] The authors do not routinely employ fenoldopam. As previously discussed, alternative contrast agents also may be considered to decrease the incidence of CN in patients with preexisting renal insufficiency.

Intravascular administration of iodinated contrast media to patients who are receiving metformin (dimethyl-biguanide), an oral antidiabetic agent, can result in lactic acidosis. This rare complication occurs only if CN occurs and the patient continues to take metformin in the presence of impaired renal function. Metformin is excreted primarily by the kidneys; continued intake in the setting of renal dysfunction may result in a toxic accumulation and subsequent lactic acidosis. The Contrast Media Safety Committee of the European Society of Urogenital Radiology has published practical guidelines on the use of contrast agents in diabetic patients taking metformin.[39] In brief, preprocedure serum creatinine levels always should be measured in these patients, and low-osmolality contrast agents must be used. In patients with a normal serum creatinine that remains stable after the procedure, metformin must be withheld from the time of administration of the contrast agent until 48 hours afterward. There is no scientific justification for withholding metformin for 48 hours before administration of the contrast medium in patients with normal renal function, as currently recommended in the package insert. In patients with baseline chronic renal insufficiency, the metformin should be held 48 hours before the procedure and may be re-started 48 hours later, if renal function and serum creatinine remain unchanged. In emergent cases with patients having abnormal renal function, alternative imaging may be considered. If the study is necessary, metformin should be stopped; the patient should be hydrated (100 mL/hr) for about 24 hours after the procedure; and renal function, serum lactic acid, and arterial pH should be monitored carefully. The clinical symptoms of lactic acidosis include vomiting, somnolence, nausea, epigastric pain, anorexia, lethargy, diarrhea, and thirst. A confirmatory arterial pH of less than 7.25, serum lactic acid of greater than 5 mmol, increased anion gap to greater than 15 mEq/L, and an increase in the lactate-to-pyruvate ratio may confirm the diagnosis.

■ CHOOSING A CONTRAST AGENT

Given an informed choice, patients would prefer to undergo angiography with a non-ionic contrast agent, primarily because of the lessened discomfort involved. Non-ionic contrast agents can be considerably more expensive than ionic agents, however (see Table 18-1). Health care providers,

Table 18-4 Medicare-accepted Indications for Use of Non-ionic Contrast Media

Previous history of contrast reaction (beyond a sensation of heat, flushing, or a single episode of nausea or vomiting)
History of asthma
History of other allergies (e.g., foods, drugs, pollens)
Presence of significant cardiac dysfunction (e.g., recent cardiac decompensation, unstable angina, severe arrhythmia, recent myocardial infarction, pulmonary hypertension)
Presence of generalized severe debilitation (e.g., diabetes mellitus, renal failure, multiple myeloma, shock, respirator dependency, paralysis, cachexia, dehydration, leukemia, COPD)
Presence of sickle cell anemia

COPD, chronic obstructive pulmonary disease.

Adapted from the Medicare Hospital Manual, Section 443g 1 and 2. Available at http://www.cms/gov/manuals/10_hospital/ho441.asp.

including Medicare, are becoming more insistent on documentation of "need" to justify the use of non-ionic agents. Although "acceptable" indications may vary from provider to provider, Table 18-4 lists conditions generally believed to justify the use of non-ionic contrast preparations.[108]

From the clinician's perspective, non-ionic agents are also the agents of choice because patient comfort during the procedure translates to an easier and less stressful examination. Contrast-related pain, "hot flashes," and muscle spasm often result in patient movement with resultant image degradation. This degradation can be particularly problematic during filming of diseased distal lower extremity vasculature where transit times are slow. Movement occurring after contrast material has entered the field of view is difficult to negate by remasking or pixel shifting. Stepped or staged multiple-field DSA studies, by virtue of the time span between procurement of the contrast material and mask images, may be impossible to perform because of excessive movement. Last, the reduction in overall adverse reaction rates with non-ionic, iso-osmolar agents simplifies the physician's role and facilitates the conduct of an expeditious examination. A meta-analysis[24] of pooled data from 31 clinical trials evaluating the nephrotoxicity of high-osmolality versus low-osmolality radiographic contrast agents found the use of low-osmolality agents to be beneficial to patients with renal insufficiency. More recently, a randomized, prospective, multicenter study comparing two low ionic agents, one an iso-osmolar agent and the other a low-osmolar medium, showed a significant reduction of CN with the use of the iso-osmolar agent in patients with chronic diabetic nephropathy.[25] These authors found that use of the iso-osmolar contrast agent was associated with a 3% incidence of CN, defined by an increase in serum creatinine of at least 0.5 mg/dL, versus 26% with the use of a low-osmolar agent. Lowering the threshold for the definition of CN to 1 mg/dL, the incidence of CN was 0% in the iso-osmolar group and 15% in the low-osmolar group.[25] Consequently, low ionic, iso-osmolar agents should be the preferred angiographic medium for high-risk patients.

■ CONTRAST ADMINISTRATION

Angiographic evaluation of large high-flow vessels, such as the aortic arch, abdominal aorta, or vena cava, requires relatively large volumes of contrast material infused over a brief period. Full-strength contrast material typically is required in these locations because of the dilutional effect of the bloodstream. Consequently, it is not generally feasible to inject the necessary quantities of relatively viscous dye by hand, and a power injector is used. These devices allow infusion of pre-set volumes of contrast material over selected periods, typically large volumes within several seconds. Pressure limits also can be set to ensure that an inappropriately forceful and potentially injurious jet of contrast material is not injected or to prevent catheter rupture in the event of a kink in the catheter. Typical contrast injection volumes, methods, and rates are detailed in Tables 18-5 and 18-6. In contrast to angiography of high-flow vessels, in which power injection is typically required, the reduced volume and concentration of contrast material needed for selective catheter studies makes hand injection feasible and offers several advantages. Chief among these is the efficiency of effecting catheter placement and proceeding directly with filming rather than having to switch from the hand-held syringe to the power injector each time a filming run is performed, while still allowing for heparinized flushing of the catheter after contrast injections if a manifold system is being used (Fig. 18-11). This is particularly advantageous with tenuous catheterizations in which delays and extraneous movements may result in dislodgment of the catheter. Hand injection allows the

Table 18-5 Typical Contrast Injection Volumes, Methods, and Rates for Various Vascular Regions

LOCATION	SUGGESTED METHOD	INJECTION RATE (mL/sec)	TOTAL VOLUME (mL)
Aortic arch	Power injection	20	40
Selective carotid	Hand or power	5-10	10
Selective vertebral	Hand injection	3-5	5
Selective subclavian/brachial	Hand or power	5-10	10
Abdominal aorta	Power injection	20	40
Renal/mesenteric	Hand injection	5-10	10
Iliac artery	Hand or power injection	10	10
Infrainguinal segments	Hand or power injection	5-10	10
Aorta to pedals, stepped run	Power injection	20	90*

*Full-strength contrast agent; all others typically performed with half-strength contrast agent when using digital subtraction angiography. Gadolinium injections are usually full strength.

Table 18-6 Recommended Radiographic Filming Projections for Optimal Branch Separation

LOCATION	RECOMMENDED FILMING PROJECTION
Aortic arch	30° left anterior oblique
Cervical carotids	AP and lateral
Intracranial carotids	AP and lateral
Vertebrobasilar system	AP and lateral
Right subclavian	Right anterior oblique
Renal artery origins	AP ± 10°
Celiac/SMA origins	Lateral
Iliac bifurcation	20° contralateral anterior oblique
Femoral bifurcation	20° ipsilateral anterior oblique
Trifurcation and tibials	Anatomic AP (or 20° ipsilateral anterior oblique with feet in the neutral supine position)

AP, anteroposterior; SMA, superior mesenteric artery.

contrast volume and infusion rate to be varied during the examination as needed to achieve the desired opacification. An additional advantage is the ability to vary the concentration of contrast material used with each injection by mixing different proportions with saline when refilling the syringe. Because power injectors generally hold 200 mL of contrast solution, when they are filled, it is more difficult to alter the concentration from run to run. As with all selective catheter injections, care must be taken during hand injections to ensure that the force of the stream of dye exiting the end of the catheter does not propel the catheter out of the selected vessel or cause injury to the vessel by the jet effect of fluid out the distal end-hole. The chief disadvantage of hand injection angiography in situations suitable for either power or hand injection is the increased radiation exposure to the physician who is in closer proximity to the x-ray source than would be necessary with the power injection technique.

For distal evaluations using a proximally placed catheter, pre-injection of contrast before image acquisition can reduce radiation exposure by eliminating pointless filming before the arrival of the contrast agent. The delay between contrast injection and initiation of filming depends on the severity of intervening occlusive disease and the cardiac output of the patient. The location of the catheter relative to the area of interest is another variable to take into consideration, with more selective (distal) catheterizations resulting in earlier and more complete vascular opacification. Ultimately, judgment about the significance of each of these factors and their effect on contrast transit time develops with experience and guides the angiographer's decisions about proper timing of the injection and filming. Even with selective catheterization, more concentrated dye may be required to achieve adequate opacification of distal vessels, particularly if there is significant upstream occlusive disease that slows contrast transit and permits greater contrast dilution during transit through collateral vessels. If opacification remains suboptimal despite use of full-strength contrast media and a selectively positioned catheter, visualization may be enhanced by larger dye loads, mechanical or pharmacologic reactive hyperemia, or occlusion balloon angiography. These techniques are described in Chapter 51.

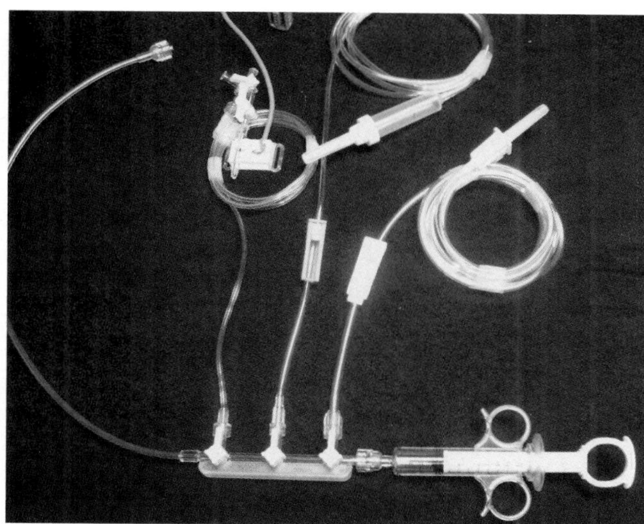

FIGURE 18-11 Rapid and convenient setup for selective angiography contrast mixing and delivery. The control syringe and manifold setup facilitate reloading after each contrast injection with one hand operating the syringe and the other regulating the proportions of contrast material and saline in the final mixture via the stopcocks on the manifold. Between injections, the saline line can be left on flush to keep the catheter irrigated. The third three-way stopcock allows continuous pressure monitoring when connected to a transducer and alternatively may be used to fill the contrast container in a retrograde fashion from remnants of contrast material in the power injector. After the contrast container is reloaded, the system is connected back to pressure.

SOURCES OF ERROR WITH ANGIOGRAPHY

The detrimental effects of patient movement on image quality and methods to correct for it already have been thoroughly discussed. Motion artifacts remain, however, the most common source of image degradation encountered during angiography. Other factors also can lead to confounding images and associated errors. Most important, the presence of tissues with radiodensity similar to the contrast agent in use frequently compromises the quality of the rendered image. The tissue most commonly responsible for this degradation of image quality is bone, although calcified plaque can have a similar effect. Although filming at different angles may succeed in separating the bone from the vessel, this may not be possible with calcified plaque or in areas with multiple or diffuse osseous structures, such as the pelvis or lower leg. Usually a combination of views can succeed, however, in minimizing the artifact and showing the luminal characteristics of the vessel of interest. Contrast in superimposed vessels also can obscure visualization of luminal irregularities in the overlapping regions; this frequently occurs near vascular bifurcations, where occlusive lesions are also common. It is incumbent on the angiographer to search for views that separate the vessels and allow visualization of all areas. Although this usually is achieved through different oblique projections, the use of cranial or caudal rotation is often helpful, particularly in areas of anterior or posterior angulation (Fig. 18-12). The typical configuration of the iliac and femoral bifurcations is best splayed out in the contralateral and ipsilateral anterior

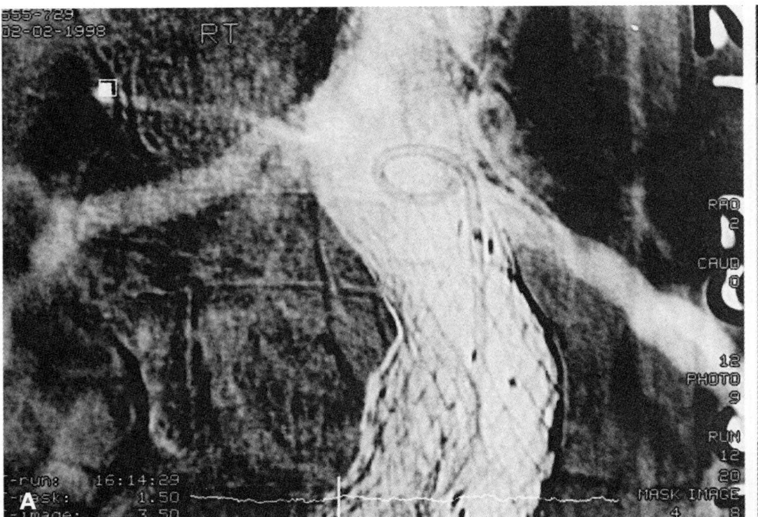

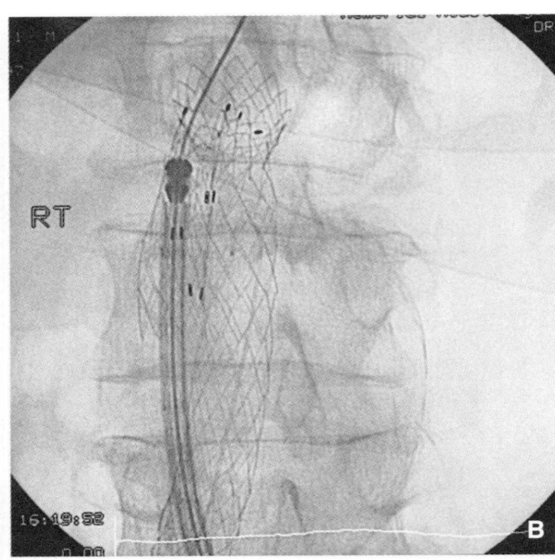

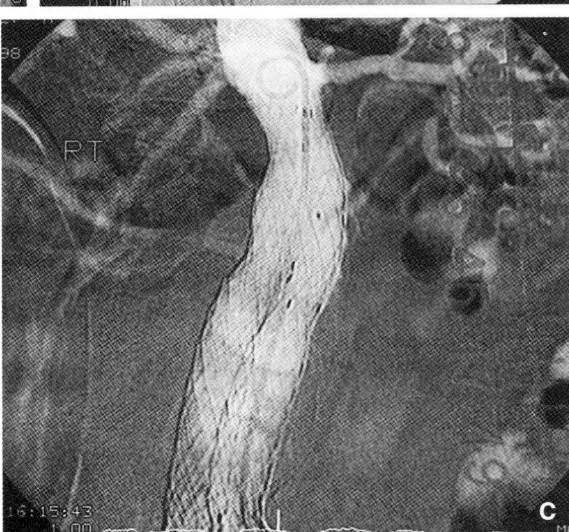

FIGURE 18-12 **A,** Completion aortic endograft angiogram in the anteroposterior projection giving the appearance of overriding of the endograft on the left renal artery. **B,** Unsubtracted visualization of the endograft stent rings revealing them to be out of alignment, consistent with anterior angulation of the aortic neck. **C,** Completion angiogram obtained in the 36-degree cranial projection, which aligns the front and back apices of the endograft and reveals that the endograft is well clear of the left renal artery.

oblique projections (Fig. 18-13). The aortic arch is best viewed in the left anterior oblique projection (Fig. 18-14), whereas the celiac axis and superior mesenteric arteries are visualized best in the lateral position (Fig. 18-15). The renal arteries can arise directly laterally or slightly anterior or posterior on the aorta (Fig. 18-16). It is incumbent on the angiographer to determine the most appropriate view to visualize the origin of the vessel of interest so that an orificial lesion is not missed.

An additional source of error being encountered more frequently since the advent of endoluminal grafting procedures is the artifact produced when tortuous vessels are straightened by stiff guide wires (Fig. 18-17). The size and rigidity of these devices require the use of stiff guide wires for the device to track through the iliac system. Angiograms obtained when these wires are in place may give the appearance of luminal stenoses or dissections produced by the unnatural course the vessel is forced into by the stiff guide wire. This can be particularly concerning at the completion of a procedure when it is conceivable that passage of the device has damaged the vessel. Although the appearance is characteristic, it is best to exchange the stiff guide wire for a softer one, then re-evaluate the situation.

■ BASICS OF RADIATION SAFETY

Because exposure to ionizing radiation is an unavoidable aspect of angiography, no review of the topic would be complete without a discussion of means of minimizing this hazard. There are two basic mechanisms to achieve this goal: (1) reduce the output of radiation or (2) shield the operator from exposure. The requisite close proximity of the operator to the x-ray source during fluoroscopy-guided catheter and guide wire manipulation translates into fluoroscopy being the greatest source of occupational radiation exposure in medicine today.[109,110] With increasingly complex percutaneous angioplasty and stenting, inferior vena cava filter placements, thrombolytic procedures, endoluminal grafting, and vascular embolization being performed more frequently, fluoroscopy times have increased substantially and so has the potential for excessive radiation exposure. Cases of fluoroscopically induced dermatitis and severe burns have been reported in patients and physicians.[111-117] In September 1994, the FDA released guidelines for physicians and other health care professionals concerning the avoidance of serious x-ray-induced skin injuries to patients during fluoroscopic procedures.[118] The

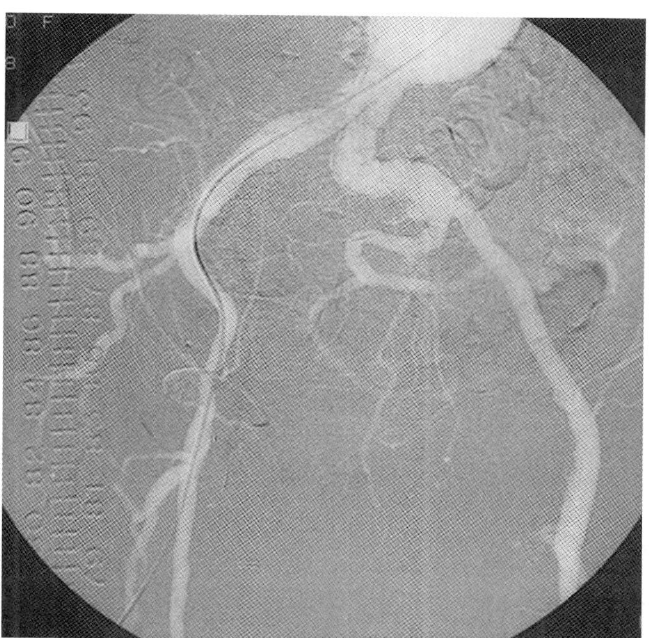

FIGURE 18-13 Pelvic arteriogram taken in the 30-degree right anterior oblique position, which splays out the contralateral iliac and ipsilateral femoral bifurcations.

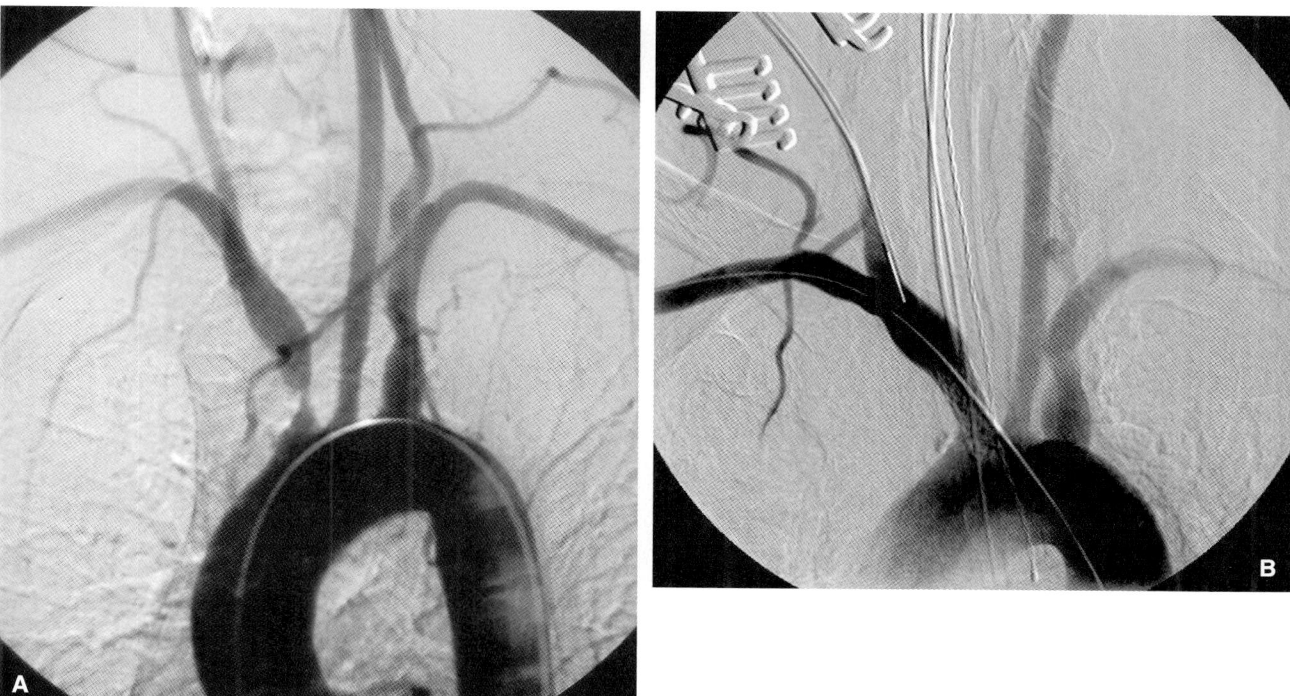

FIGURE 18-14 **A,** Aortic arch arteriogram with 30-degree left anterior oblique angulation displays a high-grade innominate artery stenosis. The origin of the right subclavian artery is obscured by the common carotid artery. It is essential to obtain a run with a right anterior oblique angulation to display the origin of the right subclavian artery. **B,** Completion arteriogram after angioplasty and stenting of the innominate with an 8 × 20 mm balloon expandable stent and cerebral protection with a surgical cut-down occlusion of the common carotid artery for right-hand claudication.

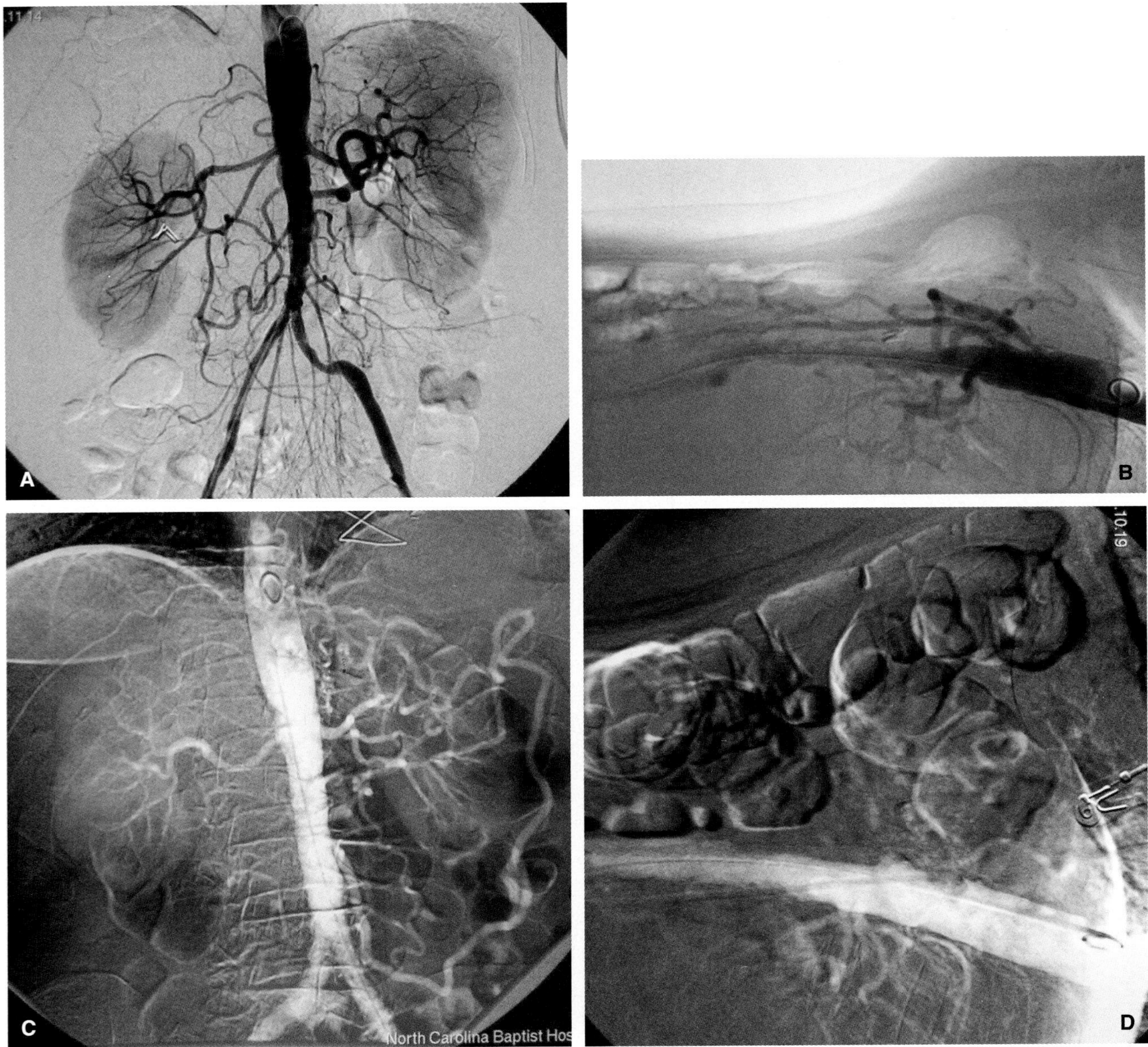

FIGURE 18-15 **A,** Anteroposterior aortogram shows a prominent splenic vessel and readily apparent superior mesenteric artery arcade. No apparent meandering mesenteric artery or large collateral between the mesenteric circulations was appreciated. Note patent bilateral common iliac stents and absent flow through the hypogastric arteries bilaterally. **B,** A lateral aortogram reveals a patent celiac axis with an approximately 50% to 60% stenosis at its origin. The superior mesenteric artery shows no significant occlusive disease. The inferior mesenteric artery is not visualized. **C,** Anteroposterior arteriogram shows single renal arteries to both kidneys. The inferior mesenteric artery is noted with large collaterals to the marginal artery of Drummond and a prominent ascending meandering artery of Riolan. The distal superior mesenteric artery appeared to reconstitute at the mid-portion by retrograde filling from ileal and jejunal branches. **D,** Lateral mesenteric view shows occluded celiac and superior mesenteric vessels. The celiac stump can be identified by the presence of heavy calcific plaque in its anatomic position.

following recommendations for facilities in which invasive procedures are performed were made:

1. Establish standard operating procedures and clinical protocols for each specific type of procedure performed
2. Know the radiation dose rates for the specific fluoroscopy systems and for each mode of operation used during the clinical protocol
3. Assess the impact of each procedure's protocol on the potential for radiation injury to the patient
4. Modify protocols when appropriate
5. Minimize cumulative adsorbed dose to any specific skin area and use equipment that aids in minimizing adsorbed dose

All practitioners who use fluoroscopic radiation should be required to be knowledgeable about the basics of radiation physics, biology, and safety. In brief, the simplest means of reducing radiation produced during fluoroscopy is judicious attention to its use. Inattentive and inexperienced

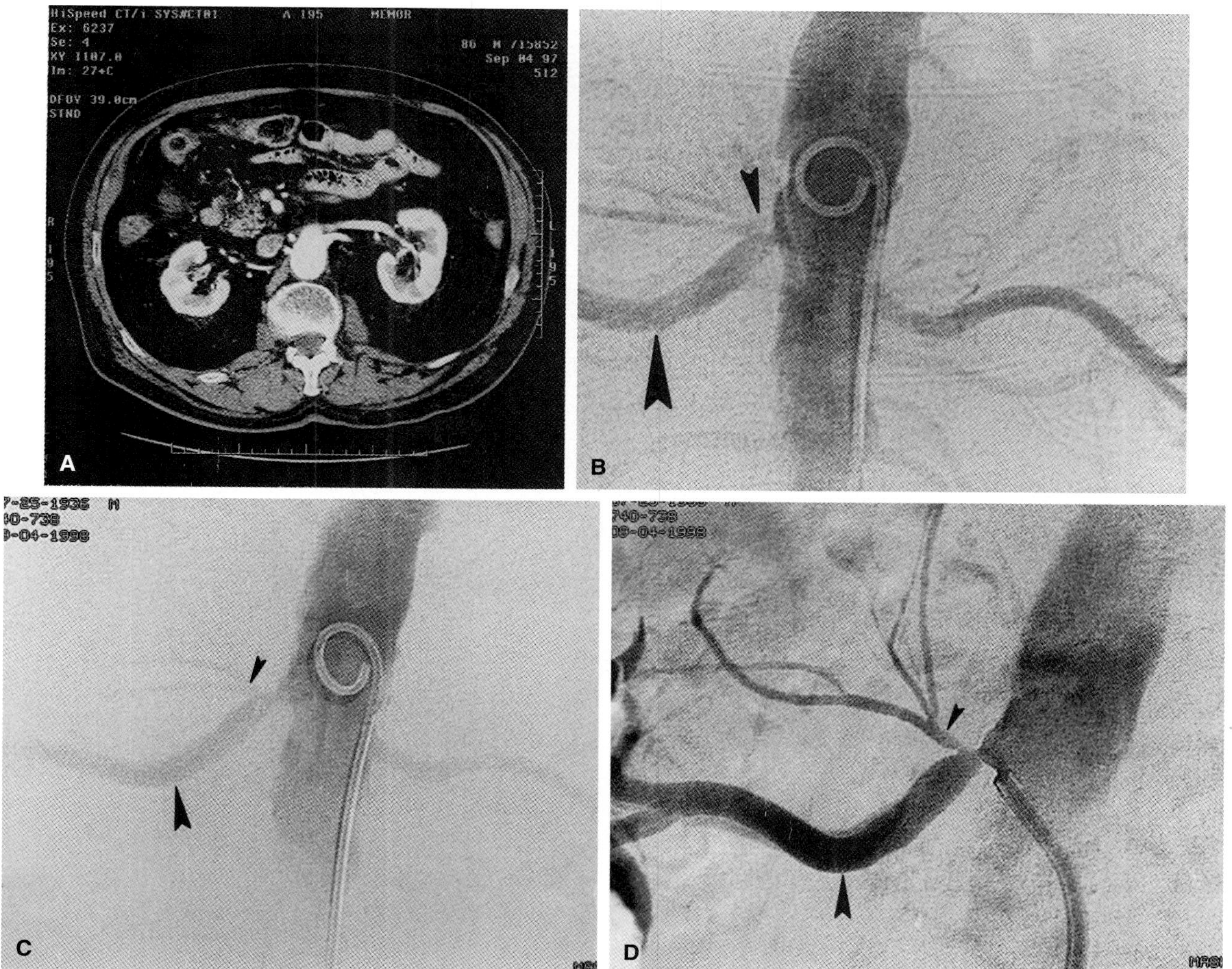

FIGURE 18-16 **A,** CT scan shows right and left renal arteries arising off of the anterior surface of the aorta. The best radiographic view for each of these would be the 10- to 15-degree contralateral anterior oblique position. **B,** Flush aortogram in the anteroposterior position suggesting a right renal artery *(large arrow)* stenosis at the renal orifice. Also noted is a branch vessel *(small arrow)*, which, in this view, appears to arise from the aorta itself. **C,** Flush aortogram in the 15-degree left anterior oblique position to evaluate better the origin of the right renal artery. This projection reveals that the right renal artery *(large arrow)* stenosis is not truly orificial, suggesting that the branch vessel *(small arrow)* arises from the renal artery directly. **D,** Selective right renal angiogram obtained in the 15-degree left anterior oblique position, producing the best opacification and characterization of the renal artery stenosis and delineation of the origin of the branch vessel.

operators tend to continue fluoroscopy long after completing the technical maneuver at hand. If the operator is not looking at the video monitor, there is no need for fluoroscopy to be on. When performing radiographic imaging, the run should be terminated as soon as the relevant information has been obtained. It is common for an inexperienced operator to "study" the fluoroscopic image in real time when a static image on the monitor from a single acquired image from fluoroscopy would suffice and reduce radiation output substantially.

When dealing with rectangular areas of interest, such as in extremity evaluations, the sides of the beam of radiation also can be collimated (narrowed) to reduce radiation output and scatter. The collimation technique has no detrimental effect on image quality and simplifies the radiographic exposure by eliminating areas with large variations in radiodensity, decreasing radiation scattering to personnel. Another mechanism to reduce radiation output is the use of pulsed rather than continuous fluoroscopy. The image quality in this mode can be diminished and noticeably choppy. For this reason, it is not used often in most practices. Finally, increasing the distance of the operator from the source of radiation decreases the dose of radiation received precipitously. The dose of radiation at 2 m is 25% the dose at 1 m. From the patient's perspective, as the distance from the x-ray tube to the patient's skin increases, the x-ray intensity is reduced and so is the potential for radiation damage. In units with a variable distance between the tube and the image intensifier, the image intensifier should be kept as close as possible to the patient below and the tube as far as possible from the patient above; this would yield the least possible radiation dose to the skin.

Despite reducing excessive radiation output, there will always be a need to shield the patient, operator, and other

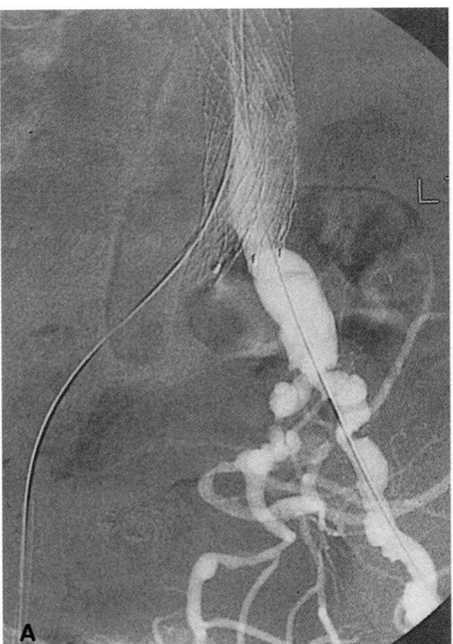

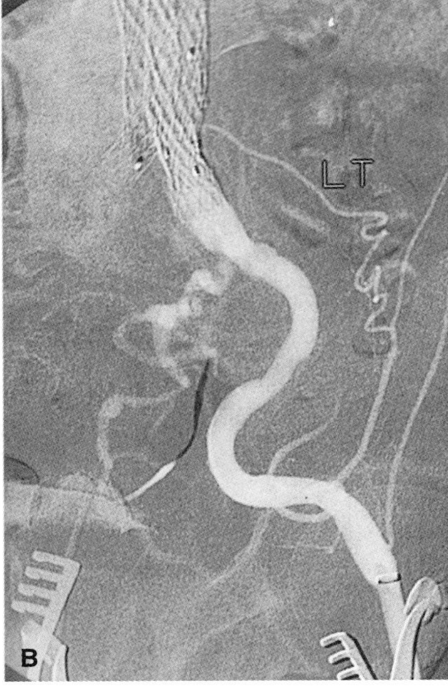

FIGURE 18-17 A, Left iliac angiogram obtained after aortic endografting, with an Amplatz superstiff guide wire in place through the iliac system. Forced straightening of the external iliac artery produces the appearance of multiple luminal stenoses. **B,** Same left iliac angiogram immediately after removal of the guide wire shows that when the iliac arteries resume their natural configuration, the "stenoses" resolve.

personnel from hazardous ionizing radiation produced during the conduct of endovascular procedures. Lead aprons and thyroid shields are universally used to shield patients' and operators' radiation-sensitive organs: the thyroid, gonads, breasts, and red bone marrow. The concept of using a sterile disposable protective drape has been introduced.[119] Although the use of leaded glass screens and collimation would be expected to reduce radiation exposure, in actual clinical practice no statistically significant effect on over-lead or under-lead monitoring badge doses were found for these variables.[120] It has been well documented that the thickness of lead aprons worn is the only variable to affect significantly the amount of radiation recorded on monitoring badges worn underneath them, with the best protection coming from aprons providing 1-mm thickness of lead in front.[120] Many active endovascular therapists wear leaded glasses with side-shields during endovascular procedures to reduce the risk of cataract formation from exposure to ionizing radiation. Finally, x-ray–attenuating surgical gloves may provide some x-ray protection to the operator, but are not likely to protect from a hand placed directly under the field.

CONCLUSION

Although the role of arteriography in the diagnosis of vascular disease may be diminished by new technologies under development, it remains the gold standard and an integral component of the rapidly developing endovascular therapies. It is incumbent on vascular surgeons to understand the basic principles of radiographic imaging and arteriographic evaluation and be able to apply them safely and effectively in their practices. The information presented in this chapter should allow vascular surgeons to make informed decisions about radiographic equipment and techniques and avoid the common pitfalls of these procedures. To put this information to good use, vascular surgeons must persevere in the pursuit of access to the best available radiographic facilities. With this combination of knowledge and facilities, vascular surgeons would be well positioned to render the best available endovascular and surgical care to their patients and participate actively in the development, evaluation, and application of new technologies.

REFERENCES

1. Aaron JO, Hesselink JR, Oot R, et al: Complications of intravenous DSA performed for carotid artery disease: A prospective study. Radiology 153:675-678, 1984.
2. Reilly LM, Ehrenfeld WK, Stoney RJ: Carotid digital subtraction angiography: The comparative roles of intra-arterial and intravenous imaging. Surgery 96:909-918, 1984.
3. Henretta JP, Hodgson KJ, Mattos MA, et al: Feasibility of endovascular repair of abdominal aortic aneurysms with local anesthesia with intravenous sedation. J Vasc Surg 29:793-798, 1999.
4. Hawkins IF: Carbon dioxide digital subtraction arteriography. AJR Am J Roentgenol 139:19-24, 1982.
5. Frankhouse JH, Ryan MG, Papanicolaou G, et al: Carbon dioxide/digital subtraction arteriography-assisted transluminal angioplasty. Ann Vasc Surg 9:448-452, 1995.
6. Harward TR, Smith S, Hawkins IF, Seeger JM: Follow-up evaluation after renal artery bypass surgery with use of carbon dioxide arteriography and color-flow duplex scanning. J Vasc Surg 18:23-30, 1993.
7. Shifrin EG, Plich MB, Verstandig AG, Gomori M: Cerebral angiography with gaseous carbon dioxide (CO_2). J Cardiovasc Surg (Torino) 31:603-606, 1990.
8. Spinosa DJ, Matsumoto AH, Angle JF, et al: Gadolinium-based contrast and carbon dioxide angiography to evaluate renal transplants for vascular causes of renal insufficiency and accelerated hypertension. J Vasc Interv Radiol 9:909-916, 1998.
9. Spinosa DJ, Angle JF, Hagspiel KD, et al: Lower extremity arteriography with use of iodinated contrast material or gadodiamide to supplement CO_2 angiography in patients with renal insufficiency. J Vasc Interv Radiol 11:35-43, 2000.
10. Weaver FA, Pentecost MJ, Yellin AE: Carbon dioxide digital subtraction arteriography: A pilot study. Ann Vasc Surg 4:437-441, 1990.

11. Weaver FA, Pentecost MJ, Yellin AE, et al: Clinical applications of carbon dioxide/digital subtraction arteriography. J Vasc Surg 13:266-273, 1991.
12. Gahlen J, Hansmann J, Schumacher H, et al: Carbon dioxide angiography for endovascular grafting in high-risk patients with infrarenal abdominal aortic aneurysms. J Vasc Surg 33:646-649, 2001.
13. Caridi JG, Hawkins IF Jr, Cho K, et al: CO_2 splenoportography: Preliminary results. AJR Am J Roentgenol 180:1375-1378, 2003.
14. Hawkins IF Jr, Caridi JG, Klioze SD, Mladinich CR: Modified plastic bag system with O-ring fitting connection for carbon dioxide angiography. AJR Am J Roentgenol 176:229-232, 2001.
15. Lang EV, Gossler AA, Fick LJ, et al: Carbon dioxide angiography: Effect of injection parameters on bolus configuration. J Vasc Interv Radiol 10:41-49, 1999.
16. Coffey R, Quisling RG, Mickle JP, et al: The cerebrovascular effects of intraarterial CO_2 in quantities required for diagnostic imaging. Radiology 151:405-410, 1984.
17. Dimakakos PB, Stefanopoulos T, Doufas AG, et al: The cerebral effects of carbon dioxide during digital subtraction angiography in the aortic arch and its branches in rabbits. AJNR Am J Neuroradiol 19:261-266, 1998.
18. Rundback JH, Shah PM, Wong J, et al: Livedo reticularis, rhabdomyolysis, massive intestinal infarction, and death after carbon dioxide arteriography. J Vasc Surg 26:337-340, 1997.
19. Caridi JG, Hawkins IF Jr, Klioze SD, Leveen RF: Carbon dioxide digital subtraction angiography: The practical approach. Tech Vasc Interv Radiol 4:57-65, 2001.
20. Boyd-Kranis R, Sullivan KL, Eschelman DJ, et al: Accuracy and safety of carbon dioxide inferior vena cavography. J Vasc Interv Radiol 10:1183-1189, 1999.
21. Manske CL, Sprafka JM, Strony JT, Wang Y: Contrast nephropathy in azotemic diabetic patients undergoing coronary angiography. Am J Med 89:615-620, 1990.
22. Hall KA, Wong RW, Hunter GC, et al: Contrast-induced nephrotoxicity: The effects of vasodilator therapy. J Surg Res 53:317-320, 1992.
23. Smith DC, Yahiku PY, Maloney MD, Hart KL: Three new low-osmolality contrast agents: A comparative study of patient discomfort. AJNR Am J Neuroradiol 9:137-139, 1988.
24. Barrett BJ, Carlisle EJ: Metaanalysis of the relative nephrotoxicity of high- and low-osmolality iodinated contrast media. Radiology 188:171-178, 1993.
25. Aspelin P, Aubry P, Fransson SG, et al: Nephrotoxic effects in high-risk patients undergoing angiography. N Engl J Med 348:491-499, 2003.
26. Ailawadi G, Stanley JC, Williams DM, et al: Gadolinium as a nonnephrotoxic contrast agent for catheter-based arteriographic evaluation of renal arteries in patients with azotemia. J Vasc Surg 37:346-352, 2003.
27. Berg KJ, Lundby B, Reinton V, et al: Gadodiamide in renal transplant patients: Effects on renal function and usefulness as a glomerular filtration rate marker. Nephron 72:212-217, 1996.
28. Schild HH, Weber W, Boeck E, et al: [Gadolinium-DTPA (Magnevist) as contrast medium for arterial DSA]. Rofo Fortschr Geb Rontgenstr Neuen Bildgeb Verfahr 160:218-221, 1994.
29. Spinosa DJ, Matsumoto AH, Angle JF, Hagspiel KD: Use of gadopentetate dimeglumine as a contrast agent for percutaneous transluminal renal angioplasty and stent placement. Kidney Int 53:503-507, 1998.
30. Spinosa DJ, Angle JF, Hagspiel KD, et al: Feasibility of gadodiamide compared with dilute iodinated contrast material for imaging of the abdominal aorta and renal arteries. J Vasc Interv Radiol 11:733-737, 2000.
31. Spinosa DJ, Hagspiel KD, Angle JF, et al: Gadolinium-based contrast agents in angiography and interventional radiology: Uses and techniques. J Vasc Interv Radiol 11:985-990, 2000.
32. Gemery J, Idelson B, Reid S, et al: Acute renal failure after arteriography with a gadolinium-based contrast agent. AJR Am J Roentgenol 171:1277-1278, 1998.
33. Terzi C, Sokmen S: Acute pancreatitis induced by magnetic-resonance-imaging contrast agent. Lancet 354:1789-1790, 1999.
34. Hamasaki O, Nakahara T, Katoh Y, et al: [Experience of cerebral angiography using gadolinium for renal insufficiency]. No To Shinkei 55:167-171, 2003.
35. Murphy KP, Szopinski KT, Cohan RH, et al: Occurrence of adverse reactions to gadolinium-based contrast material and management of patients at increased risk: A survey of the American Society of Neuroradiology Fellowship Directors. Acad Radiol 6:656-664, 1999.
36. Schenker MP, Solomon JA, Roberts DA: Gadolinium arteriography complicated by acute pancreatitis and acute renal failure. J Vasc Interv Radiol 12:393, 2001.
37. Sam AD 2nd, Morasch MD, Collins J, et al: Safety of gadolinium contrast angiography in patients with chronic renal insufficiency. J Vasc Surg 38:313-318, 2003.
38. Bettmann MA: Ionic versus nonionic contrast agents for intravenous use: Are all the answers in? Radiology 175:616-618, 1990.
39. Thomsen HS, Morcos SK: Contrast media and the kidney: European Society of Urogenital Radiology (ESUR) guidelines. Br J Radiol 76:513-518, 2003.
40. Morcos SK, Thomsen HS, Webb JA: Prevention of generalized reactions to contrast media: A consensus report and guidelines. Eur Radiol 11:1720-1728, 2001.
41. Webb JA, Stacul F, Thomsen HS, Morcos SK: Late adverse reactions to intravascular iodinated contrast media. Eur Radiol 13:181-184, 2003.
42. Lasser EC: Pretreatment with corticosteroids to prevent reactions to i.v. contrast material: Overview and implications. AJR Am J Roentgenol 150:257-259, 1988.
43. Lasser EC, Berry CC, Mishkin MM, et al: Pretreatment with corticosteroids to prevent adverse reactions to nonionic contrast media. AJR Am J Roentgenol 162:523-526, 1994.
44. Lasser EC, Berry CC, Talner LB, et al: Pretreatment with corticosteroids to alleviate reactions to intravenous contrast material. N Engl J Med 317:845-849, 1987.
45. Lasser EC, Berry CC, Talner LB, et al: Protective effects of corticosteroids in contrast material anaphylaxis. Invest Radiol 23(Suppl 1): S193-S194, 1988.
46. Lasser EC, Lang J, Sovak M, et al: Steroids: Theoretical and experimental basis for utilization in prevention of contrast media reactions. Radiology 125:1-9, 1977.
47. Greenberger PA, Patterson R: The prevention of immediate generalized reactions to radiocontrast media in high-risk patients. J Allergy Clin Immunol 87:867-872, 1991.
48. Greenberger PA, Patterson R, Tapio CM: Prophylaxis against repeated radiocontrast media reactions in 857 cases: Adverse experience with cimetidine and safety of beta-adrenergic antagonists. Arch Intern Med 145:2197-2200, 1985.
49. Katayama H, Yamaguchi K, Kozuka T, et al: Adverse reactions to ionic and nonionic contrast media: A report from the Japanese Committee on the Safety of Contrast Media. Radiology 175:621-628, 1990.
50. Yamaguchi K, Katayama H, Takashima T, et al: Prediction of severe adverse reactions to ionic and nonionic contrast media in Japan: Evaluation of pretesting: A report from the Japanese Committee on the Safety of Contrast Media. Radiology 178:363-367, 1991.
51. Freed KS, Leder RA, Alexander C, et al: Breakthrough adverse reactions to low-osmolar contrast media after steroid premedication. AJR Am J Roentgenol 176:1389-1392, 2001.
52. Morcos SK: Contrast media-induced nephrotoxicity—questions and answers. Br J Radiol 71:357-365, 1998.
53. Morris TW, Sahler LG, Violante M, Fischer HW: Work in progress: Reduction of calcium activity by radiopaque contrast media. Radiology 148:55-59, 1983.
54. Bergstra A, van Dijk RB, Brekke O, et al: Hemodynamic effects of iodixanol and iohexol during ventriculography in patients with compromised left ventricular function. Catheter Cardiovasc Interv 50:314-321, 2000.

55. Morcos SK, Dawson P, Pearson JD, et al: The haemodynamic effects of iodinated water soluble radiographic contrast media: A review. Eur J Radiol 29:31-46, 1998.
56. Dawson P: Cardiovascular effects of contrast agents. Am J Cardiol 64:2E-9E, 1989.
57. Morcos SK: Effects of radiographic contrast media on the lung. Br J Radiol 76:290-295, 2003.
58. Fay WP, Parker AC: Effects of radiographic contrast agents on thrombin formation and activity. Thromb Haemost 80:266-272, 1998.
59. Al Dieri R, Beguin S, Hemker HC: The ionic contrast medium ioxaglate interferes with thrombin-mediated feedback activation of factor V, factor VIII and platelets. J Thromb Haemost 1:269-274, 2003.
60. Sakariassen KS, Buchmann M, Hamers MJ, Stormorken H: Iohexol, platelet activation and thrombosis: II. Iohexol-induced platelet secretion does not affect collagen-induced or tissue-factor-induced thrombus formation in blood that is anticoagulated with heparin and aspirin. Acta Radiol 39:355-361, 1998.
61. Farrehi PM, Zhu Y, Fay WP: An analysis of mechanisms underlying the antifibrinolytic properties of radiographic contrast agents. J Thromb Thrombolysis 12:273-281, 2001.
62. Bettmann M: Ionic versus nonionic contrast agents and their effects on blood components: Clinical summary and conclusions. Invest Radiol 23(Suppl 2):S378-S380, 1988.
63. Kopko PM, Smith DC, Bull BS: Thrombin generation in nonclottable mixtures of blood and nonionic contrast agents. Radiology 174:459-461, 1990.
64. Weinstein JM, Heyman S, Brezis M: Potential deleterious effect of furosemide in radiocontrast nephropathy. Nephron 62:413-415, 1992.
65. Stevens MA, McCullough PA, Tobin KJ, et al: A prospective randomized trial of prevention measures in patients at high risk for contrast nephropathy: Results of the P.R.I.N.C.E. Study. Prevention of Radiocontrast Induced Nephropathy Clinical Evaluation. J Am Coll Cardiol 33:403-411, 1999.
66. Katholi RE, Woods WT Jr, Taylor GJ, et al: Oxygen free radicals and contrast nephropathy. Am J Kidney Dis 32:64-71, 1998.
67. Weisberg LS, Kurnik PB, Kurnik BR: Risk of radiocontrast nephropathy in patients with and without diabetes mellitus. Kidney Int 45:259-265, 1994.
68. Kini AS, Mitre CA, Kim M, et al: A protocol for prevention of radiographic contrast nephropathy during percutaneous coronary intervention: Effect of selective dopamine receptor agonist fenoldopam. Catheter Cardiovasc Interv 55:169-173, 2002.
69. Shammas NW, Kapalis MJ, Harris M, et al: Aminophylline does not protect against radiocontrast nephropathy in patients undergoing percutaneous angiographic procedures. J Invasive Cardiol 13:738-740, 2001.
70. Rich MW, Crecelius CA: Incidence, risk factors, and clinical course of acute renal insufficiency after cardiac catheterization in patients 70 years of age or older: A prospective study. Arch Intern Med 150:1237-1242, 1990.
71. Levy EM, Viscoli CM, Horwitz RI: The effect of acute renal failure on mortality: A cohort analysis. JAMA 275:1489-1494, 1996.
72. Gruberg L, Mintz GS, Mehran R, et al: The prognostic implications of further renal function deterioration within 48 h of interventional coronary procedures in patients with pre-existent chronic renal insufficiency. J Am Coll Cardiol 36:1542-1548, 2000.
73. Gruberg L, Weissman NJ, Pichard AD, et al: Impact of renal function on morbidity and mortality after percutaneous aortocoronary saphenous vein graft intervention. Am Heart J 145:529-534, 2003.
74. Byrd L, Sherman RL: Radiocontrast-induced acute renal failure: A clinical and pathophysiologic review. Medicine (Baltimore) 58:270-279, 1979.
75. Hodgson KJ, Mattos MA, Mansour A, et al: Incorporation of endovascular training into a vascular fellowship program. Am J Surg 170:168-173, 1995.
76. White RA, Hodgson KJ, Ahn SS, et al: Endovascular interventions training and credentialing for vascular surgeons. J Vasc Surg 29:177-186, 1999.
77. Dawson P: Contrast agent nephrotoxicity: An appraisal. Br J Radiol 58:121-124, 1985.
78. Deray G, Jacobs C: Radiocontrast nephrotoxicity: A review. Invest Radiol 30:221-225, 1995.
79. Heyman SN, Fuchs S, Brezis M: The role of medullary ischemia in acute renal failure. New Horiz 3:597-607, 1995.
80. Quader MA, Sawmiller C, Sumpio BA: Contrast-induced nephropathy: Review of incidence and pathophysiology. Ann Vasc Surg 12:612-620, 1998.
81. Rudnick MR, Berns JS, Cohen RM, Goldfarb S: Nephrotoxic risks of renal angiography: Contrast media-associated nephrotoxicity and atheroembolism—a critical review. Am J Kidney Dis 24:713-727, 1994.
82. Rudnick MR, Berns JS, Cohen RM, Goldfarb S: Contrast media-associated nephrotoxicity. Semin Nephrol 17:15-26, 1997.
83. Morcos SK, Thomsen HS: European Society of Urogenital Radiology guidelines on administering contrast media. Abdom Imaging 28:187-190, 2003.
84. Gerlach AT, Pickworth KK: Contrast medium-induced nephrotoxicity: Pathophysiology and prevention. Pharmacotherapy 20:540-548, 2000.
85. Parfrey PS, Griffiths SM, Barrett BJ, et al: Contrast material-induced renal failure in patients with diabetes mellitus, renal insufficiency, or both: A prospective controlled study. N Engl J Med 320:143-149, 1989.
86. Gupta RK, Kapoor A, Tewari S, et al: Captopril for prevention of contrast-induced nephropathy in diabetic patients: A randomised study. Indian Heart J 51:521-526, 1999.
87. Kapoor A, Sinha N, Sharma RK, et al: Use of dopamine in prevention of contrast induced acute renal failure—a randomised study. Int J Cardiol 53:233-236, 1996.
88. Kurnik BR, Weisberg LS, Cuttler IM, Kurnik PB: Effects of atrial natriuretic peptide versus mannitol on renal blood flow during radiocontrast infusion in chronic renal failure. J Lab Clin Med 116:27-36, 1990.
89. Sketch MH Jr, Whelton A, Schollmayer E, et al: Prevention of contrast media-induced renal dysfunction with prostaglandin E1: A randomized, double-blind, placebo-controlled study. Am J Ther 8:155-162, 2001.
90. Briguori C, Manganelli F, Scarpato P, et al: Acetylcysteine and contrast agent-associated nephrotoxicity. J Am Coll Cardiol 40:298-303, 2002.
91. Wang A, Holcslaw T, Bashore TM, et al: Exacerbation of radiocontrast nephrotoxicity by endothelin receptor antagonism. Kidney Int 57:1675-1680, 2000.
92. Frantz RP, Edwards BS, Olson LJ, et al: Effects of pentoxifylline on renal function and blood pressure in cardiac transplant recipients: A randomized trial. Transplantation 63:1607-1610, 1997.
93. Katholi RE, Taylor GJ, Woods WT, et al: Nephrotoxicity of nonionic low-osmolality versus ionic high-osmolality contrast media: A prospective double-blind randomized comparison in human beings. Radiology 186:183-187, 1993.
94. Steinberg EP, Moore RD, Powe NR, et al: Safety and cost effectiveness of high-osmolality as compared with low-osmolality contrast material in patients undergoing cardiac angiography. N Engl J Med 326:425-430, 1992.
95. Mueller C, Buerkle G, Buettner HJ, et al: Prevention of contrast media-associated nephropathy: Randomized comparison of 2 hydration regimens in 1620 patients undergoing coronary angioplasty. Arch Intern Med 162:329-336, 2002.
96. Louis BM, Hoch BS, Hernandez C, et al: Protection from the nephrotoxicity of contrast dye. Ren Fail 18:639-646, 1996.
97. Eisenberg RL, Bank WO, Hedgock MW: Renal failure after major angiography can be avoided with hydration. AJR Am J Roentgenol 136:859-861, 1981.
98. Solomon R, Werner C, Mann D, et al: Effects of saline, mannitol, and furosemide to prevent acute decreases in renal function induced by radiocontrast agents. N Engl J Med 331:1416-1420, 1994.
99. Barrett BJ, Parfrey PS: Prevention of nephrotoxicity induced by radiocontrast agents. N Engl J Med 331:1449-1450, 1994.

100. Trivedi HS, Moore H, Nasr S, et al: A randomized prospective trial to assess the role of saline hydration on the development of contrast nephrotoxicity. Nephron Clin Pract 93:29-34, 2003.
101. Huber W, Schipek C, Ilgmann K, et al: Effectiveness of theophylline prophylaxis of renal impairment after coronary angiography in patients with chronic renal insufficiency. Am J Cardiol 91:1157-1162, 2003.
102. Taylor AJ, Hotchkiss D, Morse RW, McCabe J: PREPARED: Preparation for Angiography in Renal Dysfunction: A randomized trial of inpatient vs outpatient hydration protocols for cardiac catheterization in mild-to-moderate renal dysfunction. Chest 114:1570-1574, 1998.
103. Tepel M, van der Giet M, Schwarzfeld C, et al: Prevention of radiographic-contrast-agent-induced reductions in renal function by acetylcysteine. N Engl J Med 343:180-184, 2000.
104. Kay J, Chow WH, Chan TM, et al: Acetylcysteine for prevention of acute deterioration of renal function following elective coronary angiography and intervention: A randomized controlled trial. JAMA 289:553-558, 2003.
105. Diaz-Sandoval LJ, Kosowsky BD, Losordo DW: Acetylcysteine to prevent angiography-related renal tissue injury (the APART trial). Am J Cardiol 89:356-358, 2002.
106. Shyu KG, Cheng JJ, Kuan P: Acetylcysteine protects against acute renal damage in patients with abnormal renal function undergoing a coronary procedure. J Am Coll Cardiol 40:1383-1388, 2002.
107. Allaqaband S, Tumuluri R, Malik AM, et al: Prospective randomized study of N-acetylcysteine, fenoldopam, and saline for prevention of radiocontrast-induced nephropathy. Catheter Cardiovasc Interv 57:279-283, 2002.
108. Hartnell GG, Gates J, Underhill J: Implementing HCFA guidelines on appropriate use of nonionic contrast agents for diagnostic arteriography: Effects on complication rates and management costs. Acad Radiol 5(Suppl 2):S359-S361, 1998.
109. Bush WH, Jones D, Brannen GE: Radiation dose to personnel during percutaneous renal calculus removal. AJR Am J Roentgenol 145:1261-1264, 1985.
110. Lowe FC, Auster M, Beck TJ, et al: Monitoring radiation exposure to medical personnel during percutaneous nephrolithotomy. Urology 28:221-226, 1986.
111. Sajben FP, Schoelch SB, Barnette DJ: Fluoroscopic-induced radiation dermatitis. Cutis 64:57-59, 1999.
112. Aerts A, Decraene T, van den Oord JJ, et al: Chronic radiodermatitis following percutaneous coronary interventions: A report of two cases. J Eur Acad Dermatol Venereol 17:340-343, 2003.
113. Rosenthal LS, Beck TJ, Williams J, et al: Acute radiation dermatitis following radiofrequency catheter ablation of atrioventricular nodal reentrant tachycardia. Pacing Clin Electrophysiol 20:1834-1839, 1997.
114. Schecter AK, Lewis MD, Robinson-Bostom L, Pan TD: Cardiac catheterization-induced acute radiation dermatitis presenting as a fixed drug eruption. J Drugs Dermatol 2:425-427, 2003.
115. Koenig TR, Mettler FA, Wagner LK: Skin injuries from fluoroscopically guided procedures: Part 2. Review of 73 cases and recommendations for minimizing dose delivered to patient. AJR Am J Roentgenol 177:13-20, 2001.
116. Sovik E, Klow NE, Hellesnes J, Lykke J: Radiation-induced skin injury after percutaneous transluminal coronary angioplasty: Case report. Acta Radiol 37(3 Pt 1):305-306, 1996.
117. Shope TB: Radiation-induced skin injuries from fluoroscopy. Radiographics 16:1195-1199, 1996.
118. Food and Drug Administration: Advisory: Avoidance of serious x-ray-induced skin injuries to patients during fluoroscopically-guided procedures. Communication. Rockville, Md, Food and Drug Administration, 1994.
119. King JN, Champlin AM, Kelsey CA, Tripp DA: Using a sterile disposable protective surgical drape for reduction of radiation exposure to interventionalists. AJR Am J Roentgenol 178:153-157, 2002.
120. Marx MV, Niklason L, Mauger EA: Occupational radiation exposure to interventional radiologists: A prospective study. J Vasc Interv Radiol 3:597-606, 1992.

Chapter 19

Principles of Venography

MICHAEL A. McKUSICK, MD
PETER GLOVICZKI, MD

Section IV

■ LOWER EXTREMITIES

Ascending Venography

The diagnosis of lower extremity deep venous thrombosis (DVT) was largely a clinical one until the 1960s, when contrast venography became a part of standard medical practice.[19] First introduced by Berberich and Hirsch[7] in 1923, lower extremity venography was used by dos Santos[17] in 1938 to confirm a clinically suspected diagnosis of DVT. The technique evolved over many years and became the "gold standard" for the diagnosis of DVT.[35] In 1940, Bauer[5] published details of normal venographic anatomy and of the venographic appearance of acute and chronic DVT (Figs. 19-1 to 19-6). Early leg venography required venous cut-down for access to the deep venous system, but this technique was modified by Welch and coworkers,[39] who recommended contrast injection into a superficial vein in the foot with a tourniquet applied above the ankle to prevent filling of the superficial veins, which often obscured the deep system. Diagnostic criteria for DVT were established in 1963 by DeWeese and Rogoff,[16] who reported their review of 100 positive leg venograms.

In past decades, the technique used for lower extremity ascending venography has been modified many times.[18,23,26,27,32,35] Even as the technique has been refined and the examination has been made safer and less painful with the use of modern contrast agents, it remains a

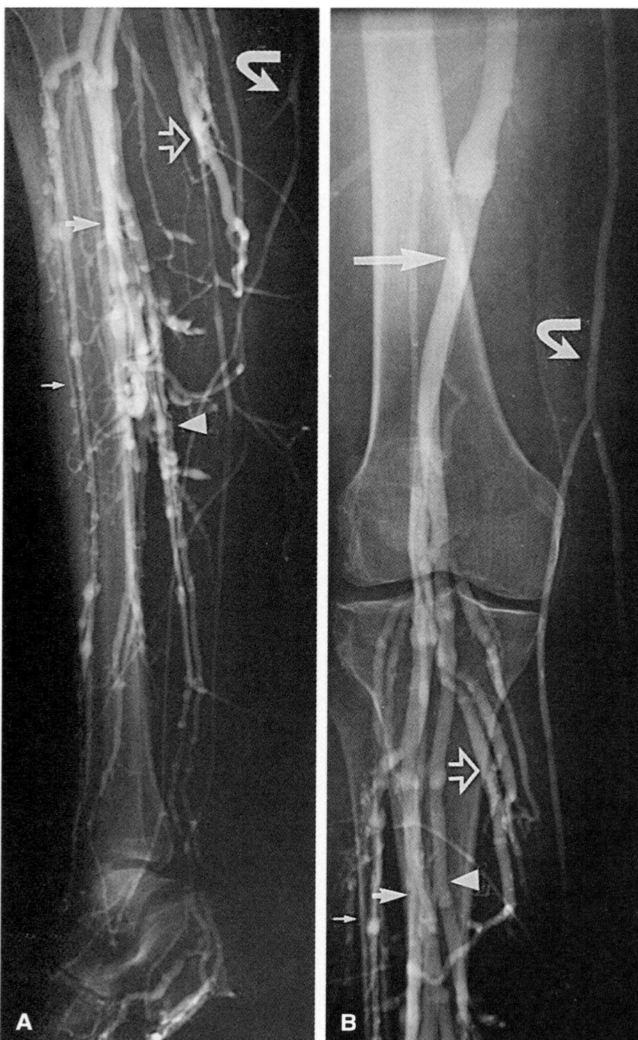

FIGURE 19-1 Normal right leg venogram. **A,** Lateral calf projection. **B,** Anteroposterior knee. Anterior tibial veins *(small arrow)*, peroneal veins *(short arrow)*, posterior tibial veins *(arrowhead)*, gastrocnemius veins *(open arrow)*, great saphenous vein *(curved arrow)*, and popliteal vein *(long arrow)*.

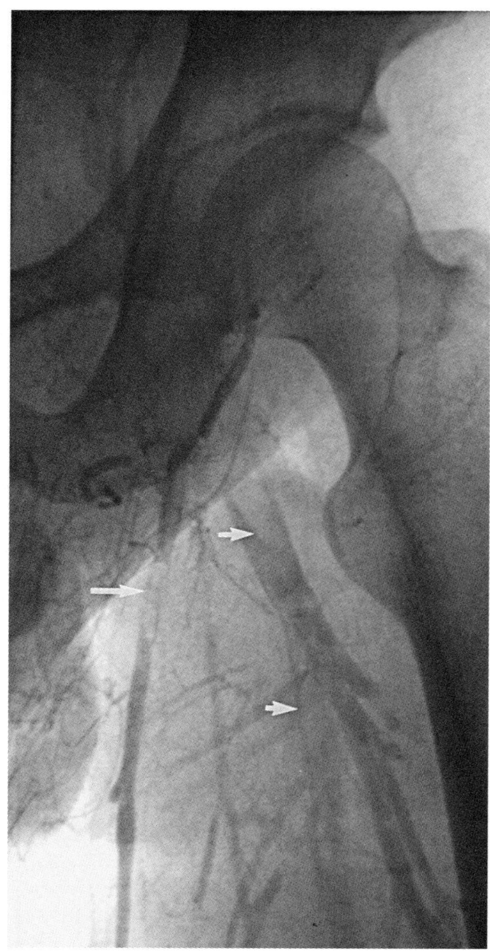

FIGURE 19-2 Acute thrombus in the deep femoral and great saphenous veins. The deep femoral vein *(short arrows)* and great saphenous vein *(long arrow)* are shown. The femoral vein is occluded.

relatively invasive study that requires an often painful venipuncture, injection of iodine-based contrast agents, and exposure of the patient to ionizing radiation. For this reason, venous duplex imaging with compression was developed as a noninvasive alternative to venography for the diagnosis of acute DVT. With sensitivities and specificities of greater than 95% in symptomatic patients with acute DVT, venous duplex imaging has overtaken contrast venography as the study of choice for evaluating patients with suspected leg vein thrombosis.[10,14] Even in suspected calf vein thrombosis, ultrasonography has shown sensitivities of 95% and specificities of 100% in experienced hands and is now trusted by many clinicians as the diagnostic test of choice.[6,9,10]

With the emergence of ultrasonography as the primary diagnostic tool for evaluation of acute leg DVT, the number of lower extremity venograms performed in our practice has decreased from 450 patients in 1982 to only 40 patients in 1997. Because of this dramatic decrease in patient numbers, it is difficult to train residents in the performance and interpretation of leg venography, a fact that will decrease further the availability and accuracy of the examination for future practitioners.

Indications and Accuracy

Properly performed and interpreted, lower extremity venography remains a powerful tool in the evaluation of acute and chronic DVT and is unsurpassed in its vivid depiction of venous anatomy and morphology. Ascending leg venography is indicated when a high clinical suspicion of thrombosis is present in the setting of negative or equivocal noninvasive tests.[40] With high diagnostic accuracy, a leg venogram is immediately useful for evaluation of the presence of deep venous disease. This so-called gold standard is uninterpretable, however, in 5% to 15% of patients because of poor technique.[27] The number of poor-quality examinations is likely to increase in the future as

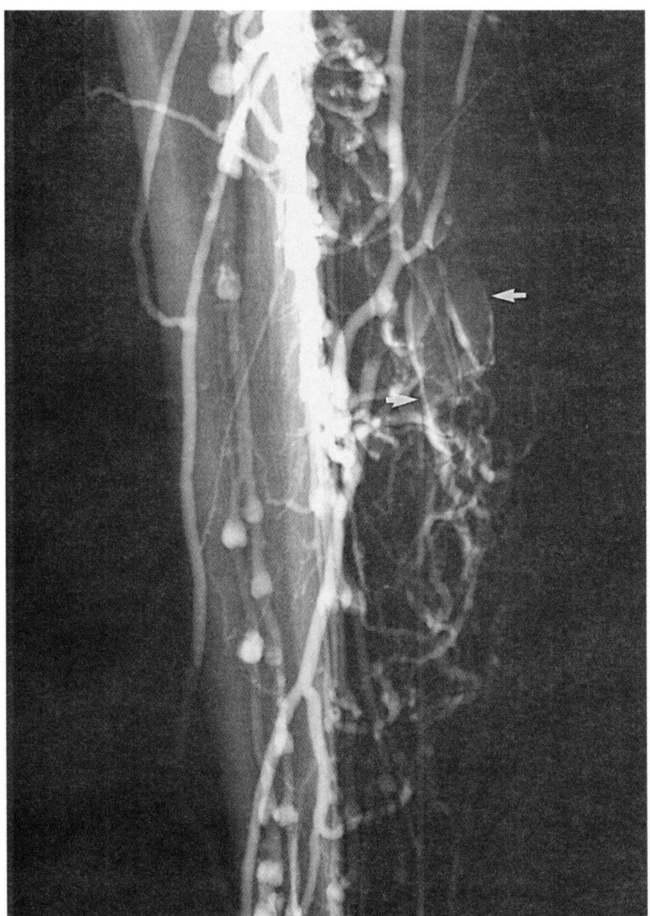

FIGURE 19-3 Acute thrombosis of the soleal veins. *Arrows* indicate fresh thrombus filling the soleal veins.

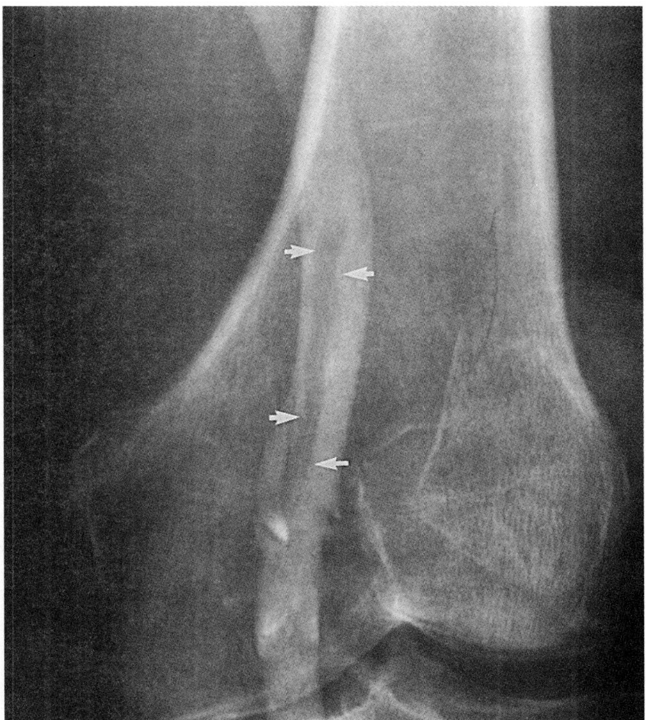

FIGURE 19-4 Subacute thrombus in the popliteal vein. *Arrows* denote retracted thrombus indicating subacute thrombosis.

patient numbers continue to decline, and this will only further diminish the utility of the examination.

Technique

Good-quality ascending venography is not difficult to accomplish, but it does call for a relatively cooperative patient. Patients should fast for 3 to 4 hours and should be well hydrated to avoid the risks of emesis and renal toxicity, which can be associated with intravenous contrast administration. Patients with significant leg swelling may benefit from an Ace wrap to displace edema fluid and to make venous cannulation easier. Warm packs to the dorsum of the foot also may facilitate venous access.

A 22-gauge plastic intravenous cannula is placed into a dorsal vein of the foot. The saphenous vein also can be used, but a tourniquet is essential to drive contrast material into the deep system. The patient is positioned on a radiographic fluoroscopy table with tilt capability and a footrest to enable positioning in the 40- to 60-degree upright position. The contralateral leg is supported with a small platform so that no weight is borne on the leg to be examined. Side grip handles are placed on the table so that the patient feels secure in the semi-upright position. Either digital spot films or regular cut films can be used for acquisition.

If the patient is examined for venous valvular incompetence, a 100-cm ruler with opaque markers is placed along the lateral aspect of the leg to determine the correct distance of incompetent perforating veins from the ankle. A tourniquet above the ankle is needed in these cases to prevent filling of the superficial veins, and fluoroscopic evaluation with videotaping is performed to capture the location of incompetent perforating veins. In a patient with acute DVT, we do not routinely use the marker system, and fluoroscopy is used to optimize visualization of the presence and location of thrombus. Because the anterior tibial, sural, and gastrocnemius veins fill better without a tourniquet, this is not applied in the setting of acute DVT unless no deep filling occurs.[22]

The examination is begun with the patient in the 40- to 60-degree semi-upright position. Intravenous contrast material with an organically bound iodine concentration of 200 mgI/mL is used to decrease pain and to minimize endothelial damage by the hypertonic contrast agent.[1] As contrast material is injected, fluoroscopic evaluation is performed to ensure against extravasation and to optimize deep vein opacification. Spot films are taken as the deep system fills. At least two projections are needed in the tibial and popliteal locations.

As contrast ascends, additional filming of the deep and superficial femoral veins is performed. About 60 to 80 mL of contrast material is needed to fill the deep venous system adequately from the ankle to the groin. For visualization of

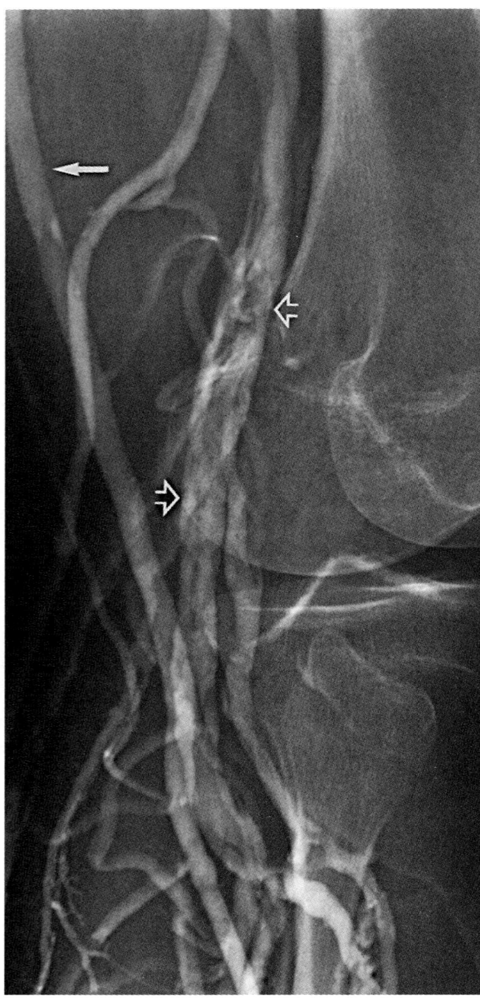

FIGURE 19-5 Chronic popliteal venous thrombosis. Note extensive recanalization of the popliteal vein *(open arrows)* and relatively large caliber of the great saphenous vein *(solid arrow)*.

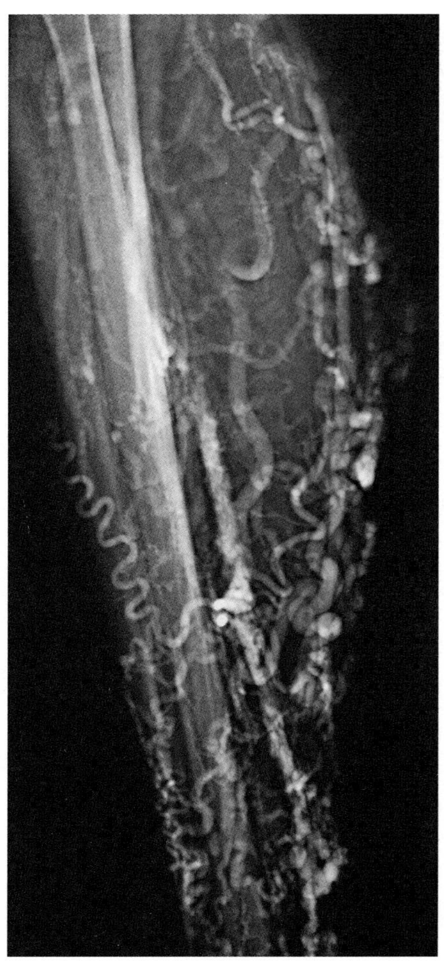

FIGURE 19-6 Chronic deep venous thrombosis. Note extensive collateral channels and nonvisualization of normal deep venous structures.

the iliocaval region, the fluoroscopy table is lowered to a flat position, and the patient is asked to hold the breath while the leg is elevated 6 inches from the tabletop. Fluoroscopy is performed to determine maximal opacification of the veins, and a spot film is obtained. In most patients, it is easy to visualize from the low inferior vena cava (IVC) down to the common femoral bifurcation on one image.

With completion of the examination, the veins are flushed with 50 mL of 0.45 normal saline to minimize contrast contact with the venous endothelium. In most patients, this technique yields beautiful, diagnostic-quality images. Additional contrast material can be injected, as needed, to visualize problem areas, and if any questions remain, a focused ultrasound study is ordered to complement venography.

In patients undergoing evaluation primarily for venous valvular incompetence, the fluoroscopic examination is recorded on videotape rather than spot films (Fig. 19-7). This medium lends itself to a graphic demonstration of incompetent perforating veins. With marker ruler in place, it is simple to translate information from the recorded image

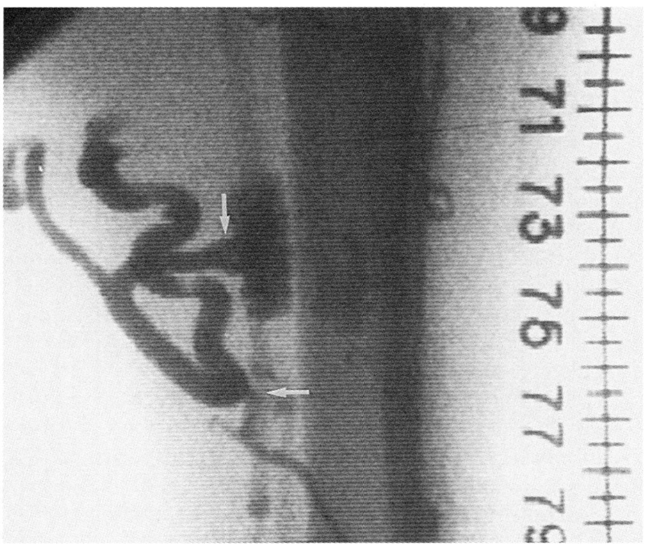

FIGURE 19-7 Incompetent medial calf perforating veins. Single-frame image of a videotape shows free flow of contrast material from the posterior tibial vein through the incompetent perforating veins *(arrows)* into the superficial varicose veins.

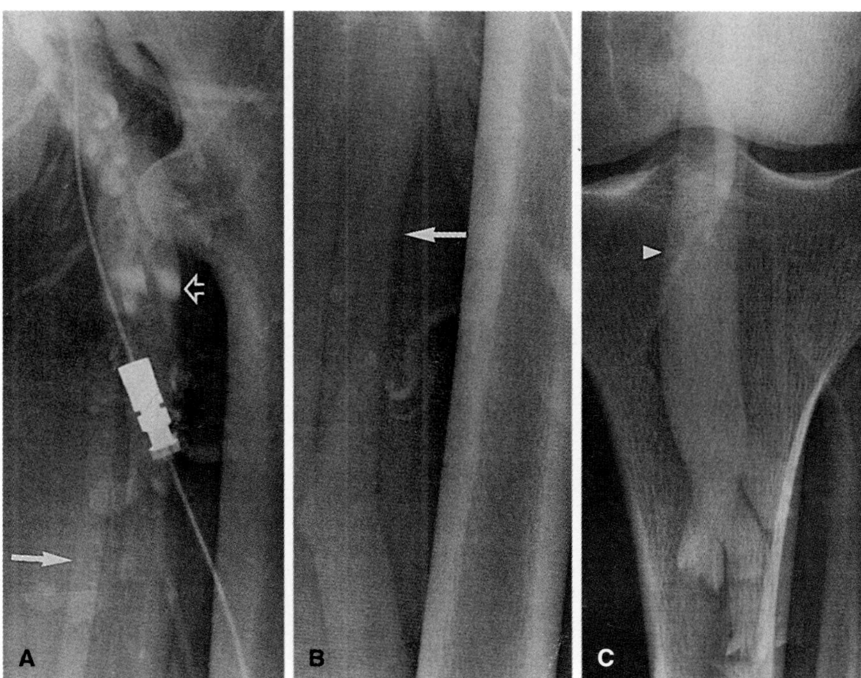

FIGURE 19-8 A-C, Descending left leg venogram shows grade 4 reflux. Note lack of valves in the femoral vein *(solid arrow)* and the large caliber of the popliteal vein *(arrowhead).* The deep femoral vein *(open arrow)* is shown.

to location on the leg, in centimeters, from the ankle. We have found this a satisfactory way to study patients who need presurgical diagnostic imaging before ligation of incompetent perforating veins is considered.

Descending Venography

As with ascending venography, lower extremity descending venography has been largely replaced by duplex scanning in the evaluation of patients with suspected deep venous incompetence. Color duplex sonography has shown good agreement with descending venography in the grading of deep and superficial vein reflux.[3] For this reason, we perform descending contrast venography only in patients with significant deep venous occlusive disease who are candidates for venous bypass, venous valve repair, or valve transplantation.

Indications and Interpretation

Descending venography is used in concert with ascending venography to distinguish primary valvular incompetence from thrombotic disease. The ascending venogram shows the location and extent of post-thrombotic disease, as manifested by occlusion, venous recanalization, collateral channels, and superficial varicosities. The descending venogram identifies the level of deep venous reflux and morphology of the venous valves (Fig. 19-8). We use the classification outlined by Kistner and colleagues[25] to categorize the severity of deep venous reflux (Table 19-1).

Although reflux may occur into the saphenous vein, isolated superficial venous reflux is relatively uncommon in symptomatic patients with advanced chronic venous disease.[30] Most patients with symptoms of chronic venous insufficiency who undergo venography in our practice have reflux into the deep venous system with or without associated saphenous vein reflux. With the use of descending venography, candidates are selected for deep venous valve repair or transplant, which is offered to patients with grade 3 or 4 reflux who have recurrent symptoms of venous insufficiency after treatment of superficial varicosities and perforator venous incompetence.

Technique

Descending venography is performed on a tilt radiographic table to allow for examination in the 40- to 60-degree upright position. Venous access is obtained via sterile Seldinger technique through the common femoral vein. A short 4F or 5F straight catheter with multiple side holes is positioned in the external iliac vein. If both legs are to be studied, the contralateral leg is imaged by means of a 65-cm Simmons II catheter (Cordis Corp, Miami, Fla) with side holes. The Simmons II catheter can be negotiated easily over a guide wire across the iliac bifurcation into the opposite external

Table 19-1 Venographic Categories of Deep Venous Reflux

GRADE	
0	Normal valvular function with no reflux
1	Minimal reflux confined to the upper thigh
2	More extensive reflux, which may reach the lower thigh; a competent valve is present in the popliteal vein, and there is no reflux to the calf level
3	Reflux as above, but associated with popliteal valvular incompetence and leakage of contrast material into the calf veins
4	Virtually no valvular competence with immediate and dramatic reflux distally into the calf; this type of reflux often opacifies incompetent calf perforators

From Kistner RL, Ferris EB, Rawdhawa G, et al. A method of performing descending venography. J Vasc Surg 4:464-468, 1986.

iliac vein. The catheter is fixed to the groin with sterile adhesive strips to prevent dislodgment when the patient is upright. The contralateral leg is supported with a small platform, as with ascending venography, so that no weight is borne on the limb to be examined.

With the patient in the semi-upright position, contrast material is injected by hand through the femoral catheter. Iodinated contrast, 20 to 30 mL, with a concentration of 200 mgI/mL is used. As the contrast material is injected, the patient is asked to perform a sustained Valsalva maneuver to enhance evidence of valvular incompetence. We record the study by videotaping the live fluoroscopic examination as the patient undergoes evaluation from the femoral region to the knee and below. Specific areas of interest can be studied further with sequential contrast injections to optimize image capture of valve location and function and extent of reflux. The videotape format is ideal for this examination, and we no longer take spot films during descending venography.

■ UPPER EXTREMITY VENOGRAPHY

Venography of the upper extremity is normally performed for evaluation of the central veins of the arms and chest. Although primary axillary-subclavian vein thrombosis is relatively uncommon (<2% of all DVT), the incidence of central venous occlusion is still rising because of the increasing use of long-term central venous catheters and transvenous cardiac pacers (Fig. 19-9).[15,33,38]

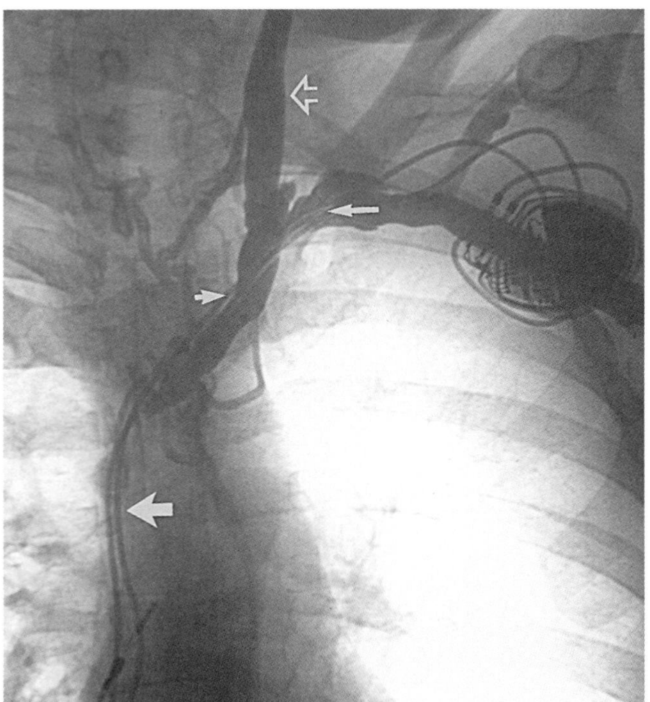

FIGURE 19-9 Chronic thrombosis of the superior vena cava, the innominate veins, and the subclavian veins caused by cardiac pacer wires. Chronic subclavian venous thrombosis *(long arrow)*, innominate vein *(short arrow)*, and expected location of the superior vena cava *(wide arrow)* are shown. Note reflux of contrast material up the left internal jugular vein *(open arrow)*.

Upper extremity venography remains the procedure of choice for most clinicians in the evaluation of central thoracic venous disease, especially in the setting of axillary-subclavian vein thrombosis caused by thoracic outlet compression.[36] In these cases, venography is performed in conjunction with thrombolytic therapy. Prelysis venography establishes the extent and location of the disease, and the postlysis examination shows residual thrombosis and extrinsic compression requiring further treatment. In patients with signs and symptoms of upper extremity thrombosis caused by neoplasm, central venous catheters, or thrombophilic state, however, compression ultrasound and magnetic resonance angiography (MRA) have proved accurate in establishing a diagnosis.[20,34] MRA is especially helpful in showing patency of the central veins and allows planning of central venous catheter placement in patients with a history of central venous occlusion.

Indications

We currently perform upper extremity venography in patients with primary axillary-subclavian venous thrombosis who are candidates for thrombolytic therapy. The examination is performed to show the extent of thrombosis and to guide placement of infusion catheters for administration of the lytic agent (Fig. 19-10). The postlysis study, as mentioned, is needed to detect the presence of residual thrombus and, when performed with thoracic outlet maneuvers, to determine the degree of extrinsic compression. This information is crucial to determine the need for additional therapy for prevention of recurrent thrombosis.

Patients with suspected central venous occlusion who are not candidates for MRA (e.g., because of a cardiac pacemaker or claustrophobia) also are studied with upper extremity venography. By far, however, the major indication for upper extremity venography at our institution is placement of a peripherally inserted central catheter (PICC) using fluoroscopic and intravenous contrast guidance.

Technique

Originally described by Lea Thomas and Andress in 1971,[28] the technique used for upper extremity venography has changed significantly with the dissemination of digital subtraction equipment.[2,31] Digital techniques allow the examination to be performed more quickly and with less contrast material than is used with cut-film studies. We do

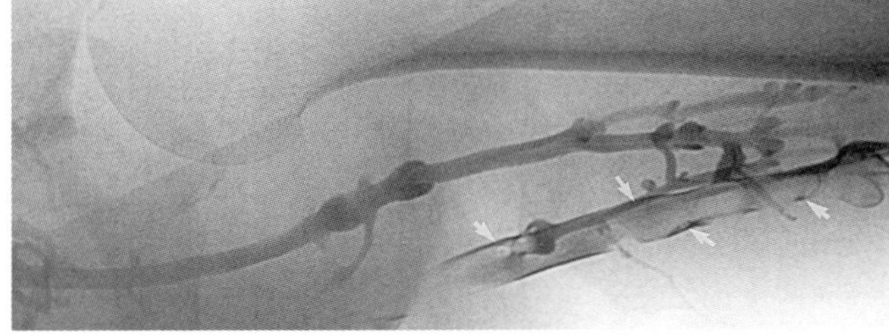

FIGURE 19-10 Acute thrombosis of the left brachial vein. *Arrows* denote fresh thrombus in the brachial vein.

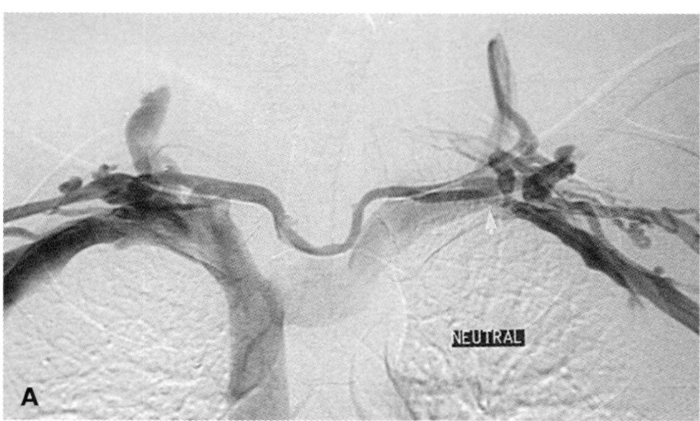

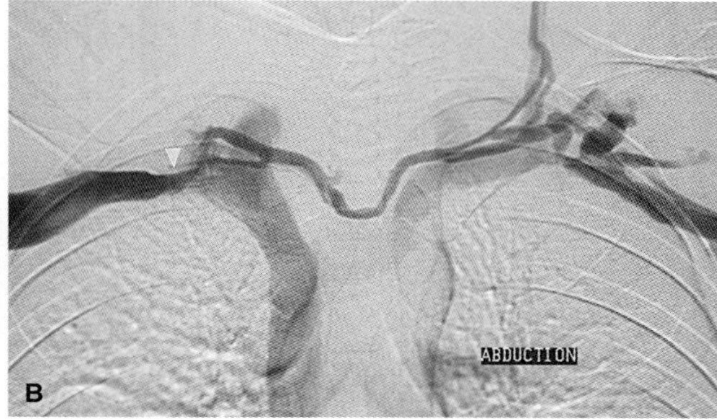

FIGURE 19-11 Bilateral upper extremity venogram in a patient with bilateral thoracic outlet syndrome. **A,** Neutral position. Note chronic thrombosis of left subclavian vein *(arrow)*. **B,** Abduction view. *Arrowhead* denotes impingement of the right subclavian vein at level of the first rib.

all upper extremity venography procedures using digital imaging equipment and firmly believe that this is the current standard of practice.

For evaluation of the central veins of the thorax, we perform venography by injecting through an intravenous site in the antecubital fossa or forearm with the arm in a neutral position at the patient's side. Contrast material, 20 to 30 mL, with a concentration of 200 mgI/mL is injected by hand for each projection needed. Digital imaging of the axillary region and mediastinum is acquired at one image per second as the patient suspends respiration. Adequate imaging of the superior vena cava (SVC) in some patients requires bilateral injections; this helps to compensate for contrast washout in the SVC by unopacified blood from the opposite innominate vein. Alternatively, although less effective, the arm being studied can be elevated slightly during the injection to facilitate contrast inflow to the SVC.

For evaluation of extrinsic compression of the axillary-subclavian junction, the patient is studied in neutral and abducted positions (Fig. 19-11). The arm is abducted by bending it at the elbow and by tucking the hand behind the patient's head. Imaging of the axillary and subclavian vein regions is obtained during maximal thoracic outlet compression.

During fluoroscopic placement of a PICC, a small intravenous cannula in the patient's hand or forearm is injected with contrast material to opacify the deep veins in the arm. Fluoroscopy is used to guide needle puncture of a deep vein suitable for catheter placement. Before a PICC is placed, the central veins of the thorax are evaluated with this technique to confirm patency and suitability for catheter advancement into the SVC.

■ CENTRAL ABDOMINAL VENOGRAPHY

Venography of the central veins of the abdomen has largely been replaced by cross-sectional imaging techniques, such as ultrasonography, computed tomography, and magnetic resonance imaging. These noninvasive modalities not only are less costly, but also usually provide a great deal more diagnostic information than can catheter venography. For this reason, the number of central venographic studies performed in our practice for diagnostic purposes has dwindled markedly in recent years.

Indications

The most common central abdominal venographic examination that we perform is a contrast study of the IVC before placement of an IVC filter. This is done to provide details of renal vein anatomy to allow for proper positioning of the filter in the infrarenal cava. Often, selective renal venography is performed in addition to the cavography to distinguish ascending lumbar veins from anomalous circumaortic left renal veins (Fig. 19-12).[21] Theoretically, it is important to place the caval filter below the origin of a large anomalous renal vein to prevent pulmonary emboli from propagating around the filter through this potential collateral vessel.[37] Hepatic venography also is commonly performed in conjunction with wedge and free pressure measurements in patients with suspected portal hypertension or Budd-Chiari syndrome.[13]

Technique

Most venographies of the central veins of the abdomen are performed from either a common femoral or an internal jugular vein approach using standard Seldinger technique. Real-time ultrasound guidance is helpful for the internal jugular approach in patients with poorly palpable carotid pulses or obesity. To image the IVC, a catheter with multiple side holes is inserted into the cava and positioned at the iliac bifurcation. Contrast material with an iodine concentration of 370 mgI/mL is administered with a power injector at a rate of 20 mL/sec for 2 seconds. Digital image acquisition is at two per second for 5 seconds with centering over the area of interest (Figs. 19-13 and 19-14).

Selective renal or hepatic venous catheterization is performed by means of a variety of catheter shapes according to the anatomy at hand and the approach. If hepatic venography is done in conjunction with a biopsy, the transjugular route is chosen; if no biopsy is needed, femoral access is adequate. The downward acute angle of the origins of the hepatic veins from the IVC from the femoral approach is markedly different from the obtuse angle generated by

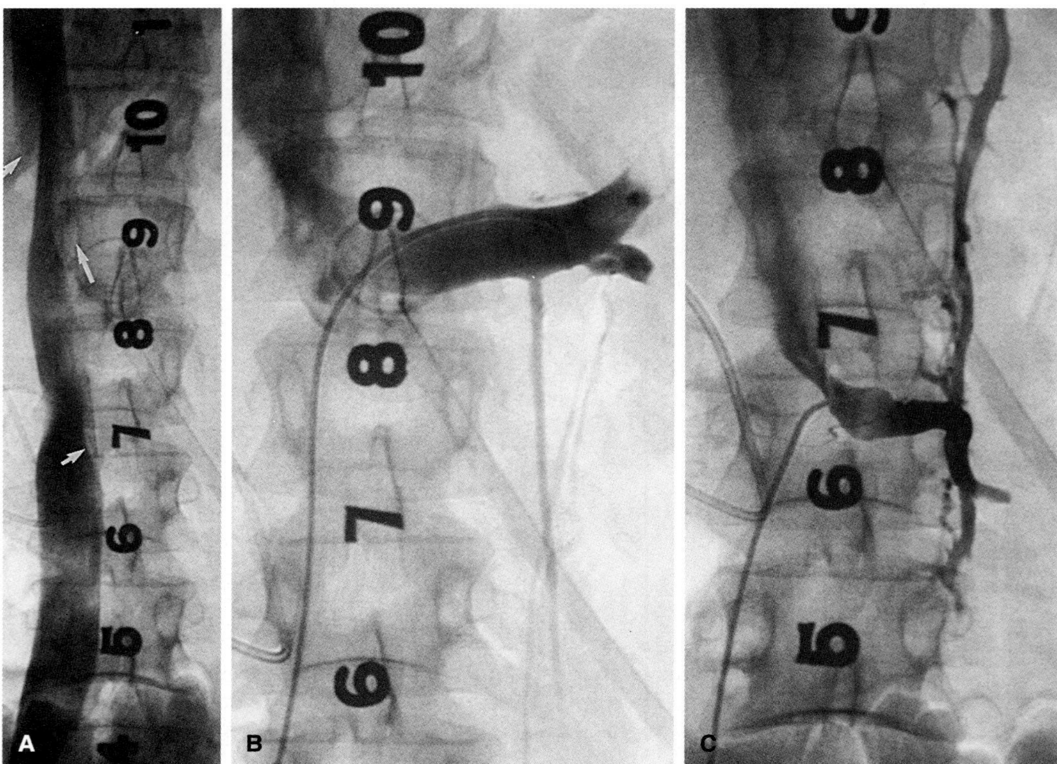

FIGURE 19-12 Normal inferior vena cavogram. **A,** Note wash-in of unopacified blood from the renal veins *(long arrows)* and the left ascending lumbar veins *(small arrow)*. **B,** Selective left renal venogram confirms location of the renal vein. **C,** Selective left lumbar venogram.

jugular access, and catheters for selective injections are chosen appropriately. The same is true for renal venous catheterization. Although the amount of contrast material used for imaging depends on vein size and flow, a total of 20 mL at 5 to 8 mL/sec generally opacifies most renal or hepatic venous structures (Figs. 19-15 and 19-16). Digital images are obtained at a rate of two per second.

■ COMPLICATIONS

Most of the complications of venography result from the side effects of the iodinated contrast material used for the examination; few complications arise from catheter placement. These complications can be grouped into three categories:

- Problems related to the toxic effect of the contrast material on vascular endothelium
- Allergic reactions to administration of contrast material
- Nephrotoxicity of iodine-based contrast agents

High-osmolar contrast material (HOCM) is hypertonic, with a concentration of six times the osmolality of human plasma. When used for lower extremity venography, this agent causes patient discomfort at the injection site. This contrast material also is thought to induce endothelial cell damage, which may result in venous thrombosis. The reported incidence of postvenography phlebitis caused by use of HOCM ranges from 9% to 31%.[8] This incidence has been decreased by (1) dilution of the contrast material with saline solution (reducing the agent's osmolality) or (2) use of modern *low-osmolar contrast material* (LOCM).

Low-osmolar agents have an osmolality of about one third that of HOCM but are still hypertonic, with a concentration of about double that of plasma. A prospective study using LOCM for ascending leg venography reported no postvenography DVT in 102 consecutive patients who underwent follow-up duplex ultrasonography.[1] In the same study, minor adverse reactions, such as nausea, local pain, or dizziness, occurred in 11 (7%) of 157 patients examined.

Allergic reactions to contrast material administration are uncommon but are potentially severe and can lead to cardiopulmonary collapse and death. Reactions to contrast material are categorized as mild, moderate, or severe. Most reactions require no treatment; non–life-threatening reactions (e.g., urticaria, mild laryngeal edema, bronchospasm) can be treated easily.

Severe contrast reactions are true medical emergencies. They are defined as anaphylaxis, hypotension, or hypertension requiring intervention, angina, cardiac arrhythmia, pulmonary edema, or laryngeal edema/spasm or bronchospasm sufficient to cause airway obstruction. These reactions are related in part to the contrast material used and are known to be less severe with the use of LOCM. A meta-analysis of the risks of severe reactions, including death, comparing HOCM versus LOCM found a rate of severe reaction of 157 per 100,000 patients with HOCM and a rate of 31 per 100,000 patients with LOCM.[12] The use of LOCM reduces the risk of a severe reaction by approximately 80%.

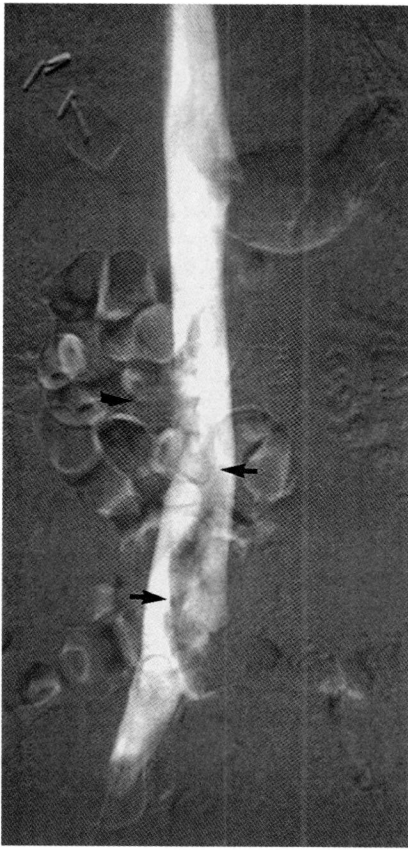

FIGURE 19-13 Inferior vena cavogram. *Arrows* indicate extension of a thrombus from the left common iliac vein into the inferior vena cava.

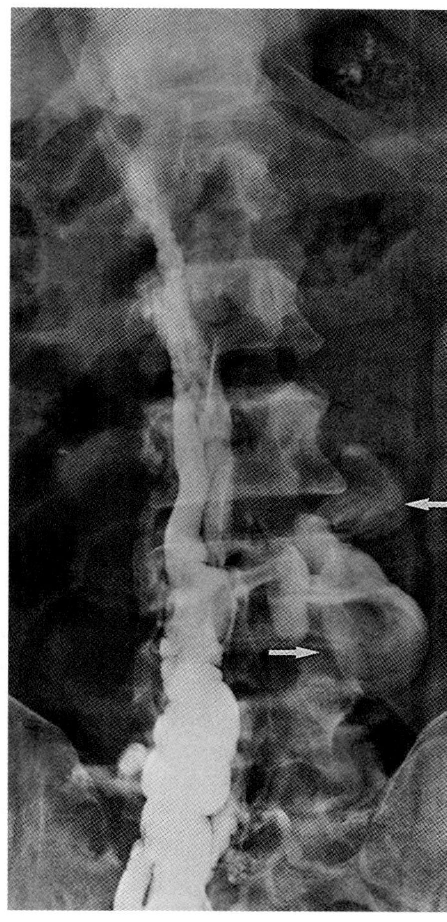

FIGURE 19-14 Chronic occlusion of the inferior vena cava. Note extensive recanalization of the inferior vena cava and large ascending lumbar collateral channels *(arrows)*.

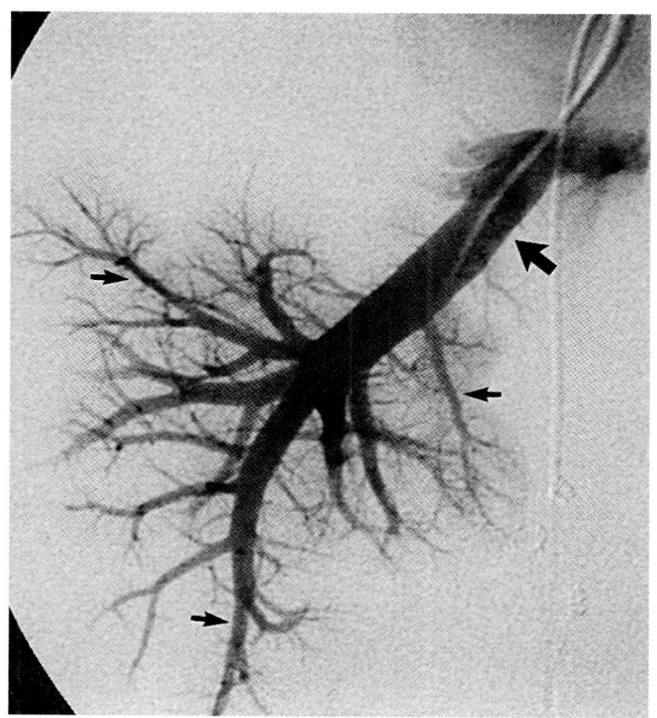

FIGURE 19-15 Digital subtraction right hepatic venogram. Note the main right hepatic vein *(large arrow)* and detail of the hepatic venous branches *(small arrows)*.

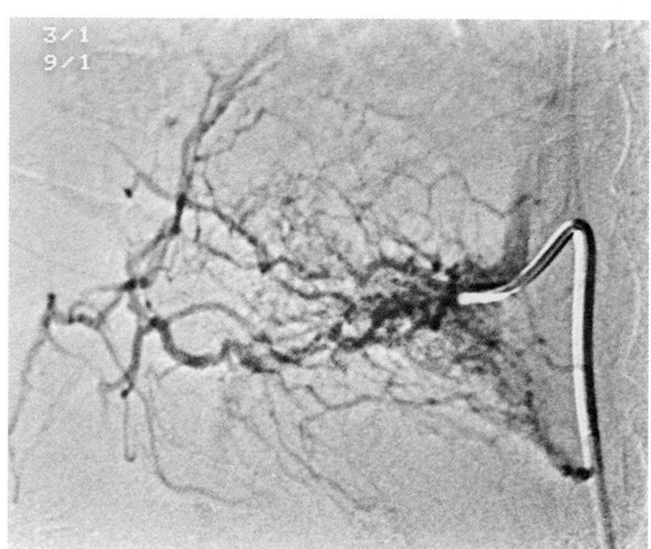

FIGURE 19-16 Budd-Chiari syndrome. Right hepatic venogram shows occlusion of the central hepatic venous channel with multiple intrahepatic collaterals.

The rate of death remains identical with either agent at about 0.9 per 100,000 patients.

In our practice, patients with known contrast allergies undergo a pretreatment regimen of 50 mg of prednisone by mouth 13 hours, 7 hours, and 1 hour before the study. Diphenhydramine hydrochloride (Benadryl), 50 mg, and ephedrine, 25 mg, also are given 1 hour before the examination. LOCM agents always are used in these patients. Patients who experience a severe contrast reaction are given appropriate intravenous doses of hydrocortisone sodium succinate (Solu-Cortef), epinephrine, and antihistamines and are admitted to the hospital for observation and supportive therapy.

Iodine-based contrast material is known to be nephrotoxic, also apparently because of its hypertonicity. Patients with preexisting renal insufficiency, diabetes, or dehydration are at most risk for contrast-induced renal failure. Although the matter is controversial, the data suggest that LOCM is less nephrotoxic than HOCM, as shown by decreased changes in serum creatinine or glomerular filtration rate after administration of LOCM.[4,24,29] Patients with preexisting renal insufficiency of any cause seem to be at higher risk for nephrotoxicity with HOCM than with LOCM.[29] This may justify the use of LOCM in this patient population.

The relatively high cost of LOCM compared with HOCM prevents these newer agents from being used exclusively in everyday practice. Many insurance carriers do not reimburse for the use of LOCM; the medical literature partially supports this stance on a cost-benefit analysis basis. One study showed that a total substitution of LOCM for HOCM would not decrease mortality rates at all and that each severe reaction would be prevented at a cost of $62,000 per event.[11] Most radiologists have concluded that LOCM use should be restricted to patients at high risk for an untoward event from contrast administration. In our practice, this category includes the following situations:

- A documented allergy to contrast material
- A history of iodine intolerance
- Advanced cardiac, pulmonary, or renal disease
- Asthma requiring steroid use

In addition, pediatric patients and older patients would be excluded.

It is hoped that with technologic improvements, manufacturers' costs will diminish and that these savings will be passed on to hospital and physician consumers in the form of less expensive contrast agents. Until it makes economic sense to switch totally to LOCM, each practitioner must determine which patients should receive these admittedly superior contrast agents.

REFERENCES

1. Abu Rahma AF, Powell M, Robinson PA: Prospective study of safety of lower extremity phlebography with nonionic contrast medium. Am J Surg 171:255-257, 1996.
2. Andrews JC, Williams DM, Cho KJ: Digital subtraction venography of the upper extremities. Clin Radiol 38:423-424, 1987.
3. Baldt MM, Bohler K, Zontsich T, et al: Preoperative imaging of lower extremity varicose veins: Color coded duplex sonography or venography? J Ultrasound Med 15:143-154, 1996.
4. Barrett BJ, Carlisle EJ: Meta-analysis of the relative nephrotoxicity of high- and low-osmolality iodinated contrast media. Radiology 188:171-178, 1993.
5. Bauer G: A venographic study of thromboembolic problems. Acta Chir Scand Suppl 61, 1940.
6. Baxter GM, Duffy P, Partridge E: Colour flow imaging of calf vein thrombosis. Clin Radiol 46:198-201, 1992.
7. Berberich J, Hirsch S: Die rontgenographische Darstellung der Arterien und Venen am lebenden Menschen. Klin Wschr 2:2226, 1923.
8. Bettman MA, Salzman EW, Rosenthal D, et al: Reduction of venous thrombosis complicating phlebography. AJR Am J Roentgenol 134:1169-1172, 1980.
9. Bradley MJ, Spencer PA, Alexander L, et al: Colour flow mapping in the diagnosis of calf deep vein thrombosis. Clin Radiol 47:399-402, 1993.
10. Burn PR, Blunt DM, Sanson HE, et al: The radiological investigation of suspected lower limb deep vein thrombosis. Clin Radiol 52:626-628, 1997.
11. Caro JJ, Trindade E, McGregor M: The cost-effectiveness of replacing high-osmolality with low-osmolality contrast media. AJR Am J Roentgenol 159:869-874, 1992.
12. Caro JJ, Trindade E, McGregor M: The risks of death and severe nonfatal reactions with high- vs low-osmolality contrast media: A meta-analysis. AJR Am J Roentgenol 156:825-832, 1991.
13. Cavaluzzi JA, Sheff R, Harrington DP, et al: Hepatic venography and wedge pressure measurements in diffuse liver disease. AJR Am J Roentgenol 129:441-446, 1977.
14. Comerota AJ, Katz ML, Hashemi HA: Venous duplex imaging for the diagnosis of acute deep venous thrombosis. Haemostasis 23(Suppl)1: 61-71, 1993.
15. Coon WW, Willis PW: Thrombosis of axillary and subclavian veins. Arch Surg 94:657-663, 1967.
16. DeWeese JA, Rogoff SM: Phlebographic patterns of acute deep venous thrombosis of the leg. Surgery 53:99-108, 1963.
17. dos Santos JC: La phlebographie directe. J Int Chir 3:625, 1938.
18. Greitz T: The technique of ascending phlebography of the lower extremity. Acta Radiol 42:421-441, 1954.
19. Hager K: Problems of acute deep venous thrombosis: I. The interpretation of signs and symptoms. Angiology 20:219-223, 1969.
20. Hartnell GG, Hughes LA, Finn JP, et al: Magnetic resonance angiography of the central chest veins: A new gold standard? Chest 107:1053-1057, 1995.
21. Hicks ME, Malden ES, Vesely TM, et al: Prospective anatomic study of the inferior vena cava and renal veins: Comparison of selective renal venography with cavography and relevance in filter placement. J Vasc Interv Radiol 6:721-729, 1995.
22. Kalebo P, Anthmyr B-A, Eriksson BI, et al: Optimization of ascending phlebography of the leg for screening of deep vein thrombosis in thromboprophylactic trials. Acta Radiol 38:320-326, 1997.
23. Kamida CB, Kistner RL, Eklof B, Masuda EM: Lower extremity phlebography. In Gloviczki P, Yao JS (eds): Handbook of Venous Disorders. London, Chapman & Hall, 1996, pp 152-167.
24. Katholi RE, Taylor GJ, Woods WT, et al: Nephrotoxicity of nonionic low-osmolality versus ionic high-osmolality contrast media: A prospective double-blind randomized comparison in human beings. Radiology 186:183-187, 1993.
25. Kistner RL, Ferris EB, Rawdhawa G, et al: A method of performing descending venography. J Vasc Surg 4:464-468, 1986.
26. Kistner RL, Kamida CB: 1994 Update on phlebography and varicography. Dermatol Surg 21:71-76, 1995.
27. Lea Thomas M: Techniques of phlebography: A review. Eur J Radiol 11:125-130, 1990.
28. Lea Thomas M, Andress MR: Axillary phlebography. AJR Am J Roentgenol 113:713-721, 1971.
29. Moore RD, Steinberg EP, Powe NR, et al: Nephrotoxicity of high-osmolality versus low-osmolality contrast media: Randomized clinical trial. Radiology 182:649-655, 1992.
30. Morano JU, Raju S: Chronic venous insufficiency: Assessment with descending venography. Radiology 174:441-444, 1990.

31. Natu JC, Sequeira JC, Weitzman AF: An improved technique for axillary phlebography. Radiology 142:529-530, 1982.
32. Nicolaides AN: Diagnosis of venous thrombosis by phlebography. In Bergan JJ, Yao JS (eds): Venous Problems. Chicago, Year Book Medical Publishers, 1978, pp 123-140.
33. Phibbs B, Marriot HJL: Complications of permanent transvenous pacing. N Engl J Med 3112:1428-1432, 1985.
34. Prandoni P, Polistena P, Bernardi E, et al: Upper-extremity deep vein thrombosis: Risk factors, diagnosis and complications. Arch Intern Med 157:57-62, 1997.
35. Rubinov K, Paulin S: Roentgen diagnosis of venous thrombosis of the leg. Arch Surg 104:134-144, 1972.
36. Rutherford RB, Hurlbert SN: Primary subclavian-axillary vein thrombosis: Consensus and commentary. Cardiovasc Surg 4:420-423, 1996.
37. Vesely T: Interventional radiologist at work: Question and answer. J Vasc Interv Radiol 2:225-226, 1997.
38. Warden GD, Wilmore DW, Pruitt BA: Central venous thrombosis: A hazard of medical progress. Trauma 13:620, 1973.
39. Welch CE, Faxon HH, McGahey CE: The application of phlebography to the therapy of thrombosis and embolism. Surgery 12:162, 1942.
40. Wheeler HB, Hirsch J, Wells P, et al: Diagnostic tests for deep vein thrombosis: Clinical usefulness depends on probability of disease. Arch Intern Med 154:1921-1928, 1994.

Chapter

20

3D Image Processing

HUGH G. BEEBE, MD

Section IV

Blood vessels and the lesions that affect them exist in three dimensions. Ideal imaging methods for vascular diagnosis or therapeutic procedure guidance ought to provide three-dimensional (3D) representations for clinical and research activities. Since November 1895, when Roentgen made pictures of his wife's hand by x-ray beams, two-dimensional (2D) imaging has flourished using ionizing radiation and a variety of other methods. This practice has long worked well when such 2D images were interpreted by physicians well trained in recognizing and overcoming their limitations. What enhanced value does 3D image processing provide that makes it worth the time, trouble, and cost? Among the advantages of 3D image processing are the following:

1. Intuitively more obvious images that can be understood and evaluated with greater ease and efficiency by the observer
2. Reduced requirements for professional trainees learning image interpretation for the purpose of clinical decision making
3. Greater accuracy for measurement of lesions or disease effects on blood vessels
4. New imaging interpretation and analysis methods that are not possible without 3D data
5. Potential improvement of endovascular procedures by making them more intuitively familiar and less subject to artifacts and errors of 2D images

To achieve 3D graphic presentation of indirectly visualized structures requires processing acquired imaging data into a subsequent form by a variety of methods. Today the availability of computer programs to accomplish this is widespread, but there must be careful and sophisticated evaluation of the process of transforming images into 3D models to validate the process. It is not correct to assume that a 3D result is useful for medical purposes without proof through empirical testing that what is shown accurately represents anatomic structures. The borderline between "art" and science can be approached when competition between commercial enterprises results in marketing efforts that may degrade anatomic truth in favor of visually appealing images. The clinician or researcher evaluating image processing must evaluate proof of accuracy in addition to other features, such as image quality and measurement tools.

This chapter reviews 3D image processing from a clinical perspective as it is currently used to enhance the value of vascular images generated from radiographic, magnetic resonance, and ultrasound sources. This chapter should be read in conjunction with Chapter 21, which has a more technical focus, but also gives examples of 3D imaging. These examples illustrate general principles that apply to other sources of medical imaging data as well.

■ REAL 3D VERSUS "FAKE" 3D

An image may be "3D" in perspective without truly being 3D, and it is important for clinicians to distinguish images that present length, breadth, and depth appearance but really lack 3D data. One of the easiest ways to understand this distinction and its significance for clinical use is to consider two images both of which appear to be 3D, but one of them is not.

Consider first an image created by a 19th-century stereoscope. This simple device uses a pair of 2D photographs, each taken from the same point but at a slightly different angle. When placed side-by-side and viewed through a simple lens system similar to binoculars, the images can be caused to align in register even though seen separately by each eye. The observer's brain processes these image data as if he or she were looking at the natural object with physiologic parallax, and it appears to be a 3D image

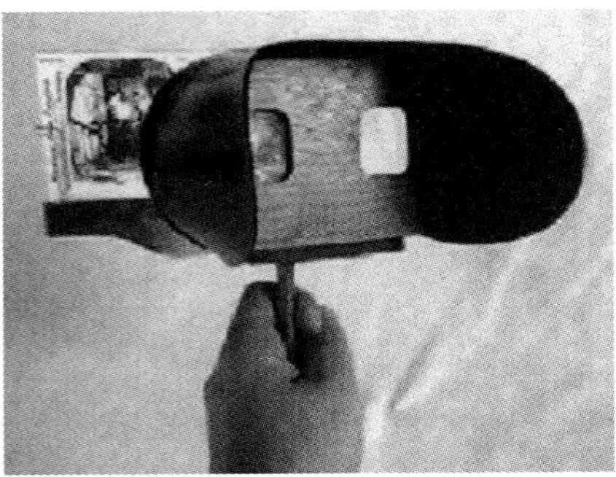

FIGURE 20-1 This 19th-century device, called the "stereoscope," used 2D images of a single object with parallax differences. A 3D impression was achieved by introducing the images separately into each eye. In effect, the visual cortex of the brain is doing 3D processing when the images are perceived as one.

(Fig. 20-1). This is a "fake" 3D appearance, however, resulting from a *trompe l'oeil* maneuver because there are no data that actually exist in 3D in the system. It is possible to achieve a 3D appearance of medical images through processing 2D data in a similar way. If one wanted to measure volume of a structure, such as an aortic aneurysm or an arterial plaque, however, it could not be done because the data would not actually exist in three dimensions.

Consider the difference between an image created by the stereoscope and a 3D image obtained by computerized postprocessing of a series of 2D computed tomographic (CT) scan slices. When this type of postprocessing is done, the CT slices are blended together in a single file using a computer algorithm that assigns an "address" within a theoretical space. Each of the smallest information segments is called a "pixel" when it exists as data from a single CT slice in two dimensions. When data from more than one CT slice are added to the file, each of the smallest data units now is given an address in three dimensions—*X, Y,* and *Z*. Pixels are now transformed into "voxels." A voxel is best conceived as the smallest unit of graphic information having a 3D address in the theoretical space of the computer program. Another way of describing this is to say that the voxel is a point surrounded by a consistent volume. When such a file of CT slices is fully assembled, the data actually exist within the computer program in three dimensions. The significance of this is that the user of this information now may perform a variety of tasks and calculations, such as rotating the object to view it from any perspective, creating a "fly through" video image that allows endoluminal viewing of an artery, and calculating the volume of atherosclerotic plaque within a blood vessel (Fig. 20-2). Other examples are shown in Figs. 21-10 through 21-12. The value of using an accurate 3D model such as this has been widely recognized because it overcomes most of the errors and artifacts of conventional 2D imaging that encumbered the early use of aortic stent grafts.[1-3]

■ 3D COMPUTED TOMOGRAPHY

The use of spiral tomographic data facilitates 3D reconstruction of graphic images because the data are acquired in a file made of voxels from the outset. Computer algorithms can rapidly generate shaded surface display and volume rendering images as an automatic result of the imaging equipment. The need for so-called postprocessing is driven by end-user requirements that cannot be met with the usual software built into scanners. The most common examples in a vascular context arise from endovascular graft treatment of aortic aneurysm. The crucial task of patient selection is largely imaging driven and requires evaluating numerous anatomic features to determine whether a patient is suitable for stent graft treatment, to determine which device might be best for individual anatomy, and to plan the procedure at a fairly high level of detail before its occurrence. If 3D images can be readily viewed and anatomic measurements obtained efficiently with accurate tools built into the imaging software, this single imaging method suffices for safe procedure planning without arteriography, as has become widely practiced in recent years.[4,5]

The general practice of image postprocessing to extract greater value from basic image data can be applied to all forms of medical imaging. Although it has been applied

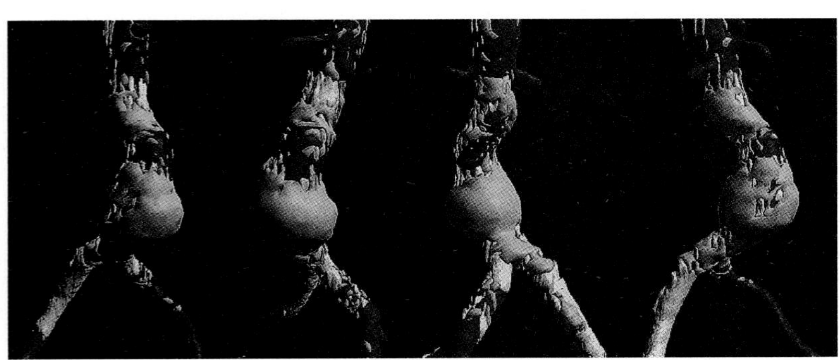

FIGURE 20-2 The appearance of an aortic aneurysm with a stent graft as it is rotated within 3D processing software on a personal computer. Assembling the 2D axial CT data to create a "rotatable object" enables the anatomy to be viewed continuously from any angle.

most commonly to CT scanning, various methods of image rendering are considered here.[6] These same techniques are increasingly applied to magnetic resonance imaging (MRI) and ultrasound. Perception differences between diagnostic radiologists and procedure-based specialists, usually surgeons, of the value of 3D imaging became apparent in the mid-1980s, when volume rendering software came into practical application for movies and medical imaging. Radiologists would often say, "it's a pretty picture, but there's no more information there than is contained in the original CT scan." In a literal sense, this was true. Radiologists synthesize a virtual 3D image in their minds from 2D data and are trained to do so. Surgeons, as end users of the imaging result less concerned with the process of obtaining it, could see an efficiency and ease of interpretation inherent in 3D images and intuitively sensed patient care value in 3D presentations of complex anatomy. Even if one interpreter of 2D information has understood it in a 3D sense, subsequent viewers of the original data, typically a series of films with CT slices on them, are required to repeat the process for themselves to understand the data in terms of a volume of tissue because it does not exist in a retrievable archive.

Experts in the field of 3D medical imaging now believe that an important new interface between the hardware and software that acquire and produce medical imaging and the interpreting physician has been reached that requires 3D processing to extract greatest potential benefit.[7] In other words, the image-generating process is now sufficiently complex and voluminous that 2D interpretation techniques are inadequate in efficiency and productivity and in communicating the imaging result to others.[8]

The advent of multislice CT scanner technology or multidetector CT scanning has produced a higher resolution capability that greatly improves precision and accuracy and other important aspects, such as isotropic data acquisitions that are technical and beyond this discussion. Multidetector CT is not simply incremental improvement of spiral CT that began in the early 1990s. Rather, it is a qualitative leap forward in image acquisition from many aspects marking a new era for vascular imaging.[9] This technique also results in many hundreds and even thousands of images for an individual examination, however, and presents a challenge for management of the data and its interpretation. The resolution of this challenge leading to enhanced productivity of the overall examination is now achieved through affordable and quick computing power and the assembly of the imaging data within sophisticated 3D software that provides rotatable objects that can be viewed in a variety of ways.

There are some real barriers to the use of computer workstations for 3D processing, however. Many radiologists have been reluctant to generate views that they are capable of visualizing mentally because of the practical difficulties associated with using 3D workstations, such as time, lack of reimbursement, and a perception of "icing on the cake" that they do not need. Most workstations have difficulty receiving, accepting, or processing data from different manufacturers' scanners or alternative imaging methods, such as between CT and MRI. It is also important to understand something about the differences between three basic methods of 3D display: surface rendering, maximum intensity projection (MIP), and volume rendering.

Surface Rendering

Surface rendering today is commonly a routine part of 3D medical image processing software built into radiology equipment. Each voxel within a dataset can be selected as a part of or not a part of the object of interest by using selected intensity values within a narrow threshold range. The appropriate isointensity surface of the object can be selected by a skilled operator, and the remaining data can be discarded. This selection requires important segmentation of the original dataset to establish the object of interest. Surface contours can be displayed and enhanced with the appearance of surface shading through use of so-called ray casting software (Fig. 20-3). Many medical presentations at meetings and published illustrations show excellent images that are striking and require little interpretation to understand. This method of image processing can be inaccurate if the surface is difficult to determine precisely, and it does not show vessel calcification distinctly.[10] Various maneuvers to enhance the inclusiveness of the shaded surface display image are described in Chapter 21 along with the dangers of introducing error. There are many opportunities for underestimating or overestimating arterial stenosis because of the arbitrary selection of image processing parameters; best use of this method may be through viewing at an interactive computer workstation rather than static images.[11]

The principal advantages of shaded surface display are the greatly reduced computing requirements compared with other processing methods because of a reduced dataset to be processed resulting in fast rendering of the finished image. The images are easily understood because of the intuitively obvious appearance. A disadvantage of this technique is that selection of too high a radiodensity threshold can result in false impressions of stenosis or too low a false minimizing of lesion significance. Another important disadvantage is that by itself there is little that can be done to use the image in quantitative measurement and serial comparison for individual patient care or pooling data for research interests (see Fig. 21-8).

Maximum Intensity Projection

MIP has been used extensively to create angiographic images from CT and MRI data. The computer algorithm creating a MIP image selects the maximum voxel intensity value along a line through the dataset as the value of the corresponding display pixel. Because the radiodensity of blood vessels containing angiographic contrast material is usually greatly different from adjacent tissue, MIP has been widely used in vascular imaging and is generally thought to be more accurate in determining actual shape of the vessel lumen than surface display rendering. MIP uses actual radiodensity differences rather than simulated light reflection generated by the computer algorithm. It is a preferred way of showing the overall amount of calcification within a vessel. When dense concentration of radiopaque contrast material is present, however, it is best viewed at a

FIGURE 20-3 **A,** An axial CT slice shows a large abdominal aortic aneurysm with thrombus filling most of the lumen *(arrows)*. **B,** An image of this aorta processed by shaded surface display shows an aneurysm that is intuitively obvious. The extent of the aneurysm is not accurately shown because of arbitrary selection of image processing variables.

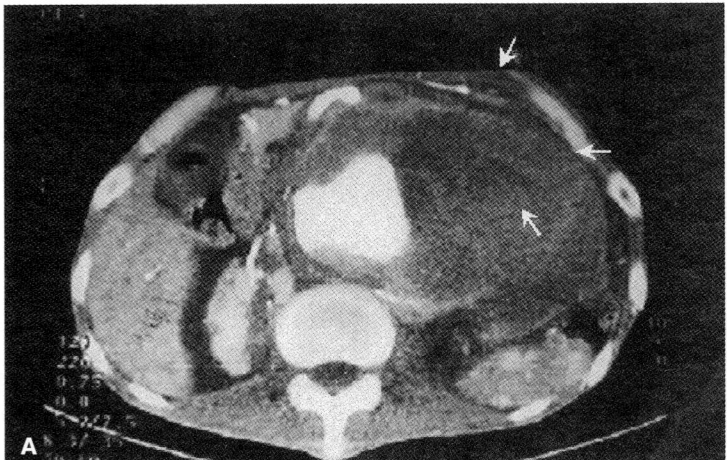

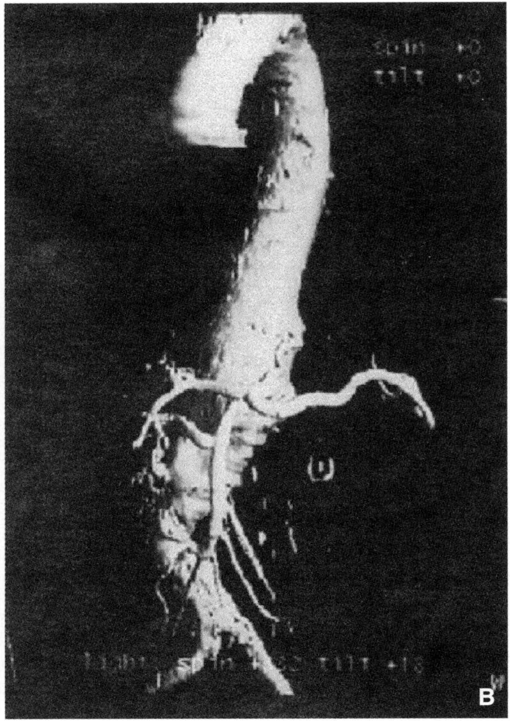

computer workstation that provides for adjustment in radiodensity "windowing" of the image to take advantage of small differences. It can be used to take advantage of radiodensity differences to display discrete objects (blood vessels) within a thick section of tissue to show the course of an artery or vein without the detrimental effects of volume averaging (Fig. 20-4). MIP usually requires greater interpretation skill than surface rendering because the three-dimensionality of the image is not as obvious. Objects seen as overlapping because of the method of their selection are not as readily interpreted in a plane. Artifacts can arise from calcification and volume averaging errors distorting vessels passing obliquely through a volume.

Volume Rendering

With volume rendering, the entire volume dataset is interpolated, and the computer program sums the contributions of each voxel to the final displayed image. Each voxel is assigned values for opacity by comparison with a tissue histogram and may be color-coded for ease of interpretation. Because the entire original dataset is contained in the working file, a variety of useful images can be obtained by use of voxel, intensity, position, spatial gradient, and other factors. The use of perspective volume rendering can provide amazingly powerful views of complex anatomic relationships. The impact of such software has become

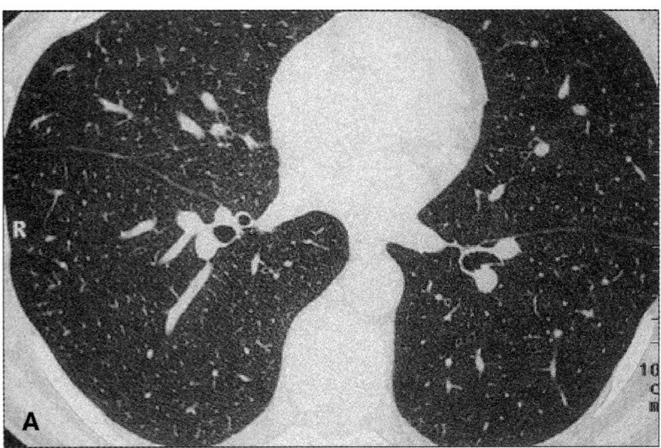

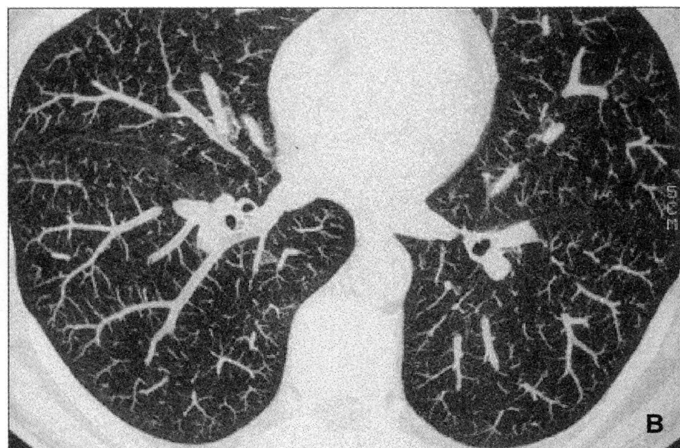

FIGURE 20-4 These two MIP images of a normal pulmonary circulation show the striking effect of slice thickness on the information conveyed by the image. **A,** A 1-mm-thick reconstruction of the CT scan shows relatively little of the blood vessels within the lung. **B,** An 8-mm-thick slice shows a more accurate depiction of the vasculature by including a large tissue volume with an appropriately chosen radiodensity window.

familiar because many motion pictures in the late 1980s created special effects through volume rendering techniques that can also be applied to medical images. Because the dataset is much larger than for other techniques, more powerful computing is required. Volume rendering is not generally available except through the use of adjunctive workstations at present, but the likelihood is that this will change as part of the evolution toward multidetector CT scanning. Advantages of volume rendering include the ability to see more detailed endoluminal information and objects outside the lumen threshold that surface display cannot offer, the ability to produce virtual reality simulation of high quality limited by computing power rather than the dataset being used, and the ability to vary perspective through a broad range to create unique views of special interest using interactive workstations. The disadvantages are mostly practical ones, such as individual access to or resistance to use of workstations, added cost and time, and the need for technical training and familiarity. Many of these issues may be resolved or reduced in the foreseeable future as the benefits of virtual reality imaging become integrated into clinical practice.[12]

■ 3D MAGNETIC RESONANCE ANGIOGRAPHY

The 3D processing of magnetic resonance data to form vascular studies is similar to CT scanning in the concepts of image processing.[13,14] There are data acquisition differences between the two imaging techniques, and these are amplified by the advent of multidetector CT scanners. Differences of consequence include the importance of signal voids that may show arterial stenosis improperly. This artifact has led to gadolinium-enhanced magnetic resonance angiography, together with the appeal of a shorter image acquisition time with its use and widespread application in vascular imaging. Questions have been raised about the accuracy of such contrast-enhanced magnetic resonance angiography, and data are emerging that it may overestimate the extent of arterial stenosis.[15]

Magnetic resonance is unable to show calcification and has difficulty depicting moving or unstable structures, such as the membrane of aortic dissection. Magnetic resonance can produce 3D images within its limitations, however, which achieve the same functions as described earlier. An example of excellent 3D MRI is shown in Figure 20-5, which depicts an endoluminal view of the aorta in a patient with an aortic aneurysm. This is only one static image of what was a series of images creating an endoluminal "fly through" or virtual angioscopic view of the aortoiliac segment.[16] The value of this type of 3D processing in providing an intuitive familiarity with anatomy may lie in assessment of complex anatomic features, such as aortic dissection, or in endovascular training.

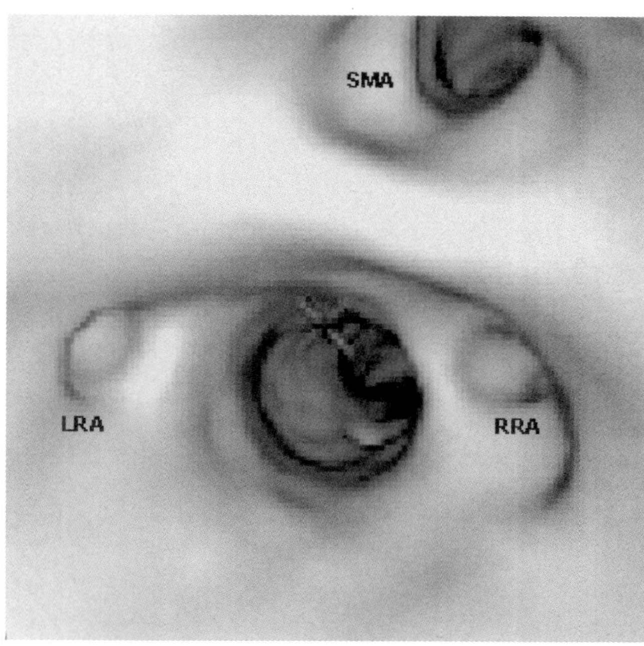

FIGURE 20-5 A still image from an endoluminal motion series shows the aortoiliac segment of a patient with abdominal aortic aneurysm. The relationship between visceral artery branches at the level of the proximal infrarenal aorta can be readily appreciated. LRA, left renal artery; RRA, right renal artery; SMA, superior mesenteric artery.

■ 3D VASCULAR ULTRASOUND

This discussion refers only to conventional external, noninvasive ultrasound, albeit with increasingly sophisticated technology, which is separate from intravascular ultrasound as presented in Chapter 23. From a theoretical perspective, ultrasound has much to recommend it for vascular imaging. It is a method capable of providing structural information in three dimensions and has the built-in capability of generating physiologic data, such as blood flow velocity, shear rate, and quantification of turbulence. In addition, it has practical qualities of being a low-cost, risk-free, and readily repeatable imaging method. Other practical factors make the accomplishment of fully useful 3D vascular ultrasound difficult, however. These factors include the positional variability of data acquisition through hand-held transducers, relatively long data acquisition time, and inherent limitations of ultrasound visualization of deep structures in the abdomen. An alternative that is making progress is real-time 3D ultrasonography using an electronically steered ultrasound beam that is considerably faster than reconstructed 3D images.[17]

Advances in genuine 3D processing have been achieved, the most visually striking example being the now commonplace pictures of a fetus in utero.[18] Examining why this obstetric application is so successful while vascular ultrasound remains challenging is instructive. Because the fetus floats in a fluid sac and fairly close to the body surface, it is an ideal ultrasound target. A lightly placed probe can be maintained in a fixed position, acquiring a sector of data without deforming the object of interest. Studying the femoropopliteal or carotid arterial segments requires moving the ultrasound transducer over a significant length and inducing some element of pressure deformity of the tissue being imaged. During image data acquisition, the hand-held transducer moves in all three axes, and this creates a major registration challenge for assigning the

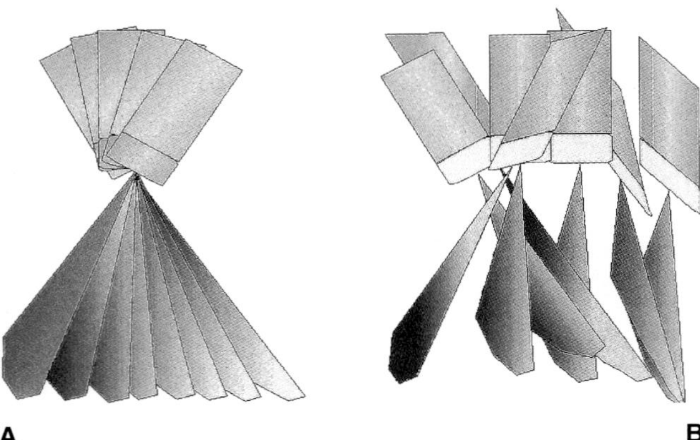

FIGURE 20-6 **A,** Schematic representation of the usual way in which an ultrasound transducer is moved during image acquisition by rocking back and forth to change the beam angle. **B,** Schematic representation of the problems in image registration created when acquiring an ultrasound image using "freehand" motion over a region.

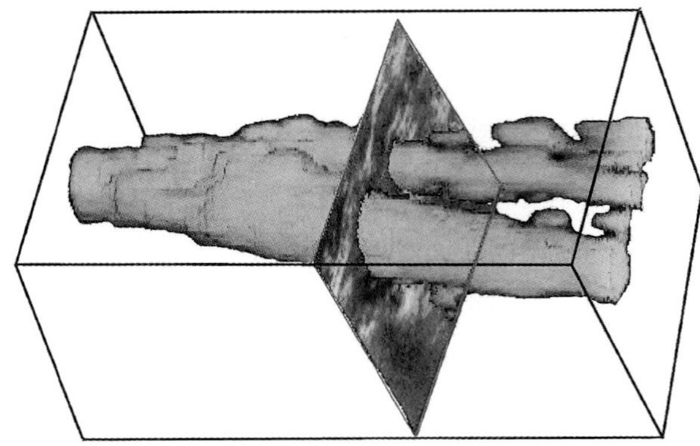

FIGURE 20-7 A 3D image of a carotid artery bifurcation created by freehand scanning with position registration together with software that "stacks" transverse ultrasound images to create a 3D object. One representative slice is shown in the model.

correct spatial "address" for each point of one image in relation to adjacent images that would need to be processed together to create the 3D object (Fig. 20-6). Added to this is the fact that blood vessels change size and shape during the cardiac and respiratory cycles. There are three basic techniques available for 3D quantitative ultrasonography: (1) stacking 2D cross-sectional images to create a 3D data set, (2) free scanning with an electromagnetic probe-position sensor, and (3) motorized probe with moving elements.

Stacking depends on devices to secure a vertical position of the probe in relation to the body, linear movement, and determination of probe positioning for each 2D image recorded (Fig. 20-7). When images are transformed into a cubic dataset resulting in a "stacked" 3D object, measurement operations on the data can be performed, for example, the calculation of the object's volume.

Keeping track of the multiaxis (X, Y, and Z) address to achieve useful registration of many images acquired during freehand scanning has been approached by use of a transmitter that produces an electromagnetic field around the patient during the ultrasound examination. A device is attached to the ultrasound probe, and changes in the electromagnetic field are used to sense the probe's 3D position. This position information is used to create a 3D address within the computer's image-processing software. Another approach has been taken through use of a proprietary system (Voluson; General Electric, Milwaukee, WI) that has a sector probe with an inner motor that rotates the piezoelectric imaging sensors. At the end of a 6-second scan, a 3D trapezoid dataset is generated.

Significant effort is ongoing to solve the problems of registration and ultrasound image processing, and it is likely that success will be achieved to enable 3D ultrasound to become a clinically useful tool at least in certain applications. One could imagine potential value in being able to obtain 3D images of carotid arteries that could be viewed in a "fly through" mode that might enhance clinical decisions and follow-up for endovascular treatment. The cervical carotid artery is readily imaged and lies in a relatively narrow plane, making image registration easier (Fig. 20-8). A variety of ultrasound laboratories already have shown this on a research basis.[18-20]

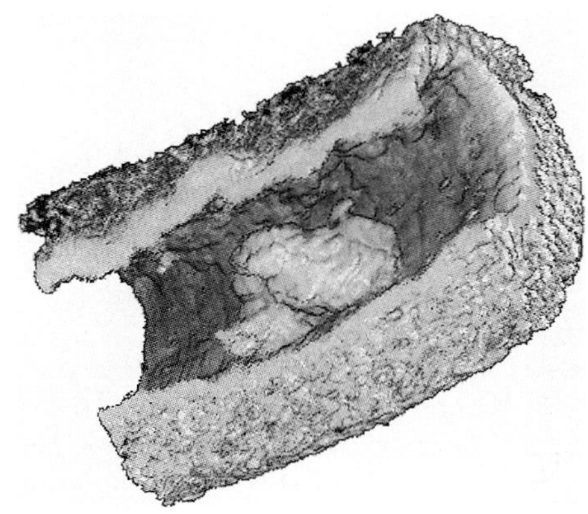

FIGURE 20-8 This 3D model of a carotid artery with a localized lesion was created by moving the ultrasound transducer on a motorized gantry across the region of interest. With precise image acquisition, plaque volume can be measured.

Another application of 3D ultrasound has been shown in the evaluation of aortic aneurysm, especially in the context of endografting. Work has shown sophisticated measurement of shear stress influence on vein grafts that is not possible without use of 3D tools.[21] In addition, the follow-up of endograft-excluded aortic aneurysm may be provided most sensitively through use of a single imaging test that, through postprocessing, provides multiple types of data, such as abdominal aortic aneurysm volume, endograft shape and alignment, and changes in shape of attachment zones (Fig. 20-9). Ultrasound might be a method of achieving this follow-up in the future through use of a low-cost, radiation-free method.[22]

■ CONCLUSION

3D processing of medical images provides a pathway to a variety of user-defined functions that extract greater value

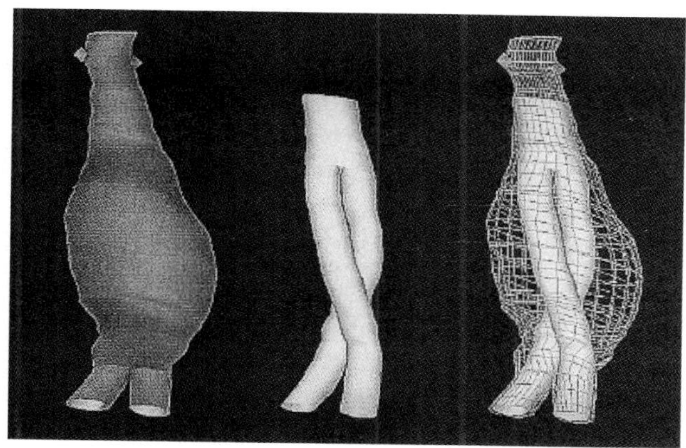

FIGURE 20-9 These images of an abdominal aortic aneurysm after endografting were made by external ultrasound by stacking a series of transverse images. On the *left* is the abdominal aortic aneurysm sac, in the *middle* is a surface display of the endograft, and on the *right* is a mesh view created by computerized image processing that shows the stent graft within the abdominal aortic aneurysm.

than can be derived from a series of 2D images. This fact together with improved resolution and accuracy of image acquisition and the universal availability of appropriate computing power to perform transforming operations on the image dataset make it increasingly likely that viewing vascular structures in three dimensions will be the routine clinical standard in the near future.

■ REFERENCES

1. Aziz I, Lee J, Lee JT, et al: Accuracy of three-dimensional simulation in the sizing of aortic endoluminal devices. Ann Vasc Surg 17:129-136, 2003.
2. Beebe HG, Jackson T, Pigott JP: Aortic aneurysm morphology for planning endovascular grafts: Limitations of conventional imaging methods. J Endovasc Surg 2:139-148, 1995.
3. Aarts NJ, Schruink GW, Schultze Kool LJ, et al: Abdominal aortic aneurysm measurements for endovascular repair: Intra- and inter-observer variability of CT measurements. Eur J Vasc Endovasc Surg 18:475-480, 1999.
4. Beebe HG, Kritpracha B, Serres S, et al: Endograft planning without preoperative arteriography: A clinical feasibility study. J Endovasc Ther 7:8-15, 2000.
5. Wyers MC, Fillinger MF, Schermerhorn ML, et al: Endovascular repair of abdominal aortic aneurysm without preoperative arteriography. J Vasc Surg 38:730-738, 2003.
6. Remy-Jardin M, Remy J: Spiral CT angiography of the pulmonary circulation. Radiology 212:615-636, 1999.
7. Lawler LP, Fishman EK: Multi-detector row CT of thoracic disease with emphasis on 3D volume rendering and CT angiography. Radiographics 21:1257-1273, 2001.
8. Beebe HG, Kritpracha B: Imaging of abdominal aortic aneurysm: Current status. Ann Vasc Surg 17:111-118, 2003.
9. Lawler LP, Fishman EK: Multidetector row computed tomography of the aorta and peripheral arteries. Cardiol Clin 21:607-629, 2003.
10. Sharma U, Ghai S, Paul SB, et al: Helical CT evaluation of aortic aneurysms and dissection: A pictorial essay. J Clin Imaging 27:273-280, 2003.
11. Takahashi M, Ashtara M, Papp Z, et al: CT angiography of carotid bifurcation: Artifacts and pitfalls in shaded-surface display. Am J Radiol 168:813-817, 1997.
12. Calhoun PS, Kuszyk BS, Heath DG, et al: Three-dimensional volume rendering of spiral CT data: Theory and method. Radiographics 19:745-764, 1999.
13. Mallouhi A, Schocke M, Judmaier W, et al: 3D MR angiography of renal arteries: Comparison of volume rendering and maximum intensity projection algorithms. Radiology 223:509-516, 2002.
14. Glockner JF: Three-dimensional gadolinium-enhanced MR angiography: Applications for abdominal imaging. Radiographics 21:357-370, 2001.
15. Townsend TC, Saloner D, Pan XM, et al: Contrast material-enhanced MRA overestimates severity of carotid stenosis, compared with 3D time-of-flight MRA. J Vasc Surg 38:36-40, 2003.
16. Glockner JF: Navigating the aorta: MR virtual vascular endoscopy. Radiographics 23:e11, 2003.
17. Stetten G, Tamburo R: Real-time three-dimensional ultrasound methods for shape analysis and visualization. Methods 25:221-230, 2001.
18. Forsberg F, Rawool NM, Merton JB, et al: Contrast enhanced vascular three-dimensional ultrasound imaging. Ultrasonics 40:117-122, 2002.
19. Dajani KF, Salles Cunha SX, Beebe HG, et al: Ultrasound volumetry of atherosclerotic plaques. J Vasc Technol 26:89-97, 2004.
20. Landry A, Fenster A: Theoretical and experimental quantification of carotid plaque volume measurements made by three-dimensional ultrasound using test phantoms. Med Phys 29:2319-2327, 2002.
21. Leotta DF, Primozich JF, Beach KW, et al: Remodeling in peripheral vein graft revisions: Serial study with three-dimensional ultrasound imaging. J Vasc Surg 37:798-807, 2003.
22. Leotta DF, Paun M, Beach KW, et al: Measurement of abdominal aortic aneurysms with three-dimensional ultrasound imaging. J Vasc Surg 33:700-707, 2001.

Chapter 21

Computed Tomography, CT Angiography, and 3D Reconstruction for the Evaluation of Vascular Disease

MARK F. FILLINGER, MD
DAVID R. WHITTAKER, MD

Since the 1990s, there has been a trend in preoperative imaging for vascular surgery primarily toward less invasive techniques. It was previously believed that preoperative angiography was necessary for repair of abdominal aortic aneurysms (AAAs),[1] but technologic advances ultimately led many surgeons to perform open AAA repair on the basis of computed tomography (CT) alone.[2,3] Ironically the less invasive technique of endovascular aneurysm repair led to a new requirement for preoperative angiography, but this problem also has been solved by advanced imaging techniques.[4] Similar trends toward eliminating preoperative angiography have occurred (or are occurring) with carotid endarterectomy and lower extremity arterial bypass procedures.[5,6] As with many technologic advances, however, the process of image creation continues to become more difficult for the average end-user to understand. Although the typical vascular surgeon can perform clinical evaluation and decision making without an understanding of the basic principles behind CT, these concepts remain important. A firm grasp of the basic concepts of CT technology is necessary so that the limitations, artifacts, and opportunities for image optimization are not overlooked. A better grasp of the image creation process and terminology also aids collaboration between radiologists creating the images and the surgeons who use the images to plan surgical intervention. Last, an understanding of the basic concepts enhances the ability of the surgeon to understand technologic advances as they become the new standard of care.

■ BASIC CONCEPTS AND TECHNOLOGY

Conventional CT

Computed tomography is aptly named—a structure is mapped and displayed as graphic "slices" with the assistance of computer technology. Work in the 1960s by Hounsfield eventually led to production of the first clinical CT scanner, produced by Elector-Musical Instruments Limited and installed in Atkinson Morleys Hospital, Wimbledon, England, in 1971.[7] Many of the principles used in this "first-generation" CT scanner are still in use today and provide a framework for understanding the technology. As with most imaging modalities, the fundamental unit for this CT scanner consists of an *emitter* and a *detector*—an x-ray beam is transmitted through the tissue and detected on the other side. The emitter produces a thin (highly collimated) x-ray beam that sweeps in linear fashion across the body cross-section (Fig. 21-1). The detector moves simultaneously with the emitter as a unit, recording data from 160 separate, parallel, and immediately adjacent beams. The emitter and detector units are mounted within a *gantry,* which is rotated 1 degree before another linear, transverse sweep takes place. This process is repeated through 180 degrees of rotation, producing the data necessary to form a 160 × 160 *matrix* for a single cross-sectional image.

The data collected by the detector is the *attenuation* of the x-ray beam. Attenuation is the rate of reduction of x-ray energy recorded at the detector. Attenuation increases with increased thickness, density, or atomic number of the material the beam passes through, and attenuation decreases with increased peak kilovoltage (kVp) of the x-ray beam. X-ray energy interacts with tissue to produce attenuation by means of atomic ionization events via the photoelectric and Compton effects. The importance of these effects is beyond the scope of this text, but suffice it to say that the energy levels used in CT indicate that soft tissue interactions involve primarily the Compton effect. Images are mostly a result of the physical density and electron density of the tissue being imaged and the energy of the x-ray beam. The *CT number* was defined to simplify quantification of the linear attenuation coefficient (μ) produced by a tissue at a given x-ray beam energy by normalizing it against the attenuation coefficient of water. The CT number is defined as: $K(\mu - {}^{\mu}H_2O)/{}^{\mu}H_2O$, where K is a constant, μ is the attenuation coefficient of the tissue, and ${}^{\mu}H_2O$ is the attenuation coefficient of water. When a scaling constant (K) of 1000 is used, the CT number is said to be expressed in *Hounsfield units (H)*.

Clinically, CT numbers range from the extremes of air (−1000 H) to dense bone (1000 H), but fat (−20 to −100 H), water (0 H), and muscle and blood (40 to 60 H) tend to lie in a much narrower range.[8] Differences in factors such

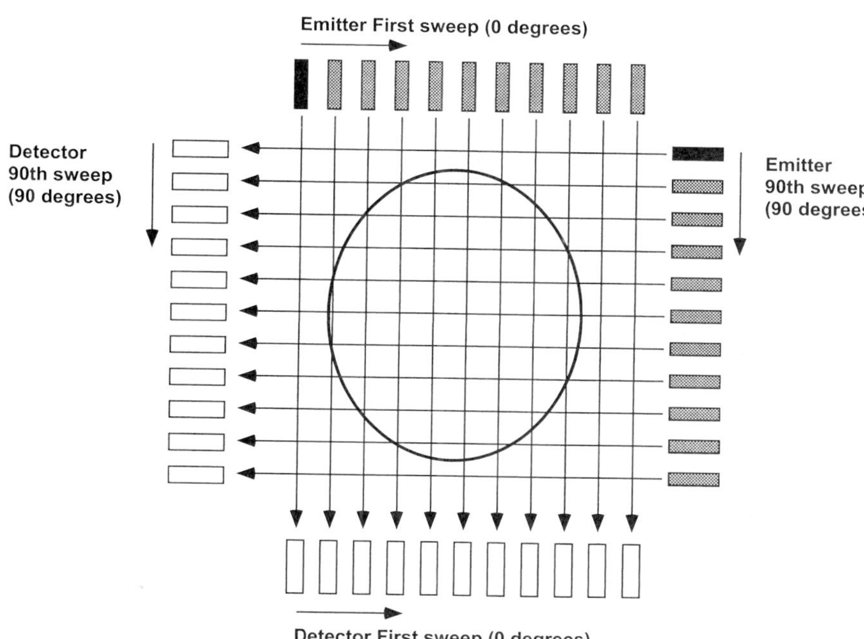

FIGURE 21-1 Principle of operation for a first-generation CT scanner.

as the energy level of the beam and tissue thickness prevent the density in Hounsfield units from being absolutely uniform from one CT scan to another, but the ranges are similar. When the range of CT numbers for a scan is determined, it can be broken up into smaller ranges for graphic display by a set of gray-scale values. In the chest, CT numbers approaching 1000 H (bone) typically are assigned values close to pure white, and CT numbers approaching −1000 H (air) typically are assigned values close to pure black. CT numbers between −1000 H and +1000 H would be displayed as graduated shades of gray.

This concept appears simple until one realizes that the x-ray emitter/detector combination works in a fashion similar to conventional x-ray film. The detector measures the attenuation of x-rays through the *entire path traversed by the beam*. So how can the attenuation coefficient for each small area on the matrix be calculated and displayed separately for each of the 160 × 160 = 25,600 data points in the matrix? This problem is solved using a computer. Digital data are collected from the attenuation of multiple x-ray beams traversing the same point in the matrix from different angles. An ingenious method is used to calculate *backward* to the density that must be present at each location in the matrix. A combination of hardware, mathematical algorithms, and computer software results in the cross-sectional images of CT scans. This was such a leap forward in imaging technology that Hounsfield and Cormack shared the Nobel Prize in 1980.

A first-generation CT scanner is capable of producing a cross-sectional image with a 160 × 160 matrix. Each data point in the matrix is mapped to a gray scale for display and is known as a *pixel* because it represents a "picture element." When displayed as a whole, this matrix of gray squares becomes an interpretable image, just as different densities of black and white dots are used to create photographs in a newspaper. In this manner, the first-generation CT scanner could create a cross-sectional image of the human body—an impressive accomplishment. This process required approximately 5 minutes to create a single cross-section. Early CT scans were applicable only to parts of the body with limited motion (e.g., the head) because the back-calculation algorithm depends on the subject remaining in one position while data are collected for the entire cross-section.

To obtain useful scans in areas such as the chest and abdomen, subsequent generations of CT scanners were designed to decrease the time required to obtain a complete cross-sectional image. The second-generation CT scan used an emitter that produced a broader fan-shaped x-ray beam and an array of 30 detectors instead of a single detector. These innovations greatly reduced the number of emitter locations required to complete a single transverse sweep and reduced the number of transverse sweeps (1-degree increments were no longer required for a complete cross-sectional image). The time for a single cross-sectional scan was reduced to approximately 15 seconds. Present-day CT uses third-generation and fourth-generation scanners. In a third-generation scanner, the emitter produces a wider fan-shaped x-ray beam, and there are hundreds of detectors arranged in an arc (Fig. 21-2). Because the beam/detector combinations cover the entire patient, no transverse sweep is required—the emitter and the detector array rotate in a continuous 180-degree or 360-degree arc to produce a complete cross-sectional scan in 1 second. In a fourth-generation CT scanner, the detector array covers the entire 360-degree arc, and only the emitter rotates. At present, scan times are similar for third-generation and fourth-generation scanners, and there is no clear clinical advantage for either type.[9] Finally, *multidetector* scanners have multiple rows of detectors, all covering the entire 360-degree arc, so that the volume to be scanned can be covered more quickly. A single-slice detector acquires one slice per rotation, whereas currently available multidetector CT scanners (with 4, 8, or

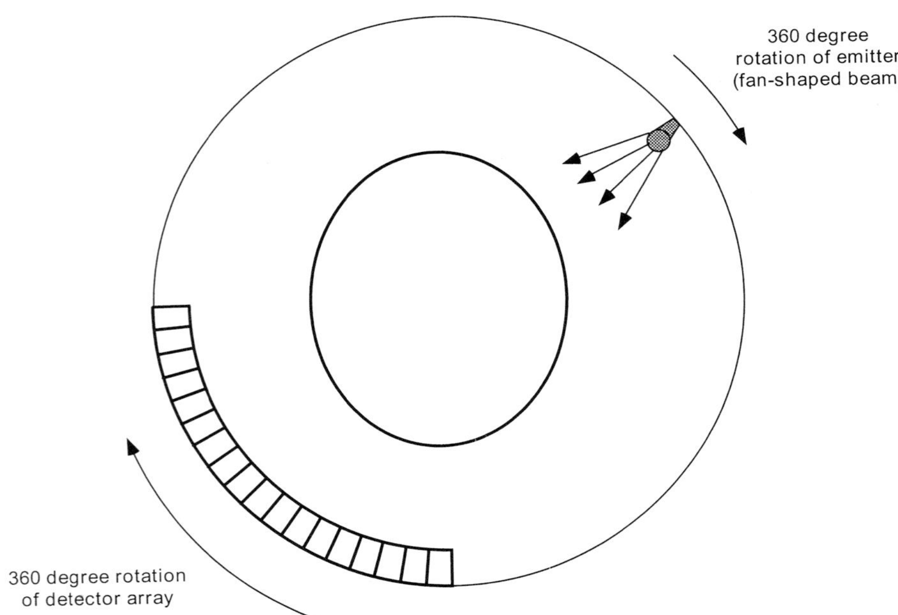

FIGURE 21-2 Principle of operation for a third-generation CT scanner.

16 detector rows or arrays) are capable of acquiring up to 16 separate slices per 360 degrees of rotation. Each slice can be acquired at 1 mm or even submillimeter thickness, with rotation times in the range of 0.5 second. Complete imaging of the abdominal vasculature can be acquired in a fraction of the time required with previous generation scanners; this can diminish or eliminate many artifacts or compromises that must be dealt with in single-row detector scanners, as discussed subsequently. For this reason, multidetector or multirow scanners are rapidly replacing the earlier generation single-row scanners.

Advances in hardware and computer software technology have also greatly improved the graphic image display despite the reduction in scan times. A first-generation CT scanner produced a cross-sectional image with a 160 × 160 matrix, but current scanners typically generate a 512 × 512 or 1024 × 1024 matrix. Each data point in the matrix is mapped to a gray scale for display so that the size of the matrix and the *field of view* (FOV) have a direct impact on the *resolution* of the display (the smallest distinguishable element). Data points are *displayed* as a two-dimensional (2D) picture, and each point in the display matrix is a *pixel* (picture element). Data points are *acquired* in three dimensions, however, and each data point in the matrix actually represents a *voxel* (volume element) that has a thickness equal to the thickness of the x-ray beam (Fig. 21-3). One current advantage of CT over magnetic resonance imaging (MRI) is that CT is typically displayed in a 512 × 512 matrix or greater, with resolutions of 0.2 to 1 mm^2 for each pixel. MRI is generally limited to a 256 × 256 matrix, and resolution in the axial plane is roughly half that of CT. The pixel for a CT display represents a voxel that may be 1 to 10 mm thick, however, and MRI typically has better resolution along the longitudinal axis.

Spiral CT

The most recent advance to achieve widespread clinical application is spiral or helical CT technology. Although the scan time needed to produce a single cross-sectional

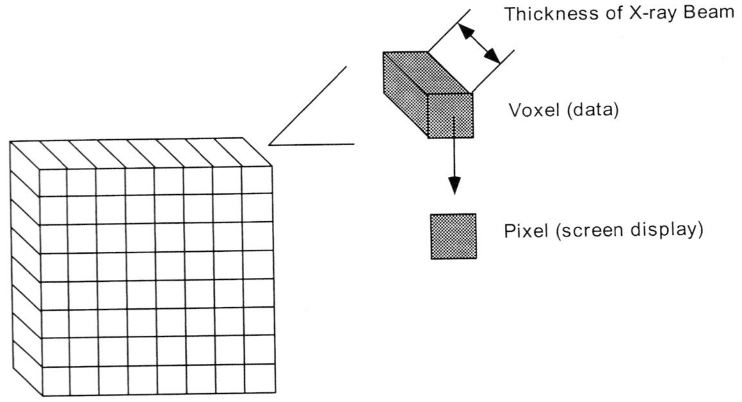

FIGURE 21-3 Data acquisition versus data display.

image is greatly reduced in third-generation and fourth-generation CT scanners, the rotating elements on the gantry (the detector array or the emitter or both) are still limiting if they are attached to power cables. Power cables attached to the rotating elements force the unit to perform a cross-sectional scan in one direction, stop, and then scan in the reverse direction for the next cross-section (to unwind the cables); this increases the time needed to scan the volume of interest and makes motion artifact more likely. The development of the *slip-ring gantry* eliminated cables by allowing the rotating elements to receive power via sliding rings that make electrical contact with stationary brushes. The emitter and detector array can rotate continuously in the same direction. More importantly, the computer can acquire data continuously because there is no need to stop and reverse direction. With conventional CT, there would still be a pause in data acquisition while the table (patient) moves to a new position for the next cross-section to be scanned. If the table moves in a continuous linear motion through the gantry while the x-ray emitter and detector rotate continuously over 360 degrees, data can be acquired in a single sweep over the entire volume of interest. In this technique, the emitter traces out a spiral relative to the patient and is referred to as a *spiral CT* or *helical CT* scan (Fig. 21-4).

Spiral or helical CT technology has several important ramifications beyond a simple decrease in scan time. A spiral CT scan collects data over a continuous *volume* rather than discontinuous slices (Fig. 21-5). The most obvious advantage of acquiring data over a continuous volume is that thin axial slices can be reconstructed from the digital dataset at arbitrarily small intervals *without additional radiation exposure*. Conventional CT can produce similar overlapping or adjacent axial slices, but the tradeoff is increased scan time and additional radiation exposure. Cross-sectional images typically are produced at 10-mm intervals in conventional CT, but at 3- to 5-mm intervals with spiral CT. In spiral CT terminology, this typically is referred to as the *reconstruction interval*. When attempting to ascertain fine detail, such as a potential renal artery stenosis, a reconstruction interval as small as 1 mm might be used.

Multiplanar Reformats and CT Angiography

Another advantage of data acquisition over an entire volume is the ability to *reconstruct* or *reformat* the data in arbitrary planes. Reformatting CT data into coronal, sagittal, or other nonaxial planes often is referred to as *multiplanar reformatting* or *multiplanar reconstruction (MPR)*. A schematic representation of this process is shown in Figure 21-6. Although this reformatting is theoretically possible with conventional CT, it is not practical because of considerations of scan time, motion artifact, and radiation exposure. In many cases, a spiral CT scan covers the volume of interest during a single breath-hold. Because structures in the volume of interest have not moved during the scan, multiplanar reformats produce useful images with minimal motion artifact (Fig. 21-7).

The ability of spiral CT to view the data in coronal, sagittal, or arbitrarily defined planes often gives more insight into vascular anatomy than axial views alone. Evaluation of

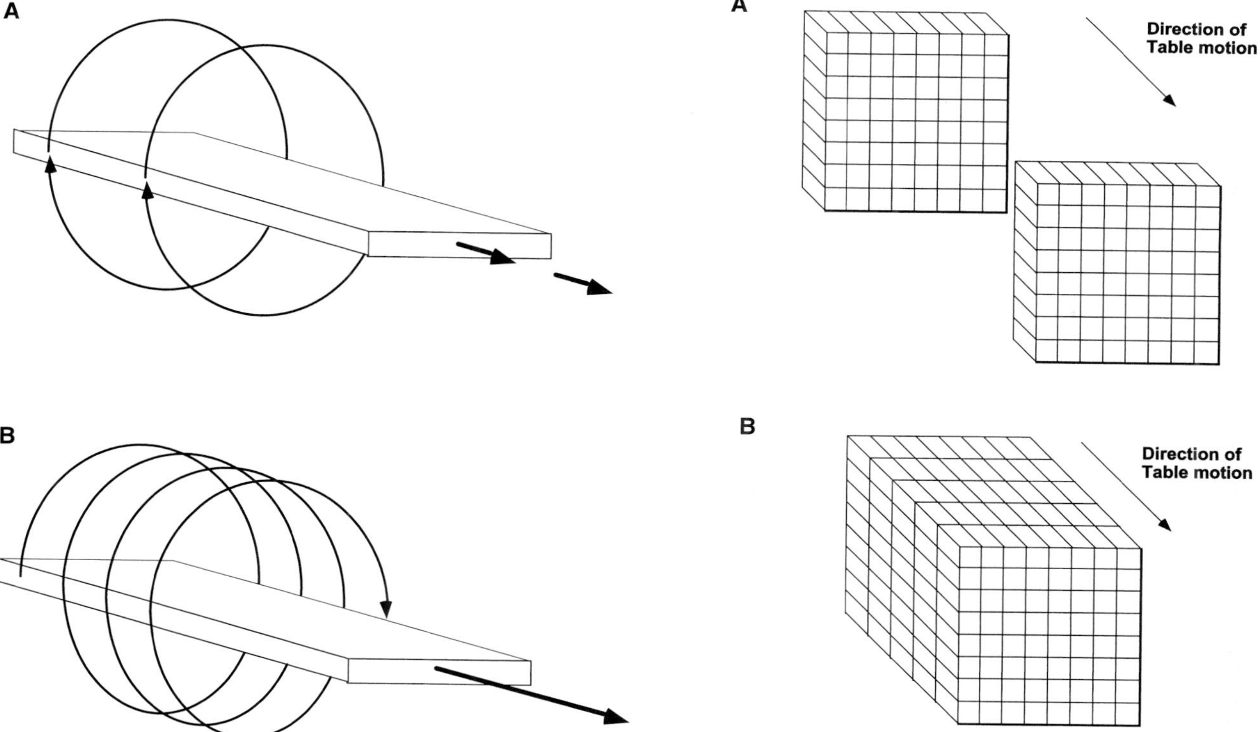

FIGURE 21-4 Conventional versus spiral CT scan gantry motion.

FIGURE 21-5 A and **B,** Discontinuous versus continuous data for conventional and spiral CT.

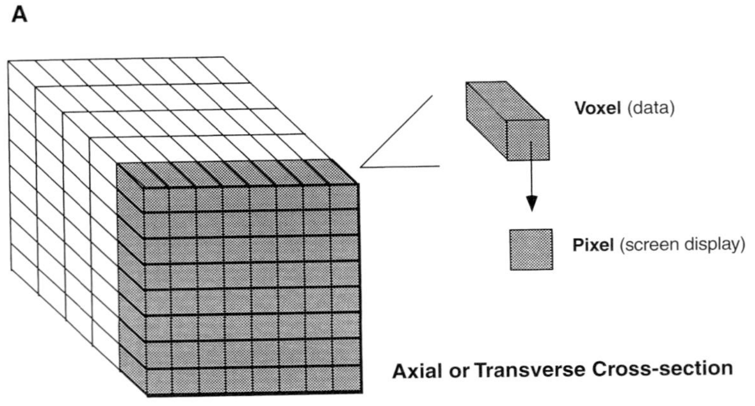

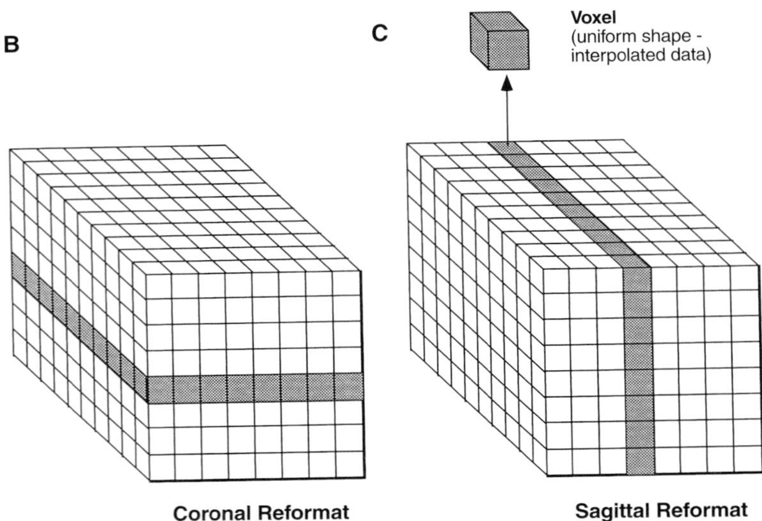

FIGURE 21-6 A-C, Because spiral CT data are acquired and stored over a continuous volume, they can be used to create axial, coronal, and sagittal sections. For display purposes, the nonuniform voxel can be interpolated into a cube, but the quality of the data still depends on the length of the original voxel (which is determined by the collimation). Reformatting CT data into coronal, sagittal, or other nonaxial planes is often referred to as *multiplanar reformatting*.

potential renal artery occlusive disease is performed best in axial and coronal sections, whereas the celiac and superior mesenteric arteries are seen best in axial and sagittal planes. Reformats along curved planes also may be useful for evaluating tortuous iliac arteries or aortic branch vessels, but should be interpreted with caution because this reformat is in an arbitrary and unnatural "warped" plane (Fig. 21-7C, D). Spiral CT reveals more anatomic detail than conventional CT by combining rapid CT data acquisition during a single breath-hold, a focus on vascular structures during a single intravenous (IV) contrast bolus, small reconstruction intervals, and multiplanar reformatting. The resulting images sometimes resemble angiography, and the process is often referred to as *CT angiography (CTA)*. CTA has greatly enhanced the ability of CT to evaluate vascular occlusive disease of aortic branches and iliac arteries (see clinical applications sections).[10,11]

3D Reconstruction

The combination of rapid scanning over the volume of interest, new software algorithms, and advances in computer technology have made it possible to create striking three-dimensional (3D) reconstructions from spiral CT data. If CT creates images by a process analogous to slicing a loaf of bread, 3D reconstruction is like putting the slices in the loaf of bread back together. In this case, however, the reconstruction can be limited to individual structures that meet certain parameters, such as density or location within the scan volume. If bony structures are of primary interest, the computer algorithm can reconstruct only the elements of the CT (voxels) that are of bone density (i.e., CT numbers or attenuation coefficients of bone). For vascular structures, CTA produces contrast density within the vessel lumen at the appropriate time so that 3D reconstruction of the vessel lumen can be performed. When creating this type of 3D reconstruction (or 3D model), the density (CT numbers) of vascular contrast and bone may overlap. Bone structures are either included in the model or are "cut away" using a tool sometimes referred to as an *electronic scalpel*. Calcium within the vessel wall cannot be cut away easily, however, and is usually included in a reconstruction of the contrast-enhanced vessel lumen. This produces the typical computer-generated 3D reconstruction, which most often is displayed as a *shaded surface display (SSD)*. In a SSD, the exterior of the structure is opaque and shaded to provide an appreciation of depth (Fig. 21-8). The 3D reconstruction can greatly aid the interpretation of difficult anatomy. Although it lacks

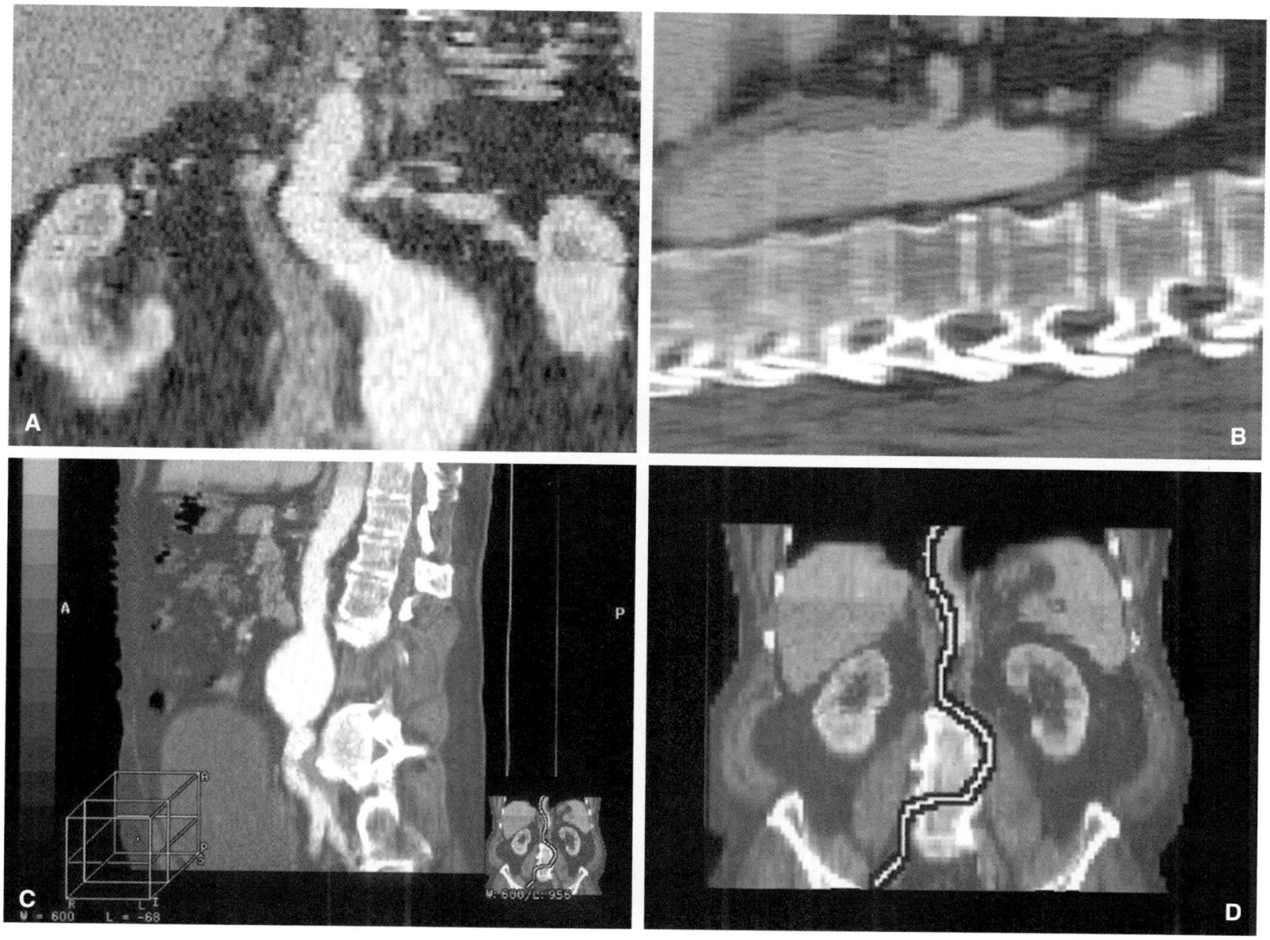

FIGURE 21-7 Clinical examples of multiplanar reformatting. **A,** Coronal reformat displaying the aorta of a patient with an infrarenal aneurysm. The more proximal aorta is not seen because it is out of the plane of this CT slice. The renal arteries are seen, but it is unclear whether they are stenotic or whether the origin of both renal arteries would be seen in a different section (hence the need to view multiple coronal and axial CT slices). The left renal artery origin is actually stenotic, but the right is not. **B,** Sagittal reformat of the abdominal aorta, showing the celiac artery. The superior mesenteric artery is seen in a different sagittal section. **C,** Curvilinear reformat. To see a long segment of the aorta and the right iliac artery together on one CT slice, the data are reformatted along a warped plane corresponding to the lumen. A cursor is used to plot a line through the tortuous lumen of the aorta seen in **A,** and the data are reformatted along this highly curved plane *(inset)*. **D,** Magnified view of the *inset* from **C,** showing how tortuous the reformatted CT plane would appear if viewed "end on" from a coronal section. The curvilinear reformat can produce a helpful display but must be interpreted with caution because tortuous structures appear to be relatively straight, and surrounding structures are distorted (note the lumbar spine moving in and out of the reformatted plane).

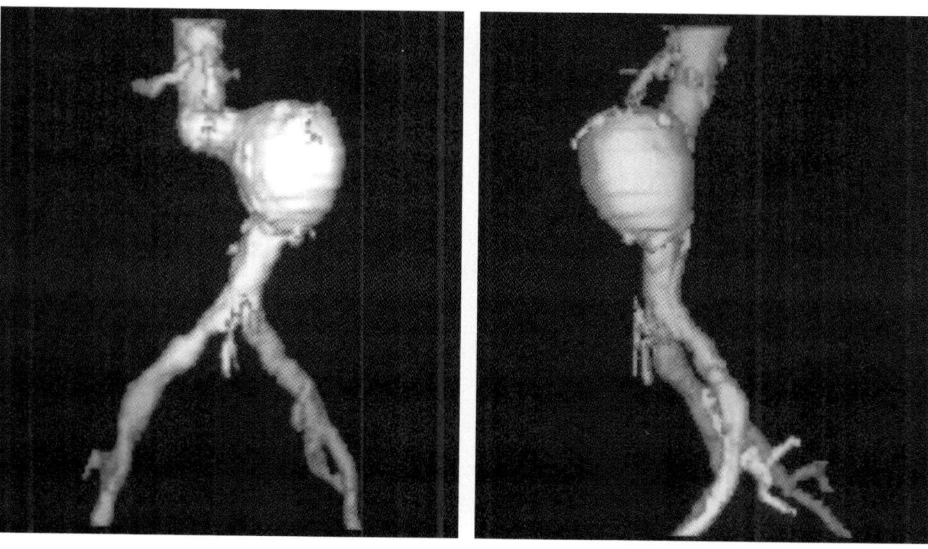

FIGURE 21-8 Computer-generated SSD of CT data. The 3D relationships of the aneurysm and surrounding structures are immediately apparent in these anteroposterior and left lateral views. In this typical single-object 3D SSD, the threshold for reconstruction is the density of contrast-enhanced blood. Because calcified plaque is denser than contrast-enhanced blood, it is included in the reconstruction. The spine was removed electronically before making the 3D reconstruction. An infinite number of views are possible on the workstation used to create the views, but a limited number of views are printed as hardcopy to show the anatomy.

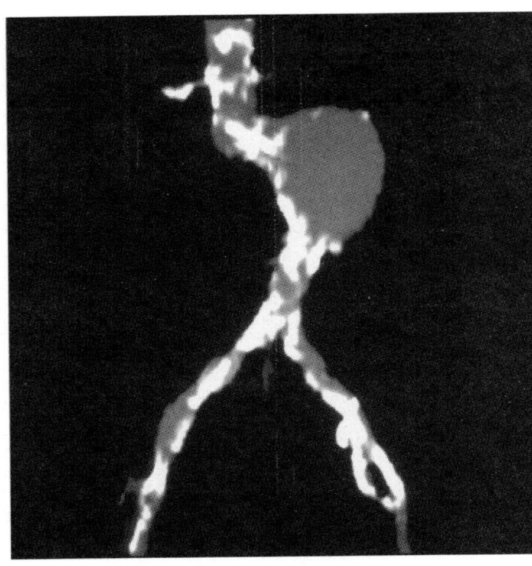
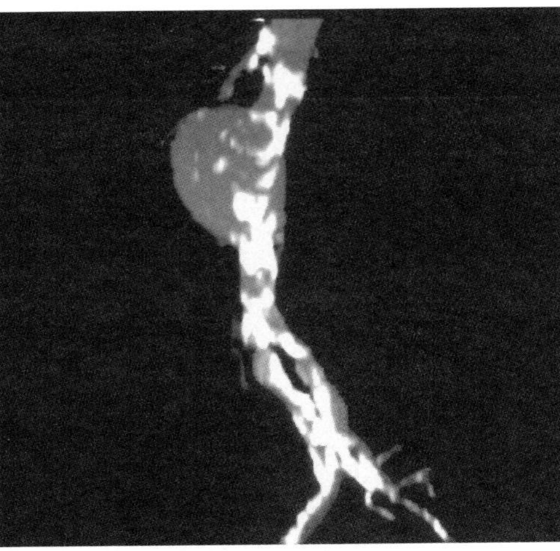

FIGURE 21-9 MIP images of the same AAA shown in Figure 21-8, anteroposterior *(left)* and left lateral *(right)* views. This reconstruction represents a 2D projection of the structure along a line defined in 3D space so that the MIP appears similar to an arteriogram. Only the structure with maximum intensity is projected, so calcified plaque is displayed prominently. MIP images display calcified plaque well, but this same feature can obscure the residual lumen in locations where the vessel is heavily calcified (note the iliac arteries in particular).

the detail of the CT scans, morphology within the 3D image is easily recognizable in far less time than it takes to review the CT data. This depiction of 3D relationships is probably most helpful in surgical planning for complicated open procedures or endovascular procedures.[3,12-14]

One problem with SSD of 3D models is that the bulk of structures, such as calcified plaque, cannot be fully appreciated because all CT numbers (physical densities) included in the model are given the same opaque color in the display. One method that better displays different physical densities is called *maximum intensity projection (MIP)*. MIP images display the 2D projection that would result if one could see only the densest structures (structures that project the maximum intensity). Although a MIP image is created from the 3D volume data, it is a projection—similar to an angiogram—and must be defined from a particular point of view (Fig. 21-9). MIP images are relatively familiar to surgeons and interventional radiologists, and they display calcified plaque well. Adequate evaluation of the structure requires many views, however, and even then a heavily calcified vessel may obscure important details regarding the vessel lumen and the degree of stenosis.

Another method developed to improve the display of structures with different physical densities involves SSD of multiple objects simultaneously. This process is based on determining which densities are relevant to interpretation of the image and coding or *segmentation* of those CT densities as separate objects; this allows separate 3D reconstructions or color-coded display of the pertinent CT densities. In vascular surgery, the most clinically relevant structures are the contrast-enhanced vessel lumen, calcified plaque, noncalcified plaque, and thrombus. Noncalcified atherosclerotic plaque and thrombus have essentially identical CT numbers and cannot be distinguished as separate objects. The latter two structures are distinct from contrast-enhanced blood flow, however, and blood flow can be distinguished from calcified plaque to a reasonable degree. With proper CT protocols and software algorithms, these structures can be displayed separately on the basis of density. Because there is some density overlap, and the edge-detection abilities of the human eye are far superior to computer algorithms at present, the "segmentation" process used to create a multiple-object SSD is usually semiautomated (i.e., it requires some human intervention and review to ensure accurate segmentation on the computer). Although the process is currently more time-consuming, the resulting 3D reconstructions display information that is not available in any other imaging modality (Fig. 21-10). Because the separate elements can be viewed in combination or separately, this type of reconstruction has the advantages of single-object SSD and MIP without most of their disadvantages. This 3D method can display best the extent of an aneurysm (because thrombus is visible), degree of calcification, and lumen narrowing secondary to plaque (especially if structures of differing density can be made invisible or transparent [Fig. 21-11]). Plaque can be made invisible electronically to simulate an angiogram or included to plan a surgical procedure. As with any 3D reconstruction, however, the 3D model must always be interpreted in the context of the actual CT data and the potential artifacts that may occur. With some types of software, CT slices can be displayed simultaneously within the 3D reconstruction, which may help provide context for the data (Fig. 21-12). If available, this ability to show the CT slice within the 3D model can also be used to verify the accuracy of the 3D reconstruction and show that it is an accurate representation of the data.

Image Optimization and Common Artifacts Related to Spiral CT

Knowledge of the physical concepts behind creation of CT images allows an understanding of concepts related to image optimization and image artifacts. These concepts are dealt with on a daily basis by radiologists, and they are useful for surgeons interested in improving routine vascular CT scanning, CT protocols for unique situations, and differentiation of artifacts from pathology.

Although spiral CT technology has led to numerous advances in imaging, it is not without drawbacks. Because the data are acquired in one continuous sweep, tube overheating limits the distance that can be covered with each "spiral." This is probably the most limiting factor for spiral or helical CT in the abdomen and pelvis and drives most of the image optimization strategies for aortic applications. The distance covered during a CT "spiral" is determined by the duration of the scan (approximately 30 to 60 seconds),

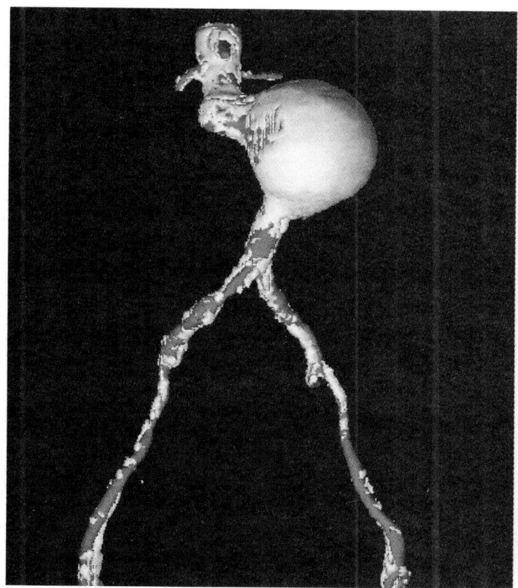
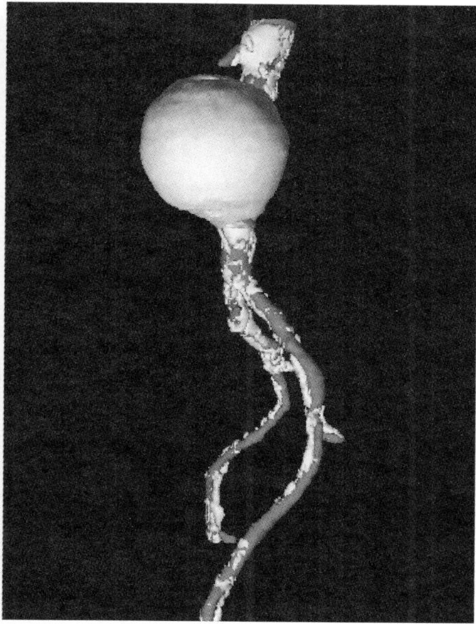

FIGURE 21-10 Multiple-object SSD, anteroposterior *(left)* and left lateral *(right)* views of the same AAA seen in Figures 21-8 and 21-9. Contrast-enhanced blood flow is displayed in red, thrombus and noncalcified plaque are yellow, and calcified plaque is white. In this type of 3D reconstruction, all the components of the aneurysm are seen. Multiple views are helpful, and it is preferable if the display can be rotated and viewed at will on a computer screen. This type of display is most helpful in determining the true extent of an aneurysm because thrombus is clearly visible. (See Color Figure in this section.)

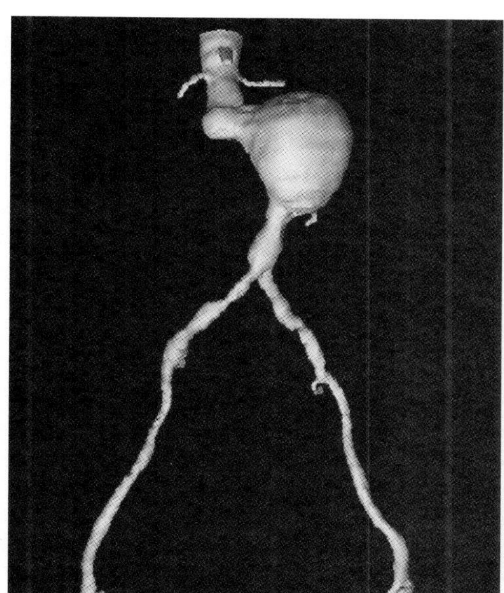
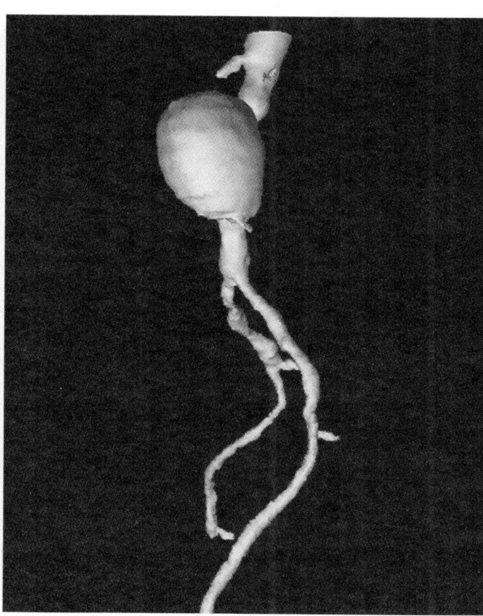

FIGURE 21-11 Multiple-object SSD from Figure 21-10 with all structures made invisible except blood flow, using the same anteroposterior *(left)* and left lateral *(right)* views. With calcified plaque made invisible, the degree of occlusive disease becomes apparent in the iliac arteries. A key point is that calcified plaque was modeled separately and has been made invisible so that this 3D reconstruction does *not* have the same appearance as the typical single-object SSD shown in Figure 21-8. For surgical planning, it is preferable if the objects can be made visible or invisible at will on a computer screen. An alternative is to print hardcopy images in multiple views with the various components sequentially highlighted, transparent, or invisible.

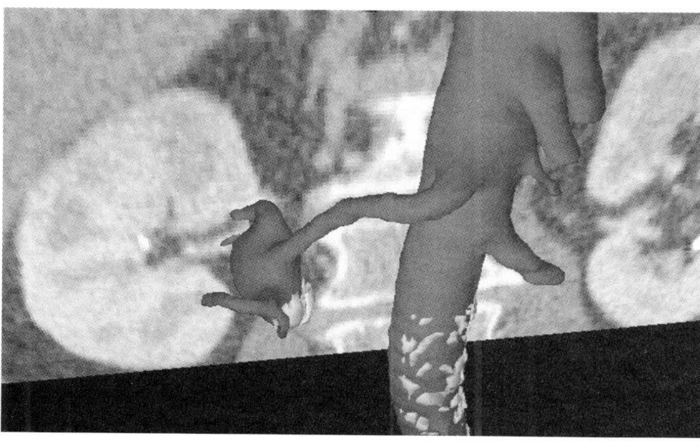

FIGURE 21-12 Multiple-object SSD with a CT slice displayed in the context of the model in 3D space. The right renal artery aneurysm is displayed with its branches heading toward the CT display of the right kidney. The central branch exiting the aneurysm is cut off as it disappears into the CT slice. (See Color Figure in this section.)

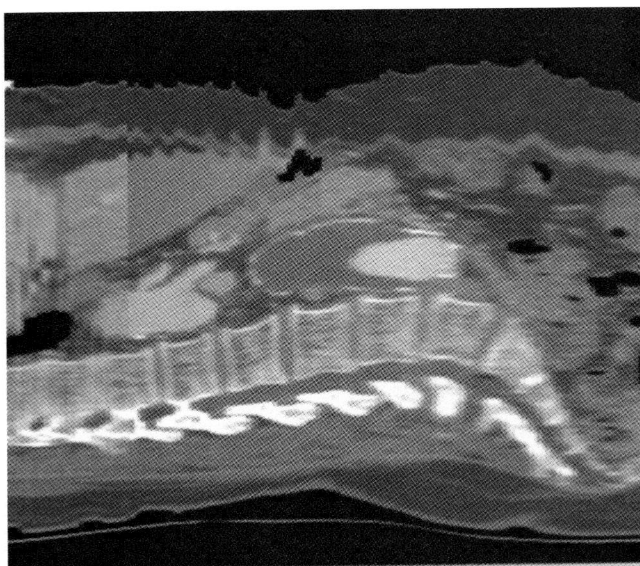

FIGURE 21-13 Importance of slice thickness (collimation) with regard to quality of multiplanar reformat. In this sagittal section, three "spirals" are apparent. The spiral in the central third of the scan has 3-mm collimation, and the spiral in the proximal third of the scan has 7-mm collimation (in the thoracic aorta, where the longitudinal resolution is less crucial in this patient). Note the difference in resolution and clarity for the spine and disk spaces. The transition point between these two spiral acquisitions was planned above the celiac axis so that potential motion artifact would be less likely to affect the quality of MPRs in a key location. Also note the motion artifact at the skin surface, which does not affect the relatively fixed aorta. The celiac and superior mesenteric artery origins are well seen, and the apparent narrowing at the celiac artery origin is not artifact—it is also seen in other CT slices.

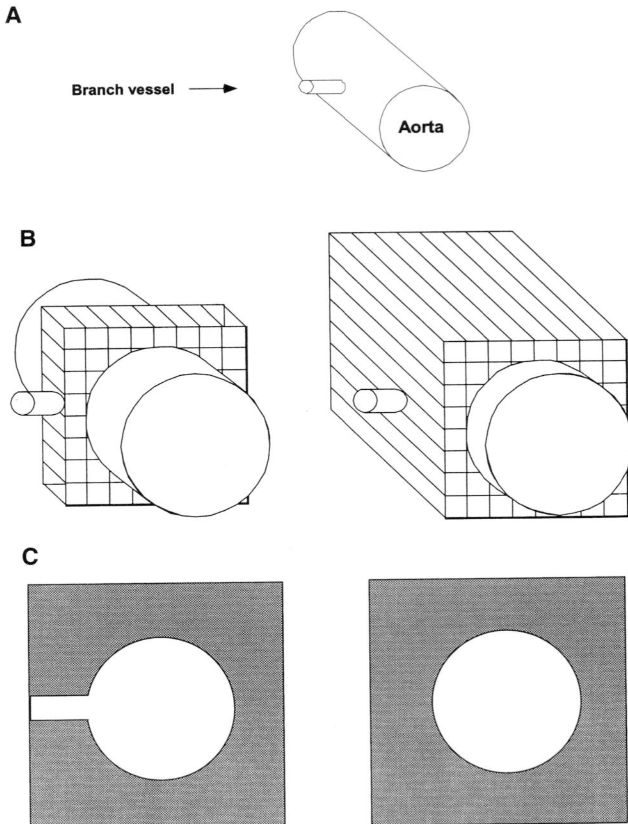

FIGURE 21-14 Importance of slice thickness with regard to detection and display of small vessels. **A,** Schematic diagram of a branch vessel arising from the aorta. **B,** The same vessels depicted during data acquisition using thin collimation *(left)* or thicker collimation *(right)*. **C,** Axial display of the data acquired in **B**. The branch vessel is seen clearly when it is in the center of a CT slice with thin collimation *(left)* because there is minimal averaging with data from low-density soft tissue in the same slice *(right)*.

the speed of rotation (usually 1 rotation/second), the *collimation* (beam thickness or slice thickness, 1 to 10 mm, but usually 3 to 7 mm), and the *pitch* (ratio of table speed to slice thickness). Balancing these factors is essentially a compromise between data quality and the distance that can be covered in a single spiral. One way to increase the distance covered during a single spiral scan is to decrease power so that the tube heats less quickly and the duration of the scan can be maximized. The problem is that the image may degrade if power is inadequate (a problem called *photopenia*).

Another way to cover more distance during the time it takes for a tube to reach its heat capacity is to widen the collimation (slice thickness). Increasing the slice thickness compromises the longitudinal resolution and the quality of multiplanar reformats and 3D reconstructions (Fig. 21-13). Increased slice thickness also compromises the ability to detect small structures, such as accessory renal arteries, because of *averaging artifact*. With this type of averaging artifact, the attenuation from contrast within a 1-mm accessory renal artery is averaged with the attenuation from surrounding soft tissue. If the slice is thick, the attenuation from the artery is lost because it represents only a small portion of the slice. The small vessel is less likely to be missed with a thinner slice (Figs. 21-14 and 21-15). Thin slices decrease the volume covered by the scan, however. During a typical 30-second scan (1 rotation/sec, pitch of 1), using a collimation of 3 mm translates into only 9 cm covered along the longitudinal axis.

One strategy to work around this problem is to use fine collimation for portions of the scan where it is needed to detect small vessels (e.g., in the visceral segment of the aorta) and "thicker" collimation for areas where it is less noticeable (e.g., the iliac arteries). *Collimation* and *reconstruction interval* are *not* interchangeable terms. Collimation is the width of the x-ray beam (slice thickness over which data are collected), and reconstruction interval is the interval at which cross-sections are created for display. When the volume is scanned and the data stored, axial cross-sections can be reconstructed at arbitrary intervals. Up to a point, increasing the reconstruction interval improves the quality of a scan because it creates overlapping slices, increases longitudinal resolution, and decreases some types of artifact. The optimal ratio of reconstruction interval to collimation is at least 2:1, and 3:1 is preferable for MPR and 3D reconstruction.[15]

Another way to cover more distance over the duration of the scan is to increase pitch (the ratio of table speed to slice thickness). The best image quality is obtained with

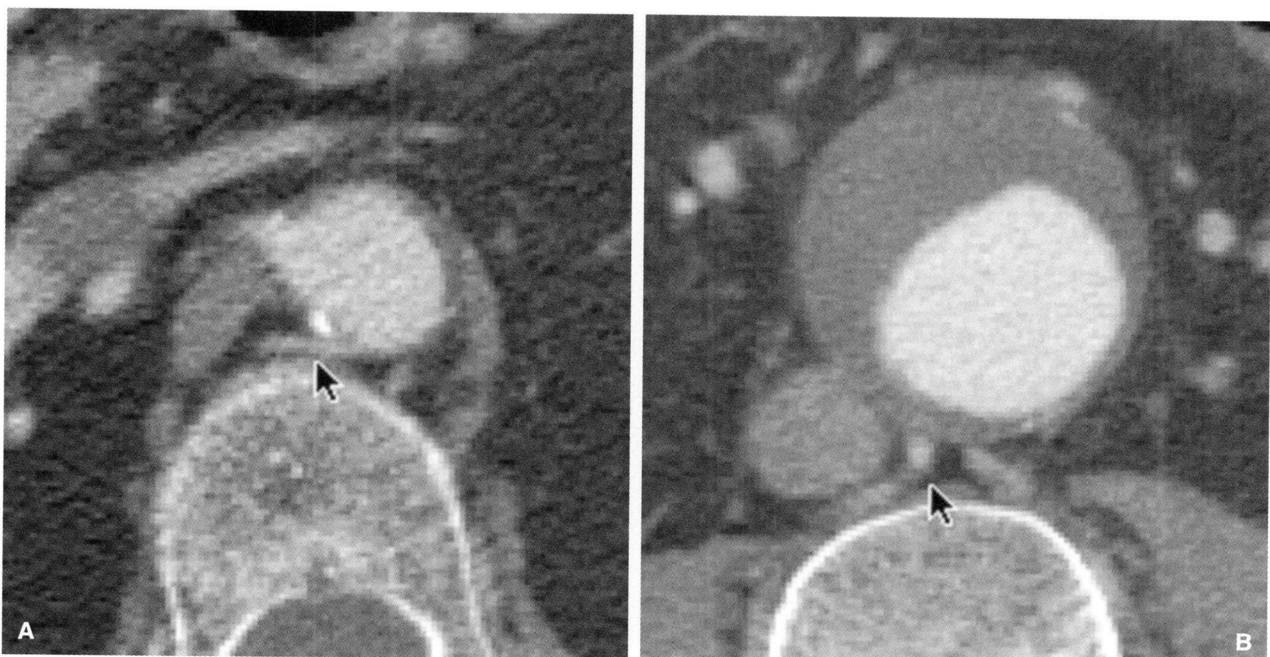

FIGURE 21-15 Clinical example of the effects of collimation for the display of small vessels. **A,** Small lumbar artery is seen easily in a CT slice at a location where the collimation is 3 mm *(arrow)*. The contrast density is similar to the aorta. **B,** This larger lumbar artery *(arrow)* should be more prominent relative to the contrast within the aortic lumen, but at this location the collimation is 7 mm. With 7-mm or thicker collimation, a small lumbar artery or a small accessory renal artery can be missed easily.

a pitch of 1 (e.g., 3 mm/sec table speed and 3-mm collimation), but this limits the distance that can be covered. With the use of 180-degree linear interpolation algorithms instead of the original 360-degree interpolation algorithms, images of relatively good quality still can be obtained with a pitch greater than 1.[15-17] Longitudinal resolution also is improved by 180-degree linear interpolation algorithms. There are tradeoffs. Noise is increased by 180-degree interpolation algorithms and higher pitch ratios. The degradation in image quality is relatively slight. The current upper limit on pitch is 2 (also designated 2:1, e.g., 6 mm/sec table speed and 3-mm collimation).

Ultimately, only so much can be done to maximize the distance covered during a single spiral scan. Many scanners are able to combine multiple "spirals" (i.e., multiple acquisitions) with a short interval to allow patient breathing between scans. This technique can increase the total duration of the scan and the distance covered (e.g., from a single 30-second spiral to three 15-second spirals). Many scanners also permit different parameters for each spiral so that pitch, power, and collimation can be optimized for each spiral. Combining multiple spiral scans is the only way to obtain adequate coverage of the thoracic and the abdominal aorta. It also is useful when coverage is desired from the celiac artery to the femoral arteries (e.g., for evaluation before endovascular AAA repair, in which the access path anatomy is nearly as important as the AAA anatomy). One downside of this technique is that the patient is more likely to move between spirals and may find it difficult to resume breath-hold at the same position for each spiral. Both of these scenarios make *motion artifact* more likely (Fig. 21-16).

Although these types of motion artifact might not affect the quality of axial reformats, they may create obvious discontinuities in multiplanar reformats or 3D reconstructions. For this reason, it is important to plan the transition point between breath-holds so that it will not be in a crucial area (see Fig. 21-13). It is important to educate the patient and obtain his or her cooperation to reduce motion artifact. Most vascular structures are in areas where shallow breathing can be allowed for patients who cannot hold their breath for an entire spiral acquisition. In most vascular patients, the vessels also are quite stiff and move little during a cardiac cycle. The aortic arch of a young patient is a notable exception, however, and motion artifact sometimes can simulate the appearance of a traumatic injury or aortic dissection owing to distortion of the lumen.[18]

Motion artifacts and problems caused by tradeoffs between collimation and pitch may be greatly reduced or eliminated as next-generation scanners become more widely available, using electron beams or multidetector arrays or both to image the volume more quickly.[18] Although electron-beam scanners are extremely rapid, the tissue penetration and images are still not adequate for many applications. Multidetector arrays are already in fairly widespread clinical use, however, with 4- to 16-array models. As briefly outlined earlier, *multidetector* scanners have multiple rows of detectors so that the volume to be scanned can be covered more quickly. The simultaneous acquisition of multiple slices, thinner beam collimation (slices), and faster emitter rotational speed dramatically shorten overall acquisition time, while still allowing higher z-axis resolution. As may be ascertained by the discussion to this point, multidetector

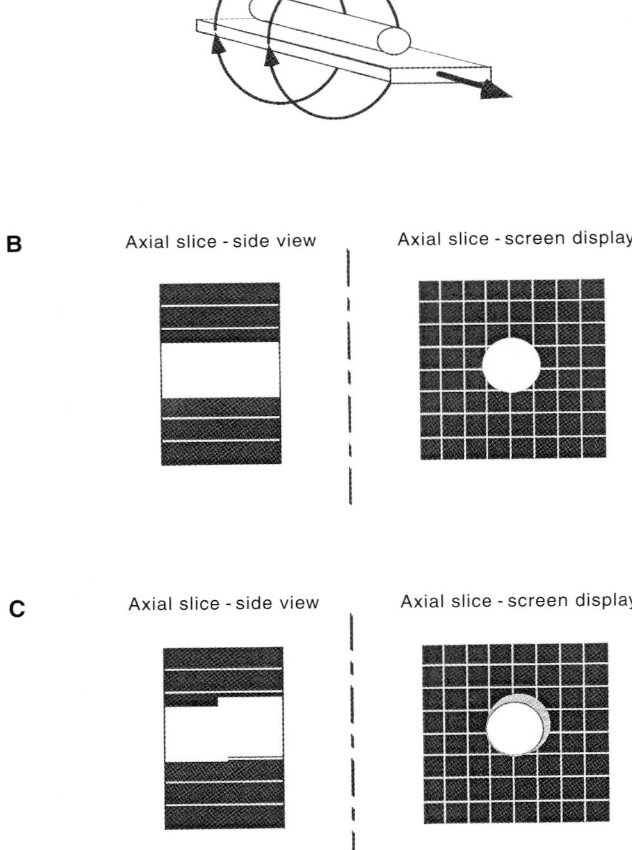

FIGURE 21-16 The decrease in the time needed for a spiral CT scan to cover the volume of interest decreases *motion artifact,* which distorts the object of interest. **B,** Without motion, the structure of interest is depicted clearly. **C,** If motion occurs, overlapping slices are less helpful because the organ, tumor, or vessel of interest has moved from one cross-sectional scan to the next, resulting in a distorted representation of the object. This type of motion can create a distortion of the aorta that can be mistaken for an intimal flap or dissection.

scanners have several advantages. First, they optimize the data acquired during the initial circulation of a contrast injection, possibly reducing contrast load. Second, a greater distance can be covered during a single breath-hold, which is particularly helpful in reducing respiratory motion artifacts and enhancing postprocessing features, such as multiplanar reformats and 3D reconstruction. Finally, the increased speed of acquisition reduces radiation exposure for the patient and results in less CT emitter-tube heating.[19-21] These attributes have greatly enhanced the ability to perform CT evaluation of smaller, more distal vasculature than was previously possible (see the clinical section on extremities).[20,21] Another technique that would diminish motion artifact is electrocardiogram-gated scanning. This technique is starting to be used clinically for MRI, but has had limited use so far for CT because it increases radiation dose significantly in single-detector scanner applications. Gated CT acquisition is likely to be more clinically applicable, however, as 16-array multidetector scanners achieve more widespread use. With 16–detector row scanners, stenoses already can be detected in vessels as small and mobile as coronary arteries with reasonable sensitivity and good specificity.[22]

Other Common Artifacts

Streak artifact or *scatter artifact* arises from interfaces between materials with large differences in density from the surrounding structures. This artifact is commonly seen with dense materials such as prosthetic hips or metallic stents in endografts. Different materials cause varying levels of artifact. Tantalum and gold stents cause significant beam-like artifacts, whereas platinum has almost no influence on the image. Steel lies in the middle of the spectrum. These artifacts can result in the erroneous interpretation of vessel lumen narrowing—sometimes 25% to 50%. Tantalum and gold cause few effects on MRI images. A knowledge of the type of stent helps to determine the preferable imaging modality.[23] Scatter also can occur secondary to dense IV contrast material in the subclavian or brachiocephalic veins because dense contrast material is often infused rapidly into these veins during the scan, and they may be adjacent to air-filled lung parenchyma. This scatter can complicate CT scans for evaluation of aortic arch vessels, so the contrast infusion should come from the arm opposite the vessel of interest or from a lower extremity.

Averaging artifact already has been mentioned with regard to "missing" a small vessel because of surrounding soft tissue, but it can also work in the opposite fashion. In this type of artifact, the large attenuation from a small piece of calcified plaque within a CT slice "averages" with thrombus-density material to produce a display with an intermediate density—similar to intraluminal contrast. This artifact often occurs within aortic aneurysms and should be suspected when contrast-density material appears with no apparent inflow or outflow vessel, and there is a piece of calcium or metal nearby. This type of artifact is reduced by using a small reconstruction interval.

Stair-step artifact occurs when the reconstruction interval on a spiral CT scan is too large, creating a stepped appearance in the vessels. This artifact is most likely to occur in vessels oriented away from the direction of the scan (e.g., renal or iliac arteries). If such an appearance is noted in a multiplanar reformat, it is difficult to evaluate potential occlusive disease. Some of these artifacts are shown in Figure 21-17. As with other artifacts, the frequency of stair-step artifact is markedly diminished with state-of-the-art CT hardware and software.

Field of View

The last important parameter to discuss in relation to image optimization is FOV. As mentioned previously, the size of the display matrix and the FOV have a direct impact on the axial resolution of the display. By keeping the FOV to the minimum necessary, pixel size is decreased. If the FOV is 30 cm and the matrix size is 512 × 512, each pixel in the display of axial slices is 0.6 mm. If the FOV is reduced to 20 cm, pixel size is improved to 0.4 mm. In general, this degree of refinement would not be an important consideration except possibly when detailed

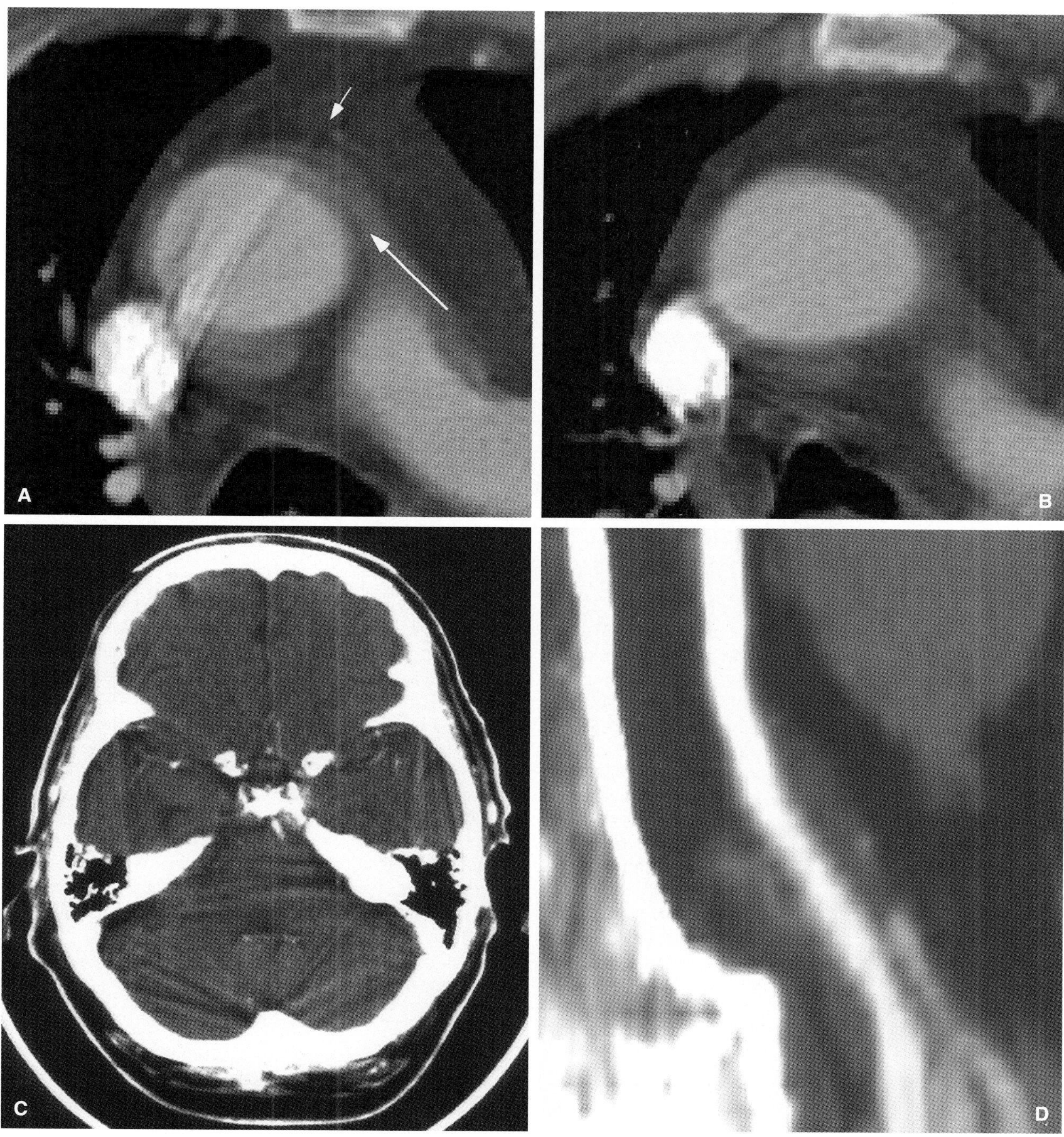

FIGURE 21-17 CT artifacts. **A,** Motion artifact described schematically in Figure 21-16 is shown here in the thoracic aorta creating the impression of an intimal flap or dissection *(longer arrow)*. The position of these artifacts is usually due to aortic motion from the left anterior to the right posterior position. Streak artifact also is seen arising from dense contrast within the superior vena cava. The longer streak is clearly artifact because it extends beyond the vessel wall *(shorter arrow)*, but the shorter streak could be misinterpreted as an intimal flap. One clue is the appearance of an obvious streak artifact in the same vessel. Another clue is the interface between structures with large differences in density. Other clues to the true nature of the aorta come from the benign patient history and the immediately adjacent CT slice. **B,** The apparent pathology (artifacts) shown in **A** is not present in this immediately adjacent CT slice. **C,** Intracranial streak artifact can make it difficult to detect infarcts in locations surrounded by dense bone. Beam- hardening artifact also is common on head CT and occurs when low-energy portions of the x-ray beam are absorbed by thick, dense structures, such as the skull. The residual beam that proceeds through the dense bone has a higher energy and may cause a small area of adjacent tissue to appear less dense (darker) than it should be. This can create an artifact resembling an ischemic infarct immediately adjacent to the skull. **D,** Stair-step artifact creates a stepped appearance in the vessel (see text). This artifact is unique to spiral or helical CT.

measurements are necessary (e.g., in endovascular surgery or calculation of carotid artery stenosis). In general, however, factors such as contrast density, timing of contrast, window level, and window width more strongly affect the ability to distinguish different structures and the edges of those structures (see sections on post hoc image optimization and scan protocols).

Post Hoc Image Optimization

As described earlier, the CT number in Hounsfield units can range from −1000 to +1000 H. For convenience, current workstations typically display the range of CT numbers as a positive integer ranging from 0 to 4096 (using a 12-bit digital computer display, $2^{12} = 4096$ possible shades of gray). Ideally the area of interest would not encompass an extremely wide range of CT numbers because the number of gray-scale values detectable by the human eye is limited to approximately 40 shades of gray.[24] The boundaries between fat (−20 to −100 H) and muscle (40 to 60 H) would be much more difficult to detect if the entire gray-scale display (from white to black) spanned from −1000 H to +1000 H instead of −100 H to +100 H. For an ideal display, the center of the gray-scale display range would be set to the average of the CT numbers in the structure of interest, and the limits of gray-scale representation would be set to the smallest possible range of CT numbers. This can be done post hoc by the CT technician or radiologist. The range of values for gray-scale representation is known as the *window width* for the display, and the center of this range is called the *window level*. The window level and width are adjusted on the CT workstation before hardcopies are printed, but they still can be altered on the workstation as long as the dataset is retained in electronic format. Although this may seem clinically unimportant, adjustment of the window level with visual feedback in real time can be useful in areas with wide variations in contrast density. Clinically, this variation often occurs when trying to determine the true lumen in a calcified vessel or when trying to determine whether there is perigraft flow around or through dense metallic areas of an endovascular stent graft. Review of magnified images on a workstation with a radiologist may help the clinician to see detail that is far beyond the capabilities of the traditional small hardcopy images.

CT Protocols

All of the concepts and considerations mentioned previously are ultimately used to form a scan protocol. Although multidetector scanners are rapidly becoming the standard at large centers, many centers still have single-detector scanners in use. Following is a single-detector CT scan protocol that might be used for a CT scan of the abdomen and pelvis for evaluation of AAA before endovascular repair. This protocol covers the distance from the celiac artery to the distal external iliac arteries, while still maintaining good image quality and contrast. It is modified from the protocol used in the Department of Radiology, Dartmouth-Hitchcock Medical Center, Hanover, New Hampshire.

Scan parameters: 120 kVp, 280 mA (minimum), 1 second
Length of helical exposure: >30 seconds
Pitch: 1:1
Collimation and sequence: First scan with no contrast, 7-mm collimation, 100 mA to localize the celiac artery, then two to three spirals of varying technique depending on the volume covered:
- First spiral: 3 mm—celiac artery to below renal arteries (90 mm distance)
- Second spiral: 7 mm—distal aorta to common femoral or external iliac arteries
- Third spiral: 7 mm—thoracic aorta above celiac artery (optional)

Patient instructions: Coached with hyperventilation. Breath-hold in mid-inspiration; breathe slowly if necessary (with breathing pause mid-scan when using split helix)
Contrast: non-ionic 300 mg/mL
Contrast volume: 140 mL (more may be acceptable)
Route of administration: IV, arm vein
Rate: 2 to 2.5 mL/sec
Scan delay: 25 seconds (or use SmartPrep or similar utility)
Reconstruction algorithm: standard
Reconstruction interval: 1 or 2 mm
FOV: ≥28 cm FOV for entire scan—must ensure inclusion of external iliac or common femoral arteries or both distally

An alternative might be to use a pitch of 2:1 with 3-mm collimation to scan from the celiac artery to the pelvis. If necessary, a second spiral at 5-mm collimation could be added at a pitch of 1.5 to 2 and lower power (e.g., 200 to 220 mA). In each case, the tradeoff is between collimation (beam thickness) and pitch (ratio of table speed to collimation) to cover the distance necessary before the emitter tube overheats. Changes in FOV can affect other parameters as well, but the ability to change this is limited by the structure to be imaged. The FOV also could be reduced to 22 cm, but likely would need to increase to 28 cm on the distal (second) spiral to ensure inclusion of both external iliac arteries. For comparison, following is a protocol for a multidetector scanner (for four rows or arrays):

Scan parameters: 120 KVp, 320 mA, auto mA
Length of helical exposure: 20 to 25 seconds
Pitch: 6
Speed: 15
Collimation and sequence: First perform anteroposterior and lateral scout views. Scan 2.5-mm images from the dome of the diaphragm through the symphysis pubis
Patient instructions: Breath-hold
Contrast: non-ionic 350 mg/mL
Contrast volume: 140 mL (more or less may be acceptable)
Route of administration: IV, arm vein
Rate: 3 to 5 mL/sec
Scan delay: use SmartPrep or similar utility
Reconstruction algorithm: standard
Reconstruction interval: 2 mm
FOV: ensure inclusion of both common femoral arteries distally

The multidetector scanner covers the same distance (or volume) in less time despite a narrower collimation. Recalling the basic principles already outlined, this results in better ability to discriminate small structures, shorter breath-hold for the patient, less motion artifact, and higher quality multiplanar reformats and 3D reconstructions.

Contrast Material

Notably, the rapid infusion of contrast material and the large distances covered for CTA generally requires a significant infusion of contrast material. A typical CTA study from the celiac artery to the external iliac arteries may require 120 to 180 mL of 60% ionic or 300 mg/mL non-ionic contrast,[9] which is similar to the dose of contrast material for an aortogram with runoff. Although the risk of renal damage may be less than for direct aortic injection of full-strength contrast material through a catheter positioned adjacent to the renal arteries, it is nonetheless a limitation for patients with significant renal impairment. For patients with a creatinine level that is twice normal, the protocol can be performed in a well-hydrated patient with lower doses of low-osmolar contrast, and less clarity can be accepted in the iliac arteries (where adjunctive duplex ultrasound can be used if necessary). Diabetes and preexisting renal disease are clear risk factors for contrast-induced renal dysfunction. If the creatinine is 2.5 to 3 times normal, a "screening" CT scan can be performed without contrast, or MR angiography (MRA) with gadolinium contrast is used. We have performed CT with gadolinium, but gadolinium is expensive, and the enhancement is notably less than with iodinated contrast material. In selected cases, however, gadolinium can provide acceptable imaging if the goal is simply to differentiate the lumen from thrombus (which is frequently all that is necessary). In some cases, MRA cannot be used (e.g., if the patient is claustrophobic or has an implanted device). The distance covered also is limited with current magnetic resonance technology, and resolution is approximately half that of CT, but good delineation of anatomy and useful 3D reconstructions usually can be obtained. Patients on dialysis can have contrast-enhanced CT if it is timed with dialysis to prevent problems from the volume load. For patients with chronic renal insufficiency (creatinine >2.4 mg/dL), the use of *N*-acetyl cysteine before and after the procedure has been shown to prevent the reduction in postprocedure renal function secondary to the iodinated contrast material.[25] It is proposed that the antioxidant effect of *N*-acetyl cysteine counters the toxic effect of the contrast material on the nephrons. Because of the almost nonexistent side effects of this protocol and the potential benefits for patients, we routinely use this protocol in patients "at risk" before contrast-enhanced CT or conventional angiography.

The other limitation for iodinated contrast material is allergic reactions, but true allergic reactions to contrast material are extremely rare. Severe reactions (hypotension, dyspnea, loss of consciousness) occur at a rate of approximately 0.22% with ionic contrast material and 0.04% with non-ionic contrast material.[26] Reactions requiring hospitalization or the care of an anesthesiologist are even less frequent (0.04% with ionic contrast and 0.004% with non-ionic contrast). Patients with allergies to other substances or asthma are approximately twice as likely to have a contrast reaction, and patients with a previous contrast reaction have roughly five times the average risk. Clinical judgment is required, but in most cases of suspected allergy, pretreatment with antihistamines and corticosteroids can reduce the incidence of reactions significantly, even if non-ionic contrast material is used.[27] Although the dosing recommendation varies, currently published guidelines recommend methylprednisolone (or equivalent), 32 mg orally 12 and 2 hours before contrast administration.[28] Using these techniques, most patients can undergo a contrast-enhanced CT scan safely.

■ CLINICAL APPLICATIONS

The role of CT in the evaluation and treatment of vascular disease has changed dramatically since the 1990s. The advent of improved computer software and hardware for CT scanners has led to CTA and capture of vascular contrast with adequate resolution for evaluating occlusive disease. Sophisticated postprocessing computer modeling software allows a more accurate depiction of the 3D vascular anatomy, relationships of intra-abdominal structures, and simulation of endovascular interventions.[3,4,29-31] All of these changes are revolutionizing the noninvasive evaluation of patients with vascular disease. Anomalies and complicated anatomy that previously were difficult to trace on the axial slices of a CT scan, such as aneurysms, aortoiliac occlusive disease, and renal or visceral artery stenosis, now can be visualized with clarity and understanding. To display and discuss clinical applications, it is probably best to cover them in anatomic "compartments," at least to a degree.

Head and Neck

Intracranial Hemorrhage Versus Infarction

The first clinical application of CT was for the evaluation of intracranial structures, and CT continues to have an important role in this area. Differentiation of cerebral infarction from intracranial hemorrhage has important diagnostic and therapeutic implications for patients presenting with acute neurologic symptoms. In the treatment of an acute stroke, most therapeutic agents require administration as quickly as possible, making rapid diagnosis crucial. Thrombolytic therapy must be administered within 3 hours to achieve a favorable balance between decreased rates of infarction versus increased intracranial hemorrhage.[32] Acute intracranial hemorrhage is a contraindication to thrombolytic therapy, however, and must be ruled out before initiating therapy. It also is important to rule out intracranial hemorrhage when a neurologic deficit occurs after carotid endarterectomy.

CT has a diagnostic accuracy of approximately 90% in the evaluation of acute intracranial hemorrhage, whereas the changes associated with intracranial hemorrhage on MRI take several days to develop.[33,34] Conversely, CT changes associated with acute ischemic infarction may take several days to develop, and only larger infarcts are apparent within the first 24 hours. The relative sensitivity for infarction within the first 24 hours after the clinical event is approximately 50% for CT and 80% for MRI.[35] MRI also seems to be more sensitive to late changes associated with infarction and hemorrhage[34-36] and less affected by bone-related artifacts when evaluating lesions in the brainstem or cerebellum. For acute presentations, CT remains a more rapid and less expensive diagnostic test that is applicable in most clinical situations. Acute hemorrhage is determined on a CT scan *without* IV contrast and should not be confused with "luxury perfusion" around an infarct or contrast enhancement of a tumor (Fig. 21-18). Acute intracranial hemorrhage is detected on CT without IV contrast because the intact red blood cells initially have a high protein content, are more dense than the surrounding structures, and produce a high-density lesion (see Fig. 21-18). In later stages after the acute hemorrhage, the red blood cells lyse and lose hemoglobin, and the area becomes isodense with the surrounding tissue on CT (MRI is more useful at this point).

Intracranial and Extracranial Vasculature

Although MRA has been more popular for imaging intracranial vasculature, the advent of spiral CT with CTA and 3D reconstruction has made it possible to obtain useful images of intracranial and extracranial vessels as well.[9] Imaging of the intracranial circulation with CT is made more difficult by contrast timing and interference from dense bone in some areas, but with some effort, useful images can be produced. Spiral CT is extremely accurate in detecting cerebral aneurysms greater than 3 mm in size[37,38] and can be useful in following intracranial dissections.[39] For extracranial vessels, excellent CT scans can be obtained without exceptional difficulty. CT scanning for extracranial vessels is easier than for intracranial vessels because

1. The carotid arteries are not contained within dense bone structures.
2. Contrast timing for scans from the upper thorax to the skull base is not too difficult.
3. The FOV is small.
4. The vessels are oriented perpendicular to the axial plane.

MRA has been relatively popular for the evaluation of extracranial cerebrovascular occlusive disease, but it tends to overestimate the severity of stenoses to some degree.[40] CT for evaluation of carotid occlusive disease has not been studied as extensively, but in 1982, Riles and coworkers[41] showed that spiral CT could be *more* accurate than angiography for carotid occlusions. More recently, it has been shown that spiral CT has a high degree of accuracy in determining the degree of carotid stenosis,[42] and this accuracy may be enhanced using CT reformats perpendicular to the vessel lumen.[43] In addition to providing a familiar display, 3D reconstruction portrays more than just the vessel lumen, making it easy to assess rapidly the extent of disease at the carotid bifurcation (Fig. 21-19). Despite the utility of the images, 3D reconstructions should be used to enhance, not replace, evaluation and measurements from the source (CT) images.[44]

Most surgeons use the carotid duplex as the sole preoperative imaging modality before performing a carotid endarterectomy. The duplex results depend, however, on the skill of the technician and the patient's anatomy. Ultrasonography can fail to provide accurate results in the presence of a high carotid bifurcation, a short neck, abundant calcifications, or a tortuous course of the internal carotid artery. It is routinely difficult for ultrasonography to interrogate intrathoracic lesions that may alter the carotid flow characteristics. These situations impede the ability of the ultrasonographer to obtain accurate velocity measurements, making determination of the degree of stenosis difficult. Spiral CT offers an operator-independent modality to visualize this difficult anatomy. Current spiral CT techniques provide excellent correlation with ultrasound findings and the degree of stenosis.[45] At the cost of a contrast injection for the patient, CT can be used in a complementary fashion to ultrasonography in atypical clinical situations. This complementary study may directly guide surgical planning and approach. The relationship of the carotid bifurcation to bone structures (e.g., the cervical vertebrae) can reveal preoperatively potential difficulties with surgical exposure (Fig. 21-20).[46,47]

Proximal Lesions (Arch Vessel Disease)

Although angiography remains the "gold standard" for evaluating intracranial and aortic arch occlusive disease, improvement in CT (and MRI) is leading to strategies that provide a more thorough vascular evaluation than duplex ultrasound without the morbidity or cost of angiography.[48] As a result of improvements in noninvasive imaging modalities and a stroke risk of 0.6% to 1.2% with angiography,[49,50] the role of diagnostic angiography before carotid endarterectomy is becoming limited.[5] Figure 21-21 compares arteriography, MRI, and CT with 3D reconstruction for an innominate artery lesion and shows some of the potential benefits of CT for arch lesions. This case also illustrates the problem of detecting calcified lesions on MRI and MRA. Nonetheless, caution should be used when evaluating arch lesions on CT because of the potential for motion artifact from aortic pulsation and streak artifact from concentrated contrast infusion in veins immediately adjacent to suspected occlusive disease. Some of these problems can be avoided by using lower concentrations of contrast material and infusions into the upper extremity opposite from the suspected arterial lesion. Infusion of contrast material into a lower extremity vein can be used if necessary, but is less appealing.

Thorax

Aortic Arch and Thoracic Outlet

Clinical applications for CT of the thorax include every major vessel in the chest. Imaging of the aortic arch vessels can be useful for the evaluation of occlusive disease, as shown in Figure 21-21; CT also can show important arch anomalies. The utility of these images continues to improve with refinement of scanning protocols for these vessels. We have found that CT can show relatively subtle lesions, such as arteritis of the subclavian arteries, if caution is used to avoid artifact from IV infusions of contrast material. Because the subclavian arteries generally travel perpendicular to the direction of table movement, spiral CT is needed to evaluate these lesions using multiplanar reformats or 3D reconstructions. CT protocols for evaluation of the thoracic outlet have shown the arterial and venous deformation that occurs with upper extremity abduction, and this may become a useful study for patients with suspected thoracic outlet syndrome (Fig. 21-22).[51]

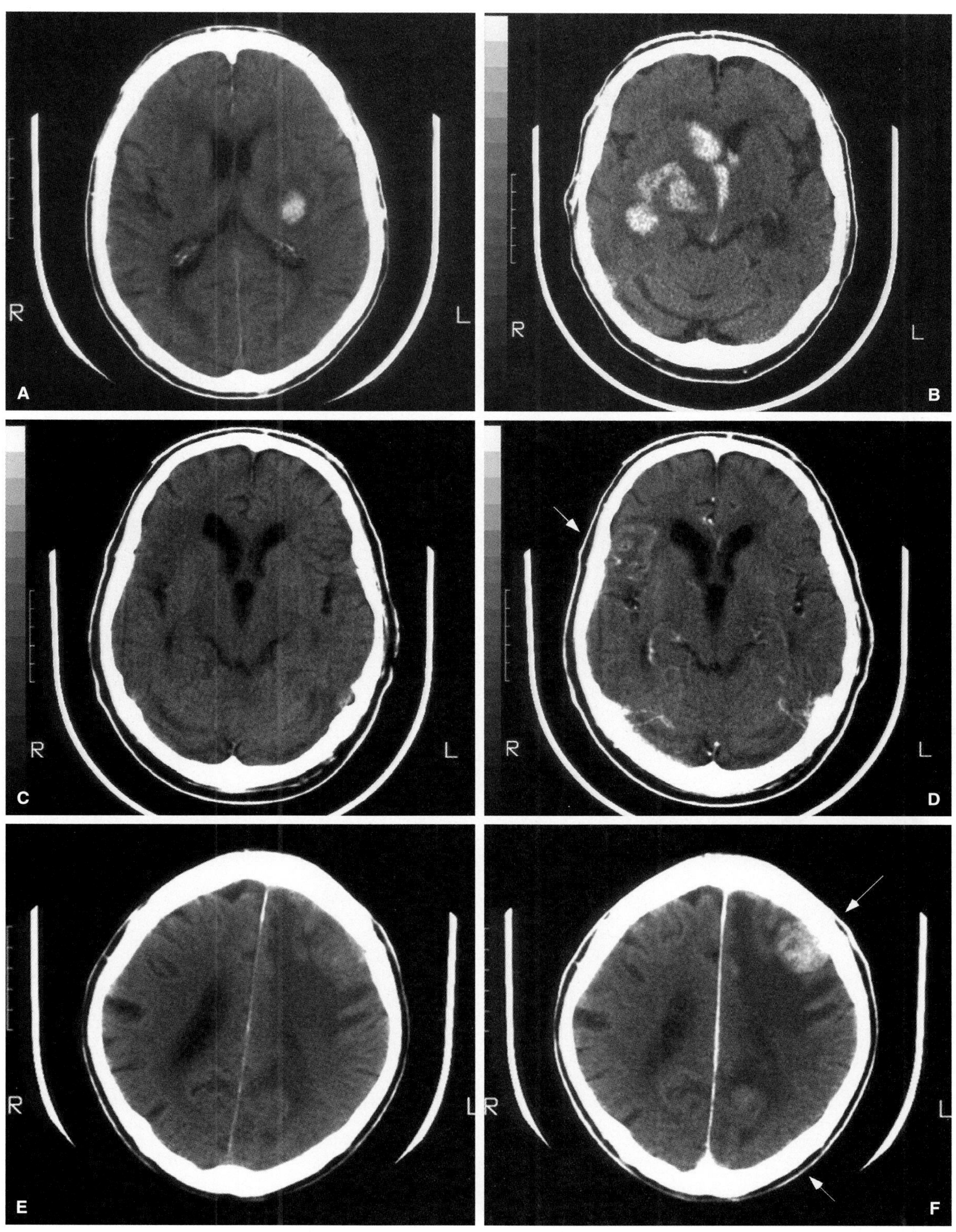

FIGURE 21-18 Demonstration of lesions on head CT that can be misinterpreted without expert help. **A,** Head CT without IV contrast shows hemorrhage in a patient with severe hypertension. **B,** A much larger intracranial hemorrhage with a midline shift and blood in the ventricle on a CT scan, again without IV contrast. A CT scan without IV contrast is the imaging modality of choice when acute hemorrhage is suspected. **C,** Right middle cerebral artery distribution ischemic infarct on a head CT scan with no IV contrast. The lesion is relatively subtle. **D,** The same infarct shown in **C,** but this time IV contrast was used. This contrast enhancement is characteristic of an ischemic infarction and is classically gyriform. It is generally thought to be due to breakdown of capillary barriers with leakage of contrast material or due to "luxury perfusion" around the infarct itself. This finding is usually absent 3 to 6 months postinfarction. **E,** Another hypodense lesion on a non–contrast-enhanced CT. This is not an ischemic infarction, but rather edema from a tumor. **F,** IV contrast enhancement of the tumor *(longer arrow)* helps show the large amount of edema characteristic of an intracranial neoplasm. The shorter arrow points to another lesion in this patient with metastatic lung cancer. It is less dense in this CT slice because it is smaller and not in the center of the slice (it is well seen in an adjacent slice).

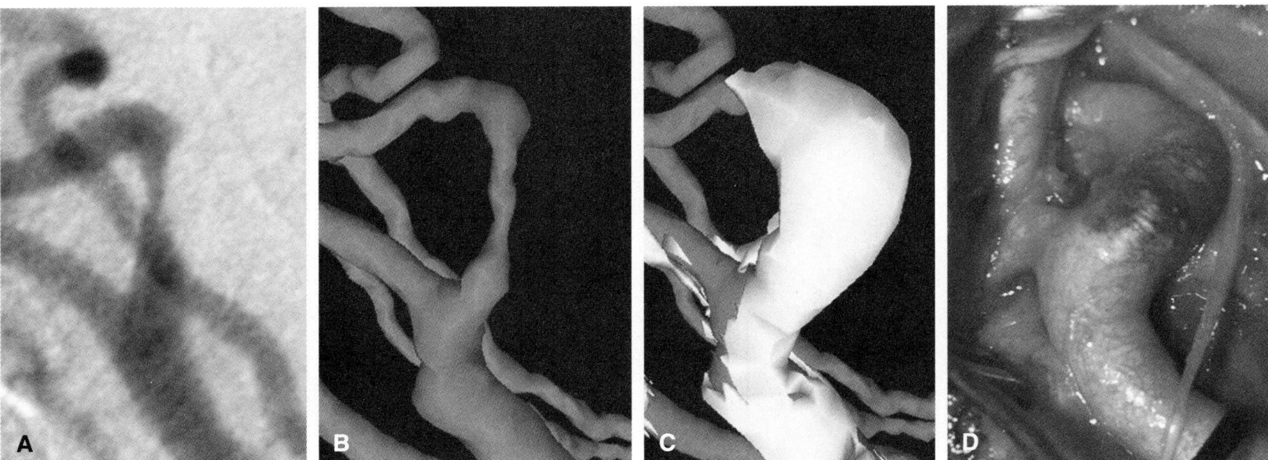

FIGURE 21-19 Demonstration of carotid artery disease. **A,** Angiogram of an internal carotid artery stenosis. **B,** 3D reconstruction of blood flow (red) in the same location. **C,** 3D reconstruction of blood flow and plaque/thrombus (yellow). **D,** Intraoperative photograph of the same location. There is a striking similarity despite rotation of the head and neck in the operative photograph. (See Color Figure in this section.)

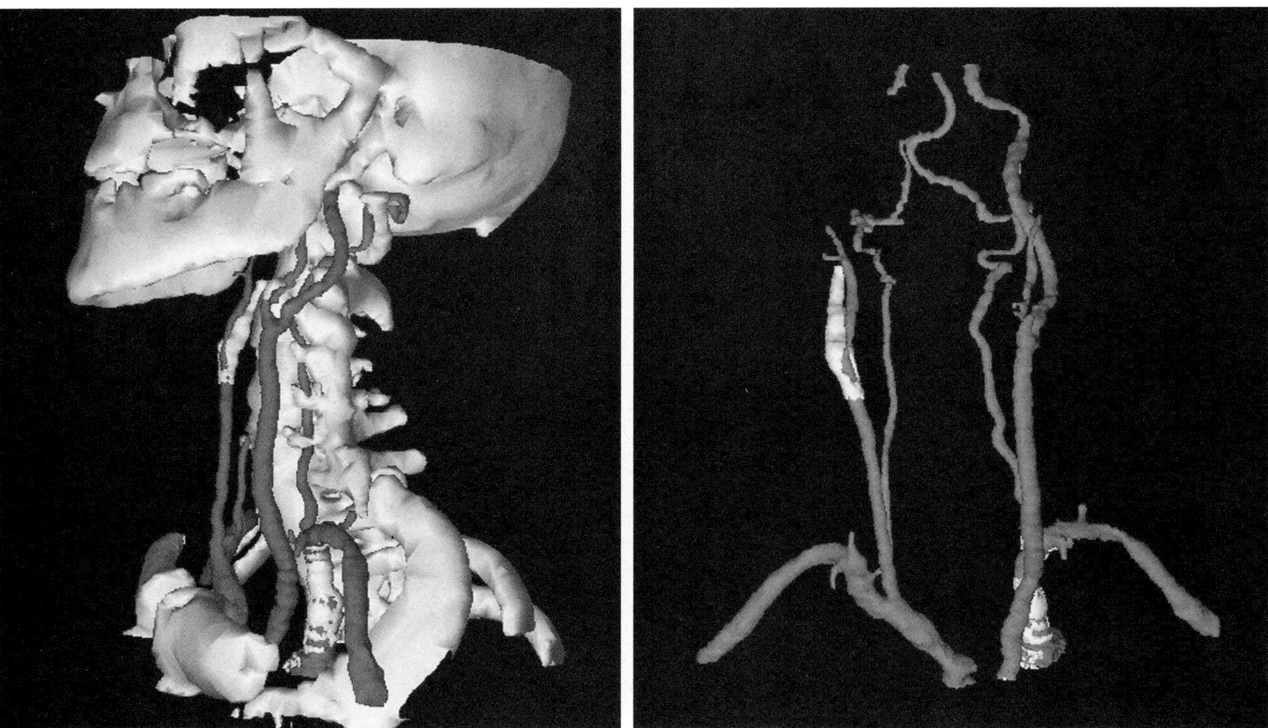

FIGURE 21-20 Multiple-object 3D reconstruction can show the relationship of the extracranial vessels and the bony structures as an aid to surgical planning. Although previously tedious and difficult, such images now are much easier to create with commercially available postprocessing software. (See Color Figure in this section.)

Aortic Dissections

With the advent of fast scanners and spiral techniques, CT has become the study of choice in most cases of thoracic dissection.[52-54] The sensitivity and specificity of spiral CT for dissection of the thoracic aorta seems to be equal to or better than transesophageal echocardiography and MRA, and it is superior for diagnosing dissection of the arch vessels.[53] With proper timing of the contrast bolus, the true and false lumina are opacified and can be seen to spiral down along the thoracic aorta (Fig. 21-23). Curvilinear artifacts simulating an aortic dissection most commonly occur in the ascending aorta (35% of cases have some artifact in this location). These artifacts usually can be distinguished from genuine pathology (see Fig. 21-17). With CT, the false lumen can be visualized even if it is thrombosed, with evidence provided by a spiraling crescent of thrombus density within the aorta. Other evidence of thoracic dissection includes displacement of calcium with

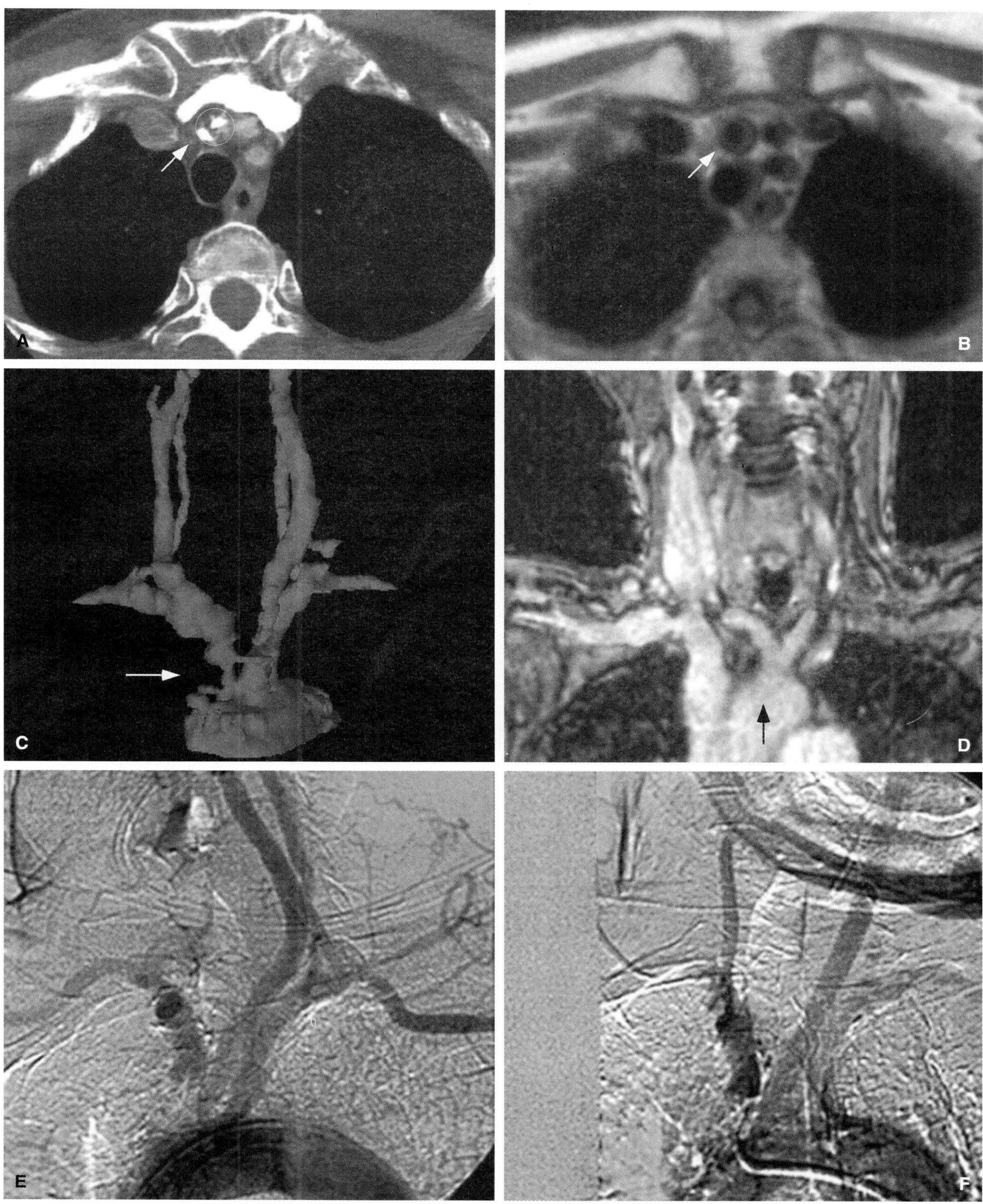

FIGURE 21-21 Comparison of CT, MRI, CT with 3D reconstruction, and arteriography for an innominate artery lesion. **A,** Axial CT scan shows two areas of dense calcification within the innominate artery *(arrow and thin circle)*. The contrast-enhanced lumen at this location is extremely small. **B,** Axial MRI at the same location illustrates the problem of detecting the calcified lesions at the same location on MRI *(arrow)*. Note the density of surrounding bony structures. **C,** Multiple-object 3D reconstruction with all objects invisible except contrast-enhanced blood flow. The innominate artery stenosis is shown. The irregularity of the adjacent arch is mostly due to defects from plaque that were made invisible on the computer-generated display. **D,** The resolution and location of the plane of reconstruction on gadolinium-enhanced MRA results in a less accurate depiction of the anatomy. **E** and **F,** Arch aortogram shows the innominate lesion, with such slow flow that the carotid bifurcation could not be visualized well despite selective injection **(F)**. The carotid bifurcation is better visualized in **C** and was relatively free of disease, as depicted on the 3D reconstruction.

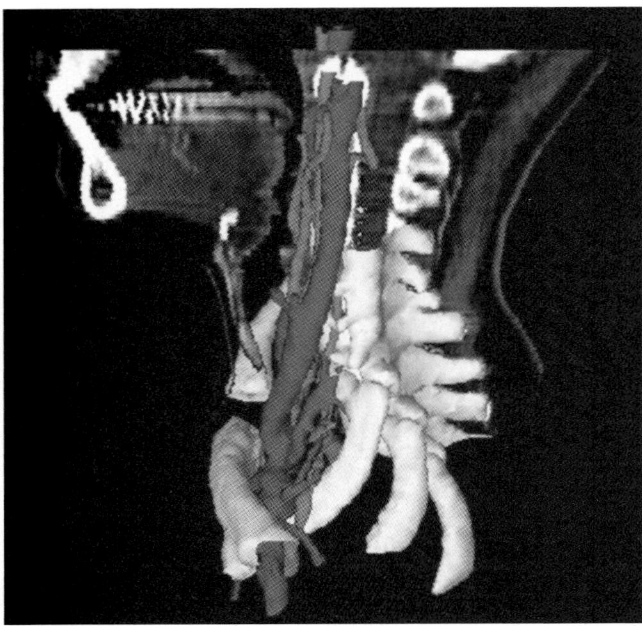

FIGURE 21-22 3D reconstruction of the bony and vascular structures of the thoracic outlet. (See Color Figure in this section.)

the vessel wall, aneurysm, atelectasis, and hemothorax. Because MRI has difficulty with depiction of calcifications or thrombus density material, it does not show aortic dissection well if one lumen is thrombosed.

Traumatic Aortic Injury

Traumatic aortic injury from blunt or penetrating sources is difficult to diagnose on the basis of clinical examination alone. The latest generation of high-speed spiral CT scanners can perform a total-body, contrast-enhanced protocol trauma scan in less time than it used to take to obtain a single segmental scan. CTA with single-detector and multidetector scanners is being used to diagnose aortic and great vessel injuries accurately. As the technology advances, the diagnostic accuracy of CT continues to improve, and large series have shown diagnostic accuracy of 75% to 99% for CT in traumatic aortic injury.[55-57] Most centers use CT as the first imaging modality to rule out aortic injury in patients with a low-probability, but concerning mechanism of injury.[58] It is the primary study of choice for pediatric patients because of vessel size and time considerations.[59] In many cases, the CT evidence is definitive enough to operate without aortography, but many centers still require aortography to rule out traumatic aortic injury requiring intervention.[57] The high resolution of current CT scans even allows the cavitating trajectory of a thoracic projectile to be tracked, facilitating a determination of the projectile's proximity to the aorta and great vessels and the potential for injury. If the potential for injury is high, but the CT scan is not illustrative, the patient can undergo formal aortography in an effort to better delineate the anatomy (Fig. 21-24).[60] With better CT technology and the trend toward endovascular repair of traumatic injuries, however, CTA is becoming the standard for evaluation and decision making in traumatic aortic injury.[61-63]

Thoracic Aneurysms

Traditionally, thoracic aneurysms have been evaluated by a combination of CT and angiography, but advances in CT technology are beginning to change this area as well. Depiction of the aneurysm as a 3D reconstruction can make interpretation of the extent of aneurysm more rapid and accurate.[12,13,52,64] With the advent of spiral CT and protocols using thin slices, we have also been able to identify the number and location of patent intercostal arteries. This information can be useful when planning the cross-clamp location and the potential for reimplantation of intercostal arteries (Fig. 21-25). CT with 3D reconstruction has transformed the evaluation for endovascular repair of AAA and is equally applicable to endovascular repair of thoracic injuries, dissections, and aneurysms (see later).

Pulmonary Vessels

The diagnosis of pulmonary embolus is a promising new CT application that is made possible by the dynamic contrast bolus and rapid acquisition of volume data provided in spiral CT. It has been shown that spiral CT can detect pulmonary emboli even in patients without clinically suspected disease.[65] It also may be more accurate and more specific than ventilation-perfusion scans.[66,67] As a result of promising results at several centers, spiral CT may become the primary noninvasive imaging study for pulmonary embolus. Currently, however, its true sensitivity and specificity are still undetermined. It is hoped that the results of the PIOPED (Pulmonary Embolism Diagnosis) II study will help determine the extent to which CT may be used in the diagnosis and workup of patients with suspected pulmonary embolisms.[68] In the interim, many centers have made this their standard approach, however, owing to speed, noninvasiveness, the fact that in 70% of cases an alternative etiology of respiratory problems is uncovered (20% to 30% of patients actually have pulmonary embolism), and accuracy on the order of 90% with multidetector scanners.[69-71] A workstation-based search, "scrolling" through the dataset in cinematic fashion, improves the pulmonary embolus detection rate over traditional hardcopy review (which should be abandoned), and preliminary studies indicate multidetector scanners have better accuracy.[65] The role of 3D reconstruction in pulmonary applications remains to be determined, but it seems to be helpful in the treatment of pulmonary arteriovenous malformations, understanding the postoperative reorientation of the pulmonary vessels, surgical planning regarding pulmonary tumors, and the diagnosis of marginated thromboembolic disease.[72] An example of a pulmonary embolus on spiral CT cross-sectional imaging is shown in Figure 21-26, showing why this noninvasive method has almost eliminated conventional angiography for pulmonary embolus evaluation in many centers.

Abdomen and Pelvis

One of the most important roles for CT in vascular surgery is the evaluation of AAA before repair. A thorough knowledge of the anatomic aspects of the aneurysm and the surrounding structures is necessary to ensure the correct

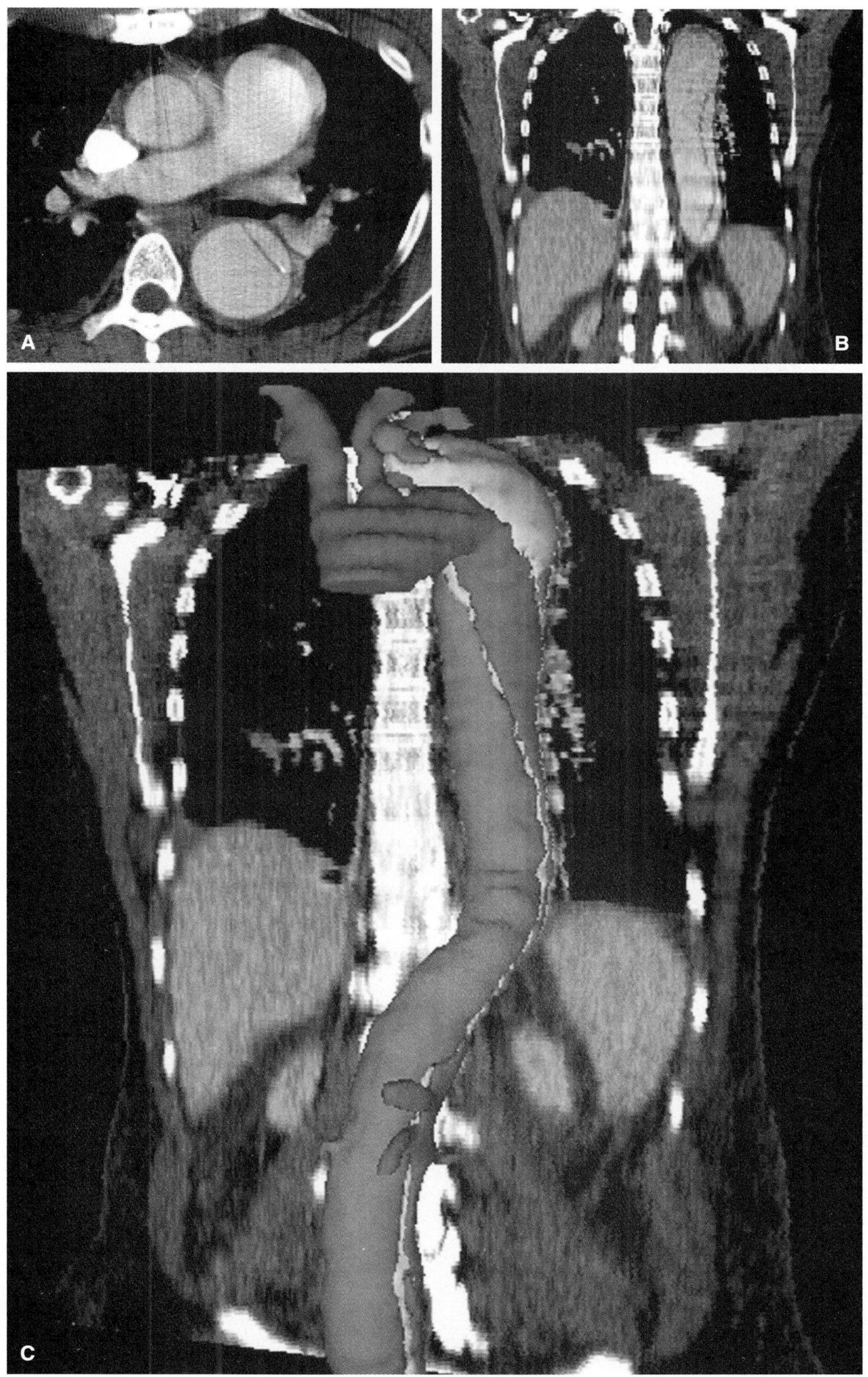

FIGURE 21-23 Dissection of the thoracic aorta. **A,** Axial CT scan shows dissection within the descending thoracic aorta. Compare this picture with the artifacts in Figure 21-17. CT artifacts can create the impression of a dissection, but these usually can be distinguished from genuine pathology. **B,** Coronal reformat shows the dissection in a consistent manner over a long segment of aorta. **C,** 3D reconstruction depicts the blood from the true lumen supplying the celiac artery, superior mesenteric artery, and left renal artery (red); blood from the false lumen involving the left subclavian artery and supplying the right renal artery (magenta); and thrombus (yellow). This shows how a 3D reconstruction can convey a large amount of information rapidly. A coronal CT slice has been placed within the model at the appropriate location to lend context.

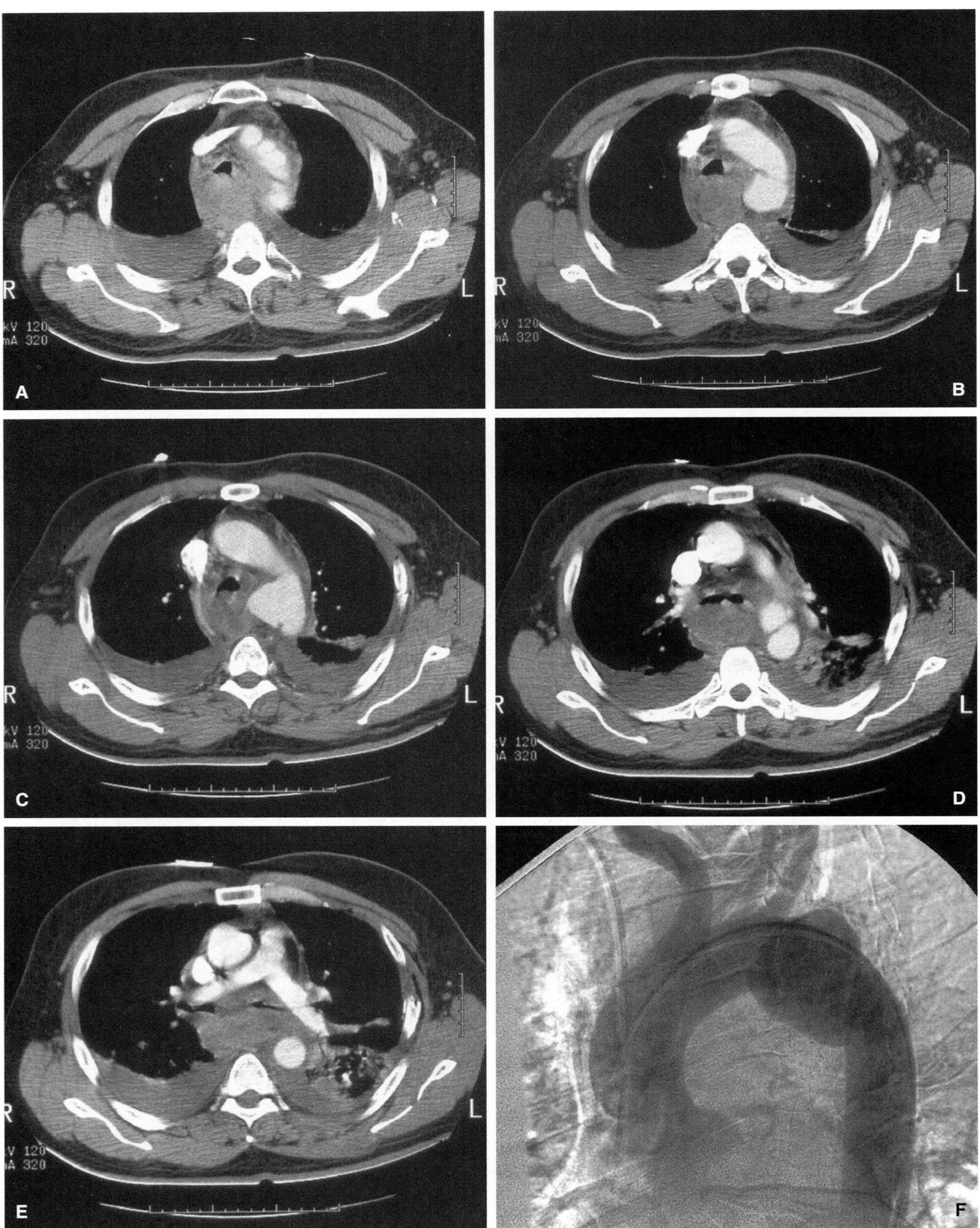

FIGURE 21-24 Traumatic aortic injury. **A,** Dissection beginning at the level of the left subclavian artery. **B-D,** Continuation of the dissection or transection and apparently abnormal dilatation of the aorta (especially inferomedially). **E,** The more distal descending aorta appears relatively normal, although the associated atelectasis, effusion, and mediastinal hematoma are still present. **F,** Aortogram shows the aneurysmal portion of the injury.

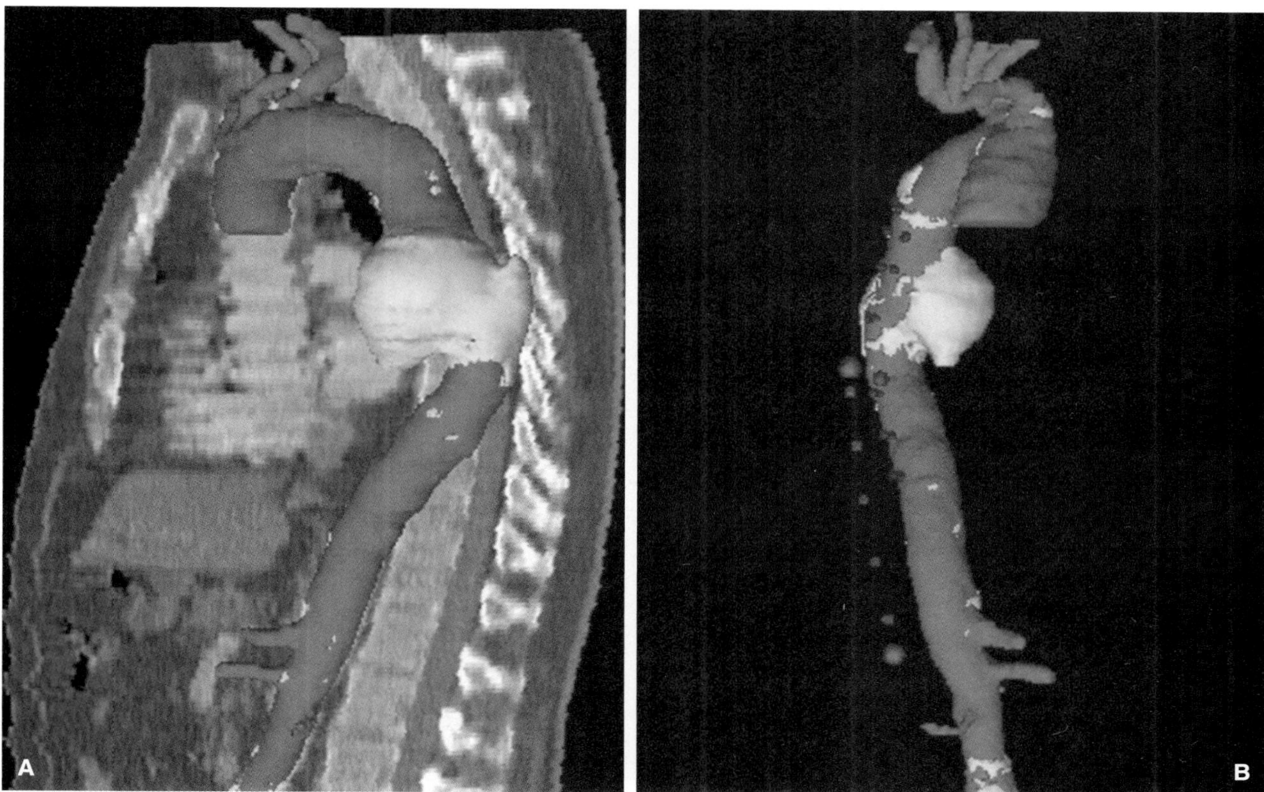

FIGURE 21-25 **A,** Aneurysm of the thoracic aorta shown using 3D reconstruction with simultaneous display of a sagittal CT slice to lend context. Motion artifact is much greater around the heart and proximal ascending aorta. The focal blebs displayed in the model were verified at the time of surgery. **B,** Intercostal arteries are marked on the CT slices and are displayed on the 3D model using interactive software (blue marks). The red marks were placed to denote the top of the 8th thoracic vertebra (T8) and the bottom of the 12th thoracic vertebra. The large intercostal artery near the top of T8 was identified and preserved at the time of operation. (See Color Figure in this section.)

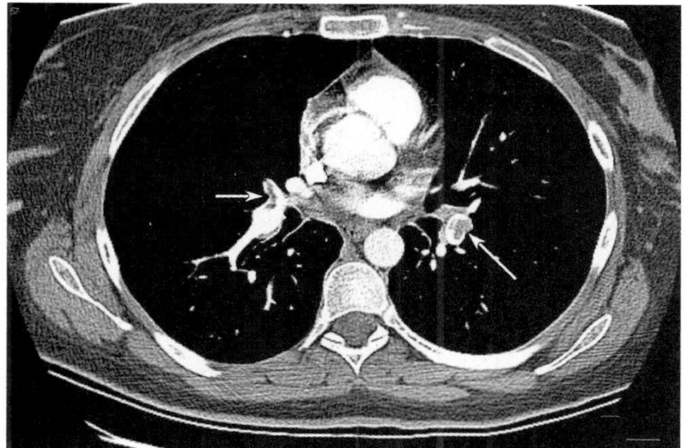

FIGURE 21-26 Pulmonary embolus as seen with spiral CT cross-sectional imaging (*arrow*). 3D reconstruction of the pulmonary arteries is not needed for routine pulmonary embolus studies.

selection and performance of a repair. Even "minor" anatomic features, such as venous anomalies, patency of the inferior mesenteric artery, number and location of patent lumbar arteries, and degree of calcified or noncalcified plaque at the sites of intended anastomoses, can alter the operative plan or the risk-to-benefit ratio of the procedure. Although most of these anatomic features can be dealt with at the time of a traditional open AAA repair, the advent of endovascular repairs has made these preoperative considerations essential to the success of the repair. The current technologic state of 3D CT reconstructions has created a new gold standard for preoperative planning.[3,4,14,31,73,74] Appropriate evaluation of an aneurysm for potential repair includes the following:

1. The extent and nature of the aneurysm
2. Involvement of the iliac arteries
3. Pathology or aberrancy of the renal or visceral vessels
4. Evaluation of other abdominal or pelvic pathology indicative of vascular issues
5. Precise measurement, planning, and simulation of deployed devices for endovascular repairs
6. Ensuring an accurate and reproducible means of follow-up

Extent and Nature of Abdominal Aortic Aneurysm

Perhaps the most important morphologic consideration for repair of an AAA is the proximal and distal extent of disease. Evaluating the extent of an aneurysm is difficult with angiography owing to the potential for a thrombus-filled lumen. MRA display of thrombus continues to improve, but calcified plaque is still not visualized on MRA, with the possible exception of cutting-edge research facilities. CT avoids both of these problems (Fig. 21-27). It is apparent from Figure 21-27 that an angiogram of the contrast-filled lumen does not reveal the aneurysmal nature of the aorta at the level of the renal arteries because much of the aneurysm is occupied by thrombus. CT generally is recognized as the best imaging modality for ascertaining the proximal and distal extent of an aortic aneurysm and identifying issues, such as calcification, that may affect clamping or sewing the aorta. This is especially true in terms of spiral CT and perspectives via multiplanar reformats and 3D reconstructions (see Fig. 21-27).[12,13]

In our center, patients with AAA are evaluated with spiral CT, including MPR and 3D reconstruction. Although less common than in the past, some patients with suprarenal or thoracoabdominal aneurysms are referred with conventional CT and angiograms or have adjunctive arteriography. In patients with suprarenal aneurysms especially, conventional CT and angiography often fail to predict the true extent of the aneurysm or the optimal cross-clamp location. In our experience, however, preoperative spiral CT with 3D reconstruction has revealed the correct proximal and distal extent of the aneurysm compared with operative findings. Spiral CT with 3D reconstruction also seems to be superior to spiral CT alone, and this does not seem to be a finding unique to our center.[12,13,64] It has been suggested that CT sometimes overestimates the extent of aneurysmal disease, but in our experience, this has not been the case. Even in unique situations, such as with inflammatory aneurysms or poor contrast administration, in which an overestimation or underestimation of aneurysm size may occur, comparison of the 3D reconstructions with the CT axial and reformatted images has ensured that the segmentation used in the 3D reconstruction is portrayed correctly.

Iliac Artery Aneurysm Extent and Pathology

Determining the extent of an aneurysm includes evaluation of potential iliac artery aneurysms, either as an extension of an aortic aneurysm or as isolated disease. In many cases, conventional CT has been poor in this regard, and even relatively modern series have reported error rates of 16% for detecting iliac aneurysms.[75] More recent series using spiral CT with MPR alone have noted accuracy of greater than 90%, however, for the detection of iliac aneurysms.[10] In our series of AAA evaluated by spiral CT with thin collimation, MPR, and 3D reconstruction, we have not missed an iliac artery aneurysm as confirmed during open repair over many years. We also have found this technique to be highly valuable in determining the extent of aneurysm disease for endovascular repair.[74]

The ability of the modern spiral CT scan to provide higher resolution and intricate detail is a key factor in the evaluation of iliac occlusive disease. Numerous thin axial slices make it more likely that a stenosis will be seen clearly on axial slices alone and improve the quality of multiplanar reformats and 3D reconstructions. With appropriate scan protocols and adequate timing of the vascular contrast bolus, evaluation of iliac occlusive disease with spiral CT is far superior to conventional CT and rivals angiography.[10,11] In our institution, spiral CT with MPR and 3D reconstruction is more accurate than spiral CT with axial slices alone or even angiography for evaluation of iliac artery occlusive disease.[4] The accuracy of angiography is enhanced when multiple views are available, but even so, a multiple-object 3D reconstruction can reveal details about plaque and relative stenosis with viewpoints from any desired angle. Compare the occlusive disease shown on an angiogram (Fig. 21-28) with the multiple-object 3D reconstruction from a CT scan of the same patient (see Figs. 21-10 and 21-11). The principal advantage of angiography for iliac artery occlusive disease is the capability to perform a "pull-back pressure," measure enhanced gradients, and perform therapeutic maneuvers that are impossible with the less invasive CT study. Generally, these maneuvers are to be avoided before endovascular repair because any stent may interfere with device deployment (and should be placed after delivery systems are withdrawn). In some cases, therapeutic maneuvers are helpful before open repair, however.

Nature of the Aneurysm Wall

Occasionally, it is important to detect the pathology of an aneurysm in addition to its extent. CT traditionally has been an excellent study for showing *ruptured, inflammatory, and mycotic* aneurysms. Clinical history and physical examination are important to differentiate these symptomatic aneurysms; the clinical aspects are discussed in other chapters. For more subtle presentations, however, CT frequently aids the diagnosis. *Inflammatory* aneurysms typically have a thickened wall described as an outer "rind" that is enhanced by the uptake of intravascular contrast material (Fig. 21-29A). *Mycotic* aneurysms also may have inflammatory aspects, but these are less circumscribed and tend to extend into adjacent soft tissues. Mycotic aneurysms also are more likely to have an irregular shape or a focal ulceration with a "punched-out" appearance (Fig. 21-29B). *Ruptured* aneurysms usually have clear extravasation of water or blood-density material that obscures the vessel wall, but this is usually not contrast enhanced in a stable patient (Fig. 12-29C). Although a ruptured aneurysm may have an obvious break in the aortic wall shown by calcifications, discontinuity within the wall can occur in asymptomatic aneurysms without evidence of infection. These focal aortic outpouchings are called *blebs* or *blisters*. Aortic blebs on an AAA have a thinner wall than the surrounding aneurysm or normal aorta and may represent a higher risk for rupture (Fig. 21-29D).[76] Infrarenal aortic dissections and isolated iliac artery dissections are uncommon, but we have been able to show this pathology on more than one occasion using spiral CT with MPR and 3D models. For iliac artery dissections, multiplanar reformats perpendicular to the vessel are especially helpful (Fig. 21-30).

Pathology or Aberrancy of the Renal or Visceral Vessels

Involvement of renal or visceral vessels increases the complexity of an aneurysm repair. An accurate understanding of anatomic considerations is important to obtain a successful result. The evaluation of occlusive disease in the renal and mesenteric vessels is more difficult than evaluation of iliac

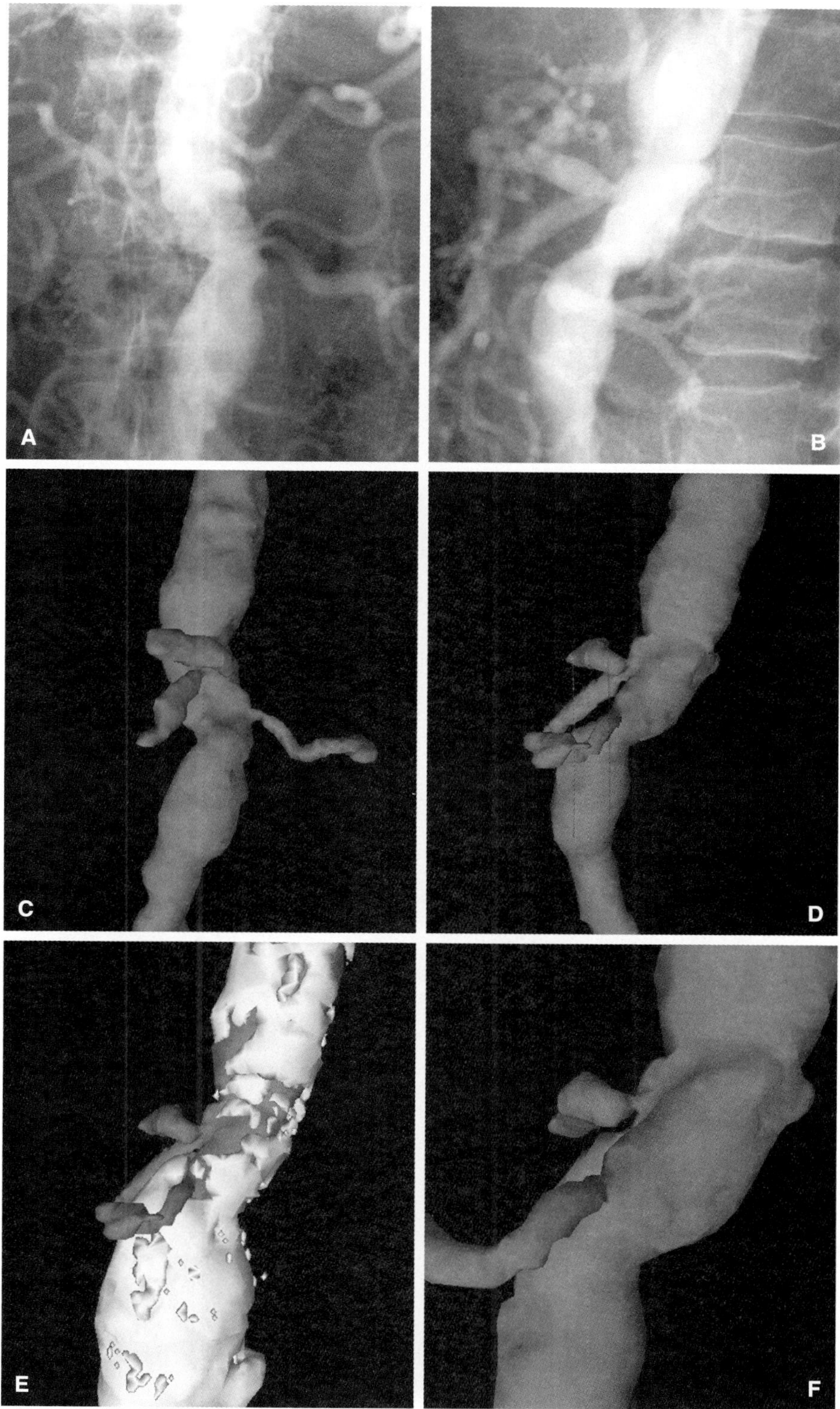

FIGURE 21-27 **A** and **B,** Anteroposterior aortogram **(A)** and lateral aortogram **(B)** of what appears to be an infrarenal AAA. The right renal artery is occluded, and the left renal artery has a mild stenosis. **C** and **D,** Anteroposterior and lateral 3D reconstruction of only the contrast-enhanced blood flow shows the same findings. **E,** Multiobject 3D reconstruction with calcified plaque (white) and thrombus (yellow) made visible shows that the AAA actually involves the suprarenal aorta, including the origin of the superior mesenteric artery. This was confirmed at operation. This view of the reconstruction was useful for determining a good location for the aortic cross-clamp (proximal to the celiac artery) and determining that a beveled anastomosis would be performed along the relatively normal aorta. The left renal artery was reimplanted on an aortic patch after endarterectomy of the plaque at the renal artery origin. **F,** Celiac artery stenosis is shown on a magnified and rotated 3D reconstruction with only blood flow made visible. The lesion was confirmed at operation. The celiac stenosis was missed by angiography because it overlapped the superior mesenteric artery on the lateral view. (See Color Figure in this section.)

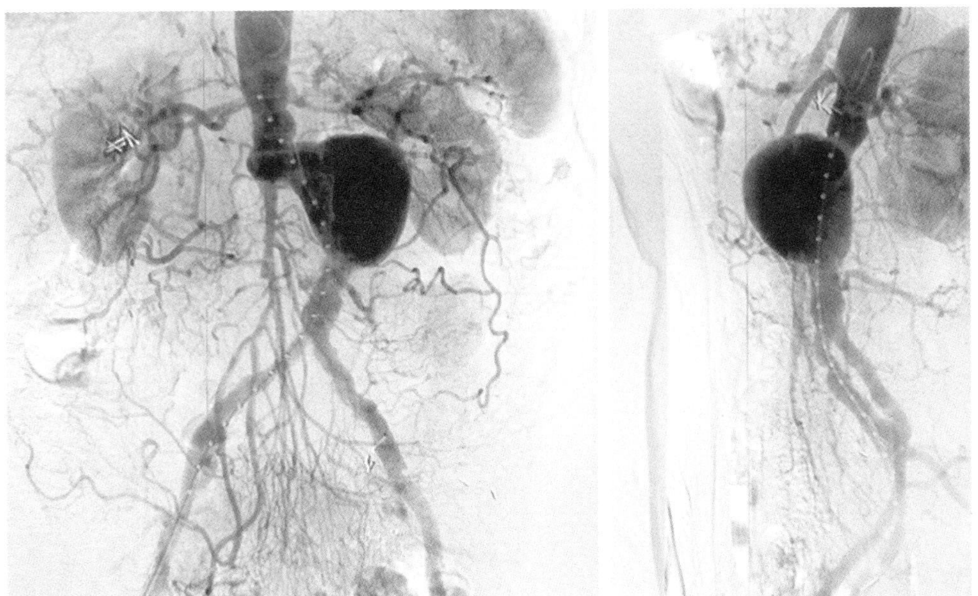

FIGURE 21-28 Iliac artery occlusive disease. Compare the right common iliac artery occlusive disease shown on this arteriogram with the multiple-object 3D reconstruction from a CT scan of the same patient (see Fig. 21-11). The angiogram catheter is in the right common iliac artery, and the lesion also can be seen on the lateral view. The right common iliac artery occlusive disease is displayed appropriately using the 3D reconstruction technique in Figure 21-11, but the inclusion of calcified plaque in a single-object SSD produces a less accurate representation of the anatomy (see Fig. 21-8).

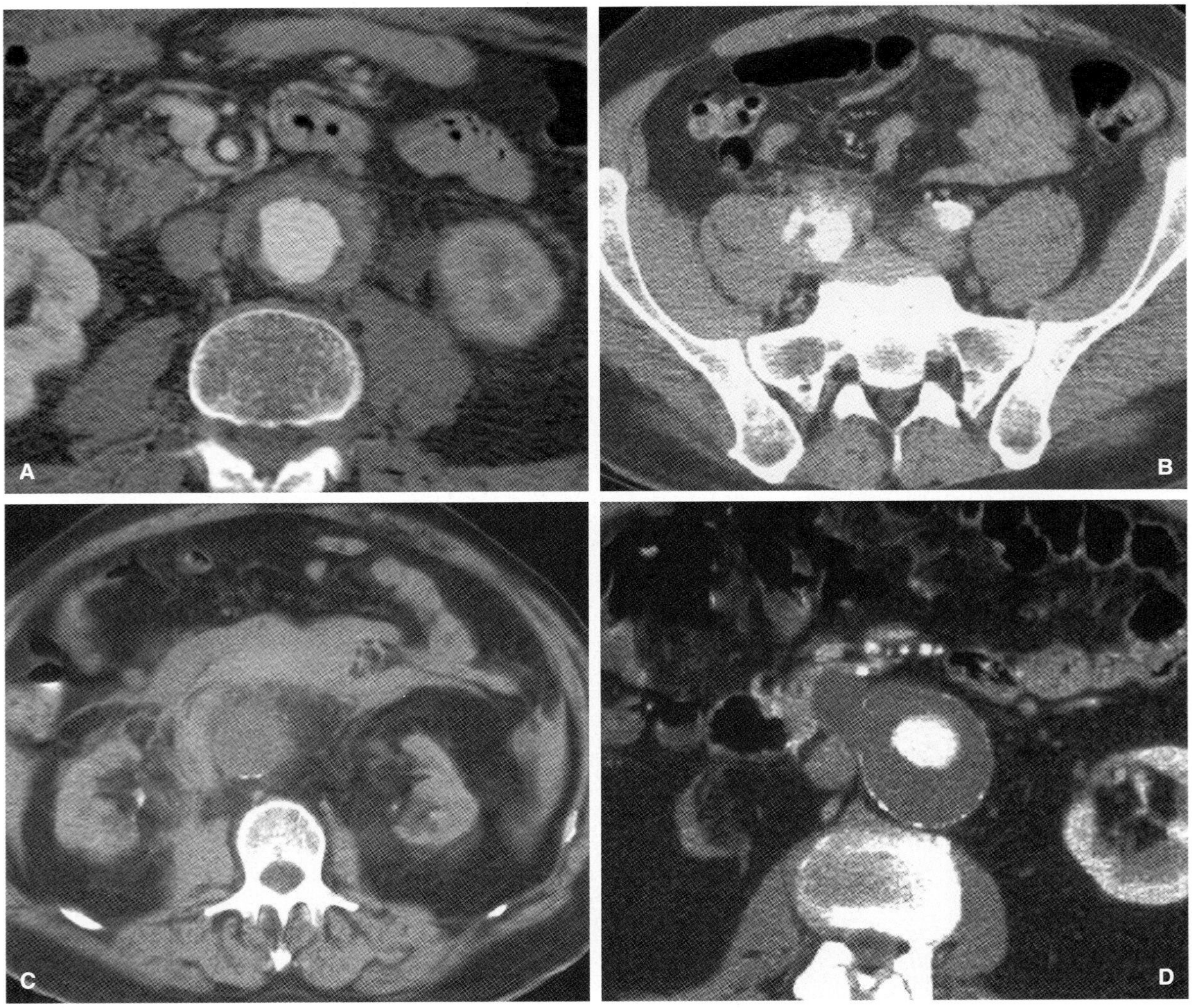

FIGURE 21-29 Variations in aneurysm pathology. **A,** Inflammatory AAA. In this case, there is a thickened wall (or rind) that shows mild contrast enhancement. Even when the rind is only mildly enhanced as in this case, it is distinctly different than the intraluminal thrombus within the AAA. **B,** Mycotic right common iliac artery aneurysm. There also is inflammation around mycotic aneurysms, but in this case it is more diffuse and blurs the surrounding tissue planes. Note the irregular, ulcerated lumen. **C,** Ruptured AAA. Blood and water-density material associated with a ruptured aneurysm also may blur soft tissue planes, but frequently the blood dissects extensively through the soft tissue. A focal rupture of the aortic wall may be seen if there is calcification within the wall of the AAA, but often the precise point of rupture is not easily identified. **D,** Focal outpouching from an aneurysm wall commonly called a *bleb* or *blister*. Absence of calcification is noted in this portion of the aortic wall, but this patient was completely asymptomatic at elective referral more than 1 week after the CT scan.

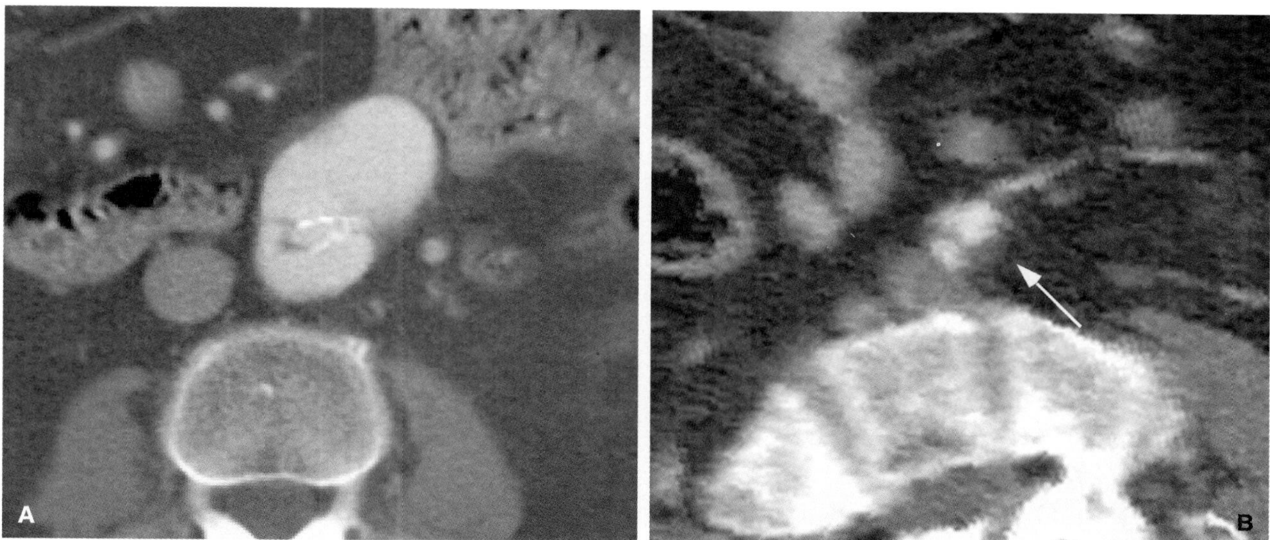

FIGURE 21-30 **A,** Infrarenal aortic dissection with calcified web shown on axial CT. This dissection extended into both common iliac arteries. **B,** Isolated left common iliac artery dissection *(arrow)* on a CT slice reformatted perpendicular to the vessel. There was no aortic dissection in this patient, and the isolated iliac artery dissection was not seen on standard CT reformats. The dissection was confirmed at the time of operation. If a reformat perpendicular to the vessel had not been obtained, the patient would have had an aortic tube graft AAA repair instead of an aorto-bi-iliac repair.

occlusive disease. The vessels are smaller, the stenotic areas are often short, and the vessels may be oriented perpendicular to conventional axial slices. Spiral CT is superior to conventional CT (which is rapidly becoming a historical context for comparison), owing to the availability of extremely thin (1 to 2 mm) axial slices and MPR on spiral CT. The visceral segment is evaluated best by views or slices perpendicular to the long axis of the vessel. The renal arteries are evaluated best with axial, coronal, and 3D reconstructions, whereas the celiac and superior mesenteric arteries are depicted best in axial, sagittal, and 3D reconstructions. CT artifacts are possible, including motion artifacts and partial volume averaging artifact (e.g., signal averaging from dense structures, such as calcium, causing a small rim of adjacent thrombus to have the appearance of contrast-enhanced blood flow). MPR is often helpful in this regard, and confidence is increased when a stenosis appears consistently in multiple views. The utility of spiral CT with 3D reconstruction for the evaluation of renal artery stenosis is illustrated in Figure 21-31. We have found spiral CT with 3D reconstruction to be accurate compared with angiography and direct inspection at the time of surgery. In a pilot study evaluating the renal and visceral arteries for stenoses greater than 50%, spiral CT with MPR and interactive 3D reconstructions had an accuracy of 97% relative to operative findings, which compared well with the 93% accuracy of angiography (unpublished data). Other investigators have also found a high degree of accuracy for renal artery stenoses using spiral CT and MPR alone,[10,77-79] although sensitivities in the 90% range are not universal.[80,81] In general, however, the accuracy of spiral CT is uniformly superior to reported values for conventional CT, and old attitudes about CT for evaluation of occlusive disease are no longer relevant in institutions with up-to-date technology.[82] Similarly, the depiction of visceral artery stenosis seems to be accurate in most studies.[10,80]

Typically, arteriography has been necessary to evaluate atypical pathology, such as a replaced right hepatic artery arising from the superior mesenteric artery or visceral artery aneurysms, but this type of pathology now can be clearly depicted by 3D reconstruction of CT data (Fig. 21-32). 3D reconstructions for assessment of renal or visceral artery pathology should not be interpreted in the absence of the actual CT data.[81] Any abnormality on the 3D model should be correlated with the CT images at the same location. A complete CT evaluation of visceral or renal artery occlusive disease should include a thorough study of all available axial slices and MPRs, preferably using magnified views in a "scrolling" or "cine" format on a workstation or personal computer. If 3D reconstructions are available, magnified and rotated views with and without plaque highlighted are helpful (see Figs 21-27 and 21-32). Software that allows the CT slice to be inserted into the appropriate location on the 3D model (for simultaneous viewing) makes correlation easier. Care should be taken when evaluating single-object SSD, which may include calcified plaque as part of the contrast-enhanced blood flow (compare Figs. 21-8 through 21-11 and Fig. 21-28 for iliac artery occlusive disease). Appropriate scanning protocols and detailed evaluation are needed to obtain high-quality results, and adjunctive studies, such as duplex, can be helpful. With the latest generation technology, however, angiography would rarely be necessary for the preoperative evaluation of AAA and pathology near the origin of the visceral arteries.

It also has traditionally been difficult for conventional CT to detect accessory renal arteries and the inferior mesenteric artery consistently. With appropriate protocols, however, spiral CT is good at detecting the presence and patency of these vessels. 3D reconstruction also is helpful in this regard, but the key to accuracy in imaging these vessels involves thin collimation, axial reconstructions, and MPR in small intervals, and the ability to scroll through every axial

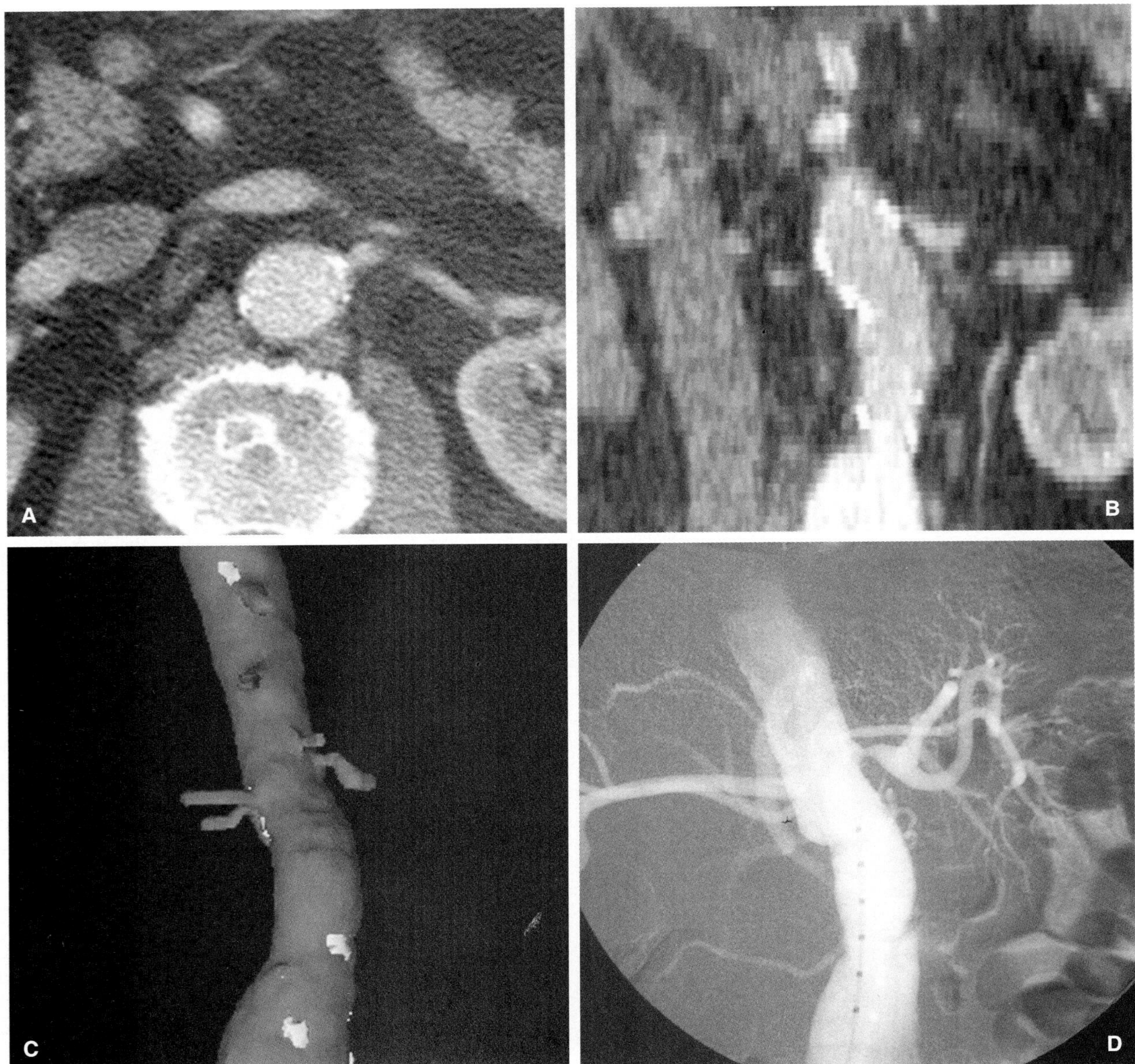

FIGURE 21-31 Spiral CT with 3D reconstruction for the evaluation of renal artery stenosis. **A,** Axial CT scan suggests a left renal artery stenosis, but multiple slices above and below this location must be reviewed because the apparent discontinuity also could be caused by a tortuous artery moving in and out of the plane of the axial CT slice. **B,** Coronal reformat suggests stenosis also, but multiple slices must be reviewed because the apparent stenosis could be caused by the artery moving in and out of the plane of the reformatted CT slice. **C,** 3D reconstruction shows a stenosis in the lower left renal artery near its origin. A left upper pole accessory renal artery and two right renal arteries also are seen. The stenosis and the multiple renal arteries were confirmed by reviewing the entire set of CT slices (as would be done normally when evaluating this type of stenosis). The depiction of the stenosis cannot be assumed accurate until it is confirmed by the CT review, but when this is accomplished the 3D reconstruction is excellent for preoperative planning because it can be viewed from any desired angle on the computer screen. **D,** Angiogram depicts the left lower renal artery stenosis, the left upper pole accessory renal artery, and two right renal arteries.

slice in magnified view looking for the presence of these small vessels. With 1- to 2-mm reconstructions, a typical spiral CT scan for AAA evaluation generates hundreds of axial slices. It is not adequate to review only the 20 to 40 hardcopy images that might be printed from a single scan. It is necessary for the radiologist or surgeon to use the CT workstation (or more recent remote digital viewing software) to review every axial slice. In our institution, the surgeon uses special software to review each individual slice on a personal computer within the context of a 3D reconstruction or remote terminal viewing software. Automated 3D reconstruction algorithms are unreliable for these small vessels because the contrast enhancement may be poor (another form of partial volume averaging; see Figs. 21-14 and 21-15).

Our current CT scan protocol uses 2.5-mm collimation through the visceral/renal segment; 1-mm axial reconstructions; scrolling through each of the axial sections (including

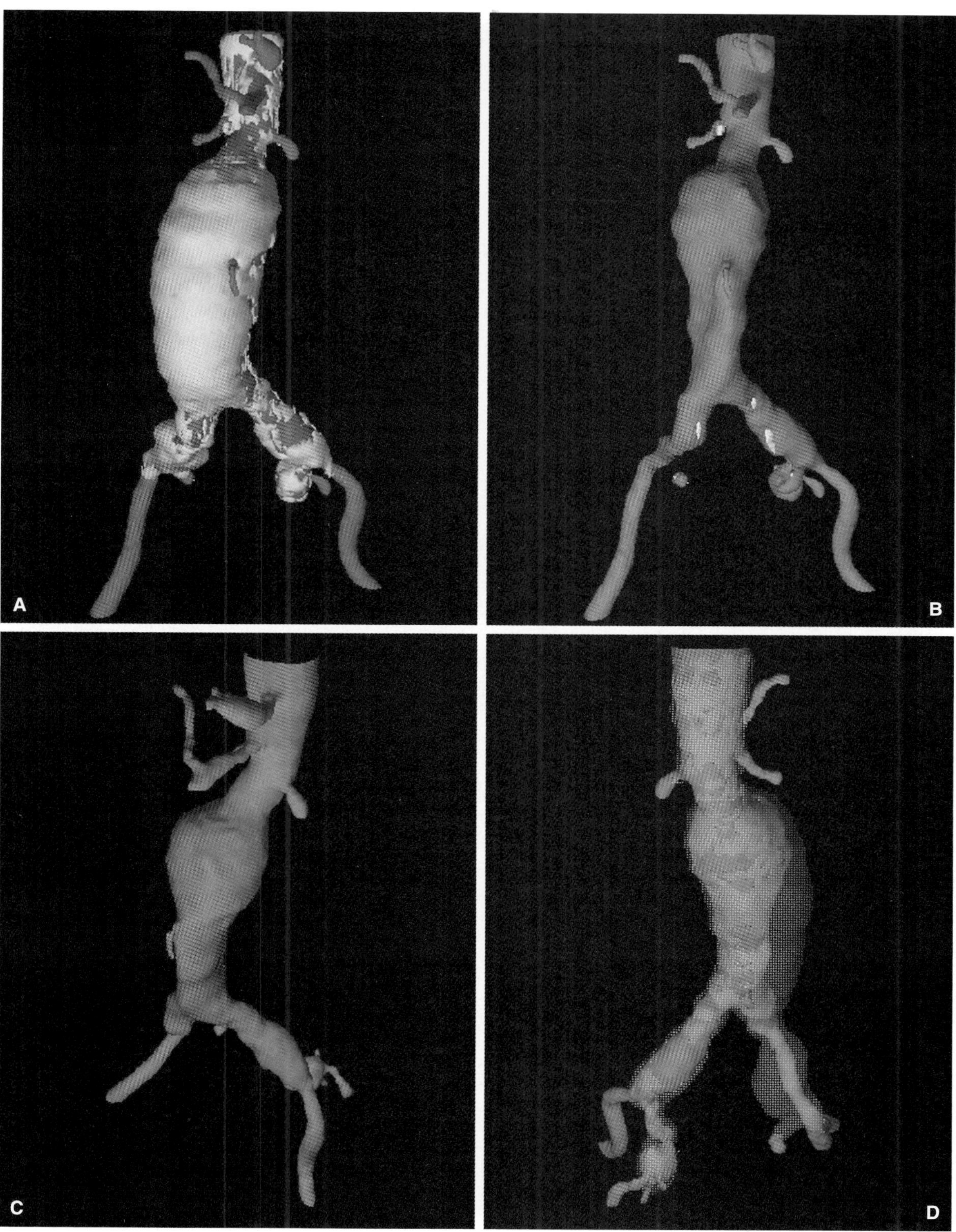

FIGURE 21-32 Several abnormalities on one 3D reconstruction are shown, highlighting the utility of multiple views and a multiple-object display. This study was obtained to evaluate a possible infrarenal AAA and revealed a celiac artery aneurysm, a replaced right hepatic artery arising from the superior mesenteric artery, multiple iliac artery aneurysms, and a right internal iliac artery occlusion. The various abnormalities are best understood by rotating the model and changing the visibility of thrombus, which can be done in real time on a workstation or a personal computer with specialized software. **A,** Anteroposterior view of a multiple-object 3D reconstruction with blood flow (red), thrombus/noncalcified plaque (yellow), and calcified plaque (white) all included in the model. **B,** 3D reconstruction with thrombus made invisible shows the right internal iliac artery occlusion. **C,** Oblique view of the 3D reconstruction shows the celiac artery aneurysm and the replaced right hepatic artery better than other views. **D,** The outflow branches of the left internal iliac artery aneurysm are best seen on a posterior view with thrombus made transparent. (See Color Figure in this section.)

magnified views); use of MPR to view the vessels in two or three planes; and (usually) 3D reconstructions capable of displaying the blood flow, thrombus, and calcified plaque as separate objects. The separate objects in the multiple-object 3D models also can be viewed individually and rotated to view the structure from any angle. We have found this technique to be extremely accurate for detecting the number, location, and patency of accessory renal arteries. When compared with operative findings, we have identified patent accessory renal arteries with nearly 100% accuracy. Other groups have noted an accuracy of 96% to 100% for the detection of accessory renal arteries.[78,81,83] We also have found this technique to be more accurate than angiography in the determination of inferior mesenteric artery patency.

Evaluation of Other Abdominal or Pelvic Pathology Indicative of Vascular Issues

CT has traditionally been found to aid in the detection of unusual structures, such as horseshoe kidney (Fig. 21-33), retroaortic renal vein, circumaortic renal vein, and duplicate or left-sided vena cava (Fig. 21-34).[75] Because of the technical advantages of spiral CT, it is excellent for detection of these anomalies. For more complex anomalies, 3D reconstruction is particularly useful because a large amount of information about spatial relationships is learned rapidly using this technology. Tortuous vessels and venous pathology in particular are much more obvious. Because of the dynamic nature of spiral CT, it also can show an aortocaval fistula, which is usually seen in association with an AAA or a history of back surgery.[84,85] Preoperative diagnosis of aortocaval fistula is important because of the high mortality rate when the diagnosis is not made preoperatively.[86] In the presence of an aortocaval fistula, aortic contrast suddenly decreases distal to the fistula. A sudden decrease in *aortic* contrast also can occur, however, owing to poor timing of the contrast infusion. The key to detection of an aortocaval fistula is to appreciate the dramatic density of contrast material within the inferior vena cava at the site of the fistula and at more proximal locations. As a result of the fistula, the aorta and vena cava have similar levels of intravascular contrast material, and *both* display a sudden decrease in intravascular contrast at precisely the same location (Fig. 21-35). Spiral CT with MPR and interactive 3D reconstructions also can identify accurately infrarenal aortic dissections, iliac artery dissections, the number and location of patent lumbar arteries, and the degree of calcified or noncalcified plaque at the sites of potential anastomoses.

Precise Measurement, Planning, and Simulation of Deployed Devices for Endovascular Repairs

Endovascular aneurysm repair requires precise and thorough preoperative planning and evaluation to a higher degree than traditional open aneurysm repairs, in which graft sizing, decision making, and troubleshooting more easily occur "on the table." Subtle differences in vessel angulation, diameter, or length can have profound impacts on the success or failure of endovascular repair. Some endograft sizing errors can be corrected without conversion to open repair, but many cannot. Numerous measurements must be performed accurately before endovascular AAA repair, including diameter and length of the aortic "neck," diameter and length of the aortic or iliac "cuffs," length of the graft in relation to the "seal zones," and diameter of the access vessels. Even small errors in any one of these measurements can lead to major problems, such as the inability to deploy the endograft, graft migration, inappropriate occlusion of branch vessels, inadequate sealing (endoleak), and subsequent aneurysm rupture.

Because of these stringent requirements, preoperative imaging algorithms for endovascular AAA repair traditionally have included CT and angiography. CT scans are used to screen candidates for endovascular repair, to determine the extent of the aneurysm, and to obtain diameter measurements. Angiograms are used for length measurements and evaluation of occlusive disease. Although this system has been used successfully in centers of excellence, it has potential pitfalls. Simple axial CT slices often do not cut through planes perpendicular to the vessel, resulting in elliptical cross-sections that can make diameter measurements difficult (Fig. 21-36). Generally, the narrowest diameter of the elliptical cross-section is the "true" arterial diameter, but this is not always the case because the aorta does not always have a simple cylindrical or conical shape. Conventional CT may lead to a slight overestimation of diameter on axial slices, whereas spiral CT slices reconstructed perpendicular to the vessel tend to be more accurate.[3,4,14,31,87] Simply using sagittal or coronal reconstruction is not always adequate because these sections may not be perpendicular to the vessel either or may not cut through the center of the vessel over an adequate length. Curvilinear reformats continue to improve, but these make length measurements difficult and straighten out angles that may affect an endovascular repair. Spiral CT with 3D reconstruction and CT reformats perpendicular to the vessel lumen eliminate the diameter measurement problems associated with the other techniques (see Fig. 21-36).[3,4,14,31,87]

CTA with 3D reconstruction offers several other important benefits that are key for imaging before endovascular surgery. In conjunction with spiral CTA and MPR, 3D reconstruction speeds assimilation of the CT data and makes the extent of the aneurysm rapidly apparent.[12,13] More important, specialized measurement software and unique aspects of the 3D reconstruction can eliminate most of the measurement problems associated with conventional techniques.[3,4,14,31,87] Software algorithms can be used to display the centerline of the blood flow channel in the infrarenal aorta and iliac arteries and allow length measurements along the vessel centerline in tortuous aortic or iliac segments. In some systems, graft paths along a line other than the centerline can be also defined by the user, which is necessary because an endovascular graft may not follow the centerline of the blood flow channel throughout its entire course. We have used such a system for many endovascular AAA repairs and find it to be extremely accurate. In test phantoms and in our clinical experience, the centerline and user-defined graft path innovations described herein have eliminated length measurement problems.[3,4,29,73]

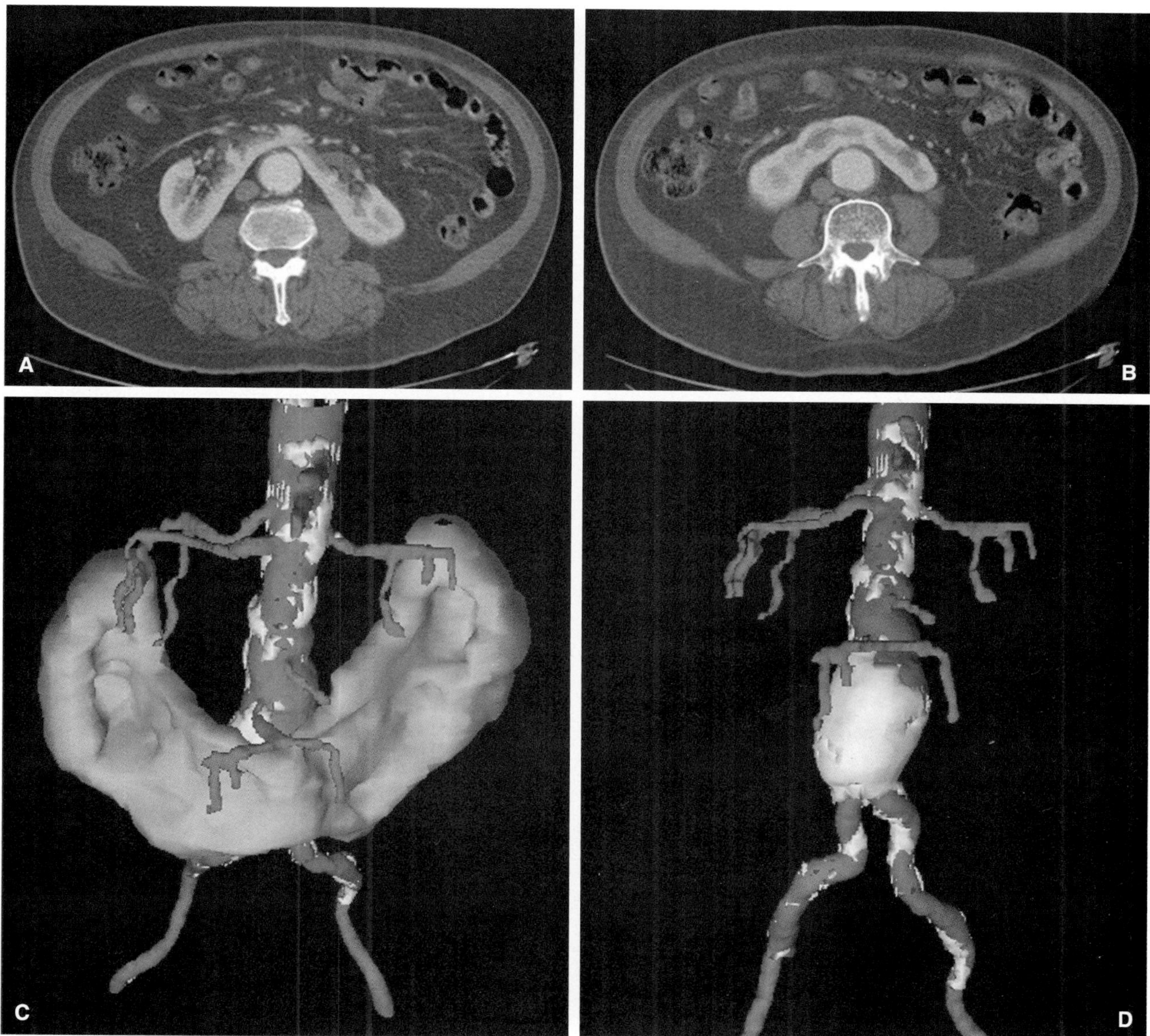

FIGURE 21-33 **A,** Horseshoe kidney on axial CT. **B,** The portion of the horseshoe kidney that crosses the midline is often relatively thin, but in this case the parenchyma does not appear to be attenuated. **C,** 3D reconstruction with the horseshoe kidney and associated complex blood supply clearly visible. The reconstruction is rotated slightly to show a stenosis in the lowest midline renal artery near its origin. A large amount of information is learned rapidly using this technology, as it would be extremely difficult to trace the renal arteries through their course on CT slices. Angiography does not provide a 3D perspective of the renal parenchyma. **D,** Anteroposterior view of the 3D reconstruction with the kidney made invisible, showing a small AAA arising just distal to the lowest renal artery (which is in the midline). (See Color Figure in this section.)

Several similar systems are commercially available or in development, and at least two have reported success using this type of specialized software for length measurements.[3,4,14,29] In a comparative study using life-size models with shapes similar to actual AAA, we compared spiral CT alone, angiography with a 1-cm graduated catheter, intravascular ultrasound, and CTA with interactive 3D reconstructions and specialized measurement software. Although all of these methods produced reasonable results in experienced hands by taking care to avoid pitfalls, CTA with interactive 3D reconstructions was the only imaging method that was accurate for diameter *and* length measurements, allowing it to be used reliably as the sole preoperative imaging modality.[4,73,87] This technique (CTA/3D) is also less invasive and less expensive than the combination of CTA and intravascular ultrasound that otherwise would be necessary.

Another unique innovation made possible by CTA with interactive 3D reconstructions and specialized software is a technology we have termed "the virtual graft," in which the diameter, length, and path of a proposed endograft can be simulated in 3D space.[29] This simulated graft can be displayed within the 3D model of the AAA and used to investigate potential problems with endograft sizing, kinking, and stenosis (Fig. 21-37). Our institution reported the absence of complications or endoleak development

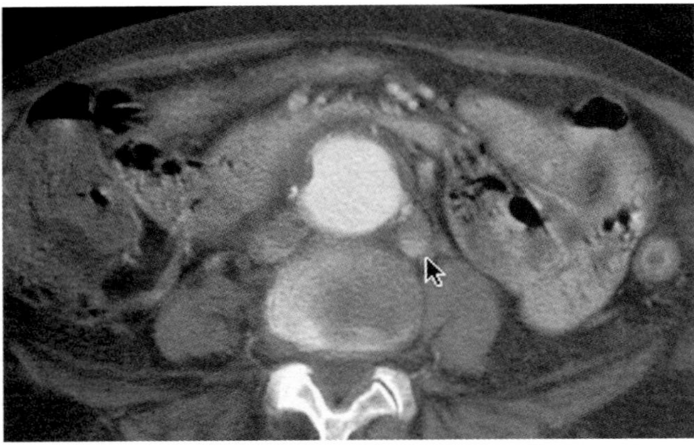

FIGURE 21-34 Duplicate vena cava seen on axial CT slice *(arrow)*.

when the internal iliac artery was covered, not coiled, during endovascular aneurysum repair.[74] This success is based on an adequate seal zone of the endo-limb with the most distal 5 mm of common iliac artery and proximal 15 mm of external iliac artery. The increasing number of available graft configurations and sizes offer many potential solutions. The use of a virtual graft in the preoperative period facilitates an accurate determination of whether or not an adequate seal-zone would be attainable with a particular graft. It also is useful to determine the diameter, length, degree of overlap, and number of components needed for modular endografts. We have used other aspects of this system to evaluate the proposed access path for the delivery system, including iliac artery tortuosity, diameter, and calcification and have found it to be extremely helpful in predicting which cases are amenable to an entirely percutaneous access.[4,31,73,74]

In our institution, spiral CTA with interactive 3D reconstruction has almost entirely eliminated the need for angiography before endovascular AAA repair and produces results comparable to the best series using angiography or other noninvasive options.[4] CTA with interactive 3D reconstruction has reliably shown important anatomic features that either were unclear or were not shown on conventional CT or angiography. We have found graft sizing to be extremely accurate and reliable using CTA with interactive 3D reconstructions and have found that angiographic measurements can be misleading. This technique does require special software and a dedicated team, including a radiologist, technologist, and surgeon, to produce quality results. Nonetheless, it seems that the spiral CT with 3D reconstruction technique that we have termed *computer-aided measurement, planning, and simulation* (3D CAMPS) has become the gold standard for the preoperative evaluation of patients before endovascular AAA repair. The key for this modality is to have good CT protocols, 3D reconstruction software that has been validated in phantoms and in clinical use, and proper training in the use of the software. Although this chapter is about CT, these techniques are applicable to MRI also, with the major issues being lower resolution of MRI and poor imaging of calcium with most current MRI technology.

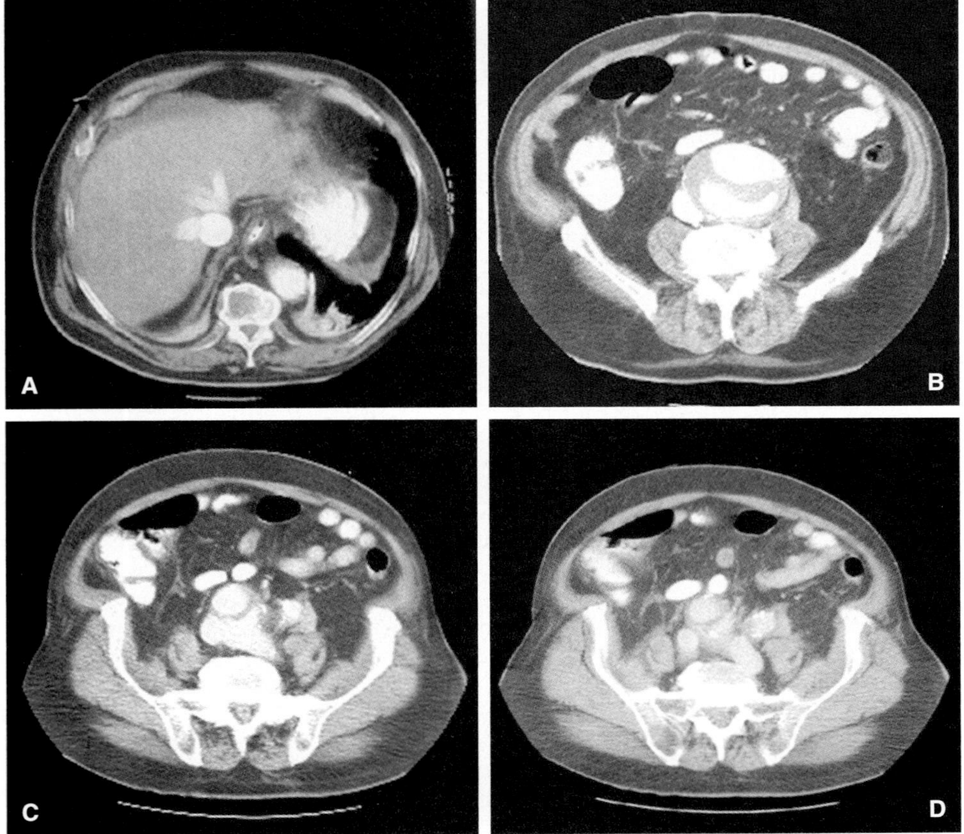

FIGURE 21-35 Aortocaval fistula associated with AAA on axial CT. The key to detection of an aortocaval fistula is to appreciate the dramatic change in contrast within the inferior vena cava at the site of the fistula and at more proximal locations. **A,** The vena cava is dramatically enhanced by intravascular contrast material, even at locations quite proximal to the fistula. **B,** Central portion of the AAA shows continued bright enhancement of the vena cava and an aortic web or dissection. **C,** Axial CT just proximal to the site of the fistula. The aortic web is still present, and the contrast enhancement of the vena cava is still similar to that of the aorta. **D,** Axial CT just distal to the fistula. The bowel opacification has not changed, so the dramatic change in intraluminal contrast is not due to a change in the CT window level. If the change in contrast were due simply to poor timing of the IV contrast bolus, the aortic contrast might decrease suddenly, but there would not be a simultaneous change from dense contrast to dilute contrast within the vena cava at the same location.

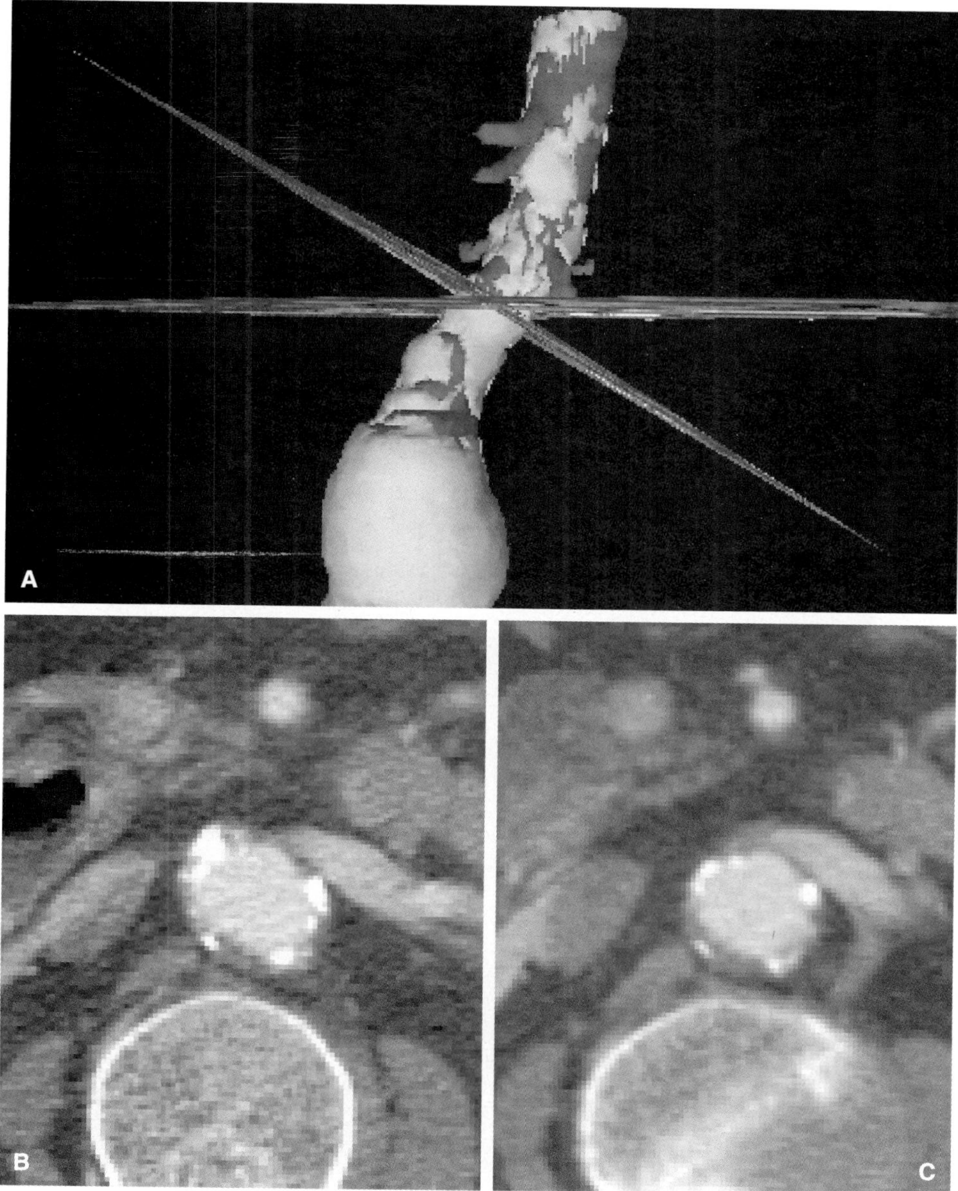

FIGURE 21-36 Diameter measurement issues and solutions using CT. **A,** 3D reconstruction with simultaneous display of CT slices in 3D space. The CT slices shown here are a standard axial reformat and a reformat perpendicular to the aorta. The 3D model was rotated to show the intersection of the two CT slices at the same location on the aorta. **B,** The same axial CT slice shown in **A**. The axial slice does not intersect the aortic neck perpendicular to its axis, creating an elliptical cross-section. Although the smaller diameter (minor axis of the ellipse) is usually similar to the true diameter, elliptical cross-sections also occur in noncylindrical vessels and at the margins of aneurysms. Viewing multiple cross-sections in sequence can help with this problem, but evaluation is still difficult. **C,** The CT slice reformatted perpendicular to the aorta (shown in **A**) accurately depicts the essentially circular lumen and provides a diameter measurement without ambiguity. This cross-section of the aorta also provides a more correct impression of thrombus thickness, which is artifactually enhanced on an elliptical cross-section. The renal vein and vertebrae help verify the magnification, location, and orientation of the slices.

Postoperative Follow-up for Open and Endovascular Abdominal Aortic Aneurysm Repair

CT is important for periodic follow-up after standard open AAA repair (for pseudoaneurysms and degeneration of adjacent aortoiliac segments), and can detect critical problems (Fig. 21-38). Owing to lower durability for endovascular aneurysm repair, however, CT follow-up has been crucial during the current development of endograft technology. If there is no perigraft flow or endoleak after endograft placement, the natural history is a decrease in aneurysm size.[79,88,89] An aneurysm occasionally enlarges without apparent endoleak, however, and ruptures can occur in this situation.[90,91] Aneurysms can also develop a late, secondary endoleak, which can lead to rupture.[92,93] Late stent-graft deformation is an important issue for long-term follow-up because it can also lead to late secondary endoleak, aneurysm rupture, or graft thrombosis.[92,93]

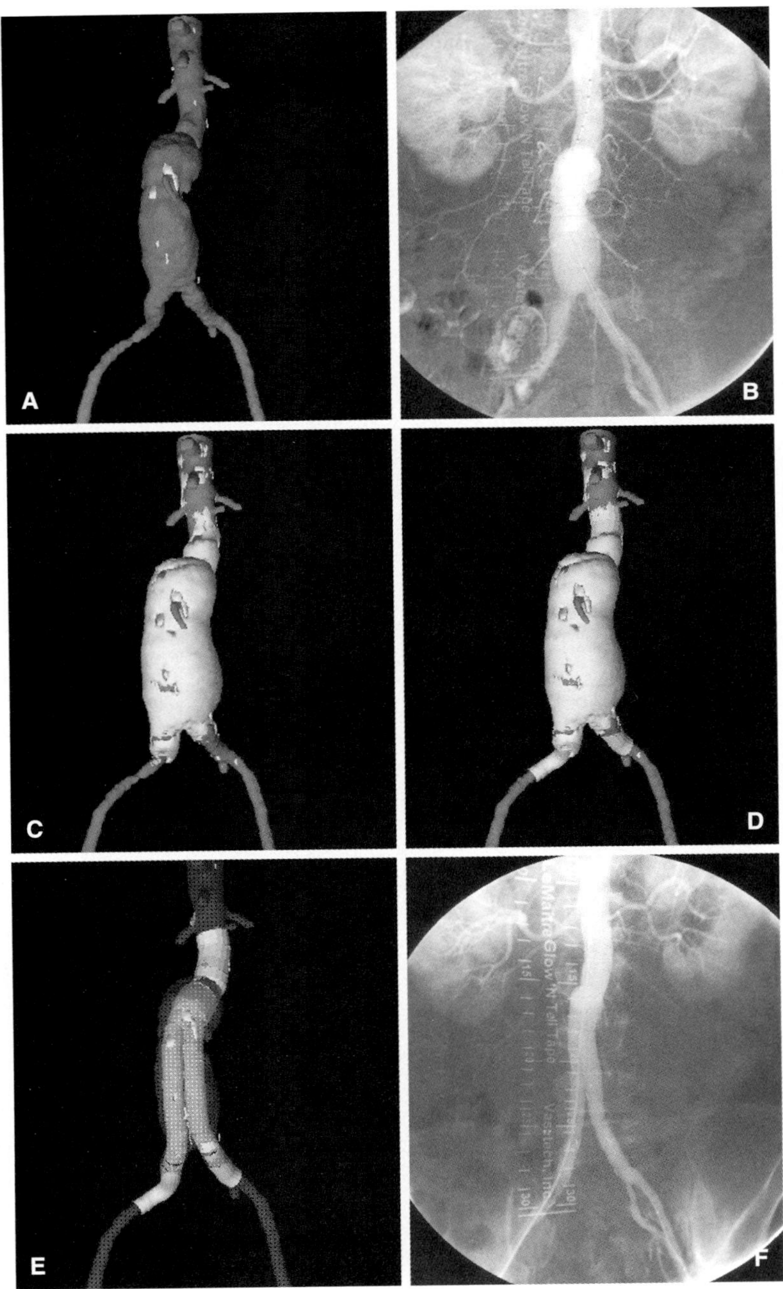

FIGURE 21-37 Use of CT with 3D reconstruction and specialized software in endovascular AAA repair. **A,** Preoperative 3D reconstruction shows contrast-enhanced blood flow (red) and calcified plaque (white). Owing to the accuracy of this technique, preoperative angiograms are not necessary. **B,** Angiogram performed on the operating table at the time of the procedure is necessary to deliver the device even if a preoperative angiogram had been performed. Note the similarity to the 3D reconstruction. **C,** Preoperative 3D reconstruction including thrombus shows the need for CT before endovascular repair. The iliac arteries are aneurysmal proximally, especially on the left. The endograft cannot be implanted into thrombus and must be long enough to achieve a seal in the normal common iliac artery. **D,** Preoperative planning with a "virtual graft," which is displayed in bright yellow. The brighter yellow of the simulated endograft protrudes beyond the red blood flow and the lighter yellow of the thrombus for sufficient lengths proximally and distally so that this 3D reconstruction shows that the proposed graft is appropriately oversized to achieve a seal at the neck of the infrarenal aorta and in the iliac arteries. This view rapidly provides a check to ensure that the proposed endograft is not too small or excessively oversized. It also graphically shows the quality and length of the "seal zone." **E,** Preoperative simulation using the virtual endograft, in this case with thrombus invisible and blood flow made transparent to show better the anticipated course of the proposed endograft. The prediction here is that the endograft will dilate as it exits the aortic neck (consistent with the degree of oversizing) and deviate slightly at the same location because it must follow the aortic lumen. It is anticipated that some deviation and constriction of the limbs will occur at the aortic bifurcation, but this does not appear to be excessive. This same technology and display is used to evaluate graft length along the centerline of the lumen or along a user-defined path. In this case, the length and diameter of the endograft were simulated to coincide with an available graft size. An endograft of this length is anticipated to end just above the left internal iliac artery origin and extend beyond the right iliac artery stenosis if it is deployed appropriately (with the proximal endograft just below the renal arteries). **F,** Completion angiogram at the time of the procedure verifies the accuracy of the preoperative computer simulation. The endograft was deployed just below the renal arteries and ends just above the left internal iliac artery origin. The endograft also extends beyond the right iliac stenosis, which is no longer apparent. (See Color Figure in this section.)

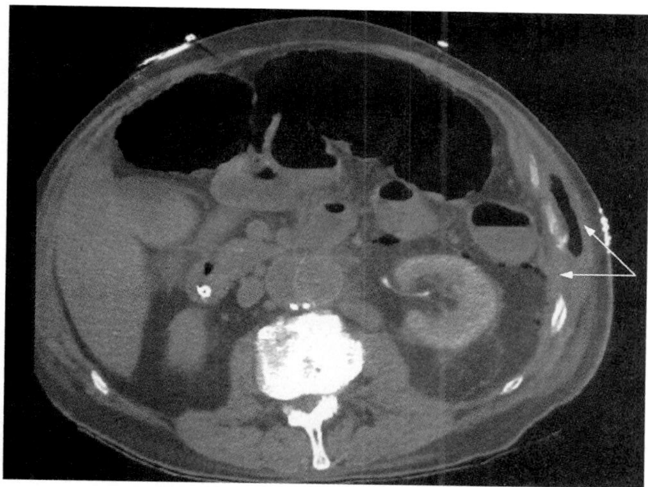

FIGURE 21-38 Abdominal air 1 week after suprarenal AAA repair via a left retroperitoneal approach *(arrows)*. This finding may represent trapped air in the early postoperative period after an AAA repair, but it should be taken seriously. In this case, it was due to a perforation in the sigmoid colon. The air surrounding Gerota's fascia anterior to the kidney is in a tissue plane that was not dissected at the time of initial surgery.

Spiral CT is a key imaging modality to follow endovascular AAA repairs. Although there remains some controversy on this subject, CT is generally believed to be more accurate for endoleaks than duplex,[30] and CT provides more accurate and reproducible diameter measurements than duplex, provided that the measurements are performed on an electronic workstation and not hardcopies.[94,95] Using a CT workstation or specialized software, highly magnified views of axial reconstructions or multiplanar reconstructions can be viewed in rapid sequence to "follow" a suspected endoleak to potential inflow and outflow sources. The latter technique is strongly recommended over simple review of selected small hardcopy images, in which subtle endoleaks may be missed. Delayed scans after contrast infusion also improve accuracy when trying to detect an endoleak.[30,96] Specialized MRI techniques are becoming useful for detection of slow endoleaks in cases in which the diagnosis remains in doubt or in patients who would not tolerate iodinated contrast material.[97,98] When specialized software is available for 3D reconstruction of spiral CT (or MRI) data, it is helpful for visualization of aneurysm and endograft deformation. 3D reconstruction also aids in characterization of endoleak by showing the inflow and outflow sources in a single image, even if they are subtle or difficult to interpret on individual CT scans (Fig. 21-39).

Volume Measurements

3D reconstructions can be used to calculate the volume of any structure in the 3D model, and data regarding imaging for tumors and other 3D structures indicate volume measurements are much more sensitive to size change than maximal diameter measurements.[99,100] Multiple institutions have confirmed that volume measurements are much more sensitive than maximum diameter for the detection of AAA size changes after endovascular AAA repair, and it seems

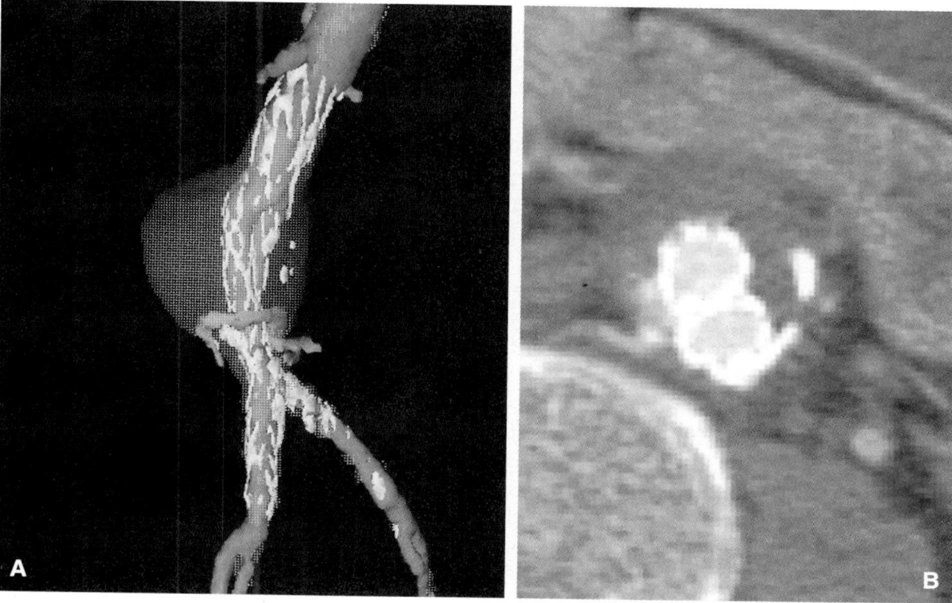

FIGURE 21-39 Perigraft flow (endoleak) after endovascular AAA repair, as displayed on 3D reconstruction **(A)** and axial CT **(B)**. The 3D reconstruction (created from the CT data) is rotated to a posterolateral view. Multiple-object 3D display includes the densities consistent with contrast-enhanced lumen (red), thrombus and noncalcified plaque (yellow, made transparent to display the endoleak), calcified plaque and metallic stent (white), and contrast-enhanced endoleak (magenta). The 3D display shows that the endoleak is associated with a patent lumbar artery and a patent inferior mesenteric artery (IMA). The axial CT cross-section shows the endograft, contrast enhancement outside the lumen of the endograft (endoleak), the patent lumbar connecting to the endoleak, and a contrast-enhanced IMA. From a single axial slice, it is impossible to decipher the connection to the IMA, which could be filling via collateral flow. The 3D reconstruction immediately conveys the relationship of the endoleak to the other structures in a much more intuitive way than scrolling through multiple CT slices. (See Color Figure in this section.)

that volume is the gold standard for early detection and accuracy regarding aneurysm growth or shrinkage.[30,101-104] The early detection of aneurysm enlargement can be crucial in follow-up for endovascular repair because it indicates the aneurysm is still at risk for rupture and usually precedes evidence of endoleak or overt rupture.[79,88-91] CT volume measurements may become a standard postoperative test for aneurysm exclusion or risk of rupture either routinely or if the aneurysm is not clearly shrinking.[30,101-104] These same studies indicate that there also may be a role for early volume measurements within the first 6 months, to identify more clearly decreasing aneurysms that may need less frequent imaging or may be able to avoid secondary interventions.

Vascular Disease in the Extremities

The use of CT for evaluating infrainguinal vascular disease has been increasing with increased use of spiral CT, CTA, and multidetector scanners. Although duplex and MRA have dominated noninvasive imaging of the lower extremities, CT has a role in selected cases. CT is useful for the evaluation of femoral and popliteal artery aneurysms. With the use of CTA or 3D reconstructions or both, CT can effectively show the location and extent of aneurysmal disease (Fig. 21-40). In conjunction with the history and physical examination, CT can rule out significant occlusive disease in the superficial femoral or popliteal arteries, but it is not the most cost-effective study in this regard, unless CT is already needed for some other reason, such as evaluation of an aneurysm. CT can be useful for unusual pathology, such as popliteal entrapment syndrome[105,106] and adventitial cystic disease (Fig. 21-41).[105,107] Spiral CT evaluation of vascular disease in the thigh and popliteal fossa, including occlusive disease, seems to be more accurate than angiography.[105,107] CT evaluation of tibial-level disease is much more difficult, however, because it is hard to time the IV contrast delivery in a manner that enhances the arteries sufficiently without also enhancing the adjacent veins to a similar extent. Arteriovenous malformations in the lower extremity present similar difficulties—they can be imaged by CT, but as with tibial-level occlusive disease, these traditionally have been better delineated by MRA.

Some of these "truths" about extremity imaging are changing with the advent of multidetector array scanners. Ofer and colleagues[20] performed multidetector CTA from the superior mesenteric artery to the pedal arteries on 18 patients who had undergone prior standard digital subtraction angiography. The CT vascular findings were grouped according to the amount of stenosis determined in the peripheral vasculature. These findings were compared with the angiograms and found to yield a multidetector CT sensitivity of 91% and a specificity of 92% for recognition and classification of peripheral vascular disease.[20] A similar study of 41 patients was performed by Martin and colleagues.[21] Their results showed a multidetector CT sensitivity and specificity for detecting lesions with a stenosis of at least 75% to be 92% and 97%. These investigators also found that CT was able to image more vascular segments in the calf vessels than angiography.[21] Multidetector CT scanners offer a significant advantage in the evaluation and diagnosis of lower extremity vascular

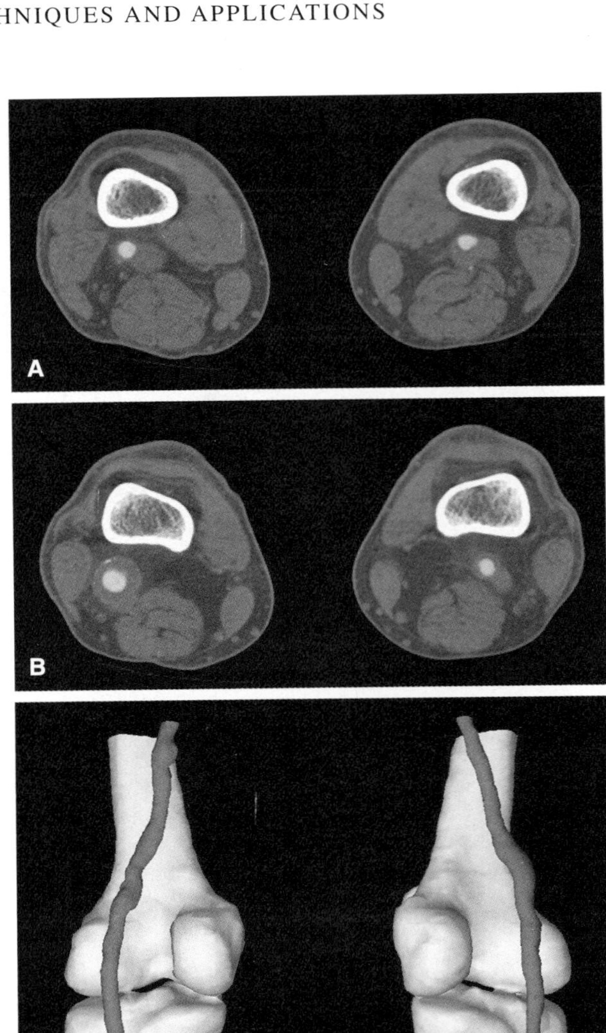

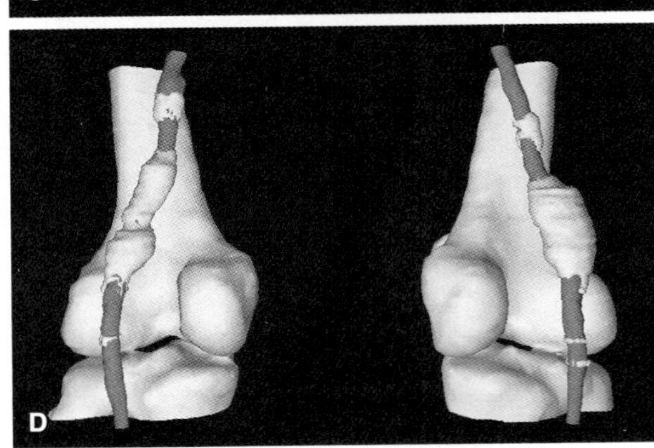

FIGURE 21-40 Bilateral popliteal aneurysms. **A,** The lumen can have a variable appearance, as shown by the eccentric cross-section on the patient's left (right side of the illustration). **B,** This axial CT cross-section shows a more characteristic circular lumen with circumferential thrombus (patient's right, which is the left side of illustration). As with other aneurysms, the diameter of the contrast-enhanced lumen does not correlate with the outer diameter of the vessel, making angiography a poor diagnostic modality. **C,** Posterior view of the 3D reconstruction with only the contrast-enhanced blood flow (red) and bones (white) made visible. This view is similar to an angiogram and would not depict the full extent of the aneurysms. The patient had no occlusive disease by ultrasound or ankle-brachial indices. **D,** This posterior view of the 3D reconstruction with thrombus and plaque added depicts the full extent of the aneurysms. In this case, bypass of the lesions could be performed without angiography.

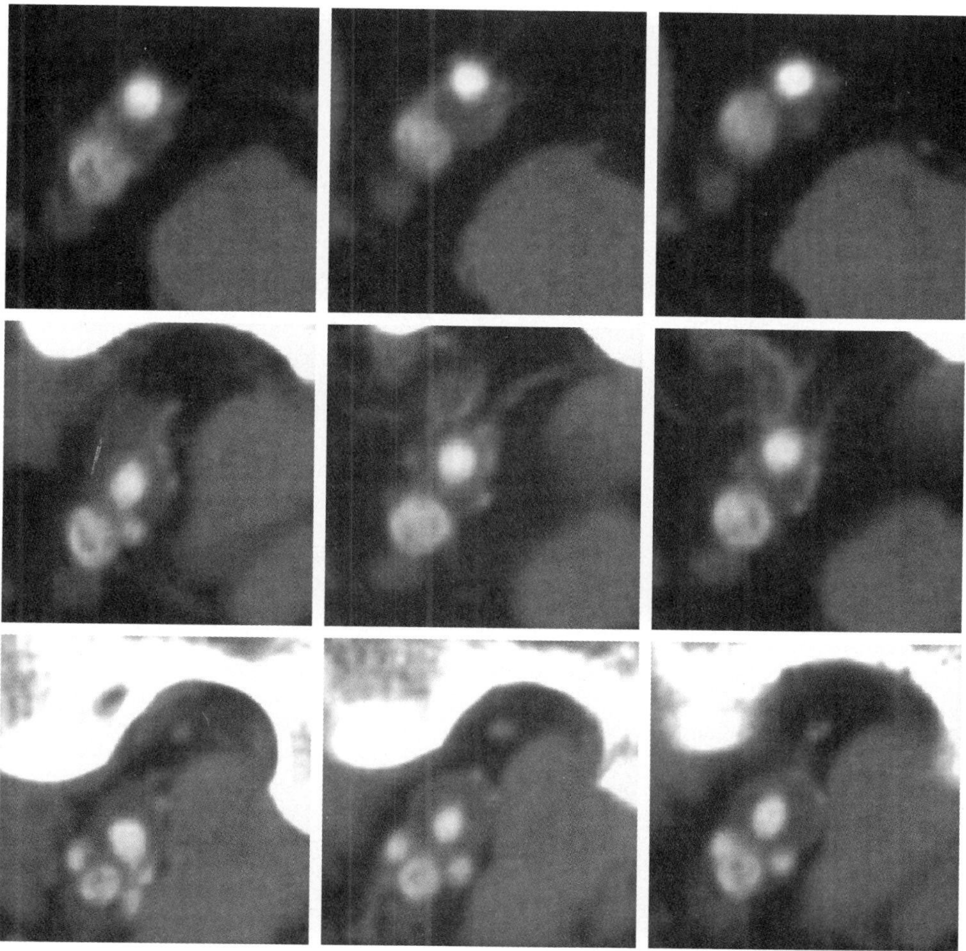

FIGURE 21-41 Adventitial cystic disease. Sequential axial CT slices through the popliteal fossa reveal the varied appearance of adventitial cystic disease in a single patient. Some locations have a circular cross-section with the cyst surrounding the entire circumference, giving the appearance of a popliteal aneurysm. In other locations, the cysts have a characteristic multiloculated appearance. The panel in the second row, far right, shows a portion of the cyst extending toward the joint space. Bony structures and the joint space are at the top in each panel.

disease, and evaluations are proceeding rapidly in other areas of the vasculature as well.

The data regarding CT for the management of upper extremity vascular disease is not as extensive, but there are potential applications. We have found that CT can show relatively subtle lesions, such as arteritis of the subclavian arteries, if caution is used to avoid artifact from IV infusions of contrast material. Because the subclavian arteries generally travel perpendicular to the direction of table movement, spiral CT is needed to evaluate these lesions using MPR or 3D reconstructions. CT protocols for evaluation of the thoracic outlet have shown the arterial and venous deformation that occurs with upper extremity abduction, and this may become a useful study for patients with suspected thoracic outlet syndrome (see Fig. 21-22).[51] Finally, upper extremity vascular trauma may be observed with a high sensitivity on dedicated CTA examinations.[108]

Venous Pathology

Throughout the clinical applications section, we have documented the use of CT to evaluate venous pathology. CT is most useful for showing venous anomalies around arterial structures of interest (e.g., a retroaortic renal vein, circumaortic renal vein, duplicate vena cava, left-sided vena cava, or aortocaval fistula). The utility of spiral CT for pulmonary embolus seems promising, as discussed earlier. Although MRI generally delineates arteriovenous malformations better than CT, spiral CT can be useful in selected cases.[109,110] CT has a sensitivity of 85% in detection of esophageal varices compared with endoscopy and has the advantage of showing collateral pathways and large portosystemic shunts with greater sensitivity than angiography.[111] In selected cases, CT also is useful for the evaluation of portal, mesenteric, caval, or iliac vein thrombosis.[112-114]

■ FUTURE CONSIDERATIONS

Estimation of Aneurysm Rupture Risk

One of the most exciting potential applications for CT (or MRI) technologies is the analysis of an aneurysm as a 3D biomechanical structure. Although aneurysm rupture is correlated with increasing vessel diameter, it is far from ideal. From a biomechanical "engineering" standpoint, rupture occurs when the stress on the structure exceeds its strength. As part of this process, it has been suggested that a mathematical analysis of AAA geometry is theoretically a better way to estimate wall stress and the risk of rupture. Because of the complexity of the shape of an aneurysm, the only way to analyze this in mathematical terms is to break down the structure into small "finite" elements, with discrete

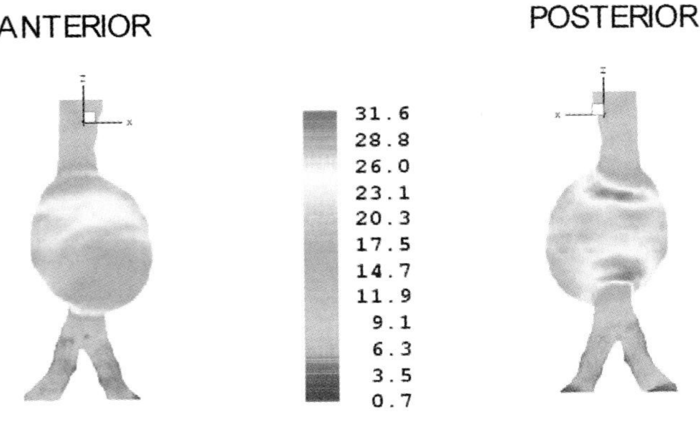

FIGURE 21-42 3D stress map on an AAA created from an AAA finite element model of wall stress using CT data. Stress is mapped onto the surface of the 3D reconstruction using color gradients to represent stress gradients. The highest stresses are shown in red, and the lowest stresses are shown in blue.

loads and boundaries that enable a computer-aided solution (by iteration on literally thousands of equations). Known as *finite element analysis,* this method was first applied to theoretical AAA by analysis of simple geometric shapes that approximated an AAA in a 2D model.[115] The method has been refined over time to include theoretical 3D shapes and later to actual AAA shapes obtained from CT data.[116-121] Although the details are beyond the scope of this chapter, the discussion of the basic principles earlier should make it obvious how well suited CT technology is to this concept. In a typical stress analysis, the individual element stresses are portrayed via a 3D reconstruction similar to those shown earlier and result in an intuitive representation of the location and amount of wall stress in an aortic aneurysm (Fig. 21-42).

Ultimately, after overcoming issues such as boundary condition artifacts, defining the necessary CT resolution, and creating a semiautomated process to perform the analysis on a large scale, a large series of AAAs with and without rupture was analyzed using a 3D finite-element analysis technique.[122,123] The first of these studies indicated that AAAs at or near the time of rupture have much higher peak wall stress than electively repaired aneurysms *of the same diameter*.[122] Our second study showed that these elevated stresses can be identified well in advance of the time of rupture, and peak wall stress estimates rupture risk better than maximum AAA diameter.[123] Although much work remains to be done in this area (e.g., evaluation of wall strength noninvasively), the technology already seems superior to diameter, and a multicenter evaluation of the clinical predictive value of AAA wall stress is currently under way.

Other Applications for the Future

So-called "fifth-generation" and "sixth-generation" CT scanners have been developed, in which the x-ray beam is moved electronically, and the detector array encompasses 360 degrees so that there are no physical components to rotate in the gantry. These scanners offer the promise of scan times so rapid that even cardiac motion would not be problematic. Because of the speed of beam movement, tube overheating also should be less problematic because 32 complete (360 degree) cross-sections can be done in 1 second. Technology and physics still limit the intensity of the beam and the quality of the images in this modality, however. The addition of multirow detectors in the z direction to improve longitudinal resolution and scanning time is now commonplace, and the trend will be toward increased numbers of rows (16 rows or arrays is not unusual in large institutions already). 3D reconstruction is already commonplace, and this will continue to become more sophisticated and easier to perform. Interactive 3D reconstruction is now available, and research is being performed that incorporates these interactive models into fluoroscopic images in real time. This form of *enhanced reality* may be used to enhance angiography and other invasive procedures. Research also is being performed that uses 3D reconstruction in advanced simulators, which may be useful for teaching or learning new techniques. The extent to which these advances would be clinically useful remains to be seen, but current computer technology is allowing rapid advancement in these elements of imaging technology. Despite advances in CT, MRI will continue to have a role for certain types of pathology, such as intracranial lesions and arteriovenous malformations. MRI is limited, however, by patient tolerance, implanted devices, resolution, display of calcified plaque, display of thrombus, availability, and expense. CT will remain the imaging modality of choice for pathology that is displayed in a similar manner on CT and MRI (with the exception of the small percentage of patients with severe renal insufficiency who are not on dialysis).

■ SUMMARY

Spiral CT, CTA, 3D display, postprocessing techniques, and simulation continue to increase the clinical role of CT in vascular surgery. Techniques such as MPR and 3D reconstruction are helpful in many cases and crucial in others. Traditionally, delineation of key anatomic features has required a combination of conventional CT and angiography, but state-of-the-art spiral CT with MPR is all that is necessary in many cases. When "basic" CTA is not sufficient, more recent advances increase the utility even further. Reformats perpendicular to the vessel lumen are helpful when precise measurements of vessel diameter or interpretation of tortuous anatomy are needed. The addition of 3D reconstruction provides further insight, especially if thrombus and calcified plaque are depicted as separate objects. Access to a CT workstation or specialized software is helpful for many anatomic features and is crucial for evaluations such as visceral artery occlusive disease, accessory renal arteries and inferior mesenteric artery patency, and preoperative planning in endovascular surgery. With appropriate protocols, spiral CT with MPR and 3D reconstruction seems to be more accurate than conventional CT or angiography in the evaluation of patients with suprarenal aortic aneurysms, for evaluating the potential for endovascular aneurysm repair, for endograft sizing, for delineating complex anatomy, and for the evaluation of suspected occlusive disease. As this technology becomes more widely available and more thoroughly evaluated, it is eliminating the need for preoperative angiography in most cases. Angiography will be reserved for highly selected patients and become oriented toward a therapeutic rather than diagnostic role.

Acknowledgments I would like to thank Robert F. Jeffrey, MD, John Weaver, MD, and Richard A. Morse, MD (Department of Radiology, Dartmouth-Hitchcock Medical Center and White River Junction VA Hospital, White River Junction, Vermont), who have diligently worked on optimizing spiral CT protocols for our institution and providing technical assistance in formatting spiral CT data for 3D reconstruction. I would also like to acknowledge Medical Media Systems, West Lebanon, New Hampshire (including David T. Chen, PhD), for providing technical assistance and co-development of software that allowed creation of many of the 3D images shown here. I appreciate the assistance of Peter J. Robbie, MFA, in collecting and assembling many of the images. Last, I would like to thank individuals who helped provide CT data or images (or both) for illustrations, including Richard A. Morse, MD, from White River Junction VA Hospital, White River Junction, Vermont; Robert F. Jeffrey, MD, David Langdon, MD, and Christopher J. Kuhn, MD, from Dartmouth-Hitchcock Medical Center, Lebanon, New Hampshire (at the time images were rendered); John Edwards, MD, from University of Cincinnati, Cincinnati, Ohio; and Werner Lang, MD, from Friedrich-Alexander Universitat, Erlangen, Germany.

■ REFERENCES

1. Brewster DC, Retana A, Waltman AC, Darling AC: Angiography in the management of aneurysms of the abdominal aorta: Its value and safety. N Engl J Med 292:822-825, 1975.
2. Simoni G, Perrone R, Cittadini G, et al: Helical CT for the study of abdominal aortic aneurysms in patients undergoing conventional surgical repair. Eur J Vasc Endovasc Surg 12:354-358, 1996.
3. Fillinger M: Utility of spiral CT in the preoperative evaluation of patients with abdominal aortic aneurysms. In Whittemore A (ed): Advances in Vascular Surgery. St. Louis, Mosby, 1997, pp 115-131.
4. Wyers MC, Fillinger MF, Schermerhorn ML, et al: Endovascular repair of abdominal aortic aneurysm without preoperative arteriography. J Vasc Surg 38:730-738, 2003.
5. Zwolak RM: Carotid endarterectomy without angiography: Are we ready? Vasc Surg 31:1-9, 1997.
6. Grassbaugh JA, Nelson PR, Rzucidlo EM, et al: Blinded comparison of preoperative duplex ultrasound scanning and contrast arteriography for planning revascularization at the level of the tibia. J Vasc Surg 37:1186-1190, 2003.
7. Hounsfield G: Computerized transverse axial scanning (tomography): I. Description of system. Br J Radiol 46:1016-1022, 1973.
8. Webster J: Encyclopedia of Medical Devices and Instrumentation. New York, Wiley, 1988.
9. Zeman R, Brink J, Costello P, et al: Helical/Spiral CT: A Practical Approach. New York, McGraw-Hill, 1995.
10. Raptopoulos V, Rosen M, Kent K, et al: Sequential helical CT angiography of aortoiliac disease. AJR Am J Roentgenol 166:1347-1354, 1996.
11. Rieker O, Düber C, Neufang A, et al: CT angiography versus intra-arterial digital subtraction angiography for assessment of aortoiliac occlusive disease. AJR Am J Roentgenol 169:1133-1138, 1997.
12. Rubin G, Walker P, Dake M, et al: Three-dimensional spiral computed tomographic angiography: An alternative imaging modality for the abdominal aorta and its branches. J Vasc Surg 18:656-665, 1993.
13. Balm R, Eikelboom B, van Leeuwen M, Noordzij J: Spiral CT-angiography of the aorta. Eur J Vasc Surg 8:544-551, 1994.
14. Broeders I, Blankensteijn J, Olree M, et al: Preoperative sizing of grafts for transfemoral endovascular aneurysm management: A prospective comparative study of spiral CT angiography, arteriography, and conventional CT imaging. J Endovasc Surg 4:252-261, 1997.
15. Wang G, Vannier M: Optimal pitch in spiral computed tomography. Med Phys 24:1635-1639, 1997.
16. Wang G, Vannier M: Spatial variation of section sensitivity profile in spiral computed tomography. Med Phys 21:1491-1497, 1994.
17. Brink J, Heiken J, Wang G, et al: Helical CT: Principles and technical considerations. Radiographics 14:887-893, 1994.
18. Duvernoy O, Coulden R, Ytterberg C: Aortic motion: A potential pitfall in CT imaging of dissection in the ascending aorta. J Comput Assist Tomogr 19:569-572, 1995.
19. Computed Tomography, Lightspeed Series, vol 2004. GE Medical Systems, 2003. Available at www.gemedicalsystems.com ed.
20. Ofer A, Nitecki SS, Linn S, et al: Multidetector CT angiography of peripheral vascular disease: A prospective comparison with intraarterial digital subtraction angiography. AJR Am J Roentgenol 180:719-724, 2003.
21. Martin ML, Tay KH, Flak B, et al: Multidetector CT angiography of the aortoiliac system and lower extremities: A prospective comparison with digital subtraction angiography. AJR Am J Roentgenol 180:1085-1091, 2003.
22. Cademartiri F, Mollet N, van der Lugt A, et al: Non-invasive 16-row multislice CT coronary angiography: Usefulness of saline chaser. Eur Radiol 14:178-183, 2004.
23. Maintz D, Tombach B, Juergens K, et al: Revealing in-stent stenoses of the iliac arteries: Comparison of multidetector CT with MR angiography and digital radiographic angiography in a phantom model. AJR Am J Roentgenol 179:1319-1322, 2002.
24. Castleman K: Digital Image Processing. Englewood Cliffs, NJ, Prentice-Hall, 1979.
25. Tepel M, Vand der Giet M, Schwarzfeld C, et al: Prevention of radiographic-contrast-agent-induced reductions in renal function by acetylcysteine. N Engl J Med 343:180-184, 2000.
26. Katayama H, Yamaguchi K, Kozuka T, et al: Adverse reactions to ionic and nonionic contrast media: A report from the Japanese Committee on the Safety of Contrast Media. Radiology 175:621-628, 1990.
27. Lasser E, Berry C, Mishkin M, et al: Pretreatment with corticosteroids to prevent adverse reactions to nonionic contrast media. AJR Am J Roentgenol 162:523-526, 1994.
28. Morcos S, Thomsen H, Webb J: Prevention of generalized reactions to contrast media: A consensus report and guidelines. Eur Radiol 11:1720-1728, 2001.
29. Fillinger M, Robbie P, McKenna M, et al: The "virtual" graft: Preoperative simulation of endovascular grafts using spiral CT with interactive three-dimensional reconstructions. J Endovasc Surg 4(Suppl I):10, 1997.
30. Fillinger MF: Postoperative imaging after endovascular AAA repair. Semin Vasc Surg 12:327-338, 1999.
31. Fillinger MF, Weaver JB: Imaging equipment and techniques for optimal intraoperative imaging during endovascular interventions. Semin Vasc Surg 12:315-326, 1999.
32. Tong D, Yenari M, Albers G: Intravenous thrombolytic therapy in acute stroke. Vasc Med 2:51-60, 1997.
33. Lim S, Sage D: Detection of subarachnoid blood clot and other thin flat structures by computed tomography. Radiology 123:79-84, 1977.
34. Meyer J, Gorey MT: Differential diagnosis of nontraumatic intracranial hemorrhage. Neuroimaging Clin N Am 8:263-293, 1998.
35. Yuh W, Crain M, Loes D, et al: MR imaging of cerebral ischemia: Findings in the first 24 hours. AJNR Am J Neuroradiol 12:621-629, 1991.
36. Crain M, Yuh W, Greene G, et al: Cerebral ischemia: Evaluation with contrast-enhanced MR imaging. AJNR Am J Neuroradiol 12:631-639, 1991.
37. Strayle-Batra M, Skalej M, Wakhloo A, et al: Three-dimensional spiral CT angiography in the detection of cerebral aneurysm. Acta Radiol 39:233-238, 1998.

38. Young N, Dorsch N, Kingston R, et al: Spiral CT scanning in the detection and evaluation of aneurysms of the circle of Willis. Surg Neurol 50:50-60, 1998.
39. Lanzino G, Kaptain G, Kallmes D, et al: Intracranial dissecting aneurysm causing subarachnoid hemorrhage: The role of computerized tomographic angiography and magnetic resonance angiography. Surg Neurol 48:477-481, 1997.
40. Riles T, Eidelman E, Litt A, et al: Comparison of magnetic resonance angiography, conventional angiography, and duplex scanning. Stroke 23:341-346, 1992.
41. Riles T, Posner M, Cohen W, et al: The totally occluded internal carotid artery: Preliminary observations using rapid sequential computerized tomographic scanning. Arch Surg 117:1185-1188, 1982.
42. Cinat M, Lane C, Pham H, et al: Helical CT angiography in the preoperative evaluation of carotid artery stenosis. J Vasc Surg 28:290-300, 1998.
43. Wise S, Hopper K, Ten Have T, Schwartz T: Measuring carotid artery stenosis using CT angiography: The dilemma of artifactual lumen eccentricity. AJR Am J Roentgenol 170:919-923, 1998.
44. Papp Z, Patel M, Ashtari M, et al: Carotid artery stenosis: Optimization of CT angiography with a combination of shaded surface display and source images. AJNR Am J Neuroradiol 18:759-763, 1997.
45. Corti R, Ferrari C, Roberti M, et al: A novel diagnostic approach for investigation for the extracranial cerebral arteries and its complementary role in duplex ultrasononography. Circulation 98:984-989, 1998.
46. Fisher D, Clagett G, Parker J, et al: Mandibular subluxation for high carotid exposure. J Vasc Surg 1:727-733, 1984.
47. Mock C, Lilly M, McRae R, Carney W: Selection of the approach to the distal internal carotid artery from the second cervical vertebra to the base of the skull. J Vasc Surg 13:846-853, 1991.
48. Patel M, Kuntz K, Klufas R, et al: Preoperative assessment of the carotid bifurcation: Can magnetic resonance angiography and duplex ultrasonography replace contrast arteriography? Stroke 26:1753-1758, 1995.
49. Brott T, Toole J: Medical compared with surgical treatment of asymptomatic carotid artery stenosis. Ann Intern Med 123:720-722, 1995.
50. National Institute of Neurological Disorders and Stroke: Carotid endarterectomy for patients with asymptomatic internal carotid artery stenosis. J Neurol Sci 129:76-77, 1995.
51. Matsumura J, Rilling W, Pearce W, et al: Helical computed tomography of the normal thoracic outlet. J Vasc Surg 26:776-783, 1997.
52. Bradshaw K, Pagano D, Bonser R, et al: Multiplanar reformatting and three-dimensional reconstruction: For pre-operative assessment of the thoracic aorta by computed tomography. Clin Radiol 53:198-202, 1998.
53. Sommer T, Fehske W, Holzknecht N, et al: Aortic dissection: A comparative study of diagnosis with spiral CT, multiplanar transesophageal echocardiography, and MR imaging. Radiology 199:347-352, 1996.
54. Quint LE, Platt JF, Sonnad SS, et al: Aortic intimal tears: Detection with spiral computed tomography. J Endovasc Ther 10:505-510, 2003.
55. Fabian T, Richardson J, Croce M, et al: Prospective study of blunt aortic injury: Multicenter trial of the American Association for the Surgery of Trauma. J Trauma 42:374-380, 1997.
56. Gavant M, Menke P, Fabian T, et al: Blunt traumatic aortic rupture: Detection with helical CT of the chest. Radiology 197:125-133, 1995.
57. Wicky S, Capasso P, Meuli R, et al: Spiral CT aortography: An efficient technique for the diagnosis of traumatic aortic injury. Eur Radiol 8:828-833, 1998.
58. Mayberry J: Imaging in thoracic trauma: The trauma surgeon's perspective. J Thorac Imaging 15:76-86, 2000.
59. Trachiotis G, Sell J, Pearson G, et al: Traumatic thoracic aortic rupture in the pediatric patient. Ann Thorac Surg 62:724-731, 1996.
60. Leblang S, Dolich M: Imaging of penetrating thoracic trauma. J Thorac Imaging 15:128-135, 2000.
61. Downing SW, Sperling JS, Mirvis SE, et al: Experience with spiral computed tomography as the sole diagnostic method for traumatic aortic rupture. Ann Thoracic Surg 72:495-501, 2001.
62. Fattori R, Napoli G, Lovato L, et al: Indications for, timing of, and results of catheter-based treatment of traumatic injury to the aorta. AJR Am J Roentgenol 179:603-609, 2002.
63. Berthet JP, Marty-Ane CH, Veerapen R, et al: Dissection of the abdominal aorta in blunt trauma: Endovascular or conventional surgical management? J Vasc Surg 38:997-1003, 2003.
64. Fillinger MF: Imaging of the thoracic and thoracoabdominal aorta. Semin Vasc Surg 13:247-263, 2000.
65. Gosselin M, Rubin G, Leung A, et al: Unsuspected pulmonary embolism: Prospective detection on routine helical CT scans. Radiology 208:209-215, 1998.
66. Garg K, Welsh C, Feyerabend A, et al: Pulmonary embolism: Diagnosis with spiral CT and ventilation-perfusion scanning—correlation with pulmonary angiographic results or clinical outcome. Radiology 208:201-208, 1998.
67. Cross J, Kemp P, Walsh C, et al: A randomized trial of spiral CT and ventilation perfusion scintigraphy for the diagnosis of pulmonary embolism. Clin Radiol 53:177-182, 1998.
68. Gottschalk A, Stein P, Goodman L, Sostman H: Overview of prospective investigation of pulmonary embolism diagnosis II. Semin Nucl Med 32:173-182, 2002.
69. Remy-Jardin M, Mastora I, Remy J: Pulmonary embolus imaging with multislice CT. Radiol Clin North Am 41:507-519, 2003.
70. Powell T, Muller NL: Imaging of acute pulmonary thromboembolism: Should spiral computed tomography replace the ventilation-perfusion scan? Clin Chest Med 24:29-38, 2003.
71. MacDonald SL, Mayo JR: Computed tomography of acute pulmonary embolism. Semin Ultrasound CT MR 24:217-231, 2003.
72. Remy J, Remy-Jardin M, Artaud D, Fribourg M: Multiplanar and three-dimensional reconstruction techniques in CT: Impact on chest diseases. Eur Radiol 8:335-351, 1998.
73. Fillinger MF: New imaging techniques in endovascular surgery. Surg Clin North Am 79:451-475, 1999.
74. Wyers MC, Schermerhorn ML, Fillinger MF, et al: Internal iliac occlusion without coil embolization during endovascular abdominal aortic aneurysm repair. J Vasc Surg 36:1138-1145, 2002.
75. Todd G, Nowygrod R, Benvenisty A, et al: The accuracy of CT scanning in the diagnosis of abdominal and thoracoabdominal aortic aneurysms. J Vasc Surg 13:302-310, 1991.
76. Faggioli G, Stella A, Gargiulo M, et al: Morphology of small aneurysms: Definition and impact on risk of rupture. Am J Surg 168:131-135, 1994.
77. Galanski M, Prokop M, Chavan A, et al: Renal arterial stenoses: Spiral CT angiography. Radiology 189:185-192, 1993.
78. Van Hoe L, Baert A, Gryspeerdt S, et al: Supra- and juxtarenal aneurysms of the abdominal aorta: Preoperative assessment with thin-section spiral CT. Radiology 198:443-448, 1996.
79. Balm R, Kaatee R, Blankensteijn J, et al: CT-angiography of abdominal aortic aneurysms after transfemoral endovascular aneurysm management. Eur J Vasc Endovasc Surg 12:182-188, 1996.
80. Cikrit D, Harris V, Hemmer C, et al: Comparison of spiral CT scan and arteriography for evaluation of renal and visceral arteries. Ann Vasc Surg 10:109-116, 1996.
81. Rubin G, Dake M, Napel S, et al: Spiral CT of renal artery stenosis: Comparison of three-dimensional rendering techniques. Radiology 190:181-189, 1994.
82. Salaman R, Shandall A, Morgan R, et al: Intravenous digital subtraction angiography versus computed tomography in the assessment of abdominal aortic aneurysm. Br J Surg 81:661-663, 1994.
83. Costello P, Gaa J: Spiral CT angiography of abdominal aortic aneurysms. Radiographics 15:397-406, 1995.
84. Brewster D, Cambria R, Moncure A, et al: Aortocaval and iliac arteriovenous fistulas: Recognition and treatment. J Vasc Surg 13:253-264, 1991.
85. Davis P, Gloviczki P, Cherry K Jr, et al: Aorto-caval and ilio-iliac arteriovenous fistulae. Am J Surg 176:115-118, 1998.

86. Schmidt R, Bruns C, Walter M, Erasmi H: Aorto-caval fistula—an uncommon complication of infrarenal aortic aneurysms. Thorac Cardiovasc Surg 42:208-211, 1994.
87. Farber A, Fillinger M, Connors J, et al: Comparison of angiography, intravascular ultrasound and three dimensional CT for morphologic evaluation in a three dimensional aneurysm model. Unpublished data, 2004.
88. Matsumura J, Pearce W, McCarthy W, Yao J: Reduction in aortic aneurysm size: Early results after endovascular graft placement. EVT Investigators. J Vasc Surg 25:113-123, 1997.
89. May J, White G, Yu W, et al: A prospective study of changes in morphology and dimensions of abdominal aortic aneurysms following endoluminal repair: A preliminary report. J Endovasc Surg 2:343-347, 1995.
90. May J, White G, Yu W, et al: A prospective study of anatomico-pathological changes in abdominal aortic aneurysms following endoluminal repair: Is the aneurysmal process reversed? Eur J Vasc Endovasc Surg 12:11-17, 1996.
91. Torsello G, Klenk E, Kasprzak B, Umscheid T: Rupture of abdominal aortic aneurysm previously treated by endovascular stentgraft. J Vasc Surg 28:184-187, 1998.
92. Matsumura J, Moore W: Clinical consequences of periprosthetic leak after endovascular repair of abdominal aortic aneurysm. J Vasc Surg 27:606-613, 1998.
93. Alimi Y, Chafke N, Rivoal R, et al: Rupture of an abdominal aortic aneurysm after endovascular graft placement and aneurysm size reduction. J Vasc Surg 28:178-183, 1998.
94. Thomas P, Shaw J, Ashton H, Scott R: Accuracy of ultrasound in a screening programme for abdominal aortic aneurysms. J Med Screening 1:3-6, 1994.
95. Lederle F, Wilson S, Johnson G, et al: Variability in measurement of abdominal aortic aneurysms. Abdominal Aortic Aneurysm Detection and Management Veterans Administration Cooperative Study Group. J Vasc Surg 21:945-952, 1995.
96. Schurink G, Aarts N, Wilde J, et al: Endoleakage after stent-graft treatment of abdominal aortic aneurysm: Implications on pressure and imaging—an in vitro study. J Vasc Surg 28:234-241, 1998.
97. Faries P, Agarwal G, Lookstein R, et al: Use of cine magnetic resonance angiography in quantifying aneurysm pulsatility associated with endoleak. J Vasc Surg 38:652-656, 2003.
98. Lookstein R, Goldman J, Pukin L, Marin M: Time-resolved magnetic resonance angiography as a noninvasive method to characterize endoleaks: Initial results compared with conventional angiography. J Vasc Surg 39:27-33, 2004.
99. Riccabona M, Nelson T, Pretorius D, Davidson T: In vivo three-dimensional sonographic measurement of organ volume: Validation in the urinary bladder. J Ultrasound Med 15:627-632, 1996.
100. Wheatley J, Rosenfield N, Feldstein D, et al: Validation of a technique of computer-aided tumor volume determination. J Surg Res 59:621-626, 1995.
101. Wever JJ, Blankensteijn JD, Mali WPTM, Eikelboom BC: Maximal aneurysm diameter follow-up is inadequate after endovascular abdominal aortic aneurysm repair. Eur J Vasc Endovasc Surg 20:177-182, 2000.
102. Singh-Ranger R, McArthur T, Corte MD, et al: The abdominal aortic aneurysm sac after endoluminal exclusion: A medium-term morphologic follow-up based on volumetric technology. J Vasc Surg 31:490-500, 2000.
103. White RA, Donayre CE, Walot I, et al: Computed tomography assessment of abdominal aortic aneurysm morphology after endograft exclusion. J Vasc Surg 33(2 Suppl):S1-10, 2001.
104. Lee JT, Aziz IN, Haukoos JS, et al: Volume regression of abdominal aortic aneurysms and its relation to successful endoluminal exclusion. J Vasc Surg 38:1254-1263, 2003.
105. Beregi J, Djabbari M, Desmoucelle F, et al: Popliteal vascular disease: Evaluation with spiral CT angiography. Radiology 203:477-483, 1997.
106. Takase K, Imakita S, Kuribayashi S, et al: Popliteal artery entrapment syndrome: Aberrant origin of gastrocnemius muscle shown by 3D CT. J Comput Assist Tomogr 21:523-528, 1997.
107. Rizzo R, Flinn W, Yao J, et al: Computed tomography for evaluation of arterial disease in the popliteal fossa. J Vasc Surg 11:112-119, 1990.
108. Soto J, Munera F, Cardoso N, et al: Diagnostic performance of helical CT angiography in trauma to large arteries of the extremities. J Comput Assist Tomogr 23:188-196, 1999.
109. Kurihashi A, Tamai K, Saotome K: Peroneal arteriovenous fistula and pseudoaneurysm formation after blunt trauma: A case report. Clin Orthop 304:218-221, 1994.
110. Rauch R, Silverman P, Korobkin M, et al: Computed tomography of benign angiomatous lesions of the extremities. J Comput Assist Tomogr 8:1143-1146, 1984.
111. Taylor C: Computed tomography in the evaluation of the portal venous system. J Clin Gastroenterol 14:167-172, 1992.
112. Kuszyk B, Osterman F Jr, Venbrux A, et al: Portal venous system thrombosis: Helical CT angiography before transjugular intrahepatic portosystemic shunt creation. Radiology 206:179-186, 1998.
113. Baldt M, Zontsich T, Kainberger F, et al: Spiral CT evaluation of deep venous thrombosis. Semin Ultrasound CT MR 18:369-375, 1997.
114. Rijs J, Depreitere B, Beckers A, et al: Mesenteric venous thrombosis: Diagnostic and therapeutic approach. Acta Chir Belg 97:247-249, 1997.
115. Stringfellow MM, Lawrence PF, Stringfellow RG: The influence of aorta-aneurysm geometry upon stress in the aneurysm wall. J Surg Res 42:425-433, 1987.
116. Mower WR, Quinones WJ, Gambhir SS: Effect of intraluminal thrombus on abdominal aortic aneurysm wall stress. J Vasc Surg 26:602-608, 1997.
117. Inzoli F, Boschetti F, Zappa M, et al: Biomechanical factors in abdominal aortic aneurysm rupture. Eur J Vasc Surg 7:667-674, 1993.
118. Elger DF, Blackketter DM, Budwig RS, Johansen KH: The influence of shape on the stresses in model abdominal aortic aneurysms. J Biomech Eng 118:326-332, 1996.
119. Raghavan ML, Webster MW, Vorp DA: Ex vivo biomechanical behavior of abdominal aortic aneurysm: Assessment using a new mathematical model. Ann Biomed Eng 24:573-582, 1996.
120. Vorp DA, Raghavan ML, Webster MW: Mechanical wall stress in abdominal aortic aneurysm: Influence of diameter and asymmetry. J Vasc Surg 27:632-639, 1998.
121. Raghavan ML, Vorp DA, Federle MP, et al: Wall stress distribution on three-dimensionally reconstructed models of human abdominal aortic aneurysm. J Vasc Surg 31:760-769, 2000.
122. Fillinger MF, Raghavan ML, Marra SP, et al: In vivo analysis of mechanical wall stress and abdominal aortic aneurysm rupture risk. J Vasc Surg 36:589-597, 2002.
123. Fillinger MF, Marra SP, Raghavan ML, Kennedy FE: Prediction of rupture risk in abdominal aortic aneurysm during observation: Wall stress versus diameter. J Vasc Surg 37(4):724-732, 2003.

Section IV

Chapter 22

Magnetic Resonance Imaging and Angiography

ERIK K. INSKO, MD, PHD
JEFFREY P. CARPENTER, MD

Over the past several years, magnetic resonance imaging (MRI) and angiography (MRA) have become standard methods of evaluation for several vascular disorders. The most common indications for MRA are evaluation of renovascular disease[1-3] and peripheral vascular disease.[4-9]

MRA has become an accepted standard of evaluation for renovascular and peripheral vascular disease because it has been demonstrated to be accurate,[1,2,5,7,8] cost-effective,[10] and increasingly available and simple to perform. The complications associated with catheter angiography are well known.[11-13] MRA has the advantage of being entirely noninvasive. In addition, this modality utilizes a contrast agent that is non-nephrotoxic and is associated with a much lower incidence of allergic reactions.[14-18] Finally, with MRA, ionizing radiation and its possible complications are avoided.[19] Other differences in the method of image formation allow MRA to be even more accurate than catheter angiography in the identification of patent runoff vessels.[20]

As a result of the accuracy and ease of the MRA examination, in combination with its advantages over traditional catheter angiography, MRA is establishing itself as a standard method of evaluation for many other types of vascular disease. They include such common disorders as carotid stenosis[21-24] and thoracic and abdominal aneurysms or dissections.[25-27] In addition to these more common disorders, MRA and magnetic resonance venography (MRV) have also demonstrated usefulness in the evaluation of central venous thrombosis,[28,29] deep venous thrombosis (DVT),[30-32] mesenteric arterial[33] and venous disease,[34] thoracic outlet syndrome,[35] potential renal donors,[36,37] and postoperative transplant grafts.[38,39] Even more esoteric diseases, such as large-vessel vasculitis,[40] connective tissue disorders,[41] and pulmonary arteriovenous malformations (AVMs),[42,43] can be accurately diagnosed and assessed by MRA.

If noninvasive and rapid methods of imaging vascular disease can yield accurate diagnostic information, the role of invasive forms of diagnostic vascular evaluation may diminish. Catheter angiography will rightfully remain the "gold standard" for evaluation of vascular disease, but its complications, combined with the power of MRA, predict that the use of catheter angiography for purely diagnostic purposes may soon be outdated.

■ MAGNETIC RESONANCE IMAGING

Creating MR Images

MRI is performed with the use of a large external magnetic field, external magnetic field gradients, and an applied oscillating magnetic field known as the *radiofrequency field* or RF field. The combination of these three types of applied magnetic fields allows the operator to produce signals from inside patients that, in turn, can be used to create MR images.

The details of the external magnetic field, the magnetic field gradients, and the RF field determine many of the characteristics of MR images. The goal of the external magnetic field is to magnetize the subject by making the protons within the subject align parallel with the external field. The physical characteristics of the protons and the size of the external magnetic field define the resonance frequency of the proton. If the external magnetic field is uniform, all the protons resonate at the same frequency.

Most MRI machines operate with an external field strength of 1.5 tesla (T). Systems with lower field strength (less than 1.0 T) tend to produce images at a slower rate or a lower resolution than is typically desirable. Generally, higher field strengths are desirable, but imagers with field strengths higher than 3.0 T have other technical problems beyond the scope of this discussion.

The magnetic field gradients are used to alter the otherwise uniform external magnetic field in a linear fashion in any one of three directions. The gradients "ramping" on and off produce the noise heard when an MR image is being made. When the gradient fields are applied, the protons resonate at a frequency that is now a function of its position. This is exactly analogous to the frequency of a radio station corresponding to a specific position on a radio's dial.

The speed and strength of the gradients determine the size of the images and may be a rate-limiting step in imaging speed. For angiographic imaging, it is generally true that faster and stronger gradients are a desirable feature of the MRI system.

Resonant coils placed adjacent to the region of interest produce the RF field. These fields are tuned to match the resonant frequency of the protons inside the patient. The applied RF in combination with the gradients is used to manipulate the protons inside the patient to produce a signal. This signal is detected with a receiver RF coil also tuned to the resonant frequency of the protons. Once detected, the signal is sent to an amplifier and receiver, where it is digitized and processed with a mathematical algorithm known as a Fourier transform to produce the MR image.

Characteristics of MR Images

The contrast in MR images depends on the characteristics of the object being imaged as well as on the specifics of the sequence itself. Images are typically referred to as either T1- or T2-weighted. T2-weighted images display simple fluids such as urine, bile, and cerebrospinal fluid as bright and other tissues with lower signal. T2-weighted imaging is one of the basic sequences for tumor imaging but is not used for angiographic imaging. MRA and MRV examinations are performed with T1-weighted image sequences. Things that are bright on T1-weighted images are often seen on MR angiographs as well; examples are fat, methemoglobin, flow effects, and MRI contrast agent.

MR Pulse Sequences

The *MR pulse sequence* is a label that refers to the particular combination of RF and gradients that are used to create the image. There are a disturbing number of acronyms for MR pulse sequences, but it is nearly true that all MR images are variations of either a spin-echo sequence or a gradient-echo sequence. The spin-echo pulse sequence methods utilize RF alone to produce the MR signal or echo. Gradient-echo pulse sequences, however, use RF and the applied gradient field to produce the echo signal. As a rough generalization, spin-echo pulse sequences are used to produce T2-weighted images, and gradient-echo sequences are used to create T1-weighted images. In particular, MRA and MRV typically are performed with T1-weighted, gradient-echo pulse sequences.

Pulse Sequence Parameters

The characteristics of a tissue that determine its appearance on MR images are the T1 and T2 values of the tissue. Some tissues are bright on T1-weighted images, and others on T2-weighted images. How then do we create a T1- or T-weighted image? All pulse sequences have fundamental parameters, known as echo time (TE) and repetition time (TR), that determine the image contrast. T2-weighted images have a longer TE, in the range of 80 milliseconds (msec) or greater. These sequences also have a longer TR time, in the range of several seconds or more. Because TE and TR times are both longer, these sequences are slower and are not appropriate for contrast-enhanced angiography. T1-weighted images have very short TR and TE times. The TE may be close to 1 msec or even less, and the TR may range from hundreds of milliseconds to less than 10 msec for angiographic sequences. T1-weighted gradient-echo sequences are fast and are used for angiographic examinations.

Other parameters used in all MR image sequences are the field-of-view (FOV) and the image matrix. The FOV is the size of the imaged region. In a two-dimensional image, it may be 40 by 30 cm with a slice thickness of 5 mm. The resolution of the image in that 5-mm slice then depends on the number of pixels within the 30 × 40-cm region. The number of pixels is the image matrix. The image resolution (voxel size) for an image matrix 256 by 192 pixels would be 1.56 mm (40 cm ÷ 256) by 3.26 mm (30 cm ÷ 192). Usually, however, MRA is performed with a three-dimensional (3D) image sequence. In that case the FOV is specified with three dimensions as 40 cm by 30 cm by 30 cm. For an image matrix of 256 by 192 by 64 pixels, the voxel size is 1.56 mm by 3.26 mm by 4.7 mm. Image postprocessing is usually performed on 3D data to make the last dimension twice as small as specified by the pulse sequence. In this case, such processing would yield a voxel size of 1.56 mm by 3.26 mm by 2.35 mm.

■ MAGNETIC RESONANCE ANGIOGRAPHY AND VENOGRAPHY

Time-of-Flight MR Angiography

MR angiography and MR venography are performed with T1-weighted gradient-echo pulse sequences. The angiographic methods may be divided into two basic categories, noncontrast methods and contrast-enhanced methods. The noncontrast methods include phase contrast and time-of-flight (TOF) angiography. Phase contrast is not commonly used in clinical practice and is not addressed here. TOF imaging, however, is often utilized in clinical practice even though contrast-enhanced MRA has proved itself superior in most cases.[1,39,44-46]

TOF angiography utilizes a rapid T1-weighted pulse sequence in either sequentially acquired 2D slices or a 3D imaging slab. For purposes of description, we will concentrate on the 2D TOF sequence, which is the most commonly used. In a single-slice image for which data are gathered rapidly, the protons within the slice lose much of their magnetization. Thus, there is much less signal from those protons, and the corresponding tissues are not well seen. The rapid imaging does not degrade any protons outside the slice, however. When those fully magnetized protons in a vessel flow into the slice of interest, they produce much greater signal than the surrounding tissue. The result is an image in which the blood flowing into the slice is very bright and the surrounding tissue is relatively dark.

For example, if the image is obtained in an axial slice through the midabdomen, the aorta and inferior vena cava (IVC) as well as some of the mesenteric arteries and veins are bright. In order to remove either the arteries or the veins, a special RF pulse is applied to the tissue either above or below the slice; this eliminates magnetization from the tissue. If an inferior saturation pulse is utilized in this example image, only the protons flowing into the slab from above (the aorta and mesenteric arteries) are bright. A series of such images obtained sequentially produce a 2D TOF abdominal angiogram.

TOF imaging is becoming less useful as contrast-enhanced methods become more and more sophisticated.[1,39,44-46] However, TOF is a robust method that can be used in cases in which contrast agent cannot be administered or as a complementary method to contrast angiography.

Contrast-Enhanced MR Angiography

All currently approved MR contrast agents are variants of Gd-DTPA, in which the rare earth element gadolinium (Gd) is chelated with diethylenetriaminepentaacetic acid (DTPA). These agents are designed to shorten the T1 value of the protons in the local vicinity, thereby making them more conspicuous on T1-weighted imaging sequences.

There are several important differences between MR contrast material and the iodinated contrast material used for computed tomography angiography (CTA) or catheter angiography. First, as suggested, MRI is designed to image not the agent itself but its effect on the protons in the surrounding water. This fact has a subtle implication that is important in certain circumstances. That is, a very small amount of MR contrast agent may be detected from its effect on multiple water molecules, whereas an equivalently small amount of iodinated contrast agent is simply not detectable directly on CTA or catheter angiography. This is one reason why the volume of MR contrast agent can be much smaller than that of an iodinated contrast agent used in CTA or a diagnostic angiogram. Other advantages of gadolinium-based contrast agents are decreased nephrotoxicity and a lower incidence of reactions to the contrast agent, as mentioned earlier.[14-18]

Three-Dimensional Image Reconstruction

Contrast-enhanced MRA is performed as a 3D imaging sequence. 3D imaging sequences are typically faster and have higher resolution than 2D, noncontrast angiograms with the same coverage. A 3D image can be viewed as a stack of 2D images, but the higher resolution of 3D methods allows for the use of multiplanar reformatting (MPR). MPR is a manipulation of the data to create images from multiple views that optimize the visualization of anatomy or disease. Images can be processed with many types of algorithms to display the 3D data to best advantage. Because contrast within vessels is designed to have the highest intensity, an algorithm that displays the maximum intensity of the voxels, known as maximum intensity projection[47] (MIP), is the most commonly used algorithm for reconstructing 3D MRA images.

Clinical Applications of MR Angiography

The primary use of MRA is to detect and assess the complications of atherosclerotic disease. MRA has become a standard method to evaluate both renal artery stenosis[48] and peripheral vascular disease.[49] Increasingly, MRA is becoming an accepted standard for evaluation of carotid atherosclerosis as well. MRA has become a standard diagnostic test for atherosclerotic disease because it has continued to improve in diagnostic performance. In the realm of atherosclerosis, there is no sign that this improvement is slowing. Current MR research into atherosclerosis and particularly into the detection of unstable plaques[24,50] has the potential to elevate the care of patients with atherosclerosis to a new level.

Renovascular Disease

3D gadolinium-enhanced MRA has become a clinical standard for the evaluation of renovascular disease.[48] The most common such disease is atherosclerotic renal artery stenosis. As MRA has matured as a technique, however, it has shown itself to be a powerful technique for evaluating more subtle renal vascular conditions, such as fibromuscular dysplasia, renal artery aneurysms, and accessory renal arteries.[1] The detection of accessory arteries is particularly important for the assessment of potential living kidney donors.[36,37]

Approximately 25% of the middle-aged white and African-American populations in the United States have high blood pressure.[51] Renal artery stenosis is the most common cause of secondary hypertension, and approximately 1% of people with hypertension have renal artery stenosis.[52] Because renal artery stenosis is so common and potentially curable,[53-55] appropriate screening tests for those at risk are critical. A large meta-analysis demonstrated that 2D TOF MRA of the renal arteries has a sensitivity of 94% and a specificity of 85% compared with catheter angiography.[1] 3D contrast-enhanced MRA, however, is even better, with a sensitivity of 94% and a specificity of 93%. In addition, it has been shown that when MRA is used to plan a renal artery intervention, both the number of pretreatment angiograms and the total amount of contrast agent are reduced.[56]

As shown in Figure 22-1, the majority of renal artery stenoses are in the ostial or proximal segments of the renal arteries.[57] As methods for 3D contrast-enhanced MRA have improved, diseases that are not typically near the renal artery origin have been more commonly diagnosed by MRA. They include another curable cause of hypertension, fibromuscular dysplasia[58,59] (Fig. 22-2).

2D MRA, although 82% sensitive for the detection of accessory renal arteries, does not match the sensitivity of the higher-resolution 3D MRA (95%).[1] Accessory renal arteries occur in nearly 45% of cases,[60] and their detection can be important in the screening of candidates for kidney donation.[36,37] MRI and MRA have been shown to be very cost-effective methods of evaluating potential kidney donors.[61] Figure 22-3 demonstrates an individual with a total of six renal arteries.

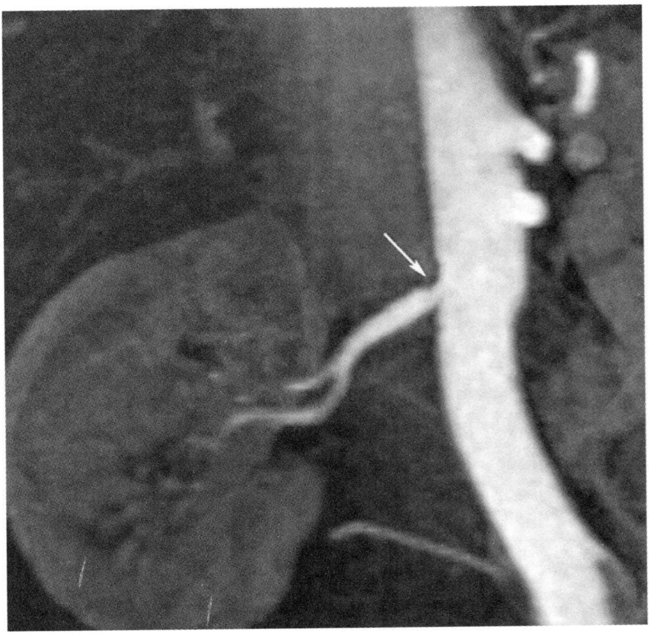

FIGURE 22-1 Coronal 3D MR angiogram showing an ostial renal artery plaque (*arrow*).

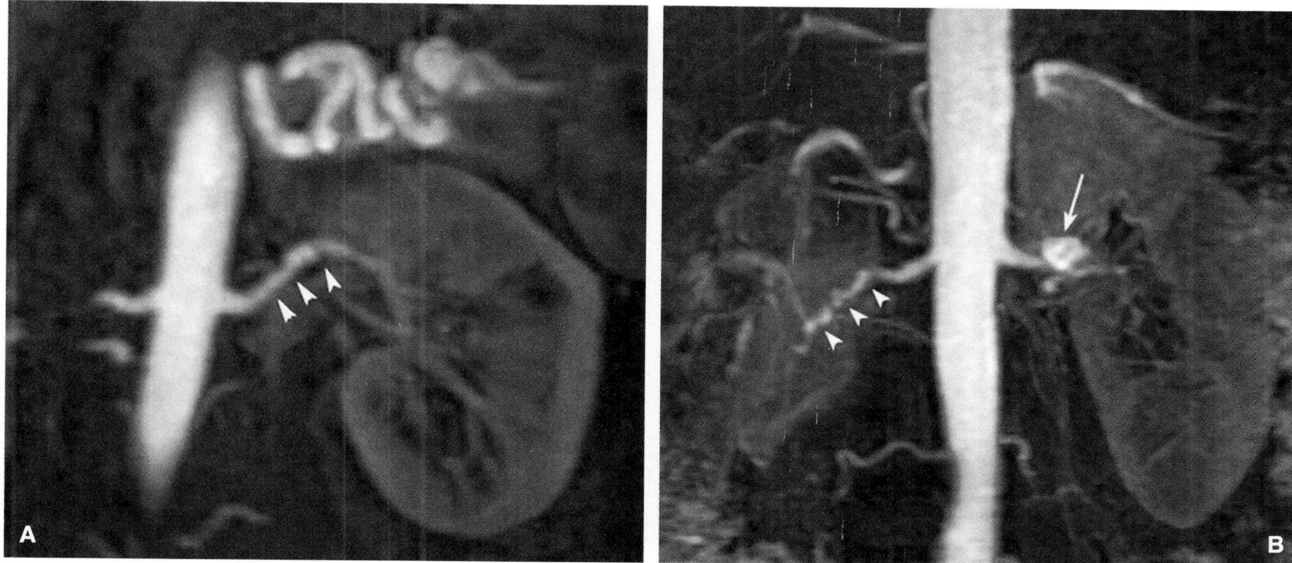

FIGURE 22-2 Coronal 3D MR angiograms. **A,** Subtle fibromuscular dysplasia can be seen (*arrowheads*). Note that the disease is isolated to the distal portion of the main renal artery. **B,** Right-sided fibromuscular dysplasia (*arrowheads*) and a left-sided renal artery aneurysm (*arrow*). Renal artery aneurysms may occur in patients with fibromuscular dysplasia.

Peripheral Vascular Disease

MRA has become a standard method of evaluation for peripheral vascular disease.[49] Peripheral vascular disease is extremely common in the middle-aged and elderly people. The prevalence is approximately 3% in those older than 55 years but increases to 11% for those older than 65 and to 20% for those older than 70 years.[62] MRA has been demonstrated to be effective in the preoperative evaluation of patients[5,63,64] with peripheral vascular disease, including imaging of the inflow vessels[65] and evaluation of any stenoses[66] (Figs. 22-4 and 22-5). The sensitivity of MRA for detecting hemodynamically significant stenoses is 99.5%, and the specificity is 98.8%, compared with digital subtraction angiography (DSA).[66] In addition, MRA is effective in imaging suitable target vessels, including vessels not seen on catheter angiography.[20,66] MRA is also a cost-effective method for evaluating a patient with peripheral vascular disease.[67,68] In many patients, MRA may be the only option for pretreatment evaluation of peripheral vascular disease because of baseline renal insufficiency and the potential nephrotoxicity of iodinated contrast agents.[15] However, we believe that MRA can and should be the sole method of preoperative imaging in almost all patients for whom vascular reconstruction or intervention is being planned.

With the continued improvement in MR technology, the MRA evaluation of peripheral vascular disease also advances.[6,45,46,69,70] Improvements in stepping table examinations have increased the speed and resolution of the examination, allowing for better visualization of smaller distal vessels as well as for arterial phase–dedicated imaging of the feet (Fig. 22-6). As mentioned previously, MRA has been shown to be superior to DSA in the evaluation of distal vessels in some cases.[20,66] A study of 37 patients showed that MRA depicts significantly more vascular segments in the foot than DSA ($P \sim .0001$).[70] This report is further evidence that MRA should be the sole method of preoperative imaging in patients with peripheral vascular disease.

In addition to its value for diagnosis and pretreatment planning, MRA may be utilized in the evaluation of patients after therapy.[71-73] MRA can be used to assess patency and stenosis of a graft (Figs. 22-7 and 22-8). This modality is also a powerful technique for demonstrating complications of graft placement, such as pseudoaneurysm formation (Fig. 22-9). Even very small grafts with very distal touchdown can be evaluated with MRA (Fig. 22-10).

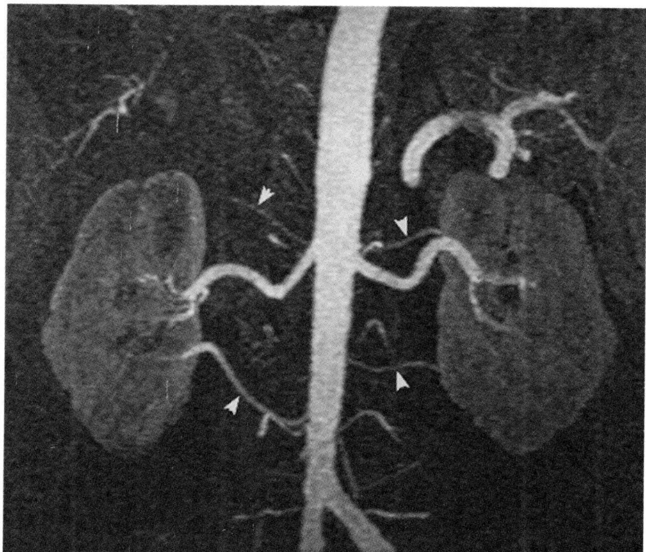

FIGURE 22-3 Coronal 3D MR angiogram showing two main renal arteries and four accessory arteries (*arrowheads*). Note that accessory arteries may enter the renal hilum or perforate the cortex.

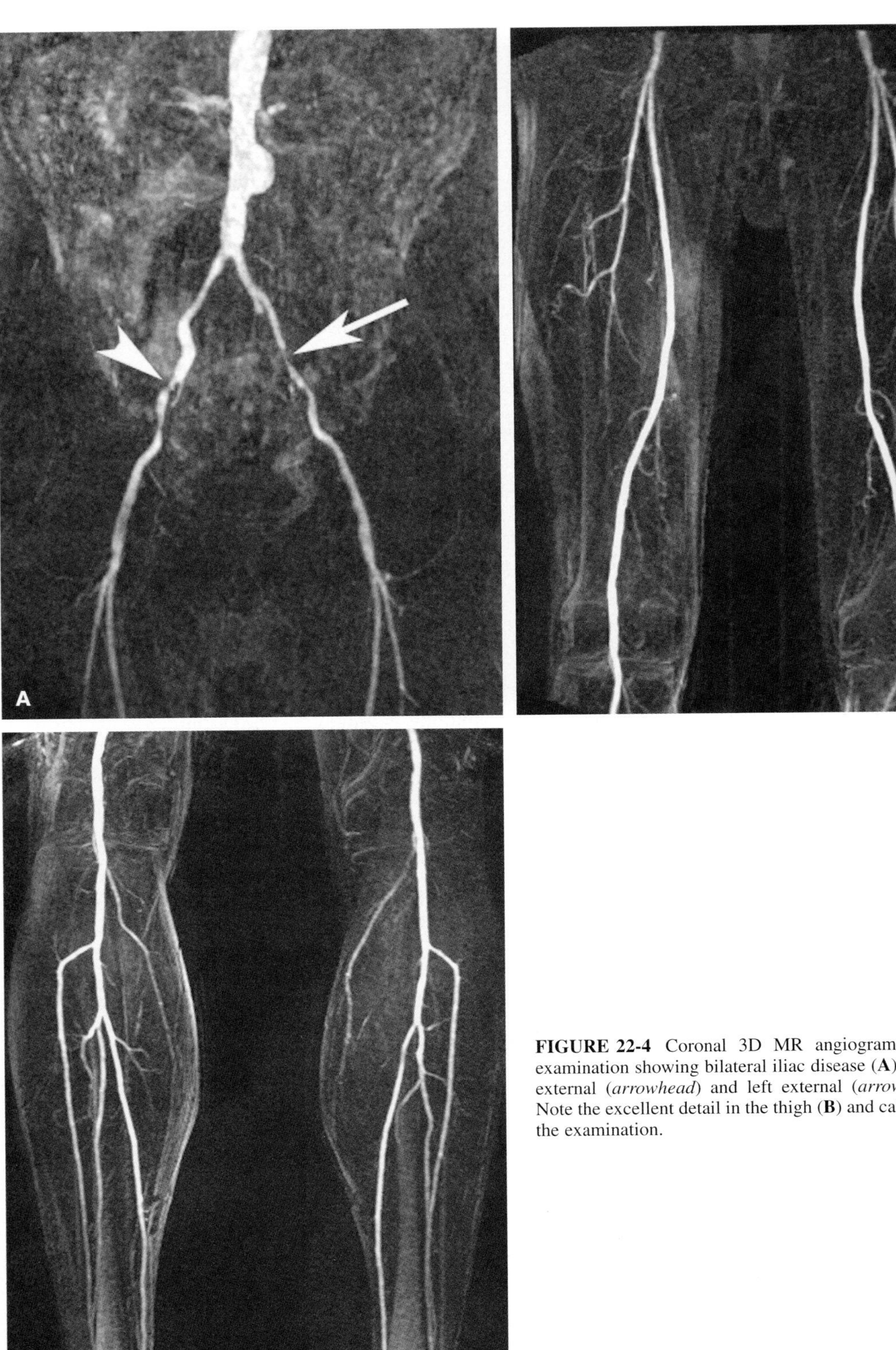

FIGURE 22-4 Coronal 3D MR angiogram stepping table examination showing bilateral iliac disease (**A**) within the right external (*arrowhead*) and left external (*arrow*) iliac arteries. Note the excellent detail in the thigh (**B**) and calf (**C**) stations of the examination.

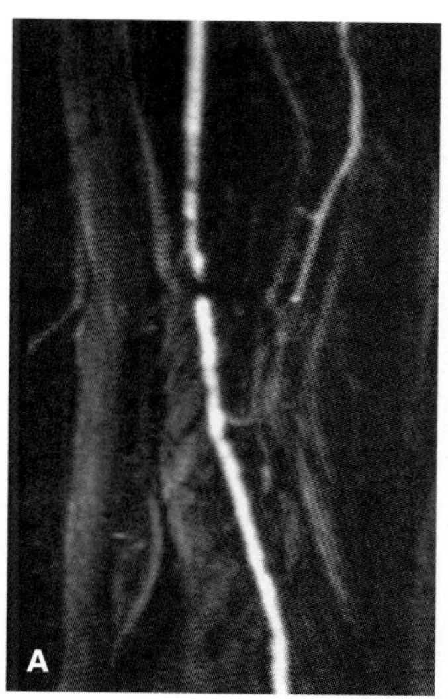

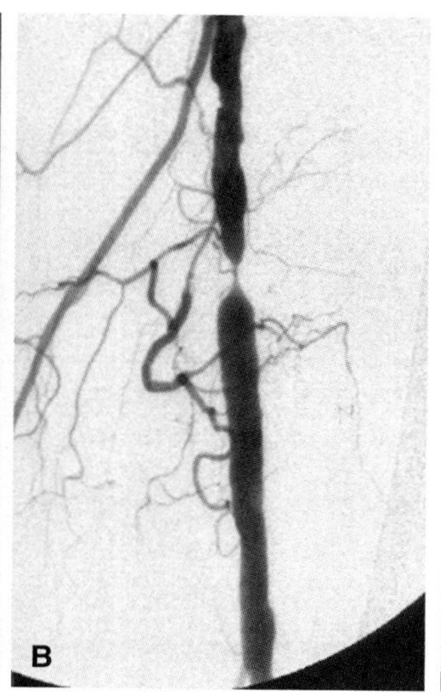

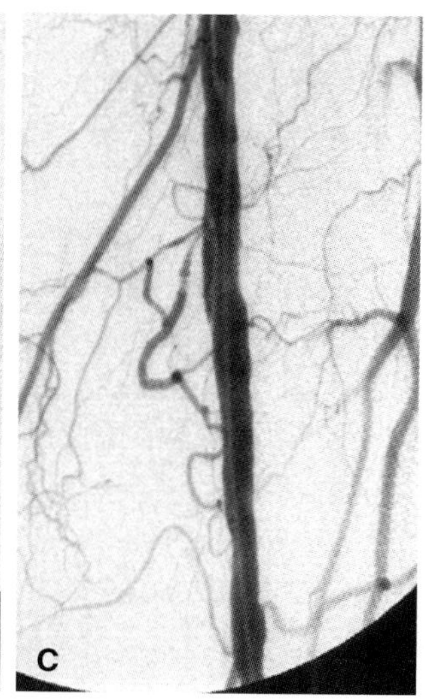

FIGURE 22-5 **A,** 3D MR angiogram showing high-grade stenosis in the above-knee popliteal artery. **B,** There is excellent correlation between findings of the pretreatment MR angiogram and DSA. **C,** An excellent result has been achieved by angioplasty.

Carotid Vascular Disease

MRA is increasingly used to evaluate carotid artery atherosclerosis, as it has proved to be a very sensitive method of detecting significant stenoses. For stenosis of between 70% and 99% narrowing, MRA has a reported sensitivity of 95% and a specificity of 90%.[21] For all stenoses, MRA has a reported sensitivity of 98% and a specificity of 86%.[22] Several researchers conclude that the performance of MRA warrants its use as a tool to plan operative or interventional revascularization.[23,74] A 3D MR angiogram of the carotid and vertebral arteries is shown in Figure 22-11.

Owing to the size of the vessels and their proximity to the skin, the carotid arteries are some of the easiest vessels to assess with high-resolution MRI. MRI assessments of the carotid arteries have shown promise in detecting complex or unstable plaque.[24,50,75] This work may advance the evaluation of atherosclerotic plaque beyond that of a simple assessment of stenosis to a more sophisticated assessment of both plaque stability and anatomic narrowing.

Aortic Vascular Disease

Contrast-enhanced 3D MRA has been used to assess the aorta in patients with many different types of disease.[25,76-78] The assessment of the aortic arch with contrast-enhanced MRA may be superior to any other technique[79] (Fig. 22-12). Other diseases that are routinely evaluated with MRA at some centers are aortic dissection[25,80-82] (Fig. 22-13) and aneurysms.[25,83] MRA has been used to evaluate patients with connective tissue disorders[40] (Fig. 22-14), to assess for aortic stent graft placement,[26,84] and to search for endoleaks in patients with nitinol-based stent-grafts.[85,86]

Mesenteric Vascular Disease

The most common use of MRA to evaluate mesenteric vascular disease is in patients with suspected intestinal angina or chronic mesenteric ischemia.[7,87] MRA is between 95% and 97% accurate for characterizing proximal disease of the superior mesenteric artery[88] in cases of chronic mesenteric ischemia.

MRA is also useful to assess more complex diseases of the mesenteric vasculature. The median arcuate ligament passes anterior to the descending aorta near the T12 level. During end-expiration, the ligament can compress the proximal portion of the celiac axis, leading to a false impression of proximal celiac stenosis. MRA can be useful in demonstrating the effect of the arcuate ligament during a single examination[89] (Fig. 22-15).

In cases of suspected mesenteric venous thrombosis, MRV can be extremely useful and has even been suggested to be superior to mesenteric catheter angiography.[90] MRV is particularly successful because of the ease of detecting small amounts of MR contrast agent. A central injection of MR contrast agent is easily visualized in the veins even after several cycles of circulation. Figure 22-16, an example of post–contrast enhancement 2D MRI, clearly depicts the portal vein, splenic vein, superior mesenteric vein, and even the inferior mesenteric venous branches occluded with thrombus.

Venous Vascular Disease

MRV is a powerful technique to evaluate both central[28,29] and deep[30-32] venous structures. Central venous structures, in particular the superior vena cava (SVC), can be evaluated with 3D methods, which have 100% sensitivity for the detection of thrombus compared with DSA.[29] For pelvic and deep venous structures, 2D TOF angiography is more commonly used.[30,31] In a series of patients with suspected DVT, this method detected pelvic DVT that could not be diagnosed by ultrasound in 20% of patients.[31] This same study also demonstrated that in cases of known pulmonary embolism and negative lower extremity Doppler ultrasound findings, 29% of patients had residual pelvic DVT.

Figure 22-17 shows 2D TOF images of an IVC thrombus with corresponding 2D post–contrast enhancement MRI images. Both types of imaging are useful for imaging DVT of the abdomen, pelvis, and lower extremities.

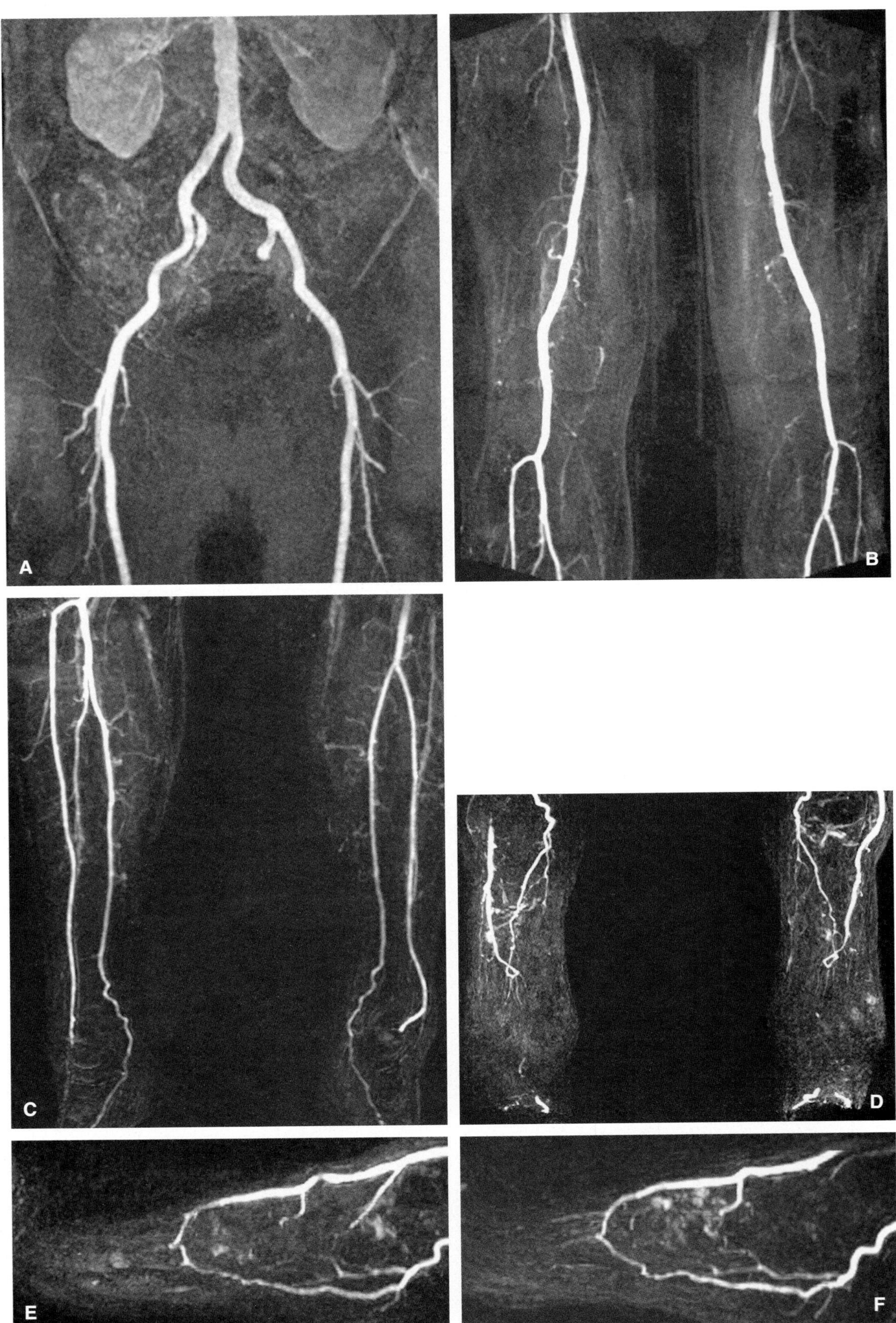

FIGURE 22-6 A five-station stepping table examination showing (**A**) normal inflow vessels to the lower extremities, (**B**) normal thigh vessels, (**C**) normal calf vessels, and (**D**) normal vessels in both feet. The high-resolution 3D data allow for reformatting of the circulation of each foot in the sagittal plane (**E** and **F**), showing a patent plantar arch in each.

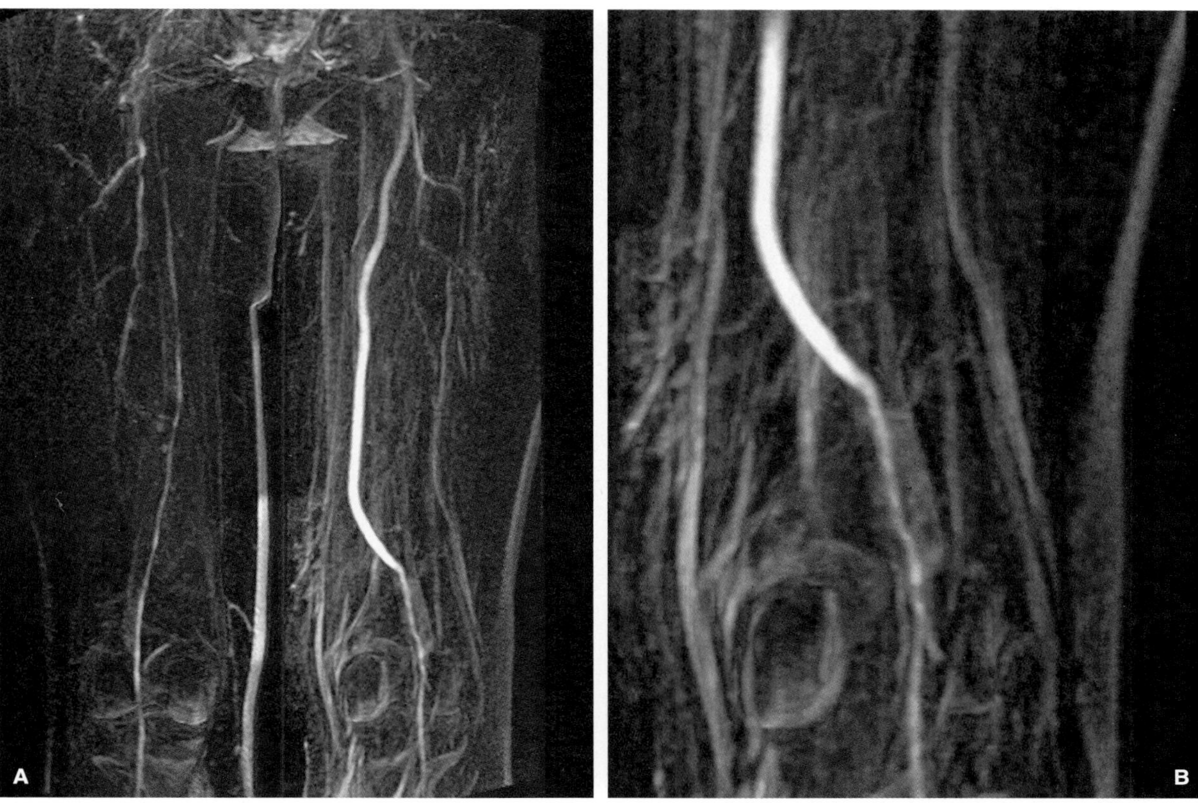

FIGURE 22-7 **A,** Thigh-station coronal 3D MR angiogram of a femoral-to-popliteal bypass graft. Note the contralateral disease of the superficial femoral artery. **B,** An oblique reformatted image shows the normal touchdown of the graft.

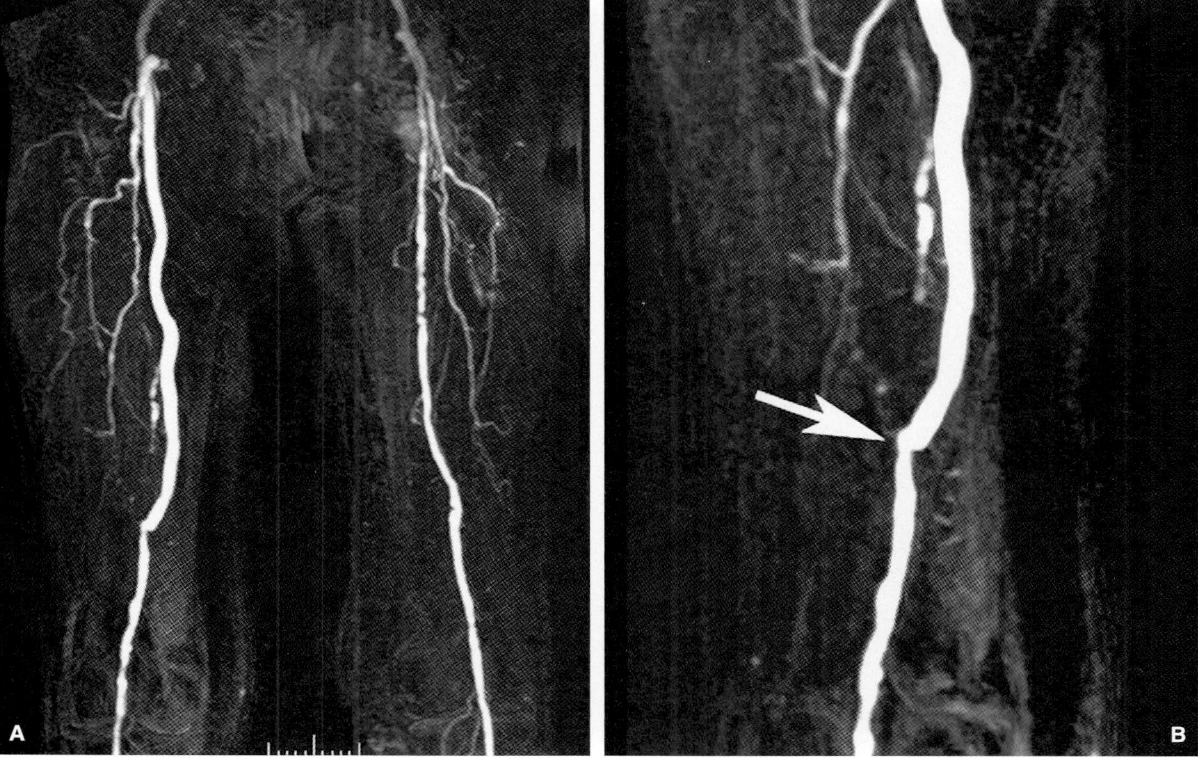

FIGURE 22-8 **A,** Thigh-station coronal 3D MR angiogram of a femoral-to-popliteal bypass graft. Note the contralateral disease of the superficial femoral artery. **B,** An oblique reformatted image shows the narrowing at the touchdown of the graft (*arrow*).

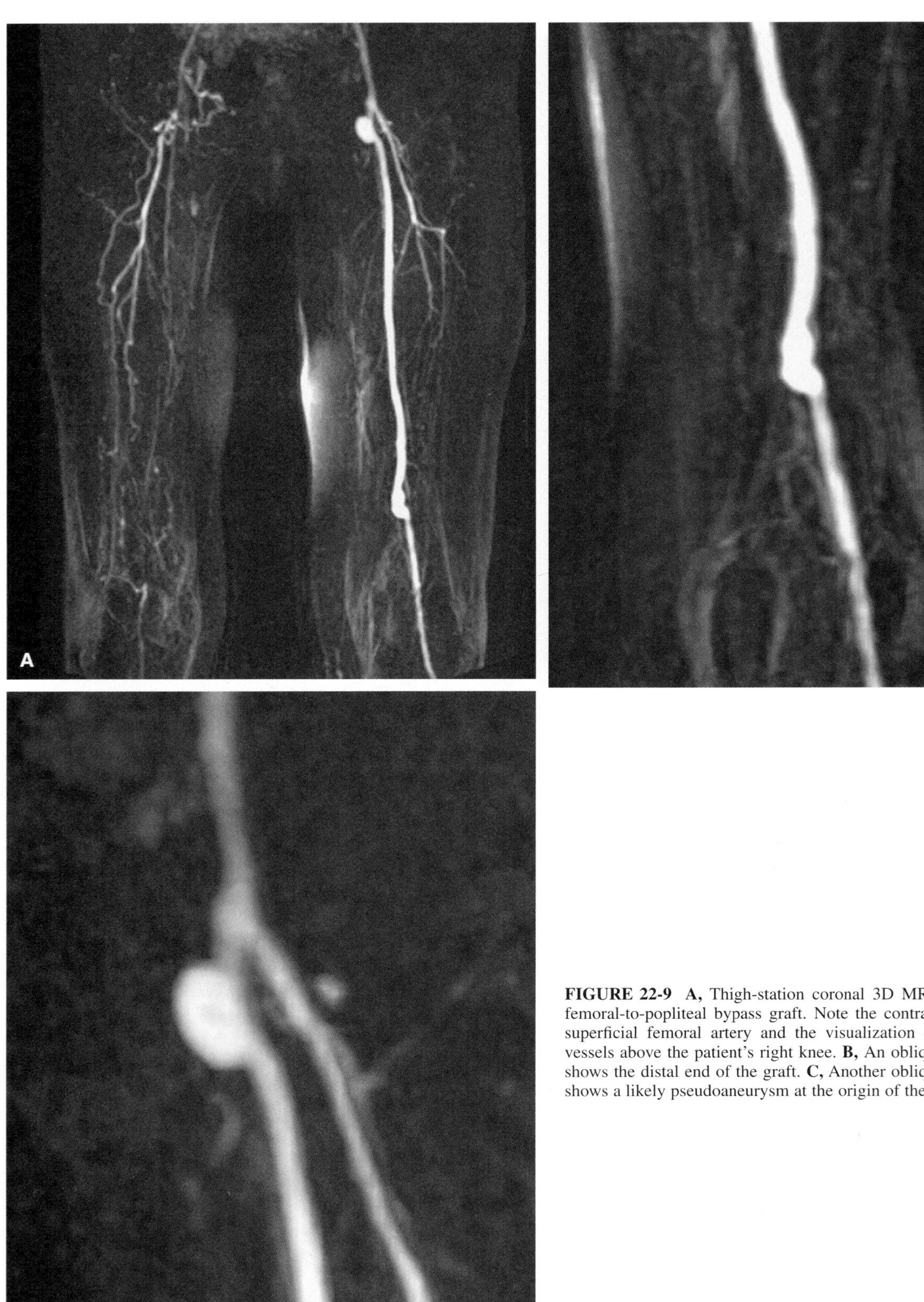

FIGURE 22-9 **A,** Thigh-station coronal 3D MR angiogram of a left femoral-to-popliteal bypass graft. Note the contralateral disease of the superficial femoral artery and the visualization of multiple collateral vessels above the patient's right knee. **B,** An oblique reformatted image shows the distal end of the graft. **C,** Another oblique reformatted image shows a likely pseudoaneurysm at the origin of the graft.

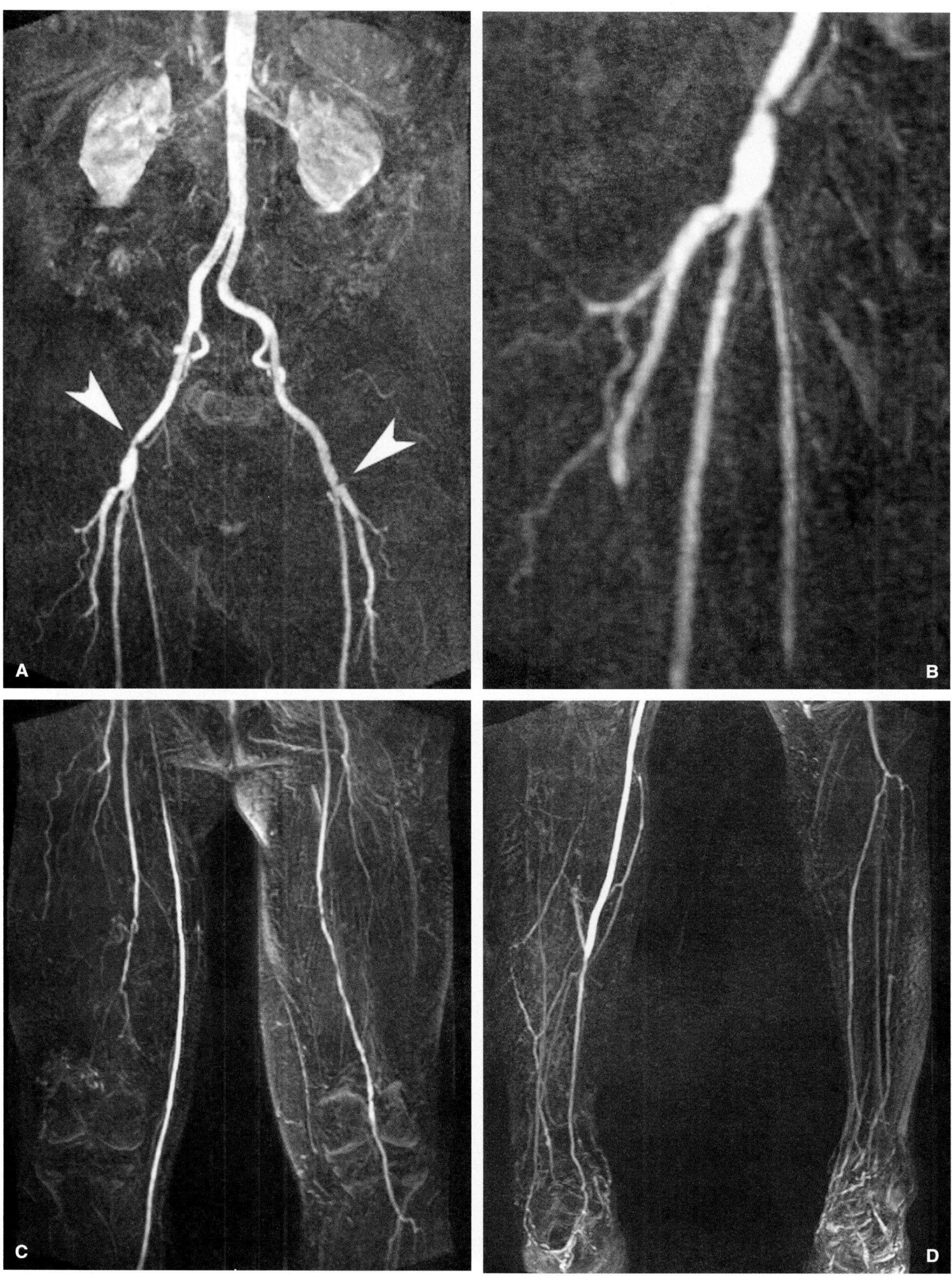

FIGURE 22-10 Coronal 3D MR angiograms. **A,** Bilateral common femoral disease (*arrowheads*) and the origin of a right saphenous vein graft. **B,** The origin of the graft and disease in the distal common femoral artery. **C,** The course of the vein graft, thigh-station image. **D,** The touchdown of the graft on the posterior tibialis artery, calf-station image.

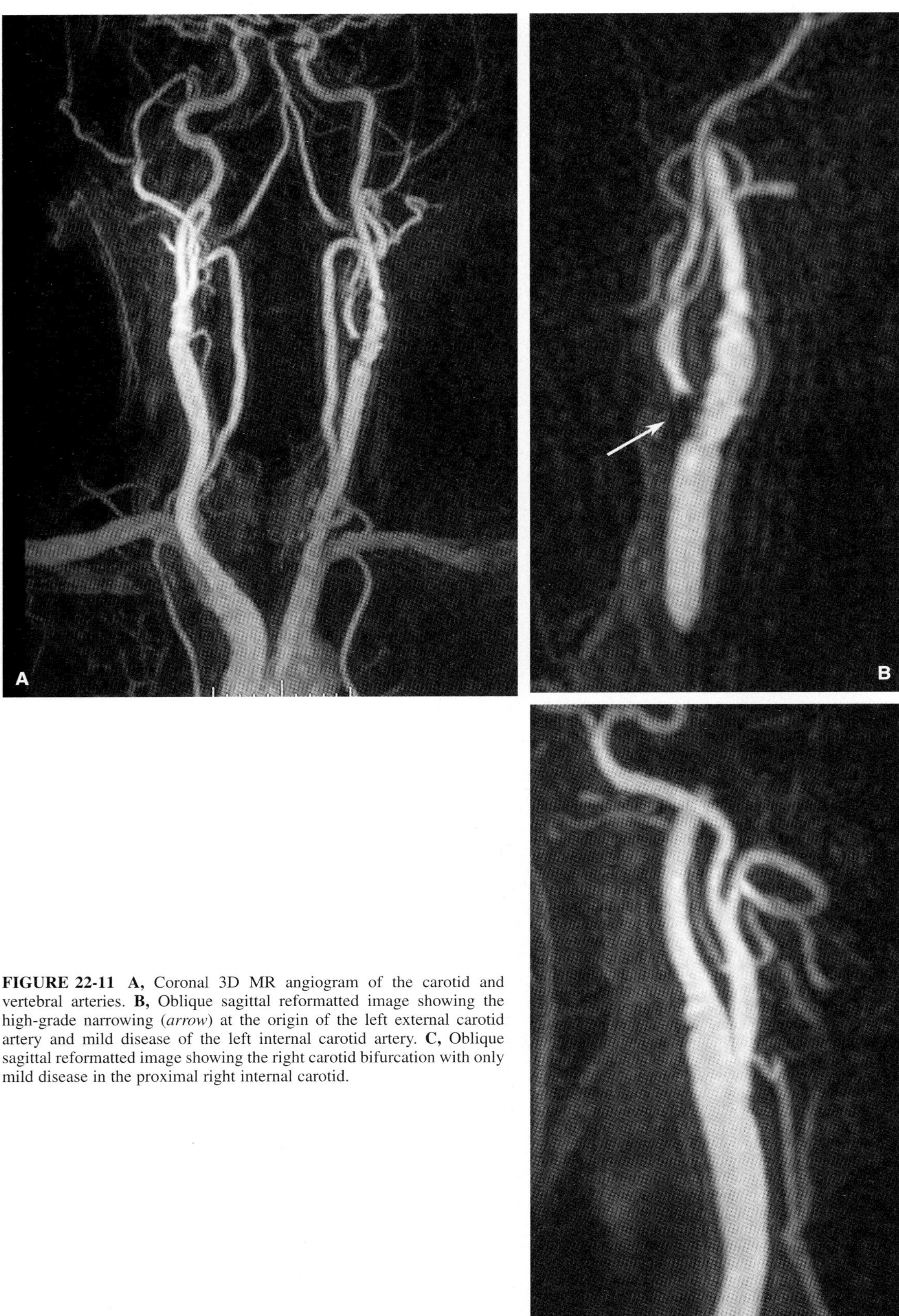

FIGURE 22-11 **A,** Coronal 3D MR angiogram of the carotid and vertebral arteries. **B,** Oblique sagittal reformatted image showing the high-grade narrowing (*arrow*) at the origin of the left external carotid artery and mild disease of the left internal carotid artery. **C,** Oblique sagittal reformatted image showing the right carotid bifurcation with only mild disease in the proximal right internal carotid.

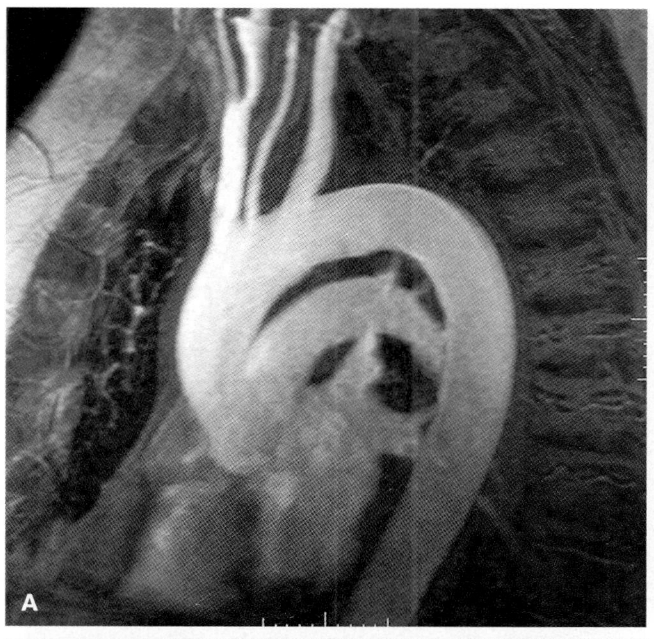

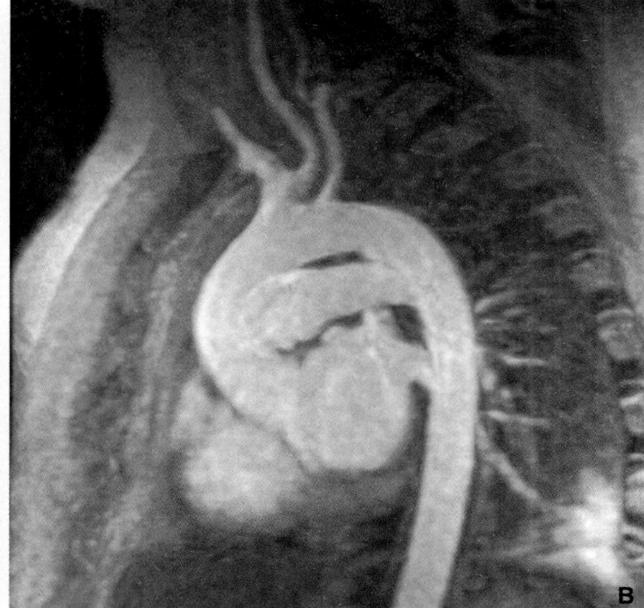

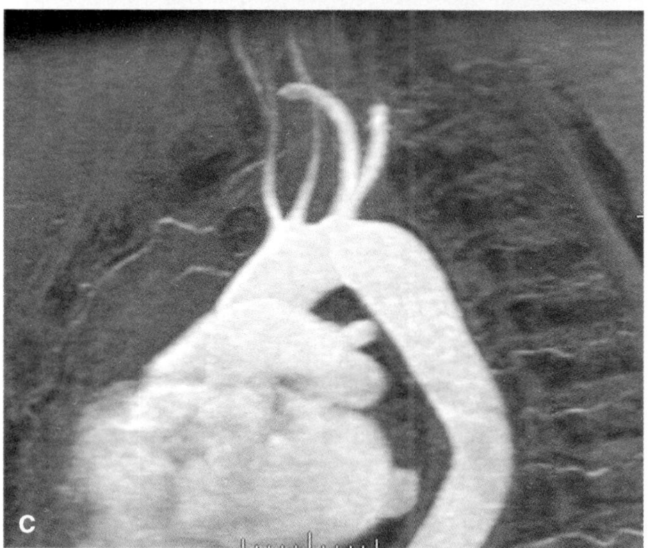

FIGURE 22-12 Sagittal oblique reformatted MR angiograms. **A,** A normal aortic arch. **B,** A bovine arch. **C,** A very rare arch anomaly, bicarotid truncus. In this anomaly, all four vessels arise separately from the arch, carotids anteriorly and the subclavians posteriorly.

Other Vascular Applications

A large variety of vascular conditions may be evaluated by MRA. The capability to perform the evaluation may depend on the experience of the physicians and technologists conducting the examination. For example, as in the case of assessment for arcuate ligament impingement on the celiac axis, MRA may be performed to assess patients with suspected thoracic outlet syndrome if the appropriate image sequences can be combined with maneuvers to elicit the symptoms.[35] In thoracic outlet syndrome (Fig. 22-18), MRA shows clear compression of the subclavian vein when the ipsilateral arm is raised above the head.

As mentioned previously, MRA is very useful for the assessment of potential kidney donors.[36,37,61] In addition, MRA can be useful in the evaluation of suspected failure of the arterial or venous anastomoses of the transplant graft.[38,39] Figure 22-19 shows the MRA evaluation of a pancreas transplant graft in the postoperative phase and in a later phase, when graft rejection was occurring.

MRA is also useful to assess what some may regard as esoteric diseases—for example, to diagnose and assess the response to therapy in large vessel vasculitis,[40] such as Takayasu's arteritis (Fig. 22-20). Another example of more esoteric disease that has been easily assessed by MRA is pulmonary AVMs[42,43] (Fig. 22-21). This modality has 100% sensitivity for pulmonary AVMs larger than 5 mm and is also able to characterize all feeding arteries and draining veins.[43]

Artifacts and Pitfalls of MR Angiography

Several common artifacts and pitfalls are associated with MR angiography. Knowledge of these limitations enables the educated user to approach the diagnostic MRA with greater sophistication and confidence that any abnormal findings do represent actual disease.

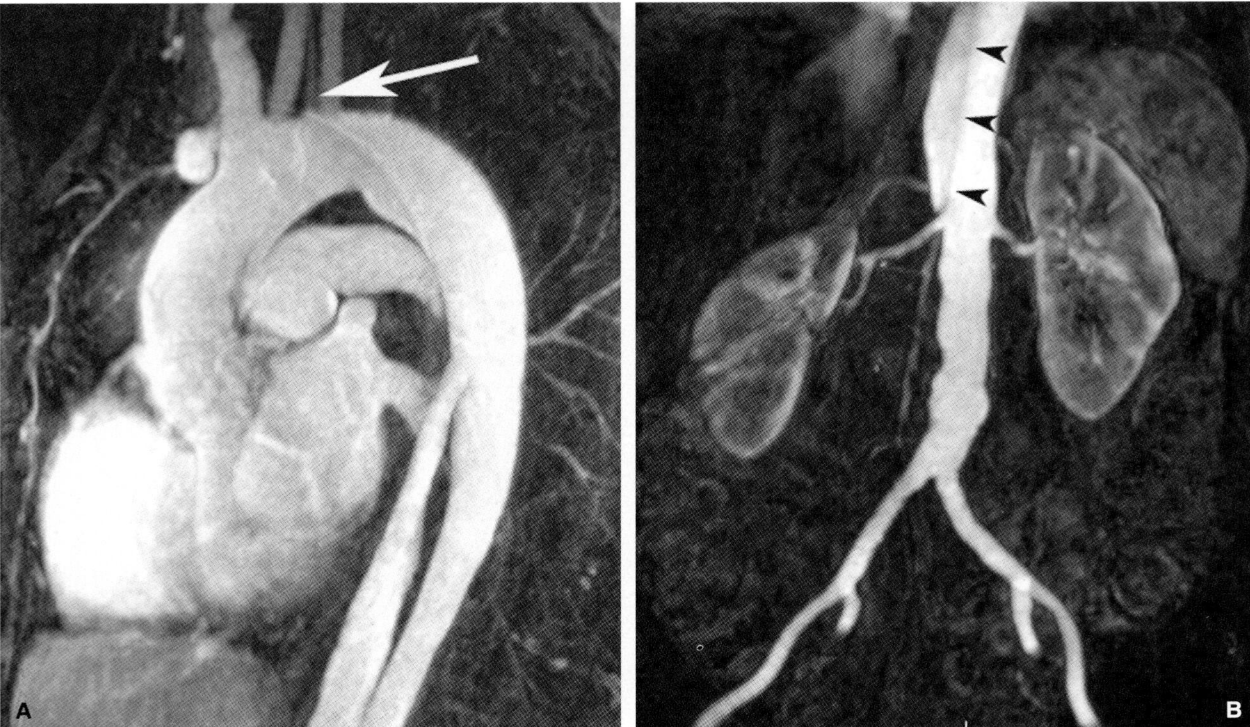

FIGURE 22-13 **A,** Sagittal oblique reformatted MR angiogram showing a type B dissection. The origin of the flap and filling of the proximal false lumen can be seen. A separate origin of the left vertebral artery from the aortic arch can also be seen (*arrow*). **B,** Coronal 3D MR angiogram obtained during the same examination at the chest station using the stepping table technique. The dissection flap (*arrowheads*) terminates just above the origin of the right renal artery.

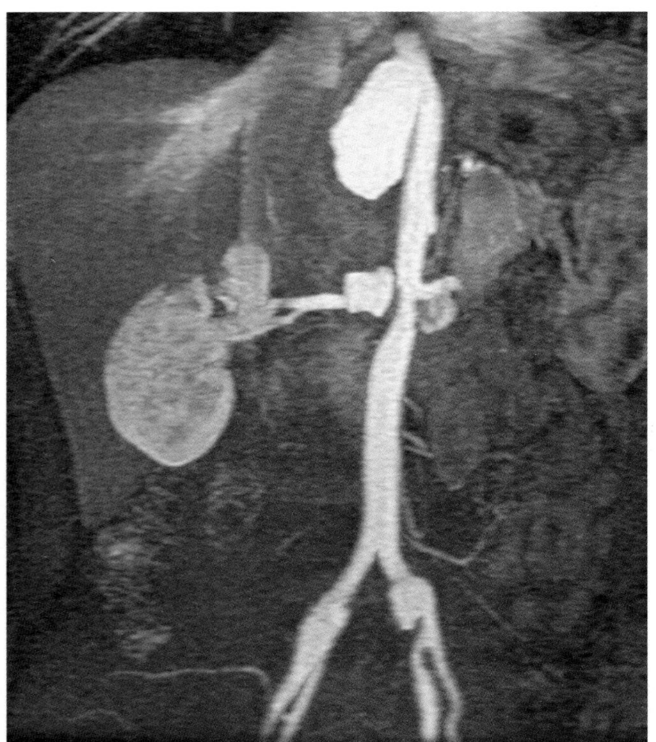

FIGURE 22-14 Coronal 3D MR angiogram in a patient with suspected Ehlers-Danlos syndrome. Saccular aneurysms from the upper abdominal aorta and both renal arteries can be seen. An irregular fusiform aneurysm of the left common iliac is also present.

Fat Saturation in Chest MR Angiography

Suppressing the signal from fat may be advantageous, because fat has high signal on the T1-weighted images used for MRA. The so-called "fat sat" method uses an RF suppression pulse to take advantage of the small difference in resonance frequency between water protons and the protons that are part of long-chain hydrocarbon fat groups. Within the chest are intravascular water protons, which are in blood vessels directly adjacent to the lungs. When such geometry exists, the resonance frequency of the water protons may be shifted to the precise range at which the fat protons normally resonate. In this case, the selective method of fat suppression actually results in suppression of the water signal instead.[91] Thus, a vessel that is entirely patent may appear entirely occluded or a vessel that is occluded may not be accurately assessed (Fig. 22-22).

Susceptibility Artifact from Concentrated Gadolinium

MRA contrast agents contain a chelated form of the rare earth element gadolinium. The chelate serves several different purposes in the formulation. First, it isolates the gadolinium, because in its unbound form gadolinium is toxic. Second, the chelate provides multiple binding sites at which surrounding water molecules may remagnetize. Hence, the chelate potentiates the T1 relaxation effects of the gadolinium. In addition, however, unbound gadolinium would not only shorten the T1 of water, it would also shorten

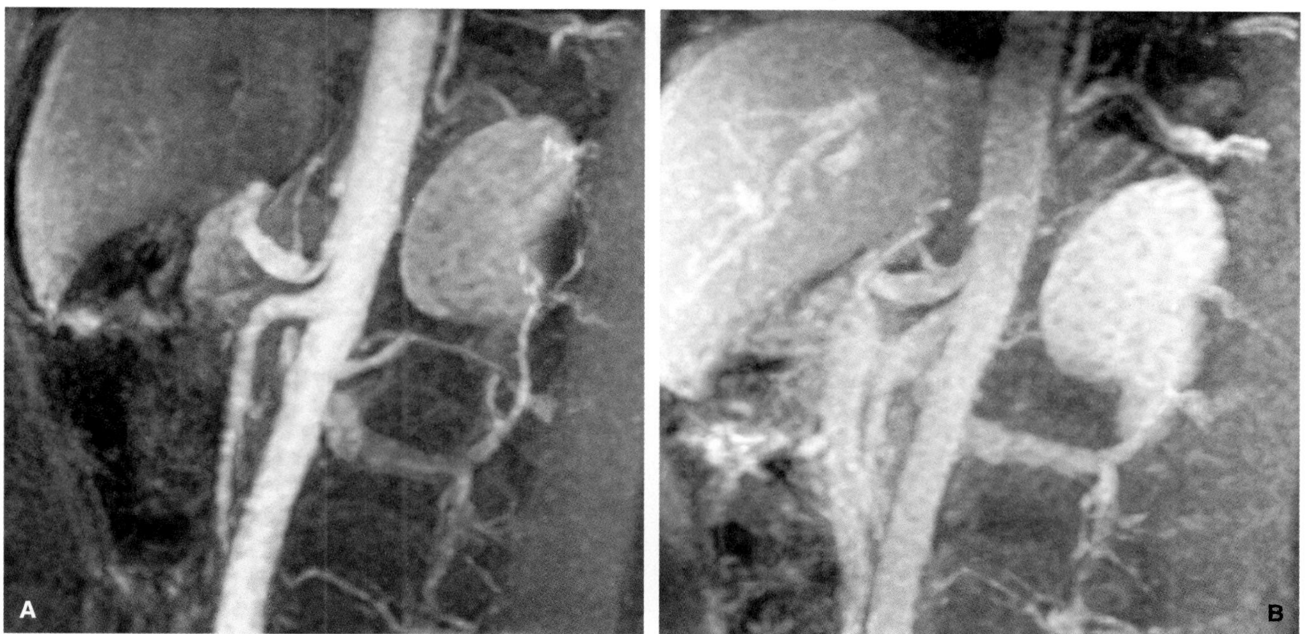

FIGURE 22-15 **A,** Arterial-phase sagittal 3D MR angiogram at end-expiration showing the impression of the arcuate ligament just proximal to the origin of the left gastric artery. Note the quality of the evaluation of the proximal superior mesenteric artery as well. **B,** Venous-phase sagittal 3D MR angiogram at end-inspiration showing no narrowing of the proximal celiac axis. During the delayed phase, the contrast enhancement within the aorta and branch vessels is adequate for visualization.

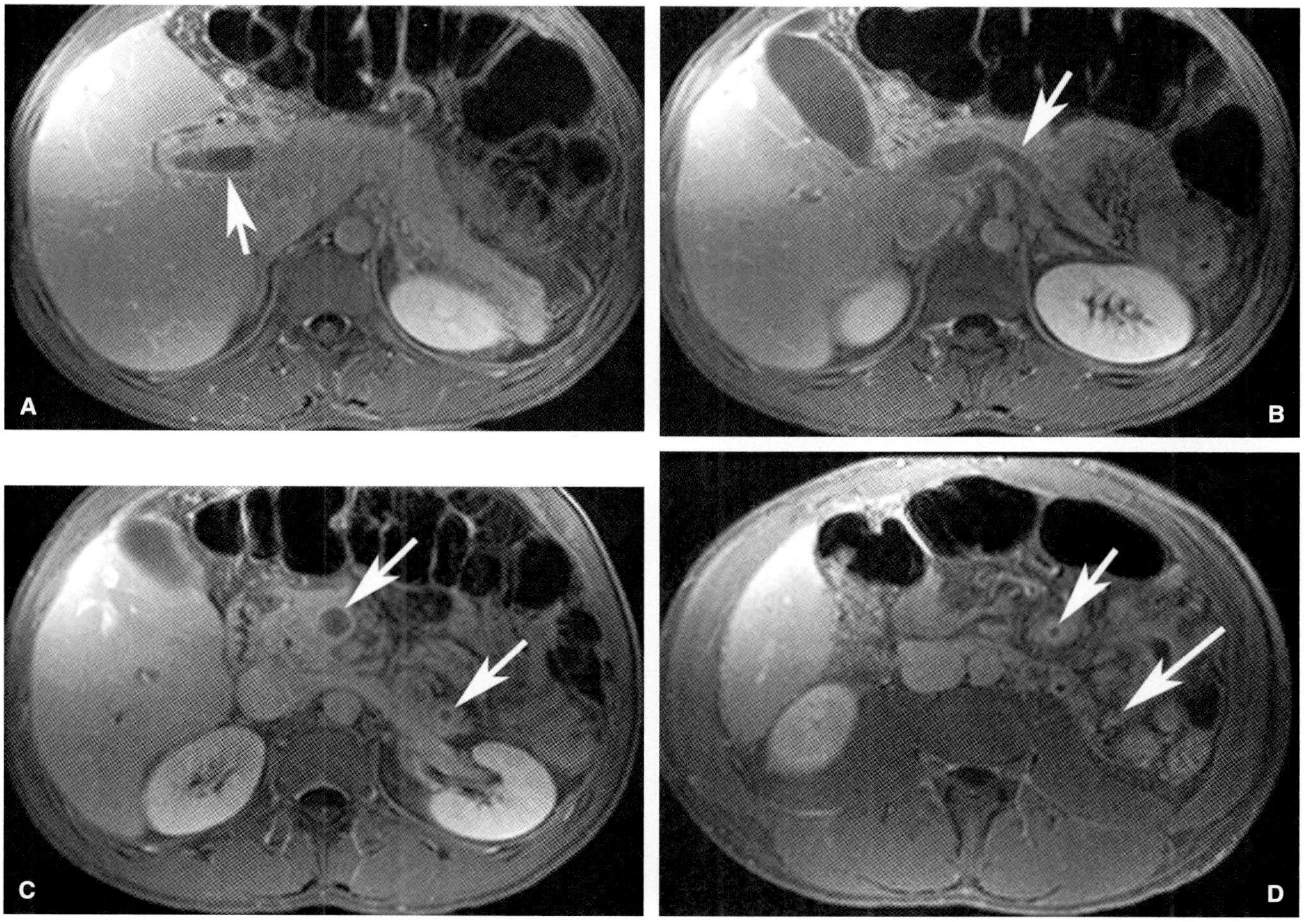

FIGURE 22-16 2D, T1-weighted post–contrast enhancement MR images **A,** Portal venous thrombus (*arrow*). **B,** Splenic venous thrombus (*arrow*). **C,** Superior mesenteric vein (SMV) and inferior mesenteric vein (IMV) thrombus (*arrows*). **D,** Small distal branches of the SMV and IMV filled with thrombus (*arrows*).

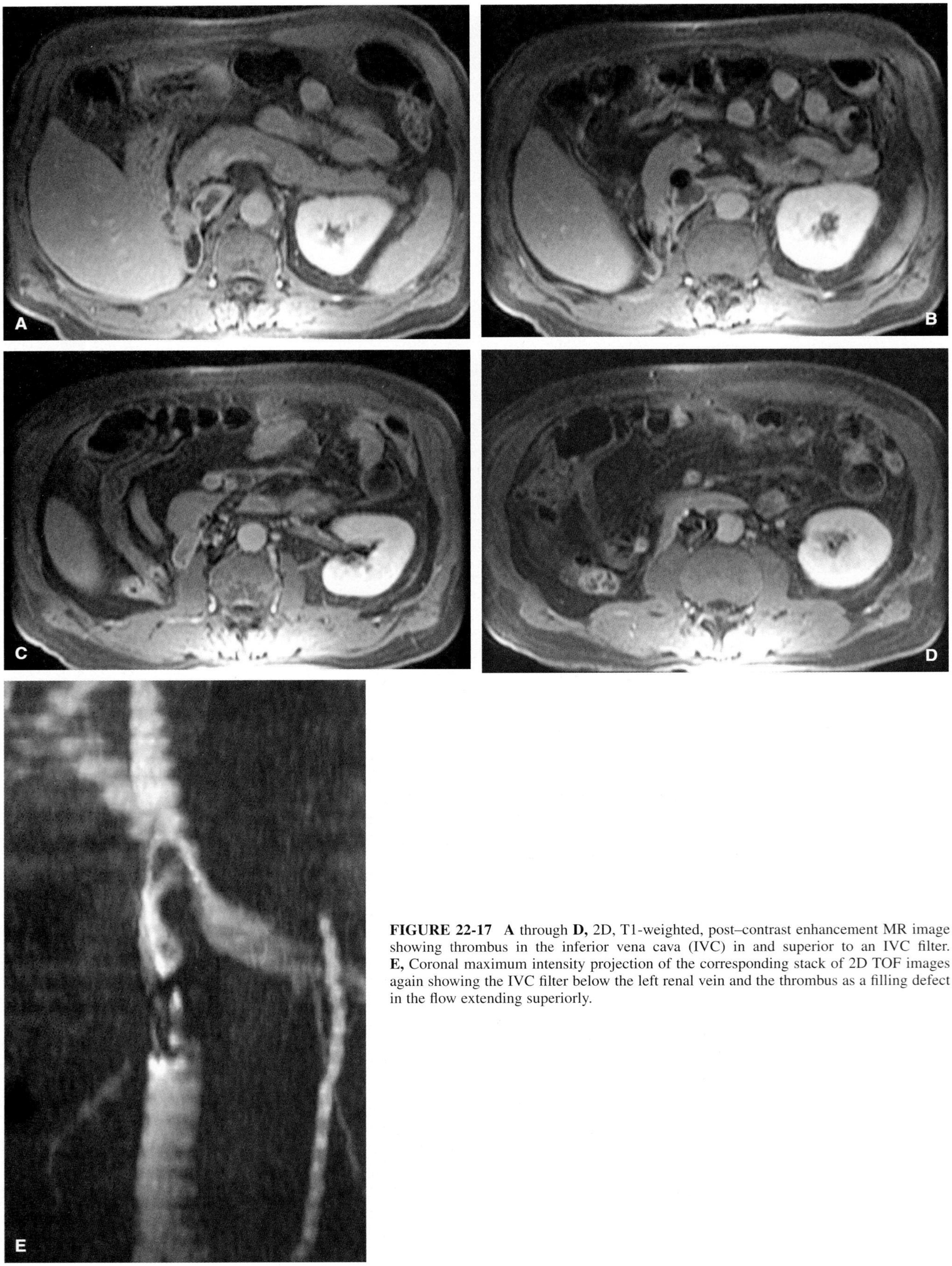

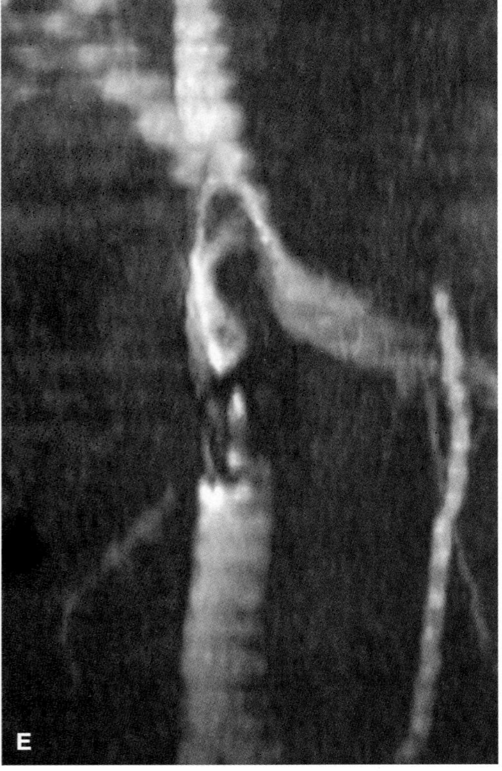

FIGURE 22-17 **A** through **D,** 2D, T1-weighted, post–contrast enhancement MR image showing thrombus in the inferior vena cava (IVC) in and superior to an IVC filter. **E,** Coronal maximum intensity projection of the corresponding stack of 2D TOF images again showing the IVC filter below the left renal vein and the thrombus as a filling defect in the flow extending superiorly.

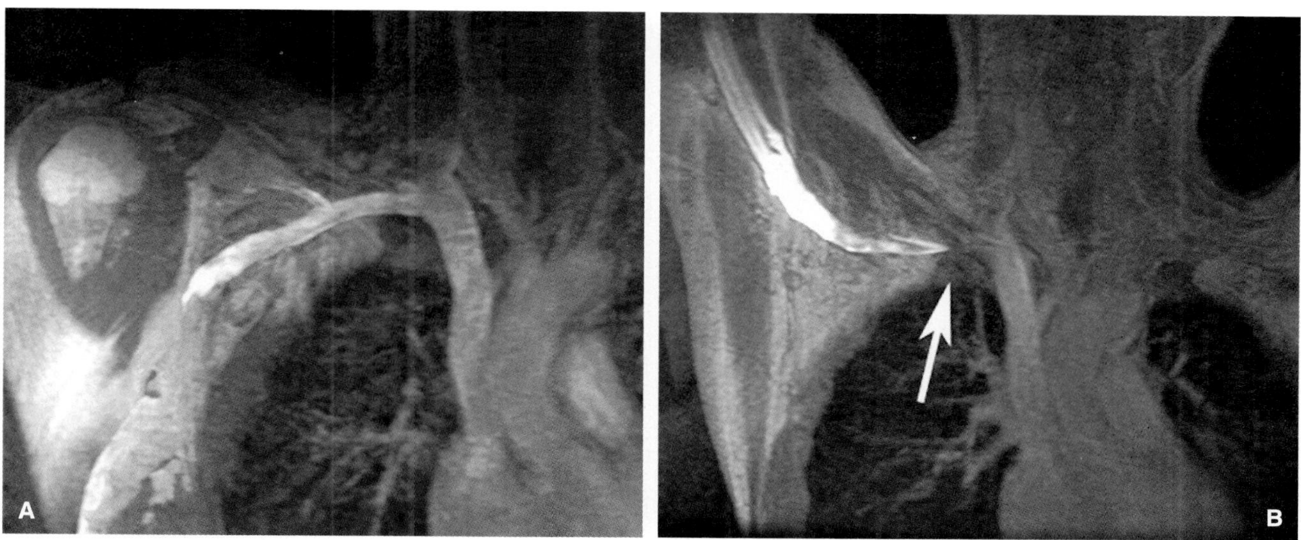

FIGURE 22-18 Coronal 3D MR angiograms of thoracic outlet syndrome. **A,** Normal right subclavian vein with the patient's arm lowered. **B,** Occlusion of the subclavian vein near the junction with the axillary vein (*arrow*). Note the pooling of very concentrated contrast agent in the arm.

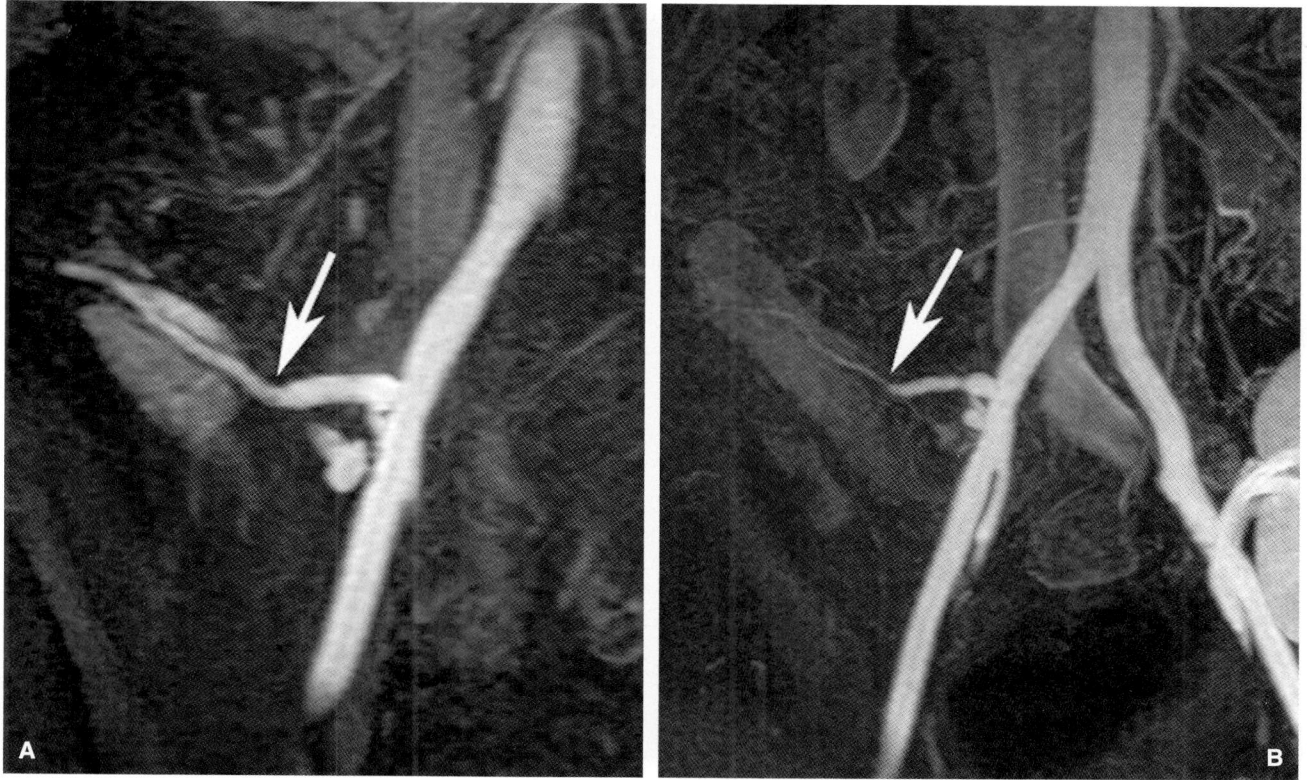

FIGURE 22-19 Coronal 3D MR angiograms of a pancreatic transplant graft. **A,** The anastomosis between the donor external iliac limb of the y-graft and the donor splenic artery that feeds the pancreatic body can be seen (*arrow*). **B,** Angiogram performed later, during transplant rejection, shows the narrowing of the donor splenic artery (*arrow*). A renal transplant can be partially seen in the left hemipelvis.

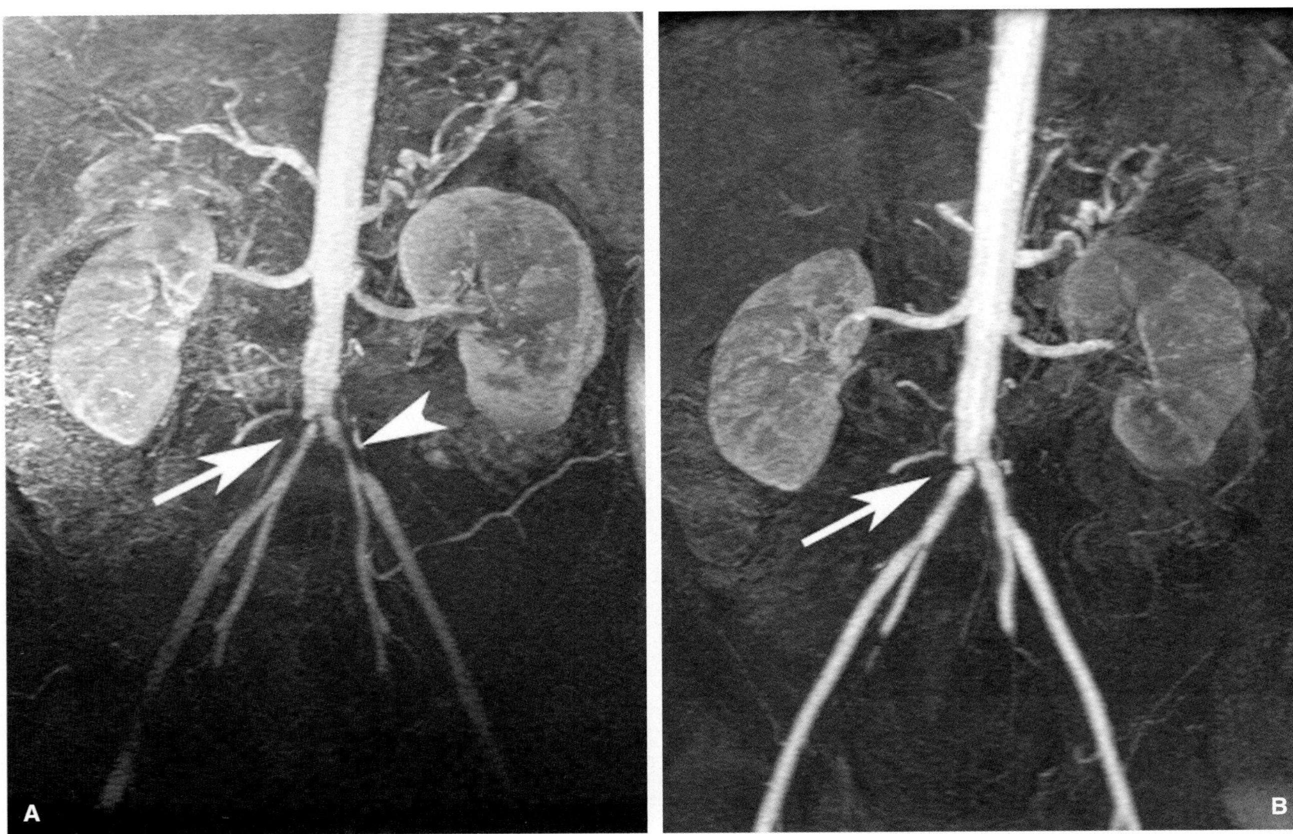

FIGURE 22-20 Coronal 3D MR angiograms. **A,** Bilateral narrowing of the proximal common iliac arteries (*arrow* and *arrowhead*). **B,** Complete resolution of the left common iliac narrowing with residual disease in the right common iliac (*arrow*).

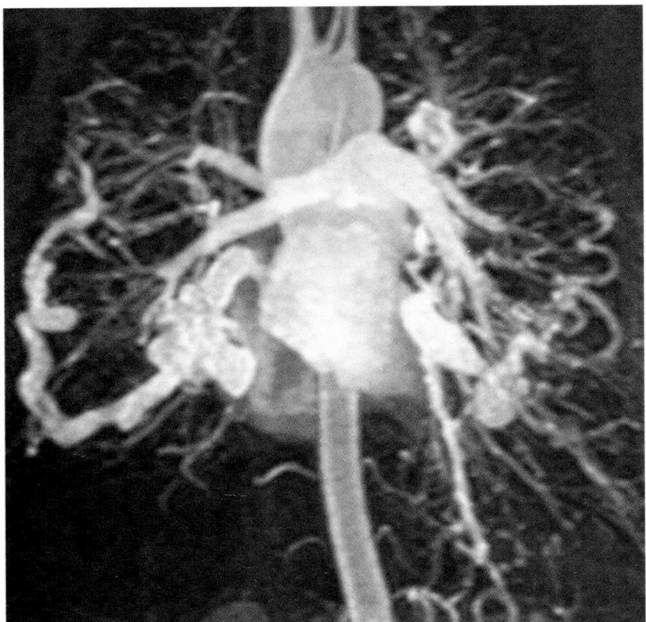

FIGURE 22-21 Coronal 3D MR angiogram showing a large right-sided pulmonary arteriovenous malformation (AVM) and several smaller left sided AVMs.

the T2 of the surrounding water. The chelate prevents close contact between the water and the gadolinium, thus minimizing the T2-shortening effects of the gadolinium. However, when the contrast agent is at high enough concentrations, there is still a T2-shortening effect that reduces the MR signal. In effect, at high concentrations, MR contrast agent behaves like a small piece of metal, producing a susceptibility artifact on the surrounding tissues. These concentrations only occur during the injection of pure contrast agent and are typically seen in the area of the origin of the great vessels[92] or in the subclavian artery[93] (Fig. 22-23).

High Intravascular Signal from Thrombus Containing Methemoglobin

Clotted blood has a widely varying appearance on MR images, depending on both the oxidation-reduction state of the hemoglobin molecule and the integrity of the red blood cell wall. At a certain stage in its evolution, clotted blood passes through a state of either intracellular or extracellular methemoglobin. This state typically occurs in the subacute phase (1 to 14 days) of a blood clot.[94] When the clot contains large amounts of methemoglobin, particularly extracellular methemoglobin, the signal may be quite high on the T1-weighted images used in MRA. This signal can be high enough to mimic intravascular contrast

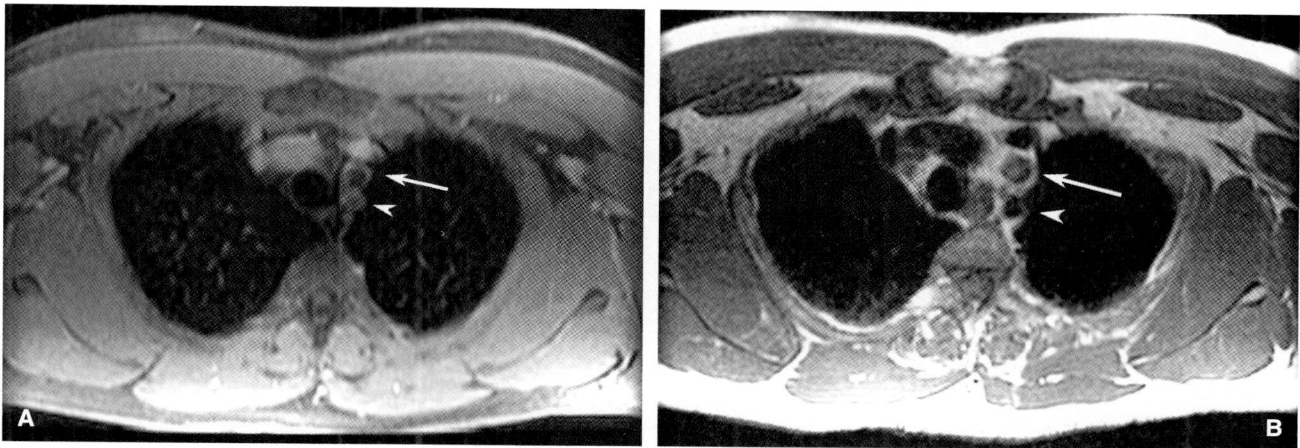

FIGURE 22-22 **A,** Axial 2D, post–contrast enhancement, fat-saturated, T1-weighted MR image showing no contrast within the left subclavian and left common carotid arteries in a patient with a type A dissection. **B,** Axial, T2-weighted, dark blood image showing a flow void within the left subclavian but signal within the left common carotid, indicating thrombosis.

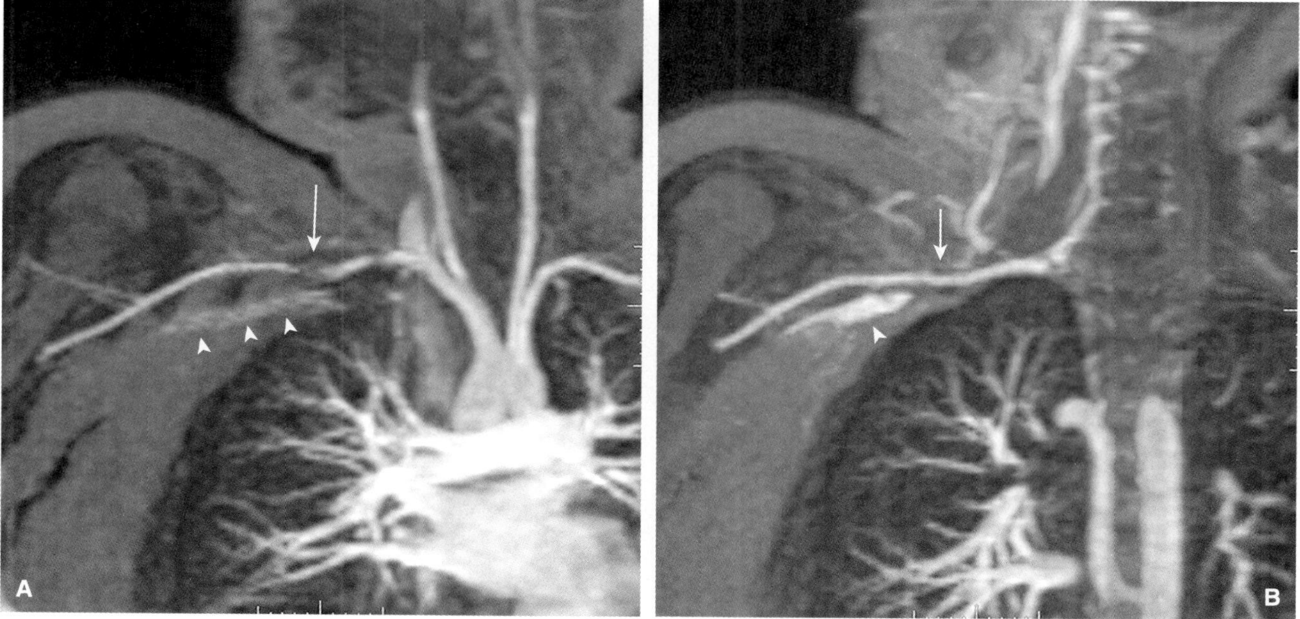

FIGURE 22-23 **A,** Arterial-phase coronal 3D MR angiogram showing apparent stenosis (*arrow*) in the right subclavian artery. Note that the signal from the pure contrast agent in the left subclavian vein (*arrowheads*) is not as high as the signal from the dilute contrast agent in the adjacent artery. **B,** Delayed-phase 3D MR angiogram showing no stenosis in the subclavian artery (*arrow*). Note that the signal from the dilute venous contrast agent is now much higher than that from the pure contrast agent (*arrowhead*).

agent (Fig. 22-24). The use of pre–contrast enhancement T1-weighted imaging can identify such a thrombus.

Contraindications to MR Imaging

Although MRI is extremely safe, the level of safety can be ensured only by maintaining the appropriate environment around the magnet and by careful screening of the patients.[95] A number of implanted metallic devices are not safe near an MRI magnet, the more common being implanted cardiac pacemakers or defibrillators, implanted pumps or neurostimulators, some cochlear implants, some aneurysm clips, and a few older heart valves. Because there are a large variety of implanted devices, sources of information regarding which ones are safe have been developed; they include books, published articles, and websites (e.g., http://www.fda.gov/cdrh/safety/mrisafety.html).[96,97]

■ CONCLUSION

MRA has become an accepted standard examination for evaluation of both renovascular and peripheral vascular

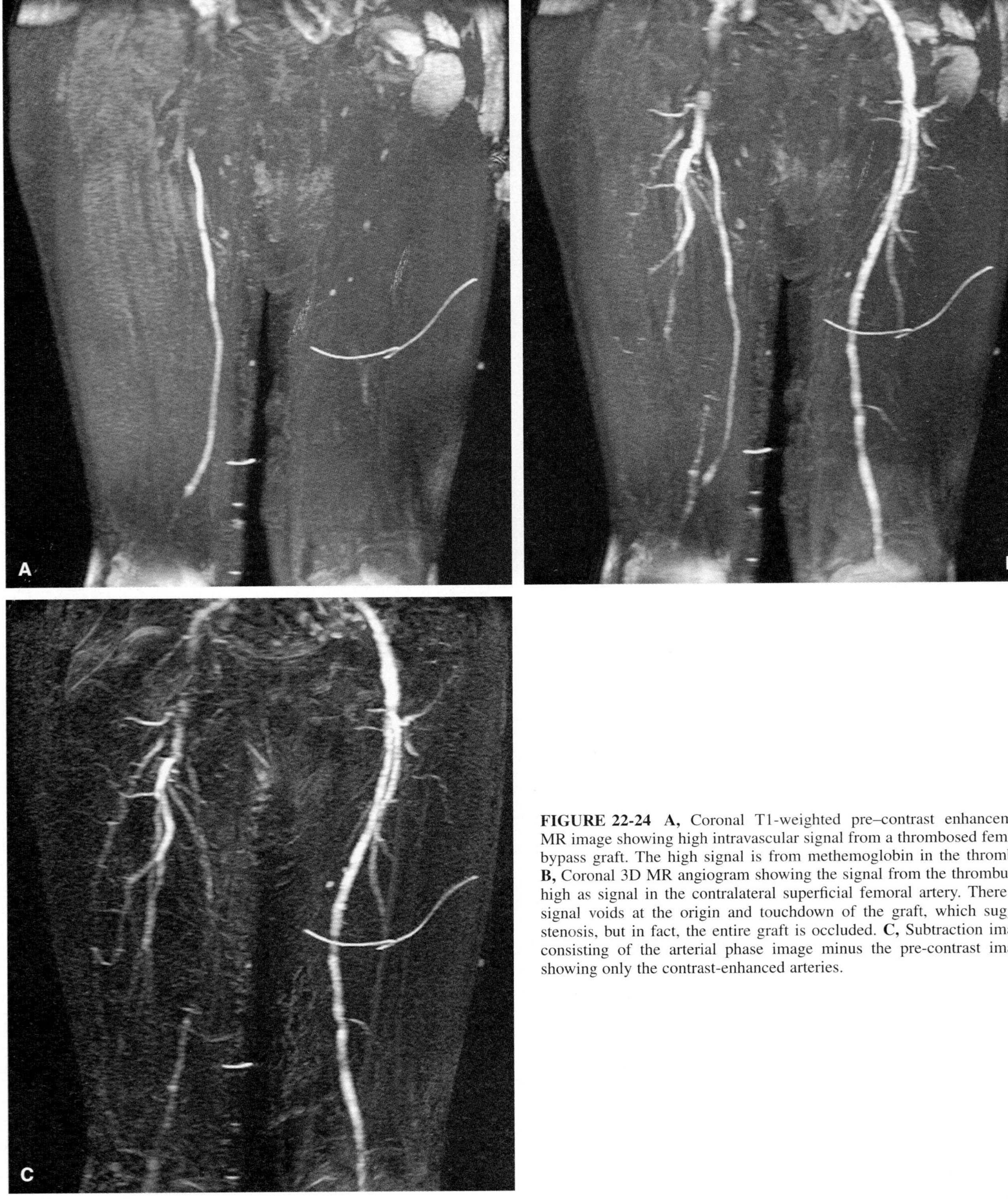

FIGURE 22-24 **A,** Coronal T1-weighted pre–contrast enhancement MR image showing high intravascular signal from a thrombosed femoral bypass graft. The high signal is from methemoglobin in the thrombus. **B,** Coronal 3D MR angiogram showing the signal from the thrombus as high as signal in the contralateral superficial femoral artery. There are signal voids at the origin and touchdown of the graft, which suggest stenosis, but in fact, the entire graft is occluded. **C,** Subtraction image, consisting of the arterial phase image minus the pre-contrast image, showing only the contrast-enhanced arteries.

disease. At some centers, MRA has become the standard method of evaluation for many other types of vascular disease, such as aneurysm and dissection. Continued research into more advanced techniques and different applications make it likely that MRA will become a standard diagnostic examination for many different types of vascular disease.

REFERENCES

1. Tan KT, van Beek EJ, Brown PW, et al: Magnetic resonance angiography for the diagnosis of renal artery stenosis: A meta-analysis. Clin Radiol 57:617-624, 2002.
2. Vosshenrich R, Fischer U: Contrast-enhanced MR angiography of abdominal vessels: Is there still a role for angiography? Eur Radiol 12:218-230, 2002.
3. Leung DA, Hagspiel KD, Angle JF, et al: MR angiography of the renal arteries. Radiol Clin North Am 40:847-865, 2002.
4. Goyen M, Ruehm SG, Debatin JF: MR angiography for assessment of peripheral vascular disease. Radiol Clin North Am 40:835-846, 2002.
5. Khilnani NM, Winchester PA, Prince MR, et al: Peripheral vascular disease: Combined 3D bolus chase and dynamic 2D MR angiography compared with x-ray angiography for treatment planning. Radiology 224:63-74, 2002.
6. Konkus CJ, Czum JM, Jacobacci JT: Contrast-enhanced MR angiography of the aorta and lower extremities with routine inclusion of the feet. AJR Am J Roentgenol 179:115-117, 2002.
7. Koelemay MJ, Lijmer JG, Stoker J, et al: Magnetic resonance angiography for the evaluation of lower extremity arterial disease: A meta-analysis. JAMA 285:1338-1345, 2001.
8. Reid SK, Pagan-Marin HR, Menzoian JO, et al: Contrast-enhanced moving-table MR angiography: Prospective comparison to catheter arteriography for treatment planning in peripheral arterial occlusive disease. J Vasc Interv Radiol 12:45-53, 2001.
9. Rofsky NM, Adelman MA: MR angiography in the evaluation of atherosclerotic peripheral vascular disease. Radiology 214:325-338, 2000.
10. Visser K, Kuntz KM, Donaldson MC, et al: Pretreatment imaging workup for patients with intermittent claudication: A cost-effectiveness analysis. J Vasc Interv Radiol 14:53-62, 2003.
11. Young N, Chi KK, Ajaka J, et al: Complications with outpatient angiography and interventional procedures. Cardiovasc Intervent Radiol 25:123-126, 2002.
12. Singh H, Cardella JF, Cole PE, et al: Quality improvement guidelines for diagnostic arteriography. J Vasc Interv Radiol 13:1-6, 2002.
13. Waugh JR, Sacharias N: Arteriographic complications in the DSA era. Radiology 194:757-764, 1992.
14. Spinosa DJ, Angle JF, Hartwell GD, et al: Gadolinium-based contrast agents in angiography and interventional radiology. Radiol Clin North Am 40:693-710, 2002.
15. Srodon P, Matson M, Ham R: Contrast nephropathy in lower limb angiography. Ann R Coll Surg Engl 85:187-191, 2003.
16. Rieger J, Sitter T, Toepfer M, et al: Gadolinium as an alternative contrast agent for diagnostic and interventional angiographic procedures in patients with impaired renal function. Nephrol Dial Transplant 17:824-828, 2002.
17. Freed KS, Leder RA, Alexander C, et al: Breakthrough adverse reactions to low-osmolar contrast media after steroid premedication. AJR Am J Roentgenol 176:1389-1392, 2001.
18. Lieberman PL, Seigle RL: Reactions to radiocontrast material: Anaphylactoid events in radiology. Clin Rev Allergy Immunol 17:469-496, 1999.
19. Katritsis D, Efstathopoulos E, Betsou S, et al: Radiation exposure of patients and coronary arteries in the stent era: A prospective study. Cathet Cardiovasc Interv 51:259-264, 2000.
20. Owen RS, Carpenter JP, Baum RA, et al: Magnetic resonance imaging of angiographically occult runoff vessels in peripheral arterial occlusive disease. N Engl J Med 326:1577-1581, 1992.
21. Nederkoorn PJ, van der Graaf Y, Hunink MG: Duplex ultrasound and magnetic resonance angiography compared with digital subtraction angiography in carotid artery stenosis: A systematic review. Stroke 34:1324-1332, 2003.
22. Lenhart M, Framme N, Volk M, et al: Time-resolved contrast-enhanced magnetic resonance angiography of the carotid arteries: Diagnostic accuracy and inter-observer variability compared with selective catheter angiography. Invest Radiol 37:535-541, 2002.
23. Westwood ME, Kelly S, Berry E, et al: Use of magnetic resonance angiography to select candidates with recently symptomatic carotid stenosis for surgery: Systematic review. BMJ 324(7331):198-222, 2002.
24. Mitsumori LM, Hatsukami TS, Ferguson MS, et al: In vivo accuracy of multisequence MR imaging for identifying unstable fibrous caps in advanced human carotid plaques. J Magn Reson Imaging 17:410-420, 2003.
25. Roberts DA: Magnetic resonance imaging of thoracic aortic aneurysm and dissection. Semin Roentgenol 36:295-308, 2001.
26. Engellau L, Albrechtsson U, Dahlstrom N, et al: Measurements before endovascular repair of abdominal aortic aneurysms: MR imaging with MRA vs. angiography and CT. Acta Radiol 44:177-184, 2003.
27. Beebe HG, Kritpracha B: Screening and preoperative imaging of candidates for conventional repair of abdominal aortic aneurysm. Semin Vasc Surg 12:300-305, 1999.
28. Kroencke TJ, Taupitz M, Arnold R, et al: Three-dimensional gadolinium-enhanced magnetic resonance venography in suspected thrombo-occlusive disease of the central chest veins. Chest 120:1570-1576, 2001.
29. Thornton MJ, Ryan R, Varghese JC, et al: A three-dimensional gadolinium-enhanced MR venography technique for imaging central veins. AJR Am J Roentgenol 173:999-1003, 1999.
30. Stern JB, Abehsera M, Grenet D, et al: Detection of pelvic vein thrombosis by magnetic resonance angiography in patients with acute pulmonary embolism and normal lower limb compression ultrasonography. Chest 122:115-121, 2002.
31. Spritzer CE, Arata MA, Freed KS: Isolated pelvic deep venous thrombosis: Relative frequency as detected with MR imaging. Radiology 219:521-525, 2001.
32. Evans AJ, Sostman HD, Witty LA, et al: Detection of deep venous thrombosis: Prospective comparison of MR imaging and sonography. J Magn Reson Imaging 6:44-51, 1996.
33. Chow LC, Chan FP, Li KC: A comprehensive approach to MR imaging of mesenteric ischemia. Abdom Imaging 27:507-516, 2002.
34. Bradbury MS, Kavanagh PV, Bechtold RE, et al: Mesenteric venous thrombosis: Diagnosis and noninvasive imaging. Radiographics 22:527-541, 2002.
35. Demondion X, Bacqueville E, Paul C, et al: Thoracic outlet: Assessment with MR imaging in asymptomatic and symptomatic populations. Radiology 227:461-468, 2003.
36. Hussain SM, Kock MC, Jzermans JN, et al: MR imaging: A "one-stop shop" modality for preoperative evaluation of potential living kidney donors. Radiographics 23:505-520, 2003.
37. Israel GM, Lee VS, Edye M, et al: Comprehensive MR imaging in the preoperative evaluation of living donor candidates for laparoscopic nephrectomy: Initial experience. Radiology 225:427-432, 2002.
38. Fang YC, Siegelman ES: Complications of renal transplantation: MR findings. J Comput Assist Tomogr 25:836-842, 2001.
39. Atalay MK, Bluemke DA: Magnetic resonance imaging of large vessel vasculitis. Curr Opin Rheumatol 13:41-47, 2001.
40. Kawamoto S, Bluemke DA, Traill TA, Zerhouni EA: Thoracoabdominal aorta in Marfan syndrome: MR imaging findings of progression of vasculopathy after surgical repair. Radiology 203:727-732, 1997.
41. Goyen M, Ruehm SG, Jagenburg A, et al: Pulmonary arteriovenous malformation: Characterization with time-resolved ultrafast 3D MR angiography. J Magn Reson Imaging 13:458-460, 2001.
42. Maki DD, Siegelman ES, Roberts DA, et al: Pulmonary arteriovenous malformations: Three-dimensional gadolinium-enhanced MR angiography—initial experience. Radiology 219:243-246, 2001.

43. Meaney JF: Magnetic resonance angiography of the peripheral arteries: Current status. Eur Radiol 13:836-852, 2003.
44. Hood MN, Ho VB, Foo TK, et al: High-resolution gadolinium-enhanced 3D MRA of the infrapopliteal arteries: Lessons for improving bolus-chase peripheral MRA. Magn Reson Imaging 20:543-549, 2002.
45. Sharafuddin MJ, Stolpen AH, Sun S, et al: High-resolution multiphase contrast-enhanced three-dimensional MR angiography compared with two-dimensional time-of-flight MR angiography for the identification of pedal vessels. J Vasc Interv Radiol 13:695-702, 2002.
46. Johnson DB, Lerner CA, Prince MR, et al: Gadolinium-enhanced magnetic resonance angiography of renal transplants. Magn Reson Imaging 15:13-20, 1997.
47. Sun Y, Parker DL: Performance analysis of maximum intensity projection algorithm for display of MRA images. IEEE Trans Med Imaging 18:1154-1169, 1999.
48. Marcos HB, Choyke PL: Magnetic resonance angiography of the kidney. Semin Nephrol 20(5):450-455, 2000.
49. Velazquez OC, Baum RA, Carpenter JP: Magnetic resonance angiography of lower-extremity arterial disease. Surg Clin North Am 78:519-537, 1998.
50. Fayad ZA: MR imaging for the noninvasive assessment of atherothrombotic plaques. Magn Reson Imaging Clin North Am 11:101-113, 2003.
51. He J, Klag MJ, Appel LJ, et al: Seven-year incidence of hypertension in a cohort of middle-aged African Americans and whites. Hypertension 31:1130-1135, 1998.
52. Derkx FHM, Schalekamp MADH: Renal artery stenosis and hypertension. Lancet 344:237-239, 1994.
53. Baumgartner I, von Aesch K, Do DD, et al: Stent placement in ostial and nonostial atherosclerotic renal arterial stenoses: A prospective follow-up study. Radiology 216:498-505, 2000.
54. Bush RL, Najibi S, MacDonald MJ, et al: Endovascular revascularization of renal artery stenosis: Technical and clinical results. J Vasc Surg 33:1041-1049, 2001.
55. Henry M, Amor M, Henry I, et al: Stents in the treatment of renal artery stenosis: Long-term follow-up. J Endovasc Surg 6:42-51, 1999.
56. Sharafuddin MJ, Stolpen AH, Dixon BS, et al: Value of MR angiography before percutaneous transluminal renal artery angioplasty and stent placement. J Vasc Interv Radiol 13:901-908, 2002.
57. Kaatee R, Beek FJ, Verschuyl EJ, et al: Atherosclerotic renal artery stenosis: Ostial or truncal? Radiology 199:637-640, 1996.
58. Birrer M, Do DD, Mahler F, et al: Treatment of renal artery fibromuscular dysplasia with balloon angioplasty: A prospective follow-up study. Eur J Vasc Endovasc Surg 23:146-152, 2002.
59. Gilfeather M, Holland GA, Siegelman ES, et al: Gadolinium-enhanced ultrafast three-dimensional spoiled gradient-echo MR imaging of the abdominal aorta and visceral and iliac vessels. Radiographics 17:423-432, 1997.
60. Debatin JF, Sostman HD, Knelson M, et al: Renal magnetic resonance angiography in the preoperative detection of supernumerary renal arteries in potential kidney donors. Invest Radiol 28:882-889, 1993.
61. Nelson HA, Gilfeather M, Holman JM, et al: Gadolinium-enhanced breathhold three-dimensional time-of-flight renal MR angiography in the evaluation of potential renal donors. J Vasc Interv Radiol 10:175-181, 1999.
62. Dillavou E, Kahn MB: Peripheral vascular disease: Diagnosing and treating the 3 most common peripheral vasculopathies. Geriatrics 58:37-42, 2003.
63. Sharafuddin MJ, Wroblicka JT, Sun S, et al: Percutaneous vascular intervention based on gadolinium-enhanced MR angiography. J Vasc Interv Radiol 11:739-746, 2000.
64. Carpenter JP, Baum RA, Holland GA, Barker CF: Peripheral vascular surgery with magnetic resonance angiography as the sole preoperative imaging modality. J Vasc Surg 20:861-871, 1994.
65. Carpenter JP, Owen RS, Holland GA, et al: Magnetic resonance angiography of the aorta, iliac and femoral arteries. Surgery 116:17-23, 1994.
66. Steffens JC, Schafer FK, Oberscheid B, et al: Bolus-chasing contrast-enhanced 3D MRA of the lower extremity: Comparison with intraarterial DSA. Acta Radiol 44:185-192, 2003.
67. Visser K, Kuntz KM, Donaldson MC, et al: Pretreatment imaging workup for patients with intermittent claudication: A cost-effectiveness analysis. J Vasc Interv Radiol 14:53-62, 2003.
68. Yin D, Baum RA, Carpenter JP, et al: Cost-effectiveness of MR angiography in cases of limb-threatening peripheral vascular disease. Radiology 194:757-764, 1995.
69. Morasch MD, Collins J, Pereles FS, et al: Lower extremity stepping-table magnetic resonance angiography with multilevel contrast timing and segmented contrast infusion. J Vasc Surg 37:62-71, 2003.
70. Hofmann WJ, Forstner R, Kofler B, et al: Pedal artery imaging—a comparison of selective digital subtraction angiography, contrast enhanced magnetic resonance angiography and duplex ultrasound. Eur J Vasc Endovasc Surg 24:287-292, 2002.
71. Heverhagen JT, Wagner HJ, Bandorski D, et al: Magnetic resonance phase contrast velocity measurement for non-invasive follow up after percutaneous transluminal angioplasty. Vasa 31:235-240, 2002.
72. Heverhagen JT, Kalinowski M, Schwarz U, et al: Quantitative human in vivo evaluation of high resolution MRI for vessel wall morphometry after percutaneous transluminal angioplasty. Magn Reson Imaging 18:985-989, 2000.
73. Coulden RA, Moss H, Graves MJ, et al: High resolution magnetic resonance imaging of atherosclerosis and the response to balloon angioplasty. Heart 83:188-191, 2000.
74. Cosottini M, Pingitore A, Puglioli M, et al: Contrast-enhanced three-dimensional magnetic resonance angiography of atherosclerotic internal carotid stenosis as the noninvasive imaging modality in revascularization decision making. Stroke 34:660-664, 2003.
75. Murphy RE, Moody AR, Morgan PS, et al: Prevalence of complicated carotid atheroma as detected by magnetic resonance direct thrombus imaging in patients with suspected carotid artery stenosis and previous acute cerebral ischemia. Circulation 107:3053-3058, 2003.
76. Carr JC, Finn JP: MR imaging of the thoracic aorta. Magn Reson Imaging Clin North Am 11:135-148, 2003.
77. Ho VB, Corse WR: MR angiography of the abdominal aorta and peripheral vessels. Radiol Clin North Am 41:115-144, 2003.
78. Vogt FM, Goyen M, Debatin JF: MR angiography of the chest. Radiol Clin North Am 41:29-41, 2003.
79. Carpenter JP, Holland GA, Golden MA, et al: Magnetic resonance angiography of the aortic arch. J Vasc Surg 25:145-151, 1997.
80. Fernandez GC, Tardaguila FM, Duran D, et al: Dynamic 3-dimensional contrast-enhanced magnetic resonance angiography in acute aortic dissection. Curr Probl Diagn Radiol 31:134-145, 2002.
81. Leiner T, Elenbaas TW, Kaandorp DW, et al: Magnetic resonance angiography of an aortic dissection. Circulation 103:E76-E78, 2001.
82. Hartnell GG: Imaging of aortic aneurysms and dissection: CT and MRI. J Thorac Imaging 16:35-46, 2001.
83. Anbarasu A, Harris PL, McWilliams RG: The role of gadolinium-enhanced MR imaging in the preoperative evaluation of inflammatory abdominal aortic aneurysm. Eur Radiol 12(Suppl 3):S192-S195, 2002.
84. Neschis DG, Velazquez OC, Baum RA, et al: The role of magnetic resonance angiography for endoprosthetic design. J Vasc Surg 33:488-494, 2001.
85. Cejna M, Loewe C, Schoder M, et al: MR angiography vs CT angiography in the follow-up of nitinol stent grafts in endoluminally treated aortic aneurysms. Eur Radiol 12:2443-2450, 2002.
86. Insko EK, Kulzer LM, Fairman RM, et al: MR imaging for the detection of endoleaks in recipients of abdominal aortic stent-grafts with low magnetic susceptibility. Acad Radiol 10:509-513, 2003.
87. Cognet F, Salem DB, Dranssart M, et al: Chronic mesenteric ischemia: Imaging and percutaneous treatment. Radiographics 22:863-880, 2002.
88. Carlos RC, Stanley JC, Stafford-Johnson D, Prince MR: Interobserver variability in the evaluation of chronic mesenteric ischemia with gadolinium-enhanced MR angiography. Acad Radiol 8:879-887, 2001.

89. Lee VS, Morgan JN, Tan AGS, et al: Celiac artery compression by the median arcuate ligament: A pitfall of end-expiratory MR imaging. Radiology 228:437-442, 2003.
90. Bradbury MS, Kavanagh PV, Bechtold RE, et al: Mesenteric venous thrombosis: Diagnosis and noninvasive imaging. Radiographics 22:527-541, 2002.
91. Siegelman ES, Charafeddine R, Stolpen AH, Axel L: Suppression of intravascular signal on fat-saturated contrast-enhanced thoracic MR arteriograms. Radiology 217:115-118, 2000.
92. Tirkes AT, Rosen MA, Siegelman ES: Gadolinium susceptibility artifact causing false positive stenosis isolated to the proximal common carotid artery in 3D dynamic contrast medium enhanced MR angiography of the thorax: A brief review of causes and prevention. Int J Cardiovasc Imaging 19:151-155, 2003.
93. Neimatallah MA, Chenevert TL, Carlos RC, et al: Subclavian MR arteriography: Reduction of susceptibility artifact with short echo time and dilute gadopentetate dimeglumine. Radiology 217:581-586, 2000.
94. Insko EK, Siegelman ES, Stolpen AH: Subacute clot mimicking flow in a thrombosed arterial bypass graft on two-dimensional time-of-flight and three-dimensional contrast-enhanced MRA. J Magn Reson Imaging 11:192-194, 2000.
95. Dempsey MF, Condon B, Hadley DM: MRI safety review. Semin Ultrasound CT MR 23:392-401, 2002.
96. Shellock FG, Kanal E: Magnetic Resonance: Bioeffects, Safety, and Patient Management, 2nd ed. Philadelphia, Lippincott Williams & Wilkins, 1996.
97. Shellock FG: Magnetic resonance safety update 2002: Implants and devices. J Magn Reson Imaging 16:485-496, 2002.

Chapter 23

Intravascular Ultrasound

GEORGE E. KOPCHOK, BS
RODNEY A. WHITE, MD

The concept of catheter-based ultrasound imaging was first introduced in the early 1970s.[1] Since its inception, the catheters and computer-driven imaging platforms have transformed the technology into a user-friendly tool. Today's catheters are designed to track over conventional guidewires and require minimal preparation. Likewise, the intravascular ultrasound (IVUS) images produced by the new software make image interpretation easier for the novice. In this chapter, we describe the different IVUS catheters available to the clinician as well as the clinical utility of the modality during endovascular interventions. It is our hope that clinicians will explore the technology to gain experience that will enable them to use and interpret the technology in more difficult and sometimes troublesome cases. We believe that IVUS is an important adjuvant in any endovascular specialist's armamentarium.

■ INTRAVASCULAR ULTRASOUND IMAGING

Ultrasound consists of the transmission of sound energy through a medium. The frequency of the sound wave is a function of the transmission speed through a given medium. The relationship between speed of transmission on any given medium and the frequency is as follows:

$$\text{Wavelength} = \text{Velocity of sound} \div \text{Frequency}$$

In air, the speed of sound is 330 m/sec. In saline and collagen, the speeds are 1560 m/sec and 1680 m/sec, respectively.[2] Ultrasound utilizes a very high frequency, 0.5 to 40 MHz.

Once an ultrasonic pulse is emitted from a transducer, the amplitude or intensity of the reflected signal depends on the interference or echo of a given tissue type. With A mode ultrasound imaging, this reflection is converted into a pulse that identifies amplitude and distance from the transducer (Fig. 23-1). B mode scans are obtained by converting the A mode signal into a signal that replaces amplitude with brightness. The resultant differences in individual intensities of dots forms the black-white shading known as *gray scale*. In order to obtain a 360-degree cross-sectional image, the ultrasound beam is scanned through a full circle, and the beam's direction and deflection are synchronized on the radial display. This can be achieved by mechanically rotating the imaging elements or by using electronically switched arrays.

Spatial or image resolution is the ability to distinguish between two points along the ultrasound beam and is a direct function of transducer frequency. It is approximately equal to one half of the pulse width. Therefore, a higher-frequency signal will have a shorter pulse width and greater resolution. The limitation with this relationship is that the depth of tissue penetration is inversely proportional to the transducer frequency. Thus, the higher the frequency, the shallower the tissue penetration. The current 8- to 30-MHz IVUS transducers used to image large to medium-sized vessels have a resolution of approximately 0.1 to 0.15 mm and a radial depth of penetration from 40 to 10 mm, respectively. For aortic type procedures, 8- to 12-MHz catheters are normally required to visualize the entire aortic circumference; 20- and 30-MHz catheters are normally used for iliac and cardiac vessels, respectively. Newly developed 40- to 50-MHz transducers provide resolution of less than 100 μm and are normally limited to coronary procedures because of the limited depth of penetration. With

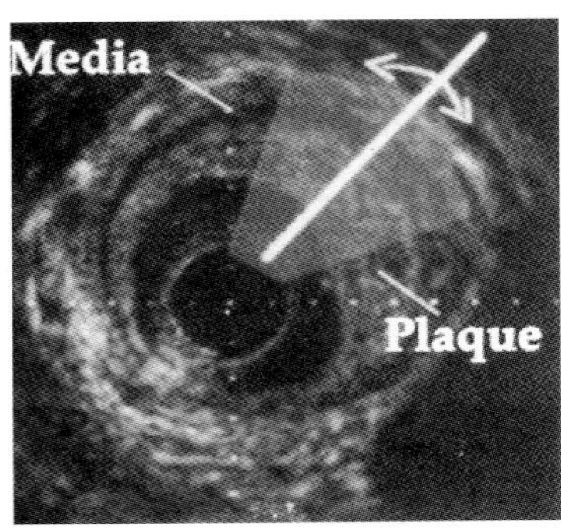

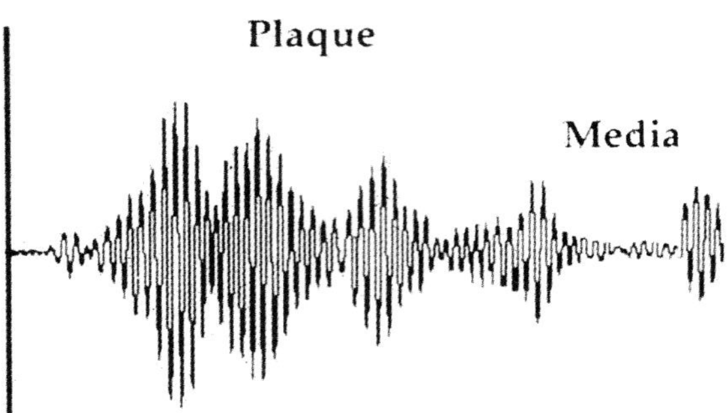

FIGURE 23-1 Different tissue types reflect the ultrasound signal at different amplitudes. The image on the right is a sample of the raw radiofrequency information corresponding to the white line on the left image. (From Yock PG, Fitzgerald PJ, Sudhir K, Ports TA: Clinical applications of intravascular ultrasound imaging. In Bernstein EF, et al [eds]: Vascular Diagnosis. Chicago, Mosby-Year Book, 1993.)

this spectrum of visualization capabilities, the technology is rapidly advancing to provide accurate imaging in all vascular beds.

Electronically Switched Phased-Array Transducers

Phased-array transducers use the principle of electronically switched or rotated arrays. A linear array of stationary elements (up to 64) on the tip of the catheter are electronically activated, producing real-time cross-sectional intraluminal images in a plane perpendicular to the long axis of the catheter. Current catheters incorporate miniature integrated circuits at their tips; such circuits provide sequenced transmission and reception without the need for numerous electrical circuits traveling the full length of the catheter (Fig. 23-2). In addition to reducing the electronic noise, this modification simplifies the manufacturing complexity and improves the flexibility of the catheter.

Current phased-array intravascular ultrasound catheters utilize frequencies in the range of 10 to 40 MHz. The catheter most commonly used for aortoiliac intervention is the 8.2 Fr, 10-MHz catheter. It tracks over a 0.035-inch (up to 0.038 inch) guidewire and can be quickly prepared, introduced, and exchanged with other catheters.

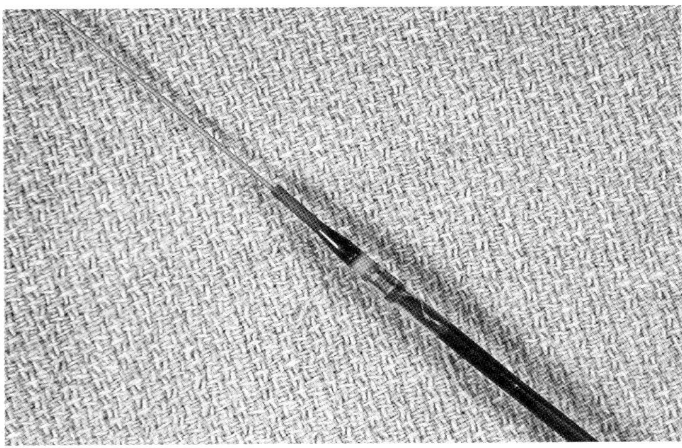

FIGURE 23-2 The Volcano Visions PV8.2F catheter, a phase-array, 8.2 Fr, 10-MHz IVUS catheter, over an 0.035-inch guidewire. The catheter tracks concentrically over the guidewire, thus eliminating guidewire image interference and improving tractability. The gold band near the tip of the catheter houses 64 linear array crystals. (Courtesy of Volcano Therapeutics, Rancho Cordova, CA.)

One limitation of these imaging catheters—common to all high-frequency ultrasound devices to some extent—is the inability to image structures in the immediate vicinity of the transducer, that is, in the "near field." This near-field effect causes a bright circumferential artifact known as the "ring down" surrounding the catheter. The ring-down artifact can be electronically removed, but structures within the region that is masked cannot be seen. Near-field effect is more apparent in phased-array configurations than in mechanical systems, because the imaging crystals may come in almost direct contact with the structure being imaged. However, this is not usually a problem in medium- to large-diameter vessels because the clinician can usually rotate the catheter or reposition the guidewire to move the catheter off the vessel wall.

Color-Flow Imaging

Color-flow duplex imaging has proved valuable in vascular interventions and has been used for many years.[3] Color-flow duplex scanning is based on differences in the ultrasound frequency transmitted by the probe and the signal reflected from moving blood, known as the *Doppler shift*. The velocity of blood is proportional to this frequency shift.[4] This imaging modality works best when the ultrasound signal is directed forward from the probe and at an angle other than perpendicular to the blood flow. These requirements limit the use of the Doppler shift principle for intravascular ultrasound. However, advances in computer technology have combined with phased-array image processing to produce real-time color-flow or Chromaflo (Volcano Therapeutics, Rancho Cordova, CA) imaging.[5] This program compares sequential axial images (at up to 30 frames per second) and records any differences in the position of echogenic blood particles between images. A larger difference is interpreted as a greater flow rate (Fig. 23-3). The software colorizes the flow accordingly and displays the results in axial and longitudinal views. Although the color differential may be substantial, actual flow velocities cannot be measured with this technique.

Mechanical Transducers

Mechanical transducers use one of two basic configurations: either the transducer itself or an acoustic mirror is rotated at the tip of the catheter with a flexible, high torque cable that extends the length of the device. However, the majority of mechanical devices currently utilize the rotating transducer.

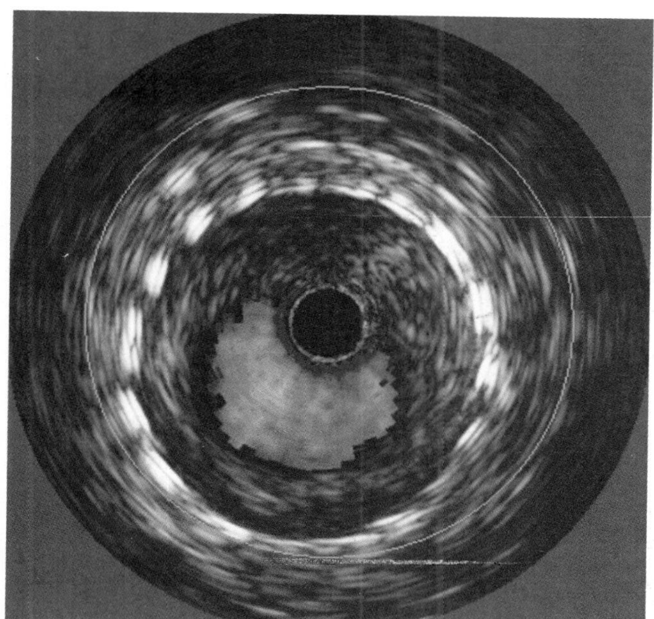

FIGURE 23-3 Color flow IVUS image demonstrating restenosis of a stent at 1 year. Image produced with a Visions PV0.018 FX catheter (Volcano Therapeutics, Rancho Cordova, CA). (Courtesy of EB Diethrich, Arizona Heart Hospital, Phoenix, AZ.) (See Color Figure in this section.)

The transducer, which is angled slightly forward of perpendicular, produces a cone-shaped ultrasound beam, resulting in an image of the vessel slightly forward or in front of the transducer assembly. These catheters utilize ultrasound frequencies between 10 and 30 MHz; some experimental devices using frequencies up to 45 MHz produce excellent images of human arteries.[6]

In the rotating transducer, and as with the phased-array devices, a part of the ring-down region and near-field zone of the beam occur outside the catheter, so that it is not possible to image clearly in this area. However, the mechanical imaging catheters suffer from less image loss due to these problems because the distance between the inner chamber and the outside of the catheter is short.[7]

In devices with a distally placed transducer and proximal rotating mirror, an electrical connecting wire must pass along the side of the imaging assembly. This wire produces an artifact that occupies approximately 15 degrees of the image cross-section. Although this artifact is of little concern in standard IVUS images, it does present a problem for the smaller high-frequency catheters used in coronary applications. For these catheters as well as for some new aortic-size catheters, a guidewire channel now serves the dual purpose of gaining catheter access across a lesion with a guidewire (Fig. 23-4A). The guidewire is then withdrawn from the catheter lumen, and the IVUS crystal is advanced through the same lumen. The IVUS crystal can be moved up and down the length of the catheter lumen to evaluate the artery. When the IVUS evaluation is completed, the crystal is withdrawn, and the guidewire is re-advanced through the working lumen. The IVUS catheter can then be withdrawn, leaving the guidewire in position.

Other potential disadvantages of mechanical systems relate to imaging chamber flushing, mechanical artifacts, miniaturization, and use with guidewires. Current mechanical catheters require a saline- or water-filled imaging chamber. This chamber must be rendered and maintained free of bubbles to allow adequate imaging, and continuous low-pressure irrigation is required. Should a bubble appear, the image is distorted or destroyed, necessitating removal of the catheter from the vessel and manual clearing of the bubble from the chamber (Fig. 23-4B).

■ CATHETER TECHNIQUES: OPTIMIZING IMAGE QUALITY AND ACCURACY

Although there are differences between mechanical and multiple-element array catheters, the techniques for obtaining optimal intravascular ultrasound images are applicable to both. It should be noted that phased-array devices are generally more flexible and do not require the careful flushing that is needed with mechanical transducers.

Most of the IVUS catheters can be passed over a guidewire (0.009 to 0.035 inch in diameter) that allows more controlled maneuvering of the device within the lumen of the vessel from a remote introduction site, particularly in tortuous or tightly stenotic vessels. Because the configuration of mechanical rotating catheters prevents a central guidewire channel, these catheters use a variety of monorail and coaxial lumen options for over-the-wire applications. Passing some of these catheters through tortuous anatomy is difficult because the catheters have a tendency to veer off of the guidewire around tight turns. Multiple-element array devices utilize a central guidewire channel, which may offer an advantage for passing catheters

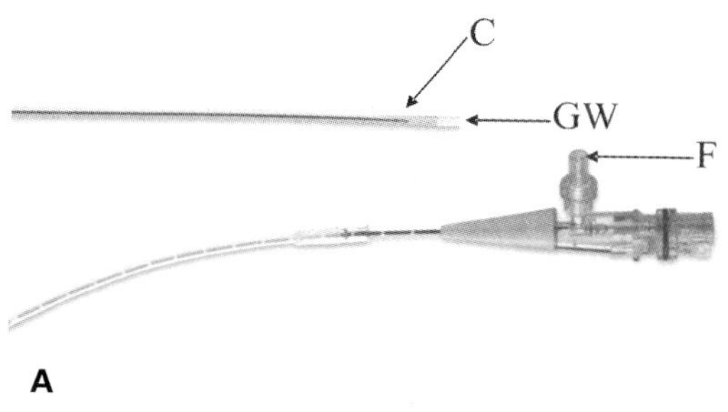

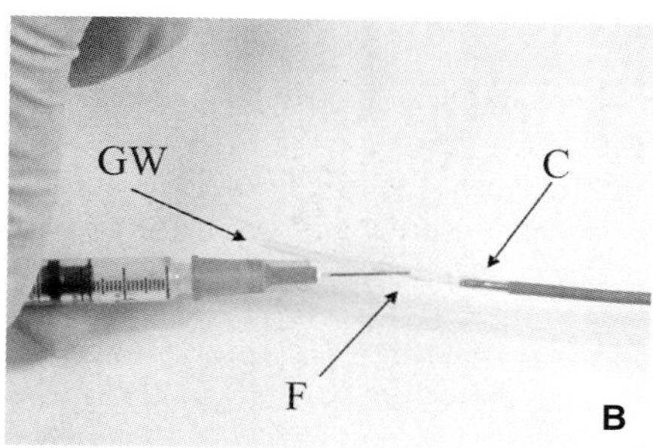

FIGURE 23-4 **A,** Atlantis PV catheter with dual-purpose lumen. **B,** Sonicath Ultra Imaging catheter demonstrating flush technique. C, the imaging crystal that rotates during use; F, the flush port or needle; GW, the guidewire lumen. (Courtesy of Boston Scientific, Natick, MA.)

through tortuous or narrowed vessels. When intravascular ultrasound is used to image vessels before and after interventions such as balloon angioplasty and stent deployment, a guidewire is essential to allow manipulation of the catheters and repeated crossing of the lesion without further disruption of the angioplasty or stent site.

Rotational Orientation

It may be important to orient the intravascular ultrasound image within the vessel so that anteroposterior accuracy can be achieved. This will also make vessel identification and interpretation easier for the clinician. The most successful method of maintaining orientation is to use anatomic landmarks. For example, as the catheter crosses the aortic bifurcation, the IVUS display can be electronically rotated so that the common iliac arteries are positioned side-by-side, in a correct anatomic location. Occasionally this anatomic arrangement is not true, especially in tortuous, dilated vessels, and the alignment must be checked against other parameters. The location of anterior visceral vessels—celiac or superior mesenteric vessels and the renal vein—is also useful for imaging in the abdominal aorta. For the iliac bed, the posteromedial position of the internal iliac artery orifices can be used to adjust angulations.

Longitudinal Reconstruction of Gray-Scale Images

A longitudinal gray-scale image is an option on most of the newer IVUS units. The longitudinal image is obtained by mechanically withdrawing the catheter through the vessel at a controlled rate. The cross-sectional images are then stacked by the processing unit and rotated 90 degrees to produce a longitudinal view of the vessel that is very similar to an angiogram. Theoretically, distances can then be measured from one point to another. Unfortunately, this option is currently limited to cardiac applications because of the slow speed of current pull-back devices. For most peripheral endovascular procedures, newer pull-back mechanisms that pull the catheters over longer distances at slightly greater speeds must be developed by the manufacturers.

An important feature of two-dimensional (2D) longitudinal reconstruction is that it displays an image of the entire length of the vessel, similar to contrast angiography. However, instead of only the luminal profile that contrast angiography achieves, the 2D reconstruction provides detailed cross-sectional wall morphology next to the longitudinal image. A tract ball can allow the user to evaluate the vessel over its entire length.

Catheter Selection

Using an IVUS catheter of the appropriate size and frequency is essential to optimizing visualization. The clinician must make a compromise between the highest frequency, the depth of penetration, and catheter size. Another consideration is the diameter of the guidewire being utilized for the procedure. Ideally, the IVUS catheter should readily work over the applicable guidewire, making guidewire exchanges unnecessary. Fortunately, this is one area in which the manufacturers have adequately addressed the issues. The IVUS catheters utilized for most aortic and iliac procedures can be advanced over a 0.0350-inch guidewire. The catheters range in size from 6 to 8 Fr and in frequency from 8 to 20 MHz. For aortic procedures, the clinician should stick to a frequency range of 8 to 12 MHz to ensure adequate circumferential imaging. Table 23-1 lists the currently available catheters applicable to peripheral vascular procedures.

Table 23-1 Intravascular Ultrasound Catheters for Peripheral Vascular Imaging

MANUFACTURER	SIZE (French)	FREQUENCY (MHz)	GUIDEWIRE LUMEN (Inches)
Volcano Therapeutics, Rancho Cordova, CA, USA	3.4*	20	0.018
	8.2*,†	10	0.038
Boston Scientific, Natick, MA, USA	8†	15	0.035
	9†	9	NA
	3.2	20	0.018
	6†	12.5	0.035
	6	20	0.035

*The only peripheral catheter currently available with color-flow imaging; the 8.2F catheter is currently under investigation for color-flow utility.
†Catheters commonly used for aortic endovascular interventions.

Image quality is best when the catheter is parallel to the vessel wall, that is, when the ultrasound beam is directed at 90 degrees to the luminal surface; minor angulations may affect the luminal shape and dimensional accuracy. Eccentric positioning causes the vessel wall nearer the imaging chamber to appear more hyperechoic than the distant wall, resulting in an artifactual difference in wall thickness. Angulations may also result in an elliptical image of the vessel lumen, especially in tortuous aortas and the thoracic arch. When this occurs, the minimal diameter (minor axis) should be used as the vessel diameter. In two studies, investigators have demonstrated that the minor axis is an accurate measurement in angled images or tortuous anatomy.[8,9]

■ INTERPRETATION OF IMAGES

The images produced by IVUS catheters not only outline the luminal and adventitial surfaces of normal arterial segments but also have the potential to discriminate between normal and diseased vessel wall.

In muscular arteries, distinct sonographic layers are visible, with the media appearing as an echolucent layer sandwiched between the more echodense intima and adventitia.[10] The internal and external elastic laminae and adventitia are considered the backscatter substrates for the inner and outer echodense zones.[11] Smooth muscle in the media is echolucent, whereas collagen in the adventitia and elastin in the intima are echodense. Small intimal lesions are also quite well-defined in muscular arteries because of the fibrous tissue content, although large or complex plaques may compress or shadow the medial detail. The three-layer vessel image seen in muscular arteries may be lost in smaller distal arteries and larger elastic arteries, because the higher elastin content makes the media echodense. In medium-sized

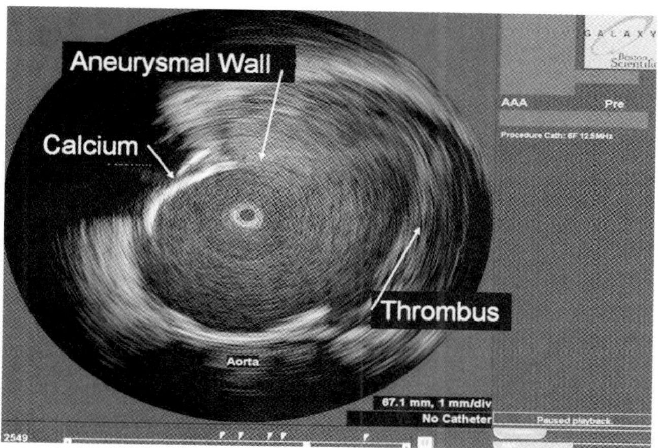

FIGURE 23-5 IVUS image of abdominal aortic aneurysm demonstrating normal and calcified wall as well as thrombus in the aneurysmal sac. Image produced with the Galaxy 2 System and an Atlantis PV mechanical rotating catheter. (Courtesy of John Tirado, Boston Scientific, Natick, MA.)

vessels such as the femoral artery, the media is visible but is thinner than in more central vessels.

Gussenhoven and colleagues[11] have described four basic plaque components that can be distinguished with 40-MHz intravascular ultrasound in vitro:

- Echolucent—lipid deposit, lipid "lake"
- Soft echoes—fibromuscular tissue, intimal proliferation, including varying amounts of diffusely dispersed lipid
- Bright echoes—collagen-rich fibrous tissue
- Bright echoes with acoustic shadowing—calcified tissue

In addition to characterization of atherosclerotic plaque, intravascular ultrasound can frequently distinguish thrombus from normal vessel wall or minimal occlusive disease. Fresh thrombus usually appears as a highly echogenic homogeneous mass with varying shadowing (image attenuation) beyond its location. Older thrombus can be difficult to differentiate from a fibrous atheromatous lesion but is usually less echogenic and very homogeneous.

For soft tissue, the absorption coefficient for ultrasound energy is proportional to the frequency, whereas for hard tissue, the coefficient is proportional to the square of the frequency.[12] Intravascular ultrasound devices therefore are sensitive in differentiating calcified and noncalcified vascular lesions. Because the ultrasound energy is strongly reflected by calcific plaque, it appears as a bright image with dense acoustic shadowing behind it (Fig. 23-5). For this reason, the exact location of the media and adventitia cannot be seen in segments of vessels containing heavily calcific disease, and dimensions must be estimated by interpolation of adjacent size data.

Dimensional Morphology and Lesion Distribution

Several investigators have observed that intraluminal ultrasound determines the dimensions of the luminal diameters and wall thickness of normal or minimally diseased arteries both in vitro and in vivo and have found the method to be accurate within 0.05 mm.[10-12] Determination of the outside diameter of the vessels may be less accurate, with a margin of error in some cases being 0.5 mm. Additional studies have compared the ability of intravascular ultrasound and uniplanar angiography in determining the luminal dimensions of normal and moderately atherosclerotic human arteries.[13,14] Uniplanar angiography can be quite accurate in defining vessel lumen cross-sectional area if the vessel is circular, as it is in most normal and mildly diseased arteries. Clinically significant atherosclerotic occlusive diseased is usually eccentrically positioned in the arterial lumen, and the lumen may be either circular or elliptical, although most are circular.[15] In instances in which the lumen is elliptical, biplanar angiograms are needed to more accurately define luminal cross-sectional areas and calculate a percentage area stenosis.[16] In elliptical lumina, the cross-sectional area calculated from angiograms is usually greater than that measured with intravascular ultrasound.

In addition to the limitations of angiography in defining luminal dimensions of elliptical vessels, the modality gives no information about vessel wall morphology aside from calcification or aneurysms visualized on the plain radiographs.

Clinical Applications

Diagnostic

IVUS is an invasive procedure. Thus, it is normally limited to functioning as an adjuvant to other procedures, such as contrast angiography and balloon angioplasty. However, when contrast agents are contraindicated or contrast-enhanced computed tomography (CT) scans are inconclusive, IVUS can serve as a useful tool for prediagnostic evaluation. This is especially true for evaluating patient suitability for abdominal or thoracic endoluminal graft (ELG) procedures. Figure 23-6 shows a longitudinal grayscale image of a patient being evaluated for treatment of a thoracic aneurysm in whom use of a contrast agent was contraindicated. The IVUS pull-through identifies the diameter and length of the proximal and distal graft fixation points as well as the overall length between the origins of the subclavian artery and celiac artery. On the basis of this information, the patient was successfully treated with an aortic ELG.

Balloon Angioplasty

IVUS can provide useful information for both preprocedural and postprocedural assessment of balloon angioplasty. It provides intraluminal cross-sectional measurements along with precise determination of the arterial morphology and lesion pathology. Postprocedural assessment also yields an accurate evaluation of the end result and may help determine whether a stent is needed to improve the overall result. In one study showing that postprocedural assessment with IVUS improves the overall results of percutaneous coronary angioplasty, IVUS guidance during percutaneous coronary interventions improved long-term outcome and cost-effectiveness of the procedure.[17]

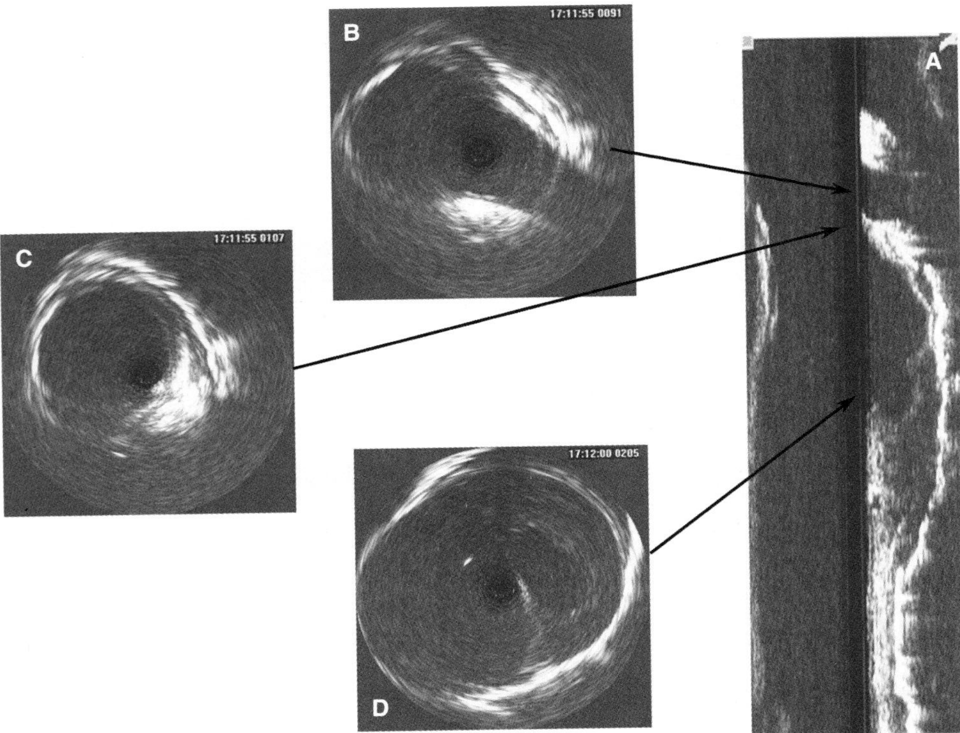

FIGURE 23-6 Evaluation of proximal and distal fixation points for treatment of thoracic aneurysm. **A,** A real-time longitudinal reconstruction of the thoracic aorta demonstrating the subclavian orifice (**B**), the proximal fixation point (**C**), and the aneurysm (**D**). Images produced with a Visions PV8.2F catheter. (Courtesy of Volcano Therapeutics, Rancho Cordova, CA.)

Stent Deployment

As with balloon angioplasty, IVUS is useful for determining accurate diameters and exact locations for stent deployment. Arteriography, regarded as the "gold standard" for assessing endovascular therapy, has limitations in evaluation of stent-based procedures. Specifically, the uniplanar images produced with arteriography detail only the outer edges of the artery and stent. This limits the ability to adequately evaluate stent-to-vessel apposition. In one study, vessel size and lumen diameter were underestimated 62% of the time with arteriography and 40% of the stents placed in the iliac arterial system were under-deployed, possibly leading to related failure of treatment.[18,19] Figure 23-7 shows IVUS images from two cases of inadequately deployed iliac stents. In both cases, because of the anteroposterior plane of the angiogram, the completion angiogram demonstrated widely patent stents with good apposition; the IVUS image, however, revealed poorly apposed stents that needed further balloon dilatation.

Endoluminal Grafts for Abdominal Aortic Aneurysm

As with stenting, IVUS can be an important adjuvant in the deployment of ELGs for the treatment of abdominal aortic aneurysm (AAA). Although most of the preprocedural evaluations can be adequately performed using contrast-enhanced spiral CT imaging, IVUS can be used to validate

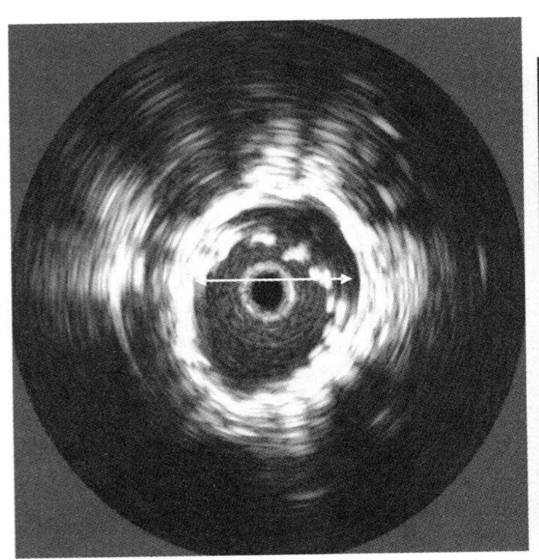

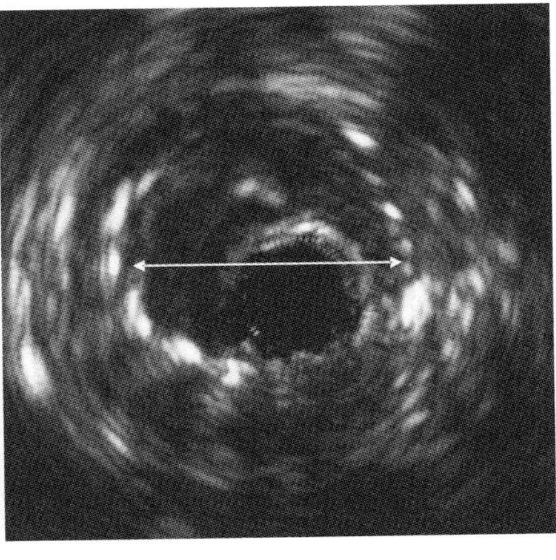

FIGURE 23-7 IVUS images of a maldeployed iliac stent. On angiography (*left*) the contrast agent conformed to the outer walls, demonstrating a well-apposed stent. IVUS evaluation (*right*) revealed poorly apposed stents, which were further dilated to maximize wall apposition. Images produced with a Visions PV8.2F catheter. (Courtesy of Volcano Therapeutics, Rancho Cordova, CA.)

measurements of proximal and distal fixation points, ensure healthy arterial wall and distribution of atherosclerotic lesions, and determine the optimal device length.[20-22] In our practice, we commonly use an aortic diagram shown in Figure 23-8. The major landmarks are found with IVUS in relation to a radiopaque scale placed behind the patient. At each given point, the IVUS catheter is centered on the fluoroscopic screen to eliminate fluoroscopic parallax. Each landmark's location is then identified and its diameter measured. If the aorta is tortuous, the minor diameter is used as described earlier. The catheter is then advanced or retracted to the next landmark and measurement repeated. This technique allows the interventionalist to interrogate the entire aortoiliac system with minimal fluoroscopy time and no contrast. It also verifies the results of the CT scan and enables the physician to further examine the fixation points. Several times in our experience the normal aortic wall seen on the CT scan was aneurysmal or

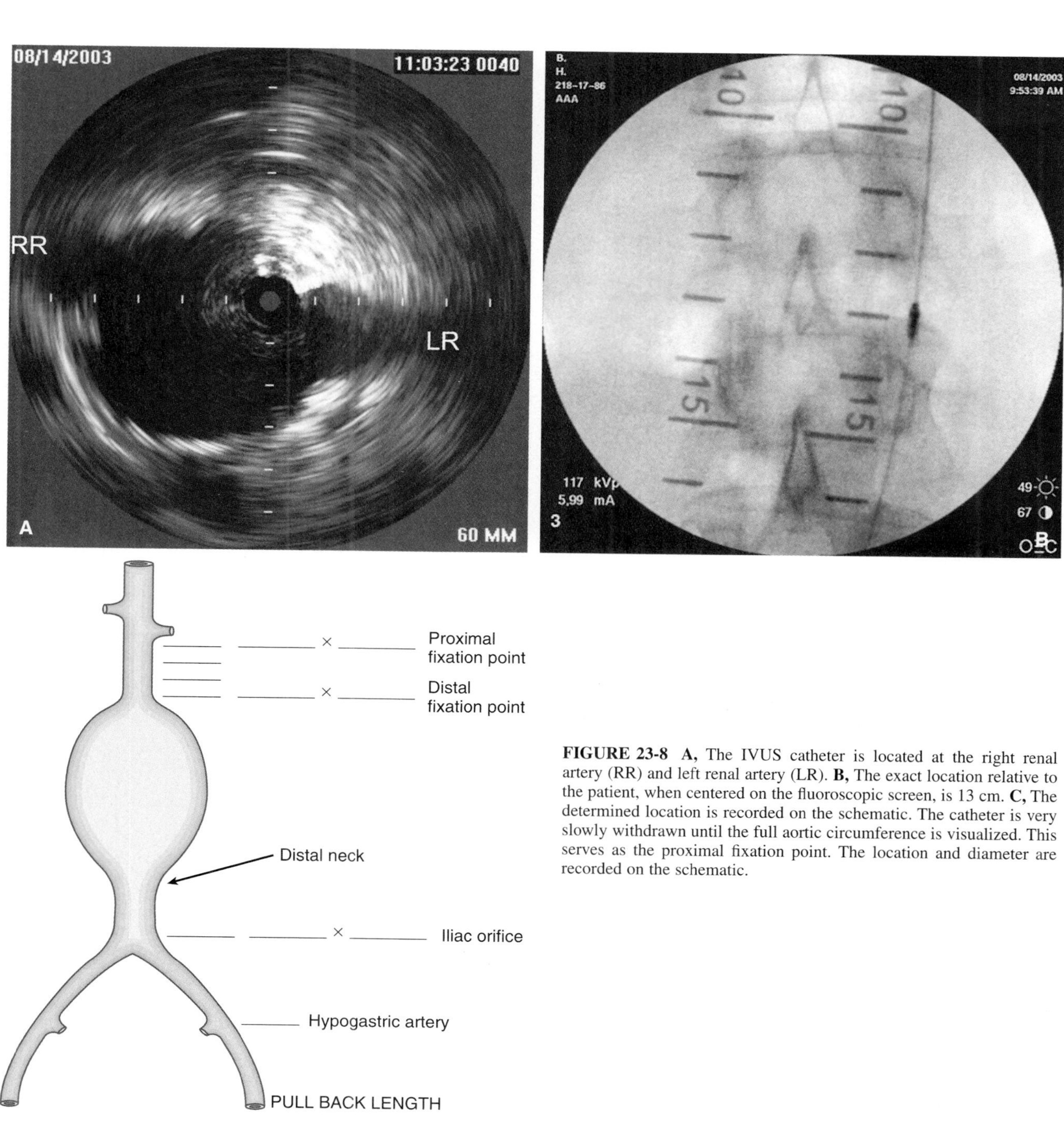

FIGURE 23-8 **A,** The IVUS catheter is located at the right renal artery (RR) and left renal artery (LR). **B,** The exact location relative to the patient, when centered on the fluoroscopic screen, is 13 cm. **C,** The determined location is recorded on the schematic. The catheter is very slowly withdrawn until the full aortic circumference is visualized. This serves as the proximal fixation point. The location and diameter are recorded on the schematic.

had evidence of a pseudoaneurysm on IVUS evaluation (Fig. 23-9). Once the landmarks are located and measured, the investigator can verify the length from the infrarenal fixation point to the iliac bifurcation and the external iliac orifice. This is accomplished placing the IVUS catheter at the level of the distal renal orifice and grasping the IVUS catheter as it exits the access sheath. The catheter can then be withdrawn to the level of the iliac orifice and the distance between the sheath and fingers measured. Leaving the fingers in place, the catheter can be withdrawn to the external iliac artery and the overall length measured. When using this technique however, it is important to avoid prograde catheter movement. The catheter should always be pulled in a distal direction. If it is advanced, it should be advanced beyond the point of interest and withdrawn distally to eliminate the catheter flex or backlash and consequent error in measurement.

Once the anatomy is interrogated, the physician may elect to perform localized angiograms to confirm renal and hypogastric artery locations and patency. In our practice, we routinely confirm the ipsilateral hypogastric artery and then advance the ELG device into the approximate location. An

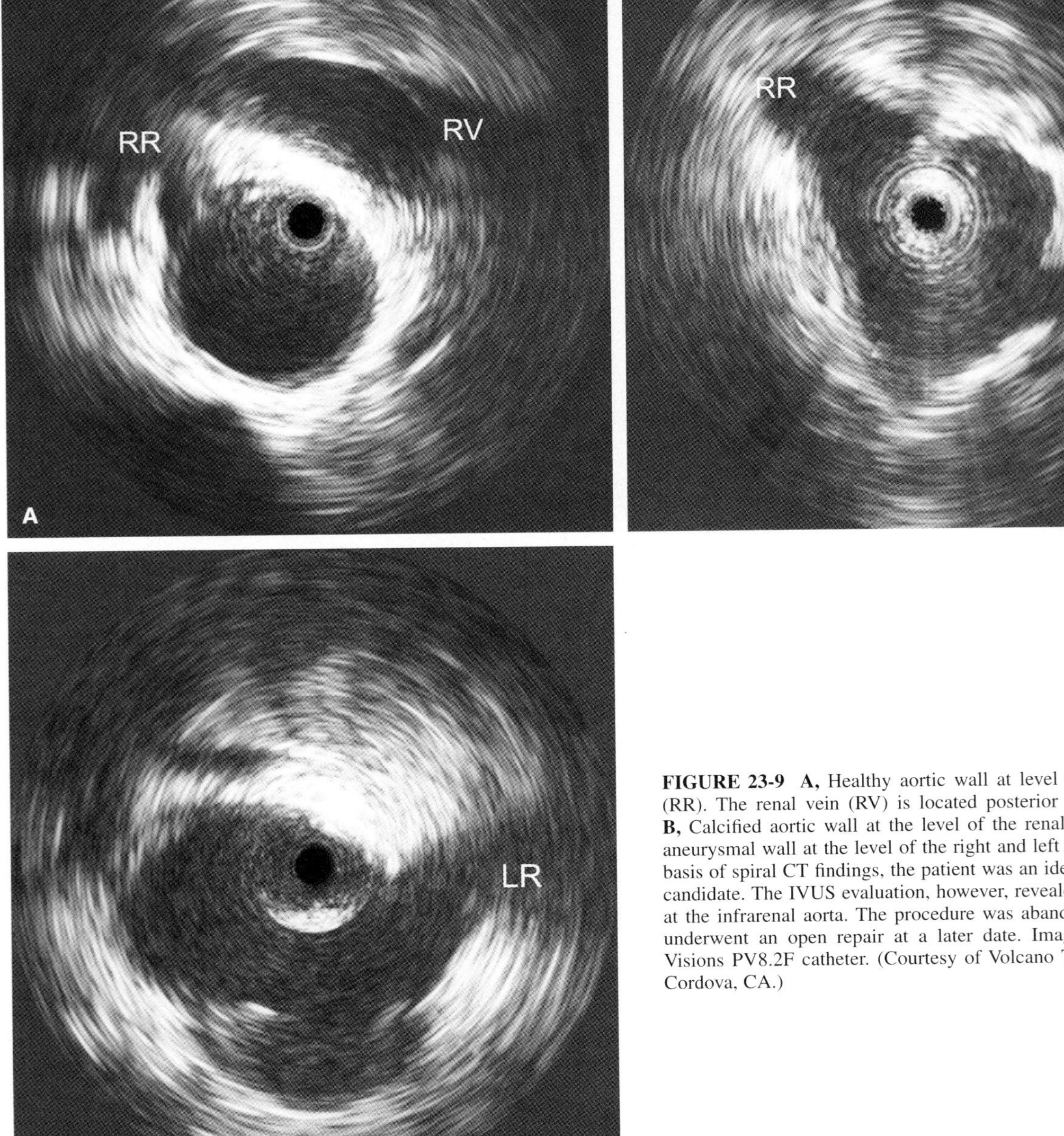

FIGURE 23-9 **A,** Healthy aortic wall at level of right renal orifice (RR). The renal vein (RV) is located posterior to the renal arteries. **B,** Calcified aortic wall at the level of the renal orifices. **C,** Pseudoaneurysmal wall at the level of the right and left renal orifices. On the basis of spiral CT findings, the patient was an ideal endovascular graft candidate. The IVUS evaluation, however, revealed a pseudoaneurysm at the infrarenal aorta. The procedure was abandoned and the patient underwent an open repair at a later date. Images produced with a Visions PV8.2F catheter. (Courtesy of Volcano Therapeutics, Rancho Cordova, CA.)

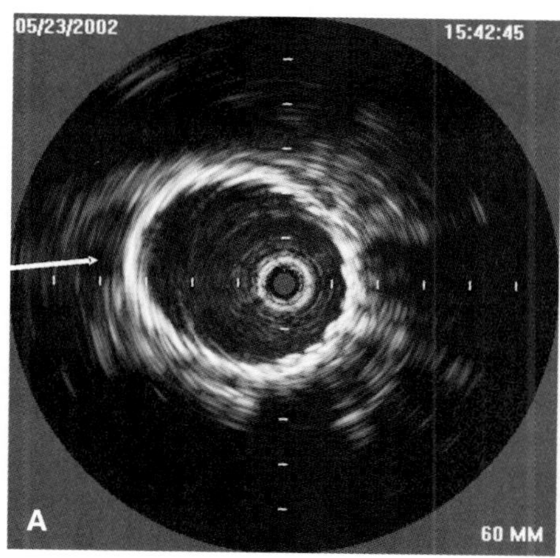

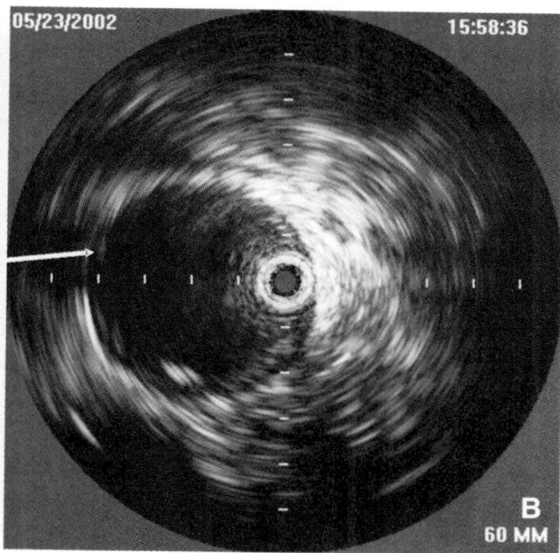

FIGURE 23-10 **A,** Endoluminal graft covering the right renal orifice. On angiogram, the right renal artery was patent, but slow filling, due to graft porosity. **B,** The endoluminal graft was pulled distally with an over-the-bifurcation technique, and the renal ostium was re-evaluated with IVUS.

angiographic catheter is positioned along side the device and a small bolus of contrast injected to confirm the infrarenal fixation point relative to the ELG.

Once the ipsilateral device is deployed, the angiographic catheter is withdrawn into the aneurysmal sac and used with a soft tip guidewire to cannulate the contralateral limb. IVUS is then used to verify proper positioning of the guidewire in the main graft body and to evaluate proximal graft apposition as well as location relative to renal arteries. Several times in our practice, the guidewire was found between the ELG and aortic wall on IVUS examination. In these cases, it was very easy to withdraw the guidewire and reposition in the correct lumen. Once guidewire location is confirmed, the contralateral limb can be deployed. Following deployment, IVUS may be used to further evaluate device location and apposition, especially if contrast is not being used of if there is an endoleak apparent on the completion angiogram. Proximity to the renal artery can also be evaluated as seen in Figure 23-10. In this case, the renal arteries appeared patent but slow filling on the completion angiogram. IVUS evaluation revealed that the ELG was covering the right renal orifice. The device was pulled distally, using a guidewire over the bifurcation technique, and the renal ostium re-evaluated with IVUS.[23,24]

In many cases, the preprocedural spiral CT evaluation is inconclusive regarding the common iliac artery diameter and location relative to the hypogastric orifice. In these cases IVUS is invaluable for measuring length and diameter of the distal fixation point, to determine if the device should be extended into the external iliac artery and whether the hypogastric artery needs coil embolization.

Although cinefluoroscopy and IVUS are complementary in enabling expedient placement of ELGs, an additional important aspect supporting the use of IVUS in this application is that fluoroscopy time and contrast usage can be reduced significantly during the procedures, minimizing the exposure of both personnel and the patient. In fact, several investigators have reported deploying both thoracic and abdominal ELGs without the use of contrast agents.[5,25]

One study that utilized IVUS, digital subtraction angiography, and spiral CT scans to evaluate patients preoperatively found that IVUS may identify patients at risk of major adverse complications following endovascular repair.[26] In this study, investigators found that in addition to providing precise measurements, IVUS provided important qualitative information on luminal morphology, including atherosclerotic plaque, calcification, fibrous lesions, and intraluminal thrombus. Investigators found that high-grade atheromatous burden at the level of the aortic neck may lead to increased risk of embolic complications. The presence of thrombus within the neck was associated with increased risk of complications such as immediate and delayed proximal endoleak, graft migration, and distal embolization (Fig. 23-11).[27]

Thoracic Dissections

Endovascular treatment of aortic dissection was first described in 1999.[28,29] Since then, improvements of the ELG design and delivery systems have broadened their utility

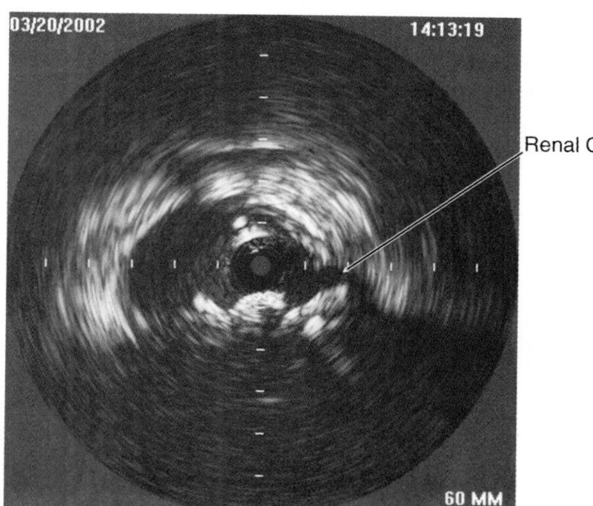

FIGURE 23-11 Heavy plaque burden at the level of the proximal neck may raise risk of embolic complications.

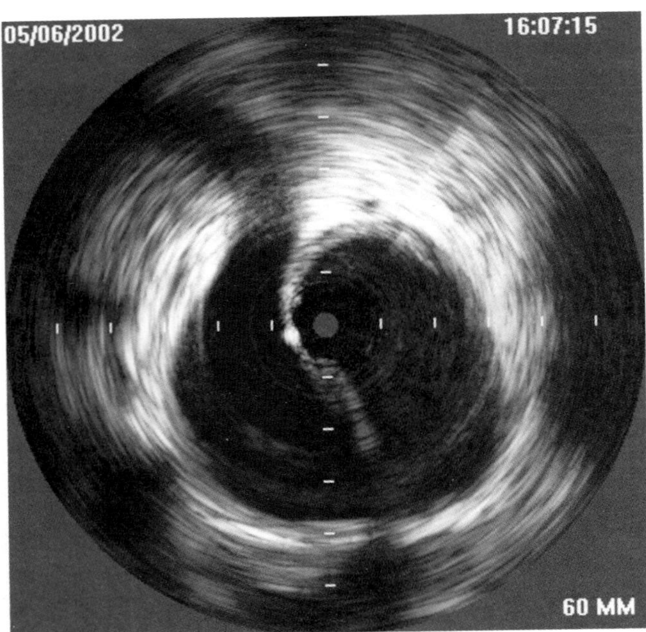

FIGURE 23-12 Major vessels can be readily evaluated to determine source of blood flow. If necessary, IVUS can also be used to evaluate the location for fenestration of dissection flaps as well as to provide real-time guidance of the fenestration device.

throughout the world. However, many challenges remain in device design.[30] These challenges include (1) The ability to accurately deploy the device around the tortuous curvature of aortic arch and proximal descending aorta. Numerous problems have been described with stent struts not conforming to the curvature of the arch, many times leading to disruption of the ascending aorta.[31] (2) Delivery system size. Due to the large diameter stents needed to treat the thoracic aorta, devices currently range from 20 to 25 Fr. (3) Concern over long-term durability of the treatment.

Accurate screening and evaluation are critical to the decision-making process for treatment of aortic dissections. Multiple-slice spiral CT and magnetic resonance imaging (MRI) have been proved to provide detailed information on thoracic aneurysms and dissections.[30,32] However, once the decision has been made to intervene with an endovascular graft, these imaging modalities are limited during the actual deployment. Preliminary investigations confirm the utility of IVUS in identifying and reconfirming the important parameters required for successful treatment of acute aortic dissection by endoluminal stents.[33,34] These parameters are (1) site of proximal entry point and distal extent of the dissection, (2) relationship of the false lumen to major aortic branches, (3) measurement of aortic dimensions to allow selection of correct stent size, (4) confirmation that the stent is being deployed in the true lumen to obliterate the false lumen, and (5) confirmation that blood supply to major branch vessels has not been compromised during deployment of the device. As with AAA intervention, IVUS can be used to identify these landmarks and confirm that the morphology has not changed in the time between initial evaluation and treatment.

Proximal and distal dissection points can be readily identified with IVUS examination. The use of color-flow imaging may also enhance the ability to evaluate flow through the false lumen and the above-mentioned dissection points. If the dissection propagates into the branch vessels, perfusion of end organs must be maintained (Fig. 23-12). Although this status can generally be determined before the intervention, the relationship of major branch vessels to true and false lumens should be reconfirmed before exclusion of the proximal entry point. IVUS can be used to evaluate this relationship at the time of the endovascular intervention.[30] Figure 23-13A demonstrates a celiac artery that is being supplied by the true and false lumens. In this patient, the dissection extended to the superior mesenteric artery and ended above the renal arteries. The dissection flap can be seen in Figure 23-13B. An ELG was placed over the flap, and device apposition was verified with IVUS at completion of the procedure (Fig. 23-13C). No contrast agent was used in this endovascular procedure.

Access to the true lumen is essential for the treatment of thoracic dissections. Many times this lumen is compromised and difficult to confirm on fluoroscopy and angiography. IVUS has been useful in our practice to guide the guidewire past the distal entry point into the true lumen of the proximal aorta. Figure 23-14 demonstrates a case in which the guidewire continually advanced into the false lumen. The IVUS catheter was introduced and used to sequentially guide the guidewire into the true lumen. It must be noted that the tip of the IVUS catheter is very stiff and could potentially puncture the aortic wall. Therefore, the guidewire must always be advanced first, and the IVUS advanced over it, to confirm location. If the wire is still in the false lumen, both the IVUS catheter and guidewire are pulled distal to the dissection, and then the guidewire is manipulated and re-advanced through the dissection.

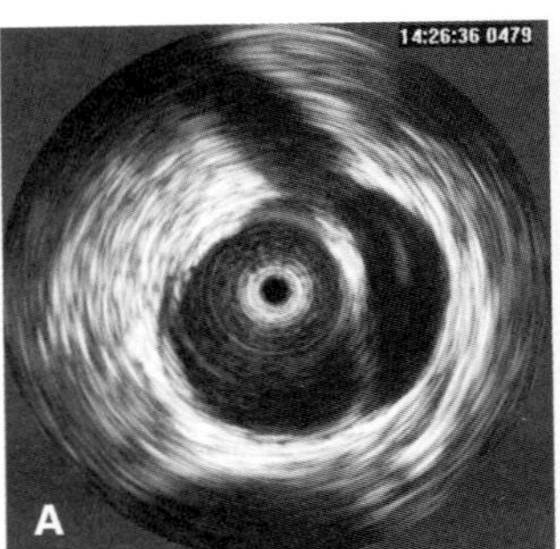

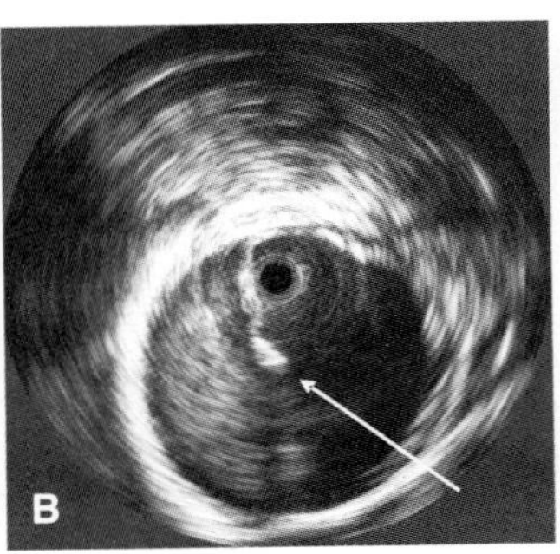

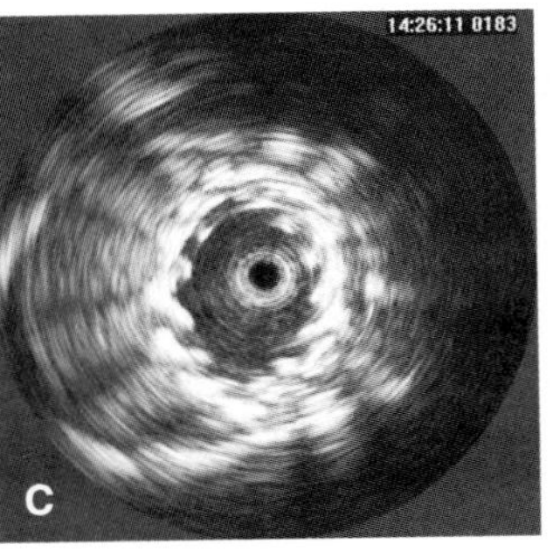

FIGURE 23-13 A, IVUS image demonstrates the dissection flap at the celiac orifice. Note that the true and false lumina are supplying blood to the artery. **B,** IVUS image of the proximal entry point of the flap of the dissection (*arrow*). In real-time imaging, these flaps were pulsating independently. **C,** An endoluminal graft was placed across the dissection flap, and its placement confirmed with IVUS.

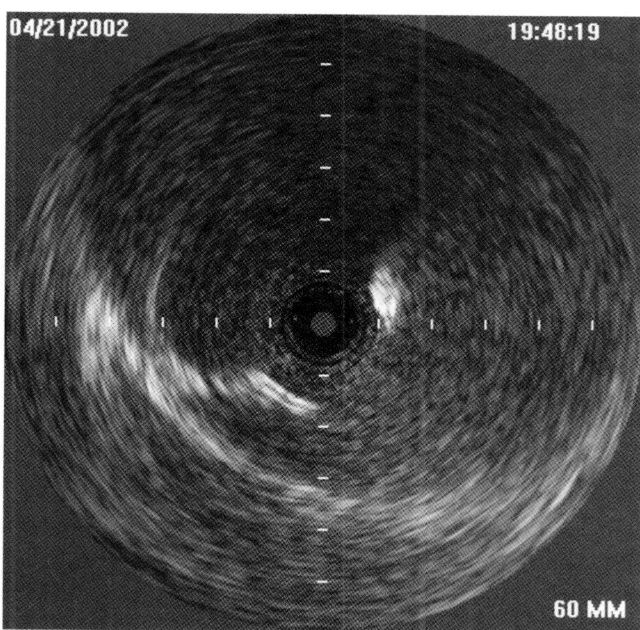

FIGURE 23-14 IVUS image of the entry point of a thoracic dissection. In this case, the guidewire continually advanced into the false lumen. The IVUS catheter was introduced and used to sequentially guide the guidewire into the true lumen. Image produced with Visions PV8.2F catheter. (Courtesy of Volcano Therapeutics, Rancho Cordova, CA.)

Thoracic Aneurysms and Ulcerations

The treatment of thoracic aneurysms and ulcerations is a little more straightforward and is generally associated with favorable primary success rates compared with aortic dissections.[35] However, given the high flow of the thoracic aorta, IVUS can be very useful for delineating the extent of the aneurysm, to confirm healthy aortic wall for proximal and distal fixation, and to identify the site for deployment of the ELG.[36] All of these predeployment assessments can readily be performed without the use of contrast agent, as previously demonstrated in Figure 23-6.

Troubleshooting and Postprocedural Assessments

As noted earlier, IVUS is an invaluable tool in the assessment of ELG apposition after graft deployment. Although it is usually difficult to image an ELG along its length because of the air in the pores of the graft material, IVUS can be very useful to assess proximal and distal fixation points. Assessment can be accomplished by advancing and retracting the IVUS catheter over the transition area. Any gap between the device and arterial wall verifies poor apposition and a potential endoleak.

Any time guidewire access through an ELG is compromised or if a re-intervention is being performed in a previously deployed device, luminal position should be verified. IVUS is very useful to confirm access through a device and to ensure that the guidewire is not trapped between the device and aorta. Figure 23-15 demonstrates the limitation of fluoroscopy for the purpose. Fluoroscopic examination shows the guidewire to be in the device's lumen. However, the IVUS images clearly show that the guidewire and catheter are positioned between the device and the aorta. In this case, guidewire access was temporarily lost while a thoracic ELG was being withdrawn.

Bedside Vena Caval Filter Placement

Pulmonary thromboembolism continues to a major complication in the treatment of critically ill patients.[37,38] Vena caval filters have been shown to reduce the incidence of pulmonary embolization in patients prone to development of deep venous thrombosis. In this regard, there has been a growing interest in the "bedside" placement of vena caval filters with IVUS guidance. In these cases, IVUS has been used to ensure correct guidewire position and to evaluate the inferior vena cava (IVC). The renal veins can usually be identified from their proximity to the renal artery. The artery appears as a dark structure crossing directly underneath the vena cava. The renal veins are usually located within a few centimeters of the artery (Fig. 23-16). After the anatomy is defined with IVUS, the same guidewire is used to deliver

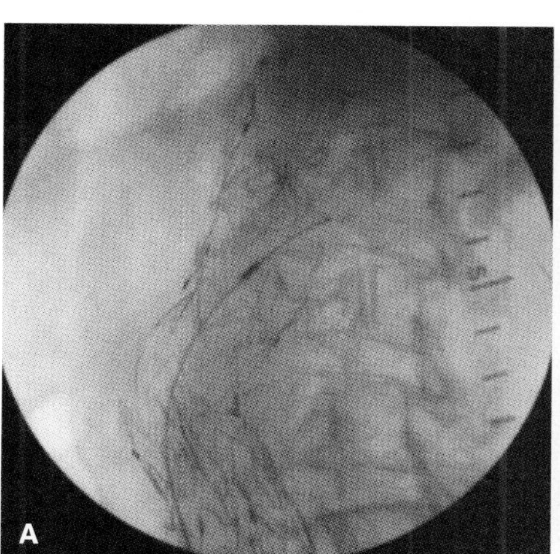

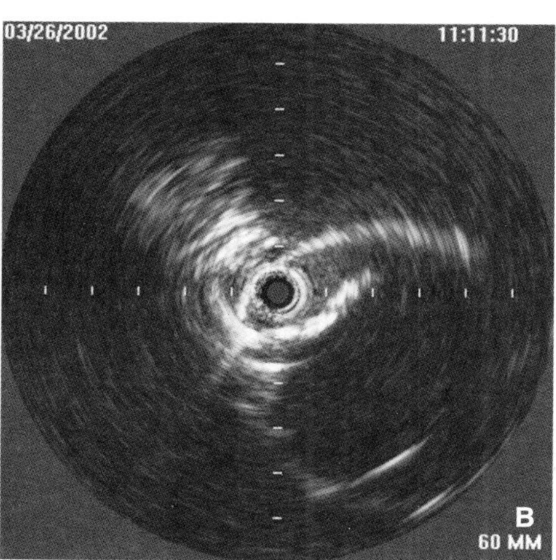

FIGURE 23-15 **A,** Fluoroscopic image demonstrating the position of the guidewire and IVUS catheter within the endoluminal device. **B,** IVUS image demonstrating that the guidewire and IVUS catheter are between the device and aortic wall. Image produced with Visions PV8.2F catheter. (Courtesy of Volcano Therapeutics, Rancho Cordova, CA.)

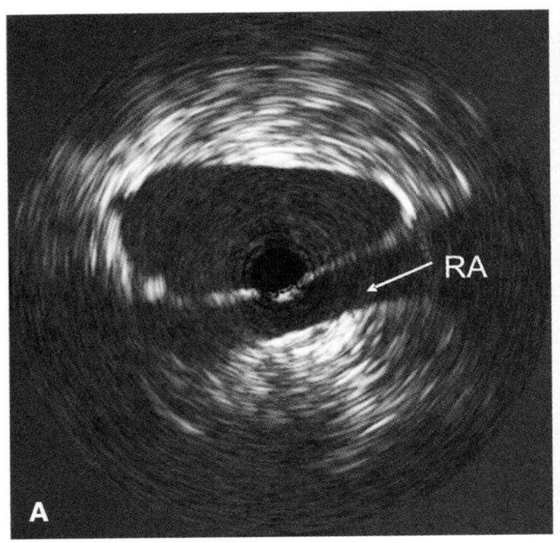

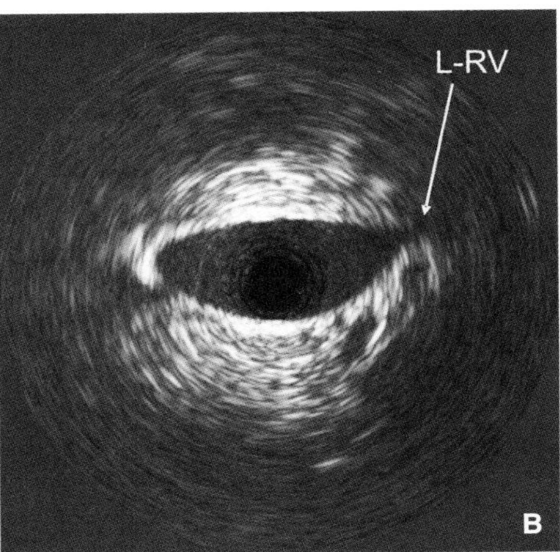

FIGURE 23-16 **A,** IVUS image of the vena cava, demonstrating the posterior renal artery (RA). **B,** The renal veins are usually within close proximity to the renal artery. L-RV, left renal vein. Image produced with Visions PV8.2F catheter. (Courtesy of Volcano Therapeutics, Rancho Cordova, CA.)

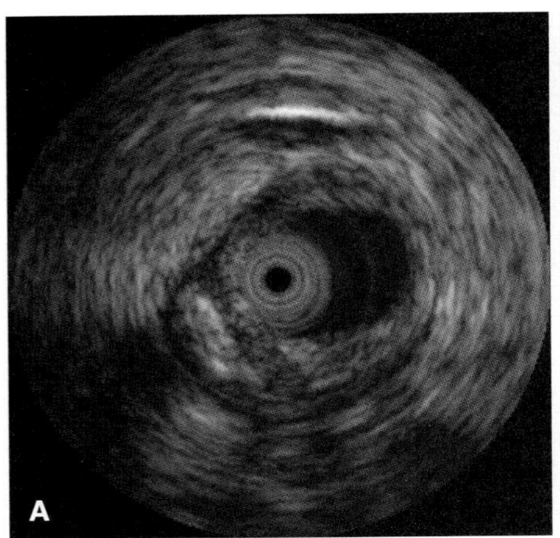

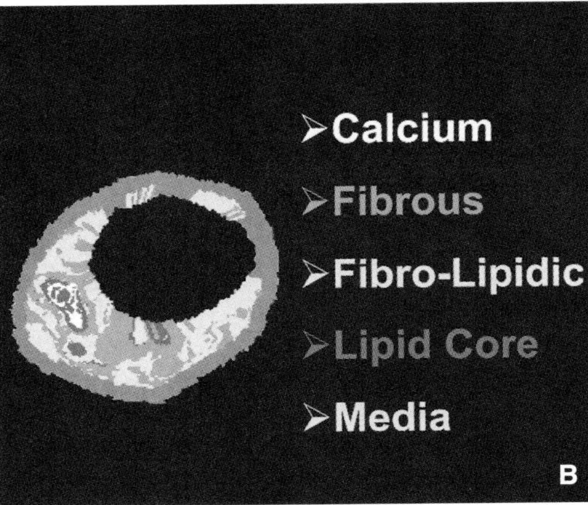

FIGURE 23-17 The frequency shift of the IVUS image can be interpreted as different tissue types, and a color assigned to each type. This approach may enable clinicians to identify troublesome plaque burdens. (Courtesy of Volcano Therapeutics, Rancho Cordova, CA.) (See Color Figure in this section.)

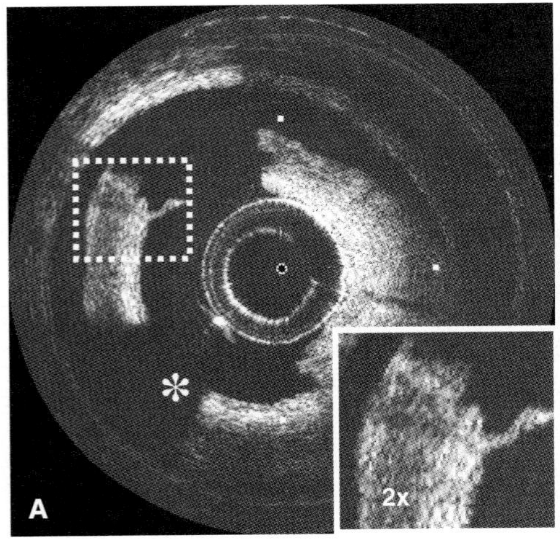

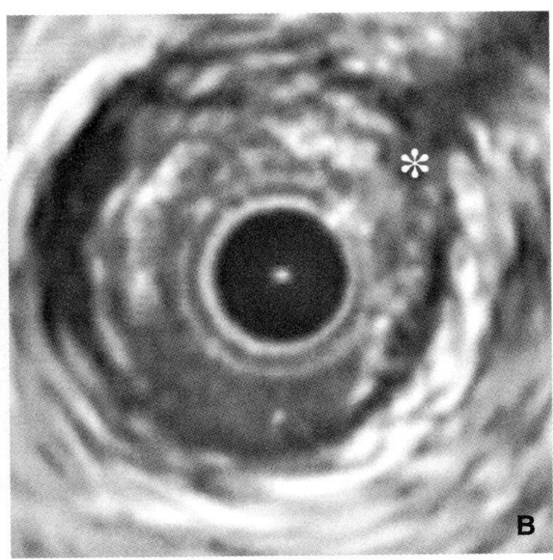

FIGURE 23-18 Optical coherence tomography (OCT) measures the intensity returning from a tissue. The OCT image of a coronary artery (**A**) demonstrates 10-μm resolution, compared with resolution of 100 to 150 μm for the IVUS image (**B**). (Courtesy of G. J. Tearney, MD, PhD, I. K. Jang, MD, PhD, and B. E. Bouma, PhD.)

the IVC filter at the appropriate distance from the access sheath. A flat plate abdominal radiograph is used to confirm satisfactory position of the IVC. This technique allows filter deployments to be performed in the intensive care unit or in morbidly obese patients with minimal radiographic equipment, thus avoiding the complications associated with transporting and imaging of such patients.

FUTURE ADVANCES

Two advances in ultrasound technology are currently being evaluated for their clinical utility. The first is a plaque identification algorithm that can assign different types of vascular diseases different colors on the IVUS image. This modality uses the standard IVUS radiofrequency signal and analyzes amplitude as well as frequency changes. Different plaque compositions reflect at different frequencies. These frequency shifts can be analyzed and used to identify different tissue types.[39] Accurate in vivo identification of plaque components may allow the detection of vulnerable atheroma before rupture (Fig. 23-17).

The second advancement finding its way through the clinical arena is optical coherence tomography (OCT).[40,41] This technology measures the intensity of light returning from within a sample. Samples that have a higher heterogeneity of optical index of refraction exhibit stronger optical scattering and therefore a stronger OCT signal. The resulting images have an improved resolution, at 10 μm. IVUS has a resolution of 100 to 150 μm. Initial clinical studies have reported that OCT demonstrated dissections, prolapse, and incomplete stent apposition more often than IVUS (Fig. 23-18). These evaluations were performed in patients undergoing coronary stenting. One current limitation of this modality for larger vessels is the need to temporarily displace blood with a hand injection of saline.

REFERENCES

1. Bom N, Lancee CT, Van Egmond FC: An ultrasonic intracardiac scanner. Ultrasonics 10:72, 1972.
2. Wells PNT: Basic physics. In deVlieger M, Holmes JH, Kazner E, et al (eds): Handbook of Clinical Ultrasound. New York: John Wiley & Sons, 1978, p 15.
3. Currie GR, White DN: Color-coded ultrasonic differential velocity arterial scanner (Echoflow). Ultrasound Med Biol 14:27, 1978.
4. Nelson TR, Pretorius DH: The Doppler signal: Where does it come from and what does it mean? AJR Am J Roentgenol 151:439, 1998.
5. Irshad K, Reid DB, Miller PH, et al: Early clinical experience with color three-dimensional ultrasound in peripheral interventions. J Endovasc Ther 8:329, 2001.
6. Lockwood GR, Ryan LK, Foster FS: High frequency intravascular ultrasound imaging. In Cavaye DM, White RA (eds): Arterial Imaging: Modern and Developing Technologies. London, Chapman & Hall, 1993, p 125.
7. Yock PG, Linker DT, Angelsen BAJ: Two-dimensional intravascular ultrasound: Technical development and initial clinical experience. J Am Soc Echocardiogr 2:296, 1989.
8. Geselschap JH, Heilbron MJ, Hussain FM, et al: The effect of angulation on intravascular ultrasound imaging observed in vascular phantoms. J Endovasc Surg 5:126, 1998.
9. Cavaye DM: Intravascular ultrasound imaging. In Cavaye DM, White RA (eds): Intravascular Ultrasound Imaging. New York, Raven Press, 1993, p 45.
10. Gussenhoven EJ, Essed CE, Lancee CT: Arterial wall characteristics determined by intravascular ultrasound imaging: An in-vitro study. J Am Coll Cardiol 14:947, 1989.
11. Gussenhoven WJ, Essed CE, Frietman P, et al: Intravascular echographic assessment of vessel wall characteristics: A correlation with histology. Int J Card Imaging 4:105, 1989.
12. West AI: Endovascular ultrasound. In Moore WS, Ahn SS (eds): Endovascular Surgery. Philadelphia, WB Saunders, 1989, p 518.
13. Nissen SE, Gurley JC, Grines CL, et al: Intravascular ultrasound assessment of lumen size and wall morphology in normal subjects and patients with coronary artery disease. Circulation 84:1087, 1991.
14. Tabbara MR, White RA, Cavaye DM, Kopchok GE: In-vivo comparison of intravascular ultrasound and angiography. J Vasc Surg 14:496, 1991.
15. Zarins C, Zatura MA, Glagov S: Correlation of postmortem angiography with pathologic anatomy: Quantitation of atherosclerotic lesions. In Bond MG, Insull W, Glagov S, et al (eds): Clinical Diagnosis of Atherosclerosis. New York, Springer-Verlag, 1983, p 283.
16. Sumner DS, Russell JB, Miles RD: Pulsed Doppler arteriography and computer assisted imaging of carotid bifurcation. In Bergan JJ, Yao JST (eds): Cerebrovascular Insufficiency. New York, Grune & Stratton, 1983, p 115.
17. Gaster AL, Skjoldberg US, Larsen J, et al: Continued improvement of clinical outcome and cost effectiveness following intravascular ultrasound guided PCI: Insights from a prospective, randomized study. Heart 89:1043, 2003.
18. Arko F, Mettauer M, McCollough R, et al: Use of intravascular ultrasound improves long-term clinical outcome in the management of atherosclerotic aortoiliac occlusive disease. J Vasc Surg 27:614, 1998.
19. Lee SD, Arko FR, Buckley CJ: Impact of intravascular ultrasonography in the endovascular management of aortoiliac occlusive disease. J Vasc Nurs 16:57, 1998.
20. van Essen JA, van der Lugt A, Gussenhoven EJ, et al: Intravascular ultrasonography allows accurate assessment of abdominal aortic aneurysm: An in vitro validation study. J Vasc Surg 27:347, 1998.
21. van Essen JA, Gussenhoven EJ, Blankensteijn JD, et al: Three dimensional intravascular ultrasound assessment of abdominal aortic aneurysm necks. J Endovasc Ther 7:380, 2000.
22. White RA, Donayre C, Kopchok GE: Utility of intravascular ultrasound in peripheral interventions. Tex Heart Inst J 24:28, 1997.
23. Ruckert RI, Romaniuk P, Umscheid T, et al: A method for adjusting a malpositioned bifurcated aortic endograft. J Endovasc Surg 5:261, 1998.
24. Kopchok G, White RA, Donayre C: Troubleshooting maldeployed aortic endografts. J Endovasc Surg 5:266, 1998.
25. Nishanian G, Kopchok GE, Donayre CE, White RA: The impact of intravascular ultrasound (IVUS) on endovascular interventions. Semin Vasc Surg 12:4:285, 1999.
26. Slovut DP, Ofstein LC, Bacharach JM: Endoluminal AAA repair using intravascular ultrasound for graft planning and deployment. J Endovasc Ther 10:463, 2003.
27. Thompson MM, Smith J, Naylor AR, et al: Microembolization during endovascular and conventional aneurysm repair. J Vasc Surg 25:179, 1997.
28. Dake MD, Kato N, Mitchell RS, et al: Endovascular stent-graft placement for treatment of acute aortic dissection. N Engl J Med 340:1546, 1999.
29. Nienaber CA, Fattori R, Lund G, et al: Nonsurgical reconstruction of thoracic aortic dissection by stent graft placement. N Engl J Med 340:1539, 1999.
30. Greenberg RK, Haulon S, Khwaja J, et al: Contemporary management of acute aortic dissection. J Endovasc Ther 10:476, 2003.

31. Hansen CJ, Bui H, Donayre CE, et al: Complications of endovascular repair of high-risk and emergent ascending thoracic aortic aneurysms and dissections. J Vasc Surg 40:228, 2004.
32. Quint LE, Platt JF, Sonnad SS, et al: Aortic intimal tears: Detection with spiral computer tomography. J Endovasc Ther 10:505, 2003.
33. Waller BF: The eccentric coronary atherosclerotic plaque: Morphologic observations and clinical relevance. Clin Cardiol 12:14, 1989.
34. White RA, Donayre C, Walot I, et al: Regression of a descending thoracoabdominal aortic dissection following staged deployment of thoracic and abdominal aortic endografts. J Endovasc Ther 9(Suppl): II92-II97, 2002.
35. Chabbert V, Otal P, Bouchard L, et al: Midterm outcomes of thoracic aortic stent-grafts: Complications and imaging techniques. J Endovasc Ther 10:494, 2003.
36. Woody JD, Walot I, Donayre CE, et al: Endovascular exclusion of leaking thoracic aortic aneurysms. J Endovasc Ther 9:79, 2002.
37. Oppat WF, Chiou AC, Matsumura J: Intravascular ultrasound-guided vena cava filter placement. J Endovasc Surg 6:285, 1999.
38. Matsuura JH, White RA, Kopchok GE, et al: Vena cava filter placement by intravascular ultrasound. Cardiovascular Surg 9:571, 2001.
39. Nair A, Kuban BD, Tuzcu EM, et al: Coronary plaque classification with intravascular ultrasound radiofrequency data analysis. Circulation 106:2200, 2002.
40. Bouma BE, Tearney GJ: Power-efficient nonreciprocal interferometer and linear-scanning fiber-optic catheter for optical coherence tomography. Optics Lett 24:531, 1999.
41. Bouma BE, Tearney, Yabushita H, et al: Evaluation of intracoronary stenting by intravascular optical coherence tomography. Heart 89:317, 2003.

Section

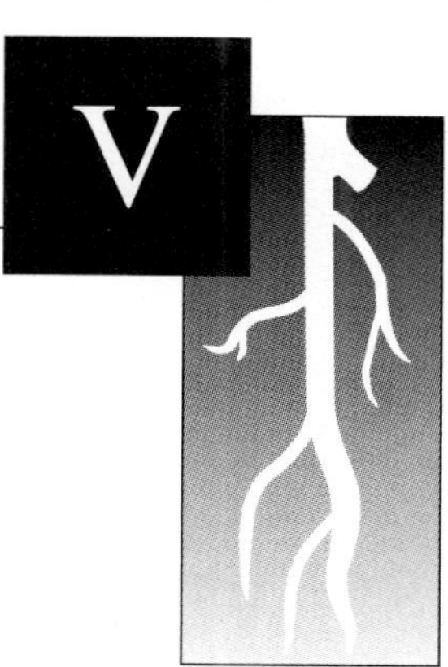

ARTERIAL DISEASES: BASIC CONSIDERATIONS

R. JAMES VALENTINE, MD

Chapter 24

Atherosclerosis: Plaque Characteristics and Concepts of Evolution

RALPH G. DEPALMA, MD, FACS

Vascular and cardiac surgeons treat patients with complicated atherosclerotic plaques that cause limb loss, stroke, and myocardial infarction. This chapter describes evolution, pathology and theories of pathogenesis, characteristics, and localization of atherosclerotic plaques. Medical treatment for atherosclerosis is discussed elsewhere; however, in considering surgical interventions, surgeons recognize that an understanding of plaque morphology and natural history is critical for making treatment choices. For example, a stenotic lesion composed of smooth muscle and collagen that is located in the superficial femoral artery at the adductor hiatus is a "safer" lesion than the typical carotid or coronary plaque with an unstable core of atheromatous debris beneath a tenuous cap. Variations in the patterns, stages, and rates of lesion progression[1,2] have important therapeutic implications as well.

This overview cannot consider atherosclerosis as comprehensively as might be wished; several thousand citations appear each year in the literature. Describing a common pathway of evolution to a stereotypic lesion is a convenient oversimplification. Several pathways likely lead to atherosclerotic lesions. This chapter describes concepts of plaque evolution from early to later stages. Considering atherosclerosis as a single entity is also convenient for describing its evolution; however, owing to its complex and variable pathology and related variable clinical presentations, some authorities have described atherosclerosis as a polypathogenic process encompassing a group of closely related vascular disorders.[3,4] Growing familiarity with the pathology of this disease, along with advances beyond arteriography in imaging plaques in the arterial wall, promise a better understanding of plaque evolution and opportunities for more precise treatment options.

■ PATHOLOGY

Atheroma is derived from the Greek *athere*, meaning porridge or gruel. *Sclerosis* means induration or hardening. Arterial plaques typically have a gruel-like color and a soft consistency, with variable amounts of induration or hardening that differ among patients, individual plaques, and stages of disease. In 1755, von Haller[5] first applied the term atheroma to a common type of plaque that, on sectioning, exuded yellow pultaceous content from its core. Figure 24-1 illustrates a typical fibrous plaque containing a central atheromatous core beneath a fibrous or fibromuscular cap, macrophage accumulation, and round cell adventitial infiltration. This lesion characterizes disease in its active phase and may be more common in younger rather than older individuals, whose lesions are more likely to be fibrotic and calcified. Although a classic definition of atherosclerotic plaque described a "variable combination of changes in the intima of arteries consisting of focal accumulation of lipids, complex carbohydrates, blood and blood products, fibrous tissue and calcium deposits," [6] this outdated description fails to encompass the spectrum of atherosclerotic lesions. The process involves the entire arterial wall. Advanced plaques invade the media, and atheromas at certain stages tend to produce bulging or even enlarged arteries. Round cell infiltration, medial changes, and neovascularization characterize advanced atherosclerotic lesions. The descriptions that follow consider

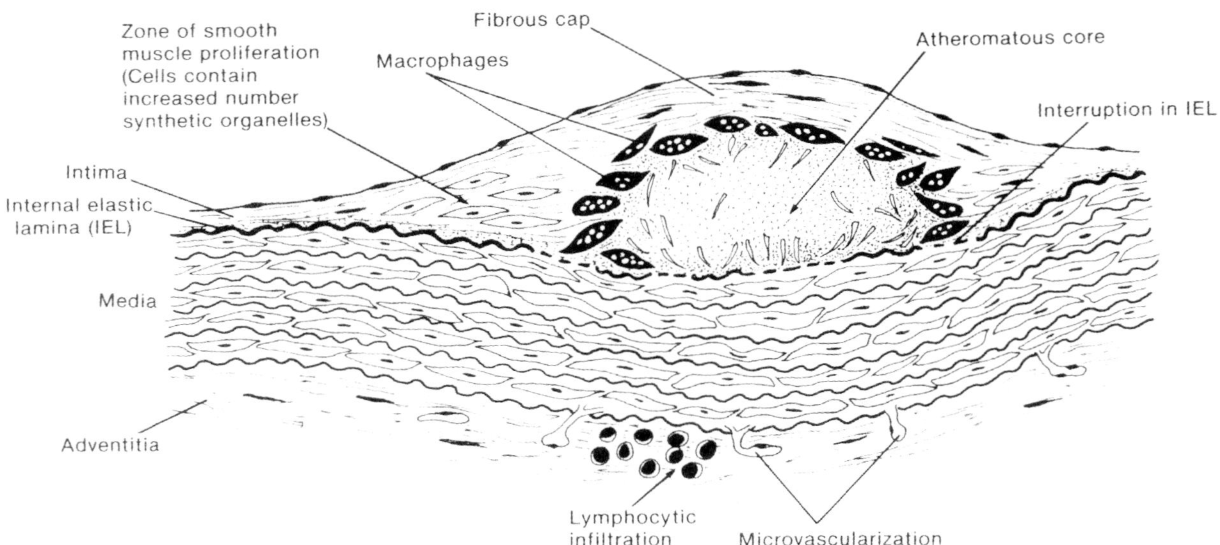

FIGURE 24-1 Schema of prototypical atheroma type IV lesion. Note the central lipid core, the fibrous cap, the macrophage accumulations, and the zone of synthetically active muscle at the shoulders of the lesion. Lymphocytic infiltration in adventitia is usually more marked than shown. (Modified from DePalma RG: Pathology of atheromas. In Bell PRF, Jameson CW, Ruckley CV [eds]: Surgical Management of Vascular Disease. London, WB Saunders, 1992, p 21.)

progressively severe types of plaque, accepted under the rubric of atheromas. All lesions, as mentioned, might not evolve in the same way.

The development and role of the lipid atherosclerotic core and its relationship to the cap have been recognized in the cause of plaque complications. An important insight is the finding that a "core" develops early in atherosclerosis, accumulating in the deep aspect of early lesions before actual fibrous plaque formation begins.[7] Another important insight is recognition of the role of inflammation along with immune reactions in atherogenesis in both early[8] and later stages.[9] An inflammatory cascade in these settings includes the interaction of proinflammatory cytokines such as interleukin-6 (IL-6), and anti-inflammatory cytokines such as IL-10, within arterial tissue. Lipid accumulation appears to attract inflammatory cells that produce cytokines locally; these cytokines can be also detected systemically in atherosclerotic subjects. For example, in persons with stable claudication, plasma concentrations of inflammatory cytokines tumor necrosis factor-α (TNF-α) and IL-6 are elevated, whereas those of the anti-inflammatory IL-10 are reduced.[10] Elevations of cytokines such as TNF-α have also been shown to affect the arterial wall.[11-13] The atherosclerotic plaque contains leukocytes, of which approximately 80% are monocytes or monocyte-derived macrophages. Lymphocytes, predominantly memory T cells,[14] compose 5% to 20% of this cell population. Inflammation, size, and composition of the lipid core are now thought to determine plaque vulnerability, promoting sudden expansion, rupture, release of distal emboli, and vascular occlusion.

Fatty Streaks

Fatty streaks are gross, minimally raised, yellow lesions found commonly in the aortas and coronary arteries of infants and children worldwide. In Western cultures, these lesions tend to progress to more advanced lesions. The early lesions contain lipids deposited intracellularly in macrophages and in smooth muscle cells. A report by a World Health Organization study group[6] defined initial fatty streaks and intermediate lesions of atherosclerosis as follows: Type I lesions in children are the earliest microscopic lesions, consisting of an increase in intimal macrophages with the appearance of foam cells.[15] Type II lesions are grossly visible; in contrast to type I lesions, type II lesions stain with Sudan III or IV stain. Fatty streaks are characterized by foam cells, lipid droplets in intimal smooth muscle cells, and heterogeneous droplets of extracellular lipids. Type III lesions are considered intermediate lesions; they are usually the bridge between the fatty streak and the prototypical atheromatous fibrous plaque, the type IV plaque[16] illustrated in Figure 24-1. Type III lesions occur in plaque expression–prone localities in the arterial tree,[17,18] that is, sites exposed to forces such as low shear stress that cause increased influx of low-density lipoprotein (LDL).[19]

The fatty steak type II lipids are chemically similar to those of the plasma.[13] Plasma lipids might enter the arterial wall in several ways.[20] LDL accumulation may occur for a number of reasons: alterations in the permeability of the intima, increases in the interstitial space in the intima, poor metabolism of LDL by vascular cells, impeded transport of LDL from the intima to the media, increased plasma LDL concentrations, and specific binding of LDL to connective tissue components, particularly proteoglycans in the arterial intima. Experimental studies show that LDL cholesterol accumulates in the intima even before lesions develop and in the presence of intact endothelium. These observations are quite similar to those of early lesion formation described by Aschoff[21] early in the 20th century and Virchow[22] in the 19th century.

In early atherogenesis, as shown in animal experiments, monocytes bind to the endothelial lining, with subsequent diapedesis into the subintimal layer to become tissue macrophages.[23-25] Experimentally, fatty streaks are populated mainly by monocyte-derived macrophages. These lipid-engorged scavenger cells become the foam cells that characterize fatty streaks and other lesions. According to the lipid hypothesis theory (see later), LDL plays a central role in atherogenesis. An important observation is that LDL must be altered by oxidation or acetylation to be taken up by the macrophages to form foam cells.[26] Oxidized LDL (OxLDL) is a powerful chemoattractant for monocytes. Another aspect of this theory suggests that the endothelium somehow modifies LDL to promote foam cell formation.

The interactions of plasma LDL levels with the arterial wall are the subject of intense interest. LDLs traverse the endothelium mostly through receptor-independent transport but also through cell breaks.[27] Endothelial cells,[28] smooth muscle cells,[29] and macrophages[30] are all capable of oxidizing LDL. The OxLDL, in turn, further attracts monocytes into the intima and promotes their transformation into macrophages. Macrophages produce platelet-derived growth factor (PDGF), transforming growth factor-β (TGF-β), and cytokines such as IL-1 and other interleukins. OxLDL also induces gene products ordinarily unexpressed in normal vascular tissue. A notable example is tissue factor (TF), the cellular initiator of the coagulation cascade expressed by atheroma monocytes and foam cells.[31] Expression of TF requires the presence of bacterial lipopolysaccharides, suggesting that hypercoagulability in atherosclerosis could be enhanced by endotoxemia.

The large numbers of macrophages and T lymphocytes in the lesion suggest a cellular immune response; oxidized lipoproteins, heat shock proteins, and microorganisms are likely antigens. Study of endarterectomy specimens with immunohistochemistry and reverse transcription–polymerase chain reaction showed proinflammatory T cell cytokines, IL-2, and interferon-7 in a large proportion of plaques.[9] A helper T-cell 1 (Th1-type) cellular immune response takes place in the atherosclerotic plaque.

Endothelium

Animal studies show that endothelial cells tend to become oriented away from the direction of flow, exhibiting proliferation, increased stigmata or stomata, and decreased microfilament bundles. During atherogenesis in humans and animals, endothelial cells become polyhedral or rounded. In humans, greater formation of multinucleated cells and cilia has been observed. Animal studies reveal increased proliferation and cell death with retraction and exposure of subendothelial foam cells. The endothelium becomes more permeable to macromolecules in experimental models; in humans, it exhibits increased mural thrombus formation and TF expression. Leukocyte adherence rises with expression of monocyte adhesion molecules (vascular cell adhesion molecule [VCAM-1]) and others. Endothelium-derived relaxing factor and prostacyclin release diminish, and vasoconstriction is enhanced.

Media

Experimentally, smooth muscle is seen to proliferate, and the cells demonstrate increased rough endoplasmic reticulum phenotype change, with consequent higher production of altered intracellular and extracellular protein matrices. In humans, these changes include increased expression of type I and type III collagen, dermatan sulfate, proteoglycans, and stromelysins. Smooth muscle cells also produce cytokines, including macrophage colony-stimulating factor (M-CSF), TNF, and monocyte chemoattractant protein-1 (MCP-1). Myocytes accumulate native and modified lipoproteins through both native receptor pathways and nonspecific phagocytosis; these cells also express increased lipoprotein lipase activity and, in experimental models, display a scavenger receptor similar to that of foam cells.

Macrophages

Macrophages proliferate and express MCP-1, M-CSF, TNF, IL-1 and other interleukins; PDGF; CD immune antigens; and TF,[26] as mentioned previously. Macrophages acquire larger amounts of free and esterified cholesterol, acetyl coenzyme A (CoA), cholesterol acyltransferase, and acid cholesterol ester hydrolase. Neutral cholesterol ester hydrolase is decreased. The altered cells also express the scavenger receptor 15-lipoxygenase and exhibit increased lipoprotein oxidation products in humans and in animal models. The extensive changes just summarized indicate the complexity of the morphologic, functional, biochemical, and genetic expressions of the arterial wall in early atherosclerosis. The reader is referred to the original report for comprehensive details,[16] with references for the described cellular alterations.[27]

Gelatinous Plaques

Another type of atheroma precursor is the intimal gelatinous lesion. This was first described in 1856 by Virchow[22] and later underscored by Haust[32] as an important progenitor of advanced atherosclerosis. A methodical study of these lesions has been neglected, but Smith[33] has described their identification and composition. The important point here is that virtually all plasma proteins, particularly hemostatic components, are capable of entering the arterial intima and initiating the formation of gelatinous plaques. Gelatinous lesions are translucent and neutral in color, with central grayish or opaque areas. Certain lesions are characterized by finely dispersed, perifibrous lipid along with collagen strands around the lesions. On gross examination, gelatinous lesions feel soft. With gentle lateral pressure, the plaque "wobbles." Gelatinous plaques can be observed during arterial surgery, especially in heavy smokers. The gelatinous material separates easily from the underlying arterial wall without entering the usual endarterectomy plane. Gelatinous plaques are commonly seen in the aorta and occur as extensive areas of flat, translucent thickenings, particularly in the lower abdominal segment. These lesions are characterized by low lipid content and high fluid content. Protein content is variable, but in some plaques, numerous smooth muscle cells are present and gelatinous plaques contain substantial amounts of cross-linked fibrin.

Fibrous Plaque: The Prototypical Atheroma

Figure 24-1 typifies the fibrous or type IV plaque. Fibrous plaques contain smooth muscle cells and connective tissue that form a fibrous cap over an inner yellow atheromatous core. The soft core contains cholesterol esters, mainly cholesteryl oleate and palmitate, believed to be derived from disrupted foam cells. A second type of particle contains both free cholesterol and cholesterol linoleate. The core in early lesions is associated with vesicular lipids rich in free cholesterol.[7] These particles are thought to be derived directly from LDL, possibly by modification of LDL by specific lipolytic enzymes capable of hydrolyzing LDL cholesterol esters.[20] Lipoprotein aggregation and fusion are likely the chief pathways of cholesterol ester accumulation. Fibrous plaques have large numbers of active smooth muscle cells, connective tissue cells, and macrophages. The composition and integrity of the cap have been emphasized because this structure stabilizes the atheroma, preventing intraluminal rupture of its soft core.[34]

Fibrous plaques appear later than, and often in locations similar to those of, the earlier fatty streaks. Many, but not all, fibrous plaques may derive from fatty streaks; other precursors, such as the gelatinous plaques and injured arterial areas, can also lead to fibrous plaque formation. Mural thrombi can also evolve to become atheromas, as demonstrated experimentally by long-term intra-arterial catheter implantation.[35]

In fixed cut sections, fibrous plaques protrude into the arterial lumen; however, when arteries are fixed at arterial pressure, plaques can often produce an abluminal or external bulge. For example, coronary plaques in vivo have been described as occupying at least 40% of the arterial wall before angiographic detection is possible[36]; atheroma growth is compensated for by arterial enlargement within certain limits.[37] Remodeling of coronary arteries in subhuman primates and humans in response to atherogenesis has been observed.[38] Lesion expansion, ulceration, rupture, or overlying thrombosis can ultimately compromise the arterial lumen. When luminal compromise occurs, distal ischemia develops. A unique adaptive response consisting of dilatation and atheromatous involvement of the entire arterial wall likely predisposes to aneurysm formation. Lytic inflammatory cells and immunologically active T lymphocytes participate in this process.

During evolution from fatty steak in early stages to fibrous plaque, cholesterol esters first appear in the form of ordered arrays of intracellular lipid crystals. In intermediate type II and fibrous plaques, the lipids assume isotropic forms and appear extracellularly.[39] Irritating cholesterol esters and oxysterols cause severe inflammatory reactions in connective tissue[40]; these likely provoke similar responses within the arterial wall. Thus, periarterial inflammation, fibrosis, and lymphocytic infiltration are common reactions during lipid accumulation. Advancing neovascularization from the adventitia characterizes intermediate fibrofatty and fibrous plaque lesions. Atherosclerotic lesions contain immunoglobulin G (IgG) in large quantities as well as other immunoglobulins and complement components. The contained IgG recognizes epitopes characteristic of OxLDL, indicating immunologic processes typical of advanced atherosclerotic plaques.[41] This local process is associated with systemic effects: patients with carotid atherosclerosis, and probably those with other areas of atherosclerosis, have higher antibody ratios of anti-OxLDL and IgG than comparable controls without atherosclerosis.[42] Some experiments suggest that atherogenesis is related to chronic inflammation driven mainly by activation of the complement and monocyte-macrophage systems.[43] In this view, enzymatic degradation may be the central event promoting plaque progression.

Complicated Plaques

Fibrous plaques are complicated by calcification, ulceration, intraplaque hemorrhage, or extensive necrosis. These late developments are associated with the clinical complications of stroke, gangrene, and myocardial infarction. Aneurysm formation, as mentioned previously, likely represents a unique genetic or immune interaction of the atherosclerotic process with host tissue, particularly in association with inflammation and elastolysis. Alternatively, aneurysms have been viewed as nonspecific arterial responses, and certainly, other pathologic processes such as medial degeneration cause aneurysm formation. Patients with abdominal aortic aneurysms have a high prevalence of atherosclerotic risk factors and concurrent atherosclerotic involvement of other arteries,[44] suggesting a unique response to atherosclerosis in this arterial segment in certain individuals.

Like early lesions,[15] the advanced lesions of atherosclerosis have been described and classified according to pathologic characteristics.[16] The type IV lesion, the atheroma emphasized in this chapter, is capable of producing symptoms. Extracellular lipid is the precursor of the core that characterizes type IV lesions. A thick layer of overlying fibrous connective tissue characterizes type V lesions, whereas type VI lesions are plaques with fissures, hematoma, or thrombus. Type V lesions have been further described as largely calcified (type Vc) or consisting mainly of connective tissue with little or no lipid or calcium (type Vb). Note that this definition of advanced atherosclerosis includes a subset of aneurysms, a notion important to the consideration of the pathogenesis of these lesions.

■ THEORIES OF ATHEROGENESIS

Lipid Hypothesis

Virchow[22] originally postulated that cellular changes characterizing atherosclerosis were reactive responses to lipid infiltration. Later, Aschoff[21] remarked, "From plasma of low cholesterin content no deposition of lipids will occur even though mechanical conditions are favorable." As can be seen from fatty streak and fibrous plaque evolution, lipids, particularly LDL cholesterol, play a pivotal role in lesion morphology, composition, and evolution. By producing atherosclerosis in cholesterol-fed rats, early experiments by Anitschkow[45] appeared to validate a simple "lipid filtration hypothesis." However, the reader now recognizes that the situation is pathogenically much more complex. Nevertheless, atherosclerosis develops in various species and individuals in proportion to the ease with which an experimental regimen displaces the normal lipid pattern toward hypercholesterolemia, particularly hyperbetalipoproteinemia. At the same time, arterial susceptibility and inflammatory responses vary among location, species, and individuals, and unique factors influence plaque evolution.

Canine and subhuman primate (rhesus and cynomolgus monkey) models of atherosclerosis consistently show plaque progression in response to dietary manipulation[46-54] with plaque regression in response to serum cholesterol lowering. However, lesion production in susceptible species is not the result of simple dietary cholesterol overload. Any diet that causes hypercholesterolemia induces experimental atherosclerosis. The presence of excess, or even any, cholesterol is not necessary in atherogenic diets. In the developmental subhuman primate feeding experiments my colleagues and I conducted, reduction of cholesterol content to 0.5% combined with sugar and eggs produced rapidly progressive plaques, but addition of high cholesterol content (up to 7% by weight) did not.[47,48] In rabbits, a variety of semipure, purified cholesterol-free diets with various mixtures of amino acids induced hypercholesterolemia and atherosclerosis.[55] Thus, elevations of plasma cholesterol, not excess dietary cholesterol, represent the significant atherogenic influence.

Epidemiologic observations provide important circumstantial evidence linking hyperlipidemia to atherosclerosis.[56] Compelling evidence for the view that elevated LDL cholesterol is a key etiologic factor for atherogenesis is demonstrated by genetic hyperlipidemia, despite objections that highly cellular lipid-laden atheromas in these afflicted patients may be different or atypical lesions.[57] These metabolic disorders are most often due to lack or abnormality of LDL receptors on hepatocytes. LDL receptors are necessary to internalize and metabolize LDL, a fundamental observation that earned Brown and Goldstein[58] a Nobel Prize. Patients with abnormal LDL receptors have markedly elevated serum cholesterol concentrations early in life; individuals with the homozygous condition die prematurely from atherosclerosis, rarely living beyond the age of 26 years. Unfortunately, the heterozygous condition is not uncommon, with apparently healthy individuals exhibiting total cholesterol levels ranging up to 350 mg/dL. Such individuals account for 1 in 500 live births[59] and, if they do not receive treatment, will suffer from premature atherosclerosis, generally in middle age. I have observed that the atheromas of these patients are similar in morphology to those seen in individuals with the acquired hyperlipidemia or premature atherosclerosis associated with heavy smoking.

This natural genetic experiment is powerful evidence that elevated LDL cholesterol is a relentless etiologic factor in plaque inception and rapid progression of atherosclerosis to lethal consequences. Familial hypercholesterolemias are characterized by autosomal dominant disorders produced by at least 12 different molecular defects of LDL receptors.[60] Familial abnormalities of high-density lipoprotein (HDL), a negative risk factor for atherosclerosis, also exist. Not only is the status of LDL and HDL metabolism important in pathogenesis; surface proteins of lipoprotein complexes or apoproteins are also relevant.

Thrombogenic Hypothesis

In the mid-19th century, Rokitansky[61] postulated that fibrinous substances deposited on the arterial intimal surface as a result of abnormal hemostatic elements in the blood undergo metamorphosis into atheromatous masses containing cholesterol crystals and globules. The Rokitansky theory held that typical atheromatous lesions resulted mainly from degeneration of blood proteins (i.e., fibrin essentially deposited in the arterial intima). Duguid[62] repopularized this theory in 1946. In particular experimental models, usually with rabbits, indwelling arterial catheters or arterial injury[63] initiates cholesterol accumulation in lesions without the necessity of added dietary cholesterol. Gelatinous plaques also evolve in these circumstances, so that accumulation of blood proteins dominates early lesion development.[32,33]

Mesenchymal Hypothesis: Hemodynamic Effects

Some consider proliferation of smooth cells in the intima and subsequent production by cells of connective tissue elements to be primary and crucial steps in atherogenesis.[64,65] Proteoglycan, an important arterial wall element, might trap infiltrated LDL, even when LDL is not elevated in the blood. Collagen is the other space-filling component of advanced atherosclerotic lesions. Haust and colleagues[66] proposed that the migration of smooth muscle cells from the media to the intima, with proliferation and production of connective tissue, is a nonspecific reaction of the artery to any injury and imply that atherosclerosis simply reflects a generic arterial response. Chisolm and colleagues[20] called this the "nonspecific" mesenchymal hypothesis. Such scenarios are analogous to wound-healing sequences in response to any injury. In part, this theory attempts to explain why physical factors such as shear stress, vasoactive agents, and different types of injuries induce similar sequences of events in the vessel wall.

Stehbens,[57] highly skeptical of the lipid hypothesis, stated that "atherosclerosis constitutes a degenerative and reparative process consequent upon the hemodynamically induced engineering fatigue of the blood vessel wall." He postulated that "the vibrations consisting of the pulsations associated with cardiac contractions and the vortex shedding generated in the blood vessels at branching, unions, curvatures, and fusiform dilatations (carotid sinus) over a lifetime are responsible for fatigue failure after a certain, but individually variable, number of vibrations." In this view, atherosclerosis is a process of wear and tear that becomes an inexorable process associated with aging, a notion that would seem to offer little hope for meaningful interventions. The theory, however, does offer a rationale: Hypertension and tachycardia induced in experimental animals during atherogenic feeding causes accelerated plaque development, whereas bradycardia induced by sinoatrial node ablation in monkeys reduces coronary and carotid atherosclerosis.[67-69]

Monoclonal Hypothesis: Smooth Muscle Proliferation

The morphologic similarity of smooth muscle proliferation in some atherosclerotic lesions to uterine smooth muscle myomata led Benditt and Benditt[64] to suggest that atherosclerotic lesions are derived from a single or, at most, a few mutated smooth muscle cells. Like tumor cells, these mutated cells proliferate in an unregulated fashion. This theory is based on the finding of only one allele for glucose-6-phosphate dehydrogenase (G6PD) in lesions from heterozygotes. A homology exists between the B chain of human PDGF and the protein product of the v-sis oncogene, which is a tumor-causing gene derived from simian sarcoma virus. Tumor-forming cells in culture express the genes for one or both of the PDGF chains and secrete PDGF into the medium.[20] This hypothesis again regards smooth muscle cell proliferation as critical in atherogenesis. Growth factors either stimulate or inhibit cell proliferation, depending on macrophage-derived cytokine activity and other circumstances. The presence of TGF-β receptors in human atherosclerosis[70] provides evidence for an acquired resistance to apoptosis. Resistance to apoptosis may lead to proliferation of resistant cell subsets associated with lesion progression. Many factors influence smooth muscle proliferation, transformation, and collagen secretion. Because all arterial cells (endothelium, macrophages, and smooth muscle) elaborate chemotactic and growth factors, this hypothesis likely relates more to reactive or response mechanisms than to first causes.

Response-to-Injury Hypothesis

Ross and Glomset[71] initially proposed two pathways promoting atheroma formation. In the first pathway, arterial injury is induced by extrinsic factors such as hypercholesterolemia. In this pathway, monocyte and macrophage migration occur without endothelial denudation. In some instances, focal endothelial loss might occur with carpeting of bare areas by platelets. In this event, platelets would stimulate proliferation of smooth muscle by releasing PDGF. However, most plaques were later observed to develop beneath morphologically intact endothelium, which was originally thought to be relatively inert.

In the second postulated pathway, the endothelium acts in an intermediary role by releasing growth factors in response to injury, stimulating smooth muscle proliferation. Examples are experimental rabbit models in which regrowing endothelium induces abundant myointimal proliferation beneath its advancing edges, stimulating accumulation of collagen[72] and glycosaminoglycans.[73] As mentioned previously, stimulated smooth muscle itself releases growth factors, leading to continued autocrine proliferative responses. In the initial iteration of this theory, the second pathway was believed to be relevant to atheromas stimulated by diabetes, possibly in relation to insulin-derived growth factors, as well as to cigarette smoking or hypertension. Although hypertension causes endothelial injury, striking differences can be observed between the behaviors of smooth muscle cells in atherosclerosis and in hypertension, which causes thickening of the arterial wall by virtue of greater protein synthesis without an increase in cell numbers.[74]

Although most spontaneous lesions develop beneath what appears to be an intact endothelium, the reasons for examining the relationship between atherosclerosis and arterial wall injury are evident, particularly to vascular surgeons and interventionalists. Physical injury leads to platelet adherence, secretion of PDGF,[75] and subsequent smooth muscle proliferation.[76] This process, coupled with response to other mitogenic stimuli,[77,78] results in development of an intrusive lesion. Well-known examples of arterial trauma are clamping and balloon injuries, which produce stenoses and initiate a range of lesions from myointimal hyperplasia to typical atheromas.[79-82] These unfavorable arterial tissue responses are accentuated by deep or severe injuries and by the presence of hyperlipidemia.[79,83,84]

Lesion Arrest or Regression

When examining pathogenesis and, more importantly, treatment, one must consider plaque regression and stabilization. Figure 24-2 presents a highly simplified pictorial sequence of processes ultimately leading to complicated

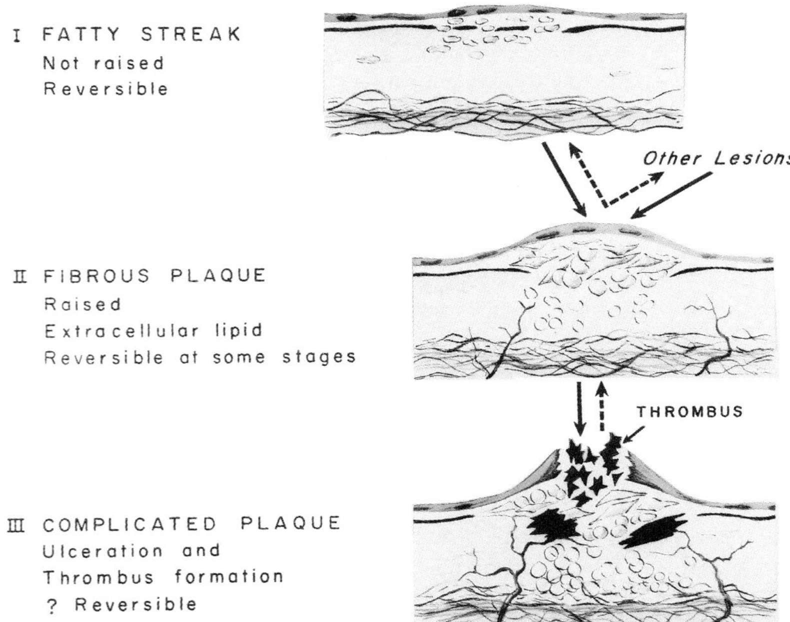

FIGURE 24-2 Simplified schema of plaque evolution from fatty streak to complicated plaque, indicating potentially reversible early stages.

plaques as well as to potential regressive changes at early stages. Plaque regression in response to threshold lowering of serum cholesterol has been demonstrated in autopsy studies of dietarily deprived humans,[21] in animal models,[85] and in early angiographic trials[86] that combined cessation of smoking with lipid reduction. Changes in carotid plaque composition with loss of lipid core and increased fibrous tissue have been demonstrated with magnetic resonance imaging (MRI).[87] Clinical trials using vascular endpoints have demonstrated impressive regression in coronary atheromas in some patients but only slight reductions of plaque bulk with arrest of progression in most. Such angiographic changes, though minimal, have been associated with significant reductions in rates of coronary events,[88] findings that correlate with predicted expectations of benefit generated from experimental studies of plaque regression.

In experimental animals, plaque bulk is reduced mainly by lipid egress, a process amply demonstrated in hypercholesterolemic dogs[46-48] and subhuman primates.[49-51] The precise mechanisms of plaque development and regression, as previously described, are incompletely understood, particularly the role of inflammatory and immune responses and the myriad factors that influence them. However, my colleagues and I[51] have demonstrated unequivocal regression of plaques using serial observations and measurements of plaque size. These findings correlated with lessened luminal encroachment, as shown by edge defects demonstrated with sequential angiography, as well as lessened plaque lipids and altered fibrous protein content, which were observed histologically and chemically. As an important technical aspect of this research, these regressive changes were validated with autopsy or direct surgical observations and measurements in affected arteries. These changes correlated strongly with observed regressive angiographic changes.[49,52] Stary[89] has further characterized regressive changes in rhesus monkeys. Drastic reduction of blood cholesterol for 42 months resulted in disappearance of macrophages, macrophage-derived foam cells, and lymphocytes as well as reduction of extracellular lipid from advanced lesions. However, calcium deposits in the arterial wall were not visibly changed, indicating a limit to regression in the presence of calcification.

Correlative observations such as these are not readily obtained in humans. In spite of adaptive wall responses, lessening of luminal intrusion on angiographic images experimentally coincides with generally decreased plaque bulk and lessened lipid content. The use of MRI or intravascular ultrasound (IVUS) promises a means of observing plaques to characterize what has become known as the "unstable plaque."[90] In some experiments, fibrous protein increased during regression, but in other instances, this plaque component decreased. Although fibrosis limits reduction of plaque bulk, it also converts a soft and unstable plaque into a more stable one. Active unstable lesions, particularly in the coronary arteries, are not necessarily the most occlusive ones. And although the edge regression in response to treatment, as demonstrated by angiographic imaging, can be minimal, clear-cut reduction in rates of coronary events has been associated with presumed plaque stabilization in these circumstances. Experimentally, serum cholesterol levels exist above which lesions inevitably progress.[46,53] This threshold appears to approximate a total serum cholesterol of 150 mg/dL or an LDL level of 100 mg/dL. Roberts[91] has cited populations with values below these levels in whom atherosclerosis is virtually absent. However, in extrapolating experimental data to human treatment, one should keep in mind that inflammatory changes are promoted by other factors, such as smoking, even when lipid levels are putatively normalized.

■ LOCALIZATION AND TYPES OF PLAQUE INVOLVEMENT

Atherosclerosis is a systemic process, but its clinical manifestations relate to segmental patterns of involvement. Plaques develop in the aorta, the coronary and carotid arteries, and the arteries of the lower extremities. Although the arteries of the upper extremities are often spared, the origins of the arch vessels develop plaques, most commonly at the inception of the left subclavian artery, followed in decreasing prevalence by the left carotid and innominate arteries. Early recognition of this typical pattern of involvement made direct surgical (and now endovascular) approaches so clinically effective.[1,2] Vascular surgeons are familiar with the immediate efficacy of the treatment of segmental disease.

Investigators led by Zarins and Glagov[18,92] have provided important insights into the hemodynamic factors promoting plaque localization. Interactions of risk factors promoting atherosclerosis, including hyperlipidemia, cigarette smoking, and diabetes—alone or in combination—are associated with unique and predictable disease localization patterns. These interactions influence treatment choices as well as prognosis.[1,2,93-95] Particular types and localizations of plaques tend to occur in specific arterial segments as a result of unique local features. Examples are the unstable type IV plaques of the outer wall of the carotid bulb, fibrous hyperplasic lesions of the superficial femoral artery at the adductor hiatus, diffuse aortic ulceration, occlusion or aneurysms of the infrarenal aortic segment, and lesions at the origins of its visceral arteries.

The definition of *atherosclerosis*—porridge-like and scarring or fibrotic—helps us comprehend the variability of plaque composition and pathology. This variation has given rise to the concept of preemptive interventions for unstable or "vulnerable plaques."[90,96,97] Advances in arterial wall imaging[98-100] now offer expanded prospects for accurate diagnosis that may affect treatment. This is of particular relevance to carotid and coronary plaques, particularly those that are asymptomatic or appear only minimally intrusive on conventional arteriography. Newer imaging techniques have an advantage over arteriography in detecting arterial wall change, particularly compensatory arterial enlargement and remodeling.[37] These changes initially limit the stenosing effect of atherosclerotic plaques through adaptive responses of the arterial wall to increased flow, direct effects of the atherosclerotic process, or remodeling of the arterial wall itself. Early adaptive changes can be appreciated in early primate atherosclerosis as beading or abluminal bulging of the arterial wall.[52] At this stage, conventional arteriography fails to show luminal intrusion.

As noted previously, arterial plaque progression eventually exceeds the potential for adaptive enlargement, and the artery can no longer compensate for the intrusive plaque. This leads to development of stenosis, a process that may bring the patient to clinical attention. Sudden plaque growth and thrombosis of the involved segment may follow acute plaque events such as hemorrhage and rupture, especially in the carotid and coronary arteries. In fact, cap fissuring with thrombosis proves to be the most common process promoting acute myocardial infarction.[34] These events are thought to relate to an extensive lipid core and to inflammatory responses promoting plaque instability. Using angiography and IVUS, Wentzel and coworkers[101] confirmed an inverse relationship between wall thickness and average low shear stress related to signaling that tended to maintain lumen dimension. However, the documented disappearance of this relationship with lumen narrowing suggested development of plaque progression that was not related to stress shear but was due to sudden events associated with plaque progression.

Localization and Hemodynamics

The hemodynamics of plaque localization has been extensively described; the reader is referred to cited reviews[19,92] and Chapter 10 in this volume. Among the variables of shear stress—flow separation and stasis, oscillation of shear stress vectors, turbulence, and increased lateral wall pressure—*low shear stress* emerges as the most important variable promoting preferential plaque localization and, interestingly, also for development of myointimal hyperplasia. Flow separation and stasis in the carotid bulb with longer residence time of blood stream factors promote plaques in this site, which is characteristically located opposite the flow divider. Carotid artery intima-media thickness (IMT) is sometimes used as a surrogate measure to suggest early atherosclerosis. In a comparison of young athletes with matched controls, carotid IMT increases were found in athletes; this increase was postulated to be due to the effect of exercise hypertension with intermittent elevation in carotid wall stress.[102] Interestingly, this effect was not found in the femoral artery IMT. The investigators in this study suggest caution in interpreting carotid IMT as a surrogate for early atherosclerosis. Observations using in vivo MRI quantification[103,104] confirm adverse hemodynamic conditions within the abdominal aorta, including flow recirculation and low wall shear stress. Exercise, by increasing aortic flow, improves these adverse hemodynamic conditions; older subjects show greater increases in mean wall stress and greater decreases in wall shear stress oscillations than younger subjects.

Localization and Risk Factors

The previous discussion suggests sedentary lifestyle as a potential risk factor for aortic localization of plaques. The interaction of risk factors, including hypertension, hyperlipidemia, sex, smoking, and diabetes (alone or in combination), contributes to unique and characteristic plaque localizations. Figure 24-3 shows three patterns of localization influenced by the risk factors diabetes, smoking, and hyperlipidemia.[93] The past three decades of experience have repeatedly confirmed that the type L pattern predominates in diabetics. Overall, the superficial femoral artery is the artery most commonly affected in the lower extremity. Smoking

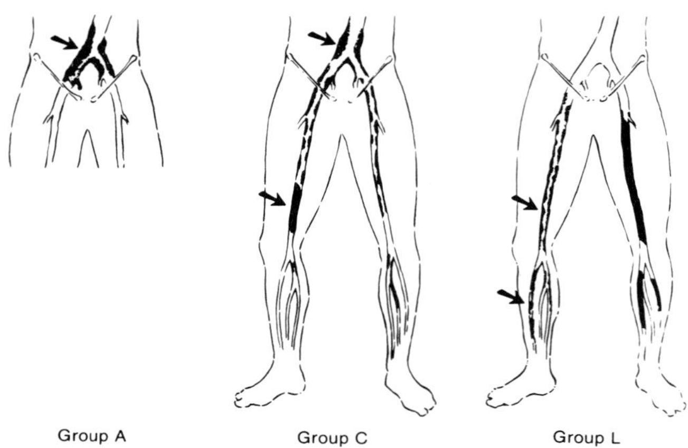

FIGURE 24-3 Anatomic patterns of infrarenal aortic and lower extremity atherosclerosis. Group A is principally aortic atherosclerosis, group C is a combined pattern, and Group L is atherosclerosis principally of the lower extremity. (From Rosen AB, DePalma RG, Victor Y: Risk factors in peripheral atherosclerosis. AMA Arch Surg 107:303, 1973.)

and hyperlipidemia predispose to combined patterns, particularly aortic and superficial femoral disease. Nonsmoking diabetics characteristically have involvement of the calf vessels below the knee, often with sparing of the foot arteries. Similar arterial patterns appear in hypertensive African Americans[95]; some of these individuals are found to have occult type 2 diabetes, with the burdens presented by that condition.[105] Interestingly, therapy with insulin enhancers has been shown to improve brachial artery reactivity in these diabetics.[106] Sidawy and colleagues[107-109] investigated factors predisposing infragenicular plaque localization by using cell culture of infragenicular arteries. Infragenicular smooth muscle cells from diabetics were unique in demonstrating an inability to relax in response to pharmacologic and physiologic stimuli. These cells proliferate in response to high levels of both insulin and glucose as well as to the inflammatory cytokine IL-1β.

Figure 24-4 depicts the zones of the profunda femoris artery; here, diabetes is significantly associated with localization in zones 3 through 7,[2,110] as shown in Table 24-1. This peculiar involvement has not been well emphasized or understood and needs further study. Physiologically, the impaired vasoreactivity of diabetic arteries might also affect this vessel. Perhaps plaque distribution in this end artery relates, somehow, to impaired runoff in the extensive muscular beds of the thigh served by the profunda femoris. Flow in the superficial femoral artery, a long conduit, encounters runoff resistance in the infragenicular arteries. Although lesions are often diffuse in the superficial femoral artery, some of the occlusions relate to retrograde thrombosis from a localized plaque at the adductor hiatus.

Other patterns and associations are clinically noteworthy. For example, cross-sectional and longitudinal studies have shown a close association between carotid and coronary atherosclerosis.[111,112] Interestingly, recurrent cardiovascular events were associated with radiolucent plaques, presumably those with active cores.[112] Virtually all patients with peripheral arterial disease (PAD) have coronary atherosclerosis and are on average a decade or two older than those presenting with coronary disease. In contrast,

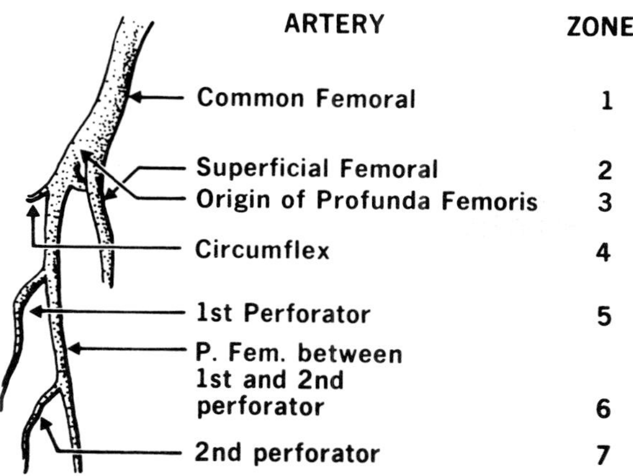

FIGURE 24-4 Anatomic zones of the profunda femoris (P. Fem.) artery. (From King TA, DePalma RG, Rhodes RS: Diabetes mellitus and atherosclerotic involvement of the profunda femoris artery. Surg Gynecol Obstet 159:553, 1984.)

PAD is uncommon in younger patients with coronary disease. Hyperlipidemia is more likely to be associated with symptomatic coronary disease. However, coronary disease is less common and less intense in older patients who present with PAD and low HDL levels.[113] Because the major causes of vascular death in patients with PAD are myocardial infarction and stroke, plaque localization in peripheral vessels indicates a need for active treatment. In the future, therapy will address the inflammatory responses, both systemic and local, that exist in atherosclerotic patients.

■ NEW HORIZONS IN THE STUDY OF ATHEROSCLEROTIC PLAQUES

The dynamic interaction between the lipid core and inflammation provides more avenues of study. This view resulted from examination of the roles of atherosclerotic tissue components as well as the discovery of novel systemic responses in atherosclerotic individuals.[114] Descriptive pathology has addressed the inflammatory nature of plaques, including macrophage accumulation and T-cell infiltration, central lipid core characteristics, and the host of biochemical reactions within plaques and arterial tissues. Plaques are rich in chemokines, which in turn attract inflammatory cells.[115] Matrix-degrading enzymes such as the metalloprotease (MMP) family are expressed by activated macrophages, whereas tissue inhibitors of the metalloprotease family (TIMPs) also are present.[116,117] TNF-α receptors at the local level may be responsible for an inflammatory response as well. Activated macrophages cause LDL oxidation and are likely to further the inflammatory response elicited by irritating cholesterol esters of the atherosclerotic core. Macrophages have been found to produce neutrophil elastase, an enzyme capable of digesting elastin and fibrillar and nonfibrillar collagen as well as modulating cytokine and MMP activity.[118] This serine protease likely plays a role in adaptive remodeling, vascular enlargement, and aneurysm formation. Leukotrienes are established inflammatory mediators; 5-lipoxygenase–derived leukotrienes have been suggested as mediators of atherosclerotic inflammation.[119]

Plaque components such as MMP-9[120,121] and inflammatory cytokines are detected within the systemic circulation[10] as markers of disease severity, as is C-reactive protein (CRP).[122] Conversely, systemic inflammatory components such as infection, high levels of TNF-α,[11,12] and inflammatory cytokines such as IL-6 entering the circulation are thought to *cause* plaque development. The relevance of these associations needs study to determine whether elevated serum or plasma cytokines incite arterial tissue damage, whether they reflect a heavy burden of circulating activated macrophages and T cells, or whether the cytokines enter the circulation as a result of widespread atheromatous changes in the arterial tissue. In a surprisingly oblique set of observations, periodontal disease, which is linked epidemiologically to atherosclerosis,[123] potentially relates to atherosclerosis by raising circulating cytokine levels, thereby promoting a proatherogenic endothelial cell phenotype with loss of antithrombotic, growth inhibitory, and vasodilator properties. Subjects with periodontal disease, along with diabetics, show impaired brachial artery dilatation.[124] Oral infection in an experimental model with the periodontal pathogen *Porphyromonas gingivalis* has been shown to increase IL-6 levels and accelerate atherosclerosis.[125] A randomized trial of periodontal treatment in individuals with both periodontal disease and atherosclerosis (Periodontitis and Vascular Events–PAVE) is in a pilot stage.[126]

Table 24-1 Comparison of Normal, Minimally Involved, and Severely Involved Profunda Femoris Artery in Nondiabetic and Diabetic Patients

	NONDIABETIC PATIENTS		DIABETIC PATIENTS		
ZONE	Normal or Minimally Involved	Severely Involved*	Normal or Minimally Involved	Severely Involved*	*P* VALUE
1	27	11	32	10	.7191
2	23	17	10	32	.0716
3	38	0	37	5	.0002†
4	36	2	37	5	.0119†
5	38	0	39	3	.0238†
6	38	0	37	54	.0043†
7	38	0	38	—	.0015†

*Stenosis greater than 50% or occlusion.
†Difference significant between diabetics and nondiabetics on basis of chi-square test.

Adapted from DePalma RG: Patterns of peripheral atherosclerosis: Implications for treatment. In Shepard J: Atherosclerosis: Developments, Complications, Treatment. New York, Elsevier, 1987, p 161.

The organism *Chlamydia pneumoniae* or its DNA has been detected in atherosclerotic plaques, with varying frequency. The reliability of detection of the organism depends on careful sampling technique requiring a minimum of 15 sections to ensure a 95% chance of detecting all true-positive cases.[127] Chlamydial heat shock protein colocalizes in plaques with *C. pneumoniae*–specific antigen,[128] leading to the hypothesis that macrophages infected with *C. pneumoniae*, upon entering the intima, mediate inflammatory and autoimmune responses by producing chlamydial heat shock protein-60.[129,130] In addition to *C. pneumoniae*, cytomegalovirus, *Helicobacter pylori*, and herpes virus have been proposed to play a role in the pathogenesis of atherosclerotic plaques. The deleterious effects of infection presumably relate to inflammation and bacterial heat shock proteins that produce arterial inflammatory and autoimmune reactions. Antibiotic trials testing these hypotheses are in progress; some trials suggest benefit,[131] but results of others are equivocal[132] or negative.[133]

Treatment Implications of Plaque Studies

The concept of the unstable plaque is important for medical and surgical decision-making about treatment,[90,96] but application of imaging techniques to detect unstable plaques remains far from routinely available. At present, the decision to select conservative versus operative intervention relies on clinical judgment using concepts based on theory. Plaques that produce symptoms are considered to be unstable, requiring prompt surgical intervention. Inflammation predisposes to progression and complications independently of blood lipid levels. These new concepts provide insights into the benefits of aspirin as an inflammatory inhibitor and into the deleterious effects of tropical oils, which stimulate inflammatory responses. Recently recognized genetic variants of toll-like receptors confer differences in the inflammatory responses elicited by bacterial lipopolysaccharides[134]; individuals capable of mounting brisk pro-inflammatory responses are more susceptible to atherosclerosis. The inflammatory cascades include interactions of pro-inflammatory and anti-inflammatory cytokines within the arterial wall. Specific means of influencing these responses have yet to be discovered. However, inhibition of MMP activity using tetracycline-like derivatives to retard aneurysmal dilatation, reported within the last decade,[135-140] is a novel effort based on experimental data that awaits final judgment. Tissue studies have shown successful inhibition of glucose and insulin-mediated growth of infragenicular arterial smooth muscle cells.[141] Although this finding has important implications for diabetics, the hypothesis has yet to be tested clinically.

The ability to lessen the burden of the lipid core with treatment at particular stages of atherogenesis is a salient finding. A randomized, placebo-controlled trial of simvastatin showed reduction of adverse cardiovascular outcomes when the agent was used for both primary and secondary prevention. The beneficial effect extended to patients without abnormal elevations of lipid concentrations, presumably owing to lessened inflammation.[142] The anti-inflammatory effect of statins has been documented by decreased levels of CRP, independent of LDL reduction.[143] Thus, lipid reduction and reduced inflammation support the utility of statin treatment of established atherosclerotic plaques within the crucible of the clinical trial. Similar rationale at the tissue level exists for clinical treatment using angiotensin-converting enzyme (ACE) inhibition; angiotensin II, a pro-inflammatory mediator, acts at several steps in plaque development.[144] Angiotensin II induces the inflammatory cytokine IL-6, which co-localizes with angiotensin receptors at strategic sites within coronary plaques.[145] In many ways, the novel findings of cell biology in plaque pathology point the way to and reinforce biologically plausible treatment selections for testing in clinical trials. Other means of reducing pro-oxidant stress, for example from ferrous iron,[146] CRP itself,[147] and cytokines promoting formation of peroxidases, need investigation at the tissue level. The delineation of these reactions, occurring in nanoseconds, will be more challenging and may be as important as the dynamics of plaque lipid core.

Acknowledgments The author wishes to acknowledge Carol Walton and Virginia W. Hayes at the Sierra Nevada Health Care Network, Reno, Nevada, for assistance in preparation of this chapter.

■ REFERENCES

1. DeBakey ME, Lawrie GM, Glaeser DH: Patterns of atherosclerosis and their surgical significance Ann Surg 201:115, 1985.
2. DePalma RG: Patterns of peripheral atherosclerosis: Implications for treatment. In Shepard J (ed): Atherosclerosis: Developments, Complications, Treatment. New York, Elsevier, 1987, p 161.
3. McMillan GC: Development of atherosclerosis. Am J Cardiol 31:542, 1973.
4. DeBakey ME: Atherosclerosis: Patterns and rates of progression. In Gotto AM Jr, South LL, Allen B (eds): Atherosclerosis Five: Proceedings of the Fifth International Symposium. New York, Springer-Verlag, 1980, p 3.
5. Haimovici H, DePalma RC: Atherosclerosis: Biologic and surgical considerations. In Haimovici H, Ascer E, Hollier LH, et al (eds): Vascular Surgery Principles and Techniques, 4th ed. Cambridge, Mass, Blackwell Science, 1996, p 127.
6. Report of Study Group: Classifications of Atherosclerotic Lesions. WHO Technical Report Series 143. Geneva, World Health Organization, 1958.
7. Guyton JR, Kemp KF: Development of the lipid-rich core in human atherosclerosis. Arterioscler Thromb Vasc Biol 164:11, 1996.
8. Ross R: Atherosclerosis is an inflammatory disease. Am Heart J 138:S419, 1999.
9. Frostegard J, Ulfgren A-K, Nyberg P, et al: Cytokine expression in advanced human atherosclerotic plaques: Dominance of proinflammatory (Th1) and macrophage-stimulating cytokines. Atherosclerosis 145:33, 1999.
10. DePalma RG, Hayes VW, Cafferata HT, et al: Cytokine signatures in atherosclerotic claudicants. J Surg Res 111:215, 2003.
11. Desfaits AC, Serri O, Renier G: Normalization of lipid peroxides, monocyte adhesion, and tumor necrosis factor-alpha production in NIDDM patients after gliclazide treatment. Diabetes Care 21:487, 1998.
12. Winkler G, Lakatos P, Nagy Z, et al: Elevated serum TNF-alpha level as a link between endothelial dysfunction and insulin resistance in normotensive obese patients. Diab Med 16:207, 1999.
13. Fazio S, Linton MF: The inflamed plaque: Cytokine production and cholesterol balance in the vessel wall. Am J Cardiol 88:122E, 2001.
14. Gerszten RE, Mach F, Sauty A, et al: Chemokines, leukocytes, and atherosclerosis. J Lab Clin Med 136:87, 2000.

15. Stary HC, Chandler AB, Glagov S, et al: A definition of initial fatty streak and intermediate lesions of atherosclerosis: A report from the Committee on Vascular Lesions of the Council on Atherosclerosis, American Heart Association. Arterioscler Thromb 14:840, 1994.
16. Stary HC, Chandler AB, Glagov S, et al: A definition of advanced types of atherosclerotic lesions and a histological classification of atherosclerosis: A report from the Committee on Vascular Lesions of the Council on Atherosclerosis, American Heart Association. Arterioscler Thromb Vasc Biol 15:1512, 1995.
17. Cornhill JF, Hederick EE, Stary HC: Topography of human aortic sudanophilic lesions. Monogr Atheroscler 15:13, 1990.
18. Glagov S, Zarins C, Giddens DP, et al: Hemodynamics and atherosclerosis: Insights and perspectives gained from studies of human arteries. Arch Pathol Lab Med 112:1018, 1988.
19. Insull W Jr, Bartch GE: Cholesterol, triglycerides and phospholipid content of intima, media and atherosclerotic fatty streak in human thoracic aorta. J Clin Invest 45:513, 1966.
20. Chisolm GM, DiCarleto PE, Erhart LA, et al: Pathogenesis of atherosclerosis. In Young JR, Graor RA, Olin JW, Bartholomew JR (eds): Peripheral Vascular Disease. St. Louis, Mosby-Year Book 1991, p 137.
21. Aschoff L: Atherosclerosis. In: Lectures on Pathology. New York, Hoeber, 1924, p 131.
22. Virchow R: Gesammelte Abhandlungen zur Wissenschaftlichen Medicin. Frankfurt, John Meidinger, 1856, p 496.
23. Fagiotto A, Ross R, Harker L: Studies of hypercholesterolemia in nonhuman primate. I: Changes that lead to fatty streak formation. Arterioscler Thromb Vasc Biol 4:323, 1984.
24. Fagiotto A, Ross R: Studies of hypercholesterolemia in the nonhuman primate. II: Fatty streak conversion to fibrous plaque. Arterioscler Thomb Vasc Biol 4:341, 1984.
25. Gerrity RG: The role of monocytes in atherogenesis. I: Transition of blood borne monocytes into foam cells in fatty lesions. Am J Pathol 103:181, 1981.
26. Steinberg D, Parthasarathy S, Carew TE, et al: Beyond cholesterol: Modifications of low-density lipoprotein that increase its atherogenicity. N Engl J Med 320:915, 1989.
27. Wildund O, Carew TF, Steinberg D: Role of the low-density lipoprotein receptor in the penetration of low-density lipoprotein into the rabbit aortic wall. Arterioscler Thromb Vasc Biol 5:135, 1985.
28. Steinbrecher UP: Role of superoxide in endothelial-cell modification of low-density lipoprotein. Biochim Biophys Acta 959:20, 1988.
29. Heinecke JW, Baker I, Rosen I, Chait A: Superoxide mediates modification of low-density lipoprotein by arterial smooth muscle cells. J Clin Invest 77:757, 1986.
30. Parthasarathy S, Printz DJ, Boyd D, et al: Macrophage oxidation of low-density lipoproteins generates a form recognized by the scavenger receptor. Arterioscler Thromb Vasc Biol 6:505, 1986.
31. Brand K, Banka CL, Mackman N, et al: Oxidized LDL enhances lipopolysaccharide induced tissue factor expression in human adherent monocyte. Arterioscler Thromb Vasc Biol 14:790, 1994.
32. Haust MD: The morphogenesis and fate of potential and early atherosclerotic lesions in man. Hum Pathol 2:1, 1971.
33. Smith EB: Fibrin in the arterial wall. Atherosclerosis 70:186, 1988.
34. Davies MJ, Thomas A: Thrombosis and acute coronary artery lesions in sudden cardiac ischemic death. N Eng J Med 310:1137, 1984.
35. Moore S: Thromboatherosclerosis in normolipemic rabbits: A result of continued endothelial damage. Lab Invest 29:478, 1973.
36. Stiel GN, Stiel LSG, Schofer J, et al: Impact of compensatory enlargement of atherosclerotic arteries on angiographic assessment. Circulation 80:1603, 1989.
37. Glagov S, Weisenberg E, Zarins C, et al: Compensatory enlargement of human atherosclerotic coronary arteries. N Engl J Med 316:1371, 1987.
38. Clarkson TB, Prichard RW, Morgan TM, et al: Remodeling of coronary arteries in human and nonhuman primates. JAMA 271:289, 1994.
39. Hata Y, Hower J, Insull W Jr: Cholesterol ester-rich inclusions from human aortic fatty streak and fibrous plaque lesions of atherosclerosis. Am J Pathol 75:423, 1974.
40. Baranowski A, Adams CWM, Bayliss-High OB, et al: Connective tissue responses to oxysterols. Atherosclerosis 41:255, 1982.
41. Yla-Herttuala S, Palinksi W, Butler S, et al: Rabbit and human atherosclerotic lesions IgG that recognizes epitopes of oxidized LDL. Arterioscler Thromb Vasc Biol 13:32, 1993.
42. Maggi E, Chiesa R, Milissano G, et al: LDL oxidation in patients with severe carotid atherosclerosis: A study of in vitro and in vivo oxidation markers. Arterioscler Thromb Vasc Biol 14:1892, 1994.
43. Schmiedt W, Kinscherf R, Deigner HP, et al: Complement CG deficiency protects against diet-induced atherosclerosis in rabbits. Arterioscler Thromb Vasc Biol 18:1790, 1998.
44. DePalma RG, Sidawy AN, Giordano JM: Associated etiological and atherosclerotic risk factors in abdominal aneurysms. In Greenhalgh RM, Mannick JA (eds): The Cause and Management of Aneurysm. London, WB Saunders, 1990, p 37.
45. Anitschkow R: Experimental atherosclerosis in animals. In Cowdry V (ed): Arteriosclerosis: Review of Problems. New York, Macmillan, 1933.
46. DePalma RG, Hubay CA, Insull W Jr, et al: Progression and regression of experimental atherosclerosis. Surg Gynecol Obstet 131:633, 1970.
47. DePalma RG, Insull W Jr, Bellon EM, et al: Animal models for study of progression and regression of atherosclerosis. Surgery 72:268, 1972.
48. DePalma RG, Bellon EM, Insull W Jr, et al: Studies on progression and regression of experimental atherosclerosis: Techniques and application to the rhesus monkey. Med Primatol 3:313, 1972.
49. DePalma RG, Bellon EM, Klein L, et al: Approaches to evaluating regression of experimental atherosclerosis. In Manning GM, Haust MD (eds): Atherosclerosis: Metabolic, Morphologic and Clinical Aspects. New York, Plenum Press, 1977, p 459.
50. DePalma RG, Bellon EM, Koletsky S, et al: Atherosclerotic plaque regression in rhesus monkeys induced by bile acid sequestrant. Exp Mol Pathol 31:423, 1979.
51. DePalma RG, Klein L, Bellon EM, et al: Regression of atherosclerotic plaques in rhesus monkeys. Arch Surg 115:1268, 1980.
52. DePalma RG: Angiography in experimental atherosclerosis: Advantages and limitations. In Bond JG, Insull W Jr, Glagov S, et al (eds): Clinical Diagnosis of Atherosclerotic Lesions: Quantitative Methods of Evaluation. New York, Springer-Verlag, 1983, p 99.
53. DePalma RG, Koletsky S, Bellon EM, et al: Failure of regression of atherosclerosis in dogs with moderate cholesterolemia. Atherosclerosis 27:297, 1977.
54. DePalma RG, Bellon EM, Manalo PM, Bomberger RA: Failure of antiplatelet treatment in dietary atherosclerosis: A serial intervention study. In Gallo LL, Vahouny GV (eds): Cardiovascular Disease: Molecular and Cellular Mechanisms, Prevention, Treatment. New York, Plenum Press, 1987, p 407.
55. Kritchevsky D: Atherosclerosis and nutrition. Nutrition 2:290, 1986.
56. La Rosa JC: Cholesterol lowering, low cholesterol and mortality. Am J Cardiol 72:776, 1993.
57. Stehbens WE: The Lipid Hypothesis of Atherosclerosis. Austin, TX, RG Landes, 1993.
58. Brown MS, Goldstein JL: Lipoprotein receptors in the liver: Control signals for plasma cholesterol traffic. J Clin Invest 72:743, 1983.
59. Schonfeld G: Inherited disorders of lipid transport. Endocrinol Metab Clin North Am 19:211, 1990.
60. Hoeg JM: Familial hypercholesterolemia: What the zebra can teach us about the horse. JAMA 271:543, 1994.
61. Rokitansky C von: A Manual of Pathological Anatomy, translated by GE Dan. London, Sydenham Society, 1852.
62. Duguid JB: Thrombosis as a factor in the pathogenesis of coronary atherosclerosis. J Pathol 58:207, 1946.
63. Bjorkerud JS, Bondjers G: Arterial repair and atherosclerosis after mechanical injury. II: Tissue response after induction of a total necrosis (deep longitudinal injury). Atherosclerosis 14:250, 1971.
64. Benditt EP, Benditt JM: Evidence for a monoclonal origin of human atherosclerotic plaques. Proc Natl Acad Sci U S A 70:1753, 1973.
65. Schwartz SM: Cellular proliferation in atherosclerosis and hypertension. Proc Soc Exp Biol Med 173:1, 1983.

66. Hauss WH, Junge-Hulsing G, Hollanden HJ: Changes in metabolism of connective tissue associated with aging and arterio- or atherosclerosis. J Atherosclerosis Res 6:50, 1992.
67. Koletsky S, Roland C, Rivera-Velez JM: Rapid acceleration of atherosclerosis in hypertensive rats on a high fat diet. Exp Mol Pathol 9:322, 1968.
68. Beere PA, Glagov S, Zarins CK: Retarding effects of a lowered heart rate on coronary atherosclerosis. Science 226:180, 1989.
69. Beere PA, Glagov S, Zarins CK: Experimental atherosclerosis at the carotid bifurcation of the cynomolgus monkey: Localization compensatory enlargement and sparing effect of lowered heart rate. Arterioscler Thromb Vasc Biol 12:1245, 1992.
70. McCaffrey TA, Du B, Fu C, et al: The expressions of TGF-beta receptors in human atherosclerosis: Evidence for acquired resistance to apoptosis due to receptor imbalance J Mol Cell Cardiol 31:1627, 1999.
71. Ross R, Glomset JA: The pathogenesis of atherosclerosis. N Eng J Med 295:369, 1976.
72. Chidi CC, DePalma RG: Collagen formation by transformed smooth muscle after arterial injury. Surg Gynecol Obstet 152:8, 1981.
73. Wight TV, Curwen KD, Litrenta MM, et al: Effects of endothelium on glycosaminoglycan accumulation in the injured rabbit aorta. Am J Pathol 113:156, 1983.
74. Schwartz SM, Ross R: Cellular proliferation in atherosclerosis and hypertension. Prog Cardiovasc Dis 26:355, 1984.
75. Ross R, Glomset F, Kariya B, et al: A platelet dependent factor that stimulates the proliferation of arterial smooth muscle cells in vitro. Proc Natl Acad Sci U S A 71:1207, 1974.
76. Ross R: The pathogenesis of atherosclerosis: A perspective for the 1990's. Nature 362:801, 1993.
77. Anderson TJ, Gerhard MD, Meridith IT, et al: Systemic nature of endothelial dysfunction in atherosclerosis. Am J Cardiol 75:7113, 1995.
78. Lindner V, Lappi DA, Baird A, et al: Role of basic fibroblast growth factor in vascular lesion formation. Circ Res l68:106, 1991.
79. DePalma RG, Chidi CC, Sternfeld WC, Koletsky S: Pathogenesis and prevention of trauma provoked atheromas. Surgery 82:429, 1977.
80. Campbell-Bodwell M, Robertson AL Jr: Effects of angiotensin II and vasopressin on human smooth muscle cells in vitro. Exp Med Pathol 35:265, 1981.
81. Itoh H, Mukuyawa M, Pratt RE, et al: Multiple autocrine growth factors modulate vascular smooth muscle in response to angiotensin II. J Clin Invest 91:2268, 1993.
82. Viswanathan M, Stromberg C, Seltzer A, et al: Balloon angioplasty enhances expression of angiotensin II: ATI receptors in neointima of rat aorta. J Clin Invest 90:1707, 1992.
83. Stevens SL, Hilgarth K, Ryan US, et al: The synergistic effects of hypercholesterolemia and mechanical injury on intimal hyperplasia. Ann Vasc Surg 6:55, 1992.
84. Baumann DS, Doblas M, Dougherty A, et al: The role of cholesterol accumulation in prosthetic vascular graft anastomotic intimal hyperplasia. J Vasc Surg 19:435, 1994.
85. St Clair RSW: Atherosclerosis regression in animal models: Current concepts of cellular and biochemical mechanisms. Prog Cardiovasc Dis 26:109, 1983.
86. Blankenhorn DH, Hodis HN: Arterial imaging and atherosclerosis reversal. Arterioscler Thromb Vasc Biol 14:177, 1994.
87. Zhao XQ, Yuan C, Hattsukami TS, et al: Effects of prolonged intensive lipid lowering therapy on the characteristics of carotid atherosclerotic plaques in vivo by MRI: A case-control study. Arterioscler Thromb Vasc Biol 21:1623, 2001.
88. La Rosa JC: Lipid lowering. In LaRosa JC (ed): Medical Management of Atherosclerosis. New York, Marcel Dekker, 1998, p 1.
89. Stary HC: The development of calcium deposits and their persistence after lipid regression. Am J Cardiol 88:16E, 2001.
90. Fuster V: Plaque stabilization: Present and future trends. In Fuster V (ed): The Vulnerable Atherosclerotic Plaque: Understanding, Identification and Modification. Armonk, NY, Futura, 1999, p 393.
91. Roberts WC: Atherosclerotic risk factors: Are there ten or is there only one? Am J Cardiol 64:552, 1989.
92. Giddens DP, Zarins CK, Glagov S: Response of arteries to near wall fluid dynamic behavior. Appl Mech Rev 43:S96, 1990.
93. Rosen AB, DePalma, Victor Y: Risk factors in peripheral atherosclerosis. Arch Surg 107:303, 1973.
94. Menzoian JO, LaMorte WW, Paniszyn CC, et al: Symptomatology and anatomic patterns of peripheral vascular disease: Differing impact of smoking and diabetes. Ann Vasc Surg 3:224, 1989.
95. Sidawy AN, Schweitzer EJ, Neville RF, et al: Race as a risk factor in the severity of infragenicular occlusive disease: Study of an urban hospital patient population. J Vasc Surg 11:537, 1990.
96. Fuster V, Corti R, Fayad ZA, et al: Integration of vascular biology and magnetic resonance imaging in the understanding of atherothrombosis and acute coronary syndromes. J Thromb Haemost 1:1410, 2003.
97. Toussaint JF: MRI characterization of atherosclerotic arteries: Diagnosis of plaque rupture. J Neuroradiol 29:223, 2002.
98. Choi CJ, Kramer CM: MR imaging of atherosclerotic plaque. Radiol Clin North Am 40:887, 2002.
99. MacNeil BD, Lowe HC, Takano M, et al: Intravascular modalities for detection of vulnerable plaque: Current status. Arterioscler Thromb Vasc Biol 23:1333, 2003.
100. Helft G, Worthley SG, Fuster V, et al: Progression and regression of atherosclerotic lesions: Monitoring with serial non-invasive magnetic resonance imaging. Circulation 105:993, 2002.
101. Wentzel JJ, Janssen E, Vos J, et al: Extension of increased atherosclerotic wall thickness into high shear stress regions is associated with loss of compensatory remodeling. Circulation 108:17, 2003.
102. Mayet J, Stanton AV, Chapman N, et al: Is carotid artery intima-media thickening a reliable marker of early atherosclerosis? J Cardiovasc Risk 9:77, 2002.
103. Cheng CP, Herfkens RJ, Taylor CA: Comparison of abdominal aortic hemodynamics between men and women at rest and during lower limb exercise. J Vasc Surg 37:118, 2003.
104. Cheng CP, Herfkens RJ, Taylor CA: Abdominal hemodynamics in healthy subjects aged 50-70 at rest and during lower limb exercise: In vivo quantification using MRI. Atherosclerosis 168:323, 2003.
105. Avena R, Curry KM, Sidawy AN, et al: The effect of occult diabetic status and oral glucose intake on brachial artery vasoactivity in patients with peripheral vascular disease. Cardiovasc Surg 6:584, 1998.
106. Avena R, Mitchell ME, Nylen ES, et al: Insulin action enhancement normalizes brachial artery vasoactivity in patients with peripheral vascular disease and occult diabetes. J Vasc Surg 28:1024, 1998.
107. Jones BA, Aly HM, Forsyth EA, Sidawy AN: Phenotypic characterization of human smooth muscle cells derived from atherosclerotic tibial and peroneal arteries. J Vasc Surg 24:883, 1996.
108. Forsyth EA, Aly HM, Neville RF, Sidawy AN: Proliferation and extracellular matrix production by human infragenicular smooth muscle cells in response to interleukin-1 beta. J Vasc Surg 26:1002, 1997.
109. Carmody BJ, Arora S, Wakefield MC, et al: Progesterone inhibits human infragenicular muscle cell proliferation induced by high glucose and insulin concentrations. J Vasc Surg 36:833, 2002.
110. King TA, DePalma RG, Rhodes RS: Diabetes mellitus and atherosclerotic involvement of the profunda femoris artery. Surg Gynecol Obstet 159:553, 1984.
111. Crouse JR 3rd, Tang R, Espeland MA, et al: Associations of extracranial atherosclerosis progression with coronary status and risk factors in patients with and without coronary artery disease. Circulation 106:2061, 2002.
112. Liapis CD, Kakisis JD, Dimitoulis DA, Kostakis AG: The impact of carotid plaque type on restenosis and future cardiovascular events: A 12-year prospective study. Eur J Vasc Endovasc Surg 24:239, 2002.
113. Seeger FM, Silverman SH, Flynn TC: Lipid risk factors in patients requiring arterial reconstruction. J Vasc Surg 10:418, 1989.
114. Ridker PM, Stampfer MJ, Rifai N: Novel risk factors for systemic atherosclerosis. JAMA 285:2481, 2001.
115. Burke-Gaffney A, Brooks AV, Bogle RG: Regulation of chemokine expression in atherosclerosis. Vasc Pharmacol 38:283, 2002.

116. Lee WH, Kim SH, Lee Y: Tumor necrosis factor receptor superfamily 14 is involved in atherogenesis by inducing proinflammatory cytokines and matrix metalloproteases. Arterioscler Thromb Vasc Biol 21:1873, 2001.
117. Sitzer M, Trostdorf F: The unstable carotid stenosis: Definition and biological processes. Hamostaseologie 23:61, 2003.
118. Dollery CM, Owen CA, Sukhova GK: Neutrophil elastase in human atherosclerotic plaques: Production by macrophages. Circulation 107:2829, 2003.
119. Radmark O: 5-Lipoxygenase-derived leukotrienes: Mediators also of atherosclerotic inflammation. Arterioscler Thromb Vasc Biol 23:1140, 2003.
120. Kalela A, Koivu TA, Sisto T, et al: Serum matrix metalloprotease-9 concentration in angiographically assessed coronary artery disease. Scand J Clin Lab Invest 62:337, 2002.
121. Beyzade S, Zhang S, Wong YK, et al: Influences of matrix metalloprotease-3 gene variation on extent of coronary atherosclerosis and risk of myocardial infarction. J Am Coll Cardiol 18:2130, 2003.
122. Ridker PM, Bassuk SS, Toth PP: C-reactive protein and risk of cardiovascular disease: Evidence and clinical application. Curr Atheroscler Rep 5:341, 2003.
123. Pussinen PJ, Jousilanti P, Alfthan G, et al: Antibodies to periodontal pathogens are associated with coronary heart disease. Arterioscler Thromb Vasc Biol 23:1250, 2003.
124. Amar S, Gokce N, Morgan S, et al: Periodontal disease is associated with brachial artery endothelial dysfunction and systemic inflammation. Arterioscler Thromb Vasc Biol 23:1245, 2003.
125. Lalla E, Lamster IB, Hofman MA, et al: Oral infection with a periodontal pathogen accelerates early atherosclerosis in apolipoprotein E-null mice. Arterioscler Thromb Vasc Biol 23:1405, 2003.
126. Haynes WG, Stanford C: Periodontal disease and atherosclerosis: From dental to arterial plaque. Arterioscler Thromb Vasc Biol 23:1309, 2003.
127. Cochrane M, Pospichal A, Walker P, et al: Distribution of *Chlamydia pneumoniae* DNA in atherosclerotic carotid arteries: Significance for sampling procedures. J Clin Microbiol 41:1454, 2003.
128. Kuroda S, Kobayashi T, Ishii N, et al: Role of *Chlamydia pneumoniae*-infected macrophages in atherosclerosis developments of the carotid artery. Neuropathology 23:1, 2003.
129. Lowe GD: The relationship between infection, inflammation and cardiovascular disease: An overview. Ann Periodontol 6:1, 2001.
130. Lamb DJ, El-Sankary W, Ferns GA: Molecular mimicry in atherosclerosis: A role for heat shock proteins in immunisation. Atherosclerosis 167:177, 2003.
131. Wiesli P, Czerwenka W, Meniconi A: Roxithromycin treatment prevents progression of peripheral arterial occlusive disease in *Chlamydia pneumoniae* seropositive men: A randomized, double blind, placebo-controlled trial. Circulation 105:2646, 2002.
132. Brassard P, Bourgault C, Brophy J: Antibiotics in primary prevention of myocardial infarction among elderly patients with hypertension. Am Heart J 145:E20, 2003.
133. Zahn R, Schneider S, Frilling B, et al: Antibiotic therapy after myocardial infarction: A prospective randomized study. Circulation 107:1253, 2003.
134. Kiechl S, Lorenz E, Reindl M, et al: Toll-like receptor 4 polymorphisms and atherogenesis. N Engl J Med 347:185, 2002.
135. Petrinec D, Liao S, Holmes DR, et al: Doxycycline inhibition of aneurysmal degeneration in an elastase induced rat model of abdominal aortic aneurysm. J Vasc Surg 23:336, 1996.
136. Boyle JR, McDermott E, Crowther M, et al: Doxycycline inhibits elastin degradation and reduces metalloprotease activity in a model of aneurysmal disease. J Vasc Surg 27:354, 1998.
137. Curci JA, Mao D, Bohner DG, et al: Preoperative treatment with doxycycline reduces aortic wall expression and activation of matrix metalloproteases in patients with abdominal aortic aneurysm. J Vasc Surg 31:325, 2000.
138. Mosorin M, Juvonen J, Biancari F, et al: Use of doxycycline to decrease the growth rate of abdominal aortic aneurysms: A randomized, double blind, placebo-controlled study. J Vasc Surg 34:606, 2001.
139. Baxter BT, Pearce WH, Waltke EA, et al: Prolonged administration of doxycycline in patients with small asymptomatic abdominal aortic aneurysms: Report of a prospective (phase II) multicenter study. J Vasc Surg 36:1, 2002.
140. Manning MW, Cassis LA, Daugherty A: Differential effects of doxycycline, a broad-spectrum matrix metalloprotease inhibitor, on angiotensin II-induced atherosclerosis and abdominal aortic aneurysm. Arterioscler Thromb Vasc Biol 23:483, 2003.
141. Avena R, Arora S, Carmody BJ, et al: Thiamine (vitamin B1) protects against glucose and insulin-mediated proliferation of human infragenicular arterial smooth muscle cells. Ann Vasc Surg 14:37, 2000.
142. Heart Protection Study Collaborative Group: MRC/BHF Heart Protection Study of cholesterol lowering with simvastatin in 20,536 high-risk individuals: A randomised placebo-controlled trial. Lancet 360:7, 2002.
143. Ridker PM, Rifai N, Lowenthal SP: Rapid reduction in C-reactive protein with cerivastatin among 785 patients with primary hypercholesterolemia. Circulation 6:1191, 2001.
144. Phillips MI, Kagiyama S: Angiotensin II as a proinflammatory mediator. Curr Opin Invest Drugs 3:569, 2002.
145. Scheiffer B, Scheiffer E, Hilfiker-Kleiner D, et al: Expression of angiotensin II and interleukin 6 in human coronary atherosclerotic plaques: Potential implications for inflammation and plaque instability. Circulation 101:1372, 2000.
146. Zacharski LR, Chow B, Lavori PW, et al: The Iron (Fe) and Atherosclerosis Study (FeAST): A pilot study of body iron stores in peripheral vascular disease. Am Heart J 139:337, 2000.
147. Seiichi K, Inoue N, Ohashi Y, et al: Interaction of oxidative stress and inflammatory response in coronary plaque instability. Arterioscler Thromb Vasc Biol 23:1398, 2003.

Chapter

25

Thromboangiitis Obliterans (Buerger's Disease)

JEFFREY W. OLIN, DO

Section V

Thromboangiitis obliterans (TAO) is a nonatherosclerotic, segmental inflammatory disease that most commonly affects the small and medium-sized arteries and veins in the upper and lower extremities. Although it is classified pathologically as a vasculitis, TAO differs from the more commonly encountered vasculitides in the following three important ways:

1. There is often a highly inflammatory thrombus with relative sparing of the blood vessel wall.
2. Acute phase reactant levels are normal except in the presence of acute infarction.
3. Markers of immunoactivation are absent.

In the early published reports, TAO was most commonly encountered in young men. However, in the later Western literature, the incidence of TAO appears to be rising in women. Virtually all patients are users of tobacco, usually cigarettes.

In 1879, von Winiwater[1] reported pathologic findings in a 57-year-old man with a 12-year history of foot pain that eventually progressed to gangrene and amputation. The pathologic specimen demonstrated intimal proliferation, thrombosis, and fibrosis. von Winiwater[1] was the first to suggest that the endarteritis and endophlebitis present in the amputated specimen were distinct from atherosclerosis. Twenty-nine years, later Leo Buerger[2] (born the year von Winiwater's original report was published) provided a detailed and accurate pathologic description of the endarteritis and endophlebitis in 11 amputated limbs. On the basis of his pathologic examination, Buerger called the disease "thromboangiitis obliterans." He emphasized the differences in the clinical and pathologic features of TAO from those of atherosclerosis.

Shortly after the publication of Buerger's comprehensive monograph,[3] Allen and Brown[4] reported on 200 cases of TAO evaluated at the Mayo Clinic from 1922 to 1926. Most of their patients were Jewish men who were heavy cigarette smokers. These investigators noted that these patients experienced foot claudication as well as trophic changes "such as excessive callosities in the weight bearing areas, or … gangrenous ulcers of the digits or gangrene involving the toes or the entire foot."[4] Although pathologically the description was identical to that in Buerger's original report, Allen and Brown[4] suggested that TAO was a disease of infectious origin, a hypothesis that has never been proved.

■ EPIDEMIOLOGY

Buerger's disease has a worldwide distribution, but it is more prevalent in the Middle East, Near East, and Far East regions than in North America and Western Europe.[5,6] The incidence of Buerger's disease has declined in the United States and Europe, possibly owing to the adoption of stricter diagnostic criteria. At the Mayo Clinic, the prevalence rate of patients with the diagnosis of Buerger's disease has steadily declined from 104 per 100,000 patient registrations in 1947 to 12.6 per 100,000 patient registrations in 1986.[5,6]

There are widely varying prevalence rates of Buerger's disease in patients with peripheral arterial disease in Europe and Asia. For example, the rates of TAO among all patients with peripheral arterial disease have been reported as 0.5% to 5.6% in Western European countries, 3% in Poland, 6.7% in East Germany, 11.5% in Czechoslovakia, 39% in Yugoslavia, 80% in Israel (Ashkenazim), 45% to 63% in India, and 16% to 66% in Korea and Japan.[7,8] These rates were calculated from highly selected series of patients treated at specialized institutions, not from the general population.

In 1973, Hill and colleagues[9] described an analysis of 106 patients with Buerger's disease in Java, Indonesia. All patients were cigarette smokers from the lowest socioeconomic sector of the community; only one was a woman. The researchers concluded that the environmental factors of significance in this disease as it occurred in Java appeared to be tobacco, cold injury, and a previous history of mycotic infection.

In 1976, the Buerger's Disease Research Committee of the Ministry of Health and Welfare of Japan[10] analyzed 3034 patients(2930 men and 104 women) with the disease from all over Japan and estimated its incidence to be about 5 per 100,000 population. In 1986, the Epidemiology of Intractable Disease Research Committee of the Ministry of Health and Welfare of Japan estimated that 8858 patients with the disease were treated at various medical institutions (5 per 100,000 population)[11] and that the prevalence among manual laborers was not significantly greater. The number of new patients with Buerger's disease in Japan seems to be decreasing slightly, but the number of the patients under the care of a physician remains almost unchanged owing to frequent recurrences.[11,12]

Buerger's Disease in Women

The reported incidence of Buerger's disease in women was 1% to 2% in most published series of cases before 1970. In the 1990s, several large series demonstrated a much higher occurrence in women. Women accounted for 26 (23%) of 112 patients with Buerger's disease evaluated between1970 and 1987 at the Cleveland Clinic Foundation.[13] From 1988 to 1996, an additional 40 patients with Buerger's disease were treated, 30% of whom were women.[14] Other series have confirmed the higher female prevalence in TAO; women accounted for 12 (11%) of 109 cases from 1981 to 1985 in Rochester, Minnesota[15]; 5 (19%) of 26 patients in a 1987 study from the University of Oregon[16]; 48 (14%) of 355 cases from 1975 to 1984 in Yugoslavia[17]; and 12 (22.6%) of 53 patients in a Swiss study.[18] The reason for the apparent increase in number of women with Buerger's disease is unknown, but the rise in the number of women smokers is a likely cause. The prevalence of Buerger's disease in Japanese women remains relatively low compared with the higher number of female smokers,[12] and in a study of 89 patients from Hong Kong all were men.[19] The problem with all of these statistics is that prevalence of TAO in a given population varies with the criteria used to make the diagnosis.

■ ETIOLOGY AND PATHOGENESIS

The etiology of Buerger's disease is unknown. Although TAO is a type of vasculitis,[20] important features distinguish Buerger's disease from other forms of vasculitis. Pathologically, the thrombus in TAO is highly cellular, with much less intense cellular activity in the wall of the blood vessel and a preserved internal elastic lamina. In addition, TAO differs from many other types of vasculitis in that the usual immunologic markers—elevation of acute phase reactants such as Westergren sedimentation rate and C-reactive protein, circulating immune complexes, and autoantibodies such as antinuclear antibody, rheumatoid factor, and complement levels—are usually normal or negative.

Smoking

There is an extremely strong association between heavy tobacco use and TAO.[13,14] Kjeldsen and Mozes[21] have demonstrated that patients with TAO have higher tobacco consumption and carboxyhemoglobin levels than patients with atherosclerosis and than control subjects without vascular disease. There have been occasional cases of TAO in users of smokeless tobacco or snuff.[22-24] It is possible that there is an abnormal sensitivity or allergy to some component of tobacco and that this sensitivity in some way leads to an inflammatory small vessel occlusive disease.[25-27] The incidence of TAO is higher in countries where the consumption of tobacco is large. There is a higher incidence of TAO in India among individuals of a low socioeconomic class who smoke bidis (unprocessed, low-grade tobacco).[27,28] In a case-control study in Bangladesh, 35% of patients with TAO and 69.1% of controls were cigarette smokers, while 65% of TAO cases and 30.1% of control subjects were bidi smokers. With the use of logistic regression analysis and the smoking of approximately 10 cigarettes per day as a reference, people who smoked more than 20 bidis per day (odds ratio [OR] = 34.76; 95% confidence interval (CI), 6.11-197.67) or 11 to 20 bidis per day (OR = 7.12; 95% CI, 2.35-21.63) had a greater risk of TAO after adjustment of data for confounding factors.[29]

It is not known whether cigarette smoking causes or only contributes to the development of Buerger's disease. However, tobacco use is a major factor in disease activity. The progression and continued symptoms associated with TAO are closely linked with continued use of tobacco.[8] Although passive smoking (secondary smoke) has not been shown to be associated with the onset of TAO, it may be an important factor in the continuation of symptoms during the acute phase of Buerger's disease. Matsushita and associates[30] have shown a very close relationship between active smoking and an active course of Buerger's disease, using the urine level of cotinine (a metabolite of nicotine) as a measurement of active smoking.

Virtually all investigators believe that smoking or tobacco use in some form is a requirement for the diagnosis of TAO. There has never been a well-documented case of TAO occurring in the absence of tobacco use. Lie[31] described one case of pathologically proven Buerger's disease affecting the upper extremities of a 62-year-old man who had "allegedly" discontinued smoking 15 years earlier. However, this report did not contain measurements of urinary nicotine or serum cotinine or carboxyhemoglobin. Therefore, it is possible that the subject of this report was still smoking.

Purified tobacco glycoprotein (TGP) could be related to changes in vascular reactivity that may occur in cigarette smokers.[32] Papa and colleagues[33] demonstrated that there was no difference in the humoral response among patients with TAO, healthy smokers, and nonsmokers, and that the two groups of smokers had the same cellular response to tobacco glycoprotein antigen but nonsmokers did not respond at all.

Tobacco use or exposure is central to initiation and progression of the disease. However, only a small number of smokers worldwide eventually have TAO; therefore, other etiologic factors must play roles as triggering mechanisms for the development of TAO in susceptible individuals.

Genetics

There may be a predisposition to development of TAO, although no gene has been identified to date. There is no consistent pattern in HLA haplotypes among patients with Buerger's disease. In the United Kingdom, there was a preponderance of HLA-A9 and HLA-B5 antigens, whereas other HLA haplotypes were more common in patients with TAO from Japan, Austria, and Israel.[34-37] This finding may be based on genetic differences in various populations as well as methodologic differences in each of the studies cited.[33] Mills and colleagues[16] performed HLA testing in 11 patients with TAO and could not identify a distinctive pattern.

Hypercoagulability

Although some studies have failed to identify a specific hypercoagulable state in patients with Buerger's disease, others have shown one or more abnormalities.[38-41]

Choudhury and colleagues[40] demonstrated that the level of urokinase-plasminogen activator was twofold higher, and that of free plasminogen activator inhibitor I was 40% lower in patients with TAO than in healthy volunteers. After venous occlusion, tissue plasminogen activator antigen was increased in patients with Buerger's disease and in healthy volunteers, but the increase was much more pronounced in the control group. This finding suggests some form of endothelial derangement in patients with Buerger's disease, characterized by greater urokinase-plasminogen activator release and reduced plasminogen activator inhibitor I release.

An increased platelet response to serotonin is described in patients with Buerger's disease.[17] Platelet contractile force (PCF) was found to be 82% higher in one TAO patient than in a normal control, and 340% higher in a second patient.[42] Elevated PCF has been seen in a variety of conditions, such as coronary artery disease and diabetes mellitus, in which endothelial function is abnormal. Whether high PCF values play a role in the pathogenesis of these diseases or simply serve as markers of enhanced platelet function, endothelial dysfunction, or both, is not known.

Brodmann and colleagues[43] reported the presence of factor V Leiden mutation in 2 of 28 (7.1%) of patients with TAO compared with 9 of 262 (3.4%) of controls ($P = .65$) and prothrombin gene mutation 20210A in 1 of 28 (3.6%) of patients with TAO compared with 25 of 262 (9.4%) of controls ($P = .48$). However, another case-control study demonstrated that the odds ratio for prothrombin 20210A allele compared with G allele was 7.98 (95% CI, 2.45-25.93). This mutation was the only prothrombotic genetic factor associated with a risk of TAO ($P = .032$).[44,45]

Interest has grown in two other factors that may predispose to abnormal thrombosis. Elevated plasma homocysteine has been reported in patients with TAO.[14,46] This rise may be related to the high prevalence of heavy cigarette smoking or may in some way be directly connected to the disease itself. Patients with TAO who have elevations of homocysteine may also have a higher amputation rate than those who have normal homocysteine levels.[14] There have been several reports of increased anticardiolipin antibody titers in patients with Buerger's disease. A study involving patients with TAO (n = 47), patients with premature atherosclerosis (pASO) (n = 48), and otherwise healthy individuals (n = 48) demonstrated a higher prevalence of elevated anticardiolipin antibody titers in patients with TAO (36%) than in patients with pASO (8%; $P = .01$) and healthy individuals (2%; $P < .001$).[47] Patients with TAO and high antibody titers tended to be younger and to suffer a significantly higher rate of major amputations than those without the antibody (100% versus 17%; $P = .003$). Because there were several methodologic problems with this study, further research is needed to confirm this observation.[48] Another study did not show such findings.[14]

Endothelial Dysfunction

Eichhorn and associates[49] measured a panel of autoantibodies—antineutrophil cytoplasmic antibodies against proteinase 3 (cANCAs), ANCAs against myeloperoxidase (pANCAs), antinuclear antibodies, anti-Ro antibodies, and anticardiolipin antibodies—in 28 patients with TAO. These autoantibody levels were normal in all patients. However, 7 patients with active disease had anti–endothelial cell antibody (AECA) titers of 1857 ± 450 arbitrary units (AU) compared with 126 ± 15 AU in 30 normal control subjects ($P < .001$) and 461 ± 41 AU in 21 patients with TAO in remission ($P < .01$). Antibodies from the sera of patients with active disease reacted not only with surface epitopes but also with sites within the cytoplasm of human endothelial cells. If these findings are corroborated, assays that measure AECA titers may prove to be useful in following disease activity in patients with TAO.

Makita and colleagues[50] demonstrated impaired endothelium-dependent vasorelaxation in the peripheral vasculature of patients with Buerger's disease. Forearm blood flow (FBF) was measured plethysmographically in the nondiseased limb after the infusion of acetylcholine (endothelium-dependent vasodilator), after infusion of sodium nitroprusside (endothelium-independent vasodilator), and after occlusion-induced reactive hyperemia. The rise in FBF response to intra-arterial acetylcholine was lower in patients with TAO (14.1 ± 2.8 mL/min per dL of tissue volume) than in healthy controls (22.9 ± 2.9 mL/min per dL) ($P < 0.01$). There was no significant increase in FBF response to sodium nitroprusside (13.1 ± 4 mL/min per dL in patients with TAO; 16.3 ± 2.5 mL/min per dL in controls). Also there was no significant difference between the two groups after reactive hyperemia. These data indicate that endothelium-dependent vasodilatation is impaired even in the nondiseased limb of patients with TAO.

Immunologic Mechanisms

Several studies have examined the immunologic mechanisms in patients with TAO. Adar and colleagues[51] studied 39 patients with Buerger's disease and measured the cell-mediated sensitivity for type I and III collagen using an antigen-sensitive thymidine incorporation assay. They found higher cellular sensitivity to type I and type III collagen (normal constituents of human arteries) in patients with TAO than in patients with atherosclerosis and healthy male controls. There was a low but significant level of anti-collagen antibody in 7 of 39 serum samples from patients with TAO, whereas this antibody was not detected in the control group of patients. Circulating immune complexes have been found in the peripheral arteries of some patients with TAO.[52-54]

Additional data from three publications suggest that immunologic activation may, at least in part, be an important pathogenetic factor in TAO. Roncon de Albuquerque and coworkers[54] analyzed the arteries of 9 patients with Buerger's disease (33 specimens) histologically, including immunophenotyping of the infiltrating cells, to elucidate the nature of this unusual type of vasculitis. The general architecture of vessel walls was well-preserved regardless of the stage of disease, and cell infiltration was observed mainly in the thrombus and the intima. Among infiltrating cells, $CD3^+$ T cells greatly outnumbered $CD20^+$ B cells. $CD68^+$ macrophages or S-100^+ dendritic cells were detected, especially in the intima during acute and subacute stages. All but one case showed infiltration of the intima by the

HLA-DR antigen–bearing macrophages and by dendritic cells. Immunoglobulin (Ig) G, IgA, IgM, and complement factors 3d and 4c (C3d, C4c) were deposited along the internal elastic lamina. These investigators concluded that Buerger's disease is an endarteritis that is introduced by T cell–mediated cellular immunity and by B cell–mediated humoral immunity associated with activation of macrophages or dendritic cells in the intima.[55]

Lee and associates[56] performed immunohistochemical and terminal deoxyribonucleotidyl transferase (TDT)–mediated deoxyuridine triphosphate (dUTP)–digoxigenin nick-end labeling (TUNEL) studies in specimens from 8 patients with TAO (7 occluded arteries and one patent artery) (1) to phenotype the infiltrating cells with CD4 (helper T cell), CD8 (cytotoxic T cell), CD56 (natural killer cell), and CD68 (macrophage); (2) to identify cell activation with vascular cell adhesion molecule-1 (VCAM-1) and insoluble nitric oxide synthase (i-NOS); (3) for identification of cell death with TUNEL analysis; and (4) to detect inflammatory cytokine with reverse transcriptase–polymerase chain reaction (RT-PCR).[56] The T-cell infiltration was localized mainly in thrombus, intima, and adventitia. Among infiltrating cells, CD4 T cells greatly outnumbered CD8 cells. VCAM-1 and i-NOS were expressed in endothelial cells around the intima (patent segment) or vaso vasorum (occluded segment). On the basis of these data, Lee and associates[56] concluded that T cell–mediated immune inflammation is a significant event in the development of TAO.

In surgical biopsy specimens obtained from femoral and iliac arteries of patients with TAO, Halacheva and colleagues[57] conducted histochemical light and electron microscope analysis to investigate the presence of tumor necrosis factor-α (TNF-α) and expression of intercellular adhesion molecule-1 (ICAM-1), VCAM-1, and E-selectin.[57] Expression of ICAM-1, VCAM-1, and E-selectin was increased on the endothelium and some inflammatory cells within the thickened intima in all specimens. The authors further report the following: "Ultrastructural immunohistochemical analysis revealed contacts between mononuclear blood cells and ICAM-1–, and E-selectin–positive endothelial cells. These endothelial cells showed morphologic signs of activation. The present data indicate that endothelial cells are activated in TAO and that vascular lesions are associated with TNF-α secretion by tissue-infiltrating inflammatory cells, ICAM-1, VCAM-1, and E-selectin expression on endothelial cells and leukocyte adhesion via their ligands. The preferential expression of inducible adhesion molecules in microvessels and mononuclear inflammatory cells suggests that angiogenesis contributes to the persistence of the inflammatory process in TAO."[57]

In summary, no single etiologic mechanism is present in all patients with TAO. Tobacco seems to play a central role in both the initiation and continuation of the disease. Other etiologic factors, such as genetic predisposition, immunologic mechanisms, endothelial dysfunction, and coagulation abnormalities, may play a role in some patients.

■ PATHOLOGY

In Buerger's disease, an inflammatory thrombosis affects both arteries and veins. The histopathology of the involved blood vessels varies according to the chronologic age of the disease at which the tissue sample is obtained for examination. The histopathology is most likely to be diagnostic at the acute phase of the disease. At the intermediate or subacute phase, histopathologic changes evolve, being consistent with or suggestive of the disease in the appropriate clinical setting; however, the histopathology becomes virtually indeterminate at the end-stage or chronic phase, when all that remains is organized thrombus and fibrosis of the blood vessels.[2,6,58-60]

Dible[60] stated that the pathologic diagnosis of Buerger's disease was by no means always secure: "There is so much variation from case to case, depending upon the stage of the disease and the characteristic capriciousness of the lesions, that it is difficult to give a succinct account of the histology." Nevertheless, Dible believed that the histologic distinction between Buerger's disease and atherosclerosis was so clear-cut that a differentiation could be made with a high degree of accuracy through simple examination of tissue sections containing digital arteries and veins. The small blood vessels in the hand and foot are not usually affected by atherosclerosis. A 2000 review reinforces some of the concepts that Dible described 40 years ago.[61]

The *acute phase* lesion is characterized by acute inflammation involving all coats of the vessel wall, especially of the veins, in association with occlusive thrombosis. Around the periphery of the thrombus, there are often polymorphonuclear leukocytes with karyorrhexis, the so-called microabscesses, in which one or more multinucleated giant cells may be present (Fig. 25-1). This histologic finding

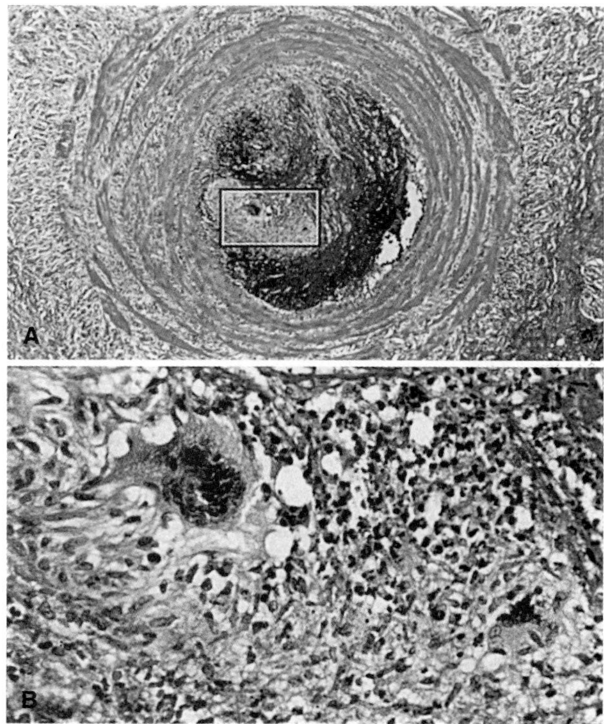

FIGURE 25-1 **A,** Typical acute histologic lesion of Buerger's disease in a vein with intense thromboangiitis (H&E staining; ×64). **B,** Close-up of the boxed area in **A,** showing microabscess in the thrombus and two multinucleated giant cells (H&E; ×400). (From Lie JT: Thromboangiitis obliterans [Buerger's disease] revisited. Pathol Annu 23:257-291, 1988.)

in superficial thrombophlebitis is most characteristic of, but may not be specific for, Buerger's disease.[62] The striking inflammatory thrombotic lesion occurs with greater regularity in veins than in arteries (Fig. 25-2).

Whether the vascular lesions of Buerger's disease are primarily thrombotic or primarily inflammatory is not known. In either event, the intense inflammatory infiltration and cellular proliferation seen in the acute stage lesions is distinctive, especially when veins are involved. If the acute and often tender nodular subcutaneous phlebitic lesion undergoes biopsy at an early stage, one may observe several coexisting lesions in different segments of the same affected vein. Findings include acute phlebitis without thrombosis, acute phlebitis with thrombosis, and acute phlebitis with thrombus containing microabscess and giant cells.

The acute phase is followed by an *intermediate phase*, in which there is progressive organization of the occlusive thrombus in the arteries and veins (see Fig. 25-2). At this stage, there is often a prominent inflammatory cell infiltrate within the thrombus and much less inflammation in the vessel wall. The *chronic phase* or end-stage lesion is characterized by organization of the occlusive thrombus with extensive recanalization, prominent vascularization of the media, and adventitial and perivascular fibrosis (Fig. 25-3).

In all three phases, the normal architecture of the vessel wall subjacent to the occlusive thrombus and including the internal elastic lamina remains essentially intact. These findings distinguish TAO from arteriosclerosis and from other systemic vasculitides, in which there is usually more striking disruption of the internal elastic lamina and the media, disproportional to the disruptions attributable to aging change.[63]

Buerger's disease is segmental in distribution; "skip" areas of normal vessel between diseased segments are common, and the intensity of the periadventitial reaction may be quite variable in different segments of the same vessel. These skip areas may be observed both angiographically and histopathologically.

The histopathology of Buerger's disease is often inconclusive in the intermediate or chronic lesions. A characteristic finding in TAO, however, is the marked cellular proliferation and inflammatory infiltrate in the thrombus. This feature is unique to Buerger's disease and is rarely seen in arterial or venous thrombosis from other causes. Lymphohistiocytic cells and, to a much lesser extent, granulocytic leukocytes contribute to the inflammatory infiltrates. Eosinophils may be present[64] but seldom in excess numbers. Another unique feature of Buerger's disease is that the elastic laminae usually remain intact, whereas other forms of vasculitis may cause disruption of the elastic laminae (Fig. 25-3B).

The end-stage or chronic lesions are the least distinctive of the three morphologic stages of Buerger's disease. It is

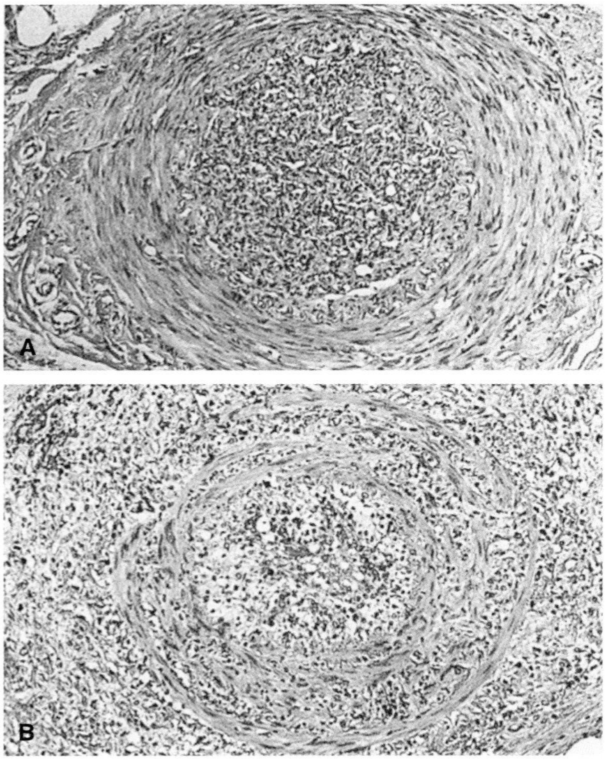

FIGURE 25-2 Digital artery (**A**) and digital vein (**B**) of intermediate stage in Buerger's disease. Note the prominent inflammatory infiltrate and early organization of the thrombus (H&E; ×64). (From Lie JT: Thromboangiitis obliterans [Buerger's disease] revisited. Pathol Annu 23:257-291, 1988.)

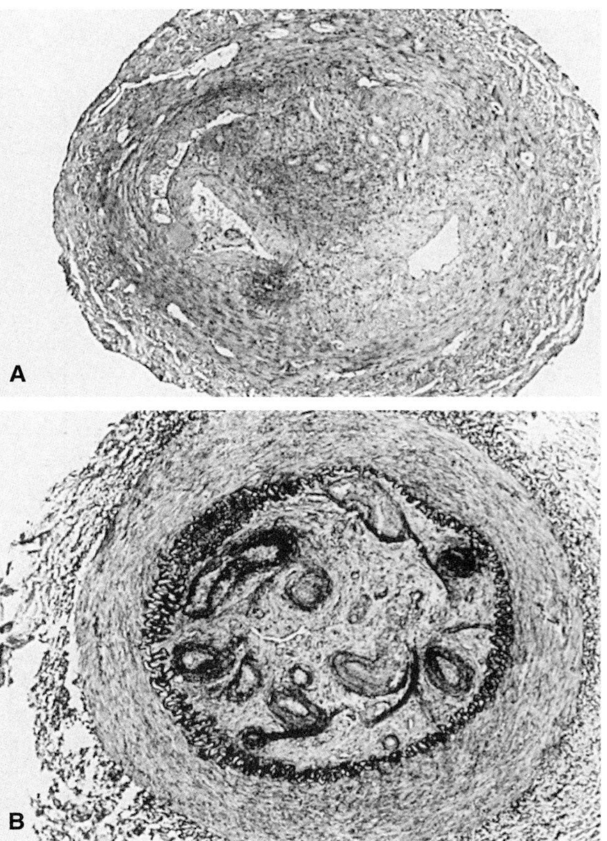

FIGURE 25-3 Chronic phase lesion of Buerger's disease in a radial artery. Note the extensive recanalization of the organized thrombus with prominent vascularization of the media, intact internal elastic lamina, and some residual lymphomononuclear cell infiltrate. (**A,** H&E, ×64; **B,** elastin–Van Gieson stain; ×64). (From Lie JT: Thromboangiitis obliterans [Buerger's disease] revisited. Pathol Annu 23:257-291, 1988.)

important to remember that in some patients, especially those older than 40 years, both Buerger's disease and arteriosclerosis may coexist and thus create further diagnostic uncertainty and controversy. Buerger's disease does not confer immunity to atherosclerosis. In fact, the history of heavy tobacco use in most patients with TAO may actually increase the likelihood of eventual development of atherosclerosis.

The process of thrombus organization in TAO is essentially identical to that in ordinary thrombosis, but with an added inflammatory component. The invasion of organizing smooth muscle cells from the media of the blood vessel is more intensified, resulting in a hypercellular thrombus with rapid organization. Prominent inflammatory cell infiltrate in organized thrombus is a hallmark of Buerger's disease. Preservation of the internal elastic lamina is another feature that distinguishes TAO from atherosclerosis and necrotizing vasculitis.

Buerger's Disease of Blood Vessels in Unusual Locations

Buerger's disease, as already noted, is almost exclusively a disease of the small and medium-sized blood vessels in the lower and upper limbs. There have been only occasional reports of involvement of large elastic arteries such as the aorta, the pulmonary artery,[65] and iliac arteries.[66] Although Buerger[3] had noted that vascular obliteration could affect blood vessels other than those of the limbs, involvements of the cerebral arteries,[67] coronary arteries,[68,69] renal arteries, mesenteric arteries,[70-76] and internal thoracic arteries[68,77] have been documented in occasional patients, almost all as single case reports. There have also been reports, although rare, of multiple-organ involvement in Buerger's disease.[78] An extreme example of Buerger's disease with combined peripheral and visceral involvement occurred in an 18-year-old male cigarette smoker who, over the next 15 years, underwent bilateral lumbar and dorsal sympathectomies, two bowel resections, and 13 amputations, including bilateral above-elbow and above-knee amputations, before he succumbed at 33 years to another episode of bowel infarction from recurrent Buerger's disease of the mesenteric arteries and veins.[79]

The histopathology of visceral TAO is identical to that observed in blood vessels of the limbs with involvement of both arteries and veins. There are even rarer instances of Buerger's disease in a saphenous vein arterial graft[80] and in the temporal arteries of young smokers.[64] Also not widely known is the occurrence of Buerger's disease in testicular and spermatic arteries and veins, as was originally described by Buerger.[3] These reports of Buerger's disease in unusual locations are viewed with skepticism by some investigators. A diagnosis of TAO in unusual locations should be made only when the histopathologic findings are classic for the acute phase lesion and the clinical presentation is consistent with the diagnosis of Buerger's disease. Although TAO occurs most commonly in the infrapopliteal and infrabrachial arteries, it is not uncommon to see involvement of the superficial femoral artery. Less commonly, Buerger's disease affects the brachial artery. The iliac artery may also be involved, but not commonly.[66]

■ CLINICAL FEATURES

The classic presentation of Buerger's disease is in a young male smoker with the onset of symptoms before the age of 40 to 45 years. One report described a case of TAO in a 19-year-old woman who had been smoking for only 3 years.[81] The incidence of TAO appears to be rising in women according to some reports.[13,15,16,82] This does not appear to be the case, however, in the Asian literature.[12,19] Buerger's disease usually begins with ischemia of the distal small arteries and veins. As the disease progresses, it may involve more proximal arteries. Large artery involvement has been reported in TAO but is unusual and rarely occurs in the absence of small vessel occlusive disease.[66] A study from Japan determined the distribution of arterial involvement in TAO on the basis of a nationwide survey carried out in 1993.[83] The subjects were 749 men and 76 women, with a mean age of 50.8 ± 0.4 years. In 42 patients (5.1%), involvement was limited to upper extremity arteries; in 616 patients (74.7%), disease was limited to the lower extremity; 167 patients (20.2%) showed involvement of both upper and lower extremities. The most frequently affected arteries were the anterior (41.4%) or posterior (40.4%) tibial arteries in the lower extremities, and the ulnar artery (11.5%) in the upper extremities. In this report, approximately 25% of the patients had upper extremity involvement[83]; other studies show a higher prevalence of upper extremity involvement.[13,84]

Patients may present with claudication of the feet, the legs, and, occasionally, the arms and hands. Foot or arch claudication may be the presenting manifestation and is often mistaken for an orthopedic problem, resulting in a considerable delay before the correct diagnosis is made. Later in the course of the disease, patients may have ischemic ulcerations in the distal portion of the toes or fingers.

At the Cleveland Clinic Foundation, 112 patients with Buerger's disease were evaluated between 1970 and 1987.[13] The presenting clinical signs and symptoms are shown in Table 25-1. Intermittent claudication occurred in 70 patients (63%). The age and gender distribution and the presenting

Table 25-1 Thromboangiitis Obliterans: Demographic Characteristics, Presenting Symptoms, and Signs in Patients from 1970 to 1987*

Patients (n)	112
Mean age (years)	42
Men	86 (77%)
Women	26 (23%)
Intermittent claudication	70 (63%)
Rest pain	91 (81%)
Ischemic ulcers	85 (76%)
Upper extremity	24 (28%)
Lower extremity	39 (46%)
Both	22 (26%)
Thrombophlebitis	43 (38%)
Raynaud's phenomenon	49 (44%)
Sensory findings	77 (69%)
Abnormal Allen test	71 (63%)

Data from Olin JW, Young JR, Graor RA, et al: The changing clinical spectrum of thromboangiitis obliterans (Buerger's disease). Circulation 825(Suppl):IV3-IV8, 1990.

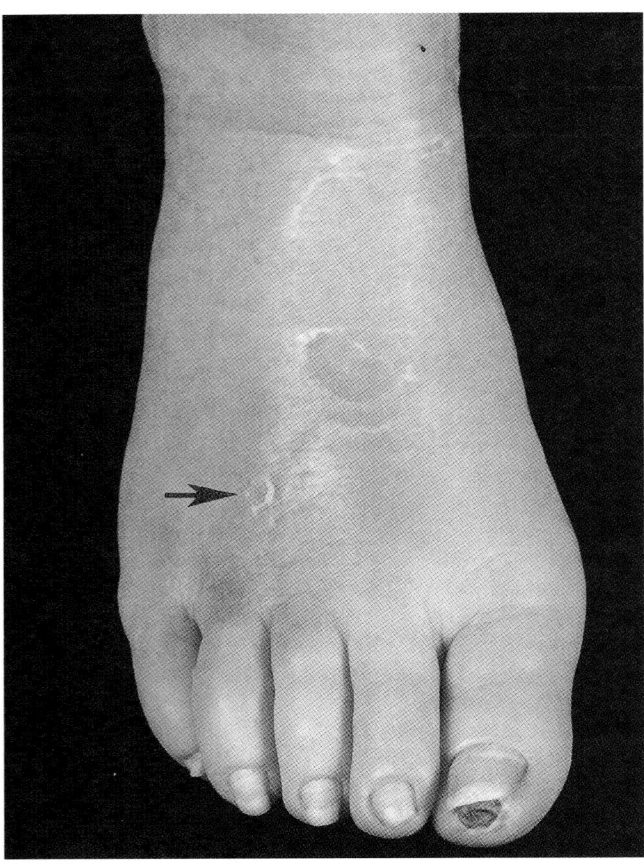

FIGURE 25-4 Ischemic ulcer on the distal portion of the right great toe in a young man with acute Buerger's disease. Note the superficial thrombophlebitis on the dorsum of the foot (*arrow*) with marked erythema around the phlebitis. (From Olin JW, Lie JT: Thromboangiitis obliterans [Buerger's disease]. In Cooke JP, Frohlich ED [eds]: Current Management of Hypertensive and Vascular Disease. Philadelphia, BC Decker, 1992, pp 265-271.)

signs and symptoms were virtually identical in a follow-up series of 40 other patients evaluated from 1988 to 1996.[14] The initial location of claudication was the arch of the foot in many patients. As the disease progressed, claudication often moved proximally to cause typical calf claudication. Seventy-six percent of patients had ischemic ulcerations at the time of presentation.[13] However, with heightened awareness of the early manifestations of TAO (foot or arch claudication), many patients could be identified sooner and treated before ischemic ulcerations develop (Fig. 25-4).

Two or more limbs are almost always involved in Buerger's disease.[8,12,22] In the series reported by Shionoya,[12] two limbs were affected in 16% of patients, three limbs in 41%, and all four limbs in 43% of patients. Because of the proclivity of TAO to involve more than one limb, it has been the author's practice to perform an arteriogram of both upper extremities, both lower extremities, or all extremities in patients who present with involvement of only one limb. It is quite common to see angiographic abnormalities consistent with Buerger's disease in limbs that are not yet clinically involved. With the availability of better noninvasive imaging, such as gadolinium-enhanced magnetic resonance angiography (MRA) and multidetector computed tomographic angiography (CTA), catheter angiography may not always be necessary in the evaluation of patients with TAO.

In patients with lower extremity ulceration in whom Buerger's disease is a consideration, an Allen's test should be performed to assess the circulation in the hands and fingers (Fig. 25-5).[85,86] An abnormal Allen's test result in a young smoker with lower extremity ulcerations is highly suggestive of TAO because it demonstrates small vessel involvement in both the upper and lower extremities. In the Cleveland Clinic series, 63% of all patients had an abnormal Allen's test result.[13] The distal nature of TAO and involvement of the lower and upper extremity help differentiate this disease from atherosclerosis. Except in

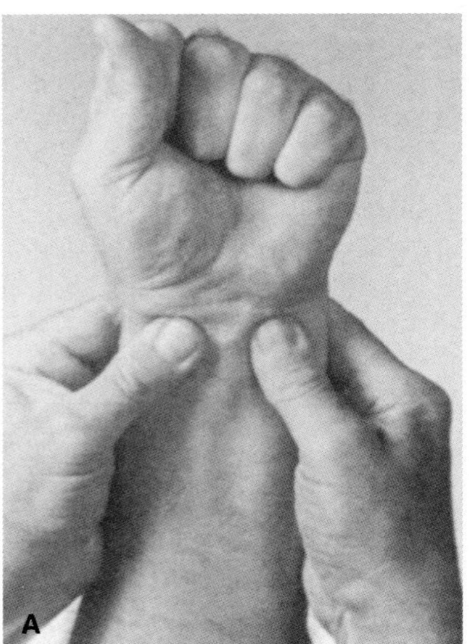

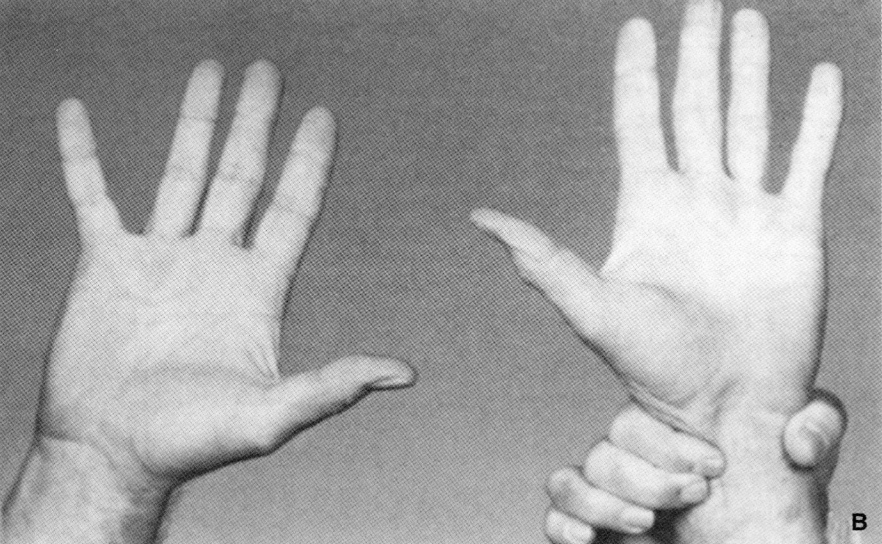

FIGURE 25-5 **A,** Allen's test with occlusion of the radial and ulnar pulse by compression. The pressure on the ulnar pulse is released, while the radial is still compressed. **B,** The hand does not fill with blood; note the paleness of the hand on the right compared with the left, indicating occlusion of the ulnar artery. (From Olin JW, Lie JT: Thromboangiitis obliterans [Buerger's disease]. In Cooke JP, Frohlich ED [eds]: Current Management of Hypertensive and Vascular Disease. Philadelphia, BC Decker, 1992, pp 265-271.)

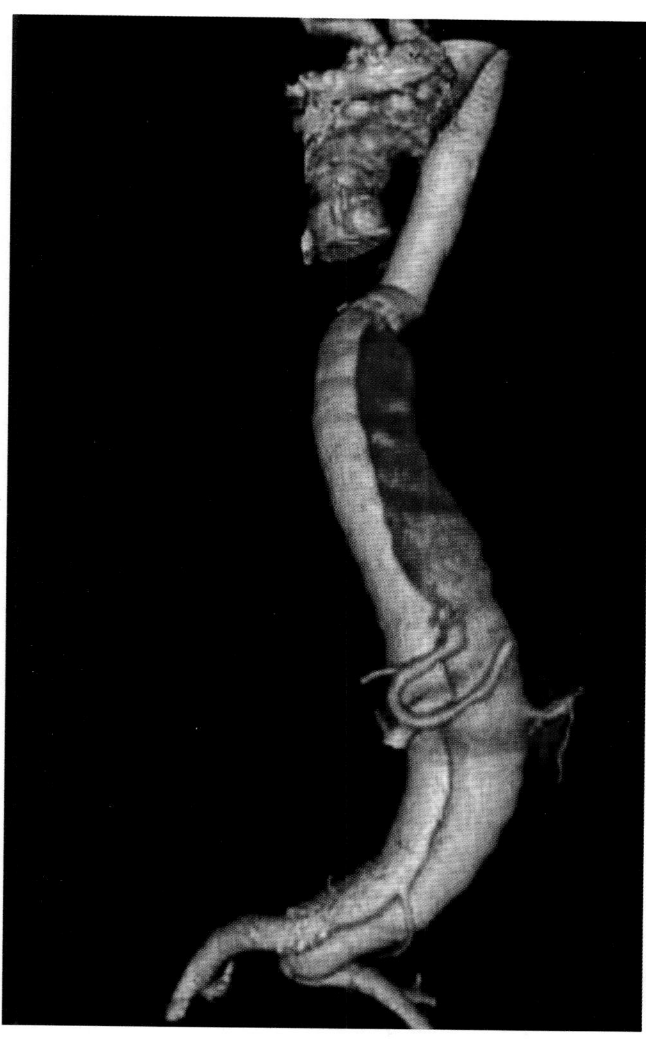

FIGURE 28-9 A 45-year-old woman with Marfan syndrome, after repair of type I ascending aortic dissection with composite graft and aortic valve replacement. The patient's brother had previously died of aortic rupture.

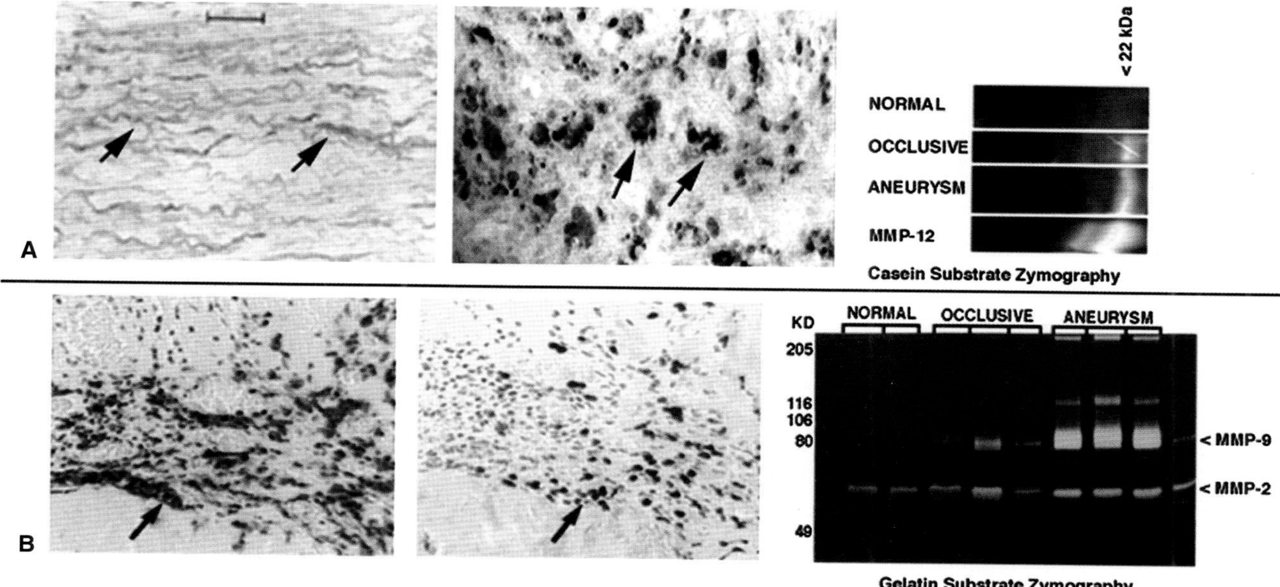

FIGURE 29-2 Histologic and zymographic evidence of representative active enzymes of the matrix metalloproproteinase (MMP) family in human aneurysm wall. **A,** Presence of MMP-12 (*arrows*) by immunohistology, in-situ hybridization, and casein zymography. **B,** Presence of MMP-9 (*arrows*) by immunohistology, in-situ hybridization, and gelatin zymography.

patients with end-stage renal disease and diabetes, atherosclerosis does not occur in the hand and rarely occurs distal to the subclavian artery.

Superficial thrombophlebitis occurs in approximately 40% of patients with TAO.[13] The thrombophlebitis may be migratory and may parallel disease activity.[87] Biopsy of an acute superficial thrombophlebitis often demonstrates the typical histopathologic lesions of acute Buerger's disease (see Figs. 25-1 and 25-2).

Cold sensitivity is common and may be one of the earliest manifestations of TAO. It may be related to ischemia or to markedly increased muscle sympathetic nerve activity, as has been demonstrated in patients with TAO compared with a control group.[88] Typical Raynaud's phenomenon has been reported in approximately 40% of patients. The extremities of patients with Buerger's disease often have an erythematous or cyanotic appearance.[89] A wide variety of other rheumatologic symptoms have also been reported in patients with TAO.[82]

Sensory findings are common in TAO and occurred in 69% of cases in the Cleveland Clinic series.[13] Many of these sensory abnormalities are due to ischemic neuropathy, which occurs late in the course of TAO. Gross and microscopic pathologic examinations have shown the nerve fibers to be encased with the inflammatory or fibrotic material in Buerger's disease, thus accounting for some of the sensory abnormalities.

■ LABORATORY AND ARTERIOGRAPHIC FINDINGS

There are no specific laboratory tests to aid in the diagnosis of TAO. A complete serologic profile to exclude other diseases that may mimic TAO should be obtained. The tests to be performed are as follows:

- Complete blood count with differential
- Liver function tests
- Renal function tests
- Fasting blood glucose measurement
- Urinalysis
- Measurements of acute phase reactants (Westergren sedimentation rate and C-reactive protein level), antinuclear antibodies, rheumatoid factor, and complement
- Measurements of serologic markers for the CREST syndrome (calcinosis, Raynaud's phenomenon, esophageal disease, sclerodactyly, telangiectasia) and scleroderma (anticentromere antibody and SCL-70)
- A complete hypercoagulability screen

A proximal source of emboli should be excluded with echocardiography (two-dimensional and/or transesophageal) and arteriography. Noninvasive imaging such as gadolinium-enhanced MRA or CTA may be used instead of catheter angiography to assess the proximal vessels. However, the resolution of these newer imaging techniques is still not good enough to visualize the detail necessary to evaluate the small arteries of the hands and feet. The angiographic features of Buerger's disease are summarized in Table 25-2.[90-92] Although the findings on arteriography may be consistent with the diagnosis of TAO, there are no pathognomonic angiographic features.

Table 25-2 Angiographic Findings in Thromboangiitis Obliterans

Involvement of small and medium-sized vessels:
- Digital arteries of fingers and toes
- Palmar, plantar, tibial, peroneal, radial, and ulnar arteries

Segmental occlusive lesions: diseased arterial segments interspersed with normal-appearing segments
More severe disease distally
Collateralization around areas of occlusion: "corkscrew collaterals"
Normal proximal arteries: no atherosclerosis
No source of embolus

Proximal arteries should show no evidence of atherosclerosis, aneurysm, or other source of proximal emboli. The disease has been rarely reported in the proximal arteries,[8] but in most cases, the proximal arteries should be normal. A pathologic specimen is needed to diagnose Buerger's disease in cases of proximal artery involvement. As noted previously, the disease is confined most often to the distal circulation and is almost always infrapopliteal in the lower extremities and distal to the brachial artery in the upper extremities. Involvement of small and medium-sized vessels affects such locations as the digital arteries in the fingers and toes, the palmar and plantar arteries in the hand and foot, and the tibial, peroneal, radial, and ulnar arteries (Figs. 25-6 and 25-7).[63,87] Because diabetes is exclusionary for the diagnosis of TAO (in the absence of a pathologic

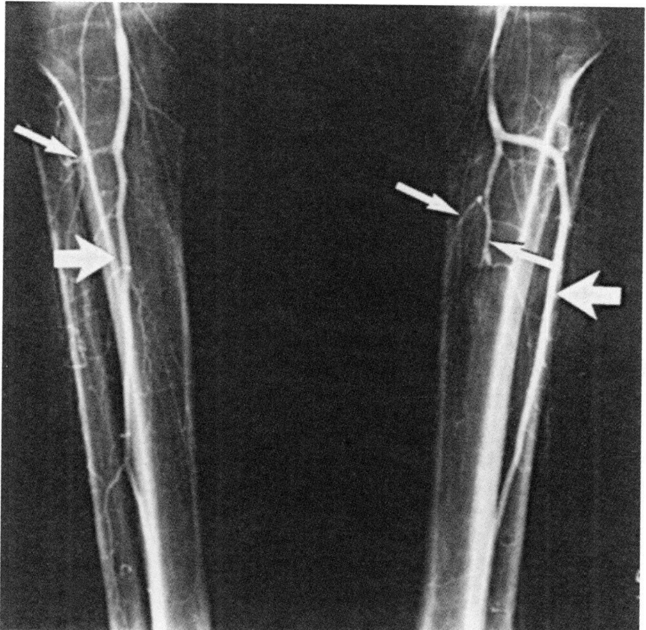

FIGURE 25-6 There is bilateral disease of the popliteal and infrapopliteal arteries in a patient with thromboangiitis obliterans. In the patient's right leg, the anterior tibial artery (*small arrow*) and the posterior tibial artery are occluded at their origin. The peroneal artery is patent (*large arrow*). In the patient's left leg, the anterior tibial artery is patent (*large arrow*), but the posterior tibial and peroneal artery (*small arrows*) are occluded proximally. (From Olin JW, Lie JT: Thromboangiitis obliterans [Buerger's disease]. In Cooke JP, Frohlich ED [eds]: Current Management of Hypertensive and Vascular Disease. Philadelphia, BC Decker, 1992, pp 265-271.)

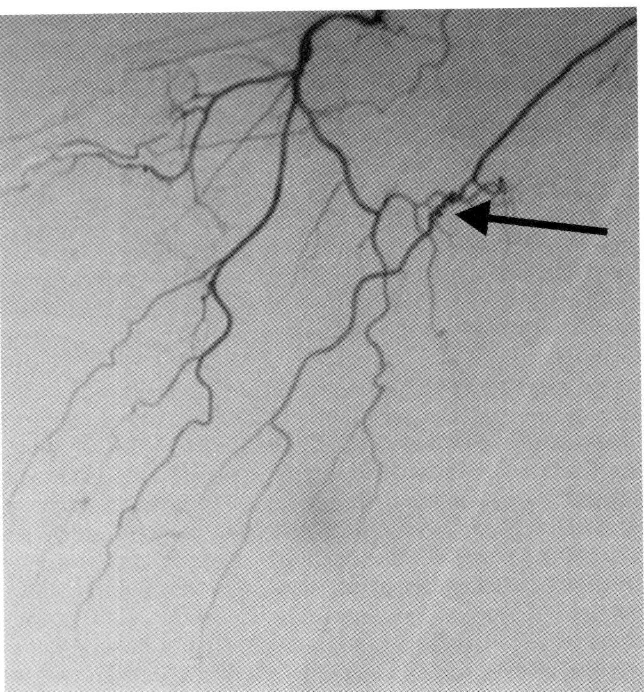

FIGURE 25-7 Arteriogram of the hand demonstrating multiple digital artery occlusions with collateralization ("corkscrew collaterals") (*arrow*) around areas of occlusion. (From Olin JW: Thromboangiitis obliterans [Buerger's disease]. In Coffman J [ed]: Peripheral Arterial Disease: Diagnosis and Treatment. Totowa, NJ, The Humana Press, pp 303-318.)

Table 25-3 Diagnostic Evaluation for Thromboangiitis Obliterans (TAO)

1. Confirmation of tobacco use.
2. Distal extremity ischemic symptoms and signs:
   a. Claudication.
   b. Ischemic rest pain.
   c. Ischemic ulcerations.
   d. Gangrene.
3. Documentation of distal nature of disease:
   a. Segmental blood pressures and pulse volume recordings.
   b. Magnetic resonance angiography (MRA).
   c. Computed tomography angiography (CTA).
   d. Intra-arterial digital subtraction angiography (IADSA).
4. Laboratory tests to exclude connective tissue diseases and hypercoagulable states.
5. Exclusion of proximal sources of emboli:
   a. MRA.
   b. CTA.
   c. IADSA.
   d. Echocardiography (transthoracic and transesophageal).
6. Consistent arteriographic findings.
7. Treatment for TAO. Biopsy indicated only for unusual features:
   a. Age >45 years at onset.
   b. Disease in unusual location:
      i. Proximal disease.
      ii. Central nervous system disease.
   c. History of tobacco use not consistent with diagnosis.

specimen), there should be no confusion between these two diseases.

Arteriographically (and pathologically), TAO is a segmental disorder, demonstrating areas of diseased vessel interspersed with normal segments of blood vessel. There is often evidence of multiple vascular occlusions with collateralization around the obstructions, or "corkscrew collaterals" (see Fig. 25-7). Corkscrew collateral vessels are not pathognomonic of Buerger's disease because they may be present in other small vessel occlusive, diseases such as CREST syndrome and scleroderma. In fact, the arteriographic appearance of Buerger's disease may be identical to that seen in patients with scleroderma, CREST syndrome, systemic lupus erythematosus, rheumatoid vasculitis, mixed connective tissue disease, and antiphospholipid antibody syndrome. The clinical and serologic manifestations of these other immunologic diseases, however, should help differentiate them from TAO. If the diagnostic evaluation is conducted in the proper order, the diagnosis of TAO can be made with a high degree of certainty, and the tissue confirmation will rarely be needed (Table 25-3).

■ DIAGNOSTIC CRITERIA

Several different diagnostic criteria have been offered for the diagnosis of TAO. Papa and Adar[87] have proposed various clinical, angiographic, histopathologic, and exclusionary criteria, and in a second report, they suggested a point scoring system to help make the diagnosis of Buerger's disease.[93] Mills and Porter[24] have proposed major and minor diagnostic criteria for the diagnosis of Buerger's disease. Their major criteria include the following: onset of distal extremity ischemic symptoms before age 45 years; tobacco abuse; undiseased arteries proximal to the popliteal or brachial level; objective documentation of distal occlusive disease by four-limb plethysmography; arteriography, histopathology, or both; and exclusion of proximal embolic sources, trauma, autoimmune diseases, hypercoagulable states, and atherosclerosis (diabetes, hyperlipidemia, renal failure, hypertension). Their minor criteria included migratory superficial phlebitis, Raynaud's syndrome, upper extremity involvement, and instep claudication.

Classifying the criteria as major and minor serves no useful purpose. It does not help diagnose TAO or enhance understanding of the pathophysiology or formulation of a treatment plan. In addition, a growing number of patients fulfill all of the major criteria for TAO but also have the exclusionary criteria for hypertension or hyperlipidemia. Some of these individuals may develop typical atherosclerosis 15 or 20 years after the original diagnosis of TAO. Therefore, if patients meet the criteria of distal extremity involvement, tobacco use, exclusion of a proximal source of emboli or atherosclerosis, in the absence of a definable hypercoagulable state, the finding of hyperlipidemia or hypertension should not exclude the diagnosis of TAO (Table 25-4).

■ DIFFERENTIAL DIAGNOSIS

The diagnosis of TAO should not be difficult if diseases that mimic TAO are excluded. The most important diseases to exclude are atherosclerosis, emboli, and autoimmune diseases, as discussed previously. Under most circumstances, atherosclerosis and emboli can be excluded on

Table 25-4 Criteria for the Diagnosis of Thromboangiitis Obliterans

SHIONOYA CRITERIA[12]	OLIN CRITERIA[13]
Onset before age 50	Onset before age 45
Smoking history	Current (or recent past) tobacco use
Infrapopliteal arterial occlusions	Distal extremity ischemia (infrapopliteal and/or infrabrachial), such as claudication, rest pain, ischemic ulcers, gangrene documented with noninvasive testing
Upper limb involvement or phlebitis migrans	Laboratory tests to exclude autoimmune or connective tissue diseases and diabetes mellitus
Absence of atherosclerotic risk factors other than smoking	Exclude a proximal source of emboli with echocardiography and arteriography
	Demonstrate consistent arteriographic findings in the involved and clinically noninvolved limbs

A biopsy is rarely needed to make the diagnosis unless the patient presents with an unusual characteristic, such as large artery involvement or age greater than 45 years.

Adapted from Olin JW: Current treatment of thromboangiitis obliterans (Buerger's disease). Harrison's On Line, 2001. Available on line at www3.accessmedicine.com/updatesContent.aspx?aID=395615&search Str=olin#searchTerm.

echocardiography and arteriography with a high degree of clinical certainty.

The diagnosis in patients who have scleroderma or the CREST syndrome is usually obvious from a clinical examination of the skin, a history of the other systemic features that occur in these diseases, and the presence of serologic markers such as SCL-70 or anticentromere antibodies. Nail-fold capillaroscopy is usually quite distinctive in patients with CREST or scleroderma.

A careful search should be undertaken to exclude systemic lupus erythematosus, rheumatoid arthritis, mixed connective tissue disease, antiphospholipid antibody syndrome, and other types of vasculitis. Serologic markers often help eliminate the possibility of these conditions. Patients with the antiphospholipid antibody syndrome may present with evidence of both arterial and venous thrombotic events. These patients may have a prolonged activated partial thromboplastin time, a positive test result for circulating "lupus type" anticoagulant, high titers of anticardiolipin antibodies, or a combination of these findings. Several cases of typical Buerger's disease have been encountered with elevated anticardiolipin antibody levels, but the pathogenetic significance of such a finding is uncertain.[14,38,47,48] A pathologic specimen would clearly differentiate these two entities, because antiphospholipid antibody syndrome is a vasculopathy, signified by thrombus with no inflammatory components as opposed to the typical highly inflammatory thrombus of Buerger's disease. The author and colleagues[14] have also demonstrated that some patients with Buerger's disease have markedly elevated levels of plasma homocysteine; preliminary data suggest that elevated homocysteine levels may be a poor prognostic sign and may identify cases that ultimately require amputation.

It should not be difficult to differentiate patients with TAO from those with Takayasu's arteritis or giant cell arteritis. Whereas patients with TAO manifest distal extremity ischemia, patients with Takayasu's arteritis or giant cell arteritis present with proximal vascular involvement. The arteriographic features of Takayasu's arteritis or giant cell arteritis are very distinctive. Many patients with Takayasu's arteritis have elevations of acute phase reactants (erythrocyte sedimentation rate and C-reactive protein), but this finding is not invariable and may not correlate with disease activity.[94]

In the presence of lower extremity involvement, the possibility of popliteal artery entrapment syndrome or cystic adventitial disease should be considered, both of which should be readily apparent on arteriography, computed tomography, or magnetic resonance imaging. An aneurysm of the popliteal artery should be easily diagnosed by physical examination.

A careful history should be taken for the possibility of ergotamine use (abuse), which may cause severe distal ischemia in multiple limbs. Like TAO, ergotamine ingestion may cause both lower and upper extremity ischemia. Even if the patient denies a history of migraine headaches or previous ergotamine use, ergotamine blood measurements should be obtained in some patients to exclude this condition. If there is isolated involvement of the upper extremity, occupational hazards such as use of vibratory tools and hypothenar hammer syndrome should be considered.

An emerging body of literature demonstrates that ischemia induced by cocaine and cannabis ingestion can closely mimic TAO.[95-98] Marder and Mellinghoff [97] published a detailed case report of heavy cocaine use masquerading as Buerger's disease. In addition to the other serologic tests already recommended, blood tests for cocaine, amphetamine, and cannabis may be indicated in the evaluation of some patients. Disdier and associates[98] reported on 10 men with a mean age of 23.7 years in whom subacute distal ischemia of lower or upper limbs developed, leading to necrosis of toes, fingers, or both and even to distal limb gangrene in some patients.[98] Two of the patients also presented with venous thrombosis, and three patients had Raynaud's phenomenon. Arteriographic evaluation in all cases revealed distal abnormalities in the arteries of feet, legs, forearms, and hands resembling those seen in Buerger's disease. All patients were moderate tobacco smokers and regular cannabis users. Despite treatment, five amputations were necessary in four patients. It has been shown that Δ8- and Δ9-tetrahydrocannabinols may induce peripheral vasoconstrictor activity. Cannabis arteritis resembles Buerger's disease or may in fact be a precipitating factor in addition to tobacco use. Therefore, all patients should be questioned about cannabis use.

■ THERAPY

Various therapies available for the treatment of TAO are shown in Table 25-5. However, the cornerstone of therapy is the complete discontinuation of cigarette and cannabis smoking or of the use of tobacco in any form. It has been demonstrated in many case reports and series that complete

Table 25-5 Treatment of Thromboangiitis Obliterans

1. Patient to discontinue using tobacco in any form *and* to avoid passive smoking as much as possible.
2. Treatment of local ischemic ulcerations and pain:
   a. Foot care:
      i. Lubrication of skin with moisturizer.
      ii. Lamb's wool between toes.
      iii. Avoidance of trauma (heel protectors, orthotics for shoes).
   b. If vasospasm present, trial of dihydropyridine calcium channel blocker, such as amlodipine or nifedipine.
   c. Trial of cilostazol (Pletal) in attempt to heal ischemic ulcers.
   d. Prostaglandin analogue (PGI or PGE).
   e. Revascularization (via percutaneous transluminal angioplasty or surgery) if anatomically feasible and patient has stopped smoking completely.
   f. Sympathectomy.
   g. Intermittent pneumatic compression pump.[129]
3. As last resort before amputation:
   a. Implantable spinal cord stimulator *or*
   b. Entry of patient into a therapeutic angiogenesis trial.
4. Treatment of cellulitis with antibiotics and superficial phlebitis with nonsteroidal anti-inflammatory agents.
5. Amputation if all else fails.

abstinence from tobacco is really the only way to halt the progression of Buerger's disease and avoid future amputations.[13,99,100] Even one or two cigarettes a day is enough to keep the disease active. In patients with documented TAO, smokeless tobacco (chewing tobacco or snuff) has also been reported to cause Buerger's disease and to keep it active once symptoms have occurred.[22,23] Of 152 patients with Buerger's disease treated at the Cleveland Clinic from 1970 to 1996, adequate long-term follow-up was obtained in 120 patients (Fig. 25-8).[13,14] Fifty-two patients (43%) discontinued cigarette smoking. Patients who did not have gangrene when they discontinued smoking did not require amputation; overall, 49 patients (94%) avoided amputation in the ex-smoking group. Of the 68 patients who continued smoking, 29 patients (43%) required one or more amputations. The mean follow-up in the original series was 91.6 ± 84 months (range 1 to 460 months),[13] and the mean follow-up in a further 40 patients was 31 months (range 1.6 to 89.7 months).[14] Chi-square testing showed these data to be highly significant.[13]

Some researchers have suggested that it is extremely difficult to get patients with TAO to discontinue smoking.[24] The author has found that it may be easier to persuade patients with Buerger's disease to stop smoking than patients with atherosclerosis. As noted, 43% of the 120 patients with long-term follow-up at the Cleveland Clinic were able to discontinue smoking.[13,14] The correlation of smoking cessation with disease activity (healing of ischemic ulcerations and avoidance of amputation) is so strong that if a patient claims to have stopped using tobacco products but still has active disease, urine nicotine and cotinine levels should be measured to determine whether the patient is being truthful about the claim or is being exposed to large amounts of environmental (secondary) tobacco smoke. One can tell from the level of urine nicotine and cotinine whether a patient is still smoking. These tests can also determine whether a patient is using other nicotine products, such as nicotine gum or patches, or is in an environment with high levels of smoke.[30] In addition, such patients should be investigated for cannabis or cocaine use.

Because smoking cessation is so closely tied to disease activity and future amputation, it is extremely important for the physician to educate and counsel the patient on the importance of discontinuing the use of all tobacco products (Fig. 25-9). Some investigators have recommended using anecdotes or photographs of patients who have undergone amputations or having the patient attend group meetings with other patients with TAO to persuade the patient to stop smoking.[22] Education is probably the most important aspect of this issue. Patients can be reassured that if they are able to discontinue tobacco use, the disease will remit and amputations will not occur as long as critical limb ischemia (gangrene and tissue loss) has not already occurred.[8] However, if arterial segments are occluded, patients should understand that they may continue to have intermittent claudication, Raynaud's phenomenon, or both.

It is unclear whether involuntary smoking (secondary smoke) can cause TAO. The author recommends that patients with active TAO avoid as much involuntary smoking as possible until the disease becomes quiescent.

Forms of therapy other than discontinuation of cigarette smoking are palliative. Fiessinger and Schafer[101] conducted a prospective, randomized, double-blind trial comparing a 6-hour daily infusion of iloprost (a prostaglandin analogue) with aspirin. All patients entered into the study had critical limb ischemia—defined as ischemic rest pain in a limb with or without tissue necrosis for which continuous analgesics in the hospital were required for at least 7 days. Iloprost was superior to aspirin at 28 days in achieving total relief of rest pain and complete healing of all trophic changes. At 6 months, 88% of the patients receiving iloprost showed response to therapy compared with 21% of those receiving aspirin. Only 6% in the iloprost group ultimately required amputations, compared with 18% in the aspirin group. Thus, iloprost appears to be useful in helping patients with critical

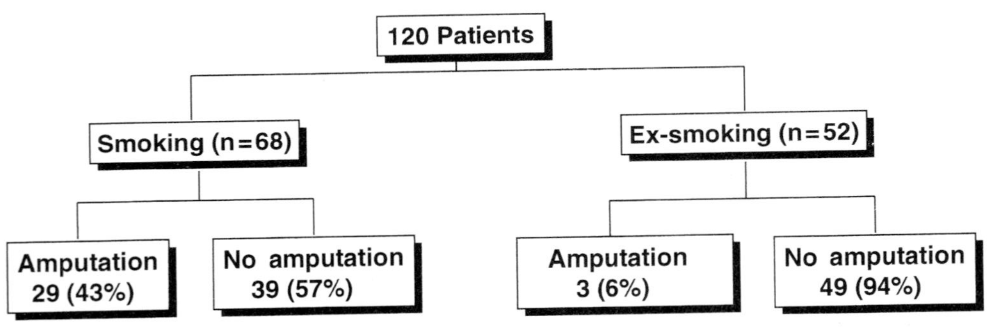

FIGURE 25-8 Smoking status related to amputation. (Adapted from Olin JW, Young JR, Graor RA, et al: The changing clinical spectrum of thromboangiitis obliterans [Buerger's disease]. Circulation 82[Suppl]:IV3-IV8, 1990; and Olin JW, Childs MB, Bartholomew JR, et al: Anticardiolipin antibodies and homocysteine levels in patients with thromboangiitis obliterans. Arthritis Rheum 39:S-47, 1996.)

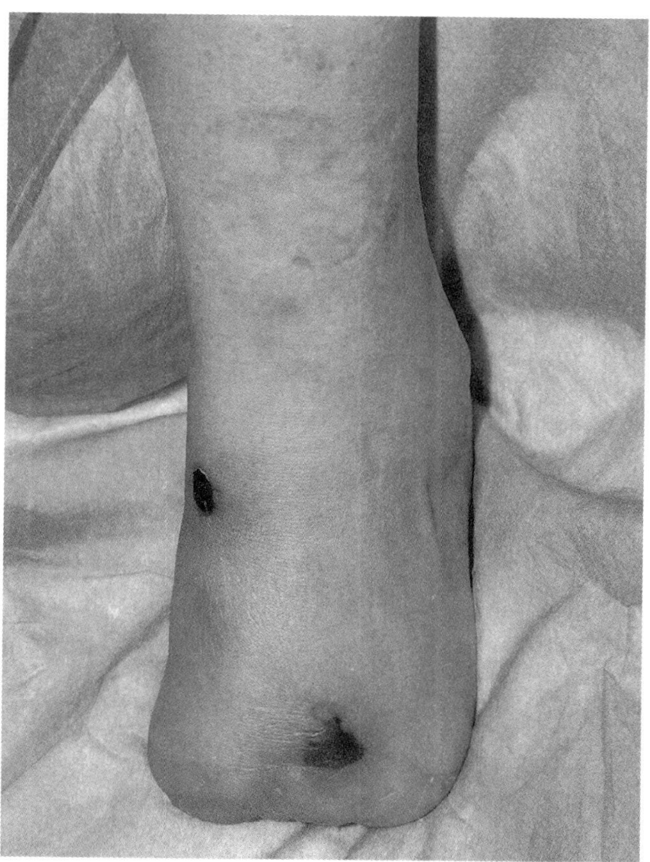

FIGURE 25-9 The foot of a patient who underwent a transmetatarsal amputation in the past. He continued to smoke, and several areas of ischemic ulceration have now developed on the foot. (From Olin JW, Lie JT: Thromboangiitis obliterans [Buerger's disease]. In Cooke JP, Frohlich ED [eds]: Current Management of Hypertensive and Vascular Disease. Philadelphia, BC Decker, 1992, pp 265-271.)

limb ischemia get through the early time, when they first discontinue cigarette smoking. An oral extended-release preparation of iloprost is pharmacologically equivalent to the intravenous form.[102]

On the basis of these findings, the European TAO Study Group conducted a double-blind, randomized trial comparing oral iloprost with placebo.[103] Three hundred and nineteen patients from six European countries, all of whom had rest pain or trophic lesions, were randomly assigned to receive oral iloprost (100 or 200 μg) or placebo twice a day for 8 weeks. There was also a 6-month follow-up period. The primary endpoint was total healing of the most important lesion. The secondary endpoint was total relief of rest pain without the need for analgesics. The combined endpoint consisted of the patient's being alive with no major amputation, no lesions, no rest pain, and no analgesic use. Iloprost was significantly more effective than placebo for relief of rest pain without the need for analgesics and for a combined endpoint at 6 months of follow-up, but there was no significant effect on total healing of lesions.[103] Thus, it appears that the intravenous form of iloprost is more effective than the oral form in ulcer healing.[104]

There is no substitute for good general vascular care in the treatment of patients with severe ischemia. A reverse Trendelenburg (vascular) position should be used in patients who have severe ischemic rest pain. Adequate narcotics should be made available during the period of severe ischemia. Anticoagulation has never been demonstrated to be effective in TAO. However, if other options are not available, some investigators use anticoagulants in an attempt to "buy time" while collateral flow develops in a severely ischemic limb. Good foot and hand care is paramount. If significant vasospasm is present, a dihydropyridine calcium channel blocking agent, such as nifedipine or amlodipine, should be used.[8] Pentoxifylline has not been adequately studied in patients with TAO; in the author's experience, its clinical benefit, if any, is modest. There have been several reports of the successful treatment of ischemic ulcerations with cilostazol when no other revascularization strategies were possible.[105,106]

The role of sympathectomy in preventing amputations or in treating pain is unclear. Sympathetic nerve activity is not increased in some patients with TAO, thus providing further indirect evidence of a local vascular abnormality in the disease.[107,108] Twenty-three patients from the Cleveland Clinic Foundation underwent sympathectomy, and there was no difference in the amputation rate between those undergoing sympathectomy and those not undergoing the procedure.[13] Sympathectomy may occasionally help the healing of superficial ischemic ulcerations. Two reports have demonstrated that sympathectomy can be safely and effectively carried out laparoscopically in the lower[109] and upper extremities.[110]

There are a few anecdotal reports in the literature on the use of implantable spinal cord stimulators in patients with Buerger's disease. The author's group has treated one patient with this modality, resulting in complete healing of all upper extremity ulcerations.[111] Other reports have demonstrated similar success.[112,113] It may be worthwhile to consider a spinal cord stimulator to help decrease pain and avoid amputation in patients in whom surgical revascularization is not an option and when other forms of therapy are not effective.

One group used therapeutic angiogenesis to treat the ischemic manifestations of TAO. Seven limbs in six patients (3 men, 3 women; mean age, 33 years; age range, 33 to 51 years) who satisfied the criteria for TAO and had signs or symptoms of critical limb ischemia were treated twice, 4 weeks apart, with 2 mg or 4 mg of vascular endothelial growth factor (phVEGF165), administered by direct intramuscular injection at four sites in the ischemic limb.[114] Ulcers that had not healed for more than 1 month before therapy healed completely in three of five limbs after the intramuscular phVEGF165 gene therapy. Nocturnal rest pain was relieved in the remaining two patients, although both continued to have claudication. Evidence of improved perfusion to the distal ischemic limb included an increase of more than 0.1 in the ankle brachial index in three limbs, an improved flow shown with magnetic resonance imaging in all seven limbs, and newly visible collateral vessels shown with serial contrast angiography in all seven limbs. The only adverse consequence of the therapy was transient ankle or calf edema in three limbs. Two patients with advanced distal forefoot gangrene ultimately required below-knee amputation despite the evidence of improved perfusion. This preliminary report suggests that therapeutic angiogenesis with phVEGF165 gene transfer, if instituted before the development of gangrene, may provide an effective therapy for patients with advanced Buerger's disease that is unresponsive to standard medical or surgical treatment methods.[114] A case of upper limb salvage after autologous bone marrow to stimulate blood vessel growth through therapeutic angiogenesis has also been reported.[115]

There is little information regarding the use of intra-arterial thrombolytic therapy as an adjunct for the treatment of Buerger's disease. In one series, selective low-dose intra-arterial streptokinase (10,000-unit bolus followed by 5000 units/hr) was administered to 11 patients with long-standing Buerger's disease who had gangrene or pregangrenous lesions of the toes or feet.[116] Many of these patients had previously undergone a lumbar sympathectomy. The investigators reported an overall success rate (defined as avoidance or alteration of amputation) of 58.3%.

Kubota and associates[117] treated a patient with superselective infusion of urokinase into the dorsalis pedis artery and demonstrated recanalization of this artery and healing of an ischemic toe ulcer; at the time of the report, the patient had remained asymptomatic for 4 years. The author's experience with thrombolytic therapy has not been as successful as that reported by Hussein and Dorri[116] and Kubota and associates.[117] Thrombi in the superficial femoral artery have been successfully lysed, but the author has found that severe distal occlusive disease is often resistant to thrombolysis. From a pathologic standpoint, there is a highly inflammatory thrombus that quickly becomes encased with connective tissue and fibrous material. Therefore, thrombolytic therapy may not be effective in many cases. However, if the patient is facing amputation, a short trial of catheter-directed thrombolytic therapy is reasonable as long as there are no contraindications to its use.

Surgical revascularization for Buerger's disease is not usually a viable alternative, owing to the diffuse segmental involvement and extreme distal nature of the disease. Often no distal blood vessel is available for bypass surgery. However, if the patient is severely ischemic and a distal infrapopliteal blood vessel is available for terminal anastomosis, bypass surgery using autologous vein should be considered.[24] Inada and associates[118] demonstrated that of their 236 patients with Buerger's disease, only 11 (4.6%) patients had lesions that were amenable to surgical revascularization. In the 11 patients who underwent surgical revascularization, the bypass remained patent for 4 months to 7 years, with a mean time of 2.8 years. Other investigators reported a 29% early success rate for arterial reconstruction in patients with TAO.[119]

Sayin and colleagues[120] described the results of surgical treatment of 216 patients with Buerger's disease. This group represented 9.7% of all of the patients treated in the Department of Cardiovascular Surgery at Istanbul University Cerrahpasa Medical School from 1981 to 1991. Lumbar sympathectomy was performed in 183 (85%) of the 216 patients. Twenty-one patients underwent direct arterial reconstruction, consisting of thromboendarterectomy with patch angioplasty,[5] aortofemoral or iliofemoral bypass grafting,[5] femoropopliteal bypass grafting,[6] or femorocrural bypass grafting.[5] Thirty-three patients underwent amputation. These investigators noted that four of the five endarterectomized segments had occluded by the 7-year follow-up. One iliofemoral, three femoropopliteal, and two femorocrural bypasses were also occluded. On the basis this experience, Sayin and colleagues[120] suggested that the long-term patency of such grafts is not good but, in many instances, the short-term patency is sufficient to allow healing of the ulcerations associated with TAO.

Sasajima and coworkers[121] evaluated the role of infrainguinal bypass over an 18-year period in patients with disease. Seventy-one autogenous vein bypasses were performed in 61 patients. Fifty-nine percent of patients were operated on for an ischemic ulcer or gangrene, and 41% for claudication. Virtually all patients were heavy smokers. Eighty-five percent of the bypasses were to the crural arteries or to arteries below the ankle. There were 38 graft failures, the main causes being poor distal vessels, progression of disease, and vein graft stenosis. Of the 38 failed grafts, 10 were restored to patency with surgical revision. The primary patency rate was 48.8%, and the secondary patency rate 62.5% at 5 years. At 10 years, primary and secondary patency rates were 43% and 56%, respectively. Patency rates were 66.8% in the group that stopped smoking and 34.7% in the group that continued to smoke ($P < .05$). Of the 28 patients with secondary graft failures, 11 underwent amputation, and 14 had disabling claudication. Some of the patients in this series may not actually have had TAO; 10 patients were older than 50 years, and 41% were operated on for claudication.

Dilege and associates[122] reported on 27 of their 36 (81%) patients with TAO eligible for revascularization who actually underwent revascularization procedures. During a 36-month follow-up, the patency rates at 12, 24, and 36 months were 59.2%, 48%, and 33.3%, respectively. However, the limb salvage rate was 92.5%. Although the patency rates do not seem promising, the limb salvage rate was quite satisfactory in this and other series.[122,123]

Another surgical approach in patients with Buerger's disease is that of omental transfer.[124-128] Singh and Ramteke[124] reported on 50 patients with TAO who underwent omental transfer for rest pain, nonhealing ischemic ulcers, or both. All patients showed an improvement in skin temperature. Rest pain decreased in 36 patients, claudication distance increased in 48 patients, and ulcers healed in 32 of the 36 patients who had ulcers. This surgical technique has not been utilized in Western Europe and the United States.

■ SUMMARY

Thromboangiitis obliterans is a nonatherosclerotic, segmental, inflammatory disease that affects the small and medium-sized arteries and veins in the lower and upper extremities. Both the initiation of disease and the continuation of symptoms and signs are causally related to tobacco use. However, there may be other factors important in the pathogenesis of TAO. Discontinuation of tobacco use is the mainstay of treatment. Patients who successfully stop smoking almost never need amputation.

■ REFERENCES

1. von Winiwarter F: Ueber eine eigenthumliche form von endarteritis und endophlebitis mit gangran des fusses. Arch Klin Chir 23:202-226, 1879.

2. Buerger L: Thromboangiitis obliterans: A study of the vascular lesions leading to presenile spontaneous gangrene. Am J Med Sci 136:580, 1908.
3. Buerger L: The Circulatory Disturbance of the Extremities: Including Gangrene, Vasomotor and Trophic Disorders. Philadelphia, WB Saunders, 1924.
4. Allen EV, Brown GE: Thrombo-angiitis obliterans: A clinical study of 200 cases. Ann Intern Med 1:535-549, 1928.
5. Lie JT: The rise and fall and resurgence of thromboangiitis obliterans (Buerger's disease). Acta Pathol Jpn 39:153-158, 1989.
6. Lie JT: Thromboangiitis obliterans (Buerger's disease) revisited. Pathol Annu 23:257-291, 1988.
7. Matsushita M, Nishikimi N, Sakurai T, Nimura Y: Decrease in prevalence of Buerger's disease in Japan. Surgery 124:498-502, 1998.
8. Olin JW: Thromboangiitis obliterans (Buerger's disease). N Engl J Med 343:864-869, 2000.
9. Hill GL, Moeliono J, Tumewu F, et al: The Buerger syndrome in Java: A description of the clinical syndrome and some aspects of its aetiology. Br J Surg 60:606-613, 1973.
10. Buerger's Disease Research Committee of Ministry of Health and Welfare of Japan: Annual Report. Tokyo, The Ministry, 1976.
11. Nishikimi N, Shionoya S, Mizuno S: Result of national epidemiological study of Buerger's disease. J Jpn Coll Angiol 27:1125-1130, 1987.
12. Shionoya S: Buerger's disease (thromboangiitis obliterans). In Rutherford RB (ed): Vascular Surgery, 3rd ed. Philadelphia, WB Saunders, 1989, pp 207-217.
13. Olin JW, Young JR, Graor RA, et al: The changing clinical spectrum of thromboangiitis obliterans (Buerger's disease). Circulation 825(Suppl):IV3-IV8, 1990.
14. Olin JW, Childs MB, Bartholomew JR, et al: Anticardiolipin antibodies and homocysteine levels in patients with thromboangiitis obliterans. Arthritis Rheum 39:S-47, 1996.
15. Lie JT: Thromboangiitis obliterans (Buerger's disease) in women. Medicine (Baltimore) 66:65-72, 1987.
16. Mills JL, Taylor LM Jr, Porter JM: Buerger's disease in the modern era. Am J Surg 154:123-129, 1987.
17. Pietraszek MH, Choudhury NA, Koyano K, et al: Enhanced platelet response to serotonin in Buerger's disease. Thromb Res 60:241-246, 1990.
18. Leu HJ: Thromboangiitis obliterans Buerger: Pathologische-anatomische analyse von 53 Fallen. Schweiz Med Wochenschr 115:1080-1086, 1985.
19. Lau H, Cheng SW: Buerger's disease in Hong Kong: A review of 89 cases. Aust N Z J Surg 67:264-269, 1997.
20. Lie JT: Diagnostic histopathology of major systemic and pulmonary vasculitis syndromes. Rheum Dis Clin North Am 16:269-292, 1990.
21. Kjeldsen K, Mozes M: Buerger's disease in Israel: Investigations on carboxyhemoglobin and serum cholesterol levels after smoking. Acta Chir Scand 135:495-498, 1969.
22. Joyce JW: Buerger's disease (thromboangiitis obliterans). Rheum Dis Clin North Am 16:463-470, 1990.
23. Lie JT: Thromboangiitis obliterans (Buerger's disease) and smokeless tobacco. Arthritis Rheum 316:812-813, 1988.
24. Mills JL, Porter JM: Buerger's disease: A review and update. Semin Vasc Surg 6:14-23, 1993.
25. Harkavy J: Tobacco sensitivities in thromboangiitis obliterans, migratory phlebitis, and coronary artery disease. Bull N Y Acad Med 9:318-322, 1933.
26. Westcott FN, Wright IS: Tobacco allergy and thromboangiitis obliterans. J Allergy 9:555-564, 1938.
27. Grove WJ, Stansby GP: Buerger's disease and cigarette smoking in Bangladesh. Ann R Coll Surg Engl 74:115-117, 1992.
28. Jindal RM, Patel SM: Buerger's disease and cigarette smoking in Bangladesh. Ann R Coll Surg Engl 74:436-437, 1992.
29. Rahman M, Chowdhury AS, Fukui T, et al: Association of thromboangiitis obliterans with cigarette and bidi smoking in Bangladesh: A case-control study. Int J Epidemiol 29:266-270, 2000.
30. Matsushita M, Shionoya S, Matsumoto T: Urinary cotinine measurement in patients with Buerger's disease—effects of active and passive smoking on the disease process. J Vasc Surg 14:53-58, 1991.
31. Lie JT: Thromboangiitis obliterans (Buerger's disease) in an elderly man after cessation of cigarette smoking—a case report. Angiology 38:864-867, 1987.
32. Becker CG, Dublin T, Wiedman A: Hypersensitivity to tobacco antigen. Proc Natl Acad Sci USA 73:1712-1716, 1976.
33. Papa M, Bass A, Adar R, et al: Autoimmune mechanisms in thromboangiitis obliterans (Buerger's disease): The role of tobacco antigen and the major histocompatibility complex. Surgery 111:527-531, 1992.
34. Otawa T, Jugi T, Kawano N, et al: HL-A antigens in thromboangiitis obliterans [letter]. JAMA 230:1128, 1974.
35. McLoughlin GA, Helsby CR, Evans CC, Chapman DM: Association of HLA-A9 and HLA-B5 with Buerger's disease. Br Med J 2(6045): 1165-1166, 1976.
36. Numano F, Sasazuki T, Koyama T, et al: HLA in Buerger's disease. Exp Clin Immunogenet 3:195-200, 1986.
37. Smolen JS, Youngchaiyud U, Weidinger P, et al: Autoimmunological aspects of thromboangiitis obliterans (Buerger's disease). Clin Immunol Immunopathol 11:168-177, 1978.
38. Casellas M, Perez A, Cabero L, et al: Buerger's disease and antiphospholipid antibodies in pregnancy. Ann Rheum Dis 523:247-248, 1993.
39. Craven JL, Cotton RC: Haematological differences between thromboangiitis obliterans and atherosclerosis. Br J Surg 54:862-867, 1967.
40. Choudhury NA, Pietraszek MH, Hachiya T, et al: Plasminogen activators and plasminogen activator inhibitor 1 before and after venous occlusion of the upper limb in thromboangiitis obliterans (Buerger's disease). Thromb Res 66:321-329, 1992.
41. Siguret V, Alhenc-Gelas M, Aiach M, et al: Response to DDAVP stimulation in thirteen patients with Buerger's disease. Thromb Res 86:85-87, 1997.
42. Carr ME Jr, Hackney MH, Hines SJ, et al: Enhanced platelet force development despite drug-induced inhibition of platelet aggregation in patients with thromboangiitis obliterans: Two case reports. Vasc Endovascular Surg 36:473-480, 2002.
43. Brodmann M, Renner W, Stark G, et al: Prothrombotic risk factors in patients with thromboangiitis obliterans. Thromb Res 99:483-486, 2000.
44. Avcu F, Akar E, Demirkilic U, et al: The role of prothrombotic mutations in patients with Buerger's disease. Thromb Res 100:143-147, 2000.
45. Avcu F, Akar N, Akar E, et al: Prothrombin gene 20210 G→A and Factor V Arg 506 to Gln mutation in a patient with Buerger's disease: A case report. Angiology 51:421-423, 2000.
46. Caramaschi P, Biasi D, Carletto A, et al: Three cases of Buerger's disease associated with hyperhomocysteinemia. Clin Exp Rheumatol 18:264-265, 2000.
47. Maslowski L, McBane R, Alexewicz P, Wysokinski WE: Antiphospholipid antibodies in thromboangiitis obliterans. Vasc Med 7:259-264, 2002.
48. Olin JW: Are anticardiolipin antibodies really important in thromboangiitis obliterans (Buerger's disease)? Vasc Med 7:257-258, 2002.
49. Eichhorn J, Sima D, Lindschau C, et al: Antiendothelial cell antibodies in thromboangiitis obliterans. Am J Med Sci 315:17-23, 1998.
50. Makita S, Nakamura M, Murakami H, et al: Impaired endothelium-dependent vasorelaxation in peripheral vasculature of patients with thromboangiitis obliterans (Buerger's disease). Circulation 94(Suppl): II211-II215, 1996.
51. Adar R, Papa MZ, Halpern Z, et al: Cellular sensitivity to collagen in thromboangiitis obliterans. N Engl J Med 308:1113-1116, 1983.
52. Gulati SM, Madhra K, Thusoo TK, et al: Autoantibodies in thromboangiitis obliterans (Buerger's disease). Angiology 33:642-651, 1982.
53. Gulati SM, Saha K, Kant L, et al: Significance of circulatory immune complexes in thromboangiitis obliterans (Buerger's disease). Angiology 35:276-281, 1984.
54. Roncon de Albuquerque R, Delgado L, Correia P, et al: Circulating immune complexes in Buerger's disease: Endarteritis obliterans in young men. J Cardiovasc Surg (Torino) 30:821-825, 1989.

55. Kobayashi M, Ito M, Nakagawa A, et al: Immunohistochemical analysis of arterial wall cellular infiltration in Buerger's disease (endarteritis obliterans). J Vasc Surg 29:451-458, 1999.
56. Lee T, Seo JW, Sumpio BE, Kim SJ: Immunobiologic analysis of arterial tissue in Buerger's disease. Eur J Vasc Endovasc Surg 25:451-457, 2003.
57. Halacheva K, Gulubova MV, Manolova I, Petkov D: Expression of ICAM-1, VCAM-1, E-selectin and TNF-alpha on the endothelium of femoral and iliac arteries in thromboangiitis obliterans. Acta Histochem 104:177-184, 2002.
58. Leu HJ: Early inflammatory changes in thromboangiitis obliterans. Pathol Microbiol (Basel) 432:151-156, 1975.
59. Williams G: Recent views on Buerger's disease. J Clin Pathol 22:573-578, 1969.
60. Dible JH: The Pathology of Limb Ischemia. Edinburgh, Oliver & Boyd, 1966.
61. Kurata A, Franke FE, Machinami R, Schulz A: Thromboangiitis obliterans: Classic and new morphological features. Virchows Arch 436:59-67, 2000.
62. Leu HJ, Bollinger A: Phlebitis saltans sive migrans. Vasa 7:440-442, 1978.
63. Olin JW, Lie JT: Thromboangiitis obliterans (Buerger's disease). In Loscalzo J, Creager MA, Dzau VJ (eds): Vascular Medicine. Boston, Little, Brown, 1996, pp 1033-1049.
64. Lie JT, Michet CJ Jr: Thromboangiitis obliterans with eosinophilia (Buerger's disease) of the temporal arteries. Hum Pathol 19:598-602, 1988.
65. Alpaslan M, Akgun G, Doven O, Oral D: Thrombus in the main pulmonary artery of a patient with thromboangiitis obliterans: Observation by transthoracic echocardiography. Eur J Echocardiogr 2:139-140, 2001.
66. Shionoya S, Ban I, Nakata Y, et al: Involvement of the iliac artery in Buerger's disease (pathogenesis and arterial reconstruction). J Cardiovasc Surg (Torino) 19:69-76, 1978.
67. Bozikas VP, Vlaikidis N, Petrikis P, et al: Schizophrenic-like symptoms in a patient with thrombo-angiitis obliterans (Winiwarter-Buerger's disease). Int J Psychiatry Med 31:341-346, 2001.
68. Donatelli F, Triggiani M, Nascimbene S, et al: Thromboangiitis obliterans of coronary and internal thoracic arteries in a young woman. J Thorac Cardiovasc Surg 113:800-802, 1997.
69. Becit N, Unlu Y, Kocak H, Ceviz M: Involvement of the coronary artery in a patient with thromboangiitis obliterans: A case report. Heart Vessels 16:201-203, 2002.
70. Deitch EA, Sikkema WW: Intestinal manifestation of Buerger's disease: Case report and literature review. Am Surg 47:326-328, 1981.
71. Rosen N, Sommer I, Knobel B: Intestinal Buerger's disease. Arch Pathol Lab Med 109:962-963, 1985.
72. Cho YP, Kwon YM, Kwon TW, Kim GE: Mesenteric Buerger's disease. Ann Vasc Surg 17:221-223, 2003.
73. Kobayashi M, Kurose K, Kobata T, et al: Ischemic intestinal involvement in a patient with Buerger disease: Case report and literature review. J Vasc Surg 38:170-174, 2003.
74. Arkkila PE, Kahri A, Farkkila M: Intestinal type of thromboangiitis obliterans (Buerger disease) preceding symptoms of severe peripheral arterial disease. Scand J Gastroenterol 36:669-672, 2001.
75. Hassoun Z, Lacrosse M, De Ronde T: Intestinal involvement in Buerger's disease. J Clin Gastroenterol 32:85-89, 2001.
76. Siddiqui MZ, Reis ED, Soundararajan K, Kerstein MD: Buerger's disease affecting mesenteric arteries: A rare cause of intestinal ischemia—a case report. Vasc Surg 35:235-238, 2001.
77. Hoppe B, Lu JT, Thistlewaite P, et al: Beyond peripheral arteries in Buerger's disease: Angiographic considerations in thromboangiitis obliterans. Catheter Cardiovasc Interv 57:363-366, 2002.
78. Harten P, Muller-Huelsbeck S, Regensburger D, Loeffler H: Multiple organ manifestations in thromboangiitis obliterans (Buerger's disease): A case report. Angiology 47:419-425, 1996.
79. Cebezas-Moya R, Dragstedt LRI: An extreme example of Buerger's disease. Arch Surg 101:632-634, 1970.
80. Lie JT: Thromboangiitis obliterans (Buerger's disease) in a saphenous vein arterial graft. Hum Pathol 18:402-404, 1987.
81. Matsushita M, Kuzuya A, Kobayashi M, et al: Buerger's disease in a 19-year-old woman. J Vasc Surg 38:175-179, 2003.
82. Ehrenfeld M, Adar R: Rheumatic manifestations in patients with thromboangiitis obliterans (Buerger's disease). J Rheumatol 27:1818-1819, 2000.
83. Sasaki S, Sakuma M, Kunihara T, Yasuda K: Distribution of arterial involvement in thromboangiitis obliterans (Buerger's disease): Results of a study conducted by the Intractable Vasculitis Syndromes Research Group in Japan. Surg Today 30:600-605, 2000.
84. Pokrovskii AV, Kuntsevich GI, Dan VN, et al: Diagnosis of occlusive lesions of upper extremity arteries in patients with thromboangiitis obliterans. Angiol Sosud Khir 9:86-94, 2003.
85. Allen EV: Thromboangiitis obliterans: Methods of diagnosis of chronic occlusive arterial lesions distal to the wrist with illustrative cases. Am J Med Sci 178:237-244, 1929.
86. Olin JW, Lie JT: Thromboangiitis obliterans (Buerger's disease). In Cooke JP, Frohlich ED (eds): Current Management of Hypertensive and Vascular Disease. Philadelphia, BC Decker, 1992, pp 265-271.
87. Papa MZ, Adar R: A critical look at thromboangiitis obliterans (Buerger's disease). Vasc Surg 5:1-21, 1992.
88. Yamamoto K, Iwase S, Mano T, Shionoya S: Muscle sympathetic outflow in Buerger's disease. J Auton Nerv Syst 44:67-75, 1993.
89. Kimura T, Yoshizaki S, Tsushima N, et al: Buerger's colour. Br J Surg 77:1299-1301, 1990.
90. Lambeth JT, Yong NK: Arteriographic findings in thromboangiitis obliterans with emphasis on femoropopliteal involvement. Am J Roentgenol Radium Ther Nucl Med 109:553-562, 1970.
91. McKusick VA, Harris WS, Ottsen OE: Buerger's disease: A distinct clinical and pathologic entity. JAMA 181:93-100, 1962.
92. McKusick VA, Harris WS, Ottsen OE, Goodman RM: The Buerger's syndrome in the United States: Arteriographic observations with special reference to involvement of the upper extremities and the differentiation from atherosclerosis and embolism. Bull Johns Hopkins Hosp 110:145-176, 1962.
93. Papa MZ, Rabi I, Adar R: A point scoring system for the clinical diagnosis of Buerger's disease. Eur J Vasc Endovasc Surg 11:335-339, 1996.
94. Jaff MR, Olin JW, Young JR: Failure of acute phase reactants to predict disease activity in Takayasu's arteritis. J Vasc Med Biol 4:223-227, 1994.
95. Noel B: Cocaine- and arsenic-induced Raynaud's phenomenon. Clin Rheumatol 21:343-344, 2002.
96. Noel B: Vascular complications of cocaine use. Stroke 33:1747-1748, 2002.
97. Marder VJ, Mellinghoff IK: Cocaine and Buerger disease: Is there a pathogenetic association? Arch Intern Med 160:2057-2060, 2000.
98. Disdier P, Granel B, Serratrice J, et al: Cannabis arteritis revisited: Ten new case reports. Angiology 52:1-5, 2001.
99. Corelli F: Buerger's disease: Cigarette smoker disease may always be cured by medical therapy alone: Uselessness of operative treatment. J Cardiovasc Surg (Torino) 14:28-36, 1973.
100. Gifford RW, Hines EA Jr: Complete clinical remission in thromboangiitis obliterans during abstinence from tobacco: Report of a case. Proc Staff Mtgs Mayo Clinic 26:241-245, 1951.
101. Fiessinger JN, Schafer M: Trial of iloprost versus aspirin treatment for critical limb ischaemia of thromboangiitis obliterans: The TAO Study. Lancet 335:555-557, 1990.
102. Hildebrand M: Pharmacokinetics and tolerability of oral iloprost in thromboangiitis obliterans patients. Eur J Clin Pharmacol 53:51-56, 1997.
103. Oral iloprost in the treatment of thromboangiitis obliterans (Buerger's disease): A double-blind, randomised, placebo-controlled trial. The European TAO Study Group. Eur J Vasc Endovasc Surg 15:300-307, 1998.
104. Melian EB, Goa KL: Beraprost: A review of its pharmacology and therapeutic efficacy in the treatment of peripheral arterial disease and pulmonary arterial hypertension. Drugs 62:107-133, 2002.

105. Dean SM, Satiani B: Three cases of digital ischemia successfully treated with cilostazol. Vasc Med 6:245-248, 2001.
106. Dean SM, Vaccaro PS: Successful pharmacologic treatment of lower extremity ulcerations in 5 patients with chronic critical limb ischemia. J Am Board Fam Pract 15:55-62, 2002.
107. Iwase S, Okamoto T, Mano T, et al: Skin sympathetic outflow in Buerger's disease. Auton Neurosci 87:286-292, 2001.
108. Ronconde Albuquerque R, Serrao P, Vale-Pereira R, et al: Plasma catecholamines in Buerger's disease: Effects of cigarette smoking and surgical sympathectomy. Eur J Vasc Endovasc Surg 24:338-343, 2002.
109. Watarida S, Shiraishi S, Fujimura M, et al: Laparoscopic lumbar sympathectomy for lower-limb disease. Surg Endosc 16:500-503, 2002.
110. De Giacomo T, Rendina EA, Venuta F, et al: Thoracoscopic sympathectomy for symptomatic arterial obstruction of the upper extremities. Ann Thorac Surg 74:885-888, 2002.
111. Swigris JJ, Olin JW, Mekhail NA: Implantable spinal cord stimulator to treat the ischemic manifestations of thromboangiitis obliterans (Buerger's disease). J Vasc Surg 29:928-935, 1999.
112. Chierichetti F, Mambrini S, Bagliani A, Odero A: Treatment of Buerger's disease with electrical spinal cord stimulation: Review of three cases. Angiology 53:341-347, 2002.
113. Pace AV, Saratzis N, Karokis D, et al: Spinal cord stimulation in Buerger's disease. Ann Rheum Dis 61:1114, 2002.
114. Isner JM, Baumgartner I, Rauh G, et al: Treatment of thromboangiitis obliterans (Buerger's disease) by intramuscular gene transfer of vascular endothelial growth factor: Preliminary clinical results. J Vasc Surg 28:964-973, 1998.
115. Taguchi A, Ohtani M, Soma T, et al: Therapeutic angiogenesis by autologous bone-marrow transplantation in a general hospital setting. Eur J Vasc Endovasc Surg 25:276-278, 2003.
116. Hussein EA, el Dorri A: Intra-arterial streptokinase as adjuvant therapy for complicated Buerger's disease: Early trials. Int Surg 78:54-58, 1993.
117. Kubota Y, Kichikawa K, Uchida H, et al: Superselective urokinase infusion therapy for dorsalis pedis artery occlusion in Buerger's disease. Cardiovasc Intervent Radiol 20:380-382, 1997.
118. Inada K, Iwashima Y, Okada A, Matsumoto K: Nonatherosclerotic segmental arterial occlusion of the extremity. Arch Surg 108:663-667, 1974.
119. Mills JL, Porter JM: Buerger's disease (thromboangiitis obliterans). Ann Vasc Surg 5:570-572, 1991.
120. Sayin A, Bozkurt AK, Tuzun H, et al: Surgical treatment of Buerger's disease: Experience with 216 patients. Cardiovasc Surg 1:377-380, 1993.
121. Sasajima T, Kubo Y, Inaba M, et al: Role of infrainguinal bypass in Buerger's disease: An eighteen-year experience. Eur J Vasc Endovasc Surg 13:186-192, 1997.
122. Dilege S, Aksoy M, Kayabali M, et al: Vascular reconstruction in Buerger's disease: Is it feasible? Surg Today 32:1042-1047, 2002.
123. Nishikimi N: Fate of limbs with failed vascular reconstruction in Buerger's disease patients. Int J Cardiol 75(Suppl 1):S183-S185, 2000.
124. Singh I, Ramteke VK: The role of omental transfer in Buerger's disease: New Delhi's experience. Aust N Z J Surg 66:372-376, 1996.
125. Talwar S, Jain S, Porwal R, et al: Free versus pedicled omental grafts for limb salvage in Buerger's disease. Aust N Z J Surg 68:38-40, 1998.
126. Talwar S, Jain S, Porwal R, et al: Pedicled omental transfer for limb salvage in Buerger's disease. Int J Cardiol 72:127-132, 2000.
127. Talwar S, Choudhary SK: Omentopexy for limb salvage in Buerger's disease: Indications, technique and results. J Postgrad Med 47:137-142, 2001.
128. Talwar S, Prasad P: Single-stage lumbar sympathectomy and omentopexy: A new surgical approach towards patients with Buerger's disease. Trop Doctor 31:73-75, 2001.
129. Montori VM, Kavros SJ, Walsh EE, Rooke TW: Intermittent compression pump for nonhealing wounds in patients with limb ischemia: The Mayo Clinic experience (1998-2000). Int Angiol 21:360-366, 2002.

Chapter 26

Takayasu's Disease:
Nonspecific Aortoarteritis

DAVID A. RIGBERG, MD
WILLIAM QUINONES-BALDRICH, MD

Takayasu's arteritis (TA) is a disease of unknown etiology with a constellation of clinical findings primarily resulting from effects on the aorta and its branches. TA varies geographically in incidence, distribution, and presentation, and these differences affect the treatment and prognosis of patients.[1-3] Although TA is classified pathologically as a giant cell vasculitis, there is no pathognomonic histopathologic finding.[4] Various names used to describe the condition have been based on associated clinical findings: middle aortic syndrome, "pulseless" disease, young female arteritis, nonspecific aortoarteritis, and aortic arch syndrome.[5] TA is not common, and the diagnosis is often delayed or unclear at the time of referral. Vascular surgeons should be familiar with the condition because it can manifest as arterial occlusions, stenoses, or aneurysms that require treatment. The systemic nature of the process must be recognized and adequately managed while these local issues are addressed.

■ HISTORY AND CRITERIA FOR DIAGNOSIS

Takayasu's arteritis is named in honor of Dr. Mikito Takayasu, a Japanese ophthalmologist who in 1908 presented his findings of arteriovenous changes of the ocular papilla in a 21-year-old woman.[6] Interestingly, two other physicians at the same meeting presented similar findings, noting also the absence of radial pulses in their patients.[7] Yasuzo Shinmi gave credit to Takayasu and used the name Takayasu's

Table 26-1 Original Criteria for Takayasu's Arteritis

CRITERIA	DEFINITION
All patients < 40 years old	Age < 40 years at diagnosis or at onset of symptoms
Two major criteria:	
(1) Left mid–subclavian artery lesion	Severe stenosis or occlusion in midportion from 1 cm proximal to the vertebral artery origin to a point 3 cm distal to the origin
(2) Right mid–subclavian artery lesion	Severe stenosis or occlusion in the midportion from right vertebral artery origin to a point 3 cm distal to the origin
Nine minor criteria:	
(1) Elevated erythrocyte sedimentation rate (ESR)	Unexplained ESR > 20 mm/hr
(2) Carotid tenderness	Unilateral or bilateral tenderness of common carotid artery on palpation; differentiate from muscle tenderness
(3) Hypertension	Persistent elevation of blood pressure, 140/90 mm Hg (brachial) or 160/90 mm Hg (popliteal)
(4) Aortic regurgitation/annular disease	By auscultation, echocardiography, or angiography
(5) Pulmonary artery disease	Lobar or segmental artery occlusion or equivalent; stenosis, aneurysm, luminal irregularity in pulmonary trunk or pulmonary arteries
(6) Left mid–common carotid lesion	Severe stenosis or occlusion in midportion 5 cm in length from a point 2 cm distal to its origin
(7) Distal brachiocephalic trunk lesion	Involves distal third
(8) Descending aortic lesion	Narrowing, dilatation or aneurysm, luminal irregularity, or combination of these findings involving thoracic aorta
(9) Abdominal aortic lesion	Narrowing, dilatation or aneurysm, luminal irregularity, or combination of these findings involving abdominal aorta plus the absence of distal aortic (last 2 cm) and iliac disease

Adapted from Ishikawa K: Diagnostic approach and proposed criteria for the clinical diagnosis of Takayasu's arteriopathy. J Am Coll Cardiol 12:964-972, 1988; and Vanoli M, Bacchiani G, Origg L, Scorza R: Takayasu's arteritis: A changing disease. J Nephrol 14:497-505, 2001.

arteritis in describing a patient in 1939.[6] In 1969, Ueda and colleagues[8] suggested both the autoimmune component of the disorder and the nature of the aortitis in these cases. In 1975, the Japanese Department of Heath and Welfare officially bestowed the name Takayasu's arteritis on the disorder (the reader is referred to Dr. Numano's excellent review of this history[6]).

Because of the syndromic nature of TA as well as the absence of pathognomonic findings, several sets of diagnostic criteria have been used over the last two decades. Ishikawa's criteria, published in 1988, have been used, albeit in a modified form, by many clinicians (Table 26-1). He based them on a Japanese patient population, limiting their application in other geographic areas. To be diagnosed with TA in this schema, patients must be younger than 40 years old and have any combination of the following: both of the major criteria (midsubclavian lesions), one major criterion and 2 minor criteria, or four minor criteria only.[9]

In 1990, The American College of Rheumatology published a similar system based on findings in North American patients.[10] One point of difference is the absence of age younger than 40 as an obligatory finding for the diagnosis (Table 26-2). Many writers believed that this system was too restrictive, and Sharma and associates[11] published their modifications of the original Ishikawa system in 1995 (Table 26-3). Of note, the age criterion was removed from this list entirely, a change that could possibly lead to overlap of patients with TA and those with temporal arteritis. It is not entirely clear at this time which system is best, and the choice of system most likely depends on the population being evaluated. Several comparisons of the classification systems have been published, and efforts to evaluate the criteria are ongoing.[12,13]

■ PATHOGENESIS

Although it is not fully understood, many observations have been made regarding the pathogenesis of TA. From a clinical standpoint, the process is focused on the aorta and great vessels, although involvement of other vessels is sometimes seen.[14] At the histologic level, TA is a process that appears to begin with destruction of the elastic component of the

Table 26-2 American College of Rheumatology Criteria for Takayasu's Arteritis (TA)*

CRITERIA	DEFINITION
Age at disease onset in years	Symptoms/findings of TA at < 40 years
Claudication	Lower or upper extremity muscle fatigue during exercise
Decreased brachial artery pulse	Unilateral or bilateral
Blood pressure (BP) difference > 10 mm Hg	Measured systolic BP between upper extremities
Bruit over subclavian arteries or aorta	One or both subclavians or abdominal aorta
Angiographic abnormalities	Narrowing or occlusion of aorta, primary branches, or the large arteries in proximal extremities; must not be secondary to arteriosclerosis, fibromuscular dysplasia, or other causes; usually focal or segmental

*If three or more of these criteria are present, Takayasu's arteritis can be diagnosed with a specificity of 97.8% and a sensitivity of 90.5%.

Adapted from Arend WP, Michel BA, Bloch DA: The American College of Rheumatology 1990 criteria for the classification of Takayasu's arteritis. Arthritis Rheum 33:1129-1134, 1990; and Vanoli M, Bacchiani G, Origg L, Scorza R: Takayasu's arteritis: A changing disease. J Nephrol 14:497-505, 2001.

Table 26-3 Sharma's Criteria for Takayasu's Arteritis*

CRITERION	DEFINITION
Three major criteria:	
(1) Left mid–subclavian artery lesion	Severe stenosis or occlusion in midportion from 1 cm proximal to the vertebral artery origin to a point 3 cm distal to the origin
(2) Right mid–subclavian artery lesion	Severe stenosis or occlusion in the midportion from right vertebral artery origin to a point 3 cm distal to the origin
(3) Characteristic signs and symptoms of at least 1 month's duration	May include the following: claudication, decrease/absence of pulses, > 10 mm Hg blood pressure (BP) differences between limbs, fever, neck pain, amaurosis fugax, blurred vision, syncope, dyspnea, palpitations
Ten minor criteria:	
(1) Elevated erythrocyte sedimentation rate (ESR)	Unexplained ESR > 20 mm/hr
(2) Carotid tenderness	Unilateral or bilateral tenderness of common carotid artery on palpation; differentiate from muscle tenderness
(3) Hypertension	Persistent elevation of BP, 140/90 mm Hg (brachial) or 160/90 mm Hg (popliteal)
(4) Aortic regurgitation/annular disease	By auscultation, echocardiography, or angiography
(5) Pulmonary artery disease	Lobar or segmental artery occlusion or equivalent; stenosis, aneurysm, luminal irregularity in pulmonary trunk or pulmonary arteries
(6) Left mid–common carotid lesion	Severe stenosis or occlusion in midportion 5 cm in length from a point 2 cm distal to its origin
(7) Distal brachiocephalic trunk lesion	Involves distal third
(8) Descending aortic lesion	Narrowing, dilatation or aneurysm, luminal irregularity, or combination of these findings involving thoracic aorta
(9) Abdominal aortic lesion	Narrowing, dilatation or aneurysm, luminal irregularity, or combination of these findings involving abdominal aorta
(10) Coronary artery lesion	Angiographically documented in patient < 30 years old and without risk factors such as hyperlipidemia and diabetes mellitus

*Diagnosis of TA requires two major elements *or* one major and two minor elements *or* four minor elements.

Adapted from Sharma BK, Iliskovic NS, Singal PK: Takayasu's arteritis may be underdiagnosed in North America. Can J Cardiol 11:311-316, 1995; and Vanoli M, Bacchiani G, Origg L, Scorza R: Takayasu's arteritis: A changing disease. J Nephrol 14:497-505, 2001.

media and subsequent fibrosis of the medial smooth muscle. The "pan-arteritic" nature of the lesion is reflective of extension of the process to the other layers of the arterial wall.[15] One explanation for the formation of aneurysms in TA is that the destructive process in the media occurs too rapidly, before fibrosis of smooth muscle can develop.[16]

Many of the steps in the pathophysiologic process have been elucidated. Although inflammation initially involves the vasa vasorum, studies have shown early infiltration of the media by lymphocytes, granulocytes, and other inflammatory cells.[17] The subsequent elaboration of pro-inflammatory cytokines has also been characterized.[18] Noris and coworkers[19] demonstrated increased levels of interleukin-6 (IL-6) in patients with active stage TA compared with controls; these levels were further found to correlate with the level of disease activity. RANTES (regulated on activation, normal T cell expressed and secreted) is another chemokine whose expression correlates with disease activity.[19] Measurements of these substances may become useful tests for assessing disease activity.

At the levels of cellular and humoral immunity, there are several interesting findings in TA. Affected patients have elevated numbers of activated lymphocytes, although the significance of this finding is not clear.[20,21] These cells play a role in blood vessel destruction and are in all likelihood directed and bound by activated endothelial cells in an HLA-dependent process.[22] The steps leading to this endothelial cell activation are not well understood, but endothelial cell antibodies are elevated in patients with TA, suggesting that these antibodies may play a pivotal role in the process.[23] The autoimmune nature of TA is further suggested by associated conditions. For example, several rheumatologic disorders have been linked to TA, including Still's disease, rheumatoid arthritis, ankylosing spondylitis, Cogan's disease, and systemic lupus erythematosus.[24-28] Idiopathic conditions with colitis (ulcerative colitis and Crohn's disease) have also been linked.[29] In most cases, however, TA occurs as an isolated disease.

The aforementioned HLA associations imply a genetic component to TA. This issue has been investigated, but no clear consensus has been reported.[30] There is also geographic diversity in the reported HLA findings. For example, HLA-B39.2 is expressed frequently in Asian patients but not in Western patients.[29,31] Finally, several other conditions have been inconsistently linked to TA, including tuberculosis, rheumatic fever, and other streptococcal infections.[32,33] The significance of these associations has not been established but does suggest the possibility that multiple insults may be capable of triggering TA in the susceptible patient.

■ INCIDENCE AND DEMOGRAPHICS

TA is an uncommon disease, although its incidence depends highly on geography. In the United States, an accepted figure is 2.6 cases per 1 million people, whereas Japanese autopsy data reflects a number of 1 case per 3000.[31,34] Reports of TA in Africa and Europe have also been published.[35,36] In all published series, there are more women than men with the disease, although the ratio of women to men also depends on the region studied. Several series have reported 100% female patients,[37,38] whereas the series reported by Kumar and associates[39] from India had just over 25% male patients.

Although the majority of patients present before age 40, slightly more than 10% present after this age. Data from a National Institutes of Health (NIH) study in the United States showed that 13% of patients present after age 40.[40] Deletion of age as a diagnostic criterion has led to increased sensitivity, but decreased specificity in diagnosis of TA.[41] Differences in age of presentation are also subject to geographic diversity. In the United States, the only ethnic group with a disproportionate prevalence of TA is Asian Americans.[39] In a review of 44 consecutive patients with TA from Mexico, 43 were Mexican mestizos, and the remaining patient was white.[42] Most of the patients in this series were women,[38] and most of the serious morbidity in these patients was from hypertension and cardiac compromise.

■ PRESENTATION

A variety of clinical syndromes are attributable to TA. In a global sense, prior consensus held that TA had a predictable course with three identifiable stages: (1) an early systemic phase characterized by vague malaise and constitutional symptoms, (2) a phase marked by vascular inflammation leading to vessel damage, and (3) the "burned out" phase. This pattern of disease is not the rule. For example, it has been demonstrated that biopsy specimens from patients with "inactive" disease often demonstrate active inflammation.[43] In addition, a sizable minority of patients never report undergoing the initial systemic phase of TA.[39] Finally, when erythrocyte sedimentation rate (ESR) is used to assess disease activity, it is elevated in only 72% of patients with active inflammation but also in 56% of patients with clinically "inactive" disease. Despite these factors, it is useful to consider the different phases to aid in the differential diagnosis for a variety of clinical situations.

The diagnosis of TA is usually made after arterial damage has become manifest.[44] Thus, the presentation depends on the arteries involved, and this feature varies considerably from series to series. Again, the pattern of disease also varies with geography. In this regard, patients in the United States and Japan are similar, with mostly upper extremity and cerebrovascular manifestations.[45,39] Review of series of patients with TA from India and China shows more involvement of the distal aorta.[46,47] The reasons underlying these differences are not known.

Upper extremity arterial insufficiency may be the most common manifestation, and this possibility is supported by angiographic evidence of disease distribution. The left subclavian artery is most often involved, with some series reporting as many as 90% of patients having such a lesion.[48] This involvement may manifest as a decreased pulse (73%) or even upper extremity "claudication" (52%).[49] Some investigators believe that subclavian steal symptoms are rare because the lesions usually affect the subclavian vessel both proximal and distal to the origin of the vertebral artery. However, angiographic evidence from a series reported by Yamato and colleagues[50] demonstrated that almost 80% of left subclavian lesions were proximal to the vertebral artery origin. Cerebrovascular involvement in the form of carotid or brachiocephalic disease is common (Fig. 26-1). A review of NIH data showed that 20% of patients with TA initially presented with stroke.[51] Likewise, patients can also present with visual changes, fleeting blindness, syncope, or dizziness.

Hypertension is a common presenting factor, affecting more than 70% of patients in some series.[32,52,53] Interestingly, bilateral subclavian artery lesions can commonly mask the diagnosis of hypertension; therefore, the clinician should also check lower extremity pressures in patients in whom TA is suspected. Most cases of hypertension in TA are due to renal artery stenoses, although aortic coarctation should be considered if there is no evidence of renal disease. Aggressive treatment of hypertension in TA is clearly indicated, because the sequelae of hypertension in this disease can be devastating. In a 14-year follow-up of patients with TA, Ishikawa and Maerani[45] reported overall survival as 96% in patients judged to be free of major disease complications, compared with 66% in those with complications. Of these complications, hypertension was a key factor, as were retinopathy and aortic incompetence, both of which are adversely affected by hypertension.

Lower extremity claudication secondary to infrarenal aortic disease is another, albeit less common, presenting complaint (Fig. 26-2).[54] The lesions of TA typically do not lead to rest pain or tissue loss, although the claudication can be particularly severe in young and otherwise active patients. TA lesions usually spare the distal aorta, iliac arteries, and runoff vessels. No data are available to indicate whether conservative treatment methods can improve exercise tolerance in patients with TA and claudication. Clinicians usually treat the condition more aggressively than would be expected in the presence of atherosclerotic disease, likely because of the younger age of these patients.

Involvement of the pulmonary arteries in TA is common, with angiographically evident disease in roughly 50% of patients.[51] This involvement is not commonly symptomatic and is an unusual initial presentation. However, pulmonary hypertension may be encountered and can be quite severe.[55]

Aneurysmal degeneration is often reported in patients with TA, although the frequency with which this complication occurs is unclear. There is geographic diversity in the incidence of aneurysmal TA, which appears to be particularly unusual in the United States.[50] In contrast, series from both South Africa and Japan report incidences of 70% and 32%, respectively.[56,57] The risk of rupture of these aneurysms is not known, although it is probably lower than that for typical nonarteritic aneurysms.[54] Although aneurysms of the aorta are most common, there are reports of degeneration of the arch branches and iliac, renal, and visceral vessels.[58] For unknown reasons, common carotid aneurysms have a predilection for the right side.[59] In the unusual situation in which a patient's initial presentation is aneurysmal disease, it is important to rule out other causes, such as syphilis, bacterial and giant cell arteritis, and Reiter's syndrome, with appropriate laboratory and pathologic studies.

Visceral artery involvement is seen in 20% to 30% of patients with TA, although the incidence of clinically significant disease is substantially lower (Fig. 26-3).[40,60] TA can have numerous cardiac sequelae, including direct coronary involvement and aortic insufficiency with resultant congestive heart failure.[61-63] Coronary arteritis is not common but, when present, tends to affect the ostia.

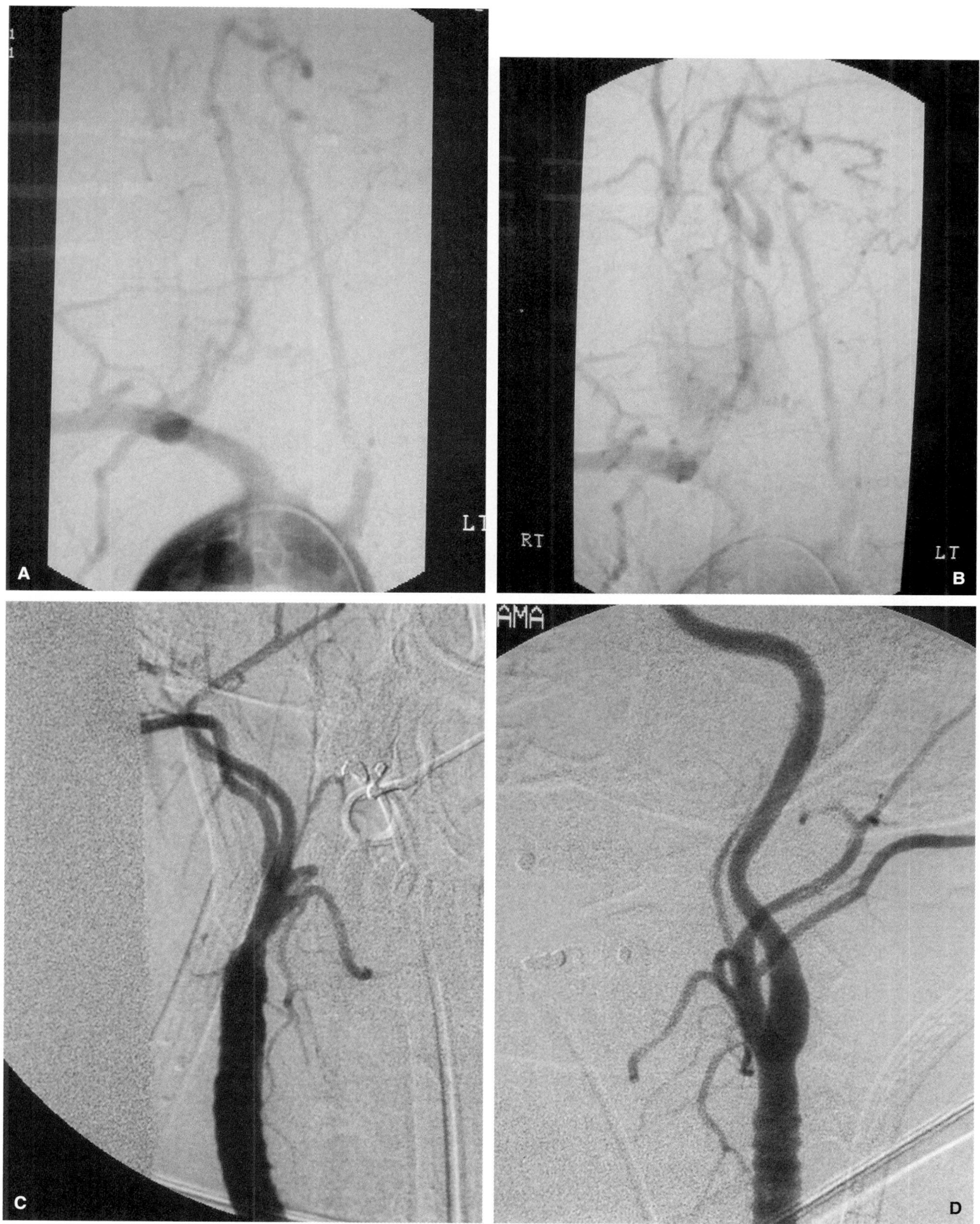

FIGURE 26-1 Preoperative films from a 35-year-old woman with TA and bilateral common carotid occlusions. **A,** The vertebral arteries can be seen at their origins from the aortic arch. **B,** On a delayed film, distal reconstitution of the common carotids can be seen. **C** and **D,** Reconstruction was performed via a Dacron aorto–bicarotid bypass with a 14 by 7–mm graft.

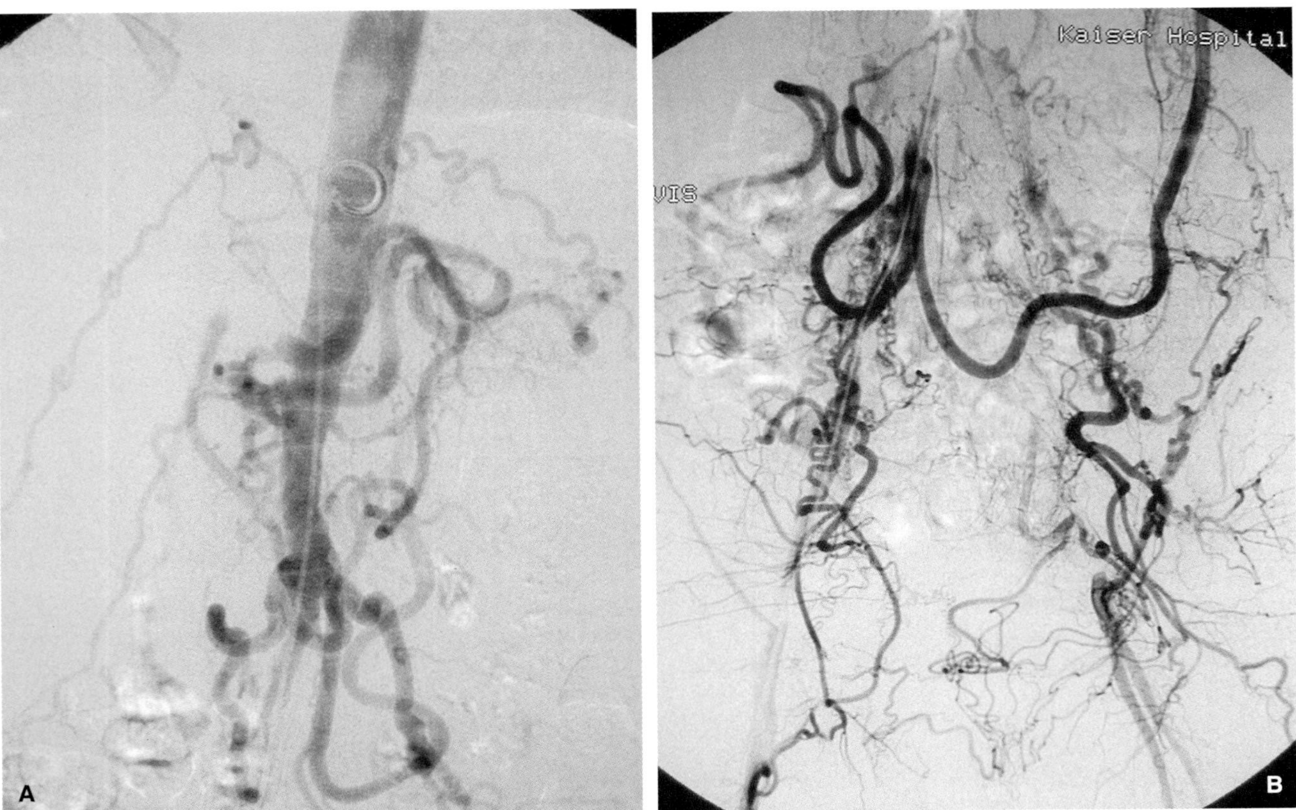

FIGURE 26-2 **A,** Abdominal aortogram in a 43-year-old woman with claudication and renal failure requiring hemodialysis. Note occlusion of the superior mesenteric artery as well as of the bilateral renal and iliac arteries. The patient underwent aortobifemoral grafting both to treat her symptoms and to allow an inflow source for a subsequent renal transplant. **B,** Note the reconstitution of the iliac arteries via hemorrhoidal and mesenteric collateral vessels.

■ CLASSIFICATION

To be clinically useful, a classification system for TA must take into account regions of disease activity (Table 26-4). Ueno's classification, first published in 1967, divided TA into three types on the basis of arterial involvement.[64] Type I described disease of the arch and its branches; type II, disease of the descending thoracic and abdominal aorta and branches; and type III, the combination of these two, which is the most common variant (Fig. 26-4). With recognition of pulmonary artery involvement in TA, Lupi-Herrera and colleagues[65] defined type IV disease as any TA with this feature. In 1994, at the Tokyo International Conference on Takayasu Arteritis, a new classification system was proposed; it was published later that year.[66] Type I disease affects only the innominate, carotid, and subclavian arteries. Type IIa involves the ascending aorta, aortic arch, and great vessels, whereas IIb includes the former plus the descending thoracic aorta. Type III describes diseases affecting the descending thoracic aorta as well as the abdominal aorta and its branches. Type IV involves only the abdominal aorta and its branches. Finally, type V disease affects the entire aorta and branches. This system is further subclassified to indicate coronary or pulmonary involvement with a C(+) or P(+), respectively.

Classification systems also exist to stratify the severity of disease. Ishikawa's prognostic criteria are used most commonly in modern series.[67] This system is based on three factors: (1) presence of major complications (microaneurysm formation, severe hypertension, severe aortic regurgitation, aortic aneurysm); (2) the nature of progression of the disease (crescendo symptom pattern or nonprogressive course); and (3) the ESR. There are other systems for classifying specific physical findings in TA. For example, the Uyama-Asayama system uses retinal findings to take into account central nervous system circulatory disturbances.[68]

■ RADIOLOGIC EVALUATION

Various invasive and noninvasive studies are available for both the diagnosis and classification of TA. Catheter angiography remains an important technique, but as in other areas, noninvasive tests are becoming more important and more useful. Unfortunately, no specific laboratory test is available to confirm the diagnosis of TA. Thus, evaluation of the patient in whom the disease is suspected must rely on radiologic studies.

Since the mid 1960s, many authorities on TA have recommended complete angiography of all possibly affected sites in patients who might have TA.[69,70] This dictum was put forth by the American College of Radiology as recently as 1990.[10] Clearly, when intervention is being considered, formal angiography is warranted. In early stages of the disease, however, other modalities are more sensitive in

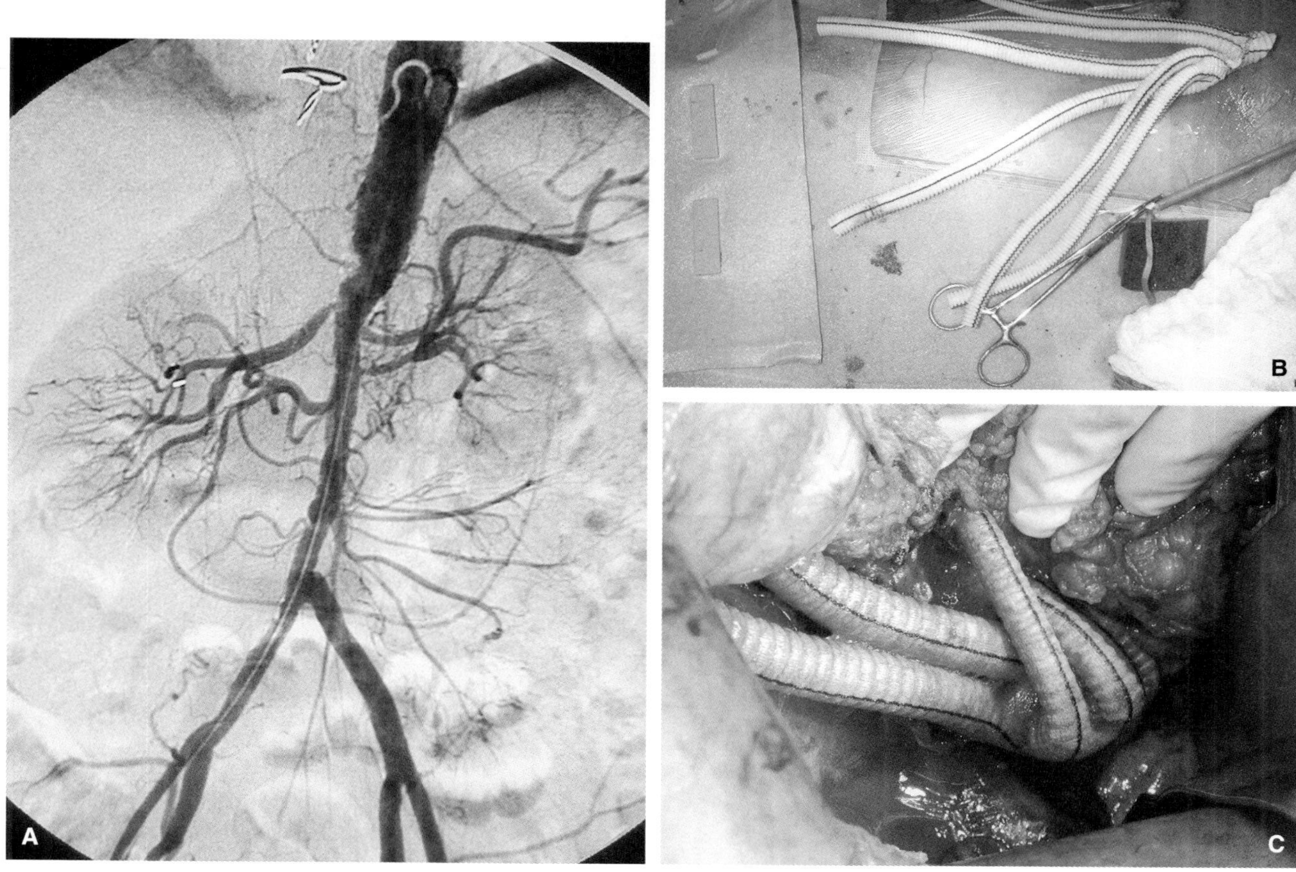

FIGURE 26-3 **A,** Aortogram from a 54-year-old woman with mesenteric steal who experienced abdominal pain with ambulation. Note lesions of both renal arteries, superior mesenteric artery, and celiac and iliac arteries. **B** and **C,** Intraoperative photographs. Reconstruction via aorto–bi-iliac bypass grafting was carried out with separate limbs to each of the diseased branches. This patient also had aortic arch disease, which was asymptomatic and so was not addressed.

Table 26-4 Comparison of Various Classification Systems for Takayasu's Arteritis

Ueno classification:	
Type I	Disease of the aortic arch and its branches
Type II	Disease confined to the descending thoracic and abdominal aorta
Type III	Combination of types I and II
Type IV	Any of the above features with pulmonary artery involvement (Lupi-Herrera modification)
Nasu classification:	
Type I	Disease limited to vessels originating from the aortic arch
Type II	Also involves aortic root and arch
Type III	Localized to subdiaphragmatic aorta
Type IV	Entire aorta and its branches involved
Tokyo International Conference on Takayasu's Arteritis classification*:	
Type I	Aortic arch branches alone
Type IIa	Ascending aorta, arch and branches
Type IIb	IIa plus descending thoracic aorta
Type III	Descending thoracic aorta and abdominal aorta/branches
Type IV	Abdominal aorta/branches
Type V	Entire aorta and branches

*Modification of any with C(+) for coronary and P(+) for pulmonary artery involvement, respectively.

detecting TA. Before there are obvious stenotic, occlusive, or aneurysmal changes, the earliest radiographic finding is thickening of the involved vessel walls. Cross-sectional images obtained by both computed tomography (CT) and magnetic resonance imaging (MRI) can demonstrate these changes.[48] In addition, both of these techniques can be used during medical therapy of TA to assess response to treatment.[71,72] These findings are usually present in the aorta, the pulmonary artery, or both.

Once arterial lesions have progressed, angiography, CT, MRI, and ultrasound all have applications. CT and MR angiography (MRA) can commonly be used in place of formal angiography or as screening tests before catheter angiography is contemplated. Duplex scanning has also been found useful in the diagnosis and evaluation of TA, particularly in patients with carotid artery involvement. Common carotid disease with homogeneous, long, and concentric lesions that spare the bifurcation is highly suggestive of TA.[73,74] Cantu and associates[75] evaluated 21 consecutive patients with TA using a combination of MRA, duplex imaging, and transcranial Doppler ultrasound examination. These investigators were able to demonstrate at least one

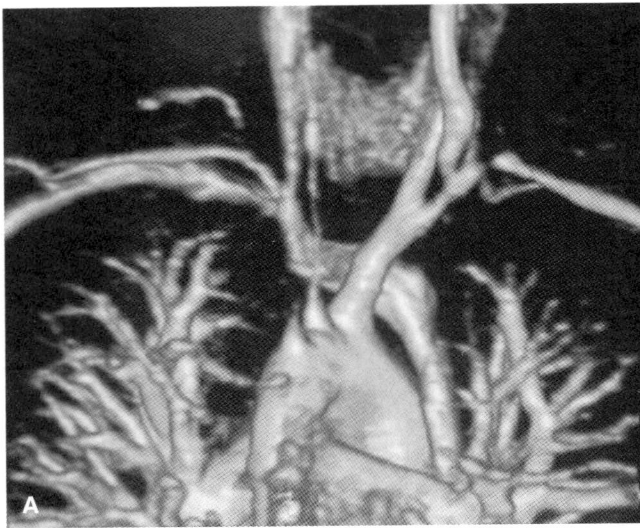

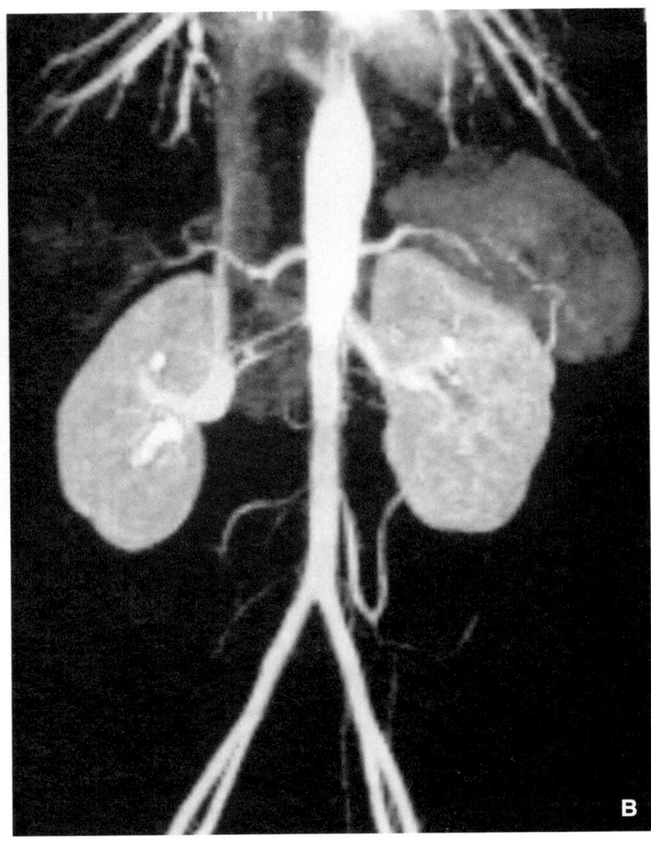

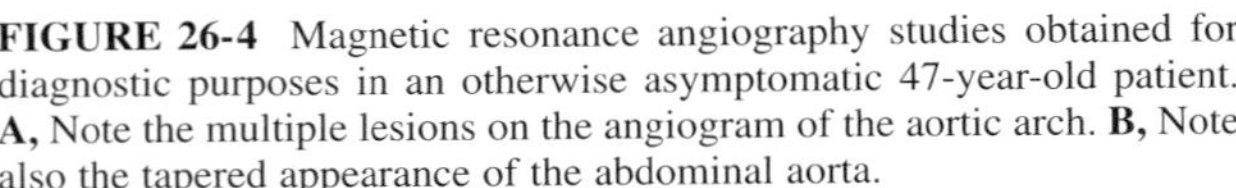

FIGURE 26-4 Magnetic resonance angiography studies obtained for diagnostic purposes in an otherwise asymptomatic 47-year-old patient. **A,** Note the multiple lesions on the angiogram of the aortic arch. **B,** Note also the tapered appearance of the abdominal aorta.

abnormality of the extracranial or intracranial vessels in 95% of the patients. The main limitation of sonography in this setting is that some patients with TA have no carotid involvement; the technique is not as useful in evaluating the more commonly involved subclavian system. Waveform analysis can indirectly demonstrate proximal lesions, and likewise can frequently be used to evaluate the abdominal aorta and visceral and renal branches. When properly performed and focused, these noninvasive studies can be used as screening and diagnostic tests for TA.[76,77]

■ TREATMENT

In addressing treatment strategies for TA, it is useful to consider two distinct clinical problems, with the understanding that there may be significant overlap in their occurrence. In patients diagnosed early in the course of the disease, treatment is directed at the systemic inflammatory response. Most cases respond favorably to steroid therapy. However, a large number of patients do not stay in remission when these drugs are discontinued.[40] In addition, there is some evidence that control of symptoms at this stage of disease does not necessarily preclude the development of arterial sequelae.[78] These lesions and their complications make up the second group of clinical problems requiring treatment.

Steroids are effective in treating the acute inflammation of TA. Numerous reports support steroid therapy, using a variety of techniques to measure disease response.[79-81] There is regional variability in treatment regimens. Ishikawa reports a large series of patients from Japan who received prednisolone (30 to 50 mg/day); dosage was tapered using the ESR as an index of disease activity.[80] Most patients continued their treatment for several years, staying on doses as high as 15 mg/day. A decade after starting therapy, half of the patients were still taking prednisolone. The NIH series in the United States differs in several regards, the most important of which are the use of prednisone (1 mg/kg/day) and the early addition of a cytotoxic drug if either steroids were not effective or the steroid dosage could not be tapered and stopped after 90 days.[40,82] As in the Japanese series, more than half of the patients in the U.S. study did not stay in remission when drug therapy was discontinued.

Cytotoxic drugs used for TA include cyclophosphamide, methotrexate, and azathioprine. "Lessons" reported by Hoffman[78] from the NIH experience suggest that methotrexate may be especially effective and may have many fewer side effects than the other agents. When considering medical therapy, both the clinician and the patient must recognize the limitations of treatment but also realize that some patients attain stable remission with therapy. Indeed, flareup is unusual if remission lasting 5 years can be attained.[83]

A critical issue in the evaluation of medical therapy is the difficulty in assessing disease activity in TA. As has already been discussed, ESR alone is commonly a poor indicator of TA progression. Some of the newer measurements available, such as of IL-6 and RANTES, have not yet been studied conclusively in the clinical realm. Thus, the clinician is left with ESR, signs of ischemia or other arterial damage, radiographic changes, and presence of systemic features such as fevers, myalgias, and other vague symptoms.[40] Refinements of these parameters and incorporation of new techniques may lead to more objective evaluation of disease activity in TA.

Open surgical intervention has been the mainstay of treatment for many years, but catheter-based procedures are finding greater application. The most significant problem with the latter is the absence of long-term information about results. Clearly, any number of clinical conditions can arise from TA, and the incidence of the various problems has already been addressed. To a much greater extent than atherosclerosis, TA requires tailoring of therapy to the individual patient. In addition, the systemic nature of the disease must be included in the treatment. Reported experience suggests a higher risk of surgical complications when the operations are undertaken during active disease.[53] In addition, despite the fact that patients with TA are generally younger than those with atherosclerosis, cardiac risk is significantly higher for patients with TA than for age-matched controls.[84-86] In the series reported by Hall and colleagues,[32] more than 25% of the patients had coronary disease with significant ischemia, and almost 60% had hypertension. Almost 80% of patients in the study reported by Panja and coworkers had a cardiac ejection fraction of less than 45%.[61]

Fortunately, most surgical and interventional procedures can be performed electively in patients with TA, allowing for appropriate consideration of cardiac and other issues during preoperative planning. There has historically been concern about using diseased vessels as target vessels. It is advisable to avoid using grossly involved arteries. However, several studies have documented the presence of histologically involved vessel margins in up to 40% of those deemed on gross examination to be free of disease.[42,87,88] This finding was challenged by Robbs and associates, who showed that gross inspection correlated well with pathologic findings[56]; their experience has not been repeated in other reports. It is not clear what effect microscopic disease has on later complications, but it is not thought to be a contraindication to arterial reconstruction. Vessel suitability can be determined on the basis of angiographic appearance and gross inspection. A series with 20-year follow-up reported an overall anastomotic aneurysm rate of 12.5% in TA; multivariate analysis showed treatment of aneurysmal lesions to be the only predictor of false aneurysm formation.[89] Bypass remains the standard operative approach to most TA lesions.[51] Endarterectomy is a poor choice because of the extensive inflammation and transmural nature of the disease process.

One of the primary indications for intervention in TA is cerebrovascular disease. Stroke in this setting is generally regarded to be due to decreased flow, not embolism.[50] There are no data to confirm this belief, although some angiographic data in patients with TA and stroke show the presence of complete occlusive lesions of carotid or innominate arteries.[90] Thus, patients with severe stenoses or occlusion of the innominate or carotid arteries are considered candidates for operative reconstruction. This treatment usually takes the form of a bypass graft from the ascending aorta to an uninvolved distal target site. The ascending aorta is chosen because of the relative infrequency with which it is involved in the disease process. A 10-mm synthetic graft can be sewn after the placement of a side-biting clamp, and additional limbs can be added if necessary for bypass to other vessels.

Interest has focused on the use of balloon angioplasty and stents for cerebrovascular disease in TA. Early reports of angioplasty alone suggested that restenosis rates compared unfavorably with those seen in the treatment of atherosclerotic disease.[91,92] Series with stenting are small, but successful cases have been reported.[92a] Takahashi and associates[93] reported their experience in stenting of bilateral common carotid arteries, innominate artery, and left subclavian artery in a patient with severe TA. Although the patient had periods of active inflammatory disease during the 2-year follow-up, no restenosis was reported. In addition, Sharma and colleagues[94] reported on six patients who underwent carotid angioplasty and stenting. The procedure was successful in five patients, the one failure representing failure to cross the lesion with a guidewire. Two of the patients had recurrence of symptoms within 5 months with extensive in-stent restenosis. Our own experience with angioplasty and stenting also suggests a high rate of recurrent symptoms and restenosis. Clearly, more data and longer follow-up are required before definitive conclusions can be drawn about the treatment of TA cerebrovascular disease by these means.

Overlap in treatment exists between the cerebrovascular disease and subclavian–upper extremity symptoms. Disease of the subclavian artery is usually approached as previously described, the disease-free ascending aorta being used for proximal blood supply and the distal subclavian or infraclavicular axillary artery as the target. Sharma and colleagues reported their angioplasty experience with subclavian disease in five patients with TA.[94] Six lesions were treated, half with stents and the other half with angioplasty alone. In their reported period of follow-up (4 to 10 months), there were no complications, and all patients were without clinical evidence of treatment failure. Other series suggest that stents are beneficial in this position.[88,89] This procedure may be a useful treatment modality, but larger series with longer follow-up are needed.

In patients with lower extremity symptoms due to ischemia, it is important to remember that TA, unlike atherosclerotic disease, often involves the midsegment of the infrarenal aorta. Thus, inflow frequently must be re-established from a suprarenal source. Giordano has recommended distal thoracic aorta to iliac bypasses in this setting.[51] Others use the supraceliac segment of the abdominal aorta, bypassing to a single iliac artery with retrograde perfusion of the contralateral limb via the disease-free distal aorta and bifurcation. Of course, therapy must be tailored to the individual patient, and at times, standard aortofemoral or aortoiliac grafts are more appropriate. Rarely, extensive stenosis of the aorta can be treated with endarterectomy if visceral and renal disease must also be treated. However, as discussed previously, endarterectomy can be particularly challenging because of the extensive inflammation encountered in TA.

Less invasive endovascular therapy has been reported for treatment of lower extremity symptoms. Keith and associates[95] presented their experience with angioplasty and stenting of a descending aortic coarctation in a woman with both severe refractory hypertension and claudication. At 2-year follow-up, the patient's hypertension was well controlled and she was no longer experiencing claudication. Sharma and coworkers reported on nine patients undergoing aortic angioplasty for claudication, four of whom also had stent placement.[94] All patients were reportedly doing well at 6-month follow-up, although one required additional stent placement to cover a saccular aneurysm. As with other areas, more data and longer follow-up are needed before this approach can be universally recommended.

Renal stenosis and renal artery hypertension in patients with TA have traditionally been treated with vein bypass, often with the same inflow limitations encountered in the planning of aortic bypass. Experience with balloon angioplasty is more extensive for TA renal artery disease than for other areas. Initial technical success can be obtained in roughly 90% of patients.[96] Also, better midterm information is available. S. Sharma and coworkers published their experience with 96 lesions (66 patients) and a mean follow-up of 22 months (range 4 to 84 months).[94] There was an 89% "clinical" success rate, which these investigators defined as either improvement or cure. At follow-up, there was a 16% rate of restenosis. Complications in this series were two groin hematomas and a renal vein injury. In B.K. Sharma's series of 6 lesions in 5 patients with TA and renal artery stenosis, 4 lesions were treated with angioplasty alone, and 2 received stents.[92a] Initial success was attained in all cases, and improvement or cure of hypertension was reported at 6-month follow-up.

It is not yet clear whether primary stenting should be performed in all cases of renal artery angioplasty in TA. The transmural nature of these lesions suggests that there is a theoretical benefit to stent placement. In cases for which catheter-based therapies are unsuccessful, traditional surgical modalities should be pursued. Weaver and coworkers[97] reported their experience with 36 renal revascularization procedures in 27 patients with TA, demonstrating 5-year primary and secondary patency rates of 79% and 89%, respectively. All but two of these procedures were either aortorenal bypasses or renal artery re-implantations. Average postoperative blood pressure was reduced to 132 mm Hg systolic/79 mm Hg diastolic, with significant increases in glomerular filtration rates. It is not known whether catheter-based therapies will be able to match these results. Longer follow-up is needed in this younger group of patients in order to determine the role of angioplasty and stenting in TA.

The indications for repair of aneurysms in TA probably mirror those for non-TA aneurysms. Although the incidence of rupture is probably lower for TA aneurysms, these lesions also occur in a much younger patient population, yielding a higher overall risk of rupture over a lifetime.[55] Long-term surveillance of these patients is of particular importance, given the probable higher incidence of anastomotic disruption after TA aneurysm repair.

Intervention may also be required for a variety of other conditions. Clinically significant aortic regurgitation may occur in up to 44% of patients with TA, and aortic valve repair or replacement is being performed more commonly for this condition.[98,99] Conventional coronary revascularization may also have to be undertaken, although in the excellent review of 106 patients with TA requiring surgery published by Miyata and colleagues, none required coronary artery bypass grafting.[101] Although the ascending aorta is typically spared, there are reports of aneurysm repairs in this location.[102] Other procedures may be indicated, and the individual patient's presentation must always be considered.

Long-term outcomes after operative intervention for TA are generally limited to small series. However, Miyata and colleagues recently reported long-term follow-up on survival of patients with TA who required surgery.[101] This study included patients undergoing operation between 1955 and 1995 at the Second Department of Surgery, The University of Tokyo. Patients were followed for between 8 months and almost 42 years. The study group was classified as to type of disease by Ueno's criteria and to severity using the Ishikawa system as previously described. Primary 10-year patency rates were 88% for carotid grafts, 64% for subclavian grafts, 100% for aorto-aortic grafts, 68% for renal grafts, and 67% for mesenteric grafts. There were 31 late deaths in the series, the most common causes of which were congestive heart failure (13 patients) and anastomotic false aneurysm (5 patients). Overall survival for patients surviving their initial operation (there were three operative deaths) was 73.5% 20 years after surgery. Interestingly, the Ishikawa classification system had no effect on overall survival for these patients. When the data were subjected to Cox regression analysis, age at the time of operation was the only factor associated with survival outcome. Patients older than 35 years at the time of surgery had a 2.74-fold higher risk of dying than younger patients.

■ CONCLUSIONS

TA has a varied presentation leading to a host of clinical problems for which the vascular surgeon may be consulted. Because it is an uncommon disorder, many of the treatment decisions must be made based on limited information, particularly with regard to the newer catheter-based interventions. Both the immediate vascular sequelae and the systemic nature of the illness must be taken into account before one embarks on treatment. A multidisciplinary approach is appropriate, and careful long-term follow-up is necessary for this diverse and challenging group of patients.

■ REFERENCES

1. Numano F: Differences in clinical presentation and outcome in different countries for Takayasu's arteritis. Curr Opin Rheumatol 9:12-15, 1997.
2. Kerr GS: Takayasu's arteritis. Rheum Dis Clin North Am 21:1041-1058, 1995.
3. Sharma BK, Jain S, Sagar S: Systemic manifestations of Takayasu's arteritis: The expanding spectrum. Int J Cardiol 54(Suppl):S173-S176, 1996.
4. Weyland CM, Goronzy JJ: Medium- and large-vessel vasculitis. N Engl J Med 349:160-169, 2003.
5. Vanoli M, Bacchiani G, Origg L, Scorza R: Takayasu's arteritis: A changing disease. J Nephrol 14:497-505, 2001.
6. Numano F: The story of Takayasu arteritis. Rheumatology 41:103-106, 2002.
7. Numano F, Kakuta T: Takayasu arteritis—five doctors in the history of Takayasu arteritis. Int J Cardiol 54(Suppl):S1-S10, 1996.

8. Ueda H, Morooka S, Ito I, et al: Clinical observation of 52 cases of aortitis syndrome. Jpn Heart J 10:227-284, 1969.
9. Ishikawa K: Diagnostic approach and proposed criteria for the clinical diagnosis of Takayasu's arteriopathy. J Am Coll Cardiol 12:964-972, 1988.
10. Arend WP, Michel BA, Bloch DA: The American College of Rheumatology 1990 criteria for the classification of Takayasu's arteritis. Arthritis Rheum 33:1129-1134, 1990.
11. Sharma BK, Iliskovic NS, Singal PK: Takayasu's arteritis may be underdiagnosed in North America. Can J Cardiol 11:311-316, 1995.
12. Cid MC, Font C, Coll-Vincent B, et al: Large vessel vasculitides. Curr Opin Rheumatol 10:18-28, 1998.
13. Sharma BK, Jain S, Suri S, et al: Diagnostic criteria for Takayasu's arteritis. Int J Cardiol 54(Suppl):S141-S147, 1996.
14. Noris M: Pathogenesis of Takayasu's arteritis. J Nephrol 24:506-513, 2001.
15. Sekiguchi M, Suzuki JI: An overview of Takayasu's arteritis. Heart Vessels Suppl 7:6-10, 1992.
16. Numano F, Kishi Y, Tanaka A, et al: Inflammation and atherosclerosis: Atherosclerotic lesions in Takayasu's arteritis. Ann N Y Acad Sci 902:65-76, 2000.
17. Inder SJ, Bobryshev YV, Cherian SM, et al: Accumulation of lymphocytes, dendritic cells, and granulocytes in the aortic wall affected by Takayasu's disease. Angiology 51:565-579, 2000.
18. Seko Y, Sato O, Takagi, et al: Restricted usage of T-cell receptor Valpha-Vbeta genes in infiltrating cells in aortic tissues in patients with Takayasu's arteritis. Circulation 93:1788-1790, 1996.
19. Noris M, Daina E, Gamba S, et al: Interleukin-6 and RANTES in Takayasu's arteritis: A guide for therapeutic decisions? Circulation 100:427-451, 1999.
20. Dhar J, Ganguly NK, Kumari S, et al: Role of calcium and protein kinase C in the activation of T cells in Takayasu's arteritis. Jpn Heart J 36:341-348, 1995.
21. Grunewald NJ, Lefvert AK: A bias in the alpha beta T cell receptor variable region gene usage in Takayasu's arteritis. Clin Exp Immunol 107:261-268, 1997.
22. Van Seveter G, Shimizu Y, Horgan K: The LFA-1 ligand ICAM-1 provides an important costimulatory signal for T cell receptor-mediated activation of resting T cells. J Immunol 144:4579-4582, 1990.
23. Eichhorn J, Sima D, Thiele B, et al: Anti-endothelial antibodies in Takayasu's arteritis. Circulation 94:2396-2401, 1996.
24. DeBandt M, Kahn MF: Takayasu's arteritis associated with Still's disease in an adult. Clin Exp Rheumatol 9:639-640, 1991.
25. Soloway M, Moir TW, Linton DS: Takayasu's arteritis: Report of a case with unusual findings. Am J Cardiol 25:258-263, 1970.
26. Magaro M, Altomonte L, Mirone L, et al: Seronegative spondarthritis associated with Takayasu's arteritis. Ann Rheum Dis 47:595-597, 1988.
27. Raza K, Karokis D, Kitas GD: Cogan's syndrome with Takayasu's arteritis. Br J Rheumatol 37:369-372, 1998.
28. Igarashi T, Nagaoka S, Matsunaga K, et al: Aortitis syndrome associated with systemic lupus erythematosus. J Rheumatol 17:1251-1252, 1990.
29. Owyang C, Miller LJ, Lie JT, et al: Takayasu's arteritis in Crohn's disease. Gastroenterology 76:825-828, 1979.
30. Khraisis MM, Gladman DD, Dagenais P, et al: HLA antigens in North American patients with Takayasu's arteritis. Arthritis Rheum 35:573, 1992.
31. Yoshida M, Kimura H, Date Y, et al: Comprehensive analysis of HLA genes in Takayasu's arteritis in Japan. Int J Cardiol 54(Suppl):S65-S73, 1996.
32. Hall S, Barr W, Lie JT, et al: Takayasu's arteritis: A study of 32 North American patients. Medicine 64:89-99, 1985.
33. Sagar S, Ganguly NK, Koicha M, et al: Immunopathogenesis of Takayasu's arteritis. Heart Vessels Suppl 7:S85-S90, 1992.
34. Nasu T: Takayasu's truncoarteritis in Japan: A statistical observation of 76 autopsy cases. Pathol Microbiol 43:140-143, 1975.
35. Turkoglu C, Memis A, Payzin S: Takayasu's arteritis in Turkey. Int J Cardiol 54(Suppl):S119-S120, 1996.
36. Vanoli M, Miani S, Amft N, et al: Takayasu's arteritis in Italian patients. Clin Exp Rheumatol 13:45-50, 1995.
37. Waern AU, Andersson P, Hemmingsson A, et al: Takayasu's arteritis: A hospital region based study on occurrence, treatment and prognosis. Angiology 34:311-320, 1983.
38. Di Giacomo V, Meloni F, Transi MG, et al: Takayasu's disease in middle aged women: A clinicopathological study. Angiology 36:70-74, 1985.
39. Kumar S, Subramanyan R, Ravi Mandalam K: Aneurysmal form of aortoarteritis (Takayasu's disease): Analysis of 30 cases. Clin Radiol 42:342-347, 1990.
40. Kerr GS, Hallahan CW, Giordano J, et al: Takayasu arteritis. Ann Intern Med 120:919-928, 1994.
41. Marooka S, Saito Y, Nonaka Y, et al: Clinical features of arteritis syndrome in Japanese women older than 40 years. Am J Cardiol 53:859-863, 1984.
42. Robles M, Reyes PA: Takayasu's arteritis in Mexico: A clinical review of 44 consecutive cases. Clin Exp Rheumatol 4:381-388, 1994.
43. Lagneau P, Michel JB, Vuong PN: Surgical treatment of Takayasu's disease. Ann Surg 205:157-166, 1986.
44. Procter CD, Hollier LH: Takayasu's arteritis and temporal arteritis. Ann Vasc Surg 6:195-198, 1992.
45. Ishikawa K, Maerani S: Long-term outcome for 120 Japanese patients with Takayasu's disease: Clinical and statistical analysis of related prognostic factors. Circulation 90:1855-1860, 1994.
46. Subramanyan R, Joy J, Balakrishnan KG: Natural history of aortoarteritis (Takayasu's disease). Circulation 80:429-437, 1989.
47. Deyu Z, Dijun F, Lisheng L: Takayasu's arteritis in China: A report of 53 cases. Heart Vessels Suppl 7:S32-S36, 1992.
48. Angeli E, Angelo V, Massimo V, et al: The role of radiology in the diagnosis and management of Takayasu's arteritis. J Nephrol 14:514-524, 2001.
49. Massimo V, Giulia B, Origg L, et al: Takayasu's arteritis: A changing disease. J Nephrol 14:497-505, 2001.
50. Yamato M, Lecky JW, Hiramatsu K, et al: Takayasu's arteritis: Radiographic and angiographic findings in 59 patients. Radiology 161:329-334, 1986.
51. Giordano JM: Surgical treatment of Takayasu's arteritis. Int J Cardiol 75:S123-S128, 2000.
52. Lupi-Herrera E, Sanchez-Torres G, Marcushamer J, et al: Takayasu's arteritis: Clinical study of 107 cases. Am Heart J 93:94-103, 1977.
53. Hall S, Buchbinder R: Takayasu's arteritis. Rheum Dis Clin North Am 16:411-422, 1990.
54. Weaver FA, Yellin AE, Campen DH, et al: Surgical procedures in the management of Takayasu's arteritis. J Vasc Surg 12:429-437, 1990.
55. Haas A, Stiehm ER: Takayasu's arteritis presenting as pulmonary hypertension. Am J Dis Child 140:372-374, 1986.
56. Robbs JV, Abdoll-Carrim A, Kadwa AM: Arterial reconstruction for nonspecific arteritis (Takayasu's disease). Eur J Vasc Surg 8:401-407, 1994.
57. Matsumura K, Hirano T, Takeda K, et al: Incidence of aneurysms in Takayasu's arteritis. Angiology 42:308-315, 1991.
58. Chieh JL, Brevetti LS, Scholz PM, et al: Multiple isolated aneurysms in a case of "burned out" Takayasu aortitis. J Vasc Surg 37:1094-1097, 2002.
59. Tabata M, Kitagawa T, Saito T, et al: Extracranial carotid aneurysm in Takayasu's arteritis. J Vasc Surg 34:739-742, 2001.
60. Park JH, Han MC, Kim SH: Takayasu's arteritis: Angiographic findings and results of angioplasty. Am J Radiol 153:1069-1074, 1989.
61. Panja M, Kar AK, Dutta AL, et al: Cardiac involvement in non-specific aorto-arteritis. Int J Cardiol 34:289-295, 1992.
62. Panja M, Sarkar C, Kar AK, et al: Coronary artery lesions in Takayasu's arteritis: Clinical and angiographic study. J Assoc Physicians India 46:678-681, 1998.

63. Amano J, Suzuki A, Tanaka H, Sunamori M: Surgical treatment for annuloaortic ectasia in Takayasu arteritis. Int J Cardiol 66:S197-S202, 1998.
64. Ueno A, Awane Y, Wakabayashi A, et al: Successfully operated obliterative brachiocephalic arteritis (Takayasu's) associated with elongated coarctation. Jpn Heart J 8:538-554, 1967.
65. Lupi-Herrera E, Sanches-Torres G, Horwitz S: Pulmonary artery involvement in Takayasu's arteritis. Chest 67:69-74, 1975.
66. Hata A, Makoto N, Moriwaki R, et al: Angiographic findings of Takayasu arteritis: New classification. Int J Cardiol 54:S155-S163, 1996.
67. Ishikawa K: Patterns of symptoms and prognosis in occlusive thromboaortopathy (Takayasu's disease). J Am Coll Cardiol 8:1041-1046, 1986.
68. Uyama M, Asayama K: Retinal vascular changes in Takayasu's disease (pulseless disease)—occurrence and evolution of the lesion. Doc Ophthalmol Proc 9:549-554, 1976.
69. Grollma JH Jr, Hanafee W: The roentgen diagnosis of Takayasu's arteritis. Radiology 83:387-395, 1964.
70. Lande A, Berkman YM: Aortitis: Pathologic, clinical, and arteriographic review. Radiol Clin North Am 14:219-240, 1976.
71. Hayashi K, Fukushima T, Matsunage N, et al: Takayasu's arteritis: Decrease in aortic wall thickening following steroid therapy, documented by CT. Br J Radiol 59:281-283, 1986.
72. Tanigawa K, Eguchi K, Kitamura Y: Magnetic resonance imaging detection of aortic and pulmonary artery with CT angiography. Radiology 196:89-93, 1995.
73. Sun Y, Yip P, Jeng J: Ultrasonographic study and long-term follow-up of Takayasu's arteritis. Stroke 27:2178-2182, 1996.
74. Maeda H, Handa N, Matsumoto M: Carotid lesions detected by B-mode ultrasonography in Takayasu's arteritis: Macaroni sign as an indicator of the disease. Ultrasound Med Biol 17:695-701, 1991
75. Cantu C, Pineda C, Barinagarrementeria F, et al: Noninvasive cerebrovascular assessment of Takayasu arteritis. Stroke 31:2197-2202, 2000.
76. Angeli E, Salvioni M, Venturini M: Diagnosis of Takayasu's arteritis with color Doppler sonography: Comparison with angiographic findings. Presented at the11th European Congress of Radiology (ECR), Vienna, March 7-12, 1999.
77. Antoniou A, Vlahos L, Mourikis D: Abdominal Takayasu's arteritis: Imaging with color duplex sonography. Eur Radiol 8:547-549, 1998.
78. Hoffman GS: Takayasu's arteritis: Lesson from the American National Institutes of Health experience. Int J Cardiol 54(Suppl):S83-S86, 1996.
79. Fraga A, Mintz JB, Valle L, et al: Takayasu's arteritis: Frequency of systemic manifestations and favorable response to maintenance steroid therapy with adrenocorticosteroids. Arthritis Rheum 15:617-624, 1972.
80. Ishikawa K: Effects of prednisolone therapy on arterial angiographic features in Takayasu's disease. Am J Cardiol 68:410-413, 1991.
81. Shelhamer JH, Volkman DJ, Parrillo JE, et al: Takayasu's arteritis and its therapy. Ann Intern Med 103:121-126, 1985.
82. Hoffman GS, Leavitt RY, Kerr GS, et al: Treatment of glucocorticoid-resistant or relapsing Takayasu's arteritis with methotrexate. Arthritis Rheum 37:578-582, 1994.
83. Sabbadini MG, Bozzolo E, Baldissera E, et al: Takayasu's arteritis: Therapeutic strategies. J Nephrol 14:525-531, 2001.
84. Talwar KD, Kumar K, Copra P, et al: Cardiac involvement in non-specific aortoarteritis (Takayasu's arteritis). Am Heart J 122:1666-1670, 1991.
85. Jolly M, Bartholomew JR, Flamm SD, et al: Angina and coronary ostial lesions in a young woman as a presentation of Takayasu's arteritis. Cardiovasc Surg 7:443-446, 1999.
86. Kathirvel S, Chavan S, Arya VK, et al: Anesthetic management of patients with Takayasu's arteritis: A case series and review. Anesth Analg 93:60-65, 2001.
87. Kieffer E, Piquois AL, Bertal A, et al: Reconstructive surgery of the renal arteries in Takayasu's disease. Ann Vasc Surg 4:156-165, 1990.
88. Sparks SR, Chock A, Seslar S, et al: Surgical treatment of Takayasu's arteritis: Case report and literature review. Ann Vasc Surg 14:125-129, 2000.
89. Miyata T, Sato O, Deguchi J, et al: Anastomotic aneurysms after surgical treatment of Takayasu's arteritis: A 40-year experience. J Vasc Surg 27:438-445, 1998.
90. Giordano J, Leavitt RY, Hoffman G, et al: Experience with surgical treatment of Takayasu's disease. Surgery 109:252-258, 1991.
91. Joseph S, Mandalam KR, Rao VR, et al: Percutaneous transluminal angioplasty of the subclavian artery in nonspecific aortoarteritis: Results of long-term follow-up. J Vasc Intervent Radiol 5:573-580, 1994.
92. Tyagi S, Verma PK, Gambhir DS, et al: Early and long-term results of subclavian angioplasty in aortoarteritis (Takayasu disease): Comparison with atherosclerosis. Cardiovasc Intervent Radiol 21:219-224, 1998.
92a. Sharma S, Gupta H, Saxena A, et al: Results of renal angioplasty in nonspecific aorto-arteritis. J Vasc Intervent Radiol 9:429-435, 1998.
93. Takahashi JC, Nobuyuki S, Manaka H, et al: Multiple supra-aortic stenting for Takayasu arteritis: Extensive revascularization and two-year follow-up. Am J Neuroradiol 23:790-793, 2002.
94. Sharma BK, Jain S, Bali HK, et al: A follow-up study of balloon angioplasty and de-novo stenting in Takayasu arteritis. Int J Cardiol 75:S147-S152, 2000.
95. Keith DS, Markey B, Schiedler M: Successful long-term stenting of an atypical descending aortic coarctation. J Vasc Surg 35:166-167, 2002.
96. Sharma S, Saxena A, Talwar KK, et al: Renal artery stenosis caused by nonspecific arteritis (Takayasu's disease): Results of treatment with percutaneous transluminal angioplasty. Am J Radiol 158:417-422, 1982.
97. Weaver FA, Kumar SR, Yellin AE, et al: Renal revascularization in Takayasu arteritis-induced renal artery stenosis. J Vasc Surg 39:749-757, 2004.
98. Isomura T, Hisatomi K, Yanagi I, et al: The surgical treatment of aortic regurgitation secondary to aortitis. Ann Thorac Surg 45:181-185, 1988.
99. Suzuki A, Amano J, Tanaka H, et al: Surgical consideration of aortitis involving the aortic root. Circulation 80:I222-I232, 1989.
100. Amano J, Suzuki A: Coronary artery involvement in Takayasu's arteritis: Collective review and guideline for surgical treatment. J Thorac Cardiovasc Surg 102:554-560, 1991.
101. Miyata T, Sato O, Koyama H, et al: Long-term survival after surgical treatment of patients with Takayasu's arteritis. Circulation 108:1474-1480, 2003.
102. Sasaki S, Yasuda K, Takigami K, et al: Takayasu's arteritis complicating annuloaortic ectasia (AAE) treated with modified Bentall procedure. J Cardiovasc Surg 38:381-384, 1997.

Chapter

27

Arterial Fibrodysplasia

JAMES C. STANLEY, MD
THOMAS W. WAKEFIELD, MD

Arterial fibrodysplasia encompasses a heterogeneous group of nonatherosclerotic occlusive and aneurysmal diseases. Principal forms of arterial fibrodysplastic stenoses include (1) intimal fibroplasia, (2) medial hyperplasia, (3) medial fibroplasia, and (4) perimedial dysplasia.[129] The first two entities represent distinctly different pathologic processes, whereas the latter two appear to represent a continuum of disease. Compounding this classification are hypoplastic dysplastic vessels occurring as true developmental lesions. Various combinations of dysplastic lesions exist, as do other less easily categorized vessel wall derangements. It is important to distinguish primary arterial dysplasia from secondary dysplasia associated with earlier inflammatory events, physical insults, and other distinct disease entities.

Dysplastic diseases are known to affect the following:

- Renal arteries
- Extracranial and intracranial cerebral arteries
- Axillary, subclavian, and brachial arteries
- Celiac, superior mesenteric, and inferior mesenteric arteries and their branches
- Iliac, femoral, popliteal, tibial, and peroneal arteries
- Aorta

Venous involvement has been reported in the superficial veins of the lower extremity, as well as in the renal vein.[36,56,105] Dysplastic disease of the pulmonary arteries has been reported and is exceedingly rare.[11] Existence of primary venous fibrodysplasia is controversial.

Complications of arterial fibrodysplasia, namely macroaneurysms, dissections, and arteriovenous fistulae, should be classified as "secondary" events and differentiated from the primary fibrodysplastic lesion. Arterial dysplasia, or the predisposition to this disease, represents a systemic arteriopathy in most instances, although discussions on this subject usually focus on the specific vessels involved.[73,74] The purpose of this chapter is to present salient pathologic and clinical features of arterial fibrodysplasia in specific vessels. Treatment options are considered elsewhere in this text.

■ RENAL ARTERIES

The renal artery is the most common site of arterial dysplasia. The precise incidence of renal artery dysplastic disease in the general population is unknown, but it generally has been said to be less than 0.5%. The frequency among black hypertensive patients appears to be even lower.[108] Differences in the definition of this disease may explain variances in reported estimates of its frequency. In a review of otherwise healthy candidates to become kidney donors, the incidence of fibromuscular dysplasia was 4.4%.[4] One might anticipate that the incidence of renal artery dysplasia in patients with hypertension would be even greater.

Renal artery dysplasia, first described in 1938,[64] is second only to atherosclerosis as the most common cause of surgically correctable hypertension. The entire spectrum of dysplastic disease affects the renal artery. The specific types of renal artery fibrodysplasia warrant separate consideration.

Forms of Renal Artery Fibrodysplasia

Intimal fibroplasia of the renal artery affects male and female patients with equal frequency. This lesion accounts for approximately 5% of all dysplastic renal artery stenoses and is observed in infants, adolescents, and young adults more often than in older people. Primary intimal fibroplasia is usually unilateral and most often affects the main renal artery, usually occurring as a smooth focal stenosis (Fig. 27-1A). Segmental vessel involvement is a less common manifestation of intimal disease. The latter usually presents as weblike lesions (Fig. 27-1B). Primary intimal fibroplasia is characterized by subendothelial mesenchymal cells that are irregularly arranged within a loose matrix of fibrous connective tissue and project into the vessel lumen (Fig. 27-2). The internal elastic lamina, although occasionally disrupted, is always identifiable. Primary intimal proliferation is usually circumferential. The cause of primary intimal fibroplasia is unknown. In some cases, it appears to represent persistent fetal arterial musculoelastic cushions, similar to the intimal cushions occurring at cerebral artery bifurcations in adults. Lipid-containing foam cells and inflammatory cells are not part of this disease. Medial and adventitial tissues are usually normal in these dysplastic vessels.

Secondary intimal fibroplasia is often difficult to differentiate from primary intimal disease. Some secondary lesions occur with developmental ostial lesions or advanced medial dysplasia as a likely consequence of altered flow through these stenoses (Fig. 27-3). More than half these lesions are bilateral. Blunt vascular trauma or intraluminal insults following thrombosis may contribute to other secondary lesions, with medial and adventitial structures in such cases appearing relatively uninvolved (Fig. 27-4). Long, tubular stenoses may represent secondary disease occurring as a consequence of recanalization of a previously thrombosed artery (Fig. 27-5). In this regard, certain cases

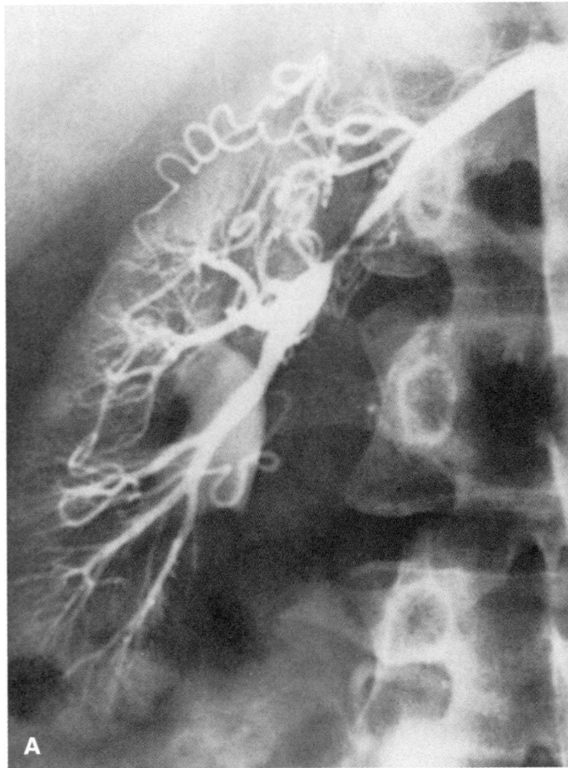

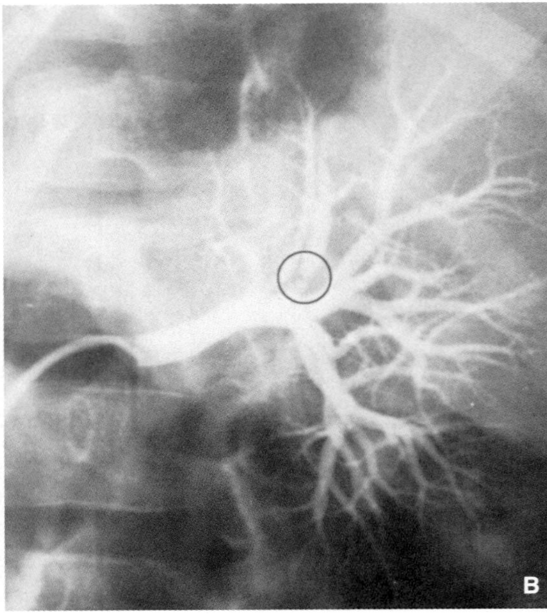

FIGURE 27-1 Primary intimal fibroplasia. **A,** Focal stenosis of the mid-portion of the main renal artery in a young adult. **B,** Intraparenchymal weblike stenosis of a segmental artery in a child. (**A,** From Stanley JC, Fry WJ: Renovascular hypertension secondary to arterial fibrodysplasia in adults: Criteria for operation and results of surgical therapy. Arch Surg 110:922-928, 1975. **B,** From Stanley JC, Fry WJ: Pediatric renal artery occlusive disease and renovascular hypertension: Etiology, diagnosis, and operative treatment. Arch Surg 116:669-676, 1981.)

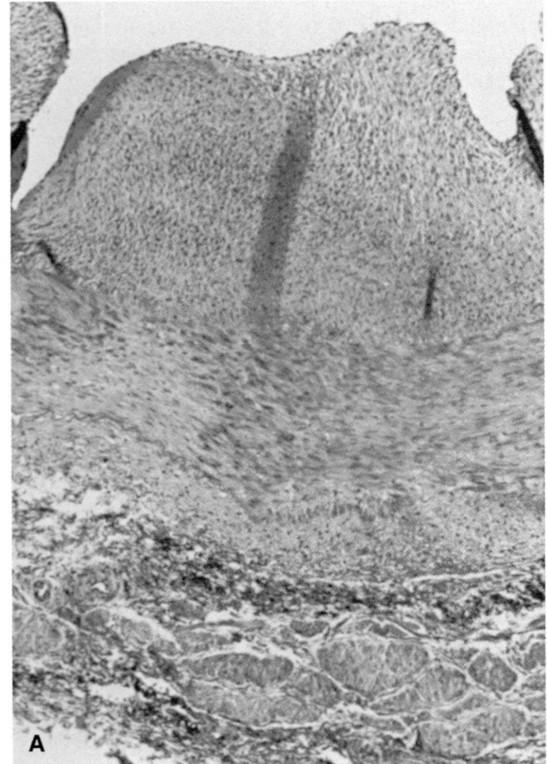

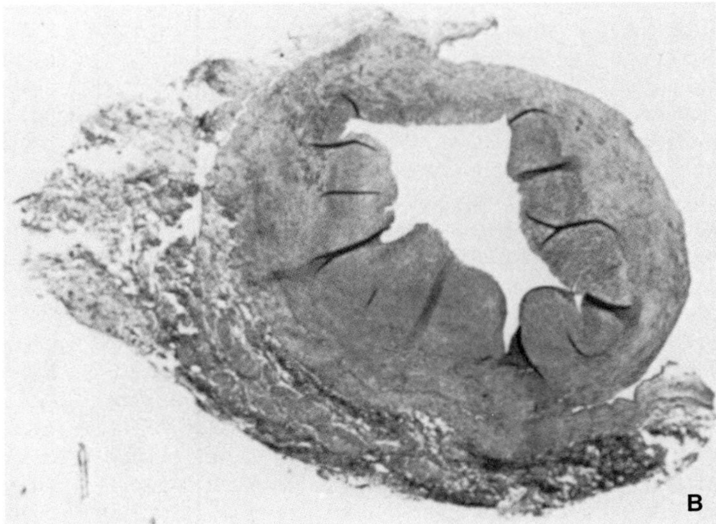

FIGURE 27-2 Primary intimal fibroplasia. **A,** Subendothelial mesenchymal cells within a loose fibrous connective tissue matrix are noted above an intact internal elastic lamina, a normal media, and normal adventitial tissues (×100). **B,** Luminal encroachments by this primary form of intimal fibroplasia are usually circumferential (×35). (**A** and **B,** Hematoxylin & eosin.) (**A,** From Stanley JC: Morphologic, histopathologic, and clinical characteristics of renovascular fibrodysplasia and arteriosclerosis. In Bergan JJ, Yao JST [eds]: Surgery of the Aorta and Its Body Branches. New York, Grune & Stratton, 1979, pp 355-376. **B,** From Stanley JC: Pathologic basis of macrovascular renal artery disease. In Stanley JC, Ernst CB, Fry WJ [eds]: Renovascular Hypertension. Philadelphia, WB Saunders, 1984, pp 46-74.)

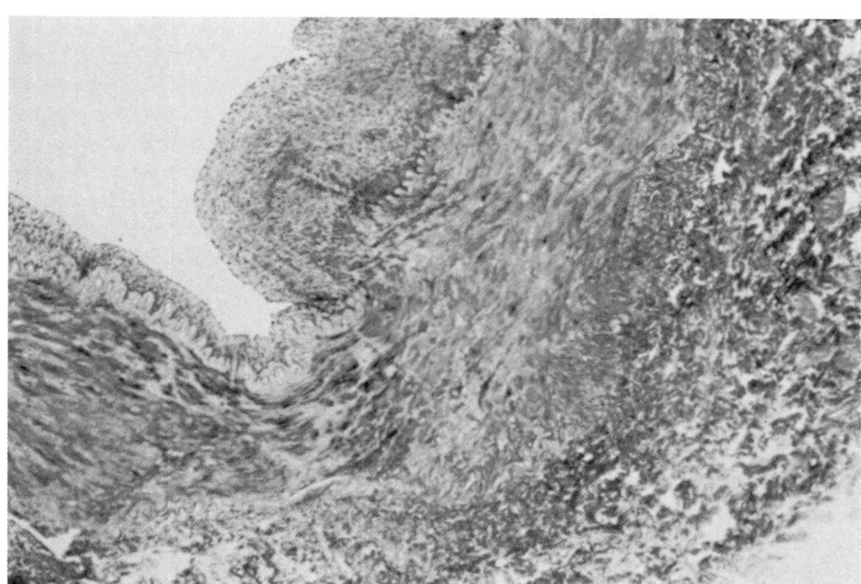

FIGURE 27-3 Secondary intimal fibroplasia. Cellular subendothelial tissue in an artery exhibiting advanced medial fibroplasia (Masson, ×80). (From Stanley JC: Pathologic basis of macrovascular renal artery disease. In Stanley JC, Ernst CB, Fry WJ [eds]: Renovascular Hypertension. Philadelphia, WB Saunders, 1984, pp 46-74.)

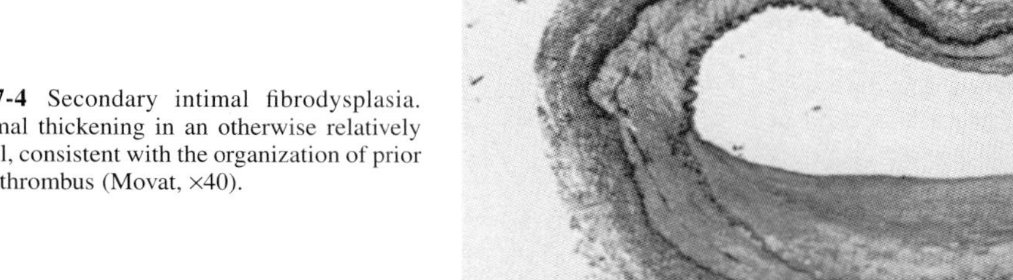

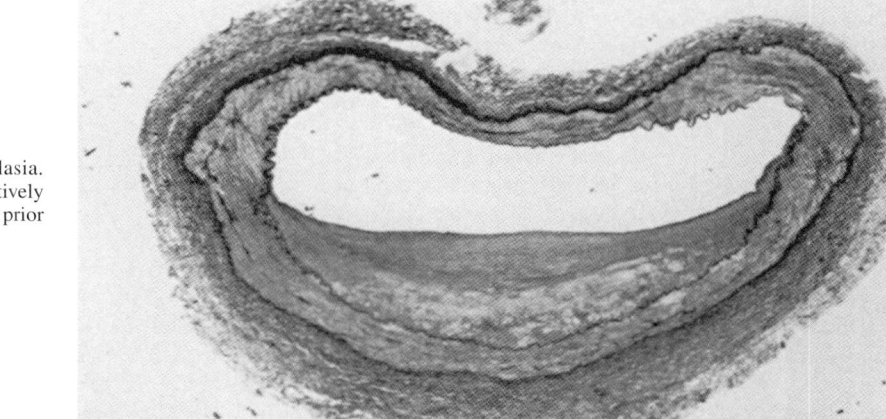

FIGURE 27-4 Secondary intimal fibrodysplasia. Marked intimal thickening in an otherwise relatively normal vessel, consistent with the organization of prior intraluminal thrombus (Movat, ×40).

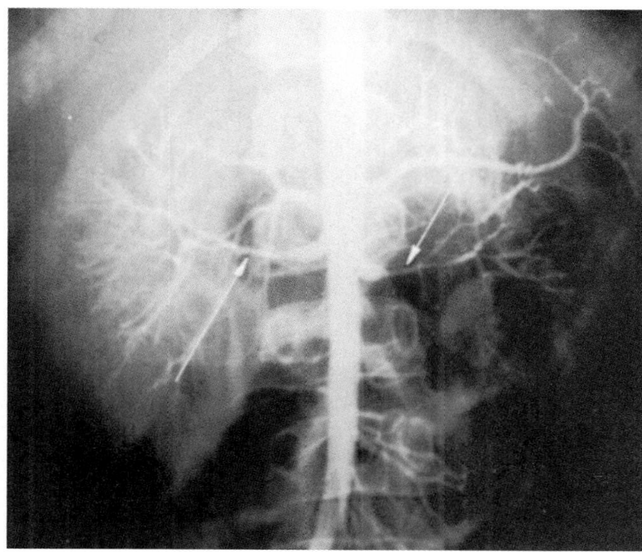

FIGURE 27-5 Secondary intimal fibroplasia. Long tubular stenoses (*arrows*) in the main distal renal arteries of an infant. (From Whitehouse WM Jr, Cho KJ, Coran AS, Stanley JC: Pediatric arterial disease. In Neiman HL, Yao JST [eds]: Angiography of Vascular Disease. New York, Churchill Livingstone, 1985, pp 289-306.)

of intimal fibroplasia have been suggested to represent a resolved arteritis, such as might occur with rubella.[133] An infectious-immunologic theory has been supported by evidence of immunoglobulin deposition within intimal tissues of certain stenotic vessels.[28]

Once a hemodynamically important arterial stenosis develops, progression of intimal fibroplasia appears a likely consequence of abnormal surface blood flow, even if the initiating etiologic factors have resolved. The specific cellular messengers responsible for this tissue proliferation have not been identified.

Medial hyperplasia without associated fibrosis is an unusual cause of renal artery stenosis. In fact, the existence of this particular dysplastic disease is subject to debate. In certain instances, oblique sections of the arterial wall or specimens near bifurcations may misleadingly portray an increase in medial thickness. Similarly, unusually large amounts of smooth muscle separated by recognizable excesses of ground substance are more likely to represent medial fibrodysplasia[20] than medial hyperplasia. Medial hyperplasia of the renal artery has been most often described in women during their 4th and 5th decades of life. If this type of lesion actually exists, it will certainly account for less than 1% of dysplastic renovascular lesions. Focal stenoses caused by medial hyperplasia usually involve the mid-portion of the renal artery, not its branches or segmental vessels (Fig. 27-6). Increases in smooth muscle cell numbers with minimal disorganization and the absence of ground substance excesses characterize these stenoses (Fig. 27-7). Intimal and adventitial structures are usually normal, although in severe stenoses, intimal fibroplasia may occur as a secondary event. Medial hyperplasia of the renal artery has not been associated with any clearly recognized cause. Contributing to the controversy surrounding this lesion is the fact that a non-neoplastic increase in smooth muscle elsewhere within the vascular system is unusual.

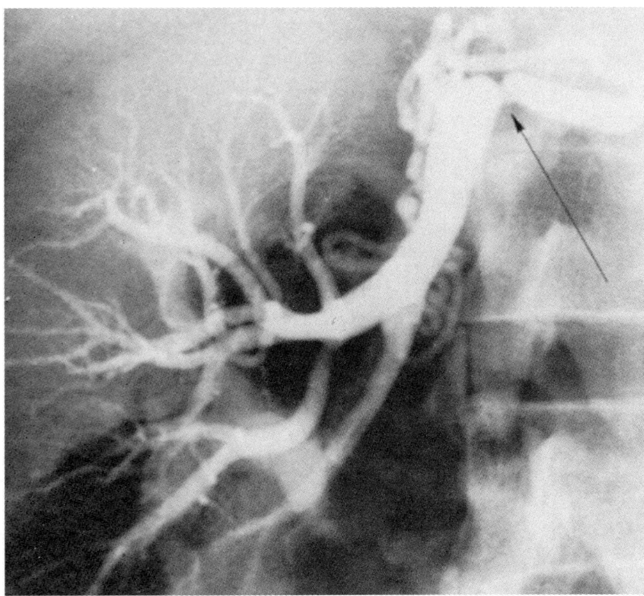

FIGURE 27-6 Medial hyperplasia. Focal stenosis (*arrow*) affecting the mid-portion of the main renal artery.

Medial fibrodysplasia accounts for nearly 85% of dysplastic renovascular disease. More than 90% of patients with medial fibrodysplasia are women. This dysplastic lesion is exceedingly uncommon among African Americans. The disease is diagnosed most often during the 4th and 5th decades of life. Although medial fibrodysplasia is considered to be a systemic arteriopathy, clinically overt arterial involvement is usually limited to the renal, extracranial internal carotid, and external iliac vessels.

The morphologic appearance of renal artery medial fibrodysplasia ranges from a solitary focal stenosis to its more common presentation as a series of stenoses with intervening aneurysmal outpouchings (Fig. 27-8). The latter, which causes a string-of-beads appearance, has not been observed in female patients before menarche, with the exception of a single case report.[97] The thin-walled mural aneurysms are often grossly evident, as are the distinct webs that project internally (Fig. 27-9). Medial fibrodysplasia most commonly affects the distal main renal artery, with extensions into first-order segmental branches occurring in approximately 25% of cases. Bilateral disease occurs in 60% to 70% of patients, but only 15% are functionally important.

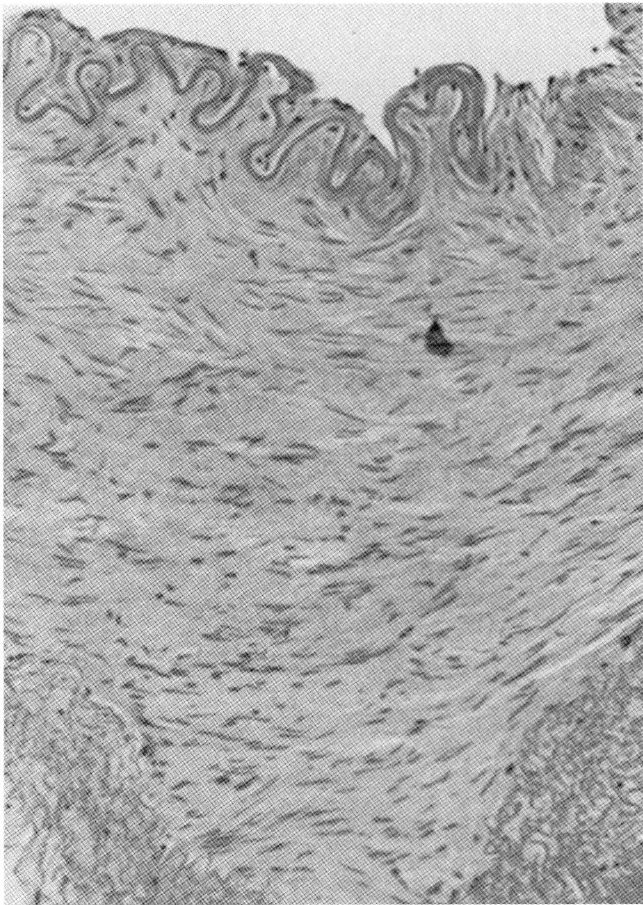

FIGURE 27-7 Medial hyperplasia. Unusual dysplastic lesion with excessive medial smooth muscle in an otherwise normal vessel (Hematoxylin & eosin, ×120). (From Stanley JC: Morphologic, histopathologic, and clinical characteristics of renovascular fibrodysplasia and arteriosclerosis. In Bergan JJ, Yao JST [eds]: Surgery of the Aorta and Its Body Branches. New York, Grune & Stratton, 1979, pp 355-376.)

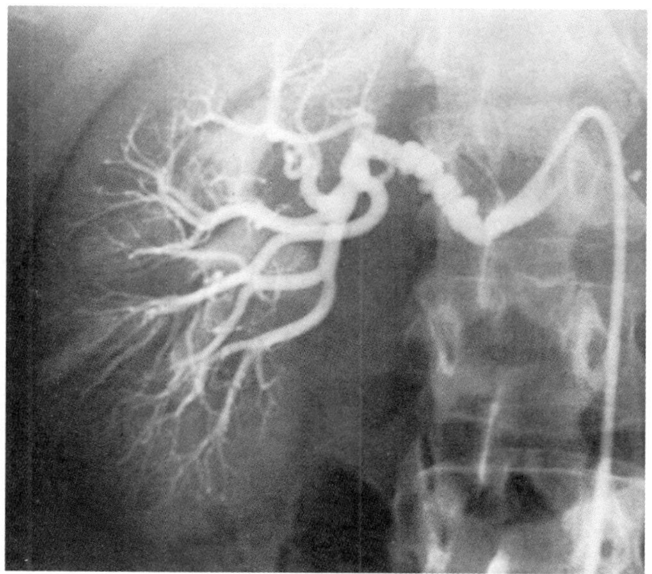

FIGURE 27-8 Medial fibrodysplasia. Serial stenoses alternating with mural aneurysms, producing a string-of-beads appearance in the mid-portion and distal main renal artery. (From Stanley JC, Graham LM: Renovascular hypertension. In Miller DC, Roon AJ [eds]: Diagnosis and Management of Peripheral Vascular Disease. Menlo Park, CA, Addison-Wesley, 1981, pp 231-235.)

Progression of medial fibrodysplasia appears to occur in 12% to 66% of patients with main renal artery lesions.[40,84,118,126] Some have suggested that the initial changes of this disease represent smooth muscle transformations, and that over time a fibrotic process occurs that has a more ominous prognosis than the earlier changes.[2] Progression is generally thought to be more common in premenopausal women, but some authors have noted no differences related to age.[116] Among a group of 71 potential kidney donors with angiographic evidence of renal artery fibrodysplasia, hypertension developed in 26% over an average follow-up of 7.5 years.[21] Hypertension developed in only 6% of an age-matched and sex-matched group of control patients. In these instances, blood pressure increases were considered to be a reflection of progressive renal artery disease. Sudden changes in fibrodysplastic renal vessels are relatively uncommon, although in one unique series 18% had progressed to occlusion.[31] Regression of renal artery dysplastic stenoses has been reported,[91] although the validity of such an event has been challenged.[82]

Two histologic forms of renal artery medial fibrodysplasia are well recognized (Fig. 27-10). The first type causes disease to the outer media (*peripheral* form), and the second exhibits disease throughout the entire media (*diffuse* form). The second form is noted twice as often as the first. Gradations between these extremes have been observed in the same vessel, supporting the tenet that they represent the same disease process. The peripheral form of medial fibrodysplasia is usually encountered in younger patients. It is possible that with the passage of time, more advanced disease evolves to affect the entire media. Consistent with this hypothesis are observed changes in the arteriographic appearance of these lesions, with multiple severe stenoses in series and true macroaneurysms developing in many patients who initially had a solitary lesion or a few stenoses of minimal severity.

Peripheral medial fibrodysplasia is characterized by compact fibrous connective tissue replacing smooth muscle in the outer media. Less obvious findings are moderate accumulations of collagen and ground substances separating disorganized smooth muscle within the inner media. Intimal tissues and the internal elastic lamina are rarely affected in these peripheral lesions. Although continuity of the external elastic lamina is frequently lost, the adventitia is usually normal. Certain peripheral forms of medial fibrodysplasia have been erroneously classified as perimedial or subadventitial disease.[45,80,81]

Diffuse medial fibrodysplasia is characterized by more severe disorganization and disruption of normal smooth muscle architecture. Occasionally, the diffuse form of dysplasia results in an amorphous-like media (Fig. 27-11). In other vessels, excessive medial accumulations of fibrous tissue alternate with areas of marked medial thinning (Fig. 27-12). In some instances, the media is nearly absent;

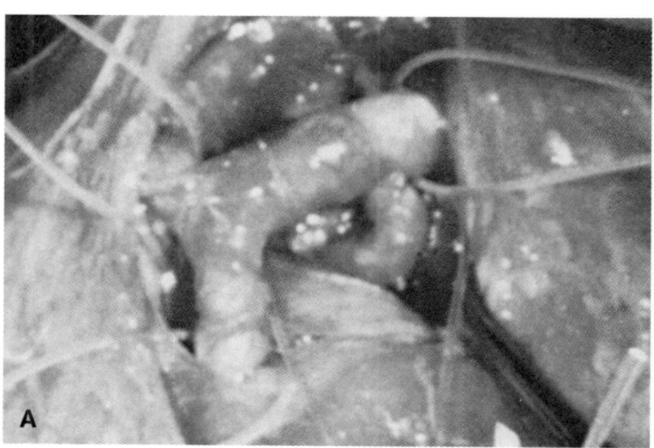

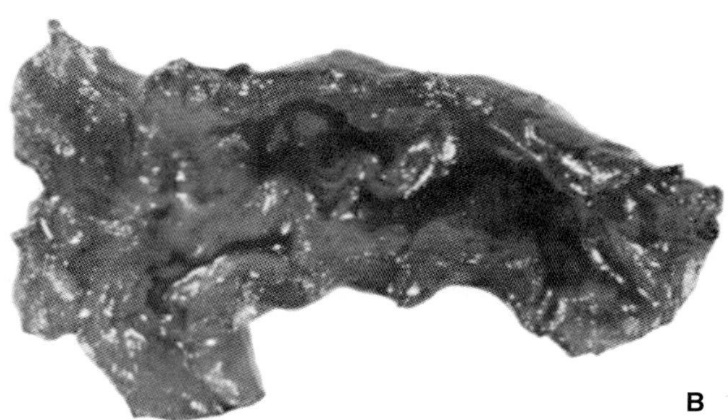

FIGURE 27-9 Medial fibrodysplasia. **A,** Gross appearance of mural aneurysms characteristic of this type of renal artery dysplasia. **B,** Internal appearance of webs projecting into the lumen of an excised main renal artery specimen. (**A** and **B,** From Stanley JC: Pathologic basis of macrovascular renal artery disease. In Stanley JC, Ernst CB, Fry WJ [eds]: Renovascular Hypertension. Philadelphia, WB Saunders, 1984, pp 46-74.)

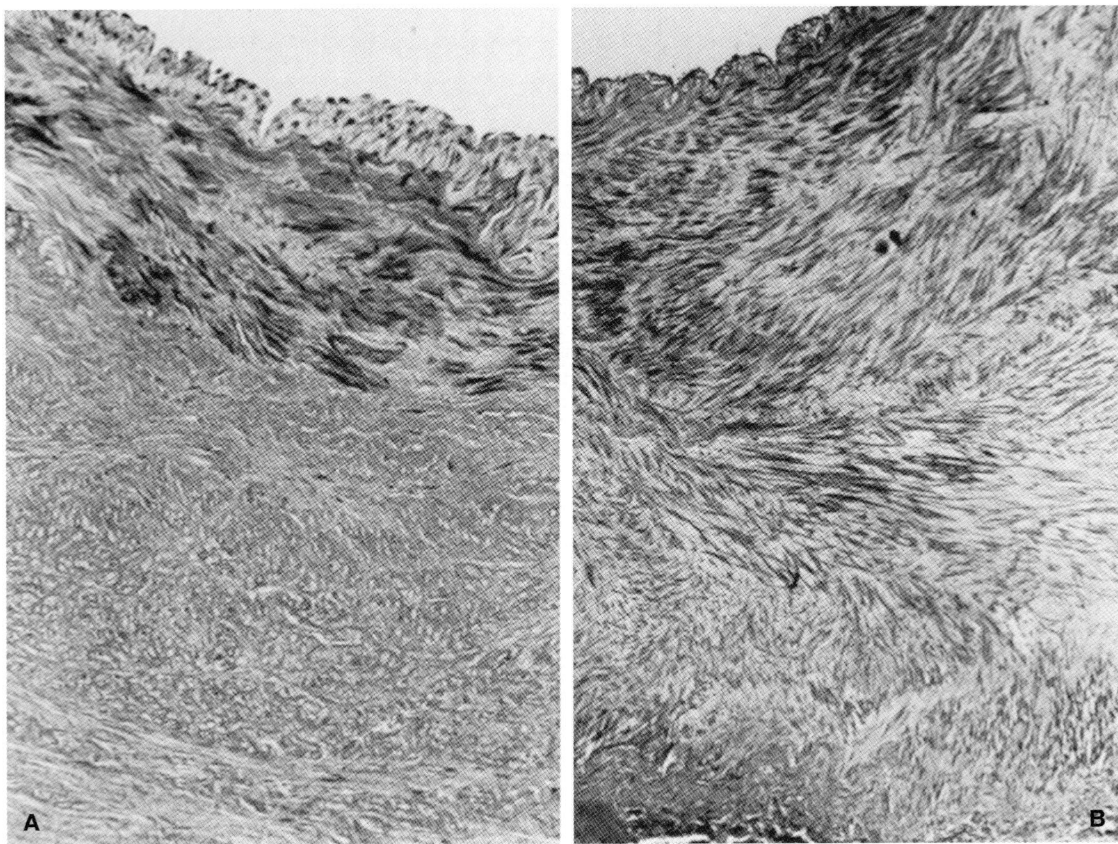

FIGURE 27-10 **A,** Peripheral form of medial fibrodysplasia. Dense fibrous connective tissue in the outer media, with disordered inner medial smooth muscle and normal intimal tissues. **B,** Diffuse form of medial fibrodysplasia. Total replacement of the media by disorganized cellular tissue (myofibroblasts) surrounded by fibrous connective tissue (Masson, ×120). (**A** and **B,** From Stanley JC: Morphologic, histopathologic, and clinical characteristics of renovascular fibrodysplasia and arteriosclerosis. In Bergan JJ, Yao JST [eds]: Surgery of the Aorta and Its Body Branches. New York, Grune & Stratton, 1979, pp 355-376.)

FIGURE 27-11 Diffuse form of medial fibrodysplasia. Amorphous appearance of excessive ground substances and fibrous connective tissue throughout the media (Masson, ×80, longitudinal section). (From Stanley JC: Pathologic basis of macrovascular renal artery disease. In Stanley JC, Ernst CB, Fry WJ [eds]: Renovascular Hypertension. Philadelphia, WB Saunders, 1984, pp 46-74.

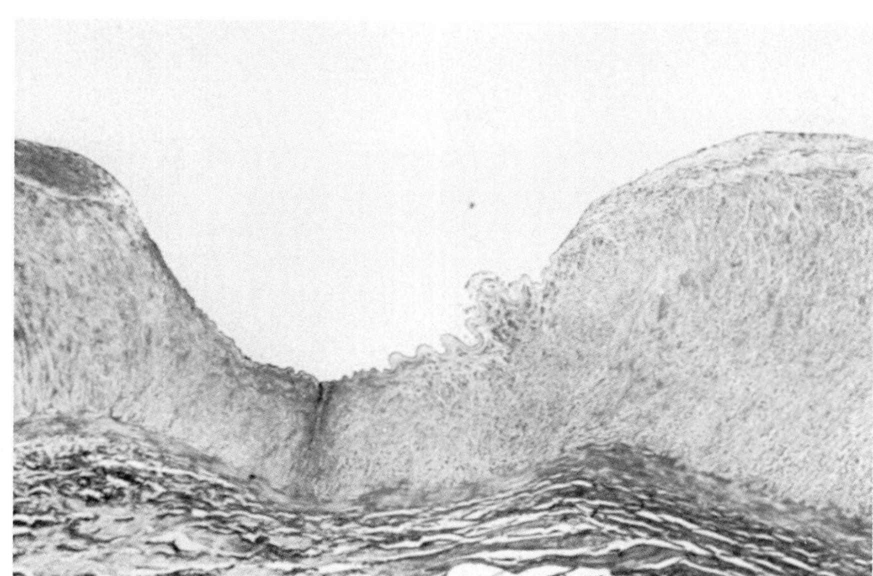

FIGURE 27-12 Diffuse form of medial fibrodysplasia. Regions of excessive fibroproliferation with intervening area of medial thinning (Masson, ×60, longitudinal section). (From Stanley JC: Morphologic, histopathologic, and clinical characteristics of renovascular fibrodysplasia and arteriosclerosis. In Bergan JJ, Yao JST [eds]: Surgery of the Aorta and Its Body Branches. New York, Grune & Stratton, 1979, pp 355-376.)

FIGURE 27-13 Medial fibrodysplasia. Extensive fragmentation and distortion of the internal elastic lamina with dissection (Movat, ×160).

these regions account for the vessel's mural aneurysmal dilations. Internal elastic lamina fragmentation and subendothelial fibrosis may also be evident. These latter two changes are considered secondary events in instances of more advanced medial fibrodysplasia. Adventitial tissues are relatively uninvolved in medial fibrodysplasia.

Extensive fragmentation and distortion of the internal elastic lamina occur in some renal arteries (Fig. 27-13). Disruptions within the vessel wall may extend into middle and outer medial structures as limited dissections (Fig. 27-14A), or they may progress as large intramural hematomas that compress the vessel lumen (Fig. 27-14B).[44] Loss of vessel integrity at bifurcations and with alterations in elastic tissue are thought to lead to the development of renal artery macroaneurysms (Fig. 27-15).[131]

Perimedial dysplasia is the dominant abnormality affecting approximately 10% of dysplastic renal arteries. It may coexist with medial fibrodysplasia. Most patients exhibiting perimedial dysplasia have been women, usually in their 5th decade of life. Bilateral disease occurs in 50% of patients. These lesions present as either focal stenoses or multiple constrictions involving the mid-portion of the main renal artery without mural aneurysms (Fig. 27-16A). Excessive elastic tissue at the junction of the media and the adventitia is the distinguishing feature of perimedial dysplasia (Fig. 27-16B). This appears as a homogeneous collar of elastic tissue adjacent to the outer media. The lesion is further characterized by minimal increases in medial ground substance surrounding intact smooth muscle cells, with little alteration of intimal tissues (Fig. 27-17).

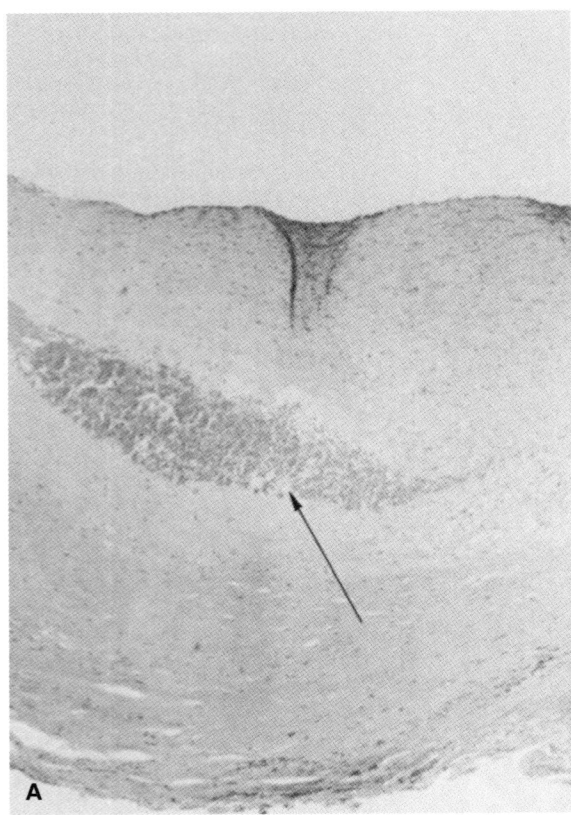

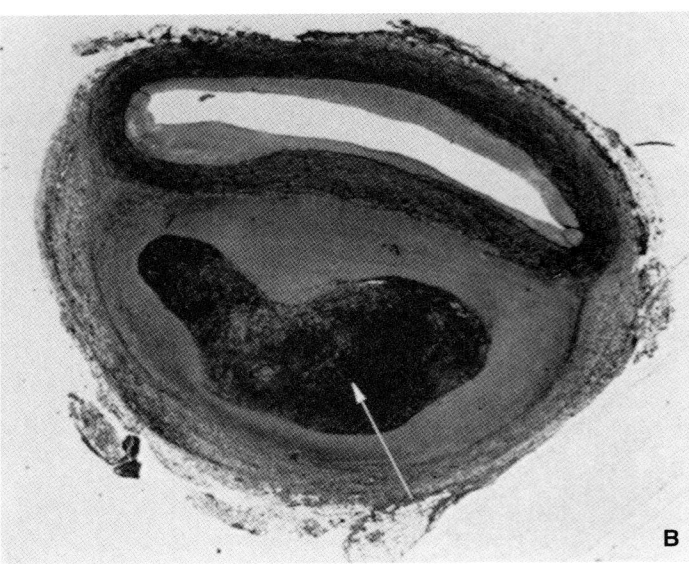

FIGURE 27-14 Dissections complicating medial fibrodysplasia. **A,** Intramedial dissection with limited hemorrhage (*arrow*) (×120). **B,** Deep medial dissection with large intramural hematoma (*arrow*) compressing the vessel lumen (×60). (**A** and **B,** Hematoxylin & eosin.) (**A** and **B,** From Stanley JC: Pathologic basis of macrovascular renal artery disease. In Stanley JC, Ernst CB, Fry WJ [eds]: Renovascular Hypertension. Philadelphia, WB Saunders, 1984, pp 46-74.)

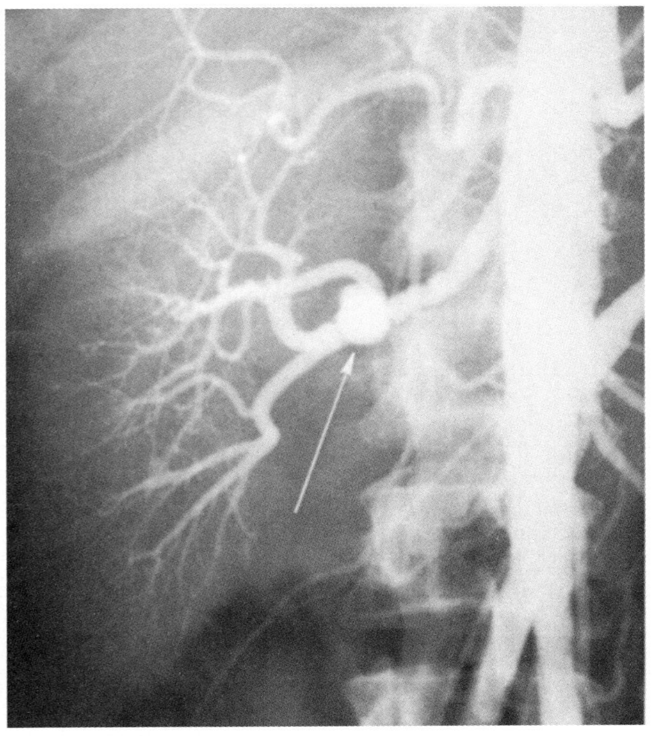

FIGURE 27-15 Macroaneurysms and medial fibrodysplasia. Large macroaneurysm (*arrow*) at a bifurcation of the renal artery. (From Ernst CB, Stanley JC, Fry WJ: Multiple primary and segmental renal artery revascularization utilizing autogenous saphenous vein. Surg Gynecol Obstet 137:1023, 1973.)

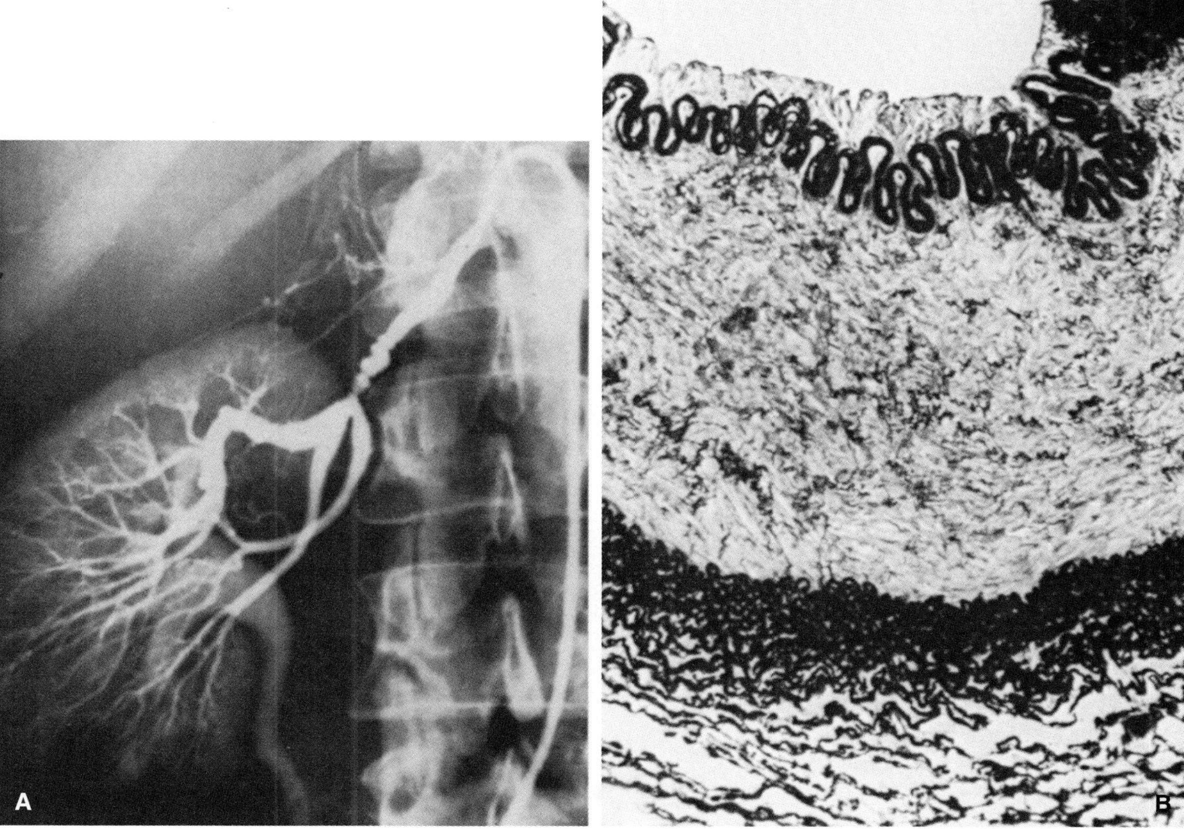

FIGURE 27-16 Perimedial dysplasia. **A,** Multiple stenoses without mural aneurysms in the mid-portion of the renal artery are characteristic of these lesions. **B,** These stenoses are due to excessive accumulations of elastic tissue at the medial-adventitial junction (Verhoeff, ×120). (**A** and **B,** From Stanley JC: Morphologic, histopathologic, and clinical characteristics of renovascular fibrodysplasia and arteriosclerosis. In Bergan JJ, Yao JST [eds]: Surgery of the Aorta and Its Body Branches. New York, Grune & Stratton, 1979, pp 355-376.)

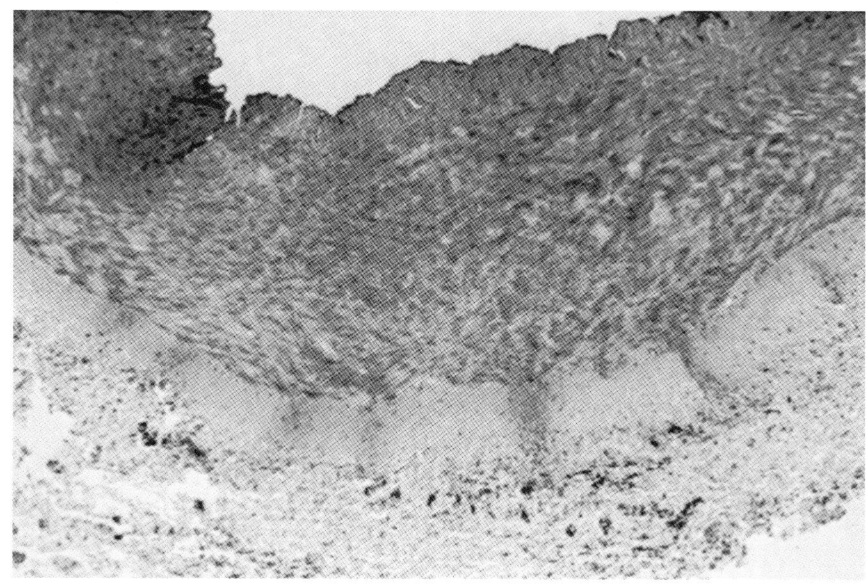

FIGURE 27-17 Perimedial dysplasia. Homogeneous collar of elastic tissue adjacent to the outer media is the dominant feature of this lesion (Hematoxylin & eosin, ×80). (From Stanley JC: Pathologic basis of macrovascular renal artery disease. In Stanley JC, Ernst CB, Fry WJ [eds]: Renovascular Hypertension. Philadelphia, WB Saunders, 1984, pp 46-74.)

Certain ultrastructural features are common to medial fibrodysplasia and perimedial dysplasia.[124] Both exhibit accumulations of ground substance and fibrous elements. Perimedial dysplasia is differentiated by collections of amorphous material and elastic tissue at the adventitial-medial border. Most important, both manifest a spectrum of change within the cellular composition of the media, ranging from near-normal smooth muscle to myofibroblasts. Fibroblasts are not a usual component of the media and are infrequently observed in these diseased tissues. Similarly, inflammatory cells such as macrophages and leukocytes are not evident in either medial fibroplasia or perimedial dysplasia. Normal smooth muscle cells are characterized by (1) close apposition of cytoplasmic processes; (2) a deeply indented and convoluted ovoid nucleus surrounded by a modest number of cellular organelles; (3) orderly arranged thick and thin myofilaments parallel to the longitudinal cell axis, with electron-dense bodies at their attachment to the plasma lamina; (4) basal laminations; and (5) scattered micropinocytotic vesicles.

The earliest alterations in the smooth muscle ultrastructure of dysplastic vessels are focal myofilament reductions as well as perinuclear sublemmal and cytoplasmic vacuolations (Fig. 27-18). In areas of advanced dysplasia, certain smooth muscle cells exhibit extreme deterioration, whereas others become fibroblast-like in appearance. The former are invariably isolated from surrounding cells by excessive amounts of ground substance (Fig. 27-19A). In these tissues, long, slender cytoplasmic processes reflect decreased cell volumes. Cell membranes are often indistinct, and the nucleus is usually pyknotic, containing dense chromatin material. Confluences of micropinocytotic vesicles are common, and subcellular organelles are sparse. Myofilaments appear dense and homogeneous in these cells. Transformation of medial smooth muscle cells to fibroblast-type cells represents a continuum

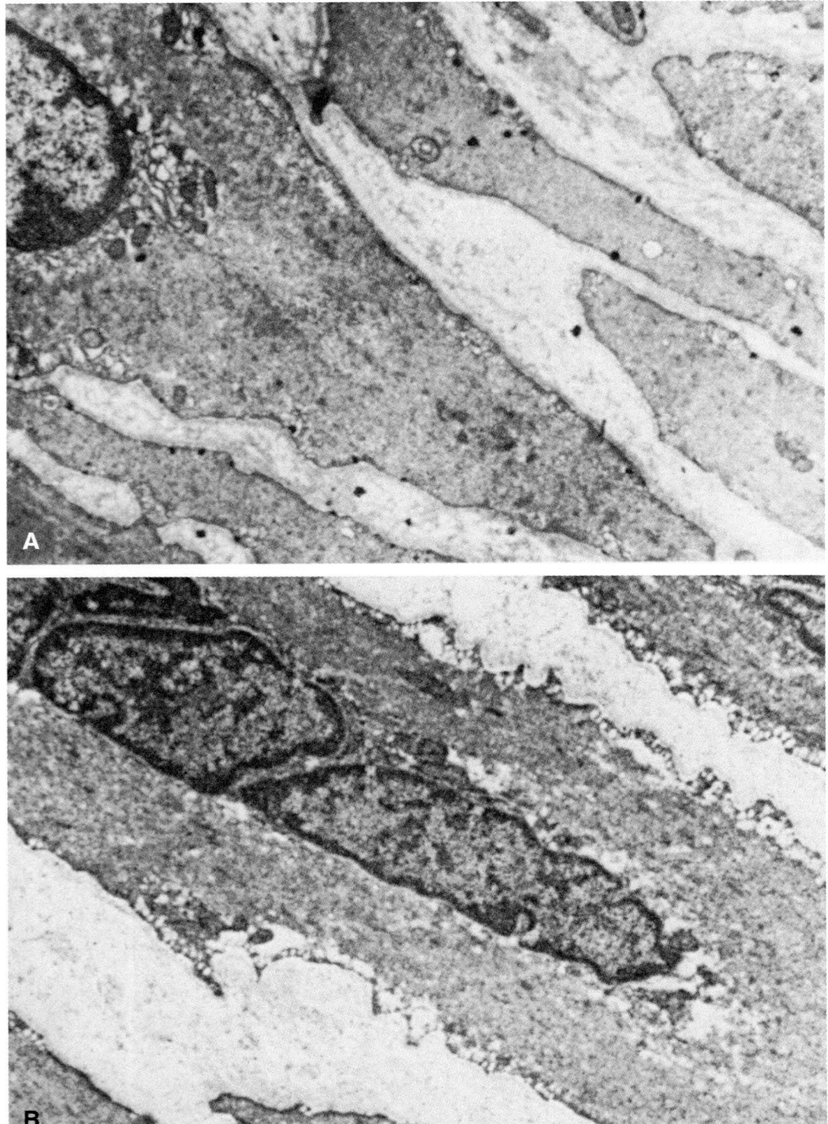

FIGURE 27-18 Smooth muscle cell. **A,** In a region of minimal fibrodysplasia, a relatively normal ultrastructure is seen, except for the focal reduction in myofilaments and the appearance of perinuclear, sublemmal, and cytoplasmic vacuoles (×18,000). **B,** In a region of moderate fibrodysplasia, more extensive perinuclear and peripheral vacuolation is evident. Loss of organelles and basement membrane and indistinct myofilaments characterize this type of cell (×12,000). (**A** and **B,** Transmission electron microscopy.) (**A** and **B,** From Stanley JC: Pathologic basis of macrovascular renal artery disease. In Stanley JC, Ernst CB, Fry WJ [eds]: Renovascular Hypertension. Philadelphia, WB Saunders, 1984, pp 46-74.)

within dysplastic tissues. Alterations in nuclear contour, loss of myofilaments, and increases in free ribosomes, rough endoplasmic reticulum, Golgi complexes, and mitochondria seemingly parallel altered function from one of contractility to one of secretion.

Myofibroblasts are the end product of smooth muscle transformation. Typical of these cells is a convoluted nucleus with numerous indentations and evaginations (Fig. 27-19B). Major juxtanuclear increases in subcellular organelles and the presence of peripherally located cytoplasmic filaments are characteristic of myofibroblasts. Myofilaments are scant and poorly defined. Active exopinocytotic deposition of proteinaceous matter may be evident in some cells (Fig. 27-20).

Vasa vasorum within the media of diseased arteries are usually widely separated from adjacent cellular tissue by fibrous material and homogeneous mucoid substances. The type of surrounding connective tissue appears to be related to the category of arterial dysplasia. Vasa vasorum within medial fibrodysplasia are predominantly surrounded by collagen bundles, whereas those in perimedial dysplasia are usually surrounded by amorphous mucoid substances consistent with elastic tissue.

The pathogenesis of *medial fibrodysplasia* and *perimedial dysplasia* has been the subject of much speculation.[60,129] Hormonal effects on smooth muscle, mechanical stresses on vessel walls, and the peculiar distribution of vasa vasorum in arteries exhibiting these lesions all are considered to be contributing factors. The exact relation of these events to each other, or their association with other unrecognized pathogenic mechanisms, remains unknown. Certain other factors may not cause the disease but may contribute to a worsening of it. Among the latter is antitrypsin deficiency, resulting in the loss of a potent proteinase inhibitor. Patients with medial fibrodysplasia having this deficiency exhibit more severe manifestations of their dysplasia.[7]

Because of the occasionally reported familial nature of medial fibrodysplasia, a genetic-related autosomal dominant etiology with incomplete penetrance has been suggested; however, confirmatory arteriographic or histologic evidence to firmly establish such a contention has not been presented.[39,77,89,106,112] In fact, the absence of a female predilection in much of the genetic data lessens the validity of that contention. Nevertheless, the familial frequency of multifocal medial dysplastic diseases supports the tenet that a genetic predisposition or cause exists.[8,96] In this regard, the ACE I allele occurs with greater frequency in patients with medial fibrodysplasia.[9] This gene affects the function of angiotensin II, which modulates smooth muscle cell proliferation and synthetic activity.

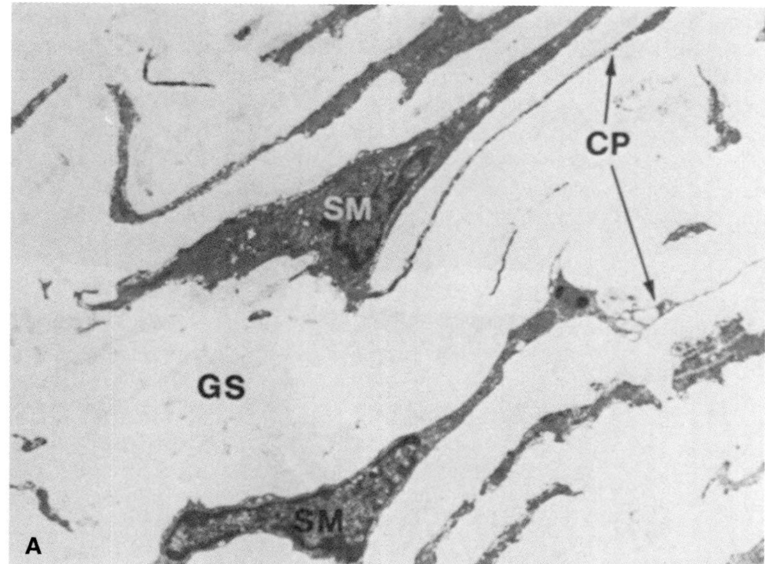

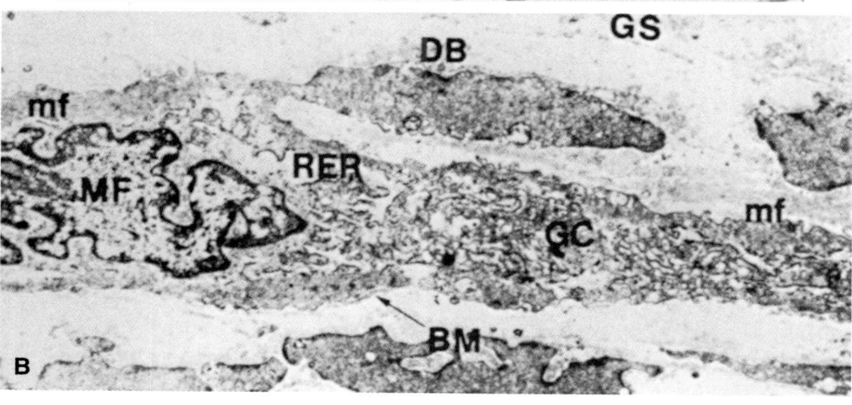

FIGURE 27-19 A, Smooth muscle cell in an area of advanced fibrodysplasia. Isolation of slender cytoplasmic processes by excesses in ground substances and pyknotic nuclei are typical of these markedly abnormal cells (×6000). **B,** Myofibroblast associated with medial fibroplasia. The convoluted nucleus is typical of smooth muscle, but increased numbers of centrally located organelles reflect the change in function from one of contractility to secretion (×8000). (**A** and **B,** Transmission electron microscopy.) SM, smooth muscle; GS, ground substance; CP, cytoplasmic processes; mf, myofilament; DB, dense body; RER, rough endoplasmic reticulum; MF, myofibroblast; GC, Golgi complex; BM, basement membrane. (**A** and **B,** From Sottiurai VS, Fry WJ, Stanley JC: Ultrastructure of medial smooth muscle and myofibroblasts in human arterial dysplasia. Arch Surg 113:1280-1288, 1978.)

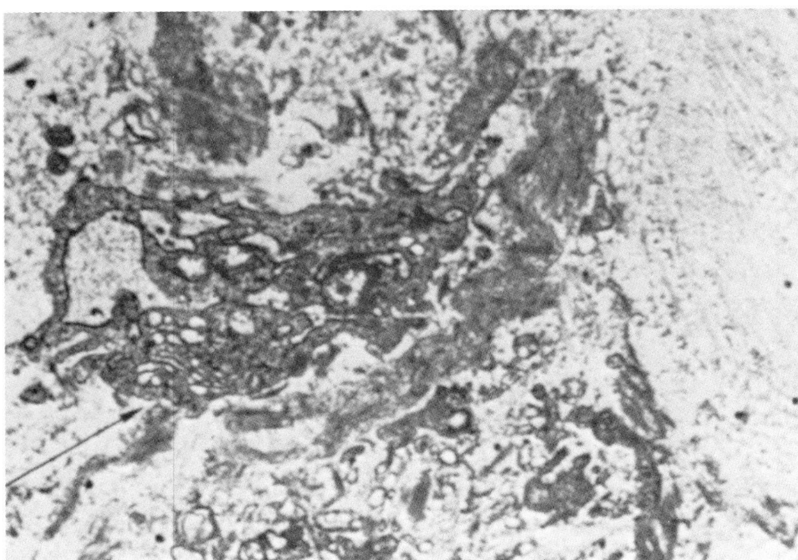

FIGURE 27-20 Myofibroblast in a region of extensive fibroplasia, exhibiting exopinocytotic secretion of proteinaceous matter (*arrow*) (transmission electron microscopy, ×25,000). (From Stanley JC: Pathologic basis of macrovascular renal artery disease. In Stanley JC, Ernst CB, Fry WJ [eds]: Renovascular Hypertension. Philadelphia, WB Saunders, 1984, pp 46-74.)

Hormonal influences seem likely in view of arterial dysplasia's unusual female predilection. More than 95% of patients exhibiting medial and perimedial disease are women. Pregnancy is known to cause rather profound vascular wall changes, including alterations in medial structures (especially elastic tissue), but it is not a recognized etiologic factor in arterial fibrodysplasia. The reproductive histories of patients in a large series with this arteriopathy did *not* reveal gravity or parity rates different from those in the general population.[129]

Antiovulants are also known to affect the arterial wall. However, the use of such drugs by fewer than half the female patients in the Michigan series does not support any obvious cause-effect association of progestins with arterial dysplasia.[129] A similar lack of association with oral contraceptive use has been reported in a case-control study.[112] Certain smooth muscle cells and fibroblasts exposed to estrogens demonstrate increased synthesis of proteinaceous substances, including collagen. It is speculated that physiologic preconditioning of vascular smooth muscle cells to a secretory state by normal circulating estrogens associated with the reproductive cycle may account for the more frequent occurrence of medial dysplastic disease in women.

Unusual physical stresses due to ptosis of the kidneys may be associated with fibrodysplastic changes in the renal arteries (Fig. 27-21). Comparable stretch or traction forces are less likely to occur in similar-sized vessels unaffected by this disease. Ptotic kidneys are common among patients with renal artery dysplastic lesions.[22,59] In some cases, positional changes causing greater ptosis have been correlated with increases in blood pressure.[140] The fact that the right kidney is usually more ptotic than the left may account for the known greater severity of right-sided disease in most adults with bilateral medial fibroplasia. In addition, in the case of unilateral lesions, 80% involve the right renal arteries. The greater mobility and lower positioning of kidneys in patients with fibrodysplasia may be evident in the more acute angulation of their renal artery's aortic origin compared with those without dysplastic vessels (81% vs. 64%).[38]

Cyclic stretching of smooth muscle cells in tissue culture causes an unusually large synthesis of collagen and certain acid mucopolysaccharides.[67] Although the existence of similar mechanisms in vivo is speculative, the predilection for dysplastic disease to occur most often in vessels subjected to peculiar mechanical forces may reflect an important pathogenic phenomenon. It is cautionary to note that in one case-control study, renal mobility was not greater in patients with renovascular fibrodysplasia.[112]

A final etiologic factor may be related to mural ischemia in dysplastic arteries. Vasa vasorum of muscular arteries usually originate from branchings of parent vessels. The renal, extracranial internal carotid, and external iliac arteries

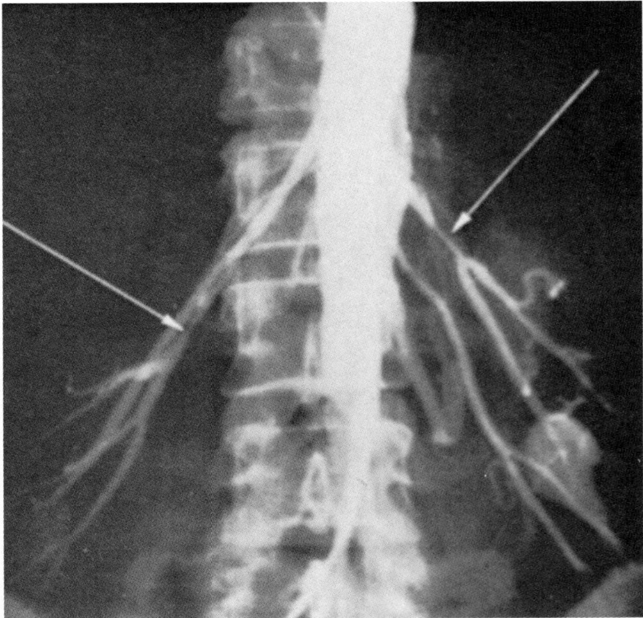

FIGURE 27-21 Medial fibrodysplasia manifesting as irregular narrowings (*arrows*) affecting the mid-portion of the main renal arteries to ptotic kidneys, which appear stretched during upright aortography.

are the three vessels most likely to develop medial fibrodysplasia. The latter two arteries, in particular, have relatively few branches compared with similar-sized vessels. These vessels have a sparsity of vasa vasorum; compromise of this nutrient supply may lead to significant mural ischemia. Vasospasm may occur in these cases and further exacerbate vessel wall ischemia.[34,98,121] Destruction of the media may be a consequence of such an ischemic injury and account for histologic changes present in arterial fibrodysplasia.[69,121] The concept that insufficient vessel wall nourishment causes dysplastic changes is supported by the common involvement of the outermost part of the media in the peripheral form of medial fibroplasia. It is precisely in this region that ischemia from inadequate vasa vasorum blood flow would be predictably greatest. Fibrodysplasia limited to the inner part of the media has never been reported. Vasa vasorum in these vessels have exhibited both dilation[46] and isolation from adjacent medial smooth muscle cells.[76] Experimental occlusion of the vasa vasorum produces a dysplastic lesion in animals similar to that seen in humans, which supports the tenet that mural ischemia may be a factor in the evolution of arterial dysplasia.[123]

Tissue hypoxia per se may be the inciting event in stimulating fibroplasia, but altered tissue pH, accumulation of metabolites, and other factors may be just as important. Cigarette smoking has been considered a potential contributing factor in fibromuscular dysplasia.[112] The observations that smokers with this disease have been recognized at a younger age and are more likely to exhibit kidney atrophy, suggest that smoking does indeed influence the development and progression of renal artery dysplasia.[8] Smooth muscle cells are central to the dysplastic process. Medial smooth muscle cells are considered by some investigators to represent multifunctional mesenchymal cells. The duration and exact degree of ischemia necessary to stimulate myofibroblasts are unknown. Myofibroblasts have been observed to develop in other tissues after very brief hypoxic events.[75] No evidence exists that myofibroblasts evolve from dormant mesenchymal cells, although this is a remote possibility.

Developmental Renal Artery Stenoses

Developmental renal artery stenoses are a unique form of renal artery dysplasia. There is no apparent gender predilection for this entity, and its exact frequency is unknown. Among patients with pediatric renovascular hypertension, nearly 40% appear to have developmental renal artery lesions,[127,132] and many have coexisting lesions of the mesenteric and carotid arteries.[110,132] Among adults with intimal fibroplastic renal artery disease, approximately 20% have stenoses that appear to represent growth or developmental defects. Similarly, some adults with isolated renal arteriosclerosis may have had preexisting developmentally narrowed vessels.

Thus, developmental renal artery occlusive disease appears to be an uncommon, but not rare, entity in the general hypertensive population. Conversely, nearly 80% of patients with abdominal aortic developmental lesions have coexisting renal artery stenoses and renovascular hypertension.[33] Developmental stenoses of the renal arteries are usually hypoplastic in character. As such, they have an external appearance of an hourglass constriction. Most developmental lesions occur at the origin of the vessel (Fig. 27-22).

The histologic character of most of these lesions, especially when they are recognized in pediatric patients, usually reveals abnormalities in more than one of the three layers of the vessel.[24,127,130,132] Sparse medial tissue and intimal fibroplasia are the most common characteristics of these stenoses (Fig. 27-23A). Fragmentation with duplication of the internal elastic lamina is a frequent finding, and excesses in adventitial elastic tissue may be present (Fig. 27-23B). Similarly, irregular deficiencies in medial tissue may be observed in these diminutive vessels (Fig. 27-23C). In some cases, especially those associated with neurofibromatosis, abnormal proliferative changes within the media are apparent.[43,86,117] Occasionally, rather amorphous post-stenotic aneurysms affect the main renal artery in patients exhibiting central aortic coarctations and renal artery occlusive disease.

Developmental renal artery narrowings appear to be related to specific in-utero events. Under normal circumstances, the paired dorsal aortas fuse and all but one of the lateral branches to each kidney regress during the same period of embryonic development, leaving a solitary renal artery. Events that alter transition of mesenchyme to medial smooth muscle tissue at this time, or its later condensation and growth, may cause aortic or renovascular anomalies. This may explain the unusual occurrence of these lesions in neurofibromatosis as well as in other genetic disorders occasionally encountered in isolated kindred.[42,132]

Several theories exist with regard to the cause of these lesions. One proposes that the constrictive lesions follow lack of, or unequal fusion of, the two dorsal aortas, with subsequent obliteration of one of these channels and constriction of the associated renal artery. The basis for such an event is unknown. It may follow an acquired insult in utero or an event during early life that arrests the growth of an otherwise normal aorta. In some instances, this insult may be viral. The fact that certain viruses, including the rubella virus, are cytocidal as well as inhibitory to cell replication supports this theory.[100] Examples of aortic hypoplasia and renal artery stenosis associated with gestational rubella have been observed.[120] In such instances, inhibition of smooth muscle cell mitoses may preclude normal aortic growth and produce renal artery ostial stenoses.

Renal arteries originate within mesenchymal tissue near the two dorsal aortas. They are initially represented by a caudally located group of vessels to the mesonephros that are replaced during fetal growth with a more cephalad group of vessels to the metanephros. A solitary artery to the primitive kidney usually evolves from each of these lateral vessel groups. Development of a single dominant vessel apparently occurs because of its obligate hemodynamic advantage over adjacent channels. Flow changes due to an evolving aortic coarctation in the region in which single renal arteries might normally arise may give coexisting polar channels hemodynamic advantages that cause their persistence. In support of such a hypothesis of renal artery occlusive disease in this subgroup of patients is the fact that central abdominal aortic coarctation and hypoplasia are frequently associated with multiple stenotic renal arteries.[41,130,132]

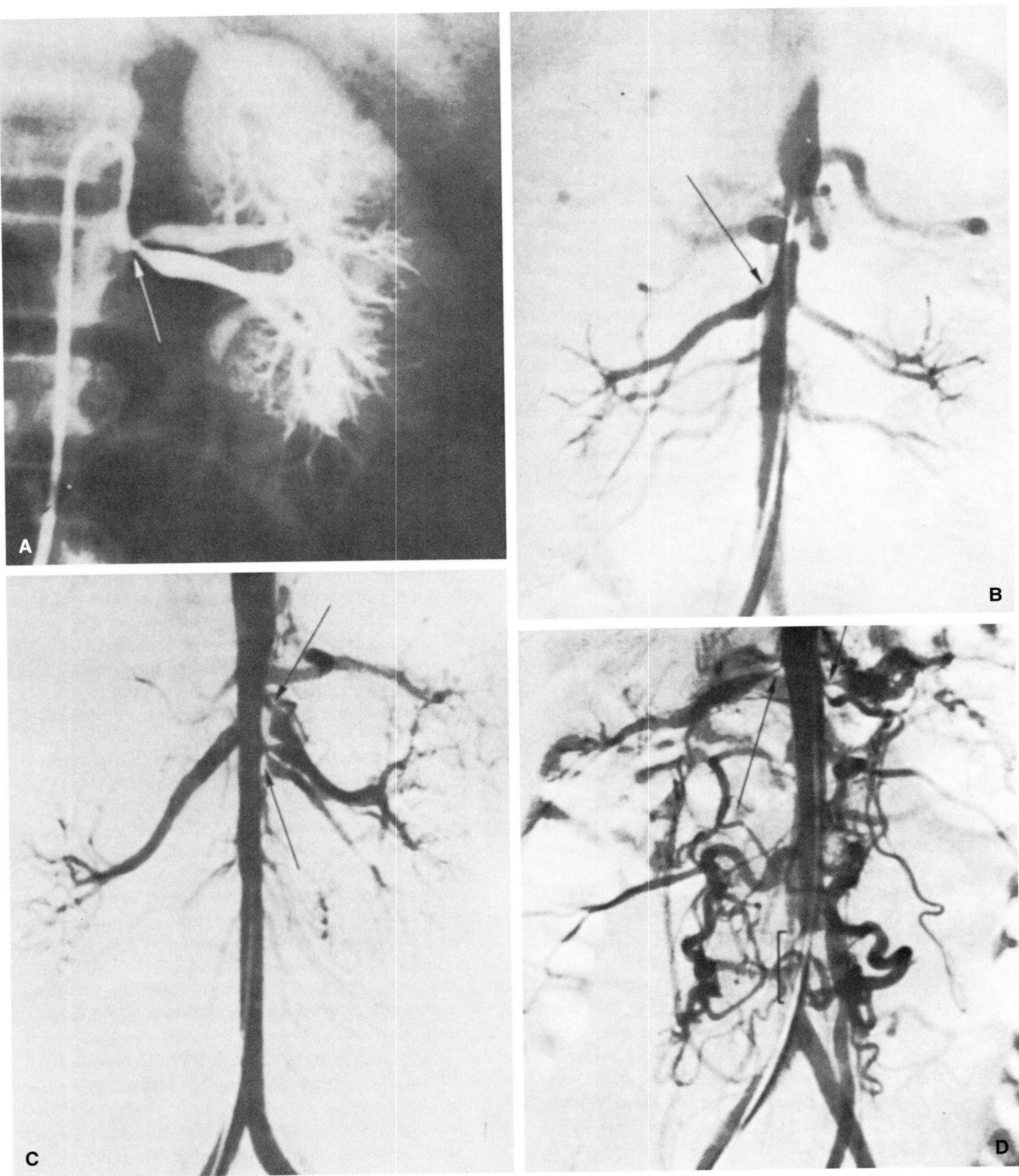

FIGURE 27-22 Developmental renal artery stenoses. **A,** Proximal stenosis (*arrow*) in a patient with neurofibromatosis. **B,** Proximal stenosis (*arrow*) in a patient with multiple renal arteries and mid-abdominal coarctation. **C,** Multivessel stenoses (*arrows*) in a patient with aortic hypoplasia. **D,** Bilateral proximal stenoses (*arrows*) in a patient with focal infrarenal aortic coarctation (*bracket*). (**A,** From Stanley JC, Fry WJ: Pediatric renal artery occlusive disease and renovascular hypertension: Etiology, diagnosis, and operative treatment. Arch Surg 116:669-676, 1984. **B** and **C,** From Graham LM, Zelenock GB, Erlandson EE, et al: Abdominal aortic coarctation and segmental hypoplasia. Surgery 86:519, 1979.)

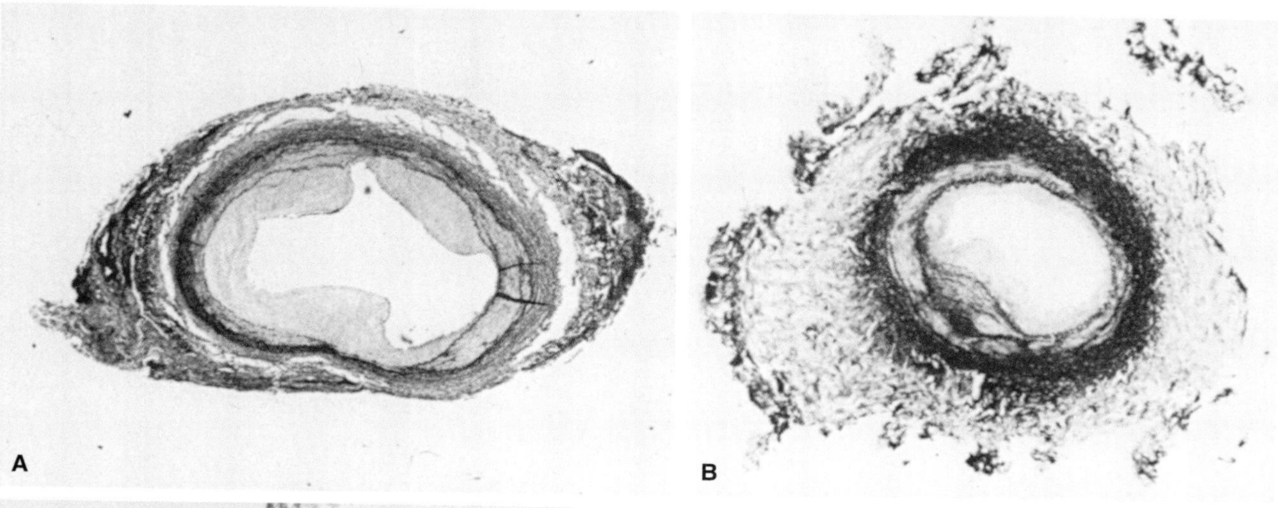

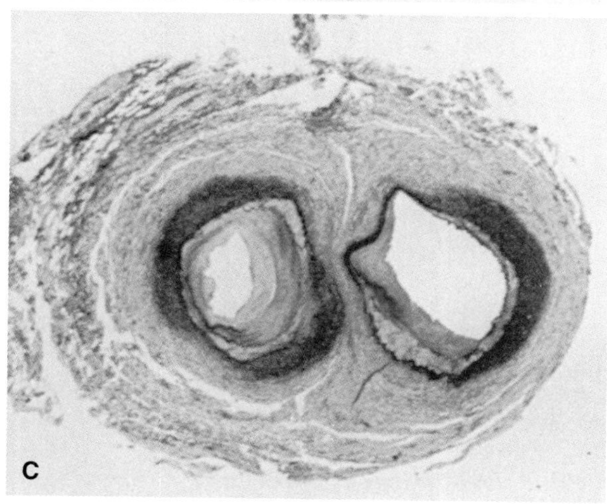

FIGURE 27-23 Hypoplastic developmental renal artery stenoses. **A,** Secondary intimal fibroplasia, fragmentation of the internal elastic lamina, and diminutions in medial tissue are typical features of this stenotic lesion. The greatest luminal dimension is 2 mm (×80). **B,** Marked fragmentation and duplication of the internal elastic lamina and attenuation of medial tissues characterize this vessel. Intimal fibroplasia encroaches on the vessel lumen, which is less than 1 mm in diameter. Adventitial elastic tissues appear excessive (×100). **C**, Diminutive paired renal arteries at their aortic origin exhibiting deficient media (×100). (**A-C,** Movat.) (**A** and **B,** From Stanley JC, Graham LM, Whitehouse WM Jr, et al: Developmental occlusive disease of the abdominal aorta, splanchnic, and renal arteries. Am J Surg 142:190, 1981.)

■ EXTRACRANIAL AND INTRACRANIAL CEREBRAL ARTERIES: CAROTID AND VERTEBRAL ARTERIES

Arterial fibrodysplasia of the extracranial and intracranial cerebral vasculature is a clinical entity of potential importance, although controversy exists beyond the simple assertion that certain lesions cause cerebral ischemic symptoms. The precise incidence of this disease is incompletely defined, although lesions of the extracranial internal carotid artery (ECICA) in the Michigan experience affected 0.42% of 3600 patients undergoing cerebral arteriographic examinations.[128] This finding was nearly identical to the 0.4% reported from the Mayo Clinic.[114] Many of these former examinations were performed for suspected cerebrovascular disease, and thus the true frequency of ECICA fibrodysplasia in the general population would be expected to be lower. Unfortunately, the much lower 0.02% incidence of this disease among necropsy examinations is likely to be too low because of the uncommon removal of distal segments of the ECICA during routine autopsies.[114] Vertebral artery disease is even less common, having been noted in approximately 20% of patients manifesting ECICA fibrodysplasia.[122,128]

Various pathologic processes have been categorized as ECICA fibrodysplasia.[93,114] This fact makes interpretation of the existing literature difficult. The two major subgroups of cerebrovascular lesions include (1) intimal fibroplasia and (2) medial fibrodysplasia. The intimal form is often associated with elongation, kinking, and coiling of the carotid artery and appears for the most part to be a secondary rather than a primary dysplastic process. This seems particularly to be true of intracranial intimal fibroplasia.[49] Occasional atypical lesions appear as isolated webs of the ECICA.[63,146]

Medial fibrodysplasia of the ECICA was first documented arteriographically and histologically more than 3 decades ago.[19,95] These lesions invariably occur in female patients, with mean patient age at the time of recognition being approximately 55 years.[18,122,128] Classic lesions of this type in childhood have been rare,[72] and when present, they often affect intracranial vessels.[25,65,119] If previous definitions of medial fibrodysplasia are rigidly applied, this particular subgroup has rarely been described in men.[1] Similarly, these lesions, like those of the renal artery, have been infrequently recognized among African American patients.[68,87]

Medial fibrodysplasia of the ECICA typically involves a 2- to 6-cm segment of the mid-carotid artery adjacent to the second and third cervical vertebrae (Fig. 27-24). The serial stenoses are often evident on examination of the external

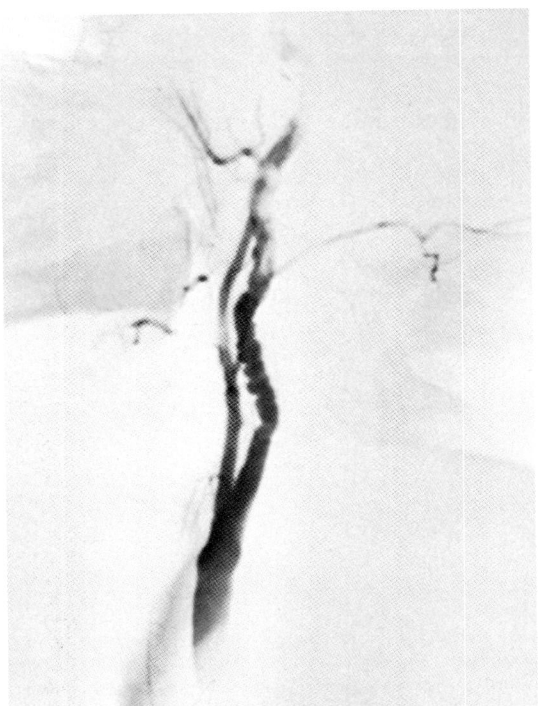

FIGURE 27-24 Medial fibrodysplasia of the extracranial internal carotid artery adjacent to the second and third cervical vertebrae, with characteristic serial stenoses alternating with mural aneurysms. (From Stanley JC, Fry WJ, Seeger JF, et al: Extracranial internal carotid and vertebral artery fibrodysplasia. Arch Surg 109:215-222, 1974.)

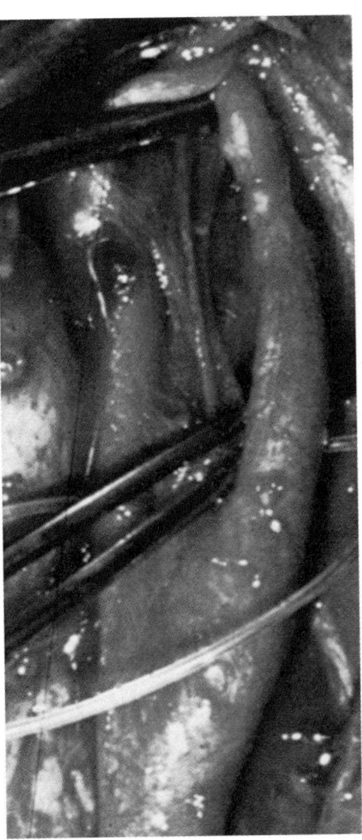

FIGURE 27-25 Medial fibrodysplasia of the extracranial internal carotid artery. Operative exposure of the artery reveals an external beaded appearance due to serial narrowings.

surface of the artery (Fig. 27-25). Bilateral disease has been reported to occur in 35% to 85% of patients with these lesions, with an average incidence of approximately 65%.[15,18,20,122,128,134] Carotid arteries affected by medial fibrodysplasia are often elongated, and kinking occurs in approximately 5% of cases (Fig. 27-26). Similar disease of the external carotid artery or its branches has been reported but is exceedingly rare.[48] Medial fibrodysplastic lesions of the anterior intracranial arteries are uncommon.[37,65,90,103,139]

Vertebral artery disease, in the form of either multiple stenoses (Fig. 27-27) or nonocclusive mural aneurysms (Fig. 27-28), has often been overlooked. These lesions develop in the lower vertebral artery at the level of the fifth cervical vertebra, or higher, at the level of the second cervical vertebra. They exhibit marked irregularities and are often accompanied by eccentric mural aneurysms, but they do not manifest the typical string-of-beads appearance noted in other muscular vessels affected with medial fibrodysplasia. Dysplastic lesions of the basilar artery are an uncommon form of intracranial medial fibrodysplasia.[113]

Noncerebrovascular medial fibrodysplasia occurs in many patients who present with ECICA lesions. Renal artery involvement affects as many as 25% of these individuals.[30,128] The frequency of ECICA lesions in patients presenting with renal artery dysplasia may be even higher, and it has been reported to be 50% in patients who underwent arteriographic assessments of both vessels.[32] Coexistence with lesions in the external iliac and superior mesenteric arteries have also been observed.[30]

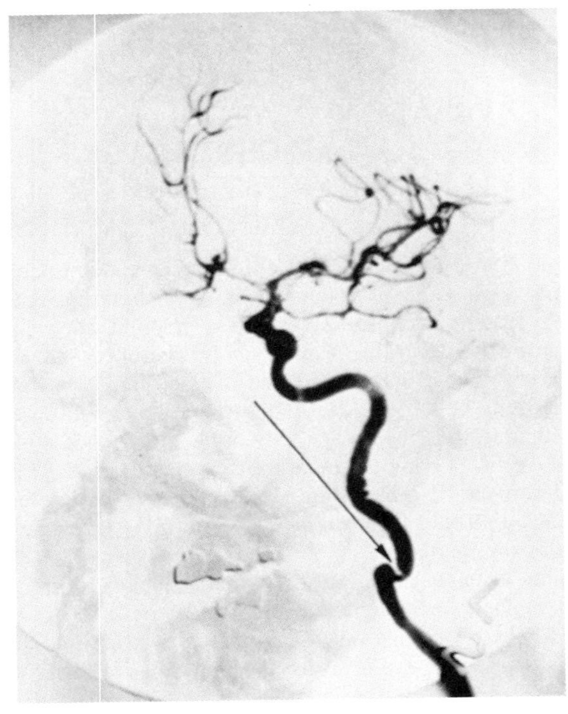

FIGURE 27-26 Medial fibrodysplasia of the extracranial internal carotid artery with angulation (*arrow*) affecting a tortuous elongated segment. (From Stanley JC, Fry WJ, Seeger JF, et al: Extracranial internal carotid and vertebral artery fibrodysplasia. Arch Surg 109:215-222, 1974.)

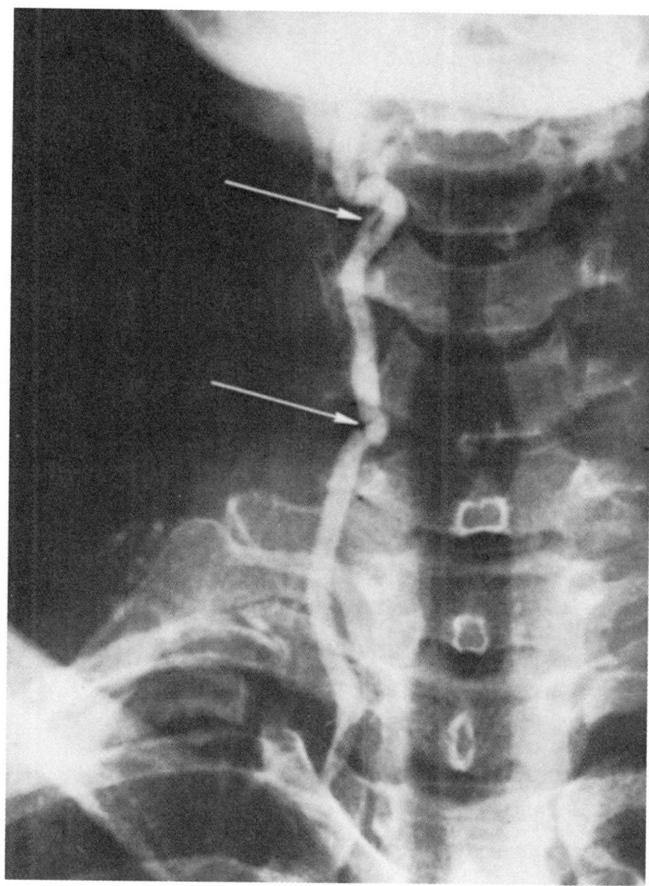

FIGURE 27-27 Medial fibrodysplasia of the vertebral artery with irregular stenoses (*arrows*).

Coexistent intracranial aneurysms have been documented in 12% to 25% of patients with ECICA medial fibrodysplasia.[15,20,37,87,128,145] Solitary intracranial aneurysms are present in 80% of these patients, with multiple aneurysms occurring in the remaining 20% of patients. A meta-analysis of 18 series, excluding those with subarachnoid hemorrhage, revealed a 7.3% prevalence of cerebral aneurysms in patients with carotid or vertebral fibrodyslasia.[17] Although intracranial arteries are occasionally the site of dysplastic disease, aneurysms seemingly do not develop in the involved vessel.[17,58] Instead, they may appear to evolve as a generalized dysplastic arteriopathy, manifested by weakening in arterial branches, which increases the likelihood of berry aneurysm formation.[79,94,131] These aneurysms tend to occur on the same side as the ECICA disease.[88] The anatomic distribution of aneurysms in patients with medial fibrodysplasia is the same as that in patients not affected with dysplastic ECICA.[128] Hypertension may contribute to the evolution of these aneurysms, but it has not been identified as a dominant factor in their pathogenesis.

Complications occurring with medial fibrodysplasia of the ECICA appear to be related to (1) encroachment on the lumen that causes flow reductions, (2) occasional collection of thrombi[68] within the cul-de-sacs, (3) potential distal embolization, and (4) dissections and rupture with arteriovenous fistula formation.[12,101] The precise incidence of these complications has not been determined, but they appear to occur in fewer than 10% of cases. Frequently, dissections obliterate clear evidence of the underlying fibrodysplastic process, and many individuals experiencing this complication are thought to have suffered from spontaneous dissections.[3] Progression of ECICA medial fibrodysplasia may approach 30%, but the exact rate of change has yet to be defined.[111,122,128,133,148] Complications occurring with medial fibrodysplasia of the vertebral arteries are rare and are usually related to thromboembolism or dissections.[99,143]

The pathogenesis of ECICA medial fibrodysplasia is poorly understood, but it appears to be similar to that occurring in the renal vessels. The role of mural ischemia may be greater because very few muscular branches originate from the extracranial portion of the internal carotid artery, thus reducing the number of intrinsic vasa vasorum in this vessel. Unusual traction or stretch stresses that occur with hyperextension and rotation of the neck appear to be other dominant factors in the development of these lesions.

Trauma has been cited as an etiologic factor in instances of vertebral artery fibrodysplasia.[52] In fact, unrecognized adventitial bleeding due to vertebral artery injury during birth may be important in the later development of these dysplastic lesions.[149]

■ ILIAC, FEMORAL, POPLITEAL, AND TIBIAL ARTERIES

The third most common vessel to be affected with medial fibrodysplasia is the external iliac artery.[144] Serial stenoses with intervening mural aneurysms typically affect the proximal third of this vessel (see Fig. 27-28). These lesions are similar to those of the renal and ECICA vessels and may in fact occur in patients with lesions in these other locations.[30,138,141,144] Fibroproliferative processes primarily involve the medial tissue adjacent to areas of relative thinning (Fig. 27-29). Occasionally, fibrodysplastic lesions of the iliac vessels appear as solitary dilations. Complications of external iliac artery fibrodysplasia usually reflect encroachment on the lumen, with restriction of blood flow or the development of mural microthrombi that embolize peripherally.[85] Acute dissection may occur with these lesions, but it is not common.[10,138] Most individuals with medial fibrodysplasia of the iliac vessels have been women in their 5th to 7th decade of life, being 10 to 20 years older than those presenting with similar renovascular disease.[50,51,136] This same pathologic lesion has been observed in an adolescent African American male, in association with a peculiar shortening of the affected lower extremity.[76]

Although rare, similar lesions reflecting the systemic nature of medial fibroplasia have been reported to affect the femoral, popliteal, and tibial vessels of the lower extremity.[56,115,142] In some instances, these extremity lesions have thrombosed[142]; in others they have been associated with aneurysmal changes.[34,47,92,104,135] The etiology of dysplastic lesions of the iliac or femoral arteries may be related more to the paucity of vasa vasorum than to any physical stretch or traction stresses. Indeed, the latter causes would be unlikely to affect any of these lower extremity

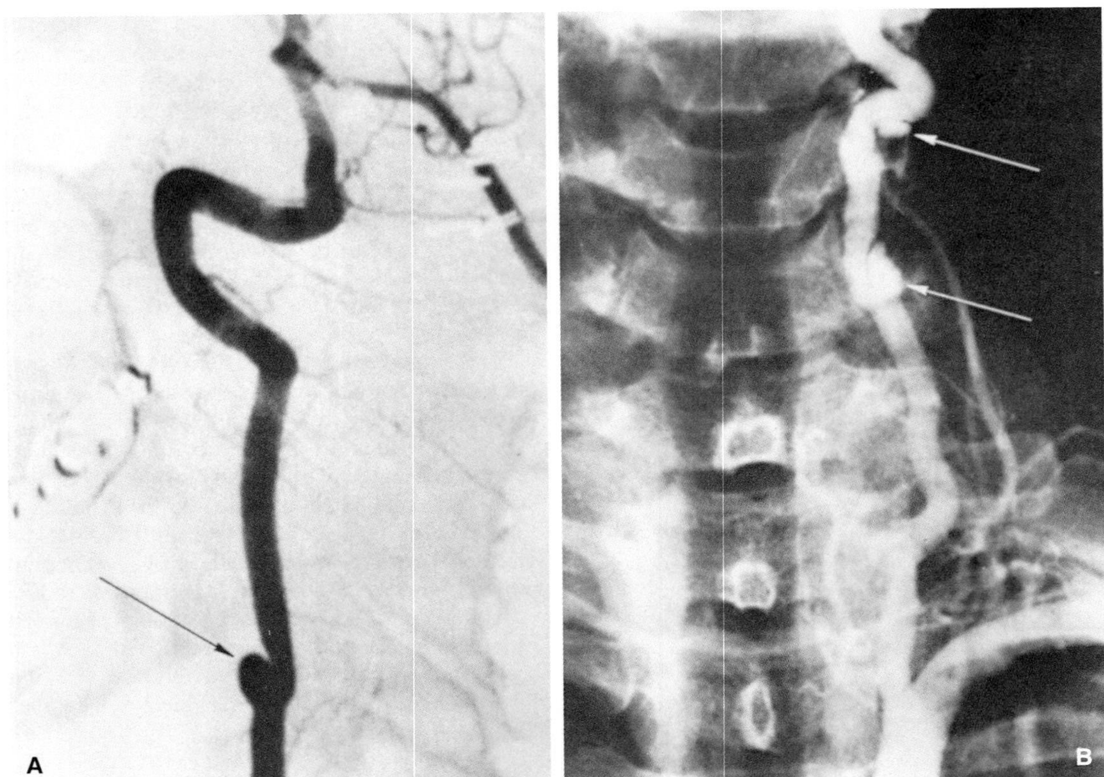

FIGURE 27-28 Medial fibrodysplasia of the vertebral artery. **A,** Isolated saccular intramural aneurysm (*arrow*). **B,** Multiple lesions (*arrows*) suggesting dissection and aneurysm formation. (**A** and **B,** From Stanley JC, Fry WJ, Seeger JF, et al: Extracranial internal carotid and vertebral artery fibrodysplasia. Arch Surg 109:215-222, 1974.)

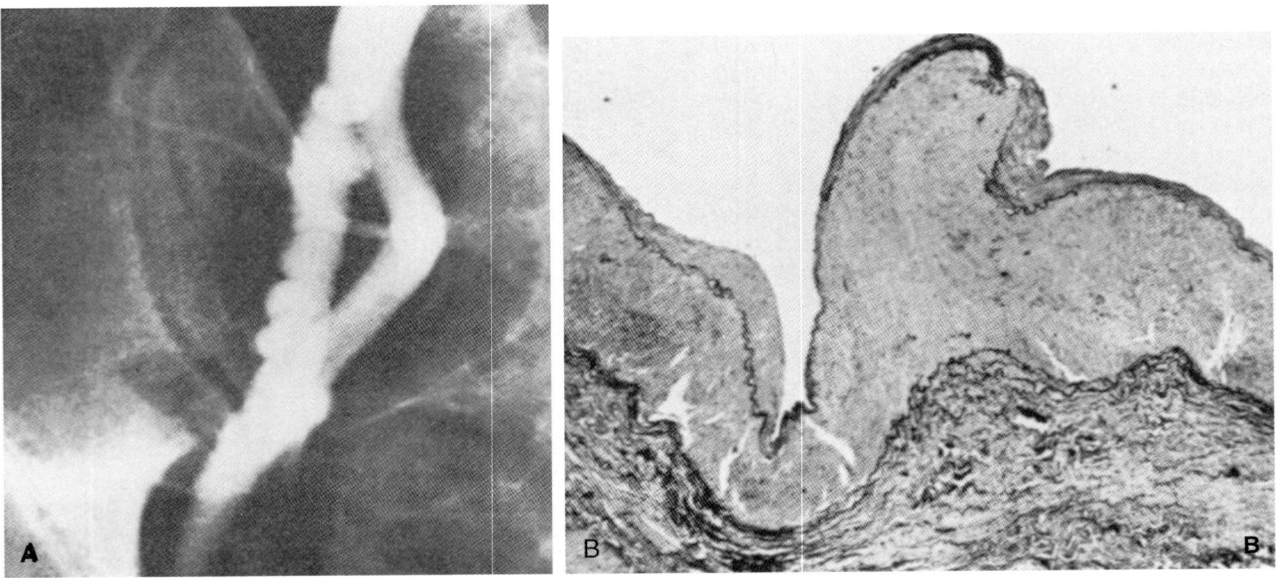

FIGURE 27-29 Medial fibrodysplasia of the external iliac artery. **A,** Multiple stenoses with intervening mural dilations. **B,** Irregular proliferative changes within the media and minimal intimal fibroplasia (elastic van Gieson, ×20, longitudinal section). (**A** and **B,** From Walter JF, Stanley JC, Mehigan JT, et al: External iliac artery fibrodysplasia. AJR Am J Roentgenol 131:125, 1978.)

muscular vessels. The incidence of external iliac artery fibrodysplasia in the general population is unknown, but this condition has been reported to occur in 1% to 6% of patients with renal artery fibrodysplasia.

Intimal fibroplasia of the external iliac artery, as well as that of the femoral, popliteal, and tibial vessels, is usually considered to be a secondary pathologic phenomenon rather than a primary etiologic process. Although most instances of intimal disease affecting these vessels may be the consequence of prior trauma, the result of thrombo-embolism with recannulation of intraluminal thrombus, or the sequela of a prior arteritis, certain cases appear to represent primary intimal fibroplasia.[33]

■ AXILLARY, SUBCLAVIAN, AND BRACHIAL ARTERIES

The most common dysplastic lesion affecting upper extremity vessels appears to be intimal fibroplasia, which is usually manifested by smooth focal or long tubular stenoses. There is a slight predominance of women among patients with these dysplastic lesions. Speculation exists as to the etiology, although the most likely underlying cause is related to an arteritis, frequently affecting all mural elements. The difficulties in differentiating some of these lesions from resolved Takayasu's arteritis are considerable. Indeed, only in the presence of obvious aortic arch, brachiocephalic, or more distal abdominal aortic disease consistent with an inflammatory aortoarteritis can the existence of this secondary form of transmural disease be easily considered. Other intimal fibroplastic lesions affecting the subclavian and axillary vessels may be a consequence of injury (i.e., that associated with repetitive subclavian trauma at the thoracic outlet from costoclavicular entrapment) or of abnormal flow associated with anatomic bands causing vascular narrowing in the same region. Axillary artery involvement may also be the consequence of blunt trauma, with manifestations occurring many years after the actual vascular injury.

Dysplastic disease compatible with medial fibroplasia, with characteristic dilations and constrictions or histologic confirmation of this form of dysplasia, may affect the subclavian,[13,29] brachial,[14,16,27,56,71,102] and radial and ulnar arteries.[61] These lesions appear to reflect a generalized systemic arteriopathy. One reported patient with brachial artery disease had generalized lesions of the iliac, carotid, and vertebral arteries, as well as a maternal history of similar disease.[136] Dysplastic lesions of the upper extremity arteries are too uncommon to be rigorously classified as to type and clinical importance.

■ SPLANCHNIC ARTERIES: CELIAC AND MESENTERIC ARTERIES

Intimal fibroplasia may affect the origins of the three principal splanchnic vessels: (1) the celiac artery, (2) the superior mesenteric artery, and (3) the inferior mesenteric artery. The basis of these lesions is unknown, but fibrodysplasia may represent a secondary phenomenon occurring in developmentally narrowed vessels. Ostial fibrodysplastic lesions are quite common in patients with intestinal angina and often exhibit associated atherosclerotic changes.[54] Intimal fibroplasia tends to occur more often in women than in men, with nearly equal involvement of the celiac and superior mesenteric arteries. The hepatic, splenic, and iliac vessels all have demonstrated fibrodysplastic tubular stenoses, which may represent the outcome of prior arteritis or resolved thrombosis. Occasional patients demonstrate more distal disease in the celiac or superior mesenteric circulatory beds. A dilated appearance of the celiac artery just beyond an eccentric stenosis due to median ligament compression is relatively common. Although earlier reports attributed this particular lesion to medial fibrodysplasia, it may simply represent chronic fibrosis of the "trapped" proximal vessel with post-stenotic dilation.

Characteristic medial fibrodysplasia is rare within the splanchnic circulation, although histologic evidence of it has been reported.[83] When present, this form of splanchnic vascular disease is often associated with similar renal or carotid lesions.[83,109] Histologic evidence of medial dysplasia is also common among patients having splenic artery aneurysms.[62,125] In fact, the development of these aneurysms may be a reflection of compromised vascular integrity due to the disruptive dysplastic process. Similar aneurysms have been noted in other splanchnic vessels, including the superior mesenteric artery.[23] The proximal superior mesenteric artery may exhibit medial fibrodysplastic occlusive disease a few centimeters beyond its origin as it emerges beneath the pancreas over the top of the duodenum. The basis of these latter lesions has not been established, although unusual stretch forces at the root of the mesentery may contribute to dysplastic changes. Involvement of smaller mesenteric branches has been reported but is considered rare.[107,147]

Intestinal branch narrowings that have been considered dysplastic in character usually represent intimal lesions resulting from an earlier inflammatory process, such as arteritis, or an adjacent inflammatory process, such as pan-creatitis. The occurrence of splanchnic arterial fibrodys-plasia is so uncommon as to prevent any firm conclusions about its natural history.

■ OTHER VESSELS

Medial fibrodysplasia also affects the coronary arteries, exhibiting dissections as well as thromboses.[5,53,70,137] Intimal fibroplasia is common in other less affected arteries among patients of all ages, from neonates to the elderly. These lesions may affect arteries of all sizes, ranging from large arteries the size of the aorta to very small vessels such as the coronary sinus node artery.[26,48,55,57,78] Certain aortic lesions may represent developmental webs or consequences of a prior intraluminal thrombotic event. Many of the latter lesions do not appear arteriographically to be very distinct from focal arteriosclerosis.[66] It is unlikely that the changes in these vessels represent a systemic arteritis in its active stage, although they may represent an end stage of an earlier arteritis. Again, experience with these rare forms of arterial dysplasia is so meager as to preclude rendering of any firm conclusions about their etiology or clinical relevance.

REFERENCES

1. Abdul-Rahman AM, Salih A, Brun A, et al: Fibromuscular dysplasia of the cervico-cephalic arteries. Surg Neurol 9:216, 1978.
2. Alimi Y, Mercier C, Pellissier J-F, et al: Fibromuscular disease of the renal artery: A new histopathologic classification. Ann Vasc Surg 6:220, 1992.
3. Andersen CA, Collins GJ Jr, Rich NM, McDonald PT: Bilateral internal carotid arterial occlusions associated with fibromuscular dysplasia. Vasc Surg 13:349, 1979.
4. Andreoni KA, Weeks SM, Gerber DA, et al: Incidence of donor renal fibromuscular dysplasia: Does it justify routine angiography? Transplantation 73:1112, 2002.
5. Arey JB, Segal R: Fibromuscular dysplasia of intramyocardial coronary arteries. Pediatr Pathol 7:97, 1987.
6. Bader H: The anatomy and physiology of the vascular wall. In Hamilton WF (ed): Handbook of Physiology, Vol 2. Washington, DC, American Physiological Society, 1963, pp 865-889.
7. Bofinger A, Hawley C, Fisher P, et al: Alpha-1-antitrypsin phenotypes in patients with renal arterial fibromuscular dysplasia. J Hum Hypertens 14:91-94, 2000.
8. Bofinger AM, Hawley CM, Fisher PM, et al: Increased severity of multifocal renal arterial fibromuscular dysplasia in smokers. J Hum Hypertens 13:517-520, 1999.
9. Bofinger A, Hawley C, Fisher P, et al: Polymorphisms of the renin-angiotensin system in patients with multifocal renal arterial fibromuscular dysplasia. J Hum Hypertens 15:185, 2001.
10. Burri B, Fontolliet C, Ruegsegger C-H, Mosimann R: External iliac artery dissection due to fibromuscular dysplasia. Vasa 12:76, 1983.
11. Campman SC, Holmes JF, Sokolove PE, et al: Pulmonary arterial fibromuscular dysplasia: A rare cause of fulminant lung hemorrhage. Am J Forensic Med Pathol 21:69, 2000.
12. Canova A, Esposito S, Patricolo A, et al: Spontaneous obliteration of a carotid-cavernous fistula associated with fibromuscular dysplasia of the internal carotid artery. J Neurosurg Sci 31:37, 1987.
13. Chambers JL, Neale ML, Appleberg M: Fibromuscular hyperplasia in an aberrant subclavian artery and neurogenic thoracic outlet syndrome: An unusual combination. J Vasc Surg 20:834,1994.
14. Cheu HW, Mills JL: Digital artery embolization as a result of fibromuscular dysplasia of the brachial artery. J Vasc Surg 14:225,1991.
15. Chiche L, Bahnini A, Koskas F, et al: Occlusive fibromuscular disease of arteries supplying the brain: Results of surgical treatment. Ann Vasc Surg 11:496, 1997.
16. Ciocca RG, Madson DL, Wilkerson DK, et al: Fibromuscular dysplasia of the brachial artery: An endovascular approach. Am Surg 61:161, 1995.
17. Cloft HJ, Kallmes DF, Kallmes MH, et al: Prevalence of cerebral aneurysms in patients with fibromuscular dysplasia: A reassessment. J Neurosurg 88:436, 1998.
18. Collins GJ Jr, Rich NM, Clagett GP, et al: Fibromuscular dysplasia of the internal carotid arteries: Clinical experience and follow-up. Ann Surg 194:89, 1981.
19. Connett M, Lansche JM: Fibromuscular hyperplasia of the internal carotid artery: Report of a case. Ann Surg 162:59, 1965.
20. Corrin LS, Sandok BA, Houser OW: Cerebral ischemic events in patients with carotid artery fibromuscular dysplasia. Arch Neurol 38:616, 1981.
21. Cragg AH, Smith TP, Thompson BH, et al: Incidental fibromuscular dysplasia in potential renal donors: Long-term clinical follow-up. Radiology 172:145, 1989.
22. de Deeuw D, Donker AJM, Burema J, et al: Nephroptosis and hypertension. Lancet 1:213, 1977.
23. den Butter G, Bockel JH, Aarts JC: Arterial fibrodysplasia: Rapid progression complicated by rupture of a visceral aneurysm into the gastrointestinal tract. J Vasc Surg 7:449, 1988.
24. Devaney K, Kapur SP, Patterson K, Chandra RS: Pediatric renal artery dysplasia: A morphologic study. Pediatr Pathol 11:609, 1991.
25. DiFazio M, Hinds SR II, Depper M, et al: Intracranial fibromuscular dysplasia in a six-year-old child: A rare cause of childhood stroke. J Child Neurol 15:559, 2000.
26. Dominguez FE, Tate LG, Robinson MJ: Familial fibromuscular dysplasia presenting as sudden death. Am J Cardiovasc Pathol 2:269, 1988.
27. Dorman RL Jr, Kaufman JA, LaMuraglia GM: Digital emboli from brachial artery fibromuscular dysplasia. Cardiovasc Intervent Radiol 17:95, 1994.
28. Dornfeld L, Kaufman JJ: Immunologic considerations in renovascular hypertension. Urol Clin North Am 2:285, 1975.
29. Drury JK, Pollock JG: Subclavian arteriopathy in the young patient. Br J Surg 68:617, 1981.
30. Effeney DJ, Ehrenfeld WK, Stoney RJ, Wylie EJ: Why operate on carotid fibromuscular dysplasia? Arch Surg 115:1261, 1980.
31. Ekelund L, Gerlock J, Molin J, Smith C: Roentgenologic appearance of fibromuscular dysplasia. Acta Radiol 19:433, 1978.
32. Ehrenfeld WK, Wylie EJ: Fibromuscular dysplasia of the internal carotid artery. Arch Surg 109:676, 1974.
33. Esfahani F, Rooholamini SA, Azadeh B, Daneshbod K: Arterial fibrodysplasia: A regional cause of peripheral occlusive vascular disease. Angiology 40:108, 1989.
34. Fiche M, Patra P, Chaillou P: Medial fibrodysplasia and aneurysm of the popliteal artery. Ann Vasc Surg 5:456, 1991.
35. Fievez ML: Fibromuscular dysplasia of arteries: A spastic phenomenon? Med Hypotheses 13:341, 1984.
36. Finley JL, Dabbs DJ: Renal vascular smooth muscle proliferation in neurofibromatosis. Hum Pathol 19:107, 1988.
37. Frens DB, Petajan JH, Anderson R, Deblanc HJ Jr: Fibromuscular dysplasia of the posterior cerebral artery: Report of a case and review of the literature. Stroke 5:161,1974.
38. Garcier JM, Macheda B, Therre T, et al: Radioanatomic study of the angle of origin of dysplastic renal arteries. J Radiol 80:927, 1999.
39. Gladstien K, Rushton AR, Kidd KK: Penetrance estimates and recurrence risks for fibromuscular dysplasia. Clin Genet 17:115, 1980.
40. Goncharenko V, Gerlock AJ, Shaff MI, Hollifield SW: Progression of renal artery fibromuscular dysplasia in 42 patients as seen on angiography. Radiology 139:45, 1981.
41. Graham LM, Zelenock GB, Erlandson EE, et al: Abdominal aortic coarctation and segmental hypoplasia. Surgery 86:519, 1979.
42. Grange DK, Balfour IC, Chen SC, et al: Familial syndrome of progressive arterial occlusive disease consistent with fibromuscular dysplasia, hypertension, congenital cardiac defects, bone fragility, brachysyndactyly, and learning disabilities. Am J Med Genet 75:469, 1998.
43. Halperin M, Currarino G: Vascular lesions causing hypertension in neurofibromatosis. N Engl J Med 273:248, 1965.
44. Harrison EG Jr, Hunt JC, Bernatz PE: Morphology of fibromuscular dysplasia of the renal artery in renovascular hypertension. Am J Med 43:97, 1967.
45. Harrison EG, McCormack LJ: Pathologic classification of renal artery disease in renovascular hypertension. Mayo Clin Proc 46:161, 1971.
46. Hata J-I, Hosoda Y: Perimedial fibroplasia of the renal artery: A light and electron microscopy study. Arch Pathol Lab Med 103:220, 1979.
47. Herpels V, Van de Voorde W, Wilms G, et al: Recurrent aneurysms of the upper arteries of the lower limb: An atypical manifestation of fibromuscular dysplasia—a case report. Angiology 38:411, 1987.
48. Hill LD, Antonius JI: Arterial dysplasia. Arch Surg 90:585, 1965.
49. Hirsch CS, Roessmann U: Arterial dysplasia with ruptured basilar artery aneurysm: Report of a case. Hum Pathol 6:749, 1975.
50. Horne TW: Fibromuscular hyperplasia of the iliac arteries. Aust N Z J Surg 45:415, 1975.
51. Houston C, Rosenthal D, Lamis PA, Stanton PE Jr: Fibromuscular dysplasia of the external iliac arteries: Surgical treatment by graduated internal dilatation technique. Surgery 85:713, 1979.
52. Hugenholtz H, Pokrupa R, Montpetit VJA, et al: Spontaneous dissecting aneurysm of the extracranial vertebral artery. Neurosurgery 10:96, 1982.

53. Imamura M, Yokoyama S, Kikuchi K: Coronary fibromuscular dysplasia presenting as sudden infant death. Arch Pathol Lab Med 121:159, 1997.
54. Insall RL, Chamberlain J, Loose HWC: Fibromuscular dysplasia of visceral arteries. Eur J Vasc Surg 6:668, 1992.
55. Ishikawa Y, Sekiguchi K, Akasaka Y, et al: Fibromuscular dysplasia of coronary arteries resulting in myocardial infarction associated with hypertrophic cardiomyopathy in Noonan's syndrome. Hum Pathol 34:282-284, 2003.
56. Iwai T, Konno S, Hiejima K, et al: Fibromuscular dysplasia in the extremities. J Cardiovasc Surg 26:496, 1985.
57. James TN: Morphologic characteristics and functional significance of focal fibromuscular dysplasia of small coronary arteries. Am J Cardiol 65:12G, 1990.
58. Kalyanaraman UP, Elwood PW: Fibromuscular dysplasia of intracranial arteries causing multiple intracranial aneurysms. Hum Pathol 11:481, 1980.
59. Kaufman JJ, Maxwell MH: Upright aortography in the study of nephroptosis, stenotic lesions of the renal artery, and hypertension. Surgery 53:736, 1963.
60. Kelly TF Jr, Morris GC: Arterial fibromuscular dysplasia: Observations on pathogenesis and surgical management. Am J Surg 143:232, 1982.
61. Khatri VP, Gaulin JC, Amin AK: Fibromuscular dysplasia of distal radial and ulnar arteries: Uncommon cause of digital ischemia. Ann Plast Surg 33:652, 1994.
62. Kojima A, Shindo S, Kubota K, et al: Successful surgical treatment of a patient with multiple visceral artery aneurysms due to fibromuscular dysplasia. Cardiovasc Surg 10:157, 2002.
63. Kubis N, Von Langsdorff D, Petitjean C, et al: Thrombotic carotid megabulb: Fibromuscular dysplasia, septae, and ischemic stroke. Neurology 52:883, 1999.
64. Leadbetter WF, Burkland CE: Hypertension in unilateral renal disease. J Urol 39:611, 1938.
65. Lemahieu SF, Marchau MMB: Intracranial fibromuscular dysplasia and stroke in children. Neuroradiology 18:99, 1979.
66. Letsch R, Kantartzis M, Sommer T, Garcia M: Arterial fibromuscular dysplasia: Report of a case with involvement of the aorta and review of the literature. Thorac Cardiovasc Surg 28:206, 1980.
67. Leung DYM, Glagov S, Matthews MB: Cyclic stretching stimulates synthesis of matrix components by arterial smooth muscle cells in vitro. Science 191:475, 1976.
68. Levien LJ, Fritz VU, Lurie D, et al: Fibromuscular dysplasia of the extracranial carotid arteries. S Afr Med J 65:261, 1984.
69. Lie JT: Segmental mediolytic arteritis: Not an arteritis but a variant of arterial fibromuscular dysplasia. Arch Pathol Lab Med 116:238, 1992.
70. Lie JT, Berg KK: Isolated fibromuscular dysplasia of the coronary arteries with spontaneous dissection and myocardial infarction. Hum Pathol 18:654, 1987.
71. Lin WW, McGee GS, Patterson BK, et al: Fibromuscular dysplasia of the brachial artery: A case report and review of the literature. J Vasc Surg 16:66, 1992.
72. Llorens-Terol J, Sole-Llelnas J, Tura A: Stroke due to fibromuscular hyperplasia of the internal carotid artery. Acta Paediatr Scand 72:299, 1983.
73. Luscher TF, Keller HM, Imhof HG, et al: Fibromuscular hyperplasia: Extension of the disease and therapeutic outcome. Results of the University Hospital Zurich cooperative study on fibromuscular hyperplasia. Nephron 44:109, 1986.
74. Luscher TF, Lie JT, Stanson AW, et al: Arterial fibromuscular dysplasia. Mayo Clin Proc 62:931, 1987.
75. Madden JW, Carlson EC, Hines J: Presence of modified fibroblasts in ischemic contracture of the intrinsic musculature of the hand. Surg Gynecol Obstet 140:509, 1975.
76. Madiba TE, Robbs JV: Fibromuscular dysplasia of the external iliac artery in association with congenital short leg and mesodermal malformation: A case report. S Afr J Surg 27:139, 1989.
77. Major P, Genest J, Cariter P, Kuchel O: Heredity fibromuscular dysplasia with renovascular hypertension. Ann Intern Med 86:583, 1977.
78. Maresi E, Becchina G, Ottoveggio G, et al: Arrhythmic sudden cardiac death in a 3-year-old child with intimal fibroplasia of coronary arteries, aorta, and its branches. Cardiovasc Pathol 9:43, 2001.
79. Masuzawa T, Nakahara N, Kobayashi S: Intracranial multiple berry aneurysms associated with fibromuscular dysplasia and mixed connective tissue disease. Neurol Med Chir (Tokyo) 27:42, 1987.
80. McCormack LJ, Noto TJ Jr, Meaney TF, et al: Subadventitial fibroplasia of the renal artery: A disease of young women. Am Heart J 73:602, 1967.
81. McCormack LJ, Poutasse EF, Meaney TF, et al: A pathologic arteriographic correlation of renal arterial disease. Am Heart J 73:602, 1967.
82. McGrath TW: Fibromuscular dysplasia versus catheter-induced renal artery spasm [Letter]. AJR Am J Roentgenol 148:651, 1987.
83. Meacham PW, Brantley B: Familial fibromuscular dysplasia of the mesenteric arteries. South Med J 80:1311, 1987.
84. Meaney TF, Dustan HF, McCormack LJ: Natural history of renal arterial disease. Radiology 91:881, 1968.
85. Mehigan JT, Stoney RJ: Arterial microemboli and fibromuscular dysplasia of the external iliac arteries. Surgery 81:484, 1977.
86. Mena E, Bookstein JJ, Holt JF, Fry WJ: Neurofibromatosis and renovascular hypertension in children. AJR Am J Roentgenol 118:39, 1973.
87. Mettinger KL: Fibromuscular dysplasia and the brain: II. Current concept of the disease. Stroke 13:53, 1982.
88. Mettinger KL, Ericson K: Fibromuscular dysplasia and the brain: Observations on angiographic, clinical, and genetic characteristics. Stroke 13:46, 1982.
89. Morimoto S, Kuroda M, Uchida K, et al: Occurrence of renovascular hypertension in two sisters. Nephron 17:314, 1976.
90. Nakamura M, Rosahl SK, Vorkapic P, et al: De novo formation of an aneurysm in a case of unusual intracranial fibromuscular dysplasia. Clin Neurol Neurosurg 102:259, 2000.
91. Nemcek AA, Holmburg CE: Reversible renal fibromuscular dysplasia. AJR Am J Roentgenol 147:737, 1986.
92. Neukirch C, Bahnini A, Delcourt A, et al: Popliteal aneurysm due to fibromuscular dysplasia. Ann Vasc Surg 10:578, 1996.
93. Osborn AG, Anderson RE: Angiographic spectrum of cervical and intracranial fibromuscular dysplasia. Stroke 8:617, 1977.
94. Ouchi Y, Tagawa H, Yamakado M, et al: Clinical significance of cerebral aneurysm in renovascular hypertension due to fibromuscular dysplasia: Two cases in siblings. Angiology 40:581, 1989.
95. Palubinskas AJ, Ripley HR: Fibromuscular hyperplasia in extra-renal arteries. Radiology 82:451, 1964.
96. Pannier-Moreau I, Grimbert P, Fiquet-Kempf B, et al: Possible familial origin of multifocal renal artery fibromuscular dysplasia. J Hypertens 15:1797, 1997.
97. Park SH, Chi JG, Choi Y: Primary intimal fibroplasia with multiple aneurysms of renal artery in childhood. Child Nephrol Urol 10:51, 1990.
98. Paulson GW: Fibromuscular dysplasia, antiovulant drugs, and ergot preparations. Stroke 9:172, 1978.
99. Perez-Higueras A, Alvarez-Ruiz F, Martinez-Bermejo A, et al: Cerebellar infarction from fibromuscular dysplasia and dissecting aneurysm of the vertebral artery. Stroke 19:521, 1988.
100. Plotkin SA, Boue A, Boue JG: The in vitro growth of rubella virus in human embryo cells. Am J Epidemiol 81:71, 1965.
101. Reddy SV, Karnes WE, Earnest F IV, Sundt TM Jr: Spontaneous extracranial vertebral arteriovenous fistula with fibromuscular dysplasia. J Neurosurg 54:399, 1981.
102. Reilly JM, McGaw DJ, Sicard GA: Bilateral brachial artery fibromuscular dysplasia. Ann Vasc Surg 7:483, 1993.
103. Rinaldi I, Harris WO Jr, Kopp JE, Legier J: Intracranial fibromuscular dysplasia: Report of two cases, one with autopsy verification. Stroke 7:511, 1976.

104. Ritota P, Quirke TE, Keys RC, et al: A rare association of fibromuscular dysplasia of the femoral artery with aneurysm and occlusion treated alternatively. J Cardiovasc Surg 35:239, 1994.
105. Rosenberger A, Adler O, Lichtig H: Angiographic appearance of the renal vein in a case of fibromuscular dysplasia of the artery. Radiology 118:579, 1976.
106. Rushton AR: The genetics of fibromuscular dysplasia. Arch Intern Med 140:233, 1980.
107. Safioleas M, Kakisis J, Manti C: Coexistence of hypertrophic cardiomyopathy and fibromuscular dysplasia of the superior mesenteric artery. N Engl J Med 344:1333, 2001.
108. Salifu MO, Gordon DH, Friedman EA, Delano BG: Bilateral renal infarction in a black man with medial fibromuscular dysplasia. Am J Kid Dis 36:284, 2000.
109. Salmon PJM, Allan JS: An unusual case of fibromuscular dysplasia. J Cardiovasc Surg 29:756, 1988.
110. Sandmann W, Schulte KM: Multivisceral fibromuscular dysplasia in childhood: Case report and review of the literature. Ann Vasc Surg 14:496, 2002.
111. Sandok BA: Fibromuscular dysplasia of the internal carotid artery. Neurol Clin 1:17, 1983.
112. Sang CN, Whelton PK, Hamper UM, et al: Etiologic factors in renovascular fibromuscular dysplasia. Hypertension 14:472, 1989.
113. Saygi S, Bolay H, Tekkok IH, et al: Fibromuscular dysplasia of the basilar artery: A case with brain stem stroke. Angiology 41:658, 1990.
114. Schievink WI, Bjornsson J: Fibromuscular dysplasia of the internal carotid artery: A clinicopathological study. Clin Neuropathol 15:2, 1996.
115. Schneider PA, LaBerge JM, Cunningham CG, et al: Isolated thigh claudication as a result of fibromuscular dysplasia of the deep femoral artery. J Vasc Surg 15:657, 1992.
116. Schreiber MJ, Pohl MA, Novick AC: The natural history of atherosclerotic and fibrous renal artery disease. Urol Clin North Am 11:383, 1984.
117. Schurch W, Messerli FH, Genest J, et al: Arterial hypertension and neurofibromatosis: Renal artery stenosis and coarctation of abdominal aorta. Can Med Assoc J 113:878, 1975.
118. Sheps SG, Kincaid OW, Hunt JC: Serial renal function and angiographic observations in idiopathic fibrous and fibromuscular stenoses of the renal arteries. Am J Cardiol 30:55, 1972.
119. Shields WD, Ziter FA, Osborn AG, Allen J: Fibromuscular dysplasia as a cause of stroke in infancy and childhood. Pediatrics 59:899, 1977.
120. Siassi B, Glyman G, Emmanouilides GC: Hypoplasia of the abdominal aorta associated with the rubella syndrome. Am J Dis Child 120:476, 1970.
121. Slavin RE, Saeki K, Bhagavan B, et al: Segmental arterial mediolysis: A precursor to fibromuscular dysplasia? Mod Pathol 8:287, 1995.
122. So EL, Toole JF, Dalal P, Moody DM: Cephalic fibromuscular dysplasia in 32 patients: Clinical findings and radiologic features. Arch Neurol 38:619, 1981.
123. Sottiurai VS, Fry WJ, Stanley JC: Ultrastructural characteristics of experimental arterial medial fibrodysplasia induced by vasa vasorum occlusion. J Surg Res 24:169, 1978.
124. Sottiurai VS, Fry WJ, Stanley JC: Ultrastructure of medial smooth muscle and myofibroblasts in human arterial dysplasia. Arch Surg 113:1280, 1978.
125. Stanley JC, Fry WJ: Pathogenesis and clinical significance of splenic artery aneurysms. Surgery 76:898, 1974.
126. Stanley JC, Fry WJ: Renovascular hypertension secondary to arterial fibrodysplasia in adults: Criteria for operation and results of surgical therapy. Arch Surg 110:922, 1975.
127. Stanley JC, Fry WJ: Pediatric renal artery occlusive disease and renovascular hypertension: Etiology, diagnosis, and operative treatment. Arch Surg 116:669, 1981.
128. Stanley JC, Fry WJ, Seeger JF, et al: Extracranial internal carotid and vertebral artery fibrodysplasia. Arch Surg 109:215, 1974.
129. Stanley JC, Gewertz BC, Bove EL, et al: Arterial fibrodysplasia: Histopathologic character and current etiologic concepts. Arch Surg 110:561, 1975.
130. Stanley JC, Graham LM, Whitehouse WM Jr, et al: Developmental occlusive disease of the abdominal aorta, splanchnic, and renal arteries. Am J Surg 142:190, 1981.
131. Stanley JC, Rhodes EL, Gewertz BL, et al: Renal artery aneurysms: Significance of macroaneurysms exclusive of dissections and fibrodysplastic mural dilatations. Arch Surg 110:1327, 1975.
132. Stanley JC, Zelenock GB, Messina LM, et al: Pediatric renovascular hypertension: A thirty-year experience of operative treatment. J Vasc Surg 21:212, 1995.
133. Stewart DR, Price RA, Nebesar R, Schuster SR: Progressing peripheral fibromuscular hyperplasia in an infant: A possible manifestation of the rubella syndrome. Surgery 73:374, 1973.
134. Stewart MT, Moritz MW, Smith RB III, et al: The natural history of carotid fibromuscular dysplasia. J Vasc Surg 3:305, 1986.
135. Stinnett DM, Graham JM, Edwards WD: Fibromuscular dysplasia and thrombosed aneurysm of the popliteal artery in a child. J Vasc Surg 5:769, 1987.
136. Suzuki H, Daida H, Sakurai H, Yamaguchi H: Familial fibromuscular dysplasia of bilateral brachial arteries. Heart 82:251, 1999.
137. Tanaka M, Watanabe T, Tomaki S, et al: Revascularization in fibromuscular dysplasia of the coronary arteries. Am Heart J 125:1167, 1993.
138. Thevenet A, Latil JL, Albat B: Fibromuscular disease of the external iliac artery. Ann Vasc Surg 6:199, 1992.
139. Tripathi M, Santosh V, Nagaraj D, et al: Stroke in a young man with fibromuscular dysplasia of the cranial vessels with anticardiolipin antibodies: A case report. Neurol Sci 22:31, 2001.
140. Tsukamoto Y, Komuro Y, Akutsu F, et al: Orthostatic hypertension due to coexistence of renal fibromuscular dysplasia and nephroptosis. Jpn Circ J 52:1408, 1988.
141. Twigg HL, Palmisano PJ: Fibromuscular hyperplasia of the iliac artery: A case report. AJR Am J Roentgenol 95:418, 1965.
142. Van den Dungen JJAM, Boontje AH, Oosterhuis JW: Femoropopliteal arterial fibrodyplasia. Br J Surg 77:396, 1990.
143. Vles JSH, Hendriks JJE, Lodder J, Janevski B: Multiple vertebrobasilar infarctions from fibromuscular dysplasia-related dissecting aneurysm of the vertebral artery in a child. Neuropediatrics 21:104, 1990.
144. Walter JF, Stanley JC, Mehigan JT, et al: External iliac artery fibrodysplasia. AJR Am J Roentgenol 131:125, 1978.
145. Wesen CA, Elliott BM: Fibromuscular dysplasia of the carotid arteries. Am J Surg 151:448, 1986.
146. Wirth FP, Miller WA, Russell AP: Atypical fibromuscular hyperplasia: Report of two cases. J Neurosurg 54:685, 1981.
147. Yamaguchi R, Yamaguchi Q, Isogai M, et al: Fibromuscular dysplasia of the visceral arteries. Am J Gastroenterol 91:1635, 1996.
148. Yamamoto I, Kageyama N, Usui K, Yoshida J: Fibromuscular dysplasia of the internal carotid artery: Unusual arteriographic changes with progression of clinical symptoms. Acta Neurochir (Wien) 50:293, 1979.
149. Yates PO: Birth trauma to the vertebral arteries. Arch Dis Child 109:215, 1974.

Chapter 28

Uncommon Arteriopathies

ROGER F. J. SHEPHERD, MB, BCH
THOM ROOKE, MD

Section V

A busy vascular specialist encounters a wide range of arterial disease. In most patients the underlying disorder is atherosclerosis resulting from risk factors of advancing age, complications of obesity with diabetes and dyslipidemia, and nicotine dependence. Some patients, however, present with unusual and puzzling arterial disorders, raising the question of an uncommon arteriopathy.

The uncommon arteriopathies are a vast and diverse group of primarily nonatherosclerotic disorders that cause arterial disease. Despite different etiologies, these disorders have in common similar consequences, including (1) arterial obstruction (causing tissue and organ ischemia) and (2) arterial expansion (with risk of dissection and rupture). This chapter deals with some of the less common but fascinating disorders that can cause arterial disease (Table 28-1) and focuses on the following: Marfan syndrome, Ehlers-Danlos type IV, pseudoxanthoma elasticum, neurofibromatosis type 1, Behçet's disease, unusual presentations of vasculitis, and drug- and radiation-induced arterial disease. Established diagnostic criteria are outlined for each disorder and salient features are discussed, including the genetic etiology for all inherited arteriopathies, typical clinical features, unusual vascular manifestations, and guidance in the management of disease complications.

In general, one should consider unusual arteriopathy in a patient who is *young* or does not have traditional *cardiovascular risk* factors for atherosclerosis. For example, the finding of an ascending aortic aneurysm or spontaneous arterial dissection in a *previously healthy* patient should arouse suspicion of a collagen disorder such as Marfan syndrome. A positive *family history* of death at an early age from arterial dissection or aneurysm rupture also suggests an inherited arteriopathy. A pediatric patient with severe arterial hypertension might have renovascular disease, perhaps due to congenital renal artery dysplasia. *Unusual patterns or location* of occlusive disease in arteries may reflect an uncommon arteriopathy. A young smoker with Raynaud's syndrome and digital artery occlusions raises the question of thromboangiitis obliterans. An *unusual aneurysm,* such as one involving the pulmonary arteries in a young adult, may be due to Behçet's disease or Takayasu's arteritis. Occlusive or aneurysmal arterial disease in the setting of a *multisystem illness* should lead to the consideration of a systemic cause such as unusual infection, vasculitis, or paraneoplastic syndrome.

Table 28-1 Incidence of Some Uncommon Arteriopathies

ARTERIOPATHY	INCIDENCE
Heritable collagen vascular disorders	
Marfan syndrome	1:5,000-10,000
Ehlers-Danlos type IV	1:5000 (estimated)
Pseudoxanthoma elasticum	1:70,000-160,000
Neurofibromatosis	1:3000
With vascular disease	1:60,000
Behçet's disease	<1:100,000

Adapted from Shepherd RFJ, Rooke T: Uncommon arteriopathies: What the vascular surgeon needs to know. Semin Vasc Surg 16:240-251, 2003.

Whenever a vascular clinician encounters something out of the ordinary, a rare arteriopathy should be considered. However, patients with uncommon arterial disorders often present to the vascular specialist with common problems such as intermittent claudication, stroke, myocardial infarction, renovascular hypertension, Raynaud's phenomenon, and aneurysmal disease. Failure to consider the diagnosis of a less common arteriopathy may lead to a delay in care for the patient or lead to suboptimal therapy and poor surgical outcomes. The clinician needs to be aware of the natural history of the disease; the risk of disease recurrence; and specific indications for anticoagulation, immunosuppression, and surgical intervention. For example, patients with Behçet's disease are at increased risk of native artery and bypass graft occlusion, but anticoagulation can lead to death from fatal hemoptysis associated with an undetected pulmonary artery aneurysm. Preoperative immunosuppression should be considered to reduce complications in a patient with active giant cell arteritis; unfortunately, the diagnosis is sometimes missed until the time of surgery.

Compared to patients with atherosclerosis, those with uncommon arteriopathies are more likely to present with life-threatening conditions such as spontaneous arterial dissection or aneurysm rupture. Arterial surgery may be associated with significant operative risk. For example, aneurysm repair in a patient with a connective tissue disorder can be fraught with the technical difficulties of reconstructing fragile tissues. Patients with uncommon arteriopathies are not only more likely to need prophylactic elective surgery but also they are high-risk surgical patients with an increased risk of native artery and bypass graft obstruction. In every case, the natural history of the disease needs to be carefully balanced against the surgical risks and expected outcomes of the procedure. This review emphasizes the differential diagnoses to be considered when encountering an unusual vascular case. For purposes of discussion, these disorders are grouped into the following categories: (1) diseases that cause premature atherosclerosis in the absence of traditional risk factors, (2) drug-induced arterial insufficiency, (3) uncommon causes of aortic aneurysms, (4) unusual presentations of vasculitis, and (5) rare causes of renovascular disease.

■ DISEASES THAT CAUSE ATHEROSCLEROSIS IN THE ABSENCE OF TRADITIONAL RISK FACTORS

Arteriopathies in the absence of traditional risk factors can be classified as inflammatory, noninflammatory, inherited, congenital, and acquired. Acquired causes may be traumatic or drug-, radiation-, or environmentally induced. The present section deals with radiation arteritis and pseudomyxoma elasticum. Inflammatory, congenital, and drug-induced arteriopathies are discussed later in this chapter. Other uncommon arteriopathies such as those associated with homocystinemia and hypercoagulable states are discussed elsewhere in this text.

Radiation Arteritis

Arteritis may develop as a late sequela of radiation therapy for treatment of malignancy. There is often a latency period of more than 10 years before symptoms of vascular damage become apparent.[1,2] Any major vessel that happens to be in the irradiated field may be affected. Aortic, renal, and mesenteric arterial damage may result from abdominal or pelvic radiation for treatment of abdominal malignancy such as lymphoma. External iliac disease may occur after therapeutic radiation for cervical cancer.

Subclavian, axillary, innominate, and carotid artery injury can result after radiation treatment for breast cancer, lymphoma, or lung cancer (Fig. 28-1).[1-7] Radiation-induced vascular damage causes premature atheromatous changes that may be indistinguishable from other causes of atherosclerosis. Endothelial damage from radiation may make the artery more susceptible to hypercholesterolemia, hyperglycemia, tobacco, and other risk factors, leading to accelerated atherosclerosis.[2] Histologic features of radiation arteritis include injury to the vasa vasorum with ischemic necrosis of the vessel wall, fibrosis of the internal elastic lamina, fibrin deposition, and thickening of the adventitia and vessel wall with luminal narrowing or obliteration.[8] The angiographic appearance of radiation-induced arteritis ranges from focal irregularity to diffuse arterial stenosis and occlusion. Radiation-induced arteritis may mimic large-vessel vasculitis with long, smooth, tapered stenosis. Arterial encasement from recurrent tumor may have a similar angiographic appearance. Radiation can be implicated as the primary cause of accelerated atherosclerosis when the site of disease is limited to the field of radiation and the location is atypical for atheromatous disease.

Clinical manifestations are similar to those associated with atherosclerotic arterial occlusive disease, including claudication of an extremity, stroke, and hypertension. Severe disease with friable plaque also predisposes to distal microembolization.[9] Radiation-induced stenosis of the coronary arteries can present with unstable angina in a young patient.[10] Radiation damage may also result in pericardial thickening with cardiac constriction, as well as diastolic dysfunction due to myocardial fibrosis.

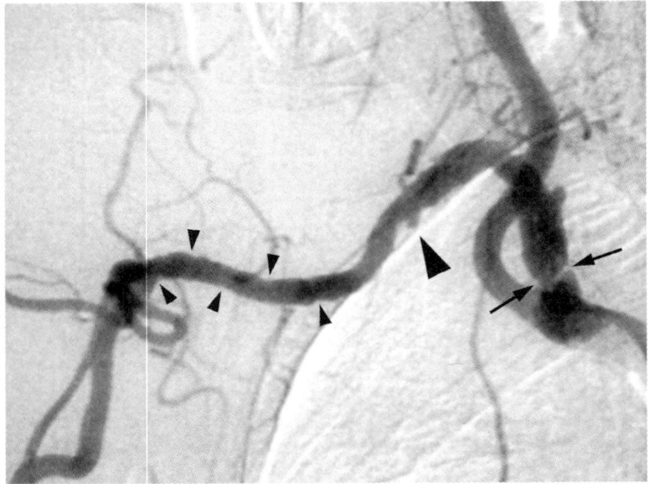

FIGURE 28-1 Angiogram of a 66-year-old patient presenting with acrocyanosis of the fingers and livedo of the skin occurring 21 years after local adjuvant radiation therapy for breast adenocarcinoma. This view of the aortic arch and right upper extremity demonstrates radiation-induced atherosclerosis with an ulcerated plaque at the origin of the subclavian artery *(arrows)* with diffuse atheromatous changes in the area of prior radiation *(arrowheads)*. (From Rubin DI, Schomberg PJ, Shepherd RF, Panneton JM: Arteritis and brachial plexus neuropathy as delayed complications of radiation therapy. Mayo Clin Proc 76:849-852, 2001.)

Radiation arteritis may require treatment with open surgical reconstruction or percutaneous transluminal angioplasty with stenting. In the Mayo Clinic experience, reported graft patency with venous or synthetic conduits was similar to patency rates for patients with atherosclerosis obliterans or Takayasu's arteritis.[11] Patients can benefit from aggressive surgical revascularization with good outcomes.[1] However, the rate of surgical complications, including delayed major infections, is significantly higher in patients with radiation-induced arteritis.[11,12] Local wound healing may also be a major problem in patients with radiation-induced arteritis; lesions with short stenotic segments should be considered for endovascular therapy (Figs. 28-2 and 28-3).[13]

Pseudoxanthoma Elasticum

Pseudoxanthoma elasticum is an inherited disorder of connective tissue causing degeneration of elastic fibers. It is a rare disorder with a prevalence between 1 in 70,000 and 1 in 160,000; however, modern prevalence rates are expected to be higher due to increased awareness of this disorder.[14] Between 1938 and 1951, 74 cases were seen at the Mayo Clinic.[15] Pseudoxanthoma elasticum involves many organ systems, including the skin, eye, and cardiovascular system. The disease is known for its characteristic skin changes with small yellow papules (xanthomas) along lines of flexion such as the neck, groin, and cubital or popliteal fossae.[16] The appearance has been likened to a "plucked chicken" (Fig. 28-4). In the eye, chorioretinal angioid streaks are

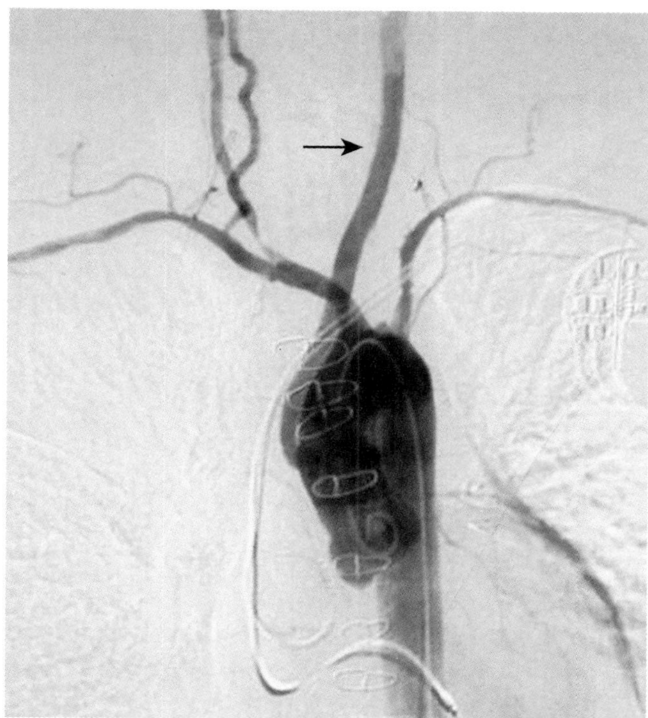

FIGURE 28-2 Radiation-induced coronary, carotid, and subclavian disease occurring 12 years after radiation treatment for lymphoma in a 35-year-old patient. The angiogram shown was obtained after a left aortic arch-to-carotid artery bypass (*arrow*).

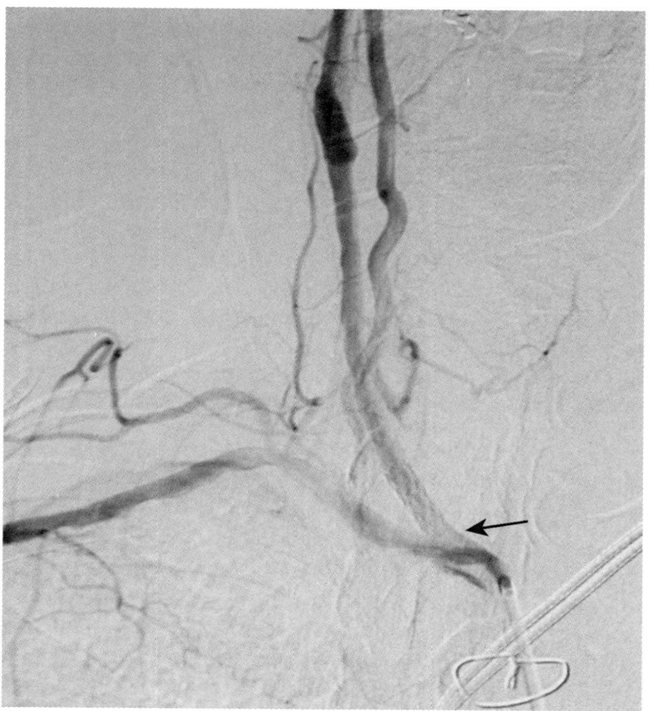

FIGURE 28-3 In the same patient as in Figure 28-2, right common carotid artery stenosis was successfully treated with percutaneous transluminal angioplasty and stent (*arrow*).

associated with decreased visual acuity at an early age. Progressive loss of vision with eventual blindness results from spontaneous retinal hemorrhages. Laser photocoagulation may delay loss of vision in some patients. Of the four subtypes, type I has autosomal dominant inheritance and produces the most severe cutaneous and vascular complications. The responsible gene has been mapped to chromosome 16.[17] Vascular manifestations account for the most devastating complications of this disorder. Diffuse arteriosclerosis occurs in the 3rd or 4th decade of life. Pseudoxanthoma elasticum is a slowly progressive disorder with clinical manifestations relevant to the involved area. Although pseudoxanthoma elasticum may spare the aorta, it often involves the renal arteries, causing hypertension. The leg arteries are commonly involved, resulting in typical symptoms of claudication that progress slowly with time.[18] Acute leg ischemia is uncommon due to the tendency for abundant collateral formation.[19,20] Severe cerebrovascular disease may lead to stenosis or occlusion of carotid and vertebral vessels. Angina pectoris is common: in one series, half of all patients had symptoms of myocardial ischemia at a mean age of 38 years. Coronary artery disease has been reported as early as childhood and has required bypass at 18 years of age in one female patient.[21] Although myocardial infarction has also been reported at an early age, it is uncommon.[22] Myocardial involvement may lead to congestive heart failure; cardiac restriction and valvular damage with mitral valve prolapse have also been reported.[23]

Pseudoxanthoma elasticum should be suspected in a young patient without obvious risk factors or radiation exposure who presents with symptoms of coronary artery disease or peripheral vascular disease. Seventy percent of patients with peripheral arterial disease associated with pseudoxanthoma elasticum are younger than 35 years of age.[19] The diagnosis is suggested by clinical features and may be confirmed by histopathology showing elastic fiber calcification. Calcification of soft tissue and vessels occurs commonly and has been noted as early as 9 years of age. Soft tissue calcification occurs most commonly at the elbow, hip, and phalanges and should be differentiated from that associated with trauma, scleroderma, and hyperparathyroidism.[20]

Typical angiographic findings include diffuse arterial disease with prominent collaterals. Occlusive disease is often amenable to surgical revascularization or angioplasty. Lower extremity revascularization for incapacitating claudication can improve the patient's lifestyle. Correction of renovascular hypertension may be indicated for uncontrolled hypertension. The vascular surgeon should be aware of the very high likelihood of severe multivessel coronary artery disease and the progressive nature of this disorder. The cardiac surgeon should consider using the saphenous vein rather than the internal thoracic artery for a coronary artery bypass conduit owing to the possible involvement of all native arteries in pseudoxanthoma elasticum.[21]

■ DRUG-INDUCED ARTERIOPATHIES

Many drugs are known to cause arterial occlusion due to vasoconstriction or direct arterial damage. A number of medications have properties that can cause reversible vaso-

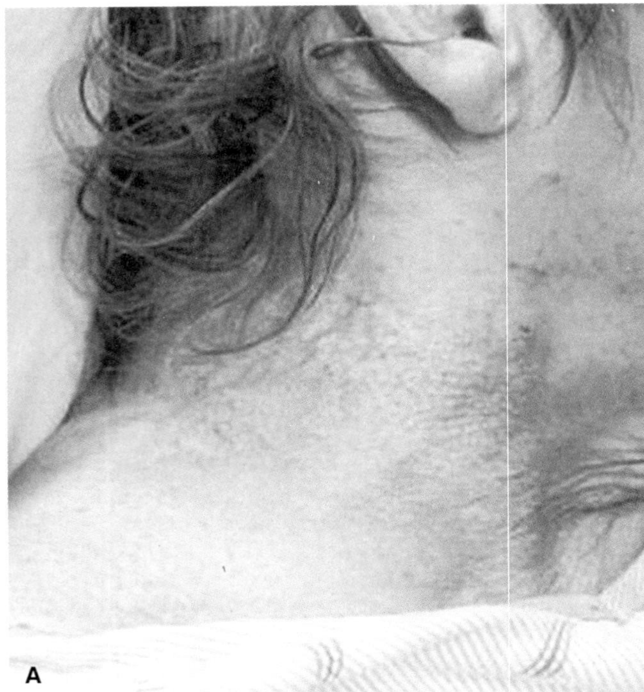

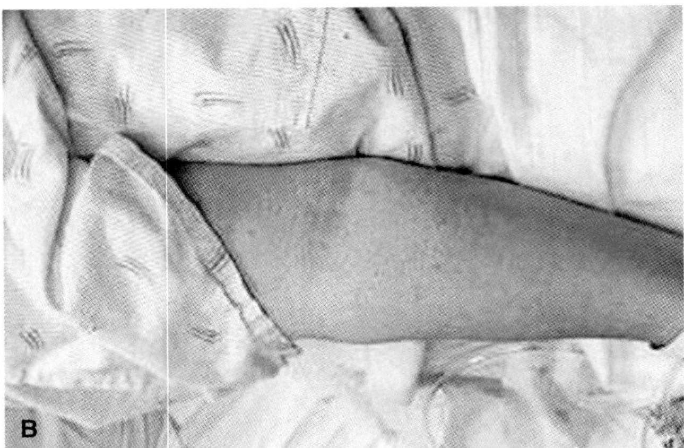

FIGURE 28-4 Pseudoxanthoma. Multiple small, slightly raised, whitish to yellow papules are typically seen along the lines of skin flexion in the neck (**A**) and the cubital fossa of the elbow (**B**).

constriction. β-Adrenergic blockers can induce vasoconstriction by preventing β_2-mediated vasodilation. Although these agents may aggravate Raynaud's phenomenon due to reversible digital artery vasospasm, they are not associated with large-vessel vasoconstriction, nor do they worsen preexisting claudication. Sympathomimetic pressor agents such as dopamine, ephedrine, epinephrine, mephentermine, metaraminol, norepinephrine, and phenylephrine cause direct peripheral vasoconstriction. Intense, prolonged vasoconstriction can lead to necrosis and gangrene of the extremities, especially in critically ill patients with low-flow states and in those with preexisting peripheral arterial disease.

Direct arterial damage may be the consequence of inadvertent intra-arterial injection that leads to arterial spasm, endothelial damage, vessel thrombosis, and occlusion. This complication was first reported in 1942, with the accidental injection of pentothal sodium into an aberrant ulnar artery in a patient undergoing induction of general anesthesia.[24] In severe cases, ischemic muscle necrosis can result with extremity gangrene and limb loss. Limb swelling often occurs as a result of distal venous obstruction. Medical management consists of supportive care with heparin anticoagulation to prevent further thrombosis, intravenous hydration to prevent renal failure from rhabdomyolysis, analgesia for pain control, and local skin care. Intra-arterial thrombolysis has rarely been used. Vasodilators may be used but are unlikely to be of benefit in patients with fixed occlusive disease. Development of compartment hypertension mandates fasciotomy. Vascular reconstruction is rarely indicated.[25]

Drugs of abuse, such as *amphetamines* and *cocaine*, are well known to cause arterial damage. Aortic dissection has been associated with both cocaine and methamphetamine.[26] Cocaine abuse may cause a variety of vascular diseases, including venous thrombosis, lower extremity vasospasm, mesenteric artery thrombosis, renal infarction, and aortic vasculitis.[27-29] Although most lesions are inflammatory in nature, accelerated atherosclerosis has been reported.[30] Modern reports estimate that cocaine accounts for up to 25% of cases of acute myocardial infarction in patients 18 to 45 years of age.[31] Cocaine causes coronary artery spasm due to increased adrenergic activity in addition to platelet aggregation with coronary thrombosis.[32] Methamphetamine is another potent sympathomimetic that has been linked to myocardial infarction and stroke.[33] Intravenous drug abuse can lead to a number of specific vascular complications including septic thrombophlebitis, aortic dissection, arteriovenous fistulae, and necrotizing fasciitis with gangrene of extremities.[34] The most frequent vascular complications in drug addicts are infected pseudoaneurysms of the femoral, brachial, or radial arteries. Surgical repair requires ligation and resection of the aneurysm, but this may be complicated by lack of vein for bypass in intravenous drug users. Use of a prosthetic graft in these circumstances is associated with an increased risk of graft infection and occlusion.[25]

Ergotism

Ergotism is a rare but important cause of arterial insufficiency. In the Middle Ages, epidemics of gangrene occurred from ingestion of food grains contaminated by a fungus, *Claviceps purpura*. Outbreaks of ergot poisoning occurred throughout Europe and Russia in 1926, Ireland in 1929, and France in 1953. Affected individuals called this affliction *Saint Anthony's fire* because the skin turned black like charcoal, as if consumed by the "holy fire."[36,37]

Today, ergot preparations are used successfully in the treatment of migraine headaches. Unfortunately, the vasoconstrictor action of ergot is not always limited to the

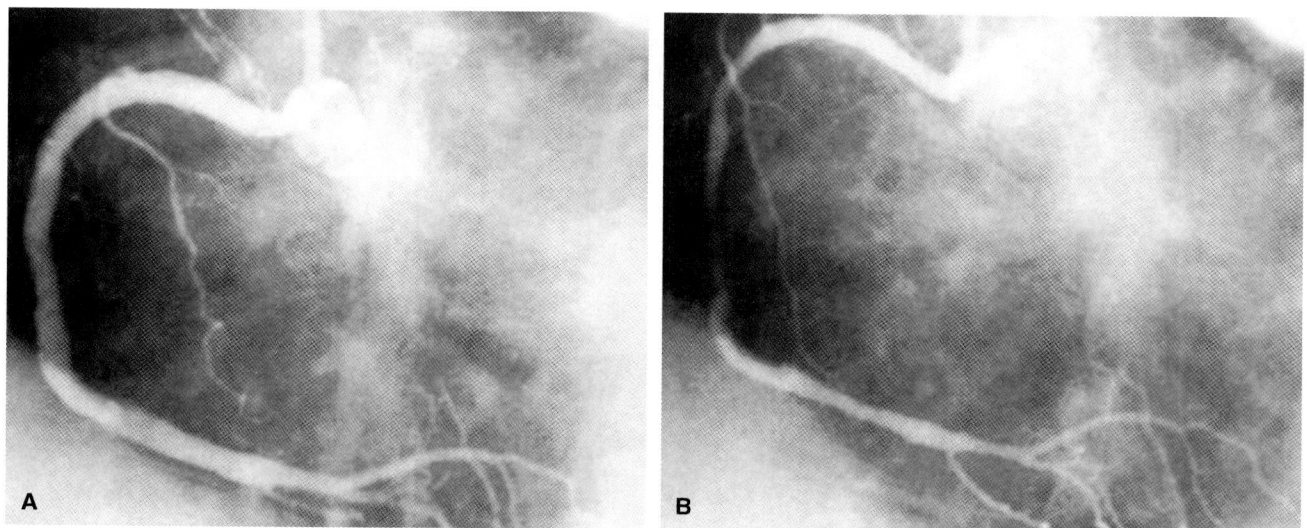

FIGURE 28-5 Ergonovine-induced constriction of the right coronary artery before (**A**) and after (**B**) intracoronary administration of ergonovine. (**A** and **B,** From Bove A, Viletstra R: Spasm in ectatic coronary arteries. Mayo Clin Proc 60:822-826, 1985.)

cerebral vessels, and ergot preparations have potential to cause widespread systemic arterial vasoconstriction. There are many case reports documenting involvement of almost all major arteries by ergotism, including upper and lower extremity arteries, renal and mesenteric arteries, and the coronary circulation.[38-43]

Ergotism most commonly involves the extremities, in particular the femoral and brachial arteries.[38] Initial symptoms can include subjective feeling of coolness, pallor, cyanosis, and numbness of the hands and feet. On examination, the distal arterial pulses may be absent. Intermittent claudication is a common feature, but unlike fixed occlusive disease, the claudication distance and severity of symptoms can vary depending on when the patient last took ergot. In severe cases, intense vasospasm in leg or arm arteries results in critical ischemia and, in rare instances, the limb requires amputation due to gangrene.

Ergotism can also result in organ ischemia. Coronary artery vasospasm may cause angina pectoris; acute myocardial infarction has been reported (Fig. 28-5).[44,45] Mesenteric artery vasospasm may cause abdominal pain and lead to bowel infarction.[41,46,47] Hypertension and renal failure can result from renal artery constriction or occlusion.[48]

Ergotism has been called the "great masquerader" because it can be mistaken for more common disease entities including atherosclerosis obliterans, aortic dissection, and thromboembolic arterial occlusion.[36,47,49] Angiographic findings have been confused with vasculitis because the appearance of vasospasm may be similar to the smooth, tapered stenoses often seen in Takayasu's disease and extracranial giant cell arteritis (Fig. 28-6). As a result of misdiagnosis, patients have undergone unnecessary surgical bypasses for ergotism. In one report, a 62-year-old farmer who was taking an ergot preparation for headaches was thought to have a thrombotic occlusion of the brachial artery. Three days after withdrawal of ergot, forearm pulses remained absent and he underwent saphenous vein bypass. A repeat angiogram 10 days later showed that the native brachial artery was open with a patent vein graft.[50]

At the Mayo Clinic, we have identified 38 patients with ergotism between 1945 and 1985. Eight patients had typical claudication, and four had rest pain. Some patients underwent surgical procedures including bypass operations, abdominal explorations, and sympathectomies.[1] Unusual clinical presentations included mesenteric ischemia with small bowel infarction, isolated arm ischemia, and pseudoclaudication due to spinal cord ischemia. Several patients had recurrent ischemic episodes, even though all ergot preparations had been discontinued by the physician. Continued surreptitious use was confirmed in one patient who had three hospital admissions over a 1-year period for painful cyanotic fingers and calf claudication due to vasospasm.[36] Most published cases have involved use of ergotamine suppositories for treatment of migraine headaches, but some have been due to parenteral dihydroergotamine for prophylaxis of deep venous thrombosis and, less frequently, oral ergot.[51]

Treatment depends on the severity of symptoms. In mild cases, symptoms usually respond to drug withdrawal. After cessation of medication, several days may be required for full reversal of vasospasm. Calcium-channel blockers such as nifedipine are variably successful in some patients, but these agents do not reverse severe vasospasm.[38] Nitroprusside causes direct relaxation of smooth muscle and is the agent of choice for patients with severe ischemia.[43,52] Although angioplasty has been described, arterial vasospasm due to ergotism should be reversible; therefore, revascularization is unnecessary unless there is concern for tissue necrosis and gangrene. Supportive measures include adequate hydration and anticoagulation.

■ UNCOMMON CAUSES OF AORTIC ANEURYSM

Most thoracic and abdominal aortic aneurysms occur in older people and are the result of atherosclerosis. In younger patients, alternative etiologies should be considered, including inherited connective tissue disorders (Marfan or

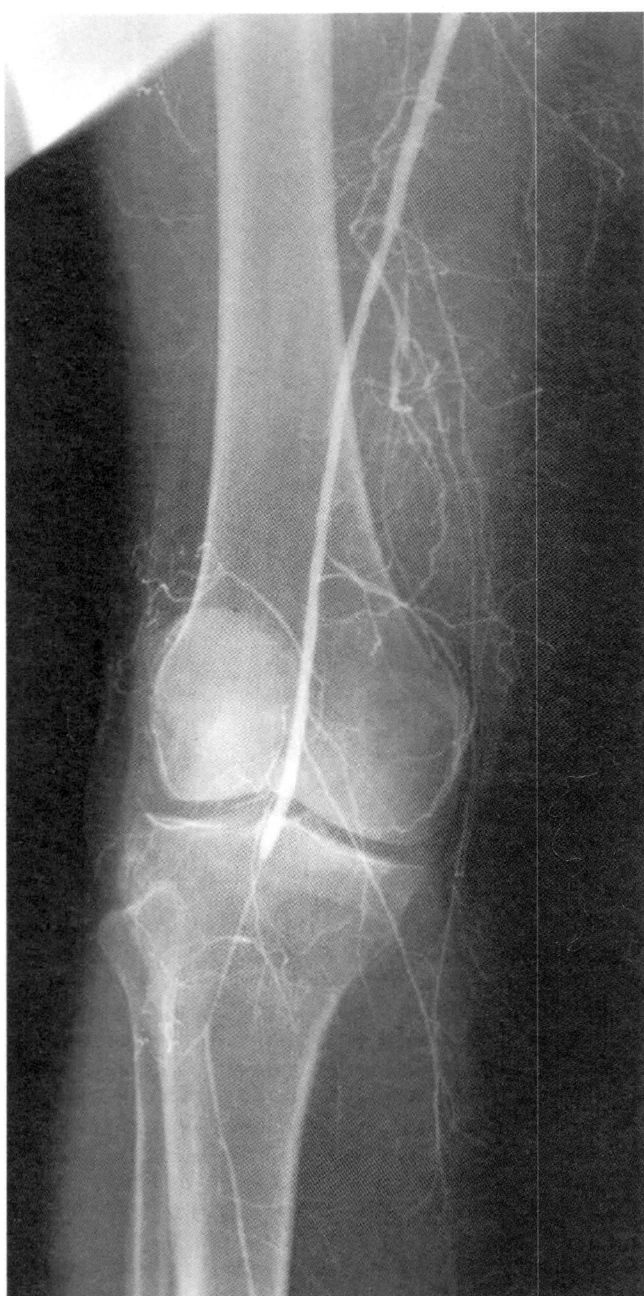

FIGURE 28-6 A 54-year-old woman with migraine headaches treated with Cafergot presented with sudden lower extremity numbness and cyanosis with absent pulses. The angiogram demonstrated severe vasospasm of the infrapopliteal arteries. Nitroprusside is the agent of choice in severe ischemia due to ergot, but it may take more than 24 hours for full reversal of the arterial vasospasm. (From Shepherd RF: Ergotism. In White RA, Hollier LH [eds]: Vascular Surgery: Basic Science and Clinical Correlations. Philadelphia, JB Lippincott, 1994, pp 177-191.)

Ehlers-Danlos syndrome), large artery vasculitis, Behçet's disease, infection, and trauma. The large-vessel arteritides include Takayasu's arteritis and temporal arteritis. Ten percent of those with temporal arteritis have extracranial arterial manifestations. Neurofibromatosis type 1 may be complicated by aneurysms of the abdominal aorta and stenotic disease affecting aortic branch vessels, especially the renal arteries. Behçet's disease is an usual vasculitis that affects medium and large arteries and is an uncommon cause of pulmonary artery aneurysms. Sudden deceleration injury from a car accident can cause an aortic tear, most commonly in the proximal descending aorta. Local or systemic infections may lead to mycotic aneurysms. Rare infectious causes of aneurysms include syphilis and tuberculosis (usually seen in older patients). Human immunodeficiency virus (HIV) infection has also been recognized as a cause of aneurysms. Noninfectious causes include periaortitis and inflammatory aneurysm, which are associated with marked wall thickening of the thoracic and abdominal aorta and are more common in older individuals (Fig. 28-7). Diseases that affect the ascending aorta are less common than those that affect the abdominal and descending thoracic segments. Ascending aortic disease often results from degeneration of the aortic media, a condition termed *cystic medial necrosis* by Erdheim. Medial necrosis occurs as a part of normal aging and results in fragmentation, loss of elastic fibers, and loss of smooth muscle cells. Cystic medial necrosis, also a part of normal aging and hypertension, is characterized by elastic fiber degeneration and accumulation of mucoid material in the medial layer of the aorta. Although the loss of smooth muscle cells give a pseudocyst appearance, there is no true cyst or necrosis depletion of cellular elements.[53] Aortic root dilation also occurs in Turner's syndrome, a sex-linked (45,XO) abnormality due to loss of one of the two X chromosomes. Affected individuals have short stature, neck webbing, broad chest with widely spaced nipples, and coarctation of the aorta. Some patients have a bicuspid aortic valve (BAV), and others have concomitant hypertension. Aortic root dilation may occur in 40% of patients. The incidence of Turner's syndrome is 1 in 5000.

BAV is a common congenital heart defect (frequency of 1% of the population) associated with an autosomal dominant inheritance pattern. Nine percent of patients with BAV have a first-degree relative with BAV. Both unicuspid and bicuspid valve abnormalities predispose to aortic root enlargement and dissection (Fig. 28-8).

Aneurysms due to Inherited Connective Tissue Diseases

Marfan Syndrome

In 1896, Antoine Marfan presented the case of a 5-year-old child with unusually long extremities who died in early adolescence. Over the next 50 years additional features of Marfan syndrome were described, including dislocation of the lens (1914) and autosomal dominant inheritance (1931). In 1943, Taussig reported the association of a congenital aneurysm of the aorta with arachnodactyly.[54] Today, Marfan syndrome is recognized as an inherited disorder of connective tissue with skeletal, ocular, and cardiovascular manifestations.

Marfan syndrome is inherited in an autosomal dominant pattern, although one fourth have no family history due to variable expression and/or spontaneous mutation. The prevalence is 1 to 3 per 10,000 individuals.[55] Molecular analysis has shown that Marfan syndrome is caused by a mutation in the gene for fibrillin 1 (*FBN1*), which is located

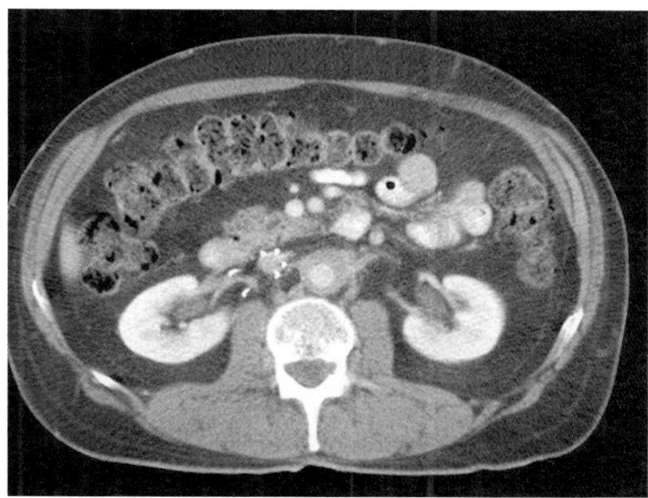

FIGURE 28-7 Inflammatory aortitis causing inferior vena cava (IVC) obstruction. Note the thick rind of tissue around the abdominal aorta and the IVC filter.

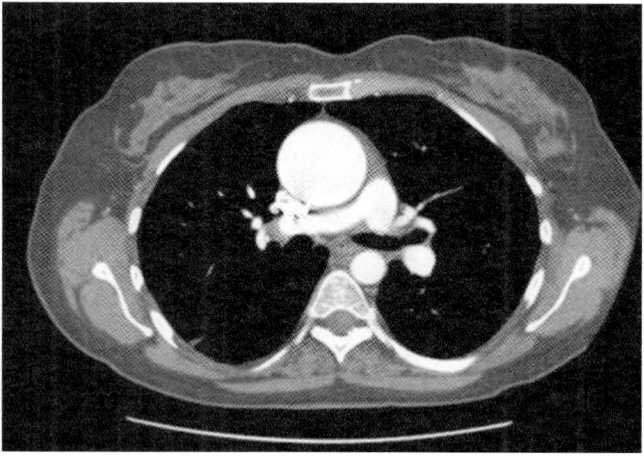

FIGURE 28-8 Ascending aortic aneurysm associated with bicuspid aortic valve and progressive aortic valve regurgitation.

on chromosome 15. This gene encodes for fibrillin-1, a 350-kd glycoprotein that is the major structural component of the elastin 10- to 12-nm microfibril and is necessary for the elastic qualities of connective tissue. Fibrillin mutations may occur from cysteine substitutions or mutations at calcium-binding sites that affect the structure of fibrillin 1.[56,57]

Genetic testing with molecular analysis may be helpful to identify individuals at risk, but the presence of a *FBN1* mutation without specific clinical features does not by itself make the diagnosis of Marfan syndrome. More than 240 different mutations in the *FNB1* gene have been reported to the International Marfan Database, and these produce a number of type 1 fibrillinopathies.[53] The large number of genetic mutations results in a wide variability in phenotypic expressions. As a result, the Marfan syndrome phenotype is a disease continuum, ranging from very mild cases that blend into the normal population to more severe cases that have multisystem involvement. Relying on a fibrillin mutation alone for diagnosis of Marfan syndrome would result in overdiagnosis. Fibrillin 1 mutations are not detected in up to 34% of patients with definite Marfan syndrome as determined by clinical criteria; therefore, relying on this gene mutation alone could result in misdiagnosis.[58]

There are a number of Marfan-like syndromes, including congenital contractural arachnodactyly and familial thoracic aortic aneurysm syndrome. Congenital contractural arachnodactyly is due to mutations in the gene for fibrillin 2. Affected patients have a marfanoid appearance and share many other features with Marfan syndrome, including joint contractures, ear abnormalities, and an autosomal dominant inheritance. However, patients with familial contractural arachnodactyly do not have the same risk of cardiovascular complications.[53] Familial thoracic aortic aneurysms, previously called *Erdheim's cystic medial necrosis*, is distinct from Marfan syndrome. In most families the phenotype for familial thoracic aortic aneurysms is also inherited in an autosomal dominant pattern, but it is not associated with any known genetic syndrome.[53,55]

Clinical Features The classic patient with Marfan syndrome is tall and thin, with long arms and legs—the so-called marfanoid habitus. The arm span exceeds the height by a ratio of greater than 1.05. The upper-to-lower body segment ratio is less than 0.86, which means that the legs are longer compared to the upper body. The lower body segment can be measured from the symphysis pubis to the floor and the upper segment measurement is obtained by subtracting the lower segment from the height. *Arachnodactyly* refers to abnormally long fingers, and two signs are considered diagnostic. The "wrist sign of Walker and Murdoch" is positive when the patient grabs the opposite wrist and the thumb overlaps the terminal phalanx of the fifth digit. The "thumb sign of Steinberg" is positive when making a fist (wrapping the fingers over the thumb) and the entire thumbnail is noted to project beyond the ulnar border of the hand.[55,58]

Skeletal abnormalities include pectus carinatum or excavatum (from overgrowth of the ribs) and spinal scoliosis. Facial features include flattened malar bones with retrognathia. A high arched palate and flat feet may be present. These skeletal features can be variable, and many patients with Marfan syndrome may have some or none these features. Ectopia lentis occurs as a result of stretching of the lenticular zonular filaments leading to displacement of the lens. Myopia causes refractive difficulties seeing distant objects.

Defective elastic tissue in the ascending aorta results in the most devastating consequences of Marfan syndrome: aortic dilation, dissection, and rupture with sudden death often before 40 years of age. The ascending aorta is involved in 80% to 90% of patients. Progressive dilation of the aorta begins at the aortic root, resulting in aortic valve incompetence. The risk of dissection and rupture increases with aneurysmal expansion. Mitral valve prolapse is found in more than 50% of patients and may cause significant mitral regurgitation requiring surgery in up to 10% of patients.[18]

The diagnosis of Marfan syndrome is based on established clinical and genetic criteria that were redefined in 1996 and referred to as the *Ghent nosology* (Table 28-2).[55]

In the Ghent nosology, clinical features constituting major criteria include aortic dissection, ectopic lens, skeletal abnormalities, and lumbosacral-dural ectasia diagnosed by computed tomography (CT) or magnetic resonance imaging (MRI). Family and genetic history comprise major criteria if a first-degree relative meets the diagnostic criteria of Marfan syndrome or genetic testing documents the presence of a mutation in the *FBN1* gene known to cause Marfan syndrome. Overly strict interpretation of the Ghent nosology may cause underdiagnosis of Marfan syndrome.[56]

Despite advances in the molecular understanding of the disease, the diagnosis of Marfan syndrome is primarily clinical. The initial evaluation of a patient with suspected Marfan syndrome should include a personal history, family history, and clinical examination, including an eye examination. Cardiac and vascular imaging should be performed with echocardiography, MRI, or CT. Echocardiography can image the ascending aorta and the aortic valve to evaluate for aortic incompetence and ascending aortic aneurysm. MRI and CT imaging are useful to exclude aortic dissection and look for aneurysms elsewhere. Blood tests including inflammatory markers should be normal in Marfan syndrome. Elevated erythrocyte sedimentation rate may suggest an inflammatory cause of aneurysm such as giant cell arteritis or another systemic disorder. A slit-lamp examination can identify a dislocated lens. Genetics counseling should be considered for all confirmed cases because the disorder has autosomal dominant inheritance and may affect 50% of offspring. Continued surveillance should be done at least annually to look for new cardiovascular complications.

Medical Management Prophylactic beta blockers are recommended for all patients with Marfan syndrome to reduce the risk of aortic dilation and dissection. Beta-blocker therapy was first considered in the early 1970s, when it was discovered that propranolol reduced the risk of aortic rupture in turkeys prone to dissection.[59] Shortly thereafter, the prophylactic use of beta blockers was suggested in patients with Marfan syndrome who were at risk of aortic dissection.[60]

In Marfan syndrome, aortic stiffness is increased owing to elastic fiber degeneration. As a result of decreased aortic distensibility, the aortic wall is less able to absorb the pulse pressure wave resulting from aortic ejection. Beta-blocker therapy may reduce the systolic ejection impulse velocity (the rate of change of arterial pressure with time [dP/dT]). The negative inotropic effect reduces the dP/dT by decreasing pulse pressure; the negative chronotropic effect on the heart lengthens the aortic ejection time. Beta blockers may have additional properties of increasing cross-linking of collagen or decreasing collagen degradation. These effects are not shared with other classes of antihypertensive medication. Vasodilator medications may lower blood pressure to the same extent, but they are not protective against rupture due to adverse effects of increased heart rate and pulse pressure.

Aortic distensibility (compliance) can be assessed noninvasively by gated MRI or by echocardiogram. When studied by MRI, patients with Marfan syndrome have decreased aortic distensibility and increased pulse wave velocity compared with controls. Some studies have documented the benefit of beta blockers in improving aortic

Table 28-2 Diagnostic Criteria for Marfan Syndrome*

ORGAN SYSTEM	MAJOR CRITERIA	MINOR CRITERIA
Genetic findings	Fibrillin 1 mutation known to cause Marfan syndrome	
Skeletal	At least 4 of the following needed for a major criteria: Pectus carinatum Pectus excavatum—requiring surgery Upper segment-to-lower segment ratio <0.86 Arm span-to-height ratio >1.05 Wrist or thumb signs Scoliosis Reduced elbow extension Pes planus Protrusio acetabulae Lumbosacral dural ectasia	Pectus excavatum Joint hypermobility High arched palate Facial appearance
Ocular	Lens dislocation	Flat cornea Increased axial length of globe with myopia
Cardiovascular	Dilation of aortic root Dissection of ascending aorta	Mitral valve prolapse Calcified mitral annulus Pulmonary artery dilation
Others	—	Pulmonary Spontaneous pneumothorax Apical blebs Skin Stria atrophicae Recurrent or incisional hernia

*Requires *one major criteria in two organ systems* and involvement of a third system.

Adapted from De Paepe A, Devereuz RB, Dietz HC, et al: Revised diagnostic criteria for the Marfan syndrome. Am J Med Genet 62:417-426, 1996.

compliance with increased distensibility and a lower pulse wave velocity. In other studies of short- and long-term administration of beta blockers, the results are less clear with a heterogeneous response; short-term administration may actually increase aortic stiffness in some patients with more dilated aortas.[61,62]

In clinical trials, prophylactic β-adrenergic blockers have been shown to reduce the rate of aortic dilation and the risk of aortic dissection in patients with Marfan syndrome. In the only randomized, prospective trial of beta-blocker treatment in Marfan syndrome, 32 patients were treated with propranolol and 38 did not receive the drug. Both groups were followed for 10 years. Endpoints were aortic root dimensions and clinical events including dissection, surgery, and death. The study showed that the rate of aortic dilation was lower in the propranolol treatment group (5 with clinical endpoints versus 9 in the untreated group). Risk of aortic dissection was reduced by half (4 patients in the control group and 2 in the propranolol treatment group).[63] Other retrospective studies (using historical controls) have also found a reduced rate of aortic root dilation in patients treated with atenolol or propranolol, and it is likely other beta blockers will have similar benefit.

The long-term benefit of beta blockers is greatest in young patients with Marfan syndrome who have only mild to moderate dilation of the aortic root.[63,64] Early institution of beta blockade is therefore recommended in Marfan patients, because there may be less benefit in those with more severely dilated aortic roots and with aortic regurgitation. There is no evidence that beta blockers decrease aortic incompetence once it develops. Lifelong prophylactic therapy with beta blockers is recommended for all patients with Marfan syndrome, even after surgical repair, owing to the risk of recurrent aneurysms. Relative contraindications to beta blockers include a history of asthma, conduction system disease, and severe bradycardia. Most beta blockers are generally well tolerated with few side effects. Adverse symptoms such as fatigue can be minimized by using selective beta blockers and avoiding maximal dosages.

A number of other pharmacologic agents may prove to be of benefit in Marfan syndrome. Vascular remodeling of aortic aneurysms may involve smooth muscle cell apoptosis. Angiotensin-converting enzyme inhibitors and angiotensin II receptor blockers inhibit smooth muscle cell apoptosis in cultured aortic media cells from patients with Marfan syndrome; these agents may prove to have a beneficial role in Marfan syndrome.[65]

Surgical Management Advances in medical and surgical management have markedly improved the longevity of patients with Marfan syndrome. Before the advent of open heart surgery, most patients with Marfan syndrome died from rupture of the aorta before 40 years of age.[54]

Aortic root dilation is progressive in all patients; the risk of dissection and rupture increases as the aorta expands. Aneurysms of 6 to 6.9 cm have an 8.8-fold higher risk of rupture compared with aneurysms of 4.0 to 4.9 cm. In one review, of 675 patients at 10 surgical centers, almost half of patients presenting with acute dissection had aortic diameters of 6.5 cm or smaller.[54] There is general consensus that patients with Marfan syndrome should undergo elective replacement of ascending aorta and aortic sinus when the aortic root diameter in an adult reaches 5 to 5.5 cm.[54,66] Earlier repair should be considered in higher-risk individuals, in particular those who have a strong family history of sudden death due to dissection at a young age, rapid aortic aneurysm expansion, or contemplated pregnancy.

Aortic dilation usually begins at the sinus of Valsalva and usually does not extend past the proximal ascending aorta. Surgical repair usually requires replacement of the aortic root with a composite graft or else there is a risk of recurrent aneurysm with continued aortic root dilation (Fig. 28-9).

Elective operations have been associated with a mortality rate as low as 2% or less.[54,67] Operative mortality is much higher for patients presenting with acute dissection. In one large multicenter review, the mean age of patients requiring surgical repair was 34 years but ranged from 4 to 73 years. Twelve percent also needed mitral valve repair. Following aortic repair, the overall 10-year survival was 75% and was 59% at 20 years.[54]

In 1968, Bentall and De Bono[68] reported a technique for replacement of the ascending aorta and aortic valve using a composite graft anastomosed to the aortic annulus. In this technique, the coronary arteries were reimplanted, and the aortic valve was replaced and sewn into the lower end of the graft. The Bentall procedure with a composite valve graft has the benefit of completely removing the aortic root segment that is most prone to dissection and rupture. In the 1990s, aortic valve-sparing operations were introduced. Preservation of the native aortic valve avoids the need for long-term anticoagulation. These procedures either remodeled the aortic root or resuspended the native aortic valve in the Dacron graft.[69] Remodeling of the aortic root corrects aortic incompetence; however, in some studies, the aortic annulus diameter continues to expand after repair. Resuspension of the native aortic valve in the ascending aortic graft has proved to be highly successful. Excellent results have been reported: up to 96% of patients survived the aortic valve-sparing procedures over 10 years without reoperations.[70] A Mayo Clinic study of 71 patients undergoing aortic root reconstruction with either preservation or reimplantation of the aortic valve found both techniques to be successful. Sixty-three of 71 patients had normal valve function or only mild aortic regurgitation. A higher failure rate was found among those with a large annulus (>25 mm) and those needing aortic cusp repair.[71]

With severe aortic regurgitation due to valve degeneration, valve-sparing techniques may not be possible, and a mechanical valve is necessary. Postsurgical follow-up for all Marfan patients should include a full clinical examination done at least annually with history, examination, and serial transthoracic echocardiogram. Reoperation may be necessary in up to 70% of patients due to development of a second aneurysm. Avoidance of contact sports and avoidance of isometric exercise such as weight lifting is advised.

Marfan Syndrome and Pregnancy There are several special concerns for patients with Marfan syndrome who become pregnant. The risk of aortic dissection is significantly increased during pregnancy. Aortic root enlargement greater than 4 cm during pregnancy or rapid aortic dilation during pregnancy is associated with increased rupture risk.[72] This may be due to relaxation of tissues or hyper-

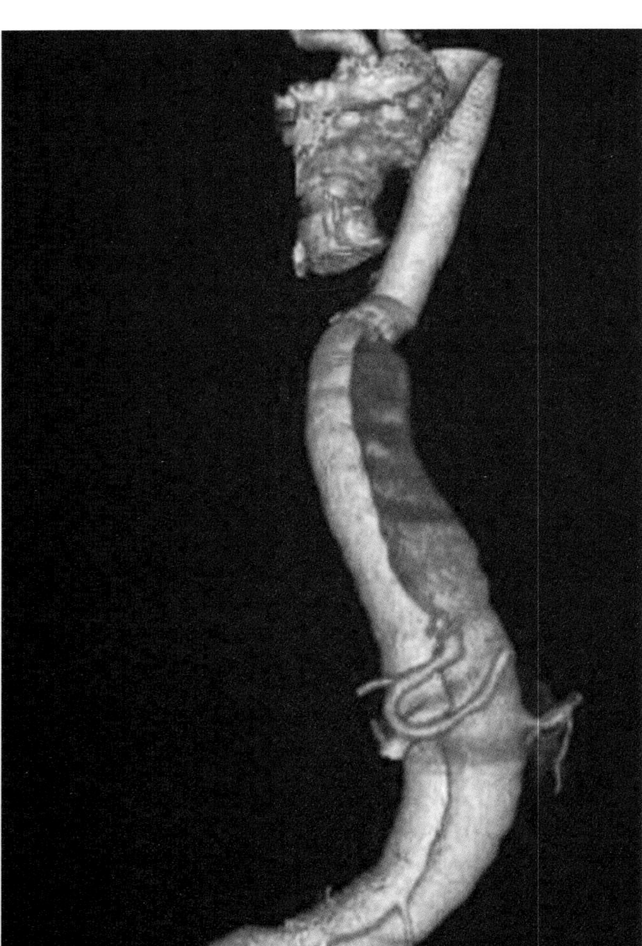

FIGURE 28-9 A 45-year-old woman with Marfan syndrome, after repair of type I ascending aortic dissection with composite graft and aortic valve replacement. The patient's brother had previously died of aortic rupture. (See Color Figure in this section.)

dynamic state. Control of gestational hypertension and preeclampsia is important; beta blockers should be continued throughout pregnancy. Because there is a 50% risk of transmission of Marfan syndrome fibrillin mutation to the fetus, genetic counseling should be offered to all women of childbearing age.

■ EHLERS-DANLOS SYNDROME

Ehlers-Danlos syndrome (EDS) is an inherited connective tissue disorder with an estimated prevalence of 1 in 5000 to 25,000.[18] Ehlers in 1901 and Danlos in 1908 defined the triad of classic features including skin hyperelasticity, joint hypermobility, and increased fragility of the skin. Sack (1936) and Barabas (1967) described the arterial-ecchymotic subtype (type IV, or the vascular type), which is the most fatal form due to arterial rupture and hemorrhage.[14] In contrast to Marfan syndrome, the aortic root can be involved, but rupture or dissection occurs primarily in the descending aorta or in medium-sized arteries.[73] EDS is now recognized as a heterogeneous group of genetically, biochemically, and clinically diverse disorders. Advances in molecular biology have led to a better understanding of specific defects in the collagen biosynthetic pathway causing EDS.

There are five types of collagen based on their composition.[74] *Type I* collagen is the most common type (90%) and is found in tendons, ligaments, and bone. *Type II* is found in hyaline cartilage. *Type III* is found in vascular structures, including colon and blood vessels. *Types IV* and *V* are found in basement membrane and connective tissue matrix. Genetic defects involving one or more different collagen genes produce clinically distinct forms of EDS.

In 1988, classification of the different clinical presentations led to the Berlin nomenclature that defined 11 EDS subtypes.[75] With the identification of specific mutations in the genes encoding collagen types I, III, and V and associated collagen-processing enzymes, a revised nomenclature was proposed in 1997. This so-called Villefranche classification condensed and simplified the previous 11 groups into six main subtypes. These are based on clinical syndromes associated with specific genetic abnormalities.[76] (See Table 28-3 for details of the Villefranche classification.) Between 40% and 50% of cases of classic EDS are due to mutations in one of the two genes that code for type V collagen (*COL5A1* and *COL5A2*). This results in abnormal production of alpha-1(V) and alpha-2(V) chains of type V collagen, adversely affecting the strength and integrity of the collagen fibril assembly.[77]

The *COL3A1* gene is responsible for the formation of type III collagen; a mutation of this gene results in the "vascular type" of EDS (Berlin IV). A mutation in the *COL1A1* and *COLIA2* genes causes the "arthrochalasia type" of EDS (Berlin type VIIA and B) with primary features of hyperextensible joints.[78]

A deficiency of collagen-processing enzymes may also cause EDS. In type VI, a deficiency of lysyl-hydroxylase causes inability to hydroxylate lysine residues and prevents cross-linking of collagen trimers. In type VII the absence of procollagen peptidase prevents cleavage of the NH_2-terminus of procollagen chains in EDS type VI. Both of these compromise the strength of the collagen fibril.[78] The most common type of EDS is now termed the "classic type" (Berlin types I and II). Affected individuals typically have stretchy skin and joint laxity. Joint hypermobility can be demonstrated by passive dorsiflexion of the little finger beyond 90 degrees or apposition of the thumb to the flexor aspect of the forearm. There may be hyperextension of knees and elbows. The patient may be able to put the palm of the hands flat on the floor while standing and bending forward without flexing the knees. In the hypermobility type (Berlin III) there is increased susceptibility to sprains, subluxations, and dislocations. Joint complications are particularly common in the shoulder, elbow, and jaw.

Ehlers-Danlos Syndrome Type IV—The Vascular Ecchymotic Type

EDS type IV (the vascular type) is rare, with a prevalence of less than 1 per 100,000. It accounts for only 4% of all 11

Table 28-3 Classification of Ehlers-Danlos Syndrome*

VILLEFRANCHE CLASSIFICATION (1997)	BERLIN CLASSIFICATION (1988)	CLINICAL FEATURES	INHERITANCE	MOLECULAR DEFECTS
Classic type	I Gravis II Mitis	Skin hyperelasticity; joint hypermobility; easy bruising; thin, atrophic scars; varicose veins; thin face	AD	Mutation in *COL5A1* or *COL5A2* gene that codes for alpha-1(V) and alpha-2(V) chains of type V collagen
Hypermobility type	III	Large joint hypermobility	AD	Not known
Vascular type	IV Arterial-ecchymotic	Thin, translucent skin with visible veins; easy bruising; characteristic facies; arterial, bowel, and uterine rupture	AD	Mutations in *COL3A1*; abnormal type III collagen synthesis, secretion
Kyphoscoliosis type	VI	Scoliosis; muscle hypotonia; joint laxity; hyperextensible skin	AR	Lysyl-hydroxylase deficiency or absence of procollagen peptidase prevents cleavage of procollagen chain
Arthrochalasia type	VIIA, VIIB Arthrochalasia multiplex	Congenital hip dislocation; severe joint hypermobility; soft skin with or without abnormal scarring	AD	Mutation in *COL1A1* (type A) or *COL1A2* (type B) gene
Dermatosporaxis type	VIIC	Severe skin fragility; sagging, redundant skin	—	Recessive mutations in type 1 collagen N-peptidase

*Includes rare forms (types V, VIII, and X) from the 1988 Berlin classification that have been described in only a few families.[76]
AD, autosomal dominant; AR, autosomal recessive.
Adapted from Beighton P, de Paepe A, Steinmann B, et al: Ehlers-Danlos syndromes: Revised nosology, Villefranche, 1997. Ehlers-Danlos National Foundation (USA) and Ehlers-Danlos Support Group (UK). Am J Med Genet 77:31-37, 1998.

types of EDS but is the major cause of mortality in EDS due to associated aneurysmal dilation and arterial rupture.[18] Inheritance is autosomal dominant. EDS type IV is caused by a mutation of the *COL3A1* gene that encodes for the proα1(III) chain resulting in abnormal or reduced secretion of type III collagen. Type III collagen is composed of a triple helix of three procollagen (alpha) chains, each containing 1029 amino acids. EDS type IV has been associated with single or multiple exon deletions in addition to numerous different single-point mutations that result in the substitution of another amino acid for glycine in the triple helix. In one study of 135 patients with EDS type IV, most were found to have many different point mutations leading to substitution of an amino acid in the helical chain. A single-exon deletion accounted for 41 mutations. There was no correlation between the nature of the mutation and the type of complications.[79] The net result of the myriad genetic abnormalities is reduced or abnormal production of type III collagen. Defective synthesis of type III collagen causes decreased tissue strength; this results in fragile blood vessels and leads to the vascular complications associated with EDS type IV.[74,78]

Clinical Features and Diagnosis The diagnosis of EDS type IV is made on the basis of clinical features and confirmed by laboratory testing (Table 28-4). Diagnosis of EDS type IV requires the presence of at least two of four major diagnostic criteria: thin, translucent skin; rupture of arteries, intestine, or uterus; easy bruisability; and a characteristic facial appearance. The diagnosis should be confirmed by DNA studies that document a mutation in the *COL3A1* gene or by skin biopsy for cultured fibroblasts that demonstrate production of abnormal type III procollagen.[76,79]

Typical facial features in EDS type IV may be present with thinness of the face, hollow cheeks due to lack of subcutaneous adipose tissue, prominent eyes, thin lips, and a narrow nose. EDS type IV patients have thin, translucent skin and visible veins. The venous pattern may be most marked over the chest.

Easy bruisability due to tissue fragility occurs in 66% of individuals. Spontaneous ecchymoses often recur in the same area and can be a lifelong tendency. It is important to exclude an inherited coagulation factor deficiency in anyone with spontaneous hemorrhage; however, in EDS type IV, coagulation testing is normal. Scars may widen with a thin, atrophic "cigarette paper" appearance; wound healing is impaired. Hypermobility of the joints in EDS type IV is limited to the fingers, and hyperelastic skin may be less prominent.[76] Complications in other organ systems are common: patients are prone to intestinal perforation (especially rupture of the sigmoid colon), uterine rupture, spontaneous pneumothorax, and musculotendinous disruption. Vascular complications include varicose veins, peripheral arteriovenous fistula, carotid-cavernous fistula, and large artery rupture.[80,81]

EDS type IV should be suspected when a young patient presents with multiple arterial aneurysms or spontaneous arterial rupture. Arterial rupture is the most common cause of death, and the peak incidence of this complication is seen in the 2nd to 3rd decade of life. In one review of 36 patients, the mean age at presentation of aneurysm or rupture was 26 years; two thirds were younger than 30 years of age.[82] Another study reported that one fourth of patients had their first complication by age 20 years, and 80% had a major complication by age 40 years. Median survival was age 48 years.[79]

Simple procedures may precipitate arterial rupture. For example, fatal arterial rupture has occurred after reduction of a dislocated shoulder. Arterial dissection is a major concern during any arterial instrumentation. Rupture of the gastrointestinal tract is likely to occur at an earlier age than arterial rupture. Many patients with EDS type IV, however, are not aware of their disease until catastrophic spontaneous rupture of an artery or intestine occurs. Only 16% of patients

Table 28-4 Diagnostic Criteria for Ehlers-Danlos Syndrome (EDS) Type IV (Vascular Type)*

Major criteria: Two or more is highly indicative of EDS type IV
Arterial rupture or intestinal, uterine rupture
Extensive bruising
Thin, translucent skin
Characteristic facial appearance
Minor criteria
Acrogeria
Hypermobility of small joints (fingers)
Tendon and muscle rupture
Clubfoot
Varicose veins of early onset
Arteriovenous malformation
Carotid-cavernous sinus fistula
Pneumothorax or hemothorax
Positive family history of sudden death

*The diagnosis of EDS type IV is made on the basis of clinical features and should be confirmed by obtaining a skin biopsy for cultured fibroblasts to document production of abnormal type III procollagen or the presence of mutations in the *COL3A1* gene.

Adapted from Beighton P, de Paepe A, Steinmann B, et al: Ehlers-Danlos syndromes: Revised nosology, Villefranche, 1997. Ehlers-Danlos National Foundation (USA) and Ehlers-Danlos Support Group (UK). Am J Med Genet 77:31-37, 1998.

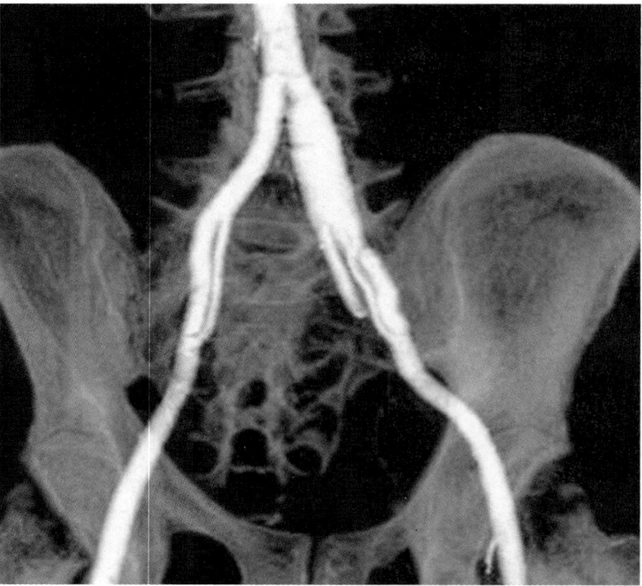

FIGURE 28-10 Spontaneous left iliac artery dissection in Ehlers-Danlos syndrome.

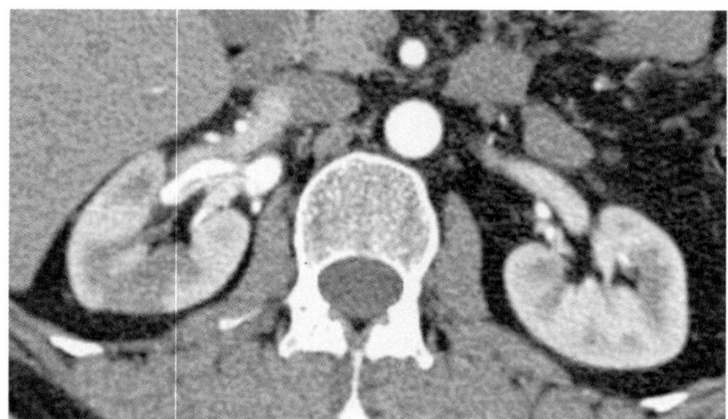

FIGURE 28-11 Right renal artery dissection in Ehlers-Danlos syndrome managed conservatively.

had symptoms suggesting EDS before a vascular event occurred.

Medium-sized arteries are most commonly involved, but any-sized vessel can rupture. Approximately 50% of patients have underlying aneurysms, but in others dissection of normal-sized vessels is a prominent feature. Many sites of arterial rupture or hemorrhage have been reported, including the abdominal aorta and iliac, femoral, popliteal, subclavian, brachial, carotid, and vertebral arteries. Visceral vessels including splenic, hepatic, renal, celiac, and mesenteric arteries can spontaneously dissect and rupture.[80,82,83] Acute abdominal, flank, or back pain with cardiovascular collapse may herald arterial rupture and requires urgent evaluation (Figs. 28-10 to 28-12).

Peripheral rupture often manifests with localized pain, hematoma, and ecchymosis.[80] Peripheral rupture may be associated with the development of unusual compartment syndromes such as sciatic neuropathy after gluteal artery rupture. Carotid artery rupture is a frequent complication of EDS type IV. This can result in a carotid-cavernous fistula associated with the sudden onset of retro-orbital pain, proptosis, periorbital edema, and visual loss.[81]

Patients with EDS type IV should be evaluated with MRI or CT. Arterial punctures should be avoided because of high risk of uncontrolled bleeding and retroperitoneal hematoma. In one report, arteriography was associated with a 67% complication rate in 8 of 12 patients and a 17% mortality rate![82] Catheter-induced arterial damage in patients with EDS type IV has included false aneurysm formation, intimal flaps, fatal dissection of the ascending aorta, and renal artery rupture.[82]

The prognosis in spontaneous arterial perforation is poor, with 44% of patients dying before any surgical procedure; 19% die during or after the operation, for a total mortality of 63%.[82] When surgical intervention is unavoidable for a vascular emergency, ligation of an aneurysm or bleeding vessel is preferable to arterial bypass. Conventional arterial repair with suture or graft may be difficult: sutures often tear through the arterial wall, preventing creation of anastomoses. Tourniquets are suggested for arterial occlusion because arterial clamps may also tear arteries. Wound dehiscence after surgery due to impaired wound healing is common. Endovascular stents have been used successfully for management of arteriovenous fistula, arterial aneurysms, and active hemorrhage; although these devices may one day become the treatment of choice, further experience is needed.[81]

The diagnosis of EDS should prompt a number of practical recommendations. Patients should be advised not to participate in any contact sports. Potential trauma from occupation or lifestyles should be minimized, and nonessential surgery should be avoided. The decision for pregnancy should be weighed very carefully. Pregnancy can be complicated by uterine rupture, and women have been reported to have a 11.5% to 25% risk of death with each pregnancy.[79,82] Autosomal dominant inheritance means there is a 50% risk of transmission of the EDS gene from

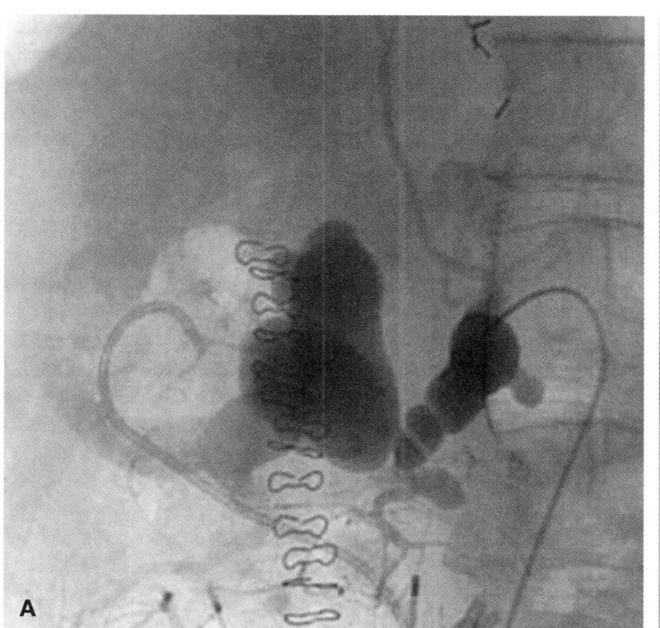

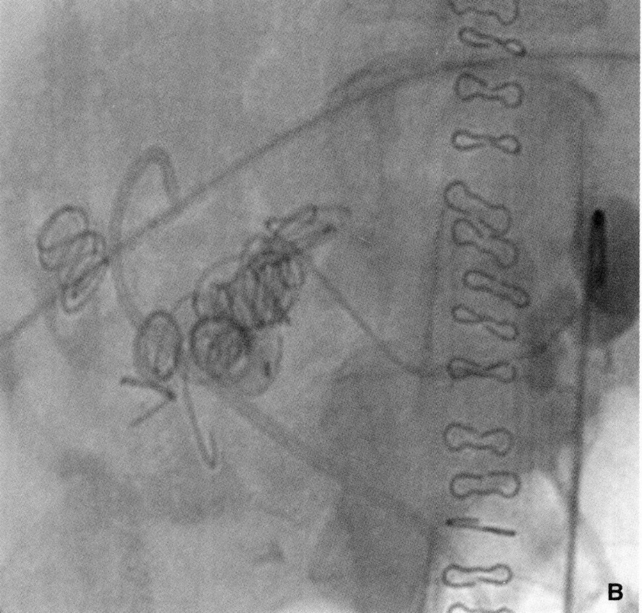

FIGURE 28-12 Coil occlusion of hepatic artery aneurysm in a patient with multiple aneurysms and clinical diagnosis of Ehlers-Danlos type IV, shown before (**A**) and after (**B**) the coil occlusion.

affected individuals to the offspring. Therefore, genetic evaluation and counseling should be offered to all patients.

■ VASCULITIS

Vessels of any size or location can be affected by vasculitis. By definition, vasculitis implies inflammation of the vessel wall, which produces arterial damage with resultant stenosis or aneurysm formation.

Classification of the arteritides is complex, in part because of the wide spectrum and overlap of clinical manifestations. Many vasculitides have similar constitutional symptoms such as malaise, fever, weight loss, myalgias, and arthralgias. Laboratory testing is often helpful but may be nonspecific: acute-phase reactants such as C-reactive protein and erythrocyte sedimentation rate are often elevated in other inflammatory disorders. The clinical and pathologic features are variable and dependent on the site and type of blood vessel affected.[84] Most classifications are based on size of the involved artery (referred to as *large-*, *medium-*, or *small-vessel vasculitis*). Arteritis can be further classified by the presence or absence of antineutrophil cytoplasmic antibodies (ANCA) (Table 28-5). These are autoantibodies formed against enzymes found in the primary granules of neutrophils. Those diseases with an antibody against proteinase 3 (PR3) show cytoplasmic immunofluorescent staining and are classified as c-ANCA. Those with an antibody directed against myeloperoxidase have perinuclear staining and are classified as p-ANCA.[84]

Large-Vessel Vasculitis

The large-vessel vasculitides include Takayasu's arteritis and temporal arteritis, which are collectively referred to as *giant cell arteritis*. Although the two disorders have similar histology, they have distinct clinical features.[85]

Takayasu's arteritis is the most common large-vessel vasculitis.[86] It is a disease of young individuals often younger than 30 years and causes both stenotic and aneurysmal disease. The diagnosis is suggested by multiple arterial bruits with diminished pulses in a young patient. Owing to frequent involvement of aortic branch vessels, it is also known as the "pulseless disease" (Fig. 28-13).[87] Arterial hypertension occurs in 33% to 88% of patients and is often due to renal artery stenosis. The diagnosis of hypertension can be missed unless blood pressure is measured in both arms.[88]

Takayasu's arteritis can also present as an isolated aortic aneurysm.[89] Ascending aortic dilation with aortic regurgitation occurs in 20% or more of patients with Takayasu's arteritis.[90]

Diagnosis During the initial inflammatory stage, there may be nonspecific symptoms of myalgias, arthralgias, and anemia. The diagnosis may not be made until later, during the chronic occlusive phase. Inflammatory markers are elevated in most patients with active vasculitis; however, in up to 10% with active disease, the erythrocyte sedimentation rate and C-reactive protein inflammatory markers are normal.[91]

In some patients, the diagnosis of vasculitis is not made until the time of surgery, for example, when unsuspected inflammation and thickened aortic tissue are encountered at the time of ascending aortic aneurysm repair.[89] Surgical reconstruction of active vasculitis should be avoided owing to the high risk of failure associated with recurrent stenosis and aneurysm formation. Concomitant steroid immunosuppression should be used when urgent revascularization is unavoidable due to severe cerebral, abdominal, or limb

Table 28-5 Classification of Vasculitis*

SIZE OF VESSEL INVOLVED	ANCA NEGATIVE	ANCA POSITIVE
Large	Takayasu's arteritis Giant cell arteritis	—
Medium	Kawasaki's disease Polyarteritis nodosa Behçet's disease Drug abuse vasculitis	Churg-Strauss angiitis
Small	Henoch-Schönlein purpura Essential cryoglobulinemia Arteritis of connective tissue	Wegener's granulomatosis Microscopic polyangiitis

*Classification by size of vessel and antineutrophil cytoplasmic antibody (ANCA) status.

From Jayne D: Update on the European Vasculitis Study Group Trials. Curr Opin Rheumatol 13:48-55, 2001.

ischemia. A retrospective review at the Mayo Clinic showed that patients with active arteritis can safely undergo aortic valve replacement with good outcomes as long as the patient receives adequate steroid suppression during the postoperative period.[92]

The pulmonary arteries may be involved in Takayasu's arteritis, and this should be suspected in a patient with unexplained exertional dyspnea (Fig. 28-14). The diagnosis of pulmonary arteritis may be missed unless specifically evaluated. In the past, pulmonary angiography was the most definitive imaging modality for the pulmonary arteries, but this has largely been replaced by CT and MR angiography.

Temporal (giant cell) arteritis can manifest as a localized stenosis or occlusion in the brachial or superficial femoral artery (Fig. 28-15).[93] In a Mayo Clinic study of 248 patients with temporal arteritis, 34 were found to have vasculitis involving the aorta or its branches. The diagnosis of temporal arteritis was made at autopsy in 4 patients who died of aortic rupture.[94]

In contrast to Takayasu's arteritis, temporal arteritis affects the elderly and is not seen in patients younger than 50 years of age. Its name relates to the frequent involvement of external carotid artery branches, resulting in symptoms of headache and jaw claudication. Classic clinical findings include thickened, ropy, and tender temporal arteries. The most devastating complication is blindness due to ophthalmic artery involvement that progresses to retinal ischemia. Blindness may be irreversible if ophthalmic arteritis is treated too late. Symptoms sometimes may be nonspecific and may raise concern for malignancy, in particular lymphoma or myeloma. Fifteen percent may develop a fever of unknown origin. Polymyalgia rheumatica is a frequent symptom that presents as myalgias causing diffuse pain or stiffness of the shoulders, back, or hips. Jaw claudication occurs in 50% of patients.

The criteria for diagnosis of temporal arteritis have been developed by the American College of Rheumatology. Diagnosis requires three of the following five criteria[95]: age older than 50 years at disease onset; localized headache; temporal artery tenderness or abnormal examination; erythrocyte sedimentation rate higher than 50; and temporal artery biopsy demonstrating arteritis with giant cells.

The diagnosis of temporal arteritis is sometimes difficult: up to 20% of patients with active arteritis have a normal temporal artery. Biopsy (of one or both temporal arteries) findings may also be negative: as shown in one study, temporal artery biopsies were negative in 42% of patients with aortic arch syndromes.[38]

In patients with extracranial arteritis, the diagnosis of vasculitis is supported by angiographic findings of long, smooth, tapered narrowing of affected arteries in the absence of atheromatous disease. In a patient without cardiovascular risk factors, unexplained absent extremity pulses should raise suspicion for temporal arteritis and prompt angiographic evaluation.

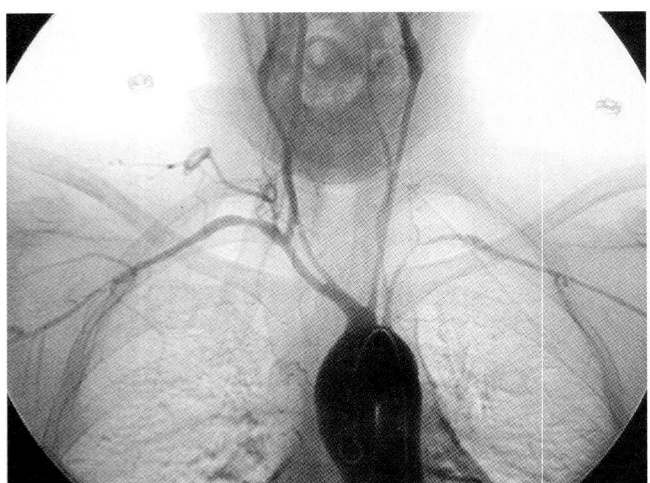

FIGURE 28-13 Takayasu's arteritis involving aortic arch vessels, including both carotid and subclavian arteries.

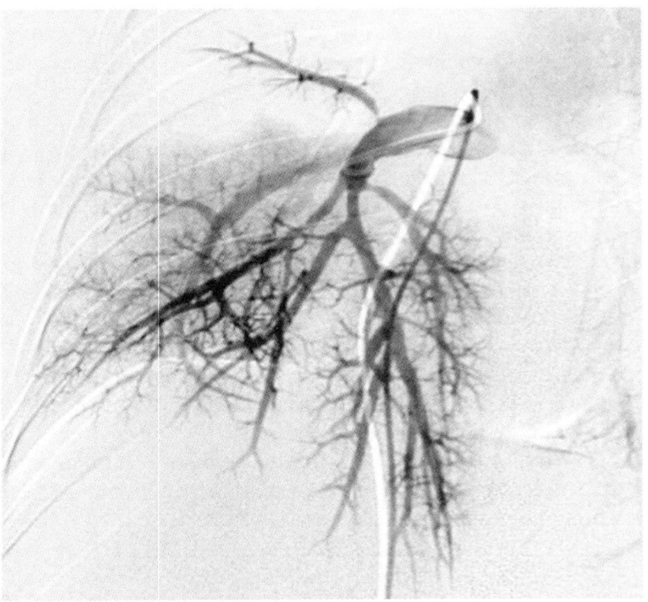

FIGURE 28-14 Stenoses of pulmonary artery branches due to Takayasu's arteritis.

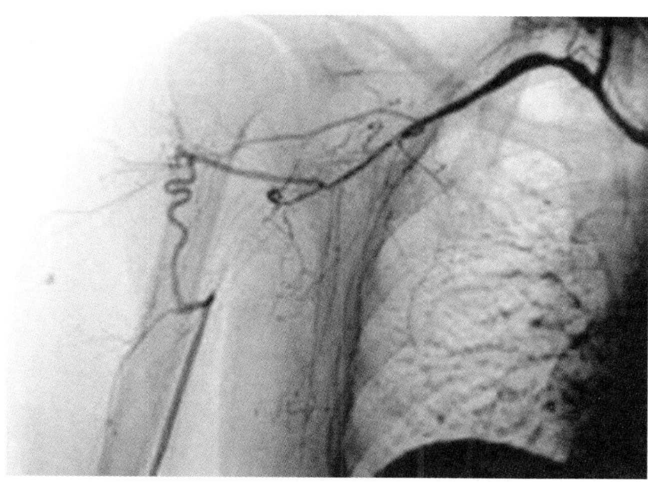

FIGURE 28-15 Giant cell arteritis of the right subclavian and axillary artery. Note collateral refilling of the brachial artery.

Medium- and Small-Vessel Vasculitis

Behçet's Disease

Behçet's disease is a systemic vasculitis of unknown etiology with hallmark features of oral and genital ulcers and relapsing uveitis. Behçet's disease was reported less than 70 years ago but most likely has been present for hundreds of years, and the original description of this disease has been traced to the Hippocratic third book of disease.[96] The disease derives its name from Hulusi Behçet, a Turkish dermatologist, who in 1936 published a series of three patients presenting with recurrent orogenital ulcerations and relapsing iritis with hypopyon (a visible layer of pus in the eye).[97]

Behçet's disease presents in young adults aged 20 to 40 years. Although uncommon, Behçet's disease has important ophthalmic, neurologic, renal, pulmonary, cardiac, and vascular manifestations.[98,99] Ophthalmic complications occur in up to 80% of affected patients. Blindness may result from uveitis and macular edema.[100] Vascular manifestations include arterial and venous thrombosis and unusual aneurysms of systemic and pulmonary arteries.

Behçet's disease is seen worldwide but is most prevalent in the Mediterranean countries, the Middle East, and the Far East. Turkey has the highest prevalence at 80 to 370 cases per 100,000 population. It is not surprising that much of the world's literature on Behçet's disease comes from Turkey.[98] Western countries have a much lower prevalence: 0.64 per 100,000 in the United Kingdom and 0.12 to 0.33 per 100,000 in the United States.[98] In the United States, males and females are affected equally. In Japan and Korea there is a slight female preponderance.[98]

The exact cause of Behçet's disease is unknown, but genetic, infectious, and toxic factors have been implicated. In the Middle East, 10% to 15% of cases are familial, but in the rest of the world, familial cases account for only 2% to 5% of cases. The HLA-B51 allele is more prevalent among Asian and Japanese patients with Behçet's disease, and the disease severity is worse if the HLA-B51 allele is present.[98]

An infectious etiology has also been considered. Viruses such as herpes simplex virus, hepatitis C, and parvovirus B19 have been implicated, but none has been proved to cause Behçet's disease. Skin lesions in Behçet's disease are remarkable for neutrophil infiltration despite lack of infection. It has been postulated that the neutrophils produce lysosomal enzymes that cause tissue injury. Increased levels of a number of cytokines have been found in Behçet's disease, including tumor necrosis factor α, interleukin 2, and interleukin 1β.[101] These cytokines are believed to activate neutrophils, leading to enhanced adherence to endothelial cells and increased expression of adhesion molecules that cause vascular damage.[98]

Clinical Features There is no specific laboratory test for Behçet's disease, and there are no serologic markers to assess the severity and activity of the disease. The diagnosis of Behçet's disease is based on clinical criteria established by the International Study Group for Behçet's Disease (Table 28-6).

Behçet's disease has a number of unique clinical features, as follows:

- *Pathergy* is considered to be one of the diagnostic criteria for Behçet's disease. Pricking the skin with a needle results in development of a small pustule at the site of injury within 24 to 48 hours. This has been thought to be pathognomonic of Behçet's disease, but some studies found sensitivity of this test to be as low as 10%.[102]
- *Oral aphthous ulcers* are present in all patients at some time during the course of the disease, but the lesions may be missed because they usually resolve in 10 to 14 days. These ulcers most commonly involve the buccal mucosa, gums, lips, tongue, and pharynx; they are shallow and painful with a sharp, round, erythematous border and a yellow fibrinous base.
- Genital ulcers resembling oral aphthae occur on the scrotum and penis in men and on the vulva in women. These are also self-limiting.
- *Ocular lesions* can occur in both the anterior and posterior chambers of the eye. Up to 25% of patients with ocular lesions become blind. Anterior uveitis presents with symptoms of blurred vision, floaters, and eye pain. Hypopyons are seen in some patients due to pus in the anterior chamber that sediments into a visible layer. Episcleritis can cause a red painful eye. Posterior eye disease can affect the retina and result in a painless decrease in visual acuity from retinal vascular damage associated with hemorrhages and exudates. Neovascularization of the iris and retina may also occur as late complications.
- *Skin lesions* are frequently found in patients with oral ulcers. More than one half of patients have cutaneous findings, most commonly a papulopustular skin lesion resembling acne or pseudofolliculitis. The initial skin lesion may have pathergic features that may start as a pustule precipitated by trauma.[97] Other skin lesions include erythema nodosum, with erythematous nodules that typically involve the legs.
- *Joints*: Nonerosive arthritis occurs in one half of patients and is typically associated with pain and swelling of knees, ankles, wrists, and elbows.
- *Gastrointestinal system:* Abdominal pain, diarrhea, and melena result from ulcers that occur in any area of

Table 28-6 Criteria* for the Diagnosis of Behçet's Disease

DIAGNOSTIC CRITERIA†	CLINICAL FINDINGS
Mandatory for diagnosis: Recurrent oral ulceration	Painful, shallow oral ulcer with round, sharp erythematous border and yellow fibrinous base, which recurred at least three times over a 12-month period
Minor criteria (need two):	
Recurrent genital ulceration	Aphthous ulceration/scarring
Eye lesions	Anterior or posterior uveitis or retinal vasculitis
Skin lesions	Erythema nodosum, pseudofolliculitis, or papulopustular lesions; or acneiform nodules
Pathergy	Sterile pustule at the site of a needle stick occurring 24-48 hours after injury

*The diagnosis of Behçet's disease is based on clinical criteria established by the International Study Group for Behçet's Disease.[148] There is no specific laboratory test for Behçet's disease, and there are no serologic markers.

†Diagnosis requires recurrent oral ulcerations and two minor criteria.

Adapted from MacCormack M, Phillips T: Behçet's disease: A clinical review. Wounds 14:275-283, 2002.

the small and large bowel. These lesions resemble inflammatory bowel disease with risk of perforation.

- *Central nervous system:* Up to 20% of patients with Behçet's disease have central nervous system involvement. Manifestations include meningitis, seizures, motor or brain stem symptoms, and cranial nerve palsies.[98]
- *Renal* involvement is unusual, but 7.5% may develop a glomerulonephritis.
- *Cardiac:* The heart is involved in only 3% to 6% of patients, but affected individuals may develop pericarditis, myocarditis, coronary artery disease, and intracardiac thrombus.

Vascular Involvement Vascular involvement in Behçet's disease ranges between 7.7% and 60% of affected patients. Lesions can result in both venous and arterial manifestations.[101] The risk of thrombosis is markedly increased in Behçet's disease. In one report, 27% of patients with Behçet's disease had arterial or venous thrombosis.[103]

Venous Thrombosis Up to 50% of patients with Behçet's disease have a history of prior venous thrombosis.[104] Thrombosis can involve the superficial and deep veins of the lower and upper extremity but may also involve central large veins, especially the superior and inferior vena cava. Less common manifestations include hepatic vein thrombosis causing Budd-Chiari syndrome, mesenteric vein thrombosis, renal vein thrombosis, and intracranial thrombosis involving the dural sinus.[103] Pulmonary artery thrombosis and intracardiac thrombus have also been reported.[105]

The increased thrombogenicity in patients with Behçet's disease has been attributed to prothrombotic states, endothelial injury, and defective fibrinolysis. A wide range of coagulation abnormalities have been reported in patients with Behçet's disease. Factor V Leiden mutation appears to be more frequent in patients with Behçet's disease and has been found in 37% of affected patients with a history of venous thrombosis. Prothrombin gene *G20210A* has been found in 31% of patients with thrombosis. In one study, 40% of patients had elevated IgG anticardiolipin antibodies.[106] Although all these may be contributing factors to an underlying prothrombotic state, no single abnormality has been consistently identifiedto explain the prothrombotic tendency associated with Behçet's disease.

Aneurysms and Occlusive Disease Both occlusive arterial disease and aneurysm formation occur as manifestations of Behçet's disease. Aneurysms are especially concerning due to the increased risk of rupture and sudden death. Although the frequency of arterial involvement in Behçet's disease has been reported to range from 2% to 34%, the true incidence may be less than 5%.[107,108] Arterial disease usually manifests 3 to 8 years after the initial diagnosis, at a mean age of 30 years.[107,109,110] Vascular complications occur less frequently in pediatric patients.

Occlusive arterial disease can involve both upper and lower extremities. When indicated, surgical revascularization such as iliofemoral or femoropopliteal bypass can be successful in relieving symptoms of limb ischemia. However, there is increased risk of graft failure due to thrombosis. This concern should not be considered a contraindication to surgery. Bypass patency using either prosthetic or autologous grafts can be enhanced by the use of postoperative anticoagulation.[107]

Behçet's disease is also well known for its propensity for *unusual arterial aneurysms* of systemic and pulmonary arteries. Arterial aneurysms are often multiple and are characterized by a saccular configuration with increased risk of unexpected rupture, thrombosis, and aneurysm recurrence. Occlusive lesions have a better prognosis than aneurysms, but arterial aneurysms occur more frequently than occlusive disease.[111] The abdominal aorta is the most common site of aneurysm formation, followed in decreasing order by the pulmonary, femoral, popliteal, brachial, and iliac arteries. Rare cases involving the carotid, vertebral, and coronary arteries have been reported.

Patients with pulmonary artery aneurysms can present with symptoms of dyspnea, cough, chest pain, and hemoptysis. Pulmonary artery aneurysms are frequently multiple and are especially worrisome because they can lead to massive and fatal hemoptysis. Aneurysm rupture is the leading cause of death in patients with Behçet's syndrome. In one literature review of 42 patients with pulmonary artery aneurysms, one third of patients died of fatal pulmonary hemorrhage within 2 years after diagnosis.[108]

Behçet's disease has been associated with intracranial aneurysms. In one report a 38-year-old man presented with a subdural hematoma due to a ruptured 5-mm fusiform aneurysm of the superior cerebellar artery. The diagnosis of Behçet's disease was made 5 months after repair of the ruptured aneurysm when he presented with painful oral aphthae and genital ulcers. He was subsequently found to have a pulmonary artery aneurysm on CT scan. Another 55-year-old man presented with a subarachnoid hemorrhage due to a dissecting pseudoaneurysm of the vertebral artery. Both were successfully treated with endovascular artery occlusion.[112]

The indications for surgery are similar to the indications with other aneurysms: repair of systemic aneurysms should be considered based on aneurysm size, rapid growth, or symptoms. Surgical treatment may be complicated by recurrent aneurysms in the operated artery or in arteries adjacent to arterial bypasses. Reoperation is frequent in Behçet's disease due to the occurrence of anastomotic aneurysms and thrombosis. In some series more than one half of patients required another operation within 4 years. Arterial aneurysms may also occur after minor arterial trauma such as arterial puncture for angiography.

Immunosuppressive Therapy Initially, the histology of Behçet's disease is characterized by an active vasculitis stage with inflammatory cell infiltration in the media and adventitia. This is later replaced by a scar stage with fibrous thickening and loss of elastic and muscle fibers.

Immunosuppression is clearly indicated for ophthalmic and neurologic complications of Behçet's disease; however, there is no consensus regarding the optimal pharmacologic treatment, and therapy remains empirical.[113] There are no serologic markers to follow to assess disease activity and severity.

The benefit of using prophylactic immunosuppression in asymptomatic patients is less clear. Postoperative corticosteroid therapy (initial dose 0.5 to 1 mg/kg/day) may prevent recurrent arterial lesions, but 86% of treated patients have been reported to relapse by 6 years.[107] Combining therapy with corticosteroids and immunosuppressant agents (especially azathioprine) has been advocated in some patients.[107]

As in other forms of vasculitis, the mainstay of medical therapy for Behçet's disease is high-dose corticosteroids (1 mg/kg/day in single or divided doses). Not all patients respond to corticosteroids, and many need a second or alternative agent. Large-vessel arteritis is treated with corticosteroids in combination with cytotoxic and immunosuppressive drugs (azathioprine, chlorambucil, cyclophosphamide, and methotrexate). Although these agents have been shown to induce and maintain remissions, relapses are frequent, and the drugs have potential side effects that may be severe.[108,114] Despite treatment with corticosteroid and immunosuppressive therapy, the mortality rate remains high.

A number of newer pharmacologic agents may have promise in Behçet's disease.[115,116] *Cyclosporine* may be of benefit in patients who are refractory to steroids.[113] Close monitoring is necessary for common adverse effects including severe hypertension and nephrotoxicity. *Thalidomide* is effective for oral and genital ulcers and has been approved for treatment of Behçet's disease.[117] Owing to the risk of teratogenicity and birth defects, use in female patients should be limited to those who have undergone hysterectomy or tubal ligation. Polyneuropathy can occur in up to 50%.[118] There is little information with regard to the use of thalidomide in vascular disease. Newer agents that may have potential benefit in Behçet's disease but have not yet been studied include tacrolimus and siroliminus.

Polyarteritis Nodosa

Polyarteritis nodosa (PAN) is a systemic necrotizing vasculitis of medium- and small-sized arteries. It can cause aneurysms, thrombosis, hemorrhage, and tissue infarction in almost every organ. Abdominal pain due to visceral ischemia is a common symptom in young adults. Affected patients may present with manifestations of appendicitis, cholecystitis, or intestinal perforation.[119] Laboratory tests demonstrate hepatitis B antigen in 30% of patients with PAN. The sedimentation rate is typically elevated, and ANCA is negative. The disease should be suspected clinically, but confirmation of the diagnosis often requires biopsy of affected tissue. Angiography documenting multiple small aneurysms in the mesenteric and parenchymal renal arteries may also be diagnostic.

Drugs of abuse including intravenous cocaine and methamphetamine can cause a panarteritis that resembles PAN.[120] HIV infections may also be associated with vasculitis. Although large-vessel involvement is uncommon, HIV can present with multiple aneurysms or occlusions of carotid, femoral, and popliteal arteries. Although some of these aneurysms are caused by opportunistic infections associated with HIV, aneurysm wall cultures are negative for infection in others.[32]

Kawasaki's Disease

Kawasaki's disease is a vasculitis affecting infants and children younger than 5 years of age. It was first described in Japan in 1967 but now is found worldwide with an incidence of 10.3 per 100,000 in the United States. It is well known as a cause of coronary aneurysms. These occur in 20% to 30% of patients and can cause other cardiac manifestations including pericardial effusion, mitral incompetence, and cardiac failure. As the child grows up, aneurysms may be found involving the aorta and iliac, axillary, brachial, mesenteric, or renal arteries.[121]

Wegener's Granulomatosis

Wegener's granulomatosis is characterized by a necrotizing or granulomatous vasculitis affecting small- to medium-sized vessels that classically involves the kidney along with the upper and lower respiratory tract. These patients may present to the vascular surgeon with an ischemic digit and clinical signs of nail fold infarcts and digital ulcerations. In Wegener's granulomatosis, c-ANCA is positive in 90% with active disease. Microscopic polyangiitis and Churg-Strauss syndrome are associated with a positive p-ANCA.[84,122,123]

■ RARE CAUSES OF HYPERTENSION AND RENOVASCULAR DISEASE

Fibromuscular Dysplasia

Fibromuscular dysplasia (FMD) is a noninflammatory abnormality that affects medium-sized arteries and is the

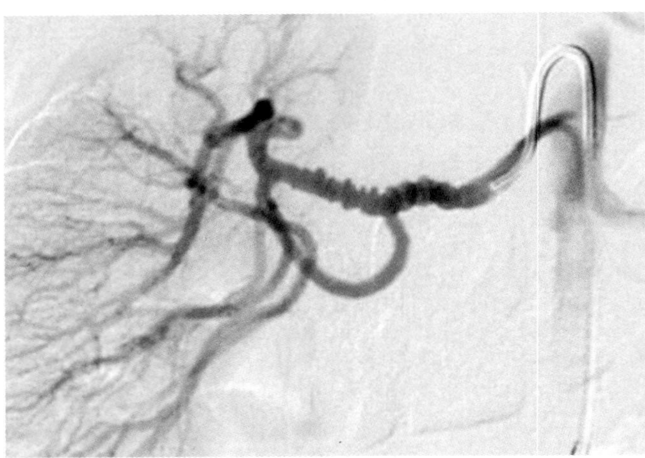

FIGURE 28-16 Medial fibromuscular dysplasia involving the right renal artery.

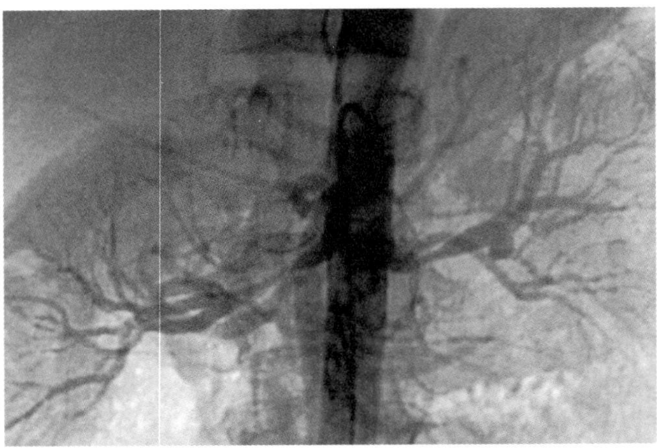

FIGURE 28-17 Intimal fibromuscular dysplasia involving the right renal artery in a 20-year-old patient with severe hypertension cured by surgical revascularization.

most common cause of renovascular hypertension in children. After atherosclerosis, it is the second most common correctable cause of renovascular hypertension in all age groups.[124] Although the renal arteries represent the most common site of involvement, FMD has been found in most vascular territories. FMD can produce symptoms due to arterial stenosis restricting renal perfusion, arterial dissection, or associated aneurysm rupture. FMD is classified according to the vessel layer involved (i.e., adventitial, medial, or intimal). Medial dysplasia accounts for 95% of FMD. The classic angiographic appearance is a "string of beads" that usually involves the mid and distal renal artery (Fig. 28-16).[125]

Intimal FMD is a rare variant that can cause severe hypertension, especially in children. Typical lesions appear as long, smooth, tapered narrowing of the proximal renal artery. Histologically, there is circumferential deposition of collagen in the intima without evidence of inflammation. These histologic features allow it to be distinguished from Takayasu's arteritis, which is a panarteritis associated with giant cells.[126] The angiographic appearance of intimal fibroplasia can be mimicked by arteritis, trauma, radiation, and neurofibromatosis (Fig. 28-17).

Aortic Coarctation

Coarctation of the aorta is one of the most common congenital aortic diseases. Owing to developmental abnormalities, coarctation of the thoracic aorta usually occurs in the region of the ductus arteriosus but in 2% can affect the abdominal aorta. A narrowing of the descending thoracic or abdominal aorta may manifest with a pulse and systolic blood pressure differential between the arms and legs. *Takayasu's arteritis* may cause arterial hypertension in 33% to 83% of patients as a result of thoracic or abdominal coarctation or from renal artery stenosis (Fig. 28-18).[90,127]

Neurofibromatosis

Neurofibromatosis (NF) may also cause severe hypertension due to abdominal aortic coarctation or to renal artery stenosis. NF is an autosomal dominant–inherited disorder characterized by cutaneous neurofibromas and café-au-lait spots. Manifestations may involve the skin and central nervous, ocular, and cardiovascular systems. Although primarily a disease of neurocutaneous tissues, vascular involvement can occur in 3.6% of individuals.

Vasculopathy associated with NF has been recognized for many years since first reported in the 1940s by Reubi and Feyrtr.[128] Arterial manifestations include renovascular hypertension, aortic stenosis, aneurysms, and occlusive disease. NF is divided into two types based on genetic and clinical features. NF type 1 (NF-1) is the most common type and was previously known as von Recklinghausen's disease because von Recklinghausen first reported this disorder in 1882. NF-1 affects 1 in 2500 individuals and is caused by a genetic defect localized to chromosome 17, which encodes for a protein, neurofibromin.[129,130] Cardinal diagnostic features include café-au-lait spots, Lisch nodules of the iris, and cutaneous neurofibromas.[129] Other features can include learning disabilities and shorter stature. The risk of malignancy is increased.[131]

Typical pigmented skin lesions include café-au-lait spots (diagnostic if ≥ six are present and are at least 2 cm in diameter) and skin freckling in non-sun-exposed areas such as the axilla. Neurofibromas are benign, rubbery, flat, or pedunculated subcutaneous tumors of peripheral nerves that are composed of Schwann cells and fibroblasts. These lesions can cause symptoms from local compression of adjacent structures and rarely turn into malignant sarcomas. Pheochromocytoma is also a tumor of neuroectodermal origin and can occur in association with NF and multiple endocrine neoplasia type 2B. In a 1972 study from the Mayo Clinic, NF was found in 3 of 132 patients with pheochromocytoma.[132] Others indicate the incidence of pheochromocytoma with NF may be less than 1%.[133]

NF-2 is less common, resulting from a genetic defect located on chromosome 22 and is characterized by the development of neurofibromas and schwannomas that affect the central and peripheral nervous system. NF-2 causes hearing loss with tinnitus in 90% of individuals due to a schwannoma of the acoustic nerve. Acoustic schwannomas

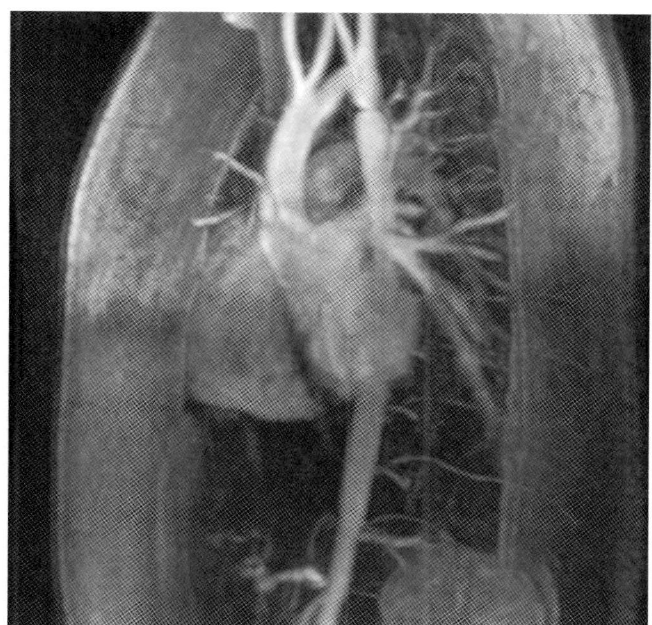

FIGURE 28-18 Aortic coarctation causing severe hypertension.

are frequently bilateral. Complete deafness can occur before age 30 years. There is an increased incidence of brain tumors, including meningiomas and tumors affecting the spinal nerves. Skeletal system involvement can result in scoliosis, tibial bowing, and pseudoarthrosis of joints. Typical skin lesions may be less apparent in NF-2.[130]

The incidence of blood vessel involvement is quite variable in NF-1, and it can cause aneurysmal dilation or occlusion of small-, medium-, and large-sized arteries. The most common vascular manifestations are stenosis or aneurysms of the abdominal aorta and aortic branch vessels (Fig. 28-19).[134]

Severe hypertension can occur at a young age owing to aortic coarctation or renal artery stenosis.[128,135-139] Renovascular hypertension is often severe and resistant to multiple medications. In contrast with medial FMD that involves the mid and distal artery, NF-1 is more likely to involve the origin of the renal artery. Angiographically, the stenoses have a distinctive appearance with diffuse involvement and narrowings that are elongated, smooth, and funnel shaped. Nonvascular manifestations should help differentiate between NF and other causes of renovascular hypertension such as congenital coarctation of the aorta, Takayasu's arteritis, radiation therapy, and intimal FMD. A complete family history and skin inspection are mandatory in young patients with renal artery stenosis.[126] Arterial hypertension has been cured by renal revascularization[140,141] but also by balloon angioplasty.[142,143]

Schurch and coworkers reported a 10-year-old girl with arterial hypertension, coarctation of the aorta, and multiple stenoses at the origin of each renal artery.[128] She underwent surgical repair with reimplantation of renal arteries into the aorta and her blood pressure subsequently normalized. Four years later hypertension recurred and angiography showed progression of disease to include abdominal aortic coarctation and restenosis of renal arteries. Histology showed eccentric intimal proliferation extending into the lumen with proliferation of smooth muscle and fibrous tissue.[128]

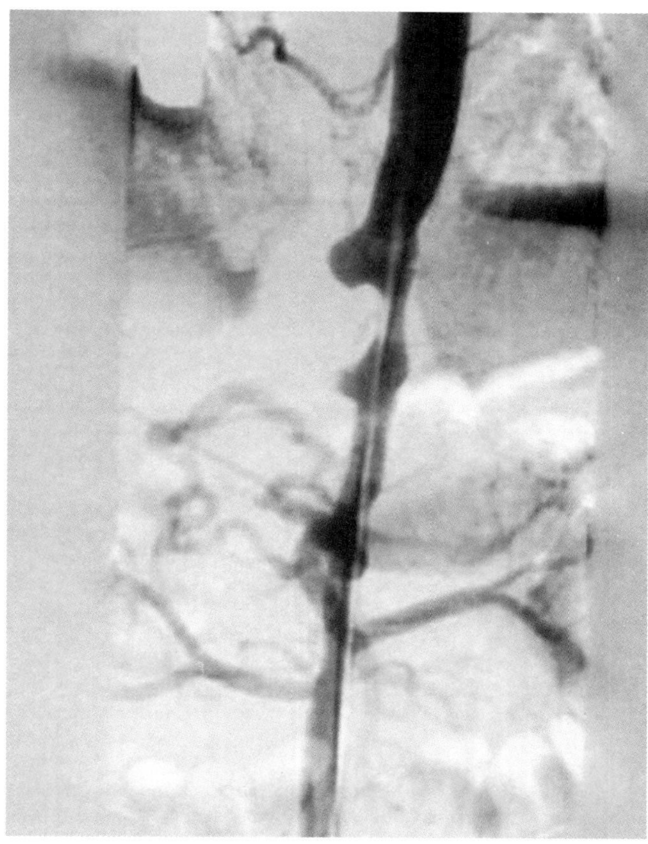

FIGURE 28-19 Neurofibromatosis with multiple thoracic and abdominal aneurysms in a young patient. Arterial hypertension can result from suprarenal aortic stenosis (as in this patient) or from renal artery stenosis.

Aortic branch vessels can be involved in patients with NF-1, including celiac, mesenteric, iliac, subclavian, pulmonary, and cervical and cerebral arteries. Pseudoaneurysms of femoral and popliteal arteries with occlusion of the superficial femoral artery have been reported. Often more than one site may be involved: the combination of aortic and renal artery involvement is common.[134]

Other vascular complications have been associated with NF. There are a number of reports in the literature describing fatal or life-threatening vascular disease in young persons with NF. Intramural hematoma of the thoracic aorta associated with NF has been reported.[144] Aneurysms may occur in small vessels including the radial artery and branches of the renal artery.[145] Arterial rupture associated with neurofibromas of the arterial adventitia and media has been described. Rupture of subclavian and intercostal arteries has been reported in patients with NF-1 at the site of a neurofibroma. Brachial artery rupture during pregnancy has required extremity amputation.[14] Rupture of a carotid artery in the postpartum period in a patient known to have NF-1 has been reported and was successfully repaired by a stented endograft.[147]

REFERENCES

1. Andros G, Schneider PA, Harris RW, et al: Management of arterial occlusive disease following radiation therapy. Cardiovasc Surg 4:135-142, 1996.
2. Himmel PD, Hassett JM: Radiation-induced chronic arterial injury. Semin Surg Oncol 2:225-247, 1986.
3. Chun YS, Cherry KJ: Radiation arteritis. J Am Coll Surg 196:482, 2003.
4. Hashmonai M, Elami A, Kuten A, et al: Subclavian artery occlusion after radiotherapy for carcinoma of the breast. Cancer 61:2015-2018, 1988.
5. Tashiro T, Ikota T, Yamashita K, et al: [A case of bilateral carotid radiation angiopathy]. Rinsho Hoshasen 30:909-912, 1985.
6. Ghosh AK, Lundstrom CE, Edwards WD: Radiation arteritis following treatment for Wilms' tumor: An unusual case of weight loss. Vasc Med 7:19-23, 2002.
7. Melliere D, Becquemin JP, Hoehne M, et al: [True and false radiation arteritis]. J Mal Vasc 8:321-327, 1983.
8. Fajardo LF, Berthrong M: Vascular lesions following radiation. Pathol Annu 23:297-330, 1988.
9. Rubin DI, Schomberg PJ, Shepherd RF, et al: Arteritis and brachial plexus neuropathy as delayed complications of radiation therapy. Mayo Clin Proc 76:849-852, 2001.
10. Tenet W, Missri J, Hager D: Radiation-induced stenosis of the left main coronary artery. Cathet Cardiovasc Diagn 12:169-171, 1986.
11. Rhodes JM, Cherry KJ Jr, Clark RC, et al: Aortic-origin reconstruction of the great vessels: Risk factors of early and late complications. J Vasc Surg 31:260-269, 2000.
12. Melliere D, Becquemin JP, Kassab M, et al: [Natural and corrected history of obliterative radiation arteritis: Apropos of 14 case reports]. J Mal Vasc 15:73-81, 1990.
13. Melliere D, Desgranges P, Berrahal D, et al: [Radiation-induced aorto-ilio-femoral arterial arteritis: Mediocrity of the long-term results after conventional surgery]. J Mal Vasc 25:332-335, 2000.
14. Fann JI, Dalman RL: Heritable arteriopathy. Semin Vasc Surg 6:46-55, 1993.
15. Connor PJ Jr, Juergens JL, Perry HO, et al: Pseudoxanthoma elasticum and angioid streaks: Review of 106 cases. Am J Med 30:537-543, 1961.
16. Sane D, Vidaillet H, Burton C: Cutaneous signs of cardiopulmonary disease: Pitfalls of chest pain. Chest 91:134-135, 1987.
17. Pyeritz RE: Pseudoxanthoma elasticum. In Goldman L, Ausiello D (eds): Cecil Textbook of Medicine, 22nd ed. Philadelphia, WB Saunders, 2000, pp 1640-1641.
18. Fann JI, Dalman RL, Harris EJ Jr: Genetic and metabolic causes of arterial disease. Ann Vasc Surg 7:594-604, 1993.
19. Korn S, Seilnacht J, Huth C, et al: [Cardiovascular manifestations of pseudoxanthoma elasticum (Gronblad-Strandberg syndrome)]. Thorac Cardiovasc Surg 35:191-194, 1987.
20. James AE Jr, Eaton SB, Blazek JV, et al: Roentgen findings in pseudoxanthoma elasticum (PXE). AJR Am J Roentgenol 106:642-647, 1969.
21. Kevorkian JP, Masquet C, Kural-Menasche S, et al: New report of severe coronary artery disease in an eighteen-year-old girl with pseudoxanthoma elasticum: Case report and review of the literature. Angiology 48:735-741, 1997.
22. Slade AK, John RM, Swanton RH: Pseudoxanthoma elasticum presenting with myocardial infarction. Br Heart J 63:372-373, 1990.
23. Mendelsohn G, Bulkley BH, Hutchins GM: Cardiovascular manifestations of pseudoxanthoma elasticum. Arch Pathol Lab Med 102:298-302, 1978.
24. Van Der Post CW: Report of a case of mistaken injection of pentothal sodium into aberrant ulnar artery. S Afr Med J 16:182, 1942.
25. Woodburn KR, Murie JA: Vascular complications of injecting drug misuse [Comment]. Br J Surg 83:1329-1334, 1996.
26. Swalwell CI, Davis GG: Methamphetamine as a risk factor for acute aortic dissection. J Forens Sci 44:23-26, 1999.
27. Bacharach JM, Colville DS, Lie JT: Accelerated atherosclerosis, aneurysmal disease, and aortitis: Possible pathogenetic association with cocaine abuse. Int Angiol 11:83-86, 1992.
28. Chen JC, Hsiang YN, Morris DC, et al: Cocaine-induced multiple vascular occlusions: A case report. J Vasc Surg 23:719-723, 1996.
29. Raso AM, Visentin I, Zan S, et al: [Vascular pathology of surgical interest in drug addicts]. Minerva Cardioangiol 48:287-296, 2000.
30. Kloner RA, Rezkalla SH: Cocaine and the heart [Comment]. N Engl J Med 348:487-488, 2003.
31. Weber JE, Shafer FS, Larkin GL et al: Validation of a brief observation period for patients with cocaine-associated chest pain [Comment]. N Engl J Med 348:510-517, 2003.
32. Kontos MC, Jesse RL, Tatum JL, et al: Coronary angiographic findings in patients with cocaine-associated chest pain. J Emerg Med 24:9-13, 2003.
33. Perez JA Jr, Arsura EL, Strategos S: Methamphetamine-related stroke: Four cases. J Emerg Med 17:469-471, 1999.
34. Gonzalez MH: Necrotizing fasciitis and gangrene of the upper extremity. Hand Clin North Am 14:635-645, ix, 1998.
35. Buchanan N, Cane RD, Miller M: Symmetrical gangrene of the extremities associated with the use of dopamine subsequent to ergometrine administration. Intensive Care Med 3:55-56, 1977.
36. Shepherd RF: Ergotism. In White RA, Hollier LH (eds): Vascular Surgery: Basic Science and Clinical Correlations. Philadelphia, JB Lippincott, 1994, pp 177-191.
37. Merhoff G, Porter J: Ergot intoxication: History, review, and description of unusual clinical manifestations. Ann Surg 180:773, 1974.
38. Seifert KB, Blackshear WM Jr, Cruse CW, et al: Bilateral upper extremity ischemia after administration of dihydroergotamine-heparin for prophylaxis of deep venous thrombosis. J Vasc Surg 8:410-414, 1988.
39. McKiernan TL, Bock K, Leya F, et al: Ergot-induced peripheral vascular insufficiency: Noninterventional treatment. Cathet Cardiovasc Diagn 31:211-214, 1994.
40. Hagen B: [Vascular changes in sporadic ergotism: Epidemiology, pathogenesis, clinical picture, and diagnosis with particular considera-tion of angiographic documentation]. Radiologe 26:388-394, 1986.
41. Greene FL, Ariyan S, Stansel HC Jr: Mesenteric and peripheral vascular ischemia secondary to ergotism. Surgery 81:176-179, 1977.
42. Magee R: Saint Anthony's fire revisited: Vascular problems associated with migraine medication. Med J Aust 154:145-149, 1991.
43. Wells K, Steed DL, Zajko AB, et al: Recognition and treatment of arterial insufficiency from Cafergot. J Vasc Surg 4:8, 1986.
44. Carr P: Self-induced myocardial infarction. Postgrad Med 57:654, 1981.
45. Goldfisher JD: Acute myocardial infarction secondary to ergot therapy. N Engl J Med 262:280, 1960.
46. Katz J, Vogel RM: Abdominal angina as a complication of methysergide maleate therapy. JAMA 199:160, 1967.
47. Kempczinski RF, Buckley CJ, Darling RC: Vascular insufficiency secondary to ergotism. Surgery 79:597-600, 1976.
48. Fedotin M, Hartman C: Ergotamine poisoning producing renal arterial spasm. N Engl J Med 283:518, 1970.
49. Abercrombie D, Oehlert W: Ergotism as a cause of acute vasospastic disease with features mimicking severe atherosclerosis. Ok State Med Assoc 77:86, 1984.
50. Herlache J, Hoskins P, Schmidt C: Unilateral brachial artery throm-bosis secondary to ergotamine tartrate. Angiology 24:369, 1973.
51. van den Berg E, Rumpf KD, Frohlich H, et al: Vascular spasm during thromboembolism prophylaxis with heparin-dihydroergotamine. Lancet 2:268-269, 1982.
52. Carliner N, Denune DP, Finch CS Jr, et al: Sodium nitroprusside treatment of ergotamine-induced peripheral ischemia. JAMA 227:308, 1974.
53. Hasham SN, Guo DC, Milewicz DM: Genetic basis of thoracic aortic aneurysms and dissections. Curr Opin Cardiol 17:677-683, 2002.
54. Gott VL, Greene PS, Alejo DE, et al: Replacement of the aortic root in patients with Marfan's syndrome [Comment]. N Engl J Med 340:1307-1313, 1999.
55. De Paepe A, Devereuz RB, Dietz HC, et al: Revised diagnostic criteria for the Marfan syndrome. Am J Med Genet 62:417-426, 1996.

56. Loeys B, Nuytinck L, Delvaux I, et al: Genotype and phenotype analysis of 171 patients referred for molecular study of the fibrillin-1 gene *FBN1* because of suspected Marfan syndrome [Comment]. Arch Intern Med 161:2447-2454, 2001.
57. Comeglio P, Evans AL, Brice G, et al: Identification of *FBN1* gene mutations in patients with ectopia lentis and marfanoid habitus. Br J Ophthalmol 86:1359-1362, 2002.
58. Dean JC: Management of Marfan syndrome. Heart 88:97-103, 2002.
59. Simpson CF, Boucek RJ, Noble NL: Influence of D-, L-, and DL-propranolol, and practolol on beta-amino-propionitrile-induced aortic ruptures of turkeys. Toxicol Appl Pharmacol 38:169-175, 1976.
60. Halpern BL, Char F, Murdoch JL, et al: A prospectus on the prevention of aortic rupture in the Marfan syndrome with data on survivorship without treatment. Johns Hopkins Med J 129:123-129, 1971.
61. Groenink M, de Roos A, Mulder BJ, et al: Changes in aortic distensibility and pulse wave velocity assessed with magnetic resonance imaging following beta-blocker therapy in the Marfan syndrome. Am J Cardiol 82:203-208, 1998.
62. Haouzi A, Berglund H, Pelikan PC, et al: Heterogeneous aortic response to acute beta-adrenergic blockade in Marfan syndrome. Am Heart J 133:60-63, 1997.
63. Shores J, Berger KR, Murphy EA, et al: Progression of aortic dilation and the benefit of long-term (beta) adrenergic blockade in Marfan's syndrome. N Engl J Med 330:1335-1341, 1994.
64. Rios AS, Silber EN, Bavishi N, et al: Effect of long-term beta-blockade on aortic root compliance in patients with Marfan syndrome. Am Heart J 137:1057-1061, 1999.
65. Nagashima H, Sakomura Y, Aoka Y, et al: Angiotensin II type 2 receptor mediates vascular smooth muscle cell apoptosis in cystic medial degeneration associated with Marfan's syndrome. Circulation 104(Suppl 1):I282-I287, 2001.
66. Coady MA, Rizzo JA, Hammond GL, et al: What is the appropriate size criterion for resection of thoracic aortic aneurysms? J Thorac Cardiovasc Surg 113:476-491, 1997.
67. Gott VL, Cameron DE, Alejo DE, et al: Aortic root replacement in 271 Marfan patients: A 24-year experience. Ann Thorac Surg 73:438-443, 2002.
68. Bentall H, De Bono A: A technique for complete replacement of the ascending aorta. Thorax 23:338-339, 1968.
69. Miller DC: Valve-sparing aortic root replacement in patients with the Marfan syndrome [Comment]. J Thorac Cardiovasc Surg 125:773-778, 2003.
70. De Oliveira NC, David TE, Ivanov J, et al: Results of surgery for aortic root aneurysm in patients with Marfan syndrome [Comment]. J Thorac Cardiovasc Surg 125:789-796, 2003.
71. Burkhart HM, Zehr KJ, Schaff HV, et al: Valve-preserving aortic root reconstruction: A comparison of techniques. J Heart Valve Dis 12:62-67, 2003.
72. Immer FF, Bansi AG, Immer-Bansi AS, et al: Aortic dissection in pregnancy: Analysis of risk factors and outcome. Ann Thorac Surg 76:309-314, 2003.
73. Wenstrup RJ, Meyer RA, Lyle JS, et al: Prevalence of aortic root dilation in the Ehlers-Danlos syndrome. Genet Med 4:112-117, 2002.
74. Maltz SB, Fantus RJ, Mellet MM, et al: Surgical complications of Ehlers-Danlos syndrome type IV: Case report and review of the literature. J Trauma 51:387-390, 2001.
75. Beighton P, de Paepe A, Danks D, et al: International Nosology of Heritable Disorders of Connective Tissue, Berlin, 1986. Am J Med Genet 29:581-594, 1988.
76. Beighton P, de Paepe A, Steinmann B, et al: Ehlers-Danlos syndromes: Revised nosology, Villefranche, 1997. Ehlers-Danlos National Foundation (USA) and Ehlers-Danlos Support Group (UK). Am J Med Genet 77:31-37, 1998.
77. Michalickova K, Susic M, Willing MC, et al: Mutations of the alpha2(V) chain of type V collagen impair matrix assembly and produce Ehlers-Danlos syndrome type I. Hum Mol Genet 7:249-255, 1998.
78. Mao JR, Bristow J: The Ehlers-Danlos syndrome: On beyond collagens. J Clin Invest 107:1063-1069, 2001.
79. Pepin M: Clinical and genetic features of Ehlers-Danlos syndrome type IV, the vascular type. N Engl J Med 342:673, 2000.
80. Meldon S, Brady W, Young JS: Presentation of Ehlers-Danlos syndrome: Iliac artery pseudoaneurysm rupture. Ann Emerg Med 28:231-234, 1996.
81. Chuman H, Trobe JD, Petty EM, et al: Spontaneous direct carotid-cavernous fistula in Ehlers-Danlos syndrome type IV: Two case reports and a review of the literature [Comment]. J Neuroophthalmol 22:75-81, 2002.
82. Cikrit DF, Miles JH, Silver D: Spontaneous arterial perforation: The Ehlers-Danlos specter. J Vasc Surg 5:248-255, 1987.
83. Parfitt J, Chalmers RT, Wolfe JH: Visceral aneurysms in Ehlers-Danlos syndrome: Case report and review of the literature. J Vasc Surg 31:1248-1251, 2000.
84. Savage COS, Harper L, Adu D: Primary systemic vasculitis. Lancet 439:553-557, 1997.
85. Stone JH, Calabrese LH, Hoffman GS, et al: Vasculitis: A collection of pearls and myths. Rheum Dis Clin North Am 27:677-749, 2001.
86. Arend WP, Michel BA, Bloch DA, et al: The American College of Rheumatology 1990 criteria for the classification of Takayasu arteritis. Arthritis Rheum 33:1129-1134, 1990.
87. Gibbs CR, Lip GY: Takayasu's pulseless disease. Clin Cardiol 23:293-294, 2000.
88. Banks MJ, Erb N, George P, et al: Hypertension is not a disease of the left arm: A difficult diagnosis of hypertension in Takayasu's arteritis. J Hum Hypertens 15:573-575, 2001.
89. Evans JM, Bowles CA, Bjornsson J, et al: Thoracic aortic aneurysm and rupture in giant cell arteritis: A descriptive study of 41 cases. Arthritis Rheum 37:1539-1547, 1994 [erratum in: Arthritis Rheum 38:290, 1995].
90. Johnson S, Lock R, Gompels M: Takayasu arteritis: A review. J Clin Pathol 55:481-486, 2002.
91. Salvarani C, Hunder GG: Giant cell arteritis with low erythrocyte sedimentation rate: Frequency of occurrence in a population-based study [Comment]. Arthritis Rheum 45:140-145, 2001.
92. Nishimura S, Toubaru T, Ootaki E, et al: Follow-up study of aortic-valve replacement surgery in patients with Takayasu's disease complicated by aortic regurgitation. Circulation 66:564-566, 2002.
93. Ninet J, Bachet P, Dumontet CM, et al: Subclavian and axillary involvement in temporal arteritis and polymyalgia rheumatica. Am J Med 88:13-20, 1990.
94. Klein R, Hunder GG, Stanson AW, et al: Large artery involvement in giant cell (temporal) arteritis. Ann Intern Med 83:806-812, 1975.
95. Hunder GG, Arend WP, Block DA, et al: The American College of Rheumatology 1990 criteria for the classification of giant cell arteritis. Arthritis Rheum 33:1122-1128, 1990.
96. Cheng TO: Behçet's disease. N Engl J Med 342:588-589, 2000.
97. MacCormack M, Phillips T: Behçet's disease: A clinical review. Wounds 14:275-283, 2002.
98. Sakane T, Takeno M, Suzuki N: Behçet's disease. N Engl J Med 341:1284-1291, 1999.
99. Ehrlich G: Behçet's disease: Now you see it, now you don't. Compr Ther 18:25-27, 1992.
100. Whallett AJ, Thurairajan G, Hamburger J, et al: Behçet's syndrome: A multidisciplinary approach to clinical care. Q J Med 92:727-740, 1999.
101. Besbas N, Ozyurek E, Balkanci F, et al: Behçet's disease with severe arterial involvement in a child. Clin Rheumatol 21:176-179, 2002.
102. Davies PG, Fordham JN, Kirwan JR, et al: The pathergy test and Behçet's syndrome in Britain. Ann Rheum Dis 43:70-73, 1984.
103. Kiraz S, Ertenli I, Ozturk MA, et al: Pathological haemostasis and "prothrombotic state" in Behçet's disease. Thromb Res 105:125-133, 2002.
104. Kuzu A, Koksoy C, Ozaslan C, et al: Evaluation of peripheral vascular system disorders in vascular symptom-free Behçet's disease. Cardiovasc Surg 4:381-383, 1996.
105. Mogulkoc N, Burgess MI, Bishop PW: Intracardiac thrombus in Behçet's disease: A systematic review [Comment]. Chest 118:479-487, 2000.

106. Mader R, Ziv M, Adawi M, et al: Thrombophilic factors and their relation to thromboembolic and other clinical manifestations in Behçet's disease. J Rheumatol 26:2404-2408, 1999.
107. Le Thi Huong D, Weschler B, Papo T, et al: Arterial lesions in Behçet's disease: A study in 25 patients. J Rheumatol 22:2103-2113, 1995.
108. Christensen PA, Twedegaard E, Strandgaard S, et al: Behçet's syndrome presenting with peripheral arterial aneurysms. Scand J Rheumatol 26:386-388, 1997.
109. De Jesus H, Rosa M, Queiroz MV: Vascular involvement in Behçet's disease: An analysis of twelve cases. Clin Rheumatol 16:220-221, 1997.
110. Ko GY, Byun JY, Choi BG, et al: The vascular manifestations of Behçet's disease: Angiographic and CT findings. Br J Radiol 73:1270-1274, 2000.
111. Tuzun H, Sayin A, Karaozbek Y, et al: Peripheral aneurysms in Behçet's disease. Cardiovasc Surg 1:220-224, 1993.
112. Kizilkilic O, Albayram S, Adaletli I, et al: Endovascular treatment of Behçet's disease-associated intracranial aneurysms: Report of two cases and review of the literature. Neuroradiology 45:328-334, 2003.
113. Yazici H, Yurdakul S, Hamuryudan V: Behçet's disease. Curr Opin Rheumatol 13:18-22, 2001.
114. Kaklamani V, Kaklamanis P: Treatment of Behçet's Disease: An update. Semin Arthritis Rheum 30:299-231, 2001.
115. Yazici H: Behçet's syndrome: An update. Curr Rheumatol Rep 5:195-199, 2003.
116. Hamuryudan V, Ozyazgan Y, Freska Y, et al: Interferon alfa combined with azathioprine for the uveitis of Behçet's disease: An open study [comment]. Israel Med Assoc J 4(11 Suppl): 928-930, 2002.
117. Hamuryudan V, Mat C, Saip S, et al: Thalidomide in the treatment of the mucocutaneous lesions of Behçet's syndrome: A randomized, double-blind, placebo-controlled trial. Ann Intern Med 128:443-459, 1998.
118. Hamza M: Treatment of Behçet's disease with thalidomide. Clin Rheumatol 5:365-371, 1986.
119. London NJM: Commentary: Arteritis in western surgical practice. Postgrad Med 76:412, 2000.
120. Mockel M, Kampf D, Lobeck H, et al: Severe panarteritis associated with drug abuse. Intensive Care Med 25:113-117, 1999.
121. Dillon MJ, Ansell BM: Vasculitis in children and adolescents. Rheum Dis Clin North Am 21:1115-1136, 1995.
122. Jayne D: Update on the European Vasculitis Study Group Trials. Curr Opin Rheumatol 13:48-55, 2001.
123. Xiao H, Heeringa P, Hu P, et al: Antineutrophil cytoplasmic autoantibodies specific for myeloperoxidase cause glomerulonephritis and vasculitis in mice [Comment]. J Clin Invest 110:955-963, 2002.
124. Daniels SR, Loggie JM, McEnery PT, et al: Clinical spectrum of intrinsic renovascular hypertension in children. Pediatrics 80:698-704, 1987.
125. Luscher TF, Lie JT, Stanson AW, et al: Arterial fibromuscular dysplasia. Mayo Clin Proc 62:931-952, 1987.
126. Lie JT: Histopathologic specificity of systemic vasculitis. Rheum Dis Clin North Am 21:883-909, 1995.
127. Kerr GS: Takayasu's arteritis. Rheum Dis Clin North Am 21:1041-1058, 1995.
128. Schurch W, Messerli FH, Genest J, et al: Arterial hypertension and neurofibromatosis: Renal artery stenosis and coarctation of abdominal aorta. Can Med J 8:879-883, 1975.
129. Ruggieri M: The different forms of neurofibromatosis. Childs Nerv Syst 15:295-308, 1999.
130. Karnes PS: Neurofibromatosis: A common neurocutaneous disorder. Mayo Clin Proc 73:1071-1076, 1998.
131. Rasmussen SA, Yang Q, Friedman JM: Mortality in neurofibromatosis 1: An analysis using U.S. death certificates. Am J Hum Genet 68:1110-1118, 2001.
132. Lynch JD, Sheps SG, Bernatz PE, et al: Neurofibromatosis and hypertension due to pheochromocytoma or renal-artery stenosis. Minn Med 55:25-31, 1972.
133. Manger WM, Gifford RW: Clinical and Experimental Pheochromocytoma, 2nd ed. Cambridge, Mass, Blackwell Science, 1996, pp 144-146.
134. Ilgit ET, Vural M, Oguz A, et al: Peripheral arterial involvement in neurofibromatosis type 1—a case report. Angiology 50:955-958, 1999.
135. Sobata E, Ohkuma H, Suzuki S: Cerebrovascular disorders associated with von Recklinghausen's neurofibromatosis: A case report. Neurosurgery 22:544-549, 1988.
136. Virdis R, Balestrazzi P, Zampolli M, et al: Hypertension in children with neurofibromatosis. J Hum Hypertens 8:395-397, 1994.
137. Pilmore HL, Na Nagara MP, Walker R.J: Neurofibromatosis and renovascular hypertension presenting in early pregnancy. Nephrol Dial Transplant 12:187-189, 1997.
138. Nakhoul F, Green J, Angel A, et al: Renovascular hypertension associated with neurofibromatosis: Two cases and review of the literature. Clin Nephrol 55:322-326, 2001.
139. Rybka SJ, Novick AC: Concomitant carotid, mesenteric, and renal artery stenosis due to primary intimal fibroplasia. J Urol 129:798-800, 1983.
140. Morin JE, Hutchinson TA, Lisbona R: Long-term prognosis of surgical treatment of renovascular hypertension: A fifteen-year experience. J Vasc Surg 3:545-549, 1986.
141. Chien GW, Gritsch HA, Quinones-Baldrich WJ: Simple surgical repair of bilateral renal artery stenosis in a patient with neurofibromatosis. J Urol 167:1811-1812, 2002.
142. Yune HY, Klatte EC, Grim CE, et al: Transluminal balloon dilatation of renal artery stenosis causing hypertension: 18 months' experience. Clin Sci 59(Suppl 6):483s-485s, 1980.
143. Lovaria A, Nicolini A, Meregaglia D, et al: Interventional radiology in the treatment of renal artery stenosis. Ann Urol 33:146-155, 1999.
144. Ali OA, Okike N, Hogan RG, et al: Intramural hematoma of the thoracic aorta in a woman with neurofibromatosis. Ann Thorac Surg 73:958-960, 2002.
145. Singh S, Riaz M, Wilmshurst AD, et al: Radial artery aneurysm in a case of neurofibromatosis. Br J Plast Surg 51:564-565, 1998.
146. Tidwell C, Copas P: Brachial artery rupture complicating a pregnancy with neurofibromatosis: A case report. Am J Obstet Gynecol 179:832-834, 1998.
147. Smith BL, Munschauer CE, Diamond N, et al: Ruptured internal carotid aneurysm resulting from neurofibromatosis: Treatment with intraluminal stent graft. J Vasc Surg 32:824-828, 2000.
148. International Study Group for Behçet's Disease: Criteria for diagnosis of Behçet's disease. Lancet 335:1078-1080, 1990.

Chapter

29

Arterial Aneurysms: Etiologic Considerations

JOHN A. CURCI, MD
B. TIMOTHY BAXTER, MD
ROBERT W. THOMPSON, MD

Section V

Aneurysm is a more or less impaired or wholly suspended cohesion, at some point, of the contractile villi that compose the texture of the arteries ... from which cause there arises either a pulsating tumor of the artery or a violent efflux of blood out of the artery. But since the weakened cohesion of these fibers may come about in many ways, I consider that, to ensure clear instruction about this, we must divide this class of malady into its differing species and then subdivide them.

Giovanni Maria Lancisi, *De Aneurysmatibus (Aneurysms)*, 1745[1]

Arterial aneurysms have captured the attention of physicians and surgeons for centuries. An arterial aneurysm is a pathologic entity strictly defined by a gross measurable anatomic change in the geometry of the blood vessel wall, namely localized dilatation. The precise amount of dilatation necessary for a definition of "aneurysm" is of some debate, but it is generally held to require an increase in arterial diameter of at least 50% compared to a "normal" baseline. The nature of this dilation may be either fusiform or saccular, but it involves the entire wall of the vessel. These lesions are therefore distinguished from "pseudoaneurysms," which result from a transmural disruption of the arterial wall with blood contained by periarterial tissues.

The etiology of arterial aneurysms is extremely diverse, but it has become clear that there are a number of fundamental pathologic changes that can be considered common to aneurysms in general. Most aneurysms develop slowly over a period of years and are clinically silent until late in their natural history, with symptoms arising only from dramatic complications, such as rupture, dissection, thrombosis, embolization, and compression or erosion of adjacent structures. The propensity for any of these complications to develop in a particular aneurysm is partly the result of the anatomic location of the aneurysm and the underlying pathophysiologic process driving the disease. The purpose of this chapter is to review current knowledge of the pathophysiologic processes responsible for aneurysm disease, both in the abdominal aorta as well as in other locations.

■ GENERAL PATHOPHYSIOLOGIC CONSIDERATIONS

Arterial Architecture

The central function of the aorta and all muscular arteries is to act as an efficient and durable conduit for pulsatile blood flow. As such, these vessels must preserve a nonthrombogenic lumen free of obstruction and maintain their structural integrity over a lifetime of cyclic hemodynamic stresses. The loss of structural integrity is the fundamental cause of aneurysm formation and ultimate rupture. Unlike occlusive atherosclerotic disease, development of an arterial aneurysm involves changes in all three layers of the arterial wall. To understand the etiopathology of arterial aneurysms, it is therefore necessary to consider the microscopic anatomy of not just the intima, but the media and adventitia—the outer layers of the arterial wall responsible for maintaining tensile strength.

The media of muscular arteries is dominated by extracellular matrix elements and vascular smooth muscle cells (SMCs). The matrix components include well-organized bundles of elastin, collagen, and proteoglycans. Microscopically, this arrangement is characterized by concentric layers of elastic fibers organized into thick lamellae, alternating with layers of vascular smooth muscle. As originally described by Wolinsky and Glagov, each layer of elastic fibers and its associated SMCs constitute a "lamellar unit" of medial structure.[2] This organization gives the vessel the necessary degree of circumferential resilience to resist permanent deformation under normal hemodynamic stresses.

The adventitia is composed of a loose network of interstitial collagen fibers and fibroblasts, as well as nerves and capillary-sized blood vessels. Although adventitial collagen fibers do not appear to be under maximal tension during normal physiologic conditions, they undergo more linear alignment with the development of aneurysmal dilation. This observation suggests that increased wall stress in aneurysms leads to stretch of adventitial collagen fibers to the limits of their tensile strength.

In normal vessels, the elastic media likely bears most of the stress of pulsatile blood pressure. Moreover, the inherent structure of the aortic wall provides a substantial amount of biomechanical reserve and reparative capacity. Although it is possible to remove a substantial portion of the media during endarterectomy without causing aneurysm formation or arterial wall failure, disruption of the normal structure of elastin and collagen in the outer arterial wall is central to the pathologic alterations that lead to aneurysm development. This suggests that two events must occur for an aneurysm to develop: (1) there must be a near complete loss of the normal medial lamellar structure and (2) there must be interruption of the normal compensatory and reparative mechanisms that maintain vascular wall integrity.

Elastin

The elastic fiber is the most stable extracellular matrix component in the arterial wall, with a biologic half-life typically measured in decades.[3] Elastin is also extremely durable in physical terms, and it can withstand the harsh chemical and thermal techniques required for its isolation.[4,5] Elastic fibers are composed of amorphous elastin and an array of microfibrils measuring 10 to 12 nm in diameter.[4,5] Microfibrils appear earlier during development than amorphous elastin and are typically oriented along the length of the growing elastic fiber; thus, they are thought to serve as a biologic scaffold for proper elastic fiber assembly. Elastin undergoes little if any metabolic turnover in the adult, and it remains unclear whether the synthesis and assembly of elastic fibers are necessary once development is complete, or even if these events can occur in a biologically efficient fashion in adults.

Tropoelastin messenger RNA (mRNA) (3.5 kilobase [kb]) is derived from a 45-kb gene on human chromosome 7 (*ELN*) and is subject to extensive alternative splicing. Because the coding sequences for the cross-linking and hydrophobic domains of tropoelastin are encoded by separate exons, the primary transcript can be spliced in cassette-like fashion while maintaining the correct reading frame.[6,7] The rubber-like biophysical properties of elastin are attributed to the hydrophobic regions in polymerized tropoelastin.[4,5] Polymerization of tropoelastin allows cross-linking of individual monomers through oxidative condensation of lysine residues on adjacent molecules. This reaction is catalyzed by lysyl oxidase, and results in the modified amino acids, desmosine and isodesmosine, which are unique to elastin.

Although there is no evidence that inherited defects in elastin result in arterial aneurysms, recent studies demonstrate that elastin has a significant impact on arterial development and function. Humans with a hemizygous deficiency of *ELN* develop a syndrome associated with supravalvular aortic stenosis.[8] Both in patients and in genetically engineered mice with a similar defect ($ELN^{+/-}$), the elastin content of the aortic wall is reduced to only 50% of normal, and the thickness of each elastic lamina is reduced to a similar extent.[8] Nevertheless, developmental compensation results in an increased number of elastic lamellae, which serve to maintain normal arterial integrity.

Collagen

Collagen accounts for approximately 20% of the total protein in the normal aorta. Most aortic wall collagen is made up of type I (75%) and type III interstitial collagens. Additional collagen is present in arteries as type IV collagen occurring within the endothelial basement membrane and surrounding SMCs and fibroblasts. Interstitial collagens are responsible for maintaining aortic wall tensile strength, and they are organized into discrete fibrillar bundles that range from 10 to 200 nm in diameter.[9-11]

Individual procollagen molecules are composed of three intertwined polypeptide (α) chains assembled within the cell to form a stable triple-helix.[9-12] Type I collagen consists of two α_1(I) procollagen chains coupled with one α_2(I) procollagen chain, whereas type III collagen contains three identical α_1(III) procollagen chains. A large fraction of the proline residues are converted to hydroxyproline by the action of proline hydroxylase. The assembly of procollagen α chains is initially mediated within the cell by interactions between the aminoterminal and carboxyterminal globular domains of each procollagen molecule.[9-11]

After secretion, nascent procollagen chains undergo extensive intermolecular cross-linking in the extracellular space. These cross-links are formed at hydroxyproline and lysine residues through the action of lysyl oxidase. This cross-linking results in a rigid fiber, which contributes to the high tensile strength and minimal elasticity of collagen in tissue. Inhibition of lysyl oxidase results in immature, poorly cross-linked collagen fibers and blood vessel fragility. This can be accomplished pharmacologically with lathyrogens such as beta-amino-propionitrile, forming the basis for some early animal models of aneurysm development.[13-15]

Smooth Muscle Cells and Fibroblasts

Not to be overlooked in the anatomy of the normal artery are the mesenchymal cells responsible for producing the exquisitely organized extracellular matrix. Although the matrix itself is responsible for maintaining arterial wall integrity, maintenance of the matrix falls on the resident SMCs and fibroblasts. This is exemplified by attempts to use decellularized arterial conduits in vascular reconstruction. Although such vessels may serve as useful replacements in the arterial system, they eventually undergo progressive dilation and ultimate aneurysm formation.

■ CLASSIFICATION OF ANEURYSM DISEASE

Arterial aneurysms have historically been classified by a combination of their anatomic location and associated clinical diseases. This system is inadequate because it does not take into account pathologic patterns that occur in different types of aneurysms. This has limited our ability to devise novel forms of therapy. Although novel classification systems are being developed to reflect current understanding of the pathologic basis of aneurysms, classification of aneurysm disease remains a challenge for several reasons. First, aneurysms occur in a diverse array of clinical settings and anatomic locations. Second, many types of aneurysms are quite rare and tissue is scarce, making it difficult to provide precise classifications based solely on pathologic criteria. Third, even the most well-studied forms of aneurysm disease appear to result from a complex interaction of genetic, local, and systemic factors, frustrating attempts to define a single or unifying etiology.

Despite these limitations there are some underlying pathologic consistencies that appear to be central to aneurysm development. For example, in most arterial aneurysms there are extensive matrix changes within the media and adventitia of the vessel, with particularly severe damage to the elastic lamina. There is also prominent inflammatory cell infiltration, a factor believed to be associated with the elaboration of matrix-degrading enzymes. Finally, there is frequently depletion of the mesenchymal cell populations generally responsible for matrix repair. Each of the processes affects other pathways in such a way that once established, these pathophysiologic changes are progressive and likely to be self-propagating (Fig. 29-1). Because the most common form of aneurysm disease occurs in the infrarenal aorta, abdominal aortic aneurysms (AAAs) are the most thoroughly investigated form of aneurysm disease. The pathologic features of AAAs thereby serve as a basis by which to evaluate and compare less common aneurysms occurring in other locations.

Many different events have been proposed to initiate the cycle of matrix injury and inflammation involved in aneurysm formation. The aneurysms arising from these diverse mechanisms can be divided into several groups. As seen in Figure 29-1, mechanical injury of the vessel wall, such as post-stenotic aneurysms or aneurysms associated with an arteriovenous fistula, can lead to direct injury to the extracellular matrix, but mechanical injury also appears to affect the function and viability of mesenchymal cells within the arterial wall. Congenital defects in structural matrix proteins can also predispose to aneurysm development, as is the case with inherited diseases such as Marfan syndrome (MFS) (fibrillin-1) and type IV Ehlers-Danlos syndrome (EDS) (type III procollagen). Infections and other inflammatory conditions can also predispose to arterial aneurysms as a direct result of inflammatory cell recruitment into the vessel wall. In many common types of aneurysm disease, including infrarenal AAAs, these processes appear to be initiated by several different mechanisms.

■ ABDOMINAL AORTIC ANEURYSMS

Because AAAs are the most common type of aneurysm disease and because AAAs cause the greatest disability to the population, research efforts to determine the pathobiology of arterial aneurysms have focused primarily on this problem. As noted earlier, the pathobiology of AAAs also serves as a useful reference point for studies on other types of aneurysms. Since the first investigations on AAAs as a disease process potentially distinct from atherosclerosis over 20 years ago,[16,17] there has been an exponential increase in our understanding of the pathobiology underlying AAAs. This has been due to increasingly detailed study of human AAA tissues and facilitated by development of successful animal models that rapidly recapitulate a disease that otherwise takes many years to develop in humans. Based in part on work done in these models, we are already on the threshold of establishing new medical therapies for early stages of aneurysm disease that were unthinkable a short time ago.[18,19]

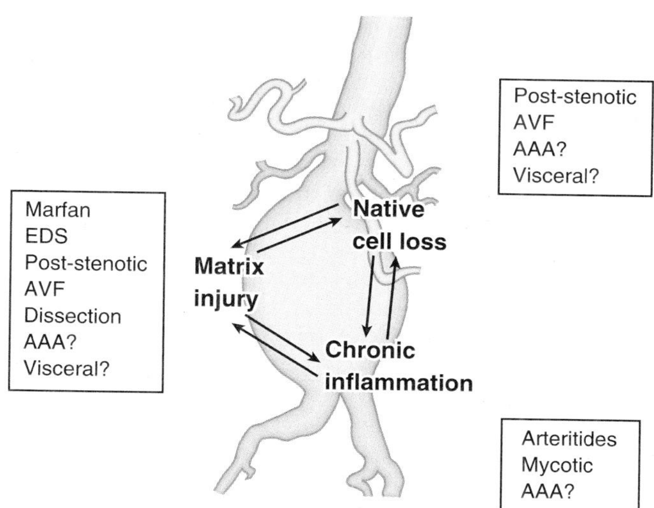

FIGURE 29-1 The interrelationship of pathophysiologic features of aneurysmal degeneration. Boxed diseases represent potential entry points into the cycle. EDS, Ehlers-Danlos syndrome; AAA, abdominal aortic aneurysm; AVF, arteriovenous fistula.

Genetics and Environment

Because the development of AAAs is asymptomatic and occurs over the course of many years, determination of the proximate cause of these lesions has required creative investigation. Case reports of familial clustering of AAAs were reported as early as the 1970s,[20] and the propensity for AAAs to occur in families was first systematically recognized and documented by Tilson and Seashore.[21] Based on these studies, an autosomal dominant pattern of inheritance was proposed.

Because approximately 15% of patients with an AAA exhibit a family history,[22,23] it has been suggested that these patients may harbor an inherited deficiency that affects the structural integrity of the vascular extracellular matrix. However, the disease patterns of patients with known errors of matrix synthesis are distinct from those seen in families with AAAs (see sections on MFS and EDS type IV). After 2 decades of study, it now appears most likely that the development of AAAs occurs in the setting of multiple genetically determined predisposing factors in concert with certain environmental factors, with only rare examples of monogenic predisposition. There is a known association between AAAs and genetic variation on the long arm of chromosome 16, and several candidate genes are located in the region of interest.[24] Furthermore, AAAs are now known to be associated with certain HLA isotypes.[25,26] This suggests that aneurysm disease may result, at least in part, from genetic factors modulating the immune response. Finally, while it is well established that AAAs occur considerably more frequently in males, the specific genetic mechanism underlying this association remains unknown.[27] Table 29-1 lists some of the risk factors for AAAs that have been identified in recent studies. It is clear that one of the most important and consistent environmental factors associated with aortic aneurysms is tobacco smoking.[28-31] Compared with the association of smoking and either coronary artery disease or cerebrovascular disease, the association of smoking with AAAs is 2.5 and 3.5 times as great, respectively.[32] Although cigarette smoking has an even greater impact on the likelihood of developing chronic obstructive lung disease and lung cancer, it remains the most important epidemiologic risk factor for AAAs yet identified.

Other epidemiologic associations of aneurysm development and rupture have focused on associations with known risk factors for atherosclerosis, such as hypertension and hyperlipidemia. Although in some studies these risk factors have shown weak associations with aneurysm development, it is often difficult to control for the coexistence of atherosclerosis. An important and notable exception is diabetes, which is strongly associated with atherosclerosis but negatively associated with AAAs. The potential protection against aneurysmal degeneration that might be afforded by diabetes remains an intriguing and unexplained observation.

The direct relationship between AAA and associated atherosclerosis has been difficult to determine. One feature of atherosclerosis that may be related to aneurysm development is the phenomenon of expansive remodeling. In response to the formation of an intimal plaque, arteries can compensate for the luminal loss by increasing the artery diameter through remodeling of the arterial matrix.[33-35] Although there are similarities based on the presence of inflammation and enzymatic loss of medial structure, these processes lead to intraluminal disruption in expansively remodeled arteries, as opposed to external rupture in aneurysms.[36,37]

Enzymes in Abdominal Aortic Aneurysms

In studies using human and canine arteries excised and subjected to ex-vivo perfusion with enzyme solutions, Dobrin and associates first demonstrated that elastin degradation is sufficient to cause aneurysmal dilation, whereas collagen degradation is required for aneurysm rupture.[17,38] Based on similar studies it has been estimated that only 0.22% to 0.77% of aortic wall collagen is actually placed under full load-bearing conditions in the normal artery,[39] suggesting that elastin normally bears the vast majority of the hemodynamic load. Given the biologic durability of elastic fibers, the near complete loss of elastin in aneurysm tissues has drawn significant attention from researchers, with a major effort directed toward identifying the specific proteinases responsible for elastin degradation in AAAs.

Both constitutive and inducible production of elastolytic enzymes can be identified within human AAA tissues. Following initial observations by Busuttil and associates,[16] early studies attributed the primary elastolytic activity in AAAs to one or more serine proteases.[40] It is now clear that enzymes of the matrix metalloproteinase (MMP) family likely make an even greater contribution to the elastolytic process seen in aneurysm tissues.

Table 29-1 Epidemiologic Factors Associated with Abdominal Aortic Aneurysms (AAAs)

FACTORS	ODDS RATIO
Permissive	
Ever smoked	5.1
Current smoker	7.4
Age (per 7-year increase)	1.7
Age 75-84 years	3.3
Family history of AAA	1.9
Symptomatic atherosclerosis	1.7
Hypercholesterolemia	1.4
Protective	
Female sex	0.2
Black race	0.5
Diabetes mellitus	0.5

Matrix Metalloproteinases in Aortic Aneurysms

MMPs are a structurally-related family of connective tissue-degrading enzymes implicated in a variety of normal and pathologic tissue remodeling processes, including embryonic development, wound healing, cancer, and arthritis.[41] The members of the MMP family (of which there are now > 25) are characterized at the protein level by several similarities, including a signal peptide, an aminoterminal propeptide, and a catalytic domain featuring a zinc-binding site. Individual MMPs are named and characterized in part by their substrate specificities, but acting together they can degrade virtually all stromal, structural, and basement membrane proteins of the extracellular matrix. Several MMPs are known for their activity against interstitial collagen fibers, including fibroblast collagenase (MMP-1), neutrophil collagenase (MMP-8), and the more recently described MMP-13. At least four MMPs are capable of degrading cross-linked elastin fibers, including the 72-kd and 92-kd gelatinases (MMP-2 and MMP-9, respectively), matrilysin (MMP-7), and macrophage metalloelastase (MMP-12).

MMPs are secreted as zymogens (pro-MMPs) and are maintained in an inactive state by the presence of the aminoterminal propeptide domain. Enzymatic cleavage of the propeptide is the most likely mechanism of MMP activation in vivo, indicating that extracellular processing of pro-MMPs is required to achieve full catalytic activity. Various proteases have been implicated in this process, such as plasmin, urokinase plasminogen activator (u-PA), and other MMPs. In some cases, spontaneous autoactivation can occur (e.g., macrophage elastase).[42]

The regulation of MMP activities is critical to prevent widespread tissue destruction, both in normal tissues undergoing remodeling and in disease.[41,43,44] MMPs are thereby controlled at several levels, including the induction and suppression of MMP gene transcription, extracellular activation, and interaction with natural inhibitors. Inflammatory mediators such as cytokines play an important role in the modulation of MMP gene transcription as well as in the transcriptional induction of their inhibitors and activators.

Elastolytic MMPs

Gelatinase A (MMP-2) is constitutively expressed by a variety of mesenchymal cell types, such as vascular endothelium, SMCs, and fibroblasts. Its expression can be further induced in and by inflammatory cell types (i.e., mononuclear phagocytes and lymphocytes). The principal matrix substrates of MMP-2 include type IV (basement membrane) collagen and denatured interstitial collagens (gelatin), although MMP-2 is also capable of acting on intact elastin. Recent evidence also indicates that MMP-2 can act as an interstitial collagenase. Increased expression of MMP-2 is associated with aortic aneurysms, atherosclerosis, and intimal hyperplasia, and it has been suggested that MMP-2 activity is required for SMC migration across elastin-rich matrices.[45]

The presence of elevated amounts of immunoreactive MMP-2 in human AAA tissue was first demonstrated by Vine and Powell,[46] followed by a series of reports confirming and extending this observation. Freestone and colleagues[47] reported that MMP-2 may be particularly elevated in small AAAs, suggesting a potential role in early stages of aneurysmal degeneration. MMP-2 production was also spatially associated with the inflammatory response, an observation consistent with evidence that fibroblasts and SMCs produce increased amounts of MMP-2 in response to inflammatory cytokines and other macrophage products.[48] In a recent study using sequential extraction of aortic tissues with different solvents, Davis and coworkers[49] showed that large amounts of MMP-2 are bound to the extracellular matrix. A large portion of this matrix-bound MMP-2 is found in the activated form, suggesting that MMP-2 is activated in AAAs and tightly sequestered within the extracellular space.

Gelatinase B (MMP-9) is one of the most prominently expressed MMPs in aortic aneurysms and other inflammatory conditions.[50-55] MMP-9 has attracted particular interest because it can degrade elastin fibers[50,56-58] and because it is abundantly produced by human AAA tissues in vitro.[54] Although protein studies have demonstrated that MMP-9 is selectively increased to a greater extent in AAAs than in atherosclerotic disease, MMP-9 mRNA is also expressed by aneurysm-infiltrating macrophages located at the site of tissue damage (Fig. 29-2B).[53,54] Studies using mice with targeted gene deletion of MMP-9 indicate that this enzyme plays a critical role in experimental aneurysmal degeneration.

Elevated levels of MMP-9 have been shown to occur in the circulation of patients with AAAs,[59] and the level of MMP-9 expression in tissue and circulation appears to be proportional to aneurysm size.[55,60] These observations have fostered the idea that MMP-9 (and perhaps other metalloproteinases) might provide useful biologic markers of aortic aneurysm disease, as well as potential targets for pharmacologic therapy in patients with small asymptomatic AAAs.[61,62]

Stromelysin-1 (MMP-3) is not elevated to as great an extent in aneurysms as that of other proteases, but this enzyme may play a specific role in activating the proenzyme form of other MMPs, particularly MMP-9.[63] Stromelysin has been detected in human AAAs by immunoblotting and mRNA analysis,[51,52,64,65] but its exact role in aneurysm development remains unclear.

Human macrophage elastase (HME; MMP-12) is a recently described homolog of mouse macrophage elastase (MME).[66,67] Macrophage elastase accounts for at least half of the elastolytic activity secreted by human alveolar macrophages obtained from cigarette smokers[66] and is essential for macrophage-mediated proteolysis and matrix invasion in vitro.[68] Unlike other MMPs, there is evidence that pro-HME can undergo spontaneous autocatalytic conversion to its activated form. In addition, it degrades a particularly broad spectrum of other matrix substrates.[69] These diverse functions of HME have resulted in studies that have suggested that macrophage expression of HME may have an important role in pulmonary emphysema and other

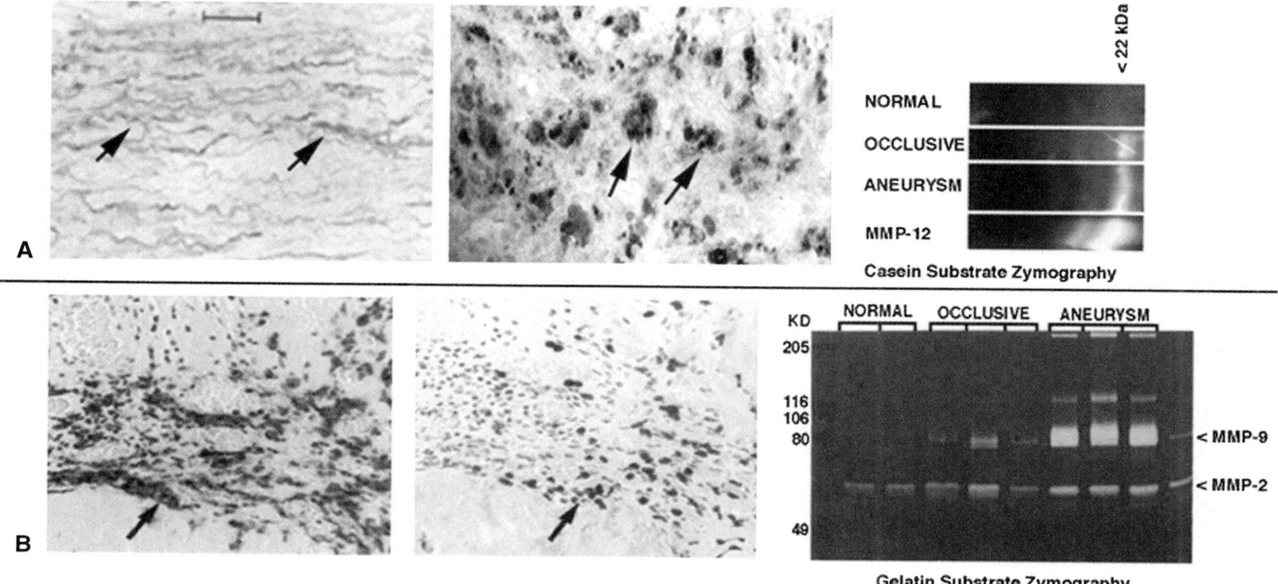

FIGURE 29-2 Histologic and zymographic evidence of representative active enzymes of the matrix metalloproproteinase (MMP) family in human aneurysm wall. **A,** Presence of MMP-12 (*arrows*) by immunohistology, in-situ hybridization, and casein zymography. **B,** Presence of MMP-9 (*arrows*) by immunohistology, in-situ hybridization, and gelatin zymography. (See Color Figure in this section.)

degenerative disorders associated with elastin degradation, including AAAs.[68,70,71]

Elevated amounts of enzymatically active HME are produced in human AAA tissue and, like MMP-9, HME is expressed by aneurysm-infiltrating macrophages in vivo.[71] Macrophage elastase is prominently localized to residual elastin fiber fragments within aneurysm tissue by immunohistochemistry, a pattern distinct from other elastolytic MMPs (Fig. 29-2A). The elevated production of HME and its unique localization to fragmented aortic elastin suggests a particularly important role for this enzyme in aneurysmal degeneration.

Collagenolytic MMPs

Because interstitial collagen is the last line of defense in the aneurysmal aorta, collagenases are thought to play a particularly important role in the events leading to aneurysm rupture. Previous studies have demonstrated the expression of MMP-1 (fibroblast collagenase) in aortic aneurysms by immunoblotting, immunohistochemistry, and mRNA analysis.[46,65,72] However, the expression of MMP-1 is highly variable in these tissues, and it has often been difficult to demonstrate an excess of collagenase activity in soluble tissue extracts.[73-77] Because MMP-2 has been described to have collagenase activity, this enzyme might also play a role in collagen degradation in AAAs. More recent studies reveal another collagenase, MMP-13, to be abundantly expressed in both atherosclerotic lesions and in AAAs.[78] MMP-13 is localized to vascular SMC in aneurysm tissue, and, moreover, it is consistently expressed by human aortic vascular SMC in culture. These results suggest for the first time that increased local production of MMP-13 may play a prominent role in the collagen degradation associated with atherosclerosis and aneurysmal degeneration.

Inhibitors of MMPs

The expression of MMPs is often accompanied by the presence of naturally occurring inhibitors, such as plasma-derived α_2-macroglobulin and a family of locally produced tissue inhibitors of metalloproteinases (TIMPs).[41,43,44,79] TIMP-1 is a 25-kd secreted polypeptide capable of inhibiting most MMPs, whereas TIMP-2 (30 kd) is quite specific for MMP-2. A third member of this family, TIMP-3, appears to be unique in that it exists primarily in association with the extracellular matrix.[79] In addition to its MMP-inhibiting activity, TIMP-3 was recently found to induce SMC apoptosis in vitro.[80]

In experimental aneurysm models, reduction of TIMP expression has been associated with increased aneurysm formation.[81-83] However, despite an early report suggesting that the amount of TIMP-1 present in human AAA tissue might be decreased,[84] there are no abnormalities in the TIMP-1 protein expressed in AAAs.[85] Indeed, there is now substantial evidence that the production of TIMPs is actually increased within the aneurysm wall.[53,54,64,65,77,86] This finding is consistent with elevated levels of antiproteases found in other matrix-degrading diseases, suggesting a function in endogenous regulation that typically prevents widespread or indiscriminate matrix damage.

Activation of Pro-MMPs

Regulation of MMP activity in tissues is often orchestrated by controlling activation of the proenzyme forms of the secreted proteinases. Although some of these enzymes can undergo autoactivation, in general this is inefficient. Cleavage of the propeptide is most likely mediated by other enzymes in the local tissue environment, such as plasminogen activators (PAs). In addition to accelerating plasmin-mediated degradation of fibrin, PAs may directly activate the zymogen form of various MMPs. Increased production of PAs within the aortic wall may therefore participate in a local cascade of proteinases involved in structural protein breakdown. The presence of immunoreactive plasmin was first detected in extracts of AAA tissue by Jean-Claude and associates,[87] with a 10-fold increase in AAAs versus normal aorta. These investigators also demonstrated strong staining of macrophages in AAAs by immunohistochemistry for plasmin,[87] and u-PA appeared to colocalize with macrophages expressing MMP-3 and MMP-9.[51] Protein blotting and immunohistochemistry both provide evidence that increased expression of tissue plasminogen activator (t-PA) and u-PA occurs in AAAs, as first presented by Reilly and colleagues.[88] These findings were subsequently extended by Schneiderman and coworkers using in-situ hybridization.[89] Shireman and associates have further demonstrated that PA expression is quantitatively increased in AAAs compared with other types of aortic tissue,[90] and Louwrens and colleagues have shown that AAA-derived SMC actively produce u-PA in culture.[91]

The discovery of membrane-type MMP (MT1-MMP or MMP-14) led to recognition that this enzyme can bind and activate pro-MMP-2 on cell surfaces. MT1-MMP is now believed to play a crucial role in regulating MMP-2 activation in a number of circumstances. Nollendorfs and associates[92] have recently provided further evidence that MMP-2 is involved in AAAs by demonstrating that MT1-MMP is similarly increased in human aneurysm tissues, especially in regions where mesenchymal cells are in close contact with inflammatory infiltrates. This suggests that paracrine modulation of MMP-2 activity may be an important mechanism in AAAs.[92]

Other Proteases in Abdominal Aortic Aneurysms

As noted earlier, the serine elastase, neutrophil elastase, was the first enzyme to be associated with aneurysmal degeneration. Cohen and colleagues demonstrated increased serine elastase activity in human AAA tissues, as well as in the circulation of patients with AAA.[40,93] They have also presented intriguing data indicating that the amount of elastase produced by circulating neutrophils is elevated in cigarette smokers and is particularly high in those with AAAs who continue to smoke.[94] Given the infrequent presence of neutrophils in established AAA tissues, the precise role of serine elastases in aneurysm disease remains to be determined.

Several investigators have recently begun to examine a potential role for cysteine and aspartate proteinases as matrix-degrading enzymes in AAAs.[95-97] Although a broad range of cathepsin family proteases have been shown to be present in AAA,[96] Sukhova and associates[97] recently demonstrated the abundant expression of two elastolytic cysteine proteinases, cathepsins S and K, in human atheroma. Human SMC in culture displayed no immunoreactivity for cathepsin K or cathepsin S and exhibited little or no elastolytic activity when incubated with insoluble elastin. On the other hand, cytokine-stimulated SMC secreted active cathepsin S and degraded substantial amounts of insoluble elastin. It is also notable that circulating levels of cystatin C, the primary endogenous inhibitor of cathepsins, are lower in individuals with aortic dilation than in control subjects. These intriguing findings indicate that cathepsins likely play an important role in aneurysmal degeneration, perhaps equal to that of MMPs, but further studies are needed to verify this hypothesis.

Inflammation in Abdominal Aortic Aneurysms

Transmural inflammatory cell infiltration is one of the pathologic hallmarks of aortic aneurysms. The inflammatory cells present in AAAs consist of monocytes, macrophages, T cells, B lymphocytes, and plasma cells. The pattern of inflammation varies between individual patients and in different areas within a given specimen of AAA tissue. Medial degeneration therefore occurs in the midst of a complex interplay among the various inflammatory cells present, the soluble mediators they produce, and resident aortic wall cells such as SMCs, fibroblasts, and microvascular endothelial cells.

The chronic inflammation observed in established AAA tissues includes components of both innate (nonspecific) inflammatory responses and adaptive (antigen-driven) immune responses. Monocytes recruited to the outer aorta undergo local activation and differentiation to tissue macrophages, which appear to act as the primary effectors of destructive matrix remodeling. Lymphocytes accompany monocytes, either as part of a nonspecific immune response or in response to local generation of antigens. Lymphocytes may thereby serve to either amplify or regulate macrophage activities.

It has long been recognized that the predominant inflammatory infiltrate consists of macrophages, T cells, and B cells.[98-100] In most animal models of aneurysm disease, arterial dilation is associated with inflammatory cell infiltration. However, in certain experimental conditions, inflammation can occur without development of aneurysmal dilation. Therefore, it appears that inflammatory infiltration is a necessary but not sufficient condition for the development of AAA.[101]

In atherosclerotic plaque, regional subclassification into lipid core, shoulder area, and so forth has resulted in the recognition that specialized pathology occurs in these distinct areas. In giant cell arteritis, another arterial disease where transmural inflammation occurs, macrophages take on distinct phenotypes depending on where they are located within the wall.[102] Although not nearly as well developed, it is now recognized that the protease expression in aneurysms is also likely to be similarly regionalized.

Histologically, the distribution and character of the inflammatory infiltrates in AAA are not uniform throughout the media. A simple classification system for aneurysm tissue has been published that divides the changes in the media into three areas: active, inflammatory, and amorphous.[71] In this system, inflammatory media is characterized by a high local concentration of T and B cells with a few macrophages and neutrophils. Areas of active media seem to be focused where there are fragmented elastic fibers; the cellular constituents are predominantly SMCs and macrophages. Finally, amorphous media generally appears extremely hypocellular and lacks the usual laminar organizational pattern.

Initiation of Inflammation

Many different antigenic stimuli have been proposed as initiators of inflammation in AAAs. It has been of some interest that the degradation products of elastolysis can stimulate an inflammatory response.[103] This, of course, begs the question of the initial elastolytic event. Some investigators have identified a single antigen or group of antigens that were believed to result in a specific immune response in aneurysms.[104-106] However, recent studies on T-cell clonality suggest that the infiltrate is generally polyclonal or at best oligoclonal in nature.[107-109]

As in atherosclerosis, infection with *Chlamydia pneumoniae* has been proposed to stimulate the immune response that results in the matrix breakdown.[110-112] Supporting evidence includes the identification of reactive T-cells against *C. pneumoniae* in human aneurysms, and facilitation of development of experimental aneurysms with *C. pneumoniae* infection.[113,114] High titers of serum immunoglobulin A antibodies against *Chlamydia* are present in 83% of men with AAA; this was found to be a significant independent predictor of rapid aneurysm expansion.[115,116] However, its exact role remains elusive because not all aneurysms appear to be infected, and the presence of *C. pneumoniae* is not associated with increased metalloproteinase production.[117,118] Furthermore, the relationship between serum markers and actual aortic infection has been brought into question.[119-121]

Antigenic stimulation of inflammation appears to play an important role in the development of human aneurysms. Based on our current knowledge, this mechanism of inflammation is not sufficient to initiate aneurysm formation; rather, it may be a permissive factor in aneurysm development. Therapies designed to disrupt the antigen-mediated response in aneurysms may present a novel intervention to prevent or inhibit aneurysmal degeneration.

Inflammatory Mediators—Chemokines, Cytokines, and Others

Once initiated, the inflammatory response is maintained for many years as a human aneurysm develops. The maintenance and effects of this inflammatory response depend on the elaboration of mediators. These mediators include cytokines, chemokines, and their activators and receptors. Identification of mediators central to aneurysm development may offer an opportunity to interrupt this destructive inflammatory process, thereby reducing or preventing aneurysm growth and rupture. However, anecdotal clinical evidence demonstrates that general immunosuppression, such as that used for transplantation, does not eliminate the development and progression of AAAs.[122-125]

Because of the prominent role of MMPs in aneurysm development, much research on inflammatory mediators in aneurysm disease has been focused on positive regulators of MMP expression or secretion. Many of these have previously been shown to be important to the development of intimal atherosclerosis, a common feature of the intima of the aortic aneurysm. To compensate for this potential confounder, age-matched aortas of patients with severe atherosclerosis are frequently used as controls to identify cytokine profiles specific for aneurysms. Unfortunately, this approach has not yielded an entirely clear understanding of cytokine-mediated enzyme production in aneurysms.

Some potent inducers of MMP-9 production that are believed to play an important role in atherosclerotic disease include interleukin (IL)-1β and tumor necrosis factor (TNF)-α. These have both been shown to be increased in AAA as compared to normal aortic tissue.[126] However, when compared with specimens of occlusive aorta, aneurysm specimens were found to have significantly *less* TNF-α protein, whereas IL-1β levels were not significantly different.[127] Paradoxically, TNF-α (but not IL-1β) mRNA is significantly increased by reverse transcription polymerase chain reaction (RT-PCR) in aneurysms as opposed to occlusive aortas.[128] Further confusing the role of these cytokines is the fact that circulating levels of IL-1β *and* TNF-α are increased in serum from aneurysm patients compared with age-matched patients with known coronary disease.[129]

Some clarification of the role of TNF-α and IL-1β may come from animal models of aneurysm disease. In the elastase perfused rat model, administration of antagonists of TNF (TNF-binding protein) blocked aneurysm development, whereas an antagonist of IL-1 (IL-1 receptor antagonist) did not. These data suggest that TNF-α may play an important role in aneurysm development despite the lower levels of protein extracted.[130] The implications for human disease are difficult to discern with confidence since general anti-inflammatory agents, such as prednisone and cyclosporine, inhibit aneurysm formation in these models.[131]

Interferon (INF)-γ is another mediator that plays an important role in regulating extracellular matrix repair and remodeling. INF-γ has been shown in early studies to be elevated in human aneurysm tissue, and has been hypothesized to contribute to aneurysm formation by impairing the process of matrix synthesis and repair.[132] More recent studies of aneurysm tissue have not consistently supported this finding at the protein or mRNA level from aortic extracts.[127,133] However, based on circulating levels, it has been suggested that IFN-γ may be particularly associated with aneurysms that are rapidly expanding.[129]

One recent study looked at a broad range of cytokines by Western blot of whole tissue extracts as a means of establishing the predominant T-helper cell population in aneurysm tissue as compared with extracts of carotid plaque. The findings of this study are summarized in Table 29-2. Based on this information, the authors concluded that the T-helper response in aneurysms is primarily T_H2, compared with the primarily T_H1 response characteristic of atherosclerotic plaque.[133] This is an important observation for our understanding of arterial disease. As mentioned earlier, the interplay between atherosclerotic disease and aneurysm formation has been a central question in arterial pathophysiology. Both forms of arterial pathology segregate with a similar demographic in the population, namely elderly men. Because patients with aneurysms invariably have some degree of aortic atherosclerosis, aneurysm formation was long thought to merely represent an exuberant extension of the intimal disease of atherosclerosis. Although evidence for a distinct pathophysiologic response in aneurysm disease has been mounting, this study by Schonbeck and coworkers[130] further develops the distinction.

Yet, just as it was an oversimplification to consider aneurysm disease an extension of atherosclerosis, it may be just as egregious to consider aneurysm disease entirely independent of the atherosclerotic process. Because all AAAs have intimal atherosclerotic disease, it is difficult to interpret a dichotomy in cytokine expression based on Western blotting of whole tissue. Further, the regional heterogeneity of the aneurysm media suggests that different collections of cytokines may be locally expressed in varying proportions resulting in the distinct collections of cells observed.

In addition to the T_H2 response-associated cytokines, several other cytokines and chemokines are known to be present in aneurysms, although their role is not well understood. For example, high levels of IL-6 mRNA production in AAA[128] do not correlate with the relatively low levels of IL-6 protein extracted from aneurysm tissue.[127] Increased IL-6 can be seen circulating in patients with AAA, and the levels correlate with aneurysm size.[134,135] One recent study using a mouse model of aneurysm disease suggests that the CC chemokines monocyte chemoattractant protein (MCP)-1 and regulated on activation normal T-cell expressed and secreted (RANTES) are upregulated and that these chemokines are expressed by elastase stimulated aortic SMCs in vitro.[136] Increased levels of MCP-1 and the CXC chemokine, IL-8, are also found in human aneurysm extracts.[137]

The activities of the MMPs are also likely to play a role in the inflammatory response in aneurysms, particularly the activity of MMP-9. The function of IL-8 can be enhanced by specific cleavage by MMP-9. The truncated IL-8 molecule is 10 times more potent as an inducer of MMP-9 release by granulocytes.[138] The activity of MMP-9 is also known to activate pro-IL-1β and to generate neoepitopes during

Table 29-2 Summary of Western Blot Data by Schonbeck and Colleagues*

ANTIGEN	WESTERN BLOT Carotid	AAA
IL-4	0	+++
IL-5	+	++
IL-10	+	+++
IL-2	+++	0
IL-12	+++	+
IL-15	++	+
IL-18	+++	+
INF-γ	++	+

*Schonbeck U, Sukhova GK, Gerdes N, Libby P: T_H2-predominant immune responses prevail in human abdominal aortic aneurysm. Am J Pathol 161:499, 2002.

AAA, abdominal aortic aneurysm; IL, interleukin; INF, interferon.

matrix degradation. Neoepitopes include elastin peptides, which can accelerate an immune response.[139]

The immune response in AAA results from a complex interplay of enzymes, soluble mediators, and cellular responses. The result is a histologically diverse infiltration of inflammatory cells and variable matrix destruction. General interruption of the inflammatory response is successful in preventing animal models of aneurysms; however, this does not appear to be the case with human aneurysms. Therapies that target immune mechanisms specific to AAA may be more successful.

Smooth Muscle Cell Loss

Increased proteolytic activity is now widely accepted as a major factor in the pathogenesis of AAAs. However, it is also becoming apparent that impaired connective tissue repair may be of equal importance, either in the gradual progression of disease or in precipitating aneurysm rupture. The stability of established AAAs is likely to be dependent on a substantial increase in collagen production, given the enormous increase in tensile wall stress as the aorta dilates. Adventitial fibroblasts and medial SMCs are the principal collagen- and elastin-producing cell types within the aortic wall, and several recent studies have emphasized that depletion of medial SMCs may be a previously overlooked factor in aneurysmal degeneration.

Initial evaluation of the medial SMC population in human aortic specimens by Lopez-Candales and colleagues[140] demonstrated that medial SMC density was not significantly different between normal aorta and atherosclerotic occlusive disease, but it was reduced by 74% in AAA. Light and electron microscopy revealed ultrastructural changes consistent with SMC apoptosis, and up to 30% of SMCs in AAAs exhibited fragmented DNA. Henderson and coworkers[141] extended these observations, finding higher levels of DNA fragmentation in AAAs than in controls, with AAAs containing more cells bearing markers of apoptosis than normal aorta.

In a separate study, tissue samples of aneurysmal, occlusive, and normal human infrarenal aorta were evaluated by methods to detect DNA fragmentation. Immunohistochemistry was also used to measure SMC density and apoptotic cell death.[142] Although SMC density was only slightly lower in aneurysmal aortas compared with control tissues, SMC apoptosis was threefold greater within AAAs (11.7 ± 1.5 cells per high-powered field [HPF]) compared with both occlusive aortas (3.3 ± 0.8 cells per HPF) and normal aortas (3.75 ± 4.6 cells per HPF). Collectively, these observations suggest that macrophages and T lymphocytes infiltrating the aneurysm wall can produce cytotoxic mediators such as cytokines, perforin, and Fas/FasL. These death-promoting products of activated immune cells may contribute to elimination of SMCs.[141,143]

It also appears that the remaining cells within the aneurysm wall do not replicate normally. Liao and associates[144] cultured medial SMCs from 15 patients undergoing AAA repair and compared them with SMCs obtained from a segment of the adjacent (nonaneurysmal) inferior mesenteric artery as a control. Explantation of these cells suggested abnormal SMC growth, because sustainable cultures were established from all inferior mesenteric artery explants but from only 9 of 15 AAAs. The interval required to achieve primary explant growth was longer for AAAs than inferior mesenteric arteries (16.4 ± 2 vs. 6.4 ± 1 days) Serum-stimulated uptake of radiolabeled thymidine was also reduced by 54.9% ± 7% in AAA-derived SMCs, but flow cytometry revealed no differences in SMC viability, apoptosis, or necrosis. These differences appear to reflect an intrinsic alteration in SMC growth capacity that is independent of age alone.

Hemodynamics and Abdominal Aortic Aneurysms

Elastin and collagen determine the passive mechanical properties of the aorta. Vascular smooth muscle has the capacity to contract and relax in response to various stimuli and to thereby modulate aortic wall mechanics; however, this appears to be of little practical importance with respect to aortic function, at least in the abdominal segment.[145,146] The more distensible elastin is the principal load bearer at low pressures and small distentions; both elastin and the stiffer collagen are load bearing at higher pressures and large distentions. In a series of elegant and influential studies, Dobrin and associates examined the relative contributions made by elastin and collagen to the biophysical properties of the aortic wall.[17,38] These findings have fostered the notion that elastin degradation plays a key step in the development of aneurysmal dilation but that collagen degradation is ultimately required for aneurysm rupture.

Hemodynamic forces can exert diverse effects on the arterial wall. The unique anatomy of the infrarenal aorta results in increased hemodynamic stress and decreased shear stress. This leads to the potential for wall weakening and aneurysm development. The localization of hemodynamic stress in the infrarenal aorta is due to three factors: (1) distal tapering of the aorta, (2) progressive stiffening of the aortic wall, especially as it enters the abdomen, and (3) the additive effects of retrograde pressure waves reflecting from the iliac bifurcation combining with the incoming antegrade pressure wave.[147,148] These hemodynamic characteristics thereby contribute to a region of relatively high hemodynamic stress in the infrarenal aorta. At the same time, the infrarenal aorta has a reduced capacity to withstand pulsatile load because there are fewer elastic lamellae relative to the wall thickness at this level. These considerations may result in direct matrix injury secondary to the high stress load per unit of matrix.

Hemodynamic forces can also directly affect cellular physiology. Cultured vascular SMCs undergo specific phenotypic changes in response to reductions in antegrade and oscillatory shear conditions.[149-151] These changes can include increased expression of proinflammatory and oxidative mediators as well as reductions in cellular viability. In animal models of AAA, increased local shear stress results in smaller aneurysms and increased cellularity of the aneurysm wall.[152] Aneurysms under increased shear stress also appear to reduce the expression of reactive oxygen species that are thought to be proinflammatory.[153]

Animal Models of Aortic Aneurysms

Difficulties in studying human tissue, including sample procurement, has led to the development of animal models of AAA. These models have been important in generating new insights into aneurysm development, particularly in the past decade. These experimental systems have also provided essential tools to evaluate the potential for new therapeutic strategies to suppress aneurysmal degeneration in vivo.

Direct injury of rat or mouse aorta has been the primary means of modeling aneurysm development. These models are generally characterized by a single intervention resulting in mild matrix injury but are adequate to initiate the cycle of inflammation, mesenchymal cellular changes, and matrix loss similar to the changes seen in human disease. Although these represent the best studied models to date, the development of murine genetic mutants prone to aortic aneurysmal degeneration will likely result in new insights as they become better characterized.

Elastase-induced Abdominal Aortic Aneurysm in the Rat and Mouse

Short perfusion of an isolated segment of rat aorta with a dilute elastase solution was shown by Anidjar and coworkers to result in progressive aneurysmal dilation over about a week.[154] The delayed onset of aneurysmal dilation appears to be associated with the development of a chronic (mononuclear) inflammatory response and subsequent degradation of the medial elastic lamellae. Halpern and associates[155] initially examined the potential role of endogenous proteinases in experimental aneurysm development. These investigators demonstrated that elastase perfusion induces the sequential production of several different metalloproteinases within the elastase-injured rat aorta. The production of endogenous proteinases was temporally correlated with the onset of aortic wall inflammation.

Others have also demonstrated that the endogenous proteinases produced in elastase-induced AAAs are equivalent to the elastolytic and collagenolytic MMPs produced by infiltrating macrophages in human aneurysms. The most prominent of these is MMP-9.[156] Petrinec and colleagues[157] subsequently used the elastase-induced rat model to provide the first experimental evidence that pharmacologic inhibition of MMPs with doxycycline has the potential to suppress aneurysmal degeneration in vivo. These investigations and others have stimulated interest in the clinical evaluation of MMP inhibitors, particularly tetracyclines, to potentially reduce aneurysm expansion in patients with small AAAs.

This model also recapitulates the inadequate reparative capacity of the aortic mesenchymal cells once the aneurysm cycle is established. To assess the functional importance of connective tissue repair during experimental aneurysmal degeneration, Huffman and coworkers[158] examined a series of rats undergoing elastase perfusion. In one group, aortic diameter was measured before elastase perfusion and up to 14 days later, and aortic wall concentrations of desmosine (Des) and hydroxyproline (OHP) were measured at each interval. The expression of tropoelastin (TE), α_1(I) procollagen (PC), and lysyl oxidase genes was also evaluated by RT-PCR. This study demonstrated that aortic wall Des concentration decreases markedly during aneurysm development, reaching as low as 3% of normal by day 14. Aortic wall OHP decreases to only 68% of normal at the same interval. TE and PC expression were undetectable in healthy aorta, but they both increased by day 7; while TE expression decreased again by day 14, PC continued to rise. Lysyl oxidase expression progressively decreased at all intervals after elastase perfusion. These findings indicate that the development of elastase-induced AAAs is accompanied by an active process of connective tissue repair that is ultimately insufficient to prevent aneurysm progression.

This model has now been adapted to the mouse with aneurysmal development and similar histologic changes occurring within 14 days of elastase perfusion.[159] This model has now been applied to genetically altered animals deficient in the murine homologs of the matrix enzymes associated with human aneurysm disease. Mice with targeted deletion of the MMP-9 gene (MMP-$9^{-/-}$) exhibit a significant suppression of aneurysmal dilation as compared to wild-type (MMP-$9^{+/+}$) background controls. Although this reduction in AAAs was associated with preservation of the medial elastic lamellae by light microscopy, there was no demonstrable suppression of inflammatory cell infiltration into the aortic wall. This finding supports the notion that MMP-9 plays a critical role in matrix degradation. A similar inhibition of aneurysm development was not seen with animals lacking the MMP-12 gene.

Transplantation Models

Allaire and colleagues developed a novel model of guinea pig to rat aortic xenografts to examine the mechanisms underlying aneurysmal degeneration.[160] Similar to other models, aneurysm development in this model is accompanied by loss of elastin, medial invasion by mononuclear inflammatory cells, and MMP upregulation. Transfection with a retroviral vector encoding TIMP-1 resulted in local overexpression of TIMP-1, as well as a decrease in MMP-9, the activated fraction of MMP-2, and a 28-kd elastolytic activity corresponding to MMP-12. Moreover, TIMP-1 overexpression was associated with preservation of medial elastin, and it prevented aneurysmal degeneration or rupture.[83]

Genetic Alterations of Mice and Model Aneurysms

A number of recent mouse models based on genetic alterations have become especially informative regarding the molecular mechanisms involved in aneurysmal degeneration. Certain alterations are designed to mimic specific human arterial diseases with known inherited defects of the extracellular matrix, such as MFS and EDS. Also coming to light are several genetic mutants without a known human correlate that result in aneurysm formation.

Nagai and associates[161] established heat shock protein (HSP)-47 knockout mice and found that these animals are severely deficient in the mature, propeptide-processed form of α_1(I) collagen and fibril structures in mesenchymal tissues. The molecular form of type IV collagen was also affected, and basement membranes were discontinuously disrupted in the homozygous deficient mice. The homozygous mice did not survive beyond 11.5 days of embryonic development, displaying abnormally orientated epithelial tissues and rupture of blood vessels.

Induced mutations in the apoE protein have provided an invaluable mouse model of complex atherosclerosis.[162] In early studies characterizing this model, Nakashima and colleagues[162] noted that the complex atherosclerotic plaques were often associated with aortic wall infiltration by foamy macrophages, fracturing of the elastic lamellae, and mild aneurysmal dilation. Daugherty and associates have recently expanded the role of the apoE knockout mouse to develop a particularly interesting model of AAAs, based in part on the role of angiotensin (AT)-II in promoting atherogenesis and vascular wall inflammation.[163] ApoE-deficient mice infused with AT-II developed pronounced aortic aneurysms located in the suprarenal portion of the abdominal aorta. These AAAs exhibited two major histopathologic characteristics: (1) an intact artery surrounded by a large remodeled adventitia and (2) medial breaks with pronounced dilation and more modestly remodeled adventitial tissue.

Summary of Abdominal Aortic Aneurysm Pathology

The development of the AAA results from three pathologic insults: (1) unique transmural matrix disruption, (2) inflammatory infiltration, and (3) depletion of mesenchymal cells. The mechanisms of interplay are beginning to be understood in greater detail, especially with the development of murine models of aneurysm development. Specifically, the activity of matrix metalloproteases and their regulation are likely to play a central role in aneurysm development.

■ THORACIC AORTIC ANEURYSMS

Aneurysms of thoracic aorta have not been studied in the same detail as those of the infrarenal aorta, and some investigators have implied that similar processes may be occurring in the two diseases.[164] In general, detailed descriptions of thoracic aortic aneurysm pathology is sparse. There is some evidence that aneurysms of the proximal aorta, from the aortic valve to the origin of the brachiocephalic artery, may be unique. For example, it is well recognized that there are certain genetic and anatomic associations that form subsets of these ascending thoracic aortic aneurysms (ATAAs), in particular those that are secondary to MFS[165] and those that occur in association with a bicuspid aortic valve (BAV).[166]

In MFS, the genetic defect is known to occur in the gene for fibrillin-1, an important component of the extracellular matrix participating in the organization of elastin into elastic fibers and in collagen networks (see later).[167] Like MFS, aortic disease associated with a BAV has also been associated with the histologic finding of "cystic medial necrosis."[168] This has been described microscopically as a localized loss of elastic fibers that are replaced by a disorganized matrix lacking cellular structures.[169,170] Another similarity between MFS and BAV is the relatively frequent occurrence of intramural dissection of the aorta—a feature not seen with AAA, where frank rupture is the rule.

Although the histology has been qualitatively described in some detail, little has been done to quantify changes in specific elements of the aneurysmal wall in patients with ATAA.[167] Defects in fibrillin production and their impact on the aortic wall are becoming better understood, but less is understood about the changes found in ATAA associated with BAV. Whittle,[171] Cattell,[172] and their colleagues have previously identified significantly decreased collagen and elastin concentrations in areas of dissection of the thoracic aorta obtained from autopsy in patients with fatal dissections. More recently, a link between the similar histology of MFS and BAV was presented by Nataatmadja and colleagues.[173] This group was able to demonstrate increased accumulation of extracellular matrix proteins within the resident SMCs and increased levels of SMC apoptosis. This suggested that there may be a defect in extracellular matrix protein transport that links these two diseases.[173]

One recently published paper has led to improved understanding of the association between abdominal and thoracic aneurysm development. Using specimens of normal aortic tissue and aneurysms of the ascending thoracic aorta and the infrarenal aorta, a complementary DNA array analysis was performed.[174] In this study, differential expression of more than 100 genes was seen in the aneurysm tissue when compared with normal aortic tissue. However, only four of these genes were concordantly differentially expressed in both AAA and ATAA: MMP-9, v-*yes*-1 oncogene, mitogen-activated protein kinase 9, and intracellular adhesion molecule-1. This suggests that although some central commonalities may exist, there may be significant heterogeneity in the pathogenesis of these aneurysms, even within different areas of the aorta.

■ ILIAC-FEMORAL-POPLITEAL ANEURYSMS

Aneurysms of the iliac, popliteal, and femoral arteries (in descending frequency) are clinically well-described entities with a close clinical association with aneurysms of the abdominal aorta. Despite the frequent association of aneurysms of the common and internal iliac arteries with AAA, it is exceedingly rare to develop an aneurysm of the external iliac artery either in isolation or in association with an AAA. The basis for resistance of the external iliac artery to aneurysmal degeneration is not known.[175,176]

Because of the close clinical association of these peripheral aneurysms with AAA, it has been presumed that the etiology is similar. Histologically, these aneurysms are characterized by elastin fragmentation, inflammatory cell infiltrate, and loss of SMCs; however, they have not been studied to the same level of detail as AAAs.[143,177]

■ MESENTERIC ANEURYSMS

Aneurysms of the mesenteric circulation are rare, and pathologic study of these aneurysms has not been performed in a systematic way. Aneurysms can occur in the renal, splenic, hepatic, superior mesenteric, inferior mesenteric, and celiac arteries.[178] However, certain of these aneurysms have a known etiology or clinical association. For example, most aneurysms of the superior mesenteric artery are mycotic. In addition, aneurysms of the renal and splenic circulation are seen more frequently in association with women of childbearing age, and these aneurysms have much increased risks of rupture during pregnancy.[178,179]

ARTERITIS-ASSOCIATED ANEURYSMS

Several diseases are known to affect large arteries with a direct inflammatory response, and some are believed to be autoimmune in origin. In Takayasu's disease, the most frequently involved vessels are the aorta and its branches. Although the disease is characterized primarily by stenoses, aneurysms can also occur in up to 31% of patients. Pathologically, the disease is associated with chronic inflammatory infiltrates, medial elastin loss, neovascularization, and loss of SMCs.[180] Studies of the immunology of Takayasu's disease suggest that the 65-kd HSP is strongly expressed in aortic tissue. It is also recognized that there is restricted usage of the $V\gamma V\delta$ genes associated with infiltrating $\gamma\delta$T cells that are known to respond to this HSP.[181-183]

Giant cell and temporal arteritis are pathologically similar diseases that can also result in aneurysm formation. In general, there is destruction of the normal structure of the large elastic arteries associated with a chronic inflammatory cellular infiltration. It has been suggested that uncontrolled activation of local dendritic cells may be important to the maintenance of this persistent inflammatory state.[184] The explanation for the peculiar anatomic predilection of these various arteritides has yet to be discovered.

Other inflammatory processes that can involve the arterial system and result in aneurysm formation include Behçet's syndrome, periarteritis nodosa, and Kawasaki's disease. These diseases are quite rare; in fact, immunoinflammatory responses in the arterial media are quite unusual, both in clinical vascular disease and in experimental models. In light of this, Dal Canto and associates[185,186] recently reported a series of experiments in mice with immunocompromise due to INF-γ receptor deficiency. Following infection with murine gamma-herpesvirus (γ–HV)-68, these animals developed a chronic viral arteritis specifically localized—and restricted—to the great elastic arteries. These lesions were associated with pronounced inflammatory infiltrates in the intima and adventitia, similar to the lesions seen in Takayasu's arteritis and Kawasaki's disease, and they exhibited prolonged viral infection in medial SMCs.[185] Immunocompetent wild-type animals also developed a similar pattern of great vessel arteritis with γ–HV-68, albeit with much larger inoculating doses of the virus, as well as persistent SMC infection lasting up to 5 months. In additional studies, it was demonstrated that persistence of viral disease in the great vessels is due to inefficient clearance of viral infection from the elastic media compared with other organs and tissues; this is associated with failure of macrophages and T cells to enter the virus-infected elastic media.[186] These findings suggested for the first time that the elastic media of the great vessels might actually be an "immune-privileged" site. Because this phenomenon appears to be based on a limited capacity of inflammatory cells to enter the normal elastic media, this observation may have important implications for the cellular mechanisms underlying the development of chronic inflammation in AAAs, where the elastic lamellae are destroyed and the immunoinflammatory response is particularly well localized to the aortic media.

INFECTIOUS (MYCOTIC) ANEURYSMS

Although it has been suggested that the development of an arteritis is secondary to a viral infectious source, it has long been clear that bacterial infections of an artery can lead to aneurysm formation. Historically, bacterial endocarditis and syphilis were the most common causes of mycotic aneurysms; however, in the modern antibiotic area, direct trauma of the arterial wall is a more common means of bacterial seeding of an artery. This has been termed *microbial arteritis with aneurysm* to distinguish it from the embolic sources of infected aneurysms. Approximately 1% of all aortic aneurysms are associated with an arterial infection.[187]

In the setting of an arterial infection, aneurysms apparently develop secondary to local matrix destruction. The source of the responsible enzymes originates partially from the acute inflammatory response, but matrix destruction may also be due to degradation of the tissues by bacterial enzymes. In contrast with the metalloproteases of a typical AAA, one study has shown that the predominant enzyme species found in mycotic aneurysms are serine proteases released from neutrophilic infiltration.[188]

As noted earlier, penetrating arterial trauma is now the most common source of arterial infection. This is related to the use of arterial cannulation by narcotic users and the several-fold increase in procedures performed via a transarterial puncture in modern practice.[189] The predominant organisms in these cases are gram-positive cocci of *Streptococcus* and *Staphylococcus* species.[190] Septic emboli, generally from an intracardiac source, can also be a source of arterial infection. Direct extension of a local infectious process to an adjacent large vessel can also result in aneurysm formation. The organisms in these cases can be varied and can include gram-negative and anaerobic organisms, as well as occasional yeast and fungi in immunocompromised patients.

Mycotic aneurysms that result from noncontinuous and nonembolic sources are termed *cryptogenic mycotic aneurysms*. The propensity of *Salmonella* species to establish an infection that leads to aneurysm formation is particularly noteworthy. In one clinical study, up to 10% of patients older than 50 years of age with *Salmonella* bacteremia can be expected to develop an arterial infection.[191]

ANEURYSMS ASSOCIATED WITH INHERITED MATRIX DEFECTS

Aneurysms associated with inherited matrix defects result from intrinsic or mechanically acquired defects in the extracellular matrix structure of the artery. The two classic acquired matrix deficiencies that result in aneurysm formation are MFS and EDS.

Marfan Syndrome

MFS is a connective tissue disorder that results in a heterogeneous clinical picture. Generally, MFS affects the musculoskeletal, ocular, and cardiovascular organ systems. Noncardiovascular abnormalities include limb disproportion, arachnodactyly, and hypermobile joints; many affected individuals have ectopic lenses. The cardiovascular complications of MFS represent a significant source of mortality in these patients. These include aortic aneurysms, aortic dissection, mitral valve prolapse, and aortic valvular incompetence. Aortic aneurysms can form anywhere, but these lesions are usually first noted in the ascending aorta.

MFS underscores the complex interplay of proteins that is required in the development of a functionally normal extracellular matrix. MFS is the prototype for a group of diseases that result from defects in fibrillins. Fibrillins comprise a group of matrix glycoproteins that form the microfibrillar network in the extracellular space. This extracellular network provides signals and scaffolding for the orderly deposition of collagen and elastin. Microfibrils may also be load bearing. MFS results from mutations in the fibrillin-1 gene, which disrupts the extensive scaffolding of proteins and prevents the orderly deposition of collagen and elastin into functional units. The fibrillin-1 gene lies on the long arm of chromosome 15, and more than 500 mutations in the gene have been identified in patients diagnosed with MFS.[192]

Animal models of mutations in the fibrillin-1 gene exhibit disruption and disorganization of the medial elastic lamellae. The animals often succumb to aortic dissection. Ultrastructural analysis reveals loss of connections between elastic fibers and medial SMCs, and the aortic disease is accompanied by chronic inflammation. These findings suggest a pattern of aortic disease that is surprisingly similar to that of degenerative AAA and implies a role for chronic inflammation and proteolytic degradation of aortic elastin.

The variability in clinical presentation of patients with MFS can partially be explained by the diversity of genetic mutations. However, MFS remains a clinical diagnosis requiring a specific set of clinical and/or genetic traits. The presence of a fibrillin-1 defect is not necessary nor specific for MFS, because some patients who carry a diagnosis of MFS do not have fibrillin-1 defects. Similarly, other diseases may also be associated with defects in fibrillin-1. For example, isolated thoracic aortic aneurysms in some patients may result from inherited mutations in fibrillin-1.[193,194]

Ehlers-Danlos Syndrome and Others

EDS comprises a family of heritable disorders of extracellular matrix characterized by hyperextensible skin, tissue fragility, and joint hypermobility. Individuals with EDS type IV (vascular EDS) have a propensity for vascular fragility and aneurysm formation. Spontaneous rupture of vessels in the thorax, abdomen, or extremities can occur with or without prior aneurysmal development. These patients are also prone to spontaneous ruptures of the colon or uterus. The skin in these patients is not as extensible as in classic EDS.[195]

A defect in type III collagen production or deposition is the common denominator for all patients with vascular EDS. Type III collagen is a homotrimer of α_1(III) procollagen and an essential component of the walls of arteries and intestine. The single gene encoding for α_1(III) procollagen is on the long arm of chromosome 2 and is known as *COL3A1*. Proper production of type III collagen requires that all strands have equal lengths of their triple-helix domain. Therefore, errors in production of α_1(III) from one allele affect the total production of type III collagen, making this a dominantly inherited trait. Nevertheless, up to 50% of cases are the result of new mutations of *COL3A1*.[195,196]

Liu and coworkers[197] inactivated the *COL3A1* gene in embryonic stem cells by homologous recombination. About 10% of the homozygous mutant animals survived to adulthood, but these animals had a much shorter life span compared with wild-type mice. The major cause of death in mutant mice was rupture of the major blood vessels, similar to patients with type IV EDS. Ultrastructural analysis of tissues from mutant mice also revealed that type III collagen is essential for normal collagen type I fibrillogenesis in the cardiovascular system and other organs.

Several other diseases that appear to generate defects in extracellular matrix rarely may be associated with the development of arterial aneurysms. These include tuberous sclerosis, gonadal dysgenesis, and Menkes' kinky hair syndrome.

■ MECHANICAL FORCE-RELATED ANEURYSMS

As noted for AAA, the mechanical forces applied to the infrarenal portion of the aorta may be large relative to the wall structure, suggesting an anatomic and hemodynamic contribution to aneurysm development in this region. The direct impact of hemodynamic changes on the matrix has not been well characterized. Some indirect evidence of the association of hypertension and aneurysm development has been seen in a mouse that overproduces AT-II.[198] At 6 weeks of age, experimental mice and controls were given either 1% sodium chloride ("salt-loaded") drinking water or tap water for 30 days. Salt-loaded experimental mice, but not controls, suffered frequent thoracic or abdominal cavity hemorrhage. The mortality after 7 days of salt loading was 23%; after 30 days of salt loading, mortality rose to 67%. Hemorrhage was due to rupture of aneurysms that developed at the aortic arch or in the aorta near the renal arteries. These aneurysms were associated with structural degeneration of the aortic media.

In addition, there is a group of aneurysms that develop primarily in response to abnormal mechanical forces applied to the artery. These aneurysms include those produced in response to proximal stenoses, and those that result from changes in wall stress for other reasons. One of the first aneurysm models relied on surgical creation of an arterial stenosis to induce the formation of a post-stenotic aneurysm. It has been well documented that arterial dilations can develop after flow-limiting stenoses. Many of these dilations remain asymptomatic. One exception is subclavian artery aneurysms that develop distal to an extrinsic compression of the subclavian artery associated with thoracic outlet syndrome. The specific pathophysiology of these aneurysms is not well described, although histologically there is medial elastin degeneration and usually an intimal ulcerative lesion.[199]

■ SUMMARY

The pathobiologic changes associated with aneurysms are diverse, but some important universal characteristics are beginning to be better understood. Common to all aneurysms is a degradation of the arterial extracellular matrix associated with a dysfunction of the normal counter-regulatory and synthetic mechanisms. In general, immune recruitment and activation appear to be either a primary or secondary event in aneurysmal development as well. The anatomic localizations of individual aneurysms and their peculiar clinical manifestations have not been well understood, in part because many aneurysms are rare and tissue has been difficult to obtain. As our understanding of these processes continues to improve, we can look forward to the development of novel diagnostic and therapeutic modalities.

■ REFERENCES

1. Lancisi GM: De Aneurysmatibus. Rome, MacMillan, 1952.
2. Wolinsky H, Glagov S: Nature of species differences in the medial distribution of aortic vasa vasorum in mammals. Circ Res 20:409, 1967.
3. Shapiro SD, Endicott SK, Province MA, et al: Marked longevity of human lung parenchymal elastic fibers deduced from prevalence of D-aspartate and nuclear weapons-related radiocarbon. J Clin Invest 87:1828, 1991.
4. Parks WC, Pierce RA, Lee KA, Mecham RP: Elastin. Adv Mol Cell Biol 6:133, 1993.
5. Mecham RP, Heuser JE: The elastic fiber. In Hay ED (ed): Cell Biology of Extracellular Matrix, 2nd ed. New York, Plenum Press, 1991, p 79.
6. Indik Z, Yeh H, Ornstein-Goldstein N, Rosenbloom J: Structure of the elastin gene and alternative splicing of elastin mRNA. In Sandell L, Boyd C (eds): Genes for Extracellular Matrix Proteins. New York, Academic Press, 1990, p 221.
7. Parks WC, Deak SB: Tropoelastin heterogeneity: Implications for protein function and disease. Am J Respir Cell Mol Biol 2:399, 1990.
8. Arteaga-Solis E, Gayraud B, Ramirez F: Elastic and collagenous networks in vascular diseases. Cell Struct Funct 25:69, 2000.
9. Prockop DJ, Kivirikko KI, Tunderman L, Guzman NA: The biosynthesis of collagen and its disorders: I. N Engl J Med 301:13, 1979.
10. Prockop DJ, Kivirikko KI, Tunderman L, Guzman NA: The biosynthesis of collagen and its disorders: II. N Engl J Med 301:77, 1979.
11. Linsenmayer TF: Collagen. In Hay ED (ed): Cell Biology of Extracellular Matrix, 2nd ed. New York, Plenum Press, 1991, p 7.
12. Olsen BR: Collagen biosynthesis. In Hay ED (ed): Cell Biology of Extracellular Matrix, 2nd ed. New York, Plenum Press, 1991, p 177.
13. Brophy CM, Tilson JE, Tilson MD: Propranolol delays the formation of aneurysms in the male blotchy mouse. J Surg Res 44:687, 1988.
14. Brophy CM, Tilson JE, Tilson MD: Propranolol stimulates the cross-linking of matrix components in skin from the aneurysm-prone blotchy mouse. J Surg Res 46:330, 1989.
15. Moursi MM, Beebe HG, Messina LM, et al: Inhibition of aortic aneurysm development in blotchy mice by beta-adrenergic blockade independent of altered lysyl oxidase activity. J Vasc Surg 21:792, 1995.
16. Busuttil R, Rinderbriecht H, Flecher A, Carnack C: Elastase activity: The role of elastase in aortic aneurysm formation. J Surg Res 32:214, 1982.
17. Dobrin PB, Baker WH, Gley WC: Elastolytic and collagenolytic studies of arteries: Implications for the mechanical properties of aneurysms. Arch Surg 119:405, 1984.
18. Mosorin M, Juvonen J, Biancari F, et al: Use of doxycycline to decrease the growth rate of abdominal aortic aneurysms: A randomized, double-blind, placebo-controlled pilot study. J Vasc Surg 34:606, 2001.
19. Baxter BT, Pearce WH, Waltke EA, et al: Prolonged administration of doxycycline in patients with small asymptomatic abdominal aortic aneurysms: Report of a prospective (phase II) multicenter study. J Vasc Surg 36:1, 2002.
20. Clifton MA: Familial abdominal aortic aneurysms. Br J Surg 64:765, 1977.
21. Tilson MD, Seashore MR: Fifty families with abdominal aortic aneurysms in two or more first-order relatives. Am J Surg 147:551, 1984.
22. Verloes A, Sakalihasan N, Koulischer L, Limet R: Aneurysms of the abdominal aorta: Familial and genetic aspects in three hundred thirteen pedigrees. J Vasc Surg 21:646, 1995.
23. Kuivaniemi H, Tromp G: Search for aneurysm susceptibility gene(s). In Keen RR, Dobrin PB (eds): Development of Aneurysms. Georgetown, TX, Landes Bioscience, 2000, p 219.
24. Powell JT, Bashir A, Dawson S, et al: Genetic variation on chromosome 16 is associated with abdominal aortic aneurysm. Clin Sci 78:13, 1990.
25. Hirose H, Takagi M, Miyagawa N, et al: Genetic risk factor for abdominal aortic aneurysm: HLA-DR2(15), a Japanese study. J Vasc Surg 27:500, 1998.
26. Rasmussen TE, Hallett JW Jr, Metzger RL, et al: Genetic risk factors in inflammatory abdominal aortic aneurysms: Polymorphic residue 70 in the *HLA-DR B1* gene as a key genetic element. J Vasc Surg 25:356, 1997.
27. Lederle FA, Johnson GR, Wilson SE, et al: Relationship of age, gender, race, and body size to infrarenal aortic diameter. The Aneurysm Detection and Management (ADAM) Veterans Affairs Cooperative Study Investigators. J Vasc Surg 26:595, 1997.
28. Lederle FA, Johnson GR, Wilson SE, Aneurysm Detection and Management Veterans Affairs Cooperative Study: Abdominal aortic aneurysm in women. J Vasc Surg 34:122, 2001.
29. Lederle FA, Johnson GR, Wilson SE, et al: The Aneurysm Detection and Management Study screening program: Validation cohort and final results. Aneurysm Detection and Management Veterans Affairs Cooperative Study Investigators. Arch Intern Med 160:1425, 2000.
30. Singh K, Bonaa KH, Jacobsen BK, et al: Prevalence of and risk factors for abdominal aortic aneurysms in a population-based study: The Tromso Study. Am J Epidemiol 154:236, 2001.
31. Blanchard JF, Armenian HK, Friesen PP: Risk factors for abdominal aortic aneurysm: Results of a case-control study. Am J Epidemiol 151:575, 2000.
32. Lederle FA, Nelson DB, Joseph AM: Smokers' relative risk for aortic aneurysm compared with other smoking-related diseases: A systematic review. J Vasc Surg 38:329, 2003.
33. Zarins CK, Weisenberg E, Kolettis G, et al: Differential enlargement of artery segments in response to enlarging atherosclerotic plaques. J Vasc Surg 7:386, 1988.
34. Glagov S, Weisenberg E, Zarins CK, et al: Compensatory enlargement of human atherosclerotic coronary arteries. N Engl J Med 316:1371, 1987.
35. Post MJ, de Smet BJ, van der Helm Y, et al: Arterial remodeling after balloon angioplasty or stenting in an atherosclerotic experimental model. Circulation 96:996, 1997.
36. Pasterkamp G, Schoneveld AH, Hijnen DJ, et al: Atherosclerotic arterial remodeling and the localization of macrophages and matrix metalloproteases 1, 2, and 9 in the human coronary artery. Atherosclerosis 150:245, 2000.
37. Virmani R, Kolodgie FD, Burke AP, et al: Lessons from sudden coronary death: A comprehensive morphological classification scheme for atherosclerotic lesions. Arterioscler Thromb Vasc Biol 20:1262, 2000.
38. Dobrin PB, Mrkvicka R: Failure of elastin or collagen as possible critical connective tissue alterations underlying aneurysmal dilatation. Cardiovasc Surg 2:484, 1994.
39. Dobrin PB: Elastin, collagen, and the pathophysiology of arterial aneurysms. In Keen RR, Dobrin PB (eds): Development of Aneurysms. Georgetown, TX, Landes Bioscience, 2000, p 43.

40. Cohen JR, Mandell C, Wise L: Characterization of human aortic elastase found in patients with abdominal aortic aneurysms. Surg Gynecol Obstet 165:301, 1987.
41. Birkedal-Hansen H, Moore WGI, Bodden HK, et al: Matrix metalloproteinases: A review. Crit Rev Oral Biol Med 4:197, 1993.
42. Nagase H: Activation mechanisms of matrix metalloproteinases. Biol Chem 378:151, 1997.
43. Matrisian LM: Metalloproteinases and their inhibitors in matrix remodeling. Trends Genet 6:121, 1990.
44. Woessner JF Jr: Matrix metalloproteinases and their inhibitors in connective tissue remodeling. FASEB J 5:2145, 1991.
45. McMillan WD, Patterson BK, Keen RR, Pearce WH: In situ localization and quantification of seventy-two-kilodalton type IV collagenase in aneurysmal, occlusive, and normal aorta. J Vasc Surg 22:295, 1995.
46. Vine N, Powell J: Metalloproteinases in degenerative aortic disease. Clin Sci 81:233, 1991.
47. Freestone T, Turner RJ, Coady A, et al: Inflammation and matrix metalloproteinases in the enlarging abdominal aortic aneurysm. Arterioscler Thromb Vasc Biol 15:1145, 1995.
48. Lee E, Grodzinsky AJ, Libby P, et al: Human vascular smooth muscle cell-monocyte interactions and metalloproteinase secretion in culture. Arterioscler Thromb Vasc Biol 15:2284, 1995.
49. Davis V, Persidskaia R, Baca-Regen L, et al: Matrix metalloproteinase-2 production and its binding to the matrix are increased in abdominal aortic aneurysms. Arterioscler Thromb Vasc Biol 18:1625, 1998.
50. Reilly JM, Brophy CM, Tilson MD: Characterization of an elastase from aneurysmal aorta which degrades intact aortic elastin. Ann Vasc Surg 6:499, 1992.
51. Newman KM, Jean-Claude J, Li H, et al: Cellular localization of matrix metalloproteinases in the abdominal aortic aneurysm wall. J Vasc Surg 20:814, 1994.
52. Newman KM, Ogata Y, Malon AM, et al: Identification of matrix metalloproteinases 3 (stromelysin-1) and 9 (gelatinase B) in abdominal aortic aneurysm. Arterioscler Thromb Vasc Biol 14:1315, 1994.
53. McMillan WD, Patterson BK, Keen RR, et al: In situ localization and quantification of mRNA for 92-kD type IV collagenase and its inhibitor in aneurysmal, occlusive, and normal aorta. Arterioscler Thromb Vasc Biol 15:1139, 1995.
54. Thompson RW, Holmes DR, Mertens RA, et al: Production and localization of 92-kilodalton gelatinase in abdominal aortic aneurysms: An elastolytic metalloproteinase expressed by aneurysm-infiltrating macrophages. J Clin Invest 96:318, 1995.
55. McMillan WD, Tamarina NA, Cipollone M, et al: Size matters: The relationship between MMP-9 expression and aortic diameter. Circulation 96:2228, 1997.
56. Senior RM, Griffin GL, Fliszar CJ, et al: Human 92- and 72-kilodalton type IV collagenases are elastases. J Biol Chem 266:7870, 1991.
57. Shipley JM, Doyle GA, Fliszar CJ, et al: The structural basis for the elastolytic activity of the 92-kDa and 72-kDa gelatinases: Role of the fibronectin type II-like repeats. J Biol Chem 271:4335, 1996.
58. Mecham RP, Broekelman TJ, Fliszar CJ, et al: Elastin degradation by matrix metalloproteinases: Cleavage site specificity and mechanisms of elastolysis. J Biol Chem 272:18071, 1997.
59. Hovsepian DM, Ziporin SJ, Sakurai MK, et al: Elevated plasma levels of matrix metalloproteinase-9 in patients with abdominal aortic aneurysms: A circulating marker of degenerative aneurysm disease. J Vasc Interv Radiol 11:1345, 2000.
60. McMillan WD, Pearce WH: Increased plasma levels of metalloproteinase-9 are associated with abdominal aortic aneurysms. J Vasc Surg 29:122, 1999.
61. Thompson RW: Basic science of abdominal aortic aneurysms: Emerging therapeutic strategies for an unresolved clinical problem. Curr Opin Cardiol 11:504, 1996.
62. Shah PK: Inflammation, metalloproteinases, and increased proteolysis: An emerging pathophysiological paradigm in aortic aneurysm. Circulation 96:2115, 1997.
63. Ogata Y, Enghild JJ, Nagase H: Matrix metalloproteinase 3 (stromelysin) activates the precursor for the human matrix metalloproteinase 9. J Biol Chem 267:3581, 1992.
64. Elmore JR, Keister BF, Franklin DP, et al: Expression of matrix metalloproteinases and TIMPs in human abdominal aortic aneurysms. Ann Vasc Surg 12:221, 1998.
65. Tamarina NA, McMillan WD, Shively VP, Pearce WH: Expression of matrix metalloproteinases and their inhibitors in aneurysms and normal aorta. Surgery 122:264, 1997.
66. Shapiro SD, Kobayashi DK, Ley TJ: Cloning and characterization of a unique elastolytic metalloproteinase produced by human alveolar macrophages. J Biol Chem 268:23824, 1993.
67. Belaaouaj A, Shipley JM, Kobayashi DK, et al: Human macrophage metalloelastase: Genomic organization, chromosomal location, gene linkage, and tissue-specific expression. J Biol Chem 270:14568, 1995.
68. Shipley JM, Wesselschmidt RL, Kobayashi DK, et al: Metalloelastase is required for macrophage-mediated proteolysis and matrix invasion in mice. Proc Natl Acad Sci U S A 93:3942, 1996.
69. Gronski TJJ, Martin RL, Kobayashi DK, et al: Hydrolysis of a broad spectrum of extracellular matrix proteins by human macrophage elastase. J Biol Chem 272:12189, 1997.
70. Churg A, Wang RD, Tai H, et al: Macrophage metalloelastase mediates acute cigarette smoke-induced inflammation via tumor necrosis factor-alpha release. Am J Respir Crit Care Med 167:1083, 2003.
71. Curci JA, Liao S, Huffman MD, et al: Expression and localization of macrophage elastase (matrix metalloproteinase-12) in abdominal aortic aneurysms. J Clin Invest 102:1900, 1998.
72. Irizarry E, Newman KM, Gandhi RH, et al: Demonstration of interstitial collagenase in abdominal aortic aneurysm disease. J Surg Res 54:571, 1993.
73. Busuttil RW, Abou-Zamzam AM, Machleder HI: Collagenase activity of the human aorta: A comparison of patients with and without abdominal aortic aneurysms. Arch Surg 115:1373, 1980.
74. Webster MW, McAuley CE, Steed DL, et al: Collagen stability and collagenolytic activity in the normal and aneurysmal human abdominal aorta. Am J Surg 161:635, 1991.
75. Evans CH, Georgescu HI, Lin CW, et al: Inducible synthesis of collagenase and other neutral metalloproteinases by cells of aortic origin. J Surg Res 51:399, 1991.
76. Menashi S, Campa JS, Greenhalgh RM, Powell JT: Collagen in abdominal aortic aneurysm: Typing, content, and degradation. J Vasc Surg 6:578, 1987.
77. Herron GS, Unemori E, Wong M, et al: Connective tissue proteinases and inhibitors in abdominal aortic aneurysms: Involvement of the vasa vasorum in the pathogenesis of aortic aneurysms. Arterioscler Thromb Vasc Biol 11:1667, 1991.
78. Mao D, Lee JK, Van Vickle SJ, Thompson RW: Expression of collagenase-3 (MMP-13) in human abdominal aortic aneurysms and vascular smooth muscle cells in culture. Biochem Biophys Res Commun 261:904, 1999.
79. Gomez DE, Alonso DF, Yoshiji H, Thorgeirsson UP: Tissue inhibitors of metalloproteinases: Structure, regulation and biological functions. Eur J Cell Biol 74:111, 1997.
80. Baker AH, Zaltsman AB, George SJ, Newby AC: Divergent effects of tissue inhibitor of metalloproteinase-1, -2, or -3 overexpression on rat vascular smooth muscle cell invasion, proliferation, and death in vitro: TIMP-3 promotes apoptosis. J Clin Invest 101:1478, 1998.
81. Allaire E, Muscatelli-Groux B, Mandet C, et al: Paracrine effect of vascular smooth muscle cells in the prevention of aortic aneurysm formation. J Vasc Surg 36:1018, 2002.
82. Silence J, Collen D, Lijnen HR: Reduced atherosclerotic plaque but enhanced aneurysm formation in mice with inactivation of the tissue inhibitor of metalloproteinase-1 (TIMP-1) gene. Circ Res 90:897, 2002.
83. Allaire E, Forough R, Clowes M, et al: Local overexpression of TIMP-1 prevents aortic aneurysm degeneration and rupture in a rat model. J Clin Invest 102:1413, 1998.
84. Brophy CM, Marks WH, Reilly JM, Tilson MD: Decreased tissue inhibitor of metalloproteinases (TIMP) in abdominal aortic aneurysm tissue: A preliminary report. J Surg Res 50:653, 1991.

85. Tilson MD, Reilly JM, Brophy CM, et al: Expression and sequence of the gene for tissue inhibitor of metalloproteinases in patients with abdominal aortic aneurysms. J Vasc Surg 18:266, 1993.
86. Thompson RW, Parks WC: Role of matrix metalloproteinases in abdominal aortic aneurysms. Ann N Y Acad Sci 800:157, 1996.
87. Jean-Claude J, Newman KM, Li H, et al: Possible key role for plasmin in the pathogenesis of abdominal aortic aneurysms. Surgery 116:472, 1994.
88. Reilly JM, Sicard GA, Lucore CL: Abnormal expression of plasminogen activators in aortic aneurysmal and occlusive disease. J Vasc Surg 19:865, 1994.
89. Schneiderman J, Bordin GM, Engelberg I, et al: Expression of fibrinolytic genes in atherosclerotic abdominal aortic aneurysm wall: A possible mechanism for aneurysm expansion. J Clin Invest 96:639, 1995.
90. Shireman PK, McCarthy WJ, Pearce WH, et al: Elevations of tissue-type plasminogen activator and differential expression of urokinase-type plasminogen activator in diseased aorta. J Vasc Surg 25:157, 1997.
91. Louwrens HD, Kwaan HC, Pearce WH, et al: Plasminogen activator and plasminogen activator inhibitor expression by normal and aneurysmal human aortic smooth muscle cells in culture. Eur J Vasc Endovasc Surg 10:289, 1995.
92. Nollendorfs A, Greiner TC, Nagase H, Baxter BT: The expression and localization of membrane type-1 matrix metalloproteinase in human abdominal aortic aneurysms. J Vasc Surg 34:316, 2001.
93. Cohen JR, Keegan L, Sarfati I, et al: Neutrophil chemotaxis and neutrophil elastase in the aortic wall in patients with abdominal aortic aneurysms. J Invest Surg 4:423, 1991.
94. Murphy EA, Danna-Lopes D, Sarfati I, et al: Nicotine-stimulated elastase activity release by neutrophils in patients with abdominal aortic aneurysms. Ann Vasc Surg 12:41, 1998.
95. Gacko M, Chyczewski L: Activity and localization of cathepsin B, D, and G in aortic aneurysm. Int Surg 82:398, 1997.
96. Gacko M, Glowinski S: Cathepsin D and cathepsin L activities in aortic aneurysm wall and parietal thrombus. Clin Chem Lab Med 36:449, 1998.
97. Sukhova GK, Shi GP, Simon DI, et al: Expression of the elastolytic cathepsins S and K in human atheroma and regulation of their production in smooth muscle cells. J Clin Invest 102:576, 1998.
98. Koch AE, Haines GK, Rizzo RJ, et al: Human abdominal aortic aneurysms: Immunophenotypic analysis suggesting an immune-mediated response. Am J Pathol 137:1199, 1990.
99. Satta J, Soini Y, Mosorin M, Juvonen T: Angiogenesis is associated with mononuclear inflammatory cells in abdominal aortic aneurysms. Ann Chir Gynaecol 87:40, 1998.
100. Satta J, Laurila A, Paakko P, et al: Chronic inflammation and elastin degradation in abdominal aortic aneurysm disease: An immunohistochemical and electron microscopic study. Eur J Vasc Endovasc Surg 15:313, 1998.
101. Pyo R, Lee JK, Shipley JM, et al: Targeted gene disruption of matrix metalloproteinase-9 (gelatinase B) suppresses development of experimental abdominal aortic aneurysms. J Clin Invest 105:1641, 2000.
102. Weyand CM, Wagner AD, Bjornsson J, Goronzy JJ: Correlation of the topographical arrangement and the functional pattern of tissue-infiltrating macrophages in giant cell arteritis. J Clin Invest 98:1642, 1996.
103. Hance KA, Tataria M, Ziporin SJ, et al: Monocyte chemotactic activity in human abdominal aortic aneurysms: Role of elastin degradation peptides and the 67-kD cell surface elastin receptor. J Vasc Surg 35:254, 2002.
104. Hirose H, Ozsvath KJ, Xia S, et al: Immunoreactivity of adventitial matrix fibrils of normal and aneurysmal abdominal aorta with antibodies against vitronectin and fibrinogen. Pathobiology 66:1, 1998.
105. Hirose H, Ozsvath KJ, Xia S, Tilson MD: Molecular cloning of the complementary DNA for an additional member of the family of aortic aneurysm antigenic proteins. J Vasc Surg 26:313, 1997.
106. Ozsvath KJ, Hirose H, Xia S, et al: Expression of two novel recombinant proteins from aortic adventitia (kappafibs) sharing amino acid sequences with cytomegalovirus. J Surg Res 69:277, 1997.
107. Yen HC, Lee FY, Chau LY: Analysis of the T cell receptor V beta repertoire in human aortic aneurysms. Atherosclerosis 135:29, 1997.
108. Seko Y, Takahashi N, Sato O, et al: Restricted usage of T-cell receptor Valpha-Vbeta genes in infiltrating cells in the aortic tissue of a patient with atherosclerotic aortic aneurysm. Int Angiol 17:89, 1998.
109. Walton LJ, Powell JT, Parums DV: Unrestricted usage of immunoglobulin heavy chain genes in B cells infiltrating the wall of atherosclerotic abdominal aortic aneurysms. Atherosclerosis 135:65, 1997.
110. Juvonen J, Juvonen T, Laurila A, et al: Demonstration of *Chlamydia pneumoniae* in the walls of abdominal aortic aneurysms. J Vasc Surg 25:499, 1997.
111. Blasi F, Denti F, Erba M, et al: Detection of *Chlamydia pneumoniae* but not *Helicobacter pylori* in atherosclerotic plaques of aortic aneurysms. J Clin Microbiol 34:2766, 1996.
112. Petersen E, Boman J, Persson K, et al: *Chlamydia pneumoniae* in human abdominal aortic aneurysms. Eur J Vasc Endovasc Surg 15:138, 1998.
113. Halme S, Juvonen T, Laurila A, et al: *Chlamydia pneumoniae* reactive T lymphocytes in the walls of abdominal aortic aneurysms. Eur J Clin Invest 29:546, 1999.
114. Tambiah J, Powell JT: *Chlamydia pneumoniae* antigens facilitate experimental aortic dilatation: Prevention with azithromycin. J Vasc Surg 36:1011, 2002.
115. Lindholt JS, Juul S, Vammen S, et al: Immunoglobulin A antibodies against *Chlamydia pneumoniae* are associated with expansion of abdominal aortic aneurysm. Br J Surg 86:634, 1999.
116. Lindholt JS, Ashton HA, Scott RA: Indicators of infection with *Chlamydia pneumoniae* are associated with expansion of abdominal aortic aneurysms. J Vasc Surg 34:212, 2001.
117. Petersen E, Boman J, Wagberg F, Angquist KA: Presence of *Chlamydia pneumoniae* in abdominal aortic aneurysms is not associated with increased activity of matrix metalloproteinases. Eur J Vasc Endovasc Surg 24:365, 2002.
118. Lindholt JS, Ostergard L, Henneberg EW, et al: Failure to demonstrate *Chlamydia pneumoniae* in symptomatic abdominal aortic aneurysms by a nested polymerase chain reaction (PCR). Eur J Vasc Endovasc Surg 15:161, 1998.
119. Porqueddu M, Spirito R, Parolari A, et al: Lack of association between serum immunoreactivity and *Chlamydia pneumoniae* detection in the human aortic wall. Circulation 106:2647, 2002.
120. Schillinger M, Domanovits H, Mlekusch W, et al: Anti-*Chlamydia* antibodies in patients with thoracic and abdominal aortic aneurysms. Wien Klin Wochenschr 114:972, 2002.
121. Vammen S, Vorum H, Ostergaard L, et al: Immunoblotting analysis of abdominal aortic aneurysms using antibodies against *Chlamydia pneumoniae* recombinant MOMP. Eur J Vasc Endovasc Surg 24:81, 2002.
122. Forbes TL, DeRose G, Kribs S, et al: Endovascular repair of abdominal aortic aneurysm with coexisting renal allograft: Case report and literature review. Ann Vasc Surg 15:586, 2001.
123. Reber PU, Vogt B, Steinke TM, et al: Surgery for aortoiliac aneurysms in kidney transplant recipients. J Cardiovasc Surg 41:919, 2000.
124. Ierardi RP, Coll DP, Kumar A, et al: Abdominal aortic aneurysmectomy after kidney transplantation: Case report and review of the literature. Am Surg 62:961, 1996.
125. Panneton JM, Gloviczki P, Canton LG, et al: Aortic reconstruction in kidney transplant recipients. Ann Vasc Surg 10:97, 1996.
126. Pearce WH, Sweis I, Yao JS, et al: Interleukin-1-beta and tumor necrosis factor-alpha release in normal and diseased human infrarenal aortas. J Vasc Surg 16:784, 1992.
127. Davis VA, Persidskaia RN, Baca-Regen LM, et al: Cytokine pattern in aneurysmal and occlusive disease of the aorta. J Surg Res 101:152, 2001.

128. Shteinberg D, Halak M, Shapiro S, et al: Abdominal aortic aneurysm and aortic occlusive disease: A comparison of risk factors and inflammatory response. Eur J Vasc Endovasc Surg 20:462, 2000.
129. Juvonen J, Surcel H-M, Satta J, et al: Elevated circulating levels of inflammatory cytokines in patients with abdominal aortic aneurysm. Arterioscler Thromb Vasc Biol 17:2843, 1997.
130. Hingorani A, Ascher E, Scheinman M, et al: The effect of tumor necrosis factor binding protein and interleukin-1 receptor antagonist on the development of abdominal aortic aneurysms in a rat model. J Vasc Surg 28:522, 1998.
131. Dobrin PB, Baumgartner N, Anidjar S, et al: Inflammatory aspects of experimental aneurysms: Effect of methylprednisolone and cyclosporine. Ann N Y Acad Sci 800:74, 1996.
132. Szekanecz Z, Shah MR, Pearce WH, Koch AE: Human atherosclerotic abdominal aortic aneurysms produce interleukin (IL)-6 and interferon-gamma but not IL-2 and IL-4: The possible role for IL-6 and interferon-gamma in vascular inflammation. Agents Actions 42:159, 1994.
133. Schonbeck U, Sukhova GK, Gerdes N, Libby P: T_H2-predominant immune responses prevail in human abdominal aortic aneurysm. Am J Pathol 161:499, 2002.
134. Rohde LE, Arroyo LH, Rifai N, et al: Plasma concentrations of interleukin-6 and abdominal aortic diameter among subjects without aortic dilatation. Arterioscler Thromb Vasc Biol 19:1695, 1999.
135. Jones KG, Brull DJ, Brown LC, et al: Interleukin-6 (IL-6) and the prognosis of abdominal aortic aneurysms. Circulation 103:2260, 2001.
136. Colonnello JS, Hance KA, Shames ML, et al: Transient exposure to elastase induces mouse aortic wall smooth muscle cell production of MCP-1 and RANTES during development of experimental aortic aneurysm. J Vasc Surg 38:138, 2003.
137. Koch AE, Kunkel SL, Pearce WH, et al: Enhanced production of the chemotactic cytokines interleukin-8 and monocyte chemoattractant protein-1 in human abdominal aortic aneurysms. Am J Pathol 142:1423, 1993.
138. Van den Steen PE, Proost P, Wuyts A, et al: Neutrophil gelatinase B potentiates interleukin-8 tenfold by aminoterminal processing, whereas it degrades CTAP-III, PF-4, and GRO-alpha and leaves RANTES and MCP-2 intact. Blood 96:2673, 2000.
139. Schonbeck U, Mach F, Libby P: Generation of biologically active IL-1 beta by matrix metalloproteinases: A novel caspase-1-independent pathway of IL-1 beta processing. J Immunol 161:3340, 1998.
140. Lopez-Candales A, Holmes DR, Liao S, et al: Decreased vascular smooth muscle cell density in medial degeneration of human abdominal aortic aneurysms. Am J Pathol 150:993, 1997.
141. Henderson EL, Gang YJ, Sukhova GK, et al: Death of smooth muscle cells and expression of mediators of apoptosis by T lymphocytes in human abdominal aortic aneurysms. Circulation 99:96, 1999.
142. Rowe VL, Stevens SL, Reddick TT, et al: Vascular smooth muscle cell apoptosis in aneurysmal, occlusive, and normal human aortas. J Vasc Surg 31:567, 2000.
143. Jacob T, Hingorani A, Ascher E: Examination of the apoptotic pathway and proteolysis in the pathogenesis of popliteal artery aneurysms. Eur J Vasc Endovasc Surg 22:77, 2001.
144. Liao S, Curci JA, Kelley B, et al: Accelerated replicative senescence of medial smooth muscle cells derived from abdominal aortic aneurysms as compared to the adjacent inferior mesenteric artery. J Surg Res 92:85, 2000.
145. Dobrin PB: Vascular mechanics. In Shepard JT, Abbound FM (eds): Handbook of Physiology: Part I. Peripheral Circulation and Organ Blood Flow. Baltimore, Williams & Wilkins, 1983, p 65.
146. Sonesson B, Vernersson E, Hansen F, Lanne T: Influence of sympathetic stimulation on the mechanical properties of the aorta in humans. Acta Physiol Scand 159:139, 1997.
147. Dobrin PB: Pathophysiology and pathogenesis of aortic aneurysms. Surg Clin North Am 69:687, 1989.
148. Newman DL, Gosling RG, Bowden NLR: Pressure amplitude increase and matching the aortic iliac junction of the dog. Cardiovasc Res 7:6, 1973.
149. Wasserman SM, Mehraban F, Komuves LG, et al: Gene expression profile of human endothelial cells exposed to sustained fluid shear stress. Physiol Genomics 12:13, 2002.
150. Gimbrone MA Jr, Topper JN, Nagel T, et al: Endothelial dysfunction, hemodynamic forces, and atherogenesis. Ann N Y Acad Sci 902:230, 2000.
151. Topper JN, Gimbrone MA Jr: Blood flow and vascular gene expression: Fluid shear stress as a modulator of endothelial phenotype. Mol Med Today 5:40, 1999.
152. Hoshina K, Sho E, Sho M, et al: Wall shear stress and strain modulate experimental aneurysm cellularity. J Vasc Surg 37:1067, 2003.
153. Nakahashi TK, Hoshina K, Tsao PS, et al: Flow loading induces macrophage antioxidative gene expression in experimental aneurysms. Arterioscler Thromb Vasc Biol 22:2017, 2002.
154. Anidjar S, Salzmann JL, Gentric D, et al: Elastase induced experimental aneurysms in rats. Circulation 82:973, 1990.
155. Halpern VJ, Nackman GB, Gandhi RH, et al: The elastase infusion model of experimental aortic aneurysms: Synchrony of induction of endogenous proteinases with matrix destruction and inflammatory cell response. J Vasc Surg 20:51, 1994.
156. Thompson RW, Liao S, Petrinec D, et al: Sequential expression of metallogelatinases during elastase-induced aneurysmal degeneration of the rat aorta: Correlations with aortic dilatation and the destruction of medial elastin [Abstract]. FASEB J 9:A967, 1995.
157. Petrinec D, Liao S, Holmes DR, et al: Doxycycline inhibition of aneurysmal degeneration in an elastase-induced rat model of abdominal aortic aneurysm: Preservation of aortic elastin associated with suppressed production of 92-kD gelatinase. J Vasc Surg 23:336, 1996.
158. Huffman MD, Curci JA, Moore G, et al: Functional importance of connective tissue repair during the development of experimental abdominal aortic aneurysms. Surgery 128:429, 2000.
159. Pyo R, Lee JK, Shipley JM, et al: Targeted gene disruption of matrix metalloproteinase-9 (gelatinase B) suppresses development of experimental abdominal aortic aneurysms. J Clin Invest 105:1641, 2000.
160. Allaire E, Guettier C, Bruneval P, et al: Cell-free arterial grafts: Morphologic characteristics of aortic isografts, allografts, and xenografts in rats. J Vasc Surg 19:446, 1994.
161. Nagai N, Hosokawa M, Itohara S, et al: Embryonic lethality of molecular chaperone HSP-47 knockout mice is associated with defects in collagen biosynthesis. J Cell Biol 150:1499, 2000.
162. Nakashima Y, Plump AS, Raines EW, et al: ApoE-deficient mice develop lesions of all phases of atherosclerosis throughout the arterial tree. Arterioscler Thromb Vasc Biol 14:133, 1994.
163. Daugherty A, Manning MW, Cassis LA: Angiotensin II promotes atherosclerotic lesions and aneurysms in apolipoprotein E-deficient mice. J Clin Invest 105:1605, 2000.
164. Baxter BT, Davis VA, Minion DJ, et al: Abdominal aortic aneurysms are associated with altered matrix proteins of the nonaneurysmal aortic segments. J Vasc Surg 19:797, 1994.
165. McKusick V: The defect in Marfan syndrome. Nature 352:279, 1991.
166. Ando M, Okita Y, Morota T, Takamoto S: Thoracic aortic aneurysm associated with congenital bicuspid aortic valve. Cardiovasc Surg 6:629, 1998.
167. Dingemans KP, Teeling P, Lagendijk JH, Becker AE: Extracellular matrix of the human aortic media: An ultrastructural histochemical and immunohistochemical study of the adult aortic media. Anat Rec 258:1, 2000.
168. Roberts CS, Roberts WC: Dissection of the aorta associated with congenital malformation of the aortic valve. J Am Coll Cardiol 17:712, 1991.
169. Saruk M, Eisenstein R: Aortic lesion in Marfan syndrome: The ultrastructure of cystic medial degeneration. Arch Pathol Lab Med 101:74, 1977.
170. Segura AM, Luna RE, Horiba K, et al: Immunohistochemistry of matrix metalloproteinases and their inhibitors in thoracic aortic aneurysms and aortic valves of patients with Marfan's syndrome. Circulation 98:II331, 1998.

171. Whittle MA, Hasleton PS, Anderson JC, Gibbs AC: Collagen in dissecting aneurysms of the human thoracic aorta: Increased collagen content and decreased collagen concentration may be predisposing factors in dissecting aneurysms. Am J Cardiovasc Pathol 3:311, 1990.
172. Cattell MA, Hasleton PS, Anderson JC: Increased elastin content and decreased elastin concentration may be predisposing factors in dissecting aneurysms of human thoracic aorta. Cardiovasc Res 27:176, 1993.
173. Nataatmadja M, West M, West J, et al: Abnormal extracellular matrix protein transport associated with increased apoptosis of vascular smooth muscle cells in Marfan syndrome and bicuspid aortic valve thoracic aortic aneurysm. Circulation 108:329, 2003.
174. Absi TS, Sundt TM III, Tung WS, et al: Altered patterns of gene expression distinguishing ascending aortic aneurysms from abdominal aortic aneurysms: Complementary DNA expression profiling in the molecular characterization of aortic disease. J Thorac Cardiovasc Surg 126:344, 2003.
175. McCready RA, Pairolero PC, Gilmore JC, et al: Isolated iliac artery aneurysms. Surgery 93:688, 1983.
176. Richardson JW, Greenfield LJ: Natural history and management of iliac aneurysms. J Vasc Surg 8:165, 1988.
177. Faggioli GL, Gargiulo M, Bertoni F, et al: Parietal inflammatory infiltrate in peripheral aneurysms of atherosclerotic origin. J Cardiovasc Surg 33:331, 1992.
178. Stanley JC: Mesenteric arterial occlusive and aneurysmal disease. Cardiol Clin 20:611, 2002.
179. Messina LM, Shanley CJ: Visceral artery aneurysms. Surg Clin North Am 77:425, 1997.
180. Inder SJ, Bobryshev YV, Cherian SM, et al: Immunophenotypic analysis of the aortic wall in Takayasu's arteritis: Involvement of lymphocytes, dendritic cells and granulocytes in immuno-inflammatory reactions. Cardiovasc Surg 8:141, 2000.
181. Seko Y, Takahashi N, Tada Y, Yagita H, et al: Restricted usage of T-cell receptor Vγ-Vδ genes and expression of costimulatory molecules in Takayasu's arteritis. Int J Cardiol 75:S77, 2000.
182. Seko Y, Sato O, Takagi A, et al: Restricted usage of T-cell receptor Vα-Vβ genes in infiltrating cells in aortic tissue of patients with Takayasu's arteritis. Circulation 93:1788, 1996.
183. Johnston SL, Lock RJ, Gompels MM: Takayasu arteritis: A review. J Clin Pathol 55:481, 2002.
184. Weyand CM, Goronzy JJ: Medium- and large-vessel vasculitis. N Engl J Med 349:160, 2003.
185. Dal Canto AJ, Virgin HW, Speck SH: Ongoing viral replication is required for γ herpesvirus 68-induced vascular damage. J Virol 74:11304, 2000.
186. Dal Canto AJ, Swanson PE, O'Guin AK, et al: IFN-gamma action in the media of the great elastic arteries, a novel immunoprivileged site. J Clin Invest 107:R15, 2001.
187. Chan P, Tsai CW, Huang JJ, et al: Salmonellosis and mycotic aneurysm of the aorta: A report of 10 cases. J Infect 30:129, 1995.
188. Buckmaster MJ, Curci JA, Murray PR, et al: Source of elastin-degrading enzymes in mycotic aortic aneurysms: Bacteria or host inflammatory response? Cardiovasc Surg 7:16, 1999.
189. Brown SL, Busuttil RW, Baker JD, et al: Bacteriologic and surgical determinants of survival in patients with mycotic aneurysms. J Vasc Surg 1:541, 1984.
190. Reddy DJ, Smith RF, Elliott JP Jr, et al: Infected femoral artery false aneurysms in drug addicts: Evolution of selective vascular reconstruction. J Vasc Surg 3:718, 1986.
191. Benenson S, Raveh D, Schlesinger Y, et al: The risk of vascular infection in adult patients with nontyphi *Salmonella* bacteremia. Am J Med 110:60, 2001.
192. Collod-Beroud G, Boileau C: Marfan syndrome in the third millennium. Eur J Hum Genet 10:673, 2002.
193. Milewicz DM, Chen H, Park ES, et al: Reduced penetrance and variable expressivity of familial thoracic aortic aneurysms/dissections. Am J Cardiol 82:474, 1998.
194. Milewicz DM, Michael K, Fisher N, et al: Fibrillin-1 (Fbn1) mutations in patients with thoracic aortic aneurysms. Circulation 94:2708, 1996.
195. Pepin M, Schwarze U, Superti-Furga A, Byers PH: Clinical and genetic features of Ehlers-Danlos syndrome type IV, the vascular type. N Engl J Med 342:673, 2000.
196. Germain DP: Clinical and genetic features of vascular Ehlers-Danlos syndrome. Ann Vasc Surg 16:391, 2002.
197. Liu X, Wu H, Byrne M, et al: Type III collagen is crucial for collagen I fibrillogenesis and for normal cardiovascular development. Proc Natl Acad Sci U S A 94:1852, 1997.
198. Nishijo N, Sugiyama F, Kimoto K, et al: Salt-sensitive aortic aneurysm and rupture in hypertensive transgenic mice that overproduce angiotensin II. Lab Invest 78:1059, 1998.
199. Dobrin PB: Poststenotic dilatation. Surg Gynecol Obstet 172:503, 1991.

Section VI

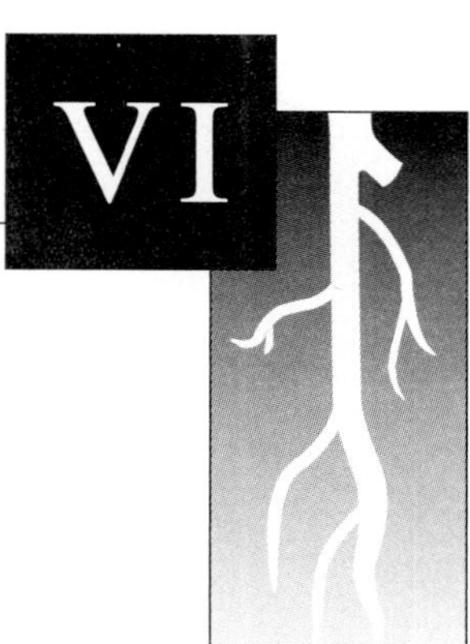

BLEEDING AND CLOTTING: FUNDAMENTAL CONSIDERATIONS

THOMAS W. WAKEFIELD, MD

Chapter 30

Normal and Abnormal Coagulation

JAWED FAREED, PhD
DEBRA A. HOPPENSTEADT, PhD
OMER IQBAL, MD
MICHELLE FLORIAN-KUJAWSKI, BS
MAHMUT TOBU, MD
RODGER L. BICK, MD, PhD
TAQDEES SHEIKH, MD
WALTER JESKE, PhD

OVERVIEW OF BLOOD COAGULATION

Hemostasis as defined by Virchow in the last century is a fine balance among blood flow, humoral factors, and cellular elements of the vascular system. Today, molecular and cellular biology has advanced our understanding of the thrombotic and hemostatic processes and their regulation. Thrombotic and bleeding disorders are the most frequent causes of death. To manage thrombosis, heparin and warfarin have remained the sole antithrombotic agents. However, specific sites in the thrombotic network at both plasmatic and cellular sites can now be targeted, and specific drugs based on the inhibition of factors Xa and IIa have been developed. Antibodies against specific platelet receptors as well as specific antitissue factor, antithrombin, and anti-Xa agents are being developed. Mutations of endogenous inhibitors have been identified as causes of congenital thrombophilias. The use of heparin has also greatly advanced with the availability of low-molecular-weight heparins (LMWHs). Several newer approaches to treat bleeding diatheses, including the use of recombinant factors VIII and VIIa, have evolved. Heparin is no longer solely a surgical anticoagulant but is used to treat a variety of conditions including venous thrombosis, unstable angina, and myocardial infarction and in procedures such as angioplasty and stent implantation. The mechanism of heparin's action has become more complex with the discovery of tissue factor pathway inhibitor (TFPI), thrombin-activatable fibrinolytic inhibitor (TAFI), selectins, and other cellular targets where the drug is able to produce its effects.

Blood normally is maintained in the fluid state so that nutrients can be delivered to the various tissues of the body. When the integrity of the vascular system has been compromised, it becomes necessary for the blood to clot. As shown in Figure 30-1, the initial response to a break in the continuity of the vasculature is the formation of the platelet plug. Platelets in the flowing blood rapidly adhere to the exposed subendothelial vessel wall matrix and become activated. During this activation process, components of the platelet α and β granules (adenosine triphosphate [ATP], adenosine diphosphate [ADP], factor V, 5-hydroxytryptamine [5-HT]) are released, causing further platelet aggregation. Also during these morphologic changes, activated platelets express protein and cell receptors and procoagulant phospholipids are expressed on their surface. The damaged

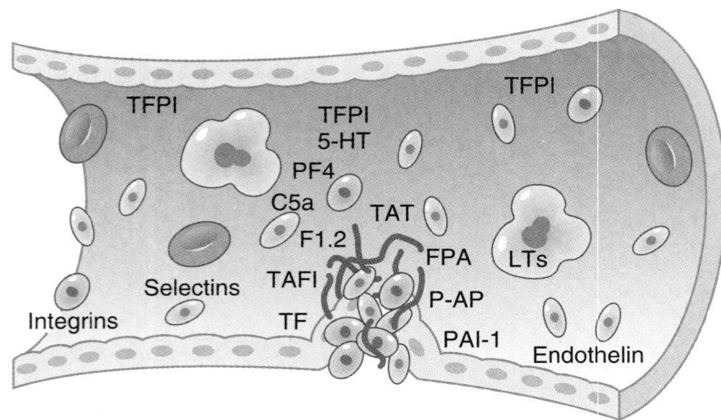

FIGURE 30-1 Formation of the platelet plug. TFPI, tissue factor pathway inhibitor; 5-HT, 5-hydroxytriptamine; TAT, thrombin-antithrombin complex; FPA, fibrinopeptide A; PF4, platelet factor 4; C5a, complement 5a; LT, leukotriene; P-AP, plasminogen-γ-antiplasmin complex; PAI-1, plasminogen activator inhibitor 1; TAFI, thrombin activatable fibrinolytic inhibitor; TF, tissue factor.

endothelium is also capable of releasing certain procoagulant substances and down-regulating the fibrinolytic process, inflammation, complement activation, and the kallikrein system.

The negatively charged phospholipid phosphatidylserine is asymmetrically distributed in mammalian cell membranes, primarily on the inner leaflet. On exposure to collagen or thrombin, the distribution of phospholipids changes with increasing phosphatidylserine in the external membrane leaf.[1] The increased expression of phosphatidylserine on the outer leaflet of the membrane creates a procoagulant surface on which several steps of the coagulation cascade take place.

The platelet plug initially arrests the loss of blood. This, however, is not a permanent blockade. The formation of a fibrin-based clot acts to stabilize the initial platelet plug. The coagulation system is a complex network of zymogens that must be activated to ultimately form the fibrin strands of the blood clot. On activation, most of these coagulation proteins are converted into active serine proteases, which are similar to trypsin and chymotrypsin. Traditionally, coagulation has been viewed as having two distinct branches: the intrinsic and the extrinsic pathways.[2,3] Today it has been widely accepted that the two pathways are linked prior to the generation of factor Xa.[4] A schematic of the coagulation cascade is depicted in Figure 30-2.

Intrinsic Pathway of Coagulation

In the intrinsic pathway, factor XII becomes activated in the contact phase of coagulation. This occurs when factors XII and XI, prekallikrein, and high-molecular-weight kininogen come together on a negatively charged surface. Although this reaction can take place in the laboratory on a negatively charged surface such as glass or kaolin, the physiologic surface is unknown. It has been proposed that this could be a tissue rich in collagen or sulfatides.[5] By binding to the negatively charged surface, factor XII is converted to its active form through an unknown mechanism. The formation of factor XIIa is amplified by a positive feedback loop. Factor XIIa is capable of converting prekallikrein to

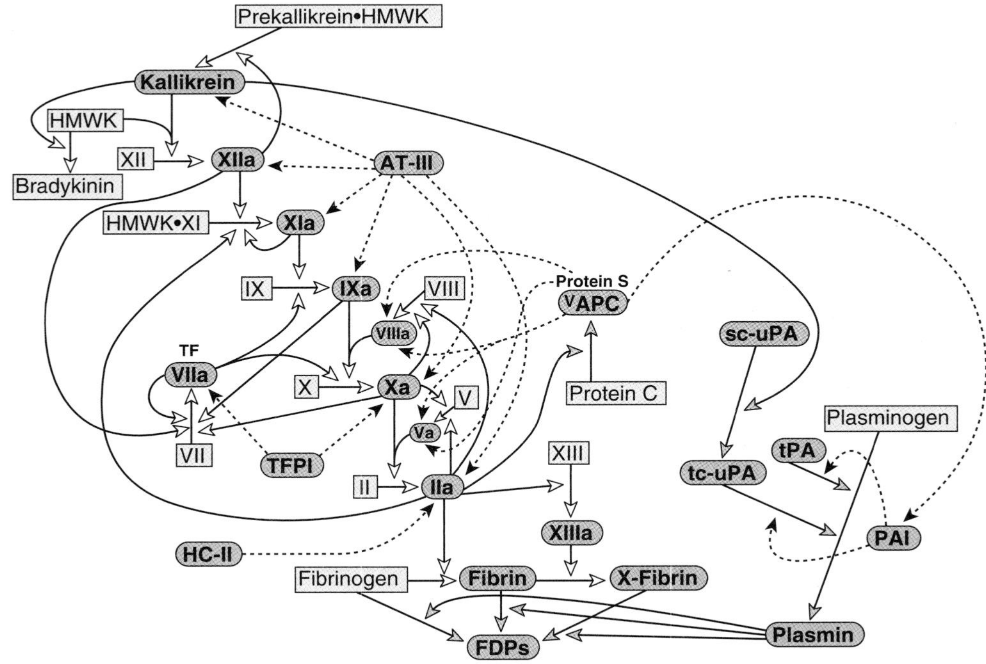

FIGURE 30-2 Coagulation cascade. Protease network in coagulation, fibrinolysis, and kallikrein-kinin systems. HMWK, high-molecular-weight kininogen; AT-III, antithrombin III; TF, tissue factor; TFPI, tissue factor pathway inhibitor; HC-II, heparin cofactor II; FDPs, fibrinogen degradation products; PAI, plasminogen activator inhibitor; sc-uPA, single-chain urokinase plasminogen activator; APC, activated protein C; tPA, tissue plasminogen activator.

kallikrein. Likewise, kallikrein converts factor XII to its active form. Factor XIIa also converts factor XI to factor XIa, which in turn activates factor IX. Factor IX along with its cofactor factor VIII, calcium ions, and phospholipid membranes forms the "tenase" complex, which converts factor X to factor Xa, thereby initiating the common pathway of coagulation. The phospholipid membrane in these complexes serves to lower the Michaelis-Menteu constant (Km) of the reaction. The phospholipid allows the enzyme to become saturated more easily and serves to localize the coagulation response to where it is most needed. The cofactor, factor V, increases the catalytic efficiency of the enzyme.[6] Factor Xa joins with its cofactor factor Va, calcium ions, and phospholipid membranes to form the prothrombinase complex. The prothrombinase complex then acts to convert prothrombin into the active enzyme thrombin. Factors V and VIII are activated through proteolytic cleavage by factor Xa or thrombin. They are not, however, active proteases. Factor Va is believed to have two rate-enhancing effects on the prothrombinase complex. In the prothrombinase complex, factors Xa and Va are present in stoichiometric amounts, resulting in an unknown alteration in the active site of factor Xa that increases its catalytic efficiency.[7] Factor Va also binds to prothrombin, thus sequestering it at the site of assembly of the prothrombinase complex. Overall, these two actions of factor Va result in a 300,000-fold increase in the rate of prothrombin conversion.

Thrombin serves many functions in coagulation. First, thrombin cleaves the soluble protein fibrinogen to generate the insoluble fibrin monomer. Fibrinogen circulates as a disulfide-linked dimer containing two A-alpha chains, two B-beta chains, and two gamma chains. Cleavage of fibrinogen by thrombin results in the release of fibrinopeptides A and B and the exposure of charged domains at opposite ends of the molecule.[8] Exposure of these charged domains leads to polymerization of the monomers. The release of fibrinopeptides A and B occur at different rates, with fibrinopeptide A preferentially removed in mammalian systems.[9,10] Removal of fibrinopeptide A leads to end-to-end fibrin polymerization, whereas loss of fibrinopeptide B allows side-to-side polymerization of the end-to-end linked monomers.[11] It is these monomers that are cross-linked by the transaminase factor XIIIa to form the meshwork of the thrombus. Thrombin also acts to augment its own generation by being a part of several positive feedback loops in the coagulation cascade. In these loops, thrombin activates factors XII, XI, VIII, and V. By activating the precursors to its own generation, thrombin greatly amplifies its own generation. Thrombin also activates platelets,[12] activates the inhibitor protein C through binding with thrombomodulin,[13] and stimulates activated endothelial cells to release tissue plasminogen activator.[14]

Extrinsic Pathway of Coagulation

The extrinsic pathway of coagulation is activated when circulating factor VII encounters tissue factor. Tissue factor is a transmembrane glycoprotein (GP) that is normally expressed by subendothelial fibroblast-like cells that surround the blood vessel. An intact endothelium normally shields the circulating blood from exposure to tissue factor. The tissue factor molecule consists of a 219-amino acid hydrophilic extracellular domain, a 23-amino acid hydrophobic region that spans the membrane, and a 21-amino acid cytoplasmic tail that anchors the molecule to the cell membrane.[15,16] Other sites of tissue factor expression include activated monocytes, activated endothelial cells, and atherosclerotic plaques.

Factor VII exhibits a weak procoagulant activity on its own, typically accounting for about 1% to 2% of the total factor VII/VIIa activity.[17] On binding to tissue factor, a 10,000,000-fold increase in factor VIIa enzymatic activity is observed.[18] Both factors VII and VIIa bind to tissue factor with equal affinity.[19] How factor VII is initially activated is not known, though it is hypothesized that factor Xa can activate factor VII in a back-activation reaction. The factor VIIa-tissue factor complex can then activate factor X, leading to the generation of thrombin and ultimately to the formation of fibrin strands.

It was shown in 1977 and has been more recently appreciated that the tissue factor-factor VIIa complex also activates factor IX to factor IXa, thus interacting with "intrinsic" pathway enzymes.[4] This is believed to be important for maintaining the clotting process. Direct activation of factor X by factor VIIa-tissue factor can rapidly initiate coagulation, but both of these enzymes are quickly inhibited by the endogenous inhibitor TFPI. By activating factor IX, the tissue factor-VIIa complex initiates two pathways for thrombin generation. The small amounts of factor Xa generated prior to TFPI inhibition are sufficient to cleave prothrombin and generate a small amount of thrombin. This thrombin is then capable of back-activating factors V, VIII, and possibly XI, thereby sustaining clot formation through generation of thrombin via the intrinsic pathway. It has been observed that the activation of factor X by the factor IXa-VIII complex in the presence of calcium and phospholipids is 50 times greater than by the tissue factor-VIIa complex.[20] Factor XI activation has been shown to occur in the presence of thrombin and a polyanion cofactor.[21,22] Activation with the cofactor has been observed to be poor. A physiologic cofactor has not been elucidated. It has been reasoned that if the direct activation of factor X by VIIa-tissue factor is the sole source of thrombin generation, there would be no manifestation of hemophilia, a genetic deficiency of either factor IX or factor VIII.

Role of Platelets

Platelets are disc-shaped, anuclear particles that circulate in a nonadhesive state in the undamaged circulation.[23] Platelets contain a contractile system and a number of storage granules. The α storage granules contain platelet factor 4, β-thromboglobulin, platelet-derived growth factor, P-selectin, fibrinogen, factor V, and von Willebrand's factor.[24] The dense or β granules contain ATP, ADP, and serotonin.[25,26]

The first step toward platelet aggregation is platelet adhesion. Normally, platelets do not adhere to the vessel walls due to the nonthrombogenic properties of the endothelium. Endothelial cells produce heparan sulfate (to activate antithrombin), thrombomodulin (for activation of protein C), plasminogen activators (to induce fibrin degradation) and TFPI (to inhibit tissue factor activity). In addition, these cells also produce prostacyclin (prostaglandin I_2), which inhibits platelet activation by raising platelet cyclic adenosine monophosphate levels and endothelial-derived relaxing factor (nitric oxide), which inhibits platelet activation through a cyclic guanosine monophosphate-dependent mechanism. When this antithrombotic continuum of cells is interrupted by vascular injury, platelets adhere to the exposed subendothelial tissues.

Following adhesion, platelets become activated. In this activation process, there is a morphologic shape change in the platelet, with pseudopod formation observed. This brings about a change in the conformation of the GP-IIb/IIIa receptor on the platelet surface, which allows for fibrinogen binding.[23] Fibrinogen binding serves as a bridge that links individual platelets into larger aggregates. An increase in cytosolic calcium levels leads to activation of internal platelet enzymes with the subsequent release of platelet granule contents. The formation of these platelet aggregates is the process of primary hemostasis, the first step to arrest blood loss.

The release of platelet granule contents leads to further platelet activation and aggregation and an activation of coagulation. Most of the known aggregating agents cause release of the storage granule contents. These agonists include thrombin, ADP, collagen, thromboxane A_2, platelet-activating factor, serotonin, epinephrine, immune complexes, and fibrinogen.[23] Thrombin is the most potent aggregating agent, capable of causing platelet aggregation without any contribution from thromboxane A_2 or ADP.[23] Serotonin and epinephrine do not induce aggregation on their own but synergistically promote aggregation induced by other agents.[27-29]

Platelet membranes contain a variety of receptors for the various agonists including the thrombin receptor, the thromboxane A_2 receptor, 5-HT_2 receptors, and α_2-adrenergic receptors. In addition, a number of GPs present on the membrane serve as receptors for collagen (GP-Ia/IIa), fibrinogen (GP-IIb/IIIa), von Willebrand factor (GP-Ib), and fibronectin (GP-IIb/IIIa).[27-29] A high-molecular-weight chondroitin sulfate proteoglycan has been shown to be released from the surface of the platelet during the aggregation process. This proteoglycan contains homopolymers of 4-O chondroitin sulfate that inhibit ADP-induced aggregation of platelets.[30]

Activated platelets also provide a procoagulant surface on which several reactions of the coagulation cascade take place. Unstimulated platelets provide only a minimally effective surface on which the tenase and prothrombinase complexes can assemble.[31-33] This is due to the bilayer partitioning of various phospholipids. In unstimulated platelets, the outer leaflet of the membrane consists of mostly phosphatidylcholine, whereas the inner leaf contains most of the phosphatidylserine. Two mechanisms have been proposed for maintaining this distribution.[34,35] When platelets are stimulated to release their granular contents, the procoagulant phospholipids are brought to the surface as the granules fuse to the membranes.[31] This expression of phosphatidylserine on the outer leaflet along with factor V release from the α granule greatly accelerates the formation of thrombin.[36-38]

Platelet activation leads to the formation of platelet derived microparticles derived from the platelet surface. These microvesicles typically account for 25% to 30% of platelet procoagulant activity and factor V binding sites.[34,39]

Role of Platelet Integrins

A number of the GPs on the surface of the platelet belong to the superfamily of adhesive protein receptors known as *integrins*. Integrins are α/β heterodimer protein complexes that are present on the surface of adherent cells of most species.[40-42] These integrins mediate cell-cell and cell-matrix interactions involved in a diverse number of biologic functions.[43,44] Integrins are divided into subfamilies based on the identity of the β subunit. The first two subfamilies of integrins, the very late antigen (VLA) complexes and the Leu-Cams, are found on white blood cells and mediate various leukocyte aggregation responses.[45,46] Platelets contain two members of the third subfamily of integrins, GP-IIb/IIIa, and the vitronectin receptor.[47,48]

Integrins function by interacting with a number of extracellular GP ligands such as fibronectin, laminin, collagen, vitronectin, fibrinogen, and von Willebrand's factor.[49] Integrins are capable of binding several ligands, and the nature of the ligand specificity is not known.

Platelet membranes contain five integrin-like receptors that are involved in the formation of the primary hemostatic plug. These include VLA-2, VLA-5, VLA-6, GP-IIb/IIIa, and the vitronectin receptor. Of these, GP-IIb/IIIa is the most abundant.[50] VLA-2 (GP-Ia/IIa) is the binding site for collagen on the platelet surface.[51] VLA-5 and VLA-6 are responsible for the binding to vitronectin and laminin, respectively.[45] The extent to which these receptors contribute to platelet adhesion in vivo is not known. The physiologic function of the vitronectin receptor is not known.

Platelet aggregation requires that platelets become activated by at least one platelet agonist, the presence of functional GP-IIb/IIIa molecules and the presence of at least one GP-IIb/IIIa ligand.[52] Lack of GP-IIb/IIIa complexes leads to the congenital bleeding disorder known as *Glanzmann's thrombasthenia*.[53] In nonactivated platelets, GP-IIb/IIIa is capable of binding only immobilized fibrinogen. Platelet activation allows plasma-borne adhesive proteins to bind to GP-IIb/IIIa complexes.[54] The activation of the GP-IIb/IIIa complex occurs by an unknown mechanism, though the number of receptors on the membrane is not altered by activation.[50] Fibrin polymers bind to the activated GP-IIb/IIIa complexes and anchor the platelet plug in place.

Recent studies have shown that the binding of ligands to GP-IIb/IIIa also activates a number of cellular processes important for platelet stimulation,[50] including the synthesis of 3-phosphorylated phosphatidylinositols, the release of arachidonic acid, and the increase in plasma calcium levels. Stimulation of these processes allows for bidirectional signaling between the intracellular and extracellular compartments.

Role of Leukocytes

Leukocytes typically express minimal amounts of procoagulant activity in the unstimulated state.[55] Cytokines such as interleukin (IL)-1 and tumor necrosis factor (TNF) can elicit the expression of tissue factor on endothelial and mononuclear cells.[56] Monocyte procoagulant activity is also induced by endotoxin, the complement system, phorbol esters, prostaglandins, and a number of other agonists.[57] Procoagulant activity associated with leukocytes is not limited to the expression of tissue factor. Several monocyte/macrophage-derived procoagulant activities have been characterized. These include tissue factor,[58-60] factor VII,[60] and factor XIII.[61] In addition, some monocytes and macrophages have been shown to express functional factor V/Va[62] and to possess binding sites for factor X.[63] The factor Xa binding site on leukocytes has been shown to be the integrin CD11b/CD18.[63] Not only does this integrin bind factor X but it also proteolytically activates factor X to Xa, allowing for initiation of coagulation on the surface of the monocytes and neutrophils.[63] Monocytes have also been shown to contain a receptor for the factor IXa-VIII complex, which allows the reactions of the intrinsic pathway of coagulation to take place on the surface of the monocyte.[64]

Prothrombin has been shown to be efficiently activated on the cell surface of monocytes and lymphocytes.[65] As with platelets, the prothrombinase activity on monocytes is increased with activated monocytes as compared to the nonactivated cells.[66]

It has been stated that when coagulation takes place on the surface of leukocytes, it "assumes the aspects of a broad inflammatory mechanism, directly influencing cellular motility and adhesion, phagocytosis, cell-cell communication, and normal or deregulated cellular growth."[63] Fibrin formation not only forms the basis for a blood clot but can also serve to limit the inflammatory response. In addition, products of the coagulation process such as thrombin, fibrinopeptides, and fibrin degradation products have chemotactic and mitogenic properties.[67,68]

Studies have indicated that leukocytes play a critical role in the activation of coagulation in patients with septicemia and in animal models of acute lung injury.[69] One study has presented direct evidence indicating the role of tissue factor expression on activated endothelial cells in in-vivo thrombogenesis.[70] Additionally, procoagulant microparticles have been found to be produced from activated leukocytes with P-selectin binding to its receptor PSGL-1, and these microparticles have been thought to be related to thrombogenesis.[71,72]

Role of the Endothelium

The endothelium plays a relatively important role in the modulation of overall coagulation, fibrinolytic, and platelet-dependent processes. Endothelial cells are reactive to various physiologic and pathologic states and release various mediators that modulate plasmatic processes. The role of endothelial function in mediating the overall coagulation process can be summarized by the following:

1. Regulation of thrombin function by binding to thrombomodulin
2. Release of fibrinolytic mediators in the regulation of the fibrinolytic system
3. Release of prostaglandin derivatives in the control of platelet function and vascular hemodynamics
4. Release of nitric oxide, TFPI, and other substances to mediate various functions

Under normal conditions, endothelial cells play a regulatory role in balancing the cellular and plasmatic reactions. However, in pathologic states such as ischemia and occlusive states (thrombotic or restenotic), endothelial function changes markedly, with endothelial cells producing various substances that mediate the pathologic changes. Some of these functions are summarized in the following:

1. Release of tissue factor to initiate the clotting process
2. Release of plasminogen activator inhibitor (PAI) to inhibit the fibrinolytic response
3. Generation of procoagulant proteins and von Willebrand's factor to activate thrombogenesis

It is therefore important to consider the endothelium as a major player in the overall regulation of hemostasis.

■ ENDOGENOUS INHIBITORS OF COAGULATION AND FIBRINOLYSIS

Antithrombin

Antithrombin is a single-chain GP with a molecular weight of approximately 58,000 Da.[73] The primary structure of this serine protease inhibitor (SERPIN) has been determined by protein and complementary DNA (cDNA) sequencing of clones from several species.[74] Normal plasma levels of antithrombin are approximately 2 to 3 μM.[75]

In the beginning of the century, it was suspected that a natural inhibitor of thrombin was present in the plasma.[76] The first hints of antithrombin's existence were detected shortly after the discovery of heparin when it was discovered that heparin required a cofactor to exhibit its anticoagulant activity.[77,78] At this point, the molecule was termed *heparin cofactor*.[78] It was not until the late 1960s that Abildgaard demonstrated that the proteins antithrombin and heparin cofactor were one and the same.[79]

Antithrombin is a member of the SERPIN superfamily of proteins, which includes the inhibitors α_2-antiplasmin, α_1-antichymotrypsin, and α_1-proteinase inhibitor.[80] Antithrombin is considered to be the primary inhibitor of coagulation[81] and targets most coagulation proteases as well as the enzymes trypsin, plasmin, and kallikrein.[82] Inhibition takes place when a stoichiometric complex between the active site serine of the protease and the ARG^{393}-SER^{294} bond of antithrombin forms.[83,84] The tertiary structure of antithrombin resembles α_1-antitrypsin in that it is folded into *N*-terminal domain helices and β sheets. This tertiary structure is maintained by the formation of three disulfide bonds.[73] Four glycosylation sites exist on human antithrombin, two of which are suspected to actually contain carbohydrate chains. The glycosylation of these sites appears to effect heparin binding to the inhibitor.[85] The efficient inhibition of proteases by antithrombin requires heparin as a cofactor. Without heparin, the inhibition rate constants for thrombin and factor Xa have been estimated to be 1×10^3 and 3×10^3 L/mol.sec^{-1}, respectively. In the presence of heparin, these rates of inhibition are accelerated to 3×10^7 and 4×10^6 L/mol·sec^{-1}, respectively, for thrombin and factor Xa.[86] The binding site for heparin is located on the *N*-terminal domain of the molecule.

Two mechanisms have been proposed to account for heparin's ability to catalyze the antiprotease actions of antithrombin. The first suggests that heparin binds to antithrombin and causes a conformational change at the active site.[83] The second model, the ternary complex or template model, proposes that heparin acts catalytically by binding both antithrombin and the serine protease, thereby bringing them in close proximity.[82] Both models may be operative, depending on the serine protease being inhibited. Conformational changes of antithrombin on heparin binding have been observed spectroscopically.[83] Furthermore, the ability of a pentasaccharide region of heparin to promote the antithrombin-mediated inhibition of factor Xa supports this model. The inhibition of thrombin appears to be better explained by the template model. Conformational changes induced by heparin binding do not alter the reactivity of antithrombin toward thrombin.[87] In addition, heparin pentasaccharides do not promote thrombin inhibition. Rather, chains of more than 18 saccharide units are needed for this inhibition. Kinetic studies indicate that heparin must bind both thrombin and antithrombin.[88] It is not clear if one binding must precede the other for optimal inhibition to occur.[83,85,88]

Deficiency of antithrombin predisposes the patient to thrombotic complications. Antithrombin deficiencies can be the result of low protein levels or due to functionally abnormal molecules. Low protein levels can be brought about by reduced synthesis or an increased turnover of the molecule. Functional deficiencies can be brought about by mutations in either the reactive site or heparin-binding sites. A number of such mutations have been documented.[82,87,88]

Heparin Cofactor II

Heparin cofactor II is a second plasma SERPIN that has resemblance to antithrombin in that it is activatable by glycosaminoglycan binding. This protein has also been called *dermatan sulfate cofactor* and *human leuserpin 2*.[89] The existence of this second inhibitor and heparin cofactor was first shown by Briginshaw and Shanberge in 1974.[90] Although antithrombin is observed to have progressive antithrombin activity and to also inhibit factor Xa, the second cofactor exhibits only weak progressive activity and does not inhibit factor Xa. Tollefsen and Blank observed two different thrombin inhibitor complexes, one of which could not be identified with antisera to known protease inhibitors.[91] Several clinical studies observed a discrepancy between heparin cofactor activity levels and plasma antithrombin antigen levels.[91] The existence of the inhibitor was confirmed when the protein was isolated from human plasma and from Cohn fraction IV.[91] The heparin cofactor II protein has a molecular weight of 62,000 to 72,000 Da, depending on the methodology used.[91]

Like antithrombin, heparin cofactor II inhibits proteases by forming a 1:1 stoichiometric complex with the enzyme. The protease attacks the reactive site of heparin cofactor II located on the C-terminus, resulting in the formation of a covalent bond. Heparin cofactor II has a higher protease specificity than antithrombin. Of the coagulation enzymes, heparin cofactor II is known only to inhibit thrombin.[92] Additionally, heparin cofactor II has been shown to inhibit chymotrypsin[93] and leukocyte cathepsin G.[94] This protease specificity appears to be due to the active site bond present in heparin cofactor II. Although antithrombin contains an Arg-Ser bond as its active site, heparin cofactor II is unique in containing a Leu-Ser bond. This suggests that another portion of the heparin cofactor II molecular may be required for protease binding.

As in the case of antithrombin, the inhibition of protease activity by heparin cofactor II is promoted by glycosaminoglycan binding. Whereas the activation of antithrombin is dependent on the presence of a specific sequence in the heparin chain, heparin cofactor II can be activated by a wide variety of agents. Heparins, heparans, and dermatan sulfate all promote thrombin inhibition via heparin cofactor II. In the absence of glycosaminoglycan, thrombin variants recognize antithrombin and heparin cofactor II to a similar degree, indicating that neither the autolysis loop nor the β loop of thrombin is required for SERPIN/protease interaction. On the addition of heparin, the interaction of antithrombin with the thrombin variants is not altered, suggesting the importance of the anion-binding exosite II for the heparin bridge between thrombin and antithrombin. These same studies indicate the importance of anion-binding exosite I for the inhibition of thrombin by heparin cofactor II because gamma thrombin, lacking this site, is not inhibited. Based on these results, a complex double-bridge mechanism for heparin cofactor II–mediated thrombin inhibition has been postulated. In this mechanism, heparin or dermatan sulfate binds to the glycosaminoglycan-binding site on heparin cofactor II and anion-binding site I on thrombin. On heparin binding to heparin cofactor II, the acidic domain is displaced and is free to interact with the β-loop region of the anion-binding exosite of thrombin, facilitating its rapid inhibition.

The normal plasma level of heparin cofactor II is approximately 1.4 ± 0.2 μM.[90] Two patients to date have been described as having heparin cofactor II deficiency related to thrombosis.[95]

Tissue Factor Pathway Inhibitor

TFPI is one of the coagulation protease inhibitors found endogenously within the vasculature. TFPI has alternately been known as *lipoprotein-associated coagulation inhibitor* or *extrinsic pathway inhibitor*. This 42-kDa inhibitor has been shown to contain three Kunitz domains tandemly linked between a negatively charged amino terminus and a positively charged carboxyterminus.[96] The active site of the first Kunitz domain binds to the active site of the VIIa-tissue factor complex, whereas the active site of the second Kunitz domain binds to the active site of factor Xa. Mutation of the active site of the third Kunitz domain has no effect on the inhibition of either factor VIIa or factor Xa. Both of these proteins are produced by recombinant methods and can be used for the study of thrombosis in simulated conditions. Modification of the second Kunitz domain has also been shown to result in a loss of inhibition of tissue factor-VIIa activity. In experiments where the third Kunitz domain has been truncated, TFPI still inhibits factor VIIa-tissue factor complexes on cell surfaces in culture.[97] The carboxyterminus of TFPI is required for the optimal inhibition of factor Xa, perhaps affecting the rate at which TFPI can bind to factor Xa. No difference is observed between the inhibition of factor VIIa-tissue factor by full-length TFPI or by a truncated form of TFPI.[98] Two studies have examined the kinetics of TFPI inhibition of factor Xa.[99,100] Both studies have indicated that more than just the second Kunitz domain is required for factor Xa binding because the association rate constants for full-length TFPI are higher than for carboxyterminus or Kunitz 3-truncated TFPI. The third Kunitz domain has recently been shown to contain a second heparin-binding site.[101]

In normal tissues of the vasculature, TFPI is produced by megakaryocytes and the endothelium.[102] Once produced, this TFPI is stored in three intravascular pools. These pools are located in the plasma and in platelets and are bound to the endothelium.[103] The smallest pool of TFPI is found in the platelets, accounting for less than 2.5% of the intravascular total. This small pool of TFPI is released on platelet activation.[104] Ten percent to 50% of the intravascular TFPI is in the plasma. Most plasma-based TFPI is bound to plasma lipoproteins.[104,105] Approximately 5% of the plasma pool of TFPI circulates in the free form.[103-105] The lipoprotein-bound TFPI is reported to be of relatively low inhibitory activity.[104] The largest pool of TFPI is found bound to the endothelial surface.[103,104,106] This pool can account for 50% to 90% of the total intravascular TFPI.

The TFPI pool bound to the endothelium has been shown to be heparin releasable in a number of studies.[104,106] Venous occlusion and agents such as DDAVP that induce exocytosis of endothelial granular proteins do not cause the release of TFPI.[106] Repeated heparin administration is observed to release similar amounts of TFPI with no tachyphylaxis.[106] It is believed that the endothelial pool of TFPI is bound to glycosaminoglycans on the surface of the endothelium. Heparin injection, then, is thought to displace TFPI from the endogenous glycosaminoglycans. The amount of TFPI in the plasma following heparin administration is determined by the heparin concentration. TFPI levels 2- to 10-fold baseline have been reported following heparin and LMWH administration. The chemical nature of the LMWH also affects the degree of TFPI release. It has been shown that when different LMWHs are administered at the same anti-Xa unit dosage, plasma TFPI levels vary by as much as 30%. Neutralization of heparin by protamine sulfate or protamine chloride results in a dramatic decrease in plasma TFPI levels.[103,107]

TFPI acts in vitro as an anticoagulant when measured by a number of assays. Both the thromboplastin-induced clotting time and the activated partial thromboplastin time (aPTT) are prolonged by TFPI.[103] Factor Xa-based assays such as the Heptest and the amidolytic anti-Xa assay are also affected by recombinant TFPI.[107] Higher amounts of TFPI are required in the prothrombin time (PT) and aPTT for prolongation of the clotting time than are needed in the Heptest. The PT is a more sensitive assay for the anticoagulant effects of TFPI than is the aPTT, suggesting that the main in-vitro inhibitory effect of TFPI is the inhibition of factor VIIa.[103] Cosupplementation of heparin and recombinant TFPI to plasma in vitro has differing effects depending on the assay used. Kristensen observed that heparin and recombinant TFPI additively prolong the Heptest clotting time.[107a] It has been shown that the prolongation of the aPTT and PT assays by heparin and TFPI is synergistic.[103-107] A study by Nordfang and associates, however, suggested that the increased effect of TFPI in the presence of heparin is due to heparin-antithrombin complexes because the addition of heparin exhibited no effect in antithrombin-deficient plasma.[98] The rate of Xa inhibition by recombinant TFPI was observed to increase 2.5-fold on the addition of heparin, though not with full-length TFPI.[105]

TFPI, when administered to rabbits, has been shown to have an antithrombotic effect when thromboplastin was used as a thrombogenic challenge.[108] TFPI was also shown to be an effective inhibitor when thrombosis was induced in rabbit jugular veins by endothelial destruction and restricted blood flow. The antithrombotic and antiprotease actions of TFPI have been tested in several other animal models. Warn-Cramer and Rapaport investigated the effect of immunodepletion of TFPI in factors VIIa- and Xa-induced coagulation in rabbits.[109] These rabbits were observed to be sensitized to the procoagulant effects of factor VIIa but not factor Xa in the absence of factor VIIa. Two studies have indicated that TFPI administration reduces the lethal effects of *Escherichia coli* administration in a septic shock model in baboons.[110] These studies also indicated that TFPI may have an anti-inflammatory effect because an attenuation of the IL-6 response was also observed. Administration of TFPI has been observed to prevent reocclusion of arteries in dogs following clot lysis with tissue plasminogen activator. Topical administration of TFPI has been shown to prevent thrombosis in a rabbit model of vascular trauma.[111]

Protein C

The protein C pathway is one of the natural anticoagulant systems that keeps blood in the fluid state. When thrombin is formed, it stimulates coagulation and its own formation by activating factors V and VIII through proteolytic cleavage.[112] Factors VIIIa and Va bind to negatively charged phospholipids on activated platelets and act as binding sites for factors IXa and Xa, respectively, allowing for formation of the tenase and prothrombinase complexes.[20]

Thrombin can also act to limit its own procoagulant activity. When thrombin is in circulation, it binds a high-affinity receptor on the endothelium known as *thrombomodulin*.[33] The dissociation constant (k_d) for this binding is 0.2 to 0.5 × 10^{-9} M.[113] Thrombomodulin is a membrane-spanning protein containing multiple functional domains and a molecular weight of approximately 60,000 Da.[114] When thrombin binds to thrombomodulin, a change in substrate specificity is noted. Although this complex is a potent activator of protein C, the bound thrombin no longer cleaves fibrinogen, is not able to activate other coagulation proteases such as factors V and VIII, and does not activate platelets.[33,113] The thrombin-thrombomodulin complex is a 20,000-fold better activator of protein C than is free thrombin.[33,113] Thrombomodulin is present on the endothelium in most arteries, veins, and capillaries.[115,116]

Protein C is a vitamin K-dependent zymogen identified by Stenflo that has been shown to be identical to autoprothrombin IIa.[116,117] On activation, protein C exhibits anticoagulant properties.[118] Alterations of thrombin's substrate specificity on binding to thrombomodulin are thought to be due both to steric hindrance of thrombin's active site and to conformational changes in the active site.[116-118] Protein C is made up of disulfide-linked heavy and light chains and has a molecular weight of approximately 62,000 Da.[119] Protein C derives its anticoagulant properties from its ability to cleave and inactivate membrane-bound forms of factors Va and VIIIa.[33] Factors V and VIII as well as non–membrane-bound forms of factors Va and VIIIa are not cleaved by protein C.

Protein C requires two cofactors to express its anticoagulant activity: protein S and factor V. Protein S is another vitamin K-dependent plasma protein whose free form expresses protein C cofactor activity for the degradation of factors Va and VIIIa.[114] Protein S is a single-chain, 70,000-Da GP that has the highest affinity for negatively charged phospholipids among vitamin K-dependent proteins.[114] Protein S forms a 1:1 complex with protein C on the lipid membrane, which may account for its ability to increase the affinity of activated protein C for such membranes.[120] Though the mechanism of action of protein S is not completely understood, it may be related to its ability to make factors Va and VIIIa available for proteolytic cleavage by activated protein C.[121] Less is known about factor V's role as an activated protein C cofactor, though it is hypothesized that factor V and protein S may synergistically act to localize protein C activity to the surface of membranes.[114]

Because low levels of protein C activation peptide are found in healthy individuals, it is suggested that protein C is constantly activated to a small degree.[122] Protein C administration has been shown to inhibit both arterial and venous thrombosis in animal models.[123] Heterozygous protein C deficiency or activated protein C resistance due to factor V mutation is thought to explain 60% to 70% of the cases of familial thrombophilia.[114]

Protease Nexins

Protease nexins 1 and 2 are endogenous SERPINs that have molecular weights of 43 and approximately 100 kDa, respectively.[124] Both protease nexin 1 and protease nexin 2 have effects on the coagulation system. Based on cell culture studies, protease nexin 1 appears to be produced by fibroblasts, smooth muscle cells, and epithelial cells.[125,126] Protease nexin 1 has a 30% sequence homology with antithrombin III, and like antithrombin III, has a high-affinity heparin-binding site. Heparin binding to protease nexin 1 accelerates protease inhibition.[125,126] Protease nexin 1 appears to be limited to the extravascular compartment because human plasma contains only small amounts of this inhibitor (20 pM).[124] Protease nexin 1 inhibits several serine proteases, including thrombin, urokinase, plasminogen activator, and activated protein C.[124,126] On formation of a stable complex with the target protease, the complex binds back to the cells, where it is internalized and degraded.[125] The physiologic role of protease nexin 1 appears to be related to protection of the extracellular matrix from degradation by urokinase and plasminogen activator.[127] This is supported by the fact that protease nexin 1 binds tightly to the extracellular matrix, thereby localizing its activity.

Protease nexin 2 is identical to the secreted form of the amyloid precursor protein containing the Kunitz-type SERPIN domain.[126,127] Protease nexin 2 circulates in blood stored as a platelet α-granule protein that is secreted on platelet activation.[125] Protease nexin 2 inhibits trypsin- and chymotrypsin-like serine proteases and is also a potent inhibitor of factor XIa.[124-126] Its location in platelets and its ability to inhibit factor XIa suggest a role in regulating blood coagulation for protease nexin 2.

Other Serine Protease Inhibitors

A number of other SERPINs are known to play a role in modulating physiologic functions. PAIs serve to limit the normal activation of the fibrinolytic process. High levels of PAI-1 are associated with an increased risk of thromboembolic disease.[127] PAI-1 has also been shown to regulate the degradation of extracellular matrix, which may be important in modulating cancer invasion. α_2-Antiplasmin rapidly inhibits the fibrinolytic activity of plasmin.[128] α_2-Macroglobulin has been described as a "panproteinase inhibitor" in light of evidence that it interacts with nearly any proteinase.[129] In addition, α_2-macroglobulin may play a role in inflammation and immune reactions through its ability to regulate the distribution and activity of numerous cytokines, including transforming growth factor β, TNF-α, platelet-derived growth factor, and several ILs.[130] The complement and contact systems are regulated by C1-esterase inhibitor through the inhibition of complement components C1r and C1s.[131] Deficiency of C1-esterase inhibitor is associated with angioedema.[132] Histidine-rich GP has been shown to bind to plasminogen and interfere with its interaction with fibrin.[133] Additionally, histidine-rich GP is known to bind to heparin and related glycosaminoglycans.[133] High levels of this protein have not been definitively linked to thrombosis.[134]

Thrombin Activatable Fibrinolytic Inhibitor

TAFI was discovered by two independent groups as a basic carboxypeptidase present in fresh serum obtained from clotted human blood and was characterized to be distinct from the constitutive basic carboxypeptidase.[135] Because of its relative instability, this enzyme was also designated as *carboxypeptidase U* (unstable). It was also found that arginine residues from such substrates as fibrin strands were digested more efficiently than lysine and thus it was also designated as *carboxypeptidase R* (arginine). Subsequent studies on cDNA encoding revealed TAFI to be a zymogen with a high degree of homology to pancreatic procarboxypeptidase.[136] The amino acid sequence of TAFI is also reported to be identical to plasma procarboxypeptidase B, U, and R. Beside thrombin-thrombomodulin, TAFI can be activated by plasmin. Activated TAFI inhibits fibrin clot lysis by removing the carboxyl terminal lysine residues from partially degraded fibrin that mediate positive feedback in the fibrinolytic cascade. TAFI has been shown to remove the carboxyl terminal arginine from thrombin and a variety of polypeptides such as anaphylatoxins and kinins.[135,137] More recently, it has been demonstrated that TAFI is an acute-phase protein. Injections of bacterial lipopolysaccharide elicit fibrinolytic deficit and increases in hepatic

TAFI messenger RNA.[138] Recent data have demonstrated that TAFI is upregulated in rats with burn injury and septic shock. A recent publication also reported on the modulation of TAFI gene expression in acute-phase and other inflammatory states in HepG2 cells by Northern blot analysis and on TAFI promoter activity by transient transfection into HepG2 cells with luciferase reporter plasmids harboring the TAFI 5′-flanking region.[139] These observations may have a direct impact on the pathogenesis of both the acute and chronic events leading to ischemic and occlusive processes that are involved in the pathogenesis of acute coronary syndromes and ischemic and thrombotic vascular deficit.

Elevated TAFI levels have been found in men with symptomatic coronary artery disease.[140] TAFI is also reported to be a risk factor for deep venous thrombosis (DVT). A recent report on the high levels of TAFI in the acute phase of ischemic stroke revealed not only the high levels but an incremental increase in TAFI with the degree of neurologic deterioration.[141] Therefore, the observation on the acute-phase nature of this protein requires further validation. In addition, it has been stated that there is a correlation between TAFI levels and cardiovascular risk factors.[142] Animal models may be needed to truly validate studies on TAFI upregulation and its relation to thrombosis.

■ ABNORMAL HEMOSTASIS

There are a number of conditions that can contribute to states of abnormal hemostasis. Many of these have medical implications, and the vascular surgeon or vascular medicine specialist will not likely encounter them primarily. These include thrombotic thrombocytopenic purpura, hemolytic-uremic syndrome, alloimmune thrombocytopenia, drug-induced thrombocytopenia, and immune thrombocytopenic purpura. In this section, we concentrate on the conditions that the vascular specialist will likely encounter.

Heparin-Induced Thrombocytopenia

Heparin-induced thrombocytopenia (HIT) occurs in approximately 5% of patients receiving heparin for at least 5 days. The diagnosis of this condition is clinical. Platelet counts drop below 100,000/μL or there is more than a 50% drop of the baseline platelet count following the administration of heparin. This occurs independent of the route of administration and is not associated with any other explanation for the thrombocytopenia. Some of the patients developing HIT go on to develop heparin-induced thrombocytopenia/thrombosis syndrome (HITTS). The incidence of HIT or HITTS may be lower with LMWHs; however, the cross-reactivity of the LMWHs can cause HIT. Although the incidence of HIT is approximately 5%, the morbidity and mortality rates are so high that failure to diagnose early can result in catastrophic complications.[143,144] The terminology *HIT type I* is used to indicate HIT via nonimmune platelet-activating mechanism. *HIT type II* is indicated for immune-mediated syndrome. The pathophysiology of HIT is still not completely understood. It is hypothesized that binding of heparin complexes to platelets triggers the platelet activation. The IgG antibodies react with a complex of heparin and platelet factor 4 forming an immune complex, which binds to an unknown site on the platelet surface. The platelet activation is triggered when the Fc portion of the IgG antibody bound to the heparin–platelet factor 4 complex reacts with the Fc receptor on adjacent platelets.[145] The laboratory testing for confirmation of HIT diagnosis can be performed by platelet aggregation, serotonin release, enzyme-linked immunosorbent assay (ELISA) (platelet IgG), ELISA (platelet factor 4-heparin), platelet activation, and lumi-aggregometry. Once the diagnosis is confirmed, heparin administration in any form should be completely stopped.

The U.S. Food and Drug Administration (FDA) has approved argatroban and recombinant hirudin to be used as alternate anticoagulants in such patients. Although antihirudin antibodies may be formed that can neutralize hirudin, jeopardizing the anticoagulant management, no such antibodies have been detected with the use of argatroban in HIT patients. Overlap of parenteral and oral anticoagulation may be required to avoid paradoxical hypercoagulable complications of warfarin. Antithrombin drugs are known to prolong the International Normalized Ratio (INR). However, danaparoid does not interfere with the INR. In patients with HIT, warfarin should not be started until the patient is adequately anticoagulated and the platelet count has risen above 100,000/μL with a parenteral anticoagulant such as danaparoid, argatroban, or recombinant hirudin. Rising of the platelet count to 100,000/μL indicates that the patient is responding to the alternate anticoagulant. For patients in whom HIT has not been diagnosed until treatment with warfarin has commenced, it is advised to stop the warfarin, since it prolongs both the INR and aPTT. In this case, suboptimal anticoagulation with antithrombin drugs may result due to aPTT-based monitoring. Furthermore, aPTT is not a specific test for the monitoring of direct thrombin inhibitors. Instead, ecarin clotting time should be used in the monitoring of antithrombin drugs. In patients treated with danaparoid, there is no need to stop warfarin since danaparoid does not interfere with the INR. For patients who are on recombinant hirudin and where initiation of warfarin is required, it is recommended to reduce the dose of hirudin until the aPTT is at the lower end of the therapeutic range before starting warfarin.[146]

Thrombocytosis

Platelet counts higher than 400,000/μL are referred to as *thrombocytosis*. Thrombocytosis is classified as being either primary or secondary. Primary thrombocytosis, or essential thrombocythemia, is associated with chronic myeloproliferative disorders such as chronic myeloid leukemia, polycythemia vera, and agnogenic myeloid metaplasia. Exclusion-based diagnosis of essential thrombocythemia is made when patients present with characteristic findings of autonomous proliferation of platelets by megakaryocytes or by the presence of megakaryocytes that are hypersensitive to thrombopoietin.[147] Thrombopoietin binds to the c-Mpl receptors on the surface of platelet membranes, and is first internalized and then degraded.[148] The salient features of essential thrombocythemia include platelet count higher than 600,000/μL, hemoglobin level of 13 g/dL, failure of iron supplementation to normalize the platelet count, absence of Philadelphia chromosome, and collagen fibrosis without splenomegaly and leukoerythroblastosis and no known cause for reactive thrombocytosis.[149] Cytoreductive therapy with hydroxyurea; anagrelide; interferon α; alkylating agents such as busulfan, chlorambucil, pipobroman and thiotepa; radioactive phosphorus; or plateletpheresis is indicated for patients who are likely to develop thrombosis or bleeding. Smoking cessation and proper management of diabetes and hypertension are important in the management of hypercoagulability. Secondary, or reactive, thrombocytosis due to increased megakaryocyte production of platelets is stimulated by various cytokines, including IL-1, IL-3, IL-6, and IL-11, and is more commonly seen than the primary. Although increased levels of IL-1, IL-6, IL-4, and C-reactive protein are found in secondary thrombocytosis, normal levels are found in primary thrombocytosis.[150-152]

Qualitative platelet disorders are defined as both the congenital and acquired disorders of platelet function. Congenital disorders of platelet function include defects in platelet-vessel wall interaction (von Willebrand's disease with deficiency of von Willebrand's factor) and Bernard-Soulier syndrome (defect in GP-Ib), disorders of aggregation, disorders of platelet secretion and signal transduction, abnormalities in arachidonic acid pathways, and disorders of platelet coagulant-protein interaction. Bernard-Soulier syndrome is an autosomal recessive disorder due to abnormality in platelet GP-Ib–factor IX-V complex that mediates the binding of von Willebrand's factor to platelets during adhesion, Glanzmann's thrombasthenia is an autosomal recessive disorder characterized by impaired platelet aggregation, a prolonged bleeding time, and mucocutaneous bleeding.

The acquired disorders of platelet function arise by different mechanisms. In most of the conditions the mechanisms of platelet dysfunction are not understood. Several disorders may result from disorders in platelet adhesion, aggregation, secretion, and platelet coagulant activities. In myeloproliferative disorders including essential thrombocythemia, polycythemia vera, chronic myelogenous leukemia, and agnogenic myeloid dysplasia, the platelet abnormalities result from their generation from an abnormal clone of stem cells or secondary to enhanced platelet activation resulting in qualitative platelet defects, leading to bleeding and thromboembolic complications. Conditions in which acquired disorders of platelet function are recognized include uremia, acute leukemia and myelodysplastic syndrome, dysproteinemias, cardiopulmonary bypass, acquired von Willebrand's disease, acquired storage pool disease, liver disease, antiplatelet antibodies, and drugs.

Several disorders of coagulation factors and fibrinolysis have been identified that lead to thrombosis or bleeding. These include von Willebrand's disease, hemophilia, coagulation factor deficiencies, acquired or congenital inhibitors of coagulation, and antiphospholipid syndrome.

A number of other conditions are mentioned only because they are referred to in other chapters. Von Willebrand's disease, hemophilia, and factor deficiency states are discussed in Chapter 33, whereas antiphospholipid syndrome is well described in Chapter 34.

Thrombotic Disorders

The thrombotic disorders include atherothrombosis, endothelial dysfunction, hypercoagulable states, and the thrombophilias. Atherothrombosis or atherosclerosis is a systemic disease of the vessel wall that occurs in the aorta, carotid, coronary, and peripheral arteries. Inflammatory response is mediated by macrophages and T lymphocytes with continued smooth muscle cell proliferation. The levels of endothelin (ET)-1, an extremely potent smooth muscle cell mitogen, acting through Gi protein-coupled ET_A and ET_B receptors are increased in atherosclerosis.[153] ET blockade inhibits fatty streak formation and restores nitric oxide-mediated endothelial function. Nitric oxide may promote smooth muscle cell apoptosis. Recently, it was shown that the plasma levels of inflammatory markers were higher in patients with coronary artery disease and peripheral arterial disease than in patients with coronary artery disease alone.[154] Although increased levels of C-reactive protein are linked to increased cardiovascular risk, the coexistence of peripheral arterial disease adds additional risk of mortality to coronary artery disease patients. Besides the C-reactive protein, other markers of inflammation include cell adhesion molecules, cytokines, and proatherogenic enzymes. The T-786 endothelial nitric oxide synthase genotype has recently been reported in the Genetic and Environmental Factors in Coronary Atherosclerosis (GENICA) study as a novel risk factor for coronary artery disease in whites.[155] Nitric oxide, a major mediator of endothelium-dependent vasodilatation, made in the endothelium by endothelial nitric oxide synthase, not only plays a key role in the regulation of vascular tone and blood pressure but is also involved in atherogenesis. The stable plaque becomes vulnerable when the fibrous cap is thin and the plaque is in imminent danger of rupture. Once ruptured, the procoagulant material released would cause thrombosis.

The endothelium is the largest endocrine, paracrine, and autocrine gland known. The endothelium plays a key role in vascular homeostasis. Endothelial activation or endothelial dysfunction results in increased expression of adhesion molecules such as E-selectin, intercellular adhesion molecule 1, and vascular cell adhesion molecule 1. Endothelial dysfunction also leads to increased production of monocyte chemotactic protein 1, IL-8, platelet-derived growth factor, and mononuclear cell-stimulating factor. The endothelial cells serve regulatory functions in maintaining vascular integrity. Therefore, with endothelial dysfunction there is a disturbance in these regulatory functions leading to vasospasm, thrombosis, inflammation, intimal growth, plaque activation, and plaque rupture and resulting in atherothrombosis, ischemia, and infarction. Endothelial dysfunction is associated with aging, atherosclerosis, and associated conditions such as hyperhomocysteinemia, infectious diseases, inflammatory cytokines, vascular injury, ischemia, and reperfusion. Although endothelial dysfunction causes downregulation of nitric oxide leading to vasoconstriction, platelet adhesion, vascular smooth muscle cell proliferation, and leukocyte adhesion, expression of adhesion molecules results in monocyte adhesion, foam cell formation, and plaque inflammation. Endothelial dysfunction also leads to decreased prostacyclin and production of ET and carbon monoxide. Furthermore, endothelial dysfunction also causes decreased tissue plasminogen activator and PAI-1 leading to impaired fibrinolysis. Understanding of the earliest changes in endothelial dysfunction may provide strategies to modulate them in a timely fashion. Reversing endothelial dysfunction reduces the risk of cardiovascular disease. Newer therapies known to improve endothelial function have been advocated, including lipid-lowering therapy, smoking cessation, exercise, angiotensin-converting enzyme inhibitors, hormone replacement therapy, angiotensin receptor blockers, control of blood glucose in diabetics, and combination antioxidants.[156] The recently commenced Multiethnic Study of Atherosclerosis (MESA) will evaluate some the predictive value of several measures of endothelial dysfunction and other markers of atherosclerosis.[157] The precise mechanism of endothelial dysfunction remains to be elucidated.

Hypercoagulable states, which can be inherited or acquired, are discussed in detail in Chapter 34, whereas disseminated intravascular coagulation is discussed in Chapter 33.

Hemostatic Problems During and After Pregnancy

The inherited bleeding disorders include von Willebrand's disease, the less common factor deficiencies, and inherited platelet disorders. The acquired disorders that manifest before the pregnancy include immune thrombocytopenic purpura and clotting factor inhibitors. The conditions that are associated with pregnancy are disseminated intravascular coagulation and the hemolysis with elevated liver functions and low platelets (HELLP) syndrome. Obstetric complications include placenta previa, abruptio placentae, ectopic pregnancy, abortion, miscarriage, and retained products of conception. Normal pregnancy is a procoagulant state with altered coagulation and fibrinolysis. Concentrations of some coagulation factors and also PAI-1 increase. Factor VIII and von Willebrand's factor increase steadily during the pregnancy.[158] Since HELLP invariably leads to postpartum complications and thrombosis, heparin administration postpartum is considered reasonable. The risk of venous thromboembolic events in pregnant women is approximately six times greater than in nonpregnant women, amounting to greater morbidity and mortality during pregnancy and puerperium. Untreated DVT resulting in pulmonary embolism, occurring in approximately 16%, is the most common cause of maternal mortality.[159]

Thrombotic and Embolic Disorders

Twenty-five percent of thrombophilic patients develop thrombosis at unusual sites resulting in cerebral venous thrombosis, mesenteric vein thrombosis, hepatic venous thrombosis, retinal vein thrombosis, purpura fulminans, splenic vein thrombosis, portal vein thrombosis, renal vein thrombosis, and axillary vein thrombosis. The thrombotic disorders may involve inflammatory and other localized factors that contribute to the vascular deficit. In addition, embolic events also play a role in the development of these thrombotic complications.

Sepsis

Sepsis, a systemic inflammatory syndrome, is a response to infection, and when it is associated with multiorgan dysfunction, it is termed *severe sepsis*. It remains a leading cause of mortality in the critically ill. The response to the invading microorganisms may be considered as a balance between a proinflammatory and an anti-inflammatory reaction. Although inadequate proinflammatory reaction and a strong anti-inflammatory response could lead to overwhelming infection and the death of the patient, a strong and uncontrolled proinflammatory response, manifested by the release of proinflammatory mediators, may lead to microvascular thrombosis and multiorgan failure. Endotoxin triggers sepsis via the release of various mediators such as TNF-α and IL-1. These cytokines activate the complement and coagulation systems, release adhesion molecules, prostaglandins, leukotrienes, reactive oxygen species, and nitric oxide. Other mediators involved in sepsis syndrome include IL-6 and IL-8, arachidonic acid metabolites, platelet-activating factor, histamine, bradykinin, angiotensin, complement components, and vasoactive intestinal peptide. These inflammatory responses are counteracted by IL-10. Most of the trials targeting the different mediators of the proinflammatory response have failed due to a lack of a correct definition of sepsis. Understanding the exact pathophysiology of the disease will enable more advanced treatment options. Targeting the coagulation system with various anticoagulant agents, including activated protein C, and TFPI is a rational approach. Many clinical trials have been conducted to evaluate these agents in severe sepsis. Although trials on antithrombin and TFPI were not too successful, the double-blind, placebo-controlled phase III trial of recombinant human activated protein C, Worldwide Evaluation in Severe Sepsis (PROWESS), was more successful, with a significant decrease in mortality when compared to the placebo group. A better understanding of the pathophysiologic mechanism of severe sepsis will provide better treatment options, and combination antithrombotic treatment may provide a multipronged approach for the treatment of severe sepsis.

HIV- and AIDS-Associated Thrombocytopenia and Thrombosis

A serious complication of human immunodeficiency virus (HIV) infection is HIV-associated thrombocytopenia. This results from immune-mediated platelet destruction and decreased and defective platelet production due to infection of megakaryocytes with HIV-1.[160] HIV-related thrombocytopenia may have an accelerated progression to acquired immunodeficiency syndrome (AIDS) and decreased survival rates. Hence, management of thrombocytopenia in AIDS patients is crucial to prevent severe complications. Severe bleeding complications in HIV-infected hemophilia patients treated with protease inhibitors is quite frequent. Ritonavir, indinavir, and saquinavir have been associated with this increased bleeding due to inhibition of cytochrome P450, which plays an important role in arachidonic acid metabolism interfering with platelet function. The frequency of thrombosis in HIV patients is 2.6/1000 patient-years. Leg swellings or tenderness should be evaluated by Doppler ultrasound to clear the doubt of thrombosis. Anticoagulants are generally well tolerated by HIV patients. Prophylactic anticoagulants may be left at the discretion of the clinician. AIDS-associated thrombotic microangiopathy may be managed by reducing the amounts of circulating von Willebrand's factor. Plasma infusion or exchange using fresh frozen plasma, cryoprecipitate-depleted fraction of plasma (cryosupernatant), or solvent/detergent-treated plasma for replacement may be considered as the treatment of choice of thrombotic thrombocytopenic purpura.[161]

Neuraxial Anesthesia and Anticoagulation

Regional anesthesia and analgesia comprise central neuraxial (epidural or spinal) and peripheral nerve block. The most serious complication of neuraxial block is spinal hematoma and the resulting paraplegia. Based on the pharmacokinetic and pharmacodynamic data of a particular antithrombotic drug, the hematologist can formulate a dosage strategy that minimizes the risk of thrombosis and bleeding and at the same time provides the most appropriate anesthesia and analgesia. Enoxaparin, a LMWH, was approved in the United States for the prophylaxis of venous thromboembolism after total hip replacement surgery. Several cases of spinal hematomas were reported with neuraxial anesthesia.[162] The incidence of spinal hematoma due to enoxaparin is estimated to be 1 in 3100 continuous epidural anesthetics and 1 in 4100 spinal anesthetics.[163] The median age of the patients was 78 years, and 78% were women. Some patients had some preexisting spinal abnormalities, and a third was using nonsteroidal anti-inflammatory agents (NSAIDs). It is well known that NSAIDS impair hemostasis. Despite the frequent use of neuraxial anesthesia in Germany, the reported incidence of spinal hematoma is low.[164,165] LMWH is increasingly being used as "bridging" therapy for chronically anticoagulated patients who need anticoagulation reversal for an operative procedure. Neuraxial anesthesia should be well timed and delayed for at least 24 hours after the last subcutaneous administration of LMWH. For patients with renal dysfunction (≥ 2.0 serum creatinine levels), the LMWH clearance is delayed. Hence neuraxial anesthesia should be delayed longer for these patients such that the anti-Xa level is not higher than 0.1 IU/mL.

Table 30-1 Incidence of DVT in Various Patient Groups

PATIENT GROUP	DVT INCIDENCE, %
Stroke	56
Elective hip replacement	51
Multiple trauma	50
Total knee replacement	47
Hip fracture	45
Retropubic prostatectomy	32
General surgery	25
Spinal cord injury	35
Neurosurgery	22
Gynecologic surgery, malignancy	22
Myocardial infarction	22
General medical	17
Gynecologic surgery	14
Geriatric	9
Transurethral prostatectomy	9

DVT, deep venous thrombosis.

Data from Collins R, Scrimgeour A, Yusuf S, Peto R: Reduction in fatal pulmonary embolism and venous thrombosis by perioperative administration of subcutaneous heparin: Overview of results of randomized trials in general, orthopedic, and urologic surgery. N Engl J Med 318:1162-1173, 1988.

Inferior Vena Caval Interventions in Thromboembolic Disease

Inferior vena caval filters were designed to prevent a thrombus embolizing from the deep veins of the legs to the pulmonary vessel causing pulmonary embolism. Pulmonary embolism is the third leading cause of death in the United States. Most filters are placed in the inferior vena cava, but they may also be placed in the superior vena cava. Anticoagulation is used to treat the underlying DVT and to prevent the hypercoagulable state and the development of clots in the filter. Temporary filters are being evaluated for their safety. There might be some patients who cannot for some reason receive the anticoagulation, and for such patients these temporary filters may be placed until anticoagulation becomes safe for them. The tethered filters and the retrievable filters are the two main temporary filters available. Temporary filters with trapped emboli may pose a problem. Lysis of the thrombus before removal of the thrombus and placement of a permanent filter above the temporary one may be tried.

Surgery and Thrombosis

Surgery and trauma could increase the risk of thrombosis up to 100-fold. Patients with thrombophilic conditions are more prone to develop postsurgical thrombosis, whereas hemophiliac patients may bleed profusely from surgical interventions. Tables 30-1 to 30-4 provide data from the International Consensus Statement on patients who undergo surgical interventions and the relative risk of thromboembolic complications.[166-169] Several factors contribute to this risk, which is increased by age, obesity, malignancy, thrombophilic states, varicose vein, and previous history of thrombosis. This risk is also increased by the duration of surgery, type of anesthetic used, presurgical and postsurgical immobility, level of hydration, and the presence of sepsis and inflammation.[170] Results of the studies in patients who have undergone general surgery and arthroplasty indicate

Table 30-2 Frequency of Proximal DVT in the Absence of Prophylaxis Diagnosed by Surveillance with Objective Methods*

PATIENT GROUP	DVT INCIDENCE, %
General surgery	6.9
Elective hip surgery	23
Total knee replacement	7.6

*Fibrinogen uptake test or phlebography.
DVT, deep venous thrombosis.

Date from Clagett GP, Reisch JS: Prevention of venous thromboembolism in general surgical patients: Results of meta-analysis. Ann Surg 208:227-240, 1988.

Table 30-3 Frequency of Clinical Pulmonary Embolism in the Absence of Prophylaxis

PATIENT GROUP	DVT INCIDENCE, %
General surgery	1.6
Elective hip surgery	4
Traumatic orthopedic surgery	6.9

DVT, deep venous thrombosis.

Data from Bergentz SE: Dextran in the prophylaxis of pulmonary embolism. World J Surg 2:19-25, 1978; Colditz GA, Tuden RL, Oster G: Rates of venous thrombosis after general surgery: Combined results of randomised clinical trials. Lancet 2:143-146, 1986; and Gallus AS: Anticoagulants in the prevention of venous thromboembolism. Baillieres Clin Haematol 3:651-684, 1990.

Table 30-4 Frequency of Fatal Pulmonary Embolism Without Prophylaxis

PATIENT GROUP	DVT INCIDENCE, %
General surgery	0.87
Elective hip surgery	1.65
Fractured neck of femur	4.0

DVT, deep venous thrombosis.

Data from Bergentz SE: Dextran in the prophylaxis of pulmonary embolism. World J Surg 2:19-25, 1978; Colditz GA, Tuden RL, Oster G: Rates of venous thrombosis after general surgery: Combined results of randomised clinical trials. Lancet 2:143-146, 1986; and Gallus AS: Anticoagulants in the prevention of venous thromboembolism. Baillieres Clin Haematol 3:651-684, 1990.

that the thrombotic risk remains even after hospital discharge. Thus, prolonged thromboprophylaxis with anticoagulants may decrease the venographically detected DVT.

Pharmacologic Management of Thrombosis

Over the past decade, interest in anticoagulant and thrombolytic drugs has grown dramatically as evidenced by a continual increase in the number of drugs introduced for both preclinical and clinical development.[171,172] These drugs include the new heparins, synthetic heparinomimetic agents, antithrombin agents, anti-Xa agents, biotechnology-derived antithrombotic proteins, antiplatelet drugs, and novel thrombolytic agents. The newer drugs represent a wide array of chemical and biologic classes with both structural and functional diversity, as shown in Figure 30-3. The outstanding scientific research and development activities in the academic centers and pharmaceutical industry have resulted in a steady flow of many of the new products.

Third-party validation of developed products and extensive clinical trials have been carried out globally to validate the claims on the safety and efficacy of the newer drugs. The results of these studies constitute a significant portion of the progress reported at various scientific forums. Through their fast track and revised policies, the regulatory bodies such as the European Medicine Evaluation Agency, the FDA, and other regional agencies have continually contributed to the timely evaluation and approval of new drugs by providing input at various stages of drug development. Such close interactions have clarified various issues related to drug development and in fact have accelerated the approval process of many new drugs such as LMWHs, synthetic heparin pentasaccharide (fondaparinux [Arixtra]), newer antithrombin agents, and activated protein C (Xigris). Many of the new antiplatelet drugs and thrombolytic agents have also gained approval for multiple indications. The concept of polytherapy including combination of different drugs has been introduced.

Owing to the dramatic development and the relatively defined chemical and biologic profile of the newer drugs, it is now widely believed that the conventional anticoagulants such as the heparins, warfarin, and aspirin will eventually be replaced by newer drugs. This is partly due to the problems with their use and the associated adverse reactions.

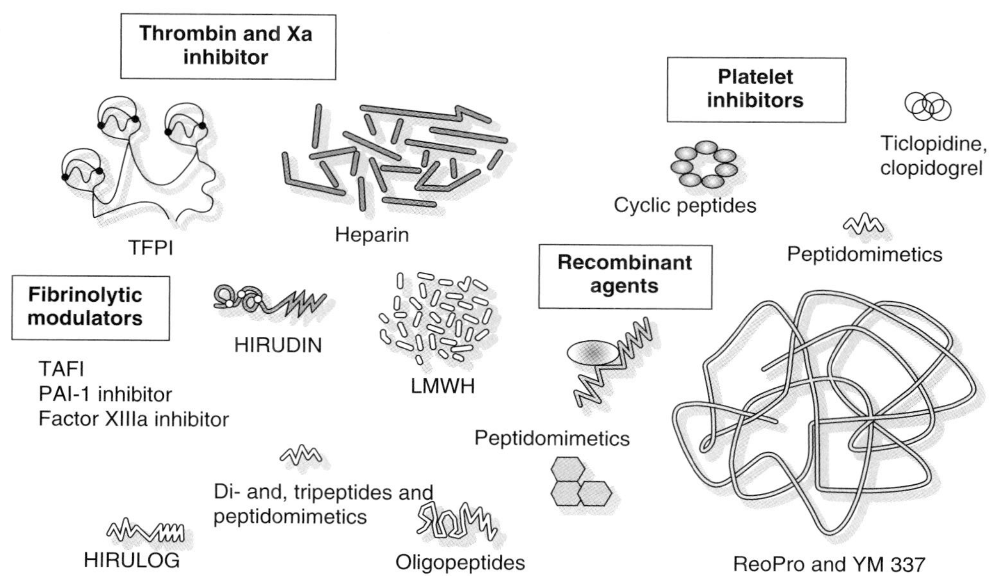

FIGURE 30-3 Anticoagulant and antithrombotic drugs. TFPI, tissue factor pathway inhibitor; LMWH, low-molecular-weight heparin; TAFI, thrombin-activatable fibrinolytic inhibitor; PAI-1, plasminogen activator inhibitor-1.

Unfractionated heparin has been in use for nearly 50 years. It is the only anticoagulant drug with an antidote. In many countries this anticoagulant still remains the main drug for the anticoagulant management of thrombosis.

The use of unfractionated heparin has been optimized by developing the LMWHs. Therefore, the LMWHs actually represent an optimized use of heparin. This is mainly due to our current understanding of the chemistry and biology of heparin. Antithrombin drugs such as hirudin, argatroban, and hirulog have been in development for many years. These drugs are useful as a substitute for heparin in such conditions as HIT; however, they do not have any antidote and cannot be used for surgical indications at this time. The anti-Xa drugs and the heparinomimetics do not have any direct effect on thrombin and produce minimal anticoagulant effects; therefore, these drugs may or may not be useful in the management of patients who have heparin compromise, and the long-term use of these agents requires further clinical validation. Heparin represents a polytherapeutic drug, but the newer drugs are usually monotherapeutic. Thus, their indications will be somewhat limited.

The oral anticoagulant drugs such as warfarin have been in use for the management of thrombotic and cardiovascular disorders for more than 40 years. Response variation, need for monitoring, and delayed onset/cessation are some of the problems associated with its use. More recently, the oral antithrombin drugs, such as ximelagatran, have been developed as potential substitutes for warfarin. Although this agent has been shown to be effective and in some cases not inferior to warfarin, its use has been associated with an increase in liver enzyme levels, and this agent passes the placental and blood-brain barriers. Furthermore, the thrombin inhibitors may compromise the regulatory function of this enzyme.

Aspirin has been in clinical use for more than 100 years. The antiplatelet effect of this agent was recognized about 40 years ago. Since then aspirin has been a life-saving drug for several types of thrombotic indications. Several newer formulations of aspirin have been developed. It now represents a universal antithrombotic drug in both thrombotic and cardiovascular indications. The newly developed cyclooxygenase inhibitors represent some specific effects of aspirin and may or may not exhibit the potential therapeutic effects in thrombosis. As a matter of fact, due to the specificity of these agents, they exhibit thrombotic complications. Table 30-5 shows a comparison between aspirin and ADP receptor inhibitors. In comparison with aspirin, the ADP receptor inhibitors are single-target drugs. The selective ADP receptors, when combined with aspirin, exhibit superior efficacy compared with monotherapy. However, their clinical spectrum without aspirin will be limited, and the same is true for the phosphodiesterase inhibitors.

Table 30-5 Aspirin Versus ADP Receptor Inhibitors

ASPIRIN	ADP RECEPTOR INHIBITOR
Polypharmacologic effects	Single-receptor targeting agent
Produces both platelets and vascular effects	Produces only platelet-mediated responses
Multiple actions (analgesic, anti-inflammatory)	Produces only inhibition of platelets

ADP, adenosine diphosphate.

The coming years will witness dramatic developments in the management of thrombotic and cardiovascular disorders. Synthetic and recombinant approaches will provide cost-effective and clinically useful drugs. LMWHs and synthetic heparin analogs are expected to have significant effects on the overall management of thrombotic and cardiovascular disorders. Factors such as managed care, regulatory issues, polytherapy, and combined pharmacologic and mechanical approaches will redirect the focus in management of DVT, myocardial infarction, and thrombotic stroke. The direct antithrombin agents such as hirudin and bivalirudin (Angiomax) will be of great value for surgical anticoagulation and various acute indications. Postsurgical control of thrombotic processes may require combination therapy and heparin-derived agents such as pentasaccharide and non-heparin glycosaminoglycans such as dermatan sulfate. Biotechnology-derived heparin analogs will also be developed as potential replacements for heparins.

It is now widely believed that the days for the classic anticoagulants are numbered, and in the foreseeable future these drugs may not exist. However, this is not the case when one reads the recommendations of the American College of Chest Physicians (ACCP) and the approval labels for the drugs.[173] Considering the results of several new clinical trials, the ACCP and the International Union of Angiology consensus conferences on antithrombotic therapy have included definitive recommendations on the clinical effectiveness of the classic drugs in both arterial and venous diseases. In addition, these recommendations include specific guidelines on additional indications for these drugs. Thus, it is highly likely that heparin, warfarin, and aspirin will continue to be important drugs in the treatment of hematologic and oncologic disorders for some time.

When the classic anticoagulants are described in some of the recent publications, they are often labeled as "bad" drugs with many adverse effects. In fact, the classic anticoagulants may not have any more adverse effects than the new drugs. Needless to say, all pharmacologic agents have their limitations. Heparin, aspirin, and warfarin certainly have issues, some of which have already been addressed, and improvements have been made.

The development of LMWHs is an example of the optimized use of a pharmacologic agent. Their use has nearly eliminated the risk of HIT, and these drugs have achieved standard of care status for many venous and arterial thrombosis indications. LMWHs have gradually replaced heparin in subcutaneous indications and are currently being examined for their effectiveness as surgical and interventional anticoagulation. Improved monitoring and dosage optimization are currently being pursued. Another example is the Stroke Prevention Using Oral Thrombin Inhibitors in Atrial Fibrillation (SPORTIF) trial in which the oral anticoagulant warfarin was found to be essentially equivalent to the new oral antithrombin agent ximelagatran, but without risk of significant bleeding. Moreover, warfarin use was not associated with elevation of liver enzyme levels.

Despite the reported problem of HIT, heparin has remained the drug of choice for surgical anticoagulation.

Table 30-6 Key Questions on the Fate of Conventional Anticoagulants and Antithrombotics

QUESTION	ANSWER
Will aspirin be replaced by newer antiplatelet drugs or drug combinations?	No—aspirin will remain the no. 1 antiplatelet drug for some time
Will warfarin be replaced by oral antithrombin and anti-Xa agents?	Only in some qualified indications
Will unfractionated heparin use be obsolete in the near future?	Unlikely—it will remain an anticoagulant of choice for surgical and interventional use

This is due to the high bleeding risk associated with the new antithrombin agents when used at higher doses coupled with the lack of an antagonist. To the contrary, the heparin-protamine combination has been used with much success for many years. Therefore, currently unfractionated heparin is the only reliable anticoagulant that can be used in surgical and interventional indications.

Thrombosis is a polycomponent syndrome that optimally requires a multitarget therapeutic approach. However, with the advanced understanding of the molecular and vascular biology of thrombotic disorders, only monotherapeutic drugs that have a single target of action have been developed. These monotherapeutic agents such as fondaparinux, ximelagatran, and clopidogrel are molecularly and functionally defined. Their applications have been validated in well-designed, sponsored clinical trials for specific indications. But, like the classic drugs, these new drugs were also found to have adverse effects. Bleeding and lack of dose response as well as monitoring and antidotes for overdosage remain problematic issues.

Table 30-6 shows some of the key questions on the fate of these conventional drugs. Conventional drugs such as heparin, oral anticoagulants, and aspirin will remain the "gold standard" despite their known drawbacks. They require further optimization and can be used for various indications in a cost-effective manner. The newer drugs, however, provide alternatives that in the next few years may lead to improved, cost-compliant treatments. The actions of the non-anticoagulant drugs such as the cholesterol-lowering agents (statins), specific inhibitors of cyclooxygenase, drugs capable of donating nitric oxide or upregulating its mediators, and drugs modulating endothelial function will also impact the combination therapy of thrombotic and cardiovascular diseases.

■ SUMMARY

The process of blood coagulation is no longer considered to be a simple transformation of fibrinogen to fibrin by the action of thrombin. Rather, this remarkably complex process is a result of several transformations that are mediated by enzymes, activators, inhibitors, and cellular contributors. The process of coagulation contributes significantly to thrombogenesis; however, it is no longer considered to be the sole event. The role of platelets, leukocytes, and endothelial cells has gradually been accepted to be crucial in the overall regulation of thrombogenesis.

Surgical interventions inflict a major stimulus for coagulation through the release of large amounts of tissue factor, enzyme, and platelet activation from the extracorporeal circulation and endothelial distress resulting in a procoagulant environment. This necessitates the use of anticoagulant and antithrombotic agents to keep blood coagulation under control. The understanding of the activation processes has led to the development of newer approaches to inhibit the coagulation process. Furthermore, the physiologic means such as hypothermia and blood salvage techniques have added to the restoration approaches during cardiovascular surgical procedures. Endogenous inhibitors such as antithrombin, protein C, and TFPI have also played a major role in the control of thrombogenesis. Heparin and warfarin have been crucial in controlling the thrombotic process both during and after surgical procedures. Alternate anticoagulant drug development will continue to provide new drugs to control the coagulation process. However, clinical studies on the long-term safety and efficacy will be needed prior to replacement of the conventional anticoagulants such as heparin and oral anticoagulant drugs.

Bleeding risk is also a major factor contributing to the mortality and morbidity in patients undergoing surgical procedures. Appropriate hemostatic measures, optimized use of anticoagulants, and identification of predisposing factors in a given patient may be helpful in minimizing surgical bleeding. The available plasma-derived hemostatic factor, recombinant factors VIII and VIIa, and antifibrinolytic agents such as aprotinin and lysine analogs (epsilon-aminocaproic and tranexamic acid) are useful in the control of surgical bleeding.

Advances in both the molecular understanding of the hemostatic process and the pathogenesis of hemostatic disorders leading to the application of genomics and proteomics will have a major impact on the risk stratification of surgical patients and profiling their potential bleeding and thrombotic complications. This will also be helpful in tailoring the use of anticoagulant and prohemostatic agents to facilitate improved clinical outcome.

■ REFERENCES

1. Bevers EM, Rosing J, Zwaal RFA: Development of procoagulant binding sites on the platelet surface. In Westweek J, Scully MF, McIntyre DE, Kakkar VV (eds): Mechanisms of Stimulus Response Coupling in Platelets. New York, Plenum Press, 1986, pp 359-372.
2. Davie EW, Ratnoff OD: Waterfall sequence for intrinsic blood clotting. Science 145:1310-1312, 1964.
3. MacFarlane RG: An enzyme cascade in the blood clotting mechanism and its function as a biochemical amplifier. Nature 202:498-499, 1964.
4. Osterud B, Rapaport SI: Activation of factor IX by the reaction product of tissue factor and factor VII: Additional pathway for initiating blood coagulation. Proc Natl Acad Sci U S A 74:5260-5264, 1977.
5. Scully MF: The biochemistry of blood clotting: The digestion of a liquid to form a solid. Essays Biochem 27:17-36, 1992.
6. Hemker HC, Kessels H: Feedback mechanisms in coagulation. Haemostasis 21:189-196, 1991.
7. Mann KG, Jerry RJ, Krishnaswamy S: Cofactor proteins in the assembly of blood clotting enzyme complexes. Annu Rev Biochem 57:915-956, 1988.
8. Hogg DH, Blomback B: The fibrinogen-thrombin reaction. Thromb Diath Haemorrh 34:328, 1975.

9. Blomback B, Vestermark A: Isolation of fibrinopeptides by chromatography. Arkiv Kemi 12:173-182, 1958.
10. Shainoff JR, Dardik BN: Fibrinopeptide B and aggregation of fibrinogen. Science 204:200-202, 1979.
11. Laurent TC, Blomback B: On the significance of the release of two different peptides from fibrinogen during clotting. Acta Chem Scand 12:1875-1877, 1958.
12. Coughlin SR, Vu TKH, Hung DT, Wheaton VI: Characterization of a functional thrombin receptor: Issues and opportunities. Clin Invest 89:351-353, 1992.
13. Esmon CT: The roles of protein C and thrombomodulin in the regulation of blood coagulation. J Biol Chem 264:4743-4761, 1989.
14. Olsen ST, Bjork I: Regulation of thrombin activity by antithrombin and heparin. In Berliner LJ (ed): Thrombin: Structure and Function. New York, Plenum Press, 1992, pp 159-217.
15. Bach R, Konigsberg W, Nemerson Y: Human tissue factor contains thioester linked palmitate and stearate on the cytoplasmic half cystine. Biochemistry 27:4227-4231, 1988.
16. McVey JH: Tissue factor pathway. Baillieres Clin Haematol 7:469-484, 1994.
17. Morrissey JH, Mack BG, Neuenschwander PF, Comp PC: Quantitation of activated factor VII levels in plasma using a tissue factor mutant selectively deficient in promoting factor VII activation. Blood 81:734-744, 1993.
18. Edgington TS, Mackman N, Brand K, et al: The structural biology of the expression and function of tissue factor. Thromb Haemost 66:67, 1991.
19. Nemerson Y: Tissue factor and haemostasis. Blood 71:1-8, 1988.
20. Mann KG, Nesheim ME, Church WR, et al: Surface-dependent reactions of the vitamin K-dependent enzyme complexes. Blood 76: 1-16, 1990.
21. Naito K, Fujikawa K: Activation of human blood coagulation factor XI independent of factor XII: Factor XI is activated by thrombin and factor XIa in the presence of negatively charged surfaces. J Biol Chem 66:7353-7358, 1991.
22. Gailani D, Broze GJ: Factor XI activation in a revised model of blood coagulation. Science 253:909-912, 1991.
23. Packham MA: Role of platelets in thrombosis and hemostasis. Can J Physiol Pharmacol 72:278-284, 1994.
24. Kaplan KL: Platelet granule proteins: Localization and secretion. In Gordon AS (ed): Platelets in Biology and Pathology, Vol 5. Amsterdam, Elsevier, 1981, p 77.
25. Holmsen H: Platelet secretion. In Colman RW, Hirsh J, Marder VJ, Salzman EW (eds): Hemostasis and Thrombosis. Philadelphia, Lippincott, 1987, p 606.
26. Niewiarowski S, Holt JC: Biochemistry and physiology of secreted platelet proteins. In Colman RW, Hirsh J, Marder VJ, Salzman EW (eds): Hemostasis and Thrombosis. Philadelphia, Lippincott, 1987, pp 618-630.
27. Coller B: Platelets in cardiovascular thrombosis and thrombolysis. In Fozzard UA, Haber E, Jennings RB, Katz AM, Morgan HE (eds): The Heart and Cardiovascular System, 2nd ed. New York, Raven Press, 1992, pp 219-273.
28. Hourani SMO, Cusack NJ: Pharmacological receptors on blood platelets. Pharmacol Rev 43:243-298, 1991.
29. Siess W: 1989: Molecular mechanisms of platelet activation. Physiol Rev 69:58-178, 1989.
30. Nader HB: Characterization of heparan sulfate and a peculiar chondroitin 4-sulfate proteoglycan from platelets: Inhibition of the aggregation process by platelet chondroitin sulfate proteoglycan. J Biol Chem 266 (16):10518-10523, 1991.
31. Zwaal RFA, Bevers EM, Comfurius P, et al: Loss of membrane phospholipid asymmetry during activation of blood platelets and sickled red cells: Mechanisms and physiological significance. Mol Cell Biochem 91:23-31, 1989.
32. Wiedmer T, Esmon CT, Sims PJ: Complement proteins C5b-9 stimulate procoagulant activity through platelet prothrombinase. Blood 68:875-880, 1986.
33. Esmon CT: Molecular events that control the protein C anticoagulant pathway. Thromb Haemost 70:29-35, 1993.
34. Sandberg H, Bode AP, Dombrose FA, et al: Expression of coagulant activity in human platelets: Release of membranous vesicles providing platelet factor 1 and platelet factor 3. Thromb Res 39:63-79, 1985.
35. Tilly RHJ, Senden JMG, Comfurius P, et al: Increased aminophospholipid translocase activity in human platelets during secretion. Biochim Biophys Acta 1029:188-190, 1990.
36. Tracy PB, Nesheim ME, Mann KG: Platelet factor Xa receptor. Meth Enzymol 215:329-360, 1992.
37. Miletich JP, Jackson CM, Majerus PW: Interaction of coagulation factor Xa with human platelets. Proc Natl Acad Sci U S A 74:4033-4036, 1977.
38. Ittyerah TR, Rawala R, Colman RW: Immunochemical studies of factor V of bovine platelets. Eur J Biochem 120:235-241, 1981.
39. Sims PJ, Wiedmer T, Esmon CT, et al: Assembly of the platelet prothrombinase complex is linked to vesiculation of the platelet plasma membrane. J Biol Chem 264:17049-17057, 1989.
40. Bogaert TN, Brown N, Wilcox M: The *Drosophila* PS2 antigen is an invertebrate integrin that, like the fibronectin receptor, becomes localized to muscle attachments. Cell 51:929-940, 1987.
41. DeSimone DW, Hynes RO: *Xenopus laevie* integrins: Structural conservation and evolutionary divergence of integrin beta. J Biol Chem 263:5333-5340, 1988.
42. Marcantonio EE, Hynes RO: Antibodies to the conserved cytoplasmic domain of the integrin beta 1 subunit react with proteins in vertebrates, invertebrates, and fungi. J Cell Biol 106:1765-1772, 1988.
43. Hynes RO: Integrins: A family of cell surface receptors. Cell 48:549-554, 1987.
44. Takada Y, Strominger JL, Hemler ME: The very late antigen family of heterodimers is part of a superfamily of molecules in adhesion and embryogenesis. Proc Natl Acad Sci U S A 84:3239-3243, 1987.
45. Hemler ME, Crouse C, Takada Y, Sonnenberg A: Multiple very late antigen (VLA) heterodimers on platelets: Evidence for distinct VLA-2, VLA-5 (fibrinogen receptor) and VLA-6 structures. J Biol Chem 263:7660-7665, 1988.
46. Anderson DC, Springer TA: Leukocyte adhesion deficiency: An inherited defect in the Mac-1, LFA-1, and P150 glycoproteins. Annu Rev Med 38:175-194, 1987.
47. Cheresh DA, Spiro RC: Biosynthetic and functional properties of an Arg-Gly-Asp directed receptor involved in human melanoma cell attachment to vitronectin, fibrinogen, and von Willebrand factor. J Biol Chem 262:17703-17711, 1987.
48. Lam SC, Plow EW, D'Souza SE, et al: Isolation and characterization of a platelet membrane protein related to the vitronectin receptor. J Biol Chem 264:3742-3749, 1989.
49. Kuijpers MJ, Schulte V, Oury C, et al: Facilitating roles of murine platelet glycoprotein Ib and alphaIIbbeta3 in phosphatidylserine exposure during vWF-collagen-induced thrombus formation. J Physiol 558(Pt 2):403-415, 2004.
50. Phillips DR, Chaio IF, Scarborough RM: GPIIB/IIIa: The responsive integrin. Cell 65:359-362, 1991.
51. Kunicki TJ: Platelet membrane glycoproteins and their function: An overview. Blut 59:30-34, 1989.
52. Shattil SJ, Bennett JS: Platelets and their membranes in hemostasis: Physiology and pathophysiology. Ann Intern Med 94:108-118, 1981.
53. Bennett JS, Vilaire G: Exposure of platelet fibrinogen receptors by ADP and epinephrine. J Clin Invest 64:1393-1401, 1979.
54. Jackson SP, Yuan Y, Schoenwaelder SM, Mitchell CA: Role of the platelet integrin glycoprotein IIb-IIIa in intracellular signalling. Thromb Res 71:159-168, 1993.
55. Drake TA, Morissey JH, Edgington TS: Selective expression of tissue factor in human tissues. Am J Pathol 134:1087-1097, 1989.
56. Carlsen E, Flatmark A, Prydz H: Cytokine-induced procoagulant activity in monocytes and endothelial cells: Further enhancement by cyclosporine. Transplantation 46:575-580, 1988.
57. Edwards RL, Rickles FR: The role of leukocytes in the activation of blood coagulation. Semin Hematol 29:202-212, 1992.
58. Gregory SA, Morissey JH, Edgington TS: Regulation of tissue factor gene expression in the monocyte procoagulant response to endotoxin. Mol Cell Biol 9:2752-2755, 1989.
59. McGee MP, Devlin R, Saluta G, Koren H: Tissue factor and factor VII

messenger RNAs in human alveolar macrophages: Effects of breathing ozone. Blood 75:122-127, 1990.
60. McGee MP, Wallin R, Devlin R, Rothberger H: Identification of mRNA coding for factor VII protein in human alveolar macrophages: Coagulant expression may be limited due to postribosomal processing. Thromb Haemost 61:170-174, 1989.
61. Weisberg LJ, Shin DT, Conkling PR: Identification of normal human peripheral blood monocytes and liver as sites of synthesis of coagulation factor XIII alpha chain. Blood 70:579-582, 1987.
62. Rothberger H, McGee MP: Generation of coagulation factor V activity by cultured rabbit alveolar macrophages. J Exp Med 160:1880-1890, 1984.
63. Altieri DA: Coagulation assembly on leukocytes in transmembrane signaling and cell adhesion. Blood 81:569-579, 1993.
64. McGee MP, Li LC: Functional difference between intrinsic and extrinsic coagulation pathways: Kinetics of factor X activation on human monocytes and alveolar macrophages. J Biol Chem 266:8079-8085, 1991.
65. Tracy PB, Eide LL, Mann KG: Human prothrombinase complex assembly and function on isolated peripheral blood cell populations. J Biol Chem 260:2119-2124, 1985.
66. Robinson RA, Worfolk L, Tracy PB: Endotoxin enhances expression of monocyte prothrombinase activity. Blood 79:406-416, 1992.
67. Perdue JF, Lubenskyi W, Kivity E, et al: Protease mitogenic response of chick embryo fibroblasts and receptor binding/processing of human a-thrombin. J Biol Chem 256:2767-2776, 1981.
68. Senior RM, Skogen WF, Griffin GL, Wilner GD: Effects of fibrinogen derivatives upon the inflammatory response. J Clin Invest 77:1014-1019, 1986.
69. Car BD, Suyemoto M, Neilsen NR, Slauson DO: The role of leukocytes in the pathogenesis of fibrin deposition in bovine acute lung injury. Am J Pathol 138:1191-1198, 1991.
70. Nawroth P, Handley D, Esmon C, Stern DM: Interleukin 1 induces endothelial cell procoagulant while suppressing cell surface anticoagulant activity. Proc Natl Acad Sci U S A 83:3460-3464, 1986.
71. Hrachovina I, Cambien B, Hafezi-Moghadam A, et al: Interaction of P-selectin and PSGL-1 generates microparticles that correct hemostasis in a mouse model of hemophilia A. Nat Med 9:1020-1025, 2003.
72. Falati S, Liu Q, Gross P, et al: Accumulation of tissue factor into developing thrombi in vivo is dependent upon microparticle P-selectin glycoprotein ligand 1 and platelet P-selectin. J Exp Med 197:1585-1598, 2003.
73. Mourey L, Samama JP, Delarue M, et al: Antithrombin III: Structural and functional aspects. Biochemie 72:599-608, 1990.
74. Chandra T, Stackhouse R, Kidd VJ, Woo SLC: Isolation and sequence characterization of a cDNA clone of human antithrombin III. Proc Natl Acad Sci U S A 80:1845-1848, 1983.
75. Conrad J, Brosstad F, Larsen ML, et al: Molar antithrombin concentration in normal human plasma. Haemostasis 13:363-368, 1983.
76. Howell WH: The coagulation of blood. In The Harvey Lectures, Vol 12. Philadelphia, Lippincott, 1918, pp 272-323.
77. Howell WH: The purification of heparin and its presence in blood. Am J Physiol 71:553-562, 1925.
78. Brinkhous KM, Smith HP, Warmer ED, Seegers WH: The inhibition of blood clotting: An unidentified substance which acts in conjunction with heparin to prevent the conversion of prothrombin into thrombin. Am J Physiol 125:683-687, 1939.
79. Abildgaard U: Highly purified antithrombin III with heparin cofactor activity prepared by disc electrophoresis. Scand J Clin Lab Invest 21:89-91, 1968.
80. Pizzo SV: The physiologic role of antithrombin III as an anticoagulant. Semin Hematol 31:4-7, 1994.
81. Pratt CW, Church FC: Antithrombin: Structure and function. Semin Hematol 28:3-9, 1991.
82. Bjork I, Danielsson A: Antithrombin and related inhibitors of coagulation proteinases. In Barrett AJ, Salvesen GS (eds): Proteinase Inhibitors. Amsterdam, Elsevier, 1986, pp 489-513.
83. Rosenberg RD, Damus PS: The purification and mechanism of action of human antithrombin–heparin cofactor. J Biol Chem 248:6490, 1973.
84. Damus PS, Hicks M, Rosenberg RD: Anticoagulant action of heparin. Nature 246:355-357, 1973.
85. Brennan SO, George PM, Jordan RE: Physiological variant of antithrombin III lacks carbohydrate side chain at ASN 135. FEBS Lett 219:431-436, 1987.
86. Jordan RE, Oosta GM, Gardner WT, Rosenberg RD: The kinetics of hemostatic enzyme-antithrombin interactions in the presence of low molecular weight heparins. J Biol Chem 255:10081-10090, 1980.
87. Peterson CB, Morgan WT, Blackburn MN: Histidine-rich glycoprotein modulation of the anticoagulant activity of heparin. J Biol Chem 262:7567-7574, 1987.
88. Nesheim M, Blackburn MN, Lawler CM, Mann KG: Dependence of antithrombin III and thrombin binding stoichiometries and catalytic activity on the molecular weight of affinity purified heparin. J Biol Chem 261:3214-3221, 1986.
89. Abildgaard U, Larsen ML: Assay of dermatan sulfate cofactor (heparin cofactor II) activity in human plasma. Thromb Res 35:257-266, 1984.
90. Briginshaw GF, Shanberge JN: Identification of two distinct heparin cofactors in human plasma: Inhibition of thrombin and activated factor X. Thromb Res 4:463-477, 1974.
91. Tollefsen DM, Blank MK: Detection of a new heparin dependent inhibitor of thrombin in human plasma. J Clin Invest 68:589, 1981.
92. Travis J, Salvesen GS: Human plasma proteinase inhibitors. Annu Rev Biochem 52:655-709, 1983.
93. Church FC, Noyes CM, Griffith MJ: Inhibition of chymotrypsin by heparin cofactor II. Proc Natl Acad Sci U S A 82:6431-6434, 1985.
94. Parker KA, Tollefsen DM: The protease specificity of heparin cofactor II: Inhibition of thrombin generated during coagulation. J Biol Chem 260:3501-3503, 1987.
95. Sie P, DuPouy D, Pichon J, Boneu B: Constitutional heparin cofactor II deficiency associated with recurrent thrombosis. Lancet 2:414-416, 1985.
96. Girard TJ, Warren LA, Novotny WF, et al: Functional significance of the Kunitz-type inhibitory domains of lipoprotein-associated coagulation inhibitor. Nature 338:518-520, 1989.
97. Hamamoto T, Yamamoto M, Nordfang O, et al: Inhibitory properties of full-length and truncated tissue factor pathway inhibitor (TFPI). J Biol Chem 268:8704-8710, 1993.
98. Nordfang O, Kristensen HI, Valentin S, et al: The significance of TFPI in clotting assays: Comparison and combination with other anticoagulants. Thromb Haemost 70:448-453, 1993.
99. Lindhout T, Willems G, Blezer R, Hemker HC: Kinetics of the inhibition of human factor Xa by full-length and truncated recombinant tissue factor pathway inhibitor. Biochem J 297:131-136, 1994.
100. Huang ZF, Wun TC, Broze GJ: Kinetics of factor Xa inhibition by tissue factor pathway inhibitor. J Biol Chem 268:26950-26955, 1993.
101. Enjyoji K, Miyaya T, Kamikubo Y, Kato H: Effect of heparin on the inhibition of factor Xa by tissue factor pathway inhibitor: A segment, Gly 212–Phe 243, of the third Kunitz domain is a heparin binding site. Biochemistry 34:5725-5735, 1995.
102. Lindahl AK, Abildgaard U, Larsen ML, et al: Extrinsic pathway inhibitor (EPI) and the post-heparin anticoagulant effect in tissue thromboplastin induced coagulation. Thromb Res Suppl 14:39-48, 1991.
103. Lindahl AK, Sandset PM, Abildgaard U: The present status of tissue factor pathway inhibitor. Blood Coag Fibrinol 3:439-449, 1992.
104. Novotny WF, Palmier MO, Wun TC, et al: Purification and properties of heparin releasable lipoprotein-associated inhibitor. Blood 78:394-400, 1991.
105. Broze GJ, Miletich JP: Isolation of tissue factor inhibitor produced by HEPG2 hepatoma cells. Proc Natl Acad Sci U S A 84:1886-1890, 1987.
106. Sandset PM, Abildgaard U, Larsen ML: Heparin induces release of extrinsic pathway inhibitor (EPI). Thromb Res 50:803-813, 1988.
107. Hoppensteadt DA, Fasanella A, Fareed J: Effect of protamine on heparin releasable TFPI antigen levels in normal volunteers. Thromb Res 79:325-330, 1995.
107a. Kristensen HI, Ostergaard PB, Nordfang O, et al: Effect of tissue factor pathway inhibitor (TFPI) in the Heptest assay and in an amidolytic anti-factor Xa assay for LMW heparin. Thromb Haemost 68:310-314, 1992.

108. Day KC, Hoffman LC, Palmier MO, et al: Recombinant lipoprotein-associated coagulation inhibitor inhibits tissue thromboplastin-induced intravascular coagulation in the rabbit. Blood 76:1538-1545, 1990.
109. Warn-Cramer BJ, Rapaport SI: Studies of factor Xa/phospholipid-induced intravascular coagulation on rabbits: Effects of immunodepletion of tissue factor pathway inhibitor. Arterioscler Thromb Vasc Biol 13:1551-1557, 1993.
110. Creasey AA, Chang ACK, Feigen L, et al: Tissue factor pathway inhibitor reduces mortality from *Escherichia coli* septic shock. J Clin Invest 91:2850-2860, 1993.
111. Khouri RK, Koudsi D, Fu K, et al: Prevention of thrombosis by topical application of tissue factor pathway inhibitor in a rabbit model of vascular trauma. Ann Plast Surg 30:398-404, 1993.
112. Kane WH, Davie EW: Blood coagulation factors V and VIII: Structural and functional similarities and their relationship to hemorrhagic and thrombotic disorders. Blood 71:539-555, 1988.
113. Owen WG, Esmon CT: Functional properties of an endothelial cell cofactor for thrombin catalyzed activation of protein C. J Biol Chem 256:5532-5535, 1981.
114. Dahlback B: The protein C anticoagulant system: Inherited defects as basis for venous thrombosis. Thromb Res 77:1-43, 1995.
115. Maruyama I, Bell CE, Majerus PW: Thrombomodulin is found on endothelium of arteries, veins, capillaries, lymphatics and syncytioblasts of human placenta. J Cell Biol 101:363-371, 1985.
116. Stenflo J: A new vitamin K-dependent protein. J Biol Chem 251:355-363, 1976.
117. Seegers WH, Novoa E, Henry RL, Hassouna HI: Relationship of "new" vitamin K-dependent protein C and "old" autoprothrombin II-A. Thromb Res 8:543-552, 1976.
118. Kisiel W, Canfield WM, Ericsson LN, Davie EW: Anticoagulant properties of bovine plasma protein C following activation by thrombin. J Biol Chem 16:5824-5831, 1977.
119. Beckman RJ, Schmidt RJ, Santerre PF, et al: The structure and evolution of a 461-amino acid human protein C precursor and its messenger RNA, based upon the DNA sequence of cloned human liver cDNAs. Acids Res 13:5233-5247, 1985.
120. Walker FJ, Fay PJ: Regulation of blood coagulation by the protein C system. FASEB J 6:2561-2567, 1992.
121. Solymoss S, Tucker MM, Tracy PB: Kinetics of inactivation of membrane-bound factor V by activated protein C. J Biol Chem 263:14884-14890, 1988.
122. Bauer KA, Kass BL, Beeler DL, Rosenberg RD: The detection of protein C activation in humans. J Clin Invest 74:2033-2041, 1994.
123. Gruber A, Hanson SR, Kelly AB, et al: Inhibition of thrombus formation by activated recombinant protein C in a primate model of arterial thrombosis. Circulation 82:578-585, 1990.
124. Preissner KT: Anticoagulant potential of endothelial cell membrane components. Haemostasis 18:271-273, 1988.
125. Baker JB, Low DA, Simmer RL, Cunningham DD: Protease nexin: A cellular component that links thrombin and plasminogen activator and mediates their binding to cells. Cell 21:37-45, 1980.
126. Eaton DL, Baker JB: Evidence that a variety of cultured cells secrete protease nexin and produce a distinct cytoplasmic serine protease-binding factor. J Cell Physiol 117:175-182, 1983.
127. Reilly TM, Mousa SA, Seetharam R, Racanelli AL: Recombinant plasminogen activator inhibitor type 1: A review of structural, functional, and biological aspects. Blood Coag Fibrinol 5:78-83, 1994.
128. Edelberg J, Pizzo SV: Lipoprotein (a) regulates plasmin generation and inhibition. Chem Phys Lipids 67-68:363-368, 1994.
129. Borth W: Alpha-2 macroglobulin, a multifunctional binding protein with targeting characteristics. FASEB J 6:3345-3353, 1992.
130. LaMarre J, Wollenberg GK, Gonias SL, Hayes MA: Cytokine binding and clearance properties of proteinase-activated alpha-2 macroglobulins. Lab Invest 65:3-14, 1991.
131. Hack CE, Ogilvie AC, Eisele B, et al: Initial studies on the administration of C1-esterase inhibitor to patients with septic shock or with a vascular leak syndrome induced by interleukin-2 therapy. Prog Clin Biol Res 388:335-357, 1994.
132. Carreer FM: The C1 inhibitor deficiency. Eur J Clin Chem Clin Biochem 30:793-807, 1992.
133. Lijnen HR, Hoylaerts M, Collen D: Isolation and characterization of human plasma protein with high affinity for lysine binding sites in plasminogen. J Biol Chem 225:10214-10222, 1980.
134. Engesser L, Kluft C, Briet E, Brommer E: Familial elevation of plasma histidine-rich glycoprotein in a family with thrombophilia. Br J Haematol 67:355-358, 1987.
135. Campbell W, Okada N, Okada H: Carboxypeptidase R is an inactivator of complement-derived inflammatory peptides and an inhibitor of finbrinolysis. Immunol Rev 180:162-167, 2001.
136. Bajzar L: Thrombin activatable fibrinolysis inhibitor and an antifibrinolytic pathway. Thromb Vasc Biol 20:2511-2518, 2000.
137. Tan AK, Eaton DL: Activation and characterization of procarboxypeptidase B from human plasma. Biochemistry 34:5811-5816, 1995.
138. Sato T, Miwa T, Asatsu H, et al: Pro-carboxypeptidase R is an acute phase protein in the mouse, whereas carboxypeptidase N is not. J Immunol 165:1053-1058, 2000.
139. Boffa MB, Hamill JD, Maret D, et al: Acute-phase mediators modulate thrombin-activable fibrinolysis inhibitor (TAFI) gene expression in HepG2 cells. J Biol Chem 278:9250-9257, 2003.
140. Bajzar L: Thrombin activatable fibrinolysis inhibitor and an antifibrinolytic pathway. Arterioscler Thromb Vasc Biol 20:2511-2518, 2000.
141. Kakkar VV, Hoppensteadt DA, Fareed J, et al: Randomized trial of different regimens of heparins and in vivo thrombin generation in acute deep vein thrombosis. Blood 99:1965-1970, 2002.
142. Lau HK, Segev A, Hegele RA, et al: Thrombin-activatable fibrinolysis inhibitor (TAFI): A novel predictor of angiographic coronary restenosis. Thromb Haemost 90:1187-1191, 2003.
143. Demasi R, Bode AP, Knupp C, et al: Heparin-induced thrombocytopenia. Am Surg 60:26-29, 1994.
144. Weisman RE, Tobin RW: Arterial embolism occurring in systemic heparin therapy. Arch Surg 76:219-226, 1958.
145. Aster RH: Heparin-induced thrombocytopenia and thrombosis. N Engl J Med 332:1374-1376, 1995.
146. Hoechst Marion Roussel, prescribing information (as of March 1998) for Refludan. HMR: The Pharmaceutical Company of Hoechst, Kansas City, MO.
147. Axelrad AA, Eskinazi D, Amato D: Hypersensitivity of circulating progenitor cells to megakaryocyte growth and development of factor (PEG-rHu MGDF) in essential thrombocythemia. Blood 92(Suppl 1):488a, 1998.
148. Kaushansky K: Thrombopoietin. N Engl J Med 339:746-753, 1998.
149. Murphy S, Iland H, Rosenthal D, et al: Essential thrombocythemia: An interim report from the Polycythemia Vera Study Group. Semin Hematol 23:177-182, 1986.
150. Rodeghiero F, Castaman G, Dini E: Epidemiological investigation of the prevalence of von Willebrand's disease. Blood 69:454-459, 1987.
151. Miller CH, Graham JB, Goldin LR, Elston RC: Genetics of classic von Willebrand's disease: I. Phenotype variation within families. Blood 54:117-136, 1979.
152. Di Paola J, Frederici AB, Mannucci PM, et al: Low-platelet alpha-2-beta-1 levels in type I von Willebrand disease correlate with impaired platelet function in a high shear stress system. Blood 93:3578-3582, 1999.
153. Barton M: Endothelial dysfunction and atherosclerosis: Endothelin receptor antagonists as novel therapeutics. Curr Hypertens Rep 2:84-91, 2000.
154. Brevetti G, Piscione F, Silvestro A, et al: Increased inflammatory status and higher prevalence of three-vessel coronary artery disease in patients with concomitant coronary and peripheral atherosclerosis. Thromb Haemost 89:1058-1063, 2003.
155. Rossi GP, Cesari M, Zanchetta M, et al: The T-786 endothelial nitric oxide synthase genotype is a novel risk factor for coronary artery disease in Caucasian patients for the GENICA Study. J Am Coll Cardiol 41:930-937, 2003.

156. Widlansky ME, Gokce N, Keaney JF Jr: The clinical implications of endothelial dysfunction. J Am Coll Cardiol 42:1149-1160, 2003.
157. Bild DE, Bluemke DA, Burke GL, et al: Multi-ethnic study of atherosclerosis: Objectives and design. Am J Epidemiol 156:871-881, 2002.
158. Bennett B, Oxnard SC, Douglas AS, et al: Studies on antihaemophilic factor (AHF, factor VIII) during labor in normal women, in patients with premature separation of the placenta, and in a patient with von Willebrand's disease. J Clin Lab Med 84:851-860, 1974.
159. Greer IA: Thrombosis in pregnancy: Maternal and fetal issues. Lancet 353:1258-1265, 1999.
160. Zucker-Franklin D, Cao YZ: Megakaryocytes of human immunodeficiency virus-infected individuals express viral RNA. Proc Natl Acad Sci U S A 86:5595-5599, 1989.
161. Viale P, Pagani L, Alberici F: Clinical features and prognostic factors of HIV-associated thrombotic microangiopathies. Eur J Haematol 60:262-263, 1998.
162. Horlocker TT, Heit JA: Low molecular weight heparin: Biochemistry, pharmacology, perioperative prophylaxis regimens, and guidelines for regional anesthetic management. Anesth Analg 85:874-885, 1997.
163. Schroeder DR: Statistics: Detecting a rare adverse drug reaction using spontaneous reports. Reg Anesth Pain Med 23(Suppl 2):183-189, 1998.
164. Bergquist D, Lindblad B, Matzsch T: Low molecular weight heparin for thromboprophylaxis and epidural/spinal anesthesia: Is there a risk? Acta Anesthesiol Scand 36:605-609, 1992.
165. Tryba M: European practice guidelines: Thromboembolism prophylaxis and regional anesthesia. Reg Anesth Pain Med 23(Suppl 12):178-182, 1998.
166. Collins R, Scrimgeour A, Yusuf S, Peto R: Reduction in fatal pulmonary embolism and venous thrombosis by perioperative administration of subcutaneous heparin: Overview of results of randomized trials in general, orthopedic, and urologic surgery. N Engl J Med 318:1162-1173, 1988.
167. Clagett GP, Reisch JS: Prevention of venous thromboembolism in general surgical patients: Results of meta-analysis. Ann Surg 208:227-240, 1988.
168. Bergentz SE: Dextran in the prophylaxis of pulmonary embolism. World J Surg 2:19-25, 1978.
169. Colditz GA, Tuden RL, Oster G: Rates of venous thrombosis after general surgery: Combined results of randomised clinical trials. Lancet 2:143-146, 1986.
170. Nicolaides A, Bergquist D, Hull R: International Consensus Statement: Prevention of Venous Thrombosis. London, UK, Med-Orion, 1997.
171. Fareed J, Hoppensteadt DA, Bick RL: Management of thrombotic and cardiovascular disorders in the new millennium. Clin Appl Thromb Hemost 9:101-108, 2003.
172. Fareed J, Hoppensteadt DA: The management of thrombotic and cardiovascular disorders in the 21st century. In Sasahara AA, Loscalzo J (eds): New Therapeutic Agents in Thrombosis and Thrombolysis, 2nd ed. New York, Marcel Dekker, 2002, pp 687.
173. Dalen JE, Hirsh J, Guyatt GH: Sixth ACCP Consensus Conference on Antithrombotic Therapy. Chest 119:1S-370S, 2001.

Chapter 31

Antithrombotic Therapy

MARK H. MEISSNER, MD

Thrombosis plays a key role in almost all cardiovascular disorders, and antithrombotic agents are among the most important drugs used in vascular medicine and surgery. They are critical in the prophylaxis and treatment of many arterial and venous diseases as well as being important adjuncts to a variety of reconstructive procedures. Thrombosis involves the interaction of the vascular wall, platelets, and the coagulation system, and from a functional standpoint most antithrombotic agents are directed toward inhibiting coagulation or preventing platelet aggregation. Arterial thrombi consist of platelet aggregates with small amounts of fibrin, whereas venous thrombi consist largely of fibrin and red blood cells. Accordingly, antithrombotic therapy for arterial disease usually includes antiplatelet agents, with anticoagulants used as an adjunct to prevent fibrin deposition, whereas anticoagulants are the primary therapy for the prevention and treatment of venous and arterial thromboembolism.[1]

Potential antithrombotic strategies include inhibiting the initiation of anticoagulation, blocking thrombin generation, directly inhibiting thrombin once formed, and blocking platelet aggregation (Fig. 31-1). Heparin, warfarin, and aspirin represent the classic anticoagulants, and each has multiple sites of action on the coagulation system. Although the low-molecular-weight heparins (LMWHs) have more recently become available, they still represent a relatively nonselective approach to anticoagulation. In contrast, newer agents continue to be developed that provide a more targeted, or monotherapeutic, approach to anticoagulation (Table 31-1). Although the newer monotherapeutic drugs provide a range of options for anticoagulation, it is becoming clear that they cannot be precisely substituted for older polytherapeutic approaches and that many disorders may require a more directed, yet still multifaceted approach to inhibiting thrombosis.[2]

■ THE COAGULATION SYSTEM

The appropriate selection and use of antithrombotic agents requires some understanding of coagulation. The mechanisms of coagulation are discussed in detail in Chapter 30, but a brief review is required prior to considering therapeutic

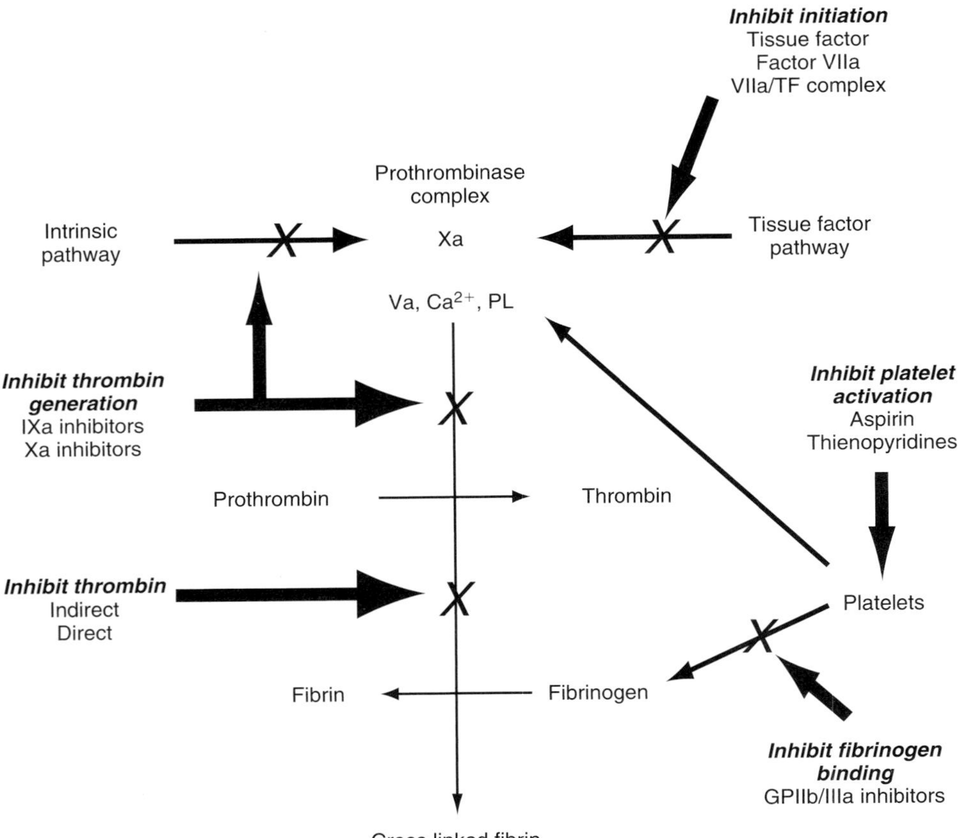

FIGURE 31-1 Mechanisms of action of anticoagulants may include inhibiting the initiation of anticoagulation through the tissue factor pathway, blocking thrombin generation, and directly inhibiting thrombin once formed. Currently available antiplatelet agents are directed toward blocking platelet activation or inhibiting GP-IIb/IIIa-mediated fibrinogen binding. Ca^{2+}, ionized calcium; PL, platelet-derived phospholipid; TF, tissue factor; GP, glycoprotein.

Table 31-1 Antithrombotic Agents

TYPE OF AGENT	MECHANISM OF ACTION	FDA APPROVED	IN DEVELOPMENT
Anticoagulants	IIa/Xa inhibitors	Unfractionated heparin	SNAC: heparin
	Xa > IIa inhibitors	LMWHs	SNAD: LMWH
	Xa inhibitors	Fondaparinux	Idraparinux
	IIa inhibitors	Lepirudin Bivalirudin Argatroban	PEG-hirudin Ximelagatran r-TAP
	Tissue factor pathway inhibitors	—	r-TFPI r-NAPc2
	IXa inhibitors	—	Anti-IX/IXa antibodies Active site-blocked IXa
	Vitamin K antagonists	Warfarin	—
Antiplatelet Agents	Cyclooxygenase inhibitors	Aspirin	—
	Phosphodiesterase inhibitors	Dipyridamole	—
	ADP antagonists	Ticlopidine Clopidogrel	—
	GP-IIb/IIIa antagonists	Abciximab Tirofiban Eptifibatide	Sibrafiban Orbofiban

FDA, U.S. Food and Drug Administration; GP, glycoprotein; SNAC, sodium-*N*-[8-(2-hydroxybenzoyl) amino] caprylate; SNAD, sodium-*N*-[10-(2-hydroxybenzoyl) amino]-decanoate; PEG, polyethylene glycol; r-TAP, recombinant tick anticoagulant peptide; r-TFPI, recombinant tissue factor pathway inhibitor; r-NAPc2, recombinant NAPc2; LMWH, low-molecular-weight heparin; ADP, adenosine diphosphate.

anticoagulation. Normal hemostasis requires the complex interaction of more than 100 procoagulant, inhibitory, and fibrinolytic proteins, platelets, and the endothelium.[3] Primary hemostasis results in the immediate formation of a platelet plug at sites of vascular injury. The platelet plug is then stabilized by a secondary fibrin thrombus organized on the surface of activated platelets. The generation of thrombin (factor IIa), the key effector enzyme of coagulation, and the conversion of soluble fibrinogen to insoluble fibrin is the primary goal of the coagulation system.

Coagulation is initiated either by mechanical injury or cytokine-induced activation of endothelial cells and monocytes. In either case, tissue factor (TF), a single-chain receptor for factor VII, is exposed as a membrane protein.[4] The TF, or extrinsic pathway, is the most important physiologic pathway for initiation of coagulation in response to injury.[5,6] Exposed TF binds both inactive factor VII and activated factor VIIa, a small amount of which circulates in blood. The TF-VIIa complex (TF-VIIa) in turn autoactivates factor VII as well as activating factors IX and X.[4,5] Feedback amplification occurs as factor VII bound to TF is activated by factors VIIa, IXa, and Xa.

Subsequent formation of the prothrombinase complex, composed of phospholipid-bound prothrombin (factor II), factor Xa, and its factor Va cofactor, results in the generation of thrombin from prothrombin. There appears to be a threshold response in which a certain level of initiating procoagulant stimulus (TF-VIIa) is required to produce effective thrombin generation.[7,8] Once this threshold is reached, the amount of thrombin generated is independent of the initiating stimulus. Thrombin in turn activates factors V, VIII, and XI, which in turn cause feedback amplification through further activation of factor IX. The thrombin-mediated conversion of pro-cofactors V and VIII is particularly important because the active cofactors serve to assemble the prothrombinase and tenase complexes. Thrombin-mediated activation of factor V may in fact be the rate-limiting step in coagulation.[9]

Phospholipid membranes are critical to the formation of the procoagulant TF-VIIa, prothrombinase, and tenase complexes. Platelets are the primary source of these phospholipids and therefore play a critically important role in propagating coagulation, amplifying the process by several orders of magnitude.[10] Once activated, either through their interaction with collagen or by binding to fibrin in coagulating plasma,[11] negatively charged phosphatidylserine residues are translocated to the outer platelet membrane. The coagulation factors involved in formation of these complexes depend on 9 to 12 amino-terminal γ-carboxyglutamic acid residues for interaction with the phospholipid surface.[12] These residues, formed post-translationally in a vitamin K-dependent process, are required for calcium binding and correct folding for interaction with the phospholipid membrane.[5]

Various models suggest that the TF pathway of coagulation can be functionally divided into two phases.[10,13] During the initiation phase, nanomolar amounts of thrombin and femto- to picomolar quantities of factors VIIa, IXa, Xa, and XIa are generated.[13] However, most important, this phase leads to quantitative activation of the Va and VIIIa cofactors. The prothrombin time (PT) and activated partial thromboplastin time (aPTT) measure only the initiation phase of coagulation. The propagation phase is characterized by explosive prothrombin activation and thrombin generation. This phase is largely driven by the tenase complex-mediated activation of factor X.[13] Most of the major congenital deficiencies and clinically effective anticoagulants have their major effect during the propagation phase.[10] The efficacy of most anticoagulants therefore depends on their ability to inhibit thrombin after formation of the initial fibrin-platelet clot.

The physiologic importance of the intrinsic coagulation pathway, through which coagulation is initiated by a combination of factor XII, high-molecular-weight kininogen, prekallikrein, and factor XI, remains unclear.[5] The less important role of the intrinsic pathway is suggested by the observation that few deficiencies of the intrinsic pathway are associated with bleeding.[10] However, thrombin-induced activation of factor XIa is likely important in the propagation of coagulation, generating sufficient IXa to prevent severe bleeding after the TF pathway has been terminated by its natural inhibitors.[4,8,11,12]

Negative regulators of coagulation include TF pathway inhibitor (TFPI), which regulates the initiation phase of coagulation, and the antithrombin (AT) and the protein C systems, which regulate the propagation phase.[10] A TFPI-Xa complex binds TF-VIIa to form an inactive quaternary complex, limiting the initiation phase but allowing sustained activation through factors VIIIa, IXa, and XIa.[7,8,10,12,14] The protein C system is initiated by the interaction of thrombin with endothelial-bound thrombomodulin. Thrombomodulin-bound thrombin undergoes a conformational change, losing its activity toward fibrinogen and factors V, VIII, and XIII and activating the vitamin K-dependent zymogen protein C.[12] Activated protein C (APC), together with its protein S cofactor, cleaves phospholipid bound factors VIIIa and Va. AT is a serine protease inhibitor, present in significant molar excess to its target proteases, that inhibits factors IIa, VIIa, IXa, Xa, XIa, and XIIa.[8] In contrast to the protein C pathway, AT acts as a scavenger and preferentially inhibits circulating, rather than membrane-bound, factors IIa and Xa.[8] Thrombin bound to fibrin clot is relatively protected from the action of AT.[4] These pathways function synergistically to more effectively limit the response to TF than any single mechanism alone. For example, TPFI potentiates the effects of AT by decreasing the rate of formation of thrombin (prolonging the initiation phase) as AT inactivates the thrombin generated (decreasing the rate and amplitude of the propagation phase).[8] The combination of TFPI and AT is 70-fold more potent than either inhibitor alone.

■ INDIRECT THROMBIN INHIBITORS

Unfractionated Heparin

Compounds that inhibit thrombin by potentiating the action of AT, such as unfractionated heparin (UFH) and the LMWHs, are known as *indirect thrombin inhibitors*. UFH, discovered by McLean in 1916, is one of the oldest, most effective, and widely administered drugs still in clinical use. Its introduction predates establishment of the U.S. Food and Drug Administration (FDA).[15] Although the use of bovine products has declined with the appearance of bovine spongiform encephalopathy,[15] UFH is prepared from tissue extracts of porcine intestine or bovine lung. Commercially available products are a heterogeneous mixture of glycosaminoglycans composed of alternating D-glucosamine and uronic acid residues having molecular weights ranging from 5000 to more than 40,000 d (mean 15,000 d).[9,15,16] These are large, sulfated, highly acidic molecules with a net negative charge.

Pharmacology and Mechanism of Action

Although AT and heparin cofactor II are the primary regulatory proteins affected by heparin, the role of heparin cofactor II is insignificant except at very high heparin concentrations.[8,16] Heparin acts primarily to catalyze the AT-mediated inhibition of thrombin (factor IIa) and factors IXa, Xa, and XIIa, the greatest clinical effect being on factors IIa and Xa.[17] In the absence of a catalyst, either endothelial heparan sulfates or exogenous heparin, AT inactivates thrombin and factor Xa at a low basal rate. Heparin binding to AT causes a 9000- and 17,000-fold increase in inhibitory activity against thrombin and factor Xa, respectively.[18] However, as discussed earlier, neither UFH nor the LMWHs are able to inactivate phospholipid-bound factor Xa or fibrin-bound thrombin.[16] Fibrin-bound thrombin is protected from the action of AT by formation of heparin-thrombin-fibrin complexes that render it inaccessible to AT-bound heparin.[19]

The structure and size of the individual heparin chains determine their ability to catalyze inhibition of thrombin and factor Xa. The catalytic effect of heparin depends on the binding of a unique pentasaccharide sequence to a specific site on AT, producing a conformational change that exposes its reactive center.[4,16,18] This pentasaccharide sequence is present in only 20% to 50% of UFH chains and even fewer LMWH chains.[15] AT-mediated inactivation of factor Xa requires only the presence of the appropriate pentasaccharide sequence, whereas binding to IIa further requires a flanking chain 15 to 16 saccharide units in length and containing a second domain that electrostatically attracts the AT-reactive site (Fig. 31-2).[6,15] Heparin chains must therefore have a minimum molecular weight of approximately 5400 d for thrombin binding.[20,21] Anti-IIa activity increases with the size of the heparin molecule while anti-Xa activity remains stable.[9] The anti-Xa and anti-IIa activity of UFH is approximately equal. The effect of heparin on the aPTT primarily reflects its anti-IIa, rather than anti-Xa, activity. Oligosaccharide chain length is also an important determinant of clearance, longer chains—those with greater anti-IIa activity and influencing the aPTT—being cleared more rapidly than shorter chains.[16]

Both UFH and LMWH also have anticoagulant properties independent of AT. Both agents cause the release of TFPI from the vascular endothelium, leading to inhibition of factor X activation and subsequent thrombin generation.[9,14] These drugs also enhance APC inactivation of factor V, but not Va, in an AT-independent manner.[9,17] Such an effect could downregulate thrombin production by decreasing the amount of membrane-bound factor V capable of conversion to Va and blocking the factor V/Va site with inactive factor V.[17] UFH also causes the release of platelet factor 4 from activated platelets.[9,22] Finally, heparin has several biologic effects unrelated to its anticoagulant action. These include osteoblast suppression/osteoclast activation associated with osteopenia, inhibition of vascular smooth muscle cell proliferation, and increased vascular permeability.[16] Heparin also binds, stabilizes, and potentiates the activities of several growth factors and cell adhesion glycoproteins (GPs).[23]

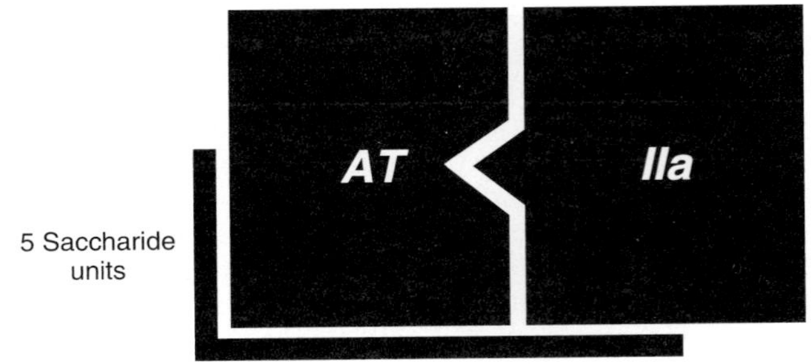

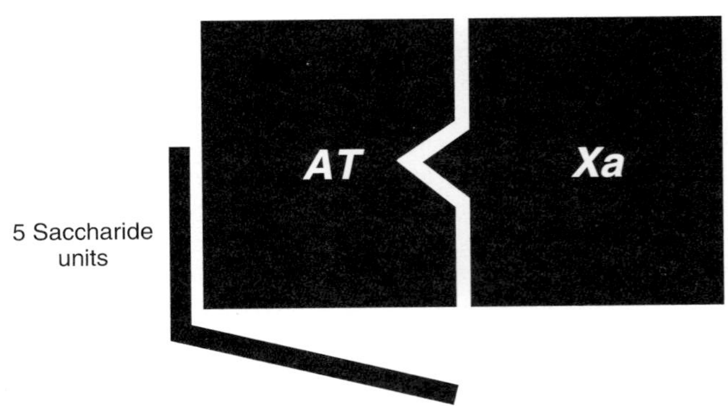

FIGURE 31-2 The catalytic effect of heparin depends on the binding of a unique pentasaccharide sequence to antithrombin (AT). Although inactivation of factor Xa requires only the presence of this pentasaccharide sequence, inactivation of factor IIa further requires the presence of a 15- or 16-unit saccharide chain to form a heparin-AT-IIa ternary complex.

In addition to its specific binding to AT, heparin also binds nonspecifically to several plasma proteins, endothelial cells, and macrophages.[16] Many heparin-binding proteins, such as vitronectin and fibronectin, are acute-phase reactants, contributing to the variable anticoagulant effect of heparin.[19] Binding to platelet factor 4 and multimers of von Willebrand's factor may be particularly important because it clears higher-molecular-weight chains from the circulation, renders them ineffective as anticoagulants, and lowers the effective heparin concentration at sites of vascular injury.[9,22] The platelet factor 4–heparin complexes are also one of the antigens responsible for heparin-induced thrombocytopenia (HIT). Nonspecific protein binding significantly affects the clearance of heparin, resulting in a bioavailability of only about 30%, as well as causing variability in dose response and heparin resistance in some patients.[20,24]

UFH is cleared from the plasma in two phases: (1) a rapid, saturable phase due to endothelial and macrophage binding and (2) slower, unsaturable renal clearance. The clearance of therapeutic doses of heparin is therefore dose related. The half-life of heparin increases from 30 minutes following an intravenous bolus of 25 U/kg to 60 minutes following a dose of 100 U/kg.[16] At therapeutic doses the half-life of plasma heparin activity is 63 ± 19 minutes, whereas that of the heparin-induced change in aPTT is 84 ± 71.5 minutes.[25] However, it is now realized that heparin also has some postdrug effects, such as the release of TFPI, that may not follow the pharmacokinetics of the drug.[9]

Dose and Administration

Heparin may be administered by continuous intravenous, intermittent intravenous, or intermittent subcutaneous injection. Continuous intravenous administration is most commonly used, and trials evaluating the safety and efficacy of intermittent subcutaneous injection have often been contradictory.[26] Although heparin is a large, highly anionic molecule that is poorly absorbed from the gastrointestinal tract, carrier molecules that increase passive intestinal absorption and enable oral administration have also been developed. Oral liquid UFH uses sodium-*N*-[8-(2-hydroxybenzoyl) amino] caprylate (SNAC) as a carrier molecule to increase bioavailability to approximately 20%. A similar carrier molecule for LMWH, sodium-*N*-[10-(2-hydroxybenzoyl) amino]-decanoate (SNAD), has also been developed. Both carriers are synthetic amido compounds that noncovalently bind heparin or LMWH, making it more lipophilic and enabling absorption across the intestinal mucosa.[27] SNAC:heparin has been shown to increase both the aPTT and anti-Xa activity in a dose-dependent fashion.[28] Unfortunately, the agent requires three-times-daily dosing and ongoing monitoring. Unlike oral heparin, the oral LMWHs do not require monitoring. Both SNAC:heparin and SNAD:LMWH have been shown to reduce thrombus formation in animal models.[27] More recently, one phase III trial has shown SNAC:heparin to be as effective as low-dose subcutaneous UFH in the prevention of deep venous thrombosis (DVT) after hip arthroplasty.[29] However, the development of newer oral anticoagulants makes the future of oral heparin and LMWH unclear.

Heparin is measured in terms of the United States Pharmacopeia unit, defined as the amount of heparin causing 1 mL of sheep blood to half-clot when kept at 20° C for 1 hour.[15] However, because UFH is a heterogeneous mixture of compounds with variable biologic activity, absolute dosages are irrelevant to its toxic and therapeutic effects.[9] The anticoagulant response varies among patients, and the use of UFH therefore requires laboratory monitoring, most often using the aPTT.[25] Differences in anticoagulant response are due to both individual differences in the clearance of heparin as well as in the aPTT response to a given amount of heparin.[25] For the treatment of venous thromboembolism (VTE), a therapeutic aPTT range of 1.5 to 2.5 times the control value has been previously recommended. However, ratios near the lower end of this target range are associated with subtherapeutic heparin levels.[30] Furthermore, the responsiveness of different aPTT reagents to heparin is variable, and there is no equivalent to the International Normalized Ratio (INR) used to adjust for variability in PT reagents.[30] The use of a fixed therapeutic range for the aPTT is therefore no longer acceptable. Current recommendations are that heparin dose be adjusted to achieve an aPTT equivalent to a heparin level of 0.2 to 0.4 U/mL measured by protamine titration.[30,31] Although at least some data suggest that the aPTT response is poorly related to the therapeutic outcome in VTE and myocardial infarction,[16] the aPTT should be checked 6 hours after an intravenous bolus dose and approximately 3 hours after a subcutaneous dose of UFH. Unfortunately, heparin can be a difficult drug to titrate, and failure to achieve a therapeutic aPTT is among the most common errors associated with use of the drug. Although some have suggested that failure to achieve a therapeutic aPTT within the first 24 hours is associated with a substantially higher risk of recurrent VTE, others have found no difference in 3-month recurrence rates among those achieving (5.3% to 7%) or not achieving (6.3% to 7.8%) a therapeutic aPTT within 24 hours if initial heparin doses exceed 30,000 U per 24 hours.[31,32] Monitoring anti-Xa levels is an alternative in patients with lupus anticoagulant or factor XII deficiency in which the aPTT may be unreliable.[20]

For the treatment of VTE, most recent studies have used an initial heparin bolus dose of 5000 U followed by a starting infusion rate of 30,000 to 35,000 U per 24 hours.[31] However, weight-based nomograms have been shown to outperform other approaches to UFH administration, increasing the aPTT above the therapeutic threshold more rapidly, better estimating eventual heparin requirements, and requiring fewer dosage adjustments.[33] Current consensus recommendations for VTE include initial treatment with 80 U/kg heparin intravenously followed by a maintenance infusion of 18 U/kg with subsequent dosage adjustment to maintain an aPTT in the therapeutic range.[16,34] Nomograms for VTE have incorporated a somewhat higher dose than for unstable angina because the bleeding risk is higher among patients receiving thrombolytic therapy or GP-IIb/IIIa antagonists. However, variability in laboratory reagents requires that the appropriate therapeutic range and dosage adjustments be locally determined.

Owing to their rapid onset of action, UFH and the LMWHs are currently the anticoagulants of choice when immediate anticoagulation is required. Established indications for UFH include the prevention and treatment of VTE; periprocedural use in cardiac surgery, vascular surgery, and coronary angioplasty; as an adjunct to coronary stents; and in the treatment of disseminated intravascular coagulation.[16] The only randomized trial comparing initial anticoagulation with heparin versus no anticoagulation in the treatment of VTE was stopped after enrolling only 35 patients due to the high mortality and recurrence rate in the untreated group.[35] Among the 19 patients randomized to no treatment, 5 died and 5 others had nonfatal recurrent pulmonary embolus in comparison to 1 death and no recurrences in the 16 treated patients. A 5-day course of intravenous UFH, when followed by oral anticoagulation, has been shown to be sufficient for the treatment of VTE. The incidence of recurrent thromboembolism during or within 1 week of heparin therapy is 1.4%.[36] UFH administered in a dose of 5000 U subcutaneously every 8 to 12 hours has also been shown effective in the prevention of VTE in general surgery patients and seriously ill medical patients.[16] UFH is usually combined with antiplatelet agents (aspirin or GP-IIb/IIIa inhibitors) or thrombolytic agents in the treatment of acute coronary syndromes.

Complications

Bleeding is the most common complication associated with anticoagulant therapy. The risk of major bleeding associated with UFH and the LMWHs has been reported to be 0% to 7% and 0% to 3%, respectively.[37] Others have noted major bleeding in 4% to 6% of patients treated with UFH,[26,36] with fatal bleeding in 1% to 2% of patients with major bleeding.[38] Although approximately half of patients with a major bleeding event will have a supratherapeutic aPTT within 24 hours of hemorrhage,[36] the aPTT is poorly predictive of bleeding complications. In contrast, 24-hour heparin dose per square meter of body surface area is significantly related to bleeding. The aPTT-independent bleeding risk associated with heparin may be due to its other effects, such as those on platelet function.[38] Most major bleeding episodes during treatment for VTE have been noted to occur near the end of initial heparin treatment when the INR is approaching the therapeutic range.[36] A body surface area ≥ 2 m^2 (odds ratio, 2.3; confidence interval [CI], 1.2 to 4.4) and malignancy (odds ratio, 2.4; CI, 1.1 to 4.9) are independent risk factors for bleeding while receiving parenteral anticoagulants.[38]

Other risks associated with UFH include elevated liver function tests, HIT, and osteopenia with long-term administration. Increased plasma levels of liver enzymes have been reported in 18% to 89% of patients receiving heparin and are also seen in association with LMWH.[39]

Based on etiology and the risk of complications, HIT is often divided into types I and II.[40] Type I HIT derives from the intrinsic proaggregatory effect of heparin and is generally asymptomatic, characterized by a drop in platelet count within the first 3 days of therapy and rarely associated with platelet counts below 100,000/mL.[40] The platelet count often returns to the normal range despite continued heparin therapy. Type II HIT is the most common drug-induced immune-mediated thrombocytopenia, occurring in 1% to 3% of patients receiving heparin for more than 5 days.[41,42] Thrombocytopenia results from antibodies directed against multimolecular complexes of platelet factor 4 and heparin chains longer than 12 to 14 saccharide units.[16,42] The heparin-platelet factor 4-IgG complex binds to platelet Fc receptors, causing antibody-mediated platelet activation and inducing platelet-derived procoagulant microparticles.[16,41] The antibody may also bind similar epitopes on endothelial cells,[42] potentially resulting in immune-mediated endothelial injury.[40] Heparin antibodies have been noted in up to 40% of patients undergoing cardiac surgery.[43]

Early manifestations of type II HIT include a fall in platelet count of more than 50%, often to less than 100,000/mL, and skin lesions at injection sites.[16] Thrombocytopenia is usually first seen after 5 to 10 days of heparin therapy but can be seen within hours in previously exposed patients. Manifestations can occur after heparin is administered in any dose by any route but are most frequently observed in patients receiving heparin as postoperative prophylaxis. In one series of 127 patients with HIT, 73.2% were receiving heparin for prophylactic indications.[41] Several laboratory tests for HIT have been developed.[40] Platelet-associated IgG is almost always elevated but has low specificity. The ^{14}C-serotonin platelet release assay to detect heparin-dependent IgG antibodies is both sensitive and specific (>90%) for HIT, but results are not immediately available. Commonly accepted diagnostic criteria for HIT include (1) a decline in platelet count to less than 150,000/mL 5 or more days after beginning heparin and (2) a positive platelet ^{14}C-serotonin release assay.[41]

In contrast with other immune-mediated thrombocytopenias,[42] type II HIT is associated with a high risk of thrombosis. Arterial or venous thrombosis may develop in 50% to 75% of patients and the mortality rate is as high as 25% to 30%.[16,44] HIT is recognized prior to the occurrence of a thrombotic event in only half of patients.[41] Although some have reported arterial events to be more common, others[41] have reported a 4.3:1 ratio of venous to arterial events. Arterial thrombi usually consist primarily of platelets, giving rise to their description as white clot syndrome.[40]

If platelet counts fall precipitously or reach levels of less than 100,000/mL, heparin should be stopped and alternative anticoagulants, such as lepirudin or argatroban, used until the patient has a therapeutic effect with warfarin. For patients with asymptomatic HIT, the 30-day cumulative thrombosis rate is 52.8%.[41] As thrombosis may occur even after withdrawal of heparin, even asymptomatic patients should be therapeutically anticoagulated with alternative agents until the platelet count has normalized.[16] Others have suggested that asymptomatic patients be treated until the HIT antibody can no longer be detected.[44] Because there is a high incidence of cross-reactivity with heparin-dependent antibodies, the LMWHs should not be used in patients with type II HIT. Furthermore, occasional reports of venous gangrene associated with decreased protein C levels suggest that warfarin, without an alternative parenteral anticoagulant, should not be used as initial monotherapy for acute HIT.[16,20,40]

The long-term administration of UFH may also be associated with osteopenia. Osteopenia is of greatest concern among patients requiring long-term prophylaxis and pregnant women receiving prophylactic or therapeutic doses of heparin for VTE, mechanical heart valves, or the antiphospholipid antibody syndrome. This most commonly arises in the setting of pregnancy, in which oral vitamin K antagonists are contraindicated, and symptomatic vertebral fractures have been noted in 2% to 3% of patients receiving heparin for longer than 1 month.[16,45] Fractures have been noted both in women receiving high-dose and low-dose heparin thromboprophylaxis.[45] Animal models have similarly shown heparin to stimulate resorption at doses as low as 25 μg/mL.[23] Bone loss with the use of UFH is secondary to both increased bone resorption and decreased bone formation. Increased osteoclast activity in animal models appears to be mediated by an osteoclast resorption-stimulating activity present in serum and is related to both the degree of sulfation and molecular size.[23] Accordingly, the LMWHs cause less osteopenia and are associated only with decreased osteoblast activity and bone formation. Perhaps due to heparin binding to matrix proteins, bone loss in animal models is not rapidly reversible.

Low-Molecular-Weight Heparin

The LMWHs were specifically developed to provide an agent that was more specific than heparin, separating its anti-IIa and anti-Xa activity, and that might reduce the hemorrhagic side effects.[15] They are derived from the chemical or enzymatic depolymerization of UFH to produce a heterogeneous mixture of species with mean molecular weights of 4500 to 5000 d.[16] The methods of depolymerization and species produced differ substantially between LMWH preparations. By definition, the LMWHs have a mean molecular weight of less than 8000 d with at least 60% of all molecules having a molecular weight of less than 8000 d.[15] Up to 30% of the components of UFH are low-molecular-weight chains.[2]

The biologic difference between UFH and the LMWHs arises from their predominant inactivation of factor Xa and reduced cellular and protein binding.[9] Owing to their shorter chain length, most LMWH species are unable to form the ternary complex required for the inactivation of thrombin, although they retain their ability to inactivate factor Xa. Among the eight LMWHs approved for use in the world (four in the United States), the anti-Xa:anti-IIa ratio varies between 1.5 and 4 in comparison to 1 for UFH.[15,16] Furthermore, because the affinity of heparin for plasma proteins depends on chain length, the LMWHs have substantially reduced protein binding.[19] Because of reduced binding to cells and plasma proteins, they are primarily renally cleared and have less interaction with macrophages, platelets, and osteoblasts. Corresponding clinical advantages of the LMWHs include 90% to 100% bioavailability, allowing once- or twice-daily subcutaneous injection; a more predictable dose-response, permitting weight-based dosing without the need for laboratory monitoring; a longer half-life; and less risk of osteopenia and HIT.[46] However, due to the high incidence of cross-reactivity, the LMWHs should not be substituted for UFH in patients with HIT. Although early animal studies suggested the LMWHs may have a wider therapeutic window and lower risk of bleeding, this has not been confirmed clinically and there are no significant differences in bleeding rates between UFH and LMWH.[9,47]

As the aPTT primarily reflects anti-IIa activity, it is not useful for monitoring the anticoagulant activity of the LMWHs. However, monitoring is unnecessary in most patients and is usually considered only in clinical situations where the dosage is poorly defined or difficult to predict. The potency of the LMWHs is most often measured by chromogenic assays for anti-Xa activity. For twice-daily administration in the treatment of DVT, anti-Xa levels of 0.6 to 1 IU/mL measured 4 hours after a subcutaneous dose appear to be adequate. Monitoring of anti-Xa levels may be appropriate in children and pregnant women, obese patients (>110 kg), and those with renal failure.[20] However, possibly because plasma assays measure only the ability to inactivate free factor Xa rather than that within the prothrombinase complex, the relationship between anti-Xa activity and in-vivo efficacy or complications is poor.[9] In the treatment of DVT, the degree of thrombus regression after 10 days of LMWH, however, appears weakly related to anti-Xa levels.[48]

Depending on the preparation and indication, the LMWHs can be administered subcutaneously once or twice daily based on total body weight. Established indications for the LMWHs include the prophylaxis and treatment of VTE and the early treatment of unstable angina.[16] In comparison with UFH, the use of LMWHs in the treatment of unstable angina or non-Q wave myocardial infarction is associated with a 15% to 20% relative risk reduction in myocardial infarction or death during the first 7 to 14 days, although this benefit is not sustained in the long term.[16] Other benefits of the LMWHs are either unclear (in combination with thrombolysis in the treatment of Q wave myocardial infarction) or doubtful (prevention of restenosis after coronary angioplasty).

■ FACTOR Xa INHIBITORS

Factor Xa may be a particularly suitable target for directed anticoagulants, since it is located at the convergence of the intrinsic and extrinsic pathways and is higher in the coagulation cascade than other potential targets. Specific inhibitors of factor Xa that are currently available or in clinical trials include various pentasaccharide derivatives. In contrast with heparin and the LMWHs, these drugs are homogeneous synthetic agents with isolated pharmacologic targets, selectively inhibiting factor Xa without a corresponding effect on factor IIa.[39] The pentasaccharide sequence corresponds to the minimal binding sequence on the heparin chain required for interaction with AT.[49] These agents thus indirectly inhibit the activity of factor Xa through AT and, unlike heparin, do not prolong the aPTT.

Fondaparinux (Arixtra) is a synthetic pentasaccharide, composed of three D-glucosamine units separated by single D-glucuronic acid and L-iduronic acid units, that reversibly binds the heparin-binding site of AT, increasing its antifactor Xa activity more than 270-fold.[50] Because it interacts only with the heparin-binding site, the drug is ineffective against thrombin but has high antifactor Xa activity.[22] Free factor Xa rather than Xa bound in the prothrombinase complex appears to be the primary target of the drug.[22] Because the agent inhibits thrombin generation, but not thrombin itself, the thrombin-mediated amplification loops are preserved and these agents do not compromise thrombin or adenosine diphosphate (ADP)-induced platelet aggregation.[49] There is, however, some experimental evidence that in the presence of fondaparinux, AT is also able to inhibit factor VIIa bound to TF.[51]

A terminal methyl group prevents nonspecific binding to plasma proteins, giving fondaparinux a predictable pharmacologic response.[52,53] No changes in the pharmacokinetic properties of the drug have been noted with concomitant administration of aspirin, warfarin, and some nonsteroidal anti-inflammatory drugs.[53] Furthermore, unlike UFH, fondaparinux is relatively insensitive to platelet-derived heparin neutralizing proteins.[22] Limited data suggest that fondaparinux does not form complexes with platelet factor 4 and does not cross-react with antibodies from patients with type II HIT.[54] The drug is 100% available after subcutaneous injection with an elimination half-life of about 17 hours, allowing once-daily subcutaneous administration in a fixed dose without monitoring.[52,53] Because the drug is not metabolized and is primarily renally excreted, precautions may be necessary in patients with renal dysfunction.

Fondaparinux is currently approved for major orthopedic prophylaxis and in a meta-analysis of 7344 patients undergoing hip replacement, major knee surgery, or surgery for hip fracture, fondaparinux 2.5 mg once daily started postoperatively reduced the odds of VTE by 55.2% in comparison with enoxaparin (6.8% vs. 13.7%).[55] However, major bleeding events were more common among those receiving fondaparinux (2.7% vs. 1.7%). In comparison with placebo after an initial 7-day course of fondaparinux in patients undergoing hip fracture surgery, extended prophylaxis for 21 days reduced the incidence of VTE at 4 weeks from 35% to 1.4%.[53] In the treatment of acute DVT, early results of phase II and III trials suggest that fondaparinux at a dose of 7.5 mg once daily is comparable in safety and efficacy to initial treatment with LMWH.[50,53] Among 2213 patients with acute symptomatic pulmonary embolism randomized to receive fondaparinux or UFH followed by a vitamin K antagonist, there was no difference in the incidence of either recurrent thromboembolism (3.8% vs. 5%) or major bleeding (1.3% vs. 1.1%).[56] Early phase II studies have also shown fondaparinux to be at least equal to UFH as an adjunct to coronary thrombolysis and angioplasty.[52,53]

The half-lives of pentasaccharide derivatives depend on their binding affinity for AT, the concentration of AT, and the elimination half-life of AT.[49] Accordingly, pentasaccharide analogs differing in their binding affinity to AT and half-life have been developed. These include an *O*-methylated, *O*-sulfated pentasaccharide with an affinity for AT 34-fold higher than that of fondaparinux.[49] The half-life of this drug is thus prolonged to as much as 61.9 hours in nonhuman primates and as much as 80 hours in humans. Idraparinux is a long-acting antifactor Xa pentasaccharide in phase III clinical trials for the treatment of VTE. The drug can be administered as a weekly subcutaneous dose. Phase III studies evaluating the efficacy of idraparinux in VTE and atrial fibrillation are in progress or planned.[53]

■ WARFARIN

Pharmacology and Mechanism of Action

The vitamin K antagonists are currently the most widely used oral anticoagulants. Vitamin K was initially discovered as an antihemorrhagic factor designated *Koagulations-vitamin*, or clotting vitamin.[57] *Vitamin K* refers to several related compounds having a methylated naphthoquinone ring structure and differing in intestinal absorption, transport, tissue distribution, and bioavailability.[57] Phylloquinone (vitamin K_1) is the most abundant dietary form of vitamin K, occurring in green vegetables such as kale, spinach, broccoli, and Brussels sprouts. Vitamin K is converted to the active hydroquinone form (KH_2), which functions as a cofactor for γ-glutamylcarboxylase in the post-translational carboxylation of glutamate residues into γ-carboxyglutamate (Fig. 31-3). These γ-carboxyglutamate residues are required for the function of their respective proteins. The active coenzyme, KH_2, is oxidized to the 2,3 epoxide form (KO) in the carboxylation reaction.[57] The epoxide is subsequently recycled to KH_2 by the enzyme KO reductase (see Fig. 31-3).

Vitamin K-dependent coagulation proteins include factors II, VII, IX, and X, as well as proteins C and S. All except protein S are synthesized exclusively in the liver. In all cases, the γ-carboxyglutamate residues function to accelerate thrombin formation by binding calcium ions, causing the protein to undergo a conformational change that exposes the platelet phospholipid-binding domain.[57] Vitamin K-dependent proteins are also involved in other regulatory processes, including bone metabolism and

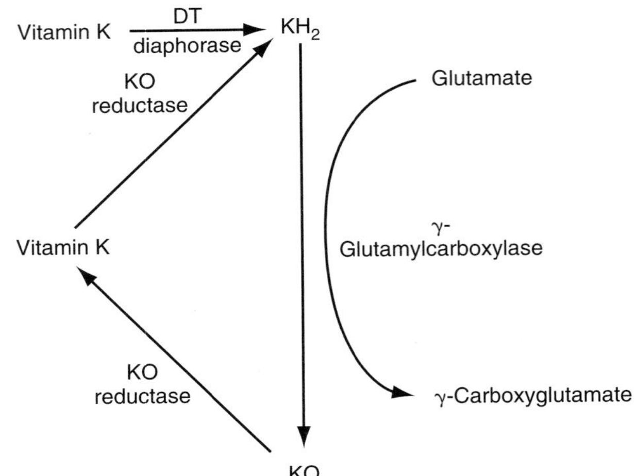

FIGURE 31-3 Vitamin K hydroquinone (KH_2) functions as the active coenzyme for γ-carboxyglutamate, which mediates the post-translational carboxylation of glutamate residues on factors II, VII, IX, and X. The carboxylation reaction oxidizes KH_2 into vitamin K 2,3 epoxide (KO). KO is then recycled in a two-stage reaction through vitamin K mediated by KO reductase. Inhibition of KO reductase allows generation of KH_2 through an alternate enzyme, DT-diaphorase, although the epoxide cannot be recycled. The vitamin K antagonists interfere with KO reductase and block the recycling of KO to KH_2. (Adapted from Vermeer C, Schurgers LJ: A comprehensive review of vitamin K and vitamin K antagonists. Hematol Oncol Clin North Am 14:339-353, 2000.)

vascular wall homeostasis, and the vitamin K antagonists interfere with physiologic processes other than those related to coagulation.[57]

The vitamin K antagonists are derived from 4-hydroxycoumarin and include warfarin, phenprocoumon, and acenocoumarol. All interfere with KO reductase and block the recycling of KO to the active hydroquinone (KH_2).[57,58] Deficiency of the active form of vitamin K causes production of partially carboxylated and decarboxylated proteins with decreased procoagulant activity. Warfarin is the most widely used vitamin K antagonist, being the 11th most frequently prescribed drug in the United States.[59] It is a racemic mixture of R and S enantiomers that are differentially metabolized, S-warfarin being approximately three times more potent.[60] Warfarin circulates bound to plasma proteins and has a half-life of 36 to 42 hours.[58]

The anticoagulant effect of warfarin is notoriously variable and is influenced by factors affecting the metabolism of warfarin; dietary and gastrointestinal factors influencing the availability and absorption of vitamin K_1; and factors such as acute illness that alter the synthesis and metabolism of vitamin K-dependent procoagulants. A reduced response to warfarin may occur in those with a diet high in green vegetables or receiving vitamin K supplements, whereas the effect my be potentiated in patients receiving intravenous antibiotics or with fat malabsorption. Drugs that have been associated with potentiation or inhibition of the anticoagulant effects of warfarin are shown in Table 31-2. Given the diversity of drug interactions, more frequent monitoring of the INR is warranted when new medications are added or withdrawn. Genetic factors may also play a role in the anticoagulant response to warfarin. Hereditary resistance to warfarin, with

Table 31-2 Warfarin Drug and Food Interactions

WARFARIN INTERACTION WITH	POTENTIATION	INHIBITION
Drugs	Amiodarone, acetaminophen, acetylsalicylic acid, anabolic steroids, cefamandole, cefazolin, chloral hydrate, cimetidine, ciprofloxacin, clofibrate, cotrimoxazole, dextropropoxyphene, disopyramide, disulfiram, erythromycin, fluconazole, fluorouracil, flu vaccine, gemfibrozil, heparin, ifosfamide, indomethacin, isoniazid, itraconazole, ketoprofen, lovastatin, metolazone, metronidazole, miconazole, moricizine, nalidixic acid, norfloxacin, ofloxacin, omeprazole, phenylbutazone, phenytoin, piroxicam, propafenone, propoxyphene, propranolol, sulindac, sulfinpyrazone, sulfisoxazole, tamoxifen, tetracycline, tolmetin, quinidine	Azathioprine, barbiturates, carbamazepine, chlordiazepoxide, cholestyramine, cyclosporine, dicloxacillin, etretinate, griseofulvin, nafcillin, rifampin, sucralfate, trazodone
Dietary	Alcohol (if concomitant liver disease)	Foods high in vitamin K, enteral feeding

Adapted from Hirsh J, Dalen JE, Anderson DR: Oral anticoagulants: Mechanism of action, clinical effectiveness, and optimal therapeutic range. Chest 119(Suppl 1):8S-21S, 2001.

affected patients requiring up to 2.6 mg/kg/day of warfarin, has been reported.[61] Such patients require high plasma levels of warfarin for adequate anticoagulation but have otherwise normal warfarin pharmacokinetics. Conversely, genetic heterogeneity for cytochrome P450 CYP2C9, the enzyme responsible for converting S-warfarin to its inactive hydroxyl forms, is associated with decreased dose requirements. Patients with a low warfarin dose requirement (<1.5 mg/day) are six times more likely to have a variant CYP2C9 allele associated with impaired S-warfarin metabolism.[60] These individuals have been noted to have more problems on induction of warfarin therapy and a 3.7-fold higher rate of major bleeding complications. Other mutations, such as those in the carboxylase recognition site of the factor IX propeptide, are also associated with an increased risk of bleeding during initiation of oral anticoagulation but are substantially less common.[62]

The anticoagulant effect of warfarin is most commonly measured using the PT, which is sensitive to reductions in three of the four vitamin K-dependent procoagulants (factors II, VII, and X). Unfortunately, thromboplastin reagents used in the PT assay vary in their responsiveness to the anticoagulant effects of warfarin, which in the past led to clinically important differences in recommended oral anticoagulant doses. This has largely been rectified by standardizing thromboplastins according to their International Sensitivity Index (ISI), which measures the responsiveness of a given thromboplastin to a reduction in vitamin K-dependent factors in comparison to a reference standard. The effect of warfarin-induced anticoagulation is now standardized by converting the PT measured with local thromboplastin reagents to an INR[58] calculated as

$$\text{INR} = (\text{patient PT} \div \text{mean normal PT})^{\text{ISI}}$$

Unfortunately, at least some evidence suggests that the anticoagulant effects of warfarin, as measured by the PT, are disassociated from the antithrombotic effects during the induction of treatment. This observation arises from the fact that prolongation of the PT early after initiating warfarin primarily reflects reductions in factor VII, which has the shortest half-life. However, the antithrombotic effect is more closely related to the level of prothrombin, which has a half-life of 96 hours in comparison with 6 to 24 hours for factors VII and IX.[58] The delayed reduction in prothrombin levels is the basis for overlapping heparin and warfarin treatment.

Dose and Administration

Randomized clinical trials have established the effectiveness of warfarin in the primary and secondary prevention of VTE; for the prevention of embolism in patients with prosthetic heart valves or atrial fibrillation; for the prevention of stroke, recurrent myocardial infarction, and death in patients with anterior myocardial infarction; for the prevention of anterior myocardial infarction in patients with peripheral vascular disease; and for the prevention of myocardial infarction in high-risk males.[58] Other commonly recognized indications include rheumatic mitral valve disease, mitral valve prolapse, mitral annular calcification, nonrheumatic mitral regurgitation, mobile aortic atheromas or plaques larger than 4 mm, and systemic thromboembolism of unknown etiology.[63] One large randomized trial has shown oral anticoagulants to be more effective than aspirin in preventing thrombosis of infrainguinal vein, but not prosthetic grafts.[64]

Clinical trials have demonstrated a moderate intensity of anticoagulation (INR, 2.0 to 3.0) to be appropriate for most indications. Although there is limited evidence that less intense anticoagulation may have a role in some settings, the therapeutic effect of warfarin is significantly reduced at INR values lower than 2. An INR of 1.3 to 2.0 may reduce myocardial ischemic events when used as primary prevention in men without ischemic heart disease.[58] However, despite the observation that low-intensity warfarin (INR, 1.5 to 2.0) is more effective than placebo in the long-term prevention of recurrent VTE[65] after a standard course of anticoagulation, conventional-intensity therapy (INR, 2.0 to 3.0) is associated with fewer recurrent episodes (0.7 vs. 1.9 per 100 person-years) and a similar risk of bleeding (0.9 vs. 1.1 events per 100 person-years) in comparison with low-intensity therapy.[66] There are some settings, including some types of mechanical prosthetic heart valves and some patients with antiphospholipid antibody syndrome, in which more intense anticoagulation may be appropriate. Data from retrospective studies have suggested an improved outcome in patients with antiphospholipid antibodies anticoagulated to an INR of 2.5 to 3.5. However, this has not been confirmed in clinical trials in which there was no significant difference in the incidence of recurrent thromboembolic events among patients randomized to moderate- (INR, 2.0 to 3.0) or high- (INR, 3.1 to 4.0) intensity warfarin.[67]

The appropriate initial warfarin dose remains controversial, although initiating warfarin at a dose of 5 mg, rather than with a loading dose of 10 mg, is often recommended. As noted earlier, the antithrombotic effect of warfarin is most closely related to prothrombin levels, which are equivalently reduced by a 5- or 10-mg dose.[58] A therapeutic INR can usually be achieved within 4 to 5 days after initiating warfarin at 5 mg/day. Adverse effects of loading doses of warfarin include a more rapid reduction in protein C and a higher risk of over-anticoagulation. Higher initial doses should be avoided in those at risk of bleeding or with a known deficiency of protein C or S, in whom the risk of skin necrosis is higher.[63] Although parenteral anticoagulants can be avoided when instituting anticoagulation for chronic atrial fibrillation,[63] heparin should be simultaneously administered for 4 to 5 days, until the INR is in the therapeutic range on two measurements at least 24 hours apart, if urgent anticoagulation is required for the treatment of thromboembolic disease.[68] Simultaneous initiation of heparin and warfarin is safe and not associated with more frequent recurrence or hemorrhage.[63] Several studies have demonstrated that the use of adjuvants such as computer-driven protocols and nomograms can improve the initiation and maintenance of anticoagulation with vitamin K antagonists.[63]

Complications

Although effective in preventing thrombosis, warfarin has a very narrow therapeutic window. Several factors, including widespread adoption of the INR, decreased intensity of anticoagulation, and the organization of anticoagulation clinics, has increased the safety of long-term oral anticoagulation.[69] However, bleeding remains the most important associated complication and is closely related to the intensity of anticoagulation. Clinical trials have established that the bleeding risk increases as the INR is increased from 2.0-3.0 to 3.0-4.5 and rises exponentially as the INR increases above 5.0.[68] However, total time in the therapeutic range is also an important determinant of bleeding risk as well as anticoagulant efficacy. Risk factors for bleeding include a history of hemorrhage, previous stroke, and comorbid conditions such as renal insufficiency or hypertension. The independent risk of bleeding associated with age remains controversial, but at least some data suggest that elderly patients can be safely anticoagulated if closely monitored in the setting of an anticoagulation clinic. The overall rate of major bleeding during a 3-month course of warfarin to maintain an INR of 2.0 to 3.0 is ≤ 3%.[37] Various clinical trials have reported major bleeding rates between 0.5 and 4.2 per 100 patients, whereas cohort studies have reported somewhat higher rates of 1.2 to 7.0 episodes per 100 patients.[63] The risk of bleeding is increased when high-intensity warfarin (INR, 3.0 to 4.5) is used in combination with aspirin.[58] However, increased rates of minor bleeding have also been reported with lower-intensity regimens.

Nonhemorrhagic adverse effects of warfarin include an associated embryopathy and warfarin-induced skin necrosis. Oral anticoagulants cross the placenta and are associated with a characteristic embryopathy, central nervous system deficits, and increased rates of fetal death. The coumarin derivatives interfere with calcium deposition, causing irregular deposition in areas that are not normally calcified, and approximately 30% of babies born to mothers taking these drugs have serious bone defects.[57] Although the incidence of embryopathy is highest during the first 6 to 12 weeks of gestation, fetal bleeding and death may occur throughout pregnancy.[68] Although warfarin is contraindicated during pregnancy, it can be safely administered to nursing mothers.[68] Warfarin-induced skin necrosis is a rare complication associated with large loading doses of warfarin and presumably occurs when the introduction of warfarin causes a more rapid reduction in protein C levels than in the other vitamin K-dependent procoagulants.[70] Its incidence is estimated to be between 1:100 and 1:10,000 and is more common in women with a predilection for the breast, thighs, and buttocks.[71] Patients with deficiencies of the protein C pathway may be particularly susceptible to skin necrosis, although this complication may also occur in nondeficient individuals. Introducing warfarin gradually while the patient is receiving therapeutic doses of parenteral anticoagulants can minimize the potential for this complication.

■ DIRECT THROMBIN INHIBITORS

Thrombin has multiple roles in coagulation including conversion of fibrinogen to fibrin, amplification of the coagulation cascade, and activation of platelets.[5,10] Given its central role in coagulation and cardiovascular disease, the treatment of many thrombotic disorders is directed toward blocking the action of thrombin. Heparin has historically been used as a primary treatment of such disorders, although it has several limitations including extensive protein binding and an inability to inactivate platelet-bound factor Xa and fibrin-bound thrombin.

This last consideration may be particularly important. The thrombin molecule contains three binding sites including the catalytic site responsible for the cleavage of substrates (active site); a substrate recognition site that also functions as the binding site for the AT component of the heparin-AT complex (exosite 1); and a heparin-binding domain (exosite 2).[19,24] Heparin bound to exosite 2 bridges more fibrin onto thrombin and renders the heparin-fibrin-thrombin complex inaccessible to inhibition by AT.[19] Such fibrin-bound thrombin serves as a reservoir of thrombogenic activity capable of converting factors V and VIII to their active form; generating fibrin from fibrinogen; activating factor XIII; and attenuating fibrinolysis.[21] Bound thrombin also continues to activate platelets through thromboxane A_2-independent mechanisms that are not inhibited by aspirin.[72] Platelet-bound factor Xa is similarly resistant to inactivation by the heparin-AT complex, serving as a source of further thrombin generation.[21] Drugs such as heparin therefore incompletely attenuate the thrombotic process, a potentially important concern at sites of arterial injury.

The direct thrombin inhibitors offer several potential advantages over heparin. These agents act independently of AT, either blocking the active site or preventing interaction with its substrates. Several direct thrombin inhibitors have been developed and can be classified as being natural substrate analogs, recombinant derivatives, or synthetic inhibitors; as being directed against the active site or exosites; and as being reversible or irreversible inhibitors.[21,44] Three parenteral direct thrombin inhibitors—lepirudin, bivalirudin, and argatroban—are currently available and oral direct thrombin inhibitors, such as ximelagatran, are on the horizon. Lepirudin and argatroban are approved for the treatment of HIT, whereas bivalirudin is approved as an adjunct to coronary angioplasty. These agents can typically be monitored with the aPTT.[44]

Fibrin binding does not compromise agents directed against the active site. Although inhibitors that also bind exosite 1 compete with fibrin, the fibrin-thrombin interaction is of low affinity in the absence of heparin.[21] The lower-molecular-weight thrombin inhibitors are more effective against fibrin-bound thrombin, presumably because of better diffusion into the thrombus.[19] In addition to inhibiting the action of thrombin on fibrinogen, the direct thrombin inhibitors block amplification of coagulation through activation of factors V and VIII as well as fibrin stabilization by factor XIII.[44] These agents do not bind plasma proteins, resulting in a more predictable dose-response than heparin.[1,19] Additionally, unlike heparin, these drugs are not neutralized by platelet factor 4 and multimers of von Willebrand's factor, large quantities of which may be present at sites of arterial plaque rupture.[21] Finally, the direct thrombin inhibitors do not promote the platelet release reactions and inactivate thrombin-induced platelet activation.[73] The combined ability to inhibit fibrin-bound thrombin without inducing platelet aggregation may be particularly important in the management of acute coronary syndromes.[74] In a meta-analysis including 35,970 patients, the use of direct thrombin inhibitors in the setting of acute coronary syndromes was associated with a 15% reduction in death or myocardial infarction in comparison with heparin.[72] It was estimated that 125 patients would need to be treated with a direct thrombin inhibitor to avoid one event. Although not currently supported by any data, similar concerns may exist in the patient with peripheral vascular disease.

Despite similar advantages, there are potentially important differences in the anticoagulant profiles of the direct thrombin inhibitors, and they should not be regarded as pharmacologically equivalent.[21] These agents do vary in their specificity, and at least some are capable of inhibiting other serine proteases.[75] Additionally, the theoretical observation that some of these drugs, particularly the tripeptide derivatives, may interfere with fibrinolysis is of unknown significance.[44,75]

Hirudin Derivatives

Hirudin, a 65-amino acid polypeptide derived from salivary extracts of the medicinal leech (*Hirudo medicinalis*), is the prototype direct thrombin inhibitor. Various recombinant derivatives of hirudin have been developed. Lepirudin is a recombinant derivative of hirudin lacking a sulfated tyrosine at residue 63 and is therefore known as a *desulfatohirudin* or *deshirudin*.[19,76] A long-acting polyethylene glycol (PEG)-complexed hirudin derivative (PEG-hirudin) has also been developed and evaluated in phase II trials.[72] Both native and recombinant hirudins form an essentially irreversible 1:1 complex with both the active site and exosite, although the deshirudins have a 10-fold lower affinity for thrombin.[19,21] Although most direct thrombin inhibitors have a predictable anticoagulant response, hirudin's narrow therapeutic window mandates monitoring.[21]

Lepirudin has a half-life of 1.3 hours, is renally excreted, and can be monitored using the aPTT.[16] An initial bolus infusion of 0.4 mg/kg followed by a continuous infusion of 0.15 mg/kg/hr with subsequent adjustments to maintain the aPTT between 1.5 and 2.5 times baseline has been recommended.[20] As it is renally cleared, strict dosage adjustment in renal failure is required.[20] Lepirudin is approved for the treatment of HIT. Clinical trials have also demonstrated hirudin to be at least as safe and effective as heparin in the management of unstable angina, as an adjunct to thrombolytic therapy, and in the prophylaxis and treatment of VTE.[19] However, there remain concerns that hirudin's narrow therapeutic window may limit its application in acute coronary syndromes, where high doses are often required and bleeding rates may be higher.[21,72,74]

Hirulogs

The hirulogs inhibit thrombin by binding to both the catalytic site and the anion binding exosite.[44,76] Bivalirudin (Angiomax) is a 20-amino acid synthetic analog of hirudin. Unlike hirudin, inhibition by bivalirudin is reversed by cleavage of the amino terminus by thrombin, thereby freeing the active site and leaving only the low-affinity interaction between the carboxyterminus and exosite 1. Because it is a reversible inhibitor, bivalirudin may have a wider therapeutic window than hirudin.[21] Bivalirudin has a half-life of 25 minutes and is eliminated both by renal clearance and by proteolytic cleavage.[24] Clearance is reduced in patients with renal insufficiency. Although bivalirudin causes dose-dependent increases in the activated clotting time (ACT), aPTT, PT, and thrombin time, point of care monitoring with the ACT is the most often used. For percutaneous coronary intervention (PCI), dose adjustment to maintain an ACT of 350 seconds or greater has been recommended.[24]

Bivalirudin is the only direct thrombin inhibitor approved for the management of acute coronary syndromes, demonstrating superiority to UFH in the frequency of death, myocardial infarction, or revascularization at 7 and 90 days after coronary angioplasty.[24] Among 4312 patients undergoing angioplasty for unstable or postinfarction angina, the incidence of death, myocardial infarction, or revascularization was lower among patients randomized to bivalirudin than in those receiving heparin both at 7 days (6.2% vs. 7.9%) and 30 days (9.0% vs. 10.4%).[77] The incidence of clinically significant bleeding was also less in the bivalirudin cohort (3.5% vs. 9.3%). A meta-analysis of trials evaluating the use of bivalirudin in acute coronary syndromes and percutaneous intervention showed bivalirudin to be at least as effective as UFH in reducing the incidence of death or myocardial infarction but with a significant reduction in major hemorrhage.[74] Other meta-analyses have similarly suggested the use of bivalirudin to be associated with a reduced risk of major bleeding.[72] In comparison with heparin, the use of bivalirudin was associated with one fewer bleeding event for every 21 patients treated.[72] This uncoupling of efficacy and bleeding after angioplasty is unique to bivalirudin.

Small-Molecule Direct Thrombin Inhibitors

Small-molecule direct thrombin inhibitors have also been developed. These include a number of tripeptide derivatives or peptidomimetic compounds such as argatroban, melagatran, efegatran, inogatran, and napsagatran.[78] Most are characterized by a strongly basic group interacting with the active site of thrombin, have low oral bioavailability, have short plasma half-lives, and are hepatically metabolized. All produce predictable anticoagulation measurable by common coagulation assays with minimal drug interactions. Plasma levels and anticoagulant response tend to be linearly related to dose with little intraindividual variation. However, because of interactions, the PT/INR cannot be used to monitor the introduction of oral vitamin K antagonists while receiving parenteral direct thrombin inhibitors.[78] As for UFH, a coagulation rebound phenomenon has been observed with the parenteral direct thrombin inhibitors. In comparison with other direct thrombin inhibitors used in the treatment of acute coronary syndromes, the univalent inhibitors are associated with a borderline increased risk of myocardial infarction and lower rates of major bleeding.[72]

Of the parenteral small-molecule direct thrombin inhibitors, argatroban (Acova) is the only agent that is currently FDA approved. Argatroban is an arginine derivative that functions as a reversible, competitive inhibitor at the catalytic site of thrombin. Unlike heparin, argatroban does not cause release of TFPI, which may contribute to its predictability and relatively low incidence of bleeding.[44] It has a half-life of 30 to 45 minutes and is hepatically metabolized by hydroxylation and aromatization of the 3-methyltetrahydroquinolone ring with subsequent biliary excretion.[19,20,79] Hepatic insufficiency is associated with a fourfold decrease in the total clearance of argatroban and a twofold to threefold increase in half-life.[78,79] In contrast with the other available direct thrombin inhibitors, the clearance and half-life of argatroban are independent of renal function.[79] The anticoagulant effect of argatroban is predictable with a low coefficient of variability between healthy subjects. However, the response is dose dependent and requires monitoring with either the aPTT or ACT.[73]

Ximelagatran (H 376/95) is the orally available prodrug of melagatran, a dipeptide direct thrombin inhibitor. The prodrug is 170 times more lipophilic than melagatran, allowing oral administration and absorption.[80] In contrast with other small-molecule inhibitors, ximelagatran has an oral bioavailability of 18% to 24% with minimal protein binding and low variability in plasma levels.[78,80] Ximelagatran is biotransformed to melagatran after oral administration and competitively and reversibly binds to the active site of thrombin. Active melagatran is cleared by the kidneys with a half-life of 3 hours.[19] It can be administered twice daily and has a predictable pharmacokinetic effect that is not influenced by age, gender, or weight, thus requiring no monitoring.[81] The drug has no relevant interactions with food or drugs metabolized by cytochrome P-450.[82]

Several clinical trials evaluating the safety and efficacy of ximelagatran in VTE and atrial fibrillation are currently underway or have recently been reported. In comparison with dalteparin (5000 IU once daily), the combination of subcutaneous melagatran (3 mg twice daily) started preoperatively and oral ximelagatran (24 mg twice daily) postoperatively reduced the frequency of VTE in orthopedic patients from 28.2% to 15.1%, although the frequency of excessive bleeding was somewhat higher (5.0% vs. 2.4%).[83] Ximelagatran in a dose of 24 mg twice daily has also shown efficacy comparable to that of enoxaparin in preventing VTE after total knee replacement.[84] In contrast, ximelagatran at a dose of 36 mg twice daily was significantly more effective than warfarin in reducing the incidence of VTE and death (20.3% vs. 27.6%) in patients undergoing total knee replacement.[82] No increased bleeding was observed in patients receiving 36 mg of ximelagatran twice daily. Ximelagatran has also shown promise in the extended treatment of a first episode of VTE. After completion of a 6-month course of anticoagulation, ximelagatran (24 mg twice daily) reduced the incidence of recurrent thromboembolism from 12.6% to 2.8% at 18 months.[85] There was no increased bleeding among patients receiving ximelagatran, although increased transaminase levels were more frequent (6.4% vs. 1.2%) than in those receiving placebo. Ximelagatran has also shown promise in the prevention of stroke in patients with nonvalvular atrial fibrillation, and clinical trials evaluating the usefulness of this approach are in progress.[86] In comparison with aspirin alone in patients with acute coronary syndromes, ximelagatran and aspirin for 6 months significantly reduced the incidence of death, nonfatal myocardial infarction, and severe recurrent ischemia from 16.3% to 12.7%.[87] Such extended treatment may provide effective secondary prophylaxis as well as protection against rebound events after UFH or LMWH are discontinued. The incidence of major bleeding did not differ between groups, although elevated transaminase levels were more common among those receiving ximelagatran. Transaminase elevation appears to be dose related, to occur within 2 to 6 months of treatment, and to be asymptomatic.[87] Other phase II trials have noted a 4.3% incidence of self-limited transaminase elevation.[86] Given the limitations of warfarin, it is anticipated that these drugs will replace vitamin K antagonists in the chronic treatment of atrial fibrillation and VTE.

■ ANTIPLATELET AGENTS

Platelets also play a significant role in most cardiovascular disorders and are an attractive target both for reducing long-term morbidity and mortality and as an adjunct to intervention. Platelets are involved in the development and progression of atherosclerosis and arterial and graft thrombosis as well as of restenosis after surgery and percutaneous intervention.[88] Endothelial injury is the first step in atherogenesis and leads to the exposure of subendothelial collagen and von Willebrand's factor. Interaction of subendothelial collagen and von Willebrand's factor with the GP-Ia/IIa and Ib-IX complex, respectively, results in platelet adhesion.[88] Shear forces at sites of stenosis also induce platelet aggregation through the binding of von Willebrand's factor to GP-Ib. Following platelet adhesion, a number of agonists including collagen, thrombin, thromboxane A_2, epinephrine, serotonin, and ADP interact with specific surface receptors to induce platelet activation.[89]

Platelet activation causes a conformational change in the GP-IIb/IIIa receptor, increasing its affinity for fibrinogen and von Willebrand's factor. Fibrinogen-mediated cross-linking of activated platelets, a process dependent on fibrinogen binding to GP-IIb/IIIa, is the final common pathway of platelet aggregation.[21,76,89] Platelet activation also causes the release of platelet granules, including ADP. ADP amplifies the response to other agonists, induces further platelet aggregation, and leads to generation of thromboxane A_2. P-selectin, contained in the alpha granules, also rapidly appears in the platelet membrane after activation. P-selectin expression and fibrinogen binding are increased in patients with peripheral vascular disease, suggesting enhanced platelet activation in these patients.[88] There is also evidence of platelet activation during angiography and angioplasty of peripheral arteries.[88,90]

Antiplatelet agents have a number of potential uses in vascular surgery, including reducing cardiovascular morbidity and as an adjunct to vascular intervention. Currently approved antiplatelet agents include aspirin; the ADP antagonists clopidogrel and ticlopidine; and the GP-IIb/IIIa antagonists abciximab, eptifibatide, and tirofiban.[2] A number of clinical trials have established that antiplatelet therapy reduces the risk of myocardial infarction and stroke by one third and vascular death by one sixth among patients with ischemic coronary or cerebrovascular disease.[91,92] Aspirin, ticlopidine, and clopidogrel also appear effective in reducing the risk of stroke, myocardial infarction, and vascular death among patients with peripheral vascular disease. Meta-analysis of several randomized trials, including patients with vascular disease, suggests a 25% reduction in the odds of sustaining an important vascular event (stroke, myocardial infarction, or vascular death) with the use of antiplatelet agents.[93] Perhaps as a consequence, limited data suggest that improved medical management, including the widespread use of antiplatelet agents, has improved the mortality rate in patients with peripheral arterial disease. In comparison to a historical mortality rate of 7.06 deaths per 100 patient-years, recent data suggest a mortality rate of 4 per 100 patient-years, with cardiovascular disease accounting for a smaller proportion of deaths.[94] Based on such data, the TransAtlantic Intersociety Consensus (TASC) panel recommends that all patients with peripheral arterial disease be considered for treatment with aspirin or other approved antiplatelet agent.[95]

Aspirin has been the most widely studied antiplatelet agent. It acts to permanently inactivate the cyclooxygenase (COX) activity of prostaglandin H synthase-1 and synthase 2 (COX-1 and COX-2) by acetylation of the COX site in the enzymatic domain.[96] These isozymes catalyze the first step leading from arachidonic acid to thromboxane A_2, which induces platelet aggregation and vasoconstriction, and prostaglandin I_2, which inhibits platelet aggregation and causes vasodilatation. Aspirin undergoes extensive first-pass hepatic metabolism to salicylate, a weak reversible COX inhibitor.[97] Despite its short half-life (15 to 20 minutes), once-daily dosing is able to completely inhibit platelet thromboxane A_2 production through irreversible inhibition of COX-1 and has proved equally effective in low (50 to 100 mg/day) and high (900 to 1500 mg/day) doses.[92] In contrast, endothelial prostaglandin I_2 production is derived from both COX-1 and COX-2 activity, COX-2-dependent synthesis being relatively aspirin resistant.[96] Nevertheless, even chronic low doses of aspirin do reduce basal and stimulated prostacyclin production.[97] Although the clinical relevance of reduced prostacyclin production remains controversial, use of the lowest effective dose may maximize efficacy and minimize toxicity.[96] Aspirin does have other effects at high doses, including an anti-inflammatory action and suppression of plasma coagulation, but it is doubtful that these effects are as clinically relevant as suppression of platelet thromboxane A_2 production.[96] As the mean life span of circulating platelets is 10 days, approximately 50% of platelets remain functional 5 to 6 days after treatment.

Aspirin has been shown to be beneficial in preventing fatal and/or nonfatal vascular events in the settings of acute myocardial infarction, chronic stable angina, unstable angina, prior myocardial infarction, acute ischemic stroke, and transient ischemic attack or minor stroke.[96] Aspirin, at an initial dose of 162 mg administered for at least 30 days, has the best benefit-risk ratio of any therapy for acute myocardial infarction and should be administered to virtually all patients with evolving myocardial infarction.[98] Aspirin at a dose of 75 to 325 mg per day has been recommended for secondary prevention of vascular events in the other high-risk groups. It has also proved to be useful in primary prevention, reducing the risk of a first myocardial infarction in otherwise healthy physicians from 32% to 44%.[98] However, despite these promising results, the data regarding the use of aspirin for primary prophylaxis in healthy persons are currently regarded as insufficient and should be guided by clinical judgment.[96,98]

The clinical role of dipyridamole, an inhibitor of cyclic nucleotide phosphodiesterase that increases cyclic adenosine monophosphate levels within platelets, remains controversial.[76] Although its efficacy remains in doubt, recent studies have suggested a benefit in patients with prior stroke or transient ischemic attacks in comparison with aspirin alone.[96]

Ticlopidine and clopidogrel are thienopyridine derivatives that selectively inhibit ADP-induced platelet aggregation through permanent alteration of a postulated ADP receptor.[96] Both can be considered prodrugs, being hepatically metabolized to an active transient metabolite, and are considered to act through similar mechanisms.[76,99] Both increase the bleeding time, with a maximal effect after 5 to 6 days of oral administration.[76]

At least some trials have suggested that the antiplatelet effect of ticlopidine may be delayed for up to 2 weeks, and ticlopidine may be a suboptimal agent when immediate antiplatelet effects are required. Ticlopidine is approved for the treatment of cerebral ischemia when aspirin has failed, is contraindicated, or is not tolerated.[96] Although hypercholesterolemia and neutropenia may mitigate its beneficial effects,[92] ticlopidine is also effective in claudicants, reducing mortality by 29.1% in comparison with controls.[100] Potentially severe complications of ticlopidine include bone marrow suppression (leukopenia, thrombocytopenia, pancytopenia), aplastic anemia, and thrombotic thrombocytopenic purpura. Careful monitoring is therefore required during the first 3 months of therapy.

Clopidogrel is six times more potent and has a better safety profile than ticlopidine[76] and may be more effective than aspirin among patients with symptomatic peripheral arterial disease. Clopidogrel is rapidly hepatically metabolized to an active platelet inhibitor with a short half-life.[99] Similar to aspirin, the active metabolite of clopidogrel is thought to permanently alter platelet function, with cumulative inhibition on repeated daily dosing.[96] At doses of 50 to 100 mg, clopidogrel requires 4 to 7 days to reach a steady state of 50% to 60% inhibition of ADP-induced platelet aggregation. However, loading doses of the drug (300 mg) result in much more rapid inhibition.[96] Approximately 7 days are required for platelet function to return to normal after cumulative doses are stopped. The bleeding risk associated with clopidogrel is approximately equivalent to that of aspirin, although aspirin is more likely to cause gastrointestinal bleeding.[101]

Clopidogrel is approved for the reduction of cardiovascular events in patients with peripheral vascular disease, recent stoke, or recent myocardial infarction.[96] In this group, clopidogrel was associated with a 23.8% reduction in the risk of stroke, myocardial infarction, or vascular death in comparison with aspirin (3.71% vs. 4.86% per year).[102] Limited data suggest that the complementary mechanisms of aspirin and clopidogrel may provide additive benefits in high-risk patients.[96] In comparison with aspirin alone in patients with acute coronary syndromes without ST-segment elevation, the combination of aspirin and clopidogrel reduced the incidence of cardiovascular death, nonfatal myocardial infarction, or stroke from 11.4% to 9.3%.[103] Major bleeding, mostly from gastrointestinal hemorrhage and bleeding at puncture sites, was more common in the clopidogrel group (3.7% vs. 2.7%). In contrast, in comparison with placebo, the combination of aspirin and clopidogrel was found to increase the risk of bleeding (24% vs. 42%) without a reduction in thrombotic events in patients with expanded polytetrafluoroethylene hemodialysis grafts.[101]

Unfortunately, aspirin and the thienopyridines target only thromboxane A_2 and ADP-mediated platelet aggregation, leaving the action of other agonists intact. It is now recognized that the integrin αIIbβ3 (GP-IIb/IIIa) is the final common pathway of platelet aggregation and that receptor antagonists are potent inhibitors of platelet aggregation.[96] Expression of the GP-IIb/IIIa integrin mediates fibrinogen binding to platelets through the Arg-Gly-Asp (RGD) and Arg-Gly-Asp-Ser (RGDS) amino acid sequences of fibrinogen, von Willebrand's factor, and fibronectin.[76] A number of GP-IIb/IIIa inhibitors have been developed including monoclonal antibodies, peptides containing the RGD sequence, and RGD mimetics. The monoclonal antibodies are noncompetitive antagonists, whereas the peptides and peptidomimetics are competitive inhibitors.[89] In addition to their antiplatelet effects, these agents diminish thrombin generation through reduced phosphatidylserine exposure and factor V binding.[11] For unclear reasons, antibody antagonists of GP-IIb/IIIa are better inhibitors of thrombin generation than are the peptide inhibitors.[11]

Abciximab (ReoPro) is a mouse/human chimeric Fab that binds the GP-IIb/IIIa receptor. A 0.25 mg/kg bolus of abciximab reduces ADP-induced platelet aggregation to less than 20%. Although platelet aggregation returns to higher than 50% within 24 hours, blockade can be maintained for 12 hours by following the bolus with a 10-μg/min infusion. Several large trials have demonstrated significant reductions in death, myocardial infarction, or urgent revascularization in patients undergoing PCI as well as a reduction in 1-year mortality.[89] Although bleeding with the use of abciximab remains a concern, recent trials have shown that when used in conjunction with carefully managed heparin and early removal of arterial sheaths, major bleeding rates are as low as, or lower than with heparin alone.[89] Current recommendations include reducing the heparin dose to 70 U/kg with a target ACT between 200 and 250 seconds. Because all of the parenteral GP-IIb/IIIa inhibitors may be associated with thrombocytopenia, platelet counts should be monitored over 24 hours after initiating therapy.

Other GP-IIa/IIIb antagonists include tirofiban (Aggrastat), a nonpeptide tyrosine derivative, and eptifibatide (Integrilin), a synthetic cyclic heptapeptide. Abciximab is approved for the treatment of patients with unstable angina expected to undergo coronary intervention (PCI) within 18 to 24 hours, whereas tirofiban and eptifibatide are approved for use in patients with acute coronary syndromes to be managed medically or with PCI.[96] A number of oral, nonpeptide GP-IIb/IIIa inhibitors have also been developed (sibrafiban, orbofiban), although their role in the long-term management of coronary artery disease remains unclear.[89]

Although lacking the voluminous data supporting their use in cardiology, antiplatelet agents also have a unique role in the management of vascular surgery patients. Aspirin appears to delay the angiographic progression of arterial occlusive disease, likely due to inhibition of plaque-associated thrombosis,[104] and to reduce the risk of peripheral arterial surgery.[105] In a randomized trial of patients undergoing carotid endarterectomy, low-dose aspirin (81 to 325 mg/day) was associated with a twofold reduction in the risk of stroke, myocardial infarction, or death at 30 and 90 days in comparison to higher dose regimens (650 to 1300 mg/day).[106]

Although there is no evidence to suggest that antiplatelet agents are effective in preventing restenosis of lower extremity reconstructions, some drugs may have a role in prolonging graft patency through other mechanisms.[104,107,108] These drugs may reduce the thrombogenic potential of grafts, particularly prosthetic conduits that take up platelets to a much greater extent than vein grafts. Aspirin has been the most widely studied drug, and although the results of randomized trials are conflicting, they do suggest that antiplatelet therapy begun preoperatively may improve graft patency, especially in prosthetic conduits.[109] Although oral anticoagulants were more effective in patients with autologous infrainguinal grafts, one large randomized trial showed aspirin to be more effective in preventing occlusion of prosthetic grafts.[64] Approximately 15 patients with prosthetic grafts need to be treated to prevent one occlusion. At least five other randomized, controlled trials have supported the role of aspirin, with or without dipyridamole, in preventing occlusion after infrainguinal bypass.[88] Current consensus recommendations are that aspirin 325 mg/day be started preoperatively for all prosthetic conduits; grafts to the tibial-peroneal arteries; complex reconstructions requiring composite grafts or endarterectomy; and suboptimal bypasses with limited runoff or requiring a compromised conduit.[104] In comparison to placebo, one randomized trial has also shown ticlopidine to significantly prolong the patency of lower extremity saphenous vein bypass grafts.[110] Although the risk of oral anticoagulants may outweigh the benefits in uncomplicated infrainguinal bypasses, the combination of aspirin 325 mg/day and warfarin to maintain an INR of 2 to 3 appears to improve the patency of high-risk grafts.[104] Among such patients, the combination of warfarin and aspirin was associated with 3-year primary graft patency and limb salvage rates of 74% and 81%, respectively, in comparison with 51% and 31% for those treated with aspirin alone.[111]

NOVEL ANTICOAGULANTS

In addition to the strategies discussed earlier, other agents under development selectively target the inhibition of the TF-VIIa pathway, factor Xa, and factor IXa. None of these agents are currently available, although many are in early-phase clinical trials. Because TF appears to be important in atherogenesis and arterial thrombosis, it is an attractive target for blocking the initiation phase of anticoagulation.[112] Various inhibitors of this pathway have been developed, including anti-TF antibodies, TF mutants, and analogs that bind factor VIIa but inhibit TF-VIIa catalytic activity, active site blocked factor VIIa (recombinant VIIai), and TFPI.[113] Animal studies have suggested that exogenous TFPI can prevent venous thrombosis, ameliorate intravascular coagulation in response to TF or endotoxin, reduce mortality from sepsis, and prevent restenosis in balloon angioplasty models.[14] Various recombinant forms of TFPI, a 276-amino acid polypeptide, have been developed that have antithrombotic activity in animal models and may have a role in arterial thrombosis.[76] Recombinant nematode anticoagulant protein (r-NAPc2) inhibits the TF-VIIa complex after initially forming a complex with zymogen or activated factor X.[112] The recombinant protein has a half-life of 50 hours or longer and is bioavailable after a subcutaneous dose. r-NAPc2 has been shown to be safe when administered in conjunction with heparin, aspirin, and clopidogrel in the setting of coronary angioplasty and to suppress thrombin generation to a greater extent than the other three drugs combined with placebo.[112]

Factor IXa plays an important role in the amplification and propagation of coagulation. Strategies for inhibiting factor IX include antibodies directed against either the activation of factor IX or factor IXa-mediated activation of factor X and active site-blocked factor IXa (factor IXai).[1,113] Active site-blocked factor IXa competes with IXa for incorporation into the tenase complex. Both have shown antithrombotic activity in animal models.

Agents targeting inhibition of factor Xa potentially avoid the inability of heparin to inactivate fibrin-bound thrombin as well as preventing thrombin-mediated amplification of coagulation. Unlike heparin, many of these agents are able to inactivate factor Xa bound to phospholipid surfaces. In addition to the indirect factor Xa inhibitors discussed earlier, these include a number of synthetic and natural inhibitors that block factor Xa in an AT-independent manner.[1] Recombinant tick anticoagulant peptide is a 60-amino acid peptide that binds to the factor Xa active site with high affinity after initial binding to an exosite.[76] Several other oral and parenteral direct factor Xa inhibitors have been developed and are in early-phase clinical trials.[1]

Augmenting the natural inhibitors of anticoagulation is another novel antithrombotic strategy. Both recombinant human thrombomodulin, which lacks the transmembrane moiety and cytoplasmic tail of native thrombomodulin, and human APC have demonstrated antithrombotic efficacy in animal models.[76]

A variety of novel antiplatelet agents including GP-Ib antagonists, thromboxane synthetase inhibitors, thromboxane receptor antagonists, and prostacyclin analogs have been developed but are of unclear clinical use.[76] Finally, the use of inflammatory inhibitors, such as antibodies or antagonists to the selectins and their receptors, have demonstrated antithrombotic activity in animal models of venous thrombosis.[114-117]

REVERSING THE ACTION OF ANTICOAGULANTS

Heparin and the Low-Molecular-Weight Heparins

The anticoagulant effect of UFH can be reversed by the administration of protamine, a cationic heparin-binding protein. Protamine is administered in a neutralizing dose of 1 mg per 100 units of UFH.[16] The 60-minute half-life of heparin must be considered in calculating the protamine dose. Risks of protamine administration include bradycardia and hypotension, which can be reduced by slow administration, and allergic reactions associated with previous exposure including protamine containing insulin, vasectomy, and fish allergies. Although protamine is effective in reversing heparin's anti-IIa activity and reducing the aPTT, it binds less well to shorter heparin chains and only partially neutralizes anti-Xa activity. Protamine sulfate can be used in patients with clinical bleeding while they are receiving LMWH but is less effective than with UFH.[118] Standard doses of protamine have been shown to acutely reverse only 42% of the factor Xa activity and 92% of the anti-factor IIa activity after a subcutaneous dose of tinzaparin.[119] However, because of the subcutaneous depot, there is a gradual return of both anti-factor IIa and Xa activities.

Warfarin

There are three approaches to correcting a supratherapeutic INR: discontinuing warfarin; administration of vitamin K_1; and infusion of fresh frozen plasma or prothrombin concentrate.[68,120] All have disadvantages, including slow reversal and transient warfarin resistance for vitamin K and the risk of viral transmission for the plasma-derived products. The appropriate approach to an individual patient depends on the INR, the presence of bleeding, and the need for invasive procedures. The risk of bleeding is significantly increased at an INR higher than 4.0 to 5.0, and in the nonbleeding patient the INR should optimally be corrected below this range but not into the subtherapeutic range.[120] Oral vitamin K significantly reduces the INR within 24 hours. Low-dose (0.5 to 2.5 mg) intravenous vitamin K is also effective, although higher doses (≥10 mg) are associated with temporary warfarin resistance on reintroducing oral anticoagulants.[120] Although occasionally associated with anaphylaxis,[121] intravenous administration of small doses (0.5 mg) of vitamin K_1 to excessively anticoagulated patients reduces the INR to less than 5.5 within 24 hours without causing excessive delay when reinstituting anticoagulation.[122]

Current recommendations include lowering or omitting a dose in patients with an INR less than 5.0 and no bleeding. For nonbleeding patients with an INR higher than 5.0 but less than 9.0, withholding one or two doses with or without administering 1 to 2.5 mg of oral vitamin K is acceptable. For patients with an INR higher than 9.0, 3 to 5 mg of oral vitamin K_1 will reduce the INR within 24 to 48 hours. For patients with serious bleeding, fresh frozen plasma or prothrombin concentrate should be administered in conjunction with 10 mg of vitamin K_1 by slow intravenous infusion.

Management of the patient undergoing surgery or other invasive procedure also requires special attention. The anticoagulant effects of warfarin require several days to recede after the drug is stopped and several days to become therapeutic after restarting the drug. Most patients require about 4 days to reach an INR less than 1.5 after warfarin is stopped.[123] For patients at low risk for bleeding, reducing the INR to 1.3 to 1.5 prior to invasive procedures is acceptable.[120,123] Postoperative intravenous heparin therapy has been estimated to cause major bleeding in 3% of patients, and approximately 3% of these episodes will be fatal or disabling.[123] It is currently recommended that the management of anticoagulated patients undergoing invasive procedures be guided by the underlying risks of thrombosis and bleeding.[68]

For VTE, preoperative therapeutic UFH or LMWH is warranted once the INR is less than 2.0 in those with an event within 1 month of surgery, whereas postoperative therapeutic anticoagulation is appropriate for those with an event within the preceding 3 months.[123] For cardiogenic arterial thromboembolism, preoperative therapeutic anticoagulation with UFH or LMWH is recommended only for those undergoing surgery within 1 month of an event. Postoperative heparin anticoagulation should be considered in such patients only if the risk of bleeding is low.[123] For patients with a low risk of thrombosis, such as those with a remote (>3-month) history of DVT or atrial fibrillation without stroke, warfarin can be discontinued preoperatively, the procedure performed with appropriate postoperative prophylaxis when the INR has returned to normal, and warfarin restarted. For intermediate-risk patients, warfarin should be discontinued approximately 4 days preoperatively, the procedure performed when the INR normalizes, and the patient covered perioperatively beginning 2 days before surgery with low-dose UFH or LMWH. For patients with a high risk of thrombosis, such as those with recent DVT, prosthetic mitral valves, or older mechanical valves, warfarin should be discontinued approximately 4 days preoperatively and the patient bridged with full-dose UFH or LMWH as the INR falls below the therapeutic range approximately 2 days preoperatively. The risk of thromboembolism exceeds that of bleeding in patients undergoing dental procedures, and warfarin need not be discontinued in patients at low risk for bleeding. The risk of bleeding not controlled by local measures among anticoagulated patients undergoing dental surgery (extractions, gingival surgery, alveolar surgery) is less than 2%, and there are no well-documented cases of serious bleeding in patients receiving therapeutic levels of anticoagulation.[124] Rinsing the mouth with antifibrinolytic agents such as tranexamic acid may further reduce the risk of bleeding after dental procedures.[63]

Newer Anticoagulants

Unfortunately, no effective antidote exists for many of the newer anticoagulants. There is no specific antidote for the pentasaccharide derivative factor Xa inhibitors, although limited data suggest that recombinant factor VIIa normalizes the thrombin generation time in healthy volunteers.[53] Protamine does not reverse the effects of the direct thrombin inhibitors.[24] Potential thrombin-inhibitor antagonists including 1-deamino-8-D-arginine vasopressin (DDAVP), factor VIIa, factor VIII, and activated prothrombin complex have been suggested.[44] Fortunately, most of the direct thrombin inhibitors have a half-life of only 30 to 45 minutes in normal individuals.[44] Although lepirudin should not be used in patients with renal insufficiency, accidental overdosage in these patients can be managed with dialysis using a polymethyl-methyl acrylate (PMMA) membrane.[19] Bivalirudin is also approximately 25% cleared by hemodialysis.[24]

■ SUMMARY

Although the target organ is variable, the pathophysiologic events involved in many thrombotic disorders are similar. VTE disorders are generally managed with anticoagulant drugs alone, while arterial disorders often require the combined use of anticoagulant and antiplatelet agents. UFH, warfarin, and aspirin have historically served as the primary antithrombotic drugs. However, despite their efficacy, each of these drugs has limitations. UFH is highly protein bound, has unfavorable interactions with platelets, is associated with a variable anticoagulant response, and is unable to inhibit fibrin-bound thrombin. Warfarin has a narrow therapeutic window and multiple drug and dietary interactions. Additionally, such drugs represent a relatively nonselective approach to antithrombotic therapy.

Accordingly, the development of targeted anticoagulant strategies is receiving great attention and has led to the development of several new antithrombotic agents. The LMWHs were among the first of these drugs, reducing the anti-IIa activity of UFH in favor of increased anti-Xa activity. The improved pharmacologic profile of the LMWHs has led to their broad acceptance in the prevention and treatment of VTE. Newer agents have subsequently become available that provide an even more selective approach than the LMWHs. Synthetic pentasaccharide derivatives, representing the minimal sequence required for interaction with AT, have been developed as specific inhibitors of factor Xa. The direct thrombin inhibitors act independently of AT and offer a favorable pharmacologic profile, the ability to inhibit fibrin bound thrombin, and the possibility of a safer oral alternative to warfarin. Several new antiplatelet agents targeting sites other than the COX pathway have also been developed and have efficacy superior to aspirin in specific clinical settings.

It is increasingly appreciated that cardiovascular events are frequently multifactorial and that optimal efficacy may require combined therapeutic approaches, such as those involving anticoagulants in combination with antiplatelet and thrombolytic agents. These approaches require the clinician to have an improved understanding of the coagulation system and the mechanisms of action and associated toxicities of several new drugs. Ultimately, much remains to be learned about the role of coagulation in cardiovascular disease, and new knowledge will continue to stimulate the development of new antithrombotic drugs and strategies.

■ REFERENCES

1. Weitz JI, Hirsh J: New anticoagulant drugs. Chest 119(1 Suppl):95S-107S, 2001.
2. Fareed J, Hoppensteadt DA, Bick RL: An update on heparins at the beginning of the new millennium. Semin Thromb Hemost 26(Suppl 1): 5-21, 2000.
3. Oldenburg J, Schwaab R: Molecular biology of blood coagulation. Semin Thromb Hemost 27:313-324, 2001.
4. Colman RW, Hirsh J, Marder VJ, Clowes AW: Overview of coagulation, fibrinolysis, and their regulation. In Colman RW, Hirsh J, Marder VJ, et al (eds): Hemostasis and Thrombosis: Basic Principles and Clinical Practice, 4th ed. Philadelphia, Lippincott Williams & Wilkins, 2001, p 17-20.
5. Dahlback B: Blood coagulation. Lancet 355:1627-1632, 2000.
6. Gallus AS, Lee LH, Coghlan DW: New aspects of the blood coagulation cascade, anticoagulants and vein thrombosis in Asia. Ann Acad Med Singapore 31:685-696, 2002.
7. Butenas S, van't Veer C, Mann KG: "Normal" thrombin generation. Blood 94:2169-2178, 1999.
8. van't Veer C, Mann KG: Regulation of tissue factor-initiated thrombin generation by the stoichiometric inhibitors tissue factor pathway inhibitor, antithrombin-III, and heparin cofactor-II. J Biol Chem 272:4367-4377, 1997.
9. Morris TA: Heparin and low-molecular-weight heparin: Background and pharmacology. Clin Chest Med 24:39-47, 2003.
10. Mann KG: Biochemistry and physiology of blood coagulation. Thromb Haemost 82:165-174, 1999.
11. Heemskerk JW, Bevers EM, Lindhout T: Platelet activation and blood coagulation. Thromb Haemost 88:186-193, 2002.
12. Davie EW: Biochemical and molecular aspects of the coagulation cascade. Thromb Haemost 74:1-6, 1995.
13. Butenas S, van 't Veer C, Cawthern K, et al: Models of blood coagulation. Blood Coagul Fibrinolysis 11(Suppl 1):S9-13, 2000.
14. Broze GJ: Tissue factor pathway inhibitor. Thromb Haemost 74:90-93, 1995.
15. Linhardt RJ, Gunay NS: Production and chemical processing of low molecular weight heparins. Semin Thromb Hemost 25(Suppl 3):5-16, 1999.
16. Hirsh J, Warkentin TE, Shaughnessy SG, et al: Heparin and low-molecular-weight heparin: Mechanisms of action, pharmacokinetics, dosing, monitoring, efficacy, and safety. Chest 119(1 Suppl):64S-94S, 2001.
17. Petaja J, Fernandez JA, Gruber A, Griffin JH: Anticoagulant synergism of heparin and activated protein C in vitro: Role of a novel anticoagulant mechanism of heparin, enhancement of inactivation of factor V by activated protein C. J Clin Invest 99:2655-2663, 1997.
18. Whisstock JC, Pike RN, Jin L, et al: Conformational changes in serpins: II. The mechanism of activation of antithrombin by heparin. J Mol Biol 301:1287-1305, 2000.
19. Weitz JI, Crowther M: Direct thrombin inhibitors. Thromb Res 106:V275-284, 2002.
20. Billett HH: Direct and indirect antithrombins: Heparins, low molecular weight heparins, heparinoids, and hirudin. Clin Geriatr Med 17:15-29, 2001.
21. Bates SM, Weitz JI: Direct thrombin inhibitors for treatment of arterial thrombosis: Potential differences between bivalirudin and hirudin. Am J Cardiol 82:12P-18P, 1998.
22. Beguin S, Choay J, Hemker HC: The action of a synthetic pentasaccharide on thrombin generation in whole plasma. Thromb Haemost 61:397-401, 1989.
23. Fuller K, Chambers TJ, Gallagher AC: Heparin augments osteoclast resorption-stimulating activity in serum. J Cell Physiol 147:208-214, 1991.
24. Wiggins BS, Spinler S, Wittkowsky AK, Stringer KA: Bivalirudin: A direct thrombin inhibitor for percutaneous transluminal coronary angioplasty. Pharmacotherapy 22:1007-1018, 2002.
25. Hirsh J, van Aken WG, Gallus AS, et al: Heparin kinetics in venous thrombosis and pulmonary embolism. Circulation 53:691-695, 1976.
26. Hommes DW, Bura A, Mazzolai L, et al: Subcutaneous heparin compared with continuous intravenous heparin administration in the initial treatment of deep vein thrombosis: A meta-analysis. Ann Intern Med 116:279-284, 1992.
27. Money SR, York JW: Development of oral heparin therapy for prophylaxis and treatment of deep venous thrombosis. Cardiovasc Surg 9:211-218, 2001.
28. Baughman RA, Kapoor SC, Agarwal RK, et al: Oral delivery of anticoagulant doses of heparin: A randomized, double- blind, controlled study in humans. Circulation 98:1610-1615, 1998.
29. Berkowitz SD, Marder VJ, Kosutic G, Baughman RA: Oral heparin administration with a novel drug delivery agent (SNAC) in healthy volunteers and patients undergoing elective total hip arthroplasty. J Thromb Haemost 1:1914-1919, 2003.
30. Brill-Edwards P, Ginsberg JS, Johnston M, Hirsh J: Establishing a therapeutic range for heparin therapy. Ann Intern Med 119:104-109, 1993.
31. Anand S, Ginsberg JS, Kearon C, et al: The relation between the activated partial thromboplastin time response and recurrence in patients with venous thrombosis treated with continuous intravenous heparin. Arch Intern Med 156:1677-1681, 1996.
32. Anand SS, Bates S, Ginsberg JS, et al: Recurrent venous thrombosis and heparin therapy: An evaluation of the importance of early activated partial thromboplastin times. Arch Intern Med 159:2029-2032, 1999.
33. Raschke R, Reilly B, Guidry J, et al: The weight-based heparin dosing nomogram compared with a "standard care" nomogram: A randomized controlled trial. Ann Intern Med 119:874-881, 1993.
34. Hyers TM, Agnelli G, Hull RD, et al: Antithrombotic therapy for venous thromboembolic disease. Chest 119(1 Suppl):176S-193S, 2001.
35. Barritt DW, Jordan SC: Anticoagulant drugs in the treatment of pulmonary embolism: A controlled trial. Lancet 1:1309-1312, 1960.
36. Zidane M, Schram MT, Planken EW, et al: Frequency of major hemorrhage in patients treated with unfractionated intravenous heparin for deep venous thrombosis or pulmonary embolism: A study in routine clinical practice. Arch Intern Med 160:2369-2373, 2000.
37. Levine MN, Raskob G, Landefeld S, Kearon C: Hemorrhagic complications of anticoagulant treatment. Chest 119(1 Suppl):108S-121S, 2001.
38. Wester JP, de Valk HW, Nieuwenhuis HK, et al: Risk factors for bleeding during treatment of acute venous thromboembolism. Thromb Haemost 76:682-688, 1996.
39. Reiter M, Bucek RA, Koca N, et al: Idraparinux and liver enzymes: Observations from the PERSIST trial. Blood Coagul Fibrinolysis 14:61-65, 2003.
40. Gupta AK, Kovacs MJ, Sauder DN: Heparin-induced thrombocytopenia. Ann Pharmacother 32:55-59, 1998.
41. Warkentin TE, Kelton JG: A 14-year study of heparin-induced thrombocytopenia. Am J Med 101:502-507, 1996.
42. Greinacher A, Potzsch B, Amiral J, et al: Heparin-associated thrombocytopenia: Isolation of the antibody and characterization of a multimolecular PF4-heparin complex as the major antigen. Thromb Haemost 71:247-251, 1994.

43. Spiess B, Warkentin T, Francis J, Koster A: Advances in the understanding and treatment of heparin-induced thrombocytopenia in patients undergoing cardiac surgery. Clin Adv Hematol Oncol August:3-11, 2003
44. Fareed J, Callas D, Hoppensteadt DA, et al: Antithrombin agents as anticoagulants and antithrombotics: Implications in drug development. Semin Hematol 36(Suppl 1):42-56, 1999.
45. Dahlman TC: Osteoporotic fractures and the recurrence of thromboembolism during pregnancy and the puerperium in 184 women undergoing thromboprophylaxis with heparin. Am J Obstet Gynecol 168:1265-1270, 1993.
46. Hirsh J, Warkentin TE, Raschke R, et al: Heparin and low-molecular-weight heparin: Mechanisms of action, pharmacokinetics, dosing considerations, monitoring, efficacy, and safety. Chest 114(5 Suppl):489S-510S, 1998.
47. Dolovich LR, Ginsberg JS, Douketis JD, et al: A meta-analysis comparing low-molecular-weight heparins with unfractionated heparin in the treatment of venous thromboembolism. Arch Intern Med 160:181-188, 2000.
48. Harenberg J, Stehle G, Blauth M, et al: Dosage, anticoagulant, and antithrombotic effects of heparin and low-molecular-weight heparin in the treatment of deep vein thrombosis. Semin Thromb Hemost 23:83-90, 1997.
49. Herbert JM, Herault JP, Bernat A, et al: Biochemical and pharmacological properties of SANORG 34006, a potent and long-acting synthetic pentasaccharide. Blood 91:4197-4205, 1998.
50. Treatment of proximal deep vein thrombosis with a novel synthetic compound (SR90107A/ORG31540) with pure anti-factor Xa activity: A phase II evaluation. The Rembrandt Investigators. Circulation 102:2726-2731, 2000.
51. Lormeau JC, Herault JP, Herbert JM: Antithrombin-mediated inhibition of factor VIIa-tissue factor complex by the synthetic pentasaccharide representing the heparin binding site to antithrombin. Thromb Haemost 76:5-8, 1996.
52. Petitou M, Duchaussoy P, Herbert JM, et al: The synthetic pentasaccharide fondaparinux: First in the class of antithrombotic agents that selectively inhibit coagulation factor Xa. Semin Thromb Hemost 28:393-402, 2002.
53. Koopman MM, Buller HR: Short- and long-acting synthetic pentasaccharides. J Intern Med 254:335-342, 2003.
54. Amiral J, Lormeau JC, Marfaing-Koka A, et al: Absence of cross-reactivity of SR90107A/ORG31540 pentasaccharide with antibodies to heparin-PF4 complexes developed in heparin-induced thrombocytopenia. Blood Coagul Fibrinolysis 8:114-117, 1997.
55. Turpie AG, Bauer KA, Eriksson BI, Lassen MR: Fondaparinux vs. enoxaparin for the prevention of venous thromboembolism in major orthopedic surgery: A meta-analysis of four randomized double-blind studies. Arch Intern Med 162:1833-1840, 2002.
56. Buller HR, Davidson BL, Decousus H, et al: Subcutaneous fondaparinux versus intravenous unfractionated heparin in the initial treatment of pulmonary embolism. N Engl J Med 349:1695-1702, 2003.
57. Vermeer C, Schurgers LJ: A comprehensive review of vitamin K and vitamin K antagonists. Hematol Oncol Clin North Am 14:339-353, 2000.
58. Hirsh J, Dalen JE, Anderson DR, et al: Oral anticoagulants: Mechanism of action, clinical effectiveness, and optimal therapeutic range. Chest 119 (Suppl 1):8S-21S, 2001.
59. Shapiro SS: Treating thrombosis in the 21st century. N Engl J Med 349:1762-1764, 2003.
60. Aithal GP, Day CP, Kesteven PJ, Daly AK: Association of polymorphisms in the cytochrome P450 CYP2C9 with warfarin dose requirement and risk of bleeding complications. Lancet 353:717-719, 1999.
61. Alving BM, Strickler MP, Knight RD, et al: Hereditary warfarin resistance: Investigation of a rare phenomenon. Arch Intern Med 145:499-501, 1985.
62. Oldenburg J, Kriz K, Wuillemin WA, et al: Genetic predisposition to bleeding during oral anticoagulant therapy: Evidence for common founder mutations (FIXVal-10 and FIXThr-10) and an independent CpG hotspot mutation (FIXThr-10). Thromb Haemost 85:454-457, 2001.
63. Schulman S: Clinical practice: Care of patients receiving long-term anticoagulant therapy. N Engl J Med 349:675-683, 2003.
64. Efficacy of oral anticoagulants compared with aspirin after infrainguinal bypass surgery. The Dutch Bypass Oral Anticoagulants or Aspirin Study: A randomised trial. Lancet 355:346-351, 2000.
65. Ridker PM, Goldhaber SZ, Danielson E, et al: Long-term, low-intensity warfarin therapy for the prevention of recurrent venous thromboembolism. N Engl J Med 348:1425-1434, 2003.
66. Kearon C, Ginsberg JS, Kovacs MJ, et al: Comparison of low-intensity warfarin therapy with conventional-intensity warfarin therapy for long-term prevention of recurrent venous thromboembolism. N Engl J Med 349:631-639, 2003.
67. Crowther MA, Ginsberg JS, Julian J, et al: A comparison of two intensities of warfarin for the prevention of recurrent thrombosis in patients with the antiphospholipid antibody syndrome. N Engl J Med 349:1133-1138, 2003.
68. Ansell J, Hirsh J, Dalen J, et al: Managing oral anticoagulant therapy. Chest 119(1 Suppl):22S-38S, 2001.
69. Mannucci PM: Genetic control of anticoagulation. Lancet 353:688-689, 1999.
70. Stewart AJ, Penman ID, Cook MK, Ludlam CA: Warfarin-induced skin necrosis. Postgrad Med J 75:233-235, 1999.
71. Sallah S, Abdallah JM, Gagnon GA: Recurrent warfarin-induced skin necrosis in kindreds with protein S deficiency. Haemostasis 28:25-30, 1998.
72. Direct thrombin inhibitors in acute coronary syndromes: Principal results of a meta-analysis based on individual patients' data. Lancet 359:294-302, 2002.
73. Matsuo T, Koide M, Kario K: Development of argatroban, a direct thrombin inhibitor, and its clinical application. Semin Thromb Hemost 23:517-522, 1997.
74. Kong DF, Topol EJ, Bittl JA, et al: Clinical outcomes of bivalirudin for ischemic heart disease. Circulation 100:2049-2053, 1999.
75. Callas D, Bacher P, Iqbal O, et al: Fibrinolytic compromise by simultaneous administration of site-directed inhibitors of thrombin. Thromb Res 74:193-205, 1994.
76. Verstraete M, Zoldhelyi P: Novel antithrombotic drugs in development. Drugs 49:856-884, 1995.
77. Bittl JA, Chaitman BR, Feit F, et al: Bivalirudin versus heparin during coronary angioplasty for unstable or postinfarction angina: Final report reanalysis of the Bivalirudin Angioplasty Study. Am Heart J 142:952-959, 2001.
78. Hauptmann J: Pharmacokinetics of an emerging new class of anticoagulant/antithrombotic drugs: A review of small-molecule thrombin inhibitors. Eur J Clin Pharmacol 57:751-758, 2002.
79. Swan SK, Hursting MJ: The pharmacokinetics and pharmacodynamics of argatroban: Effects of age, gender, and hepatic or renal dysfunction. Pharmacotherapy 20:318-329, 2000.
80. Gustafsson D, Nystrom J, Carlsson S, et al: The direct thrombin inhibitor melagatran and its oral prodrug H 376/95: Intestinal absorption properties, biochemical and pharmacodynamic effects. Thromb Res 101:171-181, 2001.
81. Giugliano RP, Braunwald E: Improving antithrombotic treatment in patients after myocardial infarction. Lancet 362:757, 2003.
82. Francis CW, Berkowitz SD, Comp PC, et al: Comparison of ximelagatran with warfarin for the prevention of venous thromboembolism after total knee replacement. N Engl J Med 349:1703-1712, 2003.
83. Eriksson BI, Bergqvist D, Kalebo P, et al: Ximelagatran and melagatran compared with dalteparin for prevention of venous thromboembolism after total hip or knee replacement: The METHRO II randomised trial. Lancet 360:1441-1447, 2002.
84. Heit JA, Colwell CW, Francis CW, et al: Comparison of the oral direct thrombin inhibitor ximelagatran with enoxaparin as prophylaxis against venous thromboembolism after total knee replacement: A phase 2 dose-finding study. Arch Intern Med 161:2215-2221, 2001.

85. Schulman S, Wahlander K, Lundstrom T, et al: Secondary prevention of venous thromboembolism with the oral direct thrombin inhibitor ximelagatran. N Engl J Med 349:1713-1721, 2003.
86. Petersen P, Grind M, Adler J: Ximelagatran versus warfarin for stroke prevention in patients with nonvalvular atrial fibrillation. SPORTIF II: A dose-guiding, tolerability, and safety study. J Am Coll Cardiol 41:1445-1451, 2003.
87. Wallentin L, Wilcox RG, Weaver WD, et al: Oral ximelagatran for secondary prophylaxis after myocardial infarction: The ESTEEM randomised controlled trial. Lancet 362:789-797, 2003.
88. Cassar K, Bachoo P, Brittenden J: The role of platelets in peripheral vascular disease. Eur J Vasc Endovasc Surg 25:6-15, 2003.
89. Ferguson JJ, Zaqqa M: Platelet glycoprotein IIb/IIIa receptor antagonists: Current concepts and future directions. Drugs 58:965-982, 1999.
90. Barani J, Gottsater A, Mattiasson I, Lindblad B: Platelet and leukocyte activation during aortoiliac angiography and angioplasty. Eur J Vasc Endovasc Surg 23:220-225, 2002.
91. Collaborative overview of randomised trials of antiplatelet therapy: I. Prevention of death, myocardial infarction, and stroke by prolonged antiplatelet therapy in various categories of patients. Antiplatelet Trialists' Collaboration. BMJ 308:81-106, 1994.
92. Patrono C, Coller B, Dalen JE, et al: Platelet-active drugs: The relationships among dose, effectiveness, and side effects. Chest 114(5 Suppl):470S-488S, 1998.
93. Secondary prevention of vascular disease by prolonged antiplatelet treatment. Antiplatelet Trialists' Collaboration. BMJ 296:320-331, 1988.
94. Fiotti N, Altamura N, Cappelli C, et al: Long-term prognosis in patients with peripheral arterial disease treated with antiplatelet agents. Eur J Vasc Endovasc Surg 26:374-380, 2003.
95. Dormandy JA, Rutherford RB: Management of peripheral arterial disease (PAD): TASC Working Group. TransAtlantic Inter-Society Consensus (TASC). J Vasc Surg 31:S83, 2000.
96. Patrono C, Coller B, Dalen JE, et al: Platelet-active drugs: The relationships among dose, effectiveness, and side effects. Chest 119(1 Suppl):39S-63S, 2001.
97. Clarke RJ, Mayo G, Price P, FitzGerald GA: Suppression of thromboxane A_2 but not of systemic prostacyclin by controlled-release aspirin. N Engl J Med 325:1137-1141, 1991.
98. Hennekens CH, Dyken ML, Fuster V: Aspirin as a therapeutic agent in cardiovascular disease: A statement for healthcare professionals from the American Heart Association. Circulation 96:2751-2753, 1997.
99. Savi P, Pereillo JM, Uzabiaga MF, et al: Identification and biological activity of the active metabolite of clopidogrel. Thromb Haemost 84:891-896, 2000.
100. Janzon L, Bergqvist D, Boberg J, et al: Prevention of myocardial infarction and stroke in patients with intermittent claudication: Effects of ticlopidine. Results from STIMS, the Swedish Ticlopidine Multicentre Study. J Intern Med 227:301-308, 1990.
101. Kaufman JS, O'Connor TZ, Zhang JH, et al: Randomized controlled trial of clopidogrel plus aspirin to prevent hemodialysis access graft thrombosis. J Am Soc Nephrol 14:2313-2321, 2003.
102. A randomised, blinded trial of clopidogrel versus aspirin in patients at risk of ischaemic events (CAPRIE). CAPRIE Steering Committee. Lancet 348:1329-1339, 1996.
103. Yusuf S, Zhao F, Mehta SR, et al: Effects of clopidogrel in addition to aspirin in patients with acute coronary syndromes without ST-segment elevation. N Engl J Med 345:494-502, 2001.
104. Jackson MR, Clagett GP: Antithrombotic therapy in peripheral arterial occlusive disease. Chest 114(5 Suppl):666S-682S, 1998.
105. Goldhaber SZ, Manson JE, Stampfer MJ, et al: Low-dose aspirin and subsequent peripheral arterial surgery in the Physicians' Health Study. Lancet 340:143-145, 1992.
106. Taylor DW, Barnett HJ, Haynes RB, et al: Low-dose and high-dose acetylsalicylic acid for patients undergoing carotid endarterectomy: A randomised controlled trial. ASA and Carotid Endarterectomy (ACE) Trial Collaborators. Lancet 353:2179-2184, 1999.
107. Davies MG, Hagen P-G: Pathophysiology of vein graft failure: A review. Eur J Endovasc Surg 9:7-18, 1995.
108. Bauters C, Meurice T, Hamon M, et al: Mechanisms and prevention of restenosis: From experimental models to clinical practice. Cardiovasc Res 31:835-846, 1996.
109. Watson HR, Belcher G, Horrocks M: Adjuvant medical therapy in peripheral bypass surgery. Br J Surg 86:981-991, 1999.
110. Becquemin JP: Effect of ticlopidine on the long-term patency of saphenous-vein bypass grafts in the legs. Etude de la Ticlopidine apres Pontage Femoro-Poplite and the Association Universitaire de Recherche en Chirurgie. N Engl J Med 337:1726-1731, 1997.
111. Sarac TP, Huber TS, Back MR, et al: Warfarin improves the outcome of infrainguinal vein bypass grafting at high risk for failure. J Vasc Surg 28:446-457, 1998.
112. Moons AH, Peters RJ, Bijsterveld NR, et al: Recombinant nematode anticoagulant protein c2, an inhibitor of the tissue factor/factor VIIa complex, in patients undergoing elective coronary angioplasty. J Am Coll Cardiol 41:2147-2153, 2003.
113. Moll S, Roberts HR: Overview of anticoagulant drugs for the future. Semin Hematol 39:145-157, 2002.
114. Myers DD Jr, Henke PK, Wrobleski SK, et al: P-selectin inhibition enhances thrombus resolution and decreases vein wall fibrosis in a rat model. J Vasc Surg 36:928-938, 2002.
115. Myers DD Jr, Schaub R, Wrobleski SK, et al: P-selectin antagonism causes dose-dependent venous thrombosis inhibition. Thromb Haemost 85:423-429, 2001.
116. Downing LJ, Wakefield TW, Strieter RM, et al: Anti-P-selectin antibody decreases inflammation and thrombus formation in venous thrombosis. J Vasc Surg 25:816-827, 1997.
117. Wakefield TW, Strieter RM, Schaub R, et al: Venous thrombosis prophylaxis by inflammatory inhibition without anticoagulation therapy. J Vasc Surg 31:309-324, 2000.
118. Turpie AGG: Customizing our approach in deep vein thrombosis and pulmonary embolism treatment: Overview of our clinical experience. Blood Coagul Fibrinolysis 10(Suppl 2):S107-S115, 1999.
119. Holst J, Bergqvist D, Garre K, et al: Protamine neutralization of intravenous and subcutaneous low-molecular-weight heparin (tinzaparin, Logiparin): An experimental investigation in healthy volunteers. Blood Coagul Fibrinolysis 5:795-803, 1994.
120. Fan J, Armitstead JA, Adams AG, Davis GA: A retrospective evaluation of vitamin K_1 therapy to reverse the anticoagulant effect of warfarin. Pharmacotherapy 23:1245-1250, 2003.
121. Martin JC: Anaphylactoid reactions and vitamin K. Med J Aust 155:851, 1991.
122. Shetty HG, Backhouse G, Bentley DP, Routledge PA: Effective reversal of warfarin-induced excessive anticoagulation with low dose vitamin K_1. Thromb Haemost 67:13-15, 1992.
123. Kearon C, Hirsh J: Management of anticoagulation before and after elective surgery. N Engl J Med 336:1506-1511, 1997.
124. Wahl MJ: Dental surgery in anticoagulated patients. Arch Intern Med 158:1610-1616, 1998.

Chapter

32

Thrombolytic Agents and Their Actions

ANTHONY J. COMEROTA, MD
TERESA L. CARMAN, MD

Section VI

■ BACKGROUND

Thrombolytic therapy is the pharmacologic basis for major advances in the management of patients with acute arterial and venous thrombotic disorders. Early restoration of patency to acutely occluded coronary arteries reduces the mortality of acute myocardial infarction (MI), reduces morbidity, and prolongs survival.[1] Treating patients with acute ischemic stroke with thrombolytic agents significantly reduces neurologic morbidity.[2] Thrombolytic therapy reduces the short-term morbidity of pulmonary embolism (PE), improves right ventricular function, and reduces mortality of massive PE.[3] In patients with acute arterial and graft occlusion, catheter-directed thrombolysis reduces the need for major surgical intervention, reduces hospital stay, and may improve amputation-free survival.[4,5] In patients with extensive deep venous thrombosis, successful thrombolysis reduces post-thrombotic morbidity and improves quality of life.[6,7] The function of indwelling central venous catheters is prolonged,[8] dialysis access is preserved,[9] and a variety of other thrombotic complications are reversed with appropriate use of thrombolytic agents on the arterial and on the venous side of the circulation.[10-15] Recognizing that these benefits can occur from the timely use and appropriate application of thrombolytic agents in patients suffering the consequences of acute arterial and venous thromboembolism underscores the need for vascular specialists to have a good understanding of the fibrinolytic system and the agents that activate it.

■ HISTORY OF THROMBOLYTIC THERAPY

An observation was made by the members of the Hippocratic School almost 400 B.C: When performing postmortem examinations, they found blood was liquefied, not clotted.[16] Morgagni[17] subsequently described that after death there was a transition of blood from the initial, early clotted phase to liquefaction. In the early part of the 20th century, it was observed that when postmortem blood was combined with blood from a healthy living person, fibrin and fibrinogen in the normal blood was destroyed.[18] These observations established that there were elements in blood that not only contributed to the blood maintaining a fluid state, but also were powerful enough to dissolve established clot. The observation that an exogenous compound could dissolve clotted blood was made by Much[19] in 1908, when he reported that *Staphylococcus aureus* contained a clot-dissolving compound, which he named *staphylokinase*.

The concept that clotted blood could be treated and the clot dissolved arose from a serendipitous observation by Tillett and Garner.[20] They incidentally observed that test tubes of calcified plasma (clotted blood) subsequently were liquefied after addition of broth from a streptococcal culture, but not the addition of a control medium. This led to the discovery of streptococcal fibrinolysin, later named *streptokinase,* and the beginning of investigations of the therapeutic benefit of fibrinolysis. The earliest use of a thrombolytic agent for therapeutic fibrinolysis was by Tillett and Sherry[21] in 1949 and Sherry and colleagues[22] in 1950 when they used intrapleural streptokinase in patients with a clotted hemothorax or empyema to break up the loculated thoracic coagulant and allow liquefaction and subsequent drainage by thoracentesis.

The major interest in the development of clot-dissolving drugs was the potential for their use in patients with acute thrombotic disorders, most notably acute coronary thrombosis. The team led by Sherry was the first to treat patients with acute MI with a thrombolytic agent, using a large dose and prolonged (30 hours) infusion of streptokinase.[23] They observed that patients treated early after symptom onset had a lower hospital mortality rate, whereas patients treated more than 20 hours after symptom onset had a mortality rate similar to untreated patients.

Cardiologists did not pursue thrombolytic therapy for MI at that time because they no longer accepted coronary thrombosis as a causative mechanism for acute MI. They mistakenly thought the ischemic event was the result of sustained coronary artery spasm and the presence of underlying atherosclerotic disease.

Perhaps the most important contribution to understanding of thrombolysis was identifying the basic mechanism of clot dissolution. This mechanism was described by Alkjaersig and colleagues[24] when they made the seminal observation that clot lysis occurred as a result of penetration of the clot by a plasminogen activator, which then broke down plasminogen that was bound to fibrin during clotting.

In addition to streptokinase, the late 1950s and early 1960s witnessed the development and purification of urokinase, which initially was derived from human urine.[25,26] The urokinase preparations were nonantigenic, could induce similar thrombolytic activity as streptokinase when given intravenously, but were associated with a milder hemostatic effect than streptokinase.

The development of pulmonary angiography and the objective assessment of pulmonary emboli supported the interest in evaluating lytic therapy for pulmonary emboli and led to two National Institutes of Health (NIH)–sponsored trials—UPET (Urokinase Pulmonary Embolism Trial)[27] and USPET (Urokinase Streptokinase Pulmonary Embolism Trial).[28] Perhaps the most meaningful stimulus to the clinical investigation and further development of thrombolytic agents was provided by DeWood and associates[29] when they confirmed that acute thrombotic occlusion of the coronary arteries was the cause of acute MI. Although lytic therapy for acute MI evolved from catheter-directed thrombolysis to systemic thrombolysis, the opposite was true for the management of patients with acute arterial and graft occlusion and acute deep venous thrombosis. It became evident that direct delivery of the plasminogen activator into the thrombus accelerated thrombus dissolution, improved success, and reduced complications. Since the 1980s, thrombolytic therapy has developed at a rapid pace not only in the identification and development of thrombolytic agents with characteristics designed to meet specifications thought to be advantageous (high fibrin specificity, long half-life), but also in the clinical evaluation of multiple applications of lytic agents for patients with acute arterial and venous occlusion.

■ FIBRINOLYTIC SYSTEM AND ITS COMPONENTS

Overview

The primary purpose of the fibrinolytic system in humans is the physiologic dissolution of thrombi. Fibrinolysis is initiated by plasminogen activators, which activate the zymogen plasminogen to plasmin, the key enzyme in this system. At least two distinct physiologic plasminogen activators have been identified, tissue-type plasminogen activator (t-PA) and urokinase-type plasminogen activator (u-PA).

There are at least two physiologic pathways that activate plasminogen to plasmin. The intrinsic activators consist of components normally found in the blood and include proteins of the contact phase of blood coagulation, such as factor XII and kallikrein, which can interact and generate plasmin, at least in vitro. The physiologic relevance of these mechanisms is uncertain. The extrinsic activators arise from cells and tissues, including vascular endothelial cells and neoplastic cells, and are the main physiologic activators. These include t-PA and u-PA. The plasmin generated by these pathways is the principal mechanism the body calls on to dissolve intravascular thrombi; however, the rate at which this occurs may be too slow to resolve pathologic thrombus. The overall goal of pharmacologic manipulation of the fibrinolytic system is to supply sufficient quantities of exogenous plasminogen activators in a well-controlled manner to induce rapid lysis of intravascular thrombi and restore blood flow to minimize or avoid the consequences of compromised perfusion; this has been the topic of several excellent reviews.[30,31]

Plasminogen

Plasminogen is synthesized in the liver and found in human plasma and serum in an average concentration of 21 mg/dL. It is a single-chain polypeptide with a molecular weight of 92 kD and contains 790 amino acids with 24 disulfide bonds.[32,33] In addition, there are five homologous triple-loop structures called *kringles*. Plasminogen circulates in two forms. The amino-terminal 76 residue of native plasminogen (Glu-plasminogen) constitutes the predominant form of the activation peptide that is released by the liver and exists in high concentrations in plasma. A smaller molecule containing an amino-terminal lysine called *LYS-plasminogen*[34] results from partial proteolysis of Glu-plasminogen. LYS-plasminogen has a much higher affinity for binding to fibrin in purified systems and in plasma and is found in high concentration in thrombus and has greater reactivity with plasminogen activators.[35] Plasminogen binding sites are present on fibrin molecules, are exposed by proteolysis, and have a particular affinity for LYS-plasminogen.[36] Activators convert plasminogen to the two-chain plasmin molecule by cleavage of a single peptide bond (arginine 560–valine 561 bond), which splits the molecule into the heavy and light chains. The formation of LYS-plasminogen and its binding to fibrin accelerates and improves the efficiency of plasmin formation when exposed to plasminogen activators, with subsequent fibrin dissolution; this is the physiologic basis for intrathrombus infusion of plasminogen activators via catheter delivery techniques. The heavy chain portion of the molecule contains the kringles, which contribute to fibrin binding and interaction with plasminogen activators.[33,37]

Plasmin

Plasmin is a serine protease composed of two polypeptide chains linked by disulfide bonds. The light chain contains the enzyme's catalytic site.[38] Because plasminogen (LYS-plasminogen) usually is bound to fibrin, it can be converted by plasminogen activators to plasmin at the localized site of fibrin deposition, which becomes the primary focus of fibrinolytic activity.[39] Any plasminogen activation that occurs in the surrounding fluid phase is promptly neutralized by α_2-antiplasmin. Physiologic thrombolysis is a well-controlled and localized process. Plasmin cleaves protein and peptide molecules at arginyl-lysyl bonds. In addition to fibrin and fibrinogen, plasmin hydrolyzes the coagulation factors V and VIII, components of serum complement, corticotropin (adrenocorticotropic hormone), growth hormone, and glucagon. Plasmin also cleaves the activation peptide from plasminogen, which serves to accelerate further plasmin formation from LYS-plasminogen.

Inhibitors

Plasmin's wide-ranging activity can have a profound effect on many plasma proteins. Human plasma contains inhibitors designed to regulate the activity of proteolytic enzymes.[40-42] α_2-Antiplasmin is the principal physiologic inhibitor of plasmin. It is fast acting and has the strongest affinity for plasmin, creating inactive plasmin–α_2-antiplasmin complexes.[43] It is present in plasma in concentrations of 1 μmol/L. A much slower acting inhibitor, α_2-macroglobulin, exists in a concentration of approximately 3 μmol/L.[43] The primary function of α_2-macroglobulin is to bind plasmin after α_2-antiplasmin is depleted. Although the plasmin–α_2-macroglobulin complexes are active, they are removed rapidly from the circulation. Other plasmin inhibitors include α_1-antitrypsin, antithrombin, and C-1 esterase inhibitor, but they have a minimal physiologic effect in the blood. Plasminogen activator inhibitors (PAIs) also are important in the control of fibrinolysis. Inhibitors of t-PA and u-PA have been identified in human plasma[44] and derived from human platelets.[45] Other inhibitors have been obtained from cultured endothelial cells, human umbilical vein, hepatoma cells, liver, placenta, monocytes, and human fibroblasts.

Breakdown Products of Fibrinolysis

Under physiologic conditions, the action of plasmin is limited to the site of fibrin deposition.[46] Circulating inhibitors bind to plasmin and form inactive complexes, preventing breakdown of fibrinogen, clotting factors, and other circulating proteins. With the exogenous administration of plasminogen activators or under certain pathologic conditions, plasmin levels exceed the inhibitor's capacity, resulting in a systemic plasminemia with breakdown of plasma proteins, especially fibrinogen. The action of plasmin on fibrinogen results in the segmental formation of several peptides, including fragment X (250 kD), which is degraded to yield fragments Y (150 kD) and D (100 kD). Fragment Y is degraded to yield fragments D and E (50 kD).[46,47]

Plasmin's action on non–cross-linked fibrin is identical to that on fibrinogen in the rate of breakdown and the end products except that BB 15-42 peptide rather than BB 1-42 peptide is produced on cleavage of the BB chain of fibrin. These peptides have been used to assess specific breakdown of fibrinogen versus fibrin by plasmin. Mature fibrin contains factor XIIIa–induced intramolecular bonds, causing a slower degradation by plasmin and different end products. D Dimer is a unique derivative of the proteolysis of cross-linked moieties from adjacent fibrin monomers, which have been covalently bound by factor XIIIa.[48,49]

■ THROMBOLYTIC AGENTS

Thrombolytic agents currently belong to the family of drugs called *plasminogen activators*. These agents act indirectly to break down plasminogen to form plasmin, the active enzyme that dissolves clots and degrades other biologically active plasma proteins, particularly the coagulation and complement proteins. Direct-acting agents are currently under investigation and include alfimeprase and plasmin. These drugs have direct proteolytic activity, in contrast to the currently available plasminogen activators.

Plasminogen Activators

Ideal Thrombolytic Agent

The characteristics of an ideal thrombolytic agent have been discussed frequently, often within the context of treating patients with MI. The characteristics of an ideal agent for MI[50] may not be considered ideal, however, for treating patients with extensive deep venous thrombosis (DVT). Some parameters of an ideal agent can be agreed on easily, such as rapid lysis and a low risk of bleeding complications with the elimination of the risk of intracranial hemorrhage. Intravenous administration is an attractive characteristic, but may be realistic only for acute ischemic events caused by limited, small-volume thrombus (MI) or thrombus that has a large blood contact surface area–to–thrombus volume ratio (PE).

High fibrin specificity has been considered an attractive feature, with the goal being to limit activation of circulating plasminogen, limiting breakdown of fibrinogen and other clotting factors. High fibrin specificity may render "hemostatic thrombi" more susceptible to dissolution compared with less fibrin-specific agents, however, increasing the risk of a distant bleeding complication. Several prospective studies evaluating the use of intra-arterial thrombolytic therapy for lower extremity ischemia have documented a survival benefit in patients receiving lytic agents that had a systemic fibrinolytic effect reflected by a decrease in fibrinogen. Because fibrinogen is a risk factor for cardiovascular mortality, its breakdown as a result of a transient systemic lytic effect may be beneficial to these high cardiovascular risk patients. It is probably too simplistic to think that fibrinogen alone is responsible for this phenomenon; rather it is likely to be associated with other procoagulant proteins, which are diminished by systemic plasminemia.

Resistance to neutralization by plasminogen activator inhibitor-1 (PAI-1) would improve the effectiveness and potency of a systemically delivered agent, but this may not be considered beneficial during intrathrombus infusion. During intrathrombus infusion, the desirable effect of the plasminogen activator is achieved locally. In the event of escape of the plasminogen activator into the systemic circulation, neutralization by PAI-1 may be desirable to limit its effect where treatment was not intended.

All would agree that the lytic agent should not generate procoagulant activity, should not be antigenic, and should have a reasonable cost. Recognizing the varying needs of the divergent patients having acute ischemic events, it seems unlikely that a single thrombolytic agent would be able to meet the requirements for all of the thrombotic disease states. Multiple agents would be required. Adjunctive use of other agents, such as direct thrombin inhibitors and low-molecular-weight heparins, has improved outcome. Further investigation of these agents, second-generation platelet inhibitors, pentasaccharides, and other antithrombotics would refine treatment further to meet patient needs.

Streptokinase

Background Streptokinase was discovered in 1933 by Tillett and Garner[51] and was the first thrombolytic agent approved for clinical use. Streptokinase is a nonenzyme protein containing 415 amino acids with a molecular weight of 43.7 kD, produced by group C β-hemolytic streptococci.[52] Streptokinase alone is incapable of directly converting plasminogen to plasmin and is not an enzyme. It indirectly activates plasminogen by forming a 1:1 complex with human plasminogen. This complex undergoes a conformational change to expose an active site on the plasminogen molecule. The plasminogen-streptokinase complex is capable of catalyzing plasminogen to plasmin. Streptokinase is then proteolytically degraded. The various degradation products are streptokinase fragments ranging from 10 to 40 kD, all of which also are able to complex with plasminogen. These fragments have 50% to 60% of the activating potential of the parent molecule.

Streptokinase has various systemic effects on the plasma coagulation and fibrinolytic systems and on platelets. Circulating levels of plasminogen and fibrinogen are markedly decreased during streptokinase therapy. Systemic fibrinogenolysis is associated with increased hemorrhagic complications. Concomitantly, there is a decrease in plasma plasminogen and plasma α_2-antiplasmin. In addition, there is evidence that platelets are altered.[53] These effects are noted without exception with all of the thrombolytic agents, although streptokinase seems to have a more pronounced effect than urokinase and recombinant tissue plasminogen activator (rt-PA). Another major disadvantage of streptokinase is its bacterial origin and antigenicity, which results in antibody formation in all patients, precluding reuse of streptokinase within at least 6 months.

Streptokinase is highly antigenic and has the potential for causing allergic reactions. Patients with recent exposure to streptococci and patients recently treated with streptokinase have a high level of circulating antistreptococcal antibodies capable of neutralizing streptokinase. Patients who are resistant to streptokinase therapy at standard doses may respond to higher doses if the saturation point of existing antibodies is exceeded. In vivo the activator complex formed by streptokinase has a half-life of approximately 23 minutes.[54] In vitro testing is available to determine the streptokinase dose needed to achieve systemic fibrinogenolysis, although 95% of patients achieve a lytic state by the standard recommended doses.

Clinical Experience Streptokinase initially was approved for the management of patients with PE. In the NIH-sponsored trials, streptokinase was shown to resolve arteriographically proven pulmonary emboli significantly faster than anticoagulation and showed more rapid restoration of cardiopulmonary hemodynamics. Although bleeding complications were increased, these observations led to the initial approval of streptokinase for clinical use. Subsequently, randomized trials showed significant reduction of mortality when patients with acute MI were treated early after symptom onset, leading to its indication for use in these patients. Its application in patients with acute arterial and graft occlusion naturally followed, incorporating the technique of intra-arterial catheter–based delivery. Although substantial benefit was observed in many patients, unpredictable and severe bleeding complications also were observed.

In 1999, the U.S. Food and Drug Administration (FDA) warned of increasing life-threatening events associated with the use of streptokinase and anistreplase. Current trends in thrombolytic therapy involve the use of more promising recombinant-type agents, such as alteplase, reteplase, and recombinant prourokinase. Because of its antigenicity, clinical unpredictability, and complication rate, streptokinase has fallen into disfavor and has been replaced by other lytic agents in most medical centers in the United States.

Urokinase

Background Urokinase was first isolated by MacFarlane and Pilling in 1946[55] and subsequently by Williams in 1951.[56] Urokinase is a double-chain, trypsin-like protease with a molecular weight of 54 to 57 kD. It was observed early by several investigators that urokinase could exist in several molecular weights of approximately 22 kD, 33 kD, and 54 kD. The lower molecular weight molecules are fragments of the larger ones. The complete primary amino acid sequence of urokinase has been characterized.[57] Plasmin and kallikrein cleave prourokinase at position 156, producing urokinase in its two-chain form. The two chains are held together by a disulfide bond that is important for the fibrinolytic activity of urokinase.

The preparations of urokinase used therapeutically either are extracted from human urine—although this method is largely obsolete—or are isolated from cultures of human fetal kidney cells. Urokinase also can be produced by recombinant genetic engineering in *Escherichia coli.* The problem in the production of urokinase from urine is the need for large quantities to produce adequate amounts of enzyme; 1500 L of urine is required for the production of enough enzyme to treat one patient. The tissue culture techniques shown by Bernik and Kwaan[58] indicated that improved production of urokinase could be achieved and that the best fibrinolytic activity was seen in cultures from cells taken from fetal kidneys at 26 to 32 weeks of gestational age.

Urokinase converts the inactive forms of plasminogen to plasmin, with greater affinity for the fibrin-bound LYS-plasminogen. The conversion is due to the cleavage of a single arginine 560–valine bond.[38] Activation of the fibrin-bound plasminogen allows fibrinolysis to occur in a relatively inhibitor-free environment because there are no competing substrates for fibrin-bound plasmin. Urokinase is cleared rapidly by the liver, with about 3% to 5% cleared by the kidneys. It has a short half-life of about 16 minutes, which might be prolonged in patients with hepatic dysfunction.

Although urokinase induces systemic fibrinogenolysis, its systemic effect is not as intense as that of streptokinase. Owing to the production costs of urokinase, its price is five to eight times that of streptokinase per patient treatment.

Clinical Experience The favorable results of patients treated for PE in UPET and USPET led to the approval of urokinase for the treatment of patients with PE. During the 1980s, it became evident that urokinase was safer and more effective than streptokinase for the management of patients with acute peripheral arterial and venous thromboembolism. By the late 1980s and throughout the 1990s, urokinase became the preferred thrombolytic agent for vascular surgeons and interventional radiologists, used predominantly for intrathrombus infusion via catheter-directed techniques. At the doses used, it seemed to have a better safety profile and became the preferred lytic agent for intraoperative use.[59,60]

In 1999, Abbott Laboratories removed urokinase from the market in response to concerns expressed by the FDA regarding the potential for viral contamination and the donor source being outside of the United States. These concerns have since been addressed. The production and purification process for urokinase currently exceeds the specifications established (good manufacturing practices), and donors are identified through cooperation with the transplantation community. Urokinase is produced from cultured neonatal kidney cells, for which there is currently no other use. Production efficiency is such that a year's supply of urokinase can be obtained from four to six neonatal kidneys. Urokinase was reintroduced to the marketplace in October 2002.

Recombinant Tissue Plasminogen Activator (Alteplase)

Background t-PA is an endogenous plasminogen activator synthesized and secreted by endothelial cells. t-PA is a glycosylated single-chain serine protease. The carboxyterminal end of the protein is a protease domain containing the enzymatic activity. The amino-terminal end of the protein chain contains four distinct domains that are significant to the binding function of the protein: a fibronectin finger-type domain, an epidermal growth factor domain, and two kringle domains (kringle 1 and kringle 2) (Table 32-1). Endogenous single-chain t-PA is converted to a two-chain molecule by plasmin. The single-chain and the two-chain forms of the protein possess enzymatic activity. The proteolytic activity of t-PA is enhanced by fibrin binding.[61] At the site of a thrombus, t-PA binds to fibrin and locally converts the fibrin-bound plasminogen to plasmin, activating the endogenous fibrinolytic system; this allows preferential activation of fibrin-bound plasminogen as opposed to free, fluid-phase plasminogen. t-PA is inactivated primarily by PAI-1.

rt-PA was produced in the 1980s. Alteplase (Activase; Genentech, South San Francisco, Calif) is produced in a Chinese hamster ovarian cell line using recombinant DNA technology. Alteplase is a mixture of single-chain and two-chain rt-PA. Approximately 80% of rt-PA produced is in the glycosylated single-chain form.[61] Alteplase is metabolized through the liver. In vivo the half-life is approximately 4 to 5 minutes. In contrast to streptokinase, rt-PA is not considered antigenic. Case reports of allergic reactions have been published, however.

Table 32-1 Native Tissue Plasminogen Activator Structural/Functional Domains

DOMAIN	FUNCTION
Finger domain	Involved in t-PA to fibrin binding
Epidermal growth factor	Binds to hepatic t-PA receptor increasing t-PA clearance
Kringle 1	Minor component of fibrin binding (?)
Kringle 2	Involved in fibrin/fibrinogen binding
Carboxyterminal catalytic site	Serine protease catalytic domain

Clinical Experience Approved indications for systemic thrombolysis with rt-PA include MI, acute ischemic stroke, and PE. In addition, alteplase has shown efficacy in restoring function to occluded central venous access devices.[62] For catheter clearance, alteplase is marketed under the name Cathflo Activase and is supplied as a 2-mg vial containing lyophilized powder. The approved dosing regimen is 2 mg for patients weighing 30 kg or more and a dose of 110% of the catheter lumen volume for patients weighing 10 kg or more, but less than 30 kg. rt-PA has been used for thrombolysis in several other clinical settings, including peripheral arterial occlusion, venous thrombosis, and dialysis access thrombosis. In addition, there are published data on the use of alteplase in children.[63]

Alteplase has been studied in numerous thrombolytic trials for MI. The TIMI-1 (Thrombolysis in Myocardial Infarction) trial was the first comparative trial between alteplase and streptokinase. A phase I trial showed a 90-minute reperfusion rate of 62% with alteplase compared with 31% with streptokinase.[64] One of the largest trials, GUSTO-1 (Global Utilization of Streptokinase and t-PA for Occluded Coronary Arteries) randomized approximately 41,000 patients to four different regimens of thrombolysis.[65] Accelerated rt-PA with intravenous heparin administered over 90 minutes was compared with streptokinase (1.5 million U) administered with either intravenous or subcutaneous heparin or a combination of rt-PA and streptokinase. The 90-minute reperfusion rate for rt-PA was significantly better than for either regimen of streptokinase (81.3% versus 59% and 53.5%; $P < .0001$). The 30-day mortality was decreased with alteplase compared with streptokinase (6.3% versus 7.3%). There was no significant difference in the intracranial hemorrhage rates (0.7% versus 0.6% and 0.5%).[65]

There are two approved dosing regimens for MI. Alteplase may be dosed either using a 90-minute accelerated regimen (a 15-mg bolus followed by infusion of the remainder of the dose) or a 3-hour infusion regimen (typically administered as a front-loaded infusion). In either regimen, the dose is decreased in patients weighing less than approximately 65 kg, and the total dose should not exceed 100 mg. Heparin typically is administered concomitantly for at least 24 hours. In addition, most patients receive aspirin as part of the MI regimen.

The National Institute of Neurological Disorders and Stroke study group published the results of a two-part, double-blind, placebo-controlled trial in patients with acute ischemic stroke.[66] For entry into the trial, patients had to have a clearly defined time of onset of stroke symptoms (<180 minutes) and no contraindications to thrombolytic therapy. Part one of the trial enrolled 291 patients; 144 received alteplase, and 147 received placebo. Using the NIH Stroke Scale (NIHSS), part one was designed to determine if there was clinical improvement or resolution of the stroke symptoms in the initial 24 hours after presentation. There was no significant difference in 24-hour improvement between the groups receiving t-PA or placebo (47% versus 57%). In addition, there was no difference in the median NIHSS scores. For t-PA, the median score was 8 (range 3 to 17), and for placebo, the median score was 12 (range 6 to 19; $P = .21$).[66] Part two enrolled 333 patients and was designed to assess clinical outcome at 3 months based on standardized scores of clinical function and recovery. At 3 months, the patients receiving t-PA within 180 minutes of stroke symptom onset showed improvement in the evaluated indices, including the NIHSS score, compared with placebo. Similarly, secondary analysis of the patients enrolled in part one confirmed the 3-month benefits in these patients according to the functional and recovery indices.[66] There was a significant increase in intracranial hemorrhage in patients treated with thrombolytics (15.4% versus 6.4% in patients treated with placebo; $P < .01$). There was no significant difference, however, between the groups in mortality. All-cause mortality at 90 days was 17.3% in patients treated with alteplase and 20.5% in patients receiving placebo.[66]

A meta-analysis reviewed data from eight randomized, controlled trials of rt-PA in patients with nonhemorrhagic stroke.[67] From this analysis, six trials enrolling 2830 patients collectively showed a benefit favoring the use of rt-PA with respect to death and disability (odds ratio 0.80, confidence interval 0.69 to 0.93). The cumulative analysis of eight trials in 2955 patients showed an increased risk of symptomatic intracranial hemorrhage (odds ratio 3.13, confidence interval 2.34 to 4.19).[67]

The currently approved dose of rt-PA for acute ischemic stroke is 0.9 mg/kg. The total dose should not exceed 90 mg. It is administered as an infusion with 10% of the dose given as an initial bolus. In contrast to MI, the concomitant use of anticoagulants or aspirin has not been addressed.

Alteplase was first used in PE in the 1980s.[68] Goldhaber and coworkers[68] published their results using a 100-mg intravenous bolus of rt-PA compared with urokinase infusion. A total of 45 patients were randomized. The primary endpoints were angiography clot lysis at 2 hours and pulmonary reperfusion at 24 hours. At 2 hours, 82% of patients receiving rt-PA showed improvement compared with 48% of urokinase-treated patients ($P = .008$). The improvement in the lung scan at 24 hours was identical between the groups.[68] Several other trials compared alteplase with streptokinase and with placebo.[69,70] Thrombolysis in PE has been shown to improve thrombus resolution,[68] improve lung scan findings,[68] and produce a more rapid improvement in hemodynamics.[70,71] No trial has convincingly shown significant improvement in mortality, however. The approved dose of rt-PA for treating PE is 100 mg administered over a 2-hour period.

The use of rt-PA for peripheral arterial occlusion and venous thrombolysis has been reviewed.[72,73] The use of rt-PA increased in both settings after the withdrawal of urokinase in 1998. In one review, the authors identified 46 clinical studies that used rt-PA for peripheral arterial occlusion thrombolysis. They concluded that there is no generally accepted dose or technique for conducting catheter-directed peripheral arterial thrombolysis. Although many studies have shown benefits from the technique, there are few prospective, randomized trials and a lack of standardized protocols and endpoints.[72] The use of thrombolysis in venous disease remains debated and requires further study.[73] Further evaluations of the techniques employed for peripheral arterial occlusion and venous thrombolysis are discussed in Chapters 53 and 150.

TNK-t-PA (Tenecteplase)

Background After the recombinant production of rt-PA, several novel plasminogen activators were designed and produced using recombinant technology. TNK-t-PA is a bioengineered mutant of t-PA. The mutations include a glycosylated amino acid substitution T103N, a deglycosylation substitution N117Q, and a tetra-alanine substitution at position 296-299 (KHRR [296-299] AAAA). These three alterations of native t-PA produced a molecule with a longer plasma half-life, increased fibrin specificity, and increased resistance to PAI-1 (Table 32-2).[74,75] The goal of these alterations is to create an agent that can be administered by a single bolus or perhaps double bolus and has less systemic plasminogen/plasmin activation, allowing a more rapid reperfusion with potentially fewer bleeding complications. This compound was designed specifically to treat patients with acute MI.

Human and rabbit studies have been performed to analyze the pharmacokinetics of TNK-t-PA.[75,76] Early rabbit studies showed a clearance rate of 1.9 mL/min/kg for TNK-t-PA compared with 16.1 mL/min/kg for t-PA. In addition, TNK-t-PA showed a 14-fold increase in fibrin specificity and an 80-fold increase in resistance to PAI-1 compared with t-PA.[75] In a human MI trial, the mean plasma clearance was 125 ± 25 to 216 ± 98 mL/min depending on the dose of the agent. Clearance decreased as the dose was increased. The clearance was modestly slower in women, patients with a lower weight, and older patients.[76] Tenecteplase is metabolized by the liver, and the metabolites are excreted in the urine. It has been suggested that the dose-dependent clearance is due to saturation of the hepatic receptors. Similar dose-dependent clearance is seen with t-PA.[76]

Clinical Experience Most of the randomized trials to date have been performed in patients with acute MI. The TIMI-10A trial, a multicenter, open-label, dose-ranging trial using single-bolus TNK-t-PA, enrolled 113 patients with acute MI. Objective frame count showed that 62% and 68% of patients receiving 30 mg and 50 mg had TIMI grade 3 coronary artery flow at 90 minutes.[77] From the results of this trial, TIMI-10B was designed as a multicenter, dose-ranging, randomized, open-label trial comparing 30-mg, 40-mg, and 50-mg single bolus administration of TNK-t-PA versus front-loaded alteplase.[78] Early in this study, an excessive number of intracranial hemorrhages led to adjustments in the TNK-t-PA dosing and the heparin dose. The 50-mg TNK-t-PA dose was replaced with a 40-mg dose, and the heparin protocol was altered. The 90-minute TIMI grade 3 flow was the same between the alteplase group (62.8%) and the 40-mg TNK-t-PA group (62.7%, P = not significant).[78] Based on the results of TIMI-10A and TIMI-10B and the safety data from ASSENT-1 (Assessment of the Safety and Efficacy of a New Thrombolytic), the phase III ASSENT-2 trial was initiated. ASSENT-2 was a multicenter, international, randomized, double-blind, controlled trial comparing tenecteplase with alteplase. The trial enrolled nearly 17,000 patients to either weight-based dosing with tenecteplase or front-loaded alteplase; 30-day mortality was the primary endpoint. There was no difference between the agents with respect to 30-day mortality (6.179% with tenecteplase versus 6.151% with alteplase); equivalency was determined.[79] The rate of hemorrhagic stroke was the same between the two groups. Fewer bleeding complications were experienced by the tenecteplase group, however. Major noncerebral bleeding occurred in 4.7% of patients receiving tenecteplase compared with 5.9% (P = .002) in the alteplase group.[79] Tenecteplase currently is approved for the treatment of acute MI using a weight-based single bolus dose.

There is limited experience using tenecteplase for peripheral thrombolysis. Burkart and colleagues[80] published their initial experience in 18 patients, 13 with arterial occlusion and 5 with venous thrombosis. Tenecteplase was infused at a rate of 0.25 mg/hr through a multi-sidehole catheter. Technical success (restoration of flow) was achieved in all patients; clinical success with respect to limb salvage or relief of symptoms or both was achieved in 11 of 13 (85%) arterial cases and 4 of 5 (80%) venous cases. Bleeding at the vascular access site requiring transfusion occurred in one patient; there were no intracranial bleeding complications.[80]

Recombinant Plasminogen Activator (Reteplase)

Background Reteplase is a single-chain recombinant plasminogen activator structurally similar to rt-PA. It possesses a kringle 2 and protease domain, but the epidermal growth factor, finger, and kringle 1 domains have been deleted. The molecule is produced by *E. coli* and as such also lacks glycosylated side-chains. It is manufactured by Boehringer Mannheim as Retavase, Rapilysin, and Ecokinase.[81]

Reteplase, similar to rt-PA, is considered a fibrin-specific plasminogen activator and preferentially activates plasminogen in the presence of fibrin as opposed to fluid-phase plasminogen. The structural changes of recombinant plasminogen activator confer a decrease in affinity for fibrin binding, however, and a decrease in endothelial cell binding. The fibrin binding of reteplase is similar to urokinase and only about 30% of that of rt-PA.[82]

In contrast to rt-PA, reteplase is eliminated by renal and hepatic metabolism. No studies have been performed to determine whether dose adjustments are necessary in patients with renal impairment.[82] Compared with rt-PA, reteplase has a longer half-life (14 to 18 minutes) and is administered by bolus dosing.

Reteplase was designed for and is currently approved for use in MI. The FDA-approved MI dosing regimen for reteplase is a 10-U bolus administered over 2 minutes with a second 10-U bolus to be repeated in 30 minutes. This double-bolus dosing regimen was established in phase I trials.

Clinical Experience RAPID-I was a multicenter, open-label, parallel-group study that compared three reteplase dosing regimens with a front-loaded, 100-mg alteplase infusion. The 10-U double-bolus reteplase TIMI grade 3 flow at 90 minutes was 63% compared with 49% (P = .019) with alteplase, without an increased incidence of adverse events.[83] RAPID-II compared 10 U plus 10 U reteplase with front-loaded alteplase in 324 patients in a multicenter, open-label, parallel-group study. At 90 minutes, TIMI grade 3 perfusion was obtained in 59.9% of patients with reteplase compared with 45.2% (P = .011) with alteplase. Total patency rate at 90 minutes (TIMI grade 2 or TIMI grade 3 flow) was improved significantly with reteplase (83.4%) compared with alteplase (73.3%; P = .031).[84] Reperfusion was achieved more rapidly with reteplase. At 60 minutes, TIMI grade 2 or TIMI grade 3 flow was observed in 81.8% of reteplase-treated patients compared with 66.1% of alteplase-treated patients (P = .032). In addition, there were significantly fewer secondary interventions required to restore normal flow in the reteplase-treated patients (13.6% versus 26.5% with alteplase; P = .004).[84] Mortality was not significantly decreased (4.1% versus 8.4%). There was no significant difference in bleeding complications.[84]

Two large mortality studies have been performed with reteplase, INJECT (International Joint Efficacy Comparison of Thrombolytics) and GUSTO III.[85,86] The INJECT trial was a European, multicenter trial that enrolled approximately 6000 patients with acute MI in a randomized, double-blind comparison between double-bolus reteplase and streptokinase. The primary endpoint was 35-day outcome. The 35-day mortality was 9% in the reteplase group compared with 9.5% in the streptokinase group (P = not significant). In addition, there was no significant difference in the 6-month mortality rates (11% versus 12%). The rates of hemorrhagic and embolic stroke were similar, and there was no difference in bleeding events.[85]

Table 32-2 Comparison of the Structural Changes of the Recombinant Plasminogen Activators

DRUG	FINGER DOMAIN	EGF DOMAIN	KRINGLE 1	KRINGLE 2	PHARMACOLOGY
rt-PA	X	X	X	X	Good fibrin specificity Short half-life
TNK-t-PA	X	X	X	X	3 positional mutations Increased half-life Increased fibrin specificity Resistance to PAI-1 inactivation
rt-PA				X	Good fibrin specificity Prolonged half-life

EGF, epidermal growth factor; PAI-1, plasminogen activator inhibitor-1.

GUSTO III compared double-bolus reteplase with alteplase in an international, multicenter, randomized, double-blind trial in approximately 15,000 patients. The primary endpoint was 30-day mortality. The 30-day mortality rate in patients treated with reteplase was 7.5% compared with 7.2% in patients receiving alteplase ($P = .61$). Similar to the INJECT trial, there was no difference between the groups with respect to hemorrhagic or embolic stroke or bleeding events.[86]

Since FDA approval, reteplase has been studied in expanded applications, including PE and arterial and venous thrombosis. Tebbe and coworkers[87] compared reteplase with alteplase in an open-label trial of 36 patients with clinical symptoms of massive PE. Double-bolus reteplase (10 U + 10 U) was administered in 23 patients, and 13 patients received 100 mg of alteplase administered as a 10-mg bolus with the remainder infused over 2 hours. All patients received concomitant heparin infusion. Although initial improvements in pulmonary resistance and pulmonary artery pressure seemed to favor the reteplase-treated group, at 24 hours there was no significant difference in the hemodynamic parameters between the groups. Many patients experienced adverse events: 18 of 23 patients (78%) and 9 of 13 patients (69%) with reteplase and alteplase.[87]

Several investigators have published experiences using reteplase for peripheral arterial or venous thrombolysis. Kiproff and associates[88] showed the efficacy of reteplase infused via "pulse-spray" catheter in 18 patients with lower extremity arterial occlusion. Heparin was coadministered in all patients. The infusion was initiated at 0.5 U/hr in 15 of 18 patients. Dose adjustments or alternatives were at the discretion of the interventionist. Clinical success with restoration of patency and relief of symptoms was achieved in 16 of 18 (89%) patients. The average time for thrombolysis was 26.9 hours (range 12 to 44 hours), and the average dose required of reteplase was 13.3 U (range 6.2 to 41.5 U). Percutaneous intervention with angioplasty or stent placement was used as an adjunct in seven patients. One patient experienced a major hemorrhagic complication requiring surgical evacuation and transfusion. Four patients (22%) experienced minor bleeding complications.[88]

Castaneda and coworkers[89] evaluated 101 arterial occlusions in 87 patients using three different dosing regimens of reteplase: 0.5 U/hr, 0.25 U/hr, and 0.125 U/hr. Concomitant heparin was infused in all patients. Thrombolytic success was achieved in 86.7%, 83.8%, and 85.3% of the groups. The 0.5 U/hr group received more reteplase ($P < .001$) and had more bleeding complications, and the 0.125 U/hr group required a longer infusion time compared with the other groups ($P < .05$).

There is limited experience using reteplase for venous thrombolysis.[90,91] Using doses ranging from 0.5 to 2 U/hr, successful thrombolysis was achieved in 10 of 11 (90.9%) of the patients; bleeding complications occurred in 27% (3 of 11).[91] Another pilot study treated 25 patients with acute or chronic DVT of the upper extremity (7), lower extremity (14), or vena cava (4), with successful thrombolysis observed in 92% (23 of 25) of the patients. Major bleeding developed in 1 patient.[90]

Additional study in patients with peripheral arterial and venous thrombosis is warranted. Data comparing reteplase with other available thrombolytic agents in these clinical circumstances are lacking.

Prourokinase

Background A single-chain precursor to high-molecular-weight urokinase, prourokinase was isolated from urine in 1979[92] and is also termed *single-chain urokinase plasminogen activator*. Prourokinase has been identified in human plasma, cultures of endothelial cells, explants of fetal organs, and various malignant cell lines.[93] This proenzyme is derived from human urine or genetically manipulated *E. coli* and has a molecular weight of approximately 54 kD.

Prourokinase is converted to high-molecular-weight urokinase by hydrolysis of the lysine 158–isoleucine 159 peptide bond after its binding to fibrin. Prourokinase is not effective as a plasminogen activator, but this cleavage converts prourokinase into its two-chain structure and increases its activity 500-fold to 1000-fold.[94] Prourokinase differs from urokinase in several characteristics, mainly in its higher fibrin affinity, lower specific activity, and stability

Table 32-3 Characteristics of Thrombolytic Agents

AGENT	MOLECULAR WEIGHT (kD)	HALF-LIFE (APPROXIMATE)	FIBRIN SPECIFICITY	APPROVED INDICATIONS
Streptokinase	47	23 min	+	AMI, PE, DVT, arteriovenous cannula occlusion, arterial thrombosis/embolism
Urokinase	32-54	16 min	++	PE, venous catheter occlusion
Alteplase	68	4-5 min	+++	AMI, stroke, PE, venous catheter occlusion
Tenecteplase	65	20-24 min	++++	AMI
Reteplase	9.6	14 min	++	AMI
Prourokinase	54	7 min	++	NA
Staphylokinase	16.5	6 min	+++++	NA
Desmoteplase	52	40-50× t-PA*	+++++	NA
Alfimeprase	23	NA	+++++	NA
Plasmin	92†	0.1 sec‡	+++++	NA

*Derived from animal models.
†Molecular weight of human plasminogen.
‡Half-life of systemic plasmin.
AMI, acute myocardial infarction; DVT, deep venous thrombosis; NA, not available; PE, pulmonary embolism.

in plasma. Fibrin specificity of prourokinase does not depend on actual fibrin binding as with t-PA, and the mechanism of clot lysis is different between the two.[93] The half-life of prourokinase is approximately 7 minutes.

Studies with prourokinase in rabbits, dogs, and baboons showed fibrin-selective clot lysis without fibrinogenolytic effects or hemorrhagic complications.[48] Prourokinase testing in dogs also revealed that although prourokinase had superior fibrin specificity, it was equal to urokinase in efficacy.[95]

Clinical Experience The initial clinical application of prourokinase in humans was for acute MI. A small pilot study followed by a multicenter study of acute MI showed a 60% reperfusion rate in patients with proven coronary artery thrombosis. Prourokinase, 50 mg, was used, with a mean time of lysis of approximately 55 minutes. Increasing the dose to 70 to 80 mg increased reperfusion to almost 70%; however, time to lysis was prolonged, and systemic fibrinogenolysis developed in several patients.[93] No hemorrhagic effects were noted. Additional studies combining urokinase and prourokinase and t-PA and prourokinase showed a synergistic response between these agents because of complementary mechanisms of action.[96] Recombinant prourokinase currently is being evaluated in clinical trials with acceptable results.

Staphylokinase

Background A century ago, the clot-dissolving capability of *S. aureus* was recognized.[19] It took an additional 40 years for further study to reveal that the agent now called *staphylokinase* did not lyse fibrin directly, but rather acted as a plasminogen activator.[97] The reason for the delay is related to the valuable actions of plasminogen activators in different animal species and to assumptions made based on observations of other plasminogen activators. Remarkable variation among species to activation of plasminogen and fibrin dissolution was observed with staphylokinase.[98] Staphylokinase was found to activate human, dog, cat, rabbit, and guinea pig plasminogen; however, it did not activate rat or bovine plasminogen.

Early experiments with staphylokinase conducted with dogs resulted in high rates of bleeding and mortality.[99] In addition, a wide range of inhibitor activity was found in humans, which was attributed to staphylokinase-neutralizing antibodies (known to occur with streptokinase), and it was presumed that these antibodies would interfere with a fixed dosing schedule of staphylokinase, rendering staphylokinase treatment unpredictable and potentially ineffective. The need to improve thrombolytic strategies and the high fibrin specificity of staphylokinase along with recombinant technology allowed increased production of staphylokinase relative to exotoxins, which renewed interest in the clinical evaluation of this product.

Staphylokinase is a bacterial profibrinolytic agent consisting of a 136-amino acid protein secreted by *S. aureus*. Because staphylokinase is only one third the size of streptokinase, it was anticipated that thrombus penetration would be better. Because of its high affinity for fibrin, the biologic half-life is extended beyond its plasma half-life, improving its effectiveness. Linking staphylokinase with polyethylene glycol reduces plasma clearance and immunogenicity.

Similar to streptokinase, staphylokinase is an indirect plasminogen activator and forms a 1:1 stoichiometric complex with plasminogen, which then activates other plasminogen molecules. Many biochemical mechanisms contribute to its fibrin selectivity. In contrast to the streptokinase-plasminogen complex, the staphylokinase-plasminogen complex is rapidly neutralized by α_2-antiplasmin in plasma (if fibrin is not present), avoiding systemic plasminogen activation and a systemic fibrinolytic state. If fibrin is present, however, the staphylokinase-plasminogen binds to the clot at the lysine binding site of the plasminogen molecule. When bound to fibrin, the staphylokinase-plasminogen complex is no longer capable of being neutralized, allowing preferential plasminogen activation to occur on the surface of the clot. Similar to streptokinase, staphylokinase dissociates from the complex when it is activated after binding to fibrin to recirculate and bind with other plasminogen molecules. In vivo models have shown that staphylokinase can induce clot lysis rapidly without fibrinogen breakdown or α_2-antiplasmin consumption, documenting its high fibrin selectivity.[100]

Immunogenicity experiments showed marked differences from streptokinase and from what was anticipated. Weekly administration of streptokinase to baboons showed increased antibody production, which was associated with hypertension and diminished thrombolytic efficacy on repeat administration. Similar experiments with staphylokinase showed approximately one quarter of the antibody production as with streptokinase and preserved thrombolytic efficacy with no hypertension or allergic reactions on repeat administration.[101]

Clinical Experience There has been a limited, albeit optimistic clinical experience with staphylokinase. The initial clinical application was in 10 patients with acute MI.[102,103] In the pilot study, 9 of 10 patients recanalized their infarct-related artery after receiving a 1-mg bolus and an infusion of 9 mg over 30 minutes. A subsequent dose-ranging, multicenter trial of staphylokinase versus rt-PA was performed comparing 10-mg and 20-mg doses (with a 10% bolus) with weight-adjusted rt-PA in patients with acute MI.[104] Results of staphylokinase patients were similar to the results in patients receiving rt-PA; however, the 20-mg dose seemed to have improved efficacy. Staphylokinase proved to be highly fibrin specific, preserving plasma fibrinogen, plasminogen, and α_2-antiplasmin levels, whereas rt-PA resulted in a significant decrease in each of these variables. Complication rates were equivalent between staphylokinase and rt-PA patients. Subsequent double-bolus staphylokinase and single-bolus polyethylene glycol–staphylokinase studies in patients with acute MI confirmed efficacy and fibrin selectivity. Ongoing acute MI trials are designed to identify the optimal dose and safety profile of polyethylene glycol–staphylokinase.

Catheter-directed delivery of staphylokinase for lower extremity arterial and graft occlusion also showed favorable results. Lytic success was documented in 83% of patients treated; 12% had major bleeding complications.[105] Likewise, five of six patients treated for iliofemoral DVT had successful lysis.[106] Staphylokinase treatment did not alter fibrinogen, plasminogen, or α_2-antiplasmin levels significantly despite prolonged infusion.

Desmoteplase

Background Four plasminogen activators have been identified in the saliva of the vampire bat (*Desmodus rotundus*). Collectively, these are referred to as *Desmodus rotundus* plasminogen activators (DSPAs). They are designated *DSPA*α_1, *DSPA*α_2, *DSPA*β, and *DSPA*γ. Most research and development has focused on one of the four proteins, DSPAα_1. Desmoteplase is a recombinant analogue of DSPAα_1. DSPAα_2 is usually referred to in the literature as *Bat-PA*. Desmoteplase and Bat-PA have structural similarity to t-PA with four distinct structural domains: a finger domain, epidermal growth factor domain, kringle domain, and protease domain. DSPAβ and DSPAγ lack the finger and epidermal growth factor domains.

The catalytic activity of desmoteplase requires a cofactor, either fibrinogen or fibrin. Fibrinogen increases the catalytic activity of desmoteplase by 8-fold, whereas fibrin increases the catalytic activity by approximately 10^5-fold. This specificity for fibrin is unique to desmoteplase compared with other plasminogen activators. Comparative values for t-PA are an 8-fold and 550-fold increase in activity in the presence of fibrinogen and fibrin.[107] The finger and kringle domains are likely responsible for this fibrin binding.[107]

This fibrin specificity promotes plasminogen activation at the interface of the thrombus and less systemic plasminogen activation. In vivo and in vitro studies show that fibrinogen and plasminogen consumption are significantly less with desmoteplase compared with other plasminogen activators. In addition, α_2-antiplasmin is conserved because there is little systemic conversion of plasmin[108,109]; this may translate into fewer bleeding complications. In the rabbit cuticle bleeding time model, comparable doses of Bat-PA and t-PA were administered by intravenous bolus. Cuticle bleeding time was minimally elevated after Bat-PA administration (1.6-fold; P = not significant), whereas t-PA increased the cuticle bleeding time by 6.2-fold ($P < .05$).[110] Another study using a rabbit ear puncture model did not show any difference between Bat-PA and t-PA with respect to bleeding time or rebleeding from hemodynamically stable sites. Other investigators have shown, however, that rabbits treated with Bat-PA had a greater number of prolonged primary bleeding and rebleeding episodes that lasted longer than 10 minutes (63% with Bat-PA versus 36% with t-PA) or greater than 30 minutes (30% with Bat-PA versus 10% with t-PA).[111]

Another difference between desmoteplase and the other plasminogen activators is the prolonged half-life. Desmoteplase has a much longer half-life; plasma clearance is approximately five to nine times slower than t-PA. The long half-life makes single bolus administration an option for arterial events, such as stroke or MI. In addition, the prolonged half-life may decrease the incidence of post-thrombolysis reocclusion.

Clinical Experience Desmoteplase currently is being investigated and developed through PAION (Aachen, Germany). Phase I clinical trials have been completed, and no significant changes in hematology or chemistry parameters were observed, no antibody formation was detected, and no adverse effects on coagulation were noted.[112] Initial phase II trial results of patients with acute MI were obtained in a nonrandomized, open-label, prospective, dose-finding study. Twenty-six patients were enrolled. TIMI grade 3 perfusion was documented in 17 of 26 patients (65%) at 90 minutes. Late patency was confirmed in 21 of 26 patients. Three patients died within 8 hours of inclusion.[112] Two phase II trials in acute stroke are currently under way. DIAS (Desmoteplase In Acute ischemic Stroke) is ongoing in Europe, and DEDAS (Dose Escalation study of Desmoteplase in Acute ischemic Stroke) has been initiated in the United States. DIAS is a multicenter, multinational, double-blind, placebo-controlled, randomized trial comparing desmoteplase at three fixed doses (25 mg, 37.5 mg, and 50 mg) with placebo in patients with acute ischemic stroke within 3 to 9 hours of symptom onset. Initial results with respect to clinical improvement showed a trend favoring desmoteplase; however, the trial design was modified because of excess of symptomatic intracranial hemorrhage in patients receiving desmoteplase. The fixed dosing regimen was replaced by a weight-based dosing regimen (62.5 μg/kg); the trial currently is enrolling patients. A similar trial began enrollment in November 2002. DEDAS is a similar multicenter, multinational, double-blind, placebo-controlled, randomized trial enrolling patients with acute ischemic stroke symptoms present for 3 to 9 hours.

Direct-Acting Agents

To date, thrombolytic therapy has used plasminogen activators to generate the enzymatically active plasmin. Alfimeprase and plasmin represent a new class of thrombolytic agents that do not require substrate plasminogen. Both are direct-acting thrombolytic agents. Because they are neutralized rapidly by circulating α_2-antiplasmin, intrathrombus infusion is necessary, as systemic infusion would be ineffective. Both agents have the promise of an improved safety profile compared with available plasminogen activators and experimental evidence suggesting rapid thrombus dissolution. Clinical trials are currently under way.

Alfimeprase

Background Fibrolase is a fibrinolytic zinc metalloprotease isolated from southern copperhead snake venom (*Agkistrodon contortrix contortrix*). A recombinant analogue of fibrolase, alfimeprase is currently under investigation and production through the cooperative efforts of Nuvelo Incorporated (Sunnyvale, Calif) and Amgen Incorporated (Thousand Oaks, Calif). Alfimeprase differs from fibrolase at the amino-terminal sequence of the protein, where three amino acid residues were replaced with a single serine.[113]

Thrombolytic agents, such as streptokinase, urokinase, rt-PA, recombinant plasminogen activator, and TNK-t-PA, rely on the activation of the endogenous plasminogen-plasmin system. Alfimeprase is not a plasminogen activator, and the mode of action and the physiologic clearance and inactivation of alfimeprase are significantly different from the available thrombolytic agents. Based on these differences, it is anticipated that alfimeprase will have clinical benefits over the available plasminogen activators when it is used for thrombolysis, including a more rapid lytic response and reduced bleeding.

Plasminogen activators convert systemic or thrombus-associated plasminogen to an active enzyme, plasmin, which is capable of degrading fibrinogen and fibrin. In contrast, alfimeprase has direct fibrinolytic activity and does not rely on the activation of plasmin for fibrinolysis. The proteolytic activity of alfimeprase is directed against the α-chain of fibrinogen/fibrin with limited β-chain proteolysis and no significant activity against the γ-chain.[114,115] Alfimeprase has been studied in several animal models. Data from numerous animal studies have indicated that the time to thrombolysis is more rapid with alfimeprase compared with other plasminogen activators (t-PA and urokinase) without excess bleeding.[116,117] In one study using piglets, induced common carotid artery thrombi were lysed approximately fourfold faster with recombinant fibrolase infusion compared with t-PA. In addition, no excess bleeding was observed compared with a control saline infusion.[117] In a similar rat model, the time to thrombolysis was approximately fivefold faster with alfimeprase compared with urokinase.[117] Another study investigated the use of recombinant fibrolase in electrically induced carotid artery occlusions in dogs. All thrombi were lysed successfully. The addition of an experimental platelet glycoprotein IIb/IIIa receptor antagonist monoclonal antibody maintained patency in four of five animals. No effect on platelet count, hemoglobin, hematocrit, or activated partial thromboplastin time was observed.[118]

In contrast to plasminogen activators, alfimeprase is bound and inactivated in the plasma by α_2-macroglobulin. α_2-Macroglobulin is a mammalian protease inhibitor capable of inhibiting several classes of proteases, including metalloproteases. In the systemic circulation, alfimeprase rapidly binds to α_2-macroglobulin in a 1:1 molar ratio. A covalent bond is formed between the two molecules, and this complex is not dissociable. The alfimeprase–α_2-macroglobulin complex is cleared by the reticuloendothelial system. This rapid and irreversible binding limits the systemic effect of alfimeprase. The hemorrhagic complications associated with plasminogen activators should not be experienced with alfimeprase.

There is a finite amount of α_2-macroglobulin available in the circulation; the clearance mechanism for alfimeprase is saturable. Experiments designed to exceed the plasma α_2-macroglobulin binding capacity caused hypotension in animal models. The hypotensive response was observed to be rapid, but capable of spontaneously correcting. Pharmacologic studies showed that this response could be blocked by a bradykinin receptor antagonist. The proposed etiology of the response is the cleavage of bradykinin from low-molecular-weight kininogen by alfimeprase.[116] Clinical dosing regimens need to be developed to avoid depletion of the α_2-macroglobulin binding capacity.

Failed thrombolysis and re-thrombosis can frustrate physicians using fibrinolytic therapy. The activity of the plasminogen activators is inhibited by α_2-antiplasmin and PAI-1. Elevated PAI-1 levels may contribute to inadequate thrombolysis and re-thrombosis.[119,120] In addition, plasmin is a known platelet activator; it is proposed that the platelet activation and aggregation promoted by plasmin contributes to a thrombogenic state and may be implicated in re-thrombosis. Alfimeprase does not rely on the activity of plasmin; there is no inhibition by α_2-antiplasmin, and there is no plasmin-associated platelet activation. In addition, alfimeprase is not inhibited by PAI-1. It may be anticipated that thrombolysis would be more successful and a prothrombotic state and re-thrombosis would be less likely to occur after thrombolysis with alfimeprase (Table 32-3).

Clinical Experience A phase I clinical trial performed in 20 patients with peripheral arterial occlusive disease has been completed. This trial was a multicenter, open-label, dose-escalation study designed to evaluate the safety and pharmacokinetics of alfimeprase. The reportedly positive results should be forthcoming. Phase II trials in peripheral arterial occlusive disease are being initiated. Another phase II multicenter trial of alfimeprase for central venous catheter occlusion currently is enrolling patients. This trial is investigating three different doses of alfimeprase compared with the approved dose of rt-PA in a randomized, double-blind fashion. The primary endpoints of the study are the safety and efficacy of alfimeprase for restoring catheter function.

Plasmin

Background Plasmin is in a new class of thrombolytic agents that do not require substrate plasminogen. As reviewed earlier, plasmin is a serine protease with wide proteolytic activity, is prone to autodegradation, is extremely rapidly inactivated by α_2-antiplasmin, and is unstable at physiologic pH.

During the developmental era of thrombolytic therapy, plasmin was recognized as the important fibrinolytic enzyme with potential clinical application.[121] Because the thrust of all thrombolytic therapy at the time was systemic intravenous infusion, however, and knowing that plasmin was neutralized rapidly by circulating α_2-antiplasmin, it was natural that the development of the plasminogen activators streptokinase and urokinase took priority. With the evolution of lytic therapy to catheter-directed intrathrombus infusion for most patients with acute arterial and venous thrombosis, the limitations of plasmin, specifically the inactivation by circulating α_2-antiplasmin, might provide a distinct mechanism of safety from bleeding complications. Plasmin is produced from human plasma. Its structural integrity is preserved by the use of 50% glycerol and a low pH. For a more in-depth description of the production process, the reader is referred to Novokhatny and colleagues.[122]

Animal Experiments Animal experiments were designed to test the hypothesis that purified plasmin could bind and dissolve clot locally and that plasmin that escaped into the circulation would be neutralized rapidly by α_2-antiplasmin, avoiding remote bleeding at sites of vascular injury.[123] Most of the experiments were performed on rabbits. Efficacy of the thrombolytic fusion was evaluated using the rabbit aorta thrombolysis model,[123] by isolating the distal abdominal aorta and injecting fresh autologous blood. Two variations of the aortic thrombolysis model were used—one allowing full antegrade flow and the other with occluded inflow.

The efficacy of the fibrinolytic agent was evaluated after a 1-hour infusion or two 30-minute infusions separated by a 15-minute observation period. Varying doses of plasmin were used and compared with varying doses of t-PA.

Distant bleeding was evaluated using a standardized rabbit ear puncture rebleed model, in which a 3.5-mm full-thickness puncture was made with a no. 11 surgical blade at 30 minutes, 10 minutes, and immediately before the infusion of plasmin or the comparator plasminogen activator, which was t-PA in most experiments. In vitro models of lysis also were used to compare efficacy of lysis of retracted clots (clots with low plasminogen concentration) and the impact of delivery of endogenous plasminogen.[122]

These experiments showed that plasmin and t-PA lyse acute (15-minute) plasminogen-rich thrombi equally well. Plasmin was significantly more effective, however, than t-PA and urokinase in dissolving retracted (plasminogen-poor) clot. There was a dose-dependent efficacy of plasmin; this was not the case with t-PA. Plasminogen supplementation significantly improved the lytic efficacy of t-PA on retracted clot, whereas there was no effect of supplemental plasminogen on plasmin-treated clots.[122] Plasmin seemed to be more effective than t-PA for acute clot lysis in the impeded blood flow model, whereas in the unimpeded model of acute arterial thrombosis, t-PA and plasmin had equal efficacy.[123] This difference likely reflected plasminogen supplementation during infusion of t-PA.

Bleeding from distant sites was not observed with routine doses of plasmin of 6 mg/kg; however a plasmin dose of 8 mg/kg caused distant bleeding in 60% of animals, suggesting a threshold for bleeding rather than a dose effect.[124] Animals receiving t-PA had distant bleeding, but it occurred in a dose-dependent fashion. Progressively higher doses of t-PA showed no dose-dependent effect on fibrinogen, although there was a stepwise increase in bleeding. Plasmin caused a dose-dependent decrease in fibrinogen, but there was a threshold effect relative to observed distant bleeding. It was evident that when fibrinogen and factor VIII were depleted by plasmin, hemostatic protection was breached, which allowed bleeding. This breach occurred at the highest doses of plasmin, which seemed to overwhelm α_2-antiplasmin, resulting in the proteolytic effects observed on fibrinogen and factor VIII.

Clinical Experience On the basis of animal experimentation, it is anticipated that most clinical arterial thromboembolic occlusions can be treated successfully with doses of 50 mg or less of plasmin. The average plasma concentration of α_2-antiplasmin is 1 μmol/L^{-1} (70 mg/L^{1}). A 70-kg individual should have 175 mg of α_2-antiplasmin in the circulation available for neutralization of any free plasmin that escapes from the site of the thrombus. Anticipating that the total dose of locally delivered plasmin is lower than the available endogenous α_2-antiplasmin, and knowing the rapid kinetics of inactivation of plasmin by α_2-antiplasmin, unwanted systemic proteolytic activity should be avoided with a substantial margin of safety from distant bleeding complications.

Animal experiments have shown that plasmin can be produced in a highly purified form that is essentially free of plasminogen activators. It is prepared from human plasma and stabilized at low pH, which is designed to have a low buffering capacity. This formulation is essentially reversibly inactivated plasmin, which becomes effective when infused into blood clots. Clinical trials are under way.

■ ULTRASOUND THROMBOLYSIS

Background

An innovative use of ultrasound is to accelerate dissolution of intravascular thrombus. Techniques have used endovascular approaches by delivering ultrasound energy via an intraluminal catheter and by the external application of ultrasound to augment thrombolysis. Depending on the intensity and the frequency of the sound waves delivered, the mechanisms of thrombus resolution vary between mechanical disruption (fragmentation) of thrombus and acceleration of enzymatic thrombolysis.

One advantage of ultrasound thrombolysis is that the effects are limited to the insonated region, and active lysis is focused at the site of thrombosis, limiting or eliminating systemic complications. The power of the ultrasound device may deliver sufficient energy to damage the vessel wall, however, through thermal injury or mechanical disruption of the artery wall. The ultrasound energy is powerful enough to recanalize vessels with atherosclerotic occlusion even in the presence of calcification.[125] Excessive energy has resulted in vessel wall damage and perforation.[125,126]

The effective delivery and distribution of plasminogen activators to the thrombus is the most important determinant of the rapidity of thrombolysis.[127] Francis and associates[128] studied the effect of insonification on the distribution of radiolabeled t-PA placed in the fluid around clot. They showed that t-PA uptake was significantly faster in the presence of ultrasound. Other investigators observed significantly deeper penetration of the plasminogen activator into clot,[129] which should result in more rapid fibrinolysis. It also has been shown that ultrasound causes reversible disaggregation of fibrin fibers into smaller fibers, which would alter flow resistance and create additional binding sites for plasminogen activators, which should improve the efficacy of lysis further.[130] Additionally, others have shown that ultrasound improves binding affinity of t-PA, increases the maximum binding of t-PA to fibrin, and improves access of t-PA to fibrin binding sites.[131]

Ultrasound-accelerated thrombolysis has been shown to increase platelet aggregation, resulting in increased reocclusion[132] and increased platelet accumulation around the periphery of thrombus.[133] Aspirin pretreatment seems to be beneficial in reducing reocclusion.[132]

Clinical Experience

The major use of ultrasound in humans has been via percutaneous delivery with a wire. Percutaneous ultrasound angioplasty has been studied by many investigators.[134-140] Most clinical experience has been gained through small studies evaluating percutaneous delivery of ultrasound to atherosclerotic arteries having significant stenosis or occlusion. Most investigators have delivered ultrasound energy in the frequency range of 19 to 20 kHz, with some increasing the frequency to 41 to 45 kHz. The transducer power output was in the range of 16 to 35 W/cm^2. The results observed in these small series have been gratifying, showing recanalization of occluded arteries in 80% and reduction of high-grade stenoses to less severe, moderate lesions. These observations go beyond the effects of thrombolysis, indicating that percutaneously delivered ultrasound can be used on atherosclerotic lesions to disobliterate occluded arteries and reduce the degree of stenosis in nonoccluded, stenotic vessels. Fourteen of 20 patients with occluded saphenous vein grafts were successfully recanalized using an ultrasound thrombolysis device with a 1.6-mm tip and a 7F guiding catheter operated at 41 kHz and 18 W.[141] As might be expected, adjunctive balloon angioplasty or stenting or both were required in all patients.

It is intriguing to consider the possibilities of ultrasound-accelerated thrombolysis during catheter delivery of plasminogen activators. If the ultrasound energy can be delivered transcutaneously to the thrombus without heat damage to the soft tissues, the success rates of thrombolysis should increase substantially, the cost of thrombolysis should be reduced considerably, and the number of patients having a contraindication to this form of therapy should be few.

■ REFERENCES

1. Rentrop KP: Development and pathophysiological basis of thrombolytic therapy in acute myocardial infarction: Part IV. In Timmis GC (ed): Thrombolytic Therapy. Armonk, NY, Futura Publishing, 1999, pp 59-72.
2. Kaste M: Thrombolysis in ischemic stroke—present and future: Role of combined therapy. Cerebrovasc Dis 11(Suppl 1):55-59, 2001.
3. Goldhaber S: Thrombolytic therapy for pulmonary embolism. In Comerota AJ (ed): Thrombolytic Therapy for Peripheral Vascular Disease. Philadelphia, JB Lippincott, 1995, pp 161-174.
4. The STILE Investigators: Results of a prospective randomized trial evaluating surgery versus thrombolysis for ischemia of the lower extremity. The STILE trial. Ann Surg 220:251-268, 1994.
5. Ouriel K, Veith FJ, Sasahara AA, et al, for the Thrombolysis or Peripheral Arterial Surgery (TOPAS) Investigators: A comparison of recombinant urokinase with vascular surgery as initial treatment for acute arterial occlusion of the legs. N Engl J Med 338:1105-1111, 1998.
6. Comerota AJ: Thrombolytic therapy for acute deep vein thrombosis. In Comerota AJ (ed): Thrombolytic Therapy for Peripheral Vascular Disease. Philadelphia, JB Lippincott, 1995, pp 175-195.
7. Comerota AJ, Throm RC, Mathias S, et al: Catheter-directed thrombolysis for iliofemoral deep venous thrombosis improves health-related quality of life. J Vasc Surg 32:130-137, 2000.
8. Haire WD, Atkinson JB, Stephens LC, et al: Urokinase versus recombinant tissue plasminogen activator in thrombosed central venous catheters: A double-blind, randomized trial. Thromb Haemost 72:543-547, 1994.
9. Falk A, Mitty H, Guller J, et al: Thrombolysis of clotted hemodialysis grafts with tissue-type plasminogen activator. J Vasc Interv Radiol 12:305-311, 2001.
10. McNamara TO, Fischer JR: Thrombolysis of peripheral arterial and graft occlusions: Improved results using high dose urokinase. AJR Am J Roentgenol 144:769-775, 1985.
11. Weaver FA, Comerota AJ, Youngblood M, et al: Surgical revascularization versus thrombolysis for nonembolic lower extremity native artery occlusions: Results of a prospective randomized trial. J Vasc Surg 24:513-523, 1996.
12. Machleder HI: The role of thrombolytic agents for acute subclavian vein thrombosis. Semin Vasc Surg 5:82, 1992.
13. Kohner EM, Pettit JE, Hamilton AM, et al: Streptokinase in central retinal vein occlusion: A controlled clinical trial. BMJ 1:550-553, 1976.
14. Chang R, Cannon RO, Chen CC, et al: Daily catheter-directed single dosing of t-PA in treatment of acute deep venous thrombosis of the lower extremity. J Vasc Interv Radiol 12:247-252, 2001.
15. Comerota AJ, Rao AK, Throm RC, et al: A prospective, randomized, blinded, and placebo-controlled trial of intraoperative intra-arterial urokinase infusion during lower extremity revascularization: Regional and systemic effects. Ann Surg 218:534-541, 1993.
16. Gross R: Fibrinolyse and thrombolyse. Panorama September:4, 1962.
17. Morgagni JB: De Sedibus et Causis Morborum per Anatomen Indagatis, 2nd ed. 1761. Translated by Alexander B: The Seats and Causes of Diseases Investigated by Anatomy, vol 3, book 4. London, Millar, 1769.
18. Morawitz P: Ner einige postmortale blutveranderungen beitr zur chem Physiol Patho. Braunschweig 8:1, 1906.
19. Much H: Uber eine Vorstufe des Fibrinfermentes in Kulturen von *Staphylokokkus aureus*. Biochemische Zeitschrift 14:143-155, 1908.
20. Tillett WS, Garner RL: The fibrinolytic activity of hemolytic streptococci. J Exp Med 58:485-502, 1933.
21. Tillett WS, Sherry S: The effect in patients of streptococcal fibrinolysin (streptokinase) and streptococcal deoxyribonuclease on fibrinous, purulent and sanguineous pleural exudations. J Clin Invest 28:173, 1949.
22. Sherry S, Tillett WS, Read CT: The use of streptokinase-streptodornase in the treatment of hemothorax. J Thorac Surg 20:393, 1950.
23. Fletcher AP, Alkjaersig N, Smyrniotis FE, et al: Treatment of patients suffering from early myocardial infarction with massive and prolonged streptokinase therapy. Trans Assoc Am Physicians 71:287-296, 1958.
24. Alkjaersig N, Fletcher AP, Sherry S: The mechanism of clot dissolution by plasmin. J Clin Invest 38:1086-1095, 1959.
25. White WF, Barlow GH, Mozen MM: The isolation and characterization of plasminogen activators (urokinase) from human urine. Biochemistry 5:2160-2169, 1966.
26. Lesuk A, Terminiello L, Traver JH: Crystalline human urokinase: Some properties. Science 147:880-882, 1965.
27. The Urokinase Pulmonary Embolism Trial: A national cooperative study. Circulation 47(Suppl II):II1-II108, 1973.
28. Urokinase-Streptokinase Pulmonary Embolism Trial: Phase II results: A cooperative study. JAMA 229:1606-1613, 1974.
29. DeWood MA, Spores J, Notske R, et al: Prevalence of total coronary occlusion during the early hours of transmural myocardial infarction. N Engl J Med 303:897-902, 1980.
30. Marder VJ, Sherry S: Thrombolytic therapy: Current status (I). N Engl J Med 318:1512-1520, 1988.
31. Marder VJ, Butler FO, Barlow GH: Antifibrinolytic therapy. In Colman RW, Hirsh J, Marder VJ, Salzman EW (eds): Hemostasis and Thrombosis: Basic Principles and Clinical Practice, 2nd ed. Philadelphia, JB Lippincott, 1987, p 380.
32. Sottrup-Jensen L, Claeys H, Zajdel M, et al: The primary structure of human plasminogen: Isolation of two lysine-binding fragments and one "mini"-plasminogen (MW, 38,000) by elastase-catalyzed specific limited proteolysis. In Davidson JF, Rowan RM, Samama MM, Desnoyers PC (eds): Progress in Chemical Fibrinolysis and Thrombolysis, vol 3. New York, Raven Press, 1978, p 191.
33. Dayhoff MO: Atlas of Protein Sequence and Structure, vol 5, suppl 3. Silver Spring, MD, National Biomedical Research Foundation, 1978.
34. Walther PJ, Steinman HM, Hill RL, et al: Activation of human plasminogen by urokinase: Partial characterization of a preactivation peptide. J Biol Chem 249:1173-1181, 1974.
35. Wallen P, Wiman B: Characterization of human plasminogen: II. Separation and partial characterization of different molecular forms of human plasminogen. Biochim Biophys Acta 257:122-134, 1972.
36. Varadi A, Patthy L: Location of plasminogen-binding sites in human fibrin(ogen). Biochemistry 22:2240-2246, 1983.

37. Markus G, DePasquale JL, Wissler FC: Quantitative determination of the binding of epsilon-aminocaproic acid to native plasminogen. J Biol Chem 253:727-732, 1978.
38. Robbins KC, Summaria L, Hsieh B, et al: The peptide chains of human plasmin: Mechanism of activation of human plasminogen to plasmin. J Biol Chem 242:2333-2342, 1967.
39. Alkjaersig N, Fletcher AP, Sherry S: The mechanism of clot dissolution by plasmin. J Clin Invest 38:1086-1095, 1959.
40. Mullertz S: Natural inhibitors of fibrinolysis. In Davidson JF, Rowan RM, Samama MM, Desnoyers PC (eds): Progress in Chemical Fibrinolysis and Thrombolysis, vol 3. New York, Raven Press, 1978, p 213.
41. Aoki N: Natural inhibitors of fibrinolysis. Prog Cardiovasc Dis 21: 276-286, 1979.
42. Wiman B: Human alpha-2-antiplasmin. Methods Enzymol 80:395, 1981.
43. Mullertz S, Clemmensen I: The primary inhibitor of plasmin in human plasma. Biochem J 159:545-553, 1976.
44. Thorsen S, Philips M: Isolation of tissue-type plasminogen activator-inhibitor complexes from human plasma: Evidence for a rapid plasminogen activator inhibitor. Biochim Biophys Acta 802:111-118, 1984.
45. Erickson LA, Ginsberg MH, Loskutoff DJ: Detection and partial characterization of an inhibitor of plasminogen activator in human platelets. J Clin Invest 74:1465-1472, 1984.
46. Francis CW, Marder VJ: Concepts of clot lysis. Annu Rev Med 37:187-204, 1986.
47. Budzynski AZ, Marder VJ, Shainoff JR: Structure of plasmic degradation products of human fibrinogen: Fibrinopeptide and polypeptide chain analysis. J Biol Chem 249:2294-2302, 1974.
48. Francis CW, Marder VJ, Martin SE: Plasmic degradation of cross-linked fibrin: I. Structural analysis of the particulate clot and identification of new macromolecular-soluble complexes. Blood 56:456-464, 1980.
49. Kopec M, Tesseyre E, Dudek-Wojciechowska G, et al: Studies on "double D" fragment from stabilized bovine fibrin. Thromb Res 2:283, 1973.
50. Van deWerf FJ: The ideal fibrinolytic agent: Can drug design improve clinical results? Eur Heart J 20:1452-1458, 1999.
51. Tillet WS, Garner RL: The fibrinolytic activity of hemolytic streptococci. J Exp Med 58:485, 1933.
52. Kwaan HC: Hematologic aspects of thrombolytic therapy. In Comerota AJ (ed): Thrombolytic Therapy. Orlando, Grune & Stratton, 1988, p 17.
53. Coller BS: Platelets and thrombolytic therapy. N Engl J Med 322:33-42, 1990.
54. Sherry S: Pharmacology of anistreplase. Clin Cardiol Suppl 5:V3-V10, 1990.
55. MacFarlane RG, Pilling J: Fibrinolytic activity of normal urine. Nature 159:779, 1947.
56. Williams JRB: The fibrinolytic activity of urine. Br J Exp Pathol 32:520, 1951.
57. Gunzler WA, Steffens GJ, Otting F, et al: The primary structure of high molecular mass urokinase from human urine: The complete amino acid sequence of the A chain. Hoppe Seylers Z Physiol Chem 363:1155-1165, 1982.
58. Bernik MB, Kwaan HC: Origin of fibrinolytic activity in cultures of the human kidney. J Lab Clin Med 70:650-651, 1967.
59. Comerota AJ, Rao AK, Throm RC, et al: A prospective, randomized, blinded, and placebo-controlled trial of intraoperative intraarterial urokinase infusion during lower extremity revascularization: Regional and systemic effects. Ann Surg 218:534, 1993.
60. Comerota AJ: Intraoperative intraarterial thrombolytic therapy. In Comerota AJ (ed): Thrombolytic Therapy for Peripheral Vascular Disease. Philadelphia, JB Lippincott, 1995, pp 313-328.
61. Froehlich J, Stump DL: Recombinant tissue plasminogen activator. In Comerota AJ (ed): Thrombolytic Therapy for Peripheral Vascular Disease. Philadelphia, JB Lippincott, 1995, pp 103-114.
62. Semba CP, Deitcher SR, Li X, et al: Treatment of occluded central venous catheters with alteplase: Results in 1,064 patients. J Vasc Interv Radiol 13:1199-1205, 2002.
63. Browne M, Newall F, Campbell J, et al: Thrombolytic therapy with tissue plasminogen activator (tPA), analysis of safety and outcome in children. J Thromb Haemost 1(Suppl 1):1488, 2003.
64. The TIMI Study Group: The Thrombolysis in Myocardial Infarction (TIMI) trial: Phase I findings. N Engl J Med 312:932-936, 1985.
65. The GUSTO Investigators: An international randomized trial comparing four thrombolytic strategies for acute myocardial infarction. N Engl J Med 329:673-682, 1993.
66. The National Institute of Neurological Disorders and Stroke rt-PA Stroke Study Group: Tissue plasminogen activator for acute ischemic stroke. N Engl J Med 333:1581-1587, 1995.
67. Wardlaw JM, Sandercock PA, Berge E: Thrombolytic therapy with recombinant tissue plasminogen activator for acute ischemic stroke: Where do we go from here? A cumulative meta-analysis. Stroke 34:1437-1442, 2003.
68. Goldhaber SZ, Kessler CM, Heit J, et al: Randomized controlled trial of recombinant tissue plasminogen activator versus urokinase in the treatment of acute pulmonary embolism. Lancet 2:293-298, 1988.
69. Konstantinides S, Geibel A, Heusel G, et al, for the Management Strategies and Prognosis of Pulmonary Embolism-3 Trial Investigators: Heparin plus alteplase compared with heparin alone in patients with submassive pulmonary embolism. N Engl J Med 347:1143-1150, 2002.
70. Meneveau N. Schiele F, Vuillemenot A, et al: Streptokinase vs alteplase in massive pulmonary embolism: A randomized trial assessing right heart haemodynamics and pulmonary vascular obstruction. Eur Heart J 18:1141-1148, 1997.
71. Meneveau N, Schiele F, Metz D, et al: Comparative efficacy of a two-hour regimen of streptokinase versus alteplase in acute massive pulmonary embolism: Immediate clinical and hemodynamic outcome and one-year follow-up. J Am Coll Cardiol 31:1057-1063, 1998.
72. Semba CP, Murphy TP, Bakal CW, et al, and the advisory panel: Thrombolytic therapy with use of alteplase (rt-PA) in peripheral arterial occlusive disease: Review of the clinical literature. J Vasc Interv Radiol 11:149-161, 2000.
73. Forster A, Wells P: Tissue plasminogen activator for the treatment of deep venous thrombosis of the lower extremity: A systematic review. Chest 119:572-579, 2001.
74. McCluskey ER, Refino CJ, Zioncheck TF, et al: Tenecteplase: Biochemistry, pharmacology, and clinical experience. In Sasahara AA, Loscalzo J (eds): New Therapeutic Agents in Thrombosis and Thrombolysis, 2nd ed. New York, Marcel Dekker, 2003, pp 501-511.
75. Keyt BA, Paoni NF, Refino CJ, et al: A faster-acting and more potent form of tissue plasminogen activator. Proc Natl Acad Sci U S A 91:3670-3674, 1994.
76. Modi NB, Eppler S, Breed J, et al: Pharmacokinetics of a slower clearing tissue plasminogen activator variant, TNK-tPA, in patients with acute myocardial infarction. Thromb Haemost 79:134-139, 1998.
77. Cannon CP, McCabe CH, Gibson CM, et al: TNK-tissue plasminogen activator in acute myocardial infarction: Results of the Thrombolysis in Myocardial Infarction (TIMI) 10A dose-ranging trial. Circulation 95:351-356, 1997.
78. Cannon CP, Gibson CM, McCabe CH, et al, for the Thrombolysis in Myocardial Infarction (TIMI) 10B investigators: TNK-tissue plasminogen activator compared with front-loaded alteplase in acute myocardial infarction: Results of the TIMI 10B trial. Circulation 98:2805-2814, 1998.
79. Assessment of the Safety and Efficacy of a New Thrombolytic investigators: Single bolus tenecteplase compared with front-loaded alteplase in acute myocardial infarction: The ASSENT-2 double-blind randomised trial. Lancet 354:716-722, 1999.
80. Burkart DJ, Borsa JJ, Anthony JP, et al: Thrombolysis of occluded peripheral arteries and veins with tenecteplase: A pilot study. J Vasc Interv Radiol 13:1099-1102, 2002.

81. Verstraete M: Third-generation thrombolytic drugs. Am J Med 109:52-58, 2000.
82. Waller M, Mack S, Martin U, et al: Clinical and preclinical profile of the novel recombinant plasminogen activator reteplase. In Sasahara AA, Loscalzo J (eds): New Therapeutic Agents in Thrombosis and Thrombolysis, 2nd ed. New York, Marcel Dekker, 2003, pp 479-500.
83. Smalling RW, Bode C, Kalbfleisch J, et al, the RAPID Investigators: More rapid, complete and stable coronary thrombolysis with bolus administration of reteplase compared with alteplase infusion in acute myocardial infarction. Circulation 91:2725-2732, 1995.
84. Bode C, Smalling RW, Berg G, et al, for the RAPID II Investigators: Randomized comparison of coronary thrombolysis achieved with double-bolus reteplase (recombinant plasminogen activator) and front-loaded, accelerated alteplase (recombinant tissue plasminogen activator) in patients with acute myocardial infarction. Circulation 94:891-898, 1996.
85. International Joint Efficacy Comparison of Thrombolytics (INJECT): Randomized, double-blind comparison of reteplace double-bolus administration with streptokinase in acute myocardial infarction (INJECT): Trial to investigate equivalence. Lancet 346:329-336, 1995.
86. The Global Use of Strategies To Open occluded coronary arteries (GUSTO III) investigators: A comparison of reteplase with alteplase for acute myocardial infarction. N Engl J Med 337:1118-1123, 1997.
87. Tebbe U, Graf A, Kamke W, et al: Hemodynamic effects of double bolus reteplase versus alteplase infusion in massive pulmonary embolism. Am Heart J 138:39-44, 1999.
88. Kiproff PM, Yammine K, Potts JM, et al: Reteplase infusion in the treatment of acute lower extremity occlusions. J Thromb Thrombolysis 13:75-79, 2002.
89. Castaneda F, Swischuk JL, Li R, et al: Declining-dose study of reteplase treatment for lower extremity arterial occlusions. J Vasc Interv Radiol 13:1093-1098, 2002.
90. Castaneda F, Li R, Young K, et al: Catheter-directed thrombolysis in deep venous thrombosis with use of reteplase: Immediate results and complications from a pilot study. J Vasc Interv Radiol 13:577-580, 2002.
91. Ouriel K, Katzen B, Mewissen M, et al: Reteplase in the treatment of peripheral arterial and venous occlusions: A pilot study. J Vasc Interv Radiol 11:849-854, 2000.
92. Husain SS, Lipinski B, Gurewich V: Isolation of plasminogen activators useful as therapeutic and diagnostic agents (single-chain, high-fibrin affinity urokinase). US patent no. 4 381 346 (filed November 13, 1979; issued April 1983).
93. Gurewich V: Tissue plasminogen activator and pro-urokinase. In Comerota AJ (ed): Thrombolytic Therapy. Orlando, Grune & Stratton, 1988, p 209.
94. Gurewich V, Pannell R, Louie S, et al: Effective and fibrin-specific clot lysis by a zymogen precursor form of urokinase (pro-urokinase): A study in vitro and in two animal species. J Clin Invest 73:1731-1739, 1984.
95. Collen D, Stump D, van de Werf F, et al: Coronary thrombolysis in dogs with intravenously administered human pro-urokinase. Circulation 72:384-388, 1985.
96. Gurewich V, Pannell R: A comparative study of the efficacy and specificity of tissue plasminogen activator and pro-urokinase: Demonstration of synergism and of different thresholds of non-selectivity. Thromb Res 44:217-228, 1986.
97. Lack CH: Staphylokinase: An activator of plasma protease. Nature 161:559-560, 1948.
98. Lewis JH, Ferguson JH: A proteolytic enzyme system of the blood: III. Activation of dog serum profibrinolysin by staphylokinase. Am J Physiol 166:594-602, 1951.
99. Lewis JH, Kerber CW, Wilson JH: Effects of fibrinolytic agents and heparin on intravascular clot lysis. Am J Physiol 207:1044-1048, 1964.
100. Lijnen HR, De Cock F, Matsuo O, et al: Comparative fibrinolytic and fibrinogenolytic properties of staphylokinase and streptokinase in plasma of different species in vitro. Fibrinolysis 6:33-37, 1992.
101. Collen D, De Cock F, Stassen JM: Comparative immunogenicity and thrombolytic properties toward arterial and venous thrombi of streptokinase and recombinant staphylokinase in baboons. Circulation 87:996-1006, 1993.
102. Collen D, Van de Werf F: Coronary thrombolysis with recombinant staphylokinase in patients with evolving myocardial infarction. Circulation 87:1850-1853, 1993.
103. Vanderschueren S, Collen D, Van de Werf F: Coronary reperfusion in patients with an acute myocardial infarction following intravenous administration of recombinant staphylokinase [abstract]. J Am Coll Cardiol 315A, 1994.
104. Vanderschueren S, Barrios L, Kerdsinchai P, et al: A randomized trial of recombinant staphylokinase versus alteplase for coronary artery patency in acute myocardial infarction. The STAR trial group. Circulation 92:2044-2049, 1995.
105. Heymans S, Vanderschueren S, Verhaeghe R, et al: Outcome and one year follow-up of intra-arterial staphylokinase in 191 patients with peripheral arterial occlusion. Thromb Haemost 83:666-671, 2000.
106. Heymans S, Verhaeghe R, Stockx L, et al: Feasibility study of catheter-directed thrombolysis with recombinant staphylokinase in deep venous thrombosis. Thromb Haemost 79:517-519, 1998.
107. Bringmann P, Gruber D, Liese A, et al: Structural features mediating fibrin selectivity of vampire bat plasminogen activators. J Biol Chem 270:25596-25603, 1995.
108. Gardell SJ, Ramjit DR, Stabilito II, et al: Effective thrombolysis without marked plasminemia after bolus intravenous administration of vampire bat salivary plasminogen activator in rabbits. Circulation 84:244-253, 1991.
109. Hare TR, Gardell SJ: Vampire bat salivary plasminogen activator promotes robust lysis of plasma clots in a plasma milieu without causing fluid phase plasminogen activation. Thromb Haemost 68:165-169, 1992.
110. Mellott MJ, Ramjit DR, Stabilito II, et al: Vampire bat salivary plasminogen activator evokes minimal bleeding relative to tissue-type plasminogen activator as assessed by a rabbit cuticle bleeding time model. Thromb Haemost 73:478-483, 1995.
111. Montoney M, Gardell SJ, Marder VJ: Comparison of the bleeding potential of vampire bat salivary plasminogen activator versus tissue plasminogen activator in an experimental rabbit model. Circulation 91:1540-1544, 1995.
112. Schleuning WD, Downer P: *Desmodus rotundus* (vampire bat) plasminogen activator DSPA α_1: A superior thrombolytic created by evolution. In Sasahara AA, Loscalzo J (eds): New Therapeutic Agents in Thrombosis and Thrombolysis, 2nd ed. New York, Marcel Dekker, 2003, pp 605-625.
113. Randolph A, Chamberlain SH, Chu HL, et al: Amino acid sequence of fibrolase, a direct-acting fibrinolytic enzyme from *Agkistrodon contortrix contortrix* venom. Protein Sci 1:590-600, 1992.
114. Ahmed NK, Tennant KD, Markland FS, et al: Biochemical characteristics of fibrolase, a fibrinolytic protease from snake venom. Haemostasis 20:147-154, 1990.
115. Retzios AD, Markland FS Jr: A direct-acting fibrinolytic enzyme from the venom of *Agkistrodon contortrix contortrix*: Effects on various components of the human blood coagulation and fibrinolysis systems. Thromb Res 52:541-552, 1988.
116. Toombs CF: Alfimeprase. In Sasahara AA, Loscalzo J (eds): New Therapeutic Agents in Thrombosis and Thrombolysis, 2nd ed. New York, Marcel Dekker, 2003, pp 627-650.
117. Toombs CF, Lott FD, Guo P, et al: Rapid thrombolysis and reduced hemorrhagic complications with fibrolase and a novel acting thrombolytic (NAT): Comparison to plasminogen activators in piglets and rats [abstract 235]. Blood 96:56A, 2000.
118. Markland FS, Friedrichs GS, Pewitt SR, et al: Thrombolytic effects of recombinant fibrolase or APSAC in a canine model of coronary artery thrombosis. Circulation 90:2448-2456, 1994.
119. Vaughan DE, Declerck PJ, Van Hotte E, et al: Reactivated recombinant plasminogen activator inhibitor-1 (rPAI-1) effectively prevents thrombolysis in vivo. Thromb Haemost 68:60-63, 1992.

120. Hamsten A, Faire U, Walldius G, et al: Plasminogen activator inhibitor in plasma: Risk factor for recurrent myocardial infarction. Lancet 2:3-9, 1987.
121. Ambrus JL, Ambrus CM, Back N, et al: Clinical and experimental studies on fibrinolytic enzymes. Ann N Y Acad Sci 68:97-102, 1957.
122. Novokhatny V, Taylor K, Zimmerman TP: Thrombolytic potency of acid-stabilized plasmin: Superiority over tissue-type plasminogen activator in an in-vitro model of catheter-assisted thrombolysis. J Thromb Haemost 1:1034-1041, 2003.
123. Marder VJ, Landskroner K, Novokhatny V, et al: Plasmin induces local thrombolysis without causing hemorrhage: A comparison with tissue plasminogen activator in the rabbit. Thromb Haemost 86:739-745, 2001.
124. Stewart D, Kong M, Novokhatny V, et al: Distinct dose-dependent effects of plasmin and tPA on coagulation and hemorrhage. Blood 101:3002-3007, 2003.
125. Siegel RJ, Fishbein MC, Forrester J, et al: Ultrasonic plaque ablation: A new method for recanalization of partially or totally occluded arteries. Circulation 78:1443-1448, 1988.
126. Ernst A, Schenk EA, Gracewski SM, et al: Ability of high-intensity ultrasound to ablate human atherosclerotic plaques and minimize debris size. Am J Cardiol 68:242-246, 1991.
127. Diamond SL, Anand S: Inner clot diffusion and permeation during fibrinolysis. Biophys J 65:2622-2643, 1993.
128. Francis CW, Blinc A, Lee S, et al: Ultrasound accelerates transport of recombinant tissue plasminogen activator into clots. Ultrasound Med Biol 21:419-424, 1995.
129. Sakharov DV, Barrett-Bergshoeff M, Hekkenberg RT, et al: Fibrin specificity of a plasminogen activator affects the efficiency of fibrinolysis and responsiveness to ultrasound: Comparison of nine plasminogen activators in vitro. Thromb Haemost 81:605-612, 1999.
130. Braaten JV, Goss RA, Francis CW: Ultrasound reversibly disaggregates fibrin fibers. Thromb Haemost 78:1063-1068, 1997.
131. Siddiqi F, Odrljin TM, Fay PJ, et al: Binding of tissue-plasminogen activator to fibrin: Effects of ultrasound. Blood 91:2019-2025, 1998.
132. Chater BV, Williams AR: Platelet aggregation induced in vitro by therapeutic ultrasound. Thromb Haemost 38:640-651, 1977.
133. Riggs PN, Francis CW, Bartos SR, et al: Ultrasound enhancement of rabbit femoral artery thrombosis. Cardiovasc Surg 5:201-207, 1997.
134. Siegel RJ, Gaines P, Crew JR, et al: Clinical trial of percutaneous peripheral ultrasound angioplasty. J Am Coll Cardiol 22:480-488, 1993.
135. Rosenschein U, Rozenszajn LA, Kraus L, et al: Ultrasonic angioplasty in totally occluded peripheral arteries: Initial clinical, histological, and angiographic results. Circulation 83:1976-1986, 1991.
136. Goyen M, Kroger K, Buss C, et al: Intravascular ultrasound angioplasty in peripheral arterial occlusion: Preliminary experience. Acta Radiol 41:122-124, 2000.
137. Siegel RJ, Gunn J, Ahsan A, et al: Use of therapeutic ultrasound in percutaneous coronary angioplasty: Experimental in vitro studies and initial clinical experience. Circulation 89:1587-1592, 1994.
138. Eccleston DS, Cumpston GN, Hodge AJ, et al: Ultrasonic coronary angioplasty during coronary artery bypass grafting. Am J Cardiol 78:1172-1175, 1996.
139. Rosenschein U, Roth A, Rassin T, et al: Analysis of coronary ultrasound thrombolysis endpoints in acute myocardial infarction (ACUTE Trial): Results of the feasibility phase. Circulation 95:1411-1416, 1997.
140. Hamm CW, Steffen W, Terres W, et al: Intravascular therapeutic ultrasound thrombolysis in acute myocardial infarctions. Am J Cardiol 80:200-204, 1997.
141. Rosenschein U, Gaul G, Erbel R, et al: Percutaneous transluminal therapy of occluded saphenous vein grafts: Can the challenge be met with ultrasound thrombolysis? Circulation 99:26-29, 1999.

Chapter 33

Perioperative Considerations: Coagulopathy and Hemorrhage

MATTHEW EAGLETON, MD
KENNETH OURIEL, MD

Bleeding in the surgical patient is common. The occurrence is variable, but occasionally bleeding can be anticipated and planned for, depending on the specific operation being performed and the patient's comorbidities. Sometimes the onset of perioperative hemorrhage is unexpected. The surgeon needs to understand the causes of perioperative hemorrhage, the methods of diagnosing the underlying etiology, and the currently available treatments to meet the challenges of unexpected perioperative hemorrhage. A thorough understanding of normal hemostasis is required to understand fully the pathophysiology of the various coagulopathies and their therapies. This topic is discussed in depth in Chapter 30 and is not reviewed here. This chapter reviews the pathophysiology, diagnosis, and treatment of perioperative hemorrhage.

■ TESTS OF COAGULATION

To understand, diagnose, and treat hemorrhagic problems, knowledge of common clinically available tests of coagulation is essential (Table 33-1).

Prothrombin Time

The prothrombin time (PT) is a rough assessment of the extrinsic pathway of coagulation and is measured by subjecting citrated plasma to clotting in response to tissue factor (TF), phospholipid, and calcium. The PT is highly sensitive to the function of the four vitamin K–dependent factors—II, VII, IX, and X—and factor V.[1-3] Vitamin K–dependent factors are inhibited by warfarin, and the resultant therapeutic anticoagulation is monitored most

Table 33-1 Tests of Coagulation*

TEST	MEASURES	COMMON CAUSES OF ABNORMALITIES	CLINICAL USEFULNESS
Prothrombin time (PT)	II, V, VII, IX, and X (proteins C and S)	Warfarin use, liver dysfunction, malnutrition, consumptive coagulopathy	Monitor warfarin effect, ID coagulopathy
Activated partial thromboplastin time (aPTT)	Most factors	Heparin use, consumptive coagulopathy, lupus anticoagulant	Monitor heparin, argatroban effect, ID argatroban effect, ID coagulopathy
Activated clotting time (ACT) monitoring	Global clotting function	Heparin use	Intraoperative
Thrombin time (TT)	Fibrinogen function	Fibrinolysis or dysfibrinogenemia, heparin, consumptive coagulopathy	Monitor systemic fibrinolysis
Bleeding time (BT)	Platelet number and function	Antiplatelet medication, uremia, thrombocytopenia	Assess platelet dysfunction
Euglobulin clot lysis time (ECLT)	Fibrinolysis	Primary fibrinolysis	ID primary fibrinolysis
Fibrinogen, FDP	Fibrinolysis	Consumptive coagulopathy	ID coagulopathy
Platelet Aggregation	Platelet aggregation	Rare platelet disorders	Specific disorders
Thromboelastography (TEG)	Clotting kinetics	Multiple	Liver transplantation

*This list is not meant to be all-inclusive.
FDP, fibrin(ogen) degradation products; ID, identify.

easily by the PT and its more accurate derived value, the International Normalized Ratio (INR), used to lessen interlaboratory variability.

Elevations in the PT are usually due to iatrogenic warfarin use, vitamin K deficiency (most commonly malnutrition or biliary obstruction), disseminated intravascular coagulation (DIC), and liver dysfunction and can best be corrected by administration of fresh frozen plasma (FFP) or vitamin K. PT also can be elevated in the setting of high doses of heparin or argatroban because of factor II inhibition.[4]

Activated Partial Thromboplastin Time

The activated partial thromboplastin time (aPTT) roughly measures function of the intrinsic pathway and is sensitive, in varying degrees, to most factors other than factor VII.[3] Mild deficiencies of a single factor may not prolong the aPTT, but the effect of multiple factor deficiencies seems to be exponential. aPTT is measured by subjecting citrated plasma to clotting after exposure to a partial thromboplastin phospholipid alone or with a contact factor activator (aPTT).[2,3] The aPTT is consistently elevated during heparin and argatroban administration secondary to factor II inhibition, but because low-molecular-weight (LMW) heparin has relatively little antithrombin III (AT III) and anti–factor II activity, it affects the aPTT in a less predictable way, and the aPTT may not be elevated at all.[5,6]

The aPTT often is elevated as part of a global coagulopathy and often responds to protamine administration even if heparin has not been given or has been adequately reversed. If the aPTT is abnormal, either a factor deficiency or a circulating anticoagulant (e.g., heparin or lupus anticoagulant) is present. If the aPTT normalizes with the addition of normal plasma, the factor deficiency exists; if not, a circulating anticoagulant should be suspected.

The PT and aPTT, as relatively global tests of overlapping factor function (Fig. 33-1), often co-vary in the setting of coagulopathy, and high doses of any anticoagulant (warfarin, heparin, or other) usually increase both values. If the PT is elevated but the aPTT is normal, a factor VII deficiency must exist, usually secondary to vitamin K deficiency (biliary obstruction or malnutrition) or inhibition (warfarin use). In contrast, if the aPTT is elevated, but the PT is normal, this indicates either hemophilia or the presence of a low-to-moderate dose of heparin or the presence of an inhibitor.[3]

Activated Clotting Time

Closely related to the aPTT is the activated clotting time (ACT). The ACT is a gross measure of the time needed for whole blood to clot when exposed to a coagulant-accelerating matrix, often diatomaceous earth. The ACT is helpful because it takes only a few minutes, and it is most useful in the operating room to assess adequacy of elective heparinization.

Thrombin Time

The thrombin time (TT) measures the thrombin-induced conversion of fibrinogen to fibrin and, as such, is a sensitive method to assess function of the end of the coagulation pathway (see Fig. 33-1). The TT can be normal even with severe "upstream" coagulopathy (e.g., hemophilia or liver disease), but it is sensitive to low levels or abnormal forms of fibrinogen and to circulating inhibitors, such as heparin or fibrin(ogen) degradation products (FDPs) associated with DIC.[3] The TT is abnormal in the setting of inherited dysfibrinogenemias, in DIC (caused by hypofibrinogenemia and FDP), and in the presence of heparin, and it has been recommended by some authors to be the most clinically useful test to monitor therapeutic fibrinolysis (assuming heparin is not being infused).[7]

In our experience, other, more commonly obtained tests (fibrinogen and FDP levels) are as useful in this setting, and the TT is rarely used. Standard fibrinogen assays require the absence of anticoagulant and are notoriously inaccurate during therapeutic fibrinolysis as a result of circulating FDPs or concurrent heparin administration. Also, aprotinin is necessary within the collection tube so that the agent does not degrade fibrinogen within the tube.

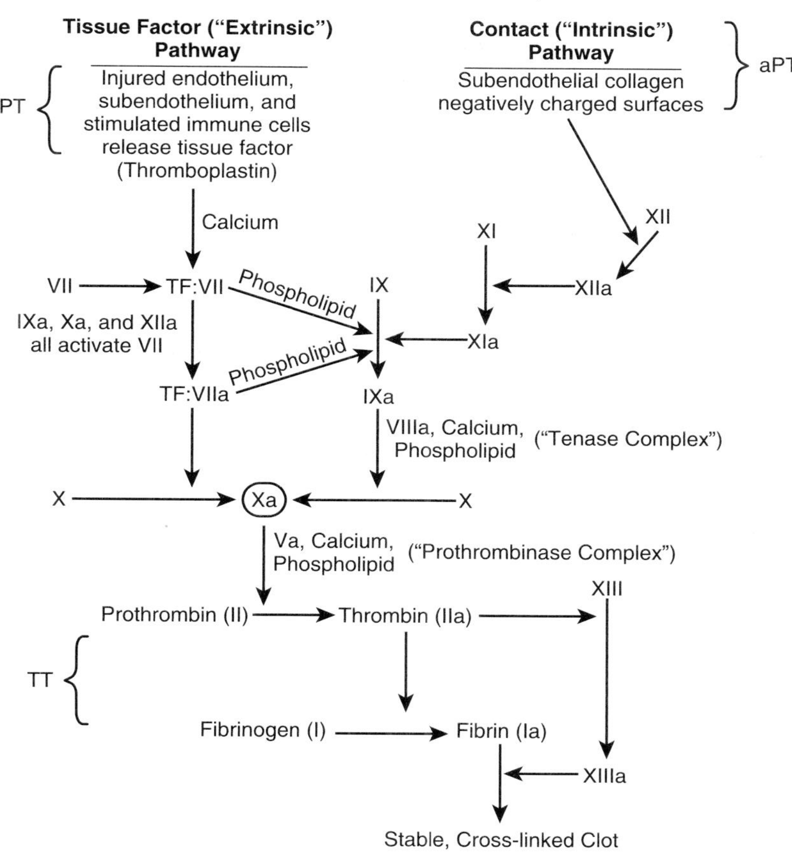

FIGURE 33-1 Schematic representation of the coagulation cascade. The prothrombin time (PT) and activated partial thromboplastin time (aPTT) are relatively global tests of overlapping function, whereas an isolated elevation of the PT is more indicative of a deficiency isolated to the "extrinsic" or tissue factor pathway. If only the aPTT is elevated, this is more indicative of a defect affecting only the "intrinsic" pathway. Defects in the common final pathway are indicated by elevations of the thrombin time (TT).

Bleeding Time

The bleeding time (BT) is the time needed for a superficial wound to clot and assesses primary hemostasis (platelet plug formation). It is sensitive to platelet number, platelet function, and, although not clinically relevant, vasoconstriction. Because the platelet number can be measured easily, the BT is most valuable as a test of platelet function. The BT can be elevated whenever platelet function is abnormal (e.g., during aspirin use, uremia, or von Willebrand disease [vWD]) or when thrombocytopenia exists, and it can be lengthened by decreased fibrinogen and factor V levels. Heparin also can increase the BT, probably because of platelet inhibition and interactions with von Willebrand factor (vWF).[8]

The BT is measured by making a controlled wound with a template in the forearm (Ivy) or earlobe (Duke); the time needed to clot is measured with a timer.[9] Values greater than 5 minutes are typically abnormal. BT is not useful as a preoperative screening test and should be reserved for specific indications.[10]

Euglobulin Clot Lysis Time

The euglobulin clot lysis time (ECLT) assesses the time needed for a clot to lyse in a test tube (<2 hours is abnormal). Adequate clot formation is required in the first place. The ECLT usually is not helpful in the setting of DIC, in which clot formation and lysis are abnormal. It can be quite helpful, however, when a primary fibrinolytic state is suspected.[11-13]

Thromboelastography

Thromboelastography is a qualitative means of measuring overall coagulation and fibrinolytic function. Blood is placed in an oscillating chamber, and the changing resistive forces created by the clotting and lysing blood are expressed as a function of time. With values derived from the plot, it is possible to measure or estimate whole-blood clotting time, platelet and factor function, fibrinolysis, and hypercoagulability.[14,15] Although interesting in concept, thromboelastography has not gained widespread acceptance, primarily because it is cumbersome and technician dependent, and the information it yields can be obtained more simply by judicious use of the aforementioned tests. It is probably most useful during liver transplantation, when multiple channels can be run simultaneously as the cause of coagulopathy changes with different phases of the operation.[16]

Other Tests

Several other tests are commonly used. Fibrinogen levels are used to assess systemic proteolysis during fibrinolysis, whether therapeutic (e.g., intra-arterial urokinase) or

Table 33-2 Replacement Resources*

RESOURCE	CONTAINS OR REPLENISHES	COMMON USES	DOSE AND EFFECTS†
Packed red blood cells	Red blood cells	Replace oxygen-carrying capacity	1 U (350 mL) increases hematocrit 3%
Platelets	Platelets; substantial clotting factors	Replace deficient or abnormal platelets; treat undefined clotting factor deficiency	1 U (50 mL) increases platelets 10/μL)
Fresh frozen plasma	Most clotting factors except V and VIII	Treat elevated PT	250 mL/U
Cryoprecipitate	Rich in VIII, vWF, fibrinogen	Treat hypofibrinogenemia	20 mL contains 200 mg fibrinogen, 70 U VIII
DDAVP	Stimulates vWF release	Treat uremic platelet dysfunction	0.3-0.4 μg/kg
Vitamin K	Stimulates II, VII, IX, and X	Treat elevated PT, hepatic dysfunction, warfarin overdosage	10-20 mg IM, SC, or IV
Protamine sulfate	Heparin antagonist	Reverse heparin, treat elevated aPTT	1 mg/100 U heparin
Aminocaproic acid (Amicar)	Plasminogen inhibitor	Treat primary fibrinolysis	0.1 g/kg load, 1 g/hr
Aprotinin	Plasmin inhibitor	Treat primary fibrinolysis	3.75 mg/kg
Specific factors	Treat specific deficiencies	Most are now available in recombinant form with zero risk of disease transmission	

*Table is not all-inclusive.
†Doses, effects, and volumes are approximate and can vary by institution, indication, or formulation.
aPTT, activated partial thromboplastin time; DDAVP, desmopressin acetate (1-deamino-8-D-arginine vasopressin); IM, intramuscular; IV, intravenous; PT, prothrombin time; SC, subcutaneous; vWF, von Willebrand's factor.

pathologic (DIC); ongoing lysis lowers the fibrinogen level. Equally useful is measurement of the degradation products of fibrin and fibrinogen, such as FDP and D dimers. Specific factors also can be measured and are invaluable in the diagnosis of specific factor deficiencies. Platelet aggregability is used for diagnosis and characterization of rare platelet disorders.

■ REPLACEMENT RESOURCES

To prevent or treat bleeding rationally, it is important to understand what options are available and what specific functions the various replacement resources have (Table 33-2). The reader is referred to several consensus statements and editorials on the use of blood products in the modern era for medical and surgical indications.[17-23]

Packed Red Blood Cells

Packed red blood cells (PRBCs) are used to restore oxygen-carrying capacity. Their use as a volume expander has all but disappeared because of blood-borne transmissible diseases. Apparently as a result of an article published in 1942, for years the "gold standard" was to transfuse until a hemoglobin level of 10 mg/dL (a hematocrit of roughly 30%) was reached.[24,25] Given the risk of disease transmission, along with the increasing realization that outcome is acceptable with a lower hematocrit (in part owing to the beneficial effects of lowered blood viscosity), current consensus is that lower levels are safe. The National Institutes of Health consensus conference recommendations are that otherwise healthy patients should have hemoglobin levels maintained at 7 mg/dL or more. Treatment must be individualized, and alternative strategies for blood conservation, such as preoperative autologous donation, erythropoietin use, acute normovolemic hemodilution, and intraoperative cell-saver devices, should be considered in appropriate circumstances.[17,18,23,26]

Fresh Frozen Plasma

Most coagulation factors, with the exception of factor VIII, are replaced adequately with FFP. FFP is most useful when an elevated PT is present, often after warfarin administration or when liver dysfunction or a global coagulopathy is present. Because of the risk of blood-borne diseases, FFP should not be used as a volume expander, but rather reserved for situations in which multiple factor deficiencies are present or ongoing factor destruction exists (e.g., consumptive coagulopathy) or for the acute reversal of warfarin.[27] There is widespread consensus that physicians currently overuse FFP.[18,22] FFP is immunogenic and should be given in an ABO, Rh-specific manner. FFP is the agent of choice for treatment of isolated factor deficiencies when a specific factor (e.g., factor V) is not available, but safe, recombinant factors VIII and IX have made FFP obsolete for treatment of the hemophilias.[22,28-30]

Platelets

Platelets should be transfused for thrombocytopenia and probably used as the first prophylactic option during massive hemorrhage.[18] They are especially useful in the latter situation because the resultant thrombocytopenia is usually the most important cause of resultant bleeding and because platelet concentrates contain a substantial amount of FFP and factor V. Although a platelet count of approximately 20/μL is usually adequate for maintenance of normal hemostasis, in the setting of active bleeding a target of 50/μL to 70/μL (even higher at times, to allow for ongoing loss or destruction) is usually recommended.[19]

Cryoprecipitate

Cryoprecipitate is rich in factor VIII, vWF, and fibrinogen.[31,32] It is used most commonly to increase fibrinogen levels during consumptive coagulopathy or when troublesome bleeding occurs during therapeutic thrombolysis. One bag (usually about 20 mL) contains about 200 to 250 mg of fibrinogen and 70 U of factor VIII.

Desmopressin

Desmopressin acetate (1-deamino-8-D-arginine vasopressin [DDAVP]) is a synthetic vasopressin analogue. Although it has little vasoconstrictor activity, it has powerful hematologic effects. DDAVP increases factor VIII and vWF levels and improves platelet adhesiveness to injured endothelium.[33,34] Levels of both factors increase quickly, and tachyphylaxis occurs, suggesting that DDAVP stimulates release of preformed molecules. DDAVP is especially useful in patients with uremic platelet dysfunction,[35] in patients after cardiopulmonary bypass,[36] and in patients with mild type I vWD (who have low levels of vWF with normal vWF receptors), shortening the BT and reducing bleeding in each condition.[37,38] Although prophylactic DDAVP use should be considered when major blood loss is anticipated, its effects have not been consistent.[39-41] DDAVP retains some antinatriuretic properties, and sodium and water balance should be monitored carefully in patients requiring large doses.[32]

Vitamin K

Vitamin K acts to carboxylate already synthesized factors stored in hepatocytes, which are released within about 6 hours after parenteral infusion. The PT usually normalizes within 18 to 24 hours.[38,42] FFP is best for rapid correction of warfarin effect; the action of vitamin K is slower but more durable, making it harder for the patient to become anticoagulated again.

Protamine Sulfate

Protamine, which is positively charged, reverses the activity of a negatively charged heparin molecule by binding to it and restoring AT III to its native, relatively inactive state. A ratio of approximately 1 mg of protamine to 100 U of heparin is usually used for reversal, but with increasing time after heparin administration, less protamine is needed because of heparin's relatively short half-life. We titrate protamine administration to the ACT or observed intraoperative bleeding; if none is present, protamine need not be given. This is an issue because of protamine's potential side effects (systemic hypotension, pulmonary hypertension, frank anaphylaxis, and death) and because of a report of worsened outcome after carotid endarterectomy when protamine had been given.[43-45]

Side effects related to protamine have been associated with fish allergy (presumably because protamine is derived from salmon semen), prior vasectomy (presumably because of cross-reactive autoantibodies), and previous insulin use (possibly because of sensitization to the protamine contained in neutral protamine Hagedorn [NPH] insulin).[43,46-49] "Designer" variants have been created to reduce the incidence of these problems, but they are not clinically available.[50] Protamine itself can have anticoagulant properties because of TF inhibition.[51] Late bleeding can occur after initially adequate reversal, but it is unclear whether this is due to a "heparin rebound" effect or to protamine's anticoagulant effects.[52,53]

Antifibrinolytic Agents

If primary fibrinolysis is suspected, direct antifibrinolytic agents, such as aminocaproic acid (Amicar), tranexamic acid (Cyklokapron), and aprotinin (Trasylol), all of which block plasminogen directly or block the action of plasmin on fibrin and fibrinogen, can be considered.[53-56] Their use is contraindicated, however, in consumptive coagulopathy. In this setting, the fibrinolysis is secondary to widespread microvascular thrombosis, and clot lysis, crucial for removing capillary thrombus, should not be inhibited.

Specific Factors

Specific factors, especially factors VIII and IX, are available for specific deficiencies. These are most often used electively when surgery must be performed on a patient with a known deficiency and usually are given in collaboration with a hematologist. A variety of factor concentrates are currently available to treat hemophilia A and B. These can be divided into factor concentrates that are plasma derived and factor concentrates that are non–plasma derived.[57] Pooled plasma factors previously carried a high risk of disease transmission, but now are treated to inactivate human immunodeficiency virus and hepatitis B virus effectively.[32,58] They are prepared by fractionation of large pools of thousands of units of donor plasma. Factor concentrates produced by recombinant DNA technology are currently available and have the highest level of purity and safety, but they are more costly than plasma-derived products. Recombinant activated factor VII was developed for the treatment of bleeding in hemophilia patients.[59,60] It has been shown to be effective in treating nonhemophiliac patients who have developed antibodies against factor VIII; patients with platelet function deficiencies; and patients bleeding secondary to trauma, surgery, and gastrointestinal conditions. Recombinant factor VIIa may be an effective and safe method to induce hemostasis in patients with factor deficiencies and platelet dysfunction.

■ PREOPERATIVE SCREENING

The history and physical examination are excellent preoperative screening tools for potential perioperative hemorrhage. A series of carefully directed questions to elicit a personal or family history of bleeding can alert the surgeon in advance of possible bleeding complications and offers an opportunity to correct underlying defects or postpone the proposed procedure. The patient should be questioned specifically regarding prolonged bleeding from skin or mucosal surfaces after injury; excessive gynecologic or obstetric bleeding; bleeding into or swelling of joints; easy bruising; prolonged bleeding during prior surgical or dental procedures; blood transfusion reactions; family history of bleeding diathesis; and ingestion of any medication that might affect hemostasis, such as aspirin, nonsteroidal anti-inflammatory drugs, or warfarin. Similarly the physical examination should be directed toward the identification of

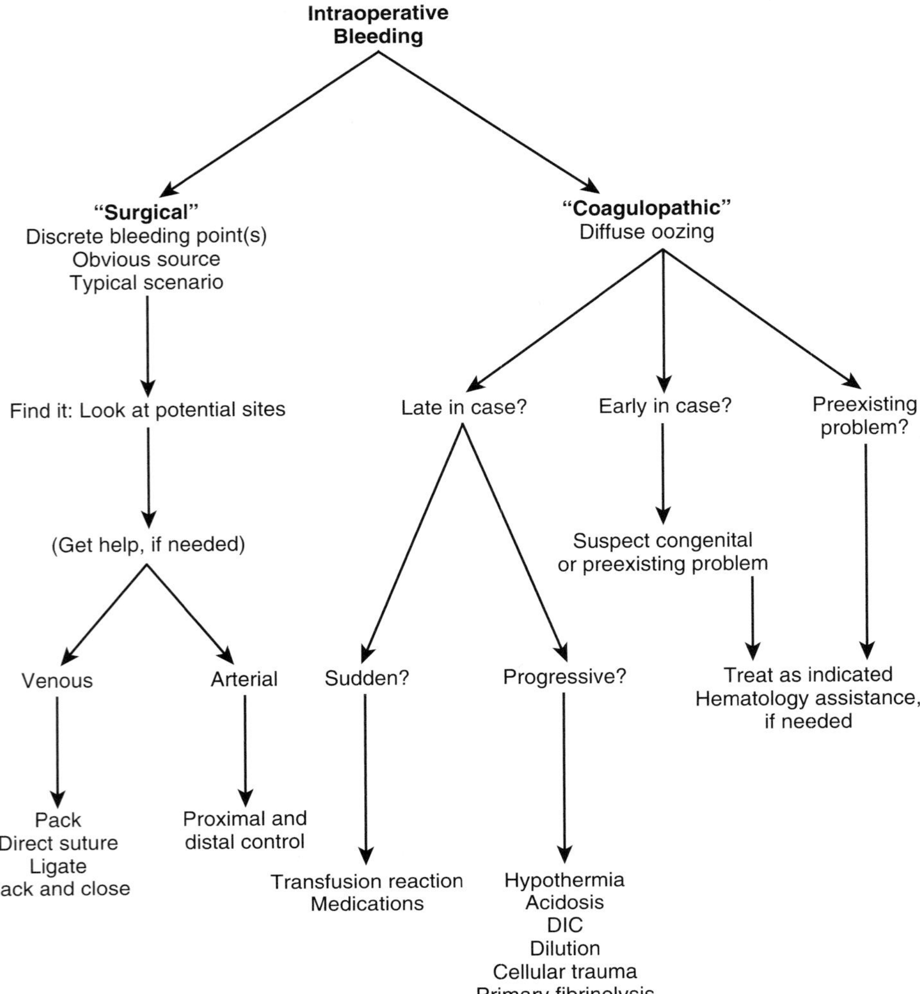

FIGURE 33-2 Algorithm for management of intraoperative bleeding. A nonsurgical coagulopathy that occurs late in a case, especially if slowly progressive, is likely due to a problem that is relatively resistant to treatment, such as disseminated intravascular coagulation (DIC), acidosis, hypothermia, dilution, or injury to proteins and cells. In this situation, terminating the operation to allow resuscitation in an intensive care unit assumes higher priority as time goes on.

any sign of a bleeding tendency, such as the presence of petechiae or bruises, hepatosplenomegaly, joint effusions, or occult blood on rectal examination.

Repeated studies and consensus statements uniformly agree that nondirected, "shotgun" laboratory screening is of no benefit (in terms of clinical efficacy or cost-effectiveness) in otherwise healthy patients without historical factors to suggest bleeding problems.[10,61-63] From the results of the history and physical examination, however, one can apply the practical guidelines put forth by Rapaport[64] regarding the likelihood of increased bleeding risk.

In *level 1,* the history and physical findings are negative, and the proposed procedure is minor; no further testing is required. In *level 2,* the patient has a negative history and physical examination result, but the proposed procedure is major. aPTT and platelet count are indicated to screen for occult disorders. *Level 3* applies to patients who have a history suspicious for major bleeding diathesis and whose proposed procedure would result in significant bleeding (e.g., open abdominal aortic aneurysm repair), altered hemostatic mechanisms (e.g., cardiopulmonary bypass), or large areas of raw surface or critical requirements for hemostasis (e.g., craniotomy). Tests recommended for patients at level 3 include aPTT, platelet count, PT, and BT. *Level 4* includes patients whose history strongly suggests a major hemostatic defect. Testing in these patients should include BT, specific factor assays for factors VIII and IX (patients with mild forms of hemophilia A and B may have a normal aPTT), and a TT to rule out dysfibrinogenemia. Consultation with a hematologist is strongly recommended as well.

When a specific defect has been identified, treatment can be tailored to the patient, including consideration of the medical necessity of the procedure. The surgeon and patient may decide that the risks outweigh the benefits of a femoropopliteal bypass for claudication in a level 4 situation.

■ INTRAOPERATIVE BLEEDING

Despite the most aggressive attempts to identify and correct potential bleeding problems preoperatively, it is inevitable that eventually serious intraoperative bleeding occasionally arises. When faced with unexpected intraoperative bleeding, the basic strategy is first to identify the cause and then to treat it appropriately. The simplest strategy is to determine whether the bleeding is due to a global coagulopathy or surgical bleeding—treatments differ considerably (Fig. 33-2).

Coagulopathies represent the most complex causes of hemorrhage in the perioperative period. These entities are discussed in more detail subsequently. The most common cause of intraoperative hemorrhage is mechanical bleeding from surgically correctable sites, which are usually easily handled, as described in more detail later. Surgically correctable bleeding is usually localized, may be torrential, and is often (if arterial) manifested by a visible jet. In contrast, bleeding due to coagulopathy is often diffuse and manifests as a slow ooze that cannot be controlled by local methods.

Coagulopathies and Treatments

There are a multitude of etiologies for bleeding diatheses. They can be caused by defects in specific cell lines; factors within the coagulation cascade; and physiologic alterations, such as changes in body temperature, calcium levels, and pH. Causes of bleeding disorders can be divided into two main categories: inherited defects in normal hemostasis and acquired defects.

Inherited Disorders of Coagulation

Platelet Disorders Inherited defects in platelets are rare diseases that have varying degrees of phenotypic severity. Platelet defects can be subclassified into disorders of adhesion, aggregation, secretion, and procoagulant activity depending on the platelet function affected.[65] Table 33-3 summarizes the major inherited diseases affecting platelets, the mode of inheritance, the platelet defect present, and the general treatment.

Bernard-Soulier syndrome (BSS) is inherited as an autosomal recessive trait that is associated with a prolonged BT, thrombocytopenia, diminished platelet longevity, and the presence of giant platelets. Platelet counts range from 20×10^3 to normal, and on peripheral smears they can reach 20 μ in diameter. BSS is characterized by a defect in the membrane glycoprotein (GP) Ib-IX-V complex, which is a primary adhesion receptor of platelets.[66,67] Defects of the *GPIbα* gene are the most frequent causes of BSS, although defects in the other components also exist because the receptor is composed of four separate gene products (Ibα, Ibβ, IX, and V). Clinical manifestations of BSS commonly include frequent episodes of epistaxis, gingival and cutaneous bleeding, and hemorrhage associated with trauma. Heterozygotes may exhibit no or mild bleeding diathesis. Initial assessment involves measurement of blood cell counts and evaluation of the blood smear for evidence of enlarged platelets and thrombocytopenia, followed by aggregometry and confirmation with biochemical analysis. Precise definition of the defect can be made by molecular genotyping. The general management of these patients involves education and avoidance of minor trauma. If hemorrhage occurs, platelet transfusion usually is required.

Platelets from patients with Glanzmann's thrombasthenia lack the integrin αIIbβ (IIb/IIIa), which results in the virtual absence of platelet aggregation.[65] Glanzmann's thrombasthenia is characterized by a prolonged BT, normal platelet count, and absent macroscopic platelet aggregation. αIIbβ3 on activated platelets binds soluble proteins, such as fibrinogen and vWF. In patients with this disease, platelets are unable to aggregate because, although they are able to attach to exposed endothelium, platelet-to-platelet interactions and platelet spreading do not occur. Glanzmann's thrombasthenia is inherited in an autosomal recessive fashion, and a large series of mutations responsible for this disease, most involving splice defects and point mutations, have been described.[68] Episodes of bleeding present in a fashion similar to that of BSS; Glanzmann's thrombasthenia also is treated with platelet transfusion.

Defects in platelet secretion can occur secondary to alterations in one or more of the four types of secretory granules: alpha granules, dense granules, lysosomes, and microperoxisomes. Alpha granules contain a variety of proteins that either are synthesized in the megakaryocyte or are endocytosed from plasma. A variety of defects can exist that are due to inherited defects of the platelet-secreted protein, and these are discussed later. Two disorders unique to alpha granules are gray platelet syndrome and Quebec platelet disorder. Gray platelet syndrome is a mild bleeding disorder inherited in an autosomal recessive fashion. It is named for the gray appearance of the platelets on a Wright-stained blood smear and the absence of alpha granule proteins. The alpha granules are present, but the proteins are absent, suggesting an inability of the platelet to target proteins to these structures.[69] Patients have lifelong problems with mucosal bleeding, but hemorrhage can be more severe when associated with trauma. In addition to abnormal blood smears, patients with gray platelet syndrome have moderate thrombocytopenia and prolonged

Table 33-3 Inherited Platelet Disorders

DISORDER	INHERITANCE	DEFECT	CAUSE	TREATMENT
Bernard-Soulier syndrome	AR	Platelet adhesion	GP Ib-IX-V deficiency	Platelet transfusion
Glanzmann's thrombasthenia	AR	Platelet aggregation	αIIbβ3 integrin	Platelet transfusion
Gray platelet syndrome	AR	Platelet secretion (alpha granule)	α-granule proteins are absent	Platelet transfusion, DDAVP
Quebec platelet disorder	AD	Platelet secretion (alpha granule)	Alpha granule proteins are degraded	Platelet transfusion, DDAVP
Wiskott-Aldrich syndrome	XR	Platelet secretion (dense granule)	Defect in dense granule secretion due to absence of WASP	Platelet transfusion, DDAVP, cryoprecipitate
Hermansky-Pudlack syndrome	AR	Platelet secretion (dense granule)	Ceroid-lipofuscin–like lysosomal storage disease	Platelet transfusion, DDAVP, cryoprecipitate
Chédiak-Higashi syndrome	AR	Platelet secretion (dense granule)	Presence of giant inclusion bodies	Platelet transfusion, DDAVP, cryoprecipitate

AD, autosomal dominant; AR, autosomal recessive; DDAVP, desmopressin acetate (1-deamino-8-D-arginine vasopressin); GP, glycoprotein; XR, X-linked recessive.

BT. Quebec platelet disorder is an autosomal dominant bleeding disorder characterized by mild thrombocytopenia and prolonged BT. In contrast to gray platelet syndrome, the alpha granules in Quebec platelet disorder appear morphologically normal.[70] Although the alpha granule structure is preserved, there appears to be degradation of the alpha granule proteins owing to the presence of increased concentrations of urokinase-type plasminogen activator.[70] Treatment of bleeding in both of these disorders requires the transfusion of platelets, although DDAVP has been used as prophylaxis in patients before invasive procedures.[71]

Dense granules are the storage sites for serotonin, calcium, pyrophosphate, and various nucleotides. Dense granule storage pool disease represents a heterogeneous group of disorders with dense granule abnormalities as the common feature.[72] Wiskott-Aldrich syndrome is an X-linked recessive disease characterized by thrombocytopenia, immunodeficiency, eczema, and recurrent infections.[73] There is a genetic defect in the Wiskott-Aldrich syndrome protein, which is an important regulator of the actin cytoskeleton mediating communication between guanosine triphosphatases and a variety of proteins.[74] Hermansky-Pudlak and Chédiak-Higashi syndromes are autosomal recessive diseases in which a dense granule deficiency leads to a bleeding diathesis and is accompanied by a lack of skin and hair pigmentation, albinism, and defective lysosomal function.[75] Most patients with a dense granule deficiency present with mild-to-moderate bleeding as has been characterized previously. Platelet counts and cell morphology are normal, but BT generally is prolonged.[76] Bleeding is generally controllable with platelet transfusions, DDAVP, and cryoprecipitate.[77,78]

von Willebrand Disease vWD is a complex disorder caused by the quantitative or qualitative defect of vWF. vWF promotes platelet adhesion to injured blood vessels, and it is a carrier for factor VIII in plasma. vWD is the most commonly inherited bleeding disorder, with an estimated incidence of 1% to 2% based on several epidemiologic studies.[79,80] The clinical manifestations of vWD are predominantly symptoms of easy bruising, prolonged epistaxis, bleeding after dental procedures, mucous membrane bleeding, and gastrointestinal bleeding. In women, menorrhagia may be the main finding.[81] With the heterogeneity of the disease, patients with only mild deficiency may present with a range of symptoms from none to symptoms more commonly associated with severe disease.

vWD is classified into three main types based generally on the deficiency of vWF. In type 1 disease, there are decreased amounts of vWF; in type 2 disease, there are qualitative defects in vWF independent of the amount of factor present; and in type 3 disease, vWF is essentially absent. Type 2 is subclassified further into four groups.[82,83] In type 2A, patients have decreased platelet-dependent functions due to a loss of high-molecular-weight multimers. Type 2B refers to variants with an increased affinity for platelet GP Ib. Type 2M is characterized by vWF platelet-dependent functional deficits without loss of high-molecular-weight multimers. Type 2N has defective factor VIII binding to VWF.

Diagnosing vWD is extremely challenging because, depending on which epitope is abnormal, only a subset of tests may be abnormal.[81] Testing can be divided into screening tests and confirmatory tests. The BT is an excellent screening test that reflects quantitative or qualitative defects (or both) of platelets and vWF, but it can be variable in mild forms of vWD. Because of this variability, the BT often is replaced by modern filter methods. Confirmatory tests include factor VIII activity, vWF antigen, ristocetin cofactor activity, collagen binding capacity, and epitope-specific vWF antigen enzyme-linked immunosorbent assays. The results of these tests vary based on the type of vWD present.

Patients rarely require treatment, unless they present with bleeding. DDAVP is effective in patients with type 1 vWD and normal platelets, but is less effective in patients with low platelet vWF content.[81] The response in patients with type 2 vWD is variable depending on the subset, and it is ineffective in patients with type 3 vWD.[84,85] Cryoprecipitate can be used in patients unresponsive to DDAVP or in whom it is contraindicated. VWF-containing concentrates also are available and include products such as Haemate-P, Factane, and Facteur Willebrand (LFB); not all of these are available in the United States.[86] Factor VIII/vWF concentrates are equally as effective.[81] Some patients, particularly patients with type 3 vWD, may require additional platelet transfusions.[87]

Hypofibrinogenemia/Afibrinogenemia Disorders of fibrinogen structure and function (hypofibrinogenemia and dysfibrinogenemia) can be hereditary or acquired and are variable in expression. Diagnosis is based on identification (with specialized reagents) of low fibrinogen levels and prolonged clotting times. Disorders involving fibrinogen also affect platelet function. Patients with congenital afibrinogenemia rarely manifest spontaneous bleeding.

Hemophilia A variety of disorders involve defects in the coagulation cascade factors (Table 33-4). The two most common are loss of factor VIII (hemophilia A) and factor IX (hemophilia B). Hemophilia A is an X-linked recessive disorder that occurs in 1 in 5000 men.[88] Hemophilia B also is an X-linked recessive disorder, but accounts for only 20% of cases of hemophilia. The two disorders are clinically indistinguishable. Hemophilia A is due to a deficiency in factor VIII, whereas hemophilia B is due to a deficiency in factor IX. Hemophilia A is caused by numerous mutations in the gene for factor VIII, but the most common defect affects 45% of the patients with the severe form of the disease.[89] Hemophilia B is due to a mutation in the gene for factor IX. There are more than 2100 known mutations for factor IX, most of which are point mutations.[89] Both disorders can be diagnosed based on family history and the presentation of abnormal bleeding. A factor IX deficiency measured with a factor IX assay confirms the diagnosis of hemophilia B, whereas altered levels of factor VIII by assay measurement suggest hemophilia A. Hemophilia A must be distinguished from severe forms of vWD, however, which also may produce low levels of factor VIII.

Hemophilia A and B are classified as mild, moderate, or severe based on factor levels. Levels less than 1% are classified as severe, levels between 1% and 5% are considered moderately severe, and levels between 6% and 25% are considered mild.[90] Classification predicts bleeding

Table 33-4 Inherited Defects of Coagulation Factors

DISEASE	FACTOR DEFICIENCY	INHERITANCE	DIAGNOSIS	TREATMENT
Hemophilia A	VIII	XR	Specific factor assay	Factor VIII
Hemophilia B	IX	XR	Specific factor assay	Factor IX
Hemophilia C	XI	AR	Specific factor assay	Factor XI
Fibrinogen disorders	I	Variable	Fibrinogen levels and analysis	Cryoprecipitate
Abnormal prothrombin	II	Variable	Specialized assays	Variable replacements
Parahemophilia	V	AR	Specific factor assay	FFP
Factor VII deficiency	VII	AR	Specific factor assay	Factor VII
Stuart-Prower factor deficiency	X	AR	Specific factor assay	FFP, prothrombin complex concentrates
Hageman factor deficiency	XII	AR	Specific factor assay	
Factor XIII deficiency	XIII	AR	Specific factor assay	Factor XIII, cryoprecipitate

AR, autosomal recessive; FFP, fresh frozen plasma; XR, X-linked recessive.

Table 33-5 Characteristics of the Various Clotting Factors Required for Safe Surgical Hemostasis

FACTOR	IN VIVO HALF-LIFE	LEVEL REQUIRED FOR OPERATIVE HEMOSTASIS	STABLE IN PLASMA IF	BEST OPTIONS FOR REPLACEMENT
I	3-4 days	100 mg/dL	4°C	FFP, cryoprecipitate
II	2-5 days	20-40%	4°C	FFP, concentrates
V	15-36 hr	<25%	Frozen	FFP, platelets
VII	4-7 hr	10-20%	4°C	Concentrates, FFP
VIII	9-18 hr	≥80%	Frozen	Concentrates, cryoprecipitate, FFP
IX	20-24 hr	≥50%	4°C	Concentrates, FFP
X	32-48 hr	10-20%	4°C	FFP, prothrombin complex concentrates
XI	40-80 hr	15-25%	4°C	Concentrates, FFP
XII	48-52 hr	None	4°C	Not necessary
XIII	12 days	<5%	4°C	Concentrates, cryoprecipitate, FFP
vWF	Few hours	25-50%	Frozen	Concentrates, cryoprecipitate, FFP

FFP, fresh frozen plasma; vWF, von Willebrand's factor.

Adapted from Edmunds LH: Hemostatic problems in surgical patients. In Colman RW, Hirsh J, Marder VJ, et al (eds): Hemostasis and Thrombosis: Basic Principles and Clinical Practice, 4th ed. Philadelphia, JB Lippincott, 2001, p 1031.

risk, guides the optimal management strategy, and predicts outcome. The hallmark of severe hemophilia A and B is repeated bleeds into joints and muscles. Persistent or recurrent joint bleeding results in synovial hypertrophy and predisposes the patient to recurrent episodes of hemorrhage.[91] Muscle bleeds may threaten the patient's limb as a result of nerve and blood vessel compression.

Therapy for hemophilia A and B has evolved considerably over the past few years. Currently, concentrated forms of specific factors, generally obtained through recombinant technology, are used almost exclusively to treat hemophilia (Table 33-5). In the absence of bleeding, the factor VIII concentration required to maintain hemostatic integrity and to prevent spontaneous hemorrhage is only about 3%. In the presence of bleeding, a factor VIII level of approximately 30% is necessary to achieve cessation of minor hemorrhage, and a level of 50% is necessary to control major bleeding.

For patients undergoing elective surgical procedures, it is desirable to achieve a factor VIII level of 80% to 100% preoperatively and to maintain the level to at least 30% for 2 weeks after the procedure. The dose required is determined by the patient's baseline factor VIII level; each unit of factor VIII infused increases the plasma level by 2%. Half the initial dose should be given every 8 to 12 hours (the half-life of factor VIII).[58,92-94] Continuous infusion of factor VIII concentrates has been proved to provide easier monitoring and more constant coagulation factor levels in the perioperative period.[95,96] In patients with hemophilia B, the desired plasma levels of factor IX are 20% to 30% for minor bleeding and 50% to 100% for major hemorrhage and surgery, and a level of 20% to 40% should be maintained for 2 weeks postoperatively. The half-life of factor IX is 24 hours, and it can be given half as frequently as factor VIII.[94,97] Because of the risk of specific antifactor inhibitors, factor activity should be measured before surgery is begun to verify adequate hemostasis. Recombinant activated factor VII induces hemostasis in major surgery and in acute bleeding episodes in hemophiliacs who have developed antibodies to the replacement factors. It is administered as 90 to 110 μg/kg boluses dosed every second hour.[60] For major surgery, administration is continued for 24 hours, at which point longer intervals between boluses can be used. Recombinant activated factor VII also can be given as a constant infusion of 50 μg/kg/hr with similar outcomes.[98]

Factor XI deficiency, also known as hemophilia C, is a less common disorder that is autosomally inherited.[99] It is particularly common among Ashkenazi Jews.[100] Affected individuals have an unpredictable bleeding tendency, which makes clinical management more difficult than in patients with hemophilia A and B. The reason for this variability is unknown. Patients who are homozygotes for the defect have more severe deficiencies than patients who are heterozygotes.[99,101,102] Patients with severe deficiencies are more likely to bleed after surgery, particularly with procedures prone to fibrinolysis, such as oropharyngeal and urogenital surgery. Spontaneous bleeding is rare. FFP had been the treatment of choice in patients with bleeding episodes until the advent of factor XI concentrates. These concentrates must be used with caution in elderly patients and in patients with preexisting cardiovascular disease and coagulopathy activation.[99]

In all of the hemophilias, bleeding can be treated as it occurs, or treatment can be given regularly to prevent bleeds from occurring. Prophylaxis, begun in childhood, has been effective at decreasing the incidence of joint bleeds and their long-term consequences.[103-105] Hemophilia is a prime disease targeted for gene therapy. There have been several attempts at trials of this form of therapy with some success in decreasing the amount of factor replacement required.[106-108] Gene therapy likely represents the future for treatment of patients with hemophilia.

Other Inherited Hemostatic Defects Other inherited disorders of prothrombin conversion include abnormalities and deficiencies of factors II (prothrombin), V, VII, and X, all of which are synthesized in the liver and (with the exception of factor V) require vitamin K for synthesis of active factors. The clinical features of these rare disorders are similar to those of the hemophilias, including variable penetrance and clinical severity. Disorders involving prothrombin itself (hypoprothrombinemia and the dysprothrombinemias) are characterized by variable elevations of the PT and aPTT, with normal TT. Definitive diagnosis involves functional and immunologic prothrombin assays.

Deficiencies of factor V, the essential procoagulant cofactor for factor Xa, are transmitted in an autosomal recessive pattern and are definitively diagnosed by factor V assay. Patients with factor VII deficiency have an unusually variable clinical presentation and characteristically exhibit prolonged PT with normal aPTT and TT; definitive diagnosis depends on performance of a specific assay for factor VII. Factor X deficiency results in prolongation of the PT and aPTT and is diagnosed by specific factor assay. Hageman factor (factor XII) deficiency, although it is associated with a prolonged aPTT, may predispose to thrombus formation and is not associated with a bleeding diathesis.[109] Factor XIII deficiency is rare and inherited as an autosomal recessive trait and can be divided into two entities based on the underlying genetic defect.[110] The most characteristic clinical feature is perinatal umbilical stump bleeding, but the sequelae associated with the other hemophilias are common in later life.

Treatment of inherited and acquired disorders of prothrombin conversion depends on the severity of the disorder. FFP, 10 to 20 mL/kg, is sufficient to restore hemostasis in most cases, unless bleeding is severe (see Table 33-5). Isolated factor replacement can be used in these extreme cases. The frequency and volume of replacement with FFP vary based on the factor deficiency.[111]

Acquired Disorders of Hemostasis

Table 33-6 lists some common nonhereditary causes of abnormal bleeding, tests designed to make the diagnoses, and general treatment strategies.

Platelet Disorders Acquired platelet disorders comprise a wide variety of abnormalities, including functional, anatomic, and quantitative defects. Thrombocytopenia is the most common manifestation. These disorders are usually part of a larger disease process, such as uremia, hypersplenism, hematologic malignancies (and their treatment), immune thrombocytopenic purpura, and thrombotic thrombocytopenic purpura.

Table 33-6 Common Acquired Causes of Bleeding and Treatment Strategies*

SITUATION	CAUSE	DIAGNOSIS	TREATMENT
Heparin use	Antifactor II (via AT III)	Elevated aPTT (and PT)	Protamine
Argatroban/hirudin use	Direct anti-II	Elevated aPTT (and PT)	FFP
Warfarin use, hepatic failure, malnutrition, biliary obstruction	Inhibition of II, VII, IX, and X	Elevated PT (with normal aPTT)	FFP, vitamin K
Dilution	Fewer molecules and cells	Clinical situation, global dysfunction	Replace missing substances
Marrow failure	Thrombocytopenia	Thrombocytopenia, smear, marrow biopsy	Platelet transfusion
Acidosis	Diminished enzyme function	Clinical situation, global dysfunction	Correct the cause, replace as needed
Hypothermia	Diminished enzyme and platelet function	Clinical situation, global dysfunction	Warm
DIC	Global activation of entire clotting system	Clinical situation, laboratory finding dependent on stage	Correct the cause, replace as needed
Thrombolytic therapy	Reduced fibrinogen, clot lysis	Clinical situation, elevated FDP, TT, ECLT	Cryoprecipitate
Primary fibrinolysis	Reduced fibrinogen, clot lysis	Clinical situation, elevated FDP, TT, ECLT	Antifibrinolytics
Uremia	Impaired platelet/endothelial binding	Lengthened BT	DDAVP
Aspirin use	Permanent platelet dysfunction	Lengthened BT	Platelet transfusion
GP IIb/IIIa inhibitor	Permanent platelet dysfunction	Lengthened BT	Platelet transfusion
Specific inhibitors	Antifactor (usually VIII)	Resistance to factor replacement	High doses, immunosuppression

*Table is not all-inclusive.
aPTT, activated partial thromboplastin time; AT III, antithrombin III; BT, bleeding time; DDAVP, desmopressin acetate (1-deamino-8-D-arginine vasopressin); ECLT, euglobulin clot lysis time; FDP, fibrin(ogen) degradation products; FFP, fresh frozen plasma; PT, prothrombin time; TT, thrombin time.

Acquired von Willebrand's Disease Acquired vWD is a rare bleeding disorder that usually occurs in elderly patients.[112] Patients generally have no history of a bleeding disorder, but they have various underlying disease processes, including hematoproliferative disorders and myeloproliferative disorders. Drug-induced acquired vWD also has been reported with medications, such as ciprofloxacin and valproate; disease resolves with discontinuation.[113,114] Acquired vWD has been associated with hypothyroidism and autoimmune disorders.[115,116] The pathogenesis of acquired vWD is not understood but may involve several different processes, including autoantibodies against vWF, adsorption of vWF by tumor cells, and nonimmunologic mechanisms of destruction.[112]

Patients generally present with mucocutaneous bleeding or bleeding in the postoperative setting without a history of bleeding disorders. Laboratory testing includes the BT and other screening tests of coagulation. Generally, BT and aPTT are prolonged with a normal PT. The most specific tests are measurements of plasma vWF antigen and ristocetin cofactor activity. Distinguishing between acquired and congenital vWD involves measurement of vWF propeptide.[112] Clinical management involves control of bleeding using desmopressin and concentrates of vWF. In addition, treatment of the underlying concomitant disease is necessary.

Acquired Hemophilia Inhibitors to specific procoagulant proteins can be acquired, and catastrophic bleeding can arise if surgery is undertaken in such a patient. These inhibitors arise in 3% to 15% of persons with hemophilia (more commonly hemophilia A and when no native protein activity is present; i.e., the most severely affected patients), and for this reason, surgery should not be performed in persons with hemophilia or other individuals who lack specific clotting activities until laboratory tests confirm that the substitution or replacement therapy given before the operation is adequate to support surgical hemostasis.

Acquired hemophilia is a coagulopathy that generally affects the elderly, patients with autoimmune disorders, and occasionally women in the postpartum period. The most common disorder is caused by autoantibodies against specific domains of the factor VIII protein. These autoantibodies inhibit factor VIII's ability to bind with vWF, activated factor IX, and negatively charged phospholipids.[117] Although these autoantibodies are the most frequently encountered, antibodies against factors V, VII, IX, XI, and XIII also exist.[28,29,58,92,118-123] The pathogenesis of these inhibitors is unclear. A genetic predisposition is suggested by twin studies.[119] Patients present with major bleeding episodes in 80% to 90% of the cases with a 10% to 22% mortality rate.[124] The remainder of patients present with anemia secondary to occult bleeding. Most patients were previously healthy, although some have associated autoimmune or lymphoproliferative disorders. The appearance of acquired hemophilia in the postpartum period is a rare but serious condition affecting primiparas within 3 months of delivery.[125]

In patients with antibodies against factor VIII, the aPTT is prolonged, factor VIII levels are low, and mixing studies indicate the presence of an inhibitor. To confirm the depletion of a specific coagulation factor, factor assays must be performed. The method used for quantification of factor VIII inhibitors is the Bethesda assay.[126] Management of patients with acquired hemophilia depends on the severity of bleeding and the results of the Bethesda assay. Increasing factor VIII levels with human factor VIII concentrates to achieve 50% of normal should control most bleeding. This treatment is effective only when the Bethesda units are less than 5. With higher levels of inhibitors (Bethesda units >5), patients usually respond only to porcine factor VIII, recombinant factor VIIa, or activated prothrombin complex concentrates.[117] Corticosteroids can eradicate autoantibodies in more than half of the patients, and cyclophosphamide may induce remission in the remainder.[127]

If the presence of an inactivating inhibitor is not identified preoperatively but suspected intraoperatively (i.e., in the setting of sudden collapse of hemostasis without other cause), cryoprecipitate should be the first-line therapy. Cryoprecipitate contains factor VIII, which is the target of the specific inhibitors in most cases. Cryoprecipitate also contains vWF and factor XIII and is the only source of concentrated fibrinogen. When the specific inhibitor has been identified, overwhelming amounts of the target factor should be administered until hemostasis has been achieved.[58,97,118] If only tenuous hemostasis can be achieved, clotting activity can be supplemented by exchange transfusion with normal FFP, usually via plasmapheresis.

Alternatively, preparations of procoagulants isolated and concentrated from pooled donors can be infused. These preparations are designed to bypass the inhibited activity and trigger the sequence of clotting enzyme reactions beyond the inhibited activity, generating thrombin. If factor VIII coagulant activity is inhibited, concentrates from the prothrombin complex isolated from plasma (factors II, VII, IX, and X) can be infused in an attempt to bypass the barrier of factor VIII inhibition. Recombinant activated factor VII may play a significant role in obtaining hemostasis in these scenarios.

Global Inhibitors The specific antibodies described earlier must be differentiated from global, nonspecific inhibitors. Nonspecific inhibitors are immunoglobulins directed against phospholipids and are generally called *antiphospholipid antibodies* (APAs). Because APAs were seen first in patients with systemic lupus erythematosus and originally diagnosed by their ability to prolong aPTT in vitro, they originally were named *lupus anticoagulants*. This name is a double misnomer. APAs are procoagulants in vivo, and lupus anticoagulants are merely a special case within the general family of APAs, which also includes anticardiolipin antibodies.[30,118,119]

Because APAs act against the phospholipids added ex vivo in the aPTT test, they prolong the aPTT by interfering with multiple steps in the coagulation pathway. Analysis shows a variably decreased activity of factors XII, XI, and occasionally IX. This decrease is rarely (if ever) complete, and usually 30% to 50% of the activity remains, and thrombin generation is not impaired. The effect of this interference is to prevent the factors from interacting with one another in vitro, but not to inhibit any specific clotting activity in vivo. Normal hemostasis with its intense procoagulant focus overrides this interference; as a result, these APAs usually are associated with hypercoagulation in vivo and do not show an increased risk of bleeding. Only antibodies targeted toward a specific clotting factor jeopardize hemostasis. The mechanism whereby the antibodies act as procoagulants in vivo is poorly understood. Hypotheses include platelet activation, endothelial damage or inhibition of prostacyclin secretion, and interference with fibrinolysis.[118,119]

Uremia The primary hemostatic abnormality in patients with renal failure involves poor platelet function or other defects of primary hemostasis. Mechanisms are numerous and incompletely understood, but they include abnormalities within the platelets themselves and impaired excretion of toxins that impede platelet function; some hemorrhagic tendencies correct with dialysis, whereas others persist. Possible platelet defects in uremia include abnormal GP IIb/IIIa, functional cyclooxygenase defect due to abnormal prostaglandin synthesis; abnormal platelet serotonin, cyclic adenosine monophosphate, and storage pool adenosine diphosphate (ADP) levels; and elevated platelet calcium content. Uremic products adversely affecting platelet function include inhibitors of glucose utilization, fibrinolysis, serotonin release, aggregation, and thromboxane production.[128,129]

Because the hemostatic defect in renal failure involves intrinsic platelet abnormalities and inhibitors, treatment is aimed at both factors. In patients with anemia, simple transfusion to a hematocrit of 30% can improve hemostasis through hemodynamic effects by improving platelet margination and enhancing platelet-endothelial contact and interaction. Erythropoietin has a similar, although more delayed, benefit. Dialysis is effective in removing circulating inhibitors of platelet function, but it is seldom successful in restoring hemostasis completely.

Platelet function also can be boosted temporarily by the administration of DDAVP. In addition to its previously stated effects, DDAVP promotes elevated concentrations of norepinephrine in the circulating plasma for 1 to 4 hours after infusion. This action results in improved platelet-endothelial interactions, probably by sensitizing or activating the α-adrenergic receptors of platelets. Infusion of 10 U of cryoprecipitate results in immediate and nearly complete hemostatic competence that lasts 4 to 12 hours; cryoprecipitate should be used preoperatively in all uremic patients in whom major operative intervention is planned.[33-35]

Vitamin K–Related Disorders Factors II, VII, IX, and X, the four vitamin K–dependent clotting factors, must undergo γ-carboxylation to become active, and vitamin K acts as the essential cofactor. These factors are inactive without vitamin K, and reduced vitamin K availability can precipitate coagulopathy.[1,38,42,130] Vitamin K is fat soluble and depends on adequate bile secretion, nutrition, and gut absorptive function to be assimilated into the bloodstream. Biliary obstruction, malnutrition, gut bacterial overgrowth, and other functional disturbances are common causes of bleeding problems in hospitalized patients.

Coagulopathy caused by vitamin K deficiency, whether due to malabsorption or warfarin administration, is usually relatively easy to correct. FFP quickly restores the PT to normal because of direct factor replacement. Parenteral vitamin K also restores factor levels by the carboxylation of presynthesized molecules. This restoration can be quite fast (6 to 24 hours), but it makes re-anticoagulation slower.

Liver Disease The liver is the sole or primary site of synthesis for essentially all of the important coagulation factors, proteins C and S, plasminogen, α_2-antiplasmin, plasminogen activator inhibitor-1 (PAI-1), and other regulatory proteins such as AT III and C1 inhibitor. In addition, the liver plays a major role in the clearance of activated coagulation factors and plasminogen activators. Reduced synthesis of the four vitamin K–dependent factors contributes substantially to bleeding in patients with liver failure, but abnormal fibrinogen synthesis, thrombocytopenia, functional platelet defects, and low-grade, chronic DIC also contribute significantly.[128,130-135] In the operating room, the relatively high portal pressure and resultant fragile, extensive collateralization also increase the risk of hemorrhage.

In mild hepatic insufficiency, it is possible to replace the coagulation factors by an infusion of FFP. In frank liver failure, however, this replacement is rarely possible, especially if there is ongoing consumption because the coagulopathy associated with hepatic failure is usually multifactorial. Hepatic insufficiency often is associated with compromised renal function, which limits the volume that can be infused. For patients with hepatic insufficiency who must undergo operation, an infusion of plasma is begun 2 to 3 hours before the procedure. It is preferable to use FFP rather than stored plasma because FFP contains all the coagulation factors, including higher levels of the labile factors V and VIII, complement, and cold insoluble globulin. Primary fibrinolysis occasionally is caused by liver disease. A 24-hour infusion of aminocaproic acid or tranexamic acid, beginning just before surgery and continuing during and after surgery, may be beneficial in this circumstance. Administration of recombinant activated factor VII in high doses may compensate for the lack of the different coagulation patterns, although its use to date in this scenario has been limited.[59]

Disseminated Intravascular Coagulation DIC is a syndrome that is always secondary to an underlying disorder.[136] It is characterized by the systemic activation of the coagulation cascade resulting in the production of fibrin and resulting in microvascular thrombosis. Continued consumption of the coagulation proteins and platelets depletes the body's stores of these factors, and the syndrome evolves into a state of coagulopathy and bleeding—hence its alternate name, *consumptive coagulopathy*. Alterations in the fibrinolytic system exist concomitantly and contribute to further intravascular clot formation and accelerated fibrinolysis and bleeding. Patients with DIC can present with thrombus formation and vessel occlusion in addition to bleeding. DIC complicates many known clinical disorders. It is seen most commonly in bacterial sepsis, occurring in 30% to 50% of these patients with equal prevalence in gram-negative and gram-positive infections.[130,137] Severe trauma also can initiate the development of DIC, and it occurs in 50% to 70% of these patients.[138,139] A variety of mechanisms may contribute to its development in the trauma patient.

Solid and hematologic malignancies can be complicated by DIC for reasons that are not entirely understood. Obstetric complications, such as placental disruption and amniotic fluid emboli, can activate DIC.[136] Vascular disorders also can cause DIC. These include giant hemangiomas and aortic aneurysms, in which activated coagulation factors overflow into the systemic circulation.[140,141]

DIC is initiated with TF-mediated thrombin generation with concomitant dysfunction in the coagulation cascade inhibitory mechanisms; this leads to enhanced fibrin formation and deposition. In addition, fibrin removal is impaired because of alterations in the fibrinolytic system.[142] All of the aforementioned stimuli, either directly or via cytokines such as interleukin-1 or tumor necrosis factor, cause release of TF from subendothelium or other cells. Thrombocytopenia usually coincides with or precedes the triggering of the coagulation cascade, as platelets are consumed peripherally at the site of infection or tissue damage or coated with immunoglobulin G or specific antibodies. The resultant membrane damage and partial or complete activation causes the membranes either to transform into procoagulant surfaces (generally called *platelet factor 3*) or to express TF. This uncontrolled and ongoing release of TF causes widespread activation of factor VII and the formation of TF–factor VIIa complex, which leads to generation of factor Xa, which triggers an intense exponential "explosion" of thrombin production.[130,143,144]

The regulating pathways of coagulation activation are impaired and contribute to continued fibrin formation. AT III levels are low in patients with DIC. The etiology of these low AT III levels is attributable to a combination of consumption during ongoing thrombus formation, degradation by elastases released from activated neutrophils, and impaired synthesis.[136] In addition, there is a significant depression in the protein C and S system. Thrombomodulin is downregulated during sepsis, leading to diminished protein C activity and the development of a procoagulant state. The fibrinolytic system is largely inactive at the time of maximal coagulation activation. This phenomenon is due to suppression of the fibrinolytic system by a sustained increase in plasma levels of PAI-1.[145]

Although there is a diminution in the natural anticoagulants, the coagulation factors also are relatively protected from inhibition while on procoagulant surfaces. The excess thrombin diffuses to create larger and larger zones of activation, upstream and downstream, and further amplifies fibrin production. Plasmin is produced to compensate for the widespread fibrin production. This plasmin originally plays a protective role by lysing microvascular clot. Excessive plasminogen activation can outstrip its restraints and inhibitors, however, to result in attack on the coagulation factors themselves.[146] The progressive consumption of fibrinogen, factor V, and factor VII by unrestricted activation and their destruction by plasmin as part of plasma proteolysis worsen the situation. If the original pathologic stimuli are sustained, the reserves of coagulation factors are exhausted, and the production of fresh coagulation factors finally is outstripped by their consumption.

If thrombin generation and fibrin accumulation continue to be amplified, fibrin microthrombi are produced. These microthrombi lodge in the microcirculation, especially in the vascular beds of the kidney, brain, lung, adrenal glands, and skin, impairing blood flow, nutrient delivery, and organ function. Polymerization of fibrin monomers initiates compensatory plasmin activation and (secondary) fibrinolysis. The degree of organ damage from occlusion of the microcirculation by these fibrin-rich microthrombi depends on the balance between their formation and lysis by plasmin. The secondary fibrinolysis that occurs as part of DIC is crucial and should not be inhibited.[146,147] This necessary fibrinolysis further impairs hemostasis because the products of fibrinogen and fibrin degradation (FDPs, D dimers, and various fibrinopeptides) themselves are anticoagulants in large quantities, acting as antithrombins, potentiating thrombolysis, and interfering with fibrin polymerization.[148,149]

DIC can be distinguished from simpler disturbances, in a philosophical but clinically important sense, by the fact that it tends to be resistant to correction when it is in full bloom. This is for several reasons:

1. The insult that leads to DIC is often relatively chronic and is often persistent despite all efforts to the contrary.
2. Activation is usually widespread, ongoing, and massive, exceeding the ability of the body to replace needed factors.
3. Many of the degradation products produced by the syndrome are active anticoagulants (notably FDP), which easily initiate a positive-feedback loop.

Prevention is crucial.

DIC is a continuously progressing process, and it can be divided into three clinical phases.[150] Phase 1 is the compensated activation of the hemostatic system. In this phase, clinical findings are generally absent, but because of the underlying disease process, the development of DIC is suspected or anticipated. In this phase, tests to measure activation of coagulation should be performed. The PT, aPTT, TT, and platelet counts are within normal limits. The prothrombin fragment F_{1+2} and thromin-antithrombin complexes are elevated, whereas antithrombin is slightly decreased. Phase 2 is decompensated activation of the hemostatic system. In this phase, the PT and aPTT are prolonged with a normal TT because fibrinogen levels at this stage still may be normal. Repeated analysis is necessary during this stage because components can change rapidly. Platelet counts, fibrinogen concentration, coagulation factor activities, and antithrombin levels are decreased or continuously decreasing. Phase 3 is "full-blown DIC."[150] This phase is characterized by extremely prolonged, or unclottable, PT, aPTT, and TT. Platelet counts also are extremely low, and coagulation factor activities, fibrinogen levels, and antithrombin levels are less than 50% normal.

DIC usually arises in characteristic clinical settings. The usual scenario is that of a gradual deterioration in previously adequate hemostasis in a critically ill patient (e.g., with sepsis, trauma, or uncontrolled bleeding), with generalized bleeding, particularly from previously hemostatic areas. Primary fibrinolysis usually occurs in patients with cirrhosis or liver failure from other causes in whom PAI synthesis and tissue plasminogen activator (t-PA) clearance are impaired. Relevant to vascular surgery, it also occurs in the setting of hepatic hypoperfusion resulting from supraceliac clamping.[13,151]

DIC is probably not an "all-or-nothing" event; it commonly arises from previous, inadequately treated problems. In a patient who is cold and underperfused, coagulopathy initially may be simply an enzymatic dysfunction. If the initial insult is not corrected and bleeding persists, however, the worsened hypothermia, acidosis, and toxemia induced by ischemic tissue may push the coagulation system into true DIC.

Because DIC, when established, is often extraordinarily resistant to treatment, prevention is paramount. Early recognition is crucial because of DIC's propensity to become autonomous and self-perpetuating. When DIC is established, general support while the underlying problem is corrected is the best option. In the short-term, measures designed to reduce operative time, maintain perfusion, and keep the patient warm and at normal physiologic parameters are important, as discussed earlier. In the longer term, maintenance of adequate nutrition, control of undrained spaces and débridement of ischemic tissues, control of pain, and control of systemic infectious problems are of equal importance. Clotting factors and platelets should be replaced at the rate they are consumed, as determined by frequent laboratory testing, and continued administration of FFP, platelets, cryoprecipitate to increase fibrinogen levels, and, as directed, more exotic factors is recommended. Antifibrinolytic agents probably should seldom, if ever, be used because the secondary fibrinolysis occurring during DIC is beneficial, cleaning the capillaries of thrombus and restoring perfusion. The mainstay of treatment is correction of the underlying stimulus directly, while halting the vicious circle and replacing cells and factors as fast as they are consumed.

Primary Fibrinolysis Primary fibrinolysis should be distinguished from the secondary fibrinolysis seen as part of DIC. In DIC, fibrinolytic activation occurs as a secondary event, acting to lyse intravascular microthrombi. As such, it is therapeutic, it is vital to tissue perfusion, and it should not be inhibited. In contrast, in primary fibrinolytic states, fibrinolysis occurs de novo as the primary problem, and direct inhibition is often beneficial.[130,146]

The mechanism by which bleeding occurs differs from that of DIC. In primary fibrinolysis, direct plasminogen activation is the primary problem rather than being secondary to high thrombin and fibrin clot levels as it is in DIC. Plasmin saturates its inhibitors, especially PAI-1 and α_2-antiplasmin, so that free plasmin builds up in the circulation (Fig. 33-3). "Upstream" substances (factors V and VIII), fibrin, and fibrinogen are destroyed. Plasmin generated on the surface of platelets and endothelial cells and within clot attacks the cell membranes and their receptors and inappropriately lyses hemostatic plugs. Compensatory thrombin generation is quickly amplified, and platelets are recruited in an effort to restore endothelial competence and hemostasis. Fibrin monomers and FDPs are created. In both circumstances, microvascular coagulation occurs when the reticuloendothelial and macrophage-phagocyte systems become overwhelmed. Thus occurs the paradoxical development of microvascular thrombosis and massive hemorrhage observed in DIC and primary fibrinolysis.[131,152,153]

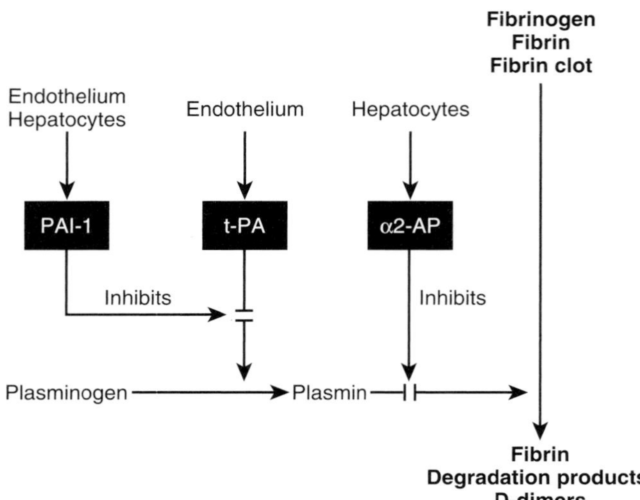

FIGURE 33-3 Fibrinolytic molecules and their inhibitors. Tissue plasminogen activator (t-PA) and other physiologic and therapeutic molecules lyse clot indirectly by cleaving plasminogen to plasmin. Plasminogen activator inhibitors (PAIs), the most common being PAI-1, inhibit t-PA and other plasminogen inhibitors, whereas α_2-antiplasmin (α_2-AP) directly inhibits plasmin's action on fibrin(ogen). (From Illig KA, Green RM, Ouriel K, et al: Primary fibrinolysis during supraceliac clamping. J Vasc Surg 25:245, 1997.)

Primary fibrinolysis is caused by high levels of fibrinolytic enzymes in the circulation and occurs in several situations. Best described is the elevation in t-PA seen in cirrhosis and liver failure, possibly resulting from deficient synthesis of competent PAI-1 and other barriers to plasminogen activation or to inadequate clearance of plasminogen activators, and during the anhepatic phase of liver transplantation.[16,131,133,154] Rapid synthesis and release of activators by various neoplasms also can occur, and several venomous snakes secrete antifibrinolytics.[131,155] More relevant to the vascular surgeon are, however, the iatrogenic administration of fibrinolytic agents for arterial and venous thrombosis and the elevation in t-PA levels seen during supraceliac aortic clamping for paravisceral and thoracoabdominal aneurysm repairs, presumably resulting from hepatic hypoperfusion.[13,151] t-PA is metabolized rapidly by the liver; restoring hepatic perfusion and stopping any infused agent are usually adequate, especially if the duration of insult is short.[156]

Treatment of primary fibrinolysis requires replacement therapy and the use of fibrinolytic inhibitors. Target substrates of plasmin fibrinogen, factor V, and, to a lesser extent, factor VIII must be replaced. Platelet infusions may be necessary to supply factor V. Fibrinolytic inhibitors, such as aminocaproic acid, tranexamic acid, and aprotinin, can be beneficial.

Drug-Induced Disorders of Hemostasis In many instances, patients requiring either elective or emergency operation are receiving antithrombotic or thrombolytic agents. Decisions must be made on an individual basis regarding whether the agent should be discontinued before the procedure. Chapter 31 presents a thorough review of the mechanisms of actions of many of these medications, so only a brief review is presented here.

Heparins Heparin is a naturally occurring glycosaminoglycan, with a molecular weight ranging from 2000 to 40,000 d. It binds to and dramatically increases the ability of AT III to inactivate the components of the intrinsic coagulation cascade, factors IXa, Xa, XIa, and XIIa and especially thrombin. Heparin anticoagulation results in prolonged aPTT and ACT, but in moderate doses it does not affect BT or PT. Heparin generally is administered parenterally, either intravenously or subcutaneously, but oral heparins are being investigated. Its half-life is predictable when the intravenous route is used (approximately 1.5 hours), but is less so when the subcutaneous route is selected (because of slower absorption and altered metabolism). The effect of heparin administered by the subcutaneous route may persist 8 hours.[50,157] As previously stated, heparin can be reversed with protamine at a dose of 1 mg of protamine for every 100 U of heparin.

LMW heparin (4000 to 8000 d) is being used instead of unfractionated heparin with increasing frequency. Advantages of LMW heparin include the ability to provide full anticoagulation and prophylaxis via the subcutaneous route without the need to monitor coagulation parameters. Because its bioavailability and metabolism are more predictable, LMW heparin acts primarily by inhibition of factor Xa and has a much higher anti-Xa-to-anti-IIa activity ratio than does conventional heparin. As such, LMW heparin does not affect the aPTT as reliably as conventional heparin does.[5,6,158] Acute reversal of LMW heparin effect is difficult. Protamine can be used, but it does not neutralize LMW heparin completely.[159]

Thrombin Inhibitors Direct thrombin inhibitors have several potential benefits over heparin. Fibrin-bound thrombin is relatively immune to inactivation by heparin, whereas bound thrombin can be inhibited by direct thrombin inhibitors.[160] Direct thrombin inhibitors produce a more predictable response because of their lack of plasma protein binding. These inhibitors include hirudin and its derivatives, noncovalent inhibitors, naturally occurring thrombin inhibitors, covalent inhibitors of thrombin's active site, and thrombin-binding DNA aptamers.[161] Hirudin is a polypeptide that originally was isolated from the salivary glands of the leech *Hirudo medicinalis*. It is currently available through recombinant DNA technology. Hirudin is a potent and specific inhibitor of thrombin.[162] It has no antidote, is cleared by the kidneys, and has a plasma half-life of 40 minutes after intravenous injection. Bivalirudin is a semisynthetic thrombin inhibitor that produces only a transient inhibition of the active site of thrombin.

Noncovalent inhibitors bind noncovalently to the active site of thrombin and act as a competitive inhibitor.[4] Argatroban is the prototypical noncovalent inhibitor and is in clinical use. Other agents, including napsagatran, inogatran, melagatran, and their derivatives, currently are being investigated and hold promise in that some are orally bioavailable.[163,164] Covalent inhibitors, such as D-Phe-Pro-Arg chloromethyl ketone (PPACK); natural thrombin inhibitors, such as bothrojaracin; and DNA aptamers are currently in investigational phases only.

Warfarin Warfarin, an orally administered anticoagulant, interferes with the action of vitamin K on the hepatic synthesis of factors II, VII, IX, and X. Vitamin K is responsible for γ-carboxylation and generation of calcium-binding sites on these factors; without vitamin K, they are synthesized in a nonfunctional form. Anticoagulation with warfarin requires concomitant use of heparin for the first several days, for two reasons:

1. The half-life of prothrombin (factor II), responsible for the anticoagulant effects of warfarin, is longer than that of factor VII, which is most responsible for elevations in the PT. Although the PT may be elevated within 24 hours, a therapeutic anticoagulant state may not yet be in effect.
2. Warfarin also inhibits the anticoagulant proteins C and S, which also have short half-lives. Early after warfarin administration, a paradoxical hypercoagulable state can occur, especially in patients with protein C or S deficiency—causing small vessel thrombosis and "warfarin-induced skin necrosis."[1,165]

Antiplatelet Agents Antiplatelet agents commonly are administered to patients with vascular disease. Aspirin, clopidogrel, and ticlopidine irreversibly inhibit platelet aggregation. Aspirin inactivates platelet cyclooxygenase, inhibiting platelet synthesis of thromboxane A_2, whereas clopidogrel and ticlopidine alter the platelet membrane structure, decreasing expression of GP IIb/IIIa by blocking the ADP receptor. The effects of these agents usually persist for 4 to 7 days after medication is stopped, until enough new, functional platelets have been synthesized.[166]

Although individual response is variable, most authors and clinicians still recommend that elective operation not take place unless the platelet count (assuming normal function) exceeds 50/µL to 70/µL.[167] Aspirin use is similarly controversial. Although many investigators believe aspirin causes clinically relevant bleeding, study results are inconsistent.[166,168,169] Aspirin clearly improves graft patency and cerebrovascular and coronary morbidity and mortality in a variety of settings; we recommend that patients specifically receive aspirin the night before operation and continue taking aspirin afterward.[170-173] If cessation is desired, the aspirin should be stopped at least 3 or 4 days preoperatively to allow restoration of platelet function through new platelet production (although the life span of a platelet is 7 to 10 days, after 3 to 4 days enough new platelets are available). Patients taking clopidogrel or ticlopidine should be treated in a similar fashion and have these medications discontinued at least 3 to 4 days before surgery.[174] Nonsteroidal medications act similarly, but because their effects on platelets are only temporary, they pose even less of a problem intraoperatively.[166]

GP IIb/IIIA receptor inhibitors are a powerful new class of drugs that provide immediate relief in ongoing arterial thrombosis. They also eliminate excessive platelet reactivity in diseased vessels, preventing occlusive thrombi and restenosis.[175] Abciximab (ReoPro; Centocor, Malvern, Pa), a GP IIb/IIIa receptor antibody, is capable of inhibiting platelet aggregation and prolongs the BT after a single bolus injection. Although this drug has an initial half-life of only 10 minutes and a second half-life of approximately 30 minutes, platelet function does not recover fully for approximately 2 days. One side effect of this treatment has been thrombocytopenia, which is reversible with recovery taking several days. Eptifibatide (Integrilin; Key Pharmaceuticals, Kenilworth, NJ), a synthetic disulfide-linked cyclic heptapeptide with a high specificity for inhibition of GP IIb/IIIa, has been shown to diminish platelet aggregation and prolong bleeding times successfully after its administration.[176] It has a half-life of approximately 2.5 hours. Tirofiban (Aggrastat; Merck, West Point, Pa) is a synthetic drug designed to mimic a peptide sequence of fibrinogen, allowing an alternative site to which GP IIb/IIIa can bind.[177] It binds in a reversible fashion, and its antiplatelet activity reverses within a few hours of bolus administration. Oral agents of this class of drug, such as roxifiban, also are available.[178] There are no antidotes to these agents.

Bleeding is the most common complication with the use of GP IIb/IIIa receptor inhibitors, particularly when used in conjunction with heparin and thrombolytic agents. No reversal agent is available, and patients with ongoing bleeding should receive platelet transfusions as necessary.[179] Platelet transfusions are effective only for abciximab, however, and not for eptifibatide or tirofiban.

Therapeutic Thrombolysis All presently available thrombolytic agents, including streptokinase, urokinase, and t-PA, act indirectly, through conversion of plasminogen to plasmin. As such, the agents are called *plasminogen activators,* and they lack activity in the absence of plasminogen. When administered systemically, two events occur. First, nonpathologic and pathologic thrombi are dissolved. The useful fibrin-platelet plug sealing a recent trivial defect in an intracerebral vessel is just as susceptible to thrombolytic dissolution as the pathologic thrombus obstructing a coronary artery. Second, systemic thrombolytic therapy produces widespread conversion of plasminogen to plasmin, producing systemic plasminemia, which leads to nonspecific proteolysis, including breakdown of circulating fibrinogen (see Fig. 33-3).

In the ideal situation, therapeutic peripheral arterial fibrinolysis is localized to the site of pathologic clot, usually by catheter-directed infusion, and systemic lysis does not occur. The doses required to achieve rapid clot dissolution are high enough to produce a systemic proteolytic state similar to that observed with systemic therapy, and it must be assumed that any individual receiving or having recently received peripheral thrombolytic therapy may have a systemic lytic state. The pathophysiology is similar to that of primary fibrinolytic states, with low fibrinogen levels and high degradation products. The PT and aPTT may be normal (if factors have not been attacked by the excess plasmin), but the TT is prolonged and the ECLT is abnormally shortened.[180]

An increased risk of bleeding may occur from the unavoidable leakage of a thrombolytic agent into the systemic circulation (a cause of primary fibrinolysis). The bleeding ceases quickly as the agents are rapidly metabolized. A longer lasting effect may occur, however, from circulating anticoagulants (FDPs) released as fibrin is degraded. FDPs are probably the most frequent and troublesome cause of bleeding complications during therapeutic thrombolysis. Hypofibrinogenemia alone is not usually responsible for abnormal bleeding (patients with congenital afibrinogenemia rarely manifest spontaneous bleeding); diminished fibrinogen levels are corrected easily with FFP or cryoprecipitate. We believe the most common cause of bleeding, however, is the lytic dissolution of desirable thrombi in the brain, in the gastrointestinal tract, or at the site of catheter insertion.

Hypothermia Clotting factors are enzymes and, similar to all enzymes, function optimally within a narrow range of temperature and pH, centered around normal values (Fig. 33-4). When these ranges are exceeded, most commonly secondary to hypothermia or acidosis, function is impaired, and clotting progressively becomes abnormal. Intraoperative hypothermia usually is encountered with prolonged operative time (owing to heat loss to the environment), global hypoperfusion (often due to critical illness or injury), and intraoperative replacement with nonwarmed fluids in large volumes.[181] Because many laboratories measure clotting tests with samples warmed to 37°C, a clinically obvious coagulopathy in a cold patient may be associated with apparently normal test results.[182] Hypothermia also can cause platelet dysfunction and precipitate full-blown DIC.[183,184] The decreased temperature alters enzyme kinetics, lowering enzyme activity, particularly the activity of enzymes involved in the polymerization process of platelets and fibrin.[185]

Similar to many situational factors causing coagulopathy, the resultant bleeding leads to worsened perfusion, greater fluid requirements, and a longer operation, creating a vicious circle. In addition, hypothermia is notoriously difficult to correct when it is established. Prevention is absolutely crucial. Operative time is often relatively fixed by the problem at hand. Although speed is not the goal, if quality is preserved, a short operation is better than a long one. If a "high-risk" situation can be identified beforehand (e.g., a ruptured aneurysm or trauma victim with a prolonged extrication time), warming the room before the patient arrives seems prudent. When fluid requirements are

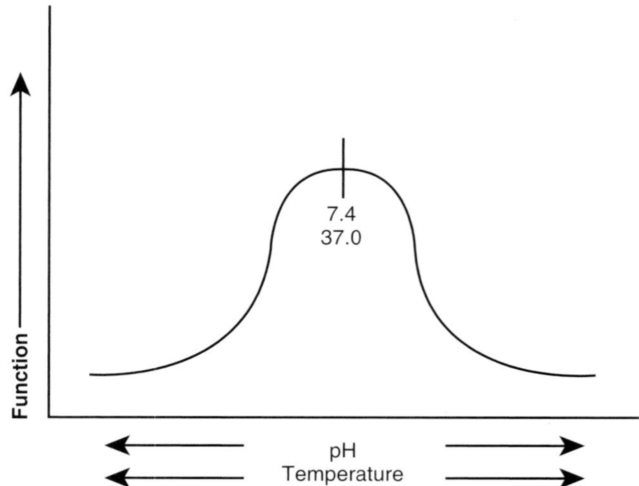

FIGURE 33-4 Schematic curve of enzyme activity (in this case, coagulation factors) versus pH and temperature. Function is maximal at normal physiologic values (7.4 and 37), but declines as these values change on either side of the norm. Platelet function also is adversely affected, at least by hypothermia, but its relation to pH is less well characterized.

expected to be more than minimal, infusion through fluid warmers is required.

Although not all agree whether warming inspired air is helpful, systems that deliver warmed air to exposed parts of the body not in the surgical field (Bair Hugger, Arizant Healthcare, Eden Prairie, MN) are of value. Finally, although maintaining optimal global perfusion is a crucial goal for many reasons, it aids in maintaining temperature and reducing the stimulus for elaboration of anticoagulant and fibrinolytic factors.

Acidosis Acidosis is a common problem in vascular surgery. It is seen most commonly in the setting of significant bacteremia, in global or local hypoperfusion, and after reperfusion of a large ischemic area. The best treatment is prevention by correcting ischemic problems early and maintaining global hemodynamics and by predicting situations that cannot be prevented and treating them quickly. When a large mass of tissue (e.g., a leg or the small bowel) has been ischemic for more than a short time, acidosis (and hyperkalemia, myoglobinemia, and high levels of other anticoagulant toxins) results when perfusion is restored. In this situation, treatment ideally should coincide with or even precede the event. Respiratory and metabolic alkalosis can be established before arterial clamp removal. In addition, unusually close attention should be paid to clinical and laboratory evidence of coagulopathy, and the operation should not be terminated until hemostasis is adequate.

Dilution Dilution also is a common problem, but one that is often overlooked in the "heat of the battle." With massive transfusion, defined as transfusion of 1 to 2 full blood volumes in a finite time span, platelets and factors are lost, and their levels decline as the result of dilution with the crystalloid necessary to maintain cardiac filling and output. There is no consensus as to how clinically significant this loss is. Although thrombocytopenia is usually the major change observed after massive transfusion, there is no specific cutoff that predicts bleeding, and FFP and platelets probably should be transfused only for specific deficiencies. Even in the face of massive blood loss, enough coagulation proteins almost always remain to maintain function.[2,25] The best strategy is to be aware of this possibility and to measure platelet count and factor function (by PT, aPTT, and ACT) frequently if massive blood loss occurs. Occasionally, loss is so rapid that waiting for laboratory testing before transfusion may not be in the patient's best interest.

Mechanical Trauma to Clotting Factors and Platelets Mechanical trauma can occur, usually iatrogenically while the patient is on cardiopulmonary bypass or using a cell-saver device.[26,186,187] Autotransfusion devices, in which the cells are washed before they are returned to the patient, may reduce the risk of DIC, but they result in removal of important coagulation factors. In contrast, the non–cell-washing devices return all the blood proteins, but also may return certain triggers of DIC, such as activated complement and damaged cellular elements. The use of extracorporeal circulation results in several abnormalities of hemostasis; qualitative and quantitative platelet abnormalities and, less commonly, significant reductions in factors V and VIII occur. Rarely, DIC may occur. The most important coagulation abnormalities may result from the massive doses of heparin required to prevent thrombosis within the perfusion system. Treatment of bleeding associated with cardiopulmonary bypass is best addressed by reversal of the two most important factors, thrombocytopenia and high levels of heparin.

Other Problems Other, less common causes of coagulopathy in the operating room need to be considered. An iatrogenic coagulopathy, such as overheparinization or warfarin administration, should be suspected in the appropriate clinical setting; correction usually is accomplished easily by appropriate doses of protamine sulfate, FFP, and vitamin K, as appropriate. If bleeding occurs in a uremic patient, DDAVP should be given as discussed earlier. LMW dextrans interfere with coagulation because of effects on the fibrin clot, hemodilution, and platelet function.[2] Platelet number and function are adversely affected after placement of a large vascular prosthesis[188,189]; this is not usually a problem in the operating room, however, and in our experience it is solely a laboratory finding. Although increasingly rare, a transfusion reaction should be suspected if abnormal, diffuse bleeding abruptly occurs while the patient is receiving blood products. The transfusion should be stopped immediately and consideration given to aborting the operation, depending on the clinical situation.

Finally, hereditary disorders occasionally are first detected during an operative procedure. Although relatively rare, such a disorder should be suspected if other causes do not seem to be present. In this setting (e.g., coagulopathic bleeding occurring early in an otherwise uneventful procedure), a full battery of coagulation tests, including TT and factor levels, should be obtained, and intraoperative consultation with a hematologist should be considered.

Surgical Bleeding

The cause of surgically correctable bleeding, by definition, is an open vessel. An open vessel can occur for several reasons: spontaneously (a ruptured aneurysm), as the result of prehospital injury, or as the result of iatrogenic, intraoperative injury. Management, although differing in detail, is conceptually the same in all situations. First, in all but the most minor situations, two things are crucial: exposure and assistance. Packing or digital control often can buy time to improve both, and if bleeding can be controlled temporarily, the situation can be thought through, a plan developed, and the problem addressed in an unhurried, logical fashion. Of all parameters, adequate, properly trained help is probably the best resource available—four hands and eyes are better than two.

Arterial and venous bleeds are approached differently. In all but the most minor arterial injuries, the first priority should be obtaining direct proximal and distal control. Often this is best accomplished by proximal control at a remote site, allowing dissection away from the hematoma or site of temporary control, and distal control with the same technique or a balloon occlusion catheter from within the opened lumen. If bleeding is localized, the patient is stable, and bleeding is expected to be handled easily; heparinization is advisable. If the risk of coagulopathy is great, however, as typified by many ruptured aneurysms, the risks of heparinization may exceed its benefits. When controlled, the injury can be exposed, explored, and repaired. Simple injuries, including stab wounds, often can be sutured directly. More complex wounds usually require more complex repair, however, as discussed elsewhere.

Venous bleeding is often approached differently. Because of large size, thin walls, and abundant feeding tributaries, proximal and distal control can often be more problematic and injury can be more diffuse. Because of low venous pressure, spontaneous thrombosis is more likely. For both of these reasons, simple packing, especially when the injury is difficult to expose, is often the best option. Essentially, any vein with the exception of the suprarenal vena cava or right renal vein can be ligated; this is a reasonable option if bleeding is vigorous, and the patient's life is at risk.[190,191]

More commonly encountered in elective surgery is surgical bleeding from less obvious sources. The first step is to conduct a thorough, systematic search. Several sources are common and specifically should be sought out. After aneurysm repair, previously patent but nonbleeding vessels, such as the lumbar or inferior mesenteric arteries or even the cut edge of the aneurysm sac, can bleed as distal perfusion is restored. The splenic bed is a potential source after splenectomy and should be inspected routinely. The spleen itself is often injured (25% of cases) during left medial visceral rotation and should be inspected routinely after this exposure. If the spleen is injured after a complex aortic repair, the surgeon should have a low threshold for splenectomy to reduce the risk of missing or misinterpreting postoperative hemorrhage.

After any vascular anastomosis, whether bleeding or not, all parts of all suture lines should be inspected. If bleeding is found from the suture line itself, repair sutures are placed. Repair sutures usually should be placed in a mattress fashion, over a pledget if any weakness or gap exists, to reduce strain on the surrounding tissues. After the hole has been identified, the inflow artery can be reclamped and the graft decompressed. Caution is required, however, because ill-placed pledgets can obscure visualization of and access to continued bleeding points, if not controlled the first time. Areas that are relatively inaccessible, such as the back wall of a proximal aortic anastomosis, should be inspected carefully before the distal anastomosis is fashioned and access is lost.

If any doubt exists as to the integrity of the tissue, pledgets should be used during initial anastomotic construction. In difficult situations, such as with diffusely friable tissues, a long strip of fabric can be used to reinforce the cuff while the anastomosis is sewn. This reinforcement has the effect of distributing the force of the suture itself over a wider area, and it can protect friable tissues from the sutures pulling through.

Needle hole bleeding is a different situation. Almost exclusively, this bleeding is seen after bypass using polytetrafluoroethylene. If needle hole bleeding is seen after a polyester (Dacron) graft has been used, a careful search should be made for gaps, especially related to crimps in the fabric. The surgeon can reduce needle hole bleeding by paying extra attention to following the curve of the needle and by using the best match between suture and needle diameter. True needle hole bleeding almost always stops within 5 or 10 minutes, especially if the hemostatic function is normal (e.g., after protamine administration). Although patience and mechanical control, such as packing with oxidized cellulose gauze (Surgicel, Johnson & Johnson, Somerville, NJ), are usually adequate, rarely a repair suture is required. A repair suture creates more needle holes; maneuvers such as using adjacent bits of tissue as a pledget and not passing through the full thickness of the polytetrafluoroethylene are valuable. Another cause of bleeding after graft placement, especially if Dacron is used, is inadequate preclotting or abnormal bleeding from the interstices. This bleeding almost always stops within a few minutes if coagulation is otherwise normal.

Operative Management

If abnormal bleeding occurs in the operating room, the first step is to identify the cause. If the cause is mechanical, the source should be identified and corrected expeditiously with exposure, local or remote control, and adequate assistance. Several mechanical resources are available. As discussed, packing is an excellent technique, especially for relatively inaccessible venous injuries. Surgicel, although not directly hemostatic, provides an excellent mechanical scaffolding for platelet and fibrin deposition. It is inexpensive and probably the first line of therapy for troublesome but minor bleeding that is expected to stop (e.g., needle hole bleeding).

More specific pharmacologic therapies are available. Topical bovine thrombin (Gentrac), especially when combined with an absorbable gelatin sponge (Gelfoam), is directly hemostatic and relatively inexpensive. Microfibrillar collagen (Avitene) is a powder that can be sprinkled on diffuse, raw, oozing areas and is quite effective, especially when combined with packing. Fibrin sealants, or fibrin glues, are surgical hemostatic agents derived from human plasma and are designed to reproduce the final steps of the coagulation cascade producing a stable fibrin clot. Fibrin sealants have been used in vascular surgery, cardiovascular surgery, and hepatic surgery with a significant reduction in blood loss, time to hemostasis, and frequency of postoperative hemorrhage.[192]

Occasionally the surgeon may encounter bleeding that is uncontrollable despite all possible measures. In this setting, packing, cessation of surgery, and transfer to the intensive care unit (ICU) with a temporary abdominal closure for resuscitation with planned repeat operation may be lifesaving. Most widely explored by trauma surgeons, this "bail-out" technique assumes that the best resuscitation (warmth, correction of acid-base problems and coagulopathy) can be carried out in the ICU.[193] This technique is applicable only for coagulopathy and when mechanical bleeding, usually venous, cannot be quickly controlled surgically but can be controlled with packing. It is not applicable when major arterial bleeding is present.

■ POSTOPERATIVE BLEEDING

Postoperative bleeding can be encountered as a continuation of intraoperative coagulopathy or as a new, unexpected problem. The first step is diagnosis, and an appropriate level of suspicion is required. In a patient who tolerates an otherwise uneventful operation without bleeding (i.e., no intraoperative coagulopathy is present), new postoperative bleeding is almost certainly surgical. In other words, unless a specific cause is present (e.g., consumptive coagulopathy or transfusion), de novo postoperative bleeding should be assumed to be due to an open blood vessel.

There are two questions to answer: (1) Is bleeding occurring? (2) What is the cause? Most bleeding can be diagnosed easily by observation of the patient's clinical course, including unexplained tachycardia, and basic laboratory parameters, such as the hematocrit, PT, aPTT, and platelet count. If consumptive coagulopathy is suspected, fibrinogen levels, FDPs, and TT should be followed as well. ECLT can identify primary fibrinolysis. Monitoring the hematocrit, PT, aPTT, platelet count, and fibrinogen levels every 6 hours is probably optimal to allow time for correction between repeated testing. Bleeding that affects these variables faster than this should be clinically obvious.

The benefit of treating a coagulopathy in the ICU is to allow for resuscitation. Warmth is crucial, as discussed earlier. An ICU allows warming by means of air blankets, radiant heaters, and infused fluids. Probably the most important reason for moving the patient to the ICU is that the patient's skin has been closed and the patient has been removed from the usually cold operating room. Acid-base status can be monitored closely and corrected, and global tissue perfusion and hemodynamic status can be optimized, all of which shift platelet and clotting enzyme function toward normalcy.

Finally, ongoing stimuli for bleeding can be identified better and corrected in the ICU. All dead tissue should be removed, by means of débridement or formal amputation, when benefit exceeds risk. An irreversibly ischemic foot in a critically ill patient with thrombocytopenia probably can be left alone for the time being, whereas a cadaveric leg with no other cause of DIC in which DIC is developing should be amputated expeditiously. Abscesses must be drained, and pain must be relieved.

Although the best way to "cure" a coagulopathy is to remove stimuli for its existence and to restore general homeostasis, ongoing replacement therapy is often required (see Table 33-5). Most commonly needed are blood, platelets, and clotting factors. PRBCs are used for restoring oxygen-carrying capacity. As discussed earlier, although tissue oxygenation is excellent at much lower levels, a hematocrit of 30% is still the target in the setting of ongoing bleeding to allow a margin for error with ongoing loss. In general, 1 U of PRBCs increases the hematocrit by 3%. If the increase is less than this, ongoing loss (or dilution) should be suspected. Platelets should be transfused for low platelet counts. Although a count of approximately 20/μL is usually adequate for maintenance of normal hemostasis, with active bleeding a target of 50/μL to 70/μL (even higher at times to allow for ongoing loss or destruction) is usually recommended. An elevated PT is usually correctable by administration of FFP (to restore new factors) and vitamin K (to counteract liver dysfunction and warfarin effects), whereas an elevated aPTT, often associated with global coagulopathy, may be corrected with protamine, even if heparin was not given or apparently was adequately reversed.

If bleeding is ongoing, the next step is to look for rarer causes, to rule out surgical bleeding, or to look for correctly identified but inadequately treated problems. Cryoprecipitate restores factor VIII and fibrinogen levels, and DDAVP improves platelet-endothelial interactions via an increase in vWF. DDAVP is especially useful in uremia and after cardiopulmonary bypass. If primary fibrinolysis is suspected, antifibrinolytic agents can be considered, but their use is contraindicated in DIC.

In general, replacement therapy should be directed by laboratory parameters. Two general exceptions exist:

1. When a defined coagulopathy is known to be present, such as DIC, primary fibrinolysis, or a hereditary disorder. In this setting, initial treatment can be empirical, specifically directed against the presumed problem, while laboratory workup is pending.
2. When coagulopathy is massive and immediately life-threatening. Laboratory evaluation should be expeditious, but before the answer is found, treatment should be empirical. An old aphorism is "give them everything you can spell." Although not scientific, this "shotgun" approach usually does more good than harm.

The most common things should be treated first (with PRBCs, platelets, and FFP, often in massive doses) while the laboratory tests are pending.

■ SUMMARY

The development of perioperative bleeding can be daunting, particularly when it is not anticipated. A thorough understanding of the hemostatic system and the potential causes of hemorrhage allow the surgeon to come quickly to the diagnosis of its etiology and provide an effective treatment. Although the potential causes are numerous, generally the patient's history, clinical scenario, and basic coagulation laboratory studies provide sufficient data on which effective treatment strategies can be based.

■ REFERENCES

1. Liem T, Silver D: Coumadin: Principles of use. Semin Vasc Surg 9:354, 1996.
2. Weaver DW: Differential diagnosis and management of unexplained bleeding. Surg Clin North Am 73:353, 1993.
3. White GC, Marder VJ, Colman RW, et al: Approach to the bleeding patient. In Colman RW, Hirsh J, Marder VJ, et al (eds): Hemostasis and Thrombosis: Basic Principles and Clinical Practice. Philadelphia, JB Lippincott, 1994, p 1134.
4. Hilpert K, Ackerman J, Banner DW, et al: Design and synthesis of potent and highly selective thrombin inhibitors. J Med Chem 37:3889, 1994.
5. Rosenberg RD: Biochemistry and pharmacology of low molecular weight heparin. Semin Hematol 34(Suppl 4):2, 1997.
6. Kessler CM: Low molecular weight heparins: Practical considerations. Semin Hematol 34(Suppl 4):35, 1997.
7. Conrad J, Samama M: Theoretic and practical consideration on laboratory monitoring of thrombolytic therapy. Semin Thromb Hemost 13:212, 1987.
8. Heiden D, Mielke CH, Rodvien R: Impairment of heparin of primary haemostasis and platelet [^{14}C] 5-hydroxytryptamine release. Br J Haematol 36:427, 1987.
9. Bowie EJ, Owen CA: The bleeding time. Prog Hemost Thromb 2:249, 1974.

10. Peterson P, Hayes TE, Arkin CF, et al: The preoperative bleeding time test lacks clinical benefit: College of American Pathologists' and American Society of Clinical Pathologists' position article. Arch Surg 133:134, 1998.
11. Francis RB Jr: Clinical disorders of fibrinolysis: A critical review. Blut 59:1, 1989.
12. Blix S: Studies on the fibrinolytic system in the euglobulin fraction of human plasma. Scand J Clin Lab Invest 13(Suppl):3, 1961.
13. Illig KA, Green RM, Ouriel K, et al: Primary fibrinolysis during supraceliac clamping. J Vasc Surg 25:244, 1997.
14. Overview of Thrombelastograph Coagulation Analyzer: A unique analytical device. Morton Grove, Ill, Haemoscope Corporation, 1991.
15. DeNicola P, Mazetti GM: Evaluation of thrombelastography. Am J Clin Pathol 25:447, 1955.
16. Kang YG, Martin DJ, Marquez J, et al: Intraoperative changes in blood coagulation and thrombelastographic monitoring in liver transplantation. Anesth Analg 64:888, 1985.
17. NIH Consensus Conference: Perioperative red blood cell transfusion. JAMA 260:2700, 1988.
18. NIH Consensus Conference: Fresh frozen plasma: Indications and risks. JAMA 253:551, 1985.
19. NIH Consensus Conference: Platelet transfusion therapy. JAMA 257:1777, 1987.
20. American College of Physicians: Practice strategies for elective red blood cell transfusion. Ann Intern Med 116:403, 1992.
21. Consensus Conference: Blood management and surgical practice guidelines. Am J Surg 170(Suppl):1S, 1995.
22. Avoiding the misuse of fresh frozen plasma [editorial]. BMJ 307:395, 1993.
23. Spence RK: Emerging trends in surgical blood tranfusion. Semin Hematol 34(Suppl):48, 1997.
24. Adams RC, Lundy JS: Anesthesia in cases of poor surgical risk. Surg Gynecol Obstet 74:1011, 1942.
25. Lipsett PA, Perler B: The use of blood products for surgical bleeding. Semin Vasc Surg 9:347, 1996.
26. Ouriel K, Shortell CK, Green RM, et al: Intraoperative autotransfusion in aortic surgery. J Vasc Surg 18:16, 1993.
27. Triulzi DJ: Plasma alternatives. Transfusion Medicine Updates, Institute for Transfusion Medicine, Pittsburgh PA, 1997.
28. Cahill MR, Colvin BT: Haemophilia. Postgrad Med J 73:201, 1997.
29. Berntorp E, Boulyjemnkov V, Brettler D, et al: Modern treatment of haemophilia. Bull WHO 73:691, 1995.
30. Khamashta MA, Cuadrado MJ, Mujic F, et al: The management of thrombosis in the antiphospholipid antibody syndrome. N Engl J Med 332:993, 1995.
31. Rutledge R, Sheldon GF, Collins ML: Massive transfusion. Crit Care Clin 2:791, 1986.
32. Ratnoff OD: Some therapeutic agents influencing hemostasis. In Colman RW, Hirsch J, Marder VJ, et al (eds): Hemostasis and Thrombosis: Basic Principles and Clinical Practice. Philadelphia, JB Lippincott, 1994, p 1104.
33. Mannucci PM, Ruggeri ZM, Pareti FI, et al: 1-Deamino-8-D-arginine vasopressin: A new pharmacologic approach to the management of hemophilia and von Willebrand's disease. Lancet 1:869, 1987.
34. Sakarisen KS, Catteneo M, Van Den Berg A, et al: DDAVP enhances platelet adherence and platelet aggregate grown on human artery subendothelium. Blood 64:229, 1984.
35. Mannucci PM, Remuzzi G, Pusineri F, et al: Deamino-8-D-arginine vasopressin shortens the bleeding time in cardiac surgery. N Engl J Med 308:8, 1983.
36. Salzman EW, Weinstein MJ, Reilly D, et al: Adventures in hemostasis: Desmopressin in cardiac surgery. Arch Surg 128:212, 1993.
37. Nichols WC, Ginsburg D: von Willebrand disease. Medicine 76:1, 1997.
38. Shearer MJ: Vitamin K. Lancet 345:229, 1995.
39. Clagett GP: Desmopressin, hemostasis, and vascular surgery. Semin Vasc Surg 9:340, 1996.
40. Clagett GP, Valentine J, Myers SI: Does desmopressin improve hemostasis and reduce blood loss from aortic surgery? A randomized, double-blind study. J Vasc Surg 22:223, 1995.
41. Kobrinsky NL, Letts RM, Patel LR, et al: 1-Deamino-8-D-arginine vasopressin (desmopressin) decreases operative blood loss in patients having Harrington rod spinal fusion surgery. Ann Intern Med 107:446, 1987.
42. Thorp JA, Gaston L, Caspers DR, et al: Current concepts and controversies in the use of vitamin K. Drugs 49:376, 1995.
43. Gupta S, Veith FJ, Ascer E, et al: Anaphylactoid reactions to protamine: An often lethal complication in insulin-dependent patients undergoing vascular surgery. J Vasc Surg 9:342, 1989.
44. Morel DR, Zapol WM, Thomas SJ, et al: C5a and thromboxane generation associated with pulmonary vaso- and bronchoconstriction during protamine reversal of heparin. Anesthesiology 66:597, 1987.
45. Mauney MC, Buchanan SA, Lawrence WA: Stroke rate is markedly reduced after carotid endarterectomy by avoidance of protamine. J Vasc Surg 22:264, 1995.
46. Knape JT, Schuller JL, de Hann P, et al: An anaphylactic reaction to protamine in a patient allergic to fish. Anesthesiology 55:324, 1981.
47. Samuel T: Antibodies reacting with salmon and human protamines in sera from infertile men and from vasectomized men and monkeys. Clin Exp Immunol 30:181, 1977.
48. Levy J, Zaiden JR, Faraj B: Prospective evaluation of risk of protamine reactions in patients with NPH insulin dependent diabetes. Anesth Analg 65:739, 1986.
49. Levy J, Schweiger IM, Zaiden JR, et al: Evaluation of patients at risk for protamine reactions. J Thorac Cardiovasc Surg 98:200, 1989.
50. Wakefield T, Stanley JC: Intraoperative heparin anticoagulation and its reversal. Semin Vasc Surg 9:296, 1996.
51. Anderson MN, Mendelow M, Alfano GA: Experimental studies of heparin-protamine activity with special reference to protamine inhibition of clotting. Surgery 46:1060, 1959.
52. Teoh KH, Young E, Bradley CA, et al: Heparin binding proteins: Contribution to heparin rebound after cardiopulmonary bypass. Circulation 88:II-420, 1993.
53. Sherry S, Marder VJ: Therapy with antifibrinolytic agents. In Colman RW, Hirsch J, Marder VJ, et al (eds): Hemostasis and Thrombosis: Basic Principles and Clinical Practice. Philadelphia, JB Lippincott, 1994, p 335.
54. Alkjaersig N, Fletcher AP, Sherry S, et al: Epsilon-aminocaproic acid: An inhibitor of plasminogen activation. J Biol Chem 234:832, 1959.
55. de Peppo AP, Pierri MD, Scafuri A, et al: Intraoperative antifibrinolysis and blood-saving techniques in cardiac surgery: Prospective trial of 3 antifibrinolytic agents. Tex Heart Inst J 22:231, 1995.
56. Robert S, Wagner BKJ, Boulanger M, et al: Aprotinin. Ann Pharmacother 30:372, 1996.
57. Fritsma MG: Use of blood products and factor concentrates for coagulation therapy. Clin Lab Sci 16:115, 2003.
58. Seremetis SV, Aledort LM: Congenital bleeding disorders: Rational treatment options. Drugs 45:541, 1993.
59. Erhardtsen E: To general haemostasis—the evidence-based route. Pathophysiol Haemost Thromb 32(Suppl):47, 2002.
60. Hedner U: Recombinant factor VIIa (NovoSeven) as a hemostatic agent. Dis Mon 49:39, 2003.
61. Golub R, Cantu R, Sorrento J, et al: Efficacy of preadmission testing in ambulatory surgical patients. Anesth Analg 163:565, 1992.
62. Narr BJ, Hansen TR, Warner MA: Preoperative laboratory screening in healthy Mayo patients: Cost-effective elimination of tests and unchanged outcomes. Mayo Clin Proc 66:155, 1991.
63. Velanovich V: Preoperative laboratory evaluation. J Am Coll Surg 183:79, 1996.
64. Rapaport SI: Preoperative hemostatic evaluation: Which tests, if any? Blood 61:229, 1983.
65. Nurden AT, Nurden P: Inherited defects of platelet function. Rev Clin Exp Hematol 5:314, 2001.

66. Clemetson KJ, McGregor JL, James E, et al: Characterization of the platelet membrane glycoprotein abnormalities in Bernard-Soulier syndrome and comparison with normal by surface-labeling techniques and high-resolution two-dimensional gel electrophoresis. J Clin Invest 70:304, 1982.
67. Lopez JA, Andrews RK, Afshar-Kharghan V, et al: Bernard-Soulier syndrome. Blood 91:4397, 1998.
68. Nair S, Ghosh K, Kulkami B, et al: Glanzmann's thrombasthenia: Updated. Platelets 13:387, 2002.
69. Levy-Toledano S, Caen JP, Breton-Gorius J, et al: Gray platelet syndrome: α-granule deficiency: Its influence on platelet function. J Lab Clin Med 98:831, 1981.
70. Hayward CP, Cramer EM, Kane WH, et al: Studies of a second family with the Quebec platelet disorder: Evidence that the degradation of the alpha-granule membrane and its soluble contents are not secondary to a defect in targeting proteins to alpha-granules. Blood 89:1243, 1997.
71. Pfueller SL, Howard MA, White JG, et al: Shortening of bleeding time by 1-deamino-8-arginine vasopressin (DDAVP) in the absence of platelet von Willebrand factor in Gray platelet syndrome. Thromb Haemost 58:1060, 1987.
72. Weiss HJ, Lages B, Vicic W, et al: Heterogeneous abnormalities of platelet dense granule ultrastructure in 20 patients with congenital storage pool deficiency. Br J Haematol 83:282, 1993.
73. Remold-O'Donnell E, Rosen FS, Kenney DM: Defects in Wiskott-Aldrich syndrome blood cells. Blood 87:2621, 1996.
74. Oda A, Ochs HD: Wiskott-Aldrich syndrome protein and platelets. Immunol Rev 178:111, 2000.
75. Huizig M, Anikster V, Gahl WA: Molecular genetics of the Hermansky-Pudlack and Chediak-Higashi syndromes. Thromb Haemost 86:234, 2001.
76. Nieuwenhuis HK, Akkeman JW, Sixma JJ: Patients with a prolonged bleeding time and normal aggregation tests may have storage pool deficiency: studies on one hundred six patients. Blood 70:620, 1987.
77. Nieuwenhuis HK, Sixma JJ: 1-Desamino-8-D-arginine vasopressin (desmopressin) shortens the bleeding time in storage pool deficiency. Ann Intern Med 108:65, 1988.
78. Gerritsen SW, Akkerman JW, Sixma JJ: Correction of the bleeding time in patients with storage pool deficiency by infusion of cryo-precipitate. Br J Haematol 40:153, 1978.
79. Rodeghiero F, Castaman GC, Dini E: Epidemiological investigation of the prevalence of von Willebrand's disease. Blood 69:454, 1987.
80. Miller CH, Lenzi R, Breen C: Prevalence of von Willebrand's disease among US adults. Blood 70:377, 1987.
81. Budde U, Schneppenheim R: von Willebrand factor and von Willebrand disease. Rev Clin Exp Hematol 5:335, 2001.
82. Sadler EJ: A revised classification of von Willebrand disease. Thromb Haemost 71:520, 1994.
83. Sadler EJ, Gralnick HR: Commentary: A new classification for von Willebrand disease. Blood 84:676, 1994.
84. Mauz-Korholz C, Budde U, Korholz D, et al: DDAVP treatment in a child with von Willebrand disease type 2M. Eur J Pediatr 158:S174, 1999.
85. Mazurier C, Gaucher C, Jorieaux S, et al: Biological effect of desmopressin in eight patients with type 2N von Willebrand disease. Br J Haematol 45:36, 1994.
86. Mannucci PM, Lattuada A, Ruggeri ZM: Proteolysis of von Willebrand factor in therapeutic plasma concentrates. Blood 83:3018, 1994.
87. Castillo R, Monteagudo J, Escolar G, et al: Hemostatic effect of normal platelet transfusion in severe von Willebrand disease. Blood 77:1901, 1991.
88. Hoyer LW: Hemophilia A. N Engl J Med 330:38, 1994.
89. Bolton-Maggs PHB, Pasi KJ: Haemophilias A and B. Lancet 361:1801, 2003.
90. Klinge J, Ananyeva NM, Hauser CAE, et al: Hemophilia A—from basic science to clinical practice. Semin Thromb Hemost 28:309, 2002.
91. Rodriguez-Merchan EC: Common orthopedic problems in hemophilia. Hemophilia 5:53, 1999.
92. Shopnick RI, Brettler DB: Hemostasis: A practical review of conservative and operative care. Clin Orthop 328:34, 1996.
93. Post M, Telfer MD: Surgery in hemophiliac patients. J Bone Joint Surg Am 57A:1136, 1975.
94. Hermens WT: Dose calculation of human factor VIII and factor IX concentrates for infusion therapy. In Brinkhous KM, Hemker HC (eds): Handbook for Hemophilia. New York, Elsevier America, 1975, p 569.
95. Tagariello G, Davoli PG, Gajo GB, et al: Safety and efficacy of high-purity concentrates in haemophiliac patients undergoing surgery by continuous infusion. Haemophilia 5:426, 1999.
96. Dingli D, Gastineau DA, Gilchrist GS, et al: Continuous factor VIII infusion therapy in patients with haemophilia A undergoing surgical procedures with plasma-derived or recombinant factor VIII concentrates. Haemophilia 8:629, 2002.
97. Roberts HR, Eberst ME: Current management of hemophilia B. Hematol Oncol Clin North Am 7:1269, 1993.
98. Ludlam CA, Smith MP, Morfini M, et al: A prospective study of recombinant activated factor VII administered by continuous infusion to inhibitor patients undergoing elective major orthopaedic surgery: A pharmacokinetic and efficacy evaluation. Br J Haematol 120:808, 2003.
99. Bolton-Maggs PHB: The management of factor XI deficiency. Haemophilia 4:683, 1998.
100. Seligsohn U: Factor XI deficiency. Thromb Haemost 70:68, 1993.
101. Rapaport SI, Proctor RR, Patch MJ, et al: The mode of inheritance of PTA deficiency: Evidence for the existence of major PTA deficiency and minor PTA deficiency. Blood 18:149, 1961.
102. Leiba H, Ramot B, Many A: Heredity and coagulation studies in ten families with factor XI (plasma thromboplastin antecedent) deficiency. Br J Haematol 11:654, 1965.
103. Yee TT, Beeton K, Griffioen A, et al: Experience of prophylaxis treatment in children with severe haemophilia. Haemophilia 8:76, 2002.
104. Van Den Berg HM, Fischer K, Van Der Bom JG, et al: Effects of prophlyactic treatment regimens in children with severe haemophilia: A comparison of different strategies. Haemophilia 8:43, 2003.
105. Miners AH, Sabin CA, Tolley KH, et al: Assessing the effectiveness and cost-effectiveness of prophylaxis against bleeding in patients with severe haemophilia and severe von Willebrand's disease. J Intern Med 244:515, 1998.
106. Kay MA, Manno CS, Ragni MV, et al: Evidence for gene transfer and expression of factor IX in hemophilia B patients treated with an AAV vector. Nat Genet 24:257, 2000.
107. Roth DA, Tawa NE, O'Brien J, et al: Non-viral transfer of the gene encoding coagulation factor VIII in patients with severe hemophilia A. N Engl J Med 344:1735, 2001.
108. Powell JS, Ragni MV, White GC, et al: Phase I trial of FVIII gene transfer for severe hemophilia A using a retroviral construct administered by peripheral intravenous injection. Thromb Haemost 86(Suppl):OC2489, 2001.
109. Lodi S, Isa L, Pollini E, et al: Defective intrinsic fibrinolytic activity in a patient with severe factor XII-deficiency and myocardial infarction. Scand J Haematol 33:80, 1984.
110. Loewy AG, McDonargh J, Mikkola H, et al: Structure and function of factor XIII. In Colman RW, Hirsch J, Marder VJ, et al (eds): Hemostasis and Thrombosis: Basic Principles and Clinical Practice. Philadelphia, Lippincott Williams & Wilkins, 2001, p 231.
111. Roberts HR, Lefkowitz JB: Inherited disorders of prothrombin conversion. In Colman RW, Hirsch J, Marder VJ, et al (eds): Hemostasis and Thrombosis: Basic Principles and Clinical Practice. Philadelphia, JB Lippincott, 1994, p 314.
112. Kumar S, Pruthi RK, Nichols WL: Acquired von Willebrand disease. Mayo Clin Proc 77:181, 2002.

113. Castaman G, Lattuada A, Mannucci PM, et al: Characterization of two cases of acquired transitory von Willebrand syndrome with ciprofloxacin: Evidence for heightened proteolysis of von Willebrand factor. Am J Hematol 49:83, 1995.
114. Kreuz W, Linde R, Funk M, et al: Induction of von Willebrand disease type I by valproic acid. Lancet 335:1350, 1990.
115. Bruggers CS, McElligott K, Rallison ML: Acquired von Willebrand disease in twins with autoimmune hypothyroidism: Response to desmopressin and L-thyroxine therapy. J Pediatr 125:911, 1994.
116. Yoshida H, Arai K, Wakashin M: Development of acquired von Willebrand's disease after mixed connective tissue disease. Am J Med 85:445, 1988.
117. Boggio LN, Green D: Acquired hemophilia. Rev Clin Exp Hematol 5:389, 2001.
118. Sallah S: Inhibitors to clotting factors. Ann Hematol 75:1, 1997.
119. Feinstein DI: Immune coagulation disorders. In Colman RW, Hirsch J, Marder VJ, et al (eds): Hemostasis and Thrombosis: Basic Principles and Clinical Practice. Philadelphia, JB Lippincott, 1994, p 881.
120. Chong L, Wong Y: A case of factor V inhibitor. Am J Hematol 19:395, 1985.
121. Weisdorf D, Hasegawa D, Fair D: Acquired factor VII deficiency associated with aplastic anaemia: Correction with bone marrow transplantation. Br J Haematol 71:409, 1989.
122. Daly H, Carson P, Smith J: Intracerebral haemorrhage due to acquired factor XIII inhibitor—successful response to factor XIII concentrate. Blood Coagul Fibrinolysis 2:507, 1991.
123. Reece EA, Clyne LP, Romero R, et al: Spontaneous factor XI inhibitors: Seven additional cases and a review of the literature. Arch Intern Med 114:525, 1984.
124. Green D, Lechner K: A survey of 215 non-hemophilic patients with inhibitors to factor VIII. Thromb Haemost 45:200, 1981.
125. Hauser I, Schneider B, Lechner K: Post-partum factor VIII inhibitors: A review of the literature with special reference to the value of steroid and immunosupressive treatment. Thromb Haemost 73:1, 1995.
126. Kasper C, Aledort L, Counts R: A more uniform measurement of factor VIII inhibitors. Thromb Diath Haemorrh 34:869, 1975.
127. Green D, Rademaker A, Briet E: A prospective, randomized trial of prednisone and cyclophosphamide in the treatment of patients with factor VIII autoantibodies. Thromb Haemost 70:753, 1993.
128. Fuse I: Disorders of platelet function. Crit Rev Oncol Hematol 22:1, 1996.
129. Remuzzi G: Bleeding in renal failure. Lancet 1:1205, 1988.
130. Baglin T: Disseminated intravascular coagulation: Diagnosis and treatment. BMJ 312:683, 1996.
131. Francis RB: Clinical disorders of fibrinolysis: A critical review. Blut 59:1, 1989.
132. Lechner K, Niessner H, Thaler E: Coagulation abnormalities in liver disease. Semin Thromb Hemost 4:40, 1977.
133. Hersh S, Kunelis T, Francis RB, et al: Pathogenesis of accelerated fibrinolysis in liver cirrhosis. Blood 69:1315, 1987.
134. Rock WA: Laboratory assessment of coagulation disorders in liver disease. Clin Lab Med 4:419, 1984.
135. Joist JH: Hemostatic abnormalities in liver disease. In Colman RW, Hirsch J, Marder VJ, et al (eds): Hemostasis and Thrombosis: Basic Principles and Clinical Practice. Philadelphia, JB Lippincott, 1994, p 906.
136. Levi M, de Jonge E, van der Poll R, et al: Disseminated intravascular coagulation. Thromb Haemost 82:695, 1999.
137. Bone RC: Gram-positive organisms and sepsis. Arch Intern Med 154:26, 1994.
138. Gando S: Disseminated intravascular coagulation in trauma patients. Semin Thromb Hemost 27:585, 2001.
139. Scherer RU, Spangenberg P: Procoagulant activity in patients with isolated head trauma. Crit Care Med 26:156, 1998.
140. Gibney EJ, Bouchier-Hayes D: Coagulopathy and abdominal aortic aneurysm. Eur J Vasc Surg 4:557, 1990.
141. Szlachetka DM: Kasabach-Merrit syndrome: A case review. Neonat Network 17:7, 1998.
142. ten Cate H, Timmerman JJ, Levi M: The pathophysiology of disseminated intravascular coagulation. Thromb Haemost 82:713, 1999.
143. Thijs LG, de Boer JP, de Groot MCM, et al: Coagulation disorders in septic shock. Intensive Care Med 19(Suppl):S8, 1993.
144. Levi M, van der Poll R, ten Cate H, et al: The cytokine-mediated imbalance between coagulant and anticoagulant mechanisms in sepsis and endotoxaemia. Eur J Clin Invest 27:3, 1997.
145. Biemond BJ, Levi M, ten Cate H, et al: Plasminogen activator and plasminogen activator inhibitor I release during experimental endotoxaemia in chimpanzees: Effect of interventions in the cytokine and coagulation cascades. Clin Sci 88:587, 1995.
146. Williams E: Disseminated intravascular coagulation. In Loscalzo J, Schafer A (eds): Thrombosis and Hemorrhage. Boston, Blackwell Science, 1994, p 1023.
147. Hesselvik JF, Blomback M, Brodin B, et al: Coagulation, fibrinolysis, and kallikrein systems in sepsis. Crit Care Med 17:724, 1989.
148. Atik M: Hemostasis and thr ıbosis. In Peters RM, Peacock EE, Benfield JR (eds): The Scientific Management of the Surgical Patient. Boston, Little, Brown, 1983, p 229.
149. Weitz JI, Leslie B, Ginsberg J: Soluble FDP potentiates tissue plasminogen activator-induced fibrinogen proteolysis. J Clin Invest 87:1082, 1991.
150. Muller-Berghaus G, ten Cate H, Levi M: Disseminated intravascular coagulation: Clinical spectrum and established as well as new diagnostic approaches. Thromb Haemost 82:706, 1999.
151. Eagleton MJ, Illig KA, Riggs PN, et al: Visceral perfusion ameliorates primary fibrinolysis during supraceliac aortic cross-clamping. Surg Forum 48:419, 1997.
152. Declerck PJ, Juhan-Vague I, Felez J, et al: Pathophysiology of fibrinolysis. J Intern Med 236:425, 1994.
153. Francis CW, Marder VJ: Mechanisms of fibrinolysis. In Beutler E, Lichtman MA, Coller BS, et al (eds): Williams' Hematology. New York, McGraw-Hill, 1995, p 1252.
154. Dzik WH, Arkin CF, Jenkins RL, et al: Fibrinolysis during liver transplantation in humans: Role of tissue-type plasminogen activator. Blood 71:1090, 1988.
155. Illig KA, Ouriel K: Ancrod: Understanding the agent. Semin Vasc Surg 9:303, 1996.
156. Collen D, Lijnen HR, Todd PA, et al: Tissue-type plasminogen activator: A review of its pharmacology and therapeutic use as a thrombolytic agent. Drugs 38:346, 1989.
157. Hirsch J, Raschke R, Warkentin TE, et al: Mechanisms of action, pharmacokinetics, dosing considerations, monitoring, efficacy, and safety. Chest 108(Suppl):258S, 1995.
158. Donayre CE: Current use of low molecular weight heparins. Semin Vasc Surg 9:362, 1996.
159. Makris M, Hough RW, Kitchen S: Poor reversal of low molecular weight heparin by protamine. Br J Haematol 108:884, 2000.
160. Weitz JI, Leslie B, Hudoba M: Thrombin binds to soluble fibrin degradation products where it is protected from inhibition by heparin-antithrombin but susceptible to inactivation by antithrombin-independent inhibitors. Circulation 97:544, 1998.
161. Weitz JI, Hirsh J: New anticoagulant drugs. Chest 119(Suppl):95S, 2001.
162. Nowak G: Pharmacology of recombinant hirudin. Semin Thromb Hemost 28:415, 2002.
163. Gustafsson D, Nystrom J-E, Carlsson S, et al: Pharmacodynamic properties of H376/95, a prodrug of the direct thrombin inhibitor melagatran, intended for oral use. Blood 94:26a, 1999.
164. Brady SF, Stauffer KJ, Lumma WC, et al: Discovery and development of the novel potent orally active thrombin inhibitor N-(9-hydroxy-9-

fluorenecarboxy)prolyl trans-4-aminocyclohexyl-methyl amide (L-372,460): Coapplication of structure-based design and rapid multiple analogue synthesis on solid support. J Med Chem 41:401, 1998.
165. Hirsch J, Dalen JE, Deykin D, et al: Oral anticoagulants: Mechanism of action, clinical effectiveness, and optimal therapeutic range. Chest 108(Suppl):231S, 1995.
166. Schafer AI: Effects of nonsteroidal antiinflammatory drugs on platelet function and systemic hemostasis. J Clin Pharmacol 35:209, 1995.
167. Limentani SA, Furie BC, Furie B, et al: The biochemistry of factor IX. In Colman RW, Hirsch J, Marder VJ, et al (eds): Hemostasis and Thrombosis: Basic Principles and Clinical Practice. Philadelphia, JB Lippincott, 1994, p 94.
168. Tuman KJ, McCarthy RJ, O'Connor CJ, et al: Aspirin does not increase allogenic blood transfusion in reoperative coronary artery surgery. Anesth Analg 83:1178, 1996.
169. Ferraris VA, Ferraris SP: Preoperative aspirin ingestion increases operative blood loss after coronary artery bypass grafting (update). Ann Thorac Surg 59:1036, 1995.
170. Antiplatelet Trialists' Collaboration: Collaborative overview of randomized trials of antiplatelet therapy: II. Maintenance of vascular graft or arterial patency by antiplatelet therapy. BMJ 308:159, 1994.
171. Hobson RW, Krupski WC, Weiss DG: Influence of aspirin in the management of asymptomatic carotid artery stenosis. J Vasc Surg 17:257, 1993.
172. ISIS-2 (Second International Study of Infarct Survival) Collaborative Group: Randomised trial of intravenous streptokinase, oral aspirin, both, or neither among 17,187 cases of suspected acute myocardial infarction: ISIS-s. Lancet 2:349, 1988.
173. Steering Committee of the Physicians' Health Study Research Group: Final report on the aspirin component of the ongoing physicians' health study. N Engl J Med 321:129, 1989.
174. Merritt JC, Bhatt DL: The efficacy and safety of perioperative antiplatelet therapy. J Thromb Thrombolysis 13:97, 2002.
175. Nurden AT, Poujol C, Durrieau-Jais C, et al: Platelet glycoprotein IIb/IIIa inhibitors: Basic and clinical aspects. Arterioscler Thromb Vasc Biol 19:2835, 1999.
176. Harrington RA, Kleiman NS, Kottke Marchant K, et al: Immediate and reversible platelet inhibition after intravenous administration of a peptide glycoprotein IIb/IIIa inhibitor during percutaneous intervention. Am J Cardiol 76:1222, 1995.
177. Hamm CW: Anti-integrin therapy. Annu Rev Med 54:425, 2003.
178. Vorchheimer DA, Fuster V: Oral platelet glycoprotein IIb/IIIa receptor antagonists: The present challenge is safety. Circulation 97:312, 1998.
179. Blankenship JC: Bleeding complications of glycoprotein IIb-IIIa receptor inhibitors. Am Heart J 138:S287-S296, 1999.
180. Kandarpa K: Complications of local intraarterial thrombolysis for lower extremity occlusions. In Ouriel K (ed): Lower Extremity Vascular Disease. Philadelphia, WB Saunders, 1995, p 359.
181. Ferrera A, MacArthur JD, Wright HK, et al: Hypothermia and acidosis worsen coagulopathy in the patient requiring massive transfusion. Am J Surg 160:515, 1990.
182. Reed RL, Johnston TD, Hudson JD, et al: The disparity between hypothermic coagulopathy and clotting studies. J Trauma 33:465, 1992.
183. Yoshihara H, Yamamoto T, Mihara H: Changes in coagulation and fibrinolysis occurring in dogs during hypothermia. Thromb Res 37:503, 1985.
184. Valeri CR: Hypothermia-induced reversible platelet dysfunction. Ann Surg 205:175, 1987.
185. Watts DD, Trask A, Soeken K, et al: Hypothermic coagulopathy in trauma: Effect of varying levels of hypothermia on enzyme speed, platelet function, and fibrinolytic activity. J Trauma 44:846, 1998.
186. Edmunds LH: Blood-surface interactions during cardiopulmonary bypass. J Card Surg 8:404, 1993.
187. Woodman RC, Harker LA: Bleeding complications associated with cardiopulmonary bypass. Blood 76:1680, 1990.
188. Clagett GP, Russo M, Hufnagel H: Platelet changes after placement of aortic prosthesis in dogs: I. Biochemical and functional alterations. J Lab Clin Med 97:345, 1981.
189. Harker LA, Slichter SJ, Sauvage LR: Platelet changes after placement of aortic prostheses: The effects of endothelialization and pharmacologic inhibition of platelet function. Ann Surg 186:594, 1977.
190. Mullins RJ, Huckfeldt R, Trunkey DD: Abdominal vascular injuries. Surg Clin North Am 76:813, 1996.
191. Aucar JA, Hirshberg A: Damage control for vascular injuries. Surg Clin North Am 77:853, 1997.
192. Mankad PS, Odispoti MC: The role of fibrin sealants in hemostasis. Am J Surg 182(Suppl):21S, 2001.
193. Rotondo MF, Zonies DH: The damage control sequence and underlying logic. Surg Clin North Am 77:761, 1997.

Chapter

34

Vascular Thrombosis Due to Hypercoagulable States

PETER K. HENKE, MD
ALVIN SCHMAIER, MD
THOMAS W. WAKEFIELD, MD

Section VI

Thrombosis is a major of cause of death throughout the world. Myocardial infarction (MI) and stroke, which are arterial thromboses, are the number one and two causes of death worldwide and the number one and three causes of death in developed nations. Arterial and venous thrombosis represents a shift in the balance in regulation between procoagulant, anticoagulant, and fibrinolytic systems. The molecular causes of thrombosis also are influenced by blood flow rates, pressure, and vessel origin. The genesis of thrombosis may be due to various organ, tissue, cellular, protein, or molecular defects. Clinical investigations have shown several molecular defects that increase a patient's risk for the clinical manifestation of thrombosis in 18% to 30% of all cases of venous thromboembolism (VTE).[61,108,110] Although atherosclerosis and venous thrombosis are associated,[96] arterial thromboses are less likely to be due to inherited hypercoagulability than to environmental and acquired risk factors.

Causes for thrombosis can be classified on the basis of the anatomic site (arterial versus venous), frequency, or likelihood for thrombosis when there is a predisposing factor (Tables 34-1 and 34-2). There is increased awareness of the fact that many hypercoagulable states are multigenetic; however, environmental factors contribute to when, how, and to what extent these states manifest as a thrombotic clinical event. This fact is highlighted by the realization that many hemostatic factor–genetic polymorphisms exist, but few have clinically perceptible consequences.[34,61,64,108] One may argue that the presentation of thrombosis is the summation of risk factors. Treatment decisions depend on the specific hypercoagulable disorder and the severity of risk causing the thrombotic event. The combination of age, genetic predisposition, and environmental factors contributes to the presentation of clinical manifestations.[100,110] The clinical presentation of thrombosis is a multifactorial event, demonstrating the breakdown of many fail-safe mechanisms preserving the constitutive anticoagulant nature of the intravascular compartment.

To begin to understand the mechanisms that account for abnormal hypercoagulability, it is important to recall the normal coagulant and fibrinolytic pathways depicted in Figure 34-1.[109] In this schematic, the known potential factor abnormalities in the balance of the coagulation and fibrinolytic systems are highlighted.[17] In the coagulation system, elevations of coagulant factors and fibrinogen are associated with increased risk for thrombosis on an epidemiologic basis. Alternatively in the fibrinolytic system, abnormal plasminogens (dysplasminogenemia) and elevations of plasminogen activator inhibitor 1 (PAI-1) are associated with increased risk for thrombosis. Although defects or deficiencies in tissue plasminogen activator (t-PA)

Table 34-1 Thrombosis Due to Hypercoagulable States

ARTERIAL	ARTERIAL AND VENOUS	VENOUS
Elevated fibrinogen	Hyperhomocysteinemia	Antithrombin
Abnormal platelet aggregation	HIT/HITTS Antiphospholipid Ab	Protein C Protein S
Atherosclerosis	Elevated PAI-1	Factor V Leiden
Lipoprotein(a)		Prothrombin G20210A Dysfibrinogenemia Elevated factors XI, IX, VIII

HIT/HITTS, heparin-induced thrombocytopenia/heparin-induced thrombocytopenia and thrombosis syndrome; PAI-1, plasminogen activator inhibitor 1.

Table 34-2 Venous Thromboembolism Due to Hypercoagulable States

FREQUENCY	SEVERITY
Factor V Leiden (20-60%)	**High Risk for Thrombosis**
Hyperhomocysteinemia (10%)	Antithrombin deficiency
Prothrombin G20210A (4-6%)	Protein C deficiency
Protein C deficiency (3-5%)	Protein S deficiency
Protein S deficiency (2-3%)	HIT/HITTS
Dysfibrinogenemia (1-3%)	Antiphospholipid Ab syndrome
Antithrombin (1-2%)	
Dysplasminogenemia (<1%)	**Lower Risk for Thrombosis**
	Factor V Leiden
	Hyperhomocysteinemia
	Prothrombin G20210A
	Dysfibrinogenemia
	Dysplasminogenemia
	Elevated factors VIII, IX, XI

HIT/HITTS, heparin-induced thrombocytopenia/heparin-induced thrombocytopenia and thrombosis syndrome.

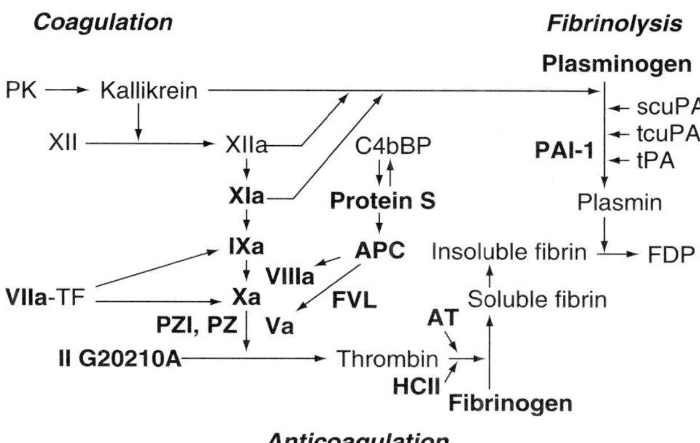

FIGURE 34-1 The biochemistry of thrombosis. This figure represents the proteins that participate in the biochemistry of venous thrombosis and indicates the proteins of the coagulation, fibrinolytic, and anticoagulant systems whose deficiencies, defects, or elevations are associated with increased risk for thrombosis. The proteins whose alteration in structure or increase or decrease in their level is associated with increased risk for venous thromboembolism are shown in bold. APC, activated protein C; AT, antithrombin; C4bBP, C4b binding protein; FDP, fibrin degradation products; FVL, factor V Leiden; HCII, heparin cofactor II; II G20210A, prothrombin G20210A; IXa, activated factor IX; PAI-1, plasminogen activator inhibitor-1; PK, prekallikrein, kallikrein, plasma kallikrein; PZ, protein Z; PZI, protein Z inhibitor; scuPA, single-chain urokinase plasminogen activator; tcuPA, two-chain urokinase plasminogen activator; tPA, tissue-type plasminogen activator; Va, activated factor V, VIIa-TF, activated factor VII in complex with tissue factor; VIIIa, activated factor VIII; Xa, activated factor X; XII, factor XII; XIa, activated factor XI; XIIa, activated factor XII.

and urokinase plasminogen activator have not been described in humans to date, alterations in these proteins also could contribute to thrombosis.

Changes in the natural anticoagulant system also contribute to thrombosis. The major anticoagulant system in vivo is the protein C and S system. Deficiencies or defects in protein C result in an enzyme that is less capable of degrading the activated cofactors, factors VIIIa and Va, which serve to create more thrombin. Activated protein C (APC) binds to endothelial cell protein C receptor to activate protease-activated receptor 1, resulting in increased fibrinolysis from t-PA liberation. Likewise, defects or deficiencies in protein S result in a reduced cofactor role of this protein to support APC from degrading factors VIIIa and Va. The anticoagulation system also consists of a group of SERPINS, serine protease inhibitors, which are important modulators of the hemostatic and fibrinolytic systems. Antithrombin (AT), formerly called *antithrombin III,* is the major SERPIN regulator of the hemostatic system. In the presence of heparin, AT inhibits factors IIa (thrombin), Xa, IXa, VIIa, XIa, and XIIa and plasma kallikrein.[17] Heparin cofactor II in the presence of dermatan sulfate is a specific inhibitor of thrombin. Protein Z inhibitor (PZI) in the presence of the vitamin K–dependent protein, protein Z (PZI), is a specific inhibitor of factor Xa. Tissue factor pathway inhibitor, also called *lipoprotein-associated coagulation inhibitor,* inhibits factor VIIa–tissue factor in a quaternary complex with factor X or Xa.[28] Although much is known about the biochemistry related to thrombosis, much less is known about the factors that contribute to the thrombotic event. This chapter focuses on the evaluation and treatment of prothrombotic disorders as they relate to pathologic venous and, to a lesser extent, arterial thrombosis.

ARTERIAL VERSUS VENOUS THROMBOSIS

Histologically, arterial thrombi typically are termed "white clots" because they are platelet rich.[45] In low-flow vessels, such as veins, the initial platelet plug may not be detected, and the clots are red, based on the trapping of red blood cells in the fibrin strands. As first described by Virchow in the 1850s,[129] most individuals who present with VTE have one or more clinical risk factors, such as vessel wall damage, stasis of blood, or activation of the coagulation (or reduction of fibrinolytic activation).

Hypercoagulability and stasis have a lesser role in arterial thrombosis but a major role in VTE. Possible specific risk factors for arterial thromboses include elevations of factor VII, fibrinogen, lipoprotein (a), and homocysteine metabolism.[50,60] Arterial thrombosis usually manifests with large vessel occlusions that result in MI, stroke, peripheral vascular occlusive disease, and other end-organ ischemic insults. Although numerous coagulation factor genetic polymorphisms exist that may be related to an increased risk of arterial thromboembolism, few have proved to be predictive in large population analyses.[60,61,64] When factor VII has been found to be elevated, no consistent clinical manifestation pattern in venous or arterial thrombosis has emerged.[60] Also, a comparison of specific factor VII polymorphisms and MI have shown protective polymorphisms, but none associated with increased thrombotic risk.[38] Overall, primary arterial thrombosis in a healthy vessel is rare. Arterial thromboses are associated with atherosclerotic vessel changes, in a setting of specific risk factors, such as diabetes, hyperlipidemia, or tobacco use. Arterial thrombosis also is seen in acquired procoagulant states, such as antiphospholipid antibody syndromes or heparin-induced thrombocytopenia and thrombosis syndrome (HITTS), also known as heparin-induced thrombocytopenia (HIT).

The classic protein deficiencies associated with VTE include AT and protein C and S deficiencies. More common protein and gene defects associated with thrombosis but having a less prothrombotic state include resistance to APC (factor V Leiden), hyperhomocysteinemia, and prothrombin G20210A. Resistance to APC and prothrombin G20210A often co-segregates, which increases the risk of VTE significantly.[5,20,108,110] Less common causes for thrombosis include abnormal fibrinogens and plasminogens.[85] Elevation of factors XI, IX, and VIII also are associated with increased risk for VTE in population studies. Lastly, a subset of hypercoagulable disorders that are not discussed in this chapter includes hematologic conditions, such as thrombotic thrombocytic purpura, hemolytic uremic syndrome, disseminated intravascular coagulation (DIC), and the myeloproliferative disorders polycythemia vera and essential thrombocythemia.

ACQUIRED RISK FACTORS FOR VENOUS THROMBOSIS

The acquired risk factors for VTE are well known (Table 34-3) and include advanced age,[106,108] prolonged immobility, obesity, chronic neurologic disease, cardiac disease, pregnancy, oral contraceptive use,[137] hormone supplemental therapy,[135] surgery,[100] trauma, malignancy,[89] nephrotic syndrome, and prior VTE. Subclinical hypoxemia induces an endothelial cell procoagulant response that may be exacerbated by a postsurgical state or advanced age.[136] Specific surgical procedures that are associated with increased risk include orthopedic procedures, such as knee and hip replacement; thoracoabdominal procedures; and urologic and gynecologic procedures. A strong relationship exists between VTE and malignancy, and occult cancer may be present in 0.5% to 5.8% of patients who present primarily with a VTE.[6] Idiopathic VTE is associated with a threefold increased likelihood of presenting with malignancy within 3 years, and 19% of cancer patients have clinical thrombotic events.[89] Chemotherapeutic treatment for malignancy also increases the risk of recurrent VTE, especially if the patient is neutropenic,[72] by elevating thrombus potential through tissue factor and E-selectin expression.[6,62]

A careful history and physical examination allow the physician to decide best whom to test for a hypercoagulable state (Table 34-4) and what tests to order (Fig. 34-2).[18,24,52,110] Last, screening of relatives of thrombophilic patients, especially patients with defects considered high risk for thrombosis, may be worthwhile, especially to administer prophylaxis during high-risk periods, rather than prophylactic lifelong therapy.[65]

DEFECTS WITH HIGH RISK FOR THROMBOSIS

Antithrombin Deficiency

Site

Venous more likely than arterial.

Mechanism

AT is a serine protease inhibitor (SERPIN) of thrombin; kallikrein; and factors Xa, IXa, VIIa, XIIa, and XIa that is synthesized in the liver. It has a half-life of 2.8 days. AT

Table 34-3 Acquired Risk Factors for Venous Thrombosis

Old age
Prolonged immobility
Obesity
Chronic neurologic disease
Cardiac disease
Pregnancy
Oral contraceptives
Hormones
Surgery
Trauma
Malignancy
Nephrotic syndrome
Prior venous thromboembolism

Table 34-4 Markers for and Components of Laboratory Evaluation for Hypercoagulable States

MARKERS	COMPONENTS OF LABORATORY EVALUATION
Unusual thrombus location	Antithrombin activity and antigen assay
Recurrent idiopathic VTE	Protein C activity and antigen assay
VTE at an early age (≤30)	Free protein S antigen assay
Strong family history and first event	APC resistance assay and factor V Leiden by PCR
Women with multiple stillbirths or abortions	Prothrombin G20210A by PCR
	Homocysteine level
	Antiphospholipid or anticardiolipin antibodies
	β_2 glycoprotein I antibodies
	Clottable fibrinogen and fibrinogen antigen
	Dilute Russell viper venom time
	Tissue thromboplastin inhibition time
	Lipoprotein (a) level
	aPTT
	PT
	D dimer

APC, activated protein C; aPTT, activated partial thromboplastin time; PCR, polymerase chain reaction; PT, prothrombin time; VTE, venous thromboembolism.

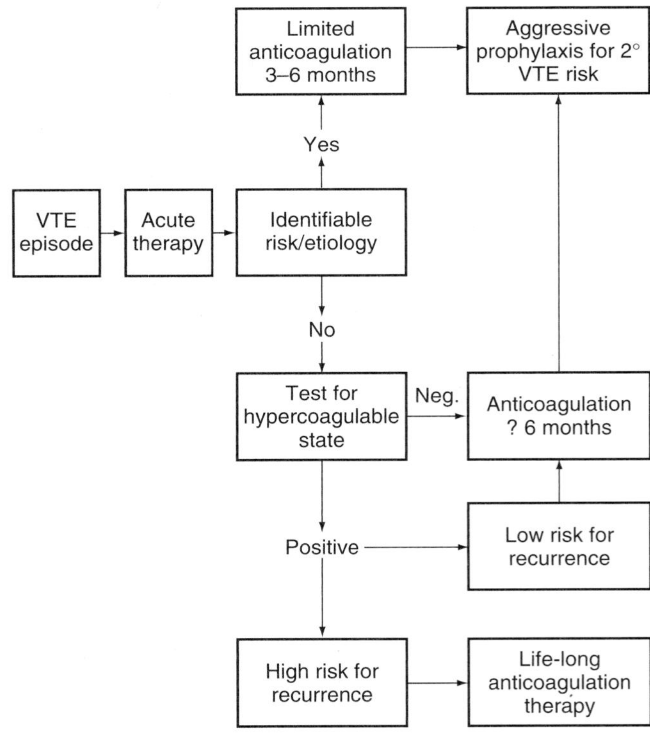

FIGURE 34-2 A suggested algorithm for treatment of patients with suspected hypercoagulable states. When a venous thromboembolism (VTE) episode is defined, standard-of-care anticoagulation is started. If a risk factor is identified, generally 3 to 6 months of oral anticoagulation is recommended. If no identifiable risk factor is present, a laboratory-based evaluation for a hypercoagulable state should be done (see Table 34-4). If negative, the diagnosis is "idiopathic," and at least 6 months of oral anticoagulation is completed. If a hypercoagulable state is identified, duration of oral anticoagulation (6 months or lifelong) depends on the specific state, the risk of recurrence, and patient-specific states. All patients with one VTE episode need aggressive prophylaxis to prevent VTE recurrence in high-risk situations (e.g., major surgery and prolonged immobility).

deficiency, either congenital (autosomal dominant) or acquired, accounts for approximately 1% to 2% of episodes of VTE and may occur at unusual anatomic sites, such as mesenteric or cerebral veins. Instances of arterial and graft thrombosis also have been described in AT deficiency.[32,118] This defect is a significant risk factor for recurrent, life-threatening thrombosis with manifestations early in life, with most cases apparent by 50 years of age.[93] Heparin is an anticoagulant because of its ability to potentiate the anticoagulant effects of AT.[48] AT deficiency is suspected if heparin is unable to produce anticoagulation or heparin fails to prevent thrombus recurrence or extension. Homozygous individuals usually die in utero, whereas heterozygous patients usually have AT levels less than 70% of normal. Causes of acquired AT deficiency include liver disease, malignancy, sepsis,[95] DIC, malnutrition, and renal disease.[32] The nephrotic syndrome is associated with AT (relative molecular mass [M_r] = 59 kD) deficiency because of the loss of intermediate-sized proteins into the urine along with albumin (M_r = 68 kD), with potential thrombosis of renal veins and arterial bypass grafts.[112] Less frequent causes of AT deficiency include defective AT activity with normal quantitative levels (an abnormal protein) and AT deficiency with an abnormal interaction between AT and heparin.[26]

Diagnosis

The diagnosis should be suspected in a patient who cannot be adequately anticoagulated on heparin (i.e., heparin resistant) or who develops thrombosis while taking heparin. The diagnosis is made by measuring AT antigen and activity levels when a patient has not been exposed to heparin or related compounds for at least 2 weeks. Heparin therapy decreases AT levels 30%, and this effect can be seen 10 days after stopping intravenous heparin therapy.[18] Conversely, warfarin may increase AT levels.

Treatment

Anticoagulation with heparin usually requires the administration of fresh frozen plasma to provide AT, 2 U every 8 hours, decreasing to 1 U every 12 hours, followed by the administration of oral anticoagulants. AT concentrates also are available.[84] Anticoagulant with a direct thrombin inhibitor, such as hirudin, argatroban, or bivalirudin, is a reasonable alternative (extrapolated from its success in heparin-induced thrombocytopenia).[76] Aggressive prophylaxis against VTE even in childhood is recommended during the perioperative period, and lifelong anticoagulation therapy is required after a first VTE.[110]

Protein C and S Deficiencies

Site

Venous more likely than arterial.

Mechanism

Protein C and its cofactor protein S are vitamin K–dependent factors synthesized in the liver with half lives of 4 to 6 hours and 12 to 14 hours. APC functions as an anticoagulant by inactivating factors Va and VIIIa in the coagulation prothrombinase and Xase (tenase) complexes.[11] Protein C is activated by thrombin when bound to the endothelial cell receptor, thrombomodulin, which localizes protein C for thrombin cleavage.[28] The net effect of protein C activation is less thrombin formation. Additionally, APC, through activation of protease-activated receptor 1 on endothelial cells, stimulates t-PA liberation, increasing the fibrinolytic potential of blood. Most cases of protein C or protein S deficiency are inherited as autosomal dominant traits and present with VTE, often in young patients 15 to 30 years old.[7,110] Protein C and S deficiency states are responsible for 3% to 5% (protein C) and 2% to 3% (protein S) of patients with VTE. Some cases of arterial thrombosis have been reported, however.[25] When present as a homozygous state at birth, infants usually die from unrestricted clotting and fibrinolysis, a condition of extreme DIC that is termed *purpura fulminans*. Patients heterozygous for protein C deficiency usually have antigenic protein C levels less than 60% of normal.[18,34] Acquired deficiency states for protein C occur with liver failure, DIC, and nephrotic syndrome.

Protein S is a cofactor to APC and is regulated by complement C4b binding protein, with free protein S being functionally active as an anticoagulant. The deficiency results in a clinical state identical to protein C deficiency. Nephrotic syndrome also can lead to a reduction in free protein S (M_r = 42 kD) levels and acquired hypercoagulable state.[112] Inflammatory states, such as systemic lupus erythematosus, can result in an elevation of C4b binding protein, which complexes with protein S and reduces free protein S.

Diagnosis

The diagnosis of protein C or S deficiency is made by plasma protein C and S measurements.[46,52] For protein C, antigen and activity levels are measured, whereas for protein S, only antigen levels are measured because the coagulant assay on most commercial assays has a high coefficient of variation. Protein S antigen in plasma is measured only after the plasma is adsorbed with polyethylene glycol to remove C4b binding protein, a protein S binder. Only free protein S not bound to C4b binding protein is available to act as an APC cofactor. A condition also exists in which there is an abnormality in the function of the protein C molecule itself, resulting in a decrease in protein C activity without a decline in antigenic protein C.[7]

Treatment

When the diagnosis is made in the setting of a thrombotic event, treatment consists of anticoagulation, initially with heparin, followed by lifelong oral anticoagulation. Not all patients with low levels of these factors develop VTE, however, and there have been reports that in large populations of asymptomatic blood donors, low protein C levels may be found in asymptomatic patients. Many heterozygous family members of homozygous protein C–deficient infants also are unaffected.[28] The institution of anticoagulation therapy in patients should occur only after they manifest the phenotype of thrombosis, but aggressive anticoagulant prophylaxis during perioperative periods or high-risk environmental situations is a must for asymptomatic heterozygote carriers.

With the initiation of oral anticoagulation, blood may become transiently hypercoagulable as the vitamin K–dependent factors with short half-lives are inhibited (factor VII, protein C) before the other vitamin K–dependent factors (factors II, IX, and X).[17] In a patient already partially deficient in protein C or S, the levels of these anticoagulant factors diminish even further with the initiation of warfarin, resulting in a temporary hypercoagulable state. This situation can result in thrombosis in the microcirculation and the syndrome of warfarin-induced skin necrosis.[12] The syndrome leads to full-thickness skin loss, especially over fatty areas where blood supply is poor to begin with, such as the breasts, buttocks, and abdomen. To prevent this devastating complication, warfarin therapy always should be initiated under the protection of systemic heparin anticoagulation (standard heparin or low-molecular-weight heparin) or a direct thrombin inhibitor in patients in whom the indication for anticoagulation is VTE.

Heparin-Induced Thrombocytopenia and Thrombosis Syndrome

Site

Venous more likely than arterial.

Mechanism

HITTS/HIT, also known as heparin-associated thrombocytopenia, occurs in 0.6% to 30% of patients in whom heparin is administered, although severe thrombocytopenia associated with thrombosis (HITTS) is seen much less frequently.[3,4] About 50% of HITTS/HIT patients have thrombosis that is observable clinically or is recognized with duplex interrogation. In an analysis of 11 prospective studies, the incidence was reported to be 3%, with thrombosis in 0.9%.[9] Morbidity and mortality rates of 61% and 23% have been reported.[113] With early diagnosis and appropriate treatment, morbidity and mortality rates have declined to 6% and 0%.[2] HITTS/HIT is caused by a heparin-dependent antibody IgG, which, when bound to platelet factor 4, induces platelets via Fc receptors to aggregate when exposed to heparin.[55,130] The antibody may not be heparin specific, as the degree of sulfonation of the heparin-like compound has been suggested to be crucial for aggregation.[42] Bovine and porcine standard unfractionated heparins and low-molecular-weight heparins have been associated with HITTS/HIT.[132] HITTS/HIT usually begins 3 to 14 days after heparin administration. Arterial and venous thromboses have been reported, and even small exposures to heparin, as with the heparin coating on indwelling catheters or tubing, have been known to cause the syndrome.[3,66,130]

Diagnosis

The diagnosis should be suspected in a patient who experiences a 50% decrease in platelet count or when there is a decrease in platelet count to less than 100,000/μL during heparin therapy or in any patient who experiences thrombosis, particularly in unusual sites, during heparin administration.[3,36,51,133] HITTS/HIT may be a difficult diagnosis to make because many hospitalized patients have multiple reasons for declines in the platelet count, such as sepsis or DIC. The laboratory diagnosis of HITTS/HIT is made by numerous assays. The serotonin release assay (SRA) was the "gold standard." In the SRA, donor platelets are radiolabeled with ^{14}C-5-hydroxytryptamine. Patient plasma is mixed with variable concentrations of heparin (or low-molecular-weight heparin if it is the offending agent), and the degree of serotonin release is measured when the heparinized patient's plasma is mixed with donor platelets. This aggregation test has sensitivity and specificity of 94% and 100%.[111] An enzyme-linked immunosorbent assay (ELISA) detecting the antiheparin antibody in the patient's plasma directed against the heparin–platelet factor 4 complex is used more commonly today to detect this disorder.[3,41] The ELISA is less specific, but easier to perform and interpret than the SRA.

Treatment

Cessation of heparin is essential, including heparin intravenous flushes and catheters.[66] Because these patients have circulating platelet microparticles, they have an ongoing prothrombotic state. Warfarin is contraindicated in this condition until an adequate alternative anticoagulant has been started in the patient because a prothrombotic state similar to that seen when warfarin is given in patients with protein C or S deficiency occurs, which may lead to venous limb gangrene.[131] Low-molecular-weight heparins (enoxaparin and dalteparin) have 92% cross-reactivity with standard heparin antibodies on the SRA and should not be substituted for standard heparin in patients with HITTS/HIT, although some have suggested that if a low-molecular-weight heparin tests negative in vitro, it may be used clinically.[115]

Many new anticoagulants are now available. The direct thrombin inhibitors hirudin (lepirudin [Refludan]) and argatroban are the treatments of choice.[3,43,69,76] These agents show no cross-reactivity to heparin antibodies. The glycoprotein platelet IIb/IIIa receptor antagonist abciximab (ReoPro) has been used to prevent platelet activation[71] but has not become standard therapy.

Lupus Anticoagulant/Antiphospholipid Syndrome (Antiphospholipid Antibody Syndrome)

Site

Venous more likely than arterial.

Mechanism

It is a misnomer to name the antiphospholipid antibody syndrome an "anticoagulant" syndrome because it is associated with a prothrombotic state. The antiphospholipid antibody syndrome consists of the presence of an elevated antiphospholipid antibody titer in association with episodes of thrombosis, recurrent fetal loss, thrombocytopenia, and livedo reticularis.[73,74] Stroke, MI, visceral infarction, and extremity gangrene also may occur. Although the lupus anticoagulant has been reported in 5% to 40% of patients with systemic lupus erythematosus, it can exist in patients without lupus and can be induced in patients by medications, cancer, and certain infectious diseases.[56]

This syndrome is associated with antiphospholipid antibodies (to the acidic and neutral phospholipids, such as phosphatidyl serine, choline, and ethanolamine) that are most commonly IgG against β_2 glycoprotein I and prothrombin. Antiphospholipid antibody syndrome is a particularly virulent type of hypercoagulable state that results in a 5-fold to 16-fold greater risk of arterial and venous thrombosis.[27,35,56] Many possible thrombotic mechanisms have been suggested, including (1) inhibition of prostacyclin synthesis or its release from endothelial cells,[10] (2) inhibition of protein C activation by thrombin/thrombomodulin,[13] (3) increased PAI-1 levels,[127] (4) direct platelet activation,[128] (5) coexistence of endothelial cell activation with antiphospholipid antibodies,[31] and (6) interference with the endothelial cell–associated anticoagulant activity of annexin V.[98] Increased tissue factor expression on monocytes and low free protein S plasma levels also have been noted in patients with antiphospholipid syndrome and a history of thrombosis.[101]

Thrombosis can involve the arterial and venous circulations, especially peripheral vessels of the extremities.[134] At least one third of patients with lupus anticoagulants have a history of one or more thrombotic events, with more than 70% as VTE.[40] Arterial thrombosis is seen as well. Graft thrombosis has been observed in 27% to 50% of patients positive for antiphospholipid antibody, including late follow-up.[1,87] The incidence of antiphospholipid antibodies also was found to be elevated (26%) in a group of young white men (≤45 years old) with chronic lower leg ischemia compared with control patients (13%).[122] In contrast, a prospective comparison of elective infrainguinal bypass grafting revealed that although one third of patients were positive for antiphospholipid antibodies, there was minimal difference in primary or assisted patency rates, limb salvage, or survival rates between positive and negative patients.[68]

Diagnosis

The diagnosis is suspected in a patient with a prolonged activated partial thromboplastin time (APTT) with other standard coagulation tests within normal limits and the presence of an increased antiphospholipid or anticardiolipin antibody titer and elevation of β_2 glycoprotein I.[18,46] The prolongation in the APTT is strictly a laboratory phenomenon. The antiphospholipid antibody interacts with the anionic phospholipids in the APTT assay, prolonging the assay. The finding that a prolonged dilute Russell viper venom time is shortened by the addition of excess phospholipids confirms the presence of a lupus anticoagulant.

There is imperfect agreement between diagnostic tests for this abnormality. Approximately 80% of patients with a prolonged APTT have a positive ELISA antiphospholipid antibody, but only 10% to 50% of patients with a positive ELISA antiphospholipid antibody have a prolonged APTT.[77] Patients with both tests positive are reported to have the same thrombotic risk as patients with either test positive alone.

Treatment

Heparin followed by anticoagulation with warfarin (International Normalized Ratio >3) has been recommended to treat antiphospholipid syndrome.[40,56] For recurrent fetal loss, heparin or low-molecular-weight heparin use throughout the pregnancy is recommended. In patients with lupus anticoagulants, heparin therapy is monitored by anti–factor Xa levels.

■ DEFECTS WITH LOWER RISK FOR THROMBOSIS

Resistance to Activated Protein C (Factor V Leiden)

Site

Venous more likely than arterial.

Mechanism

Resistance to APC has been reported to be present in 20% to 60% of cases of idiopathic VTE and 1% to 2% of the general population.[102,107,116] It is the most common underlying abnormality associated with a VTE, although it alone confers a relatively low risk. The syndrome is much more common in whites than in nonwhite Americans.[102] It arose in the Near East and spread through present-day Europe. The hypercoagulability is conferred by resistance to inactivation of factor Va by APC as a result of the substitution of a single amino acid, glutamine for arginine, at position 506 in the protein for factor V (termed *factor V Leiden*) caused by a nucleotide substitution of guanine for adenine at 1691 in factor V gene.[53,81,114] Additionally, by impaired factor Va inactivation, less factor VIIIa is interfered with, compounding the procoagulant state. The complexity of APC interactions is only more recently starting to be understood.[16,86] Thrombotic manifestations are noted in individuals either homozygous or heterozygous for this mutation. The relative risk for VTE in patients heterozygous for factor V Leiden is 7-fold, whereas in patients homozygous for factor V Leiden, the relative risk for thrombosis is 80-fold.[110] In contrast to factor deficiency hypercoagulable states, persons homozygous for this mutation usually do not die in infancy. Additionally, the incidence of thrombosis is correlated with the presence of additional acquired risk factors for thromboses, especially oral contraceptive use, pregnancy, and coexistent hyperhomocysteinemia.[20,37,81]

Combined defects with other hypercoagulable states, such as protein C and S deficiency or prothrombin G20210A, markedly increase thrombotic risk.[57,58] In addition to the many cases of VTE caused by this defect, recurrent VTE is more common in patients with this entity, with an increase in a recurrent venous thrombosis relative risk of 2.4-fold.[116] Although VTE predominates in patients with this syndrome, arterial thrombosis, especially involving lower extremity revascularizations, also has been reported.[92] The prevalence of this abnormality has been suggested to be increased in patients with peripheral vascular occlusive disease, measured by the functional assay[25] and by genetic analysis.[33]

Diagnosis

The diagnosis of APC resistance is made by a clot-based assay with the addition of APC (modified APTT). Additionally, genetic analysis should be done to confirm heterozygosity versus homozygosity because treatment decisions may be affected. If the patient has a known lupus anticoagulant syndrome, this entity may interfere with the clot-based APC resistance assay,[123] and genetic analysis is more accurate.

Treatment

Treatment options for APC resistance after a VTE include anticoagulation, initially heparin, followed by oral anticoagulation. The long-term use of warfarin is controversial. No data exist to suggest that long-term warfarin should be given after a first episode of VTE in a patient with this syndrome, especially if heterozygous for the mutation.[49] The fact that APC resistance is a relatively low risk for recurrent thrombosis (2.4-fold) suggests that not all patients after their first episode of VTE need long-term anticoagulant treatment and that patients must be evaluated in light of their overall risk for thrombosis, including age, clinical circumstances, other risk factors, and medications.[110]

Hyperhomocysteinemia

Site

Arterial roughly equal to venous.

Mechanism

Hyperhomocysteinemia has been known to be a risk factor for atherosclerosis and vascular disease since the 1970s, although a direct cause-and-effect relationship has not been established outside of familial hyperhomocysteinemia.[19,21,22] A meta-analysis suggests the risk of VTE with elevated homocysteine to be 2.5-fold,[23] however, and hyperhomocysteinemia is responsible for 10% of cases of VTE. Elevated serum homocysteine ($\geq$11 μmol/L) may occur because of defects in two enzymes, N^5, N^{10}-methylene tetrahydrofolate reductase (MTHFR), or cystathionine beta synthase.[67] Deficiencies in vitamins B_6 and B_{12} and folate contribute to elevation of plasma homocysteine. Mutations are common in these enzymes and may exist in 35% of patients. The common polymorphism in MTHFR alone is not a factor, however, in the elevation of plasma homocysteine or thrombosis.[61] Hyperhomocysteinemia also has been found to be a risk factor for VTE in people younger than 40 years old[29] and women[19] and for recurrent venous thrombosis in people 20 to 70 years old,[21] but this finding has not been confirmed by all.[67] The combination of hyperhomocysteinemia and factor V Leiden has been suggested to result in an increased risk of venous and arterial thromboses.[80] Elevated plasma homocysteine principally results in abnormal endothelial function. In hyperhomocysteinemic patients, there is reduced protein C activation on thrombomodulin, reduced plasminogen binding to endothelial cells, reduced t-PA activation of bound plasminogen, increased factor V expression on endothelium, and impaired endothelium-dependent vasodilatation (nitric oxide dependent).[47,75,105,117,121] Elevated homocysteine also increases lipid peroxidation, which impairs nitric oxide synthetase and directly degrades nitric oxide[8,99] and increases thromboxane B_2, while decreasing prostacyclin levels.[39] The sum of these seemingly varied mechanisms of the prothrombotic effects of homocysteine can be understood by the fact that homocysteine elevation injures endothelial cells.

Diagnosis

Fasting homocysteine levels are determined from serum, usually on two occasions. Serum measurements may be done after a methionine oral loading regimen.[36,120]

Treatment

Elevation of homocysteine is treated with folate supplements. Although the association between hyperhomocysteinemia and VTE has been established, treatment to lower homocysteine levels using folic acid, vitamin B_6, or vitamin B_{12} and the long-term effects of such treatment on procoagulant activity have yet to be validated.[19] The downside of a daily multivitamin seems to be little, as long as moderation is practiced.

Prothrombin G20210 Polymorphism

Site

Venous more likely than arterial.

Mechanism

Prothrombin (factor II) is a vitamin K–dependent factor synthesized in the liver. When activated, it becomes thrombin, the main clotting enzyme. A more recently recognized genetic polymorphism in the distal 3′ untranslated region of the prothrombin gene has been described in patients with VTE and results in a normal prothrombin, but at increased levels.[7,20,126] This base-pair polymorphism, G20210A, confers a 2-fold to 7-fold increased risk for VTE, and it is associated with 4% to 6% of patients with VTE.[14,79,110] This genotype does not confer increased risk in patients with arterial occlusive disease,[30] unless co-morbid risk factors, such as tobacco use, exist.[52] This thrombosis risk is increased in pregnant women[37] and in women with early MIs[103] and is synergistic with factor V Leiden.[20] Most patients are heterozygous for this mutation, which affects whites more often and almost never patients of Asian or African descent.[103]

Diagnosis

Genetic analysis for the 20210 (G-to-A) mutation is the sole marker for this abnormality. Measurement of plasma factor II activity is not a reliable predictor of the presence of this polymorphism.[82]

Treatment

Patients who present with VTE should be treated according to current standards of care. Recurrent episodes of VTE in individuals with prothrombin G20210A mandate lifelong anticoagulation. Lifelong anticoagulation also is required in patients with a primary VTE and coexistence with factor V Leiden.[20]

■ OTHER DISORDERS ASSOCIATED WITH THROMBOSIS

Defective Fibrinolysis, Dysfibrinogenemia, and Lipoprotein (a)

Site

Arterial roughly equal to venous.

Mechanism

Abnormal plasminogens (dysplasminogenemias), although rare (<1%), have been described in cases of spontaneous arterial thromboembolism or VTE.[100] Other defects in fibrinolysis that are not well defined may affect 10% of the normal population.[119] Abnormal fibrinogens may account for 1% to 3% of patients with venous thrombosis and patients presenting with digital ischemia.[63] Numerous molecular defects have been classified, and the abnormal fibrinogen may have defective thrombin binding or may be resistant to plasmin-mediated breakdown.[104] Although not clearly documented, defects in availability or function of the plasminogen activators, t-PA or urokinase plasminogen activator, may precipitate thrombotic events (see Fig. 34-2).[88] Elevated PAI-1 has been associated with deep venous thrombosis and MI in epidemiologic studies.[100] Although the relationship between VTE and abnormal fibrinolysis is debated, it is clear that there is a relationship between impaired postoperative fibrinolysis and VTE.[97,100,125] Additionally, secretion of PAI-1 is upregulated by thrombin, endotoxin, and interleukin-1, explaining the elevated circulating levels of PAI-1 during certain infections.[94] Lipoprotein (a), associated with low-density lipoprotein, is atherogenic and prothrombotic.[50,70,122] It prevents plasminogen from binding to cells or fibrin and inhibits plasminogen activation from initiating fibrinolysis.[44] Elevated levels of lipoprotein (a) have been associated with VTE in childhood, although it is considered a weak thrombotic risk factor in adults.[90]

Diagnosis

A confirmatory test for a dysfibrinogenemia includes a fibrinogen clotting activity-to-antigen ratio. Dysfibrinogenemia also may be detected by a prolonged thrombin clotting or reptilase time.[15] Abnormal plasminogens are detected by the presence of reduced activity-to-antigen ratios. PAI-1 levels have to be measured directed by activity or antigen assay. Lipoprotein (a) is measured in serum.

Treatment

When an individual with thrombosis presents with one of the aforementioned diagnoses, the standards of anticoagulation therapy need to be applied. There have been too few documented patients to know the severity of the prothrombotic risk factor.[85,108]

Abnormal Platelet Aggregation

Site

Arterial more likely than venous.

Mechanism

It has been recognized for some time that there is a subset of patients who have thrombosis and may have hyperactive or hyperresponsive platelets. This clinical entity is poorly defined. Diabetes mellitus, which is known to be associated with hyperactive platelets and hyperlipidemic states, may be a contributor to these conditions. There are two clinical settings in which abnormal platelet aggregation has been associated with thrombosis: advanced malignancy of the lung and uterus and after carotid endarterectomy. Hyperactive platelets also have been seen during graft thrombosis in peripheral vascular reconstructions.[27] Assays to detect hyperaggregable platelets have not been developed. Some studies suggest that these platelets would respond to doses of platelet agonists (e.g., adenosine diphosphate, epinephrine, or collagen) at concentrations lower than that usually seen. Because there is not a good way to assess the more highly activated platelet, the incidence and importance of platelets in relation to thrombosis are unknown.

Diagnosis

Most hospital laboratories do not routinely have quantitative platelet function testing. Hyperactive platelets are detected by determining if patient platelets respond to concentrations of platelet agonists below the lower limit of the normal range. Bleeding time measurements are not specific and are not recommended for this diagnosis.

Treatment

Standard heparin followed by warfarin anticoagulation has been used for treatment, but few data exist regarding specific treatment. Aspirin and the thienopyridine derivatives, such as clopidogrel, may be useful.[45]

Elevated Procoagulant Factors: VIII, IX, XI

Site

Venous more likely than arterial.

Mechanism

Elevated prothrombotic factors have only more recently been associated with increased primary and recurrent

VTE.[54,110] A dose-response effect has been observed, and elevated factor VIII has been the best studied.[54,59,91] Factor VIII:C above the 90th percentile is associated with a fivefold increased risk of VTE.[78,91] Factor VIII:C elevation also is affected by blood type and race. Elevation of factor XI above the 90th percentile also was associated with a two-fold increase in VTE compared with controls and was independent of other hypercoagulability factors.[83] Similar increases in VTE risk have been observed with elevated factor IX.[124] In an analogous situation to the prothrombin G20210A mutation, acquired and environmental factors precipitate VTE in patients with elevation of these factors, in contrast to the inherited deficiencies of AT, protein C, and protein S, which confer higher VTE risk.[64]

Diagnosis

Direct measurement of these factors with activity assays is the diagnostic procedure of choice; however, in the individual patient, how to handle a specific elevated value is unknown.

Treatment

If VTE occurs, standard-of-care management should be instituted.[108]

■ REFERENCES

1. Ahn SS, Kalunian K, Rosove M, et al: Postoperative thrombotic complications in patients with the lupus anticoagulant: Increased risk after vascular procedures. J Vasc Surg 7:749, 1988.
2. Almeida J, Coats R, Liem TK, Silver D: Reduced morbidity and mortality rates of the heparin-induced thrombocytopenia syndrome. J Vasc Surg 27:309, 1998.
3. Alving B: How I treat heparin-induced thrombocytopenia and thrombosis. Blood 101:31-37, 2003.
4. Ansell JE, Price JM, Shah S, et al: Heparin-induced thrombocytopenia: What is its real frequency? Chest 88:878, 1985.
5. Bavikatty NM, Killeen AA, Akel N, et al: Association of the prothrombin G20210A mutation with factor V Leiden in a Midwestern American population. Am J Clin Pathol 114:272, 2000.
6. Bick RL: Coagulation abnormalities in malignancy: A review. Semin Thromb Hemost 18:353, 1992.
7. Bick RL: Prothrombin G20210A mutation, antithrombin, heparin cofactor II, protein C, and protein S defects. Hematol Oncol Clin North Am 17:9-36, 2003.
8. Blom HJ, Kleinveld HA, Boers GH, et al: Lipid peroxidation and susceptibility of low-density lipoprotein to in vitro oxidation in hyperhomocysteinemia. Eur J Clin Invest 25:149, 1995.
9. Cancio LC, Cohen DJ: Heparin-induced thrombocytopenia and thrombosis. J Am Coll Surg 186:76, 1998.
10. Carreras LO, Defreyn G, Machin SJ, et al: Arterial thrombosis, intra-uterine death, and "lupus" anticoagulant: Detection of immunoglobulin interfering with prostacyclin formation. Lancet 1:244, 1981.
11. Clouse LH, Comp PC: The regulation of hemostasis: The protein C system. N Engl J Med 314:1298, 1986.
12. Cole MS, Minifee PK, Wolma FJ: Coumadin necrosis: A review of the literature. Surgery 103:271, 1988.
13. Comp PC, DeBault LE, Esmon NL, Esmon CT: Human thrombomodulin is inhibited by IgG from two patients with non-specific anticoagulants [abstract]. Blood 62(Suppl 1):299a, 1983.
14. Cumming AM, Keeney S, Salden A, et al: The prothrombin gene G20210A variant: Prevalence in a U.K. anticoagulant clinic population. Br J Haematol 98:353, 1997.
15. Cunningham MT, Brandt JT: Laboratory diagnosis of dysfibrinogenemia. Arch Pathol Lab Med 126:499-505, 2002.
16. Dahlbäck B: Activated protein C resistance and thrombosis: Molecular mechanisms of hypercoagulable state due to FVR506Q mutation. Semin Thromb Hemost 25:273-289, 1999.
17. Dahlbäck B: Blood coagulation. Lancet 355:1627, 2000.
18. de Moerloose P, Bounameaux HR, Mannucci PM: Screening tests for thrombophilic patients: Which tests, for which patient, by whom, when, and why? Semin Thromb Hemost 24:321-327, 1998.
19. de Stefano V, Casorelli I, Rossi E, et al: Interaction between hyperhomocysteinemia and inherited thrombophilic factors in venous thromboembolism. Semin Thromb Hemost 26:305-311, 2000.
20. de Stefano V, Martinelli I, Mannucci PM, et al: The risk of recurrent deep venous thrombosis among heterozygous carriers of both Factor V Leiden and the G20210A prothrombin mutation. N Engl J Med 341:801, 1999.
21. den Heijer M, Blom HJ, Gerrits WB, et al: Is hyperhomocysteinaemia a risk factor for recurrent venous thrombosis? Lancet 345:882, 1995.
22. den Heijer M, Koster T, Blom HJ, et al: Hyperhomocysteinemia as a risk factor for deep-vein thrombosis. N Engl J Med 334:759, 1996.
23. den Heijer M, Keijzer M: Hyperhomocysteinemia as a risk factor for venous thrombosis. Clin Chem Lab Med 39:710, 2001.
24. Donaldson MC, Weinberg DS, Belkin M, et al: Screening for hypercoagulable states in vascular surgical practice: A preliminary study. J Vasc Surg 11:825, 1990.
25. Donaldson MC, Belkin M, Whittemore AD, et al: Impact of activated protein C resistance on general vascular surgical patients. J Vasc Surg 25:1054, 1997.
26. Eby CS: A review of the hypercoagulable state. Hematol Oncol Clin North Am 7:1, 1993.
27. Eldrup-Jorgensen J, Flanigan DP, Brace L, et al: Hypercoagulable states and lower limb ischemia in young adults. J Vasc Surg 9:334, 1989.
28. Esmon CT: The regulation of natural anticoagulant pathways. Science 235:1348, 1987.
29. Falcon CR, Cattaneo M, Panzeri D, et al: High prevalence of hyperhomocyst(e)inemia in patients with juvenile venous thrombosis. Arterioscler Thromb 14:1080, 1994.
30. Ferraresi P, Marchetti G, Legnani C, et al: The heterozygous 20210 G/A prothrombin genotype is associated with early venous thrombosis in inherited thrombophilias and is not increased in frequency in artery disease. Arterioscler Thromb Vasc Biol 17:2418, 1997.
31. Ferro D, Pittoni V, Quintarelli C, et al: Coexistence of antiphospholipid antibodies and endothelial perturbation in systemic lupus erythematosus patients with ongoing prothrombotic state. Circulation 95:1425, 1997.
32. Flinn WR, McDaniel MD, Yao JS, et al: Antithrombin III deficiency as a reflection of dynamic protein metabolism in patients undergoing vascular reconstruction. J Vasc Surg 1:888, 1984.
33. Foley PW, Irvine CD, Standen GR, et al: Activated protein C resistance, factor V Leiden and peripheral vascular disease. Cardiovasc Surg 5:157, 1997.
34. Franco RF, Reitsma PH: Genetic risk factors of venous thrombosis. Hum Genet 109:369, 2001.
35. Galli M, Luciani D, Bertolini G, et al: Lupus anticoagulants are stronger risk factors for thrombosis than anticardiolipin antibodies in the antiphospholipid syndrome: A systematic review of the literature. Blood 101:1827, 2003.
36. George JN, Alving B, Ballem P: Platelets. In McArthur JR, Benz EJ (eds): Hematology—1994: The Educational Program of the American Society of Hematology. Washington, DC, American Society of Hematology, 1994, p 66.
37. Gerhardt A, Scharf RE, Beckmann MW, et al: Prothrombin and Factor V mutations in women with a history of thrombosis during pregnancy and the puerperium. N Engl J Med 342:374, 2000.
38. Girelli D, Russo C, Ferraresi P, et al: Polymorphism in the Factor VII gene and the risk of myocardial infarction in patients with coronary artery disease. N Engl J Med 343:774, 2000.
39. Graeber JE, Slott JH, Ulane RE, et al: Effect of homocysteine and homocystine on platelet and vascular arachidonic acid metabolism. Pediatr Res 16:490, 1982.
40. Greenfield LJ: Lupus-like anticoagulants and thrombosis. J Vasc Surg 7:818, 1988.

41. Greinacher A, Michels I, Kiefel V, et al: A rapid and sensitive test for diagnosing heparin-associated thrombocytopenia. Thromb Haemost 66:734, 1991.
42. Greinacher A, Michels I, Mueller-Eckhardt C: Heparin-associated thrombocytopenia: The antibody is not heparin specific. Thromb Haemost 67:545, 1992.
43. Greinacher A, Volpel H, Janssens U, et al: Recombinant hirudin (Lepirudin) provides safe and effective anticoagulation in patients with heparin-induced thrombocytopenia. Circulation 99:73, 1999.
44. Griffin JH, Fernández JA, Deguchi H: Plasma lipoproteins, hemostasis, and thrombosis. Thromb Haemost 86:386, 2001.
45. Harker LA: Platelets in thrombotic disorder: Quantitative and qualitative platelet disorders predisposing to arterial thrombosis. Semin Hematol 35:241, 1998.
46. Hassouna HI: Laboratory evaluation of hemostatic disorders. Hematol Oncol Clin North Am 7:1161, 1993.
47. Hayashi T, Honda G, Suzucki K: An atherogenic stimulus homocysteine inhibits cofactor activity of thrombomodulin and enhances thrombomodulin expression in human umbilical vein endothelial cells. Blood 79:2930, 1992.
48. Hirsh J, Raschke R, Warkentin TE, et al: Heparin: Mechanism of action, pharmacokinetics, dosing considerations, monitoring, efficacy, and safety. Chest 108:258S, 1995.
49. Hooper WC, Evatt BL: The role of activated protein C resistance in the pathogenesis of venous thrombosis. Am J Med Sci 316:120, 1998.
50. Ishibashi S: Lipoprotein (a) and atherosclerosis. Arterioscler Thromb Vasc Biol 21:1, 2001.
51. Jackson MR, Krishnamurti C, Aylesworth CA, et al: Diagnosis of heparin-induced thrombocytopenia in the vascular surgery patient. Surgery 121:419, 1997.
52. Jennings I, Cooper P: Screening for thrombophilia: A laboratory perspective. Br J Biomed Sci 60:39, 2003.
53. Kalafatis M, Mann KG: Factor V Leiden and thrombophilia. Arterioscler Thromb Vasc Biol 17:620, 1997.
54. Kamphuisen PW, Lensen R, Houwing-Duistermaat JJ, et al: Heritability of elevated Factor VIII antigen levels in Factor V Leiden families with thrombophilia. Br J Haematol 109:519, 2000.
55. Kelton JG, Smith JW, Warkentin TE, et al: Immunoglobulin G from patients with heparin-induced thrombocytopenia binds to a complex of heparin and platelet factor 4. Blood 83:3232, 1994.
56. Khamashta MA, Cuadrado MJ, Mujic F, et al: The management of thrombosis in the antiphospholipid-antibody syndrome. N Engl J Med 332:993, 1995.
57. Koeleman BP, Reitsma PH, Allaart CF, et al: Activated protein C resistance as an additional risk factor for thrombosis in protein C-deficient families. Blood 84:1031, 1994.
58. Koeleman BP, van Rumpt D, Hamulyak K, et al: Factor V Leiden: An additional risk factor for thrombosis in protein S deficient families? Thromb Haemost 74:580, 1995.
59. Koster T, Blann AD, Briët E, et al: Role of clotting Factor VIII in effect of von Willebrand factor on occurrence of deep venous thrombosis. Lancet 345:152, 1995.
60. Koster T, Rosendaal FR, Reitsma PH, et al: Factor VII and fibrinogen levels as risk factors for venous thrombosis. Thromb Haemost 71:719, 1994.
61. Kottke-Marchant K: Genetic polymorphisms associated with venous and arterial thrombosis. Arch Pathol Lab Med 126:295, 2002.
62. Kuenen BC, Levi M, Meijers JCM, et al: Analysis of coagulation cascade and endothelial cell activation during inhibition of vascular endothelial growth factor/vascular endothelial growth factor receptor pathway in cancer patients. Arterioscler Thromb Vasc Biol 22:1500, 2002.
63. Kwaan HC, Levin M, Sakurai S, et al: Digital ischemia and gangrene due to red blood cell aggregation induced by acquired dysfibrinogenemia. J Vasc Surg 26:1061, 1997.
64. Lane DA, Grant PJ: Role of hemostatic gene polymorphisms in venous and arterial thrombotic disease. Blood 95:1517, 2000.
65. Langlois NJ, Wells PS: Risk of venous thromboembolism of symptomatic probands with thrombophilia: A systematic review. Thromb Haemost 90:17, 2003.
66. Laster J, Silver D: Heparin-coated catheters and heparin-induced thrombocytopenia. J Vasc Surg 7:667, 1988.
67. Legnani C, Palareti G, Grauso F, et al: Hyperhomocysteinemia and a common methylenetetrahydrofolate reductase mutation (Ala[223] Val MTHFR) in patients with inherited thrombophilic coagulation defects [abstract]. Arterioscler Thromb Vasc Biol 17:2924, 1997.
68. Lee RW, Taylor LM Jr, Landry GJ, et al: Prospective comparisons of infrainguinal bypass grafting in patients with and without antiphospholipid antibodies. J Vasc Surg 24:524, 1996.
69. Lewis BE, Iaffaldano R, McKiernan TL, et al: Report of successful use of argatroban as an alternative anticoagulant during coronary stent implantation in a patient with heparin-induced thrombocytopenia and thrombosis syndrome. Cathet Cardiovasc Diagn 38:206, 1996.
70. Liao JK, Shin WS, Lee WY, et al: Oxidized low-density lipoprotein decreases the expression of endothelial nitric oxide synthase. J Biol Chem 270:319, 1995.
71. Liem TK, Teel R, Shukla S, et al: The glycoprotein IIb/IIIa antagonist c7E3 inhibits platelet aggregation in the presence of heparin-associated antibodies. J Vasc Surg 25:124, 1997.
72. Lin J, Proctor MC, Varma M, et al: Factors associated with recurrent thromboembolic events in patients with malignancy. J Vasc Surg 37:970, 2003.
73. Lockshin MD: Antiphospholipid antibody syndrome. JAMA 268:1451, 1992.
74. Lockshin MD: Antiphospholipid antibody: Babies, blood clots, biology. JAMA 277:1549, 1997.
75. Loscalzo J: The oxidant stress of hyperhomocyst(e)inemia. J Clin Invest 98:5, 1996.
76. Lubenow N, Greinacher A: Hirudin in heparin-induced thrombocytopenia. Semin Thromb Hemost 28:431, 2002.
77. Lynch A, Marlar R, Murphy J, et al: Antiphospholipid antibodies in predicting adverse pregnancy outcome: A prospective study. Ann Intern Med 120:470, 1994.
78. Mansvelt EPG, Laffan M, McVey JH, et al: Analysis of the F8 gene in individuals with high plasma factor VIII:C levels and associated venous thrombosis. Thromb Haemost 80:561, 1998.
79. Martinelli I, Sacchi E, Landi G, et al: High risk of cerebral vein thrombosis in carriers of a prothrombin gene mutation and in users of oral contraceptives. N Engl J Med 338:1793, 1998.
80. Mandel H, Brenner B, Berant M, et al: Coexistence of hereditary homocystinuria and factor V Leiden-effect on thrombosis. N Engl J Med 334:763, 1996.
81. Mann KG, Kalafatis M: Factor V: A combination of Dr. Jekyll and Mr. Hyde. Blood 101:20, 2003.
82. McGlennen RC, Key NS: Clinical and laboratory management of the prothrombin G20210A mutation. Arch Pathol Lab Med 126:1319, 2002.
83. Meijers JC, Tekelenburg WL, Bouma BN, et al: High levels of coagulation Factor XI as a risk factor for venous thrombosis. N Engl J Med 342:696, 2000.
84. Menache D: Antithrombin III concentrates. Hematol Oncol Clin North Am 6:1115, 1992.
85. Mosesson MW: Dysfibrinogenemia and thrombosis. Semin Thromb Hemost 25:311, 1999.
86. Nicolaes AF, Dahlbäck B: Factor V and thrombotic disease: Description of a Janus-faced protein. Arterioscler Thromb Vasc Biol 22:530, 2002.
87. Nielsen TG, Nordestgaard BG, von Jessen F, et al: Antibodies to cardiolipin may increase the risk of failure of peripheral vein bypasses. Eur J Vasc Endovasc Surg 14:177, 1997.
88. Nilsson IM, Ljungner H, Tengborn L: Two different mechanisms in patients with venous thrombosis and defective fibrinolysis: Low concentrations of plasminogen activator or increased concentration of plasminogen activator inhibitor. Br Med J Clin Res Ed 290:1453, 1985.
89. Nordström J, Lindblad B, Anderson H: Deep venous thrombosis and occult malignancy: An epidemiological study. BMJ 308:891, 1994.
90. Nowak-Göttl U, Junker R, et al: Increased lipoprotein (a) is an important risk factor for venous thromboembolism in childhood. Circulation 100:743, 1999.
91. O'Donnell J, Mumford AD, Manning RA, et al: Elevation of FVIII:C in venous thromboembolism is persistent and independent of the acute phase response. Thromb Haemost 83:10, 2000.
92. Ouriel K, Green RM, DeWeese JA, et al: Activated protein C resistance: Prevalence and implications in peripheral vascular disease. J Vasc Surg 23:46, 1996.

93. Pabinger I, Schneider B: Thrombotic risk in hereditary antithrombin III, protein C, or protein S deficiency. Arterioscler Thromb Vasc Biol 16:742, 1996.
94. Paramo JA, Perez JL, Serrano M, et al: Types 1 and 2 plasminogen activator inhibitor and tumor necrosis factor alpha in patients with sepsis. Thromb Haemost 64:3, 1990.
95. Perry DJ: Review: Acquired antithrombin deficiency in sepsis. Br J Haematol 112:26, 2001.
96. Prandoni P, Bilora F, Marchiori A, et al: An association between atherosclerosis and venous thrombosis. N Engl J Med 348:1435, 2003.
97. Prins MH, Hirsh J: A clinical review of the evidence supporting a relationship between impaired fibrinolytic activity and venous thromboembolism. Arch Intern Med 151:1721, 1991.
98. Rand JH, Wu XX, Andree HA, et al: Pregnancy loss in the antiphospholipid-antibody syndrome—a possible thrombogenic mechanism. N Engl J Med 337:154, 1997.
99. Rees MM, Rodgers GM: Homocysteinemia: Association of a metabolic disorder with vascular disease and thrombosis. Thromb Res 71:337, 1993.
100. Reiner AP, Siscovick DS, Rosendaal FR: Hemostatic risk factors and arterial thrombotic disease. Thromb Haemost 85:584, 2001.
101. Reverter JC, Tassies D, Font J, et al: Hypercoagulable state in patients with antiphospholipid syndrome is related to high induced tissue factor expression on monocytes and to low free protein S. Arterioscler Thromb Vasc Biol 16:1319, 1996.
102. Ridker PM, Miletich JP, Hennekens CH, et al: Ethnic distribution of factor V Leiden in 4047 men and women: Implications for venous thromboembolism screening. JAMA 277:1305, 1997.
103. Ridker PM, Hennekens CH, Miletich JP: G20210A mutation in prothrombin gene and risk of myocardial infarction, stroke, and venous thrombosis in a large cohort of US men. Circulation 99:999, 1999.
104. Roberts HR: Review of the dysfibrinogenemias. Br J Haematol 114:249, 2001.
105. Rodgers GM, Conn MT: Homocysteine, an atherogenic stimulus, reduces protein C activation by arterial and venous endothelial cells. Blood 75:895, 1990.
106. Rosendaal FR: Thrombosis in the young: Epidemiology and risk factors, a focus on venous thrombosis. Thromb Haemost 78:1-6, 1997.
107. Rosendaal FR, Koster T, Vandenbroucke JP, et al: High risk of thrombosis in patients homozygous for factor V Leiden (activated protein C resistance). Blood 85:1504, 1995.
108. Rosendaal FR: Venous thrombosis: A multicausal disease. Lancet 353:1167, 1993.
109. Schmaier AH: Evaluation of thrombosis. In Schmaier AH, Petruzzelli LM (eds): Hematology for the Medical Student. Philadelphia, Lippincott Williams & Wilkins, 2003, pp 121-126.
110. Seligsohn U, Lubetsky A: Genetic susceptibility to venous thrombosis. N Engl J Med 344:1222-1231, 2001.
111. Sheridan D, Carter C, Kelton JG: A diagnostic test for heparin-induced thrombocytopenia. Blood 67:27, 1986.
112. Siddiqi FA, Tepler J, Fantini GA: Acquired protein S and anti-thrombin III deficiency caused by nephrotic syndrome: An unusual cause of graft thrombosis. J Vasc Surg 25:576, 1997.
113. Silver D, Kapsch DN, Tsoi EK: Heparin-induced thrombocytopenia, thrombosis and hemorrhage. Ann Surg 198:301, 1983.
114. Simioni P, Prandoni P, Lensing AW, et al: The risk of recurrent venous thromboembolism in patients with an Arg^{506}→Gln mutation in the gene for factor V (factor V Leiden). N Engl J Med 336:399, 1997.
115. Slocum MM, Adams JG Jr, Teel R, et al: Use of enoxaparin in patients with heparin-induced thrombocytopenia syndrome. J Vasc Surg 23:839, 1996.
116. Svensson PJ, Dahlbäck B: Resistance to activated protein C as a basis for venous thrombosis. N Engl J Med 330:517, 1994.
117. Tawakol A, Omland T, Gerhard M, et al: Hyperhomocyst(e)inemia is associated with impaired endothelium-dependent vasodilation in humans. Circulation 95:1119, 1997.
118. Towne JB, Bernhard VM, Hussey C, et al: Antithrombin deficiency—a cause of unexplained thrombosis in vascular surgery. Surgery 89:735, 1981.
119. Towne JB, Bandyk DF, Hussey CV, et al: Abnormal plasminogen: A genetically determined cause of hypercoagulability. J Vasc Surg 1:896, 1984.
120. Ueland PM, Refsum H, Brattstrom L: Plasma homocysteine and cardiovascular disease. In Francis RB Jr (ed): Atherosclerotic Cardiovascular Disease, Hemostasis, and Endothelial Function. New York, Marcel Dekker, 1993, p 183.
121. Upchurch GR, Welch GN, Randev N, et al: The effect of homocysteine on endothelial nitric oxide production [abstract]. FASEB J 9:A876, 1995.
122. Valentine RJ, Kaplan HS, Green R, et al: Lipoprotein (a), homocysteine, and hypercoagulable states in young men with premature peripheral atherosclerosis: A prospective, controlled analysis. J Vasc Surg 23:53, 1996.
123. Van Cott EM, Soderberg BL, Laposata M: Activated protein C resistance, the Factor V Leiden mutation, and a laboratory testing algorithm. Arch Pathol Lab Med 126:577, 2002.
124. van Hylckama V, Van der Linden IK, Bertina RM, et al: High levels of Factor IX increase the risk of venous thrombosis. Blood 95:3678, 2000.
125. van Tilburg NH, Rosendaal FR, Bertina RM: Thrombin activatable fibrinolysis inhibitor and the risk for deep venous thrombosis. Blood 95:2855, 2000.
126. Vicente V, González-Conejero R, Rivera J, et al: The prothrombin gene variant 20210A in venous and arterial thromboembolism. Haematologica 84:356, 1999.
127. Violi F, Ferro D, Valesini G, et al: Tissue plasminogen activator inhibitor in patients with systemic lupus erythematosus and thrombosis. BMJ 300:1099, 1990.
128. Vermylen J, Blockmans D, Spitz B, et al: Thrombosis and immune disorders. Clin Haematol 15:393, 1986.
129. Virchow R: Phlogose und Thrombose im Gefäßsystem. Gesammelte Abhandlungen zur Wissenschaftlichen Medizin. Frankfurt, Germany, Staatsdruckerei, 1856.
130. Walenga JM, Jeske WP, Messmore HL: Mechanisms of venous and arterial thrombosis in heparin-induced thrombocytopenia. J Thromb Thrombolysis 10:S13, 2000.
131. Warkentin TE, Elavathil LJ, Hayward CP, et al: The pathogenesis of venous limb gangrene associated with heparin-induced thrombocytopenia. Ann Intern Med 127:804, 1997.
132. Warkentin TE, Levine MN, Hirsch J, et al: Heparin-induced thrombocytopenia in patients treated with low-molecular-weight heparin or unfractionated heparin. N Engl J Med 332:1330, 1995.
133. Warkentin TE: Heparin-induced thrombocytopenia: A clinicopathologic syndrome. Thromb Haemost 82:439, 1999.
134. Williams FM, Hunt BJ: The antiphospholipid syndrome and vascular surgery. Cardiovasc Surg 6:10, 1998.
135. Writing Group for the Women's Health Initiative Investigators: Risks and benefits of estrogen plus progestin in healthy postmenopausal women. JAMA 288:321, 2002.
136. Yan SF, Mackman N, Kisiel W, et al: Hypoxia/hypoxemia-induced activation of the procoagulant pathways in the pathogenesis of ischemia-associated thrombosis. Arterioscler Thromb Vasc Biol 19:2029, 1999.
137. World Health Organization: Venous thromboembolic disease and combined oral contraceptives: Results of international multicenter case-control study. World Health Organization Collaborative Study of Cardiovascular Disease and Steroid Hormone Contraception. Lancet 346:1575, 1995.

Section VII

NONOPERATIVE MANAGEMENT OF PATIENTS WITH VASCULAR DISEASES

RUSSELL H. SAMSON, MD

Chapter 35

Overview:
Medical Management in a Vascular Surgery Practice

RUSSELL H. SAMSON, MD

This sixth edition of *Vascular Surgery* initiates a new section devoted to the medical management of the vascular patient. By so doing, the editors acknowledge the central role vascular surgeons can play in the treatment of arterial and venous disorders. Vascular surgery has evolved dramatically with the explosion of noninvasive diagnostic tools and endovascular techniques for the management of vascular conditions. Vascular surgeons are now actively involved in all these technical aspects of care. Many surgeons relegate much, if not most, of the medical management of their patients to physician colleagues. Vascular surgeons are rarely involved in preventive measures. As a result, although we may skillfully bypass or open up blocked arteries and repair aneurysms with minimally invasive techniques, patients continue to die from the other cardiovascular consequences of their underlying disease. The assumption that the family physician, internist, or cardiologist will take care of these aspects is not correct. Many reports have shown that atherosclerotic risk factors in patients with peripheral arterial disease (PAD) are treated less intensively than in patients with coronary artery disease.[1-3] In a review of 195 PAD patients discharged from a tertiary care hospital in Canada, Anand and colleagues[2] reported that fewer than half were sent home with antiplatelet medication. Only 20% were taking beta blockers, and only 16% were taking cholesterol-lowering medications. In a review of 2500 patients referred to our vascular laboratory for carotid duplex scans, only 7% were at goal blood pressure (<130 mm Hg systolic); this represents a failure to apply established and needed preventive care.

Many explanations may be offered as to why vascular surgeons do not become involved in the nonoperative management of patients, including insufficient knowledge; lack of time outside the operating room or endovascular suite; concern they may alienate the referring physician by becoming involved in that physician's management of the atherosclerotic process; or as previously stated, the assumption that the primary physician will do it well, or even better. Some of the above-mentioned impediments may be valid in a given vascular surgeon's practice, but vascular surgeons at least should know what is appropriate care for their patients' underlying disease, if only to ensure it is being properly applied. This chapter offers suggestions on how to overcome such impediments and incorporate medical management into a vascular surgery practice, busy as it may be.

■ LACK OF TIME

The modern vascular surgeon tends to spend most of his or her time in the operating room or endovascular suite, leaving limited time for an office practice. What office time is available is often taken up with evaluating new patients and following up patients who have had prior procedures. There may be little time for the in-depth patient counseling required to achieve the goals of "medical" therapy. Such a predicament can be overcome by improved office efficiency.

To improve office efficiency, the vascular surgeon needs to use physician extenders. Physician assistants (PAs) are interdependent, semiautonomous clinicians practicing in partnership with physicians and are found in almost every medical and surgical specialty.[4-9] PAs perform tasks similar to their physician partners, including examination, diagnosis, diagnostic testing, treatment (including referral), and prescribing. Research evaluating the effectiveness of PAs has shown them to be capable of providing care comparable to that of physicians for similar services.[8] Traditionally, PAs consider themselves as part of the physician-led team. In contrast, nurse practitioners (NPs) come from a nursing background and feel closer to nursing. Although PAs generally are broadly trained in many specialty areas, many NPs are trained in just one special area, such as women's health. Despite these stereotypical differences, however, PAs and NPs can be trained in vascular surgery and the nonoperative management of vascular disease. A physician extender can be used to interview new patients and participate in the follow-up of established patients, affording the physician the time to become meaningfully involved in patients' nonoperative management. Using routines developed by the vascular surgeon, the physician extender can help greatly in providing medical management under the direction of the surgeon.

Not to be overlooked as extenders of the vascular surgeon are vascular laboratory technicians who work in the surgeon's office. These professionals have sufficient knowledge to be able to monitor, by noninvasive methods, the patients already in the practice, and if guidelines of significant change from baseline are followed, the surgeon may not need to see these patients as frequently. The technician who performs a follow-up noninvasive examination can augment this with pertinent clinical information and assess whether a patient needs to be seen by the vascular surgeon or safely can wait for a later visit. This use of vascular laboratory technicians alleviates the surgeon's office burden, allowing more time for involvement in "medical" management.

■ ALIENATING REFERRING PHYSICIANS

Vascular surgery remains a tertiary care specialty with most surgeons obtaining patients by referral from other physicians. In the event that the referring internist, family practitioner, cardiologist, or, in the case of a diabetic patient, endocrinologist is willing and able to provide the referred patient with appropriate medical care of the underlying vascular disease and related conditions, the vascular surgeon's role should be to reinforce the treatment program. This reinforcement would involve counseling the patient about the risks of dietary indiscretion, lack of exercise, and smoking and the need to continue to take prescribed medications. It has been well documented that such positive reinforcement is a major stimulus for patients to follow medical advice.[10]

Many referred patients are not managed adequately, presenting to the vascular surgeon with uncontrolled hypertension, atherosclerotic risk factors, and diabetes. The surgeon's dilemma is that in interfering in the patient's treatment, albeit with best intentions and to the patient's benefit, he or she may alienate the referring physician and potentially limit future referrals. Some referring physicians may welcome positive input from the surgeon. Sounding out the physician's approach to the medical management of the underlying vascular condition or co-morbidities is recommended to avoid misunderstanding (Fig. 35-1). We have found that most referring physicians are happy to have the vascular surgeon help in their patients' management. In most cases, when discussion has been initiated, the

Dear Referring Doctor,

As you know, despite all our best surgical efforts, many of the patients referred to us for treatment of vascular disease will ultimately suffer and even die from complications related to their underlying disease. Accordingly, we have included in our practice a strong commitment to helping the patient reduce the risk of these complications through a better understanding of their condition and the importance of proper diet, exercise, and risk factor control medications. It is not our goal to take over their care. In most cases, we will simply be reinforcing your treatment plans. However, when we encounter patients who could benefit from more intensive therapy, we would appreciate your input as to how we should deal with these patients. Please circle the response you feel is most appropriate for your patients so that we may comply with your wishes.

1. Notify me by phone so that we can discuss the issues.
2. Notify me in writing so that I can make the appropriate treatment decision.
3. Start what you think is appropriate treatment and I will adjust it as necessary.
4. Manage as you deem necessary, but keep me informed.
5. Do not treat and do not involve yourself in this aspect of my patient's care.
6. Other response (please outline) ________________________________.

Thank you for your continued trust in our practice,

Yours sincerely,

____

FIGURE 35-1 An example of a letter that can be used to sound out a referring physician's approach to the medical management of a patient's underlying vascular condition or co-morbidities.

physician incorporates our suggestions into the patient's treatment plan, limiting the need for intensive follow-up by us. If PAs or NPs are used to manage these medical conditions, it is imperative that the surgeon be completely informed and can assure the referring physician that he or she is responsibly involved in all treatment decisions.

■ INSUFFICIENT KNOWLEDGE

Proper knowledge of aspects of nonoperative care, and medical management of patients with vascular diseases may not have been obtained in a vascular surgeon's training or updated in continuing medical education courses. This section's chapters are intended to provide such information. The following chapters provide an up-to-date review of the various medical options available to treat the diseases commonly seen in patients with vascular diseases. The contributing authors were asked to provide their information in such a way that the practicing vascular surgeon could readily incorporate the information into their practices. These chapters, as summarized here, inform the medically inclined vascular surgeon on how to decrease low-density lipoprotein (LDL) to less than 100 mg/dL, increase high-density lipoprotein (HDL) to greater than 40 mg/dL, reduce triglycerides to less than 150 mg/dL and reduce postprandial lipemia, decrease lipoprotein (a) to less than 20 mg/dL, decrease oxidation of LDL particles and increase LDL particle size, reduce homocysteine levels, correct hyperglycemia and insulin resistance, normalize blood pressure, improve endothelial function, stop patient smoking, minimize symptoms of claudication, and control associated pain.

Medical Management of Atherosclerosis: Control of Risk Factors (Chapter 36)

Fundamental to all treatment approaches to arterial pathology is an understanding of the role of lipids in atherosclerosis. It is now well known that there is more to cholesterol than good and bad varieties, and medical treatment must be targeted at each abnormality differently. Although statins are the dominant medications, not all statins are equal, and there are other drugs that may prove valuable. The beneficial effects of these drugs may go beyond changes in lipid content. Some patients with PAD potentially can benefit from these medications even if they have "normal" lipid levels when first screened (especially patients with insulin resistance, family history of atherosclerosis and its complications, truncal obesity, and low HDL or high triglycerides). The vascular surgeon who wishes to be more than a technician and appropriately treat PAD beyond intervening for extremity ischemic complications needs to be aware of such nuances and other key considerations in managing the underlying atherosclerosis process. This awareness includes the value of exercise, good nutrition, and smoking cessation.

Circulation-Enhancing Drugs (Chapter 37)

Medications to treat claudication have been available for many years but until more recently have been of dubious clinical benefit. Currently, new agents are being used in Europe, and the role of available medications is being defined. It is becoming increasingly clear that the surgeon and the patient have to have a realistic expectation of what these medications can do. Overreliance on these agents can delay appropriate treatment. As a corollary, failure to try these drugs in mild claudicants can lead to unnecessary interventions.

Diabetes, Dysmetabolic Syndrome, and the Vascular Patient (Chapter 38)

Diabetes is well recognized as a major risk factor for arterial disease. It is increasingly being recognized, however, that insulin resistance may be a precursor to type 2 diabetes and that it also is associated with atherosclerotic vascular disease. This condition, variously known as *syndrome X, insulin resistance syndrome,* or *dysmetabolic syndrome,* is now reaching epidemic proportions in many parts of the world, and the implications for vascular surgeons are expected to be enormous. It is important that the vascular surgeon recognize this condition. Although there is no known cure, there are many therapies to alleviate it and early evidence that it can be prevented.

Hypertension and the Vascular Patient (Chapter 39)

Hypertension also is intricately entwined in vascular pathology and morbidity. Vascular surgeons have been involved in treating the renovascular etiology, but seldom do we become actively involved in its medical management. Yet, uncontrolled blood pressure is a leading cause of cardiovascular mortality. Many of the medications used to control high blood pressure may have a direct impact on the development of atherosclerosis and vascular injury. Some, such as angiotensin-converting enzyme inhibitors, may even help patients who are not hypertensive. Many patients present to the vascular surgeon with uncontrolled blood pressure elevation. Positive reinforcement by the vascular surgeon about the benefits of blood pressure control may have a significant impact on the patient's willingness to comply with medications. Hypertensive emergencies can complicate many vascular procedures, so the surgeon also should be familiar with medications that can alleviate this often fatal complication.

Pain Management (Chapter 40)

Despite our best efforts to prevent or control vascular disease, many patients go on to suffer painful complications. Neuropathy, phantom pain, postsympathectomy neuralgia, and ischemic rest pain all can be intractable and debilitating. In some patients with limb-threatening ischemia, control of pain can delay amputation for months or years. Pain management can be especially important in patients with atheroembolism, in whom pain relief can allow ischemic areas to demarcate, allowing more distal amputation than would be required if performed early for pain control. It behooves the vascular surgeon not to ignore patients' pain, but rather to become actively involved in its control.

■ SUMMARY

In addition to the common or generic aspects dealt with in this section, many other, more specific aspects of medical treatment and nonoperative care are addressed elsewhere in other sections of this textbook: prevention of thrombosis by inhibiting platelet function (Chapter 31), management of hypercoagulable states (Chapter 34), screening and prevention of cardiac complications (Chapter 56), prevention and management of respiratory (Chapter 57) and renal (Chapter 58) complications, combating infection (Chapter 59), nonoperative management of lower extremity ischemia (Chapter 77), management of foot lesions in diabetics (Chapter 87), management of vasospastic disease (Chapter 93), prevention and medical treatment of deep venous thrombosis (Chapter 149), nonoperative management of chronic venous insufficiency (Chapter 156), and nonoperative managemnt of chronic lymphedema (Chapter 168). Taken together, these chapters provide strong support for vascular surgeons who wish to become, or continue to be, the "complete" vascular surgeon who should be able to offer all aspects of care, including surgery, endovascular interventions, and medications. In some areas of the United States, we may alleviate our responsibilities by practicing in so-called centers of vascular excellence, where the vascular surgeon, interventionalist, and vascular internist cooperate in a multispecialty vascular clinic. The modern vascular surgeon, however, educated in all aspects of vascular disease, should be able to function as a Center of Excellence of *one,* someone who is able to *operate, dilate, and medicate*.

■ REFERENCES

1. Bismuth J, Klitfod L, Sillesen H: The lack of cardiovascular risk factor management in patients with critical limb ischaemia. Eur J Vasc Endovasc Surg 21:143, 2001.
2. Anand SS, Kundi A, Eikelboom J, et al: Low rates of preventive practices in patients with peripheral vascular disease. Can J Cardiol 15:1259, 1999.
3. McDermott MM, Mehta S, Ahn H, et al: Atherosclerotic risk factors are less intensively treated in patients with peripheral arterial disease than in patients with coronary artery disease. J Gen Intern Med 12:209, 1997.
4. DeLamielleure JL: The impact of surgical physician assistants on the delivery of modern healthcare. Best Pract Benchmarking Healthc 2:136, 1997.
5. Detmer DE, Perry HB: The utilization of surgical physician assistants: Policy implications for the future. Surg Clin North Am 62:669, 1982.
6. Terry K: How "physician extenders" can strengthen your practice. Med Econ 70:57, 1993.
7. Jones PE, Cawley JF: Physician assistants and health system reform: Clinical capabilities, practice activities, and potential roles. JAMA 271:1266, 1994.
8. Mittman DE, Cawley JF, Fenn WH: Physician assistants in the United States. BMJ 325:485, 2002.
9. Perry K: Patient survey: Physician extenders. Why patients love physician extenders. Med Econ 72:58, 1995.
10. Berlowitz DR, Ash AS, Hickey EC, et al: Inadequate management of blood pressure in a hypertensive population. N Engl J Med 339:1957, 1998.

Chapter 36

Atherogenesis and the Medical Management of Atherosclerosis

WILLIAM R. HIATT, MD

Section VII

Atherosclerosis is the cause of peripheral arterial disease (PAD) as well as vascular diseases affecting the coronary and cerebral circulations. Patients with PAD commonly present for treatment because of symptoms of intermittent claudication or critical leg ischemia. However, there is significant overlap of these disorders, in that patients with PAD have concomitant and severe coronary and cerebral disease. Thus, treatment goals must focus on both the effects of atherosclerosis in the peripheral circulation and the systemic nature of the disease, which is associated with a markedly increased risk of cardiovascular events leading to cardiovascular morbidity and mortality. Thus, all patients presenting for treatment of lower extremity atherosclerosis must undergo rigorous assessment of cardiovascular risk factors, and appropriate therapies must be instituted to reduce the risks of both PAD progression and cardiovascular events. This chapter evaluates both the common as well as newly described risk factors for peripheral atherosclerosis, summarizes the pathogenesis of atherosclerosis, and describes the medical management of this disorder.

■ EPIDEMIOLOGIC CONSIDERATIONS

PAD affects 12% of the general population and 20% of individuals older than 70 years.[1,2] As discussed previously, PAD is a marker of systemic atherosclerosis and thus is associated with a markedly increased risk of cardiovascular events.[3] Understanding the systemic nature of this disease and the higher risk of cardiovascular events associated with it emphasizes the importance of aggressive risk factor modification and use of antiplatelet therapies.

Table 36-1 Mortality Risk in Peripheral Arterial Disease

			ALL-CAUSE MORTALITY (EVENT RATE/YEAR)			CVD MORTALITY (EVENT RATE/YEAR)		
STUDY (YEAR)*	**NO.**	**GROUP**	**Control**	**PAD**	**RR (95% CI)**	**Control**	**PAD**	**RR (95% CI)**
Criqui et al (1992)[3]	565	Men	1.7	6.2	3.1 (1.9-4.9)	0.8	4.2	5.9 (3.0-11.4)
		Women	1.2	3.3		0.4	1.8	
Vogt et al (1993)[4]	1492	Women	1.1	5.4	3.1 (1.7-5.5)	0.4	3.0	4.0 (1.7-9.1)
Leng et al (1996)[6]	1498	Symptomatic	2.0	3.8	1.6 (0.9-2.8)	0.7	2.7	2.7 (1.3-5.3)
		Asymptomatic	2.0	6.1	2.4 (1.6-3.7)	0.7	2.3	2.1 (1.1-3.8)
Leng et al (1996)[7]	1592	All patients	2.1	4.4	1.8 (1.3-2.4)	0.1	2.4	2.3 (1.5-3.6)
Newman et al (1997)[5]	1537	Men	1.5	5.3	3.0 (2.8-5.3)	0.5	2.2	3.4 (1.3-8.9)
		Women	1.3	3.8	2.7 (1.6-4.6)	0.4	1.6	3.3 (1.3-8.6)
Total No./Average Rate	6674		1.6	4.8	2.5	0.5	2.5	3.4

*Superscript numbers indicate chapter references.
CI, confidence interval; CVD, cardiovascular disease; PAD, peripheral arterial disease; RR, relative risk.

Table 36-1 lists selective natural history studies evaluating risk of all-cause and cardiovascular disease mortality rates in patients with PAD.[3-7] In all of these studies, cases of PAD were identified with the ankle/brachial index as a screening tool or other appropriate hemodynamic measures. Patients with PAD were then monitored for the occurrence of cardiovascular events. This table demonstrates that on average, an age-matched control group had an all-cause mortality rate of 1.6% per year, whereas in patients with PAD the mortality was 4.8% per year, a 2.5-fold rise in risk. Cardiovascular mortality rates are similarly affected, with an overall event rate of 0.5% per year in controls and 2.5% per year in patients with PAD, a 3.4-fold increase. Importantly, women are at only slightly less risk than men, and even asymptomatic individuals have a markedly higher risk of cardiovascular events. In patients with known coronary artery disease, the presence of PAD is an independent risk factor for death, raising the risk 25% even when other known risk factors are controlled for in the model.[8]

This higher event rate in patients with PAD underlies the importance of intensive medical management to reduce the risk of cardiovascular morbidity and mortality. Importantly, patients with PAD are under-recognized by primary care physicians and, thus, are also undertreated for their risk factors.[9] All vascular specialists and primary care physicians must improve their awareness of the problem and become more aggressive in management of affected patients.

■ RISK FACTORS

Table 36-2 lists the major and minor risk factors for PAD. The major risk factors have been determined from large epidemiologic studies and are highly concordant with the risk factors for coronary and cerebral vascular disease. Studies have confirmed that four major risk factors—diabetes, smoking, hypertension, and hyperlipidemia—account for 80% to 90% of all cardiovascular disease in the United States.[10,11] The minor risk factors have been determined from smaller observational studies but are of interest to clinicians who desire a comprehensive risk assessment in this patient population. When evaluated together with multivariate modeling techniques, the following risk factors emerge as primarily important in the development of PAD: age, diabetes mellitus, current smoking status, C-reactive protein (CRP) value, alterations in lipid metabolism, hypertension, elevations in plasma homocysteine values, and elevations in fibrinogen values. Also, for any number of risk factors found in an individual patient, the presence or absence of cigarette smoking nearly doubles the risk in progression of PAD independent of other risk factor associations.[12] Further discussions of these risk factors follow.

Age

All forms of cardiovascular disease become more prevalent with age, and thus, it is not surprising that PAD is more common in the elderly. In several studies, the risk of PAD increased 1.5- to 2.0-fold for every 10-year rise in age.[2,12,13]

Diabetes Mellitus

Diabetes has been long recognized as a major risk factor for PAD. In the Framingham Study with a 16-year follow-up, the age-adjusted risk ratio for development of intermittent claudication was fivefold higher in diabetic men than in controls and threefold higher in diabetic women.[14-16] In other epidemiologic studies in which PAD was defined by the ankle/brachial index, diabetes increased the risk by approximately threefold.[2,17] The peripheral atherosclerosis observed in patients with diabetes is typically more distal in distribution and often more extensive. Diabetes is also

Table 36-2 Risk Factors for Peripheral Arterial Disease

Major risk factors	Age Diabetes Cigarette smoking C-reactive protein Hyperlipidemia Hypertension Homocysteine Fibrinogen
Minor risk factors	Gender Race Diet Hypercoagulable states Alcohol Asymmetric dimethylarginine

associated with peripheral neuropathy and inability to appropriately respond to infections, leading to a complicated and serious compromise of the lower extremity that may result in diabetic foot ulcers.

Although diabetes is highly associated with peripheral atherosclerosis, the degree of glycemic control, defined by blood glucose concentration or hemoglobin A_1C concentration at any given time point, has not been strongly associated with the severity of the peripheral atherosclerosis.[18] Thus, diabetes is a critical risk factor in the development of PAD, particularly in conjunction with other risk factors.

Cigarette Smoking

Cigarette smoking and diabetes are perhaps the most potent risk factors for peripheral atherosclerosis.[19-22] In general, cigarette smoking is associated with an approximate 3-fold increase in risk for peripheral atherosclerosis.[2,12,13] Current smokers are at greater risk than former smokers, and higher numbers of pack-years are associated with more severe disease. For example, ex-smokers had a 7-fold higher risk of PAD, but current smokers had a 16-fold higher risk.[23]

In addition to being a major risk factor for PAD, current cigarette smoking also significantly affects PAD outcomes. Table 36-3 lists several of these major outcomes. For example, progression from intermittent claudication to ischemic rest pain occurs significantly more frequently in patients who are using tobacco than in those who are abstinent.[24-26] Graft patency results are also significantly affected by cigarette smoking, in terms of both prosthetic and vein bypass grafts.[24,27] Amputation rates are also driven by current smoking status, being approximately double to triple the rates in nonsmokers.[28] Finally, a patient's survival is significantly worse if he or she continues to smoke rather than become abstinent.[24]

Table 36-3 Effects of Tobacco on Outcome of Peripheral Arterial Disease (PAD)

CLINICAL EVENT	TOBACCO USE*	TOBACCO ABSTINENCE*
PAD Clinical Progression		
Claudication to rest pain; 5-year rest progression	18	0
Revascularization Procedure Success Rates		
Vein graft patency at 1 year	70	90
"Reconstruction success"	19	81
Vein graft patency at 3 years	50	90
Patency rate at 3 years	78	94
Prosthetic bypass patency rate at 1 year	65	85
Cumulative patency rate at:		
1-12 months	66.7	75.4
1-2 years	55.2	65.5
2-3 years	52.6	63.6
3-4 years	48.6	60.8
4-5 years	48.6	55.7
Secondary graft patency at:		
1 month	70	91
12 months	40	75
Vein graft patency (femoropopliteal) at 2 years	60	90
Vein/Dacron graft patency (aortofemoral) at 4 years	75	90
Vein graft patency at 1 year	63	84
Amputation Rates		
Amputation rate	23	10
Cumulative limb loss rate at:		
1-12 months	2.7	2.0
1-2 years	14.9	3.3
2-3 years	22.8	6.5
3-4 years	28.1	6.5
4-5 years	28.1	10.9
Patient Survival		
Survival at:		
1 year	85	100
3 years	40	67
5 years	36	66

*All values and rates shown as percentages.

Adapted from Hirsch AT, Treat-Jacobson D, Lando HA, et al: The role of tobacco cessation, antiplatelet and lipid-lowering therapies in the treatment of peripheral arterial disease. Vasc Med 2:243-251, 1997.

Hyperlipidemia

Alterations in lipid metabolism are a major risk factor for all forms of atherosclerosis. Several large epidemiologic trials have conclusively shown that elevations in total cholesterol and low-density lipoprotein (LDL) cholesterol levels and decreases in high-density lipoprotein (HDL) cholesterol levels are significantly and independently associated with cardiovascular mortality.[29-31] LDL cholesterol levels are positively correlated with increased risk, whereas HDL cholesterol levels are associated with protection from cardiovascular events. For example, a 1-mg/dL increase in HDL cholesterol concentration is associated with a 2% to 3% decrease in coronary heart disease risk and a 4% to 5% decrease in cardiovascular disease mortality rate.[31] The role of triglyceride elevations has been debated, but later studies have conclusively shown that elevations of fasting triglyceride values are also a strong and independent predictor of ischemic heart disease and PAD.[32-34] More recently recognized lipid risk factors are apolipoprotein B in very-low-density lipoprotein (VLDL) cholesterol, apolipoprotein C-III in VLDL and LDL cholesterol, and apolipoprotein E in HDL cholesterol, all of which are strong predictors of cardiovascular events.[35] LDL cholesterol particle size has also been considered a risk (smaller particles are more atherogenic)[36]; however, this assumption has been challenged.[37]

In PAD, several lipid fractions are critically important in determining the presence and progression of peripheral atherosclerosis. Independent risk factors for PAD include elevations of total cholesterol, LDL cholesterol, triglycerides, and Lp(a) lipoprotein.[2,12,38] Protective against PAD are increases in HDL cholesterol and apolipoprotein A-I.[38] For every 10-mg/dL increase in total cholesterol concentration, the risk of PAD rises approximately 10%.[2]

Elevations in Lp(a) lipoprotein are a newly recognized independent risk factor for coronary and PAD, particularly in men.[39-41] In studies of coronary disease, elevations in

Lp(a) lipoprotein increase the risk approximately twofold. Similar results have been observed in patients with PAD. In patients with critical leg ischemia, Lp(a) lipoprotein levels are a predictor of mortality.[42] Critical levels are 30 mg/dL or greater.[41] As discussed later, treatment options for modifying this lipid fraction are limited, but its role in peripheral atherosclerosis has now become well recognized.

Lipid screening should begin with the standard lipid profile measured after a 12- to 14-hour fast. Total cholesterol, HDL cholesterol, and triglycerides are measured, and LDL cholesterol concentration is calculated from these findings.[43] In the majority of patients being evaluated or managed for PAD, this information is sufficient to make treatment decisions by targeting LDL cholesterol, HDL cholesterol, and triglycerides for treatment. If these lipid fractions could be brought to established treatment goals, the morbidity and mortality risk of PAD would be greatly reduced.[44]

Hypertension

Hypertension is also a well-recognized risk factor for atherosclerotic diseases, particularly stroke and ischemic heart disease.[45] In PAD, hypertension increases risk approximately twofold to threefold.[2,12,13,46,47] Hypertension has also been found to be an independent risk factor but, perhaps, of less importance than the other risk factors already listed.[48]

Homocysteine

Alterations in homocysteine metabolism are an important independent risk factor for all forms of atherosclerosis, particularly PAD.[49-54] In epidemiologic studies, elevations in homocysteine values are strongly associated with the development of premature coronary carotid and peripheral atherosclerosis.[55] The relative risk is in general approximately increased twofold. Plasma levels of homocysteine are regulated, in part, by B vitamins, and vitamin supplementation has been shown to lower plasma homocysteine levels.[56] Thus low levels of folate and vitamin B_6 levels are also associated with the risk of PAD, perhaps through the modulation of homocysteine levels.[57]

Homocysteine works through a variety of putative mechanisms.[58] An amino acid, homocysteine can react with LDL cholesterol to form oxidized LDL cholesterol, which is often found in foam cells and early atherosclerotic lesions. Through the formation of reactive oxygen species, homocysteine can promote endothelial dysfunction, proliferation of vascular smooth muscle cells, lipid peroxidation, and oxidation of LDL cholesterol. Homocysteine also inhibits nitric oxide (NO) production by endothelial cells and promotes endothelial dysfunction.[59] Homocysteine is also a well-recognized risk factor for thrombophlebitis and thus promotes both venous and arterial thrombosis. All these mechanisms then lead to acceleration of atherosclerosis. Elevations in homocysteine values may be due to genetic defects in homocysteine metabolism typically caused by cystathionine β-synthase deficiency. The homozygous form of the disease is quite rare and results in life-threatening manifestations of arterial and venous thrombosis at an early age. Homocysteine concentrations are approximately twofold to fourfold higher in heterozygotes for this deficiency than in unaffected individuals. Alterations in B_{12} metabolism are also associated with rises in homocysteine levels. Perhaps the most common cause of elevations in homocysteine is nutritional deficiencies of B vitamins, particularly folic acid and vitamins B_6 and B_{12}.

C-Reactive Protein

Inflammation has been associated with the development of atherosclerosis and also the risk of cardiovascular events. In particular, CRP is independently associated with PAD, even in patients with normal lipid levels.[60,61] In the Physicians Health Study, an elevated CRP value was a risk factor for the development of symptomatic PAD as well as a risk for peripheral revascularization.[62] In patients with established PAD, CRP is an independent predictor of future cardiovascular events.[63] The measurement of CRP may also guide lipid therapy, in that statin drugs lower CRP levels and such a reduction may contribute to the benefits of statin drugs.[64]

Fibrinogen and Alterations in Blood Rheology

Elevations of fibrinogen concentration have been recognized as a cardiovascular risk factor for many years.[65] In a meta-analysis, an elevation in fibrinogen levels was associated with an approximately twofold to fourfold higher risk of myocardial infarction or stroke.[66] Rises in blood fibrinogen level are also associated with increases in blood viscosity. Thus, in the evaluation of patients with PAD, increases in fibrinogen and viscosity were independent predictors of peripheral atherosclerosis.[67,68] In addition to their relationship to the presence of PAD, increases in fibrinogen levels and blood viscosity are associated with worsening claudication symptoms.[69] In one study, patients with the worst symptoms of claudication and the lowest levels of physical activity had the highest fibrinogen levels.[70] Conversely, increased physical activity through exercise training may lead to symptomatic improvement, in part by lowering fibrinogen levels.[71] Claudication symptoms may be related to fibrinogen levels through an increase in viscosity, which leads to microcirculatory defects in oxygen delivery. Thus, greater elevations of these variables are associated with worse claudication symptoms. Treatment has not yet been established for elevations in blood viscosity and fibrinogen concentration.

Hypercoagulable States

Alterations in coagulation are commonly associated with the development of venous thrombosis and thromboembolism. However, except for changes in homocysteine metabolism, hypercoagulable states have been less well evaluated in patients with PAD. In one study, presence of the lupus anticoagulant was associated with peripheral atherosclerosis.[72] Also, markers of platelet activation, such as increases in β-thromboglobulin levels, are also associated with PAD.[73] However, the frequency of these abnormalities is low and has not been fully substantiated, so screening is not warranted.

Alcohol

Alcohol has been well recognized to both decrease and increase the risk of cardiovascular disease and cardiovascular events. When taken in small amounts (< 1 drink/day), ethanol is associated with higher HDL cholesterol levels, which may be protective for atherosclerosis.[74] However, when taken in large amounts (≥ 4 drinks/day), alcohol raises blood pressure substantially and also predisposes to cardiac arrhythmias, leading to a higher risk of cardiovascular events.[75] Thus, the effects of alcohol vary widely according to dose but not to type of alcohol consumed.[76,77]

The Physicians Health Study was conducted as a primary prevention trial of the use of aspirin and antioxidants in preventing cardiovascular disease in physicians. One of its findings was that moderate alcohol consumption (approximately 1 drink/day) was associated with a slightly lower risk for the development of PAD.[78] Similar results were observed in the Framingham Study, in terms of alcohol's reducing the risk for development of intermittent claudication.[79]

Miscellaneous Risk Factors

Diet may be a risk factor for PAD. For example, an increase in the consumption of fiber-containing foods was found to be associated with a higher ankle/brachial index, and increased consumption of meat products with a lower ankle/brachial index.[80] In particular, low serum concentrations of vitamin C are associated with higher levels of CRP and more severe PAD.[81] Supplementation with vitamins C and E may slow the progression of peripheral atherosclerosis, although large clinical trials have not shown a benefit of vitamin E therapy.[82]

The formation of NO is critical to maintaining normal endothelial function, and alterations in endothelial function are well-described in patients with atherosclerosis. In patients with PAD, NO synthesis can be inhibited by the endogenous compound asymmetric dimethylarginine (ADMA). The levels of ADMA in PAD patients are directly correlated with inhibition of NO synthesis and the severity of claudication symptoms.[83] Potentially, this inhibition of NO synthesis can be reversed by dietary supplementation with L-arginine.

■ PATHOGENESIS OF ATHEROSCLEROSIS

Risk Factors and Atherogenesis

Atherosclerosis, in part, develops in response to injury to the endothelium. However, the mechanisms by which hypercholesterolemia and the other risk factors alter the endothelium have not been determined. Experimental models of hypertension, hypercholesterolemia, diabetes mellitus and tobacco exposure are characterized by common endothelial abnormalities, such as increased generation of superoxide anion and reductions in bioactivity, synthesis, or both of endothelium-derived NO.[84-87]

Role of Endothelial Dysfunction

The aberrations of endothelial function represent an oxidative stress to the cells and occur within minutes to hours of exposure to the noxious stimuli. Oxidative stress perturbs the cell membrane and increases endothelial permeability. Moreover, the greater endothelial elaboration of oxygen-derived free radicals activates oxidant-sensitive transcriptional proteins such as nuclear factor κB (NFκB). Activated NFκB translocates to the nucleus, where it induces the expression of adhesion molecules (e.g., vascular cell adhesion molecule 1 [VCAM-1]) and chemokines (such as monocyte chemoattractant peptide 1 [MCP-1]) that participate in monocyte adhesion and infiltration (Fig 36-1).[88-92] The expression of these adhesion molecules and chemokines may explain the observation that within several days of the start of a high-cholesterol diet, monocytes adhere to the endothelium, particularly at intercellular junctions.[92] Therefore, the endothelial injury that triggers atherosclerosis may be intracellular oxidative stress (precipitated by hypercholesterolemia and other risk factors).

The monocytes migrate into the subendothelium, where they begin to accumulate lipid and become foam cells. This is the earliest event in the formation of the fatty streak. These activated monocytes (macrophages) release mitogens and chemoattractants that recruit additional macrophages as well as vascular smooth muscle cells into the lesion. In addition, they generate reactive oxygen species that increase

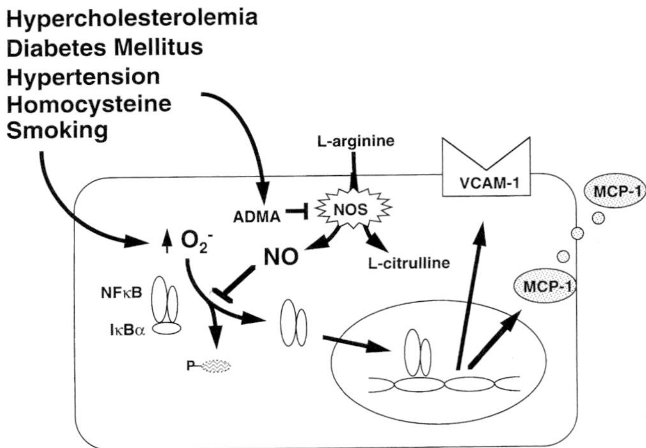

FIGURE 36-1 Atherosclerotic risk factors such as hypercholesterolemia, hypertension, tobacco, and diabetes mellitus lead to increased free radical production and decreased nitric oxide (NO) activity in endothelial cells. Endothelial dysfunction has not only acute effects on vascular tone, but also chronic effects on vessel structure. Increased superoxide anion leads to activation of nuclear factor κB (NFκB) via phosphorylation and degradation of the inhibitor protein (IκBα). NFκB is then free to translocate into the nucleus to initiate transcription of pro-atherogenic genes such as vascular cell adhesion molecule 1 (VCAM-1) and monocyte chemoattractant peptide 1 (MCP-1). Nitric oxide can inhibit these processes by inhibiting superoxide production, directly scavenging superoxide anions, as well as increasing the transcription and activity of IκBα. Moreover, because NO is a paracrine factor, it can have important inhibitory effects on circulating leukocytes and underlying smooth muscle cells. ADMA, asymmetric dimethylarginine.

oxidative stress within the vessel wall and accelerate oxidation of LDL cholesterol trapped in the subintimal space. The oxidation of LDL cholesterol particles in the subintimal space promotes foam cell formation,[89,92] because the oxidized LDL cholesterol is taken up via the scavenger receptor. Unlike the receptor for native LDL cholesterol, the scavenger receptor is not downregulated by intracellular levels of cholesterol. Accordingly, oxidized LDL cholesterol continues to be taken up by the macrophage via the scavenger receptor, with the result that the macrophages become grossly swollen with lipid, giving them a characteristic "foamy" appearance on microscopy. As foam cells accumulate in the subendothelial space, they distort the overlying endothelium and eventually may even rupture through the endothelial surface.[92]

In these areas of endothelial ulceration, platelets adhere to the vessel wall, releasing epidermal growth factor, platelet-derived growth factor, and other mitogens and cytokines that contribute to smooth muscle migration and proliferation. These factors induce smooth muscle cells in the vessel wall to proliferate and migrate into the area of the lesion. The vascular smooth muscle cells undergo a change in phenotype from "contractile" cells to "secretory" cells. The secretory vascular smooth muscle cells elaborate extracellular matrix (e.g., elastin), which transforms the lesion into a fibrous plaque. Extracellular matrix may contribute significantly to growth of the lesion. Indeed, a genetic variant of the stromelysin promoter that causes reduced degradation of extracellular matrix is associated with accelerated progression of atherosclerosis.[93] In addition to elaborating extracellular matrix, the smooth muscle cells may become engorged with lipid to form foam cells. The lesion grows with the recruitment of more cells, the elaboration of extracellular matrix, and the accumulation of lipid until it is transformed from a fibrous plaque to a complex plaque.

The complex plaque typically is characterized by a fibrous cap overlying a necrotic core ("necrotic" core may be a misnomer, because apoptosis undoubtedly contributes in a significant way to cell death and is likely involved in the formation of the cell-free, lipid-rich area in the interior of a complex plaque). The necrotic core is composed of cell debris and cholesterol and contains a high concentration of the thrombogenic tissue factor secreted by macrophages. In later-stage lesions, calcification may occur. Calcifying vascular cells in the vessel wall can transform into osteoblast-like cells and secrete bone proteins such as osteopontin.[94] Microscopic examination of these areas shows histologic characteristics very similar to those of bone tissue. Oxidized lipoprotein stimulates the elaboration of bone protein by these vascular cells. By contrast, oxidized lipoprotein reduces bone formation by osteoblasts.[94] This intriguing finding may account for the clinical observation that some patients with atherosclerosis (typically, elderly women) appear on radiographs to have nearly as much calcium in their aortas as in their spines.

Cellular Mechanisms that Oppose Atherogenesis

Most of the research defining the pathophysiology of atherosclerosis has focused on those factors that precipitate vascular disease. However, a number of endogenous mechanisms oppose atherogenesis. HDL may participate in reverse cholesterol transport (from the vessel to the liver) and also contains enzymes that metabolize platelet-activating factor (PAF) (i.e., paraoxonase and PAF acetylhydrolase).[95] Tissue plasminogen activator is produced by endothelial cells,[96] and, by inducing fibrinolysis, may reduce the accretion of thrombus onto the vessel wall. Intracellular superoxide dismutase detoxifies oxygen-derived free radicals. Endothelium-derived NO and prostacyclin (prostaglandin I_2 [PGI_2]) inhibit several processes that lead to development of an atherosclerotic plaque.[97] These compounds are vasodilators and they inhibit the adherence of platelets and leukocytes to the endothelium. In addition, both NO and PGI_2 (1) inhibit the proliferation of vascular smooth muscle cells and macrophages and (2) suppress the generation of oxygen-derived free radicals. The reduction in oxidative stress turns off the oxidant-responsive genes (e.g., MCP-1 and VCAM-1) that mediate monocyte binding and infiltration into the vessel wall.[96]

It is well established that hypercholesterolemia reduces the bioactivity of endothelium-derived NO.[98,99] In parallel, the endothelium begins to generate superoxide anion.[85] This greater endothelial generation of superoxide anion induced by hypercholesterolemia in a rabbit model can be reversed by starting the animals on a low-cholesterol diet.[100] The reduction in superoxide anion generation is associated with an improvement in endothelium-dependent vasodilator function. In addition to inducing the generation of superoxide anion, hypercholesterolemia causes a decline in tissue glutathione levels and, thereby, increases susceptibility to oxidative damage.[101]

Multiple mechanisms may account for the abnormalities in the L-arginine–NO pathway induced by hypercholesterolemia. They include reduced availability of L-arginine; abnormalities of endothelial receptor–G protein coupling; decreased levels of cofactors such as tetrahydrobiopterin; reduced NO synthase expression and activity; increased degradation of NO by superoxide anion or oxidized lipoproteins and the formation of a circulating inhibitor of NO synthase.[102] Accumulating evidence indicates that endogenous methylarginines inhibit the activity of NO synthase. One of these, ADMA, is a competitive inhibitor of NO synthase and is elevated in patients with either atherosclerosis or risk factors for it.[83,103] The elevation in ADMA probably explains the observation that administration of L-arginine to individuals with atherosclerosis or risk factors for it restores endothelial vasodilator function and can even reduce symptoms of coronary or PAD.[104-107] Given long term, L-arginine supplementation enhances vascular NO production, reduces superoxide anion generation, suppresses monocyte adherence, and inhibits (and even reverses) intimal lesion formation in hypercholesterolemic rabbits.[108-112] By contrast, pharmacologic inhibition of NO synthase or genetic deletion of the enzyme accelerates atherogenesis in animal models.

Plaque Vulnerability and Rupture

Plaque rupture is accepted as the major cause of acute coronary syndromes[113] and likely plays an important role in the progression of PAD. Plaque rupture is accepted to have a role in acute coronary syndromes, in aortic atheroembolism,

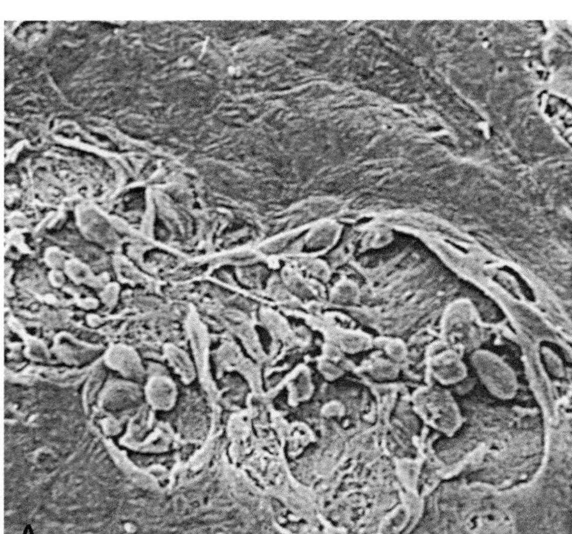

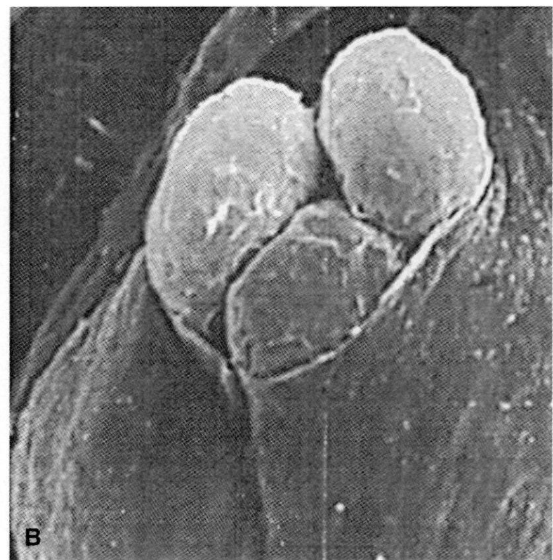

FIGURE 36-2 Scanning electron microphotographs from the coronary artery of a rabbit fed a high cholesterol diet for 10 weeks. **A,** Area of endothelial ulceration. **B,** Lipid-laden microphage, apparently emerging from the subintimal space.

and in symptomatic carotid artery disease. The contribution of plaque rupture to acute exacerbation of PAD, or to its gradual progression, is very likely but has not yet received definitive support. Plaque rupture and thrombosis are often asymptomatic but contribute to the rapid growth of lesions as the thrombus undergoes fibrosis. Histopathologic studies show that plaque rupture is noted at the site of a coronary thrombosis in two thirds of cases.[113,114] The remaining cases appear to be due to thrombosis occurring at the site of endothelial denudation.[114]

Areas of endothelial denudation in the coronary artery of the hypercholesterolemic rabbit are typically associated with collections of macrophages subjacent to the injured endothelium (Fig. 36-2A). Moreover, in adjacent areas, single macrophages or collections of macrophages may be observed to be emerging through microulcerations in the endothelial surface (Fig. 36-2B).

A number of characteristics differentiate stable plaque from plaque that is likely to rupture or that has ruptured. A common feature of the ruptured plaque is thinning of the overlying fibrous cap. The fibrous cap is largely composed of vascular smooth cells and extracellular matrix. In ruptured plaques, the fibrous cap appears to be eroded at the shoulder of the lesion (where the fibrous cap meets the intima of the normal segment of the vessel wall). This is the area that is affected by the greatest hemodynamic stress and where rupture typically occurs.[115]

Another commonality is a large necrotic core filled with lipid and cell debris. The lipid core has a semifluid consistency at body temperature, a feature that likely plays a role in plaque stability; the more fluid the core, the greater mechanical stress the fibrous plaque must bear.[116] Another characteristic feature of the ruptured plaque is intraplaque and intraluminal thrombosis.[117] Angioscopic studies have demonstrated that patients with unstable angina characteristically have complex ulcerated lesions with associated thrombosis, whereas those with stable angina typically have obstructed lesions with an unperturbed endothelial surface.[118] Finally, another common feature of ruptured plaques is an intense infiltration with macrophages (Fig. 36-3).[114] A wealth of data now indicate that macrophages within the plaque play a key role in determining many of the characteristic features of vulnerable plaque and in predisposing the lesion to rupture.

Role of the Macrophages

Accumulating evidence indicates that macrophages are responsible for some key features of the vulnerable plaque, including endothelial denudation, thin fibrous cap, large acellular core, and thrombogenicity of the plaque contents. In the normal vessel, synthesis and degradation of extracellular matrix are remarkably slow, with collagen turnover being measured in years.[119] However, in the diseased vessel, extracellular matrix degradation is increased and can lead to structural weakening of the fibrous cap. An intense infiltration of macrophages is invariably observed at the site of plaque rupture, where the fibrous cap appears to be undermined. In addition to cathepsins, these macrophages are synthesizing abundant amounts of metalloproteinases (MMP-1, MMP-3, and MMP-9).[120-122] These MMPs degrade extracellular matrix, weakening the fibrous cap.[123-125]

In addition to an increased degradation of extracellular matrix, inflammatory cells may reduce the synthesis of collagen by vascular smooth muscle cells. T cells in the region of the fibrous cap elaborate interferon-γ, a potent inhibitor of collagen synthesis.[126] Furthermore, interferon-γ is known to induce apoptosis of vascular smooth muscle cells.[126] The vascular smooth muscle cells may also be under attack from hydrochlorous acid and peroxynitrate anion produced by the macrophages, both of which free radicals may induce apoptosis.[127-130] The increased apoptosis may account for the observation that fibrous caps that have ruptured have half as many smooth muscle cells as unruptured fibrous caps.[115] Macrophages contribute to the thrombotic nature of the vulnerable plaque. The

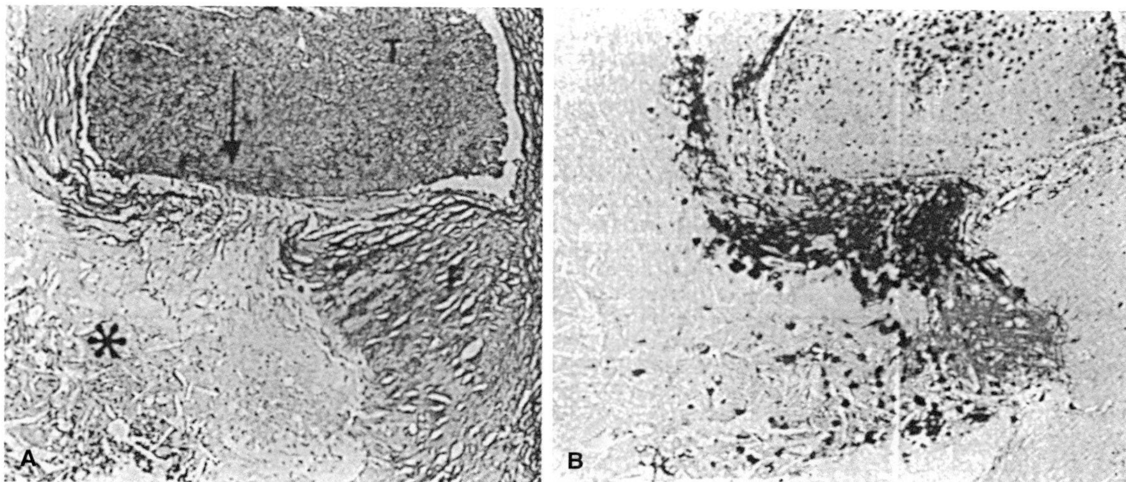

FIGURE 36-3 **A,** A microphotograph of a cross-section through a ruptured plaque in a human coronary artery. Note the thrombus in the lumen (T) and the point of plaque rupture (*arrow*). At this point, the fibrous cap appears to have been thinned, exposing the lumen to the contents of the necrotic core (*asterisk*). **B,** An adjacent cross-section has been stained using a monoclonal antibody directed at macrophage antigen. Note the intense accumulation of macrophages in the area of rupture.

macrophages in the lesion are a rich source of tissue factor, which can be found in the acellular core as well as in the vascular smooth muscle of the fibrous cap.[131,132] Macrophage content and expression of tissue factor correlate with rupture of the human atherosclerotic plaque.[132-134] Macrophage and tissue factor content is greater in coronary atherectomy specimens from patients with unstable angina than in those from patients with stable angina.[134]

Role of Infection

The causative factors initiating inflammation of the fibrous cap are unknown. However, there is mounting circumstantial evidence that implicates infection in the progression of atherosclerosis.[135,136] Seroepidemiologic and immunohistochemical evidence shows that infectious agents such as cytomegalovirus, herpes virus, and *Chlamydia pneumoniae* are associated with atherosclerotic vascular disease and vascular events.[137-140] Such infections may trigger plaque rupture by increasing hemodynamic stress (e.g., tachycardia and higher cardiac output that may accompany a febrile illness) or may directly affect the vascular biology of the plaque. Infection localizing to the plaque may activate endothelial cells to express adhesion molecules, may stimulate vascular cells to undergo proliferation, and may induce resident inflammatory cells to elaborate cytokines that promote further local inflammation.[136]

Imaging Modalities to Detect Vulnerable Plaque

It is apparent from the preceding discussion that an imaging modality to detect vulnerable plaque would be useful for the identification (and appropriate management) of patients at the greatest risk for a catastrophic vascular event. Unfortunately, no current imaging modalities are adequate to detect vulnerable plaque. Angiography can detect stenoses, but this information is not useful in predicting vulnerability to rupture. Indeed, 50% to 75% of plaque ruptures leading to coronary thrombosis occur at sites where the plaque caused less than 50% narrowing of the lumen.[133,141,142] Furthermore, intravascular ultrasound studies show that the volume of the intimal lesion may often be underestimated on angiography.[143] Intravascular ultrasonography is superior to angiography in assessing plaque burden and can provide some information about the characteristics of the lesion; however, the currently available two-dimensional visual images cannot provide the tissue characterization that could reproducibly differentiate stable from unstable atheroma. Although angioscopy and intravascular ultrasonography can identify the presence of thrombosis and some of the lipid-rich plaques, these techniques are invasive and are not practical in evaluating the prognosis in the majority of individuals who have minimal or no symptoms.

Noninvasive tests for determining the risk of acute coronary syndromes are needed. Current noninvasive tests are neither sensitive nor specific. In one study of patients with coronary artery disease, all patients were prospectively evaluated with angiography, exercise testing, and ambulatory monitoring. However, none of these tests nor their combination was effective in predicting acute events.[144] This is probably because severity of stenosis (which is assessed by these technologies) is unrelated to acute events.[145]

Ultrafast computed tomography is noninvasive and is useful in measuring calcium content in the vessel wall, but no clinical studies have been performed to indicate a positive correlation between calcium content and clinical events; indeed, in patients with stroke, the risk of recurrent vascular events is negatively correlated with aortic calcium content.[146] Magnetic resonance angiography may replace angiography to detect stenoses but is currently ineffective at detecting vulnerable plaques. However, one study of carotid artery lesions evaluated with surface coils before endarterectomy has shown that magnetic resonance imaging, with future refinements, may be capable of effectively discriminating lipid core, fibrous caps, calcification, and normal media and adventitia.[147]

Triggers of Acute Vascular Events

There is a circadian pattern of acute myocardial infarction and sudden death, with most heart attacks occurring in the morning during arousal from sleep or shortly thereafter.[148,149] A similar circadian pattern is observed in certain physiologic parameters, with increases in heart rate, blood pressure, and platelet aggregability also occurring in the morning hours.[150] The circadian variation in hemodynamic stress and blood coagulability probably accounts for the increase in vascular events in the morning hours and is probably driven by greater sympathetic nerve flow during arousal from sleep.[150] In addition to this circadian variation, there is also a weekly variation, with more events occurring on Monday in workers but not in retired persons.[151]

The sympathetic nervous system is also activated by fear, anger, and strenuous exertion, possibly accounting for the higher risk of myocardial infarction with emotional or physical stress. The Determinants of Myocardial Infarction Onset Study showed that the risk of myocardial infarction was twofold higher after an outburst of anger, after heavy exertion, or after sexual activity.[152-154] Several other external events have been reported as possible triggers, including earthquakes, blizzards, heat waves, and missile strikes.[155-159] All of these triggers are likely exerting their effects via the sympathetic nervous system, a probability that may explain the observation that β-adrenergic antagonists confer longevity in patients with atherosclerotic coronary artery disease. Because most patients with PAD have co-existing coronary artery disease (CAD), β-adrenergic drugs should be utilized to reduce the risk of myocardial ischemia, hypertension, and arrhythmia.

■ TREATMENT

Patients with peripheral atherosclerosis who present for evaluation and treatment of leg complaints must first be considered for aggressive risk factor modification. As already discussed, these patients are at high risk for cardiovascular events because of the systemic nature of their disease. The following discussion addresses specific approaches to risk factor modification. Much of the data presented in this section have been derived from larger clinical trials of treatment of patients either with known coronary disease or at high risk for coronary and cerebral vascular events. Where available, clinical trials evaluating risk factor modification in PAD are also discussed.

Diabetes

Aggressive control of blood glucose and treatment of insulin resistance are essential in the management of diabetes. Several strategies are well established and are not discussed in detail here. Caloric restriction and exercise are the most important lifestyle changes that can be made, and they may even prevent the development of diabetes.[160] Patients whose type 2 diabetes is not controlled with these recommendations typically are started on oral hypoglycemic medications and newer agents such as metformin and troglitazone to improve insulin sensitivity. Insulin therapy is reserved for patients whose disease cannot be managed on these first-line therapies. Unfortunately, there are no data about the effects of improved glycemic control on the prevention of peripheral atherosclerosis.[161] As already mentioned, excellent glycemic control may not be sufficient in the treatment of atherosclerosis. Therefore, the clinician must address the other cardiovascular risk factors—smoking, hypertension, and hyperlipidemia—in the diabetic patient in addition to treating the diabetes.

Hypertension

A critical factor in the management of diabetes is the control of hypertension. In patients with diabetes, the presence of hypertension significantly increases the risk of the development of PAD as well as several other cardiovascular complications.[162] Treatment of hypertension should be addressed in all patients with diabetes with a goal of the lowest tolerated blood pressure. In a study of patients with type 2 diabetes and PAD, the reduction of blood pressure from a baseline of 135 mm Hg systolic/84 mm Hg diastolic to 128/75 mm Hg was associated with a marked reduction in cardiovascular events. Improved cardiovascular outcomes have been observed in patients with diabetes in trials of lipid-lowering agents, in that lowering of cholesterol in these patients is beneficial in reducing coronary heart disease mortality. These results are discussed later.

Foot Care

In addition to the treatment of diabetes per se and its attendant risk factors, another important aspect is good foot care. Establishing foot care programs in primary care medical clinics has demonstrated benefit in preventing infections and even amputation in persons with diabetes. Such interventions have been shown to prevent the progression to foot ulceration in such patients.[163]

Smoking Cessation Strategies

Smoking cessation remains the cornerstone of PAD treatment. In fact, smoking cessation in the general population has been associated with a 36% reduction in all-cause mortality.[164] Several approaches have been advocated to modify smoking behavior in patients with cardiovascular diseases. They have ranged from physician advice to nicotine replacement to specific drug therapies, and the results are summarized in Table 36-3. It is well recognized that the rate of spontaneous smoking cessation in the population remains low because of the addictive nature of tobacco. Therefore, more structured programs have been recommended to focus on behavior modification and physician advice. Physician advice and behavioral modification therapies result in abstinence rates of approximately 15% at 1 year, but in general, these quit rates are considered inadequate.[24,165] In one large study involving 16,000 men at high risk for coronary disease, enrollment in a clinical trial and recommendations to stop smoking resulted in a 25% quit rate in the intervention group compared with 17% in the control group over 4 years.[166]

Nicotine Replacement

Nicotine replacement therapies in addition to behavior modification are slightly more effective than behavior modification alone. A meta-analysis of several placebo-controlled trials showed cessation rates of 23% to 27% over 6 to 12 months for the use of a nicotine patch, compared with 13% to 18% for placebo.[167] Also, in patients with medical diseases, transdermal nicotine patches have been shown to be safe even in high-risk populations. Thus, this strategy should be considered for patients with PAD.

Antidepressant Therapy

Observations suggest an association between tobacco dependence and depression. Thus, antidepressant therapy may be effective in helping patients quit smoking. Several studies have evaluated the use of the antidepressant bupropion as an aid to smoking cessation in addition to established therapies already discussed. In one large study, use of this antidepressant was associated with a quit rate of 50% at 1 year.[168] These results suggest that combined therapies of behavior modification, nicotine replacement, and antidepressants may be necessary to obtain acceptable quit rates in smokers with PAD.

Summary

An aggressive and multifactorial approach must be implemented to persuade patients with PAD to quit smoking. Table 36-3 presents the benefits of tobacco cessation compared with continued tobacco use regarding both life and limb. At a minimum, this approach should include a behavior modification program and nicotine replacement. The use of other pharmacologic interventions may be warranted in this highly addicted population..

Treatment of Hyperlipidemia

Several effective therapies have been developed to treat patients with hyperlipidemias. Dietary restriction of cholesterol and saturated fats has only a modest effect on LDL cholesterol levels. However, caloric restriction and weight loss can lead to substantial decreases in triglyceride levels, which are important in the management of PAD. Low-cholesterol diets can also be supplemented by high intakes of soluble fiber. In particular, when fiber is ingested in the form of psyllium, there are additional small but significant decreases in total and LDL cholesterol levels, in the range of 5% to 7%.[169,170] This effect is independent of other macronutrients in the diet. In patients with mild elevations in cholesterol, these dietary interventions may be sufficient to effectively reduce cholesterol levels.

The statin drugs have become a well-established means of reducing LDL cholesterol levels. In general, large decreases in LDL cholesterol concentration can be achieved with this form of therapy. Gemfibrozil, a fibrate, has been shown to lower LDL cholesterol concentration with the added benefit of a mild increase in HDL cholesterol concentrations. A more potent means of modifying HDL cholesterol concentration is the use of niacin, which, when combined with a statin, can have substantial benefit on several lipid fractions. For example, when extended-release niacin was combined with lovastatin in one study, there was a greater than 40% reduction in LDL cholesterol and triglyceride levels and a 33% rise in HDL cholesterol levels.[171] In addition, this combination of medications improved Lp(a) lipoprotein, apolipoprotein B, and apolipoprotein A-1 levels and increased LDL particle size. These changes would be expected to be particularly important in patients with PAD, who have abnormalities in all these lipid fractions. The Arterial Disease Multiple Intervention Trial demonstrated the safety and efficacy of niacin in the PAD population.[172] In patients with refractory elevations in LDL cholesterol levels, stepped care should include the addition of a statin drug, then drugs that inhibit cholesterol absorption such as ezetimibe or cholestyramine, and finally a fibrate. The practicality of this approach has been well established and may be necessary in a minority of patients, although often with significant side effects.[173]

Effect of Cholesterol Lowering on Cardiovascular Events

Several very large, well-controlled trials have been conducted in patients who have underlying coronary disease or increased risk for coronary events, to determine the benefits of cholesterol lowering. The major compounds tested were simvastatin and pravastatin. The populations of patients studied included patients with coronary disease and established hyperlipidemia as well as patients with coronary artery disease and cholesterol levels in the "normal" range. In patients with coronary heart disease, the reduction in cholesterol levels with the above-mentioned therapies has been strongly associated with improvements in coronary event rates.

One of the early large studies of lipid-lowering therapy was the Helsinki Heart Study, which was conducted in 4081 men at risk for coronary events. Treatment with gemfibrozil was associated with an increase in HDL cholesterol levels and a decrease in LDL cholesterol levels. The study also showed a 34% reduction in the incidence of coronary heart disease events without an effect on total mortality.[174]

The Scandinavian Simvastatin Survival Study (4S) was the first lipid-lowering trial that demonstrated a very significant decrease in both total mortality and CAD mortality with use of a lipid-lowering agent.[175,176] The study enrolled patients who had experienced a prior myocardial infarction and had an elevated total cholesterol value. More than 4000 patients participated in this secondary prevention trial and were monitored for an average of 5.4 years. Total cholesterol level was decreased in the active drug arm by 25% and LDL cholesterol level by 35%, with a rise in HDL cholesterol level of 8%. The results of the study showed a 30% reduction in total mortality and 42% reduction in risk of major coronary events. The benefits were strongly correlated with on-treatment reductions in total and LDL cholesterol levels as well as apolipoprotein B levels.[177]

The Cholesterol And Recurrent Events (CARE) Trial studied patients who had experienced a myocardial infarction but whose lipid values were in the normal range.[178] More than 4000 patients with total cholesterol levels less than 240 mg/dL and LDL cholesterol levels ranging from 115 to 174 mg/dL were enrolled in the study. Pravastatin was shown to significantly improve lipid profiles (20% decrease in total cholesterol and a 28% decrease in LDL cholesterol; mean LDL cholesterol concentration with therapy was less than 100 mg/dL). Treated patients had a 24% decrease in fatal and nonfatal myocardial infarction rates but no difference in total mortality. Additional benefits were reductions in the need for coronary bypass surgery and in the rate of stroke. The major benefits of pravastatin were seen in patients who experienced a reduction in LDL cholesterol levels down to 125 mg/dL, with less benefit in those with lower LDL cholesterol levels.[179]

The results of all the cholesterol-lowering trials have been evaluated by several meta-analyses.[180,181] These studies have clearly shown that in patients with cardiovascular diseases, such as coronary disease with PAD, the target LDL cholesterol level should be 100 mg/dL or less. In these trials, for every 10% reduction in total cholesterol, coronary heart disease mortality risk was reduced by 15% and total mortality risk by 11%.[180] This benefit has also been shown to be rather universal and not to be restricted to any particular group of patients. For example, a subanalysis of the Scandinavian (4S) study has shown that cholesterol-lowering therapy is effective in both women and elderly patients; therefore, these therapies should not be restricted to any particular cardiovascular population.[182]

On the basis of the results of these and other studies, the National Cholesterol Education Program recommends that patients with underlying cardiovascular disease begin cholesterol-lowering therapy if their LDL cholesterol level exceeds 130 mg/dL, with a target goal of 100 mg/dL or less. These data have been driven particularly by the finding that patients with a beginning LDL cholesterol level of 125 mg/dL or higher experience a benefit from cholesterol-lowering therapy.

Cholesterol Reduction in Peripheral Arterial Disease

In patients with peripheral atherosclerosis, cholesterol-lowering therapies have been associated with stabilization or regression of atherosclerosis. For example, in the carotid circulation, the carotid wall thickness measurement on ultrasonography has been shown to be affected positively by reductions in cholesterol levels.[183,184] In patients with PAD, the use of colestipol and niacin therapy has also been shown to stabilize or regress femoral atherosclerosis.[185]

The observations that cholesterol-lowering therapy would potentially improve the peripheral circulation resulted in several clinical trials. The Program on the Surgical Control of the Hyperlipidemias (POSCH) used ileal bypass surgery to lower lipid concentrations and included a 10-year follow-up.[186] This program showed that lowering cholesterol levels was associated with a slowed rate of progression of PAD. Specifically, the risk of development of an abnormal ankle-brachial index (<0.95) was reduced by 44%, and the risk of development of clinical manifestations of PAD was reduced by 30%, in the group receiving cholesterol-lowering therapy compared with the control group. In 4S, the reduction in cholesterol concentration by simvastatin therapy was also associated with a reduction in the risk of new or worsening intermittent claudication symptoms by 38% compared with placebo.[187] Thus, cholesterol-lowering therapy has been associated with major reductions in cardiovascular morbidity and mortality as well as in progression and symptoms of PAD in patients with systemic atherosclerosis. These results clearly indicate the critical need for cholesterol-lowering therapy in all patients with atherosclerosis.

Until recently, there was no direct evidence of the mortality benefits of using statin drug therapy in patients with PAD. Thus, data from the Heart Protection Study (HPS) are an important addition to our understanding of the role of lowering LDL cholesterol levels in this population.[188] The HPS enrolled more than 20,500 subjects at high risk for cardiovascular events, including 6748 patients with PAD. Simvastatin at a dose of 40 mg was associated with a 12% reduction in total mortality, a 17% reduction in vascular mortality, a 24% reduction in rate of coronary heart disease events, a 27% reduction in rates of all strokes, and a 16% reduction in the rate of noncoronary revascularization procedures. Similar results were obtained in the PAD subgroup, whether or not they had evidence of coronary disease at baseline. Thus, the HPS demonstrated that in patients with PAD (even in the absence of a prior myocardial infarction or stroke), aggressive LDL lowering was associated with a marked reduction in rates of cardiovascular events (myocardial infarction, stroke, revascularization, and vascular death). This is the first large, randomized trial of statin therapy to demonstrate that aggressive lipid modification can significantly improve outcomes in the PAD population. A limitation of HPS was that the evidence in PAD was derived from a subgroup analysis, and we still do not have a trial exclusively evaluating patients with PAD. Despite these limitations, LDL cholesterol levels in all patients with PAD should be lowered to less than 100 mg/dL.

As discussed previously, Lp(a) lipoprotein is also an independent risk factor for PAD, but there are no effective drug therapies to treat this lipid abnormality. In one study, patients with CAD who had elevations in total cholesterol as well as Lp(a) lipoprotein were randomized to receive either simvastatin therapy alone or simvastatin with biweekly apheresis in an attempt to further lower Lp(a) lipoprotein levels.[189] The apheresis therapy used a system to selectively absorb lipoproteins that contain apolipoprotein B, which was expected to reduce the levels of VLDL, LDL cholesterol, and Lp(a) lipoprotein. This study clearly showed that treatment with simvastatin alone had no effect on Lp(a) lipoprotein levels, whereas patients randomly assigned to receive simvastatin with apheresis had a 19% reduction in Lp(a) lipoprotein levels. Changes in PAD were assessed with duplex imaging of the femoral and tibial vessels. Patients who received simvastatin therapy alone experienced an increase in the number of occlusive lesions in the peripheral circulation, whereas those receiving simvastatin plus apheresis showed a decrease. Thus, although apheresis is not a practical means to treat hyperlipidemia, this study does suggest that (1) Lp(a) lipoprotein levels are critical in the development of peripheral atherosclerosis and (2) when Lp(a) lipoprotein concentration is reduced, there is an improvement in the peripheral circulation.

Symptomatic Benefits

Patients with PAD have a marked reduction in exercise performance, as evidenced by a 50% or greater reduction in peak oxygen uptake compared with age-matched healthy controls.[190,191] Patients with claudication have shorter community walking speed and distance, have lower physical function scores on standardized questionnaires, have shorter 6-minute walk distances and speeds, and even have alterations in balance and coordination.[192,193] Thus, an important treatment goal, as stated previously, is to improve exercise performance, walking ability, and functional status in such patients.

Several drugs have been developed for claudication, the most effective of which is cilostazol.[194] Later studies have tested the hypothesis that statins may improve endothelial function and other aspects of PAD, leading to improvement in clinical symptoms. In a small single-center study, patients with PAD were randomly assigned to receive either placebo or simvastatin, and the primary endpoint was changes in peak walking performance on the treadmill.[195] Patients with PAD were enrolled who had very high LDL cholesterol levels, in the 190 mg/dL range, at baseline, which suggested a marked abnormality in lipid metabolism. After 3 months of therapy (simvastatin or placebo), patients receiving statin had an improvement in peak walking time on the treadmill, manifested as a decrease in claudication symptoms. A second study with simvastatin also demonstrated improvements in initial claudication distance on the treadmill.[196]

A third trial evaluated the effects of atorvastatin on treadmill performance.[197] In this study, patients with PAD were randomly assigned to three groups, receiving placebo or two different doses of atorvastatin for 1 year. Patients treated with either dose of drug demonstrated a trend toward improvement in peak walking time and significant increases in claudication onset time. The treadmill findings were supported by a parallel improvement in physical function determined by questionnaires.

At least three randomized trials now suggest that statins may improve limb function. Further evidence emerged from the assessment of the relationship between statin use and limb functioning in a cross-sectional study.[198] This study also supported the concept that statins may improve limb functioning. Thus, the weight of evidence suggests that statins may be an important modulator of symptoms as well as systemic risk. On the basis of this concept, several trials are now under way or are ongoing to look at the overall clinical benefit of statins and other lipid-modifying agents in treating the symptoms of claudication.

Summary

Patients with PAD are at high risk for myocardial infarction and ischemic strokes. Cholesterol-lowering therapies, based primarily on statin drugs, can be expected to cause a significant reduction in cardiovascular event rates. Further, there may be positive effects on the peripheral circulation, although these results are less well established. A number of therapies are available for patients with PAD—diet and soluble fiber supplements for those with modest elevations in LDL cholesterol concentration, and the addition of simvastatin and other agents for those with need for more intensive therapy.

Hypertension Therapy

All patients with cardiovascular disease and hypertension should undergo aggressive lowering of both systolic and diastolic blood pressure. Initial management should include dietary modification with restrictions in sodium, alcohol, and fat intake and increases in exercise and intake of both fruits and vegetables are associated with modest reductions in blood pressure.[199] In addition to lifestyle modification, extensive guidelines have been published for the detection and treatment of hypertension by the Joint National Committee on Detection, Evaluation, and Treatment of High Blood Pressure.[200,201] These guidelines, which give clinicians a detailed approach to pharmacologic treatment of hypertension, are not repeated here. However, it is important to recognize that many effective medications are available to lower blood pressure in patients with cardiovascular disease.

A number of very large clinical trials have been performed to establish the benefits of anti-hypertensive therapy. Perhaps the best summary of these trials can be found in a meta-analysis that summarizes the results in 20,820 women and 19,975 men.[202] The main treatments were thiazide diuretics and beta blockers. Lowering of blood pressure reduced rates of cardiovascular death by 14%, of fatal and nonfatal strokes by 38%, and of all major cardiovascular events by 26% in women; and rates of cardiovascular deaths by 29%, of fatal and nonfatal strokes by 34%, and of all major cardiovascular events by 22% in men. Another meta-analysis summarized the data in 15,559 elderly patients.[203] All patients were older than 59 years, and the main treatments were thiazide diuretics and beta blockers. Analysis showed that the treatment reduced all-cause mortality by 12%, stroke mortality by 36%, and coronary heart disease mortality by 25%. These results are important because most patients with PAD are older than 59 years.

Hypertension Therapy in Peripheral Arterial Disease

In patients with PAD, there has been an historical concern that the use of beta blockers potentially worsens the symptoms of claudication. However, several studies have shown that this class of drugs is safe in patients with claudication and are an acceptable choice for blood pressure lowering.[204] Nevertheless, large reductions of systolic pressure and leg perfusion by any class of antihypertensive agent may result in modest worsening of claudication symptoms.[205]

The angiotensin-converting enzyme (ACE) inhibitor drugs have also shown benefit beyond blood pressure lowering in high-risk groups. The Heart Outcomes Prevention Evaluation (HOPE) included 4046 patients with PAD.[206] In this subgroup, there was a 22% risk reduction in patients randomly assigned to receive ramipril compared with placebo that was independent of lowering of blood pressure. On the basis of this finding, the U.S. Food and

Drug Administration (FDA) has now approved ramipril for its cardioprotective benefits in patients at high risk, including those with PAD. Thus, as a drug class, the ACE inhibitors would certainly be recommended in such patients.

Thus the goals of treating hypertension in patients with PAD should be similar to those in populations of patients with other cardiovascular diseases. As discussed previously, any class of antihypertensive therapy would be appropriate and would be guided by individual patient needs.

Treatment of Elevated Homocysteine Levels

Most patients with elevated homocysteine levels can be easily treated by supplementation with B vitamins. In fact, folic acid has been approved for supplementation in cereal-grain products, and modification of diet has been shown to lower homocysteine levels. Levels of folic acid obtained by this means are sufficient to significantly reduce plasma homocysteine levels, an effect that may have therapeutic efficacy.[207,208] If folate is prescribed as a supplement, 0.8 mg per day appears to be the minimally effective dose.[56] In older patients, caution should be used to not treat patients with vitamin B_{12} deficiencies solely with folic acid, which could precipitate the peripheral neuropathy unless vitamin B_{12} is also provided.

Despite this ease of therapy, no clinical trials have demonstrated efficacy of folic acid in reducing homocysteine levels.[209,210] Clinicians may consider screening for elevated homocysteine levels in young patients presenting with PAD, but no other cardiovascular risk factors for premature peripheral atherosclerosis. These patients may be candidates for B vitamin supplementation if their homocysteine values are elevated. However, clinical recommendations on treatment of homocysteine elevations must await clinical trial results.

Estrogen Treatment

Although women are generally protected from cardiovascular disease, this protection is lost after menopause. This fact has led to several trials using estrogen-progesterone replacement to prevent the development of cardiovascular disease. The results have been disappointing. For example, the Heart and Estrogen/Progestin Replacement Study evaluated the effects of hormone therapy in 2763 postmenopausal women with CAD.[211] Rates of peripheral arterial events (defined as aortic or carotid surgery, lower extremity revascularization, or amputation) were unaffected by hormone therapy. In addition, hormone therapy has been associated with a reduced graft patency in women undergoing femoropopliteal bypass surgery, possibly in relation to the prothrombotic effects of the therapy.[212] Therefore, administration of estrogen for postmenopausal women should be avoided.

Exercise Therapy

Exercise clearly has a role in the treatment of patients with claudication to improve their symptoms and walking ability.[213,214] The effects of routine exercise on cardiovascular mortality has not been studied in PAD. However, other studies have shown a positive association between physical activity and reduced mortality.[215] Thus, exercise may have multiple benefits in the treatment of patients with PAD.

Antiplatelet Therapy

In addition to risk factor modification, antiplatelet therapies have been shown to slow the progression of peripheral atherosclerosis as well as to decrease cardiovascular morbidity and mortality. Aspirin is the primary antiplatelet drug with the most evidence supporting its use. The Antithrombotic Trialists' Collaboration meta-analysis concluded that when patients with cardiovascular disease were given aspirin, there was a consistent 25% odds reduction in subsequent cardiovascular events.[216] This latest meta-analysis has also clearly demonstrated that low-dose aspirin (75 to 160 mg) is protective and probably safer in terms of gastrointestinal bleeding than higher doses of aspirin. For patients with PAD, the meta-analysis of all antiplatelet trials (including studies of aspirin, clopidogrel, ticlopidine, dipyridamole, and picotamide) has demonstrated a 23% odds reduction in ischemic events.[216]

What is remarkable is that specific studies in the PAD population using aspirin have not shown a statistically significant reduction in cardiovascular events.[217] Thus, although antiplatelet drugs are clearly indicated in the overall management of PAD, aspirin does not have FDA approval for use in this patient population.[218]

In contrast to aspirin, clopidogrel has good evidence for prevention of myocardial infarction, stroke, and vascular death in PAD.[219] In the PAD subgroup of the Clopidogrel versus Aspirin in Patients at Risk of Ischaemic Events (CAPRIE) study, there was a 23.8% lower risk in patients receiving clopidogrel than in those undergoing aspirin therapy (see Fig. 36-5).

Both aspirin and clopidogrel have potential side effects. Aspirin causes gastrointestinal disturbances in some patients, although it is well tolerated by the majority of patients. In the CAPRIE study, patients taking clopidogrel had a higher incidence of diarrhea, rash, and pruritus than those taking aspirin but a lower incidence of gastrointestinal disturbances and upper gastrointestinal bleeds. This was true even though aspirin-intolerant patients were excluded from the trial. Clopidogrel, although closely related to ticlopidine, does not have the increased risk of neutropenia; therefore, far less hematologic monitoring is required for this new drug.

Given that PAD is a systemic atherosclerotic disease and that patients with the disease have a strong and independent risk of cardiovascular morbidity and mortality, such patients should be treated with antiplatelet agents unless contraindicated. Given the current data, with lack of clinical trial evidence of the benefits of aspirin in patients with PAD, clopidogrel would be the preferred antiplatelet agent in this patient population.

Complementary Therapies

A number of descriptive and case-control studies have shown an association between antioxidant vitamin intake and reductions in cardiovascular events.[220] Antioxidants may make LDL cholesterol resistant to oxidation, making that lipid fraction less atherogenic. In addition, the effects on

LDL cholesterol and other mechanisms may improve endothelium-dependent vasodilatation by reducing the oxidative degradation of NO.[220]

Vitamins C, E, and betacarotene have been the most popular of the antioxidant supplements. However betacarotene has fallen out of favor because several large trials have failed to show a benefit of betacarotene in reducing cardiovascular events; moreover, there is a possible excess rate of lung cancer events with its use.[221,222] More importantly, several large clinical trials that have included vitamin E in the treatment (the Heart Protection Study and the Heart Outcomes Prevention Evaluation) did not show any clinical benefit or reduction in risk with vitamin supplementation.[188,223] Therefore, at least vitamin E cannot be recommended in patients with PAD at this time.

■ CONCLUSIONS

In summary, patients with peripheral atherosclerosis have a very high risk of cardiovascular morbidity and mortality. A reduced ankle/brachial index is an independent predictor of mortality and an indicator of systemic atherosclerosis. The primary causes of death in patients with PAD are cardiovascular and are due to myocardial infarctions and strokes. Despite these alarming figures, very few studies have attempted to look at the benefits of risk factor modification or antiplatelet therapy in reducing these systemic events in patients with PAD.

Despite the lack of data, patients with PAD should not be ignored. This discussion has advocated an aggressive approach to risk factor modification, including normalization of LDL cholesterol levels, smoking cessation, treatment of diabetes and associated risk factors, and lowering of blood pressure. These guidelines were derived primarily from large studies conducted in patients at risk for CAD, and the results extrapolated to the PAD population. Finally, all patients with PAD should receive antiplatelet therapy. Clopidogrel would be the preferred agent; if it is not available, then at a minimum, aspirin should be advocated. An overall strategy for risk reduction is presented in Figure 36-4. The evidence for pharmacologic risk reduction therapies is shown in Figure 36-5.

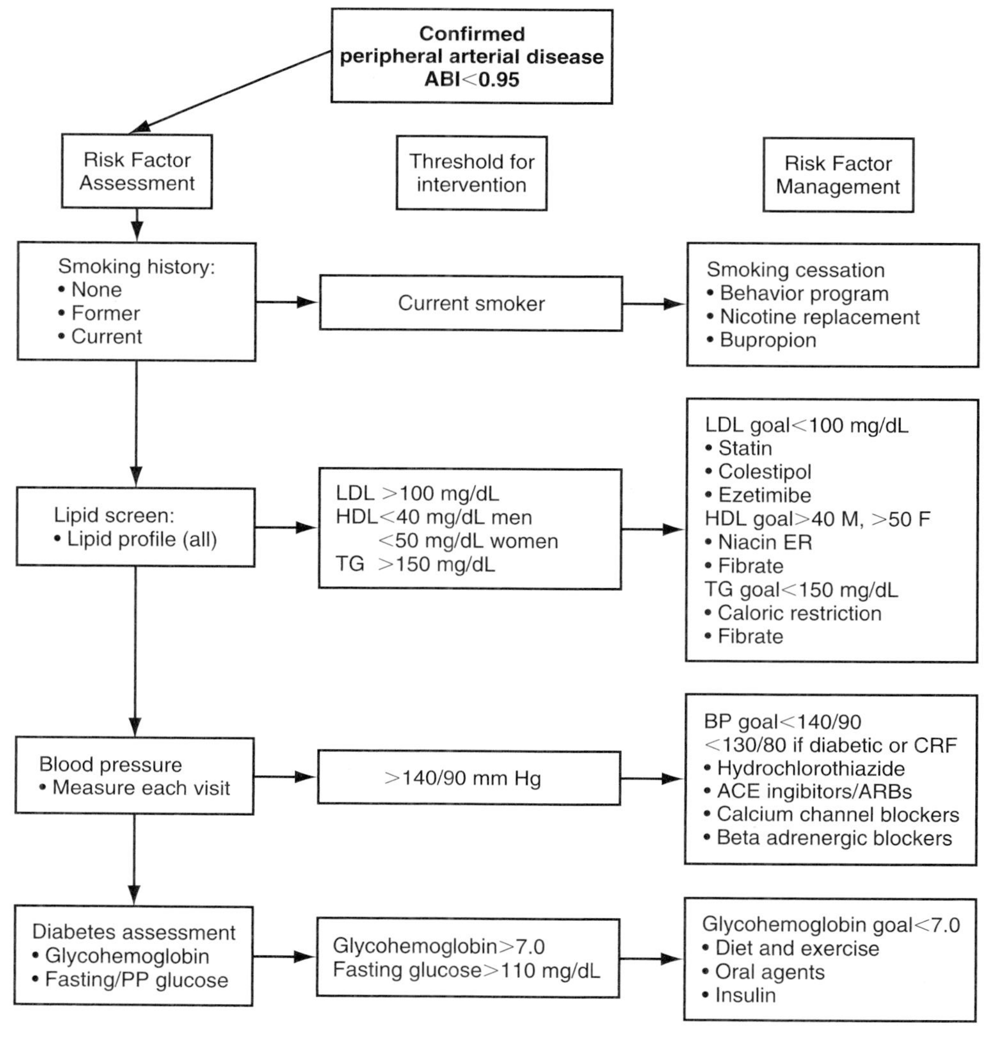

FIGURE 36-4 An overall strategy for detection and management of risk factors for peripheral arterial disease. ABI, ankle brachial index; ACE, angiotensin-converting enzyme; ARBs, angiotensin II receptor blockers; BP, blood pressure; HDL, high-density lipoprotein; LDL, low-density lipoprotein; TG, triglycerides.

Evidence-based drug treatment for PAD

Drug	*Control*	*Rate/yr*	*RRR*	*NNT*
Aspirin				
CV events	control	4.6%	15%	140
Patency	control	15.7%	40%	17
Clopidogrel				
CV events	aspirin	4.8%	24%	94
Ramipril				
CV events	placebo	4.4%	26%	88
Simvastatin (PAD only)				
CV + revasc	placebo	6.1%	21%	86

0.25 0.5 0.75 1.0

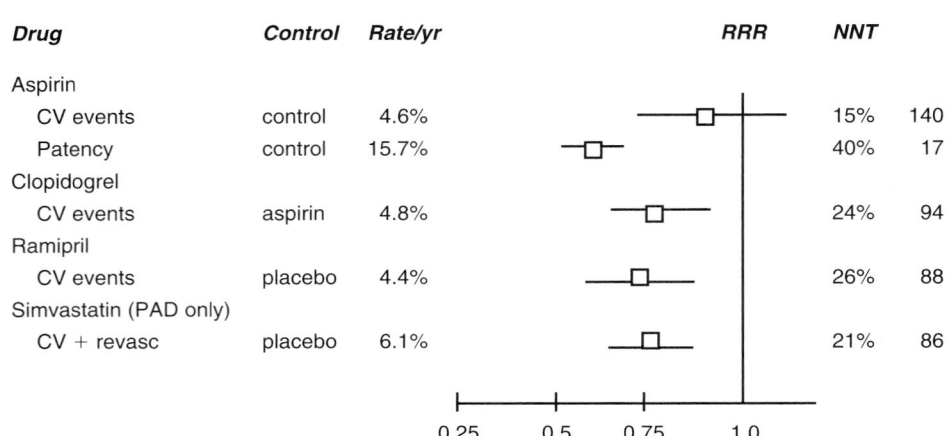

FIGURE 36-5 Evidence-based drug treatment for peripheral arterial disease. (PAD). (BMJ 308:81-106, 1994; Lancet 348:1329-1339, 1996. N Engl J Med 342:145-153, 2000; Lancet 360:7-22, 2002.)

■ REFERENCES

1. Criqui MH, Fronek A, Barrett-Connor E, et al: The prevalence of peripheral arterial disease in a defined population. Circulation 71:510-515, 1985.
2. Hiatt WR, Hoag S, Hamman RF: Effect of diagnostic criteria on the prevalence of peripheral arterial disease: The San Luis Valley Diabetes Study. Circulation 91:1472-1479, 1995.
3. Criqui MH, Langer RD, Fronek A, et al: Mortality over a period of 10 years in patients with peripheral arterial disease. N Engl J Med 326:381-386, 1992.
4. Vogt MT, Cauley JA, Newman AB, et al: Decreased ankle/arm blood pressure index and mortality in elderly women. JAMA 270:465-469, 1993.
5. Newman AB, Tyrrell KS, Kuller LH: Mortality over four years in SHEP participants with a low ankle-arm index. J Am Geriatr Soc 45:1472-1478, 1997.
6. Leng GC, Fowkes FG, Lee AJ, et al: Use of ankle brachial pressure index to predict cardiovascular events and death: A cohort study. BMJ 313:1440-1444, 1996.
7. Leng GC, Lee AJ, Fowkes FG, et al: Incidence, natural history and cardiovascular events in symptomatic and asymptomatic peripheral arterial disease in the general population. Int J Epidemiol 25:1172-1181, 1996.
8. Eagle KA, Rihal CS, Foster ED, et al: Long-term survival in patients with coronary artery disease: Importance of peripheral vascular disease. The Coronary Artery Surgery Study (CASS) Investigators. J Am Coll Cardiol 23:1091-1095, 1994.
9. McDermott MM, Mehta S, Ahn H, et al: Atherosclerotic risk factors are less intensively treated in patients with peripheral arterial disease than in patients with coronary artery disease. J Gen Intern Med 12:209-215, 1997.
10. Khot UN, Khot MB, Bajzer CT, et al: Prevalence of conventional risk factors in patients with coronary heart disease. JAMA 290:898-904, 2003.
11. Greenland P, Knoll MD, Stamler J, et al: Major risk factors as antecedents of fatal and nonfatal coronary heart disease events. JAMA 290:891-897, 2003.
12. Murabito JM, D'Agostino RB, Silbershatz H, et al: Intermittent claudication: A risk profile from The Framingham Heart Study. Circulation 96:44-49, 1997.
13. Vogt MT, Cauley JA, Kuller LH, et al: Prevalence and correlates of lower extremity arterial disease in elderly women. Am J Epidemiol 137:559-568, 1993.
14. Kannel WB, McGee DL: Diabetes and cardiovascular disease: The Framingham study. JAMA 241:2035-2038, 1979.
15. Kannel WB, McGee DL: Update on some epidemiologic features of intermittent claudication: The Framingham study. J Am Geriatr Soc 33:13-18, 1985.
16. Kannel WB, D'Agostino RB, Wilson PW, et al: Diabetes, fibrinogen, and risk of cardiovascular disease: The Framingham experience. Am Heart J 120:672-676, 1990.
17. Hooi JD, Kester AD, Stoffers HE, et al: Incidence of and risk factors for asymptomatic peripheral arterial occlusive disease: A longitudinal study. Am J Epidemiol 153:666-672, 2001.
18. Beach KW, Strandness DE: Arteriosclerosis obliterans and associated risk factors in insulin-dependent and non-insulin-dependent diabetes. Diabetes 29:882-888, 1980.
19. Kannel WB, McGee DL, Castelli WP: Latest perspectives on cigarette smoking and cardiovascular disease: The Framingham study. J Cardiac Rehabil 4:267-277, 1984.
20. Kannel WB, Shurtleff D, National Heart and Lung Institute, et al: The Framingham study: Cigarettes and the development of intermittent claudication. Geriatrics 28:61-68, 1973.
21. Krupski WC, Rapp JH: Smoking and atherosclerosis. Perspect Vasc Surg 1:103-134, 1988.
22. Krupski WC: The peripheral vascular consequences of smoking. Ann Vasc Surg 5:291-304, 1991.
23. Cole CW, Hill GB, Farzad E, et al: Cigarette smoking and peripheral occlusive disease. Surgery 114:753-757, 1993.
24. Hirsch AT, Treat-Jacobson D, Lando HA, et al: The role of tobacco cessation, antiplatelet and lipid-lowering therapies in the treatment of peripheral arterial disease. Vasc Med 2:243-251, 1997.
25. Jonason T, Bergstrom R: Cessation of smoking in patients with intermittent claudication. Acta Med Scand 221:253-260, 1987.
26. Quick CRG, Cotton LT: The measured effect of stopping smoking on intermittent claudication. Br J Surg 69(Suppl):S24-S26, 1982.
27. Myers KA, King RB, Scott DF, et al: The effect of smoking on the late patency of arterial reconstructions in the legs. Br J Surg 65:267-271, 1978.
28. Stewart CP: The influence of smoking on the level of lower limb amputation. Prosthet Orthot Int 11:113-116, 1987.
29. Martin MJ, Hulley SB, Browner WS, et al: Serum cholesterol, blood pressure, and mortality: Implications from a cohort of 361,662 men. Lancet 2(8513):933-936, 1986.
30. Pekkanen J, Linn S, Heiss G, et al: Ten-year mortality from cardiovascular disease in relation to cholesterol level among men with and without preexisting cardiovascular disease. N Engl J Med 322:1700-1707, 1990.

31. Gordon DJ, Probstfield JL, Garrison RJ, et al: High-density lipoprotein cholesterol and cardiovascular disease: Four prospective American studies. Circulation 79:8-15, 1989.
32. Burchfiel CM, Laws A, Benfante R, et al: Combined effects of HDL cholesterol, triglyceride, and total cholesterol concentrations on 18-year risk of atherosclerotic disease. Circulation 92:1430-1436, 1995.
33. Jeppesen J, Hein HO, Suadicani P, et al: Triglyceride concentration and ischemic heart disease: An eight-year follow-up in the Copenhagen Male Study. Circulation 97:1029-1036, 1998.
34. Drexel H, Steurer J, Muntwyler J, et al: Predictors of the presence and extent of peripheral arterial occlusive disease. Circulation 94(Suppl I):II199-II205, 1996.
35. Sacks FM, Alaupovic P, Moye LA, et al: VLDL, apolipoproteins B, CIII, and E, and risk of recurrent coronary events in the Cholesterol and Recurrent Events (CARE) trial. Circulation 102:1886-1892, 2000.
36. Stampfer MJ, Krauss RM, Ma J, et al: A prospective study of triglyceride level, low-density lipoprotein particle diameter, and risk of myocardial infarction. JAMA 276:882-888, 1996.
37. Campos H, Moye LA, Glasser SP, et al: Low-density lipoprotein size, pravastatin treatment, and coronary events. JAMA 286:1468-1474, 2001.
38. Johansson J, Egberg N, Hohnsson H, et al: Serum lipoproteins and hemostatic function in intermittent claudication. Arterioscler Thromb 13:1441-1448, 1993.
39. Bostom AG, Cupples LA, Jenner JL, et al: Elevated plasma lipoprotein(a) and coronary heart disease in men aged 55 years and younger: A prospective study. JAMA 276:544-548, 1996.
40. Lupattelli G, Siepi D, Pasqualini L, et al: Lipoprotein (a) in peripheral arterial occlusive disease. Vasa 23:321-324, 1994.
41. Valentine RJ, Kaplan HS, Green R, et al: Lipoprotein (a), homocysteine, and hypercoagulable states in young men with premature peripheral atherosclerosis: A prospective, controlled analysis. J Vasc Surg 23:53-61, 1996.
42. Cheng SW, Ting AC: Lipoprotein (a) level and mortality in patients with critical lower limb ischaemia. Eur J Vasc Endovasc Surg 22:124-129, 2001.
43. Guidelines for using serum cholesterol, high-density lipoprotein cholesterol, and triglyceride levels as screening tests for preventing coronary heart disease in adults. American College of Physicians. Part I. Ann Intern Med 124:515-517, 1996.
44. Executive Summary of the Third Report of the National Cholesterol Education Program (NCEP) Expert Panel on Detection, Evaluation, and Treatment of High Blood Cholesterol in Adults (Adult Treatment Panel III). JAMA 285:2486-2497, 2001.
45. Stokes J, Kannel WB, Wolf PA, et al: The relative importance of selected risk factors for various manifestations of cardiovascular disease among men and women from 35 to 64 years old: 30 years of follow-up in the Framingham Study. Circulation 75:V65-V73, 1987.
46. Sutton KC, Wolfson SKJ, Kuller LH: Carotid and lower extremity arterial disease in elderly adults with isolated systolic hypertension. Stroke 18:817-822, 1987.
47. Safar ME, Laurent S, Asmar RE, et al: Systolic hypertension in patients with arteriosclerosis obliterans of the lower limbs. Angiology 38:287-295, 1987.
48. Juergens JL, Barker NW, Hines EA: Arteriosclerosis obliterans: A review of 520 cases with special reference to pathogenic and prognostic factors. Circulation 21:188-195, 1960.
49. Clarke R, Daly L, Robinson K, et al: Hyperhomocysteinemia: An independent risk factor for vascular disease. N Engl J Med 324:1149-1155, 1991.
50. Molgaard J, Malinow MR, Lassvik C, et al: Hyperhomocyst(e)inaemia: An independent risk factor for intermittent claudication. J Intern Med 231:273-279, 1992.
51. Taylor LM, DeFrang RD, Harris EJ, et al: The association of elevated plasma homocyst(e)ine with progression of symptomatic peripheral arterial disease. J Vasc Surg 13:128-136, 1991.
52. Brattstrom L, Israelsson B, Norrving B, et al: Impaired homocysteine metabolism in early-onset cerebral and peripheral occlusive arterial disease. Atherosclerosis 81:51-60, 1990.
53. Malinow MR, Kang SS, Taylor LM, et al: Prevalence of hyperhomocyst(e)inemia in patients with peripheral arterial occlusive disease. Circulation 79:1180-1188, 1989.
54. Hoogeveen EK, Kostense PJ, Beks PJ, et al: Hyperhomocysteinemia is associated with an increased risk of cardiovascular disease, especially in non-insulin-dependent diabetes mellitus: A population-based study. Arterioscler Thromb Vasc Biol 18:133-138, 1998.
55. Mansoor MA: Redox status and protein binding of plasma homocysteine and other aminothiols in patients with hyperhomocysteinemia due to cobalamin deficiency. Am J Clin Nutr 76:631-635, 1994.
56. Wald DS, Bishop L, Wald NJ, et al: Randomized trial of folic acid supplementation and serum homocysteine levels. Arch Intern Med 161:695-700, 2001.
57. Robinson K, Arheart K, Refsum H, et al: Low circulating folate and vitamin B6 concentrations: Risk factors for stroke, peripheral vascular disease, and coronary artery disease. European COMAC Group. Circulation 97:437-443, 1998.
58. Welch GN, Loscalzo J: Homocysteine and atherothrombosis. N Engl J Med 338:1042-1050, 1998.
59. Stuhlinger MC, Oka RK, Graf EE, et al: Endothelial dysfunction induced by hyperhomocyst(e)inemia: Role of asymmetric dimethylarginine. Circulation 108:933-938, 2003.
60. Ridker PM, Hennekens CH, Buring JE, et al: C-reactive protein and other markers of inflammation in the prediction of cardiovascular disease in women. N Engl J Med 342:836-843, 2000.
61. Ridker PM, Stampfer MJ, Rifai N: Novel risk factors for systemic atherosclerosis: A comparison of C-reactive protein, fibrinogen, homocysteine, lipoprotein(a), and standard cholesterol screening as predictors of peripheral arterial disease. JAMA 285:2481-2485, 2001.
62. Ridker PM, Cushman M, Stampfer MJ, et al: Plasma concentration of C-reactive protein and risk of developing peripheral vascular disease. Circulation 97:425-428, 1998.
63. Rossi E, Biasucci LM, Citterio F, et al: Risk of myocardial infarction and angina in patients with severe peripheral vascular disease: Predictive role of C-reactive protein. Circulation 105:800-803, 2002.
64. Ridker PM, Rifai N, Clearfield M, et al: Measurement of C-reactive protein for the targeting of statin therapy in the primary prevention of acute coronary events. N Engl J Med 344:1959-1965, 2001.
65. Cortellaro M, Cofrancesco E, Boschetti C, et al: Increased fibrin turnover and high PAI-1 activity as predictors of ischemic events in atherosclerotic patients: A case-control study. The PLAT Group. Arterioscler Thromb 13:1412-1417, 1993.
66. Ernst E, Resch KL: Fibrinogen as a cardiovascular risk factor: A meta-analysis and review of the literature. Ann Intern Med 118:956-963, 1993.
67. Dormandy JA, Hoare E, Khattab AH, et al: Prognostic significance of rheological and biochemical findings in patients with intermittent claudication. Br Med J 4:581-583, 1973.
68. Lee AJ, Lowe GDO, Woodward M, et al: Fibrinogen in relation to personal history of prevalent hypertension, diabetes, stroke, intermittent claudication, coronary heart disease, and family history: The Scottish Heart Health Study. Br Heart J 69:338-342, 1993.
69. Lowe GDO, Fowkes FGR, Dawes J, et al: Blood viscosity, fibrinogen, and activation of coagulation and leukocytes in peripheral arterial disease and the normal population in the Edinburgh Artery Study. Circulation 87:1915-1920, 1993.
70. Killewich LA, Gardner AW, Macko RF, et al: Progressive intermittent claudication is associated with impaired fibrinolysis. J Vasc Surg 27:645-650, 1998.
71. Gardner AW, Killewich LA: Association between physical activity and endogenous fibrinolysis in peripheral arterial disease: A cross-sectional study. Angiology 53:367-374, 2002.
72. Donaldson MC, Weinberg DS, Belkin M, et al: Screening for hypercoagulable states in vascular surgical practice: A preliminary study. J Vasc Surg 11:825-831, 1990.

73. Catalano M, Russo U, Libretti A: Plasma beta-thromboglobulin levels and claudication degrees in patients with peripheral vascular disease. Angiology 37:339-342, 1986.
74. Steinberg D, Pearson TA, Kuller LH: Alcohol and atherosclerosis. Ann Intern Med 114:967-976, 1991.
75. Notzon FC, Komarov YM, Ermakov SP, et al: Causes of declining life expectancy in Russia. JAMA 279:793-800, 1998.
76. Mukamal KJ, Conigrave KM, Mittleman MA, et al: Roles of drinking pattern and type of alcohol consumed in coronary heart disease in men. N Engl J Med 348:109-118, 2003.
77. Gaziano JM, Hennekens CH, Godfried SL, et al: Type of alcoholic beverage and risk of myocardial infarction. Am J Cardiol. 83:52-57, 1999.
78. Camargo CAJ, Stampfer MJ, Glynn RJ, et al: Prospective study of moderate alcohol consumption and risk of peripheral arterial disease in US male physicians. Circulation 95:577-580, 1997.
79. Djousse L, Levy D, Murabito JM, et al: Alcohol consumption and risk of intermittent claudication in the Framingham heart study. Circulation 102:3092-3097, 2000.
80. Donnan PT, Thomson M, Fowkes FGR, et al: Diet as a risk factor for peripheral arterial disease in the general population: The Edinburgh Artery Study. Am J Clin Nutr 57:917-921, 1993.
81. Langlois M, Duprez D, Delanghe J, et al: Serum vitamin C concentration is low in peripheral arterial disease and is associated with inflammation and severity of atherosclerosis. Circulation 103:1863-1868, 2001.
82. Salonen RM, Nyyssonen K, Kaikkonen J, et al: Six-year effect of combined vitamin C and E supplementation on atherosclerotic progression: The Antioxidant Supplementation in Atherosclerosis Prevention (ASAP) Study. Circulation 107:947-953, 2003.
83. Boger RH, Bode-Boger SM, Thiele W, et al: Biochemical evidence for impaired nitric oxide synthesis in patients with peripheral arterial occlusive disease. Circulation 95:2068-2074, 1997.
84. Rajagopalan S, Kurz S, Munzel T, et al: Angiotensin II-mediated hypertension in the rat increases vascular superoxide production via membrane NADH/NADPH oxidase activation: Contribution to alterations of vasomotor tone. J Clin Invest 97:1916-1923, 1996.
85. Ohara Y, Peterson TE, Harrison DG: Hypercholesterolemia increases endothelial superoxide anion production. J Clin Invest 91:2546-2551, 1993.
86. Tesfamariam B, Cohen RA: Free radicals mediate endothelial cell dysfunction caused by elevated glucose. Am J Physiol 263:H321-H326, 1992.
87. Tsao PS, Buitrago R, Chang H, et al: Effects of diabetes on monocyte-endothelial interactions and endothelial superoxide production in fructose-induced insulin-resistant and hypertensive rats. Circulation 92:A2666, 1995.
88. Cybulsky MI, Gimbrone MAJ: Endothelial expression of a mononuclear leukocyte adhesion molecule during atherogenesis. Science 251:788-789, 1991.
89. Berliner JA, Navab M, Fogelman AM, et al: Atherosclerosis: Basic mechanisms. Oxidation, inflammation, and genetics. Circulation 91:2488-2496, 1995.
90. Tsao PS, Buitrago R, Chan JR, et al: Fluid flow inhibits endothelial adhesiveness: Nitric oxide and transcriptional regulation of VCAM-1. Circulation 94:1682-1689, 1996.
91. Tsao PS, Wang B, Buitrago R, et al: Nitric oxide regulates monocyte chemotactic protein-1. Circulation 96:934-940, 1997.
92. Ross R: Cellular and molecular studies of atherosclerosis. Atherosclerosis 131:S3-S4, 1997.
93. Ye S, Eriksson P, Hamsten A, et al: Progression of coronary atherosclerosis is associated with a common genetic variant of the human stromelysin-1 promoter which results in reduced gene expression. J Biol Chem 271:13055-13060, 1996.
94. Parhami F, Morrow AD, Balucan J, et al: Lipid oxidation products have opposite effects on calcifying vascular cell and bone cell differentiation: A possible explanation for the paradox of arterial calcification in osteoporotic patients. Arterioscler Thromb Vasc Biol 17:680-687, 1997.
95. Zimmerman GA, McIntyre TM, Prescott SM: Adhesion and signaling in vascular cell-cell interactions. J Clin Invest 100:S3-S5, 1997.
96. Vaughan DE: The renin-angiotensin system and fibrinolysis. Am J Cardiol 79:12-16, 1997.
97. Cooke JP, Dzau VJ: Nitric oxide synthase: Role in the genesis of vascular disease. Annu Rev Med 48:489-509, 1997.
98. Heistad DD, Armstrong ML, Marcus ML, et al: Augmented responses to vasoconstrictor stimuli in hypercholesterolemic and atherosclerotic monkeys. Circ Res 54:711-718, 1984.
99. McLenachan JM, Williams JK, Fish RD, et al: Loss of flow-mediated endothelium-dependent dilation occurs early in the development of atherosclerosis. Circulation 84:1273-1278, 1991.
100. Ohara Y, Peterson TE, Sayegh HS, et al: Dietary correction of hypercholesterolemia in the rabbit normalizes endothelial superoxide anion production. Circulation 92:898-903, 1995.
101. Ma XL, Lopez BL, Liu GL, et al: Hypercholesterolemia impairs a detoxification mechanism against peroxynitrite and renders the vascular tissue more susceptible to oxidative injury. Circ Res 80:894-901, 1997.
102. Cooke JP, Dzau VJ: Derangements of the nitric oxide synthase pathway, L-arginine, and cardiovascular diseases. Circulation 96:379-382, 1997.
103. Boger RH, Bode-Boger SM, Sxuba A, et al: Asymmetric dimethylarginine (ADMA): A novel risk factor for endothelial dysfunction: Its role in hypercholesterolemia. Circulation 98:1842-1847, 1998.
104. Drexler H, Fischell TA, Pinto FJ, et al: Effect of L-arginine on coronary endothelial function in cardiac transplant recipients: Relation to vessel wall morphology. Circulation 89:1615-1623, 1994.
105. Clarkson P, Adams MR, Powe AJ, et al: Oral L-arginine improves endothelium-dependent dilation in hypercholesterolemic young adults. J Clin Invest 97:1989-1994, 1996.
106. Lerman A, Burnett JCJ, Higano ST, et al: Long-term L-arginine supplementation improves small-vessel coronary endothelial function in humans. Circulation 97:2123-2128, 1998.
107. Bode-Boger SM, Boger RH, Alfke H, et al: L-Arginine induces nitric oxide-dependent vasodilation in patients with critical limb ischemia: A randomized, controlled study. Circulation 93:85-90, 1996.
108. Cooke JP, Singer AH, Tsao P, et al: Antiatherogenic effects of L-arginine in the hypercholesterolemic rabbit. J Clin Invest 90:1168-1172, 1992.
109. Wang BY, Singer AH, Tsao PS, et al: Dietary arginine prevents atherogenesis in the coronary artery of the hypercholesterolemic rabbit. J Am Coll Cardiol 23:452-458, 1994.
110. Boger RH, Bode-Boger SM, Mugge A, et al: Supplementation of hypercholesterolaemic rabbits with L-arginine reduces the vascular release of superoxide anions and restores NO production. Atherosclerosis 117:273-284, 1995.
111. Tsao PS, McEvoy LM, Drexler H, et al: Enhanced endothelial adhesiveness in hypercholesterolemia is attenuated by L-arginine. Circulation 89:2176-2182, 1994.
112. Candipan RC, Wang BY, Buitrago R, et al: Regression or progression: Dependency on vascular nitric oxide. Arterioscler Thromb Vasc Biol 16:44-50, 1996.
113. Fuster V, Lewis A: Conner Memorial Lecture: Mechanisms leading to myocardial infarction: Insights from studies of vascular biology. Circulation 90:2126-2146, 1994.
114. van der Wal AC, Becker AE, van der Loos CM, et al: Site of intimal rupture or erosion of thrombosed coronary atherosclerotic plaques is characterized by an inflammatory process irrespective of the dominant plaque morphology. Circulation 89:36-44, 1994.
115. Falk E: Why do plaques rupture? Circulation 86:III30-III42, 1992.
116. Loree HM, Tobias BJ, Gibson LJ, et al: Mechanical properties of model atherosclerotic lesion lipid pools. Arterioscler Thromb 14:230-234, 1994.
117. Stary HC, Chandler AB, Dinsmore RE, et al: A definition of advanced types of atherosclerotic lesions and a histological classification of atherosclerosis: A report from the Committee on Vascular Lesions of

the Council on Arteriosclerosis, American Heart Association. Arterioscler Thromb Vasc Biol 15:1512-1531, 1995.
118. Sherman CT, Litvack F, Grundfest W, et al: Coronary angioscopy in patients with unstable angina pectoris. N Engl J Med 315:913-919, 1986.
119. Tikkanen MJ, Laakso M, Ilmonen M, et al: Treatment of hypercholesterolemia and combined hyperlipidemia with simvastatin and gemfibrozil in patients with NIDDM: A multicenter comparison study. Diabetes Care 21:477-481, 1998.
120. Henney AM, Wakeley PR, Davies MJ, et al: Localization of stromelysin gene expression in atherosclerotic plaques by in situ hybridization. Proc Natl Acad Sci U S A 88:8154-8158, 1991.
121. Nikkari ST, O'Brien KD, Ferguson M, et al: Interstitial collagenase (MMP-1) expression in human carotid atherosclerosis. Circulation 92:1393-1398, 1995.
122. Brown DL, Hibbs MS, Kearney M, et al: Identification of 92-kD gelatinase in human coronary atherosclerotic lesions: Association of active enzyme synthesis with unstable angina. Circulation 91:2125-2131, 1995.
123. Galis ZS, Sukhova GK, Libby P: Microscopic localization of active proteases by in situ zymography: Detection of matrix metalloproteinase activity in vascular tissue. FASEB J 9:974-980, 1995.
124. Shah PK, Falk E, Badimon JJ, et al: Human monocyte-derived macrophages induce collagen breakdown in fibrous caps of atherosclerotic plaques: Potential role of matrix-degrading metalloproteinases and implications for plaque rupture. Circulation 92:1565-1569, 1995.
125. Lendon CL, Davies MJ, Born GV, et al: Atherosclerotic plaque caps are locally weakened when macrophage density is increased. Atherosclerosis 87:87-90, 1991.
126. Geng YJ, Wu Q, Muszynski M, et al: Apoptosis of vascular smooth muscle cells induced by in vitro stimulation with interferon-gamma, tumor necrosis factor-alpha, and interleukin-1 beta. Arterioscler Thromb Vasc Biol 16:19-27, 1996.
127. Beckman JS, Koppenol WH: Nitric oxide, superoxide, and peroxynitrite: The good, the bad, and the ugly. Am J Physiol 271:C1424-C1437, 1996.
128. Heinecke JW: Mechanisms of oxidative damage of low density lipoprotein in human atherosclerosis. Curr Opin Lipidol 8:268-274, 1997.
129. Isner JM, Kearney M, Bortman S, et al: Apoptosis in human atherosclerosis and restenosis. Circulation 91:2703-2711, 1995.
130. Geng YJ, Libby P: Evidence for apoptosis in advanced human atheroma: Colocalization with interleukin-1 beta-converting enzyme. Am J Pathol 147:251-266, 1995.
131. Marmur JD, Thiruvikraman SV, Fyfe BS, et al: Identification of active tissue factor in human coronary atheroma. Circulation 94:1226-1232, 1996.
132. Moreno PR, Bernardi VH, Lopez-Cuellar J, et al: Macrophages, smooth muscle cells, and tissue factor in unstable angina: Implications for cell-mediated thrombogenicity in acute coronary syndromes. Circulation 94:3090-3097, 1996.
133. Little WC, Constantinescu M, Applegate RJ, et al: Can coronary angiography predict the site of a subsequent myocardial infarction in patients with mild-to-moderate coronary artery disease? Circulation 78:1157-1166, 1988.
134. Annex BH, Denning SM, Channon KM, et al: Differential expression of tissue factor protein in directional atherectomy specimens from patients with stable and unstable coronary syndromes. Circulation 91:619-622, 1995.
135. Benditt EP, Barrett T, McDougall JK: Viruses in the etiology of atherosclerosis. Proc Natl Acad Sci U S A 80:6386-6389, 1983.
136. Libby P, Egan D, Skarlatos S: Roles of infectious agents in atherosclerosis and restenosis: An assessment of the evidence and need for future research. Circulation 96:4095-4103, 1997.
137. Melnick JL, Adam E, DeBakey ME: Possible role of cytomegalovirus in atherogenesis. JAMA 263:2204-2207, 1990.
138. Grattan MT, Moreno-Cabral CE, Starnes VA, et al: Cytomegalovirus infection is associated with cardiac allograft rejection and atherosclerosis. JAMA 261:3561-3566, 1989.
139. Saikku P, Leinonen M, Mattila K, et al: Serological evidence of an association of a novel *Chlamydia*, TWAR, with chronic coronary heart disease and acute myocardial infarction. Lancet. 2:983-986, 1988.
140. Minick CR, Fabricant CG, Fabricant J, et al: Atheroarteriosclerosis induced by infection with a herpesvirus. Am J Pathol 96:673-706, 1979.
141. Davies MJ, Thomas A: Thrombosis and acute coronary-artery lesions in sudden cardiac ischemic death. N Engl J Med 310:1137-1140, 1984.
142. Ambrose JA, Winters SL, Arora RR, et al: Coronary angiographic morphology in myocardial infarction: A link between the pathogenesis of unstable angina and myocardial infarction. J Am Coll Cardiol 6:1233-1238, 1985.
143. Pinto FJ, Chenzbraun A, Botas J, et al: Feasibility of serial intracoronary ultrasound imaging for assessment of progression of intimal proliferation in cardiac transplant recipients. Circulation 90:2348-2355, 1994.
144. Mulcahy D, Husain S, Zalos G, et al: Ischemia during ambulatory monitoring as a prognostic indicator in patients with stable coronary artery disease. JAMA 277:318-324, 1997.
145. Mann JM, Davies MJ: Vulnerable plaque: Relation of characteristics to degree of stenosis in human coronary arteries. Circulation 94:928-931, 1996.
146. Cohen A, Tzourio C, Bertrand B, et al: Aortic plaque morphology and vascular events: A follow-up study in patients with ischemic stroke. FAPS Investigators. French Study of Aortic Plaques in Stroke. Circulation 96:3838-3841, 1997.
147. Toussaint JF, Lamuraglia GM, Southern JF, et al: Magnetic resonance images lipid, fibrous, calcified, hemorrhagic, and thrombotic components of human atherosclerosis in vivo. Circulation 94:932-938, 1996.
148. Muller JE, Stone PH, Turi ZG, et al: Circadian variation in the frequency of onset of acute myocardial infarction. N Engl J Med 313:1315-1322, 1985.
149. Willich SN, Linderer T, Wegscheider K, et al: Increased morning incidence of myocardial infarction in the ISAM Study: Absence with prior beta-adrenergic blockade. ISAM Study Group. Circulation 80:853-858, 1989.
150. Muller JE, Tofler GH, Stone PH: Circadian variation and triggers of onset of acute cardiovascular disease. Circulation 79:733-743, 1989.
151. Willich SN, Lowel H, Lewis M, et al: Weekly variation of acute myocardial infarction: Increased Monday risk in the working population. Circulation 90:87-93, 1994.
152. Mittleman MA, Maclure M, Sherwood JB, et al: Triggering of acute myocardial infarction onset by episodes of anger: Determinants of Myocardial Infarction Onset Study Investigators. Circulation 92:1720-1725, 1995.
153. Mittleman MA, Maclure M, Tofler GH, et al: Triggering of acute myocardial infarction by heavy physical exertion: Protection against triggering by regular exertion. Determinants of Myocardial Infarction Onset Study Investigators. N Engl J Med 329:1677-1683, 1993.
154. Muller JE, Mittleman A, Maclure M, et al: Triggering myocardial infarction by sexual activity: Low absolute risk and prevention by regular physical exertion. Determinants of Myocardial Infarction Onset Study Investigators. JAMA 275:1405-1409, 1996.
155. Trichopoulos D, Katsouyanni K, Zavitsanos X, et al: Psychological stress and fatal heart attack: The Athens (1981) earthquake natural experiment. Lancet 1(8322):441-444, 1983.
156. Leor J, Poole WK, Kloner RA: Sudden cardiac death triggered by an earthquake. N Engl J Med 334:413-419, 1996.
157. Meisel SR, Kutz I, Dayan KI, et al: Effect of Iraqi missile war on incidence of acute myocardial infarction and sudden death in Israeli civilians. Lancet 338:660-661, 1991.

158. Semenza JC, Rubin CH, Falter KH, et al: Heat-related deaths during the July 1995 heat wave in Chicago. N Engl J Med 335:84-90, 1996.
159. Glass RI, Zack MMJ: Increase in deaths from ischemic heart disease after blizzards. Lancet 1(8114):485-487, 1979.
160. Knowler WC, Barrett-Connor E, Fowler SE, et al: Reduction in the incidence of type 2 diabetes with lifestyle intervention or metformin. N Engl J Med 346:393-403, 2002.
161. Intensive blood-glucose control with sulphonylureas or insulin compared with conventional treatment and risk of complications in patients with type 2 diabetes (UKPDS 33). UK Prospective Diabetes Study (UKPDS) Group. Lancet 352:837-853, 1998.
162. Mehler PS, Jeffers BW, Estacio R, et al: Associations of hypertension and complications in non-insulin-dependent diabetes mellitus. Am J Hypertens 10:152-161, 1997.
163. Litzelman DK, Slemenda CW, Langefeld CD, et al: Reduction of lower extremity clinical abnormalities in patients with non-insulin-dependent diabetes mellitus: A randomized, controlled trial. Ann Intern Med 119:36-41, 1993.
164. Critchley JA, Capewell S: Mortality risk reduction associated with smoking cessation in patients with coronary heart disease: A systematic review. JAMA 290:86-97, 2003.
165. Fiore MC, Jorenby DE, Baker TB: Smoking cessation: Principles and practice based upon the AHCPR Guideline, 1996. Ann Behav Med 19:213-219, 1997.
166. Hjermann I, Velve BK, Holme I, et al: Effect of diet and smoking intervention on the incidence of coronary heart disease: Report from the Oslo Study Group of a randomised trial in healthy men. Lancet 2(8259):1303-1310, 1981.
167. Joseph AM, Norman SM, Ferry LH, et al: The safety of transdermal nicotine as an aid to smoking cessation in patients with cardiac disease. N Engl J Med 335:1792-1798, 1996.
168. Pasternak M: Sustained-release bupropion for smoking cessation. N Engl J Med 338:619-620, 1998.
169. Jenkins DJ, Wolever TM, Rao AV, et al: Effect on blood lipids of very high intakes of fiber in diets low in saturated fat and cholesterol. N Engl J Med 329:21-26, 1993.
170. Sprecher DL, Harris BV, Goldberg AC, et al: Efficacy of psyllium in reducing serum cholesterol levels in hypercholesterolemic patients on high- or low-fat diets. Ann Intern Med 119:545-554, 1993.
171. Bays HE, Dujovne CA, McGovern ME, et al: Comparison of once-daily niacin extended-release/lovastatin with standard doses of atorvastatin and simvastatin (the ADvicor Versus Other Cholesterol-Modulating Agents Trial Evaluation [ADVOCATE]). Am J Cardiol 91:667-672, 2003.
172. Elam MB, Hunninghake DB, Davis KB, et al: Effect of niacin on lipid and lipoprotein levels and glycemic control in patients with diabetes and peripheral arterial disease: The ADMIT study: A randomized trial. Arterial Disease Multiple Intervention Trial. JAMA 284:1263-1270, 2000.
173. Pasternak RC, Brown LE, Stone PH, et al: Effect of combination therapy with lipid-reducing drugs in patients with coronary heart disease and "normal" cholesterol levels: A randomized, placebo-controlled trial. Harvard Atherosclerosis Reversibility Project (HARP) Study Group. Ann Intern Med 125:529-540, 1996.
174. Frick MH, Elo O, Haapa K, et al: Helsinki Heart Study: Primary-prevention trial with gemfibrozil in middle-aged men with dyslipidemia: Safety of treatment, changes in risk factors, and incidence of coronary heart disease. N Engl J Med 317:1237-1245, 1987.
175. Randomised trial of cholesterol lowering in 4444 patients with coronary heart disease: The Scandinavian Simvastatin Survival Study (4S). Lancet 344:1383-1389, 1994.
176. Kjekshus J, Pedersen TR: Reducing the risk of coronary events: Evidence from the Scandinavian Simvastatin Survival Study (4S). Am J Cardiol 76:64C-68C, 1995.
177. Pedersen TR, Olsson AG, Faergeman O, et al: Lipoprotein changes and reduction in the incidence of major coronary heart disease events in the Scandinavian Simvastatin Survival Study (4S). Circulation 97:1453-1460, 1998.
178. Kramer JR, Proudfit WL, Loop FD, et al: Late follow-up of 781 patients undergoing percutaneous transluminal coronary angioplasty or coronary artery bypass grafting. Am Heart J. 118:1144-1153, 1989.
179. Sacks FM, Moye LA, Davis BR, et al: Relationship between plasma LDL concentrations during treatment with pravastatin and recurrent coronary events in the Cholesterol And Recurrent Events trial. Circulation 97:1446-1452, 1998.
180. Gould AL, Rossouw JE, Santanello NC, et al: Cholesterol reduction yields clinical benefit: Impact of statin trials. Circulation 97:946-952, 1998.
181. Grundy SM: Statin trials and goals of cholesterol-lowering therapy. Circulation 97:1436-1439, 1998.
182. Miettinen TA, Pyorala K, Olsson AG, et al: Cholesterol-lowering therapy in women and elderly patients with myocardial infarction or angina pectoris: Findings from the Scandinavian Simvastatin Survival Study (4S). Circulation 96:4211-4218, 1997.
183. Furberg CD, Adams HPJ, Applegate WB, et al: Effect of lovastatin on early carotid atherosclerosis and cardiovascular events: Asymptomatic Carotid Artery Progression Study (ACAPS) Research Group. Circulation 90:1679-1687, 1994.
184. Hodis HN, Mack WJ, LaBree L, et al: Reduction in carotid arterial wall thickness using lovastatin and dietary therapy: A randomized controlled clinical trial. Ann Intern Med 124:548-556, 1996.
185. Blankenhorn DH, Azen SP, Crawford DW, et al: Effects of colestipol-niacin therapy on human femoral atherosclerosis. Circulation 83:438-447, 1991.
186. Buchwald H, Bourdages HR, Campos CT, et al: Impact of cholesterol reduction on peripheral arterial disease in the Program on the Surgical Control of the Hyperlipidemias (POSCH). Surgery 120:672-679, 1996.
187. Pedersen TR, Kjekshus J, Pyorala K, et al: Effect of simvastatin on ischemic signs and symptoms in the Scandinavian Simvastatin Survival Study (4S). Am J Cardiol 81:333-335, 1998.
188. Heart Protection Study Collaborators Group: MRC/BHF Heart Protection Study of cholesterol lowering with simvastatin in 20,536 high-risk individuals: A randomised placebo-controlled trial. Lancet 360:7-22, 2002.
189. Kroon AA, van Asten WN, Stalenhoef AF: Effect of apheresis of low-density lipoprotein on peripheral vascular disease in hypercholesterolemic patients with coronary artery disease. Ann Intern Med 125:945-954, 1996.
190. Hiatt WR, Nawaz D, Brass EP: Carnitine metabolism during exercise in patients with peripheral vascular disease. J Appl Physiol 62:2383-2387, 1987.
191. Bauer TA, Regensteiner JG, Brass EP, et al: Oxygen uptake kinetics during exercise are slowed in patients with peripheral arterial disease. J Appl Physiol 87:809-816, 1999.
192. Vogt MT, Cauley JA, Kuller LH, et al: Functional status and mobility among elderly women with lower extremity arterial disease: The Study of Osteoporotic Fractures. J Am Geriatr Soc 42:923-929, 1994.
193. Khaira HS, Hanger R, Shearman CP: Quality of life in patients with intermittent claudication. Eur J Vasc Endovasc Surg 11:65-69, 1996.
194. Regensteiner JG, Ware JE Jr, McCarthy WJ, et al: Effect of cilostazol on treadmill walking, community-based walking ability, and health-related quality of life in patients with intermittent claudication due to peripheral arterial disease: Meta-analysis of six randomized controlled trials. J Am Geriatr Soc 50:1939-1946, 2002.
195. Mondillo S, Ballo P, Barbati R, et al: Effects of simvastatin on walking performance and symptoms of intermittent claudication in hypercholesterolemic patients with peripheral vascular disease. Am J Med 114:359-364, 2003.
196. Aronow WS, Nayak D, Woodworth S, et al: Effect of simvastatin versus placebo on treadmill exercise time until the onset of

intermittent claudication in older patients with peripheral arterial disease at six months and at one year after treatment. Am J Cardiol 92:711-712, 2003.

197. Mohler ER III, Hiatt WR, Creager MA: Cholesterol reduction with atorvastatin improves walking distance in patients with peripheral arterial disease. Circulation 108:1481-1486, 2003.
198. McDermott MM, Guralnik JM, Greenland P, et al: Statin use and leg functioning in patients with and without lower-extremity peripheral arterial disease. Circulation 107:757-761, 2003.
199. Appel LJ, Moore TJ, Obarzanek E, et al: A clinical trial of the effects of dietary patterns on blood pressure: DASH Collaborative Research Group. N Engl J Med 336:1117-1124, 1997.
200. The 1988 report of the Joint National Committee on Detection, Evaluation, and Treatment of High Blood Pressure. Arch Intern Med 148:1023-1038, 1988.
201. Sheps SG, Dart RA: New guidelines for prevention, detection, evaluation, and treatment of hypertension: Joint National Committee VI. Chest 113:263-265, 1998.
202. Gueyffier F, Boutitie F, Boissel JP, et al: Effect of antihypertensive drug treatment on cardiovascular outcomes in women and men: A meta-analysis of individual patient data from randomized, controlled trials. The INDANA Investigators. Ann Intern Med 126:761-767, 1997.
203. Insua JT, Sacks HS, Lau TS, et al: Drug treatment of hypertension in the elderly: A meta-analysis. Ann Intern Med 121:355-362, 1994.
204. Hiatt WR, Stoll S, Nies AS: Effect of β-adrenergic blockers on the peripheral circulation in patients with peripheral vascular disease. Circulation 72:1226-1231, 1985.
205. Solomon SA, Ramsay LE, Yeo WW, et al: β blockade and intermittent claudication: Placebo controlled trial of atenolol and nifedipine and their combination. BMJ 303:1100-1104, 1991.
206. Effects of an angiotensin-converting-enzyme inhibitor, ramipril, on cardiovascular events in high-risk patients. The Heart Outcomes Prevention Evaluation Study Investigators. N Engl J Med 342:145-153, 2000.
207. Appel LJ, Miller ER III, Jee SH, et al: Effect of dietary patterns on serum homocysteine: Results of a randomized, controlled feeding study. Circulation 102:852-857, 2000.
208. Malinow MR, Duell PB, Hess DL, et al: Reduction of plasma homocyst(e)ine levels by breakfast cereal fortified with folic acid in patients with coronary heart disease. N Engl J Med 338:1009-1015, 1998.
209. Stampfer MJ, Malinow MR: Can lowering homocysteine levels reduce cardiovascular risk? N Engl J Med 332:328-329, 1995.
210. Liem A, Reynierse-Buitenwerf GH, Zwinderman AH, et al: Secondary prevention with folic acid: Effects on clinical outcomes. J Am Coll Cardiol 41:2105-2113, 2003.
211. Hsia J, Simon JA, Lin F, et al: Peripheral arterial disease in randomized trial of estrogen with progestin in women with coronary heart disease: The Heart and Estrogen/Progestin Replacement Study. Circulation 102:2228-2232, 2000.
212. Timaran CH, Stevens SL, Grandas OH, et al: Influence of hormone replacement therapy on graft patency after femoropopliteal bypass grafting. J Vasc Surg 32:506-518, 2000.
213. Hiatt WR, Regensteiner JG, Hargarten ME, et al: Benefit of exercise conditioning for patients with peripheral arterial disease. Circulation 81:602-609, 1990.
214. Hiatt WR, Wolfel EE, Meier RH, et al: Superiority of treadmill walking exercise vs. strength training for patients with peripheral arterial disease: Implications for the mechanism of the training response. Circulation 90:1866-1874, 1994.
215. Hakim AA, Petrovitch H, Burchfiel CM, et al: Effects of walking on mortality among nonsmoking retired men. N Engl J Med 338:94-99, 1998.
216. Collaborative meta-analysis of randomised trials of antiplatelet therapy for prevention of death, myocardial infarction, and stroke in high risk patients 1. BMJ 324:71-86, 2002.
217. Collaborative overview of randomised trials of antiplatelet therapy—I: Prevention of death, myocardial infarction, and stroke by prolonged antiplatelet therapy in various categories of patients. Antiplatelet Trialists' Collaboration. BMJ 308:81-106, 1994.
218. 63 Federal Register 56802-56819 (1998).
219. A randomised, blinded trial of Clopidogrel versus Aspirin in Patients at Risk of Ischaemic Events (CAPRIE). CAPRIE Steering Committee. Lancet 348:1329-1339, 1996.
220. Diaz MN, Frei B, Vita JA, et al: Antioxidants and atherosclerotic heart disease. N Engl J Med 337:408-416, 1997.
221. Hennekens CH, Buring JE, Manson JE, et al: Lack of effect of long-term supplementation with beta carotene on the incidence of malignant neoplasms and cardiovascular disease. N Engl J Med 334:1145-1149, 1996.
222. Omenn GS, Goodman GE, Thornquist MD, et al: Effects of a combination of beta carotene and vitamin A on lung cancer and cardiovascular disease. N Engl J Med 334:1150-1155, 1996.
223. Yusuf S, Dagenais G, Pogue J, et al: Vitamin E supplementation and cardiovascular events in high-risk patients. The Heart Outcomes Prevention Evaluation Study Investigators [see comments]. N Engl J Med 342:154-160, 2000.

Chapter

37

Medical Treatment of Intermittent Claudication

SAMUEL R. MONEY, MD, MBA, FACS
W. CHARLES STERNBERGH III, MD

Section VII

The term *claudication* is derived from the Latin word *claudere,* "to limp." Claudius, a Roman emperor, was born with a deformed foot and was named after the resulting physical impairment. *Intermittent claudication* is a clinical condition of ischemic extremity muscular discomfort induced by exercise and relieved by short periods of rest. Although intermittent claudication is usually a manifestation of peripheral arterial disease (PAD) most often due to atherosclerosis, untreated it most often does not result in limb loss. Most medical treatment plans have been directed at the symptom complex itself, rather than the underlying disease process. The most conservative and perhaps most appropriate treatment for mild-to-moderate intermittent claudication is directed at lifestyle modification and attempting to lengthen pain-free and maximal walking distance by walking exercise programs. The only nonoperative treatment consistently shown to improve intermittent claudication has been the strict adoption of a structured supervised exercise regimen. Other lifestyle modifications include smoking cessation and dietary restrictions aimed at reducing hyperlipidemias.

Enthusiasm for pharmacologic treatments for claudication has varied since physicians first diagnosed that the painful cramping in the lower extremity was a result of reduced blood flow to the musculature. Claudication historically has been treated by many different modalities with mixed results. The medical treatment of claudication has included vasodilator therapy, antiplatelet agents, hemorheologic agents, anticoagulants, and agents directed at improving the metabolic handling of oxygen within ischemic tissue. Since the 1970s, scientific evaluation of the efficacy of these agents has been based increasingly on objective data and not simply subjective or anecdotal reports. Objective data have been related to improvement in walking ability during standardized treadmill testing. Specifically the two endpoints of interest that have been used when evaluating treadmill testing are pain-free walking distance (PFWD), or initial claudication distance, and maximal walking distance (MWD), or absolute claudication distance. PFWD is the point at which the patient starts to feel pain in the affected muscular group. MWD represents the maximal or absolute distance a patient can walk until the pain becomes so severe that the patient must stop walking to rest and relieve the pain. Claudication also has numerous effects on the patient's life and lifestyle with secondary psychological impacts affecting overall quality of life. In an effort to grade some of the subjective data that claudication can affect, questionnaires regarding quality of life have been used. Generic and disease-specific questionnaires have been used. Questionnaires have included the Walking Impairment Questionnaire and the SF-36 form. These instruments of quality-of-life measurements also have been used to evaluate pharmacologic interventions.

Because intermittent claudication is usually a manifestation of a generalized atherosclerotic process, treatment of that disease process and its general systemic consequences is an integral part of any medical regimen. This aspect of medical management is discussed fully elsewhere in this textbook. Although strict medical control of these co-morbid conditions has been shown to reduce the risk of coronary artery disease, its success in slowing the progression of PAD and improving intermittent claudication has not been proved by statistically significant valid clinical trials.[1] The current chapter reviews advances in the pharmacologic treatment of the pain syndrome of intermittent claudication. The chapter also summarize some past treatments that have fallen out of favor.

■ PLATELET INHIBITORS

Aspirin

Aspirin has well-proven effects as a cost-effective medication to reduce secondary events in patients with atherosclerotic disease. Other reports have shown a reduction in the need for peripheral arterial procedures in patients who routinely use aspirin.[2,3] Numerous other studies also have shown that aspirin improves vascular graft patency, reducing secondary procedures on these grafts and ultimately reducing limb loss. Despite these results, aspirin has not been shown to improve walking distance or symptoms in patients with intermittent claudication. Aspirin is effective in preventing secondary events and should be considered in all patients with PAD. Aspirin is not currently indicated, however, for the treatment of the symptoms of intermittent claudication.

Clopidogrel

Clopidogrel (Plavix) is an antiplatelet agent that has been shown to be more potent than aspirin in reducing secondary events in patients with atherosclerotic disease. In the

CAPRIE (Clopidogrel versus Aspirin in Patients at Risk of Ischemic Events) trial, clopidogrel was associated with an overall reduction in primary endpoints (i.e., stroke, myocardial infarction, or death from other vascular causes).[4] Although overall percentage reduction was 8.7%, the absolute change was only 0.5% (5.32% versus 5.83%). This benefit was statistically different, however, from that observed in patients receiving aspirin. In treating patients with vascular disease, closer scrutiny of the CAPRIE trial is important. If one were to break down the patients enrolled in the CAPRIE trial based on their previous cardiovascular event, patients with peripheral vascular disease had a higher rate of protection from secondary events compared with patients who enrolled because of myocardial infarction or cerebrovascular disease. The CAPRIE trial did show significant results in terms of reducing secondary events, and this reduction was more pronounced in patients with PAD. There is no evidence, however, to suggest that the symptoms of claudication are reduced by long-term treatment with clopidogrel.

■ VASODILATORS

Initial attempts at improving blood flow to the extremities involved the use of vasodilators, especially papaverine.[5] Vasodilator use was based on the concept that by dilating blood vessels, more blood would flow to the ischemic limb. As understanding of the pathophysiology of blood flow has advanced, however, this theory has been discredited. Ischemic extremity tissue releases metabolic by-products that lead to a maximal dilatation of the local vasculature distal to an obstructing lesion. The addition of vasodilator therapy has little effect on what is already a maximally dilated distal vascular bed. When vasodilator therapy is given, vessels proximal to the stenotic or occlusive lesion and vessels parallel to the lesion dilate and improve blood flow to that neighboring vascular bed. This improvement leads to a steal proximal to the stenotic or occlusive lesion, reducing blood flow from the already ischemic distal tissue. Vasodilators also have the capacity to reduce overall systemic vascular resistance, leading to a reduction in perfusion pressure. This reduction in perfusion pressure in conjunction with the steal phenomenon increases the ischemic insult to the underperfused extremity. This concept of enhancing blood flow by giving vasodilators systemically is probably incorrect.

Use of calcium channel blockers as vasodilators may suggest other mechanisms. Bagger and colleagues[6] conducted a double-blind, random crossover study in which 44 patients had undergone a previous period of titration testing. During the titration period, patients were given increasing doses of verapamil (120 mg, 240 mg, 360 mg, and 480 mg) over 4 weeks to identify the dose of the drug that would be associated with the longest MWD. These doses were specific for each individual patient. After a washout period, each patient was given the previously identified drug dose. These researchers found that verapamil increased the pain-free walking distance by 29% and the mean MWD by 49% ($P < .01$ and $P < .001$). There was no change in ankle/brachial index, suggesting that it was not purely secondary to blood flow. A theory that has evolved from this study is that the calcium channel blocker has a secondary effect—that of changing the oxygen extraction/utilization capacity. Calcium channel blockers may improve the efficiency of oxygen use in the extremity. Despite this fairly small study, more recent data from other studies have found the effects of other calcium channel vasodilator therapy to be inconclusive. At present, the treatment of intermittent claudication with pure vasodilators cannot be recommended.

Pentoxifylline

In 1984, the first drug specifically indicated for the treatment of claudication was granted U.S. Food and Drug Administration (FDA) approval. Pentoxifylline (Trental) is a methylxanthine derivative that has numerous effects. Its primary effect was thought to be an improvement in red blood cell deformability. Other effects include a decrease in blood viscosity, platelet aggregation inhibition, and a reduction in fibrinogen levels. Numerous trials have reported mixed results concerning pentoxifylline's effects in the treatment of intermittent claudication. The two major randomized double-blind studies highlight these inconsistencies.[7,8] The first of these two trials compared pentoxifylline with placebo over a 24-week period. A total of 128 patients were randomized in this trial. Patients given pentoxifylline showed a 22% greater improvement in the PFWD from baseline compared with the placebo group.[7] The pentoxifylline-treated group had an improvement in PFWD (45% versus a 23% improvement in patients given placebo; $P = .02$) and MWD (32% versus 20% improvement in patients treated with placebo; $P = .04$). Several observations regarding this trial are noteworthy. First, the placebo effect of merely enrolling a patient in a trial improved PFWD by 23%. This result is common in studies using treadmill testing. Second, despite significant improvements in PFWD and MWD, subjective assessment of cramping, tiredness, and pain was not improved in the pentoxifylline group. Specific subjective testing for walking impairment was not used, however.

A second large trial randomized 150 patients to 1200 mg/day of pentoxifylline ($n = 76$) or placebo ($n = 74$).[8] In contrast to the findings of the previous study, these investigators found no improvement in PFWD and only a trend that suggested an improvement in MWD in patients given pentoxifylline ($P = .09$). It is possible, however, that this study incorporated a type II error and that more patients would have made MWD reach significance. In doing a post hoc subset analysis, certain subpopulations of patients showed significant improvement in PFWD and MWD compared with placebo. Patients with moderate versus mild disease tended toward significance, and patients with a chronic duration of the disease greater than 1 year also tended toward significance.

To add to the confusion, Ernst and associates[9] speculated that the beneficial effects of pentoxifylline may wear off with long-term administration. In their study, MWD at certain time intervals during the study period showed significant improvement (1 and 8 weeks). No significant benefit in PFWD or MWD was observed, however, after 12 weeks of pentoxifylline therapy.

Although the above-mentioned trials failed to agree conclusively on a statistically significant benefit gained with pentoxifylline therapy, these results do suggest that there is a small beneficial effect in patients with intermittent claudication. Meta-analyses by Hood and coworkers[10] and Girolami and associates[11] support these beneficial findings, but agree that the magnitude of the benefits of using pentoxifylline is small. The major problem is that this mild increase in walking distance may not be appreciated subjectively by the patient. The purpose of treating intermittent claudication is not simply to increase walking distance, but to improve the quality of life of the patient. If the medication fails to improve quality of life, yet the patient can walk an additional 50 m, is it reasonable to prescribe this medication? In the author's personal experience, occasional patients have been treated with long-term pentoxifylline and have reported a significant improvement in quality of life. Whether this is a true or placebo effect of the medication cannot be differentiated. These patients have been maintained on this medication.

The use of pentoxifylline in patients using other methylxanthine derivatives (aminophylline, theophylline) require special attention. Concurrent use may result in increased drug levels and activity. Frequent monitoring of the blood levels is essential.

Cilostazol

In January 1999, the second drug for the treatment of patients with intermittent claudication was granted approval by the FDA. Cilostazol (Pletal) is a phosphodiesterase type III inhibitor that is thought to exert its mechanism of action by inhibiting cyclic adenosine monophosphate (cAMP) phosphodiesterase. By increasing the levels of cAMP in platelets and blood vessels, there is a resultant inhibition of platelet aggregation and a promotion of smooth muscle cell relaxation. Other additional pharmacologic properties include a positive lipid effect, increasing high-density lipoprotein cholesterol and decreasing triglycerides.[12] In vitro studies have shown that there may be a reduction in smooth muscle cell proliferation.[13]

No claudication medication has been studied in as many prospective placebo, double-blind trials as has cilostazol. More than 2700 patients were involved in the numerous phase III double-blind trials.[12,14,15] The data presented in this paragraph were compiled from these trials. The mean age and ankle/brachial index of the patients was 63.3 years and 0.64. Most patients were men (76%), and 92% of the total patient population were either previous or current smokers. Of the patients, 60% had hypertension, 25% had diabetes, and 22% had coronary artery disease (previous history of myocardial infarction). The dosage most commonly used in these studies was 100 mg orally twice a day versus placebo. Numerous studies showed increasing MWD ranging from a low of approximately 30% to a high of greater than 100% improvement. Patients who received cilostazol walked on average 140 m more than they did at baseline.

As already mentioned, the symptoms of claudication are mainly subjective. It is important for patients to perceive the subjective improvement that the medication may offer. Such perceived benefit was noted in the drug studies of cilostazol (51% versus 30% for placebo). The variation in response with this medication necessitates that the prescribing physician educate the patient before starting cilostazol. A patient's expectation of going from claudication after walking half a block to being able to walk five to seven blocks is not a realistic goal. To go from one and a half blocks to two and a half blocks or from one block to two blocks is probably within the realm of what cilostazol is capable of achieving.

Numerous side effects occur with the long-term use of cilostazol that the prescribing physician should understand. The most common side effect is headache. Patients frequently develop headaches during the early or "ramp-up" phase of this drug. Headache is probably secondary to the drug's vasodilatory properties. Discussing this side effect with the patient beforehand and possibly starting with a lower dose, such as 50 mg once a day, then after approximately 1 week, increasing to 50 mg twice a day, and then increasing to the recommended dosage of 100 mg twice a day may alleviate most of these headaches. Many headaches also respond to nonprescription medications, such as acetaminophen. Gastrointestinal problems, specifically diarrhea and large bulky stools, are also common side effects. Most patients who experience this side effect can tolerate it fairly well. Occasionally, there is a patient in whom the change in bowel habits is so severe that the drug needs to be discontinued. Palpitations are another side effect, with the average patient's heart rate increasing by approximately 4 beats/min. Most patients tolerate this increase if they are warned of this potential side effect before starting therapy.

Other phosphodiesterase inhibitors, but not cilostazol specifically, have been shown to decrease survival rate compared with placebo in patients with New York Heart Association class 3 to class 4 congestive heart failure.[16] Cilostazol is contraindicated in patients with congestive heart failure of any severity.

Cilostazol is partially metabolized in the liver by the CYP3A4 or the CYP2C19 enzymes. Because of this metabolism, other drugs that rely on these specific hepatic enzymes may increase cilostazol levels. Examples include antifungals, erythromycin, some selective serotonin reuptake inhibitors, and omeprazole. Although the concurrent use of these medications is not discouraged, one may want to consider reducing the daily dose of cilostazol to 50 mg twice a day.

Cilostazol is a drug that can improve PFWD and MWD in patients with symptoms secondary to PAD. Physician and patient expectations must be realistic, however. As described, approximately half of patients generate subjective improvements in their symptoms. A patient who feels subjectively improved and has no significant side effects from the drug should stay on the drug indefinitely. The patient should be re-evaluated routinely, however, for the development of congestive heart failure, and if this does develop, the drug should be discontinued.

Naftidrofuryl

Naftidrofuryl (Praxilene) is a serotonin antagonist that has been available and has been used by numerous vascular specialists in Europe since the 1980s. The proposed mechanisms of action include vasodilatory properties and improved efficiency of aerobic mechanism. In a multicenter study, naftidrofuryl use was associated with a significant improvement in mean PFWD over placebo (35% over placebo) in patients treated for 12 weeks ($P < .02$).[17] A later multicenter randomized prospective study duplicated these findings, showing a similar (32%) increase in PFWD in patients treated with the active drug for 6 months.[18] There was no significant difference, however, in the increase in MWD with the active drug. This difference in effect is unexplained. The main adverse reactions are gastrointestinal complaints, such as gas and abdominal pain. This drug is currently not available for use in the United States, and it is not undergoing active clinical investigation.

Levocarnitine

It is proposed that levocarnitine's mechanism of action is to improve the availability of substrates required for energy production, increasing efficiency in the Kreb cycle. In contrast to previously mentioned pharmacologic therapies, there is no significant increase in blood flow to ischemic tissues, red blood cell deformability, or blood viscosity changes. There have been numerous small studies using levocarnitine; however, the best study is by Brevetti and colleagues.[19] This small double-blind, crossover trial showed significant improvement in PFWD in patients receiving oral levocarnitine. PFWD improved by approximately 70% over baseline during therapy, but returned back to baseline when patients were converted back to placebo. Patients additionally reported improvements in subjective symptoms while receiving levocarnitine. In an effort to elucidate the mechanism, investigators found reductions in lactate/pyruvate levels in patients treated with levocarnitine when samples were obtained from the popliteal vein. In another study, a longer acting carnitine analogue, propionyl levocarnitine, was found to improve MWD by 27% over placebo after 6 months of therapy ($P = .03$).[20] Improvements in PFWD in patients receiving the longer acting propionyl levocarnitine were almost double that experienced by patients in the placebo group. Changes in PFWD did not reach significance but approached it. A comparison study between levocarnitine and propionyl levocarnitine showed greater increases in walking capacity in patients receiving propionyl levocarnitine.[21] Propionyl levocarnitine has not been statistically proved, however, to be better than levocarnitine or consistently statistically better than placebo in other large studies.

Improving the metabolic efficiency of ischemic skeletal muscle is a unique approach to the treatment of intermittent claudication. Although these studies show only small improvements, they are encouraging and suggest that this supplement may truly be helpful.[22] Carnitine supplements are available in most health food stores across the United States and Canada. There is no suggested recommended dosage for the treatment of intermittent claudication, and full scientific data proving its efficacy are lacking. In addition, the potential side effects and drug interactions have not been fully delineated. For these reasons, despite the potential for levocarnitine to help patients with intermittent claudication, its use cannot currently be scientifically supported.

Chelation

Chelation therapy refers to the administration of an agent that binds with calcium by forming complexes with calcium-containing divalent cations (Ca^{2+}); this theoretically prevents the progression and possibly reverses atherosclerotic disease. The drug used most commonly is ethylenediaminetetraacetic acid (EDTA). Numerous poorly controlled and poorly planned studies suggested that chelation therapy would improve walking distance and overall quality of life. More well controlled and better performed studies found chelation therapy to have no benefit in PFWD or MWD, however.[23-25] In addition, no differences in subjective assessment of quality of life were identified after these studies.

More recently, a meta-analysis of randomized placebo-controlled, double-blind clinical trials found that EDTA was not an effective treatment for intermittent claudication and concluded that chelation therapy should be considered obsolete. Rare potentially fatal reductions in plasma cations are of concern, and close chemical and hematologic monitoring is required when patients undergo this therapy. Despite these convincing results against chelation, many practitioners continue to advocate its use for intermittent claudication.[26] Many patients question the vascular specialist about the success and long-term use of chelation therapy. It has been proposed that chelation therapy may benefit atherosclerosis by acting as an antioxidant. This proposal has prompted the FDA to start a randomized study to evaluate this pharmaceutical so that its benefit or lack of benefit finally can be determined (http://nccam.nih.gov/news/2002/chelation/pressrelease.htm). Currently, chelation therapy cannot be recommended for treatment of claudication.

Arginine

Arginine is an amino acid that is the precursor for nitric oxide formation. A randomized trial compared the intravenous use of arginine (8 mg twice a day), prostaglandin E_1 (40 mg twice a day), and placebo for the treatment of patients with PAD.[27] Patients were evaluated by improvements in PFWD and MWD. In this study, both treatments resulted in significant improvements in both of these endpoints. Patients receiving arginine and prostaglandin E_1 compared favorably with the control patients, who surprisingly experienced no increase in walking ability; as previously mentioned, many studies that use a control group show a significant increase in walking ability in the control group by the end of the study. There was no difference found between the two experimental active treatment groups. The only adverse reaction was erythema and pain seen at the area of injection with the prostaglandin E_1. Further studies are needed to validate these results. Arginine is available in most health food stores as an oral supplementation, but it is currently difficult to be assured as to the purity of the substance. In addition, we believe more well-controlled clinical trials are needed before this supplement can be recommended for the treatment of patients with intermittent claudication.

Ginkgo biloba

The use of herbal medicines has become fashionable in the treatment of many illnesses. *Ginkgo biloba* extract is a popular herbal medicine. A literature review identified a meta-analysis of randomized double-blind, placebo controlled trials comparing *Ginkgo biloba* with placebo for the treatment of intermittent claudication.[28] Although meta-analyses are prone to obvious criticisms, this analysis suggests that *Ginkgo biloba* did improve PFWD and MWD in patients with intermittent claudication. The studies did not suggest that there seemed to be consistent adverse reactions, but gastrointestinal complaints were reported most commonly. More large-scale, well-controlled clinical trials using *Ginkgo biloba* are needed before it can be recommended for the treatment of intermittent claudication.

Buflomedil

Buflomedil is a vasoactive drug that has effects not only on the vasculature, but also on platelet inhibition and red blood cell deformability. It also has a suggestive mechanism of improving the efficiency of muscle cell metabolism. Trübestein and associates[29] showed significant improvements in PFWD and MWD compared with placebo in patients treated with 600 mg of active buflomedil daily for 12 weeks ($P < .001$ and $P < .01$). Mild and transient side effects included gastrointestinal disorders, headaches, dizziness, erythema, and pharyngitis. Buflomedil is currently available in Europe and some Latin American countries but is not available in the United States. No large-scale clinical trial has yet to be reported showing the efficacy of this drug in North American patient populations.

Ketanserin

Ketanserin is a serotonin S-2 receptor antagonist. This drug has been tested extensively in Europe on almost 4000 patients. In a subset analysis, 594 patients were evaluated for its effects on treating PFWD for more than 1 year of treatment.[30] No increases in walking distance occurred in patients receiving ketanserin. Other serotonin antagonists, such as naftidrofuryl, are used in numerous countries to treat patients with claudication. Currently the use of ketanserin cannot be suggested to treat patients with symptoms of intermittent claudication.

Niacin and Lovastatin

A large clinical trial has started to evaluate the effects of combined extended-release niacin and lovastatin on the symptoms of intermittent claudication. The hypothesis behind the use of this combination is that the positive effects on total cholesterol, low-density lipoproteins, triglycerides, and high-density lipoproteins in combination with a reduction in the fibrinogen levels would compare favorably with placebo in terms of improvement of walking ability in patients with PAD. Inositol niacinate is a derivative of niacin. This medication has been used in three small studies to treat patients with intermittent claudication. It showed significant increases in PFWD compared with placebo. Safety data from these studies revealed that this drug was well tolerated; gastrointestinal symptoms were the most commonly reported side effect. One side effect of niacin and niacin derivatives that is well known is flushing. It is too early to evaluate the true effects of niacin and lovastatin combinations on PAD; however, the large-scale results of the trial should be forthcoming shortly.

■ CONCLUSION

Mild-to-moderate claudication not only impairs walking ability, but also can result in numerous and sometimes serious lifestyle consequences. Primarily, treatment should be aimed at lifestyle modification and, most important, at the implementation of a routine walking exercise program. Compliance is poor with these methods of management. Treatment of claudication with medicines is an effective way to improve PFWD and MWD, but this should be viewed as supplementary Currently, FDA approval for the treatment of intermittent claudication is limited to pentoxifylline and cilostazol; the latter seems to be more effective in increasing PFWD and MWD. These results must be viewed in perspective. Many patients may simply exhibit a placebo effect, and although many patients show an improvement, only half report subjective improvement in their quality of life after treatment with cilostazol. Many other medications that are used in Europe, Latin America, and Asia have shown promising results, but further clinical evaluation is necessary. New treatment regimens are under evaluation; they should be accepted only after they have been proved beneficial by appropriately conducted, scientifically based clinical trials.

■ REFERENCES

1. Hiatt WR: Medical treatment of peripheral arterial disease and claudication. N Engl J Med 344:1608-1621, 2001.
2. Goldhaber SZ, Manson JE, Stampfer MJ, et al: Low-dose aspirin and subsequent peripheral arterial surgery in the Physician's Health Study. Lancet 340:143-145, 1992.
3. Collaborative overview of randomized trials of antiplatelet therapy II: Maintenance of vascular graft or arterial patency by antiplatelet therapy. BMJ 308:159-168, 1994.
4. CAPRIE Steering Committee: A randomized, blinded trial of clopidogrel versus aspirin in patients at risk of ischemic events (CAPRIE). Lancet 348:1329-1339, 1996.
5. Coffman JD: Vasodilator drugs in peripheral vascular disease. N Engl J Med 300:713-717, 1979.
6. Bagger JP, Helligsoe P, Randsbaek F, et al: Effect of verapamil in intermittent claudication. Circulation 95:411-414, 1997.
7. Porter JM, Culter BS, Lee BY, et al: Pentoxifylline efficacy in the treatment of intermittent claudication: Multicenter controlled double blind trial with objective assessment of chronic occlusive arterial disease patients. Am Heart J 104:66-72, 1982.
8. Lindgärde F, Jelnes R, Björkman H, et al: Conservative drug treatment in patients with moderately severe chronic occlusive peripheral arterial disease. Circulation 80:1549-1556, 1989.
9. Ernst E, Kollár L, Resch KL: Does pentoxifylline prolong the walking distance in exercised claudicants? A placebo-controlled double-blind trial. Angiology 42:121-125, 1992.

10. Hood SC, Moher D, Barber GG: Management of intermittent claudication with pentoxifylline: Meta-analysis of randomized controlled trials. Can Med Assoc J 155:1053-1059, 1996.
11. Girolami B, Bernardi E, Prins MH, et al: Treatment of intermittent claudication with physical training, smoking cessation, pentoxifylline or nafronyl: A meta-analysis. Arch Intern Med 159:337-345, 1999.
12. Money SR, Herd JA, Isaacsohn JL, et al: Effect of cilostazol on walking distances in patients with intermittent claudication caused by peripheral vascular disease. J Vasc Surg 27:267-275, 1998.
13. Takahashi S, Oida K, Fujiwara R, et al: Effect of cilostazol, a cyclic AMP phosphodiesterase inhibitor, on the proliferation of rat aortic smooth muscle cells in culture. J Cardiovasc Pharmacol 20:900-906, 1992.
14. Beebe HG, Dawson DL, Cutler BS, et al: A new pharmacological treatment for intermittent claudication: Results of a randomized, multicenter trial. Arch Intern Med 159:2041-2050, 1999.
15. Dawson DL, Cutler BS, Meissner MH, et al: Cilostazol has beneficial effects in treatment of intermittent claudication. Circulation 98:678-686, 1998.
16. Packer M, Carver JR, Rodeheffer RJ, et al: Effect of oral milrinone on mortality in severe chronic heart failure. The PROMISE study research group. N Engl J Med 325:1468-1475, 1991.
17. Trübestein G, Böhme H, Heidrich H, et al: Naftidrofuryl in chronic arterial disease: Results of a controlled multicenter study. Angiology 35:500-505, 1984.
18. Adhoute G, Bacourt F, Barral M, et al: Naftidrofuryl in chronic arterial disease: Results of a six month controlled multicenter study using Naftidrofuryl tablets 200mg. Angiology 37:160-169, 1986.
19. Brevetti G, Chiariello M, Ferulano G, et al: Increases in walking distance in patients with peripheral vascular disease treated with L-carnitine: A double-blind, cross-over study. Circulation 77:767-773, 1988.
20. Brevetti G, Perna S, Sabba C, et al: Propionyl-L-carnitine in intermittent claudication: Double-blind, placebo-controlled, dose titration, multicenter study. J Am Coll Cardiol 26:1411-1416, 1995.
21. Brevetti G, Perna S, Sabba C, et al: Superiority of L-propionyl carnitine to L-carnitine in improving walking capacity in patients with peripheral vascular disease: An acute, intravenous, double-blind, cross-over study. Eur Heart J 13:251-255, 1992.
22. Brevetti G, Perna S, Sabba C, et al: Effect of propionyl-L-carnitine on quality of life in intermittent claudication. Am J Cardiol 79:777-780, 1997.
23. Olszewer E, Carter JP: EDTA chelation therapy in chronic degenerative disease. Med Hypotheses 28:41-49, 1988.
24. Guldager B, Jelnes R, Jørgensen SJ, et al: EDTA treatment of intermittent claudication—a double-blind, placebo-controlled study. J Intern Med 231:261-267, 1992.
25. van Rij AM, Solomon C, Packer SGK, Hopkins WG: Chelation therapy for intermittent claudication: A double-blind, randomized, controlled trial. Circulation 90:1194-1199, 1994.
26. Chappell LT, Miranda R, Hancke C, et al: EDTA chelation treatment for peripheral vascular disease. J Intern Med 237:429-434, 1995.
27. Böger RH, Bode-Böger SM, Thiele W, et al: Restoring vascular nitric oxide formation by L-arginine improves the symptoms of intermittent claudication in patients with peripheral arterial occlusive disease. J Am Coll Cardiol 32:1336-1341, 1998.
28. Pittler MH, Ernst E: Ginkgo biloba extract for the treatment of intermittent claudication: A meta-analysis of randomized trials. Am J Med 108:276-281, 2000.
29. Trübestein G, Balzer K, Bisler H, et al: Buflomedil in arterial occlusive disease: Results of a controlled multicenter study. Angiology 35:500-505, 1984.
30. PACK Claudication Substudy Investigators: Randomized placebo-controlled, double-blind trial of ketanserin in claudicants. Circulation 80:1544-1548, 1989.

Chapter 38

Hyperglycemia, Diabetes, and Syndrome X

JONATHAN M. WEISWASSER, MD
ANTON N. SIDAWY, MD, MPH

The importance of disorders of glucose metabolism is well recognized by vascular surgeons. Not only does diabetes affect perioperative management and outcome of surgical procedures; the disorder and its related conditions, such as syndrome X are major risk factors for the development of atherosclerotic disorders. Accordingly, it is imperative that the modern vascular surgeon be more aware of these metabolic conditions.

Proper glucose homeostasis and disposal rely on both adequate secretion of insulin by the pancreatic beta cell and a responsive population of insulin receptors on the target cellular surface. The ability of the individual to maintain normoglycemia when given a glucose load depends on the extent to which the pancreas can produce insulin. Indeed, insulin-mediated glucose uptake varies about tenfold among healthy subjects. Elevated serum glucose values can be observed in normal, healthy individuals with seemingly normal oral glucose tolerance test results, who also have elevated insulin values, reflective of some degree of insulin resistance.[1] It is a generally accepted phenomenon that glucose homeostasis can be maintained as long as the pancreas can increase its production of insulin. As soon as this compensatory production is exhausted, however, we can expect the onset of type 2 diabetes.[2] What is becoming more evident are the roles that *insulin* per se and resistance to insulin have in the development of disease.

Several large, longitudinal studies have examined the development of insulin resistance and diabetes and have confirmed the supposition that insulin intolerance represents a spectrum of entities, with mildly exaggerated insulin responses on the one end, true insulin resistance with the ability to maintain normal glucose homeostasis somewhere in the middle, and frank type 2 diabetes mellitus on the other extreme. These studies also demonstrate that the existence of insulin resistance often predates the development of type 2 diabetes.[3-5] Although the relationship between type 2 diabetes and insulin resistance may be clear, the converse is not, because only a minority of patients with insulin resistance experience type 2 diabetes, instead overcoming their defect by overproducing insulin. Their glucose homeostasis may ultimately remain controlled, but the observation that this subset of patients suffers medical co-morbidities has led many authorities to believe that insulin plays a significant role in the development of such complications.

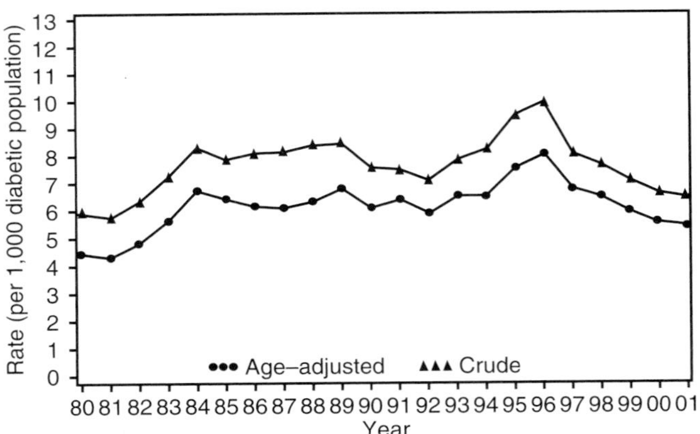

FIGURE 38-1 Nontraumatic lower extremity amputation with diabetes. (From Centers for Disease Control and Prevention: Diabetes Surveillance System: Crude and Age-standardized Rate of Hospital Discharge for Nontraumatic Lower Extremity Amputation per 1000 Diabetic Population, United States, 1980-2001.)

■ DIABETES MELLITUS

Epidemiology

Hyperglycemia, its metabolic sequelae, and the ultimate development of diabetes mellitus constitute markers on a spectrum of disease resulting from abnormal glucose disposal. The epidemiology of this disorder, however, is overwhelming. As of 2000, more than 17 million, or 6.2% of the population of the United States, were estimated to have diabetes, of which only 11 million were diagnosed.[6,7] In 1999, 450,000 individuals died of their disease, so that diabetes accounted for 19% of deaths in the U.S. among those older than 25 years.[8] Although the disease constituted the sixth leading cause of death, it conferred a twofold to fourfold rise in the rate of heart disease–related deaths among adults with diabetes and accounted for more than 60% of nontraumatic lower extremity amputations. From 1997 to 1999, about 82,000 nontraumatic lower limb amputations were performed each year among people with diabetes. Finally, diabetes is the leading cause of treated end-stage renal disease, accounting for more than 43% of new cases on a yearly basis. The estimated direct and indirect monetary cost of diabetes in the U.S. as of 2002 was $132 billion.[9]

Although the global effects that diabetes can inflict upon its patient population cannot be overlooked, the vascular surgeon is all too keenly aware of the manifestations of disease in the lower extremity in particular. Advances in the detection and treatment of lower extremity disease continue, but little epidemiologic evidence supports the notion that these maneuvers are improving the rates of limb salvage. The current rate of 6.5 discharges for lower extremity amputation per 1000 hospital discharges is little changed from 20 years ago, emphasizing what we prefer to interpret as a fault in aggressive detection and timely treatment of the disease rather than the results of therapy (Fig. 38-1). Below-knee amputations followed toe amputations as the most common level of amputation site, at 1.9 per 1000 per year.

Diagnosis

According to the *Definition, Diagnosis and Classification of Diabetes Mellitus*, published by the World Health Organization (WHO) in 1999, diabetes mellitus (DM) is defined as "a metabolic disorder of multiple aetiology characterized by chronic hyperglycemia with disturbances of carbohydrate, fat and protein metabolism resulting from defects in insulin secretion, insulin action, or both."[10] The constellation of "neuropathy, nephropathy, and retinopathy" remains a bulwark of the late-stage manifestations of the disease, but as is all too familiar to the vascular surgeon, the addition of vasculopathy seems appropriate. Diabetes classically causes the characteristic symptoms of blurring of vision, weight loss, polyuria, and thirst. In extreme DM, the metabolic effects include ketoacidosis and nonketotic hyperosmolarity, which in turn can lead to stupor, coma, and death. More commonly, the presence of chronic hyperglycemia predates the diagnosis of true diabetes. Over the long term, retinopathy leading to blindness, nephropathy resulting in renal failure, and neuropathy resulting in Charcot's foot are all common to the diabetic patient whose disease is untreated. Diabetics are also at significantly greater risk for development of cardiovascular, peripheral vascular, and cerebrovascular diseases.[10]

The diagnosis of true DM requires very careful consideration, not just for the nuances of what can be a subtle disease but also because of the prognosis for the patient's future health that accompanies the diagnosis. The diagnostic approach to the patient with hyperglycemia can be divided according to whether the patient has severe symptoms or asymptomatic hyperglycemia. The presence of infection, recent trauma, or other systemic insult, any of which leads to the phenomena of transitory hyperglycemia, should not suggest the diagnosis of diabetes. Moreover, hyperglycemia detected on a single blood test should *never* lead the physician to brand the patient a diabetic. Rather, the diagnosis of diabetes is made only on the basis of serial blood glucose levels, measured either after fasting, randomly, or after an oral glucose tolerance test (OGTT), that are in the diabetic range. Factors such as age, ethnicity, family history, and obesity may dictate the regularity of blood glucose surveillance in a patient with normal results of an OGTT or similar study. An alternative to the OGTT has been the measure of glycosylated hemoglobin. This test, which determines average glycemia over the course of

Table 38-1 Values for Diagnosis of Diabetes Mellitus and Other Categories of Hyperglycemia

	GLUCOSE CONCENTRATION, mmol l^{-1} (mg dL^{-1})		
	Whole Blood		
	Venous	*Capillary*	Plasma,* Venous
Diabetes mellitus:			
Fasting *or* 2-hr postglucose load	≥ 6.1 (≥ 110) ≥ 10.0 (≥ 180)	≥ 6.1 (≥ 110) ≥ 11.1 (≥ 200)	≥ 7.0 (≥ 126) ≥ 11.1 (≥ 200)
Impaired glucose tolerance (IGT):			
Fasting (if measured) *and* 2-hr postglucose load	< 6.1 (< 110) and ≥ 6.7 (≥ 120)	< 6.1 (< 110) and ≥ 7.8 (≥ 140)	< 7.0 (< 126) and ≥ 7.8 (≥ 140)
Impaired fasting glycemia (IFG):			
Fasting	≥ 5.6 (≥ 100) and < 6.1 (< 110)	≥ 5.6 (≥ 100) and < 6.1 (< 110)	≥ 6.1 (≥ 110) and < 7.0 (< 126)
and (if measured) 2-hr postglucose load	< 6.7 (< 120)	< 7.8 (< 140)	< 7.8 (< 140)

*Corresponding values for capillary plasma are: for diabetes mellitus, fasting ≥ 7.0 (≥ 126); 2-hr ≥ 12.2 (≥ 220); for impaired glucose tolerance, fasting < 7.0 (< 126) and 2-hr ≥ 8.9 (≥ 160) and ≥ 12.2 (≥ 220); and for impaired fasting glycemia ≥ 6.1 (≥ 110) and < 7.0 (< 126) and if measured, 2-hr < 8.9 (< 160).

For epidemiologic or population screening purposes, the fasting of 2-hr value after 75 g oral glucose may be used alone. For clinical purposes, the diagnosis of diabetes should always be confirmed by repeating the test on another day unless there is unequivocal hyperglycemia with acute metabolic decompensation or obvious symptoms.

Glucose concentrations should not be determined on serum unless red cells are immediately removed; otherwise glycolysis will result in an unpredictable underestimation of the true concentrations. It should be stressed that glucose preservatives do not totally prevent glycolysis. If whole blood is used, the sample should be kept at 0-4 °C or centrifuged immediately, or assayed immediately.

Adapted from World Health Organization, Department of Noncommunicable Disease Surveillance: Definition, Diagnosis and Classification of Diabetes Mellitus. Geneva, WHO, 1999.

weeks, has been demonstrated to be as sensitive and specific as an OGTT.[11]

Diagnosis of diabetes from the OGTT result is presented in Table 38-1. For the primary care physician, the OGTT is considered in the patient in whom randomly measured blood glucose levels are in the uncertain range and fasting levels are normal or below those necessary for the diagnosis. A typical OGTT is performed through measurement of plasma glucose levels after fasting and then 2 hours after the administration of a 75-g oral glucose load.

Treatment

Of paramount importance in the management of the patient with diabetes is glycemic control, which has been demonstrated to substantially reduce the development and progression of microvascular disease.[12] Hemoglobin A_{1C} (HbA_{1C}), hemoglobin A_1, and total glycosylated hemoglobin should be checked every 6 months to monitor the effect of therapy. If changes are being made to the drug regimen, the testing interval should be shortened to 3 months. The extent to which "tight" glycemic control is pursued depends on several factors in the patient's medical history and lifestyle and ultimately represents a balance between the risk of hypoglycemia and the benefit of glycemic control to the microvasculature. Factors such as congestive heart failure, end-stage renal disease, limited life expectancy, and financial constraints may favor less aggressive therapy.[13]

Diet and exercise remain the mainstay of first-line treatment. Although no formal "diabetic diet" has been suggested by the American Diabetes Association, the patient's diet should be designed to help attain desired treatment goals. Referral to a nutritionist is strongly suggested for this aspect of therapy.[14] Moderate weight loss has beneficial effects, not only in terms of glycemic control but also on the presence of hypertension and dyslipidemia.[15] Failing this approach, pharmacologic therapy is indicated.

The options for pharmacologic therapy have multiplied and now include oral hypoglycemics, such as sulfonylureas, biguanides, α-glucosidase inhibitors, thiazolidinediones, meglitinides (Table 38-2), and subcutaneous insulins (Table 38-3).

Sulfonylureas

Sulfonylureas have traditionally been used as a first-line therapy in the pharmacologic treatment of patients with DM type 2.[16] These agents act by both increasing pancreatic output of insulin and enhancing receptor sensitivity.[17] Older, long-acting agents such as chlorpropamide, which could cause hypoglycemia, have been replaced with second-generation, shorter-acting agents (glipizide, glyburide, and glimepiride). The dose of a sulfonylurea is gradually increased from a low baseline at weekly intervals until the highest recommended dose is attained. At that dose, if normoglycemia is not obtained, consideration is given to combining the sulfonylurea with one of the other oral hypoglycemics or insulin. Of note is that the sulfonylureas carry a warning that their use may raise the risk of cardiovascular death. This warning is based on a study published in 1970, in which a now discontinued sulfonylurea, tolbutamide, was shown to increase cardiovascular mortality to two and a half times that seen with diet alone.[18]

Biguanides

Metformin, the prototype biguanide, may also be used as a first-line therapy in the treatment of diabetics in whom nonpharmacologic therapy has failed.[19] By increasing peripheral glucose uptake and utilization and decreasing hepatic glucose production, metformin is able to lower blood glucose but carries with it risk of fatal lactic acidosis in patients with renal, hepatic, or cardiac dysfunction.[20] In order to prevent this complication, metformin should be

Table 38-2 The Oral Hypoglycemics*

CLASS	GENERIC NAME	TRADE NAME	FREQUENCY
Sulfonylureas	chlorpropamide glipizide glyburide glimepiride	Diabinese Glucotrol Glucotrol XL Micronase Glynase DiaBeta Amaryl	1-2/day before meals
Biguanides	metformin	Glucophage	BID
α-Glucosidase inhibitors	acarbose miglitol	Precose Glyset	With the first bite of the meal
Thiazolidinediones	rosiglitazone troglitazone pioglitazone	Avandia Rezulin Actos	QD or BID with food
Meglitinides	repaglinide nateglinide	Prandin Starlix	Before each meal
Sulfonylurea/ biguanide combination	glyburide/ metformin	Glucovance	1-2/day before meals

*There is no fixed dosage regimen for the management of diabetes mellitus with any hypoglycemic agent. Some elderly patients may require initiating therapy with half pills. In addition to the usual monitoring of urinary glucose, the patient's blood glucose must also be monitored periodically to determine the minimum effective dose for the patient; to detect primary failure, i.e., inadequate lowering of blood glucose at the maximum recommended dose of medication; and to detect secondary failure, i.e., loss of an adequate blood glucose lowering response after an initial period of effectiveness. Glycosylated hemoglobin levels may also be of value in monitoring the patient's response to therapy.

temporarily discontinued when intravenous radiologic contrast agents are used or when major surgery or septic conditions may result in hypoperfusion. The biguanides are also not without side effects, as up to 30% of patients taking them experience severe gastrointestinal side effects, such as diarrhea, nausea, and anorexia. As with the sulfonylureas, dosing begins low and is gradually increased until the target control is reached; the addition of other agents and insulin is reserved for those in whom the maximum dose of biguanide does not achieve the target glucose level.

α-Glucosidase Inhibitors

The class of oral hypoglycemics known as α-glucosidase inhibitors, including acarbose and miglitol, may be used in conjunction with diet control to lower blood glucose.[21] These agents decrease postprandial plasma glucose by slowing the digestion of carbohydrates and delaying the absorption of glucose into the bloodstream. Diarrhea, flatulence, and abdominal pain are common side effects and often lead to the discontinuance of these drugs. However, with continued use of these agents, many of the side effects may diminish, leading to the recommendation that α-glucosidase inhibitors be initiated at low doses to help encourage patient compliance with therapy.[22]

Thiazolidinediones

Thiazolidinediones are also often referred to as the "glitazones." Troglitazone, the first of the thiazolidinediones, is thought to act by enhancing the action of both endogenous insulin and exogenous insulin by improving sensitivity to insulin in muscle and adipose tissue and by inhibiting hepatic glucose production.[23] Initially, troglitazone was approved only for use in patients with type 2 diabetes who require insulin therapy and was not approved for monotherapy use. Severe side effects, including significant liver dysfunction and failure and neutropenia, led to the withdrawal of troglitazone from the market. However, rosiglitazone and pioglitazone, approved for use by the U.S. Food and Drug Administration (FDA) in 1997, have become important elements in the treatment of type 2 diabetes and perhaps in the prevention and management of syndrome X, described later in this chapter.

Meglitinides

Two drugs in the class known as meglitinides are now available—repaglinide, derived from benzoic acid and approved by the FDA in 1997, and nateglinide, derived from D-phenylalanine and approved in 2000. These agents raise insulin levels rapidly by stimulating the beta cells via mechanisms different from those seen with sulfonylureas. Meglitinides enhance insulin release from the pancreas over a short time only when the glucose level is high. Therefore, the risk of hypoglycemia is lower than with sulfonylureas. Their activity more closely mimics normal first-phase insulin release when food is eaten by a person without diabetes. Peak drug activity is seen in 1 hour, and their short action time (3 hours) makes these agents ideal for matching the glucose load imposed after a carbohydrate-rich meal.

Insulins

Exogenous subcutaneous insulin remains a mainstay for the patient with refractory type 2 diabetes (see Table 38-3). Hypoglycemia, the most common adverse effect reported by those who take insulin, has been reported to occur in up to 26% of patients, with a mean of approximately two episodes per year.[24] Additionally, one can expect considerable weight gain with the commencement of insulin therapy.[24] Further, rapid glucose control with aggressive insulin administration can exacerbate proliferative retinopathy in 5% of patients. Current recommendations for patients with diabetic retinopathy call for reductions in HbA_{1C} by 2% per year with retinal examinations every 6 months to avoid this complication.[26]

Insulin absorption variability contributes most to the inability to mimic physiologic insulin secretion. The duration and onset of action of the different types of insulin vary greatly when mixed and, interestingly, with site of administration.[27] Human insulins behave differently when administered in large doses from insulin analogues, and it is not uncommon to observe vast variation in the level of hypoglycemic effects according to location of administration (e.g., abdomen versus thigh) and type of insulin used (e.g., NPH [neutral protamine Hagedorn] insulin versus NPH insulin combined with a shorter-acting agent).[28] Insulin pens, a means by which the patient can purchase cartridges with premeasured doses or combinations, offer the advantage of greater reliability of dosing but carry significantly higher cost. Insulin pumps, which are supposed

Table 38-3 Insulins

INSULIN	TYPE
Rapid-acting (onset less than 15 minutes):	
Humalog (insulin lispro)	Analogue
Humalog cartridges	Analogue
NovoLog (insulin aspart)	Analogue
Short-acting (onset ½-2 hours):	
Humulin R (regular)	Human
Iletin II Pork Regular	Pork
Humulin R cartridges (1.5 mL)	Human
Novolin R (regular)	Human
Velosulin Human (regular) (buffered)	Human
Intermediate-acting (onset 2-4 hours):	
Humulin L (lente)	Human
Humulin N (NPH [neutral protamine Hagedorn])	Human
Iletin II Pork Lente	Pork
Iletin II Pork NPH	Pork
Humulin N Cartridges (1.5 mL)	Human
Novolin N (NPH)	Human
Long-acting (onset 4-6 hours):	
Humulin-U (ultralente)	Human
Very-long-acting (24+ hours):	
Lantus (insulin glargine, formerly HOE901)	Analogue
Mixtures:	
Humalog Mix 75/25 (75% insulin lispro protamine suspension and 25% insulin lispro injection (recombinant DNA origin)	Analogue
Humalog Mix 75/25 pen (75% insulin lispro protamine suspension and 25% insulin lispro injection (recombinant DNA origin)	Analogue
Humulin 50/50 (50% NPH, 50% regular)	Human
Humulin 70/30 (70% NPH, 30% regular)	Human
Humulin 70/30 cartridges (1.5 mL)	Human
Novolin 70/30 (70% NPH, 30% regular)	Human

to mimic physiologic insulin levels, require attention to access site and tubing and may raise the risks of hypoglycemia. Patients with insulin pumps must also have traditional insulin delivery mechanisms available.

Insulin may be administered as rapid-acting insulin (insulin lispro, insulin aspart), short-acting insulin (regular insulin), intermediate-acting insulin (NPH), and long-acting insulin (ultralente, insulin glargine) (see Table 38-3). Traditional therapy consisted of the use of a combination of a "longer-acting" agent to mimic the basal physiologic insulin state combined with a shorter-acting agent (e.g., regular human insulin) to account for prandial variation in blood glucose. Administered twice per day, this combination required rather strict consistency of meal timing and ignored the effects of each insulin type on both basal insulin levels and postprandial requirements. Delay of lunch, for example, could be associated with hypoglycemia, causing many patients to add a "meal between meals" to account for the overlapping effects. As a result, current recommendations favor the administration of a basal insulin (NPH or ultralente) at regular twice-daily intervals, and postprandial supplementation with short-acting agents (regular insulin). Although this regimen requires more frequent injections, surveys of diabetics demonstrate that this is more preferable to the dietary restrictions of the former approach.[29] The American Diabetes Association recommends self-monitoring of blood glucose levels at a frequency of three times per day.[27]

Insulin therapy commences in patients with type 2 diabetes when oral therapy has failed, which is signified by HbA_{1C} levels approaching 8% despite optimal oral therapy.[31] Many such patients resist the addition of insulin administration because of the perception that it represents a failure of therapy, yet several studies have demonstrated a significant benefit in terms of patient satisfaction, general well-being, and quality of life.[32,33] Optimal management continues the oral agent in conjunction with insulin therapy. The majority of patients benefit from the addition of a sulfonylurea or metformin in combination with insulin, and this regimen generally reduces insulin dose by approximately 25% and by as much as 50% in some individuals. Emphasis is placed on target HbA_{1C} level, reduced hypoglycemia, and reduced weight gain, not lower insulin dose. Despite the additional secretagogue effects of the sulfonylureas, endogenous insulin production can be expected to decline, and with this decline, the beneficial effects of oral therapy are lost.[34] Failing natural insulin production can be ascertained by measuring C-peptide levels. When insulin is initially synthesized by the pancreatic beta cells, it is produced as a large molecule and then cleaved. The intermediate segment, C-peptide, is released at the same time but it has no known function. Normal levels are 0.5 to 2.0 ng/mL, and low levels result from failing insulin production.

■ INSULIN RESISTANCE AND SYNDROME X

A combination of clinical phenomena associated with diabetes was first described by Vague[35] more than 40 years ago and was re-examined and refined in 1988 by Reaven,[36] who defined syndrome X as a constellation of clinical entities that seemed to group together. Insulin resistance, glucose intolerance, hypertension, and an adverse cholesterol profile could be clinically as well as statistically linked, an observation that has produced the hypothesis that as a syndrome, these phenomena may have a common clinical ancestor. Though the term *syndrome X* is the most common appellation, "syndrome X plus,"[37] the "deadly quartet,"[38] "metabolic syndrome,"[39] and the "insulin resistance syndrome"[40] are also used to describe the syndrome, depending on the emphasis and inclusion of certain phenotypes. The WHO defined the metabolic syndrome, or syndrome X, in 1998 as listed in Table 38-4.[41] As a result of broader longitudinal studies, a later definition has emerged in the *Third Report of the National Cholesterol Education Program Expert Panel on Detection, Evaluation, and Treatment of High Blood Cholesterol in Adults* (ATP-III), a National Institutes of Health-sponsored document that adopted the definition of the metabolic syndrome as the presence of three or more of the following: (1) waist circumference greater than 102 cm in men and 88 cm in women, (2) serum triglyceride level at least 150 mg/dL, (3) high-density lipoprotein (HDL) cholesterol level less than 40 mg/dL in men and less than 50 mg/dL in women, (4) blood pressure of at least 130/85 mm Hg, and (5) fasting serum glucose value of at least 110 mg/dL.[42]

As more experimental and clinical evidence emerges from the examination of this syndrome, hyperinsulinemia and glucose intolerance appear to engender metabolic,

Table 38-4 World Health Organization Definition of the Metabolic Syndrome (Syndrome X)

1. Glucose intolerance, impaired glucose tolerance, and/or insulin resistance:
   a. Hyperinsulinemic under euglycemic conditions.
   b. Glucose uptake below lowest quartile for background population.

Plus two or more of the following:

2. Raised arterial pressure (> 160 mm Hg systolic/90 mm Hg diastolic).
3. Raised plasma triglycerides (> 1.7 mmol/L; 150 mg/dL) and/or low high-density lipoprotein cholesterol (< 0.9 mmol/L, 35 mg/dL men; < 1.0 mmol/L, 39 mg/dL women).
4. Central obesity (men: waist-to-hip ratio > 0.90; women: waist-to-hip ratio > 0.85) and/or body mass index > 30 kg/m^2.
5. Microalbuminuria (urinary albumin excretion rate ≥ 20 μg/min or albumin-to-creatinine ratio ≥ 20 mg/L).

Adapted from Alberti KG, Zimmet PZ: Definition, diagnosis and classification of diabetes mellitus and its complications. Part I: Diagnosis and classification of diabetes mellitus. Provisional report of a WHO consultation. Diabet Med 15:539-553, 1998.

hemodynamic, and vascular sequelae. Although these sequelae are often observed in patients with non–insulin-dependent diabetes mellitus, the presence of syndrome X implies that therapy for the consequences of hyperinsulinemia and glucose intolerance should commence earlier in the patient's lifetime.

Etiology

Several researchers have embarked on defining a cause-and-effect relationship between insulin and the components of syndrome X. A major obstacle in the discussion of the syndrome remains measuring and defining insulin resistance, however, because no consensus exists as to what is "normal." The epidemiology of the syndrome suggests that the disorder is more common in certain ethnic groups, such as Asian Indians and Chinese, Australian Aborigines, African-Americans, Mexican-Americans, Polynesians, and Micronesians.[43,44] Perhaps the most notable etiology for the syndrome is the purely statistical association of its components.[45] The convenience of attributing the facets of the syndrome to one common etiologic entity has been investigated through several analyses that consistently demonstrate that more than one factor seems to be involved.[46-49] At best, hyperinsulinemia could be considered the common etiologic agent, yet this relationship is not absolutely borne out when one examines this relationship in different populations.[2,50] Among differing populations in whom the syndrome is prevalent, affected individuals demonstrate correlation between elements of syndrome X, yet the strength of these correlations varies in different populations.

Physiologically, several hypotheses have emerged to explain the development of syndrome X. Some have implicated the pancreatic beta cell and its response and function in the presence of various glucose and other stimulatory exercises by demonstrating that in a defined population of patients, a relationship exists between the syndrome and abnormal parameters of pancreatic function.[51] Mitrakou and colleagues,[52] assessing glucose tolerance in normal and obese individuals, demonstrated that the 30-minute response to oral glucose was inversely related to the degree of hyperglycemia. In this study, adiposity was controlled to minimize variability, and the results seemed to suggest a role for beta cell dysfunction in the development of insulin resistance.[52] Further studies in animal models corroborate the finding that single molecular defects in the action of insulin lead to hyperinsulinemia but not to glucose intolerance.[53] Beta cell dysfunction, however, induces hyperglycemia.[54]

As a method for determining the etiology for some of the hemodynamic effects of syndrome X, the sympathetic nervous syndrome has been implicated in the development of hypertension among individuals with hyperinsulinemia.[55] Insulin-mediated glucose uptake in central hypothalamic neurons regulates sympathetic activity as a response to dietary intake, perhaps linking dietary intake and glucose disposal with a prohypertensive effect mediated by renal modulation and cardiovascular changes. The Normative Aging Study demonstrated a significant correlation between insulin concentration and urinary norepinephrine level.[56] In patients below the 50th percentile in terms of urinary epinephrine and plasma insulin values 2 hours after stimulation, only 15% had hypertension; 37% of patients above the 50th percentile had hypertension. These findings carried through the analysis even after control of the data for variables such as basal metabolic index and body distribution of fat. Additionally, adrenal medullary activity, as assessed by 24-hour urinary epinephrine excretion, seems to play a significant role in dyslipidemia resembling that found in syndrome X, after correction for the effect of insulin. Epinephrine levels were inversely correlated to favorable lipid patterns.[57,58]

Other metabolic factors, in particular those that relate to metabolism and modulation of fatty tissue, have been associated with syndrome X. Some researchers have shown that leptin has been positively correlated with total body fat and, acting through a hypothalamic receptor, increases thermogenesis and decreases food intake.[59] Leptin carries a strong correlation with fasting insulin levels as well, and its behavior suggests that it may act in concert with insulin levels to promote syndrome X.[60] Interestingly, leptin may play a role in the modulation of insulin activity and sensitivity and may represent the link between diabetes and obesity. This relationship between elevated leptin values and insulin resistance occurs independently of body weight.[61] Other investigators have postulated that certain types of fatty tissue elaborate substances that interfere with normal glucose disposal and insulin action. The presence of increased "visceral" fat as a percentage of fat mass was positively correlated with insulin resistance and hepatic glucose production.[62] In rats, the production of tumor necrosis factor-α and leptin by all fatty tissue was found to be dramatically reduced with the surgical removal of visceral fat; this phenomenon may provide another link in the association with obesity and insulin resistance.

Hemodynamic Effects

Welborn and associates[63] first described the association of elevated insulin with hypertension in 1966. Several larger studies have since established the association of insulin resistance and hyperinsulinemia with essential hypertension.[64,65] Although the prevalence of essential hypertension among patients with glucose intolerance is high, the prevalence of glucose intolerance among patients with essential hypertension remains at a level that does not suggest that insulin is causative in the development of routine essential hypertension.[66] Thus, insulin resistance and hyperinsulinemia are not uniquely required for hypertension to develop. As with the development of type 2 diabetes, in which the ability of the pancreas to compensate is lost, a theory has emerged postulating that hypertension develops much like diabetes—that is, hypertension, through a currently unknown mechanism that relies on insulin, develops when the compensatory mechanisms that regulate the adverse effects of insulin are stretched beyond their means.[67] Reaven and coworkers[68] propose a mechanism for the development of hypertension through hyperinsulinemia that employs the sympathoadrenal route.

Perhaps some of the most convincing data has emerged from several larger-scale studies, including that by the European Group for the Study of Insulin Resistance. In this study, 333 normotensive patients underwent extensive investigation of the relationship between fasting insulin concentration and blood pressure. Independent of age, gender, and degree of obesity, blood pressure was directly related to the level of insulin resistance and the plasma insulin concentration.[69] Additionally, it has also been established that hypertension cannot be implicated in the development of hyperinsulinemia.[70] The first-degree relatives of patients with essential hypertension are more likely to be insulin resistant and to have elevated insulin plasma values than a similar cohort without the history of hypertension, independent of age, gender, and obesity.[71] Lastly, several prospective studies have demonstrated that hyperinsulinemia is a risk factor in the development of hypertension, independent of gender and obesity type.[72-74]

In summary, these studies strongly suggest that insulin and overexpression of insulin as part of a compensatory mechanism contribute significantly to the development of essential hypertension. Because essential hypertension can develop without hyperinsulinemia, we cannot conclude that there is a pure cause-and-effect relationship between insulin and hypertension. However, these data demonstrate the strong association between hyperinsulinemia and hypertension and, thus, establish hypertension as one feature of syndrome X.

Metabolic Effects

Although the majority of the discussion so far has focused on hyperinsulinemia and the effects of elevated insulin levels and ensuing hyperglycemia on homeostasis, the effects of insulin on modulation of fat disposition now requires attention. Insulin clearly plays a role in both hepatic synthesis and degradation of circulating lipoproteins by both the liver and skeletal muscle.[75] Just as glucose-intolerant individuals require exceedingly greater concentration of insulin to maintain euglycemia, glucose intolerance also results in elevations of free fatty acids and apolipoprotein B levels, even after adjustment for age and basal metabolic rate.[76] Thus, "insulin resistance" includes resistance to both insulin-mediated glucose disposal and free fatty acid suppression.

The dyslipidemia associated with syndrome X is characterized by an elevation in triglycerides, a diminution of HDL cholesterol, and an enhancement of postprandial lipemia.[77,78] Perhaps more alarming is the association of insulin resistance with cholesterol particle size. There is considerable evidence to demonstrate that insulin sensitivity and cholesterol particle size are directly correlated. Patients with insulin resistance have small, dense low-density lipoprotein (LDL) cholesterol particles. The significance of particle size and density relates to the association of cholesterol particle size with elevated cardiac risk[79] (and is detailed in Chapter 36). High levels of LDL cholesterol have been correlated with greater intimal media thickness of the carotid artery and with insulin resistance as well. In a large-scale Swedish study (an arm of the Atherosclerosis and Insulin Resistance Study), subjects who met the criteria for diagnosis of the metabolic syndrome also had greater intimal media thickness in the carotid artery, carotid bulb, and femoral arteries as well as a preponderance of smaller LDL cholesterol particles.[80] Other investigators have stated that the presence of insulin resistance is as much a risk factor for carotid thickening as an elevation of LDL cholesterol.[81]

Perhaps as important as the dyslipidemia associated with syndrome X is the effect that hyperinsulinemia has on excretion of homocysteine and urinary nitrate. The most convincing evidence of this relationship is provided by an arm of the Framingham study, which looked at more than 2000 patients in the fifth examination of the study who did not have diabetes. More than 12% of these patients had hyperinsulinemia, and 15% had traits associated with syndrome X. There was a significant increase in the mean plasma homocysteine level in patients who manifested signs of syndrome X, and as the individuals demonstrated additional phenotypes consistent with the disease, their homocysteine levels rose.[82] Although other, smaller studies have refuted this association,[83] the strong association of hyperhomocysteinemia with syndrome X may contribute to our understanding of the endothelial dysfunction associated with the disease. The effects of homocysteinemia on the vascular system are more fully detailed in Chapter 36.

Last, hypercoagulability and impairment of fibrinolysis may compound the risk of development of atherosclerosis in insulin-resistant individuals.[84] High fibrinogen levels have been correlated with myocardial infarction and stroke in nondiabetic subjects.[85] In addition, there is a strong correlation between levels of fibrinogen and plasminogen activator inhibitor-1 (PAI-1) and levels of insulin and its precursors,[86] suggesting an additional mechanism by which hyperinsulinemia might contribute to the development of coronary disease.

Syndrome X and the Vasculature

What is evident from the discussion of syndrome X and its effects is that hyperinsulinemia, even in the presence of what could be considered near-normal glucose concentrations, breeds entities that bear significant cardiovascular risk, namely hypertension and adverse cholesterol and free fatty acid levels. There is additional evidence that insulin, independently and in high concentration, can have adverse effects on the vasculature.

The effect of insulin on vascular smooth muscle has been a subject of great interest and debate. We have shown that insulin and glucose synergistically increase the proliferation of infragenicular arterial smooth muscle cells. Since the usual distribution of diabetic atherosclerotic disease is primarily in the infragenicular vasculature, we used cells harvested from tibial and peroneal arteries during below-knee amputations for non-reconstructible arterial disease. Insulin and glucose separately and in combination significantly increased the proliferation of these cells.[87] Although the metabolic effect of insulin is mediated by the insulin receptor (IR), Avena and colleagues[88] have shown that its growth-promoting effect on the infragenicular smooth muscle cells is mediated by the insulin-like growth factor-1 receptor (IGF-1R); the proliferative effects of insulin were inhibited by antibody to the IGF-1R and not by IR antibody.[88]

The importance of this finding becomes evident when we consider the search for a substance that has the metabolic effects of insulin but does not interact with the IGF-1R. Such a substance, demethylasterriquinone B1 (DMAQB1), was described by Zhang and associates,[89] who found that DMAQB1, extracted from the *Pseudomassaria* fungus found in Kinshasa, Africa, is more stimulatory to the IR than insulin and does not bind with the IGF-1R.[89] Weber and coworkers[90] have shown that, like insulin, DMAQB1 actively incorporates glucose in human infragenicular smooth muscle cells; but in contrast to insulin, DMAQB1 did not cause increased cell proliferation in a milieu of high concentrations of insulin and glucose.[90] In addition, some materials inhibited the proliferation of human infragenicular arterial smooth muscle cells in response to insulin and glucose. Thiamine (vitamin B_1), for example, inhibited combined insulin and glucose-induced proliferation of these cells, indicating a possible role for this vitamin in preventing the atherosclerotic complication of diabetes.[91]

In addition to possibly contributing to the formation of vessel disease, insulin and hyperinsulinemia affect vessel function and mediators of vasoreactivity. Avena and colleagues[92] have shown that brachial artery vasoreactivity improves with administration of insulin sensitizers in patients with peripheral vascular disease and abnormal glucose tolerance tests.[92] Furthermore, nitric oxide levels have been demonstrated to be higher in healthy patients with insulin resistance.[93] This finding may represent a compensatory response by the vasculature to overcome the untoward vascular effects of hyperinsulinemia outlined above. Insulin resistance has also been correlated with elevations of asymmetric dimethylarginine (ADMA), an endogenous nitric oxide synthase inhibitor.[94] Elevation of ADMA, which has been associated with an increased risk of cardiovascular disease, was found to be positively related to insulin resistance even after accounting for other factors associated with the development of cardiovascular disease.[95] More interesting was the finding that the rise in ADMA level was attenuated by the administration of rosiglitazone, an insulin-enhancing drug. Ultimately, the effects of hyperinsulinemia on ADMA, through its effects on nitric oxide production, may explain much of the endothelial dysfunction associated with insulin resistance and syndrome X.

Treatment

Being continuously revised without a consensus definition and lacking evidence-based results from clinical trials, the treatment of syndrome X is currently evolving. A keen awareness of the patients at risk and the associated manifestations of the syndrome is most important. For example, insulin resistance varies directly with adult body mass index but inversely with this ponderal index at birth. Foremost is the emphasis on avoidance of obesity and, especially, abdominal obesity. The importance of lifestyle interventions (weight loss from diet and exercise) has been established, with the reduction observed in the incidence of new onset of type 2 diabetes being significantly more effective in groups applying these interventions than in parallel groups receiving metformin or placebo.[96] Indeed, simple measures such as weight loss and regular exercise can have a dramatic effect on plasma insulin levels[97] and should be the mainstays of treatment.

Glucose transport is the rate-limiting step in glucose metabolism, which is mediated by glucose transporter 4 (GLUT 4). Molecular disruption of this transporter results in insulin resistance and glucose intolerance.[98] Furthermore, exercise appears to improve insulin sensitivity by increasing levels of GLUT 4.[99] Exercise for as little as 20 minutes three times per week has been demonstrated to improve serum insulin levels. Reduction in the incidence of type 2 diabetes involved exercise for at least 150 min/week in one study,[70] whereas more intensive exercise—360 to 450 minutes per week—resulted in a greater loss of abdominal fat than of midthigh fat in another.[100] Weight loss has also been clearly shown to improve hypertension, especially in patients with syndrome X.[101]

Consideration should also be given to the avoidance of obesity-provoking medications, such as anti-epileptic drugs and, especially, antipsychotic agents (olanzapine).[102] Manifestations of syndrome X have been reported with the use of retinoic acid for acne,[103] and in patients with acquired immune deficiency syndrome (AIDS) receiving highly active antiretroviral treatment (HAART) with the lipodystrophy syndrome.[104] Improvement in dietary intake has been repeatedly proved to favorably affect LDL cholesterol and triglyceride levels. In addition, some benefit may be provided by substituting monounsaturated and polyunsaturated fats for saturated fat in the diet insofar as LDL cholesterol concentrations are concerned. Patients with syndrome X should also be encouraged to include viscous fiber and plant stanol or sterol esters in the diet. What is decidedly worse is the recommendation for a high-carbohydrate diet, which clearly provokes the secretion of insulin.

In addition to primary treatment with diet and exercise, therapeutic use of pharmacotherapy should be considered. Reaven and associates[105] have shown that the enteric lipase inhibitor orlistat can have a favorable impact on weight loss and lipid profiles in patients with syndrome X. Subjects with syndrome X who lost additional weight with orlistat had a significantly favorable change in plasma triglyceride levels, insulin levels, and LDL levels. These researchers suggest that orlistat can enhance weight loss and can favorably affect cholesterol profiles in patients with syndrome X, results that might decrease the overall risk of coronary heart disease in these patients. Weight loss can also be achieved by the use of the anorexiants sibutramine and metformin. The latter is commonly used as a form of insulin sensitizer in type 2 diabetes, reducing levels of HbA_{1C} as well as improving lipid profile. In nondiabetics, metformin can favorably affect the abnormal metabolic profile, including hypertension, that is common to syndrome X.[106] Thiazolidinediones such as rosiglitazone and pioglitazone, acting on the peroxisome proliferator–activated receptor (PPAR), are another type of insulin sensitizer with the potential to benefit many of the abnormal aspects of insulin resistance.[67] α-Glucosidase inhibitors, such as acarbose and miglitol, inhibit conversion of carbohydrates into monosaccharides and slow the absorption of glucose with a decrease in postprandial glucose and improve insulin action in type 2 diabetes.

Statins used to lower LDL cholesterol have also been shown to improve insulin sensitivity. Simvastatin was shown to particularly benefit those subjects in the Scandinavian Simvastatin Survival Study (4S) with the metabolic syndrome profile,[107] and pravastatin was found to reduce the incidence of diabetes by 30% in another study, suggesting a new role for these pleiotropic agents.[108] Another group of antilipemic agents, the fibrates are more potent than the statins in raising HDL cholesterol levels and lowering triglyceride levels, abnormalities of which are often seen in syndrome X.

Other therapeutic options for patients with syndrome X are the use of angiotensin-converting enzyme inhibitors, which have been shown to inhibit the development of both microvascular and macrovascular disease in diabetics and are also relatively more insulin-sensitizing than other blood pressure–lowering drugs. Importantly, use of the angiotensin-converting enzyme inhibitor ramipril in diabetics was associated with significant protective effects on the vasculature and a reduction in the appearance of new-onset diabetes.[109] The use of aspirin, the avoidance of cigarette smoking, and, perhaps, the use of light-to-moderate intake of alcohol[30] would also be potentially beneficial.

Finally, additional agents under investigation may prove to be beneficial in syndrome X. They include the insulin sensitizer D-chiro-inositol,[25] glucagon-like peptide-1 (an incretin agent promoting the release of endogenous insulin), and growth hormone, which has beneficial effects on body mass index.

■ SUMMARY

The association of diabetes and insulin resistance syndromes with peripheral vascular disease is now well established. Therefore, the vascular surgeon needs to be aware of these conditions and medical treatment options to supplement surgical treatment. Diet and exercise are important first-line efforts, but medications are often required. Prevention of hypoglycemia, insulin overactivity, or both may significantly diminish the incidence of peripheral vascular disease.

■ REFERENCES

1. Reaven GM, Brand RJ, Chen YD: Insulin resistance and insulin secretion are determinants of oral glucose tolerance in normal individuals. Diabetes 42:1324-1332, 1993.
2. Shen SW, Reaven GM, Farquhar JW: Comparison of impedance to insulin mediated glucose uptake in normal and diabetic subjects. J Clin Invest 49:2151-2160, 1970.
3. Sicree RA, Zimmet PZ, King OM, et al: Plasma insulin response among Nauruans: Prediction of deterioration in glucose tolerance over 6 years. Diabetes 36:179-186, 1987.
4. Warram JH, Martin BC, Krolewski AS, et al: Slow glucose removal rate and hyperinsulinemia precede the development of type 2 diabetes in the offspring of diabetic parents. Ann Intern Med 113:909-915, 1990.
5. Haffner SM, Stern MP, Mitchell HP, et al: Incidence of type 2 diabetes in Mexican-Americans predicted by fasting insulin and glucose levels, obesity, and body fat distribution. Diabetes 39:283-288, 1990.
6. Centers for Disease Control and Prevention, National Center for Chronic Disease Prevention and Health Promotion: United States Diabetes Statistics. Atlanta, CDC, 2003.
7. National Diabetes Data Group: Diabetes in America, 2nd ed. (NIH Publication no. 95-1468.) Bethesda, MD, National Institutes of Health, 1995.
8. Centers for Disease Control and Prevention, National Center for Chronic Disease Prevention and Health Promotion: National Diabetes Fact Sheet, 2003.
9. Hogan P, Dall T, Nikolov P: Economic costs of diabetes in the US in 2002. Diabetes Care 26:917-932, 2003.
10. World Health Organization, Department of Noncommunicable Disease Surveillance: Definition, Diagnosis and Classification of Diabetes Mellitus. Geneva, WHO, 1999.
11. McCance DR, Hanson RL, Charles MA, et al: Comparison of tests for glycated hemoglobin and fasting and two hour plasma glucose concentrations as diagnostic methods for diabetes. BMJ 308:1323-1328, 1994.
12. The effect of intensive treatment of diabetes on the development and progression of long-term complications in insulin-dependent diabetes mellitus. The Diabetes Control and Complications Trials Research Group. N Engl J Med 329:977-983, 1993.
13. Vijan S, Stevens DL, Herman WH, et al: Screening, prevention, counseling, and treatment for the complications of type II diabetes mellitus: Putting evidence into practice. J Gen Intern Med 12:567-580, 1997.
14. Franz MJ, Monk A, Barry B, et al: Effectiveness of medical nutrition therapy provided by dietitians in the management of non-insulin-dependent diabetes mellitus: A randomized, controlled clinical trial. J Am Diet Assoc 95:1009-1017, 1995.
15. Wing RR, Koeske R, Epstein LH, et al: Long-term effects of modest weight loss in type II diabetic patients. Arch Intern Med 147:1749-1753, 1987.
16. Gerich JE: Oral hypoglycemic agents. N Engl J Med 321:1231-1245, 1989.
17. Lebovitz HE: Sulfonylurea drugs. In Lebovitz HE (ed): Therapy for Diabetes and Related Disorders, 2nd ed. Alexandria, VA, American Diabetes Association, 1995, pp 116-123.
18. Meinert CL, Knatterud GL, Prout TE, et al: A study of the effects of hypoglycemic agents on vascular complications in patients with adult-onset diabetes. II: Mortality results. Diabetes 19(Suppl):789-830, 1970.
19. DeFronzo RA, Goodman AM: Efficacy of metformin in patients with non-insulin-dependent diabetes mellitus. The Multicenter Metformin Study Group. N Engl J Med 333:541-549, 1995.
20. Stumvoll M, Nurjhan N, Periello G, et al: Metabolic effects of metformin in non-insulin dependent diabetes mellitus. N Engl J Med 333:550-555, 1995.
21. Chiasson JL, Josse RG, Hunt JA, et al: The efficacy of acarbose in the treatment of patients with non-insulin-dependent diabetes mellitus: A multicenter controlled clinical trial. Ann Intern Med 1221:928-935, 1994.
22. Lebovitz HE: A new oral therapy for diabetes management: Alpha-glucosidase inhibition with acarbose. Clin Diabetes Nov/Dec:99-103, 1995.
23. Saltiel AR, Olefsky JM: Thiazolidinediones in the treatment of insulin resistance and type II diabetes. Diabetes 45:1661-1669, 1996.
24. Intensive blood-glucose control with sulfonylureas or insulin compared to conventional treatment and risk of complications in patients with type 2 diabetes (UKPDS 33). Lancet 352:837-853, 1998.

25. Nestler JE, Jakubowicz DJ, Reamer P, et al: Ovulatory and metabolic effects of D-chiro-inositol in the polycystic ovary syndrome. N Engl J Med 340:1314-1320, 1999.
26. Chantelau E, Kohner EM: Why some cases of retinopathy worsen when diabetes control improves. BMJ 315:1105-1106, 1997.
27. Insulin administration. Diabetes Care 23(Suppl 1):S86-S89, 2000.
28. Galloway JA, Rost MA, Rathmacher RP, et al: A comparison of acid regular and neutral regular insulin. Diabetes 22:471-479, 1973.
29. Training in flexible, intensive insulin management to enable dietary freedom in people with type 1 diabetes. BMJ 325:746, 2002.
30. Facchini F, Chen YDI, Reaven GM: Light-moderate alcohol intake is associated with enhanced insulin sensitivity. Diabetes Care 17:115-118, 1994.
31. DeWitt DE, Irl HB: Outpatient insulin therapy in type 1 and type 2 diabetes mellitus. JAMA 289:2254-2263, 2003.
32. Taylor R, Davies R, Fox C, et al: Appropriate insulin regimes for type 2 diabetes. Diabetes Care 23:1612-1618, 2000.
33. Taylor R, Foster B, Kyne-Grzebalski D, et al: Insulin regimens for the non-insulin dependent. Diabet Med 11:551-557, 1994.
34. DeWitt DE, Hirsch IB: Outpatient insulin therapy in type 1 and type 2 diabetes mellitus. JAMA 287:2254-2264, 2003.
35. Vague J: The degree of masculine differentiation of obesity: A factor determining predisposition to diabetes, arteriosclerosis, gout and uric calculus disease. Am J Clin Nutr 4:20-34, 1956.
36. Reaven GM: Role of insulin resistance in human disease. Diabetes 37:1595-1607, 1988.
37. Zimmet P: Non-insulin dependent (type 2) diabetes mellitus—does it really exist? Diabet Med 6:728-735, 1989.
38. Kaplan NM: The deadly quartet: Upper-body obesity, glucose intolerance, hypertriglyceridemia, and hypertension. Arch Intern Med 149:1514-1520, 1989.
39. Zimmet PZ: The pathogenesis and prevention of diabetes in adults. Diabetes Care 18:1050-1064, 1995.
40. Defronzo R, Ferrannini E: Insulin resistance: A multifaceted syndrome responsible for NIDDM, obesity, hypertension, dyslipidemia and atherosclerotic cardiovascular disease. Diabetes Care 14:173-194, 1991.
41. Alberti KG, Zimmet PZ: Definition, diagnosis and classification of diabetes mellitus and its complications. Part I: Diagnosis and classification of diabetes mellitus. Provisional report of a WHO consultation. Diabet Med 15:539-553, 1998.
42. Third Report of the National Cholesterol Education Program Expert Panel on Detection, Evaluation, and Treatment of High Blood Cholesterol in Adults (Adult Treatment Panel III). (NIH Publication 01-3670.) Bethesda, MD, National Institutes of Health, 2001.
43. Zimmet P, Alberti G: The changing face of macrovascular disease in non-insulin dependent diabetes mellitus in different cultures: An epidemic in progress. Lancet 350(Suppl 1):S1-S4, 1997.
44. Zimmet P: Challenges in diabetes epidemiology—from West to the rest. Diabetes Care 15:232-252, 1992.
45. Reaven GM: Insulin resistance: A chicken that has come to roost. Ann N Y Acad Sci 892:45-57, 1999.
46. Leyva FI, Godsland IF, Ghatei M, et al: Hyperleptinemia as a component of metabolic syndrome of cardiovascular risk. Arterioscler Thromb Vasc Biol 18:928-933, 1997.
47. Austin MA, Edwards KL: Small, dense low density lipoproteins, the insulin resistance syndrome and noninsulin-dependent diabetes. Curr Opin Lipidol 7:167-171, 1996.
48. Edwards KL, Austin MA, Newman B, et al: Multivariate analysis of the insulin resistance syndrome in women. Arterioscler Thromb 14:940-945, 1994.
49. Edwards KL, Burchfiel CM, Sharp DS, et al: Factors of the insulin resistance syndrome in nondiabetic and diabetic elderly Japanese-American men. Am J Epidemiol 147:441-447, 1998.
50. Ferrannini ES, Haffner M, Mitchell BD, et al: Hyperinsulinaemia: The key feature of a cardiovascular and metabolic syndrome. Diabetologia 34:416-422, 1991.
51. Porte D: Mechanisms for hyperglycemia in the metabolic syndrome: The key role of beta cell dysfunction. Ann N Y Acad Sci 892:72-83, 1999.
52. Mitrakou A, Kelley D, Mokan M, et al: Role of reduced suppression of glucose production and diminished early insulin release in impaired glucose tolerance. N Engl J Med 326:22-29, 1992.
53. Araki E, Lipes MA, Patti ME, et al: Alternative pathway of insulin signaling in mice with targeted disruption of the IRS-1 gene. Nature 372:186-190, 1994.
54. Terauchi Y, Sakura H, Yasuda K, et al: Pancreatic beta-cell-specific targeted disruption of glucokinase gene: Diabetes mellitus due to defective insulin secretion to glucose. J Biol Chem 270:30253-30256, 1995.
55. Landsberg L: Role of the sympathetic adrenal system in the pathogenesis of the insulin resistance syndrome. Ann N Y Acad Sci 892:84-90, 1999.
56. Ward KD, Sparrow D, Landsberg L, et al: The influence of obesity, insulin, and sympathetic nervous system activity on blood pressure [abstract]. Clin Res 41:168A, 1993.
57. Ward KD, Sparrow D, Landsberg L, et al: The relationship of epinephrine excretion to serum lipid levels: The Normative Aging Study. Metabolism 43:509-513, 1994.
58. Ward KD, Sparrow D, Vokonas PS, et al: The relationships of abdominal obesity, hyperinsulinemia and saturated fat intake to serum lipid levels: The Normative Aging Study. Int J Obesity 18:137-144, 1994.
59. Maffei M, Halaas J, Ravussin E, et al: Leptin levels in human and rodent: Measurement of plasma leptin and *ob* RNA in obese and weight-reduced subjects. Nat Med 1:1155-1161, 1995.
60. Zimmet P, Hodge A, Nicolson M, et al: Serum leptin concentration, obesity, and insulin resistance in Western Samoans: Cross sectional study. Br Med J 313:965-969, 1996.
61. Zimmet P, Boyko EJ, Collier GR, et al: Etiology of the metabolic syndrome: Potential role of insulin resistance, leptin resistance, and other players. Ann N Y Acad Sci 892:25-44, 1999.
62. Barzilai N, Gaurav G: Interaction between aging and syndrome X: New insights on the pathophysiology of fat distribution. Ann N Y Acad Sci 892:58-72, 1999.
63. Welborn TA, Breckenridge AH, Rubinstein CT, et al: Serum-insulin in essential hypertension and in peripheral vascular disease. Lancet 1(7451):1136-1137, 1966.
64. Ferrannini E, Buzzigoli G, Bonadona R: Insulin resistance in essential hypertension. N Engl J Med 317:350-357, 1987.
65. Swislocki AL, Hoffman BB, Reaven GM: Insulin resistance, glucose intolerance and hyperinsulinema in patients with hypertension. Am J Hypertens 2:419-423, 1989.
66. Zavaroni I, Mazza S, Dall'Aglio E, et al: Prevalence of hyperinsulinemia in patients with high blood pressure. J Intern Med 231:235-240, 1992.
67. Reaven GM: Insulin resistance: A chicken that has come to roost. Ann N Y Acad Sci 892:45-57, 1999.
68. Reaven GM, Lithell H, Landsberg L: Mechanisms of disease: Hypertension and associated metabolic abnormalities—the role of insulin resistance and the sympathoadrenal system. N Engl J Med 334:374-381, 1996.
69. Ferrannini E, Natali A, Capaldo B, et al: Insulin resistance, hyperinsulinemia, and hypertension: The role of age and obesity. Hypertension 30:1144-1149, 1992.
70. Shamiss A, Carroll J, Rosenthal T: Insulin resistance in secondary hypertension. Am J Hypertens 5:26-28, 1992.
71. Facchini F, Chen YD, Clinkingbeard C, et al: Insulin resistance, hyperinsulinemia, and dyslipidemia in individuals with a family history of hypertension. Am J Hypertens 5:694-699, 1992.
72. Skarfors ET, Lithell HO, Selinus I: Risk factors for the development of hypertension: A 10-year longitudinal study in middle aged men. J Hypertens 9:217-223, 1991.
73. Schmidt MI, Brancati FL, Duncan BB, et al: A metabolic syndrome in whites and African-Americans: The Atherosclerosis Risk in Communities Baseline Study. Diabetes Care 19:414-419, 1996.

74. Taittonen L, Uhari M, Nuutinen M, et al: Insulin and blood pressure among healthy children. Am J Hypertens 9:193-199, 1996.
75. Pollare T, Vessby B, Lithell H: Lipoprotein lipase activity in skeletal muscle is related to insulin sensitivity. Arterioscler Thromb 11:1192-1203, 1991.
76. Laws A, Hoen HM, Selby JV, et al: Differences in insulin suppression of free fatty acid levels by gender and glucose tolerance status: Relation to plasma triglyceride and apoprotein B concentrations. Arterioscler Thromb Vasc Biol 17:64-71, 1997.
77. Zavaroni I, Mazza S, Luchetti L, et al: High plasma insulin and triglyceride concentrations and blood pressure in offspring of people with impaired glucose tolerance. Diabet Med 7:494-498, 1990.
78. Laws A, Reaven GM: Evidence for an independent relationship between insulin resistance and fasting plasma HDL-cholesterol, triglyceride and insulin concentration. J Intern Med 231:25-30, 1992.
79. Swinkels DW, Demacker PN, Hendriks JC, et al: The relevance of protein-enriched low density lipoprotein as a risk for coronary heart disease in relation to other known risk factors. Atherosclerosis 77:59-67, 1989.
80. Hulthe J, Bokemark L, Wilkstrand J, et al: The metabolic syndrome, LDL particle size, and atherosclerosis. The Atherosclerosis and Insulin Resistance (AIR) Study. Arterioscler Thromb Vasc Biol 20:2140-2147, 2000.
81. Wang PW, Liou CW, Wang ST: Relative impact of low-density lipoprotein-cholesterol concentration and insulin resistance on carotid wall thickening in nondiabetic, normotensive volunteers. Metabolism 51:255-259, 2002.
82. Meigs JB, Jacques PF, Selhub J, et al: Fasting plasma homocysteine levels in the insulin resistance syndrome: The Framingham offspring study. Diabetes Care 24:1403-1410, 2001.
83. Godsland IF, Rosankiewicz JR, Proudler AJ, et al: Plasma total homocysteine concentrations are unrelated to insulin sensitivity and components of the metabolic syndrome in healthy men. J Clin Endocrinol Metab 86:719-723, 2001.
84. Juhan-Vague I, Alessi MC, Vague P: Thrombogenic and fibrinolytic factors and cardiovascular risk in NIDDM. Ann Med 28:371-380, 1996.
85. Ernst E, Resch KL: Fibrinogen as a cardiovascular risk factor: A meta-analysis and review of the literature. Ann Intern Med 118:956-963, 1993.
86. Festa A, D'Agostino R, Mykkanen L, et al: Relative contribution of insulin and its precursors to fibrinogen and PAI-1 in a large population with different states of glucose tolerance: The Insulin Resistance Atherosclerosis Study (IRAS). Arterioscler Thromb Vasc Biol 19:562-568, 1999.
87. Avena R, Mitchell ME, Neville RF, Sidawy AN: The additive effects of glucose and insulin on the proliferation of infragenicular vascular smooth muscle cells. J Vasc Surg 28:1033-1039, 1998.
88. Avena R, Mitchell ME, Carmody BJ, et al: Insulin-like growth factor-1 receptors mediate infragenicular VSMC proliferation in response to glucose and insulin. Am J Surg 178:156-161, 1999.
89. Zhang B, Salituro G, Szalkowski D, et al: Discovery of a small molecule insulin mimetic with antidiabetic activity in mice. Science 284:974-977, 1999.
90. Weber MA, Lidor A, Arora S, et al: A novel insulin mimetic without a proliferative effect on vascular smooth muscle cells. J Vasc Surg 32:1118-1126, 2000.
91. Avena R, Arora S, Carmody BJ, et al: Thiamine (vitamin B1) protects against high glucose and insulin mediated proliferation of human infragenicular arterial smooth muscle cells. Ann Vasc Surg 14:37-43, 2000.
92. Avena R, Mitchell ME, Marc E, et al: Insulin action enhancement normalizes brachial artery vasoreactivity in patients with peripheral vascular disease and occult diabetes. J Vasc Surg 28:1024-1032, 1998.
93. Zavaroni I, Platti PM, Monti LD, et al: Plasma nitric oxide concentrations are elevated in insulin resistant healthy subjects. Metabolism 49:959-961, 2000.
94. Stuhlinger M, Abbasi F, Chu J, et al: Relationship between insulin resistance and an endogenous nitric oxide synthase inhibitor. JAMA 287:1420-1426, 2002.
95. Cooke JP: Does ADMA cause endothelial dysfunction? Arterioscler Thromb Vasc Biol 20:2032-2037, 2000.
96. Knowler WC, Barrett-Conner E, Fowler SE, et al: Reduction in the incidence of type 2 diabetes with lifestyle intervention or metformin. N Engl J Med 346:393-403, 2002.
97. Reaven G: Syndrome X. Curr Treat Options Cardiovasc Med 3:323-332, 2001.
98. Zisman A, Peroni OD, Abel ED, et al: Targeted disruption of the glucose transporter 4 selectively in muscle causes insulin resistance and glucose intolerance. Nat Med 6:924-928, 2000.
99. Sato Y: Diabetes and life-styles: Role of physical exercise for primary prevention. Br J Nutr 84:S187-S190, 2000.
100. Despres JP, Pouliot MC, Moorjani S, et al: Loss of abdominal fat and metabolic response to exercise training in obese women. Am J Physiol 261:E159-E167, 1991.
101. Su HY, Sheu WH, Chin HM, et al: Effect of weight loss on blood pressure and insulin resistance in normotensive and hypertensive obese individuals. Am J Hypertens 8:1067-1071, 1995.
102. Allison DB, Carey DE: Antipsychotic-induced weight gain: A review of the literature. J Clin Psychiatry 62:22-31, 2001.
103. Rodoni N, Darioli R, Ramelet AA, et al: High risk of hyperlipidemia and the metabolic syndrome after an episode of hypertriglyceridemia during 13-cis retinoic acid therapy for acne: A pharmacogenetic study. Ann Intern Med 136:582-589, 2002.
104. Shevitz AH, Knox TA: Nutrition in the era of highly active antiretroviral therapy. Clin Infect Dis 33:1769-1775, 2001.
105. Reaven G, Segal K, Hauptman J, et al: Effect of Orlistat-assisted weight loss in decreasing coronary heart disease risk in patients with syndrome X. Am J Cardiol 87:827-831, 2001.
106. Giugliano D, De Rosa N, DiMarco G, et al: Metformin improves glucose, lipid metabolism, and reduces blood pressure in hypertensive, obese women. Diabetes Care 16:1387-1390, 1993.
107. Ballantyne CM, Olsson AG, Cook TJ, et al: Influence of low high-density lipoprotein cholesterol and elevated triglyceride on coronary heart disease events and response to simvastatin therapy in 4S. Circulation 104:3046, 2001.
108. Freeman DJ, Norrie J, Sattar N, et al: Pravastatin and the development of diabetes mellitus: Evidence for a protective effect in the West of Scotland Coronary Prevention Study. Circulation 103:357-362, 2001.
109. Effects of ramipril on cardiovascular and microvascular outcomes in people with diabetes mellitus: Results of the HOPE study and MICRO-HOPE substudy. Heart Outcomes Prevention Evaluation Study Investigators. Lancet 355:253-259, 2000.

Chapter

39

Hypertension and Patients with Vascular Disorders

RUSSELL H. SAMSON, MD

■ EPIDEMIOLOGY OF HYPERTENSION

Hypertension is reaching epidemic proportions, with more than 1 billion people believed to be hypertensive.[1] The Third National Health and Nutrition Examination Survey (NHANES III)[2] estimated that the age-adjusted prevalence of hypertension in the United States is 32% in non-Hispanic blacks and 23% in non-Hispanic white and Mexican Americans. In patients older than 60 years, these numbers increase to 65% and 80% in non-Hispanic black men and women, respectively, and 55% and 65% in non-Hispanic white men and women, respectively. Despite this prevalence, NHANES III estimated that adequate blood pressure control was achieved in only 25% of non-Hispanic blacks and whites and in only 14% of Mexican Americans. In our practice, when treating patients with diagnosed peripheral arterial disease (PAD), we have found that only 32% of patients are normotensive during their office visits or vascular laboratory evaluations.[3]

■ HYPERTENSION DEFINITIONS

According to the Seventh Joint National Committee on Prevention, Detection, Evaluation, and Treatment of High Blood Pressure (JNC 7),[1] the following definitions can be used in the evaluation of blood pressure:

- *Normal blood pressure*: < 120 mm Hg systolic and < 80 mm Hg diastolic
- *Prehypertension*: 120 to 139 mm Hg systolic or > 80 to 89 mm Hg diastolic
- *Hypertension*: Stage 1—140 to 159 mm Hg systolic or > 90 to 99 mm Hg diastolic; Stage 2—> 160 mm Hg systolic or > 100 mm Hg diastolic

Prehypertension is a new category that has been added based on the recognition that epidemiologic studies have demonstrated that there is a gradual increase in cardiovascular risk as blood pressure increases above even "normal" values of 110/75 mm Hg.[1,4-7] Further, patients in this category are likely to develop overt hypertension, with those in the 130/80 to 139/89 mm Hg category being twice as likely to become hypertensive.[1]

Isolated systolic hypertension refers to patients who have systolic hypertension yet maintain diastolic pressures of less than 90 mm Hg.

Hypertension due to a recognized cause is referred to as *secondary hypertension,* whereas idiopathic or primary hypertension is referred to as *essential hypertension*. Patients with essential hypertension may also be subdivided according to their renin activity, with approximately 25% of patients having what is referred to as *low-renin essential hypertension*.[8] Whether such patients have a distinct form of essential hypertension or whether they are just part of a continuum of hypertensives is not clear. However, it is likely that such patients will be more salt sensitive,[9] at a lower risk for myocardial infarction,[10] less likely to respond to weight reduction,[11] be African American or elderly,[12] and may show a more pronounced response to diuretics and calcium-channel blocker agents.[13]

Secondary hypertension is beyond of the scope of this chapter; however, the possibility that this exists in an individual should always be borne in mind. Further, in the atherosclerotic patient with PAD or cerebrovascular disease, renal artery stenosis may often play a role in the patient's blood pressure control. The most common other causes of secondary hypertension are primary renal disease; pheochromocytoma; primary hyperaldosteronism; Cushing's syndrome; hypothyroidism or hyperthyroidism; hyperparathyroidism; oral contraceptives; sleep apnea syndrome; and coarctation of the aorta.

Ambulatory hypertension is defined as a 24-hour average blood pressure higher than 135/85 mm Hg or a daytime average of 140/90 mm Hg. This is measured using devices that measure the blood pressure throughout the day at predetermined intervals. It is often recommended to evaluate so-called white coat hypertension, in which patients are noted to have elevated pressure in the physician's office but not at home (see later).

Resistant hypertension is usually defined as a diastolic blood pressure higher than 95 to 100 mm Hg despite use of three or more antihypertensive medications.

Malignant hypertension is marked hypertension associated with ophthalmic findings of retinal hemorrhage, exudates, or papilledema.

■ INCREASE IN BLOOD PRESSURE AND CARDIOVASCULAR RISK

Hypertension is the predominant risk factor for atherosclerosis.[14] As noted earlier, epidemiologic studies have demonstrated that there is a gradual increase in cardiovascular risk as blood pressure increases above even "normal" values of 110/75 mm Hg.[1,4-7] For individuals aged 40 to 70 years, each increase of 20 mm Hg in systolic blood pressure or 10 mm Hg in diastolic blood pressure doubles the risk of cardiovascular disease (CVD).[1] There do appear to be variations in risk dependent on the populations studied, however, with risk being higher in the United States and Northern Europe in comparison with countries such as Japan and southern Europe.[15] Further, lowering blood pressure has been shown to improve outcome in hypertensive patients.[16-18] In clinical trials, antihypertensive therapy has been associated with 35% to 40% mean reductions in stroke incidence; 20% to 25% in myocardial infarction; and more than 50% in heart failure.[19] It is estimated that in patients with stage 1 hypertension and additional CVD risk factors, lowering systolic blood pressure 12 mm Hg for 10 years will prevent one death for every 11 patients treated. If CVD or PAD is present or target end-organ damage has occurred, only 9 patients would require this treatment to prevent one death.[20]

Blood pressure lowering has also been shown to be effective in patients who are prehypertensive, especially if they have associated conditions such as chronic renal failure and diabetes.[1] Pulse pressure has also been associated with increased risk.[16-18] In the elderly vascular patient, a decrease in arterial compliance may lower diastolic pressure and increase systolic pressure. This may explain why systolic and pulse pressure may be more predictive of risk in this elderly population,[16] who often may exhibit only isolated systolic hypertension. In fact, some of the most beneficial results of antihypertensive therapy may be seen in this group of elderly patients even with short-term therapy.[21,22] In patients between the ages of 50 and 60 years, systolic hypertension is also the best predictor of cardiovascular risk, whereas in patients younger than 50 years diastolic blood pressure has the best predictive value.[16]

Control of diastolic blood pressures above 105 mm Hg has been demonstrated to significantly reduce the incidence of cardiovascular events (55% vs. 17% at 5 years).[23] However, the benefit may not be as marked in patients with mild diastolic hypertension of 90 to 100 mm Hg. In a study of somewhat short duration by Hebert et al,[24] treatment of mild diastolic hypertension for 4 to 5 years prevented a coronary event in 0.7% of patients and a cerebrovascular event in 1.3%. Cardiovascular death was reduced by only 0.8%. It is conceivable that with long-term therapy the benefit of treatment may be even better. In fact, in the overall experience of the Framingham Heart Study, the risk of cardiovascular death for treated versus untreated patients was 0.4% over 10 years.[25]

■ EVALUATION OF THE HYPERTENSIVE PATIENT

The diagnosis of hypertension should be based on two or more correctly performed measurements at each of two or more visits after an initial screen. The JNC 7 suggests that the correct method for examining blood pressure is to have the patient sitting comfortably in a chair with the feet on the floor and the arm supported at heart level. Systolic blood pressure is where the first of two or more sounds are heard and diastolic is the point before the disappearance of sounds. If there is a disparity between systolic and diastolic measurements, the higher value determines the severity of hypertension.

Once a diagnosis has been made, the physician should attempt to define whether a curable cause for hypertension is active. Once this has been excluded, target organ damage must be evaluated and the patient's risk factors and cardiovascular status defined. The workup of most of the secondary causes of hypertension is beyond the scope of this chapter. However, certain fundamental studies should be performed in all new hypertensive patients. These include a complete blood count, blood urea nitrogen, blood glucose, calcium, creatinine, and electrolyte determinations. A lipid profile should be ordered to assess other risk factors for atherosclerosis. Because diuretics may result in hyperuricemia, a baseline level should also be drawn. Further, uric acid may prove to be an independent risk factor for atherosclerosis.[26] Urinalysis should also be routinely requested, especially in the diabetic patient where microalbuminuria is an early manifestation of nephropathy and is associated with an increased risk of developing CVD.[27] Plasma renin activity is seldom measured except in patients with low-renin forms of hypertension such as primary hyperaldosteronism, which is suggested by unexplained hypokalemia. Although patients who may have low-renin essential hypertension may respond better to diuretics and calcium-channel blockers, measurement of renin activity is seldom suggested because many of these patients are elderly or black, in which case these agents are most likely to be prescribed anyway.

An electrocardiogram may show evidence of left ventricular hypertrophy (LVH), although an echocardiogram may prove to be more sensitive and may identify patients who otherwise may not have been treated based on blood pressure measurements alone.[28]

The role of ambulatory blood pressure monitoring remains controversial, and some insurance carriers do not reimburse for this study. However, it has been suggested that as many as 20% of patients have white coat hypertension, exhibiting elevation in blood pressure only in the physician's office.[29] Some have claimed that even these patients require treatment, but in many patients with this condition, ambulatory pressure measurements exclude hypertension as occurring at any other time. Ambulatory measurements may also be helpful in investigating resistance to treatment or postural symptoms. Also, most patients' blood pressure falls 10% to 20% during sleep. Those who do not demonstrate this fall are at increased risk for CVD events.[1]

The workup for renovascular hypertension is detailed in another chapter in this text. However, if this disorder is suspected because of sudden onset or exacerbation of hypertension or the presence of an abdominal bruit, aneurysm, or aortic atherosclerosis, Doppler ultrasonography is usually the first-line test. Magnetic resonance angiography or spiral computed tomographic scan may also obviate the need for arteriography.

■ TREATMENT RECOMMENDATIONS

In general, the treatment of hypertension can be separated into pharmacologic and nonpharmacologic regimens. The latter involve little or no risk and often produce improvements in health unrelated to blood pressure control. As such, these should be initiated as the first-line treatment for this condition and can achieve blood pressure reduction of 2 to 20 mm Hg.[1] Nonpharmacologic treatments include weight reduction, adoption of the so-called DASH[30] diet (fruits and vegetables, low-fat dairy products with reduced levels of saturated and total fat), reduction in dietary sodium (2.4 g of sodium or 6 g of sodium chloride), increased physical activity at least 30 minutes for most days of the week, and a reduction in alcohol to one or two drinks per day.[1] The role of salt reduction in treating hypertension is well established. However, its role in prevention of hypertension is less clear, with sodium reduction causing only a 1.9/1.1 mm Hg reduction in blood pressure in normotensive individuals.[31] Smoking cessation has not been shown to improve hypertension but clearly mitigates many of its complications.

Pharmacologic therapy, on the other hand, although often more effective and necessary to achieve goal blood pressure, is often associated with side effects, some of which (hypokalemia and hyperlipidemia) may actually increase coronary risk. Accordingly, it is generally recommended that in the absence of end-organ damage or extreme hypertension medications should be reserved for patients in whom lifestyle modification has failed to achieve goal blood pressure after three to six visits. In nondiabetic patients or patients who have normal renal function, antihypertensive medication is usually begun with pressures higher than 140/90 mm Hg.

Current recommendations suggest the use of diuretics as the first line of drug therapy. Initial therapy with two drugs should be considered when the blood pressure is 20/10 mm Hg above goal. In patients with diabetes or chronic renal failure, antihypertensive medications should be considered if the blood pressure is higher than 130/80 mm Hg, although a benefit may not be seen in patients excreting more than 1 to 2 g of protein per day. In these patients, three drugs may often be necessary.[1]

Some patients may exhibit white coat hypertension, exhibiting increased blood pressure only when in the office. Under such circumstances ambulatory blood pressure measurements may be required to define the patient's true blood pressure status. It has been recommended that patients without evidence of end-organ damage should be treated only when hypertension is confirmed by repeat measurement over three to six visits or when confirmed by ambulatory pressure measurements. Hartley et al[32] showed that patients with initial white coat hypertension had a subsequent reduction in blood pressure of 15/7 mm Hg by the third visit with a new physician. Further, although patients with white coat hypertension may be at risk of developing true hypertension, the risk of developing cardiovascular complications is low provided that they do not have ambulatory hypertension.[11]

Patients with prehypertension are usually not treated with antihypertensives because there are currently no clinical data to support pharmacologic therapy. However, they should be monitored frequently because they are at high risk to progress to true hypertension.

In a number of other circumstances, which are dealt with separately, antihypertensive medications may be prescribed for their effects on other aspects of cardiovascular health. In particular, such medications may be used for the treatment of heart failure and post-myocardial infarction, for the prevention of cardiac events during surgery, and to prevent the onset of diabetes and its vascular complications.

GUIDELINES FOR THE PHARMACEUTICAL TREATMENT OF ESSENTIAL HYPERTENSION

Initial Therapy

A variety of different classes of drugs can be used to initiate therapy. These include the following:

- Diuretics
- Beta blockers
- α_1-Adrenergic blockers
- Calcium-channel blockers
- Angiotensin-converting enzyme (ACE) inhibitors
- Angiotensin II receptor blockers (ARBs)

However, until recently there has been no uniform agreement as to which antihypertensive agent should be given for initial therapy. The JNC 7 guidelines suggest initiating therapy with a thiazide diuretic in patients with uncomplicated hypertension,[1] reserving the use of two drugs for patients whose blood pressure is more than 20/10 mm Hg above goal. This is based largely on the Antihypertensive and Lipid-Lowering Treatment to Prevent Heart Attack Trial (ALLHAT), which is the largest controlled trial ever performed in the treatment of hypertension.[33] That study comparing chlorthalidone (diuretic), lisinopril (ACE inhibitor), amlodipine (calcium-channel blocker), and doxazosin (α_1 blocker) demonstrated similar protection for the first three medications when analyzing the primary endpoint of coronary death and nonfatal myocardial infarction. Chlorthalidone, which is not only the least expensive of the four, also had a lower rate of heart failure. (This is not surprising because this drug is also a first-line therapy for heart failure and was not used in the other drug arms of the study.)

However, major drug trials[34,35] have shown benefits specific to the other agents that may suggest using some of them, in specific circumstances, as first-line therapy or adding them to diuretics initially. The Heart Outcomes Prevention Evaluation (HOPE) trial[34] demonstrated that the ACE inhibitor ramipril reduced the incidence of cardiovascular events in patients with coronary artery disease (CAD) or PAD or who had at least one CAD risk factor. Hypertension was not an entry criterion for this study, and the benefit was independent of its blood pressure-lowering effect (although this claim has been subsequently challenged).[36] However, the ALLHAT trial[33] demonstrated a higher event rate with the ACE inhibitor lisinopril (but the dose of that agent may not have been optimal). The Losartan Intervention for Endpoint (LIFE) trial[35] studying patients with severe hypertension with electrocardiographic evidence of LVH demonstrated that the ARB losartan was associated with a significantly lower composite cardiovascular endpoint (primarily due to stroke reduction) than the beta blocker atenolol. This was especially notable in diabetic patients, in whom there was also a reduction in total mortality. Furthermore, there has been conflicting evidence demonstrating in a group of elderly Australian patients that ACE inhibitors may be superior to diuretics after all.[37] All three trials were performed on largely white groups, and so extrapolating these results to blacks is problematic, especially because it is recognized that blacks with hypertension do not respond as well to ACE inhibitors.[38] Despite this caveat, the findings that ACE inhibitors are of benefit to patients with prior myocardial infarction or stroke, heart failure, type 1 diabetic nephropathy, and nondiabetic proteinuric chronic renal failure independent of their antihypertensive effects suggest that they should be considered for first-line therapy in these situations. These indications may well hold true for ARBs as well. Certainly they should be considered for patients who cannot tolerate ACE inhibitors usually because of cough or angioneurotic edema. The LIFE trial has also shown a benefit for ARBs in patients with severe hypertension and LVH[35] and in type 2 diabetics with microalbuminuria or nephropathy.[39]

Beta blockers should be considered for stable patients with heart failure; after an acute myocardial infarction; or for patients with angina, atrial fibrillation, or asymptomatic LVH. ACE inhibitors should be added in patients with unstable angina or acute myocardial infarction. Alpha blockers may be considered for elderly male patients at low risk who have symptoms of prostate enlargement. Calcium-channel blockers may be considered for initial use in black patients because they may not respond as well as whites to ACE inhibitors or beta blockers. Further, they are two to four times as likely as whites to develop angioedema with ACE inhibitors.[40] Calcium-channel blockers may also be useful in patients with obstructive airways disease or third-degree heart block because beta blockers can aggravate these conditions. They can also be used as an alternative to beta blockers in patients with ischemic heart disease. Aldosterone-receptor blockers should be considered in patients with heart failure or after myocardial infarction[41] but should be avoided in patients with potassium values above 5 mEq/L. ACE inhibitors and ARBs should be avoided during pregnancy.

Achieving Goal

Goal blood pressure depends on the patient's age and whether target organ damage has occurred. Coexistent morbidities may also change goal expectations. In general, treatment is targeted at the higher value of systolic or diastolic hypertension. The JNC 7 suggests that in patients with diabetes mellitus and chronic renal failure, blood pressures lower than 130/80 mm Hg should be sought.[1] In patients with uncomplicated hypertension, goal pressures should be at or below 140/90 mm Hg. However, in the 65-year-and-older patient population that is often seen by vascular surgeons, isolated systolic hypertension is increasingly being recognized. These patients may be prone to stroke if attempts to lower systolic hypertension inadvertently lower diastolic pressure below 65 mm Hg.[42,43] Because the elderly may have sluggish baroreceptors and sympathetic nervous system responses as well as impaired cerebral autoregulation, it is suggested that drug therapy be initiated at lower doses than used for young patients and that blood pressure lowering be gradual. Only in extremely hypertensive patients should rapid lowering of blood pressure be attempted because cerebrovascular and cardiovascular complications may occur.

Once therapy has been initiated, patients should return at least monthly for office visits until goal is achieved. Serum potassium and creatinine levels should be measured at least once or twice a year, especially if chlorthalidone is used. Once blood pressure is controlled, follow-up visits can be at 3- to 6-month intervals unless co-morbidities warrant more intensive follow-up.

Despite the fact that most agents are roughly equally effective, producing an adequate blood pressure-lowering effect in 40% to 60% of patients,[38] there remains a wide variability in individual patients' response to treatment. This may account for the lack of clear guidelines for the management of hypertension that is refractory or does not respond to single-drug therapy. Three approaches have been tried, as discussed in the following sections.

Increase the First Drug to Maximum Dosage This method can lead to increased side effects that are often dose dependent and still may not be effective because most responders will do so at relatively low doses.[44]

Add a Second Drug This is especially useful when rapid control of blood pressure is required; however, caution should be exercised when two agents are used initially, especially in patients at risk for orthostatic hypotension such as diabetics and the elderly. However, most patients prefer to use fewer medications, and use of two can also increase side effects. Despite patient preference, with the advent of the JNC 7 guidelines, it is anticipated that this method will become increasingly common, with many patients being placed on a diuretic and another family of antihypertensives. Further, a low dose of a thiazide diuretic often enhances the response rate of other agents,[45,46] and the second agent such as an ACE inhibitor may mitigate some of the metabolic effects of the diuretic such as hypokalemia, hyperuricemia, and hyperlipidemia. Combination of an ACE inhibitor and a calcium-channel blocker may decrease the incidence of edema seen with the calcium-channel blocker.[47] These findings support the rationale for some of the combination agents that are increasingly being marketed (Table 39-1).[44,48] Further, although monotherapy is preferred, evidence suggests that most patients require two drugs.[49,50] Combining two drugs into one pill may increase patient compliance.

Use Sequential Monotherapy This has been the favored method of adjusting treatment because it may minimize side effects and increase patient compliance. Patients who do not respond to the first agent have a 50% chance of responding to a different agent. Ultimately, using this technique, 80% of mildly hypertensive patients become normotensive with just one agent.[51]

Even with the physician's best intentions, achieving goal can be problematic. Failure is usually multifactorial but is most often due to the physician not increasing the hypertensive therapy.[52] Patient noncompliance is the next most frequent cause. This can result from a lack of understanding of the seriousness of their condition, especially in the absence of symptoms or clinical findings. Patient

Table 39-1 Combination Antihypertensive Drugs

COMBINATION TYPE	FIXED-DOSE COMBINATION, mg*	TRADE NAME
ACE inhibitors and CCBs	Amlodipine/benazepril hydrochloride (2.5/10, 5/10, 5/20, 10/20)	Lotrel
	Enalapril maleate/felodipine (5/5)	Lexxel
	Trandolapril/verapamil (2/180, 1/240, 2/240, 4/240)	Tarka
ACE inhibitors and diuretics	Benazepril/hydrochlorothiazide (5/6.25, 10/12.5, 20/12.5, 20/25)	Lotensin HCT
	Captopril/hydrochlorothiazide (25/15, 25/25, 50/15, 50/25)	Capozide
	Enalapril maleate/hydrochlorothiazide (5/12.5, 10/25)	Vaseretic
	Lisinopril/hydrochlorothiazide (10/12.5, 20/12.5, 20/25)	Prinzide
	Moexipril HCl/hydrochlorothiazide (7.5/12.5, 15/25)	Uniretic
	Quinapril HCl/hydrochlorothiazide (10/12.5, 20/12.5, 20/25)	Accuretic
ARBs and diuretics	Candesartan cilexetil/hydrochlorothiazide (16/12.5, 32/12.5)	Atacand HCT
	Eprosartan mesylate/hydrochlorothiazide (600/12.5, 600/25)	Teveten HCT
	Irbesartan/hydrochlorothiazide (75/12.5, 150/12.5, 300/12.5)	Avalide
	Losartan potassium/hydrochlorothiazide (50/12.5, 100/25)	Hyzaar
	Telmisartan/hydrochlorothiazide (40/12.5, 80/12.5)	Micardis HCT
	Valsartan/hydrochlorothiazide (80/12.5, 160/12.5)	Diovan HCT
Beta blockers and diuretics	Atenolol/chlorthalidone (50/25, 100/25)	Tenoretic
	Bisoprolol fumarate/hydrochlorothiazide (2.5/6.25, 5/6.25, 10/6.25)	Ziac
	Propranolol LA/hydrochlorothiazide (40/25, 80/25)	Inderide
	Metoprolol tartrate/hydrochlorothiazide (50/25, 100/25)	Lopressor HCT
	Nadolol/bendroflumethiazide (40/5, 80/5)	Corzide
	Timolol maleate/hydrochlorothiazide (10/25)	Timolide
Centrally acting drug and diuretic	Methyldopa/hydrochlorothiazide (250/15, 250/25, 500/30, 500/50)	Aldoril
	Reserpine/chlorothiazide (0.125/250, 0.25/500)	Diupres
	Reserpine/hydrochlorothiazide (0.125/25, 0.125/50)	Hydropres
Diuretic and diuretic	Amiloride HCl/hydrochlorothiazide (5/50)	Moduretic
	Spironolactone/hydrochlorothiazide (25/25, 50/50)	Aldactone
	Triamterene/hydrochlorothiazide (37.5/25, 50/25, 75/50)	Dyazide, Maxzide

*Some drug combinations are available in multiple fixed doses. Each drug dose is reported in milligrams.
ACE, angiotensin-converting enzyme; ARB, angiotensin receptor blocker; CCB, calcium-channel blocker; HCl, hydrochloride; HCT, hydrochlorothiazide; LA, long acting.

From Chobanian AV, Bakris GL, Black HR, et al: The Seventh Report of the Joint National Committee on Prevention, Detection, Evaluation, and Treatment of High Blood Pressure: The JNC 7 report. JAMA 289:2560-2572, 2003.

compliance issues also relate to the dosing schedule. A twice-daily regimen at half the dose results in a lesser peak effect, but the response is sustained for 24 hours. However, patients usually prefer once-a-day regimens. Yet, even with so-called long-acting agents, blood pressure may start to increase in the early hours of the morning, resulting in nocturnal and early morning hypertension. Early morning abrupt elevations in blood pressure may result in increased cardiovascular events. Therefore, patients should be taught to evaluate their pressure in the morning prior to the next dose to ensure that such early morning hypertension is not occurring. Adverse side effects, cost, and complexity of care are also significant contributing factors to patient noncompliance. Accordingly, all members of the health care team must work together to influence the patient to maintain lifestyle changes and adhere to recommended medical therapy. The vascular surgeon, who often cares for hypertensive patients with advanced PAD and CAD, plays a critical role in helping these patients realize the benefits of achieving goal blood pressure.

■ THE MEDICATIONS

A detailed description of the medications used to control hypertension is beyond the scope of this chapter. Following is a brief outline of the method of action, primary indication for use, and side effects of the major types of antihypertensives. Tables 39-1 and 39-2 summarize some of the common oral and combination antihypertensive drugs and their usual doses.

Diuretics

A diuretic is usually the drug of choice for the initial treatment of hypertension with the addition of potassium-sparing agents if hypokalemia is noted during the first 6 months of treatment. They are also commonly used as adjuncts to other antihypertensive drugs[53] and are especially useful in patients with hypercalciuria, calcium stones, and osteoporosis because they decrease calcium excretion. The first group of diuretics includes the thiazides, of which the prototype is hydrochlorothiazide, and chlorthalidone, the diuretic studied in the ALLHAT trial. They have been the most widely used and cheapest drugs in the treatment of hypertension. Lower dose thiazides are quite effective but usually take 3 to 4 weeks to reduce blood pressure. The second group of drugs includes the loop diuretics, of which the prototype is furosemide. Although the latter has been used in the direct treatment of hypertension, it usually is used in individuals who are azotemic where volume or cardiac failures are issues. If the serum creatinine level is less than 1.8 mg/dL, the thiazide diuretics are usually effective, but when renal function is worse (serum creatinine of 2.5 to 3 mg/dL, i.e., a glomerular filtration rate of < 30 mL/min/1.73m^2), the use of a loop diuretic is often required.

Diuretic actions are somewhat complex. Their effect, with modest renal Na^+ loss, appears related to reduced vascular responsiveness to vasoconstrictors such as norepinephrine. This results in a reduction of peripheral vascular resistance. In addition, the reductions in extracellular fluid volume and lesser circulating volume

Table 39-2 Oral Hypertensive Drugs*

CLASS	DRUG (TRADE NAME)	USUAL DOSE, RANGE, mg/day	DAILY FREQUENCY
Thiazide diuretics	Chlorothiazide (Diuril)	125-500	1
	Chlorthalidone (generic)	12.5-25	1
	Hydrochlorothiazide (Microzide, HydroDIURIL)†	12.5-50	1
	Polythiazide (Renese)	2-4	1
	Indapamide (Lozol)†	1.25-2.5	1
	Metolazone (Mykrox)	0.5-1	1
	Metolazone (Zaroxolyn)	2.5-5	1
Loop diuretics	Bumetanide (Bumex)†	0.5-2	2
	Furosemide (Lasix)†	20-80	2
	Torsemide (Demadex)†	2.5-10	1
Potassium-sparing diuretics	Amiloride (Midamor)†	5-10	1-2
	Triamterene (Dyrenium)	50-100	1-2
Aldosterone receptor blockers	Eplerenone (Inspra)	50-100	1-2
	Spironolactone (Aldactone)†	25-50	1-2
Beta blockers	Atenolol (Tenormin)†	25-100	1
	Betaxolol (Kerlone)†	5-20	1
	Bisoprolol (Zebeta)†	2.5-10	1
	Metoprolol (Lopressor)†	50-100	1-2
	Metoprolol extended release (Toprol XL)	50-100	1
	Nadolol (Corgard)†	40-120	1
	Propranolol (Inderal)†	40-160	2
	Propranolol long acting (Inderal LA)†	60-180	1
	Timolol (Blocadren)†	20-40	2
Beta blockers with intrinsic sympathomimetic activity	Acebutolol (Sectral)†	200-800	2
	Penbutolol (Levatol)	10-40	1
	Pindolol (generic)	10-40	2
Combined alpha and beta blockers	Carvedilol (Coreg)	12.5-50	2
	Labetalol (Normodyne, Trandate)†	200-800	2
ACE inhibitors	Benazepril (Lotensin)†	10-40	1-2
	Captopril (Capoten)†	25-100	2
	Enalapril (Vasotec)†	2.5-40	1-2
	Fosinopril (Monopril)	10-40	1
	Lisinopril (Prinivil, Zestril)†	10-40	1
	Moexipril (Univasc)	7.5-30	1
	Perindopril (Aceon)	4-8	1-2
	Quinapril (Accupril)	10-40	1
	Ramipril (Altace)	2.5-20	1
	Trandolapril (Mavik)	1-4	1
Angiotensin II antagonists	Candesartan (Atacand)	8-32	1
	Eprosartan (Teveten)	400-800	1-2
	Irbesartan (Avapro)	150-300	1
	Losartan (Cozaar)	25-100	1-2
	Olmesartan (Benicar)	20-40	1
	Telmisartan (Micardis)	20-80	1
	Valsartan (Diovan)	80-320	1
Calcium-channel blockers—non-dihydropyridines	Diltiazem extended release (Cardizem CD, Dilacor XR, Tiazac)†	180-420	1
	Diltiazem extended release (Cardizem LA)	120-540	1
	Verapamil immediate release (Calan, Isoptin)†	80-320	2
	Verapamil long acting (Calan SR, Isoptin SR)†	120-360	1-2
	Verapamil-coer (Covera HS, Verelan PM)	120-360	1
Calcium-channel blockers—dihydropyridines	Amlodipine (Norvasc)	2.5-10	1
	Felodipine (Plendil)	2.5-20	1
	Isradipine (DynaCirc CR)	2.5-10	2
	Nicardipine sustained release (Cardene SR)	60-120	2
	Nifedipine long acting (Adalat CC, Procardia XL)	30-60	1
	Nisoldipine (Sular)	10-40	1
$Alpha_1$ blockers	Doxazosin (Cardura)	1-16	1
	Prazosin (Minipress)†	2-20	2-3
	Terazosin (Hytrin)	1-20	1-2
Central α_2 agonists and other centrally acting drugs	Clonidine (Catapres)†	0.1-0.8	2
	Clonidine patch (Catapres TTS)	0.1-0.3	1 weekly
	Methyldopa (Aldomet)†	250-1000	2
	Reserpine (generic)	0.05-0.25	1‡
	Guanfacine (generic)	0.5-2	1
Direct vasodilators	Hydralazine (Apresoline)†	25-100	2
	Minoxidil (Loniten)†	2.5-80	1-2

*Dosages may vary from those listed in the *Physicians' Desk Reference*, which may be consulted for additional information.
†Are now or will soon become available in generic preparations.
‡A 0.1-mg dose may be given every other day to achieve this dosage.
ACE, angiotensin-converting enzyme.

From Chobanian AV, Bakris GL, Black HR, et al: The Seventh Report of the Joint National Committee on Prevention, Detection, Evaluation, and Treatment of High Blood Pressure: The JNC 7 report. JAMA 289:2560-2572, 2003.

reductions associated with an early diuresis contribute to the initial antihypertensive action in some patients but is probably not a mechanism explaining the long-term effectiveness of these drugs. Diuretics reduce pressure more effectively in an elderly, salt-sensitive black patient than in a white patient.[54] Most diuretics usually result in a somewhat flat dose response, meaning that a markedly increased dose does not result in a markedly increased antihypertensive effect. Further, such increases usually significantly increase the number and severity of side effects.

Complications and Side Effects

Complications and side effects associated with diuretics used for long-term management of hypertension include (1) hypokalemia with the K^+-wasting kaliuretic effect of the thiazides, especially chlorthalidone; (2) an increased risk of hyperuricemia, with uric acid and the diuretic competing for tubular secretion, resulting in subsequent gout attacks; and (3) an average 6% to 7% elevation of blood lipids, particularly low-density lipoproteins. Similarly, increases in blood glucose occur, although there seems to be little evidence that these sulfonamide derivative drugs (thiazides) should be avoided altogether with hyperglycemia. Also, hyperglycemia may be related to potassium losses, and this may be ameliorated to some degree by potassium supplementation. Nevertheless, it is important to weigh the benefits of treatment in the elderly with the recognition that these diuretics may worsen glucose tolerance and precipitate problems with blood sugar control in diabetics. Finally, one should be cautious regarding the risk of hypovolemia, especially in patients with modestly severe carotid, coronary, or renal artery disease in whom the effects of organ hypoperfusion may prove hazardous. Diuretics may also be associated with impotence.[55] However, most of these side effects can generally be avoided and the antihypertensive effect maintained by the use of low doses such as 12.5 to 25 mg of hydrochlorothiazide and 12.5 mg of chlorthalidone daily.

Beta-Adrenergic Blockers

Beta blockers are quite effective at lowering blood pressure and have received wide approval for the first-line treatment of hypertension.[56] These agents reduce cardiac contractility and output and reduce renin release. For most patients, this results in a return toward normotension because these effects outweigh the tendency for the blood pressure to rise due to peripheral vascular $beta_2$ blockade, impeding the vasodilator component of epinephrine's actions. There are a number of subclasses of beta blockers, including the nonselective ($beta_1$, $beta_2$) agents, of which propranolol is the most commonly recognized, and the cardioselective agents that may have a greater $beta_1$ and $beta_2$ affinity, evident in atenolol and metoprolol. Cardioselectivity seems to be dose dependent and is less with higher doses. There are also some beta blockers that have weak alpha-blocking activity, such as labetalol and carvedilol, yet appear to have the same efficacy as selective beta blockers.[57]

Beta blockers are effective when used alone or as adjunct to other agents, the latter usually to inhibit the reflex tachycardia caused by other drugs. They may be preferred for use in patients who have angina, tachycardia, a history of a prior myocardial infarction, hypothyroidism, glaucoma, or migraine headaches. Preliminary data have suggested that beta blockers may slow the rate of aneurysm expansion more than other antihypertensive drugs, and they may be preferred in individuals having aneurysms if there are no contraindications to using these agents. They are also important adjuncts in patients who are undergoing major surgery.[58]

Complications and Side Effects

The blunted cardiac stimulation after exercise accompanying use of beta blockers often results in reduced tolerance to physical activities in many individuals who were otherwise quite physically active. It is commonly believed that beta blockers worsen the symptoms of claudication, but this concept has been challenged.[59,60] A meta-analysis documented that only 1 of 11 studies confirmed that beta blockers worsened the claudication in patients with peripheral arterial occlusive disease.[59] Nevertheless, certain individuals describe claudication for the first time shortly after beginning beta-blocker treatment of their hypertension. If this is noted, it is reasonable to discontinue these agents and treat the hypertension with other drugs. Occasionally, patients with lower extremity occlusive disease causing rest pain that is not amenable to operative intervention may have their beta blockers discontinued with the hope that amputation may not be necessary, although hard data suggesting that this would be the case are nonexistent in the literature.

Other complications associated with beta blockers include exacerbations of asthma and breathing difficulty in emphysema. This is related to the blocking of $beta_2$ receptors that mediate adrenergic bronchodilation. Side effects also include reduced high-density lipoprotein cholesterol, elevated triglyceride levels, insulin resistance, exacerbations of congestive heart failure, and potentiation of cardiac conduction disorders in patients with known atrioventricular block or bradycardia. In insulin-dependent diabetics, these drugs may mask hypoglycemic symptoms and increase the hypertensive response to hypoglycemia.

One should never discontinue beta blockers abruptly because there is a significant rebound increase in heart rate on re-exposure to norepinephrine after receptor up-regulation due to long-term use of these agents.

Calcium-Channel Blockers

Calcium-channel blockers have frequently been administered to control mild or modest hypertension.[61] These drugs interfere with angiotensin II and α_2-adrenergic-mediated vasoconstriction, and they may also affect α_1-adrenergic vasoconstriction by blocking cellular Ca^{2+} entry. These drugs work well in both black and white patients.

There are two major types of calcium-channel blockers: the dihydropyridines (e.g., nifedipine and amlodipine), which are potent vasodilators and the non-dihydropyridines (e.g., verapamil), which have cardiac depressant activity, and diltiazem, which has both less vasodilator activity than nifedipine and less cardiac depression than verapamil. Although these differences result in different kinds of side effects, the degree of blood pressure control tends to be roughly equivalent.[62] The dihydropyridines are the most powerful vasodilators, but this hypotensive effect is partially attenuated by activation of the sympathetic nervous and renin-angiotensin systems. Calcium-channel blockers tend to moderately increase sodium excretion, and in contrast with most other antihypertensive agents, their efficacy is usually not significantly enhanced by dietary salt restriction.[63] Accordingly, they may be valuable in patients who will not restrict their salt intake. They may also be useful in patients who take nonsteroidal anti-inflammatory agents. The latter medications, by decreasing vasodilator prostaglandins, can increase blood pressure in patients on antihypertensives other than calcium-channel blockers.[64]

The non-dihydropyridine agents reduce cardiac contractility as well as peripheral vasoconstriction. Their use has been most often as an effective alternative to beta blockers. The dihydropyridine class has selective vasodilators, do not have the significant cardiac-depressive effects, and may be more appropriate for use when cardiac depression is to be avoided or when mild cardiac stimulation might prove beneficial. Their effect on arteriolar vasodilatation occurs without affecting venoconstriction, a factor contributing to peripheral edema. Renal insufficiency does not have a major effect on the pharmacokinetics of these drugs.

Calcium-channel blockers are effective antihypertensive agents that do not produce hyperlipidemia or insulin resistance and do not interfere with sympathetic function. They may also be beneficial in patients with Raynaud's syndrome.

Complications and Side Effects

Important side effects of these agents include depression of cardiac contractility, rate, automaticity, and impulse conduction, all of which have made these drugs potentially hazardous in patients with second- or third-degree heart block (verapamil and diltiazem) and congestive heart failure with moderate to marked systolic dysfunction. Several trials have demonstrated an increased mortality rate when large doses of *short-acting* calcium-channel blockers are used in patients immediately after an acute myocardial infarction.[63]

The concomitant use of beta blockers with these agents is discouraged in patients with preexisting slow heart rates, and if they must be used, the dihydropyridine drugs are favored. These drugs however can cause flushing due to vasodilatation. In addition, many patients incur constipation as a side effect of the non-dihydropyridines. Finally, these drugs, especially the dihydropyridine agents, may cause, as previously noted, considerable peripheral edema resulting from increased transcapillary pressure gradients.

Angiotensin-Converting Enzyme Inhibitors

ACE inhibitors are advantageous in the treatment of hypertension in that they are broadly effective in all patient groups, lack the adverse lipid and glycemic effects of high doses of thiazides and beta blockers, and have few serious side effects. Most important, they may also have beneficial effects on plaque stabilization independent of their antihypertensive action. This was demonstrated in the HOPE trial, which randomized 3577 at-risk patients with diabetes (among a total of almost 10,000 participants) to either ramipril or placebo.[65] At a mean follow-up of 4.5 years, ramipril therapy significantly lowered the incidence of myocardial infarction, stroke, and total mortality by 22%, 33%, and 24%, respectively. This benefit remained after adjustments for the small decrease in blood pressure (2 mm Hg) observed with active therapy. The benefit was similar to that in the United Kingdom Prospective Diabetes Study, in which much larger differences in blood pressure control were achieved (10/5 mm Hg).[66]

These agents directly or indirectly inhibit angiotensin II synthesis in a transient manner and indirectly inhibit aldosterone release. In addition, these pluripotent drugs also inhibit the breakdown of bradykinin, a naturally occurring vasodilator whose activities include stimulating the production of endothelium-derived relaxing factor (EDRF) and prostacyclin. The chemical moiety of ACE is identical to kinase II, a bradykinase. The dose-response curve with ACE inhibitors is relatively flat.

ACE inhibitors are rarely effective as monotherapy and so are most often used as an adjunct to other antihypertensive drugs. They are particularly useful when treating patients with congestive heart failure.[67] ACE inhibitors may also act synergistically with thiazide diuretics by limiting the increase in renin that may occur with hypovolemia.[68] The ACE inhibitors and ARBs as well as certain calcium-channel antagonists appear to reduce proteinuria and may lessen the progression of renal insufficiency in the elderly hypertensive patient.[69] These drugs significantly reduce the mortality and morbidity associated with hypertension and its secondary complications, especially in type 2 diabetic patients.[65] They also may increase sensitivity to insulin and may reduce the onset of type 2 diabetes.[70]

Complications and Side Effects

The most common side effect of ACE inhibitors, affecting as many as 20% of patients, is a dry cough, believed to be related to increased bradykinin or substance P. It is especially noted in women. In patients with renal artery stenotic disease or severe congestive heart failure, loss of the renal efferent arteriolar tone may cause the glomerular filtration rate to fall, and renal failure may become clinically evident.[19] This is almost always reversible with discontinuation of the drug. Rarely, patients may experience angioedema that may be life threatening. When used with diuretics because of their synergistic effects, excessive hypotension may occur. Finally, these agents indirectly decrease aldosterone levels, which may indirectly result in hyperkalemia, such that the use of K^+-sparing diuretics or oral K^+ supplements must be used cautiously, if at all, with ACE inhibitors. A major contraindication for the use of any of the ACE inhibitors is the potential for severe or fatal fetal developmental anomalies, especially of the urinary tract, and thus patients who might become pregnant or are pregnant should not be treated with these drugs.[71]

Angiotensin-II Receptor Blockers

Although not as extensively studied as ACE inhibitors, ARBs appear to have similar efficacy both as antihypertensives and as medications that can decrease cardiovascular morbidity and mortality in high-risk patients.[72] They have also been shown to have similar benefit in high-risk type 2 diabetic patients and may preserve renal function in this group. Two major trials—the Irbesartan Diabetic Nephropathy trial and the Reduction in End Point in Noninsulin-Dependent Diabetes Mellitus with the Angiotensin II Antagonist Losartan (RENAAL) trial—demonstrated a clear benefit in terms of renoprotection with ARBs in patients with nephropathy due to type 2 disease.[73,74]

These receptor blockers are a reasonable alternative to ACE inhibitors, with fewer or no typical ACE inhibitor side effects.[75,76] Their action in blocking angiotensin II receptors results in the reduction of angiotensin II-mediated vasoconstriction and a secondary decrease in aldosterone release. The angiotensin I receptor is selectively blocked with these agents, and it is this receptor that mediates most all of the actions of angiotensin II. These ARBs lack the potential beneficial effects of enhancing bradykinin metabolism accompanying ACE inhibitors. These ARBs may be particularly useful in reducing proteinuria in nephrotic states. Like the ACE inhibitors, diuretics are a logical drug to be added to these receptor blockers to control hypertension in many patients.

As with ACE inhibitors, ARBs are contraindicated during pregnancy. It is the angiotensin II receptor in fetal development that appears to mediate programmed cell death that may be interfered with using these blockers. Currently, cost is the main objection to their widespread use.

Selective α_1 Blockers

Selective α_1 blockers block sympathomimetic-induced vasoconstriction and other α-mediated responses in the periphery by way of postsynaptic α_1 blockade, with essentially no effect on presynaptic α_1 receptors.[77,78] Their effectiveness depends on the degree of sympathetic activation, being more potent when patients are upright rather than supine. They may be first-choice drugs for use in patients with severe hyperlipidemia, because the α blockers may actually lower low-density and increase high-density lipoproteins and improve insulin sensitivity.[79] They are also useful in patients with benign prostatic hypertrophy in whom a smooth muscle-relaxing effect may lessen the manifestations of obstructive uropathy.

These agents are unassociated with impotence. The most important side effects of these agents relate to first-dose syncope and orthostatic hypotension, especially when used in patients who are volume depleted because of prior use of a diuretic and when used long term. They may also be associated with a reflex tachycardia, with a need to add a beta blocker, as well as a compensatory renal Na^+ retention with a need to add a diuretic in some patients. Two related drugs, terazosin and doxazosin,[80] allegedly have lower risks of orthostatic hypotension than prazosin. However, the ALLHAT trial did show an increased rate of heart failure when compared with chlorthalidone (8.1% vs. 4.5%).[33]

Centrally Acting Alpha Antagonists

Centrally acting α-antagonist drugs have a central α_2-antagonist action in the ventrolateral medulla that reduces sympathetic activity within the periphery.[81,82] Diuretics are usually added to block the Na^+ and water retention that often accompanies their use. Side effects include a dry mouth and impotence. There are major rebounds in blood pressure and heart rate when the drug is abruptly discontinued. The latter is exceedingly hazardous, and caution with gradual withdrawal of this agent must be considered. The use of transdermal clonidine patches has a lingering effect of 8 to 24 hours after removed. Rebound hypertension with discontinuance of this drug is best managed with beta blockers.

Methyldopa is an alternative drug with a somewhat lower efficacy as a peripheral α antagonist compared to norepinephrine, therefore resulting in decreased vasoconstriction. However, it is considered one of the preferred agents for managing hypertension during pregnancy. It does carry a risk of hepatotoxicity, although the incidence is quite low. Hemolytic anemia may also be a side effect of this drug.

Catecholamine Depletor

Reserpine, which is the prototype catecholamine depletor, depletes peripheral neuronal norepinephrine resulting in decreased vasoconstriction and heart rate as well as contractility by decreasing the sympathetic cardiac drive.[83] Catecholamine depletors are used mainly as second-line drugs for the control of hypertension. Their side effects include bradycardia, orthostatic hypotension, and occasional congestive heart failure. Fatigue and drowsiness are infrequent but notable side effects. Their use has become limited with the advent of ACE inhibitors, calcium-channel blockers, and ARBs.

Direct Vasodilators

Direct vasodilators are used when other drugs prove ineffective and in instances when afterload reduction for severe congestive heart failure is needed. Hydralazine has a relatively rapid vasodilatory effect, perhaps releasing or activating EDRF. Side effects include tachycardia, renal Na^+ retention, and a lupus-like syndrome. Hydralazine also interferes with vitamin D_6 metabolism and in rare occasions has been associated with a peripheral neuritis. A related drug, minoxidil, is seldom used because of the adverse side effects of hirsutism, pulmonary fibrosis, and cardiac myocyte damage. Minoxidil should always be administered with a beta blocker and potent diuretic, usually a loop diuretic.[84,85]

■ TREATMENT OF MALIGNANT HYPERTENSION

If malignant hypertension is uncontrolled, hypertensive encephalopathy and hypertensive nephrosclerosis can result. As blood pressure rises, autoregulation in the arteriolar bed prevents transmission of the elevated blood pressure into the capillary bed, preventing endothelial destruction. Patients with chronic hypertension usually develop arteriolar hypertrophy, which minimizes pressure transmission into the capillaries. Accordingly, malignant hypertension is seen only when diastolic blood pressure goes above 130 mm Hg.

However, encephalopathy could occur in previously normotensive patients if diastolic blood pressure were to rise suddenly above 100 mm Hg or in patients in whom autoregulation may be disordered, such as diabetic patients.

Slow onset of action and an inability to control the degree of blood pressure reduction have limited the use of oral antihypertensive agents in the therapy of hypertensive crises. They may, however, be useful when there is no rapid access to the parenteral medications described later. Both sublingual nifedipine (10 mg) and sublingual captopril (25 mg) can substantially lower the blood pressure within 10 to 30 minutes in many patients.[86] The major risk with these drugs is ischemic symptoms (e.g., angina pectoris, myocardial infarction, or stroke) due to an excessive and uncontrolled hypotensive response.[87] Thus, their use should generally be avoided in the treatment of hypertensive crises unless more suitable and controllable agents are not available.

Because of the seriousness of this condition, parenteral medications listed later often are necessary.[88] All of the following have a rapid onset, although nitroprusside is the most immediate:

- Nitroprusside is an arteriolar and venous dilator, given as an intravenous infusion with an initial dose of 0.25 to 0.5 mg/kg/min and a maximum dose of 8 to 10 mg/kg/min. Nitroprusside acts within seconds and has duration of action of only 2 to 5 minutes. Accordingly, hypotension can be easily reversed by temporarily discontinuing the infusion, providing an advantage over the drugs listed subsequently. However, prolonged use can lead to cyanide poisoning, particularly in patients with renal insufficiency. Another disadvantage is that the medication is light sensitive. It can be used in most hypertensive emergencies.
- Nitroglycerine is a coronary vasodilator and direct venodilator with variable arterial effects given as an infusion of 5 to 100 μg/min. Like nitroprusside it has a short duration of action. Prolonged use can lead to methemoglobinemia and tolerance. It is especially indicated in patients with coronary ischemia.
- Nicardipine is an arteriolar dilator calcium-channel blocker given as an intravenous infusion with an initial dose of 5 mg/hr and a maximum dose of 15 mg/hr with duration of action of 1 to 4 hours. It should be avoided in patients with acute heart failure and coronary ischemia. It is light stable but has the slowest onset of the vasodilators (5 to 10 minutes).
- Fenoldopam is a peripheral dopamine$_1$ receptor agonist given as an intravenous infusion with an initial dose of 0.1 μg/kg/min. The dose is then titrated at 15-minute intervals, depending on the blood pressure response. It can be used in most emergencies but should be used with caution in patients with glaucoma. It has the added advantage of being somewhat renal protective.
- Hydralazine is rarely used except in patients with eclampsia or in someone in whom intravenous access cannot be obtained. It is given as an intravenous bolus of 10 to 20 mg or intramuscular dose of 10 to 50 mg. Onset is the slowest of all these agents, occurring at 10 to 20 minutes with the intravenous route or 20 to 30 minutes with the intramuscular route. It can aggravate angina.
- Enalaprilat is an ACE inhibitor given intravenously at a dose of 1.25 to 5 mg every 6 hours. It also has a slow onset of action at 15 to 30 minutes and can cause a precipitous fall in blood pressure in high-renin states. It should be avoided in patients with an acute myocardial infarction but may be advantageous in patients with acute left ventricular failure.[88]
- Labetalol is an α- and β-adrenergic blocker given as an intravenous bolus or infusion with a bolus of 20 mg initially, followed by 20 to 80 mg every 10 minutes to a total dose of 300 mg. Infusion is then maintained at 0.5 to 2 mg/min. It should be avoided in patients with acute heart failure.
- Esmolol is an adrenergic inhibitor given at a rate of 200 to 500 μg/kg/min for 4 minutes, then 5 to 300 μg/kg/min. It has been recommended for use in the perioperative setting and in patients with aortic dissection.[88]
- Trimethaphan is a ganglion blocker that has been recommended for aortic dissections associated with hypertension. It is given at a dose of 0.5 to 5 mg/min.
- Phentolamine, an adrenergic inhibitor, is given in an intravenous dose of 5 to 15 mg.

PERIOPERATIVE MANAGEMENT OF HYPERTENSION

Preoperative hypertension is, unfortunately, common and may be a significant risk factor for postoperative mortality. In one study of 76 patients who died of a cardiovascular cause within 30 days of elective surgery, a preoperative history of hypertension was four times more likely than among 76 matched controls.[89] This increase in mortality seems to occur only when the diastolic blood pressure is higher than 110 mm Hg[90] or when hypertension has caused end-organ damage.[91] Systolic hypertension higher than 200 mm Hg prior to surgery has also been associated with an increase in postoperative cerebrovascular complications following carotid endarterectomy.[92] Blood pressure and heart rate can increase significantly with surgery, and this is even more prone to occur in hypertensive patients. Further, labile hypertension with periods of hypotension is also more commonly seen in these patients.[93] Accordingly, it is suggested that elective vascular procedures be postponed if the blood pressure is higher than 170/110 mm Hg.[94] If the procedure is emergent, then a parenteral medication should be chosen to reduce the blood pressure preoperatively.

Preoperative Management

Preoperative antihypertensive medications should be maintained until and including the day of surgery. Because many patients will be taking diuretics, preoperative volume and potassium levels should be checked. There are some theoretical reasons to possibly withhold ACE inhibitors, ARBs, and calcium-channel blockers the day before surgery, but this has not been generally accepted. The former can blunt the compensatory activation of the renin-angiotensin system during surgery, resulting in prolonged hypotension. This has been supported by a study of 150 patients undergoing vascular surgery that showed that hypotension during induction was noted less frequently when these medications were stopped the evening before surgery.[95] Those data would support discontinuing those medications if the indication for their use is congestive heart failure and not hypertension. Calcium-channel blockers can increase postoperative bleeding[96] due to platelet inhibition. However, abrupt withdrawal can cause coronary vasospasm, and so it is not recommended that they be discontinued.

Acute withdrawal is also especially dangerous for beta blockers and the centrally acting sympatholytic drugs.[97,98] Further, beta blockers in the perioperative period decrease mortality in high-risk cardiac patients[99] and should be considered for all patients undergoing major vascular surgery.

Postoperative Hypertension and Its Management

Postoperative hypertension is more common in patients who are hypertensive preoperatively and is especially common in patients undergoing vascular procedures. Goldman and Caldera[91] reported that postoperative hypertension occurred in 57% of abdominal aortic aneurysm resections and 29% of other vascular procedures compared with 8% of other nonvascular procedures. Hypertension is also a potentially serious complication following carotid endarterectomy.[92] Paradoxically, some patients may experience normalization of their blood pressure for many months after major surgery, although it seldom persists.[100]

Hypertensive emergencies should be treated as outlined earlier. Other causes of hypertension specific to the postoperative period (pain, agitation, hypoxia, bladder distention, and hypervolemia) all should be addressed. Patients unable to take their customary oral agents should be started on a parenteral equivalent. For example, patients on diuretics can receive intravenous furosemide or bumetanide; beta blockers (propranolol, labetalol, or esmolol); ACE inhibitors (enalaprilat); and calcium-channel blockers such as nicardipine. (Sublingual nifedipine should never be used, because it can cause severe hypotension and cardiac ischemia.[87]) However, there are currently no scientific data to recommend resuming the same class of drug except in the case of beta blockers and clonidine, which should not be stopped acutely. Accordingly, if another class of drugs is more suitable or if rapid action is required, another class of drugs satisfying these requirements can be used.

Management of Hypertension After a Thromboembolic Stroke

Although reducing blood pressure is advantageous in preventing stroke, hypertension following a thromboembolic stroke is believed to be cerebroprotective by maintaining flow to hypoperfused areas.[101] In fact, elevation in blood pressure is often noted for the first 10 days after such a stroke. Because of these findings, it is usually recommended that antihypertensive therapy be stopped after a thrombotic stroke unless the patient has cardiac failure, aortic dissection, or diastolic blood pressure higher than 120 mm Hg or systolic pressure higher than 220 mm Hg.[101] Under such circumstances, labetalol may be preferred because it can be adjusted readily. Nitroprusside should be carefully used because it can increase intracranial pressure.

■ SUMMARY

Control of hypertension in the vascular patient is clearly a priority. However, these patients often have significant comorbidities that may influence the choice of medication. Whenever possible, monotherapy should be attempted first, although in selected circumstances combination therapy may be more appropriate, such as diuretics and ACE inhibitors or ARBs in high-risk diabetic patients. Some antihypertensives may also have beneficial results separate from their blood pressure-lowering effects. Unfortunately, the choice of medication may be limited by cost or health plan directives.

Preoperatively, medications should be continued up to and including the morning of surgery. Procedures should be postponed only if the blood pressure is higher than 180/110 mm Hg. Postoperative hypertension can usually be managed by use of a variety of intravenous medications.

■ REFERENCES

1. The Seventh Report of the Joint National Committee on Prevention, Detection, Evaluation, and Treatment of High Blood Pressure. The JNC 7 report. JAMA 289:2560, 2003.
2. Burt VL, Whelton P, Roccella EJ, et al: Prevalence of hypertension in the U.S. adult population: Results from the Third National Health and Nutrition Examination Survey, 1988-1991. Hypertension 25:305, 1995.
3. Samson RH, Showalter DP, Liss E: Incidence of hypertension in patients referred for vascular laboratory testing. In press.
4. Lewington S, Clarke R, Qizilbash N, et al: Age-specific relevance of usual blood pressure to vascular mortality: A meta-analysis of individual data for one million adults in 61 prospective studies. Lancet 360:1903, 2002.
5. MacMahon S, Peto R, Cutler J, et al: Blood pressure, stroke, and coronary heart disease: I. Prolonged differences in blood pressure: Prospective observational studies corrected for the regression dilution bias. Lancet 335:765, 1990.
6. Vasan RS, Lerson MG, Leip EP, et al: Impact of high-normal blood pressure on the risk of cardiovascular disease. N Engl J Med 345:1291, 2001.
7. Borghi C, Dormi A, Ambrosioni E, Gaddi A: Relative role of systolic, diastolic, and pulse pressure as risk factors for cardiovascular events in the Brisighella Heart Study. J Hypertens 20:1737, 2002.
8. Buhler FR, Bolli P, Kiowski W, et al: Renin profiling to select antihypertensive baseline drugs. Am J Med 77:36,1984.
9. Trenkwalder P, James GD, Laragh JH, Sealey JE: Plasma renin activity and plasma prorenin are not suppressed in hypertensives surviving to old age. Am J Hypertens 9:621, 1996.
10. Alderman MH, Madhavan S, Ooi WL, et al: Association of the renin-sodium profile with the risk of myocardial infarction in patients with hypertension. N Engl J Med 324:1098, 1991.
11. Cavallini MC, Roman MJ, Pickering TG, et al: Is white coat hypertension associated with arterial disease or left ventricular hypertrophy? Hypertension 26:413, 1995.
12. Blaufox MD, Lee HB, Davis B, et al: Renin predicts the blood pressure response to nonpharmacologic and pharmacologic therapy. JAMA 267:1221, 1992.
13. Bühler FR: Calcium antagonists as first-choice therapy for low-renin essential hypertension. Kidney Int 36:295, 1989.

14. Wilson PW: Established risk factors and coronary artery disease: The Framingham Study. Am J Hypertens 7:7S, 1994.
15. van den Hoogen PC, Feskens EJ, Nagelkerke NJ, et al: The relation between blood pressure and mortality due to coronary heart disease among men in different parts of the world. Seven Countries Study Research Group. N Engl J Med 342:1, 2000.
16. Franklin SS, Larson MG, Khan SA, et al: Does the relation of blood pressure to coronary heart disease risk change with aging? The Framingham Heart Study. Circulation 103:1245, 2001.
17. Benetos A, Thomas F, Bean K, et al: Prognostic value of systolic and diastolic blood pressure in treated hypertensive men. Arch Intern Med 62:577, 2002.
18. Strandberg TE, Salomaa VV, Vanhanen HT, et al: Isolated diastolic hypertension, pulse pressure, and mean arterial pressure as predictors of mortality during a follow-up of up to 32 years. Hypertension 20:399, 2002.
19. Neal B, MacMahon S, Chapman N: Effects of ACE inhibitors, calcium antagonists, and other blood pressure-lowering drugs: Results of prospectively designed overviews of randomised trials. Blood Pressure-Lowering Treatment Trialists' Collaboration. Lancet 356:1955, 2000.
20. Ogden LG, He J, Lydick E, Whelton PK: Long-term absolute benefit of lowering blood pressure in hypertensive patients according to the JNC VI risk stratification. Hypertension 35:539, 2000.
21. Wang JG, Staessen JA: Antihypertensive drug therapy in older patients. Curr Opin Nephrol Hypertens 10:263, 2001.
22. Kostis JB, Davis BR, Cutler J, et al: Prevention of heart failure by antihypertensive drug treatment in older persons with isolated systolic hypertension. JAMA 278:212, 1997.
23. Veterans Administration Cooperative Study Group on Antihypertensive Agents. Effects of treatment on morbidity in hypertension: Results in patients with diastolic blood pressure averaging 90 through 114 mmHg. JAMA 213:47, 1970.
24. Hebert PR, Moser M, Mayer J, et al: Recent evidence on drug therapy of mild to moderate hypertension and decreased incidence of coronary heart disease. Arch Intern Med 153:578, 1993.
25. Sytkowski PA, D'Agostino RB, Behanger AJ, et al: Secular trends in long-term sustained hypertension, long-term treatment, and cardiovascular mortality. The Framingham Heart Study, 1950 to 1990. Circulation 93:697, 1996.
26. Culleton BF, Larson MG, Kannel WB, Levy D: Serum uric acid and risk for cardiovascular disease and death: The Framingham Heart Study. Ann Intern Med 131:7, 1999.
27. Rosa TT, Palatini P: Clinical value of microalbuminuria in hypertension. J Hypertens 18:645, 2000.
28. Cuspidi C, Lonati L, Macca G, et al: Cardiovascular risk stratification in hypertensive patients: Impact of echocardiography and carotid ultrasonography. J Hypertens 19:375, 2001.
29. O'Brien E, Beevers G, Lip GY: ABC of hypertension: Blood pressure measurement: Part III, Automated sphygmomanometry: Ambulatory blood pressure measurement. BMJ 322:1110, 2001.
30. Sacks FM, Svetkey LP, Vollmer WM, et al: Effects on blood pressure of reduced dietary sodium and the Dietary Approaches to Stop Hypertension (DASH) diet. DASH-Sodium Collaborative Research Group. N Engl J Med 344:3, 2001.
31. Cutler JA, Follmann D, Allender PS: Randomized trials of sodium reduction: An overview. Am J Clin Nutr 65 (Suppl):643S, 1997.
32. Hartley RM, Velez R, Morris RW, et al: Confirming the diagnosis of mild hypertension. BMJ 286:287, 1983.
33. Major outcomes in high-risk hypertensive patients randomized to angiotensin-converting enzyme inhibitor or calcium channel blocker vs. diuretic: The Antihypertensive and Lipid-Lowering Treatment to Prevent Heart Attack Trial (ALLHAT). JAMA 288:2981, 2002.
34. Effects of an angiotensin-converting-enzyme inhibitor, ramipril, on cardiovascular events in high-risk patients. N Engl J Med 342:145, 2000.
35. Dahlof B, Devereux RB, Kjeldsen SE, et al: Cardiovascular morbidity and mortality in the Losartan Intervention for Endpoint reduction in hypertension study (LIFE): A randomised trial against atenolol. Lancet 359:995, 2002.
36. Svensson P, de Faire U, Sleight P, et al: Comparative effects of ramipril on ambulatory and office blood pressures: A HOPE substudy. Hypertension 38:E28, 2001.
37. Wing LM, Reid CM, Ryan P, et al: A comparison of outcomes with angiotensin-converting-enzyme inhibitors and diuretics for hypertension in the elderly. N Engl J Med 348:583, 2003.
38. Materson BJ, Reda DJ, Cushman WC, et al: Single-drug therapy for hypertension in men: A comparison of six antihypertensive agents with placebo. N Engl J Med 328:914, 1993; correction 1994; 330:1689, 1994.
39. Lindholm LH, Ibsen H, Dahlof B, et al: Cardiovascular morbidity and mortality in patients with diabetes in the Losartan Intervention for Endpoint reduction in hypertension study (LIFE): A randomised trial against atenolol. Lancet 359:1004, 2002.
40. ALLHAT Officers and Coordinators for the ALLHAT Collaborative Research Group: Major outcomes in high-risk hypertensive patients randomized to angiotensin converting enzyme inhibitor or calcium channel blocker vs diuretic: The Antihypertensive and Lipid-Lowering Treatment to Prevent Heart Attack Trial (ALLHAT). JAMA 288:2981, 2002.
41. Pitt B, Zannad F, Remme WJ, et al: The effect of spironolactone on morbidity and mortality in patients with severe heart failure. Randomized Aldactone Evaluation Study Investigators. N Engl J Med 341:709, 1999.
42. Voko Z, Bots ML, Hofman A, et al: J-shaped relation between blood pressure and stroke in treated hypertensives. Hypertension 34:1181, 1999.
43. Somes GW, Pahor M, Shorr RI, et al: The role of diastolic blood pressure when treating isolated systolic hypertension. Arch Intern Med 159:2004, 1999.
44. Epstein M, Bakris G: Newer approaches to antihypertensive therapy: Use of fixed-dose combination therapy. Arch Intern Med 156:1969, 1996.
45. Neutel JM, Black HR, Weber MA: Combination therapy with diuretics: An evolution of understanding. Am J Med 101 (Suppl):61S, 1996.
46. Moser M: Current recommendations for the treatment of hypertension: Are they still valid? J Hypertens 20(Suppl 1):S3, 2002.
47. Gradman AH, Cutler NR, Davis PJ, et al: Combined enalapril and felodipine extended release (ER) for systemic hypertension. Am J Cardiol 79:431, 1997.
48. de Leeuw PW, Notter T, Zilles P: Comparison of different fixed antihypertensive combination drugs: A double-blind, placebo-controlled parallel group study. J Hypertens 15:87, 1997.
49. Cushman WC, Ford CE, Cutler JA, et al: Success and predictors of blood pressure control in diverse North American settings: The Antihypertensive and Lipid-Lowering Treatment to Prevent Heart Attack Trial (ALLHAT). J Clin Hypertens (Greenwich) 4:393, 2002.
50. Black HR, Elliott WJ, Neaton JD, et al: Baseline characteristics and elderly blood pressure control in the CONVINCE trial. Hypertension 37:12, 2001.
51. Materson BJ, Reda DJ, Preston RA, et al: Response to a second single antihypertensive agent used as monotherapy for hypertension after failure of the initial drug. Arch Intern Med 155:1757, 1995.
52. Berlowitz DR, Ash AS, Hickey EC, et al: Inadequate management of blood pressure in a hypertensive population. N Engl J Med 339:1957, 1998.
53. O'Donovan RA, Muhammedi M, Puschett JB: Diuretics in the therapy of hypertension: Current status. Am J Med Sci 304:312, 1992.
54. Jamerson KA: Prevalence of complications and response to different treatments of hypertension in African Americans and white Americans in the U.S. Clin Exp Hypertens 15:979, 1993.
55. Grimm RH Jr, Grandits GA, Prineas RJ, et al: Long-term effects on sexual function of five antihypertensive drugs and nutritional hygienic treatment of hypertensive men and women. Hypertension 29:8, 1997.

56. Frishman WH, Sonnenblick EH: β-Adrenergic blocking drugs and calcium-channel blockers. In Alexander RW, Schlant RC, Fuster V (eds): Hurst's The Heart, 9th ed. New York, McGraw-Hill, 1998, p 1583.
57. Moser M, Frishman W: Results of therapy with carvedilol, a β-blocker vasodilator with antioxidant properties, in hypertensive patients. Am J Hypertens 11 (Suppl):15S, 1998.
58. Mangano DT, Layug EL, Wallace A, et al, for the Multicenter Study of Perioperative Ischemia Research Group: Effect of atenolol on mortality and cardiovascular morbidity after noncardiac surgery. N Engl J Med 335, 1996.
59. Radack K, Deck C: β-Adrenergic blocker therapy does not worsen intermittent claudication in subjects with peripheral disease: A meta-analysis of randomized, controlled trials. Arch Intern Med 151:1769, 1991.
60. Roberts DH, Tsao Y, McLoughlin GA, et al: Placebo-controlled comparison of captopril, atenolol, labetalol, and pindolol in hypertension complicated by intermittent claudication. Lancet 2:650, 1987.
61. Kaplan NM: Calcium entry blockers in the treatment of hypertension: Current status and future prospects. JAMA 262:817, 1989.
62. Nicholson JP, Resnick LM, Laragh JH: The antihypertensive effect of verapamil at extremes of dietary sodium intake. Ann Intern Med 107:329, 1987.
63. Furberg CD, Psaty BM, Meyer JV: Nifedipine: Dose-related increase in mortality in patients with coronary heart disease. Circulation 92:1326, 1995.
64. Sahloul MZ, al-Kiek R, Ivanovich P, et al: Nonsteroidal anti-inflammatory drugs and antihypertensives: Cooperative malfeasance. Nephron 56:345, 1990.
65. Effects of ramipril on cardiovascular and microvascular outcomes in people with diabetes mellitus: Results of the HOPE study and MICRO-HOPE substudy. Heart Outcomes Prevention Evaluation (HOPE) Study Investigators. Lancet 355:253, 2000.
66. Efficacy of atenolol and captopril in reducing risk of macrovascular and microvascular complications in type 2 diabetes: UKPDS 39. UK Prospective Diabetes Study Group. BMJ 317:713, 1998.
67. The SOLVD Investigators: Effect of enalapril on survival in patients with reduced left ventricular ejection fractions and congestive heart failure. N Engl J Med 325:293, 1991.
68. Townsend RR, Holland OB: Combination of converting enzyme inhibitor with diuretic for the treatment of hypertension. Arch Intern Med 150:1175, 1990.
69. Giatras I, Lau J, Levey SS: Effect of angiotensin-converting enzyme inhibitors on the progression of nondiabetic renal disease: A meta-analysis of randomized trials. Ann Intern Med 127:337, 1997.
70. Alkharouf J, Nalinkumari K, Corry D, Tuck M: Long-term effects of the angiotensin converting enzyme inhibitor captopril on metabolic control in non-insulin-dependent diabetes mellitus. Am J Hypertens 6:337, 1993.
71. Shotan A, Widerhorn J, Hurst A, Elkayam U: Risks of angiotensin-converting enzyme inhibition during pregnancy: Experimental and clinical evidence, potential mechanisms, and recommendations for use. Am J Med 96:451, 1994.
72. Dahlof B, Devereux RB, Kjeldsen SE, et al: Cardiovascular morbidity and mortality in the Losartan Intervention For Endpoint reduction in hypertension study (LIFE): A randomised trial against atenolol. Lancet 359:995, 2002.
73. Lewis EJ, Hunsicker LJ, Clarke WR, et al: Renoprotective effect of the angiotensin receptor antagonist irbesartan in patients with nephropathy due to type 2 diabetes. N Engl J Med 345:851, 2001.
74. Brenner BM, Cooper ME, de Zeeuw D, et al: Effects of losartan on renal and cardiovascular outcomes in patients with type 2 diabetes and nephropathy. N Engl J Med 345:861, 2001.
75. Bermann MA, Walsh MF, Sowers JR: Angiotensin II biochemistry and physiology:Update on angiotensin-II receptor blockers. Cardiovasc Rev 15:75, 1997.
76. Weber MA: Angiotensin II receptor antagonists in the treatment of hypertension. Cardiol Rev 5:72, 1997.
77. Graham RM: Selective α_1-adrenergic antagonists: Therapeutically relevant antihypertensive agents [Abstract]. Am J Cardiol 53:16A, 1984.
78. Izzo JL Jr, Licht MR, Smith RJ, et al: Chronic effects of direct vasodilation (pinacidil), alpha-adrenergic blockade (prazosin) and angiotensin-converting enzyme inhibition (captopril) in systemic hypertension. Am J Cardiol 60:303, 1987.
79. Khouri AF, Kaplan NM: Alpha-blocker therapy of hypertension. JAMA 266:394, 1991.
80. Neaton JD, Grimm RH Jr, Prineas RJ, et al: Treatment of Mild Hypertension Study: Final results. JAMA 270:713, 1993.
81. Oster JR, Epstein M: Use of centrally acting sympatholytic agents in the management of hypertension. Arch Intern Med 151:1638, 1991.
82. MacMillan LB, Hem L, Smith MS, et al: Central hypotensive effects of the alpha-2a-adrenergic receptor subtype. Science 273:801, 1996.
83. Participating Veterans Administration Medical Centers: Low doses vs. standard dose of reserpine: A randomized, double-blind, multiclinic trial in patients taking chlorthalidone. JAMA 248:2471, 1982.
84. Campese VM: Minoxidil: A review of its pharmacological properties and therapeutic use. Drugs 22:257, 1981.
85. Zacest R, Gilmore E, Koch-Weser J: Treatment of essential hypertension with combined vasodilation and β-adrenergic blockage. N Engl J Med 286:617, 1972.
86. Angeli P, Chiesa M, Caregaro U, et al: Comparison of sublingual captopril and nifedipine in immediate treatment of hypertensive emergencies: A randomized, single-blind clinical trial. Arch Intern Med 151:678, 1991.
87. Grossman E, Messerli FH, Grodzicki T, et al: Should a moratorium be placed on sublingual nifedipine capsules for hypertensive emergencies or pseudoemergencies? JAMA 276:1328, 1996.
88. The Sixth Report of the Joint National Committee on Detection, Evaluation, and Diagnosis of High Blood Pressure (JNC VI). Arch Intern Med 157:2413, 1997.
89. Howell SJ, Sear YM, Yeates D, et al: Hypertension, admission blood pressure, and perioperative cardiovascular risk. Anaesthesia 51:1000, 1996.
90. Wolfsthal SD: Is blood pressure control necessary before surgery? Med Clin North Am 77:349, 1993.
91. Goldman L, Caldera DL: Risks of general anesthesia and elective operation in the hypertensive patient. Anesthesiology 50:285, 1979.
92. Towne JB, Bernhard VM: The relationship of postoperative hypertension to complications following carotid endarterectomy. Surgery 88:575, 1980.
93. Prys-Roberts C, Meloche R, Foex P: Studies of anesthesia in relation to hypertension: Part I, Cardiovascular responses of treated and untreated patients. Br J Anaesth 43:112, 1971.
94. Fleisher LA: Preoperative evaluation of the patient with hypertension. JAMA 287:2043, 2002.
95. Coriat P, Richer C, Douraki T, et al: Influence of chronic angiotensin-converting enzyme inhibition on anesthetic induction. Anesthesiology 81:299, 1994.
96. Zuccala G, Pahor M, Landi F, et al: Use of calcium antagonists and need for perioperative transfusion in older patients with hip fracture: Observational study. BMJ 314:643, 1997.
97. Psaty BM, Koepsell TD, Wagner EH, et al: The relative risk of incident coronary heart disease associated with recently stopping the use of β-blockers. JAMA 263:1653, 1990.
98. Houston MC: Abrupt cessation of treatment in hypertension: Consideration of clinical features, mechanisms, prevention, and management of the discontinuation syndrome. Am Heart J 102:415, 1981.
99. Mangano DT, Layug EL, Wallace A, et al: Effect of atenolol on mortality and cardiovascular morbidity after noncardiac surgery. N Engl J Med 335:1713, 1996.
100. Kaplan NM: Treatment of hypertension: Drug therapy. In: Clinical Hypertension, 7th ed. Baltimore, Williams & Wilkins, 1998, p 181.
101. Lavin P: Management of hypertension in patients with acute stroke. Arch Intern Med 146:66, 1986.

Chapter

40

Vascular Pain

KAJ JOHANSEN, MD, PHD

Section VII

Although vascular disease manifests in diverse ways, pain in one form or another is a common manifestation of arterial, venous, or lymphatic problems. Indeed, in some cases, the nature and location of pain complaints may be virtually diagnostic of the underlying vascular condition. Alternatively, pain arising from nonvascular conditions may mimic that associated with various vascular states, thereby delaying or complicating diagnosis and therapy. And the relief of vascular pain is commonly a hallmark of the success of the medical or surgical therapy of vascular diseases. Accordingly, this chapter explores the mechanisms and pathophysiology of vascular pain and its relief. This chapter consists of a discussion of basic neuroanatomy and neurophysiology relevant to vascular pain, a compilation of different vascular pain syndromes, and a review of various interventions for pain of vascular origin.

Because of the central nature of pain as a presenting feature of vascular disease and its therapy, topics covered herein necessarily share an interface with numerous other chapters in this text. Information provided here is, however, intended to be supplementary to or expansive of material in those chapters rather than duplicative. For more detailed discussions of pain, the reader is referred to comprehensive sources on this subject.[1-4]

■ BASIC NEUROANATOMIC AND NEUROPHYSIOLOGIC CONSIDERATIONS

A brief review of the neuroanatomy and neurophysiology of vascular structures and the organs and parts they serve helps inform an understanding of the way vascular disease results in pain. This issue is further clarified by an enunciation of the way pain is stimulated peripherally and transmitted and appreciated centrally.

The International Association for the Study of Pain defines *pain* as "an unpleasant sensory and emotional experience associated with actual or potential tissue damage, or described in terms of such damage."[5] A patient's pain perception is a consequence of many variables, including previous and current pain experiences, level of consciousness, and emotional state.

Nociceptive pain is that uncomfortable sensation associated with injurious stimulation, whereas *neuropathic* pain arises and is transmitted in the absence of such injury. From a teleologic perspective, pain's "purpose" is to signal the presence of (and presumably to prevent) tissue damage and is thus one aspect of homeostasis. Only when it becomes chronic, or is a manifestation of the postoperative state, is pain unhelpful.

Pain can be characterized by its location, duration, quality, and severity or intensity. Qualities of pain include the descriptive terms "aching," "burning," "spasmodic," "radiating," "lancinating," "dull," and "sharp." *Local pain* is noted at the site of injury, but *diffuse pain* is more characteristic of deep structures. *Radicular pain* radiates along peripheral nerve pathways, not uncommonly in concert with motor or sensory neurologic deficits. *Referred pain* is perceived at a site remote from where the noxious stimulation is actually occurring and results from a misplaced cortical appreciation of pain. Referred pain generally follows spinal segmental enervation and must be differentiated from *radicular pain*, which generally follows specific dermatomal distributions. *Visceral pain* is dull and aching and has an agonizing, "sickening" component.

Pain can result from numerous physical stimuli, including pressure, puncture, squeeze, tension, and extreme heat or cold. Pain can also result from chemical effects such as those resulting from a marked change in pH or the presence of various mediators, including histamine-like materials, serotonin, bradykinin, and other similar polypeptides. Endogenous prostanoids can lower the pain threshold as a consequence of certain stimuli; local acidosis can enhance the perception of pain. Local mediators, such as substance P, are released at sites of injury, and the neural stimulation that results can be interpreted as pain.

Nociceptive receptors are usually free nerve endings, and pain is transmitted in the small unmyelinated A delta and C nerve fibers. These afferent nerves' cell bodies are located in the dorsal root ganglia and their axons enter the spinal cord through the dorsal roots. These axons synapse in the dorsal gray of the cord with second-order neurons. Most pain is transmitted in the crossed lateral spinothalamic tract up the cord to third-order neurons in the thalamus. The paleospinothalamic tract, including the periaqueductal gray region of the brainstem, is relevant to more diffuse, longer-lasting pain and, probably, neuropathic pain. Interestingly, the precise central nervous system (CNS) location for pain perception remains obscure.

Large and medium-sized arteries have two types of innervation—afferent (sensory) nerves and autonomic (sympathetic) nerves. Pain is the primary sensation transmitted via nociceptive afferents in arteries and veins: Position, temperature, and other such sensations do not appear to be transmitted via the innervation of blood vessels. In large and medium-sized arteries, these receptors appear to be stimulated by direct trauma (e.g., an arteriography needle), stretch (as noted with balloon dilatation or stent placement), or shear (as in arterial dissection). Nociception in large and medium-sized veins is due to pain receptors in the venous adventitia, which appear to respond primarily to stretch (as in venous distention or engorgement due to downstream thrombosis or other obstruction).

As demonstrated in extensive neuroanatomic work by Pick,[6] sympathetic and sensory fibers enter the arterial (and venous) adventitia to form an intrinsic neural network ("adventitial plexus"), mostly composed of sensory afferents. From this plexus, bundles of nonmyelinated fibers (mostly sympathetic) approach the media ("border plexus"), and extensions of this network ramify within the media ("muscular plexus").

The basis for neuropathic pain, and how it is sustained, remain obscure. Such pain also appears to be transmitted by sensory afferents but, unlike nociceptive pain, has autonomic (sympathetic nerve) components as well, resulting in the well-established (although poorly understood) role of sympathetic modulation for neuropathic pain by pharmacologic or anesthetic blockade or by sympathectomy. Recognition, diagnosis, and management of various forms of sympathetically mediated or sympathetically sustained pain—formerly termed "causalgia" or "reflex sympathetic dystrophy" (RSD) but now subsumed, by fiat of expert panels,[7] under the umbrella term *complex regional pain syndrome* (CRPS)—is discussed in detail in Chapter 75.

Most nociceptive pain is relieved, according to teleologic definition, by resolution of the underlying noxious stimulus. Upon occasion, the presence or severity of nociceptive pain warrants consideration of more invasive procedures to effect pain relief. Such procedures are characterized as *neuroablative* or neural *augmentation.* Although this chapter is not intended to detail such procedures exhaustively, analysis of these procedures' results, in both the near term and the long term, provides insight into the way peripheral pain is transmitted and appreciated.

When used for the management of pain, neuroablative procedures appear to be more effective the more centrally they are performed. Peripheral *neurectomy* rarely works, and also, because most peripheral nerves are mixed motor and sensory, peripheral nerve section may result in loss of motor function as well as anesthesia-analgesia. *Rhizotomy* involves ablation of the sensory nerve root. In order for rhizotomy to be effective, at least three nerve roots must be transected; unfortunately, sacrifice of more than two sensory nerve roots for an extremity can result in loss of function, even though motor capacity is preserved.[8] *Dorsal root entry zone* (DREZ) lesioning, usually with an electrode-based radiofrequency current, involves electrocoagulation of Lissauer's tract and the underlying dorsal horn gray matter, thereby interrupting second-order neurons involved in the sensory and pain pathway. DREZ lesioning works best for pain due to spinal cord injury and plexus transection or avulsion.[9] *Cordotomy* involves section or radiofrequency coagulation of the spinothalamic tract itself, usually percutaneously and under stereotactic control in the awake patient; it works best in patients with unilateral trunk or lower extremity pain.[10]

Intracranial neuroablative procedures include midbrain *tractotomy* (lesioning of the spinothalamic tract at the level of the midbrain, including the periaqueductal gray, as well as the paleospinothalamic pathway—which is thought to mediate the emotional response to chronic pain) and *thalamotomy* (which exploits the fact that the ventrocaudal nucleus of the thalamus is the terminus of the lateral spinothalamic tract); lesions in the medial thalamus can produce substantial pain relief without demonstrable analgesia.[11] *Prefrontal leukotomy (cingulotomy)* can be particularly effective for pain associated with head and neck malignancy or other upper body pain problems, particularly when depressive symptoms are a major component of the patient's suffering.[12]

Sympathectomy is a unique form of neuroablative procedure that has an important role to play for various forms of sympathetically mediated or sympathetically sustained pain (see Chapters 75 and 85). Sympathectomy also can relieve certain types of visceral pain because afferent nerve fibers from the abdominal and pelvic viscera travel in the sympathetic nervous system. Pain relief after sympathectomy presumably results from the following observations: Afferent fibers to the extremities travel with the sympathetic nerves, abnormal efferent activity in sympathetic nerves maintains pain, and connections occur between sympathetic and somatic fibers.

The rationale for neural augmentation procedures is based on the gate control theory of pain. This hypothesis, initially advanced by Melzack and Wall[13] in 1965 and extensively investigated subsequently, suggests that substantial modulation of nociception may occur via interaction between myelinated and unmyelinated fibers within the dorsal horn of the spinal cord. The interplay of ascending, descending, and interneural interactions at this level governs the net level of nociception transmitted centrally via the spinothalamic tracts.

Stimulation of the spinal cord or of peripheral nerves can block pain, because unmyelinated pain fibers have a high electrical resistance and remain unstimulated but pain-modulatory activity can result from stimulation of lower-resistance myelinated neural tissue. Such a neuromodulatory imbalance can result in a mitigation of central nociceptive transmission, resulting in reduced pain.

This observation (which, parenthetically, validates the gate theory of Melzack and Wall[13]) is the basis for the use of spinal cord stimulation (SCS) and transcutaneous electrical nerve stimulation (TENS) for pain mitigation. SCS is usually performed by percutaneous placement of an epidural electrode in close proximity to the dorsal column. The electrode then can be connected to a subcutaneously implanted receiver or to a pulse generator similar to a cardiac pacemaker. SCS has been used for treatment of chronic pain resulting from peripheral nerve injuries, CRPSs of various sorts, postamputation pain, deafferentation phenomena, and multiple sclerosis.[14]

TENS, initially a noninvasive means of screening patients for SCS, is now used as a means of long-term pain relief, often in the physical therapy setting.[15] The underlying physiology appears to be based on the aforementioned differential electrical impedance in myelinated and nonmyelinated pain fibers that can result in modulation of central pain transduction.

Perhaps of greatest importance in the management of chronic pain has been the development and maturation, over the past 25 years, of the use of intrathecal and epidural opiate narcotics.[16] Morphine (or one of its congeners) can be delivered into the intrathecal or epidural space by means of an implanted programmable pump. Certain patients with cancer have been kept pain free in this fashion for up to 3 years. The use of this technique for noncancer pain is controversial. Tolerance occurs over time, with a doubling or tripling of the required dose being demonstrated within the first 1 to 2 years after catheter insertion. Non-narcotic agents such as local anesthetics (e.g., bupivacaine), gamma-aminobutyric acid (GABA) or somatostatin agonists, *N*-methyl-D-aspartame (NMDA) receptor agonists, and calcium channel blockers may have a role to play in chronic intraspinal infusion modes.[17]

The neurophysiology undergirding the use of epidural and intrathecal opiates is as follows. Modulation of afferent nociceptive input occurs in the dorsal horn via several neurotransmitters. Receptors for various endogenous opioid systems (enkephalins and endorphins) regulate descending modulatory activity, usually in an inhibitory fashion, and multiple receptors for these substances are present in both the central and peripheral nervous systems. Such receptors are the basis for the favorable effect on pain of exogenously administered opioid analgesics.

■ VASCULAR PAIN SYNDROMES

As previously noted, pain in one form or another is a common manifestation of various vascular disorders, and the location, quality, and natural history of such pain may be crucial to the diagnosis or treatment of the condition. For example, sudden tearing interscapular pain is virtually diagnostic of an acute type B thoracic aortic dissection; mitigation of this pain is a hallmark of satisfactory "medical" management of this condition by means of antihypertensive therapy with beta blockers. A compendium of the types of pain associated with various arterial, venous, and lymphatic conditions follows.

Intermittent Claudication

Claudication is one of the commonest pain complaints seen by vascular specialists. As noted in Chapters 37 and 77, the pathophysiology of arterial claudication is based on a reduction of arterial perfusion to an extent that, although it permits basal (resting) skeletal muscle metabolism, it is inadequate to meet the needs of working muscles. The clinical phenomenon is seen most commonly in the gastrocnemius-soleus muscle group distal to atherosclerotic occlusion of the superficial femoral artery but can also be seen in more proximal muscle groups with aortoiliac occlusive disease or in the upper extremities with chronic brachiocephalic arterial stenoses or occlusion. Rarely patients may note claudication of the gluteal or lumbar paraspinal muscles in association with pelvic arterial insufficiency, and claudication of the masseter muscles with mastication is almost diagnostic of involvement of the external carotid artery by giant cell arteritis.[18]

The quality and pattern of the pain associated with intermittent claudication are stereotypical. The pain is never present with rest, occurring only after exertion of a specific amount and disappearing quickly after cessation of exertion. That the phenomenon is a consequence of inadequate blood supply to working muscles is demonstrated by the parallel course of the development of symptoms and the decline in skeletal muscle perfusion as measured by ankle-arm Doppler arterial pressure indices during treadmill walking and by symmetric improvement in symptoms and limb perfusion when such exercise is halted.

The pain associated with the claudication of arterial insufficiency is localized to the working muscles and is characterized as "burning," "cramping," or "aching." The muscles are not particularly tender, and because basal blood supply is adequate, no trophic lesions occur. At the cellular level, such claudication pain likely results from a combination of ischemic neuropathy (particularly of small unmyelinated A delta and C sensory fibers) and a localized lactic acidosis resulting from the anaerobic metabolism of ischemia, perhaps heightened by elaboration of substance P.

Several types of intermittent *pseudo*claudication exist and contribute to an important differential diagnosis among patients presenting with walking-related extremity pain. The most important and most commonly seen of these alternative diagnoses is *neurogenic claudication,* which results from one form or another of lumbosacral neurospinal compression syndrome—spinal stenosis, arachnoiditis, spondylolisthesis, and the like. Initially the affected patient's complaints may appear to be very similar to those of subjects with arterial insufficiency, to the extent that patients with such symptoms are occasionally subjected to revascularization when they actually needed laminectomies (or vice versa).

Fortunately, a careful history frequently solves this diagnostic conundrum. Because the basis for neurogenic claudication involves compression of nerve roots by a diffuse fibrotic or inflammatory process in the region of the lower spinal cord or the cauda equina, the condition is more commonly bilateral than arterial insufficiency. Further, the pain of neurogenic claudication is more diffuse, frequently extending from buttocks to feet, and commonly has a deeper, more aching, or burning quality, not infrequently associated with distal paresthesias or numbness.

The subject with neurogenic claudication frequently finds relief from the steadily worsening symptoms by bending over while walking; when hip and leg pain forces the subject to halt, symptoms are commonly relieved only with sitting. Unlike the individual with arterial claudication, who can walk the same distance on the level or on the treadmill over and over again with equal interspersed rest periods, the individual with neurogenic claudication who attempts to walk very far achieves shorter and shorter walking distances at the expense of longer and longer periods of sitting.

The pain of neurogenic claudication is believed to result from both ischemia and reactive swelling of nerve roots at their site of compression, a diagnosis confirmed by studies utilizing intrathecal fibroscopy during treadmill walking in patients with neurogenic claudication.[19] Temporary relief of the pain of neurogenic claudication by various postural changes, or by sitting, appears to result from the fact that flexion of the hip and back relieves lumbosacral nerve root compression and allows decongestion of the epidural veins in the region.

Substantial diagnostic confusion can result from the fact that older patients with lower extremity claudication may have both atherosclerotic arterial occlusive disease *and* degenerative lumbosacral spine disease. Minimal or no change in the Doppler ankle pressure index despite the development of lower extremity symptoms during treadmill exercise excludes (or at least reduces the likelihood of) arterial occlusive disease as a cause of a patient's claudication.

Several other, much less common causes of intermittent claudication are proximal venous occlusive disease of the lower extremities, resulting in a characteristic sense of "bursting" discomfort and engorgement of the exercising extremity ("venous claudication")[20] as well as various forms of myositis, the most common of which is an iatrogenic muscle inflammation and necrosis that results from the administration of various statin medications to treat hyperlipidemia.[21]

Lower extremity claudication in younger individuals should bring to mind two diagnoses—*popliteal entrapment syndrome* and (when exercise-induced pain is localized to the anterolateral aspect of the leg) *chronic compartment syndrome*. The intermittent claudication seen in young people (often athletes or military recruits) associated with popliteal artery entrapment syndrome has the same pathophysiologic mechanism as that associated with atherosclerotic lower extremity arterial occlusive disease.[22] The cellular basis for the anterior muscle compartment pain associated with chronic compartment syndrome is ischemia resulting from diminution of the muscular arteriovenous pressure differential due to venous congestion and compartment tissue hypertension.[23]

Aortic and Other Large Artery Pain

A substantial number of pain receptors populate the media of large and medium-sized arteries. As noted previously, these receptors can respond to direct stimulation, for example, by a needle or other penetrating device; they also may respond to stretch or shear. Sensory nerve fibers do not appear in or near the arterial intima, perhaps explaining why atherosclerosis, even when it is "biologically active,"[24] is not painful. Chronic slow dilatation of arteries, such as occurs with abdominal aortic aneurysm (AAA), does not appear to stimulate intra-arterial pain fibers. Palpation of an AAA occasionally results in a diffuse deep sickening ache, but in the author's experience, this occurs with equivalent frequency after deep palpation of normal nonaneurysmal aortas. Stimulation of periaortic autonomic fibers by such palpation may contribute to this characteristic sensation.

The pain associated with aortic aneurysmal rupture, usually into the peritoneal cavity, the retroperitoneum, or (rarely) the pleural space, is generally described as sudden, steady, burning, and penetrating in nature. Such pain likely arises as a consequence of nociception at several levels, including stimulation of pain fibers in the torn aorta, in the stretched or torn peritoneum or pleura, and from extravasation and hematoma expansion in an enclosed pleura or retroperitoneum (tellingly, free rupture of an AAA into the abdominal cavity is commonly characterized only by transient pain followed by rapid loss of consciousness as the patient expires from hypovolemic shock).

Pain—characteristically "tearing," "ripping," "boring," and located in a substernal or interscapular location—is a hallmark of aortic dissection. Similar burning pain in the lateral neck characterizes extracranial carotid arterial dissection. Shearing of nociceptive receptors in the aortic or carotid media by progression of the pulsatile hematoma within the media is the likely explanation for this pain. Except for patients with Marfan's or Ehlers-Danlos syndrome, whose aortic or arterial dissections may occur asymptomatically, pain is a constant consequence of arterial dissection. Relief of such pain with hypotensive therapy is believed to indicate satisfactory control of an aortic dissection, whereas persistent pain suggests that such therapy is inadequate, requiring that such therapy either be augmented or be replaced by a more invasive intervention (operation or endovascular repair).

Vasculitic inflammatory involvement of large and medium-sized arteries is uncommon but not rare. The most common such involvement of the aorta is the development of an inflammatory aneurysm, usually of the abdominal aorta. The pathophysiology of this process remains obscure, but its presentation is stereotypically as a thickened "rind" of chronically inflamed fibrofatty perianeurysmal tissues, frequently with an adhesive involvement of the ureters or the duodenum that can significantly complicate open aneurysmal repair. Patients with inflammatory AAAs commonly complain of diffuse aching midback discomfort, and their aneurysms are dully tender to palpation.

Besides the aforementioned jaw claudication often associated with giant cell arteritis,[18] inflammatory vasculitis of patients with the disorder can be associated with diffuse pain and tenderness over the affected arteries—especially the superficial temporal artery, biopsy (or duplex scanning)[25] of which may be diagnostic of the underlying condition. As for inflammatory AAA and arteritis of other large and medium-sized vessels, the diffuse and poorly localized pain seen in this condition is likely due to inflammatory involvement of nociceptors found both in the arterial media and adventitia and in periarterial connective tissue. That the pain associated with this condition is inflammatory is borne out by its resolution after administration of anti-inflammatory agents (particularly corticosteroids).

Rest Pain, Ulcers, and Gangrene

Advanced, critical, or chronic arterial insufficiency is associated—usually in the lower extremities—with characteristic symptoms and signs that signal impending limb loss. Indeed, virtually all patients with rest pain, ischemic ulcers, or gangrene require a surgical intervention—either an arterial reconstruction operation or an amputation. Such patients' arterial occlusive disease is severe and multilevel ("tandem"), and their mortality rate exceeds 50% over the next 5 years, usually consequent to premature, aggressive coronary artery disease.

Rest pain, which is characterized by a diffuse, ill-localized aching or burning pain in the distal foot, generally is present initially when the subject is recumbent or the leg and foot are elevated; symptoms dissipate if the leg is hung over the edge of the bed or the subject arises and limps around. The pathophysiology of rest pain is likely that of an ischemic neuropathy, with positional malperfusion of small sensory nerves in the distal foot. The symptoms of rest pain (or other advanced arterial insufficiency) necessarily develop in the most distal small arteries, those farthest away from the heart. Thus, pain at rest does not occur above foot level in the more proximal lower extremity (with one cardinal exception—rest pain may develop in concert with severe ischemia of a below-knee or above-knee amputation stump).

Arterial ulceration in the nondiabetic patient is characterized by a shallow, nonhealing, pallid erosion of the skin in the distal foot—in a distribution similar to that of rest pain. The pain of such ulcerations is unremitting and severe, occasionally refractory even to high-dose oral narcotic analgesic agents, and is optimally treated only by urgent revascularization or amputation. The pain of such ulcerations is described as aching or burning and arises not only from the chronic severe ischemic neuropathy, which gives rise to ischemic rest pain, but also from actual necrosis of sensory nerves in the skin at the site of the arterial ulcer.

Gangrenous changes of the toes or heel are indications, of course, that tissue death has occurred. Associated pain complaints are thus a summation not only of ischemic neuropathy but also of the consequences of skin and subcutaneous tissue necrosis, osteomyelitis, and ascending infection. The pain of patients with arterial ulceration may be severe and unremitting; unlike in patients with rest pain and arterial ulceration, necrosis of sensory nerves may actually make such gangrenous distal feet insensate and anesthetic, paradoxically resulting in less pain than would be anticipated from the degree of tissue destruction present.

Atheroembolism, usually to the toes or distal foot ("blue toe syndrome"[26]) occurs because of digital or branch artery occlusion from debris—clot, atheroma—that has embolized into the distal circulation from a proximal source (e.g., an aortoiliac or popliteal aneurysm or an ulcerated atherosclerotic plaque). For the syndrome to occur, the proximal arteries must be patent, and the distal limb is usually not ischemic. Pain is therefore uncommon until digital ischemia is severe enough to result in sensory nerve damage.

The diabetic foot (see Chapters 38 and 87) is a special circumstance wherein chronic lower extremity and foot pain, nonhealing ulceration, and toe gangrene may be present yet the underlying pathogenesis revolves around not ischemia but, rather, diabetic neuropathy, structural changes in the foot, and the inability of diabetic patients to combat bacterial infection of the soft tissues. Indeed, most diabetic foot lesions are *not* ischemic,[27] and revascularization is uncommonly required as part of their management. Widespread loss of distal foot and even lower leg sensation in diabetic persons consequent to diabetic neuropathy makes pain due to ulceration, gangrene, or infection relatively uncommon among diabetics, although neuropathic pain is frequent (see later).

Pain Syndromes After Stroke

Pain is uncommon in association with cerebrovascular accident (CVA), except in patients whose cerebrovascular ischemia results from intracranial hemorrhage or tumor. Stroke survivors sometimes experience what appears to be a centrally mediated pain ipsilateral to the neurologic deficit.[28]

Pain Associated with Diseases Involving Small Arteries

Numerous local, regional, or systemic disorders include involvement of small arteries. In the extremities, such conditions commonly manifest coolness, pallor, numbness, cyanosis, and pain—manifestations of Raynaud's syndrome.[29] Often, such symptoms and signs result simply from abnormal arterial reactivity—such as occurs in the benign form of Raynaud's disease (developing primarily in young and middle-aged women or as a consequence of chronic vibratory tool use, primarily in young male laborers). Dull aching digital pain is noted by such patients during periods of extreme vasoconstriction; with the hyperemia of digital reperfusion, when vasoconstriction is replaced by vasodilatation, this dull aching pain is commonly replaced by a burning "fiery" pain as the digits are suffused via vasodilated digital arteries.

A more ominous form of small artery involvement associated with Raynaud's syndrome (termed Raynaud's *phenomenon* in this setting) results from digital arterial occlusions due to one or another form of various rheumatoid conditions, especially scleroderma.[30] To these individuals' pain syndrome, which is associated with digital vasoconstriction and then vasodilatation, is added a severe pain associated with fingertip ulceration or necrosis. Such patients' distal digital pain is frequently severe and unremitting, not uncommonly refractory even to large doses of opiate analgesic medications, and amputation may be required for pain relief. Pathophysiologically, these lesions are similar to those of advanced chronic lower extremity arterial insufficiency.

Another form of small artery involvement resulting in severe pain is that associated with Buerger's disease (thromboangiitis obliterans [TAO]), a condition most commonly seen in young male tobacco addicts. TAO is a nonatherosclerotic necrotizing process involving arteries, veins, and nerves, primarily in the extremities.[31] Because only the tibial arteries in the lower extremity, or the distal radial and ulnar arteries of the upper extremity, are commonly involved, patients with TAO have excellent arterial inflow but poor collateralization, and their ability to heal refractory ulcerations or areas of gangrene is poor. These patients' foot or hand pain is described as severe, unremitting, aching, burning, and agonizing.

Pain Associated with Venous Disorders

Venous disease is common and is frequently undiagnosed, in part because one major component of venous disease—deep venous thrombosis (DVT)—commonly occurs in a relatively vegetative, bland fashion associated with only minimal inflammation. Such patients' first symptom may be painless lower extremity edema or, upon occasion, the chest pain and cardiorespiratory collapse associated with pulmonary embolus. Pain is only inconsistently associated with superficial venous disease. Patients with primary or secondary venous varicosities may note diffuse aching or burning pain associated with their venous varicosities, a discomfort likely secondary to stretch stimulation of nociceptors in and around the venous adventitia and media or in the surrounding soft tissue.

Patients who have suffered a prior lower extremity DVT have a substantial likelihood of manifesting symptoms and signs of the postphlebitic (post-thrombotic) syndrome. Symptoms and signs that characterize this condition are chronic lower extremity edema, secondary venous varicosities, and characteristic skin changes, including stasis pigmentation and eczema, subcutaneous atrophy, and, in advanced stages, skin breakdown and chronic nonhealing ulcerations. These stasis ulcerations, which usually are relatively small and shallow but occasionally are circumferential and extend from ankle to midleg, are in the author's experience notably *not* painful—often manifesting only mild itching or burning. When significant pain occurs in a stasis ulcer, a secondary diagnosis should be entertained—invasive infection (usually streptococcal) or (rarely), ischemia, osteomyelitis or cancers.

Superficial phlebitis generally results from chemical irritation of the intima of peripheral veins due to intravenous infusions of various agents, sterile inflammation secondary to indwelling catheters or other foreign bodies, or bacterial infection. Such phlebitis is characterized by marked localized tenderness with overlying cellulitis, a palpable "cord" along the course of the vein, and, rarely, systemic toxicity. Pain, characteristically well-localized along the vein and burning in nature, results not only from stimulation of vein-wall nociceptive receptors but, even more, from perivenous inflammation, with elaboration of acidic inflammatory or infectious mediators that thereby stimulate perivenous nociceptors.

Pain Associated with Lymphatic Diseases

The most common lymphatic disorder is *lymphedema praecox*—idiopathic bland nonvenous swelling, usually of a lower extremity. Other forms of lymphedema either are iatrogenic (consequent to lymphadenectomy or irradiation) or result from infections of various sorts. The lymphatics are not innervated, so most forms of lymphedema are painful only when cellulitis or lymphangitis—an unfortunately common complication of lymphedema—supervenes.

Pain Associated with Amputation

Commonly performed because of intractable pain in a nonsalvageable limb, amputation itself often results in pain of various types. They can be classified as being either acute, appearing at the time of the amputation, or chronic, occurring weeks, months or even (upon occasion) years after the initial procedure.

Acute postamputation pain may be related to the surgical procedure itself or to incompletely understood phenomena arising from the patient's preoperative pain status. Such pain may result from the obligatory section of major nerves during limb amputation. The incisional and wound pain that results from transtibial or transfemoral amputation (much less commonly with through-knee amputation) commonly resolves within a week or so after amputation—sooner in many surgeons' experience if a rigid dressing is applied to the residual limb.[32] Other relatively straightforward amputation pain issues occurring early in the postoperative period include those related to stump hematoma or to actual stump necrosis, because the amputation was performed too far distally or because of acute thrombosis of the stump's residual arterial blood supply. The latter complication generally requires re-amputation at a higher level.

Early postamputation pain problems unrelated to the wound itself include the development of several neuropathic phenomena, including phantom limb *sensation* and phantom limb *pain*. Virtually all amputees experience the sense that the amputated limb is still present, for example, that it itches and needs to be scratched. Phantom limb sensation is generally considered benign and self-limited. Phantom limb pain, however, can frequently be severe and upon occasion even incapacitating, although patients can be reassured that the phenomenon generally diminishes or disappears within months to a year after amputation. Treatment with anti-seizure medications, tricyclic antidepressants, regional sympathetic blockade with long-acting local anesthetic agents, TENS units, sympathectomy, spinal cord stimulation,[33] or even DREZ sectioning[34] may be considered for persistent or severe phantom limb pain. Issues related to the management of acute postamputation phenomena are discussed in greater detail in Section XXIII.

Late postamputation pain most commonly results from poorly fitted prostheses, and an experienced prosthetist's opinion is invaluable in this setting. Other, less common but important causes of late postamputation stump pain are progressive stump ischemia, DVT, progressive autonomic dysfunction (CRPs), and neuroma formation—the last of which is best prevented by ensuring that large nerves sectioned at the time of the original amputation are buried in muscle, well away from cut bone ends and the skin flap.

■ DIFFERENTIATING VASCULAR AND NONVASCULAR PAIN

It is clinically self-evident that a large overlap occurs between the pain syndromes arising from vascular and nonvascular diseases. The not infrequent misdiagnoses of a ruptured abdominal aortic aneurysm as ureteral or biliary colic, of an aortic dissection as a myocardial infarction or gastroesophageal reflux, or of lower extremity ischemic pain arising from arterial occlusive disease as lumbar spinal stenosis, all point to the importance of considering the entire constellation of diagnostic possibilities in patients presenting with various forms of pain.

The scope of this chapter precludes an exhaustive discussion of those disease states in which the misdiagnosis of vascular for nonvascular disease (or, as important, the converse) can occur; the reader is referred to seminal general surgical differential diagnostic texts for further details.[35-37] Those intent upon formalizing the divergence of vascular surgery from general surgery,[38,39] both in the context of resident training and as a separate specialty, must make every effort to ensure that future vascular surgeons and their general surgery colleagues are exposed to a shared body of clinical knowledge and judgment in this context.

■ THE RELIEF OF VASCULAR PAIN

The relief (or at least the mitigation) of pain is the sine qua non of the rationale for many vascular interventions, to the extent that failure to achieve pain relief may be tantamount to failure—either of the original diagnosis or of the intervention itself. The patient who continues to experience calf claudication after a technically successful femoropopliteal bypass may well have benefited if more preoperative attention had been paid to the status of his or her lumbosacral spine. The return of claudication after a period of pain-free walking suggests the progressive deterioration of the original revascularization.

Relief of several types of aortic pain can take both "medical" and surgical forms. As previously intimated, the presence of tearing central truncal pain is a hallmark of aortic dissection. All type A aortic dissections require immediate referral to a cardiothoracic surgeon for urgent open or endovascular intervention (see Chapter 104). However, type B aortic dissections' natural history, as well as their indications for operative or endovascular intervention, depends heavily on the relief of this lesion's characteristic pain by pharmacologic therapy—specifically, the administration of beta-blocker agents, whose effect is to halt the medial hematoma's dissection by lowering systolic and mean blood pressure as well as left ventricular systolic ejection rate (dV/dt).[40]

The pain associated with an expanding, leaking, or ruptured abdominal or thoracic aortic or iliac aneurysm is relieved by successful graft interposition, either open or by means of a stent-graft. Graft repair of aneurysms eroding into the spine commonly relieves the pain resulting from such bony erosion. Similarly, and for obscure reasons, graft repair of inflammatory abdominal aortic aneurysms resolves the characteristic inflammatory "rind" around the aorta and with it the diffuse, poorly localized, boring, midabdominal-to-midback ache patients with such aneurysms commonly note. Interestingly, the use of corticosteroids, administered systemically or by injection, can also diminish the pain associated with an inflammatory aneurysm,[41] although such therapy may raise the risk of aneurysm expansion and rupture.[42]

Most pain resulting from vascular disease arises from inadequate tissue oxygenation, most commonly with exertion or other increased nutritive blood flow demands but occasionally from basal blood flow states in which tissue viability itself is threatened. Many vascular interventions focus on restoring tissue perfusion to (or toward) normal—not only various revascularization procedures, such as open or endovascular, but also pharmacologic or hygienic measures as simple as the encouragement of smoking cessation or aerobic exercise or the administration of hemorheologic medications. Although such interventions are most commonly carried out for the symptomatic consequences of lower extremity atherosclerotic occlusive disease, the principle of relieving vascular pain by improving tissue nutrition can be relevant for nonatherosclerotic diseases of the upper extremities as well—for example, the salutary effects of the administration of cilostazol in patients with various small artery occlusive phenomena of the digits[43] or the relief of dialysis access–associated rest pain of the hand by the performance of distal revascularization–interval ligation.[44]

In unusual circumstances, revascularization by conventional operative or pharmacologic means may not be feasible or may not provide tissue reperfusion adequate to relieve pain or other ischemic manifestations. In such circumstances the observation, initially popularized by Leriche, that sympathectomy can increase skin perfusion[45] may offer a therapeutic alternative. Ipsilateral lumbar sympathectomy (most effectively by operative excision, although a therapeutic effect can result from phenol or absolute alcohol ablation) can heal shallow ischemic skin lesions and relieve associated ischemic rest pain. This probably results through the combined effects of increased skin blood flow and interruption of afferent pain fibers traveling within the lumbar sympathetic chain.[46,47] Patients subjected to such therapy risk development of a sometimes debilitating though transient burning pain termed *postsympathectomy neuralgia*.[48]

Revascularization to treat severe ischemia may not be possible or, even if technically feasible, may not be successful in relieving pain. When tissue loss—advanced ischemic ulceration or gangrene—supervenes, amputation is indicated. However, in that subset of patients who have far-advanced, refractory ischemia in which significant tissue loss has not yet developed but pain is severe and unremitting, Jacobs and colleagues[49] have extensively investigated the possibility that neural augmentation techniques such as SCS might relieve pain and forestall amputation as a pain relief measure. Initial enthusiasm for this approach, based on nonrandomized studies demonstrating improved microcirculatory blood flow in subjects with advanced non-reconstructible lower extremity arterial disease, has waned with publication of less favorable results from later prospective trials of SCS.[50] At present, the role of SCS in the management of subjects with advanced chronic limb ischemia appears to be restricted to those with relatively preserved microcirculatory skin perfusion.[50]

Pain associated with venous disease of various sorts is ubiquitous, although rarely severe or incapacitating. The central role of vein wall distention as the proximate cause of lower extremity venous symptoms associated with saphenous or deep venous insufficiency is perhaps best demonstrated by the almost universal symptomatic improvement associated with such "low-tech" maneuvers as limb elevation and the donning of elastic support stockings. The "swollen" or "bursting" sensations associated with significant large vessel lower extremity venous obstruction ("venous claudication") may be effectively treated only with bypass (Palma-Dale or Husni procedures; see Section XXI) or endovascular relief of proximal venous occlusions.[51] The pain associated with acute venous thrombosis, either deep or superficial, is both congestive and inflammatory and is optimally treated with limb elevation, compression, or both plus anti-inflammatory medications.

The management of acute pain is central to the cultural identity of most medical specialties. Unfortunately, published research has repeatedly documented that most medical professionals have inadequate training, experience, and understanding of the proper management of acute or chronic pain. Pharmacologic (or other) management of chronic or severe pain of any origin is increasingly the domain of specialists, commonly with an anesthesiology background, in a multidisciplinary pain clinic setting.

■ SUMMARY

The proper management of the manifold types of vascular pain is a vast and, to date, incompletely illuminated topic. Vascular pain's multifactorial nature confounds simple or stereotypical prescriptions for its relief. In a large majority of cases, restoration to (or toward) normalcy of the underlying arterial or venous condition resolves or improves associated vascular pain. Chronic vascular pain is closely allied with neuritic or neuropathic abnormalities, for the management of which involvement of specialist consultants in chronic pain is appropriate.

■ REFERENCES

1. Loeser JD (ed): Bonica's Management of Pain, 3rd ed. Philadelphia, Lippincott Williams & Wilkins, 1998.
2. Wall PD, Melzack R (eds): Textbook of Pain, 4th ed. Edinburgh, Churchill Livingstone, 1999.
3. Raj PP (ed): Practical Management of Pain, 3rd ed. St. Louis, Mosby, 2000.
4. Aronoff GM (ed): Evaluation and Treatment of Chronic Pain, 3rd ed. Baltimore, Williams & Wilkins, 1998.
5. Mersky H: Classification of chronic pain: Description of chronic pain syndromes and definition of pain terms. Pain Suppl 3:S1, 1986.
6. Pick J: The Autonomic Nervous System: Morphological, Comparative, Clinical and Surgical Aspects. Philadelphia, JB Lippincott, 1970.
7. Harden RN, Bruehl S, Galer BS, et al: Complex regional pain syndrome: Are the IASP diagnostic criteria valid and sufficiently comprehensive? Pain 83:211, 1999.
8. Van Kleef M, Spaans F, Dingemans A, et al: Effects and side effects of a percutaneous thermal lesion of the dorsal root ganglion in patients with cervical pain syndrome. Pain 52:49, 1993.
9. Nashold BS Jr, El-Naggar AO, Ovelmen-Levitt J, Muwaffak A: A new design of radiofrequency lesion electrodes for use in the caudalis nucleus DREZ operation. J Neurosurg 80:1116, 1994.
10. Lahuerta J, Bowsher D, Lipton S, Buxton PH: Percutaneous cervical cordotomy: A review of 181 operations on 146 patients with a study on the location of "pain fibers" in the C-2 spinal cord segment of 29 cases. J Neurosurg 80:975, 1994.
11. Shieff C, Nashold BS Jr: Stereotactic mesencephalotomy. Neurol Surg Clin North Am 1:825, 1990.
12. Cosgrove GR, Rauch SL: Stereotactic cingulotomy. Neurosurg Clin North Am 14:225, 2003.
13. Melzack R, Wall PD: Pain mechanisms: A new theory. Science 150:97, 1965.
14. North RB, Kidd DH, Zahurak M, et al: Spinal cord stimulation for chronic, intractable pain: Experience over two decades. Neurosurgery 32:384, 1993.
15. Meyler WJ, de Jongste MJ, Rolf CA: Clinical evaluation of pain treatment with electrostimulation: A study on TENS in patients with different pain syndromes. Clin J Pain 10:22, 1994.
16. Gorecki JP: Intrathecal narcotic analgesia. In Wilkins RH, Rengachary SS (eds): Neurosurgery. New York, McGraw-Hill, 1995.
17. Krames E: Implantable devices for pain control: Spinal cord stimulation and intrathecal therapies. Best Pract Res Clin Anaesthesiol 16:619, 2002.
18. Smetana GW, Shmerling RH: Does this patient have temporal arteritis? JAMA 287:92, 2002.
19. Binder DK, Schmidt MH, Weinstein PR: Lumbar spinal stenosis. Semin Neurol 22:157, 2002.
20. Delis KT, Bountouroglou D, Mansfield AO: Venous claudication in iliofemoral thrombosis: Long-term effects on venous hemodynamics, clinical status, and quality of life. Ann Surg 239:118, 2004.
21. Rosenson RS: Current overview of statin-induced myopathy. Am J Med 116:408, 2004.
22. Levien LJ: Popliteal artery entrapment syndrome. Semin Vasc Surg 16:223, 2003.
23. Turnipseed WD: Diagnosis and management of chronic compartment syndrome. Surgery 132:613, 2002.
24. Danesh J, Whincup P, Walker M, et al: Low-grade inflammation and coronary heart disease: Prospective study and updated meta-analyses. Br Med J 321:199, 2000.
25. LeSar CJ, Meier GH, DeMasi RJ, et al: The utility of color duplex ultrasonography in the diagnosis of temporal arteritis J Vasc Surg 36:1154, 2002.
26. Renshaw A, McCowen T, Waltke EA, et al: Angioplasty with stenting is effective in treating blue toe syndrome. Vasc Endovasc Surg 36:155, 2002.
27. Reiber GE, Vileikyte L, Boyko EJ, et al: Causal pathways for incident lower-extremity ulcers in patients with diabetes from two settings. Diabetes Care 22:157, 1999.
28. Widar M, Ek AC, Ahlstrom G: Coping with long-term pain after a stroke. J Pain Symptom Manage 27:215, 2004.
29. Wigley FM: Raynaud's phenomenon. N Engl J Med 347:1001, 2002.
30. Pope J, Fenlon D, Thompson A, et al: Iloprost and cisaprost for Raynaud's phenomenon in progressive systemic sclerosis. Cochrane Database Syst Rev CD000953, 2000.
31. Ohta T, Ishioashi H, Hosaka M, Sugimoto I: Clinical and social consequences of Buerger disease. J Vasc Surg 29:176, 2004.
32. Smith DG, McFarland LV, Sangeorzan BJ, et al: Postoperative dressing and management strategies for transtibial amputation: A critical review. J Rehabil Res Dev 40:213, 2003.
33. Katayama Y, Yamamoto T, Kobayashi K, et al: Motor cortex stimulation for phantom limb pain: Comprehensive therapy with spinal cord and thalamic stimulation. Stereotact Funct Neurosurg 77:159, 2001.
34. Prestor B: Microsurgical junctional DREZ coagulation for treatment of deafferentation syndromes. Surg Neurol 56:259, 2001.
35. Greenfield LJ (ed): Surgery: Scientific Principles and Practice, 3rd ed. Philadelphia, Lippincott Williams & Wilkins, 2001.
36. Schwartz SL (ed): Principles of Surgery, 7th ed. New York, McGraw-Hill, 1999.
37. Corson JD, Williamson RCN (eds): Surgery. London, Mosby, 2001.
38. Veith FJ: The case for an independent American Board of Vascular Surgery. J Vasc Surg 32:619, 2000.
39. Stanley JC: The discipline of vascular surgery at the close of the millennium, the American Board of Surgery Sub-Board for Vascular Surgery, and the wisdom of evolving a conjoint board of vascular surgery: One surgeon's perspective. J Vasc Surg 31:831, 2000.
40. Westaby S: Management of aortic dissection. Curr Opin Cardiol 10:505, 1995.
41. Stotter AT, Grigg MJ, Mansfield AO: The response of peri-aneurysmal fibrosis—the "inflammatory" aneurysm—to surgery and steroid therapy. Eur J Vasc Surg 4:201, 1990.
42. Reilly JM, Savage EB, Brophy CM, Tilson MD: Hydrocortisone rapidly induces aortic rupture in a genetically susceptible mouse. Arch Surg 125:707, 1990.
43. Rajagopalan S, Pfenninger D, Somers E, et al: Effects of cilostazol in patients with Raynaud's syndrome. Am J Cardiol 92:1310, 2003.
44. Diehl L, Johansen K, Watson J: Operative management of distal ischemia complicating upper extremity dialysis access. Am J Surg 186:17, 2003.
45. Ewing M: The history of lumbar sympathectomy. Surgery 70:791, 1971.
46. Mailis A, Furlan A: Sympathectomy for neuropathic pain. Cochrane Database Syst Rev CD002918, 2003.
47. AbuRahma AF, Robinson PA, Powell M, et al: Sympathectomy for reflex sympathetic dystrophy: Factors affecting outcome. Ann Vasc Surg 8:372, 1994.
48. Kramis RC, Roberts WJ, Gillette RG: Post-sympathectomy neuralgia: Hypotheses on peripheral and central neuron mechanisms. Pain. 65:1, 1996.

49. Jacobs MJ, Jorning PJ, Beckers RC, et al: Post salvage and improvement of microvascular flow as a result of epidural spinal cord electrical stimulation. J Vasc Surg 12:354, 1990.
50. Ubbink DT, Spincemaille GH, Prins MH, et al: Microcirculatory investigations to determine the effect of spinal cord stimulation for critical leg ischemia: The Dutch Multicenter randomized controlled trial. J Vasc Surg 30:236, 1999.
51. Raju S, Owen S Jr, Neglen P: The clinical impact of iliac venous stents in the management of chronic venous insufficiency. J Vasc Surg 35:8, 2002.

OPEN VASCULAR SURGERY: BASIC CONSIDERATIONS

JOHN J. RICOTTA, MD, FACS

Chapter 41

General Strategies:
Choice of Procedure and Technique

JOHN J. RICOTTA, MD, FACS

The ability to expertly select and perform open vascular procedures will continue to be the single feature that distinguishes vascular surgeons from other "vascular specialists." Although vascular surgeons have been the leaders, and often the sole providers, in noninvasive diagnostic techniques and the diagnosis and management of nonsurgical vascular conditions, there has been increasing activity in these areas on the part of diagnostic and interventional radiologists as well as other medical specialists, particularly vascular internists and cardiologists. Percutaneous and endoluminal therapies have, appropriately, become a major part of the contemporary practice of vascular surgery, but this area, too, is shared with interventional radiology and cardiology.

Nevertheless, no other specialty claims the mastery of open surgical procedures for management of patients with a wide spectrum of vascular disease. The ability to perform open vascular operations requires a thorough knowledge of vascular anatomy, which is provided in Chapter 42, and mastery of the techniques featured in Chapters 43 through 45. As any experienced vascular surgeon knows, however, the technical ability to perform an operation is often less important than the ability to determine when such an operation is indicated or to choose which of several options is most appropriate for a given clinical situation. Learning to match the procedure with the patient's clinical condition is a major focus of vascular fellowship training and of ongoing education in vascular surgery. Specific vascular techniques are described in detail by Ouriel and Rutherford.[1] This chapter focuses on the factors that influence the selection of open vascular procedures and the appropriate strategies to apply to this selection process. Some of the more general considerations in this aspect of management have already been covered in Chapter 2.

Vascular disease is diffuse and relentless. By the time it has become manifest clinically, the disease process has been ongoing for decades. Despite recent pharmacologic developments that prevent disease progression, there is no established therapy to reverse clinically manifest vascular disease. Management of patients with vascular disease must take these factors into consideration. First, patients with clinical manifestations of vascular disease must be assumed to have more widespread and advanced disease than is clinically apparent, involving multiple vascular beds (and multiple organ systems). Assessment of end-organ dysfunction in other critical circulations (e.g., coronary, carotid, renal) is crucial prior to selection of the proper therapeutic alternative. Second, the expected mortality of the "signature" operations of vascular surgery (2% to 5%) exceeds expected mortality for all but the most complex elective surgical operations. Thorough assessment and careful perioperative management, along with careful selection and conduct of the operative procedure, are essential to minimize complications. Vascular intervention is often prophylactic and always palliative.

Third, the life expectancy of patients with clinically manifest vascular disease is significantly limited compared with the general population. In addition, each intervention has its own limited functional life span. Finally, vascular operations are associated with a narrow margin for error. The ill-conceived or technically flawed intervention is poorly tolerated by the typical patient with clinically manifest disease and has potential for immediate and significant morbidity. Thus, it is incumbent on the practitioner of vascular surgery to be familiar with multiple alternative approaches, now including both open and endoluminal interventions, and to select the most appropriate one for a given patient. Only by objectively considering all possible alternatives for a given clinical situation and selecting the most appropriate one without bias can the vascular surgeon properly serve the patient.

■ GENERAL CONSIDERATIONS

Several factors are important in the selection of open surgical alternatives. They include the medical condition of the patient (e.g., co-morbidities), specific anatomic factors that might dictate approach, and the durability associated with a given intervention. In principle, patients in good medical condition with long life expectancy have the lowest perioperative risk. They should be offered the operation that provides the most durable long-term result. In contrast, patients at higher risk of perioperative complication or those with limited life expectancy may be offered operations that are less durable but more easily tolerated.

The decision process involved in selecting open or endovascular repair for aortic aneurysm is a good example. These two alternative techniques have been shown to have equivalent perioperative morbidity in patients who are candidates for either intervention. However, it is generally appreciated that endovascular repair is better tolerated by the elderly and high-risk patients than open repair.[2] Endovascular repair is less durable and requires more frequent monitoring and secondary intervention than conventional open repair.[3] It follows that endovascular aneurysm repair is preferable in the elderly who have higher perioperative morbidity and more limited life expectancy, even though the late intervention rate may be higher. Conversely, open repair is recommended in younger, fit patients with a longer life expectancy, because of the established durability of the approach.[4] Deciding between direct and extra-anatomic bypass for aortic occlusive disease involves a similar process. Although extra-anatomic approaches (e.g., axillofemoral, femorofemoral) are less durable than in-line "anatomic" reconstructions (e.g., aortofemoral bypass), they avoid intracavitary exposure and may be preferred in patients with significant medical co-morbidities, "hostile" abdominal conditions or body habitus, or prior operative procedures.

In some cases, durability may be sacrificed for short-term efficacy, such as choosing between alternative approaches in lower extremity reconstruction. The "gold standard" for infrainguinal reconstruction remains autologous saphenous vein bypass. However, even this conduit has a significant failure rate at 5 years.[5-7] Moreover, saphenous vein may be in short supply or of poor quality in up to 30% of patients who need surgery. The vascular surgeon, therefore, must often choose from among a number of less than perfect alternatives—spliced vein, arm vein, prosthetic conduits, modified biologic grafts, and endoluminal techniques. The relative benefits of these conduits are discussed in Chapter 46. Clinical decisions are directed by indications for surgery, objectives (e.g., limb salvage or relief of claudication) and required durability of the reconstruction. Operations for claudication often return patients to their preoperative status when failure occurs, and in patients with long life expectancy, a second operative intervention within 5 years may almost be assumed. For the treatment of claudication, there is a growing interest in percutaneous interventions, which not only avoid a major operation but also preserve saphenous vein for possible use in the future in distal reconstruction for critical limb ischemia.

Frail patients who require intervention for critical limb ischemia may be considered for operations that sacrifice multiyear patency for immediate success with minimal morbidity. Nonautogenous grafts that are readily available "off the shelf" may be preferred to vein, which must be harvested (and often spliced) from remote sites (arm, lesser saphenous vein, contralateral leg). For such patients, infrainguinal angioplasty, a procedure associated with reasonable short-term efficacy but only modest midrange durability, may be appropriate.[8,9] Interventions that can improve arterial inflow long enough to heal a small offending ulcer or to institute a vigorous walking program in a patient with claudication may be appropriate.[9] Similar arguments have been made in the past to favor above-knee prosthetic bypass, with the goal of "saving" the vein for later use.[10,11] Although this approach has many critics,[12] the principle of long-range planning in the management of the patient with peripheral occlusive disease is a sound one. One must embark on each procedure with the twin goals of maximizing immediate success and leaving as many options as possible open for the future.

■ DISEASE DISTRIBUTION AND CHOICE OF PROCEDURE

The anatomic distribution of vascular disease has a major influence on the choice of surgical procedure. The success of arterial reconstruction relies on adequacy of inflow and outflow. Relative benefits of different endarterectomy techniques are described in Chapter 45. All types of endarterectomy are best suited for discrete localized arterial lesions in which the origin and endpoint of the offending atheroma can be identified. Remote endarterectomy, by either eversion or use of an intraluminal stripper, can be applied to longer vascular lesions but requires more extensive dissection than bypass and is associated with inferior results except when employed by persons with extensive experience. Remote endarterectomy and eversion endarterectomy are best used in dirty or infected fields or when there are short (>10 cm) occlusions in the common carotid superficial femoral artery or external iliac artery, as alternatives to either bypass or angioplasty.[13,14] Occasionally, the superficial femoral artery can be excised and "disobliterated" by eversion endarterectomy for use as a bypass conduit.

The guiding principle—and Achilles' heel—of endarterectomy procedures is the management of the distal endpoint. Failure to evaluate and secure this endpoint satisfactorily is a prescription for failure. This is the major reason that endarterectomy has been abandoned for reconstruction of arterial segments with more generalized disease. Although the procedure has the advantage of a direct approach to the offending lesion, it requires more skill, particularly in the renal position, than bypass and may lead to more prolonged distal ischemia if the distal end of the lesion does not have a nice, abrupt transition to relatively normal artery. The latter consideration has led many surgeons to prefer bypass to endarterectomy for most renal lesions.[15] However, the procedure should be part of the armamentarium of every vascular surgeon. The techniques of endarterectomy are well described in Chapter 45.

Like endarterectomy, balloon angioplasty is also best suited to discrete lesions and is now its major competition. Good results with lesions up to 10 cm in length have been reported.[16,17] The indications for angioplasty are discussed in more detail in Chapters 84, 131, and 140. Angioplasty has been most successful in larger-diameter (>5 mm) arteries and those that are not heavily calcified. Complex calcified lesions are more likely to recur ("arterial recoil") after angioplasty or to manifest perioperative complications such as dissection, embolization, and perforation. Angioplasty is recommended as the primary treatment of short stenoses or occlusions in the aortoiliac segment.[17] Good results after angioplasty of short hyperplastic lesions have led many to employ this procedure in the treatment of recurrent stenoses after carotid endarterectomy or infrainguinal bypass.[18] Inferior early and late results of angioplasty of smaller arteries and long, complex lesions have limited the efficacy of this approach in primary infrainguinal reconstruction (see Chapter 84).

Arterial bypass is the most common and most versatile reconstructive technique. The proximal anastomosis of an arterial bypass should originate above any significant occlusive or aneurysmal disease. Failure to adhere to this principle leads to early thrombosis, perioperative embolization, or anastomotic dehiscence. Outflow should be to a vessel with minimal or mild atherosclerosis and good communication with the distal arterial tree (runoff); in the case of bypasses ending at the groin, this vessel is the deep femoral artery. In more distal bypasses, such as tibial reconstructions, good communication with the distal arterial tree may be an elusive goal. In such circumstances, preoperative duplex ultrasound scanning can be used to select the most appropriate outflow vessel and the site of distal anastomosis.[19] Successful arterial bypass requires an adequate arterial conduit. In general, large vessel reconstructions can be reliably undertaken with either prosthetic or autogenous material. Short bypasses to moderate-size arteries (e.g., renal, mesenteric, carotid, subclavian) can also be made with prosthetic material with excellent results, especially if they have relatively high flow.[20] In the preceding circumstances, the most important feature is selecting a conduit of appropriate diameter. In cases of infrainguinal bypass, autogenous tissue is preferred over prosthetic or nonautogenous biologic grafts. A more thorough discussion of choice of arterial conduit is presented in Chapter 46.

■ PATIENT CHARACTERISTICS AND CHOICE OF PROCEDURE

Some examples of how patient characteristics influence the choice of operative procedure have been mentioned previously. In general, transabdominal operations are more difficult in obese patients, and the risk of surgical infection, particularly when a groin incision is also required, is higher. In such patients, the retroperitoneal approach to the aorta may be more direct and preferred to standard transabdominal approaches.[21,22] Incisions that traverse the groin crease are avoided whenever possible in obese patients, especially if prosthetic materials are being used. When such incisions are unavoidable, placing the incision transversely above the groin crease, as has become popular for endovascular aneurysm repair, is useful if only a limited access to the common femoral artery is required. When an infrainguinal bypass is contemplated in an obese patient, use of the superficial femoral or even the profunda femoris artery as the inflow source can avoid an incision at or near the groin crease.

Patients who have had prior surgery are also candidates for alternative vascular approaches. The general principle in such cases is to perform as much of the reoperative procedure through "virgin territory" as possible. Extra-anatomic routing of a bypass may be helpful for secondary reconstructions or in patients with a "hostile abdomen." Reoperative aortic surgery is simplified by the retroperitoneal approach, which avoids intra-abdominal adhesions and facilitates exposure of the perirenal aorta.[21] Similarly, using a suprainguinal incision to expose the external iliac artery for inflow[23] or, less frequently, a high thigh incision to expose the second portion of the deep femoral artery[24] can facilitate "redo" lower extremity procedures. Lateral exposure of the popliteal or tibial vessels may facilitate a distal anastomosis through clean tissue planes. These issues are discussed in detail in Chapter 83.

■ INDICATIONS FOR SPECIFIC SURGICAL APPROACHES

Retroperitoneal Versus Transperitoneal Approach to the Aorta

The transperitoneal approach, which is usually through a midline abdominal incision (though some surgeons prefer a transverse or even paramedian incision), is familiar and affords broad exposure of the abdomen and its contents. This issue is important in the patient in whom there is concern about other intra-abdominal disease, for evaluation of the viscera after vascular reconstruction, or for access to visceral or right iliac vessels beyond their origin. Although transperitoneal exposure of the perirenal and suprarenal segments of the aorta is possible, it requires more dissection than retroperitoneal approach. The transperitoneal approach can also be difficult in patients who have adhesions from prior abdominal surgery.

There are reports that the retroperitoneal approach may be advantageous in patients who are obese or have chronic obstructive pulmonary disease and for surgery of inflammatory aortic aneurysm.[21,22,25] The major benefits of this technique, however, are (1) the ability to expose the aorta from the renal arteries to above the celiac axis and (2) its suitability for reoperative aortic surgery. In the aneurysm with a short neck or a reoperation with suprarenal clamping, the retroperitoneal approach may facilitate reconstruction. The major disadvantages of this approach are the limited exposure it provides of the anterior and right-sided aspects of the aorta and its branches, the extensive retroperitoneal dissection required (as opposed to intraperitoneal exposure), and the incidence of "flank bulge" from denervation of the lateral abdominal muscles.

Problems with each approach may be overcome by specific technical maneuvers. Medial visceral rotation may be used to access the visceral aortic segment transperitoneally. Similarly, counter-incisions in the right lower quadrant may be used to access the right iliac artery when a retroperitoneal exposure is chosen.[21] Darling and associates[15] have described exposure of extended portions of the visceral vessels via the retroperitoneal approach. That this can be done, however, is not the issue. Rather, matching the benefits of each approach to the clinical situation should be the goal. My colleagues and I prefer the retroperitoneal aortic approach for exposure of the upper abdominal aorta, "redo" aortic procedures, and surgery that involves the left renal or iliac artery. We are inclined to use this approach in obese patients and in patients with significant pulmonary compromise if there are no other contraindications, because we believe that it facilitates their postoperative recovery. We avoid the retroperitoneal approach in patients with extensive right iliac and visceral disease, and we rely on transabdominal exposure for the routine open aortic aneurysm.

Alternatives for Visceral Reconstruction

Although reconstruction of the visceral (renal, celiac, and mesenteric) vessels is infrequently required, patients in whom reconstruction is needed often have significant atherosclerotic and other co-morbidities. Visceral stenotic disease usually involves both the visceral aorta and the origins of the visceral vessels. Options for open visceral reconstruction include endarterectomy and bypass via prograde, retrograde, and extra-anatomic approaches.

Endarterectomy of the visceral vessels is the most direct and satisfying approach with proper patient selection. However, a number of criteria must be met before we choose this procedure for a given patient. The disease must be relatively limited to the visceral aorta and the origins of the visceral vessels. If the disease is too extensive, a distal endpoint will not be achieved. As noted in Chapter 45, presence of aneurysmal degeneration in the aorta is a contraindication to this procedure. Anatomic factors alone make endarterectomy unsuitable in many patients. Medical co-morbidities are also important. Transaortic endarterectomy requires suprarenal and often supraceliac clamping with attendant increases in cardiac afterload and visceral ischemia. Consequently, we avoid this procedure in patients with significant preoperative cardiac dysfunction and any degree of renal insufficiency. Paradoxically, this procedure may be optimal for patients with bilateral renal orifice disease that is localized, because the total renal ischemia time of a limited transaortic renal endarterectomy may be shorter than that of bilateral bypass. However, these patients are increasingly rare in our current practice, and most are now treated by renal angioplasty and stenting.

Arterial bypass remains the most common method of visceral revascularization. It is usually performed for lesions not amenable to angioplasty (occlusions), those in which there is fear of distal embolization due to degeneration of the visceral aorta, or when intraoperative evaluation of the viscera is desirable at the time of revascularization. Inflow for the bypass can be obtained from the aorta (*anatomic*) or from an iliac or visceral vessel (*extra-anatomic*). If an anatomic bypass is chosen, the character of the aorta determines the site of origin. It is important that a significantly disease-free segment of the aorta be available to avoid either embolization or occlusion of the bypass from an intimal flap at the aortic clamp site. The infrarenal aorta is often heavily involved by atherosclerosis and may not be suitable for a retrograde bypass. The supraceliac and lower thoracic segments of aorta are usually relatively free of disease.

Proximal (*prograde*) bypass from the supraceliac or thoracic aorta has the additional advantage of more hemodynamic antegrade flow with reduced turbulence and risk of kinking. *Retrograde* bypasses are more prone to these problems. However, prograde bypass requires supraceliac clamping, with its attendant risks. In general, the time for clamping is less than that associated with endarterectomy, and the visceral ischemia is well tolerated. However, the hemodynamic changes associated with clamping and unclamping of the aorta are real and may be dangerous in elderly patients with cardiac dysfunction. If a good segment of supraceliac aorta is available for clamping and the patient has relatively normal left ventricular function, we prefer a prograde bypass originating from the supraceliac aorta. This is exposed transabdominally by cutting of the crus of the diaphragm when mesenteric reconstruction is required. On the rare occasion that isolated reconstruction of the left renal artery is performed, a left retroperitoneal approach is ideal.[15] We reserve use of the thoracic aorta for young patients in whom the supraceliac aorta is not usable. In these cases, a thoracoabdominal approach is required; this is extremely rare in our practice.

When a prograde anatomic reconstruction is not feasible, our next choice is extra-anatomic bypass, particularly for renal reconstruction.[26] These procedures are discussed in Chapter 129. Inflow can be from the splenic, hepatic, or superior mesenteric bypass with saphenous vein or prosthetic vessel. Use of visceral vessels as the inflow source allows the surgeon to avoid clamping the aorta, a particularly useful feature in elderly patients. This procedure is well tolerated with minimal physiologic disturbance. Such a bypass is most often used for the renal arteries, because reconstructions for mesenteric ischemia are not undertaken in the absence of multiple vessel involvement.

Our third option is retrograde bypass from the common iliac artery or distal aorta. We choose this option when we judge that prograde bypass is not indicated and the visceral arteries are not suitable for bypass. The infrarenal aorta is the preferred origin of our bypass graft. Complete cross-clamping, not partial occlusion, is performed in a portion of the aorta that is relatively disease-free. Occasionally, a local endarterectomy and placement of a patch are required to ensure suitable inflow. When the infrarenal aorta is degenerated but has no hemodynamically significant occlusions, we do not hesitate to use the iliac arteries as an inflow source if they are suitable. Through matching of the approach with the anatomy and physiology of each patient, visceral reconstruction can be done with excellent results.

Revascularization of the Supra-aortic Trunk Vessels

With the exception of carotid bifurcation endarterectomy, operation on other branches of the aortic arch is uncommon. Operative options include endarterectomy and anatomic or extra-anatomic bypass. Treatment of each vessel is discussed separately. Indications for surgery are beyond the scope of this chapter; rather, the discussion focuses on factors that influence the choice of operation.

Isolated lesions of the innominate artery are usually operated on for stenosis with embolization rather than occlusion with hemodynamic compromise. This is because the abundant collateral vessels, which supply both the subclavian and right carotid distributions, usually compensate for occlusion of the innominate artery. As a consequence, the embolic lesions must be addressed, either directly or by exclusion with extra-anatomic bypass. Assessing the risk of median sternotomy and clamping of the aortic arch in an individual patient dictates the approach to isolated lesions of the innominate artery. Direct reconstructions (bypass or endarterectomy) are preferred in younger, fit patients because of their greater long-term durability. However, in patients with prior median sternotomy, chronic obstructive pulmonary disease, heavily calcified aorta, or other risk factors that might make a transthoracic approach more dangerous, an extrathoracic (extra-anatomic) approach is preferred.

Focal lesions of the origin of the innominate artery, with aortic "spillover" (but without extensive aortic atherosclerosis), represent the best indication for transthoracic innominate endarterectomy with excellent long-term results. This approach avoids the need for bypass grafts, which may become compressed and are subject to late occlusion. Recurrence after innominate endarterectomy is rare. Percutaneous angioplasty has been reported for isolated innominate lesions.[27] Indications for angioplasty depend on the character of the innominate lesions—calcification, embolic potential, orificial versus intrinsic disease.

Extra-anatomic revascularization for isolated innominate disease is rarely required. It is indicated in patients with symptomatic innominate lesions who are not candidates for median sternotomy. When performed, extra-anatomic revascularization usually involves a subclavian-to-subclavian (or, less commonly, an axillary-to-axillary) bypass. Although it is possible to use the left common carotid as the inflow source, this maneuver is avoided when possible because it interferes with prograde cerebral flow. Bypass from one subclavian artery to another has the advantage of a short bypass; also, the right common carotid can be implanted directly into the bypass, thereby excluding an embolic source. If axilloaxillary bypass is chosen, some allowance for retrograde perfusion of the right common carotid must be made.

Isolated lesions of the common carotid arteries are usually treated with a bypass or transposition using the subclavian artery as the donor vessel. These operations, which predominantly involve the left common carotid artery, can be done through a transcervical approach. Transposition is preferred because it avoids use of a prosthetic and possible kinking of the bypass. Extensive common carotid disease can be addressed by eversion endarterectomy of the common carotid artery with re-implantation of the disobliterated vessel into the subclavian in an effort to avoid bypass. If a bypass is performed, it should originate proximally on the subclavian artery and ascend as close to the common carotid as possible, to avoid kinking when a more diagonal retrograde course is taken in the patient in whom common carotid disease occurs with disease of the carotid bifurcation.

Bifurcation endarterectomy can be combined with proximal retrograde balloon angioplasty if the disease in the common carotid artery is focal in nature.[28] If the disease is more diffuse, bifurcation endarterectomy can be combined with bypass or re-implantation of an endarterectomized common carotid artery, with use of the subclavian as the inflow source. Some investigators have advocated using the distal anastomosis of a subclavian carotid bypass as an "onlay patch" to close the bifurcation endarterectomy. We prefer to separate the bifurcation endarterectomy, which is patched, from the bypass, transecting the common carotid below the bifurcation arteriotomy and performing an end-to-end bypass from the subclavian to the common carotid. Alternatively, the common carotid can be transected at the thoracic inlet, and eversion endarterectomy can be performed with a separate incision for the bifurcation endarterectomy (Figs. 41-1 and 41-2).

Isolated lesions of the subclavian artery can be treated in the same manner as common carotid lesions, that is, with transposition or bypass. Transposition is our preferred approach, although the proximal dissection is a bit more involved. Bypass is preferred when a heavily calcified proximal subclavian artery would make transection and proximal ligation difficult, diffuse subclavian disease would require extensive endarterectomy, or in patients with "coronary steal syndrome" in whom proximal clamping of the subclavian may interfere with flow through an internal mammary artery bypass graft. The bypass should originate low on the common carotid artery and should parallel the subclavian artery as much as possible. Lesions of the subclavian artery have been treated successfully by endarterectomy (see Chapter 45). Isolated subclavian lesions have also been treated successfully with angioplasty. Transfemoral and retrograde transbrachial approaches have both been reported to have success.[29]

Reconstruction of the proximal vertebral artery is discussed in Chapter 141. Our preference, in the rare cases in which we have performed this operation, is re-implantation into the common carotid artery.

When aortic atherosclerosis is more diffuse, and when there are multiple lesions of the arch vessels, endarterectomy is not indicated. If a transthoracic approach is possible, a bypass graft originating from the ascending aorta to the innominate artery (and extending to the left common carotid and subclavian if needed) provides the best method for revascularization of multiple lesions of the supra-aortic trunk vessels.[30] This approach is also advantageous in cases of a "bovine arch" because it allows perfusion through one carotid to continue while anastomosis is performed to either the innominate or left common carotid artery. Extra-anatomic bypass in the case of diffuse disease is individualized. Inflow vessels may include the subclavian,

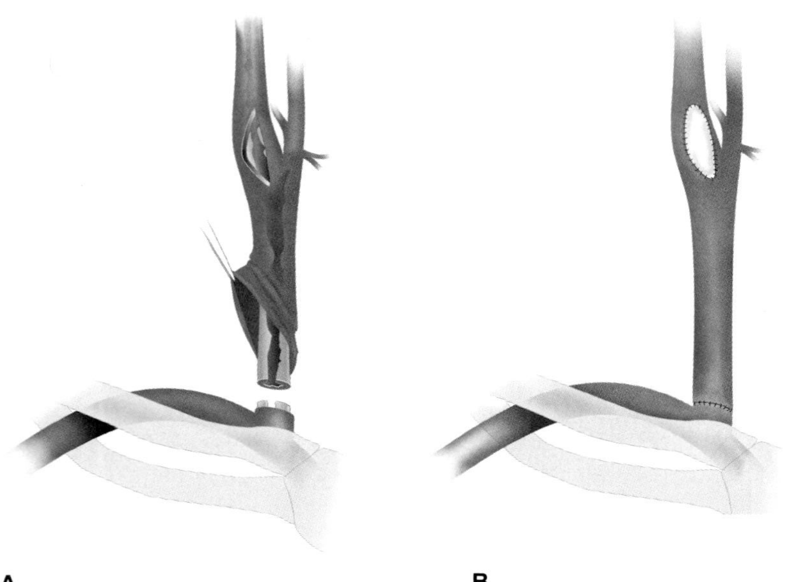

FIGURE 41-1 **A,** Option for dealing with extensive common carotid artery and carotid bifurcation disease. Common carotid artery is transected below the disease and common carotid plaque is removed by eversion endarterectomy. Carotid bifurcation plaque is addressed by a separate incision. **B,** Arterial continuity is restored by end-to-end anastomosis of the common carotid artery and patch closure of the bifurcation.

common carotid, and even the femoral artery. Carotid-to-carotid bypass using a retropharyngeal approach has been useful when there is diffuse arch vessel disease[31] and the patient is believed not to be a suitable candidate for transthoracic reconstruction. In this case, lesions involving the subclavian vessels (and thereby preventing them from serving as inflow sources) are not addressed because they are rarely symptomatic.

Lower Extremity Reconstruction

Alternative methods for open lower extremity reconstruction are discussed in detail later in this text. Choice of vascular conduits is discussed in Chapter 46. The evolving role of angioplasty in infrainguinal disease is discussed in Chapter 84. Comments here are restricted to choosing among alternative approaches for lower extremity arterial bypass procedures. Anatomic tunneling is performed in reconstructions that originate or terminate in the above-knee popliteal artery, because in-situ techniques would require excessive lengths of saphenous vein and put the conduit at risk of thrombosis from external compression by the adductor muscles of the thigh. Subcutaneous tunneling, which makes follow-up with duplex scanning and revisions of stenoses easier, is our preferred method when the originating or terminating vessels are below the knee. Nonreversed translocated vein has advantages when there are significant discrepancies in proximal and distal vein diameter and in-situ grafting is not possible. When the vein is removed from its bed and is isodiametric, we prefer to use it in a reversed position, because doing so removes the need for valve lysis and eliminates potential problems with retained valves.

An extra-anatomic position for the bypass graft is preferred in some situations. They include reoperation, for either infection or multiple failed procedures, and operations in which the target is the proximal or mid–anterior tibial artery. In these cases, a tunnel on the lateral aspect of the leg may be required. We find this step preferable to crossing anterior to the tibia (except when done at the level of the ankle). When prosthetic graft is used, we prefer externally supported rings, particularly when the groin or knee is being crossed.

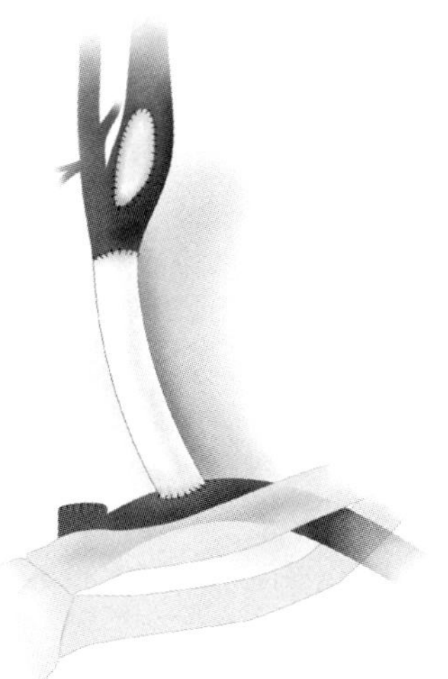

FIGURE 41-2 When disease in the common carotid artery (CCA) is too extensive for eversion endarterectomy, a bypass from the subclavian artery is done to the distal CCA. The bifurcation is addressed by a separate arteriotomy and patch closure.

■ COMBINING OPEN AND ENDOVASCULAR TECHNIQUES

An evolving area in vascular surgery, and one that will by necessity remain the province of the vascular surgeon, is the combination of open and endovascular techniques. Such combinations may allow a safer and more definitive approach to a clinical situation than the use of either open or endoluminal approaches in isolation. The most common example is angioplasty of proximal lesions of the aorta and iliac arteries combined with infrainguinal bypass.[32] Open thromboembolectomy for acute ischemia is another area in which endoluminal techniques can be combined with a limited femoral exposure to provide improved perfusion in a rapid manner (see Chapter 44). Because many patients with acute ischemia have significant coronary co-morbidities, this combined approach offers advantages over more extensive operation and more time-consuming thrombolysis.

Open and endovascular techniques can be combined for the treatment of complex aortic aneurysm disease. Combining surgical bypass of important branch vessels (renal, mesenteric, arch vessels) with endoluminal aneurysm exclusion may allow these aneurysms of the thoracic and visceral aorta to be treated with less patient morbidity. Ellozy and coworkers[33] have described such combined approaches for the treatment of aneurysms of the thoracic aorta involving the arch vessels. Similar approaches can be used in patients with aneurysms involving the pararenal and visceral aorta, who are not candidates for open aortic surgery. Extra-anatomic renal and visceral artery bypass may allow endoluminal grafts to traverse the native origins of these vessels, facilitating endovascular repair.

■ SUMMARY

Open vascular techniques remain the exclusive domain of the vascular surgeon. Mastery of these techniques is the essence of what distinguishes the vascular surgeon from other "vascular interventionalists." Such mastery is based on a thorough knowledge of vascular anatomy and clinical experience with alternative techniques, both open and endovascular. The exposures and techniques described in Chapters 42 to 45 should be familiar to all practicing vascular surgeons. Each has advantages that may be brought to bear in specific circumstances for the benefit of our patients.

■ REFERENCES

1. Ouriel K, Rutherford RB: Atlas of Vascular Surgery: Operative Procedures. Philadelphia, WB Saunders, 1998.
2. Hill BB, Wolf YG, Lee WA, et al: Open versus endovascular AAA repair in patients who are morphological candidates for endovascular treatment. J Endovasc Ther 9:255-261, 2002.
3. Conner MS 3rd, Sternbergh WC 3rd, Carter G, et al: Secondary procedures after endovascular aortic aneurysm repair. J Vasc Surg 36:992-996, 2002.
4. Brewster DC, Cronenwett JL, Hallett JW, et al: Guidelines for the treatment of abdominal aortic aneurysms: Report of a subcommittee of the Joint Council of the American Association for Vascular Surgery and Society for Vascular Surgery. J Vasc Surg 37:1106-1117, 2003.
5. Faries PL, LoGerfo FW, Arora S, et al: A comparative study of alternative conduits for lower extremity revascularization: All-autogenous conduit versus prosthetic grafts. J Vasc Surg 32:1080-1090, 2000.
6. Byrne J, Darling RC 3rd, Chang BB, et al: Infrainguinal arterial reconstruction for claudication: Is it worth the risk? An analysis of 409 procedures. J Vasc Surg 29:259-269, 1999.
7. Shah DM, Leather RP, Darling RC 3rd, et al: Long-term results of using the in situ saphenous vein bypass. Adv Surg 30:123-140, 1996.
8. Becquemin JP, Favre JP, Marzelle J, et al: Systematic versus selective stent placement after superficial femoral artery balloon angioplasty: A multicenter prospective randomized study. J Vasc Surg 37:487-494, 2003.
9. Nasr MK, Taylor PJ, Horrocks M: Vascular training in the U.K.: Femorodistal bypass, an index procedure? Eur J Vasc Endovasc Surg 25:135-138, 2003.
10. Quinones-Baldrich WJ, Prego AA, Ucelay-Gomez R, et al: Long-term results of infrainguinal revascularization with polytetrafluoroethylene: A ten-year experience. J Vasc Surg 16:209-217, 1992.
11. Quinones-Baldrich WJ, Busuttil RW, Baker JD, et al: Is the preferential use of polytetrafluoroethylene grafts for femoropopliteal bypass justified? J Vasc Surg 8:219-228, 1988.
12. Roddy SP, Darling C, Mehta M, et al: Infrainguinal reconstruction to the above knee popliteal artery using prosthetic: Is the vein really saved [abstract]? American Association of Vascular Surgery Plenary Session, Chicago, June 8-11, 2003.
13. Smeets L, Ho GH, Hagenaars T, et al: Remote endarterectomy: First choice in surgical treatment of long segmental SFA occlusive disease? Eur J Vasc Endovasc Surg 25:583-589, 2003.
14. Ouriel K, Smith CR, DeWeese JA: Endarterectomy for localized lesions of the superficial femoral artery at the adductor canal. J Vasc Surg 3:531-534, 1986.
15. Darling RC 3rd, Shah DM, Chang BB, et al: Retroperitoneal approach for bilateral renal and visceral artery revascularization. Am J Surg 168:148-151, 1994.
16. Management of peripheral arterial disease (PAD): TransAtlantic Inter-Society Consensus (TASC). Section B: Intermittent claudication. Eur J Vasc Endovasc Surg 19(Suppl A):S47-S114, 2000.
17. Dormandy JA, Rutherford RB: Management of peripheral arterial disease (PAD). TASC Working Group. TransAtlantic Inter-Society Consensus (TASC). J Vasc Surg 31:S1-S296, 2000.
18. Bandyk DF, Novotney ML, Back MR, et al: Expanded application of in situ replacement for prosthetic graft infection. J Vasc Surg 34:411-420, 2001.
19. Mazzariol F, Ascher E, Hingorani A, et al: Lower-extremity revascularisation without preoperative contrast arteriography in 185 cases: Lessons learned with duplex ultrasound arterial mapping. Eur J Vasc Endovasc Surg 19:509-515, 2000.
20. Paty PS, Darling RC 3rd, Lee D, et al: Is prosthetic renal artery reconstruction a durable procedure? An analysis of 489 bypass grafts. J Vasc Surg 34:127-132, 2001.
21. Shepard AD, Scott GR, Mackey WC, et al: Retroperitoneal approach to high-risk abdominal aortic aneurysms. Arch Surg 121:444-449, 1986.
22. Williams GM, Ricotta J, Zinner M, Burdick J: The extended retroperitoneal approach for treatment of extensive atherosclerosis of the aorta and renal vessels. Surgery 88:846-855, 1980.
23. Ascher E, Scheinman M, Mazzariol F, et al: Comparison between supra- and infrainguinal inflow sites for infrapopliteal PTFE bypasses with complementary arteriovenous fistula and vein interposition. Eur J Vasc Endovasc Surg 19:138-142, 2000.
24. Darling RC 3rd, Shah DM, Chang BB, et al: Can the deep femoral artery be used reliably as an inflow source for infrainguinal reconstruction? Long-term results in 563 procedures. J Vasc Surg 20:889-895, 1994.
25. Sicard GA, Reilly JM, Rubin BG, et al: Transabdominal versus retroperitoneal incision for abdominal aortic surgery: Report of a prospective randomized trial. J Vasc Surg 21:174-183, 1995.
26. Geroulakos G, Wright JG, Tober JC, et al: Use of the splenic and hepatic artery for renal revascularization in patients with atherosclerotic renal artery disease. Ann Vasc Surg 11:85-89, 1997.
27. Korner M, Baumgartner I, Do DD, et al: PTA of the subclavian and innominate arteries: Long-term results. Vasa 28:117-122, 1999.
28. Grego F, Frigatti P, Lepidi S, et al: Synchronous carotid endarterectomy and retrograde endovascular treatment of brachiocephalic or common carotid artery stenosis. Eur J Vasc Endovasc Surg 26:392-395, 2003.
29. Sullivan TM, Gray BH, Bacharach JM, et al: Angioplasty and primary stenting of the subclavian, innominate, and common carotid arteries in 83 patients. J Vasc Surg 28:1059-1065, 1998.

30. Brewster DC, Moncure AC, Darling RC, et al: Innominate artery lesions: Problems encountered and lessons learned. J Vasc Surg 2:99-112, 1985.
31. Abou-Zamzam AM Jr, Moneta GL, Edwards JM, et al: Extrathoracic arterial grafts performed for carotid artery occlusive disease not amenable to endarterectomy. Arch Surg 134:952-957, 1999.
32. Siskin G, Darling RC 3rd, Stainken B, et al: Combined use of iliac artery angioplasty and infrainguinal revascularization for treatment of multilevel atherosclerotic disease. Ann Vasc Surg 13:45-51, 1999.
33. Ellozy SH, Carroccio A, Minor M, et al: Challenges of endovascular tube graft repair of thoracic aortic aneurysm: Midterm follow-up and lessons learned. J Vasc Surg 38:676-683, 2003.

Chapter

42

Anatomy of Commonly Exposed Arteries

R. JAMES VALENTINE, MD
GARY G. WIND, MD

Vascular surgeons must become intimately acquainted with anatomy of the vascular tree before embarking on correction of vessel disease. This anatomy is complex and cannot be understood with a superficial overview. A thorough grasp of the anatomic relationships among arteries, veins, and their surrounding structures is fundamental to obtaining adequate operative exposure and avoiding complications. Inadvertent injury to adjacent structures, such as nerves, may be disastrous. Vascular surgeons must also be aware of common anatomic variations and congenital anomalies. Failure to recognize variant anatomy may result in a spectrum of problems ranging from incomplete repair to exsanguination.

The purpose of this chapter is to convey the regional anatomy of arteries that are commonly exposed by vascular surgeons. Developmental anatomy is described in Chapter 7. The continuity of the vascular tree is assumed, but the descriptions are organized by body regions in order to maintain clinical relevancy. A complete and detailed description of all aspects of vascular anatomy is beyond the scope of a single chapter, and the reader is referred to anatomic texts and atlases for study in greater depth.

■ EXTRACRANIAL CIRCULATION OF THE HEAD AND NECK

Fascial Layers of the Neck

The platysma muscle represents the superficial fascia in the neck, covering cutaneous nerves and superficial veins. The deep fascia consists of three specific layers:

1. The investing fascia, the most superficial layer of the deep fascia, extends from the posterior midline and splits to envelop the trapezius and sternocleidomastoid muscles.
2. The middle layer of the deep fascia is also known as the visceral or pretracheal fascia. It encloses the viscera and strap muscles in the central neck.
3. The prevertebral fascia is the deepest layer and covers the paraspinous muscles, the origins of the cervical nerves, the roots of the brachial plexus, and the subclavian artery. Lateral to the first rib, the prevertebral fascia extends to form the axillary sheath.

The deep fascial layers contribute to the aggregation of connective tissue known as the carotid sheath. This sheath is not a discrete fascial sheet. It is bounded by the visceral fascia medially, the prevertebral fascia posteriorly, and the sternocleidomastoid muscle anterolaterally. The contents of the carotid sheath are the carotid artery, the internal jugular vein, and the vagus nerve. The cervical sympathetic chain is embedded within the posterior fibers of the sheath, and the ansa cervicalis is located within the anterior fibers of the sheath.

Carotid Artery

The common carotid artery enters the base of the neck posterior to the sternoclavicular joint and ascends medial to the internal jugular vein. The carotid bifurcation is usually located at the level of the superior border of the thyroid cartilage, but the bifurcation may occur as high as the hyoid bone or as low as the cricoid cartilage. A high bifurcation, which is more common than a low bifurcation,[1] may prompt the surgeon to consider maneuvers such as mandibular subluxation to enhance exposure in the distal neck.[2] The carotid bifurcation is usually crossed anteriorly by the common facial vein, which must be divided in order to obtain exposure. Two small receptors lie intrinsic to the medial wall of the bifurcation: (1) a chemoreceptor known as the carotid body and (2) a baroreceptor known as the carotid sinus. Nerve twigs to the carotid body from the

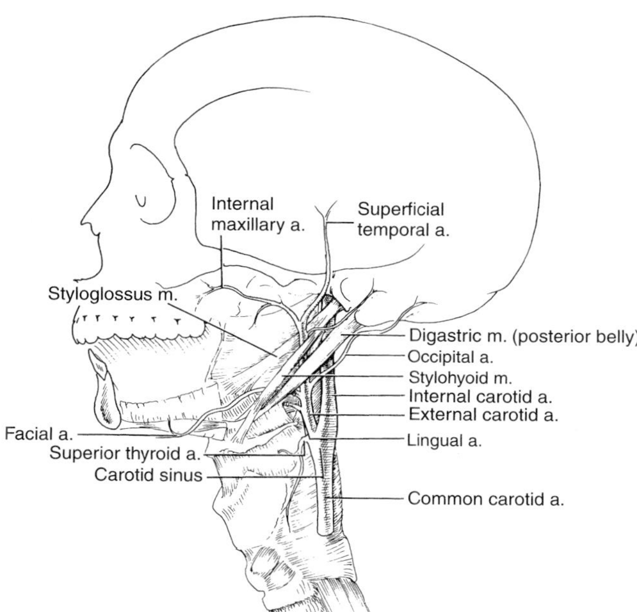

FIGURE 42-1 The relationship between the posterior suspensory muscles of the pharynx and the internal and external carotid arteries. (From Valentine RJ, Wind GG: Anatomic Exposures in Vascular Surgery, 2nd ed. Philadelphia, Lippincott Williams & Wilkins, 2003, p 34.)

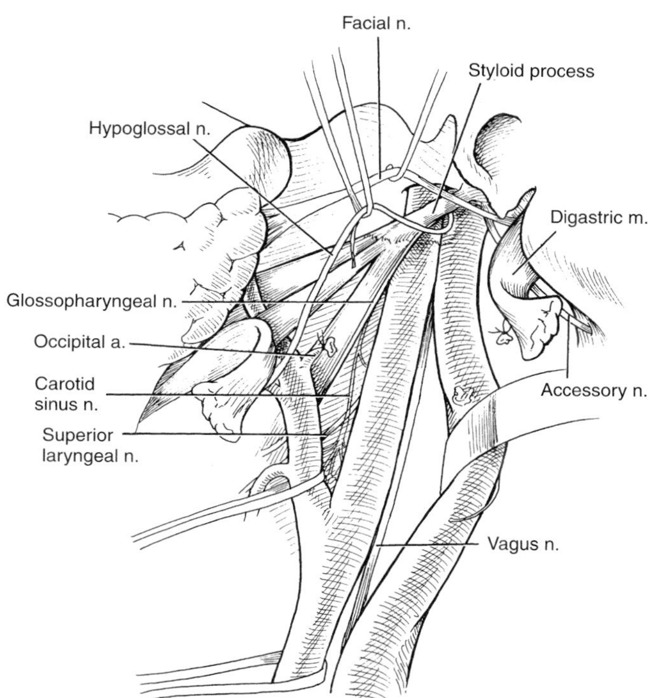

FIGURE 42-2 The internal carotid artery passes deep to the hypoglossal nerve, the occipital artery, and the posterior belly of the digastric muscle. The glossopharyngeal nerve is prone to injury during division of the styloid process. (From Valentine RJ, Wind GG: Anatomic Exposures in Vascular Surgery, 2nd ed. Philadelphia, Lippincott Williams & Wilkins, 2003, p 48.)

glossopharyngeal, vagus, and superior cervical sympathetic nerves lie between the internal and external carotid branches. The carotid sinus nerve arises from the baroreceptors at the carotid bifurcation and ascends between the internal and external carotid branches to join the glossopharyngeal nerve. Surgical manipulation of the carotid sinus nerve may cause reflex bradycardia and hypotension.

The external carotid artery supplies the extracranial structures of the head. It gives off several branches before its terminal bifurcation into the maxillary and superficial temporal arteries. These include the superior thyroid, ascending pharyngeal, lingual, facial, occipital, and posterior auricular arteries (Fig. 42-1).

The internal carotid artery ascends vertically in the neck to enter the carotid canal at the base of the skull just anterior to the jugular vein. In its distal ascent, the internal carotid is crossed laterally by pharyngeal tributaries of the internal jugular vein, the hypoglossal nerve, the occipital artery, and the posterior belly of the digastric muscle (Fig. 42-2). Venous tributaries should be carefully controlled and ligated to avoid troublesome bleeding during exposure of the internal carotid artery. The hypoglossal nerve can be carefully mobilized away from the artery. The sternocleidomastoid branch of the occipital artery tethers the hypoglossal nerve and should be divided to free the nerve completely. The occipital artery crosses the internal carotid artery at the inferior border of the digastric muscle. Division of the occipital artery and the digastric muscle allows exposure of the internal carotid artery to within 2 cm of the skull base. In its most distal cervical portion, the internal carotid artery passes deep to the styloid process and all associated structures to reach the base of the skull. Exposure of the highest segment of the cervical internal carotid artery is accomplished by dividing the stylohyoid ligament and the stylohyoid, stylopharyngeus, and styloglossus muscles to allow removal of the styloid process.[3]

A number of cranial nerves lie in proximity to the carotid artery and its branches. The facial nerve arises posterior to the base of the styloid process and passes anterolaterally to enter the parotid gland, where it is prone to injury during extreme distal exposure of the internal carotid artery. The marginal mandibular branch of the facial nerve, located deep to the platysma, emerges below the angle of the mandible and runs across the ramus of the mandible. It is subject to retractor injury during exposure of the carotid, causing a visible defect in the ipsilateral orbicularis oris muscle. The hypoglossal nerve descends from the hypoglossal canal and passes lateral to the internal and external carotid arteries before turning anteromedially toward the base of the tongue. Injury to the hypoglossal nerve causes paralysis of the ipsilateral tongue musculature and deviation of the tongue.

The accessory, glossopharyngeal, and vagus nerves exit the skull from the jugular foramen. The accessory nerve passes medial to the styloid process and passes obliquely to the upper fibers of the sternocleidomastoid muscle, then to the trapezius muscle. The glossopharyngeal nerve runs along the posterior edge of the stylopharyngeus muscle and passes superficial to the internal carotid artery. Loss of its sensory and motor fibers to the tongue and posterior pharynx result in severe complications from inability to swallow and chronic aspiration. The vagus nerve descends vertically in the neck between the jugular vein and the internal carotid artery superiorly and the common carotid artery inferiorly.

Table 42-1 Perioperative Cranial Nerve Injuries Documented in 1415 Surgical Subjects Participating in the North American Symptomatic Carotid Endarterectomy Trial

NERVE	CASES OF MILD INJURY*	CASES OF MODERATE INJURY**	TOTAL
Hypoglossal	50 (3.5%)	2 (0.2%)	52 (3.7%)
Vagus/recurrent laryngeal	31 (2.2%)	5 (0.4%)	36 (2.5%)
Facial	28 (2.0%)	3 (0.2%)	31 (2.2%)
Spinal accessory	3 (0.2%)	0	3 (0.2%)

*No delay in discharge; recovery documented in follow-up.
**Delay in discharge or documentation that deficit never recovered.

Adapted from Ferguson GG, Eliasziw M, Barr H, et al: The North American Symptomatic Carotid Endarterectomy Trial: Surgical results in 1415 patients. Stroke 30:1751, 1999.

The superior laryngeal nerve originates from the vagus nerve in the neck and runs posterior to the internal and external carotid branches to supply the upper larynx. The recurrent laryngeal nerve almost always branches from the vagus nerve within the mediastinum, loops around the subclavian artery on the right side or the ascending aorta on the left, and then ascends in the neck in the tracheo-esophageal groove. In rare cases, a nonrecurrent laryngeal nerve branches directly from the vagus nerve in the neck and crosses laterally to the carotid bifurcation, making it prone to injury during exposure of the carotid.[4] This anomaly is more common on the right side (0.6%) than on the left (0.04%); a right nonrecurrent laryngeal nerve may be associated with an aberrant right subclavian artery. Injury to either the vagus nerve or the recurrent laryngeal nerve produces hoarseness and loss of an effective cough mechanism as a result of ipsilateral vocal cord paralysis.

Careful examination of patients who have undergone carotid endarterectomy shows cranial nerve injury in 8% to 14% of cases.[5-7] Detailed examination by neurologists participating in the North American Symptomatic Carotid Endarterectomy Trial (NASCET) discovered cranial nerve injuries in 122 (8.6%) of 1415 patients who underwent carotid endarterectomy (Table 42-1).[7] Although the frequency of individual nerve injuries remains controversial, most investigators report that either the hypoglossal or the recurrent laryngeal nerve is the most commonly injured.[5-7] Fortunately, the majority of nerve injuries are transient.

Vertebral Artery

The vertebral arteries are located beneath the prevertebral fascia in the deep neck. In the proximal third, each artery ascends from its subclavian artery origin to the transverse process of the sixth cervical vertebra, which is known as the carotid tubercle or Chassaignac's tubercle. In this extraosseous course, the arteries bisect an angle formed by the anterior scalene and longus colli muscles. Under the hood of the inverted V formed by these muscles, the vertebral arteries penetrate the prevertebral fascia and enter the transverse process of C6 (Fig. 42-3). The phrenic nerves lie on the ventral surfaces of the anterior scalene muscles and are subject to injury during exposure of the vertebral arteries. The distal two thirds of the extracranial vertebral arteries lie within the bony canal formed by the transverse processes of C1 through C6. In this canal, the arteries cross anterior to the roots of the cervical nerves (Fig. 42-4). Extensive venous tributaries accompany the arteries within the canal, making exposure of the interosseous segment somewhat treacherous. In order to reduce the risk of venous injury, the surgeon should control the vertebral artery by entering the bony canal rather than attempting to isolate the artery between the transverse processes.[8] After exiting the transverse processes of the atlas, the arteries enter the cranium through the foramen magnum and converge to form the basilar artery at the lower border of the pons.

The paired anatomic arrangement of the vertebral arteries provides a well-collateralized circulation to the posterior brain. However, developmental variation may limit collateral flow in some individuals. Hypoplastic vertebral arteries occur in approximately 15% of people, more commonly on the right side.[9] In the intracranial portion, the arteries do not unite 5% of the time: The vertebral artery terminates as a posterocerebellar artery on the right in 3.1% of cases, and on the left in 1.8%.[9]

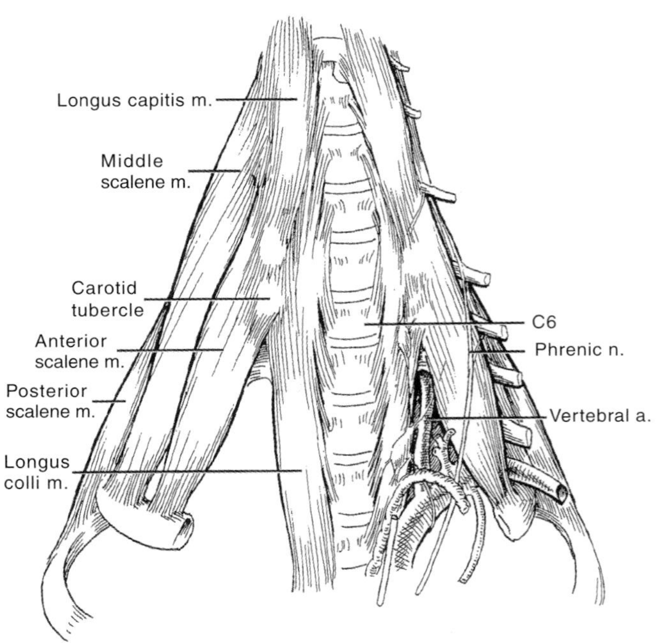

FIGURE 42-3 The vertebral arteries bisect an angle formed by the longus colli and anterior scalene muscles. (From Valentine RJ, Wind GG: Anatomic Exposures in Vascular Surgery, 2nd ed. Philadelphia, Lippincott Williams & Wilkins, 2003, p 51.)

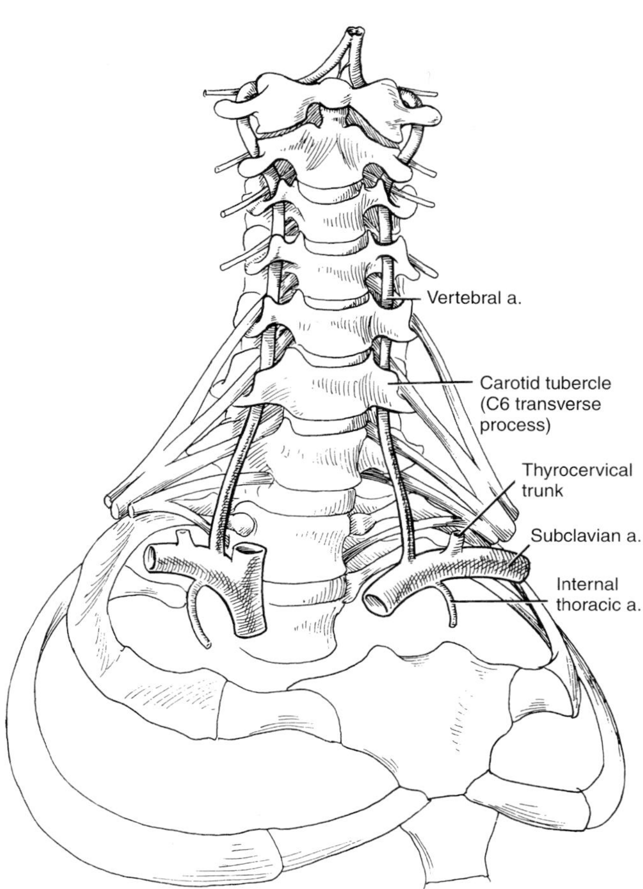

FIGURE 42-4 The vertebral arteries enter the bony canal formed by the transverse processes at the level of C6. (From Valentine RJ, Wind GG: Anatomic Exposures in Vascular Surgery, 2nd ed. Philadelphia, Lippincott Williams & Wilkins, 2003, p 52.)

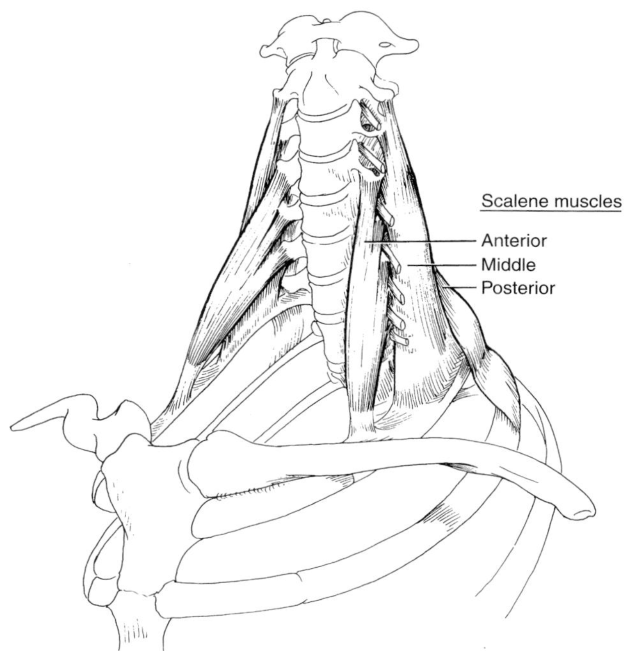

FIGURE 42-5 Two scalene muscles insert onto the first rib. The subclavian vein lies anterior to the anterior scalene muscle, and the subclavian artery lies between the anterior and middle scalene muscles. (From Valentine RJ, Wind GG: Anatomic Exposures in Vascular Surgery, 2nd ed. Philadelphia, Lippincott Williams & Wilkins, 2003, p 115.)

■ VESSELS OF THE THORACIC OUTLET AND SHOULDER

Anatomy of the Thoracic Outlet

The thoracic outlet is bounded by the bony structures of the superior thorax, which comprise the spinal column, first ribs, and sternum. Immediately adjacent to the thoracic outlet, the clavicles arch over the medial portions of the first ribs and articulate with the manubrium. Two scalene muscles originate from the vertebral column and insert on the first ribs (Fig. 42-5). The anterior scalene muscles originate from the transverse processes of C3-C6 and insert on the inner borders and superior surfaces of the first ribs, just anterior to the grooves for the subclavian arteries. The middle scalene muscles arise from the transverse processes of the lower six cervical vertebrae and insert broadly on the posterior aspects of the first ribs. Coursing ventral to the anterior scalene muscles, the subclavian veins constitute the most anterior vascular structures of the superior aperture. The subclavian arteries and the roots of the brachial plexus emerge between the anterior and middle scalene muscles. The entire neurovascular bundle traverses the costoclavicular passage underneath the middle third of the respective clavicle to reach the axillary space.

A number of developmental anomalies have been associated with neurovascular compression syndromes in the thoracic outlet. In a study of 200 transaxillary surgical procedures performed in 175 patients with symptoms of thoracic outlet compression, Makhoul and Machleder[10] recognized nontraumatic causes in 66%; the distribution of thoracic outlet anomalies in their study is shown in Table 42-2. The most common reported anomalies are related to ligamentous and muscular attachments that insert on the first rib, prompting the rationale for first rib resection to treat all causes of thoracic outlet compression.[11]

Table 42-2 Anomalies of the Thoracic Outlet Found in 200 Transaxillary Surgical Procedures Performed for Neurovascular Compression Syndromes

ABNORMALITY	NO. OF CASES
None found	68 (34%)
Anomaly of scalene muscle	86 (43%)
Anomaly of subclavius tendon	39 (19.5%)
Scalenus minimus abnormality	20 (10%)
Cervical rib	17 (8.5%)
Fibrous structures or ligamentous abnormalities	15 (7.5%)
Total	200

Adapted from Makhoul RG, Machleder HI: Developmental anomalies at the thoracic outlet: An analysis of 200 consecutive cases. J Vasc Surg 16:534, 1992.

Cervical ribs are reported to occur in approximately 1% of the normal population, and they are bilateral 50% of the time.[11,12] Only 5% to 10% of patients with cervical ribs have symptoms of thoracic outlet compression.[13] Although the majority of cervical ribs are rudimentary or incomplete, most have ligamentous attachments to the first rib. Cervical ribs are most commonly embedded in the fibers of the middle scalene muscle and displace both the subclavian artery and the brachial plexus.

Subclavian Artery

The subclavian arteries ascend in the mediastinum and course over the first ribs behind the anterior scalene muscles. The right subclavian artery originates most frequently from the brachiocephalic artery, and the left subclavian artery originates as the third branch of the aortic arch. In approximately 1% of the population, the right subclavian artery originates on the left side of the mediastinum as the most distal branch of the aortic arch (Fig. 42-6).[14] Proximal vascular control of the right subclavian artery in its normal position can be obtained via median sternotomy. The trajectory of the aortic arch renders the left subclavian too far posterior to be accessible through a median sternotomy approach; proximal vascular control is best obtained through a lateral thoracotomy. Direct exposure of the more distal subclavian arteries can be obtained through supraclavicular incisions.

The branches of the subclavian artery are the vertebral, internal thoracic, thyrocervical, costocervical, and dorsal scapular arteries:

1. The vertebral arteries arise from the superoposterior aspect of the subclavian arteries proximal to the medial border of the anterior scalene muscles.
2. The internal thoracic arteries arise opposite the vertebral arteries, on the inferior border of the subclavian arteries.
3. The short, wide thyrocervical trunks originate from the subclavian arteries near the medial border of the anterior scalene muscles and branch immediately into the inferior thyroid, superficial cervical, and suprascapular branches.
4. Costocervical trunk and dorsal scapular artery branches arise from the posterior aspect of both subclavian arteries as they course behind the anterior scalene muscles.

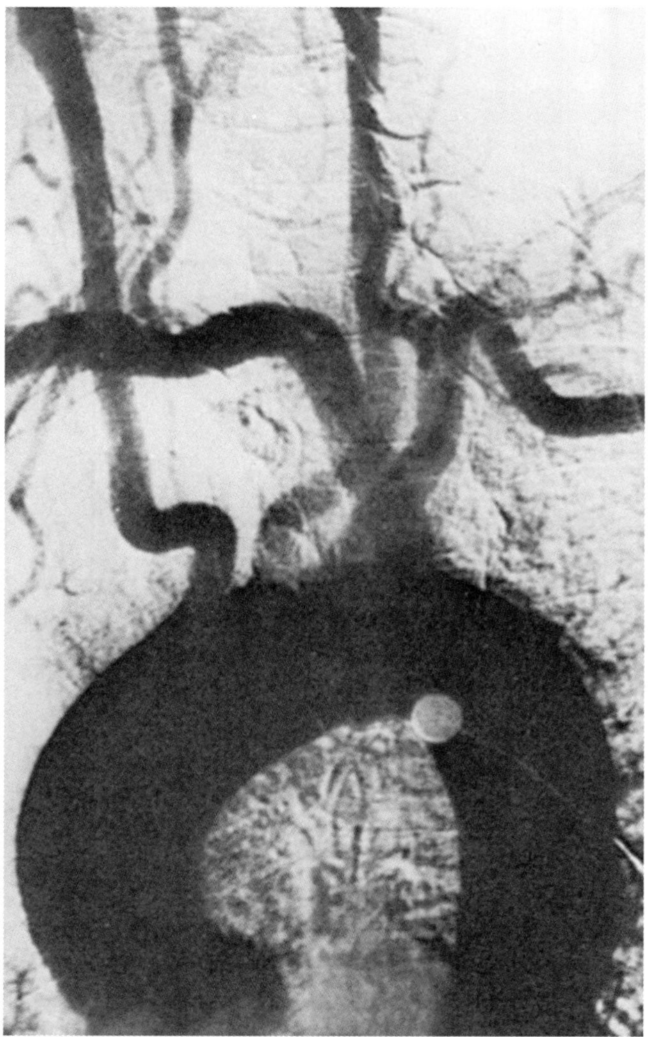

FIGURE 42-6 Arteriogram demonstrating an aberrant right subclavian artery originating as the most distal branch of the aortic arch. (From Valentine RJ, Carter DJ, Clagett GP: A modified extrathoracic approach to the treatment of dysphagia lusoria. J Vasc Surg 5:498, 1987, with permission from the Society for Vascular Surgery and the American Association for Vascular Surgery.)

A number of surrounding structures are prone to injury during subclavian artery exposure. The subclavian veins cross ventral to the anterior scalene muscles; large venous tributaries should be carefully ligated during arterial exposure to prevent troublesome bleeding. On the left side, the thoracic duct arches over the subclavian artery to reach the posterior aspect of the subclavian-jugular vein confluence. To prevent chylous leak, the surgeon should identify and ligate this duct. The vagus and phrenic nerves also lie adjacent to the subclavian arteries and must be protected during arterial exposure. The right vagus nerve descends lateral to the right common carotid artery and crosses anterior to the right subclavian artery near its origin. After looping around the inferior border of the subclavian artery, the recurrent laryngeal branch of the right vagus nerve ascends into the neck in the tracheoesophageal groove. The left vagus nerve descends on the lateral border of the left common carotid artery, crosses anterior to the aortic arch, and loops under the arch to ascend posterior to the aorta. The phrenic nerves descend from the neck on the anteromedial surface of the anterior scalene muscles. After crossing anterior to the subclavian arteries, the nerves enter the thorax by passing anteromedial to the internal thoracic arteries. Injury to a phrenic nerve at the time of subclavian artery exposure is most likely to occur during division of the anterior scalene muscle.

Axillary Artery

The lateral border of the first rib is the anatomic boundary marking the transition between the subclavian and axillary

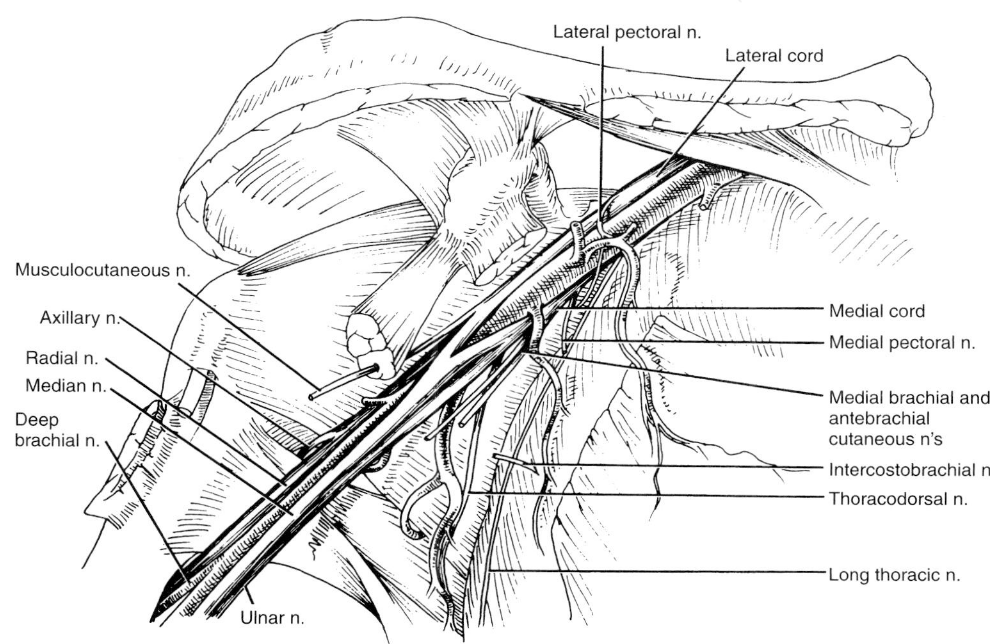

FIGURE 42-7 Divisions and cords of the brachial plexus surround the axillary artery as it emerges beneath the costoclavicular passage. The brachial plexus evolves into its final nerve form at the artery's distal third. (From Valentine RJ, Wind GG: Anatomic Exposures in Vascular Surgery, 2nd ed. Philadelphia, Lippincott Williams & Wilkins, 2003, p 158.)

arteries. There the artery is joined by divisions and cords of the brachial plexus (Fig. 42-7). The lateral, posterior, and medial cords of the brachial plexus surround the axillary artery as it emerges from beneath the costoclavicular passage. These neural structures exchange fibers around the artery as the neurovascular bundle courses through the axilla under the pectoralis minor muscle, evolving into their final nerve form at the artery's distal third. Throughout their course, the axillary artery and accompanying neural structures are covered by a thin fascia known as the axillary sheath, which is separated from the axillary vein by a fat pad. The distal extent of the axillary artery is marked by the lateral edge of the teres major muscle.

The axillary artery is divided into three anatomic sections as follows:

- The first part extends from the lateral border of the first rib to the medial border of the pectoralis minor.
- The second part is that portion behind the pectoralis minor muscle.
- The third part extends beyond the muscle's lateral border.

The first part of the axillary artery is the simplest to expose because it is medial to the pectoralis muscle and has only one branch, the supreme thoracic artery. Two branches arise from the second part, the thoracoacromial artery and the lateral thoracic artery. Exposure of the second part requires division of the pectoralis minor muscle, risking injury to the medial and lateral pectoral nerves.[15] These nerves are important because they innervate the large pectoralis major muscle, and injury may result in significant cosmetic and functional chest wall defects.

The third part of the axillary artery gives origin to three branches: the subscapular artery, the medial humeral circumflex artery, and the lateral humeral circumflex artery. At this level, the brachial plexus has assumed the final configuration of nerves to the arm. Relative to the axillary artery, the median nerve is located anterior, the radial nerve is posterior, and the ulnar nerve is inferior within the axillary sheath.

■ ARTERIES OF THE ABDOMEN AND PELVIS

Supraceliac Aorta

The aorta enters the abdomen behind the diaphragm at the level of the lower border of the 12th thoracic vertebra. It is crossed ventrally by the converging diaphragmatic crura at a site known as the median arcuate ligament, deep to the esophagogastric junction. Limited exposure of the aortic segment above the celiac axis can be gained through the lesser sac by dividing the fibers of the median arcuate ligament.[16] This area is usually free of plaque disease and is an excellent alternative site for placement of a proximal anastomosis during bypass construction.[17] In order to gain adequate length of aorta to accommodate vascular clamps, the surgeon should divide the median arcuate ligament and the diaphragmatic crura as far proximally as possible.

The proximal abdominal aorta is surrounded by a number of visceral and vascular structures. The esophagus enters the abdomen through an opening at the level of the 10th thoracic vertebra, a little to the left and in front of the aortic opening. The cisterna chyli is located on the right posterolateral surface of the aorta, and the connecting thoracic duct ascends into the chest through the aortic aperture in the same plane. More laterally, the inferior vena cava and caudate lobe of the liver limit access to the supraceliac aorta from the right side. Because this aortic segment is covered only by the diaphragmatic crus on the left side, easy access can be obtained through a left retroperitoneal approach.[18]

Visceral Aorta and Mesenteric Arteries

The closely spaced and ventrally located visceral arteries prevent ready access to this segment of the abdominal aorta from an anterior approach (Fig. 42-8). The celiac trunk is framed by the median arcuate ligament superiorly and by the superior border of the pancreas inferiorly. It arises directly from the ventral surface of the aorta and is surrounded by tough lymphatic and nerve plexuses. Following a short anterior course, the celiac trunk divides into main arterial branches supplying the circulation of the foregut.

Most commonly, three branches emanate from a trifurcation: the common hepatic artery, the splenic artery, and the left gastric artery. These branches lie deep to the retroperitoneum of the lesser sac. The common hepatic artery passes to the right and enters the hepatoduodenal ligament immediately above the pylorus. The splenic artery passes to the left and follows a serpentine course along the superior border of the pancreas to give off numerous pancreatic and short gastric branches before terminating at the spleen. The right and left gastroepiploic arteries connect the splenic and hepatic circulations, forming a collateral circulation that preserves arterial flow to the spleen when the splenic artery is ligated medial to the left gastroepiploic artery (Fig. 42-9). The left gastric artery ascends beneath the peritoneum to reach the lesser curvature of the stomach.

The origin of the superior mesenteric artery forms a sharp caudal angle with the anterior surface of the aorta. Lying within this angle are the left renal vein, the uncinate process of the pancreas, and the third portion of the duodenum. The proximal part of the superior mesenteric artery is crossed by the neck of the pancreas, and the superior mesenteric vein lies on the right side of the artery at the inferior border of the pancreatic neck. These two structures course over the uncinate process and third portion of the duodenum to run side by side in the small bowel mesentery. The superior mesenteric artery supplies the intestine from the second part of the duodenum to the midtransverse colon.

The renal arteries arise laterally from the aorta between 2 cm above and below the L1-L2 disk space. Single renal arteries are present in 70% of individuals.[19] Two hilar vessels occur in approximately 25%, and three hilar vessels occur in approximately 3%. Among patients with single renal arteries, the left is usually slightly more cephalad than the right. The left renal vein crosses anterior to the aorta in 96% of individuals[20] and is considered a reliable marker for locating the left renal artery. In a study of 57 postmortem subjects, the left renal artery was located directly behind the left renal vein in 52%, below (caudal to) the left renal vein in 14%, and above (cephalad to) the left renal vein in 34%.[21] The right renal artery crosses posterior to the inferior vena cava and is usually located directly behind the right renal vein. Both renal veins may receive a lumbar venous tributary, which should be ligated during mobilization to avoid hemorrhage. In addition, the left renal vein receives the left adrenal and gonadal veins.

The inferior mesenteric artery arises on the anterior surface of the aorta approximately 3 to 4 cm above the aortic bifurcation. It is closely applied to the aorta as it courses inferiorly and to the left into the mesentery of the left colon. The inferior mesenteric artery supplies the left third of the transverse colon, the descending and sigmoid colon, and most of the rectum.

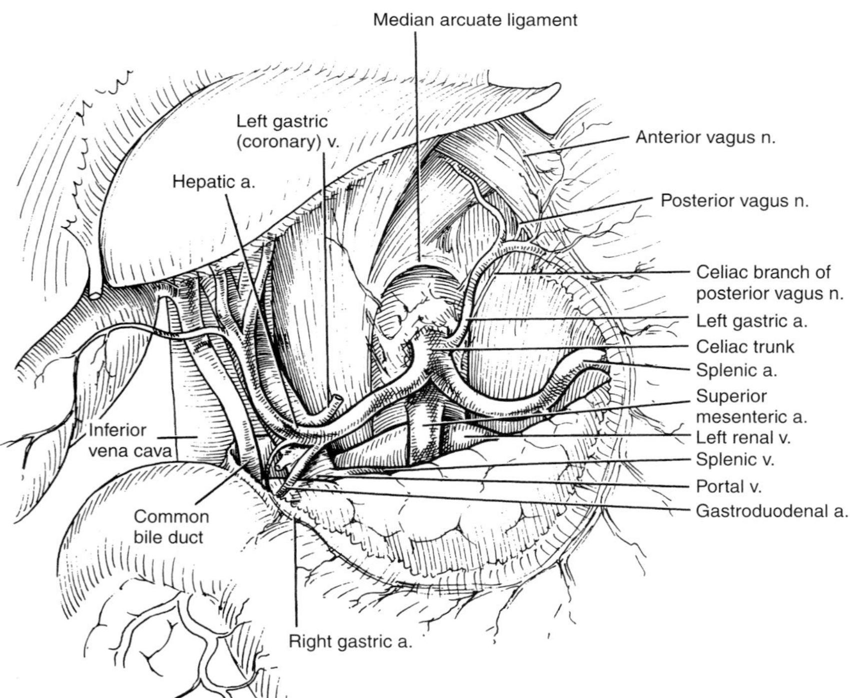

FIGURE 42-8 The celiac trunk and superior mesenteric artery lie deep to the posterior peritoneum of the omental bursa. (From Valentine RJ, Wind GG: Anatomic Exposures in Vascular Surgery, 2nd ed. Philadelphia, Lippincott Williams & Wilkins, 2003, p 268.)

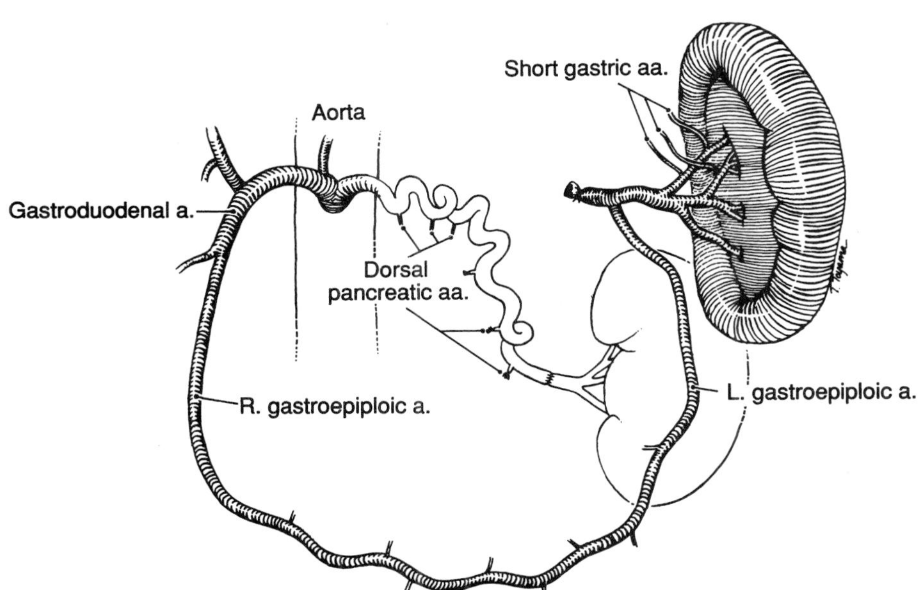

FIGURE 42-9 Collateral circulation to the spleen after splenorenal bypass. (From Valentine RJ, Rossi MB, Myers SI, Clagett GP: Splenic infarction after splenorenal bypass. J Vasc Surg 17:602, 1993, with permission from the Society for Vascular Surgery and the American Association for Vascular Surgery.)

Collateral Mesenteric Circulation

The three major arteries of the mesenteric circulation are interconnected by a network of branches that form a rich collateral circulation in the event of segmental occlusion.[22] Arising as the second branch of the common hepatic artery, the gastroduodenal artery gives off a retroduodenal branch, which continues as the posterior superior pancreaticoduodenal artery. The gastroduodenal artery then divides into the anterior superior pancreaticoduodenal and right gastroepiploic arteries. The anterior and posterior superior branches anastomose with corresponding branches arising from the superior mesenteric artery. The inferior pancreaticoduodenal vessels arise either separately or as a single trunk from the superior mesenteric artery as it emerges near the inferior border of the pancreas. This collateral network between the celiac axis and superior mesenteric artery is known as the pancreaticoduodenal arcade (Fig. 42-10).

A variable collateral circulation between the superior and inferior mesenteric arteries is located in the mesentery of the left colon. The middle colic artery arises as the second branch of the superior mesenteric artery and enters the transverse mesocolon. The left branch of the middle colic artery continues adjacent to the left colon and is usually continuous with the marginal artery, also known as the artery of Drummond. The ascending branch of the left colic artery, a branch of the inferior mesenteric artery, is also usually continuous with the marginal artery and completes the anastomotic network (Fig. 42-11). Normally present medial anastomotic channels between the superior and inferior mesenteric circulations can enlarge into a major vessel in the presence of major trunk narrowing. This potential connection (the arc of Riolan) may prevent colon necrosis in individuals with incomplete marginal arteries.[23] It is formed by an early branch of the left colic artery that ascends directly to join the left branch of the middle colic artery. Known also as the meandering mesenteric artery, this collateral may enlarge and become tortuous within the mesentery of the left colon in individuals with occlusion of either the inferior or superior mesenteric arteries (Fig. 42-12).

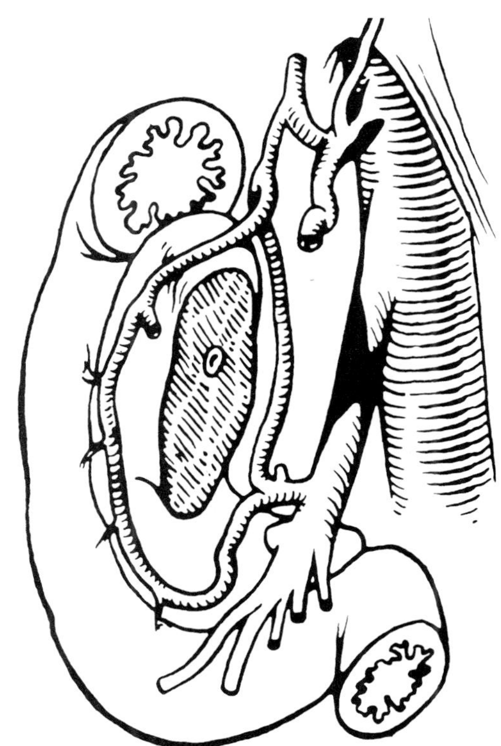

FIGURE 42-10 The pancreaticoduodenal arcade as viewed from a sagittal perspective. This network provides collateral blood flow between the celiac axis and superior mesenteric artery circulations when one or the other is occluded. (From Fisher DF Jr, Fry WJ: Collateral mesenteric circulation. Surg Gynecol Obstet 164: 487, 1987. By permission of Journal of the American College of Surgeons.)

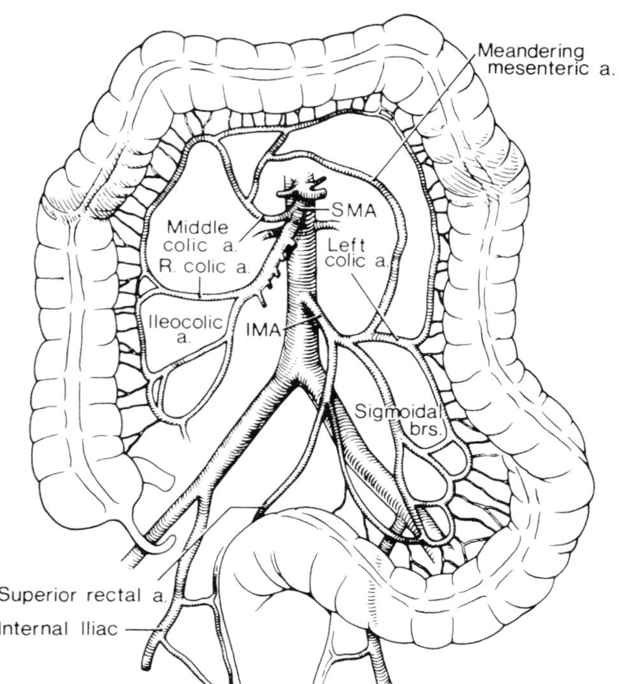

FIGURE 42-11 Arterial circulation of the mesentery. Note the medial anastomotic channels between the superior and inferior mesenteric arteries (SMA and IMA), which may enlarge to become the meandering mesenteric artery in chronic ischemic states. (From Fisher DF Jr, Fry WJ: Collateral mesenteric circulation. Surg Gynecol Obstet 164:487, 1987. By permission of Journal of the American College of Surgeons.)

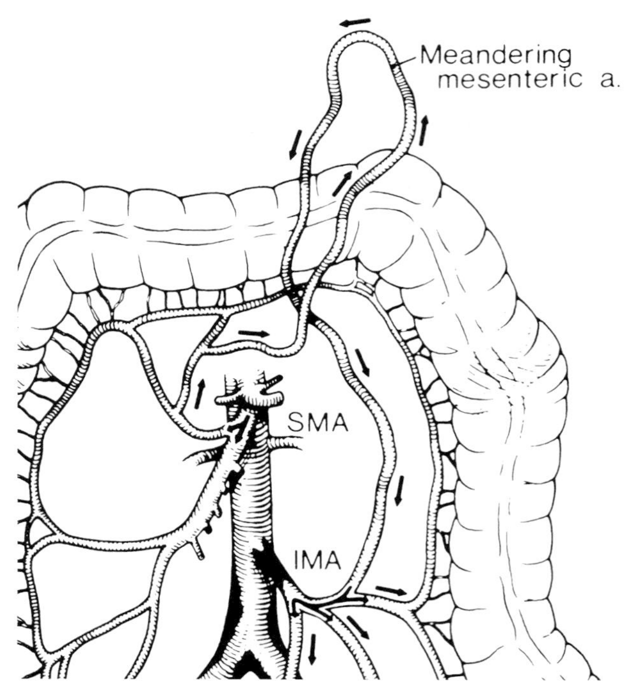

FIGURE 42-12 Chronic ischemia may result in enlargement and tortuosity of the medial anastomotic channel. This channel serves as an important collateral between the superior (SMA) and inferior (IMA) mesenteric arterial circulations. (From Fisher DF Jr, Fry WJ: Collateral mesenteric circulation. Surg Gynecol Obstet 164:487, 1987. By permission of Journal of the American College of Surgeons.)

Infrarenal Aorta and Iliac Arteries

The distal abdominal aorta below the renal arteries lies slightly to the left of midline and immediately anterior to the vertebral bodies of L1 through L4. The third and fourth portions of the duodenum overlie the aorta and must be reflected to the patient's right side during exposure of the aorta. The surgeon can gain more proximal exposure near the renal arteries by dividing the ligament of Treitz. Anteriorly, the aorta is covered by lymphatic tissue, which should be ligated to prevent chylous leak.[24] Paired lumbar arteries originate from the posterolateral aortic wall and wrap around the vertebral bodies, dividing into branches supplying the dorsal abdominal wall and spine. A variable plexus of segmental lumbar veins lie between the dorsal surface of the aorta and the anterior surface of the vertebral bodies. These friable venous structures are easily torn and must be carefully avoided during maneuvers to encircle the aorta. A retroaortic left renal vein exists in up to 2.5% of individuals[20] and is also subject to injury during aortic mobilization. Anomalies of the inferior vena cava may also create technical difficulties during aortic exposure (Table 42-3).

The aorta bifurcates at the level of the fourth lumbar vertebra into right and left common iliac arteries. The right common iliac artery crosses anterior to the confluence of the common iliac veins at the inferior vena cava. The right common iliac vein courses posterior to the right common iliac artery, and the left common iliac vein courses deep to the inferior surface of the left common iliac artery (Fig. 42-13). The aortic bifurcation is separated from the fourth vertebra by the left common iliac vein. Adhesions commonly form between the bifurcations of the aorta and vena cava, making manipulation or separation of these structures extremely hazardous. The common iliac arteries

Table 42-3 Anomalies of the Inferior Vena Cava (IVC) and Left Renal Vein (LRV)

ANOMALY	INCIDENCE (%)	LOCATION
Duplication of IVC	0.2-3.0	Large veins run on both sides of aorta, joining anteriorly at level of renal arteries
Left-sided IVC	0.2-0.5	Left-sided IVC crosses anterior to aorta at level of renal arteries, then courses on right side of aorta
Absence of IVC	Very rare	Veins from lower extremity drain toward diaphragm via ascending lumbar and azygous veins
Retroaortic LRV	1.2-2.4	LRV posterior to aorta
Circumaortic LRV	1.5-8.7	Venous collar around aorta

Adapted from Trout HH, Giordano JM: Anomalies of the inferior vena cava. J Vasc Surg 3:924, 1986.

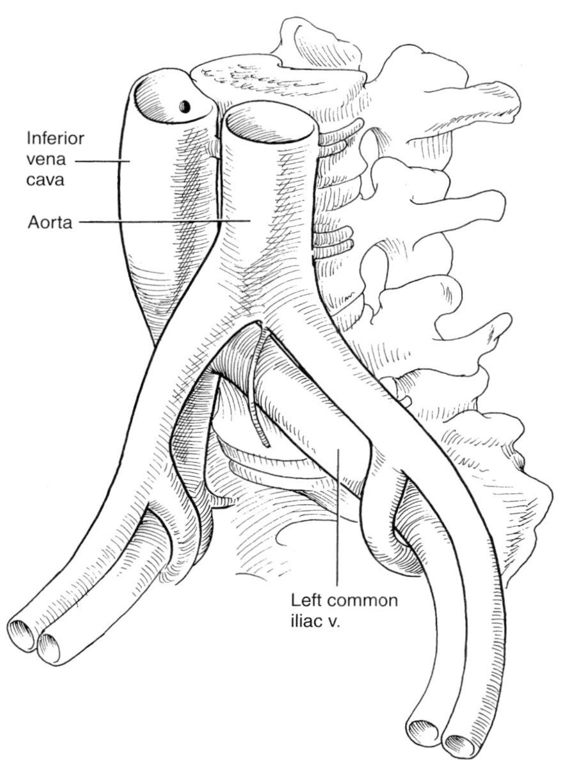

FIGURE 42-13 The aortic bifurcation overrides the bifurcation of the vena cava. (From Valentine RJ, Wind GG: Anatomic Exposures in Vascular Surgery, 2nd ed. Philadelphia, Lippincott Williams & Wilkins, 2003, p 311.)

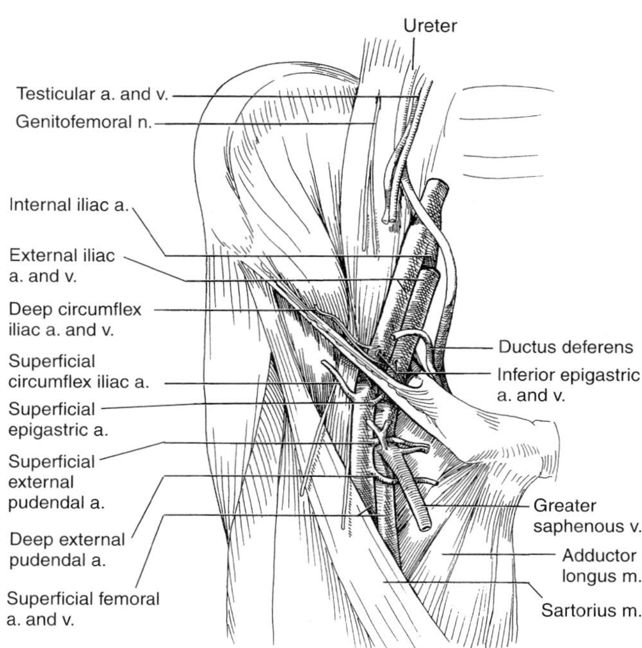

FIGURE 42-14 After passing beneath the inguinal ligament, the femoral vessels course within Scarpa's triangle. Note the relationship of the other retroperitoneal structures to the vessels. (From Valentine RJ, Wind GG: Anatomic Exposures in Vascular Surgery, 2nd ed. Philadelphia, Lippincott Williams & Wilkins, 2003, p 378.)

give small branches to the psoas major muscle and adjacent nerves. These branches should be ligated at the time of iliac artery mobilization.

The common iliac arteries bifurcate at the lip of the true pelvis. Crossing on the ventral surface of the iliac bifurcation, the gonadal vessels and ureters enter the pelvis on the anterior surface of the internal iliac arteries. The external iliac arteries pass obliquely along the pelvic brim medial to the psoas muscles, giving off inferior epigastric and deep circumflex iliac branches near the inguinal ligament. The external iliac veins lie medial and deep to the corresponding arteries.

Each internal iliac artery branches into anterior and posterior trunks. Branches of the anterior trunk are (1) the superior and inferior vesical arteries, (2) the middle rectal artery, (3) the obturator artery, (4) the internal pudendal artery, and (5) the inferior gluteal artery. The posterior trunk branches are (1) the iliolumbar artery, (2) the lateral sacral artery, and (3) the superior gluteal artery.

■ ARTERIES OF THE LEG

Femoral Arteries

The inguinal ligament marks the boundary between the external iliac and common femoral artery. A fibrous covering, known as the femoral sheath, wraps around the common femoral artery and vein, which are separated within the sheath by a well-developed septum. The femoral sheath is perforated by the saphenous vein on the medial aspect. The femoral vessels course within a triangular space defined by muscular boundaries known as Scarpa's triangle. This space is bounded on the lateral side by the sartorius muscle, on the medial side by the adductor longus muscle, and on the superior side by the inguinal ligament (Fig. 42-14). Within the triangle, the common femoral vein is located medially, the femoral nerve is located laterally, and the common femoral artery is located in between.

Several branches of the common femoral artery may be encountered during dissection near the inguinal ligament, including the superficial epigastric artery, the superficial circumflex iliac artery, and the superficial external pudendal artery. The deep external pudendal branch arises medially and crosses under the saphenous vein near the saphenofemoral junction. The saphenous vein enters Scarpa's triangle through a medial opening in the fascia lata known as the fossa ovalis. One group of superficial lymph nodes lies directly over the fossa ovalis. Another group of superficial inguinal lymph nodes lies more cephalad in the path of an anterior groin incision to the femoral artery. Ligation of all lymphatics associated with superficial lymph nodes at the time of arterial exposure reduces the risk of a postoperative lymphocele.[25]

The common femoral artery divides into the deep (profunda) and superficial femoral arteries approximately 4 cm distal to the inguinal ligament. Originating on the lateral side of the parent vessel, the deep femoral artery courses posterior to the superficial femoral artery and vein on the medial side of the femur. Near its origin, the deep femoral

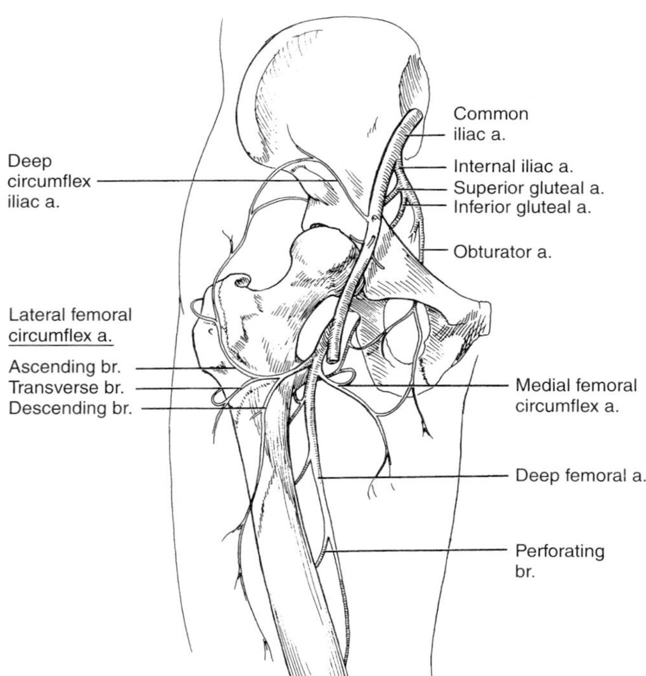

FIGURE 42-15 The deep femoral artery contributes to a rich collateral circulation around the hip joint and proximal femur. (From Valentine RJ, Wind GG: Anatomic Exposures in Vascular Surgery, 2nd ed. Philadelphia, Lippincott Williams & Wilkins, 2003, p 389.)

artery is crossed by the lateral femoral circumflex vein, which can be injured during dissection in the "crotch" formed by the origins of the deep and superficial femoral arteries. Early in its course, the deep femoral artery gives medial and lateral femoral circumflex branches (Fig. 42-15). The descending branch of the lateral femoral circumflex artery anastomoses with genicular branches at the knee, providing an important source of collateral blood flow when the superficial femoral artery is occluded. The medial femoral circumflex artery supplies the proximal adductor compartment.

In approximately 20% of cases, the medial or lateral femoral circumflex artery originates directly from the common femoral artery and may be a cause of significant backbleeding from an opened, cross-clamped femoral artery. In its continuation, the deep femoral artery enters the plane posterior to the adductor longus muscle, sending four perforating branches through the adductor magnus along its tendinous insertion to the linea aspera of the femur. These perforators anastomose with each other and provide blood supply to the muscles of the flexor compartment. The second perforator provides a nutrient artery to the femur, and the fourth perforator is the termination of the deep femoral artery.

The superficial femoral artery is the direct continuation of the common femoral artery beyond the deep femoral branch. It enters the aponeurotic tunnel in the thigh known as the adductor (Hunter's) canal at the apex of Scarpa's triangle. This tunnel is bounded by the vastus medialis on the anterolateral surface, by the adductor longus on the posterior surface, and by a strong aponeurosis between the adductors and the vastus medialis on the anteromedial surface. Coursing within the canal are the superficial femoral artery and vein, the saphenous nerve, and the nerve to the vastus medialis. The vessels give off a number of variably sized muscular branches, which should be preserved for their potential as collateral vessels during exposure within the adductor canal. The saphenous nerve leaves the canal at the adductor hiatus to course with the saphenous vein to the medial ankle and foot.

Popliteal Artery

The anatomic boundary separating the superficial femoral and popliteal artery is the adductor hiatus. From this opening in the adductor magnus, the popliteal artery courses distally between the femoral condyles and passes deep to the soleus muscle, where the artery soon gives off an anterior tibial branch. A number of muscular and genicular branches arise from the popliteal artery as it passes through the popliteal fossa. The sural arteries arise at the level of the knee joint and supply the gastrocnemius, soleus, and plantaris muscles. The paired superior, middle, and inferior genicular arteries form a rich collateral anastomosis around the knee.

The popliteal artery is separated from the posterior surface of the femur by a fat pad.

The popliteal vein courses around the artery, so that the vein lies posterolateral to the artery at the adductor hiatus, dorsal to the artery between the heads of the gastrocnemius muscle, and medial to the artery in its distal extent. The small saphenous vein joins the popliteal vein in the popliteal fossa between 3 and 7.5 cm above the knee joint.[26] The tibial nerve enters the popliteal fossa between the semimembranosus and biceps femoris muscles. It lies on the lateral aspect of the popliteal vessels at the level of the knee joint, then crosses the vessels posteriorly to become the most superficial midline structure encountered during posterior exposure of the popliteal artery. The peroneal nerve branch follows the medial border of the biceps femoris tendon toward the fibular head (Fig. 42-16).

Infrapopliteal Arteries

The popliteal artery divides into two separate bifurcations below the knee. The term "trifurcation" is a misnomer because the popliteal artery trunk divides into three separate branches in only 0.4% of cases.[27] The artery first bifurcates into anterior tibial and tibioperoneal branches between 3 and 7 cm below the knee joint. The second bifurcation occurs between 2 and 3 cm more distally, where the tibioperoneal trunk divides into posterior tibial and peroneal branches.

The anterior tibial artery passes anterolaterally and leaves the deep posterior fascial compartment through an opening in the interosseous membrane on the medial side of the fibular neck. The artery enters the anterior compartment between the tibialis anterior and extensor digitorum longus muscles (Fig. 42-17). It is joined early by the deep peroneal nerve, which enters the anterior compartment after winding around the lateral aspect of the fibular head. The neurovascular structures pass through the entire anterior compartment, coursing behind the extensor hallucis longus muscle in their distal extent to reach the dorsum of the foot.

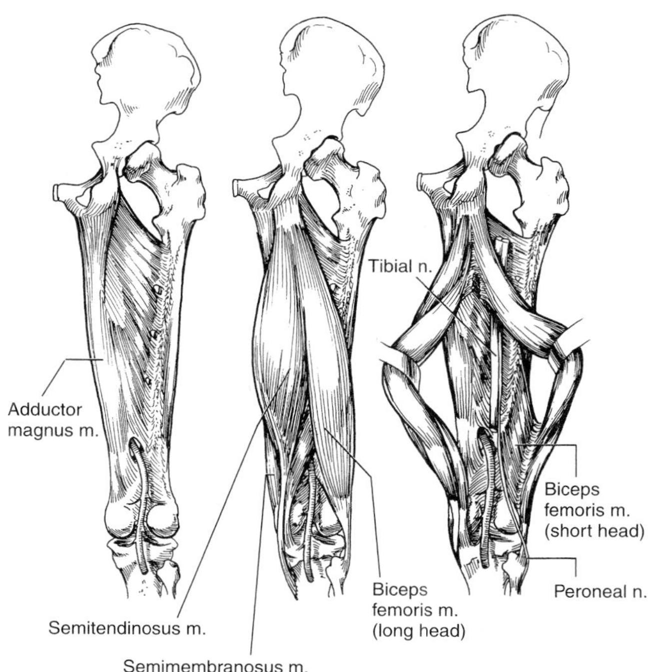

FIGURE 42-16 The peroneal nerve branch of the tibial nerve follows the medial border of the biceps femoris tendon and courses toward the fibular head. (From Valentine RJ, Wind GG: Anatomic Exposures in Vascular Surgery, 2nd ed. Philadelphia, Lippincott Williams & Wilkins, 2003, p 436.)

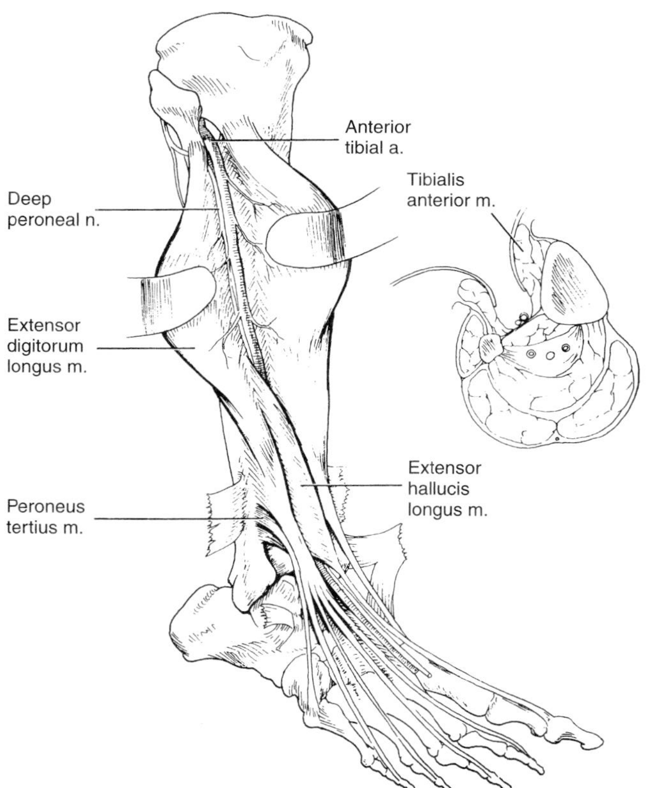

FIGURE 42-17 The anterior tibial artery and deep peroneal nerve lie between the extensor digitorum longus and tibialis anterior muscles in the anterior compartment. (From Valentine RJ, Wind GG: Anatomic Exposures in Vascular Surgery, 2nd ed. Philadelphia, Lippincott Williams & Wilkins, 2003, p 481.)

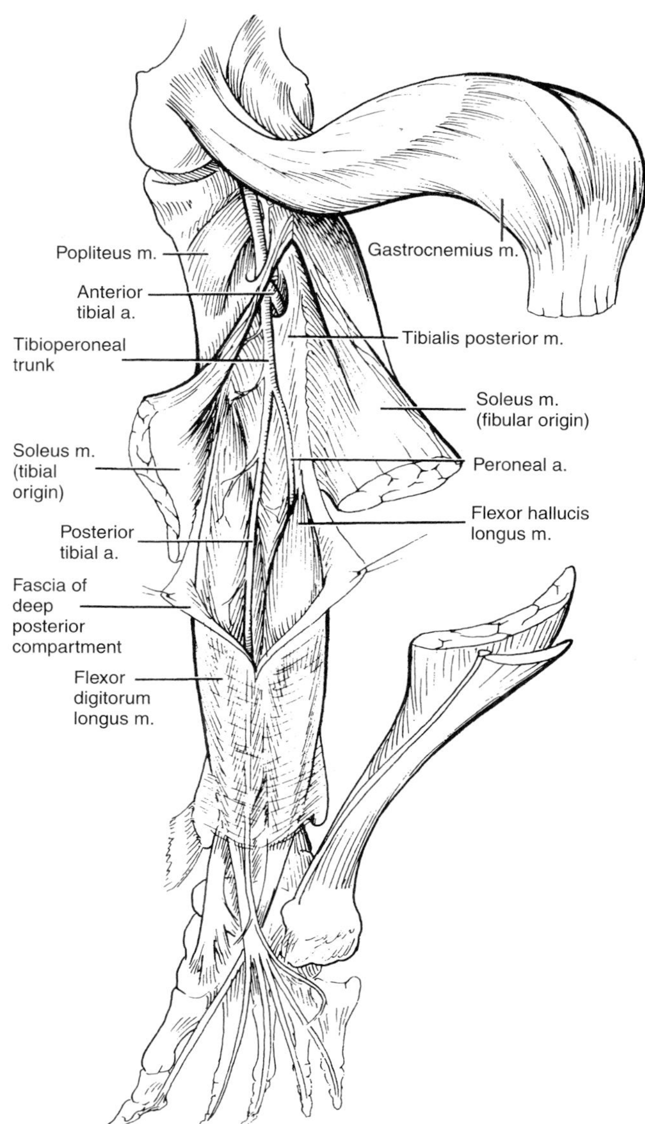

FIGURE 42-18 The peroneal and posterior tibial arteries lie in the deep posterior compartment. The posterior tibial artery courses posterior to the flexor digitorum longus muscle, whereas the peroneal artery courses anterior to the flexor hallucis longus muscle. (From: Valentine RJ, Wind GG: Anatomic Exposures in Vascular Surgery, 2nd ed. Philadelphia, Lippincott Williams & Wilkins, 2003, p 482.)

The tibioperoneal trunk lies in the deep posterior compartment on the posterior surface of the tibialis posterior muscle (Fig. 42-18). The anterior tibial vein crosses the tibioperoneal artery and should be divided to enhance exposure from a medial approach. Distal to the bifurcation of the tibioperoneal trunk, the posterior tibial artery branch is accompanied by the tibial nerve and follows an oblique medial course to reach the medial malleolus. In the distal half of the leg, these neurovascular structures lie on the posterior surface of the flexor digitorum longus muscle, just beneath the thin fascia of the deep posterior compartment (Fig. 42-19). The posterior tibial artery is easily exposed from a medial approach[28] but can also be isolated in its distal extent through a posterior approach.[29]

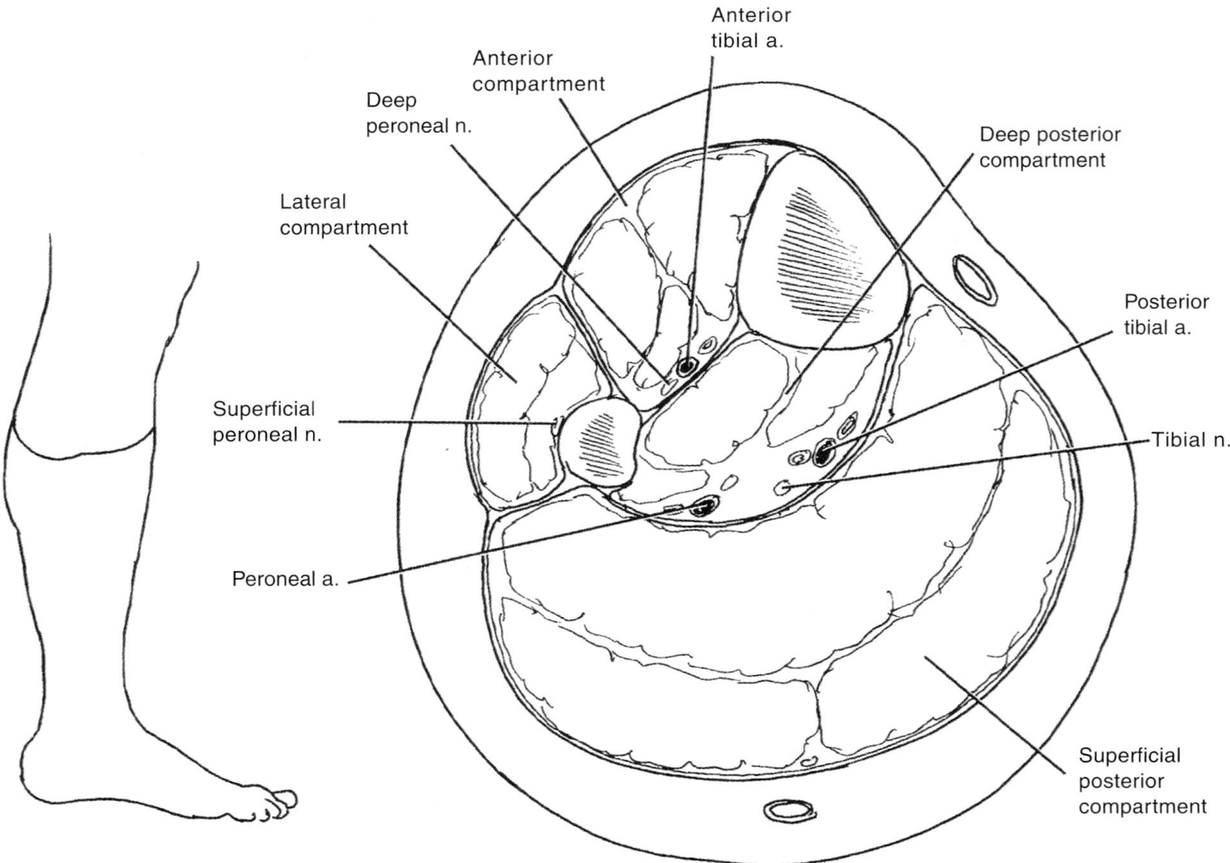

FIGURE 42-19 Relationship of the infrapopliteal arteries to the muscle compartments of the mid-leg. (From Valentine RJ, Wind GG: Anatomic Exposures in Vascular Surgery, 2nd ed. Philadelphia, Lippincott Williams & Wilkins, 2003, p 486.)

The peroneal artery courses laterally towards the ankle and lies near the medial surface of the fibula. In its distal extent, the peroneal artery lies between the tibialis posterior and flexor hallucis longus muscles. The peroneal artery can be exposed from a medial approach, but deep dissection behind the tibia sometimes limits exposure.[28] Because the peroneal artery lies just beneath the medial surface of the fibula, fibular resection may yield simpler exposure through a lateral incision.[30] Ouriel[29] has demonstrated that the most distal peroneal artery is readily exposed between the flexor hallucis muscle and the calcaneus tendon through a posterior incision.

■ REFERENCES

1. Bergman RA, Thompson SA, Afifi AK: Catalogue of Human Variation. Baltimore, Urban & Schwarzenberg, 1984, p 97.
2. Simonian GT, Pappas PJ, Padberg FT Jr, et al: Mandibular subluxation for distal internal carotid exposure: Technical considerations. J Vasc Surg 30:1116, 1999.
3. Shaha A, Phillips T, Scalea T, et al: Exposure of the internal carotid artery near the skull: The posterolateral anatomic approach. J Vasc Surg 8:618, 1988.
4. Ayerdi J, Gupta SK, Sampson LN, Deshmukh N: Recognition of a non-recurrent laryngeal nerve during carotid endarterectomy. Cardiovasc Surg 10:206, 2002.
5. Schauber MD, Fontenelle LJ, Solomon JW, Hanson TL: Cranial/cervical nerve dysfunction after carotid endarterectomy. J Vasc Surg 25:481, 1997.
6. Ballotta E, Da Giau G, Renon L, et al: Cranial and cervical nerve injuries after carotid endarterectomy: A prospective study. Surgery 125:85, 1999.
7. Ferguson GG, Eliasziw M, Barr H, et al: The North American Symptomatic Carotid Endarterectomy Trial: Surgical results in 1415 patients. Stroke 30:1751, 1999.
8. Meier DE, Brink BE, Fry WJ: Vertebral artery trauma: Acute recognition and treatment. Arch Surg 116:236, 1981.
9. Thomas GI, Anderson KN, Hain RF, Merendino KA: The significance of anomalous vertebrobasilar artery communications in operations on the heart and great vessels. Surgery 46:747, 1959.
10. Makhoul RG, Machleder HI: Developmental anomalies at the thoracic outlet: An analysis of 200 consecutive cases. J Vasc Surg 16:534, 1992.
11. Pollack EW: Surgical anatomy of the thoracic outlet syndrome. Surg Gynecol Obstet 150:97, 1980.
12. Bergman RA, Thompson SA, Afifi AK: Catalogue of Human Variation. Baltimore, Urban & Schwarzenberg, 1984, pp 201-204.
13. Roos DB: Congenital anomalies associated with thoracic outlet syndrome: Symptoms, diagnosis, and treatment. Am J Surg 132:771, 1976.
14. Valentine RJ, Carter DJ, Clagett GP: A modified extrathoracic approach to the treatment of dysphagia lusoria. J Vasc Surg 5:498, 1987.
15. Moosman DA: Anatomy of the pectoral nerves and their preservation during modified mastectomy. Am J Surg 139:883, 1980.

16. Veith FJ, Gupta S, Daly V: Technique for occluding the supraceliac aorta through the abdomen. Surg Gynecol Obstet 151:426, 1980.
17. Hagino RT, Valentine RJ, Clagett GP: Supraceliac aortorenal bypass. J Vasc Surg 26:482,1997.
18. Williams GM, Ricotta J, Zinner M, et al: The extended retroperitoneal approach for treatment of extensive atherosclerosis of the aorta and renal vessels. Surgery 88:846, 1980.
19. Valentine RJ, Wind GG: Anatomic Exposures in Vascular Surgery, 2nd ed. Philadelphia, Lippincott Williams & Wilkins, 2003, p 542.
20. Trout HH, Giordano JM: Anomalies of the inferior vena cava. J Vasc Surg 3:924, 1986.
21. Valentine RJ, MacGillivray DC, Blankenship CL, Wind GG: Variations in the relationship of the left renal vein to the left renal artery at the aorta. Clin Anat 3:249, 1990.
22. Fisher DF Jr, Fry WJ: Collateral mesenteric circulation. Surg Gynecol Obstet 164:487, 1987.
23. Gonzalez LL, Jaffe MS: Mesenteric arterial insufficiency following abdominal aortic resection. Arch Surg 93:10, 1966.
24. Garrett HE Jr, Richardson JW, Howard HS, Garrett HE: Retroperitoneal lymphocele after abdominal aortic surgery. J Vasc Surg 10:245, 1989.
25. Kwaan JH, Bernstein JM, Connaly JE: Management of lymph fistulas in the groin after arterial reconstruction. Arch Surg 114:1416, 1979.
26. Williams PL, Bannister LH, Berry MM, et al (eds): Gray's Anatomy: The Anatomical Basis of Medicine and Surgery. New York, Churchill Livingstone, 1995, p 1597.
27. Bardsley JL, Staple TW: Variations in branching of the popliteal artery. Radiology 94:581, 1970.
28. Tiefenbrun J, Beckerman M, Singer A: Surgical anatomy in bypass of the distal part of the lower limb. Surg Gynecol Obstet 141:528, 1975.
29. Ouriel K: The posterior approach to popliteal-crural bypass. J Vasc Surg 19:74, 1994.
30. Dardick H, Dardick I, Veith FJ: Exposure of the tibioperoneal arteries by a single lateral approach. Surgery 75:377, 1974.

Chapter 43

Basic Vascular Surgical Techniques

ROBERT B. RUTHERFORD, MD

Section VIII

To avoid unnecessary repetition elsewhere in this book, this chapter reviews some of the basic technical principles on which open vascular surgical operations are based, for example, (1) dissection, exposure, and control of vessels, (2) intraoperative hemostasis and anticoagulation, (3) incision and closure of blood vessels, and (4) basic anastomotic techniques. The fundamental aspects of the more specialized techniques, thromboembolectomy and endarterectomy, are presented in Chapters 44 and 45, respectively, and endovascular techniques are covered in Section IX.

HISTORICAL BACKGROUND

Everyone's view of the history of the development of vascular surgical techniques is different. This personal view is presented for the reader's appreciation of what we now take for granted: how difficult the early days must have been and how far we have come.

The first recorded vascular reconstruction was reported by Lambert in 1762. He described Hallowell's closure, in 1759, of a small opening in a brachial artery, performed with a pin around which a thread was twisted. This was a historic step; before that time, restoration of flow had always been sacrificed for the sake of hemostasis, and ligation was essentially the only vascular procedure practiced. Unfortunately, Asman's subsequent failures to achieve patency after vascular repair with similar techniques in experimental animals discouraged the surgeons of the day, and for almost a century, it was believed that suture material entering the lumen of a vessel would invariably produce an obliterating thrombosis.

By 1882, Schede had accomplished the first successful lateral vein repair. The first direct vascular anastomosis probably was Nicolai Eck's lateral anastomosis, in 1877, between the inferior vena cava and the portal vein in dogs. The opposing surfaces of the two vessels were sutured together by two rows of interrupted sutures. A suture at one corner was left untied temporarily to allow a special instrument to be inserted to slit open each vessel and allow cross-flow through the anastomosis. Although this was technically a lateral, or side-to-side, anastomosis, it was converted into an end-to-side portacaval shunt by subsequent ligation of the hepatic limb of the portal vein. It is interesting to reflect on Eck's enduring fame as a result of this experiment, considering that he had only one survivor and made no other significant contributions to surgery.

In 1899, Kummell performed the first end-to-end anastomosis of an artery in a human—if one discounts Murphy's invagination anastomosis 2 years earlier. As a background to these and other sporadic clinical successes, the decades following the beginning of the 20th century witnessed numerous experimental studies evaluating almost every conceivable suture technique. Absorbable versus nonabsorbable sutures as well as continuous versus interrupted, simple versus mattress, and everting versus edge-to-edge approximation techniques all were tried. These endeavors culminated in the classic studies by Carrel[1] and Guthrie[2] that established the principles and techniques of the modern vascular anastomosis. These investigators also were the first to achieve significant experimental success with fresh and preserved homografts and heterografts for vascular replacement and bypass.[3]

In 1906, Goyanes used a segment of popliteal vein to bridge a defect caused by the excision of an aneurysm of the accompanying artery. The next year, Lexer used the saphenous vein for arterial reconstruction after excision of an axillary artery aneurysm. Although the stage appeared to be set by the aforementioned experimental studies and by continuing, though sporadic, clinical successes such as these, widespread clinical application of these principles and techniques did not occur for almost 40 years. The reasons for this delay are not entirely clear, but the innovation of better diagnostic techniques (especially angiography and cardiac catheterization), the evolution of vascular prostheses and homograft storage methods, the development of techniques that allowed thoracotomy to be performed at reasonable risk, and the availability of heparin and type-specific, cross-matched blood were probably all important in the final launching of the "golden era of cardiovascular surgery," which began after World War II.

Before the technical explosion that followed in the 1950s, the mainstays of surgery for peripheral vascular disease were (1) arterial ligation for vascular trauma, arteriovenous fistula, or aneurysm, (2) simple vascular repair with or without local thrombectomy for acute occlusion, (3) sympathectomy for chronic ischemia, and (4) a variety of amputations. The implantation, first of arterial homografts, then of a succession of plastic prostheses culminating in the porous, knitted polyester (Dacron) graft of today; the emerging preference for fresh venous and arterial autografts for replacement of smaller arteries; and, finally, the additional availability of the human umbilical vein allograft and, after that, of various specially preserved (formaldehyde-preserved and cryopreserved) homografts and heterografts, plus the expanded polytetrafluoroethylene (PTFE) (Teflon) graft, have now provided the vascular surgeon with an adequate array of arterial substitutes for most situations. Graft choice has been further enhanced by the addition, to prosthetic grafts, of external supporting rings to prevent kinking and compression and special coatings to reduce thrombogenicity, limit initial blood loss through interstices, or resist infection Unfortunately, the concomitant development and refinement of vascular suture materials, atraumatic vascular clamps, prosthetic grafts, and endovascular devices, such as vena caval filters, balloon and mechanical thrombectomy catheters, and stents and stent-grafts, have received almost better coverage in manufacturers' brochures than in the formal surgical literature.

■ INSTRUMENTS AND SUTURE MATERIAL

The instruments essential for simpler vascular procedures, in addition to the standard instruments used in any operative dissection, comprise only the following:

- Vascular forceps
- Fine-pointed diamond-jawed needle holder
- Right-angled clamp
- Vascular scissors
- An assortment of atraumatic vascular clamps

Vascular forceps usually have fine teeth or serrations that interdigitate, allowing them to grip the vessel wall without crushing, as exemplified by the DeBakey and Swan-Brown forceps shown in Figure 43-1. Similar requirements pertain to vascular clamps, and although many different designs are available, most achieve their nonslipping, noncrushing, occlusive grip by means of several longitudinal rows of serrations or teeth on the inside of the jaw or clamp, which are offset so that they interdigitate, as shown in Figure 43-2. An assortment of such vascular clamps, of different sizes and shapes, is necessary to accommodate differences in extent of exposure, depth of wound, size of vessel, and angle of application (i.e., transverse, oblique, or tangential) (Fig. 43-3).

In addition to these vascular clamps, which have handles that allow them to be held and with which vessel position can be manipulated, there are smaller vascular clamps without handles, the jaws of which are held in the occlusive position by a spring. These so-called bulldog clamps, or large neurosurgical aneurysm clips, are useful for working

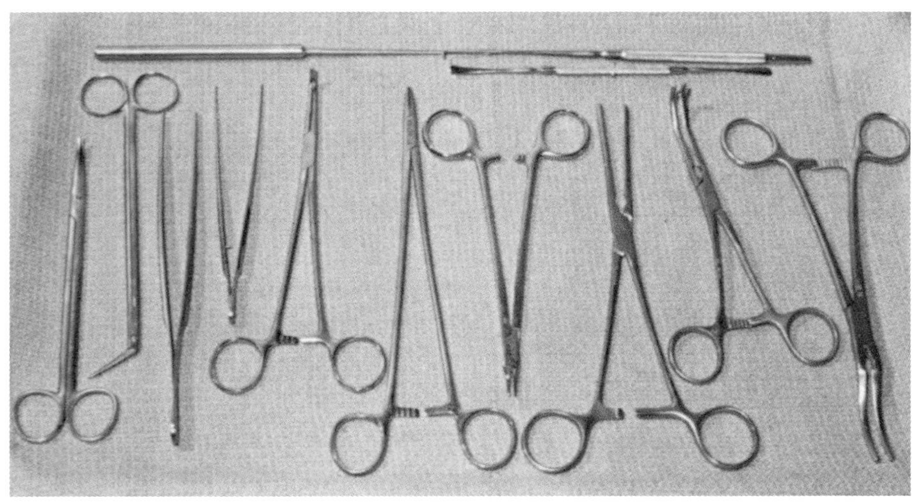

FIGURE 43-1 Some basic vascular instruments (*left to right*): Metzenbaum and angled Potts scissors; DeBakey and Swan-Brown forceps; a right-angle clamp; long and short vascular needle holders; straight, Satinsky, and spoon-shaped vascular clamps; and (*at top*) a blunted nerve hook and Penfield and Freer dissectors for endarterectomy.

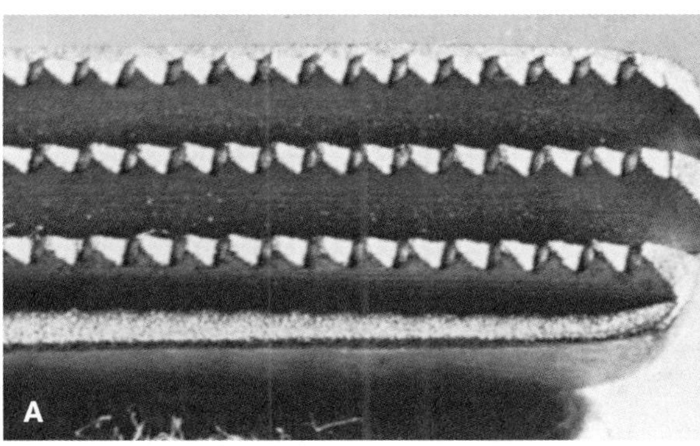

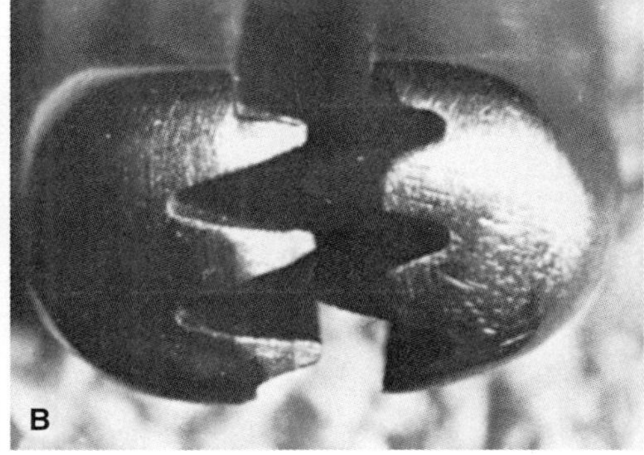

FIGURE 43-2 Magnified views show the multiple "teeth" of a typical vascular clamp. **A,** Side view of one jaw. **B,** End-on view of the jaws interdigitating.

on smaller vessels or controlling branches or tributaries, particularly when the exposure is limited (Fig. 43-4).

Moistened umbilical tapes, polymeric silicone (Silastic) loops, or thin rubber catheters are used to encircle vessels and their major tributaries during dissection and manipulation. A heavy silk suture, doubly looped around a small branch or tributary, can, through the weight of a hemostat clamped to its end, control intraoperative bleeding from these branches without crowding of the operative field with additional vascular clamps. During maneuvers to dissect, free, and encircle vessels, a right-angled clamp with fine (but not too pointed) tips is invaluable.

Small Metzenbaum scissors or (on smaller, more delicate vessels) plastic or even iris scissors are particularly suitable for dissection on or around the vessels because they do not have sharp-pointed tips and are less likely to cause inadvertent injury of the vessel. Curved, straight, or angled Potts scissors, however, are preferable for incision or excision of the vessel wall itself because they have delicately pointed tips. An assortment of balloon and irrigating catheters is useful for many purposes in addition to that of removing intravascular thrombus (see Chapter 44).

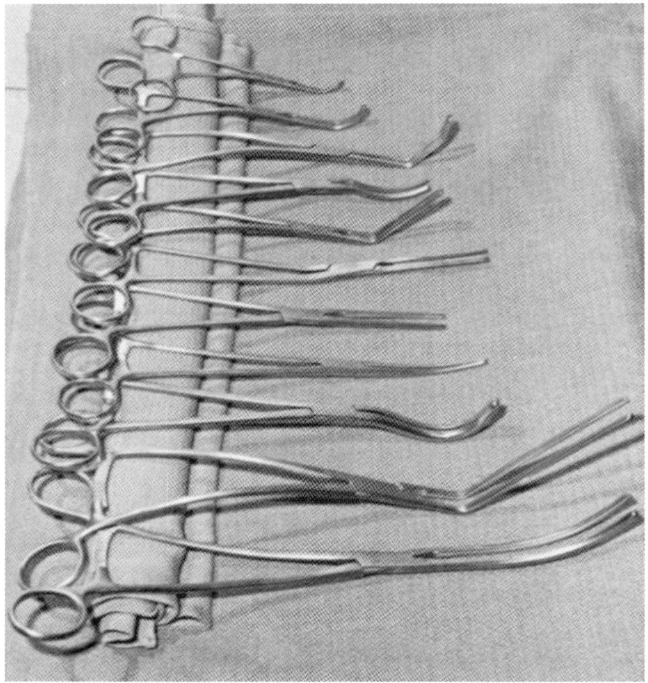

FIGURE 43-3 An assortment of vascular clamps, demonstrating the variety of shapes and sizes.

To some extent, the selection of vascular suture material, like that of vascular instruments, is an individual matter, and every surgeon has favorites. The caliber of the suture used should be as fine as possible, short of risking suture line disruption (and anastomotic aneurysm formation), to minimize hemorrhage through suture holes and the amount of suture material in contact with the vessel lumen. As a frame of reference, a range from 2-0 to 7-0 is used in most clinical practice as the surgeon progresses from the aorta centrally to the radial or crural arteries peripherally. For most peripheral anastomoses, 5-0 or 6-0 sutures are usually preferred. All vascular sutures should be swaged onto fine, one-half-circle or three-eighths-circle, round needles with tapered or slightly beveled tips. Flattening of the body of such a fine needle parallel with the radius of its curve and placing of a tapered cutting edge on the side of its tip facilitate penetration through hard arteriosclerotic plaques and avoid bending of the body of the needle during the anastomosis.

Braided fine silk, lubricated with sterile mineral oil or bone wax, handles well and is satisfactory for autogenous tissues, especially venous anastomoses, but PTFE-coated Dacron and monofilament polypropylene are usually preferred for arterial work because of their greater strength and durability and their reduced tissue reactivity. Absorbable monofilament suture with a long half-life (e.g., polydioxanone suture) is now being used instead of interrupted sutures in pediatric vascular surgery to allow anastomotic growth. It is common practice to use doubled swaged-on vascular suture (i.e., with a needle on each end) to allow more flexibility and speed in performing vascular anastomoses.

■ VASCULAR EXPOSURE AND CONTROL

Vascular exposure and control usually constitute the first order of business during any vascular operation, once the general field of operation has been exposed. Each operation

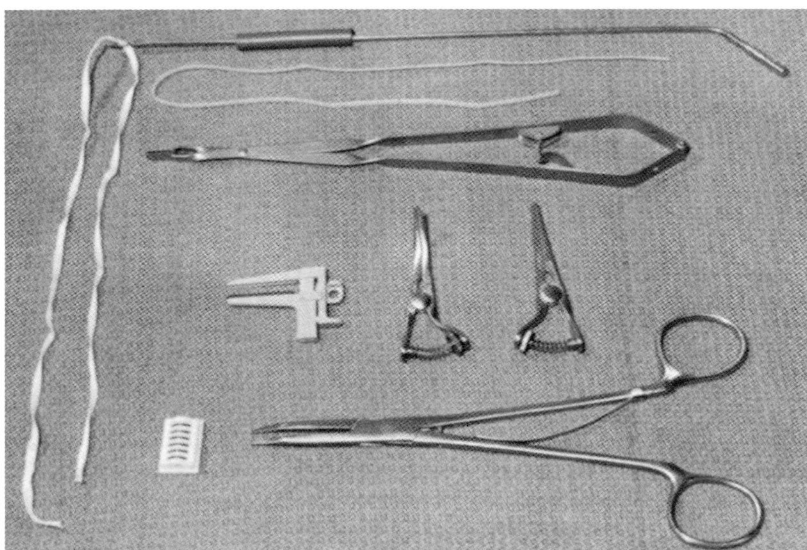

FIGURE 43-4 A variety of instruments used to control or occlude smaller arterial branches. Shown *(from top down)* are a modified Rummel tourniquet that uses umbilical tape, a polymeric silicone rubber (Silastic) "loop," a Heifitz aneurysm clip with applicator, a Fogarty clamp and two DeBakey bulldog clamps, and metal surgical clips (Ligaclips) with applicator.

has special exposures of the operative field. These are detailed in the author's atlas[4] and are also presented in Chapter 42. Only the principles of individual vessel exposure and control are discussed here. The local exposure of the blood vessels, as needed for the procedure to be performed, is attained before systemic anticoagulation is instituted to facilitate the dissection and minimize blood loss. A clear knowledge of the anatomic relationships among the involved vessels, their major collaterals or tributaries, and the surrounding structures is essential, because the procedure is often performed for occlusive disease and the surgeon does not have the luxury of dissecting toward a palpable pulse. In such a situation, however, the surgeon may be able to detect the location of an arteriosclerotic artery that is hardened or contains firm thrombosis by rolling it with the fingertip from side to side in the underlying tissues. A patent, though pulseless, artery can be located with a sterile Doppler probe; this device may be particularly helpful for dissecting through scarred or inflamed tissues.

Major vessels are usually enclosed in an identifiable fascial envelope or sheath, incision of which normally is the final step in obtaining exposure. The characteristic pattern of the vasa vasorum immediately identifies an exposed artery, and the bluish white color and the almost ballotable sensation (imparted by the rapid refilling after the quick application and release of pressure) usually makes the accompanying vein easy to recognize.

Smaller, more peripheral vessels, such as may be encountered at the wrist or ankle, may go into spasm during the dissection. This event, or the lack of arterial pulsations below an obstructive lesion, may make the distinction between an adjacent small artery and vein difficult. Observing the direction of blood flow after gentle temporary occlusion or comparing the color of microaspirates of blood taken with a tuberculin syringe and 25-gauge needle can be helpful maneuvers in these situations.

In the presence of arterial or venous occlusive disease, and especially in reoperations on the same vessels, considerable inflammatory reaction and connective tissue may surround the vessels. In this situation, the standard advice to dissect off the looser outer adventitial layers and "stay close" to the artery is particularly worthwhile. Arteries are usually approached from the direction of their closest proximity to the skin, and because they rarely give off major branches in that direction, the nearest, or uppermost, surface of the artery normally is devoid of branches, or "free." Once in the correct plane inside the loose outer investiture of the artery, and after its upper surface has been exposed fully, the surgeon should dissect a convenient segment of the artery free circumferentially in this same plane by gently spreading the tissues with a right-angle clamp, taking care not to puncture the accompanying vein, which may be closely adherent to the opposite surface, especially near bifurcations.

Next, the surgeon passes an umbilical tape or polymeric silicone loop around the artery and clamps its loose ends with a hemostat. Traction on this tape and on each additional encircling tape progressively draws the arterial structures up out of their bed, allowing restricting points of fixation and major branches to be identified, thus making the dissection progressively easier. The surgeon should proceed in this manner until an adequate length of arterial segment and all its major branches are completely free and encircled with tapes. Small branches may represent potentially significant future collateral vessels; therefore, rather than divide them, the surgeon should control such branches temporarily with a double loop of heavy braided silk or a small cerebral aneurysm clip.

To obtain control of the vessels, even in elective procedures, the surgeon does best to dissect out first the major inflow vessels and then the main outflow vessels before proceeding with lesser collaterals. Depending on the operative procedure planned, exposure and control of one or more such arterial segments may be necessary, and if a bypass graft between such segments is to be constructed, the surgeon should prepare the intervening "tunnel" or passage for the graft before heparin is given.

HEMOSTASIS AND ANTICOAGULATION

The processes of hemostasis and anticoagulation lie at the very foundation of vascular surgery. Only the simplest, most abbreviated vascular surgical procedures can be undertaken without the need to interrupt the flow of blood temporarily. In performing such interruption, the surgeon must avoid the two opposing complications of vascular surgery: exsanguinating hemorrhage and intravascular thrombosis.

Hemostasis

Hemostasis, produced spontaneously by spasm and platelet thrombi in smaller vessels and by clamping and ligature in larger vessels, is an integral part of almost every surgical dissection. Whenever the operation involves the direct transgression of major blood vessels, however, as is characteristic of vascular surgery, blood flow must be either temporarily or permanently interrupted. Temporary interruption requires the application of atraumatic vascular clamps or double-looped polymeric silicone tapes after exposure and control of the vessels have been achieved, as illustrated in Figure 43-5. A valuable alternative during bypass to small calcified distal arteries, to avoid crushing or otherwise traumatizing them, is the proximal application of a sterile pneumatic tourniquet during the distal anastomosis.

Anticoagulation

With ligation or division of major vessels, the surgeon does not ordinarily need to take any measures to prevent thrombus formation in the interrupted vessel. Thrombus formation usually occurs eventually within the blind end of the vessel and propagates back as far as the takeoff of the last major collateral. In most vascular procedures, however, the vessels are not simply divided but are explored, replaced, or bypassed. Also, to ensure restoration of flow *after* an arteriotomy or venotomy has been closed or an anastomosis has been performed, the surgeon must either (1) prevent intravascular thrombus formation while flow is interrupted or (2) remove the accumulated thrombus immediately before completion of the final suture line. If a vessel, such as the external jugular vein of the dog, is occluded temporarily between two adjacent vascular clamps or nooses, the blood trapped in the intervening segment ordinarily does not clot. If the same vessel, during this occlusion, is simply opened and then closed with fine silk sutures, thrombosis commonly does occur. Understandably, such segmental vascular thrombosis is even more likely to occur in diseased vessels during the more extensive manipulations required in vascular surgery.

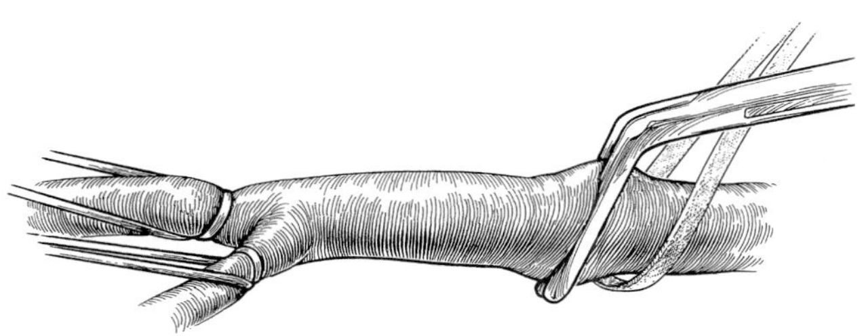

FIGURE 43-5 Two methods for obtaining temporary vascular control. A standard vascular clamp occludes the proximal inflow vessel, but less traumatic polymeric silicone (Silastic) loops are adequate for the smaller distal branches. (From Rutherford RB: Basic vascular techniques. In: Atlas of Vascular Surgery: Basic Techniques and Exposures. Philadelphia, WB Saunders, 1993, p 16.)

If the procedure is relatively simple, accumulated thrombus may be extracted with forceps or balloon catheters just before placement of the final sutures, and flow is thus restored before further clotting occurs. Although this practice is still used as an expedient in selected circumstances, it carries a small but definite risk of failure that has been made unnecessary by the introduction of heparin anticoagulation. This step is used in all but the simplest vascular procedures; the only major exception is thoracoabdominal or suprarenal aneurysm repair, in which timely flushing and irrigation are preferred to heparinization because of large anastomoses, high flows, and the risk of creating a bleeding diathesis. It is also the preference of some vascular surgeons not to heparinize during infrarenal abdominal aortic aneurysm repair, for the same reasons, but coated prostheses have significantly decreased the blood loss associated with restoring flow.

Although spontaneous clotting may be retarded by aspirin, dextran, dipyridamole, and other drugs that reduce platelet aggregation, and by coumarin drugs that lower the circulating levels of clotting factors II, VII, IX, and X, none of these drugs is reliable for preventing intravascular thrombosis during the performance of a major vascular procedure. In sufficient dosage, however, heparin does render blood incoagulable at normal temperatures and pH ranges. The action of heparin is complex, affecting platelet adhesiveness, the endothelial cells' negative charge (or zeta potential), and the early phases of clotting by inhibiting the activation of factors IX and X. The major action of heparin is believed to result from its union with a cofactor in the blood to form an antithrombin that inhibits the conversion of fibrinogen to fibrin. Given intravenously, this drug has an effective action for up to 3 to 4 hours, or even longer with higher or repeated dosage.

A satisfactory level of anticoagulation may be achieved within 5 minutes after the intravenous injection of 100 units (~1.0 mg) per kg body weight of aqueous sodium heparin. For continued, sustained anticoagulation, as required during longer vascular procedures, one third to one half of this dose may be repeated at hourly intervals. During procedures in which the blood will be exposed to large surface areas of foreign material, as during cardiopulmonary bypass, larger doses of heparin (up to 300 units/kg) are usually advisable. Using larger doses also significantly lengthens the half-life of heparin.

Rendering the blood completely incoagulable, however, is not without its disadvantages. Wound surfaces that would remain naturally hemostatic may bleed profusely, and spontaneous bleeding may occur elsewhere in the body. Fortunately, these complications are extremely rare during most vascular operations, a common exception being repair of thoracoabdominal and suprarenal aortic aneurysms.

Although the greatest risk of segmental thrombosis during a vascular procedure lies in the static circulation distal to the point of occlusion, regional heparinization cannot be achieved practically. Therefore, after dissection and exposure of the vessel have been carried out, including "tunneling," and after a porous knitted Dacron graft (if it is to be used) has been preclotted, the appropriate systemic dosage of heparin (usually 100 units/kg) is injected intravenously by the anesthesiologist at the direction of the surgeon. The time is noted so that half of this dose can be repeated in 1 to 1½ hours during longer procedures.

Whenever large tissue surfaces have been exposed during the course of the dissection or whenever there is extensive oozing of blood from the tissues or prosthesis after completion of the anastomosis, the heparin effect may be reversed before wound closure with an equivalent dose of protamine sulfate, that is, milligram for milligram, allowing for the temporal decay of heparin that was given earlier. It is important to remember that protamine (1) may cause hypotension if it is injected too rapidly and (2) may produce the opposite of the intended effect, namely, hypocoagulability, if it is administered in a dose in excess of that needed to counteract the heparin. For this reason, the surgeon usually asks the anesthesiologist to give half of the calculated dose over the first 5 minutes, and then an additional 5 mg every few minutes until the surgeon notes a decrease in oozing or the appearance of clots in the operative field. In most vascular procedures, however, protamine need not be given; instead, the effects of administered heparin are simply allowed to wear off.

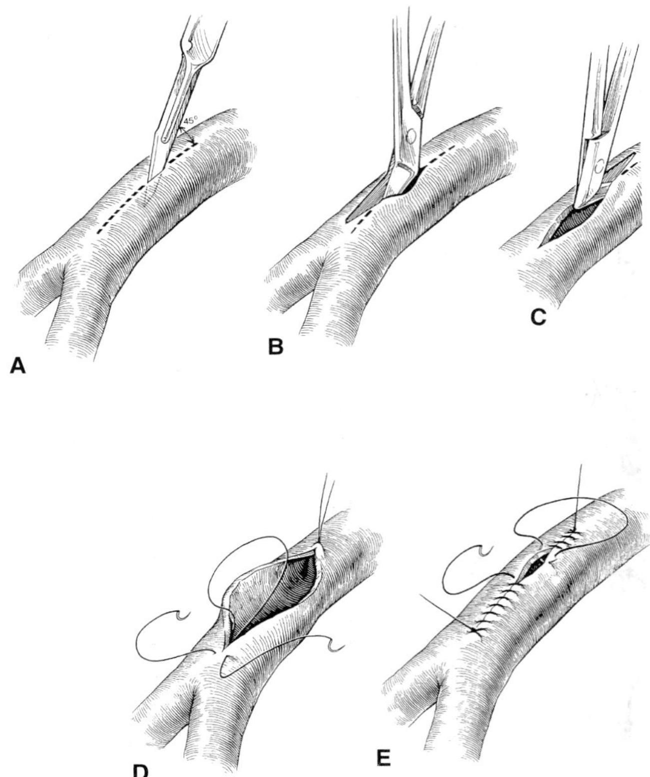

FIGURE 43-6 **A** to **E,** Longitudinal arteriotomy is begun with a sharp scalpel blade and completed with Potts scissors. Closure is accomplished with continuous suture, run from each end toward the middle. (From Rutherford RB: Basic vascular techniques. In: Atlas of Vascular Surgery: Basic Techniques and Exposures. Philadelphia, WB Saunders, 1993, p 31.)

■ VASCULAR INCISIONS AND CLOSURES

Entering a vessel through a simple lateral incision ranks only slightly above vessel ligature in complexity. The maneuver is used clinically to introduce catheters or cardiac bypass cannulas and to remove thrombi, emboli, or atheromatous deposits. Only two aspects deserve special consideration here:

- Manner of closure
- Direction of the incision

Closure of either longitudinal or transverse incisions usually produces some reduction in the cross-sectional area of the vessel. At normal systemic pressures, a reduction of almost 50% in diameter is required to produce a significant hemodynamic effect or gradient in most peripheral arteries. There may be some turbulence with lesser degrees of stenosis, however, particularly in low-flow, high-resistance situations. Furthermore, there is a tendency toward hypercoagulability in the immediate postoperative period, and these factors, combined with the break in intimal continuity and the presence of foreign (suture) material at the site of closure, may lead to thrombosis. For all these reasons, care must be taken to minimize this narrowing.

Longitudinal incisions offer good exposure and can be extended readily (Fig. 43-6). They have the additional advantage of being convertible into end-to-side anastomoses. Closure of a longitudinal incision in *smaller* (<4 mm in diameter) vessels, however, probably narrows the lumen over a greater distance than occurs with a transverse incision and therefore is more likely to produce significant stenosis and turbulence and to lead to thrombosis. For this reason, a transverse arteriotomy or venotomy is usually preferable in smaller vessels (Fig. 43-7). When a longitudinal incision is necessary, narrowing of its closure may be prevented by the insertion of an elliptical patch graft of vein or PTFE or coated Dacron into the arteriotomy (Fig. 43-8).

Placement of Vascular Sutures

Regardless of the manner in which the vascular suture is placed, two rules always should be observed:

1. Excess adventitial tissue should be excised from the outer surface of the vessel so that it will not be dragged into the anastomosis and promote thrombus formation in the suture line.
2. The suture should pass through all layers, particular care being taken always to include the intima.

Interrupted sutures are still popular for very small anastomoses and in growing children to allow anastomotic growth. A simple over-and-over suture usually is chosen for most arterial closures or anastomoses, with "bites" taken approximately 1 mm apart and 1 mm from the edges, unless the vessels are large, thick-walled, or diseased. Eversion of the edges to produce a smooth, sutureless internal surface through the placement of continuous or interrupted

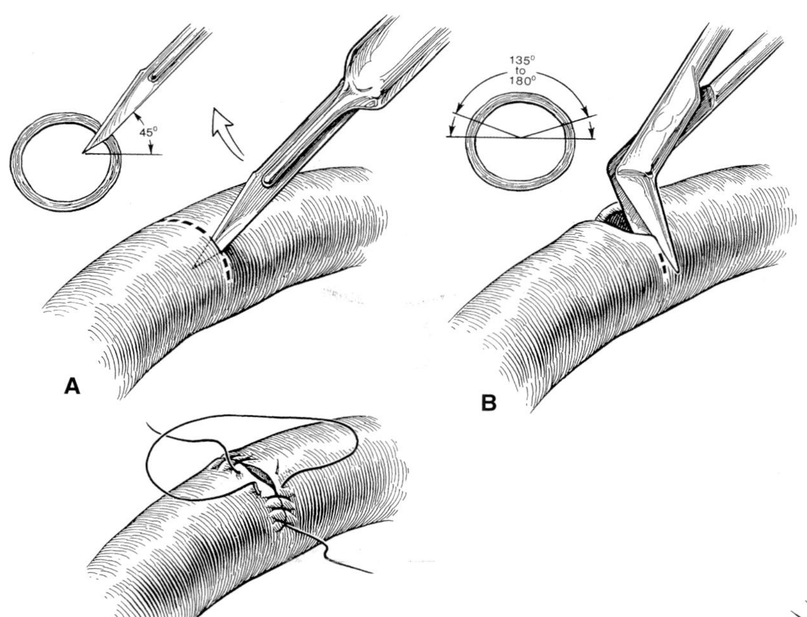

FIGURE 43-7 A to C, Transverse arteriotomy is performed first with a scalpel blade followed by enlargement to 135 to 180 degrees of the circumference using Potts scissors. Continuous closure, from both ends toward the middle, is most commonly employed. (From Rutherford RB: Basic vascular techniques. In: Atlas of Vascular Surgery: Basic Techniques and Exposures. Philadelphia, WB Saunders, 1993, p 30.)

horizontal mattress sutures has lost much of its original popularity, mainly because the theoretical advantages have not been manifested in major arterial reconstructions and because the technique tends to produce a greater narrowing at the closure or anastomosis. Even with the simpler, over-and-over continuous suture, the surgeon can achieve some eversion in most anastomoses by starting each "corner" with a horizontal mattress suture (Kunlin's technique) and then gently holding out the edges of the vessel or graft with forceps as they are first being sutured together, to develop everting edges.

Whenever possible, the direction of penetration of vessels should be from the inside out, with care being taken to include the intima. This advice is particularly important in suturing of arteriosclerotic arteries, in which penetration in the reverse direction may push a hard plaque inward rather than penetrate it, creating an intimal flap that may be dissected further by arterial flow and thus leading to occlusion. The vascular suture must be pulled and held taut continuously to avoid suture line bleeding at slack points. In this regard, vascular suture line bleeding can be stopped, in most cases, with finger tamponade, a little patience, and, occasionally, the help of a fine, superficially placed suture that draws more adventitia over the leak. If deeper sutures are required, flow should be interrupted again while they are placed; otherwise, new suture holes are created that may bleed more vigorously than the old.

The surgeon must take care as suturing nears the corner, or end, of an anastomosis to ensure that the suture is not catching the opposite side of the vessel or graft. Inserting a fine nerve hook with blunted point through the opening in the anastomosis as each stitch is placed is a useful precaution against this error. Another safeguard is the practice of always beginning at and sewing away from the corners and toward the "middle" of each suture line, using two separate sutures that are tied together there.

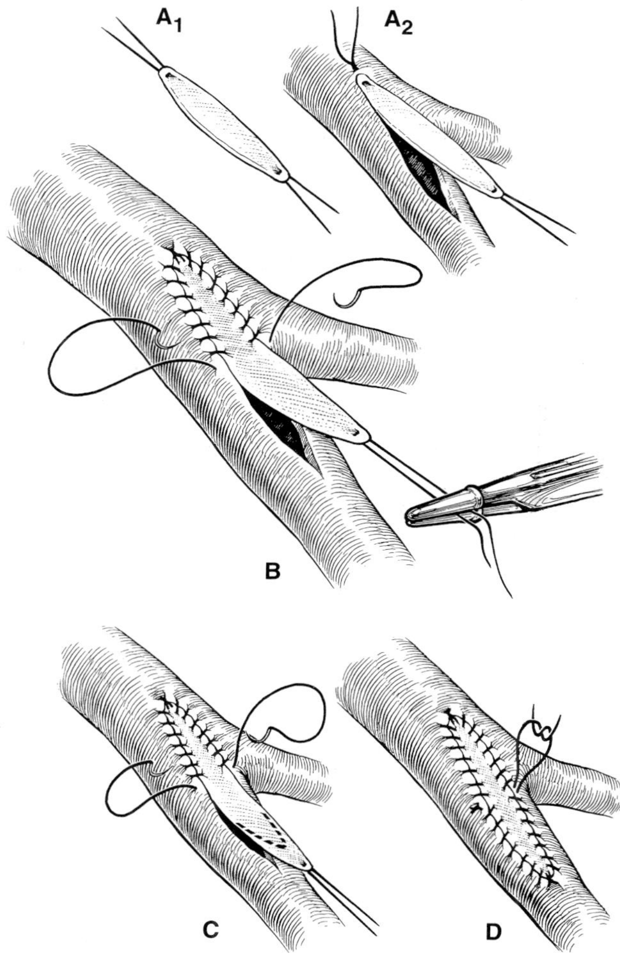

FIGURE 43-8 A to D, Patch angioplasty. A thin elliptical patch is fashioned, and mattress sutures are placed in both tips. One suture is carried into the corner of the arteriotomy and is tied to begin closure, aided by traction on the other suture. The closure is continued from each end, along the sides of the arteriotomy, toward the middle, where the sutures are tied to each other. Before the second corner is begun, the tip may have to be trimmed for better fit. (From Rutherford RB: Basic vascular techniques. In: Atlas of Vascular Surgery: Basic Techniques and Exposures. Philadelphia, WB Saunders, 1993, p 33.)

Methods of Vascular Interruption

The permanent interruption of flow through a major vessel may be accomplished in several ways (Fig. 43-9). Smaller arteries or veins may be divided between two hemostats before ligature and release of the clamps or, preferably, if there is adequate exposure, may be doubly ligated before division. In the latter approach, a curved or right-angle clamp is usually passed under the vessel after it has been dissected free, and a ligature, held taut by a clamp at its distal end, is "fed" into the grasp of the right-angle clamp and pulled around the vessel as the latter is withdrawn. This maneuver is repeated, the two ligatures then are tied, and the vessel between them is divided.

Because of the potential danger that pulsations, thrusting against the blind end of an artery that has been simply ligated and divided, eventually may force the ligatures off, it usually is advisable to ligate larger arteries doubly on *both* sides of the point of division, with the central one of each of these pairs of ligatures being a "transfixion" or "suture ligature" that is placed through the lumen of the vessel and tied on either side of it. Another alternative, which is usually reserved for the largest of vessels, is division between vascular clamps followed by a formal closure of the cut ends with continuous vascular suture.

If, however, interruption of flow is all that is desired and division of the vessel is not required, ligation-in-continuity is an acceptable alternative to the maneuvers just mentioned; furthermore, if the vessel in question is short and difficult to control with vascular clamps, this may be not only the most expedient but also the safest approach. The recommended technique for ligation-in-continuity is to place two heavy ligature circumferences around the vessel, thereby interrupting flow, and then to place a transfixion suture between them to destroy intimal continuity and promote an organized thrombotic occlusion of that segment. This precaution is designed to prevent later recanalization, the major objection to simple ligation-in-continuity.

The clinical situation that best illustrates the application of the foregoing principles is that used in correcting a patent ductus arteriosus. Indeed, the early history of cardiovascular surgery was enriched and enlivened by studies and debates centering on the most appropriate technical approach for closing this congenital anomaly.

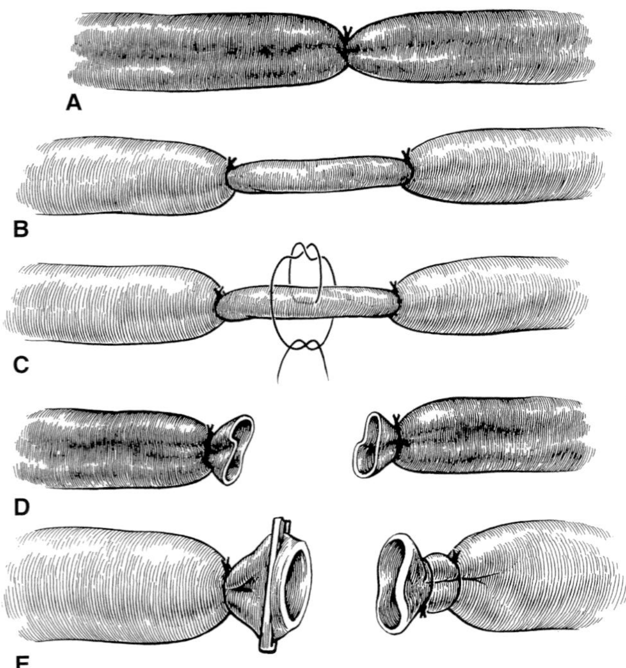

FIGURE 43-9 Vascular interruption techniques for small arteries and veins. **A,** Single ligation. **B,** Double ligation in continuity. **C,** Double ligation with intervening transfixion suture. **D,** Double ligation and division. **E,** Reinforcement of ligatured ends with a transfixion suture or metal clip. (From Rutherford RB: Basic vascular techniques. In Atlas of Vascular Surgery: Basic Techniques and Exposures. Philadelphia, WB Saunders, 1993, p 26.)

■ VASCULAR ANASTOMOSES

End-to-End Anastomosis

The end-to-end anastomosis is performed as follows:

1. It is usually begun with two corner sutures placed 180 degrees apart. Although they may be placed as simple sutures, a horizontal mattress suture results in slight eversion of the suture line and facilitates intima-to-intima approximation. If double-ended vascular sutures are used, these corner sutures are tied, the two ends being left at equal length.
2. One needle from each corner is used to "run" the suture line in a simple over-and-over fashion to the middle of each side of the anastomosis, where the ends of the two sutures are tied together, completing the anterior half of the anastomosis.
3. The surgeon then rotates the vessel ends 180 degrees by moving the vascular clamps to expose the previous "posterior" half of the anastomosis.
4. The suture line is continued in an identical fashion to complete the anastomosis (Fig. 43-10).

If the vessel ends are not sufficiently mobile for this technique, the surgeon may perform the "posterior" half of the suture line transluminally or may place the corner sutures directly anteriorly and posteriorly, instead of laterally, and sew from the posterior midline around each side to the anterior midline. With this approach, only minimal rotation of the vascular clamps is necessary to make the suture line readily visible.

A final option is "triangulation," in which the surgeon places three stay sutures 120 degrees apart and sews from one to the other much as described for the corner sutures, rotating the vessel with the clamps so that the segment being sutured is always directly anterior. This maneuver avoids catching opposite walls in the tight corners that may be created with the use of two stay sutures 180 degrees apart. Unfortunately, it is usually most needed when there is limited exposure in small vessels, and in these circumstances, the clamps may have to be reapplied rather than rotated.

If the vessels to be joined are relatively small (e.g., 2 to 5 mm in diameter), the surgeon may enlarge the anastomosis by beveling the ends 45 degrees in opposite

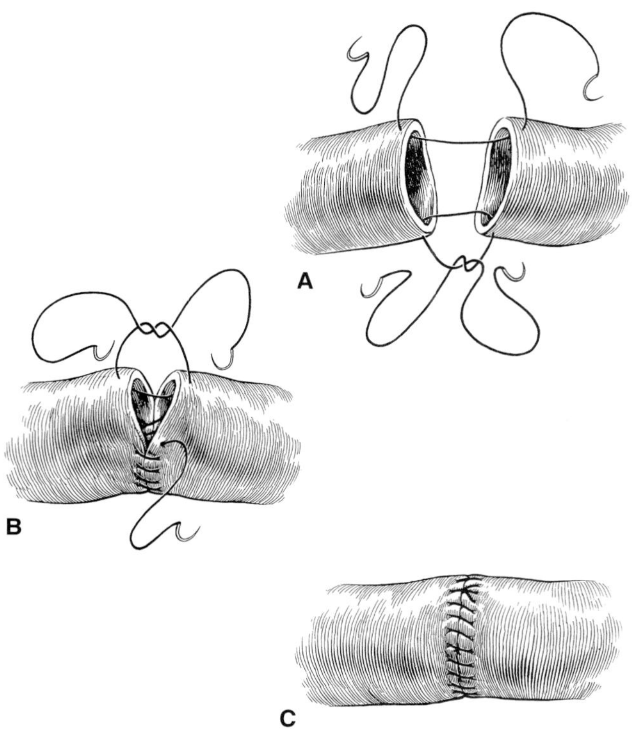

FIGURE 43-10 A to C, A simple perpendicular end-to-end anastomosis begun with two sutures 180 degrees apart and run continuously toward each other. (From Rutherford RB: Basic vascular techniques. In: Atlas of Vascular Surgery: Basic Techniques and Exposures. Philadelphia, WB Saunders, 1993, p 35.)

directions. If the vessel is thin-walled and flexible, the surgeon can slit the opposing ends longitudinally for a length approximating the vessel's diameter but 180 degrees out of phase from each other and then round off the corners (Fig. 43-11). These flanged or beveled anastomoses are designed to avoid the circumferential, constricting effect that may be produced by a simple perpendicular end-to-end anastomosis in smaller vessels.

In addition, because a continuous suture, when used for end-to-end anastomosis, may result in "purse-stringing," or circumferential narrowing of the anastomosis, interrupted sutures may be preferred for end-to-end anastomosis of smaller vessels. If smooth, monofilament vascular sutures with doubled swaged-on needles are used, the sutures can be placed and left untied before completion of the anastomosis. The vascular clamps can then be slowly released, allowing the lumen to expand and the suture to slide slightly to accommodate this expansion (Fig. 43-12). The sutures are then tied while the clamps are briefly reapplied. These techniques apply as well to the direct interposition of a segment of vein or prosthetic graft as they do to a direct end-to-end anastomosis.

End-to-Side Anastomosis

The end-to-side anastomosis has wide clinical use in placement of arterial bypass grafts. The side of the "recipient" vessel may be prepared by elliptical excision or simple longitudinal incision, and the end of the donor vessel is usually beveled to produce an acute angle of entry and to

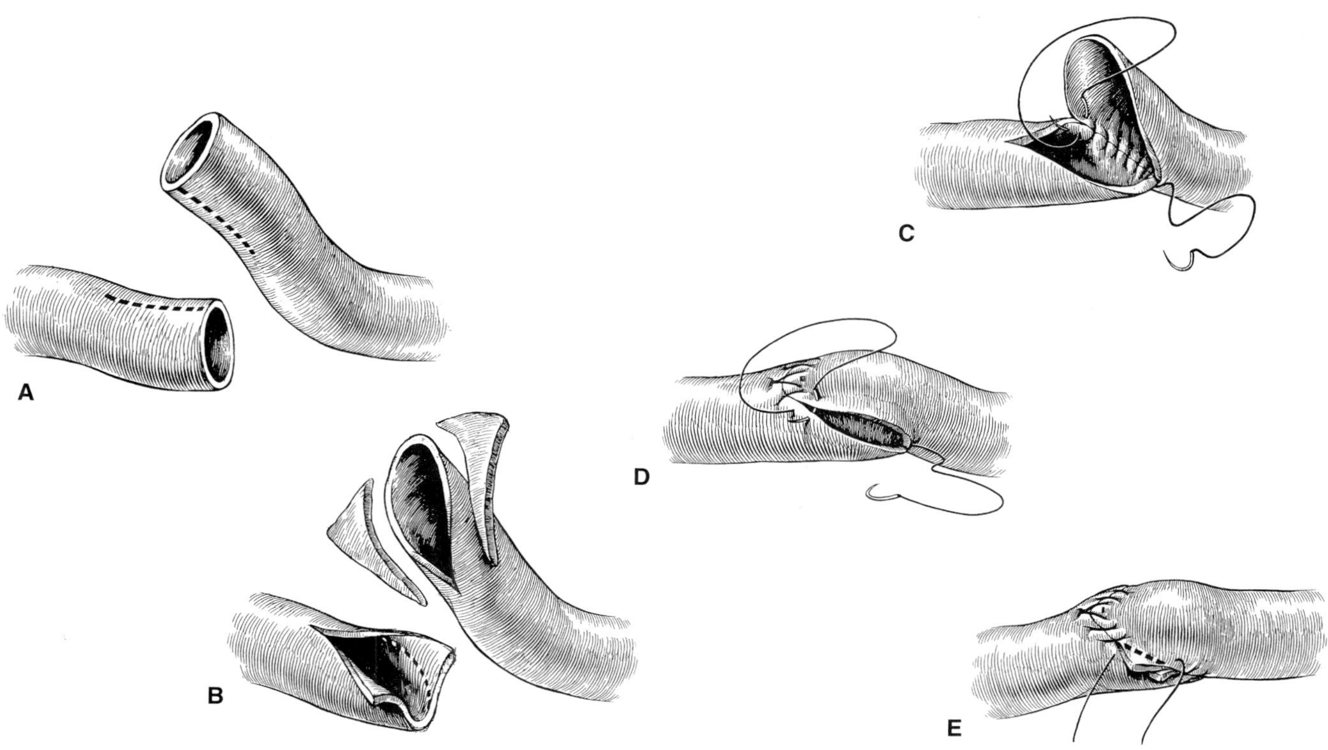

FIGURE 43-11 Technique of oblique end-to-end anastomosis. A, The two ends are slit 180 degrees apart. B, The resultant corners and adjacent lateral edges are trimmed conservatively. Anastomosis (C) is begun in one corner (head-to-toe) and (D) run to and around the opposite end and back toward the starting point. E, The other suture is run up to meet it in the middle; any remaining "angles" must be trimmed to avoid "dog ears." (From Rutherford RB: Basic vascular techniques. In: Atlas of Vascular Surgery: Basic Techniqes and Exposures. Philadelphia, WB Saunders, 1993, pp 40-41.)

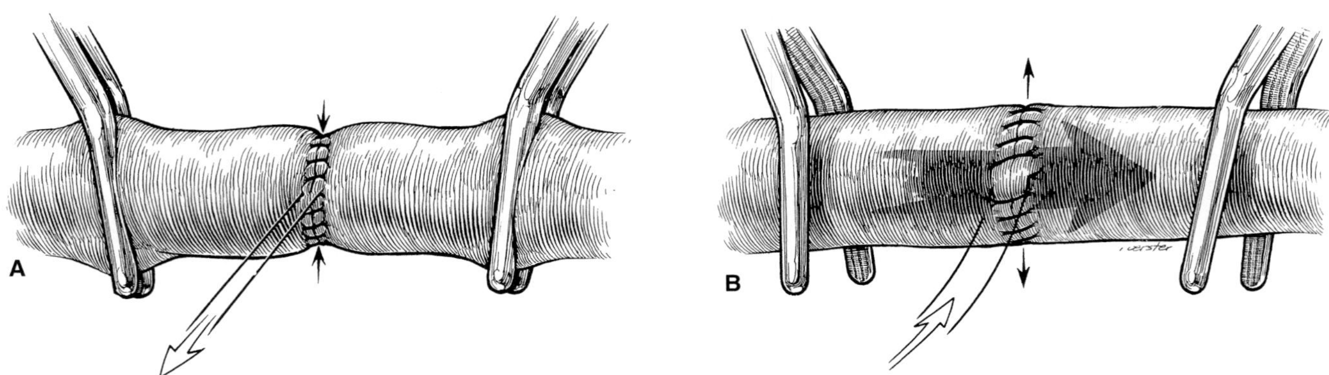

FIGURE 43-12 **A,** Pulling up and tying a continuous suture in a perpendicular end-to-end anastomosis may cause an anastomotic stricture. **B,** Briefly releasing the clamps before tying allows the monofilament suture to slide and the anastomosis to expand to a fuller diameter. (From Rutherford RB: Basic vascular techniques. In: Atlas of Vascular Surgery: Basic Techniques and Exposures. Philadelphia, WB Saunders, 1993, p 36.)

minimize turbulence. Although the optimal angle of entry for an end-to-side anastomosis depends on the velocity of flow across it, this angle should be 30 to 45 degrees or less for arterial anastomosis. Such an acute angle results in a functional approximation and minimal turbulence.

As illustrated in Figure 43-13, end-to-side anastomosis is performed as follows:

1. The end of the donor vessel (vein or prosthetic graft) is fashioned (cut, beveled, or trimmed) to fit into the lateral opening in the recipient artery or vein, whose length is at least twice the diameter of the donor vessel.
2. The "heel" of the anastomosis is started first, with a running suture carried partway along each side.

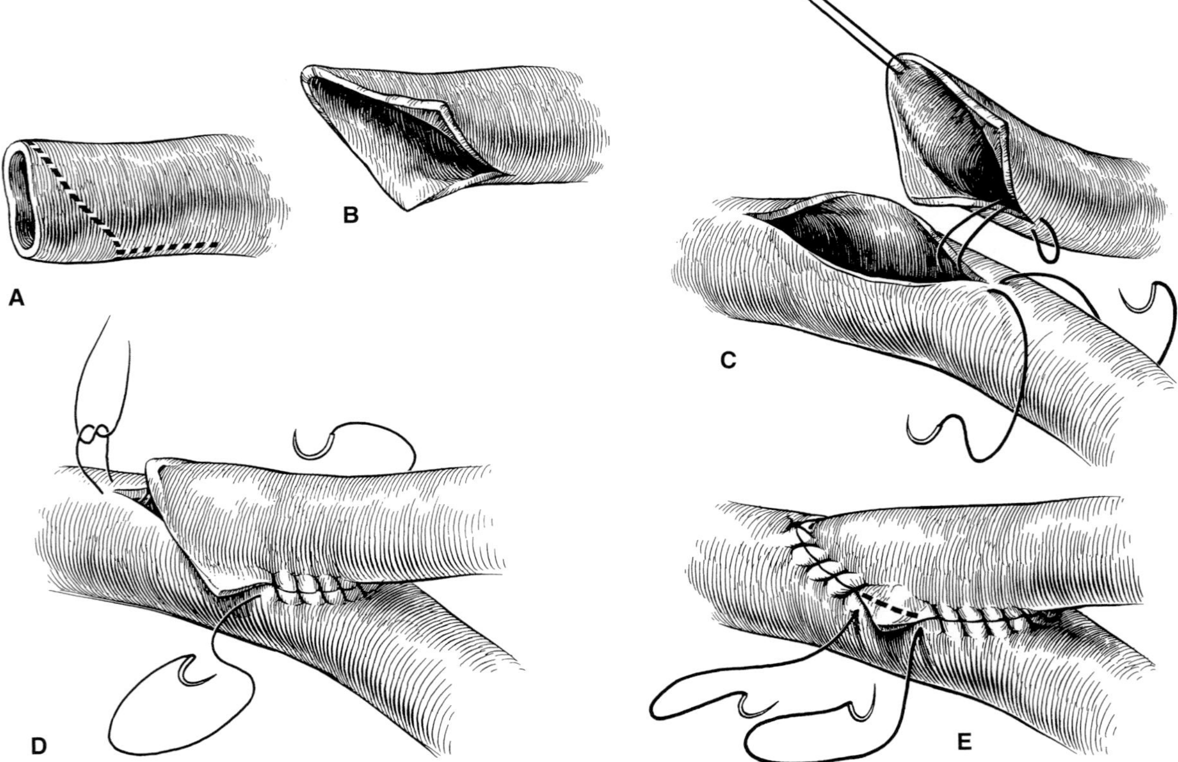

FIGURE 43-13 Typical end-to-side, prosthesis-to–recipient artery anastomosis. **A** and **B,** The graft is trimmed. **C,** The "heel" of the anastomosis is started with a mattress suture. **D,** With the heel completed, the "toe" is begun with another horizontal mattress suture. **E,** Excess edges must be trimmed before the anastomosis is completed. (From Rutherford RB: Basic vascular techniques. In Atlas of Vascular Surgery: Basic Techniques and Exposures. Philadelphia, WB Saunders, 1993, pp 50-51.)

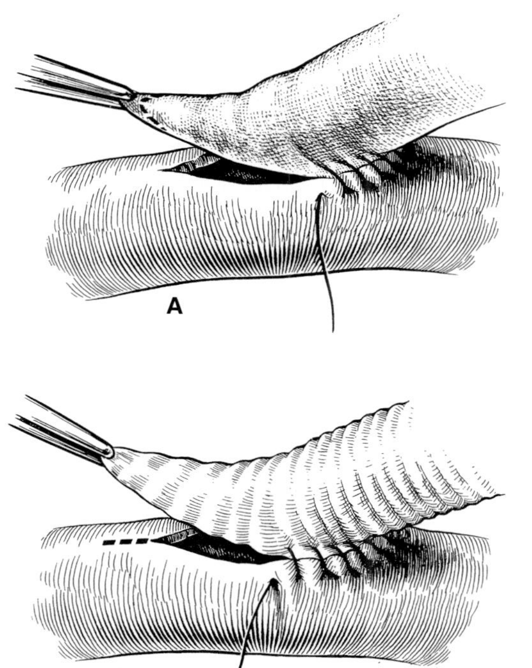

FIGURE 43-14 The advantages of the heel-first, toe-last sequence is illustrated. This method allows the surgeon to make a final length adjustment by either trimming the tip (toe) (**A**) or extending the arteriotomy (**B**). (From Rutherford RB: Basic vascular techniques. In: Atlas of Vascular Surgery: Basic Techniques and Exposures. Philadelphia, WB Saunders, 1993, p 53.)

3. The "toe" of the anastomosis is started, with continuous sutures brought along each side to meet the other sutures in the middle on both sides.

This heel-first, toe-last technique is the safest end-to-side technique. It ensures good hemostasis at the most inaccessible aspect (the heel), allows accurate suture placement at the most critical point to avoid narrowing (the toe), permits adjustments to be made in the fit of the anastomosis by trimming of the graft tip or lengthening of the arteriotomy (Fig. 43-14), and enables the final sutures to be placed quickly and accurately along the sides. Although the end-to-side anastomosis must be modified according to the nature of the host and donor vessels, it is equally applicable to the anastomosis of prosthesis to artery, vein to artery, vein to vein, and artery to artery. It is one of the most commonly used techniques in reconstructive vascular surgery.

Side-to-Side Anastomosis

Although the side-to-side anastomosis is not commonly used in clinical vascular surgery, the best-known examples of this technique probably are the side-to-side portacaval shunt, the Potts and Waterston aortopulmonary anastomosis, and arteriovenous fistulae. For this anastomosis:

1. A curved, spoon-shaped, or angled Satinsky's vascular clamp is placed laterally on adjacent segments of the two vessels to be anastomosed.
2. Matching longitudinal incisions are made in (or equal ellipses removed from) each segment.
3. The adjacent openings are sutured together with continuous suture, the posterior line being performed intraluminally.

There are many varieties of each of these basic techniques. Knowledge of them and of vascular exposures are the two major foundations of operative technique in vascular surgery. For further details of these and other basic techniques, the reader is referred to the companion volume, *Atlas of Vascular Surgery: Basic Techniques and Exposures*.[4]

■ REFERENCES

1. Carrel A: The surgery of blood vessels. Johns Hopkins Med J 18:18, 1907.
2. Guthrie CG: Heterotransplantation of blood vessels. Am J Physiol 19:482, 1907.
3. Carrel A: Heterotransplantation of blood vessels preserved in cold storage. J Exp Med 9:226, 1907.
4. Rutherford RB: An Atlas of Vascular Surgery: Basic Techniques and Exposures. Philadelphia, WB Saunders, 1993.

Chapter

44

Techniques for Thromboembolectomy of Native Arteries and Bypass Grafts

FRANK J. VEITH, MD
EVAN C. LIPSITZ, MD
NICHOLAS J. GARGIULO, MD
JACOB CYNAMON, MD

The need for thromboembolectomy of both native arteries and arterial bypass grafts almost always arises in current practice in patients who have advanced arteriosclerosis and who present with acute limb or organ ischemia (see Chapters 32, 53, 65 to 68, 122, and 134). In the past, many patients with this presentation had an embolus arising from the heart and lodging at a bifurcation within a relatively disease-free arterial tree. Surgical removal of the embolus, either directly or with the aid of balloon catheters, was deemed one of the simplest of modern-day vascular operations. This is no longer the case because the elimination of rheumatic heart disease and atrial fibrillation means that almost all patients who currently present with acute limb ischemia have advanced underlying atherosclerosis. This results in atypical localization of emboli, increased difficulty in clearly differentiating embolization from thrombosis, greater difficulty in restoring adequate distal circulation, and the need for more complex vascular surgical procedures to do so. Moreover, these procedures must often be performed in patients who are quite ill from medical co-morbidities.

Arterial embolectomy to treat acute occlusions was first attempted more than 100 years ago by Szabanajeff,[1] but it was only in 1911 when Einar Key in Stockholm and Georges Labey in Paris independently performed the first successful femoral embolectomies.[2] Labey's procedure[2] required extensive dissection to remove the embolus and its propagated thrombus. The associated morbidity and mortality did not generate much enthusiasm for the procedure, and over the next half century techniques of arterial embolectomy were sporadically reported in the literature with variable results.

The introduction of the balloon catheter technique in 1963[3] heralded an era of arterial thromboembolectomy with reduced morbidity. This technique permitted removal of thromboembolic material from sites proximal and distal to the arteriotomy with a minimum of invasiveness and tissue dissection. As the devices and the procedure became standardized, balloon thromboembolectomy became a suitable, safe, and effective method for the revascularization of an acutely occluded vessel.

Over the next 3 decades, changing trends in the etiology of acute occlusions have led to a demonstrated decline in the effectiveness of simple balloon catheter embolectomy.[4,5] Because of this change in results, various methods have been developed either to replace or to serve as an adjunct to simple balloon catheter embolectomy. Nevertheless, balloon catheter embolectomy by itself or with adjunctive techniques continues to be a valuable tool in the treatment of acute arterial occlusion. In this chapter, we describe both established and newer techniques for performing surgical thromboembolectomy when indicated in the patient population. Most of the established techniques depend on use of the single-lumen balloon thromboembolectomy catheter, although a variety of newer catheters are also described. In standard practice, all of these catheters are passed blindly through the lumen of the arterial tree, a maneuver that can be difficult or impossible when extensive arteriosclerotic plaque is present. The newer techniques use catheters, guide wires, balloons, and stents placed under digital fluoroscopic control to improve and simplify thromboembolectomy of both native arteries and grafts.

■ GENERAL CONSIDERATIONS

The first important issue when considering a thromboembolectomy is to determine the underlying cause of the acute occlusion. Since about 1960, and especially since 1970, this etiologic mechanism has changed from cardiac emboli from rheumatic heart disease to cardiac emboli from myocardial infarction or atrial fibrillation and in-situ thrombotic events secondary to generalized atherosclerosis.[5,6] The typical patient with acute arterial occlusion has changed from a young person with rheumatic heart disease to an older person with diffuse arterial disease and significant medical co-morbidities.[7] Although some authors claim that an occlusion arising from atherosclerotic thrombus has many characteristics in common with true emboli and therefore the intervention should basically be the same,[8] the etiology of the acute ischemic event (whether true

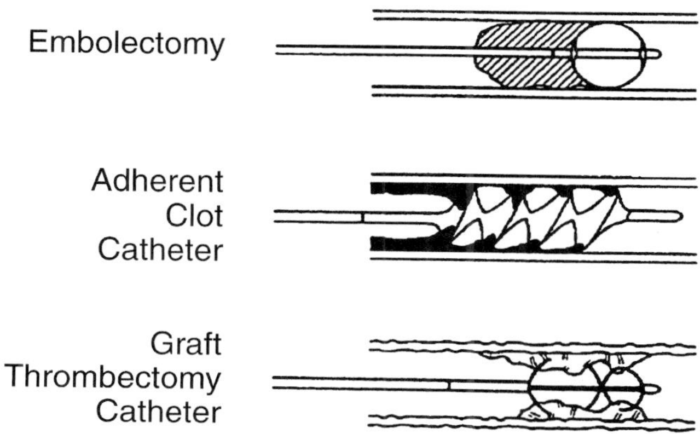

FIGURE 44-1 Types of thromboembolectomy catheters. (From Fogarty TJ, White JV: Thrombectomy, pharmacological and mechanical thrombolysis. In Ahn SS, Hodgson KJ [eds]: Handbook on Endovascular Procedures. Coursebook for NA-ISCVS/SVS Third Annual Endovascular Surgery Workshop, San Diego, June 1998.)

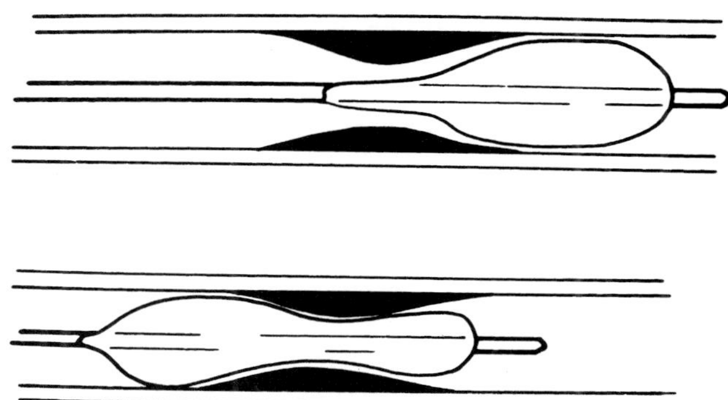

FIGURE 44-2 Compliance of the embolectomy balloon.

embolism or thrombosis in the setting of severe peripheral vascular disease) significantly influences the success or failure of a simple embolectomy.[5]

Obtaining a complete history and physical examination, including bilateral ankle-brachial indices and segmental pressures, gives an indication of the underlying presence of chronic disease. In general, full *arteriography* should be performed before operation for several reasons. Precise arteriographic localization of the occlusion helps the surgeon place the incision in the optimal site. In addition, unexpected inflow disease may be detected, and appropriate sites of inflow and outflow may be selected should a bypass be required. Nonocclusive ischemia may be excluded.[9] Finally, unsuspected second emboli may be detected and treated. Indeed, multiple sites of occlusion in locations not usually associated with chronic disease is one of the most certain pieces of evidence to support embolization as the etiologic mechanism of the acute ischemic event. The arteriogram can thus provide important information about the occlusive event and delineate the management plan accordingly.

A simple balloon embolectomy may be limb and life saving in most cases of true embolism; however, when an acute thrombotic event *is* superimposed on chronic progressive occlusive disease, this procedure by itself usually does not suffice for revascularization, and adjunctive techniques or a well-planned and well-executed bypass operation may be required to achieve a successful outcome.

The choice of instrumentation is also important. Since its introduction in 1963, the embolectomy catheter has undergone minor modifications, but the general concept behind its use has remained relatively constant.[10,11] The catheter consists of a hollow, pliable shaft with a compliant, distensible balloon at the distal end (Fig. 44-1, top). The compliant balloon is effective in extracting true emboli and the acute clot formed from stasis at a critically narrowed segment. The compliance of the balloon, although having the advantage of minimizing intimal trauma, proves disadvantageous for removal of the occlusion due to plaque from atherosclerotic disease (Fig. 44-2). For managing more adherent clots, a latex-covered spiral cable catheter has been developed that is more effective in extracting the dense, adherent, mature thrombus (see Fig. 44-1, middle). A spiral cable catheter without the latex covering is advocated for use in synthetic grafts (see Fig. 44-1, bottom). This graft thrombectomy catheter works as a ringed variable diameter device that strips out densely adherent fibrinous material associated with graft healing. Additional discussions of the causes, methods, and instrumentation for managing arterial thromboembolism are presented in Chapters 32 and 53.

It is critical to adopt a technique that ensures the least amount of arterial injury. Balloon catheter embolectomy is not without its complications and injurious effects.[12] The correlation between shear forces applied to the arterial wall during instrumentation and the degree of intimal injury resulting in intimal hyperplasia is well recognized.[13-15] Some authors have compared the different brands of balloon embolectomy catheters and their potential for injury and intimal damage.[8,9] Although differences among the various brands have been described, these differences are slight. Moreover, freedom from underlying chronic disease and the use of the proper technique may have more to do with preventing intimal damage than the choice of any particular brand of balloon catheter.[16]

■ ESTABLISHED BALLOON CATHETER THROMBOEMBOLECTOMY TECHNIQUE

Operative catheter thromboembolectomy begins with exposure of an adequate length of artery to allow control both proximal and distal to the catheter introduction site. A transverse arteriotomy was used in the past, but we now prefer a *longitudinal incision* to allow for the possibility of converting the arteriotomy to a graft anastomotic site if a bypass is required. Careful closure with or without a patch does not produce luminal narrowing, even in small diseased arteries. After opening the artery, we inspect the lumen to ensure that catheter passage does not take place subintimally.

The balloon catheter is inspected and prepared for use. The balloon is inflated with saline and checked for concentricity and leaks. Concentricity is important because an eccentric balloon displaces the catheter tip and body toward one side of the arterial wall and produces increased drag and friction.[17] Inflation and deflation of the balloon are repeated to make the balloon more pliable. This increases balloon control during the procedure. It is also worthwhile to inflate the balloon ex vivo to determine its inflated size and the volume of saline required to achieve this size. Small-bore syringes are recommended for balloon inflation, but some find that the smaller stroke distance resulting from the use of larger-bore syringes affords finer control. For smaller-diameter catheters (1 and 2 French), air is used to inflate the balloon because the inflation lumen of these catheters is too tiny to permit quick adjustments in balloon size if saline inflation is performed. When even small amounts of air may be hazardous, as in the cerebral vasculature, carbon dioxide can be used for inflation.

Before occluding arteries and introducing the balloon catheter, we give systemic heparin (100 units kg). Catheter advancement must be performed with great care. Although the pliable embolectomy catheter is designed to facilitate passage, cannulation may be difficult at times because of arterial disease or tortuosity. A common site of difficulty is the popliteal artery. Varying the angle of knee flexion may allow the catheter to pass. Persistent inability to pass the catheter indicates atherosclerotic obstruction or narrowing of the vessel, and it is more prudent to assess the area using intraoperative arteriography rather than persist in potentially damaging attempts at catheter passage. It may be advantageous to place the incision below the knee and the arteriotomy at the distal popliteal artery to perform safe embolectomy of the distal popliteal and its branches.[18] However, this usually requires regional or general anesthesia.

Catheter retrieval must be performed in a gentle manner with the least possible amount of shear force, repeated the least possible number of times that ensures complete clot extraction. When a large amount of pull force is required to remove the catheter, either the balloon has been overinflated or the lumen of the artery is being narrowed by plaque. In these cases, the balloon should be deflated and reinflated to the point where it can be withdrawn with minimal resistance On the other hand, when the balloon embolectomy catheter is withdrawn from a vessel with an increasing diameter, addition of saline may be required for the balloon to maintain arterial wall contact. Balloon overinflation causes an inordinate amount of shear force to be exerted on the arterial endothelium. Endothelial injury and plaque dislodgment may occur. Certain techniques for decreasing shear force and friction have been described. These include slowly inflating the balloon in the first 0.5 cm of catheter motion during withdrawal and allowing a small amount of heparinized blood in the lumen proximal to the point of embolic obstruction.[19]

The importance of distal catheter passage cannot be overemphasized. Distal thrombus may be discontinuous with proximal thrombus. Vigorous backflow resulting from proximal thromboembolectomy can give false assurance of distal patency. Failure to remove the distal thrombus results in the retained thrombus propagating proximally to cause reocclusion. Patency of the distal vasculature must always be confirmed by completion arteriography or return of distal pulses (pedal or radial).

■ EMBOLECTOMY IN SPECIFIC VESSELS

Aortoiliac Embolectomy

Bilateral groin incisions are made, and the common, superficial, and deep femoral arteries are isolated and controlled with vessel loops or clamps (Fig. 44-3). Prior to arteriotomy, the common femoral artery is palpated to determine the location of plaque. A longitudinal arteriotomy is made proximal to the bifurcation to allow visualization of the superficial and deep femoral arteries when they are cannulated. Distal exploration is carried out first through the superficial and deep femoral arteries. Passage of a long (15 to 20-cm) section of a 2- or 3-French embolectomy catheter ensures that the deep femoral artery, rather than one of the large circumflex branches that arise from this vessel, has been cannulated.

Following distal embolectomy, heparin-saline solution is infused into the femoral system and the common femoral artery is clamped. Embolectomy of the aorta and the ipsilateral iliac artery with a 6-French catheter is carried out while the contralateral common femoral artery is occluded to prevent clot dislodgment into the opposite distal arterial tree. The contralateral side is explored in a similar manner to exclude embolization that may have occurred to either side (see Fig. 44-3). After flow is restored, complete clearing of the arterial tree must be confirmed by the detection of pedal pulses. If these cannot be detected, completion arteriography is mandatory, and a bypass may be required.

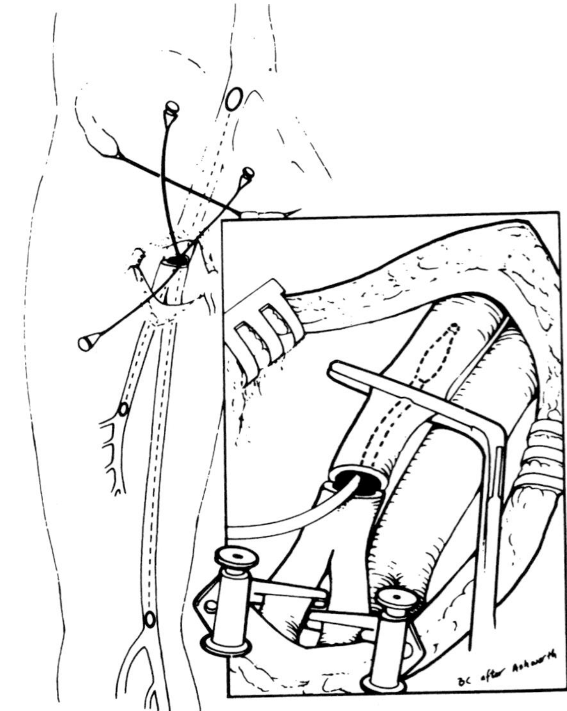

FIGURE 44-3 Cannulation of both proximal and distal vessels in aortoiliac embolectomy. Although a transverse arteriotomy may be used, a longitudinal arteriotomy is preferred.

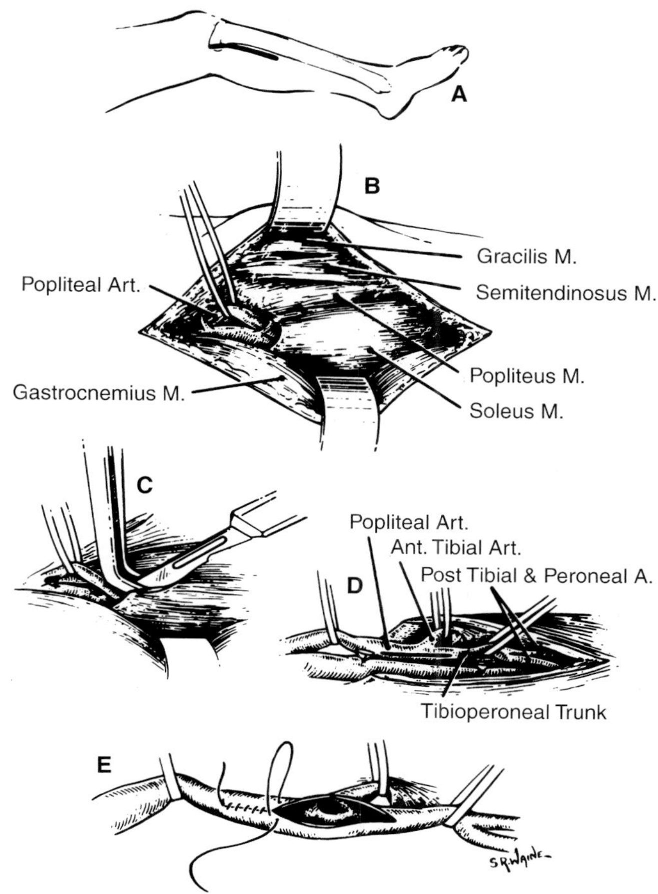

FIGURE 44-4 Embolectomy of the distal popliteal artery. **A,** Incision for exposure of the distal popliteal artery. **B,** Exposure of the vascular bundle after incision of the deep fascia and retraction of gastrocnemius muscle posteriorly. **C,** Division of overlying soleus muscle fibers. **D,** Mobilized distal popliteal artery, anterior tibial artery, and tibioperoneal trunk and position of longitudinal incision in the artery. **E,** Ostia of anterior tibial artery as seen through the arteriotomy and closure of the arteriotomy with fine vascular sutures without producing any stenosis. M, muscle; Art, artery; Ant, anterior. (From Gupta SK, Samson RH, Veith FJ: Embolectomy of the distal part of the popliteal artery. Surg Gynecol Obstet 153:254, 1981.)

Infrainguinal Embolectomy

Infrainguinal occlusions are approached through a groin incision. Catheter explorations through the superficial and deep femoral systems are carried out as just described. Two catheters (2 or 3 French) are sequentially passed into the distal lower extremity. The first catheter usually passes into the peroneal or posterior tibial artery. Inflating the balloon at the origin of the tibioperoneal trunk may allow the subsequent catheter to pass into the anterior tibial artery.[20] When occlusions involve the popliteal artery and its trifurcated branches, it is best to approach the arterial tree with a below-knee incision.[18] The arteriotomy is placed opposite the origin of the anterior tibial artery (Fig. 44-4). With this approach, it is easier to pass the catheter into all three crural arteries, and instrumentation of a patent minimally diseased superficial femoral artery is avoided.

Upper Extremity Occlusions

An arteriotomy is performed in the brachial artery just proximal to the bifurcation at the antecubital fossa to allow access and control of all three arteries.[21,22] Emboli in the proximal subclavian artery can be removed by retrograde extraction, although one must continually be aware of the possibility of fragmentation of emboli during extraction with displacement to the cerebral circulation.

Renal and Mesenteric Occlusions

The techniques for management of renal and mesenteric embolic occlusions (see Chapters 122 and 134) are similar to those described for management for peripheral occlusions, albeit with two major differences. First, because the external support provided by adjacent tissue is significantly less in the vessels supplying the viscera than in those of the peripheral vasculature, the risk of perforation is higher in these vessels. Therefore, catheter advancement and manipulations should be performed with greater care and gentleness. Second, procedures in these arterial systems must be accomplished under angiographic or fluoroscopic control and never as a blind procedure, as has been done in the past. In general, visceral and renal embolectomy is performed via a transabdominal approach. However, catheter-directed clot extraction techniques and thrombolysis may become more widely used in the future.

Graft Thrombectomy

Prosthetic graft thrombectomy (see Chapter 65) is performed in a similar manner to that done on native arteries. An initial extraction using the balloon catheter is accomplished with the extraction of soft clots, followed by passage of special catheters, described previously, that address the problem of removing the adherent thrombus that is frequently encountered in artificial conduits. The catheter is passed in the low-profile configuration until it is positioned within the region of the adherent material within the graft. The pitch of the spiral retrieval element is then adjusted to engage the adherent material, and the catheter is withdrawn through the arteriotomy or graftotomy. Fluoroscopic guidance may be most valuable during these procedures.

Intraoperative Monitoring and Postprocedure Assessment and Evaluation

The aim of surgical embolectomy is to restore the peripheral circulation to its preocclusive state. Evaluation of results must be based on restoration of pulses or completion arteriography. Complete extraction of the embolus and the propagated thrombus is absolutely necessary for the success of the procedure. One clue to the completeness of extraction is the appearance of the extracted thrombus. Usually, although not always, a smooth, tapering clot indicates adequate removal; a sharp cutoff suggests that additional thrombotic material remains. As mentioned previously, vigorous back-bleeding is not an indicator of the completeness of thromboembolectomy. The presence of a waterhammer pulse suggests distal obstruction. Even with these clues and arteriography, however, it may still be difficult to assess results in atherosclerotic patients.

Completion arteriography or fluoroscopy remains the standard for the evaluation of procedural success. It has been reported that up to 68% of thromboembolectomies clinically deemed successful required re-interventions for residual lesions detected by radiographic means.[23] Digital fluoroscopy is a valuable newer adjunct that, in addition to demonstrating the success of the procedure, can facilitate the accurate identification, localization, and treatment of significant underlying arterial lesions during the procedure.[24,25]

■ NEWER TECHNIQUES AND PROCEDURES FOR THROMBOEMBOLECTOMY

The traditional methods of thromboembolectomy have the disadvantage of being performed blindly. Information is not provided to the surgeon regarding the extent of clot removal or the localization of underlying disease. Techniques employing fluoroscopically guided catheters and guide wires eliminate the blind aspects of the procedure. These techniques allow the operator to (1) manipulate and direct the catheter through difficult, diseased arteries and branches, (2) monitor and control balloon inflation, (3) detect and retrieve any residual clot, and (4) detect and treat underlying hemodynamically significant atherosclerotic plaque.

Fluoroscopically Assisted Thromboembolectomy

Fluoroscopically guided catheter and guide wire thromboembolectomy has been used and described by our group.[25] This method uses digital cinefluoroscopy with a mobile C-arm unit and catheter-based endovascular techniques to facilitate balloon catheter passage and the accurate identification, localization, and treatment of the underlying arterial lesions. It also reduces the risk of arterial damage and intimal injury. With the use of a directional catheter and guide wires, even tortuous diseased arteries can be traversed under fluoroscopic guidance (Fig. 44-5). The balloon catheter can be inflated with contrast material and withdrawn to remove the clot while the balloon configuration is visualized fluoroscopically. This prevents overdistention of the balloon and allows identification of stenosing lesions as they distort the image of the balloon.

After the clot is removed, these lesions may be confirmed angiographically by injection into a catheter or the side arm of the hemostatic sheath. Once identified, the lesion can be treated by an angioplasty balloon or stent placement. This technique, therefore, provides immediate feedback and allows immediate interventional elimination of uncovered lesions.

To perform retrograde iliac thrombectomy, the surgeon inserts a hemostatic vascular sheath into the artery and uses a guide wire and directional catheter to cross the occluded or diseased arterial segments (Fig. 44-6; see also Fig. 44-5). The sheath is then advanced over the wire; the dilator is removed, and a standard balloon catheter is passed (see Fig. 44-5). The sheath is retracted, and the inflated balloon is withdrawn to remove the clot. Alternatively, a double-lumen balloon catheter may be inserted over the wire and passed through the occlusion (see Fig. 44-6). Under fluoroscopic guidance, the balloon is filled with dilute contrast medium until the balloon profile approaches the size of the underlying vessel lumen. Gentle withdrawal of the balloon catheter is then undertaken under fluoroscopic control. Deformities of the balloon profile caused by underlying arterial lesions are identified and the locations are noted. These lesions can be treated by repeated thrombectomy, angioplasty with or without stent placement, or surgical revascularization.

Intraoperative Thrombolysis

Certain situations may arise in which the distal outflow tract is occluded by clots that cannot be retrieved by mechanical means. In these instances, intraoperative thrombolysis may offer a viable option for revascularization.[26,27] After removal of as much thrombus as possible using mechanical extraction devices, the inflow artery is occluded and boluses of urokinase or tissue plasminogen activator are instilled distally. After 20 minutes, angiography and the bolus or lytic drug are repeated until the distal bed is cleared of clot. This procedure and the use of percutaneous catheter-directed urokinase to treat acute thromboembolic occlusions are discussed further in Chapters 32 and 53.

Aspiration Thromboembolectomy and Mechanical Clot-Removing Endoluminal Devices

Possible adjuncts or alternatives to thrombolysis and surgical embolectomy include aspiration thromboembolectomy[28,29] and the use of mechanical catheter-based devices, such as the Angiojet system, to remove clot.[30,31] These methods may be performed percutaneously or via an open arteriotomy. The aspiration technique involves passage of a 6- to 8-French sheath through which an aspiration catheter is advanced over a guide wire to the site of the occlusion. A 50-mL syringe is then used to apply suction to the end of the aspiration catheter. Withdrawal of the aspiration catheter is carried out while suction is maintained. Repeated aspirations are performed to clear the occlusion. The limitation of the technique is that it can only be used in distal peripheral acute occlusions and not in the larger arterial branches, such as the iliac arteries, because of the large volumes of material that would require aspiration in these vessels.

In the last several years, several mechanical clot-removing devices have been undergoing clinical trials.[30,31] These devices are usually inserted percutaneously through a hemostatic sheath and over a guide wire. They employ a variety of methods to fragment the clot so that it can be aspirated. Some of these devices have been used as stand-alone systems, whereas others have been used in conjunction with thrombolytic agents. At present only the Angiojet system is approved by the U.S. Food and Drug Administration for use in the periphery.

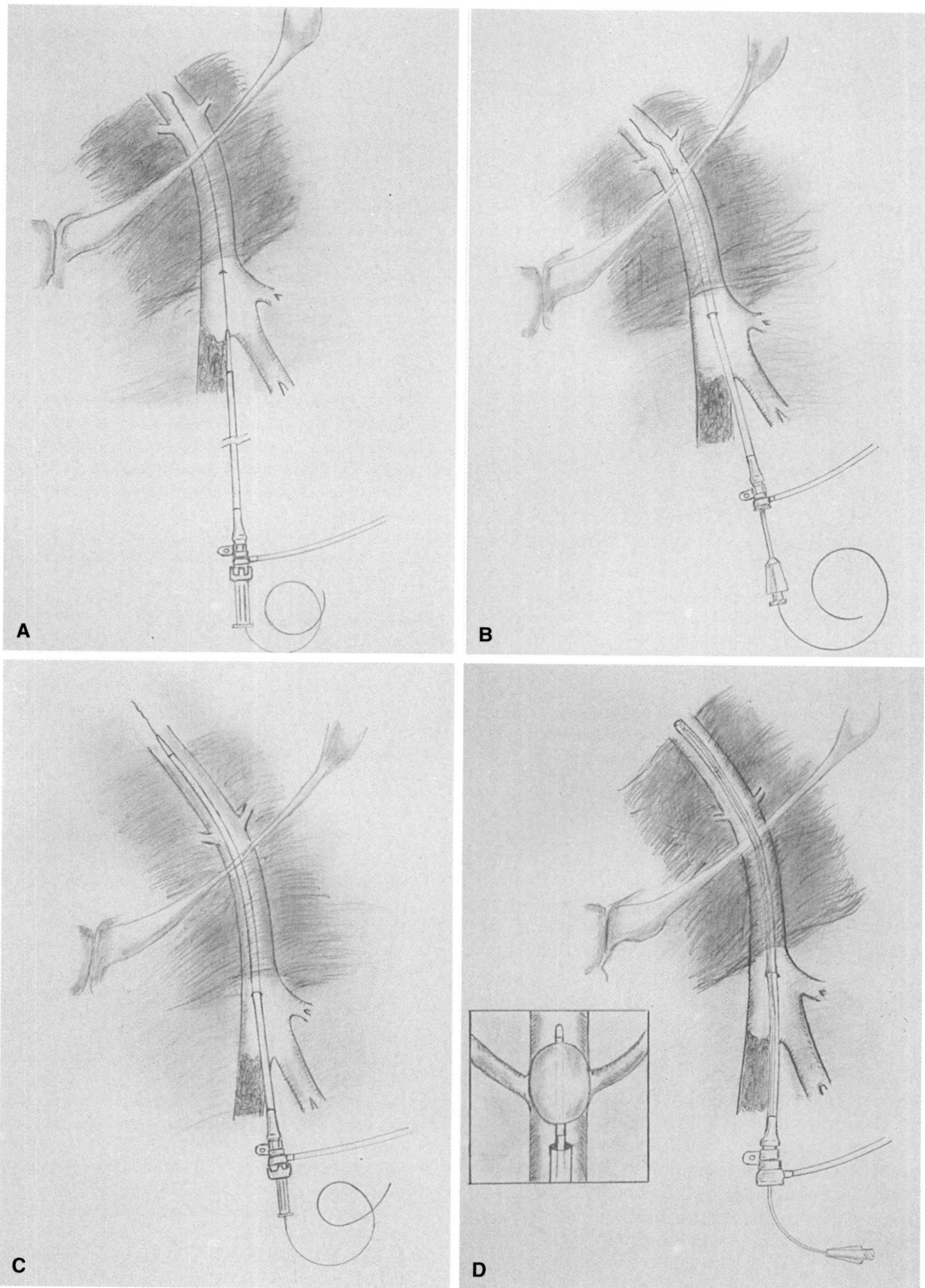

FIGURE 44-5 Diagrams illustrating fluoroscopically assisted thromboembolectomy using over-the-wire technique I. **A,** Guide wire has been inserted a short distance through a needle. The needle has been removed, and the hemostatic sheath and its dilator are being advanced over the guide wire. Entrance through arterial wall is facilitated by rotating the sheath and dilator as they are advanced as a unit. **B,** After removal of dilator, a directional catheter (Berenstein) is inserted through a sheath over the wire. Under fluoroscopic guidance, the wire is advanced well into the external iliac artery. **C,** The catheter is removed, leaving the wire and sheath in place. The dilator is replaced, and the sheath and dilator are advanced over the wire well into the external iliac artery. **D,** The dilator is removed along with the guide wire, leaving the sheath within the iliac artery. The balloon catheter is advanced within the sheath. After retracting the sheath, the balloon is inflated with dilute contrast material and withdrawn under fluoroscopic guidance to remove clot and identify lesions (*inset*). (**A-D,** Adapted from Veith FJ, Sanchez LA, Ohki T: Technique for obtaining proximal intraluminal control when arteries are inaccessible or unclampable because of disease or calcification. J Vasc Surg 27:582, 1998.)

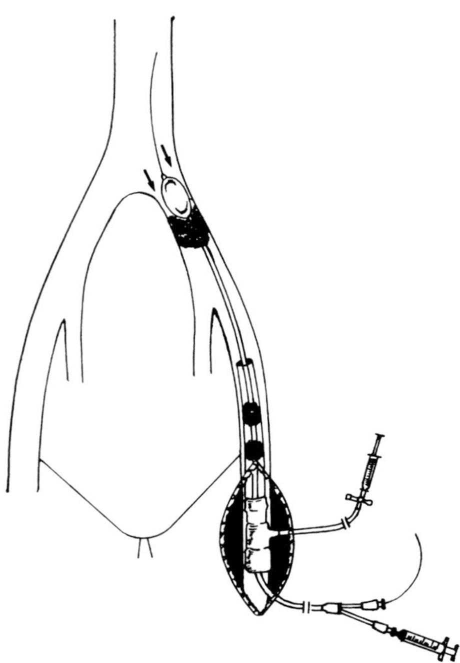

FIGURE 44-6 Diagram illustrating fluoroscopically assisted thromboembolectomy using over-the-wire technique II. Following passage of a radiographic guide wire, a balloon thrombectomy catheter equipped with two lumina is passed through a hemostatic valve in a previously placed vascular sheath. Under fluoroscopic control, the balloon is withdrawn through the vessel containing the clot, and the clot is withdrawn into the introducer sheath. Several passes of the balloon thrombectomy catheter may be made prior to the removal of the sheath containing the thrombectomized clot. (From Parsons RE, Marin ML, Veith FJ, et al: Fluoroscopically-assisted thromboembolectomy: An improved method for treating acute arterial occlusions. Ann Vasc Surg 10:201, 1996.)

■ SUMMARY

The changing trends in etiology and patient population in acute arterial occlusion dictate that the treatments be modified accordingly to achieve optimum results. Although simple balloon catheter thromboembolectomy has greatly improved the management of acute arterial occlusion, the occurrence of thromboembolic problems in patients with increasingly advanced underlying arteriosclerosis means that patients will be increasingly difficult to treat. This mandates that we improve our diagnostic and therapeutic techniques to improve results in this challenging group of patients. To this end, the use of digital cinefluoroscopy and catheter-guide wire techniques combined with endovascular treatments, such as angioplasty and stents, are important technical adjuncts that can simplify and improve balloon thromboembolectomy procedures in the future.

Acknowledgments The authors thank the Anna S. Brown Trust and the New York Institute for Vascular Studies.

■ REFERENCES

1. Szabanajeff: On the question of blood vessel suture. Russk Khir Arkh 11:625, 1895.
2. Mesney M, Dumont NJ: Embolie femorale au cours d'un retrecissement mitral pur arteriotomie. Guerison Bull Acad Med 66:358, 1911.
3. Fogarty TJ, Cranley JJ, Krause RJ, et al: A method for extraction of arterial emboli and thrombi. Surg Gynecol Obstet 116:241, 1963.
4. Hight DW, Tilney NL, Couch NP: Changing clinical trends in patients with peripheral arterial emboli. Surgery 79:172, 1976.
5. Hill SL, Donato AT: The simple Fogarty embolectomy: An operation of the past? Am Surg 60:907, 1994.
6. Braithwaite BD, Earnshaw JJ: Arterial embolectomy: A century and out. Br J Surg 81:1705, 1994.
7. Haimovici H, Moss CM, Veith FJ: Arterial embolectomy revisited. Surgery 78:409, 1975.
8. Fogarty TJ, Hermann GD: New techniques for clot extraction and managing acute thromboembolic limb ischemia. In Veith FJ (ed): Current Critical Problems in Vascular Surgery, Vol 3. St. Louis, Quality Medical, 1991, pp 197-203.
9. Dardik H, Dardik I, Spreyregen S, Veith FJ: Asymmetrical nonocclusive ischemia of the lower extremities. JAMA 227:1417, 1974.
10. Niblet PG, Fleischl JM, Campbell WB: Which balloon embolectomy catheter? Br J Surg 77:930, 1990.
11. Schwarcz TH, Dobrin PB, Mrkvicka R, et al: Balloon embolectomy catheter–induced arterial injury: A comparison of four catheters. J Vasc Surg 11:382, 1990.
12. Foster JH, Carter JW, Edwards WH, et al: Arterial injuries secondary to the use of the Fogarty catheter. Ann Surg 171:971, 1970.
13. Goldberg EM, Goldberg MC, Chowdhury LN, et al: The effects of balloon embolectomy-thrombectomy catheters on vascular architecture. J Cardiovasc Surg 24:74, 1983.
14. Chidi C, DePalma R: Atherogenic potential of the embolectomy catheter. Surgery 83:549, 1987.
15. Jorgensen RA, Dobrin PB: Balloon embolectomy catheters in small arteries: IV. Correlation of shear forces with histologic injury. Surgery 93:798, 1983.
16. Bowles CR, Olcott C, Pakter RL, et al: Diffuse arterial narrowing as a result of intimal proliferation: A delayed complication of embolectomy with the Fogarty balloon catheter. J Vasc Surg 7:487, 1988.
17. Dobrin PB, Jorgensen RA: Balloon embolectomy catheters in small arteries: III. Surgical significance of eccentric balloons. Surgery 93:402, 1983.
18. Gupta SK, Samson RH, Veith FJ: Embolectomy of the distal part of the popliteal artery. Surg Gynecol Obstet 153:254, 1981.
19. Dobrin PB, Jorgensen RA: Balloon embolectomy catheters in small arteries: A technique to prevent excessive shear forces. J Vasc Surg 2:692, 1985.
20. Santiago O, Diethrich EB, Bahadir I, et al: A double balloon occlusion technique for embolectomy in the trifurcation vessels. Surg Gynecol Obstet 174:164, 1992.
21. Haimovici H: Cardiogenic embolism of the upper extremity. J Cardiovasc Surg 23:209, 1982.
22. Dregelid E: Diameter of the brachial artery: The selection of arteriotomy site for embolectomy. Ann Chir Gynaecol 76:222, 1987.
23. Crolla RM, van de Pavoordt ED, Moll FL: Intraoperative digital subtraction angiography after thromboembolectomy: Preliminary experience. J Endovasc Surg 2:168, 1995.
24. Robicsek F: Dye-enhanced fluoroscopy-directed catheter embolectomy. Surgery 95:622, 1984.
25. Parsons RE, Marin ML, Veith FJ, et al: Fluoroscopically assisted thromboembolectomy: An improved method for treating acute arterial occlusions. Ann Vasc Surg 10:201, 1996.
26. Quinones-Baldrich WJ, Zierler RE, Hiatt JC: Intraoperative fibrinolytic therapy: An adjunct to catheter thromboembolectomy. J Vasc Surg 2:319, 1985.
27. Beard JD, Nyanekye I, Earnshaw JJ, et al: Intraoperative streptokinase: A useful adjunct to balloon catheter embolectomy. Br J Surg 80:21, 1993.

28. Murray JG, Brown AL, Wilkins RA: Percutaneous aspiration thromboembolectomy: A preliminary experience. Clin Radiol 49:553, 1994.
29. Cleveland TJ, Cumberland DC, Gaines PA: Percutaneous aspiration thromboembolectomy to manage the embolic complications of angioplasty and as an adjunct to thrombolysis. Clin Radiol 49:549, 1994.
30. Muller-Hulsbeck S, Jahnke P: Peripheral arterial applications of percutaneous mechanical thrombectomy. Tech Vasc Interv Radiol 6:22, 2003.
31. Vesely TM: Mechanical thrombectomy devices to treat thrombosed hemodialysis grafts. Tech Vasc Interv Radiol 6:35, 2003.

Chapter 45

Endarterectomy

WILLIAM C. KRUPSKI, MD
LOUIS M. MESSINA, MD
RONALD J. STONEY, MD

Section VIII

■ HISTORICAL PERSPECTIVE

Open surgical endarterectomy dates back more than 50 years to 1946, when the Portuguese surgeon Cid Dos Santos performed the first thromboendarterectomy through two arteriotomies.[10] He attributed his success to the use of the new anticoagulant drug heparin, calling the procedure *disobliteration*. Bazy and Reboul[1] later coined the term *endarterectomy* for this operation. Leriche and Kunlin[23] used the more comprehensive word *thromboendarterectomy* to describe removal of obstructing thrombus as well as the diseased arterial intima. There is no precise expression to describe this technique accurately because, when it is properly performed, the inner media is removed with the intima; however, the terms *endarterectomy* and *thromboendarterectomy*, which are interchangeable, are used most commonly.

In 1950, Dr E. J. Wylie performed the first thromboendarterectomy in the United States in San Francisco to relieve aortoiliac obstruction.[37] Soon thereafter, Wylie reported a large experience with this technique at the University of California Medical Center in San Francisco (UCSF).[35] For the ensuing half century at UCSF, endarterectomy has remained one of the preferred therapeutic options for patients with atherosclerotic peripheral arterial disease, resulting in a significant experience with this operative technique in all arterial sites where such lesions occur. Initially, thromboendarterectomy was the procedure of choice for patients with peripheral vascular occlusive disease, but the advent of bypass techniques and the development of prosthetic grafts led to a marked decline in the number of surgeons performing these technically demanding procedures. Indeed, the decline in the number of surgeons familiar with these techniques was one of the arguments used to justify the development of vascular surgical training programs in the 1970s.[20]

With the more recent development of endovascular stenting and atherectomy, thromboendarterectomy as a primary procedure in the treatment of lower extremity ischemic disease has been indicated less frequently. However, the advantages of autogenous vascular reconstruction, as well as its usefulness as an adjunctive technique for patients requiring both aortoiliac and infrainguinal revascularization, continues to make thromboendarterectomy an essential component of the vascular surgeon's armamentarium (Fig. 45-1).

The critical features that make endarterectomy feasible are the characteristic localization of atherosclerotic plaques to the intima and subjacent media of the diseased artery and the segmental distribution of plaques at areas of turbulent flow. The outer media and adventitia are spared

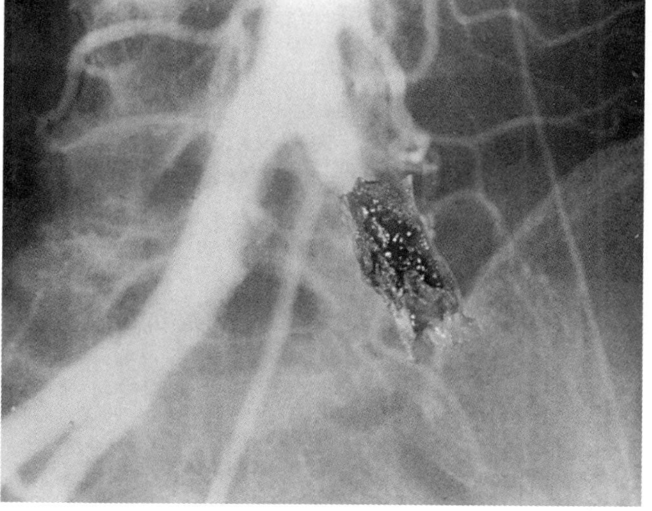

FIGURE 45-1 Aortogram with superimposed left iliac lesion removed by endarterectomy. This short lesion is ideal for thromboendarterectomy; note the virtual absence of atherosclerotic occlusive disease on the right. (Courtesy of Anthony J. Comerota, MD, Philadelphia, Pa.)

by atherosclerosis; therefore, a cleavage plane can be developed between the diseased and nondiseased zones of the arterial wall. This cleavage plane is characterized by easy separation between the two zones, and the plane is macroscopically continuous throughout the length of the lesion. When the atherosclerotic plaque is segmentally localized, the tapering distal termination of the lesion (the endpoint) makes a transition between intima-media to intima alone. This permits removal of the plaque smoothly or with only a minimal residual ledge of slightly thickened intima that is adherent to the underlying media. When such an intimal ledge is present, it can be sharply beveled to minimize the risk of an obstructing flap becoming elevated after restoration of flow. If the distal endpoint is only loosely adherent to the underlying media, it can be secured with fine "tacking" sutures tied externally (rarely required). Nearly all anatomic patterns of occlusive atherosclerosis are suitable for endarterectomy, whether the disease is localized, diffuse, degenerative, or calcific.

The immediate success of endarterectomy also depends on the characteristics of the residual arterial wall that resist dilation and eventual disruption following restoration of pulsatile flow at systemic blood pressures. It has always been of great interest that the residual outer media and adventitia left after endarterectomy have sufficient tensile strength to support the vessel wall; this is true even in the aorta, where the medial myoelastic lamellae are thought to be important to vascular integrity. However, this arterial function is destroyed if any degree of dilation or aneurysmal degeneration is present. Current information suggests that aneurysmal degeneration involves an imbalance of degradative metalloproteases and metalloprotease inhibitors throughout the arterial wall, perhaps most important in the adventitia, and that this process may be biochemically distinct from the atherosclerotic changes evident in occlusive disease patterns (see Chapters 10 and 100). Endarterectomy of such an artery, even if initially successful, predictably leads to aneurysmal dilation of the endarterectomized segment over time. For this reason, the presence of aneurysmal disease is the only specific and absolute contraindication to endarterectomy for the management of occlusive arterial disease.

■ PATTERNS OF ATHEROSCLEROSIS

There are three distinct patterns of occlusive atherosclerosis, which can be characterized according to (1) site in the arterial tree, (2) relation to sites of arterial fixation, and (3) proximity to sites of turbulence. Each pattern is associated with specific arterial lesions amenable to endarterectomy.

Sites Within the Arterial Tree

Lesions in the 10 major aortic branches are predictably located near the origin of the vessel from the aorta, are short, and terminate with a smooth transition to a nearly normal lumen within the arterial branch. Only rarely is the aortic ostia of an involved aortic branch spared, with the obstructing lesion developing within the proximal artery itself and extending distally for a variable length.

These features of aortic branch atherosclerosis make transaortic endarterectomy an important technique for improving perfusion in all vascular beds supplied by these branches, except for the three branches of the transverse aortic arch. In this location, a proximal aortic cross-clamp cannot be applied without producing intolerable cardiac strain. Therefore, transvessel retrograde endarterectomy is necessary, but the proximal occluding clamp must include the orifice of the branch (e.g., the innominate artery). The five major abdominal aortic branches (three viscerals, two renals) are ideally suited for transaortic endarterectomy.

Patterns of obstructive atherosclerotic disease affecting the infrarenal aortoiliac arteries are classically divided into two types. Patients with *type I* disease have atherosclerotic involvement of the infrarenal aorta, the common iliac artery, and the internal iliac artery. Except for the proximal 1 to 2 cm of the external iliac arteries, the remainder of these vessels and the femoral arteries are free of disease. The outflow vessels are also normal unless there has been earlier atheroembolization from the proximal lesions (Fig. 45-2). *Type II* disease includes the type I pattern in addition to involvement of the external iliac arteries and common femoral bifurcations. Often there is diffuse disease of the infrainguinal vessels as well (Fig. 45-3). Type II disease is more common than type I (in a 4:1 ratio) and affects men more often than women (male-to-female ratio for type II, 5:1; male-to-female ratio for type I, 2:1).[21]

On average, type II patients are 7 years older than type I patients.[21] Because data on the relative incidences of disease patterns have been obtained from symptomatic patients, usually with advanced disease, the true patterns of involvement in the general population may not be known.[3]

Sites of Arterial Fixation

The superficial femoral artery traverses the adductor canal in the lower third of the thigh. At this site, it is confined by the adductor magnus muscle and is locally fixed by the adductor tendon at the hiatus through which it passes as it enters the popliteal space. This normal anatomic configuration favors the development of atherosclerotic disease at this particular site in the femoropopliteal arterial segment. The superficial femoral artery is the most frequent lower extremity vessel to be involved with segmental atherosclerosis, although isolated involvement of the common femoral artery, the profunda femoris artery, or the popliteal artery may occur.[18]

Osseous or myofascial anomalies may also cause fixation of arteries in other locations, particularly near active joints. The subclavian artery near the thoracic outlet and the popliteal artery adjacent to the knee are typical examples. A cervical rib or gastrocnemius muscle entrapment produces arterial compression and eventually injury.

Repeated arterial injury of the subclavian artery produces post-stenotic aneurysm or focal atherosclerotic intimal ulceration. These can produce upper extremity microembolization or macroembolization. The focal occlusive and ulcerated lesions of the subclavian arterial tree are quite amenable to thromboendarterectomy through the affected artery; however, when either subclavian or popliteal aneurysms are present, interposition grafting is preferred.

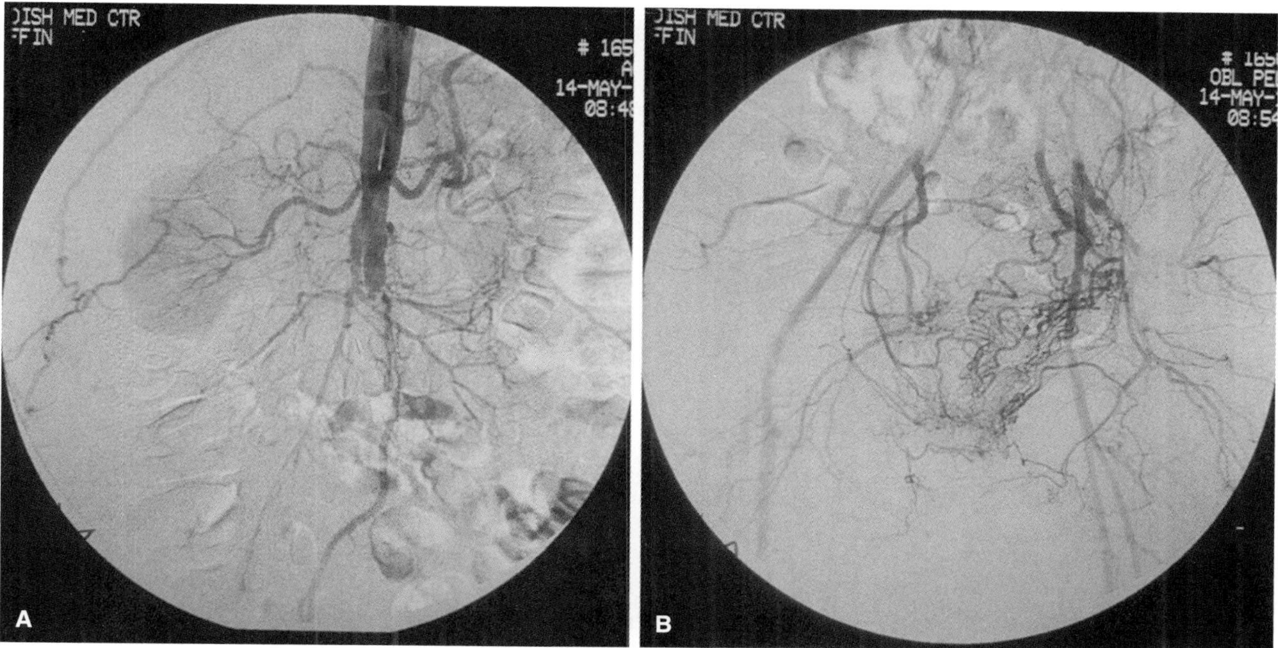

FIGURE 45-2 Digital subtraction aortogram performed via a transaxillary approach in a patient with type I aortoiliac disease. **A,** Occluded aorta just below the inferior mesenteric artery. **B,** Reconstitution of iliac artery bifurcations with external iliac arteries free of disease.

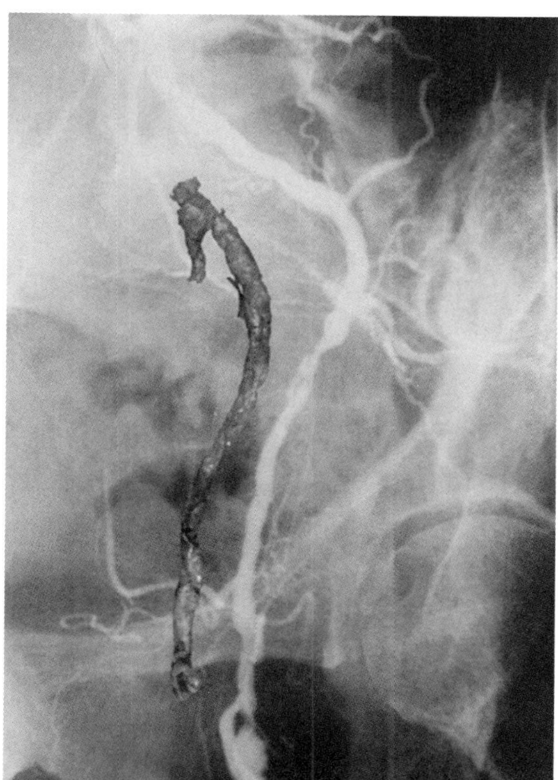

FIGURE 45-3 Aortogram showing type II aortoiliac disease with the endarterectomy specimen superimposed. The atherosclerotic changes in the common femoral bifurcation are often present in type II disease. (Courtesy of Anthony J. Comerota, MD, Philadelphia, Pa.)

Sites of Turbulence

Turbulent blood flow produces areas of low shear stress that enhance the deposition of intimal atheromatous lesions. The carotid bifurcation may be the most common example, although the bifurcations of the infrarenal aorta, common femoral, and popliteal arteries are also important in relation to lower extremity ischemia. The carotid bifurcation is the undisputed site for preferential use of open endarterectomy in vascular surgery as it is now practiced, and in many surgeons' practices it is the *only* place where this technique is employed! Currently, however, carotid stenting is being evaluated in trials with endarterectomy to treat symptomatic carotid atherosclerosis.

■ DIAGNOSIS

A detailed history and physical examination are mandatory to identify systemic and end-organ manifestations of atherosclerotic disease and to determine the specific risks of therapeutic intervention. Regardless of the anatomic location of disease, noninvasive vascular assessment is useful to (1) document the severity of stenosis, (2) identify the particular pattern of disease, and (3) document the severity of ischemia. For cerebrovascular, visceral, and renovascular disease, noninvasive testing employs duplex ultrasonography. For extremity vascular insufficiency, in addition to duplex ultrasonography, segmental pressures, arterial indices (e.g., ankle-brachial index), and arterial pulse volume waveform analyses at rest and with exercise or reactive hyperemia are the useful diagnostic studies for identifying and unmasking hemodynamically significant lesions.

Advances in duplex ultrasonography have made it a satisfactory test for the diagnosis and management of carotid artery occlusive disease, obviating the need for arteriography. In addition, this technology now permits complete arterial mapping from the juxtarenal aorta to the ankles possible and may eventually replace the need for arteriography. However, biplanar arteriography remains the "gold standard" for assessing aortoiliac and infrainguinal disease patterns and collateral circulation. Coupled with intra-arterial pressure monitoring and provocative testing with intra-arterial vasodilators, these studies can provide both anatomic and hemodynamic assessment of the arterial anatomy. Although the diagnosis and quantification of the severity of occlusive disease can be determined noninvasively, arteriography may be particularly useful in cases of atheroembolization by identifying mildly stenotic nonhemodynamic ulcerative lesions that may be the source of distal emboli. Endarterectomy can effectively remove the source of atheroemboli from accessible arteries (e.g., subclavian and aortoiliac).

■ TECHNIQUE

Most vascular surgeons are familiar with a lesion in the carotid bifurcation and perhaps portions of lesions removed to facilitate the implantation of grafts in other sites in the arterial tree. The pathologist dutifully reports the segment of atherosclerotic plaque and describes the microscopic features in relatively bland terms. To the surgeon who regularly uses the technique of endarterectomy, however, it becomes obvious that different lesions require different endarterectomy techniques.

The variation in the composition of these lesions is in part the result of metabolism of the arterial wall and the response to injury and repair and certainly the result of systemic and local factors currently unknown. Activity within an atherosclerotic plaque, such as hemorrhage, alters the composition of the lesion and its intimal surface. Finally, the location, distribution, luminal size, and contour of the atheroma vary significantly and affect not only the conduct of the endarterectomy but also the short-term and long-term results.

Five specific techniques of endarterectomy are available to the surgeon, depending on the type, extent, and location of the lesion to be removed and on his or her experience.

Open Endarterectomy

Open endarterectomy is the most commonly used technique, originally advocated by Bazy and Reboul[1] and performed through a longitudinal arteriotomy. The procedure exposes the extent of the lesion to be removed and allows direct separation of the disease from the subjacent arterial wall. A dural elevator or clamp is the instrument usually selected to separate the atheroma from the arterial wall. The cleavage plane is directly visualized for the length of the lesion, and the plaque is separated from the arterial wall. A transition zone is usually present at the distal endpoint of the plaque, where it tapers to a more superficial cleavage plane. Occasionally, the surgeon must fashion this endpoint using a Beaver blade to achieve plaque separation. Interrupted tacking mattress sutures may be necessary at the distal endpoint to prevent dissection after restoration of blood flow. Autogenous material may be used for patch angioplasty in a longitudinal arteriotomy in a relatively small vessel, in which primary closure would lead to significant vessel narrowing. The most common example is carotid bifurcation endarterectomy (Fig. 45-4).

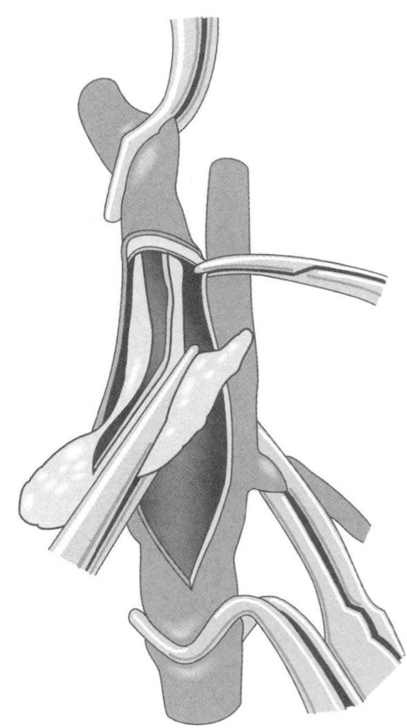

FIGURE 45-4 Eversion endarterectomy of distal internal carotid lesion beyond the end of the arteriotomy.

Semi-closed (Remote) Endarterectomy

The semi-closed technique was originally performed by Dos Santos.[10] Either transverse or longitudinal arteriotomies are placed at the proximal and distal extents of the lesion within the artery. A distal endpoint is established, and retrograde separation of the atheromatous plaque or core from the uninvolved artery proceeds in a proximal direction through the unopened vessel (Fig. 45-5). One or more intervening arteriotomies may be used to disobliterate long arterial segments. This procedure is continued to the proximal arteriotomy, where the lesion is detached and then removed; a hand-held loop stripper[6] or gas-powered or electric-powered strippers that oscillate[24] are available and may be used to traverse long distances between arteriotomies. In addition, the MollRing cutter is a modification of the original single-loop ring cutter with two shafts instead of one, which telescope into each other.[16,31,32] Two symmetric, elliptical rings are attached at a 135-degree angle to the most distal part of each shaft. The rings come in different sizes, ranging from 5- to 10-mm inner diameter. Both parallel rings have sharpened inner edges and cut like a pair of scissors when they shear across each other during telescoping the shafts. These devices maintain the separation plane between the atheroma and the residual arterial wall. The semi-closed technique is commonly used

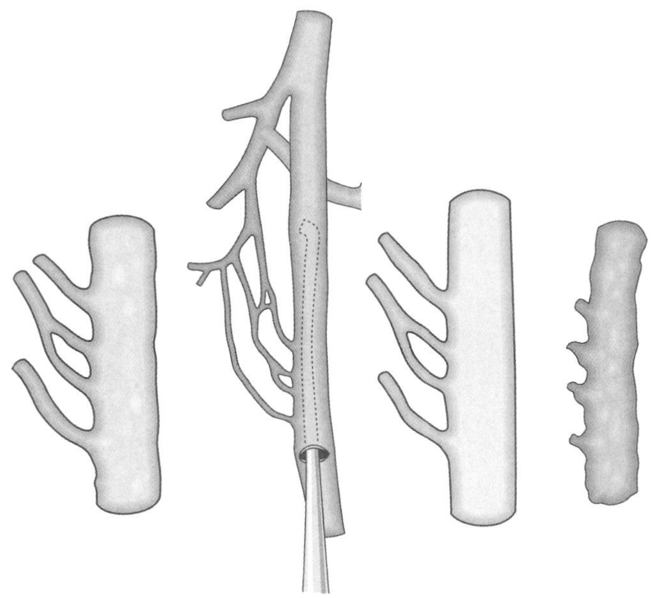

FIGURE 45-5 Semi-closed endarterectomy. Retrograde separation of plaque with loop stripper yields atheromatous core with branch artery orifices.

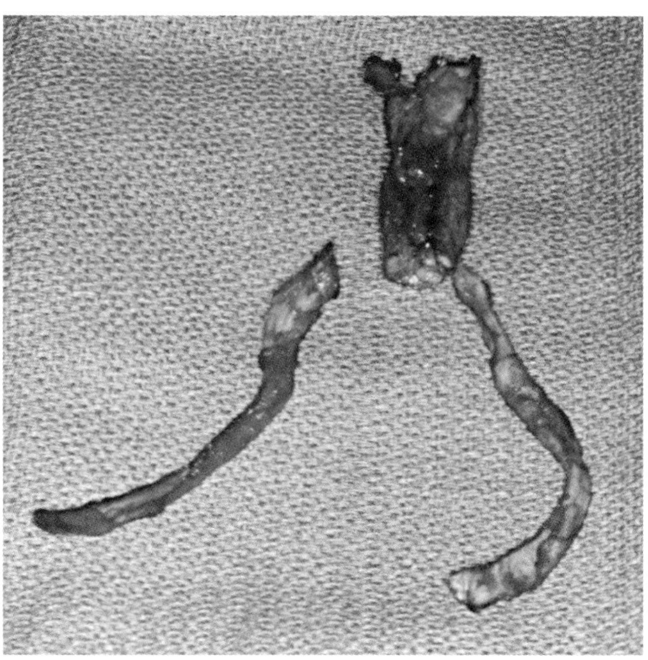

FIGURE 45-6 Operative specimen. Iliac plaques transected at aortic bifurcation to facilitate removal.

in the iliac or superficial femoral artery (Fig. 45-6).[16,31,32] It avoids the use of a long segmental patch, which would generally be required if the endarterectomy were performed in an open manner through a longitudinal arteriotomy. Adjunctive procedures employed with remote endarterectomies include angioscopy and use of intraluminal stents for fixation of distal intimal flaps.[13,15,29,30] In addition, a long intraluminal polytetrafluoroethylene graft may have use in this setting.[2]

Extraction Endarterectomy

The technique of extraction endarterectomy requires either retrograde or antegrade removal of an atheroma through a single arteriotomy, either transverse or longitudinal, in the involved vessel. It is performed using straight or slightly curved long-jawed clamps or a dural elevator. If the endarterectomy is performed retrograde, the proximal endpoint is separated by clamping the artery, which fractures or crushes the plaque. This technique is used in performing common femoral and distal external iliac endarterectomies. If the endarterectomy is performed in an antegrade direction, the distal endpoint is identified by external palpation of the artery. The surgeon gently controls and removes the atheromatous termination by grasping it in the jaws of the clamp—in effect, operating *beyond* his or her direct vision. This technique may be particularly useful in endarterectomies of lesions of hypogastric or profunda femoris origin (Fig. 45-7).

When transaortic (open) endarterectomy involves the removal of lesions from the orifices of major arterial (renal or visceral) branches, the portion of the endarterectomy conducted in the branch artery uses the extraction principle. The dissection plane is carried from the aorta into the branch circumferentially and is extended beyond the orifice. Within

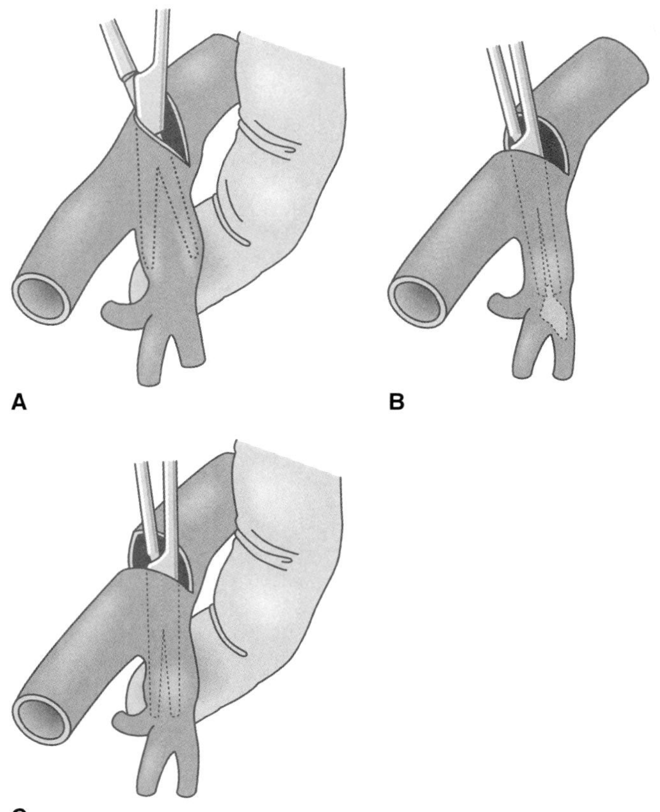

FIGURE 45-7 Hypogastric endarterectomy. **A,** Development of intimal core with hemostat. **B,** Extraction of specimen (incomplete). **C,** Removal of residual fragments.

1.5 to 3 cm, the thickened intima returns to a normal thin layer and separates cleanly. The well-mobilized branch is prolapsed toward the aorta, and simultaneous traction on the specimen permits visualization of the endpoint. Special angled extraction clamps (Figs. 45-8 and 45-9) facilitate the endarterectomy and removal of the occlusive lesion in the proximal aortic branch (Figs. 45-10 and 45-11).

Eversion Endarterectomy

The eversion technique, originally described by Harrison and associates,[14] requires distal transection of the artery beyond the site of disease and eversion or turning back of the residual proximal arterial wall on itself as traction is applied to the atheromatous core. The core of disease can be transected at its origin after the eversion is complete and the

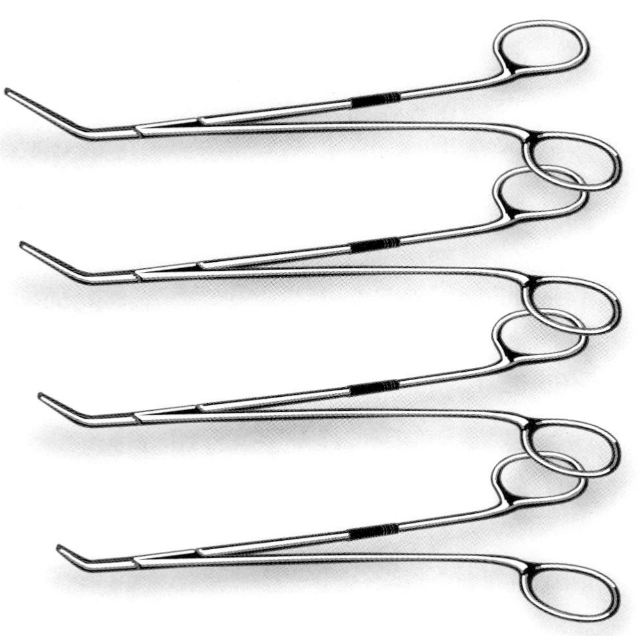

FIGURE 45-8 Special angled extraction clamps facilitate extraction endarterectomy.

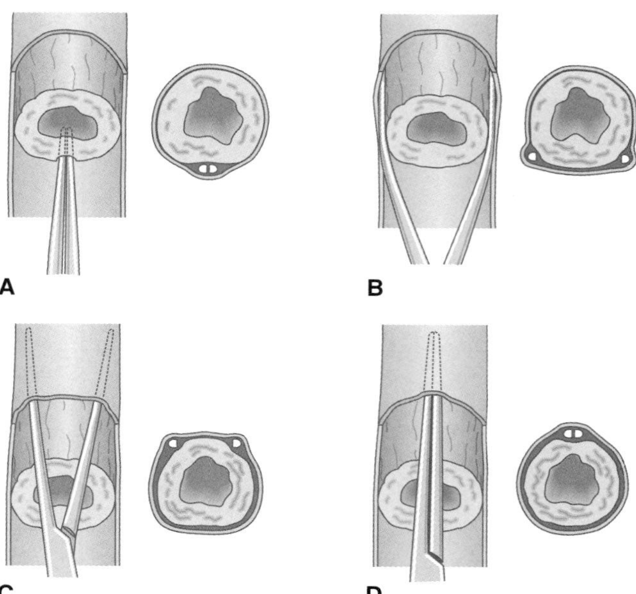

FIGURE 45-9 **A-D,** Use of angled extraction clamp to separate atheromatous core from arterial wall circumferentially during extraction endarterectomy.

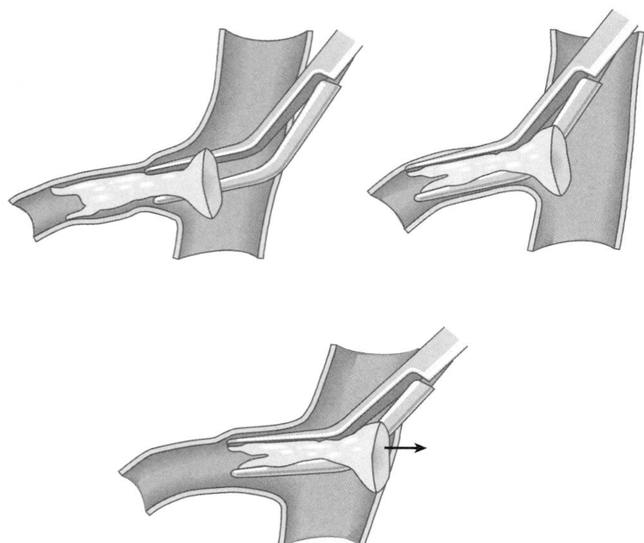

FIGURE 45-10 Angled extraction clamps allow endarterectomy of branch vessels to a disease-free endpoint.

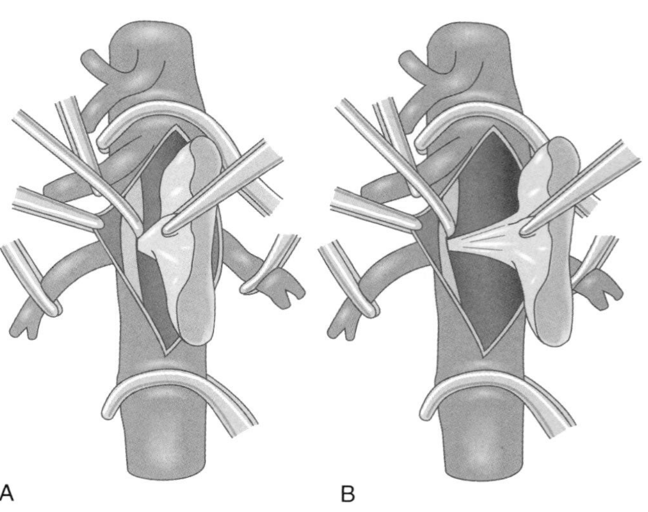

FIGURE 45-11 Removal of renal lesions. **A,** Dissection in endarterectomy plane in right renal artery after aortic portion has been completed. **B,** Endpoint of renal endarterectomy.

atheroma is removed. The arterial wall is then drawn back distally into a normal position, restoring the now patent artery to its normal location, where it can be reanastomosed to the distal arterial segment. This technique can also be used to disobliterate totally occluded excised arterial segments, which can then be employed in remote sites as arterial autografts. Common examples are the use of the internal or external iliac arteries and the occluded superficial femoral artery. In addition, eversion endarterectomy has been employed by some groups for carotid endarterectomy with good results.[9]

Selective Endarterectomy

The selective endarterectomy technique is a modification of the semi-closed endarterectomy and is used to remove discontinuous atheromatous lesions in one arterial segment. It is performed in a retrograde manner through a distal arteriotomy. The procedure requires precise sizing of the arterial loop stripper to the artery to be treated. The operator is guided during careful retrograde advancement of this instrument by the *feel* of resistance as the loop engages, separates, and then disengages the discontinuous lesion in the artery. This type of endarterectomy is often suitable in the external iliac artery.

Selective endarterectomy can be performed within the diseased arterial segment itself (e.g., superficial femoral artery), through the parent artery (e.g., the aortorenal region), or both (e.g., the carotid or common femoral bifurcation). In endarterectomy performed from the parent artery, the disease in the parent artery should always be separated before the endarterectomy plane is extended into the diseased branch (e.g., transaortic renal thromboendarterectomy) (see Fig. 45-11). In cases of disease contained in both the parent artery and its bifurcation branches, it is usually preferable to separate the disease first from the parent (proximal artery) and next from the less critical bifurcation branch, completing the endarterectomy finally in the critical bifurcation branch. An example of this is carotid bifurcation endarterectomy.

■ RESULTS

The results of endarterectomy depend, above all, on the experience of the vascular surgeon with this method of revascularization. The pattern of disease, the clinical consequences of the flow-obstructing lesion, and the characteristics of the atheroma are less important determinants of the outcome. Localized lesions with short terminations or transitions to normal or nearly normal distal arteries are ideal for endarterectomy. As in every method of revascularization, a normal inflow capable of delivering high-energy blood flow to the reconstructed vascular bed and a patent distal arterial tree that perfuses the organ or extremity provide the best characteristics for a durable endarterectomy. High-flow vascular beds (i.e., visceral, renal) are ideal for endarterectomy because their high flow rates result in extended patency.[28,33,36]

Endarterectomy, once the preferred method of revascularization in most medical centers, has gradually been replaced by bypass graft techniques. Prosthetic grafts are generally preferred for bypass of occlusive disease of the abdominal aorta and the iliac branches, and autologous vein grafts are favored for the infrainguinal arteries supplying the lower extremities. Aortofemoral and femoropopliteal bypass procedures replaced endarterectomy for lower extremity revascularization in the early 1960s, and by the mid-1970s femorotibial bypass was developed to revascularize ischemic limbs with distal tibial disease.

Table 45-1 Cumulative Patency for Aortoiliac and Aortoiliofemoral Thromboendarterectomy

SERIES, YEAR	OPERATION	PATENCY RATE, % At 5 Years	PATENCY RATE, % At 10 Years
Butcher and Jaffe, 1971[5]	AI + AIF TEA	72	—
Inahara, 1972[20]	AIF TEA	96.1	—
Inahara, 1975[22]	AI TEA	—	85
	AIF TEA	—	90
Brewster and Darling, 1978[4]	AI TEA	94	85.2
	AIF TEA	79.6	68.3
Stoney and Reilly, 1987[34]	AI TEA	95	90
	AIF TEA	85	72

AI, aortoiliac; AIF, aortoiliofemoral; TEA, thromboendarterectomy.

A number of authors have documented the safety and efficacy of aortoiliac or aortoiliofemoral endarterectomy in the treatment of patients with type I or II atherosclerotic disease patterns.[3,5,20] Operative mortality rates have ranged from 1% to 7% for the procedure, with the lower rates reflective of improvements in patient selection and anesthesia techniques. Five-year and 10-year patency rates for endarterectomy in patients with type I disease have been impressive and comparable to bypass procedures (Table 45-1). Some authors have claimed similar results for aortoiliofemoral endarterectomy in patients with type II disease patterns,[3,5,20] whereas others have reported better patency for prosthetic bypass in this setting.[3]

Proponents of inflow endarterectomy stress the importance of the following technical aspects of the procedure that ensure their long-term effectiveness:

1. The endarterectomy of the aorta should begin at the level of the renal arteries. Failure to completely clear the aorta of plaque and maintain adequate inflow will result in restenosis or occlusion of the reconstruction.
2. Endarterectomy should terminate at the iliac artery bifurcation for patients with type I disease and at the common femoral artery bifurcation in patients with type II patterns of atherosclerosis to ensure complete disobliteration of the disease process.
3. Unilateral procedures should be avoided because the atherosclerotic process below the bifurcation is essentially always bilateral.
4. The entire medial layer should be removed during the procedure to allow for enlargement of the blood vessel and to create a smooth luminal flow surface. Inahara[20,21] has noted that the external iliac and common femoral arteries will enlarge by 2 to 5 mm after the procedures and suggests that the change in vessel size contributes the most to the long-term patency of aortoiliofemoral endarterectomy.

5. Unobstructed outflow into the profunda femoris artery must be maintained by extended endarterectomy, if necessary, regardless of the patency of the superficial femoral artery, to maintain the patency of aortoiliofemoral endarterectomy for patients with type II disease.

A successful inflow endarterectomy can restore sexual potency in approximately 70% of patients with vasculogenic impotence in addition to improving lower extremity blood flow. With careful operative dissection, ejaculatory function can be retained in 80%.

Lengthy superficial femoral endarterectomy procedures were abandoned for several reasons, including (1) to minimize the dissection, (2) to shorten the procedure, and (3) to use the reliable autogenous grafts. The original technique of long endarterectomy was less than ideal. Crude devices were designed to disobliterate diseased vessels, but no standardized technique or training was available to new vascular surgeon trainees in acquiring the skill to perform such procedures. Only reports by Inahara[20] in Oregon, Imparato and colleagues[18] in New York, and Smeets and colleagues[32] in the Netherlands emphasized the excellent results that could be achieved by endarterectomy when the technique was precisely performed in the superficial femoral and popliteal arterial segments. However, early and late patency rates of femoropopliteal endarterectomies performed by others, such as the group at Dartmouth,[26] were found to be inferior to comparable bypass grafts, and the bypass graft became firmly established as the preferred method for revascularization in these arterial beds.

Although prosthetic textile grafts have performed admirably in proximal sites, namely the aorta and its terminal branches, the results with prosthetics remain inferior to those achieved with autogenous saphenous vein grafts in the lower extremity itself. Because the greater saphenous vein is suitable in only about 80% of patients, other autogenous revascularization techniques must frequently be sought. The use of autologous cephalic or lesser saphenous veins (see Chapters 81 and 83) is one alternative, and another is superficial femoropopliteal endarterectomy performed by an open or semi-closed technique.

It is therefore appropriate to consider new technologic contributions that may overcome those factors reported to cause poor results. Extensive circumferential mobilization of long segments of the arterial tree has been considered mandatory to facilitate semi-closed endarterectomy when these long occlusions are disobliterated. Circumferential fibrosis can develop throughout the length of the endarterectomized segment, causing narrowing and eventual occlusion, and this has contributed to the low late patency rate of endarterectomy. Because endarterectomy is a controlled arterial injury that ideally heals by intimal regrowth, an optimal environment is necessary for this healing to occur. Extensive mobilization of the entire length of the artery to be treated may in fact devascularize the artery, stimulating postoperative periarterial fibrosis, impaired metabolism of the arterial wall, and therefore compromised arterial healing.[6-8]

To eliminate these possible local problems arising from previous endarterectomy techniques, we have begun to evaluate new instruments and exposures that minimize trauma during semi-closed endarterectomy of long arterial segments. Although the air-driven oscillating loop device developed by Lerwick[24] and Amsco Hall has certain attractive features, it is unwieldy and awkward because of its weight, inflexibility, and immobility. Its air hose tethers the instrument and makes its use somewhat restrictive. An electric loop endarterectomy stripper that is light and flexible and adapts to various anatomic sites in the arterial tree was developed at UCSF. This device is battery powered and can be sterilized. The MollRing cutter as described earlier is another new device that has been applied to superficial femoral artery occlusive disease.[16,31,32]

Studies to assess the immediate and long-term patency rates of these technologic modifications for superficial femoropopliteal semi-closed endarterectomy have produced mixed results. Dutch investigators have reported 5-year cumulative patency rates by life-table analysis of 37 ± 6.7% and primary assisted patency rate of 47.9 ± 6.3%.[32] However, the Dartmouth group[26] reported *1-year* patency of only 28 ± 11% using a ring stripper/cutter and distal stenting. Minimal dissection and the reduced intimal trauma using the power-driven loop to create the endarterectomy cleavage plane are obvious immediate benefits of this method compared with older techniques that use the hand-held or even the oscillating Lerwick loop instruments. Rosenthal and associates[29] reported medium-term results of remote superficial femoral artery endarterectomy in a multicenter trial; at a mean follow-up of 12.9 months (range 3 to 36 months) primary cumulative patency rate by life-table analysis was 61.4 ± 9%. Primary assisted patency was more than 80%. Ouriel's group reported an overall cumulative patency rate of 66% at 3 years and 57% for endarterectomy of localized lesions of the superficial femoral artery at the adductor canal.[27]

As noted earlier, the healing of arteries subjected to endarterectomy involves a number of favorable and unfavorable cellular responses. In the past, the late development of neointimal hyperplasia was responsible for the occlusive failure of many long-segment endarterectomy techniques. Research into the cellular and molecular biology of arterial healing may now make it feasible to consider novel pharmacologic adjuncts to the performance of endarterectomy to modulate these events. For example, investigation using a well-established animal model of intimal injury has allowed Clowes and Reidy[7] to categorize arterial healing into three phases of myointimal cell response: (1) cellular *migration* into the neointimal layer, (2) myointimal cell *proliferation,* and (3) deposition of *extracellular matrix*.

The precise factors regulating each of these phases are now becoming more clear, and this may allow the use of pharmacologic adjuncts such as heparin,[8] angiotensin-converting enzyme (ACE) inhibitors,[8] and growth factor antagonists[12,25] to improve the results of endarterectomy. Limited clinical trials are now under way to evaluate the potential of heparin-like agents to limit myointimal cell migration and proliferation, ACE inhibitors to modulate myointimal cell proliferation, and other agents to limit the deposition of matrix materials. It may also be possible, owing to the exciting developments in gene transfer technology currently under way, to use these methods to manipulate the healing response of the arterial wall following endarterectomy. With the availability of these new adjunctive therapies, it would not be surprising to see endarterectomy become a more widely applied technique of arterial reconstruction for occlusive disease during the next decade.

A technically perfect endarterectomy depends on a number of instruments and new techniques now available to the vascular surgeon. Improved illumination of the field by fiberoptic headlights aids in detection and elimination of technical defects that may adversely affect the healing of the endarterectomy site. The use of angioscopy may further aid in inspecting segments of the disobliterated artery at sites remote from the arteriotomies and therefore may improve the precision with which a smooth endarterectomy plane is achieved throughout the entire length of the vessel. Finally, intraoperative duplex scanning with spectral analysis to confirm the adequacy of endarterectomy in various locations has been more accurate for intraoperative assessment of the repair than has operative arteriography.

The benefits of endarterectomy for the vascular surgeon who has mastered the technique and has the knowledge and skill to use it appropriately in the practice of vascular surgery are immeasurable. It expands the individual's understanding of atherosclerotic occlusive disease and its potential for management. This knowledge extends the vascular surgeon's ability to improve perfusion for any patient, even when the alternative, the bypass graft procedure, is either contraindicated or impossible.

■ SUMMARY

Dos Santos[10] knew the problems he faced in the battle to manage occlusive arterial disease successfully with this technique when he wrote, "At the beginning failure was usual, success occasional." The proper use of endarterectomy, after more than 50 years, is still not without controversy. However, as technical refinements, improved instrumentation, training programs offering technical opportunities in endarterectomy, and pharmacologic modification of the arterial response to injury and healing are perfected, it is our opinion that endarterectomy will assume an increasingly important role for the vascular surgeon.

Thromboendarterectomy remains the procedure of choice for extracranial carotid artery stenoses, and it is a viable alternative for aortoiliac and femoropopliteal revascularization in selected patients. Patency and limb salvage results are excellent in reports originating from vascular surgeons with experience and skill using these techniques. Because no prosthetic material is required, thromboendarterectomy carries little risk of infection, in contrast with conventional bypass grafts. If failure eventually occurs, standard bypasses can still be employed. This technique should be a part of the armamentarium of all vascular surgeons performing arterial revascularizations.

■ REFERENCES

1. Bazy L, Reboul H: Technique de l'endarterectomie desobliterate. J Int Chir 65:196, 1950.
2. Bray AE: Superficial femoral endarterectomy with intra-arterial PTFE grafting. J Endovasc Surg 2:297, 1995.
3. Brewster DC: Clinical and anatomical considerations for surgery in aortoiliac disease and results of surgical treatment. Circulation 83(Suppl):42, 1991.
4. Brewster DC, Darling RC: Optimal methods of aortoiliac reconstruction. Surgery 84:739, 1978.
5. Butcher FR, Jaffe BM: Treatment of aortoiliac disease by endarterectomy. Ann Surg 173:925, 1971.
6. Cannon JA, Barker WF: Successful management of obstructive femoral atherosclerosis by endarterectomy. Surgery 38:48, 1955.
7. Clowes AW, Reidy MA: Prevention of stenosis after vascular reconstruction: Pharmacologic control of intimal hyperplasia—a review. J Vasc Surg 13:885, 1991.
8. Clowes AW, Clowes MM, Vergel SC, et al: Heparin and cilazapril together inhibit injury-induced intimal hyperplasia. Hypertension 18(Suppl):II-65, 1991.
9. Darling RC, Mehta M, Roddy SP, et al: Eversion carotid endarterectomy: A technical alternative that may obviate patch closure in women. Cardiovasc Surg 11:347, 2003.
10. Dos Santos JC: Sur la desobstruction des thrombus arterielles anciennes. Mem Acad Chir 73:409, 1947.
11. Dos Santos JC: Late results of reconstructive arterial surgery (restoration, disobliteration, replacement with the establishment of some operative principles). J Cardiovasc Surg 5:445, 1964.
12. Ferns GAA, Raines EW, Sprugel KH, et al: Inhibition of neointimal smooth muscle accumulation after angioplasty by an antibody to PDGF. Science 253:1129, 1991.
13. Galland RB, Whiteley MS, Gibson M, et al: Maintenance of patency following remote superficial femoral artery endarterectomy. Cardiovasc Surg 8:533, 2000.
14. Harrison JH, Jordan WD, Perez AR: Eversion thromboendarterectomy. Surgery 61:26, 1967.
15. Heider P, Hofmann M, Maurer PC, von Sommoggy S: Semi-closed femoropopliteal thromboendarterectomy: A prospective study. Eur J Vasc Endovasc Surg 18:43, 1999.
16. Ho GH, Moll F, Hedeman J, et al: The MollRing cutter remote endarterectomy: Preliminary experience with a new endovascular technique for treatment of occlusive superficial artery disease. J Endovasc Surg 2:278, 1995.
17. Illig KA, Shortell CK, Zhang R, et al: Carotid endarterectomy then and now: Outcome and cost-effectiveness of modern practice. Surgery 134:705, 2003.
18. Imparato AM, Bracco A, Kim GE, et al: Comparison of three techniques for femoropopliteal arterial reconstruction. Ann Surg 117:375, 1973.
19. Imparato AM, Sanoudos G, Epstein HY, et al: Results in 96 aortoiliac reconstructive procedures: Preoperative, angiographic, and functional classifications used as prognostic guides. Surgery 68:610, 1970.
20. Inahara T: Endarterectomy for occlusive disease of the aortoiliac and common femoral arteries. Am J Surg 124:235, 1972.
21. Inahara T: Eversion endarterectomy for aorto-ilio-femoral occlusive disease. Am J Surg 138:196, 1979.
22. Inahara T: Evaluation of endarterectomy for aortoiliac and aortoilio-femoral occlusive disease. Arch Surg 110:1458, 1975.
23. Leriche R, Kunlin J: Essais de desobstruction des enteres thromboses suivant la technique de Jean Cid Dos Santos. Lyon Chir 42:475, 1947.
24. Lerwick ER: Oscillating loop endarterectomy for peripheral vascular reconstruction. Surgery 97:574, 1985.
25. Lindner V, Reidy MA: Proliferation of smooth muscle cells after vascular injury is inhibited by an antibody against basic fibroblast growth factor. Proc Natl Acad Sci U S A 88:3739, 1991.
26. Nelson PR, Powell RJ, Proia RR, et al: Results of endovascular superficial femoral endarterectomy. J Vasc Surg 34:526, 2001.
27. Ouriel K, Smith CR, DeWeese JA: Endarterectomy for localized lesions of the superficial femoral artery at the adductor canal. J Vasc Surg 3:531, 1986.

28. Rapp JH, Reilly LM, Quarfordt PG, et al: Durability of endarterectomy and antegrade grafts in the treatment of chronic visceral ischemia. J Vasc Surg 3:799, 1986.
29. Rosenthal D, Schubart PJ, Kinney EV, et al: Remote superficial femoral artery endarterectomy: Multicenter medium-term results. J Vasc Surg 34:432, 2001.
30. Rosenthal D. Wellons ED, Matsurra JH, et al: Remote superficial femoral artery endarterectomy and distal vein bypass for limb salvage: Initial experience. J Endovasc Ther 10:121, 2003.
31. Smeets L, DeBorst GJ, DeVries JP, et al: Remote iliac artery endarterectomy: Seven-year results of a less invasive technique for iliac artery occlusive disease. J Vasc Surg 38:1297, 2003.
32. Smeets L, Ho GH, Hagenaars T, et al: Remote endarterectomy: First choice in surgical treatment of long-segmental SFA occlusive disease? Eur J Vasc Endovasc Surg 25:583, 2003.
33. Stoney RJ, Ehrenfeld WK, Wylie EJ: Revascularization method in chronic visceral ischemia. Ann Surg 186:468, 1977.
34. Stoney RJ, Reilly LM: Endarterectomy for aortoiliac disease. In Ernst CG, Stanley JC (eds): Current Therapy in Vascular Surgery. Philadelphia, BC Decker, 1987, p 157.
35. Wylie EJ: Thromboendarterectomy for arteriosclerotic thrombosis of major arteries. Surgery 23:275, 1952.
36. Wylie EJ: Endarterectomy and autogenous arterial grafts in the surgical treatment of stenosing lesions of the renal artery. Urol Clin North Am 2:351, 1975.
37. Wylie EJ, Kerr E, Davis O: Experimental and clinical experiences with the use of fascia lata applied as a graft about major arteries after thromboendarterectomy and aneurysmorrhaphy. Surg Gynecol Obstet 93:257, 1951.

Chapter 46

Vascular Conduits:
An Overview

JOHN J. RICOTTA, MD

The ideal vascular conduit remains the "Holy Grail" for vascular surgeons. Properties of such a conduit include ready availability, appropriate size, easy handling, resistance to infection and thrombosis, compliance characteristics similar to native artery, and long-term durability. In short, the conduit should be similar to the artery or vein it is replacing. It is not surprising then, that autogenous arteries are the best arterial substitutes available. Experience in the coronary circulation demonstrates the superiority of both internal mammary and radial artery conduits over saphenous vein.[1] Similarly, hypogastric or external iliac artery free grafts have been shown to be the best conduits for visceral revascularization.[2] However suitable autogenous arterial substitutes are limited in quantity. This forces the vascular surgeon to rely on a series of less suitable substitutes.

The concept of "thrombotic threshold velocity," described by Lester Sauvage,[3] is important in a discussion of vascular conduit. This concept states that each vascular conduit requires a certain minimal threshold of blood flow to maintain patency. The character of the inner lining of the conduit determines this threshold. Grafts lined with viable endothelium exhibit the lowest thresholds. The ability to support viable endothelium, or myointimal ingrowths (anastomotic and interstitial), improves this thrombotic threshold velocity. Preservation of an endothelial lining in biologic grafts and modifications of the inner lining of prosthetic grafts have been undertaken with the intent of lowering this thrombotic threshold velocity.

Compliance characteristics both at implantation and during follow-up are also thought to be important. "Compliance mismatch" has been correlated with the late development of anastomotic intimal hyperplasia,[4] and stiff conduits may be difficult to handle at the time of implantation. Although considerable work has been done emphasizing the importance of compliance mismatch, several factors must be considered in determining its ultimate importance. First is the fact that the compliance of diseased arterial beds that frequently provide the inflow and outflow for vascular conduits is not the same as the compliance of normal artery and is often difficult to measure. Second is the likelihood that compliance of a conduit changes from the time of implantation through the process of arterialization and tissue incorporation. These confounders make it difficult to determine the true effect of conduit compliance on long-term results. It is likely that the major effects of compliance mismatch manifest themselves as changes in shear stress at the artery-to-conduit anastomosis.[5] Efforts to normalize such shear stress abnormalities have been associated with improvements in long-term conduit patency.[4,6] In general, conduits that handle like a native normal artery or vein are easiest to implant and intuitively would seem to have the best long-term behavior.

Ready availability in appropriate size is also of great practical importance. Harvesting of autogenous conduits remains one of the most time-consuming aspects of lower extremity revascularization and is the major contributor to postoperative morbidity of leg edema and wound complications that occur in 20% to 30% or more of infrainguinal reconstructions. Size mismatch between conduit and native artery or vein remains a source of both early and late failure in vascular reconstructions. Problems with size and availability are the two greatest difficulties with autogenous vein as a conduit. In the extremities, the size and quality of venous conduits are the most significant factors in determining long-term patency. In general, veins smaller than 2.5 mm in diameter or with evidence of intraluminal thickening or synechiae are not suitable for peripheral reconstruction (see Chapter 47). Size mismatch between artery and vein is one of the main indications for the use of vein in the nonreversed rather than reversed configuration. When size and quality are problematic, alternatives to autogenous veins must be used.

Long-term durability includes the ability to resist infection and structural deterioration over time. Resistance to infection is of great importance in a vascular conduit. Postoperative graft infection is a devastating complication of vascular surgery, compromising both life and limb. The ability to place a graft that can resist infection at the time of primary reconstruction or be placed in an infected field during a secondary revascularization is a great advantage. Structural deterioration occurs in all types of vascular conduits over time. In autogenous grafts early lesions can be expected in 10% to 20% of cases within the first 2 years of follow-up. Hyperplastic lesions may occur within the conduit itself (as an exacerbation of retained valve leaflets or unrecognized preexisting venous injury) or at the arterial anastomoses. Late deterioration of autogenous grafts occurs relatively infrequently, although its incidence may be underestimated. Long-term durability is also a problem with nonautogenous conduits, particularly biologic grafts. These conduits retain the biologic architecture of the normal artery or vein but are modified to allow implantation and early function. In the case of cryopreserved or fresh homografts, a chronic rejection process results in inexorable alteration of the vessel wall and a high degree of late thrombosis or aneurysmal dilation. In the case of glutaraldehyde-treated umbilical vein, late aneurysmal dilation remains a problem, although prosthetic external support has helped address this.[7] Prosthetic grafts also undergo late dilation and longitudinal expansion of as much as 20%,[8,9] which may lead to redundancy and thrombosis or the development of false aneurysms on late follow-up. The degree of late degeneration of prosthetic grafts is related to their initial characteristics (polytetrafluoroethlylene [PTFE], polyurethane, Dacron) as well as the tightness of the fabric "weave."

In the area of large-vessel arterial substitution, size match and durability are paramount. The flow velocities present in aortoiliac reconstruction are sufficient to maintain patency of prosthetic grafts with minimal tissue ingrowth and only limited endothelial repopulation. Resistance to infection is also a consideration in this position, although the incidence of graft infection is low in the absence of a groin incision. Compliance mismatch and shear stress are less important. The size of the femoral artery and the volumes of flow reduce the clinical importance of anastomotic intimal hyperplasia, except in cases of limited femoral outflow. For reconstruction of smaller diameter (<6-mm) arteries and veins, the ability of the conduit to remain patent at lower flows is paramount. In these cases, issues of thromboresistant inner lining, anastomotic shear stress, and long-term behavior of the conduit itself become more important. Resistance to infection remains a significant consideration, although the consequences of a peripheral graft infection are less dramatic than those of an intracavitary one. Durability is also important. However, the 5-year survival of patients who undergo infrainguinal reconstruction, particularly for critical limb ischemia, is often limited, and "long term" may be defined as 3 to 5 years rather than 5 to 10 years. With these thoughts in mind, the selection of vascular conduits by anatomic region are discussed.

■ RECONSTRUCTION OF THE AORTA AND ILIAC ARTERIES

Excellent long-term patency has been achieved with a number of prosthetic grafts, which have the advantage of being available in a variety of sizes. Use of Dacron or PTFE is generally a matter of surgeon preference. The graft should be chosen to approximate the diameter of artery (usually the aorta) at the proximal anastomosis. Discrepancy between the diameter of the graft and artery at the distal anastomosis is usually compensated by beveling the graft or by the use of a Linton patch at the distal artery. Occasionally, with small aortas or external iliac occlusive disease an end-to-side proximal configuration is preferred, but most of the time the aortic anastomosis is end to end.

Grafts should be chosen that are relatively impermeable at the time of implantation. The most permeable grafts are knitted Dacron, whereas both PTFE and woven Dacron are more hemostatic. Collagen impregnation of knitted grafts significantly reduces their porosity at the time of implantation. PTFE has the added characteristics of "needle-hole bleeding," which, although it can be reduced by some maneuvers, remains a drawback in the mind of some surgeons. Fabrication of the graft is also related to handling (stiffness), tissue incorporation, and late changes in graft fabric. The more porous grafts were designed to increase tissue incorporation over the long term. Tissue incorporation stabilizes the inner lining of the graft surface and is believed to improve resistance to late graft infection. Knitted Dacron exhibits the most tissue incorporation of the prosthetic grafts. The degree of PTFE incorporation depends on both pore size and the presence or absence of an external wrap, which is placed in some types of PTFE graft to prevent late dilation. Some PTFE demonstrates seroma formation, or sweating, both at the time of implantation and in the later postoperative period. Seromas around PTFE grafts, particularly in the extra-anatomic position, may be bothersome and occasionally require graft removal.[10] PTFE grafts do not dilate over time, whereas most Dacron grafts can be expected to increase in both diameter and length by 10% to 15% over the long term, with knitted grafts demonstrating more dilation than woven grafts. It is important to take these long-term changes into consideration when selecting graft diameter and determining graft length at the time of implantation. In general, knitted grafts handle better than woven grafts or PTFE. However, recent development of stretch and thin-walled PTFE prosthetics have reduced these differences. The inner lining of vascular grafts has been modified to improve thromboresistance by endothelial cell seeding or alteration of the chemical character of the graft-blood interface (see Chapter 49) to reduce attraction to thrombus and blood elements. This has not had a measurable clinical effect to date in aortic reconstruction.

Resistance to infection is related to the composition of the inner lining of the graft and to the presence or absence of antibiotic binding. PTFE is the most inert of the prosthetic fabrics and resists bacterial inoculation better than Dacron grafts that have been impregnated with antibacterials and antibiotics in an attempt to influence the incidence of late graft infection. Although these grafts are appealing in cases where in-situ replacement of an infected prosthesis is performed, their ultimate role in primary arterial reconstruction remains to be defined.[11-13]

Autologous deep veins of the lower extremity have been used in aortoiliac reconstruction. This approach, popularized by Clagett and associates, consists of using the superficial femoral and popliteal veins for replacement of the aorta and iliac arteries.[14] Used first to treat graft infection, these substitutes have been applied to other areas where a large vascular conduit is needed and in situations where arterial outflow is marginal, suggesting the need for a thromboresistant lumen. These conduits hold up well over time as substitutes for large arteries, and significant late changes in this conduit have been minimal in most reports. The major drawback to use of deep lower extremity veins is the increased time for operative harvest and the occurrence of edema and compartment syndrome in a significant minority of patients. Patients with evidence of preoperative arterial insufficiency and those in whom the saphenous vein has already been removed are at increased risk for these complications.[15] The presence of prior deep venous thrombosis may also limit the use of this conduit. In general, deep vein is used as a conduit most often during secondary in-situ reconstruction, occasioned either by graft infection or multiple failed revascularization.

Arterial homografts have been used for aortic and iliac reconstructions. Most often this conduit is used when the concerns for graft infection are significant. This may occur in the presence of primary graft infection or when significant intra-abdominal organ damage with local contamination exists. Koskas, Keiffer, and their colleagues[16,17] have been the main proponents of arterial homografts for reconstruction in complex cases involving the thoracic or abdominal aorta. Early results have been good, although late degeneration remains a problem in most homografts. In patients with prolonged life expectancy, late replacement of such homografts may be expected, although their use may initially be lifesaving. The major clinical role for these conduits seems to be in replacement of the thoracic and suprarenal aorta.

■ MEDIUM-SIZED ARTERIAL RECONSTRUCTION

Medium-sized arteries are in general 6 to 8 mm in diameter and include the carotid, subclavian, common femoral, and visceral vessels. The need to reconstruct these vessels is less frequent than for either the aortoiliac or infrainguinal segment. The advantages and disadvantages of each conduit type are similar to what has been described for aortoiliac reconstruction. These medium-sized vessels share several common features that influence the selection of the appropriate conduit. Each of these vessels has a relatively large diameter and flow, particularly when compared to the extremity vessels. In most cases the length of the conduit required is short (<15 cm). These two factors make prosthetic conduits an attractive choice. Data from the literature suggest that there is little difference between prosthetic and autogenous conduits in these anatomic configurations, unless arterial size (<5 mm) and runoff are compromised. In fact data in the carotid-subclavian position suggest that prosthetic conduits may be superior to autogenous saphenous vein owing presumably to restrictions in size and therefore flow of the latter conduit. In several configurations (e.g., carotid-subclavian, femoral, aortovisceral) potential kinking of autogenous conduits has led many surgeons to prefer prosthetic grafts, which are externally supported, to autogenous saphenous vein.

Major indications for the use of autogenous vein in reconstruction of medium-sized arteries include the fear of graft infection or wound complications and concern over vessel size discrepancy or limited vascular runoff. This most often arises in the case of visceral reconstruction to a small renal artery or in the presence of intra-abdominal contamination from visceral ischemia or trauma. In those case, suitably sized saphenous vein, or potentially superficial femoral vein, can be used for reconstruction.[18,19] Use of homografts in the reconstruction of medium-sized arteries has limited, if any, application owing to concerns over late degeneration.

■ EXTREMITY ARTERIAL RECONSTRUCTIONS

Although most reconstructions involve the lower extremity, the same considerations apply for both upper and lower extremity bypass. In selecting conduits for revascularization of the extremity, resistance to thrombosis and long-term durability are the prime considerations. Since the flow in extremity arteries is significantly less than that in large and medium-sized arteries, particularly during diastole, the conduit should have a thromboresistant inner lining. This is most easily accomplished by using a graft with a viable endothelium. Endothelial cells exhibit both antithrombotic and antiproliferative properties in their unperturbed state. There have been many efforts to line artificial conduits with endothelial cells,[20,21] but autogenous vein represents the most readily available conduit that meets these criteria. Preservation of autogenous venous endothelium requires meticulous attention to dissection, distention, and storage of the vein during preparation, as outlined in Chapter 47. A single segment of normal autogenous vein is the best conduit currently available for extremity reconstruction. It resists both thrombosis and infection. Handling characteristics and compliance are surpassed only by autogenous artery. Long-term durability of appropriately selected and prepared autogenous conduits is excellent. Selection of such conduits and their preparation are described in detail in Chapter 47. In the absence of autogenous vein of suitable quality or diameter, a variety of prosthetic and biologic substitutes have been developed. Thromboresistance is conferred in these conduits by either chemical modification of biologic substitutes (treatment of the intima with cryopreservatives or glutaraldehyde) or modification of the inner lining of synthetic conduits by electrical charge or heparin bonding. To date, these efforts have failed to produce a thromboresistant lining comparable to that of a normal vein. Additional adjuncts are helpful when using nonautogenous conduits, particularly in infragenicular reconstructions. These include cuffs, boots, patches, and modification of the distal end of the graft to reduce shear stress and distal arteriovenous fistula.[22-25] All such infragenicular reconstruction with nonautogenous tissue should be placed on long-term antithrombotic therapy (aspirin plus low-dose warfarin [Coumadin]).[26] All infrainguinal reconstructions, regardless of conduit type, should be accompanied by perioperative and postoperative antiplatelet therapy to reduce both graft-related and general cardiovascular events during follow-up.

A single segment of autogenous saphenous vein may not be available in 20% to 30% of individuals requiring extremity revascularization. This percentage is likely to increase as patients survive longer after both coronary bypass and prior lower extremity reconstruction. Ipsilateral saphenous utilization can be increased by selecting alternative inflow and outflow sites to minimize conduit length and/or using sequential grafting techniques or endovascular interventions to address issues of inflow or outflow, limiting conduit use to replace long segments of occluded arteries. When ipsilateral saphenous vein is not available, other sources of autogenous conduit such as contralateral saphenous vein, lesser saphenous vein, and arm vein must be considered. The decision to choose one of these alternatives over another or to use homograft or prosthetic depends on the indication for surgery and the patient's overall clinical condition. When a single segment of vein can be used for bypass, this is preferred. If a short reconstruction can be performed using a single segment of lesser saphenous vein or arm vein, this is preferred, particularly when the reconstruction is below the knee. We prefer to use a single segment of contralateral autogenous greater saphenous vein rather than constructing an autogenous composite graft by splicing vein segments together. Although good results have been shown with spliced vein, these conduits require close observation and more frequent revision than single vein segments.[24] In most such cases the indications for reconstruction are limb-threatening ischemia and the outflow is a tibial vessel. Unless there is severe ischemia in the contralateral extremity, we believe that achieving optimal results in the extremity that is immediately threatened is more important than future considerations of potential revascularization of the contralateral limb. When spliced vein grafts must be used, we agree with the approach outlined in Chapter 47.

For femoropopliteal reconstruction above the knee, prosthetic grafts give acceptable short- and mid-term results. Use of prosthetic grafts may be acceptable for patients in this anatomic configuration who have either claudication or limb-threatening ischemia when ipsilateral autogenous vein is not available. Two prospective, randomized trials demonstrate that 5-year patency of autogenous vein is superior to that of prosthetic grafts in the above-knee position.[27,28] It is our belief that if symptoms are sufficient to warrant open operative intervention, the best conduit should be chosen and the best operation performed: This is ipsilateral autogenous saphenous vein. When prosthetic is used, data suggest that a 6-mm conduit gives inferior results to larger (7- or 8-mm) prosthetics.[29] There are no data to suggest that adjuncts such as cuffs or anticoagulation improve the long-term patency of above-knee bypasses. Owing to the depth of both the inflow and outflow arteries in these cases, we prefer to use the vein in an anatomic tunneled configuration rather than in situ and favor the reversed configuration unless size discrepancies are significant.

When the target artery is the below-knee popliteal segment, saphenous vein, either in situ or reversed, is the conduit of choice. When saphenous vein is not available, adjuncts have been shown to improve the patency of prosthetics placed in this position. Such adjuncts include the use of long-term anticoagulation (aspirin plus low-dose warfarin)[26] and alteration of the distal arterial anastomosis using cuffs or patches mentioned earlier. Alterations to the prosthetic graft such as distal flow diffusers and carbon coating are discussed in Chapter 49. Although there is an intuitive tendency to use externally supported grafts in the below-knee position, this has not been supported in a prospective, randomized trial.[30] Deep femoral vein has been used for femoropopliteal reconstruction in preference to prosthetic conduits, with good results.[31] Difficulties in harvesting and size discrepancy in reconstruction may limit enthusiasm for this approach except in unusual circumstances. Cryopreserved homografts have limited applicability in these cases. Despite a wealth of reported good experience with human umbilical vein in this configuration, there has been minimal enthusiasm for its routine use (see Chapter 48).

For femorotibial reconstructions, autogenous tissue is the conduit of choice. Ipsilateral greater saphenous vein of suitable quality and diameter is preferred. With experience, the in-situ technique is often easier than removing the vein and avoids the problem of size mismatch when long segments of vein are required for reconstruction. Concerns with size mismatch may prompt the use of saphenous vein in a nonreversed, translocated fashion with ex-vivo valve lysis unless it is nearly isodiametric. Appropriate vein mapping and remote valve lysis can often avoid long incisions once thought necessary for this technique. Operative fluoroangiography or angioscopy can be used to identify side branches and residual valves. Side branches can then be marked and ligated through small incisions or coil embolized under fluoroscopic control.[32] This reduces one of the major morbidities of femorotibial bypass: local wound problems and postoperative leg edema. We believe that venous bypasses to the tibial vessels should be placed in the subcutaneous position to facilitate long-term surveillance, which is a crucial aspect of long-term management. In these cases, when long bypasses to small arteries with limited outflow are required, we use spliced vein in preference to prosthetic grafts or homografts because of our belief in the better long-term patency of these conduits. As noted earlier, spliced conduits are at increased risk for late stenosis and require diligent surveillance.

When prosthetic grafts are required for femorotibial reconstruction, the adjunctive measures used in below-knee femoropopliteal reconstruction are of even more importance. In addition, the use of a distal arteriovenous fistula may further increase the patency of such grafts by decreasing outflow resistance and improving graft flow. Several configurations of such fistulae have been reported.[33,34] Such fistulae should be used when there is concern about the quality of the outflow vessel or runoff. Modification of prosthetic grafts by endothelial cell seeding, carbon coating, or heparin bonding are discussed in Chapter 49. The role of these efforts has not yet been established.

Modified biologic grafts have their greatest role in this anatomic configuration. Choice of biologic versus prosthetic graft remains an area where physician preference often supersedes the availability of hard data. Although the best results for nonautogenous reconstruction are reported with the human umbilical vein graft, most surgeons find the graft awkward to use and the additional benefit in patency not worth the effort. Cryopreserved homografts are much easier to use and are quite convenient. However, the expense associated with their use and the occurrence of late aneurysmal deterioration have limited enthusiasm for their adoption at present. Whether or not this will change in the future remains to be seen. The discrepancy between limb salvage and graft patency seen with cryopreserved grafts (greater than that with other graft types) is unexplained and may have to do with patient selection or, alternatively, the mode of failure of these grafts. Distal embolization prior to occlusion is well described with prosthetic grafts; it is possible that this may occur to a lesser extent with the biologic substitutes. No data are available to address this question at present.

■ VENOUS RECONSTRUCTIONS

Indications for reconstruction of thrombosed or injured veins remain an area of controversy. However, when venous reconstruction is undertaken, the choice of conduit is important. Because of the velocity of venous flow, marked variations in flow during the cardiac cycle, and the compressibility of the venous system, venous reconstructions are more prone to thrombosis than reconstruction of the corresponding arteries. In general venous reconstruction is limited to central veins such as the inferior or superior vena cava and the iliofemoral segments. Venous reconstructions should be tension free, and the vascular conduit should be slightly larger in diameter than the vein it is to replace. Autogenous venous conduits generally give the best results but require significant modification in most instances. Diameter discrepancies seen with the saphenous vein require use of spiral graft construction if this is to be used for replacement of large veins such as the superior or inferior vena cava.[35-37] Deep femoral veins, when these can be removed without compromising the venous return of the extremity, may be useful for reconstruction of jugular, subclavian, and iliofemoral venous segments.

Venous homografts, either fresh or cryopreserved, have been used in experimental and clinical venous reconstruction.[38,39] Use of adjuvants to prevent thrombosis may yield reasonable results, and even when thrombosis occurs, recanalization may be expected in some proportion of cases. Increasing experience with externally supported PTFE in reconstruction of the vena cava has been encouraging.[37] Although these results are not as good as those reported using spiral vein, the marked reduction of complexity of the procedure has significant attraction. Such reconstructions may be combined with adjuvant arteriovenous fistula to improve graft patency.

■ ARTERIOVENOUS GRAFTS FOR DIALYSIS

The topic of arteriovenous grafts for dialysis is covered in detail in another section of the text; however, some general comments are relevant here. The selection of the appropriate conduit for arteriovenous access is dependent on a set of factors that differs somewhat from those used in vascular reconstructive surgery. The goal of arteriovenous access surgery is to make available a conduit that provides a high enough rate of blood flow (400 to 600 mL/min) to allow efficient hemodialysis, be durable, and resist infection. The conduit must be able to withstand the continuing trauma of cannulation two or three times per week. Furthermore, the functional life of these conduits depends to a great extent on the skill and dedication of the dialysis nurse and technician, something over which the operating surgeon has no control.

Current recommendations indicate that autogenous arteriovenous fistulae are preferred over prosthetic bridge grafts because of their long-term improved patency. However, this must be balanced by the fact that more than 30% of arteriovenous fistulae either do not mature sufficiently to be used for dialysis or require significant revisions to maintain a useful life. Furthermore, most arteriovenous fistulae cannot be used for dialysis for 2 to 3 months after implantation. This configuration works best in patients who are having their initial access and are not yet on dialysis. Refinements in preoperative evaluation and the use of vein transpositions have increased the rate of autogenous fistulae performed for dialysis. It appears that current best practice may result in two thirds to three fourths of access procedures being autogenous.

Prosthetic grafts play a major role in dialysis access. They provide reliably high flows when placed in the appropriate configuration, can be used within 2 weeks of implantation, and are easier to access than autogenous fistulae. However, the rate of intermediate failure is higher in prosthetic bridge grafts than it is in autogenous fistulae, with the primary cause being hyperplasia at and just distal to the venous anastomosis. The most common prosthetic used in current practice is PTFE, although new polyurethane grafts are available that allow immediate cannulation and appear to have similar patency rates.[40] Modifications of PTFE grafts to change the hemodynamic forces at the venous anastomosis have been reported to reduce intimal hyperplasia and prolong graft patency when placed in the upper arm.[41] In most series, however, the rate of revision and ultimate failure of prosthetic grafts is significantly higher than that of well-placed autogenous fistulae.

In this area, as in distal reconstruction, modified biologic grafts have played a niche role. These grafts are generally used when autogenous vein has been exhausted and arterial inflow or venous outflow is compromised following multiple prior access procedures. These grafts may also have a role in positions where the possibility of infection is increased (e.g., thigh grafts).

■ DURABILITY AND LONG-TERM FOLLOW-UP

The arterial autograft is the most durable of all vascular conduits. However, as noted previously, the availability of this conduit is markedly restricted and in current practice it is used almost exclusively for coronary revascularization. The next best functioning conduit is autogenous vein. As described later, although a significant subset of vein grafts undergo mid-term hyperplastic or long-term degenerative changes, most well-selected autogenous veins last for the life of the patient in whom they have been placed. Biologic grafts are subject to mid-term and late deterioration and must be monitored in an ongoing fashion for the life of the patient. Prosthetic grafts demonstrate the least deterioration of conduit but are also least tolerant of low-flow situations (i.e., highest thrombotic threshold velocity). These grafts are most prone to sudden thrombosis without warning and demonstrate the least benefit with surveillance protocols, are never fully incorporated into the host, and are a continued risk for late infection throughout the course of their implantation.

Placement of an arterial conduit commits the patient and surgeon to a program of long-term follow-up, since all types of conduits deteriorate over time and arteriosclerosis is, to date, a disease of inexorable progression. Graft failure has traditionally been separated into three categories: (1) perioperative (within 30 days); (2) midterm (up to 24 months); and (3) late (more than 24 months). Perioperative failures are due to either technical or judgmental error (e.g., selecting a poor conduit, or choice of inflow or outflow vessel). Many of these problems can be reduced by imaging of the reconstruction at the time of completion in the operating room.[42] This is usually not done for aortic reconstructions but is standard practice for infrainguinal and visceral reconstructions. Such revisions improve both early and late patency. Although angiography has been the "gold standard" for such perioperative quality control, over the last decade it has been increasingly supplanted by duplex ultrasound.

Thrombosis of a bypass conduit between 30 days and 2 years is most often the result of hyperplastic lesions, either in the conduit itself or at the vascular anastomosis. Improvement in design of prosthetic conduits has rendered them free of internal defects for the most part and failure within the conduit is usually restricted to autogenous tissues. The increasing use of in-situ saphenous vein for infrainguinal reconstruction, with the attendant possibility of retained valves and side-branch fistula, first focused the attention of vascular surgeons on detecting changes in the vein graft itself after implantation. These changes can also occur in reversed vein grafts. Changes include lesions within the graft at sites of retained valves or valve leaflets or unsuspected vein damage and changes at the proximal or distal anastomosis. For many years it has been known that vein grafts can remain patent in situations where they are extremely disadvantaged hemodynamically. This circumstance has been known variously as *pseudo-occlusion* or the *failing graft*.[43,44] The observation that these grafts could be revised and maintain near-normal patency, while revision of vein grafts after thrombosis was disappointing, prompted surgeons to look for deterioration in vein grafts before thrombosis occurs using duplex ultrasound.[45] Regular ultrasound surveillance at 3- to 6-month intervals is recommended for vein grafts after infrainguinal reconstruction. A variety of ultrasound parameters have been used to detect and characterize such lesions: In general they rely on detecting reductions in total graft flow velocity and the detection of focal elevations of velocity at the sites of narrowing. Focal defects can be repaired by open surgery or percutaneous transluminal angioplasty. Open techniques include patch angioplasty or resection of the area of narrowing or a jump graft around this area with autogenous tissue. Balloon dilation of these defects is technically easier than open surgery but less effective in anastomotic stenosis[44] and is generally reserved for short lesions within the conduit itself.

Although changes within the conduit are uncommon when prosthetic grafts are used, anastomotic hyperplasia is common with prostheses. This is caused primarily by alterations in shear stress at these anastomoses, which may be magnified by the differences in both size and compliance between the native vessel and the prosthetic graft. Altering the configuration of the proximal or distal anastomosis by the use of cuffs, boots, patches, or modified grafts with flow diffusers, as previously noted, may reduce the incidence of clinical complications. Monitoring of prosthetic grafts is more controversial, since they do not tolerate changes in graft flow the way biologic conduits do and usually close without warning. The role of surveillance of prosthetic grafts remains unsettled at present.

Biologic grafts share the propensity of autogenous tissue for degeneration over time. Particularly in the case of homografts, this can be seen within the first 2 years and may manifest itself by either aneurysm formation or development of stenosis. These grafts should be monitored for development of defects, which if detected may be repaired with some hope of success.

Late failure of the fabric of the prosthetic graft is a rare event with contemporary materials. Late pseudoaneurysm development, which has been an increasingly recognized complication of aortic grafting, is usually the result of native artery deterioration. Some authors recommend surveillance at 5-year intervals after aortic replacement to check for true or anastomotic or perianastomotic aneurysm. Late changes in autogenous vein are also unusual. In general vein grafts that remain patent beyond 36 months are unlikely to develop later lesions, and problems that occur in late follow-up are most often the result of progression of proximal or distal disease. There are some vein grafts that develop atherosclerotic accumulations after prolonged implantation. This has been best described in the coronary circulation but also occurs in peripheral bypass grafts.[46-48] These changes may manifest themselves as both stenosis and aneurysmal dilation. As a rule this phenomenon is most common in patients with persistent, uncontrolled hyperlipidemias. Biologic grafts are most prone to late degeneration owing to the modification of the conduit at the time of preparation. Cryopreserved homografts show significant deterioration by 36 months after implantation. This is more common with venous than arterial homografts. However, even current methods of preservation of arterial homografts result in significant late deterioration of this conduit. Human umbilical vein performs better in the long term than other current homografts. Although there is evidence of late aneurysmal deterioration in a small number of cases, failure due to thrombosis remains the main problem with this conduit. Patients in whom any biologic conduit is placed must undergo lifelong surveillance with the expectation that eventual replacement of the biologic graft will be necessary.

■ SUMMARY

The vascular surgeon is faced with a variety of choices for vascular reconstruction. Issues of availability, size match, and long-term performance are the major factors in determining conduit choice. Large and medium-sized arteries with high-flow states constitute the major indication for prosthetic graft use. If runoff is compromised or infection is a concern, autogenous deep vein has proved a durable second choice. For reconstruction of smaller arteries (<6 mm) and for venous reconstructions, the benefits of autogenous tissue are most obvious. These benefits, in terms of both early and late patency, are so great that prosthetic grafts are infrequently indicated in these reconstructions. When prosthetics are used, adjuvants can improve patency. Modified biologic grafts continue to represent a potential of an off-the-shelf graft that performs better than prosthetics. For the most part, this potential has not been realized, and their expense makes them a last choice in most cases. Their main indication is in cases of infection or extreme low flow.

Implantation of a graft—autogenous, biologic, or prosthetic—commits both surgeon and patient to a lifelong regimen of regular follow-up and risk factor reduction.

■ REFERENCES

1. Beghi C, Nicolini F, Budillon AM, et al: Midterm clinical results in myocardial revascularization using the radial artery. Chest 122:2075-2079, 2002.
2. Stoney RJ, Olofsson PA: Aortorenal arterial autografts: The last two decades. Ann Vasc Surg 2:169-173, 2002.
3. Sauvage LR, Berger KE, Mansfield PB, et al: Future directions in the development of arterial prostheses for small- and medium-caliber arteries. Surg Clin North Am 54:213-228, 1974.
4. Tiwari A, Cheng KS, Salacinski H, et al: Improving the patency of vascular bypass grafts: The role of suture materials and surgical techniques on reducing anastomotic compliance mismatch. Eur J Vasc Endovasc Surg 25:287-295, 2003.
5. Salacinski HJ, Goldner S, Giudiceandrea A, et al: The mechanical behavior of vascular grafts: A review. J Biomater Appl 15:241-278. 2001.
6. Greenwald SE, Berry CL: Improving vascular grafts: The importance of mechanical and haemodynamic properties. J Pathol 190:292-299, 2000.
7. Dardik H, Wengerter K, Qin F, et al: Comparative decades of experience with glutaraldehyde-tanned human umbilical cord vein graft for lower limb revascularization: An analysis of 1275 cases. J Vasc Surg 35:64-71, 2002.
8. Schepens MA: Dilation of knitted grafts in thoracic aorta. Eur J Cardiothorac Surg 20:430-431, 2001.
9. Nunn DB: Structural failure of Dacron arterial grafts. Semin Vasc Surg 12:83-91, 1999.
10. Eid A, Lyass S: Acute perigraft seroma simulating anastomotic bleeding of a PTFE graft applied as an arteriovenous shunt for hemodialysis. Ann Vasc Surg 10:290-291, 1996.
11. Bandyk DF, Novotney ML, Back MR, et al: Expanded application of in situ replacement for prosthetic graft infection. J Vasc Surg 34:411-419, 2001.
12. Earnshaw JJ: Conservative surgery for aortic graft infection. Cardiovasc Surg 4:570-572, 1996.
13. Batt M, Magne JL, Alric P, et al: In situ revascularization with silver-coated polyester grafts to treat aortic infection: Early and midterm results. J Vasc Surg 38:983-989, 2003.
14. Clagett GP, Valentine RJ, Hagino RT: Autogenous aortoiliac/femoral reconstruction from superficial femoral-popliteal veins: Feasibility and durability. J Vasc Surg 25:255-266, 1997.
15. Wells JK, Hagino RT, Bargmann KM, et al: Venous morbidity after superficial femoral-popliteal vein harvest. J Vasc Surg 29:282-289, 1999.
16. Koskas F, Plissonnier D, Bahnini A, et al: In situ arterial allografting for aortoiliac graft infection: A 6-year experience. Cardiovasc Surg 4:495-499, 1996.
17. Kieffer E, Sabatier J, Plissonnier D, Knosalla C: Prosthetic graft infection after descending thoracic/thoracoabdominal aortic aneurysmectomy: Management with in situ arterial allografts. J Vasc Surg 33:671-678, 2001.
18. Modrall JG, Joiner DR, Seidel SA, et al: Superficial femoral-popliteal vein as a conduit for brachiocephalic arterial reconstructions. Ann Vasc Surg 16:17-23, 2002.
19. Modrall JG, Sadjadi J, Joiner DR, et al: Comparison of superficial femoral vein and saphenous vein as conduits for mesenteric arterial bypass. J Vasc Surg 37:362-366, 2003.
20. Ortenwall P, Wadenvik H, Kutti J, Risberg B: Endothelial cell seeding reduces thrombogenicity of Dacron grafts in humans. J Vasc Surg 11:403-410, 1990.
21. Herring M, Smith J, Dalsing M, et al: Endothelial seeding of polytetrafluoroethylene femoral popliteal bypasses: The failure of low-density seeding to improve patency. J Vasc Surg 20:650-655, 1994.
22. Harris P, Da Silva T, How T: Interposition vein cuffs. Eur J Vasc Endovasc Surg 11:257-259, 1996.
23. Kreienberg PB, Darling RC III, Chang BB, et al: Adjunctive techniques to improve patency of distal prosthetic bypass grafts: Polytetrafluoroethylene with remote arteriovenous fistulae versus vein cuffs. J Vasc Surg 31:696-701, 2000.
24. Kreienberg PB, Darling RC III, Chang BB, et al: Early results of a prospective randomized trial of spliced vein versus polytetrafluoroethylene graft with a distal vein cuff for limb-threatening ischemia. J Vasc Surg 35:299-306, 2002.
25. Neville RF, Attinger C, Sidawy AN: Prosthetic bypass with a distal vein patch for limb salvage. Am J Surg 174:173-176, 1997.
26. Johnson WC, Williford WO: Benefits, morbidity, and mortality associated with long-term administration of oral anticoagulant therapy to patients with peripheral arterial bypass procedures: A prospective randomized study. J Vasc Surg 35:413-421, 2002.
27. Johnson WC, Lee KK: A comparative evaluation of polytetrafluoroethylene, umbilical vein, and saphenous vein bypass grafts for femoral-popliteal above-knee revascularization: A prospective randomized Department of Veterans Affairs cooperative study. J Vasc Surg 32:268-277, 2002.
28. Klinkert P, Schepers A, Burger DH, et al: Vein versus polytetrafluoroethylene in above-knee femoropopliteal bypass grafting: Five-year results of a randomized controlled trial. J Vasc Surg 37:149-155, 2003.
29. Green RM, Abbott WM, Matsumoto T, et al: Prosthetic above-knee femoropopliteal bypass grafting: Five-year results of a randomized trial. J Vasc Surg 31:417-425, 2000.
30. Gupta SK, Veith FJ, Kram HB, Wengerter KR: Prospective, randomized comparison of ringed and nonringed polytetrafluoroethylene femoropopliteal bypass grafts: A preliminary report. J Vasc Surg 13:163-172, 1991.
31. Schulman ML, Badhey MR, Yatco R: Superficial femoral-popliteal veins and reversed saphenous veins as primary femoropopliteal bypass grafts: A randomized comparative study. J Vasc Surg 6:1-10, 1987.
32. Rosenthal D, Arous EJ, Friedman SG, et al: Endovascular-assisted versus conventional in situ saphenous vein bypass grafting: Cumulative patency, limb salvage, and cost results in a 39-month multicenter study. J Vasc Surg 31:60-68, 2000.
33. Dardik H, Silvestri F, Alasio T, et al: Improved method to create the common ostium variant of the distal arteriovenous fistula for enhancing crural prosthetic graft patency. J Vasc Surg 24:240-248, 1996.

34. Kallakuri S, Ascher E, Hingorani A, et al: Hemodynamics of infrapopliteal PTFE bypasses and adjunctive arteriovenous fistulas. Cardiovasc Surg 11:125-129, 2003.
35. Dammers R, de Haan MW, Planken NR, et al: Central vein obstruction in hemodialysis patients: Results of radiological and surgical intervention. Eur J Vasc Endovasc Surg 26:317-321, 2003.
36. Doty JR, Flores JH, Doty DB: Superior vena cava obstruction: Bypass using spiral vein graft. Ann Thorac Surg 67:1111-1116, 1999.
37. Kalra M, Gloviczki P, Andrews JC, et al: Open surgical and endovascular treatment of superior vena cava syndrome caused by nonmalignant disease. J Vasc Surg 38:215-223, 2003.
38. Read RC, Thompson BW, Wise WS, Murphy ML: Mesocaval H venous homografts. Arch Surg 101:785-791, 1970.
39. Sitzmann JV, Imbembo AL, Ricotta JJ, et al: Dimethylsulfoxide-treated, cryopreserved venous allografts in the arterial and venous systems. Surgery 95:154-159, 1984.
40. Kiyama H, Imazeki T, Kurihara S, Yoneshima H: Long-term follow-up of polyurethane vascular grafts for hemoaccess bridge fistulas. Ann Vasc Surg 17:516-521, 2003.
41. Kovalic AJ, Beattie DK, Davies AH: Outcome of ProCol, a bovine mesenteric vein graft, in infrainguinal reconstruction. Eur J Vasc Endovasc Surg 24:533-534, 2002.
42. Johnson BL, Bandyk DF, Back MR, et al: Intraoperative duplex monitoring of infrainguinal vein bypass procedures. J Vasc Surg 31:678-690, 2000.
43. Smith CR, Green RM, DeWeese JA: Pseudo-occlusion of femoropopliteal bypass grafts. Circulation. 68:II88-II93, 1983.
44. O'Mara CS, Flinn WR, Johnson ND, et al: Recognition and surgical management of patent but hemodynamically failed arterial grafts. Ann Surg 193:467-476, 1981.
45. Avino AJ, Bandyk DF, Gonsalves AJ, et al: Surgical and endovascular intervention for infrainguinal vein graft stenosis. J Vasc Surg 29:60-70, 1999.
46. Motwani JG, Topol EJ: Aortocoronary saphenous vein graft disease: Pathogenesis, predisposition, and prevention. Circulation 97:916-931, 1998.
47. Sarjeant JM, Rabinovitch M: Understanding and treating vein graft atherosclerosis. Cardiovasc Pathol 11:263-271, 2002.
48. Karpe F, Taskinen MR, Nieminen MS, et al: Remnant-like lipoprotein particle cholesterol concentration and progression of coronary and vein-graft atherosclerosis in response to gemfibrozil treatment. Atherosclerosis 157:181-187, 2001.

Chapter 47

The Autogenous Vein

FRANK B. POMPOSELLI JR., MD
FRANK W. LOGERFO, MD

The greater saphenous vein is the conduit of choice for arterial reconstructive surgery in the lower extremity. Kunlin[1] first described the use of greater saphenous vein as a bypass graft for the correction of arterial occlusive disease of the superficial femoral artery in France in the middle of the 20th century. Saphenous vein grafting provided a simpler alternative to superficial femoral endarterectomy as popularized by Dos Santos[2] and was greeted with enthusiasm by a number of surgeons in the United States. Early experiences in this country with saphenous vein bypass, however, proved disappointing, with technical difficulties such as anastomotic strictures, frequently leading to graft failure in an era when specialized vascular surgical techniques, fine sutures, and instruments did not exist. Most surgeons at the time abandoned saphenous vein grafting in favor of arterial allografts, which were larger in caliber and easier to suture. Experience demonstrated that allografts frequently deteriorated, with resulting complications of aneurysm formation, occasional rupture, and frequent thrombosis or embolization.[3] Allografts gave way to the newly developed synthetic fabric prostheses, which demonstrated biologic inertness, long-term structural integrity, ease of use, and "off-the-shelf" availability.[4] For more than a decade, synthetic polyester (Dacron) grafts were the standard of care for femoropopliteal arterial reconstruction. Although early results with polyester grafts were quite acceptable, with longer follow-up thrombosis frequently occurred, especially with grafts crossing the knee joint and when distal runoff was poor.[5] A new interest in saphenous vein grafts resulted from a landmark paper by Linton and Darling,[6] demonstrating that by using meticulous handling and suturing techniques, patency rates of 70% or higher at 5 years could be achieved with vein grafts. Although the development of the expanded polytetrafluoroethylene (PTFE) prosthesis led to a renewed enthusiasm for synthetic grafts in the 1970s and 1980s,[7,8] clinical trials demonstrated clearly that even modern PTFE grafts could not match the results achieved with a saphenous vein conduit, especially to outflow target arteries distal to the knee.[9] Since that time, there has been a progressive improvement in the results of vein grafting in the lower extremity due to better harvesting and preparation; the availability of small-caliber sutures on high-quality stainless-steel needles; optical loupe magnification; and specialized, finely tooled instruments. Intra-arterial digital subtraction angiography, and, more recently, magnetic resonance angiography, has made it possible to routinely image the entire lower extremity arterial circulation from the aorta to the base of the toes, providing vascular surgeons with a complete picture of the arterial circulation and all possible bypass options. If the length and quality of available vein are found to be less than expected, based on the arteriogram, an alternative backup procedure can be chosen, using a more distal inflow site or more proximal outflow target, ensuring that only good-quality vein is used and the use of prosthetic graft is minimized. The "guesswork" of vein graft preparation has been largely eliminated with the use of preoperative duplex ultrasound vein mapping and intraoperative angioscopy. For many surgeons, intraoperative duplex ultrasound or angioscopy has replaced completion angiography as the modality to detect technical defects that cause immediate graft thrombosis. Postoperative duplex graft surveillance can identify hemodynamically significant graft strictures from intimal hyperplasia, facilitating their correction before graft thrombosis occurs. As the result of these and many other improvements in the technical aspects of the procedure, the quality of the venous conduit has become the primary determinant of long-term graft patency.

The development and evolution of cellular molecular biology have led to a new understanding of the physiology of the autogenous vein conduit, particularly the endothelium. A properly functioning endothelium is critical both to maintain blood in its fluid state and to prevent the formation of neointimal hyperplasia. Careful handling and preparation of the saphenous vein graft are critical to minimize injury to the endothelium. Investigations are now underway to determine if the endothelial surface of the vein graft can be modified to resist the formation of neointimal hyperplasia after its implantation as an arterial conduit. This chapter reviews the anatomy and physiology of autogenous vein grafts, their preparation, the technical considerations in their use as an arterial conduit, and the mechanisms leading to graft failure and their prevention.

■ HISTOLOGY AND MICROANATOMY

The saphenous vein consists of three structural components: endothelium, smooth muscle, and connective tissue. They are arranged in three concentric layers: the intima, media, and adventitia.[10] The intima is a thin structure consisting of a continuous layer of endothelial cells lying on a deep, fenestrated basement membrane, bounded by a thin, fragmented, elastic lamina.[11] The central portion of the endothelial cell contains the nucleus, which bulges into the lumen and can be distinctly seen on histologic staining. The media is composed of three layers of smooth muscle bundles. The innermost and outermost layers are oriented longitudinally, whereas the middle layer has a circular orientation. Each layer of muscle is separated by loose connective tissue and thin or thick elastic fibrils.[12] This arrangement is thought to increase contractile efficiency.[12] The circular muscle layer is most extensive at the insertion point of the valve leaflets. The adventitia is the thickest layer of the vein wall and is primarily composed of a network of collagen fibers that interlace in a longitudinal spiral and circular fashion.[11] In some locations, fibers of elastic tissue can also be found within the adventitial layer. The adventitia merges with the perivenous connective tissue and contains the vasa vasorum and adrenergic nerve fibers. The vasa vasorum provide nutrient blood flow to the vein wall. They enter the adventitia at intervals of 0.5 to 1.5 cm, and the innermost capillaries of their network penetrate to the level of the inner longitudinal muscle layer of the media.[13] Unlike the arterial wall, the entire vein wall is dependent on the vasa vasorum for its supply of oxygen and nutrients. The vasa vasorum are necessarily divided during vein harvesting, although they usually re-establish continuity with the circulation within a few weeks after arterial reconstruction.[14] In the preceding interval, the arterialized vein graft is entirely dependent on diffusion of oxygen and nutrients from the lumen to maintain viability, which is a fundamental change in vein wall physiology. The extent of the alteration in nutritive blood flow to the vein wall may be different for in-situ and reversed vein grafts and has been the subject of some debate in the past (see later). Nonetheless, it is likely that regardless of the method of implantation, the alterations in the microcirculation of the vein wall are significant and may have a profound effect on both the short- and long-term viability of the arterialized vein graft.

All veins contain valves to prevent retrograde blood flow with elevations in venous pressure.[10] The valves are composed of a thin layer of collagen and a variable amount of smooth muscle, covered on all surfaces by an endothelial layer. Valves have two components: (1) a cusp composed of concentrations of smooth muscle fibers running both circumferentially and longitudinally along the base of the cusp and (2) the two leaflets composed of collagen and endothelium. The circular fibers of the cusp reduce the vein diameter, and the longitudinal fibers shorten and thicken the cusp to help maintain vein tone in response to the increased pressure on the valve leaflets as they close in response to retrograde blood flow.[12]

The composition of vein walls varies greatly with location. As a general rule, smooth muscle content increases with more distal locations. Consequently, veins in the lower extremity have significantly more smooth muscle than the upper extremity veins, and veins of the superficial system have more smooth muscle than the deep veins.[12]

■ ANATOMY

Greater Saphenous Vein

The greater or long saphenous vein is the longest vein in the body.[10] Classically, the origin of the word *saphenous* is thought to be from the Greek word *safaina*, which means "evident." However, in a recent historical review, Caggiati and Bergan[15] submitted that *saphenous* is actually derived from the Arabic *el safin*, which means "hidden" or "concealed." The ancient Arabic physicians used the ankle portion of the saphenous vein for blood letting, but never the thigh portion, since it was not superficial enough to be clearly visible. Hence, they referred to the proximal greater saphenous vein as *el safin*. This anatomic feature is well known to any modern vascular surgeon who has struggled with exposing the greater saphenous vein in the depths of an excessively obese thigh.

The greater saphenous vein starts at the dorsal venous arch as it curves medially to become the medial marginal vein of the foot, which is an important vein for in-situ dorsalis pedis arterial reconstructions.[16] It consistently crosses the ankle joint immediately anterior to the medial malleolus and then ascends on the medial side of the lower leg with the saphenous nerve. It usually crosses the knee joint posterior to the medial condyle of the femur, where it separates from the saphenous nerve and maintains a relatively straight course through the medial aspect of the lower and mid thigh, and then angles slightly laterally and anteriorly to enter the common femoral vein at the fossa ovalis. In a detailed anatomic study of 385 limbs, using contrast phlebography, Shah and colleagues[17] demonstrated that only 38.2% of greater saphenous veins had a "conventional" configuration of a single trunk from the ankle to the groin, whereas 62.8% demonstrated significant variations. The most common variation in the thigh was a double system of equal or differing sizes, which was seen in 35% of cases. Most duplicated systems rejoined into one vein within 10 cm of the knee joint. They noted that of the 65% of veins that had a single trunk in the thigh, about 8% took a more anterolateral path than the normal position.

In the lower leg, variations were even more frequent. Although 45% had a single trunk, nearly 10% took a path 4 to 6 cm posterior to the tibia instead of the usual path 1 to 2 cm posterior to it. Forty-six percent had a double lower system, with the anterior branch most commonly dominant. Nine percent had multiple trunks or other configurations. In a more recent study[18] using duplex ultrasonography for anatomic evaluation of the greater saphenous vein in more than 1400 limbs, the same authors found strikingly similar results. The thigh portion of the greater saphenous vein consisted of a single trunk in 67%, with 8% positioned more laterally. In the calf, 65% of veins comprised a single trunk, whereas the remainder had double systems. Fifteen percent of the calf veins took a more posterior course to the usual route.

Valves are found in the saphenous vein and all other veins used in arterial reconstruction. The valves of the venous system were first described by Fabricius of Aqua Pendente (1533-1620).[12] His detailed observations described their structure and function in remarkable detail. In a contemporary study of 50 cadaver specimens, the average number of valves in the greater saphenous vein was found to be seven, with no differences noted between men and women. In the study by Shah and colleagues, saphenous veins contained an average of 6.3 ± 2.8 valves, with a range of 1 to 13.[17] The first saphenous valve is usually encountered directly at the fossa ovalis. In in-situ bypass, this valve is easily excised with Potts scissors under direct vision. The next valve is usually seen within 5 cm of the first. Saphenous vein valves are generally bicuspid, although single-cusp and tricuspid valves are occasionally seen when veins are evaluated by angioscopy. Valves are usually oriented parallel to the overlying skin, which is helpful to remember when performing valve cutting during in-situ bypass. Although gossamer thin in appearance, they are remarkably strong and can withstand pressures to 3 atmospheres.[12]

Understanding the anatomy and variations of the greater saphenous vein is critically important for any surgeon harvesting it for arterial reconstruction. Although duplex ultrasonographic vein mapping has removed much of the uncertainty in vein harvesting and preparation (see later), it is neither always available nor always correct. When a bifurcation point is encountered during vein harvesting, it is important to remember that if the exposed segment appears to be of inadequate size or caliber, there may be another larger segment running parallel to the first. When both are of equal size, they can be harvested in continuity and both used as part of the vein conduit. Similarly, if the vein is not found in its usual location, understanding where the alternate pathway is located (anterolateral in the thigh, posteriorly in the calf) often leads to the discovery of a useful conduit.

Lesser Saphenous Vein

The lesser, or short, saphenous vein begins at the lateral aspect of the dorsal venous arch of the foot. It starts its course posterior to the lateral malleolus, turning medially to cross the Achilles tendon, and then rises in the mid-portion of the posterior calf, in close proximity to the sural nerve.[12] It penetrates the deep fascia in the proximal third of the calf and terminates in the popliteal fossa, where it joins the popliteal vein. In anatomic and duplex studies, the termination point of the lesser saphenous vein is found to be quite variable. In 5% to 15% of cases, the lesser saphenous vein terminated above the level of the popliteal vein by joining the greater saphenous vein or another deep vein above the knee. In 7.8% of cases, it arborizes into multiple small branches in the lower leg and is unusable as a venous conduit.[19] Duplex studies can be extremely helpful in determining if the lesser saphenous vein will make a functional conduit, although its diameter is often underestimated by this method.

Many vascular surgeons avoid the use of the lesser saphenous vein owing to concerns about its length, caliber, and difficulties in harvesting. Studies by Chang and colleagues,[19] however, have shown that if the lesser saphenous vein appears suitable in preoperative duplex vein mapping studies, when exposed for surgery, most were quite acceptable conduits. The average diameter of harvested veins was 4.3 mm, with an average usable length of 28.6 cm, somewhat shorter than the average length reported by Rutherford and coworkers of 37.4 cm.[20] The length of one lesser saphenous vein usually suffices for the typical femoral to above-knee popliteal or popliteal to tibial bypass. Two full-length veins, spliced together end to end, can usually reach from the common femoral to the mid-tibial level or from the distal superficial femoral artery to the foot.

Harvesting the lesser saphenous vein can be accomplished by a number of methods. The patient can be positioned prone and one or both veins can be harvested, the wounds then closed, and the patient repositioned supine and prepared and draped for bypass. Although somewhat time consuming, this method allows the surgeon to work most comfortably and harvest the vein carefully and gently. Alternatively, the patient can be started in the supine position, with the lower extremity "frog legged." Harvesting the mid-portion of the lesser saphenous vein is readily accomplished by this approach, but exposing the distal and proximal portions usually requires holding the leg up in the air, with the surgeon working upward and underneath the leg, a most awkward and uncomfortable position. Both methods require the placement of an additional incision down the middle of the back of the calf, which is generally not a useful incision for arterial exposures, other than the

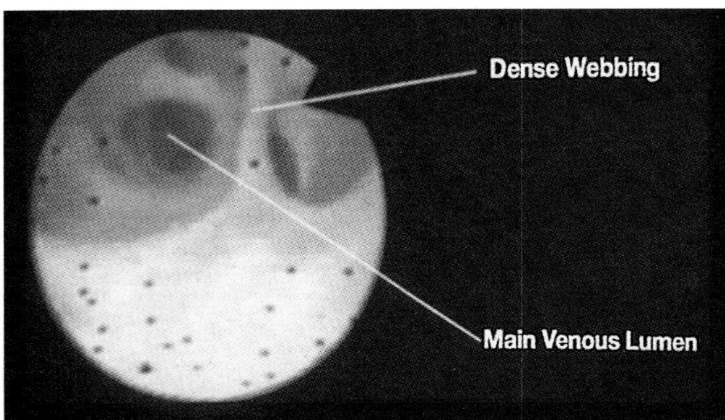

FIGURE 47-1 Digital image of the internal surface of an arm vein as seen through an angioscope. Dense webs are seen in this segment, which was discarded. When examined histologically, webs have been found to be organized thrombus, probably from previous venipuncture.

popliteal artery. A third exposure strategy first popularized by Shandal and associates[21] starts with the patient supine with a medial incision on the calf, as would be done to harvest the greater saphenous vein. This is deepened to divide the subcutaneous tissue and deep fascia, and a full-thickness flap deep to the fascia is raised until the lesser saphenous vein is exposed. The usefulness of this method is that the lesser saphenous vein can be harvested in a position comfortable and familiar to the surgeon and that both the greater and lesser saphenous veins and the popliteal and tibial arteries all can be exposed through a single incision. Careful dissection and meticulous hemostasis are important, however, when performing this flap to avoid seroma or hematoma formation, which can lead to varying amounts of flap necrosis. Chang and colleagues[19] routinely drain the space between the flap and the gastrocnemius muscle with a Jackson-Pratt drain and advise bed rest for 48 hours to help stabilize the flap and avoid this complication.

Arm Vein

Arm vein grafts have been gaining popularity among vascular surgeons as an alternative venous conduit with the increasing shortage of saphenous vein and need for redo arterial reconstructions. Although Kakkar[22] demonstrated the feasibility of the arm vein as a conduit for arterial reconstruction in 1969, it did not enjoy widespread acceptance among vascular surgeons because of concerns about durability, fragility, and difficulties in harvesting and handling. More recent studies have demonstrated that good-quality arm vein grafts perform well in the arterial circulation and that harvesting can be accomplished with minimal morbidity.[23-25] Although arm veins are generally more thin walled and fragile than saphenous vein grafts, concerns about rupture and aneurysm formation have been unfounded. A significant concern with arm vein grafts has been the presence of synechiae and webs on the luminal surface (Fig. 47-1), resulting from organized thrombus from previous venipuncture, which may lead to strictures from neointimal hyperplasia once placed in the arterial circulation. These abnormalities are not always apparent from external appearances. Some, including the authors,[26] have recommended the use of angioscopy (Fig. 47-2) prior to bypass to identify abnormal vein segments so that they may be excluded or repaired.[27] Holzenbein and associates[28] found that repaired or "upgraded" arm vein conduits performed nearly as well as good-quality arm vein conduits not requiring upgrading.

The two principal upper extremity veins used for arterial reconstruction are the cephalic and basilic veins.[23] Both can be thought of as having two parts: a distal forearm and proximal upper arm segment, connected at the elbow by the

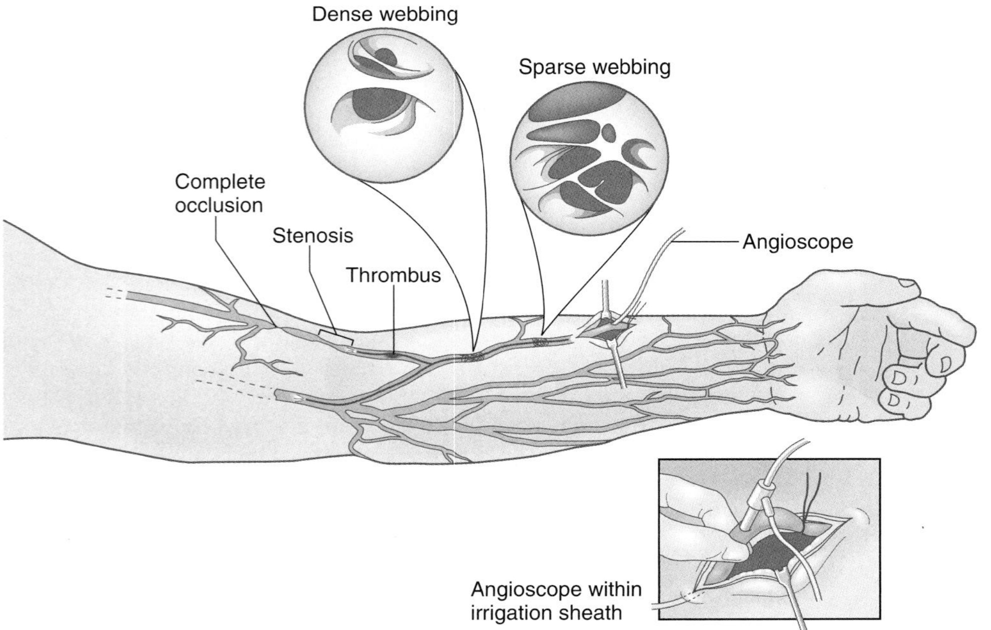

FIGURE 47-2 Schematic of intraoperative "in-situ" angioscopy of an arm vein prior to harvesting. The angioscope is inserted from the divided distal end and advanced proximally with saline irrigation via a pump to clear the field of blood. Areas of dense webbing that are encountered can be discarded or not harvested. Angioscopy can also be performed after the vein has been removed and is especially useful when performing valve lysis. (From Marcaccio EJ, Miller A, Tannenbaum GA, et al: Angioscopically directed interventions improve arm vein bypass grafts. J Vasc Surg 17:994-1002, 1993.)

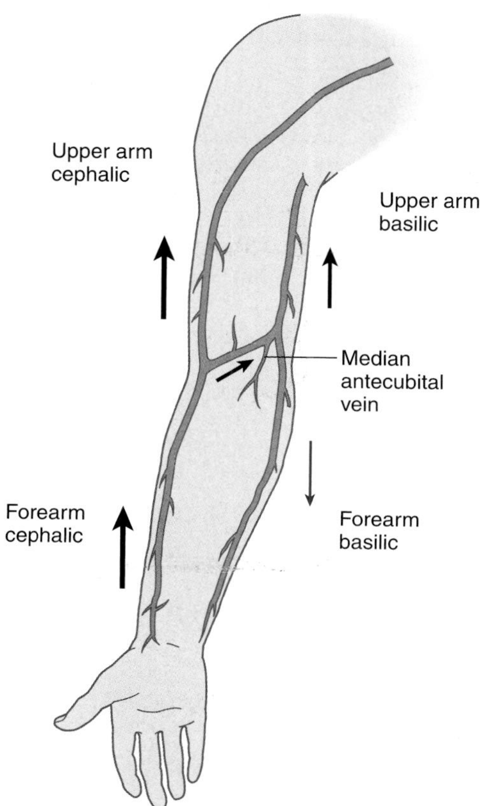

FIGURE 47-3 The "normal" pattern of upper extremity arm veins. Variations are common.

median cubital vein (Fig. 47-3). The cephalic vein starts in the wrist over the lateral aspect of the radius and then turns slightly medially, following a straight course along the volar forearm. Near the elbow, it merges with the distal basilic vein and branches of the deep system to form the median cubital vein. At the volar flexion crease of the elbow, the median cubital vein bifurcates, giving rise to the proximal portion of the cephalic vein, which ascends along the lateral aspect of the biceps muscle. At the shoulder, it enters the deltopectoral groove and then joins the axillary vein at the level of the clavicle.

The basilic vein begins in the ulnar part of the dorsal venous network of the hand.[29] It runs posteriorly on the ulnar side of the forearm but then angles anterolaterally near the elbow, where it joins the median cubital vein before ascending along the medial aspect of the biceps muscle in the upper arm. In the mid-portion of the humerus, it penetrates the deep fascia and then ultimately joins the brachial vein to form the axillary vein.

Anatomic variations are common with upper extremity veins, and the caliber of the various segments can vary widely. The length of the median cubital vein is not constant, and occasionally it may be nonexistent, demonstrating no connection between the cephalic and basilic systems. Oftentimes, forearm segments, especially the cephalic vein, are found to be unusable due to repeated trauma from previous venipuncture. In constructing an arm vein bypass conduit of suitable length, many different configurations and combinations of the various segments are possible, including single grafts comprising the lower and upper vein segments of the same system or composite grafts combining the forearm portion of one and the upper arm segment of the other system. The poor quality of forearm veins makes the use of a composite graft composed entirely of the upper arm cephalic and basilic veins joined by the median cubital vein, the upper arm "loop" graft, as described by LoGerfo and colleagues,[29] particularly useful (Fig. 47-4). Other configurations incorporating components of the lower and upper arm veins joined together by the median cubital vein are also possible (Fig. 47-5). When the median cubital vein is unusable or absent, two vein segments can be joined by end-to-end venovenostomies. When using the upper arm loop graft, one segment, usually the basilic vein, must be used nonreversed, necessitating lysis of the valves (Fig. 47-6). In other composite vein grafts, the desire to construct a conduit tapering in caliber from proximally to distally may also require valve lysis and a combination of nonreversed and reversed segments. In a recent series of more than 500 arm vein grafts, most of which were prepared with the aid of angioscopy, Faries and coworkers[30] showed that all configurations demonstrated comparable results and that valve lysis and end-to-end venovenostomies did not adversely affect patency. The authors emphasized the importance of familiarity with the preparation of reversed and nonreversed vein grafts, flexibility and creativity, and the routine use of angioscopy during conduit preparation.

Constructing arm vein grafts that require the use of angioscopy, valve lysis, and venovenostomies can be time consuming and tedious. Nonetheless, Calligaro and

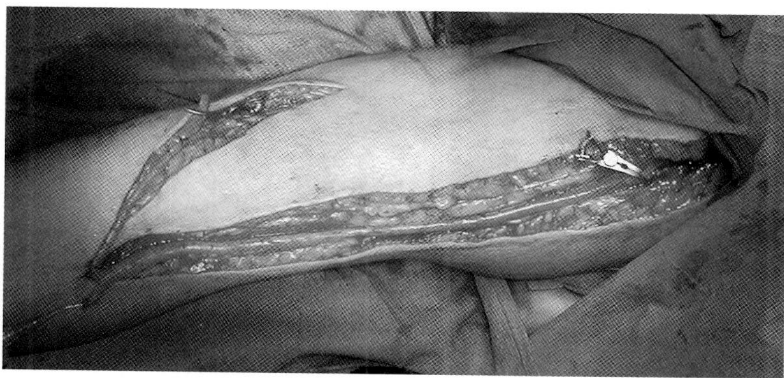

FIGURE 47-4 Intraoperative photo of the upper arm cephalic basilic loop graft. The entire length of the cephalic vein has been exposed along with half of the basilic vein and is connected by a short median cubital vein. This conduit reached from the above-knee popliteal artery to the dorsalis pedis artery.

associates[31] found the results of their arm vein bypass procedures sufficiently superior to prosthetic bypass to make them worthwhile, especially to outflow target arteries distal to the knee joint, an opinion shared by the authors. Use of two teams, one to harvest and prepare the vein and another to expose inflow and outflow arteries, preparing the vein with angioscopy and using distal inflow sites when available (which shortens the length of vein required) are all useful strategies to reduce the time and complexity of these procedures.

Superficial Femoral Vein

The superficial femoral vein is an excellent venous conduit whose caliber and durability make it an attractive in-situ replacement for infected aortofemoral prosthetic grafts and for major venous reconstructions in the thorax and abdomen.[32] It has also proved useful for lower extremity arterial reconstruction when saphenous vein is unavailable. Schulman and colleagues[33] reported patency rates in excess of 80% for lower extremity arterial bypass with superficial

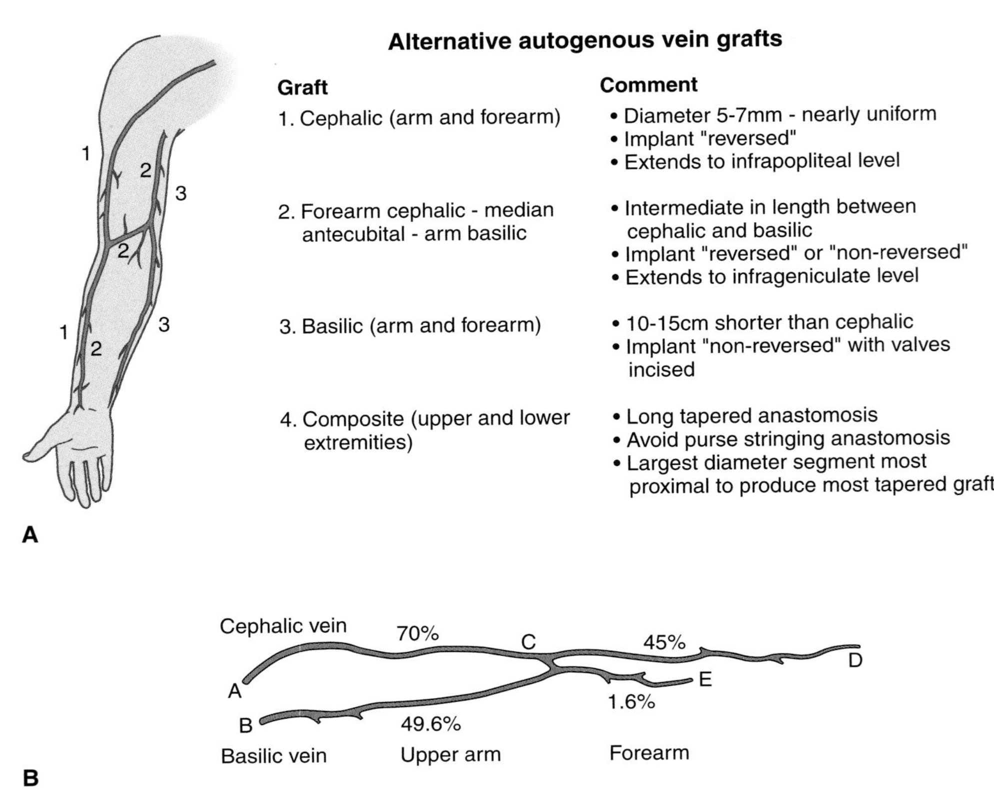

Alternative autogenous vein grafts
Graft
Comment
1. Cephalic (arm and forearm)
• Diameter 5-7mm - nearly uniform
• Implant "reversed"
• Extends to infrapopliteal level
2. Forearm cephalic - median antecubital - arm basilic
• Intermediate in length between cephalic and basilic
• Implant "reversed" or "non-reversed"
• Extends to infrageniculate level
3. Basilic (arm and forearm)
• 10-15cm shorter than cephalic
• Implant "non-reversed" with valves incised
4. Composite (upper and lower extremities)
• Long tapered anastomosis
• Avoid purse stringing anastomosis
• Largest diameter segment most proximal to produce most tapered graft
A
Cephalic vein
70%
C
45%
D
A
E
1.6%
B
49.6%
Basilic vein
Upper arm
Forearm
B

FIGURE 47-5 **A,** Alternative vein conduits of various types and configurations can be used for a variety of lower extremity arterial reconstructions when the saphenous vein is unavailable. Grafts can be used reversed or nonreversed and can usually be fashioned into a tapered conduit. Many grafts can be constructed to reach to the distal tibial or pedal level, especially when the inflow anastomosis starts at the popliteal level. **B,** In our experience, upper arm veins are more commonly usable than the forearm veins, although the forearm cephalic vein was used in 46% of arm vein bypasses. (**A,** From Bergan JJ, Yao JST: Arterial Surgery: New Diagnostic and Operative Techniques. Orlando, Grune & Stratton, 1988; **B,** From Holzenbein TJ, Pomposelli FB Jr, Miller A, et al: Results of a policy with arm veins used as the first alternative to an unavailable ipsilateral greater saphenous vein for infrainguinal bypass. J Vasc Surg 23:130-140, 1996.)

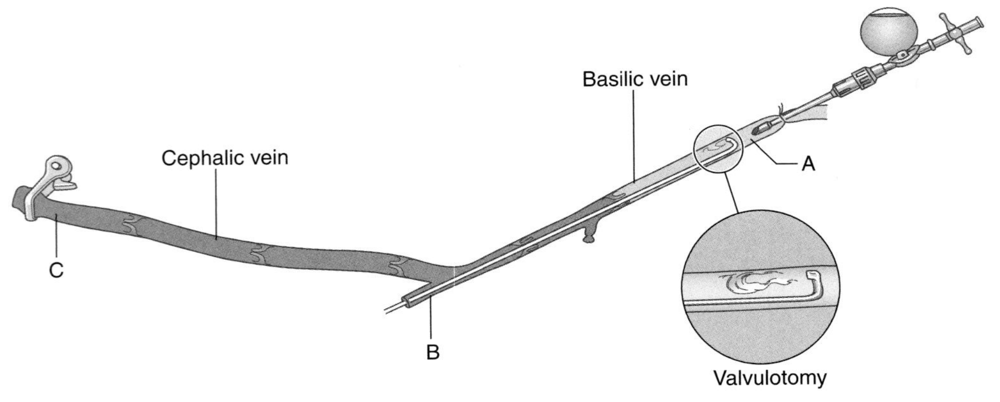

FIGURE 47-6 When constructing an upper arm vein loop graft, the valves must be cut in one segment, usually the basilic vein, to have forward blood flow.

femoral and popliteal vein grafts at 3 years and these were not significantly different from their randomized, concurrent results with reversed saphenous vein.[34] Clagett, Hagino, and their colleagues[32,35] emphasized the importance of obtaining preoperative duplex ultrasonography to assess the size and patency of the superficial femoral vein prior to harvesting.

Harvesting the superficial femoral vein can be tedious. It is best accomplished by an incision along the lateral border of the sartorius muscle, starting at the anterosuperior iliac spine and extending as far distally as needed. The superficial femoral vein can be harvested in continuity with the above-knee popliteal vein to increase length. The sartorius muscle is reflected medially, and the vein will be found in the same compartment and adjacent to the superficial femoral artery. This same incision also provides a clean plane for exposure of the distal superficial or deep femoral arteries when dealing with a prosthetic graft infection in the groin. All venous branches of the superficial femoral vein should be securely ligated or suture ligated. When possible, all crossing arterial branches should be preserved since these may be important collaterals in "redo" arterial reconstructions. It is important to preserve the junction of the profunda femoris vein with the common femoral vein when transecting the proximal end of the superficial vein to avoid excessive lower extremity venous hypertension.[36] The vein should be used in a nonreversed fashion in an end-to-end anastomosis to the aorta to optimize size match between the larger end of the vein and the aorta. This requires retrograde passage of a valvulotome or direct valve excision with the vein everted. Usually, three or four valves are encountered in the full length of the superficial femoral vein. Limb edema has been a concern with the use of superficial femoral vein grafts. However, in a study of 41 patients with aortoiliac reconstructions with superficial femoral vein, Clagett and colleagues[32] reported excellent long-term patency and limb salvage rates with only four patients suffering permanent limb edema, which was generally easily controlled with compression stockings. No patients developed venous ulcers.

■ PHYSIOLOGY

The blood vessel is no longer considered a passive conduit for flowing blood but is a complex living structure comprising connective tissues and endothelial and vascular smooth muscle cells (VSMCs) coupled together in a complex set of autocrine-paracrine interactions. Blood vessels have mechanisms to sense changes within their milieu, integrating these signals by intercellular communications and local production of mediators that influence structure and function.

The endothelium lines the luminal surface of blood vessels. It has a glistening, filmy appearance on gross inspection and comprises one layer of endothelial cells.[12] It plays an important role in maintaining blood fluidity, capillary transport, lipoprotein metabolism, angiogenesis, vasomotor function, and vascular structure. Normal endothelium secretes multiple paracrine molecules or *cytokines* to maintain a delicate balance between vasoconstriction and vasodilation, coagulation and blood fluidity, and promotion and inhibition of vascular growth. Identification of endothelial-derived cytokines and determination of their function in homeostasis and disease have been subject to intense investigation. Although they are incompletely understood, recent advances in molecular biology have led to tremendous increase in the identification of a variety of cytokines and a better understanding of how they interact with and modify the structure and function of the blood vessel wall.

Endothelial cells secrete prostacyclin (prostaglandin I_2 [PGI_2]), a potent vasodilator and inhibitor of platelet aggregation.[37-39] Conversely, they also secrete thromboxane A_2, which is a vasoconstrictor and platelet aggregation agonist.[40-42] Endothelial cells also elaborate tissue plasminogen activator (tPA), thrombomodulin, and heparin sulfates, which are antithrombogenic, but also synthesize von Willebrand's factor and tPA inhibitor, which are thrombogenic.[43-45] Endothelial cells can affect vascular smooth muscle relaxation or constriction independently of the autonomic nervous system's effect on the arterial wall (endothelial-derived relaxation or contraction). Physiologic assays of endothelial-derived vasomotor reactivity are commonly used in experiments to evaluate the integrity of endothelial function. The endothelial vasodilators are endothelial-derived relaxing factor (EDRF), now known to be nitric oxide, and PGI_2, whereas vasoconstrictors are endothelin and angiotensin II (AII). In addition to effects on vasomotor reactivity, endogenous endothelial-derived vasodilators in general suppress VSMC growth,[46,47] whereas the vasoconstrictors are VSMC growth promoters.[48] VSMC proliferation is promoted by other endothelial products such as platelet-derived growth factor (PDGF), fibroblast growth factor (FGF), and insulin-like growth factor (IGF).[49-51] The proliferative effects of PDGF, FGF, and IGF are modulated by the antimitogenic effects of endothelial transforming growth factor β (TGF-β).[52,53] These are some of the examples of the evolving understanding of the balance of biologic activity maintained by the endothelium.

In general, the functions that predominate under normal circumstances are vasodilatory, antithrombogenic, and antiproliferative. Under certain unfavorable conditions, however, the balance shifts to favor vasoconstriction, thrombosis, and VSMC proliferation. The aberrations in endothelial function that occur are probably the seminal event resulting in the development of vascular disease, especially atherosclerosis. Moreover, injuries sustained to vein grafts during harvesting can trigger alterations in endothelial function, resulting in the pathogenesis of intimal hyperplasia and atherosclerosis.

■ VEIN GRAFT PREPARATION

Although saphenous vein grafts have been clinically proved to be the best conduit for arterial reconstruction, they are hardly ideal. On the average, 15% to 25% of grafts fail within 5 years of implantation into the arterial circulation. Technical errors and intimal hyperplasia account for most early failures.[54] Intimal hyperplasia in part occurs as the result of endothelial damage that occurs during vein harvesting. Clinical and experimental studies over the past 20 years have demonstrated that three main variables—dissection technique, preparation solution, and distention pressure—influence the functional and structural injury that occurs to the endothelium during graft preparation.

Dissection Technique

Several authors have demonstrated that manipulation of the vein during harvesting can have a significant impact on its performance. Gundry and associates[55] demonstrated that clamps placed on the vein wall destroyed endothelium and fractured both the intima and the media. They also noted marked luminal stenoses in the area of vein branches where the ties were placed immediately adjacent to the arterial wall. They advised the use of a "no-touch" technique to the vein, which included minimal handling of the vein wall and tying branches a short distance away from the main vein to avoid these injuries. Dries,[56] Souza,[57] and their colleagues found that veins harvested using the no-touch technique had a better endothelial preservation on light and scanning electron microscopy than veins harvested by conventional methods, irrespective of the preparation solution used, even when excessive distention pressures were avoided.

In a prospective, randomized trial, evaluating three harvesting techniques of saphenous vein grafts for coronary bypass grafting, with graft patency by coronary angiography at 18 months as the endpoint, grafts harvested gently, with a no-touch technique, which included harvesting the vein with a surrounding layer of tissue and avoiding distention (see later), had significantly better patency than grafts harvested with conventional techniques.[58] There has been much interest recently in the use of a variety of endoscopic methods for harvesting saphenous vein grafts, particularly for coronary revascularization, although similar methods are now being applied to lower extremity bypass as well. Concerns have been raised that the required manipulation of the veins harvested with the endoscope might lead to more vein injury and graft failure. In a recent study, Alrawi and coworkers[59] found no difference in the number of viable endothelial cells cultured from saphenous vein grafts harvested by either the no-touch or endoscopic method and suggested that endoscopic harvesting is preferred for coronary revascularization, since it results in less morbidity.

Distention Pressure

During harvesting, most saphenous vein grafts usually develop some degree of vasospasm. Vascular surgeons often use pressure distention of the vein through a syringe to break areas of spasm and also to uncover leaks from vein tributaries, which were cut and left unligated when the vein was excised. Studies have demonstrated that intraluminal venous pressures as high as 700 mm Hg can be generated with careless overdistention of the vein through a syringe.[60] Many reports have demonstrated the deleterious effects of high pressure in distending the saphenous vein prior to bypass. In early animal experiments, Ramos and associates[61] and Bonchek[62] demonstrated that veins distended to 600 or 700 mm Hg demonstrated histologic and electron microscopic evidence of progressive degenerative changes in all layers of the vein wall, including endothelial cell involution and desquamation, and re-endothelialization. When the endothelial surfaces regenerated, variable degrees of subendothelial fibrosis and myoepithelial proliferation occurred. Distention with cold saline caused more damage to the endothelium than did distention with blood. LoGerfo and colleagues[63] demonstrated that in canine and human veins prepared for arterial bypass grafting, endothelial morphology was best preserved when veins were pretreated with papaverine to overcome spasm, a phosphodiesterase inhibitor that causes vasodilation by direct smooth muscle cell relaxation. They also advised the use of a warm solution for gentle distention when looking for open branches, since dilation of the vein to excessive pressures with cold solutions proved especially harmful. Kurusz and coworkers[64] demonstrated that veins distended with indiscriminant pressure showed massive endothelial disruption regardless of the solution used and concluded that limiting the distending pressure was the most important factor in minimizing endothelial disruption and injury. Adcock and associates[65] similarly found "ideally" harvested canine jugular vein grafts incorporating the use of papaverine irrigation, careful tributary ligation, and pressure distention to no greater than 100 mm Hg with heparinized blood with storage in an identical solution at 4° C in a gently distended state, demonstrated less endothelial denudation and ultrastructural alteration and less platelet aggregation and monocyte infiltration than control grafts harvested not using these techniques. In addition, even when healed, control grafts demonstrated more intimal medial thickness than ideally harvested grafts. Excessive pressure also led to alterations in venous endothelial fibrolytic activity in addition to causing deleterious ultrastructural and histologic changes. Malone and colleagues[66] demonstrated a progressive decrement in fibrolytic activity in relationship to increased change in pressure from control levels to 700 mm Hg.

Solutions

A variety of substances have been used to preserve endothelial integrity, both during harvesting of saphenous vein grafts and in the time interval where the vein graft is stored prior to implantation. The ideal storage solution should maintain endothelial cell viability and prevent vasospasm, which is deleterious to endothelial morphology. LoGerfo and coworkers[67] recommended percutaneous infiltration of papaverine along the course of the vein prior to incision to minimize the vasospasm that occurs with harvesting. Endothelial morphology was best preserved when veins were treated with papaverine before they were excised and when a warm solution was used for dilation of the vein grafts. A protective effect against injury from distention was also noted with this technique, since veins treated with papaverine appeared resistant to the adverse effects of pressure, even when they were distended to 500 mm Hg. Baumann and colleagues[68] similarly found that veins preserved with a combination of balanced electrolyte solution and papaverine showed the least degree of endothelial contraction and the best preservation of the endothelial surface. They hypothesized that the prolonged contracture of a vein in vasospasm led to endothelial protrusion and sloughing from the surface since endothelial cells cannot slide over one another as do smooth muscle cells in the media of the contracting blood vessel wall. Instead, they herniate into the lumen and are disrupted from the wall. Sottiurai and associates[69] studied the effect of high- and low-pressure distention and the effect of papaverine in a canine jugular vein model. Similar to LoGerfo and coworkers, they noted a protective effect against mechanical distention in veins pretreated with papaverine, which demonstrated less mural leukocyte infiltration, less fibrosis of the media, and reduced amounts of intimal hyperplasia. Kurusz and associates[64] demonstrated that cold (10° C) heparinized saline, heparinized blood, and heparinized cardioplegic solution all resulted in a similar morphologic appearance to the endothelium, provided that the veins were not distended to greater than 200 mm Hg.

Temperature

There has been some controversy regarding the temperature at which a saphenous vein graft should be stored prior to implantation. Intuitively, hypothermia would appear to be best, since cold temperatures decrease metabolic activity, resulting in higher degrees of cell viability during the period of ischemia between harvesting and implantation. LoGerfo and coworkers[67] suggested that the optimum storage should be 4° C. Gundry and associates[55] also found that saphenous vein grafts were best preserved at low temperatures although recommended heparinized cold blood, since cold saline solution produced mural edema. More recent studies, however, have suggested that the storage of vein grafts in cold solutions may be deleterious, particularly when experiments are designed to measure the functional state of the endothelial cell. Bush and colleagues[37] demonstrated that the endogenous production of prostacyclin by the endothelial cell was optimized when canine vein grafts were stored at 37° C, compared with veins stored at lower temperatures. Lawrie and colleagues[70] investigated the effect of temperature on endothelial-dependent relaxation in human saphenous vein grafts. Harvested fresh human saphenous veins were constricted with phenylephrine and then relaxed with the EDRF-dependent agents, calcium ionophore, or acetylcholine. Endothelial-dependent relaxation was preserved the best in vein grafts stored in heparinized, room temperature blood, or room temperature balanced salt solution. Veins stored at 2° C to 4° C had severe depression of EDRF. Excessive pressurization to 400 mm Hg also depressed EDRF function, and the use of nitroglycerin, papaverine, or verapamil produced no improvement. Cook and associates[71] measured thrombomodulin activity in paired human saphenous vein grafts for coronary artery bypass. Thrombomodulin is a membrane glycoprotein present on normal vascular endothelium, which binds circulating thrombin and is important in protein C activation. Its function contributes to the nonthrombogenic nature of endothelium. They found that thrombomodulin functional activity was not significantly changed after harvesting with relatively short periods of storage at room temperature in heparinized saline.

The results of available studies indicate that all storage solutions have advantages and shortcomings. Based on available data, the following recommendations can be made. Vein grafts should be harvested gently with a minimal amount of grasping and manipulation. Vasospasm and forcible distention must be avoided. Papaverine is an extremely valuable adjunct in reducing vasospasm and should be used topically and when flushing or distending the vein. Veins should be gently distended to no more than 200 mm Hg with a warm, physiologic solution containing heparin and papaverine, with a pH and electrolyte composition similar to human plasma. Both whole blood and balanced salt solution are acceptable. Storage times prior to implantation should be as short as possible. Storing the vein in either warm or cold solutions is reasonable, although studies suggest that while lower temperatures may increase endothelial cell viability, they also result in direct and persistent metabolic injury of the endothelial cell that can have an adverse effect on its function. These effects appear to be magnified when cold solutions are used to distend vein grafts, which should be avoided.

E_2F Oligonucleotides

After implantation, all veins grafts undergo structural changes that can be thought of as an adaptive response to the injury of implantation and the increased pressure of the arterial environment. Vein grafts demonstrate increased wall thickness with some degree of intimal hyperplasia. At the cellular level, smooth muscle cell activation, migration, and proliferation is seen. At the molecular level, there is an upregulation of numerous genes responsible for the expression of growth factors, cytokines, and adhesion molecules by the VSMCs. In its pathologic form, this adaptive response to injury and arterial pressure causes *intimal hyperplasia,*[72] which manifests itself as diffuse vein graft narrowing and thickening, or focal stenotic lesions. Intimal hyperplasia leads to reduction in blood flow and ultimate graft thrombosis. Small-caliber grafts, those injured by harvesting or valve lysis, grafts that have previously undergone thrombectomy, composite vein grafts composed of ectopic segments, arm vein grafts, and bypass grafts in "redo" distal arterial reconstructions are particularly prone to thrombosis from intimal hyperplasia.

Modifying the intimal hyperplastic response by pharmacologic means has not proved successful. A novel approach, currently under intense investigation, uses smooth muscle cell cycle blockage by ex-vivo gene therapy to inhibit the intimal hyperplastic response.[73] Either a specific gene or an entire cell cycle can be inhibited with small nucleic acid molecules, oligonucleotides, that block the translation of specific messenger RNA or the activity of regulatory proteins (transcription factors) that control gene expression. Transcription factors bind to specific sites on the DNA chromosome (promoter regions) to either turn on or turn off gene expression. A "decoy" oligonucleotide that contains the base pair sequence for attachment to the promoter region blocks the transcription factor from attaching to the gene and inhibits its function (Fig. 47-7).[74] E_2F is a pivotal transcription factor that upregulates a dozen cell cycle genes important in intimal hyperplasia.[75] In a phase I clinical study, E2F oligonucleotide was delivered to vein grafts ex vivo in a closed chamber, bathing all surfaces of the vein at 6 pounds per square inch without vein distention for 10 minutes immediately prior to implantation. A total of 41 patients were randomized to treatment of their vein grafts with placebo, E_2F decoy, or a scrambled sequence oligonucleotide. Laboratory studies demonstrated successful delivery of the decoy to more than 90% of the

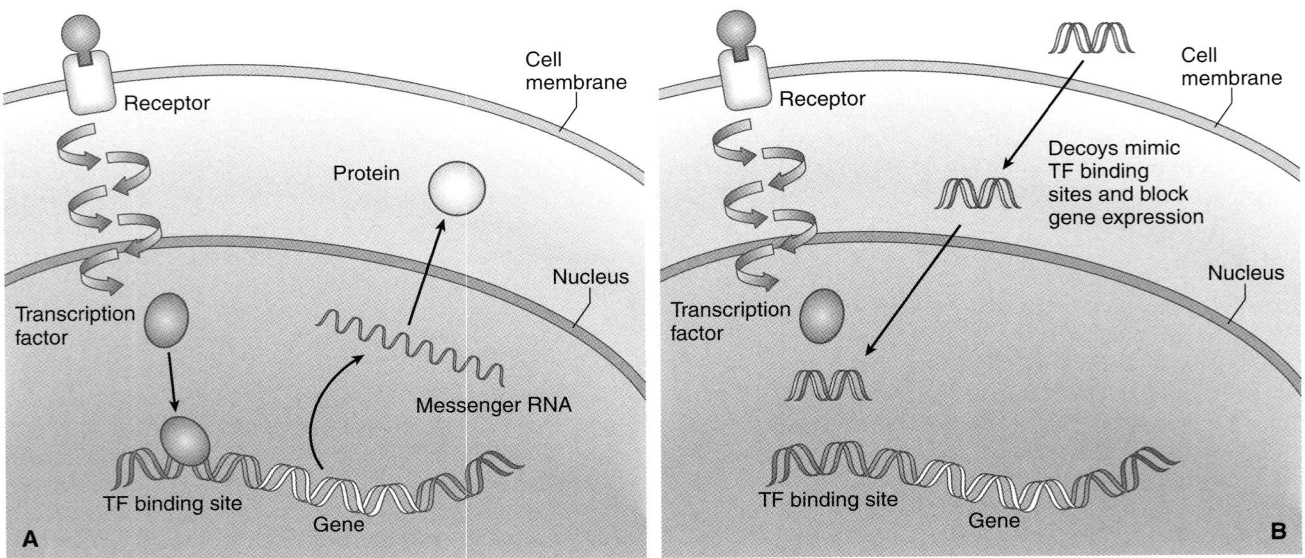

FIGURE 47-7 Schematic representation of how transcription factors (TFs) regulate gene expression. **A,** The TF binds to a specific site on the DNA strand (promoter region) to turn on messenger RNA production and ultimate protein synthesis. **B,** A decoy oligonucleotide contains the TF-binding site and binds the TF, effectively preventing gene expression. (**A** and **B,** Courtesy of Corgentech, Inc., San Francisco, Calif.)

cells in the vein wall. No systemic complications, laboratory abnormalities, or adverse events were noted. Although not designed to test clinical efficacy, a smaller number of graft revisions were needed to maintain patency in the E_2F-treated grafts compared with controls.[76] Similar findings were noted in a larger phase II trial of 200 patients undergoing coronary bypass surgery in Germany.[77] Currently, a phase III, multicenter, prospective, placebo-controlled, randomized clinical trial is underway evaluating the efficacy of E_2F decoy in preventing lower extremity vein graft failure. Recruitment of 1400 patients in 50 centers across North America began in December of 2001 and at this time is now complete.[75] The patients will be followed for up to 4 years, and the study is adequately powered to detect a 30% reduction in the primary endpoint of graft failure defined as graft thrombosis or need for interventions to maintain graft patency at 1 year.

In harvesting and preparing saphenous vein grafts, gentle handling with a no-touch or minimal-touch technique; proper ligation of side branches a slight distance away from the vein wall; the use of papaverine to overcome vasospasm, minimizing vein graft mechanical distention; or storage in warm, balanced salt solution or whole blood containing heparin and papaverine appear to be the factors that can both minimize endothelial injury and best preserve endothelial cell function. Nonetheless, even when the best efforts are made to harvest vein grafts with their structure and function intact, some injury is unavoidable. The results of the preliminary studies of vein graft pretreatment with an E_2F decoy represent an exciting advance in the preparation of vein grafts that may lead to better-quality vein grafts, decreased need for revision or replacement, and improved long-term durability. The efficacy of this novel approach awaits the results of multicenter prospective trials now underway in North America and Europe.

■ SURGICAL TECHNIQUE

Vein grafts can be used in a reversed, in-situ, or nonreversed fashion. In our experience, all are useful and should be part of every vascular surgeon's armamentarium. Flexibility in preparation of a vein graft and awareness of different potential bypass options to achieve the desired clinical outcome are critical in maximizing the use of autologous vein, which gives the most durable result. Proper handling and preparation of the vein, regardless of the configuration, is the most critical factor in both short- and long-term success.

Vein Mapping

Knowing ahead of time what length of conduit of an adequate caliber is available can decrease time in the operating room and avoid the morbidity associated with the needless exposure of inadequate and useless vein. Evaluating the status of the saphenous vein is critically important in planning an in-situ procedure using a limited incision technique to identify anatomic anomalies such as duplications and narrowed segments that might make in-situ bypass impossible. Previously, determining the status of the vein prior to surgery could only be accomplished by contrast venography.[78] In the last 15 years, venography has been replaced by the use of pre-bypass duplex ultrasonographic assessment of all vein segments that may be used, or *vein mapping*.[79] Anatomic studies of saphenous vein grafts evaluated with duplex ultrasound correlate closely with findings of earlier studies using contrast venography.[18] Veins should be scanned for patency, quality, caliber, and location. As a general rule, veins smaller than 2.5 mm in diameter, incompressible veins, and those that appear sclerotic and thick walled should not be exposed. In 51 saphenous and cephalic veins scanned prior to bypass, Seeger and associates[79] found B mode ultrasonography to be 98% accurate in determining vein adequacy. Chang and colleagues[19] found that 90% of lesser saphenous veins deemed suitable by duplex mapping were ultimately successfully used as bypass conduits. In their resting state veins are somewhat contracted, and duplex of veins may underestimate the true diameter of the vein. Davies and coworkers[80] found that the use of a blood pressure cuff on the proximal limb inflated to a pressure to obstruct venous flow to distend the vein increased the functional diameter of the saphenous vein by an average of 1 mm. Distention of 5 of 35 veins increased their diameter from less than to greater than 3 mm, making them suitable for bypass conduits. Hoballah and associates[81] found that proximal cuff occlusion with the leg placed in a dependent position significantly increased saphenous vein diameter compared with the use of dependency alone.

Reversed Saphenous Vein Graft

When harvesting the saphenous vein for a reversed vein graft, the importance of gentle handling and avoidance of vasospasm by liberal use of papaverine is critical. The perivenous space can be infiltrated with papaverine prior to incision[67] or the vein can be covered with papaverine-soaked gauze pads immediately on exposure. Incisions should be placed directly over the vein without the creation of skin flaps. Grasping the vein directly with a forceps for the purpose of countertraction during excision can be avoided by the use of a polymeric silicone loop placed around the vein or grasping the adjacent perivenous tissues (Fig. 47-8). Meticulous, sharp dissection in a plane just superficial to the adventitia decreases the chance of inadvertent injury. All vein branches should be meticulously tied with 3-0 or 4-0 silk ligatures a short distance away from the vein wall. The end of the vein branch remaining in the leg can be controlled with a small hemoclip. We avoid the use of clips on the vein, which may become inadvertently dislodged during tunneling leading to troublesome bleeding. Once removed, the vein should be gently distended with either balanced electrolyte solution or whole blood containing heparin and papaverine at room temperature to check for leaks from unligated branches. Forcible distention to overcome vasospasm should be avoided. Unligated branches can be clamped with a small Jacobsen clamp and tied or suture ligated with 6-0 or 7-0 polypropylene suture (Fig. 47-9). Prior to implantation the vein should be stored in the same solution. Solutions can be room temperature or cold according to the surgeon's preference. Storage time prior to implantation should be as brief as possible. When used as a conduit, the vein must be reversed to overcome the obstruction to flow from the valves. This necessitates the creation of an anastomosis between the smaller caliber distal end of the vein and the larger caliber proximal artery. This anastomosis may lead to creation of a stricture at the "heel" if the vein is small, especially if the arterial wall is thickened from atherosclerosis. As a general rule, we avoid the direct anastomosis of veins smaller than 3 mm to such arteries to avoid this problem. Strategies to overcome this problem include spatulating the end of the vein into a side branch to increase the vein's diameter at the anastomosis, or first closing the arteriotomy with a vein patch,[82] then making an incision in the vein patch to form the anastomosis between the vein graft and artery. Alternatively, the valves can be cut and the vein can be used in a nonreversed fashion,[83] which is our preferred method (Fig. 47-10).

In-Situ and Nonreversed Grafts

Since the landmark paper by Leather and associates[84] describing a newer and simpler technique for the construction of in-situ vein grafts, it has become a popular configuration for many vascular surgeons. Proponents of the in-situ technique tout the better size match and less manipulation in its preparation as its principal advantage. To overcome the size mismatch problem inherent to the

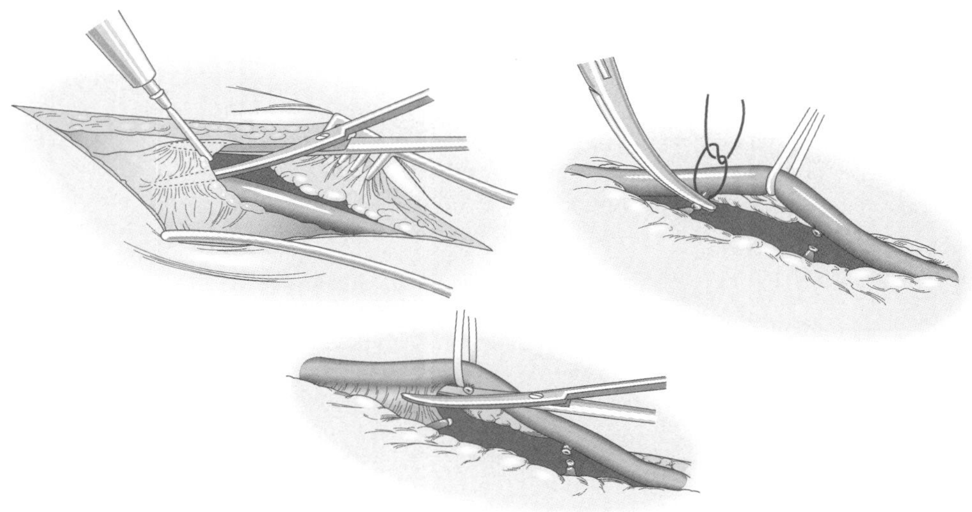

FIGURE 47-8 Veins should be handled gently during vein harvest to minimize vein wall injury. Incisions should be made directly over the vein to avoid the creation of flaps. Branches should be tied in continuity with 3-0 or 4-0 silk at least 1 mm away from the vein wall. Veins should be excised by careful sharp dissection. Countertraction is best accomplished by encircling the vein with a polymeric silicone (Silastic) vessel loop. The vein should not be grasped with the jaws of a forceps.

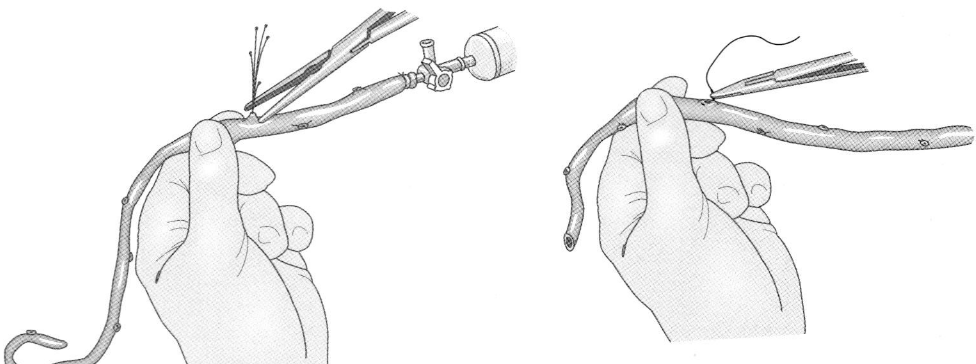

FIGURE 47-9 Once the vein has been removed, it should be gently distended to check for leaks. Forcible distention to overcome spasm should be avoided since excessive pressure can cause severe vein injury (see text). Small, unligated branches can be clamped with a fine hemostat such as a Jacobsen clamp. If a branch has been avulsed, the defect can be suture ligated with a 7-0 polypropylene suture.

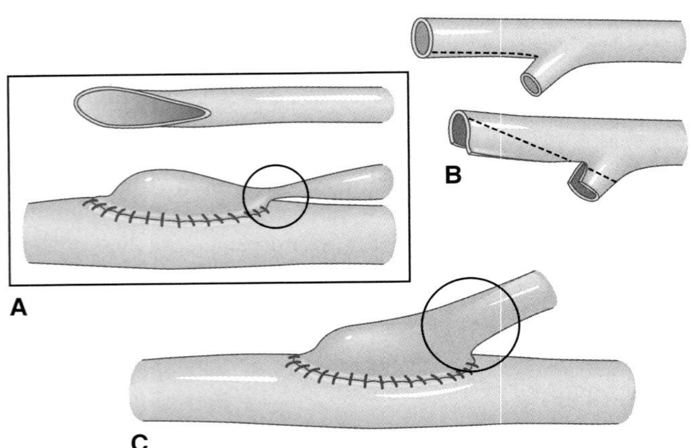

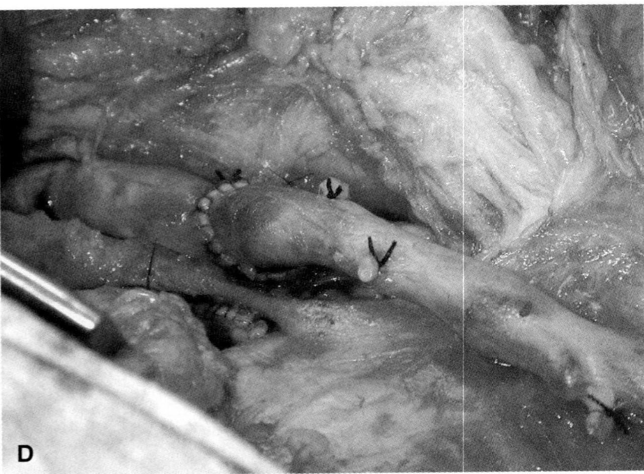

FIGURE 47-10 **A,** When using a reversed vein graft, the smaller caliber, distal end of the vein must be used for the proximal anastomosis to a large-caliber artery (*A, inset*). This can result in a stricture at the heel of the anastomosis, especially when the vein is less than 4 mm. **B** and **C**, When a branch is near the end, the vein can be spatulated through the branch to increase the effective diameter of the vein. **D**, Alternatively, the valves can be cut and the vein used nonreversed. Strictures are usually avoided since the large-caliber proximal end of the vein is used for the proximal anastomosis. (**A**, From Bergen JJ, Yao JST: Arterial Surgery: New Diagnostic and Operative Techniques. Orlando, Grune & Stratton, 1988.)

reversed vein bypass, surgeons searched for ways to render the valves incompetent while leaving the saphenous vein in situ. Early attempts at valve fracture by Rob and Kenyon proved too traumatic to the vein resulting in frequent early graft thrombosis or strictures. Hall[85] described an in-situ technique where the valve leaflets were excised via transverse venotomy. Results were acceptable, but it was too tedious and time consuming to be practical. In 1979 Leather and colleagues[84] reported their experience with a new technique of in-situ vein grafting using specialized instruments including a modified Mills valvulotome inserted retrograde from a side branch, which cut the valves precisely and expeditiously without significant trauma to the vein (Fig. 47-11). This technique has been widely accepted and made in-situ vein graft technically feasible for most vascular surgeons. Many vascular surgeons noted improved results when they adopted the in-situ technique and suggested that it possessed inherent advantages over reversed vein grafts including increased use of vein from the ability to use smaller-caliber veins due to better size match and better endothelial preservation. Studies have demonstrated that in-situ veins as small as 2.0 mm in diameter will remain patent.[86,87] Although the proponents of reversed vein grafts report similar patency and utilization rates to reported series of in-situ grafts,[88,89] others have demonstrated worse patency with veins smaller than 3.5 mm.[90] The evidence for some inherent biologic superiority of the in-situ graft based on better preservation of the endothelium has been controversial. The physiologic basis for this assumption was the more limited manipulation and preservation of vasa vasorum with the in-situ technique. In experiments using canine jugular veins, Buchbinder and associates [91] saw less endothelial sloughing and denuding with the in-situ technique, compared with reverse vein grafting. Bush and coworkers,[92] also using a canine model, noted higher levels of prostacyclin from in-situ grafts, compared to reversed veins, and postulated that this was due to a better functioning endothelium with the in-situ technique. Cambria and associates,[93] however, in comparing in-situ vein grafts with atraumatically dissected, nonreversed vein grafts observed no difference in endothelial fibrinolytic activity between the in-situ and gently handled reversed vein grafts at either

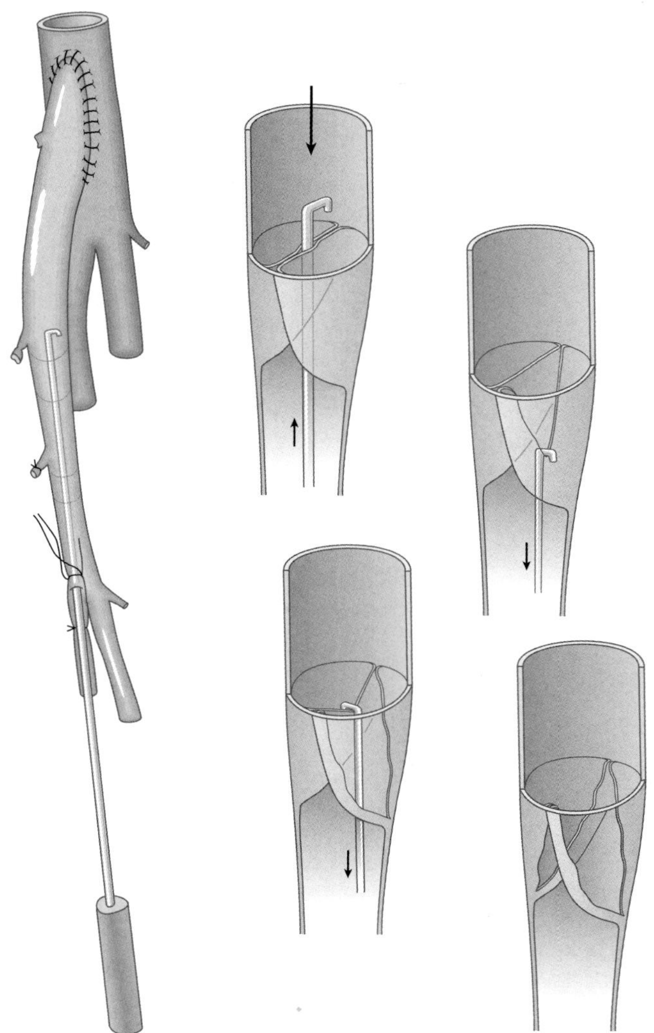

FIGURE 47-11 Schematic representation of valve lysis with a Mills valvulotome when constructing an in-situ saphenous vein graft. After the proximal anastomosis has been completed, arterial flow is re-established into the vein graft, which will stop at the first competent valve. The Mills valvulotome is inserted through a distal side branch and directed proximally through the valve and then carefully withdrawn to cut the leaflets. This procedure is usually done blindly, by "feel," and requires a significant learning curve before it can be consistently accomplished without vein injury. (From Zarins CK, Gewertz BL: Atlas of Vascular Surgery. New York, Churchill Livingstone, 1989.)

24 hours or 6 weeks after surgery. Batson and Sottiurai,[94] using a similar canine model, compared reversed, nonreversed, and in-situ grafts and could distinguish no discernible morphologic differences between the two techniques. The preponderance of available data suggests that endothelial preservation does not confer any physiologic advantage to the in-situ graft. In four prospective, randomized trials conducted in North America and Europe since 1991 comparing in-situ with reversed vein grafts in terms of graft patency and limb-salvage (Table 47-1), no discernible advantage could be seen in any study with the in-situ versus the reversed vein technique.[95-98] Nonetheless, we think the in-situ technique is particularly useful for long bypasses extending from the common femoral artery to tibial or pedal vessels. Using the vein in situ leads to a more technically satisfactory anastomosis at both ends owing to better size match and is more expeditious than removing and reversing a long saphenous vein simply for the reason of overcoming the valves. For shorter grafts however, such as those extending to the popliteal artery or those starting at the popliteal artery and terminating more distally, the in-situ technique possesses little advantage since once the proximal and distal ends are mobilized to perform the anastomosis with the artery, the actual vein segment left in situ is usually quite short. Moreover, the graft is left in the subcutaneous location and subject to the potential risk of damage from infection to the harvest wound. If there is a significant difference in size between the proximal and distal end of the vein, it can be harvested as described for reversed vein grafts but the valves cut, forming a *nonreversed* graft,[83,94] which can be placed subcutaneously or tunneled in an anatomic plane. Valve lysis can be accomplished with a modified Mills valvulotome inserted from the distal end after the proximal anastomosis has been completed using arterial blood pressure to close the valves or prior to bypass using balanced electrolyte infusion through a syringe inserted into the proximal end to close the valves as the valvulotome is withdrawn from the distal end. We prefer the use of irrigation through the angioscope to close the valves, which allows valve lysis under direct vision (see later).

Experiences with the in-situ bypass have demonstrated that it is technically more demanding and difficult to master than reverse vein bypass. Technical errors during preparation of in-situ grafts have lead to a generally higher rate of early graft defects. Valve lysis with the modified Mills valvulotome is generally done blindly, by "feel,"

Table 47-1 Prospective Trials Comparing Results of In-Situ and Reversed Vein Grafts

AUTHOR	YEAR	*N*	FOLLOW-UP, mo	PATENCY, % In Situ	PATENCY, % Reversed	*P*
VA Coop 141[98]	1988	526	24			
Fem pop				78	75	NS
Fem tib				76	67	NS
Wengerter et al[95]	1991	125	30	69	67	NS
Moody et al[97]	1992	215	60	63.5	62	NS
Watelet et al[96]	1997	100	120	64.8	70.2	NS

Fem pop, femoral to popliteal; Fem tib, femoral to tibial; NS, not significant.

and involves a significant learning curve. Injuries to the endothelium or vein wall and missed or incompletely cut valves are common technical errors, especially in smaller diameter veins. Arteriovenous (AV) fistulae can develop from vein branches inadvertently left unligated and may result in reduced graft blood flow. Identifying these problems mandates assessment of the technical result prior to leaving the operating room by angiography, duplex ultrasonography, or angioscopy.[99] Bandyk and associates [100] first used intraoperative velocity waveform analysis and duplex scanning to detect unsuspected patent AV fistulae, uncut valves, and narrowed vein segments that compromised graft blood flow to identify grafts at risk for early thrombosis. They subsequently demonstrated that intraoperative duplex scanning can improve early graft patency and, when performed at regular intervals in the postoperative period, could identify developing vein graft strictures and stenoses prior to graft thrombosis.[101] This was the first reported use of duplex vein graft surveillance, which has now become a routine for all vascular surgeons performing lower extremity arterial reconstruction with vein (see later). Shah and associates,[102] in a review of their experience with the in-situ saphenous vein in more than 2000 arterial reconstructions, reported 1-month patency of 96% and a cumulative secondary patency of 81% and 70% at 5 and 10 years, respectively, with limb salvage rates 90% or greater at all time intervals. They emphasized that their excellent technical results in the short and long term were predicated on meticulous surgical technique and regular graft surveillance in the postoperative period with duplex scanning.

We introduced the use of the angioscope with a specially designed pump irrigation system and modified long, flexible-shafted valvulotome to prepare in-situ grafts, which remains our preferred method of in-situ vein preparation (Fig. 47-12).[103] The vein is fully exposed and all side branches ligated. The proximal end is detached from the femoral vein and the distal end transected and mobilized for a distance of 5 to 10 cm. The first valve is excised with Potts scissors. The angioscope with a diameter of 1.9 mm is inserted to the proximal end of the vein. The angioscope is connected to a video camera with the image projected on a television screen analogous to the method used for laparoscopic procedures. A balanced electrolyte solution containing heparin is injected via the pump in an antegrade direction through a port in the angioscope or through a cannula inserted adjacent to it to simultaneously clear the field of blood and close the valve leaflets. A specially modified Mills valvulotome on a long flexible shaft is simultaneously inserted retrograde from the distal end of the vein to the point of the first excised valve. As the valvulotome is withdrawn, the angioscope is advanced. Irrigation fluid is infused to clear the field of blood. When a valve is encountered, irrigation through the angioscope is used to close the valve, which is then cut under direct vision, eliminating the need to work blindly (Fig. 47-13). In addition, open, unligated side branches are readily identified. The surgeon controls the rate and volume of irrigation fluid by a foot switch connected to the pump. In a prospective study comparing in-situ vein grafts prepared by the traditional "blind" technique and those prepared with the assistance of angioscopy, the authors noted a significant reduction in the number of vein wall injuries, missed uncut valves, and identified previously unsuspected areas of vein graft pathology.[103] Subsequent studies showed that the volume of solution infused rarely exceeded 1 L and did not lead to fluid overload or congestive heart failure.[104] To evaluate whether the use of completion angioscopy would improve the outcome of vein bypass grafting, the same authors conducted a prospective, randomized trial comparing completion angioscopy to angiography in 293 patients undergoing a variety of vein bypasses including in-situ grafts. Graft failure at 30 days was observed in 3.1% of grafts in the angioscopy group and 6.6% of grafts studied with angiography. Although not statistically significant, probably due to the small size of the study population, the difference demonstrated the value of vein graft preparation and monitoring with angioscopy.[105]

In addition to higher incidence of early technical problems leading to vein graft stenosis and early graft failure, wound infection is more common with in-situ grafts[106,107] and is especially worrisome due to the superficial location of the vein that may become exposed and infected. This complication can lead to vein graft disruption and hemorrhage, with potentially catastrophic outcomes. Strategies have been devised to decrease the wound complications associated with in-situ saphenous vein grafting by reducing the length of the incision required to expose and prepare the vein graft. One strategy employs the use of preoperative vein mapping; angioscopy-directed valve lysis with a long, flexible-shafted valvulotome; and multiple, small incisions to ligate tributaries and AV fistulae.[108] Another technique incorporates a specially designed steerable angioscope with a port to deploy intraluminal coils into side branches of the greater saphenous vein. Using this method, it is possible to make only a proximal and distal incision for exposure of the two ends of the vein graft and the inflow and outflow arteries. Although championed by a few who have demonstrated excellent short-term results,[109,110] this technique has not gained widespread acceptance among vascular surgeons owing to the concerns about the length of time required for preparation of vein grafts by this method, the amount of saline infused, and the costs of the specialized equipment and coils required. Moreover, the future of this technique is now in question since the manufacturer of the specialized angioscope has stopped production. Another technique for reducing the length of the incision required is the use of a commercially available, expandable, self-centering valvulotome (Fig. 47-14). In this technique the proximal and distal ends of the vein and proximal and distal outflow arteries are exposed. The first valve is removed with Potts scissors and the proximal anastomosis is performed. The self-centering, expandable valvulotome is then inserted from the distal end of the vein to a point just distal to the proximal anastomosis and then slowly withdrawn. The valvulotome has four cutting blades on metal springs that expand or contract according to the diameter of the vein. The valvulotome is designed to center itself in the lumen, ensuring that only valve leaflets are cut as they are encountered. Withdrawing the valvulotome slowly is critical to be sure that leaflets are fully closed by the antegrade flow of arterial blood as it proceeds down the vein from the lysis of more proximal valves. Two or more passages of the valvulotome may be required to ensure that all leaflets are adequately cut. Once all valves have been cut, Doppler insonation is used with

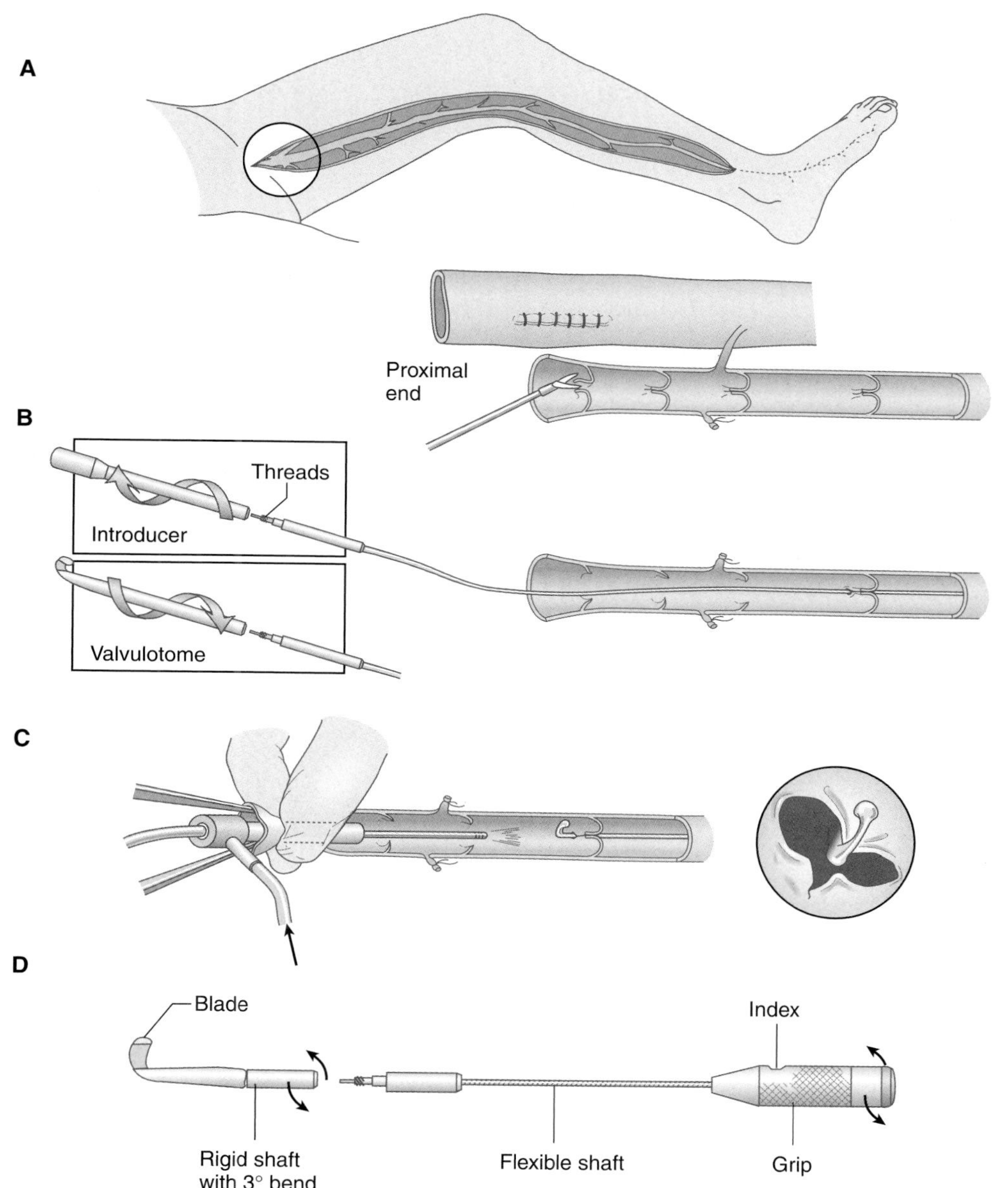

FIGURE 47-12 Schematic representation of angioscopically directed valvulotomy. **A,** The vein is fully exposed, the proximal and distal 10 cm of vein are mobilized, and all side branches are ligated to minimize blood flow into the vein graft. **B,** After being detached from the femoral vein, the first valve is excised with Potts scissors. A specially modified Mills valvulotome (**D**) on a long flexible shaft is inserted from the distal end of the vein to the proximal end. The valvulotome has a detachable blunt tip, which is used when advancing the valvulotome through the vein to avoid injury. The blunt tip is then removed and replaced with the valvulotome at the proximal end of the vein. **C,** A cannula (similar to the introducer used for a pulmonary artery catheter), connected to a roller pump irrigation system, is inserted into the proximal vein and the angioscope is inserted into the irrigation cannula. As the angioscope is advanced, a foot switch, controlled by the surgeon, turns on the pump, which injects saline irrigation into the vein to both clear the field of blood and close the valve leaflets, which can be cut under direct vision as seen on a television monitor. This process is repeated for the entire length of the vein. Newer generations of the angioscope contain an irrigation port, eliminating the need for the irrigation cannula. (**A-D,** From Miller A, Stonebridge PA, Tsoukas AI, et al: Angioscopically directed valvulotomy: A new valvulotome and technique. J Vasc Surg 13:813-820, 1991.)

the distal end of the vein graft compressed to find patent AV fistulae, which are then ligated directly under small incisions along the course of the vein graft. Gangadharan and associates[111] prepared 37 vein grafts in this fashion, with a 30-day graft failure rate of only 2.7%. An average of 3.1 incisions per limb was required to ligate hemodynamically significant AV fistulae. In follow-up ranging from 1 to 33 months, they noted that AV fistulae undetected at surgery closed spontaneously in 44% of cases, and only two symptomatic fistulae required surgical correction. There were only two anastomotic stenoses noted. Primary and secondary patency rates at 1 year were 77% and 92%, respectively. This technique has been gaining increased acceptance among vascular surgeons and has become more attractive with the technologic improvements of the latest generation of the valvulotome, which can be used safely in

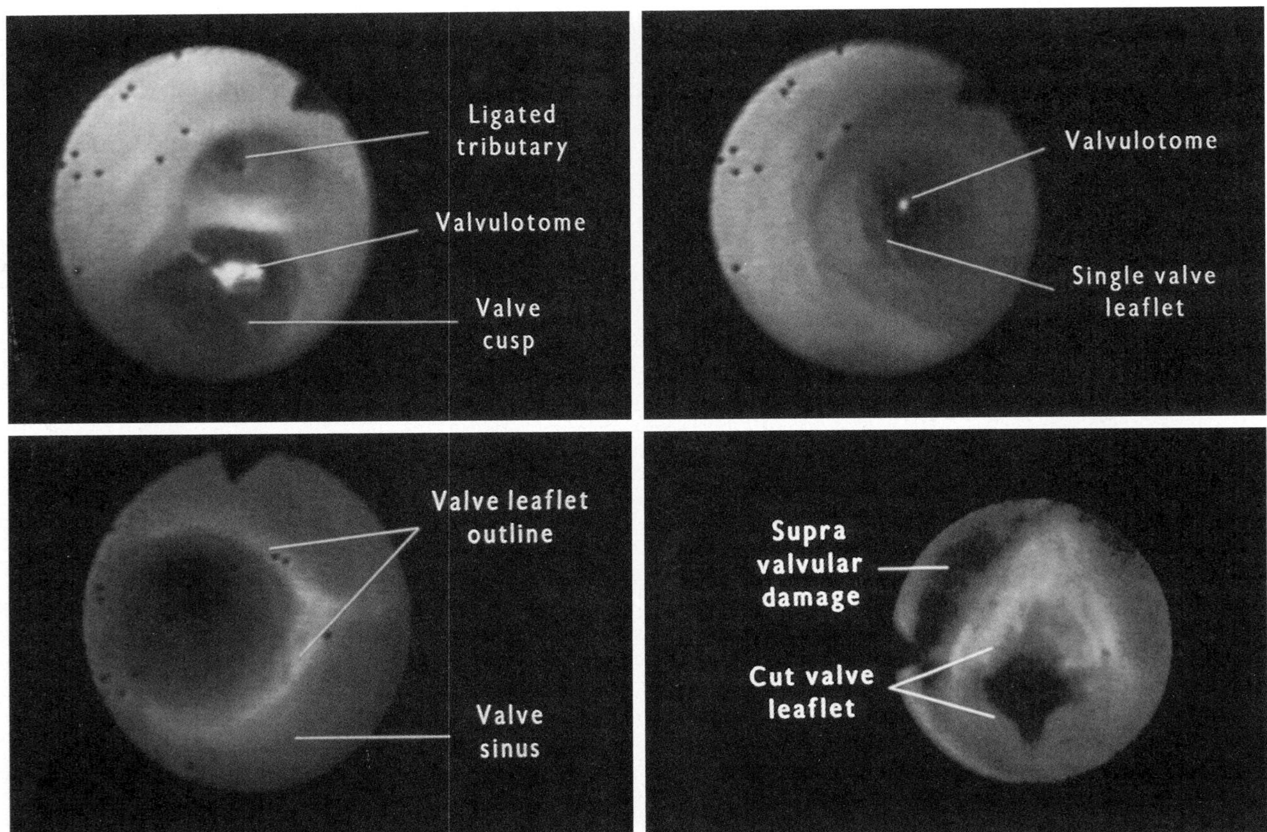

FIGURE 47-13 Digital photographs of the luminal surface of a saphenous vein graft as seen through an angioscope. **A,** The valvulotome is engaging a valve leaflet adjacent to a ligated side branch. **B,** Although usually bicuspid, single leaflet valves are occasionally seen on angioscopy. **C,** An empty valve sinus where no leaflets were seen. **D,** Damage to the adjacent vein wall from valve cutting that was too deep, extending beyond the leaflets. These injuries may result in intimal hyperplasia. When severe, they can cause early graft thrombosis. (**A-D,** From Miller A, Stonebridge PA, Tsoukas AI, et al: Angioscopically directed valvulotomy: A new valvulotome and technique. J Vasc Surg 13:813-820, 1991.)

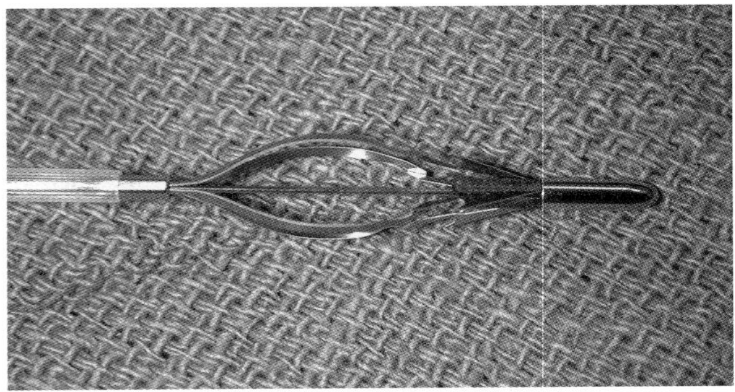

FIGURE 47-14 The distal end of the self-centering, expandable Lemaitre valvulotome. The valvulotome resides in the clear plastic sheath until it is opened in the proximal end of the vein just distal to the proximal anastomosis. The metal bands proximal to the cutters expand and contract according to the diameter of the vein to keep the four cutting blades centered in the lumen as the device is withdrawn. Arterial blood flow closes the valves. The device must be withdrawn slowly and the manufacturer recommends at least two passages of the valvulotome to ensure that all valves have been cut.

smaller caliber veins than earlier designs. We think that the self-expanding valvulotome does not adequately cut valves in veins smaller than 3 mm.

■ MECHANISMS OF VEIN GRAFT FAILURE

Vein grafts are biologic conduits. When placed into the arterial circulation they undergo a number of structural changes as they adapt to the injuries of implantation and the increased stress of supporting the pressure of arterial blood flow in the milieu of atherosclerosis. In general terms, vein grafts fail for one of three reasons: thrombosis, poor hemodynamic result, or primary graft degeneration.[101] Each of the principal causes of graft failure has unique mechanisms and a typical time course in which they occur.

Graft thrombosis is most commonly caused by a reduction in graft blood flow. As blood flows through a vein graft, a minimum velocity of flow must be maintained or thrombosis will occur. The lowest velocity at which blood flow continues is known as the *thrombotic threshold velocity*. Any mechanical problem that results in a reduction of graft flow below the thrombotic threshold can cause graft thrombosis. Within the first 30 days of surgery, poor graft blood flow leading to thrombosis usually occurs as a result of mechanical defects due to technical errors in the construction of the bypass, improper patient or procedure selection, or use of a poor-quality, small-caliber, or severely damaged vein conduit. Occasionally, grafts fail in the early postoperative period without an identifiable mechanical defect or cause. Even when there is a technical defect, it may not be identifiable once graft thrombosis has occurred. Donaldson and colleagues[112] found that many patients with unexplained early graft thrombosis had a previously undiagnosed hypercoagulability disorder.

Problems leading to graft failure between 30 days and 2 years are usually due to stenotic flow-restricting lesions from intimal hyperplasia.[72] Intimal hyperplasia may be a focal lesion, occurring at areas of vein injury such as the anastomosis; points of valve lysis or vein repair; or diffusely involve the graft, when the vein has been extensively damaged due to improper handling or preparation. Identification of flow-restricting lesions due to intimal hyperplasia is best determined by duplex ultrasonography (see later). Beyond 2 years, graft thrombosis is most likely due to stenotic lesions from progression of atherosclerosis in the inflow or outflow bed beyond the graft.

Atherosclerosis can also occur within the vein graft itself. In coronary bypass vein grafts, atherosclerosis develops frequently, causing occlusion in up to 40% of grafts 10 years after implantation, and is especially prevalent in patients with elevated cholesterol and serum lipid levels.[113] In a large multicenter, prospective Post Coronary Artery Bypass Graft Trial,[114] aggressive lowering of the low-density lipoprotein (LDL) cholesterol to less than 100 mg/dL resulted in a 31% reduction of atherosclerotic progression in vein grafts compared to patients with moderate reductions in LDL. The presence of atherosclerosis has also been demonstrated in lower extremity vein grafts and appears to also be related to both hyperlipidemia and hypertension. The likelihood of the development of atherosclerosis in vein grafts increases over time, usually developing after 4 or more years after implantation, but has been seen in grafts as early as 3 years postbypass. The incidence of atherosclerosis in lower extremity vein grafts is not well defined. Using arteriography, DeWeese and Rob[115] found atherosclerotic changes in only 3 of 18 grafts followed for 5 years or more. Reifsnyder and coworkers[116] studied 72 vein grafts functioning for 4.5 to 21.6 years with regular duplex ultrasonography and found three distinct types of abnormalities of atherosclerosis including wall plaque, discrete stenoses, and aneurysmal dilation in 57% of grafts. Forty-six percent of the stenoses were seen at sites that had been previously revised, whereas aneurysms occurred most frequently in grafts subjected to mechanical thrombectomy or thrombolysis for graft thrombosis at an average interval of 40 months' postbypass.

Hemodynamic failure is defined as a patent vein graft without resolution of ischemic symptoms.[117] This most commonly results from an error in surgical judgment when a vein graft is connected to an outflow target artery with inadequate runoff to achieve the desired result such as an isolated popliteal or tibial arterial segment. Hemodynamic failure may also occur in established, well-functioning grafts with the development of atherosclerosis in the inflow or outflow arteries of the graft. Although most prosthetic grafts usually thrombose in this situation, some vein grafts remain patent, even with severe compromise of their inflow or outflow arterial beds due to the thromboresistant effect of their endothelium.

Graft degeneration can occur at any time due to infection. Vein graft infections are uncommon and usually result from adjacent wound sepsis, which is extensive enough to involve the graft itself. Mature vein grafts may fail as a result of diffuse dilation due to aneurismal degeneration.[118] With progressive dilation, blood flow velocity decreases, ultimately causing thrombosis. Aneurysmal degeneration of vein grafts has been rare and is uniformly associated with advanced changes of atherosclerosis. Reifsnyder and associates[116] postulated that transmural ischemic injury was the cause since most aneurysms occurred in grafts previously subjected to thrombectomy. It is noteworthy that 25% of reported vein graft aneurysms have occurred in patients with lower extremity arterial or aortic aneurysms, suggesting that the same pathobiologic mechanism responsible for arterial aneurysms may affect vein grafts implanted in these patients.

Other causes of graft failure are thromboembolism and trauma.

■ PREVENTING GRAFT FAILURE—GRAFT SURVEILLANCE

Approximately 15% to 20% of vein grafts fail within the first 5 years of implantation. Clinical studies by Donaldson,[54] Mills,[119] and their coworkers demonstrated that in more than 60% of failed grafts, the culprit lesion was a focal intrinsic lesion within the graft itself. Identification and correction of vein defects prior to the occurrence of graft thrombosis are critical since most vein grafts do not maintain long-term patency after mechanical thrombectomy or graft thrombolysis.[120] Secondary arterial reconstruction performed for recurring ischemia from failure of the primary procedure is generally more technically difficult, has lower likelihood of patency or limb salvage, and is accomplished with higher rates of morbidity and mortality.[121,122] Identifying grafts at risk prior to thrombosis provides the rationale for graft surveillance protocols now in widespread use by most vascular surgeons.

In the past, the diagnosis of a failing vein graft was made clinically on the basis of history, physical examination, and serial measurement of ankle-brachial indices (ABIs). Any patient who had return of ischemic symptoms, loss or reduction of pulses on physical examination, or a reduction in the ABI of 0.2 even in the absence of symptoms underwent arteriography to detect a potentially correctable lesion. Reliance on clinical diagnosis alone, however, has proved to be unreliable. Experience has shown that grafts can fail in the absence of any warning symptoms or signs, and the positive predictive value of the ABI alone in detecting a failing graft is only 12% to 34%.[101]

Modern methods of vein graft surveillance incorporate both hemodynamic measurements (ABI) and noninvasive

Table 47-2 Stratification of Risk for Graft Thrombosis by Surveillance Data

RISK LEVEL	HIGH-VELOCITY CRITERIA		LOW-VELOCITY CRITERIA		ABI REDUCTION
Highest	PSV > 300 cm/sec or Vr > 3.5 *Or* EDV > 100 cm/sec	*and*	GFV < 45 cm/sec	*or*	>0.15
High	PSV > 300 cm/sec or Vr > 3.5	*and*	GFV > 45 cm/sec	*and*	<0.15
Intermediate	PSV 180-300 cm/sec or Vr > 2.0	*and*	GFV > 45 cm/sec	*and*	<0.15
Low	PSV < 180 cm/sec	*and*	GFV > 45 cm/sec	*and*	>0.15

ABI, ankle-brachial index; PSV, peak systolic velocity; Vr, ratio of the PSV within the lesion to the PSV in a proximal normal segment of the graft; GFV, graft flow velocity; EDV, end-diastolic velocity.

Data from Mills JL Sr: Infrainguinal vein graft surveillance: How and when. Semin Vasc Surg 14:169-176, 2001.

vascular imaging with duplex ultrasonography.[101] The timing and techniques involved take into account the important features in the development and natural history of vein graft failure described by Mills as follows[123]:

1. Eight percent of lesions develop within the first 12 months of implantation.
2. Lesions that develop early, within the first 3 months, progress rapidly and are more threatening than later developing lesions.
3. There is a 2% to 4% annual incidence of late-appearing graft stenosis in addition to a 5% to 10% lifetime risk of progression of atherosclerosis in the inflow or outflow bed of the graft that may require re-intervention.

The first evaluation of the graft should be performed prior to hospital discharge or within the first month of graft implantation. Subsequent evaluations are carried out 3 and 6 months after implantation. If the first three evaluations are normal, the surveillance studies are extended to every 6 months until 2 years after surgery. After 2 years, annual evaluations should be carried out for the life of the patient.

When a flow disturbance is identified by duplex ultrasonography, it is graded for severity by measurement of graft flow velocity (GFV), peak systolic velocity within the stenotic lesion (PSV), and a ratio of the PSV within the lesion to the PSV in a proximal normal segment of the graft (Vr). These criteria coupled with the ABI can be used to categorize lesions as low, intermediate, or high risk for graft thrombosis (Table 47-2).[123] Grafts at high risk should be revised. Grafts with low or intermediate risk lesions should be followed for progression.

When a graft at high risk for thrombosis has been identified, arteriography should be performed to identify the culprit lesion. Most often, a focal area of stenosis due to intimal hyperplasia is identified. Focal lesions (<3 cm within the body of the graft) can usually be corrected with vein patch angioplasty (Fig. 47-15). More lengthy lesions require replacement with an interposition graft. Stenotic lesions at the inflow or outflow anastomosis or in the adjacent artery are best treated with a "jump" graft to a normal more proximal or distal artery.

The fate of the revised vein graft has been good. In a series of 1498 lower extremity vein grafts implanted over 10 years from 1990 to 2000, Landry and colleagues[124] identified 330 graft revisions performed in 259 extremities. Graft surveillance was accomplished with duplex ultrasonography. Fifty-five percent of revisions were done within 1 year of surgery, 33% between the 1st and 5th year, and 12% in grafts older than 5 years. Within 1 year, 78% of stenotic lesions were located within the graft itself, with the rest equally divided between the inflow or outflow artery. After 1 year, the number of stenoses found within the graft had decreased to 60%, whereas the number of stenoses in the inflow or outflow arteries had increased to nearly 40%. Only nine patients had concurrent ischemic symptoms at the time a critical lesion was identified. The assisted primary patency and limb salvage rate for revised grafts was 87.3% and 88.6%, respectively, at 5 years and 80.3% and 75.3%, respectively, at 10 years, not appreciably different from contemporary series of lower extremity vein bypass grafts, including both revised grafts and grafts not requiring revision.

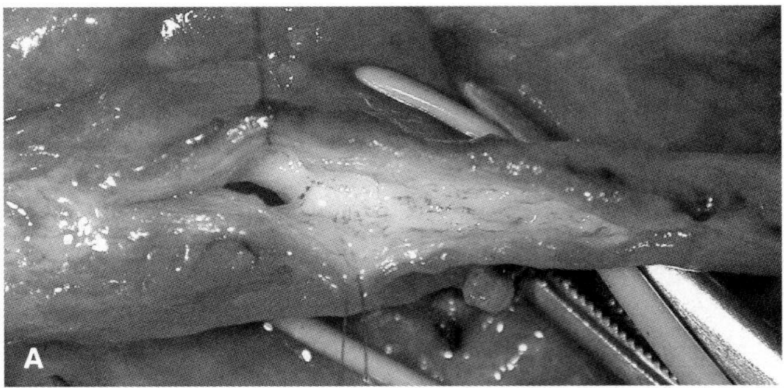

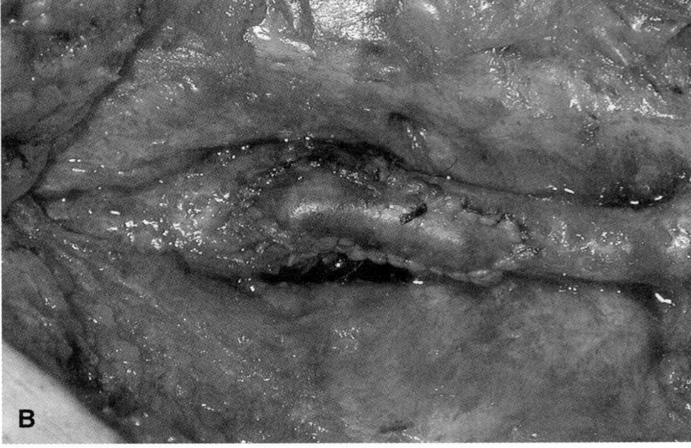

FIGURE 47-15 **A,** Typical appearance of intimal hyperplasia in a vein graft, 8 months after implantation. The wall is thickened and fibrotic. The luminal surface is glistening white and severely narrowed. **B,** Repair of the stenosis with a vein patch.

REFERENCES

1. Kunlin J: Le traitement de l'ischemie arteritique par la greffe veinuse longue. Rev Chir 70:206-235, 1951.
2. Dos Santos J: Sur la desobstruction des thromboses arterielles anciennes. Mem Acad Chir 73:409-411, 1947.
3. DeWeese JA, Dale WA: Failure of homografts as arterial replacements. Surgery 46:565, 1959.
4. Voorhees AB, Blakemore AH: The use of tubes constructed from vinyon "N" cloth in bridging arterial defects: A preliminary report. Am Surg 135:332, 1952.
5. Edwards WS: Late occlusion of femoral and popliteal fabric arterial grafts. Surg Gynecol Obstet 110:714-718, 1960.
6. Linton RR, Darling RC: Autogenous saphenous vein bypass grafts in femoropopliteal obliterative arterial disease. Surgery 51:62-73, 1962.
7. Thompson JE, Garrett WV: The role of polytetrafluoroethylene grafts in vascular surgery. Surgery 85:601-602, 1979.
8. Haimov H, Giron F, Jacobson JH II: The expanded polytetrafluoroethylene graft: Three years' experience with 362 grafts. Arch Surg 114:673-677, 1979.
9. Veith FJ, Gupta SK, Ascer E, et al: Six-year prospective multicenter randomized comparison of autologous saphenous vein and expanded polytetrafluoroethylene grafts in infrainguinal arterial reconstructions. J Vasc Surg 3:104-114, 1986.
10. Gray H: Anatomy of the Human Body, 29th ed. Philadelphia, Lea & Febiger, 1973.
11. Fuchs JC, Mitchener JS III, Hagen PO: Postoperative changes in autologous vein grafts. Ann Surg 188:1-15, 1978.
12. Goldman MP: Anatomy and Histology of the Venous System of the Leg. St. Louis, Mosby-Year Book, 1991.
13. Kachlik D, Lametschwandtner A, Rejmontova J, et al: Vasa vasorum of the human great saphenous vein. Surg Radiol Anat 24:377-381, 2003.
14. Corson JD, Leather RP, Balko A, et al: Relationship between vasa vasorum and blood flow to vein bypass endothelial morphology. Arch Surg 120:386-388, 1985.
15. Caggiati A, Bergan JJ: The saphenous vein: Derivation of its name and its relevant anatomy. J Vasc Surg 35:172-175, 2002.
16. Pomposelli FB Jr, Jepsen SJ, Gibbons GW, et al: Efficacy of the dorsal pedal bypass for limb salvage in diabetic patients: Short-term observations. J Vasc Surg 11:745-751, 1990.
17. Shah DM, Chang BB, Leopold PW, et al: The anatomy of the greater saphenous venous system. J Vasc Surg 3:273-283, 1986.
18. Kupinski AM, Evans SM, Khan AM, et al: Ultrasonic characterization of the saphenous vein. Cardiovasc Surg 1:513-517, 1993.
19. Chang BB, Paty PS, Shah DM, Leather RP: The lesser saphenous vein: An underappreciated source of autogenous vein. J Vasc Surg 15:152-156, 1992.
20. Rutherford RB, Sawyer JD, Jones DN: The fate of residual saphenous vein after partial removal or ligation. J Vasc Surg 12:422-426, 1990.
21. Shandal AA, Leather RP, Corson JD, et al: Use of the short saphenous vein in situ for popliteal-to-distal artery bypass. Am J Surg 154:240-244, 1987.
22. Kakkar VV: The cephalic vein as a peripheral vascular graft. Surg Gynecol Obstet 128:551, 1969.
23. Andros G, Harris RW, Salles-Cunha SX, et al: Arm veins for arterial revascularization of the leg: Arteriographic and clinical observations. J Vasc Surg 4:416-427, 1986.
24. Campbell DR, Hoar CS Jr, Gibbons GW: The use of arm veins in femoral-popliteal bypass grafts. Ann Surg 190:740, 1979.
25. Balshi JD, Cantelmo NL, Menzoian JO, LoGerfo FW: The use of arm veins for infrainguinal bypass in end-stage peripheral vascular disease. Arch Surg 124:1078-1081, 1989.
26. Stonebridge PA, Miller A, Tsoukas A, et al: Angioscopy of arm vein infrainguinal bypass grafts. Ann Vasc Surg 5:170-175, 1991.
27. Marcaccio EJ, Miller A, Tannenbaum GA, et al: Angioscopically directed interventions improve arm vein bypass grafts. J Vasc Surg 17:994-1002, 1993.
28. Holzenbein TJ, Pomposelli FB Jr, Miller A, et al: Results of a policy with arm veins used as the first alternative to an unavailable ipsilateral greater saphenous vein for infrainguinal bypass. J Vasc Surg 23:130-140, 1996.
29. LoGerfo FW, Paniszyn CW, Menzoian J: A new arm vein graft for distal bypass. J Vasc Surg 5:889-891, 1987.
30. Faries PL, Arora S, Pomposelli FB Jr, et al: The use of arm vein in lower-extremity revascularization: Results of 520 procedures performed in eight years. J Vasc Surg 31:50-59, 2000.
31. Calligaro KD, Syrek JR, Dougherty MJ, et al: Use of arm and lesser saphenous vein compared with prosthetic grafts for infrapopliteal arterial bypass: Are they worth the effort? J Vasc Surg 26:919-924, 1997.
32. Clagett GP, Valentine RJ, Hagino RT: Autogenous aortoiliac/femoral reconstruction from superficial femoral-popliteal veins: Feasibility and durability. J Vasc Surg 25:255-261, 1997.
33. Schulman ML, Badhey MR, Yatco R, Pillari G: An 11-year experience with deep leg veins as femoropopliteal bypass grafts. Arch Surg 121:1010-1015, 1986.
34. Schulman ML, Badhey MR, Yatco R: Superficial femoral-popliteal veins and reversed saphenous veins as primary femoropopliteal bypass grafts: A randomized comparative study. J Vasc Surg 6:1-10, 1987.
35. Hagino RT, Bengtson TD, Fosdick DA, et al: Venous reconstructions using the superficial femoral-popliteal vein. J Vasc Surg 26:829-837, 1997.
36. Coburn M, Ashworth C, Francis W, et al: Venous stasis complications of the use of the superficial femoral and popliteal veins for lower extremity bypass. J Vasc Surg 17:1005-1008, 1993.
37. Bush HL Jr, McCabe ME, Nabseth DC: Functional injury of vein graft endothelium: Role of hypothermia and distention. Arch Surg 119:770-774, 1984.
38. Eldor A, Hoover EL, Pett SB Jr, et al: Prostacyclin production by arterialized autogenous venous grafts in dogs. Prostaglandins 22:485-498, 1981.
39. Eldor A, Falcone DJ, Hajjar DP, et al: Recovery of prostacyclin production by de-endothelialized rabbit aorta: Critical role of neointimal smooth muscle cells. J Clin Invest 67:735-741, 1981.
40. Esmon CT, Owen WG: Identification of an endothelial cell cofactor for thrombin-catalyzed activation of protein C. Proc Natl Acad Sci U S A 78:2249-2252, 1981.
41. Levin EG, Loskutoff DJ: Cultured bovine endothelial cells produce both urokinase and tissue-type plasminogen activators. J Cell Biol 94:631-636, 1982.
42. Marcum JA, McKenney JB, Rosenberg RD: Acceleration of thrombin-antithrombin complex formation in rat hindquarters via heparin-like molecules bound to the endothelium. J Clin Invest 74:341-350, 1984.
43. Jaffe EA, Hoyer LW, Nachman RL: Synthesis of von Willebrand factor by cultured human endothelial cells. Proc Natl Acad Sci U S A 71:1906-1909, 1974.
44. Levin EG: Latent tissue plasminogen activator produced by human endothelial cells in culture: Evidence for an enzyme-inhibitor complex. Proc Natl Acad Sci U S A 80:6804-6808, 1983.
45. Butcher EC: Leukocyte-endothelial cell recognition: Three (or more) steps to specificity and diversity. Cell 67:1033-1036, 1991.
46. Garg UC, Hassid A: Nitric oxide-generating vasodilators and 8-bromo-cyclic guanosine monophosphate inhibit mitogenesis and proliferation of cultured rat vascular smooth muscle cells. J Clin Invest 83:1774-1777, 1989.
47. Loesberg C, van Wijk R, Zandbergen J, et al: Cell cycle-dependent inhibition of human vascular smooth muscle cell proliferation by prostaglandin E_1. Exp Cell Res 160:117-125, 1985.
48. Naftilan AJ, Pratt RE, Dzau VJ: Induction of platelet-derived growth factor A-chain and *c-myc* gene expressions by angiotensin II in cultured rat vascular smooth muscle cells. J Clin Invest 83:1419-1424, 1989.
49. Fox PL, DiCorleto PE: Regulation of production of a platelet-derived growth factor-like protein by cultured bovine aortic endothelial cells. J Cell Physiol 121:298-308, 1984.

50. Hansson HA, Jennische E, Skottner A: Regenerating endothelial cells express insulin-like growth factor-I immunoreactivity after arterial injury. Cell Tissue Res 250:499-505, 1987.
51. Vlodavsky I, Folkman J, Sullivan R, et al: Endothelial cell-derived basic fibroblast growth factor: Synthesis and deposition into subendothelial extracellular matrix. Proc Natl Acad Sci U S A 84:2292-2296, 1987.
52. Antonelli-Orlidge A, Saunders KB, Smith SR, D'Amore PA: An activated form of transforming growth factor beta is produced by cocultures of endothelial cells and pericytes. Proc Natl Acad Sci U S A 86:4544-4548, 1989.
53. Owens GK, Geisterfer AA, Yang YW, Komoriya A: Transforming growth factor beta-induced growth inhibition and cellular hypertrophy in cultured vascular smooth muscle cells. J Cell Biol 107:771-780, 1988.
54. Donaldson MC, Mannick JA, Whittemore AD: Causes of primary graft failure after in situ saphenous vein bypass grafting. J Vasc Surg 15:113-118, 1992.
55. Gundry SR, Jones M, Ishihara T, Ferrans VJ: Optimal preparation techniques for human saphenous vein grafts. Surgery 88:785-794, 1980.
56. Dries D, Mohammad SF, Woodward SC, Nelson RM: The influence of harvesting technique on endothelial preservation in saphenous veins. J Surg Res 52:219-225, 1992.
57. Souza DS, Christofferson RH, Bomfim V, Filbey D: "No-touch" technique using saphenous vein harvested with its surrounding tissue for coronary artery bypass grafting maintains an intact endothelium. Scand Cardiovasc J 33:323-329, 1999.
58. Souza DS, Dashwood MR, Tsui JC, et al: Improved patency in vein grafts harvested with surrounding tissue: Results of a randomized study using three harvesting techniques. Ann Thorac Surg 73:1189-1195, 2002.
59. Alrawi SJ, Balaya F, Raju R, et al: A comparative study of endothelial cell injury during open and endoscopic saphenectomy: An electron microscopic evaluation. Heart Surg Forum 4:120-127, 2001.
60. Adcock OT Jr, Adcock GL, Wheeler JR, et al: Optimal techniques for harvesting and preparation of reversed autogenous vein grafts for use as arterial substitutes: A review. Surgery 96:886-894, 1984.
61. Ramos JR, Berger K, Mansfield PB, Sauvage LR: Histologic fate and endothelial changes of distended and nondistended vein grafts. Ann Surg 183:205-228, 1976.
62. Bonchek LI: Prevention of endothelial damage during preparation of saphenous veins for bypass grafting. J Thorac Cardiovasc Surg 79:911-915, 1980.
63. LoGerfo FW, Quist WC, Crawshaw HM, Haudenschild C: An improved technique for preservation of endothelial morphology in vein grafts. Surgery 90:1015-1024, 1981.
64. Kurusz M, Christman EW, Derrick JR, et al: Use of cold cardioplegic solution for vein graft distention and preservation: A light and scanning electron microscopic study. Ann Thorac Surg 32:68-74, 1981.
65. Adcock GD, Adcock OT Jr, Wheeler JR, et al: Arterialization of reversed autogenous vein grafts: Quantitative light and electron microscopy of canine jugular vein grafts harvested and implanted by standard or improved techniques. J Vasc Surg 6:283-295, 1987.
66. Malone JM, Kischer CW, Moore WS: Changes in venous endothelial fibrinolytic activity and histology with in vitro venous distention and arterial implantation. Am J Surg 142:178-182, 1981.
67. LoGerfo FW, Haudenschild CC, Quist WC: A clinical technique for prevention of spasm and preservation of endothelium in saphenous vein grafts. Arch Surg 119:1212-1214, 1984.
68. Baumann FG, Catinella FP, Cunningham JN Jr, Spencer FC: Vein contraction and smooth muscle cell extensions as causes of endothelial damage during graft preparation. Ann Surg 194:199-211, 1981.
69. Sottiurai VS, Sue SL, Batson RC, et al: Effects of papaverine on smooth muscle cell morphology and vein graft preparation. J Vasc Surg 2:834-842, 1985.
70. Lawrie GM, Weilbacher DE, Henry PD: Endothelium-dependent relaxation in human saphenous vein grafts: Effects of preparation and clinicopathologic correlations. J Thorac Cardiovasc Surg 100:612-620, 1990.
71. Cook JM, Cook CD, Marlar R, et al: Thrombomodulin activity on human saphenous vein grafts prepared for coronary artery bypass. J Vasc Surg 14:147-151, 1991.
72. Imparato AM, Bracco A, Kim GE, Zeff R: Intimal and neointimal fibrous proliferation causing failure of arterial reconstructions. Surgery 72:1007-1017, 1972.
73. Braun-Dullaeus RC, Mann MJ, Dzau VJ: Cell cycle progression: New therapeutic target for vascular proliferative disease. Circulation 98:82-89, 1998.
74. Morishita R, Gibbons GH, Horiuchi M, et al: A gene therapy strategy using a transcription factor decoy of the E_2F binding site inhibits smooth muscle proliferation in vivo. Proc Natl Acad Sci U S A 92:5855-5859, 1995.
75. Conte MS, Mann MJ, Simosa HF, et al: Genetic interventions for vein bypass graft disease: A review. J Vasc Surg 36:1040-1052, 2002.
76. Mann MJ, Whittemore AD, Donaldson MC, et al: Ex-vivo gene therapy of human vascular bypass grafts with E2F decoy: The PREVENT single-centre, randomised, controlled trial. Lancet 354:1493-1498, 1999.
77. SoRelle R: Late-breaking clinical trials at the American Heart Association's scientific sessions 2001. Circulation 104:E9046-E9048, 2001.
78. Veith FJ, Moss CM, Sprayregen S, Montefusco C: Preoperative saphenous venography in arterial reconstructive surgery of the lower extremity. Surgery 85:253-256, 1979.
79. Seeger JM, Schmidt JH, Flynn TC: Preoperative saphenous and cephalic vein mapping as an adjunct to reconstructive arterial surgery. Ann Surg 205:733-739, 1987.
80. Davies AH, Magee TR, Jones DR, et al: The value of duplex scanning with venous occlusion in the preoperative prediction of femoro-distal vein bypass graft diameter. Eur J Vasc Surg 5:633-636, 1991.
81. Hoballah JJ, Corry DC, Rossley N, et al: Duplex saphenous vein mapping: Venous occlusion and dependent position facilitate imaging. Vasc Endovasc Surg 36:377-380, 2002.
82. Masser PA, Taylor LM Jr, Moneta GL, Porter JM: Technique of reversed vein bypass for lower extremity ischemia. Ann Vasc Surg 10:190-200, 1996.
83. Belkin M, Knox J, Donaldson MC, et al: Infrainguinal arterial reconstruction with nonreversed greater saphenous vein. J Vasc Surg 24:957-962, 1996.
84. Leather RP, Powers SR, Karmody AM: A reappraisal of the in situ saphenous vein arterial bypass: Its use in limb salvage. Surgery 86:453-461, 1979.
85. Hall KV: The great saphenous vein used in situ as an arterial shunt after extirpation of the vein valves: A preliminary report. Surgery 51:492-495, 1962.
86. Bergamini TM, Towne JB, Bandyk DF, et al: Experience with in situ saphenous vein bypasses during 1981 to 1989: Determinant factors of long-term patency. J Vasc Surg 13:137-147, 1991.
87. Leather RP, Shah DM, Chang BB, Kaufman JL: Resurrection of the in situ saphenous vein bypass: 1000 cases later. Ann Surg 208:435-442, 1988.
88. Mills JL, Taylor SM: Results of infrainguinal revascularization with reversed vein conduits: A modern control series. Ann Vasc Surg 5:156-162, 1991.
89. Taylor LM Jr, Edwards JM, Porter JM: Present status of reversed vein bypass grafting: Five-year results of a modern series. J Vasc Surg 11:193-205, 1990.
90. Wengerter KR, Veith FJ, Gupta SK, et al: Influence of vein size (diameter) on infrapopliteal reversed vein graft patency. J Vasc Surg 11:525-531, 1990.
91. Buchbinder D, Singh JK, Karmody AM, et al: Resident research award: Comparison of patency rate and structural changes of in situ and reversed vein arterial bypass. J Surg Res 30:213-222, 1981.

92. Bush HL Jr, Jakubowski JA, Curl GR, et al: The natural history of endothelial structure and function in arterialized vein grafts. J Vasc Surg 3:204-215, 1986.
93. Cambria RP, Megerman J, Abbott WM: Endothelial preservation in reversed and in situ autogenous vein grafts: A quantitative experimental study. Ann Surg 202:50-55, 1985.
94. Batson RC, Sottiurai VS: Nonreversed and in situ vein grafts: Clinical and experimental observations. Ann Surg 201:771-779, 1985.
95. Wengerter KR, Veith FJ, Gupta SK, et al: Prospective randomized multicenter comparison of in situ and reversed vein infrapopliteal bypasses. J Vasc Surg 13:189-197, 1991.
96. Watelet J, Soury P, Menard JF, et al: Femoropopliteal bypass: In situ or reversed vein grafts? Ten-year results of a randomized prospective study. Ann Vasc Surg 11:510-519, 1997.
97. Moody AP, Edwards PR, Harris PL: In situ versus reversed femoropopliteal vein grafts: Long-term follow-up of a prospective, randomized trial. Br J Surg 79:750-752, 1992.
98. Comparative evaluation of prosthetic, reversed, and in situ vein bypass grafts in distal popliteal and tibial-peroneal revascularization. Veterans Administration Cooperative Study Group 141. Arch Surg 123:434-438, 1988.
99. Gilbertson JJ, Walsh DB, Zwolak RM, et al: A blinded comparison of angiography, angioscopy, and duplex scanning in the intraoperative evaluation of in situ saphenous vein bypass grafts. J Vasc Surg 15:121-127, 1992.
100. Bandyk DF, Cato RF, Towne JB: A low-flow velocity predicts failure of femoropopliteal and femorotibial bypass grafts. Surgery 98:799-809, 1985.
101. Bandyk DF: Postoperative surveillance of infrainguinal bypass. Surg Clin North Am 70:71-85, 1990.
102. Shah DM, Darling RC III, Chang BB, et al: Long-term results of in situ saphenous vein bypass: Analysis of 2058 cases. Ann Surg 222:438-446, 1995.
103. Miller A, Stonebridge PA, Tsoukas AI, et al: Angioscopically directed valvulotomy: A new valvulotome and technique. J Vasc Surg 13:813-820, 1991.
104. Kwolek CJ, Miller A, Stonebridge PA, et al: Safety of saline irrigation for angioscopy: Results of a prospective randomized trial. Ann Vasc Surg 6:62-68, 1992.
105. Miller A, Marcaccio EJ, Tannenbaum GA, et al: Comparison of angioscopy and angiography for monitoring infrainguinal bypass vein grafts: Results of a prospective randomized trial. J Vasc Surg 17:382-396, 1993.
106. Wengrovitz M, Atnip RG, Gifford RR, et al: Wound complications of autogenous subcutaneous infrainguinal arterial bypass surgery: Predisposing factors and management. J Vasc Surg 11:156-161, 1990.
107. Blankensteijn JD, Gertler JP, Petersen MJ, et al: Avoiding infrainguinal bypass wound complications in patients with chronic renal insufficiency: The role of the anatomic plane. Eur J Vasc Endovasc Surg 11:98-104, 1996.
108. Maini BS, Andrews L, Salimi T, et al: A modified, angioscopically assisted technique for in situ saphenous vein bypass: Impact on patency, complications, and length of stay. J Vasc Surg 17:1041-1047, 1993.
109. Nelson PR, McEnaney PM, Callahan LA, Arous EJ: Impact of endovascular-assisted in situ saphenous vein bypass technique on hospital costs. Ann Vasc Surg 15:653-660, 2001.
110. Cikrit DF, Dalsing MC, Lalka SG, et al: Early results of endovascular-assisted in situ saphenous vein bypass grafting. J Vasc Surg 19:778-785, 1994.
111. Gangadharan SP, Reed AB, Chew DK, et al: Initial experience with minimally invasive in situ bypass procedure with blind valvulotomy. J Vasc Surg 35:1100-1106, 2002.
112. Donaldson MC, Belkin M, Whittemore AD, et al: Impact of activated protein C resistance on general vascular surgical patients. J Vasc Surg 25:1054-1060, 1997.
113. Campeau L, Enjalbert M, Lesperance J, et al: Atherosclerosis and late closure of aortocoronary saphenous vein grafts: Sequential angiographic studies at 2 weeks, 1 year, 5 to 7 years, and 10 to 12 years after surgery. Circulation 68:II1-II7, 1983.
114. The effect of aggressive lowering of low-density lipoprotein cholesterol levels and low-dose anticoagulation on obstructive changes in saphenous-vein coronary-artery bypass grafts. The Post Coronary Artery Bypass Graft Trial Investigators. N Engl J Med 336:153-162, 1997.
115. DeWeese JA, Rob CG: Autogenous venous grafts ten years later. Surgery 82:755-784, 1977.
116. Reifsnyder T, Towne JB, Seabrook GR, et al: Biologic characteristics of long-term autogenous vein grafts: A dynamic evolution. J Vasc Surg 17:207-216, 1993.
117. Veith FJ, Gupta SK, Daly VD: Femoropopliteal bypass to the isolated popliteal segment: Is polytetrafluoroethylene graft acceptable? Surgery 89:296-303, 1981.
118. Alexander JJ, Liu YC: Atherosclerotic aneurysm formation in an in situ saphenous vein graft. J Vasc Surg 20:660-664, 1994.
119. Mills JL, Fujitani RM, Taylor SM: The characteristics and anatomic distribution of lesions that cause reversed vein graft failure: A five-year prospective study. J Vasc Surg 17:195-204, 1993.
120. Gardiner GA Jr, Harrington DP, Koltun W, et al: Salvage of occluded arterial bypass grafts by means of thrombolysis. J Vasc Surg 9:426-431, 1989.
121. Robinson KD, Sato DT, Gregory RT, et al: Long-term outcome after early infrainguinal graft failure. J Vasc Surg 26:425-437, 1997.
122. Landry GJ, Moneta GL, Taylor LM Jr, et al: Comparison of procedural outcomes after lower extremity reversed vein grafting and secondary surgical revision. J Vasc Surg 38:22-28, 2003.
123. Mills JL Sr: Infrainguinal vein graft surveillance: How and when. Semin Vasc Surg 14:169-176, 2001.
124. Landry GJ, Moneta GL, Taylor LM Jr, et al: Long-term outcome of revised lower-extremity bypass grafts. J Vasc Surg 35:56-62, 2002.

Chapter

48

The Modified Biograft

LINDA M. HARRIS, MD

Section VIII

Autogenous greater saphenous vein is the preferred conduit for all infrageniculate bypasses and popliteal bypass by many surgeons. The lack of suitable access is becoming more of an issue, with increased longevity of vascular patients, and more aggressive efforts at limb salvage including second and third revascularizations. Unfortunately, the greater saphenous vein is not available in 10% to 30% of all patients needing revascularization due to previous lower extremity bypass, cardiac bypass, or vein stripping.[1-4] The saphenous vein may also be unsuitable due to small size, previous phlebitis, or varicosities. The choice of conduit when the ipsilateral saphenous vein is not present is still a subject of controversy. Many surgeons opt for the contralateral greater saphenous vein, followed by other autogenous veins, including the lesser saphenous and arm veins, sometimes used as composite grafts. The patency rates of lesser saphenous and composite autogenous grafts are inferior to that of a single segment of greater saphenous vein.[5,6] In addition, for patients requiring secondary or tertiary procedures, no suitable autogenous vein is present in up to 50% of patients.[7] When no autogenous conduit is available, the surgeon is faced with choosing between prosthetic grafts, including Dacron and polytetrafluoroethylene (PTFE), modified biologic grafts, endovascular techniques for revascularization, or limb amputation.

Prosthetic grafts have been used with reasonable success in the above-knee position but have relatively poor results when used for distal revascularizations.[8-10] Multiple techniques have been proposed to augment the patency of the prosthetic grafts, including arteriovenous fistula, or a variety of venous cuffs and patches.[11-13] Nonetheless, prosthetic grafts remain a suboptimal alternative for distal reconstruction.

The lack of a suitable prosthetic substitute for the greater saphenous vein has led to the exploration of other biologic tissues. Modified biologic grafts include human umbilical vein grafts (HUV) and fresh and cryopreserved venous and arterial homografts. The potential benefit of the biografts is the availability of an "off-the-shelf" graft of good caliber that handles in a similar fashion to autogenous tissue.

There has been variable enthusiasm about modified biologic grafts over the last several decades. Recent publications, demonstrating improved outcomes with prosthetic grafts and potential problems with biologic grafts, has diminished the role of currently available biografts for the vascular surgeon. The choice to use a biologic graft rather than prosthetic currently is influenced by the presence of tissue loss, active infection, and the caliber of vessel. There are few studies that directly compare the efficacy of modified biografts against prosthetic grafts, with or without patches or cuffs.

■ HUMAN UMBILICAL VEIN GRAFTS

The placement of glutaraldehyde-tanned umbilical grafts was first described in humans in 1976 by Dardik and Dardik.[14] Their work followed the pioneering work of Carpentier,[15] Rosenberg,[16] and their associates with treated xenografts.

The original umbilical grafts were prepared by manual stripping of the human umbilical cord tissue and stabilization of the vessel wall with glutaraldehyde. Currently umbilical vein grafts are prepared with computer-controlled mechanical lathes. The process yields grafts with a uniform wall thickness and a Dacron mesh on the outer surface, added in an attempt to prevent or delay aneurysm formation. The process of glutaraldehyde tanning produces a collagen conduit devoid of endothelium, eliminating the immunogenicity of the graft. The graft is not at increased risk of thrombosis due to rejection but also lacks the antithrombotic benefits of the endothelial lining.*

■ OPERATIVE TECHNIQUE FOR HUMAN UMBILICAL VEINS

The graft is shipped and stored in 50% ethanol and is provided on a glass mandrill. To prepare it for use, it is placed in a basin with 1 L of low-molecular-weight dextran (LMWD) and irrigated with the solution 6 to 10 times. The final irrigation is with heparinized saline (10,000 U of heparin sodium in 1 L of saline). The graft is then left in the heparinized saline until ready for use.

The HUV does not tolerate traction in the tunneling process and should be pulled through a metal conduit for tunneling to prevent ripping. The manufacturer strongly recommends against the use of standard vascular clamps and advocates tourniquet control to avoid damage to the conduit. The graft is also difficult to declot with thrombectomy catheters, should it occlude. To decrease the risk of anastomotic aneurysm formation, the manufacturer also recommends that the entire wall, including both the vein and the supporting Dacron mesh, be incorporated in the suture line.

Postoperative anticoagulation beginning with heparin 500 U/hr, increasing to 1000 U/hr or until therapeutic, and infusion of LMWD for the first 3 days is also recommended to decrease the risk of early thrombosis.

Dardik and associates[17] reported on their initial experience with 907 bypasses. They found a 5-year assisted primary patency rate of 57% for femoropopliteal and 33% for femorocrural bypasses. After further modifications of the graft,

*The current HUV graft is available from Synovis Life Technologies, Inc., St. Paul, Minn.

Table 48-1 Lifetable Analyses for Crural Patency and Limb Salvage with Human Umbilical Vein Grafts

AUTHOR (YEAR)	NO. OF GRAFTS IMPLANTED	ANEURYSM FORMATION, %	PATENCY POPLITEAL BYPASS, %	PATENCY CRURAL BYPASS AT 5 YEARS, %
Dardik et al (1988)[17]	907	57	57	33
Dardik (1995)[18]	71	—	58	36
Batt et al (1990)[26]	105	6	—	29 (3 yr)
Sato et al (1995)[27]	111	—	—	60.9
Dardik et al (2002)[25]	283	0	56	43
Sommeling et al (1990)[28]	227	37	55/57 (BK/AK)	19
Johnson et al (2000)[21]	261	1	49	—

BK/AK, below knee/above knee.

Dardik's group reported on 71 infrageniculate bypasses with a 58% primary patency for below-knee popliteal and 36% for crural reconstructions.[18] Secondary patency was 64% and 41%, respectively.

When comparing bypasses for rest pain or tissue loss, Cranley and Hafner[19] in 1982 reported a 3-year patency of 59% for saphenous vein, 35% for PTFE, and 31% for HUV endothelial cell (HUVEC) for tibial reconstructions. The New England Society of Vascular Surgery Registry in 1991[20] compared HUVEC and PTFE and found better 5-year patency with HUV than PTFE for femoral popliteal bypass both above knee (69% vs. 45%) and below knee (45% vs. 22%). The only randomized, prospective study of HUV in the United States was a Veterans Affairs study[21] in 2000. The study showed a 5-year assisted primary patency for above-knee bypasses of 53% for HUV versus 73% for greater saphenous vein and 39% for PTFE. Patients with HUV, however, were found to have the highest early thrombosis and amputation rate. Other randomized studies comparing HUV to PTFE have found higher patency rates for HUV at 3 to 6 years, ranging from 42% to 75% versus 22% to 34% for PTFE.[22,23] However, owing to the early increased rate of thrombosis, lack of familiarity with the graft, and the increased technical steps associated with preparing the graft, HUV has not become a popular conduit despite the statistics that suggest improved patency when compared to PTFE.

Complications associated with umbilical vein grafts include thrombosis, infection, and aneurysm formation. In an attempt to decrease the risk of early postoperative thrombosis, the manufacturer recommends administration of heparin and/or LMWD.

The incidence of infection for umbilical vein grafts is similar to that for saphenous grafts. Graft infection rates of 3% to 4.3% have been reported with increased risk for patients with active infection or reoperations.[18,24]

The primary concern with HUV has been related to biodegradation of the graft, with subsequent aneurysm formation. Most aneurysms have developed after 5 years. Dardik and colleagues,[17] in their initial study, found that after 5 years, up to 36% of patent grafts became aneurysmal. In response to these findings, the graft was modified in 1990. These modifications included improvement of glutaraldehyde fixation, mechanical stripping of the surrounding tissue, tighter weave of the surrounding mesh, and improved quality control mechanisms. UV-2A, or second-generation HUV, appears to have a reduced risk of biodegradation.[25] Dardik and coworkers followed patients longer than 10 years since the modification of the graft and reported on 283 lower extremity bypasses.[25] They found no aneurysmal dilation since the modification in their study versus a 57% rate of biodegradation and 2.9% rate of aneurysm formation with the earlier grafts. Limb salvage rates remained unchanged. Primary tibial bypass patency was 44% with a secondary patency rate of 53%. Three tibial grafts failed without thrombosis, 10 developed infections, 5 became stenotic, and 1 each developed dissection or pseudoaneurysm.

Despite their excellent results, of all patients in the study mentioned earlier, twenty-three were anticoagulated, and all had an arteriovenous fistula created at the distal anastomosis. Results of patency and limb salvage from recent studies of HUV are listed in Table 48-1.[17,18,20,25-28]

■ CRYOPRESERVED VASCULAR CONDUITS

The initial idea to use venous allografts as a vascular conduit was explored in 1912 by Carrel in canine experiments for aortic replacement.[29] Linton[30] in 1955 and Dye and associates[31] in 1956 reported the first clinical experiences with allografts. The concept of preserving the vein to allow for prolonged periods of storage and to create a bank of veins was initiated in the 1960s.[32] The goal of preservation is to provide a readily available graft with near-normal morphologic and physiologic capacity. The preservation process was initially thought to maintain viability of the cells while decreasing antigenicity.[32,33] Since the mid-1980s, an increase in the use of cryopreserved saphenous vein grafts has occurred, in part due to the availability of these grafts through commercial sources.

■ METHOD OF CRYOPRESERVATION

Multiple modalities have been explored for the preservation of vein grafts. The use of very cold temperatures for storage can lead to significant cellular damage and death during either the freezing or thawing process. Without cryoprotectants, the extracellular matrix of the vein freezes at 0° C while the cytoplasm remains liquid, creating a vapor pressure gradient.[34] When the temperature is decreased slowly, dehydration of the cell results, whereas with a more rapid process, membrane disruption occurs due to the sudden loss of water from the cell. Without cryoprotection, freezing results in a nonviable and structurally damaged conduit.[34-37] Studies of allograft veins stored at 4° C without cryopreservation showed a result of 90% occlusion within 5 months.[38]

Cryoprotectants enter the cell wall and decrease the vapor pressure gradient, thereby preventing cellular damage during the freezing and thawing cycles. Variables in the current techniques of cryopreservation include the type and amount of cryoprotectant, freezing temperature, cooling rate, and time of storage.[34-37] It is generally agreed that the optimal storage temperature is between −196° C and −120° C. Dimethyl sulfoxide (DMSO) is the cryoprotectant of choice, used in concentrations ranging between 10% and 20%. However, protection with DMSO alone resulted in poor survival of venous endothelium.[39,40] Chondroitin sulfate, initially used for storage of corneas, was then added to the cryopreservation solution to improve viability of the cells. The addition of chondroitin sulfate has enhanced the viability and function of the cryopreserved veins.[40]

■ CRYOPRESERVED VENOUS ALLOGRAFT PREPARATION

All allografts are tested for communicable fungal, bacterial and viral diseases (hepatitis, human immunodeficiency virus). There has been no known case of viral or bacterial transmission of infection with cryopreserved vein implants.

The greater saphenous vein is harvested from the level of the femoral vein to the ankle within 24 hours of cessation of circulation from organ donors. The vein is placed in cryoprotectants and stored in the vapor phase of liquid nitrogen between −110° C and −196° C.

Cryolife cryografts are shipped frozen in a solution of DMSO at −96° C until ready to be thawed for use. The grafts are seromatched for ABO/Rh blood type to decrease risk of rejection. After proximal and distal target vessels have been identified, the graft is thawed by submersion in a warm water bath (37° C to 42° C), which allows rapid thawing without damage to the cells. It is then rinsed in a series of three solutions provided by the manufacturer before implantation. The Cryovein handles similarly to autogenous greater saphenous vein. The graft is placed through a tunnel in similar fashion to the normal greater saphenous vein. A subcutaneous tunnel is preferred to allow for easier access for late revisions/aneurysms. Patients are heparinized and the graft is typically placed in a reversed fashion.

■ FUNCTIONAL STATUS OF THE CRYOPRESERVED VEIN

Although cryopreservation may preserve the morphologic appearance of the vein graft,[35-37,41,42] questions have remained about the biologic activity of the conduit. Most studies have documented an intact endothelium after cryopreservation. Brockbank and associates documented maintenance of overall intimal integrity despite loss of a significant number of endothelial cells.[42] Significant endothelial denudation occurs after implantation into the arterial system. Faggioli and colleagues have similarly documented some endothelial denudation after implantation in the arterial system in rabbits.[41] The maintenance of antithrombotic properties, fibrinolytic activity, and prostacyclin production has also been documented in cryopreserved veins.[43,44] Platelet adhesion is not increased in an animal model of cryopreserved vein bypasses.[45] However, cryopreserved veins do appear to accumulate low-density lipoprotein (LDL) cholesterol at a higher rate than nonpreserved veins in an in-vitro experiment suggesting some loss of endothelial integritity.[46] The ability of the graft to respond appropriately to endothelial cell-dependent relaxation to acetylcholine, thrombin, and calcium ionophore A23187 in animal studies further documents the viability of the cells after transplant.[47]

Additional evaluation of the grafts has focused on the viability and function of the smooth muscle cell (SMC) layer. The SMCs of cryopreserved veins exhibit a synthetic appearance after implantation suggestive of activated cells.[41] Brockbank and coworkers have noted a decreased secretory capacity after cryopreservation.[42] Elmore and associates noted that reactivity to prostaglandin F_2 is increased while relaxation to NO is decreased.[45] Miller and colleagues have also documented a loss of response to KCl, phenylephrine, and endothelin in the SMC.[48] The SMC layer in implanted grafts is eventually replaced by fibrotic layer a few months after implantation.[32,38,49-52] This effect is due to an immune reaction resulting in cellular destruction and fibrosis.

■ IMMUNOLOGY OF THE CRYOPRESERVED ALLOGRAFT

Transplanted organs and tissues present antigenic proteins, which result in immunologic rejection. Early investigators suggested that venous allografts might be only weakly antigenic.[33] Initial attempts at altering the antigenicity properties of allografts centered on modifying the wall, including glutaraldehyde treatment, which resulted in a nonviable conduit. Early studies of cryopreserved veins documented improved patency as compared to fresh allografts, suggesting that the cryopreservation process might confer some immunologic protection.[32,53,54] Recent studies, however, have proved that venous allografts are indeed antigenic and that the antigenicity is not modified by cryopreservation.[55-58]

According to Todd and Boctar,[59] there are three phases to the immune reaction seen in vascular allografts. The first phase occurs within 24 hours of implantation with recognition of the graft as a foreign body. The antigenicity of the vein graft derives from several components of the vein wall. Endothelial cells have the ability to express classes I and II MHC antigens when exposed to T cells and lymphokines.[60] SMCs are also able to express class II MHC antigens and participate in the immune process. The second phase is characterized by an increase in cells infiltrating the intima and adventitia, seen between 30 to 60 days after implantation. The third phase is intimal thickening and medial necrosis, which occurs between 60 and 100 days after implantation. Chronic rejection eventually leads to intimal thickening with resultant thrombosis or adventitial fibroblastic reaction and medial necrosis resulting in aneurysmal degeneration.[61]

Immunosuppression has been examined as a possible adjunct to decrease the antigenicity of the cryopreserved venous allograft and thereby increase utility of the conduit. Immunosuppression coupled with use of cryopreserved vein grafts has been shown to enhance patency in animal models.[48,61-64] Although animal models are encouraging, data on humans are quite limited. Posner and coworkers[65] evaluated a combination of low-dose cyclosporine, azathioprine, prednisone, warfarin, aspirin, and vasodilators on patency of cryopreserved vein bypasses in humans and found a significantly improved patency (59% vs. 17%) at 1 year. They continued to find a high rate of aneurysmal degeneration in patent grafts (33%). Carpenter and Tomaszewski, however, were unable to show any benefit to low-dose immunosuppression with azathioprine when compared to control with regard to graft patency or limb salvage.[58,66] The potential risks of immunosuppression are significant, and the ultimate role of immunosuppression remains uncertain.

■ CLINICAL OUTCOMES

Short-term reports have often suggested widely varying outcomes for cryopreserved allograft bypasses.[50,65-77] Fewer series are available to analyze long-term outcomes. Further confounding analysis of outcome are differences in methods of preservation. Uniformity in cryopreservation techniques still does not exist today. Although contemporary techniques are not as varied, with most cryopreserved veins being purchased from one of several major commercial sources, there are still differences between these companies that may impact on short- and long-term outcomes. Other confounding factors are (1) variability in patient population between series, including indication for surgery and location of distal anastomosis, and (2) use of pharmacologic adjuncts, including warfarin and various immunosuppressive agents.

A summary of recent series using cryopreserved venous allografts for infrainguinal bypass is presented in Table 48-2.[50,65-77] Short-term patency rates range from 28% to 80% at 1 year and fall to between 19% and 42% at 2 years. Complications related to implantation of cryopreserved venous allografts include an early failure rate (<30 days) of 17% and late aneurysm formation rate of between 5% and 33% in reported series (Table 48-3).[50,65-77] Unfortunately, there are still relatively few studies with any long-term results, thereby making conclusions from long-term patency data difficult.

The indication for bypass with cryopreserved vein is the threatened limb in the overwhelming majority of patients in all current series. Seventy-seven percent to 100% of patients are operated for rest pain or tissue loss in recent reviews, with the exception of cryopreserved veins used for revascularization in infected fields. Further, allograft bypasses are almost exclusively to tibial or pedal vessels. The indication for surgery and level of outflow do not appear to influence patency in the studies with adequate documentation (Table 48-4).[50,65-77]

It is difficult, however, to appropriately compare cryopreserved vein bypasses to prosthetic bypasses or HUV in

Table 48-2 Lifetable Analyses for Patency and Limb Salvage with Cryopreserved Vein

AUTHOR (YEAR)	NO. OF GRAFTS IMPLANTED	ABO MATCH, %	SOURCE OF VEINS	LIMB SALVAGE, %	PATENCY, %		
					1 Year	18 Months	2 Years
Shah et al (1993)[67]	43	100	CryoLife	?	—	54	—
Walker et al (1993)[68]	39	49	CryoLife	67	28 (46*)	14 (37*)	—
Harris et al (1993)[69]	25	100	CryoLife UC Chicago Cryolab Virginia Tissue Bank American Red Cross	74	36*	—	—
Carpenter and Tomaszewski (1997)[66]	40	100	CryoLife	42	13	2.5	—
Fujitani et al (1992)[50]	10	100	UC Chicago Cryolab Virginia Tissue Bank CryoLife	?	80 (14 mo)	—	—
Selke et al (1989)[70]	6	83	Virginia Tissue Bank	100	33	—	—
Leseche et al (1997)[71]‡	25	80	Noncommercial	78	52*	—	—
Posner et al (1996)[65]	21	95	Virginia Tissue Bank CryoLife	62	59.4†	—	—
Martin et al (1994)[72]	115	100	Virginia Tissue Bank CryoLife	66	37	—	19
Gournier et al (1995)[73]	20	100	Gambro‡	100	68	—	42
CryoLife (1998)[74]	424	?	CryoLife	72	41	32	32
Farber et al (2003)[75]	240	100	Cryolife	80	30	—	18
Harris et al (2001)[76]	80	100	CryoLife	62.3	36.8	—	—
Buckley et al (2000)[77]	26	100	CryoLife	80	87	82	82

*Secondary patency.
†In immunosuppressed patients.
‡Cryopreserved arteries.

Table 48-3 Graft Complications

AUTHOR (YEAR)	EARLY OCCLUSION, %	ANEURYSM FORMATION, %
Shah et al (1993)[67]	5	7
Walker et al (1993)[68]	33	?
Harris et al (1993)[69]	>13	?
Fujitani et al (1992)[50]	11	?
Carpenter and Tomaszewski (1997)[66]	17.5	2.5
Selke et al (1989)[70]	33	?
Leseche et al (1997)[71]	16	?
Posner et al (1996)[65]	14	33
Martin et al (1994)[72]	6	5
Gournier et al (1995)[73]	0	5
CryoLife (1998)[74]	20 (3 mo)	?
Harris et al (2001)[76]	18	—
Farber et al (2003)[75]	5	44

that there are no randomized trials comparing the two conduits. In historical studies, surgeons appear to preferentially use allograft vein for patients with disadvantaged outflow or more distal sites, thereby making historical comparisons questionable. Patency of prosthetic to below-knee popliteal bypass ranges from 44% to 60%[8,10] at 5 years. However, patency rates of prosthetic directly anastomosed to tibial vessels has generally been unsatisfactory, with only 12% to 22% patency at 5 years.[8] Taylor and associates[11] initially achieved good long-term results, with 54% 5-year patency, with distal PTFE bypasses by using a vein patch. Other recent studies have found improving patency rates of 48% to 63%[4,78-80] at 2 to 4 years by use of a distal vein patch. These improving patencies will further challenge the indications for biograft implantation.

Recently, arterial allografts have been suggested as an alternative to extra-anatomic revascularization for aortic infections. Vogt and colleagues[81] showed a decreased mortality to 6% and decreased hospital stay with arterial cryografts. There were no recurrent infections or late deaths in their series of 49 patients. Verhelst and coworkers,[82] however, found an early mortality rate of 17.7% with use of cryografts in infected fields. Of the surviving patients, 4.4% died of graft-related problems and 5.5% required subsequent revisions. They found the highest mortality in patients operated for enteroprosthetic fistulae (65% early, 18% late). Noel and associates[83] found no benefit for in-situ replacement with cryograft, with a 30-day mortality rate of 13%, and an overall mortality of 25%. After operation, 51% of patients had one or more complications, with 25% being graft related. Knosalla's group[84] also found that aortic arterial allografts were more resistant to reinfection than synthetic grafts after in-situ replacement of infected prosthesis. The resistance was not complete, and antibiotic loading of the allograft before cryopreservation was recommended.

Attempts to use cryopreserved veins for coronary bypass began in the 1970s[85] with initially encouraging results. However, multiple subsequent studies have found poor patency rates, clearly inferior to those with autogenous saphenous vein or internal mammary artery bypass.[86,87] Even early patency, at less than 6 months, was dismal.[88] The one area of cardiac surgery in which there has been a positive experience with cryopreserved veins is for treatment of children with heart defects in which the homograft is used for bridging therapy to more definitive treatment instead of small-diameter prosthetics.[89]

The most recent area of interest for cryografts has been for dialysis access.[90-92] However, patients receiving cryografts for access have been found to have increased panel-reactive antibody (PRB) levels that may interfere with potential for future renal transplant.[92] To address this potential problem, a new cryopreserved graft, devoid of endothelium, is being investigated in a prospective, multicenter study to determine the effect of this graft on alloimmunization and graft patency for dialysis patients

■ CONCLUSION

Although cryopreserved veins and HUV are now more readily available, problems with long-term patency and aneurysmal degeneration remain unsolved. HUV and cryopreserved veins may have a role in the threatened leg with limb salvage rates ranging from 67% to 100%.[4,20,25,28,71,77,78] Another potential use of allograft vein may be the infected field.[53,81,84,90] Despite less than optimal long-term patency, the modified biograft may allow for adequate perfusion

Table 48-4 Indications, Outflow Site, and Patency for Cryopreserved Veins

AUTHOR (YEAR)	PERCENTAGE WITH PREVIOUS PROCEDURES	OUTFLOW LEVEL		REST PAIN/ TISSUE LOSS, %	1 YEAR PATENCY
		Tibial/Pedal	Infrageniculate		
Shah et al (1993)[67]	44	42	86	88	54
Walker et al (1993)[68]	87	92	100	87	28
Harris et al (1993)[69]	76	92	100	100	36
Fujitani et al (1992)[50]	80	40	50	0‡	80
Carpenter and Tomaszewski (1997)[66]	90	93	100	100	13
Leseche et al (1997)[71]‡	33	100	100	100	52*
Posner et al (1996)[65]	87	90	100	100	59.4†
Martin et al (1994)[72]	94	88	100	80	37
Gournier et al (1995)[73]	100	55	100	100	68
CryoLife (1998)[74]	69	65	87	77	41

*Secondary patency.
†In immunosuppressed patients.
‡100% done for infection.

and treatment of infection, with subsequent replacement with prosthetic material. Recent modifications in the HUV may alter the long-term degeneration of the graft and make it more appealing for bypass.[25] Randomized studies comparing prosthetic, HUV, and cryopreserved veins to tibial and pedal vessels are needed before any of these grafts can be confidently recommended for use in other than the desperate situation.

For cryopreserved veins to be more useful for the average patient, their associated immunologic problems must be addressed. It is conceivable that appropriate immunosuppression or genetic manipulation of the conduit may significantly improve patency without causing serious adverse reactions to the patient and increase the utility of this conduit, although the practicality of this is suspect. Decellularization of the media may be a more logical approach to reducing immunogenicity, but its efficacy remains to be proved. Current use of cryopreserved veins is investigational and should be restricted to limb-threatening ischemia or revascularization caused by infection without suitable autogenous vein due to their relatively poor long-term patency results. Further studies on HUV by other investigators are necessary to confirm Dardik's more recent findings if HUV are to be considered acceptable for revascularization.

■ REFERENCES

1. Kent KC, Whittemore AD, Mannick JA: Short-term and midterm results of an all autogenous tissue policy for infrainguinal reconstruction. J Vasc Surg 9:107-114, 1989.
2. Gentile AT, Lee RW, Moneta GL, et al: Results of bypass to the popliteal and tibial arteries with alternative sources of autogenous vein. J Vasc Surg 23:272-280, 1996.
3. Taylor LM Jr, Edwards JM, Brant B, et al: Autogenous reversed vein bypass for lower extremity ischemia in patients with absent or inadequate greater saphenous vein. Am J Surg 153:505-510, 1987.
4. Neville RF, Tempesta B, Sidway AN: Tibial bypass for limb salvage using polytetrafluoroethylene and a distal vein patch. J Vasc Surg 33:266-271, 2001.
5. Chew DK, Owens DC, Belkin M, et al: Bypass in the absence of ipsilateral greater saphenous vein: Safety and superiority of the contralateral saphenous vein. J Vasc Surg 35:1085-1092, 2002.
6. Pomposelli FB, Kansal N, Hamdan AD, et al: A decade of experience with dorsalis pedis artery bypass: Analysis of outcome in more than 1000 cases. J Vasc Surg 37:307-315, 2003.
7. Brewster DC: Composite grafts. In Rutherford RB (ed): Vascular Surgery, 3rd ed. Philadelphia, WB Saunders, 1989, p 481-486.
8. Abbott WM: Prosthetic above-knee femoral-popliteal bypass: Indications and choice of graft. Semin Vasc Surg 10:3-7, 1997.
9. Veith FJ, Gupta SK, Ascer E, et al: Six-year prospective multicenter randomized comparison of autologous saphenous vein and expanded PTFE grafts in infrainguinal reconstruction. J Vasc Surg 3:104-114, 1986.
10. Dalman RL, Taylor LM: Basic data related to infrainguinal revascularization procedures. Ann Vasc Surg 4:309-312, 1990.
11. Taylor RS, Loh A, McFarland RJ, et al: Improved technique for polytetrafluoroethylene bypass grafting: Long-term results using anastomotic vein patches. Br J Surg 79:348-354, 1992.
12. Miller JH, Foreman RK, Fergusson L, et al: Interposition vein cuff for anastomosis of prosthesis to small artery. Aust N Z J Surg 54:283-285, 1984.
13. Tyrrell MR, Wolfe JHN: PTFE grafts and a venous boot. Perspect Vasc Surg 6:57-66, 1993.
14. Dardik H, Dardik I: Successful arterial substitution with modified human umbilical vein. Ann Surg 183:252-258, 1976.
15. Carpentier A, Blondeau P, Laurens P: Remplacement des valvules mitrales et tricuspides pare des heterogrefes. Ann Chir Thorac Cardiovasc 7:33-38, 1968.
16. Rosenberg N, Martinez A, Sawyer PN, et al: Tanned collagen arterial prosthesis of bovine carotid origin in man: Preliminary studies of enzyme-treated heterografts. Ann Surg 164:247-256, 1966.
17. Dardik H, Miller N, Dardik A, et al: A decade of experience with the glutaraldehyde tanned human umbilical vein graft for revascularization of the lower limb. J Vasc Surg 7:336-346, 1988.
18. Dardik H: Umbilical vein grafts for atherosclerotic lower extremity occlusive disease. In Ernst CB, Stanley JC (eds): Current Therapy in Vascular Surgery, 3rd ed. St. Louis, Mosby, 1995, pp 484-487.
19. Cranley JJ, Hafner CD: Revascularization of the femoro-popliteal arteries using saphenous vein, polytetrafluoroethylene, and umbilical vein grafts: Five- and six-year results. Arch Surg 117:1543-1550, 1982.
20. Johnson WC, Squires JW: Axillo-femoral (PTFE) and infrainguinal revascularization (PTFE and umbilical vein). Vascular Registry of the New England Society for Vascular Surgery. J Cardiovasc Surg 32:344-349, 1991.
21. Johnson WC and members of the Department of Veterans Affairs Cooperative Study 141: A comparative evaluation of polytetrafluoroethylene, umbilical vein, and saphenous vein bypass grafts for femoral-popliteal above-knee revascularization: A prospective randomized Department of Veterans Affairs Cooperative Study. J Vasc Surg 32:268-277, 2000.
22. Aalders GJ, Van Vroonhover T: Polytetrafluoroethylene versus HUV in AK femoropopliteal bypass: Six-year results of randomized clinical trial. J Vasc Surg 16:816-824, 1992.
23. Eickhoff JH, Bromme A, Ericsson BF, et al: Four years' results of a prospective randomized clinical trial comparing PTFE and modified HUV for BK femoropopliteal bypass. J Vasc Surg 6:506-511, 1987.
24. Jarrett F, Mahood BA: Long-term results of femoropopliteal bypass with umbilical vein grafts. Am J Surg 168:111-114, 1994.
25. Dardik H, Wengerter K, Qin F, et al: Comparative decades of experience with glutaraldehyde-tanned human umbilical cord vein graft for lower limb revascularization: An analysis of 1,275 cases. J Vasc Surg 35:64-71, 2002.
26. Batt M, Gagliardi JM, Avril G, et al: Human umbilical vein grafts as infrainguinal bypasses: Long-term clinical follow-up and pathological investigation of explanted grafts. Clin Invest Med 13:155-164, 1990.
27. Sato O, Okamoto H, Takagi A, et al: Biodegradation of glutaraldehyde-tanned human umbilical vein grafts. Surg Today 25:901-905, 1995.
28. Sommeling CA, Buth J, Jakimowicz JJ: Long-term behaviour of modified human umbilical vein grafts: Late aneurysmal degeneration established by colour-duplex scanning. Eur J Vasc Surg 4:89-94, 1990.
29. Carrel A: Ultimate results of aortic transplantations. J Exp Med 15:389-392, 1912.
30. Linton RR: Some practical considerations in the surgery of blood vessel grafts. Surgery 38:817-834, 1955.
31. Dye WS, Grove WJ, Olin JH, et al: Two- to four-year behavior of vein grafts in the lower extremities. Arch Surg 72:64-68, 1956.
32. Barner HB, DeWeese JA, Schenk EA: Fresh and frozen homologous venous grafts for arterial repair. Angiology 17:389-401, 1966.
33. Schwartz SI, Kutner FR, Neistadt A, et al: Antigenicity of homografted veins. Surgery 61:474-477, 1967.
34. Litvan GG: Mechanism of cryoinjury in biological systems. Cryobiology 9:182-191, 1972.
35. Lindenauer SM, Ladin DA, Burkel WE, et al: Cryopreservation of vein grafts. In Biologic and Synthetic Vascular Prostheses. New York, Grune & Stratton, 1982, pp 397-422.
36. Ladin DA, Lindenauer SM, Burkel WE, et al: Viability, immunological reaction and patency of cryopreserved venous allografts. Surg Forum 33:460-463, 1982.
37. Dent TL, Wever TR, Lindenauer SM, et al: Cryopreservation of vein grafts. Surg Forum 25:241-243, 1974.
38. Stephen M, Sheil AGR, Long J: Allograft vein arterial bypass. Arch Surg 113:591-593, 1978.

39. Brockbank KGM: Basic principles of viable tissue preservation. In Clark DR (ed): Transplantation Techniques and Use of Cryopreserved Allograft Cardiac Valves and Vascular Tissue. Boston, Adams, 1989, pp 9-23.
40. Brockbank KGM: Function of chondroitin sulfate-protected cryopreserved canine venous allografts. Cardiovasc Surg 5, 1994.
41. Faggioli GL, Gargiulo M, Giardino R, et al: Long-term cryopreservation of autologous veins in rabbits. Cardiovasc Surg 2:259-265, 1994.
42. Brockbank KGM, Donovan TJ, Ruby ST, et al: Functional analysis of cryopreserved veins: Preliminary report. J Vasc Surg 11:94-102, 1990.
43. Malone JM, Moore WS, Kischer CW, et al: Venous cryopreservation: Endothelial fibrinolytic activity and histology. J Surg Res 29:209-222, 1980.
44. Bambang LS, Mazzucotelli JP, Moczar M, et al: Effects of cryopreservation on the proliferation and anticoagulant activity of human saphenous vein endothelial cells. J Thorac Cardiovasc Surg 110:998-1004, 1995.
45. Elmore JR, Gloviczki P, Brockbank KGM, et al: Cryopreservation affects endothelial and smooth muscle function of canine autogenous vein grafts. J Vasc Surg 13:584-592, 1991.
46. Ligush J, Berceli SA, Moosa HH, et al: First results on the functional characteristics of cryopreserved human saphenous vein. Cells Materials 1:359-368, 1991.
47. Ku DD, Willis WL, Caulfield JB: Retention of endothelium-dependent vasodilatory responses in canine coronary arteries following cryopreservation. Cryobiology 27:511-520, 1990.
48. Miller VM, Bergman RT, Gloviczki P, et al: Cryopreserved venous allografts: Effects of immunosuppression and antiplatelet therapy on patency and function. J Vasc Surg 18:216-226, 1993.
49. Oschner JL, DeCamp PT, Leonard GL: Experience with fresh venous allografts as an arterial substitute. Ann Surg 173:933-939, 1971.
50. Fujitani RM, Hisham SB, Bruce LG: Cryopreserved saphenous vein allogenic homografts: An alternative conduit in lower extremity arterial reconstruction in infected fields. J Vasc Surg 15:519-526, 1992.
51. Balderman SC, Montes M, Schmartz K, et al: Preparation of venous allografts: A comparison of technique. Ann Surg 200:117-123, 1984.
52. Bank H, Schmerhl MK, Warner R, et al: Transplantation of cryopreserved canine venous allografts. J Surg Res 50:57-64, 1991.
53. Weber TR, Dent TL, Salles CA, et al: Cryopreservation of venous homografts. Surg Forum 26:291-293, 1975.
54. Tice DA, Zerbino V: Clinical experience with preserved human allografts for vascular reconstruction. Surgery 72:260-267, 1972.
55. Axthelm SC, Porter JM, Strickland S, et al: Antigenicity of venous allografts. Ann Surg 189:290-292, 1979.
56. Cochran RP, Kunzelman KS: Cryopreservation does not alter antigenic expression of aortic allografts. J Surg Res 46:597-599, 1989.
57. Nataf P, Guettier C, Hadjiisky P, et al: Evaluation of cryopreserved arteries as alternative small-vessel prostheses. Int J Artif Organs 18:197-202, 1995.
58. Carpenter JP, Tomaszewski JE: Human saphenous vein allograft bypass grafts: Immune response. J Vasc Surg 27:492-499, 1998.
59. Todd IA, Boctar ZN: Experimental homotransplantation of arteries. Transplantation 4:123-130, 1966.
60. Pober JS, Gimbrone MA, Collins T, et al: Interactions of T lymphocytes with human vascular endothelial cells: Role of endothelial surface antigens. Immunobiology 168:483-494, 1984.
61. Schmitz-Rixen T, Megerman J, Colvin RB, et al: Immunosuppressive treatment of aortic allografts. J Vasc Surg 7:82-92, 1988.
62. Augelli NV, Lupinetti FM, Khatib HE, et al: Allograft vein patency in a canine model. Transplantation 52:466-470, 1991.
63. Bandlien KO, Toledo-Peyra, Barnhart MI, et al: Improved survival of venous allografts in dogs following graft pretreatment with cyclosporine. Transpl Proc 15(Suppl):3084-3091, 1983.
64. Perloff LJ, Reckard CR, Rowlands DT Jr, et al: The venous homograft: An immunological question. Surgery 72:961-970, 1972.
65. Posner MP, Makhoul RG, Altman M, et al: Early results of infrageniculate arterial reconstruction using cryopreserved homograft saphenous conduit (Cadvein) and combination low-dose systemic immunosuppression. J Am Coll Surg 183:208-216, 1996.
66. Carpenter FP, Tomaszewski JE: Immunosuppression for human saphenous vein allograft bypass surgery: A prospective randomized trial. J Vasc Surg 26:36-42, 1997.
67. Shah RM, Faggioli GL, Mangione S, et al: Early results with cryopreserved saphenous vein allografts for infrainguinal bypass. J Vasc Surg 18:965-971, 1993.
68. Walker PJ, Mitchell RS, McFadden PM, et al: Early experience with cryopreserved saphenous vein allografts as a conduit for complex limb-salvage procedures. J Vasc Surg 18:561-569, 1993.
69. Harris RW, Schneider PA, Andros G, et al: Allograft vein bypass: Is it an acceptable alternative for infrapopliteal revascularization? J Vasc Surg 18:553-560, 1993.
70. Selke FW, Meng RL, Rossi NP: Cryopreserved saphenous vein homografts for femoral-distal vascular reconstruction. J Cardiovasc Surg 30:838-842, 1989.
71. Leseche G, Penna C, Bouttier S: Femorodistal bypass using cryopreserved venous allografts for limb salvage. Ann Vasc Surg 11:230-236, 1997.
72. Martin RS, Edwards WH, Mulherin JL Jr: Cryopreserved saphenous vein allografts for below-knee lower extremity revascularization. Ann Surg 219:664-672, 1994.
73. Gournier JP, Favre JP, Gay JL: Cryopreserved arterial allografts for limb salvage in the absence of suitable saphenous vein: Two-year results in 20 cases. Ann Vasc Surg 9(Suppl):S7-S14, 1995.
74. CryoLife, Inc., Clinical Research Department Communication, 1998.
75. Farber A, Major K, Wagner WH, et al: Cryopreserved saphenous vein allografts in infrainguinal revascularization: Analysis of 240 grafts. J Vasc Surg 38:15-21, 2003.
76. Harris L, O'Brien-Irr M, Ricotta JJ: Long-term assessment of cryopreserved bypass grafting success. J Vasc Surg 33:528-532, 2001.
77. Buckley CJ, Abernathy S, Lee SD, et al: Suggested treatment protocol for improving patency of femoral-infrapopliteal cryopreserved saphenous vein allografts. J Vasc Surg 32:731-738, 2000.
78. Kansal N, Pappas PJ, Gwertzman GA, et al: Patency and limb salvage for polytetrafluoroethylene bypasses with vein interposition cuffs. Ann Vasc Surg 13:386-392, 1999.
79. Ascer E, Gennaro M, Pollina RM, et al: Complementary distal arteriovenous fistula and deep vein interposition: A five-year experience with a new technique to improve infrapopliteal prosthetic bypass patency. J Vasc Surg 24:134-143, 1996.
80. Kreienberg PB, Darling C, Chang BB, et al: Adjunctive techniques to improve patency of distal prosthetic bypass grafts: Polytetrafluoroethylene with remote arteriovenous fistulae versus vein cuffs. J Vasc Surg 31:696-701, 2000.
81. Vogt PR, Brunner-LaRocca HP, Lachat M, et al: Technical details with use of cryopreserved arterial allografts for aortic infection: Influence on early and midterm mortality. J Vasc Surg 35:80-86, 2002.
82. Verhelst R, Lacroix V, Vraux H, et al: Use of cryopreserved arterial homografts for management of infected prosthetic grafts: A multicentric study. Ann Vasc Surg 14:602-607, 2000.
83. Noel AA, Glonzhi P, Cherry RJ Jr, et al, and Members of the United States Cryopreserved Aortic Allograft Registry: Abdominal aortic reconstruction in infected fields: Early results of the United States Cryopreserved Aortic Allograft Registry. J Vasc Surg 35:847-852, 2002.
84. Knosalla C, Goeau-Brissonniere O, Leflon V, et al: Treatment of vascular graft infection by in situ replacement with cryopreserved aortic allografts: An experimental study. J Vasc Surg 27:689-698, 1998.
85. Tice DA, Zerbino VR, Isom OW, et al: Coronary artery bypass with freeze-preserved saphenous vein allografts. J Thorac Cardiovasc Surg 71:378-382, 1976.
86. Iaffaldano RA, Lewis BE, Johnson SA, et al: Patency of cryopreserved saphenous vein grafts as conduits for coronary artery bypass surgery. Chest 108:725-729, 1995.
87. Laub GW, Muralidharan S, Clancy R, et al: Cryopreserved allograft veins as alternative coronary artery bypass conduits: Early-phase results. Ann Thorac Surg 54:826-831, 1992.

88. Sellke FW, Stanford W, Rossi NP: Failure of cryopreserved saphenous vein allografts following coronary artery bypass surgery. J Cardiovasc Surg 32:820-823, 1991.
89. Tam VK, Murphy K, Parks J, et al: Saphenous vein homograft: A superior conduit for the systemic arterial shunt in the Norwood operation. Ann Thorac Surg 71:1537-1540, 2001.
90. Fronk D: Hemodialysis graft infections treated with cryopreserved femoral vein. Cardiovasc Surg 10:561-565, 2002.
91. Matsuura JH, Johnson RH, Rosenthal D, et al: Cryopreserved femoral vein grafts for difficult hemodialysis access. Ann Vasc Surg 14:50-55, 2000.
92. Benedetto B, Liphowitz G, Madden R, et al: Use of cryopreserved cadaveric vein allograft for hemodialysis access precludes kidney transplantation because of allosensitization. J Vasc Surg 34:139-142, 2001.

Chapter 49

Prosthetic Grafts

LIAN XUE, MD, PHD
HOWARD P. GREISLER, MD

The search for artificial vascular grafts dates back to the late 1940s, when Hufnagel,[1] Donovan and Zimmerman,[2] and Moore[3] experimented with methylacrylate and polyethylene tubes for aortic replacement in animal models. In 1952, Voorhees and colleagues[4] developed the first fabric graft using woven Vinyon N. The initial failure of materials such as metal, glass, ivory, silk, and nylon brought two important criteria in focus: thrombogenicity and durability. Research was directed toward the goal of relatively inert materials that minimally interact with blood and tissue. Polyethylene terephthalate (Dacron) and expanded polytetrafluoroethylene (ePTFE) are the products of this research and are currently the standard biomaterials of prosthetic vascular grafts.

After decades of use, it may be concluded that Dacron and ePTFE grafts generally perform well at diameters greater than 6 mm, yet their limitations and less than optimal results for small-diameter (≤6 mm) applications are well recognized and continue to represent a major challenge. The mid-term to long-term failure of existing synthetic grafts is due primarily to unfavorable healing processes, including incomplete endothelialization and myointimal hyperplasia.

Dacron and ePTFE react with blood components and perigraft tissues in a manner that is beneficial and detrimental. It is likely unrealistic to seek completely nonreactive substances. Optimizing tissue-biomaterial interactions to elicit desirable results is a major emphasis of current research. Various modifications have been applied to Dacron and ePTFE grafts to improve their function. Elastic polymers have been employed in the manufacture of compliant grafts based on the notion that compliance mismatch between the synthetic graft and native artery may contribute to myointimal hyperplasia. The emergence of tissue-engineering technology has made the development of novel, biologically viable vascular substitutes feasible and may prove to be the ultimate solution for small-diameter vascular grafting.

■ GRAFT HEALING

A complex but largely predictable host response to prosthetic grafts begins immediately after restoration of circulation. The typical reaction cascade starts at the blood-biomaterial interface with the adsorption of plasma proteins, followed by the deposition and activation of platelets, the infiltration of neutrophils and monocytes, and the migration and proliferation of endothelial and smooth muscle cells. Even the most inert substances developed so far are still recognized as "foreign." The tissue-graft and blood-graft interfaces are highly complex microenvironments that are ultimately responsible for graft patency.

Protein Adsorption

The most abundant serum proteins, albumin, fibrinogen, and IgG, along with other serum proteins adsorb to the graft almost instantaneously after exposure to the systemic circulation. Then according to the Vroman effect,[5] there is a redistribution of proteins regulated by each protein's relative biochemical and electrical affinity for the graft surface and by its relative abundance. The constitution and concentration of bound protein largely determines the interaction of blood and graft and affects graft survival because the platelets and blood cells interact predominantly with the bound proteins rather than with the prosthetic material itself.

Fibrinogen, laminin, fibronectin, and vitronectin all have RGD sequence (arg-gly-asp) regions that bind to the glycoprotein IIb/IIIa receptor complex on platelet membranes. Platelet deposition and activation are influenced by prior protein adsorption. The binding of the RGD sequence to β_2 integrins expressed on the cell surface also contributes to the recruitment of circulating leukocytes to the graft. The neutrophils bound to immobilized IgG and fibrinogen show a deficiency in their ability to kill bacteria, which may contribute to the susceptibility of grafts to infections.[6]

Additional plasma proteins, including complement components, can be activated directly by synthetic surfaces. The generation of complement C5a, a monocyte chemoattractant, is greater after implantation of Dacron compared with ePTFE grafts in an animal model.[7] In addition, the rapid accumulation of coagulant proteins, such as thrombin and factor Xa, on the luminal surface after implantation contributes to the graft-associated procoagulant activity.[8]

Platelet Deposition

Early platelet deposition occurs primarily via receptor-mediated interactions with adsorbed proteins and, to a lesser extent, by direct adherence to the graft. The platelet/protein complex is mediated through von Willebrand factor and platelet membrane glycoproteins. After adherence, the platelets undergo conformational changes and degranulate, releasing a variety of bioactive substances, including serotonin, epinephrine, adenosine diphosphate, and thromboxane A_2. These substances further activate additional platelets and increase thrombin generation. A variety of growth factors, including platelet-derived growth factor (PDGF), epidermal growth factor, and transforming growth factor-β (TGF-β), are released by activated platelets. These growth factors modulate endothelial cell (EC) and smooth muscle cell (SMC) migration and proliferation and extracelluar matrix synthesis and degradation. In addition, platelets release monocyte chemoattractants, such as platelet factor 4 and β-thromboglobulin, which mediate the recruitment of monocytes to the graft.

The platelet deposition and activation continue on a long-term basis after graft implantation. Animal experiments show increased levels of thromboxane and decreased systemic platelet counts 1 year after Dacron graft implantation.[9] Human studies also have revealed an increase in indium-111–labeled platelet adhesion to grafts long after implantation.[10-12]

The thrombogenic nature of the synthetic graft surface is a major determinant of early and late graft patency. A myriad of interventions targeting the platelet deposition, aggregation, and activation have been investigated. Antiplatelet agents directly targeting platelet/graft binding molecules, such as platelet surface glycoprotein IIb/IIIa (αIIbβ3 intergrin) and different functional domains of thrombin have been shown at least transiently to decrease the accumulation of platelets on Dacron grafts.[13,14] A variety of techniques used to alter surface thrombogenicity have been studied experimentally, including the application of antiplatelet or anticoagulant substances to biomaterial surfaces, the alteration of surface electronegativity, and the radiofrequency glow discharge of plasma polymerized monomers to surfaces, in the hope of enhancing surface thromboresistance without alteration of the material's bulk properties.

Neutrophil and Monocyte Infiltration

The acute inflammatory response is mediated through potent chemoattractants, such as C5a and leukotriene B_4, which draw neutrophils to the synthetic graft surface. Neutrophils are attracted to the fibrin coagulum of the inner and outer capsule of the graft. They bind to fibrinogen deposited on the graft surface through cell surface β_2 integrins (mainly CD11b/CD18). Neutrophils also can interact with other deposited proteins, such as IgG, C3bi, and factor X.

The recruitment of phagocytic cells around prosthetic grafts does not increase infection resistance sufficiently. On the contrary, neutrophils adherent to biomaterials express a deficiency in their ability to kill and phagocytose bacteria. It has been proposed that Fc receptor ligation by immobilized IgG on the graft surface may account for this deficiency.[6]

Neutrophils adhere to the ECs in the perianastomotic region through adhesion molecule–mediated mechanisms.[15] When stimulated by agonists such as interleukin (IL)-1, tumor necrosis factor (TNF), lipopolysaccharide, and thrombin, ECs upregulate intercellular adhesion molecule-1 and vascular cell adhesion molecule-1, both of which are the ligands of the integrins on the neutrophil surface.[16,17]

Circulating monocytes also are attracted to areas of injured or regenerating endothelium, especially in areas preactivated by IL-1 and TNF. In the presence of plasma-activating factors, monocytes differentiate into macrophages and become the major participant in the body's chronic inflammatory response. The activated macrophages form multinucleated foreign-body giant cells, which are found chronically lining the synthetic polymers in a process known as "frustrated phagocytosis." Macrophages and activated neutrophils release proteases and oxygen free radicals, which can result in matrix degradation and may inhibit complete endothelialization and tissue incorporation of the vascular graft.

A variety of cytokines are released from inflammatory cells activated by biomaterials. Cultured monocytes and macrophages incubated with Dacron and ePTFE have been shown to produce different amounts of IL-1β, IL-6, and TNF-α, with higher amounts produced with Dacron than with ePTFE.[18] Macrophages grown in the presence of polyglactin 910, a bioresorbable material readily phagocytized by macrophages, synthesize fibroblast growth factor (FGF)-2 capable of stimulating the proliferation of quiescent ECs, SMCs, and fibroblasts.[19,20] Leukocyte-biomaterial interactions induce production of TNF-α, which enhances SMC proliferation.[21] Because the inflammatory reaction elicits a cascade of growth responses, it has been proposed that approaches attenuating the initial inflammatory reaction may improve the long-term patency of grafts.

Endothelial and Smooth Muscle Cell Ingrowth

Native uninjured blood vessels possess an endothelial lining that constantly secretes bioactive substances, which inhibit thrombosis, promote fibrinolysis, and inhibit SMC proliferation to help maintain normal blood flow. After graft implantation, tissue ingrowth originates primarily from the cut edge of the adjacent artery. A complete endothelialization of synthetic grafts can be observed in most animal models. Currently available grafts implanted into humans manifest only limited EC ingrowth, however, not extending beyond 1 to 2 cm of both anastomoses.

In addition to perianastomotic areas, endothelial islands also have been described in the midportions of grafts at significant distances from the anastomosis, suggesting that other EC sources for graft endothelialization may exist. Interstitial tissue ingrowth accompanied by microvessels from the perigraft tissue provides another EC source for graft flow surface endothelialization on experimental high-porosity ePTFE and on bioresorbable prostheses.[22-25] Evidence supports the notion that bone marrow–derived endothelial progenitor cells also may play a part in graft endothelialization. These progenitor cells are released into circulation in response to certain stimuli, such as ischemia and vascular trauma.[26-28] It has been shown that circulating endothelial progenitor cells participate in endothelialization of vascular grafts and injured arteries,[29-32] and in endothelial repair in the neovasculature in experimental sponge-induced granulation tissue, in wound healing, in tumors, and in ischemic hindlimbs and myocardium.[33-36] In a canine bone marrow transplant model, donor origin ECs were found on silicone rubber–coated, impervious Dacron grafts by polymerase chain reaction analysis.[29,30] Bone marrow–derived $CD34^+$ cell seeding significantly increased endothelialization of impervious Dacron grafts in canine thoracic aortas compared with the controls (92% ± 3.4% versus 26.6% ± 7.6% by 4 weeks).[37] Mobilization of bone marrow progenitor cells by granulocyte colony-stimulating factor administration also significantly enhanced endothelialization of impervious Dacron grafts in this canine model.[38]

The ECs growing onto prosthetic graft surfaces undergo phenotypic modulation. These phenotypically altered "activated" cells may secrete bioactive substances, which promote thrombogenesis and SMC growth. Activated ECs increase their PDGF synthesis and secretion, and subintimal SMC proliferation occurs predominantly in the areas with an endothelial lining (i.e., the perianastomotic region), suggesting a link between EC turnover and intimal thickening.[39] The perianastomotic region is highly complex with chronic EC injury and complex biomechanical characteristics and chronic inflammation.

SMC proliferation begins 2 days after graft implantation, then peaks by 2 weeks and subsides thereafter, although SMC turnover persists chronically at levels above those of native arteries. The SMCs within the neointima of prosthetic grafts also are functionally altered. They produce significantly higher amounts of PDGF than the SMCs of the adjacent vessel, which may contribute to the development of myointimal hyperplasia.[40] In addition to SMCs, inflammatory mononuclear phagocytes and foreign-body giant cells produce a variety of growth-modulating substances, including PDGF, FGF, and TGF-β, which perpetuate SMC proliferation and production of extracellular matrix (ECM) components. Continuous ECM synthesis increases pseudointimal volume, ultimately resulting in a stenotic lesion.[41]

The terms *myointimal, neointimal,* and *pseudointimal hyperplasia* often are used interchangeably. *Neointimal* should be reserved, however, for areas that include all normal intimal constituents, including ECs, whereas *pseudointimal* is more appropriate for the relatively acellular tissue within clinically implanted vascular grafts. *Myointimal* can be used more generically to include both types.

■ GRAFT PROPERTIES AND THEIR IMPACT ON GRAFT PERFORMANCE

General agreement exists about the desirable characteristics of a vessel substitute. A primary prerequisite is biocompatibility. The material must be free of significant toxic, allergic, and carcinogenic side effects. The second important criterion is durability. The graft should be physically stable, free from significant dilatation, aneurysm formation, rupture, or excessive elongation that could promote tortuosity and kinking. The graft should be capable of being adequately sterilized and stored as an "off-the-shelf" product and ideally should be resistant to infection. Good suturability and handling properties also are expected. The graft should be easy to penetrate with suture needles without undue resistance and should be able to retain suture adequately without tearing. It should be sufficiently pliable that it can be bent without significant kinking, a quality that is especially important in long grafts across joints or grafts that must follow curved or irregular pathways. A vascular graft needs to be impervious to blood leakage through the graft wall and ideally have minimal needle hole bleeding. The intrinsic characteristics of a vascular graft, including its surface and bulk chemical composition, construction parameters, and biomechanics, influence its interactions with the host and determine its fate.

Porosity

The important relationship between the porosity of the prosthetic graft and its performance has long been recognized.[4] The porosity of a textile graft, such as Dacron, is defined by its water permeability, whereas average internodal distance commonly is used to describe the "porosity" of ePTFE grafts. The rate of tissue ingrowth depends on graft porosity (over limited ranges, which differ in various graft types). Enhanced transinterstitial tissue ingrowth, greater EC coverage, and higher patency rate were reported with the 60-μ or 90-μ internodal distance ePTFE grafts compared with the more commonly used 30-μ internodal distance ePTFE grafts in animal models.[42,43] Human trials using the 90-μ internodal distance ePTFE have failed to show any advantage, however, over the standard 30-μ internodal distance ePTFE grafts.[44]

Compliance

Compliance is defined as the diameter change of a vessel between diastolic and systolic pressures. The compliance mismatch between arteries and grafts causes flow disruption, which has been thought to influence anastomotic neointimal hyperplasia.[45] Dacron and ePTFE grafts are relatively noncompliant. There have been attempts to design more compliant grafts, including the use of more flexible materials or by changing construction parameters. Grafts made of elastomeric polyurethane reportedly possess better compliance than ePTFE.[46] Polyurethane grafts are discussed later. Placement of venous tissue at the distal anastomosis between prosthetic graft and native artery has been shown in some reports to increase the long-term patency rates of the graft.[47-52] Improvement of the compliance mismatch at the distal anastomosis is thought to be one of the mechanisms responsible for the possible beneficial effect of this type of procedure.[53]

The extent to which the initial compliance may affect the long-term function of the graft is controversial.[54] There is a great variability in the arterial tree in that the distal small-caliber arteries are often less compliant than the larger, more central arteries. Diseases such as atherosclerosis with progressive wall thickening and calcification influence the compliance further. Additionally, it has long been realized that fibrous tissue formation within and surrounding an implanted graft would compromise graft compliance. In a follow-up study of eight patients with iliofemoral artery woven Dacron grafts, the graft average diameter variation during the cardiac cycle was 6% 1 month after implantation and decreased to 1% after 1 year.[55] The mechanical behavior of vascular grafts in vivo is governed not only by the properties of the implanted graft, but also by the nature and the amount of tissue incorporation.

Flow Surface Characteristics

The interfacial reactions between blood and the graft surface depend on the surface chemical and physical properties, such as surface charge, surface energy, and degree of roughness. A negative surface charge attenuates platelet adhesion, and a positive charge promotes it. Heterogeneity of charge density distribution also is thought to be thrombogenic. A myriad of approaches have been used to stabilize or passivate the thrombotic reaction, including modification of surface properties, incorporation of antiplatelet or anticoagulant substances onto the graft, and endothelialization of the blood-contacting surface.

■ GRAFT FAILURE AND GRAFT INFECTION

Graft Failure

Problems related to prosthetic graft failure include infection, material deterioration, anastomotic aneurysm, and occlusion. A variety of mechanisms can lead to vascular graft occlusion. Immediate graft failure is usually the result of technical problems during surgery or is due to the hypercoagulable status of the patient. Failure in the first month after graft placement is most commonly the result of thrombosis in the face of high distal resistance. Anastomotic myointimal hyperplasia is the most common reason for graft failure 6 months to 3 years after graft insertion. Late graft occlusions frequently are secondary to the progression of distal atherosclerotic disease.

Aortic reconstruction involves the placement of large-caliber Dacron or ePTFE grafts. Because of the relatively high flow rates and low outflow resistance, these grafts have an 85% to 95% 5-year patency rate.[56,57] When prosthetic grafts are used in the infrainguinal position and especially the infrapopliteal position, the results are much worse. The 1- and 3-year patency rates for ePTFE grafts used in infrainguinal bypasses to the below-knee arteries are 20% to 58% and 18% to 41%.[58-61] These small-caliber grafts are especially susceptible to anastomotic myointimal hyperplasia and are more prone to early thrombosis because of lower flow rates and higher resistance outflow vessels.

Graft Infection

Prosthetic graft infection is discussed in Chapter 59. This section focuses on the role of antibiotic bonding to prosthetic grafts. Vascular graft infection occurs in only 1% to 6% of implanted grafts,[62,63] but the consequences are often catastrophic, resulting in a 50% amputation rate and a 25% to 75% mortality rate.[64] Many attempts have been made to affix antibiotics into graft materials in the hope of increasing graft resistance to bacterial infection.[65-67] Antibiotic-bonded grafts have been used clinically for in-situ replacement in selected patients with graft infections. Some authors suggest prophylactic use of the antibiotic-bonded grafts in patients with high risk of graft infection.[68] The importance of antibiotic bonding in the prevention of graft infection is uncertain, however. Animal experiments showed that rifampicin-bonded, gelatin-sealed Dacron grafts (Sulzer Vascutek, Inchinnan, Renfrewshire, UK) increased protection against bacterial colonization and reduced the rate of reinfection when used for in-situ replacement of infected grafts.[69-71] Yet clinical studies on more than 3000 patients have failed to prove that rifampicin bonding reduces the incidence of vascular graft infection.[71-74] An Italian study of 600 patients with aortofemoral grafts reported 2-year infection rates of 1.7% with rifampicin-bonded grafts compared with 2.3% with control grafts.[72,73] A large European study examined 2522 patients having aortofemoral or femorofemoral bypass and found that rifampicin-bonded grafts had 2-year infection rates of 2% (12 of 600) versus 2.3% (7 of 304) for the control grafts.[72] A randomized multicenter study from the United Kingdom reported a 2-year infection rate for extra-anatomic bypasses of 4.5% with no difference between the rifampicin-bonded grafts and control grafts.[74] No statistical significance was achieved in any of the three trials.

■ PROSTHETIC GRAFTS

As mentioned earlier, the two standard polymers used for vascular grafts in clinical practice are Dacron and ePTFE. Both of these polymer molecules are highly crystalline and hydrophobic; these two properties protect the polymers from hydrolysis. The hydrophobicity of the polymer has important implications in predicting surface interactions with blood and tissue.

Dacron

Polyethylene terephthalate was first introduced in 1939. DuPont developed the material further and patented its widely known Dacron fiber in 1950.[75] Vascular grafts made from Dacron were first implanted by Julian in 1957 and DeBakey in 1958.[76]

Clinically available Dacron grafts are fabricated in either woven or knitted forms. In woven grafts, the multifilament Dacron threads are fabricated in an over-and-under pattern in lengthwise (warp) and circumferential (weft) directions (Fig. 49-1). This structure results in limited porosity and the best dimensional stability of the finished grafts. Woven grafts have less bleeding through interstices and less likelihood of structural deformation after implantation. The disadvantages of such grafts are less desirable handling features, reduced compliance, a tendency to fray at cut edges, and reduced tissue incorporation.

Knitted grafts employ a textile technique in which the Dacron threads are looped to form a continuous interlocking chain (Fig. 49-2). Most knitted grafts currently are manufactured with the threads predominantly oriented in a longitudinal direction (warp knitting) as opposed to a circumferential direction (weft knitting), which has been proved to be structurally unstable. Warp knits have good handling characteristics and reasonable dimensional stability. The loop structure creates greater porosity and radial distensibility. Köper knitting is a modified warp knitting patented by Vascutek (Inchinnan Renfrewshire, UK), in which the yarns are arranged perpendicular to one another on the internal graft surface in an attempt to increase the dimensional stability of the knitted graft (Fig. 49-3).

The velour technique that extends the loops of yarn on the surfaces of the fabrics (Fig. 49-4) has been employed in an attempt to increase tissue incorporation. An external velour surface permits more extensive and firmer incorporation of the graft into surrounding tissue, but the function of an internal velour structure is controversial, with suggestions that it may enhance firm anchorage of the fibrin/platelet pseudointima.[77,78]

Crimping technique is used to increase flexibility, distensibility, and kink resistance of textile grafts. It is recognized, however, that much of the initial elasticity is lost with the stretching during implantation and with later tissue incorporation. Crimping also reduces the effective internal diameter of the graft and creates an uneven luminal surface. The latter potentially can interfere with laminar blood flow, which leads to increased thrombogenicity of the graft. After implantation, the pseudointimal fibrin coagulum tends to be thicker in the concavities, effectively rendering the flow surface smooth. Although this consideration may not be crucial in large-diameter grafts, it is important in small-diameter grafts. Prosthetic rings or coils are applied to the external surface of grafts to provide external support to resist kinking and mechanical compression.

FIGURE 49-1 Woven Dacron graft. Scanning electron micrograph of the surface of a woven Dacron graft. (Original magnification, ×50.)

FIGURE 49-2 Knitted Dacron graft. Scanning electron micrograph of the surface of a knitted Dacron graft. (Original magnification, ×50.)

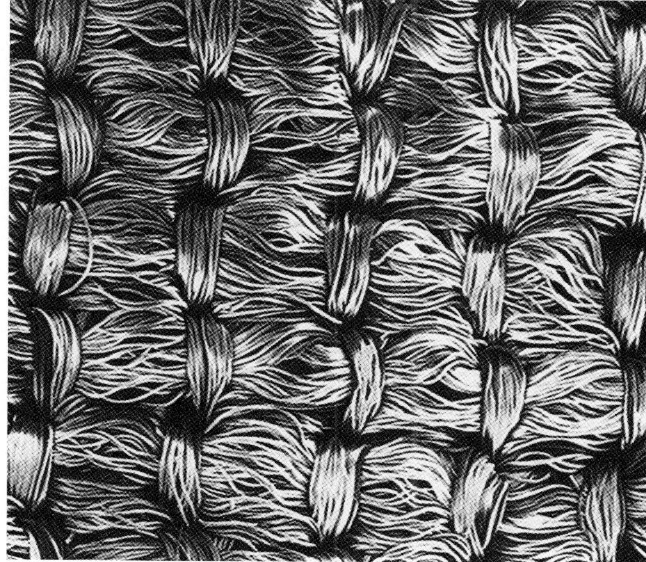

FIGURE 49-3 Köper knitting. Scanning electron micrograph of the surface of a Gelsoft knitted Dacron graft.

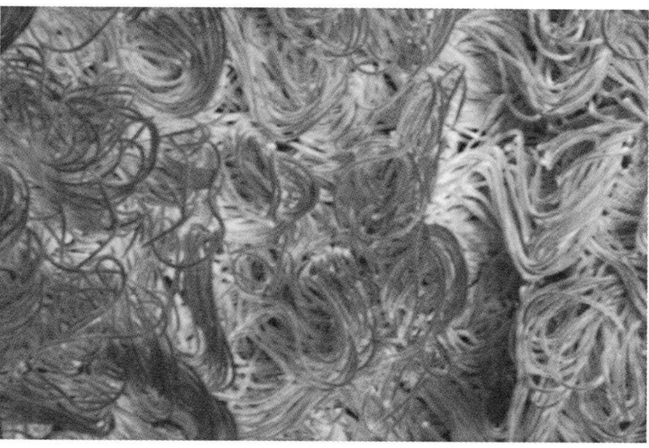

FIGURE 49-4 Scanning electron micrograph of an outer surface of a velour, knitted Dacron graft. (Original magnification, ×50.)

The high porosity of the knitted graft necessitates preclotting to prevent transmural blood extravasation. Gelatin (Vascutek, Inchinnan, Renfrewshire, UK), collagen (Boston Scientific, Oakland, NJ), and albumin (Bard Cardiovascular, Billerica, Mass) are used to seal knitted Dacron graft pores. The gelatin and collagen in the Vascutek and Boston Scientific grafts are cross-linked by low concentrations of formaldehyde, a method resulting in a weak linkage that allows the gelatin or collagen to be degraded in the body in less than 2 weeks.[79,80] Bard uses glutaraldehyde to cross-link albumin; the albumin is absorbed in 2 months.[81]

Dacron grafts, especially knitted grafts, have been shown to be prone to dilate when implanted into the arterial environment. A 10% to 20% increase in graft size on restoration of blood flow is considered to be in the expected range. A follow-up study in 95 patients 2 weeks to 138 months postoperatively (mean 33 months) showed a mean increase of 17.6% (0 to 84%) over initial graft size.[82] A direct relationship between uncomplicated graft dilatation and structural failure has not been established. Consequently, no consensus recommendation has been made on a specific degree of dilatation that constitutes a significant hazard and warrants graft replacement.

Structural failure has been reported sporadically in the literature despite advances in the design and manufacturing of grafts. In 1997, an inquiry to the U.S. Food and Drug Administration (FDA) by Wilson and associates[83] revealed 68 cases of Dacron graft failure due to structural defect with an average time to failure of 7.4 years (range 4 to 18 years). Wilson and associates[83] pointed out that the true incidence of structural failure is difficult to estimate because most patients with grafts are not followed for long periods or not evaluated periodically for graft integrity, and because cases may not be reported to avoid litigation. Many factors may contribute to the graft degradation, including the design of the textile structure, the manufacturing process, surgical handling or application of clamps during implantation, mechanical fatiguing due to cyclic stresses of pulsatile blood flow, and chemical and physical alterations associated with biodegradation. The first generation of double-velour knitted Dacron grafts introduced in the mid-1970s, such as the Microvel and Cooley Double Velour grafts (Boston Scientific Meadox, Oakland, NJ), showed excessive dilatation and rupture after implantation.[83,84] Structural failure of these grafts was believed to be related to the fabrication techniques, such as the use of trilobal filaments, insufficient strength of guideline yarns, and the weakness of connecting lines where two knitted bands joined together to form a tube.[82,85] In the 1980s, the trilobal filaments were replaced with more durable cylindrical filaments.

After implantation, a coagulum containing fibrin, platelets, and blood cells builds up during the first few hours to days and stabilizes over 6 to 18 months forming a compacted layer. The histologic characteristics observed within Dacron grafts are a compact fibrin layer on the blood-contacting surface and densely packed foreign-body giant cells between the outer layer of the graft wall and the surrounding connective tissue capsule. The fibrin layer within the mid-graft remains acellular regardless of whether the grafts are woven or knitted. Protein impregnation changes the surface properties of Dacron grafts and may induce more inflammatory reaction, but does not change the clinical patency rates of these grafts.[79,86,87]

ePTFE

PTFE was patented by DuPont in 1937 as Teflon. The expanded polymer is manufactured by heating, stretching, and extruding processes, which produce a microporous structure more supportive of firm tissue adhesion.

The PTFE molecule is biostable, and the graft made from it does not undergo biologic deterioration within the body. The surface of the graft is electronegative, which minimizes its reaction with blood components. ePTFE grafts are manufactured by stretching a melt-extruded solid polymer tube, which then cracks into a nontextile porous tube. The characteristic structure of ePTFE is a node-fibril structure in which solid nodes connect through fine fibrils with an average internodal distance of 30 μ for standard graft (Fig. 49-5).

The initial host response to ePTFE grafts is similar to the response to Dacron grafts.[77,78] A fibrin coagulum or amorphous platelet-rich material develops over a time sequence similar in both materials. Lack of luminal surface cellular coverage is found at the mid-graft region indefinitely after human implants.[88-90] In outer wrap–reinforced grafts, the wrap diminishes the infiltration of the cells from perigraft tissue.[78] The densely fabricated wrap is manufactured on the outer surface of some of the Gore-tex grafts as reinforcement to the graft wall. This wrap added important mechanical stability to the ePTFE grafts produced in the 1970s, but its importance today with current manufacturing techniques is controversial.

In addition to the standard ePTFE graft, numerous modified grafts have been developed to offer specific properties for various applications. Thin-walled grafts, which have a wall thickness of 0.2 to 0.3 mm (0.4 to 0.6 mm for the standard graft), possess better handling characteristics and compliance but with no improvement in patency rates over standard grafts.[91] Extended stretch ePTFE grafts have longitudinal extensibility that is achieved by a "micro-crimping" of the fibrils. When the stretch graft is extended, the fibrils are extended to their full length, and the microstructure of the graft is identical to that of the standard

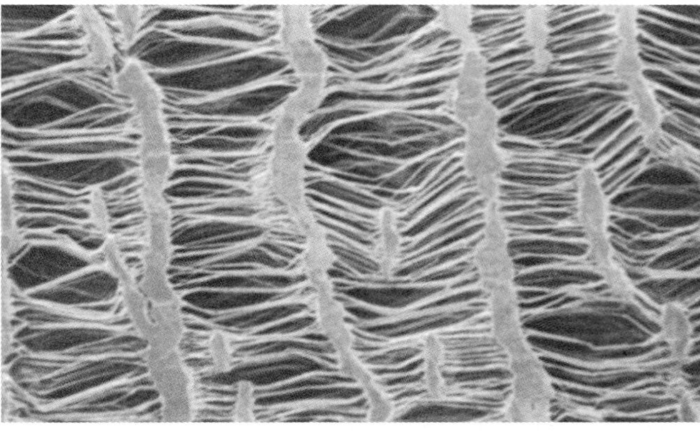

FIGURE 49-5 Expanded polytetrafluoroethylene (ePTFE) graft. Scanning electron micrograph of the surface of an ePTFE graft. (Original magnification, ×1000.)

ePTFE graft. Stretch ePTFE grafts displayed better patency rates when used for arteriovenous access. No data support such an advantage when used for peripheral reconstructions. Rings or coils are applied to the abluminal surface of the graft to provide external support to increase the graft resistance to external compression and to reduce kinking.

Attempts also have been made to increase transmural tissue ingrowth by increasing graft porosity as mentioned earlier. An ePTFE graft with an average internodal distance of 60 μm on the abluminal surface tapering down to 20 μm on the luminal surface is currently on the market (Atrium Medical Corporation, Hudson, NH) (Fig. 49-6). Only limited data are available presently. No difference has been found in the 3-year patency rates of above-knee femoropopliteal bypasses and the 18-month patency rates of arteriovenous access grafts with this type of graft compared with the conventional 30-μm internodal distance ePTFE grafts, according to data in the brochure published by the company. Another modification has focused on the luminal surface of the graft. Carbon coating (Carboflo; Bard Peripheral Vascular, Tempe, Ariz) is used to increase the surface electronegativity so as to diminish thrombus formation. Early studies showed decreased platelet deposition on carbon-coated grafts, but the overall patency rates were not improved compared with uncoated grafts.[92,93] A prospective multicenter clinical study, consisting of 81 carbon-impregnated ePTFE grafts and 79 standard ePTFE grafts for below-knee popliteal and distal bypasses, showed no difference in patency rates between the two groups 2 years after implantation.[94] A report of a multicenter trial in Europe involving 128 carbon-coated ePTFE grafts and 126 standard ePTFE grafts for infrainguinal bypasses showed significantly greater 1- and 2-year patency rates of the carbon-coated grafts versus the standard grafts by life-table analysis.[95]

Applying the concept of the vein cuff, a precuffed graft has been developed to improve the hemodynamics at the distal anastomosis.[96] The ePTFE in the "cuff" is thinner, which results in improved handling, allowing successful completion of the distal anastomoses in an often hostile anatomic environment. The graft has been tested for hemodialysis angioaccess[97] and infrapopliteal applications.[98,99] The 2-year patency rates for angioaccess were significantly higher with the precuffed graft versus the stretch ePTFE graft.[97] In a nonrandomized study by Fisher and colleagues[98] from the United Kingdom, 50 precuffed grafts (Distaflo; Bard Peripheral Vascular, Tempe, Ariz) were inserted into 46 patients with critical limb ischemia. The patency, limb salvage, and survival rates were similar to historical control groups of Miller vein cuff bypass grafts. A North American prospective randomized multicenter trial comparing the Distaflo with a standard ePTFE graft with vein modification at the distal anastomosis is currently under way. The mid-term results, with a mean follow-up of 12.7 months, showed primary patency rates of 54.35% (25 of 46) for the Distaflo graft compared with 55.81% (24 of 43) for the vein cuff ePTFE graft.[99] If the long-term data confirm the early results, the precuffed graft may offer an alternative in prosthetic femorodistal arterial reconstruction. The application of anticoagulant agents to the graft also has been explored (discussed later).

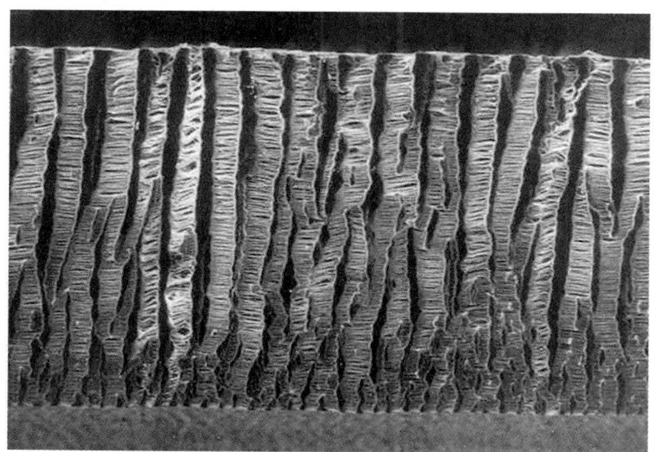

FIGURE 49-6 Cross section of Advanta expanded polytetrafluoroethylene graft. (Courtesy of Atrium Medical Corporation, Hudson, NH.)

Polyurethane

The superior elastic and compliant properties along with acceptable biocompatibility of polyurethane make it an appealing material for vascular grafts. Developing polyurethane-based, small-diameter vascular grafts has attracted great interest from industry.

The unique mechanical properties of polyurethane derive from the molecular structure of the polymer. Segmented polyurethanes are copolymers comprising three different monomers—a hard domain derived from a diisocyanate, a chain extender, and a soft domain most commonly polyol. The soft domain is mainly responsible for flexibility, whereas the hard domain imparts strength. The selection of the three monomers can produce materials with different mechanical characteristics, which makes polyurethane an attractive biomaterial. Lycra is a trade name of segmented polyether polyurethane, which was commercialized in 1962 by DuPont.

As a biomaterial, polyurethane was first used in manufacturing implantable roller pumps and left ventricular assist devices and as a coating for early artificial hearts.[100] The first generation of polyurethane vascular grafts was developed using polyester polyurethanes, such as the Vascugraft by B. Braun Melsungen AG (Melsungen, Germany). Although initial reports showed good biocompatibility,[101] the graft underwent surface chemical modification and deterioration in vivo.[102,103] A clinical trial using Vascugraft for below-knee bypass was aborted after 8 of 15 grafts had occluded in the first year.[103] It has been reported that polyurethanes with polyester polyols as soft segments are hydrolytically unstable.[104]

Next, polyether-based polyurethanes were employed, such as the Pulse-Tec (Newtec Vascular Products, North Wales, UK) vascular access graft. Polyetherurethane was relatively insensitive to hydrolysis but susceptible to oxidative degradation.[104] The Pulse-Tec graft underwent in vivo biodegradation and died in the product pipeline. Vectra (Thoratec Laboratories Corporation, Pleasanton, Calif) is another vascular access graft made with polyetherurethaneurea. The graft is manufactured with an average pore size of 15 μm and a nonporous layer under the luminal surface, which makes it impervious to liquids.[105] In a multicenter trial involving 142 patients receiving either Vectra or ePTFE vascular access grafts with a follow-up time of 12 months, no difference was found in terms of the patency rate or complications between the two grafts, but the Vectra grafts allowed earlier access.[106] The polyurethane graft elongated over time after implantation, however, and the incidence of pseudointimal thickening near the anastomosis was higher compared with ePTFE grafts.[106,107] The Vectra graft received FDA clearance in 2000. A small-diameter coronary bypass graft by the company using the same material is currently undergoing clinical trial.

The graft made of poly(carbonate-urea)urethane (Chronoflex; CardioTech International, Woburn, Mass) is expected to have better stability because the polymer has no ether/ester linkages and is hydrolytically and oxidatively stable and more resistant to biodegradation.[108] Good stability of the graft was indicated in in-vitro and in animal studies.[109-112] The graft currently is undergoing a clinical trial. Carboxylated polyurethane treatment of the graft can create a surface with reactive carboxylic acid groups to which hirudin has been covalently bound.[113] Antithrombin activity of immobilized hirudin may be expected to improve the graft performance.

Tissue reactions to polyurethane grafts are discrepant in the literature because factors such as different compositions of polymers, graft fabrication, porosity, and surface modifications all affect the results.[113-115] No conclusion can be made at this point as to whether polyurethane grafts may be functionally superior to ePTFE or Dacron grafts until more data become available.

One major concern regarding polyurethane grafts is the potential carcinogenic effect by its degradation products. In 1991, the FDA terminated the use of polyurethane foam as a surface coating material for breast implants after it had been marketed for more than 20 years. A statement issued by the FDA suggested that the implanted foam might degrade to form 2,4-toluene diamine, which has been shown to cause liver cancer in laboratory animals.[75]

Anticoagulant Affixation

As discussed earlier, early prosthetic graft failure often occurs as a consequence of thrombosis. One strategy for reducing the thrombogenicity of prosthetic materials is to apply heparin to the graft surface. A heparin-bonded Dacron graft by InterVascular (La Ciotat, France) is currently available on the market. The heparin is bound primarily through Van der Waals bonds to the polyester fiber pretreated with a cationic agent, tri-dodecil-methyl-ammonium chloride. The external third of the graft wall is coated with collagen to prevent blood extravasation.[116] In a comparative clinical trial involving 209 patients undergoing femoropopliteal bypass grafts, the heparin-bonded Dacron graft exhibited a slightly better patency at 1, 2, and 3 years of 70%, 63%, and 55% compared with untreated ePTFE graft of 56%, 46%, and 42% ($P = .044$).[117]

A heparin-bonded ePTFE graft developed by W.L. Gore is currently available in Europe. Heparin binding is through covalent endpoint attachment of the heparin to the pretreated bioactive surface of the graft. An animal study showed improved patency of the graft compared with the standard ePTFE graft in a canine carotid interposition model lasting 6 months.[118] The surface heparin activity measured by antithrombin III uptake per unit area was 24.7 ± 7.9 pmol/cm^2 at 2 weeks and remained at 15.3 ± 3.7 pmol/cm^2 by 12 weeks after implantation. No clinical data are available at this time.

Whether the anticoagulation works through continuous release of heparin from the material establishing an effective concentration at the interface between blood and the graft surface or through nonconsumptive mechanisms of active function of the heparin immobilized on the material surface is unclear. A major concern with heparinization of the graft surface is the duration of heparin function. Premature release or disturbance of functional heparin or the presence of a physical barrier due to adherent blood components implies a theoretical inefficacy of the approach. Another theoretical concern is heparin-induced adverse effects, including thrombocytopenia. Approximately 30,000 InterGard heparin-bonded grafts have been implanted in Europe over 10 years, and no adverse effects have been reported due to the implantation of heparin grafts. Caution should be observed, however, and heparin grafts should not be used in patients with known heparin sensitivity.

■ GRAFT SELECTION

Aortic Reconstruction

A variety of prosthetic grafts function adequately in the large-diameter, high-flow positions. For procedures on the thoracic aorta and for extensive thoracoabdominal aortic reconstructions, tightly woven Dacron grafts are an appropriate choice. Their long-term patency and dimensional stability have been satisfactory.

For elective infrarenal aortoiliac replacement or bypass, woven and knitted Dacron grafts have well-documented excellent long-term results.[119] Many surgeons prefer knitted grafts owing to their better handling and healing characteristics. Such features are thought to be particularly important for aortofemoral grafts done for occlusive disease that must cross the inguinal ligament, often with anastomoses made to a diseased femoral artery or profunda femoris branch alone.[120] Although Dacron grafts have long been a conventional choice, a randomized multicenter trial comparing stretch ePTFE versus knitted Dacron (collagen or gelatin coated) grafts showed no difference in 5-year patency rates among all three grafts when used for aortic bifurcation reconstructions.[121]

In general, all currently available prosthetic grafts perform well for aortic reconstructions. Issues of cost, convenience, and diminished late complications are probably the discriminating factors for graft selection.

Infrainguinal Reconstruction

It is well established that autogenous saphenous vein is the preferred choice for infrainguinal bypass, with primary patency rates of 70% at 5 years in selected populations.[58,122,123] Nevertheless, controversy exists regarding whether prosthetic grafts should be the graft of choice initially when bypass to the above-knee popliteal level is feasible. Many well-designed clinical trials showed that there were usually no significant differences in patency or limb salvage rates between vein and prosthetic grafts within 2 years; however, the 4- to 5-year patency with vein grafts was higher than with ePTFE grafts (61% to 76% versus 38% to 68%).[58-61]

The rationale for the preferential use of prosthetic grafts is that the compromised long-term survival of many of these patients may reduce the importance of long-term graft patency. It is reasoned that even if patency rates with prosthetic conduits are slightly lower, the saphenous vein still would be available for use in a second operation if this were required.[124] The patency rates of reoperations are much higher with autogenous veins than prosthetic grafts.[125-128] The advantages of initial use of prosthetic grafts are the shorter operative time and the need for less dissection, which may be advantageous in the high-risk patient population. No study has confirmed the supposed reduction in mortality and morbidity rates with prosthetic grafts. Many studies have shown that prosthetic graft failure was associated with a significantly higher incidence of limb-threatening ischemia,[129] and more second operations were required with the initial use of prosthetic grafts.[61,130] The morbidity rate and the risks of associated complications such as graft infection, which are clearly higher with second operations, also must be considered.[130]

Most surgeons currently agree that, when it is available, saphenous vein should be the first choice, especially for limb-salvage situations. Prosthetic grafts may be used preferentially in selected patients, particularly older patients undergoing operation for noncritical ischemia with fairly good runoff.

For infrapopliteal bypasses, every effort should be made to use autogenous vein because the long-term function of prosthetic grafts in this position is far less than satisfactory. The patency rates for ePTFE grafts are 20% to 58% at 1 year and 18% to 41% at 3 years.[58,131-134] Adjunctive techniques are often employed to improve the results of below-knee bypass grafts, such as the interposition of a venous cuff, patch, or boot at the anastomoses of the prosthetic conduits to the distal arterials[48-52]; the creation of prosthetic-vein composite grafts[135]; and the addition of a remote distal arteriovenous fistula.[136]

The interposition of venous tissue at the distal anastomosis between the artery and prosthetic graft has appealing theoretical advantages deriving from biologic and mechanical factors. Animal experiments have shown a decreased neointimal thickness by the presence of vein at the perianastomotic area.[53,137,138] Venous endothelium also may confer a beneficial effect through fibrinolytic and antiplatelet activity, although these effects remain unproved. Mechanically, vein interposed between a stiff prosthetic graft and a more pliable artery would buffer the compliance mismatch. It also is possible that venous tissue simply enlarges the distal anastomosis so that the formation of hyperplasia must encroach on a wider lumen before becoming clinically significant.

A variety of prosthetic grafts are currently available for lower extremity revascularization procedures, including standard and modified (thin wall, stretch, 60/20 thru-pore, carbon-coated, heparin-bond) ePTFE grafts and biologically coated knitted Dacron grafts. ePTFE grafts are more widely used mainly because of their better handling properties. Prospective comparisons between Dacron and ePTFE grafts in the above-knee femoral popliteal position confirm virtually identical results.[139] Despite all the efforts from the manufacturers, there has been no significant improvement in the long-term performance of the new products over the standard ePTFE graft.[94,140-142] Solutions for small-diameter vascular reconstructions prove to be a continuous challenge.

Extra-anatomic Grafts

Extra-anatomic reconstructions, such as axillofemoral, femorofemoral, or axilloaxillary bypasses, often involve remote, subcutaneously implanted grafts. Graft compression or kinking is a major concern, and using externally supported grafts is a common practice.

ePTFE and Dacron grafts have been shown to have equivalently good long-term patency.[143-146] The externally supported ePTFE grafts for axillobifemoral bypass have a 5-year primary patency of 71%,[143] and the externally supported, knitted Dacron grafts used for axillofemoral bypass have a primary patency rate of 78% at 5 years and 73% at 7 years.[144] Many reports have documented better patency of axillobifemoral grafts compared with axillo-unifemoral grafts, likely a result of the reduced outflow resistances provided by the second limb. The 5-year primary patency of femorofemoral crossover grafts in patients with disabling claudication is 72% with no difference between Dacron and ePTFE grafts.[145] For carotid-subclavian grafts, some authors have documented higher long-term patency rates with ePTFE or Dacron grafts than with vein grafts.[147-149]

Venous Reconstruction

Ring-reinforced ePTFE grafts commonly are used for large-caliber venous replacements in unusual circumstances, such as the replacement or bypass of the inferior or superior vena cava[150,151] or iliofemoral,[153] jugular,[154] or portal[155] veins or the construction of portosystemic shunts for portal hypertension.[156,157] The ring reinforcement in theory resists respiratory compression better and prevents graft collapse that may be a factor in promotion of thrombosis. No comparative study with nonringed grafts has been done, however, and a study is not feasible given the small numbers of patients in even the largest reports with these procedures.

Hemodialysis Vascular Access

Typically, long-term access to the vascular system is provided by an arteriovenous fistula or a bridge graft. The prosthetic bridge graft accounts for approximately half of all permanent grafts placed in patients with end-stage renal disease in the United States.[158] Only 26% of them remain patent without complication 2 years after placement.[159] The secondary 3-year patency can reach 42% to 60%.[160-162] The failure of prosthetic angioaccess grafts often is associated with stenosis at the venous anastomosis, which leads to subsequent thrombosis.

ePTFE grafts are usually the prosthetic choice for angioaccess when a primary arteriovenous fistula cannot be performed or has failed. Dacron grafts used for hemodialysis often have patency, bleeding, and wall integrity difficulties. Various modified grafts have been studied for many years in an attempt to improve the prosthetic performance for this application, including changing the wall structure, adding luminal or extramural coatings, and incorporating impervious layers.

Tordoir and colleagues[163] showed that stretched ePTFE is superior to the standard, nonstretched configurations. These investigators hypothesized that this advantage was caused by less intimal hyperplasia from poor compliance match problems. Thin-wall ePTFE grafts also commonly are used because of their better handling and flexibility, but no advantages have been proved by clinical data.[164] The tapered ePTFE graft was designed to improve the hemodynamics by changing the geometric configuration. Improved performance was reported in animal and early clinical studies,[165-167] but a more recent randomized multicenter trial showed no difference between tapered and thin-wall stretch ePTFE grafts.[168]

A common limitation for angioaccess grafts is that they require a maturation period after implantation before use. Autogenous arteriovenous fistulae typically require 6 weeks to 6 months before first cannulation, whereas prosthetic grafts are not accessed for 2 to 4 weeks to permit tissue incorporation. The Vectra polyurethane graft reportedly allows early access. It requires a significantly shorter time to reach hemostasis after puncture compared with ePTFE grafts,[106] although long-term graft survival data currently are not available. Technical complications manifested by graft kinking have been noted with this graft by several groups.[107]

Other Locations

Visceral and renal arterial reconstructions may be performed with prosthetic grafts with good results. Many surgeons prefer prosthetic grafts for these procedures. In a series of 489 renal revascularizations, Paty and associates[169] reported a patency of 97% at 7 years with ePTFE grafts. Another study by Cormier and colleagues[170] achieved 85% patency at 5 years. High blood flow, short graft length, and not being subjected to mechanical stresses around body joints are thought to account for their good patency. Autogenous veins usually are recommended for distal renal artery grafting in young adult patients with fibromuscular disease or visceral or renal procedures that involve bypass to diseased vessels with compromised distal arterial beds.

■ FUTURE DIRECTIONS

Endothelial Cell Seeding

It is well recognized that ECs perform a variety of important physiologic functions, among them being the provision of thromboresistance, with anticoagulant and fibrinolytic activities. The presence of endothelium can prevent platelet deposition and theoretically prevent the development of pseudointimal hyperplasia by reducing platelets; by releasing bioactive factors responsible for SMC migration, proliferation, and ECM synthesis; by reducing intramural inflammatory cell infiltration; and by assuming a quiescent phenotype in which ECs may release SMC growth inhibitors.

In 1978, Herring and coworkers[171] first reported that EC seeding onto a graft surface enhanced graft survival. Since then, this subject has been intensively investigated. Considerable progress has been achieved, especially related to technical problems. Initial difficulties in cell harvest, cell seeding and adhesion, and prevention of desquamation all have been largely overcome.[172,173] The ideal seeded grafts should have a confluent EC lining with their desired physiologic functions intact at the time of implantation, and the cells should be able to resist sheer stress after the restoration of circulation. One of the difficulties is the relatively low cell density initially retained by the graft. The cell density of the EC lining on a normal vein is approximately 10^3 ECs/mm^2.[174] In a completely lined vascular graft, cell density must approach this value. The initial attachment of at least 5×10^3 ECs/mm^2 is required for immediate confluent human EC coverage of a small-caliber vascular graft because of cell desquamation after exposure to flow. To maximize immediate cell inoculation density, a two-stage seeding procedure is often performed in which ECs are harvested, allowed to proliferate in vitro, and seeded and grown to confluence on the vascular graft before implantation.[173,176,177] The disadvantage of this technique is the potential for infection, the alterations of EC phenotype and function, the requirement of a 3- to 4-week waiting period for cell expansion, and the necessity of two operative procedures. Alternatively, microvascular ECs harvested from omentum have been seeded onto small-diameter grafts with a single-stage technique. The seeded graft showed confluent endothelial linings, larger thrombus-free surface area, and improved patency rates at 1 year in a canine model.[178] High-density microvascular EC application throughout the wall of ePTFE grafts has been referred to as "sodding" and extensively investigated by Williams and colleagues.[179]

ECs adhere poorly to synthetic graft materials. Many adhesive proteins, such as fibronectin, collagen, fibrin, laminin, other peptides with RGD and related sequences, and plasma, have been applied to the graft surface to improve the seeding efficiency. Studies on the kinetics of EC seeding showed that at least 20% of initially adherent cells were lost during the first hour, and 60% were lost within the first 24 hours.[180-182] Prolongation of incubation time on the grafts before exposure to flow has been suggested to induce maturation of the cytoskeleton so as to improve the cell retention on the graft surface.[183-186] Preconditioning the seeded EC monolayer with gradually loaded shear stress promotes reorganization of the EC cytoskeleton and production of ECM, which enhances the EC retention at the time of exposure to flow.[187] The inherent properties of prostheses themselves also affect EC attachment. Dacron and polyurethane permit better cell attachment than ePTFE.[184,188,189] The negative charge on PTFE obstructs the negatively charged ECs from accessing the graft surface. A technique called *electrostatic transplantation* has been developed to reverse the surface charge temporarily, inducing EC attraction to the graft surface and accelerating their morphologic maturation. It can significantly improve cell retention against shear stress.[190] A theoretical advantage of this technique is that when the graft is removed from the device, the luminal surface charge immediately reverts to its natural negative state, theoretically rendering any non-endothelialized areas less thrombogenic. This overcomes the limitation of adhesive protein coating, which may allow exposure of thrombogenic surfaces to flow when ECs do not reach complete confluence or when they desquamate from the surface. Another desirable aspect of this technique is its simplicity, which may further bring EC seeding time to a clinically acceptable range.

Animal studies have suggested EC-seeded Dacron and ePTFE grafts elicit decreased platelet deposition and increased patency rates.[191-195] Nevertheless, the seeded grafts have not been shown reproducibly to reduce anastomotic pseudointimal hyperplasia significantly.[196]

Initial clinical studies using the single-stage EC seeding technique showed mixed results. Herring and colleagues[197] reported an increased 1-year patency rate for femoropopliteal bypasses with EC-seeded ePTFE grafts compared with unseeded grafts in a nonsmoking population. Several later studies failed to show a long-term advantage, however.[198] With a two-stage EC seeding method, significantly improved early patency and decreased late amputation rates were reported in infrapopliteal (femorotibial) reconstruction patients.[199] Zilla and associates[200] also showed increased patency and decreased platelet deposition in EC-seeded ePTFE femoropopliteal bypass grafts followed for 3 years compared with unseeded grafts. The same investigators more recently reported encouraging long-term results in a clinical follow-up, multi-institutional study involving 153 endothelialized ePTFE grafts implanted in the infrainguinal position in 136 patients.[201] In the initial randomized trial, the primary patency rates were 84.7% for the endothelialized grafts and 55.4% for the control ePTFE grafts after 3 years, 73.8% versus 31.3% after 5 years, and 73.8% versus 0% after 7 years. Combining these data with the more recent additional patients who received EC-seeded grafts, the overall 7-year patency was a remarkable 62.8% for endothelialized infrainguinal ePTFE grafts.

A major concern with EC-seeded grafts in humans is the potential for intimal thickening, supported by histopathologic observations from two separate case reports. In one case with bilateral above-knee grafts seeded with cephalic vein ECs, one of the grafts developed stenosis and had to be replaced 41 months after implantation. The central part of this graft was explanted and analyzed histologically. The graft had a confluent endothelial lining on a collagen IV–positive basement membrane with a neointimal thickness of 1.21 ± 0.19 mm.[202] The unusually thick subendothelial layer also has been found in another case in which a microvascular EC-seeded Dacron graft was placed as a mesoatrial bypass and had to be resected because of external mechanical stricture 9 months after implantation.[203] The ultimate function of seeded ECs is unknown. These cells potentially can be activated by the process of manipulation or chronic exposure to an unphysiologic environment. Higher levels of PDGF and basic FGF have been measured in EC-seeded grafts, which is particularly concerning given the potential role of these growth factors in stimulating the migration and proliferation of SMCs and stimulating the development of pseudointimal hyperplasia.[204,205]

Advances in molecular biology have provided the possibility of applying genetically modified ECs with select desired functions to prosthetic grafts. The first application of this technology on vascular grafts was reported by Wilson and colleagues.[206] Dacron grafts seeded with retrovirally transduced ECs containing a *lacZ* marker gene were implanted into canine carotid arteries. Gene expression from modified ECs on the graft surface was identified for a period of 5 weeks. Tissue plasminogen activator has been successfully transfected into ECs.[207] These modified cells transiently expressed this fibrinolytic agent effectively after being seeded onto synthetic graft surfaces.[208] Gene transduction is a developing technology, however, and more prolonged expression may be achievable. The effects of gene transduction and of the vector employed on EC physiologic characteristics and on the host response introduce new variables to EC seeding, which remain to be elucidated. Controversial results have been reported in the literature related to the proliferation, adhesion, and retention of genetically modified ECs on the surface of synthetic grafts.[209-211] Genetically modified ECs have been shown in some reports to display relatively poor retention on graft surfaces in vivo. A significantly lower percent surface endothelialization was detected at 6 weeks on canine thoracoabdominal aortic ePTFE grafts seeded with *lacZ*-transduced ECs compared with grafts seeded with nontransduced control ECs.[203] Poor cell retention with tissue plasminogen activator–transduced ECs was observed when seeded onto Dacron and ePTFE grafts.[213-215] Little has been documented so far concerning the long-term benefit of genetically modified, EC-seeded grafts in vivo. The introduction of genetic engineering offers considerable potential to manipulate the function of seeded cells on graft surfaces, and the additional use of seeded subendothelial SMCs may augment the efficiency of EC seeding further and promote quiescence of that EC monolayer.

Manipulation of In-Vivo Healing Processes

Tissue incorporation is an unavoidable and a desirable process for implanted prostheses. Excessive cell proliferation and ECM deposition result in intimal hyperplasia, leading to vascular graft failure. The ideal healing process of vascular grafts would be rapid endothelialization of blood-contacting surfaces, spatially and temporally limited subendothelial SMC growth, followed by phenotypic and functional differentiation of cell components and controlled remodeling of the ECM. The expansion of knowledge concerning mechanisms responsible for cell migration and proliferation, differentiation, angiogenesis, and ECM deposition and remodeling provides the possibility of manipulating the healing process by optimizing the microenvironments of the graft and perigraft tissue.

Various bioactive substances have been integrated within or onto prosthetic grafts by many delivery methods to modulate the graft healing process. To achieve a controlled healing response, it is important to have a defined delivery system with which to apply bioactive substances to the graft and predictably release them locally with bioactivities preserved for a desired period.

Greisler and associates[216] have investigated fibrin gel delivery of growth factors onto ePTFE grafts. The FGF-1-containing fibrinogen solution is polymerized by thrombin to form a hydrogel that can be impregnated onto prosthetic grafts. Heparin is added to the system to protect the FGF-1 from proteolytic degradation. In-vivo release kinetics have shown a 13% retention of FGF-1 at 1 week and 4% at 1 month after implantation using radioactive iodine (^{125}I)–FGF-1–impregnated ePTFE grafts. The early thrombogenicity of fibrin gel–impregnated graft was assessed with indium 111–labeled platelets. Decreased platelet deposition has been observed in vitro and in vivo compared with untreated ePTFE grafts.[217,218] The fiber orientation and state of polymerization are thought to account for the altered affinity of fibrin to platelet adherence.

ePTFE grafts (60-μm internodal distance) impregnated with fibrin gel/FGF-1/heparin were evaluated in canine aortoiliac and thoracoabdominal aortic models. Compared with fibrin gel (no FGF-1)–treated or untreated ePTFE grafts, the fibrin gel/FGF-1/heparin treatment resulted in a significant early increase in surface EC proliferation and more rapid development of a confluent factor VIII–positive endothelial coverage.[216,219] Extensive transinterstitial capillary ingrowth was observed throughout the graft wall. The treatment also stimulated subendothelial myofibroblast proliferation, however, resulting in a significantly thicker neointima.

Immobilization of FGF-2 and heparin to a microporous polyurethane graft by cross-linked gelatin also has been shown to accelerate tissue regeneration on the graft in a rat aortic grafting model.[220] A consistent "neointima" of approximately 40 μm in thickness with intermittent endothelialization was observed in the mid-portion of treated grafts compared with control grafts which were covered with only a fibrin layer.

In addition to the continuing emphasis on the endothelialization of the flow surface, the function of other cell types in the vascular wall has received more attention. It has been suggested that ECs by themselves cannot produce a stable intima without SMCs or fibroblasts underneath. When applying growth factors to the graft, it is likely that ECs, SMCs, and fibroblasts all will be exposed to the stimuli. The cells respond to the exogenous stimuli and to the signaling peptides produced by other cells through autocrine and paracrine mechanisms. Intimal hyperplasia could be a sequela of such intervention. The key point is fine control of the proliferation and differentiation processes. Incorporation of a delayed-release growth inhibitor aiming at cessation of cell cycling may prove to be beneficial.

Blood Vessel Tissue Engineering

Driven by the desire to develop an ideal vascular substitute, attempts to construct a "neoartery" have been carried out. Vascular cells are seeded into three-dimensional ECM or polymer scaffolds. After implantation, these cells proliferate and produce ECM, while the scaffolds degrade and eventually are replaced by host tissue. The newly formed conduits are viable vessels with the ability to remodel to fit the hemodynamic environment and the ability to maintain many of the normal functions of the cell components, at least for the short period studied so far.

A landmark study was reported in 1986 by Weinberg and Bell.[221] They constructed a three-layered blood vessel model with collagen matrix as a scaffold for ECs, SMCs, and fibroblasts. Similar efforts have been reported by other groups.[222,223] This model failed to yield requisite mechanical strength, however, even when the vessels were reinforced with Dacron meshes. This weakness is presumed to be, at least in part, a result of lack of organization of ECM. Alternatively, L'Heureux and associates[224] cultured human vascular cells in a well-defined environment to produce organized ECM that resembles ECM in natural vessels. SMCs cultured in vitro formed a cellular sheet that was wrapped around a tubular support to produce the "media," and subsequently a similar sheet of fibroblasts was placed around the "media" to provide the "adventitia." After maturation, the tubular support was removed, and ECs were seeded onto the luminal surface. This constructed "vessel" displayed a burst strength greater than 2000 mm Hg. The SMCs expressed circumferential and longitudinal orientations with a differentiation marker, desmin, and showed contractile responses when challenged with vasoactive agonists. Abundant ultrastructurally organized collagen and elastin fibers were present in the ECM. When implanted into canine femoral arteries, intramural blood infiltration was noticed. From a practical standpoint, cell sourcing must be considered. Nonautologous cells present immunologic concerns, whereas autogenous cells require additional surgery to harvest cells and time to use them in constructing the engineered tissue.

Although much more effort is required to conquer technical obstacles, optimize the manufacturing system, and examine the long-term efficacy, the possibility of creating novel viable substitutes for vascular replacement exists. Another approach is to employ a biodegradable polymer scaffold. In a series of reports, Greisler and colleagues[225-233] showed that bioresorbable grafts constructed from lactide/glycolide copolymers, such as polyglycolic acid (PGA), and implanted into animal models induced formation of a neoartery consisting of myofibroblast-laden walls beneath endothelial monolayers at the blood-contacting surface. The cellular recruitment was primarily a transmural cell migration with proliferation induced by growth factors, primarily FGF-2, synthesized by macrophages activated by phagocytosis of the resorbable polymers. The proliferative response paralleled the kinetics of macrophage-mediated prosthetic resorption among a variety of polymers. A Harvard-MIT group constructed a tubular scaffold with woven polyglactin as an outer layer and nonwoven glycolic acid (PGA) as an inner layer.[234] Autologous cells with mixed populations from arterial explants were seeded onto the scaffolds. After 7 days of in-vitro culture, the constructed vessels were implanted into ovine pulmonary arteries. All seven were patent for 12 weeks. The polymer scaffold was replaced by cells and ECM over time. The vessels showed an increase in diameter, however. In a later report, the same investigators designed a more durable PGA/polyhydroxyalkanoate scaffold.[235] The inner layer was made of nonwoven PGA designed to degrade over 6 to 8 weeks, and the outer layer was nonporous, slower degrading polyhydroxyalkanoate. Using this scaffold, the investigators showed that all the tissue-engineered vessels were patent with no aneurysms 150 days after implantation into ovine abdominal aortas. The PGA layers were completely replaced by tissue by 3 to 4 months. Development of endothelium and of a media containing collagen with the presence of elastin fibers was evident.

Organized tissue can be generated only under appropriate mechanical conditions. Culturing SMC-seeded

PGA scaffolds under pulsatile flow for 8 weeks results in organization of SMCs into multilayer structures with orientated collagen fibrils between cells. The vessel structure displayed contractile response to vasoconstrictors, although the magnitude was only 15% to 20% of that of the native artery.[236] The ECM accumulates after exposure to in-vivo hemodynamic environments. Biochemical analysis showed that the content of elastin and proteoglycans peaked at 8 and 16 weeks after implantation after exceeding their native artery levels, then decreased, approaching that of native artery. Nevertheless, collagen content continuously increased to about five times that of the native artery by 24 weeks without decline.[237] ECM deposition is necessary for the establishment of graft strength, but excessive matrix formation indicates unfavorable tissue remodeling. Much still needs to be learned to control this balance.

The PGA polymer does not possess cell-anchoring sites. Surface modifications have been investigated to facilitate cell attachment or spatial cell distribution or both. Treatment with 1N sodium hydroxide transforms ester groups on the surface of PGA fibers to carboxylic acid and hydroxyl groups. The resultant hydrolyzed surface increased its adsorption of serum proteins and doubled seeded SMC attachment density.[238] Incorporation of the RGD sequence to the polymer surface can direct receptor-mediated cell adhesion.[239] Patel and colleagues[240] synthesized a biotinylated polylactic acid–polyethylene glycol copolymer. Biotinylated-RGD peptide was immobilized on the polymer surface by avidin. In combination with patterning technology, the authors were able to achieve a controlled directed cell distribution. ECs adhered and spread only on the RGD-functionalized lines separated by no cell zones in between. This technique and the concept of controlling specific cell distribution represent new possibilities in the tissue-engineering field.

When using bioresorbable polymers as scaffolds, in parallel to the resorption of polymer is an inflammatory process. Degradation of polymer can produce acidic products and create a low-pH microenvironment, which stimulates chronic inflammation and induces fibrocollagenous tissue formation that impairs the compliance of the graft and eventually may cause graft failure. The complete understanding and fine control of this process will be the key to the success of constructing this kind of blood vessel replacement.

■ SUMMARY

Dacron and ePTFE remain the standard materials for large-diameter vascular grafts, but no ideal alternative to autologous vein grafts is currently available for small-diameter applications. Little or only marginal clinical improvement has been achieved from various modifications of the basic grafts. We are on the verge of integrating understanding of biologic reactions to vascular grafts with principles of tissue engineering and innovations of technology to develop a new generation of vascular substitutes. A living vascular graft with predictable and desirable biologic functions likely will be constructed by culturing blood vessel cells on biologic/synthetic scaffolds in bioreactors under optimal hemodynamic and biomechanical conditions, probably supplemented with spatially and temporally controlled three-dimensional delivery of bioactive agents to induce postimplantation cell recruitment and to optimize remodeling, or by use of genetic engineering techniques. This may provide the ultimate solution for the current dismal long-term patency rates of small-caliber prosthetic grafts.

■ REFERENCES

1. Hufnagel CA: Permanent intubation of the thoracic aorta. Arch Surg 54:382, 1947.
2. Donovan TJ, Zimmerman B: The effect of artificial surface on blood coagulability, with special reference to polyethylene. Blood 4:1310, 1949.
3. Moore HD: The replacement of blood vessels by polyethylene tubes. Surg Gynecol Obstet 91:593, 1950.
4. Voorhees AB Jr, Jaretzki A, Blakemore AH: The use of tubes constructed of Vinyon N cloth in bridging arterial defects. Ann Surg 135: 332, 1952.
5. Vroman L: Methods of investigating protein interaction on artificial and natural surfaces. Ann N Y Acad Sci 516:300, 1978.
6. De La Cruz C, Haimovich B, Greco RS: Immobilized IgG and fibrinogen differentially affect the cytoskeletal organization and bactericidal function of adherent neutrophils. J Surg Res 80:28, 1998.
7. Shepard AD, Gelfand JA, Callow AD, O'Donnell TF Jr: Complement activation by synthetic vascular prostheses. J Vasc Surg 1:829, 1984.
8. Toursarkissian B, Eisenberg PR, Abendschein DR, Rubin BG: Thrombogenicity of small-diameter prosthetic grafts: Relative contributions of graft-associated thrombin and factor Xa. J Vasc Surg 25:730, 1997.
9. Ito RK, Rosenblatt MS, Contreras MA, et al: Monitoring platelet interactions with prosthetic graft implants in a canine model. ASAIO Trans 36:M175, 1990.
10. McCollum CN, Kester RC, Rajah SM, et al: Arterial graft maturation, the duration of thrombotic activity in Dacron aortobifemoral grafts measured by platelet and fibrinogen kinetics. Br J Surg 68:61, 1981.
11. Stratton JR, Thiele BL, Ritchie JL: Platelet deposition on Dacron aortic bifurcation grafts in man, quantitation with indium-111 platelet imaging. Circulation 66:1287, 1982.
12. Stratton JR, Thiele BL, Richie JL: Natural history of platelet deposition on Dacron aortic bifurcation grafts in the first year after implantation. Am J Cardiol 52:371, 1983.
13. Mazur C, Tschopp JF, Faliakou EC, et al: Selective $\alpha IIb\beta 3$ receptor blockage with peptide TP9201 prevents platelet uptake on Dacron vascular grafts without significant effect on bleeding time. J Lab Clin Med 124:589, 1994.
14. Kelly AB, Maragamore JM, Bourdon P, et al: Antithrombotic effects of synthetic peptides targeting various functional domains of thrombin. Proc Natl Acad Sci U S A 89:6040, 1992.
15. Jones DA, Smith CW, McIntire LV: Leucocyte adhesion under flow conditions, principles important in tissue engineering. Biomaterials 17:337, 1996.
16. Bevilacqua MP, Pober JS, Wheeler ME, et al: Interleukin-1 acts on cultured human vascular endothelium to increase the adhesion of polymorphonuclear leukocytes, monocytes, and related leukocyte cell lines. J Clin Invest 76:2003, 1985.
17. Gamble JR, Harlan JM, Klebanoff SJ, Vadas MA: Stimulation of the adherence of neutrophils to umbilical vein endothelium by human recombinant tumor necrosis factor. Proc Natl Acad Sci U S A 82:8667, 1985.
18. Swartbol P, Truedsson L, Parsson H, Norgren L: Tumor necrosis factor-α and interleukin-6 release from white blood cells induced by different graft materials in vitro are affected by pentoxifylline and iloprost. J Biomed Mater Res 36:400, 1997.
19. Greisler HP, Ellinger J, Henderson SC, et al: The effects of an atherogenic diet on macrophage/biomaterial interactions. J Vasc Surg 14:10, 1991.
20. Greisler HP, Petsikas D, Cziperle DJ, et al: Dacron stimulation of macrophage transforming growth factor-beta release. Cardiovasc Surg 4:169, 1996.

21. Mattana J, Effiong C, Kapasi A, Singhal PC: Leukocyte-polytetrafluoroethylene interaction enhances proliferation of vascular smooth muscle cells via tumor necrosis factor-alpha secretion. Kidney Int 52:1478, 1997.
22. Clowes AW, Kirkman TR, Reidy MA: Mechanisms of arterial graft healing: Rapid transmural capillary ingrowth provides a source of intimal endothelium and smooth muscle in porous PTFE prostheses. Am J Pathol 123:220, 1986.
23. Greisler HP, Dennis JW, Endean ED, et al: Derivation of neointima in vascular grafts. Circulation 78:I-6, 1988.
24. Golden MA, Hanson SR, Kirkman TR, et al: Healing of polytetrafluoroethylene arterial grafts is influenced by graft porosity. J Vasc Surg 11:838, 1990.
25. Onuki Y, Kouchi Y, Yoshida H, et al: Early flow surface endothelialization before microvessel ingrowth in accelerated graft healing, with BrdU identification of cellular proliferation. Ann Vasc Surg 12:207, 1998.
26. Hattori K, Dias S, Heissig B, et al: Vascular endothelial growth factor and angiopoietin-1 stimulate postnatal hematopoiesis by recruitment of vasculogenic and hematopoietic stem cells. J Exp Med 193:1005, 2001.
27. Takahashi T, Kalka C, Masuda H, et al: Ischemia- and cytokine-induced mobilization of bone marrow-derived endothelial progenitor cells for neovascularization. Nat Med 5:434, 1999.
28. Gill M, Dias S, Hattori K, et al: Vascular trauma induces rapid but transient mobilization of VEGFR2(+)AC133(+) endothelial precursor cells. Circ Res 88:167, 2001.
29. Shi Q, Rafii S, Wu MH, et al: Evidence for circulating bone marrow-derived endothelial cells. Blood 92:362, 1998.
30. Shi Q, Wu MH, Fujita Y, et al: Genetic tracing of arterial graft flow surface endothelialization in allogenic marrow transplanted dogs. Cardiovasc Surg 7:98, 1999.
31. Walter DH, Rittig K, Bahlmann FH, et al: Statin therapy accelerates reendothelialization: A novel effect involving mobilization and incorporation of bone marrow-derived endothelial progenitor cells. Circulation 105:3017, 2002.
32. Wener N, Priller J, Laufs U, et al: Bone marrow-derived progenitor cells modulate vascular reendothelialization and neointimal formation: Effect of 3-hydroxy-3-methylglutaryl coenzyme A reductase inhibition. Arterioscler Thromb Vasc Biol 22:1567, 2002.
33. Asahara T, Murohara T, Sullivan A, et al: Isolation of putative progenitor endothelial cells for angiogenesis. Science 275:964, 1997.
34. Asahara T, Masuda H, Takahashi T, et al: Bone marrow origin of endothelial progenitor cells responsible for postnatal vasculogenesis in physiological and pathological neovascularization. Circ Res 85:221, 1999.
35. Crosby JR, Kaminski WE, Schatteman G, et al: Endothelial cells of hematopoietic origin make a significant contribution to adult blood vessel formation. Circ Res 87:728, 2000.
36. Orlic D, Kajstura J, Chimenti S, et al: Bone marrow cells regenerate infracted myocardium. Nature 410:701, 2001.
37. Bhattacharya V, McSweeney PA, Shi Q, et al: Enhanced endothelialization and microvessel formation in polyester grafts seeded with CD34(+) bone marrow cells. Blood 95:581, 2000.
38. Shi Q, Bhattacharya V, Hong-De Wu M, Sauvage LR: Utilizing granulocyte colony-stimulating factor to enhance vascular graft endothelialization from circulating blood cells. Ann Vasc Surg 16:314, 2002.
39. Greisler HP: Regulation of vascular graft healing by induction of tissue incorporation. In Wise DL, Trantolo DJ, Altobelli DE, et al (eds): Human Biomaterials Applications. Totowa, NJ, Humana Press, 1996, p 227.
40. Pitsch RJ, Minion DJ, Goman ML, et al: Platelet-derived growth factor production by cells from Dacron grafts implanted in a canine model. J Vasc Surg 26:70, 1997.
41. Hamdan AD, Misare B, Contreras M, et al: Evaluation of anastomotic hyperplasia progression using the cyclin specific antibody MIB-1. Am J Surg 172:168, 1996.
42. Clowes AW, Kirkman TR, Reidy MA: Mechanisms of arterial graft healing: Rapid transmural capillary ingrowth provides a source of intimal endothelium and smooth muscle in porous PTFE prostheses. Am J Pathol 123:220, 1986.
43. Cameron BL, Tsuchida H, Connall TP, et al: High porosity PTFE improves endothelialization of arterial grafts without increasing early thrombogenicity. J Cardiovasc Surg 34:281, 1993.
44. Clowes AW, Kohler T: Graft endothelialization: The role of angiogenic mechanisms. J Vasc Surg 13:734, 1991.
45. Abbott WM, Cambria RP: Control of physical characteristics, elasticity, and compliance of vascular grafts. In Stanley JC (ed): Biological and Synthetic Vascular Prostheses. New York, Grune & Stratton, 1982, p 189.
46. Stansby G, Berwanger C, Shukla N, et al: Endothelial seeding of compliant polyurethane vascular graft material. Br J Surg 81:1286, 1994.
47. Miller JH, Foreman RK, Ferguson L, Faris I: Interposition vein cuff for anastomosis of prosthesis to small artery. Aust N Z J Surg 54:283, 1984.
48. Taylor RS, Loh A, McFarland RJ, et al: Improved technique for polytetrafluoroethylene bypass grafting: Long-term results using anastomotic vein patches. Br J Surg 79:348, 1992.
49. Yeung KK, Mills JL Sr, Hughes JD, et al: Improved patency of infrainguinal polytetrafluoroethylene bypass grafts using a distal Taylor vein patch. Am J Surg 182:578, 2001.
50. Stonebridge PA, Prescott RJ, Ruckley CV: Randomized trial comparing infrainguinal polytetrafluoroethylene bypass grafting with and without vein interposition cuff at the distal anastomosis. The Joint Vascular Research Group. J Vasc Surg 26:543, 1997.
51. Kansal N, Pappas PJ, Gwertzman GA, et al: Patency and limb salvage for polytetrafluoroethylene bypasses with vein interposition cuffs. Ann Vasc Surg 13:386, 1999.
52. Neville RF, Tempesta B, Sidway AN: Tibial bypass for limb salvage using polytetrafluoroethylene and a distal vein patch. J Vasc Surg 33:266, 2001.
53. Suggs WD, Henriques HF, Depalma RG: Vein cuff interposition prevents juxta-anastomotic neointimal hyperplasia. Ann Surg 207:717, 1988.
54. Greenwald SE, Berry CL: Improving vascular grafts: The importance of mechanical and haemodynamic properties. J Pathol 190:292, 2000.
55. Gozna ER, Mason WF, Marble AE, et al: Necessity for elastic properties in synthetic arterial grafts. Can J Surg 17:176, 1974.
56. Moore WS, Cafferata HT, Hall AD, Blaisdell FW: In defense of grafts across the inguinal ligaments: An evaluation of early and late results of aorto-femoral bypass grafts. Ann Surg 168:207, 1968.
57. Lind RE, Wright CB, Lynch TG, et al: Aortofemoral bypass grafting. Microvel Am Surg 48:89, 1982.
58. Veith FJ, Gupta SK, Ascer E, et al: Six-year prospective multicenter randomized comparison of autologous saphenous vein and expanded polytetrafluoroethylene grafts in infrainguinal arterial reconstructions. J Vasc Surg 3:104, 1986.
59. AbuRahma AF, Robinson PA, Holt SM: Prospective controlled study of polytetrafluoroethylene versus saphenous vein in claudicant patients with bilateral above knee femoropopliteal bypasses. Surgery 126:594, 1999.
60. Johnson WC, Lee KK: A comparative evaluation of polytetrafluoroethylene, umbilical vein, and saphenous vein bypass grafts for femoral-popliteal above-knee revascularization: A prospective randomized Department of Veterans Affairs cooperative study. J Vasc Surg 32:268, 2000.
61. Klinkert P, Schepers A, Burger DH, et al: Vein versus polytetrafluoroethylene in above-knee femoropopliteal bypass grafting: Five-year results of a randomized controlled trial. J Vasc Surg 37:149, 2003.
62. Leikweg WG, Greenfield LJ: Vascular prostheses graft infections: Collected experiences and results of treatment. Surgery 81:335, 1997.
63. Szilagyi DE, Smith RF, Elliot JP, Vrandecic MP: Infection in arterial reconstruction with synthetic vascular graft. Ann Surg 176:321, 1972.
64. Goldstone J, Moore WS: Infections in vascular prostheses. Am J Surg 128:225, 1974.
65. Ghiselli R, Giacometti A, Goffi L, et al: Prophylaxis against *Staphylococcus aureus* vascular graft infection with mupirocin-soaked, collagen-sealed dacron. J Surg Res 99:316, 2001.

66. Ghiselli R, Giacometti A, Goffi L, et al: Efficacy of rifampicin-levofloxacin as a prophylactic agent in preventing *Staphylococcus epidermidis* graft infection. Eur J Vasc Endovasc Surg 20:508, 2000.
67. Ghiselli R, Giacometti A, Cirioni O, et al: Quinupristin/dalfopristin bonding in combination with intraperitoneal antibiotics prevent infection of knitted polyester graft material in a subcutaneous rat pouch model infected with resistant *Staphylococcus epidermidis*. Eur J Vasc Endovasc Surg 24:203, 2002.
68. Strachan CJ, Newsom SW, Ashton TR: The clinical use of an antibiotic-bonded graft. Eur J Vasc Surg 5:627, 1991.
69. Goeau-Brissonniere O, Mercier F, Nicolas MH, et al: Treatment of vascular graft infection by in situ replacement with a rifampicin-bonded gelatin sealed Dacron graft. J Vasc Surg 19:739, 1994.
70. Vicaretti M, Hawthorne WJ, Ao PY, Fletcher JP: An increased concentration of rifampicin bonded to gelatin-sealed Dacron reduces the incidence of subsequent graft infections following a staphylococcal challenge. Cardiovasc Surg 6:268, 1998.
71. Vicaretti M, Hawthorne W, Ao PY, Fletcher JP: Does in situ replacement of a staphylococcal infected vascular graft with a rifampicin impregnated gelatin sealed Dacron graft reduce the incidence of subsequent infection? Int Angiol 19:158, 2000.
72. D'Addato M, Curti T, Freyrie A: Prophylaxis of graft infection with rifampicin-bonded Gelseal graft: 2-year follow-up of a prospective clinical trial. Italian Investigators Group. Cardiovasc Surg 4:200, 1996.
73. Pratesi C, Russo D, Dorigo W, Chiti E: Antibiotic prophylaxis in clean surgery: Vascular surgery. J Chemother 13:123, 2001.
74. Earnshaw JJ, Whitman B, Heather BP: Two-year results of a randomized controlled trial of rifampicin-bonded extra-anatomic Dacron grafts. Br J Surg 87:758, 2000.
75. Friedman DW, Orland PJ, Greco RS: Biomaterials: An historical perspective. In Greco RS (ed): Implantation Biology: The Host Response and Biomedical Devices. Boca Raton, Fla, CRC Press, 1994, p 1.
76. Hess F: History of (micro) vascular surgery and the development of small-caliber blood vessel prostheses. Microsurgery 6:59, 1985.
77. Greisler HP: Characteristics and healing of vascular grafts. In Callow AD, Ernst CB (eds): Vascular Surgery: Theory and Practice. Stamford, Conn, Appleton & Lange, 1995, p 1181.
78. Davids L, Dower T, Zilla P: The lack of healing in conventional vascular grafts. In Zilla P, Greisler HP (eds): Tissue Engineering of Vascular Prosthetic Grafts. Austin, Tex, RG Landes Company, 1999, p 3.
79. Jonas RA, Ziemer G, Schoen FJ, et al: A new sealant for knitted Dacron prostheses: Minimal cross-linked gelatin. J Vasc Surg 7:414, 1988.
80. Scott SM, Gaddy LR, Sahmel R, Hoffman H: A collagen coated vascular prosthesis. J Cardiovasc Surg (Torino) 28:498, 1987.
81. Cziperle DJ, Joyce KA, Tattersall CW, et al: Albumin impregnated vascular grafts: Albumin resorption and tissue reactions. J Cardiovasc Surg 33:407, 1992.
82. Nunn DB: Structural failure of Dacron arterial grafts. Semin Vasc Surg 12:83, 1999.
83. Wilson SE, Drug R, Muller G, Wilson L: Late disruption of Dacron aortic grafts. Ann Vasc Surg 11:383, 1997.
84. King M, Blais P, Guidoin R, et al: Polyethylene terephthalate (Dacron) vascular prostheses: Material and fabric construction aspects. In Williams DF (ed): Biocompatibility of Clinical Implant Materials. CRC Series in Biocompatibility. Boca Raton, Fla, CRC Press, 1981, p 177.
85. Chakfe N, Riepe G, Dieval F, et al: Longitudinal ruptures of polyester knitted vascular prostheses. J Vasc Surg 33:1015, 2001.
86. De Mol Van Otterloo JC, Van Bockel JH, Ponfoort ED, et al: Systemic effects of collagen-impregnated aortoiliac Dacron vascular prostheses on platelet activation and fibrin formation. J Vasc Surg 14:59, 1991.
87. Prager M, Polterauer P, Böhmig HJ, et al: Collagen versus gelatin-coated Dacron versus stretch polytetrafluoroethylene in abdominal aortic bifurcation graft surgery: Results of a seven-year prospective, randomized multicenter trial. Surgery 130:408, 2001.
88. Sottiurai VS, Yao JS, Flinn WR, Batson RC: Intimal hyperplasia and neointima: An ultrastructural analysis of thrombosed grafts in humans. Surgery 93:809, 1983.
89. Bellon JM, Bujan J, Contreras LA, et al: Similarity in behavior of polytetrafluoroethylene (ePTFE) prostheses implanted into different interfaces. J Biomed Mater Res 31:1, 1996.
90. Clowes AW, Gown AM, Hanson SR, Reidy MA: Mechanisms of arterial graft failure: 1. Role of cellular proliferation in early healing of PTFE prostheses. Am J Pathol 118:43, 1985.
91. Lenz BJ, Veldenz HC, Dennis JW, et al: A three-year follow-up on standard versus thin wall ePTFE grafts for hemodialysis. J Vasc Surg 28:464, 1998.
92. Akers DL, Du YH, Kempczinski RF: The effect of carbon coating and porosity on early patency of expanded polytetrafluoroethylene grafts: An experimental study. J Vasc Surg 18:10, 1993.
93. Tsuchida H, Cameron BL, Marcus CS, Wilson SE: Modified polytetrafluoroethylene: Indium 111-labeled platelet deposition on carbon-lined and high porosity polytetrafluoroethylene grafts. J Vasc Surg 16:643, 1992.
94. Bacourt F: Prospective randomized study of carbon-impregnated polytetrafluoroethylene grafts for below-knee popliteal and distal bypass: Results at 2 years. Ann Vasc Surg 11:569, 1997.
95. Groegler FM, Kapfer X, Meichelboeck W: Does carbon improve PTFE bypass material? 20th World Congress of the International Union of Angiology, New York, April 2002.
96. Fisher RK, How TV, Toonder IM, et al: Harnessing haemodynamic forces for the suppression of anastomotic intimal hyperplasia: The rationale for precuffed grafts. Eur J Vasc Endovasc Surg 21:520, 2001.
97. Sorom AJ, Hughes CB, McCarthy JT, et al: Prospective, randomized evaluation of a cuffed expanded polytetrafluoroethylene graft for hemodialysis vascular access. Surgery 132:135, 2002.
98. Fisher RK, Kirkpatrick UJ, How TV, et al: The distaflo graft: A valid alternative to interposition vein? Eur J Vasc Endovasc Surg 25:235, 2003.
99. Panneton JM: Midtern results of the Distaflo Trial for critical limb ischemia. Veith Symposium, New York, November 2002.
100. Boretos JW, Pierce WS: Segmented polyurethane: A new elastomer for biomedical applications. Science 158:1481, 1967.
101. Hess F, Jerusalem C, Steeghs S, et al: Development and long-term fate of a cellular lining in fibrous polyurethane vascular prostheses implanted in the dog carotid and femoral artery. J Cardiovasc Surg 33:358, 1992.
102. Marois Y, Paris E, Zhang Z, et al: Vascugraft microporous poly-esterurethane arterial prosthesis as a thoraco-abdominal bypass in dogs. Biomaterials 17:1289, 1996.
103. Zhang Z, Marois Y, Guidoin RG, et al: Vascugraft polyurethane arterial prosthesis as femoro-popliteal and femoro-peroneal bypasses in humans: Pathological, structural and chemical analyses of four excised grafts. Biomaterials 18:113, 1997.
104. Santerre JP, Labow RS, Duguay DG, et al: Biodegradation evaluation of polyether and polyester-urethanes with oxidative and hydrolytic enzymes. J Biomed Mater Res 28:1187, 1994
105. Eberhart A, Zhang Z, Guidoin R, et al: A new generation of polyurethane vascular prostheses: Rara avis or ignis fatuus? J Biomed Mater Res 48:546, 1999.
106. Glickman MH, Stokes GK, Ross JR, et al: Multicenter evaluation of a polytetrafluoroethylene vascular access graft as compared with the expanded polytetrafluoroethylene vascular access graft in hemodialysis applications. J Vasc Surg 34:465, 2001.
107. Allen RD, Yuill E, Nankivell BJ, Francis DM: Australian multicentre evaluation of a new polyurethane vascular access graft. Aust N Z J Surg 66:738, 1996.
108. Tanzi MC, Fare S, Petrini P: In vitro stability of polyether and polycarbonate urethanes. J Biomater Appl 14:325, 2000.
109. Salacinski HJ, Odlyha M, Hamilton G, Seifalian AM: Thermo-mechanical analysis of a compliant poly(carbonate-urea)urethane after exposure to hydrolytic, oxidative, peroxidative and biological solutions. Biomaterials 23:2231, 2002.
110. Salacinski HJ, Tai NR, Carson RJ, et al: In vitro stability of a novel compliant poly(carbonate-urea)urethane to oxidative and hydrolytic stress. J Biomed Mater Res 59:207, 2002.

111. Edwards A, Carson RJ, Szycher M, Bowald S: In vitro and in vivo biodurability of a compliant microporous vascular graft. J Biomater Appl 13:23, 1998.
112. Salacinski HJ, Tiwari A, Carson RJ, et al: In vivo biocompatibility and biostability of a novel compliant microporous poly(carbonate-urea)urethane vascular graft. Cardiovasc Pathol 11:24, 2002.
113. Phaneuf MD, Dempsey DJ, Bide MJ, et al: Bioengineering of a novel small diameter polyurethane vascular graft with covalently bound recombinant hurudin. ASIAO J 44:M653, 1998.
114. Bowald S, Busch C, Eriksson I: Arterial regeneration following polyglactin 910 suture mesh grafting. Surgery 86:722, 1979.
115. Yue X, van der Lei B, Schakenraad JM, et al: Smooth muscle cell seeding in biodegradable grafts in rats: A new method to enhance the process of arterial wall regeneration. Surgery 103:206, 1988.
116. Lambert AW, Fox AD, Williams DJ, et al: Experience with heparin-bounded collagen-coated grafts for infrainguinal bypass. Cardiovasc Surg 7:491, 1999.
117. Devine C, Hons B, McCollum C: Heparin-bounded Dacron or polytetrafluoroethylene for femoropopliteal bypass grafting: A multicenter trial. J Vasc Surg 33:533, 2001.
118. Begovac PC, Thomson RC, Fisher JL, et al: Improvements in Gore-tex vascular graft performance by Carmeda Bioactive Surface heparin immobilization. Eur J Vasc Endovasc Surg 25:432, 2003.
119. Quarmby JW, Burnand KG, Lockhart SJ, et al: Prospective randomized trial of woven versus collagen-impregnated knitted prosthetic Dacron grafts in aortoiliac surgery. Br J Surg 85:775, 1998.
120. Brewster DC, Darling RC: Optimal methods of aortoiliac reconstruction. Surgery 84:739, 1978.
121. Prager M, Polterauer P, Bohmig HJ, et al: Collagen versus gelatin-coated Dacron versus stretch polytetrafluoroethylene in abdominal aortic bifurcation graft surgery: Results of a seven-year prospective, randomized multicenter trial. Surgery 130:408, 2001.
122. Comparative evaluation of prosthetic, reversed, and in situ vein bypass grafts in distal popliteal and tibial-peroneal revascularization. Veterans Administration Cooperative Study Group 141. Arch Surg 123:434, 1988.
123. Bennion RS, Williams RA, Stabile BE, et al: Patency of autogenous saphenous vein versus polytetrafluoroethylene grafts in femoropopliteal bypass for advanced ischemia of the extremity. Surg Gynecol Obstet 160:239, 1985.
124. Budd JS, Langdon I, Brennan J, Bell PR: Above-knee prosthetic grafts do not compromise the ipsilateral long saphenous vein. Br J Surg 78:1379, 1991.
125. Brewster DC, LaSalle AJ, Robison JG, et al: Femoropopliteal graft failures: Clinical consequences and success of secondary reconstructions. Arch Surg 118:1043, 1983.
126. Sterpetti AV, Schultz RD, Feldhaus RJ, Peetz DJ Jr: Seven-year experience with polytetrafluoroethylene as above-knee femoropopliteal bypass graft: Is it worthwhile to preserve the autologous saphenous vein? J Vasc Surg 2:907, 1985.
127. Whittemore AD, Clowes AW, Couch NP, Mannick JA: Secondary femoropopliteal reconstruction. Ann Surg 193:35, 1981.
128. Taylor LM Jr, Edwards JM, Porter JM: Present status of reversed vein bypass grafting: Five-year results of a modern series. J Vasc Surg 11:193, 1990.
129. Jackson MR, Belott TP, Dickason T, et al: The consequences of a failed femoropopliteal bypass grafting: Comparison of saphenous vein and PTFE grafts. J Vasc Surg 32:498, 2000.
130. Michaels JA: Choice of material for above-knee femoropopliteal bypass graft. Br J Surg 76:7, 1989.
131. Charlesworth PM, Brewster DC, Darling RC, et al: The fate of polytetrafluoroethylene grafts in lower limb bypass surgery: A six year follow-up. Br J Surg 72:896, 1985.
132. Davies MG, Feeley TM, O'Malley MK, et al: Infrainguinal polytetrafluoroethylene grafts: Saved limbs or wasted effort? A report on ten years' experience. Ann Vasc Surg 5:519, 1991.
133. Whittemore AD, Kent KC, Donaldson MC, et al: What is the proper role of polytetrafluoroethylene grafts in infrainguinal reconstruction? J Vasc Surg 10:299, 1989.
134. Faries PL, LoGerfo FW, Arora S, et al: A comparative study of alternative conduits for lower extremity revascularization: All-autogenous conduit versus prosthetic grafts. J Vasc Surg 32:1080, 2000.
135. Roddy SP, Darling RC 3rd, Ozsvath KJ, et al: Composite sequential arterial reconstruction for limb salvage. J Vasc Surg 36:325, 2002.
136. Kreienberg PB, Darling RC 3rd, Chang BB, et al: Adjunctive techniques to improve patency of distal prosthetic bypass grafts: Polytetrafluoroethylene with remote arteriovenous fistulae versus vein cuffs. J Vasc Surg 31:696, 2000.
137. Kissin M, Kansal N, Pappas PJ, et al: Vein interposition cuffs decrease the intimal hyperplastic response of polytetrafluoroethylene bypass grafts. J Vasc Surg 31:69, 2000.
138. Gentile AT, Mills JL, Gooden MA, et al: Vein patching reduces neointimal thickening associated with prosthetic graft implantation. Am J Surg 176:601, 1998.
139. Abbott WM, Green RM, Matsumoto R, et al: Prosthetic above-knee femoropopliteal bypass grafting: Results of a multicenter randomized prospective trial. Above-knee Femoropopliteal Study Group. J Vasc Surg 25:19, 1997.
140. Green RM, Abbott WM, Matsumoto T, et al: Prosthetic above-knee femoropopliteal bypass grafting: Five-year results of a randomized trial. J Vasc Surg 31:417, 2000.
141. Robinson BI, Fletcher JP, Tomlinson P, et al: A prospective randomized multicentre comparison of expanded polytetrafluoroethylene and gelatin-sealed knitted Dacron grafts for femoropopliteal bypass. Cardiovasc Surg 7:214, 1999.
142. Post S, Kraus T, Muller-Reinartz U, et al: Dacron vs. polytetrafluoroethylene grafts for femoropopliteal bypass: A prospective randomised multicentre trial. Eur J Vasc Endovasc Surg 22:226, 2001.
143. Landry GJ, Moneta GL, Taylor LM Jr, Porter JM: Axillobifemoral bypass. Ann Vasc Surg 14:296, 2000.
144. El-Massry S, Saad E, Sauvage LR, et al: Axillofemoral bypass with externally supported, knitted Dacron grafts: A follow-up through twelve years. J Vasc Surg 17:107, 1993.
145. Berce M, Sayers RD, Miller JH: Femorofemoral crossover grafts for claudication: A safe and reliable procedure. Eur J Vasc Endovasc Surg 12:437, 1996.
146. Christenson JT, Broome A, Norgren L, Eklof B: The late results after axillo-femoral bypass grafts in patients with leg ischaemia. J Cardiovasc Surg (Torino) 27:131, 1986.
147. van der Vliet JA, Palamba HW, Scharn DM, et al: Arterial reconstruction for subclavian obstructive disease: A comparison of extrathoracic procedures. Eur J Vasc Endovasc Surg 9:454, 1995.
148. Ziomek S, Quinones-Baldrich WJ, Busuttil RW, et al: The superiority of synthetic arterial grafts over autologous veins in carotid-subclavian bypass. J Vasc Surg 3:140, 1986.
149. Perler BA, Williams GM: Carotid-subclavian bypass—a decade of experience. J Vasc Surg 12:716, 1990.
150. Bower TC, Nagorney DM, Toomey BJ, et al: Vena cava replacement for malignant disease: Is there a role? Ann Vasc Surg 7:52, 1993.
151. Huguet C, Ferri M, Gavelli A: Resection of the suprarenal inferior vena cava: The role of prosthetic replacement. Arch Surg 130:793, 1995.
152. Sarkar R, Eilber FR, Gelabert HA, Quinones-Baldrich WJ: Prosthetic replacement of the inferior vena cava for malignancy. J Vasc Surg 28:75, 1998.
153. Caldarelli G, Minervini A, Guerra M, et al: Prosthetic replacement of the inferior vena cava and the iliofemoral vein for urologically related malignancies. Br J Urol Int 90:368, 2002.
154. Comerota AJ, Harwick RD, White JV: Jugular venous reconstruction: A technique to minimize morbidity of bilateral radical neck dissection. J Vasc Surg 3:322, 1986.
155. Norton L, Eiseman B: Replacement of portal vein during pancreatectomy for carcinoma. Surgery 77:280, 1975.
156. Sarfeh IJ, Rypins EB, Mason GR: A systematic appraisal of portacaval H-graft diameters: Clinical and hemodynamic perspectives. Ann Surg 204:356, 1986.
157. Collins JC, Ong MJ, Rypins EB, Sarfeh IJ: Partial portacaval shunt for variceal hemorrhage: Longitudinal analysis of effectiveness. Arch Surg 133:590, 1998.

158. US Renal Data System Annual Data Report. Bethesda, Md, National Institutes of Health, 1997.
159. Gibson KD, Gillen DL, Caps MT, et al: Vascular access survival and incidence of revisions: A comparison of prosthetic grafts, simple autogenous fistulas, and venous transposition fistulas from the United States Renal Data System Dialysis Morbidity and Mortality Study. J Vasc Surg 34:694, 2001.
160. Tordoir JH, Herman JM, Kwan TS, Diderich PM: Long-term follow-up of the polytetrafluoroethylene (PTFE) prosthesis as an arterio-venous fistula for haemodialysis. Eur J Vasc Surg 2:3, 1987.
161. Palder SB, Kirkman RL, Whittemore AD, et al: Vascular access for hemodialysis: Patency rates and results of revision. Ann Surg 202:235, 1985.
162. Rosas SE, Joffe M, Burns JE, et al: Determinants of successful synthetic hemodialysis vascular access graft placement. J Vasc Surg 37:103, 2003.
163. Tordoir JH, Hofstra L, Bergmans DC, et al: Stretch versus standard expanded PTFE grafts for hemodialysis access. In Henry ML, Ferguson RM (eds): Vascular Access for Hemodialysis—IV. Chicago, WL Gore & Associates and Precept Press, 1995, p 277.
164. Lenz BJ, Veldenz HC, Dennis JW, et al: A three-year follow-up on standard versus thin wall ePTFE grafts for hemodialysis. J Vasc Surg 28:464, 1998.
165. Fillinger MF, Reinitz ER, Schwartz RA, et al: Graft geometry and venous intimal-medial hyperplasia in arteriovenous loop grafts. J Vasc Surg 11:556, 1990.
166. Keynton RS, Evancho MM, Sims RL, et al: Intimal hyperplasia and wall shear in arterial bypass graft distal anastomoses: An in vivo model study. J Biomech Eng 123:464, 2001.
167. Polo JR, Tejedor A, Polo J, et al: Long-term follow-up of 6-8 mm brachioaxillary polytetrafluorethylene grafts for hemodialysis. Artif Organs 19:1181, 1995.
168. Dammers R, Planken RN, Pouls KP, et al: Evaluation of 4-mm to 7-mm versus 6-mm prosthetic brachial-antecubital forearm loop access for hemodialysis: Results of a randomized multicenter clinical trial. J Vasc Surg 37:143, 2003.
169. Paty PS, Darling RC 3rd, Lee D, et al: Is prosthetic renal artery reconstruction a durable procedure? An analysis of 489 bypass grafts. J Vasc Surg 34:127, 2001.
170. Cormier JM, Fichelle JM, Laurian C, et al: Renal artery revascularization with polytetrafluoroethylene bypass graft. Ann Vasc Surg 4:471, 1990.
171. Herring M, Gardner A, Glover J: A single-staged technique for seeding vascular grafts with autogenous endothelium. Surgery 84:498, 1978.
172. Graham LM, Burkel WE, Ford JW, et al: Expanded polytetrafluoroethylene vascular prostheses seeded with enzymatically derived and cultured canine endothelial cells. Surgery 91:550, 1982.
173. Jarrell BE, Williams SK: Microvessel derived endothelial cell isolation, adherence, and monolayer formation for vascular grafts. J Vasc Surg 13:733, 1991.
174. Sipehia R, Martucci G, Lipscombe J: Transplantation of human endothelial cell monolayer on artificial vascular prosthesis: The effect of growth-support surface chemistry, cell seeding density, ECM protein coating, and growth factors. Artif Cells Blood Substit Immobil Biotechmol 24:51, 1996.
175. Shindo S, Takagi A, Whittemore AD: Improved patency of collagen-impregnated grafts after in vitro autogenous endothelial cell seeding. J Vasc Surg 6:325, 1987.
176. Prendiville EJ, Coleman JE, Callow AD, et al: Increased in vitro incubation time of endothelial cells on fibronectin-treated ePTFE increases cell retention in blood flow. Eur J Vasc Surg 5:311, 1991.
177. Sentissi JM, Rambnerg K, O'Donnell TF Jr, et al: The effect of flow on vascular endothelial cells grown in tissue culture on polytetrafluoroethylene grafts. Surgery 99:337, 1986.
178. Pasic M, Muller-Glauser W, von Segesser LK, et al: Superior late patency of small-diameter Dacron grafts seeded with omental microvascular cells: An experimental study. Ann Thorac Surg 58:677, 1994.
179. Williams SK, Jarrell BE, Rose DG, et al: Human microvessel endothelial cell isolation and vascular graft sodding in the operating room. Ann Vasc Surg 3:146, 1989.
180. Schneider PA, Hanson SR, Price TM, Harker LA: Preformed confluent endothelial cell monolayers prevent early platelet deposition on vascular prostheses in baboons. J Vasc Surg 8:229, 1988.
181. Rosenman JE, Kempczinski RF, Pearce WH, Silberstein EB: Kinetics of endothelial cell seeding. J Vasc Surg 2:778, 1985.
182. Vohra R, Thomson GJ, Carr HM, et al: In vitro adherence and kinetics studies of adult human endothelial cell seeded polytetra-fluoroethylene and gelatin impregnated Dacron grafts. Eur J Vasc Surg 5:93, 1991.
183. Miyata T, Conte MS, Trudell LA, et al: Delayed exposure to pulsatile shear stress improves retention of human saphenous vein endothelial cells on seeded ePTFE grafts. J Surg Res 50:485, 1991.
184. Sugawara Y, Miyata T, Sato O, et al: Rapid postincubation endothelial retention by Dacron grafts. J Surg Res 67:132, 1997.
185. Prendiville EJ, Coleman JE, Callow AD, et al: Increased in vitro incubation time of endothelial cells on fibronectin-treated ePTFE increases cell retention in blood flow. Eur J Vasc Surg 5:311, 1991.
186. Zilla P, Preiss P, Groscurth P, et al: In vitro-lined endothelium, initial integrity and ultrastructural events. Surgery 116:524, 1994.
187. Ott MJ, Ballermann BJ: Shear stress-conditioned, endothelial cell-seeded vascular grafts, improved cell adherence in response to in vitro shear stress. Surgery 117:334, 1995.
188. Vohra RK, Thomson GJ, Sharma H, et al: Effects of shear stress on endothelial cell monolayer on expanded polytetrafluoroethylene grafts using preclot and fibronectin matrices. Eur J Vasc Surg 4:33, 1990.
189. Giudiceandrea A, Seifalian AM, Krijgsman B, Hamilton G: Effect of prolonged pulsatile shear stress in vitro on endothelial cell seeded PTFE and compliant polyurethane vascular grafts. Eur J Vasc Endovasc Surg 15:147, 1998.
190. Bowlin GL, Rittgers SE, Milsted A, Schmidt SP: In vitro evaluation of electrostatic endothelial cell transplantation onto 4 mm interior diameter expanded polytetrafluoroethylene grafts. J Vasc Surg 27:504, 1998.
191. Whitehouse WM Jr, Wakefield TW, Vinter DW, et al: Indium-111 oxide labeled platelet imaging of endothelial seeded Dacron thoracoabdominal vascular prostheses in a canine experimental model. ASAIO Trans 29:183, 1983.
192. Wakefield TW, Lindblad B, Graham LM, et al: Nuclide imaging of vascular graft-platelet interactions, comparison of indium excess and technetium subtraction techniques. J Surg Res 40:388, 1986.
193. Stanley JC, Burkel WE, Ford JW, et al: Enhanced patency of small-diameter, externally supported Dacron iliofemoral grafts seeded with endothelial cells. Surgery 92:994, 1982.
194. Allen BT, Long JA, Clark RE, et al: Influence of endothelial cell seeding on platelet deposition and patency in small-diameter Dacron arterial grafts. J Vasc Surg 1:224, 1984.
195. Graham LM, Stanley JC, Burkel WE: Improved patency of endothelial-cell-seeded, long, knitted Dacron and ePTFE vascular prostheses. ASAIO J 8:65, 1985.
196. Graham LM, Brothers TE, Vincent CK, et al: The role of an endothelial cell lining in limiting distal anastomotic intimal hyperplasia of 4-mm-I.D. Dacron grafts in a canine model. J Biomed Mater Res 25:525, 1991.
197. Herring MB, Gardner A, Glover J: Seeding human arterial prostheses with mechanically derived endothelium: The detrimental effect of smoking. J Vasc Surg 1:279, 1989.
198. Jensen N, Lindblad B, Bergovist D: Endothelial cell seeded Dacron aortobifurcated grafts, platelet deposition and long-term follow-up. J Cardiovasc Surg 35:425, 1994.
199. Magometschnigg H, Kadletz M, Vodrazka M, et al: Prospective clinical study with in vitro endothelial cell lining of expanded poly-tetrafluoroethylene grafts in crural repeat reconstruction. J Vasc Surg 15:527, 1992.
200. Zilla P, Deutsch M, Meinhart J, et al: Clinical in vitro endothelialization of femoropopliteal bypass grafts, an actuarial follow-up over three years. J Vasc Surg 19:540, 1994.

201. Meinhart JG, Deutsch M, Fischlein T, et al: Clinical autologous in vitro endothelialization of 153 infrainguinal ePTFE grafts. Ann Thorac Surg 71:S327, 2001.
202. Deutsh M, Meinhart J, Vesely M, et al: In vitro endothelialization of expanded polytetrafluoroethylene grafts: A clinical case report after 41 months of implantation. J Vasc Surg 25:757, 1997.
203. Park PK, Jarrell BE, Williams SK, et al: Thrombus free, human endothelial surface in midregion of a Dacron vascular graft in the splanchnic venous circuit—observations after nine months of implantation. J Vasc Surg 11:468, 1990.
204. Graham LM, Fox PL: Growth factor production following prosthetic graft implantation. J Vasc Surg 13:742, 1991.
205. Sapienza P, di Marzo L, Cucina A, et al: Release of PDGF-BB and bFGF by human endothelial cells seeded on expanded polytetrafluoroethylene vascular grafts. J Surg Res 75:24, 1998.
206. Wilson JM, Birinyi LK, Salomon RN, et al: Implantation of vascular grafts lined with genetically modified endothelial cells. Science 244:1344, 1989.
207. Dichek DA, Nussbaum O, Degen SJ, Anderson WF: Enhancement of the fibrinolytic activity of sheep endothelial cells by retroviral-mediated gene transfer. Blood 77:533, 1991.
208. Shayani V, Newman KD, Dichek DA: Optimization of recombinant t-PA secretion from seeded vascular grafts. J Surg Res 57:495, 1994.
209. Brothers TE, Judge LM, Wilson JM, et al: Effect of genetic transduction on in vitro canine endothelial cell prostanoid production and growth. Surg Forum 41:337, 1990.
210. Jaklitsh MT, Biro S, Casscells W, Dichek DA: Transduced endothelial cells expressing high levels of tissue plasminogen activator have an unaltered phenotype in vitro. J Cell Physiol 154:207, 1993.
211. Huber TS, Welling TH, Sarkar R, et al: Effects of retroviral-mediated tissue plasminogen activator gene transfer and expression on adherence and proliferation of canine endothelial cells seeded onto expanded polytetrafluoroethylene. J Vasc Surg 22:795, 1995.
212. Baer RP, Whitehill TE, Sarkar R, et al: Retroviral-mediated transduction of endothelial cells with the lacZ gene impairs cellular proliferation in vitro and graft endothelialization in vivo. J Vasc Surg 24:892, 1996.
213. Dunn PF, Newman KD, Jones M, et al: Seeding of vascular grafts with genetically modified endothelial cells, secretion of recombinant tPA results in decreased seeded cell retention in vitro and in vivo. Circulation 93:1439, 1996.
214. Huber TS, Welling TH, Sarkar R, et al: Effects of retroviral-mediated tissue plasminogen activator gene transfer and expression on adherence and proliferation of canine endothelial cells seeded onto expanded polytetrafluoroethylene. J Vasc Surg 22:795, 1995.
215. Falk J, Townsend LE, Vogel LM, et al: Improved adherence of genetically modified endothelial cells to small-diameter expanded polytetrafluoroethylene grafts in a canine model. J Vasc Surg 27:902, 1998.
216. Greisler HP, Cziperle DJ, Kim DU, et al: Enhanced endothelialization of expanded polytetrafluoroethylene grafts by fibroblast growth factor type 1 pretreatment. Surgery 112:244, 1992.
217. Gosselin C, Ren D, Ellinger J, Greisler HP: In vivo platelet deposition on polytetrafluoroethylene coated with fibrin glue containing fibroblast growth factor 1 and heparin in a canine model. Am J Surg 170:126, 1995.
218. Zarge JI, Gosselin C, Huang P, Greisler HP: Platelet deposition on ePTFE grafts coated with fibrin glue with or without FGF-1 and heparin. J Surg Res 67:4, 1997.
219. Gray JL, Kang SS, Zenni GC, et al: FGF-1 affixation stimulates ePTFE endothelialization without intimal hyperplasia. J Surg Res 57:596, 1994.
220. Doi K, Matsuda T: Enhanced vascularization in a microporous polyurethane graft impregnated with basic fibroblast growth factor and heparin. J Biomed Mater Res 34:361, 1997.
221. Weinberg CB, Bell E: A blood vessel model constructed from collagen and cultured vascular cells. Science 231:397, 1986.
222. L'Heureux N, Germain L, Labbe T, Auger FA: In vitro construction of a human blood vessel from cultured vascular cells: A morphologic study. J Vasc Surg 17:499, 1993.
223. Ziegler T, Nerem RM: Tissue engineering a blood vessel, regulation of vascular biology by mechanical stresses. J Cell Biochem 56:204, 1994.
224. L'Heureux N, Paquet S, Labbe T, et al: A completely biological tissue-engineered human blood vessel. FASEB J 12:47, 1998.
225. Greisler HP: Arterial regeneration over absorbable prostheses. Arch Surg 117:1425, 1982.
226. Greisler HP, Kim DU, Price JB, Voorhees AB Jr: Arterial regenerative activity after prosthetic implantation. Arch Surg 120:315, 1985.
227. Greisler HP, Ellinger J, Schwarcz TH, et al: Arterial regeneration over polydioxanone prostheses in the rabbit. Arch Surg 122:715, 1987.
228. Greisler HP, Petsikas D, Lam TM, et al: Kinetics of cell proliferation as a function of vascular graft material. J Biomed Mater Res 17:955, 1993.
229. Greisler HP, Dennis JW, Endean ED, et al: Derivation of neointima in vascular grafts. Circulation 78:I-6, 1988.
230. Greisler HP, Henderson SC, Lam TM: Basic fibroblast growth factor production in vitro by macrophages exposed to Dacron and polyglactin 910. J Biomater Sci Polym Ed 4:415, 1993.
231. Zenni GC, Ellinger J, Lam TM, Greisler HP: Biomaterial-induced macrophage activation and monokine release. J Invest Surg 7:135, 1994.
232. Greisler HP, Endean ED, Klosak JJ, et al: Polyglactin 910/polydioxanone bicomponent totally resorbable vascular prostheses. J Vasc Surg 7:697, 1988.
233. Greisler HP, Tattersall CW, Klosak JJ, et al: Partially bioresorbable vascular grafts in dogs. Surgery 110:645, 1991.
234. Shinoka T, Shum-Tim D, Ma PX, et al: Creation of viable pulmonary artery autografts through tissue engineering. J Thorac Cardiovasc Surg 115:536, 1998.
235. Shum-Tim D, Stock U, Hrkach J, et al: Tissue engineering of autologous aorta using a new biodegradable polymer. Ann Thorac Surg 68:2298, 1999.
236. Niklason LE, Abbott W, Gao J, et al: Morphologic and mechanical characteristics of engineered bovine arteries. J Vasc Surg 33:628, 2001.
237. Stock UA, Wiederschain D, Kilroy SM, et al: Dynamics of ECM production and turnover in tissue engineered cardiovascular structures. J Cell Biochem 81:220, 2001.
238. Gao J, Niklason L, Langer R: Surface hydrolysis of poly(glycolic acid) meshes increases the seeding density of vascular smooth muscle cells. J Biomed Mater Res 42:417, 1998.
239. Drumheller PD, Hubbell JA: Polymer networks with grafted cell-adhesion peptides for highly biospecific cell adhesive substrates. Anal Biochem 222:380, 1994.
240. Patel N, Padera R, Sanders GHW, et al: Spatially controlled cell engineering on biodegradable polymer surfaces. FASEB J 12:1447, 1998.

Section IX

ENDOVASCULAR SURGERY: BASIC CONSIDERATIONS

KENNETH OURIEL, MD

Chapter 50

Training in Endovascular Surgery

KENNETH OURIEL, MD
RICHARD M. GREEN, MD

We live in an environment of technologic change; engineering and scientific research strives to create simpler and smaller innovations. Health care has not been exempted from this relentless progression toward less complex treatment modalities to replace more invasive procedures. This shift toward less invasive methods of treating disease should not be rejected; rather, it symbolizes a natural and desirable evolution of medical science. But the field of vascular surgery must adapt to rapidly changing technology if vascular surgeons are to continue to care for patients with peripheral vascular disease.[1] Although available treatment may involve traditional open surgical procedures in many instances, we have already witnessed a shift to percutaneous therapies and later to yet unimagined technology that will make even our percutaneous procedures obsolete. There is widespread belief throughout the community of vascular surgeons that the care for vascular problems should continue to reside, in large part, within the specialty, irrespective of what the treatment for those problems is at a particular time.[2,3]

In the last 2 decades of the 20th century, vascular practitioners recognized the usefulness of endovascular techniques to treat diseases formerly relegated to major open surgery.[4,5] We have witnessed insidious, relentless growth in the endovascular treatment of aortic aneurysms, carotid stenosis, and lower extremity occlusive disease (Fig. 50-1). The long-term outcome after less invasive treatment remains ill defined, and, even when data are available, it appears that many endovascular procedures have not yet attained the level of reliability associated with the more traditional approaches.[6] Nonetheless, patients and their physicians appear willing to accept a mild decrement in long-term outcome for the opportunity to offer a minimally invasive treatment.

Technologic change creates educational challenges for the specialty. Engineers and physician innovators create new technology; the technology is tested in preclinical benchtop and animal studies and then rolled out to a limited number of clinician investigators to evaluate in human trials. If the outcome from such trials appears reasonable, the technology is offered to the community of caregivers involved in the treatment of the specific disease. But, in many cases, the caregivers are ill prepared to deploy this technology. The technology often involves a variety of novel techniques that are unfamiliar to the practitioners. And the more advanced the technology, the wider the educational gap between current practice and the innovation.

Particular educational challenges are created when technologic change occurs at a rapid pace, fast enough that the period between introduction and acceptance is much shorter than the career life cycle of the practitioners. A small number of individuals skilled in the new technology must be identified, usually innovators who have been self-trained. Next, these innovators must transfer knowledge and technical skills to a cadre of individuals who will train our residents and fellows. And, most important, the community of vascular practitioners must be retrained so that they, too, are able to offer the new techniques to their patients.

The increasing use of interventional procedures for vascular disease was the topic of a position paper written by the Regional Vascular Society Committee on Interventional Therapy published in 1989.[7] The authors of this document noted that the physician team involved in interventional procedures should possess fundamental knowledge in the diagnosis and management of peripheral vascular disease. Further, such individuals should be skilled in the performance and interpretation of angiographic studies. The authors

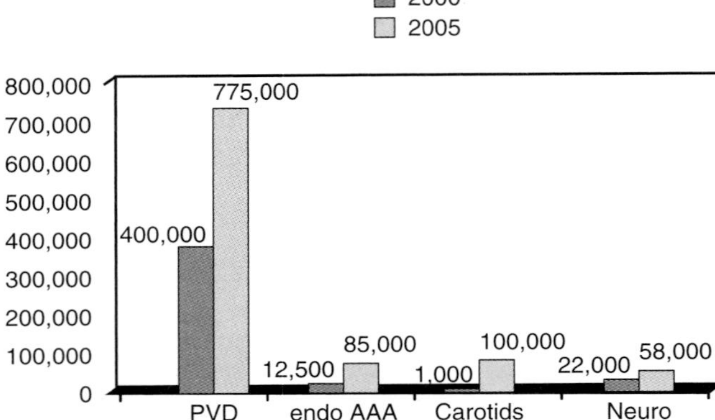

FIGURE 50-1 Projected growth in the number of endovascular procedures. PVD, peripheral vascular disease; endo AAA, endovascular abdominal aortic aneurysm. (Data from Wieslander CK, Huang CC, Omura MC, Ahn SS: Endovascular workforce for peripheral vascular disease: Current and future needs. J Vasc Surg 35:1218-1225, 2002.)

suggested that these skills should be acquired through residency and fellowship training programs, supervised preceptorships, or approved courses. It was thought to be essential for the vascular societies to take a leadership role in the development of guidelines for credentialing and quality assurance. As well, the societies were challenged to support educational programs for interventional techniques.

The same issues identified in the Regional Vascular Society Committee document still plague the vascular surgeons today.[6] As a specialty, we remain undertrained in the use of interventional techniques.[8] Endovascular training within our accredited vascular surgical fellowship programs is inconsistent. Lastly, we have not identified standard educational paradigms that are most effective for the training of endovascular-competent vascular surgeons. This chapter is designed to outline paradigms that should be considered in the training and retraining of vascular practitioners. This chapter is not meant to be specific to vascular surgeons; rather, the principles should apply to any specialty interested in providing state-of-the-art care to patients with vascular disease (Table 50-1). Although the issues change over time, the principles should remain constant. Successful incorporation of novel technology into the armamentarium of the practitioner is facilitated through the application of these principles, irrespective of the particular innovation or the specialty of the trainee.

Table 50-1 Number of Cardiovascular Specialty Training Programs and Positions

SPECIALTY	TRAINING PROGRAMS	FIRST-YEAR POSITIONS
Vascular surgery	89	100
Interventional radiology	94	240
Interventional cardiology	55	127
Cardiothoracic surgery	90	148

Data from Wieslander CK, Huang CC, Omura MC, Ahn SS: Endovascular workforce for peripheral vascular disease: Current and future needs. J Vasc Surg 35:1218-1225, 2002.

PARADIGMS FOR ENDOVASCULAR TRAINING

Clearly, the standard residency and fellowship programs comprise the most efficient venue for training in endovascular techniques. Eventually, endovascular skills will be taught concurrently with open surgical techniques, beginning early in the residency and continuing throughout the training program. In this manner, endovascular skills will be no different from open surgical skills, part and parcel of the training program.[9] Each graduating fellow will possess a continuum of skills that runs the gamut to encompass the medical care of the patient with vascular disease; diagnostic imaging to include ultrasound, computed tomography, and magnetic resonance imaging; endovascular techniques; and traditional open surgery. Although such a scenario is not possible in every fellowship program at the present time, the goals should be attainable within the next several years.

Clinical Rotations

The precise manner in which such training programs are organized is worthy of consideration. There exist two choices: (1) focused endovascular training on a dedicated endovascular service and (2) conjoined endovascular and open surgical training on the same service. Traditionally, surgical training has been conducted using the former approach, with subspecialty rotations such as urology, orthopedics, cardiothoracic surgery, and the like, interspersed throughout the first few years of a 5-year residency program. A variety of disparate techniques may be included within a given subspecialty rotation, however. For instance, residents may be taught laparoscopic cholecystectomy on the same service that they learn how to perform a hepatic resection. It appears as though the organization of training has been, in great part, dependent on the practice spectrum of the attending physician. The rotations, in general, encompass those procedures performed by the training physician on the service. When the training physician's practice is limited to a specific area of a subspecialty (e.g., endovascular surgery), it makes sense to compartmentalize the rotation to parallel the same degree of subspecialization (e.g., an endovascular rotation). By contrast, when the attending physician's practice is broader in scope (e.g., all vascular surgical procedures), it is most efficient to organize the rotation along similar lines (e.g., a combination of endovascular and open surgical procedures within a single rotation). Currently, most endovascular surgeons do not limit their practice to endovascular procedures; thus, the vascular surgical rotations encompass both endovascular and open surgery within the same rotation. There exist potential downsides to such a paradigm; the pace of learning may be slowed by a defocused rotation. A one-to-one relationship between trainee and attending physician, however, avoids the operational issues inherent when a single attending physician is assigned to more than one clinical service.

Duration of Training

The emergence of endovascular techniques greatly expanded the depth of basic knowledge and technical skills required for a vascular trainee. The traditional 1- or even

2-year vascular fellowship programs appear too brief to acquire adequate familiarity with the myriad diagnostic and treatment skills necessary for the contemporary practice of vascular and endovascular surgery. The curriculum must include a broad base in diagnostic imaging, the vascular noninvasive laboratory, the medical care of the patient with vascular disease, preventive modalities, and some exposure to research—all in conjunction with adequate exposure to a wide array of open and endovascular procedures. The duration of a vascular training that provides adequate preparation in all pertinent areas is likely to be at least 3 years in length. The addition of 3 years after a traditional 5-year general surgical training program, however, is likely to diminish interest in pursuing a vascular surgical career. With declining applications to both general and vascular surgical training programs, any change that would result in a further decrement in interest would be detrimental.

With these limitations of the current training scheme in mind, training paradigms have been considered. Each would decrease the duration of the general surgical residency, with the potential to add time in the vascular surgical fellowship. There are several issues that must be addressed when considering such changes, such as the following:

1. *Is a general surgery certificate important?* It is possible that a significant reduction in the duration of the general surgical residency would result in the inability to receive a general surgical certificate at the completion of training. The general surgical certificate may be important to those individuals who do not plan to confine their practice to vascular surgery, for example, trainees interested in seeking a rural practice setting.
2. *How long should the endovascular component be?* Proficiency, in any field, is achieved at differing rates for different individuals. That said, the complexity and broad range of endovascular techniques underlie the requirement for a significant investment in time to acquire the skills necessary to perform endovascular procedures independently. Although there exist little objective data on which to base recommendations, it appears as though a total of 1 year of dedicated but not necessarily contiguous endovascular training is usually necessary.
3. *What could be eliminated from the general surgical training?* If we agree that the necessity for training in vascular medicine, the vascular noninvasive laboratory, open surgery, and endovascular techniques mandates a minimum of 3 years of vascular fellowship and if we also assume that any training period longer than 6 years is likely to negatively impact the number of trainees choosing a vascular surgical career, it is evident that the general surgical training period cannot exceed 3 years. It is likely that the "service rotations" such as neurosurgery, otolaryngology, urology, and others, may need to be eliminated. Other rotations, including plastic surgery, cardiac surgery, and noncardiac thoracic surgery, may be of importance when treating patients with vascular problems and therefore might be retained.

Given these considerations, the most appropriate solution may be offered with a 3-year general surgical preliminary program that encompasses general surgery and other subspecialties necessary for the practice of vascular surgery. Such a paradigm would necessitate the selection of vascular surgery by the trainee early in training, preferably during medical school. Successful recruitment at this early stage would require an adequate exposure to vascular surgery during the 3rd and 4th years of medical school, as well as the promotion of the specialty to medical students by the vascular societies. Identification of the vascular surgical trainee at the beginning of residency facilitates tailoring of the 3-year general surgical experience to the requirements of the vascular resident. In fact, shifting some general surgical requirements to the later half of a 6-year training paradigm would allow certain vascular surgical experience to begin early in the residency program. Although the specifics of this paradigm remain unclear and need to be negotiated by the various national training bodies, the shift from a traditional "5 + 2" paradigm will be necessary if the trainee is to be facile with endovascular techniques at the completion of training.

■ SPECIFIC DEVICE TRAINING

As new devices are studied and approved, the practitioner must become familiar with their use. There are three possible scenarios that may arise, and training is different for each.

1. *The device is similar to predicate devices.* Often the new device is similar to older devices that the practitioner has been trained to use. An example of this scenario is the substitution of a new, improved guide wire for the older guide wire. No formal training is required in these cases. Rather, the practitioner can independently gain the necessary exposure to the device through attendance at didactic seminars, discussions with colleagues, and industry representatives and through the review of printed materials.
2. *The device is different from existing devices, but the method of use is similar.* When the new device differs from devices that the practitioner is familiar with, but the methods involved in the use of the technology are quite similar, a short period of dedicated training is required. Examples of this scenario include the use of a new nitinol stent and its delivery system by someone familiar with standard self-expanding stents, or the introduction of a new femoral artery closure device to a practitioner accustomed to the use of predicate devices. Training may necessitate hands-on experience in these instances, wherein a trained individual remains an integral part of a few procedures until the trainee has acquired adequate mastery of the new technique.
3. *The device is part of a technology that is distinct from existing technology.* When a new device represents a true paradigm shift from older treatment modalities, formal training is required. Examples of such technology include endovascular aortic aneurysm repair and carotid stenting by individuals who have never performed these procedures. In these instances, formalized training is required. The nature of the training frequently is specified at the time of approval of the device by the U.S. Food and Drug Admin-

istration, and the device manufacturer is responsible for organizing and executing the training. In some instances, proctoring is required before the practitioner is allowed to independently perform the procedure. A proctor, usually certified by the manufacturer, visits the trainee and observes the performance of several procedures. Multiple visits may be necessary until the proctor "signs off" on the individual's skills.

■ RETRAINING OF VASCULAR SURGEONS

The rapid development of effective endovascular techniques has left a large proportion of the vascular surgical workforce untrained and unable to offer these newer modalities to their patients.[6] Retraining is necessary if such individuals wish to offer the spectrum of open surgical and interventional procedures to their patient population.[10] There are several means available to accomplish retraining; the major limitation of each is the extent to which a practitioner must leave his or her practice to achieve proficiency in endovascular procedures. Over time, however, it is relatively straightforward to train the other members of a group practice once a single member has been trained.

Endovascular Minifellowships

Endovascular "minifellowship" programs offer one paradigm for retraining.[3] An individual travels to one of the institutions that offer such a program. The programs range in duration from 1 month to 1 year. Generally, a fee is charged by the training institution, a fee that has been offset by corporate sponsorship in some cases. Unfortunately, the number of endovascular minifellowship programs has been low, limiting the development of an adequate workforce of vascular surgeons who are skilled in endovascular techniques (Fig. 50-2).[3,6]

Although the completion of a minifellowship is probably the best method of retraining, several drawbacks exist. First, there can be problems with licensing of the trainee; some states allow the trainee to fall within the institution's blanket-training license used for residents and fellows. Other states require the individual to obtain a formal medical license before he or she can engage in hands-on patient activities.

A second limitation of the minifellowship paradigm relates to the effects it has on the institution's residency program. Unless there are ample endovascular cases, the experience of the vascular surgical fellows may be compromised by the minifellow. As well, there is a tendency for the minifellow to leave the nonoperative patient care activities to the residents, spending most of his or her time within the endovascular suite. The failure to actively participate in the preprocedure and postprocedure patient care negatively impacts on the minifellow's experience and may be a source of friction between the minifellow and the vascular residents.

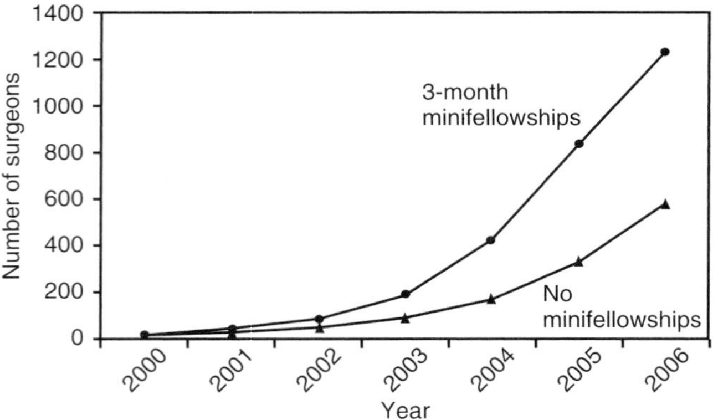

FIGURE 50-2 Number of endovascular-trained surgeons with and without the development of endovascular minifellowship training programs. (Data from Ouriel K, Kent KC: The role of the vascular surgeon in endovascular procedures. J Vasc Surg 33:902-903, 2001.)

Endovascular Preceptorships

Preceptorships are another retraining paradigm that has been employed with some success. Vascular practitioners spend 1 week (occasionally up to 1 month) at the training institution, where hands-on experience is gained in a variety of endovascular techniques. As in the minifellowships, gaining licensure can be problematic and the trainee can negatively impact the institution's formal vascular fellowship unless the case volume is adequate. Experience with preceptorships has shown that these short programs work best when the trainee arrives with some degree of baseline endovascular competence. In addition, although the programs can be focused to one specific endovascular skill set (e.g., carotid stenting), it is an unusual center that can aggregate enough cases of one particular type to provide an adequate experience. For this reason, even the training programs that are disease focused offer training in a variety of other endovascular techniques during the preceptorship.

The Role of Simulation

Computer-based simulation has been used in many high-risk areas to enhance the capabilities of training methodologies. The purpose is to provide a risk-free environment where physicians can engage themselves and their clinical team in a real-time experience. Not only can hands-on skills be practiced, but sequencing can be practiced in an environment that provides constant feedback. Cognitive decision making and management of adverse events can be learned without endangering any patients. Although the concept of simulation-based training for endovascular procedures has not been validated, experience with other videoscopic surgical procedures has been favorable.

■ CERTIFICATION OF TRAINING PROGRAMS

Incumbent on any specialty involved in the training of skilled physicians is a formal certification process for its training programs. Until recently, no such certification program was in place. Recently, however, the Society for Vascular Surgery developed the Endovascular Program Evaluation and Endorsement Committee (EV-PEEC) to evaluate training programs and determine the applicant center's endorsement status.[11] Specific aims of the EV-PEEC are to formulate guidelines for a comprehensive endovascular training program and to establish criteria by which such programs can achieve endorsement The review process is accomplished through the evaluation of submitted written materials, the performance of a personal site visit, and the review of site visit reports. Initially, the EV-PEEC was charged with the review of freestanding endovascular training programs, that is, those that offer postgraduate endovascular training for vascular surgeons. Although the review of the endovascular training components of accredited vascular fellowship programs is not presently a component of the endorsement process, such programs may benefit from the adoption of the guidelines and objectives established by the EV-PEEC.

■ CREDENTIALING FOR ENDOVASCULAR PROCEDURES

The development of new techniques creates a need for guidelines for granting privileges for individuals who wish to employ such techniques in their clinical practice. A report that addressed guidelines for hospital privileges in vascular surgery was generated by an ad hoc committee of the Joint Council of the Society for Vascular Surgery and the International Society for Cardiovascular Surgery (North American chapter).[12] This report was published in 1989, many years after the emergence of vascular surgery as a separate specialty. The document became a standard which hospital credentialing committees could reference when delineating their local criteria for vascular surgical credentialing. Since 1989, however, the growth of the endovascular therapies and their designation as an important component of vascular surgery by the Accreditation Council for Graduate Medical Education (ACGME) have rendered the original guideline document incomplete. In this setting, an updated document was created by a second ad hoc committee and was published in 2002.[13]

Components of this newer guideline document were the delineation of endovascular interventions as one of the five pillars of vascular surgery, the advocacy of endovascular surgery as an important component of all ACGME-accredited fellowships, and the delineation of several methods of acquiring adequate endovascular training. Beginning in 2004, all vascular surgical fellows from accredited fellowship programs are required to be proficient in catheter-based interventions. Fellows who graduated prior to this requirement should be required to produce a case list of endovascular procedures, and this experience should be verified by the program director. A second pathway applies for those vascular surgeons who did not gain endovascular experience in their fellowship, consisting of an "adjunctive" fellowship at a center with interest in, experience with, and commitment to endovascular surgery and education. The adjunctive training is often 3 months in duration and has been described (see earlier) as the endovascular minifellowship. As for the accredited programs, the volume of endovascular cases should be documented and verified.

The number and spectrum of endovascular procedures required before credentialing can be granted are subjects of some debate, primarily since the actual requirements differ among the various specialties. A guideline document sponsored by the Society for Vascular Surgery was published in 1999,[14] representing the revision of a document published 6 years earlier.[15] The guideline document includes a minimum general threshold of 50 angiograms and 25 interventions performed with the applicant as the primary interventionist prior to the granting of endovascular privileges (Table 50-2). These are absolute minimal guidelines, and a mentored experience should be obtained prior to the independent performance of specific procedures such as aortic endograft placement, renal stenting, carotid stenting, and others.

Other specialties have produced documents that outline somewhat different training paradigms for peripheral interventional procedures. The American College of Cardiology (ACC) has published revised recommendations for training, emanating from the Core Cardiology Training Symposium (COCATS) in 1994.[16] The COCATS-2 document, published in 2002 on the ACC website, includes a section on training in vascular medicine and peripheral catheter-based interventions.[17] Although referring specifically to cardiologists, the document outlines three levels of training. Level 1 comprises basic training required of all competent practitioners to care for patients with peripheral vascular disease. Level 2 includes additional training that enables the

Table 50-2 Number of Catheterizations and Interventions to Achieve Competence, by Specialty Society

					SVS/ISCVS*	
APPROACH	SCVIR	SCAI	ACC*	AHA*	1993	1998
Catheterizations/angiograms	200	100/50†	100	100	50†	100/50†
Interventions	25	50/25†	50/25†	50/25†	10-15†	50/25†
Live demonstration	Yes	Yes	Yes	Yes	Yes	Yes

*Includes knowledge of thrombolysis or thrombolytic therapy.
†As primary interventionist.
SCVIR, Society of Cardiovascular and Interventional Radiology; SCAI, Society for Cardiac Angiography and Interventions; ACC, American College of Cardiology; AHA, American Heart Association; SVS/ISCVS, Society for Vascular Surgery/International Society for Cardiovascular Surgery.

Data from White RA, Hodgson KJ, Ahn SS, et al: Endovascular interventions training and credentialing for vascular surgeons. J Vasc Surg 29:177-186, 1999.

practitioner to develop special expertise in the evaluation and management of vascular patients but does not include interventional treatment. Level 3 is advanced training in peripheral interventions, whereby the practitioner develops the cognitive and technical skills necessary for the interventional treatment of patients with peripheral vascular disease and can train others to perform these procedures at a high skill level. A minimum duration of 12 months of training beyond the traditional fellowship is suggested for peripheral vascular interventions. The COCATS-2 document suggests a minimum case volume of 100 diagnostic angiograms, 50 peripheral angioplasties, and 10 peripheral thrombolytic cases to achieve competence. These cases should be documented in a logbook, but the COCATS-2 document does not specify whether the trainee must be the primary operator for the procedures.

■ SUMMARY

The development of newer, less invasive methods of treating peripheral vascular diseases is a natural and desirable evolution in the field. The rapidity with which these novel techniques have appeared has created a large segment of the vascular surgical community that is untrained and unable to offer endovascular treatment modalities. Modifications in the traditional training paradigms must be made if vascular surgeons are to continue to provide the broad spectrum of care to patients with vascular disease. The traditional accredited vascular fellowships must provide adequate endovascular training such that the graduate is able to safely perform a wide variety of endovascular treatment modalities. The duration of the vascular fellowship must be increased to provide adequate endovascular training, likely with a concomitant decrease in the length of the preliminary general surgical residency. Practicing vascular surgeons who have not previously been trained in endovascular techniques should seek minifellowships or preceptorships to acquire sufficient skills. Once a single member of a group practice has been trained, this individual can train the other members of the group. Implementation of these training strategies should provide an adequate complement of vascular surgeons skilled in the performance of endovascular and open surgical procedures. An individual who has the ability to perform either an endovascular or an open surgical solution to a vascular problem is most likely to offer the patient a complete set of options, and, in this manner, the patient with vascular disease will benefit.

■ REFERENCES

1. Kashyap VS, Ahn SS, Davis MR, et al: Trends in endovascular surgery training. J Endovasc Ther 9:633-638, 2002.
2. Ricotta JJ: Presidential address: Towards competence in vascular care. J Vasc Surg 34:955-961, 2001.
3. Ouriel K, Kent KC: The role of the vascular surgeon in endovascular procedures. J Vasc Surg 33:902-903, 2001.
4. Elsey JK: Responsibilities of vascular surgeons to study and control the field of endovascular surgery. J Vasc Surg 10:213-214, 1989.
5. Rutherford RB: Endovascular surgery: The new challenge. J Vasc Surg 10:208-210, 1989.
6. Goldstone J: Cardiovascular workforce in the 21st century. J Vasc Surg 35:1301-1302, 2002.
7. String ST, Brener BJ, Ehrenfeld WK, et al: Interventional procedures for the treatment of vascular disease: Recommendations regarding quality assurance, development, credentialing criteria, and education. Regional Vascular Society Committee on Interventional Therapy. J Vasc Surg 9:736-739, 1989.
8. Wieslander CK, Huang CC, Omura MC, Ahn SS: Endovascular workforce for peripheral vascular disease: Current and future needs. J Vasc Surg 35:1218-1225, 2002.
9. Choi ET, Wyble CW, Rubin BG, et al: Evolution of vascular fellowship training in the new era of endovascular techniques. J Vasc Surg 33(2 Suppl):S106-S110, 2001.
10. Ouriel K, Kent KC: The role of the vascular surgeon in endovascular procedures. J Vasc Surg 33:902-903, 2001.
11. Hodgson KJ: Endovascular program evaluation and endorsement committee (EV-PEEC). *http://www.vascularweb.org/file/EV-PEEC_31-36.pdf*
12. Moore WS, Treiman RL, Hertzer NR, et al: Guidelines for hospital privileges in vascular surgery. J Vasc Surg 10:678-682, 1989.
13. Moore WS, Clagett GP, Veith FJ, et al: Guidelines for hospital privileges in vascular surgery: An update by an ad hoc committee of the American Association for Vascular Surgery and the Society for Vascular Surgery. J Vasc Surg 36:1276-1282, 2002.
14. White RA, Hodgson KJ, Ahn SS, et al: Endovascular interventions training and credentialing for vascular surgeons. J Vasc Surg 29:177-186, 1999.
15. White RA, Fogarty TJ, Baker WH, et al: Endovascular surgery credentialing and training for vascular surgeons [see comments]. J Vasc Surg 17:1095-1102, 1993.
16. COCATS: Guidelines for Training in Adult Cardiovascular Medicine: Core Cardiology Training Symposium, American College of Cardiology, June 27-28, 1994. J Am Coll Cardiol 25:1-34, 1995.
17. Beller GA, Bornow RO, Fuster V, et al: ACC revised recommendations for training in adult cardiovascular medicine core cardiology training II (COCATS-2). *http://www.acc.org/clinical/training/cocats2.pdf*
18. White RA, Hodgson KJ, Ahn SS, et al: Endovascular interventions training and credentialing for vascular surgeons. J Vasc Surg 29:177-186, 1999.

Chapter

51

Fundamental Techniques in Endovascular Surgery

JUAN AYERDI, MD
KIM J. HODGSON, MD

Section IX

Endovascular therapies for peripheral vascular occlusive disease have evolved over the past several decades to become viable alternative approaches to surgical revascularization. In fact, the evolution of endovascular devices to treat a myriad of peripheral vascular disease is occurring at a dizzying pace. In 1999, the U.S. Food and Drug Administration (FDA) approved the first two aortic endografts, with subsequent approval of several others, and this less invasive treatment for abdominal aortic aneurysms is now widely available. Recently, the FDA approved the first stent and cerebral protection system for performance of percutaneous carotid artery stenting, and endografts to treat thoracic aortic aneurysms are in active investigational trial. Consequently, if vascular surgeons wish to remain on the forefront of the diagnosis and treatment of peripheral vascular disease, they will need to add these techniques to their armamentarium. By doing so, they can offer comprehensive, multimodality diagnostic and therapeutic care to vascular patients, a position that allows for objective treatment decisions without the bias inherently present when the controlling physician can perform only some of the possible therapeutic procedures.

Unfortunately, though most vascular surgeons have a general familiarity with the concepts related to endovascular procedures, concepts are not the same as skills. For example, all too often surgeons try to equate central venous catheter placement with percutaneous arterial catheterization in an attempt to gain credentials to perform percutaneous endovascular interventions. In practice, however, most are quickly humbled by how challenging this seemingly simple aspect of percutaneous endovascular procedures can sometimes be. Furthermore, although the concepts of the Seldinger technique used in both procedures are analogous, neither the skills required nor the risks to the patient are comparable. Vascular surgeons need to transform concepts into skills, a feat that can be accomplished only through actual experience performing endovascular procedures.

Furthermore, the impetus for performance of an endovascular intervention is to replace a complicated, high-risk surgical procedure with a minimally invasive one having an acceptable patency and clinical success. Though not always as durable as the corresponding surgical revascularization, the low risk-benefit ratio of an endoluminal intervention and its typical repeatability often make it the procedure of choice, particularly in patients with significant or prohibitive medical co-morbidities. Although percutaneous interventions are generally considered "low risk," failures and complications are not innocuous and can result in adverse clinical outcomes. Systemic complications related to catheter manipulation, radiographic contrast material, or physiologic stress may include stroke, myocardial infarction, renal failure, limb loss, or even death. Required conversion to open procedures for salvage of an early post-procedural complication carries all the risks of an emergency procedure in a high-risk patient. For these reasons it is critical that the vascular surgeon have thorough knowledge and understanding of the pathophysiology of the condition being treated, the indications and potential complications of the therapeutic alternatives, and the training and experience in the catheter and guide wire skills necessary to perform them with good results.

This chapter reviews the fundamental concepts related to the performance of the broad spectrum of diagnostic and therapeutic endovascular procedures, with the aforementioned caveat that this is no substitute for actual human hands-on training. Specific indications, results, and complications are addressed elsewhere in this text. Guidelines concerning the characteristics and attributes of certain catheters, wires, and devices are only generalizations to be considered when approaching given clinical situations, each of which is unique and possessed of its own nuances. The ability to anticipate how a given catheter or guide wire will likely perform is based on analysis of the situation that must take into account multiple variables, including the extent of tortuosity and angulation present, the working distances involved, the characteristics of the target vessel or lesion, and many others. Ultimately, this boils down to judgment, which itself can only come from experience with similar situations. Once mastered, however, innovative applications of these basic techniques become possible and allow increasingly complex situations to be successfully addressed.

GAINING AND MAINTAINING PERCUTANEOUS VASCULAR ACCESS

By definition, all endovascular procedures require the surgeon to gain access to the lumen of the arterial or venous system in order to proceed. Although this can be performed percutaneously or by direct surgical exposure of the access vessel, the overwhelming majority of endovascular procedures can and should be performed via the percutaneous route of vascular access. Although conceptually simple, percutaneous access is actually the most uncontrolled component of any endovascular procedure, typically being performed with minimal benefit of any imaging guidance (but ultrasonographic guidance systems are now available for unusual situations). The potential for mishap is quite real and can preclude performance of the intended endovascular procedure, limit the therapeutic options available, or actually render the patients worse off than when they started.

Vessel Puncture Equipment and Techniques

There are basically two types of entry needles to choose from: single- and double-wall puncture types (Fig. 51-1). The single-wall puncture needle is most familiar to surgeons and the one most commonly used. It is a bevel-tipped 16- or 18-gauge hollow needle that accommodates a 0.035-inch guide wire. The needle is advanced toward the palpated pulse until the anterior wall of the vessel is punctured and pulsatile blood flow returns. A J-tipped guide wire is advanced through the needle into the vessel and threaded toward the target region. Theoretically, blood return out of the hub of the needle may occur while the beveled area is still within the wall of the vessel and subsequent wire passage could then dissect any plaque in the region. Therefore, it is critical to evaluate the characteristics of blood return through the needle to be assured that a central position of the needle in the vessel is likely. If blood return is inconsistent or less than would be expected on the basis of the patient's symptoms and the quality of the pulse, subtle manipulation of the needle should be performed to try to improve the quality of the blood return before attempting guide wire passage. Furthermore, fluoroscopic observation of guide wire passage, a routine for many interventionalists, should definitely be performed if any resistance to advancement is met, to ensure that the guide wire is not dissecting the wall of the vessel (Fig. 51-2). The importance of this cannot be overemphasized because it minimizes vascular injury not only at the insertion site but further along the course of the guide wire as well. Similarly, the sheath should never be advanced over the entry guide wire until radiographic evaluation has confirmed that the wire is properly positioned and without kinks.

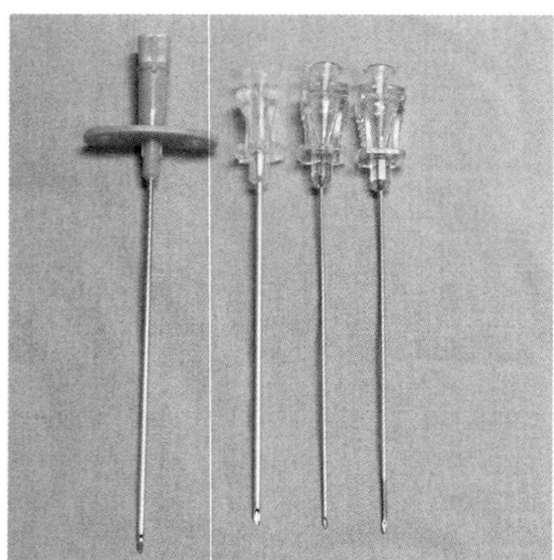

FIGURE 51-1 A double-wall puncture needle (*left*) and three single-wall needles (*right*).

A coaxial micropuncture set is a variation of the single-wall puncture needle that includes a 21-gauge needle for initial access (Fig. 51-3). After adequate back-bleeding is obtained, a 0.18-inch guide wire (either stainless steel or nitinol with a platinum tip) is advanced through the needle and the needle is removed. Because of the reduced luminal diameter of the micropuncture access needle compared with the standard 16- or 18-gauge ones, less vigorous bleeding is observed. On removal of the needle, the introducer and dilator (3 or 4 French) are inserted either as a

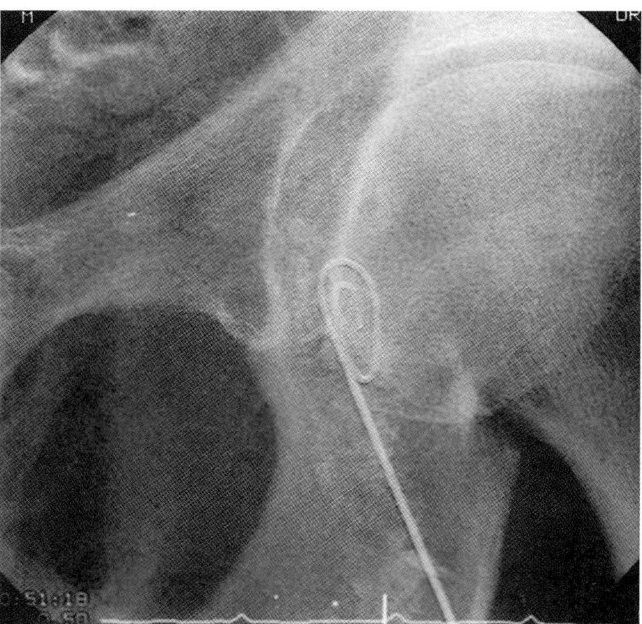

FIGURE 51-2 Extreme curling of the entry guide wire as it emerges from the puncture needle, indicating likely subintimal passage. (From Hodgson KJ, Mattos MA, Sumner DS: Access to the vascular system for endovascular procedures: Techniques and indications for percutaneous and open arteriotomy approaches. Semin Vasc Surg 10:206-221, 1997.)

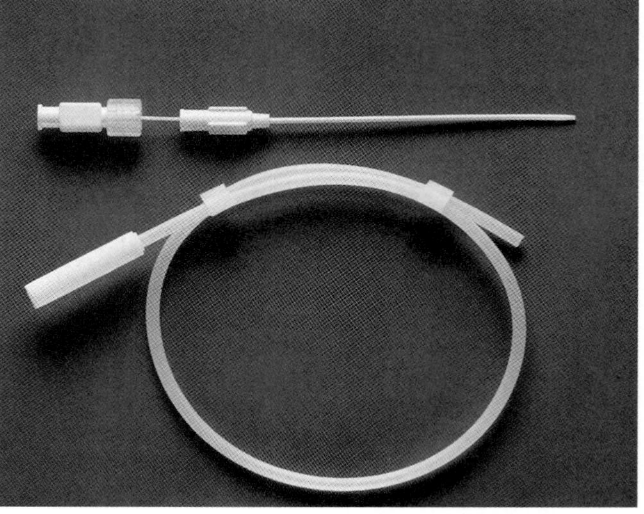

FIGURE 51-3 Micropuncture needle and sheath setup.

unit or sequentially in a coaxial sequential dilation fashion, depending on the needs. These sheaths may have a hydrophilic coating to reduce wall friction. The dilator and wire are then removed and exchanged for a standard 0.035- or 0.038-inch guide wire, over which a working introducer sheath may be exchanged. Alternatively, if only a diagnostic catheterization is required, a 4-French diagnostic catheter may be inserted without exchanging the sheath. Another recent modification to the angiographic needles has been the addition of echogenic needle bevels, for identification of the needle tip during arterial cannulation with ultrasonographic guidance.

The second major category of needles are the double-wall puncture needles, which are two component systems that combine a blunt-tipped hollow needle with a bevel-tipped stylet that projects slightly out the end of the needle (see Fig. 51-1). The double-wall puncture technique involves the intentional passage of the needle/stylet assembly through both walls of the vessel until it contacts the underlying bone. The stylet is then removed and the remaining outer needle is slowly withdrawn until blood return is noted, assuming, that is, that the target vessel was actually punctured. The needle angle is then flattened somewhat so as to direct the subsequently passed guide wire more centrally within the lumen of the vessel. Theoretically, there is less chance of guide wire-induced plaque dissection with this approach, although insufficient withdrawal or premature angulation of the needle can still result in dissection of the posterior wall. Because this technique affords little protection against dissection and creates an unnecessary puncture of the posterior wall of the vessel, it has not gained a large following among vascular surgeons, who generally prefer the less traumatic single-wall puncture technique with its instantaneous feedback at the time the vessel is punctured.

Though rarely used, there is one more type of vessel puncture system available for use that has particular advantages in situations where the target vessel is pulseless, especially if it is in close proximity to sensitive structures that could be injured by multiple needle passages. This two-component 16- or 18-gauge needle (*Smart*Needle) is designed for single-wall puncture but is constructed like a double-wall needle. The inner stylet is a Doppler probe with a 14-MHz transducer attached to an audio monitor that provides audible Doppler guidance during needle passage to assist the operator in directing the needle to the intended vessel or to avoid arterial cannulation when venous access is the intention. Once below the skin, the needle is panned side to side to locate arterial flow signals that allow the needle to be advanced directly toward the target vessel. Fluid medium is essential for Doppler signal transmission; consequently, flushing the needle after skin insertion is frequently helpful. Vessel puncture is accompanied by a significant increase in amplitude of the Doppler signal, at which time the Doppler stylet is removed, blood return is observed, and an entry guide wire is advanced as previously described. Although the *Smart*Needle may be helpful for common femoral artery (CFA) punctures below iliac artery occlusions, anatomic and radiographic landmarks are usually sufficient guidance in this situation and avoid the extra expense (Fig. 51-4). Some interventionists have reported using this system to puncture the popliteal artery for retrograde approaches to the superficial femoral artery (SFA), whereas others have advocated its use for puncturing pulseless femoral or axillary arteries and for arterial or venous vascular access in pediatric patients.[1-4] Although no definitive data document any reduced rates of complication with the *Smart*Needle, its use may reduce the risk of inadvertent brachial plexus, carotid artery, or popliteal vein injuries during accessing of the brachial artery, jugular vein, and popliteal arteries, respectively.

Maintaining Vascular Access

After vascular access has been achieved, consideration must be given as to how best to maintain it. If a purely diagnostic procedure is planned and multiple catheter and guide wire exchanges are not likely, the size of the puncture wound can be minimized by using a full-length guide wire as the entry wire and simply advancing the diagnostic catheter directly into the vessel over the guide wire. This is a reasonable approach when all imaging can be performed through flush aortography (or vena cavography) without the need for selective catheterizations, which would generally require exchanging out the pigtail catheter for one or more selective catheters. Each catheter/guide wire exchange has the potential to traumatize the vessel puncture site by enlarging it, lifting an intimal flap, or both. Furthermore, during each exchange there will be some blood that escapes from the puncture, forming a localized hematoma that may compromise effective compression after completion of the case. Therefore, unless the desired study can be accomplished with just one catheter and without a lot of manipulation, it is generally recommended that an indwelling sheath be used. Because of the higher profile and irregular surface characteristics of balloon angioplasty catheters and stents, use of a sheath is absolutely mandatory for interventional procedures to prevent device-related vessel wall injury.

Sheaths are essentially access ports to the vascular system placed at the time initial vascular access is achieved and removed after completion of the diagnostic study or intervention. Subsequent exchanges of guide wires, diagnostic catheters, and interventional catheters or devices all are performed through the lumen of the sheath, which functions to maintain access to the vascular system while minimizing trauma to the vessel wall as well as extravasation of blood from the puncture site during exchanges. Back-bleeding from the sheath itself is prevented by a hemostatic valve located in its hub, which also maintains hemostasis when catheters or guide wires are in place by sealing around these devices (Fig. 51-5). There are limits, however, to how effective the hemostatic valve can be, particularly when very small guide wires or non-coaxial intravascular ultrasound (IVUS) catheters are in place. In the former case leakage is a function of difficulty sealing around such a small device, whereas in the latter case a seal is difficult to obtain because the profile of the IVUS catheter alongside the guide wire presents an irregular shape for the valve to seal against. Very large diameter sheaths (in the 22-French range) designed to accommodate large-diameter endoluminal aortic aneurysm devices may have a clamping chamber instead of a hemostatic valve because it is problematic to design a hemostatic valve that can effectively seal around a range of sizes as great as that encountered

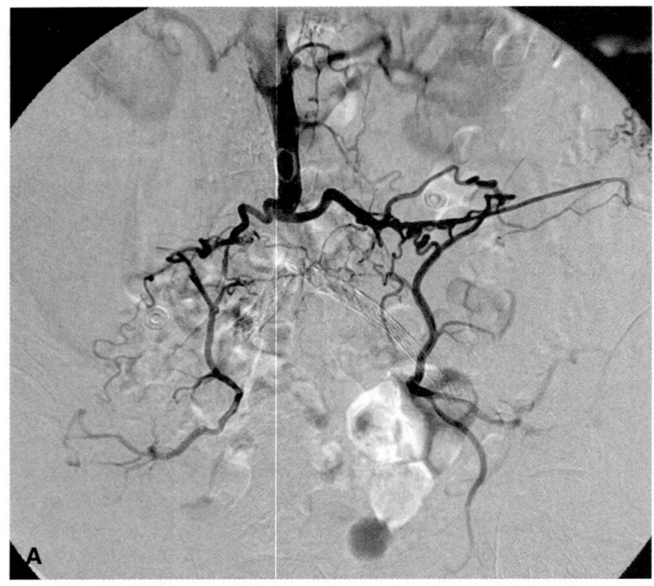

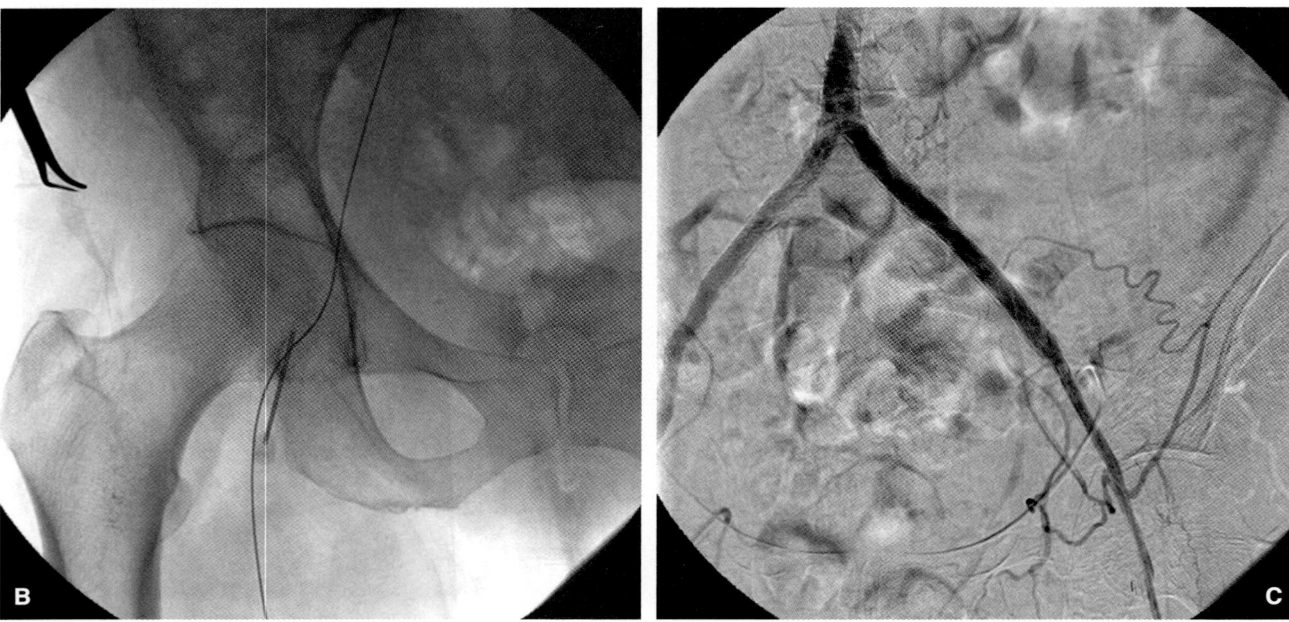

FIGURE 51-4 **A,** Distal aortic occlusion diagnosed by brachial artery catheterization. **B,** Guide wire access on the right using anatomic landmarks to cannulate the right common femoral artery. **C,** Result following bilateral common iliac artery angioplasty.

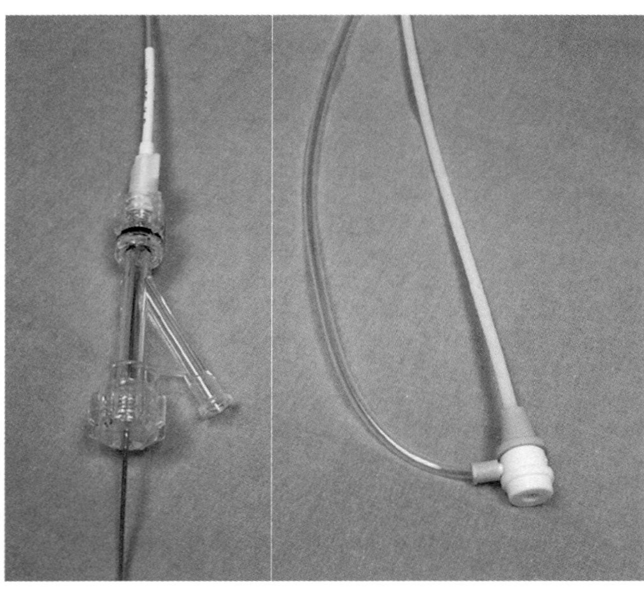

FIGURE 51-5 Y-adapter on a guiding catheter (*left*) and hemostatic valve of a sheath (*right*).

in this situation, from the 0.035-inch guide wire to the 7-mm-diameter endograft delivery system.

Sheaths come in a variety of diameters and lengths, but the diameters most commonly used are in the 5- to 6-French range (1 French = 0.33 mm or 0.013 inch), because most diagnostic and balloon catheters are of this size. Placement of stents requires the use of sheaths in the 6- to 8-French range, whereas iliac and SFA endografts require approximately 7- to 12-French sheaths and aortic endografts require sheaths as large as 22 to 25 French, if a sheath is even used at all. The size designation denotes the *internal* diameter (ID) of the sheath, as opposed to catheters which are sized in French by their *outer* diameters (OD). Accordingly, the maximal size catheter that can be placed through a 5-French sheath is a 5-French catheter. A standard 5-French sheath has an OD of approximately 6 or 7 French, which represents a 1- or 2-French increase in the size of the puncture than would be made if a sheath was not used. In practice this is not a clinically significant issue, and the benefits of sheaths far outweigh this consideration or their relatively modest cost.

Guiding catheters are preshaped interventional catheters with an atraumatic tip design that assist in directing guide wires, balloons, stents, and other devices into vessels and maintaining that selective vascular access during angiography and interventions. They are inserted through an access sheath and allow for selective catheterizations and large lumina for increased dye flow and visualization while selective catheterizations are being performed. Like diagnostic catheters, guide catheters are sized in French by their ODs, with their IDs typically provided in fractional inches (e.g., 0.086). Consequently a 6-French sheath accommodates a 6-French guide catheter that typically has an inner (working) lumen diameter of around 0.060 to 0.070 inch. Depending on the manufacturer's specifications, the ID of a guide catheter may accommodate a 1- or 2-French downsized diagnostic catheter. In selective catheterizations, sheaths may be avoided by the use of the novel guide-sheaths that have been designed with preshaped tips and hemostatic valves allowing them to function as both guiding catheters and access sheaths, thus downsizing the arterial entry site by 1 or 2 French units for the same inner working diameter.

Until recently, there were four basic length ranges for sheaths: 3 to 5, 10 to 12, 22 to 25, and 30 to 40 cm. The two longer length ranges are generally only needed for endograft placement and interventions contralateral to the side of vascular access. The 10- to 12-cm length is standard for most peripheral vascular diagnostic and interventional procedures and the 3- to 5-cm length is used mostly for dialysis graft work. Some long sheaths, referred to as *crossover sheaths*, have preshaped curved tips or kink-resistant internal support to facilitate their use over the aortic bifurcation (i.e., crossover). Some manufacturers place a radiopaque marker on the end of their sheaths that facilitates its visualization under fluoroscopic imaging. This is particularly valuable during interventional work, especially stent placement, where it is critical to know that the stent is completely outside of the sheath before beginning deployment. Guiding catheters are offered in 6 to 8 French and lengths of 55 to 90 cm. Guiding sheaths are usually available in 6 or 7 French and a standard length of 45 cm because they have been primarily promoted for renal interventions.

Another useful feature of sheaths is the side-port connection, which allows for blood sampling, pressure monitoring, vasodilator administration, or contrast injection during the procedure (see Fig. 51-5). For example, if the entry guide wire cannot be passed all the way up the vessel at the time of initial vascular access, visualization of the cause of the problem can be helpful (Fig. 51-6). Although injecting contrast medium directly through the entry needle may elucidate the nature of the obstruction, it is often better visualized by inserting the sheath a limited distance into the vessel and then performing a diagnostic study through the sheath because the small-diameter needle may not permit a sufficient volume of contrast agent to be infused rapidly enough for adequate visualization. If, however, direct injection through the needle is undertaken, attaching the dye-loaded syringe to the entry needle via a segment of intravenous extension tubing can minimize movement of the needle and, therefore, possible arterial injury during injection.

■ VASCULAR ACCESS SITES AND TECHNIQUES

Access to the arterial system is typically obtained through one of three approaches: the retrograde CFA puncture, the antegrade CFA puncture, or the retrograde axillary/brachial puncture. Occasionally, access may be gained through the radial, SFA, popliteal, and tibial arteries or by direct puncture of a graft, such as an axillobifemoral bypass (Fig. 51-7), whereas puncture of dialysis grafts is commonplace. On the venous side of the circulation, the retrograde femoral and antegrade jugular approaches are standard approaches that are well known to vascular surgeons and are not further described. In general, selecting the site in closest proximity to the target lesion provides the greatest number of therapeutic options and best catheter response as long as there is adequate working room between the puncture site and the lesion to safely inflate balloons and deploy stents. Though a common concern among surgeons, direct punctures of vascular grafts, even in their anastomotic regions, are not generally problematic.[5] However, the associated scar tissue may hinder sheath placement, requiring predilation of the access track with a dilator one or two French sizes larger than the intended sheath. That failing, exchanging out for a stiff guide wire or sheath may be required. Scarred groins can be advantageous, however, because postprocedure hematoma formation is uncommon, a consequence of the absence of a tissue space for blood to collect in.

Retrograde Common Femoral Artery Cannulation

The retrograde femoral artery puncture is the most common approach and the one with the least risk due to its relatively large size and the fact that it can be effectively compressed against the underlying osseous structures. A thorough understanding of the anatomic relationship of the femoral artery and the surrounding bony and ligamentous structures is essential, particularly if the femoral pulse is weak or absent, because the risk of puncture site bleeding is significantly increased if the puncture occurs above the inguinal ligament or on the side of the artery. The latter is

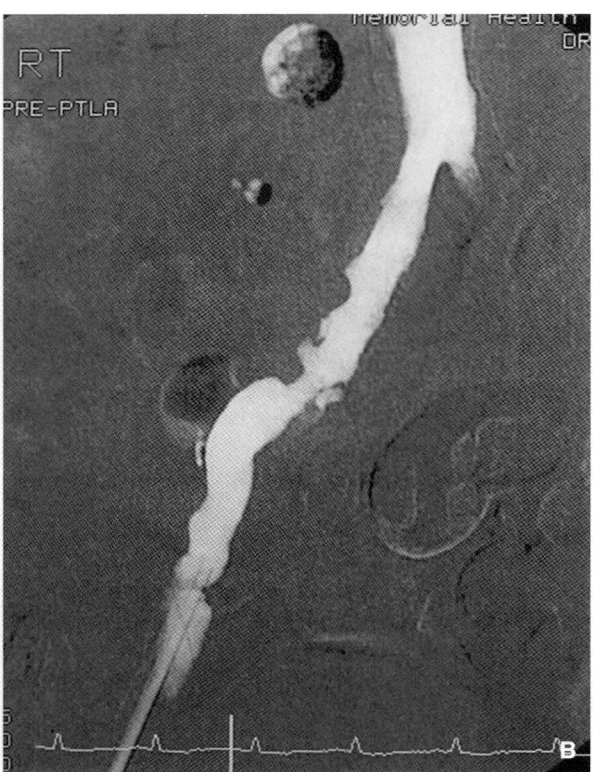

FIGURE 51-6 **A,** Entry guide wire advancement is impeded by an unknown obstacle in the iliac artery region. **B,** An adequate length of intraluminal wire allows placement of a sheath, through which this diagnostic study was performed, revealing the nature of the problem to be a stenosis in the external iliac artery (EIA). **C,** Controlled guide wire passage is now possible and subsequent dilation is performed. PTLA, percutaneous transluminal angiography; CIA, common iliac artery.

not usually a problem if there is a good pulse to guide the way, but an appreciation of the location of the inguinal ligament is critical. Difficulty in compressing the femoral artery cephalad to the inguinal ligament is responsible for the increased risk of bleeding complications, particularly retroperitoneal bleeding, observed with suprainguinal punctures.[6,7] Punctures overly distal in the CFA can also be problematic because the smaller size of the artery in this location and the more abundant plaque commonly found in the distal CFA or proximal SFA results in a greater risk of thrombosis and dissection. Furthermore, the relative abundance of arterial and venous branches and the less adherent perivascular tissues found distal to the femoral bifurcation result in an increased risk of hematomas, false aneurysms, and arteriovenous fistulae with low punctures (Fig. 51-8).[8-10]

One radiographic landmark for the CFA is the midpoint of the inguinal ligament, with the CFA typically being located within 1.5 cm on either side of this location.[11] However, palpation of the pubic tubercle and the anterior superior iliac crest is not always helpful because many elderly patients are too obese to allow for definitive localization of the structures. Furthermore, both anatomic and radiographic landmarks for the location of the inguinal

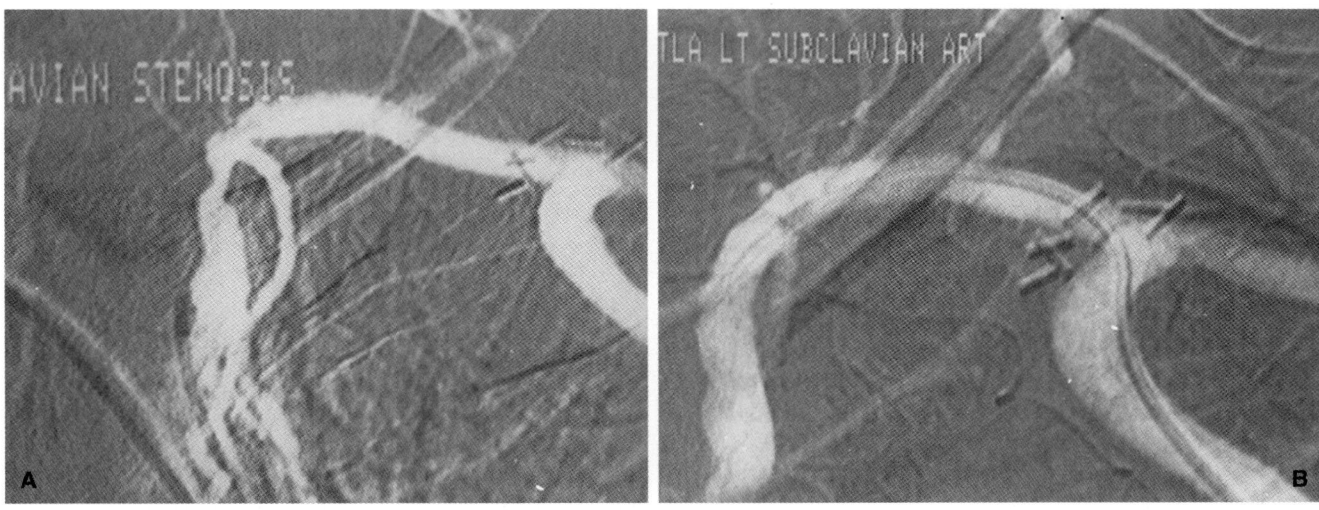

FIGURE 51-7 **A,** Stenosis of the left subclavian artery providing inflow to an axillobifemoral bypass approached via direct puncture of the graft over the anterior chest wall to avoid the risks of an axillary or brachial puncture. **B,** Completion arteriogram after balloon dilation of the left subclavian artery.

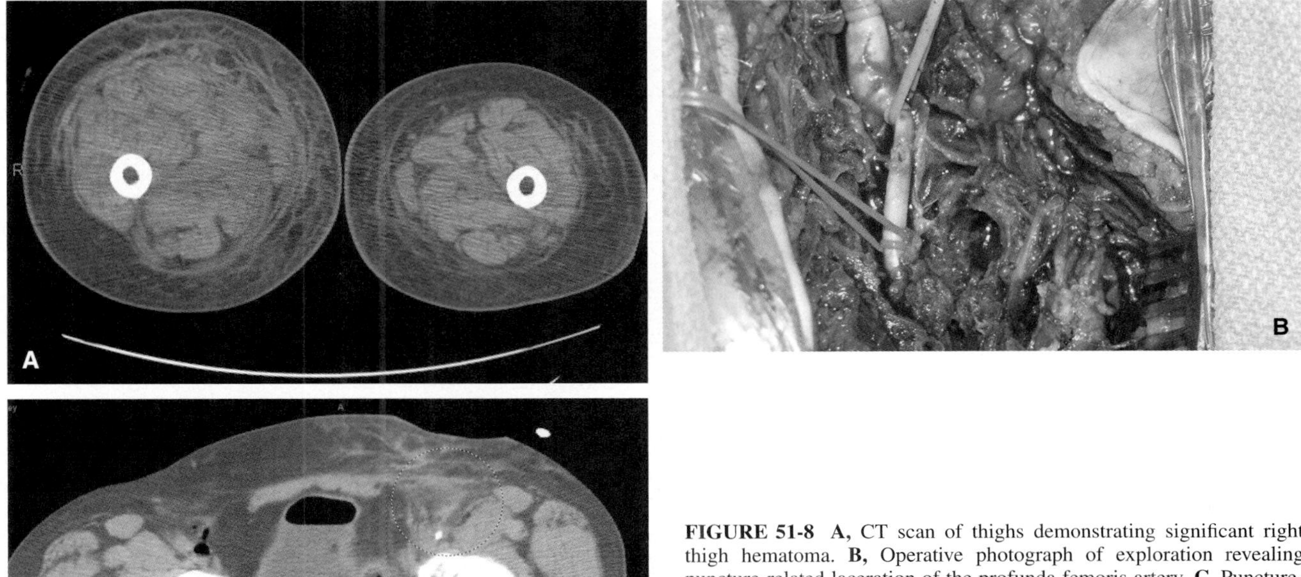

FIGURE 51-8 **A,** CT scan of thighs demonstrating significant right thigh hematoma. **B,** Operative photograph of exploration revealing puncture-related laceration of the profunda femoris artery. **C,** Puncture-associated left retroperitoneal hematoma.

ligament have been found to be poor predictors of its actual location.[12,13] The most medial cortex of the femoral head, on the other hand, has been found to be on average 14.8 mm (range, 7 to 35 mm) below the inguinal ligament[12] and 33 mm (range, 2 to 66 mm) above the femoral bifurcation.[14] In 77% to 79% of patients, at least part of the CFA lumen has been found to be located over the medial third of the femoral head.[13,14] Consequently, puncturing the femoral artery 1 cm lateral to the most medial cortex of the femoral head, as assessed radiographically, appears to be best for both retrograde and antegrade femoral artery catheterizations (see Fig. 51-4). When doing this it is important to remember that the femoral head should be centered in the field of view to avoid parallax errors that might otherwise occur. Additionally, any rotation of the patient's pelvis on the angiographic table distorts the relationship between the artery and the femoral head. Radiographic visualization of a calcific blood vessel may guide a successful puncture in patients with weak or absent femoral pulses. Obese, fully anticoagulated, and pulseless patients are at an extraordinarily high risk for complications from vascular access. Under these circumstances, the use of ultrasound guidance of the needle can reduce the incidence of complications.[15,16]

Once the site of intended needle insertion is ascertained, the skin and subcutaneous tissues are anesthetized with 1% lidocaine and a small skin nick is made with a No. 11 knife blade. The entry needle is then advanced through the skin nick toward the pulse at an angle of about 45 to 60 degrees. Keeping the artery between two fingers as one advances the needle can help guide the needle and may also stabilize the artery somewhat. If the patient experiences discomfort as the needle approaches the artery, one may inject more lidocaine through the entry needle into that region. Shooting pains down the anterior thigh may indicate femoral nerve stimulation from a laterally positioned needle that should be redirected. Although some interventionists attach a syringe to the needle and apply suction as they advance the needle, we prefer to go with an "open" needle because this allows assessment of the "quality" of the puncture and needle position by the force of the stream of blood that is expelled. For venous access, however, suction is usually required.

Once good blood return is obtained, the J-end of an entry guide wire (typically packaged with the sheath) is advanced through the needle. If *any* resistance is encountered, further advancement under fluoroscopic guidance is mandatory. Once the wire is beyond the tip of the needle and advancing smoothly it is generally best to "fluoro it up" the iliac artery. Not only does this ensure smooth passage but areas where the wire "hangs up" can be noted for further assessment. It is not uncommon for the wire to curl in the CFA or iliac arteries as it is being advanced. This can usually be resolved by slight rotation or repositioning of the needle and readvancement of the guide wire under fluoroscopic visualization. In some instances, the use of a straight "floppy-tipped" guide wire (testing with the hand first to ensure that it is the floppy end of the guide wire being inserted) may be more successful. A slight angle can usually be placed on the straight end of the wire by gently bending it over a thumbnail, giving the wire some steerability. If the entry guide wire becomes kinked or damaged, it is best to replace it. Although one can switch to a full-length diagnostic guide wire (because one will generally already be open and ready to use), it must be a metal-jacketed wire. Occasionally, significant vessel tortuosity may impair passage of the wire. Because 80% of significant iliac tortuosities are unilateral,[17] if the degree of tortuosity proves problematic or prohibitive for device passage, contralateral cannulation should be considered to minimize the risk of arterial damage. Plastic-coated guide wires, such as the Turemo glidewire, while invaluable for crossing stenoses, should *never* be used through an entry needle because the plastic coating can be shaved off by the bevel of the needle.[10,18,19]

Once the wire is successfully positioned in the iliac artery or distal aorta and there has been radiographic confirmation that there are no kinks, loops, or significant deviations in the course of the wire, the sheath may be inserted. The needle is withdrawn off the wire and pressure is held over the puncture site while an assistant threads the dilator/sheath assembly onto the wire for its subsequent advancement over the wire into the iliac artery. A firm, smooth motion is employed to advance the sheath over the wire. If resistance is met, fluoroscopy can be used to ascertain the reason. It is most important to try to advance the sheath in line with the wire because any angulation or arching creates resistance that may hinder passage. Once the sheath is advanced to the hub, it is important to evaluate the situation again radiographically before withdrawing the wire because, particularly in obese patients, the sheath may not have advanced into the artery but may be curled in the subcutaneous tissue. If the tip of the guide wire is up against a stenosis, the wire (and possibly the dilator) may have to be withdrawn a bit while the sheath is being advanced so as not to traumatize the stenotic lesion. However, the sheath should never be advanced on its own without a wire and tapering dilator leading the way.

In patients who have undergone numerous femoral catheterizations or previous femoral artery dissections, significant resistance to advancement of the sheath may be encountered. In such instances it is advisable to pass a dilator one-French size larger than the intended sheath size over the wire to create a larger track through the scar before attempting to readvance the sheath. If continued resistance is encountered, one can go up yet another French size or reinsert the previous dilator into the vessel and exchange out the guide wire for a stiffer wire, which allows the sheath to track better through the scar and into the vessel. Perisheath bleeding from overdilation is rarely a problem, and post-procedure hematomas are uncommon because the scar does not allow a place for blood to collect.

Antegrade Common Femoral Artery Cannulation

The antegrade femoral artery puncture is considerably more difficult for two basic reasons: body contours tend to interfere with access to the artery, and the close proximity of the puncture site to the origin of the SFA or lower extremity bypass grafts limits available working room between the needle puncture and the first bifurcation. The latter consideration mandates as high a puncture as possible (still entering the artery below the inguinal ligament), whereas the former often renders this quite difficult. Access can sometimes be facilitated by placing a roll of towels under the ipsilateral hip to extend it and by having an assistant retract the abdomen up and taping it out of the way. In most cases it is necessary to cannulate the SFA or a bypass graft at the time of the initial sheath placement because having to retract the sheath out of the profunda femoris artery (PFA) and trying to manipulate it into the SFA later risks inadvertent sheath removal and loss of vascular access. Consequently, passage of the entry guide wire must be carefully observed fluoroscopically and the wire must be seen to follow the anticipated course of the SFA or graft before the sheath is advanced over the wire (Fig. 51-9). When in doubt, one should perform a scout angiogram through the entry needle to identify the origin

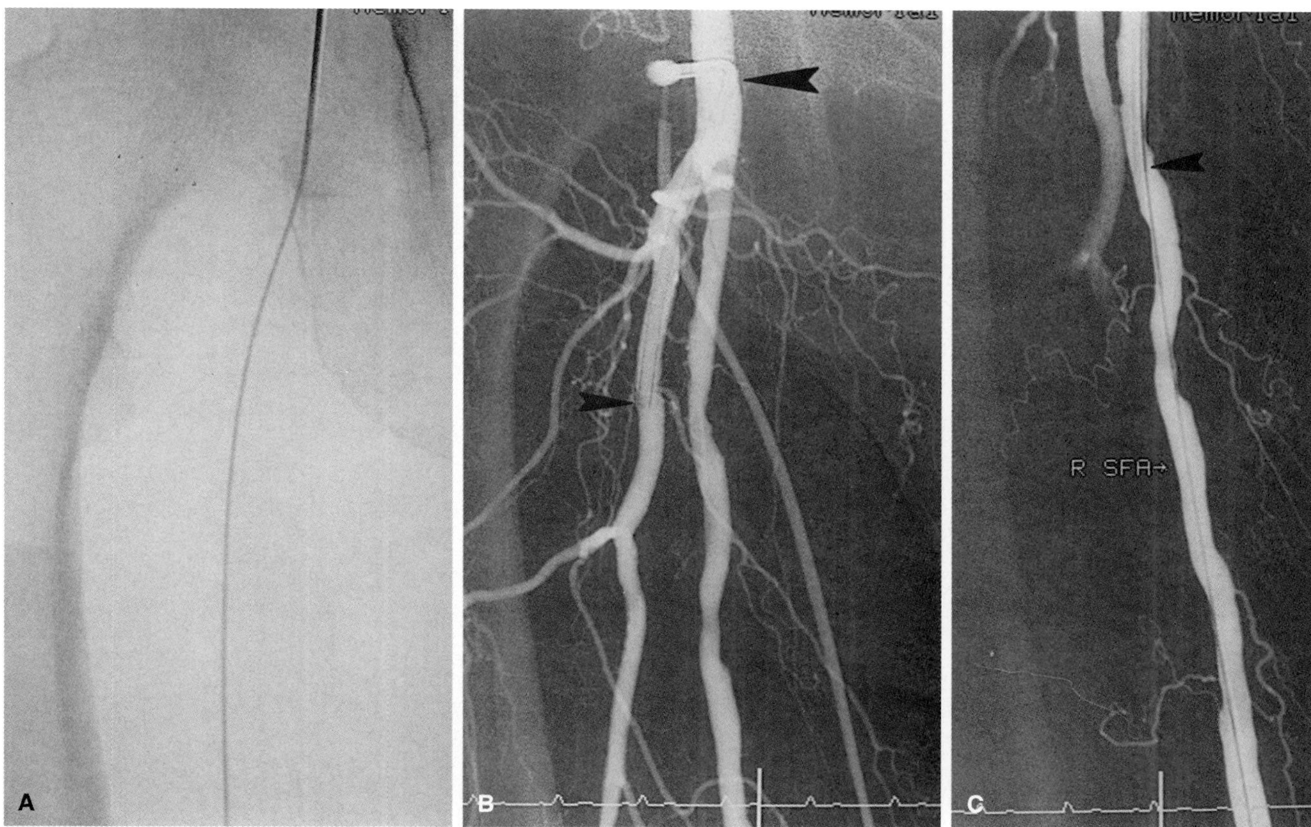

FIGURE 51-9 **A,** Initial guide wire passage during antegrade femoral artery catheterization demonstrates medial deviation of the guide wire suggestive of passage into the profunda femoris artery. **B,** Failing to appreciate this, the sheath was inserted over the guide wire, and subsequent angiography confirms its placement in the profunda femoris artery. The *upper arrowhead* indicates the puncture site, and the *lower arrowhead* indicates the distal tip of sheath in the profunda femoris artery. **C,** Nonetheless, because the puncture was sufficiently proximal to the femoral bifurcation, there was adequate working room to allow the sheath to be retracted, the guide wire redirected and advanced into the superficial femoral artery, and the sheath readvanced over the guide wire into the intended position in the superficial femoral artery. The *arrowhead* indicates the distal tip of the sheath in the superficial femoral artery (SFA). (**A-C,** From Hodgson KJ, Mattos MA, Sumner DS: Access to the vascular system for endovascular procedures: Techniques and indications for percutaneous and open arteriotomy approaches. Semin Vasc Surg 10:206-221, 1997.)

of the vessel of interest and its course (Fig. 51-10). Alternatively, a small (4-French) dilator can be advanced into the artery and an angiogram performed through it. If it turns out to be in the SFA, it can be rewired and the sheath placed in standard fashion. If it is in the PFA and the puncture site is proximal enough on the CFA to allow for guide wire manipulation, the dilator can be slowly withdrawn while an angled guide wire is manipulated through the dilator and into the SFA. A set with an extra-long puncture needle and a preshaped catheter sheath using a wing-shaped steering device may overcome some of these issues.[20,21] Any movement of the angiographic table or image intensifier between performance of the scout study and attempted wire passage should be avoided because it will alter the relationships between the anatomic and radiographic landmarks, thereby confusing the situation.

Angiographic evaluation sometimes reveals that the puncture is in the SFA itself. Providing that there is still sufficient working room to address the lesion of interest, there is no need to withdraw and repuncture. If, however, it is determined that the puncture is in the PFA or too distal in the CFA to allow wire manipulation, the needle will need to be removed, pressure held for 5 to 10 minutes, and the puncture attempt repeated. Alternatively, a closure device may be used and a new access site selected. On occasion, disease in the SFA prevents the standard entry J-wire from passing into or far enough down the SFA. In such situations a floppy-tipped wire can be used, such as a Bentson Starter or a Wholey Mallinckrodt, usually after placing a slight (~60-degree) angle on it as described earlier. The remainder of the sheath placement procedure is the same as outlined earlier. One must remember to check sheath placement radiographically prior to removing the guide wire, however, because subcutaneous curling of the sheath rather than intravascular positioning is most common with the antegrade CFA puncture.

Retrograde-to-Antegrade Femoral Artery Cannulation

Although we do not favor it, some have proposed a technique for conversion from a retrograde femoral cannulation to an antegrade approach as a means of more easily gaining antegrade femoral artery access. If one anticipates

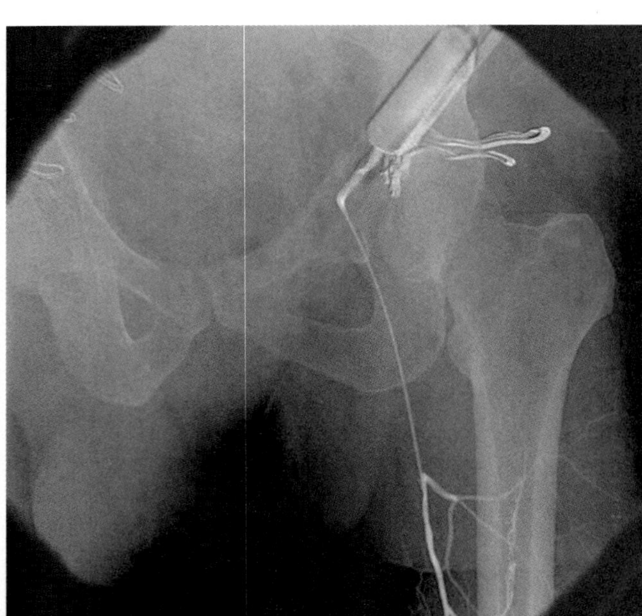

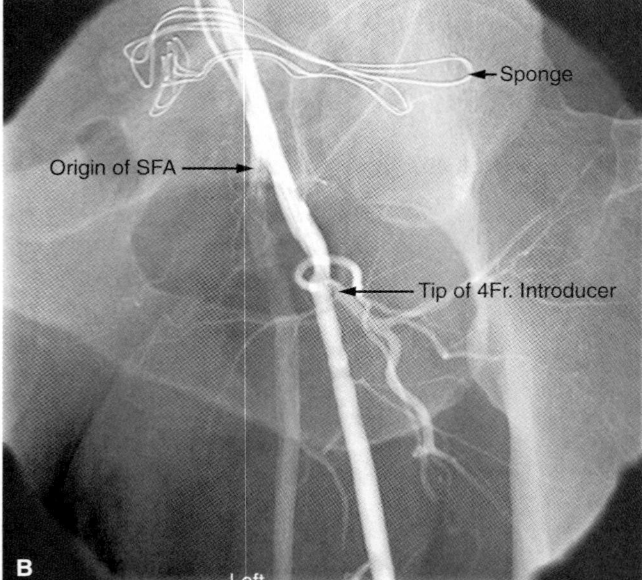

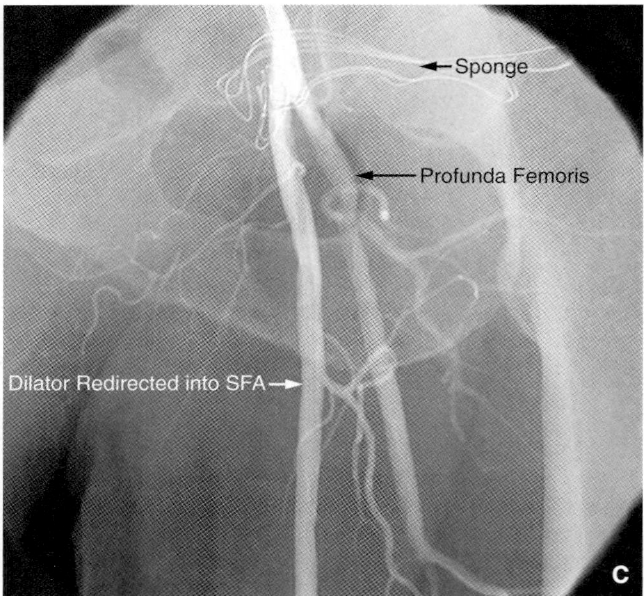

FIGURE 51-10 **A,** Scout angiograph through a 4-French dilator noted to be residing in the distal profunda femoris artery. **B,** With the dilator retracted, the femoral bifurcation is visualized. **C,** The guide wire and then sheath are redirected down the superficial femoral artery (SFA).

the need for this technique, the puncture should be relatively high on the CFA with a steep, near-vertical angle to the skin. Ultrasonographic guidance to avoid puncturing the PFA or femoral veins may be advantageous. After retrograde placement of a soft 4- or 5-French sheath in the CFA, a sidewinder catheter such as a Simmons, Omni SOS, or Visceral Selective-1 (VS-1) is formed in the abdominal aorta or ipsilateral iliac artery. The catheter is retracted into the ipsilateral SFA or bypass graft and confirmed angiographically. Wire purchase is then obtained and the access sheath and diagnostic catheter are pulled back until the secondary curve of the diagnostic catheter reaches the arterial puncture site. Once the diagnostic catheter has taken its shape, further wire purchase is obtained and a sheath is then inserted in an antegrade fashion. Drawbacks from this technique include a high risk of puncture to the PFA or veins, the potential for shear injury to the arterial access site, and kinks in the sheath. Higher radiation doses have been documented with the use of this technique[22] but no significant complications have been reported.[22-25] Proponents of this conversion technique believe that it may be have some advantages over an antegrade femoral approach, particularly in obese patients.[22]

Retrograde Popliteal and Distal Arterial Cannulations

The technique for retrograde popliteal and tibial artery cannulations is similar to that of standard CFA access, except for the use of ultrasound-guided puncture (Fig. 51-11).

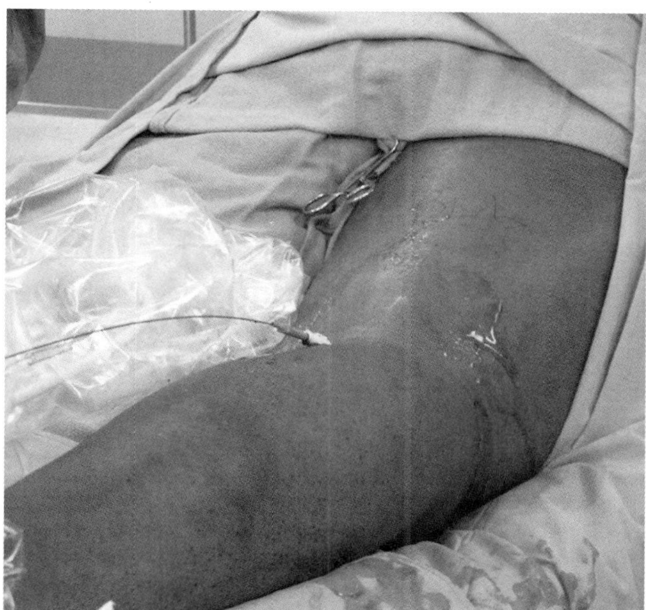

FIGURE 51-11 Percutaneous access into the right popliteal artery.

The retrograde popliteal approach is the more common of the two and has been advocated when a CFA approach is problematic or not possible; it may avoid difficult and dangerous antegrade femoral punctures in obese patients; patients with high CFA bifurcations; in patients with extra-anatomic bypass grafts; or in patients with local groin issues, such as open wounds, infection, or radiation changes. It also permits combined treatment of ipsilateral SFA and iliac lesions in the same setting or recanalization of the true lumen from a subintimal SFA angioplasty.[26,27] However, this technique requires placement of the patient in the prone position. This is usually well tolerated except for obese patients with obstructive pulmonary disease, in which case ventilatory support may be required if this particular approach is necessary.

The popliteal artery and vein are ultrasonographically imaged in their longitudinal orientation and punctured under ultrasound guidance. This technique is greatly facilitated by the use of an echogenic-tipped needle. Ultrasound can also demonstrate the healthiest possible site for access, avoiding heavily calcified plaque formations or aneurysmal arteries. The use of the *Smart*Needle for this application has been previously discussed in this chapter.[2] The greatest concern with the popliteal puncture is the creation of an arteriovenous fistula. This complication can be minimized with the routine use of ultrasound guidance. Furthermore, if distal embolization were to occur into the run-off arteries, the options for mechanical or catheter-directed pharmacologic thrombolysis are limited.

Two innovative techniques for retrograde cannulation of the tibial and peroneal arteries for limb salvage in the setting of distal lower extremity occlusive disease have been proposed.[28,29] In the report by Botti and associates,[28] retrograde percutaneous guide wire passage through the tibial arteries was successful in all six cases treated, and five of them experienced rapid wound healing. Wolosker and colleagues[29] employed an open approach through the peroneal artery to perform adjuvant SFA angioplasty during a compromised below knee-amputation with a good clinical result.

Upper Extremity Arterial Cannulation

On occasion, such as in the situation of bilateral iliac artery occlusions or in the presence of recently (<3 month) created aortoiliofemoral or femorofemoral crossover bypass grafts, arterial access must be obtained via an upper extremity approach. This can be achieved through either open or percutaneous subclavian, axillary, brachial, or radial approaches. Vascular surgeons are well familiar with the technique for open vascular access and, consequently, it is not discussed further here. Suffice to say that this is the safest approach because the neural and vascular structures are directly visualized and protected and the artery can be primarily repaired, minimizing the risks of related complications. In those less experienced in percutaneous brachial access, the open technique may be preferred because an increased incidence of complications in the occasional brachial percutaneous angiographer has been recognized.[30] A technique for catheterization of the second portion of the subclavian artery or first portion of the axillary artery has been introduced by surgeons[31]; however, it has not been broadly adopted because it is technically demanding, has a steep learning curve, and there are concerns about iatrogenic pneumothorax. This technique, when performed by expert surgeons and with the use of supraclavicular and infraclavicular pressure after removal of the catheters, has been associated with high success and low complication rates.[31]

Of the upper extremity percutaneous access techniques, the mid/high-brachial puncture is the most commonly performed and the one that we favor. Unless there is evidence of coexisting subclavian/axillary disease, the left side is the preferred upper extremity access site. This is because it is generally easier to manipulate the wire/catheter into the descending aorta from the left than the right, particularly in cases in which the innominate artery originates low on the arch (Fig. 51-12). Furthermore, when approached from the right side the catheter and wire reside in the flow path to the right vertebral and common carotid arteries, the innominate artery, and the left carotid artery, increasing the risk of neurologic embolic events.

Proper positioning of the patient is important and is best achieved by having patients place their ipsilateral hand palm-up behind their head. The brachial artery pulse is palpated lateral to the pectoralis major muscle and the overlying skin is anesthetized. The close proximity of the brachial plexus trunks mandates a careful, deliberate passage of the needle, though direct nerve injury from the needle is uncommon, occurring in less than 1% of axillary punctures.[31-33] Patient complaints of shooting pain down the arm should prompt retraction followed by redirection of the needle. The highly mobile axillary/brachial artery often benefits from manual fixation by the surgeon's second hand. Once good arterial blood return is encountered, the guide wire is advanced into the artery, after which the sheath is advanced over the entry wire as previously outlined.

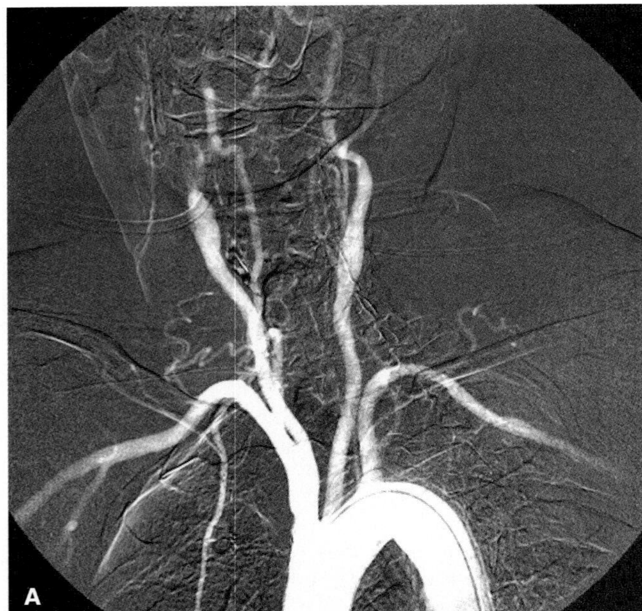

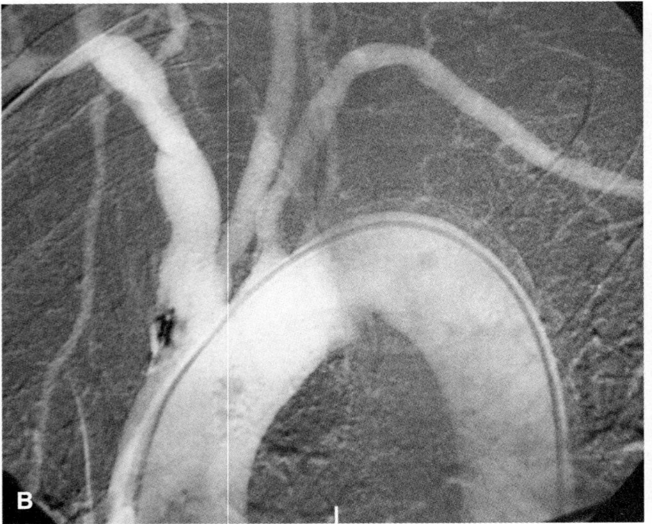

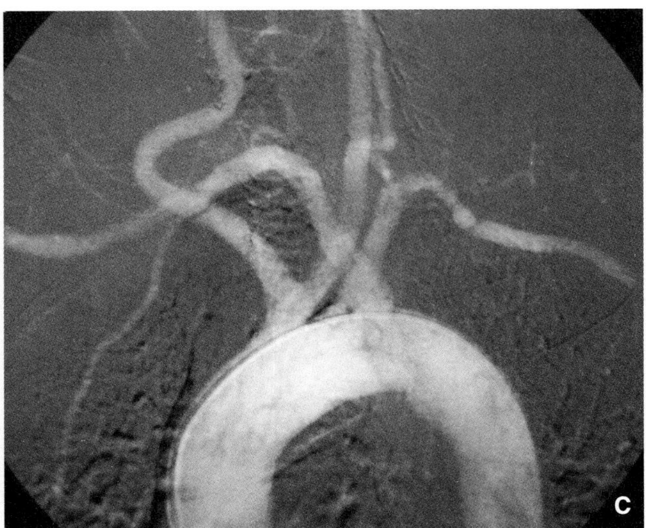

FIGURE 51-12 **A,** Normal arch anatomy. **B,** A common origin of the innominate and left common carotid arteries. **C,** Bovine arch anatomy with the left common carotid artery arising directly from the innominate artery.

Having secured arterial access, a full-length angiographic guide wire (preferably a J-wire) is then advanced through the sheath under fluoroscopic guidance and manipulated down the descending aorta, a maneuver best observed in the left anterior oblique orientation. Frequently, a pigtail catheter can be hooked at the origin of the left subclavian artery and used to direct the guide wire down the descending thoracic aorta. Nevertheless, if the wire repeatedly courses into the ascending aorta, an angled diagnostic catheter (i.e., Bernstein, Cobra, right Judkins, inferior mesenteric) can be used in coaxial concert with a guide wire to negotiate the wire into the descending aorta. From here the remainder of the procedure is performed in the usual fashion.

In general, it is advisable to use the smallest sheath possible in the upper extremity arteries because their relatively small size increases the risk of vessel thrombosis. Additionally, puncture-related hemorrhage, more common with larger punctures, has the added risk of axillary sheath hematoma with neurologic compromise, though this is reported to occur in less than 3% of brachial or axillary artery catheterizations.[34-36] This complication requires immediate recognition and surgical decompression if permanent neurologic dysfunction is to be avoided. The development of peripheral paresthesias warrants close observation, whereas any loss of motor function mandates emergent surgical attention if the risk of permanent neurologic deficit is to be minimized.[34,35] Despite attempts to minimize the puncture size, on occasion it is necessary to stent via the axillary approach and the sheath will have to be up-sized to 6 or 8 French, usually a well-tolerated situation. Brachial artery thrombosis is the most frequent major complication associated with brachial access.[36] We consider the mid/high-brachial approach preferable to an antecubital brachial artery puncture because the distal brachial artery is smaller to begin with and has a higher propensity to go into spasm, greatly increasing the risk of puncture-related thrombosis.

The merits of percutaneous radial artery access for coronary and cerebral angiography have long been recognized.[37,38] The advantages of this technique include limited patient discomfort, simple and safe postprocedural hemostasis, and early mobilization. However, this technique requires puncture of a very spastic small-diameter artery, limiting the options of sheath access. A positive Allen test is a mandatory prerequisite to the use of this technique. Additionally, this approach typically mandates the use of longer catheters to reach most peripheral target vessels.

Venous Cannulation

The only other approaches that one needs to know are those that provide access to the venous system for the performance of vena caval filter placement, renal vein renin sampling, or treatment of upper or lower extremity deep venous thrombosis (Fig. 51-13). The technique of femoral venous puncture parallels that of its corresponding artery. Basically, the femoral vein is located just medial to the artery, the pulsation of which is typically used as its landmark. If arterial pulsation is absent, the vein can be found approximately 2 cm lateral to the pubic tubercle. As with arterial punctures, it is recommended that one advance the guide wire up the iliac vein under fluoroscopic visualization to ensure against any inadvertent misplacement of the sheath. Although vena caval filters can be inserted via the contralateral femoral approach to a deep venous thrombosis, we prefer the jugular approach as an access site because it reduces the risk of instrumentation through thrombus or potential venous injury from the filter carrier that could predispose to development of deep venous thrombosis on the unaffected side.

Catheterization of the jugular vein for insertion of a vena caval filter is best performed on the right side, because this provides a "straight shot" to the infrarenal vena cava. The jugular vein is punctured just lateral to the carotid artery either anterior or posterior to the sternocleidomastoid muscle and a sheath is inserted in the typical fashion. If neither femoral access site can be used owing to proximity of the venous thrombosis process and the jugular approach is also unavailable owing to, for example, local thrombosis or a cervical collar, the subclavian or axillary veins may be a practical alternative. The subclavian vein can be approached through a supraclavicular puncture just lateral to the clavicular head of the sternocleidomastoid muscle directing the needle toward the contralateral nipple. Alternatively, the axillary vein can be punctured with ultrasonographic guidance and/or with fluoroscopically guided venography. Fluoroscopy may be performed by injecting 10 to 15 mL of 50% contrast via a peripherally placed line and the use of digital subtraction angiography (DSA). The road mapping feature available on most fluoroscopy machines can be used to guide the vein puncture. When the axillary vein is inadequately visualized to allow puncture, application of a tourniquet to the upper arm just above the elbow helps direct the contrast flow toward the deep venous system.[39]

Our preference is to routinely perform a power venacavogram prior to inferior vena caval filter insertion with a pigtail catheter positioned at the third lumbar vertebral body using 25 mL of nonionic contrast agent injected over 2 seconds. Simultaneous hand injection of 15 mL of 50% contrast via an oversized ipsilateral sheath aids in visualization of the iliac bifurcation. Because of the high incidence of suboptimal nonselective venacavograms, 68% in our experience, we advocate a low threshold for selective catheterization of the renal, iliac, and other large veins draining into the vena cava to optimize filter placement.[40]

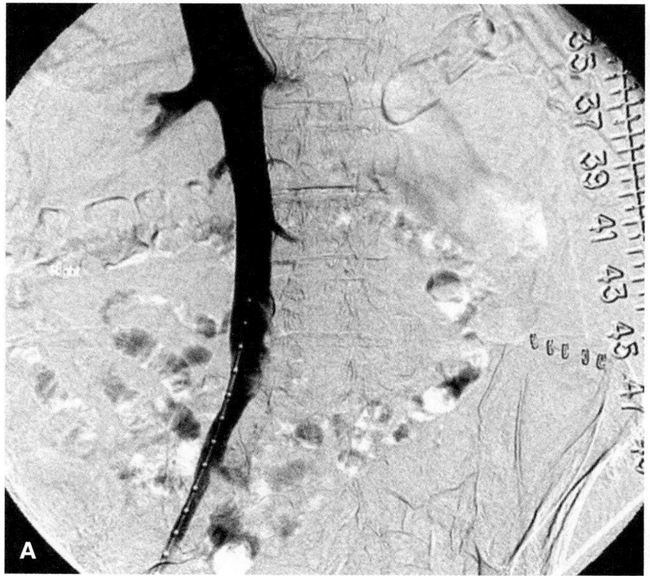

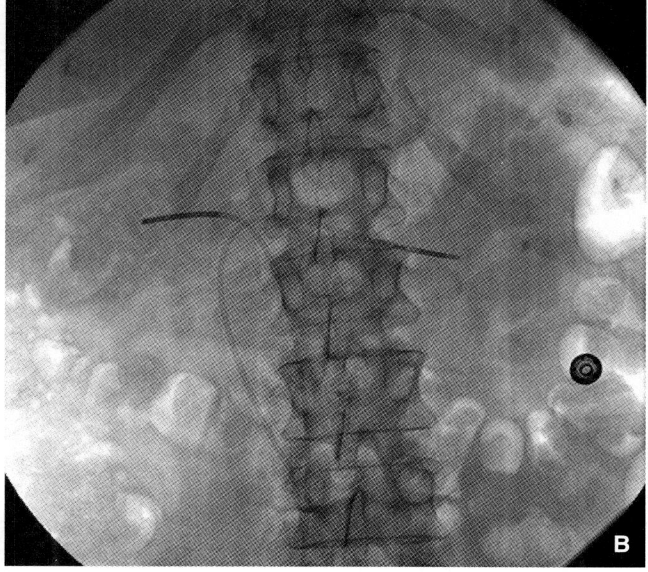

FIGURE 51-13 **A,** Venacavogram via the right common femoral approach demonstrating reflux of contrast agent into the proximal renal veins bilaterally. **B,** Simultaneous bilateral renal vein selective catheterizations.

Though less frequently performed than in the past, renin vein sampling can provide useful information in patients with bilateral moderate renal arterial stenoses, where it can help define which, if either, kidney is responsible for the elevated renin production. Similarly, in patients with an atrophic kidney and severe hypertension despite aggressive medical management, renin sampling from the atrophic kidney's effluent vein can help predict the need for and success of nephrectomy, because low renin values have been shown to predict the lack of clinical response following intervention.[41] Our protocol for renin vein sampling involves strict bed rest for 24 hours, fluid restriction and adjuvant diuresis with loop diuretics, avoidance of all antihypertensive medications other than calcium-channel blockers, and placement of bilateral 5-French sheaths for simultaneous bilateral renal vein samplings and for simultaneous suprarenal and infrarenal venous samplings. It is imperative to place the selective catheter well into the main renal vein and to withdraw blood slowly so that no blood is being aspirated from the vena cava. Additionally, the catheter tip should be past the gonadal and suprarenal branches. Following renal vein sampling the catheters are moved (one to a suprarenal and the other to an infrarenal position) and repeat samplings are obtained. At least three samples 10 minutes apart are obtained in each position.

■ ENDOVASCULAR DEVICES

Angiographic Guide Wires

Despite differences in materials and handling characteristics, all guide wires serve the same basic function of facilitating the positioning of catheters in particular locations by providing guidance and support for the catheter being advanced over them. The guide wire characteristics required to achieve this depend on the unique anatomic circumstances present, as well as the nature of the task at hand. To address these varying requirements, guide wires are available with a variety of diameters, lengths, tip shapes, tip and shaft stiffnesses, and antifriction coatings. Small-diameter wires are difficult to see under fluoroscopy, a problem sometimes addressed by using radiopaque material such as gold or platinum in the tip. Similarly, some guide wires have radiopaque markers placed at fixed distances from each other to allow calibration of the computer for subsequent measurement of vessel diameters (Fig. 51-14). *Steerability*, which refers to the degree of correlation between rotation of the shaft of the guide wire ex vivo and that of the guide wire tip in vivo, can also vary between different types of wires. Disposable "torque" devices designed to grip guide wires and facilitate manipulation are frequently necessary, especially with hydrophilic-coated wires, which are difficult to grip.

Classic guide wires are constructed of two different wire components: an inner wire called a *mandrel*, which tapers toward the tip to produce a floppier tip than shaft, and an outer stainless-steel coil wrap. There is typically a safety wire connecting the mandrel to the tip of the outer coil to prevent their separation. In some wires, the inner mandrel, which is responsible for most of the stiffness of the wire, can be moved within the outer coil to vary the stiffness and shape of the tip of the wire. Such guide wires are referred to as *movable core wires*.

With infusion guide wires the inner core wire can be removed, allowing its channel to be used to infuse dilute contrast or thrombolytic agents. The Turemo glidewire has gained popularity due to its excellent torque response and low-friction coating. Constructed of a nitinol (nickel-titanium) inner core with a polyurethane outer coating, the surface is further coated with a hydrophilic polymer, making it extremely slippery when wet. This characteristic facilitates guide wire advancement, particularly through tortuous areas, as well as catheter/guide wire exchanges, but it must be kept meticulously clean and moist to avoid becoming tacky.

To successfully serve its function, the guide wire itself, alone or with directional catheter assistance, must be able to be manipulated into the desired location without traumatizing the vessel. Tip shape plays a major role in this function, with J-tipped configurations being the least traumatic and least likely to dissect or perforate blood vessels but also the least likely to negotiate tight stenoses. The most common J-wires have either 1.5- or 3-mm arc radii, resulting in wires that lead with 3- or 6-mm prows, respectively. Guide wires also come with angled or straight tips, and most metal guide wire tips can be shaped as desired by bending them over a thumbnail. Having a shaped tip gives the guide wire directionality and facilitates its being directed into branch vessels. At times, complex anatomic curves are best negotiated with a combination of a directional catheter and guide wire, using the catheter to direct the wire into branch vessels, after which the catheter is advanced over it. Regardless of configuration, most guide wire tips are fairly floppy over a distance of 3 to 8 cm to minimize the risk of dissection and perforation.

Most guide wires in use today have some type of antifriction coating, often Teflon, to facilitate guide wire placement and catheter/wire exchanges. Nonetheless, it is important to keep guide wires clean by wiping them down after each catheter exchange. This prevents blood from drying on the wire and hindering catheter passage. The hydrophilic coating of the Turemo glidewires, as mentioned earlier, renders them extremely slippery when they are wet but quite tacky when they start to dry out. These types of wires should be wet wiped before each new catheter passage to minimize friction between the wire and the catheter, thereby reducing the risk of losing the guide wire position during the catheter exchange. In general, guide wires can be classified according to their tip characteristics as floppy, straight, and steerable or angled and to their body as standard, stiff, and super-stiff. These wire characteristics are important to recognize, because each of these varieties has different applications. As previously mentioned, such hydrophilic coatings can be shaved off if they are used through entry needles and, therefore, these types of wires are not used for initial vascular access.

The ability of a guide wire to support subsequent catheter passage, particularly around multiple turns, depends greatly on the stiffness of the shaft of the wire. To some extent this is a function of guide wire diameter, but even within the same size category, a variety of guide wire stiffnesses are available. In general, the most flexible shafted guide wire that provides sufficient support to achieve the desired catheter or device position is the one that should be used, bearing in mind that larger and stiffer devices, such as

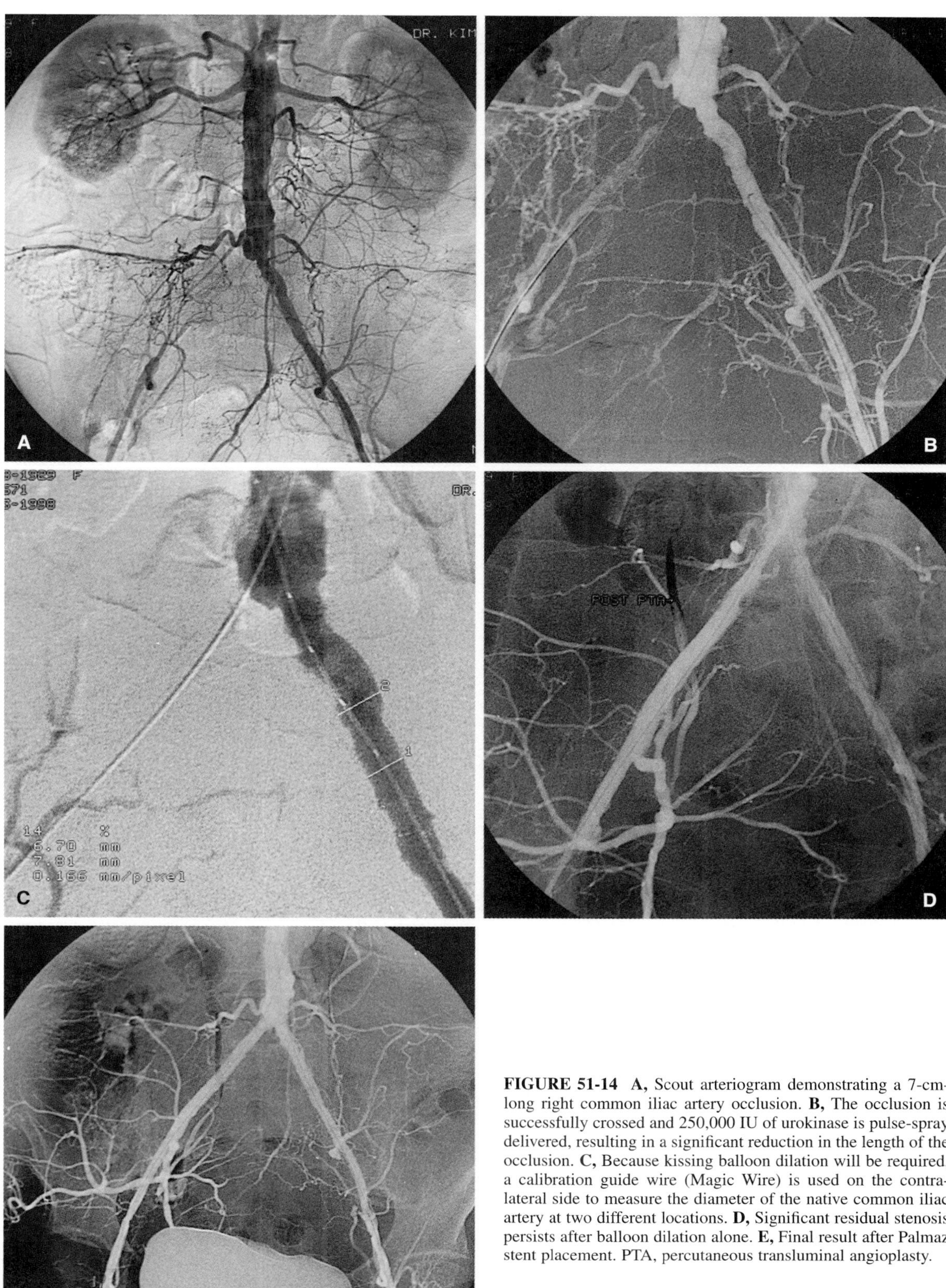

FIGURE 51-14 **A,** Scout arteriogram demonstrating a 7-cm-long right common iliac artery occlusion. **B,** The occlusion is successfully crossed and 250,000 IU of urokinase is pulse-spray delivered, resulting in a significant reduction in the length of the occlusion. **C,** Because kissing balloon dilation will be required, a calibration guide wire (Magic Wire) is used on the contralateral side to measure the diameter of the native common iliac artery at two different locations. **D,** Significant residual stenosis persists after balloon dilation alone. **E,** Final result after Palmaz stent placement. PTA, percutaneous transluminal angioplasty.

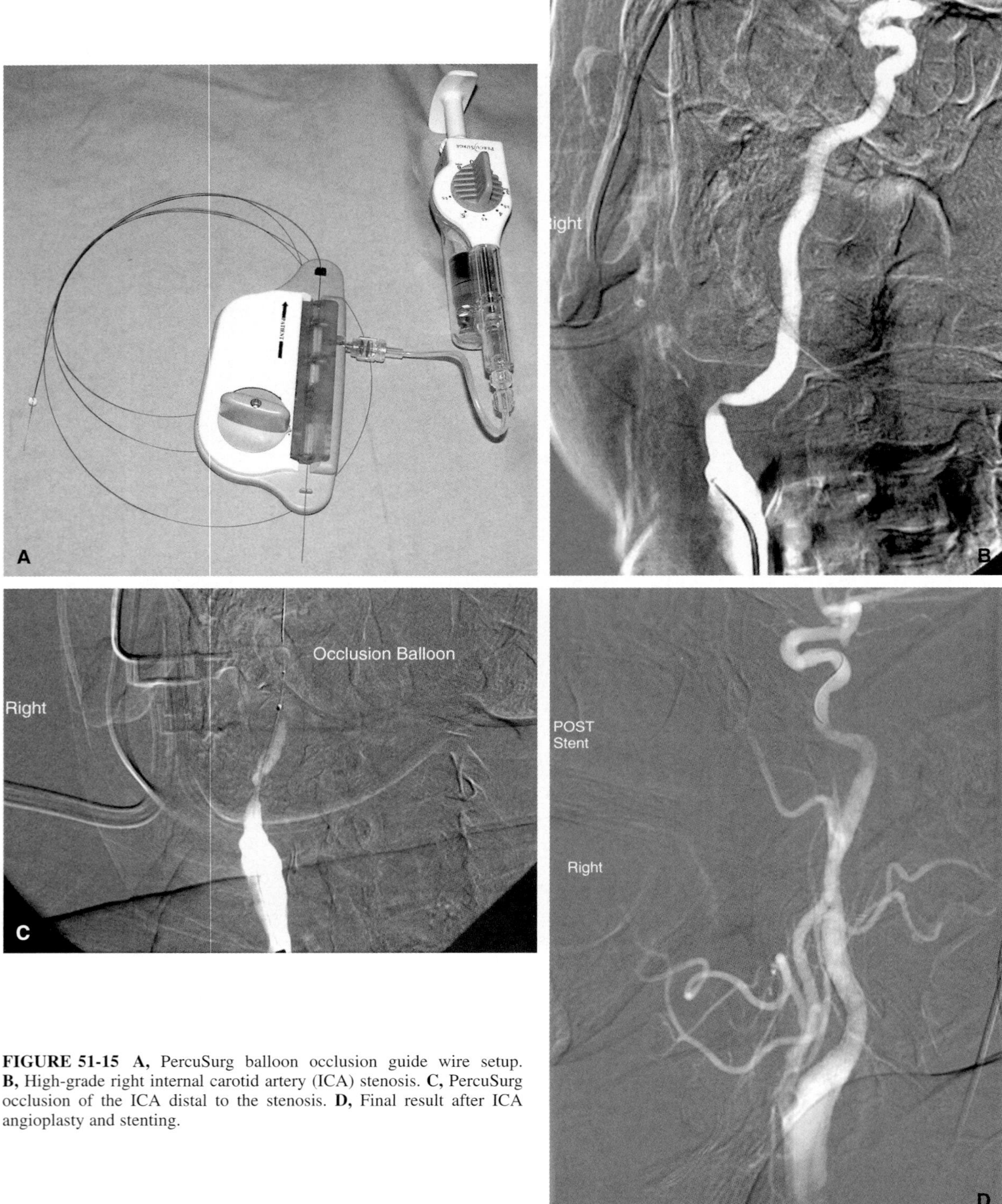

FIGURE 51-15 **A,** PercuSurg balloon occlusion guide wire setup. **B,** High-grade right internal carotid artery (ICA) stenosis. **C,** PercuSurg occlusion of the ICA distal to the stenosis. **D,** Final result after ICA angioplasty and stenting.

stents and endoluminal grafts, require stiffer wires to reliably track over. Different devices have different maximum guide wire sizes, with standard diagnostic and balloon catheters typically accepting up to a 0.035- or 0.038-inch guide wire, whereas small-vessel angioplasty catheters often accept only up to a 0.014-inch guide wire. If the guide wire alone is insufficient to provide the necessary support to achieve the desired catheter position, supplemental external support can be provided by an appropriately shaped guiding catheter or guiding sheath.

Guide wires are generally available in two different length ranges. The standard lengths range from 145 to 180 cm and are useful for positioning catheters but are not long enough to permit "exchanging out" a catheter unless

Section IX Plate 1

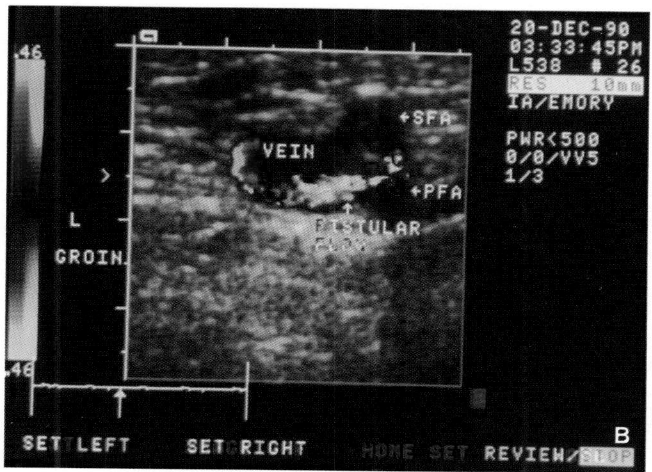

FIGURE 54-7B. Typical appearance of fistula on duplex scanning.

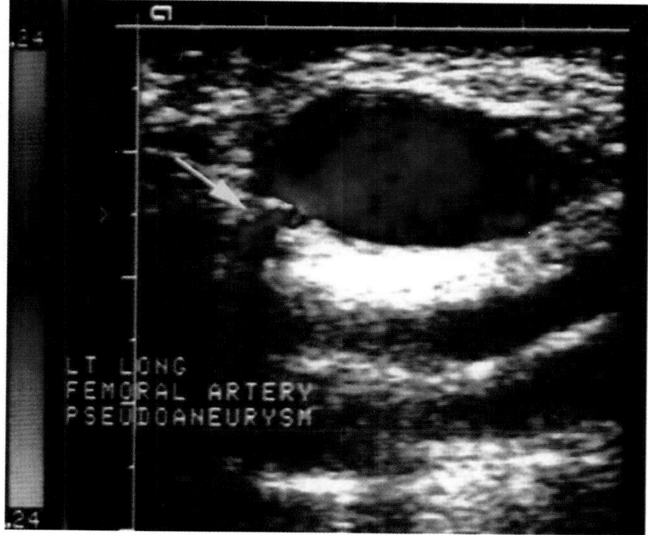

FIGURE 54-9 Duplex scanning examination of pseudoaneurysm showing tract from the femoral artery into the pseudoaneurysm cavity.

the lesion crossing to be maintained is within about 30 to 40 cm from the site of vascular access or one is using a catheter with a rapid exchange system. This maneuver, where the guide wire is left in its final desired position while one catheter is removed from over the wire and replaced with another, requires a sufficient length of wire to permit complete withdrawal of the initial catheter without having to relinquish the desired position of the guide wire or lose contact with the ex-vivo tail of the wire. Wires long enough to permit this type of exchange, referred to as *exchange-length guide wires*, are typically in the 240- to 300-cm-length range. Some guide wires have a “docking” feature that allows a standard wire to be transformed into an exchange-length wire by attaching an extension onto the standard length wire.

Guide wire diameters are specified in fractional inches, ranging from 0.012 to 0.052 inch, with 0.035 inch being the most commonly used size for peripheral work. As previously noted, given the same material and method of construction, guide wire diameter is the primary variable influencing the stiffness of the wire. Clearly, guide wires are just one component of the instrumentation system being used for a particular task, and it is important to ensure that the guide wire and catheter or device to be tracked over it have compatible sizes. Although guide wires with smaller diameters than the maximal lumen size of a catheter can be used through that catheter, the resultant diminution of support generally renders this an undesirable combination. Furthermore, when performing coil embolization it is imperative that the guide wire diameter, catheter lumen size, and embolization coil diameter be closely matched before attempting to push the coil through the catheter with the guide wire, lest the coil begin to take its shape prematurely within the catheter resulting in jamming of the coil inside the catheter. The most common situations where a smaller than maximum allowable guide wire are used is when a larger catheter is being exchanged for a smaller catheter that would only accommodate the smaller guide wire or when pressure gradients are to be measured without losing crossing of the lesion. In instances where it is desirable to be able to infuse radiographic contrast (or another liquid) through a catheter while the guide wire is in place, using a smaller than maximal possible guide wire allows some of the lumen of the catheter to remain open to transmit the contrast agent, though achievable flow rates will be small and resultant opacification frequently suboptimal. Unfortunately, compensating for this by infusing full-strength contrast rarely improves the situation because its increased viscosity inhibits its flow through the small residual lumen.

A new category of guide wire has recently emerged, driven by the desire to be able to position antiembolic balloons or filters downstream of an atherosclerotic lesion during intervention. The technical need for these wires to be both flexible and small in diameter diminishes their ability to provide firm tracking support for subsequent device passage, mandating the use of a guiding catheter or sheath in close proximity to the lesion being treated. The first embolic protection device, the GuardWire, has an occlusion balloon at the distal end and has been approved by the FDA for distal embolization protection in the coronary arteries. The balloon from these wires is positioned beyond the lesion to be treated entrapping fragments from the lesion to be treated into a proximal static column of blood, which can be aspirated with the use of an export aspiration catheter. This protection balloon has also been used off-label for renal and cerebral angioplasty (Fig. 51-15). More recent entries into this arena provide blood stream filtration rather than outflow occlusion, allowing maintained perfusion during intervention.

Ultimately, guide wire selection is a function of the task at hand and the given anatomic configuration. Initial evaluation is generally performed with a guide wire least likely to cause injury to the vessel wall, such as a J-wire. If target lesions are identified, it may be appropriate to switch to a calibrated wire for accurate sizing (Magic Torque) or to an angled (Radiofocus Terumo glidewire) or straight-tipped wire (Benson Starter) to traverse stenotic lesions. Working with relatively large or stiff devices or through tortuous vessels may mandate the use of a stiffer shafted wire to get the device to track the wire without dislodging it. Stiff wires include the Lunderquist, the Microvena, and the Amplatz Super Stiff wires. The decision should be based on the need to avoid kinking, length of the floppy end, and the degree of stiffness required. Despite these general guidelines, wire selection is often based on operator familiarity and experience, and the use of multiple wires to address different challenges during a given case is not uncommon.

■ DIAGNOSTIC CATHETERS

Diagnostic catheters are designed to facilitate the delivery of radiographic contrast to specific areas of the vascular system to permit radiographic opacification of the flow channel of these vessels. Catheters intended for contrast infusion in the aorta and vena cava are typically advanced to that location from the site of vascular access over a guide wire and are referred to as *nonselective catheters*. In contrast, “selective” catheters are designed to engage the orifices of branch vessels and may or may not be advanced further out the selected vascular tree prior to contrast infusion. Generally, optimal visualization occurs when the catheter position is close to the area of interest, thereby maximizing contrast density in this region while minimizing opacification of adjacent overlapping vessels which may obscure detail in the area of interest. Although some nonselective catheters can be used in conjunction with a guide wire support and direction to perform selective catheterizations (Fig. 51-16), this is not their primary function. Ancillary uses for selective catheters include pullback pressure measurements, the instillation of pharmacologic agents (e.g., vasodilators or sclerosants), delivery of embolic material (e.g., coil embolization), and sampling of blood from specific locations (e.g., renal vein renin sampling). Nonselective catheters would not generally be suitable for these uses.

A variety of characteristics of diagnostic catheters determine how each will behave and for what use they are best suited. Principal among these variations is the shape a catheter assumes (or can be made to assume) once it is intravascular and the leading guide wire has been removed. Other important characteristics include catheter stiffness, tip design, torque response, antifrictional properties, radiopacity, and whether they have multiple side-holes

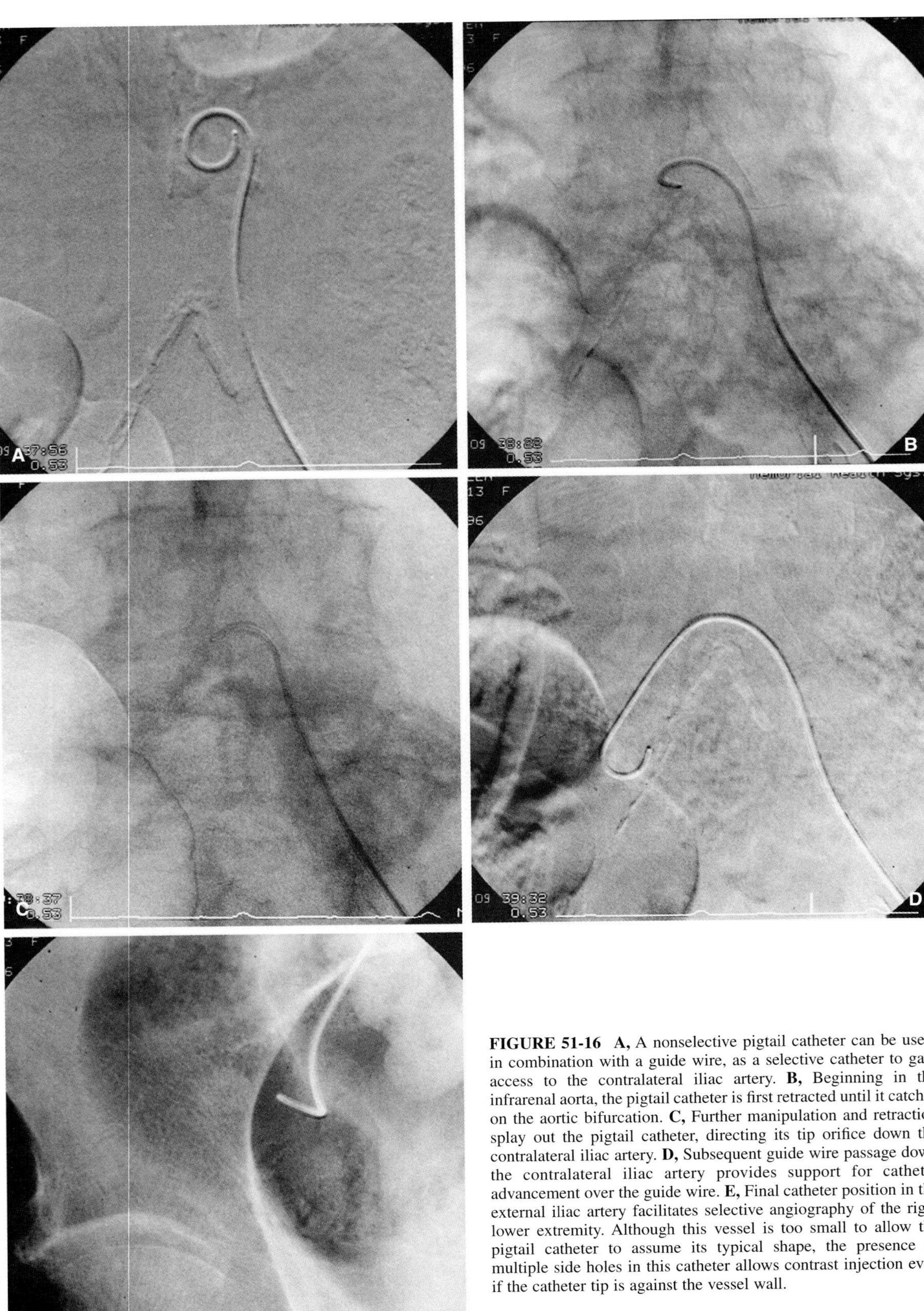

FIGURE 51-16 **A,** A nonselective pigtail catheter can be used, in combination with a guide wire, as a selective catheter to gain access to the contralateral iliac artery. **B,** Beginning in the infrarenal aorta, the pigtail catheter is first retracted until it catches on the aortic bifurcation. **C,** Further manipulation and retraction splay out the pigtail catheter, directing its tip orifice down the contralateral iliac artery. **D,** Subsequent guide wire passage down the contralateral iliac artery provides support for catheter advancement over the guide wire. **E,** Final catheter position in the external iliac artery facilitates selective angiography of the right lower extremity. Although this vessel is too small to allow the pigtail catheter to assume its typical shape, the presence of multiple side holes in this catheter allows contrast injection even if the catheter tip is against the vessel wall.

in addition to their end-hole. It goes without saying that catheter length also needs to be considered to ensure that the catheter can reach the target vessel from the selected site of vascular access. Catheters are typically available in 65- and 100-cm working lengths, with the shorter lengths being suitable for abdominal and proximal contralateral lower extremity catheter placements and the longer lengths for arch, brachiocephalic, and distal contralateral lower extremity work, assuming a CFA site of access.

In contrast with sheaths, diagnostic catheter diameters are sized (in French units) by their OD, with their ID being determined by the thickness of the catheter wall. Diagnostic catheter sizes commonly used for peripheral work range from 4 to 6 French and typically have IDs (specified in fractional inches) of 0.035 or 0.038 inch, the former being the most common. Catheters as small as 2 or 3 French (Renegade Microcatheter) are available and can be advanced through standard diagnostic catheters, acting as guiding catheters (to be discussed shortly), for superselective work. Obviously, the lumen of such small catheters only accommodates a commensurately smaller guide wire and only permits relatively low contrast infusion rates.

Catheter shape is by far the most critical characteristic to be considered in the selection of a catheter. Shaped catheters can be subcategorized in several ways depending on their many characteristics. Multiple side-hole catheters are used to infuse relatively high volumes of contrast into high-flow vessels where injection under higher pressure is required to achieve adequate opacification. The multiple holes dissipate the flow of contrast, minimizing the potentially injurious "jet effect" of the injectate on the vessel wall were it all to be injected out of a single end-hole. Furthermore, the multiple sites of injection into the flow-stream provide more uniform opacification of the vessel. Some catheters, such as the pigtail, tennis racquet, and Omni SOS catheters, have further improved on this aspect by creating catheter shapes that maximize contrast dispersion. These are typically used for aortic and vena caval studies but can be manipulated into medium-sized branch vessels, although they may not "form" (i.e., assume their predesigned shape) in these smaller vessels (see Fig. 51-16). Virtually all multiple side-hole catheters are "self-forming," meaning that they assume their shape spontaneously after removal of the guide wire in vessels of the size they are intended to be used in.

Catheters whose curves have an overall radius less than the diameter of the blood vessel are generally self-forming and are useful for selecting the origins of a number of branch vessels. Advancement of the catheter further into the branch vessel is usually performed over a guide wire, though this is not always so. Selection of tip shape is largely dependent on the angulation of the branch of interest. In contrast, catheters with too large a curve to form spontaneously need to be manipulated into their shape, usually by engaging the tip in a side-branch while advancing the body of the catheter, effectively "folding" the catheter over on itself. These catheters usually form U-turn configurations and typically can be advanced within the side branch several centimeters by withdrawing the body of the catheter once the tip has engaged the branch vessel. This improves the quality of the angiogram by minimizing contrast reflux and washout in the aorta. The technique of forming catheters is difficult to explain but critical to master (Figs. 51-17 to 51-20). Generally, the catheter is supported by a guide wire inserted to the point of the dominant curve in the catheter and, with the tip engaged in a side branch or "caught" on some plaque, the catheter body advances while the tip stays fixed, effectively manipulating the catheter into its designed shape. There is a definite risk of embolization during such catheter manipulation and consequently forming catheters in the ascending aorta should be done with extreme care. Rather, when used for brachiocephalic catheterization, they are usually formed in the distal arch or proximal descending aorta and then advanced into the ascending aorta in their formed state.

Two additional techniques for the formation of a Simmons catheter are illustrated (see Figs. 51-19 and 20). The aortic valve technique is simple and in our experience has been well tolerated; however, one should be aware of the possibility of ectopy. The suture loop technique is particularly suited for patients with shaggy aortic changes in whom there is only a small segment of healthy artery to form the Simmons catheter (see Fig. 51-20). Additionally, this suture loop technique may be desirable in circumstances in which there are difficulties finding a side branch to engage for catheter forming or in which, despite engaging in a side branch, the small vessel diameter does not allow catheter formation. Patients with a bovine arch present a formidable challenge for selective catheterization of the left carotid system. Manipulations of the Simmons catheter as described in Figure 51-21 facilitate this task. Alternatively, a diagnostic catheter with a very acute angle may be employed for selective catheterization followed by wire purchase and catheter advancement. However, the technique herein described avoids wire manipulation in the cerebral circulation (see Fig. 51-21).

Although some catheters are shaped to engage side branches while they are being pushed forward, others are designed to be most effective when being withdrawn. The endovascular surgeon has to carefully analyze the orientation of the aorta and its relevant branches and should perform all catheter manipulations under fluoroscopic guidance to reduce the risk of plaque dissection or perforation. Remember to consider the geometry of all of a catheter's curves and envision the shape the catheter will take when confined by the walls of the vessel it is being inserted in to refine the catheter selection process. Although the Cobra 2, Omni SOS, VS-1, and internal mammary artery catheters are effective in crossing the aortic bifurcation, the nonselective pigtail catheter can usually be manipulated across as well (see Fig. 51-16), saving on the cost of a catheter if the pigtail was already used for the aortogram run. The guide wire is used to partially open the curve of the pigtail so that it can be engaged in the contralateral common iliac artery. The guide wire is then advanced down the iliac artery, followed by the catheter. Table 51-1 lists catheters commonly used to access different vessels.

Most selective catheters available today are made of polyethylene, which has good torqueability (i.e., twisting of the ex-vivo portion of the catheter produces a similar degree of rotation of the in-vivo tip of the catheter) and pliability and holds its shape well. Nylon is often used in the construction of high-flow catheters, such as the pigtail,

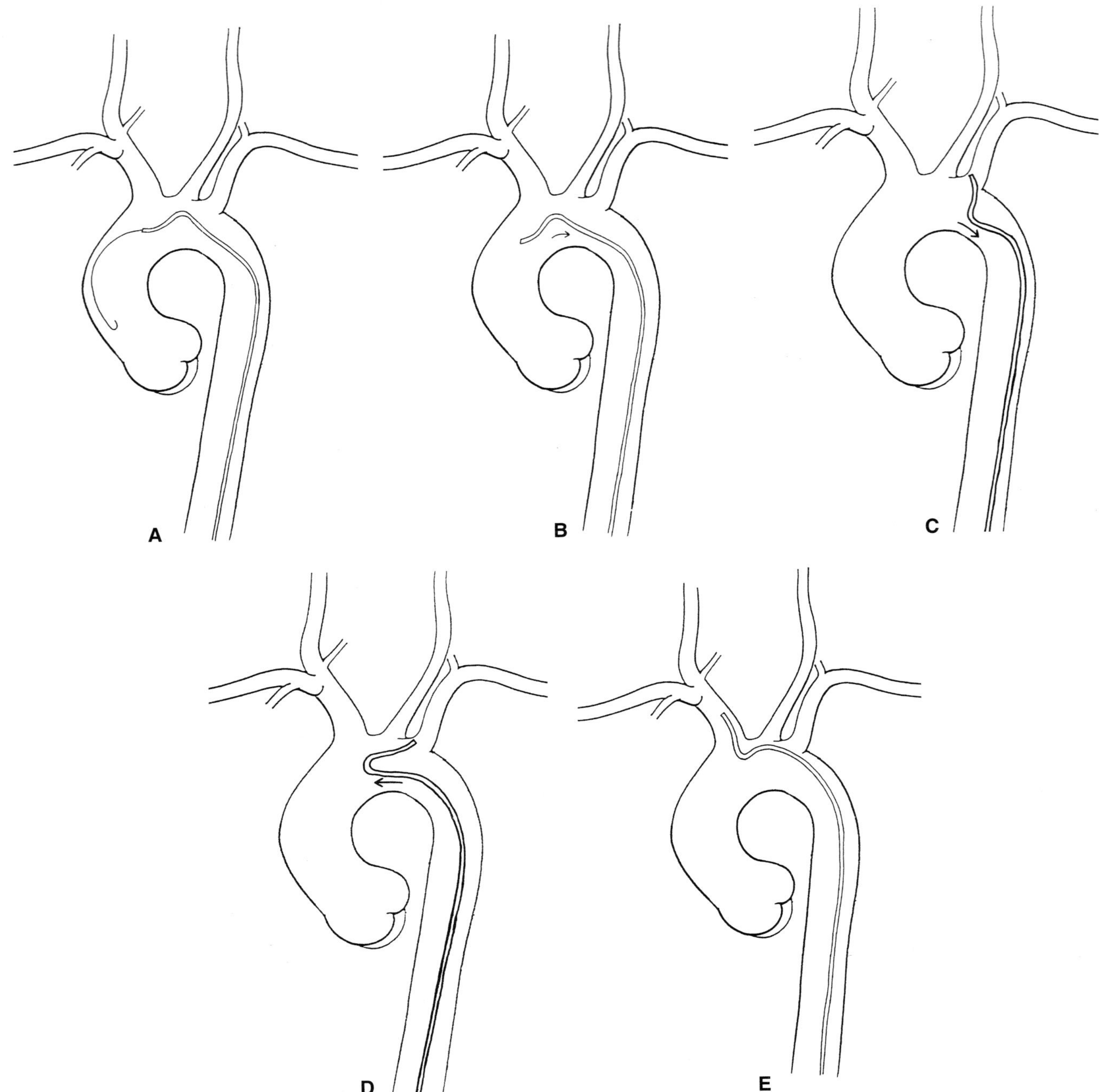

FIGURE 51-17 This series of drawings depicts how a Simmons catheter is manually formed into its preset shape. **A,** The catheter is first advanced over a guide wire into the aortic arch. **B,** The guide wire is removed, but the catheter does not spontaneously assume its U-turn shape because the aortic diameter is insufficient to allow for this. **C,** The catheter is rotated and retracted so that it engages the orifice of the left subclavian artery. **D,** The catheter is then advanced with the tip engaged, resulting in a "folding over" of the catheter, which is now in its preset shape. **E,** The catheter is then advanced beyond the origin of the innominate artery and retracted to engage the tip well up into the innominate artery for subsequent angiography or further advancement over a guide wire. *Arrows* in **B, C,** and **D** denote direction of movement described.

Table 51-1 Catheters Commonly Used for Selective Catheterizations

VESSEL	CATHETER SHAPES	CATHETER NAMES
Contralateral iliac	Self-forming Manual forming	Cobra 1, 2, or 3; IMA; pigtail Simmons 1, 2, or 3; Chuang C; crossover
Renal/mesenteric	Self-forming Manual forming Axillary approach	Cobra 1, 2, or 3; renal double curve (short or long); SMA/celiac curve Simmons 1, 2, or 3; Shepherd Hook Berenstein; Weinberg; Cobra 1 or 2
Subclavian/carotid	Self-forming Manual forming	Berenstein; Weinberg; right Judkins (JR4) Simmons 1, 2, or 3; Headhunter H3

IMA, inferior mesenteric artery; SMA, superior mesenteric artery.

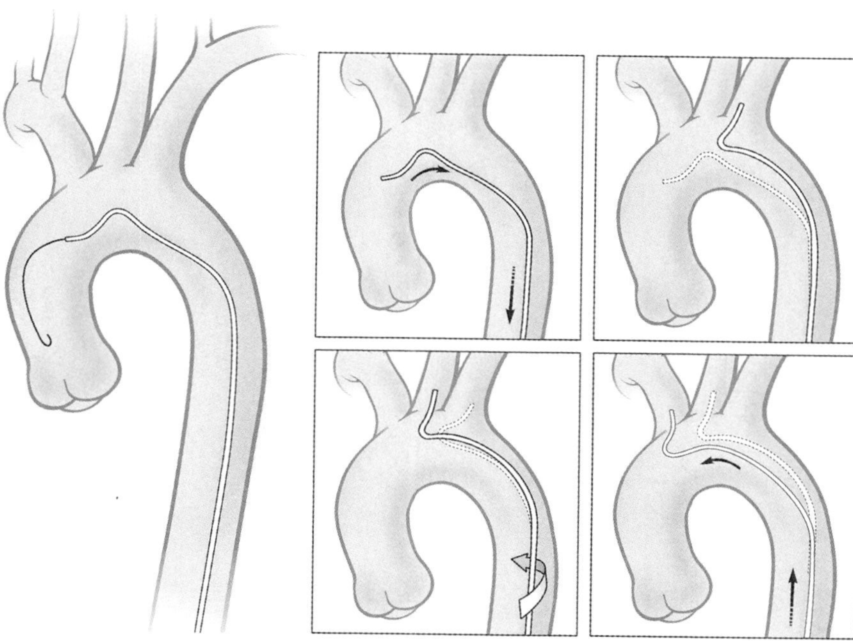

FIGURE 51-18 **A** to **E,** Technique of forming a Simmons catheter on a side-branch vessel.

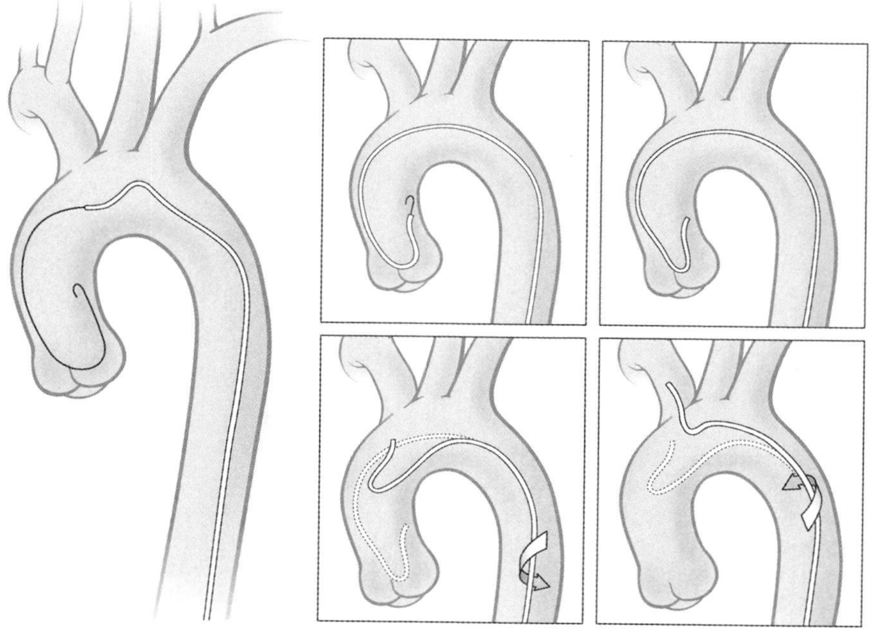

FIGURE 51-19 **A** to **E,** Technique of forming a Simmons catheter off the aortic valve.

because nylon can withstand higher infusion pressures than polyethylene. Polyurethane is a softer, more pliable material that yields catheters with poor torqueability but that track guide wires well, although the higher coefficient of friction often mandates a friction-reducing coating on either the guide wire or the lumen of the catheter. To improve torqueability of polyurethane catheters, a fine wire mesh is often incorporated into the catheter wall. Experience with various catheters is necessary to learn which ones work best in various settings.

Although referred to as *diagnostic catheters*, they are important for interventional procedures as well because they facilitate access to branch artery lesions. Although for diagnostic studies it is usually only necessary that the catheter tip be engaged in the vessel origin to obtain good images, interventional work frequently requires guide wire support well beyond the lesion being treated. Using the curve of the catheter to select a branch vessel allows for the passage of a guide wire into that branch and beyond the lesion, facilitating its subsequent treatment. Furthermore,

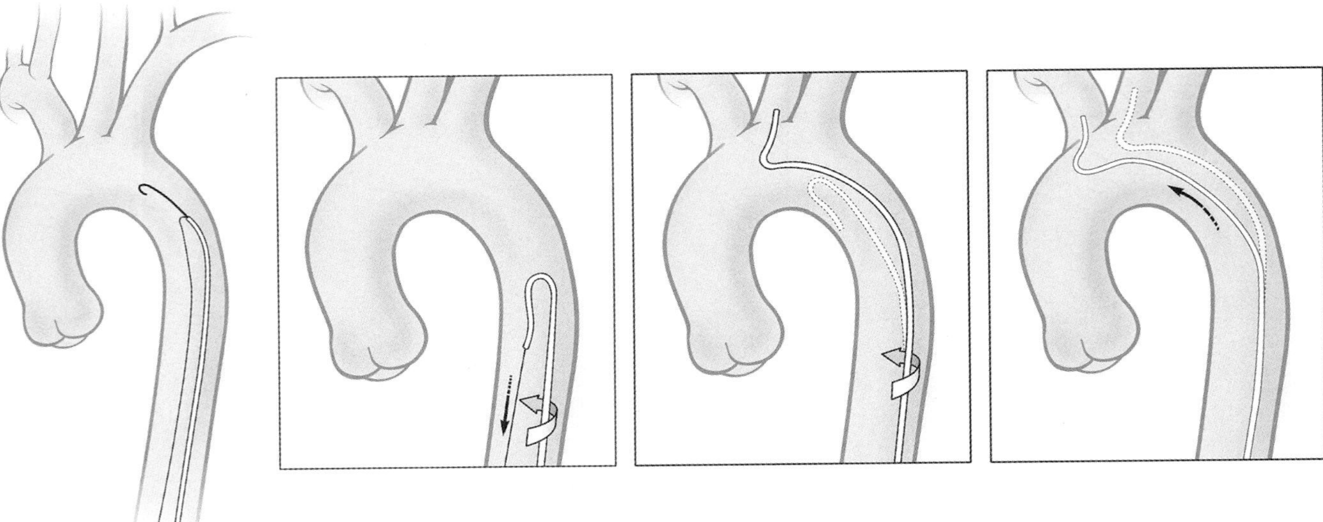

FIGURE 51-20 **A** to **D,** Technique of forming a Simmons catheter with a silk suture pull.

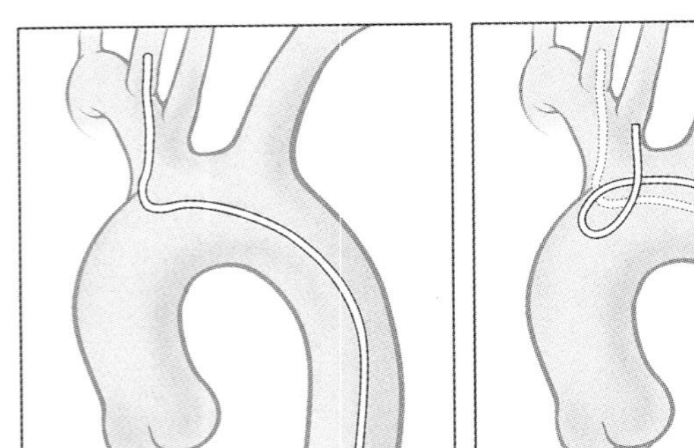

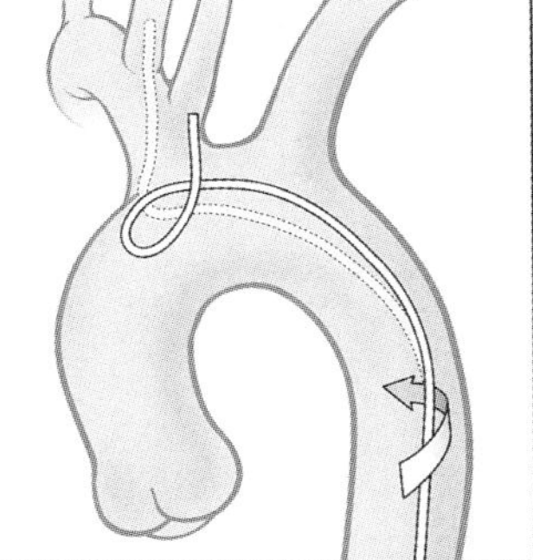

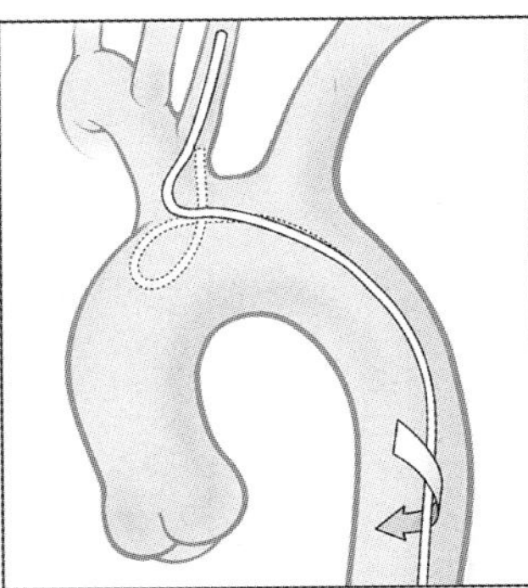

FIGURE 51-21 **A** to **C,** Manipulation of a Simmons catheter into a bovine arch left common carotid artery.

diagnostic catheters are also commonly used to perform coil embolization of branch vessels they have been manipulated into or have been used to direct microcatheters into. Specifics of coil embolization of hypogastric arteries prior to aortic endografting or for the treatment of endoleaks are beyond the scope of this chapter but are well described elsewhere.[42-45] Lastly, in a similar fashion to marker guide wires, catheters with fixed distance radiopaque markers on them are available to facilitate computer calibration and subsequent vessel diameter or length measurements.

■ GUIDING CATHETERS

Guiding catheters are larger diameter catheters, usually preshaped to one of the self-forming curves, through which balloon catheters or other interventional devices are passed. Their use has several advantages and few limitations except for the requisite larger vessel puncture necessary to accommodate the larger sheath they are used through. One use of guiding catheters during endovascular interventions is to provide a mechanism to angiographically evaluate the results of the intervention without losing access to the treated area (Fig. 51-22) because it is generally advisable that a lesion undergoing treatment remain traversed by a guide wire or catheter (referred to as maintaining *lesion crossing*) at all times until a successful interventional result has been demonstrated. Guiding catheters, by virtue of their oversized lumina, allow for contrast injection while the balloon and/or guide wire remain in position across the lesion. This is analogous to the use of crossover sheaths (previously described) for contralateral iliac and lower extremity interventions. Because the balloon material can distort the image and alter flow dynamics, it is generally withdrawn, or at least retracted into the catheter, away from the area of the vessel undergoing evaluation prior to contrast injection.

Without the use of a crossover sheath or guiding catheter, angiographic evaluation of an intervention site without losing lesion crossing requires leaving the tip of the catheter just beyond the most distal aspect of the dilated area, removing the guide wire, and forcefully injecting through the guide wire channel of the balloon catheter. In most cases a sufficient volume of contrast refluxes proximally and allows a general assessment of the adequacy of the intervention,

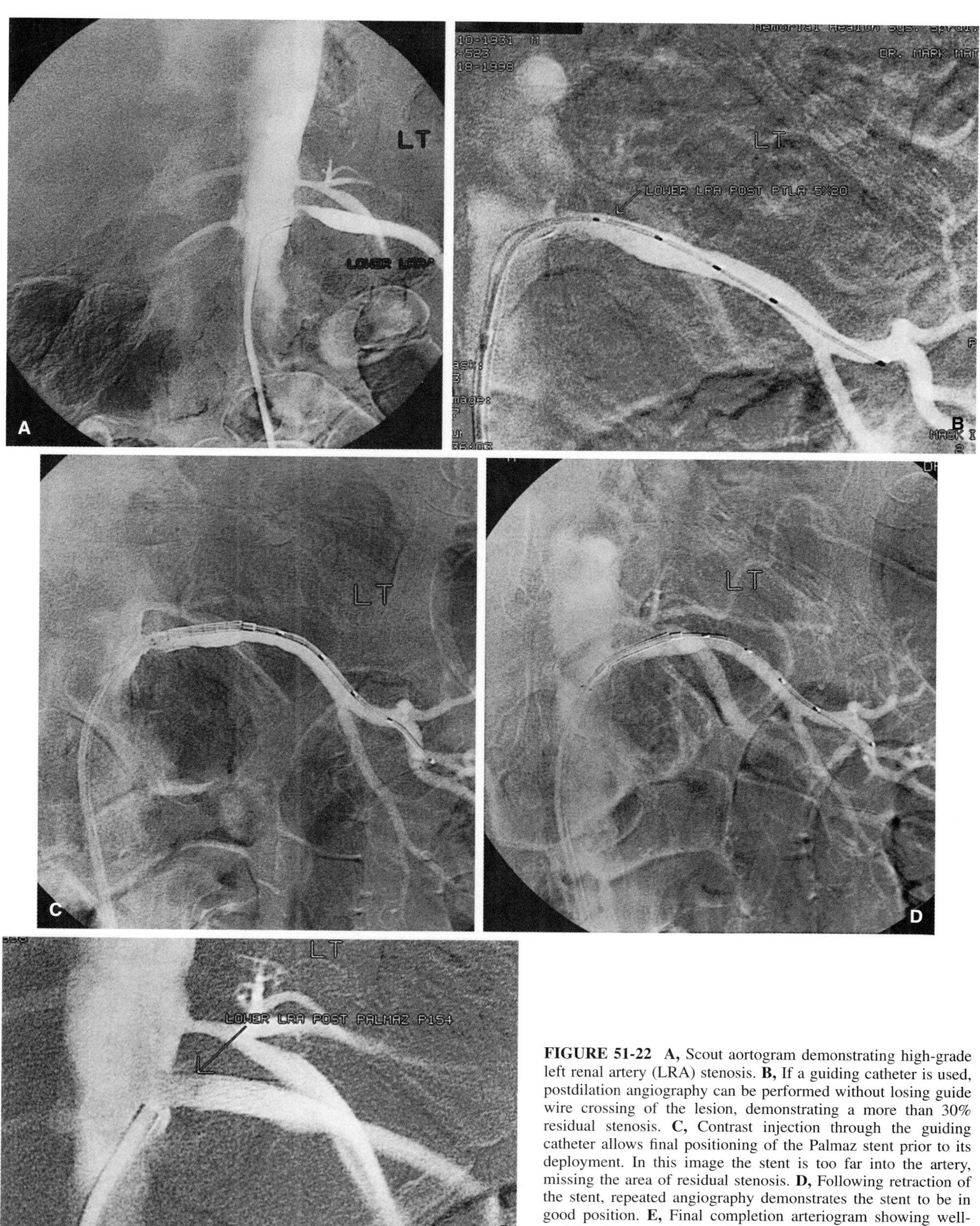

FIGURE 51-22 **A,** Scout aortogram demonstrating high-grade left renal artery (LRA) stenosis. **B,** If a guiding catheter is used, postdilation angiography can be performed without losing guide wire crossing of the lesion, demonstrating a more than 30% residual stenosis. **C,** Contrast injection through the guiding catheter allows final positioning of the Palmaz stent prior to its deployment. In this image the stent is too far into the artery, missing the area of residual stenosis. **D,** Following retraction of the stent, repeated angiography demonstrates the stent to be in good position. **E,** Final completion arteriogram showing well-positioned stent at the renal artery origin. PTLA, percutaneous transluminal angioplasty; LT, left.

although the balloon material may degrade the image somewhat. If things look good, the catheter can be withdrawn to a position upstream of the lesion and formal completion angiography performed. If a problem is revealed that requires repeat dilation after the lesion crossing has been given up, the lesion will need to be recrossed. This carries a significant risk of plaque dissection and subintimal wire passage. If this maneuver is attempted, it should be performed under fluoroscopic guidance and is most safely accomplished with a J-wire. An alternative to prematurely relinquishing guide wire crossing of the angioplasty site is to exchange out the standard guide wire for an undersized one, which may make it possible to inject dye through a slightly withdrawn balloon with the lesion crossing maintained by the undersized guide wire. In general this would require use of a wire smaller than usually necessary to accomplish the other technical requirements of the procedure. Both the "contrast reflux" and "small wire" angiography techniques may provide adequate imaging in relatively small, low-flow vessels, but obtaining adequate opacification in larger, high-flow vessels can be problematic. The use of a guiding catheter in this situation overcomes these difficulties.

A related use of guiding catheters is for determining appropriate positioning of a balloon catheter or stent prior to its inflation or deployment (see Fig. 51-21). Because contrast injection can be performed while the predeployed device is across the lesion, there is the opportunity to make any final adjustments in its position prior to completing the intervention. This is particularly critical when deploying stents at the orifice of branch vessels, such as for renal or subclavian artery lesions, because the risk of an excessive amount of the stent projecting into the aorta can be minimized. Furthermore, during interventions where the length of guide wire that can be positioned beyond the lesion is restricted, such as with renal artery stenoses, there may not be enough of the stiff part of the wire through the lesion for the interventional device to track to its intended site. In this situation, guiding catheters can provide substantial external support and guidance to the interventional device. This is particularly valuable in situations where acute vascular angulation is present.

Another advantage of using guiding catheters is their ability to facilitate performance of balloon angioplasty of very distant contralateral sites or through tortuous arteries by reducing the arterial wall friction effect on the interventional catheter passing through them. In essence, the guiding catheter acts as a reduced friction sleeve through which the interventional catheter is passed. When used over the aortic bifurcation, for example, both crossover sheaths and guiding catheters redirect the force vector of the interventional catheter being passed through them such that it is more like it was being introduced from the aorta itself, resulting in improved torqueability and pushability of the interventional catheter. In a similar fashion, guiding catheters are used to provide a smooth pathway to a lesion when implanting balloon-deployed stents. Without them, or a sheath performing a similar function, there is a risk of either vessel wall trauma or stent dislodgment from the catheter during passage of the stent to its intended site of deployment. Lastly, guiding catheters are used for passage of snares and graspers to protect the walls of the vessel along the way to the target lesion.

Guiding catheters are sized by the minimum size of the sheath through which the catheter passes, with typical sizes ranging from 6 to 10 French. Therefore, the French size of the catheter refers to its maximal outside OD. Also critical, of course, is the ID, because this determines what size devices can be passed through it and how much additional channel is available for injection of contrast. In an analogous situation to diagnostic catheters, the ID is expressed in fractional inches. These characteristics vary slightly from manufacturer to manufacturer but are typically detailed on the package, which should be reviewed prior to selection. Because of the increased diameter of these catheters, large volumes of contrast can be injected easily. Unlike sheaths, however, guiding catheters do not have hemostatic valves, mandating the use of a hemostatic plug or Y-adapter on the guiding catheter lest significant volumes of blood leak out alongside the guide wire or balloon catheter. Furthermore, in contrast to sheaths, which come with tapered dilators that create a smooth transition from the size of the guide wire to that of the sheath, most guiding catheters have no similar tapered obturator. Consequently, there is typically a significant step-off between the wire and the guide catheter (e.g., from the 0.035-inch OD of the guide wire to the 0.105-inch OD of a typical 8-French guide catheter), which can easily snag atheromatous plaque or debris during passage. Even though most guiding catheters have soft, pliable tips designed to minimize vascular trauma, it is still advisable to observe their passage under fluoroscopy to minimize this risk. Recently, manufacturers have started to provide long, tapering obturators with some of their guiding catheters, analogous to the dilators used with sheaths during their insertion, to address this concern.

■ BALLOON ANGIOPLASTY CATHETERS

Balloon angioplasty catheters are available from a number of manufacturers and differ in regard to several factors, including the balloon material, the presence of friction-reducing coatings on the balloon and/or catheter shaft, the length of catheter tip extending beyond the balloon, and the length of the "shoulder" of the balloon (that part of the balloon at each end that does not achieve the rated balloon diameter but tapers to its attachment site on the shaft of the balloon). The latter two factors, tip and shoulder length, assume relevance when dilating near branch points or in other situations where the amount of balloon or catheter shaft extending beyond the balloon needs to be limited.

Differences in balloon construction have the greatest effect on performance. Early balloons were made of polyvinylchloride (PVC) but were overly compliant, resulting in both lower burst pressures and a tendency to dilate beyond their rated size. Less compliant materials such as polyethylene (and its derivatives), polyester, and woven Dacron have essentially replaced PVC for peripheral angioplasty. Differences between these materials relate to the balloon's maximal inflation pressure, profile (how closely the balloon wraps around the catheter shaft), pliability, compliance, and resistance to perforation by calcified plaque or stents. Polyester and woven Dacron balloons are "high-pressure" balloons, usually rated to 17 atm, whereas most polyethylene balloons are rated to 12 atm. Balloons capable of withstanding higher inflation pressures are often needed for dilating heavily calcified plaques and bypass graft stenoses. The Conquest angioplasty balloon made of Gore-Tex and Nidex, has achieved a 30 mm Hg-rated bursting pressure and is currently recommended for refractory hemodialysis access cases. More recently, balloons have been designed to be variably compliant under pressure, allowing the same balloon to have, for example, a diameter of 5.0 mm at 6 atm or 5.5 mm at inflation pressures of 16 atm. Such partially compliant balloons allow the operator to fine-tune the dilation with one insertion of a balloon. There are limits, however, and typically the most one can expect at higher inflation pressures is an additional 10% of the balloon's rated diameter.

Some manufacturers have begun to apply a hydrophilic coating to the outside of their balloons, which may aid in advancing the balloon through tight stenoses, occlusions, or guiding catheters. Unfortunately, such coatings also make it difficult to securely affix stents to these balloons, and many stents have been dislodged or lost because of them. For this reason, and because such coatings were probably not necessary in the first place, their use on the balloons themselves is declining, although the catheter shaft may still be so coated. If it is necessary to mount a stent on a coated balloon, every effort should be made to remove the coating by rubbing the balloon vigorously with a gauze sponge before mounting the stent.

Having identified a lesion for dilation and selected the appropriate type of balloon, other variables that must be considered include balloon diameter and length, usable catheter length, catheter shaft diameter, and maximum size guide wire that the catheter will accept. Balloon diameters typically range from 1.5 to 18 mm, in 0.5-mm increments for balloons less than 5 mm in diameter and 1.0-mm increments for larger balloons. Ideally the balloon diameter selected should be 10% to 20% greater than the adjacent "normal" vessel diameter except for cutting balloons discussed later. When measuring off of a conventional arteriogram, the balloon should be sized to the actual measurement because the magnification factor of the filming technique generally provides this level of overdilation. If using DSA, it may be necessary to calculate the "normal" vessel diameter by calibrating the computer with a marker wire such as the Magic Wire (see Fig. 51-14C), some other standardization device such as a marked pigtail catheter, or a quarter, which is 24 mm in diameter. With experience comes the ability to judge vessel size from the DSA image without performing measurements, though caution should always be exercised in critical situations.

Balloon lengths vary among manufacturers but generally include lengths approximating 2.0, 4.0, and 10.0 cm. Although the length selected is usually gauged to allow complete dilation with a single positioning of the balloon, sometimes it is necessary to perform overlapping dilations to cover the entire lesion if the balloon length is shorter than the lesion and a longer balloon cannot be used. One reason to perform overlapping dilations rather than using a longer balloon would be in situations where the next longer size would necessitate the balloon extending into a smaller diameter branch vessel, which would be at risk for overdilation. Another situation to avoid is using a long balloon on a curved arterial segment, such as the external iliac artery, because the balloon tends to straighten out the artery when it is inflated, which may result in injury at the relatively fixed endpoints of the dilation.

Balloon catheters are available in several usable lengths (e.g., 40, 75, and 120 cm), the selection of which depends on the location of the lesion to be treated and the site of vascular access. In general, the shortest catheter that will reach the lesion is best because longer catheters are more difficult to manipulate. This is particularly true with smaller shaft-size catheters because they are inherently more floppy and typically cannot accept the larger guide wires (0.035 to 0.038 inch) that provide the support necessary to negotiate tortuous vessels over long distances. When it is necessary to use a smaller catheter and wire over a long distance, a stiff-shaft guide wire may prove helpful by providing supplemental internal support or a guiding catheter may be used for additional external support. Larger shaft balloon catheters are generally more "pushable" due to their inherent rigidity, but this may work against their negotiation of tight turns, such as when dilating an iliac artery contralateral to the site of vessel puncture.

Cutting balloons have been introduced for the treatment of coronary stenosis in circumstances where a high-pressure balloon-resistant lesion is encountered, such as with in-stent restenosis and de-novo lesions refractory to conventional angioplasty. Additionally, cutting balloon angioplasty may be appropriate for angioplasty of small vessels not ideal for stenting such as tibials or renal branch vessels, but data are still lacking for this indication. Currently, in the United States, these balloons are approved for coronary use and consequently they are available only in small diameter (2 to 4 mm) and lengths (6 to 15 mm). However, larger diameters up to 7 mm for femoral and iliac work are expected to become commercially available in the near future. Cutting balloons are available in rapid exchange (monorail) systems using a 0.14-inch guide wire. They have three or four microsurgical blades mounted longitudinally on the outer surface of the balloon (Fig. 51-23). On inflation these atherotomes score the plaque, creating controlled longitudinal incisions for plaque fracture propagation, which allows for dilation at lower pressures.

Several special considerations are important when using a cutting balloon. In contradistinction to standard angioplasty, the balloon should *not* be oversized (not to exceed a balloon-artery ratio of 1.1:1). Furthermore, these balloons should not be used in the setting of arterial occlusion, because of the risk of arterial perforation, and they should not be advanced into vessels with excessive tortuosity because the microsurgical blades make them relatively inflexible. Owing to the risk of balloon rupture and arterial perforation, the balloon inflation pressure should not exceed the rated burst pressure (10 atm), and inflation and deflation should be slow, at no more than 1 atm per 5 seconds, to allow for the blades to expand radially and folds in the balloon to shield the blades, protecting the vessel as it is manipulated to and from the lesion.

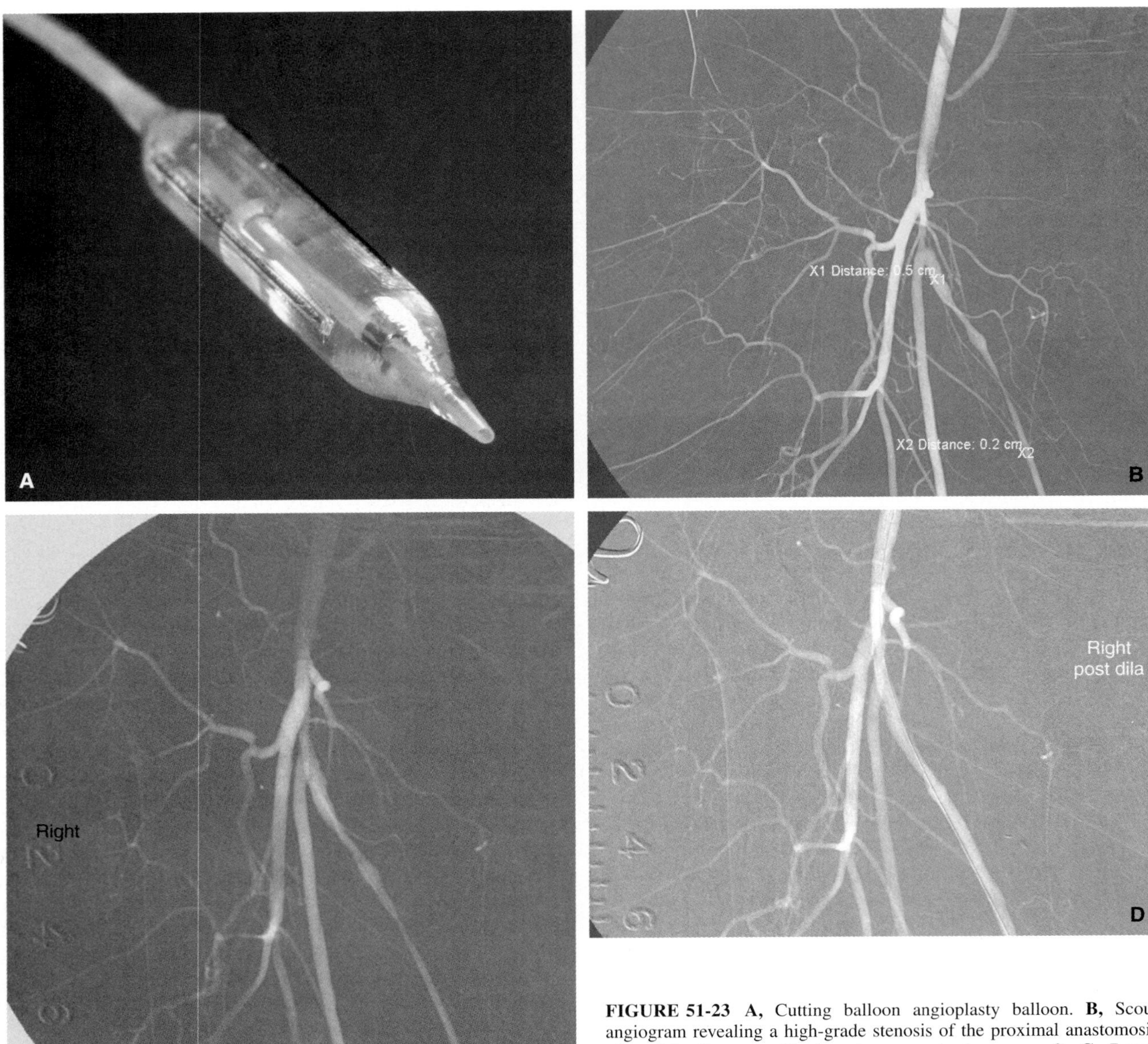

FIGURE 51-23 **A,** Cutting balloon angioplasty balloon. **B,** Scout angiogram revealing a high-grade stenosis of the proximal anastomosis of a right femoropopliteal saphenous vein bypass graft. **C,** Result following simple balloon angioplasty. **D,** Final result following cutting balloon angioplasty.

In the peripheral territory, cutting balloon angioplasty has been advocated for the settings of resistant peripheral arterial bypass graft stenosis secondary to neointimal hyperplasia,[46,47] to treat carotid in-stent restenosis,[48] resistant renal artery in-stent restenosis,[49] resistant high-grade dialysis graft stenosis,[50] and in pediatric pulmonary artery branch stenosis.[51] Even when treating restenosis in arteries larger than 4 mm, which is the largest cutting balloon currently available, cutting balloon angioplasty might cause enough of a controlled incision in the intima to allow further successful angioplasty with a high-pressure balloon such as the BlueMax (burst rate 20 atm) or the ConQuest (burst rate 30 atm). Fibrotic stenotic lesions refractory to standard angioplasty may still require supplemental stenting. In-stent restenosis refractory to standard angioplasty may require repeat stenting within the lumen of the original stent or surgical revascularization. The disadvantage of restenting is overexpansion of the arterial wall, which in turn may further stimulate fibrointimal hyperplasia. This may explain the poor long-term result of restenting in the coronary circulation.[52] The microincisions from cutting balloon angioplasty may disrupt the fibrointimal hyperplasia, minimizing the elastic recoil of these lesions. In the cardiac setting cutting balloon angioplasty has demonstrated an excellent initial technical response; however, no significant differences were demonstrated in regard to late restenosis in a recent large, multicenter, randomized clinical trial.[53] Drug-eluting stents and cryotherapy are two evolving techniques that may hold a promise to impact the rate of restenosis. Nevertheless, because this technology is advancing so rapidly, by the time long-term data become available, device evolution will likely render the data obsolete.

The reported cardiac complications from the use of a cutting balloon are rare and include arterial dissection and perforation.[53-55] In addition, there are two case reports of stent extraction due to entrapment within the blades of the cutting balloon for the treatment of in-stent restenosis.[56,57] These complications have been related to balloon oversizing. The published experience in the noncoronary circulation is limited, but no significant complications have yet been reported.

■ INTRAVASCULAR STENTS

Stents can be classified by a number of characteristics, but the most relevant include their method of deployment, flexibility, ability to be crushed by external pressure, radial strength, radiopacity, predictability of final deployment location and length, ability to be recaptured or repositioned prior to complete deployment, and the material they are constructed of. Each type of stent is generally available in a number of sizes, varying in both diameter and length. Requisite sheath sizes vary between different stents and different stent sizes within a stent family, but most require sheaths ranging from 6 to 10 French.

Perhaps the most dichotomous characteristic of stents is their method of deployment: balloon expanded or self-expanding. The Palmaz stent (Fig. 51-24) is the prototypical balloon-expandable stent. These stents are now on their fifth generation (Genesis), with premounted stents, thinner struts, and smaller cells making them more flexible while maintaining their radial strength. By virtue of its balloon expandability, the final stent diameter is variable within a range, being dependent on the size of the balloon used to expand it. This also permits subsequent dilation to a larger size if the original assessment of the necessary diameter proves to be too small. However, this restricts the ability to stent in areas where the vessel size changes, such as when going from the common to the external iliac arteries, unless different diameter balloons are used in each of these areas. Although this can be done, it significantly adds to the complexity of the procedure and risks the overdistention of the smaller of the two arteries. Furthermore, optimal vessel wall contact may not be achievable near the transition zone.

Because stents must be delivered to their intended site mounted on an angioplasty balloon, there is also the risk of dislodgment of the undeployed stent from the balloon. This usually occurs during advancement of the stent to its intended site of deployment, most often when negotiating turns in the vascular system. The occurrence of this complication has been greatly reduced with factory mounting of stents on the balloon as opposed to the hand mounting of old. Nonetheless, it is for this reason that balloon-deployed stents delivered through highly angulated tortuous vessels are best passed through delivery sheaths or guiding catheters rather than being advanced through the vascular system bare, where contact with the vessel wall could dislodge the stent or traumatize the vessel.

Once in position across the lesion, the sheath or guiding catheter is retracted to allow balloon inflation. When properly positioned on the angioplasty catheter, balloon expansion occurs at both ends of the stent first (Fig. 51-25), ensuring that the stent remains centered on the balloon and deploys at its intended site. It is critical to ensure that the stent remains reasonably centered on the balloon before initiating deployment, however, lest subsequent balloon inflation propel the stent forward or backward off the

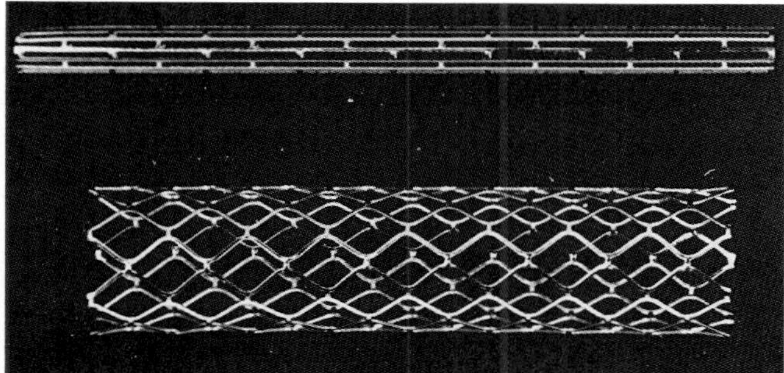

FIGURE 51-24 Palmaz P308 stent in undeployed (*top*) and deployed (*bottom*) states.

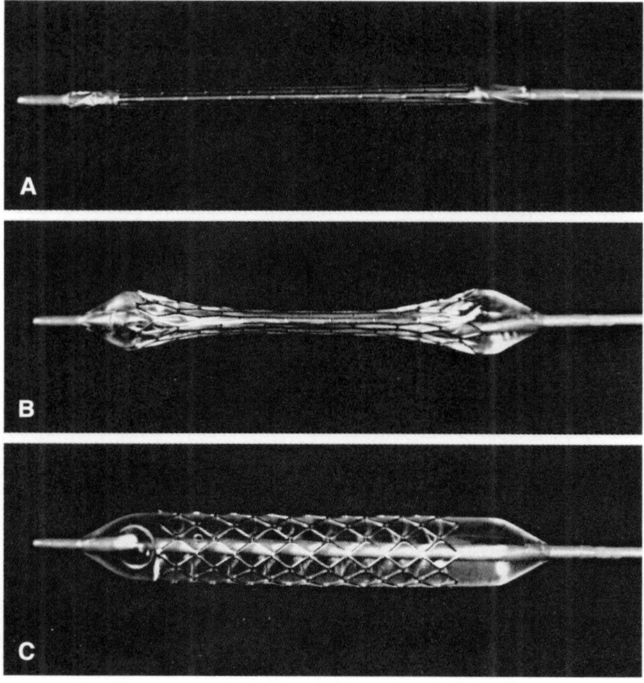

FIGURE 51-25 **A,** Expansion sequence of a Palmaz stent. The predeployed stent is centered on the balloon at the start of deployment. **B,** The balloon first inflates at the ends of the stent. **C,** Complete expansion of the stent occurs last in the center.

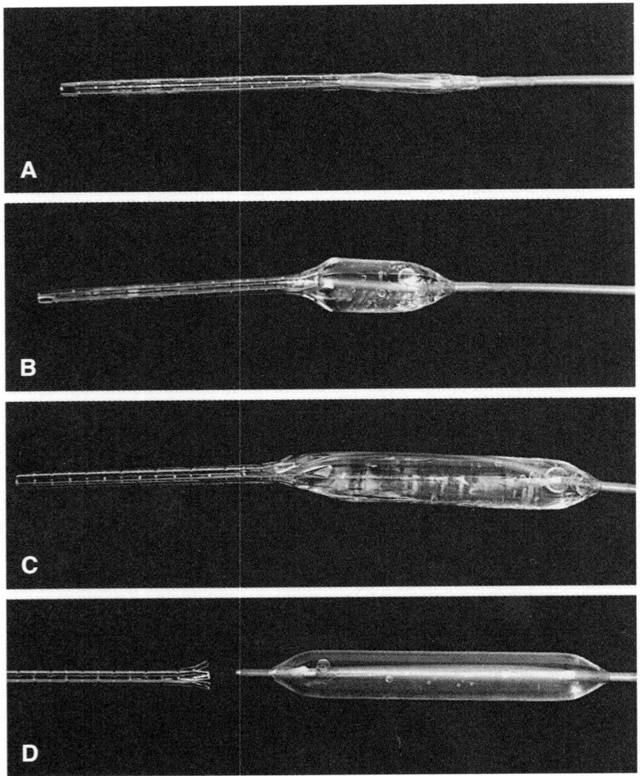

FIGURE 51-26 **A,** A predeployment Palmaz stent malpositioned on the balloon catheter. **B,** As inflation proceeds, the balloon inflates proximally first. **C** and **D,** Further inflation progressively propels the unexpanded stent off the end of the catheter.

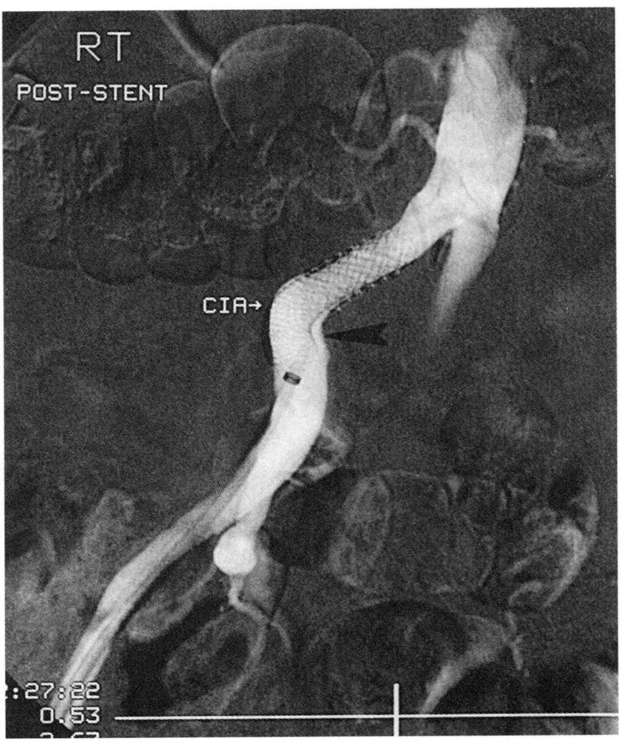

FIGURE 51-27 An undersized Wallstent not in contact with the vessel wall. CIA, common iliac artery.

balloon (Fig. 51-26). This can be a challenging situation to address because, in its undeployed state, it is difficult to reposition the balloon into the stent to permit its deployment, not only because of the stent's small internal channel but also because it is not fixed in space.

A related failure of complete deployment can occur if the balloon ruptures during deployment. Although this can often be addressed by rapid hand or power inflation of the balloon to overwhelm the leak, essentially filling the balloon faster than the fluid can leak out, at times this will be unsuccessful and a free-floating or marginally secured stent will be the result. As long as the stent has achieved a reasonable degree of fixation, the leaking balloon can usually be switched for a new balloon that can be carefully advanced into the stent to complete the deployment. It is obviously critical to maintain a guide wire through the true lumen of the stent until its final and complete expansion.

Self-expanding stents differ because they spontaneously expand once the containing delivery system is retracted and, therefore, if properly oversized, immediately achieve secure fixation within the vessel. However, if undersized for the vessel they are deployed in, they may not make adequate wall contact (Fig. 51-27) and, in contrast to balloon-expandable stents, cannot be overdilated to achieve secure fixation unless an oversized stent is placed within them to maintain their dilation beyond their rated diameter. This limitation makes accurate size selection much more critical than with balloon-expandable stents and requires a much larger inventory of stents because a given self-expanding stent has a much narrower range of expansion than a balloon-deployed type. Typically, stents are available in 1-mm-diameter increments up to 8 mm, after which subsequently larger sizes increase in 2-mm increments.

Another difference between these two categories of stents is in their conformability to changing vessel diameters, a particular asset of the self-expanding variety of stent. Furthermore, they tend to be much more flexible, accommodating tortuous vessels without imparting kinks at the endpoints of the stent. This flexibility extends to the undeployed state as well and permits self-expanding stents to be manipulated through tortuous vessels and over the aortic bifurcation much more easily than balloon-expandable stents can be. Furthermore, this flexibility allows these stents to be deployed in areas subject to significant motion that might irrevocably crush a balloon-deployed stent, such as in the internal carotid or the popliteal arteries.

Although self-expanding stents are advanced through the vascular system without requisite sheath or guiding catheter access to the lesion, in actuality they are encased by an outer catheter of their own, an integral component of their delivery system that maintains their collapsed state until it is retracted and the stent is allowed to expand. This also protects the vessels being traversed from being traumatized during passage of the catheter and prevents any stent dislodgment. Although the size of the vascular access sheath varies between stent brands and within the size range of each type of stent, most peripheral vessels can be stented

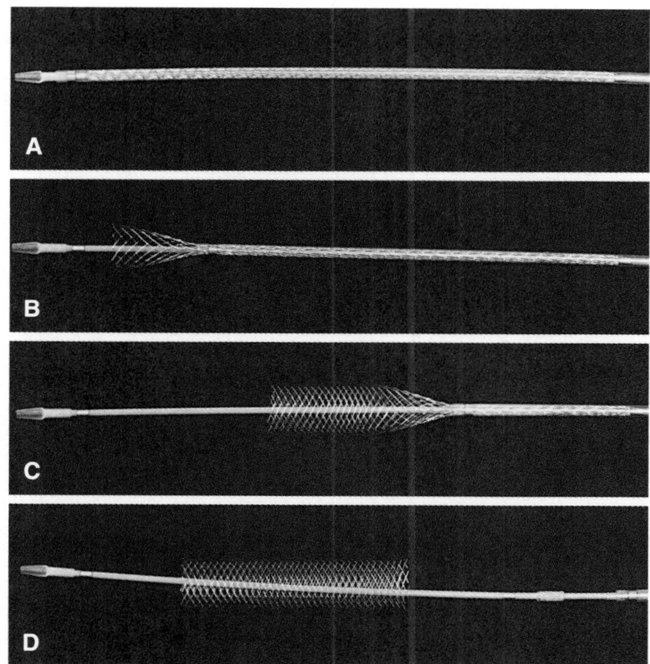

FIGURE 51-28 **A,** Sequence of deployment of a Wallstent. The collapsed Wallstent can be seen mounted on its delivery catheter over a length about twice the stent's rated length. **B,** As the outer covering component of the delivery system is retracted, the stent begins to expand in a funnel configuration that permits repositioning of the stent distally, but not proximally, once deployment has begun. **C,** After further deployment, the stent is fully expanded distally so this end point is now known and is still changeable by virtue of the reconstraining feature of the new Wallstent delivery system. **D,** After complete retraction of its outer covering, the stent is fully expanded and no longer recapturable. Note the degree of shortening of the stent from its predeployment length.

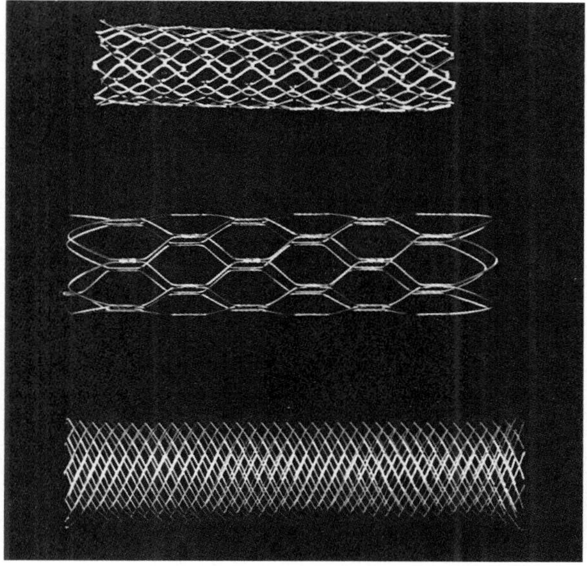

FIGURE 51-29 Comparison of stent reconstruction. From *top* to *bottom* are the balloon-expanded Palmaz stent, the self-expanding nitinol Symphony stent, and the self-expanding stainless-steel Wallstent.

through sheaths ranging from 6 to 10 French. There are two different mechanisms responsible for expansion of self-expanding stents: the method of fabrication and the material used in their construction. Although the Wallstent achieves its expansion by virtue of its stainless-steel braid method of construction (Fig. 51-28), most of the newer stents being developed rely on the self-expansion properties of the thermal memory metal nitinol (Fig. 51-29). This alloy of nickel and titanium can be manufactured to assume a specific size and shape when unconstrained at body temperature, yet be conformable enough when chilled to be compressed into a relatively small-diameter delivery system.

The principal advantage of the Nitinol stents over the braided stainless-steel construction is the predictability of the final overall length once deployed in the body. With the braided construction the stent is longer when constrained in a smaller vessel, rendering its final length of coverage difficult to predict in even uniformly sized vessels and virtually impossible to foresee in vessels with lack of uniformity in their diameter. At its longest when still contained in its delivery system, the Wallstent shortens as it is deployed and its diameter expands (see Fig. 51-28). In contrast, Nitinol stents exhibit minimal foreshortening with deployment and therefore have a much more predicable final length. Although the Palmaz stent also shortens as it is dilated to larger diameters, this is much less pronounced than with the Wallstent. For this reason, Wallstents are rarely used in situations where the final length and stent position are critical, such as near the origins of aortic branch vessels or across the origins of otherwise critical branch vessels (Fig. 51-30). Because Wallstents deploy from distal to proximal (tip to hub), it is the proximal stent endpoint location that is problematic. Furthermore, the radial strength of Wallstents at their endpoints is much less than that of the Palmaz or Nitinol stents, rendering the latter the preferred stents for branch vessel origins. However, Wallstents are one of the few presently available stents that can be recaptured during deployment (≤ 85% of total deployment), a feature that can facilitate repositioning of the stent if the apparent destined final position appears to be problematic.

An additional advantage of the self-expanding stents is their resistance to being permanently deformed by external forces such as manual pressure or flexion forces across a joint. Lacking these characteristics, balloon-expandable stents are not generally recommended for use in the region of the inguinal ligament or at the knee. Furthermore, care must be taken if operating in the vicinity of a Palmaz stent because vascular clamping near or within such a stent would likely result in a sustained collapse of the lumen of the vessel even after removal of the clamp. A final significant difference between stents pertains to their radiopacity. Although stainless-steel stents are usually relatively easy to visualize, Nitinol stents, particularly those with very open architecture, can be extremely difficult to see, particularly with portable fluoroscopy units. This can compromise their accurate positioning during deployment and appreciation of their existence during subsequent radiographic evaluations. This problem has been recognized by Nitinol stent manufacturers, who are now offering radiopaque markers on some of their stents.

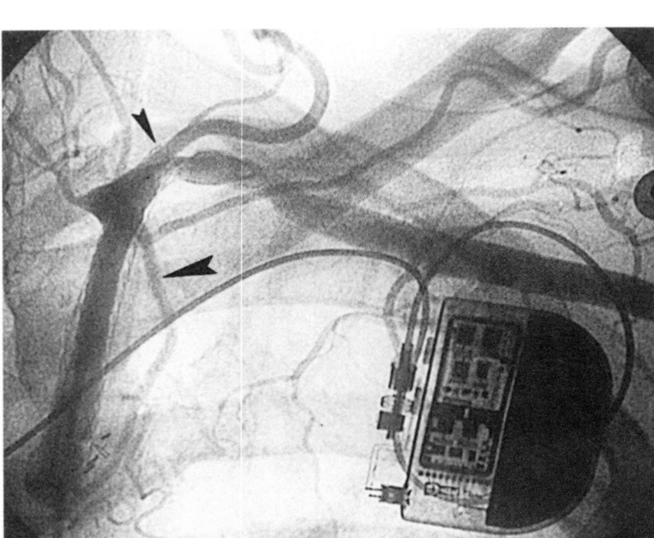

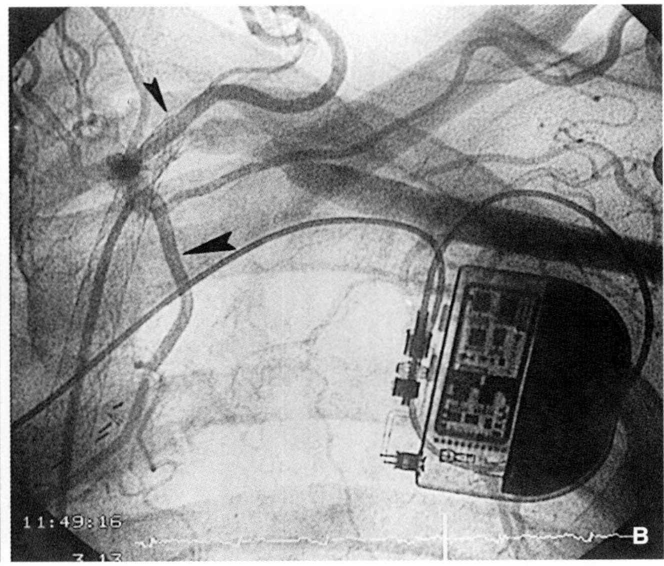

FIGURE 51-30 **A,** The patient underwent Wallstent placement (at an outlying institution) in the left subclavian artery, which is providing inflow to a mammary artery coronary graft (*bottom arrowhead*). The *top arrowhead* indicates the distal extent of the stent, which was presumably placed via the ipsilateral brachial-axillary approach. Although possibly of no consequence, placing the coronary graft at risk by overlying a stent should generally be avoided. Although this was likely purely a mistake in sizing the stent, the unpredictability of the final length of the Wallstent contributes significantly to the risk of this complication and may contraindicate use of the Wallstent in situations such as this, when critical branch vessels are in close proximity to the lesion being treated. **B,** A late-phase view of the same patient provides better visualization of the stent. The *arrowheads* are as in **A**.

Currently, there are three fabric-covered stents (Fig. 51-31) that have FDA approval for human use, albeit for tracheobronchial applications: the Wallgraft, the Viabahn, and the Fluency. These covered stent grafts have multiple arterial applications, if not FDA labeling, such as for the treatment of aneurysms, pseudoaneurysms, traumatic arterial perforations, arteriovenous communications, and even for the endovascular revascularization of the hypogastric artery during endografting of aortoiliac aneurysms.[42] Not surprisingly, covered stent grafts have a larger delivery system profile than their uncovered brethren stents, usually requiring 8- to 12-French access sheaths. Although the Wallgraft is covered with Dacron, the Viabahn and Fluency are covered with expanded polytetrafluoroethylene. At the present time, only the Fluency has radiopaque markers, but the Wallgraft, being of stainless-steel construction, is easily visualized. The Wallgraft and Fluency are deployed from tip to hub by a simple pullback mechanism, whereas the Viabahn has a cord pull mechanism with either tip-to-hub or hub-to-tip deploying mechanisms. As previously alluded to, the nitinol-based stent grafts (Viabahn and Fluency) have a much lesser degree of stent foreshortening than the Wallgraft. There are some other manufacturer-specific differences between these stentgrafts with regard to radial force, crossing profile, flexibility, and available lengths and diameters, but these characteristics are beyond the scope of this discussion.

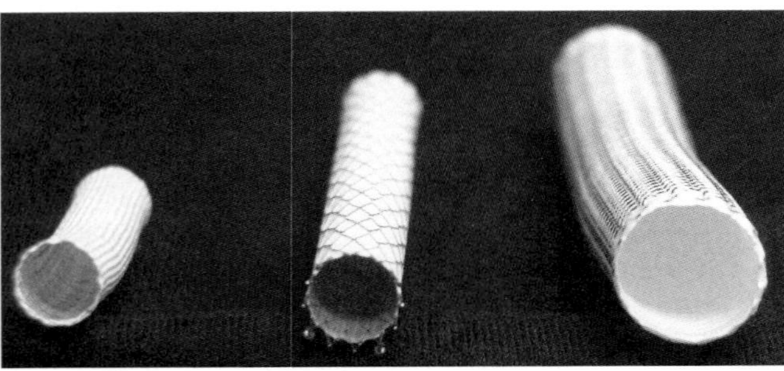

FIGURE 51-31 A selection of peripheral covered stents (endografts).

Drug-eluting stents are the latest development in stent technology aimed at overcoming the problem of in-stent restenosis. Many classes of drugs have been considered for use, including anti-inflammatories or immunomodulators, antiproliferative agents, drugs that affect migration and extracellular matrix production, and drugs that promote healing and re-endothelialization. The main drugs that have been used are paclitaxel and sirolimus.[58,59] Eluting stents have a coating substance with pores or wells that provide controlled release of the drug into the surrounding vessel wall, decreasing the humoral responses responsible for the activation of inflammatory and growth factors. Current data from cardiac trials with eluting stents suggest that early and mid-restenosis rates are significantly improved with their use.[58,59] Based on these early results, many peripheral trials are underway, and these stents are currently available in an off-label setting for peripheral interventions, albeit in coronary sizes only and at considerable expense. However, the cost and effectiveness of these new technologies should be carefully considered prior to widespread usage.

Arterial Closure Devices

Traditionally arteriographic interventions have required prolonged periods of manual pressure compression at the access site and bedrest (4 to 8 hours) following sheath removal. Arterial closure devices have recently become available to allow for briefer compression and earlier ambulation. In general these devices are either suture mediated (Perclose) or collagen based (Angio-Seal and VasoSeal). These devices are designed for the treatment of femoral arteriotomies of 8 French or less. The newer generation of the Perclose, the ProGlide, now incorporates a monofilament suture to minimize tissue response. This device is approved for immediate re-access of the original puncture site. The AngioSeal device uses an intra-arterial cap that anchors a collagen plug in the periadventitial arterial layer, whereas the VasoSeal simply applies a collagen plug to the arteriotomy site. There are many published comparisons of procedures for hemostasis with these devices.[60-62] In general these devices effectively reduce the discomfort associated with direct manual or device compression and the time to hemostasis and ambulation. However, these devices have not conclusively demonstrated a decrease in the incidence of major complications, and at least in one study arteriotomy closure devices were associated with increased incidence of vascular complications when compared with manual compression.[63] Because newer generations of these devices have continued to be released with friendlier and safer features, it is difficult to appreciate whether these modifications will result in improved complication rates. It is also possible that certain closure devices may be superior to others in specific circumstances according to clinical characteristics and femoral artery anatomy. However, device selection should be based on operator familiarity, because all of them are associated with a significant learning phase.[61-63] At the present time, due to the additional cost of these devices and the absence of strong evidence suggesting reduced complication rates, their use needs to be justified to those patients that would benefit the most from rapid ambulation and early discharge.

■ BASIC ENDOVASCULAR TECHNIQUES

Techniques for Reactive Hyperemia

It is imperative that the endovascular surgeon has an ample knowledge of the techniques to improve image quality. Not infrequently we have found patients referred from other institutions with no identifiable distal target vessel suitable for bypass. The techniques of mechanical and chemical reactive hyperemia are extremely useful in such situations. The traditional mechanical reactive hyperemia is induced by inflating a blood pressure cuff to suprasystolic pressures (20 to 50 mm Hg above the systolic blood pressure) for about 5 to 10 minutes. Rapid inflation prevents the discomfort from venous engorgement from slow or incomplete occlusion of the arterial inflow. The cuff(s) is then rapidly deflated, and within seconds contrast material is injected for imaging. Alternatively, mechanical hyperemia may be induced by local extremity or total-body warming and by the use of pneumatic boots.

All of these mechanical techniques are of largely historical interest as hyperemia is most commonly achieved pharmacologically today. Agents commonly used as vasodilators by direct injection through the diagnostic catheter include nitroglycerin, tolazoline, and papaverine; all of them are also useful in treating catheterization-associated vasospasm. Nitroglycerin stimulates a guanosine 3′,5′-monophosphate-dependent protein kinase with resultant dephosphorylation of the light chain of myosin and relaxation of the contractile state of smooth muscle. The usual intra-arterial doses of nitroglycerin in peripheral arteriography are 100 to 300 μg with a maximal vasodilatory effect within 30 seconds. In one report,[64] 72% of patients receiving nitroglycerin complained of mild headache. Tolazoline is a competitive α-adrenergic antagonist that has a predominantly α_1 dose-dependent activity and also causes the release of histamine and prostaglandin resulting in effective arterial and venous vasodilations. The arteriographic run should be delayed for approximately 6 minutes, because a paradoxical vasoconstriction within the first 30 seconds has been observed.[65] This drug causes a burning sensation and even at the recommended arteriographic doses of 25 to 50 mg has been associated with hypertension, palpitations, arrhythmias, angina, and myocardial infarction.[66] For these reasons, in our opinion, tolazoline should not be used routinely for arteriography in cardiovascular patients. Papaverine is an opioid alkaloid that produces generalized nonspecific arterial vasodilation and smooth muscle relaxation at the usual doses of 10 to 30 mg. Side effects of ventricular arrhythmia, excessive sedation, and thrombocytopenia have been reported with the intra-arterial use of papaverine.[67] In addition, there are in-vitro and clinical data indicating that papaverine precipitates in the presence of some nonionic contrast agents causing arterial thrombosis.[68-71] These findings emphasize the need for adequate flushing between the injection of medications and contrast agents. Verapamil is a calcium-channel blocker that inhibits the electromechanical coupling by calcium antagonism resulting in a predominantly arterial smooth muscle relaxation with no significant venous action. The usual doses for arteriography are between 50 and 500 μg to obtain a maximal dilation effect at 30 seconds that lasts about 6 minutes. It is generally well tolerated, but at high doses it may produce bradycardia and hypotension.[64] Intra-arterial nitroglycerin and verapamil are our preferred agents for chemical vasodilation because of their safety profile, availability, easy of use, and effectiveness.[64,72] Other vasodilators that have been investigated as angiographic adjuvants include prostaglandin E_1, sodium nitroprusside, tolmesoxide (RX71107), diazoxide, hydralazine, glyceryl trinitrate, and potassium.[73-75]

Balloon occlusion angiography is also a valuable alternative for the identification of difficult distal targets in patients with limited distal perfusion precluding adequate visualization by the standard arteriographic techniques. With this technique, inflow to the target extremity is briefly occluded with the use of an elastomeric occlusion balloon while contrast is being injected. For an ipsilateral angiographic examination, the balloon is positioned at the proximal inflow vessel and contrast is injected through an access sheath with a larger profile than the catheter's shaft. When the access site is remote from the target vessel, the occlusion balloon catheter is positioned at the inflow artery and contrast is injected through the end-hole of the catheter. The balloon is deflated immediately after the contrast is injected and images are obtained. This technique provides excellent visualization of low-flow distal arteries in patients

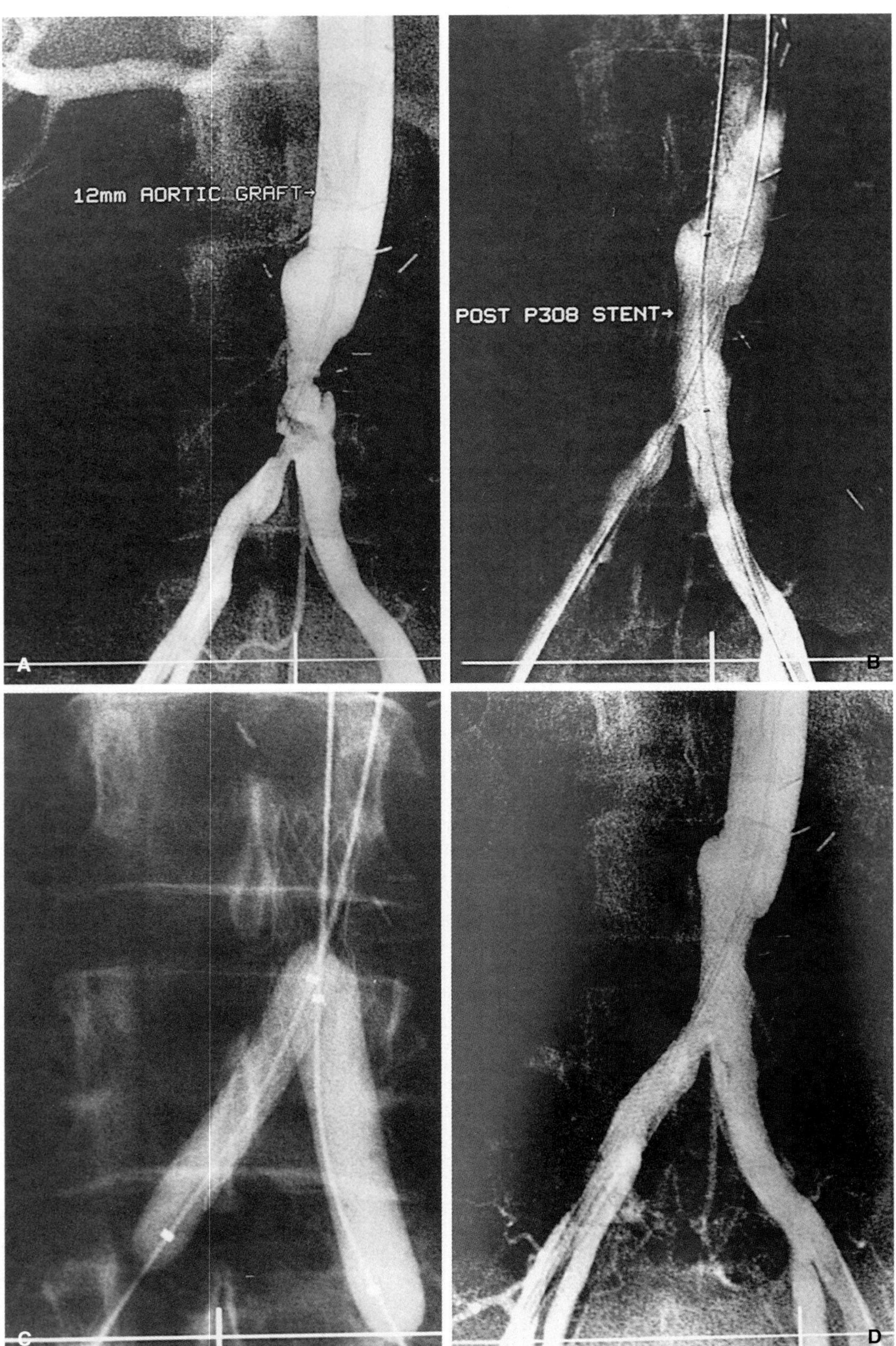

FIGURE 51-32 **A,** Complex atheromatous plaque just distal to the distal anastomosis of a descending thoracic to infrarenal abdominal aorta bypass (performed with a 12-mm Dacron graft) and extending into the iliac arteries, most notably on the right. **B,** Endovascular repair begins with dilation and primary Palmaz stenting of the distal aorta with a 12 mm × 4 cm balloon and a P308 stent. **C,** The iliac arteries are then dilated (8 mm × 4 cm on right, 10 mm × 4 cm on left) with primary Palmaz stenting of the right common iliac artery (P294) using the kissing balloon technique. **D,** Final angiographic result. Resting ankle-brachial index and exercise treadmill test scores normalized.

with severe proximal disease with smaller amounts of contrast injection. Although it would be possible to produce a balloon injury, this is unlikely with careful technique and has not been reported.[76-78]

Technique of Percutaneous Balloon Angioplasty

Patient Preparation

Percutaneous transluminal (balloon) angioplasty (PTA) is well tolerated under local anesthesia with 1% lidocaine, and the liberal use of intravenous sedation averts patient anxiety and discomfort. With the use of these measures, even major vascular, endovascular, or hybrid interventions can be performed.[79,80] All patients should have electrocardiographic and blood pressure monitoring. A urinary catheter may be considered, depending on the anticipated length of the intervention.

All patients undergoing PTA should be on antiplatelet therapy, which should be continued for at least 3 months after the procedure and preferably for life. For most interventions, aspirin therapy is sufficient, but carotid and infrageniculate dilations may benefit from supplemental clopidogrel (Plavix). After confirming intra-arterial access and before wire and catheter manipulation, systemic anticoagulation is obtained with 50 to 100 IU/kg of intravenous heparin. Although there is no strong evidence to support the prophylactic use of antibiotics in endovascular cases, if stent placement is anticipated, antibiotic prophylaxis with a first-generation cephalosporin is recommended.[81-83]

Vascular Access

The preferred site of vascular access is that which is closest to the lesion to be dilated but which allows adequate working room to complete the procedure. This optimizes catheter tracking ("pushability"), the lack of which can be a problem when working over acutely angled aortic bifurcations or through tortuous iliac arteries. Proximal iliac lesions are therefore best treated from an ipsilateral, retrograde CFA access (Fig. 51-32). Lesions of the very distal external iliac artery, CFA, or proximal SFA can be treated only from the contralateral femoral or axillary/brachial approach, because an ipsilateral puncture would not provide adequate working room for the balloon, even without a sheath. Lesions distal to the proximal third of the SFA are best approached through an ipsilateral antegrade CFA puncture. Renal arteries can be approached from either a femoral or axillary/brachial site of access, whereas mesenteric arteries are best approached from an axillary/brachial site of access.

A 5- or 6-French introducer sheath can accommodate most angioplasty catheters, but if the use of a guiding catheter or stent is anticipated, a larger diameter (7 to 10 French) sheath may be needed. For renal, subclavian, or contralateral iliac arteries, guiding catheters or long guiding sheaths are invaluable for wire/catheter stabilization and contrast injection for angiographic monitoring of the procedure. They are also required for the safe delivery of balloon-deployed stents.

Guide Wire Crossing

Successful crossing of the intended lesion with a guide wire is the next and often most difficult step in PTA. Although a J-tipped guide wire has the lowest potential for vessel injury, the large-profile, nondirectional leading element does not allow wire advancement across most severely stenotic lesions. Alternatively, a straight or angled floppy-tipped wire such as a Wholey, Terumo Glidewire, or Bentson can be used with careful fluoroscopic guidance. The Glidewire has a hydrophilic coating that renders it so slippery that extreme care must be taken to not advance the wire in a dissection plane behind the offending lesion, because subsequent dilation within the wrong plane may result in a hemodynamically significant dissection and vessel occlusion. If needed, performance characteristics of a floppy-tipped guide wire can be altered by using the additional support afforded by advancing a diagnostic catheter to within 1 or 2 cm of the end of the wire. Altering the position of the stiffening catheter relative to the tip of the guide wire can provide a variable degree of floppiness to the guide wire tip. Furthermore, the coaxial use of angle-tipped catheters adds steerability to a straight-tipped wire that can aid in directing the wire through tortuous vessel segments or angulated lesions. This may be particularly helpful when dilating renal, subclavian, or other branch vessels, and specific catheter shapes are available for all commonly encountered anatomic configurations to direct the guide wire toward the origin of the vessel of interest (see Table 51-1). Once the lesion is crossed, great care must be taken during subsequent catheter exchanges to ensure that the guide wire position across the lesion is maintained without advancing the wire far beyond the lesion where it might cause damage to branch vessels.

Crossing arterial occlusions poses additional challenges. An occlusion with a soft thrombotic core may easily allow guide wire passage. This generally mandates use of an angled or floppy-tipped Glidewire. Resistant occlusions may require extra support for the guide wire, which can be provided by a straight catheter positioned within 1 or 2 cm of the tip of the guide wire. This allows the flexible tip to probe the lesion while preventing the wire from buckling under the stress of firm forward pressure. Guide wire passage through occlusions often occurs, not surprisingly, in a subintimal plane. Therefore, it is imperative that re-entry of the guide wire into the lumen of the vessel be confirmed to ensure that dilation will re-establish continuity of the flow channel rather than extend the occlusion. Spinning the wire and observing free rotation of the angled tip, careful inspection of the course of the wire in several projections, or advancing a small catheter over the guide wire into the re-entered vessel and injection of contrast all are measures that can be employed to confirm that re-entry has occurred and in an acceptable location.

Following traversal of an occlusion a trial of thrombolytic therapy may be warranted, because a significant component of the occlusion may be thrombotic in nature and, therefore, amenable to dissolution. Not only can this reduce the overall length of the vessel requiring subsequent dilation but it also minimizes the chance of embolization of unstable thrombus during the dilation. Although the chances of successful clot lysis are significantly enhanced if the thrombus is less than 2 weeks old,[84,85] even substantially older thrombus can be successfully lysed, though less predictably so.[86] The inherent instability of acute thrombus mandates a trial of lysis prior to dilation in patients suspected of having unstable thrombus, whereas the need to attempt lysis in clinical situations suggestive of more chronic occlusions remains a subject of debate.

Balloon Angioplasty

Selection of an angioplasty balloon requires judgment and, at times, calibration and measurement of angiographic images. Once selected, the angioplasty balloon is prepared by placing it under negative pressure by a syringe containing half-strength contrast. On release of the suction, the balloon inflation channel fills with the diluted contrast, allowing visualization of the balloon inflation and minimizing the risk of air embolization were the balloon to rupture. Balloon angioplasty catheters are generally not test inflated prior to use because this would enlarge the profile of the balloon, possibly complicating its passage across a lesion. On the other hand, occlusion balloons are generally pretested to ensure reliable symmetric expansion. The guide wire channel is simply irrigated with saline.

Correct positioning of the balloon across the lesion to be dilated can be achieved by fluoroscopic reference to anatomic structures or radiopaque external markers placed at the time of the scout angiogram. Care must be taken to ensure that the marker system not be moved and that alignment of the scout and positioning images are identical. "Road mapping" or background opacification may be helpful for accurate positioning (see Chapter 18). Contrast injections through an adequately positioned and sized guiding catheter or sheath can be used to effectively monitor the position of the balloon.

It is generally preferable to inflate angioplasty balloon catheters with diluted contrast delivered by a pressure-monitoring device to ensure that safe inflation pressure limits are not exceeded. Balloon inflation is monitored fluoroscopically, and as the pressure within the balloon increases, any waist in the balloon profile disappears as the lesion dilates. The optimal number and duration of inflations is not currently known. Experimental data would suggest that inflation periods of 30 to 60 seconds are sufficient to allow for a desirable plastic deformation of the cellular components of the media.[87,88] After fluoroscopic confirmation of a complete deflation, the angioplasty balloon is withdrawn from the region and out the guiding catheter or introducer sheath.

The appreciation of pain by the patient on dilation is common and generally resolves with deflation of the balloon. Pain during PTA may be related to stretching of the adventitial nerve fibers, and failure to experience pain may indicate insufficient dilation.[89] Persistent pain after deflation of the balloon should prompt re-evaluation of the situation by contrast injection because it may indicate arterial rupture with extravasation. This further reinforces the need to maintain guide wire crossing of all lesions until their final assessment has been performed, because treatment of any vessel rupture or severe dissection endoluminally requires maintained access to the true vascular channel.

Atherosclerotic plaques occurring at bifurcations are essentially single plaques with extensions into both vessels and require special consideration because of this. Dilation of only one branch vessel can result in fracture of the plaque in the other branch, with the potential for dissection, stenosis, or occlusion. The aortic bifurcation is a common location for this situation, with atherosclerotic plaque involving the origins of both of the common iliac arteries. In such situations dilation is best accomplished with the "kissing balloon" technique, whereby both proximal common iliac arteries are dilated simultaneously from bilateral femoral artery punctures with the balloons kissing in the distal aorta (see Fig. 51-32). This approach supports both sides during dilation and is recommended for proximal common iliac lesions, even if only one of them is severe enough to warrant therapeutic dilation. At the very least, placing a guide wire across the "contralateral" vessel preserves access to that pathway should any dissection or occlusion require treatment.[90] Similarly, when the lesion to be treated is in close proximity to a branch vessel, such as in a mid-renal artery stenosis, passage of two guide wires, one into each branch, ensures access to both branches should a dissection or occlusion occur after treatment of the proximal lesion.

Dilation across branch vessel origins must be approached with caution because it may result in occlusion of the branch vessel. Although this may be of little consequence for some vessels, such as the hypogastric artery, loss of a vertebral artery during dilation of a subclavian lesion or of a polar renal branch may have more severe consequences, and good clinical judgment is warranted.

Assessment of Results

Knowing when to conclude an endovascular therapy and when to continue, perhaps with a larger balloon or placement of a stent, can be a difficult assessment. The presence of dilation-associated dissections can, at times, produce a worrisome-appearing angiogram despite actually representing an excellent therapeutic result (Fig. 51-33). As long as the dissection does not extend beyond the dilated area and does not obstruct flow, it need not, in and of itself, be considered a significant problem and should not increase the risk of restenosis. On the other hand, a satisfactory angiographic result may actually be hemodynamically suboptimal owing to the limitations of the angiographic method of assessment. The use of IVUS may provide a superior means of evaluation of the result of angioplasty but is beyond the scope of this chapter. However, the overwhelming majority of angioplasties performed today are evaluated solely on the basis of completion angiography, despite some potential shortcomings of this technique.

The accuracy of angiography can be improved by obtaining views in several different planes and by careful catheter selection and positioning to ensure adequate opacification without the introduction of contrast injection artifacts. This mandates the use of a catheter large enough to deliver an adequate volume of contrast and positioned proximal enough to the region under study to ensure thorough mixing of the contrast within the blood stream before it reaches the area of interest. When dilating a lesion from the retrograde approach, contrast material can be injected through the deflated balloon catheter (left in position across the dilated lesion to maintain lesion crossing) after removal of the guide wire. Although the wings of balloon material may degrade the image somewhat, this technique is generally adequate for a reasonable assessment of the result of the intervention and to allow a decision to be made about the need for further intervention.

In antegrade interventions the tip of the balloon catheter resides downstream of the dilated lesion. In such instances, use of a guiding catheter or sheath allows for contrast infusion from above, which provides the best opacification. Otherwise, there are only two other means of assessing the interventional result without losing "lesion crossing." The best alternative is to leave the deflated balloon catheter in place across the lesion, remove the guide wire, and forcefully inject through the balloon catheter, hoping to get sufficient reflux of contrast to opacify the area of interest. High-flow situations compromise opacification with this technique, and there is always a risk of vessel wall trauma or embolization due to the "jet effect" of forceful injection through a small-diameter end-hole catheter. Alternatively, use of a significantly undersized guide wire may allow for injection of enough contrast material through the proximally retracted balloon catheter with the wire left in position through the balloon catheter and across the lesion.

In general, a balloon dilation procedure is considered technically successful if there is less than a 30% residual stenosis present on completion of the procedure. Greater residual stenoses, though often not hemodynamically significant, correlate with early recurrence of the stenosis. In some instances hemodynamic assessment may be possible and is generally considered a more reliable measure of success than the angiographic appearance alone. Dilation of an iliac lesion from the ipsilateral approach, for example, allows for measurement of a "pull-through pressure" whereby the distal aspect of an end-hole catheter is placed proximal to the dilated area and the blood pressure is measured through the catheter as it is withdrawn through the lesion. Ordinarily there should be no discernible decrement in pressure within or on the downstream side of the dilated area, though a drop of 5 to 10 mm Hg is probably not significant.

For such a determination to be performed from a contralateral puncture, the catheter must actually be positioned across the lesion at the time that the downstream pressure is measured. Because the catheter itself may partially obstruct the flow channel, thereby producing a pressure drop, this technique has an increased false-positive rate. However, if no significant pressure differential is detected by this approach, it can generally be assumed that dilation has been successful. For SFA dilations performed from either ipsilateral or contralateral CFA punctures, this is the only way to perform a hemodynamic assessment. Unfortunately, obstruction of flow from the catheter becomes even more significant as the size of the artery decreases, introducing an even greater level of error with this approach in the SFA and renal arteries than in the iliac system.

If bilateral retrograde femoral sheaths are in place, it is possible to display simultaneous waveforms from both external iliac arteries. This allows comparison of the pressure below an iliac dilation with an index arterial pressure obtained from the contralateral iliac artery. If there is coexisting contralateral iliac disease, a catheter can be advanced into the aorta on that side to provide a true measure of "normal" arterial pressure. This method of assessing the result of intervention is particularly suited to situations where kissing balloon dilation has been performed, because bilateral sheaths will already be present.

Finally, pharmacologic provocation can be used to assess the significance of any residual stenosis by continuous pressure monitoring downstream from a treated area following injection of intra-arterial vasodilators into the ipsilateral extremity circulation (see Techniques for

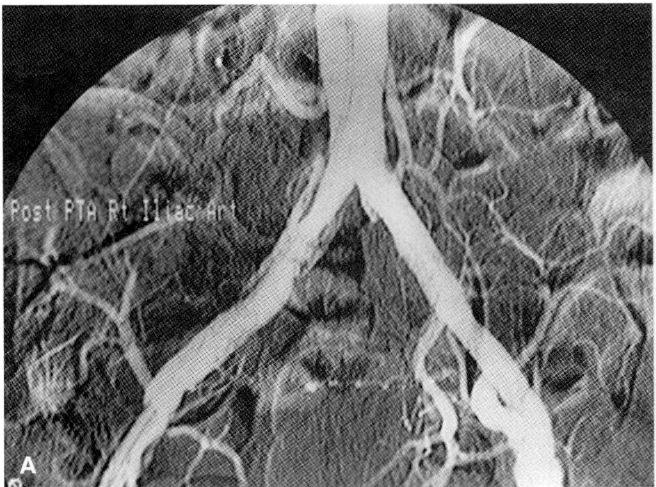

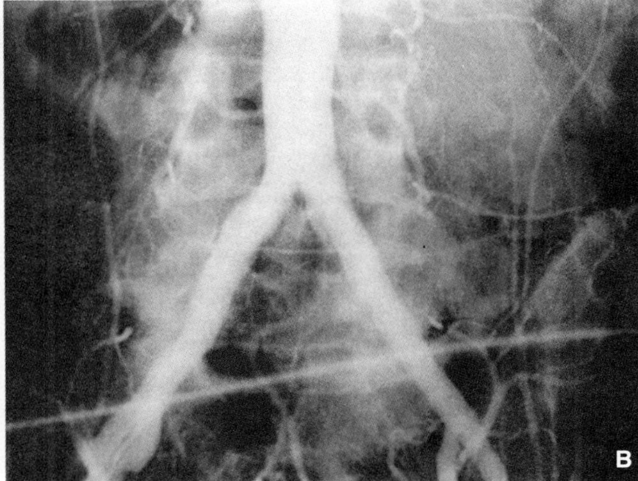

FIGURE 51-33 **A,** Severe dissection of the right common iliac artery following balloon dilation of a high-grade stenosis performed for claudication at a time prior to the availability of stents. Nonetheless, the patient's symptoms resolved and the ankle-brachial index normalized. **B,** Same artery 6 months later at the time of an unrelated angiogram. The patient maintained his clinical and hemodynamic successes as well.

Reactive Hyperemia). A drop in systolic pressure exceeding 20 mm Hg would be considered evidence that the residual stenosis was hemodynamically significant. Although the doses recommended do not usually produce a measurable drop in systemic blood pressure, this source of error is negated by measuring the contralateral iliac or aortic pressure, looking for a pressure differential of 20 mm Hg or greater. Measurement of ankle-brachial indices in the early post-treatment period may not be helpful because maximal improvement in pressure is typically not seen for at least several days. Furthermore, the presence of coexisting occlusive disease often obscures significant improvement in the treated area.

■ SURVEILLANCE AND RECOMMENDED FOLLOW-UP

Close monitoring following endovascular interventions is as important to good long-term results as in open vascular reconstructions. Treatment of a recurrent stenosis with a second endovascular procedure is more likely to be successful and durable than an attempt to restore patency of a total occlusion that might result from inadequate follow-up. A variety of modalities are used to monitor the status of endovascular interventions, applying clinical, hemodynamic, and anatomic criteria.

Duplex ultrasound is most frequently used for post-angioplasty follow-up. Because there are currently no well-defined criteria to determine a 30% degree of stenosis (our definition of initial angiographic success) with this modality, a clinically significant restenosis is usually defined by duplex criteria that identify a greater than 50% stenosis of the treated lesion. Evaluation intervals for all sites of PTA are somewhat arbitrary. In general we recommend clinical evaluation and duplex scanning at the time of discharge and at 1, 3, and 6 months, with follow-up every 6 months thereafter. Suspected restenotic lesions should be confirmed with arteriography and addressed promptly. Similar intervals can be used for the follow-up of aortic endovascular endoprosthesis.[91]

■ CONCLUSION

The explosive growth in endovascular technologies over the past 2 decades now provides a multitude of therapeutic options to patients with vascular disease. Although some may not pass the test of time and will be discarded, others have proved their worth and become standard care. Keeping current with these emerging technologies is itself a challenge. This chapter has reviewed the fundamental techniques and instrumentation relevant to presently available technologies but in no way constitutes a mechanism for the reader to become proficient in these techniques without supplemental training. However, once mastered, these basic skills will serve one well in moving forward to implement existing technologies and investigate promising new developments.

■ REFERENCES

1. Galland RB, Whiteley MS, Gibson M, et al: Remote superficial femoral artery endarterectomy: Medium-term results. Eur J Vasc Endovasc Surg 19:278-282, 2000.
2. Kluge A, Rauber K, Breithecker A, et al: Puncture of the popliteal artery using a Doppler-equipped (SMART) needle in transpopliteal interventions. Eur Radiol 13:1972-1978, 2003.
3. Blank R, Rupprecht HJ, Schorrlepp M, et al: [Clinical value of Doppler ultrasound-controlled puncture of the inguinal vessels with the "smart needle" within the scope of heart catheter examination]. Z Kardiol 86:608-614, 1997.
4. Verghese ST, McGill WA, Patel RI, et al: Comparison of three techniques for internal jugular vein cannulation in infants. Paediatr Anaesth 10:505-511, 2000.
5. Zajko AB, McLean GK, Freiman DB, et al: Percutaneous puncture of venous bypass grafts for transluminal angioplasty. AJR Am J Roentgenol 137:799-802, 1981.
6. Hessel SJ, Adams DF, Abrams HL: Complications of angiography. Radiology 138:273-281, 1981.
7. Illescas FF, Baker ME, McCann R, et al: CT evaluation of retroperitoneal hemorrhage associated with femoral arteriography. AJR Am J Roentgenol 146:1289-1292, 1986.
8. Altin RS, Flicker S, Naidech HJ: Pseudoaneurysm and arteriovenous fistula after femoral artery catheterization: Association with low femoral punctures. AJR Am J Roentgenol 152:629-631, 1989.
9. Sidawy AN, Neville RF, Adib H, Curry KM: Femoral arteriovenous fistula following cardiac catheterization: An anatomic explanation. Cardiovasc Surg 1:134-137, 1993.
10. Gibson M, Foale R, Spyrou N, al-Kutoubi A: Retrieval of detached coating of a hydrophilic guidewire from the profunda femoris artery using an Amplatz gooseneck snare. Cathet Cardiovasc Diagn 42:310-312, 1997.
11. Hunt JA, Harris JP: Is the mid-inguinal point an accurate landmark for the common femoral artery in vascular patients? Aust N Z J Surg 66:43-45, 1996.
12. Rupp SB, Vogelzang RL, Nemcek AA Jr, Yungbluth MM: Relationship of the inguinal ligament to pelvic radiographic landmarks: Anatomic correlation and its role in femoral arteriography. J Vasc Interv Radiol 4:409-413, 1993.
13. Grier D, Hartnell G: Percutaneous femoral artery puncture: Practice and anatomy. Br J Radiol 63:602-604, 1990.
14. Dotter CT, Rosch J, Robinson M: Fluoroscopic guidance in femoral artery puncture. Radiology 127:266-267, 1978.
15. Hughes P, Scott C, Bodenham A: Ultrasonography of the femoral vessels in the groin: Implications for vascular access. Anaesthesia 55:1198-1202, 2000.
16. Wacker F, Wolf KJ, Fobbe F: Percutaneous vascular access guided by color-duplex sonography. Eur Radiol 7:1501-1504, 1997.
17. Hessel SJ, Sequeira JC: Femoral artery catheterization and vessel tortuosity. Cardiovasc Intervent Radiol 4:80-82, 1981.
18. Reagan K, Matsumoto AH, Teitelbaum GP: Comparison of the hydrophilic guidewire in double- and single-wall entry needles: Potential hazards. Cathet Cardiovasc Diagn 24:205-208, 1991.
19. Kim JK, Kang HK: Percutaneous retrieval of the peeled-off plastic coating from a guide wire. J Vasc Interv Radiol 5:657-658, 1994.
20. Kikkawa K: A new antegrade femoral artery catheter needle set. Radiology 151:798, 1984.
21. Saltzman J, Probst P: A new puncture needle (Seldinger technique) for easy antegrade catheterization of the superficial femoral artery. Eur J Radiol 7:54-55, 1987.
22. Nice C, Timmons G, Bartholemew P, Uberoi R: Retrograde versus antegrade puncture for infrainguinal angioplasty. Cardiovasc Intervent Radiol 26, 2003.
23. Hartnell G: An improved reversal technique from retrograde to antegrade femoral artery cannulation. Cardiovasc Intervent Radiol 21:512-513, 1998.
24. Giavroglou CE: "Retroantegrade" catheterization of the branches of the femoral artery: Technical note. Cardiovasc Intervent Radiol 12:337-339, 1989.
25. Shenoy SS: Sidewinder catheter for conversion of retrograde into antegrade catheterization. Cardiovasc Intervent Radiol 6:112-113, 1983.

26. Yilmaz S, Sindel T, Luleci E: Bilateral transpopliteal approach for treatment of complex SFA and iliac occlusions. Eur Radiol 12:911-914, 2002.
27. Villas PA, Cohen G, Goyal A, et al: The merits of percutaneous transluminal angioplasty of a superficial femoral artery stenosis via a retrograde popliteal artery approach. J Vasc Interv Radiol 10:325-328, 1999.
28. Botti CF Jr, Ansel GM, Silver MJ, et al: Percutaneous retrograde tibial access in limb salvage. J Endovasc Ther 10:614-618, 2003.
29. Wolosker N, Nakano L, Duarte FH, et al: Peroneal artery approach for angioplasty of the superficial femoral artery: A case report. Vasc Endovasc Surg 37:129-133, 2003.
30. Hildick-Smith DJ, Khan ZI, Shapiro LM, Petch MC: Occasional-operator percutaneous brachial coronary angiography: First, do no arm. Catheter Cardiovasc Interv 57:161-165, 2002.
31. Andros G, Harris RW, Dulawa LB, et al: Subclavian artery catheterization: A new approach for endovascular procedures. J Vasc Surg 20:566-574, 1994.
32. Westcott JL, Taylor PT: Transaxillary selective four-vessel arteriography. Radiology 104:277-281, 1972.
33. McIvor J, Rhymer JC: Two hundred forty-five transaxillary arteriograms in arteriopathic patients: Success rate and complications. Clin Radiol 45:390-394, 1992.
34. Chitwood RW, Shepard AD, Shetty PC, et al: Surgical complications of transaxillary arteriography: A case-control study. J Vasc Surg 23:844-849, 1996.
35. O'Keefe DM: Brachial plexus injury following axillary arteriography: Case report and review of the literature. J Neurosurg 53:853-857, 1980.
36. Armstrong PJ, Han DC, Baxter JA, et al: Complication rates of percutaneous brachial artery access in peripheral vascular angiography. Ann Vasc Surg 17:107-110, 2003.
37. Campeau L: Percutaneous radial artery approach for coronary angiography. Cathet Cardiovasc Diagn 16:3-7, 1989.
38. Wappenschmidt J: [Demonstration of the cerebral vessels by retrograde contrast injection into the radial artery]. Fortschr Geb Rontgenstr Nuklearmed 102:575-579, 1965.
39. Chun HJ, Byun JY, Yoo SS, Choi BG: Tourniquet application to facilitate axillary venous access in percutaneous central venous catheterization. Radiology 226:918-920, 2003.
40. Danetz JS, McLafferty RB, Ayerdi J, et al: Selective venography versus nonselective venography before vena cava filter placement: Evidence for more, not less. J Vasc Surg 38:928-934, 2003.
41. Hasbak P, Jensen LT, Ibsen H: Hypertension and renovascular disease: Follow-up on 100 renal vein renin samplings. J Hum Hypertens 16:275-280, 2002.
42. Ayerdi J, McLafferty RB, Solis MM, et al: Retrograde endovascular hypogastric artery preservation (REHAP) and aortouniiliac (AUI) endografting in the management of complex aortoiliac aneurysms. Ann Vasc Surg 17:329-334, 2003.
43. Solis MM, Ayerdi J, Babcock GA, et al: Mechanism of failure in the treatment of type II endoleak with percutaneous coil embolization. J Vasc Surg 36:485-491, 2002.
44. Parra JR, Ayerdi J, McLafferty R, et al: Conformational changes associated with proximal seal zone failure in abdominal aortic endografts. J Vasc Surg 37:106-111, 2003.
45. Teruya TH, Ayerdi J, Solis MM, et al: Treatment of type III endoleak with an aortouniiliac stent graft. Ann Vasc Surg 17:123-128, 2003.
46. Engelke C, Sandhu C, Morgan RA, Belli AM: Using 6-mm cutting balloon angioplasty in patients with resistant peripheral artery stenosis: Preliminary results. AJR Am J Roentgenol 179:619-623, 2002.
47. Engelke C, Morgan RA, Belli AM: Cutting balloon percutaneous transluminal angioplasty for salvage of lower limb arterial bypass grafts: Feasibility. Radiology 223:106-114, 2002.
48. Bendok BR, Roubin GS, Katzen BT, et al: Cutting balloon to treat carotid in-stent stenosis: Technical note. J Invasive Cardiol 15:227-232, 2003.
49. Munneke GJ, Engelke C, Morgan RA, Belli AM: Cutting balloon angioplasty for resistant renal artery in-stent restenosis. J Vasc Interv Radiol 13:327-331, 2002.
50. Ryan JM, Dumbleton SA, Smith TP: Technical innovation: Using a cutting balloon to treat resistant high-grade dialysis graft stenosis. AJR Am J Roentgenol 180:1072-1074, 2003.
51. Bergersen L, Marshall AC, Lang P, et al: Follow-up results of cutting balloon angioplasty for pulmonary artery stenosis in children. J Am Coll Cardiol 41(6 Suppl B):489, 2003.
52. Galassi AR, Foti R, Azzarelli S, et al: Long-term angiographic follow-up after successful repeat balloon angioplasty for in-stent restenosis. Clin Cardiol 24:334-340, 2001.
53. Mauri L, Bonan R, Weiner BH, et al: Cutting balloon angioplasty for the prevention of restenosis: Results of the Cutting Balloon Global Randomized Trial. Am J Cardiol 90:1079-1083, 2002.
54. Marti V, Martin V, Garcia J, et al: Significance of angiographic coronary dissection after cutting balloon angioplasty. Am J Cardiol 81:1349-1352, 1998.
55. Maruo T, Yasuda S, Miyazaki S: Delayed appearance of coronary artery perforation following cutting balloon angioplasty. Cathet Cardiovasc Interv 57:529-531, 2002.
56. Kawamura A, Asakura Y, Ishikawa S, et al: Extraction of previously deployed stent by an entrapped cutting balloon due to the blade fracture. Cathet Cardiovasc Interv 57:239-243, 2002.
57. Harb TS, Ling FS: Inadvertent stent extraction six months after implantation by an entrapped cutting balloon. Cathet Cardiovasc Interv 53:415-419, 2001.
58. Grube E, Silber S, Hauptmann KE, et al: TAXUS I: Six- and twelve-month results from a randomized, double-blind trial on a slow-release paclitaxel-eluting stent for de novo coronary lesions. Circulation 107:38-42, 2003.
59. Morice MC, Serruys PW, Sousa JE, et al: A randomized comparison of a sirolimus-eluting stent with a standard stent for coronary revascularization. N Engl J Med 346:1773-1780, 2002.
60. Baim D, Pinkerton R, Schatz R: Acute results of STAND percutaneous vascular surgical device trial. Circulation 96:443-448, 1997.
61. Carey D, Martin JR, Moore CA, et al: Complications of femoral artery closure devices. Cathet Cardiovasc Interv 52:3-7, 2001.
62. Silver S, Door R, Muhling H, Konig U: Sheath pulling immediately after PTCA: Comparison of two different deployment techniques for the hemostatic puncture closure device—a prospective, randomized study. Cathet Cardiovasc Diagn 41:378-383, 1997.
63. Dangas G, Mehran R, Kokolis S, et al: Vascular complications after percutaneous coronary interventions following hemostasis with manual compression versus arteriotomy closure devices. J Am Coll Cardiol 38:638-641, 2001.
64. Stoeckelhuber BM, Suttmann I, Stoeckelhuber M, Kueffer G: Comparison of the vasodilating effect of nitroglycerin, verapamil, and tolazoline in hand angiography. J Vasc Interv Radiol 14:749-754, 2003.
65. Friedman J, Zeit RM, Cope C, Bernhard VM: Optimal use of tolazoline in arteriography. AJR Am J Roentgenol 142:817-820, 1984.
66. Hansteen V, Lorentsen E: Vasodilator drugs in the treatment of peripheral arterial insufficiency. Acta Med Scand Suppl 556:3-62, 1974.
67. Miller JA, Cross DT, Moran CJ, et al: Severe thrombocytopenia following intraarterial papaverine administration for treatment of vasospasm. J Neurosurg 83:435-437, 1995.
68. Zagoria RJ, D'Souza VJ, Baker AL: Recommended precautions when using low-osmolality or nonionic contrast agents with vasodilators. Invest Radiol 22:513-514, 1987.
69. Pilla TJ, Beshany SE, Shields JB: Incompatibility of Hexabrix and papaverine. AJR Am J Roentgenol 146:1300-1301, 1986.
70. Pallan TM, Wulkan IA, Abadir AR, et al: Incompatibility of Isovue 370 and papaverine in peripheral arteriography. Radiology 187:257-259, 1993.
71. Irving HD, Burbridge BE: Incompatibility of contrast agents with intravascular medications: Work in progress. Radiology 173:91-92, 1989.
72. Cohen MI, Vogelzang RL: A comparison of techniques for improved visualization of the arteries of the distal lower extremity. AJR Am J Roentgenol 147:1021-1024, 1986.

73. Robinson BF, Phillips RJ, Wilson PN, Chiodini PL: Effect of local infusion of ouabain on human forearm vascular resistance and on response to potassium, verapamil, and sodium nitroprusside. J Hypertens 1:165-169, 1983.
74. Robinson BF, Collier JG, Dobbs RJ: Comparative dilator effect of verapamil and sodium nitroprusside in forearm arterial bed and dorsal hand veins in man: Functional differences between vascular smooth muscle in arterioles and veins. Cardiovasc Res 13:16-21, 1979.
75. Collier JG, Lorge RE, Robinson BF: Comparison of effects of tolmesoxide (RX71107), diazoxide, hydralazine, prazosin, glyceryl trinitrate and sodium nitroprusside on forearm arteries and dorsal hand veins of man. Br J Clin Pharmacol 5:35-44, 1978.
76. Cardella JF, Smith TP, Darcy MD, et al: Balloon occlusion femoral angiography prior to in-situ saphenous vein bypass. Cardiovasc Intervent Radiol 10:181-187, 1987.
77. Welch HJ, Belkin M, Kessler R, et al: Superiority of balloon occlusion arteriography to reactive hyperemic arteriography in visualization of distal lower limb vessels. Ann Vasc Surg 7:83-87, 1993.
78. Santilli SM, Payne WD, Hunter DW, Knighton DR: Comparison of preoperative standard angiography with preoperative balloon occlusion femoral angiography of the lower extremity. J Invest Surg 6:83-95, 1993.
79. Barkmeier LD, Hood DB, Sumner DS, et al: Local anesthesia for infrainguinal arterial reconstruction. Am J Surg 174:202-204, 1997.
80. Henretta JP, Hodgson KJ, Mattos MA, et al: Feasibility of endovascular repair of abdominal aortic aneurysms with local anesthesia with intravenous sedation [see comments]. J Vasc Surg 29:793-798, 1999.
81. Paget DS, Bukhari RH, Zayyat EJ, et al: Infectibility of endovascular stents following antibiotic prophylaxis or after arterial wall incorporation. Am J Surg 178:219-224, 1999.
82. Deitch JS, Hansen KJ, Regan JD, et al: Infected renal artery pseudoaneurysm and mycotic aortic aneurysm after percutaneous transluminal renal artery angioplasty and stent placement in a patient with a solitary kidney. J Vasc Surg 28:340-344, 1998.
83. Dravid VS, Gupta A, Zegel HG, et al: Investigation of antibiotic prophylaxis usage for vascular and nonvascular interventional procedures. J Vasc Interv Radiol 9:401-406, 1998.
84. Ouriel K: Thrombolysis or operation for peripheral arterial occlusion. Vasc Med 1:159-161, 1996.
85. Ouriel K, Veith FJ, Sasahara AA: Thrombolysis or peripheral arterial surgery: Phase I results. TOPAS Investigators. J Vasc Surg 23:64-73, 1996.
86. Wholey MH, Maynar MA, Pulido-Duque JM, et al: Comparison of thrombolytic therapy of lower-extremity acute, subacute, and chronic arterial occlusions. Cathet Cardiovasc Diagn 44:159-169, 1998.
87. Castaneda-Zuniga WR, Sibley R, Amplatz K: The pathologic basis of angioplasty. Angiology 35:195-205, 1984.
88. Consigny PM, LeVeen RF: Effects of angioplasty balloon inflation time on arterial contractions and mechanics. Invest Radiol 23:271-276, 1988.
89. Korogi Y, Takahashi M, Bussaka H, Hatanaka Y: Percutaneous transluminal angioplasty: Pain during balloon inflation. Br J Radiol 65:140-142, 1992.
90. Hood DB, Hodgson KJ: Percutaneous transluminal angioplasty and stenting for iliac artery occlusive disease. Surg Clin North Am 79:575-596, 1999.
91. Karch LA, Henretta JP, Hodgson KJ, et al: Algorithm for the diagnosis and treatment of endoleaks. Am J Surg 178:225-231, 1999.

Chapter

52

Basic Techniques of Endovascular Aneurysm Repair

GEOFFREY H. WHITE, MD, FRACS
JAMES MAY, MD, MS, FRACS, FACS

This chapter discusses basic techniques of endovascular repair of abdominal aortic aneurysms (AAA). Details of patient selection, results, and complications are more fully addressed in Chapter 101. Endovascular aneurysm repair involves the transluminal placement of a graft within the aneurysm that completely excludes the aneurysm sac from the general circulation.[1-8] The graft is anchored in place by a balloon-expandable or self-expanding metal frame that supports all or part of the graft and provides a tight seal proximal and distal to the dilated segment of the artery. Because it avoids the need for laparotomy, cross-clamping of the aorta, and the obligatory blood loss associated with opening the aneurysm sac, the technique has much to recommend it. Endovascular aneurysm repair has been shown to reduce the morbidity associated with conventional open AAA repair and to extend the scope of repair to patients with severe medical co-morbidities who previously were denied treatment.

■ HISTORY OF DEVELOPMENT OF ENDOVASCULAR TECHNIQUES

Endovascular treatment of aortic aneurysms is not new.[9] In 1864, Moore is said to have attempted thrombosis of an aneurysm by introducing 75 feet of intraluminal wire into it.[10] Before antibiotics were used, most aneurysms were syphilitic in origin and saccular in morphology; this made them more amenable to treatment by wiring than the fusiform variety seen today. In 1879, Corradi modified the process by passing an electric current along an insulated wire.[11] Electrothermic coagulation of aortic aneurysm by wiring was used until 1953, when graft replacement of aneurysms was introduced.

The relatively high morbidity and mortality rates for open graft replacement of aortic aneurysms, particularly in high-risk patients, maintained the interest of researchers in developing an endovascular method of repair. Balko and colleagues[12] probably can be credited with the first reported experimental use of a stent-graft combination for the treatment of artificial aneurysms. In their experiments, a novel form of nitinol Z-stent was combined with a sleeve of polyurethane and tested in a sheep model of aortic aneurysm. The first radiographically guided aortic graft implantations were reported in 1987 by Lawrence and associates,[13] who used a chain of stainless steel Gianturco Z-stents (Cook, Bloomington, Ind) within a tube of woven polyester. Parodi and coworkers[1] did not report the first clinical use in humans of transfemoral, endovascular grafting to exclude AAA until 1991. Their concept was the use of balloon-expandable, vascular stents to replace sutures and secure the proximal and distal ends of a fabric graft within the lumen of the aorta. Since this report was published, numerous ingenious devices have been developed and tested clinically.

■ INDICATIONS FOR TREATMENT

The indications for elective repair of an AAA include asymptomatic aneurysms more than 5 cm in diameter and all symptomatic and ruptured aneurysms, provided that coexisting medical conditions do not preclude operation.[14] Endovascular repair was first used in the management of aortic aneurysms in high-risk patients who were unfit for conventional open repair. Although many high-risk patients were able to be treated, there were important implications if the endovascular technique failed and required conversion to open repair in patients denied conventional surgery because of medical co-morbidities. The mortality in patients with this clinical course proved to be high.[15] With improvements in technology and increasing experience, however, the incidence of conversion from endovascular to open operation has been reduced to a low percentage.[16] High-risk patients may continue to be considered for endovascular repair, provided that the size of the aneurysm justifies intervention and the patient understands the increased risk.

A diameter of 6 cm is about the point at which the risk of rupture begins to exceed the risk of endovascular repair in a high-risk patient. High-risk patients were defined by the Endovascular Graft Committee as "patients with large, threatening aneurysms whose operative risk is excessive, for example, in excess of three to four times normal, on the basis of heart, lung, or liver disease or previous abdominal scarring or infection."[17] This definition is important when outcomes are compared and patients are informed of the relative risks.

Now that the feasibility and relative safety of endovascular repair have been established, the procedure can be offered to selected patients who are considered fit for conventional open repair. It is important, however, that these patients understand that the long-term outcome of these procedures is unknown and that concurrent comparison of endovascular and open repair of AAA shows a significantly higher failure rate for the endovascular method after mid-term follow-up of several years.[18,19] Encouraging survival rates in patients with ruptured AAA treated by endovascular repair have been reported.[20-22] These results make it appropriate to include ruptured AAA as a relative indication in those sufficiently stable for endovascular treatment.

■ CRITERIA FOR ENDOVASCULAR TREATMENT

The previous edition of this book recommended a collar or neck of normal aorta between the renal arteries and an aneurysm of 15 mm or greater in length and a diameter of 28 mm or less, with angulation in the proximal neck being limited to 60 degrees. Heavy circumferential calcification, mural thrombus, and an inverted funnel-shaped collar were considered contraindications to the endovascular method. Although these are safe guidelines, later generations of endografts have been shown to be feasible with proximal necks that are shorter and larger in diameter.[23]

Many interventionalists, faced with patients with large aneurysms who are very high risk for open repair, have modified their criteria for endovascular repair. A patient with circumferential or eccentric mural thrombus within the proximal neck is at risk not only of peripheral embolization at operation, but also of poor device fixation and progressive dilatation of the neck because mural thrombus is a marker of preaneurysmal disease. Use of endovascular grafts in such patients is justified, provided that the patient understands that the treatment being offered is prone to complications and is available for closely supervised follow-up. For patients with a normal aortic segment at the level of the renal arteries but no suitable aortic neck, the alternative use of fenestrated grafts is being studied in trials.[24-27] Such grafts are custom made to include circular or scalloped openings in the graft fabric that extends above the renal arteries.

Because the endovascular method of aneurysm repair requires isolation of the aneurysm sac from the circulation, the presence of large patent collateral channels, such as the inferior mesenteric artery and the internal iliac arteries, communicating with the aortic or iliac sac previously was considered a relative contraindication. Experience has shown that a large inferior mesenteric artery is not a significant risk factor for successful endovascular graft procedure. Internal iliac arteries presenting this problem may be occluded by coil embolization preoperatively. Alternatively, the internal iliac artery may be ligated proximally and revascularized by transposition or bypass graft. Branched prostheses with limbs for the internal and the external iliac arteries currently are being studied in trials.[28-30] Thus, the criteria of feasibility for endovascular repair are being progressively broadened.

■ PREOPERATIVE IMAGING

Preoperative imaging is very important because patient selection and sizing of the endograft depend on it. Contrast-enhanced, spiral, multislice computed tomography (CT) is the preferred initial method of investigation. The scans are acquired rapidly, which allows uniform vascular enhancement at peak intensity with similar or lower contrast load compared with conventional CT. The contrast material allows thrombus to be distinguished from flowing blood and enables the proximal neck to be assessed for suitability for endovascular repair. The dimensions of the aortic neck can be determined accurately and the presence of calcification or mural thrombus noted. The size of the iliac arteries and the presence of aneurysm disease and calcification also can be assessed. Three-dimensional reconstruction or reformatting of the CT images is now available in many centers and has many advantages in accurate representation of the aortic anatomy (see Chapters 20 and 21).

Software packages are available that plot the axial line of the aorta and aneurysm and enable cuts to be made at right angles to that line. This capability enables more accurate measurements of the diameter of the aorta and the distance from the renal arteries to the aortic and iliac bifurcations to be made. Although the anatomy of the iliac arteries and accessory renal arteries can be shown by spiral CT, aortography is performed in some medical centers for measurement of length when the patient has been found to be suitable for endovascular repair by CT. The aortogram should be performed with a calibrated catheter to allow accurate length measurements and precise calculation of diameters. Anteroposterior and lateral views are required to show tortuosity in the neck of the aneurysm and the iliac arteries. Because the aortogram shows the lumen of the aorta, and CT shows the arterial wall in addition to the lumen, the diameter of the neck of the aneurysm is usually greater when measured by CT than by angiography.

■ PROSTHESES FOR ENDOVASCULAR REPAIR OF ABDOMINAL AORTIC ANEURYSMS

Tube Grafts, Bifurcated Grafts, and Aortoiliac Grafts

The early endovascular prostheses comprised tubular or tapered fabric grafts anchored in place by stents at each end. Hooks or barbs were incorporated in the stents to minimize migration of the device. Initially the configuration of the endografts was tubular. To increase the number of patients who were suitable for endovascular repair, endovascular aortoiliac and aortofemoral tapered grafts were combined with extravascular femorofemoral crossover grafts (Fig. 52-1).[31-33] One-piece bifurcated prostheses were developed that required the contralateral limb to be pulled across the aortic bifurcation to the contralateral side by a crossover wire. Both iliac limbs were anchored by metal stents. The limitations of these devices became apparent, and a second generation of prostheses was developed. In these, a metallic frame supported the fabric throughout to prevent kinking and to add column strength. The modular method was used to deploy bifurcated grafts, with component parts being delivered from both groins. The delivery system's internal diameter was reduced from 24F to 18F to 21F, and the flexibility was increased (Fig. 52-2).

Tube Grafts

Although tube graft repair is preferred whenever possible in open repair procedures, it has become apparent that stent-graft treatment for infrarenal AAA requires a bifurcated graft system in most cases. The anatomy of the proximal neck and the iliac arteries is the major determinant of graft selection. In most patients assessed for this procedure, the distal "neck" or aortic cuff is unsuitable to implant a tube graft successfully.[34-36] Even if the distal aortic cuff is 20 to 25 mm in length, it is often lined with thrombus and is prone to late expansion, which may result in endoleak.[37] Problems of achieving a good seal in the distal aorta are increased by the fact that accurate length determination for a tube graft may be difficult because of the curved tortuous path in which the graft must lie[38]; this aspect is not so vital if a bifurcated graft is used because there is a longer attachment site within the iliac artery. One method of overcoming this problem with tube grafts is by customizing graft length at the time of the procedure by overlap of several tube grafts.[39] This method commonly is used in endovascular treatment of thoracic aneurysms.

Several studies have shown that the percentage of patients suitable for tube grafts under current criteria is usually less than 5%.[35,40] In most series, bifurcated grafts are being used for more than 90% of endoluminal graft procedures, with aortoiliac tapered grafts making up the difference. In the abdominal aorta, tube grafts generally are restricted in use for focal saccular, anastomotic, or false aneurysms.

Bifurcated Grafts

Implanting a bifurcated graft configuration inside the aorta by remote access presents problems of how to manipulate the two graft limbs into the iliac arteries. To date, there have been two main techniques used:

1. *Single-piece bifurcated grafts,* such as the Guidant Ancure Endograft,[41] the Chuter Device,[42] and the Endologix Device,[43] feature a single-piece bifurcated graft, which is introduced initially into the aorta, with one limb (the "contralateral limb") being manipulated into position by guide wires and pull-out wires directed across the aortic bifurcation by conventional interventional techniques.
2. *Modular bifurcated grafts* are usually two-piece or three-piece designs. The various component grafts are overlapped within the aorta or iliac arteries to construct the bifurcated configuration. The second iliac limb is inserted by separate contralateral femoral artery access via antegrade puncture. Modular designs allow some degree of customization of graft component length or diameter to match individual patient anatomy.

Table 52-1 lists differences between single-piece and modular designs of bifurcated grafts. Modular component devices include the Vanguard[44,45] (Boston Scientific, Natick, Mass), AneuRx[46,47] and Talent[48] devices (Medtronic, Eden Prairie, Minn), Lifepath AAA Graft System[49,50] (Edwards Lifesciences, Irvine, Calif), Gore Excluder[51,52] (WL Gore, Flagstaff, Ariz), Fortron[53] (Cordis, NJ), and Zenith

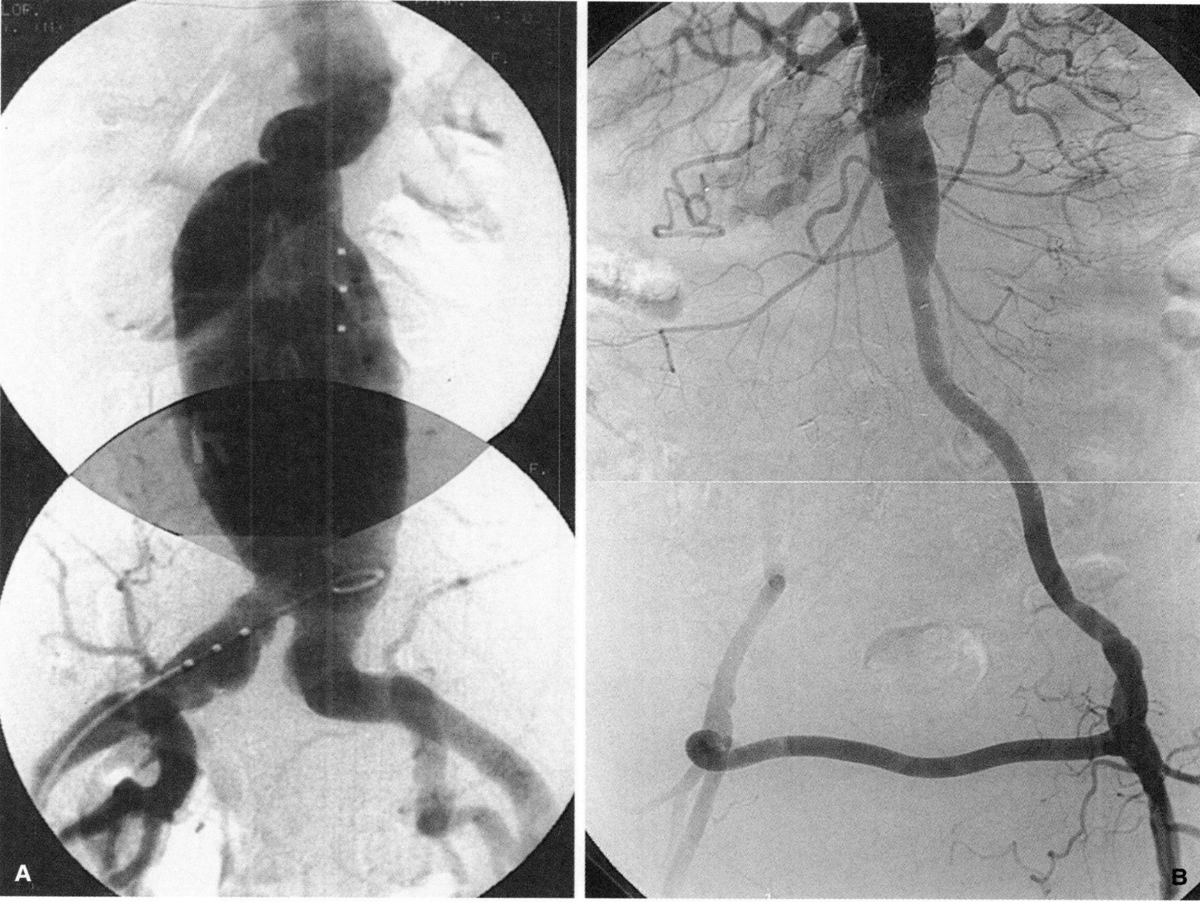

FIGURE 52-1 **A,** Aortogram shows 6.5-cm abdominal aortic aneurysm with common iliac artery ectasia. **B,** Postoperative aortogram from the same patient 2 years after endoluminal repair using an aortofemoral endograft. The right common iliac artery has been occluded by a detachable balloon, and the right limb has been revascularized by a femorofemoral crossover graft. (From May J, White GH, Yu W, et al: Repair of abdominal aortic aneurysms by the endoluminal method: Outcome in the first 100 patients. Med J Aust 165:549-551, 1996.)

endografts[54,55] (Cook Company, Bloomington, Ind). All these devices have been tested or are currently undergoing testing in clinical trials, and their design involves modularity and a metallic internal stent or wireform support ("endoskeleton") or external stent ("exoskeleton"). The Vanguard has been withdrawn because of device complications. Talent, Fortron, and Zenith endografts feature an uncovered proximal stent segment, introducing the possibility of implantation over the renal arteries ("suprarenal attachment"). Although this remains a controversial issue, such an approach has benefits for attachment of the endograft in patients with a short aortic neck.[53] The implantation procedure for bifurcated grafts is more complex, and the limbs of bifurcated grafts are more prone to thrombotic occlusion, especially if compromised by external compression or kinking secondary to tortuosity of the iliac vessels.

Table 52-1 Comparison of Single-Piece and Modular Bifurcated Endovascular Grafts

SINGLE-PIECE	MODULAR (MULTIPIECE)
Complex graft construction and delivery system	Simple graft components and delivery system
Graft dimensions determined at time of manufacture	Customized graft component selection may be available at time of procedure
Requires preliminary insertion of iliac crossover catheter	Requires guide wire access to the contralateral graft stump to place iliac limb
Single-piece construction may reduce potential for fabric leak or graft failure	Potential for leakage, disconnection, or stenosis at graft overlap zone
Difficult to deliver fully stented—may require additional stents implanted into graft limbs	Can be delivered as a fully supported stent graft

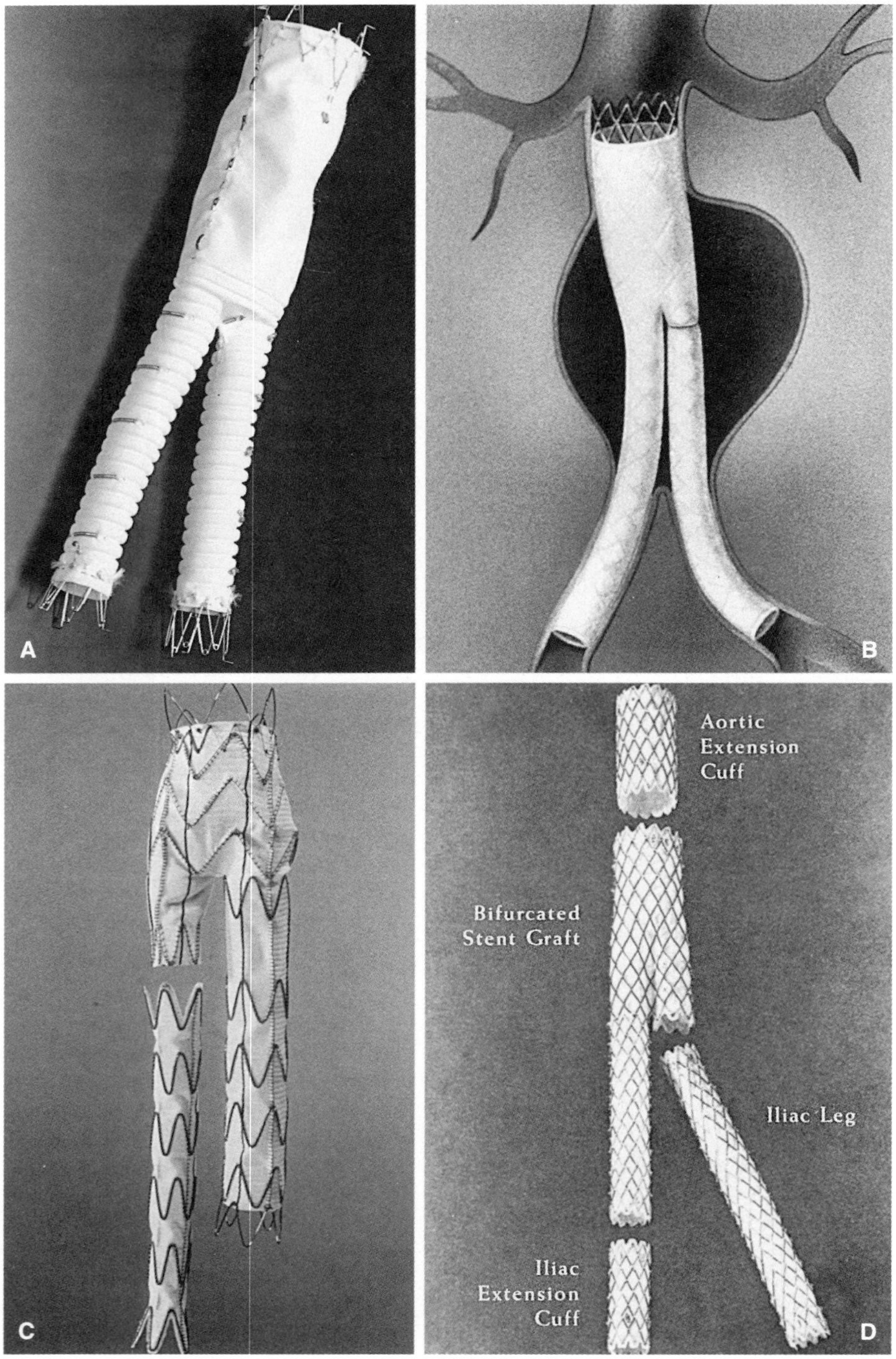

FIGURE 52-2 Endovascular techniques. **A,** One-piece bifurcated endograft. **B,** Boston Scientific modular bifurcated endograft. **C,** World Medical modular bifurcated endograft. **D,** Medtronic modular bifurcated endograft.

Aortoiliac Grafts

Commonly referred to as aortomonoiliac or aortouni-iliac grafts, these devices are usually reserved for special application in patients with difficult anatomy or for cases in which rapid deployment is desirable, such as ruptured AAA. Fixed angulation of the proximal segment of the common iliac artery, with associated stenosis and calcification (especially in patients with chronic renal failure) can present an almost impenetrable barrier to safe access to the aorta, and perforation of these segments is possible. In such cases and in some patients with stenosis or aneurysm of the iliac artery on one side or in patients with a narrow distal aorta (too narrow to accommodate both limbs of a bifurcated graft), an aortoiliac graft may be preferable, used in conjunction with femoral crossover graft.[32,33] An occluder device must be implanted into the contralateral common iliac artery, to prevent backflow of blood from the internal iliac artery on that side to the AAA sac. Use in acute or ruptured AAA is favored in some centers because of the simpler deployment of these designs.

■ TECHNIQUES OF ENDOVASCULAR ABDOMINAL AORTIC ANEURYSM REPAIR

Anatomic Measurements and Procedural Planning

Preprocedural planning is one of the most important aspects of achieving successful endovascular repair. Essentials of the patient's anatomy should be recorded on a dedicated planning sheet, including the basic dimensional details of the aortic neck (neck diameter, length, and shape) and other characteristics, such as angulation in the anteroposterior or lateral planes, wall irregularity, and thrombus. In addition, note is made of the shape and diameter of the flow lumen through the sac and the characteristics of the access arteries (iliac tortuosity, calcification, and atheroma). It is important to be aware of the number of renal arteries and their relationship to the aortic neck and the position of the lowest renal artery with respect to bony landmarks, such as the first or second lumbar vertebrae, and any significant amount of thrombus or atheroma on the aortic wall close to the renal orifices or within the aortic neck. This information is used to plan the device dimensions and the order of the procedure, including a consideration of likely difficulties or complications during the operation and a backup plan as to their management. Planning also should include the provision of reserve or extension grafts, which can be used to deal with endoleaks or inadequate coverage; this is particularly applicable in patients with a difficult aortic neck or calcified, atherosclerotic iliac arteries.

Table 52-2 presents a general guide to the anatomic requirements for successful implantation of an endovascular AAA graft. Variations in these recommendations are provided in the instructions for use of individual graft designs. Measurements of the diameter of the aortic neck and the iliac arteries in general are best obtained from the CT scans, whereas length measurements are more accurate when obtained from three-dimensional reconstructions or from calibrated angiography. When determining vessel diameters, it is important to recognize that some of the device companies recommend sizing with respect to the internal or luminal measurement of the aortic neck or iliac diameter, whereas others recommend measuring the external, adventitial diameter. Vessel diameter measurements usually assume a circular or cylindrical shape, so it is important to verify that the true shape is not ovoid or irregular by reference to the three-dimensional images. The angles of deployed devices should be anticipated, and consideration should be given as to whether this could be improved by use of a different access side or technique or by using different device components. Extra graft extensions of various sizes, balloons, access catheters, and guide wires should be available. In cases in which there may be access difficulties, an alternative technique of access should be preplanned and the patient prepared and informed.

Table 52-2 Anatomic Information Required for Endovascular Grafting of Abdominal Aortic Aneurysm

Aortic Neck
Diameter
Length
Shape
Angulation
Aortic Sac
Channel
Angulation
Distal diameter
Iliac Arteries
Diameter/patency
Length of common iliac
Shape/iliac aneurysm
Angulation
Calcification

Device Oversizing

Most endovascular device companies recommend use of a graft that is oversized by approximately 10% to 15% compared with the diameters of the attachment zones in the aortic neck and the iliac arteries. This recommendation has been empirical, based on the fact that a self-expanding graft needs to deploy to a size large enough to attain attachment and seal within these sites. There also has been an argument that allowance should be made for late spontaneous dilatation of the aortic neck,[56] although there is a contrary view that deployment of an endograft high within the aortic neck has the effect of preventing neck dilatation.[57] The true amount of oversizing that results depends on the method used for calculating the vessel diameters, for which there is no standardized technique. Usually the aortic neck diameter is calculated with respect to the external (adventitial) surface so that the true diameter of the lumen may be considerably less and the graft diameter may be oversized substantially more with respect to the lumen.

With severe oversizing, some endograft designs appear to cause dilatation of the neck because of their inherent radial expansile force. Excessive oversizing ($\geq$20%) has been shown to be associated with increased graft migration rates with at least two self-expanding device designs.[58,59] In one study, oversizing by more than 20% with the AneuRx graft resulted in late aortic neck dilatation and high rates of device migration.[58] With the Zenith graft, oversizing of 30% in a multicenter phase II trial resulted in a 14-fold increase in migration rates, increased rate of AAA sac enlargement, and early dilatation of the aortic neck at the 6-month follow-up interval, which then stabilized out to 24 months.[59] Although these changes may be device dependent, avoidance of excessive oversizing is recommended. The characteristics of the neck itself also are important factors: A short neck or aortic neck angulation greater than 40% has significant adverse effects on the outcome.[60,61]

General Technique for Modular Bifurcated Graft Deployment

This section summarizes the general techniques for implantation of modular bifurcated devices, which are now used in most AAA cases. Each commercial device has variations or additions to this general technique, and the

Table 52-3 Additional Equipment Required for Endovascular Graft Procedures

Fluoroscope with digital angiography capabilities
- C-arm or fixed unit
- Cine-loop recording and image recall facility

Radiolucent carbon-fiber procedure table
Power injector
- Recommended for intraoperative and completion fluoroscopy studies
- Radiopaque vascular contrast medium

Radiopaque ruler (centimeter increments) or marker board
Guide wires
- A selection of various guide wires of adequate length (140-260 cm), including Amplatz Super-Stiff (diameter 0.035 inch or 0.038 inch), Terumo hydrophilic nonkink guide wires, and Bentson 0.035-inch wires

Angiocatheters, access sheaths, and guiding catheters
- Assorted diameters and shapes

Angioplasty balloons
Aortic occlusion balloons
- For ruptured aneurysms

Tool kit of extension grafts, stents
Snares
IVUS catheters and IVUS machine
- Optional—for selected cases only

IVUS, intravascular ultrasound.

instructions for use for individual devices should be followed. Specific stages of the deployment procedure are described in further detail subsequently.

Endovascular repair may be performed under general, regional, or local anesthesia in an operating room or in an endovascular suite with facilities suitable for surgical cut-down approach. The operating room environment is preferred for the rare cases in which it is anticipated that there may be a requirement for conversion to open repair in the event of failed endovascular repair or severe complications needing open operation. Endovascular AAA procedures require a large amount of additional equipment that is not normally needed for open repair (Table 52-3). Apart from the stent-graft device, equipment facilities required include a radiolucent carbon-fiber operating table and a C-arm image intensifier that provides cine-loop angiography with digital subtraction capability and frame-by-frame replay. The patient is positioned so that the C-arm can be placed beneath the abdomen and lower chest without obstruction from the table. A radiopaque ruler or marker board may be placed beneath the patient as a reference point during device deployment. In general, the goal is to place the stent-graft device so that it covers the whole length of infrarenal aorta from just below the lowest renal artery orifice, down to the region of the bifurcation of the iliac arteries. The attachment length within the neck and within the iliac arteries should be as long as practical, with most device companies recommending attachment site lengths of at least 15 mm.

The common femoral arteries are exposed (or sometimes accessed percutaneously), guide wires and access sheaths are introduced, and heparin is administered. A preprocedure aortogram may be performed with a power injector; preferably with a calibrated pigtail or straight-tip catheter introduced from the designated contralateral side, with the holes positioned immediately above the level of the renal arteries. The positions of the renal arteries, aortic bifurcation, and iliac bifurcation are noted. The dimensions chosen for the device from preprocedural imaging may be confirmed by further diameter and length measurements made from this angiogram. Experienced teams often omit this full procedural aortogram, making use of preprocedural imaging and limiting angiography at this stage to localization of the renal arteries.

Typically the trunk segment of a bifurcated graft with the incorporated ipsilateral iliac limb is implanted first, via the right femoral artery. The shape of the AAA sac, the tortuosity of the iliac arteries, and the perceived risk of dislodging mural thrombus all are factors that may influence the choice of primary access side. The deployment sheath may be passed directly over the guide wire into the artery, or a transverse arteriotomy can be made in such a way that the guide wire is situated within the arteriotomy. The catheter and prosthesis within it are introduced over a super-stiff guide wire after checking the orientation of the device under the image intensifier. The catheter is advanced under radiographic control until the superior end of the prosthesis is immediately below the renal arteries. The image intensifier is moved superiorly to place the superior end of the prosthesis (and the renal arteries) in the center of the field. The angiographic catheter is withdrawn to the point where contrast material injected through it accurately locates the exact position of the renal arteries. These last maneuvers eliminate parallax and avoid errors caused by the deployment sheath straightening an angled aorta and moving the renal arteries to a different level.

The trunk and ipsilateral limb of the bifurcated prosthesis are deployed under radiographic control. After ipsilateral limb deployment, attention is directed to passing a guide wire from the contralateral femoral artery through the contralateral stump of the prosthesis; this usually can be achieved from below with an angled guiding catheter. If severe difficulty is experienced, the guide wire alternatively may be passed from the ipsilateral groin through the ipsilateral limb of the prosthesis and, again with the aid of a guiding catheter, inferiorly through the contralateral stump into the aneurysm sac. From here, it may be retrieved by a snare passed from the contralateral groin.

After cannulation of the contralateral stump, the contralateral limb graft, within its catheter, is delivered under radiographic control to a position within and overlapping the contralateral stump (see Fig. 52-2). This position is identified by clearly visible radiopaque markers on the stump and endograft limb (Fig. 52-3). The limb is now deployed, again under radiographic control. Most self-expanding devices require adjunctive balloon dilatation at this stage to ensure that the stents are fully expanded and in contact with the vessel wall. The pigtail catheter is reintroduced, and a postprocedure digital subtraction aortogram is performed. The cine loop is examined several times for the presence of endoleak, to confirm graft position and that an adequate segment of iliac artery has been covered to provide secure distal fixation. Flow of contrast material through the iliac limbs also is examined for any kinking or twisting. When successful graft implantation has been confirmed, all catheters, sheaths, and guide wires may be removed and the arteriotomy incisions repaired before closure of the groin wounds.

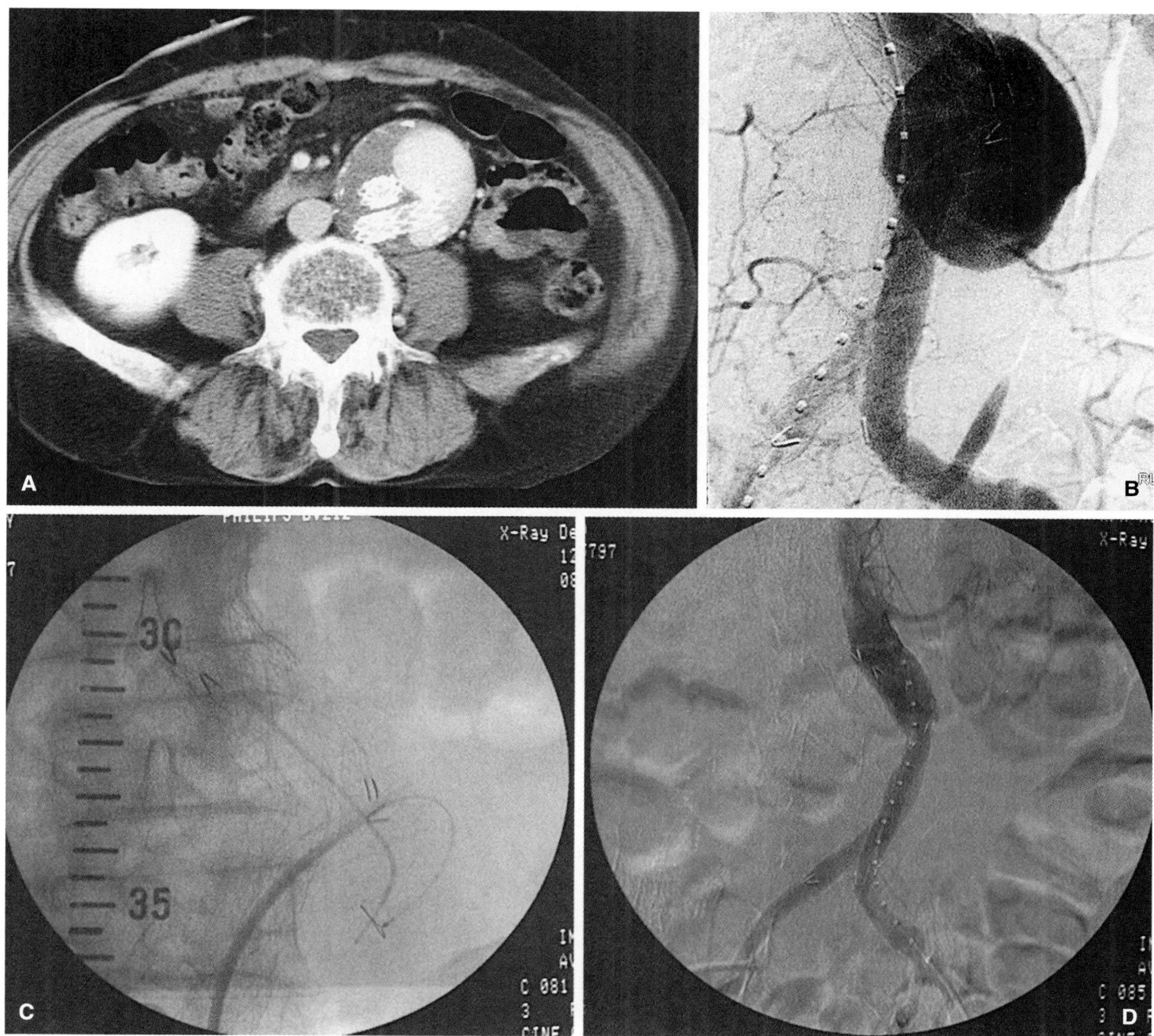

FIGURE 52-3 **A,** Contrast CT scan shows an endoleak 1 year after endoluminal repair of an abdominal aortic aneurysm with a bifurcated endograft. The right limb of the endograft is circular in cross-section, indicating vertical disposition. The left limb is lying transversely. **B,** On the table, preprocedure aortogram of the patient. A large circular endoleak due to dislocation of the left (contralateral) limb of the endograft is shown. Note the V-shaped radiopaque markers on the dislocated limb and the two vertical radiopaque markers on the contralateral stump. **C,** Hard copy from image intensifier shows a guide wire that has been passed from the left brachial artery into the endograft and out through the contralateral stump into the aneurysm sac. A snare has been passed superiorly through the dislocated contralateral limb to pull the brachial guide wire down to the femoral artery in the left groin. **D,** Postprocedure aortogram after deployment of an intrasegmental endograft to reunite the contralateral stump and contralateral limb. Note the absence of endoleak and restoration of flow through the left limb of the endograft. (From May J, White GH: Endovascular leak. In Whittemore A [ed]: Advances in Vascular Surgery, vol. 6. St. Louis, Mosby-Year Book, 1998, pp 65-79.)

Specific Aspects of Technique

Access Techniques

Access to the femoral arteries usually is achieved by an open surgical approach ("femoral cut-down"), but also may be gained by a percutaneous approach. In selected cases, a tunneled approach is made to allow a relatively straight-line entry to the artery when the femoral vessels are unduly deep because of fat, bulk, or deformity.

Femoral Cut-down Approach An oblique transverse incision is preferred by many surgeons and may have a lower incidence of postoperative seroma or lymphocele than a vertical incision.[62,63] The incision usually is limited to 3 to 4 cm in length because exposure of only the common femoral artery is required. Most access sheaths now are designed with a smooth taper so that the sheath can be inserted directly over the guide wire into the artery resulting in a gradual dilatation of the arteriotomy; use of a formal surgical arteriotomy is limited to selected vessels that are severely calcified or stenotic.

Percutaneous Approach Improvements in the profile of sheath systems potentially allow for percutaneous access, but the widespread application of this technique is limited by a lack of approved efficient devices required to achieve effective closure of the large hole formed in the arterial wall. The Perclose system (Abbott Vascular, Menlo Park, Calif) is used most commonly, applying a particular method of deploying percutaneous needles and sutures before the passage of the endograft deployment sheath.[64-67] (These devices have not yet been specifically approved for such an application in the United States.)

Tunneled Femoral Access When the femoral artery is deep, the device deployment sheath may be compromised by angulation and kinking over the ridge formed by the tissues overlying the vessel. In this situation, it is often advantageous to form a narrow subcutaneous tunnel angled gradually down to the vessel from a small skin incision 5 to 10 cm or further down the thigh.

Passage of Guide Wires and Sheaths Through the Iliac Arteries

Passage of the various guide wires and sheaths is usually straightforward, but there may be particular difficulties if the external iliac or common iliac arteries are calcified, stenotic, angulated, or tortuous. Arterial wall dissection, vascular thrombosis or occlusion, and wall perforation may occur. The access sheaths may become damaged or kinked, and progress into the aorta may be impossible. In severe cases, life-threatening arterial rupture or transection can occur.

Progress of the primary access guide wire should be monitored by fluoroscopic imaging. A guiding catheter is used if there is any difficulty caused by angulation or stenosis. When passage of the device delivery sheath is prevented by a stenotic lesion within the iliac artery, angioplasty may be performed by progressive dilatation with tapered introducers or by balloon angioplasty technique. Despite such maneuvers, some iliac vessels are so extremely atherosclerotic and tortuous that sheath passage is impossible; in such cases, alternative access via a conduit graft sutured to the common iliac artery should be considered,[2,68] or an aortomonoiliac graft should be used from the other side. Alternatively, straightening of the segment may be attempted by the use of a brachiofemoral guide wire approach, which then acts as the monorail for passage of the delivery sheath (see later).

Cannulation of the Contralateral Stump

When a modular device is used, three basic techniques are available for cannulation of the contralateral stump.

Cannulation from Below (Retrograde Cannulation) In most cases, access to the contralateral stump can be achieved expeditiously by guide wire and catheter technique retrogradely from the contralateral femoral access site. All modular devices feature a radiopaque marking system to indicate the position of this stump and facilitate the cannulation process. When the guide wire passes into the correct channel, exchange is made for a super-stiff wire, which is used for passage of the delivery sheath. Various special maneuvers may be used to verify that the wire is truly within the lumen of the contralateral stump, including rotation of a preshaped catheter tip[69] or injection of contrast material.

Crossover Cannulation (Antegrade Cannulation) An alternative technique is to pass a guide wire via an angulated guiding catheter over the graft bifurcation and down into the contralateral stump. This wire may be directed further down the iliac artery or may be retrieved by a snare catheter passed from the contralateral femoral site.

Brachial Artery Approach An approach from the left brachial artery also may be used if the two previous methods fail. A guide wire is passed from the left brachial artery and directed down the descending thoracic aorta by either a guiding catheter or a balloon catheter, which can be inflated in the aorta and carried distally by blood flow to reach the aneurysm sac via the contralateral stump. The brachial approach also may be a useful adjunct in cases of extreme tortuosity in the iliac arteries. After retrieval of the brachial guide wire in the aneurysm sac by snare, tension can be applied from the brachial and femoral ends.[70] This tension results in considerable straightening of the iliac arteries, allowing passage of the sheaths.

Technical Considerations for the Difficult Neck

Current endovascular graft designs are indicated for use in patients with a relatively straight aortic neck of length at least 15 mm. Fixation and seal of the device within the neck region are compromised by angulation, irregular wall shape, short length of the neck region, and factors such as mural thrombus or irregular atheroma inside the neck. Claims have been made that particular devices may have advantages over others in these difficult anatomies, but to date there are no reliable comparative long-term data to support such claims. Features that may improve results in difficult necks include fixation hooks or barbs, suprarenal attachment stents, balloon-expanded components, and precise deployment mechanisms. Other approaches to the difficult neck include the use of fenestrated or scalloped graft designs (see later).

Suprarenal or Infrarenal Attachment

Some endovascular graft devices feature a bare-stent segment, which projects superiorly from the top of the graft, above the level of graft fabric, with struts of these stents extending to the level of the suprarenal aorta. Such devices also may include projecting hooks designed to improve attachment and long-term fixation of the device. The postulated main advantage of suprarenal attachment is that it may protect against early or late migration of the device by improving the resistance to displacement by flowing blood and other forces. The compromise of such devices is that the stent struts may cross the orifice of the renal arteries causing significant detrimental effects on renal function, including renal failure and an increased risk of renal infarcts secondary to emboli or compromised flow.[71] Despite these concerns, some centers use suprarenal attachment devices routinely, whereas other centers are selective, using infrarenal devices for routine anatomy and reserving suprarenal attachment for selected cases with a difficult neck (short, or angulated, or containing mural thrombus).

Access Techniques for Unfavorable Iliac Arteries

Categories of difficult anatomy in the iliac segment include tortuosity, acute angulations, narrow atherosclerotic lesions, and calcified vessel wall. Iliac aneurysms present their own problems in management. Unfavorable iliac anatomy may present obstacles to access and successful deployment of aortic devices and problems in obtaining aneurysm exclusion and secure fixation. Early or late migration of iliac limb devices may occur, whereas angulation of the limbs can lead to device occlusion. As regards access, adjunctive techniques include use of super-stiff guide wires of various grades, hydrophilic delivery catheters, arterial dilatation by angioplasty balloons or tapered sheaths, and iliac conduit grafts. External manipulation of the iliac vessels through the abdominal wall sometimes may be a helpful adjunct.[72,73]

Improved fixation and seal in ectatic or aneurysmal iliac arteries usually requires the use of large-diameter extension limbs, often with flared distal ends ("bell-bottom" technique). For such cases, it is helpful to have a variety of grafts in a range of diameters and lengths to allow in-situ customizing to the anatomy of the individual patient.

■ FOLLOW-UP

Because the long-term outcome of endovascular repair is not yet well documented, careful and prolonged follow-up is required. Physical examination and contrast-enhanced CT within 1 month of operation and at 6, 12, and 18 months after operation and annually thereafter are recommended.[74] Plain abdominal x-rays also should be obtained at regular intervals. The main features to be monitored are AAA size; structural integrity of the graft; and any evidence of endoleak, sac expansion, device migration, or other complications. Color-coded duplex ultrasonography also has been used successfully, but its accuracy is operator dependent. It does have the advantages, however, of showing blood flow within the sac, not requiring contrast material, and being less costly than CT.

■ MANAGEMENT OF PERIOPERATIVE COMPLICATIONS

Complications have been divided into *remote* or *systemic* and *local* or *vascular* by the Ad Hoc Committee for uniform reporting standards of the Joint Societies of Vascular Surgery and North American Chapter of the International Society for Cardiovascular Surgery.[74,75] *Remote/systemic* complications after endoluminal AAA repair do not vary greatly from complications after open aneurysm repair and are not discussed further here. *Local/vascular* complications are important, however, because many of them are specific to the endoluminal method of aneurysm repair. These complications are listed in Table 52-4, and the more important ones are considered in detail subsequently.

Table 52-4 Complications Specific to Endovascular Grafts

Early
X-ray radiation exposure
Potential risk to patients and staff
Trauma to access arteries
Perforation, dissection, or thrombosis of femoral or iliac artery
Microembolization
Due to dislodgment of mural components or thrombus from the AAA sac
Graft displacement or misplacement
Occlusion of major branch arteries
Renal artery, accessory renal arteries, mesenteric arteries
Endoleak
AAA rupture
Postimplantation syndrome
Fever, backache, malaise
Graft limb compression, stenosis, occlusion
Contrast allergy or renal failure
Late
Graft migration
Endoleak
Endotension
Late stenosis, kink, or thrombosis of graft or graft limb
Graft tear or failure, material fatigue, stent or wire form breakage
AAA rupture

AAA, abdominal aortic aneurysm.

Injuries to Arteries of Access

The passage of comparatively large-bore catheters, containing endografts, through tortuous and diseased femoral and iliac arteries may result in dissection or rupture. Such problems may become apparent not only during the introduction of the various guide wires and catheters, but also after withdrawal of the delivery sheath. If iliac rupture occurs, the onset of bleeding often is delayed by the tamponading effect of the sheath. Although later generation prostheses are capable of being introduced through iliac arteries with a considerable degree of tortuosity, the presence of heavy circumferential calcification considerably increases the risk of rupturing the artery. When this complication is suspected, it is important to maintain guide wire access so that immediate endovascular management can be achieved by deployment of iliac extension grafts. If necessary, bleeding can be controlled by inflation of an angioplasty balloon more proximal in the iliac system while the extension graft is being prepared or while open repair is done.

If it is not technically possible to correct an iliac dissection or rupture by endovascular means, we recommend placing a prosthetic surgical bypass graft from the common iliac artery to the common femoral artery via an extraperitoneal approach. This graft allows simultaneous revascularization of the affected limb and ensures access to the common iliac artery for delivery of the endovascular device into the aneurysm.

Suprarenal arteries also are vulnerable to injury when the brachial route is used to complement access of the AAA. The seemingly harmless passage of a guide wire from the brachial artery down the descending thoracic aorta may result in substantial intraperitoneal bleeding if it

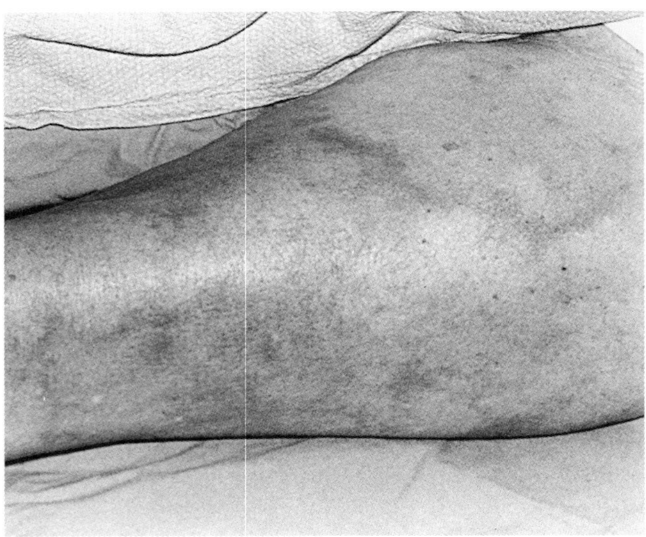

FIGURE 52-4 Skin changes in the left thigh after distal embolization in a patient with mural thrombus in the proximal neck of an abdominal aortic aneurysm treated by endoluminal repair.

passes inadvertently and unnoticed into the superior mesenteric artery and ruptures one of the terminal branches of this artery.

Embolization

Manipulation of endovascular devices within the sac of an AAA has resulted in widespread microembolization and death from renal failure.[76] Every effort should be made to reduce the catheter introduction process to one pass in which the prosthesis is delivered to the level of the renal arteries. The movement of all component parts of the catheter from this point should be in the direction of withdrawal, not advancement, to minimize the risk of thrombus dislodgment.

Embolic stroke can occur due to guide wire movements within the aortic arch. To avoid this complication, the position of the top end of the various guide wires should be monitored by fluoroscopic imaging and kept out of the arch. The straighter descending aorta is a safer place for the guide wire, but debris still may be displaced causing renal, splenic, or bowel infarcts.

Distal embolization resulting in leg ischemia also is a recognized complication (Fig. 52-4). In our experience, significant limb embolization has been limited to patients in whom an endograft has been deployed in the presence of eccentric mural thrombus or irregular atheroma in the neck of the aneurysm. It is recommended to avoid the endoluminal method in patients with this finding or to clamp both common femoral arteries during deployment if a decision is made to take a calculated risk in poor-risk patients with mural neck thrombus.

Endoleak

Angiography is always performed at the completion of device deployment to confirm wide patency of the graft and to exclude endoleak, incomplete sealing, or exclusion of the aneurysm sac by the endograft.[77-81] Digital subtraction cineangiography is performed at the level of the renal arteries and by retrograde injection at the distal ends of the iliac limbs, looking for any sign of perigraft leakage. Type II endoleaks due to retrograde flow into the AAA sac from patent lumbar arteries may be observed but do not require active treatment at this time; many of these close spontaneously over the next 1 to 3 months.[80] Type I and type III endoleaks should be treated immediately, however, by balloon dilatation of the involved graft component, endograft extension pieces or supportive stent, or combinations of these techniques.[7,80,81] Every attempt should be made to close such endoleaks before the patient leaves the operating room because the AAA remains at risk of rupture until sealed exclusion has been achieved. If endoleaks cannot be sealed successfully at the time of the procedure, we do not recommend proceeding to open repair at the same time because the patient already has undergone a prolonged operation, often with high contrast load and other factors that increase perioperative morbidity and mortality rates.

Graft Limb Stenosis or Thrombosis

Narrowing of the iliac limb grafts may occur owing to external compression, kinking within angulated iliac segments, or graft twist. Such narrowing predisposes to early or late occlusion. Early-generation endografts with unsupported fabric were prone to thrombosis of the limbs of the graft secondary to kinking and twisting within the native iliac arteries. Even with later prostheses in which the fabric is supported by a metallic frame, the problem persists. Postprocedure on-table angiography in one plane is no guarantee that kinking has not occurred. When graft limb stenosis is suspected, pressure measurements should be obtained by connecting a pressure line to the femoral sheath on that side, with comparison of the pressure with the radial line parameters. A pressure differential of more than 10 to 20 mm Hg should prompt management by adjunctive balloon dilatation, with or without stent implantation. Plain x-ray studies in anteroposterior and lateral planes in the immediate postoperative period are recommended to identify a problem in the metal frame before thrombosis occurs and while correction may be carried out by endovascular rather than open means.

Successful endoluminal repair often results in reduction in the size of the aneurysm sac and changes in its length and transverse diameter. This reduction in size may lead to kinking of the previously straight limbs of an endoluminal graft, with progression to thrombosis. Such kinking also may encourage or result in dislocation of the limbs of the endograft from the native iliac arteries or the contralateral limb from the contralateral stump of the endograft (see Fig. 52-3). Kinks in the iliac arteries and within the aneurysm sac are amenable to endovascular correction, avoiding open operation.

Conversion to Open Repair

Acute conversion to open repair may be required if aortic rupture occurs during the implantation procedure.[16] In this situation, blood loss may be reduced by inflation of an occlusion balloon at or above the level of the renal arteries. In selected situations, continuation with the endovascular technique may be a reasonable method to achieve sealing. As described earlier, immediate conversion to open repair is not recommended for management of endoleak. This conversion is best done as a separate procedure with the patient and operating team fully prepared.

Postimplant Syndrome

Postimplant syndrome is characterized by back pain and fever in the absence of leukocytosis or other evidence of infection.[82] It follows implantation directly, generally lasts 2 to 3 days but sometimes 7 days, and usually is associated with thrombosis within the aneurysm sac. The cause is unknown, and the incidence may be 50%. Despite some early reports of an associated coagulopathy, the course of postimplant syndrome generally is considered to be benign; some authors hold it to be a favorable sign signifying thrombosis of the aneurysm sac and successful endoluminal repair. Treatment is not often required and for severe cases it should be supportive, including antipyretic or anti-inflammatory medications.

■ ENDOVASCULAR GRAFT TECHNIQUES FOR RUPTURED ABDOMINAL AORTIC ANEURYSM

There has been considerable interest in the use of endoluminal graft technique for acute and ruptured AAA.[20-22,83-88] Most studies done to date have reported improved outcomes (volume of blood loss, fluid requirements, operative mortality, and major complications) compared with open repair. The basic techniques for endograft implantation are the same as for the elective situation except that in some cases supplementary techniques may be employed for control of hemorrhage by occlusion balloons. A program of endovascular repair requires ready availability of an experienced endovascular team, a range of device sizes and ancillary equipment, capability to perform rapid preoperative imaging (particularly CT), and excellent procedural imaging equipment in the operating room environment.

Special anesthetic techniques may be used; endovascular repair of acute or ruptured AAA can be done under local anesthesia, with or without intravenous sedation.[22,83,88] Fluid resuscitation may be restricted to reduce blood loss, a technique that has been termed *hypotensive hemostasis*.[84] The process generally involves rapid assessment of the patient by spiral CT to judge anatomic suitability for endovascular repair (many centers use emergency department ultrasound scanning to confirm the diagnosis initially).[87] If the blood pressure is judged to be too low during patient imaging or during the procedure, an occlusion balloon can be inserted percutaneously over a stiff guide wire and inflated at the level of the first lumbar vertebra to achieve hemostasis.[21,22,84] Alternatively, transport to the operating room may be done without CT scanning. In these cases, a brachial or femoral guide wire is placed into the supraceliac aorta under local anesthesia, and arteriography is performed. If aortoiliac anatomy is suitable, endovascular graft repair may proceed; if the anatomy is unfavorable, the aneurysm may be repaired by standard open technique.[84] If circulatory collapse occurs, an occlusion balloon is inserted and inflated over the guide wire. Alternatively, this may be an indication for conversion to open repair.[88]

The proportion of patients with ruptured AAA who are anatomically suitable for endovascular repair has been stated variously to be 40% to 80%.[85,86] Some centers routinely use an aortomonoiliac graft for acute cases, whereas others prefer bifurcated devices—this choice often depends on local factors, such as device availability and experience. An aortomonoiliac device has the advantage of relatively rapid deployment of the primary graft, whereas it also requires implantation of a contralateral occlusion plug into the iliac artery and revascularization by a femorofemoral crossover bypass.

■ TECHNIQUES FOR THORACIC ENDOGRAFT PROCEDURES

On theoretical grounds, there is much to recommend the endoluminal method for treatment of aneurysms of the descending thoracic aorta.[89-93] The mortality advantage over open repair is potentially much greater. There are no anatomic barriers, such as the renal arteries and aortic bifurcation, that exist in the abdominal aorta. The problems of deployment of endografts in the descending thoracic aorta are limited to availability of a prosthesis of sufficiently large diameter to match the aorta adjacent to the aneurysm; the difficulty of accurate graft placement in a large, high-flow artery; and the risk of paraplegia.

There are sound explanations why the risk of paraplegia should be less when the endoluminal method rather than the open method is used. The patient is more likely to be hemodynamically stable during endoluminal repair and to avoid spinal cord ischemia due to low flow in the intercostal arteries during periods of hypotension. The short period of interference with flow in the thoracic aorta during endoluminal graft deployment virtually guarantees good perfusion of the important intercostal arteries distal to the aneurysm without the complexity and complications of using a shunt. The seminal work of Dake and associates[89] in the clinical setting supports the theoretical advantages referred to earlier. Paraplegia was limited to 4 of 121 patients undergoing endoluminal repair of aneurysms of the descending thoracic aorta. All four patients previously had undergone open repair of AAA.[89]

Advances in technology seem certain to provide improved prostheses for the thoracic aorta. Applications include thoracic aortic aneurysms; transection of the aorta due to blunt trauma; aortic dissections (chronic and acute); and unusual clinical entities such as penetrating aortic ulcer, mural hematoma, and false aneurysm.[94-98] Techniques for endograft deployment are similar to those for AAA except that the devices used are tube grafts, and the access sheaths required are generally larger in diameter and length. In addition, the length of aorta to be covered by the endograft is limited by the desire not to occlude too many of the branch vessels that supply the spinal cord.

In many cases, two or more devices are deployed in overlapped orientation to aid in accurate positioning of the proximal and distal aspects of the graft at the target attachment sites. For proximal thoracic lesions, the deployment sheath becomes curved over the arch of the aorta, and there is a danger of kinking of the sheath and device, making it difficult to push the device out of the sheath. In addition, for such aneurysms or other thoracic lesions close to the aortic arch, the endograft often must be implanted close to or overlapping the origin of the left subclavian artery. Occlusion of the subclavian artery does not usually have any side effects apart from loss of pulses and lowered blood pressure measurements in the left arm. There is also an option to reperfuse the subclavian artery by an interposition graft taken from the carotid artery.

Fenestrated and branched thoracic endografts are being studied in trials; these have openings or side branches that are designed to maintain perfusion of the major branch vessels of the aortic arch. The high blood flow in the proximal aspects of the thoracic aorta can make accurate deployment and positioning of the device difficult. In some cases, a technique of induction of temporary cardiac asystole by intravenous administration of the drug adenosine may be used to assist with accurate deployment of the prosthesis.[93]

Thoracic aneurysm repair by endovascular graft techniques has many advantages over open repair, but in high-risk patients a relatively high incidence remains of serious complications, such as stroke, paraplegia, endoleak, and aortic wall trauma. As with AAA endoluminal repair, further careful long-term follow-up is required to ensure that mechanical device failure is not a limiting factor and that long-term results are satisfactory.

■ REFERENCES

1. Parodi JC, Palmaz JC, Barone HD: Transfemoral intraluminal graft implantation for abdominal aortic aneurysm. Ann Vasc Surg 5:491-499, 1991.
2. Volodos NL, Karpovich IP, Troyan VI, et al: Clinical experience of the use of self-fixing synthetic prostheses for remote endoprosthetics of the thoracic and the abdominal aorta and iliac arteries through the femoral artery and as intraoperative endoprosthesis for aorta reconstruction. Vasa 33(Suppl):93-95, 1991.
3. Parodi JC, Barone A, Piraino R, Schonholz C: Endovascular treatment of abdominal aortic aneurysms: Lessons learned. J Endovasc Surg 4:102-110, 1997.
4. Balm R, Eikelboom BC, May J, et al: Early experience with transfemoral endovascular aneurysm management (TEAM) in the treatment of aortic aneurysms. Eur J Vasc Endovasc Surg 11:214-220, 1996.
5. White GH, Yu W, May J, et al: Three-year experience with the White-Yu endovascular GAD graft for transluminal repair of aortic and iliac aneurysms. J Endovasc Surg 4:124-136, 1997.
6. Moore WS, Rutherford RB, for the EVT Investigators: Transfemoral endovascular repair of abdominal aortic aneurysm: Results of the North American EVT phase 1 trial. J Vasc Surg 23:543-553, 1996.
7. Marin ML, Veith FJ, Cynamon J, et al: Initial experience with transluminally placed endovascular grafts for the treatment of complex vascular lesions. Ann Surg 222:449-469, 1995.
8. Blum U, Voshage G, Lammer J, et al: Endoluminal stent-grafts for infrarenal abdominal aortic aneurysms. N Engl J Med 336:13-20, 1997.
9. Power D: The palliative treatment of aneurysms by "wiring" with Colt's apparatus. Br J Surg 9:27, 1921.
10. Keen WW: Surgery: Its Principles and Practice. Philadelphia, WB Saunders, 1921, pp 216-349.
11. Wiley FB: Clio Chirurgica: The Arteries Part 1. Austin, Tex, Silvergirl, 1998.
12. Balko A, Piasecki GJ, Shah DM, et al: Transfemoral placement of intraluminal polyurethane prosthesis for abdominal aortic aneurysm. J Surg Res 40:305-309, 1986.
13. Lawrence DD, Chansangavej C, Wright KC, et al: Percutaneous endovascular graft: Experimental evaluation. Radiology 163:357-360, 1987.
14. Ernst CB: Abdominal aortic aneurysm. N Engl J Med 328:1167-1172, 1993.
15. May J, White GH, Yu W, et al: Conversion from endoluminal to open repair of abdominal aortic aneurysms: A hazardous procedure. Eur J Vasc Endovasc Surg 14:4-11, 1997.
16. May J, White GH, Yu W, et al: Endovascular grafting for abdominal aortic aneurysms: Changing incidence and indications for conversion to open operation. Cardiovasc Surg 6:194-197, 1998.
17. Veith FJ, Abbott WM, Yao JST, et al: Guidelines for development and use of transluminally placed endovascular prosthetic grafts in the arterial system. J Vasc Surg 21:670-685, 1995.
18. May J, White GH, Yu W, et al: Concurrent comparison of endoluminal versus open repair in the treatment of abdominal aortic aneurysms: Analysis of 303 patients by life table method. J Vasc Surg 27:213-222, 1998.
19. May J, White GH, Waugh RC, et al: Improved survival after endoluminal repair with second generation prostheses compared with open repair in the treatment of abdominal aortic aneurysms: A 5-year concurrent comparison using life table method. J Vasc Surg 33:S21-S26, 2001.
20. Yusuf SW, Whitaker SC, Chuter TA, et al: Emergency endovascular repair of leaking aortic aneurysm. Lancet 344:1645, 1994.
21. Ohki T, Veith F, Sanchez LA, et al: Endovascular graft repair of ruptured aorto-iliac aneurysms. J Am Coll Surg 189:102-113, 1999.
22. Verhoven ELG, Prins TR, van den Dungen JJA, et al: Endovascular repair of acute AAAs under local anesthesia with bifurcated endografts: A feasibility study. J Endovasc Ther 9:729, 2002.
23. Greenberg R, Fairman R, Sivrastava S, et al: Endovascular grafting in patients with short proximal necks: An analysis of short-term results. Cardiovasc Surg 8:350-354, 2000.
24. Anderson JL, Berce M, Hartley DE: Endoluminal aortic grafting with renal and superior mesenteric artery incorporation by graft fenestration. J Endovasc Ther 8:3-15, 2001.
25. Stanley BM, Semmens JB, Lawrence-Brown MM, et al: Fenestration in endovascular grafts for aortic aneurysm repair: New horizons for preserving blood flow in branch vessels. J Endovasc Ther 8:16-24, 2001.
26. Faruqi RM, Chuter TA, Reilly LM, et al: Endovascular repair of abdominal aortic aneurysm using a pararenal fenestrated stent-graft. J Endovasc Surg 6:354-358, 1999.
27. Greenberg RK, Haulon S, Lyden SP, et al: Endovascular management of juxtarenal aneurysms with fenestrated endovascular grafting. J Vasc Surg 39:279-287, 2004.
28. Iwase T, Inoue K, Sato M, et al: Transluminal repair of an infrarenal aortoiliac aneurysm by a combination of bifurcated and branched stent grafts. Catheter Cardiovasc Interv 47:491-494, 1999.
29. Chuter TA, Buck DG, Schneider DB, et al: Development of a branched stent-graft for endovascular repair of aortic arch aneurysms. J Endovasc Ther 10:940-945, 2003.
30. Inoue K, Hosokawa H, Iwase T, et al: Aortic arch reconstruction by transluminally placed endovascular branched stent graft. Circulation 100(19 Suppl):II-316-II-321, 1999.
31. Yusuf SW, Baker DM, Hind RE, et al: Endoluminal transfemoral abdominal aortic aneurysm repair with aortouni-iliac graft and femorofemoral crossover. Br J Surg 82:916, 1995.
32. Yusuf SW, Whitaker SC, Chuter TA, et al: Early results of endovascular aortic aneurysm surgery with aortouniiliac graft, contralateral iliac occlusion and femoro-femoral bypass. J Vasc Surg 25:165-172, 1997.

33. Chuter TA, Faruqi RM, Reilly LM, et al: Aortomonoiliac endovascular grafting combined with femorofemoral bypass: An acceptable compromise or a preferred solution? Semin Vasc Surg 12:176-181, 1999.
34. Parodi JC: Endovascular repair of abdominal aortic aneurysms and other arterial lesions. J Vasc Surg 21:549-557, 1995.
35. Chuter TAM, Green RM, Ouriel K, DeWeese JA: Infrarenal aortic aneurysm structure: Implications for transfemoral repair. J Vasc Surg 20:44-50, 1994.
36. Andrews SM, Cumig R, MacSweeney STR, et al: Assessment of feasibility for endovascular prosthetic tube correction of aortic aneurysms. Br J Surg 82:917-919, 1995.
37. May J, White GH, May J, et al: Importance of graft configuration in outcome of endoluminal aortic aneurysm repair: A five year analysis by life table method. Eur J Vasc Endovasc Surg 15:406-411, 1998.
38. Lawrence-Brown MMD, Hartley D, MacSweeney STR, et al: The Perth endoluminal bifurcated graft system—development and early experience. Cardiovasc Surg 4:706-712, 1996.
39. Yu W, White GH, May J, et al: Endoluminal repair of abdominal aortic aneurysms using the Trombone technique. Asian J Surg 19:37-40, 1996.
40. Schumacher H, Eckstein HH, Kallinowski F, Allenberg JR: Morphometry and classification in abdominal aortic aneurysms: Patient selection for endovascular and open surgery. J Endovasc Surg 4:39-44, 1997.
41. Moore WS, Matsumura JS, Makaroun MS, et al, EVT/Guidant Investigators: Five-year interim comparison of the Guidant bifurcated endograft with open repair of abdominal aortic aneurysm. J Vasc Surg 38:46-55, 2003.
42. Chuter TAM, Wendt G, Hopkinson BR, et al: Transfemoral insertion of a bifurcated endovascular graft for aortic aneurysm repair: The first 22 patients. Cardiovasc Surg 3:121-128, 1995.
43. Carpenter JP, Endologix Investigators: Multicenter trial of the PowerLink bifurcated system for endovascular aortic aneurysm repair. J Vasc Surg 36:1129-1137, 2002.
44. Blum U, Voshage G: Abdominal aortic aneurysm repair using the Meadox/Vanguard prosthesis: Indications, implantation technique and results. Tech Vasc Interv Radiol 1:19-24, 1998.
45. Blum U, Voshage G, Beyersdorf F, et al: Two-center German experience with aortic endografting. J Endovasc Surg 4:137-146, 1997.
46. White RA, Donayre CE, Walot I, et al: Modular bifurcation endoprosthesis for treatment of abdominal aortic aneurysms. Ann Surg 226:381-391, 1997.
47. Zarins CK, White RA, Schwarten D, et al: AneuRx stent graft versus open surgical repair of abdominal aortic aneurysms: Multicenter prospective clinical trial. J Vasc Surg 29:292-305, 1999.
48. Uflacker R, Robinson JG, Brothers TE, et al: Abdominal aortic aneurysm treatment: Preliminary results with the Talent stent-graft system. J Vasc Interv Radiol 9:51-60, 1998.
49. May J, White GH, Yu W: Aorto-aortic prosthesis: The Baxter endovascular graft. In Yusuf W, Marin ML, Ivancev K, Hopkinson BR (eds): Operative Atlas of Endoluminal Aneurysm Surgery. Oxford, Isis Medical Media, 1998.
50. Carpenter JP, Anderson WN, Brewster DC, et al, Lifepath Investigators: Multicenter pivotal trial results of the Lifepath System for endovascular aortic aneurysm repair. J Vasc Surg 39:34-43, 2004.
51. Matsumura JS, Brewster DC, Makaroun MS, Naftel DC: A multicenter controlled clinical trial of open versus endovascular treatment of abdominal aortic aneurysm. J Vasc Surg 37:262-271, 2003.
52. Kibbe MR, Matsumura JS, Excluder Investigators: The Gore Excluder US multi-center trial: Analysis of adverse events at 2 years. Semin Vasc Surg 16:144-150, 2003.
53. Chuter TA: The choice of stent-graft for endovascular repair of abdominal aortic aneurysm. J Cardiovasc Surg (Torino) 44:519-525, 2003.
54. Lawrence-Brown MM, Hartley D, MacSweeney ST, et al: The Perth endoluminal graft system—development and early experience. Cardiovasc Surg 4:706-712, 1996.
55. Greenberg R, Zenith Investigators: The Zenith AAA endovascular graft for abdominal aortic aneurysms: Clinical update. Semin Vasc Surg 16:151-157, 2003.
56. Cao P, Verzini F, Parlani G, et al: Predictive factors and clinical consequences of proximal aortic neck dilatation in 230 patients undergoing abdominal aorta aneurysm repair with self-expandable stent-grafts. J Vasc Surg 37:86-90, 2003.
57. May J, White GH, Ly CN, et al: Endoluminal repair of abdominal aortic aneurysm prevents enlargement of the proximal neck: A 9-year life-table and 5-year longitudinal study. J Vasc Surg 37:86-90, 2003.
58. Connors MS, Sternbergh WC, Carter G, et al: Endograft migration one to four years after endovascular abdominal aortic repair with the AneuRx device: A cautionary note. J Vasc Surg 36:476-484, 2002.
59. Sternbergh WC, Money SR, Greenberg RK, Chuter TA, Zenith Investigators: Influence of endograft oversizing on device migration, endoleak, aneurysm shrinkage, and aortic neck dilation: Results from the Zenith Multicenter Trial. J Vasc Surg 39:20-26, 2004.
60. Sternbergh WC, Carter G, York JW, et al: Aortic neck angulation predicts adverse outcome with endovascular abdominal aortic aneurysm repair. J Vasc Surg 35:482-486, 2002.
61. Chaikof EL, Fillinger MF, Matsumura JS, et al: Identifying and grading factors that modify the outcome of endovascular aortic aneurysm repair. J Vasc Surg 35:1061-1066, 2002.
62. Chuter TA, Reilly LM, Stoney RJ, Messina LM: Femoral artery exposure for endovascular aneurysm repair through oblique incisions J Endovasc Surg 6:125, 1998.
63. Caiati JM, Kaplan D, Gitlitz D, et al: The value of the oblique groin incision for femoral artery access during endovascular procedures. Ann Vasc Surg 14:248-253, 2000.
64. Rachel ES, Bergamini TM, Kinney EV, et al: Percutaneous endovascular abdominal aortic aneurysm repair. Ann Vasc Surg 16:43-49, 2002.
65. Howell M, Doughtery K, Strickman N, Krajcer Z: Percutaneous repair of abdominal aortic aneurysms using the AneuRx stent graft and the percutaneous vascular surgery device. Catheter Cardiovasc Interv 55:281-287, 2002.
66. Traul DK, Clair DG, Gray B, et al: Percutaneous endovascular repair of infrarenal abdominal aortic aneurysms: A feasibility study. J Vasc Surg 32:770-776, 2000.
67. Torsello GB, Kasprzak B, Klenk E, et al: Endovascular suture versus cutdown for endovascular aneurysm repair: A prospective randomised study. J Vasc Surg 38:78-82, 2003.
68. Abu-Ghaida AM, Clair DG, Greenberg RK, et al: Broadening the applicability of endovascular aneurysm repair: The use of iliac conduits. J Vasc Surg 36:111-117, 2002.
69. Dawson DL, Terramani TT, Loberman Z, et al: Simple technique to ensure coaxial guidewire positioning for placement of iliac limb of modular aortic endograft. J Intervent Cardiol 16:223-226, 2003.
70. Criado FJ, Wilson EP, Abul-Khoudoud O, et al: Brachial artery catheterisation to facilitate endovascular grafting of abdominal aortic aneurysm: Safety and rationale. J Vasc Surg 32:1137-1141, 2000.
71. Bockler D, Krauss M, Mannsmann U, et al: Incidence of renal infarctions after endovascular AAA repair: Relationship to infrarenal versus suprarenal fixation. J Endovasc Ther 10:1054-1060, 2003.
72. Sternbergh WC, Money SR, Yoselovitz M: External transabdominal manipulation of vessels: A useful adjunct with endovascular abdominal aortic aneurysm repair. J Vasc Surg 33:886-887, 2001.
73. Ivancev K, Chuter TAM: Adjunctive manoeuvres for endovascular exclusion of abdominal aortic aneurysm. In Hopkinson B, Yusuf W, Whitaker S, Veith F (eds): Endovascular Surgery for Aortic Aneurysms. London, WB Saunders, 1997, pp 57-71.
74. Chaikof EL, Blankensteijn JD, Harris PL, et al, Ad Hoc Committee for Standardized Reporting Practices in Vascular Surgery of The Society for Vascular Surgery/American Association for Vascular Surgery: Reporting standards for endovascular aortic aneurysm repair. J Vasc Surg 35:1048-1060, 2002.
75. Ahn SS, Rutherford RB, Johnston KW, et al: Reporting standards for infrarenal endovascular abdominal aortic aneurysm repair. J Vasc Surg 25:405-410, 1997.
76. Parodi JC: Endovascular repair of abdominal aortic aneurysms and other arterial lesions. J Vasc Surg 21:549-555, 1995.

77. White GH, Yu W, May J, et al: Endoleak as a complication of endoluminal grafting of abdominal aortic aneurysms: Classification, incidence, diagnosis, and management. J Endovasc Surg 4:152-168, 1997.
78. White GH, May J, Waugh RC, Yu W: Type I and type II endoleak: A more useful classification for reporting results of endoluminal repair of AAA (Letter). J Endovasc Surg 5:189-191, 1998.
79. White GH, May J, Waugh RC, et al: Type III and type IV endoleak: Toward a complete definition of blood flow in the sac after endoluminal AAA repair. J Endovasc Surg 5:305-309, 1998.
80. Faries PL, Cadot H, Agarwal G, et al: Management of endoleak after endovascular aneurysm repair: Cuffs, coils, and conversion. J Vasc Surg 37:1155-1161, 2003.
81. Chuter TA, Faruqi RM, Sawhney R, et al: Endoleak after endovascular repair of abdominal aortic aneurysm. J Vasc Surg 34:98-105, 2001.
82. Storck M, Scharrer-Pamler R, Kapfer X, et al: Does a postimplantation syndrome following endovascular treatment of aortic aneurysms exist? Vasc Surg 35:23-29, 2001.
83. Henretta JP, Hodgson KJ, Mattos MA, et al: Feasibility of endovascular repair of abdominal aortic aneurysms with local anesthesia with intravenous sedation. J Vasc Surg 29:793-798, 1999.
84. Veith F, Ohki T, Lipsitz EC, et al: Endovascular grafts and other catheter-directed techniques in the management of ruptured abdominal aortic aneurysms. Semin Vasc Surg 16:326-331, 2003.
85. Peppelenbosch N, Yilmaz N, van Marrewijk C, et al: Emergency treatment of acute symptomatic or ruptured abdominal aortic aneurysm: Outcome of a prospective intent-to-treat by EVAR protocol. Eur J Vasc Endovasc Surg 26:303-310, 2003.
86. Reichart M, Geelkerken RH, Huisman AB, et al: Ruptured abdominal aortic aneurysm: Endovascular repair is feasible in 40% of patients. Eur J Vasc Endovasc Surg 26:479-486, 2003.
87. Willman JK, Lachat ML, von Smekal A, et al: Spiral-CT angiography to assess feasibility of endovascular aneurysm repair in patients with ruptured aortoiliac aneurysm. Vasa 30:271-276, 2001.
88. Lachat M, Pfammatter T, Bernard E, et al: Successful endovascular repair of a leaking abdominal aortic aneurysm under local anesthesia. Swiss Surg 7:86-89, 2001.
89. Dake MD, Miller DC, Semba CP, et al: Transluminal placement of endovascular stent grafts for the treatment of descending thoracic aortic aneurysms. N Engl J Med 331:1729-1734, 1994.
90. Carroccio A, Ellozy S, Spielvogel D, et al: Endovascular stent grafting of thoracic aortic aneurysms. Ann Vasc Surg 17:473-478, 2003.
91. Criado FJ, Clark NS, Barnatan MF: Stent graft repair in the aortic arch and descending thoracic aorta: A 4-year experience. J Vasc Surg 36:1121-1128, 2002.
92. Czerny M, Cejna M, Hutschala D, et al: Stent-graft placement in atherosclerotic descending thoracic aortic aneurysms: Midterm results. J Endovasc Ther 11:26-32, 2004.
93. Dorros G, Cohn JM: Adenosine-induced transient cardiac asystole enhances precise deployment of stent-grafts in the thoracic or abdominal aorta. J Endovasc Surg 3:270-272, 1996.
94. Dake MD: Endovascular stent-graft management of thoracic aortic diseases. Eur J Radiol 39:42-49, 2001.
95. Dake MD, Kato N, Mitchell RS, et al: Endovascular stent-graft placement for the treatment of acute aortic dissection. N Engl J Med 340:1546-1552, 1999.
96. Nienaber CA, Ince H, Weber F, et al: Emergency stent-graft placement in thoracic aortic dissection and evolving rupture. J Card Surg 18:464-470, 2003.
97. Nienaber CA, Fattori R, Lund G, et al: Nonsurgical reconstruction of thoracic aortic dissection by stent-graft placement. N Engl J Med 340:1539-1545, 1999.
98. Taylor PR, Bell RE, Reidy JF: Aortic transection due to blunt trauma: Evolving management using endovascular techniques. Int J Clin Pract 57:652, 2003.

Chapter 53

Intra-arterial Catheter-Directed Thrombolysis

ANTHONY J. COMEROTA, MD, FACS

■ BACKGROUND

Vascular specialists have appreciated the benefits of catheter-directed intrathrombus infusion of fibrinolytic agents for arterial and graft occlusion. Although the regional delivery of plasminogen activators was performed in the 1960s,[1] it has been a routinely accepted therapy only since the 1980s. The evolution of intra-arterial catheter-directed thrombolytic therapy is the result of increasing interest in thrombolysis for all forms of thromboembolic vascular disease, an improved understanding of the technique of delivery, rapidly improving technology and delivery systems, and expansion in the understanding and number of thrombolytic agents.

Currently, all thrombolytic agents are plasminogen activators. The goal of thrombolytic therapy is to deliver the plasminogen activator to the offending thrombus, regardless of its location. Because the primary and most efficient mechanism for thrombolysis is penetration of the plasminogen activator into the thrombus, with activation of plasminogen that was bound to fibrin during the clotting process,[2] it is intuitively evident that delivery of plasminogen activators into the thrombus should maximize lysis. When the plasminogen activator is delivered into the thrombus, it is protected from circulating plasminogen activator inhibitors, improving its efficiency. On activation of fibrin-bound plasminogen, plasmin acts within the thrombus to lyse clot, while being protected from circulating plasmin inhibitors. As regional or intrathrombus infusion continues, systemic activation of plasminogen occurs as a result of leakage of the plasminogen activator or plasmin into the bloodstream, resulting in breakdown of circulating fibrinogen, clotting factors, and other plasma proteins.

Although the medical literature is replete with clinical observations and institutional series documenting the benefit of intra-arterial catheter-directed thrombolysis compared with systemically delivered plasminogen activators for acute arterial and graft occlusion, its improved efficacy was objectively established by Berridge and colleagues[3] in a randomized study. Sixty patients with acute or subacute peripheral arterial thrombosis were randomized into a parallel group comparison of three thrombolytic regimens—intravenous recombinant tissue plasminogen activator (rt-PA), intra-arterial rt-PA, or intra-arterial streptokinase. Patients treated with intra-arterial rt-PA had the greatest degree of successful lysis and clinical improvement. Intra-arterial rt-PA was significantly better than intra-arterial streptokinase. Intra-arterial rt-PA and streptokinase were better than intravenous rt-PA. Intra-arterial rt-PA was safer than intra-arterial streptokinase ($P < .05$). This small but important study established the superiority of catheter-directed lytic therapy over intravenous therapy, and the superior efficacy and safety profile of rt-PA compared with streptokinase.

The primary objectives of catheter-directed thrombolysis are to dissolve the occluding thrombus, restore perfusion, and identify the underlying cause of arterial or graft thrombosis, allowing definitive correction (Figs. 53-1 and 53-2) Numerous investigators have emphasized the importance of identifying and correcting an underlying lesion after successful lysis. McNamara and Bomberger[4] and Gardiner and coworkers[5] showed good patency rates after successful thrombolysis when an underlying lesion was identified and corrected versus a dismal result when a lesion was not corrected (Table 53-1). Important additional goals of therapy are as follows:

1. Convert an urgent surgical procedure to an elective operative revascularization
2. Re-establish patency of an occluded but nondiseased inflow source for subsequent bypass
3. Lyse thrombi in distal arteries, restoring patency to the outflow of arteries
4. Convert a major vascular reconstruction to a limited, less extensive procedure
5. Prevent arterial intimal injury from balloon catheter thrombectomy by avoiding operative thromboembolectomy
6. Restore patency to branch vessels that are inaccessible to mechanical thrombectomy
7. Reduce the level of amputation in patients in whom complete success cannot be achieved

■ PATIENT SELECTION

The first step to successful treatment is appropriate patient selection. Randomized trials have helped to identify appropriate patients for catheter-directed thrombolysis; however, good clinical judgment with knowledge of the patient's underlying pathophysiology is most important for individual patient success. The observation that long segments of the vascular tree can be obliterated by acute thrombus precipitated by severe but relatively segmental atherosclerotic disease or neointimal fibroplasia is the underlying rationale for catheter-directed thrombolytic

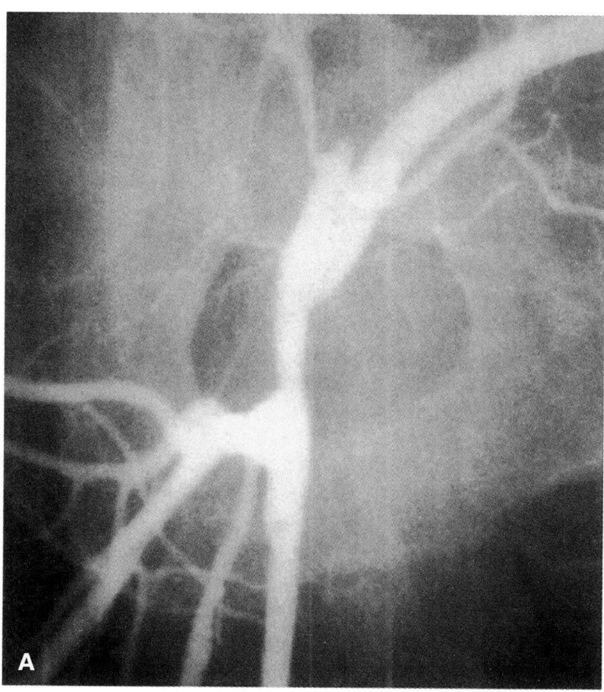

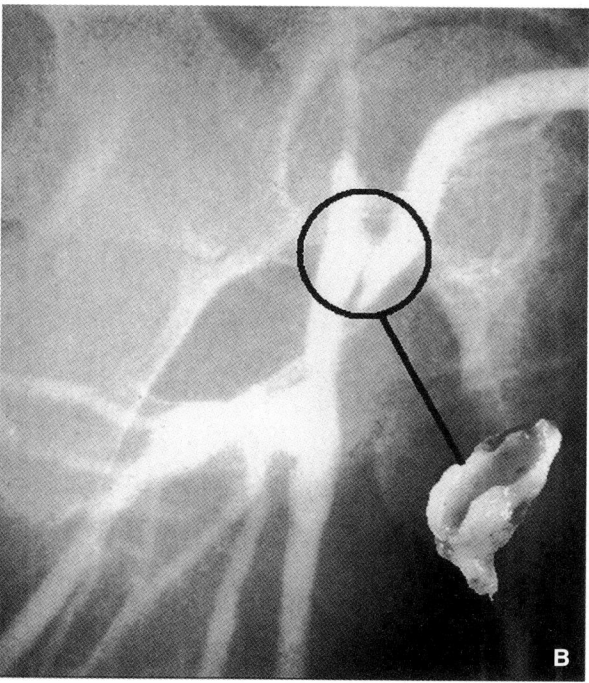

FIGURE 53-1 **A,** Completion arteriogram after catheter-directed thrombolysis of an acutely occluded iliofemoral bypass 9 months after implantation. The initial completion arteriogram shows no evidence of an underlying lesion. **B,** After repositioning the patient in a more oblique position, a repeat arteriogram shows a high-grade stenosis at the graft-to–right common femoral artery anastomosis. *Inset* shows the neointimal fibroplastic lesion, which was removed at the time of anastomotic revision.

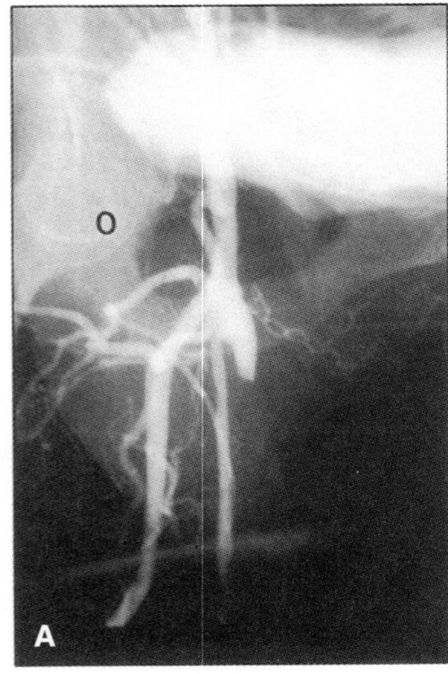

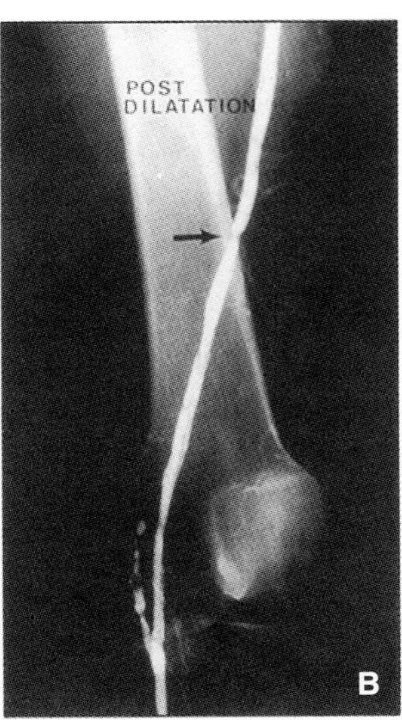

Pulse Wave and Pressure Index

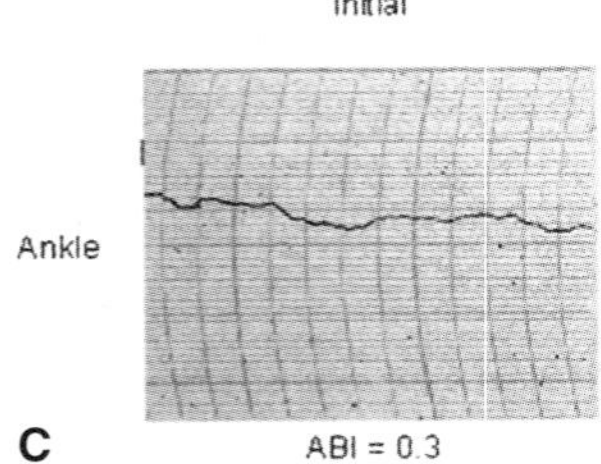

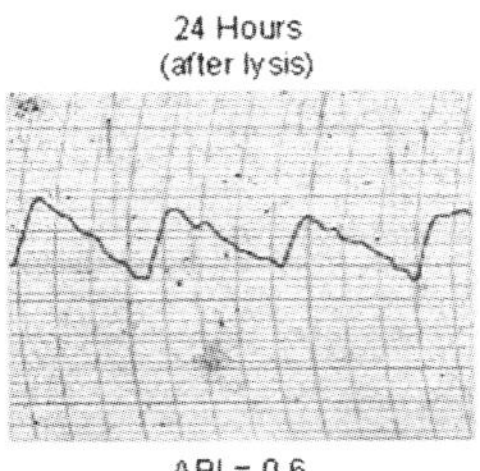

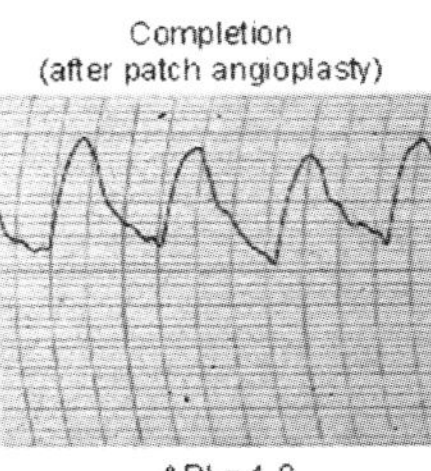

FIGURE 53-2 **A,** Initial arteriogram of a patient with an acutely occluded reversed saphenous vein femoropopliteal bypass. The bypass was functional for 3 years before thrombosis. **B,** Catheter-directed thrombolysis was patent and revealed a vein valve stenosis in the mid-graft, which was resistant to balloon dilatation. **C,** After vein patch angioplasty, normal perfusion was restored to the lower extremity. ABI, ankle/brachial index.

therapy. This rationale applies to segmental disease in native arteries and bypass grafts. Although lysis is often possible, the ability to identify and correct segmental pathology after successful thrombolysis is the key to long-term benefits.

Good Candidates for Lytic Therapy

Patients who have a high likelihood of successful reperfusion or a potentially lower complication rate with catheter-directed thrombolysis than with operative revascularization are considered good candidates for therapy. Among them are patients with the following conditions:

- Acute embolic or thrombotic occlusion of arteries inaccessible or requiring involved surgical exposure for operative thromboembolectomy
- Wound complications in a new surgical wound that would be associated with substantial additional morbidity
- Acute thrombosis of a popliteal aneurysm causing limb-threatening foot ischemia, usually associated with thrombosis of the infrapopliteal arteries
- Acute arterial thrombosis (especially in proximal arteries)
- Thrombosed saphenous vein grafts that have been functioning for 1 year or more

Table 53-1 Subsequent Patency of Lower Extremity Bypass Grafts After Successful Catheter-Directed Thrombolysis: Importance of Identifying and Correcting Underlying Lesion

	LESION CORRECTED (%)	
	Yes	**No**
McNamara and Bomberger[4]	80	7
Gardiner et al[5]	86	37

Thrombosed saphenous vein grafts that have been functioning for 1 year or more are likely to have a segmental underlying lesion responsible for graft failure.

Poor Candidates for Lytic Therapy

Patients whose underlying condition is associated with a low likelihood of success or a high complication rate or who have surgical options that offer higher success rates and fewer complications are considered poor candidates for catheter-directed thrombolysis. Among them are patients with the following conditions:

- Acute embolic occlusion of a large artery easily accessible via a limited operative procedure
- Acute postoperative bypass graft thrombosis
- Modest ischemia, producing tolerable symptoms (intermittent claudication)
- Severe limb ischemia in which viability is imminently threatened, although these patients are also at high risk for operative management

Early postoperative thrombosis is most often associated with either a technical error or poor patient selection for the bypass. For the former, operative thrombectomy is required with correction of the technical problem. For the latter, re-thrombosis is certain after any mechanical or pharmacologic thrombectomy; additional intervention with lytic agents poses needless risk without potential gain. The combined complication and failure rate of thrombolysis in these patients is excessively high. Patients with severe limb ischemia in which viability is imminently threatened are the most challenging patients, requiring the most experienced clinical judgment.

■ RANDOMIZED TRIALS

Many important randomized trials have been performed. These trials have compared catheter-directed thrombolysis with operative revascularization and one plasminogen activator with another. No trial has yet offered definitive conclusions, although many important observations have been made that can guide current therapy and assist in the design of future studies.

Catheter-Directed Thrombolysis Versus Operative Revascularization

Rochester Trial

Ouriel and colleagues[6] published an important study that has come to be known as the Rochester trial. This trial equally randomized 114 patients presenting with acute lower extremity arterial ischemia (≤7 days) to catheter-directed urokinase or operative revascularization. The primary endpoints included limb salvage and survival. Thrombolysis was successful in 70% of the patients in the urokinase group. Cumulative limb salvage was 82% in each of the treatment groups at 12 months (Table 53-2). Survival was significantly improved, however, in patients randomized to thrombolysis (84% versus 58% at 12 months; $P = .01$). The authors attributed the mortality difference to be due primarily to cardiopulmonary complications occurring as a result of surgery. The 30-day mortality was not significantly different, however, between the two groups, and on the basis of subsequent randomized trial survival data, other mechanisms responsible for improved survival may be operative in the patients receiving thrombolytic therapy.

Table 53-2 Major Observations from the Rochester Trial

	THROMBOLYTIC THERAPY ($n = 57$)	SURGICAL THERAPY ($n = 57$)	*P* VALUE
Limb salvage at 12 mo	82%	82%	1.00
Survival at 12 mo	84%	58%	.01
Hospitalization (median)	11 days	11 days	1.00
Major bleeding	11%	6%	.06
Intracranial bleed	2%	0	NS
Hospital cost	$15,672	$12,253	.02

NS, not significant.

STILE Trial

The STILE (Surgery versus Thrombolysis for the Ischemic Lower Extremity) trial[7] was designed to evaluate a strategy of catheter-directed thrombolysis versus operative revascularization and whether there were differences in outcome between rt-PA and urokinase. Patients with chronic limb ischemia (6 months) and patients with acute limb ischemia were included in this study. At the time of randomization, patients were not stratified according to duration of ischemia. Outcomes were analyzed on an intent-to-treat basis and a per-protocol basis. rt-PA initially was infused at 0.1 mg/kg/hr and decreased to 0.05 mg/kg/hr for 12 hours, or urokinase was given as a 250,000-IU bolus followed by 4000 IU/min for 4 hours, then 2000 IU/min for 36 hours. Endpoints were intended to evaluate major complications such as death, persistent (or recurrent) ischemia, major amputation, and major morbidity (major morbidity was essentially bleeding). Additional endpoints included reduction in the magnitude of a surgical procedure, the clinical outcome of the patient, length of hospitalization, and results according to the duration of ischemia at the time of randomization (acute versus chronic ischemia).

The Data and Safety Monitoring Committee halted the trial at the time of the first interim analysis because the overall outcome results met the statistical stopping rules established at the initiation of the trial. This decision was driven by the results (failure) of catheter-directed thrombolysis in patients with chronic native artery occlusion. The overall results of the STILE trial are provided in Table 53-3, which shows a significantly better outcome in patients randomized to surgery because of the greater success of the revascularization procedure. The clinical outcome at 30 days was similar in the two groups due to a successful surgical revascularization procedure after failed lytic therapy.

Important insights were obtained when the outcomes of patients with acute limb ischemia were compared with patients with chronic ischemia. In patients with acute limb ischemia (<2 weeks), there was a significant reduction in major limb amputation and significantly improved amputation-free survival in patients randomized to lysis. In patients with chronic ischemia, limb salvage was significantly better after surgical revascularization (Table 53-4).

There was a reduction in the magnitude of the surgical procedure in patients randomized to lytic therapy (59% versus 5%; $P = .001$) and a reduction in duration of hospitalization in patients with acute limb ischemia who were randomized to thrombolysis ($P < .04$). In patients with acute ischemia, failed primary lysis led to amputation in 30%, whereas a failed surgical procedure resulted in a major amputation in 68%. Detailed analysis failed to show any difference in efficacy or safety between the rt-PA and urokinase groups; however, there was a significantly shorter time to lysis in patients randomized to rt-PA (8 hours versus 16 hours; $P = .01$).

Major bleeding complications occurred more frequently in patients randomized to thrombolysis, occurring in 5.6% of the patients in the lytic group and 0.7% of the patients in the surgical group ($P = .014$). The bleeding complications occurred early in the course of lytic therapy, and the duration of therapy was no longer in patients experiencing bleeding complications compared with patients with no bleeding. The fibrinogen level was lower (188 mg/dL versus

Table 53-3 STILE Trial Results: Outcome at 1 Month by Duration of Ischemia (Intention-to-Treat Analysis)

	SURGERY (n = 135)		THROMBOLYSIS (n = 240)		
EVENT	No.	%	No.	%	*P* VALUE
Duration of Ischemia: 0-14 Days (Count)	39		73		
Composite clinical outcome	21	53.8	43	61.4	.459
Death	2	5.1	3	4.3	.810
Major amputation	7	17.9	4	5.7	.061
Ongoing/recurrent ischemia	15	38.5	34	48.6	.328
Major morbidity	10	25.6	15	21.4	.598
Life-threatening hemorrhage	0	0	4	5.7	.157
Perioperative complications	8	20.5	7	10	.098
Renal failure	0	0	0	0	—
Anesthesia complications	0	0	0	0	—
Vascular complications	1	2.6	5	7.1	.293
Postintervention wound complications	1	2.6	5	7.1	.293
Duration of Ischemia >14 Days (Count)	96		170		
Composite clinical outcome	28	29.2	107	62.9	<.001
Death	4	4.2	5	2.9	.617
Major amputation	2	2.1	9	5.3	.218
Ongoing/recurrent ischemia	20	20.8	99	58.2	<.001
Major morbidity	13	13.5	34	20	.169
Life-threatening hemorrhage	1	1.0	9	5.3	.080
Perioperative complications	5	5.2	7	4.1	.712
Renal failure	1	1	3	1.8	.618
Anesthesia complications	1	1	0	0	—
Vascular complications	4	4.2	18	10.6	.063
Postintervention wound complications	3	3.1	8	4.7	.526

310 mg/dL; $P = .01$), and the partial thromboplastin time (PTT) was longer (114 seconds versus 58 seconds; $P = .26$) in patients with a bleeding complication, suggesting a more severe induced coagulopathy in patients who bled. Three patients had intracranial bleeds, which occurred with both lytic agents.

Further analysis of the patients in the STILE trial was performed evaluating the subsets with occluded native arteries[8] and bypass grafts.[9] The trial randomized 237 patients with lower extremity ischemia due to either iliofemoral or femoropopliteal native arterial occlusion. Surgical revascularization was significantly better in patients with native arterial occlusion compared with catheter-directed thrombolysis. At 1 year, the incidence of persistent (or recurrent) ischemia (64% versus 35%; $P < .0001$) and major amputation (10% versus 0%; $P = .0024$) was increased in patients who were randomized to lysis. Factors associated with a poor lytic outcome included infrainguinal occlusion, diabetes, and critical limb ischemia. Although no difference in overall mortality was noted between the two groups, in evaluating the highest risk subset of patients, diabetics with infrapopliteal occlusive disease, there was a significant difference in 1-year mortality. Highest risk patients randomized to lysis had a 7% 1-year mortality compared with 32% randomized to surgery ($P < .05$). Although lytic therapy did not improve lower extremity perfusion in these high-risk patients, it seemed to offer a survival benefit.

Table 53-4 STILE Trial Results: Death and Amputation Outcome at 6 Months, by Duration of Ischemia

	0-14 DAYS					>14 DAYS				
	Surgery		Lysis			Surgery		Lysis		
	No.	%	No.	%	*P* Value	No.	%	No.	%	*P* Value
Intent-to-Treat (Count)	40		72			101		174		
Death/amputation	15	7.5	11	15.3	.01	10	9.9	31	17.8	.08
Death	4	10	4	5.6	.45	8	7.9	12	6.9	.81
Major amputation	12	30	8	11.1	.02	3	3	21	12.1	.01
Per-Protocol (Count)	36		50			89		143		
Death/amputation	13	36.1	7	14	.02	9	10.1	30	21	.03
Death	4	11.1	3	6	.45	7	7.9	12	8.4	.99
Major amputation	10	27.8	5	10	.04	3	3.4	20	14	.01

Also randomized were 124 patients with lower extremity bypass graft occlusion. The results of thrombolysis depended on the duration of graft occlusion. Patients presenting with acute ischemia (0 to 14 days) had better lytic success resulting in a lower 1-year amputation rate compared with patients randomized to surgery (20% versus 48%; $P = 0.026$). Patients with chronic graft occlusion (ischemia >14 days) had a better overall outcome (less ischemia) with surgical revascularization ($P = .003$). Patients with prosthetic grafts had more major morbid events compared with patients with autogenous grafts.

TOPAS Trial

The observations made in the Rochester trial of improved survival with catheter-directed thrombolysis formed the basis for the design of the TOPAS (Thrombolysis Or Peripheral Arterial Surgery for acute limb ischemia) trials. The TOPAS trials compared catheter-directed recombinant urokinase with surgical revascularization. The preliminary dose-ranging TOPAS trial[10] involved 213 patients with acute limb ischemia randomized to one of three doses of recombinant urokinase (2000 IU/min, 4000 IU/min, or 8000 IU/min) for 4 hours followed by an infusion of 2000 IU/min for 44 additional hours. The regimen of 4000 IU/min seemed to be most effective when overall efficacy and safety were considered. Although amputation-free survival was similar in the urokinase-treated patients compared with the surgical control group, patients treated with thrombolysis required fewer major surgical procedures. Bleeding complications were greater in the urokinase group, and 2.1% had an intracranial bleed.

The dose-ranging study led to a larger comparison trial of recombinant urokinase with surgical revascularization in patients with acute limb ischemia. The TOPAS trial[11] randomized 544 patients to either catheter-directed intra-arterial recombinant urokinase or surgical revascularization. All patients were randomized within 14 days of acute arterial or graft occlusion. Amputation-free survival was the primary endpoint for this trial.

The major early and 1-year results are summarized in Table 53-5. Amputation-free survival rates in the urokinase group were 72% at 6 months and 65% at 1 year compared with 75% and 70% in the surgery group. By 1 year, the surgical group had undergone 590 surgical procedures compared with 351 procedures in the urokinase group. Bleeding complications were more common in patients treated with urokinase. Major hemorrhage occurred in 13% in the urokinase group compared with 6% in the surgical group ($P = .005$), with intracranial hemorrhage occurring in 1.6% of the urokinase group but none in the surgical group. Although the primary endpoints of the STILE and TOPAS trials were different, there are consistent observations when patients with acute limb ischemia are compared (Table 53-6).

Table 53-5 TOPAS Trial: Summary of Results*

	UROKINASE (n = 272)	SURGERY (n = 272)
Early		
Recanalization	80%	—
Complete lysis	68%	—
Hospitalization (median)	10 days	10 days
Major hemorrhage	13%	6%†
Intracranial bleed	1.6%	0%
1 Year		
Major amputation	15%	13%
Death	20%	17%
Amputation-free survival	65%	70%
Open surgical procedures	351	590
Percutaneous procedures	135	70

*Percentages rounded except for intracranial bleed.
†$P = .005$.

Table 53-6 Consistent Observations from the STILE and TOPAS Trials of Catheter-Directed Thrombolysis for Acute Limb Ischemia

Patients with acute limb ischemia face a 1-year mortality of 10-20%
Treatment of occluded bypass grafts has a better outcome than treatment of native arteries
Risk of major bleeding increases with thrombolysis compared with surgical revascularization
Risk of a bleeding complication increases as coagulopathy worsens (decreased fibrinogen, prolonged PTT)
Risk of an intracranial bleed is approximately 1-2% with thrombolysis
Lytic patients require fewer open surgical procedures

PTT, partial thromboplastin time.

Randomized Trials Comparing Lytic Agents

PURPOSE Trial (Recombinant Prourokinase Versus Urokinase)

The PURPOSE (Prourokinase versus Urokinase for Recanalization of Peripheral Occlusions, Safety and Efficacy) trial[12] evaluated the potential of prourokinase offering added efficacy and safety advantages as an alternative to urokinase in patients undergoing catheter-directed thrombolysis for acute limb ischemia. Recombinant prourokinase (r-ProUK) has theoretical advantages as a fibrin-specific agent, and its fibrinolytic activity is limited to the occluding thrombus. When prourokinase is activated, however, urokinase may escape into the circulation with its attendant fibrinolytic activity (see Chapter 32). The PURPOSE trial was a well-designed, randomized, double-blind, parallel group, phase II, multicenter study comparing three doses of intra-arterial, catheter-directed r-ProUK for the initial 8-hour infusion (2 mg/hr, 4 mg/hr, or 8 mg/hr), then continuing at 0.5 mg/hr versus urokinase at 4000 IU/min for 4 hours, then 2000 IU/min. The primary endpoint was complete (>90%) lysis of the occluding thrombus after 8 hours of infusion. Amputation-free survival was also evaluated.

The results showed improved clot lysis at 8 hours, decreasing fibrinogen concentrations and increasing rates of bleeding observed as the r-ProUK dose increased from 2 mg/hr to 8 mg/hr. No intracranial bleeding events were observed in any group. Complete lysis at 8 hours, major bleeding, and amputation-free survival results are listed in Table 53-7. No significant differences in these endpoints were noted between groups. The risk of mortality was

Table 53-7 Major Results from the PURPOSE Trial*

	COMPLETE (> 95%) LYSIS AT 8 HOURS (%)	MAJOR BLEEDING (%)	AMPUTATION-FREE SURVIVAL AT 30 DAYS (%)
2 mg r-ProUK	39	15	93
4 mg r-ProUK	44	20	85
8 mg r-ProUK	56	23	86
Urokinase	49	17	83

*No significant difference between treatment groups.

significantly lower in the 2-mg r-ProUK group, however, compared with the 8-mg r-ProUK group at hospital discharge (P = .037) and at 30 days. The risk of mortality was lower in the 2-mg r-ProUK group compared with the urokinase group (0% versus 6.9%; P = .038).

An important observation from this trial is that the rate of in-hospital amputation or death was greater in patients who experienced distal embolization during therapy than in patients who did not (19% versus 9%). The PURPOSE trial showed that r-ProUK is potentially effective in the management of patients with acute limb ischemia; however, there was a dose-associated relationship of bleeding complications and fibrinogenolysis. This agent requires further investigation and dose modification to achieve an optimal efficacy/safety balance.

Recombinant Tissue Plasminogen Activator Versus Urokinase

Mahler and associates[13] conducted a prospective multicenter evaluation comparing rt-PA versus urokinase for patients undergoing catheter-directed thrombolysis for femoropopliteal occlusions. The authors integrated mechanical techniques with catheter-directed thrombolysis. Comparing lytic outcome alone, rt-PA seemed to be more effective than urokinase in restoring complete reperfusion by the end of lysis using an end-hole catheter (P = .045). When other mechanical techniques were used as adjunctive therapy, however, results improved in both groups, and there was no significant difference in final outcome.

The STILE trial[7] randomized the lysis patients to either rt-PA or urokinase. The details of the STILE trial have been reviewed in a previous section. The comparison of urokinase with rt-PA showed no differences in either efficacy or bleeding complications. There was a significant difference in speed of lysis favoring rt-PA (P < .02).

Two additional trials compared catheter-directed rt-PA versus urokinase for the management of patients with lower extremity arterial and graft occlusion.[14,15] Both studies chose relatively high doses of rt-PA to compare with moderate or low doses of urokinase. Myerovitz and colleagues[14] equally randomized 32 patients to receive rt-PA (10-mg bolus followed by 5 mg/hr for 24 hours) or urokinase (60,000-IU bolus followed by 240,000 IU/hr for 2 hours, then 120,000 IU/hr for 2 hours, then 60,000 IU/hr for 20 hours). The endpoint of 95% clot lysis was achieved more rapidly (P = .04) with rt-PA, which may not be surprising considering the high bolus dose and high infusion dose of rt-PA relative to urokinase. At 24 hours, fibrinogen levels were lower (P = .01), and there were more bleeding complications (P = .39) in the rt-PA patients. At 30 days, there was no difference in clinical success.

Schweizer and coworkers[15] randomized 120 patients with acute or subacute infrainguinal arterial thrombosis. Patients randomized to rt-PA received a 5-mg bolus and a 5 mg/hr infusion. The urokinase patients received the relatively low dose of 60,000 IU/hr infusion with no bolus. All patients received an intra-arterial heparin bolus of 5000 IU followed by an infusion of 700 to 750 IU/hr. Patients receiving rt-PA had better lytic success and more rapid lysis (P < .05) and had less severe ischemia at 6 months. Although direct comparison of lytic agents in randomized fashion is valuable, widely disparate dosing between agents is likely to alter efficacy and safety based on the dose of drug delivered, rather than inherent differences between plasminogen activators. High-dose and bolus infusion of rt-PA have been shown to reduce lysis time and increase bleeding complications compared with lower doses.[16,17] Similar observations have been made with urokinase.[18] It is imperative that comparable dosing between agents be used in trials that are designed to evaluate differences in efficacy and safety of plasminogen activators.

Technical Aspects of Catheter-Directed Thrombolysis

Although catheter-directed thrombolysis is a broadly accepted therapeutic modality for patients with acute limb ischemia, substantial differences of opinion exist regarding nuances in technique, methods of administration, and mechanics of delivery of the lytic agent. Adjunctive mechanical thrombus maceration is being investigated in an effort to restore perfusion more rapidly and reduce duration of lytic infusion; however, inherent complications are associated with thrombus maceration.

It is accepted that the "guide wire traversal test" is a good predictor of success of thrombolysis. Passage of a nonhydrophilic guide wire through the length of the occluded vessel is associated with a high likelihood of a successful outcome.[7,19]

The technique of "thrombus lacing," or giving an intrathrombus bolus dose of lytic agent, has been advocated to speed thrombolysis and shorten infusion times. This technique refers to the intrathrombus delivery of a concentrated form of lytic agent intended to saturate the thrombus with the plasminogen activator. Sullivan and colleagues[18] reported better outcomes in patients receiving high-dose intrathrombus bolus infusions of urokinase. This observation also was made in a prospective study of rt-PA infusion.[16]

Intrathrombus, intermittent high-pressure infusion refers to the "pulsed spray" technique of delivering the thrombolytic agent. This technique forcefully injects the plasminogen activator into the thrombus to fragment the thrombus and increase the surface area available for enzymatic action by the plasminogen activator. The purpose of this technique also is to accelerate lysis and shorten treatment time. It is accepted that when antegrade flow is established, there is no benefit from additional pulse-spray infusion compared with the continuous infusion technique.[20-22]

Greenberg and colleagues[23] evaluated mechanical versus chemical thrombolysis in an experimental model assessing mechanisms of thrombolysis, time to reperfusion, and completeness of thrombus resolution. Using radiolabeled (iodine 125) thrombus in a 5-cm segment of polytetrafluoroethylene graft, three treatment regimens were evaluated: a pressurized pulse spray of saline, a similar pressurized pulse spray of urokinase, and a standard continuous infusion of urokinase. A 5% dextrose in water infusion served as the control group. Time to reperfusion was significantly shorter in both of the groups using the pressurized spray technique, whereas there was no evidence of reperfusion at 90 minutes in the control group. The completeness of thrombus dissolution was higher with the continuous infusion of urokinase compared with either of the power injection groups. The amount of embolic debris produced was significantly higher in both of the power injection groups compared with the continuous infusion of urokinase. The size of the embolic particles decreased when urokinase was added to the solution used by the power injector. This well-designed in-vitro trial fits with many of the previous and subsequent clinical observations made by clinicians using pharmacomechanical thrombolysis.

Percutaneous mechanical thrombectomy techniques have become increasingly popular. This is a heterogeneous group of devices designed to clear intravascular thrombus with the use of combinations of mechanical dissolution, thrombus fragmentation, and aspiration.[24-26] It is beyond the scope of this chapter to review the variety of methods available for percutaneous mechanical thrombectomy. These techniques are used with increasing frequency, however, in high-risk patients who are not candidates for thrombolysis. They also are used to remove insoluble material or debulk thrombus in patients undergoing lytic therapy to accelerate restoration of flow and reduce the duration of lytic infusion. Several new techniques incorporate a saline jet spray with an associated Venturi effect to fragment and lyse thrombus mechanically and suction the debris. Although many clinicians routinely incorporate these mechanical devices as either primary or adjunctive techniques to catheter-directed thrombolysis, none is approved for intra-arterial use; this is also true for catheter-directed thrombolysis. Outcome data resulting from studies that incorporate two off-label techniques to achieve a single endpoint cannot be used for registration.

■ ADJUNCTIVE PHARMACOTHERAPY

Failure of catheter-directed thrombolysis occurs with disturbing frequency, as has been reported in prospective trials. Patients having successful lysis often require prolonged infusion times. Pericatheter thrombosis, ongoing thrombosis during infusion, and recurrent occlusion are problems that have yet to be fully overcome.

Because catheters are placed in occluded arteries, a low-flow situation exists during an extended part of therapy. Pericatheter thrombosis and re-thrombosis of diseased arteries and grafts as a result of their significant thrombogenic stimulus have led to the use of anticoagulants, especially heparin, during and after catheter-directed thrombolysis.

Because platelets are important in acute arterial thrombosis initially and postprocedure, it is intuitive that platelet inhibition be incorporated in all patients with significant underlying atherosclerotic disease. A new, potent class of platelet inhibitors are the glycoprotein (GP) IIb/IIIa receptor antagonists. Although not routinely used in patients with peripheral arterial disease, it is appropriate that these agents be studied in this patient group in light of the benefits observed in patients undergoing percutaneous coronary interventions.

Aspirin

Aspirin use is ubiquitous in patients with atherosclerotic disease. Aspirin use is appropriate in light of existing data showing the reduction in cardiovascular morbidity and mortality in these high-risk patients. Some thrombolytic therapy protocols routinely have incorporated aspirin for all patients entering the trial. Although there are no randomized data available evaluating the relative benefits of aspirin in patients undergoing peripheral arterial thrombolysis, it is recognized that patients with peripheral arterial disease have a twofold to threefold increase in death rate due to cardiovascular causes. Meta-analyses of numerous randomized trials have shown a 25% to 27% risk reduction of a major ischemic event if patients are given a platelet inhibitor—often aspirin.[27,28] It is appropriate that patients continue to receive aspirin while undergoing thrombolysis. The British Thrombolysis Study Group[29] showed improved outcomes in patients who were taking aspirin during catheter-directed thrombolysis.

Heparin

The beneficial effects of heparin have been elucidated in patients undergoing coronary thrombolysis. Associated with improved efficacy is the correlation, however, of hemorrhagic risk with higher heparin doses. Many observations have been made in peripheral arterial thrombolysis regarding benefits and risks of heparin. Berridge and associates[30] failed to show benefit from low-dose (250 U/hr) heparin as an adjunct to rt-PA infusion. Because the heparin was given intravenously, the anticoagulant effect in the target vessel was ineffective considering the thrombogenic stimulus. The TOPAS investigators[11] initially incorporated heparin infusion in their protocol. As a result of observations of increased bleeding with heparin and the correlation of a prolonged PTT with bleeding, their protocol was amended, and heparin was discontinued. Similar observations were made by Decrinis and coworkers.[31]

At the time the STILE protocol was written, the relative risks and benefits of heparin were controversial. The option of using heparin was left to the investigator. Heparin use was

Table 53-8 Catheter-Directed Thrombolysis with rt-PA and Urokinase: Outcome Related to Heparin Use (STILE Trial)

	HEPARIN (%)	NO HEPARIN (%)	*P* VALUE
rt-PA (*n* = 133)			
Death	5	8	.46
Successful lysis	46	25	.06
Morbidity	24	21	.75
Urokinase (*n* = 98)			
Death	3	0	.40
Successful lysis	54	25	.01
Morbidity*	19	25	.74

*Most morbidity was bleeding.

split evenly in the rt-PA and urokinase patients, and the intravenous dose was in the 800 to 1000 IU/hr range. There was a marked difference in successful thrombolysis in patients receiving heparin (Table 53-8). Bleeding complications were significantly linked with low fibrinogen levels and a trend toward a prolonged PTT; however, bleeding complications were not linked directly to heparin.

Most clinicians intuitively would agree that heparin is beneficial in reducing thrombosis if used in an amount resulting in a therapeutic effect. To deliver adequate amounts of anticoagulant to the target vessel using an intravenous infusion, however, unacceptably high doses of heparin must be given. Intra-arterial infusion of heparin into the target vessel delivers the necessary concentration to achieve benefit, while markedly reducing the systemic dose and reducing hemorrhagic risk.

Glycoprotein IIb/IIIa

The most potent platelet inhibitors are members of a new class of agents, the platelet GP IIb/IIIa receptor antagonists. These agents have been studied in clinical trials of coronary intervention and showed reduction in the short-term and long-term incidence of death, myocardial infarction, and restenosis in patients requiring coronary angioplasty.[32-37] These agents also reduced the risk of procedure-related thrombotic complications in patients with unstable angina undergoing coronary angioplasty and stenting.[38,39] To improve the results of peripheral thrombolysis, many investigators have evaluated the GP IIb/IIIa receptor antagonist, abciximab, as adjunctive pharmacotherapy. Abciximab is a chimeric (human/murine) monoclonal antibody that selectively binds to the surface GP IIb/IIIa receptor, the final pathway in platelet aggregation. It also binds to the vitronectin receptor, potentially reducing neointimal smooth muscle cell migration and proliferation.

Numerous reports more recently have surfaced in the literature.[40-44] Although the number of patients in each report is small, preliminary observations can be made that may improve the thoughtful application of patient care and should be considered in the design of future trials. Observations from the existing reports suggest an improved primary success rate with thrombolytic therapy with fewer than anticipated bleeding complications. There is also a suggestion of improved sustained benefit in patients receiving abciximab. Ouriel and colleagues[44] observed significantly reduced distal emboli when abciximab was added to reteplase during catheter-directed thrombolytic therapy for patients with acute or subacute arterial occlusion.

■ INTRAOPERATIVE INTRA-ARTERIAL THROMBOLYTIC THERAPY

Intraoperative thrombolysis has become recognized as an important and successful adjunct to open surgical thromboembolectomy. Clinical and laboratory studies have documented a high frequency of residual intraluminal thrombus after acute thrombosis and balloon catheter thrombectomy.[45-49] Residual thrombus increases the risk of re-thrombosis and failure of the revascularization procedure. A recent operation is considered a relative contraindication to thrombolytic therapy. It is recognized, however, that plasminogen activators delivered to the thrombus can lyse acute clot effectively without causing a systemic lytic effect.

In a randomized, blinded, and placebo-controlled trial in patients undergoing elective infrainguinal reconstruction, the regional and systemic effects of three doses of urokinase (125,000 IU, 250,000 IU, and 500,000 IU) were investigated.[50] Bolus infusions of urokinase into the distal arterial circulation were safe and associated with the breakdown of complexed fibrin (elevated D dimer) but not with depletion of fibrinogen. Although there was dose-related plasminogen activation, there was not significant plasminogen depletion compared with placebo. There were no additional bleeding complications in patients receiving urokinase. There was a significantly lower mortality in urokinase patients compared with controls.

After thromboembolectomy, a bolus dose of intra-arterial rt-PA or urokinase into the thrombectomized arteries is advised (distally and occasionally into the proximal arterial segments while the clamps are in place) (Fig. 53-3). The vascular volume is estimated, and 2 to 8 mg of rt-PA or 100,000 to 250,000 IU of urokinase is infused in an appropriate volume.

In patients who have extensive residual thrombus or multivessel distal thrombotic occlusion, repeated attempts at mechanical thrombectomy may be futile. In such cases, bolus dose infusion seems to be inadequate, and patients require an ongoing drip infusion.[48] Depending on the volume of residual thrombus, a 20- to 30-minute drip infusion may lyse the thrombus and restore circulation. In many of these patients, an isolated limb perfusion is more effective (Fig. 53-4). The isolated limb perfusion technique begins with exsanguinating the venous blood with a rubber bandage, applying a thigh blood pressure cuff inflated to suprasystolic pressure, and infusing the lytic agent into the distal arterial tree with a slow hand infusion or attaching the arterial catheter to a standard infusion pump while draining the venous effluent. Because the venous effluent is being drained, a large dose and volume of lytic agent can be used without any systemic lytic effect.

Another option in patients requiring isolated limb perfusion is the use of an extracorporeal pump. We have used this technique only in patients who have profound limb ischemia as a result of acute multivessel distal thrombosis,

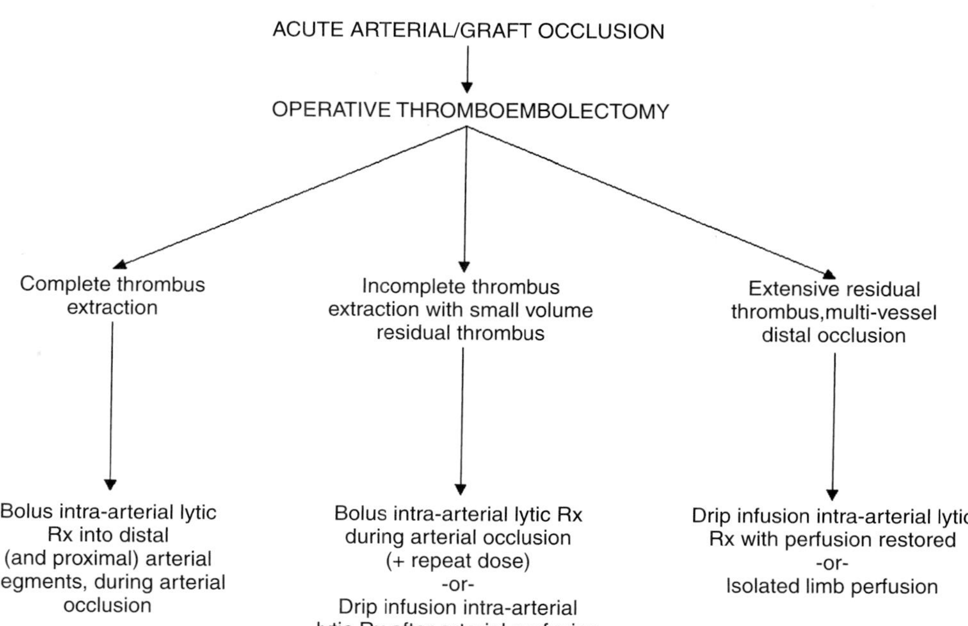

FIGURE 53-3 Suggested algorithm for intraoperative intra-arterial thrombolytic therapy.

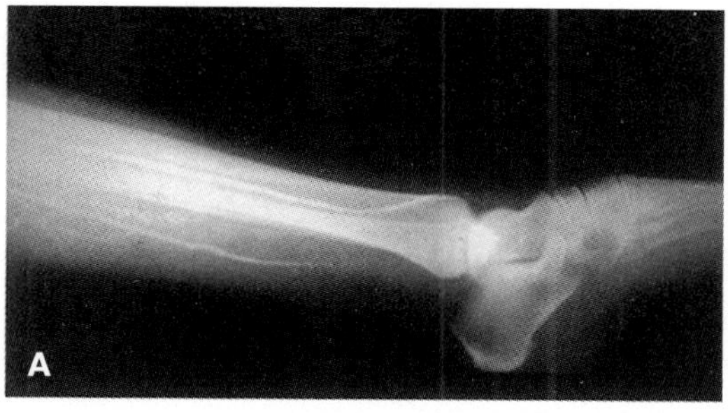

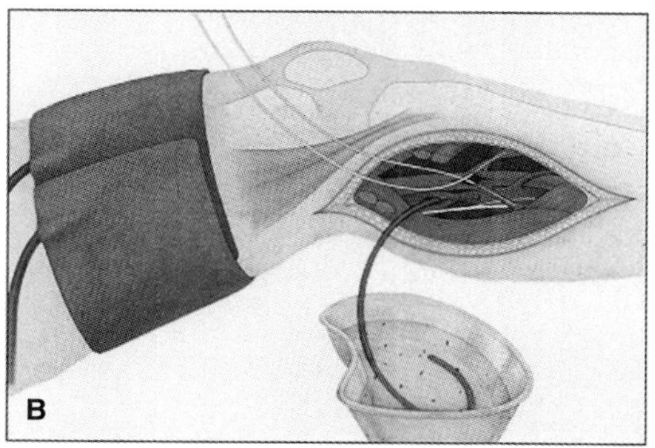

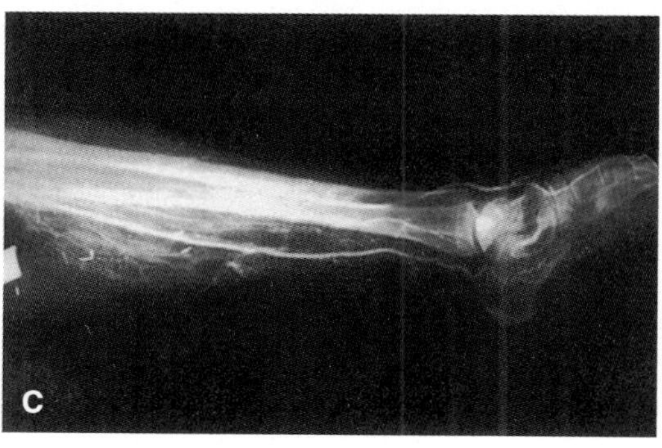

FIGURE 53-4 Technique of intraoperative high-dose isolated limb perfusion of a thrombolytic agent in a patient at high risk for bleeding from any systemic fibrinolytic effect. This patient was 2 days post emergency coronary artery bypass graft surgery. She developed multivessel distal arterial embolus/thrombosis after the percutaneous insertion and removal of an intra-aortic balloon counterpulsation pump. **A,** The intraoperative arteriogram after balloon catheter thrombectomy of the popliteal and tibial vessels shows no perfusion into the foot. After arteriotomy closure, the patient's foot remained pale and cool with no Doppler signals at the ankle. Additional thrombus could not be mechanically removed. **B,** The patient's limb was elevated and the venous blood exsanguinated with a rubber bandage. A sterile blood pressure cuff was placed on the distal thigh and inflated to 250 mm Hg. The popliteal vein was cannulated with a red rubber catheter and drained into a basin. Catheters were placed into the anterior tibial and posterior tibial arteries, and 1 million IU of urokinase was infused into the lower leg in a volume of 1 L of saline (500,000 IU/500 mL in each tibial artery) over 20 minutes. After completion of urokinase infusion, the limb was flushed with a heparin and saline solution. The red rubber catheter was removed, and the venotomy was closed primarily. The arterial catheters were removed, and the arteriotomy was closed with a patch. **C,** A postinfusion arteriogram showed significant improvement of perfusion to the foot. The patient had a palpable dorsalis pedis pulse and a pink foot after wound closure.

in whom maximal fibrinolysis was required for limb salvage, and in whom a 1-hour tourniquet time might be inadequate. In such a situation, 100 mg of rt-PA or 2 million U of urokinase would be added to the reservoir for initial infusion and replenished at a rate of 20% of the original dose every 10 minutes. The venous effluent removes most of the plasminogen activator; however, with prolonged extracorporeal isolated limb perfusion, there is likely to be some escape of plasminogen activator via the bone marrow.

The body of literature involving thrombolytic therapy for arterial and graft occlusion was reviewed and summarized by an international consensus committee. Recommendations were made ranging from appropriate definitions and pretreatment imaging to lytic therapy for acute arterial and graft occlusion and adjunctive pharmacotherapy. Although techniques are evolving, this consensus document remains a valuable reference for the management of lower limb peripheral arterial occlusion with catheter-directed thrombolysis.

■ REFERENCES

1. McNicol GP, Reid W, Bain WH, Douglas AS: Treatment of peripheral arterial occlusion by streptokinase perfusion. BMJ 1:1508, 1963.
2. Alkjaersig N, Fletcher AP, Sherry S: The mechanism of clot dissolution of plasmin. J Clin Invest 38:1086, 1959.
3. Berridge DC, Gregson RHS, Hopkinson BR, Makin GS: Randomized trial of intra-arterial recombinant tissue plasminogen activator, intravenous recombinant tissue plasminogen activator and intra-arterial streptokinase in peripheral arterial thrombolysis. Br J Surg 78:988, 1991.
4. McNamara TO, Bomberger RA: Factors affecting initial and six month patency rates after intraarterial thrombolysis with high dose urokinase. Am J Surg 152:709, 1986.
5. Gardiner GA, Harrington DP, Koltun W, et al: Salvage of occluded bypass grafts by means of thrombolysis. J Vasc Surg 9:426, 1989.
6. Ouriel K, Shortell CK, DeWeese JA, et al: A comparison of thrombolytic therapy with operative revascularization in the initial treatment of acute peripheral arterial ischemia. J Vasc Surg 19:1021, 1994.
7. The STILE Investigators: Results of a prospective randomized trial evaluating surgery versus thrombolysis for ischemia of the lower extremity: The STILE trial. Ann Surg 220:251, 1994.
8. Weaver FA, Comerota AJ, Youngblood M, et al: Surgical revascularization versus thrombolysis for nonembolic lower extremity native artery occlusions: Results of a prospective randomized trial. J Vasc Surg 24:513, 1996.
9. Comerota AJ, Weaver FA, Hosking JD, et al: Results of a prospective, randomized trial of surgery versus thrombolysis for occluded lower extremity bypass grafts. Am J Surg 172:105, 1996.
10. Ouriel K, Veith FJ, Sasahara AA: Thrombolysis or peripheral arterial surgery: Phase I results. TOPAS investigators. J Vasc Surg 23:64, 1996.
11. Ouriel K, Veith FJ, Sasahara AA: A comparison of recombinant urokinase with vascular surgery as initial treatment for acute arterial occlusion of the legs. N Engl J Med 338:1105, 1998.
12. Ouriel K, Kandarpa K, Schuerr DM, et al: Prourokinase versus urokinase for recanalization of peripheral occlusions, safety and efficacy: The PURPOSE trial. J Vasc Interv Radiol 10:1083, 1999.
13. Mahler F, Schneider E, Hess H: Recombinant tissue plasminogen activator versus urokinase for local thrombolysis of femoropopliteal occlusions: A prospective, randomized multicenter trial. For the Steering Committee, Study on Local Thrombolysis: University Hospitals of Bern and Zurich, Switzerland, and Klinik Diakoniewerk, Munich, Germany. J Endovasc Ther 8:638, 2001.
14. Myerovitz MF, Goldhaber SZ, Reagan K, et al: Recombinant tissue-type plasminogen activator versus urokinase in peripheral arterial and graft occlusions: A randomized trial. Radiology 175:34, 1990.
15. Schweizer J, Altmann E, Stoblein F, et al: Comparison of tissue plasminogen activator and urokinase in the local infiltration thrombolysis of peripheral arterial occlusions. Eur J Radiol 22:129, 1996.
16. Braithwaite BD, Buckenham TM, Galland RB, et al: A prospective randomized trial of high dose versus low dose tissue plasminogen activator infusion in the management of acute limb ischemia. Br J Surg 84:646, 1997.
17. Ward AS, Andaz SK, Bygrave S: Peripheral thrombolysis with tissue plasminogen activator: Results of two treatment regimens. Arch Surg 129:861, 1994.
18. Sullivan KL, Gardiner GA, Shapiro MJ, et al: Acceleration of thrombolysis with a high-dose transthrombus bolus technique. Radiology 173:805, 1989.
19. Ouriel K, Shortell CK, Azodo MW, et al: Acute peripheral arterial occlusion: Predictors of success in catheter-directed thrombolytic therapy. Radiology 93:561, 1994.
20. Kandarpa K, Chopra PS, Arung JE, et al: Intra-arterial thrombolysis of lower extremity occlusion: Prospective randomized comparison of forced periodic infusion and conventional slow continuous infusion. Radiology 188:861, 1993.
21. Kandarpa K, Goldhaber SZ, Myerovitz MF: Pulse-spray thrombolysis: The careful analysis. Radiology 193:320, 1994.
22. Hye RJ, Turner C, Valji K, et al: Is thrombolysis of occluded popliteal and tibial bypass grafts worthwhile? J Vasc Surg 20:588, 1994.
23. Greenberg RK, Ouriel K, Srivastava S, et al: Mechanical versus chemical thrombolysis: An in vitro differentiation of thrombolytic mechanisms. J Vasc Interv Radiol 11:199, 2000.
24. Sharafuddin MJA, Hicks ME: Current status of percutaneous mechanical thrombectomy: Part I. General principles. J Vasc Interv Radiol 8:911, 1997.
25. Sharafuddin MJA, Hicks ME: Current status of percutaneous mechanical thrombectomy: Part II. Devices and mechanisms of action. J Vasc Interv Radiol 9:15, 1998.
26. Sharafuddin MJA, Hicks ME: Current status of percutaneous mechanical thrombectomy: Part III. Present and future applications. J Vasc Interv Radiol 9:209, 1998.
27. Antiplatelet Trialists' Collaboration: Collaborative overview of randomized trials of antiplatelet therapy: I. Prevention of death, myocardial infarction, and stroke by prolonged antiplatelet therapy in various categories of patients. BMJ 308:81, 1994.
28. Antithrombotic Trialists' Collaboration: Collaborative meta-analysis of randomized trials of antiplatelet therapy for prevention of death, myocardial infarction, and stroke in high-risk patients. BMJ 324:71, 2002.
29. Braithwaite BD, Jones L, Yusuf SW, et al: Aspirin improves the outcome of intra-arterial thrombolysis with tissue plasminogen activator. Br J Surg 82:1357, 1995.
30. Berridge DC, Gregson RH, Makin GS, Hopkinson BR: Tissue plasminogen activator in peripheral arterial thrombolysis. Br J Surg 77:179, 1990.
31. Decrinis M, Pilger E, Stark G, et al: A simplified procedure for intraarterial thrombolysis with tissue-type plasminogen activator in peripheral arterial occlusive disease: Primary and long-term results. Eur Heart J 14:297, 1993.
32. The EPIC Investigators: Use of a monoclonal antibody directed against the platelet glycoprotein IIb/IIIa receptor in high-risk coronary angioplasty. N Engl J Med 330:956, 1994.
33. Topol EJ, Califf RM, Weisman HF, et al: Randomized trial of coronary intervention with antibody against platelet IIb/IIIa integrin for reduction of clinical restenosis: Results at 6 months. Lancet 343:881, 1994.
34. Topol EJ, Ferguson JJ, Weisman HF, et al: Long-term protection from myocardial ischemic events in a randomized trial of brief integrin b_3 blockade with percutaneous coronary intervention. JAMA 278:479, 1997.

35. The EPILOG Investigators: Platelet glycoprotein IIb-IIIa receptor blockade and low-dose heparin during percutaneous coronary revascularization. N Engl J Med 336:1689, 1997.
36. The PURSUIT Trial Investigators: Inhibition of platelet glycoprotein IIb/IIIa with eptifibatide in patients with acute coronary syndromes. N Engl J Med 339:436, 1998.
37. Theroux P, Kouz S, Roy L, et al: Platelet membrane receptor glycoprotein IIb/IIIa antagonism in unstable angina: The Canadian Lamifiban Study. Circulation 94:899, 1996.
38. The CAPTURE Investigators: Randomized placebo-controlled trial of abciximab before and during coronary intervention in refractory unstable angina: The CAPTURE study. Lancet 349:1429, 1997.
39. The EPISTENT Investigators: Randomized placebo-controlled and balloon-angioplasty-controlled trial to assess safety of coronary stenting with use of platelet glycoprotein-IIb/IIIa blockade. Lancet 352:87, 1998.
40. Tepe G, Schott U, Erley C, et al: Platelet glycoprotein IIb/IIIa receptor antagonist used in conjunction with thrombolysis for peripheral arterial thrombosis. AJR Am J Roentgenol 172:1343, 1999.
41. Schweizer J, Kirch W, Koch R, et al: Short and long-term results of abciximab versus aspirin in conjunction with thrombolysis for patients with peripheral occlusive arterial disease and arterial thrombosis. Angiology 51:913, 2000.
42. Haumer M, Atteneder M, Ahmadi R, et al: Co-administration of low-dose urokinase and abciximab in thrombolysis for lower limb ischemia: A safety study. Thromb Res 103:S143, 2001.
43. Duda S, Tepe G, Luz O, et al: Peripheral artery occlusion: Treatment with abciximab plus urokinase versus with urokinase alone—a randomized pilot trial (the PROMPT study). Radiology 221:689, 2001.
44. Ouriel K, Castaneda F, McNamara T, et al: Reteplase monotherapy and reteplase/abciximab combination therapy in peripheral arterial occlusive disease-results from the RELAX trial. J Vasc Interv Radiol 15:229, 2004.
45. Dunnant JR, Edwards WS: Small vessel occlusion in the extremity after periods of arterial obstruction: An experimental study. Surgery 75:240, 1973.
46. Plecha FR, Pories WJ: Intraoperative angiography in the immediate assessment of arterial reconstruction. Arch Surg 105:902, 1972.
47. Quinones-Baldrich WJ, Ziomek S, Henderson TC, et al: Intraoperative fibrinolytic therapy: Experimental evaluation. J Vasc Surg 4:229, 1986.
48. Quinones-Baldrich WJ, Zierler RE, Hiatt JC: Intraoperative fibrinolytic therapy: An adjunct to catheter thromboembolectomy. J Vasc Surg 2:319, 1985.
49. Parent FN, Berhard VW, Pabst TS, et al: Fibrinolytic treatment of residual thrombus after catheter embolectomy for severe lower limb ischemia. J Vasc Surg 9:153, 1989.
50. Comerota AJ, Rao AK, Throm RC, et al: A prospective, randomized, blinded, and placebo-controlled trial of intraoperative intraarterial urokinase infusion during lower extremity revascularization: Regional and systemic effects. Ann Surg 218:534, 1993.
51. Comerota AJ, White JV: Intraoperative, intraarterial thrombolytic therapy as an adjunct to revascularization in patients with residual distal arterial thrombus. Semin Vasc Surg 5:110, 1992.
52. Working Party on Thrombolysis in the Management of Limb Ischemia: Thrombolysis in the management of lower limb peripheral arterial occlusion—a consensus document. Am J Cardiol 81:207, 1998.

Chapter 54

Complications of Endovascular Procedures

ALAN B. LUMSDEN, MD, FACS
ERIC PEDEN, MD
RUTH L. BUSH, MD
PETER H. LIN, MD

As more endovascular techniques are performed, the number of interventionists rises, and the array of endovascular techniques continues to expand, we will increasingly encounter complications from these procedures. Some of the complications are simply a function of the access, such as arteriovenous fistula (AVF), bleeding, and pseudoaneurysm. Others are specific to the type of procedure being performed on the target vessel, such as renal artery dissection and stent migration from iliac veins. Furthermore, with each new device, unexpected and occasionally unique complications are identified and treatment strategies gradually refined; examples of device-related complications are migration of an aortic stent-graft, failure to retrieve an inferior vena cava (IVC) filter, occlusion of an embolization protection device, and femoral artery infection due to closure devices. Consequently, the interventionist must be aware of these complications and the salvage options available for them. In this chapter we describe some of the more commonly encountered complications and discuss their management.

■ ACCESS SITE COMPLICATIONS

The frequency of groin complications after an endovascular procedure varies according to the type of procedure being performed. Because of the very large number of coronary interventions performed compared with peripheral procedures, reports of groin complications tend to predominate after those interventions. The incidence of groin

Table 54-1 Type of Complications of Endovascular Procedures Requiring Surgical Intervention

COMPLICATION	INCIDENCE (%)
Pseudoaneurysm	61.2
Hematoma	11.2
Arteriovenous fistula	10.2
External bleeding	6.1
Retroperitoneal hematoma	5.1
Arterial thrombosis	3.1
Groin abscess	2.0
Mycotic aneurysm	1.0

complications is 0.05% to 0.7% after cardiac catheterization but is much higher after percutaneous transluminal angioplasty, 0.7% to 9.0%.[1-3] Peripheral vascular complications include hematoma, pseudoaneurysms, AVFs, acute arterial occlusions, cholesterol emboli, and infections; such complications occur with an overall incidence of 1.5% to 9%.[1] In descending order of frequency they are: groin hematoma, rebleeding, pseudoaneurysm, AVF, arterial occlusion, and distal embolization. Complications following intravascular interventions that require surgical repair are listed in Table 54-1. The anatomic distribution of access site complications, showing their rates within the common femoral, superficial femoris, and profunda femoris arteries, is shown in Figure 54-1. As a result of the growing use of groin closure devices, an unusual complication, arterial infection, is being reported much more frequently.[4,5] Acceptable threshold incidences for these complications have been described by the Society for Interventional Radiology (Table 54-2).[6]

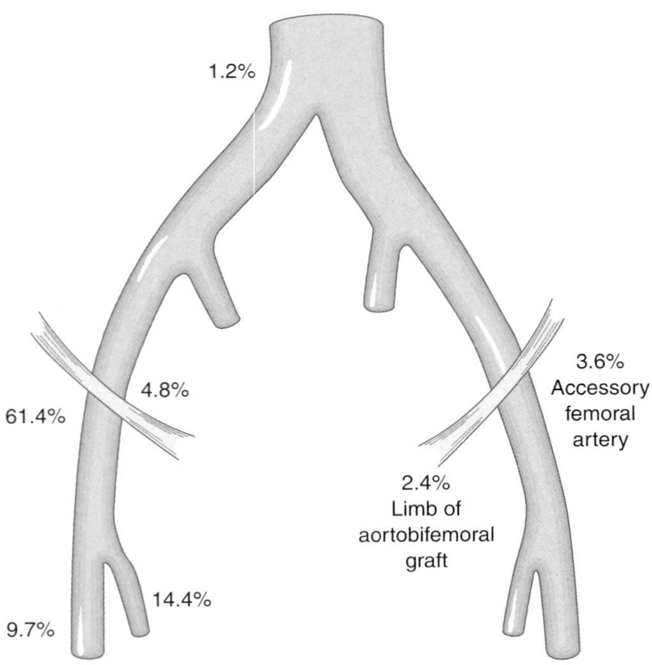

FIGURE 54-1 Distribution of puncture sites associated with groin complications.

Table 54-2 Society for Interventional Radiology's Threshold Complication Rate for Quality Assurance After Groin Puncture and Angiography

COMPLICATION	THRESHOLD (%)
Hematoma	3
Occlusion	0.5
Pseudoaneurysm	0.5
Arteriovenous fistula	0.1
Catheter-induced complications:	
Arterial dissection	2
Subintimal injection	1
Cerebral angiography:	
All neurologic complications	4
Permanent neurologic complications	1
Contrast agent reactions:	
All reactions	3
Major reactions	0.5
Contrast agent–induced renal failure	10

From Singh H, Cardella JF, Cole PE, et al: SCVIR Standards of Practice Committee, Society of Cardiovascular and Interventional Radiology: Quality improvement guidelines for diagnostic arteriography. J Vasc Interv Radiol 13:1-6, 2002.

Groin Hematoma

Groin hematoma may be trivial or potentially life threatening (Figs. 54-2 and 54-3). Sudden-onset massive bleeding can occur (Fig. 54-4). Symptoms vary from mild groin discomfort to severe pain, huge swelling, and potential necrosis of the overlying skin from pressure of the hematoma. Initially ecchymosis is minimal, but it worsens. As the patient ambulates, the ecchymosis extends down the thigh, changing to a more yellowish appearance. The patient with a hematoma that is under observation should be cautioned about these developments. Eventually the discoloration extends into the leg below the knee, a development that does not represent new bleeding. Extent of a hematoma and presence or absence of retroperitoneal extension are best determined on computed tomography (CT) (Fig. 54-5). Rarely, active bleeding can be seen on angiography, which can be associated with hemodynamic instability (Fig. 54-6).

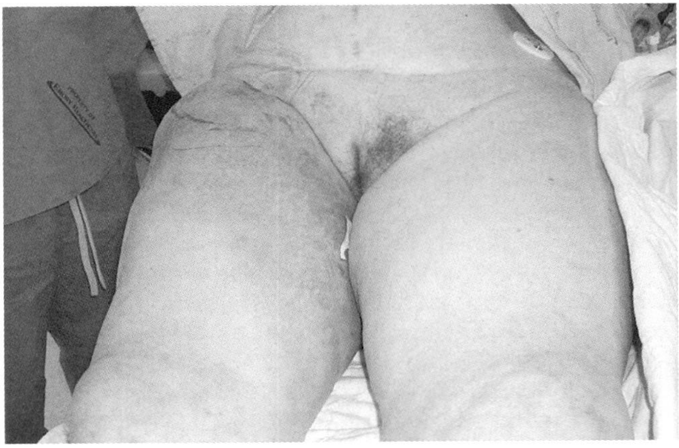

FIGURE 54-2 Thigh enlargement from a large groin hematoma. Note the minimal amount of ecchymosis at this stage.

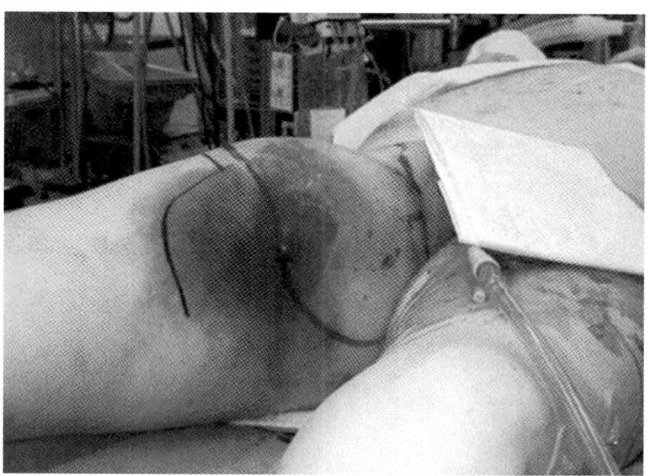

FIGURE 54-3 A tense thigh hematoma that has undergone treatment by observation. There is extensive ecchymosis and early skin compromise.

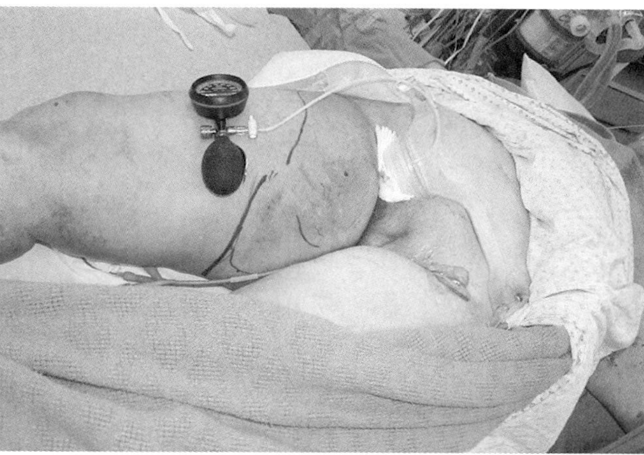

FIGURE 54-4 Massive thigh hematoma is developing despite an external compression device.

Indications for groin exploration and hematoma evacuation are severe pain, progressive enlargement, skin compromise, and evidence of femoral nerve compression (see later discussion of retroperitoneal hematoma). There is a high incidence of wound infection following hematoma evacuation. Wounds should be irrigated with antibiotic solution and drained. It is often not possible to close the underlying adipose tissue after evacuation of a large hematoma.

Arteriovenous Fistula

The most common cause of AVF is inadvertent puncture of the profunda femoris artery and the vein, which crosses between it and the superficial femoral artery. Fistulae are usually asymptomatic and detected clinically from the presence of a palpable thrill in the groin or auscultation of a continuous bruit. The overwhelming majority of AVFs do not give rise to signs of cardiac failure. Duplex ultrasonography confirms the presence of a fistula, showing the characteristic systolic-diastolic flow pattern with arterialization of the venous signal (Fig. 54-7). Kresowik and associates,[7] in a prospective duplex scanning examination of 144 patients undergoing coronary angioplasty, noted a 2.8% incidence of AVF. In contrast, Kent and coworkers,[8] who used the detection of an audible bruit as a trigger for duplex scanning, reported an incidence of 0.3%, although this approach clearly underestimates the true incidence. Fistulae usually do not close spontaneously, so operative repair is indicated when they are detected. Because AVFs

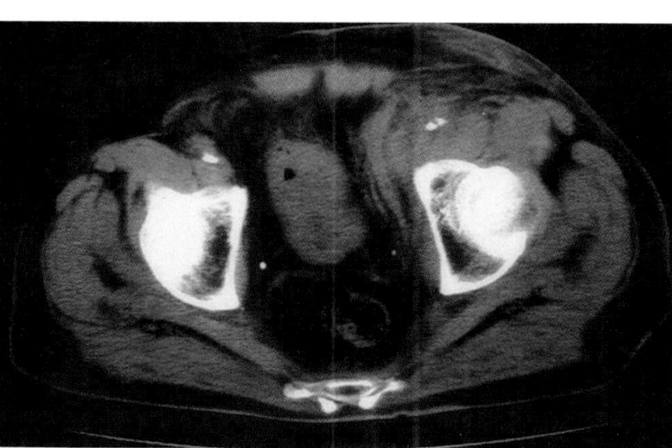

FIGURE 54-5 CT scan shows left groin hematoma around the femoral vessels and in the subcutaneous tissues.

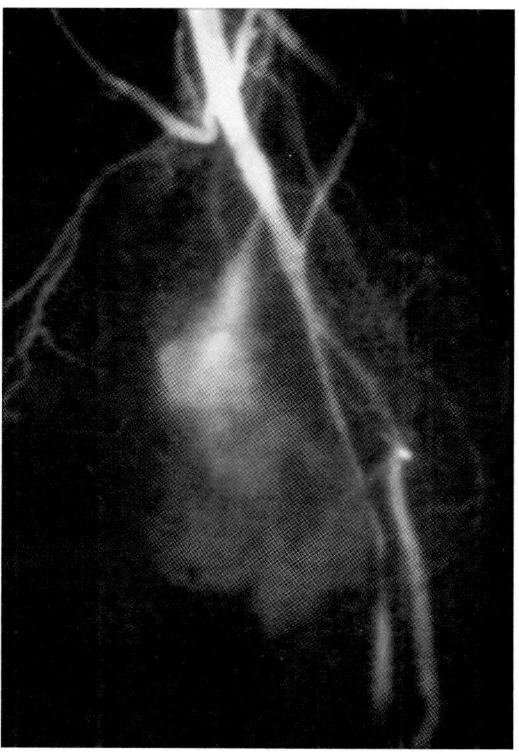

FIGURE 54-6 Rarely seen angiographic appearance of active bleeding from a puncture site in the femoral artery.

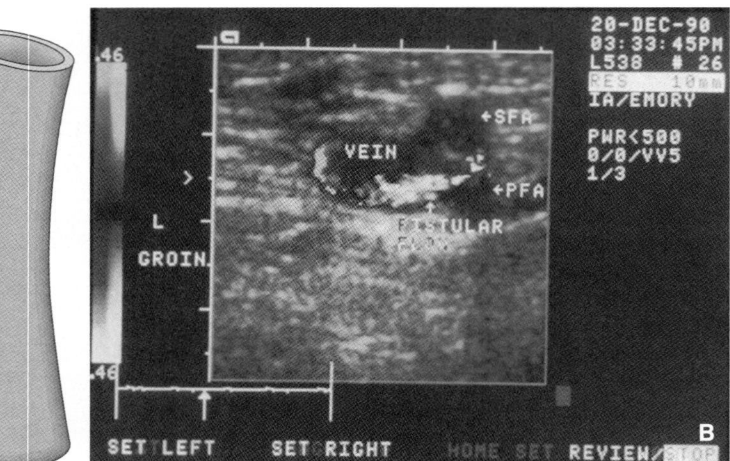

FIGURE 54-7 **A,** Diagram of an arteriovenous fistula. **B,** Typical appearance of fistula on duplex scanning. (See Color Figures in this section.)

progressively enlarge with time, expeditious intervention is warranted.

Risk factors for development of an AVF are female gender, hypertension, left femoral puncture, and periprocedural anticoagulation. The higher incidence associated with left groin puncture may be a function of the fact that the physician stands on the patient's right side so uses the wrong angle of approach, resulting in arterial and venous puncture.[9]

Surgical repair is performed through dissection of the artery until the defect is signified by brisk arterial bleeding. The artery is then controlled by either clamping or digital pressure. The venous bleeding is usually easily controlled with direct pressure until repair can be effected. The defect in the artery is repaired with interrupted polypropylene sutures first, followed by repair of the vein. Usually only one or two horizontal mattress sutures are required in each vessel.[10] In our opinion, there is no current role for the use of covered stents in the management of AVFs or pseudoaneurysms.

Some investigators have reported using stent-grafts to treat femoral AVF. Only those fistulae that are remote from the origin of the profunda femoris artery should be considered for such an approach, so that the orifice of the profunda femoris artery is not covered during stent-graft deployment. Only very short-term data currently exist for this approach. Consequently, it should remain a secondary option in patients in whom surgery would be challenging.[11]

Pseudoaneurysm

Pseudoaneurysm after arterial puncture results from failure of closure of the arteriotomy site, with contained bleeding into the soft tissue around the artery (Fig. 54-8). Blood flows in and out of the artery. Pseudoaneurysms can occur in any vessel that is punctured, although most frequently they develop in the femoral artery. Pseudoaneurysm can be difficult to detect if accompanied by a hematoma. However, the presence of expansile pulsation and tenderness should raise suspicion of pseudoaneurysm and lead to diagnosis with duplex scanning (Fig. 54-9). The duplex examination should note the size and likely source of the pseudoaneurysm. Some lesions are complex and appear to have multiple lobes; others are single, simple cavities. The neck of the pseudoaneurysm should be defined as a single wide neck or a long tortuous narrow neck (the latter is easier to compress).

Femoral pseudoaneurysms occur in approximately 1% of femoral artery punctures. Knight and colleagues[12] noted three independent risk factors for pseudoaneurysm: female gender, interventional procedures (versus diagnostic studies), and lack of a closure device. Women have smaller arteries, which may be more difficult to access and more difficult to compress. Interventions require a larger-diameter sheath than diagnostic studies. Although closure devices may reduce the risk of bleeding complications and pseudoaneurysms, they may be associated with a slight increase in the number of thrombotic and infective complications.

There are now a variety of approaches for treatment of pseudoaneurysm. Surgical repair has been the main therapy.[10,13] The rationale for prompt surgical intervention was the belief that pseudoaneurysms had a low incidence of spontaneous resolution. This concept has been challenged, and complications after groin exploration are not uncommon (Table 54-3). It was believed that an aggressive approach would result in relief of groin pain, prevention of progressive

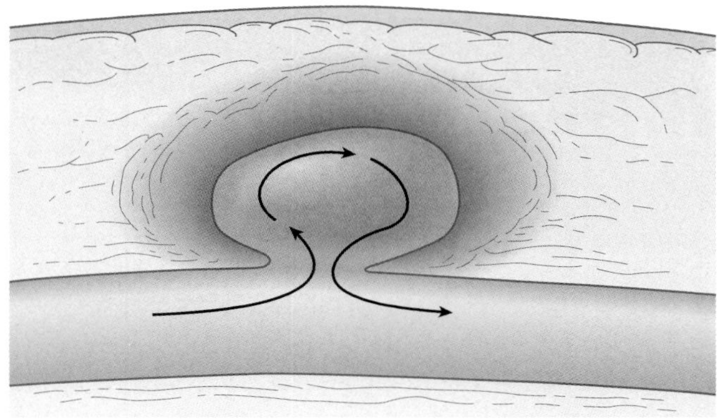

FIGURE 54-8 Diagram of typical femoral pseudoaneurysm.

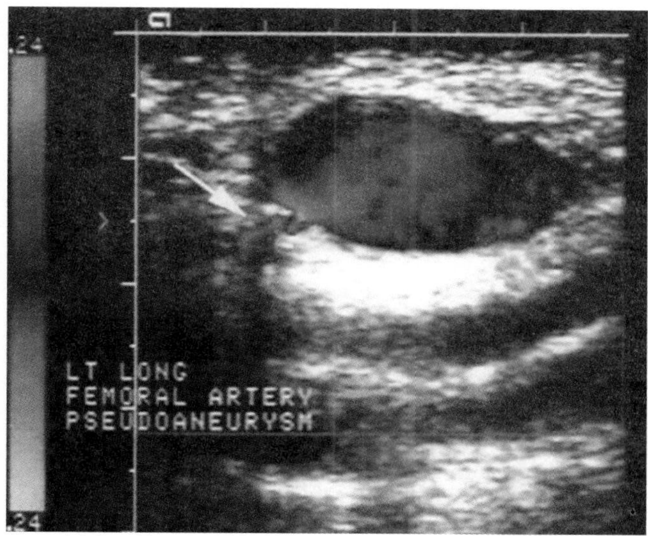

FIGURE 54-9 Duplex scanning examination of pseudoaneurysm showing tract from the femoral artery into the pseudoaneurysm cavity. (See Color Figures in this section.)

enlargement and rupture, skin necrosis, and compression neuropathy.

In this procedure, the femoral artery is exposed through a groin incision. Techniques vary, some surgeons opting to gain full control of the artery before exposing the puncture site. Proximal control can be obtained by opening the external oblique muscle and identifying the femoral artery as it enters the thigh. Rolling the inguinal ligament superiorly or dividing the external oblique fibers permits exposure of the external iliac artery. Gaining proximal control is particularly important with a large hematoma or large pseudoaneurysm. Some surgeons use an alternative approach, knowing that the arterial defect is usually only a 2- to 3-mm puncture site; they opt to enter the pseudoaneurysm directly, controlling the bleeding digitally and oversewing the puncture site with polypropylene. It is extremely important to ensure that the arterial wall is exposed before repair. A common error is to misidentify a hole in the fascia as the arterial defect and to place sutures within the fascia. This error can lead to recurrent pseudoaneurysm formation or persistent bleeding. We do not routinely explore the posterior wall of the artery.

Table 54-3 Complications After Arterial Repair

COMPLICATION	RATE (%)
Aspiration pneumonia	1.05
Neuralgia	5.25
Wound bleeding	7.35
Retroperitoneal bleeding	2.1
Lymph leak	1.05
Limb swelling	1.05
Myocardial infarction	1.05
Septicemia	2.1
Death	3.1

Observation is very reasonable management for small pseudoaneurysms that are not associated with a lot of discomfort. Most small pseudoaneurysms undergo spontaneous thrombosis within 2 to 4 weeks. It is likely, however, that concurrent anticoagulation decreases the likelihood that spontaneous thrombosis will occur.

Ultrasonography-guided compression can also be used to treat a pseudoaneurysm. The neck of the pseudoaneurysm, identified as a high-velocity jet, is localized with ultrasonography, and direct compression is applied with the transducer. Pressure is increased until the jet is obliterated and then continued for 20 minutes. Mean time to thrombosis is 22 minutes of compression, but some cases require up to 120 minutes This procedure may be associated with significant discomfort, so sedation and analgesia are always required. This approach is also very labor intensive because it requires the exclusive services of a technician to apply the pressure.

Ultrasonography-guided thrombin injection is an "off-label" use for thrombin (i.e., a use not approved by the U.S. Food and Drug Administration), but this treatment is very successful in inducing thrombosis of pseudoaneurysm and thereby avoiding surgery.[14,15]

Retroperitoneal Hematoma

Retroperitoneal hematoma (RPH) after groin puncture is an uncommon (0.15% incidence) but morbid complication.[16] It is perhaps the most feared complication of groin puncture. The term *retroperitoneal hematoma* refers to blood contained within the retroperitoneum, but several patterns occur. An *iliopsoas hematoma* occurs when bleeding enters and is confined within the fascia of the iliopsoas muscle. The psoas muscle contains the lumbar plexus, and this pattern of hematoma may be more likely to be associated with compression neuropathy (Fig. 54-10). In contrast, the space between the peritoneum and retroperitoneal structures is potentially vast and can contain huge quantities of blood, which may be very difficult to detect clinically (Fig. 54-11). Hematomas in this location can lead to dramatic elevation and compression of the ipsilateral kidney.

Lower abdominal pain that develops in any patient who has undergone groin puncture should be suspected of being due to RPH. Abdominal examination usually shows tenderness only. Occasionally, palpable fullness may be detected. Thigh pain, numbness, or quadriceps weakness should lead to suspicion of RPH and femoral nerve compression and mandates urgent CT and possible decompression. Postcatheterization anticoagulation and high arterial puncture have been identified as the principal risk factors. Early recognition is essential and should be prompted by a falling hematocrit, lower abdominal pain, or neurologic changes in the lower extremity. There should be a low threshold for performing abdominopelvic CT scans in patients with these findings. This modality is diagnostic (see Fig. 54-9).

Management of RPH must be individualized. Patients with neurologic deficits in the ipsilateral extremity need urgent decompression of the hematoma. Anticoagulation should be stopped or minimized. Evidence of hematoma progression on serial CT scans necessitates surgical evacuation and repair of the arterial puncture site.

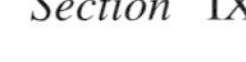

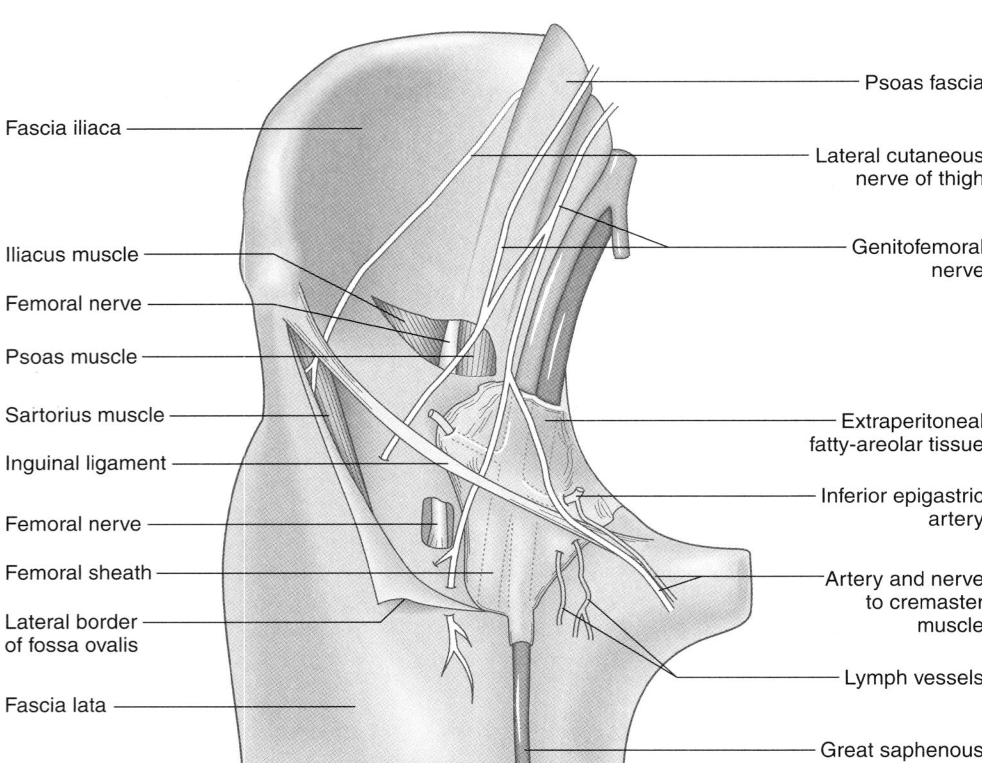

FIGURE 54-10 Anatomy of the retroperitoneal space.

Miscellaneous Complications of Femoral Puncture

Acute thrombosis of the femoral artery occurs infrequently and manifests as typical lower extremity ischemia. It has been associated with insertion of devices, but several series have reported its occurrence with groin closure devices.[17,18] Exploration of the femoral artery usually shows a large posterior plaque that has been elevated with thrombosis of the residual lumen. Femoral endarterectomy patch angioplasty with balloon catheter embolectomy of the external iliac and superficial femoral artery is the most commonly required procedure. Distal embolization is more commonly due to passage of catheters and the intervention performed than to groin puncture alone but can result in trash foot (Fig. 54-12). Rarely, catheter or wire passage can result in arterial perforation and, more rarely, in mycotic pseudoaneurysm (Fig. 54-13). Femoral endarteritis and mycotic femoral artery aneurysm have also been reported as a result of the use of percutaneous closure devices. Fortunately the incidence of this complication is low (0.7%). Obesity and diabetes mellitus raise the risk of this complication. Gram-positive cocci are the most common pathogens.[19-22]

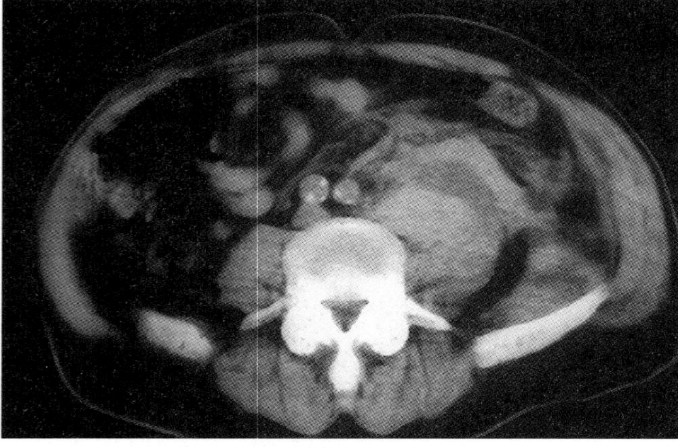

FIGURE 54-11 Hematoma lateral to the psoas major muscle within the retroperitoneal space.

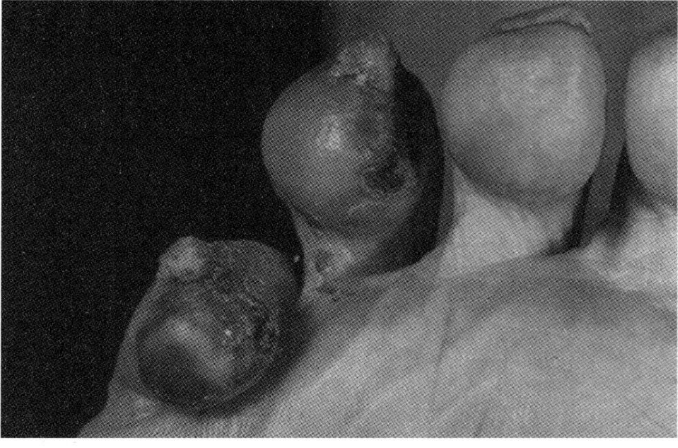

FIGURE 54-12 Toe ischemia (trash foot) as a result of distal embolization.

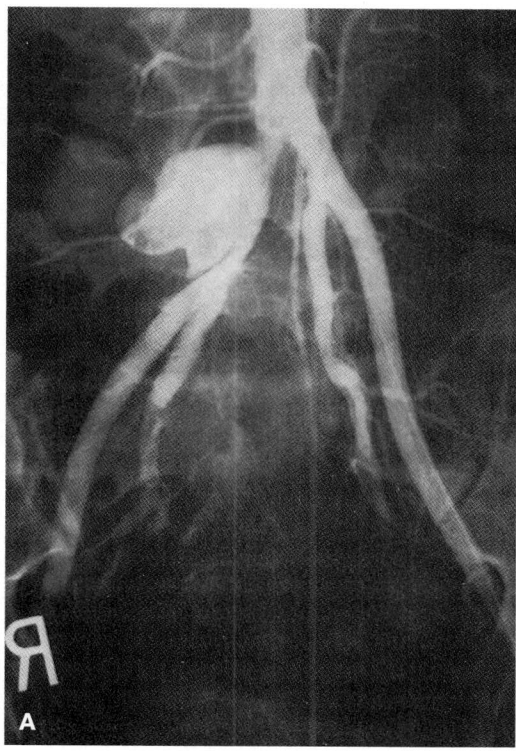

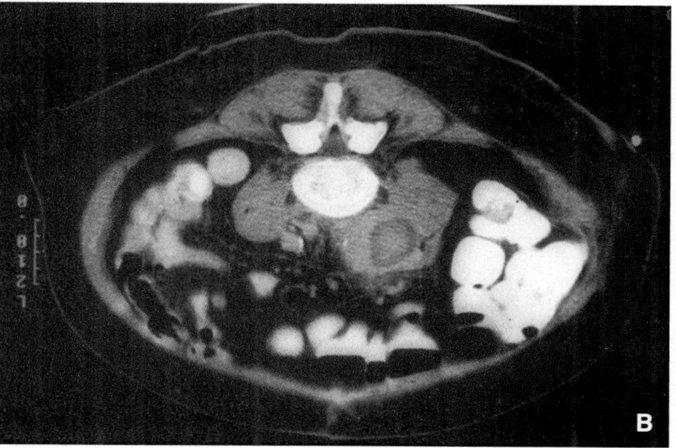

FIGURE 54-13 Mycotic pseudoaneurysm as a result of common iliac perforation and retroperitoneal hematoma.

Axillary and Brachial Artery Puncture

All of the complications previously described for femoral artery puncture have also been described complicating axillary artery and brachial arterial puncture. However, there is also a higher incidence for neuropraxia involving the median nerve or other branches of the brachial plexus. In a prospective study of cardiac catheterization via the femoral artery, damage to the adjacent femoral nerve occurred in 20 of 9585 cases (0.2%) and, although initially disabling, was reported to be almost completely reversible.[20,21] Frequency of injury to nerves of the brachial plexus ranges between 0.4% and 12.7%.[24] There are three potential mechanisms for nerve injury. Hematoma formation is likely the most common. The hematoma forms within a fascial compartment containing the neurovascular bundle, resulting in nerve compression (Fig. 54-14). Direct nerve damage can be caused by the needle, catheter, or introducer sheath. In a minority of patients, nerve damage can be due to nerve ischemia caused by varying degrees of arterial thrombosis.

Time to symptom onset varies from immediate to 3 days after the procedure (mean 12 hours).[22] Pain at the puncture site is the most common symptom of nerve injury. The pain may radiate down the arm. Muscle weakness accompanied by numbness indicates more severe symptoms and mandates immediate intervention. Swelling from a hematoma is inconsistent; even a small strategically placed hematoma can result in nerve compression (Fig. 54-15). The size of a hematoma and presence of ecchymosis does not correlate with either the severity of symptoms or the extent of nerve damage.

Surgical Therapy

The treatment principles consist of (1) awareness of the possibility of nerve compression following axillary or brachial artery puncture, (2) evaluation of the hand after the procedure for pain and sensory or motor dysfunction, and (3) early surgical decompression for any patient who has either more pain than anticipated from arterial puncture or a motor sensory deficit.

The artery is surgically exposed, any hematoma evacuated, and the puncture site repaired with polypropylene. The

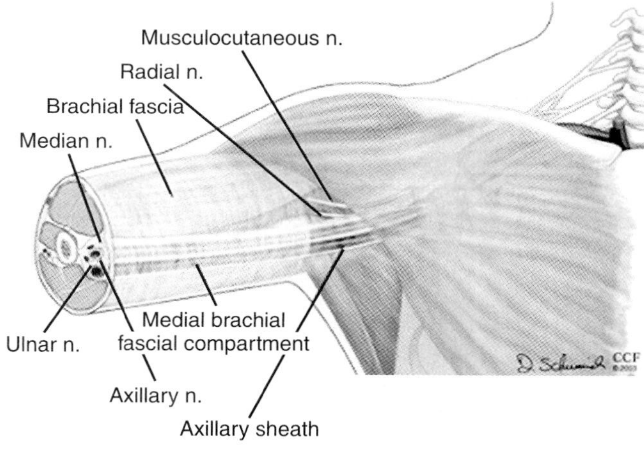

FIGURE 54-14 Anatomy of the brachial and axillary neurovascular bundles.

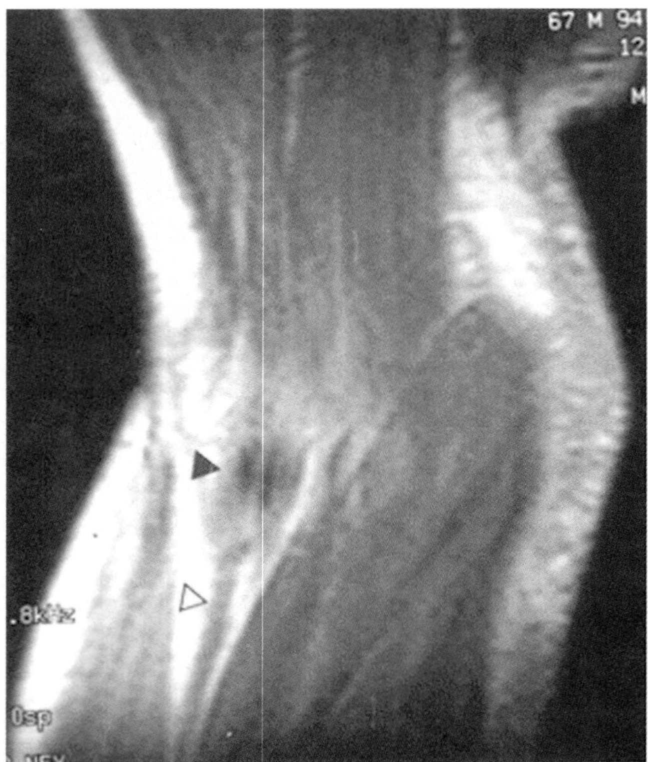

FIGURE 54-15 T1-weighed magnetic resonance image of the forearm. The *black arrow* indicates a small hematoma at the antecubital fossa, and the *white arrow* indicates the radial artery as it crosses the antecubital fossa.

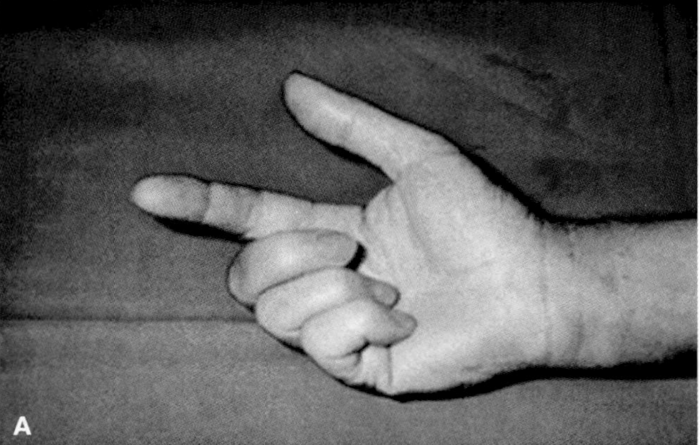

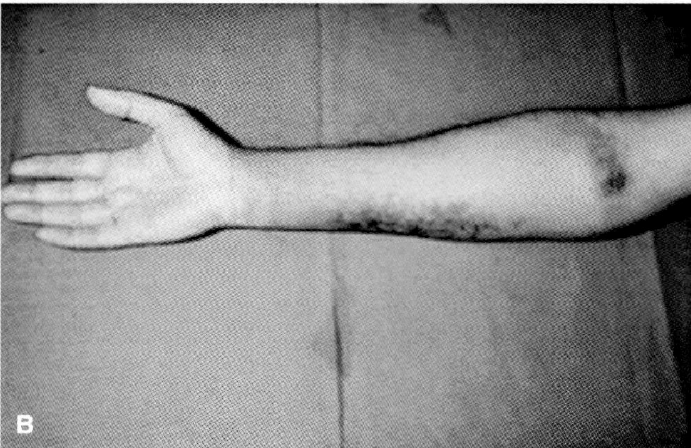

FIGURE 54-16 **A,** Orator's hand posture: The patient has been asked to make a fist. The hand is held in an "orator's hand" posture. This is typical of a high median nerve palsy, in which there is paralysis of the flexor pollicis longus and the flexor digitorum profundus of the second digit, which leads to an inability to pinch together the thumb and index finger. **B,** The extensive bruising of the right forearm was noted 2 days after the angiogram in the same patient.

fascia of the neurovascular bundle is widely opened, and any perineural hematoma is evacuated. The deep fascia of the forearm is not closed; only the subcutaneous fat and skin should be approximated.

The functional outcome from a missed nerve injury is poor, and most patients, although having some improvement, report persistent sensory or motor impairment (Fig. 54-16). A few patients experience disabling pain syndromes.[22]

■ COMPLICATIONS RELATED TO PASSAGE OF CATHETERS AND DEVICES

As a wire, catheter, or device is passed through a blood vessel, it can injure the vessel wall directly. Glidewires, for example, are notorious for entering the vessel wall and continuing to track in an intramural position. Lack of blood return through a catheter should raise suspicion of dissection. Hand injection of 3 to 5 mL of dye will confirm catheter position through the appearance of a spot of dye that fails to wash out. The catheter should be pulled back until blood return is obtained, and a wire used to navigate the true lumen. These types of dissections, when identified, are usually of no clinical consequence.

Microembolization can occur after passage of any endovascular device. It is particularly likely to happen in patients with severe atheromatous disease. Stroke from catheter manipulation in an atheromatous aortic arch is well recognized. Catheters and wires should be kept out of the arch unless access is necessary for the procedure, and manipulation should be minimized.

When wires are passed blindly, they can enter side branches or even the supra-aortic trunks. Even at the femoral access site, wires may deflect either inferiorly, down the superficial femoral or profunda femoris artery, or superiorly, up the circumflex iliac artery. Femoral arterial injury results from attempts at sheath introduction when the wire is misplaced in these positions. Good technique can avoid this complication. Imaging of the wire and control of the wire tip are fundamental. It is possible for inadvertent perforation of organs to occur—for example, renal perforation if the wire enters a renal artery and is not visualized. Wires entering the supra-aortic trunks can lead to cerebrovascular accident.

■ INTERVENTION-SPECIFIC COMPLICATIONS

Intervention-specific complications can broadly be classified as infection, bleeding, rupture, dissection, embolization, occlusion, and restenosis. These complications can occur with essentially any intervention, but the frequency and significance of each varies according to the type of intervention being performed.

Device Infection

Infection of endovascular devices has generally been rare. Given the huge number of coronary procedures performed, including stent implantation, reports on infections of these devices are remarkably uncommon. The use of antibiotic prophylaxis has been sporadic and its necessity questioned. However, the advent of stent-grafting has clearly been associated with increasing reports of device infection. Two mechanisms account for this complication: infection at the time of implantation and "seeding" of an implanted graft via bacteremia. Unlike aortic graft infections, which are indolent, slowly progressive, and present years after implantation, infections of endografts are quickly progressive, resulting in rapid conformational changes and rupture of the aneurysm. The patient shows all the classic signs of sepsis, and the device must be removed, with aortic reconstruction via the standard techniques for aortic graft infection. Fiorani and colleagues[23] reported on endovascular graft infections in an international study. They concluded that endograft infection occurs in 0.45% of cases; 65% of affected patients presented with abdominal infection, groin abscess, or septic embolization. The remaining 35% had vague symptoms only. Overall mortality rate was 27.4%. *Staphylococcus aureus* was the offending organism in 54.5% of cases.

There have also been increasing reports of infection in bare stents. This complication is particularly likely to occur if stents are placed in patients in whom catheters are placed for long times (such as for lysis).[24] Stent infection results in septic arteritis within the wall of the host artery, pseudoaneurysm formation, and rupture (Fig. 54-17). Seeding of stents also appears to occur. Usually, arterial resection and reconstruction with autogenous tissue is necessary.[25]

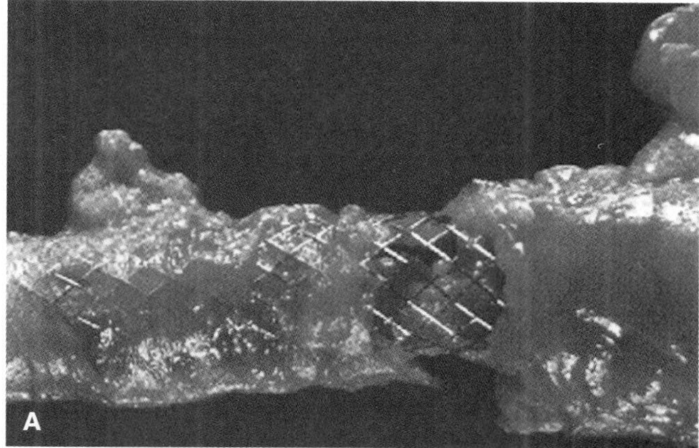

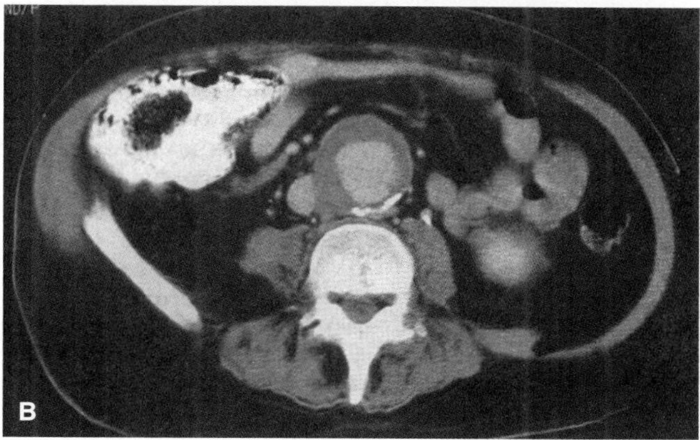

FIGURE 54-17 Mycotic aortic aneurysm complicating infection of an iliac Wallstent, which occurred after prolonged lysis followed by stent placement. Infection in the artery has resulted in destruction of the iliac artery wall and extension into the aorta. (From Hoffman AI, Murphy PT: Septic arteritis causing iliac artery rupture and aneurysmal transformation of the distal aorta after iliac artery stent placement J Vasc Interv Radiol 8:215-219, 1997.)

Fibrinolysis

Lytic agents activate plasminogen to form plasmin, which breaks fibrin into fibrin degradation products, resulting in clot lysis. In appropriately selected patient groups, complications are minor and most commonly relate to local bleeding at the site of catheter entry—hematoma, retroperitoneal bleeding, and pseudoaneurysm. In the majority of cases, these complications may be controlled by local application of pressure. There should be a high index of suspicion of retroperitoneal hematoma in any patient receiving lytic therapy who demonstrates a drop in hematocrit value and no obvious source of blood loss. The suspicion can be easily confirmed with an abdominal CT scan. Development of an RPH usually requires discontinuation of therapy. Bleeding from an anastomosis is usually a problem only in recently implanted or infected grafts. Distal embolization is, in theory, more likely during graft lysis than during lysis of native vessels because of the more extensive thrombus formation in grafts. Transgraft bleeding is a concern only in recently placed polyester (Dacron) grafts. Cerebrovascular accident is an uncommon, but dreaded, complication of lytic therapy. No specific factors raise this risk, other than a history of cerebrovascular accident. History of a cerebrovascular accident within the previous 2 months is an absolute contraindication to lytic therapy. Fibrinolytic therapy should not be used in patients with sustained systolic pressures higher than 200 mm Hg, or diastolic pressures greater than 110 mm Hg.

Aortic Stent-Grafts

Numerous complications have been described that are relatively specific to aortic stent-grafting. Iliac artery dissection and rupture can occur with insertion of a stent-graft. This is particularly likely in patients with small, calcified iliac arteries, especially those with intercurrent occlusive disease. Growing awareness of this problem has led to the development of alternative approaches, such as insertion of an iliac conduit using a retroperitoneal approach, to avoid such difficult iliac arteries. Misplacement of a stent-graft can result in coverage of the renal arteries by the device, leading to development of renal failure. Occlusion of the inferior mesenteric artery or hypogastric arteries can result in colonic ischemia. Embolization or coverage of the internal iliac arteries results in buttock claudication in 30%

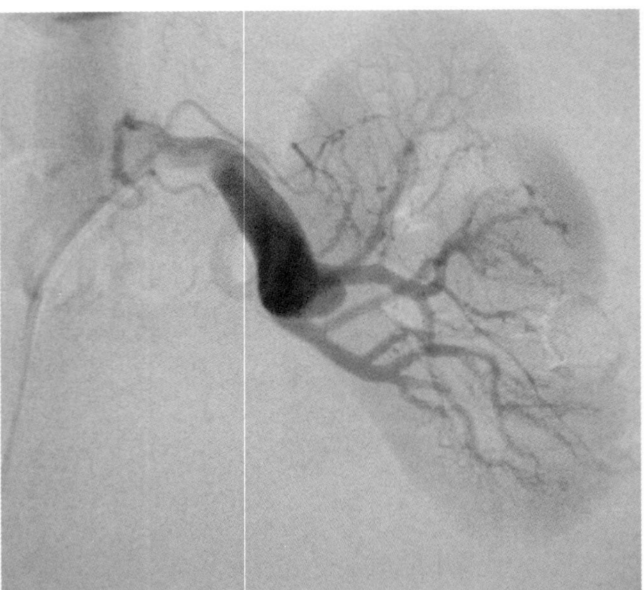

FIGURE 54-18 Left renal artery dissection and pseudoaneurysm formation (*arrow*).

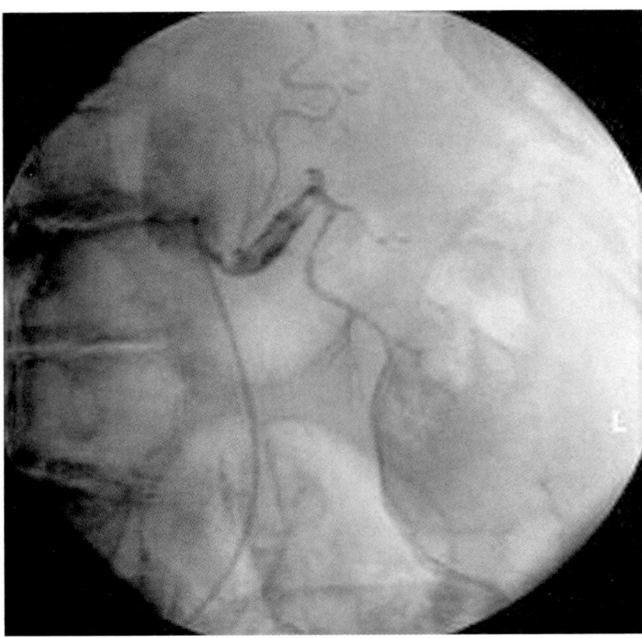

FIGURE 54-19 Thrombosis of left renal artery following percutaneous transluminal angiography. The thrombus is seen extending into the distal main renal artery.

of cases. Pelvic ischemia syndromes such as cauda equina ischemia and colon ischemia can also occur.

The number of reports of infection occurring in aortic stent-grafts has been growing. This complication is most commonly due to hematogenous seeding and leads to rapidly progressive infection, presumably because of the favorable environment of a stent-graft surrounded by thrombus. Pain, rapid aneurysm expansion, and rupture are the usual clinical sequence.

Consequences and complications of endoleaks are beyond the scope of this chapter.

Renal Angioplasty and Stenting

Renal angioplasty is one of the more difficult endovascular procedures. Gaining atraumatic access to the renal artery and establishing a stable platform for intervention are the keys to avoiding complications. Traumatic crossing of a renal stenosis can result in dissection of the renal artery, a condition that must be recognized and usually is successfully treated with renal stenting (Fig. 54-18). Failure to recognize this complication can result in renal artery thrombosis (Fig. 54-19). Renal artery occlusion threatens the viability of the kidney and mandates immediate intervention, which involves thrombolysis, stenting, and, occasionally, surgical bypass grafting.

During renal angioplasty, the tip of the guidewire should always be visible in the peripheral image field. Inadvertent advancement of the wire can result in perforation of the renal parenchyma and perinephric or subcapsular hematoma. Most such hematomas can be managed by anticoagulation reversal and observation, although branch renal vessel embolization may be required.

Microembolization may account for the deterioration in renal function that occurs in some patients after renal stenting. This is usually implied rather than documented, although cholesterol embolization has been documented on renal biopsy.

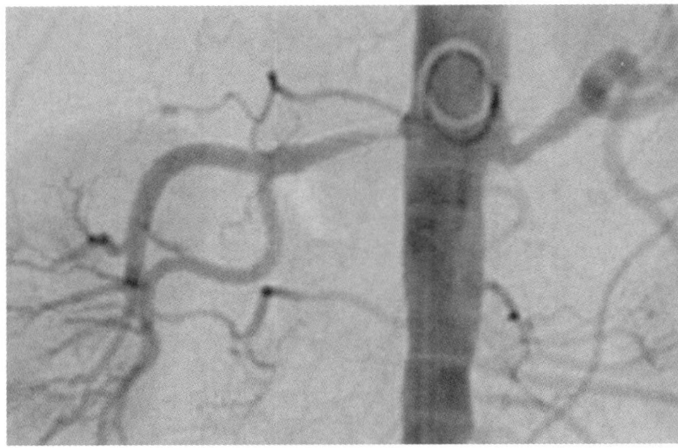

FIGURE 54-20 Restenosis of right renal stent 3 months after implantation.

Restenosis remains the Achilles' heel of renal stenting, with rates as high as 20% being reported (Fig. 54-20). This complication can result in return of hypertension or deterioration in renal function. A second angioplasty is required; surgical bypass can be significantly more complicated if stents extend well beyond the ostia of the renal arteries.

Iliac Angioplasty and Stenting

The most common problem encountered in iliac angioplasty is subintimal passage of the guidewire, which tracks up into the aortic wall. This complication is prevented if one

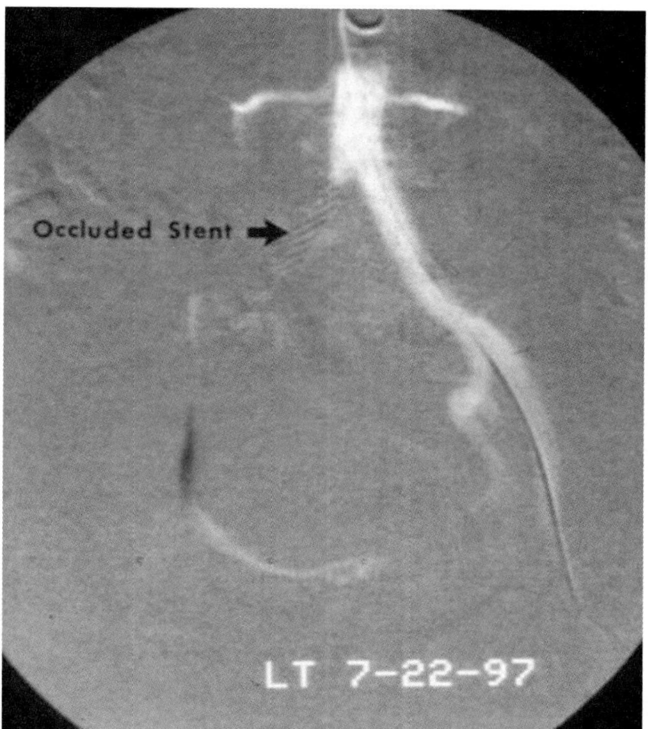

FIGURE 54-21 Occlusion of stent in right common iliac artery.

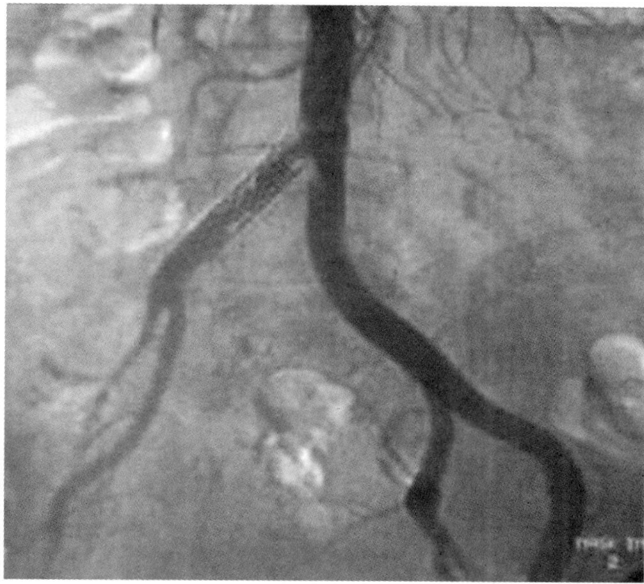

FIGURE 54-22 Thrombus has formed inside the right common iliac stent.

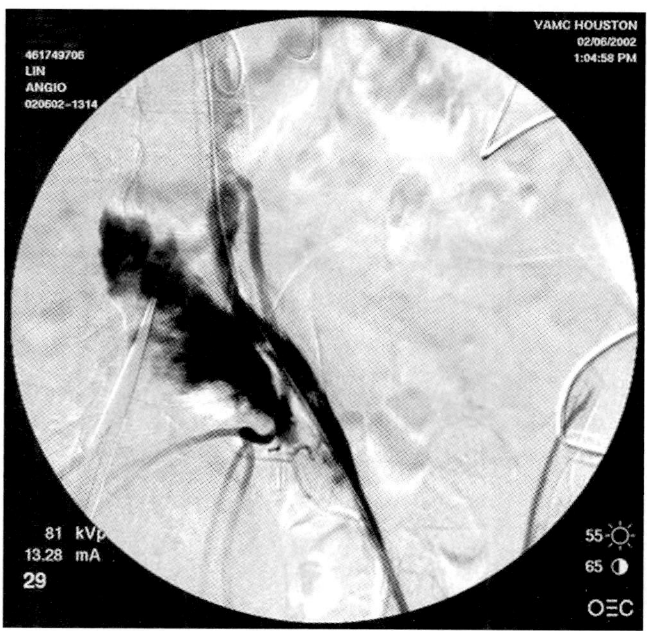

FIGURE 54-23 Iliac rupture after percutaneous transluminal angiography resulting in dye extravasation.

observes the movement of the wire as it crosses the lesion. Subintimal passage of the wire should be suspected with failure to aspirate blood from the catheter and hand injection of 2 to 3 mL of dye, which forms a spot in the aortic wall and fails to wash out. The catheter and wire are retrieved and the lesions re-crossed. Failure to recognize the subintimal location of a guidewire can lead to catastrophic problems if devices are then advanced over the wire.

Restenosis occurs in 10% to 20% of cases and can lead to complete stent occlusion (Fig. 54-21). Embolization is uncommon, but the risk is increased in recanalization of total occlusions. It can also occur as a result of thrombus formation on the implanted stent (Fig. 54-22).

Iliac rupture is remarkably uncommon in iliac angioplasty and stenting but is a particular risk in small calcified iliac arteries, especially the external iliac artery (Fig. 54-23). In such high-risk cases, a stent-graft (e.g., Viabahn, Wallgraft) should be immediately available to seal a rupture.

■ VENOUS INTERVENTIONS

Venous angioplasty and stenting is performed for central venous stenoses such as occur with dialysis access or in the left common iliac vein in May-Thurner syndrome. Venous lesions, especially those associated with dialysis access, are notoriously difficult to dilate, often require very high balloon pressures (up to 30 atmospheres), and can result in venous rupture. Most of the venous ruptures are self-limiting and seal either spontaneously or with a few minutes of balloon tamponade.

Stent deployment in central veins is associated with the highest incidence of device migration, because of the highly compliant nature of the veins and their ability to change dramatically in diameter. Careful measurement, oversizing of the stent in relation to vessel diameter, and ensuring a secure proximal anchor for the stent are important. Migrated Wallstents can usually be retrieved with a snare (Gooseneck or EN-snare); since they will compress when pulled into a sheath, they usually can be removed percutaneously.[26] Retrieval of nitinol of balloon-expanded stents usually requires a surgical cutdown.[27]

Table 54-4 Society for Interventional Radiology's Threshold Complication Rate for Use of Inferior Vena Cava (IVC) Filters

COMPLICATION	REPORTED RATE (%)	THRESHOLD (%)
Death	0.12	<1
Recurrent pulmonary embolism	0.5-6	5
IVC occlusion	2.0-30.0	10
Filter embolization	2.0-5.0	2

Grassi LJ, et al: Quality improvement guidelines for percutaneous permanent inferior vena cava filter placement for the prevention of pulmonary embolism. J Vasc Interv Radiol 12:137-141, 2001.

Table 54-5 Reported Complications of Inferior Vena Cava (IVC) Filter Placement

COMPLICATION	REPORTED RATE (%)
IVC penetration	0-41
Migration	0-18
Fracture	2-10
Access site thrombosis:	
All	0-25
Occlusive	3-10
Insertion problems	5-50

IVC filters are widely used. Specific complications of their use are IVC occlusion, vena caval penetration, filter migration, and filter maldeployment (Tables 54-4 and 54-5). Wire prolapse is unique to the bird-nest filter and is usually asymptomatic. Guidewire entrapment, usually with J-wires, is another complication unique to IVC filters. Care must be taken in advancing and retrieving guidewires in the venous system when IVC filters are present.[28]

■ REFERENCES

1. Nasser TK, Mohler ER 3rd, Wilensky RL, Hathaway DR: Peripheral vascular complications following coronary interventional procedures. Clin Cardiol 18:609-614, 1995.
2. Zahn R, Thoma S, Fromm E, et al: Pseudoaneurysm after cardiac catheterization: Therapeutic interventions and their sequelae: Experience in 86 patients. Cathet Cardiovasc Diagn 40:9-15, 1997.
3. Fransson SG, Nylander E: Vascular injury following cardiac catheterization, coronary angiography, and coronary angioplasty. Eur Heart J 15:232-235, 1994.
4. Dangas G, Mehran R, Kokolis S, et al: Vascular complications after percutaneous coronary interventions following hemostasis with manual compression versus arteriotomy closure devices. J Am Coll Cardiol 38:638-641, 2001.
5. Toursarkissian B, Mejia A, Smilanich RP, et al: Changing patterns of access site complications with the use of percutaneous closure devices. Vasc Surg 35:203-206, 2001.
6. Singh H, Cardella JF, Cole PE, et al; SCVIR Standards of Practice Committee, Society of Cardiovascular and Interventional Radiology: Quality improvement guidelines for diagnostic arteriography. J Vasc Interv Radiol 13:1-6, 2002.
7. Kresowik TF, Khoury BV, Miller BV, et al: A prospective study of the incidence and natural history of femoral vascular complications after percutaneous transluminal coronary angioplasty. J Vasc Surg 13:328-335, 1991.
8. Kent KC, McArdle B, Kennedy DS, et al: A prospective study of the clinical outcome of femoral artery pseudoaneurysms and arteriovenous fistulas induced by arterial puncture. J Vasc Surg 17:125-133, 1993.
9. Perings SM, Kelm M, Jax T, Strauer BE: A prospective study on the incidence and risk factors of arteriovenous fistulae following transfemoral cardiac catheterization. Int J Cardiol 88:223-228, 2003.
10. Lumsden AB, Miller JM, Kosinski AS, et al: A prospective evaluation of surgically treated groin complications following percutaneous cardiac procedures. Am Surg 60:132-137, 1994.
11. Baltacioglu F, Cimsit NC, Cil B, et al: Endovasculr stent-graft applications in iatrogenic vascular injuries. Cardiovasc Intervent Radiol 26:434-439, 2003.
12. Knight CG, Healy DA, Thomas RL: Femoral artery pseudoaneurysms: Risk factors, prevalence and treatment options. Ann Vasc Surg 17:503-508, 2003.
13. Perler BA: Surgical treatment of femoral pseudoaneurysm following cardiac catheterization. Cardiovasc Surg 1:118-121, 1993.
14. Hughes MJ, McCall JM, Nott DM, Padley SP: Treatment of iatrogenic femoral artery pseudoaneurysms using ultrasound-guided injection of thrombin. Clin Radiol 55:749-751, 2000.
15. Lennox AF, Delis KT, Szendro G, et al: Duplex-guided thrombin injection for iatrogenic femoral artery pseudoaneurysm is effective even in anticoagulated patients. Br J Surg 87:796-801, 2000.
16. Sreeram S, Lumsden AB, Miller JS, et al: Retroperitoneal hematoma following femoral arterial catheterization: A serious and often fatal complication. Am Surg 59:94-98, 1993.
17. Wagner SC, Gonsalves CF, Eschelman DJ, et al: Complications of a percutaneous suture-mediated closure device versus manual compression for arteriotomy closure: A case controlled study. J Vasc Interv Radiol 14:735-745, 2003.
18. Mackrell PJ, Kalbaugh CA, Langan EM, et al: Can the Perclose suture-mediated closure system be safely used in patients undergoing diagnostic and therapeutic angiography to treat lower extremity ischemia? J Vasc Surg 38:1305-1308, 2003.
19. Whitton Hollis H, Rehring TF: Femoral endarteritis associated with percutaneous suture closure: New technology, challenging complications. J Vasc Surg 38:83-87, 2003.
20. Kent KC, Moscucci M, Gallagher S, et al: Neuropathy after cardiac catherization: Incidence, clinical patterns, long term outcome. J Vasc Surg 19:1008-1014, 1994.
21. Tsao BE, Wilbourn AJ: The medial brachial fascial compartment syndrome following axillary arteriography. Neurology 61:1037-1041, 2003.
22. Kennedy AM, Grocott M, Schwartz MS, et al: Median nerve injury: An underrecognised complication of brachial artery cardiac catheterisation? J Neurol Neurosurg Psychiatry 63:542-546, 1997.
23. Fiorani P, Speziale F, Calisti A, et al: Endovascular graft infection: Preliminary results of an international inquiry. J Endovasc Ther 10:919-927, 2003.
24. Hoffman AI, Murphy PT: Septic arteritis causing iliac artery rupture and aneurysmal transformation of the distal aorta after iliac artery stent placement. J Vasc Interv Radiol 8:215-219, 1997.
25. Walton KB, Hudenko K, D'Ayala M, Toursarkissian B: Aneurysmal degeneration of the superficial femoral artery following stenting: An unusual infectious complication. Ann Vasc Surg 17: 445-448, 2003.
26. Ashar RM, Huettl EA, Halligan R: Percutaneous retrieval of a Wallstent from the pulmonary artery following stent migration from the iliac vein. J Intervent Cardiol 15:101-106, 2002.
27. Feghaly EL, Soula P, Chaiban F, et al: Endovascular retrieval of two migrated venous stents by means of balloon catheters. J Vasc Surg 28:541-546, 1998.
28. Stavropoulos SW, Itkin M, Treatola SO: In vitro study of guidewire entrapment in currently available inferior vena caval filter. J Vasc Interv Radiol 14:905-910, 2003.

Section X

COMPLICATIONS OF VASCULAR SURGERY AND ISCHEMIA: PREVENTION AND MANAGEMENT

BRUCE A. PERLER, MD

Chapter 55

Overview

BRUCE A. PERLER, MD

■ CARDIAC COMPLICATIONS: SCREENING AND PREVENTION (Chapter 56)

Prevalence

It is well accepted that there is a high prevalence of coronary artery disease among patients with significant peripheral arterial occlusive disease. It has been suggested that the vascular surgeon should assume that all patients undergoing peripheral vascular intervention have at least subclinical coronary atherosclerosis. It is estimated that approximately 50,000 non–cardiac surgical patients experience a perioperative myocardial infarction (MI) annually, and more than 50% of the 40,000 postoperative deaths that occur each year in the United States are secondary to transmural MI.[1,2] Cardiac disease continues to represent a major cause of morbidity and is one of the leading causes of mortality following vascular surgical procedures. Although the incidence of fatal MI has declined substantially in recent years, it is reported that myocardial ischemia occurs in 20% to 40% of vascular surgical patients, and all forms of cardiac adverse events occur in roughly 50%.[3-5] In addition, the severity of underlying coronary artery disease is an important consideration in electing percutaneous versus open surgical revascularization procedures.

Screening

There is no consensus on how aggressive one should be in performing preoperative cardiac evaluation in vascular surgical patients for several reasons. First, although coronary disease continues to represent a significant cause of perioperative morbidity, cardiac mortality rates have declined significantly in recent years among patients undergoing a variety of vascular surgical procedures. Since the 1990s, the rate of perioperative MI has ranged from 0% to 7% (mean 2.2%) and fatal MI has ranged from 0% to 5% (mean 1.4%) after open aortic surgery in several published series. Among patients undergoing infrainguinal bypass surgery, the reported rates of MI and fatal MI have ranged from 1.6% to 11% (mean 4%) and 0% to 4.5% (mean 1.8%). Similarly, although carotid artery disease is a sensitive marker for coronary artery disease, perioperative cardiac morbidity is low in reported series. Since 1990, the rates of perioperative MI and fatal MI have ranged from 0% to 4.2% (mean 1%) and 0% to 1.9% (mean 0.4%).

Second, evidence suggests that acute coronary syndromes may not occur in association with the most severe coronary atherosclerotic lesions. Rather, it seems that plaque erosion and rupture secondary to inflammation around the plaque may be an important factor in producing cardiac complications. Cardiac screening examinations typically identify hemodynamically significant lesions, however, which may not be vulnerable to rupture and symptomatic events.

In addition, analysis of several series failed to show a consistent benefit of aggressive preoperative coronary disease screening. Most authors would agree that cardiac risk stratification is imprecise at best. It seems that the reduction of cardiac morbidity after vascular surgical procedures among patients who undergo aggressive preoperative screening may be balanced by the morbidity associated with coronary angiography, percutaneous coronary revascularization procedures, and coronary artery bypass surgery. Also, occasionally patients have deferred undergoing the vascular surgical procedure after the coronary intervention.

Finally, it has been argued that the purported benefit of successful coronary revascularization in improving long-term survival among patients with severe coronary disease in general may not apply to the patient population with severe peripheral arterial occlusive disease. Until ongoing randomized trials are completed, it is reasonable to select patients for coronary revascularization based on their underlying symptomatic history, regardless of the need for peripheral vascular surgical intervention.[6] Widespread routine screening does not seem justified, however, on a cost efficacy basis.

Prevention

The reduction in major cardiac morbidity among vascular surgical patients in recent years reflects significant improvement in perioperative medical management. A preponderance of evidence indicates that perioperative beta blockade is associated with a significant reduction in acute and long-term cardiac mortality in vascular surgical patients. Specifically the incidence of perioperative ischemic complications, including MI, cardiac death, and overall operative mortality, is reduced among patients treated with beta blockers.[7] There is no compelling evidence, however, that the prophylactic administration of nitroglycerin intraoperatively significantly reduces the incidence of perioperative cardiac events. Likewise, it is difficult to prove a clear benefit for many other perioperative medical modalities among patients undergoing major vascular reconstructive surgery. Numerous investigations have failed to offer compelling evidence that pulmonary artery catheter–based monitoring of the patient's volume status reduces perioperative morbidity.

■ RESPIRATORY COMPLICATIONS IN VASCULAR SURGERY (Chapter 57)

Postoperative respiratory complications are a major cause of perioperative morbidity and mortality in vascular surgical patients. The most common postoperative complications include atelectasis, bronchospasm, pharmacologically induced hypoventilation, aspiration, pneumonia, pulmonary edema, and acute respiratory distress syndrome (ARDS) and respiratory failure. Nosocomial pneumonia is the leading cause of death due to hospital-acquired infections, with mortality rates ranging from 20% to 50%.[8,9] Gram-negative bacteria are responsible for approximately 60% of nosocomial pneumonias.[8] Although most cases of nosocomial pneumonia occur outside of the intensive care unit, the highest risk is in patients on mechanical ventilation.

Minimizing the incidence of respiratory complications in elderly vascular surgical patients begins in the preoperative period by identifying key risk factors, including patient-related and procedure-related variables. The most important patient-related risk factors include preexisting chronic lung disease, asthma, tobacco use, obesity, upper respiratory tract infection, metabolic derangements, and overall health status. In addition to addressing active respiratory infection and maximizing the patient's overall health status before elective vascular surgery, smoking cessation is one important potentially modifiable risk factor. Active smoking is associated with a threefold increased risk of postoperative respiratory complications.[10-12] It has been found that patients who have quit smoking recently experience an increased rate of postoperative respiratory complications compared with active smokers, although the reason for this seemingly paradoxical effect is not clear. Nevertheless, smoking cessation should occur at least 1 to 2 months before surgery to be clinically beneficial.

Procedural variables associated with an increased incidence of postoperative respiratory complications include upper abdominal or thoracic surgical site, duration of surgery longer than 3 hours, and type of anesthesia and type of neuromuscular blockade. There is ongoing controversy with respect to the impact of anesthetic method on the incidence of postoperative respiratory complications. A meta-analysis of 141 trials including nearly 10,000 patients identified a reduced incidence of pulmonary complications among patients receiving epidural or spinal anesthesia compared with patients receiving general anesthesia.[13] In a study from the Johns Hopkins Hospital, 168 patients undergoing abdominal aortic surgery were randomized to receive either thoracic epidural anesthesia combined with light general anesthesia or general anesthesia alone intraoperatively and either intravenous or epidural patient-controlled analgesia postoperatively. Epidural patient-controlled analgesia correlated with significantly shorter time to extubation, although the treatment groups experienced comparable times to intensive care unit discharge and comparable postoperative pain scores.[14]

Preoperative pulmonary function testing historically has been an important part of preoperative pulmonary risk assessment, although more recent studies have challenged its role in risk stratification. Pulmonary function testing can be useful in identifying patients for whom elective vascular surgery may be deferred or an endovascular approach selected or patients requiring open abdominal or thoracic vascular reconstruction for whom more intensive preoperative pulmonary management is indicated. In an era of increasing cost consciousness, preoperative chest x-rays are of minimal value. In a meta-analysis including more than 14,000 chest x-rays, in only 140 cases were unexpected findings identified, and in only 14 cases was management influenced by the findings.[15]

Acute respiratory failure is a general term encompassing diverse pulmonary pathologic conditions, and it implies significant ventilation, perfusion, or gas exchange abnormalities. Prevention of atelectasis, minimizing the period of postoperative mechanical ventilation, strict glucose control, and prevention of bacterial infection are some of the most important means of minimizing the development of postoperative respiratory complications. Acute respiratory failure may be hypoxic, hypercapnic, or both in etiology. The appropriate management of respiratory failure includes ruling out a mechanical cause, such as pneumothorax, hemothorax, obstructed endotracheal tube, occluded airway, or ascites, as the first step; oxygen delivery should be maximized; and oxygen consumption should be reduced by identifying and treating infection, by providing appropriate sedation, and by optimizing carbon dioxide removal. Failure to correct the underlying pathologic process adequately and persistence of an inflammatory state result in the development of ARDS. Predisposing factors for the development of ARDS include sepsis, blood transfusions, pneumonia, pulmonary contusion, cardiopulmonary bypass, pancreatitis, and other conditions. Currently, newer methods of ventilation using low tidal volumes and limiting plateau pressure may be protective to the lung and may minimize additional pulmonary injury.

■ RENAL COMPLICATIONS (Chapter 58)

Operative mortality among patients undergoing aortic surgery has declined significantly in recent decades. One important reason for this decline has been a reduced incidence of postoperative renal dysfunction. Although the incidence of postoperative renal failure seems to have declined since the 1990s, it continues to be a significant potential complication of patients undergoing aortic reconstruction, especially among patients who present with a ruptured aortic aneurysm. Postoperative renal failure continues to be associated with high operative mortality. An understanding of normal renal physiology and mechanisms of perturbation are paramount to limiting the development of this morbidity.

Aortic reconstructive surgery is associated with significant volume shifts, resulting from local tissue trauma related to operative dissection, hemodynamic changes secondary to aortic clamping and unclamping, and operative blood loss. In total, there is a decrease in intravascular volume and activation of neuroendocrine mechanisms that reduce the excretion of sodium and water by the kidneys. In addition, there is an accumulation of fluid in the extracellular "third space" as a result of shifts in the tissue acid-base balance secondary to temporary tissue ischemia, the impact of blood loss, the reduction in cardiac output perioperatively, and the systemic effects of circulating stress hormones. Recognition of this pathophysiologic process and aggressive fluid resuscitation using balanced salt solutions in the perioperative period reduce the likelihood of renal functional deterioration.[16] It has been shown that mobilization of third-space fluid does not occur for 2 to 5 days after surgery in most cases, and this must be considered in directing postoperative fluid management.

Alterations in renal function after aortic surgery may range from mild natriuresis to acute renal failure requiring dialysis, and there are several potential causes. Renal dysfunction usually is manifested by oliguria or a rise in the serum creatinine level. Prerenal factors are the most common cause of oliguria in the early postoperative period, owing to either intravascular volume depletion or cardiac dysfunction. Renal artery occlusive disease, or ischemic nephropathy, may be a factor. Postrenal factors are the least common cause of oliguria and include urethral, ureteral, or urinary catheter obstruction.

Renal parenchymal injury is a more common cause of postoperative renal dysfunction and is most likely to result in permanent renal functional compromise. *Acute tubular necrosis* refers to all parenchymal causes of acute renal failure. The most common causes of acute tubular necrosis in the vascular surgical patient include ischemic injury secondary to shock, renal artery occlusion, atheroembolism, multisystem failure, and toxic injury, most often due to contrast dye injury or myoglobinuria. The incidence of ischemic renal injury is greater after surprarenal compared with infrarenal aortic clamping and is greatest after repair of thoracoabdominal aortic aneurysms. Recovery of renal function in this setting depends on patient age and the duration of renal ischemia. Atheroembolism increasingly is being recognized as an important cause of renal dysfunction, either due to manual manipulation and clamping of the atherosclerotic aorta or in association with catheter-based procedures, but it also can occur spontaneously. Worsening renal function in a patient with known atherosclerotic disease or a patient using an angiotensin-converting enzyme inhibitor should raise the suspicion of ischemic nephropathy.[17]

There are multiple potential causes of toxic renal injury in the vascular surgical patient, including most commonly aminoglycosides, radiologic contrast media, and myoglobin. Preexisting renal dysfunction, advanced age, volume contraction, and use of other nephrotoxic agents are associated with an increased incidence of nephrotoxicity. The primary site of iodinated contrast agent nephrotoxicity is the renal tubule. Preexisting renal dysfunction, diabetes mellitus, volume depletion, and the total volume of contrast agent administered increase the risk of contrast-induced renal dysfunction in a vascular surgical patient.[18] The amount of time that the kidney tissue is exposed to the contrast agent seems to be a significant factor in mediating contrast-induced renal dysfunction. Minimizing the contrast volume and maximizing urine flow during and after angiography are useful strategies to minimize the incidence of this complication. *N*-Acetyl cysteine may protect against the development of contrast-induced renal dysfunction by scavenging reactive oxygen species.

Among patients undergoing aortic reconstruction, several strategies can be used to reduce the likelihood of postoperative renal dysfunction. The patient should be administered systemic anticoagulation with heparin before aortic cross-clamping. Mannitol (12.5 to 25 g) also should be administered before cross-clamping. This agent acts not only as an osmotic diuretic, but also as a free radical scavenger. Dopamine may be beneficial to increase renal perfusion, glomerular filtration rate, and urine output during aortic surgery, although its clinical benefit to reduce the incidence of postoperative renal failure is uncertain. A dopaminergic type 1 receptor agonist, fenoldopam, also may reduce the incidence of postoperative renal failure by increasing the glomerular filtration rate through increase of flow to the inner cortex and medulla of the kidney. At the Johns Hopkins Hospital, partial left heart bypass with distal aortic perfusion is used to minimize the period of visceral ischemia during thoracoabdominal aortic aneurysm repair, although some authors have questioned its value in preventing postoperative renal failure.

■ INFECTION IN PROSTHETIC VASCULAR GRAFTS (Chapter 59)

At a time of enormous progress in the diagnosis and treatment of peripheral vascular disease, prosthetic graft infection remains a difficult challenge for the surgeon and a potentially devastating complication for the patient. The overall incidence of prosthetic graft infection ranges from less than 1% to 5%, and the incidence varies with the anatomic location of the conduit, reoperative versus primary procedure, elective versus emergent operation, host defenses, and a variety of other patient-specific variables. Prosthetic graft infection may present at any time, from within days of the operation to many years postoperatively. In general, graft infection most commonly affects prostheses in the groin and leg. With the evolution of endovascular techniques to treat occlusive and aneurysmal disease, stents and stent grafts also are vulnerable to infection, albeit with an incidence of less than 1%. *Staphylococcus aureus* has been the organism most commonly cultured in prosthetic graft infection and is seen in 25% to 50% of cases. Reports suggest that methicillin-resistant *S. aureus* is responsible for 25% of prosthetic graft infections in contemporary practice. The prevalence of gram-negative organisms also is increasing, and these tend to be more virulent infections. Likewise, *Staphylococcus epidermidis* increasingly is being identified as a cause of graft infection, especially late graft infection.

Diagnosis

The clinical presentation of prosthetic graft infection depends on the anatomic location, the timing of presentation, and the virulence of the organism involved. As noted, most prosthetic graft infections occur in the groin, and the clinical signs may include mild cellulitis, a sinus tract, anastomotic pseudoaneurysm, or frank hemorrhage. Grafts confined to the abdomen or chest may present with a picture of systemic sepsis or general malaise. Graft enteric fistula is one manifestation of prosthetic graft infection in the abdomen (see Chapter 61).

Many radiographic studies may be valuable in making the diagnosis of graft infection. Computed tomography (CT) is most useful in evaluating thoracic or abdominal grafts. Perigraft fluid or gas, soft tissue inflammation, anastomotic pseudoaneurysms, and frank abscess formation can be identified easily and are strongly suggestive of an infected conduit. Magnetic resonance imaging is also a useful modality in assessing infection of intracavitary prostheses. Ultrasound is a cost-effective technique for evaluating possible infection of peripheral bypass grafts. Anastomotic pseudoaneurysms, perigraft fluid in a long-term graft, and frank abscess formation are strongly indicative of prosthetic graft infection. Formal arteriography confirms anastomotic breakdown, which is suggestive of infection, and may be helpful to plan operative repair.

The evaluation of possible prosthetic graft infection also may include a radiolabeled white blood cell scan, which can identify the presence of leukocytes within the perigraft tissues. Many radionuclide agents have been used, including indium 111, technetium 99m hexametazime, and gallium 67 citrate. In the author's experience, this modality can provide circumstantial evidence of infection, but there can be false-positive and false-negative results.

Treatment

The dogma that infection involving a foreign body can be eradicated only by the complete removal of that foreign body is the basis for the conventional treatment of prosthetic graft infection—complete graft excision and revascularization, if necessary, through clean tissue planes. Over the years, some of the highest rates of operative mortality and morbidity have been observed in association with this approach, and these high rates have stimulated the pursuit of less aggressive forms of therapy. The strategy elected to treat prosthetic graft infection depends on the anatomic location of the graft, the responsible organism, and the extent of graft involvement. In most cases, infection involving the entirety of an aortic graft mandates complete graft removal and performance of an extra-anatomic axillobifemoral or bilateral axillopopliteal bypass graft. Evidence suggests that staging the procedure, with performance of the extra-anatomic bypass 1 or 2 days before the abdominal procedure, reduces overall operative morbidity.[19,20] In the 1990s, several series noted an operative mortality rate ranging from 11% to 30% among patients undergoing excision of infected aortic grafts and extra-anatomic bypass. Aortic stump blowout and limb loss are mid-term and long-term potential complications. In-situ graft replacement has been successful in the setting of prosthetic graft infection with *S. epidermidis*. Infection involving one limb of an aortofemoral bypass graft usually requires complete excision of the limb and extra-anatomic reconstruction. When infection of an aortofemoral, femorofemoral, or femorodistal bypass graft seems to be localized to the groin, wide soft tissue débridement, with or without graft replacement, and coverage with a rotational muscle flap may be successful, particularly if relatively low-virulence organisms are involved.[21,22] Early experience with infection involving aortic stent grafts and arterial stents suggests that complete removal of the foreign body and reconstruction with autogenous tissue is the most appropriate strategy.

■ ANASTOMOTIC ANEURYSMS (Chapter 60)

The incidence of anastomotic aneurysms has declined in recent years secondary to improved synthetic graft material, discontinuation of silk sutures for construction of arterial anastomoses, and meticulous attention to surgical technique. The overall incidence of anastomotic aneurysms is low, and most aneurysms occur at the femoral level. In two large series, the incidence of femoral anastomotic aneurysms was 2.4% and 13.6%.[23,24] The incidence of anastomotic aneurysms increases with time after the bypass as the underlying artery develops progressive degenerative disease.

The causes of anastomotic pseudoaneurysms include suture disruption, graft deterioration, arterial degeneration, physical stress, technical imperfection, and infection. Although most anastomotic aneurysms are pseudoaneurysms, occasionally true aneurysmal degeneration of the native artery may be the underlying pathologic condition. Careful attention to surgical technique in performing an anastomosis is paramount in minimizing the incidence of anastomotic aneurysms. This attention includes taking adequate bites of the artery wall, avoiding excessive space between bites, avoiding tension on the suture line when tunneling the graft, avoiding the development of wound hematoma, and meticulous attention to sterile technique. The clinical presentation depends on the anatomic site of involvement. As noted, most present in the groin as asymptomatic palpable masses. Progressive enlargement may result in pain, leg swelling secondary to adjacent venous compression, or muscle weakness due to neural compression. Complications of anastomotic aneurysms include rupture, acute thrombosis, and distal embolization in a few cases. Indications for repair of a femoral anastomotic aneurysm include progressive enlargement, size greater than 2 to 2.5 cm in diameter, development of symptoms, or development of complications. Anastomotic aneurysms involving the aorta or iliac arteries are usually asymptomatic and identified when radiographic studies are performed for other reasons. Any patient presenting with a femoral artery anastomotic pseudoaneurysm should undergo evaluation of other anastomotic sites to rule out synchronous anastomotic breakdown. Aortic and iliac artery anastomotic aneurysms occur more commonly in patients who have undergone graft placement for aneurysm as opposed to occlusive disease. The indications for repair of an aortic anastomotic aneurysm include an aneurysm greater than 4 cm in diameter, an enlarging lesion, and symptoms such as back pain or complications secondary to the lesion. It is recommended that iliac anastomotic aneurysms merit repair if they exceed 3.5 cm in diameter.

Because infection is an increasingly important etiology for anastomotic pseudoaneurysm, sepsis must be ruled out before undertaking repair. In the absence of infection, inline graft replacement of the involved area of the graft, after securing adequate proximal and distal control, is the most appropriate and efficacious approach. Infection with *S. epidermidis* is an important cause of anastomotic pseudoaneurysms, and there is growing evidence that inline reconstruction may be successful in this scenario. With more virulent organisms, however, extra-anatomic bypass with resection of the infected tissue should be done. In some patients with aortic or iliac artery anastomotic pseudoaneurysm, endoluminal covered stent or stent graft repair may be a useful option.

■ AORTOENTERIC FISTULAE (Chapter 61)

Secondary aortoenteric fistulae (i.e., involving a previously placed aortic graft) are more common than primary fistulae and represent one of the most serious and potentially devastating complications of aortic reconstructive surgery. Most commonly, secondary aortoenteric fistulae present as a direct communication between the aorta and a bowel segment at the aortic-graft anastomosis. Less often, an aortoenteric fistula may present as a communication between the body of the graft and a bowel segment, also known as *graft enteric erosion*. More than 80% of aortoenteric fistulae involve the duodenum, but the colon, appendix, small bowel, stomach, and esophagus have been affected in rare cases. With improvement in operative technique, the incidence of aortoenteric fistula has declined in recent years and now is 1% or less. The incidence of aortoenteric fistula is roughly two times higher after repair of ruptured aortic aneurysm compared with intact aortic aneurysm repair. Aortoenteric fistula formation has been reported after aortic stent graft placement.[25]

Infection of the graft is believed to be the etiology of aortoenteric fistula development in many cases. This observation is supported by numerous clinical and laboratory studies. Pulsatile graft pressure on the adjacent duodenum and duodenal injury at the time of graft implantation are other potential etiologies of this complication. In light of this, careful attention to the technical details of operation is crucial in minimizing the development of this complication. Important considerations include eliminating breaks in sterile technique; avoiding excess tension on the duodenum and other bowel segments by fixed retraction systems; and maximizing soft tissue coverage of the newly placed graft with the aneurysm wall, retroperitoneal tissue, and omentum.

The clinical presentation of an aortoenteric fistula includes gastrointestinal bleeding, sepsis, and abdominal pain, although this complete triad is seen rarely in most patients. Three quarters of patients present with bleeding, which occasionally may be massive initially, but in most cases is self-limited and known as a "herald bleed." The evaluation must proceed expeditiously to rule out other causes of gastrointestinal bleeding because massive hemorrhage may ensue at any time after presentation. Any patient with a previous history of aortic graft placement who presents with gastrointestinal bleeding must be assumed to have an aortoenteric fistula until proved otherwise. A few patients present with signs of graft infection but without overt bleeding. Abdominal pain is relatively uncommon among patients presenting with a secondary aortoenteric fistula.

Upper gastrointestinal endoscopy is a valuable diagnostic test, largely to rule out other causes of bleeding, such as a duodenal or gastric ulcer. The examination should include the third and fourth portions of the duodenum and must be done cautiously to minimize the likelihood of disrupting a tamponading thrombus at the fistula site. Occasionally the actual graft material is visualized during the examination. More recently, contrast-enhanced CT has been shown to be a valuable diagnostic adjunct. Although the fistula often is not visualized, periaortic gas or fluid or both, an anastomotic pseudoaneurysm, bowel wall thickening, and retroperitoneal inflammatory signs all are suggestive of graft infection and possible fistula formation. Arteriography is less useful and may add unnecessary delay to carrying out the definitive treatment. If the patient presents with massive bleeding or is unstable, immediate exploration without performing diagnostic testing may be required.

Definitive management of a patient who presents with an aortoenteric fistula depends on the hemodynamic stability of the patient, the extent of sepsis in the graft bed, and the underlying arterial anatomy. If the patient is hemodynamically stable, experience suggests that performing an extra-anatomic bypass followed by staged removal of the graft and bowel repair minimizes operative mortality and morbidity, including the risk of limb amputation.[26] In the setting of ongoing hemorrhage, abdominal exploration must be carried out expeditiously. Typically a midline laparotomy is used, although if the right axillary artery can be used for inflow for the extra-anatomic bypass, a left retroperitoneal exposure would facilitate suprarenal/supraceliac aortic control, which usually is required. After graft excision and bowel repair, the abdomen is closed, and clean instruments are used to construct the extra-anatomic bypass after repeat preparation of the patient. Alternatively, in-situ reconstruction may be done using lower extremity deep veins, cryopreserved autogenous conduits, or antibiotic-soaked prosthetic grafts after aggressive retroperitoneal débridement.[27-29] There should be minimal retroperitoneal contamination. Endovascular adjuncts, such as placement of an aortic occlusion balloon to achieve proximal control or deployment of a temporizing covered stent across the fistula, have been used in some centers.[30,31]

■ ISCHEMIC NEUROPATHY (Chapter 62)

Ischemic neuropathy describes any peripheral nerve injury resulting from a decrease in blood supply, including a large or small vessel occlusive process; the ischemia may be acute or chronic. Acute ischemia may be associated with transient symptoms with complete recovery, whereas a more prolonged period of acute ischemia may eventuate in permanent nerve damage. The tolerance of nerve function to chronic ischemia has not been well studied in humans. Peripheral neuropathy develops in some patients with chronic arterial occlusive disease, and it is important to establish this neurologic etiology for the patient's symptoms before undertaking arterial reconstruction aimed at alleviating the symptoms. After an episode of severe acute ischemia, some patients continue to experience persistent neuropathic symptoms after successful revascularization. Neuropathic symptoms include pain that is burning in character and that is frequently worse at rest and at night. Neuropathic pain is unrelieved or affected by exercise. The involved extremity may be warm while the patient perceives it to be cold. There may be muscle wasting of the affected foot and abnormal reflexes. Ischemic neuropathic findings are typically asymmetric as opposed to the symmetric presentation of diabetic neuropathy or neuropathy secondary to alcohol or other etiologies.

Severe arterial insufficiency should be ruled out in evaluating severe foot pain in a patient with peripheral arterial occlusive disease. If adequate perfusion is documented, a diagnosis of ischemic neuropathy should be considered, and several diagnostic tests should be performed. The presence and severity of ischemic neuropathy can be established with several electrophysiologic studies, including motor nerve conduction and sensory nerve conduction studies and needle electrode examination. In the absence of significant arterial insufficiency, most patients with ischemic neuropathy are treated conservatively. A relatively novel approach has been the use of intramuscular gene therapy to administer vascular endothelial growth factor.[32]

Ischemic mononeuropathy is seen in association with small vessel diseases, such as diabetes and vasculitides. Scattered reports of peroneal, tibial, and femoral neuropathy secondary to large vessel occlusive disease have been reported. Multiple mononeuropathies have been described in dialysis patients after construction of arteriovenous access sites and most likely represent a "steal" phenomenon.[33] Diabetes mellitus is often a predisposing factor. Patients typically complain of pain in the affected hand and associated weakness, although the hand is usually warm. Nerve conduction studies show decreased motor and sensory evoked potentials. Ligation of the access site resolves symptoms in most cases. Finally, endovascular stent graft placement has been reported to result in many neuropathies, including lumbosacral plexus dysfunction with lower extremity weakness, sciatic neuropathy, femoral neuropathy, and autonomic neuropathy secondary to pelvic arterial flow interruption.[34-37]

■ LYMPHATIC COMPLICATIONS (Chapter 63)

Lymphatic complications are seen commonly after open vascular surgical procedures and include the development of extremity edema, lymphorrhea, lymphocele, chylous ascites, or chylothorax. Careful attention to meticulous operative dissection and early recognition and treatment of these complications are crucial to minimizing overall morbidity.

Lower extremity edema is experienced by most patients after infrainguinal bypass graft procedures and results from the increased production of lymphatic fluid and operative disruption of lymphatic drainage channels. Venous obstruction and insufficiency play a minimal role in the etiology of postbypass limb edema. Careful attention to avoiding disruption of lymphatic channels and ligation of lymphatic channels when division is necessary during the groin dissection is crucial in minimizing the development and extent of postbypass leg edema. Two prospective randomized studies showed a reduced rate of lymphatic complications using endoscopic as opposed to conventional open saphenous vein harvest.[38,39] The use of graded compression stockings continues to be the mainstay of conservative management.

Lymphatic injury in the groin also may present either with lymphorrhea or the development of a lymphocele. Most cases of lymphorrhea present within days after surgery. If the lymph drainage does not resolve quickly with conservative management, including bed rest, pressure dressings, and prophylactic antibiotics, operative intervention is indicated. The challenge is identifying the leaking lymphatic channel in the groin. The administration of isosulfan blue into the web spaces of the foot just before groin exploration often identifies the leaking lymphatic. A collection of lymph fluid in the groin, a lymphocele, often can be managed expectantly unless it is causing discomfort. Percutaneous sclerotherapy, using talcum, fibrin sealant, a variety of antibiotics, or povidone-iodine, has been shown to be effective in treating lymphoceles in many centers. If the fluid-filled mass is enlarging or in the presence of a prosthetic graft, operative repair is indicated. The key to successful repair, as with lymphorrhea, is identification of the culprit lymphatic. The sac should be closed in layers over a closed suction drain. Rarely a lymphocele may present in the retroperitoneum, or a retroperitoneal lymphocele may present with a groin lymphocele. CT-guided aspiration has been successful in treating some cases, and in others sclerotherapy is curative. When operative repair is undertaken, isosulfan blue may be useful to identify the leaking retroperitoneal lymphatic. If chyle is identified in the cyst, whipped cream may be administered via a gastric tube 4 hours before exploration to identify the source of the leak.

Chylous ascites is a rare but potentially morbid complication after abdominal aortic surgery. Symptoms include progressive abdominal distention, pain, nausea, and dyspnea, with the potential for significant malnutrition. Conservative management includes the administration of a medium-chain triglyceride diet, with total bowel rest and the use of total parenteral nutrition, and paracentesis as necessary, in the

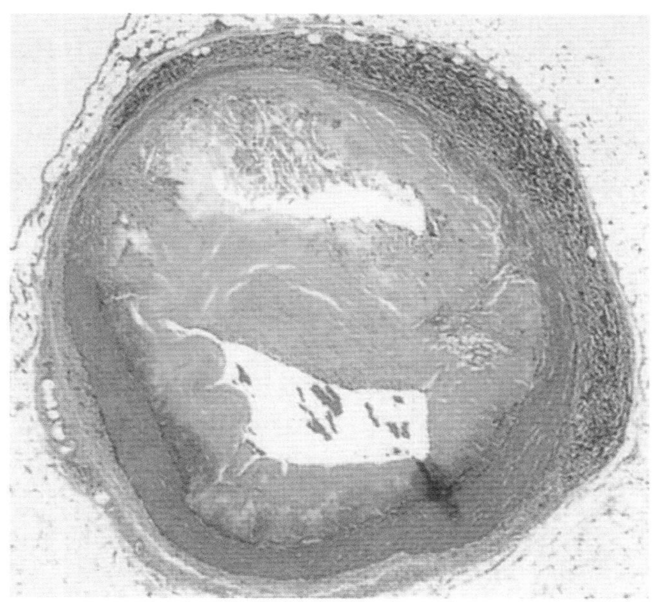

FIGURE 56-2 Buffon and colleagues[45] showed widespread coronary inflammation in unstable angina. This color electron micrograph shows extraordinary infiltration of myeloperoxidase-laden neutrophils into a section of coronary artery from a patient with unstable angina. This is a diffuse process, not localized to a single vulnerable plaque. The implications are that focused therapy (e.g., percutaneous transluminal coronary angioplasty or coronary artery bypass graft surgery) may not be protective against coronary events in the vascular patient; instead, anti-inflammatory (e.g., antiplatelet therapy) treatment, stabilization with antilipid treatments, and beta blockers to decrease myocardial oxygen consumption may be more beneficial than mechanical approaches. (From Buffon A, Fiasucci LM, Liusso G, et al: Widespread coronary inflammation in unstable angina. N Engl J Med 347:5-12, 2002.)

most severe cases. Operative ligation of the leaking para-aortic lymphatic channels is reserved for failures of conservative management. Chylothorax may be seen rarely after thoracic aortic and thoracoabdominal aortic aneurysm surgery. Chest tube drainage and nutritional management, as for chylous ascites, is successful in most cases. Patients who fail conservative management should undergo operative ligation of the thoracic duct via open surgery or thoracoscopically. Parietal pleurectomy has been reported to be successful when no discrete leak can be identified at surgery.[40] Percutaneous embolization of the cysterna chyli with coils and glue has been reported to be successful in treating patients with chylothorax.[41]

■ POSTOPERATIVE SEXUAL DYSFUNCTION AFTER AORTOILIAC INTERVENTIONS (Chapter 64)

Although rates of operative mortality, graft patency, limb salvage, and other objective metrics traditionally have been used to assess the outcome of vascular surgical procedures, in recent years increasing attention appropriately has been focused on quality-of-life outcomes. Postoperative sexual dysfunction is one such quality-of-life issue. Leriche first identified impotence as a sign of aortoiliac occlusive disease more than 80 years ago. Impotence may develop as a complication of aortoiliac reconstruction, or in some cases preexisting impotence may be improved through arterial reconstruction.

Before undertaking aortoiliac reconstruction for occlusive or aneurysmal disease, the surgeon should obtain an accurate history with respect to the patient's sexual function, and this should be well documented in the medical record. More objective evidence of penile arterial inflow can be obtained using either penile plethysmography or duplex assessment of penile flow after administration of a vasoactive agent.

Postoperative sexual dysfunction refers to impotence and ejaculatory abnormalities. Impotence after aortoiliac reconstruction typically results from interruption of internal iliac artery flow. Disruption of para-aortic autonomic nerve fibers may result in retrograde ejaculation with or without erection and orgasm, anejaculation, failure of emission, or normal erection with failure to achieve ejaculation or orgasm. Preservation or improvement of internal iliac artery flow and protection of para-aortic autonomic nerve fibers are the keys to optimizing postoperative sexual function. Dissection outside the aorta should be kept to a minimum to avoid nerve plexus injury and to minimize the risk of atheroembolism. In repairing an abdominal aortic aneurysm, the aneurysm should be entered to the right of midline, and the inferior mesenteric artery should be ligated intraluminally. Dissection at the aortic bifurcation should be avoided. Likewise, reconstruction for aortoiliac occlusive disease should be accomplished with minimal extra-aortic dissection. Among patients with preoperative impotence, reconstruction of at least one internal iliac artery should be considered. Among younger sexually active patients undergoing aortoiliac reconstruction for occlusive disease, an extra-anatomic femorofemoral bypass generally avoids sexual dysfunction.

■ POSTOPERATIVE GRAFT THROMBOSIS: PREVENTION AND MANAGEMENT (Chapter 65)

Early postoperative thrombosis of a vascular reconstruction represents a potentially devastating complication for the patient. In one series, 1 year after a failed infrainguinal bypass graft thrombosis, 50% of patients had undergone amputation of the affected limb.[42] Likewise, carotid endarterectomy site complications have been the most common cause of perioperative stroke.[43,44] Optimal patient care depends on prevention of early perioperative thrombotic complications. The causes of early vascular reconstructive failure include technical factors and patient variables. As a result of improvements in the technologic ability to assess the technical precision of arterial reconstructions intraoperatively, early graft failure is now secondary to technical imperfection in a few cases in centers of excellence.

Prevention

Numerous studies have shown that early postoperative bypass graft thrombosis is a poor prognostic sign for late graft patency and limb salvage. Every effort should be made to confirm the technical adequacy of the repair at operation. Simple palpation of the bypass graft and target vessel is a notoriously imperfect means of assessing the adequacy of the technical reconstruction, and many more objective methodologies are now available and should be liberally used. Completion arteriography has been a widely accepted "gold standard" method for assessing the technical adequacy of the bypass graft, although it has limitations. Often the proximal anastomosis is excluded from the film, and typically only a single plane of view is obtained; this may miss subtle abnormalities, such as residual platelet-fibrin debris or intimal defects. The wider availability of digital subtraction angiography, often using a C-arm or fixed angiographic unit in the operating room, obviates these limitations of completion arteriography. Continuous wave Doppler provides a quick assessment of graft flow and runoff. It is most useful for detecting residual arteriovenous fistulae in in-situ reconstructions. Although a high-frequency flow signal may indicate a technical problem in the graft or runoff, this technology provides a subjective and insensitive assessment; also, it provides no image. Intraoperative B-mode ultrasonography has been used but is limited by the inability to differentiate moving blood from fresh clot and the significant operator experience required to obtain optimal images. Duplex ultrasonography has emerged as a more valuable method to assess the technical adequacy of the infrainguinal bypass graft. Low-flow velocities or highly accelerated flow jets indicate intrinsic lesions in the graft, and imaging can confirm this pathophysiologic observation. Several studies have confirmed the value of intraoperative duplex scanning in achieving optimal bypass graft patency. Angioscopy is another modality used by some to assess bypass graft adequacy.

Likewise, the efficacy of carotid endarterectomy is predicated on a low rate of perioperative neurologic complications. The incidence of technical abnormalities identified intraoperatively ranged from 5% to 43% (mean 12%) in a review of more than 2000 carotid endarterectomy procedures.[45] Although most abnormalities were detected in the external carotid artery, the incidence of internal carotid artery defects was 6.5%. Although not uniformly practiced, the routine use of intraoperative completion arteriography has led to re-exploration in 2% to 26% of cases.[46,47]

A physiologic assessment of the endarterectomy site can be obtained using either continuous wave Doppler ultrasonography or duplex ultrasonography. Continuous wave Doppler is probably the most commonly used modality for assessing the carotid endarterectomy site. This modality seems to have acceptable sensitivity but not specificity to mandate re-exploration in the absence of a confirmatory test. There is a growing clinical experience suggesting that duplex ultrasound is a sensitive modality for identifying technical imperfections at operation, reducing the incidence of perioperative neurologic events and the incidence of residual and recurrent carotid stenoses.

Management

The etiology of infrainguinal bypass graft thrombosis depends on the timing of presentation. Occlusions that occur in the early postoperative period must be assumed to be technical in nature or due to inadequate inflow or outflow or quality of the autogenous conduit and should mandate immediate return to the operating room in all but the most exceptional cases. The patient should be administered systemic anticoagulation with heparin as soon as the diagnosis is made. In view of the liberal use of intraoperative completion studies to confirm technical adequacy at the original operation, more recent series have shown that no more than 20% of early postoperative graft occlusions are secondary to remediable technical defects. Although this fact may be gratifying for the surgeon, it portends a poor long-term graft prognosis for the patient. In some cases, thrombectomy and systemic anticoagulation has resulted in long-term graft salvage; however, this is the exception rather than the rule because most patients with grafts who undergo thrombectomy without an identifiable lesion experience early recurrent thrombosis. Early bypass graft thrombosis without apparent contributing anatomic problems should prompt a hypercoagulability evaluation.

Mid-term and long-term graft thrombosis is more likely to result from the development of vein graft lesions or progressive native arterial disease. In this scenario, initial treatment with thrombolysis may be indicated. This approach allows identification of vein graft lesions and new disease in the inflow or outflow vessels. In addition, lysis of thrombus in the outflow bed, which may be extensive when prosthetic infrainguinal bypass grafts thrombose, maximizes runoff and improves the chance that a revised or new graft will be successful. Whether the vascular surgeon replaces the failed vein graft or attempts salvage depends on many factors, such as the condition of the conduit, the timing of occlusion, and the availability of further autogenous vein. Balloon angioplasty of intrinsic vein graft stenoses seems most appropriate for focal lesions, whereas surgical revision should be considered with multiple lesions or more diffuse stenoses.

Acute postoperative thrombosis of the carotid endarterectomy site is a potentially devastating complication and warrants immediate return to the operating room for thromboembolectomy. Frequently, even with adequate restoration of carotid patency, the neurologic outcome is not good. Anecdotal experience has suggested a role for catheter-directed intracerebral thrombolysis to treat distal thromboemboli not accessible to the surgeon's balloon embolectomy catheter.[48]

■ REFERENCES

1. Mangano DT, Brower WS, Hollenberg M, et al: Association of perioperative myocardial ischemia with cardiac morbidity and mortality in men undergoing noncardiac surgery: The Study of Perioperative Ischemia Research Group. N Engl J Med 323:1781-1788, 1990.
2. Mangano DT, Goldman L: Preoperative assessment of patients with known or suspected coronary disease. N Engl J Med 333:1750-1756, 1995.
3. Landesberg G, Einav S, Christopherson R, et al: Perioperative ischemia and cardiac complications in major vascular surgery: Importance of preoperative twelve-lead electrocardiogram. J Vasc Surg 26:570-578, 1997.
4. Landesberg G, Mosseri M, Wolfe Y, et al: Perioperative myocardial ischemia and infarction: Identification by continuous 12-lead electrocardiogram with online ST-segment monitoring. Anesthesiology 96:264-270, 2002.
5. Landesberg G, Mosseri M, Zahger D, et al: Myocardial infarction after vascular surgery: The role of prolonged stress-induced ST segment depression-type ischemia. J Am Coll Cardiol 37:1839-1845, 2001.
6. Fleisher LA, Eagle KA: Clinical practice: Lowering cardiac risk in noncardiac surgery. N Engl J Med 345:1677-1682, 2001.
7. Auerbach AD, Goldman L: Beta-blockers and reduction of cardiac events in noncardiac surgery: Scientific review. JAMA 287:1435-1444, 2002.
8. Centers for Disease Control and Prevention: Guideline for prevention of nosocomial pneumonia. Respir Care 39:1191, 1994.
9. Fagon JY, Chastre J, Hance AJ, et al: Nosocomial pneumonia in ventilated patients: A cohort study evaluating attributable mortality and hospital stay. Am J Med 94:281-288, 1993.
10. Bluman LG, Mosca L, Newman N, et al: Preoperative smoking habits and postoperative pulmonary complications. Chest 113:883-889, 1998.
11. Moller AM, Maaloe R, Pedersen T: Postoperative intensive care admittance: The role of tobacco smoking. Acta Anaesthesiol Scand 45:345-348, 2001.
12. Nakagawa M, Tanaka H, Tsukama H, et al: Relationship between the duration of reoperative smoke-free period and the incidence of postoperative complications following abdominal surgery. Chest 120:705-710, 2001.
13. Rodgers A, Walker N, Shug S, et al: Reduction of postoperative mortality and morbidity with epidural or spinal anesthesia: Results from overview of randomized trials. BMJ 321:1-12, 2000.
14. Norris EJ, Beattie C, Perler BA, et al: Double-masked randomized trial comparing alternative combinations of intraoperative anesthesia and postoperative analgesia in abdominal aortic surgery. Anesthesiology 95:1054-1067, 2001.
15. Archer C, Levy AR, McGregor M: Value of routine preoperative chest x-ray: A meta-analysis. Can J Anaesth 40:1022-1027, 1993.
16. Bomberger RA, McGregor B, Depalma RG: Optimal fluid management after aortic reconstruction: A prospective study of two crystalloid solutions. J Vasc Surg 4:164-167, 1986.
17. Hansen KJ, Cherr GS, Craven TE, et al: Management of ischemic nephropathy: Dialysis-free survival after surgical repair. J Vasc Surg 32:472-482, 2000.
18. Barrett BJ: Contrast nephrotoxicity. J Am Soc Nephrol 5:125-137, 1994.
19. Yeager RA, Taylor RM, Moneta GL, et al: Improved results with conventional management of infrarenal aortic infection. J Vasc Surg 30:76-83, 1999.

20. Seeger JM, Pretus HA, Welborn MB, et al: Long-term outcome after treatment of aortic graft infection with staged extra-anatomic bypass and aortic graft removal. J Vasc Surg 32:451-461, 2000.
21. Perler BA: The conservative management of infected prosthetic grafts (pro). Adv Surg 29:17-32, 1996.
22. Perler BA, Vander Kolk CA, Manson PM, Williams GM: Rotational muscle flaps to treat prosthetic graft infection: Long-term follow-up. J Vasc Surg 18:358-365, 1993.
23. Ernst CB, Elliott JP Jr, Ryan CJ, et al: Recurrent femoral anastomotic aneurysms: A 30-year experience. Ann Surg 208:401-409, 1988.
24. van den Akker PJ, van Schilfgaarde R, Brand R, et al: Long term success of aortoiliac operation for arteriosclerotic obstructive disease. Surg Gynecol Obstet 174:485-496, 1992.
25. Abou-Zamzam AM, Bianchi C, Mazraany W, et al: Aortoenteric fistula development following endovascular abdominal aortic aneurysm repair: A case report. Ann Vasc Surg 17:119-122, 2003.
26. Reilly LM: Aortic graft infection: Evolution in management. Cardiovasc Surg 10:372-377, 2002.
27. Clagett GP, Valentine RJ, Hagino RT: Autogenous aortoiliac/femoral reconstruction from superficial femoral-popliteal veins: Feasibility and durability. J Vasc Surg 25:255-266, 1997.
28. Kieffer E, Bahnini A, Koskas F, et al: In-situ allograft replacement of infected infrarenal aortic prosthetic grafts: Results in forty-three patients. J Vasc Surg 17:349-355, 1993.
29. Young RM, Cherry KJ Jr, David PM, et al: The results of in-situ prosthetic graft replacement for infected aortic grafts. Am J Surg 159:466-469, 1999.
30. Burks JA, Faries PL, Gravereaux EC, et al: Endovascular repair of bleeding aortoenteric fistulas: A 5 year experience. J Vasc Surg 34:1055-1059, 2001.
31. Chuter TA, Lukaszewicz GC, Reilly LM, et al: Endovascular repair of a presumed aortoenteric fistula: Late failure due to recurrent infection. J Endovasc Ther 7:240-244, 2000.
32. Schratzberger P, Schratzberger G, Silver M, et al: Favorable effect of VEGF gene transfer on ischemic peripheral neuropathy. Nat Med 4:405-413, 2000.
33. Wilbourne AJ, Furlan AJ, Hulley W, Ruschhaupt W: Ischemic monomelic neuropathy. Neurology 33:447-451, 1983.
34. Dougherty MJ, Calligaro KD: How to avoid and manage nerve injuries associated with aortic surgery: Ischemic neuropathy, traction injuries, and sexual derangements. Semin Vasc Surg 14:275-281, 2001.
35. Kibria SG, Gough MJ: Ischemic sciatic neuropathy: A complication of endovascular repair of abdominal aortic aneurysm. Eur J Vasc Endovasc Surg17:266-267, 1999.
36. Kwok PC, Chung TK, Chong LC, et al: Neurologic injury after endovascular stent-graft and bilateral internal iliac embolization for infrarenal abdominal aortic aneurysm. J Vasc Interv Radiol 12:761-763, 2001.
37. Forester ND, Parry D, Kessel D, et al: Ischemic sciatic neuropathy: An important complication of embolization of a type II Endoleak. Eur J Vasc Endovasc Surg 24:462-463, 2002.
38. Allen KB, Griffith GL, Heimansohn DA, et al: Endoscopic versus traditional saphenous vein harvesting: A prospective randomized trial. Ann Thorac Surg 66:26-31, 1998.
39. Puskas JD, Wright CE, Miller PK, et al: A randomized trial of endoscopic versus open saphenous vein harvest in coronary bypass surgery. Ann Thorac Surg 68:1509-1512, 1999.
40. Browse NL, Allen DR, Wilson NM: Management of chylothorax. Br J Surg 84:1711-1716, 1997.
41. Cope C, Kaiser LR: Management of unremitting chylothorax by percutaneous embolization and blockage of retroperitoneal lymphatic vessels in 42 patients. J Vasc Interv Radiol 13:1139-1148, 2002.
42. Watson HR, Schroeder TV, Simms MH, et al: Relationship of femorodistal bypass patency to clinical outcome. Eur J Vasc Endovasc Surg 17:77-83, 1999.
43. Frawley JE, Hicks RG, Woodforth NJ: Risk factors for peri-operative stroke complicating carotid endarterectomy: Selective analysis of a prospective audit of 1000 consecutive operations. Aust N Z J Surg 70:52-56, 2000.
44. Jacobwitz GR, Rockman CB, Lamperello PJ, et al: Causes of perioperative stroke after carotid endarterectomy: Special considerations in symptomatic patients. Ann Vasc Surg 15:19-24, 2001.
45. Barnes RW, Nix ML, Nichols BT, et al: Recurrent versus residual carotid stenosis: Incidence detected by Doppler ultrasound. Ann Surg 203:652-660, 1986.
46. Courbier R, Jausseran JM, Reggi M, et al: Routine intraoperative carotid angiography: Its impact on operative morbidity and carotid restenosis. J Vasc Surg 3:343-350, 1986.
47. Donaldson MC, Ivarsson BL, Mannick JA, et al: Impact of completion angiography on operative conduct and results of carotid endarterectomy. Ann Surg 217:682-687, 1993.
48. Perler BA, Murphy K, Sternbach Y, et al: Immediate post-operative thrombolytic therapy: An aggressive strategy for neurologic salvage when cerebral thromboembolism complicates carotid endarterectomy: A case report. J Vasc Surg 31:1033-1037, 2000.

Chapter 56

Cardiac Complications: Screening and Prevention

WILLIAM C. KRUPSKI, MD

Since the landmark publication of Hertzer and colleagues[129] from the Cleveland Clinic in 1984, the coexistence of coronary artery disease (CAD) and peripheral arterial disease (PAD) has been accepted with almost religious zeal by physicians treating patients with PAD. That seminal study, in which 1000 consecutive patients undergoing operations for PAD underwent preoperative cardiac catheterizations (whether or not they had symptoms of CAD), is unlikely ever to be repeated, and the published article is one of the most widely quoted articles in the medical and surgical literature. These investigators reported that only 8% of their patients (who were roughly divided into thirds—aortic, infrainguinal, and carotid disease) had *normal* coronary arteries, and approximately one third had severe-correctable or severe-inoperable CAD. Although this study probably overestimated the prevalence of CAD in the vascular population, in part because epidemiologic studies have shown a decline in CAD in the general U.S. population,[108-111,286] CAD remains a major co-morbidity in most vascular patients. Older and more recent reports confirm that complications of CAD (principally myocardial infarctions [MIs], congestive heart failure [CHF], unstable angina, and arrhythmias) constitute the major causes of early and late morbidity and mortality in patients with PAD.[73,92,93,179] Nevertheless, approximately 25% of the reduction in the rate of death that has occurred since the 1970s is largely related to primary prevention and better understanding of the events leading to coronary deaths.[102,121,139] Despite such decreases in the incidence of new atherosclerotic disease, however, the aging of the population (the so-called baby boomers) will offset any inroads made in primary and secondary prevention of atherosclerotic disease and its complications; it has been estimated that one fifth of the U.S. population will be older than age 65 by 2030.

The reportedly high prevalence of CAD in vascular patients has led to numerous algorithms for its evaluation and management. Much controversy still exists, however. Although there are many fervent advocates for one strategy or another, there is little unanimity of opinion in many areas: (1) What events define coronary morbidity? (2) Which coronary artery lesions are most likely to produce adverse perioperative cardiac outcomes? (3) Should the strategy for cardiac evaluation and management be different depending on the location of peripheral arterial atherosclerosis (aortic, infrainguinal, or carotid)? (4) Is screening for CAD worthwhile, or is it preferable simply to assume that most vascular patients have CAD? (5) How "bad" are the adverse cardiac outcomes in vascular surgery patients with respect to early and late morbidity and mortality? (6) What are the safety and efficacy of evaluation and revascularization for CAD in PAD patients? (7) What is the role for perioperative "optimization" of patients suspected to have CAD, including the use of beta blockers? (8) Until prospective studies currently under way are completed, what are present recommendations? This chapter summarizes the available data on these topics and speculates on current and future research in this important area.

■ DEFINING CARDIAC COMPLICATIONS

Numerous undesirable cardiac events have been evaluated and considered as endpoints in clinical reviews of peripheral vascular operations, including (1) unstable angina pectoris, (2) CHF, (3) arrhythmias, (4) myocardial ischemia (overt and "silent"), (5) nonfatal MI, and (6) fatal MI.[59,178] Of these adverse events, the first four endpoints are relatively "soft" compared with the last two. Although unstable angina is included as one of the acute coronary syndromes (ACS), it does not routinely produce lasting cardiac damage, and its definition is variable, ranging from a mere change in frequency of chest pain to unrelenting pain unresponsive to standard therapeutic maneuvers, such as administration of nitroglycerin and rest. CHF may be the result of fluid overload, which often occurs after vascular procedures or the use of a narcotic agent as the primary anesthetic.[6,279] The diagnosis of CHF is often subjective with no consensus regarding the criteria required to confirm the diagnosis (jugular venous distention, dyspnea, rales, S_3, chest x-ray findings, pedal or sacral edema, objective measurement of decreased cardiac output—in variable combinations). Arrhythmias may be brief, self-limiting, hemodynamically benign, and due to factors other than cardiac disease, including hypoxia, drug toxicity, or metabolic derangements. Myocardial ischemia occurs in 20% to 40% of vascular surgery patients, and more than 50% of these patients develop clinical adverse cardiac events.[163,165,166] Numerous investigators independently have shown the importance of perioperative myocardial ischemia detected on routine Holter monitoring.[177,180,229,231-233] A report by Landesberg and associates[166] from Jerusalem showed, however, that during 11,132 patient-hours of monitoring after vascular surgery, 38 of 185 consecutive patients had 66 transient ischemic events, but only 12 patients (6.5%) sustained perioperative

MIs. In addition, Kirwin and coworkers[153] were unable to correlate silent myocardial ischemia on preoperative continuous ambulatory electrocardiogram (ECG) (Holter) monitoring with perioperative MIs in PAD patients.

Nonfatal and fatal MIs are the most important and specific "hard" outcomes in determining the cardiac morbidity of vascular procedures. Criteria for diagnosis of acute MI as defined by the World Health Organization require two of the following three features: (1) a history of prolonged typical chest pain, (2) evolutionary changes on the ECG, and (3) elevation of serial cardiac enzymes.[306] The Joint European Society of Cardiology/American College of Cardiology (ACC) Committee for the redefinition of MI has updated these criteria.[145] In postoperative patients, symptoms are atypical or absent, however, in 75% of patients who have objective evidence of MI because symptoms are masked by residual anesthetic effects, administration of analgesic agents, competing somatic stimuli such as incisional pain, and other factors.[54,60,61,147-149,155] The ECG is difficult to interpret in postoperative patients and often does not exhibit classic ST-segment elevations or development of Q waves associated with MIs.[34,44] The principal method of statistical analyses of these sorts of Committee definitions employs the BOGSAT technique—"Bunch of Guys Sitting Around a Table" (Goldstone J, personal communication, Case Western Reserve University, Cleveland, Ohio).

The traditional enzymes used to determine MIs (creatine phosphokinase [CK]) may be released from skeletal muscle secondary to surgical trauma or ischemia/reperfusion injuries, masking the isoenzyme CK-MB released from dying myocardial cells. The troponins (C, T, and I) are normal muscle proteins involved in calcium-regulated, actin-myosin interactions.[43,122] Troponin I and T, but not C, exist as distinct cardiac-specific subtypes, and qualitative and quantitative assays based on antibodies to cardiac troponin T (cTnT) and I (cTnI) have been developed and approved by the U.S. Food and Drug Administration for use in the clinical diagnosis of MI. To date, most investigations have used cTnT to determine the presence and extent of cardiac ischemia, but there is cross-reactivity with skeletal muscle troponin T.

In contrast, cTnI is found only in cardiac tissue, it is 13 times more abundant in the myocardium than CK-MB, it is not detectable in the blood of healthy individuals or in patients with renal failure (as is CK-MB and cTnT), and it may remain elevated for 7 to 10 days after an episode of myocardial necrosis.[4,295] CK and CK-MB are released only when myocardial necrosis occurs, not with transient loss of cell membrane integrity, as occurs with ischemia. Elevation of cTnI has been shown to be an independent risk factor for mortality in patients with unstable angina and non–Q wave MIs, and higher levels correlate with high mortality[103-105,213,214] and new regional wall motion abnormalities on echocardiography.[5] Each increase of 1 ng/mL in cTnI is associated with a significant increase ($P = .03$) in the risk ratio for death after adjustment for baseline characteristics.[15,288,289] Andrews and colleagues[13] showed that cTnI levels were accurate in detecting myocardial ischemia in patients undergoing vascular surgery. The currently accepted definition of MI (inapplicable to many earlier studies) has been formulated by the European Society of Cardiology/ACC in a consensus document in which an MI occurs when cTnI levels are greater than 3.1 ng/mL after prolonged ST-segment elevation.[8,294] Although much has been written regarding the importance of cTnI, ECG ST-segment changes are at least of equal importance in the diagnosis of cardiac injury after vascular operations.[164] A superb editorial by Antman[14] summarizes decision making with cardiac troponin tests.

■ PATHOPHYSIOLOGY OF ACUTE CORONARY EVENTS

It has been well accepted by most cardiologists that primary MIs in ambulatory patients most likely are caused by stenoses *less than 50%* (i.e., nonhemodynamically significant lesions), in contrast to the situation in PAD, in which higher grade lesions are most likely to produce complications (e.g., transient ischemic attacks, strokes, lower extremity ischemia).[9-11,20-22,53-55,82,83,97-100,208,273,282] In contrast to lesions of PAD, cardiac events result from *disrupted* atherosclerotic plaques, which need not be stenotic to rupture and cause occlusive thrombosis. The distribution of postoperative MIs is not in the same distribution as hemodynamically critical coronary artery lesions.[198] "Unstable" plaques have a large lipid core and a thin, weakened fibrous cap infiltrated by macrophages (Fig. 56-1). It is hypothesized that these plaques with a large lipid pool and a thin, weakened fibrous cap infiltrated by macrophages and other inflammatory cells are the most vulnerable to disruption.[56] Cytokines and proteases involved in the balance between synthesis and degradation of collagen and elastin, which determines the structural integrity of the plaque cap, play an important role in acute coronary events.

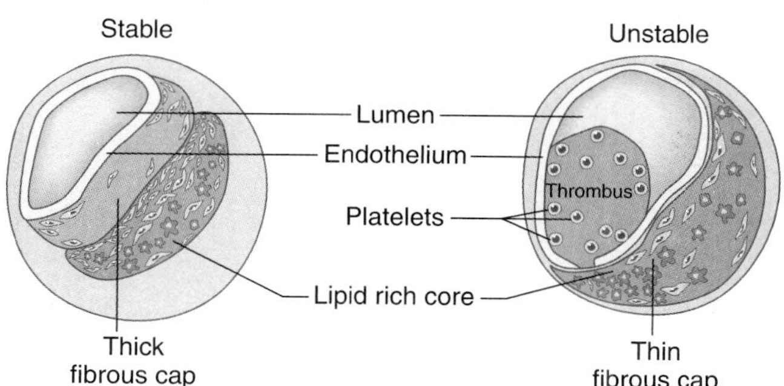

FIGURE 56-1 In contrast to atherosclerotic disease of peripheral arteries, in which complications are usually directly related to the degree of stenosis and hypoperfusion (e.g., high-grade carotid artery stenoses), lesions within the coronary arteries may cause acute events even when stenoses are not critical. This is due to relatively unstable or "vulnerable" plaques with a large lipid pool and a thin, weakened fibrous cap (shown in the second diagram) infiltrated by macrophages. These plaques are most susceptible to disruption and development of platelet-derived thrombosis. Infiltration by macrophages and other inflammatory cells produces a vulnerable cap most vulnerable to disruption. Cytokines and proteases involved in the balance between synthesis and degradation of collagen and elastin determine structural integrity and play an important role in acute coronary events. Identification of and intervention for hemodynamically significant coronary artery lesions may not provide secure protection against perioperative adverse cardiac events after vascular surgery. (From Falk E, Fuster V: Angina pectoris and disease progression. Circulation 92:2058-2065, 1995.)

There is also great interest in the role of inflammation within or surrounding the plaque as a precursor of plaque rupture. Unstable lesions may be especially prone to infection with chlamydia, cytomegalovirus, or *Helicobacter,* which may contribute to plaque instability or vulnerability. Evidence supporting the role of inflammation includes the visible presence of inflammatory cells in and around the unstable lesion, activation of metalloproteinases at the area of plaque fissures, and the finding of a variety of inflammatory mediators in and around the unstable lesion. C-reactive protein (a nonspecific indicator of active inflammation) in the plasma is important as a long-term predictor of MI risk.[135,156,199-201,203,226,235] In addition, the action of aspirin in reducing C-reactive protein levels and reducing infarcts likely relates to its antiplatelet and its anti-inflammatory actions.[81,88,203] Inflammation within vulnerable coronary artery plaques may cause acute events by promoting rupture and erosion. Buffon and colleagues[45] measured the neutrophil myeloperoxidase content in the cardiac and femoral circulations in patients with angina that was stable, recurrent, or unstable. The authors reported widespread activation of neutrophils across the coronary vascular bed in patients with unstable angina, regardless of the location of the culprit stenosis, challenging the concept of a single vulnerable plaque in ACS (Fig. 56-2). In addition, there was a significant correlation between systemic levels of C-reactive protein and the neutrophil myeloperoxidase content in blood from the great cardiac vein. C-reactive protein levels and activated neutrophils traversing the coronary circulation of patients with unstable angina are markers of widespread inflammatory processes occurring in the coronary vasculature. The possibility of widespread coronary inflammation has important implications for research and therapy and challenges the widely accepted hypothesis that a single vulnerable plaque is responsible for the development of coronary instability—questioning the logic of percutaneous transluminal coronary angioplasty (PTCA)/stenting or bypass for a presumed "index" plaque. Antiplatelet therapy may be even more effective in the big picture.[3,45,133,167]

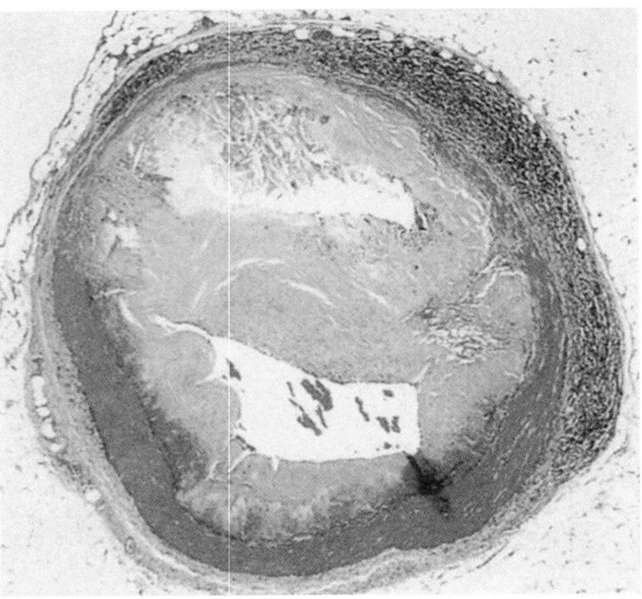

FIGURE 56-2 Buffon and colleagues[45] showed widespread coronary inflammation in unstable angina. This color electron micrograph shows extraordinary infiltration of myeloperoxidase-laden neutrophils into a section of coronary artery from a patient with unstable angina. This is a diffuse process, not localized to a single vulnerable plaque. The implications are that focused therapy (e.g., percutaneous transluminal coronary angioplasty or coronary artery bypass graft surgery) may not be protective against coronary events in the vascular patient; instead, anti-inflammatory (e.g., antiplatelet therapy) treatment, stabilization with antilipid treatments, and beta blockers to decrease myocardial oxygen consumption may be more beneficial than mechanical approaches. (See Color Figures in this section.)

Recognition of unstable or vulnerable coronary artery plaque has led to therapeutic approaches that "stabilize" plaques, such as administration of lipid-lowering medications even to individuals *with* CAD but without demonstrable hyperlipidemias using drugs such as gemfibrozil, hydroxymethylglutaryl coenzyme A reductase inhibitors (statins), and niacin.[245,246,248,250,252-258,260,281,296,302] Sacks and colleagues[251-253,256,258,281] showed that disruption of coronary artery plaques can lead to neointimal proliferation, vasoconstriction, and occlusive thrombosis. Similarly, Pitt and coworkers[221] for the Atorvastatin versus Revascularization Treatment investigators randomized 341 patients with stable CAD to medical treatment with atorvastatin versus revascularization. Low-density lipoprotein was maintained at less than 115 mg/dL versus percutaneous revascularization. In low-risk patients with stable CAD, these level 1 data showed that aggressive lipid-lowering therapy is *at least* as effective as angioplasty and usual care in reducing the incidence of ischemic events.[62] Considering the important finding that plaques do not need to be *greatly stenotic* to rupture and cause acute thrombosis, the Committee for the Mechanisms Precipitating Acute Cardiac Events has estimated that stenotic plaques are responsible for approximately one third of thrombotic events, although stenotic plaques may serve as a marker for the number of nonstenotic plaques present (i.e., "atherosclerotic burden").[198] At present, however, there are no validated invasive or noninvasive methods to identify plaques that are vulnerable to disruption in patients, casting some doubt on the relevance of the preoperative screening studies currently used because these tend to identify hemodynamically significant lesions that may or may not be unstable or vulnerable for producing ACS.

Identification of the unstable or vulnerable plaque would provide important pathophysiologic and therapeutic information for treating patients with CAD, whether or not they are undergoing noncardiac operative procedures. Depré and colleagues[69] in Belgium used directional coronary atherectomy and histologic and biochemical analysis of extracted plaque fragments to study the characteristics of coronary artery plaques; all plaque fragments retrieved from patients with stable angina were fibrous, whereas cellularity increased in patients with unstable angina in proportion to severity of the plaque instability score. These findings corroborate the hypothesis put forth by Fuster and others[96,100,101] that plaque thickness and stability is relatively "protective" against acute coronary events (see earlier). Depré and colleagues[69] concluded that the morphologic pattern of coronary atherosclerotic lesions varies at different stages of ACS; the different stages of angina correlate with an increasing prevalence of the following morphologic characteristics: thrombus, atheroma, neovascularization, and cellular hyperplasia (i.e., plaque thickness).

Lest we "throw out the baby with the bathwater," it is clear that a well-done provocative test that produces *normal* results confers a high *negative predictive value* for perioperative cardiac problems. The inescapable conclusion is that virtually all available screening tests assess hemodynamic abnormalities in cardiac perfusion. If hemodynamically significant stenoses do not reliably produce cardiac events, "positive" tests have a low *positive predictive value*—which is true. Prospective surveillance studies using screening ECGs and enzyme data report perioperative myocardial ischemia rates of 30% for ECG changes alone and 18% for ECG changes with cTnI elevations.[13] Landesberg and associates[165] reported a 32% incidence of perioperative myocardial ischemia after vascular operations. In 1996, a meta-analysis comparing intravenous dipyridamole-thallium-201 imaging and dobutamine echocardiography for risk stratification before vascular surgery concluded that cardiac event rates were low in patients without a history of CAD (1% in 176 patients) compared with patients with CAD and a normal or fixed-deficit pattern (4.8% in 83 patients) or one or more thallium-201 redistribution abnormalities (18.6% in 97 patients; $P = .0001$).[274] Because of the diffuse nature of atherosclerosis, it is not surprising that CAD occurs with great frequency in vascular surgery patients, regardless of the location of PAD. Most of the literature concerning the cardiac morbidity of vascular surgery has focused on patients requiring aortic reconstructions for either aneurysmal or occlusive disease. Myocardial damage in these patients was attributed to the stress of aortic cross-clamping, declamping hypotension, and fluid shifts associated with major abdominal operations. Investigators consistently have shown, however, strikingly high occurrences of early and late cardiac morbidity in patients requiring infrainguinal arterial operations.

A hemodynamically positive test may indicate a large coronary artery atherosclerotic "burden," and a positive screening test may warrant some concern for postoperative cardiac complications. In other words, the index lesions identified by preoperative testing may not accurately predict the precise myocardium at risk. The wide variety of available tests suggests that so far there is no one study that reliably predicts perioperative cardiac adverse consequences. Acute MIs may have been caused by plaque disruption at the site of hemodynamically insignificant coronary lesions.[119,292] Mickley[195] showed that demonstration of significant stenoses (>50%) often leads to mechanical revascularization, including PTCA or coronary artery bypass graft (CABG), but coronary angiography does not adequately predict the location of the culprit plaque that subsequently produces acute MI. These studies apply to vascular surgery patients who are found to have often relatively or completely asymptomatic CAD.

PREVALENCE OF CARDIAC COMPLICATIONS

Although the widespread prevalence of CAD in patients requiring peripheral vascular surgery is well accepted,[2,127,129] the frequency of adverse cardiac outcomes in vascular patients is more controversial. In the often-quoted Cleveland Clinic study, hemodynamically significant CAD was shown in 36% of patients with abdominal aortic aneurysms, 28% of patients with lower extremity ischemia, and 32% of patients with extracranial carotid artery disease.[129] Although these prevalence figures are hard to dispute, comparison of cardiac morbidity of vascular operations between different studies is often misleading because the frequency of cardiac complications depends on the vigor with which the diagnosis is pursued.[52] On average, retrospective reviews (using clinical criteria such as the Cleveland Clinic studies) report lower perioperative MI rates than series in which data are gathered in a proscribed prospective fashion.[132] Contemporary rates of fatal and nonfatal MIs associated with aortic, infrainguinal, and carotid vascular operations are given in Tables 56-1, 56-2, and 56-3. According to our previously published studies, early adverse cardiac outcomes occur *at least* as frequently after infrainguinal procedures as aortic operations,[137,158] and late adverse cardiac events occur about twice as often in patients requiring infrainguinal operations as patients having aortic procedures (25% adverse cardiac events in infrainguinal patients versus 8% in aortic surgery patients at 2-year follow-up; $P = .04$).[159] L'Italien and coworkers[171] reported a twofold *acute* increase in early cardiac morbidity in infrainguinal compared with aortic procedures (13% versus 6%). Fewer postoperative events usually occur after carotid operations, but even this statement has been challenged in the literature. Most investigators have reported MI rates as shown in Table 56-3, with fatal and nonfatal perioperative MI rates averaging about 1%.

In contrast, Ennix and associates[78] reported an operative mortality rate of 18.2% in 77 patients undergoing carotid endarterectomies without coronary revascularization compared with an operative mortality of only 3% in 135 patients who underwent either prior CABG or simultaneous carotid endarterectomy and CABG. Hertzer and Lees[130] reviewed their experience with 335 patients after carotid endarterectomies followed 6 to 11 years after operation. MI caused 38.5% of the deaths that occurred within 11 years. Fatal MIs accounted for 60% of early deaths within 30 days of the operation, occurring in 1.8% of the entire series. Although we have not performed a formal meta-analysis of these data, we estimate the average perioperative fatal and nonfatal MI rates associated with aortic, infrainguinal, and carotid surgery as 2.2%, 4%, and 1.2%. These estimates are far smaller than often appear in the literature—especially grant proposals with requirements for large numbers of "endpoints," hence the use of the generic term *adverse cardiac outcomes* employed in many grant proposals. Our references for each series are available to readers by accessing our sources on the Internet; in developing Tables 56-1, 56-2, and 56-3, we did our best to sort out true MI rates, but this is difficult for numerous reasons. Many studies report "adverse

Table 56-1 Incidence of Perioperative Myocardial Infarction in Elective Infrarenal Aortic Surgery

AUTHOR	SITE	YEAR	PATIENTS (No.)	MI (%)	FATAL MI (%)
Ameli et al[12]	Wellesley, Toronto	1990	105	6.7	4.7
Clark et al[58]	University of Chicago	1990	200	1.5	1.5
Mason et al[183]	Stanford	1995	144	4.2	1.4
Isaacson et al[140]	Emory, Atlanta	1990	102	2	1
Sedwitz et al[266]	VAMC, San Diego	1990	109	3.7	0
Golden et al[115]	Brigham & Women's	1990	500	3	1.2
Shah et al[270]	Albany Medical College	1991	280	—	2.5
Bunt[46]	Maricopa Medical Center	1992	156	0	0
Seeger et al[267]	University of Florida	1994	146	—	0.6
Baron et al[25]	Hopital Pitie-Salpetriere, Paris	1994	457	4.8	2.2
Lord et al[173]	St. Vincent's, Sydney	1994	329	—	1.2
Sicard et al[277]	Washington University	1995	145	—	1.4
Huber et al[136]	University of Florida	1992	722	—	1.5
Carrel et al[50]	University Hospital, Zurich	1995	216	4.6	1.9
Henderson and Effeney[126]	Princess Alexandra, Brisbane	1995	538	10	3.7
Erickson et al[79]	VAMC, Milwaukee	1996	209	3.8	1
Schueppert et al[265]	University of Iowa	1996	400	2.1	0.7
Jarvinen et al[144]	Tampere University, Finland	1996	400	4.2	2.3
D'Angelo et al[66]	Long Island Jewish	1997	113	1.8	0.9
Mingoli et al[197]	Creighton	1997	238	0.9	0.4
Berry et al[32]	Emory	2001	856	1.3	—
Hertzer[127]	Cleveland Clinic	1987	1135	1	0.3
Total			7500	2.2*	1.4*

*Of series reporting same.
MI, myocardial infarction.

Table 56-2 Incidence of Perioperative Myocardial Infarction in Lower Extremity Revascularization

AUTHOR	SITE	YEAR	PATIENTS (No.)	MI (%)	FATAL MI (%)
Taylor et al[290]	Oregon Health Science	1990	434	3.5	1.4
Mills and Taylor[196]	Lackland Air Force Base	1991	120	—	2.5
Rivers et al[242]	Albert Einstein/Montefiore	1991	213	10.8	4.2
Taylor et al[291]	Oregon Health Science	1991	498	5.2	2.2
Quinones-Baldrich et al[227]	UCLA	1992	258	—	3.5
Wengerter et al[299]	Albert Einstein/Montefiore	1992	153	8.5	3.9
Farkouh et al[87]	McMaster University, Ontario	1994	173	2.3	1.2
Fichelle et al[89]	Clinique Bizet, Paris	1995	145	—	1.4
Belkin et al[27]	Brigham & Women's	1995	300	1.7	0.3
Belkin et al[28]	Brigham & Women's	1996	661	3.5	—
Woratyla et al[305]	Albany Medical College	1997	1313	—	2.8
Byrne et al[48]	Albany Medical College	1999	409	—	0
Albertini et al[7]	Hopital d'adultes, Mareile	2000	148	—	1.3
Faries et al[85]	Beth Israel Deaconess	2000	690	1.6	—
Chew et al[55]	Brigham & Women's	2001	154	—	1.8
Jamsen et al[143]	Kuopio University, Finland	2001	263	—	1.1
Faries et al[86]	Beth Israel Deaconess	2001	126	2.4	—
Total			6058	4*	1.8*

*Of series reporting same.
MI, myocardial infarction.

cardiac outcomes" rather than documented MI rates; the problems of CHF and arrhythmias with respect to "hard" outcome measures already have been discussed. In addition, most publications report their "admirable" results; although several investigators described data to "improve" results, it is unlikely that surgeons whose patients had experienced extraordinarily high MI rates would report them.

Several important trends can be ascertained by perusal of Tables 56-1, 56-2, and 56-3: (1) The incidence of fatal and nonfatal MI after carotid surgery is the lowest of common vascular procedures[134]; these procedures are excluded from many randomized series comparing interventions for avoidance of cardiac complications, presumably because the event rates are too low to provide sufficient power for the study. The CARP (Coronary Artery Revascularization Prophylaxis) study (see later) and the zoniporide study (a potent and selective sodium-hydrogen exchanger type I inhibitor that has potential for myocardial protection during

Table 56-3 Incidence of Perioperative Myocardial Infarction in Carotid Endarterectomy

AUTHOR	SITE	YEAR	PATIENTS (No.)	MI (%)	FATAL MI (%)
Mackey et al[174]	Tufts	1990	614	2.6	—
Salenius et al[259]	Tampere University, Finland	1990	331	—	0
Maini et al[175]	Fallon Clinic, Worcester	1990	246	0.8	—
Bunt[46]	Maricopa Medical Center	1992	114	0	0
Freischlag et al[95]	UCLA	1992	141	1.4	0
NASCET[208]	Multiple	1991	328	1.2	0.3
Hobson et al[134]	VAMC Multiple	1993	211	4.2	1.9
Berman et al[31]	University of Arizona	1994	203	2.5	0
Shah et al[271]	Albany Medical College	1994	654	0.3	0.3
Ombrellaro et al[211]	University of Tennessee	1995	266	1.5	0
ACAS[80]	Multiple	1995	724	—	0.1
Mattos et al[185]	Southern Illinois University	1995	2243	—	0.7
Kerdiles et al[152]	Rennes, France	1997	912	—	0.3
Dardik et al[67]	Johns Hopkins	1997	201	2.5	0.5
Hertzer[127]	Cleveland Clinic	1987	2228	—	0.4
Samson et al[262]	Vascular Associates, Sarasota	1998	654	0.6	0.5
Barnett et al[24]	Multiple	1998	1087	—	0.2
Economopoulos et al[77]	University of Arizona	1999	190	1	1
Hamdan et al[123]	Beth Israel Deaconess	1999	1001	0.5	0.1
Zannetti et al[310]	Multiple	1999	1305	—	0.2
Bowyer et al[40]	Travis Air Force Base	2000	489	1	—
Archie[16]	Carolina Associates and Wake Medical Center	2000	1360	1.8	0.8
Chang et al[51]	Albany Medical College	2000	2233	—	0.5
Maxwell et al[187]	University of North Carolina and New Hanover Regional	2000	1970	1	0.5
Papavasiliou et al[216]	Dartmouth-Hitchcock	2000	803	0.6	0
Radak et al[234]	Belgrade University	2000	2469	0.8	0.4
McCarthy et al[188]	Royal United, Bath, UK	2001	240	0.8	0.4
Katras et al[150]	East Tennessee State	2001	322	0.6	0.3
Hayes et al[125]	Leicester Royal Infirmary, UK	2001	274	—	0.7
Aziz et al[18]	Harbor UCLA	2001	123	1.6	0.8
Rockman et al[243]	New York University	2001	2476	0.9	—
Ommer et al[212]	University of Düsseldorf	2001	2262	1.2	0.5
Scavee et al[263]	Universite Catholique de Louvain, Belgium	2001	600	0.5	0.2
Mattos et al[186]	Southern Illinois University	2001	1068	0.7	0.4
Bond et al[38]	Multiple	2001	1729	0.4	0.2
O'Hara et al[209]	Cleveland Clinic	2002	195	—	0.5
Total			28,362	1*	0.4*

*Of series reporting same.
MI, myocardial infarction.

ischemia) exclude carotid operations in their protocols. (2) MIs after aortic surgery average about 2%, and the values have remained fairly stable despite a plethora of strategies to avoid cardiac morbidity in the 1990s. (3) The average fatal and nonfatal MI rates after infrainguinal surgery (performed acutely) average approximately 4%; there seems to be a trend in decreasing rates in more recent series, perhaps suggesting that surgeons are believing the data we presented regarding the cardiac morbidity of infrainguinal bypasses in the early 1990s. Overall, improvements also may be related to more widespread use of beta blockers, optimization of anesthesia, or—an unknown—more frequent use of preoperative coronary revascularization (though we doubt it, based on our review).

■ PREOPERATIVE SCREENING TESTS

Although "outcomes research" is gaining ground rapidly, perhaps no topic related to vascular surgery has generated more articles than preoperative screening tests to assess cardiac, pulmonary, and other perioperative risks associated with vascular procedures and to attempt to decrease complications. A review article by Lee and Boucher[168] summarizes these tests in patients with stable CAD. In addition, we have summarized the strengths and weaknesses of many of these studies in previous publications.[157,160]

The principal goals of preoperative identification of patients at high risk for adverse cardiac outcomes are to permit intervention to treat underlying CAD (e.g., PTCA or CABG), use more intensive anesthetic monitoring or "safer" anesthetic techniques (e.g., use of pulmonary artery pressure monitoring catheters), administer medications to decrease cardiac morbidity (e.g., beta blockers), or change preoperative plans (e.g., performance of axillobifemoral rather than direct aortic reconstruction for aortic occlusive disease). Preoperative screening tests run the gamut from completely noninvasive (e.g., scoring systems), to minimally invasive (e.g., echocardiographic estimation of ejection fraction), to moderately invasive (e.g., dipyridamole thallium screening tests), to maximally invasive (e.g., coronary angiography). The number and variety of tests and sophisticated algorithms available underscore the absence of a consensus for optimal cardiac risk stratification in patients undergoing peripheral vascular surgery. With respect to preoperative CAD risk stratification, an abundant variety of clinical risk indices has been proposed.[1,70,107,117,118,168,169,172,215,272,275,304,309] We and others have recently reviewed the copious literature and varieties of strategies for cardiac screening.[161,204,205]

Additional recommendations for preoperative cardiac evaluation abound. Although the following list is far from inclusive, it describes some of the many proposed tests:

1. Exercise treadmill testing (e.g., the "Bruce protocol," which many vascular patients cannot perform because of claudication, congestive heart disease, or chronic lung disease)[64,65,71,145,192,268]
2. Ambulatory ECG (Holter monitoring)[158,178,202,217,231,233]
3. Radionuclide ventriculography[151,218,220]
4. Dipyridamole-thallium scintigraphy[19,33,46,68,74,154,162,206,236,274,303]
5. Dobutamine stress echocardiography (DSE) or sestamibi stress echocardiography[19,33,68,162]

Various combinations of studies to predict the occurrence of adverse cardiac outcomes also have appeared—literally by the hundreds (e.g., comparison of clinical examination, exercise testing, dobutamine stress echocardiography, and coronary arteriography by Therre and colleagues[293]).

Most authorities would agree that coronary angiography provides precise anatomic assessment of the status of CAD, but in light of current hypotheses of the pathophysiology for perioperative cardiac morbidity, as discussed earlier, it is difficult to justify routine arteriography, unless the patient's symptoms warrant revascularization on their own merits.[219] Using the technique of decision analysis, Mason and coworkers[183] from Stanford University compared three strategies to deal with CAD in vascular patients. Decision analysis found that vascular surgery without preoperative coronary angiography generally leads to better outcomes. According to these investigators, preoperative coronary angiography should be reserved for patients whose estimated mortality from vascular surgery is substantially higher than average. In contrast, Glance[112] performed a decision-tree model to compare the cost-effectiveness of four preoperative screening strategies based on data regarding patient mortality, morbidity, and costs from a literature review. He concluded that selective screening before vascular surgery may improve 5-year survival and may be cost-effective, especially compared with routine angiography. The incremental cost-effectiveness ratio for selective screening was significantly lower than for routine angiography ($44,800/years of life saved versus $93,300/years of life saved; $P < .02$). Similar cost comparisons have been described by others.[275]

As previously discussed, all of these screening tests rely heavily on development of hemodynamically related symptoms (which generally occur because of hypoperfusion) or demonstration of a hemodynamically significant stenosis. Because it has not been possible to identify the most vulnerable and unstable plaques, these tests all have failed to predict reliably postoperative myocardial events. A normal test *does* correlate with *absence* of events, most likely because of a lesser atherosclerotic—CAD—burden; hence the good "negative predictive value" of many studies but failure to predict accurately adverse cardiac outcomes. In a well-conducted study by Poldermans and associates[222] of preoperative DSE in patients who subsequently died of acute MI and who underwent autopsy by a pathologist unaware of the DSE results, there was relatively poor correlation of the anatomic location of the infarction; in 50% of the patients, the MI extended beyond the ischemic territory assessed by DSE. Poldermans and associates[222] concluded that perioperative medical therapy should be aimed at coronary plaque stabilization.

In 1996 and more recently in 2002, the ACC and the American Heart Association (AHA) appointed a task force of respected scholars to develop guidelines for perioperative cardiovascular evaluation for noncardiac surgery. Aside from the able representation of Hertzer, who was a member of the 1996 committee, surgeons generally have been underrepresented in this task force. The 2002 document is 58 pages long. In fairness to the committee, the guidelines are an attempt to be complete—akin to "Everything you ever wanted to know about cardiac disease in vascular patients." The lack of surgical input and the complexity of the document limit its utility, however. Figure 56-3 is an algorithm that summarizes the ACC/AHA guidelines. Although there is much useful information in the publication, it is limited by almost overwhelming complexity; simply trying to follow the suggested steps and arrows for a given patient is an ordeal.

Despite this complexity, numerous publications have appeared showing the apparent utility of employing the ACC/AHA Guidelines. Samain and colleagues[260] retrospectively applied the guidelines to a group of 133 patients undergoing aortic surgery. Similar to the guidelines, this study was complex; it concluded that *had* the investigators used the guidelines, at least one cardiac-related death could have been avoided, but this is pure speculation. Farid and colleagues[84] at the Cleveland Clinic found abnormal test results in 27 of 181 patients scheduled for major surgery; 2 patients declined treatment, 8 patients had primary medical management, and 17 had cardiac catheterization with a variety of findings (including two "normals"). Only 15% (27 of 180) of the patients with indications for a stress test had a positive result, and even fewer patients had any alteration of the perioperative period. It would seem from the results of this study that the authors could answer the question they posed in the title as follows "effect on perioperative outcome—very little." A prospective evaluation of implementation of the ACC/AHA Guidelines for preoperative cardiac risk assessment before aortic surgery has been completed at the University of Michigan, and results should be available soon (personal communication).

■ OUTCOME OF CARDIAC COMPLICATIONS

Much of what is known about the incidence of acute MI and fatal coronary heart disease comes from isolated community surveillance studies,[2,113,114,191] cohort studies of cardiovascular disease,[142,287] or studies of managed care programs.[193] We have already discussed the apparent decrease in deaths

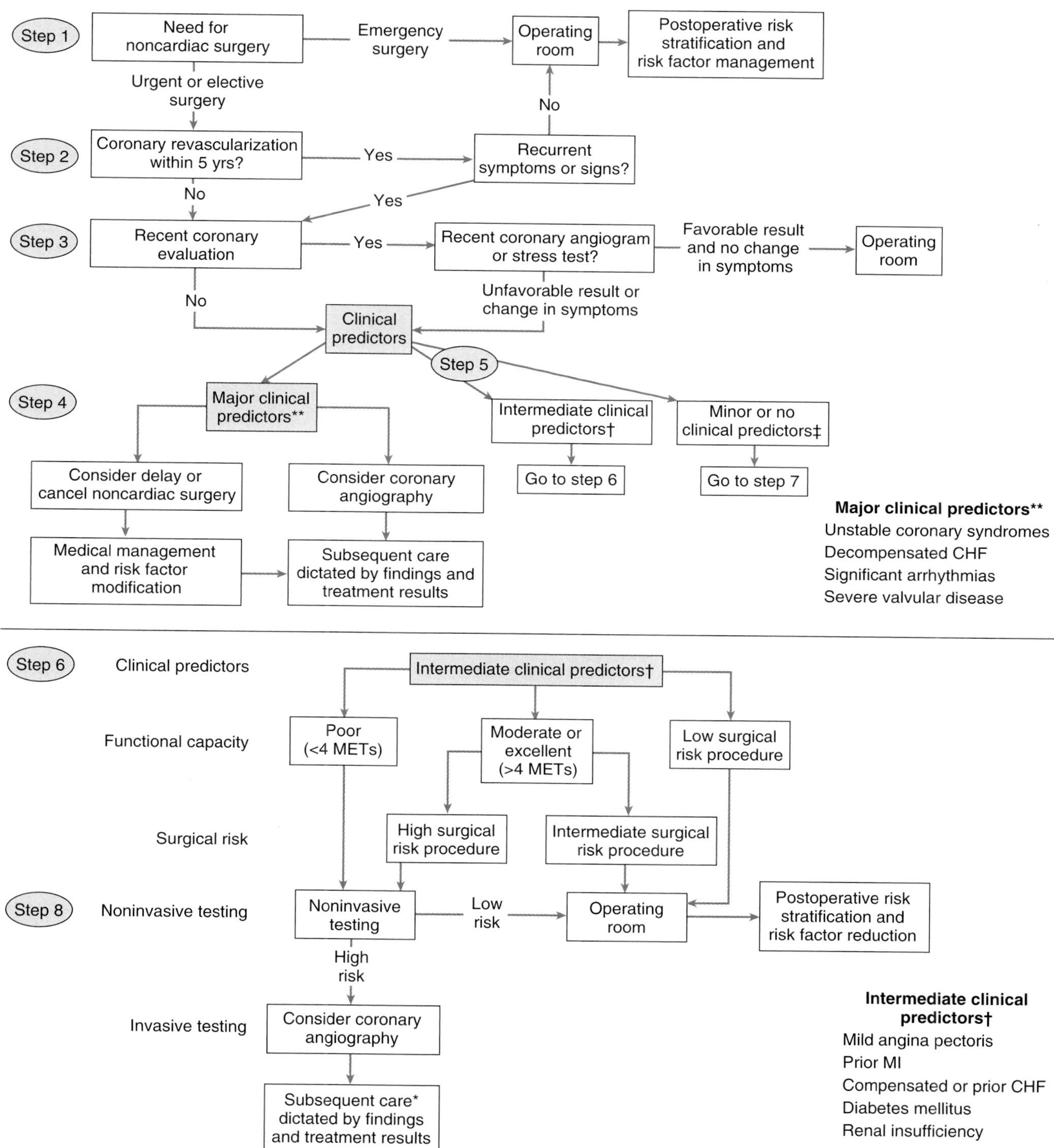

FIGURE 56-3 Algorithm recommended by the American College of Cardiology and American Heart Association (ACC/AHA) with steps to help evaluate vascular patients with presumed coronary artery disease. The ACC/AHA Guidelines is a scholarly and well-written document, but it is complex and difficult to follow. CHF, congestive heart failure; ECG, electrocardiogram; MI, myocardial infarction. (From Eagle KA, Berger PB, Calkins H, et al: ACC/AHA guideline update for a report of the American College of Cardiology/American Heart Association Task Force on Practice Guidelines (Committee to Update the 1996 Guidelines on Perioperative Cardiovascular Evaluation for Noncardiac Surgery.) Circulation 105:1257-1267, 2002.)

Continued

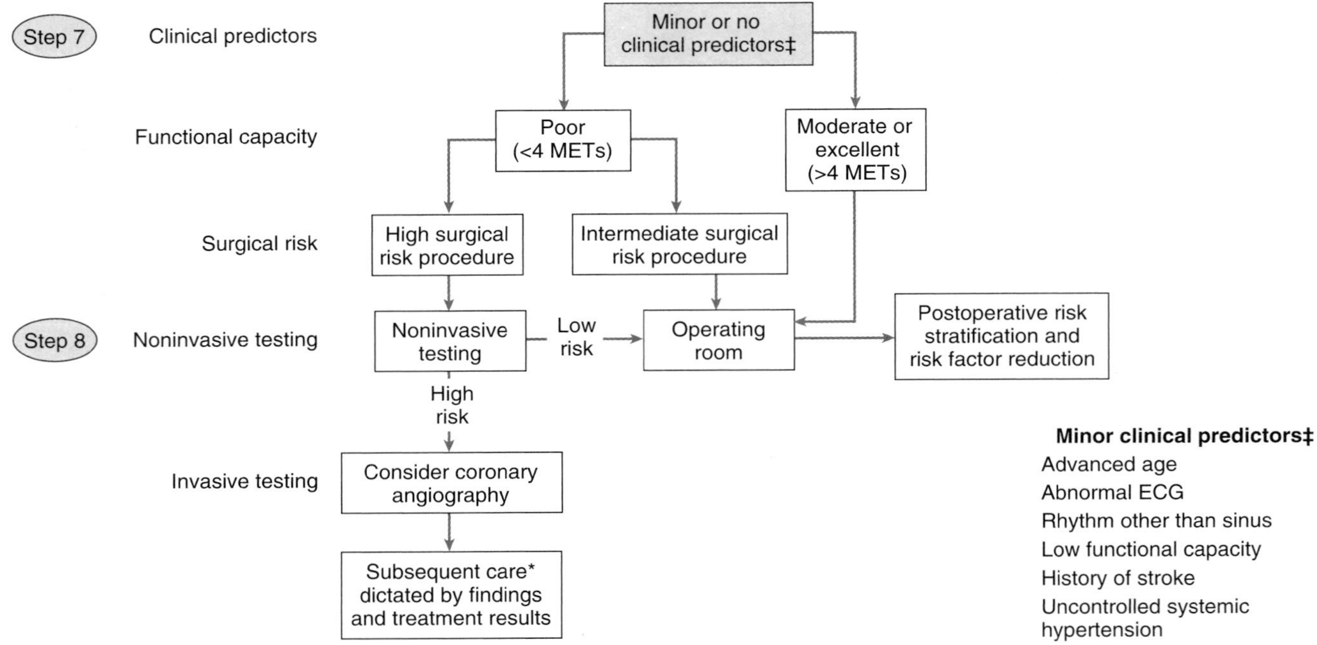

FIGURE 56-3—cont'd. Algorithm recommended by the American College of Cardiology and American Heart Association (ACC/AHA) with steps to help manage vascular patients with presumed coronary artery disease.

due to CAD in the general U.S. population.[109,244,286] In the surgical population, the adverse outcomes of transmural, Q-wave MIs in postoperative patients have been well documented.

Mangano and associates[178] indicated that of the 25 million patients who undergo noncardiac operations in the United States each year, approximately 3 million are at risk of having CAD, and approximately 50,000 of these patients have a perioperative MI. More than half of the 40,000 annual postoperative deaths are due to transmural MIs.[179] In a selective review of several thousand vascular surgical procedures, Hertzer[127] found that cardiac complications were responsible for about half of all perioperative deaths and that fatal events were nearly five times more likely to occur in the presence of standard preoperative indications of CAD. Sprung and colleagues[280] analyzed 6948 vascular operations at the Cleveland Clinic and found 107 patients with postoperative transmural MIs. The overall in-hospital mortality rate was 20.6% with the highest mortality on postoperative day 0. In a similar series, Badner and co-workers[23] reported a 17% post-MI mortality rate after non-cardiac surgery. Although these mortality rates are better than rates reported in older series (presumably owing to improved anesthetic care, beta blockers, and so forth), a death rate from MI of almost one in five is startlingly high.

The late (5-year) mortality rate for vascular patients suspected to have CAD is twice that for patients who were not suspected to have CAD (approximately 40% versus 20%).[128] We reported an adverse cardiac outcome risk of 25% among a group of patients having infrainguinal bypass in a short 2-year follow-up.[159] As Wilson[301] wrote in a provocative editorial, when Leriché termed vascular intervention the "surgery of ruins," he had in mind the shortened survival of these patients as a result of systemic atherosclerosis. Wilson went on to say, "As a rule of thumb, one can estimate a mortality rate of approximately 5% per year in patients who have undergone operation for arterial occlusive disease at any site." If anything, this estimate is probably on the low end.

Some authors have questioned the clinical importance of non–Q wave MIs (i.e., "chemical" MIs) in vascular surgery patients. Yeager and colleagues[307,308] followed 8 of 31 patients who sustained a perioperative MI with "chemical MIs" in which enzyme elevation was the sole indicator of post-operative MI. At a mean follow-up of 27.7 months, survival for patients with nonfatal perioperative MI at 1 and 4 years was 80% and 51%, which did not differ significantly from that of control patients (90% and 60%; $P > .05$) Although these investigators concluded that "a perioperative chemical MI" may not be a clinically significant event, patients surviving nonfatal perioperative MIs after peripheral vascular surgery did have a higher incidence of subsequent adverse cardiac events and subsequent coronary artery revascularization. Similarly, McFalls and coworkers[190] reported that even in vascular patients with perioperative transmural MIs, nonfatal perioperative MI was only a marginally significant independent predictor of 1-year mortality ($P = .06$), whereas the extent of vascular disease at presentation was a more important determinant of long-term survival.

Such optimism with respect to the relatively benign outcomes after "chemical" MIs is not supported by reports in the medical literature. More than half of all acute MIs in the United States occurring in ambulatory patients are non–Q wave MIs, and this proportion is increasing.[35,114,280] Several investigations have reported higher rates of early and late ischemic complications, such as reinfarction and postinfarction angina, presumably because of the presence of viable but jeopardized myocardium within the perfusion zone of the artery responsible for the infarct.[35,39,49,57,106,138,170,176,182,207,239,264] The best management approach to non–Q wave MIs is controversial. The 1987 ACC/AHA guidelines recommended routine coronary arteriography for all patients after non–Q wave MI,[2] although newer guidelines no longer endorse this approach.[221,249] To determine the optimal treatment strategy for patients with non–Q wave MIs, Boden and colleagues[35] performed a multicenter prospective randomized trial comparing invasive management (i.e., routine coronary angiography followed by myocardial revascularization) with conservative management (i.e., medical therapy and noninvasive testing). The VANQWISH (Veterans Affairs Non–Q-Wave Infarction Strategies in Hospital) trial randomized 920 patients to one of the two strategies. A substantial 28% rate of cardiac events occurred during a follow-up period of 12 to 44 months, but overall mortality did not differ significantly between patients assigned to one group or the other. Because most patients with non–Q wave MIs did not benefit from routine, early invasive management, the investigators recommended a conservative, ischemia-guided initial approach. Although the VANQUWISH study may be criticized for potential inapplicability to women, it cannot be said that patients cared for in Department of Veterans Affairs (VA) hospitals received care of poorer quality than patients cared for in non-VA hospitals. Petersen and associates[220] compared 2486 veterans discharged from 81 VA hospitals and 29,249 Medicare patients discharged from non-VA hospitals and found no difference in mortality, despite the fact that VA patients had more coexisting conditions than Medicare patients.

■ ADVISABILITY OF REVASCULARIZATION FOR CORONARY ARTERY DISEASE IN VASCULAR PATIENTS

There is no "free lunch" in the search for CAD in PAD patients. A retrospective analysis of the experience with extended cardiac evaluations and interventions before vascular surgery at the Denver VA Medical Center appeared in 2000.[161] Extended cardiac evaluation included standard screening studies plus special tests, including echocardiography, radionuclide ventriculography, dipyridamole thallium scintigraphy, and cardiac catheterization. Extended cardiac evaluations were performed in 42 patients: 9 (21%) had PTCA, and 7 (17%) had CABG. Unfavorable outcomes occurred in *one third* of candidates for vascular surgery subjected to extensive preoperative assessment of cardiac risk over a 1-year period (Table 56-4). Eight patients (20%) who were so evaluated elected not to undergo the vascular procedures for which their cardiac evaluations were undertaken. Most of these individuals (seven of eight) had a potentially life-threatening vascular disorder (abdominal aortic aneurysms). The reasons cited for refusal were multifactorial, but many patients stated something to the effect that "they had been through enough." There was no difference in cardiac morbidity between the patients who had extensive evaluations and interventions compared with patients who did not (2.4% versus 2.9%; P = not significant). The patients who ultimately refused vascular surgery were of particular interest; in the review of implementation of the ACC/AHA Guidelines by Farid and colleagues,[84] 3 of 27 patients (11%) who met ACC/AHA criteria either refused further treatment at the Cleveland Clinic or never underwent the originally planned noncardiac operations. The Denver VA Medical Center and Cleveland Clinic publications are relatively small, retrospective series and the VA medical center study did not have a defined strict protocol for determination of operative cardiac risk. Nonetheless, it is worrisome that many patients did not seem to benefit from extensive searches for CAD.

In addition to the previously discussed controversies over the best way to stratify patients for cardiac risk, what to do when severe, correctable CAD is identified remains unsettled. Advocates of coronary revascularization before peripheral vascular operations contend that it enhances the safety of the vascular procedure itself and potentially prolongs the life expectancy in these patients. We already have discussed the report by Ennix and coworkers[78] in which prophylactic CABG markedly improved long-term survival after carotid endarterectomies. Similar results have been reported for patients undergoing PAD operations in other locations.[94,128,129,189,238] Many of these reports describe large numbers of patients who did well after coronary revascularization, but they describe selected patients, and none were randomized or prospective.

Caution is warranted in widespread application of coronary revascularization before PAD surgery. The morbidity and mortality rates of CABG and PTCA in elderly patients with PAD are substantial. Cutler and Leppo[63] screened 116 patients scheduled for peripheral vascular operations with dipyridamole-thallium scintigraphy and referred 7 (6%) for CABG. One patient (14%) died after CABG, and another died awaiting CABG (14%). No operative deaths occurred after the subsequent 106 PAD operations; the 2 deaths that occurred (1.7% of total) were directly related to the cardiac screening program. A policy

Table 56-4 Adverse Outcomes in 16 of 42 Patients Undergoing Extended Cardiac Evaluations before Major Vascular Surgery in a 1-Year Period at Denver VAMC

COMPLICATION	NO. PATIENTS
Patient refused vascular surgery for which cardiac evaluation was undertaken	8
Limb loss owing to delay in vascular surgery because of cardiac evaluation	2
Prosthetic graft infection after arteriogram requiring graft removal/revision	1
Iatrogenic femoral artery pseudoaneurysm requiring surgical repair	2
Sternal wound infection after coronary artery bypass graft operation	1
Contrast-induced renal failure requiring hemodialysis	1
Anoxic brain injury after CABG	1
Total	16 (38%)

CABG, coronary artery bypass graft.

of prophylactic myocardial revascularization at the University of Iowa led to CABG procedures in 15 patients, with a mortality rate of 6.7% and postoperative complications in 20% of patients.[194,283] Mesh and colleagues[194] from Cleveland and Cincinnati, Ohio, reported 3.6-fold higher morbidity rates (39.7%) in patients with PAD who underwent CABG compared with non-PAD patients (16.7%). Often the recovery from this major morbidity either precluded or substantially delayed the peripheral vascular surgery for which the cardiac evaluation was undertaken. Even PTCA in patients with PAD carries higher morbidity and mortality than in patients without PAD.[120,136] Finally, the increased long-term survival in patients with CAD treated by coronary revascularization as proven by the CASS (Coronary Artery Surgery Study) trial, may not apply to older patients with peripheral vascular disease, which is a strong, independent predictor of long-term mortality in patients with stable CAD; in addition, the CASS patients all were significantly symptomatic, whereas that may not be true for the patient with PAD whose CAD is discovered by provocative testing (i.e., it may be unfair to extrapolate the CASS results to the PAD population).[75,76,240]

Although to date there are no prospective randomized comparisons between "aggressive" cardiac management versus best "conservative" medical care, a report by Massie and associates[184] examined the results of coronary revascularization compared with control subjects. Ischemic responses to dipyridamole scans were observed in 297 patients, of whom 70 underwent cardiac catheterization and 25 underwent coronary revascularization procedures. Adverse outcomes affected 46% of the coronary angiography group and 44% of the control group. Patients who underwent coronary angiography and were considered for cardiac revascularization had fewer cardiac events with a subsequent vascular operation than did the control subjects. Any possible benefit from invasive cardiac evaluation was offset, however, by three deaths and two MIs that complicated the cardiac evaluation. There was no significant difference between the angiography group and the matched control subjects with respect to perioperative nonfatal MI (13% versus 0%), fatal MI (4% versus 3%), late nonfatal MI (16% versus 19%), or late cardiac death (10% versus 13%). The risks of extended cardiac evaluation and treatment did not produce any improvement in either the perioperative or the long-term survival rate. The authors concluded that for most vascular surgery patients who have a positive dipyridamole-thallium scan, coronary angiography does not provide any additional useful information or benefit.

■ ROLE OF PERIOPERATIVE PULMONARY ARTERY CATHETERS AND PHARMACOLOGIC THERAPY

Intuitively, it would seem that optimizing a vascular patient's volume status by means of a perioperative use of pulmonary artery catheters would enhance the safety of vascular surgery. Neither retrospective nor prospective trials have convincingly shown this expected result. Since 1980, reports have described attempts at maintenance of optimal cardiac performance to improve results of vascular (particularly aortic) surgery. Whittemore and associates[300] suggested that this approach was responsible for the low perioperative mortality rate and improved late survival rate in their patients, but the study was retrospective and based on historical control subjects. More recent randomized, controlled trials of pulmonary artery catheters generally have failed to achieve improved outcomes. In 1997, Bender and coworkers[29] randomized 104 consecutive patients having major vascular operations to a pulmonary artery catheter versus placement of a catheter only "if clinically indicated" (introducing potential bias into this study). Except for discrepancy in the amounts of fluids administered, there were no significant differences in outcomes or surgical intensive care unit length of stay, suggesting no benefit of routine pulmonary artery catheters in elective vascular surgery patients. In 1998, Valentine and colleagues[298] performed a truly randomized trial of this technique. Valentine and colleagues[298] randomized 120 patients undergoing elective aortic surgery to placement of pulmonary artery catheters ($n = 60$) versus a control group receiving intravenous hydration on the ward ($n = 60$). These investigators found no significant differences in cardiac morbidity, renal insufficiency, pulmonary events, intensive care unit stay, or hospital stay between groups; they concluded that there was no benefit to routine use of pulmonary artery catheters. A meta-analysis of routine perioperative pulmonary artery catheterization concluded that it has no effect on rate of complications in vascular surgery patients.[26]

Although some of the articles mentioned placed pulmonary artery catheters in the intensive care unit the day before surgery, they variably attempted to "optimize" the cardiac function of the patients involved. There is even more controversy over the utility of such optimization. At least 10 studies have addressed perioperative hemodynamic optimization to improve outcomes after vascular surgery, but most have been retrospective reviews with historical controls with contradictory findings.[30,47,90,225,237,276,300] Four prospective, randomized controlled trials of preoperative hemodynamic optimization of cardiac and volume status in vascular surgery patients showed no benefit, even when the goals of maintaining optimal arterial and venous oxygen saturations were achieved.[37,146,298,311] One "positive" randomized, prospective study of the effect of deliberate perioperative increase of oxygen delivery on mortality in high-risk surgical patients using dopexamine hydrochloride showed improved outcomes, but this study was not limited to vascular operations.[41] Most randomized, prospective trials of preoperative hemodynamic optimization in vascular surgery have failed to show significant benefits, and the costs to perform this routinely would be enormous.

There have been remarkably few reports on the efficacy of administering theoretically beneficial medications to prevent cardiac complications in vascular surgical patients. Prophylactic nitroglycerin infusion during noncardiac surgery does not reduce perioperative ischemia, as shown in a prospective, randomized study from Columbia University.[72] Another impractical study examined the efficacy of a small oral dose of clonidine in patients having vascular surgery; although it appeared that this drug was beneficial, absorption of an oral agent is unpredictable in vascular surgery, and the work has not been confirmed by other studies.[285]

Table 56-5 Controlled, Randomized Trials of Perioperative Beta Blockade

AUTHOR	YEAR	No.	DRUG	FOLLOW-UP	CONTROL	BETA BLOCKERS
Stone et al[284]	1988	128	Control = 39; labetalol = 29; atenolol = 30; oxprenolol = 30	Intraoperative	28% Ischemia	2% Ischemia; $P < .001$
Mangano et al[181]	1996	200	Control = 101; atenolol = 99	2 Years	21% Mortality	10% Mortality; $P < .019$
Poldermans et al[224]	1999	112	Control = 53; bisoprolol = 59	30 Days	17% Cardiac death	3.4% Cardiac death; $P = .02$
Raby et al[230]	1999	26	Control = 11; esmolol = 15	48 Hours	73% Persist ischemia	33% Persist ischemia; $P < .05$
Urban et al[297]	2000	107	Control = 55; esmolol = 52	48 Hours	15% Ischemia; 6% MI; 16% cardiac morbidity	6% Ischemia; 2% MI; 11% cardiac morbidity; P = NS
Poldermans et al[223]	2001	101	Control = 44; bisoprolol = 57	2 Years	32% Cardiac events	12% Cardiac events; $P = .025$

MI, myocardial infarction; NS, not significant.

Finally, mivazerol, a drug with α_2-agonist properties (the "active" counterpart of a beta blocker), was evaluated in a randomized, blinded, prospective study of 1897 patients with CAD undergoing noncardiac surgery (48% vascular surgery), with no alteration in the rates of MI or cardiac death.[210] Studies of this agent in vascular patients in the United States have been discontinued.

In contrast to the absence of efficacy of the drugs discussed in the preceding paragraph, it is now well accepted that beta blockade is efficacious in reducing short-term and long-term cardiac morbidity and mortality in vascular surgery patients. Selzman and colleagues[269] published a thoughtful, thorough review article of β-adrenergic blockade as prophylaxis against perioperative cardiovascular morbidity and mortality. This publication reviews the history of β-adrenergic blockade and summarizes the pathophysiology of its mechanisms of action and the data supporting beta-blocker use in virtually all vascular patients. Beta blocker therapy is not a new concept, although its popularity had not surged until more recent prospective trials proved its efficacy. The neurohormonal stress of surgery is related in part to adrenal cortical stimulation with catecholamine release, one of the links to perioperative myocardial ischemia associated with vascular and other serious operations.[241,261] Catecholamines increase each of the four major determinants of myocardial oxygen consumption (heart rate, preload, afterload, and contractility).[42] In 1982, Smulyan and associates[278] recommended continuous propranolol infusion after abdominal surgery. Yeager and coworkers[309] reported reduction in perioperative MIs after vascular surgery using beta blockade. This work and subsequent nonrandomized studies led to five controlled, randomized, prospective trials of perioperative blockade in patients (mostly vascular) with known or probable coexistent CAD. These studies are summarized in Table 56-5, and all show a decrease in acute or chronic cardiac morbidity and mortality using beta blockade.[181,223,224,230,284,297] It is apparent that acute perioperative ischemic events, MIs, cardiac death, overall mortality, and adverse cardiac events in general are decreased in frequency by administration of beta blockers.[17] The advantageous effects of beta blockers relate to the decreased myocardial oxygen consumption they produce as illustrated in Figure 56-4, which summarizes the methods by which myocardial oxygenation may be minimized.[17,42] Administration of beta blockers in the perioperative period is safe and effective.[124]

■ RECOMMENDATIONS

This chapter has been replete with disclaimers regarding retrospective studies, absence of control data, and a notable absence of level 1 data to guide treatment protocols.[62] A randomized prospective multicenter trial currently is under way that is expected to provide extremely important information with respect to optimal management of the vascular surgery patient who may have CAD. The protocol has been approved and funded by the VA Cooperative Studies Program section, and a complete protocol has been described by McFalls and coworkers.[190] Figure 56-5 summarizes the details of randomization and algorithm of the CARP study. In brief, a sample size of 559 randomized patients will provide 90% power to detect a difference in 3.5-year survival rates of 75% versus 85%. Allowing for 10% of the patients to drop out after randomization, the final target sample size is 620 patients, which will be gathered at 18 high-quality VA medical centers. As in every VA study, the results will suffer from an excess of men versus women, and recruitment has been difficult so far. Nevertheless, the study is proceeding well, and we are about halfway to completion. Only prospective randomization of comparable patients will provide the answer whether coronary evaluation or coronary revascularization or both before elective vascular surgery would enhance the safety of vascular surgery or prolong life of patients.

Until the CARP results are available, our recommendations are to keep things simple. Rather than attempting to follow the complex ACC/AHA guidelines, we prefer to assume that most of our vascular patients have at least some degree of CAD. Because beta blockade is effective in

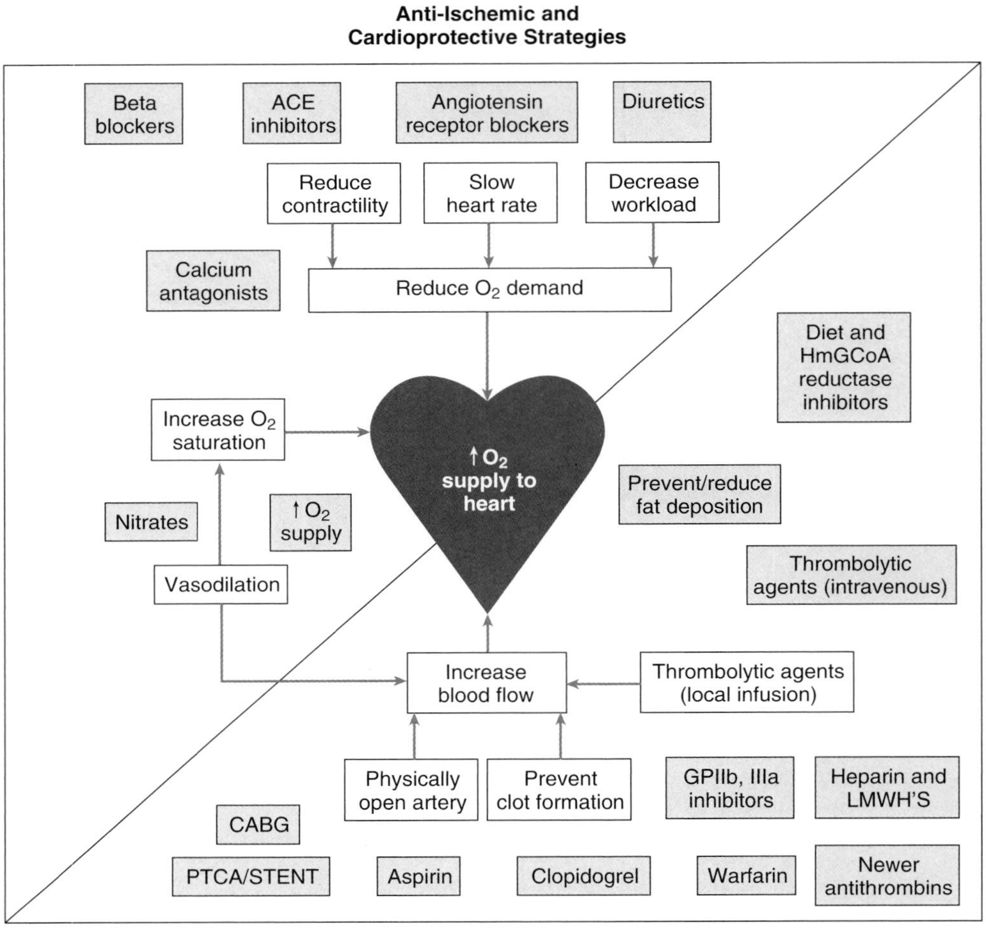

Anti-Ischemic and Cardioprotective Strategies

Beta blockers
ACE inhibitors
Angiotensin receptor blockers
Diuretics
Reduce contractility
Slow heart rate
Decrease workload
Calcium antagonists
Reduce O_2 demand
Diet and HmGCoA reductase inhibitors
Increase O_2 saturation
↑ O_2 supply to heart
Prevent/reduce fat deposition
Nitrates
↑ O_2 supply
Vasodilation
Thrombolytic agents (intravenous)
Increase blood flow
Thrombolytic agents (local infusion)
Physically open artery
Prevent clot formation
GPIIb, IIIa inhibitors
Heparin and LMWH'S
CABG
PTCA/STENT
Aspirin
Clopidogrel
Warfarin
Newer antithrombins

FIGURE 56-4 Factors that play a role in myocardial oxygen consumption. ACE, angiotensin-converting enzyme; CABG, coronary artery bypass graft; GP, glycoprotein; HMG CoA, hydroxymethylglutaryl coenzyme A; LMWH, low-molecular-weight heparin; PTCA, percutaneous transluminal coronary angioplasty.

decreasing cardiac morbidity, optimization of anesthesia and the use of beta blockers effectively decrease cardiac morbidity (see earlier). Figure 56-6 summarizes my present recommendations. Many "boxes" are identical (i.e., operate, but assume most patients have some degree of CAD, use beta blockers in virtually all patients, and optimize the rate/pressure product in anesthesia). We avoid provocative tests or coronary revascularization except in unusual cases. If patients have severe CAD, consideration should be given to modification of the planned operation or use of conservative management if possible.

Because CARP is a VA study with the disclaimers associated with most such investigations, it is likely that some controversy will persist, and well-respected and knowledgeable vascular surgeons have a variety of opinions on optimal management strategies. Fleisher and Eagle[91] have written a clinical practice guideline that concludes, "in high-risk patients scheduled to undergo noncardiac surgery, coronary-artery bypass grafting and percutaneous coronary revascularization are appropriate if they are indicated *independently* of the need for noncardiac surgery." I do not disagree with this statement. Additionally, I agree with Raby's[228] editorial, which concludes, "Is preoperative cardiac testing necessary among vascular patients? Based on the above body of evidence, the answer for most patients appears to be: No." Bodenheimer[36] has opined, "Otherwise, the tests should be skipped and the patient cleared [for vascular surgery]." I also agree with the title of the article by Itani and colleagues[141]—that "preoperative cardiac evaluation is unnecessary in most patients undergoing vascular operations." In the final analysis, as Goldman[116] has stated in an editorial, "The bad news is we still do not have all the answers. The good news is that approaches to the treatment of a cardiac patient undergoing noncardiac surgery are increasingly being driven by data, including data from randomized clinical trials."

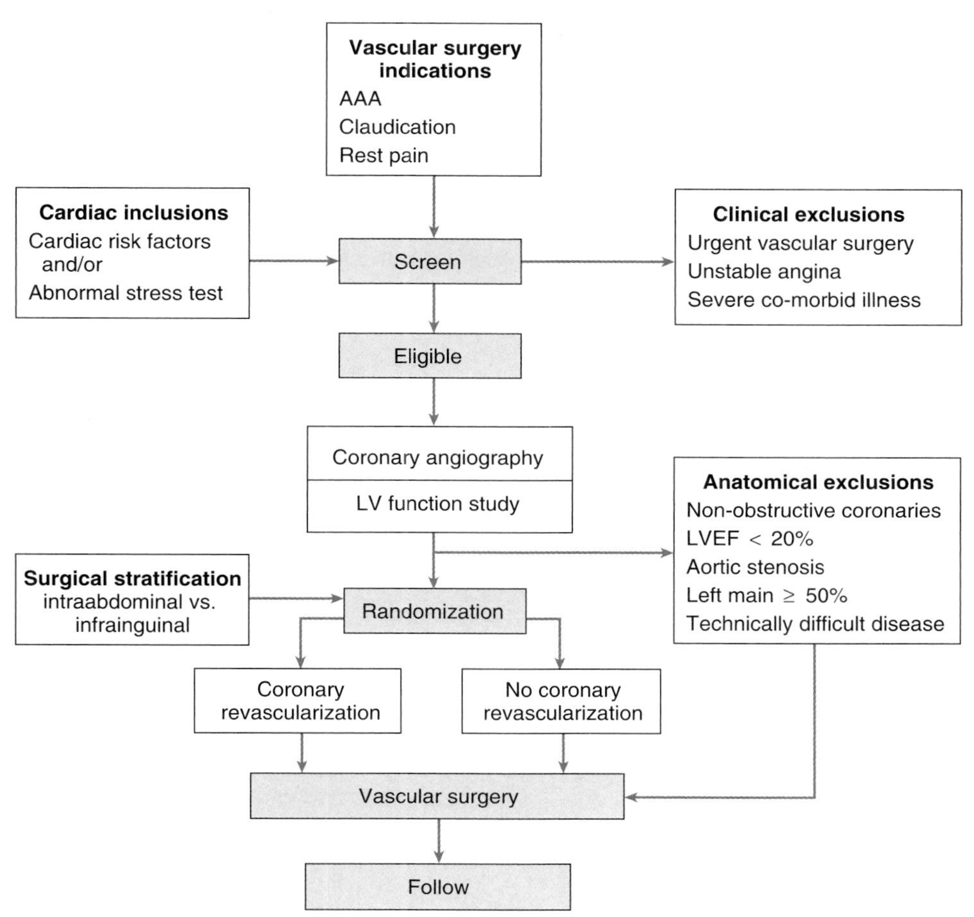

FIGURE 56-5 Algorithm of the CARP (Coronary Artery Revascularization Prophylaxis) study, a Department of Veterans Affairs–sponsored study that comprises a randomized prospective multicenter trial to answer the hypothesis that coronary artery evaluation and revascularization enhance the acute safety of peripheral arterial operations and potentially increase long-term survival of patients. AAA, abdominal aortic aneurysm; LV, left ventricular; LVEF, left ventricular ejection fraction.

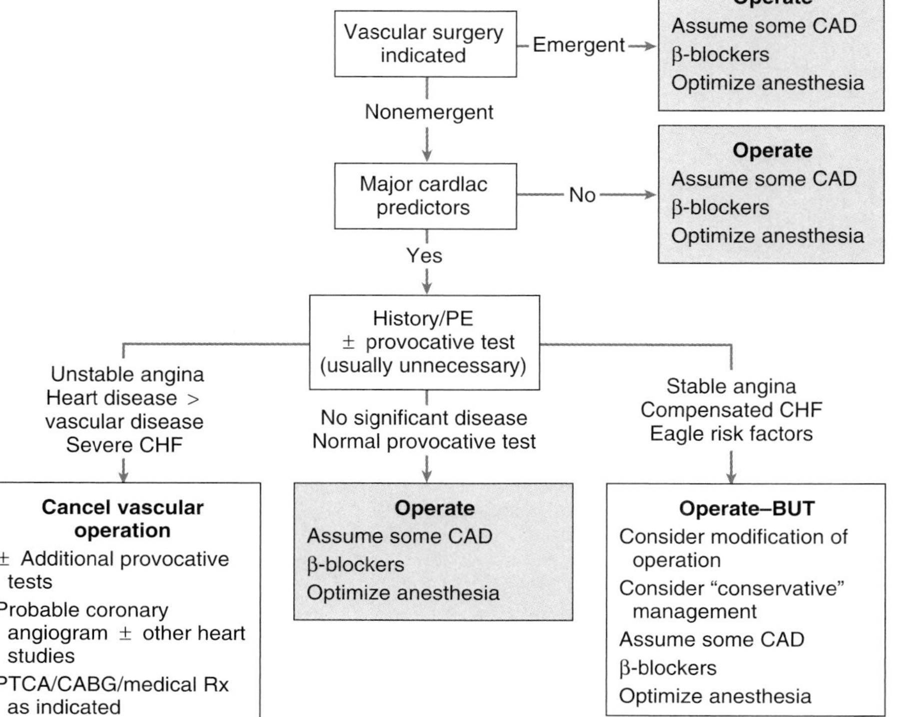

FIGURE 56-6 Until the CARP results are available (level 1—evidence-based data), recommendations by Eagle and colleagues[74] for dealing with most patients with peripheral arterial disease and (probably) coronary artery disease (CAD) in a simple, straightforward approach. The Eagle risk factors include (1) age older than 70, (2) myocardial infarction by history or Q wave on electrocardiogram, (3) angina pectoris, (4) history of congestive heart failure (CHF), (5) diabetes mellitus, and (6) ventricular ectopy requiring therapy. CABG, coronary artery bypass graft; PE, physical examination; PTCA, percutaneous transluminal coronary angioplasty. (From Eagle KA, Coley CM, Newell JB, et al: Combining clinical and thallium data optimizes preoperative assessment of cardiac risk before major vascular surgery. Ann Intern Med 119:859-866, 1989.)

REFERENCES

1. Abraham SA, Coles NA, Coley CM, et al: Coronary risk of noncardiac surgery. Prog Cardiovasc Dis 34:205-234, 1991.
2. Guidelines for coronary angiography: A report of the American College of Cardiology/American Heart Association Task Force on Assessment of Diagnostic and Therapeutic Cardiovascular Procedures (Subcommittee on Coronary Angiography). Circulation 76:963A-977A, 1987.
3. Aspirin for the primary prevention of cardiovascular events: Recommendation and rationale. Ann Intern Med 136:157-160, 2002.
4. Adams JE III, Abendschein DR, Jaffe AS: Biochemical markers of myocardial injury: Is MB creatine kinase the choice for the 1990s? Circulation 88:750-763, 1993.
5. Adams JE III, Sicard GA, Allen BT, et al: Diagnosis of perioperative myocardial infarction with measurement of cardiac troponin I. N Engl J Med 330:670-674, 1994.
6. Adriani J, Zepernick R, Harmon W, Hiern B: Iatrogenic pulmonary edema in surgical patients. Surgery 61:183-191, 1967.
7. Albertini JN, Barral X, Branchereau A, et al: Long-term results of arterial allograft below-knee bypass grafts for limb salvage: A retrospective multicenter study. J Vasc Surg 31:426-435, 2000.
8. Alpert JS, Thygesen K, Antman E, Bassand JP: Myocardial infarction redefined—a consensus document of The Joint European Society of Cardiology/American College of Cardiology Committee for the redefinition of myocardial infarction. J Am Coll Cardiol 36:959-969, 2000.
9. Ambrose JA, Fuster V: The risk of coronary occlusion is not proportional to the prior severity of coronary stenoses. Heart 79:3-4, 1998.
10. Ambrose JA, Winters SL, Arora RR, et al: Coronary angiographic morphology in myocardial infarction: A link between the pathogenesis of unstable angina and myocardial infarction. J Am Coll Cardiol 6:1233-1238, 1985.
11. Ambrose JA, Winters SL, Stern A, et al: Angiographic morphology and the pathogenesis of unstable angina pectoris. J Am Coll Cardiol 5:609-616, 1985.
12. Ameli FM, Stein M, Provan JL, et al: Predictors of surgical outcome in patients undergoing aortobifemoral bypass reconstruction. J Cardiovasc Surg (Torino) 31:333-339, 1990.
13. Andrews N, Jenkins J, Andrews G, Walker P: Using postoperative cardiac Troponin-I (cTi) levels to detect myocardial ischaemia in patients undergoing vascular surgery. Cardiovasc Surg 9:254-265, 2001.
14. Antman EM: Decision making with cardiac troponin tests. N Engl J Med 346:2079-2082, 2002.
15. Antman EM, Tanasijevic MJ, Thompson B, et al: Cardiac-specific troponin I levels to predict the risk of mortality in patients with acute coronary syndromes. N Engl J Med 335:1342-1349, 1996.
16. Archie JP Jr: A fifteen-year experience with carotid endarterectomy after a formal operative protocol requiring highly frequent patch angioplasty. J Vasc Surg 31:724-735, 2000.
17. Auerbach AD, Goldman L: Beta-blockers and reduction of cardiac events in noncardiac surgery: Scientific review. JAMA 287:1435-1444, 2002.
18. Aziz I, Lewis RJ, Baker JD, Virgilio C: Cardiac morbidity and mortality following carotid endarterectomy: The importance of diabetes and multiple Eagle risk factors. Ann Vasc Surg 15:243-246, 2001.
19. Bach DS, Eagle KA: Dobutamine stress echocardiography: Stressing the indications for preoperative testing. Circulation 95:8-10, 1997.
20. Badimon JJ, Zaman A, Helft G, et al: Acute coronary syndromes: Pathophysiology and preventive priorities. Thromb Haemost 82:997-1004, 1999.
21. Badimon L, Badimon JJ, Galvez A, et al: Influence of arterial damage and wall shear rate on platelet deposition: Ex vivo study in a swine model. Arteriosclerosis 6:312-320, 1986.
22. Badimon L, Fuster V, Dewanjee MK, Romero JC: A sensitive new method of "ex vivo" platelet deposition. Thromb Res 28:237-250, 1982.
23. Badner NH, Knill RL, Brown JE, et al: Myocardial infarction after noncardiac surgery. Anesthesiology 88:572-578, 1998.
24. Barnett HJ, Taylor DW, Eliasziw M, et al: Benefit of carotid endarterectomy in patients with symptomatic moderate or severe stenosis. North American Symptomatic Carotid Endarterectomy Trial Collaborators. N Engl J Med 339:1415-1425, 1998.
25. Baron JF, Mundler O, Bertrand M, et al: Dipyridamole-thallium scintigraphy and gated radionuclide angiography to assess cardiac risk before abdominal aortic surgery. N Engl J Med 330:663-669, 1994.
26. Barone JE, Tucker JB, Rassias D, Corvo PR: Routine perioperative pulmonary artery catheterization has no effect on rate of complications in vascular surgery: A meta-analysis. Am Surg 67:674-679, 2001.
27. Belkin M, Conte MS, Donaldson MC, et al: Preferred strategies for secondary infrainguinal bypass: Lessons learned from 300 consecutive reoperations. J Vasc Surg 21:282-293, 1995.
28. Belkin M, Knox J, Donaldson MC, et al: Infrainguinal arterial reconstruction with nonreversed greater saphenous vein. J Vasc Surg 24:957-962, 1996.
29. Bender JS, Smith-Meek MA, Jones CE: Routine pulmonary artery catheterization does not reduce morbidity and mortality of elective vascular surgery: Results of a prospective, randomized trial. Ann Surg 226:229-236, 1997.
30. Berlauk JF, Abrams JH, Gilmour IJ, et al: Preoperative optimization of cardiovascular hemodynamics improves outcome in peripheral vascular surgery: A prospective, randomized clinical trial. Ann Surg 214:289-297, 1991.
31. Berman SS, Bernhard VM, Erly WK, et al: Critical carotid artery stenosis: Diagnosis, timing of surgery, and outcome. J Vasc Surg 20:499-510, 1994.
32. Berry AJ, Smith RB III, Weintraub WS, et al: Age versus comorbidities as risk factors for complications after elective abdominal aortic reconstructive surgery. J Vasc Surg 33:345-352, 2001.
33. Bigatel DA, Franklin DP, Elmore JR, et al: Dobutamine stress echocardiography prior to aortic surgery: Long-term cardiac outcome. Ann Vasc Surg 13:17-22, 1999.
34. Blackburn H, Vasquez CL, Keys A: The aging electrocardiogram: A common aging process or latent coronary artery disease? Am J Cardiol 20:618-627, 1967.
35. Boden WE, O'Rourke RA, Crawford MH, et al: Outcomes in patients with acute non-Q-wave myocardial infarction randomly assigned to an invasive as compared with a conservative management strategy. Veterans Affairs Non-Q-Wave Infarction Strategies in Hospital (VANQWISH) Trial Investigators. N Engl J Med 338:1785-1792, 1998.
36. Bodenheimer MM: Noncardiac surgery in the cardiac patient: What is the question? Ann Intern Med 124:763-766, 1996.
37. Bonazzi M, Gentile F, Biasi GM, et al: Impact of perioperative haemodynamic monitoring on cardiac morbidity after major vascular surgery in low risk patients: A randomized pilot trial. Eur J Vasc Endovasc Surg 23:445-451, 2002.
38. Bond R, Narayan SK, Rothwell PM, Warlow CP: Clinical and radiographic risk factors for operative stroke and death in the European carotid surgery trial. Eur J Vasc Endovasc Surg 23:108-116, 2001.
39. Bosch X, Theroux P, Waters DD, et al: Early postinfarction ischemia: Clinical, angiographic, and prognostic significance. Circulation 75:988-995, 1987.
40. Bowyer MW, Zierold D, Loftus JP, et al: Carotid endarterectomy: A comparison of regional versus general anesthesia in 500 operations. Ann Vasc Surg 14:145-151, 2000.
41. Boyd O, Grounds RM, Bennett ED: A randomized clinical trial of the effect of deliberate perioperative increase of oxygen delivery on mortality in high-risk surgical patients. JAMA 270:2699-2707, 1993.

42. Braunwald E: Thirteenth Bowditch lecture: The determinants of myocardial oxygen consumption. Physiologist 12:65-93, 1969.
43. Braunwald E, Califf RM, Cannon CP, et al: Redefining medical treatment in the management of unstable angina. Am J Med 108:41-53, 2000.
44. Browner WS, Li J, Mangano DT: In-hospital and long-term mortality in male veterans following noncardiac surgery. The Study of Perioperative Ischemia Research Group. JAMA 268:228-232, 1992.
45. Buffon A, Fiasucci LM, Liusso G, et al: Widespread coronary inflammation in unstable angina. N Engl J Med 347:5-12, 2002.
46. Bunt TJ: The role of a defined protocol for cardiac risk assessment in decreasing perioperative myocardial infarction in vascular surgery. J Vasc Surg 15:626-634, 1992.
47. Bush HL Jr, Huse JB, Johnson WC, et al: Prevention of renal insufficiency after abdominal aortic aneurysm resection by optimal volume loading. Arch Surg 116:1517-1524, 1981.
48. Byrne J, Darling RC III, Chang BB, et al: Infrainguinal arterial reconstruction for claudication: Is it worth the risk? An analysis of 409 procedures. J Vasc Surg 29:259-267, 1999.
49. Cannon CP, Thompson B, McCabe CH, et al: Predictors of non-Q-wave acute myocardial infarction in patients with acute ischemic syndromes: An analysis from the Thrombolysis in Myocardial Ischemia (TIMI) III trials. Am J Cardiol 75:977-981, 1995.
50. Carrel T, Zund G, Jenni R, Turina M: Prediction of early cardiac morbidity and mortality following aorto-iliac reconstruction: Comparison between clinical scoring systems, echocardiography and dipyridamole-thallium scanning. Vasa 24:362-367, 1995.
51. Chang BB, Darling RC III, Patel M, et al: Use of shunts with eversion carotid endarterectomy. J Vasc Surg 32:655-662, 2000.
52. Charlson ME, MacKenzie CR, Ales K, et al: Surveillance for postoperative myocardial infarction after noncardiac operations. Surg Gynecol Obstet 167:407-414, 1988.
53. Chesebro JH, Toschi V, Lettino M, et al: Evolving concepts in the pathogenesis and treatment of arterial thrombosis. Mt Sinai J Med 62:275-286, 1995.
54. Chesebro JH, Zoldhelyi P, Fuster V: Pathogenesis of thrombosis in unstable angina. Am J Cardiol 68:2B-10B, 1991.
55. Chew DK, Conte MS, Donaldson MC, et al: Autogenous composite vein bypass graft for infrainguinal arterial reconstruction. J Vasc Surg 33:259-264, 2001.
56. Chesebro JH, Zoldhelyi P, Fuster V: Plaque disruption and thrombosis in unstable angina pectoris. Am J Cardiol 68:9C-15C, 1991.
57. Chung MK, Bosner MS, McKenzie JP, et al: Prognosis of patients > or = 70 years of age with non-Q-wave acute myocardial infarction compared with younger patients with similar infarcts and with patients > or = 70 years of age with Q-wave acute myocardial infarction. Am J Cardiol 75:18-22, 1995.
58. Clark ET, Gewertz BL, Bassiouny HS, Zarins CK: Current results of elective aortic reconstruction for aneurysmal and occlusive disease. J Cardiovasc Surg (Torino) 31:438-441, 1990.
59. Cohn PF: Silent ischemia. Heart Dis Stroke 1:295-297, 1992.
60. Cohn PF: Silent and symptomatic ischemia. Rev Port Cardiol 13:15-19, 1994.
61. Cohn PF, Kannel WB: Recognition, pathogenesis, and management options in silent coronary artery disease: Introduction. Circulation 75:II-1, 1987.
62. Cook D: Rules of evidence and clinical recommendations on the use of antithrombotic agents. Chest 102(Suppl):305s-311s, 1992.
63. Cutler BS, Leppo JA: Dipyridamole thallium 201 scintigraphy to detect coronary artery disease before abdominal aortic surgery. J Vasc Surg 5:91-100, 1987.
64. Cutler BS, Wheeler HB, Paraskos JA, Cardullo PA: Applicability and interpretation of electrocardiographic stress testing in patients with peripheral vascular disease. Am J Surg 141:501-506, 1981.
65. Cutler BS, Wheeler HB, Paraskos JA, Cardullo PA: Assessment of operative risk with electrocardiographic exercise testing in patients with peripheral vascular disease. Am J Surg 137:484-490, 1979.
66. D'Angelo AJ, Puppala D, Farber A, et al: Is preoperative cardiac evaluation for abdominal aortic aneurysm repair necessary? J Vasc Surg 25:152-156, 1997.
67. Dardik A, Williams GM, Minken SL, Perler BA: Impact of a critical pathway on the results of carotid endarterectomy in a tertiary care university hospital: Effect of methods on outcome. J Vasc Surg 26:186-192, 1997.
68. Day SM, Younger JG, Karavite D, et al: Usefulness of hypotension during dobutamine echocardiography in predicting perioperative cardiac events. Am J Cardiol 85:478-483, 2000.
69. Depré C, Wijns W, Robert AM, et al: Pathology of unstable plaque: Correlation with the clinical severity of acute coronary syndromes. J Am Coll Cardiol 30:694-702. 1997.
70. Detsky AS, Abrams HB, McLaughlin JR, et al: Predicting cardiac complications in patients undergoing non-cardiac surgery. J Gen Intern Med 1:211-219, 1986.
71. Do D, West JA, Morise A, et al: A consensus approach to diagnosing coronary artery disease based on clinical and exercise test data. Chest 111:1742-1749, 1997.
72. Dodds TM, Stone JG, Coromilas J, et al: Prophylactic nitroglycerin infusion during noncardiac surgery does not reduce perioperative ischemia. Anesth Analg 76:705-713, 1993.
73. Eagle KA, Berger PB, Calkins H, et al: ACC/AHA guideline update for perioperative cardiovascular evaluation for noncardiac surgery-executive summary a report of the American College of Cardiology/American Heart Association Task Force on Practice Guidelines (Committee to Update the 1996 Guidelines on Perioperataive Cardiovascular Evaluation for Noncardiac Surgery). Circulation 105:1259-1267, 2002.
74. Eagle KA, Coley CM, Newell JB, et al: Combining clinical and thallium data optimizes preoperative assessment of cardiac risk before major vascular surgery. Ann Intern Med 119:859-866, 1989.
75. Eagle KA, Rihal CS, Foster ED, et al: Long-term survival in patients with coronary artery disease: Importance of peripheral vascular disease. The Coronary Artery Surgery Study (CASS) Investigators. J Am Coll Cardiol 23:1091-1095, 1994.
76. Eagle KA, Rihal CS, Mickel MC, et al: Cardiac risk of noncardiac surgery: Influence of coronary disease and type of surgery in 3368 operations. CASS Investigators and University of Michigan Heart Care Program. Coronary Artery Surgery Study. Circulation 96:1882-1887, 1997.
77. Economopoulos KJ, Gentile AT, Berman SS: Comparison of carotid endarterectomy using primary closure, patch closure, and eversion techniques. Am J Surg 178:505-510, 1999.
78. Ennix CL Jr, Lawrie GM, Morris GC Jr, et al: Improved results of carotid endarterectomy in patients with symptomatic coronary disease: An analysis of 1,546 consecutive carotid operations. Stroke 10:122-125, 1979.
79. Erickson CA, Carballo RE, Freischlag JA, et al: Using dipyridamole-thallium imaging to reduce cardiac risk in aortic reconstruction. J Surg Res 60:422-428, 1996.
80. Executive Committee for the Asymptomatic Carotid Atherosclerosis Study: Endarterectomy for asymptomatic carotid artery stenosis. JAMA 273:1421-1428, 1995.
81. Falk E, Fernandez-Ortiz A: Role of thrombosis in atherosclerosis and its complications. Am J Cardiol 75:3B-11B, 1995.
82. Falk E, Fuster V: Angina pectoris and disease progression. Circulation 92:2058-2065, 1995.
83. Falk E, Shah PK, Fuster V: Coronary plaque disruption. Circulation 92:657-671, 1995.
84. Farid I, Litaker D, Tetzlaff JE: Implementing ACC/AHA guidelines for the preoperative management of patients with coronary artery disease scheduled for noncardiac surgery: Effect on perioperative outcome. J Clin Anesth 14:126-128, 2002.
85. Faries PL, LoGerfo FW, Arora S, et al: Arm vein conduit is superior to composite prosthetic-autogenous grafts in lower extremity revascularization. J Vasc Surg 31:1119-1127, 2000.

86. Faries PL, Brophy D, LoGerfo FW, et al: Combined iliac angioplasty and infrainguinal revascularization surgery are effective in diabetic patients with multilevel arterial disease. Ann Vasc Surg 15:67-72, 2001.
87. Farkouh ME, Rihal CS, Gersh BJ, et al: Influence of coronary heart disease on morbidity and mortality after lower extremity revascularization surgery: A population-based study in Olmsted County, Minnesota (1970-1987). J Am Coll Cardiol 24:1290-1296, 1994.
88. Fernandez-Ortiz A, Badimon JJ, Falk E, et al: Characterization of the relative thrombogenicity of atherosclerotic plaque components: Implications for consequences of plaque rupture. J Am Coll Cardiol 23:1562-1569, 1994.
89. Fichelle JM, Marzelle J, Colacchio G, et al: Infrapopliteal polytetrafluoroethylene and composite bypass: Factors influencing patency. Ann Vasc Surg 9:187-196, 1995.
90. Flancbaum L, Ziegler DW, Choban PS: Preoperative intensive care unit admission and hemodynamic monitoring in patients scheduled for major elective noncardiac surgery: A retrospective review of 95 patients. J Cardiothorac Vasc Anesth 12:3-9, 1998.
91. Fleisher LA, Eagle KA: Clinical practice: Lowering cardiac risk in noncardiac surgery. N Engl J Med 345:1677-1682, 2001.
92. Fleisher LA, Eagle KA: Guidelines on perioperative cardiovascular evaluation: What have we learned over the past 6 years to warrant an update? Anesth Analg 94:1378-1379, 2002.
93. Fleisher LA, Eagle KA, Shaffer T, Anderson GF: Perioperative- and long-term mortality rates after major vascular surgery: The relationship to preoperative testing in the Medicare population. Anesth Analg 89:849-855, 1999.
94. Foster ED, Davis KB, Carpenter JA, et al: Risk of noncardiac operation in patients with defined coronary disease: The Coronary Artery Surgery Study (CASS) registry experience. Ann Thorac Surg 41:42-50, 1986.
95. Freischlag JA, Hanna D, Moore WS: Improved prognosis for asymptomatic carotid stenosis with prophylactic carotid endarterectomy. Stroke 23:479-482, 1992.
96. Fuster V: Mechanisms of arterial thrombosis: Foundation for therapy. Am Heart J 135:S361-S366, 1998.
97. Fuster V: Understanding the coronary disease process and the potential for prevention: A summary. Prev Med 29:S9-10, 1999.
98. Fuster V, Badimon JJ, Chesebro JH: Atherothrombosis: Mechanisms and clinical therapeutic approaches. Vasc Med 3:231-239, 1998.
99. Fuster V, Badimon L, Cohen M, et al: Insights into the pathogenesis of acute ischemic syndromes. Circulation 77:1213-1220, 1988.
100. Fuster V, Fallon JT, Badimon JJ, Nemerson Y: The unstable atherosclerotic plaque: Clinical significance and therapeutic intervention. Thromb Haemost 78:247-255, 1997.
101. Fuster V, Fayad ZA, Badimon JJ: Acute coronary syndromes: Biology. Lancet 353(Suppl 2):SII-5-SII-9, 1999.
102. Fuster V, Gotto AM Jr: Risk reduction. Circulation 102:IV-94-IV-102, 2000.
103. Galvani M, Ferrini D, Puggioni R, et al: New markers for early diagnosis of acute myocardial infarction. Int J Cardiol 65(Suppl 1): S17-S22, 1998.
104. Galvani M, Nicolini FA, Ferrini D, Ottani F: [Management of acute coronary syndrome: New pharmacologic approaches]. G Ital Cardiol 29(Suppl 4):23-27, 1999.
105. Galvani M, Ottani F, Ferrini D, et al: Prognostic influence of elevated values of cardiac troponin I in patients with unstable angina. Circulation 95:2053-2059, 1997.
106. Gibson RS: Non-Q-wave myocardial infarction: Diagnosis, prognosis, and management. Curr Probl Cardiol 13:9-72, 1988.
107. Gilbert K, Larocque BJ, Patrick LT: Prospective evaluation of cardiac risk indices for patients undergoing noncardiac surgery. Ann Intern Med 133:356-359, 2000.
108. Gillum RF: Cardiovascular disease in the United States: An epidemiologic overview. Cardiovasc Clin 21:3-16, 1991.
109. Gillum RF: Trends in acute myocardial infarction and coronary heart disease death in the United States. J Am Coll Cardiol 23:1273-1277, 1994.
110. Gillum RF, Blackburn H, Feinleib M: Current strategies for explaining the decline in ischemic heart disease mortality. J Chronic Dis 35:467-474, 1982.
111. Gillum RF, Folsom AR, Blackburn H: Decline in coronary heart disease mortality: Old questions and new facts. Am J Med 76:1055-1065, 1984.
112. Glance LG: Selective preoperative cardiac screening improves five-year survival in patients undergoing major vascular surgery: A cost-effectiveness analysis. J Cardiothorac Vasc Anesth 13:265-271, 1999.
113. Goldberg RJ, Gorak EJ, Yarzebski J, et al: A communitywide perspective of sex differences and temporal trends in the incidence and survival rates after acute myocardial infarction and out-of-hospital deaths caused by coronary heart disease. Circulation 87:1947-1953, 1993.
114. Goldberg RJ, Gore JM, Alpert JS, Dalen JE: Non-Q wave myocardial infarction: Recent changes in occurrence and prognosis—a community-wide perspective. Am Heart J 113:273-279, 1987.
115. Golden MA, Whittemore AD, Donaldson MC, Mannick JA: Selective evaluation and management of coronary artery disease in patients undergoing repair of abdominal aortic aneurysms: A 16-year experience. Ann Surg 212:415-420, 1990.
116. Goldman L: Assessing and reducing cardiac risks of noncardiac surgery. Am J Med 110:320-323, 2001.
117. Goldman L: Assessment of perioperative cardiac risk. N Engl J Med 330:707-709, 1994.
118. Goldman L, Caldera DL, Nussbaum SR, et al: Multifactorial index of cardiac risk in noncardiac surgical procedures. N Engl J Med 297:845-850, 1977.
119. Goldstein JA, Demetriou D, Grines CL, et al: Multiple complex coronary plaques in patients with acute myocardial infarction. N Engl J Med 343:915-922, 2000.
120. Gottlieb A, Banoub M, Sprung J, et al: Perioperative cardiovascular morbidity in patients with coronary artery disease undergoing vascular surgery after percutaneous transluminal coronary angioplasty. J Cardiothorac Vasc Anesth 12:501-506, 1998.
121. Grundy SM, Balady GJ, Criqui MH, et al: Guide to primary prevention of cardiovascular diseases: A statement for healthcare professionals from the Task Force on Risk Reduction. American Heart Association Science Advisory and Coordinating Committee. Circulation 95:2329-2331, 1997.
122. Haggart PC, Ludman PF, Bradbury AW: Cardiac troponin: A new biochemical marker for peri-operative myocardial injury. Eur J Vasc Endovasc Surg 22:301-305, 2001.
123. Hamdan AD, Pomposelli FB Jr, Gibbons GW, et al: Perioperative strokes after 1001 consecutive carotid endarterectomy procedures without an electroencephalogram: Incidence, mechanism, and recovery. Arch Surg 134:412-415, 1999.
124. Harwood TN, Butterworth J, Prielipp RC, et al: The safety and effectiveness of esmolol in the perioperative period in patients undergoing abdominal aortic surgery. J Cardiothorac Vasc Anesth 13:555-561, 1999.
125. Hayes PD, Allroggen H, Steel S, et al: Randomized trial of vein versus Dacron patching during carotid endarterectomy: Influence of patch type on postoperative embolization. J Vasc Surg 33:994-1000, 2001.
126. Henderson A, Effeney D: Morbidity and mortality after abdominal aortic surgery in a population of patients with high cardiovascular risk. Aust N Z J Surg 65:417-420, 1995.
127. Hertzer NR: Basic data concerning associated coronary disease in peripheral vascular patients. Ann Vasc Surg 1:616-620, 1987.
128. Hertzer NR: Fatal myocardial infarction following peripheral vascular operations: A study of 951 patients followed 6 to 11 years postoperatively. Cleve Clin Q 49:1-11, 1982.
129. Hertzer NR, Beven EG, Young JR, et al: Coronary artery disease in peripheral vascular patients: A classification of 1000 coronary angiograms and results of surgical management. Ann Surg 199:223-233, 1984.

130. Hertzer NR, Lees CD: Fatal myocardial infarction following carotid endarterectomy: Three hundred thirty-five patients followed 6-11 years after operation. Ann Surg 194:212-218, 1981.
131. Hertzer NR, Mascha EJ, Karafa MT, et al: Open infrarenal abdominal aortic aneurysm repair: The Cleveland Clinic experience from 1989 to 1998. J Vasc Surg 35:1145-1154, 2002.
132. Hertzer NR, O'Hara PJ, Mascha EJ, et al: Early outcome assessment for 2228 consecutive carotid endarterectomy procedures: The Cleveland Clinic experience from 1989 to 1995. J Vasc Surg 26:1-10, 1997.
133. Hiatt WR: Preventing atherothrombotic events in peripheral arterial disease: The use of antiplatelet therapy. J Intern Med 251:193-206, 2002.
134. Hobson RW, Weiss DG, Fields WS, et al, Veterans Affairs Cooperative Study Group: Efficacy of carotid endarterectomy for asymptomatic carotid stenosis. N Engl J Med 328:221-227, 1993.
135. Horowitz GL, Beckwith BA: C-reactive protein in the prediction of cardiovascular disease. N Engl J Med 343:512-513, 2000.
136. Huber KC, Evans MA, Bresnahan JF, et al: Outcome of noncardiac operations in patients with severe coronary artery disease successfully treated preoperatively with coronary angioplasty. Mayo Clin Proc 67:15-21, 1992.
137. Huber TS, Harward TR, Flynn TC, et al: Operative mortality rates after elective infrarenal aortic reconstructions. J Vasc Surg 22:287-293, 1995.
138. Huey BL, Gheorghiade M, Crampton RS, et al: Acute non-Q wave myocardial infarction associated with early ST segment elevation: Evidence for spontaneous coronary reperfusion and implications for thrombolytic trials. J Am Coll Cardiol 9:18-25, 1987.
139. Hunink MG, Goldman L, Tosteson AN, et al: The recent decline in mortality from coronary heart disease, 1980-1990: The effect of secular trends in risk factors and treatment. JAMA 277:535-542, 1997.
140. Isaacson IJ, Lowdon JD, Berry AJ, et al: The value of pulmonary artery and central venous monitoring in patients undergoing abdominal aortic reconstructive surgery: A comparative study of two selected, randomized groups. J Vasc Surg 12:754-760, 1990.
141. Itani KM, Miller CC, Guinn G, Jones JW: Preoperative cardiac evaluation is unnecessary in most patients undergoing vascular operations. Am J Surg 176:671-675, 1998.
142. Ives DG, Fitzpatrick AL, Bild DE, et al: Surveillance and ascertainment of cardiovascular events. The Cardiovascular Health Study. Ann Epidemiol 5:278-285, 1995.
143. Jamsen T, Tulla H, Manninen H, et al: Results of infrainguinal bypass surgery: An analysis of 263 consecutive operations. Ann Chir Gynaecol 90:92-99, 2001.
144. Jarvinen O, Laurikka J, Sisto T, Tarkka MR: Intestinal ischemia following surgery for aorto-iliac disease: A review of 502 consecutive aortic reconstructions. Vasa 25:148-155, 1996.
145. Joint European Society of Cardiology: Myocardial infarction redefined—a consensus document of the Joint European Society of Cardiology/American College of Cardiology Committee for the redefinition of myocardial infarction. Eur Heart J 21:1502-1513, 2000.
146. Joyce WP, Provan JL, Ameli FM, et al: The role of central haemodynamic monitoring in abdominal aortic surgery: A prospective randomized study. Eur J Vasc Surg 4:633-636, 1990.
147. Kannel WB: Detection and management of patients with silent myocardial ischemia. Am Heart J 117:221-226, 1989.
148. Kannel WB: Prevalence and clinical aspects of unrecognized myocardial infarction and sudden unexpected death. Circulation 75:II-4-II-5, 1987.
149. Kannel WB: Silent myocardial ischemia and infarction: Insights from the Framingham Study. Cardiol Clin 4:583-591, 1986.
150. Katras T, Baltazar U, Rush DS, et al: Durability of eversion carotid endarterectomy: Comparison with primary closure and carotid patch angioplasty. J Vasc Surg 34:453-458, 2001.
151. Kazmers A, Moneta GL, Cerqueira MD, et al: The role of preoperative radionuclide ventriculography in defining outcome after revascularization of the extremity. Surg Gynecol Obstet 171:481-488, 1990.
152. Kerdiles Y, Lucas A, Podeur L, et al: Results of carotid surgery in elderly patients. J Cardiovasc Surg (Torino) 38:327-334, 1997.
153. Kirwin JD, Ascer E, Gennaro M, et al: Silent myocardial ischemia is not predictive of myocardial infarction in peripheral vascular surgery patients. Ann Vasc Surg 7:27-32, 1993.
154. Klonaris CN, Bastounis EA, Xiromeritis NC, Balas PE: The predictive value of dipyridamole-thallium scintigraphy for cardiac risk assessment before major vascular surgery. Int Angiol 17:171-178, 1998.
155. Knight AA, Hollenberg M, London MJ, et al: Perioperative myocardial ischemia: Importance of the preoperative ischemic pattern. Anesthesiology 68:681-688, 1988.
156. Krause KJ: C-reactive protein—a screening test for coronary disease? J Insur Med 33:4-11, 2001.
157. Krupski WC: Update on perioperative evaluation and management of cardiac disease in vascular surgery patients. J Vasc Surg 36:1292-1308, 2002.
158. Krupski WC, Layug EL, Reilly LM, et al: Comparison of cardiac morbidity between aortic and infrainguinal operations. Study of Perioperative Ischemia (SPI) Research Group. J Vasc Surg 15:354-363, 1992.
159. Krupski WC, Layug EL, Reilly LM, et al: Comparison of cardiac morbidity rates between aortic and infrainguinal operations: Two-year follow-up. Study of Perioperative Ischemia Research Group. J Vasc Surg 18:609-615, 1993.
160. Krupski WC, Nehler MR: How to avoid cardiac ischemic events associated with aortic surgery. Semin Vasc Surg 14:235-244, 2001.
161. Krupski WC, Nehler MR, Whitehill TA, et al: Negative impact of cardiac evaluation before vascular surgery. Vasc Med 5:3-9, 2000.
162. Lalka SG, Sawada SG, Dalsing MC, et al: Dobutamine stress echocardiography as a predictor of cardiac events associated with aortic surgery. J Vasc Surg 15:831-840, 1992.
163. Landesberg G, Einav S, Christopherson R, et al: Perioperative ischemia and cardiac complications in major vascular surgery: importance of the preoperative twelve-lead electrocardiogram. J Vasc Surg 26:570-578, 1997.
164. Landesberg G, Luria MH, Cotev S, et al: Importance of long-duration postoperative ST-segment depression in cardiac morbidity after vascular surgery. Lancet 341:715-719, 1993.
165. Landesberg G, Mosseri M, Wolf Y, et al: Perioperative myocardial ischemia and infarction: Identification by continuous 12-lead electrocardiogram with online ST-segment monitoring. Anesthesiology 96:264-270, 2002.
166. Landesberg G, Mosseri M, Zahger D, et al: Myocardial infarction after vascular surgery: The role of prolonged stress-induced, ST depression-type ischemia. J Am Coll Cardiol 37:1839-1845, 2001.
167. Lauer MS: Clinical practice: Aspirin for primary prevention of coronary events. N Engl J Med 346:1468-1474, 2002.
168. Lee TH, Boucher CA: Clinical practice: Noninvasive tests in patients with stable coronary artery disease. N Engl J Med 344:1840-1845, 2001.
169. Lee TH, Marcantonio ER, Mangione CM, et al: Derivation and prospective validation of a simple index for prediction of cardiac risk of major noncardiac surgery. Circulation 100:1043-1049, 1999.
170. Liebson PR, Klein LW: The non-Q wave myocardial infarction revisited: 10 years later. Prog Cardiovasc Dis 39:399-444, 1997.
171. L'Italien GJ, Cambria RP, Cutler BS, et al: Comparative early and late cardiac morbidity among patients requiring different vascular surgery procedures. J Vasc Surg 21:935-944, 1995.
172. L'Italien GJ, Paul SD, Hendel RC, et al: Development and validation of a Bayesian model for perioperative cardiac risk assessment in a cohort of 1,081 vascular surgical candidates. J Am Coll Cardiol 27:779-786, 1996.

173. Lord RS, Crozier JA, Snell J, Meek AC: Transverse abdominal incisions compared with midline incisions for elective infrarenal aortic reconstruction: Predisposition to incisional hernia in patients with increased intraoperative blood loss. J Vasc Surg 20:27-33, 1994.
174. Mackey WC, O'Donnell TF Jr, Callow AD: Cardiac risk in patients undergoing carotid endarterectomy: Impact on perioperative and long-term mortality. J Vasc Surg 11:226-233, 1990.
175. Maini BS, Mullins TF III, Catlin J, O'Mara P: Carotid endarterectomy: A ten-year analysis of outcome and cost of treatment. J Vasc Surg 12:732-739, 1990.
176. Maisel AS, Ahnve S, Gilpin E, et al: Prognosis after extension of myocardial infarct: The role of Q wave or non-Q wave infarction. Circulation 71:211-217, 1985.
177. Mangano DT: Dynamic predictors of perioperative risk. Study of Perioperative Ischemia (SPI) Research Group. J Card Surg 5:231-236, 1990.
178. Mangano DT, Browner WS, Hollenberg M, et al: Association of perioperative myocardial ischemia with cardiac morbidity and mortality in men undergoing noncardiac surgery. The Study of Perioperative Ischemia Research Group. N Engl J Med 323:1781-1788, 1990.
179. Mangano DT, Goldman L: Preoperative assessment of patients with known or suspected coronary disease. N Engl J Med 333:1750-1756, 1995.
180. Mangano DT, Hollenberg M, Fegert G, et al: Perioperative myocardial ischemia in patients undergoing noncardiac surgery: I. Incidence and severity during the 4 day perioperative period. The Study of Perioperative Ischemia (SPI) Research Group. J Am Coll Cardiol 17:843-850, 1991.
181. Mangano DT, Layug EL, Wallace A, Tateo I: Effect of atenolol on mortality and cardiovascular morbidity after noncardiac surgery: Multicenter Study of Perioperative Ischemia Research Group. N Engl J Med 335:1713-1720, 1996.
182. Marmor A, Sobel BE, Roberts R: Factors presaging early recurrent myocardial infarction ("extension"). Am J Cardiol 48:603-610, 1981.
183. Mason JJ, Owens DK, Harris RA, et al: The role of coronary angiography and coronary revascularization before noncardiac vascular surgery. JAMA 273:1919-1925, 1995.
184. Massie MT, Rohrer MJ, Leppo JA, Cutler BS: Is coronary angiography necessary for vascular surgery patients who have positive results of dipyridamole thallium scans? J Vasc Surg 25:975-982, 1997.
185. Mattos MA, Modi JR, Mansour MA, et al: Evolution of carotid endarterectomy in two community hospitals: Springfield revisited—seventeen years and 2243 operations. J Vasc Surg 21:719-728, 1995.
186. Mattos MA, Sumner DS, Bohannon WT, et al: Carotid endarterectomy in women: Challenging the results from ACAS and NASCET. Ann Surg 234:438-445, 2001.
187. Maxwell JG, Taylor AJ, Maxwell BG, et al: Carotid endarterectomy in the community hospital in patients age 80 and older. Ann Surg 231:781-788, 2000.
188. McCarthy RJ, Walker R, McAteer P, et al: Patient and hospital benefits of local anaesthesia for carotid endarterectomy. Eur J Vasc Endovasc Surg 22:13-18, 2001.
189. McCollum CH, Garcia-Rinaldi R, Graham JM, DeBakey ME: Myocardial revascularization prior to subsequent major surgery in patients with coronary artery disease. Surgery 81:302-304, 1977.
190. McFalls EO, Ward HB, Krupski WC, et al: Prophylactic coronary artery revascularization for elective vascular surgery: study design. Veterans Affairs Cooperative Study Group on Coronary Artery Revascularization Prophylaxis for Elective Vascular Surgery. Control Clin Trials 20:297-308, 1999.
191. McGovern PG, Pankow JS, Shahar E, et al: Recent trends in acute coronary heart disease—mortality, morbidity, medical care, and risk factors. The Minnesota Heart Survey Investigators. N Engl J Med 334:884-890, 1996.
192. McPhail N, Calvin JE, Shariatmadar A, et al: The use of preoperative exercise testing to predict cardiac complications after arterial reconstruction. J Vasc Surg 7:60-68, 1988.
193. Merenich JA, Lousberg TR, Brennan SH, Calonge NB: Optimizing treatment of dyslipidemia in patients with coronary artery disease in the managed-care environment (the Rocky Mountain Kaiser Permanente experience). Am J Cardiol 85:36A-42A, 2000.
194. Mesh CL, Cmolik BL, Van Heekeren DW, et al: Coronary bypass in vascular patients: A relatively high-risk procedure. Ann Vasc Surg 11:612-619, 1997.
195. Mickley H: Coronary arteriography and coronary angioplasty in stable ischemic heart disease: Value in the prediction and prevention of future acute myocardial infarction. Ugeskr Laeger 161:5146-5151, 1999.
196. Mills JL, Taylor SM: Results of infrainguinal revascularization with reversed vein conduits: A modern control series. Ann Vasc Surg 5:156-162, 1991.
197. Mingoli A, Sapienza P, Feldhaus RJ, et al: Aortoiliofemoral bypass graft in young adults: Long-term results in a series of sixty-eight patients. Surgery 121:646-653, 1997.
198. Muller JE, Kaufmann PG, Luepker RV, et al: Mechanisms Precipitating Acute Cardiac Events: Review and recommendations of an NHLBI workshop. National Heart, Lung, and Blood Institute, Mechanisms Precipitating Acute Cardiac Events participants. Circulation 96:3233-3239, 1997.
199. Mulvihill N, Foley JB, Ghaisas N, et al: Early temporal expression of soluble cellular adhesion molecules in patients with unstable angina and subendocardial myocardial infarction. Am J Cardiol 83:1265-1267, A9, 1999.
200. Mulvihill NT, Foley JB: Inflammation in acute coronary syndromes. Heart 87:201-204, 2002.
201. Mulvihill NT, Foley JB, Murphy R, et al: Evidence of prolonged inflammation in unstable angina and non-Q wave myocardial infarction. J Am Coll Cardiol 36:1210-1216, 2000.
202. Munoz DR, Dae MW, Ports TA, Botvinick EH: Diagnostic and prognostic value of ambulatory electrocardiographic monitoring. Am Heart J 124:1213-1219, 1992.
203. Murray WM: Inflammation, aspirin, and the risk of cardiovascular disease. N Engl J Med 337:422-424, 1997.
204. Nehler MR, Krupski WC: Cardiac complications and screening. In Rutherford RB (ed): Vascular Surgery. Philadelphia, WB Saunders, 2000, pp 626-646.
205. Nehler MR, Krupski WC: Cardiac evaluation before aortic surgery. In Gewertz BL, Schwartz LB (ed): Surgery of the Aorta and Its Branches. Philadelphia, WB Saunders, 2000, pp 51-61.
206. Nguyen TT, Amsterdam EA, Schaefer S: Risk stratification prior to vascular surgery: Does the location of a dipyridamole thallium scintigram defect provide prognostic information? Cardiology 88:569-575, 1997.
207. Nicod P, Gilpin E, Dittrich H, et al: Short- and long-term clinical outcome after Q wave and non-Q wave myocardial infarction in a large patient population. Circulation 79:528-536, 1989.
208. North American Symptomatic Carotid Endarterectomy (NASCET) collaborators: Beneficial effect of carotid endarterectomy in symptomatic patients with high-grade carotid stenosis. N Engl J Med 325:445-453, 1991.
209. O'Hara PJ, Hertzer NR, Mascha EJ, et al: A prospective, randomized study of saphenous vein patching versus synthetic patching during carotid endarterectomy. J Vasc Surg 35:324-332, 2002.
210. Oliver MF, Goldman L, Julian DG, Holme I: Effect of mivazerol on perioperative cardiac complications during non-cardiac surgery in patients with coronary heart disease: The European Mivazerol Trial (EMIT). Anesthesiology 91:951-961, 1999.
211. Ombrellaro MP, Dieter RA III, Freeman M, et al: Role of dipyridamole myocardial scintigraphy in carotid artery surgery. J Am Coll Surg 181:451-458, 1995.
212. Ommer A, Pillny M, Grabitz K, Sandmann W: Reconstructive surgery for carotid artery occlusive disease in the elderly—a high risk operation? Cardiovasc Surg 9:552-558, 2001.
213. Ottani F, Galvani M, Ferrini D, et al: Direct comparison of early elevations of cardiac troponin T and I in patients with clinical unstable angina. Am Heart J 137:284-291, 1999.

214. Ottani F, Galvani M, Nicolini FA, et al: Elevated cardiac troponin levels predict the risk of adverse outcome in patients with acute coronary syndromes. Am Heart J 140:917-927, 2000.
215. Palda VA, Detsky AS: Perioperative assessment and management of risk from coronary artery disease. Ann Intern Med 127:313-328, 1997.
216. Papavasiliou AK, Magnadottir HB, Gonda T, et al: Clinical outcomes after carotid endarterectomy: Comparison of the use of regional and general anesthetics. J Neurosurg 92:291-296, 2000.
217. Pasternack PF, Imparato AM, Bear G, et al: The value of radionuclide angiography as a predictor of perioperative myocardial infarction in patients undergoing abdominal aortic aneurysm resection. J Vasc Surg 1:320-325, 1984.
218. Pasternack PF, Imparato AM, Riles TS, et al: The value of the radionuclide angiogram in the prediction of perioperative myocardial infarction in patients undergoing lower extremity revascularization procedures. Circulation 72:II-13-II-17, 1985.
219. Pepine CJ, Allen HD, Bashore TM, et al: ACC/AHA guidelines for cardiac catheterization and cardiac catheterization laboratories. American College of Cardiology/American Heart Association Ad Hoc Task Force on Cardiac Catheterization. Circulation 84:2213-2247, 1991.
220. Petersen LA, Normand SL, Daley J, McNeil BJ: Outcome of myocardial infarction in Veterans Health Administration patients as compared with Medicare patients. N Engl J Med 343:1934-1941, 2000.
221. Pitt B, Waters D, Brown WV, et al: Aggressive lipid-lowering therapy compared with angioplasty in stable coronary artery disease. Atorvastatin versus Revascularization Treatment investigators. N Engl J Med 341:70-76, 1999.
222. Poldermans D, Boersma E, Bax JJ, et al: Correlation of location of acute myocardial infarct after noncardiac vascular surgery with preoperative dobutamine echocardiographic findings. Am J Cardiol 88:1413-1414, A6, 2001.
223. Poldermans D, Boersma E, Bax JJ, et al: Bisoprolol reduces cardiac death and myocardial infarction in high-risk patients as long as 2 years after successful major vascular surgery. Eur Heart J 22:1353-1358, 2001.
224. Poldermans D, Boersma E, Bax JJ, et al: The effect of bisoprolol on perioperative mortality and myocardial infarction in high-risk patients undergoing vascular surgery. Dutch Echocardiographic Cardiac Risk Evaluation Applying Stress Echocardiography Study Group. N Engl J Med 341:1789-1794, 1999.
225. Powelson JA, Maini BS, Bishop RL, Sottile FD: Continuous monitoring of mixed venous oxygen saturation during aortic operations. Crit Care Med 20:332-336, 1992.
226. Quinn MJ, Foley JB, Mulvihill NT, et al: *Helicobacter pylori* serology in patients with angiographically documented coronary artery disease. Am J Cardiol 83:1664-1666, A6, 1999.
227. Quinones-Baldrich WJ, Prego AA, Ucelay-Gomez R, et al: Long-term results of infrainguinal revascularization with polytetrafluoroethylene: A ten-year experience. J Vasc Surg 16:209-217, 1992.
228. Raby KE: Is preoperative cardiac testing necessary among vascular surgery patients? Vasc Med 5:1-2, 2000.
229. Raby KE, Barry J, Creager MA, et al: Detection and significance of intraoperative and postoperative myocardial ischemia in peripheral vascular surgery. JAMA 268:222-227, 1992.
230. Raby KE, Brull SJ, Timimi F, et al: The effect of heart rate control on myocardial ischemia among high-risk patients after vascular surgery. Anesth Analg 88:477-482, 1999.
231. Raby KE, Goldman L, Cook EF, et al: Long-term prognosis of myocardial ischemia detected by Holter monitoring in peripheral vascular disease. Am J Cardiol 66:1309-1313, 1990.
232. Raby KE, Goldman L, Creager MA, et al: Correlation between preoperative ischemia and major cardiac events after peripheral vascular surgery. N Engl J Med 321:1296-1300, 1989.
233. Raby KE, Selwyn AP: The role of ambulatory monitoring in assessing cardiac risk in peripheral vascular surgery. Cardiol Clin 10:467-472, 1992.
234. Radak D, Radevic B, Sternic N, et al: Single center experience on eversion versus standard carotid endarterectomy: A prospective non-randomized study. Cardiovasc Surg 8:422-428, 2000.
235. Rader DJ: Inflammatory markers of coronary risk. N Engl J Med 343:1179-1182, 2000.
236. Reifsnyder T, Bandyk DF, Lanza D, et al: Use of stress thallium imaging to stratify cardiac risk in patients undergoing vascular surgery. J Surg Res 52:147-151, 1992.
237. Reinhart K, Radermacher P, Sprung CL, et al: PA catheterization—quo vadis? Do we have to change the current practice with this monitoring device? Intensive Care Med 23:605-609, 1997.
238. Reul GJ Jr, Cooley DA, Duncan JM, et al: The effect of coronary bypass on the outcome of peripheral vascular operations in 1093 patients. J Vasc Surg 3:788-798, 1986.
239. Rich MW, Bosner MS, Chung MK, et al: Is age an independent predictor of early and late mortality in patients with acute myocardial infarction? Am J Med 92:7-13, 1992.
240. Rihal CS, Eagle KA, Mickel MC, et al: Surgical therapy for coronary artery disease among patients with combined coronary artery and peripheral vascular disease. Circulation 91:46-53, 1995.
241. Riles TS, Fisher FS, Schaefer S, et al: Plasma catecholamine concentrations during abdominal aortic aneurysm surgery: The link to perioperative myocardial ischemia. Ann Vasc Surg 7:213-219, 1993.
242. Rivers SP, Scher LA, Sheehan E, Veith FJ: Epidural versus general anesthesia for infrainguinal arterial reconstruction. J Vasc Surg 14:764-768, 1991.
243. Rockman CB, Castillo J, Adelman MA, et al: Carotid endarterectomy in female patients: Are the concerns of the Asymptomatic Carotid Atherosclerosis Study valid? J Vasc Surg 33:236-240, 2001.
244. Rosamond WD, Chambless LE, Folsom AR, et al: Trends in the incidence of myocardial infarction and in mortality due to coronary heart disease, 1987 to 1994. N Engl J Med 339:861-867, 1998.
245. Rubins HB: Target levels for low-density lipoprotein in patients with coronary heart disease. JAMA 271:101-102, 1994.
246. Rubins HB: Triglycerides and coronary heart disease: Implications of recent clinical trials. J Cardiovasc Risk 7:339-345, 2000.
247. Rubins HB, Collins D, Robins SJ: The VA HDL intervention trial: Clinical implications. Eur Heart J 21:1113-1115, 2000.
248. Rubins HB, Robins SJ: Conclusions from the VA-HIT study. Am J Cardiol 86:543-544, 2000.
249. Ryan TJ, Anderson JL, Antman EM, et al: ACC/AHA guidelines for the management of patients with acute myocardial infarction: A report of the American College of Cardiology/American Heart Association Task Force on Practice Guidelines (Committee on Management of Acute Myocardial Infarction). J Am Coll Cardiol 28:1328-1428, 1996.
250. Sacks FM: Lipid-lowering therapy in acute coronary syndromes. JAMA 285:1758-1760, 2001.
251. Sacks FM: The relative role of low-density lipoprotein cholesterol and high-density lipoprotein cholesterol in coronary artery disease: Evidence from large-scale statin and fibrate trials. Am J Cardiol 88:14N-18N, 2001.
252. Sacks FM, Alaupovic P, Moye LA, et al: VLDL, apolipoproteins B, CIII, and E, and risk of recurrent coronary events in the Cholesterol and Recurrent Events (CARE) trial. Circulation 102:1886-1892, 2000.
253. Sacks FM, Krukonis GP: The influence of apolipoprotein E on the interactions between normal human very low density lipoproteins and U937 human macrophages: Heterogeneity among persons. Vasc Med 1:9-18, 1996.
254. Sacks FM, Moye LA, Davis BR, et al: Relationship between plasma LDL concentrations during treatment with pravastatin and recurrent coronary events in the Cholesterol and Recurrent Events trial. Circulation 97:1446-1452, 1998.
255. Sacks FM, Pfeffer MA, Moyé L, et al: Rationale and design of a secondary prevention trial of lowering normal plasma cholesterol levels after acute myocardial infarction: the Cholesterol and Recurrent Events trial (CARE). Am J Cardiol 68:1436-1446, 1991.

256. Sacks FM, Pfeffer MA, Moye LA, et al: The effect of pravastatin on coronary events after myocardial infarction in patients with average cholesterol levels. Cholesterol and Recurrent Events Trial investigators. N Engl J Med 335:1001-1009, 1996.
257. Sacks FM, Rouleau JL, Moye LA, et al: Baseline characteristics in the Cholesterol and Recurrent Events (CARE) trial of secondary prevention in patients with average serum cholesterol levels. Am J Cardiol 75:621-623, 1995.
258. Sacks FM, Tonkin AM, Shepherd J, et al: Effect of pravastatin on coronary disease events in subgroups defined by coronary risk factors: The Prospective Pravastatin Pooling Project. Circulation 102:1893-1900, 2000.
259. Salenius JP, Harju E, Riekkinen H: Early cerebral complications in carotid endarterectomy: risk factors. J Cardiovasc Surg (Torino) 31:162-167, 1990.
260. Samain E, Farah E, Leseche G, Marty J: Guidelines for perioperative cardiac evaluation from the American College of Cardiology/American Heart Association task force are effective for stratifying cardiac risk before aortic surgery. J Vasc Surg 31:971-979, 2000.
261. Sametz W, Metzler H, Gries M, et al: Perioperative catecholamine changes in cardiac risk patients. Eur J Clin Invest 29:582-587, 1999.
262. Samson RH, Showalter DP, Yunis JP: Routine carotid endarterectomy without a shunt, even in the presence of a contralateral occlusion. Cardiovasc Surg 6:475-484, 1998.
263. Scavee V, Viejo D, Buche M, et al: Six hundred consecutive carotid endarterectomies with temporary shunt and vein patch angioplasty: Early and long-term results. Cardiovasc Surg 9:463-468, 2001.
264. Schechtman KB, Capone RJ, Kleiger RE, et al: Differential risk patterns associated with 3 month as compared with 3 to 12 month mortality and reinfarction after non-Q wave myocardial infarction. The Diltiazem Reinfarction Study Group. J Am Coll Cardiol 15:940-947, 1990.
265. Schueppert MT, Kresowik TF, Corry DC, et al: Selection of patients for cardiac evaluation before peripheral vascular operations. J Vasc Surg 23:802-808, 1996.
266. Sedwitz MM, Hye RJ, Freischlag JA, Stabile BE: Zero operative mortality rate in 109 consecutive elective aortic operations performed by residents. Surg Gynecol Obstet 170:385-389, 1990.
267. Seeger JM, Rosenthal GR, Self SB, et al: Does routine stress-thallium cardiac scanning reduce postoperative cardiac complications? Ann Surg 219:654-661, 1994.
268. Sekiya M, Suzuki M, Fujiwara Y, et al: Hemodynamic characteristics of patients with coronary artery disease presenting false-negative exercise stress test. Angiology 43:506-511, 1992.
269. Selzman CH, Miller SA, Zimmerman MA, Harken AH: The case for beta-adrenergic blockade as prophylaxis against perioperative cardiovascular morbidity and mortality. Arch Surg 136:286-290, 2001.
270. Shah DM, Chang BB, Paty PS, et al: Treatment of abdominal aortic aneurysm by exclusion and bypass: An analysis of outcome. J Vasc Surg 13:15-20, 1991.
271. Shah DM, Darling RC, Chang BB, et al: Carotid endarterectomy in awake patients: Its safety, acceptability, and outcome. J Vasc Surg 19:1015-1020, 1994.
272. Shah KB, Kleinman BS, Rao TL, et al: Angina and other risk factors in patients with cardiac diseases undergoing noncardiac operations. Anesth Analg 70:240-247, 1990.
273. Shah PK, Falk E, Badimon JJ, et al: Human monocyte-derived macrophages induce collagen breakdown in fibrous caps of atherosclerotic plaques: Potential role of matrix-degrading metalloproteinases and implications for plaque rupture. Circulation 92:1565-1569, 1995.
274. Shaw LJ, Eagle KA, Gersh BJ, Miller DD: Meta-analysis of intravenous dipyridamole-thallium-201 imaging (1985 to 1994) and dobutamine echocardiography (1991 to 1994) for risk stratification before vascular surgery. J Am Coll Cardiol 27:787-798, 1996.
275. Shaw LJ, Hachamovitch R, Cohen M, et al: Cost implications of selective preoperative risk screening in the care of candidates for peripheral vascular operations. Am J Manag Care 3:1817-1827, 1997.
276. Shoemaker WC, Appel PL, Kram HB, et al: Prospective trial of supranormal values of survivors as therapeutic goals in high-risk surgical patients. Chest 94:1176-1186, 1988.
277. Sicard GA, Reilly JM, Rubin BG, et al: Transabdominal versus retroperitoneal incision for abdominal aortic surgery: Report of a prospective randomized trial. J Vasc Surg 21:174-181, 1995.
278. Smulyan H, Weinberg SE, Howanitz PJ: Continuous propranolol infusion following abdominal surgery. JAMA 247:2539-2542, 1982.
279. Soto J, Sacristan JA, Alsar MJ: Pulmonary oedema due to fentanyl? Anaesthesia 47:913-914, 1992
280. Sprung J, Abdelmalak B, Gottlieb A, et al: Analysis of risk factors for myocardial infarction and cardiac mortality after major vascular surgery. Anesthesiology 93:129-140, 2000.
281. Stampfer MJ, Sacks FM, Salvini S, et al: A prospective study of cholesterol, apolipoproteins, and the risk of myocardial infarction. N Engl J Med 325:373-381, 1991.
282. Stein B, Badimon L, Israel DH, et al: Thrombosis/platelets and other blood factors in acute coronary syndromes. J Cardiovasc Clin 20:105-129, 1989.
283. Steinberg JB, Kresowik TF, Behrendt DM: Prophylactic myocardial revascularization based on dipyridamole-thallium scanning before peripheral vascular surgery. Cardiovasc Surg 1:552-557, 1993.
284. Stone JG, Foex P, Sear JW, et al: Myocardial ischemia in untreated hypertensive patients: Effect of a single small oral dose of a beta-adrenergic blocking agent. Anesthesiology 68:495-500, 1988.
285. Stuhmeier KD, Mainzer B, Cierpka J, et al: Small, oral dose of clonidine reduces the incidence of intraoperative myocardial ischemia in patients having vascular surgery. Anesthesiology 85:706-712, 1996.
286. Sytkowski PA: Declining mortality from cardiovascular disease. Compr Ther 17:39-44, 1991.
287. Sytkowski PA, D'Agostino RB, Belanger AJ, Kannel WB: Secular trends in long-term sustained hypertension, long-term treatment, and cardiovascular mortality: The Framingham Heart Study 1950 to 1990. Circulation 93:697-703, 1996.
288. Tanasijevic MJ, Antman EM: Diagnostic performance of cardiac troponin I in suspected acute myocardial infarction: Implications for clinicians. Am Heart J 137:203-206, 1999.
289. Tanasijevic MJ, Cannon CP, Antman EM: The role of cardiac troponin-I (cTnI) in risk stratification of patients with unstable coronary artery disease. Clin Cardiol 22:13-16, 1999.
290. Taylor LM Jr, Edwards JM, Porter JM: Present status of reversed vein bypass grafting: Five-year results of a modern series. J Vasc Surg 11:193-205, 1990.
291. Taylor LM Jr, Hamre D, Dalman RL, Porter JM: Limb salvage vs amputation for critical ischemia: The role of vascular surgery. Arch Surg 126:1251-1257, 1991.
292. Theroux P: Angiographic and clinical progression in unstable angina: From clinical observations to clinical trials. Circulation 91:2295-2298, 1995.
293. Therre T, Ribal JP, Motreff P, et al: Assessment of cardiac risk before aortic reconstruction: Noninvasive work-up using clinical examination, exercise testing, and dobutamine stress echocardiography versus routine coronary arteriography. Ann Vasc Surg 13:501-508, 1999.
294. Thygesen KA, Alpert JS: The definitions of acute coronary syndrome, myocardial infarction, and unstable angina. Curr Cardiol Rep 3:268-272, 2001.
295. Trinquier S, Flecheux O, Bullenger M, Castex F: Highly specific immunoassay for cardiac troponin I assessed in noninfarct patients with chronic renal failure or severe polytrauma. Clin Chem 41:1675-1676, 1995.
296. Tsevat J, Kuntz KM, Orav EJ, et al: Cost-effectiveness of pravastatin therapy for survivors of myocardial infarction with average cholesterol levels. Am Heart J 141:727-734, 2001.
297. Urban MK, Markowitz SM, Gordon MA, et al: Postoperative prophylactic administration of beta-adrenergic blockers in patients at risk for myocardial ischemia. Anesth Analg 90:1257-1261, 2000.

298. Valentine RJ, Duke ML, Inman MH, et al: Effectiveness of pulmonary artery catheters in aortic surgery: A randomized trial. J Vasc Surg 27:203-211, 1998.
299. Wengerter KR, Yang PM, Veith FJ, et al: A twelve-year experience with the popliteal-to-distal artery bypass: The significance and management of proximal disease. J Vasc Surg 15:143-149, 1992.
300. Whittemore AD, Clowes AW, Hechtman HB, Mannick JA: Aortic aneurysm repair: Reduced operative mortality associated with maintenance of optimal cardiac performance. Ann Surg 192:414-421, 1980.
301. Wilson SE: Late survival after intervention for peripheral vascular disease. J Endovasc Surg 3:361-363, 1996.
302. Wilt TJ, Rubins HB, Robins SJ, et al: Carotid atherosclerosis in men with low levels of HDL cholesterol. Stroke 28:1919-1925, 1997.
303. Wolf YG, Landersberg G, Mosseri M, et al: Preoperative dipyridamole-thallium scanning, selective coronary revascularization and long-term survival in patients with critical lower limb ischemia. J Cardiovasc Surg (Torino) 42:89-95, 2001.
304. Wong T, Detsky AS: Preoperative cardiac risk assessment for patients having peripheral vascular surgery. Ann Intern Med 116:743-753, 1992.
305. Woratyla SP, Darling RC III, Chang BB, et al: The performance of femoropopliteal bypasses using polytetrafluoroethylene above the knee versus autogenous vein below the knee. Am J Surg 174:169-172, 1997.
306. World Health Organization Task Force: Nomenclature and criteria for diagnosis of ischemic heart disease. Report of the Joint International Society and Federation of Cardiology/World Health Organization task force on standardization of clinical nomenclature. Circulation 59: 607-609, 1979.
307. Yeager RA, Moneta GL, Edwards JM, et al: Late survival after perioperative myocardial infarction complicating vascular surgery. J Vasc Surg 20:598-604, 1994.
308. Yeager R, Moneta GL, Edwards JM, et al: Reducing perioperative myocardial infarction following vascular surgery: The potential role of beta-blockade. Arch Surg 130:869-872, 1995.
309. Yeager RA, Weigel RM, Murphy ES, et al: Application of clinically valid cardiac risk factors to aortic aneurysm surgery. Arch Surg 121:278-281, 1986.
310. Zannetti S, Cao P, De Rango P, et al: Intraoperative assessment of technical perfection in carotid endarterectomy: A prospective analysis of 1305 completion procedures. Collaborators of the EVEREST study group. Eversion Versus Standard Carotid Endartectomy. Eur J Vasc Endovasc Surg 18:52-58, 1999.
311. Ziegler DW, Wright JG, Choban PS, Flancbaum L: A prospective randomized trial of preoperative "optimization" of cardiac function in patients undergoing elective peripheral vascular surgery. Surgery 122:584-592, 1997.

Chapter

57

Respiratory Complications in Vascular Surgery

JAYME E. LOCKE, MD
PAMELA A. LIPSETT, MD, FACS, FCCM

Postoperative pulmonary complications can be a major cause of morbidity and mortality in the perioperative period.[1-3] The incidence of postoperative pulmonary complications has been reported to range from 5% to 80%, depending on the patient population and criteria used to define complications.[4] A comprehensive definition of postoperative pulmonary complications could include all patients with fever and either pulmonary signs or symptoms (e.g., productive cough, rhonchi, or diminished breath sounds) or changes on chest x-ray (e.g., atelectasis, consolidation, or incomplete expansion).[4] Although such a definition is inclusive, many of these complications are of no clinical relevance; a more useful and narrow definition would comprise the problems that produce identifiable disease or dysfunction that is clinically significant and adversely affects the clinical course (Table 57-1). This chapter discusses identification and prevention of pulmonary complications with particular emphasis on identification of preoperative patient-related risk factors and newer modes of ventilator management.

Table 57-1 Common Postoperative Respiratory Complications

Atelectasis
Bronchospasm
Hypoventilation from analgesics and residual neuromuscular blockade
Infection
Aspiration
Pulmonary edema
Acute lung injury and acute respiratory distress syndrome
Respiratory failure

■ RISK FACTORS AND PREOPERATIVE OPTIMIZAITON

Risk factors for pulmonary complications can be grouped into patient-related and procedure-related risks (Table 57-2).[5-9] Although procedure-related risk factors may be the more important risk factors, except in choice of procedure, these factors may not be greatly modifiable. The potential patient-

Table 57-2 Potential Patient-Related and Procedure-Related Risk Factors for the Development of Postoperative Pulmonary Complications

PATIENT-RELATED RISK FACTORS	PROCEDURE-RELATED RISK FACTORS
Chronic lung disease	Surgical site (thoracic or upper abdominal)
Asthma	Duration of surgery (>3 hours)
Tobacco use	Type of anesthesia
Health status	Type of neuromuscular blockade
Obesity	
Age	
Upper respiratory infection	
Metabolic factors	

related factors studied include the following: (1) chronic lung disease, (2) asthma, (3) tobacco use, (4) general health status, (5) obesity, (6) age, (7) upper respiratory infection, and (8) metabolic factors. A complete history and physical examination are the most important elements of preoperative risk assessment. Significant risk factors should be identified. Evidence suggesting unrecognized chronic lung disease should be sought, including a history of exercise intolerance, unexplained dyspnea, or cough. Physical examination should be directed toward evidence for obstructive lung disease, especially noting decreased breath sounds, wheezes, rhonchi, or prolonged expiratory phase.[9]

Chronic Lung Disease

Known chronic lung disease is the most important patient-related risk factor for postoperative pulmonary complications with reported unadjusted relative risks ranging from 2.7 to 6.[6] Clinical studies using preoperative findings of decreased breath sounds, prolonged expiration, rales, wheezes, or rhonchi or chest radiographs consistent with the diagnosis of chronic obstructive pulmonary disease (COPD) have shown complications varying from 26% in patients with these findings to 8% in patients without these findings. Despite the increased risk of postoperative pulmonary complications in patients with obstructive lung disease, there seems to be no prohibitive level of pulmonary function below which surgery is absolutely contraindicated.[6,10] The benefit of surgery must be weighed against the known risks; even extremely high-risk patients may proceed to surgery if the indication is sufficiently compelling.

Preoperative Preparation

The treatments and preparation of patients who have COPD before elective surgery are the same as those in nonoperative settings.[11] Clinicians should not employ treatments because of upcoming surgery unless the treatments are otherwise indicated independent of the need for surgery. Multimodality treatment programs, including chest physical therapy, bronchodilators, smoking cessation, and antibiotics and corticosteroids (when indicated) reduce the risk of postoperative pulmonary complications in patients who have COPD.[8,9,12] Standard therapy for COPD includes use of ipratropium for patients who have daily symptoms plus the addition of inhaled β-agonists as needed for symptoms.[11,13] Theophylline use should be reserved for patients who are not responsive to other maximal therapies. Approximately 20% to 30% of patients with COPD respond to the use of systemic corticosteroids.[6] Unless a patient has been shown previously to be a nonresponder, clinicians should use systemic corticosteroids for patients who have COPD before surgery if airflow obstruction has not been maximally reduced and the patients are not at their optimal baseline despite other therapies, as determined by symptoms and peak flow. There is no role for routine antibiotics before surgery; clinicians should recommend antibiotics only if a change in the chest radiograph or the character or amount of sputum suggests lower respiratory tract infection. In these cases, elective surgery should be canceled until the patient has returned to the baseline level of function.

Asthma

Despite early reports indicating that patients with asthma had higher than expected rates of postoperative pulmonary complications, patients with asthma who are well controlled and who have a peak flow measurement of greater than 80% of predicted or personal best can proceed to surgery at average risk.[6] In a report of 706 patients having general surgery, there were no incidents of death, pneumothorax, or pneumonia in the entire sample.[14] There were 14 minor complications, including bronchospasm (12) and laryngospasm (2). One patient developed postoperative respiratory failure without sequelae.

Physicians should prepare patients who have asthma for surgery in the same fashion as optimization of airway obstruction and reactivity in the nonsurgical setting.[15] A 1-week course of systemic corticosteroids (e.g., prednisone, 40 to 60 mg daily) can be used safely as needed without an increase in the risk of respiratory infection or wound complications.[16-18] The goal of treatment is to render the patient wheeze-free and asymptomatic if possible and to achieve a peak flow rate of greater than 80% of predicted or personal best.

Smoking

Current smoking increases the risk for postoperative pulmonary complications by threefold.[19-22] This risk exists even among patients who do not have superimposed chronic lung disease. Three studies analyzed the risk of postoperative pulmonary complications attributed to smoking, and all three studies reported the same counter-intuitive result: Recent quitters have a higher rate of pulmonary complications than do current smokers. Bluman and colleagues[20] reported a relative risk of pulmonary complications of 6.7 for smokers who had recently quit or reduced cigarette use compared with current smokers undergoing noncardiac surgery. Most of these patients had quit or reduced smoking within 1 month before surgery. Patients who reduced smoking closer to the date of surgery had higher complication rates. Nakagawa and colleagues[22] likewise reported higher pulmonary complication rates among patients undergoing pulmonary surgery who had quit within 4 weeks of surgery (54%) than among current smokers (43%) or patients who had stopped smoking for more than 4 weeks (35%).

The mechanism for this repeated and seemingly paradoxical finding is unknown, but it might relate to the clinical observation that many smokers experience an increase in the quantity of cough and sputum in the 1 to 2 months after stopping cigarette use or to selection bias in that sicker patients were more likely to attempt cigarette cessation or reduction before surgery. As a practical conclusion, smoking cessation must begin at least 1 to 2 months before elective surgery to confer a reduction in pulmonary complications. Patients should be strongly encouraged to stop smoking 2 months before major elective surgery when possible.

General Health Status

Overall health status is an important determinant of pulmonary risk. The commonly used American Society of Anesthesiologists classification considers any systemic disease that affects activity or is a threat to life. This classification also would capture patients with chronic lung disease. This classification system generally has correlated with pulmonary risk: An American Society of Anesthesiologists class greater than 2 confers a 1.5-fold to 3.2-fold increase in risk.[6,23]

Obesity

Physiologic changes that accompany morbid obesity include reduction in lung volumes, ventilation-perfusion mismatch, and relative hypoxemia.[24] These findings might be expected to accentuate similar changes seen with anesthesia and increase the risk of pulmonary complications. The literature on the independent contribution of obesity to perioperative pulmonary complications is conflicting, with some studies showing increased risk and others showing no increased risk when adjustments for co-morbidities are made.[25,26] The study by Calligaro and associates[27] of 128 aortic surgery patients, 26 of whom were obese, showed a pulmonary complication rate of 27% in the obese group versus 17% in the nonobese group, an unadjusted ratio of 1.6 for obesity as a risk factor. A careful analysis would suggest that patients with co-morbidities and obesity are at increased risk, and identification of these associated diseases is important.

Age

Early studies suggested an increased risk of pulmonary complications with advanced age.[28] These studies were not adjusted for overall health status, however, or the presence of known pulmonary disease. A multivariate model for postoperative respiratory failure identified age older than 60 years as a minor risk factor.[29] The odds ratios for age 60 to 69 years and age older than 70 years were 1.51 and 1.91. The data are conflicting as to the risk due to age, but it seems that any risk due to age alone, when corrected for co-morbidities, is small.[30,31]

Upper Respiratory Infection

Data regarding the risk of pulmonary complications among adults undergoing high-risk surgical procedures with current or recent upper respiratory infection are limited. It would seem wise, however, to avoid elective surgery in this setting.

Metabolic Factors

A multifactorial risk index for postoperative respiratory failure identified two metabolic risk factors.[29] Albumin less than 3 g/dL and blood urea nitrogen greater than 30 mg/dL each predicted risk; odds ratios were 2.53 and 2.29.

■ PROCEDURE-RELATED RISK FACTORS

Surgical factors that potentially may affect pulmonary risk perioperatively include the site and duration of the operation, the method of anesthesia, and the specific use of pancuronium as a neuromuscular blocker (see Table 57-2).[6,32]

Surgical Site

Surgical site is the most important factor in predicting the overall risk of postoperative pulmonary complications; the incidence of complications is inversely related to the distance of the surgical incision from the diaphragm. The choice of incision is likely to influence respiratory muscle and diaphragmatic function.[33,34] The complication rate is significantly higher for thoracic and upper abdominal incisions than for all other procedures.[1,34,35] Complication rates for upper abdominal surgery range from 17% to 76%; for lower abdominal surgery, 0 to 5%; and for thoracic surgery, 19% to 59%.[34,35]

Duration of Surgery

Surgical procedures lasting more than 3 to 4 hours are associated with a higher risk of pulmonary complications.[36-38] A study of risk factors for postoperative pneumonia in 520 patients found an incidence of 8% for surgeries lasting less than 2 hours versus 40% for procedures lasting more than 4 hours. This observation suggests that, when available, a less ambitious, briefer procedure should be considered in an extremely high-risk patient.

Type of Anesthesia

There are conflicting data with regard to the pulmonary risk of spinal or epidural anesthesia compared with general anesthesia.[39-42] Although not specific to vascular surgery, a large review of 141 trials that included 9559 patients[39] reported a reduction in risk of pulmonary complications among patients receiving neuraxial blockade (either epidural or spinal anesthesia) compared with patients receiving general anesthesia. Patients receiving neuraxial blockade had an overall 39% reduction in the risk of pneumonia and a 59% decrease in the risk of respiratory depression. In a large clinical trial performed at our institution by Norris and colleagues,[43] 168 patients undergoing abdominal aorta surgery were randomized to receive either a thoracic epidural anesthesia combined with a light general anesthesia or general anesthesia alone intraoperatively and either intravenous or epidural patient-controlled analgesia postoperatively. Although epidural patient-controlled analgesia correlated with a significantly shorter time to extubation, the treatment groups had comparable times to intensive care unit (ICU) discharge, ward admission, first bowel sounds, first flatus, tolerance of clear liquids and regular diet, and independent ambulation. Postoperative pain scores also were comparable. This study could not identify any major advantage or disadvantage for the light general anesthesia followed by intravenous or epidural versus general anesthesia alone.

Type of Neuromuscular Blockade

Pancuronium, a long-acting neuromuscular blocker, leads to a higher incidence of postoperative residual neuromuscular blockade than do shorter acting agents. Berg and colleagues[44] performed a trial of 691 patients undergoing surgery with general anesthesia and randomized them to pancuronium (long acting), atracurium (shorter acting), and vecuronium (shorter acting) as the neuromuscular blocker. The incidence of residual neuromuscular blockade after surgery was 26% in the pancuronium group and 5% in the group receiving shorter acting agents. Among the patients receiving pancuronium who had residual neuromuscular blockade, there was a 3.5-fold increase in the risk of postoperative pulmonary complications. While this report awaits confirmation by other investigators, it is reasonable to avoid pancuronium in patients who are at high risk for pulmonary complications.

■ PREOPERATIVE TESTING

Pulmonary Function Testing

Except in pulmonary resection, there is considerable debate regarding the role of preoperative pulmonary function tests (PFTs) for perioperative risk stratification.[45-48] There are two reasonable goals that could justify the use of preoperative PFTs: (1) identification of a group of patients for whom the risk of the proposed open vascular surgical procedure is not justified by the benefit or in whom a percutaneous or endoluminal procedure would be better tolerated or (2) identification of a subset of patients at higher risk for whom aggressive perioperative management is warranted. Although a 1990 American College of Physicians consensus statement recommended liberal use of preoperative spirometry,[48] more recently available literature suggests a more limited use might be appropriate. PFTs should not be obtained routinely for patients having abdominal surgery, and they should not be used as the primary reason for denying a patient an operation. PFTs might be useful for patients with COPD or asthma if clinical evaluation cannot determine if the patient is at his or her best baseline and that airflow obstruction is optimally reduced. In this case, PFTs may identify patients who would benefit from more aggressive preoperative management. Similarly, in patients with dyspnea or exercise intolerance that remains unexplained after clinical evaluation, PFTs may be indicated. In this case, the differential diagnosis may include cardiac disease or deconditioning. The results of PFTs may change preoperative management.

Arterial Blood Gas Analysis and Chest Radiographs

No data suggest that the finding of hypercapnia identifies high-risk patients who otherwise would not have been identified based on established clinical risk factors. In addition, abnormal chest radiographs are seen with increasing frequency with age. Chest radiographs add little to the clinical evaluation in identifying healthy patients at risk for perioperative complications. A meta-analysis of studies of routine preoperative chest radiographs reached the same conclusion.[49] Of 14,390 preoperative radiographs, there were only 140 unexpected abnormalities and only 14 cases in which the chest radiograph was abnormal and influenced management. The available literature does not allow an evidence-based determination of which patients would benefit from a preoperative chest radiograph. A chest radiograph also should be performed if there has been a recent change in cardiac or pulmonary status.

■ PULMONARY RISK INDICES

Cardiac risk indices have been used widely since 1977 to stratify the risk of perioperative cardiac complications.[50] Although several studies have attempted to identify and quantify the risk for postoperative pulmonary complications, each study has significant limitations.[51-55] The most ambitious risk index was developed to predict the risk of postoperative respiratory failure in a large Veterans Administration database.[29] This index is modeled after the widely used cardiac risk indices. The authors evaluated the factors that predicted postoperative respiratory failure and assigned each factor points based on its strength in the multivariate analysis (Table 57-3). Procedure-related risk factors dominate the index, with type of surgery and emergency surgery being the most important predictors. New observations in this study included the importance of abdominal aortic aneurysm repair, emergency surgery, and metabolic factors as risk

Table 57-3 Multivariate Risk Factors for Postoperative Respiratory Failure

PREOPERATIVE PREDICTOR	POINT VALUE
Type of surgery	
Abdominal aortic aneurysm	27
Thoracic	21
Neurosurgery, upper abdominal, or peripheral vascular	14
Neck	11
Emergency surgery	11
Albumin (30 g/L)	9
Blood urea nitrogen (>30 mg/dL)	8
Partially or fully dependent functional status	7
History of chronic obstructive pulmonary disease	6
Age	
70	6
60-69	4

CLASS	POINT TOTAL	PREDICTED PROBABILITY OF POSTOPERATIVE PULMONARY FAILURE (%)
1	<10	0.5
2	11-19	2.2
3	20-27	5
4	28-40	11.6
5	>40	30.5

From Arozullah AM, Daley J, Henderson WG, Khuri SF, for the National Veterans Administration Surgical Quality Improvement Program: Multifactorial risk index for predicting postoperative respiratory failure in men after major noncardiac surgery. Ann Surg 232:242, 2000.

factors. In the validation cohort of this study, the index accurately predicted the risk of respiratory failure, with complication rates ranging from 0.5% (class 1) to 26.6% (class 4). None of the predictive factors are modifiable, other than potentially changing the proposed procedure to a less ambitious and lower risk intervention, such as an endovascular aneurysm repair. As a result, this index is more valuable to predict risk and to determine candidacy for surgery than as a tool for risk reduction strategies. A prospective index also has been published to predict perioperative risk of pneumonia.[55]

■ PERIOPERATIVE PULMONARY PHYSIOLOGY

In a normal, nonstressed individual, respiratory rate is 10 to 12 breaths/min; each breath has a tidal volume of approximately 500 mL, with a total minute ventilation of 5 to 6 L/min. Total minute ventilation consists of alveolar ventilation and the anatomic dead space, which is the portion of a breath not available for gas exchange. Anatomic dead space is roughly equal to 130 to 180 mL each breath. Gas exchange depends on alveolar ventilation rather than total minute ventilation.

Reduction in lung volumes resulting from anesthesia and surgery is the primary physiologic mechanism that contributes to the development of atelectasis and other postoperative pulmonary complications.[33,56,57] Patients, particularly after upper abdominal and thoracic surgery, typically experience a significant change in pulmonary function. The mechanisms are primarily a decrease in phrenic nerve activity and a resultant decrease in diaphragmatic function and increases in intercostal and abdominal muscle tone that occur in response to pain and spinal reflex arcs postoperatively. The most important physiologic change observed in postsurgical patients is a decrease in the functional residual capacity (FRC), the volume of air left in the lungs after normal expiration. In the absence of intervention, FRC reaches a nadir at 24 to 48 hours postoperatively and returns to normal in uncomplicated non–high-risk patients in approximately 1 week. The relationship between FRC and closing capacity (CC), the volume left in the lungs as the midsize and small airways begin to collapse, is a major determinant of postoperative pulmonary function and the resultant pulmonary morbidity. Normally, FRC is well above CC, and tidal volumes result in air distribution throughout the alveoli units. In the postoperative period, FRC decreases dramatically, whereas the CC remains unchanged. Patients who are experiencing severe pain often are not able to generate a tidal volume sufficient to overcome the CC, resulting in lack of airflow to most alveolar units, leading to atelectasis. Similarly, although patients experiencing only mild pain may be able to generate adequate peak inspiratory flow to overcome CC, the ability to oxygenate alveolar units only at the peak of inspiration leads to ventilation-perfusion abnormalities (ventilation-perfusion mismatch), contributing to postoperative hypoxemia. Adequate pain control is essential to facilitate the patient's ability to breathe more deeply (increase tidal volume and FRC) and cough more effectively (increased forced expiratory volume in 1 second), averting the worsening of pulmonary dysfunction associated with surgery and general anesthesia. Although lower abdominal surgery is associated with similar changes, but to a lesser degree, reductions in lung volumes are not seen with surgery on the extremities.

■ ATELECTASIS

Atelectasis is one of the most common pulmonary complications in the postoperative period. Clinically significant atelectasis has been reported in 20% of patients undergoing upper abdominal surgery and in 30% of patients undergoing thoracic surgery.[32] Altered compliance of lung tissue, impaired regional ventilation, and retained airway secretions contribute to the development of atelectasis.[58]

Postoperative strategies differ from the above-mentioned strategies, which reduce or avoid risk factors. Strategies after surgery involve lung expansion maneuvers and pain control; both strategies work to minimize the expected decrease in lung volumes after surgery and decrease pulmonary complication rates. Lung expansion maneuvers range from simple but effort-dependent strategies, such as incentive spirometry and deep breathing, to more complex, expensive, and effort-independent strategies, such as continuous positive airway pressure (CPAP). In a meta-analysis of different lung expansion techniques, Thomas and McIntosh[59] reported odds ratios for pulmonary complications for incentive spirometry and deep breathing exercises of 0.44 and 0.43.

Using a more rigorous study selection strategy that excluded all studies with a methodologic flaw, Overend and colleagues[60] found 35 of 46 retrieved articles on incentive spirometry to be flawed. Of the remaining 11, only 5 studies used pulmonary complications as an endpoint, and 2 of these showed a benefit of incentive spirometry. Although the literature contains flawed studies, incentive spirometry and deep breathing exercises are low risk, are inexpensive, and are recommended as a strategy to reduce risk. The combination of these two interventions is no more effective than either one alone. Postoperative CPAP is an equally effective strategy. Stock and colleagues[61] randomly assigned patients after upper abdominal surgery to postoperative CPAP, incentive spirometry, or coughing and deep breathing. Atelectasis was less common in the CPAP group than in either of the other two groups (23% versus 42%). Because CPAP is more costly and carries a small risk of barotrauma, it is reasonable to reserve this intervention for patients who are unable to cooperate with effort-dependent strategies.

Intermittent positive pressure breathing (IPPB) was used commonly in the 1960s and 1970s, but it is associated with more complications than other methods of lung expansion. This association was illustrated in a prospective study, which found that the rates of postoperative pulmonary complications in an IPPB-treated group were similar to the rates in patients receiving incentive spirometry or voluntary deep breathing exercises[62]; however, 18% of the IPPB-treated group required discontinuation of therapy because of abdominal distention. In addition, IPPB is more costly than other methods of lung expansion. IPPB should not be used for routine prophylaxis.

Pain control strategies, including epidural analgesia and intercostal nerve blocks, reduce splinting and promote the ability to take deep breaths after thoracic, aortic, and upper abdominal surgeries. Although pain control is improved with epidural analgesia and intercostal nerve blocks compared with systemic opioids, studies of their ability to reduce postoperative pulmonary complications have shown conflicting results. In a systematic review and meta-analysis, Ballantyne and colleagues[42] helped to determine the benefit of specific pain control strategies. Epidural opioids and intercostal nerve blocks showed a nonsignificant trend toward reduced pulmonary complications, whereas epidural local anesthetics reduced pulmonary infection rates (relative risk 0.36, confidence interval 0.21 to 0.65) and total pulmonary complications (relative risk 0.58, confidence interval 0.42 to 0.80).

■ ACUTE RESPIRATORY FAILURE

Acute respiratory failure is an umbrella term for many pulmonary pathologies.[63,64] In a general sense, it implies that profound ventilation, perfusion, or gas exchange abnormalities are present. Acute respiratory failure can be thought of as primarily hypoxic in origin, hypercapnic (ventilatory failure), or with both combined. Commonly the lungs of these patients are plagued by marked decreases in compliance, often requiring higher inspiratory pressures to achieve the same level of inflation and an increased work of breathing. This increased work of breathing can result in further oxygen debt or in mechanical ventilatory failure.

Shallow breathing secondary to poorly controlled pain in the postoperative patient, aspiration, bronchospasm, absorption atelectasis from anesthesia, or pneumothorax or hemothorax from central line placement all can cause alveolar collapse and decrease FRC. Alveolar collapse affects gas exchange by creating a ventilation-perfusion mismatch. Acutely, compensation occurs through pulmonary artery spasm and shunting of blood to ventilated areas. The loss of volume secondary to alveolar collapse creates a decrease in lung compliance, making it difficult to ventilate patients. Positive end-expiratory pressure (PEEP) is often used in this setting to "recruit" alveoli, increasing the size of the functional lung. This recruitment results in improved compliance, decrease in dead space, increase in oxygenation, and decrease in shunting. In the attempt to recruit collapsed alveoli, normal alveoli may become overdistended. Normal lung is vulnerable to this phenomenon because it is the most compliant. To avoid this side effect, plateau inspiratory pressures should be kept at less than 30 to 35 cm.

Pulmonary edema also results in decreased FRC, which affects gas exchange and compliance. Three main causes for pulmonary edema exist: increased hydrostatic pressure from left ventricular failure and fluid overload, decreased plasma oncotic pressure from liver failure, and increased capillary permeability as seen in burn and septic shock patients. Patients often require positive-pressure ventilation to improve gas exchange when pulmonary edema exists. This mode of ventilation limits alveolar collapse, increases surface area for water accumulation, and overcomes the effects of bronchial occlusion. Pulmonary edema is a more serious cause of acute respiratory failure than alveolar collapse alone because the protein-rich fluid makes the patient highly susceptible to infection and fibrosis.

The approach to and management of respiratory failure can be broken down simply into a four-step process:

1. Rule out mechanical causes for the failure, such as pneumothorax, hemothorax, plugged endotracheal tube, occluded airway, or ascites.
2. Optimize delivery of oxygen (see later).
3. Attempt to decrease or limit oxygen consumption by treating infection and fever and by providing adequate sedation.
4. Optimize carbon dioxide removal. Improve minute ventilation. Avoid heavy carbohydrate loads in the patient's diet.

Ultimately, if the patient's underlying disease process is not corrected and a systemic inflammatory response persists, acute respiratory failure does not reverse and culminates in a disease process known as *acute respiratory distress syndrome* (ARDS).

Oxygen delivery (Do_2) is equal to the oxygen content of the blood (Cao_2) multiplied by the cardiac output. Cao_2 is determined by the concentration of oxygen-saturated hemoglobin and dissolved oxygen in the blood (Table 57-4). Based on this equation, oxygen kinetics depend heavily on ventilation and perfusion. When delivered to the periphery, oxygen is consumed (Vo_2) at a rate of about 200 mL/min in the average adult. Vo_2 has many regulators, including catecholamines and thyroid hormones. Do_2 can be increased by improving oxygenation, correcting anemia, and optimizing cardiac output. Although optimizing Do_2 may seem a worthy goal, studies using a pulmonary artery catheter to set a specified goal (>500 mL/min) have not convincingly shown any improved patient outcomes.[65,66] This study and others were primarily of unselected, not specifically ill patient populations, however. Vascular surgery patients with abnormal Do_2 or patients with high

Table 57-4 Oxygen Measurements

MEASUREMENT	EQUATION
Arterial oxygen content (Cao_2)	$Cao_2 = (1.36 \times [Hbg] \times Sao_2) + (Pao_2 \times 0.0031)$
Mixed venous oxygen content (Cvo_2)	$Cvo_2 = (1.36 \times [Hbg] \times Svo_2) + (Pvo_2 \times 0.0031)$
Arteriovenous oxygen difference (a-vDo_2)	$a\text{-}vDo_2 = (Cao_2 - Cvo_2)$
Oxygen delivery (Do_2)	$Do_2 = ([1.36\ (Hbg) \times Sao_2] + [Pao_2 \times 0.0031]) \times CO$
Mixed venous oxygen saturation (Svo_2)	$Svo_2 = (1.36 \times [Hbg] \times Sao_2) + (Pvo_2 \times 0.0031)$
Oxygen consumption (Vo_2)	$Vo_2 = CO \times (a\text{-}vDo_2)$

Cao_2, arterial oxygen content (mL O_2/dL blood); Cvo_2, mixed venous oxygen content (mL O_2/dL blood); a-vDo_2, arteriovenous oxygen difference (mL O_2/dL blood); Do_2, systemic oxygen delivery (mL O_2/min/m^2); Vo_2, systemic oxygen consumption (mL O_2/min/m^2); CO, cardiac output (mL/min/m^2); Hbg, hemoglobin concentration (mg/dL); Sao_2, arterial oxygen saturation; Svo_2, mixed venous oxygen saturation; Pao_2, arterial partial pressure of oxygen (mm Hg); Pvo_2, mixed venous partial pressure of oxygen (mm Hg).

$\dot{V}O_2$ (abnormal DO_2-to-$\dot{V}O_2$ ratios) have not been definitively studied. As a practical matter, patients with abnormal DO_2 with low mixed venous saturations should have cardiac output or hemoglobin concentration or both modified.

■ ACUTE RESPIRATORY DISTRESS SYNDROME

In 1994, the American-European Consensus Conference on Acute Respiratory Distress Syndrome defined ARDS as a diffuse inflammatory process involving both lungs that arises as a complication of diseases that produce a severe form of systemic inflammatory response.[67] The disease must have an acute onset; the arterial partial pressure of oxygen-to-fraction of inspired oxygen ratio must be less than 200; the chest radiograph should have bilateral infiltrates, without a clinical suspicion of pneumonia; and the left atrial pressure should be normal or if suspicion of an elevated left atrial pressure is present, a pulmonary artery catheter should be placed to assess wedge pressure. A pulmonary capillary wedge pressure of less than 18 mm Hg combined with the previously stated findings would be consistent with ARDS. A European study involving 78 ICUs from nine countries noted that 7.4% had or developed acute lung injury (arterial partial pressure of oxygen-to-fraction of inspired oxygen ratio of 200 to 300) or ARDS (2.8% acute lung injury and 5.3% ARDS).[68] Epidemiologic data suggest that ARDS may account for 36,000 deaths per year in a country the size of the United States. Although there is evidence that the mortality of ARDS may be declining over time, it remains high (30% to 40%), and it is an important cause of morbidity in patients who leave the hospital. Herridge and associates[69] found that survivors of ARDS had persistent functional disability 1 year after discharge from the ICU. Despite the bleak outlook for this patient population, research in the field of critical care medicine has elucidated new treatment strategies.

Predisposing conditions for ARDS include sepsis, receipt of blood products, catheter sepsis, pneumonia, pulmonary contusion, cardiopulmonary bypass, and pancreatitis.[68] ARDS is often progressive and characterized by distinct stages with different clinicopathologic and radiographic manifestations. The acute or exudative phase is manifested by the rapid onset of respiratory failure in a patient at risk for the condition. Arterial hypoxemia that is refractory to treatment with supplemental oxygen is a characteristic feature. Computed tomography has shown that alveolar filling, consolidation, and atelectasis occur predominantly in dependent lung zones, whereas other areas may be relatively spared. Lavage of these areas reveals substantial inflammation, however. Although the disease may resolve in some patients after this acute phase, in other patients it progresses to fibrosing alevolitis with persistent hypoxemia, increased alveolar dead space, and a further decrease in pulmonary compliance.

The cellular constituents of the lung change greatly during ARDS.[70] The alveolar epithelium has extensive necrosis of type 1 cells, which slough from the alveolar surface to be replaced by proteinaceous deposits (hyaline membranes). Type 2 cells, in addition to secreting surfactant, provide a population of cells capable of replication and differentiation to replace type 1 cells. Type 2 cells are more vulnerable to the effects of stretch at day 1 of culture than at day 5. Fundamentally the lung may be more susceptible to stress/stretch–related trauma during this time.

Historically, traditional ventilator strategies have relied on tidal volumes in the range of 10 to 12 mL/kg.[71] Because of the amount of atelectasis present, delivery of a tidal volume of 10 to 12 mL/kg into this smaller actual lung volume has consequences. Dependent portions of the lung that are atelectatic do not open with this lung volume; the remaining lung of necessity accommodates this larger lung volume, causing higher peak and plateau inspiratory pressures. Portions of the lung in the midzone have alveoli that open, but become overdistended with this tidal volume, whereas alveoli that are partially collapsed may be recruited. Alveoli that are overdistended may develop shear force stress, increased vascular permeability, loss of surfactant function, cytokine production, and further local and systemic end-organ injury. This increase in lung inflammation perpetuates the systemic inflammatory response syndrome. Strategies for management with a smaller tidal volume during ARDS were developed out of these concepts. In an elegant study by Ranieri and coworkers,[72] patients were managed with a conventional tidal volume and PEEP versus a protective ventilation strategy in which PEEP and tidal volume were set between the lower and upper inflection points of the pressure-volume curve. Alevolar fluid was sampled by bronchoalveolar lavage (BAL), and serum and BAL fluid were tested for the cytokines, tumor necrosis factor (TNF), and interleukin-1 and interleukin-6. Before randomization by ventilation strategy, patients were similar in both groups. TNF levels decreased in the low tidal volume group, however, compared with conventional ventilation. Findings of the other cytokines paralleled that of TNF. Serum values and end-organ failure also were lower in the protective lung strategy.

Other authors have suggested that the high mortality rates associated with ARDS are due to direct alveolar injury from cyclic alveolar reopening and overdistention. Amato and associates[73] randomized 53 patients to conventional or protective mechanical ventilation. Protective mechanical ventilation was defined as elevated PEEP, tidal volume less than 6 mL/kg, permissive hypercapnia, and use of pressure-limited ventilator modes. Patients receiving protective mechanical ventilation compared with conventional ventilation had a lower 28-day mortality, higher rate of weaning, and decreased rate of barotrauma. It is likely that this strategy maximizes alveolar recruitment and aeration, minimizing sheer stress and decreasing inflammation in the lung tissue. Although the protective ventilation strategy in this study was associated with a substantial and significant decrease in mortality, patients with conventional ventilation had a surprisingly high baseline mortality (70%) compared with historical mortality rates for ARDS of 40%.

In a multicenter randomized trial involving 517 critically ill patients, the ARDS Network compared traditional ventilation tidal volumes, 12 mL/kg, with lower tidal volumes, 6 mL/kg, and found that the use of lower tidal volumes in patients with ARDS resulted in fewer ventilator-dependent days and decreased mortality (40% conventional versus 31% protective lung).[74] The ARDS Network has reported on the ALVEOLI trial, which confirmed the benefit of a strategy that lowers tidal volume and limits plateau pressure in patients with ARDS. The death rates of patients ventilated with high and conventional pressure end-expiratory pressure strategies were less than 30% and did not differ between the groups.[75] The optimal PEEP in patients with ARDS could not be determined. Today, patients with ARDS should be managed with a protective lung ventilation strategy that incorporates a tidal volume of 4 to 6 mL/kg with limitation of plateau pressure to 35 cm H_2O. Because lower tidal volumes are used in this protective strategy, traditional goals of gas exchange have to be modified.

Nuckton and coworkers[76] identified a pulmonary-specific risk factor for death in ARDS, the dead space fraction. In a prospective study, these authors measured the dead space fraction in 179 intubated patients and found it to be elevated early in the course of ARDS and to be higher in the patients who died. More specifically, they determined that for every 0.05 increase in pulmonary dead space, the risk of death increased by 45%. These findings are significant because the dead space fraction provides prognostic information about patients with ARDS.

■ ALTERNATIVE MODES OF MECHANICAL VENTILATION

Noninvasive Positive-Pressure Ventilation

Acute respiratory failure that is unresponsive to conservative medical therapy often requires mechanical ventilation via an endotracheal tube. Endotracheal intubation poses a risk of morbidity, however, including upper airway trauma, nosocomial pneumonia, and sinusitis. In more recent years, noninvasive positive-pressure ventilation (NPPV) (i.e., the combination of pressure support and PEEP delivered via facemask or nasal mask) has been used increasingly to avoid endotracheal intubation in patients with acute respiratory failure.[77,78] The effectiveness of NPPV depends on the etiology or indication for its use. For acute exacerbations of COPD, the clinical trial evidence strongly suggests that NPPV not only brings about rapid symptomatic and physiologic improvements, but also reduces the need for intubation, mortality rates, and, in some studies, hospital length of stay. Although NPPV may be associated with nasal bridge ulceration in less than 46% of patients, and gastric distention occasionally occurs, major complications, such as aspiration, are infrequent. A consensus opinion recommended that NPPV be considered as the ventilatory mode of first choice in selected patients with exacerbations of COPD.[78]

For asthmatic patients, the data supporting NPPV are inconclusive.[78] A reasonable approach to an asthmatic patient who does not respond promptly to initial medical therapy, but who has not developed a contraindication to NPPV, may be a trial of this therapy. Asthmatic patients may deteriorate rapidly, however, and delay of needed intubation is a risk. NPPV also may be used in patients with upper airway edema after extubation and patients with acute respiratory failure resulting from obstructive sleep apnea.

For patients with pulmonary edema, CPAP (10 cm H_2O) should be used initially, with NPPV reserved for patients with substantial hypercapnia or unrelenting dyspnea.[78] This recommendation is based on the fact that CPAP is effective and that the single randomized trial comparing CPAP and NPPV for patients with acute pulmonary edema showed an increase in myocardial infarction rate in the NPPV patients. A study of high-flow oxygen versus NPPV did not show any differences in myocardial ischemia rates, however. For selected groups of patients with severe community-acquired pneumonia, patients with chest wall restrictive diseases, and immunocompromised patients, NPPV has been administered successfully.

There is accumulating evidence that NPPV may be useful in lung resection and postgastroplasty. Specifically, one randomized trial of NPPV in lung resection patients with acute respiratory insufficiency showed significant reductions in the need for intubation, ICU length of stay, and mortality rates compared with conventionally treated subjects. Although these studies have not been conducted specifically in postoperative vascular surgery patients, it is reasonable to believe the mechanical benefits of NPPV would extend to this patient group. NPPV is contraindicated, however, after upper airway or esophageal surgery. A detailed review of the acute applications of NPPV has been published.[78]

High-Frequency Oscillatory Ventilation

Since the 1990s, case reports and observational studies of high-frequency oscillatory ventilation (HFOV) in patients failing conventional ventilation strategies have suggested improved oxygenation in adult patients with severe ARDS.[79] These reports have suggested that early initiation of HFOV (<2 days) is more likely to result in survival than delayed treatment (>7 days). In a randomized controlled trial of HFOV for ARDS versus pressure-controlled ventilation, early improvement in oxygenation (<16 hours) was seen in the HFOV group but not in the pressure-controlled ventilation group over 72 hours. Mortality at 30 days was 37% in the HFOV group and 52% in the conventional group ($P = .10$). Although HFOV is nonstandard therapy, its use in adults may be considered when fraction of inspired oxygen requirements exceed 60% and mean airway pressure is approaching 20 cm H_2O or higher. The potential role of additional adjunctive therapies with HFOV, such as prone ventilation, inhaled nitric oxide, aerosolized vasodilators, and liquid ventilation, currently is being considered.

■ NOSOCOMIAL PNEUMONIA

Nosocomial pneumonia is the leading cause of death due to hospital-acquired infections, with estimates of associated mortality ranging from 20% to 50%.[80,81] Most cases of nosocomial pneumonia occur outside of ICUs. The highest risk is in patients on mechanical ventilation (ventilator-associated pneumonia [VAP]), for an average risk of 1% per day, although the daily risk of acquisition of VAP is higher in the first week of intubation.[80]

Aspiration is thought to play a central role in the pathogenesis of nosocomial pneumonia.[82] Although some authors believe that an endotracheal tube is protective against aspiration, the presence of an endotracheal tube permits the aspiration of oropharyngeal or gastric pathogens.

Depending on the number and virulence of the organisms reaching the lung, pneumonia may ensue.

Gram-negative bacteria colonize the oropharynx within several days of admission, and 75% of severely ill patients are colonized within 48 hours.[82] In addition, the near-sterility of the stomach and upper gastrointestinal tract may be disrupted by alterations in gastric pH secondary to illness, medications, or enteric feedings. Less frequently, pneumonia can result from inhalation of infectious aerosols or from bacteremia originating in a distant focus.

Pathogens

Nosocomial pneumonias are frequently polymicrobial, with gram-negative bacilli predominating. Gram-negative bacilli cause 60% of nosocomial pneumonias, constituting six of the seven most frequently identified pathogens (Fig. 57-1).[81] In some institutions, *Acetobacter* species can be an important pathogen. Large variations in pathogens may be seen within and between institutions, and clinicians should be familiar with the specific pathogens and their sensitivity in their own institution.

Risk Factors and Prevention

The most significant risk factor for nosocomial pneumonia is mechanical ventilation. Many authors use the terms *nosocomial pneumonia* and *VAP* interchangeably. Intubation increases the risk of nosocomial pneumonia 6-fold to 21-fold.[80,82] Other risk factors are listed in Table 57-5. Some of these risk factors are easily modifiable and should be modified in all patients. A patient on mechanical ventilation should be formally assessed for suitability for weaning and extubation on a daily basis.[83] This assessment is best performed by a daily spontaneous breathing trial, usually as a T-piece trial for 30 to 120 minutes. The longer time

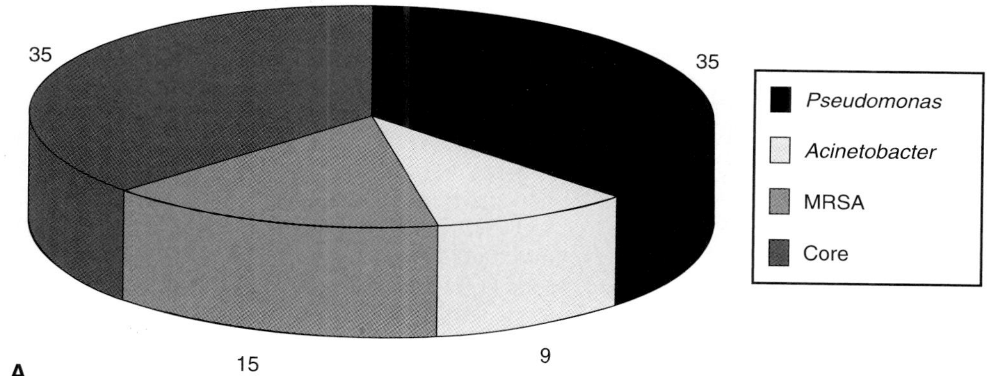

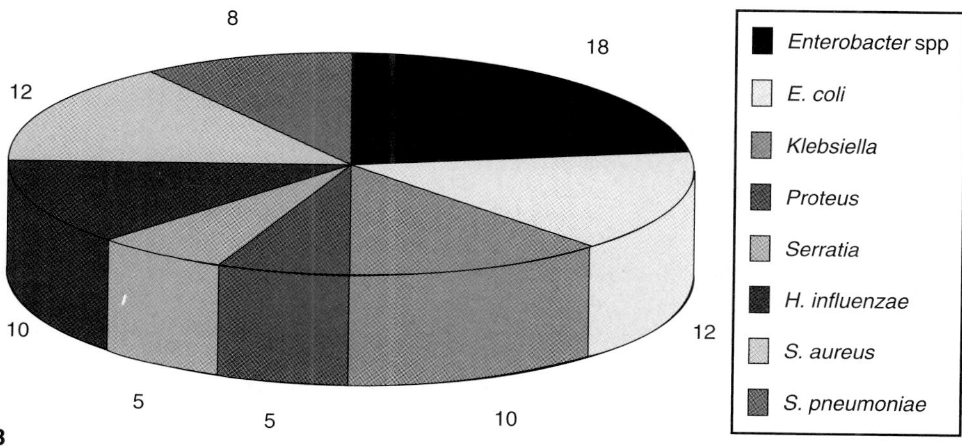

FIGURE 57-1 A, Species commonly seen in early-onset nosocomial pneumonia and referred to as "core" organisms. **B,** Species commonly seen in late-onset, often severe nosocomial pneumonia.

Table 57-5 Risk Factors for the Development of Nosocomial Pneumonia

Mechanical ventilation
Age >70 years
Chronic lung disease
Depressed level of consciousness or an intracranial pressure monitor
Large volume aspiration
Operative site on the chest wall
Frequent ventilator circuit changes
Nasogastric tube
Reintubation
Previous antibiotic therapy, especially third-generation cephalosporins
H_2 blocker or antacid therapy
Transfer to and from intensive care unit for diagnostic or therapeutic tests or procedures
Supine position
Hospitalization in fall or winter

interval may be best for marginal patients, although both time intervals have been studied and successfully predict success or failure of extubation in most patients. In addition to daily breathing trials, patients should be kept in an upright position unless there is a specific contraindication. Although tight glucose control (80 to 110 mg/dL) is not linked specifically to preventing pneumonia per se, the incidence of infection is decreased by 45%, and in ICU patients with a prolonged stay, tight glucose control should be employed.[84]

Role of Gastric pH

Several studies have suggested an increased incidence of nosocomial pneumonia when the gastric pH was increased with the use of H_2 blockers or antacids. A meta-analysis of studies published before 1990 failed to corroborate this assumption at a statistically significant level.[85] In the randomized controlled trial of ranitidine versus sucralfate, which was designed to assess specifically efficacy of prophylaxis in nosocomial pneumonia rate, no significant difference in pneumonia was seen, but surprisingly ranitidine was more efficacious in preventing stress ulcer bleeding.[86]

Decontamination of the Digestive Tract

Selective decontamination of the digestive tract (SDD) is another strategy that aims to decrease the incidence of nosocomial pneumonia by preventing oropharyngeal and gastric colonization with aerobic gram-negative bacilli and *Candida* species, without disrupting the anaerobic flora. Although the data are convincing that SDD prevents nosocomial pneumonia, SDD has not found widespread favor in North America. Although the reasons for this are many, probably the most compelling rationale for not using SDD is the fear of encouraging widespread resistant organisms.[87]

Patient Positioning

Several studies have shown that patients in the supine position are predisposed to microaspiration of gastric contents compared with patients in the semirecumbent position.[88-90] A randomized trial of positioning in 90 intubated patients was stopped early when interim analysis found a significantly lower incidence of clinically suspected and microbiologically confirmed nosocomial pneumonia in semirecumbent versus supine patients.[90] Although no effect of positioning on mortality has been shown, it seems prudent to place intubated patients preferentially in the semirecumbent position unless contraindicated.

Subglottic Drainage

Drainage of subglottic secretions also may lessen the risk of aspiration and decrease the incidence of VAP. A specially designed endotracheal tube has been developed for continuous aspiration of subglottic secretions (CASS). In a randomized clinical trial of 150 patients admitted to the ICU of a single institution, patients who underwent CASS using the most extensively employed device, the Hi-Lo Evac (Mallinckrodt Inc, Athlone, Ireland), had a lower incidence of VAP (4% versus 12%).[91] CASS using the same device did not achieve this result, however, in a larger randomized trial of 343 postoperative cardiac surgery patients.[92] The clinical role and economic impact of CASS are currently unclear.[93]

Diagnosis

Details of establishing the diagnosis of VAP or nosocomial pneumonia are beyond the scope of this chapter. Nosocomial pneumonia when diagnosed clinically is commonly treated when the condition is not clearly present and cannot be confirmed by histologic grounds. Whether an aggressive invasive strategy employing BAL should be used remains a subject of active debate. A study from France evaluated whether an invasive diagnostic approach using protected brush specimens or BAL was superior to clinical criteria in 413 ICU patients with a clinical suspicion of VAP.[94] Patients managed with the invasive strategy had a significantly lower 14-day mortality (16% versus 26%); this mortality advantage persisted at day 28 and was associated with significantly more antibiotic-free days and a lower mean number of antibiotics administered.

Treatment

Many patients are incorrectly suspected of having pneumonia, which leads to frequent overtreatment with its attendant risks of superinfection and antibiotic toxicity. Appropriate initial antibiotic therapy significantly affects survival.[95] If treatment is indicated, the choice of antibiotic should be influenced by the patient's recent antibiotic therapy (if any), the resident flora in the hospital or ICU, the presence of underlying diseases, and available culture data (interpreted with care).[96] In addition, duration of hospitalization and severity of illness should influence the choice of empirical coverage. Because increasing data suggest that initial appropriate empirical antibiotic therapy is linked to survival, the current opinion for the treatment of nosocomial therapy is with de-escalation therapy, that is, to decrease therapy as information and clinical status change.

■ SUMMARY

Pulmonary complications are frequent and potentially lethal complications for patients undergoing major vascular surgical procedures. Preoperative identification and optimization of patients with COPD and asthma can reduce postoperative complications. Prevention of atelectasis, minimizing duration of mechanical ventilation, control of glucose, and prevention of bacterial infection are the primary modalities used to minimize pulmonary complications. NPPV is expected to be an increasingly used modality for preoperative respiratory support. If ARDS develops postoperatively, new modes of ventilation that use protective lung strategies of low tidal volume and limiting plateau pressure can minimize the development of additional lung and organ system dysfunction.

■ REFERENCES

1. Lawrence VA, Hilsenbeck SG, Mulrow CD, et al: Incidence and hospital stay for cardiac and pulmonary complications after abdominal surgery. J Gen Intern Med 10:671, 1995.
2. Pronovost PJ, Jenckes MW, Dorman T, et al: Organizational characteristics of intensive care units related to outcomes of abdominal aortic surgery. JAMA 281:1310, 1999.
3. Pronovost PJ, Dang D, Dorman T, et al: Intensive care unit nurse staffing and the risk for complications after abdominal aortic surgery. Effective Clin Pract 4:199, 2001.
4. Svensson LG, Hess KR, Coselli JS, et al: A prospective study of respiratory failure after high-risk surgery on the thoracoabdominal aorta. J Vasc Surg 14:271, 1991.
5. Pedersen T: Complications and death following anesthesia: A prospective study with special reference to the influence of patient-, anaesthesia-, and surgery-related risk factors. Dan Med Bull 41:319, 1994.
6. Smetana GW: Preoperative pulmonary evaluation. N Engl J Med 340:937, 1999.
7. Hall JC, Tarala RA, Hall JL, et al: A multivariate analysis of the risk of pulmonary complications after laparotomy. Chest 99:923, 1991.
8. Gracey DA, Divertie MB, Didier EP: Preoperative pulmonary preparation of patients with chronic obstructive pulmonary disease. Chest 76:123, 1979.
9. Stein M, Cassara E: Preoperative pulmonary evaluation and therapy for surgery patients. JAMA 211:787, 1970.
10. Stein M, Cassara EL: Preoperative pulmonary evaluation and therapy for surgery patients. JAMA 211:787, 1970.
11. American Thoracic Society: Standards for the diagnosis and care of patients with chronic obstructive pulmonary disease. Am J Respir Crit Care Med 152:S77, 1995.
12. Tarhan S, Moffitt EA, Sessler AD, et al: Risk of anesthesia and surgery in patients with chronic bronchitis and chronic obstructive pulmonary disease. Surgery 74:720, 1973.
13. Sestini P, Rensoni E, Robinson, et al: Short-acting beta 2 agonists for stable chronic obstructive pulmonary disease. Cochrane Review Issue 3, 2003.
14. Warner DO, Warner MA, Barnes RD, et al: Perioperative respiratory complications in patients with asthma. Anesthesiology 85:460, 1996.
15. National Heart, Lung and Blood Institute National Asthma Education Program Expert Panel Report: Guidelines for the diagnosis and management of asthma: Part X. Special considerations. J Allergy Clin Immunol 88:425, 1991.
16. Oh SH, Patterson R: Surgery in corticosteroid-dependent asthmatics. J Allergy Clin Immunol 53:345, 1974.
17. Pien LC, Grammar LC, Patterson R: Minimal complications in a surgical population with severe asthma receiving prophylactic corticosteroids. J Allergy Clin Immunol 82:696, 1988.
18. Kabalin CS, Yarnold PR, Grammar LC: Low complication rate of corticosteroid-treated asthmatic undergoing surgical procedures. Arch Intern Med 155:1379, 1995.
19. Warner MA, Offord KP, Warner ME, et al: Role of preoperative cessation of smoking and other factors in postoperative pulmonary complications: A blinded prospective study of coronary artery bypass patients. Mayo Clin Proc 64:609, 1989.
20. Bluman LG, Mosca L, Newman N, et al: Preoperative smoking habits and postoperative pulmonary complications. Chest 113:883, 1998.
21. Moller AM, Maaloe R, Pedersen T: Postoperative intensive care admittance: The role of tobacco smoking. Acta Anaesthesiol Scand 45:345, 2001.
22. Nakagawa M, Tanaka H, Tsukuma H, et al: Relationship between the duration of the preoperative smoke-free period and the incidence of postoperative pulmonary complications after pulmonary surgery. Chest 120:705, 2001.
23. Brooks-Brunn JA: Predictors of postoperative complications following abdominal surgery. Chest 111:564, 1997.
24. Hall JC, Tarala MD, Hall JL, et al: A multivariate analysis of the risk of pulmonary complications after laparotomy. Chest 99:923, 1991.
25. Pasulka PS, Bistrian BR, Benotti PN, et al: The risks of surgery in obese patients. Ann Intern Med 104:540, 1986.
26. Thomas E, Goldman L, Mangione C, et al: Body mass index as a correlate of postoperative complications and resource utilization. Am J Med 102:277, 1997.
27. Calligaro KD, Azurin DJ, Dougherty MJ, et al: Pulmonary risk factors of elective abdominal aortic surgery. J Vasc Surg 18:914, 1993.
28. Djokovic JL, Hedley-White J: Prediction of outcome of surgery and anesthesia in patients over 80. JAMA 242:2301, 1979.
29. Arozullah AM, Daley J, Henderson WG, Khuri SF, for the National Veterans Administration Surgical Quality Improvement Program: Multifactorial risk index for predicting postoperative respiratory failure in men after major noncardiac surgery. Ann Surg 232:242, 2000.
30. Thomas DR, Ritchie CS: Preoperative assessment of older adults. J Am Geriatr Soc 43:811, 1995.
31. Polanczyk CA, Marcantonio E, Goldman L, et al: Impact of age on perioperative complications and length of stay in patients undergoing noncardiac surgery. Ann Intern Med 134:637, 2001.
32. Mohr DN, Jett JR: Preoperative evaluation of pulmonary risk factors. J Gen Intern Med 3:277, 1988.
33. Xue FS, Li BW, Zhang GS, et al: The influence of surgical sites on early postoperative hypoxemia in adults undergoing elective surgery. Anesth Analg 88:213, 1999.
34. Ford GT, Whitelaw WA, Rosenal TW, et al: Diaphragm function after upper abdominal surgery. Am Rev Respir Dis 127:431, 1983.
35. Gracey DR, Divertie MB, Didier EP: Preoperative pulmonary preparation of patients with chronic obstructive pulmonary disease. Chest 76:123, 1979.
36. Garibaldi RA, Britt MR, Coleman ML, et al: Risk factors for postoperative pneumonia. Am J Med 70:677, 1981.
37. Kroenke K, Lawrence VA, Theroux JF, et al: Operative risk in patients with severe chronic obstructive pulmonary disease. Arch Intern Med 152:967, 1992.
38. Pedersen T, Eliasen K, Henriksen E: A prospective study of risk factors and cardiopulmonary complications associated with anaesthesia and surgery: Risk indicators of cardiopulmonary morbidity. Acta Anaesthesiol Scand 34:144, 1990.
39. Rodgers A, Walker N, Schug S, et al: Reduction of postoperative mortality and morbidity with epidural or spinal anesthesia: Results from overview of randomised trials. BMJ 321:1, 2000.
40. Christopherson R, Beattie C, Frank SM, et al: Perioperative morbidity in patients randomized to epidural or general anesthesia for lower extremity vascular surgery. Perioperative Ischemia Randomized Anesthesia Trial Study Group. Anesthesiology 79:422, 1993.
41. Major CP, Greer MS, Russell WL, et al: Postoperative pulmonary complications and morbidity after abdominal aneurysmectomy: A comparison of postoperative epidural versus parenteral analgesia. Am Surg 62:45, 1996.

42. Ballantyne JC, Carr DB, de Ferranti S, et al: The comparative effects of postoperative analgesic therapies on pulmonary outcome: Cumulative meta-analysis of randomized, controlled trials. Anesth Analg 86:598, 1998.
43. Norris EJ, Beattie C, Perler BA, et al: Double-masked randomized trial comparing alternate combinations of intraoperative anesthesia and postoperative analgesia in abdominal aortic surgery. Anesthesiology 95:105, 2001.
44. Berg H, Roed J, Viby-Mogensen J, et al: Residual neuromuscular block is a risk factor for postoperative pulmonary complications: A prospective, randomised, and blinded study of postoperative pulmonary complications after atracurium, vecuronium and pancuronium. Acta Anaesthesiol Scand 41:1095, 1997.
45. Lawrence VA, Page CP, Harris GD: Preoperative spirometry before abdominal operations: A critical appraisal of its predictive value. Arch Intern Med 149:280, 1989.
46. De Nino LA, Lawrence VA, Averyt EC, et al: Preoperative spirometry and laparotomy: Blowing away dollars. Chest 111:1536, 1997.
47. Zibrak JD, O'Donnell CR, Marton K: Indications for pulmonary function testing. Ann Intern Med 112:763, 1990.
48. American College of Physicians: Preoperative pulmonary function testing. Ann Intern Med 112:793, 1990.
49. Archer C, Levy AR, McGregor M: Value of routine preoperative chest x-rays: A meta-analysis. Can J Anaesth 40:1022, 1993.
50. Goldman L, Caldera DL, Nussbaum SR, et al: Multifactorial index of cardiac risk in noncardiac surgical procedures. N Engl J Med 297:845, 1977.
51. Arslan V, Barrera R, Ginsberg R, et al: Cardiopulmonary risk index (CPRI) does not predict complications after thoracic surgery [abstract]. Am J Respir Crit Care Med 153:A676, 1996.
52. Epstein SK, Faling J, Daly BD, et al: Predicting complications after pulmonary resection: Preoperative exercise testing vs. a multifactorial cardiopulmonary risk index. Chest 104:694, 1993.
53. Castillo R, Haas A: Chest physical therapy: Comparative efficacy of preoperative and postoperative in the elderly. Arch Phys Med Rehabil 66:376, 1985.
54. Brooks-Brunn JA: Validation of a predictive model for postoperative pulmonary complications. Heart Lung 27:151, 1998.
55. Arozullah AM: Development and validation of a multifactorial risk index for predicting postoperative pneumonia after major noncardiac surgery. Ann Intern Med 153:847, 2001.
56. Wahba RM: Airway closure and intraoperative hypoxaemia: Twenty-five years later. Can J Anaesth 43:1144, 1996.
57. Rosenberg J, Rasmussen GI, Wojdemann KR, et al: Ventilatory pattern and associated episodic hypoxaemia in the late postoperative period in the general surgical ward. Anaesthesia 54:323, 1999.
58. Warner DO, Warner MA, Offord KP, et al: Airway obstruction and perioperative complications in smokers undergoing abdominal surgery. Anesthesiology 90:372, 1999.
59. Thomas JA, McIntosh JM: Are incentive spirometry, intermittent positive pressure breathing, and deep breathing exercises effective in the prevention of postoperative pulmonary complications? A systematic overview and meta-analysis. Phys Ther 74:3, 1994.
60. Overend TJ, Anderson CM, Lucy SD, et al: The effect of incentive spirometry on postoperative pulmonary complications: A systematic review. Chest 120:971, 2001.
61. Stock MC, Downs JB, Gauer PK, et al: Prevention of postoperative pulmonary complications with CPAP, incentive spirometry, and conservative therapy. Chest 87:151, 1985.
62. Celli BR, Rodriguez KS, Snider GL: A controlled trial of intermittent positive pressure breathing, incentive spirometry, and deep breathing exercises in preventing pulmonary complications after abdominal surgery. Am Rev Respir Dis 130:12, 1984.
63. Rubenfeld GD: Epidemiology of acute lung injury. Crit Care Med 31(Suppl):s276, 2003.
64. Vincent JL, Sakr Y, Ranieri VM: Epidemiology and outcome of acute respiratory failure in intensive care unit patients. Crit Care Med 31(Suppl):s296, 2003.
65. Sandham JD, Hull RD, Brant RF, et al: A randomized, controlled trial of the use of pulmonary-artery catheters in high-risk surgical patients. N Engl J Med 348:5, 2003.
66. Barone JE, Tucker JB, Rassias D, Corvo PR: Routine perioperative pulmonary artery catheterization has no effect on rate of complications in vascular surgery: A meta-analysis. Am Surg 67:674, 2001.
67. Bernard GR, Artigas A, Brigham KL, et al: The American-European Consensus Conference on ARDS: Definitions, mechanisms, relevant outcomes, and clinical trial coordination. Am J Respir Crit Care Med 149:818, 1994.
68. Ware LB, Matthay MA: The acute respiratory distress syndrome. N Engl J Med 342:1334, 2000.
69. Herridge MS, Cheung AM, Tansey CM, et al: One-year outcomes in survivors of the acute respiratory distress syndrome. N Engl J Med 348:683, 2003.
70. Pinhu L, Whitehead T, Evans T, et al: Ventilator-associated lung injury. Lancet 362:332, 2003.
71. Brower RG, Rubenfeld GD: Lung-proctective ventilation strategies in acute lung injury. Crit Care Med 31(Suppl):s312, 2003.
72. Ranieri VM, Suter PM, Tortorella C, et al: Effect of mechanical ventilation on inflammatory mediators in patients with acute respiratory distress syndrome: A randomized controlled trial. JAMA 282:54, 1999.
73. Amato MBP, Barbas CSV, Medeiros DM, et al: Effect of a protective-ventilation strategy on mortality in the acute respiratory distress syndrome. N Engl J Med 338:347, 1998.
74. Acute Respiratory Distress Syndrome Network: Ventilation with lower tidal volumes as compared with traditional tidal volumes for acute lung injury and the acute respiratory distress syndrome. N Engl J Med 342:1301, 2000.
75. ARDS Clinical Network: The Assessment of Low Tidal Volume and Elevated End-expiratory Volume to Obviate Lung Injury (ALVEOLI) trial: A prospective randomized multi-center trial of higher end-expiratory lung volume/lower FiO_2 versus lower end-expiratory lung volume/higher FiO_2 ventilation in acute respiratory distress syndrome. Available at http://hedwig.mgh.havard.edu/ardsnet/alveoli.pdf. Accessed November 6, 2002.
76. Nuckton TJ, Alonso JA, Kallet RH, et al: Pulmonary dead-space fraction as a risk factor for death in the acute respiratory distress syndrome. N Engl J Med 346:1281, 2002.
77. Lightowler JV, Wedzicha JA, Elliott MW: Non-invasive positive pressure ventilation to treat respiratory failure resulting from exacerbations of chronic obstructive pulmonary disease: Cochrane systematic review and meta-analysis. BMJ 326:1, 2003.
78. Liesching T, Kwok H, Hill N: Acute applications of noninvasive positive pressure ventilation. Chest 124:699, 2003.
79. Derdak S: High-frequency oscillatory ventilation for acute respiratory distress syndrome in adult patients. Crit Care Med 31(Suppl):s317, 2003.
80. Fagon JY, Chastre J, Hance AJ, et al: Nosocomial pneumonia in ventilated patients: A cohort study evaluating attributable mortality and hospital stay. Am J Med 94:281, 1993.
81. Centers for Disease Control and Prevention: Guideline for prevention of nosocomial pneumonia. Respir Care 39:1191, 1994.
82. Scheld WM: Developments in the pathogenesis, diagnosis and treatment of nosocomial pneumonia. Surg Gynecol Obstet 172(Suppl):42, 1991.
83. MacIntgre N, Cook DJ, Ely EW, et al: Evidence-based guidelines for weaning and discontinuing ventilatory support. A Collective Task Force Facilitated by the American College of Chest Physicians; the American Association for Respiratory Care; and the American College of Critical Care Medicine. Chest 120(Suppl):375s, 2001.
84. van den Berghe G, Wouters P, Weekers F, et al: Intensive insulin therapy in critically ill patients. N Engl J Med 345:1359, 2001.
85. Cook DJ, Laine LA, Guyatt GH, et al: Nosocomial pneumonia and the role of gastric pH: A meta-analysis. Chest 100:7, 1991.
86. Cook DJ, Guyatt GM, Marshall J, et al: A comparison of sucralfate and ranitidine for the prevention of upper gastrointestinal bleeding in patients requiring mechanical ventilation. N Engl J Med 338:791, 1998.

87. van Nieuwenhoven CA, Buskens E, van Tiel FH, et al: Relationship between methodological trial quality and the effects of selective digestive decontamination on pneumonia and mortality in critically ill patients. JAMA 286:335, 2001.
88. Torres A, Serra-Batlles J, Ros E, et al: Pulmonary aspiration of gastric contents in patients receiving mechanical ventilation: The effect of body position. Ann Intern Med 116:540, 1992.
89. Orozco-Levi M, Torres A, Ferrer M, et al: Semirecumbent position protects from pulmonary aspiration but not completely from gastroesophageal reflux in mechanically ventilated patients. Am J Respir Crit Care Med 152:1387, 1995.
90. Drakulovic MB, Torres A, Bauer TT, et al: Supine body position as a risk factor for nosocomial pneumonia in mechanically ventilated patients: A randomised trial. Lancet 354:1851, 1999.
91. Smulders K, van Der Hoeven H, Weers-Pothoff I, et al: A randomized clinical trial of intermittent subglottic secretion drainage in patients receiving mechanical ventilation. Chest 121:858, 2002.
92. Kollef MH, Skubas NJ, Sundt TM: A randomized clinical trial of continuous aspiration of subglottic secretions in cardiac surgery patients. Chest 116:1339, 1999.
93. Shorr AF, O'Malley PG: Continuous subglottic suctioning for the prevention of ventilator-associated pneumonia: Potential economic implications. Chest 119:228, 2001.
94. Fagon JY, Chastre J, Wolff M, et al: Invasive and noninvasive strategies for management of suspected ventilator-associated pneumonia: A randomized trial. Ann Intern Med 132:621, 2000.
95. Luna CM, Vujacich P, Niederman MS, et al: Impact of BAL data on the therapy and outcome of ventilator-associated pneumonia. Chest 111:676, 1997.
96. Hospital-acquired pneumonia in adults: Diagnosis, assessment of severity, initial antimicrobial therapy, and preventive strategies. A consensus statement, American Thoracic Society, November 1995. Am J Respir Crit Care Med 153:1711, 1996.

Chapter 58

Renal Complications

KIMBERLEY J. HANSEN, MD
JEFFREY D. PEARCE, MD

The complex relationships between fluid shifts and renal function that occur during aortic surgery have been the subject of intense study for 30 years. An improved understanding of these relationships has led to the ability to perform complex aortic and branch aortic reconstruction, while maintaining adequate excretory renal function. Insight into the causes of renal dysfunction complicating vascular surgery remains fragmentary, however. Despite the increased awareness of the need for fluid resuscitation and the frequent use of invasive monitoring devices, renal dysfunction is a frequent occurrence. Because of the limited ability to alter the natural history of acute tubular necrosis (ATN) and the significant mortality associated with acute renal failure (ARF), regardless of renal replacement therapy, it is imperative that vascular surgeons be familiar with measures to prevent this complication. To address the mechanism and presentation of ATN and ARF associated with vascular surgery, one first must consider normal renal physiology. From this reference point, a variety of aberrations in renal function are presented.

NORMAL RENAL FUNCTION

Although a complete discussion of normal renal physiology is beyond the scope of this chapter, a basic understanding of intrarenal and excretory renal function is necessary to understand abnormal renal function complicating the management of vascular disorders. The kidney serves as the dominant site for maintenance of normal intravascular volume and composition. Under normovolemic, unstressed conditions, the kidneys receive approximately 25% of the cardiac output. Based on a 5 L/min cardiac output, the kidneys receive approximately 900 L/day of plasma flow. Given the fact that the glomeruli filter 20% of the renal plasma flow and that the normal 24-hour urinary output for a 70-kg man is less than 1.8 L, the kidney's tubular system must reabsorb more than 99% of the 180 L/day of filtered plasma to maintain homeostasis. The initial composition of the ultrafiltrate is the electrolyte and solute concentration of plasma. Electrolytes and other solutes, such as glucose, also must be almost totally reabsorbed.[1]

Reabsorption of electrolytes from the tubular fluid occurs by active transport and by passive back-diffusion. The sodium ion is reabsorbed in the early proximal tubule by its cotransportation with organic solutes, bicarbonate, and divalent cations through an active transport mechanism. Similarly, sodium is actively transported in the late proximal tubule in combination with chloride transport. Because water freely follows this movement of solutes and ions, the tubular fluid is iso-osmotic to plasma as it enters the loop of Henle.

Depending on their location, the tubular cells of the loop of Henle vary in their permeability. This variable permeability establishes a hypotonic tubular fluid and medullary osmotic gradient. The descending loop of Henle is permeable to water but relatively impermeable to sodium and chloride, whereas the ascending loop of Henle is impermeable to water but actively transports the chloride ion, with sodium passively following. The resulting countercurrent mechanism produces a medullary osmotic gradient that regulates urine osmolarity from 50 to 1200 mOsm. Distal tubular reabsorption of sodium also is active. In the distal tubule and in the proximal collecting ducts, sodium is actively and almost completely reabsorbed under the control of aldosterone (Fig. 58-1). Of the approximately 25,000 mEq of sodium filtered daily, only 50 to 200 mEq ultimately is excreted (<1%).

Filtered potassium is almost totally reabsorbed in the proximal tubule and the loop of Henle. The electrochemical gradient and intracellular concentration of potassium promote its passive secretion by the distal tubules and early collecting ducts into the tubular lumen. Essentially all of the potassium in the urine is transported there through this process.[1,2]

Neuroendocrine Modulators of Renal Function

Intravascular volume is regulated primarily by a series of stretch receptors or baroreceptors located in the arterial tree and the atria. Because these receptors not only sense pressure or volume changes (atrial receptors), but also monitor the rates of change during the cardiac cycle, they govern the effective circulating volume. Factors that decrease cardiac performance alter the intravascular volume perceived by these receptors and alter renal function to retain salt and water, increasing the effective circulating volume. Similarly, when the concentration of circulating plasma proteins is reduced, there is a net diffusion of intravascular water into the extravascular space secondary to the decreased intravascular oncotic pressure. This net decrease in circulating volume is sensed by these same receptors, and neuroendocrine regulators of urinary output inhibit excretion of water to correct the volume deficiency.

When the baroreceptors perceive a reduction in circulating volume, their afferent signals are reduced, which decreases their tonic inhibition over the neuroendocrine system. This reduced inhibition leads to increased secretion of vasopressin, β-endorphins, growth hormone, and adrenocorticotropic hormone through the central nervous system and to an increase in release of epinephrine from the adrenal medulla. At the level of the nephron, baroreceptors within

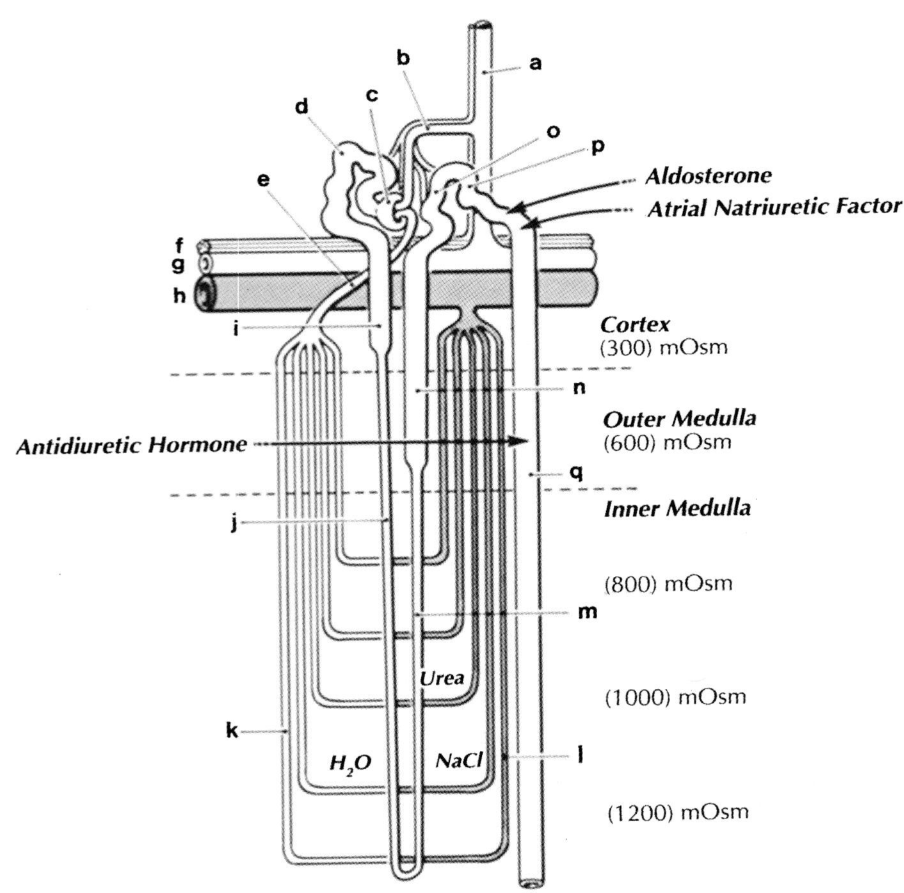

FIGURE 58-1 Anatomic depiction of the nephron and its major hormonal regulators.

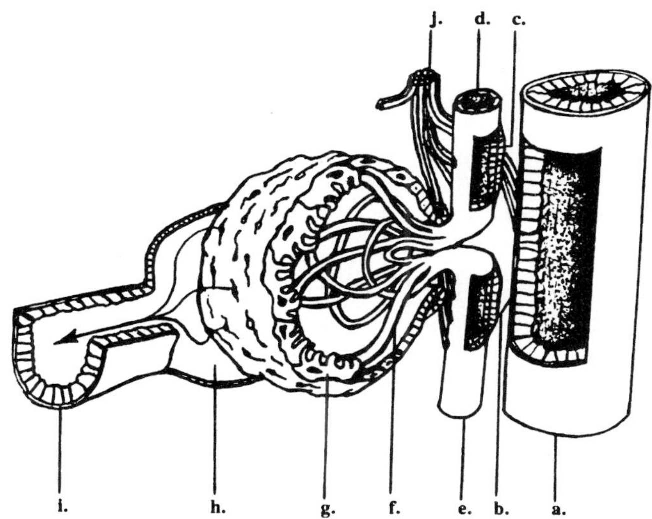

FIGURE 58-2 The juxtaglomerular apparatus of the nephron. *a,* Thick ascending loop of Henle; *b,* macula densa; *c,* juxtaglomerular cells; *d,* afferent arteriole; *e,* efferent arteriole; *f,* glomerular capillary; *g,* mesangial cell; *h,* Bowman's space; *i,* proximal convoluted tubule; *j,* renal sympathetic nerves.

the macula densa cells of the juxtaglomerular apparatus perceive a decrease in intravascular pressure or plasma ion concentration and stimulate juxtaglomerular cells to release renin (Fig. 58-2). Renin stimulates the production of angiotensin I from angiotensinogen, which ultimately forms angiotensin II. Angiotensin II functions to increase blood pressure by direct vasoconstriction and through its stimulation of aldosterone indirectly functions to increase circulating plasma volume.

The primary hormonal regulators of fluid and electrolyte balance are aldosterone, cortisol, vasopressin, and angiotensin. The interactions between insulin, epinephrine, plasma glucose concentration, acid-base balance of the plasma, and other factors play a vital role in modulating the release of these hormones and directly affect the renal tubular management of water and the respective filtered solutes.[1-3] Discussion of these interactions and their impact on renal function and fluid shifts is limited to the effects of aortic and branch aortic reconstruction.

■ FLUID SHIFTS ASSOCIATED WITH AORTIC SURGERY

Reconstruction of the abdominal aorta is associated with volume shifts within fluid compartments that differ from the unstressed state. These shifts stem from local tissue trauma that occurs with operative dissection, from hemodynamic consequences that occur with aortic clamping and unclamping, and from operative blood loss. In large part, the changes are mediated through transcapillary and transcellular movement of fluid.

The net movement of water and solutes from the intravascular, extracellular compartment (plasma) to the interstitium (extracellular or third space) normally takes place at the precapillary level secondary to increased hydrostatic pressure. The reentry of fluid back into the intravascular compartment in the distal capillaries is favored by the presence of intravascular protein—albumin—which exerts an oncotic pressure gradient. Normally, 7% of intravascular albumin arriving at the capillary level crosses the capillary membrane into the interstitial space. This extravascular protein eventually enters lymphatics and ultimately returns to the intravascular pool. The operative dissection that occurs during aortic surgery results in disruption of lymphatic channels and the release of inflammatory mediators causing local and systemic alterations in tissue perfusion, contributing to an increase in permeability of capillary membranes to albumin.[4] The exact mechanisms involved are obscure, but the resultant effects are a flux of albumin into the interstitium and subsequent decrease in water reabsorption into the intravascular space. Postoperative hypoalbuminemia is a common finding early after aortic surgery. It is mainly caused by albumin redistribution and not by metabolic changes. The net effect is a decrease in intravascular volume and activation of the neuroendocrine mechanisms that decrease renal excretion of sodium and free water. In addition, there is a net movement of sodium and water into the intracellular space from the extracellular compartment. This process is due to a relative decline in the normal cellular transmembrane potential after ischemia-reperfusion or shock or both secondary to blood loss.[5] The causes of the decline in transmembrane potential are unclear but are due in part to impaired function of the Na^+,K^+-ATPase pump and a loss of active ion transport. This cellular swelling also is governed by a change in intracellular calcium homeostasis and an increase in the intracellular level of calcium.[6] During periods of resuscitation, abnormalities of intracellular sodium concentration and water are reversed.

The normal homeostatic method of contending with a decreased circulating intravascular volume is to mobilize the extracellular (third-space) interstitial fluid. The extravascular fluid space is expanded as a consequence of the aforementioned response to the stress of aortic surgery. This excess extravascular third-space fluid might be described conceptually as "entrapped" by its greater oncotic pressure, and the functional reserve of fluid available for return to the plasma for expansion of the contracted intravascular volume is reduced. When one considers the additive impact of temporary ischemia to tissue beds during aortic surgery, the ensuing shift in acid-base balance in the involved tissue beds, the adverse impact of unreplaced blood loss, the potential reductions in cardiac performance during aortic cross-clamping, and the stimulation of stress response neuroendocrine mechanisms, one can appreciate the vicious cycle of events leading to the shift of total body water from the functional circulating blood volume into the third space.[7,8]

The determination of the intravascular volume and its associated solutes after major surgery has been of dramatic benefit to the intraoperative and early postoperative fluid management of patients undergoing major vascular surgery. The increased obligatory losses of intravascular volume associated with major surgery have led to the current use of balanced salt solutions (5% dextrose Ringer's lactate) for volume replenishment.[9] Theoretical advantages of albumin replacement therapy in the early postoperative period

Table 58-1 Inciting Events Causing Renal Dysfunction

PRERENAL	PARENCHYMAL	POSTRENAL
Low cardiac output/ cardiogenic shock	Nephrotoxic drugs	Catheter kinking
Increased vascular space	Radiologic contrast	Catheter clot
Septic shock	Myoglobinuria	Bladder clot
Hypovolemia	Acute tubular necrosis	Ureteral obstruction
Blood loss	Other causes	Renal pelvic obstruction
Dehydration		
Third-space sequestration		

have not shown clear benefit. Of equal importance in postoperative management is the appreciation that hourly parenteral fluid replacement requirements during surgery are severalfold those required during a resting state and may vary from 100 to 500 mL/hr. Even this range of additional replacement fluids is inadequate, however, during and after acute blood loss. These increased fluid replacement requirements continue in the immediate postoperative period owing to continued sequestration of fluid into the areas of the operative site and persistent effects of inflammatory mediators.[10]

Mobilization of the sequestered third-space fluid is delayed for 2 to 5 days depending on the magnitude of operative and postoperative stress, cardiac performance, and intravascular oncotic pressure. Reabsorption of third-space fluid usually begins on postoperative day 2 or 3. If not managed with appropriate reduction in maintenance parenteral fluid administration or the addition of diuretic therapy, reabsorption of third-space fluid can lead to intravascular volume overload and acute congestive heart failure.

■ RENAL DYSFUNCTION AFTER VASCULAR SURGERY

Renal dysfunction after vascular surgery varies widely in its causes and severity, ranging from a mild natriuresis to fulminant ATN and ARF requiring dialysis. For purposes of discussion, inciting events causing renal dysfunction can be classified as prerenal, renal, or postrenal in nature (Table 58-1). Although the incidence of renal dysfunction complicating vascular surgery has decreased with the development of appropriate perioperative fluid resuscitation, better surgical technique, and less nephrotoxic radiocontrast material, the mortality associated with ARF remains high, ranging from 10% to 80% depending on the associated presence of multiorgan system failure.[11,12]

Diagnosis of Renal Dysfunction

Postoperative renal dysfunction usually is identified by oliguria or increases in serum creatinine. Evaluation of the many possible causes of postoperative renal dysfunction allows the clinician to develop an organized plan of diagnosis and treatment. The general evaluation must include a thorough physical examination of the patient. Evidence of intravascular volume depletion, hemodynamic instability, sepsis, or congestive heart failure directs the differential diagnosis toward possible prerenal, renal, and postrenal causes for renal dysfunction. Prerenal causes are the most frequent source of acute renal dysfunction in the early postoperative period. An evaluation of the patient's intravascular volume status and cardiac performance is required. A patient with signs of volume depletion, such as flat neck veins, dry mucous membranes, and reduced filling pressures, requires replenishment of intravascular volume with physiologic saline. In light of the possibility of renal failure, potassium-containing solutions should be avoided. If examination reveals that diminished cardiac performance is responsible for the oliguria, as suggested by findings of distended neck veins, S_3 gallop, pulmonary edema, acute electrocardiogram changes, dysrhythmias, decreased cardiac output, and elevated filling pressures, judicious inotropic support is provided while measuring indices of cardiac performance.[13]

If correction of filling pressures or myocardial performance fails to improve urinary output, samples of urine and blood are obtained, and diuretic therapy is considered. Serum electrolytes, blood counts, and urine studies allow evaluation of other possible sources of oliguria and renal failure, such as ATN or myoglobinuria. Urine studies include urinalysis, urine sodium, urea and creatinine concentrations, urine osmolality, and estimation of fractional excretion of sodium (Table 58-2). An additional source

Table 58-2 Urinary and Blood Parameters in Renal Dysfunction

CHARACTERISTIC	PRERENAL DYSFUNCTION	RENAL PARENCHYMAL DYSFUNCTION	POSTRENAL DYSFUNCTION
Urine specific gravity	>1.020	1.010	1.012
Urine osmolarity (mOsm/L)	>400	300 ± 20	300 ± 40
U/P osmolarity	>1.5	1	1
UNa (mEq/L)	<20	>30	<30*
Fractional excretion of sodium	<1%	>1%	<1%*
UNa/[U/P Cr]	<1	>1	<1
BUN:Cr	20	10	10-20*
U/P Cr	>40	<20	<20

*First 24 hours only.
BUN, blood urea nitrogen; Cr, creatinine; UNa, urinary sodium; U/P, urine/plasma.

Adapted from Muther RS: Acute renal failure: Acute azotemia in the critically ill. In Civetta JM, Taylor RW, Kirby RR (eds): Critical Care, 2nd ed. Philadelphia, JB Lippincott, 1992, pp 1583-1598.

of prerenal dysfunction is renal artery occlusive disease. When other etiologies have been excluded, the diagnosis of bilateral renal artery stenosis or occlusion should be considered and evaluated by renal duplex sonography. We proceed with renal duplex sonography, however, only if we are prepared to follow the scan with angiographic confirmation and intervention.

Categorization of Renal Dysfunction

Prerenal Dysfunction

Prerenal causes are the most frequent source of acute renal dysfunction in the early postoperative period. Renal failure from a prerenal cause is usually the direct result of a contracted intravascular volume secondary to inadequate fluid replacement during intraoperative and postoperative fluid losses. Less commonly, it is secondary to a primary reduction in cardiac performance, which triggers neurohormonal reflexes to increase intravascular volume by increasing tubular reabsorption of sodium and water. In their pure forms, these two causes of reduced renal function are easily discernible. Hypovolemia is associated with flat neck veins, dry mucous membranes, and reduced pulmonary artery wedge pressure, whereas renal dysfunction secondary to poor cardiac performance is associated with distended neck veins, clinical fluid overload, and elevated pulmonary artery wedge pressure. The therapy for hypovolemic prerenal azotemia is to increase intravascular volume by administration of balanced salt solution and red blood cells as needed. Conversely, therapy for renal dysfunction of cardiogenic origin is directed at improving myocardial performance by administering afterload-reducing agents and inotropic agents and instituting diuretic therapy as needed to diminish the preload of the failing left ventricle.

Because an atherosclerotic patient who is undergoing major vascular surgery frequently has associated coronary artery disease and impaired left ventricular function, distinction between these two causes of prerenal dysfunction (hypovolemic versus cardiogenic) can be difficult. Preexisting heart disease may raise the baseline total body volume for an individual to higher central filling pressures, and apparently normal or low-normal cardiac filling pressures may reflect relative hypovolemia. In this clinical situation, we maintain a constant infusion of afterload-reducing agents and inotropic agents (e.g., dobutamine) and cautiously administer small boluses of balanced salt solutions, while monitoring cardiac output and pulmonary artery wedge pressure. If no urinary response is noted when filling pressures begin to increase, diuretic therapy is added. The vascular surgeon should have reliable estimates of cardiac function and filling pressures before inotropic or diuretic therapy, or exacerbation of compromised renal function may result.[14,15]

A more recently recognized prerenal cause of acute and chronic renal insufficiency is occlusive disease of the renal arteries. Also termed *ischemic nephropathy,* this diagnosis is made by exclusion of other causes. If other causes of prerenal dysfunction have been excluded, renal duplex sonography is used to determine whether there is occlusive disease of the main renal arteries. Hemodynamically significant renal artery stenosis or occlusion is characterized by focal increase in the peak systolic velocity (≥1.8 m/sec) with distal turbulent Doppler waveforms (i.e., stenosis) or absence of Doppler flow (i.e., occlusion). By contrast, because interstitial swelling from parenchymal causes of ATN may increase renal parenchymal resistance dramatically, ATN is characterized by a marked decrease in the diastolic velocity and increased resistance index measured from the renal artery spectral analysis. In the absence of acute or chronic renal parenchymal disease, the diastolic velocity is increased, reflecting a compensatory decrease in renovascular resistance.[16] When the duplex scan is positive and correction of a renovascular occlusion is contemplated, we perform contrast angiography to clarify the presence of the occlusion and to plan its correction.

Postrenal Dysfunction

Postrenal mechanisms represent the least frequent cause of postoperative oliguria leading to renal dysfunction. The pathophysiology involved in this process is obstructive and is usually at the level of the urethra or urinary catheter and less commonly at the level of the ureters. Hematuria or traumatic catheter insertion can predispose to clots and obstruction of indwelling urinary catheters, resulting in obstructive uropathy. For this reason, when rapid cessation of urine flow is detected, initial maneuvers should be directed toward catheter irrigation or replacement, which is usually successful at restoring urinary flow. Problems encountered with catheter insertion should be noted, such as the presence of clots or urethral strictures or both. Similarly, catheter kinking should be avoided because this occasionally can cause obstruction.

Postrenal oliguria also can be caused by ureteral or renal pelvic obstruction, and these mechanisms should be sought after other causes of oliguria have been excluded. Causes include iatrogenic injury or compression of the ureters associated with aortic surgery and graft placement and stone disease. Preliminary diagnosis can be suggested on the basis of renal ultrasound or isotope renography and can be confirmed using retrograde urography. Therapy may require the placement of ureteral stents or percutaneous nephrostomy to relieve such an obstruction.[13]

Acute urinary retention from obstructive uropathy rarely can accompany urinary catheter removal. Clinical situations in which acute urinary retention can arise include voiding dysfunction after urinary catheter removal in patients with epidural catheters placed for pain control and in patients with prostatic hypertrophy. Generally, we allow 6 to 12 hours to elapse after epidural analgesia is discontinued before removal of urinary catheters to avoid urinary retention. Prostatitis or traumatic urinary catheter insertion combined with general anesthetic also can precipitate acute urinary retention. Both of these problems, if recognized early, are easily treatable by catheter reinsertion and rarely progress to obstructive uropathy.

Renal Parenchymal Dysfunction

Parenchymal causes of acute renal dysfunction are diverse and pose the greatest risk for permanent compromise of excretory renal function. The associated pathophysiology depends on the specific etiology. For this discussion, it is best to categorize the types of renal failure commonly seen as they relate to vascular surgery. In the broadest sense, ATN describes all renal parenchymal causes of ARF. More specifically, the pathophysiologic mechanism of ATN involves a decrease in cellular adenosine triphosphate, which is associated with a loss in the actin cytoskeleton; this causes a loss of renal tubular cell membrane polarity with subsequent loss of intercellular tight junctions. Shedding of the apical portion of tubule cells into the tubules can cause tubular obstruction and lead to a further reduction or cessation of glomerular filtration in the nephron.[17,18] ARF ultimately results. Manifested clinically by an abrupt rise in the serum creatinine, either with or without a change in urinary output (oliguria), it is sometimes possible to detect the presence of tubular cells in the urinary sediment on microscopic urinary evaluation. Although ATN may be transient and self-limited, its causes related to vascular surgery include ischemic injury (shock, acute renal artery occlusion, multiorgan failure, and atheroembolic injury) and toxic injury (myoglobinuria and dye related injury).[13]

■ ISCHEMIC INJURY

Acute Ischemic Injury

Caused by either temporary periods of interruption of renal perfusion or periods of systemic hypoperfusion associated with major vascular procedures, the pathophysiology of acute ischemic injury is twofold. First, as a consequence of the magnitude and duration of ischemia, tubular cell swelling occurs after reperfusion. This swelling can cause tubular obstruction, leading to further reduction or cessation of glomerular filtration in the nephron. Second, tubular cells either can lose their basement membrane attachment secondary to the interstitial edema that develops after reperfusion or can undergo cell death during ischemia, subsequently being sloughed into the tubule. The medullary thick ascending loop of Henle and the pars recta of the proximal tubule seem to be the segments of the tubular epithelium that are most sensitive to ischemia. After loss of the tubular cell, a back-leak of glomerular filtrate into the renal parenchyma develops.[17-19]

The risk of renal dysfunction after vascular surgical intervention is greatest for aortic surgery. Aortic repair requiring a suprarenal cross-clamp poses a significant risk for ischemic renal insult, and the risk is greater for repair of thoracoabdominal aneurysm, in which longer periods of renal ischemia can be anticipated. Rates of ARF approaching 18% routinely have been quoted in larger series for elective repair of thoracoabdominal aneurysms (Table 58-3). Ultimate recovery of renal function after suprarenal aortic cross-clamping relates to preexisting renal dysfunction, patient age, and duration of renal ischemia. Periods of hypotension related to blood loss, myocardial dysfunction, or sepsis also can diminish renal blood flow and incite ARF.[20-22] Contemporary series report the occurrence of renal failure after infrarenal aortic aneurysm repair to range from 1% to 13%.[23-29]

Acute renal artery occlusion is discussed thoroughly in Chapter 134. It can result from emboli from a cardiac origin, trauma, or aortic or renal artery dissection. When related to a cardioembolic event, the diagnosis often is delayed, and ultimate recovery of renal function depends on the magnitude of the occlusion and the presence of preexisting collaterals to the kidneys. Back, flank, or abdominal pain; new onset of hypertension; hematuria; and elevation in serum lactate dehydrogenase may provide a clue regarding the diagnosis and treatment.[30] Traumatic renal artery occlusion is suggested by the presence of hematuria and nonvisualization of kidney on an intravenous pyelogram. Prompt angiography is necessary to confirm the process, although the success of revascularization largely depends on the ischemic period, which is frequently prolonged. Dissection of the renal artery can be caused by catheter-related injury or arise from preexisting disease (fibromuscular dysplasia). The treatment and opportunity for functional recovery are based on the extent of the dissection and, in cases of complete occlusion of the renal artery, the period of ischemia before surgical revascularization.

Vascular procedures complicated by sepsis, myocardial dysfunction, and reperfusion injury can incite transient or permanent degrees of renal dysfunction. In these instances, recovery of excretory renal function depends on elimination of the septic focus and improvement in left ventricular performance to ensure adequate renal perfusion.

Atheroembolism to the renal arteries has been increasingly recognized as a cause of ARF and can cause renal damage culminating in end-stage renal disease. Catheter-based peripheral and coronary angiography and endoluminal interventions, such as coronary artery balloon angioplasty, are well-recognized sources of renal atheroemboli. Atheromatous disease from proximal diseased aortic segments can complicate suprarenal cross-clamping or manipulation of the aorta. Atheroembolism also can occur spontaneously from these proximal sources or from renal artery atheromatous plaques. The clinical diagnosis is suggested by a deterioration in renal function in a patient who displays other extrarenal manifestations of atheroembolism (e.g., blue toe syndrome) and is highly suggested by the laboratory finding of eosinophilia (71%). Diagnosis is confirmed by renal biopsy, and treatment is supportive.[31-34]

Table 58-3 Incidence of Acute Renal Failure and Renal Replacement Therapy After Aortic Surgery

				MORTALITY	
PROCEDURE	***N***	**ARF (%)**	**RRT(%)**	**ARF (%)**	**RRT (%)**
Elective Infrarenal AAA[76]	210		2		
CrCl >45	162	8	0		
CrCl <45	48	18	7		
Infrarenal AAA[22]	166	10	2		
Suprarenal AAA[22]	39	28	3		
TAA[20]	234	18	15	49	
TAA[73]	1509	18	9	23	
TAA[107]	475	25	8	38	56
Elective TAA[21]	70		12	16	25
Ruptured TAA[21]	18		22		
Ruptured AAA[108]	112	34	6	66	86
Ruptured TAA[109]	314	29			
Ruptured AAA[110]	105	32	18		65

AAA, abdominal aortic aneurysm; ARF, acute renal failure; comb, combined mortality for ARF and RRT; CrCl; creatinine clearance in mL/min; RRT; renal replacement therapy; TAA, thoracoabdominal aneurysm.

Chronic Ischemia—Ischemic Nephropathy

Ischemic nephropathy is discussed in Chapter 130. The term *ischemic nephropathy* describes reduced renal excretory function in combination with renovascular disease. Usually the renovascular disease is bilateral in distribution or involves a solitary kidney to implicate diminished renal artery perfusion as the cause of elevated serum creatinine. The significance of this condition is that it tends to be rapidly progressive in nature and is thought to be responsible for 20% of patients becoming dialysis dependent. Uncorrected renovascular disease as a cause of end-stage renal disease is associated with a rapid rate of death during follow-up, with a median survival of only 27 months after the initiation of dialysis and a 5-year survival of only 12%. Although dialysis dependence places the patient at increased operative risk, patients who survive successful renal artery revascularization have an improved probability of long-term survival.[35]

In patients with atherosclerosis and a recent worsening of renal function along with hypertension or worsening of renal function while taking an angiotensin-converting enzyme inhibitor, the presence of ischemic nephropathy should be sought.[36] In contrast to renovascular hypertension secondary to unilateral renal artery stenosis, in which hypertension is renin dependent, the hypertension in ischemic nephropathy tends to be volume dependent. Patients with this pattern of disease present with severe hypertension, elevated serum creatinine, and volume overload. Alternatively the clinical presentation may be that of recurrent episodes of flash pulmonary edema. This entity almost always coexists with some element of intrinsic renal parenchymal disease.[36-39]

Toxic Injury and Angiography

Chemical injury to the kidney can result from many sources. Nephrotoxic agents should be identified and used with caution, particularly in a vascular patient with compromised renal clearance. Aminoglycosides are one of the most common compounds responsible for such injury in the postoperative period; myoglobin and radiologic contrast media also have been implicated. Aminoglycosides appear to exert their renal toxicity at the tubular cell by causing mitochondrial damage, cell membrane destruction, phospholipase activation, or alteration in lysosomes.[40] Because of this relationship and the frequent history of reduced renal function in postoperative vascular surgery patients, it is important to identify risk factors that can contribute to nephrotoxicity before the administration of aminoglycosides. These risk factors include preexisting renal insufficiency, advanced patient age, extracellular volume depletion, and concomitant use of other nephrotoxins. The routine use of aminoglycoside blood levels to predict or prevent nephrotoxicity is probably not warranted.[13] Although alternative antibiotics with less nephrotoxicity have reduced the use of aminoglycosides in vascular surgical patients, all pharmacologic agents should be administered with caution and the dosage adjusted for renal clearance.[40,41]

Myoglobinuria is an important cause of renal failure in patients submitted to revascularization after prolonged periods of limb ischemia. Circulating as a breakdown product of muscle death, myoglobin is filtered freely by the glomerulus. Myoglobin exerts its toxicity through direct tubular cell injury and through precipitation and obstruction of the tubule.[42] Hematuria after reperfusion of the profoundly ischemic extremity suggests pigment toxicity and should prompt urinalysis. Myoglobinuria is suggested when the urine is dipstick positive for blood, but no red blood cells are present on microscopic analysis and can be confirmed by testing the urine for myoglobin. When diagnosed, injury to the kidney may be lessened by maximizing the urine flow rate through the administration of intravenous crystalloid infusion and diuretics (mannitol) and by alkalinizing the urine (sodium bicarbonate).[43]

Of particular importance as it relates to vascular surgical practice and renal complications is contrast-induced nephrotoxicity. Conventional contrast agents have iodine incorporated into their structure to absorb x-ray photons, achieving visualization of the vasculature. The nephrotoxicity of such iodinated contrast agents has been recognized for many years. The principal site of contrast-induced nephrotoxicity is the renal tubule from transient regional renal ischemia; the effects on glomerular function seem to be mild.[44,45] The ionization and high osmolarity of early contrast agents may contribute to their nephrotoxicity. Nonionic contrast agents (e.g., iohexol) are now available that provide comparable absorption of x-ray photons yet are significantly less charged than traditional agents. It was hoped that the reduced ionic nature would decrease their nephrotoxicity, but severe adverse renal events did not differ between ionic and nonionic contrast media in a large randomized clinical trial.[46]

Renal nephrotoxicity after exposure to ionic agents occurs most commonly in patients with preexisting renal insufficiency (3.3 relative risk) alone or in combination with diabetes mellitus, especially when diabetes is juvenile onset.[46] Other risk factors, such as dehydration, volume of contrast agent used, and simultaneous exposure to other nephrotoxins, contribute to the likelihood of acute contrast nephrotoxicity.[47] Other risk factors include multiple myeloma and heavy proteinuria. Overall, the incidence of acute renal dysfunction after contrast angiography varies from 0 to 10%, although these estimates are skewed by several studies that included only juvenile diabetes patients. In one study, hospital-acquired nephropathy occurred in 12% of patients.[48] In patients with normal renal function, however, the incidence of contrast nephropathy is only 1% to 2%.[49]

The impact of diabetes on the risk of ARF after angiography seems to depend on the type of diabetes and the magnitude of secondary diabetic nephropathy. Type 1 diabetics seem to be more susceptible to contrast-induced ARF than type 2 diabetics.[50,51] Harkonen and Kjellstrand[50] found that 22 of 26 patients (76%) with a prestudy serum creatinine level of greater than 2 mg/dL who underwent excretory urography developed ARF. Weinrauch and associates[52] reported that ARF after coronary angiography developed in 12 of 13 patients (92%) with juvenile-onset diabetes and severe diabetic nephropathy. In addition, the cause of chronic renal insufficiency seems to affect recovery from contrast-induced ARF. Although diabetic and nondiabetic patients with renal insufficiency are at increased risk for contrast-induced ARF, diabetics seem to recover less often and are at greater risk of permanent dependence on dialysis as a consequence of contrast-induced ARF.[50-52]

Specific measures to minimize the risk of contrast-induced ARF are controversial, and the results from controlled studies are largely inconclusive. Nevertheless, the basic relationship between the use of contrast material and the risk of contrast nephropathy seems to be related to the amount of time the kidney is exposed to the contrast material. For this reason, maximizing urine flow rate during and immediately after angiography and limiting the quantity of contrast agent used are important considerations. Maximal urine flow rate should be achieved by preliminary intravenous hydration of the patient. Studies that examined the optimal preparation for patients with renal insufficiency indicated that hydration with 0.45% saline provides better protection against acute decline in renal function associated with radiocontrast agents than does hydration with 0.45% saline plus mannitol or furosemide.[53] We routinely admit any patient with the above-mentioned risk factors 12 hours before angiography for intravenous hydration at 1.5 mL/kg/hr. Immediately before angiography, the patient usually receives a bolus of intravenous fluid (3 to 5 mL/kg). Finally, intravenous hydration is continued for 4 to 6 hours after completion of the study.

Although attempts to calculate a safe upper limit of contrast material have met with some success, no definitive limit currently exists. Even small doses (30 to 60 mL) may induce renal failure in patients with extreme renal insufficiency (glomerular filtration rate [GFR] ≤15 mL/min). Conversely, more than 300 mL of contrast material may be administered safely to other patients with no risk factors for ARF.[54] We limit the quantity of nonionized contrast agent to less than 50 to 75 mL in patients with a significant reduction in GFR (<20 to 30 mL/min). If additional contrast material is required to complete the vascular evaluation, we postpone further study and approach the total evaluation in a sequential manner. In some instances, digital subtraction techniques have been useful in limiting the quantity of contrast material required. Nevertheless, we have found that a single midstream aortic injection, using 30 to 40 mL of nonionic contrast material and conventional cut-film techniques, is just as safe as digital subtraction angiography.

Adjuncts or alternatives to conventional angiography are appropriate in many instances. In addition to the use of digital subtraction techniques, carbon dioxide gas can be used for angiography with minimal renal risk.[55,61] Because it offers limited detail, carbon dioxide angiography often is used to identify the site of disease, which is better defined with conventional contrast agents. Other alternatives to conventional angiography that reduce or eliminate the risk of nephrotoxicity include the use of gadolinium as a contrast agent for angiography,[56,57] magnetic resonance angiography,[58] and abdominal ultrasound with visceral/renal artery duplex sonography.

By scavenging reactive oxygen species, acetylcysteine may protect against contrast-induced nephrotoxicity. Tepel and colleagues[59] studied patients with chronic renal dysfunction who required nonionic contrast administration for computed tomography. They documented a significant reduction in serum creatinine with the use of oral acetylcysteine and hydration compared with placebo and hydration.[59] Further study is needed to define better the role of acetylcysteine during aortography; however, we administer two oral doses of acetylcysteine (600 mg) before and after these studies in patients at high risk for contrast nephrotoxicity.

Finally, high-dose loop diuretics, angiotensin-converting enzyme inhibitors, and angiotensin II receptor antagonists are held for at least 72 hours before aortic reconstruction or exposure to arterial contrast agents. Selective beta blockers and calcium channel blockers are substituted when necessary.[60]

■ SPECIAL CONSIDERATIONS

Renal Failure Associated with Aortic Surgery

ARF after aortic surgery continues to be associated with an extremely high mortality. Although it is reported to have an incidence ranging from 1% to 13% in elective aortic surgery,[23-29] the occurrence of ARF depends on the clinical circumstances of the operation, level of aortic repair undertaken, preoperative renal function, intraoperative and postoperative events, and overall prior health status of the patient. The reported data from several series regarding rates of ARF after operations performed for ruptured abdominal aortic aneurysms are summarized in Table 58-3.[20-22,73,76,107-110] The incidence of ARF complicating rupture of aortic aneurysms has remained formidable despite a 20-year period of surgical and technologic advancement. Nevertheless, recognition of the clinical syndrome of multiorgan system failure has shed some light on factors that increase this mortality. In patients with postoperative renal failure as an isolated system failure, the associated mortality ranges from 25% for nonoliguric renal failure to 70% for oliguric renal failure. Determinants of outcome include the preexisting disease and precipitating events. In contrast, when renal failure is only one of several system failures, mortality is extremely high, approaching 100% for three or more organs failing simultaneously.[11,66,67] It might be surmised that one simply needs to prevent or provide improved treatment of multiorgan system failure to improve the probability of survival in this group with renal failure. To date, the prevention of multiorgan system failure has proved an illusive goal.

ARF after procedures involving the juxtarenal aorta seldom parallels pure pathophysiologic models, but rather results from a combination of underlying causes. For purposes of discussion, however, the respective causes are addressed here as independent sources of ARF with the understanding that all of these mechanisms may be active in the production of postoperative renal failure in an individual patient.

A temporary isolated period of renal ischemia caused by suprarenal aortic cross-clamping, temporary renal artery occlusion, a single episode of hypovolemic shock, post–cross-clamp hypotension, or cardiogenic shock in the perioperative period is the most common cause of acute renal dysfunction and renal failure associated with aortic surgery. Through observations of patients and use of investigative models, Myers and associates[68-71] postulated that a pathophysiologic cascade of events after temporary renal ischemia leads to ARF. Renal biopsy specimens and autopsy studies in patients with postischemic ARF have shown minimal, if any, disturbance in glomerular architecture, yet profound disruption of tubular morphology. These findings led Oliver and colleagues[72] to suggest that this form of ARF is initiated through tubular luminal obstruction caused by sloughed tubular cells as discussed earlier.

Clinically observed rates of renal failure after aortic surgery may be divided according to the level of aortic repair undertaken. Svensson and associates'[73] large series of patients undergoing thoracoabdominal aneurysm repair quoted an 18% incidence of renal failure (serum creatinine >3 mg/dL) and a 9% rate of dialysis-dependent renal failure. Series using regional renal hypothermia for renal protection and clamp-and-sew technique identified occurrence of ARF in 11.5% of patients.[74] Factors identified to predict renal dysfunction included a preoperative creatinine greater than 1.5 mg/dL and a total cross-clamp time greater than 100 minutes. These results do not seem to differ from series in which partial left heart bypass and distal aortic perfusion were used.[74] In cases of juxtarenal and suprarenal abdominal aortic aneurysms, preservation of renal function may be enhanced through the use of renal hypothermia.[75] For elective infrarenal aortic surgery, preoperative creatinine clearance less than 45 mL/min has been associated with a significant risk of subsequent renal failure. In the same series, no patient with preoperative serum creatinine less than 1.5 mg/dL required postoperative dialysis, whereas 8% of patients with a preoperative serum creatinine greater than 1.8 required postoperative dialysis support.[76]

An alternative cause of ARF in aortic surgery that may be considered a permanent form of ischemic insult is renal atheroembolism. Although this mechanism receives much less attention than the pathophysiologic consequences of temporary ischemia, it may be the dominant cause of ARF in patients without prolonged renal ischemia, excessive blood loss and hypotension, or other recognized nephrotoxic insult to renal function.[77] The quantity of microembolization produced during manipulation of the juxtarenal aorta during dissection depends on the embologenic potential of the atheromatous debris and the operative techniques employed to prevent such an event. The clinical impact of such renal microembolization depends on the quantity of functioning renal parenchyma embolized and the presence of other causes of ARF. In the absence of other factors favoring ARF and a normal mass of functioning nephron units, relatively large amounts of atheromatous microemboli can occur without an immediate impact on renal function.[78] In contrast, if there is a minimal renal reserve, the added insult of even minor microembolization can lead to decompensation and ARF.

Protection of Renal Function

Measures to protect renal function during aortic surgery should be practiced because the mortality of ARF requiring dialysis remains high. These protective measures include limiting the period of warm renal ischemia, providing adequate circulating blood volume before operation by means of preoperative intravenous fluid hydration and adequate blood volume replacement during and immediately after surgery, avoiding repetitive or prolonged renal ischemia, and maintaining maximal parameters of cardiac performance. Additional modalities include the use of mannitol, furosemide, and other diuretics; renal hypothermia; renal vasodilating drugs; and other, more investigational techniques.[79-84] Conceptually, all of these modalities are directed toward reduction of the severity or duration of renal tubular ischemia, reduction of renal tubular metabolic needs during periods of ischemia, or prevention of tubular obstruction by sloughed tubular cells. No single modality or combination of modalities entirely prevents the insult of aortic surgery on renal function, but by using these preventive measures, one can lessen the severity and duration of renal dysfunction.[85-86]

Careful attention should be given to limiting the period of warm renal ischemia. For a normally perfused kidney, less than 40 minutes of warm ischemia is well tolerated. For a chronically ischemic kidney, the duration of safe warm ischemic time is extended for an unknown period depending on the amount of collateral flow that has developed. Preoperative evaluation and intraoperative preparation can help to reduce the ischemic time and diminish the chances of time-consuming intraoperative complications.

In addition to routine heparinization and confirmation of systemic anticoagulation by measurement of activated clotting time, intravenous administration of mannitol, 12.5 to 25 g, before aortic cross-clamping is widely practiced as a routine measure to prevent ARF. Extensive investigation of its actions suggests that mannitol not only acts as an osmotic diuretic to increase urine flow rate, but also may attenuate the reduction in cortical blood flow that occurs during and immediately after aortic cross-clamping. Mannitol also acts as a free radical scavenger.[80] Compared with saline administration before aortic cross-clamping in patients undergoing infrarenal aortic aneurysm repair, mannitol causes a reduction in subclinical glomerular and renal tubular damage.[85] These results are not uniformly reproduced, however, because others have found an absence of clinical benefit from using mannitol and dopamine over volume expansion alone.[87] Profound and sustained alterations in renal hemodynamics are observed in patients with impaired renal function or when surgical occlusion of the aorta is prolonged. ARF after aortic surgery requires aggressive therapy, and goals should be aimed at correcting extracellular volume deficits. The conversion of oliguric renal failure to a nonoliguric state is associated with fewer complications and an improved survival.[66]

Dopamine is administered frequently during aortic surgery. Low-dose dopamine in healthy adults causes increases in renal perfusion, GFR, and urine output.[88] The effect of low-dose dopamine in patients undergoing aortic surgery is less well understood. During aortic reconstruction, dopamine administration may cause increased urine output through inotropic effects.[89] The clinical benefit of prophylactic dopamine administration in patients undergoing aortic surgery is unproved, however.[90,91] Because dopamine may cause tachyarrhythmias, myocardial ischemia, pulmonary shunting, or mesenteric vasoconstriction,[88] its routine use should be approached with caution.

Fenoldopam is a dopaminergic type 1 (DA_1) receptor agonist that may reduce the risk of ARF. Two dopamine receptors are found in the kidney: DA_1 and DA_2. Activation of the DA_1 receptor causes increased GFR likely mediated by increased blood flow to the inner cortex and medulla of the kidney. Activation of the DA_2 receptor causes a reduction in renal blood flow and GFR.[92] Because it is a selective DA_1 agonist, fenoldopam significantly increases renal blood flow in healthy adults.[93] It seems to maintain kidney perfusion in animal models of radiocontrast-induced nephrotoxicity[94] and aortic cross-clamping.[95] Atrial natriuretic peptide is an endogenous hormone released from the cardiac atria with vasodilatory, diuretic, and natriuretic properties.[96] Atrial natriuretic peptide and fenoldopam infusions have shown benefit in preventing contrast-induced nephropathy[94,97] and renal dysfunction after cardiac surgery.[98-101] Their role in patients undergoing aortic surgery is not yet defined clearly, however. At this time, experience with fenoldopam is limited but encouraging. Additional investigation is needed to elucidate better the role of fenoldopam and atrial natriuretic peptide during aortic surgery.

Distal aortic perfusion may be used to maintain renal perfusion during repair of thoracoabdominal aneurysms. This technique is most attractive during the repair of an isolated thoracoabdominal aneurysm[102] or when complex disease precludes prompt completion of the proximal thoracic aortic anastomosis.[103] Distal aortic perfusion may be modified with "octopus" catheters to perfuse the renal arteries directly during distal reconstruction.[104] Because the routine use of distal aortic perfusion has been associated with an increased incidence of ARF despite spinal cord protection in extensive (type II) thoracoabdominal aneurysm,[104,105] we prefer other strategies to provide renal protection.

Regional renal hypothermia has been used sporadically for many years to protect renal function during periods of ischemia. Its use is based on the valid premise that even modest decreases in core temperature significantly reduce metabolic needs. These unmet metabolic needs during ischemia lead to a series of events that produce ARF. The technique usually employs the infusion of 500 mL to 1 L of cold (4°C to 5°C) crystalloid solution with or without other additives into the isolated segment of the aorta containing the renal arteries or directly into the renal artery ostia using a handheld cannula or infusion balloon catheters. The protective effect of minimal changes in core temperature has been evaluated in rats. The first 10°C reduction in tissue temperature seems to provide the greatest protection. Postoperative serum creatinine levels and renal tubular morphology data revealed that a protective effect occurred with a minimal, sustained decrease in core temperature to 35°C.[106]

Finally, one cannot overstate the importance of operative technique in preventing microembolization of atheromatous debris during juxtarenal aortic dissection and control. One should avoid repetitive cross-clamping because this increases the risk of atheroembolization to the renal arteries from proximal atheromatous debris. Because the embologenic potential of the debris cannot be judged definitively until after the aorta is opened, one should assume the worst until it is proved otherwise. For this reason, we temporarily occlude renal artery flow immediately before the application of the aortic cross-clamp whenever the aortogram suggests the presence of complicated perirenal atherosclerosis; this applies to infrarenal and suprarenal aortic cross-clamping. Although the authors can provide only anecdotal support for this maneuver, we believe it has been an important adjunct in minimizing the incidence of postoperative ARF among our patients.

■ REFERENCES

1. Robaczewski DL, Dean RH, Hansen KJ: Pathophysiology of renovascular hypertension. In White RA, Hollier LH (eds): Vascular Surgery: Basic Science and Clinical Considerations. Armonk, NY, Futura Publishing Company, 2005, pp 180-191.
2. Valtin H, Seafer JA: Renal Function: Mechanisms Preserving Fluid and Solute Balance in Health, 3rd ed. Boston, Little Brown, 1995.
3. Shires GT III: Management of fluids and electrolytes. In Sabiston DC Jr, Lyerly HK (eds): Sabiston's Essentials of Surgery, 2nd ed. Philadelphia, WB Saunders, 1994, p 36.
4. Granger H, Dhar J, Chen, HI, et al: Structure and function of the interstitium. In: Proceedings of the Workshop on Albumin. Bethesda, Md, National Institutes of Health, 1976, p 114.
5. Smeets HJ, Kievit J, Dulfer FT, et al: Analysis of post-operative hypoalbuminemia: A clinical study. Int Surg 79:152, 1994.
6. Humes HD: Role of calcium in pathogenesis of acute renal failure. Am J Physiol 250:F579, 1986.
7. Lucas CE, Ledgerwood AM: The fluid problem in the critically ill. Surg Clin North Am 63:439, 1983.
8. Dawson CW, Lucas CE, Ledgerwood AM: Altered interstitial fluid space dynamics and post-resuscitation hypertension. Arch Surg 116:657, 1981.
9. Bomberger RA, McGregor B, Depalma RG: Optimal fluid management after aortic reconstruction: A prospective study of two crystalloid solutions. J Vasc Surg 4:164, 1986.
10. Nielsen OM, Engell HC: Effects of maintaining normal plasma colloid osmotic pressure on renal function and excretion of sodium and water after major surgery: A randomized study. Dan Med Bull 32:182, 1985.
11. Brezis M, Rosen S, Epstein FH: Acute renal failure. In Brenner BM, Rector FC (eds): The Kidney, 4th ed. Philadelphia, WB Saunders, 1991, pp 993-1061.
12. Bullock ML, Umen A, Finkelstein M, Keane WF: The assessment of risk factors in 462 patients with acute renal failure. Am J Kidney Dis 5:97, 1985.
13. Muther RS: Acute renal failure: Acute azotemia in the critically ill. In Civetta JM, Taylor RW, Kirby RR (eds): Critical Care, 2nd ed. Philadelphia, JB Lippincott, 1992, pp 1583-1598.
14. Bush HC Jr: Renal failure following abdominal aortic reconstruction. Surgery 93:107, 1983.
15. Rice CL, Hobelman CF, John DA, et al: Central venous pressure or pulmonary capillary wedge pressure as the determinant of fluid replacement in aortic surgery. Surgery 84:437, 1978.
16. Hansen KJ, Tribble RW, Reavis SW, et al: Renal duplex sonography: Evaluation of clinical utility. J Vasc Surg 12:227, 1990.
17. Molitoris BA: New insights into the cell biology of ischemic acute renal failure. J Am Soc Nephrol 1:1263, 1991.
18. Mason J, Joeris B, Welsch J, et al: Vascular congestion in ischemic renal failure: The role of cell swelling. Miner Electrolyte Metab 15:114, 1989.
19. Mohaupt M, Kramer HJ: Acute ischemic renal failure: Review of experimental studies on pathophysiology and potential protective interventions. Ren Fail 11:177, 1989-90.
20. Safi HJ, Harlin SA, Miller CC, et al: Predictive factors for acute renal failure in thoracic and thoracoabdominal aortic aneurysm surgery. J Vasc Surg 24:338, 1996.
21. Schepens MA, Defauw JJ, Hamerlijnck RP, et al: Risk assessment of acute renal failure after thoracoabdominal aortic aneurysm surgery. Ann Surg 219:400, 1994.

22. Breckwoldt WL, Mackay WC, Belkin M, et al: The effect of suprarenal cross-clamping on abdominal aortic aneurysm repair. Arch Surg 127:520, 1992.
23. Gardner RJ, Lancaster JR, Tarney TJ, et al: Five year history of surgically treated abdominal aortic aneurysms. Surg Gynecol Obstet 130:981, 1970.
24. O'Donnell D, Clarke G, Hurst P: Acute renal failure following surgery for abdominal aortic aneurysm. Aust N Z J Surg 59:405, 1989.
25. Thompson JE, Hollier JH, Patman RD, et al: Surgical management of abdominal aortic aneurysms: Factors influencing mortality and morbidity—a 20-year experience. Ann Surg 181:654, 1975.
26. Bergqvist D, Olsson P-O, Takolander R, et al: Renal failure as a complication to aortoiliac and iliac reconstructive surgery. Acta Chir Scand 149:37, 1983.
27. McCombs PR, Roberts B: Acute renal failure following resection of abdominal aortic aneurysm. Surg Gynecol Obstet 148:175, 1979.
28. Diehl JT, Cali RF, Hertzer NR, Beven EG: Complications of abdominal aortic reconstruction, an analysis of perioperative risk factors in 557 patients. Ann Surg 197:49, 1983.
29. Gornick CC Jr, Kjellstrand CM: Acute renal failure complicating aortic aneurysm surgery. Nephron 35:145, 1983.
30. Ouriel K: Renal artery embolism. In Ernst CB, Stanley JC (eds): Current Therapy in Vascular Surgery, 3rd ed. St Louis, Mosby-Year Book, 1995, p 821.
31. Lye WC, Cheah JS, Sinniah R: Renal cholesterol embolic disease: Case report and review of the literature. Am J Nephrol 13:489, 1993.
32. Blankenship JC: Cholesterol embolisation after thrombolytic therapy. Drug Saf 14:78, 1996.
33. Thadani RI, Camargo CA Jr, Xavier RJ: Atheroembolic renal failure after invasive procedures: Natural history based on 52 histologically proven cases. Medicine 74:350, 1995.
34. Sakalayan MG, Gupta S, Suryaprasad A, et al: Incidence of atheroembolic renal failure after coronary angiography: A prospective study. Angiology 48:609, 1997.
35. Hansen KJ, Cherr GS, Craven TE, et al: Management of ischemic nephropathy: Dialysis-free survival after surgical repair. J Vasc Surg 32:472, 2000.
36. Textor SC: Renal failure related to angiotensin converting enzyme inhibitors. Semin Nephrol 17:67, 1997.
37. Navis G: ACE inhibitors and the kidney: A risk benefit assessment. Drug Saf 15:200, 1996.
38. Toto RD: Renal insufficiency due to angiotensin-converting enzyme inhibitors. Miner Electrolyte Metab 20:193, 1994.
39. Kalra PA, Mamtora H, Holmes AM: Renovascular disease and renal complications of angiotensin-converting enzyme inhibitor therapy. QJM 77:1013, 1990.
40. Moore RD, Smith CR, Lipsky JJ, et al: Risk factors for nephrotoxicity in patients treated with aminoglycosides. Ann Intern Med 100:352, 1984.
41. Boucher BA, Coffey BC, Kuhl DA, et al: Algorithm for assessing renal dysfunction risk in critically ill trauma patients receiving aminoglycosides. Am J Surg 160:473, 1990.
42. Braum SR, Weiss FR, Keller AL, et al: Evaluation of the renal toxicity of hemoproteins and their derivatives: A role in the genesis of acute tubular necrosis. J Exp Med 131:443, 1979.
43. Eneas JF, Schoenfeld BY, Humphreys MH: The effect of infusion of mannitol-sodium bicarbonate on the clinical course of myoglobinuria. Arch Intern Med 139:801, 1979.
44. Donadio C, Tramonti G, Lucceshi A, et al: Tubular toxicity is the main renal effect of contrast media. Ren Fail 18:647, 1996.
45. Larson JS, Hudson K, Mertz ML, et al: Renal vasoconstriction responses to contrast medium. J Lab Clin Med 101:385, 1983.
46. Rudnick MR, Goldfarb S, Wexler L, et al: Nephrotoxicity of ionic and nonionic contrast media in 1196 patients: A randomized trial. The Iohexol Cooperative Study. Kidney Int 47:254, 1995.
47. Barrett BJ: Contrast nephrotoxicity. J Am Soc Nephrol 5:125, 1994.
48. Hou SH, Burchinsky DA, Wish JB, et al: Hospital acquired renal insufficiency: A prospective study. Am J Med 74:243, 1983.
49. Parfrey PS, Griffiths SM, Barrett BJ, et al: Contrast material-induced renal failure in patients with diabetes mellitus, renal insufficiency or both. N Engl J Med 320:143, 1989.
50. Harkonen S, Kjellstrand CM: Exacerbation of diabetic renal failure following intravenous pyelography. Am J Med 63:939, 1977.
51. Shieh SD, Hirsch SR, Boshell BR, et al: Low risk of contrast media induced acute renal failure in nonazotemic type 2 diabetes mellitus. Kidney Int 21:739, 1982.
52. Weinrauch LA, Healy RW, Leland OS, et al: Coronary angiography and acute renal failure in diabetic azotemic nephropathy. Ann Intern Med 86:56, 1977.
53. Solomon R, Werner C, Mann D, et al: Effects of saline, mannitol and furosemide to prevent acute decreases in renal function induced by radiocontrast agents. N Engl J Med 331:1416, 1994.
54. Cigarroa RG, Lang RA, Williams RH, Hillis LD: Dosing of contrast material to prevent contrast nephropathy in patients with renal disease. Am J Med 86:649, 1989.
55. Seager JM, Self S, Harward TR, et al: Carbon dioxide gas as an arterial contrast agent. Ann Surg 217:688, 1993.
56. Hammer FS, Goffette PP, Malaise J, et al: Gadolinium demeglumine: An alternative contrast agent for digital subtraction angiography. Eur Radiol 9:128, 1999.
57. Rieger J, Sitter T, Toepfer M, et al: Gadolinium as an alternative contrast agent for diagnostic and interventional angiographic procedures in patients with impaired renal function. Nephrol Dial Transplant 17:824, 2002.
58. Goyen M, Ruehm SG, Debatin JF: MR-angiography: The role of contrast agents. Eur J Radiol 34:247, 2000.
59. Tepel M, van der Giet M, Schwarzfeld C, et al: Prevention of radiographic-contrast-agent-induced reductions in renal function by acetylcysteine. N Engl J Med 343:180, 2000.
60. Bonventure JV: Mechanisms of ischemic acute renal failure. Kidney Int 43:1160, 1993.
61. Weaver FA, Pentecost MJ, Yellin AE: Carbon dioxide digital subtraction arteriography: A pilot study. Ann Vasc Surg 4:437, 1990.
62. Chawla SK, Najafi H, Ing TS, et al: Acute renal failure complicating ruptured abdominal aortic aneurysm. Arch Surg 110:521, 1975.
63. Hicks GL, Eastland MW, DeWeese JA, et al: Survival improvement following aortic aneurysm resection. Ann Surg 181:863, 1975.
64. Fielding JL, Black J, Ashton F, et al: Ruptured aortic aneurysms: Postoperative complications and their aetiology. Br J Surg 71:487, 1984.
65. Gordon AC, Pryn S, Collin J: Outcome of patients who required renal support after surgery for ruptured abdominal aortic aneurysm. Br J Surg 81:836, 1994.
66. Anderson RJ, Lines SL, Berus AS, et al: Non-oliguric acute renal failure. N Engl J Med 296:1134, 1977.
67. Mann HJ, Fuhs DW, Hemstrom CA: Acute renal failure. Drug Intell Clin Pharm 20:421, 1986.
68. Myers BD, Moran SM: Hemodynamically mediated acute renal failure. N Engl J Med 314:97, 1986.
69. Myers BD, Miller DC, Mehigan JT, et al: Nature of the renal injury following total renal ischemia in man. J Clin Invest 73:329, 1984.
70. Moran SM, Myers BD: Course of acute renal failure studied by a model of creatinine kinetics. Kidney Int 27:928, 1985.
71. Hilberman M, Myers BD, Carrie G, et al: Acute renal failure following cardiac surgery. J Thorac Cardiovasc Surg 77:880, 1979.
72. Oliver J, MacDowell M, Tracy A: Pathogenesis of acute renal failure associated with traumatic and toxic injury: Renal ischemia, nephrotoxic damage, and the ischemuric episode. J Clin Invest 30:1305, 1951.
73. Svensson LG, Crawford ES, Hess KR, et al: Experience with 1509 patients undergoing thoracoabdominal and aortic operations. J Vasc Surg 17:357, 1993.
74. Kashyap VS, Cambria RP, Davison JF, et al: Renal failure after thoracoabdominal aortic surgery. J Vasc Surg 26:949, 1997.
75. Allen BT, Anderson CB, Rubin BG, et al: Preservation of renal function in juxtarenal and suprarenal abdominal aortic aneurysm repair. J Vasc Surg 17:948, 1993.

76. Powell RJ, Roddy SP, Meier GH, et al: Effect of renal insufficiency on outcome following infrarenal aortic surgery. Am J Surg 174:126, 1997.
77. Iliopoulos JI, Zdon MJ, Crawford BG, et al: Renal microembolizatuion syndrome: A cause for renal dysfunction after abdominal aortic reconstruction. Am J Surg 146:779, 1983.
78. Smith MC, Ghose MK, Henry AR: The clinical spectrum of renal cholesterol embolization. Am J Med 71:174, 1981.
79. Miller DC, Myers BD: Pathophysiology and prevention of acute renal failure associated with thoracoabdominal or abdominal aortic surgery. J Vasc Surg 5:518, 1987.
80. Abbott WM, Abel RM, Beck CH: The reversal of renal cortical ischemia during aortic occlusion by mannitol. J Surg Res 16:482, 1974.
81. Hanley MJ, Davidson K: Prior mannitol and furosemide infusion in a model of ischemic acute renal failure. Am J Physiol 241:F556, 1981.
82. Ochsner JL, Mills NL, Gardner PA: A technique for renal preservation during suprarenal abdominal aortic operations. Surg Gynecol Obstet 159:388, 1984.
83. Hilberman M, Maseda J, Stinson EB, et al: The diuretic properties of dopamine in patients following open heart operations. Anesthesiology 61:489, 1984.
84. Lindner A, Cutler RE, Bell AJ: Attenuation of nephrotoxic acute renal failure in the dog with angiotensin-converting enzyme inhibitor (SQ-20, 881). Circ Res 51:216, 1982.
85. Salem MG, Crooke JW, McLoughlin GA, et al: The effect of dopamine on renal function during aortic cross clamping. Ann Roy Coll Surg Engl 701:9, 1988.
86. Nicholson ML, Baker DM, Hopkinson BR, et al: Randomized control trial of the effect of mannitol on renal reperfusion injury during aortic aneurysm surgery. Br J Surg 83:1230, 1996.
87. Paul MD, Mazer CD, Byrick RJ, et al: Influence of mannitol and dopamine on renal function during elective infrarenal aortic clamping in man. Am J Nephrol 6:427, 1986.
88. Denton MD, Chertow M, Brady HR: "Renal-dose" dopamine for the treatment of acute renal failure: Scientific rationale, experimental studies and clinical trials. Kidney Int 50:4, 1996.
89. De Lasson L, Hansen HE, Jugl B, et al: A randomised, clinical study of the effect of low-dose dopamine on central and renal haemodynamics in infrarenal aortic surgery. Eur J Vasc Endovasc Surg 10:82, 1995.
90. Girbes AR, Lieverse AG, Smit AJ, et al: Lack of specific renal haemodynamic effects of different doses of dopamine after infrarenal aortic surgery. Br J Anaesth 77:753, 1996.
91. Baldwin L, Henderson A, Hickman P: Effect of postoperative low-dose dopamine on renal function after elective major vascular surgery. Ann Intern Med 120:744, 1994.
92. Kebabian JW, Calne DB: Multiple receptors for dopamine. Nat Lond 277:93, 1979.
93. Mathur VS, Swan SK, Lambrecht LJ, et al: The effects of fenoldopam, a selective dopamine receptor agonist, on systemic and renal hemodynamics in normotensive subjects. Crit Care Med 27:1832, 1999.
94. Bakris GL, Lass NA, Glock D: Renal hemodynamics in radiocontrast medium-induced renal dysfunction: A role for dopamine-1 receptors. Kidney Int 56:206, 1999.
95. Halpenny M, Markos F, Snow HM, et al: The effects of fenoldopam on renal blood flow and tubular function during aortic cross-clamping in anaesthetized dogs. Eur J Anaesth 17:491, 2000.
96. Goetz KL: Physiology and pathophysiology of atrial peptides. Am J Physiol 254:E1, 1988.
97. Kurnik BR, Allgren RL, Genter FC, et al: Prospective study of atrial natriuretic peptide for the prevention of radiocontrast induced nephropathy. Am J Kidney Dis 31:674, 1998.
98. Sward K, Valson F, Ricksten SE: Long-term infusion of atrial natriuretic peptide (ANP) improves renal blood flow and glomerular filtration rate in clinical acute renal failure. Acta Anaesthesiol Scand 45:536, 2001.
99. Hayashida N, Chihara S, Kashikie H, et al: Effects of intraoperative administration of atrial natriuretic peptide. Ann Thorac Surg 70:1319, 2000.
100. Halpenny M, Lakshmi S, O'Donnell A, et al: Fenoldopam: Renal and splanchnic effects in patients undergoing coronary artery bypass grafting. Anaesthesia 56:953, 2001.
101. Halpenny M, Rushe C, Breen P, et al: The effects of fenoldopam on renal function in patients undergoing elective aortic surgery. Eur J Anaesthesiol 19:32, 2002.
102. Von Oppell U, Dunne T, DeGroot K, et al: Spinal cord protection in the absence of collateral circulation: Meta-analysis of mortality and paraplegia. J Card Surg 9:685, 1994.
103. Coselli JS: Thoracoabdominal aortic aneurysms: Experience with 372 patients. J Card Surg 9:638, 1994.
104. Safi HJ, Harlin SA, Miller CC, et al: Predictive factors for acute renal failure in thoracic and thoracoabdominal aortic aneurysm surgery. J Vasc Surg 24:338, 1996.
105. Coselli JS, LeMaire SA, Miller CC III, et al: Mortality and paraplegia after thoracoabdominal aortic aneurysm repair: A risk factor analysis. Ann Thorac Surg 69:409, 2000.
106. Pelkay TJ, Frank RS, Stanley JJ, et al: Minimal physiologic temperature variations during renal ischemia alter functional and morphologic outcome. J Vasc Surg 15:619, 1992.

Chapter 59

Infection in Prosthetic Vascular Grafts

DENNIS F. BANDYK, MD, FACS
MARTIN R. BACK, MD, FACS

The use of prostheses (grafts, metallic stents, endovascular stent-grafts) in the arterial or venous circulations has permitted palliation of a large number of disabling or fatal vascular conditions. Despite routine antibiotic prophylaxis and refinements in implantation technique, microbial infection of the vascular prosthesis can occur and eventually produce a perilous condition. Infection involving a prosthetic graft is difficult to eradicate. If not recognized or treated promptly, implant failure will occur by producing sepsis, hemorrhage, or thrombosis.[6,14,27,33,52,56] In general, surgical therapy is always required, often coupled with prosthesis excision, because antibiotics alone are insufficient to eradicate an established infectious process. Patient care requires adherence to specific criteria in selecting an appropriate treatment care plan whether the management involves graft excision alone, graft preservation within the implant wound, in-situ graft replacement, or graft excision in conjunction with extra-anatomic bypass grafting. Improved results have been reported following both graft excision coupled with extra-anatomic bypass and in-situ replacement procedures.[8,17,23,25,34,62,67,78,79] Even when treatment is successful, the morbidity associated with vascular graft infections is considerable, with outcomes often worse than the natural history of the vascular condition that led to graft implantation.

The clinical manifestations of prosthetic vascular infections vary depending on the anatomic location and the virulence of the pathogen.[6,18,21,27,35,52] The resulting clinical spectrum of graft infection mandates surgeons use a patient-specific treatment approach. Keys to successful outcome include using accurate diagnostics to identify the infecting organism and extent of graft infection, the administration of culture-specific antibiotic therapy, and a well-planned surgical intervention to excise or replace the infected graft. Since most patients present with a low-virulence graft infection, in-situ replacement therapy has evolved to be a "preferred" treatment strategy using autogenous venous conduits, cryopreserved allografts, or antibiotic-impregnated prosthesis to replace the infected grafts.[5,8,10,22,23,25,31,43,45,55,75,79] A single-stage procedure that involves excision of the infected graft with immediate in-situ replacement is appealing because it avoids the complexity and increased morbidity of staged or multiple procedures associated with graft excision and extra-anatomic bypass grafting. Regardless of the technique used to eradicate the graft infection, success is measured by patient survival, freedom from recurrent infection, patency of the revascularization, and the avoidance of major morbidity or amputation.

Epidemiology

The reported incidence of infection involving a vascular prosthesis varies, occurring after 0.2% to 5% of operations, and is influenced by the implant site, indication for intervention, underlying disease, and host defense mechanisms (Table 59-1).[6,7,21,28,30,33,36,52-57,66,71] Vascular surgeons now realize that the potential for graft infection extends well beyond the perioperative period. Aortic graft infections can develop months to years after implantation, and thus the long-term incidence is higher. During a 10-year period after prosthetic grafting of the aorta, a population-based study from the Mayo Clinic estimated the incidence of infection to be 5%.[38] Graft infection occurs much less frequently than wound infection, with the incidence of early (<30-day) graft infection being in the range of 1% of procedures. Infection is more likely to involve prosthetic grafts implanted during an emergency procedure (e.g., for ruptured abdominal aortic

Table 59-1 Incidence of Prosthetic Graft and Endovascular Device Infection Relative to Implant Site

INFECTION AND DEVICE	INCIDENCE, %
Graft Implant Site	
Descending thoracic aorta	0.7-3
Aortoiliac	0.2-1.3
Aortofemoral	0.5-3
Femorofemoral	1.3-3.6
Axillofemoral	5-8
Femoropopliteal	1-10
Femorotibial	2-3.4
Carotid patch	0.3-0.8
Carotid-subclavian	0.5-1.2
Axilloaxillary	1-4
Endovascular Device	
Aortic stent-graft	0.4-0.8
Iliac stent	<0.5
Carotid stent	<0.5

Section X

aneurysm [AAA], acute arterial ischemia) and when the prosthesis is anastomosed to the femoral artery or placed in a subcutaneous tunnel (e.g., with axillofemoral or femorofemoral bypass). In a Canadian prospective, multicenter trial of nonruptured AAA repair, the incidence of graft infection was 0.2%, which is similar to the incidence reported following endovascular stent-graft AAA repair (0.4%).[3,28,44,58] Infection can also develop following percutaneous stent angioplasty, but the incidence is low (<0.5%), with case reports suggesting colonization occurred during an episode of bacteremia.[26]

Prosthetic graft infections can be classified by appearance time, relationship to postoperative wound infection, and the extent of graft involvement (Table 59-2). An early (<4 months after graft implantation) infection correlates with a Szilagyi grade III wound infection that involves the vascular prosthesis.[71] These infections are caused by virulent hospital-acquired bacteria and present with sepsis evidenced by fever, leukocytosis, bacteremia, and an advanced wound infection. There is evidence that even Szilagyi grades I and II wound infections increase the likelihood of a late-appearing graft infection. Late infections are the result of graft colonization by "low-virulence" organisms such as *Staphylococcus epidermidis* or infrequently *Candida* species.[5-8,36,44,78] The low titer of microorganisms on graft surfaces produces an indolent infection without signs of sepsis, and cultures of perigraft fluid or tissue may yield no growth.

Bunt proposed using a standardized terminology to reflect the spectrum of graft infection and allow comparison of treatment outcomes.[14] Categories include perigraft infection (P0, P1, P2, and P3), graft-enteric erosion (GEE), graft-enteric fistula (GEF), and aortic stump infection. Most early graft infections present after discharge from the hospital, typically within 1 to 3 months, and involve an extracavitary graft. Cavitary (i.e., aortic) graft infections present as a late (>4 months) infection with a mean appearance times of more than 40 months.[5,9,56,60,66,77] Both early and late infections can present with either total (P0, P1) or partial (P2, P3) graft involvement.

Table 59-2 Clinical Classifications of Prosthetic Graft Infections

Appearance Time after Implantation

Early: <4 mo
Late: >4 mo

Szilagyi's Classification (Applicable to Postoperative Wound Infections)

Grade I: cellulitis involving wound
Grade II: infection involving subcutaneous tissue
Grade III: infection involving the vascular prosthesis

Bunt's Classification (Modified)

Peripheral graft infection
- *P0 graft infection:* infection of a cavitary graft (e.g., aortic arch; abdominal and thoracic aortic interposition; aortoiliac, aortofemoral, iliofemoral graft infections)
- *P1 graft infection:* infection of a graft whose entire anatomic course is noncavitary (e.g., carotid-subclavian, axilloaxillary, axillofemoral, femorofemoral, femorodistal; dialysis access bridge graft infections)
- *P2 graft infection:* infection of the extracavitary portion of a graft whose origin is cavitary (e.g., infected groin segment of an aortofemoral or thoracofemoral graft, cervical infection of an aortocarotid graft)
- *P3 graft infection:* infection involving a prosthetic patch angioplasty (e.g., carotid and femoral endarterectomies with prosthetic patch closure)

Graft-enteric erosion
Graft-enteric fistula
Aortic stump sepsis following excision of an infected aortic graft

PATHOGENESIS

The presence of a foreign body potentiates the infectivity of bacteria. In 1957, Elek and Conen demonstrated that a single-braided silk suture significantly reduced the inoculum of staphylococci required to produce a local infection.[32] The risk of foreign body infection can be predicted by the formula:

$$\text{Risk of biomaterial infection} = \frac{\text{Dose of bacterial contamination} \times \text{virulence}}{\text{Host resistance}}$$

The initiating event is bacterial adherence to the biomaterial surfaces, followed by colonization and development of "bacterial-laden" biofilm that resists host defenses and antibiotic penetration. Both graft and bacterial characteristics influence the likelihood of colonization. Bacterial adherence to polyester grafts is 10 to 100 times greater than to polytetrafluoroethylene (PTFE) grafts; and gram-positive bacteria, such as staphylococci, produce an extracellular glycocalyx, or "mucin," that promotes adherence to biomaterials in greater numbers than gram-negative bacteria. The increased adhesion of staphylococci to biomaterials is due to specific capsular adhesions that mediate microorganism attachment and colonization. Antibodies to these specific cell-surface glycoproteins have been developed and have been used clinically for the diagnosis of graft infection, and their application to graft surfaces can inhibit bacterial adherence.

Etiologic Factors Involved in Graft Colonization

A vascular prosthesis exposed to microorganisms (bacteria or fungi) can result in clinical infection by the following four major mechanisms:

1. Perioperative contamination via the surgical wound
2. Bacteremia seeding of the biomaterial
3. Mechanical erosion into bowel or genitourinary tract or through the skin
4. Involvement caused by a contiguous infectious process

Perioperative Contamination

Skin and lymph nodes are a major reservoir of bacteria. Biomaterial surfaces can contact microorganisms (1) by a *direct route* during implantation, (2) through the surgical wound (in the event of a healing complication), or (3) by *hematogenous* or *lymphatic* sources arising from remote sites of infection (e.g., urinary tract infection, tinea pedis, pneumonia, venous or arterial catheter sepsis, endocarditis, and ischemic foot lesions). Important potential sources of direct graft contamination include breaks in aseptic operative technique; contact with the patient's endogenous flora harbored within sweat glands, lymph nodes, diseased artery walls (e.g., atherosclerotic plaque or aneurysm thrombus), disrupted lymphatics, or intestinal bag effluents; and injury or opening of the gastrointestinal or genitourinary tract. If the surgical wound does not develop a fibrin seal or heal promptly following operation, the underlying vascular prosthesis is susceptible to colonization from any superficial wound problems (e.g., erythema, dermal necrosis, and lymphocele). Wounds with persistent drainage indicate the presence of ischemic or injured tissues, which if complicated by superficial infection can extend to deeper tissue and involve the prosthesis. Diseased artery walls and reoperative wounds are an unappreciated source of bacteria, with microbiology cultures recovering pathogenic strains of staphylococci in 10% to 20% of cases.[6] Bacteria can be harbored in the scar tissue or lymphoceles of healed wounds and contact prosthetic grafts undergoing revision or replacement for thrombosis or anastomotic aneurysm. Cultures of explanted graft material from such procedures have isolated microorganisms, typically *S. epidermidis*, from 50% to 70% of thrombosed grafts and more than 80% of grafts associated with anastomotic aneurysms.[44]

Bacteremia

Bacterial seeding of the prosthesis via a hematogenous route is an uncommon but important mechanism of graft and stent infection. Experimentally, intravenous infusion of 10^7 colony-forming units of *Staphylococcus aureus* produces a clinical graft infection in nearly 100% of animals if administered within days of implantation. Thus, bacteremia arising from infected intravascular catheters, urinary tract infections, or other remote tissue infections (e.g., pneumonia, infected foot ulcer) increases the risk of graft infection and occurs regularly in the elderly vascular patient during the postoperative period. In debilitated, leukopenic, or septic patients, it is best to avoid the use of prosthetic vascular grafts or stents. Parenteral antibiotic therapy has been shown experimentally to significantly decrease the risk of graft colonization from bacteremia and is the rationale for both antibiotic prophylaxis and culture-specific antibiotic therapy in patients with a known site of infection. As the prosthesis heals and becomes incorporated with surrounding tissue, susceptibility to bacteremic colonization decreases, but vulnerability has been documented beyond 1 year after implantation, with infection developing as the result of dental and gastrointestinal diagnostic procedures. Transient bacteremia, in combination with altered immune status, may account for graft infections occurring years after the original operation. It is also possible for a low-grade graft infection to become secondarily infected by a more virulent organism. For example, *Escherichia coli* urosepsis might inoculate an unincorporated graft involved by a *S. epidermidis* biofilm infection, converting a low-grade infection into a more virulent graft infection.

Mechanical Erosion

Erosion of a prosthetic graft through the skin or into the gastrointestinal or genitourinary tract results in a perigraft infection that then spreads along the graft length. GEE/GEF can develop as a result of pulsatile pressure transmitted via an aortic graft to the overlying adherent bowel, most commonly to the third part of the duodenum. The reported incidence after prosthetic aortic grafting is 0.4% to 2%. Three anatomic types of graft-enteric communication have been reported: (1) direct fistula to the suture line, (2) fistula to false aneurysm, and (3) prosthetic erosion into the bowel. Theoretically, this complication can be avoided by adequate coverage of the graft with retroperitoneal tissue or omentum at the time of implantation. The pathogenesis of GEF involves complex anatomy, including communication of the bowel with the graft-artery suture line, and in one half of cases a pseudoaneurysm of the aorta is present. In most patients, the clinical history indicates that the infection of the aortic prosthesis occurred first, followed by extension to involve the suture line with infection weakening the native aortic wall and subsequent pseudoaneurysm formation. The microflora associated with GEE/GEF are commonly gram-positive organisms, except in a graft segment with bile staining where *E. coli* and other coliforms are isolated. Graft erosion through intact skin is most commonly the result of a low-grade infection caused by *S. epidermidis*. The perigraft infection produces an inflammatory reaction that damages overlying skin and leads to a graft-cutaneous fistula. In rare cases, skin injury at the time of extra-anatomic graft tunneling can result in cutaneous exposure of the prosthesis.

Involvement by a Contiguous Infectious Process

Prosthetic grafts can become colonized as a result of an adjacent infection. The most common clinical scenarios are an aortofemoral graft limb infection due to diverticulitis and peripheral graft infection due to an infected lymphocele. Frequently the graft segment adjacent to the contiguous bowel or soft tissue infection may be involved. Initial treatment should be directed at drainage of the perigraft abscess and, if present, the bowel abnormality.

Pathobiology of Biomaterial-Associated Infections

The most common cause of graft infection is *microorganism contamination* of the graft during implantation or in the perioperative period. The pathogenesis of biomaterial-associated infection involves the following fundamental steps:

1. Bacterial adhesion to graft or stent surfaces
2. Microcolony formation within a bacterial biofilm
3. Activation of host defenses (neutrophil chemotaxis, complement activation)
4. Inflammatory response involving perigraft tissues and the graft-artery anastomoses

The vascular prosthesis and the adherent bacteria act together as a co-inflammatory stimulus to activate the immune system, in particular the inflammatory cytokines. The result is an inflammatory process that attempts to localize the infection but is accompanied by tissue-damaging effects, including recruitment of polymorphonuclear granulocytes, production of tumor necrosis factor α, and activation of other humoral and cellular defenses (Fig. 59-1). The prosthesis is not an "innocent

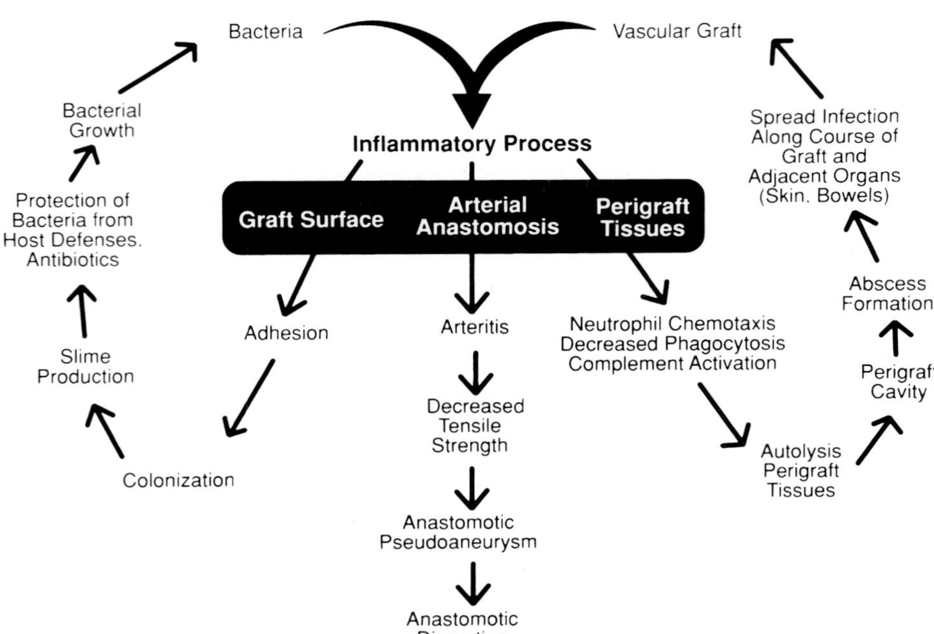

FIGURE 59-1 Pathogenesis of vascular biomaterial-associated infections.

bystander"; by eliciting an immune foreign body reaction, it produces an acidic, ischemic microenvironment conducive to bacterial biofilm formation and proliferation. Unlike autogenous grafts, implanted prosthetic grafts do not develop rich vascular connections with surrounding tissue, and this prevents host immune defenses and antibiotics from exerting maximal effect on infecting organisms. The extent of perigraft inflammation and tissue injury depends on the virulence of the infecting organism, but even with indolent infections, tissue autolysis can occur that leads to vessel wall or anastomotic disruption and hemorrhage. Initially, the perigraft tissue inflammation produces a failure of graft incorporation (healing) and formation of a perigraft cavity or abscess. As the infectious process spreads along the length of the graft, adjacent structures (e.g., adjacent artery, skin, bowel) can be involved. The pathobiology is manifested clinically with a spectrum of signs, including graft sepsis, localized perigraft abscess, anastomotic pseudoaneurysm, graft-cutaneous sinus tract, or GEE or GEF (secondary aortoduodenal fistula). Often, the only features of a low-grade, "late" graft infection are the absence of graft incorporation with surrounding tissue and perigraft fluid containing large numbers of white blood cells (WBCs).

Predisposing Factors

Graft infections are commonly associated with (1) operative events that result in bacterial contamination of the graft or (2) patient risk factors that predispose to infection (i.e., impaired host defenses) (Table 59-3). Faulty sterile surgical technique can facilitate bacterial inoculation from the patient's endogenous flora, the operating room environment, or the surgical team. Several conditions accentuate this mechanism, including prolonged preoperative hospital stay (allowing skin colonization by more resistant organisms), emergency procedures, operative procedures longer than 4 hours, and operations complicated by wound hematoma or graft thrombosis.[58] All reoperative vascular procedures are associated with an increased risk of infection due to a higher frequency of wound colonization and healing complications (e.g., hematoma, lymphocele, and dermal necrosis). Concomitant biliary (e.g., cholecystectomy), bowel (e.g., colon resection), and urologic (e.g., ureter repair) procedures also increase the risk of bacteria contacting the graft during the procedure. More often, the graft colonization occurs as a result of a postoperative complication such as bile fistula or

Table 59-3 Risk Factors for Graft Infection

Bacterial Contamination of the Graft
Faulty sterile technique
Prolonged preoperative hospital stay
Emergency surgery
Extended operative time
Reoperative vascular procedure
Simultaneous gastrointestinal procedure
Remote infection
Postoperative superficial wound infection/skin necrosis/seroma/lymphocele
Altered Host Defenses
Local factors
Biomaterial foreign body reaction
Bacterial slime production producing a protective biofilm
Systemic factors
Malnutrition
Leukopenia/lymphoproliferative disorder
Malignancy
Corticosteroid administration
Chemotherapy
Diabetes mellitus
Chronic renal failure
Autoimmune disease

anastomosis breakdown. One or more of these risk factors can be identified in more than 90% of patients who develop a graft infection.

Local and systemic conditions that diminish host defenses are also important risk factors for graft infection. All biomaterials produce a local foreign body reaction that impedes tissue ingrowth and neutrophil (WBC) bactericidal function. The architecture of prosthetic grafts permits bacterial colonization within the interstices of the biomaterial and formation of biofilms that resist both antibiotic and WBC penetration. An important virulence factor of gram-positive and gram-negative bacteria is the ability to produce an extracellular glycocalyx called *slime* that protects bacteria within adherent microcolonies. Body surface culture results indicate that most patients who undergo prosthetic graft implant procedures are colonized with slime-producing bacteria strains of staphylococci, the primary opportunists of foreign body infections. The altered immune function associated with malignancy, lymphoproliferative disorders, or drug administration (e.g., steroids or chemotherapy) can predispose patients to graft infection with low numbers of contaminating bacteria.

■ PREVENTION

Prevention of graft infection is an important concept, and the surgical team must be cognizant of preoperative, operative, and postoperative prophylactic measures. Vascular infections can be minimized if the following principles are applied:

- Avoid a prolonged preoperative hospital stay to minimize the development of skin flora resistant to commonly used antibiotics (i.e., hospital-acquired strains).
- Have patients shower or scrub with an antibacterial soap the night before the operation.
- Control any remote infection before an elective operation, especially if a prosthetic graft or stent implantation is planned.
- Remove operative site hair immediately before the operation using clippers rather than a razor to minimize skin trauma.
- Protect vascular grafts from contact with any potentially contaminating sources, especially the exposed skin adjacent to the operative field, by the use of iodine-impregnated plastic drapes or antibiotic-soaked towels.
- Avoid simultaneous gastrointestinal procedures during grafting procedures to prevent graft contamination with enteric organisms.
- Use prophylactic antibiotics whenever a prosthetic graft or stent is implanted.
- Longer (>48-hour) duration of perioperative antibiotics should also be considered when two or more patient-related risk factors for surgical wound infection are identified, including extremes of age, malnutrition, chronic illnesses (diabetes, chronic obstructive lung disease), remote infections, immunosuppression, recent operations, or prior irradiation of the surgical site.

Prophylactic antibiotics should be infused before incision of the skin, and at regular intervals during the procedure to maintain tissue drug levels above the minimal bactericidal

Table 59-4 Antibiotic Prophylaxis in Adults Undergoing Prosthetic Graft or Patch Implantation During Clean Surgical Procedures*

Cefazolin 1-2 g IV slowly prior to induction of anesthesia and repeated (1-2 g) q 8 hours for 24-48 hours, or cefuroxime 1.5 g IV and q 12 hours for total of 6 g; a single dose of cefazolin 1 g IV is recommended prior to endovascular stent deployment

When methicillin-resistant *Staphylococcus aureus* is cultured on body surfaces or is a known important pathogen in hospitalized patients, add vancomycin 1 g IV infused over 1 hour

If the patient has a cephalosporin allergy, give aztreonam 1 g IV q 8 hours for 24 hours

If patient has a vancomycin allergy, give clindamycin 900 mg IV over 20-30 minutes followed by 450-900 mg IV q 8 hours for 24 hours

*There is no evidence to support prophylaxis until central venous or Foley catheters are removed.
IV, intravenous.

concentration for expected pathogens (Table 59-4). Additional dosing may be needed during the operation depending on the rate of drug elimination and volume of distribution, larger or more frequent dosing necessary during prolonged (>4-hour) procedures or excessive changes in blood volume, fluid administration, or renal blood flow during the procedure. Culture-specific antibiotics should be prescribed for patients undergoing vascular graft implantation who have coexisting infections of the leg or another remote site. At some vascular centers, prophylactic antibiotics are continued for 3 to 5 days in patients deemed to be at high risk for infection from bacteremia, prolonged preprocedure hospitalization, or high (>10%) institutional wound infection rates.

Meticulous attention to sterile technique is imperative to avoid bacterial contact of vascular devices with implant procedures, especially during emergency or prolonged reconstructive procedures. The graft can be protected from potentially contaminating sources, especially the exposed skin, by the use of iodine-impregnated plastic drapes or antibiotic-soaked towels or sponges. Careful handling of the tissues, meticulous hemostasis to prevent hematoma formation, and closure of the groin incisions in multiple layers to eliminate dead space are important technical measures that decrease wound healing problems and subsequent infection. Irrigating wounds with topical antibiotics before closure or soaking the prosthetic has been shown to decrease wound infection rates. In a randomized clinical trial of 2522 patients, use of a rifampin-soaked (1 mg/mL) gelatin-impregnated polyester aortofemoral graft reduced groin wound infection rates (4.4% vs. 2.7% control, $P < 0.05$), but subsequent graft infection rates were similar (0.6% vs. 0.3%, controls).[11] All graft infections were caused by *S. aureus*.

Simultaneous gastrointestinal procedures should be avoided during grafting procedures to prevent graft contamination with enteric organisms. A possible exception is cholecystectomy for asymptomatic cholelithiasis. An 18% incidence of postoperative acute cholecystitis has been reported in patients following elective AAA repair, and a Mayo Clinic retrospective review of simultaneous cholecystectomy with aortic reconstruction indicated a low risk of graft infection but an overall higher procedural complication rate.[18] Cholecystectomy should be performed after aortic grafting and the retroperitoneum has been closed over the vascular prosthesis. If an unplanned enterotomy should occur during celiotomy, graft implantation should be postponed. The arterial reconstruction can be scheduled for several days later with planned implantation of an antibiotic-impregnated prosthesis, and if feasible, via a retroperitoneal approach.

After prosthetic graft implantation, patients should be informed of the potential risk for graft colonization and infection via bacteremia, especially following interventional procedures such as dental work, colonoscopy, and cystoscopy. Antibiotic prophylaxis is recommended for these procedures: amoxicillin 2 g orally 1 hour prior to the procedure or, if a penicillin allergy is present, clindamycin 500 mg orally 1 hour prior to the procedure.

■ BACTERIOLOGY

Although virtually any microorganism can infect a vascular prosthesis, *S. aureus* is the most prevalent pathogen, accounting for one fourth to one half of infections depending on the implant site (Table 59-5). Graft infections due to *S. epidermidis* or gram-negative bacteria have increased in frequency. This change in the microbiology of graft infection is the result of reporting both early- and late-appearing graft infections, including aortic graft infections associated with GEE or GEF. Surgeons have also become aware of microbiologic sampling errors in late infections owing to low numbers of bacteria present within the graft surface biofilm.[57] Graft infections associated with negative culture results are caused by *S. epidermidis* or other coagulase-negative staphylococci, and on occasion by *Candida* species. Infections due to gram-negative bacteria such as *E. coli, Pseudomonas, Klebsiella, Enterobacter,* and *Proteus* species are particularly virulent. The incidence of anastomotic dehiscence and artery rupture is high and is due to the ability of the organisms to produce destructive endotoxins (e.g., elastase and alkaline protease) that compromise wall structural integrity.[19,20] Fungal infections of grafts (e.g., with *Candida, Mycobacterium,* and *Aspergillus* species) are rare, and most patients with such infections either are severely immunosuppressed or have an established fungal infection elsewhere.

Methicillin-resistant *S. aureus* (MRSA) now accounts for one fourth of early prosthetic graft infections.[9] The recent increase in MRSA wound infections may justify use of specific antibiotic prophylaxis for all vascular device implant procedures. Gram-negative organisms such as *Proteus, Pseudomonas, Klebsiella,* and *Enterobacter* species can also be involved in early postoperative graft infections, with anastomotic bleeding most commonly associated with a *Pseudomonas aeruginosa* infection. Graft complications such as GEE or GEF typically involve infection with gram-negative enteric bacteria and occur beyond 4 months after implantation. Late-appearing graft infections are commonly associated with less virulent bacteria such as *S. epidermidis*, but the incidence of MRSA has been noted to be increasing. Coagulase-negative staphylococci are present in normal skin flora but have the ability to adhere to and colonize biomaterials where growth occurs within a biofilm on the prosthetic surfaces.

Table 59-5 Bacteriology of Prosthetic Vascular Graft Infections: Incidence from 1400 Collected Cases

	INCIDENCE (%)					
MICROORGANISM	**AEF**	**AI**	**AF**	**FD**	**TA**	**ICS**
Staphylococcus aureus	4	3	27	28	32	50
Staphylococcus epidermidis	2	3	34	11	20	15
Streptococcus species	9	3	8	11	2	3
Escherichia coli	28	30	12	7	2	5
Pseudomonas species	3	7	6	16	10	6
Klebsiella species	5	10	5	2	2	4
Enterobacter species	5	13	2	2	2	—
Enterococcus species	8	10	2	7	6	—
Bacteroides species	8	3	3	2	—	—
Proteus species	4	—	4	7	2	—
Candida species	3	—	2	1	4	5
Serratia species	1	—	1	2	—	—
Other species	3	2	3	6	2	—
No growth culture	8	13	2	2	9	12

AEF, aortoenteric fistula or erosion (n = 450); AI, aortoiliac or aortic tube graft (n = 54); AF, aortobifemoral or iliofemoral graft (n = 460); FD, femoropopliteal, femorotibial, axillofemoral, or femorofemoral graft (n = 285); TA, thoracic aorta graft (n = 65); ICS, innominate, carotid, or subclavian bypass graft or carotid patch following endarterectomy (n = 90).

■ DIAGNOSIS

Prompt diagnosis and treatment of prosthetic graft infections are essential to avoid complications (e.g., sepsis and hemorrhage) and death. Clinical manifestations are varied and may be subtle, particularly those associated with cavitary graft infections. Operative exploration is the most accurate method for confirming infection and may be necessary when clinical suspicion of GEE exists. In equivocal cases, the vascular surgeon must prove that a graft infection is not present. Most graft infections are detected more than 4 months after graft implantation,[6,7,68,77] and fewer than 20% are detected in the early postoperative period. The urgency of diagnostic evaluation depends on the presentation and the clinical status of the patient.

Clinical Evaluation

Patient History

Vascular surgeons should maintain a low threshold for proceeding with additional diagnostic testing when any symptom or sign suggests graft infection. Aortic grafts confined to the abdomen can present as unexplained sepsis, prolonged postoperative ileus, or abdominal distention as the only clinical signs. If infection involves an extracavitary graft (i.e., in leg, groin, or neck incisions), the initial sign of infection is an inflammatory perigraft process with cellulitis; the development of a cutaneous sinus tract or anastomotic pseudoaneurysm is a later sign. Any patient with gastrointestinal bleeding and an aortic graft should be considered to have graft infection and GEE until another source of bleeding is conclusively identified by endoscopy or no graft-bowel communication is verified at operation.[6,67,76]

In patients with vague symptoms suggestive of and ultrasound or computed tomography (CT) evidence of perigraft fluid, careful review of the operative history and surgical notes may furnish clues that further support the diagnosis of graft infection and provide the rationale for invasive diagnostic testing. The patient should also be queried about recent medical illnesses that may have resulted in hematogenous or lymphatic seeding of the graft with bacteria. Early graft infections due to *S. aureus* or other gram-negative bacteria typically present within weeks of the procedure as fever, leukocytosis, and obvious perigraft purulence.

Bacteremia is a sign of an advanced graft infection associated with artery wall or mural thrombus infection or the secondary development of endocarditis. Patients with a graft infection due to *S. epidermidis* typically present months to years after graft implantation with graft-healing complication (e.g., anastomotic aneurysm, perigraft cavity with fluid, or graft-cutaneous sinus tract). Systemic signs of sepsis (e.g., fever, leukocytosis, and bacteremia) are characteristically absent.

Physical Examination

The clinician should carefully examine the site or sites of graft implantation for any signs of inflammation. Surgical incisions should be carefully inspected for erythema and draining sinuses. Masses near anastomotic sites can represent perigraft abscesses or anastomotic pseudoaneurysms. The extremities should be examined for signs of septic embolization (i.e., a cluster of petechiae downstream from the infected graft). Other sources of infection, such as infected foot lesions, osteomyelitis, and infected urinary calculi, should be sought because these conditions can predispose to hematogenous bacterial seeding and graft colonization.

Diagnostic Testing

An elevated WBC count (15,000 to 18,000 cells/mL) with left-shifted differential and an increased erythrocyte sedimentation rate (>20 mm/min) are common but nonspecific findings in patients with graft infection and fever. Routine laboratory testing should also include urinalysis, blood cultures, and cultures of other clinical sites of infection, such as foot ulcers or surgical wound drainage. Positive blood cultures are uncommon (<5%) but, when present, indicate an advanced graft infection. All laboratory test results may be normal in patients with late-appearing perigraft infections due to *S. epidermidis*. In patients with suspected GEE, a stool guaiac is positive in only approximately two thirds of patients with documented lesions.

Vascular Imaging

Vascular imaging is essential for the diagnosis and treatment of graft infection and its sequelae. Anatomic signs of graft infection, such as perigraft abscess, anastomotic aneurysm, and GEE/GEF, can be accurately identified (with > 90% sensitivity) using a combination of ultrasonography, CT, magnetic resonance imaging (MRI), arteriography, or endoscopy. Functional radionuclide imaging (gallium 67 citrate, indium 111-labeled leukocyte, technetium 99m hexametazime-labeled leukocyte) can confirm the presence of a clinically suspected graft infection when anatomic signs of perigraft abscess are equivocal. The combination of anatomic and functional vascular imaging techniques is highly accurate (sensitivity, 80% to 100%; specificity, 50% to 90%) for confirming the presence of infection, planning management, and assessing operative sites for residual or recurrent infection (Fig. 59-2). Arteriography is used to develop an operative strategy for revascularization and

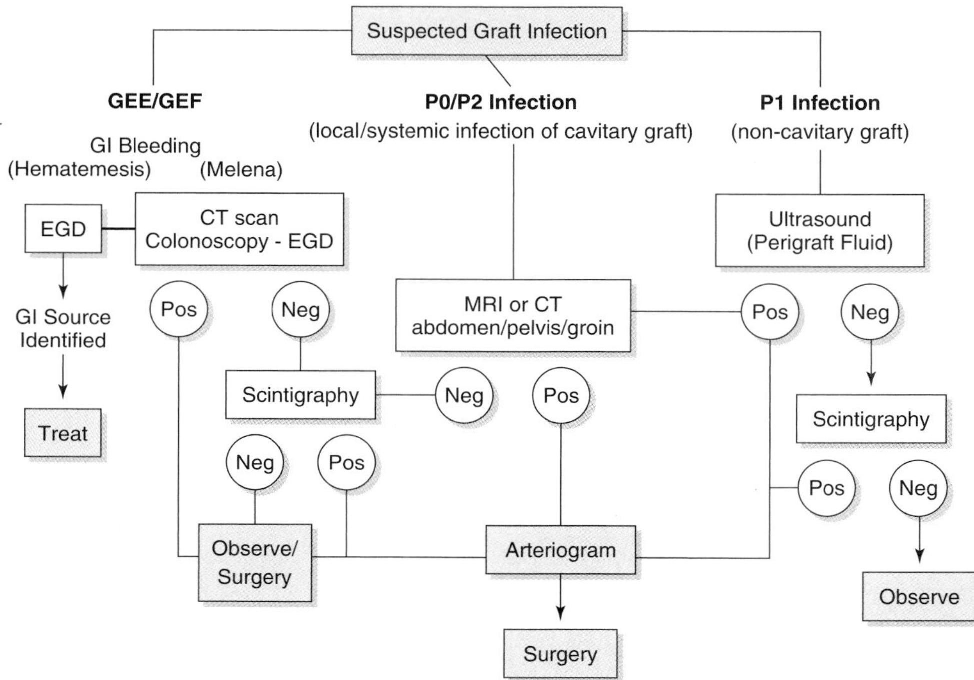

FIGURE 59-2 Algorithm for evaluation of a suspected prosthetic graft infection. GEE, graft-enteric erosion; GEF, graft-enteric fistula; EGD, esophagogastroduodenoscopy; GI, gastrointestinal; Pos, positive; Neg, negative.

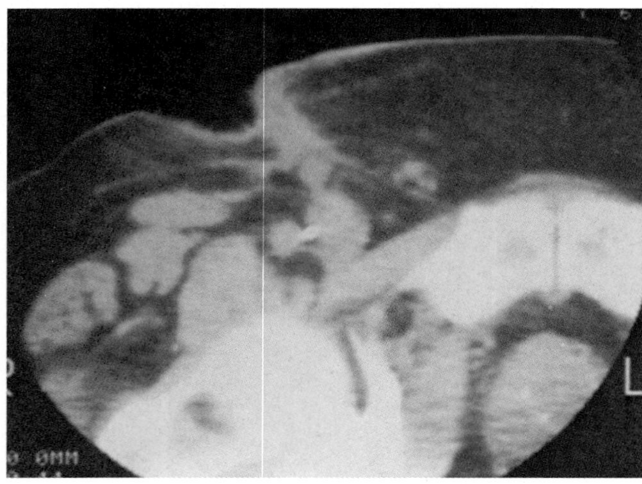

FIGURE 59-3 CT scan of an infected aortofemoral graft limb showing perigraft inflammation extending to the skin. The patient presented with groin sinus tract. Graft culture isolated *Staphylococcus epidermidis*.

should be routine. Imaging studies are performed to identify safe sites for operative exposure, to place vascular clamps, and to minimize the likelihood of injury or organ/limb ischemia due to anatomic anomalies or concomitant occlusive disease. Each imaging technique has unique diagnostic application, and the necessary extent of testing is patient specific.

Contrast-Enhanced CT

- The preferred initial imaging technique for suspected aortofemoral, abdominal aorta, or thoracic aorta (P0, P2) graft infections
- Diagnostic criteria consistent with infection include the loss of normal tissue planes of the retroperitoneal structures (indicative of inflammation); abnormal collections of fluid or gas around the graft; false aneurysm formation; hydronephrosis; adjacent vertebral osteomyelitis; and juxta-aortic retroperitoneal abscess (Fig. 59-3). Any gas in periprosthetic tissues beyond 6 months of implantation is an abnormal CT finding.
- Should be performed with intravenous and oral contrast to better identify the lumen of the graft, delineate periprosthetic abscess, and define the relationship of the duodenum and small and large bowel to the aortic prosthesis
- Testing is sufficiently fast to be useful in evaluating symptomatic but hemodynamically stable patients with suspected GEF/GEE.

Ultrasonography

- Readily available imaging technique that is suited for "portable" bedside examination
- Initial imaging study for extracavitary (P1, P2, P3) graft infections
- Color duplex scanning can reliably differentiate perigraft fluid collection from anastomotic pseudoaneurysm, hematoma, and soft tissue masses.
- Diagnostic accuracy depends on the skill of the examiner and the ability to adequately image the graft. Imaging of abdominal cavity grafts can be obscured by intestinal gas and obesity.
- Most accurate vascular imaging technique for verifying vessel or graft patency and assessing pulsatile masses adjacent to grafts in the groin and limbs

MRI

- Provides superior anatomic imaging compared with CT, including the ability to distinguish between perigraft fluid and fibrosis based on signal intensity differences between T1- and T2-weighted images
- Useful in patients with renal insufficiency since gadolinium contrast is not nephrotoxic
- Can produce angiographic images of sufficient resolution to plan surgical revascularization

Functional White Blood Cell Scanning

- All radionuclide imaging techniques are used to demonstrate abnormal accumulation of leukocytes in perigraft graft tissues.
- Type of radionuclide used (gallium 67 citrate, indium 111-labeled leukocyte, technetium 99m hexametazime-labeled leukocyte) can vary and affects diagnostic accuracy
- Not useful during the early postoperative course because of nonspecific radionuclide uptake in the perigraft tissues
- Normal scans (i.e., no labeled leukocyte accumulation) have been reported in late-appearing aortic graft infection and documented GEE cases.
- Accuracy (positive predictive value) of the functional imaging scans, especially indium 111-labeled WBC scans, approaches 80% to 90% in the detection of graft infection.
- IgG scans are preferred over leukocyte scans by some vascular groups because of the ease of preparation, the lack of staff exposure to the patient's blood, the absence of concomitant red blood cell and platelet imaging, and the long shelf life.
- Can be used with MRI and CT to delineate accurately the extent of graft involvement

Endoscopy

- An important diagnostic modality in patients with suspected GEF/GEE (Fig. 59-4)
- Essential that the entire upper gastrointestinal tract be inspected, including the third and fourth portions of the duodenum, the most common sites of GEE
- Patients with recent massive gastrointestinal hemorrhage should be examined *in the operating room*, with preparation for operation should exsanguination from the fistula be induced.
- Can sometimes (<20%) visualize the graft eroded through the bowel mucosa, but the primary goal is to rule out other sources of gastrointestinal bleeding (gastritis, ulcer disease, diverticula, cancer)
- Negative examination findings do *not* exclude the possibility of an aortoduodenal fistula.

Arteriography

- Can accurately identify infection-associated complications, such as graft rupture and anastomotic aneurysm
- Biplanar aortic angiography with visualization of lower limb runoff is recommended to assess the patency of the

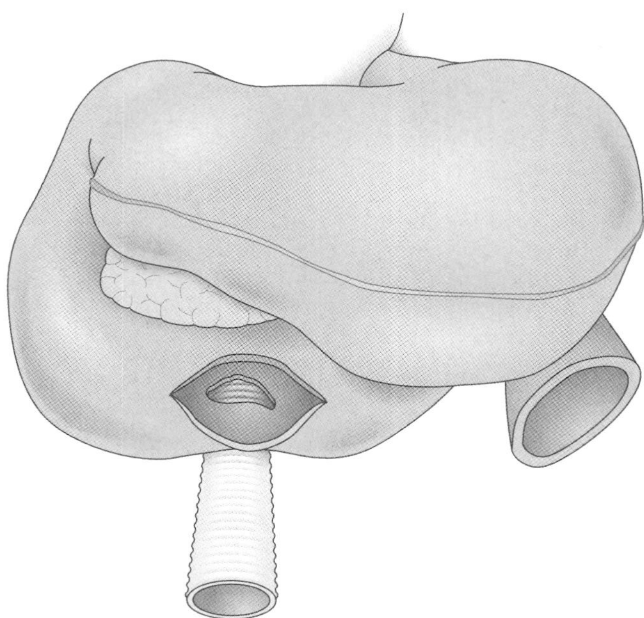

FIGURE 59-4 Graft-enteric fistula.

visceral and renal vessels and evaluate the status of the proximal aorta and distal vessels as potential sites for extra-anatomic (e.g., thoracofemoral) bypass grafts.

- Should be obtained routinely unless necessary anatomy is provided by CT or MR angiography or precluded by emergency operation

Microbiologic Methods

Recovery of microorganisms from sites of graft infection, either suspected or clinically apparent, is necessary to confirm the diagnosis and to select appropriate antibiotic therapy. Routine cultures of graft surfaces and perigraft fluid are usually adequate in patients who have graft infections associated with fever, leukocytosis, perigraft abscess, or cellulitis. Virulent organisms, such as *S. aureus*, streptococci, and gram-negative bacteria, produce systemic signs of graft sepsis and are readily identified. However, surface swabs may not recover less virulent pathogens that do not invade perigraft tissues. A Gram stain of tissue or fluid from around an unincorporated prosthetic graft showing no organisms is not sufficient to exclude the presence of a low-grade graft infection because the bacteria can reside within a surface biofilm. To reliably recover microorganisms from within the biofilm, mechanical (tissue grinding) or ultrasound disruption of the biofilm of an explanted graft segment must be performed prior to incubation in broth culture media (Fig. 59-5). Placement of the graft in a trypticase soy broth media is believed to maximize bacterial growth and recovery because the liquid medium allows submersion of the graft and optimal exposure of any adherent bacteria to the nutrient medium. The use of mechanical disruption and broth cultures is particularly useful for confirming graft infections with *S. epidermidis*. Culture tubes should be maintained for 5 to 7 days to exclude growth. These techniques overcome the sampling errors of routine culturing methods in isolating bacteria harbored in slowly growing colonies.

Operative Findings

The definitive diagnostic test for suspected graft infection is operative exploration. Exposure of the graft permits the surgeon to access graft healing and surrounding tissues for signs of infection. Exploration, graft excision, and broth culture of the graft material are often the only reliable methods of identifying the causative bacteria.[6,11] Operation is also an essential diagnostic test for patients with a history

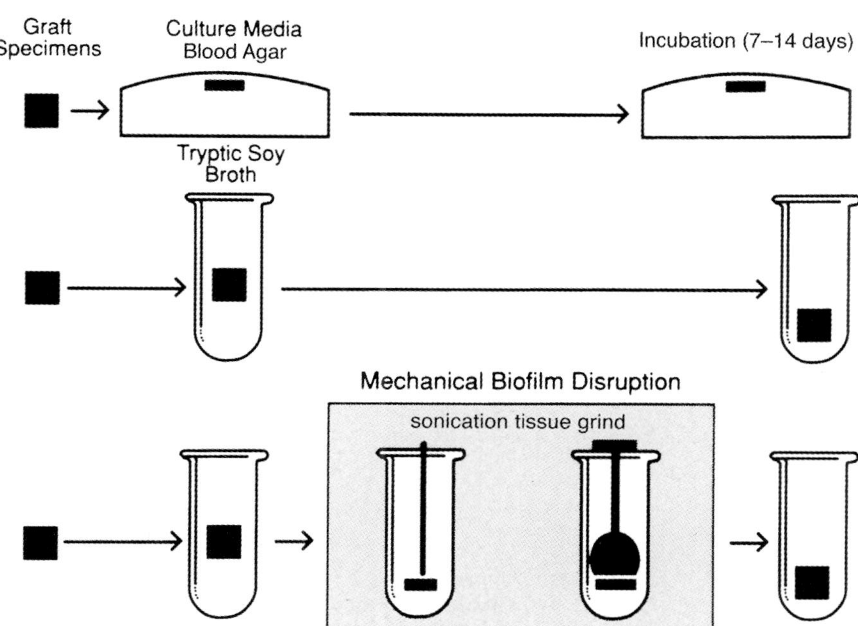

FIGURE 59-5 Culture techniques for recovery of bacteria from prosthetic vascular grafts.

of aortic surgery and gastrointestinal bleeding when all other sources of bleeding have been excluded. Approximately one half of patients with GEE/GEF are diagnosed with certainty by CT or MRI methods described previously.[66,75] Complete mobilization of the duodenum and dissection of small bowel from the retroperitoneal aortic graft is necessary to exclude GEE. The operative finding of a bowel segment adherent to the prosthetic graft and a CT scan demonstrating perigraft inflammation are pathognomonic for GEE.

■ MANAGEMENT STRATEGIES

The clinical spectrum of graft infection permits surgeons to individualize treatment. The surgeon should select a procedure that the patient can tolerate and that eradicates the clinical manifestations and potential complications of the infectious process. Available treatment options can include graft excision without revascularization, graft preservation, graft excision coupled with extra-anatomic or ex-situ bypass (conventional management), and graft replacement in situ (Fig. 59-6). Which option is selected depends on the clinical presentation and microbiology of the graft infection (Table 59-6). Observed advantages of the in-situ replacement therapy compared with conventional management are a shorter operative time, less surgical stress, reduced rate of limb loss, and improved graft patency. Judicious patient selection is key, since persistent infection is the failure mode of in-situ replacement. The lower limb deep veins (femoropopliteal vein), which are of suitable caliber for aortoiliac reconstruction, have been used successfully as in-situ replacements for infected aortoiliac and aortofemoral prosthetic grafts. The aortoiliac reconstruction with the femoral vein has demonstrated excellent durability (85% primary patency), and minimal morbidity in the donor lower limb(s). In-situ prosthetic replacement is appropriate in properly chosen patients, but autogenous reconstruction is superior in reducing the risk of reinfection. In general, the more virulent the infectious process, the higher the failure rate of any attempt to preserve the graft or in performing in-situ replacement. For patients with prohibitive risks for total graft excision, partial graft preservation may be the only viable treatment option.

General Principles

Preparing the Patient for Surgery

When a patient presents in septic shock or hypovolemia secondary to anastomotic bleeding resulting from an infected graft, there is little time for preparation. Adequate resuscitation with blood and fluid volume; perioperative cardiopulmonary monitoring; administration of broad-spectrum, high-dose antibiotics; and thoughtful planning of the surgical approach are the essential elements of urgent preoperative treatment. Delay in removing the infected graft in these critically ill patients until the sepsis is controlled is not recommended.

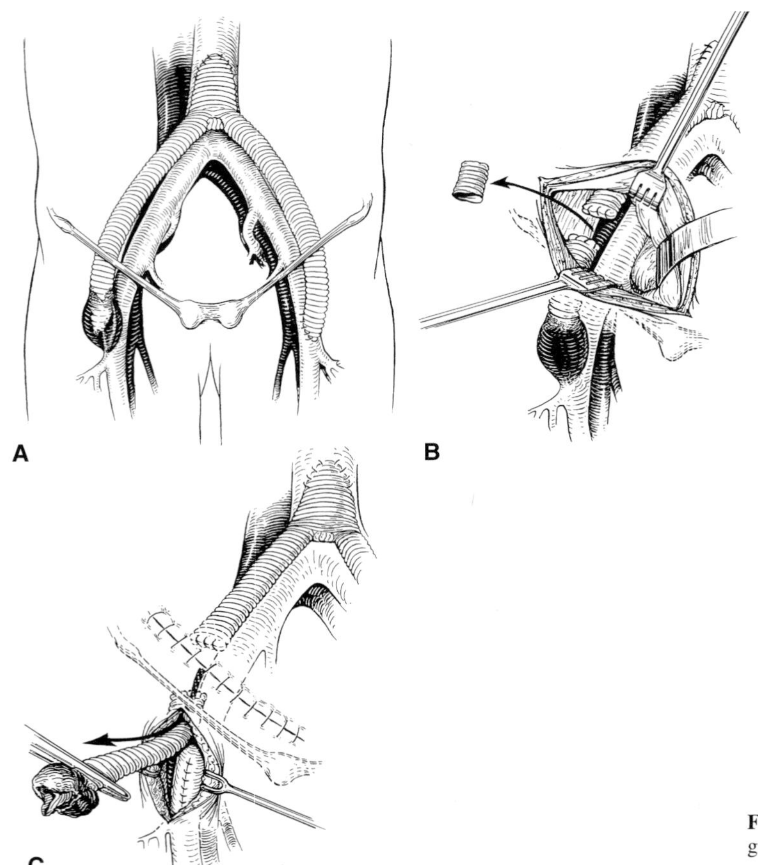

FIGURE 59-6 Excision of an infected femoral graft. **A,** Localized groin infection. **B,** Retroperitoneal exposure of noninfected graft segment. **C,** Excision of infected graft segment. (See text for details.)

Table 59-6 Patient Selection Criteria or Treatment of a Prosthetic Graft Infection by Excision, In-Situ Replacement, or Ex-Situ Bypass and Graft Excision

TREATMENT OPTION	CLINICAL PRESENTATION	MICROBIOLOGY
Graft preservation	Early infection and no sepsis	All except *Pseudomonas*
Excision alone	Graft thrombosis and adequate collaterals	Positive cultures
In-situ replacement		
Autogenous vein	Invasive graft infections without sepsis or GEE/GEF	Positive cultures
Allograft	Invasive graft infection without sepsis and no suitable autogenous conduit	Positive cultures
Rifampin-bonded graft	Localized biofilm graft infections	*Staphylococcus epidermidis*
Excision and ex-situ bypass		
Simultaneous	Unstable patient with GEE/GEF	No exclusion criteria
Preliminary—staged	Stable patient with aortic infection ± GEE/GEF	No exclusion criteria

GEE/GEF, graft-enteric erosion/fistula.

Fortunately, most cases of graft infection are discovered in time to allow adequate preoperative preparation, identification of the infecting pathogen, and determination of the extent of graft infection. Patients should be prepared, physiologically and psychologically, for the most extensive operation that may be required.

- Cardiac function should be determined, and if abnormal, cardiac index and peripheral vascular resistance should be optimized with the administration of nitrates, antiarrhythmic medications, beta blockers, and α antagonists.
- Pulmonary status should be evaluated and augmented with bronchodilators and respiratory therapy as needed.
- If the serum creatinine level is abnormal (>1.5 mg/dL), renal function should be optimized by hydration, acetylcysteine (Mucomyst) prior to contrast agent administration, or low-dose dopamine (3 to 5 mg/kg/min).
- Malnourished patients with depleted nutritional reserves or who are "anergic" to a battery of standard skin tests may benefit from supplemental enteral or parenteral nutrition, if time permits.
- Diabetic patients should have glucose levels closely monitored and controlled prior to surgery.
- The colon should be cleansed with mechanical and nonabsorbable antibiotic preparations in patients who have a cavitary graft infection.
- Arterial circulation to the upper and lower extremities should be assessed by Doppler-derived pressure measurements and arteriography performed to assess for all potential revascularization alternatives to maintain limb perfusion after graft excision.
- Venous ultrasound of lower limb deep and superficial veins to assess patency and caliber should be performed if in-situ replacement is an option.
- Systemic antibiotics should be selected according to isolated or suspected pathogens.

Determining the Extent of Graft Infection

Persistent infection of a nonexcised graft segment or in the arterial graft bed is the major reason for treatment failure and the cause of morbidity and death.[75] Local control of infection is more successful when there is no gross purulence and when culture results are negative or *S. epidermidis* is recovered. CT, MRI, and WBC radionuclide scans are helpful in localizing the infected portion of the graft, but surgical exploration remains the most reliable method of determining the extent of graft infection. The finding of hydronephrosis on abdominal imaging studies is a reliable sign of advanced aortic graft infections that denotes diffuse graft involvement.

Removing the Graft

Removal of the entire infected graft is essential to eradicating the infectious process in patients who are septic, present with anastomotic bleeding, or have complete graft involvement. Attempts at graft preservation have been reported, but infection can persist, particularly if the graft is made of Dacron. Treatment by serial wound débridement risks exsanguination from anastomotic or arterial rupture if wounds are left open. Calligaro and coworkers recommended specific criteria and treatment principles that, when adhered to, resulted in successful prosthetic graft preservation in approximately 70% of cases (Table 59-7).[16-18] Graft infection caused by *Pseudomonas* species, a virulent pathogen, represents a contraindication for management by graft preservation adjuncts. At the time of serial infected wound débridements, implantation of antibiotic (vancomycin, gentamicin)-impregnated beads for 5 to 7 days can assist in sterilization of the wound. Once wound cultures are negative, the graft can be replaced and the reconstruction covered with a muscle flap.

Table 59-7 Selection Criteria and Treatment Adjuncts for Selective Graft Preservation for Early Extracavitary Infections

Selection Criteria for Graft Preservation
Patent graft that is not constructed of polyester (Dacron)
Anastomoses are intact and not involved with infection
Patient has no clinical signs of sepsis
Treatment Adjuncts for Graft Preservation
Repeated and aggressive wound débridement in the operating room
Daily wound dressing change at 8-hour intervals using dilute povidone-iodine (1 mL of 1% povidone-iodine in 1 L normal saline)
If wound is closed between serial wound débridement, antibiotic (vancomycin, tobramycin)-impregnated methylmethacrylate beads are implanted in the subcutaneous tissue
Administration of culture-specific antibiotics
Rotational muscle coverage of the exposed prosthetic graft segment

Table 59-8 Results of Treatment for Aortic Graft Infections

PROCEDURE	OPERATIVE MORTALITY RATE, %	AMPUTATION RATE, %	REINFECTION RATE, %	SURVIVAL >1 YEAR, %	COMMENTS
Ex-situ bypass and total graft excision	11-24	5-25	3-13	73-86	Considered the gold standard, especially for GEF
In-situ replacement and total graft excision					
Deep vein	7-15	2-5	0-1	82-85	Complicated procedure; some patients are not candidates
Allograft	6-25*	5	10-15	70-80	Graft rupture and late deterioration can occur
Rifampin-polyester or PTFE graft	0-15*	<5	10-20	80-90	Bridge graft or used as in-situ replacement in biofilm infections

*Higher mortality (25-50%) when used to treat GEE/GEFs.
GEE, graft-enteric erosion; GEF, graft-enteric fistula; PTFE, polytetrafluoroethylene.

For patients with infection localized to only a portion of an aortofemoral graft, a single treatment approach is not applicable or appropriate. Excision of the entire graft and extra-anatomic bypass are associated with amputation and mortality rates of 11% to 24% (Table 59-8). Morbidity continues to be high, owing to persistent infection of the aortic stump (10% incidence), recurrent infection of the extra-anatomic bypass (5% to 10% incidence), and future secondary procedures for thrombosis of the failed extra-anatomic bypass (25% to 50% incidence). The use of staged lower limb revascularization (preliminary axillofemoral bypass) followed in 1 or 2 days by aortic graft excision is associated with reduced morbidity.

In special cases, morbidity (death, amputation) may be decreased if the surgeon excises only the infected portion of the graft (partial graft excision), with distal revascularization via remote bypass (obturator) through tissues not involved with infection. At the site of graft retention, culture specimens should be obtained and topical antibiotics instilled via wound irrigation systems or antibiotic-impregnated bone cement beads to cleanse perigraft tissues. The quantity and virulence of the pathogens, the adequacy of local and systemic host defenses, and the extent of infections are critical factors that influence decision making and treatment outcomes.

Débridement of the Arterial Wall and Perigraft Tissues and Drainage

After graft excision, débridement of all inflamed tissues and drainage of the graft bed are important principles for preventing persistence of the infectious process. The artery wall adjacent to the infected graft is a potential reservoir of bacteria, and positive artery wall culture findings increase the risk of aorta stump or artery disruption.[5,7] The artery wall and perigraft tissues should be débrided back to normal-appearing tissues, especially in the presence of purulence or false aneurysm. Adequate débridement of the aorta should be confirmed by histologic examination, and if positive wall culture results are obtained, patients should be treated with long-term antibiotic therapy.[5]

It is essential to use monofilament permanent sutures to close a ligation artery or the aortic stump. Closed-suction drainage should be positioned in the infected graft bed when gross purulence is present. Coverage of the arterial closures with viable, noninfected tissue, such as an omental pedicle or rotational muscle flaps, lessens the risk of stump blowout and separates the arterial closures from adjacent organs, the graft bed, and drains. Antibiotic-impregnated (vancomycin, tobramycin) beads can also be left in the beds of infected grafts as an adjunct for tissue sterilization. The antibiotic beads are exchanged every 7 to 10 days until deep wound cultures yield no growth.

Antibiotic Therapy

When the pathogen(s) can be identified before operation, bactericidal antibiotics should be administered in large doses preoperatively and perioperatively. If the infecting organism has not been isolated, broad-spectrum antibiotics (i.e., an aminoglycoside plus semisynthetic penicillin), a second-generation cephalosporin, or ampicillin plus sulbactam should be given. If *S. aureus* or *S. epidermidis* is the most likely pathogen, parenteral therapy with a first- or second-generation cephalosporin and vancomycin is appropriate. Once operative cultures have isolated all infecting organisms, antibiotic coverage should be modified based on antibiotic susceptibility testing of the recovered strains. The duration of antibiotic administration after treatment by graft excision is empirical, but at least 2 weeks of systemic antibiotics is recommended. Patients who received long-term antibiotics (parenteral antibiotics for 6 weeks, followed by oral antibiotics for 6 months) had significantly better results than patients treated with short-term therapy (2 weeks). Oral antibiotic treatment of MRSA infections is now possible using linezolid 600 mg orally every 12 hours.[13] The incidences of recurrent infection and aortic stump sepsis may be decreased with long-term or lifelong antibiotic administration, especially in the presence of positive arterial wall cultures. In patients with negative wound or graft cultures, parenteral antibiotics (vancomycin) should be administered for 2 to 4 weeks, followed by 3 months of oral therapy (quinolone, amoxicillin/clavulanate).

Antibiotic therapy is an adjunct to the treatment of a vascular graft infection. Surgical management of the infection site by abscess drainage, débridement of devitalized tissue, and excision of the infected graft is essential. In selected patients, with exposed grafts but no involvement of anastomotic site, preservation of the graft with serial surgical wound débridement, coupled with antibiotic therapy and early muscle flap coverage, may be possible in selected patients. Repeat wound cultures should be performed if staged procedures are used to identify any development of bacterial resistance or change in the microbial flora. Patients with virulent graft infections may require nutritional support, in addition to antibiotic therapy, for successful resolution of the infectious process.

Revascularization of Organs and Limbs

Rarely can graft excision alone, without revascularization, be performed as treatment for a patent infected prosthetic graft. Occluded grafts and grafts implanted to alleviate symptoms of claudication may be treated by total graft excision without revascularization or in combination with endovascular angioplasty. An end-to-side anastomotic configuration permits reconstruction of the native arteries after graft excision via autogenous patch angioplasty alone or in combination with endarterectomy. If a monophasic Doppler arterial signal is present at the ankle after graft excision or if arterial systolic pressure is greater than 40 mm Hg at the ankle or forearm, delayed reconstruction is an option because sufficient collaterals are present to maintain limb viability. In the presence of critical limb ischemia (i.e., when no distal Doppler signal is audible), arterial revascularization should not be delayed because of the associated morbidity from ischemic compartment syndrome and nerve ischemia.

It is preferable to perform limb revascularization before the infected graft is removed; in the presence of anastomotic bleeding and shock, however, control of hemorrhage takes precedence. Autogenous tissue grafts (greater saphenous vein, femoral vein, endarterectomized iliac or superficial femoral artery), if available, are the conduits of choice for limb or organ revascularization. If a prosthetic graft is used for an ex-situ bypass, PTFE conduits are preferred to polyester grafts, although PTFE or a polyester antibiotic-impregnated graft may be the conduits of choice for the treatment of graft infection by either in-situ replacement or extra-anatomic bypass grafting.

Several vascular groups have demonstrated decreased morbidity and mortality with staged or sequential treatment as compared with traditional treatment (i.e., total graft excision followed by immediate extra-anatomic bypass).[62,68] Preliminary revascularization can be performed without increasing the risk of death, amputation, or new graft infection, and with staged treatment (i.e., revascularization followed in 1 to 2 days by total graft excision), the overall physiologic stress on the patient may be reduced. Sequential treatment also avoids the necessity of keeping the patient heparinized during total graft excision and closure of the artery or aorta stump.

The options of graft preservation or in-situ replacement can be applied in carefully selected cases. When infection involves the thoracic aorta or visceral segment of the abdominal aorta, in-situ replacement may be the only practical approach. The perigraft infectious process should be a low-grade one, not associated with anastomotic hemorrhage, and cultures should be sterile, or the anatomic and microbiologic characteristics of the graft infection should suggest infection with *S. epidermidis*. In-situ replacement has been used successfully to treat secondary aortoduodenal fistula, with an operative mortality rate as low as 19%. Patients with GEE and minimal retroperitoneal infection fared best.

In-situ replacement appears to be a safe and durable option for patients with prosthetic graft infections caused by *S. epidermidis*. From 1987 to 2000, the authors treated 45 aortoiliofemoral and 40 extracavitary prosthetic graft infections in patients presenting with groin false aneurysm, inflammatory mass, or groin sinus tract. Selection criteria and components of surgical management are outlined in Table 59-9. No deaths or early graft failures occurred, and during follow-up, all replacement grafts remained patent and without signs of infection. Ten percent of patients required an additional graft replacement for infection that developed proximal to or involved the in-situ replacement graft. Failure of the in-situ prosthetic procedures was the result of virulent (MRSA) and antibiotic-resistant bacterial strains.

In-situ treatment of bacterial biofilm graft infections is effective treatment for localized graft healing problems, but because of the indolent nature of this type of biomaterial infection, subsequent infection of previously uninvolved graft segments may be expected. When advanced biofilm aortic graft infections are encountered (i.e., P0 graft infection), in-situ replacement using the neoaortoiliac deep femoral vein procedure or an arterial allograft is preferred (Table 59-10; see also Table 59-9). In-situ graft replacement should be avoided when GEF is the presenting problem.

Table 59-9 Selection Criteria and Treatment Components of In-Situ Prosthetic Graft Replacement for Bacterial Biofilm Graft Infection

Selection Criteria
Clinical
Presentation month to years after graft implantation
No systemic signs of infection: afebrile, normal serum white blood cell count, sterile blood culture
Anatomic
Inflammation of tissue adjacent to prosthetic graft
Perigraft cavity with absence of graft incorporation
Weakening of graft-artery anastomosis (pseudoaneurysm)
Microbiologic
Perigraft fluid Gram stain: white blood cells, no bacteria
Perigraft fluid culture: no growth
Graft biofilm culture: coagulase-negative staphylococci (*Staphyloccocus epidermidis)*
Treatment Components
Preoperative and perioperative administration of vancomycin—beginning 3 days prior to replacement
Wide débridement of inflamed (abnormal) perigraft tissue and sinus tract, if present
Excision of anastomotic sites
Cleansing/débridement of tissues and retained graft segment with wound irrigation system
Replace with rifampin-soaked (60 mg/mL) polyester gelatin or collagen-impregnated polyester vascular prosthesis
Muscle flap coverage of replacement graft segment in groin, if feasible
Prolonged (6-week) parenteral administration of culture-specific antibiotics

Table 59-10 Operative Technical Details in Using Cryopreserved Arterial Allografts for Aortic Infection

Excise infected vascular segments with perivascular débridement
Allografts are thawed and rinsed immediately before implantation
Use appropriate-length allograft to perform a tension-free anastomosis
Through-and-through ligature of allograft side branches—avoid use of metal clips
End-to-end anastomosis to native arteries or retained prosthetic graft
Anastomotic reinforcement with allograft strips
Use gentamicin-impregnated fibrin glue at suture lines
Aggressive wound drainage

Treatment of Infected Graft Sites

Aortoiliac or Aortic Interposition Graft Infections

Aortoiliac or aortic interposition graft infections are best treated by preliminary (right-sided) axillobifemoral bypass grafting through clean, uninfected tissues, followed either during the same operation or 1 or 2 days later by total graft excision of the infected aortic graft (i.e., sequential treatment). Preliminary remote bypass is safe and is associated with lower morbidity than is traditional treatment.[66,75,99] Extra-anatomic bypass grafting should be performed before the contaminated abdomen or retroperitoneum is entered. Because the aortic graft is confined to the abdomen, the distal axillofemoral anastomoses can usually be attached to the common femoral arteries bilaterally.

After completion of the extra-anatomic bypass grafting, all wounds should be closed and covered with sterile protective dressings. Celiotomy or a left-sided retroperitoneal exposure is then performed to afford excision of the infected aortic graft. Heparinization should be used during the extra-anatomic revascularization procedure but should be reversed during excision of the infected graft. In cases with proximal and distal end-to-side anastomoses, in-situ autogenous reconstruction should be considered. This scenario is uncommon, however, because most aortic interposition and aortoiliac grafts were implanted to treat aneurysmal disease rather than atherosclerotic occlusive disease. Allograft replacement of an infected aortic graft has been advocated as a "bridge," but the logistics of cadaver aorta retrieval and maintaining a vascular tissue bank are not possible at most U.S. institutions. Cryopreserved aortic allografts demonstrate reduced antigenicity and improved cellular integrity as compared to fresh homografts, but technical problems with usage, including early rupture and persistent infection, have caused graft-related mortality of 5% and 6% in two large series.

The entire infected abdominal aortic graft should be excised. Achieving proximal control at the supraceliac aorta before approaching the proximal anastomosis is of value, especially in patients who have a proximal anastomotic aneurysm or a juxtarenal anastomosis. Meticulous care is necessary to dissect adherent viscera and duodenum from the graft capsule. If GEE or GEF is present, débridement of all necrotic or inflamed bowel wall is imperative, and primary end-to-end anastomosis of the bowel is preferred. The iliac arteries distal to the graft should also be exposed for distal control before excision of the graft. Culture of explanted graft material should be performed using standard broth media and biofilm culture techniques.

The aorta should be débrided to normal-appearing wall and closed with interlocking monofilament sutures. Use of pledgets is not recommended because they increase the risk of stump infection. A pedicle of omentum should be passed through the transverse mesocolon and carefully positioned over the aortic stump and into the bed of the excised graft. When necessary, the aorta can be excised to above the level of the renal arteries, in which case renal revascularization is achieved via bypasses originating from the splenic or hepatic arteries.[63] Closed-suction drains should be placed in the infected graft bed and brought out the flank contralateral to the axillofemoral graft limb.

The distal aorta or iliac arteries should also be closed with monofilament suture. The ureter should be located and protected from injury throughout the procedure. Preoperative placement of ureteral stents can be helpful; however, they are usually not necessary unless hydronephrosis is present. The site and the method of iliac artery ligation should be chosen to maintain perfusion to the colon, the pelvis, and the buttock muscles. After infrarenal aorta ligation, pelvic circulation can be adequately maintained via retrograde blood flow from the extra-anatomic femoral bypass via the external and internal iliac arteries. Inflow to a single internal iliac artery is usually sufficient to maintain adequate pelvic perfusion because of the abundant collateral flow via the visceral and deep femoral arteries.

Aortobifemoral Graft Infections

Aortobifemoral graft infections are more difficult to treat because involvement of the groin complicates lower limb revascularization and mandates distal anastomoses of the ex-situ bypass to the deep femoral, superficial femoral, or popliteal arteries. Preoperative vascular imaging studies can identify localized aortofemoral graft limb infection, thus permitting partial graft excision, typically of the distal graft limb in the groin. Patients should have no CT evidence of perigraft infection or pseudoaneurysm at the aorta-graft anastomosis. For localized graft infection in the groin, local treatment by drainage of the perigraft abscess without graft excision, radical débridement of the perigraft tissues, and topical povidone-iodine irrigation have been successful.[56] Muscle flap coverage of the exposed graft facilitates graft coverage and wound healing.[73]

Treatment without graft excision is appropriate only in carefully selected patients and is not recommended when patients are septic, the prosthetic graft is occluded, anatomic signs of arterial infection are present, or the infecting organism is a *Pseudomonas* species.[19,20] Patients treated by graft preservation should be monitored in the intensive care unit, and persistence of perigraft purulence or systemic signs of infection should prompt the surgeon to recommend total graft excision.

If infection is localized to the femoral region of a single aortofemoral graft limb but sepsis or anastomotic involvement (e.g., femoral pseudoaneurysm or bleeding) is present, graft excision is recommended. Proximal control of the

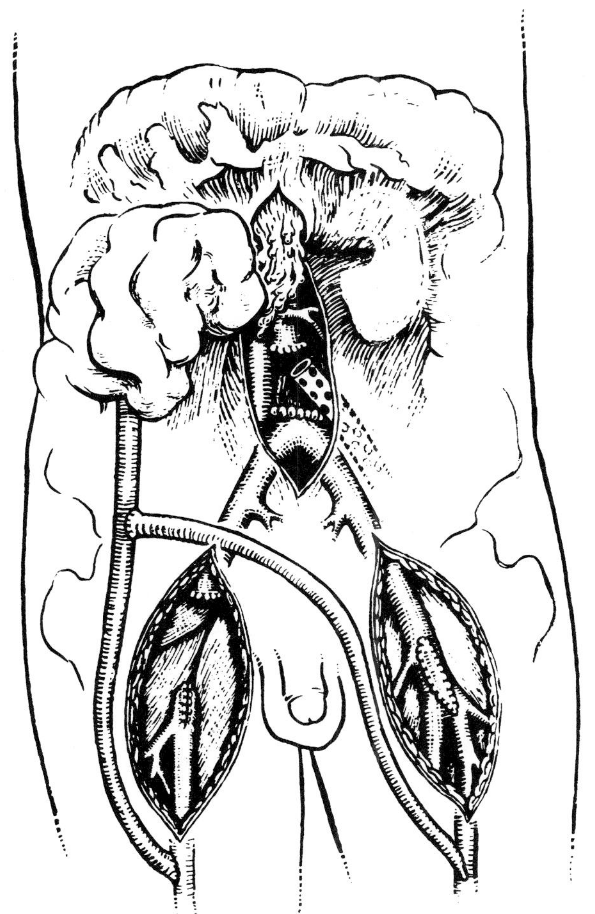

FIGURE 59-7 Excision of an infected aortobifemoral graft with extra-anatomic bypass.

aortofemoral graft via a retroperitoneal approach using an oblique, suprainguinal incision is recommended. The intracavitary graft segment can be evaluated for infection, and if found to be well incorporated, the distal graft is excised and the remainder of the graft is retained (Fig. 59-7). After division of the graft limb through the retroperitoneal approach, adjacent tissue should be interposed between the oversewn proximal and distal ends of the graft. The retroperitoneal incision should then be closed, and the infected femoral graft limb should be excised through an inguinal incision. The entire graft-artery anastomosis to the femoral artery should be excised, the adjacent artery wall débrided, and autogenous patch closure performed. Local endarterectomy may be required to facilitate closure.

Salvage of the common femoral artery is important in maintaining retrograde flow into the pelvis. If the superficial femoral artery is open, an alternative method is to anastomose the superficial femoral artery to the deep femoral artery end to end to maintain pelvic flow via collaterals from the deep femoral system (Fig. 59-8). After graft excision, all arterial ligation and anastomosis sites should be covered with viable tissue. A rotational sartorius muscle flap is particularly useful to cover the femoral artery reconstruction. The groin wound should be left open and treated with topical 0.1% povidone-iodine or antibiotic dressings.

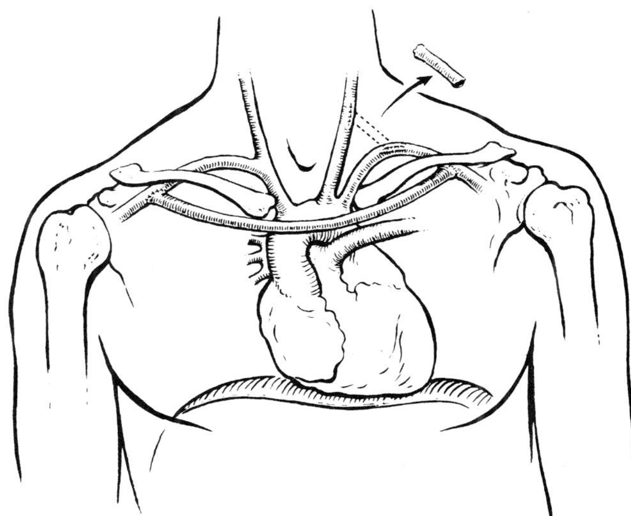

FIGURE 59-8 Excision of an infected carotid-subclavian graft with axilloaxillary bypass.

Revascularization of the limb should be performed as necessary to maintain limb viability. Alternatives to revascularization depend on the patency of the distal circulation and can be performed to the deep femoral artery, the superficial femoral artery, or the popliteal artery. Revascularization should be accomplished via noninfected tissue planes using crossover femorofemoral grafts with medial tunneling or tunneling in the retropubic or suprapubic space, obturator bypass via the obturator canal, or lateral tunneling through the psoas tunnel to course diagonally distal to the distal outflow artery. These bypasses are usually performed with PTFE conduits or saphenous vein if it is of large caliber (≥5 mm in diameter).

Carefully selected cases of aortofemoral graft limb infection that are localized to the groin, and have been demonstrated to be caused by *S. epidermidis,* may be treated by graft excision and in-situ replacement. Perioperative and postoperative use of antibiotics, both systemic and topical, is imperative with in-situ replacement therapy. Wide débridement of all inflamed perigraft tissues, including artery wall adjacent to the graft, is essential. In-situ replacement with a rifampin soaked, gelatin-impregnated PTFE prosthesis is recommended. Parenteral antibiotic therapy should continue for 4 to 6 weeks after in-situ replacement, followed by an additional 1 to 3 months of oral antibiotics.

Comparison of Treatment Outcomes

Treatment of aortic graft infections with extra-anatomic bypass and excision of the entire graft has produced improved results. The perioperative mortality of clinical series reported in the 1990s was in the range of 11% to 13%. Although early amputation rates are less than 1%, late amputation due to extra-anatomic graft failure is in the range of 10%. Aortic stump blowout is a major cause of early and late mortality, but the incidence of this complication has also decreased. Reilly and associates[61] reported a 21% decline in mortality, 19% decline in aortic stump disruption, and a 27% decline in limb loss during a treatment interval that spanned from 1980 to 1992. Improved outcomes were attributed to more aggressive débridement of infected graft beds, reduced intervals of lower limb ischemia, and advances in surgical critical care. Limb loss and failure of the extra-anatomic bypass are greater for aortofemoral graft infections than for infected aortoiliac grafts. Subsequent infection of an axillofemoral graft is associated with a significantly higher amputation rate than is an infection-free extra-anatomic bypass that fails because of repetitive thrombotic events.

Redo aortic grafting from the descending thoracic aorta or aortic stump can be performed 6 to 12 months after aortic graft removal for failure of the extra-anatomic bypass.[29] The procedure reliably relieves ischemic symptoms of the hemodynamically inadequate or thrombosed extra-anatomic bypass. Reinfection remains a risk after redo aortic procedures, especially when the indication for the procedure infection involved an extra-anatomic bypass.

In-situ replacement, an alternative to extra-anatomic bypass grafting and total graft excision, is believed by several surgical groups to be associated with less morbidity and improved long-term outcomes. More than one half of patients presenting with an aortic graft infection are candidates for in-situ replacement using either autogenous vein or an antibiotic-bonded graft. When applied to low-grade aortic graft infections without GEE or GEF, this procedure is safe (4% in-hospital mortality), durable, and is associated with a low (3%) incidence of long-term limb loss. Successful treatment by either autogenous superficial femoral-popliteal reconstruction or standard ex-situ bypass followed by graft excision is associated with long-term survival in more than 70% of patients.

Infected aortofemoral graft limb infections that are limited to the groin can be treated with local operative débridement, antibiotic therapy, and muscle flap coverage. Calligaro and associates[16-18] achieved complete graft preservation and wound healing in 73% of cases of graft infection due to gram-negative bacteria and 70% of cases due to gram-positive bacteria. The potential for treatment failure exists, and patients must be carefully monitored. All four deaths in this series (10% mortality) were due to graft sepsis; nine patients ultimately required total graft excision, and in seven patients, surgical wounds never healed. *Pseudomonas* was a particularly virulent pathogen and was associated with failure of wound healing, anastomotic disruption, and arterial bed hemorrhage. Attempts to preserve a polyester (Dacron) graft involved by infection were less successful that that of PTFE grafts. This approach has also been used in selected patients with prohibitive risks for total graft excision. Success was achieved in seven of nine patients with aortic graft infection using a strategy of percutaneous open-drain placement into perigraft abscess cavities, instillation of antibiotics three time daily, repeated débridement of infected groin wounds, and intravenous antibiotic therapy for at least 6 weeks.

Expanded application of in-situ replacement for prosthetic graft infections has been reported. Outcomes following deep venous replacement are overall better than with the use of arterial allografts or implantation of a "new" prosthetic graft. The highest mortality rate (20%) is in patients with GEF, an incidence similar to total graft excision and ex-situ bypass. Treatment of bacterial biofilm infections regardless of the replacement conduit used is associated with low mortality (<3%), high (>90%) success rate, and a long-term survival of 70%.

Endovascular Stent-Graft and Stent Infections

Infection of an endovascular stent or stent-graft is an emerging problem. The reported incidence after AAA repair is 0.2% to 0.8% (mean, 0.4%). Most infections present clinically within 3 months of implantation with sepsis, mycotic aneurysm, and/or septic emboli. *S. aureus* is the most common (56% of cases) pathogen, and CT scanning is diagnostic in more than 85% of patients with signs of retroperitoneal inflammation and periaortic fluid collections. Case reports have described infection resulting from a urinary tract infection and erosion into duodenum. Treatment should consist of device removal, antibiotic therapy, and autogenous (superficial femoral-popliteal veins) reconstruction of the involved arterial segment, if feasible. Mortality is high (30%) with conservative treatment (i.e., antibiotics and percutaneous drainage or perigraft fluid collections). Mortality with graft excision and either extra-anatomic bypass or in-situ bypass is in the range of 10% to 15%. Patient survival after successful treatment is high (>90%), and the incidence of limb loss is low (<2%). Patients treated by CT-guided drainage and antibiotic therapy fared worse with a mortality in excess of 30%, suggesting this approach should be avoided.

Femoral, Popliteal, and Tibial Graft Infections

Once the diagnosis of infrainguinal prosthetic bypass graft infection is made, excision of the entire graft is the preferred treatment. Patients who have anastomotic disruption or graft sepsis should undergo prompt intervention. Treatment principles include removal of the entire graft, radical débridement of infected perigraft tissues, closure of the arteriotomies with monofilament suture, and the administration of systemic and topical antibiotics. Often a staged approach is advantageous, beginning with drainage of the perigraft abscess, followed in 1 to 2 days by graft excision and autogenous vein bypass grafting via adjacent or remote tunneling. In-situ replacement therapy is possible in 80% of patients. The treatment of peripheral graft infections is associated with a low mortality rate but a higher amputation rate as compared with the treatment of aortic graft infections (Table 59-11).

Patients who had prosthetic grafts inserted for claudication may be treated with graft excision alone. Heparin should be administered to patients in whom limb viability is jeopardized by graft excision. Patients with limb-threatening ischemia resulting from excision of the infected bypass should have revascularization, preferably with autogenous tissue. Frequently, however, autogenous tissue is not available, and reconstruction with prosthetic graft via remote, noninfected planes should be performed in lieu of amputation. In patients with septic emboli, the muscles distal to the

Table 59-11 Results of Treatment of Femoropopliteal or Tibial Prosthetic Graft Infections

REFERENCE	NO. OF CASES	MORTALITY RATE, %	AMPUTATION RATE, %
Szilagyi et al, 1972[71]	10	0	50
Liekweg and Greenfield, 1977[52]	55	9	33
Yashar et al, 1978[77]	35	0	67
Durham et al, 1986[30]	38	0	67

graft can become infected and amputation is the only treatment option.

The local treatment of infrainguinal graft infections by aggressive perigraft tissue débridement, antibiotic use, and muscle flap coverage, without graft excision, has been successful in patients without graft sepsis or anastomotic disruption. Multiple small series[20,59,62] have shown that this alternative treatment method can result in healing in approximately 70% of cases and may not harm the patient as long as early, aggressive management by graft excision is undertaken if sepsis or anastomotic disruption or bleeding occurs.[70] In general, in-situ replacement therapy is preferred to graft preservation procedures. The morbidity and hospital length of stay are reduced, and a low (5% to 10%) amputation rate can be expected when autogenous bypass grafting can be performed.

Thoracic Aortic Graft Infections

Thoracic aortic graft infection is a grave complication (Table 59-12). The principles of graft excision and extra-anatomic bypass are not applicable to most cases of prosthetic aortic valve or ascending or transverse aortic arch graft infection.[28,46] In-situ replacement in conjunction with local antibacterial irrigation of the revascularization is required. The operative approach should be wide débridement of the infected tissues, graft excision and replacement, and coverage of the graft with viable, noninfected tissues. Pericardial fat pads; adjacent muscle, including the pectoralis major, the rectus abdominis, and the latissimus dorsi; and the greater omentum pedicle have been used for graft coverage. These principles were used by Coselli and colleagues[24] in 40 patients. There were five operative deaths: two due to coagulopathy and hemorrhage and three to cardiopulmonary and renal complications. Twenty-eight patients (70%) were alive and without any evidence of recurrent graft infection 4 months to 6.5 years later.

Infections involving prosthetic grafts in the descending thoracic aorta may be amenable to graft excision and revascularization through clean, uninfected planes. A remote bypass graft can be placed through a median sternotomy from the ascending aorta to the abdominal aorta, tunneling through the diaphragm via an uninfected route. This graft should be placed before excision of the descending thoracic graft via a left thoracotomy.[46] The aortic closure should be covered with viable tissue transferred locally.

Innominate, Subclavian, and Carotid Graft Infections

Management of infection of a bypass or patch graft of an innominate, subclavian, or carotid artery should be based on the same principles used for lower extremity graft infections. The risks of treatment of prosthetic infections at this location include not only persistent sepsis and death but also stroke (see Table 59-12). The surgical approach to a patient with prosthetic infection of a transthoracic bypass graft often requires a median sternotomy and preparation for cardiopulmonary bypass and total circulatory arrest, if needed for proximal control.[52] Treatment should include total graft excision, administration of parenteral and topical antibiotics, and remote bypass, preferably with autogenous tissue, if needed. There have been reports of successful treatment of infected prostheses with local irrigation, but this is not recommended because graft excision and remote revascularization are usually possible.

An infected transthoracic or extrathoracic bypass graft originally performed for upper extremity ischemia can often be removed without the need for immediate revascularization. Ligation of the proximal innominate or subclavian arteries, unlike ligation of the iliac or common femoral arteries, is often tolerated and does not provoke critical extremity ischemia. A subsequent bypass, if needed, can be performed after the infection clears. Upper extremity amputation following removal of a subclavian bypass graft for infection is rare; only case reports have been published.[52] When severe upper extremity ischemia results from graft excision, bypass with autogenous conduits such as the femoral or greater saphenous vein is recommended. Patients with transthoracic bypass grafts to the innominate and subclavian arteries often have multivessel disease of the aortic arch, necessitating that remote bypasses use the femoral artery, the descending thoracic aorta, or the supraceliac abdominal aorta as the inflow vessel.

Remote bypass following excision of an infected carotid-subclavian bypass can be performed with a carotid-carotid

Table 59-12 Collected Series Results of Treatment of Thoracic, Innominate, Carotid, or Subclavian Prosthetic Graft Infections

GRAFT SITE	NO. OF CASES	OPERATIVE DEATHS	PERIOPERATIVE STROKES*	PERCENT SURVIVAL > 1 YEAR†
Thoracic aorta	61	9	0	80
Innominate, carotid, or subclavian bypass graft	33	9	3	50
Carotid patch	60	4	2	80

*All patients with strokes were treated by carotid ligation without reconstruction, which resulted in four operative deaths and one late death.
†Late follow-up was not reported for 13 patients with an innominate, carotid, or subclavian bypass graft and for 1 patient with a carotid patch.

Data from Kieffer et al, 1986; 2001; Ehrenfeld et al, 1979; and Bergamini et al, 1993.

bypass using saphenous vein or an axilloaxillary bypass using vein or PTFE. After excision of an infected axilloaxillary graft, flow can be successfully re-established with a supraclavicular subclavian-subclavian bypass, a carotid-carotid bypass, or a femoroaxillary bypass.

The incidence of infection involving a prosthetic graft or patch reconstruction of the carotid artery ranges from 0.3% to 0.8%. Ligation of the carotid artery is not an option in the majority of patients due to inadequate collaterals via the circle of Willis. Transcranial Doppler testing with common carotid compression can identify the patients likely to experience a stroke if treated by ligation without reconstruction. Ligation of the common or internal carotid artery may be safely performed in patients with stump pressures higher than 70 mm Hg, but reconstruction of the artery to maintain cerebral blood flow and prevent stroke should be performed if possible.

After graft excision, revascularization is best done with autogenous tissue. The anatomy of the extracranial carotid artery often does not permit remote bypass through non-infected, uninflamed tissues, and it often requires autogenous bypass in the infected graft bed. Coverage of the bypass with muscle can be of value in this situation in preventing the recurrence of infection. Autogenous bypasses with saphenous vein, internal jugular vein, or internal iliac artery are successful alternatives.[35] Treatment of carotid prosthetic patch infections is usually best achieved by excising the patch and reconstruction with vein patch angioplasty or interposition vein grafting. Electroencephalographic monitoring and selective use of carotid shunts to maintain cerebral perfusion are useful adjuncts in these difficult, challenging procedures. The sternocleidomastoid muscle can be used as coverage for the vascular reconstruction. In general, a low (<5%) procedure mortality and stroke rate can be expected with either interposition grafting or patch angioplasty with autogenous vein. Stroke, recurrent infection, and carotid pseudoaneurysm formation are late complications in 12% of cases.[12]

FUTURE DIRECTIONS

Dissatisfaction with the morbidity and mortality of treating vascular graft infections, regardless of location, by total graft excision and remote bypass has been the impetus for the expanded application of in-situ replacement and graft preservation procedures. Clinical experience with these less aggressive treatment options is evolving and based on experimental studies that have shown in-situ replacement can be successful in a contaminated field, and continued progress can be expected. Treatment outcome depends on the virulence of the infecting organism, the extent of graft-artery infection, and the immune status of the patient. In-situ replacement of a graft infected with a virulent organism may not be safe if the immune status of the patient is also compromised.

Use of lower limb deep veins is the preferred method for replacement of large-caliber prosthetic grafts and is superior to standard therapy by staged ex-situ bypass and total graft excision in reducing the risk of reinfection and providing superior long-term graft patency. Use of infection-resistant arterial conduits, including cadaveric arterial/venous homografts and antibacterial impregnated prosthetic grafts, is a treatment option in selected patients. Clinical safety and efficacy have been demonstrated for various types of graft infection, but best results can be expected in the treatment of low-grade infections not complicated by GEF/GEE. Prophylactic use of an antibiotic-bonded graft would be of most clinical benefit in patients judged to be at increased risk for infection. Other adjuncts to sterilize the surgical wound (i.e., degradable antibiotic beads) may improve the efficacy of all in-situ replacement procedures.

REFERENCES

1. Abbott WM, Green RM, Matsumoto T, et al: Prosthetic above-knee femoropopliteal grafting: Results of a multicenter trial. J Vasc Surg 25:19, 1977.
2. Arnold PG, Pairolero PC: Intrathoracic muscle flaps in the surgical management of life-threatening hemorrhage from the heart and great vessels. Plast Reconstr Surg 81:831, 1988.
3. Baker M, Uflacker R, Robinson J: Stent-graft infection after abdominal aortic aneurysm repair: A case report. J Vasc Surg 36:180, 2002.
4. Bakker-deWekker P, Alfieri O, Vermeulin F, et al: Surgical treatment of infected pseudoaneurysms after replacement of the ascending aorta. J Thorac Cardiovasc Surg 88:447, 1984.
5. Bandyk DF, Berni GA, Thiele BL, et al: Aortofemoral graft infection due to *Staphylococcus epidermidis*. Arch Surg 119:102, 1984.
6. Bandyk DF: Vascular graft infections: Epidemiology, microbiology, pathogenesis, and prevention. In Bernhard VM, Towne JB (eds): Complications in Vascular Surgery. St. Louis, Quality Medical, 1991, pp 223-234.
7. Bandyk DF: Infection of prosthetic vascular grafts. In Rutherford RB (ed): Vascular Surgery, 5th ed. St. Louis, CV Mosby, 1995, p 566.
8. Bandyk DF, Bergamini TM, Kinney EV, et al: In situ replacement of vascular prostheses infected by bacterial biofilms. J Vasc Surg 13:575, 1991.
9. Bandyk DF, Novotney ML, Back MR: Expanded application of in situ replacement for prosthetic graft infection. J Vasc Surg 34:411, 2001.
10. Batt M, Mange JL, Alric P, et al: In situ revascularization with silver coated polyester grafts to treat aortic infection: Early and midterm results. J Vasc Surg 38:983, 2003.
11. Bergamini TM, Bandyk DF, Govostis D, et al: Identification of *Staphylococcus epidermidis* vascular graft infections: A comparison of culture techniques. J Vasc Surg 9:665, 1989.
12. Bergamini TM, Seabrook GR, Bandyk DF, et al: Symptomatic recurrent carotid stenosis and aneurysmal degeneration following endarterectomy. Surgery 113:580, 1993.
13. Branchereau A, Magnan PE: Results of vertebral artery reconstruction. J Cardiovasc Surg 31:320, 1990.
14. Bunt TJ: Synthetic vascular graft infections. Surgery 93:733, 1988.
15. Busuttil RW, Rees W, Baker JD, et al: Pathogenesis of aortoduodenal fistula: Experimental and clinical correlates. Surgery 85:1, 1979.
16. Calligaro KD, Westcott CJ, Buckley RM, et al: Infrainguinal anastomotic arterial graft infections treated by selective graft preservation. Ann Surg 216:74, 1993.
17. Calligaro KD, Veith FJ, Schwartz ML, et al: Selective preservation of infected prosthetic grafts: Analysis of a 20-year experience with 120 extra-cavitary infected grafts. Ann Surg 220:461, 1994.
18. Calligaro KD, Veith FJ, Schwartz ML, et al: Are gram-negative bacteria a contraindication to selective preservation of infected prosthetic arterial grafts? J Vasc Surg 16:337, 1992.
19. Calligaro KD, Veith FJ, Schwartz ML, et al: Differences in early versus late extracavitary arterial graft infections. J Vasc Surg 22:680, 1995.
20. Calligaro KD, Veith FJ, Yuan JG, et al: Intra-abdominal aortic graft infection: Complete or partial graft preservation in patients at very high risk. J Vasc Surg 38:1199, 2003.
21. Campbell WB, Tambeeur LJ, Geens VR: Local complications after arterial bypass grafting. Ann R Coll Surg Engl 76:127, 1994.
22. Cherry KJ, Roland CF, Pairolero PC, et al: Infected femorodistal bypass: Is graft removal mandatory? J Vasc Surg 15:295, 1992.

23. Clagett GP, Valentine RJ, Hagino RT: Autogenous aortoiliac/femoral reconstruction from superficial femoral-popliteal veins: Feasibility and durability. J Vasc Surg 25:25, 1997.
24. Coselli JS, Crawford ES, Williams TW, et al: Treatment of postoperative infection of ascending aorta and transverse aortic arch, including use of viable omentum and muscle flaps. Ann Thorac Surg 50:868, 1990.
25. Daenens K, Fourneau I, Nevelsteen A: Ten-year experience in autogenous reconstruction with the femoral vein in the treatment of aortofemoral prosthetic infection. Eur J Vasc Surg 25:240, 2003.
26. Darling RC III, Resnikoff M, Kreienberg PB, et al: Alternative approach for management of infected aortic grafts. J Vasc Surg 25:106, 1997.
27. Dean RH, Allen TR, Foster JH, et al: Aortoduodenal fistula: An uncommon but correctable cause of upper gastrointestinal bleeding. Am Surg 44:37, 1978.
28. Deiparine MK, Ballard JL, Taylor FC, Chase DR: Endovascular stent infection. J Vasc Surg 23:529, 1996.
29. Dimuzio PJ, Reilly LM, Stoney RJ: Redo aortic grafting after treatment of aortic graft infection. J Vasc Surg 24:328, 1996.
30. Durham JR, Rubin JR, Malone JM: Management of infected infrainguinal bypass grafts. In Bergan JJ, Yao JST (eds): Reoperative Arterial Surgery. Orlando, FL, Grune & Stratton, 1986, pp 359-373.
31. Ehrenfeld WK, Wilbur BG, Olcott CN, et al: Autogenous tissue reconstruction in the management of infected prosthetic grafts. Surgery 85:82, 1979.
32. Elek SD, Conen PE: The virulence of *Staphylococcus pyogenes* in man: A study of the problems of wound infection. Br J Exp Pathol 38:573, 1957.
33. Fry WJ, Lindenauer SM: Infection complicating the use of plastic arterial implants. Arch Surg 94:600, 1966.
34. Fujitani RM, Bassiouny HS, Gewertz BL, et al: Cryopreserved saphenous vein allogenic homografts: An alternative conduit in lower extremity arterial reconstruction in infected fields. J Vasc Surg 15:519, 1992.
35. Geary KJ, Tomkiewicz ZM, Harrison HN, et al: Differential effects of a gram-negative and a gram-positive infection on autogenous and prosthetic grafts. J Vasc Surg 11:339, 1990.
36. Goldstone J, Moore WS: Infection in vascular prostheses: Clinical manifestations and surgical management. Am J Surg 128:225, 1974.
37. Hagino RT, Clagett GP: Treatment of infected aortic grafts with in-situ aortic reconstruction using superficial femoral-popliteal veins. Adv Vasc Surg 6:37, 1998.
38. Hallett JW, Marshall DM, Petterson TM, et al: Graft-related complications after abdominal aortic aneurysm repair: Population-based experience. J Vasc Surg 25:277, 1977.
39. Hargrove WC III, Edmunds H Jr: Management of infected thoracic aortic prosthetic grafts. Ann Thorac Surg 37:72, 1984.
40. Huber TS, Carlton LM, O'Hern DG, et al: Financial impact of tertiary care in an academic medical center. Ann Surg 231:860, 2000.
41. Jackson MR, Joiner DR, Clagett GP: Excision and autogenous revascularization of an infected aortic stent graft resulting from a urinary tract infection. J Vasc Surg 36:622, 2002.
42. Jacobs MJHM, Reul GJ, Gregoric I, et al: In situ replacement and extra-anatomic bypass for the treatment of infected abdominal aortic grafts. Eur J Vasc Surg 5:83, 1991.
43. Johnston KW: Multicenter prospective study of nonruptured abdominal aortic aneurysm: II. Variables predicting morbidity and mortality. J Vasc Surg 9:437, 1989.
44. Kaebnick HW, Bandyk DF, Bergamini TM, Towne JB: The microbiology of explanted vascular prostheses. Surgery 102:756, 1987.
45. Kieffer E, Bahnini A, Koskas F, et al: In situ allograft replacement of infected infrarenal aortic prosthetic grafts: Results in 43 patients. J Vasc Surg 17:349, 1993.
46. Kieffer E, Petitjean C, Bahnini A: Surgery for failed brachycephalic reconstruction. In Bergan JJ, Yao JST (eds): Reoperative Arterial Surgery. Orlando, Grune & Stratton, 1986, pp 581-607.
47. Kieffer E, Sabatier J, Plissonnier D, Knosalla C: Prosthetic graft infection after descending thoracic/thoracoabdominal aortic aneurysmectomy: Management with in situ arterial grafts. J Vasc Surg 33:671, 2001.
48. Kitka MJ, Goodson SF, Rishara RA, et al: Mortality and limb loss with infected infrainguinal bypass grafts. J Vasc Surg 5:566, 1987.
49. Koskas F, Plissonier D, Bahnini A, et al: In-situ allografting for aortoiliac graft infection: A 6-year experience. J Cardiovasc Surg 4:495, 1996.
50. Kuestner LM, Reilly LM, Jicha DL, et al: Secondary aortoenteric fistula: Contemporary outcomes with use of extra-anatomic bypass and infected graft excision. J Vasc Surg 21:194, 1995.
51. Lavigne JP, Postal A, Kolh P, Limet R: Prosthetic vascular infection complicated or not by aortoenteric fistula: Comparison of treatment with and without cryopreserved allograft (homograft). Eur J Vasc Surg 25:416, 2003.
52. Liekweg WG Jr, Greenfield LJ: Vascular prosthetic infections: Collected experience and results of treatment. Surgery 81:335, 1977.
53. Lorentzen JE, Nielsen OM, Arendrup H, et al: Vascular graft infection: An analysis of sixty-two graft infections in 2411 consecutively implanted synthetic vascular grafts. Surgery 98:81, 1985.
54. Naylor AR, Payne D, London NJ, et al: Prosthetic patch infection after carotid endarterectomy. Eur J Vasc Surg 23:11, 2002.
55. Nevelsteen A, Lacroix H, Suy R: Autogenous reconstruction of the lower extremity deep veins: An alternative treatment of prosthetic infection after reconstructive surgery of aortoiliac disease. J Vasc Surg 22:129, 1995.
56. O'Hara PJ, Hertzer NR, Beven EG, et al: Surgical management of infected abdominal aortic grafts: Review of a 25-year experience. J Vasc Surg 3:725, 1986.
57. Ohki T, Veith FJ, Shaw P, et al: Increasing incidence of midterm and long-term complications after endovascular graft repair of abdominal aortic aneurysms: A note of caution based on a 9-year experience. Ann Surg 234:323, 2001.
58. Olofsson PA, Auffermann W, Higgins CB, et al: Diagnosis of prosthetic aortic graft infection by magnetic resonance imaging. J Vasc Surg 8:99, 1988.
59. O'Mara CS, Williams GM, Ernst CB: Secondary aortoenteric fistula. Am J Surg 142:203, 1981.
60. Quinones-Baldrich WJ, Hernandez JJ, Moore WS: Long-term results following surgical management of aortic graft infection. Arch Surg 126:507, 1991.
61. Reilly LM, Altman H, Lusby RJ, et al: Late results following surgical management of vascular graft infection. J Vasc Surg 1:36, 1984.
62. Reilly LM, Stoney RJ, Goldstone J, et al: Improved management of aortic graft infection: The influence of operation sequence and staging. J Vasc Surg 5:421, 1987.
63. Reul GJ Jr, Cooley DA: False aneurysms of the carotid artery. In Bergan JJ, Yao JST (eds): Reoperative Arterial Surgery. Orlando, Grune & Stratton, 1986, pp 537-553.
64. Ricotta JJ, Faggioli GI, Stella A, et al: Total excision and extra-anatomic bypass for aortic graft infection. Arch Surg 126:507, 1991.
65. Rockman CB, Su WT, Domenig C, et al: Postoperative infection associated with polyester patch angioplasty after carotid endarterectomy. J Vasc Surg 38:251, 2003.
66. Rosenthal D, Archie JP, Garcia-Rinaldi R, et al: Carotid patch angioplasty: Intermediate and long-term results. J Vasc Surg 12:326, 1990.
67. Schmitt DD, Seabrook GR, Bandyk DF, et al: Graft excision and extra-anatomic revascularization: The treatment of choice for the septic aortic prosthesis. J Cardiovasc Surg 31:327, 1990.
68. Seeger JM, Pretus HA, Welborn MB, et al: Long-term outcome after treatment of aortic graft infection with staged extra-anatomic bypass and aortic graft removal. J Vasc Surg 32:451, 2000.
69. Snyder SO, Wheeler JR, Gregory RT, et al: Freshly harvested cadaveric venous homografts as arterial conduits in infected fields. Surgery 101:283, 1987.
70. Speziale F, Rizzo L, Sabrigia E, et al: Bacterial and clinical criteria relating to the outcome of patients undergoing in-situ replacement of infected abdominal aortic grafts. Eur J Endovasc Surg 13:127, 1997.

71. Szilagyi DE, Smith RF, Elliott JP, et al: Infection in arterial reconstruction with synthetic grafts. Ann Surg 176:321, 1972.
72. Taylor SM, Mills JL, Fujitani RM, et al: The influence of groin sepsis on extra-anatomic bypass patency in patients with prosthetic graft infection. Ann Vasc Surg 6:80, 1992.
73. Thompson BW, Read RC, Campbell GS: Operative correction of proximal blocks of the subclavian or innominate arteries. J Cardiovasc Surg 21:125, 1980.
74. Trout HH, Kozloff L, Giordano JM: Priority of revascularization in patients with graft-enteric fistulas, infected arteries, or infected arterial prostheses. Ann Surg 199:669, 1984.
75. Vogt PR, Brunner-LaRocca HP, Lachat M, et al: Technical details with the use of cryopreserved arterial allografts for aortic infection: Influence on early and midterm mortality. J Vasc Surg 35:80, 2002.
76. Walker WE, Cooley DA, Duncan JM, et al: The management of aortoduodenal fistula by in situ replacement of the infected abdominal aortic graft. Ann Surg 205:727, 1987.
77. Yashar JJ, Weyman AK, Burnard RJ, et al: Survival and limb salvage in patients with infected arterial prostheses. Am J Surg 135:499, 1978.
78. Yeager RA, Taylor LM, Moneta GL, et al: Improved results with conventional management of infrarenal aortic infection. J Vasc Surg 30:76, 1999.
79. Young RM, Cherry KJ Jr, Davis PM, et al: The results of in situ prosthetic replacement for infected aortic grafts. Am J Surg 178:136, 1999.
80. Zacharoulis DC, Gupta SK, Seymour P, Landa RA: Use of muscle flap to cover infections of the carotid artery after carotid endarterectomy. J Vasc Surg 25:769, 1997.

Chapter 60

Anastomotic Aneurysms

PATRICK J. CASEY, MD
GLENN M. LAMURAGLIA, MD

One of the ways that bypass grafts can fail is through degeneration of the anastomosis over time and development into an aneurysm. Although this process can occur in the vessel or in the body of the graft adjacent to the anastomosis, the area of deterioration is more commonly the anastomosis itself. Anastomotic aneurysms generally evolve slowly over time, and in the partial or complete dehiscence of the anastomotic suture line (Fig. 60-1), a pseudoaneurysm can develop. A *pseudoaneurysm*, or false aneurysm, can be defined as a cavity without the three layers (intima, media, and adventitia) of the vessel wall. This disruption of vascular continuity results in extravasation of blood contained by scarification of surrounding tissue (Fig. 60-2). Without the integrity and strength of the vessel wall, this fibrous capsule can progressively enlarge, resulting in complications such as aneurysm rupture, erosion into or compression of contiguous structures, embolization, and vascular thrombosis. The focus of this chapter is the etiology, diagnosis, and treatment of aneurysms associated with vascular graft reconstruction.

■ INCIDENCE

The incidence of anastomotic aneurysms has been described as low and depends on several factors that can be classified under the determinants surgical technique, patient factors, or anatomic location. These factors have been most often described after prosthetic aortofemoral reconstruction for occlusive or aneurysmal disease.[1-3] The sites of anastomotic aneurysm after aortic surgery are the femoral artery, the aorta, and the iliac arteries. Ernst and colleagues[4] reported a low incidence of anastomotic aneurysms in a 30-year experience with 6090 aorto-iliofemoral anastomoses. This study tabulated incidence of anastomotic aneurysms as 2.4% in the femoral arteries, 0.4% in the aorta, and 0.8% in the iliac arteries.[4] Higher incidences were reported from a 20-year follow up of 518 patients who underwent screening for anastomotic aneurysms with ultrasonography or angiography.[3] In this study, the incidence of anastomotic aneurysms was 13.6% in the femoral artery, 4.8% in the aorta, and 6.3% in the iliac arteries. Although the rates are

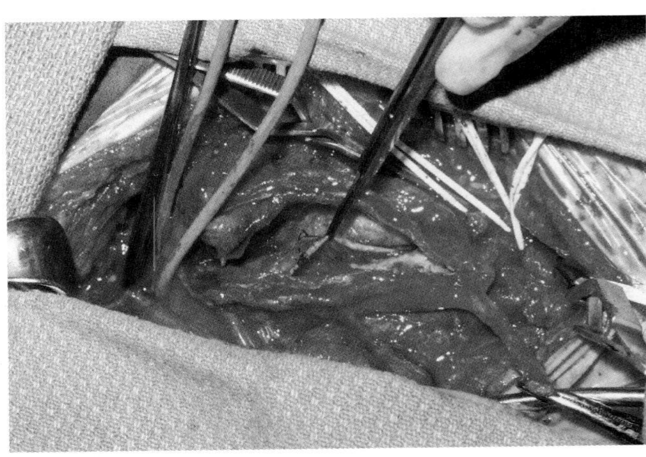

FIGURE 60-1 Photograph of the surgical exposure of an opened femoral anastomotic aneurysm with the disrupted anastomosis (forceps). Note the frayed suture line.

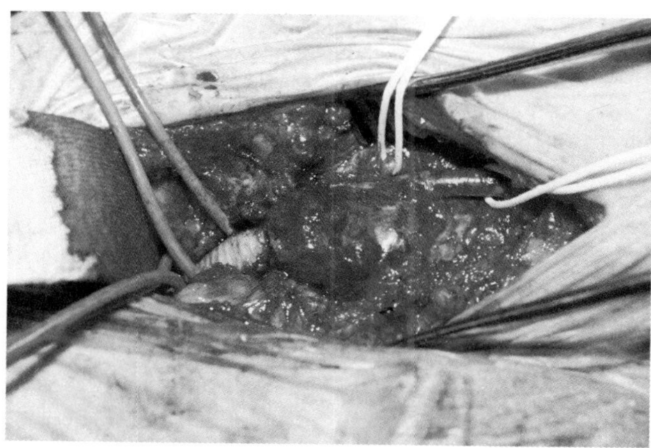

FIGURE 60-2 Photograph of the surgical exposure of a femoral pseudoaneurysm. Proximally, a large red vessel loop encircles the limb of the aortofemoral graft, and the fibrous capsule of the dehisced anastomosis has been dissected, with white vessel loops surrounding the superficial and profunda femoris arteries.

still not very high, these data suggest the need for continued late follow-up for patients who have undergone aortic and other bypass reconstructions, to identify and correct this complication in an effort to avoid clinical sequelae.

■ ETIOLOGY

Several factors, alone or in conjunction, can contribute to the pathogenesis of anastomotic aneurysms. They are suture line disruption, graft failure, arterial wall failure, infection, technical error, and physical stress.

Suture Line Disruption

Suture line disruption can occur acutely or develop over time, predisposing to anastomotic aneurysms. Because the anastomotic strength depends on the suture coaptation of the graft to the vessel wall, its integrity is paramount, especially in the early postoperative period. Autografts and some biologic grafts heal to the vessel wall, consequently resulting in diminishing dependence on the suture material to maintain apposition of the anastomosis. However, despite tissue incorporation, prosthetic grafts and the adjacent vessel never heal into a merged vessel and therefore require continued support by the suture material for integrity.

After implantation, most suture materials lose their strength over time,[5-7] and it is for this reason that careful choices must be made. Silk, originally considered a permanent suture material, was used in the early experience of vascular grafting. Although silk sutures were not problematic when biologic tissue was used, the slow absorption and focal inflammatory reaction associated with the use of silk with prosthetic grafts resulted in a very high incidence of anastomotic aneurysms within 5 to 10 years.[8] Braided Dacron sutures have withstood their strength over time, but their poor incorporation into tissue, the persistent inflammatory reaction to their presence, and the "drag" when Dacron is used for running anastomoses have decreased the popularity of this substance for anastomoses. Nylon sutures, though permanent, lose a significant amount of tensile strength over time, making nylon a poor choice for use with prosthetic grafts. However, nylon's easy physical extrusion into ultra-thin suture (9-0, 10-0) and its lack of brittle qualities make it the suture material of choice for microanastomoses. Polytetrafluoroethylene (PTFE) sutures are permanent, are easy to work with, and incite little inflammation, but they do not have the same cross-sectional strength as polypropylene. For good reason, polypropylene is the mainstay of vascular anastomoses. It is well incorporated into tissue, is minimally reactive, maintains a very high percentage of its strength over time, has a very low coefficient of friction, and does not provide a good adherent surface for bacterial biofilms. The one disadvantage is that polypropylene is brittle and must be carefully handled to avoid loss of strength or fracture.

There have been ongoing investigations into nonsuture methods of performing anastomoses. These studies have evaluated a number of techniques, including adhesives, stents, rings, vascular clips, and laser welding, in an effort to minimize damage to the vessel wall, increase efficiency, and improve patency and long-term anastomotic integrity.[9] Each method has inherent limitations and associated complications. Only vascular clips appear to provide promise for use with autogenous tissue anastomoses not involving an endarterectomy, but long-term follow-up on their use is still needed.

Graft Failure

Graft material is important to maintain anastomotic and graft integrity. Although some earlier generations of prosthetic grafts (both Dacron and expanded PTFE) that are still used today were found to deteriorate and fail over time, they have been removed from the market (see Chapter 49). A consideration worth remembering when one is using woven velour Dacron grafts is to thermally seal the edges of the cut graft or to take large enough bites of the graft, because of the potential of edge fraying that could contribute to late anastomotic disruption.

Arterial Wall Failure

As with the graft material, the vessel wall adjacent to the anastomosis can also deteriorate at the suture line and develop into a pseudoaneurysm. Alternatively, the vessel wall, of normal caliber at the time of the original anastomotic surgery, can degenerate into a recurrent aneurysm of the native artery. Often it is difficult to determine on imaging whether the problem is a true or a false aneurysm. Therefore, unless an artery wall aneurysm can be clearly identified, one should assume that the lesion is a pseudoaneurysm when deciding about surgical correction.

Inflammatory Response

One of the factors that can contribute to the degeneration of the anastomosis is an inflammatory response. This may result from the reaction to the graft or suture material, from adjacent seromas or fluid collections, or, more commonly, from an indolent subacute infection. Subacute infections can result from contamination at the time of surgical implantation or, less likely, from late inoculation. Such infections have been implicated in the formation of anastomotic pseudoaneurysms, but the timing of their clinical presentation can be quite remote—even decades later. In a study evaluating the incidence of bacterial presence in 45 operated pseudoaneurysms, bacterial culture results were positive in 60% of the resected graft material specimens; coagulase-negative staphylococcal species accounted for 89% of the organisms.[10] The most common anatomic location for infected pseudoaneurysms is the femoral anastomosis.[11]

Although less common, graft infections may also result from acute infection due to contamination from the surgical field, hematogenous spread, bowel or adjacent soft tissue infection, or needle or catheter inoculation. Such infections may be fulminant and rapidly progressive, leading to rupture of the anastomosis. Careful aseptic technique and perioperative administration of antibiotics are the optimal methods of minimizing graft infections. There is no evidence that periprocedural antibiotic therapy, as used in cardiac valve replacements, prevent hematogenous seeding of established, well-incorporated vascular grafts (see Chapter 59).

Technical Errors

Surgical technique remains an important determinant to minimize the development of anastomotic failure. Using enough number of suture loops, taking adequate bites of graft and arterial tissue during suturing, and carefully following the curve of the needle to avoid arterial disruption are important principles of surgical technique in this situation. Performing an endarterectomy at the location of a planned anastomosis must be carefully considered, because removal of the intima and media can lead to the development of an anastomotic aneurysm. In these instances, aneurysmal degeneration can lead to formation of a pseudoaneurysm or the native vessel may dilate as a true aneurysm in the region of the anastomosis. One can reduce the likelihood of this occurrence by not performing the endarterectomy too deep and by taking extra large bites of the vessel wall during suturing.

Another consideration in avoiding iatrogenic aneurysms is the arterial access close to an anastomosis, such as the distal anastomosis of an aortofemoral graft. Both arterial sheaths for diagnostic or interventional therapy[12] and intra-aortic balloon pumps[13] can be safely placed in well-incorporated grafts and may be lifesaving.

Physical Stress

Physical stresses to the anastomosis may contribute to the development of anastomotic aneurysms. Such stresses include significant hypertension, direct trauma, and compression or distraction forces that may be placed on the anastomosis with motion across a joint. Distraction forces are generally not significant if the bypasses are constructed with adequate laxity in the graft length and tunneling.[14] Another consideration is a significant compliance mismatch between the graft and the artery wall. Because a prosthetic graft is generally less compliant than the artery, the lateral forces generated at the anastomosis lead to preferential stress on the native system. Choice of proper graft size is important because lateral wall stress can also result from turbulence generated when the graft diameter greatly differs from the vessel diameter.[15,16] This issue becomes more of a factor when the anastomotic aneurysm starts to develop, because the physical stresses increase as the aneurysm enlarges.[17] Thus, the frequency of follow-up should correlate with increased size of the anastomotic aneurysm.

■ CLINICAL PRESENTATION

Anastomotic aneurysms are generally asymptomatic. They are usually identified either on physical examination as palpable pulsatile masses or as findings on imaging studies, depending on anatomic location. Occasionally, an anastomotic aneurysm can manifest regional symptoms, including fullness, pain, pulsatility, and symptoms associated with local compression (e.g., weakness from compression of an adjacent nerve).

Physical findings in an anastomotic aneurysm depend on its location as well as the patient's presentation and the body habitus. Most often, an aneurysm is identified as a palpable pulsatile mass in the area of a prior anastomosis. Rarely, the presentation comprises the clinical sequelae of the anastomotic aneurysm, and the physical findings result from the corresponding complication. These findings, which vary and depend on location, include rupture with bleeding into adjacent tissues or structures, embolization from mural thrombus, thrombosis with distal ischemia, and venous congestion or thrombosis from compression of an adjacent vein. Emergency operative intervention for repair of anastomotic aneurysms carries a higher morbidity and mortality than elective repair, underlining the importance of identification of and surveillance for these lesions in this patient population.

Although the anastomotic aneurysm can manifest any time after implantation of the graft, the median time to identification is approximately 6 years after surgery.[1,3,4,18,19] Earlier manifestation of a pseudoaneurysm should prompt consideration of an infectious etiology. Further evaluation with imaging of the whole graft by fine-cut computed tomography (CT) with and without contrast material (radioactive iodine or, for the patient with renal failure, gadolinium) and measurement of erythrocyte sedimentation rate, which should be very high in chronic inflammatory states, can help delineate the etiology (see Chapter 59).

■ ANATOMIC CONSIDERATIONS

Anastomotic aneurysms, which can occur at any location where there is an anastomosis, are more common when a prosthetic graft is used and when the anastomosis is in an end-to-side configuration. There are clinical variances based on the topography of these lesions, the more common of which are discussed here.

Femoral Artery Anastomosis

A femoral artery anastomosis is the most prevalent site for anastomotic pseudoaneurysms, occurring in approximately three fourths of cases and resulting from either an inflow or an outflow bypass.[4] Because the femoral artery is a relatively superficial location, most of the cases are diagnosed from the clinical finding of an asymptomatic pulsatile mass. With careful surveillance, such masses can be detected in up to 44% of patients[19]; less than 10% of clinically significant pseudoaneurysms require surgery, however.[4] The importance of making the diagnosis in these patients relates to (1) monitoring the aneurysm until it meets the criteria for operative repair and (2) ensuring that the patient is never catheterized through the affected groin, because this procedure could acutely precipitate hemorrhage or thrombosis. Occasionally patients present with symptoms, such as fullness, pain, leg swelling (compression of the femoral vein), and leg weakness (compression of the femoral artery).

The clinical sequelae of femoral anastomotic aneurysms include thrombosis, embolization, and, rarely, spontaneous rupture with bleeding.[8,20] These complications of the anastomotic pseudoaneurysm are related to size. Generally, the indications for operative repair are related to the presence of symptoms, the growth rate of the aneurysm (especially if within 1 to 2 years of implantation), and size (2 to 2.5 cm in a topographically symmetrical pseudoaneurysm). If the aneurysm has a topographically asymmetric relation to the graft or if the underlying anatomy is a patch and not a bypass conduit, an earlier intervention may be indicated.

With the suspicion of the diagnosis or for monitoring the size of the lesion in an asymptomatic patient, ultrasonography is adequate. Once the diagnosis of a femoral anastomotic aneurysm is made, the contralateral femoral anastomosis should be carefully evaluated to assess for the same diagnosis. In the patient with an aortofemoral or iliofemoral graft, contrast-enhanced CT (Fig. 60-3A) should be performed to determine whether an abdominal aortic pseudoaneurysm is present, because the risk factors leading to the development of one anastomotic aneurysm are likely present at all the other anastomoses. When the decision to treat the femoral anastomotic aneurysm is made, contrast-enhanced CT should be performed. Usually, this study with three-dimensional reconstructions is adequate to proceed with surgery, and catheter-based angiography is undertaken only in cases of poor distal perfusion (Fig. 60-3B).

Standard open surgical repair for these lesions is the only option, because endoluminal repair is not appropriate over a joint such as the hip. In noninfected fields, localized replacement of the graft segment is indicated.

The following surgical recommendations are worth considering:

1. Know beforehand the vessels involved in the touchdown site of the distal anastomosis. Determine whether the external iliac or common femoral artery proximal to the anastomosis is patent, and establish its importance to the pelvic circulation. Knowing the size and type of graft material used as well as the likelihood that the cause is infectious is also helpful.
2. Access to the anastomotic aneurysm should be through the previous incision. Occasionally with large aneurysms, the inguinal ligament may have to be divided through a lateral bearing incision. A separate retroperitoneal incision to obtain proximal control is very rarely needed.
3. Fixed retraction should be used (with occasional relaxation to avoid local fat necrosis) as attention is first directed to obtaining proximal control of the graft when patent (see Fig. 60-2). Dissection should be carried to the upper portion of the capsule and directed proximally in the midline to find the graft. Once the graft is identified, exposure further up should

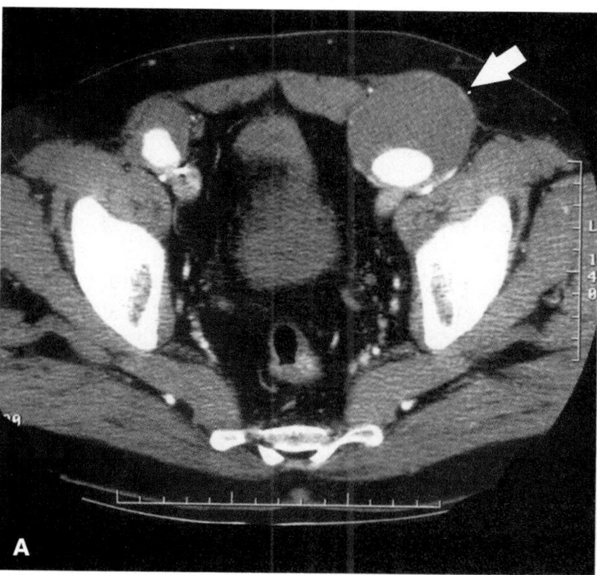

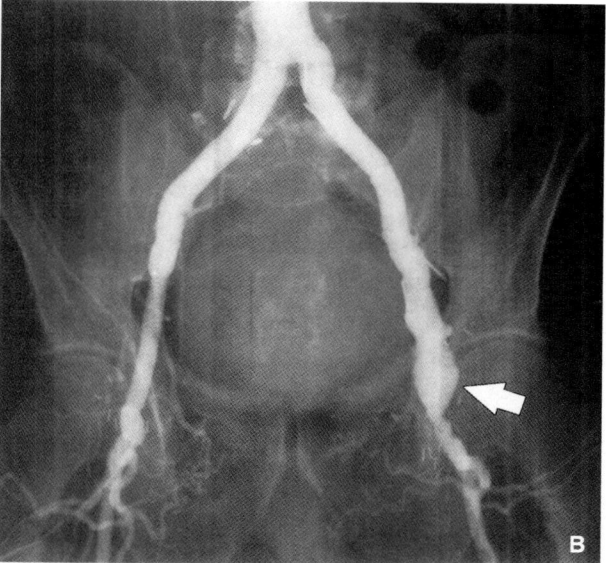

FIGURE 60-3 CT scan of a femoral anastomotic aneurysm larger than 5 cm occurring more than 15 years after aortofemoral graft placement. **A,** The aneurysm extends into the pelvis and has a significant amount of thrombus within the cavity. Note the smaller but significant 3.5-cm right femoral anastomotic aneurysm. **B,** Angiogram of a left femoral anastomotic aneurysm that requires repair, in a patient who already has a right iliofemoral bypass with resection of the right femoral anastomotic aneurysm.

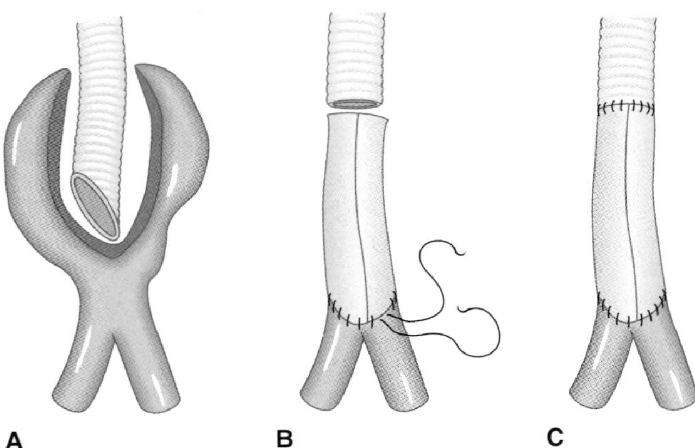

FIGURE 60-4 Depiction of the steps for surgical reconstruction of a femoral anastomotic aneurysm. **A,** After control of the vessels, the anastomotic aneurysm is entered, and the defect inspected. Débridement of tissue and the distal portion of the graft is performed, and (**B**) the distal anastomosis is undertaken but not completed, leaving a flush hole. Both grafts are transected in a perpendicular orientation while taut. Two small wedges, at 3 o'clock and 9 o'clock, have been removed from the new distal graft to permit imbrication of the distal graft just into the proximal one. **C,** The proximal anastomosis is performed, and after flushing, the distal anastomosis is completed, restoring circulation.

be obtained directly on the graft material before it is encircled with a vessel loop. Topographical information from the CT scan of the inguinal ligament structures helps identify the location of the anastomosis and avoids encircling the graft too low. Attention is then directed to the identification of the superficial femoral artery, deep femoral artery, and other major branches, which can be facilitated with the use of a handheld Doppler transducer. In an effort to avoid injury to the external iliac and common femoral veins, control of the external iliac artery, when patent, is performed only if very straightforward.

4. Once control of the vessels is obtained, systemic anticoagulation is administered, and the exposed vessels are clamped. The anastomotic aneurysm is opened (Fig. 60-4A), and any bleeding sites are controlled with small balloon catheters. The graft is proximally transected in a perpendicular fashion and stay sutures are placed at the 3- and 9-o'clock positions. The etiology of the pseudoaneurysm is determined, and if infection (see Chapter 59) is not a major consideration, graft replacement is undertaken with good arterial tissue. The decision whether the external iliac artery can be part of the reconstruction can now be made. If continuity of the external iliac artery must be preserved but cannot be incorporated into the anastomosis because of degeneration of the common femoral artery, a separate iliofemoral bypass should be constructed. This bypass should be made first in an end-to-end configuration before the inflow from the old graft is undertaken. Alternatively, depending on anatomic and clinical necessities, the proximal native system can be oversewn.
5. Once the distal anastomotic site (distal common femoral, superficial femoral, deep femoral, combination with a forked tongue configuration, or the iliofemoral graft) is prepared, preferentially an expanded PTFE graft of the same diameter as the inflow limb is sewn to the distal anastomosis but not completed, leaving a vent hole (Fig. 60-4B). Thus, with distal fixation, the graft length required can be accurately determined and the graft transected perpendicularly. After ratcheting of the new graft and removal of a small wedge of graft at the 3- and 9-o'clock positions to enable eversion of the new graft within the old graft limb—to allow for the 10% to 15% expected enlargement of the Dacron over time—the anastomosis is undertaken (Fig. 60-4C). After the proximal anastomosis is tested, with venting through the distal anastomosis, which is then completed, circulation is re-established. Assessment of the adequacy of distal perfusion is then performed in customary fashion.
6. Closure should include the pseudointima when adequate for coverage of the graft. In cases of very large aneurysms with a significant soft tissue defect, consideration should be given to swinging a sartorius muscle flap over the graft.

Abdominal Aorta Anastomosis

Anastomotic aneurysms of the aorta, which are more common in patients in whom the underlying pathology was aneurysmal disease rather than occlusive disease, occur in about 2% to 5% of patients with aortic grafts.[1,21] Therefore, an imaging study of the aorta should be performed every 5 to 10 years after aortic graft implantation.[22] Anastomotic aneurysm of the abdominal aorta is generally asymptomatic and is not identified on physical examination unless it is large and appears in a very thin patient. In the asymptomatic patient, the aortic anastomotic aneurysm is often identified like an aortic aneurysm—as an incidental finding on abdominal imaging for other diagnoses.

Occasionally patients present with vague symptoms such as back or abdominal pain or discomfort, which is often nonspecific and difficult to attribute to an aneurysm. The clinical presentation can result from one of the clinical sequelae of an aortic anastomotic aneurysm, which include rupture with hemorrhage, thrombosis or embolism, and, less commonly, erosion into an adjacent structure such as bowel or vena cava.

With identification of an aortic anastomotic aneurysm, a contrast-enhanced CT with three-dimensional reconstructions should be performed to help determine whether the lesion is a recurrent aneurysm of the aortic remnant or a pseudoaneurysm of the anastomosis. Ultrasonography can occasionally be helpful to make the diagnosis, but radiologic interpretation and sensitivity can be limited to the subtleties because of the postoperative nature of the anatomy. Contrast angiography is rarely necessary, because it does not provide additional information and because the manipulation of catheters in this scenario is not without some, though limited, risk (Fig. 60-5).

Indications for repair of aortic anastomotic aneurysms include symptomatic aneurysms, patients presenting with complications of the anastomotic aneurysm, or diameter of a truly anastomotic aneurysm either greater than twice the

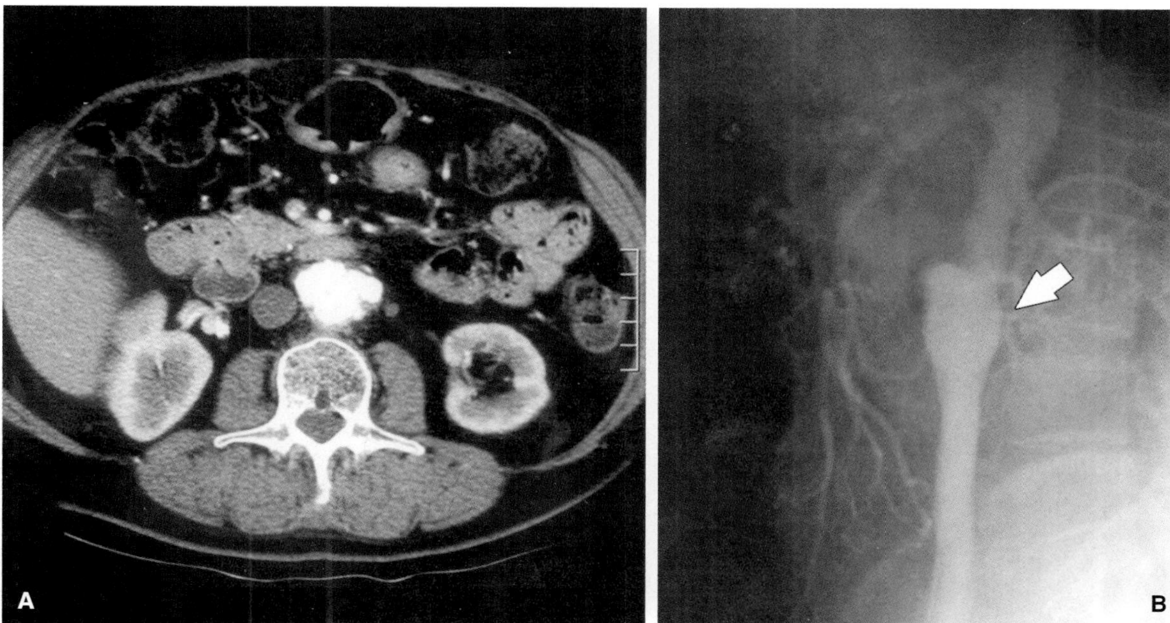

FIGURE 60-5 **A,** CT scan of an aortic anastomotic aneurysm. **B,** Aortogram showing corresponding level (*arrow*) of the CT scan. Note the characteristic lobulated appearance of the anastomotic aneurysm on the CT scan.

diameter of the graft or more than 4 cm. The presence of a saccular rather than a fusiform pseudoaneurysm would advocate for an earlier intervention.[23]

Open surgical repair of the aortic pseudoaneurysm can be a formidable undertaking. Generally, the retroperitoneal approach is preferred because it provides the best exposure for control of the suprarenal or supraceliac aorta, which is often necessary. The caveat of sewing to good-quality aorta is imperative and may require concomitant renal artery bypass and a beveled anastomosis. The distal graft-to-graft anastomosis is generally straightforward, often requiring resection of part of the original graft for length considerations.

In cases of aortic pseudoaneurysms for which infection is not a likely cause, endograft reconstruction should always be considered and should be undertaken if appropriate for the topography and the patient. There must be an adequate proximal neck length (15 mm below the lowest renal artery, with the option of extra-anatomic renal artery bypass), diameter (<30 mm with currently available devices), and angle (<60 degrees). Another challenge is the length of the body of the aortic graft. The standard aortobifemoral configuration of a short body with long limbs can make the placement of a bifurcated aortic endograft very difficult with available graft body lengths (7 cm to the flow divider). In some of these cases, the surgeon must build up the endograft from one limb, "jailing" and occluding the other limb. This problem ultimately necessitates a femorofemoral bypass to provide perfusion down both legs. The endograft procedure can be straightforward and easily tolerated. With the graft material providing an excellent distal touchdown point, the dimensions and quality of the infrarenal aortic remnant are the main determinants.

Iliac Artery Anastomosis

Anastomotic aneurysms of the iliac artery and the aorta are very similar in presentation, diagnostic evaluation, and complications. The differences include the rare instance of erosion into bowel, in which the fistula is not into the duodenum but the distal small bowel, or colon. Compression of the iliac vein can result in lower extremity swelling or deep venous thrombosis, whereas the desmoplastic reaction around the anastomotic aneurysm can lead to ureteral obstruction and hydronephrosis with its clinical presentation. Imaging evaluation of the other anastomoses should also be undertaken to exclude other anastomotic aneurysms and formulate appropriate clinical plans.

Indications for repair of iliac anastomotic aneurysms include presence of symptoms, presence of a complication, and aneurysmal size 2.5 to 3 cm. Most commonly, this lesion involves the iliac anastomosis as the distal graft anastomosis, but in the case of occlusive disease, it can also be the proximal anastomosis, usually in the common iliac artery.

Of the common anatomic locations of anastomotic aneurysms, the iliac location is the most suitable for endograft repair and thus this should always be considered and appropriately evaluated with contrast-enhanced CT (Fig. 60-6). Generally, the prior graft is proximally located, providing an ideal place to seat the endograft, and distally, the external iliac artery is devoid of branches and rarely aneurysmal, providing another good location to seal the endograft connection. However, there are several requirements for the placement of an endograft in this location: (1) there is a low probability of an infectious cause; (2) the aneurysm itself does not need to be debulked because of the clinical presentation; and (3) there is no contraindication to internal iliac artery coil embolization if this artery is

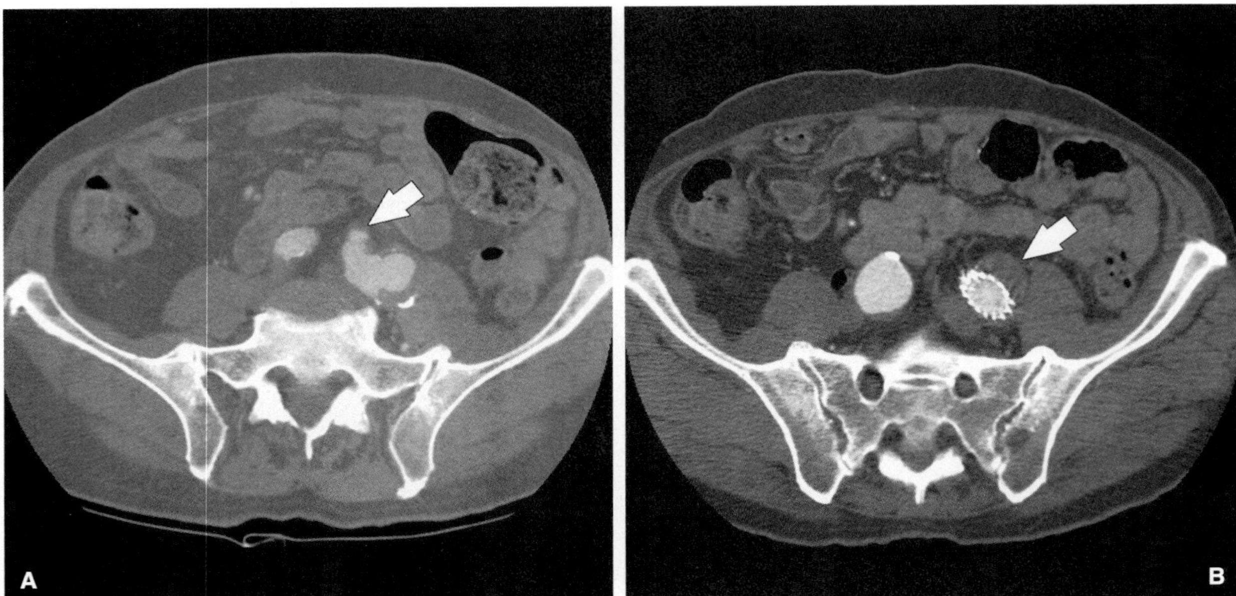

FIGURE 60-6 Axial CT scans demonstrating a large, 3.5-cm left iliac anastomotic aneurysm. **A,** The graft is delineated by the *arrow*. **B,** After placement of the stent graft, there is exclusion of the aneurysm with absence of contrast material (*arrow*) and a decrease in size.

still patent (Fig. 60-7). Alternatively, an end-to-end bypass to the internal iliac artery should be constructed at the time of endograft placement. In this fashion, an endograft can be placed to seal the aneurysm proximally and distally, and with ligation of the proximal internal iliac and distal internal iliac bypass, the pelvic circulation remains unaltered. In fact, in stable patients with acute rupture, endograft placement can be used for treatment of an iliac pseudoaneurysm by the surgeon comfortable and experienced with endovascular techniques.

Open surgical repair can be generally performed via a retroperitoneal approach with fixed retraction. When the procedure is performed to maintain pelvic circulation through the internal iliac, a separate bypass to the hypogastric artery is generally required; alternatively, this vessel can be ligated at the time of the graft to external iliac artery bypass.

Carotid Artery Pseudoaneurysms

Although rare, carotid artery pseudoaneurysms can occur at the site of a patch reconstruction. The incidence is rare, being reported as 0.6%, and may in part result from technical problems, use of poor quality vein for a patch, very bulbous reconstruction of the arteriotomy, or, in the case of

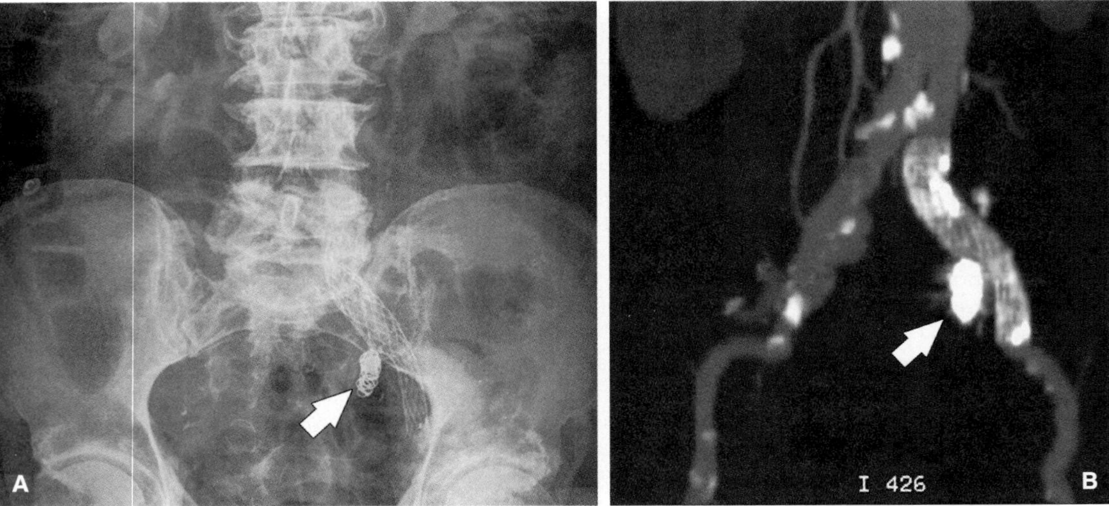

FIGURE 60-7 Abdominal radiograph (**A**) and three-dimensional reconstruction of a CT scan (**B**) after endograft repair of a left common iliac anastomotic aneurysm. After coiling of the hypogastric arteries (*arrow* in each), two stent-grafts (distal 15-mm and proximal 20-mm cuff) were used to seal the graft proximally and the external iliac artery distally to exclude the anastomotic aneurysm.

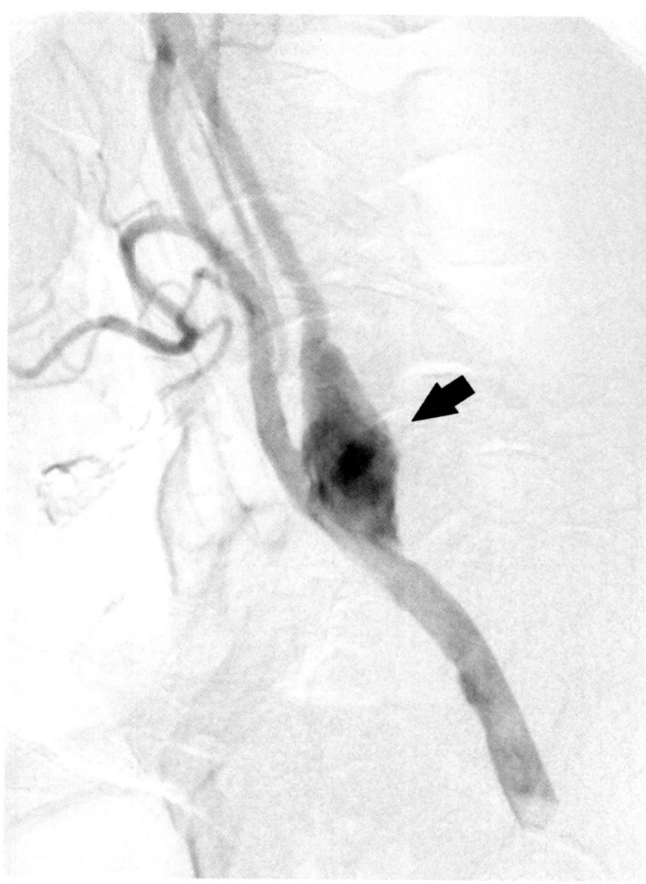

FIGURE 60-8 Angiogram of a carotid artery pseudoaneurysm. The saphenous vein patch from a prior carotid endarterectomy has degenerated into a pseudoaneurysm (*arrow*), now requiring reconstruction.

prosthetic patch, an infective process.[24] Presenting findings include an asymptomatic or painful pulsatile cervical mass and, in the setting of a previous carotid endarterectomy, transient ischemic attacks.

The diagnosis is often made on carotid duplex scanning, and contrast-enhanced CT with reconstructions can be very useful in planning the surgical intervention. The use of angiography (Fig. 60-8) generally does not add to the preoperative assessment and should be avoided in most patients, but both duplex and contrast CT scanning should be undertaken to confirm the diagnosis. Even a relatively small asymptomatic pseudoaneurysm may degenerate and produce thrombus and embolic material in the lumen and so should be considered for reconstruction.

Surgical correction with bypass replacement of the carotid artery should be the treatment of choice. Intraoperative manipulation should be minimized, and careful dissection of the vagus and hypoglossal nerves should be undertaken. With fixed retraction, often the distal internal and the proximal common carotid arteries can be dissected free, and a bypass can be performed around the aneurysm without incorporating the external carotid artery in the reconstruction. In this way, the aneurysm is debulked, and the external carotid artery is carefully oversewn from inside the aneurysmal sac.

Placement of a carotid endograft for repair of a carotid pseudoaneurysm should not be considered at this time. There is generally significant debris within the lumen of these lesions that can readily embolize and result in a stroke. Distal embolization protection devices are being developed that could capture particulate matter and protect the brain from embolic stroke. When these protection devices and appropriately sized and tapered endografts (accommodating the larger common carotid proximally and the smaller internal carotid distally) become available, this therapeutic modality should be investigated and may become a therapeutic option for treating carotid pseudoaneurysms.[25]

■ PREVENTION

There are sound surgical and endovascular principles for minimizing the occurrence of anastomotic aneurysms, although they cannot be totally prevented. The use of permanent sutures—with big bites but not long travels during suturing in the construction of the anastomosis—is important. The development of hematomas should be avoided; when they occur, such lesions should be surgically drained, hemostasis should be achieved, and the incision should be carefully reclosed. Perioperative antibiotic therapy and meticulous surgical technique help minimize the incidence of infection. Despite care to prevent the occurrence of anastomotic aneurysms, they cannot be totally avoided. Therefore, it is important to practice careful graft surveillance of patients at risk with imaging studies, when appropriate, to help reduce the clinical complications related to this entity.

■ REFERENCES

1. Edwards JM, et al: Intraabdominal para-anastomotic aneurysms after aortic bypass grafting. J Vasc Surg 15:344-353, 1992.
2. Szilagyi E, et al: A thirty-year survey of the reconstructive surgical treatment of aortoiliac occlusive disease. J Vasc Surg 3:421-436, 1986.
3. van den Akker PJ, et al: Long term success of aortoiliac operation for arteriosclerotic obstructive disease. Surg Gynecol Obstet 174:485-496, 1992.
4. Ernst CB, et al: Recurrent femoral anastomotic aneurysms: A 30-year experience. Ann Surg 208:401-409, 1988.
5. Calhoun TR, Kitten CM: Polypropylene suture—is it safe? J Vasc Surg 4:98-100, 1986.
6. Chen LE, Seaber AV, Urbaniak JR: Comparison of 10-0 polypropylene and 10-0 nylon sutures in rat arterial anastomosis. Microsurgery 14:328-333, 1993.
7. Ross G, et al: Absorbable suture materials for vascular anastomoses: Tensile strength and axial pressure studies using polyglycolic acid sutures. Am Surg 47:541-547, 1981.
8. Hollier LH, Batson RC, Cohn I Jr: Femoral anastomotic aneurysms. Ann Surg 191:715-720, 1980.
9. Zeebregts CJ, et al: Non-suture methods of vascular anastomosis. Br J Surg 90:261-271, 2003.
10. Seabrook GR, et al: Anastomotic femoral pseudoaneurysm: An investigation of occult infection as an etiologic factor. J Vasc Surg 11:629-634, 1990.
11. Dennis JW, et al: Anastomotic pseudoaneurysms: A continuing late complication of vascular reconstructive procedures. Arch Surg 121:314-317, 1986.
12. Da Silva JR, et al: Aortofemoral bypass grafts: Safety of percutaneous puncture. J Vasc Surg 1:642-645, 1984.

13. LaMuraglia GM, et al: The safety of intraaortic balloon pump catheter insertion through suprainguinal prosthetic vascular bypass grafts. J Vasc Surg 13:830-837, 1991.
14. Taylor LM Jr, et al: Axillofemoral grafting with externally supported polytetrafluoroethylene. Arch Surg 129:588-595, 1994.
15. Hasson JE, Megerman J, Abbott WM: Increased compliance near vascular anastomoses. J Vasc Surg 2:419-423, 1985.
16. Rodgers VG, et al: Characterization in vitro of the biomechanical properties of anastomosed host artery-graft combinations. J Vasc Surg 4:396-402, 1986.
17. Foster JH, et al: Comparative study of elective resection and expectant treatment of abdominal aortic aneurysm. Surg Gynecol Obstet 129: 1-9, 1969.
18. Gardner TJ, Brawley RK, Gott VL: Anastomotic false aneurysms. Surgery 72:474-478, 1972.
19. van den Akker PJ, et al: False aneurysms after prosthetic reconstructions for aortoiliac obstructive disease. Ann Surg 210:658-666, 1989.
20. Richardson JV, McDowell HA: Anastomotic aneurysms following arterial grafting: A 10-year experience. Ann Surg 184:179-182, 1976.
21. McCann RL, Schwartz LB, Georgiade GS: Management of abdominal aortic graft complications. Ann Surg 217:729-734, 1993.
22. Bastounis E, et al: The validity of current vascular imaging methods in the evaluation of aortic anastomotic aneurysms developing after abdominal aortic aneurysm repair. Ann Vasc Surg 10:537-545, 1996.
23. Taylor BV, Kalman PG: Saccular aortic aneurysms. Ann Vasc Surg 13:555-559, 1999.
24. Thompson JE: Complications of carotid endarterectomy and their prevention. World J Surg 3:155-165, 1979.
25. Criado E, et al: Endovascular repair of peripheral aneurysms, pseudoaneurysms, and arteriovenous fistulas. Ann Vasc Surg 11:256-263, 1997.

Chapter 61

Aortoenteric Fistulae

VIKRAM S. KASHYAP, MD
PATRICK J. O'HARA, MD

One of the more uncommon but devastating conditions a vascular surgeon may face is a patient presenting with an *aortoenteric fistula* (AEF). The fistula may occur in the setting of a native diseased abdominal aorta (primary AEF) or, more commonly, in the setting of a prior aortic reconstruction with prosthetic material (secondary AEF). The communication between the aorta and the bowel usually occurs between the infrarenal segment of the aorta and the third or fourth portion of the duodenum. Rarely, the fistula may occur in other enteric areas of the small bowel, colon, stomach, or esophagus. The first description of a primary AEF between the infrarenal aorta and the duodenum was published in 1829 by Sir Astley Cooper.[1] The first report of secondary AEF was made in 1953 by Brock,[2] who described a fistula between the proximal anastomosis of an aortic homograft and the duodenum. Zenker performed the first repair of a primary AEF in 1954 with primary closure.[3] MacKenzie and colleagues[4] performed the first successful repair of a secondary AEF in 1958.

Despite progress in aortic surgery over the last four decades, AEF is often a lethal condition. The rarity of the disease, combined with a presentation similar to that of other gastrointestinal (GI) bleeding diagnoses, leads this condition to often go unrecognized and be underdiagnosed. Furthermore, the limitations of our current diagnostic studies, and the physiologic stress of sepsis combined with operative treatment have contributed to the high morbidity and mortality rates of AEF. Management of this particular entity requires a high index of suspicion in any patient presenting with GI hemorrhage and a history of aortic replacement, expeditious evaluation, and appropriate clinical judgment. Furthermore, technical skill is needed to successfully stop the hemorrhage, remove the infected vascular prosthesis, and reconstruct both bowel and vascular continuity. This chapter reviews the etiology, diagnostic methods, and treatment modalities for successful management of AEFs.

■ CLASSIFICATION AND ETIOLOGY

The types of AEFs are primary and secondary. A *primary* AEF is a communication between the aorta, usually diseased, and the bowel lumen. The communication most commonly occurs between an aneurysmal infrarenal aorta and the third or fourth portion of the duodenum (83% of patients), because these structures abut each other, especially with aneurysm expansion. The fixed nature of the duodenum in the retroperitoneum due to the ligament of Treitz also allows erosive mechanical factors to play a role in fistula formation.[5,6] Occasionally, other segments of the bowel may be involved—esophagus, stomach, jejunum, ileum, appendix, and colon.[7,8]

Primary AEF occurs spontaneously in association with either aortic or GI disease. A review of more than 100 cases showed aortic aneurysm to be the dominant cause of primary AEF in more than 70% of cases.[9] Usually, the aneurysm is sterile and secondary to degeneration of the aortic wall. In the remainder of patients, aortitis or mycotic aneurysm due to *Staphylococcus* infection causes the primary AEF.[10] Other, infrequent causes of primary AEF are peptic ulcer perforation into the aorta, neoplastic erosion into the bowel and adjacent aorta, tuberculous mesenteric lymphadenitis, primary aortitis, and pancreatic pseudocyst penetration.[11-15] Unusual causes of primary AEF are ingested foreign body, diverticulitis, appendicitis, and radiation injury.[5] Of these GI causes of primary AEF, peptic ulcer disease seems to be the most prominent and has been seen in more than two dozen cases.[16] In these cases, peptic ulcer symptoms precede the formation of AEF, and continued untreated peptic ulcer disease leads to erosion of the bowel wall into the native aorta. Because affected patients often carry the diagnosis of peptic ulcer disease, their episodes of bleeding are treated as such, and the underlying AEF is not appreciated. In 9 out of 24 cases in one series, a massive hemorrhage led to death, and diagnosis of AEF was made only at autopsy.[16] Formation of primary AEF in patients who have peptic ulcer disease is not predictable, and presumably, the incidence is decreasing with the current widespread use of acid-lowering medications.

The pathogenesis of primary AEF is likely different from that of secondary AEF. Data on etiology are scarce and are derived mostly from clinical information and long-term follow-up of patients who have been observed carefully by clinicians. The etiologic factors in the pathophysiology of AEFs are displayed in Figure 61-1. Factors associated with primary AEF formation include both aortic and duodenal forces. Aortic forces causing primary AEF are mechanical compression of the duodenum by an enlarging aorta, local inflammatory changes, and primary aortic infections. All

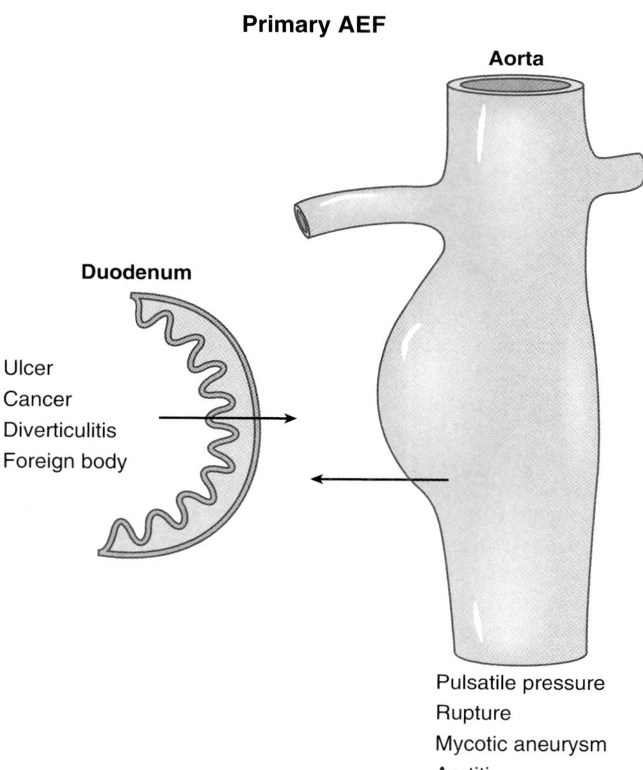

FIGURE 61-1 Etiologic factors for primary aortoenteric fistula (AEF). Pulsatile pressure from an expanding aneurysm is thought to be the predominant feature in the development of primary AEF. Other factors related to intrinsic bowel conditions may play a role in the development of primary AEF in a minority of cases.

can lead to a spontaneous communication between aorta and bowel lumen. The paramount factor in primary AEF formation is presumed to be continued pulsatile pressure from an expanding aneurysm. The argument that enteric erosion and perforation by mechanical forces from a diseased or deformed aorta may be the fundamental mechanism for the formation of primary AEF is supported by the clinical observations that in-line aortic reconstructions are only rarely complicated by infection.[9,17,18] Furthermore, there is general agreement that secondary AEF is less likely to occur after aortic reconstruction if care is taken to maintain separation of the synthetic graft and the bowel by insertion of adequate retroperitoneal tissue or omentum as a reinforcement.[19,20]

Secondary AEFs occur after prior aortic surgery. They usually follow aortic reconstructive procedures with prosthetic grafts using Dacron. Secondary AEFs have also been reported after aortic reconstruction with homografts and other procedures, including endarterectomy and aortorenal bypass.[21-23] Secondary AEFs occur in two forms, (1) a communication between the aortic lumen and bowel lumen at the aortic anastomosis and (2) the less common aortoparaprosthetic-enteric sinus or graft-enteric erosion. Secondary AEFs are more common than primary AEFs. Early reports of aortic reconstruction indicated that secondary AEFs complicated as many as 10% of aortic reconstructive procedures.[24,25] With improvements in operative technique, the incidence has declined to less than 1%.[26-29] Some features of secondary AEFs are similar to those of primary AEF, including the fact that the third or fourth portion of the duodenum is the most common location for fistula formation.

Multiple investigators have previously attempted to classify AEFs. Vollmar and Kogel[30] designated direct aortoenteric communications as *type I* fistulae with subclassification according to the absence (*type IA*) or presence (*type IB*) of an associated pseudoaneurysm. *Type II* AEFs were graft-enteric erosions. A classification based on pathologic appearance was described by Buchbinder and colleagues,[31] in which aortic disruptions were either fistulae or erosions. An AEF, whether primary or secondary, represented a direct communication between aorta and bowel, whereas a graft-enteric erosion designated a paraprosthetic sinus. A similar schema was proposed by Bunt,[26] who included graft infections and aortic stump sepsis in this spectrum of aortic complications.

The proposed etiologies for secondary AEFs may provide more insight into the pathophysiology of this condition (Fig. 61-2). As in primary AEF, both aortic and duodenal factors play a role in the causation of the fistula. The inciting event may be (1) infection of the prosthesis, (2) continued pulsatile pressure from a noncompliant prosthesis, or (3) duodenal injury.

Infection of the prosthesis as the initiating event for secondary AEF can lead to suture line disruption, local inflammatory changes, and eventual pseudoaneurysm formation. Thus, secondary AEF would represent the end stage along the spectrum of aortic graft infections (covered in Chapter 59).

The presence of prosthetic material serves as a nidus for bacterial growth and also possibly causes a foreign body inflammatory reaction. Several types of graft mate-

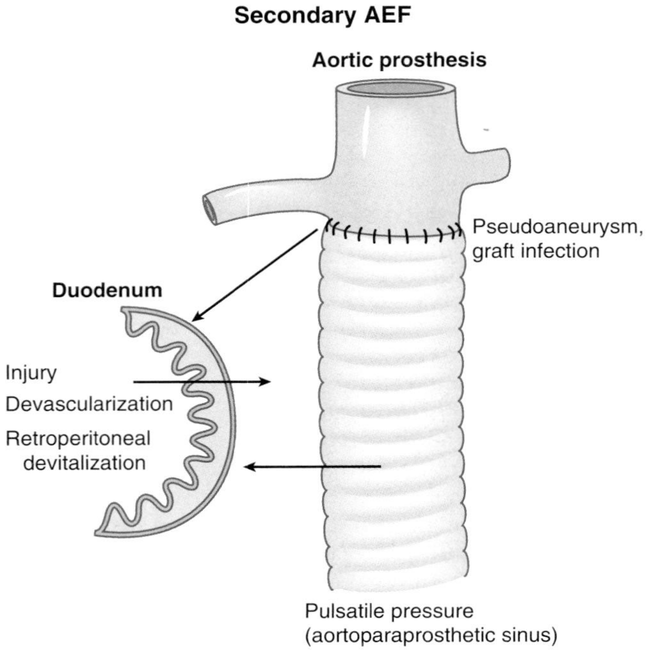

FIGURE 61-2 Etiologic factors for secondary aortoenteric fistula (AEF). Secondary AEF occurs after aortic reconstruction, and both graft factors and duodenal factors play roles in its development. Graft infection is the primary causative feature in secondary AEFs, whereas continued pulsatile pressure can erode bowel tissue and is the predominant cause of aortoparaprosthetic sinus formation.

rials have been associated with AEF, including polyester (Dacron), polytetrafluoroethylene (Teflon), nylon, and homografts.[2,20,32,33] Prosthetic grafts that are sterile at the time of delivery to the operating field may become inoculated at the time of surgical implantation owing to a break in surgical technique or contamination. At some later point, bacterial growth may occur because the patient's immunologic defense mechanism dips in strength. Supporting this possibility is the fact that most bacteria isolated from aortic graft infections are skin flora.[26] The incidence of secondary AEF rises to 40% with primary aortic graft infection.[34-36] Hematogenous spread of bacteria to a prosthetic graft may also occur late after a remote infection.

There is compelling experimental evidence that low-grade infection is an important cause of AEF. Using a model of aortic duodenal fistula in dogs, Busuttil and associates[34] found that the addition of intravenous bacteria led to fistula formation but simple fixation of the duodenum to the prosthesis did not. Other evidence of bacteria inoculation at the time of graft implantation includes the presence of bacteria in the transudation fluid that collects in the intestinal bag holding the small intestine during aortic surgery and the fact that many graft infections are due to skin flora.[37] These data suggest that the cause of secondary AEF is a primary low-grade infection that flares due to a variety of factors in play months to years after the graft procedure. The corollary is that prevention of infection may diminish the chance of this complication.

Another proposed mechanism of secondary AEF formation implicates continued pulsatile pressure on the duodenum, analogous to the etiology of primary AEF. This pressure can occur from a noncompliant prosthesis or an enlarging pseudoaneurysm causing duodenal erosion.[33] The breakdown of the proximal suture line may lead to an aortic pseudoaneurysm that eventually erodes into adjacent duodenum. The original suture line disruption may be secondary to a variety of factors, including suture fatigue, aortic wall degeneration, and hypertension.[25,38] Interestingly, events that predispose to infection increase the likelihood of anastomotic disruption, indicating that infection may still be the root cause of AEF.[39-41] Busuttil and associates[34] reported that repair of ruptured aneurysms is associated with a 1.7% incidence of AEF, compared with 0.7% after elective aneurysm resection and 0.2% after elective aortic reconstruction for aortoiliac occlusive disease.[34] The incidence of AEF development was higher in the 1950s and 1960s, when silk suture was used for arterial anastomoses; silk may be more prone to breakdown than the polypropylene in current use.[42]

A distinct entity is the *aortoparaprosthetic sinus*, also known as a *graft-enteric erosion* (GEE). In this condition, pulsatile pressure and mechanical erosion of the bowel are thought to be the primary cause, with resultant infection of the graft by enteric flora. The GEE forms in the midgraft distinct from the suture line, which is often involved in AEF. The outer connective tissue capsule of the prosthesis erodes into the bowel lumen, but there is no communication with the aortic lumen except through the interstices of the graft. The eroded edges of bowel mucosa also may be the source of bleeding. A sinus can evolve into a fistula if the sinus erodes into the aortic lumen or spreads to include the proximal or distal suture lines.[20,26] After bowel perforation, bacteria and digestive enzymes bathe the graft, causing graft infection, retroperitoneal inflammation, and formation of an aortoenteric sinus. With progression of the process and extension of the sinus, the proximal suture line eventually erodes, resulting in a true AEF.[26,31,43] Bulky, or large-diameter, synthetic grafts may be more likely to erode into adjacent bowel and predispose to AEF formation because they are more difficult to cover effectively with retroperitoneal tissue.[40,41]

GEE is not as common as the more dramatic AEF. Bunt[26] noted 38 cases of GEE compared with 256 cases of AEF. Risk factors for the occurrence of either of these lesions include emergency operations, "redo" operations, inadequate retroperitoneal coverage, and the presence of systemic sepsis.

The last factor in the formation of AEF is duodenal injury. The third or fourth portion of the duodenum is consistently the most likely sight of fistula formation, presumably because the anterior wall of the aneurysm and the posterior wall of the duodenum are in very close proximity and often adherent. However, operative trauma or ischemia to the duodenum also contributes to erosion.[20] Thus, duodenal injury or devascularization at the time of initial aortic reconstruction may be an etiologic factor in secondary AEF. It may lead to retroperitoneal adhesions or fibrosis and may initiate the process of fistula formation with the aortic prosthesis.

Anecdotally, some experienced vascular surgeons believe that AEF is distinctly unusual when a retroperitoneal approach has been utilized for aortic reconstruction. This clinical impression is unproved and might be the result of a small sample size, because AEF is an unusual complication of aortic surgery. It also, however, might indicate that the transperitoneal approach, which requires division of the parietal peritoneum to expose the aorta, may devitalize this tissue, leading to necrosis and adherence of the duodenum to the graft material. A confounding variable is that most large series of AEF management accrued at a time when the vast majority of aortic reconstructions were performed via a midline transabdominal approach. Unfortunately, the approach at initial operation has not been documented well in reports dealing with secondary AEF. Proposing a trial to study this hypothesis would be difficult because of the low incidence of the lesion.

In summary, multiple factors related to the aorta and adjacent duodenum are responsible for the formation of AEF. Presumably, in most cases, an interplay of multiple factors eventually leads to the fistulous communication.

Prevention

The available data suggest that some simple, but prudent, technical factors that, if considered at the time of the original aortic reconstruction, may have an important influence on the prevention of this devastating complication. They are as follows:

1. Careful attention should be focused upon adequate cleansing of the skin and draping of the field to avoid any initial contamination during the procedure. This practice may play a role in decreasing acute aortic prosthetic infections and latent bacterial growth.
2. During placement of fixed retraction, attention should be directed to avoiding undue compression on and ischemia of the duodenum. Moist laparotomy pads should be interposed between the bowel and the metal retractors, to help avoid devitalization of the bowel wall and the resultant periprosthetic, fibrous adhesions.
3. Most importantly, closure of the retroperitoneum after aortic reconstruction should be carefully performed. Often a large redundant aortic aneurysm wall is present and can be closed over the aortic graft. A second layer including the retroperitoneal tissue and parietal peritoneum allows complete exclusion of the prosthetic graft from the intra-abdominal viscera. When an aortic graft is placed for occlusive disease—in which an aneurysm sac is not available—the retroperitoneum should still be closed over the graft for the greatest length possible. Occasionally, when retroperitoneal tissue is insufficient for complete closure, a flap of greater omentum may be tunneled through the transverse mesocolon and carefully interposed between the graft and the duodenum.

■ CLINICAL PRESENTATION

The prevalence of primary AEF is low, but the diagnosis may be underappreciated. The prevalence is estimated to be between 0.04% and 0.07% on the basis of autopsy studies.[44] The total cases reported in the literature numbered less than 300, with only a handful reported in the last decade. A 1996 survey adds to the notion that these cases are underreported. Voorhoeve and coworkers[18] sent a questionnaire to all surgical clinics in the Netherlands, netting 29 cases of primary AEF that had been previously unpublished.

Secondary AEFs are more common. As previously mentioned, Brock[2] first described secondary AEF in 1953. In the early days of aortic reconstruction, when homografts were widely used, approximately 80% of the AEFs occurred in the body of homograft and a minority occurred at the suture line. The converse is true today: Most of the AEFs occur at the suture line. The incidence of aortic graft infection and AEF formation has been carefully documented. In a review of 3652 aortic grafts spanning the years 1961 through 1985, only 13 AEFs were found, giving an incidence of 0.326%. There were also 28 graft infections, leading to an incidence of 0.77%.[29] In another study, the incidence of AEF was found to be 1.6% in a defined community in Minnesota between 1957 and 1990. Graft infection occurred in an additional 1.3% of cases, and sterile pseudoaneurysm in 3%.[27]

Clinical presentation of AEF rarely leads to the classic triad—GI bleeding, sepsis, and abdominal pain—in a single patient.[19,26] GI bleeding, manifested as hematemesis, hematochezia, melena, or chronic anemia, is the most common presenting symptom, occurring in nearly 70% of patients. Massive hemorrhage rarely occurs at presentation, and more often, a "herald bleed" is encountered, in which the patient has an episode of small but brisk bleeding that stops. Bleeding episodes can recur as an occluding thrombus seals the fistulous tract temporarily.[17,26] Voyles and Moretz[45] reported that 27% of their patients with AEF survived less than 6 hours, 14% survived 16 to 24 hours, and 46% were alive after 24 hours.

The interval from aortic reconstruction to the onset of hemorrhage averages 2 to 6 years after graft placement.[46-48] The natural history of untreated AEF manifesting as a herald bleed is eventual GI hemorrhage even though the interval may vary. In the majority of patients, there is time before exsanguinating hemorrhage occurs for diagnostic testing to establish a definitive diagnosis. Even though AEF is rare, GI bleeding after aortic surgery is quite common. In a study of 253 patients, bleeding episodes occurred in 21%, with a total of 74 bleeding episodes between 1 and 108 months after surgery.[49] All of the patients underwent extensive evaluation, and only one AEF was diagnosed, giving an incidence of 0.4% for the grafts inserted. In the vast majority of the remaining patients, there were GI sources for bleeding, and no subsequent evidence of AEF was encountered with a mean follow-up of 28 months.

GI bleeding is often found in combination with symptoms and signs of infection. A quarter of patients present with evidence of infection alone, without any bleeding episodes. Fevers and generalized malaise are common, but the fever and leukocytosis are usually quite mild, and sepsis occurs in only 27%.[50] Signs of infection are found more commonly (60%) in patients with paraprosthetic-enteric sinuses. Septicemia results from bacterial absorption through venous or lymphatic channels, and blood cultures may test positive for enteric organisms.[51] Bacteria may translocate through the interstices of the graft, onto the prosthetic lining, and occasionally they manifest as septic emboli to the legs, which are surprisingly common (27%

of patients). Other remote manifestations of sepsis in AEF are multicentric osteomyelitis and hypertrophic osteoarthropathy.[52] In these cases, fever of unknown origin, lower extremity cellulitis, and multiple distal abscesses may be presenting complaints.

Abdominal pain is not very common with secondary AEF but is sometimes associated with primary AEF when acute aneurysm expansion occurs.[9] Paraprosthetic sinuses manifest as pain in 20% of patients with primary AEFs, whereas only 11% of patients with secondary AEFs complain of pain.[26] Graft thrombosis is another uncommon presentation of AEF. The clinical presentation is sometimes quite variable, and a high index of suspicion is required for expeditious diagnosis and management.

■ EVALUATION

The preoperative evaluation of suspected AEF depends on the tempo of bleeding and the stability of the patient. In unstable patients with ongoing hemorrhage, there is no time for any preoperative evaluation, and emergency celiotomy should be planned. In these cases, the diagnosis of AEF is made after exploration has commenced for GI bleeding and the vascular surgeon is urgently summoned to the operating room to consult. Often the hint that an AEF is present is a bile-stained prosthesis at the location of duodenal inflammation. If a patient presents with a "herald bleed" and is stable or has been stabilized, a more orderly progression of preoperative testing can be performed. Prolonged delays in preoperative evaluation can pose a hazard, however, because up to 40% of patients have another large bleed within 24 hours. Although only 50% of AEFs can be definitively diagnosed preoperatively,[53-55] an attempt should be made to identify the source of bleeding if the patient is clinically stable. Importantly, diagnostic testing may uncover other, more likely sources for GI bleeding in patients with prior aortic reconstruction.

Physical examination may demonstrate a palpable abdominal aortic aneurysm or large pseudoaneurysm. The patient may exhibit signs consistent with low-grade sepsis, and signs of septic emboli may be present in the lower extremities. Blood cultures occasionally identify enteric organisms, suggesting the presence of an AEF.

Esophagogastroduodenoscopy (EGD) is the preoperative test most commonly performed first. The first description of the use of upper endoscopy to diagnose AEF was first described by Mir-Madjlessi and colleagues[56] in 1973. A patient in whom an aortic graft had been placed 7 years previously presented with GI bleeding. The AEF was in the third portion of the duodenum, and these investigators emphasized that a complete upper endoscopy to look for AEF should include reaching the third and fourth portions of the duodenum. This procedure has to be performed by an experienced endoscopist and sometimes requires use of a pediatric endoscope to visualize the entire duodenum, because the majority of AEFs are located there (73%). Also, the presence of another source of bleeding such as gastritis or of nonbleeding peptic ulceration should not preclude completion of the EGD, because these entities may coexist with AEF. Findings of EGD suggestive of an AEF are compression of the duodenum by an extrinsic mass, ulcerations of the distal duodenum, bleeding, and, rarely, presence of graft material (Fig. 61-3). During endoscopy, the tamponading thrombus may become dislodged, precipitating sudden hemorrhage.[41] Consequently, some surgeons recommend performing endoscopy in the operating room with preparations at hand for emergency celiotomy if severe hemorrhage occurs.[10,40]

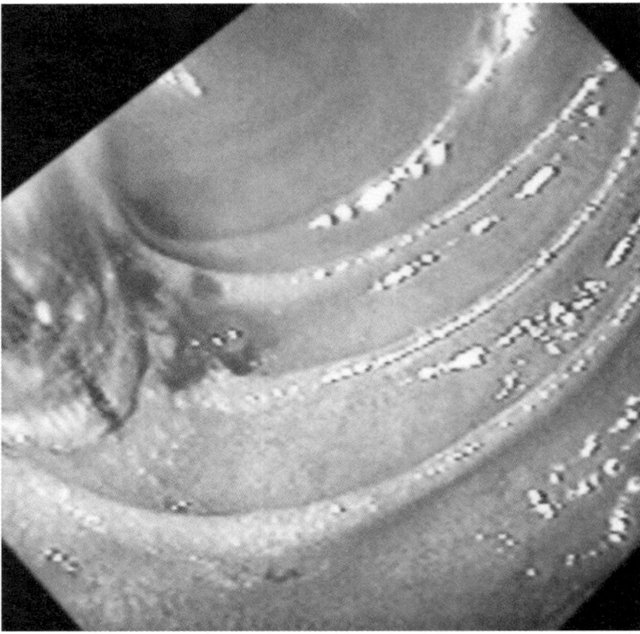

FIGURE 61-3 Esophagogastroduodenoscopy (EGD) shows an exposed Dacron graft that has eroded into the duodenum. Although this finding is unusual, EGD to visualize the fourth portion of the duodenum should be performed in most patients with gastrointestinal bleeding and previous aortic reconstruction.

Because most endoscopic studies are not definitive, contrast-enhanced computed tomography (CT) has emerged as a good complementary study. The use of CT has become widespread, and often, the surgeon encounters the CT scan before the patient in the emergency room. However, the use of CT to diagnose AEF has been documented for the last two decades.[57,58] Common findings are periaortic gas or fluid accumulation, bowel wall thickening, proximal pseudoaneurysm formation, and other signs of retroperitoneal inflammation (Fig. 61-4). Most of the CT findings are consistent with infection, and rarely is actual flow of contrast material seen in the fistula segment. CT findings are often subtle, but the sensitivity (94%) and specificity (85%) of this modality remain high, and it may be the most reliable test that we currently have.[59] Continued improvements in CT, including image acquisition, data processing, image quality, and resolution, may allow CT to replace EGD as an appropriate first evaluation in patients presenting with presumed AEF.[60] Culture specimens of perigraft fluid may be obtained with CT-guided needle aspiration to confirm infection, but this result does not confirm the presence of a fistula or graft erosion.[61,62]

Catheter angiography only rarely documents the fistula (Fig. 61-5), because in most stable patients, an occluding thrombus temporarily seals the fistula.[63,64] Also, aortography cannot document an aortoparaprosthetic sinus. However,

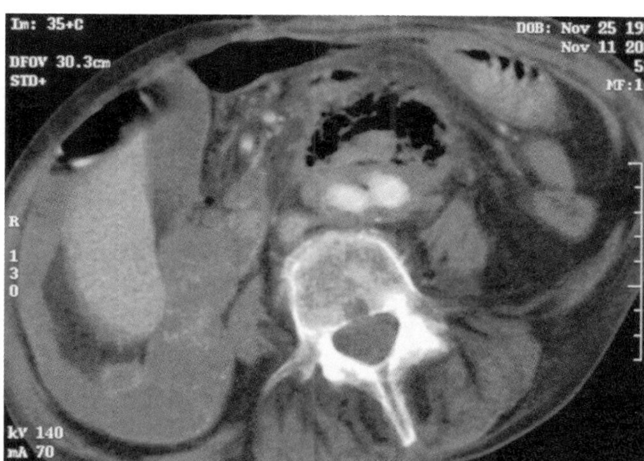

FIGURE 61-4 Contrast-enhanced CT scan of a patient with a secondary aortoenteric fistula. Note the accumulation of gas and retroperitoneal inflammation surrounding a bifurcated aortic prosthesis.

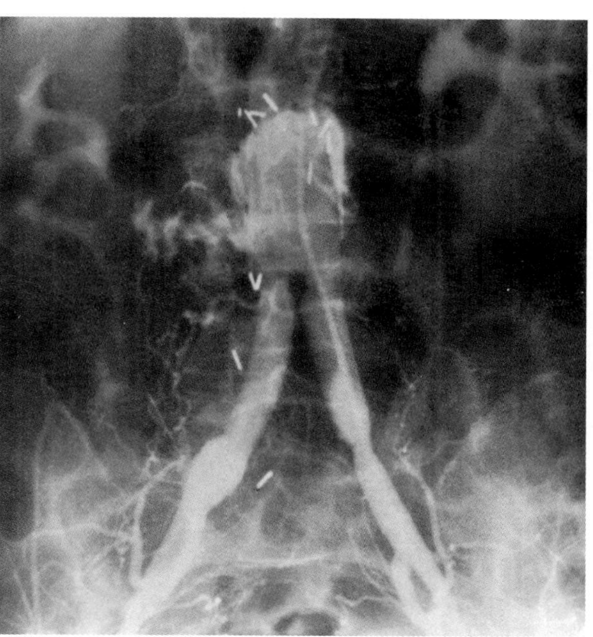

FIGURE 61-5 Aortography showing a secondary aortoenteric fistula (AEF) arising from the proximal anastomosis of a bifurcated aortic prosthesis. Note the presence of contrast agent in the bowel lumen. Angiography is useful in planning reconstruction after graft excision, but it only rarely documents an AEF, because in most stable patients, an occlusive thrombus seals the fistula. (Reprinted from O'Hara PJ: Surgical management of infected abdominal aortic grafts. In Cowgill LD [ed]: Cardiac Surgery: State of the Art Reviews. Philadelphia, Hanley and Belfus, 1987.)

angiography does provide clues that an AEF is present, such as a bulge in the proximal anastomotic region due to deterioration of the prosthetic fabric, a pseudoaneurysm, and a kink in the graft.[65] More importantly, angiography of the aorta and lower extremity vessels is useful for the planning of operative repair in the setting of AEF. The number and location of renal arteries, the patency of visceral vessels, and runoff to the legs are important anatomic factors that influence reconstruction and that can be assessed with an arteriogram.

Other tests, including nuclear scanning with radionuclide-tagged leukocytes or erythrocytes, magnetic resonance imaging (MRI), ultrasonography, and GI radiographic studies using contrast agent are potentially useful, but usually less accurate and more time intensive. Both MRI and magnetic resonance angiography (MRA) may aid in the diagnosis of graft infection and AEF[66] but are more difficult to obtain in critically ill patients. Nuclear imaging techniques using leukocytes labeled with indium 111[67] or technetium Tc 99m–hexamethyl propyleneamine oxime (HMPAO)[69] or immunoglobulin G labeled with indium 111[68] have high sensitivity in detecting graft infection, but their role in detecting AEF is less clear. Contrast GI studies should be avoided because they rarely help in making the diagnosis, are time intensive, and can obscure findings in subsequent angiographic or contrast-enhanced CT studies.

A rare type of AEF is an aortoappendiceal fistula which, given the location of the fistula and the quick transit time of blood through the large bowel, can manifest as bright red blood per rectum. In this situation, colonoscopy and nuclear scans with tagged erythrocytes may be needed to make the diagnosis.[70] Rarely, plain skeletal radiography shows changes consistent with systemic infection. Unilateral lower limb hypertropic osteoarthropathy[71,72] and multifocal osteomyelitis[52] have also been associated with an AEF.

An algorithm for the management of patients with a suspected AEF is presented in Figure 61-6. An emergency exploration is often necessary to manage the unstable patient who presents with GI hemorrhage. For the stable patient, EGD and CT are recommended as initial tests to diagnose AEF. Catheter angiography aids in operative planning. MRI and tagged nuclear scanning can be performed if results of all of the preceding evaluations are indeterminate, but a definitive diagnosis of AEF is often not made until laparotomy. Signs of graft infection combined with a clinical scenario consistent with AEF should prompt expeditious evaluation and definitive operative management.

■ TREATMENT

General Considerations

Once the diagnosis of AEF is established, conservative therapy is ineffective, surgical treatment being the only approach with the potential for success. Although the outcome of surgical therapy is influenced by the presence of the usual co-morbid medical conditions, such as associated cardiac, pulmonary, or renal disease, the timing and sequence of optimal surgical management are heavily influenced by several factors. Arguably, the most important of these are the presence of active hemorrhage, whether AEF is primary or secondary, the anatomic distribution of associated aneurysmal or occlusive disease, and the extent of associated sepsis.

The goals of treatment are first to preserve the life of the patient and then to maintain limb salvage. Ideally, both objectives can be accomplished. The fundamental principles of surgical management are control of hemorrhage, repair of the GI tract, adequate control of infection, and maintenance of adequate distal perfusion.

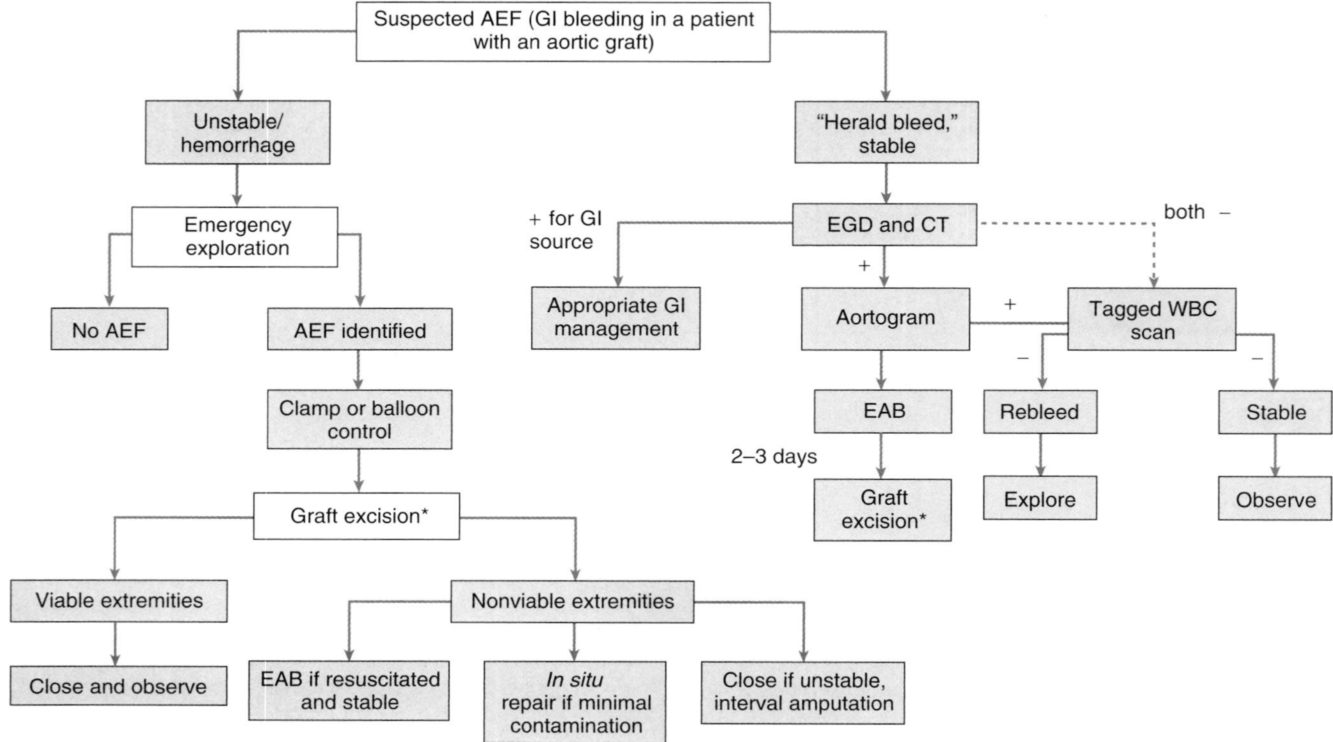

FIGURE 61-6 Algorithm for the management of patients with a suspected aortoenteric fistula (AEF). This algorithm can be used as a guideline, with the understanding that the rate of hemorrhage and the clinical stability of the patient must ultimately influence the management of the patient with suspected AEF. *Graft excision consists of (1) resection of all prosthetic graft, (2) débridement of retroperitoneum, and (3) closure of enteric defect. CT, computed tomography; EAB, extra-anatomic bypass; EGD, esophagogastroduodenoscopy; GI, gastrointestinal; WBC, white blood cell; +, positive or positive result; –, negative or negative result.

The diagnosis of AEF requires expeditious treatment, especially if there is evidence of hemorrhage. Sometimes bleeding is obvious and massive at the outset, but if a patient has presented with a herald bleed that has stabilized temporarily, surgical treatment should still be initiated expediently because subsequent GI hemorrhage in AEF can be sudden, severe, and difficult to predict. Improved survival rates are associated with prompt surgical intervention.[40] While preparations are being made for urgent operation, broad-spectrum antibiotic therapy covering gram-positive and gram-negative organisms should be initiated, adequate monitoring and intravenous access should be established, and proper volume resuscitation undertaken. If the patient has not shown evidence of GI bleeding and is stable, aortography with demonstration of runoff may be helpful to aid in the planning of arterial reconstruction, especially in the presence of associated occlusive disease. However, the decision to pursue angiography should be tempered by its availability and should be individualized with the understanding that it is disadvantageous to delay surgery in an unstable patient with a visit to the angiography suite.

Surgical Approach

The surgical strategy employed in the treatment of either primary or secondary AEF depends on whether the patient is hemodynamically stable at the time of operation, the status of which is usually clinically obvious. It also depends, however, on whether infection is present or absent in the aortic bed at the time of surgical intervention, a circumstance that may be difficult to determine with reasonable certainty at laparotomy (see Fig. 61-6).

If the patient is actively bleeding, expeditious aortic control is imperative and should be established before attempts at extra-anatomic bypass are considered, even though this approach might entail some increase in the risk of limb loss resulting from prolonged aortic clamp time. The abdomen is usually explored through a midline incision, although a left retroperitoneal approach may be used if the proximal aorta is anticipated to be difficult to control because of a short infrarenal neck. A disadvantage of the left retroperitoneal approach, however, is inferior access to the distal right common iliac artery and, potentially, less favorable exposure for the duodenal repair. Furthermore, if an extra-anatomic bypass is required, the left retroperitoneal approach may preclude use of a left axillofemoral graft.

Supraceliac aortic control should be established initially, either through isolation of the aorta through the crus of the diaphragm or by medial visceral rotation. To minimize visceral ischemic time, the clamp should be placed in position but not actually closed until it is needed to control hemorrhage. When proximal control is established, the abdomen should be carefully explored, and distal control should be established either by distal clamping of the iliac vessels or by means of occlusion balloon catheters, as the situation dictates. Dissection of all adherent bowel from the diseased aorta or prosthesis is then carefully undertaken to define the fistula and facilitate its repair. The aortic disease is then addressed, either by resection and in-situ reconstruction if no evidence of local infection is observed or anticipated or by resection with retroperitoneal débridement and drainage and subsequent extra-anatomic bypass if local infection is determined to be present. The bowel, usually but not exclusively the distal duodenum, is repaired primarily with transverse closure, resection and anastomosis, or roux-en-Y reconstruction as the anatomy dictates. Gastrostomy and feeding jejunostomy tubes are usually helpful as well, because patients undergoing the procedure usually have a prolonged postoperative course.

If no active bleeding is present and the patient is hemodynamically stable at the time of presentation, the opportunity for preliminary extra-anatomic bypass may be available. Extra-anatomic bypass has been shown to minimize the risk of amputation, especially if excision of a functioning infected graft is clearly necessary and a prolonged clamp time can be anticipated.[29,50,73,74] Cystoscopy for the placement of ureteral stents may be coordinated with the preparations for laparotomy in the stable patient and should be considered if time permits. These stents can aid in intraoperative identification of the ureters, which can be problematic in an inflamed retroperitoneum, to minimize the risk of ureteral injury during dissection of the aortoiliac arterial segment.

Primary Aortoenteric Fistula

Primary AEF is a distinctly unusual clinical entity, and consequently, experience with its treatment at a single center is usually limited, especially compared with that in the treatment of secondary AEFs. Nevertheless, if active hemorrhage either is controlled or is not a factor, the management strategy depends on whether infection is present or absent in the aortic bed at the time of surgical intervention, a circumstance that may be difficult to determine with reasonable certainty at laparotomy. In the absence of gross evidence of infection, however, some investigators have advocated repair of the duodenum and in-situ aortic reconstruction with a standard synthetic prosthesis; the good early and late results observed in limited numbers of patients may relate to the size and character of the bacterial inocula present.[5,17] Adequate débridement of the involved aortic tissue is required, and contamination with duodenal contents must be avoided at the initial operation to minimize the risk of contamination of the aortic prosthesis. Omentum or other available, well-vascularized autogenous tissue should be interposed between the duodenal closure and the prosthetic graft to minimize the risk of secondary AEF.[75] Nevertheless, if this approach is taken, it seems clear that close follow-up should be continued indefinitely and that utilization of long-term antibiotic therapy should be seriously considered, because late graft infection may become apparent only years after implantation.[76]

Although good long-term results have been reported in carefully selected patients treated with duodenal repair and in-situ synthetic graft replacement, clinical judgment is required in its application. Proximal primary AEFs involving the duodenum may be associated with less bacterial contamination than distal primary AEFs involving the sigmoid colon, because of the differing pH and bacterial flora in these locations. Furthermore, up to 30% of aneurysms associated with primary AEF formation may prove to be infected.[10] Consequently, if there is doubt about the presence or absence of local infection or if contamination with GI fluids has occurred, the preferred approach is to manage the primary AEF as though it were a secondary AEF and avoid the placement of prosthetic material in an infected bed.

Secondary Aortoenteric Fistula

Controversy exists regarding the optimal management of patients presenting with secondary AEF because many treatment options are available but all are associated with substantial risks of early or late morbidity (see Fig. 61-6). The available operative choices are (1) local repair, (2) graft excision alone, (3) in-situ replacement, (4) graft excision and reconstruction with autogenous vein, and (5) extra-anatomic revascularization and graft excision. Local drainage has been successfully used for graft infection but has no role in the treatment of AEF.[77] In most series, including our own, local repair or incomplete excision of clearly infected graft material has resulted in high mortality rates.[29,50] There is general agreement that all of the infected synthetic material must be resected if there is clear evidence of graft and retroperitoneal contamination, which is more likely with AEFs involving the distal GI tract and fistulae that have been chronic. The infected arterial tissue should be débrided back to grossly healthy tissue and closed with monofilament permanent suture material, preferably in two layers. The defect in the GI tract should be repaired, with the use of conventional techniques appropriate for the location of the fistula, and retroperitoneal drains placed to minimize the risk of persisting sepsis and consequent breakdown or pseudoaneurysm formation at the site of the arterial closure. The resulting complication of aortic stump blowout formerly accounted for approximately 30% of early deaths in the early reports but is less common in later published series.[26,50,78,79] If feasible, a flap of omentum should be placed to separate the bowel from the aortic stump closure and to fill the dead space resulting from graft excision. Others have advocated the use of serosal patch to support the aortic closure.[80]

If the excised synthetic graft has become occluded or was initially placed for occlusive disease, the patient may have sufficient collateral circulation to maintain viability of the lower extremities without revascularization. A preoperative angiogram occasionally helps in determining the extent of collateral flow present and the need for revascularization. If the proximal anastomosis of the original synthetic graft was placed in an end-to-side configuration, graft removal combined with local endarterectomy and autogenous patching of the resulting arteriotomies may be feasible as a means to preserve adequate distal perfusion. However, if the infected graft has been patent, and especially if it was originally placed to treat an aortoiliac aneurysm and the patient has palpable distal pulses, it is likely that perfusion to the lower extremities will have to be restored to avoid amputation.

The most expeditious means to accomplish revascularization, a factor important if clamp time has been lengthy, is extra-anatomic bypass through uninfected tissue performed after abdominal closure, with a new set of clean instruments after surgical skin preparation and draping have been repeated. Externally supported (ringed) polytetrafluoroethylene (PTFE) appears to be the graft material of choice in this setting.[81] If the previous aortic synthetic graft reconstruction was intra-abdominal, then axillobifemoral grafting is feasible (Fig. 61-7). However, if the graft infection has extended to the femoral arteries, as in the case of previous aortobifemoral graft placement, then bilateral axillo-unifemoral grafts tunneled laterally to the available femoral or popliteal arteries may be required (Fig. 61-8). Tunneling of the left extra-anatomic bypass may be problematic if a left retroperitoneal incision was used for the initial graft excision. A variation on this approach involves the use of a composite graft consisting of synthetic extra-anatomic graft placement in a noncontaminated tissue plane with the autogenous graft component extending to the débrided, contaminated femoral vessels. Care must be taken to avoid contamination of the synthetic component, and the surgeon should be familiar with techniques to provide adequate soft tissue coverage for the femoral vessels, such as sartorius muscle flap rotation. Appropriate antibiotic coverage is important to minimize the risk of bacterial seeding of the extra-anatomic bypass graft, which can occur in approximately 15% to 25% of patients.[29,73]

If the diagnosis of secondary AEF is clear preoperatively and the patient is hemodynamically stable, preliminary extra-anatomic bypass performed 1 to 3 days prior to graft excision has the advantage of eliminating the lower extremity ischemia associated with the long clamp times that may be required during difficult abdominal graft excision procedures (see Fig. 61-6). This approach cannot be effectively utilized in the presence of ongoing hemorrhage but, when feasible, has been shown to decrease the risk of subsequent amputation in patients undergoing surgery for secondary AEF.[29,73] The theoretical concern that occlusion of the extra-anatomic bypass graft due to competitive flow may occur during the interval between placement of the extra-anatomic bypass graft and excision of the aortic graft has not been realized in practice, probably because the interval is usually short.

Clagett and associates[82,83] have advocated an attractive and innovative approach to revascularization of the lower

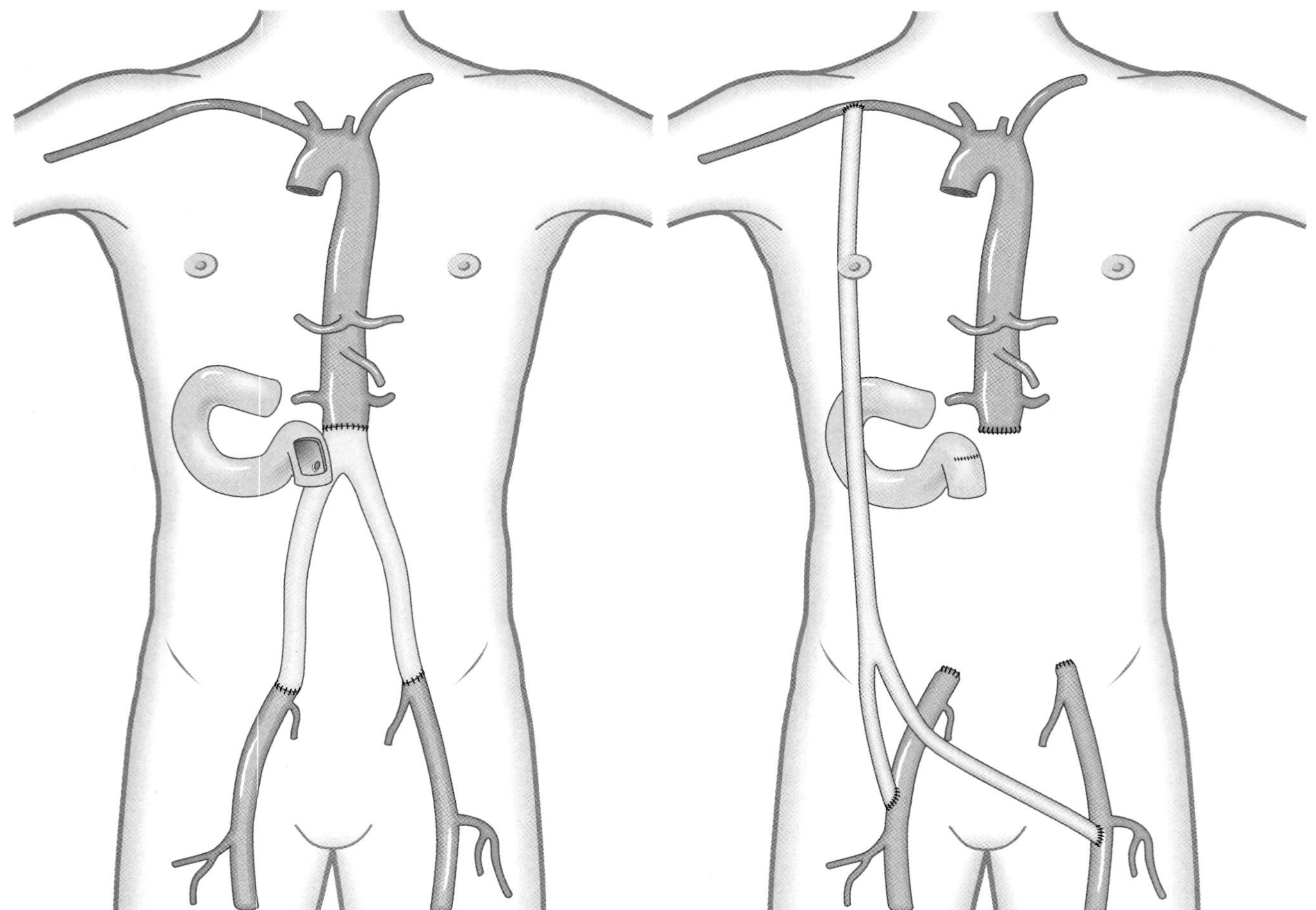

FIGURE 61-7 A, Development of secondary aortoenteric fistula after synthetic aortobi-iliac graft placement. **B,** Surgical management involves extra-anatomic bypass with an axillobifemoral graft, resection of all abdominal prosthetic material, retroperitoneal débridement, and closure of the bowel defect. (Adapted from O'Hara PJ: Surgical management of infected abdominal aortic grafts. In Cowgill LD [ed]: Cardiac Surgery: State of the Art Reviews. Philadelphia, Hanley and Belfus, 1987.)

extremities utilizing the lower extremity deep veins to reconstruct an autogenous "neo-aorto-iliac system" in the setting of an infected aortic prosthesis. This approach allows for in-situ vascular reconstruction using completely autologous tissue and has been reported to be effective and durable. The principal disadvantages are that the procedure cannot be performed as a preliminary, staged procedure and is relatively tedious and time consuming to perform. This latter feature is problematic if the lower extremities have been ischemic for a prolonged period or if hemorrhage and hemodynamic instability are an issue, but in selected patients, it may be ameliorated if multiple surgical teams are available to permit simultaneous vein harvest. Experience with this procedure in the setting of AEF has been limited.

Other investigators have used in-situ aortic graft replacement with either antibiotic-impregnated synthetic grafts or cryopreserved allografts with varying degrees of success.[75,84] These alternatives may be suitable in carefully selected cases if the residual bacterial inoculum is small after excision and débridement of the infected synthetic and autogenous tissue and bacterial colonization can be suppressed. Because cryopreserved grafts are essentially collagen tubes, these grafts may be particularly susceptible to gram-negative bacteria that produce proteolytic enzymes. The use of synthetic grafts impregnated with antibiotics for in-situ replacement of an infected aortic prosthesis is an attractive idea, but a major disadvantage of this approach is the observation that the antibiotic activity delivered by this method is currently short-lived.[85] The development of better antibiotic bonding and delivery systems may eventually make this a preferred approach. If these methods are utilized, careful long-term follow-up is imperative to detect the development of late graft infection or pseudoaneurysm formation while effective management options are still available.

General Supportive Measures

Patients with AEFs often have multiple co-morbid medical conditions, those commonly associated with the elderly population most likely to have vascular disease. Furthermore, such patients are often debilitated and most have at

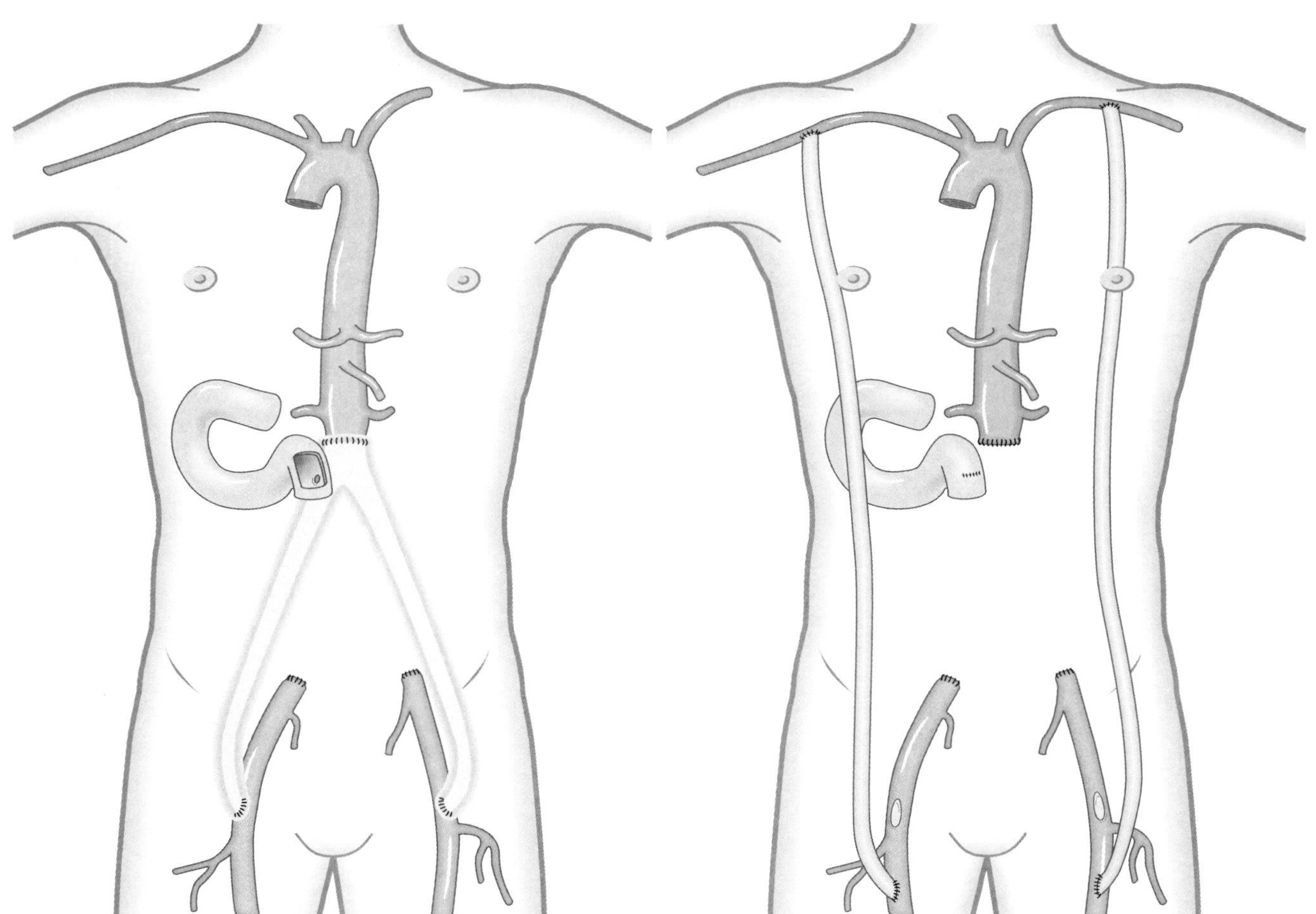

FIGURE 61-8 **A,** Development of secondary aortoenteric fistula after synthetic aortobifemoral graft placement. **B,** Surgical management involves extra-anatomic bypass with bilateral axillofemoral grafting placed through noninfected tissue, resection of all infected prosthetic material with autogenous patch closure of the femoral arteries, retroperitoneal débridement, and closure of the bowel defect. Alternatives include in-situ grafting and aortic reconstruction using autogenous deep veins from the lower extremities. (Adapted from O'Hara PJ: Surgical management of infected abdominal aortic grafts. In Cowgill LD [ed]: Cardiac Surgery: State of the Art Reviews. Philadelphia, Hanley and Belfus, 1987.)

least an element of systemic sepsis. Multisystem support in the intensive care setting is required, and a multidisciplinary team approach that involves specialists in intensive care, infectious disease, and nutrition offers the best chance of survival. Appropriate levels of organism-specific antibiotic therapy as well as parenteral nutritional support are necessary initially. Caloric requirements should be delivered via the patient's functioning GI tract as soon as feasible.

Role of Endovascular Therapy

Endovascular therapy currently has limited application in the treatment of AEFs but its role is constantly evolving.[86] In some circumstances, aortic control may be facilitated by placement of a temporary balloon occlusion catheter in the visceral aorta via either a femoral or left transbrachial approach if fluoroscopic facilities are available. Furthermore, this maneuver may temper the physiologic insult of ongoing hemorrhage. This approach is most useful if it can be carried out simultaneously with preparations for laparotomy, thus avoiding delay. In other circumstances, if the anatomy is favorable, temporary tamponade of a bleeding AEF may be achieved with placement of a covered stent-graft across the fistula. This measure may be best viewed as a temporizing one to permit hemodynamic stabilization in preparation for definitive graft excision.

Endovascular aneurysm repair might be considered for treatment of primary AEF. It seems likely, however, that a persisting communication between the enteric fistula and the endograft will lead to the development of secondary AEF formation, because omentum or other tissue would not have been interposed between the GI tract and the aorta with endovascular grafting alone.[87] As with all modes of therapy, good judgment is required to avoid wasting valuable time between the establishment of the diagnosis and the accomplishment of definitive treatment.

Interestingly, AEF after endovascular repair of an abdominal aortic aneurysm has also been reported.[18,88,89] This occurrence seems counterintuitive because the endograft is placed intraluminally. However, continued pressurization of the aneurysm by endoleak or endotension can translate to continued pulsatile pressure and erosion of the duodenum. Also, endovascular graft infection may be an etiologic factor in such cases. These cases illustrate that AEF does not affect only open aortic reconstruction and that continued vigilance is required in all patients who have undergone endovascular repair.

■ RESULTS

In primary AEF, standard aortic reconstruction with repair of the associated bowel defect has been met with success.[17-19] Hemorrhage due to mechanical erosion rather than infection seems to be the predominant factor in primary AEF.[5,18] In their collective review of 118 cases in the literature, Sweeney and Gadacz[9] reported that nonoperative management was uniformly fatal; 33 patients were treated surgically, with an operative mortality of 36%. Standard aortic reconstruction with duodenal repair was performed in the 19 of 22 survivors, with minimal long-term sequelae. Similar results have been reported for 35 other cases treated in the Netherlands, indicating that placement of a prosthesis in primary AEF appears to be safe.[18]

The natural history of untreated secondary AEFs consists of hemorrhage, continued sepsis, and eventual death.[20,26,40] Table 61-1 summarizes the operative results and survival after surgical treatment for secondary AEF from selected contemporary series. Surgical mortality ranges from 13% to 86% with an average of 30% to 40%. Amputation rates hover at 10%, and long-term survival approximates 50% at 3 years. Taken together, these results document the tremendous physiologic stress from the AEF itself and the magnitude of operative repair for AEF. It is notable that many investigators have documented higher mortality rates in patients treated for AEF rather than aortic graft infection alone (Fig. 61-9).[29,90] In a report of 61 patients with complications of abdominal aortic grafts, surgical treatment of AEF required longer hospitalization and more

Table 61-1 Results of Surgical Treatment for Secondary Aortoenteric Fistula (AEF)

STUDY	YEAR	PATIENTS (No.)	OPERATIVE MORTALITY (%)	AMPUTATION (%)	LONG-TERM SURVIVAL (%)	LENGTH OF FOLLOW-UP
O'Hara et al[29]	1986	33	51	27	25	3-yr life-table
Moulton et al[96]	1986	25	40	NR	36	1-6 yr
Thomas and Baird[28]	1986	8	25	NR	75	1-5 yr
Walker et al[75]	1987	23	22	0	65	5.2 yr
Harris et al[91]	1987	14	58	NR	36	1 yr
Vollmar and Kogel[30]	1987	15 (4, 1° AEF)	47	7	53	1-3 yr
Yeager et al[97]	1990	15	33	NR	NR	NR
Higgins et al[95]	1990	15	33	7	53	4 mo-9 yr
McCann et al[90]	1993	17	35	23	18	18 mo, life-table
Kuestner et al[50]	1995	33	18	9	71	4.4 yr
van Baalen et al[94]	1996	27	41	NR	37	1-3 yr
Bergquist et al[98]	1996	27	28	NR	42	43 mo
Nevelsteen et al[93]	1998	7	86	NR	NR	NR
Young et al[85]	1999	15	13	0	NR	NR
Seeger et al[73]	1999	10	40	10	NR	NR
Reilly[81]	2002	81	28	10.5	NR	3.9 yr

NR, not reported or results commingled with patients treated for other conditions, including graft infection without AEF.

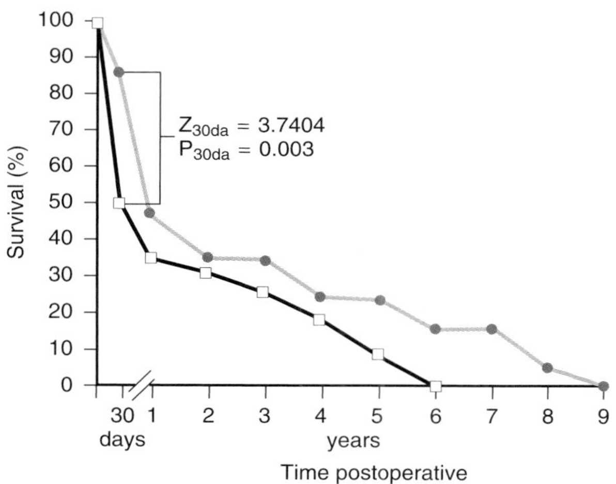

FIGURE 61-9 Cumulative survival curves for patients who underwent surgical treatment of synthetic aortic graft infection. The 30-day survival for the 33 patients with aortoenteric fistula (*squares*) was 49%, significantly lower than the 86% survival for the 51 patients without aortoenteric fistula (*circles*). (Adapted from O'Hara PJ, Hertzer NR, Beven EG, Krajewski LP: Surgical management of infected abdominal aortic grafts: Review of 25-year experience. J Vasc Surg 3:725, 1986.)

blood transfusion than that for graft infection. Furthermore, operative mortality was higher (35% versus 17%) and 12-month survival lower (25% versus 60%) in AEF than in aortic graft infection.[90]

Multiple strategies for operative repair for AEF have been advocated. Local aortic anastomotic repair is associated with high rates of re-infection and mortality rates exceeding 60%.[46,91] Graft excision without revascularization, which may be feasible in cases of aortoiliac occlusive disease, also carries a mortality greater than 70%.[46,91,92] Thus, these operative options are unacceptable except for the rare case in which aortic graft excision is being performed in the presence of occlusive disease and adequate collateralization leads to viable extremities after graft removal.

More favorable results have been reported with several other forms of treatment. Reilly and colleagues[50,74,81] have popularized staged extra-anatomic bypass and subsequent graft excision. In their latest report, consistent progress in the results of surgical treatment has been documented over three decades for both AEF and aortic graft infection. Currently, this team performs revascularization with extra-anatomic bypass followed by graft excision in 85% of cases.[81] Secondary AEFs treated with this approach were reported to have a mortality of only 18% and a 3-year cumulative cure rate of 70%.[50] The concern about infection of the newly placed prosthetic extra-anatomic bypass in the presence of an infected abdominal graft has not been realized.[29,74]

Graft excision with in-situ bypass allows a direct aortic revascularization in a single operation and avoids the potential complication of aortic stump blowout. However, this option can be applied only in the setting of a minimally infected retroperitoneum and still has the potential for re-infection of the new graft. Several conduits have been used in this approach. Autogenous deep lower extremity vein has been used very successfully for aortic graft infection, but the results in AEF have been less uniform.[82,83] The use of cadaveric allografts was associated with an operative mortality of only 12% in patients with both aortic graft infection and AEF.[84] However, cryopreserved arterial allografts worked well in aortic graft infection but poorly in AEF, with only one of seven patients with AEF surviving.[93] In-situ regrafting with prosthetic grafts has worked well for selected patients,[75,94] although these results have not been universal.[65,72,95] Also, the use of antibiotic-impregnated prosthetic grafts has shown encouraging results in selected patients.[85] The level of retroperitoneal sepsis dictates whether an in-situ approach is feasible. All of the investigators using the in-situ technique emphasize careful patient selection for this approach.

Staged revascularization followed by graft excision causes less physiologic stress and, thus, may be the preferable approach in stable patients with AEF. Unstable patients with a minimally soiled retroperitoneum may benefit from in-situ reconstruction. Regardless, the management of patients with AEF continues to require expeditious diagnosis, appropriate clinical judgment, and technical skill for successful outcomes.

■ REFERENCES

1. Cooper A: The lectures of Sir Astley Cooper on the Principles and Practice of Surgery with Additional Notes and Cases by F. Tyrell, 5th ed. Philadelphia, Haswell, Barrington, and Haswell, 1939.
2. Brock RC: Aortic homografting: A report of six successful cases. Guys Hosp Rep 102:204, 1953.
3. Heberer A: Diagnosis and treatment of aneurysms of the abdominal aorta. Ger Med Monatchr 2:203, 1957.
4. MacKenzie RJ, Buell AH, Pearson SC: Aneurysm of aortic homograft with rupture into the duodenum. Arch Surg 77:965, 1958.
5. Dossa CD, Pipinos II, Shepard AD, Ernst CB: Primary aortoenteric fistula: Part I. Ann Vasc Surg 8:113, 1994.
6. Reckless JPD, McColl I, Taylor GW: Aortoenteric fistulae: An uncommon complication of abdominal aortic aneurysms. Br J Surg 59:458, 1972.
7. Dossa CD, Pipinos II, Shepard AD, Ernst CB: Primary aortoenteric fistula: Part II. Primary aortoesophageal fistula. Ann Vasc Surg 8:207, 1994.
8. Lorimer JW, Goobie P, Rasuli P, et al: Primary aortogastric fistula: A complication of ruptured aortic aneurysm. J Cardiovasc Surg 37:363, 1996.
9. Sweeney MS, Gadacz TR: Primary aortoduodenal fistula: Manifestations, diagnosis, and treatment. Surgery 96:492, 1984.
10. Trout HH III, Kozloff L, Giordano JM: Priority of revascularization in patients with graft enteric fistulas, infected arteries, or infected arterial prostheses. Ann Surg 199:669, 1984.
11. Chaphery AD, Gupta RL, Currie RD: Carcinoma of head of pancreas with aortoduodenal fistula. Am J Surg 111:580, 1966.
12. Frosch HL, Horowitz W: Rupture of abdominal aorta into duodenum through sinus tract created by tuberculous mesenteric lymphadenitis. Ann Intern Med 21:481, 1944.
13. Morrow C, Safi H, Beall AC Jr: Primary aortoduodenal fistula caused by *Salmonella* aortitis. J Vasc Surg 6:415, 1987.
14. Sindelar WF, Mason GR: Aortocystoduodenal fistula: Rare complication of pancreatic pseudocyst. Arch Surg 114:953, 1979.
15. Sternberg A, Nava HR, Irac AT, et al: Perforation of a benign gastric ulcer into the supradiaphragmatic aorta. Am J Gastroenterol 82:579, 1987.
16. Odze RD, Begin LR: Peptic ulcer induced aortoenteric fistula: Report of case and review of the literature. J Clin Gastroenterol 113:682, 1991.

17. Daugherty M, Shearer GR, Ernst CB: Primary aortoduodenal fistula: Extra-anatomic vascular reconstruction not required for successful management. Surgery 86:399, 1979.
18. Voorhoeve R, Moll FL, Bast TJ: The primary aortoenteric fistula in The Netherlands—the unpublished cases. Eur J Vasc Endovasc Surg 11:429, 1996.
19. Bernhard VM: Aortoenteric Fistula. Orlando, FL, Grune & Stratton, 1985, pp 513-525.
20. Elliott JP, Smith RF, Szilagyi DE: Aortoenteric and paraprosthetic-enteric fistulas. Arch Surg 108:479, 1974.
21. Campbell HC Jr, Ernst CB: Aortoenteric fistula following renal revascularization. Am Surg 44:155, 1978.
22. King RM, Sterioff S, Engen DE: Renal artery graft-to-duodenum fistula: Unusual presentation of a recurrent flank abscess. J Cardiovasc Surg 26:509, 1985.
23. Sheil AGR, Reeve TS, Little JM, et al: Aortointestinal fistulas following operations on the abdominal aorta and iliac arteries. Br J Surg 56:840, 1969.
24. Donovan TJ, Bucknam CA: Aorto-enteric fistula. Arch Surg 95:810, 1967.
25. Humphries AW, Young JR, deWolfe VG, et al: Complications of abdominal aortic surgery. Arch Surg 86:43, 1963.
26. Bunt TJ: Synthetic vascular graft infections. II: Graft-enteric erosions and graft-enteric fistulas. Surgery 94:1, 1983.
27. Hallett JW Jr, Marshall DM, Petterson TM, et al: Graft-related complications after abdominal aortic aneurysm repair: Reassurance from a 36-year population-based experience. J Vasc Surg 25:277, 1997.
28. Thomas WEG, Baird RN: Secondary aorto-enteric fistulae: Towards a more conservative approach. Br J Surg 73:875, 1986.
29. O'Hara PJ, Hertzer NR, Beven EG, Krajewski LP: Surgical management of infected abdominal aortic grafts: Review of 25-year experience. J Vasc Surg 3:725, 1986.
30. Vollmar JF, Kogel H: Aorto-enteric fistulas as postoperative complication. J Cardiovasc Surg 28:479, 1987.
31. Buchbinder D, Leather R, Shah D, et al: Pathologic interactions between prosthetic aortic grafts and the gastrointestinal tract. Am J Surg 140:192, 1980.
32. Claytor H, Birch L, Cardwell ES, et al: Suture-line rupture of a nylon aortic bifurcation graft into the small bowel. Arch Surg 73:947, 1956.
33. DeWeese MS, Fry WJ: Small bowel erosion following aortic resection. JAMA 179:882, 1962.
34. Busuttil RN, Reese W, Baker JD, et al: Pathogenesis of aortoduodenal fistula: Experimental and clinical correlates. Surgery 85:1, 1979.
35. Higgins RSD, Steed DL, Zajko AB, et al: Computed tomographic scan confirmation of paraprosthetic enteric fistula. Am J Surg 162:36, 1991.
36. Reilly LM, Ehrenfeld WK, Goldstone J, et al: Gastrointestinal tract involvement by prosthetic graft infection: The significance of gastrointestinal hemorrhage. Ann Surg 202:342, 1985.
37. Lawrence PF: Management of infected aortic grafts. Surg Clin North Am 75:783, 1995.
38. Conn JH, Hardy JD, Chavez CM, et al: Infected arterial grafts. Ann Surg 171:704, 1970.
39. Fry WJ, Lindenauer SM: Infection complicating the use of plastic arterial implants. Arch Surg 94:600, 1967.
40. Kleinman LH, Towne JB, Bernhard WM: A diagnostic and therapeutic approach to aorto-enteric fistulas: Clinical experience with twenty patients. Surgery 86:868, 1979.
41. Perdue GD Jr, Smith RB, Ansley JD, et al: Impending aortoenteric hemorrhage: The effect of early recognition on improved outcome. Ann Surg 192:237, 1980.
42. Nelken N: Aortoenteric fistula. In Callow AD, Ernst CB (eds): Vascular Surgery: Theory and Practice. Stamford, CT, Appleton & Lange, 1995, pp 1311-1323.
43. O'Mara CS, Imbembo AL: Paraprosthetic enteric fistula. Surgery 81:556, 1977.
44. Hirst AE, Affeldt JE: Abdominal aortic aneurysm with rupture into the duodenum: A case report of eight cases. Gastroenterology 17:504, 1971.
45. Voyles WR, Moretz WH: Rupture of aortic aneurysms into gastrointestinal tract. Surgery 43:666, 1958.
46. Champion MC, Sullivan SN, Coles JC, et al: Aortoenteric fistula: Incidence, presentation, recognition, and management. Ann Surg 195:314, 1982.
47. Crawford ES, Manning LG, Kelly TF: "Redo" surgery after operations for aneurysm and occlusion of the abdominal aorta. Surgery 81:41, 1977.
48. Fulenwider JT, Smith RB, Johnson RW, et al: Reoperative abdominal arterial surgery: A ten-year experience. Surgery 93:20, 1982.
49. Pabst TS III, Bernhard VM, McIntyre KE Sr, et al: Gastrointestinal bleeding following aortic surgery: The place of laparotomy to rule out aortoenteric fistula. J Vasc Surg 8:280, 1988.
50. Kuestner LM, Reilly LM, Jicha DL, et al: Secondary aortoenteric fistula: Contemporary outcome with use of extra-anatomic bypass and infected graft excision. J Vasc Surg 21:184, 1995.
51. Rosenthal D, Deterling RA Jr, O'Donnell TF, et al: Positive blood culture as an aid in the diagnosis of secondary aortoenteric fistula. Arch Surg 114:1041, 1979.
52. Gordon SL, Nicholas GG, Carter SL, et al: Aortoenteric fistula presenting as multicentric osteomyelitis. Clin Orthop 131:255, 1978.
53. Baker BH, Baker MS, vander Reis L, et al: Endoscopy in the diagnosis of aortoduodenal fistula. Gastrointest Endosc 24:35, 1977.
54. Bunt TJ, Doerhoff CR: Endoscopic visualization of an intraluminal Dacron graft: Definitive diagnosis of aortoduodenal fistula. South Med J 77:86, 1984.
55. Ott DJ, Kerr RM, Gelfand DW: Aortoduodenal fistula. Gastrointest Endosc 24:296, 1978.
56. Mir-Madjlessi SH, Sullivan BH Jr, Farmer RG, et al: Endoscopic diagnosis of aortoduodenal fistula. Gastrointest Endosc 19:187, 1973.
57. Kukora JS, Rushton FW, Cranston PE: New computed tomographic signs of aortoenteric fistula. Arch Surg 119:1073, 1984.
58. Gupta RK, Rogers KE: A unique case of aortoduodenal fistula following carcinoma of cervix. Am J Obstet Gynecol 131:110, 1978.
59. Low RN, Wall SD, Jeffrey RB, et al: Aortoenteric fistula and perigraft infection: Evaluation with CT. Radiology 175:157, 1990.
60. Lemos DW, Raffetto JD, Moore TC, Menzoian JO: Primary aortoduodenal fistula: A case report and review of the literature. J Vasc Surg 37:686, 2003.
61. Cunat JS, Haaga JR, Rhodes R, et al: Periaortic fluid aspiration for recognition of infected graft: Preliminary report. AJR Am J Roentgenol 139:251, 1982.
62. Katz BH, Black RA, Colley DP: CT-guided fine-needle aspiration of a perigraft collection. J Vasc Surg 5:762, 1987.
63. O'Donnell TF Jr, Scott G, Shepard A, et al: Improvements in the diagnosis and management of aortoenteric fistulas. Am J Surg 149:481, 1985.
64. Schütte HE: Angiographic signs of aortic graft-enteric fistulae. Clin Radiol 38:503, 1987.
65. O'Mara CS, Williams GM, Ernst CB: Secondary aortoenteric fistula: A 20 year experience. Am J Surg 142:203, 1981.
66. Olofsson PA, Auffermann W, Higgins CB, et al: Diagnosis of prosthetic graft infection by magnetic resonance imaging (MRI). J Vasc Surg 8:99, 1988.
67. Lawrence PF, Dries DJ, Alazraki N, et al: Indium 111-labeled leukocyte scanning for detection of prosthetic graft infection. J Vasc Surg 2:165, 1985.
68. LaMurglia GM, Fischman AJ, Strauss HW, et al: Utility of indium-111-labeled human immunoglobulin G scan for the detection of focal vascular graft infection. J Vasc Surg 10:20, 1989.
69. Ramo OJ, Vorne M, Lantto T, et al: Postoperative graft incorporation after aortic reconstruction: Comparison between computerized tomography and Tc-99m-HMPAO labeled leucocyte imaging. Eur J Vasc Surg 7:122, 1993.
70. Alfrey EJ, Stanton C, Dunnington G, et al: Graft appendiceal fistulas. J Vasc Surg 7:814, 1988.
71. Dalinka MK, Reginato AJ, Berkowitz HD, et al: Hypertrophic osteoarthropathy as indication of aortic graft infection and aortoenteric fistula. Arch Surg 117:1355, 1982.

72. King JO: Localized clubbing in hypertrophic osteoarthropathy due to infection in an aortic prosthesis. Br Med J 4:404, 1972.
73. Seeger JM, Back MR, Albright JL, et al: Influence of patient characteristics and treatment options on outcome of patients with prosthetic aortic graft infection. Ann Vasc Surg 13:413, 1999.
74. Reilly LM, Stoney RJ, Goldstone J, et al: Improved management of aortic graft infection: The influence of operative sequence and staging. J Vasc Surg 5:421, 1987.
75. Walker WE, Cooley DA, Duncan JM, et al: The management of aortoduodenal fistula by in situ replacement of the infected abdominal aortic graft. Ann Surg 205:727, 1987.
76. Taheri SA, Kulaylat MN, Grippi J, et al: Surgical treatment of primary aortoduodenal fistula. Ann Vasc Surg 5:265, 1991.
77. Belair M, Soulez G, Oliva VL, et al: Graft infection: The value of percutaneous drainage. AJR Am J Roentgenol 171:119, 1998.
78. Bunt TJ: Vascular graft infections: A personal experience. Cardiovasc Surg 1:489, 1993.
79. Bergquist D, Alm A, Claes G, et al: Secondary aortoenteric fistulas: An analysis of 42 cases. Eur J Vasc Surg 1:11, 1987.
80. Shah DM, Buchbinder D, Leather RP, et al: Clinical use of the seromuscular jejunal patch for protection of the infected aortic stump. Am J Surg 146:198, 1983.
81. Reilly LM: Aortic graft infection: Evolution in management. Cardiovasc Surg 10:372, 2002.
82. Clagett GP, Bowers BL, Lopez-Viego MA, et al: Creation of a neo-aortoiliac system from lower extremity deep and superficial veins. Ann Surg 210:239, 1993.
83. Clagett GP, Valentine RJ, Hagino RT: Autogenous aortoiliac/femoral reconstruction from superficial femoral-popliteal veins: Feasibility and durability. J Vasc Surg 25:255, 1997.
84. Kieffer E, Bahnini A, Koskas F, et al: In-situ allograft replacement of infected infrarenal aortic prosthetic grafts: Results in forty-three patients. J Vasc Surg 17:349, 1993.
85. Young RM, Cherry KJ Jr, David PM, et al: The results of in situ prosthetic replacement for infected aortic grafts. Am J Surg 178:136, 1999.
86. Burks JA, Faries PL, Gravereaux EC, et al: Endovascular repair of bleeding aortoenteric fistulas: A 5 year experience. J Vasc Surg 34:1055, 2001.
87. Chuter TA, Lukaszewicz GC, Reilly LM, et al: Endovascular repair of a presumed aortoenteric fistula: Late failure due to recurrent infection. J Endovasc Ther 7:240, 2000.
88. Abou-Zamzam AM, Bianchi C, Mazraany W, et al: Aortoenteric fistula development following endovascular abdominal aortic aneurysm repair: A case report. Ann Vasc Surg 17:119, 2003.
89. Bertges DJ, Villela ER, Makaroun MS: Aortoenteric fistula due to endoleak coil embolization after endovascular AAA repair. J Endovasc Ther 10:130, 2003.
90. McCann RL, Schwartz LB, Georgiade GS: Management of abdominal aortic graft complications. Ann Surg 217:729, 1993.
91. Harris JP, Sheil AGR, Stephen MS, et al: Lessons learnt in the management of aortoenteric fistula. J Cardiovasc Surg 28:449, 1987.
92. Kiernan PD, Pairolero PC, Hubert JP Jr, et al: Aortic graft-enteric fistula. Mayo Clin Proc 55:731, 1980.
93. Nevelsteen A, Feryn T, Lacroix H, et al: Experience with cryopreserved arterial allografts in the treatment of prosthetic graft infections. Cardiovasc Surg 6:378, 1998.
94. van Baalen JM, Kluit AB, Maas J, et al: Diagnosis and therapy of aortic prosthetic fistulas: Trends over a 30-year experience. Br J Surg 83:1729, 1996.
95. Higgins RSD, Steed DL, Julian TB, et al: The management of aortoenteric and paraprosthetic fistulae. J Cardiovasc Surg 31:81, 1990.
96. Moulton S, Adams M, Johansen K: Aortoenteric fistula: A 7 year experience. Am J Surg 151:607, 1986.
97. Yeager RA, Moneta GL, Taylor LM Jr, et al: Survival and limb salvage in patients with aortic graft infection. Am J Surg 159:466, 1990.
98. Bergquist D, Bjorkman H, Bolin T, et al: Secondary aortoenteric fistulae: Changes from 1973 to 1993. Eur J Vasc Endovasc Surg 11:425, 1996.

Chapter 62

Ischemic Neuropathy

J. JEAN E. TURLEY, MD, FRCS(C)
K. WAYNE JOHNSTON, MD, FRCS(C)

Ischemic neuropathy is a term used to describe any injury of peripheral nerve caused by a reduction in blood supply. These disorders may be associated with diseases of large or small arteries. Large-artery lesions may be acute (e.g., those due to arterial embolism, thrombosis, or injury) or chronic (e.g., those due to atherosclerosis). Small endoneurial arteries may be involved in periarteritis nodosa, rheumatoid vasculitis, Churg-Strauss syndrome, and Wegener's granulomatosis. Capillary disease may be significant in diabetic neuropathy. For the surgeon, ischemic disorders of nerve resulting from large-artery disease are important.

■ PERIPHERAL NERVES

Anatomy and Physiology

Peripheral nerves are composed of fascicles of nerve fibers. The fascicles are made of nerve fibers, Schwann cells, collagen, small vessels, and endoneurial fluid. Nerve fibers are bathed in endoneurial fluid that is maintained within narrow metabolic limits by blood-nerve and perineurial barriers.

Structural proteins and macromolecules are produced in the nerve cell body and transported in the axon. Axon transport is energy dependent and requires oxygen and glucose,

which are supplied locally to the endoneurial fluid by endoneurial vessels. Transmission of nerve impulses is accomplished by transient depolarization of limited portions of the axonal membrane, during which time sodium and potassium diffuse across the membrane and are then restored to resting levels. This flow uses stored energy that is replenished by glycolysis in the Krebs cycle through aerobic metabolism. Although the nerve continually uses energy to maintain resting ionic gradients, the oxygen requirement of mammalian nerve is small, and even when this requirement is increased by activity, it is less than that of other tissues.[1] As a result, peripheral nerves are relatively resistant to ischemia.

Blood Supply

The metabolic needs of large nerves are met by intraneural blood vessels, the vasa nervorum, whereas those of small nerves are met by diffusion from surrounding tissues. The vasa nervorum arise from nearby major arteries and enter nerve trunks at multiple levels, frequently near joints. The epineural arteries branch, and arteriolar and precapillary branches then penetrate the perineurium to perfuse the endoneurium. There is a complete terminal network of capillaries through the perineurium that supplies blood to nerve at some distance from the nutrient arteries.[1-4] The abundant collateral circulation pattern of peripheral nerve explains why it is difficult to injure a peripheral nerve by occlusion of one or even several nutrient arteries. Regional nutrient arteries have been ligated over considerable lengths of a nerve trunk without disturbing blood supply to nerve or adversely affecting the structure and function of nerve fibers.[5] Extensive studies of the microvasculature of peripheral nerve have demonstrated that the organization of vasa nervorum is such that a total interruption of circulation in nerves is highly unlikely unless drastic interference with the blood supply is produced.[6]

The pattern of epineural vessels varies in different nerves, and some nerves may be more susceptible than others to ischemia.[5] In some cases, a single nutrient artery provides the major blood supply to a considerable length of nerve, and this may predispose to ischemic damage to the nerve trunk. At its upper end, the human sciatic nerve receives an arterial branch from the inferior gluteal artery. As the sciatic nerve enters the popliteal fossa, its blood supply is taken over by the popliteal artery and its branches. The tibial nerve is intimately related to the posterior tibial artery, which supplies a large number of direct nutrient arteries.

The peroneal nerve, in contrast, diverges from the main vessels and is supplied in the region of the fibular head by small adjacent arteries. At the neck of the fibula, the major intraneural vessels occupy a superficial position that may expose them to damage from pressure. In the calf, the posterior tibial and peroneal nerves receive branches from the anterior and posterior tibial arteries. The intraneural arterial pattern in the buttock and thigh contains several arterial channels of fairly large caliber, whereas below the knee, one major vessel usually dominates. The peroneal nerve at the knee, and perhaps the more distal portions of the peroneal and posterior tibial nerves, may therefore be more prone to ischemic damage.[5] In an animal model of large-vessel ligation, Kelly and colleagues[7] produced an ischemic neuropathy in animals, all of which showed clinical evidence of neuropathy in 1 week confirmed by nerve conduction studies. Examination of corrosion casts showed an area of underfilling of the microcirculation in the region of the proximal tibial nerve with good filling of vessels proximal and distal to this, indicating that in generalized hypoperfusion states (e.g., large-vessel occlusion) the area of poorest perfusion is a watershed zone between two adjacent nutrient vessels to the nerve.

Sympathetic nerve fibers innervate vessels in the epineurium and perineurium. High sympathetic drive may significantly reduce intraneural circulation. Sympathetically mediated vasoconstriction may be important in the pathogenesis of reflex sympathetic dystrophy and chronic pain.[3]

■ ISCHEMIC NERVES

Pathophysiology

Many studies have been carried out to determine the effect of anoxia on nerve function. A short period of experimental ischemia results in disturbed function of nerve, which can recover if circulation is restored. Severe acute ischemia appears to result in decreased or abolished conduction of impulses. Thus, if ischemia is of short duration or is mild, function in peripheral nerve can be impaired in a transient manner.[8] The slight metabolic needs of nerve and the diffusion of nutrients from surrounding tissues enable it to survive. If ischemia is prolonged or severe, damage may be permanent.[5,9]

Exactly how these functional changes of nerve occur is unknown. Obviously, ischemia impairs the metabolic processes that maintain the ionic gradient necessary for impulse transmission. Fast axoplasmic transport also depends on an adequate blood supply. The transport of material in the axon is impaired by ischemia at the same time that conduction is impaired, suggesting that both depend on the same sources of energy.[10] The block of fast axoplasmic transport becomes irreversible after 6 to 8 hours of ischemia. The permeability of endoneurial vessels during ischemia is impaired after 8 to 10 hours.[11] Metabolic factors, including anoxia, hypercapnia, hyperkalemia, and acidosis, are probably important. Potassium accumulation in the extracellular space during anoxia may cause irreversible depolarization of cell membrane.[2,12]

There is controversy about the relative vulnerabilities of nerve and muscle to ischemia. The idea is entrenched in the literature that muscle is more sensitive, and Dyck,[11] in a review of hypoxic neuropathy, still considers skeletal muscle to be more vulnerable to ischemic injury than nerve. Korthals and coworkers[13] ligated the abdominal aorta and femoral artery in cats and found necrotic changes in muscle at 2 to 3 hours, whereas no nerve lesions appeared until 5 hours of ischemia. However, a study by Chervu and associates[14] of the relative sensitivities of skeletal muscle and peripheral nerve function to ischemia and reperfusion suggests that peripheral nerve is more susceptible to ischemia than skeletal muscle.

Pathologic Changes

Pathologic studies have been performed of peripheral nerves in ischemic limbs. Farinon and colleagues,[15] examining muscle and nerve biopsy specimens from patients with chronic arterial insufficiency, found a combination of segmental demyelination and axonal degeneration. They believed that large fibers and small fibers were equally affected and further noted that the severity of the nerve pathology did not correlate well with the severity of vascular disease.

Eames and Lange[16] described the pathologic changes in sural nerve biopsy specimens from eight patients with vascular disease. They found evidence of segmental demyelination and remyelination, axonal degeneration and regeneration, and an increase in endoneurial collagen. The unmyelinated fibers were essentially normal. Rodriguez-Sánchez and associates[17] examined morphologic alterations in the sural nerve from patients with chronic atherosclerotic disease. Both axonal degeneration-regeneration and demyelination-remyelination were seen. In cases of atherosclerotic disease of large vessels, the lumina of the epineurial and endoneurial vasa nervorum in the sural nerves have been found to be markedly narrowed and the walls thickened.[16]

A later study by Nukada and coauthors[18] examined the pathology of nerves taken from amputated limbs of seven acutely and nine chronically ischemic legs. In acutely ischemic nerves, axonal degeneration of both myelinated and unmyelinated nerve fibers was prominent if ischemia was present for more than 24 hours. Chronically ischemic limbs showed demyelination, remyelination, endoneurial edema, and relative preservation of unmyelinated nerves. All changes except the high rate of demyelination and remyelination have been described in experimental models of acute ischemic and reperfusion injury. The authors concluded that "pathological alterations in chronic ischemic neuropathy may be due to the combined effects of acute ischemia/reperfusion and chronic hypoxia." [18]

Many experimental studies have examined the morphology of animal nerve.[19-23] Sladky and coworkers[24] produced 50% to 75% endoneurial blood flow reduction in rats and found that nerve conduction velocities fell by 25% to 30%; morphologic studies showed structural abnormalities at nodes of Ranvier and mild axonal atrophy. The authors suggested that reduced endoneurial blood flow insufficient to cause infarction may result in measurable functional and morphologic abnormalities in peripheral nerves. In general, large myelinated fibers, particularly in the center of nerves, seem to undergo axonal degeneration.

■ ISCHEMIC POLYNEUROPATHY

Etiology

Chronic Arterial Insufficiency

In humans, neither the effects of chronic ischemia on the structure and function of nerves nor the limit of tolerance of peripheral nerve to ischemia is well defined.

The incidence of neurologic deficits in patients with chronic peripheral vascular disease has not been ascertained. Peripheral nerve involvement in atherosclerosis is probably underestimated because neuropathic symptoms—pain, sensory changes, and even weakness—may be confused with claudication or rest pain. A number of series have reported symptoms such as painful burning and signs varying from sensory impairment to reflex loss, muscle wasting, and weakness in patients with peripheral arterial occlusive disease.

Hutchison and Liversedge found peripheral nerve dysfunction, as manifested by sensory deficits and absent reflexes, in 50% of their patients with peripheral vascular disease.[25] They believed that the presence of neuropathy was related to the severity of the vascular disease. Eames and Lange[16] found impaired sensation in 88% of their 32 atherosclerotic patients, muscle weakness in 50%, and decreased or absent reflexes in 41%. Again, the extent of the deficit was proportional to the degree of ischemia. All patients with claudication after walking less than 100 yards had a neurologic abnormality. Twenty patients had a superficial femoral artery occlusion, and the remainder had proximal vascular disease. Hunter and colleagues[26] found neurologic deficits in 22% of ischemic limbs. Miglietta[27] found decreased ankle jerks and decreased vibration sense in 54% of his patients with atherosclerosis. Weinberg and associates[28] recently evaluated 19 patients with chronic arterial limb ischemia: 84% had neuropathic symptoms (primarily pain and sensory disturbance), with only 16% reporting weakness. On clinical evaluation, 70% had reduced ankle reflexes, 75% had decreased sensation, and 63% had distal weakness. In 48 diabetic patients evaluated by Ram and colleagues,[29] vascular insufficiency has been shown to increase the severity of neuropathy.

When electrophysiologic studies are added to the clinical evaluation, neurologic abnormalities are uncovered in an even greater number of individuals who have no apparent clinical symptoms or signs. Miglietta and Lowenthal[30] found slowing of motor conduction velocity in peroneal nerves in nearly all patients with severe vascular disease and no neurologic signs, but many patients had diabetes. Hunter and colleagues[26] found abnormal peroneal nerve compound muscle action potential amplitudes in 86% and abnormal conduction velocities in the lower extremities in 36% of atherosclerotic patients, whereas only 22% had clinical neurologic abnormalities. Weber and Ziegler[31] examined nerve conduction findings in 44 limbs of 25 patients with peripheral arterial occlusion of varying severity and no other causes for neuropathy. Fifty percent had sensory symptoms, and 50% had decreased ankle reflexes in the affected limb. They found reduced sural nerve conduction velocity and reduced compound muscle action potentials in the feet and F wave abnormalities that were greater in patients with rest pain than with intermittent claudication, suggesting that the severity of the neuropathy was a function of the duration and severity of the vascular disease. A study by Pasini and coworkers[32] of 64 patients with claudication, 19 with rest pain, and 7 with distal leg ulcers revealed reduction in sural and superficial nerve conduction velocities in all patients with a progression of abnormality as the disease advanced.

Therefore, it seems that peripheral neuropathy develops in some patients with chronic occlusive vascular disease. The precise location and the severity of the requisite arterial lesion have not been defined, nor has the precise incidence. Nevertheless, there is considerable clinical importance in detecting the presence of neuropathy before surgery. If some of the patient's symptoms are neuropathic in origin, it is to be expected that improvement of vascular supply to the limb may not immediately relieve all of the symptoms, even if adequate revascularization is achieved.

Acute Arterial Insufficiency

Acute arterial occlusion due to embolism, thrombosis, or arterial injury is often associated with acute neural dysfunction. The motor and sensory deficit usually has a distal limb distribution, but selective peroneal palsy has been described.[33] The frequency of clear neurologic signs in the acutely ischemic limb has seldom been carefully analyzed. Haimovici[34] reported that 22% of his patients presented with sensory symptoms, but no data on physical signs are presented. A number of other reports[1] have documented neurologic deficits with motor signs in about 20% and sensory deficits in 50%. After acute arterial occlusion, if flow is not re-established within several hours (and this time limit has not been clearly defined), symptoms and signs of neurologic dysfunction may persist when circulation is restored and the neurologic deficit may be permanent.

The clinical features of ischemic neuropathy following trauma to major blood vessels were summarized by Sunderland.[5] He reported that sensory loss is distal and of a "stocking-and-glove" type; it is associated with distal muscle wasting and weakness and is sometimes accompanied by late fibrosis and contracture. Wilbourn and coworkers[35] subsequently described 14 cases of ischemic monomelic neuropathy in a single limb, with pain, paresthesia, and paralysis following the restoration of blood flow after acute occlusion of a proximal limb artery.

The precise incidence of ischemic neuropathy and the various factors that predispose to the development of neuropathy in an ischemic limb have not yet been characterized by the publication of a large series or by a prospective study. After an episode of severe ischemia, however, it is not unusual for patients with a satisfactorily revascularized leg to continue to complain of pain that is due to neuropathy. The neuropathic pain is burning and paresthetic in nature, is frequently worse with rest and at night, and is unaffected or relieved by walking, in marked contrast with the pain of claudication. The patient perceives the foot to be cold, although it is in fact warm. The patient may remark on loss of mobility of the toes.

Examination no longer reveals signs of significant ischemia. Instead, the small muscles of the affected foot are wasted compared with those of the normal side, and they are weak. There may be slight ankle weakness, and the ankle reflex may be depressed compared with that of the normal side. There is a unilateral stocking sensory loss, particularly to vibration sense. Unlike the findings in neuropathies caused by diabetes, uremia, drug intoxication, or alcoholism, the findings in ischemic neuropathy are asymmetrical, with sensory and motor findings exclusively or prominently in the limb that was afflicted by severe ischemia.

Diagnosis

Vascular Assessment

The severity of ischemia can be assessed clinically or may be determined more objectively by noninvasive methods, including the measurement of ankle and toe pressures and Doppler waveform recordings. If the ankle pressure is greater than 50 to 60 mm Hg or the toe pressure is greater than 30 mm Hg, ischemic rest pain is unlikely and the diagnosis of ischemic neuropathy should be suspected. Flat or monophasic Doppler waveforms confirm that the arterial disease is severe. If clinical examination and noninvasive assessment confirm that the peripheral circulation is adequate, the pain is probably not due to ischemia. If the perfusion is inadequate, the pain may be due to ischemia, neuropathy, or both, and treatment should be directed first toward improvement of the limb blood flow.

Electrophysiologic Studies

Careful electrophysiologic studies can establish the diagnosis of ischemic neuropathy and define its severity. Typically, a unilateral axonal neuropathy involving distal nerves is present.

Motor nerve conduction studies show a decrease in or an absence of the compound *muscle action potential* amplitude from the extensor digitorum brevis muscle when the peroneal nerve is stimulated and from the flexor hallucis brevis muscle when the posterior tibial nerve is stimulated in the affected foot. Frequently, the distal posterior tibial nerve is more involved than the distal peroneal nerve. The abnormality is always most severe in the distal nerves. The distal latency, if one can be recorded, and the velocity of conduction in the calf portion of the peroneal and posterior tibial nerves are relatively well preserved. These findings are in sharp contrast with those in diabetic and uremic neuropathies, in which distal latencies and conduction velocities tend to be symmetrically reduced well below normal velocities at an early stage in *both* lower limbs.

Sensory nerve conduction studies show decreased or absent sensory potential amplitudes from sural, superficial peroneal, and plantar nerves, whereas sensory conduction velocity, when recordable, is normal.

Needle electrode examination reveals the changes of muscle denervation in the small muscles of the affected foot, particularly in the sole of the foot, with fibrillation potentials at rest and large motor units of long duration in much reduced numbers. Lesser denervation changes are seen in the muscles of the calf if the ischemia has been severe.

Treatment

Once a diagnosis of ischemic neuropathy has been made by clinical and electrophysiologic investigations, what treatment can be offered? If peripheral blood flow is significantly reduced, vascular reconstructive surgery is justified. However, if perfusion is adequate, conservative treatment is indicated. Wilbourn and coworkers[35] suggested that phenytoin, tricyclic antidepressants, and analgesics are ineffective but that carbamazepine produces partial relief. Three of their patients had a sympathectomy, and two reported pain relief. Persistent pain that is uncontrolled by such drugs, if dramatically relieved by sympathetic blocks, may well deserve sympathectomy, particularly if the passage of time does not indicate spontaneous regression is taking place. Many clinicians believe that tricyclic antidepressants, sometimes in combination with small amounts of phenothiazine, are effective.

Kihara and colleagues[36,37] have produced experimental ischemic neuropathy in rat sciatic nerve, treating with hyperbaric oxygen and limb cooling. They found that hyperbaric oxygen 2 hours per day for 7 days beginning within 30 minutes of ischemia was effective in rescuing fibers from ischemic degeneration if ischemia was not extreme. In limbs with the same degree of ischemia, limbs that were hypothermic suffered less ischemic nerve fiber damage. These findings have not yet been applied clinically.

A new approach to treatment is therapy with phVEGF165 vascular endothelial growth factor gene. Trials of *VEGF* in rabbits 10 days after the induction of hind-limb ischemia restored nerve function earlier than in untreated animals.[38] A recent trial of intramuscular gene transfer for treatment of ischemic neuropathy in 17 patients with chronic limb ischemia over 6 months reported an improvement in vascular ankle-brachial index as well as improvement in clinical and nerve conduction assessment. Diabetic patients also responded. Therapeutic angiogenesis may be an effective treatment in the future.[39]

Prognosis

The prognosis of acute arterial insufficiency is uncertain. After other types of axonal nerve injury, peripheral nerves show a considerable capacity to regenerate, and regeneration has been seen in animal models after ischemia. Therefore, particularly in the absence of any other causes of neuropathy, such as diabetes, uremia, blood dyscrasias, or carcinoma, axon repair might be expected to occur slowly, with relief of symptoms.

■ ISCHEMIC MONONEUROPATHY ASSOCIATED WITH ATHEROSCLEROTIC DISEASE OF LARGE ARTERIES

Ischemic mononeuropathy is a frequent occurrence in diseases of small vessels associated with vasculitis and diabetes. Ischemic mononeuropathies that seem distinct from compressive neuropathies have occasionally been documented in the literature in association with atherosclerotic disease of large vessels.

Peroneal Neuropathy

Ferguson and Liversedge[33] reported seven cases of peroneal palsy with vascular disease: three resulted from cardiac emboli, and four were associated with atherosclerosis. The precise location of the arterial occlusions was not documented angiographically. As described earlier, the nature of the vascular supply to the peroneal nerve at the fibular head certainly predisposes to ischemic damage, although the nerve is also prone to compression in the same area.

Peroneal neuropathy presents as weakness of dorsiflexion and eversion of the ankle, with preservation of inversion and plantar flexion, which are functions of the posterior calf muscles. The sensory deficit is confined to the dorsum of the foot and perhaps to the lateral calf, and the ankle jerk is preserved. It is possible to confirm the diagnosis with nerve conduction studies, which demonstrate abnormality in peroneal function while all other nerve conduction is intact. It is usually possible to distinguish a compressive peroneal neuropathy, which produces a local area of conduction slowing and block at the fibular head, from an ischemic lesion, which is primarily axonal in nature and produces a uniform conduction velocity throughout the length of the nerve and a reduction in the motor and sensory potential amplitudes.

Tibial Neuropathy

In a recent study of 52 patients with tibial neuropathy, 19% were thought to be due to ischemia related to embolic events, compartment syndromes, or graft occlusions. Forty percent of these were isolated, and 60% were associated with a peroneal neuropathy. All had sensory loss in the sole and lateral aspect of the foot, and all had weakness of plantar flexion of the ankle and toes.[40]

Femoral Neuropathy

Whether a femoral neuropathy occurs with vascular occlusion in the absence of compression, traction, or hemorrhage is unclear. Chopra and Hurwitz[41] reported slight wasting and weakness of the quadriceps muscle in 1 of 29 patients with atherosclerosis and claudication symptoms, and Archie[42] reported a femoral neuropathy due to common iliac artery occlusion in a nondiabetic patient. D'Amour and associates[43] reported two cases of femoral neuropathy, one following surgery for abdominal aortic aneurysm with aortobifemoral bypass grafting and one following placement of an intra-aortic balloon pump.

The main trunk of the femoral artery receives nutrient arteries from the iliac branch of the iliolumbar artery, from the deep circumflex iliac artery in the iliac fossa, and from the lateral circumflex femoral artery in the femoral triangle.[5]

A femoral nerve lesion results in flaccid paralysis of the quadriceps muscle, an absent knee jerk, and loss of sensation over the anterior and medial thigh and the inner aspect of the calf down to the level of the medial malleolus. Electrophysiologic studies show decreased or absent motor-evoked response from the quadriceps muscle when the femoral nerve is stimulated in the groin and an absent saphenous sensory potential at the ankle, together with fibrillation potentials and motor unit loss, on needle electrode examination of the quadriceps muscle. Other nerves in the limb are normal. Femoral neuropathy is a frequent complication of diabetes and is presumably due to abnormalities of the vasa nervorum. The prognosis for recovery in both traumatic and diabetic femoral neuropathy is excellent. The incidence of and prognosis for ischemic femoral neuropathy await further reports.

Lumbosacral Plexus Lesions

Whether lumbosacral plexus lesions rather than lower cord or cauda equina lesions result from occlusive vascular disease is not well documented.

The lumbosacral plexus really has two parts: (1) a lumbar plexus arising from the second, third, and fourth lumbar roots and forming the femoral and obturator nerves, and (2) a sacral plexus arising from the fourth and fifth lumbar roots and the first three sacral roots and forming the superior and inferior gluteal nerves and the sciatic nerve. Blood supply to the lumbosacral plexus is through five lumbar arteries from each side of the abdominal aorta, the deep circumflex iliac artery, a branch of the external iliac artery, and the iliolumbar and gluteal branches of the internal iliac artery.[5]

Usubiaga and colleagues[44] described a lumbosacral plexus lesion after resection of an abdominal aortic aneurysm and aortobifemoral grafting. At autopsy, the plexus was totally infarcted. Voulters and Bolton[45] reported lumbosacral plexus damage following aortofemoral bypass grafting for repair of an abdominal aortic aneurysm. D'Amour and associates[43] described a number of cases, one following aortofemoral bypass grafting for stenosis of the common and external iliac arteries; one following acute occlusion of an aortobifemoral graft; one following aortofemoral bypass and femoropopliteal thrombectomy for occlusion of the common iliac, internal iliac, and superficial femoral arteries; and one following occlusion of the common iliac and femoral arteries. In these instances, the sciatic nerve seemed to be mainly involved. In two cases, neurologic symptoms appeared following vascular occlusion before surgery. Partial slow recoveries were reported. Gloviczki and coworkers[46] reported on a non-insulin-dependent diabetic patient who had bilateral leg weakness following aorta-profunda femoris bypass grafting for internal iliac disease. The patient experienced slow partial recovery. Five further cases of lumbosacral plexus injuries with reoperative aortic procedures were described by Plecha and coworkers.[47]

Clinical evaluation of the patient with unilateral lower limb dysfunction can often distinguish a lesion of the lumbosacral plexus from one affecting the spinal cord or a major peripheral nerve. When the abnormality resides in the plexus, motor and sensory loss affects more than one peripheral nerve and dermatomal segment. Weakness involves proximal muscles (the iliopsoas, hip adductors and abductors, or glutei) as well as distal muscles. The limb is flaccid and areflexic, with no response to plantar stimulation. This is in contrast with spinal lesions, which produce a spastic, hyper-reflexic limb with extensor plantar response and dissociated sensory loss. Electromyography is usually essential to confirm the diagnosis. Localization to the lumbosacral plexus depends on the unilateral absence of sensory potentials (these are preserved in cauda equina and proximal root lesions), the absence of paraspinal denervation, and the presence of denervation changes in muscles innervated by multiple nerves and roots.

It is important to attempt to distinguish the precise level of the lesion when severe unilateral limb dysfunction occurs. Although lesions of the lower spinal cord or cauda equina have a poor prognosis, there is some hope of recovery if the damage has occurred to part of the lumbosacral plexus.

■ ISCHEMIC MONOMELIC NEUROPATHY WITH VASCULAR ACCESS SURGERY

In 1983, Wilbourn and associates[48] described a group of hemodialysis patients with multiple mononeuropathies. Almost exclusively, the patients were diabetics, especially those with preexisting neuropathy or peripheral vascular disease, and symptoms occurred within minutes or hours of placement of arteriovenous access, usually in a brachiocephalic or antecubital location. They had acute pain with weakness or paralysis of muscles of the hand and forearm, particularly wrist and finger drop with distal sensory loss. The hand was usually warm, and a radial pulse may have been present. Nerve conduction studies show decreased motor and sensory-evoked responses from involved nerves with distal denervation. The antecubital fossa is a watershed for vasa nervorum of the three upper limb nerves.[49] Presumably the neuropathy is due to shunting of critical blood supply. Early diagnosis and access closure are critical to prevent hand paralysis.[50]

■ NEUROPATHY WITH ENDOVASCULAR GRAFT SURGERY

There are case reports emerging of nerve injury associated with endovascular stent-graft placement. Abnormalities have included lumbosacral dysfunction with bilateral limb weakness, sciatic neuropathy, femoral neuropathy, and autonomic neuropathy and are presumably due to occlusion of the pelvic blood flow or other supplying arteries.[51-54]

■ SUMMARY

Nerve injury due to ischemia has been discussed. Although many experimental animal studies have been published, the association of atherosclerotic disease with clinical neuropathic lesions in humans has not been as clearly reported. Occlusive vascular disease, both acute and chronic, seems capable of producing a painful unilateral axonal polyneuropathy, and major vascular occlusion may occasionally cause a mononeuropathy or lumbosacral plexus lesion. In the clinical setting, attempts should be made to detect the location and severity of the neurologic lesion precisely so that clearer therapeutic and prognostic guidelines can be established. In general, if significant ischemia is present, revascularization is indicated; if perfusion is adequate, a conservative approach is justified.

■ REFERENCES

1. Daube JR, Dyck PJ: Neuropathy due to peripheral vascular diseases. In Dyck PJ, Thomas PK, Lambert EH, et al (eds): Diseases of the Peripheral Nervous System. Philadelphia, WB Saunders, 1984, p 1458.
2. Olsson Y: The involvement of vasa nervorum in diseases of peripheral nerves. In Vinken PJ, Bruyn GW (eds): Handbook of Clinical Neurology, Vol XII. Amsterdam, North Holland Publishing, 1972, p 644.
3. Lundborg G: Intraneural microcirculation. Orthop Clin North Am 19:1, 1988.
4. Lundborg G: The intrinsic vascularization of human peripheral nerves: Structural and functional aspects. J Hand Surg 4:34, 1979.
5. Sunderland S: Nerve and Nerve Injuries. Edinburgh, Churchill Livingstone, 1978.

6. Lundborg G: Ischemic nerve injury: Experimental studies on intraneural microvascular pathophysiology and nerve function in a limb subjected to temporary circulatory arrest. Scand J Plast Reconstr Surg Suppl 6:3, 1970.
7. Kelly CJ, Augustine C, Rooney BP, et al: An investigation of the pathophysiology of ischaemic neuropathy. Eur J Vasc Surg 5:535, 1991.
8. Parry GJ, Linn DJ: Transient focal conduction block following experimental occlusion of the vasa nervorum muscle and nerve. Muscle Nerve 9:345, 1986.
9. Schmetzer JD, Zochodne E, Low PA: Ischemic and reperfusion injury of rat peripheral nerve. Proc Natl Acad Sci U S A 86:16, 1989.
10. Leone J, Ochs S: Anoxic block and recovery of axoplasmic transport and electrical excitability of nerve. J Neurobiol 9:229, 1978.
11. Dyck PJ: Hypoxic neuropathy: Does hypoxia play a role in diabetic neuropathy? The 1988 Robert Wartenberg Lecture. Neurology 39:111, 1989.
12. Fox JL, Kenmore PI: The effect of ischemia on nerve conduction. Exp Neurol 17:403, 1967.
13. Korthals JK, Maki T, Gieron MA: Nerve and muscle vulnerability to ischemia. J Neurol Sci 71:283, 1985.
14. Chervu A, Moore WS, Homsher E, et al: Differential recovery of skeletal muscle and peripheral nerve function after ischemia and reperfusion. J Surg Res 47:12, 1989.
15. Farinon AM, Marbini A, Gemignani F, et al: Skeletal muscle and peripheral nerve changes caused by chronic arterial insufficiency: Significance and clinical correlations-histological, histochemical, and ultrastructural study. Clin Neurol 3:240, 1984.
16. Eames RA, Lange LS: Clinical and pathological study of ischemic neuropathy. J Neurol Neurosurg Psychiatry 30:215, 1967.
17. Rodriguez-Sánchez C, Medina Sánchez M, Malik RA, et al: Morphological abnormalities in the sural nerve from patients with peripheral vascular disease. Histol Histopathol 6:63, 1991.
18. Nukada H, van Rij AM, Packer SG, et al: Pathology of acute and chronic ischaemic neuropathy in atherosclerotic peripheral vascular disease. Brain 119:1449, 1996.
19. Benstead TJ, Dyck PJ, Sangalang V: Inner perineurial cell vulnerability in ischemia. Brain Res 489:177, 1989.
20. Korthals JK, Korthals MA, Wisniewski HM: Peripheral nerve ischemia: II. Accumulation of organelles. Ann Neurol 4:487, 1978.
21. Parry GJ, Brown MJ: Selective fiber vulnerability in acute ischemic neuropathy. Ann Neurol 11:147, 1981.
22. Nukada H, Dyck PJ: Acute ischemia causes axonal stasis, swelling, attenuation, and secondary demyelination. Ann Neurol 22:311, 1987.
23. McManis PG, Low PA: Factors affecting the relative viability of centrifascicular and subperineurial axons in acute peripheral nerve ischemia. Exp Neurol 99:84, 1988.
24. Sladky JT, Tschoepe RL, Greenberg JH, et al: Peripheral neuropathy after chronic endoneurial ischemia. Ann Neurol 29:272, 1991.
25. Hutchison EC, Liversedge LA: Neuropathy in peripheral vascular disease: Its bearing on diabetic neuropathy. Q J Med 25:267, 1956.
26. Hunter GC, Song GW, Nayak NN, et al: Peripheral nerve conduction abnormalities in lower extremity ischemia: The effects of revascularization. J Surg Res 45:96, 1988.
27. Miglietta O: Electrophysiologic studies in chronic occlusive peripheral vascular disease. Arch Phys Med Rehabil 48:89, 1967.
28. Weinberg DH, Simovic D, Isner J, Ropper AH: Chronic ischemic monomelic neuropathy from critical limb ischemia. Neurology 57:1008-1012, 2001.
29. Ram Z, Sadeh M, Walden R, Adar R: Vascular insufficiency quantitatively aggravates diabetic neuropathy. Arch Neurol 48:1239-1242, 1991.
30. Miglietta O, Lowenthal M: Nerve conduction velocity and refractory period in peripheral vascular disease. J Appl Physiol 17:837, 1962.
31. Weber F, Ziegler A: Axonal neuropathy in chronic peripheral arterial occlusive disease. Muscle Nerve 26:471-476, 2002.
32. Laghi Pasini F, Pastorelli M, Beermann U, et al: Peripheral neuropathy associated with ischemic vascular disease of the lower limbs. Angiology 47:569-577, 1996.
33. Ferguson FR, Liversedge LA: Ischemic lateral popliteal nerve palsy. BMJ 2:333, 1954.
34. Haimovici H: Peripheral arterial embolism. Angiology 1:20, 1950.
35. Wilbourn AJ, Furlan AJ, Hulley W, et al: Ischemic monomelic neuropathy. Neurology 33:447, 1983.
36. Kihara M, McManis PG, Schmelzer JD, et al: Experimental ischemic neuropathy: Salvage with hyperbaric oxygenation. Ann Neurol 37:89, 1995.
37. Kihara M, Schmelzer JD, Kihara Y, et al: Efficacy of limb cooling on the salvage of peripheral nerve from ischemic fiber degeneration. Muscle Nerve 19:203, 1996.
38. Schratzberger P, Schratzberger G, Silver M, et al: Favorable effect of *VEGF* gene transfer on ischemic peripheral neuropathy. Nat Med 6:405-413, 2000.
39. Simovic D, Isner JM, Ropper AH, et al: Improvement in chronic ischemic neuropathy after intramuscular phVEGF165 gene transfer in patients with critical limb ischemia. Arch Neurol 58:761-768, 2001.
40. Drees C, Wilbourn AJ, Stevens GHJ: Main trunk tibial neuropathies. Neurology 59:1082-1084, 2002.
41. Chopra JS, Hurwitz LJ: Femoral nerve conduction in diabetes and chronic occlusive vascular disease. J Neurol Neurosurg Psychiatry 31:28, 1968.
42. Archie JP Jr: Femoral neuropathy due to common iliac artery occlusion. South Med J 76:1073, 1983.
43. D'Amour ML, Lebrun LH, Rabbat A, et al: Peripheral neurological complications of aortoiliac vascular disease. Can J Neurol Sci 14:127, 1987.
44. Usubiaga JE, Kolodny J, Usubiaga LE: Neurologic complications of prevertebral surgery under regional anaesthesia. Surgery 68:304, 1970.
45. Voulters L, Bolton C: Acute lumbosacral plexus neuropathy following vascular surgery. Can J Neurol Sci 10:153, 1983.
46. Gloviczki P, Cross SA, Stanson AW, et al: Ischemic injury to the spinal cord or lumbosacral plexus after aorto-iliac reconstruction. Am J Surg 162:131, 1991.
47. Plecha EJ, Seabrook GR, Freischlag JA, Towne JB: Neurologic complications of reoperative and emergent abdominal aortic reconstruction. Ann Vasc Surg 9:95-101, 1995.
48. Wilbourn AJ, Furlan AJ, Hulley W, Ruschhaupt W: Ischemic monomelic neuropathy. Neurology 33:447-451, 1983.
49. Dyck PJ, Conn DL, Okazaki H: Necrotizing angiopathic neuropathy: Three-dimensional morphology of fiber degeneration related to sites of occluded vessels. Mayo Clin Proc 47:461-475, 1972.
50. Miles AM: Upper limb ischemia after vascular access surgery: Differential diagnosis and management. Semin Dial 13:312-315, 2000.
51. Kibria SG, Gough MJ: Ischaemic sciatic neuropathy: A complication of endovascular repair of abdominal aortic aneurysm. Eur J Vasc Endovasc Surg 17:266-267, 1999.
52. Forester ND, Parry D, Kessel D, et al: Ischaemic sciatic neuropathy: An important complication of embolisation of a type II endoleak. Eur J Vasc Endovasc Surg 24:462-463, 2002.
53. Kwok PC, Chung TK, Chong LC, et al: Neurologic injury after endovascular stent-graft and bilateral internal iliac artery embolization for infrarenal abdominal aortic aneurysm. J Vasc Interv Radiol 12:761-763, 2001.
54. Dougherty MJ, Calligaro KD: How to avoid and manage nerve injuries associated with aortic surgery: Ischemic neuropathy, traction injuries, and sexual derangements. Semin Vasc Surg 14:275-281, 2001.

Chapter 63

Lymphatic Complications of Vascular Surgery

PETER GLOVICZKI, MD, FACS
ROBERT C. LOWELL, MD, FACS, RVT

Section X

Injury to the lymphatic system during open vascular surgical reconstructions is almost unavoidable. Fine lymph vessels run parallel to corresponding arteries and veins, and major groups of lymph nodes are close to major vessels. However, the ability of transected or ligated lymphatics to regenerate and re-establish normal lymphatic transport is remarkable. Lymphatic injury frequently heals spontaneously and causes minimal or no morbidity. Injury to the lymphatics, however, is a major contributor to the development of edema of a lower extremity after infrainguinal reconstruction.[1-11] Interruption of lymphatic vessels during surgical dissection may also cause a lymphatic fistula[12-17] or lymphocele.[17-27] Rarely, injury to the para-aortic or mesenteric lymphatics may result in chylous ascites,[22,28-46] and thoracic duct injury during cervical, thoracic, or thoracoabdominal aortic reconstruction[31,47-56] or after high translumbar aortography[57] may result in chylothorax. This chapter reviews the pathophysiology, diagnosis, and management of the most frequent lymphatic complications following vascular reconstructions and suggests guidelines for prevention.

■ POSTBYPASS EDEMA

Lower extremity edema occurs in 50% to 100% of patients who undergo successful open infrainguinal arterial reconstruction for chronic ischemia.[2,7] Leg swelling after femoropopliteal or femorotibial bypass becomes evident with dependency, usually when the patient resumes ambulation. Pitting edema usually subsides within 2 to 3 months after reconstruction. During this period, normal ambulation may be impaired and wound healing delayed. In some patients, the edema may become chronic and cause persistent functional disability despite successful arterial reconstruction.

Etiology and Pathogenesis

Lymphedema develops when the rate of production of protein-rich interstitial fluid exceeds the capacity of the lymphatic system to remove the increased volume of lymph. Insufficiency of lymphatic transport plays the most important role in the development of postbypass edema.[58] Lymphatic insufficiency has two main causes (Fig. 63-1). First, increased production of interstitial fluid after successful revascularization results in a significant increase in the lymphatic load. Second, the transport capacity of the lymphatic system is reduced because of lymphatic injury and obstruction of deep and superficial lymph channels during dissection in the popliteal space, lymphatic damage along the great saphenous vein, and at the groin.

Increased capillary filtration results from elevated arterial pressure after revascularization, alterations in the regulation of the microcirculatory flow, and probable endothelial and smooth muscle injury from chronic ischemia.[1,7] Decreased arterial and arteriolar smooth muscle tone as a cause of hyperemia following revascularization was first proposed in 1959 by Simeone and Husni.[59] Eickhoff,[8] however, demonstrated that abnormalities in local blood flow regulation normalized within about a week after reconstruction, whereas edema persisted much longer in these patients. Although derangement of the microcirculation contributes to postbypass edema to some degree, Eickhoff's experiments support the theory that lymphatic obstruction due to surgical injury is the most important cause of postbypass edema.

If the number of functioning major lymph channels decreases to a critical level, lymphedema develops. In one study, in which patients underwent lymphangiography after infrainguinal bypass, the average number of patent superficial lymph vessels visualized was reduced to 1.7 per patient, as compared with the normal average of 9.5.[1] In a similar series of 37 patients, edema was not significant when more than three intact superficial lymph vessels were visualized on the postoperative lymphangiogram.[4]

AbuRahma and colleagues examined the involvement of the lymphatic system in the pathophysiology of edema formation in patients undergoing femoropopliteal bypass grafting.[9] Edema developed in 29 (40%) of the 72 patients, and leg swelling occurred in 17 (85%) of 20 of the patients treated by conventional dissection of the femoropopliteal arteries. When careful dissection was performed that preserved the lymphatics, edema developed in only 2 (10%) of 20 patients. Postoperative lymphangiography showed normal anatomy in 6 of the 8 patients without edema, but the anatomy was markedly abnormal in all 8 patients with edema who underwent lymphangiography. Persson and coworkers found less edema in those patients who needed less dissection during surgery.[10] Significantly less swelling was observed in patients with prosthetic grafts than in those with vein grafts. Patients with above-knee grafts also had less edema than those with below-knee bypasses.[10]

Studies using albumin clearance in patients with post-revascularization edema also support the idea that edema is mainly lymphatic in origin. A reduction in plasma albumin level with a concomitant increase in the extremity albumin content was noted after femoropopliteal bypass.[60] The increase in albumin content was three times greater in limbs revascularized by femoropopliteal bypass than in those revascularized by aortoiliac grafts. These data correspond to the clinical observation that edema rarely develops after aortofemoral revascularization.

Although venous thrombosis has been proposed as a cause of postoperative leg edema,[61,62] studies have demonstrated a low incidence of deep venous thrombosis in patients with postbypass edema.[63,64] In one series, normal venous hemodynamics and morphology were confirmed in 41 of 45 patients with leg edema after arterial bypass.[65] The incidence of deep venous thrombosis after femoropopliteal bypass was found to be similar in patients who had edema (7%) and in those who did not (10%).[9] Deep venous thrombosis, therefore, seems to play a minor role in postbypass edema in most patients.[7,58,66]

Diagnosis

Mild, partially pitting ankle edema appears on the 2nd or 3rd postoperative day and resolves almost completely with leg elevation and bed rest. Deep venous thrombosis should be excluded as a cause of postoperative edema when there is excessive postoperative swelling, cyanosis, muscle tenderness, or unusual pain. Duplex scanning of the deep veins is the test of choice for excluding deep venous thrombosis. If the cause of the edema is still in question, lymphoscintigraphy confirms lymphedema (Fig. 63-2).

Management

Postoperatively, mild edema of the extremity should be treated with frequent elevation of the limb and some restriction of ambulation. Cardiac failure should be treated promptly to help preserve the normal pressure gradient and to allow venous return and lymph flow toward the heart. Moderate to severe postbypass edema is treated with com-

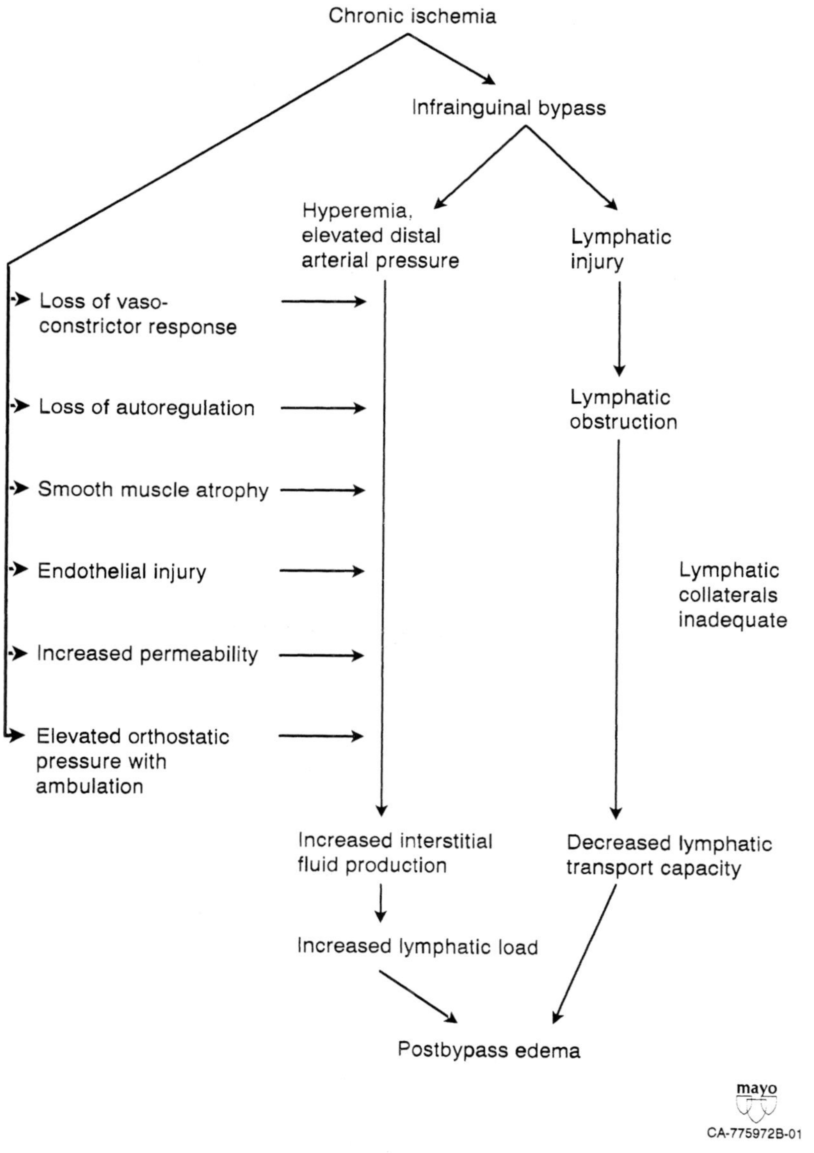

Chronic ischemia
Infrainguinal bypass
Hyperemia, elevated distal arterial pressure
Lymphatic injury
Loss of vaso-constrictor response
Loss of autoregulation
Lymphatic obstruction
Smooth muscle atrophy
Endothelial injury
Lymphatic collaterals inadequate
Increased permeability
Elevated orthostatic pressure with ambulation
Increased interstitial fluid production
Decreased lymphatic transport capacity
Increased lymphatic load
Postbypass edema

mayo
CA-775972B-01

FIGURE 63-1 Mechanism of postbypass edema. (Adapted from Gloviczki P, Bergman RT: Lymphatic problems and revascularization edema. In Bernhard VM, Towne JB [eds]: Complications in Vascular Surgery, 2nd ed. St. Louis, Quality Medical Publishing, 1991, p 366.)

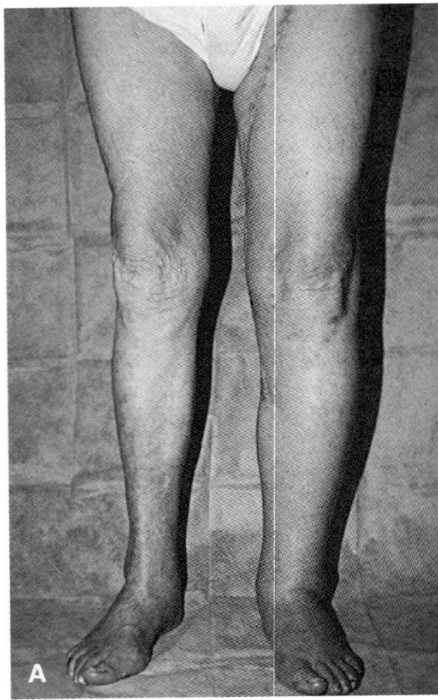

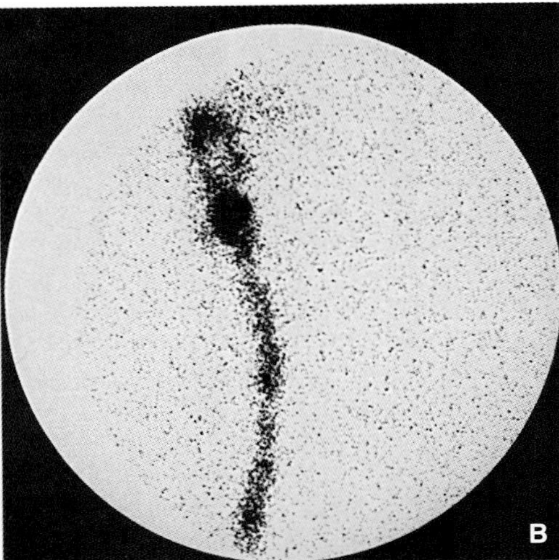

FIGURE 63-2 **A,** Edema of the left lower extremity in an 88-year-old man 4 weeks after left femoropopliteal saphenous vein bypass performed for severe chronic ischemia. **B,** Lymphoscintigraphy confirmed the severe lymphedema of the left leg with no visualization of the lymph vessels or inguinal lymph nodes. Lymphatic transport was normal on the right.

pression stockings. In general, we prescribe calf-length therapeutic elastic stockings with compression of 30 to 40 mm Hg at the ankle level. For patients with a below-knee in-situ bypass or any bypass to the distal tibial or pedal arteries, management is individualized to avoid direct compression of the subcutaneous vein graft. Attempts to prevent or limit postbypass edema pharmacologically with steroids, mannitol, terbutaline, or furosemide have not proved effective[10] and are not recommended.

Prevention

Meticulous, lymph-preserving surgical dissection is needed to minimize postbypass edema.[9,58] For infrainguinal bypass, a vertical groin incision slightly lateral to the femoral pulse should be made in an attempt to preserve the patency of lymph vessels and the integrity of lymph nodes. The inguinal lymphatics should be retracted medially, and a vertical incision should be made in the femoral sheath to dissect the femoral arteries. Loupe magnification facilitates identification of lymph nodes and lymph vessels. The lymphatics should be carefully preserved; if they must be divided, they should be ligated or cauterized to avoid lymph leakage. Attempts should be made to preserve as much lymphatic tissue as possible between the saphenofemoral junction and the femoral artery. A skin bridge should be left between the groin incision and the incision made in the thigh to dissect the more distal portion of the saphenous vein. Multiple, short skin incisions to dissect the saphenous vein disrupt fewer superficial lymphatics.[9]

Dissection around the popliteal artery should be performed with the same care to avoid lymphatic disruption. The vascular sheath should be opened longitudinally without dissection of the popliteal vein or the posterior tibial nerve in the neurovascular bundle. Fibroadipose tissue, which contains the deep lymphatics in the popliteal fossa, should be left intact.

The increasing use of minimally invasive techniques to harvest the great saphenous vein for lower extremity or coronary bypass should, it is hoped, decrease wound healing problems and associated lymphatic complications. Video-assisted saphenous vein harvest requires fewer and shorter skin incisions in the leg. In a series of 68 lower extremity bypass procedures, only one bleeding complication was related to the video-assisted harvest and two seromas developed at the arterial dissection sites.[67] The benefit of endoscopic versus open vein harvesting with a reduced rate of lymphatic complications was confirmed in prospective, randomized studies.[68,69]

■ LYMPHATIC FISTULA

Because of the rich lymphatic network of the femoral triangle, lymphatic fistulae following vascular reconstructions most often occur at the groin. In 4000 vascular operations, Kalman and associates observed lymphatic fistulae in 45 patients (incidence, 1.1%).[16] In other series, the incidence of this complication was similar, ranging from 0.8% to 6.4%.[13,70,71]

Etiology

Important factors that contribute to lymphatic leakage are failure to ligate or to cauterize divided lymphatics and failure to approximate the tissue layers properly at closure. Lymphatic leakage occurs more frequently in older diabetic patients with poor wound healing. Excessive early limb motion, infection of the operated leg or foot, reoperation, and placement of a prosthetic graft to the groin are other possible causes.[16]

Diagnosis

Persistent leakage of clear or yellow fluid from a groin incision establishes the diagnosis. Lymphoscintigraphy to confirm that the fluid is of lymphatic origin is seldom necessary when the fistula develops within days or a few weeks after the operation. When lymphatic leakage occurs several months or years after vascular reconstruction, lymphoscintigraphy is helpful; in such cases, however, computed tomography (CT), white blood cell scanning, and sometimes fistulography must be performed to exclude infection of an underlying vascular graft. CT scanning is also valuable for diagnosis of concomitant retroperitoneal lymphatic injury because retroperitoneal lymphocele or chylous ascites can present with lymphatic fistulae at the groin.[58]

Management

Early diagnosis and management of lymphatic fistula are important to prevent prolonged hospitalization and delayed wound healing. In one study[14] of 35 patients with lymphatic leakage, infection of an underlying vascular graft was not noted; however, most studies have reported a small but definite risk of deep wound infection from persistent lymph leakage.[13,16] In the first few days, conservative management is indicated and should include local wound care, administration of systemic antibiotics, and bed rest with leg elevation to reduce lymph flow.

Like other authors,[13,16] we favor surgical closure in the operating room when the fistula continues to produce large volumes despite several days of conservative management. First, 5 mL of isosulfan blue (Lymphazurin dye) is injected subcutaneously into the first and third interdigital spaces in the foot (Fig. 63-3).[15,58] The groin incision is then opened, and the site of the lymphatic injury is readily apparent by the leakage of blue fluid droplets. The area is oversewn, and the wound is closed in multiple layers over a small polyethylene drain. When it is impossible to oversew the damaged tissue, injection of fibrin glue may also be useful.

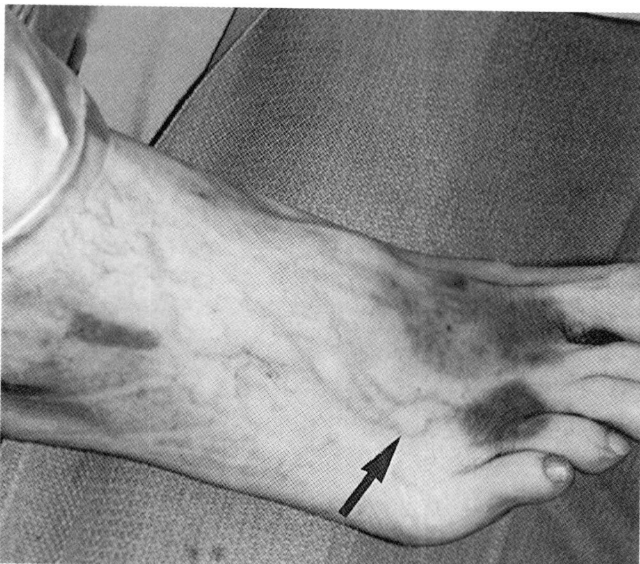

FIGURE 63-3 Injection of isosulfan blue (Lymphazurin) dye into the first and third interdigital spaces of the foot immediately visualizes the foot lymphatics *(arrow)* and during surgery helps identify the site of lymphatic injury at the groin.

■ THORACIC DUCT FISTULA

Injury to the thoracic duct may occur after dissection of the proximal left common carotid artery or after left subclavian or vertebral artery dissection.[22] Neglected cases of thoracic duct cutaneous fistula may lead to malnutrition, lymphocytopenia, anemia, or infection of an underlying prosthetic graft. Early operation with lateral closure using 7-0 or 8-0 nonabsorbable monofilament sutures is the optimal treatment. If lateral closure is not possible, ligation of the thoracic duct at the neck is an accepted alternative because the collateral lymphatic circulation is usually adequate. The incision is closed over a subcutaneous drain, which is left in place for a brief period postoperatively.

■ LYMPHOCELE

A lymphocele is a localized collection of lymph. Early after injury to the lymphatic pathways, the lymph collects between tissue planes. Unless the lymph reabsorbs spontaneously or drains through a cutaneous fistula, a pseudocapsule develops. In contrast with a seroma, a lymphocele usually has a well-localized connection with one or more of the lymphatic channels. For this reason, lymphoscintigraphy can readily demonstrate a lymphocele (Fig. 63-4).

Groin Lymphocele

As with lymphatic fistulae, the most frequent site of lymphoceles after vascular reconstructions is the groin. Most lymphoceles develop in the early postoperative period but may appear later. Large lymphoceles cause local

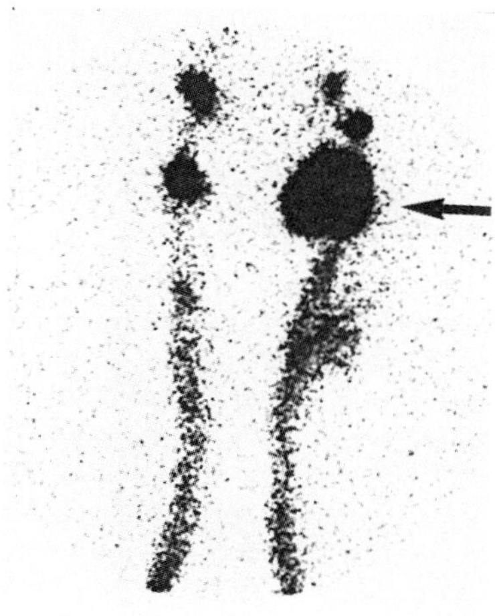

FIGURE 63-4 Bilateral lower extremity lymphoscintigraphy demonstrates a large left groin lymphocele *(arrow)* and extravasation of the colloid in the left thigh.

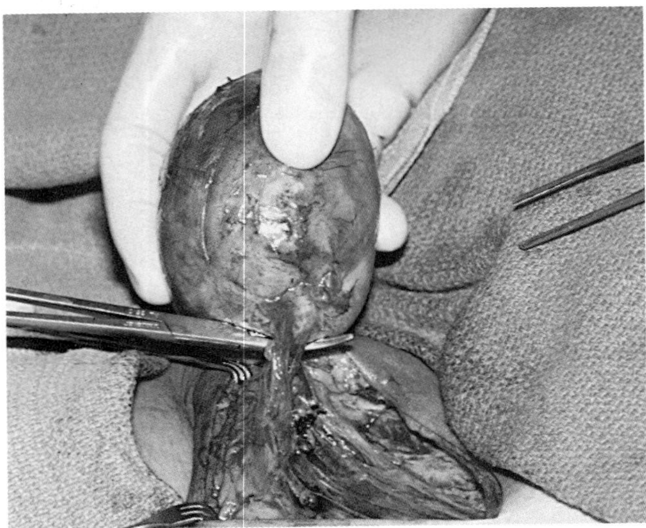

FIGURE 63-5 Intraoperative photograph of a dissected left groin lymphocele with an easily identifiable lymphatic pedicle. The pedicle was ligated, and the lymphocele was removed.

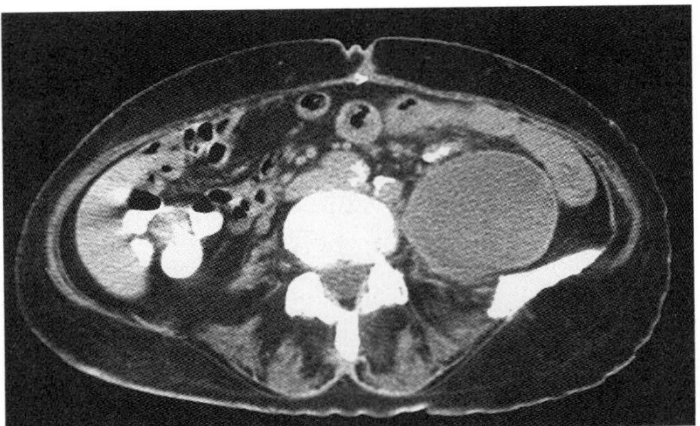

FIGURE 63-6 CT scan of a 70-year-old woman reveals a large left retroperitoneal lymphocele 9 months after repair of a thoracoabdominal aortic aneurysm.

discomfort, pain, and leg swelling. Hematoma, seroma, and wound infection should be considered in the differential diagnosis. The presence of a soft, fluid-filled cyst and intermittent drainage of clear lymph through a fistula confirms the diagnosis of lymphocele. Ultrasonography is helpful in distinguishing a solid, dense hematoma from a cystic lymphocele. CT is performed when a lymphocele develops several weeks to months after the operation. CT is helpful for excluding graft infection or for identifying retroperitoneal lymphocele extending to the groin.

Small lymphoceles can be observed because they may reabsorb spontaneously. For enlarging or symptomatic lymphoceles or lymphoceles that lie close to a prosthetic graft, we advocate early surgery to reduce the risk of graft infection. Injection of isosulfan blue into the foot is helpful for identifying the lymphatic channels supplying the lymphocele. The lymphocele is excised, and the lymphatic pedicle is ligated or oversewn (Fig. 63-5). The wound is closed in multiple layers over a small subcutaneous drain. Sclerotherapy, used more frequently for retroperitoneal lymphoceles, can also be used for groin lymphoceles.

Retroperitoneal Lymphocele

Symptomatic retroperitoneal lymphoceles are rare. In a review of more than 4000 aortic reconstructions, an incidence of 0.1% was reported by Garrett and colleagues.[25] In reviewing the literature, we found 11 well-documented cases of this complication following aortic reconstruction.[18,19,21-23,25,58] The number of unreported and asymptomatic cases is undoubtedly higher. Retroperitoneal lymphoceles have been reported more frequently after renal transplantation (incidence 0.6% to 18%).[26,72-74] In these patients, however, lymphocele develops not only because of injury to the recipient pelvic lymphatics but also because of increased lymph production and lymph leakage from the donor kidney.[26]

Diagnosis

The most common symptoms of retroperitoneal lymphocele are abdominal distention, nausea, and abdominal pain, and the most frequent finding is an abdominal or a flank mass. Although signs or symptoms may develop early, in almost half of the patients the lymphocele is discovered a year or several years after the operation.[58] Patients who present with signs or symptoms of a retroperitoneal lymphocele should be examined with CT (Fig. 63-6). In 5 of 11 published cases of retroperitoneal lymphocele, a groin mass was also present.[58] Evaluation of these patients showed a communication between the groin lymphocele and a retroperitoneal lymphocele. This observation illustrates the importance of CT when a groin mass develops after aortofemoral reconstruction. If infection is suspected, white blood cell scanning should also be performed unless CT has already confirmed graft infection. Lymphoscintigraphy can be diagnostic of a retroperitoneal lymphocele and should distinguish it from a perigraft seroma. Nevertheless, lymphoscintigraphic confirmation of a lymphocele does not rule out graft infection.

Management

For patients with a small, asymptomatic retroperitoneal lymphocele, observation with serial ultrasonography or CT is warranted. If the lymphocele increases in size or causes local compression to adjacent structures, needle aspiration under CT or ultrasound guidance is performed. This maneuver is both diagnostic and therapeutic. In 4 of 11 patients, aspiration alone was used with success.[58] Placement of an indwelling irrigation-drainage system is associated with a risk of infection. Garrett and colleagues[25] discussed two patients whose prosthetic grafts became infected after an irrigation-drainage system was placed for retroperitoneal lymphocele. Therefore, when repeated aspiration is unsuccessful, sclerotherapy or operative repair should be considered.

Abdominal exploration is performed after injection of 5 mL of isosulfan blue into the ipsilateral foot according to the technique detailed earlier. The lymphocele is

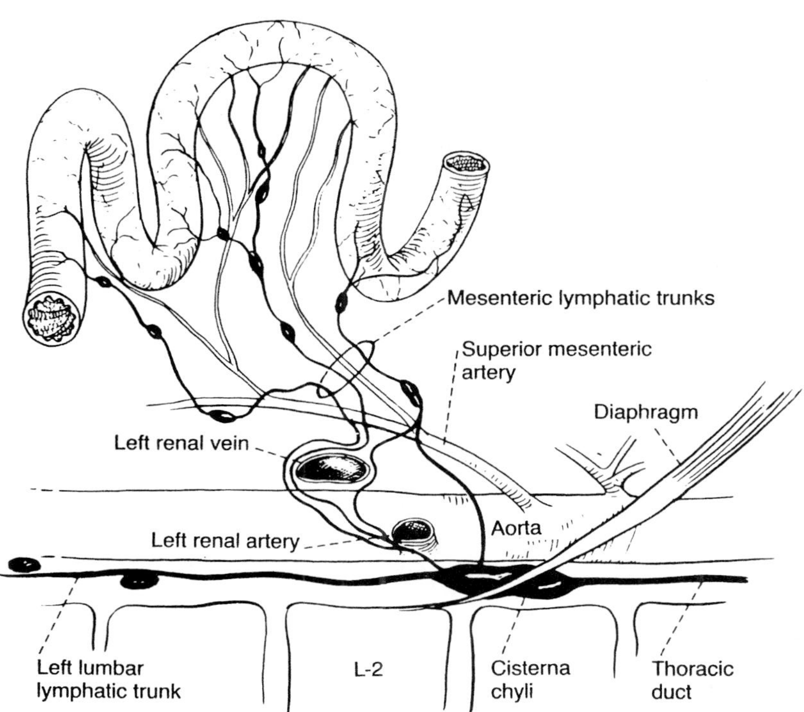

FIGURE 63-7 Anatomy of the mesenteric and ascending lumbar lymphatic trunks and the cisterna chyli. (From Gloviczki P, Bergman RT: Lymphatic problems and revascularization edema. In Bernhard VM, Towne JB [eds]: Complications in Vascular Surgery, 2nd ed. St. Louis, Quality Medical Publishing, 1991, p 366.)

unroofed, and the site of the lymphatic injury is oversewn, ligated, or both. If the prosthetic graft is exposed, it is covered by retroperitoneal tissue or omentum. When preoperative aspiration confirms the presence of chyle in the cyst, 24 ounces of whipping cream is given through a nasogastric tube 4 hours before exploration. Absorption of the cream helps to identify the site of lymphatic leakage in the mesenteric lymphatics around the left renal vein or at the cisterna chyli (Fig. 63-7). Whereas the mesenteric lymphatic trunks should be ligated or oversewn, lateral closure of the cisterna may be attempted first with loupe magnification.

For post-transplant lymphocele, peritoneal fenestration has been recommended for treatment.[72-74] Since the advent of surgical laparoscopy, however, several reports have described aspiration and peritoneal fenestration under laparoscopic visualization.[73,74] A tongue of omentum is brought down and placed through the peritoneal window to prevent premature closure and recurrence of the cyst. One study analyzed results of 12 laparoscopic and 23 open surgical internal marsupializations of pelvic lymphoceles. Laparoscopic lymphocelectomy required a longer operative time, but it resulted in shorter hospital stays, faster convalescences, and fewer recurrences of the lymphocele.[72] Laparoscopic transperitoneal drainage may become a useful addition to the vascular surgeon's armamentarium for the occasional treatment of lymphoceles after vascular reconstruction.

Percutaneous sclerotherapy has been used with increasing success as the definitive treatment of lymphoceles. The injection of talcum, bleomycin, doxicycline, povidone-iodine, fibrin sealant, and absolute alcohol has been reported, with good results in most cases.[75-82] Treatment with repeated injections may be necessary.

■ CHYLOUS ASCITES

The development of chylous ascites after abdominal aortic reconstructions is rare, but morbidity and mortality related to this complication can be significant. In reviewing the literature, we found 23 patients who were reported to have chylous ascites after aortic reconstruction.[22,28-46,74] Eighteen patients (78%) underwent repair of an abdominal aortic aneurysm, and five (22%) had surgery for occlusive disease. Ascites developed in the first 6 weeks after surgery in all but one patient.

Diagnosis

Symptoms of chylous ascites include progressive abdominal pain, dyspnea, and nausea. Abdominal distention can be significant, and the loss of proteins and fat may result in malnourishment. Lymphopenia and anemia can also develop, frequently resulting in poor immune function. Ascites can usually be detected by physical examination and confirmed by ultrasonography or CT. Paracentesis is necessary to verify the presence of chyle in the ascitic fluid. Chyle is an odorless, sterile, alkaline fluid that is milky in appearance. Its specific gravity is greater than 1012 g/dL. Its protein content is usually above 3 g/dL, and its fat content ranges from 0.4 to 4 g/dL. The fat in the fluid stains with Sudan stain.

Management

Although chylous ascites in patients with abdominal malignancies carries an ominous prognosis, the outcome when chylous ascites develops after open aortic surgery is somewhat better. Still, after open aortic surgery, 4 of 23 patients with this complication died (mortality rate, 17%).[22,31,47,83] The causes of death were sepsis in 2 patients and pulmonary embolus and malnutrition in 1 patient each.[22,31,42,83]

Most patients with chylous ascites after aortic surgery can be successfully treated without operation. The mainstay of treatment in patients with mild to moderate ascites is a medium-chain triglyceride diet to decrease chyle formation. For severe cases, however, complete bowel rest and total parenteral nutrition must be instituted. Repeated paracentesis results in resolution of the symptoms in most patients. Placement of a peritoneovenous shunt was reported in five patients, but sepsis caused death in one.[74] If repeated paracentesis is unsuccessful, exploration and closure of the site of the lymphatic injury should be performed. Larger mesenteric or para-aortic lymphatic channels should be ligated or oversewn, but lateral closure of the injured cisterna chyli can be attempted with fine monofilament sutures, as mentioned earlier. Of six reported patients who underwent exploration and surgical closure of the fistula, all recovered without recurrence.[28,34,39,41,44,45]

Prevention

Injury to the retroperitoneal and mesenteric lymphatics during aortic dissection should be carefully avoided. The cisterna chyli is formed by the right and left lumbar and the mesenteric lymphatic trunks; it is usually located at the level of the second lumbar vertebra, between the inferior vena cava and the abdominal aorta.[58] In half of patients, a well-developed cisterna chyli is absent. Several large mesenteric lymph vessels are located on the anteroinferior aspect of the left renal vein (see Fig. 63-7). Injury to these vessels results in leakage of chyle. Failure to close the divided lymphatics may lead to the development of chylous ascites or retroperitoneal lymphocele. All large lumbar, para-aortic, and mesenteric lymph vessels should be ligated or clipped when division is necessary during aortic dissection. Lateral closure of the injured cisterna chyli should be attempted with 7-0 monofilament sutures.

■ CHYLOTHORAX

Effusion of chyle into the pleural cavity after vascular procedures is uncommon; it occurs in 0.2% to 1% of cases after cardiothoracic surgery.[55] It is more common in neonates and small children operated on for congenital vascular anomalies, most frequently for aortic coarctation.[51-56] Chylothorax after repair of thoracic aortic aneurysm has been reported,[47-50] and in one patient it occurred after repair of an abdominal aortic aneurysm.[31] Chylothorax may develop as a complication of transthoracic dorsal sympathectomy[48] or after high translumbar aortography.[57]

Diagnosis

Pleural effusion is confirmed by chest radiographic studies or CT scan. Analysis of the fluid obtained through thoracentesis or through the thoracostomy tube confirms the diagnosis. Laboratory analysis of the milky or serous fluid is similar to that described for chylous ascites.

Management

Because respiratory embarrassment is frequent, drainage of the chylous fluid through a thoracostomy tube is usually necessary. The principles of treatment for decreasing chyle formation are the same as those for chylous ascites. Conservative management, consisting of closed drainage through a thoracostomy tube and nutritional support, has been effective in most cases. If a low-fat, high-protein diet with medium-chain triglyceride supplementation is not successful, intravenous hyperalimentation is started. Rarely, surgical closure of the site of the leak by oversewing or ligating the thoracic duct must be performed. Pleurodesis facilitates closure of the pleural space and decreases the potential for recurrence. Parietal pleurectomy is the most successful treatment when no distinct chylous leak can be identified.[84] Of six patients who had chylothorax after aortic aneurysm repair,[47] only one patient needed thoracotomy to treat a large chylous pseudocyst; however, one patient who was treated conservatively died after a long postoperative course that was complicated by both chylous ascites and chylothorax.[31]

Chylothorax that developed after thoracic operations was treated at the Mayo Clinic in 47 patients.[85] Nonoperative therapy was successful in one third, but 32 patients required ligation of the thoracic duct and 2 patients were treated with mechanical pleurodesis and fibrin glue. Reoperation was successful in 31 (91.2%) of the 34 patients. These authors recommended early reoperation and ligation of the thoracic duct when drainage exceeds 1000 mL/day. With progress in thoracoscopic surgery, thoracoscopic clipping of the thoracic duct has replaced open thoracotomy in many patients.[86] Real progress in the treatment has occurred recently with a report on percutaneous cannulation of the cisterna chyli and embolization of the thoracic duct using microcoils, particles, and glue.[87] Cope and Kaiser[87] reported on 42 patients who underwent percutaneous transabdominal catheter embolization or needle disruption of retroperitoneal lymphatic vessels in the treatment of high-output or unremitting chylothorax. Cure or improvement was documented in 74% of the patients. They recommend this procedure particularly in ill and high-risk patients.

Prevention

Injury to the thoracic duct during thoracic aortic dissection should be carefully avoided. The thoracic duct extends upward from the cisterna chyli and enters the posterior mediastinum through the aortic hiatus, slightly to the right of the aorta and to the left of the azygos vein (Fig. 63-8). In the posterior mediastinum, it is mostly a right-sided structure. The thoracic duct enters the superior mediastinum behind the aortic arch and subclavian artery, to the left of the esophagus. It is thus exposed to injury during dissection of the proximal thoracic aorta, the aortic arch, or the proximal subclavian artery. Once injury to the thoracic duct is recognized, an attempt at lateral closure should be made using 7-0 monofilament sutures with loupe magnification. When this is not successful, ligation of the thoracic duct should be performed. Adequate collateral lymphatic circulation usually develops.

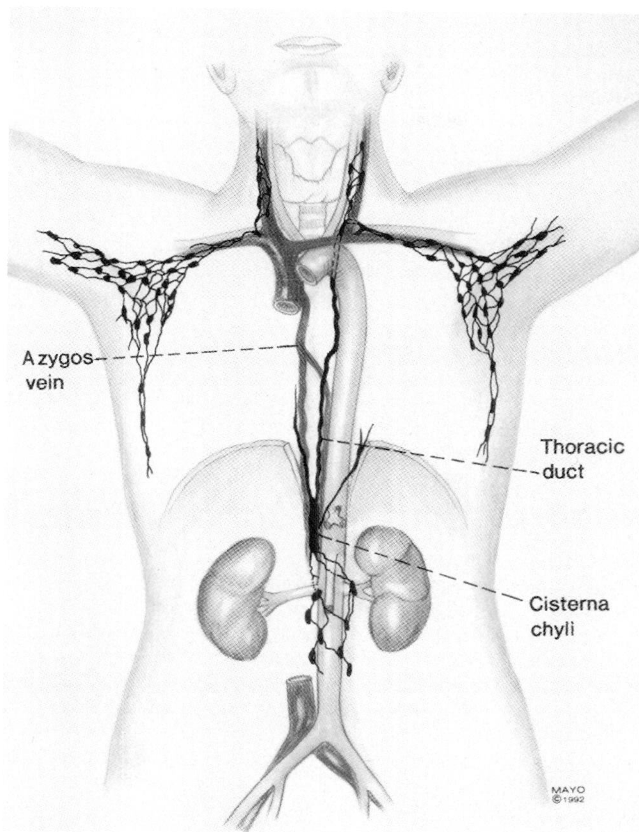

FIGURE 63-8 Anatomy of the thoracic duct. (©1992, Mayo Foundation.)

■ REFERENCES

1. Vaughan BF, Slavotinek AH, Jepson RP: Edema of the lower limb after vascular operations. Surg Gynecol Obstet 133:282, 1970.
2. Porter JM, Lindell TD, Lakin PC: Leg edema following femoropopliteal autogenous vein bypass. Arch Surg 105:883, 1972.
3. Storen EJ, Myhre HO, Stiris G: Lymphangiographic findings in patients with leg oedema after arterial reconstructions. Acta Chir Scand 140:385, 1974.
4. Schmidt KR, Welter H, Pfeifer KJ, et al: Lymphographic investigations of oedema of the extremities following reconstructive vascular surgery in the femoropopliteal territory. RoFo Fortschr Geb Rontgensr Nuklearmed 128:194, 1978.
5. Stillman RM, Fitzgerald JF, Varughese G, et al: Edema following femoropopliteal bypass: Etiology and prevention. Vasc Surg 18:354, 1983.
6. Stranden E: Edema in the lower limb following arterial reconstruction for atherosclerosis: A study of pathogenetic mechanisms. J Oslo City Hosp 34:3, 1984.
7. Schubart PJ, Porter JM: Leg edema following femorodistal bypass. In Bergan JJ, Yao JST (eds): Reoperative Arterial Surgery. Orlando, Grune & Stratton, 1986, p 311.
8. Eickhoff JH: Local regulation of subcutaneous blood flow and capillary filtration in limbs with occlusive arterial disease: Studies before and after arterial reconstruction. Dan Med Bull 33:111, 1986.
9. AbuRahma AF, Woodruff BA, Lucente FC: Edema after femoropopliteal bypass surgery: Lymphatic and venous theories of causation. J Vasc Surg 11:461, 1990.
10. Persson NH, Takolander R, Bergqvist D: Edema after lower limb arterial reconstruction: Influence of background factors, surgical technique, and potentially prophylactic methods. Vasa 20:57, 1991.
11. Esato K, Ohara M, Seyama A, et al: ^{99m}Tc-HSA lymphoscintigraphy and leg edema following arterial reconstruction. J Cardiovasc Surg 32:741, 1991.
12. Stolzenberg J: Detection of lymphaticocutaneous fistula by radionuclide lymphangiography. Arch Surg 113:306, 1978.
13. Kwaan JHM, Berstein JM, Connolly JE: Management of lymph fistulae in the groin after arterial reconstruction. Arch Surg 114:1416, 1979.
14. Murphy JL, Cole WC, White PM, et al: Lymphatic fistula after vascular reconstruction: A case control study. Can J Surg 34:76, 1991.
15. Weaver FA, Yellin AE: Management of postoperative lymphatic leaks by use of isosulphan blue [Letter]. J Vasc Surg 14:566, 1991.
16. Kalman PG, Walker PM, Johnston KW: Consequences of groin lymphatic fistulae after vascular reconstruction. Vasc Surg 25:210, 1991.
17. Khauli RB, Mosenthal AC, Caushaj PF: Treatment of lymphocele and lymphatic fistula following renal transplantation by laparoscopic peritoneal window. J Urol 147:1353, 1992.
18. Dillon ML, Postlethwait RW: The management of an abdominal mass recurring after resection of abdominal aortic aneurysm. Surg Clin North Am 50:1021, 1970.
19. Fitzer PM, Sallade RL, Graham WH: Computed tomography and the diagnosis of giant abdominal lymphocele. Va Med Q 107:448, 1980.
20. Patel BR, Burkhalter JL, Patel TB, et al: Interstitial lymphoscintigraphy for diagnosis of lymphocele. Clin Nucl Med 10:175, 1985.
21. Puyau FA, Adinolfi MF, Kerstein MD: Lymphocele around aortic femoral grafts simulating a false aneurysm. Cardiovasc Intervent Radiol 8:195, 1985.
22. Jensen SR, Voegeli DR, McDermott JC, et al: Lymphatic disruption following abdominal aortic surgery. Cardiovasc Intervent Radiol 9:199, 1986.
23. Pardy BJ, Harris P, Mourad K, et al: Case reports: Upper abdominal lymphocele following urgent aortorenal bypass grafting. J R Soc Med 79:674, 1986.
24. Scott AR: A report on the management of a lymphocyst after vascular surgery. Aust N Z J Surg 57:205, 1987.
25. Garrett HE Jr, Richardson JW, Howard HS, et al: Retroperitoneal lymphocele after abdominal aortic surgery. J Vasc Surg 10:245, 1989.
26. Malovrh M, Kandus A, Buturovic-Ponikvar J, et al: Frequency and clinical influence of lymphoceles after kidney transplantation. Transplant Proc 22:1423, 1990.
27. Velanovich V, Mallory P, Collins PS: Lower extremity lymphocele development after saphenous vein harvesting. Mil Med 156:149, 1991.
28. Bradham RR, Gregorie HB, Wilson R: Chylous ascites following resection of an abdominal aortic aneurysm. Am Surg 36:238, 1970.
29. Klippel AP, Hardy DA: Postoperative chylous ascites. Mo Med 68:253, 1971.
30. DeBartolo TF, Etzkorn JR: Conservative management of chylous ascites after abdominal aortic aneurysm repair: Case report. Mo Med 73:611, 1976.
31. Lopez-Enriquez E, Gonzalez A, Johnson CD, et al: Chylothorax and chyloperitoneum: A case report. Bol Assoc Med P R 71:54, 1979.
32. Meinke AH III, Estes NC, Ernst CB: Chylous ascites following abdominal aortic aneurysmectomy: Management with total parenteral hyperalimentation. Ann Surg 190:631, 1979.
33. Stubbe LTHFL, Terpstra JL: Chylous ascites after resection of an abdominal aortic aneurysm. Arch Chir Neerl 31:111, 1979.
34. McKenna R, Stevick CA: Chylous ascites following aortic reconstruction. Vasc Surg 17:143, 1983.
35. Savrin RA, High JR: Chylous ascites after abdominal aortic surgery. Surgery 98:866, 1985.
36. Sarazin WG, Sauter KE: Chylous ascites following resection of a ruptured abdominal aneurysm. Arch Surg 121:246, 1986.
37. Fleisher HL III, Oren JW, Sumner DS: Chylous ascites after abdominal aortic aneurysmectomy: Successful management with a peritoneovenous shunt. J Vasc Surg 6:403, 1987.
38. Schwein M, Dawes PD, Hatchuel D, et al: Postoperative chylous ascites after resection of an abdominal aortic aneurysm: A case report. S Afr J Surg 25:39, 1987.

39. Williamson C, Provan JL: Chylous ascites following aortic surgery. Br J Surg 74:71, 1987.
40. Boyd WD, McPhail NV, Barber GC: Case report: Chylous ascites following abdominal aortic aneurysmectomy: Surgical management with a peritoneovenous shunt. J Cardiovasc Surg 30:627, 1989.
41. Heyl A, Veen HF: Iatrogenic chylous ascites: Operative or conservative approach. Neth J Surg 41:5, 1989.
42. Ablan CJ, Littooy FN, Freeark RJ: Postoperative chylous ascites: Diagnosis and treatment. Arch Surg 125:270, 1990.
43. Bahner DR Jr, Townsend R: Chylous ascites after ruptured abdominal aortic aneurysm. Contemp Surg 36:37, 1990.
44. Sultan S, Pauwels A, Poupon R, et al: Ascites chyleuses de l'adulte aspects étiologiques, térapeutiques et évolutifs: A propos de 35 cas. Ann Gastroenterol Hepatol (Paris) 26:187, 1990.
45. Williams RA, Vetto J, Quinones-Baldrich W, et al: Chylous ascites following abdominal aortic surgery. Ann Vasc Surg 5:247, 1991.
46. Sanger R, Wilmshurst CC, Clyne CA: Chylous ascites following aneurysm surgery: Case report. Eur J Vasc Surg 5:689, 1991.
47. Mack JW, Heydorn WH, Pauling FW, et al: Postoperative chylous pseudocyst. J Thorac Cardiovasc Surg 77:773, 1979.
48. Kostiainen S, Meurala H, Mattila S, et al: Chylothorax: Clinical experience in nine cases. Scand J Thorac Cardiovasc Surg 17:79, 1983.
49. Okabayashi H, Tamura N, Hirose N, et al: Aortic aneurysm associated with coarctation of the aorta. Kyobu Geka 42:1032, 1989.
50. Sachs PB, Zelch MG, Rice TG, et al: Diagnosis and localization of laceration of the thoracic duct: Usefulness of lymphangiography and CT. AJR Am J Roentgenol 157:703, 1991.
51. Hallman GL, Bloodwell RD, Cooley DA: Coarctation of the thoracic aorta. Surg Clin North Am 46:893, 1966.
52. Bortolotti U, Faggian G, Livi U, et al: Postoperative chylothorax following repair of coarctation of the aorta: Report of a case with unusual clinical manifestation. Thorac Cardiovasc Surg 30:319, 1982.
53. Fairfax AJ, McNabb WR, Spiro SG: Chylothorax: A review of 18 cases. Thorax 41:880, 1986.
54. Baudet E, Al-Qudah A: Late results of the subclavian flap repair of coarctation in infancy. J Cardiovasc Surg 30:445, 1989.
55. Cooper P, Paes ML: Bilateral chylothorax. Br J Anaesth 66:387, 1991.
56. Chun K, Colombani PM, Dudgeon DL: Diagnosis and management of congenital vascular rings: A 22-year experience. Ann Thorac Surg 53:597; discussion, 602, 1992.
57. Negroni CC, Ortiz VN: Chylothorax following high translumbar aortography: A case report and review of the literature. Bol Assoc Med P R 80:201, 1988.
58. Gloviczki P, Bergman RT: Lymphatic problems and revascularization edema. In Bernhard VM, Towne JB (eds): Complications in Vascular Surgery, 2nd ed. St. Louis, Quality Medical Publishing, 1991, p 366.
59. Simeone FA, Husni EA: The hyperemia of reconstructive arterial surgery. Ann Surg 150:575, 1959.
60. Campbell H, Harris PL: Albumin kinetics and oedema following reconstructive arterial surgery of the lower limb. J Cardiovasc Surg 26:110, 1985.
61. Taylor GW: Arterial grafting for gangrene. Ann R Coll Surg Engl 31:168, 1962.
62. Hamer JD: Investigation of oedema of the lower limb following successful femoropopliteal by-pass surgery: The role of phlebography in demonstrating venous thrombosis. Br J Surg 59:979, 1972.
63. Myhre HO, Dedichen H: Haemodynamic factors in the oedema of arterial reconstructions. Scand J Thorac Cardiovasc Surg 6:323, 1972.
64. Myhre HO, Storen EJ, Ongre A: The incidence of deep venous thrombosis in patients with leg oedema after arterial reconstruction. Scand J Thorac Cardiovasc Surg 8:73, 1974.
65. Husni EA: The edema of arterial reconstruction. Circulation 35(Suppl):I-169, 1967.
66. Cass AJ, Jennings SA, Greenhalgh RM: Leg swelling after aortic surgery. Int Angiol 5:207, 1986.
67. Jordan WD, Voellinger DC, Schroeder PT, McDowell HA: Video-assisted saphenous vein harvest: The evolution of a new technique. J Vasc Surg 26:405, 1997.
68. Allen KB, Griffith GL, Heimansohn DA, et al: Endoscopic versus traditional saphenous vein harvesting: A prospective randomized trial. Ann Thorac Surg 66:26,1998.
69. Puskas JD, Wright CE, Miller PK, et al: A randomized trial of endoscopic versus open saphenous vein harvest in coronary bypass surgery. Ann Thorac Surg 68:1509,1999.
70. Skudder PA, Geary J: Lymphatic drainage from the groin following surgery of the femoral artery. J Cardiovasc Surg (Torino) 28:460, 1987.
71. Johnston KW: Multicenter prospective study of nonruptured abdominal aortic aneurysm: II. Variables predicting morbidity and mortality. J Vasc Surg 9:437, 1989.
72. Gill IS, Hodge EE, Munch LC, et al: Transperitoneal marsupialization of lymphoceles: A comparison of laparoscopic and open techniques. J Urol 153:706, 1995.
73. Melvin WS, Bumgardner GL, Davies EA, et al: The laparoscopic management of post-transplant lymphocele: A critical review. Surg Endosc 11:245, 1997.
74. Doehn C, Fornara P, Fricke L, Jocham D: Laparoscopic fenestration of post-transplant lymphoceles. Surg Endosc 16:690, 2002.
75. Sawhney R, D'Agostino HB, Zinck S, et al: Treatment of postoperative lymphoceles with percutaneous drainage and alcohol sclerotherapy. J Vasc Interv Radiol 7:241, 1996.
76. Kerlan RK Jr, LaBerge JM, Gordon RL, Ring EJ: Bleomycin sclerosis of pelvic lymphoceles. J Vasc Interv Radiol 8:885, 1997.
77. Cannon L, Walker AJ: Sclerotherapy of a wound lymphocoele using tetracycline. Eur J Vasc Endovasc Surg 14:505, 1997.
78. Seelig MH, Klingler PJ: Oldenburg WA: Treatment of a postoperative cervical chylous lymphocele by percutaneous sclerosing with povidone-iodine. J Vasc Surg 27:1148, 1998.
79. Caliendo MV, Lee DE, Queiroz R, Waldman DL: Sclerotherapy with use of doxycycline after percutaneous drainage of postoperative lymphoceles. J Vasc Interv Radiol 12:73, 2001.
80. Teiche PE, Pauer W, Schmid N: Use of talcum in sclerotherapy of pelvic lymphoceles. Tech Urol 5:52,1999.
81. Michail PO, Griniatsos J, Kargakou M, et al: Treatment of persistent lymphorrhea using bleomycin sclerotherapy. Plast Reconstr Surg 107:890, 2001.
82. Chin A, Ragavendra N, Hilborne L, Gritsch HA: Fibrin sealant sclerotherapy for treatment of lymphoceles following renal transplantation. J Urol 170:380, 2003.
83. Servelle M, Nogues CL, Soulie J, et al: Spontaneous, postoperative and traumatic chylothorax. J Cardiovasc Surg (Torino) 21:475, 1980.
84. Browse NL, Allen DR, Wilson NM: Management of chylothorax. Br J Surg 84:1711, 1997.
85. Cerfolio RJ, Allen MS, Deschamps C, et al: Postoperative chylothorax. J Thorac Cardiovasc Surg 112:1361, 1996.
86. Hirata N, Ueno T, Amemiya A, et al: Advantage of earlier thoracoscopic clipping of thoracic duct for post-operative chylothorax following thoracic aneurysm surgery. Jpn J Thorac Cardiovasc Surg 51:378, 2003.
87. Cope C, Kaiser LR: Management of unremitting chylothorax by percutaneous embolization and blockage of retroperitoneal lymphatic vessels in 42 patients. J Vasc Interv Radiol 13:1139, 2002.

Chapter 64

Postoperative Sexual Dysfunction After Aortoiliac Interventions

RALPH G. DEPALMA, MD, FACS

Impotence has interested vascular surgeons since Leriche's 1923 observation[1] that erectile dysfunction was often the first signal of aortoiliac occlusive disease, particularly in young men. In these cases erectile failure was due to compromised arterial inflow to the corpora cavernosa. Using techniques to minimize damage to the pelvic nerves and restoring flow into the internal iliac arteries, potency can be restored after aortoiliac reconstruction.[2-4] Aortoiliac reconstruction itself can also cause erectile dysfunction not present preoperatively due to failure to perfuse the internal iliac arteries or to damaged autonomic genital nerves with conventional open procedures.[5] These cases are of particular interest to vascular surgeons. The general problem of erectile dysfunction as a chief complaint has proven to be more complex and is considered in Chapter 88.

Early in the 1970s, erectile dysfunction was assumed to be due to arterial insufficiency and that this effect was progressive with aging. Beginning in the early 1980s, intracavernous injection with vasoactive agents such as papaverine[6] and phentolamine[7] was discovered to facilitate erection by relaxation of corporal smooth muscle. This provided a better understanding of the physiology of erection along with the recognition that the defect in men with the chief complaint of erectile dysfunction was more often due to failure of smooth muscle relaxation. Normal erectile function requires adequate inflow, which can be assessed using penile plethysmography in a nonerect state[8,9] or Doppler duplex measurements of penile arterial flow after injection of a vasoactive agent.[10,11]

■ SCOPE OF THE PROBLEM

A number of studies report that 25% of men regained erectile function after aortoiliac reconstructions, including open repairs for patients of varying age for both occlusive disease and aneurysms.[2,12-19] The prevalence and etiology of preoperative erectile dysfunction in various series are difficult to assess with accuracy. Erectile function depends on age, co-morbid factors including the use of drugs, as well as methods of subjective and objective documentation available to the clinician to estimate, with some degree of confidence, sexual dysfunction. In a personal series of 126 aortoiliac reconstructions, using preoperative evaluation and operative techniques previously described,[2,7,20] 53 (42%) men with an average age of 65 years had erectile dysfunction and remained impotent postoperatively, and 30 (25%) men with an average age of 57 years who were potent preoperatively remained so postoperatively. In addition, 39 (31%) men with erectile dysfunction preoperatively regained normal function and 4 (3%) men in the 4th to the 7th decades of life became impotent postoperatively. Two of these men had emergency operations for ruptured aneurysms, and in the other two, internal iliac aneurysms required ligation. These individuals were followed up to 3 years postoperatively. In all of the instances of erectile dysfunction, penile plethysmography showed flat lines, with penile brachial blood pressure ratios well below 0.5.

Flanigan and coworkers[12] stated that with planning to avoid diversion of pelvic blood flow, nerve-sparing aortoiliac dissections, and selective employment of indirect methods, iatrogenic impotence can be minimized and that a significant proportion of patients regain normal postoperative sexual function. In a retrospective series of 110 patients using direct and indirect aortoiliac revascularization, 45% of patients with preoperative vasculogenic impotence regained normal sexual function postoperatively, no patients with normal preoperative sexual function were rendered impotent, and two men developed retrograde ejaculation.

Recognizing limitations inherent in these largely retrospective series, it is useful to examine Fredburg and Mouritzen's report[21] of aortoiliac operations using conventional techniques. Eleven of 20 men with aneurysms were impotent preoperatively and 19 (95%) reported sexual dysfunction postoperatively. Among 48 patients undergoing operation for occlusive disease, 15 (31%) presented with erectile dysfunction and 29 (60%) had postoperative sexual dysfunction. Similarly, Miles and associates[16] reported that 22% of 76 patients undergoing conventional aortoiliac operations for aneurysmal or occlusive disease described preoperative sexual dysfunction, and an additional 30% were rendered impotent. Impotence was twice as common in men reporting unspecified preoperative "minor dysfunctions." It appears unlikely that prospective trials comparing conventional aortic reconstructions to nerve-sparing internal iliac revascularization techniques will surface, since attention to such technical details of these procedures imposes little additional surgical burden.

Rich interconnections of the vegetative nervous system about the aortoiliac vessels and the inferior mesenteric artery include both sympathetic and parasympathetic fibers that promote normal ejaculatory function. Damage to these fibers can cause other types of sexual dysfunction: retrograde ejaculation with or without erection and orgasm; anejaculation; failure of emission; and rarely, normal erection with failure to achieve either ejaculation or orgasm. Ejaculatory disorders have been reported to be the most prevalent sexual dysfunction, approaching 40% of men.[22] This condition is more likely encountered in urologic[23] or fertility practices and has not been a prominent compliant in my vascular practice. Ejaculatory disorders should be differentiated from erectile dysfunction, though its psychological consequences can interfere with erection in some men.

In the past, women have been considered to be less susceptible to sexual dysfunction after aortoiliac surgery.[24] In my experience, three women regained arousal, lubrication, and orgasm after aortoiliac surgery using nerve-sparing aortoiliac reconstructions that provided internal iliac flow. In this anecdotal experience, these operations were performed using the same technique as in men. The approach was done out of habit, without an intent to influence sexual function; the women only later reported favorable effects. Only scanty data have been gathered because so few females of active sexual age require aortoiliac reconstructions, and measurement methods to assess female arousal are difficult to perform. Hultgren and colleagues[25] described sexual dysfunction, based on questionnaires, in women before and after aortoiliac operation. They stressed the possibility of iatrogenic nerve damage as a cause of postoperative sexual dysfunction. Female sexual dysfunction (FSD) has been described after radical hysterectomy with ligation of the uterine arteries and ovarian collaterals.[26] Nerve-sparing hysterectomy and more limited operations have been proposed to prevent these effects.[27,28] Only recently have methodical investigations begun for the diagnosis and treatment of FSD, estimated to afflict 30% to 50% of American women.[29]

■ LARGE-VESSEL INTERVENTION TECHNIQUES

Large-vessel interventions have proved more effective and durable than microvascular penile procedures, although vascular interventions are applicable to no more than 7% of men with the chief complaint of impotence.[30,31] Therefore, preventive techniques are crucial among patients undergoing major vascular surgical reconstructions.

Surgical approaches to the aortoiliac arteries to prevent erectile failure or restore normal function are relatively straightforward. These are (1) preservation of nerve fibers in the periaortic and pelvic fields and (2) perfusion of the internal iliac arteries.

For open aneurysm repair, I prefer an inlay technique with entry into the sac well to the right, avoiding the mesenteric leaf on the left side, the inferior mesenteric artery, and the pelvic neural plate (Fig. 64-1). The inferior mesenteric artery is closed by suture of its orifice from within the sac. These maneuvers require minimal dissection and likely help avoid colon and spinal ischemia. I cannot recall a need to reimplant the inferior mesenteric artery, nor has colon ischemia been a problem. Figure 64-2 illustrates the approach to the right common iliac bifurcation. Small abdominal aneurysms, typically less than 5.5 cm in diameter, occasionally cause penile ischemia due to emboli into the internal iliac artery. Therefore, recognition of this pathophysiologic mechanism would liberalize the indications for repair of smaller aneurysms as recently described,[30] and this potential complication should be guarded against during surgical repair. We have not investigated the sexual functional effects of extraperitoneal exposure of the aorta, although the ability to dissect the nerve bundle from the aortic bifurcation and left iliac artery using this approach appears clear. Division of the inferior mesenteric artery is required, and autonomic nerves accompany this vessel into the pelvic plate.

Among patients undergoing operation for occlusive disease, a right-sided nerve-sparing approach with limited aortic mobilization is also used to preserve erectile and ejaculatory function (Fig. 64-3). Van Schaik and coworkers[32] from Leiden have contributed elegant anatomic studies of periaortic nerve plexus reproduced in Figures 64-4 and 64-5. A retroperitoneal approach to the internal iliac artery can be used when this vessel is selected as a target. While operating through a midline incision, it is important to recognize that the internal iliac arteries lie deep in the pelvis and course laterally beneath the external iliac arteries and veins. Peritoneal incisions lateral to the colon with medial retraction of the intestine and ureters can be used to expose these vessels as they exit the greater sciatic notch.

Another approach that may be selected among patients with aortoiliac occlusive disease is femorofemoral bypass, sometimes combined with transluminal dilation of a donor common iliac artery. In fact, this strategy has yielded good results in restoring penile blood flow.[33] Plethysmography results correlate with return of erectile function as reported by patients. This procedure completely avoids the aortoiliac dissection, and the long-term results of femorofemoral bypass are reasonably durable.

Transluminal dilation of the external iliac artery along with stenting also can improve penile perfusion by relieving steal through the internal iliac and gluteal arteries (Fig. 64-6). Axillofemoral bypass is more applicable to limb salvage in high-risk individuals rather than for prevention of

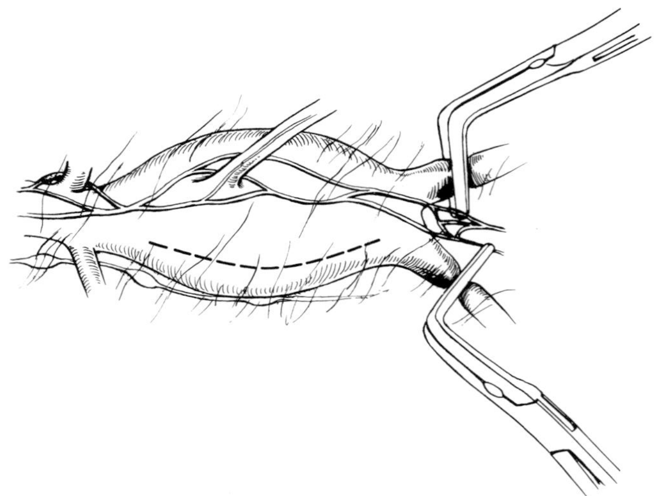

FIGURE 64-1 Right-sided approach and planned incision for abdominal aortic aneurysm and minimal dissection of common iliacs and neck. Note the application of distal clamps first.

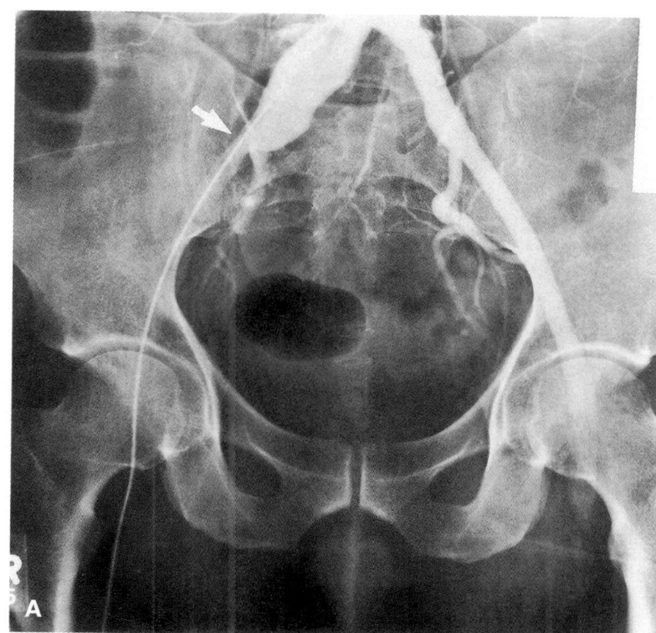

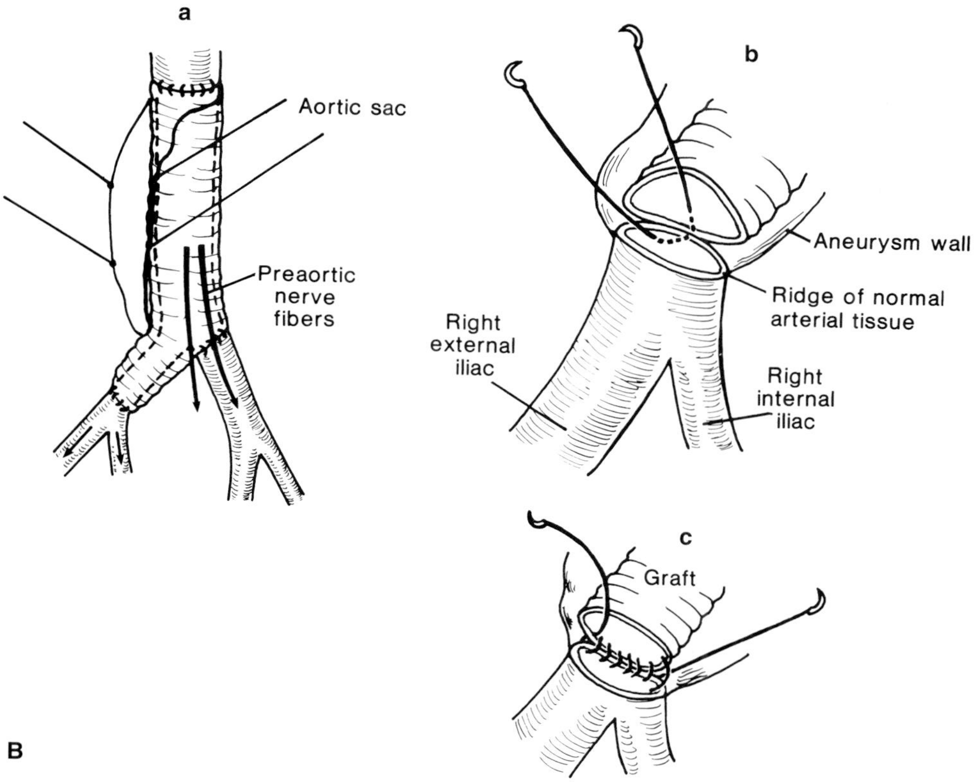

FIGURE 64-2 **A,** Preoperative arteriogram of a potent man showing details of a right iliac aneurysm (*arrow*). **B,** Method of reconstruction to preserve outflow and maintain internal iliac flow. (**B,** From DePalma RG: Management of impotence associated with aortoiliac surgery. In Haimovici H [ed]: Haimovici's Vascular Surgery. Cambridge, Mass., Blackwell Science 1996, pp 828-841.

postoperative sexual dysfunction. When axillofemoral or femorofemoral bypass is employed, it is important to ensure abundant profunda femoris flow using the hood of the graft as a patch angioplasty.

In my experience the primary focus of endovascular interventions for erectile dysfunction has been directed to the common or external iliac arteries.[34] Others have described selective dilation of the internal iliac arteries.[35] Procedures attempting endovascular interventions distal to this level, that is, in the pudendal arteries, have failed.[36] Recently, Lin and associates[37] reported pelvic ischemia and erectile dysfunction due to internal iliac embolization associated with endovascular aneurysm repair. The severity of the ischemia is related to both bilateral embolization and the

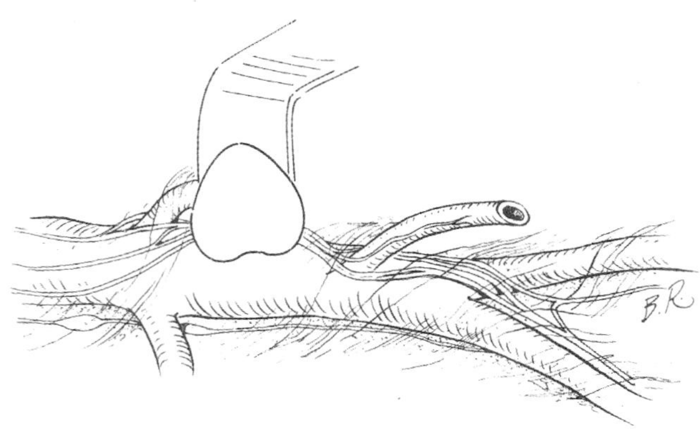

FIGURE 64-3 Right-sided approach for occlusive disease. Note limited aortic dissection, retraction of nerve bundles on the aorta, and preservation of the inferior mesenteric outflow.

presence of disease in the profunda femoris artery. The use of endovascular grafts for aneurysms may require occlusion of the orifice of one or both internal iliac arteries to achieve adequate landing sites.

Management of internal iliac artery flow deserves special emphasis. Bilateral internal iliac occlusion or ligation is associated with a risk of pelvic ischemia. Furthermore, adequate hypogastric flow, at least through one of these vessels, is related to normal sexual function. However, this risk is not absolute because femoral collaterals sometimes compensate internal iliac occlusion. Branches of the femoral artery can provide significant collateral circulation to the penis in the face of hypogastric artery occlusion.[38] Internal iliac collateral flow in the presence of acute hypogastric artery ligation is more dependent on the ipsilateral external iliac artery than it is on the contralateral internal iliac, even though abundant collateralization between the left and the right internal iliac arteries is common in chronic ischemia.[39,40] Ohshiro and Kosaki[41] suggested that preservation of the hypogastric nerve plexus is more important than preservation of internal iliac blood flow. They found little correlation existed between postoperative sexual dysfunction and the hypogastric circulation. On the other hand, Metz and colleagues[42] in a series of 28 patients did not perform nerve-sparing dissection aiming solely to preserve penile blood supply. They reported that 7 of the preoperatively potent patients remained potent and 9 preoperatively impotent became potent. No mention was made of ejaculatory dysfunction. Of 26 patients with bilateral hypogastric atherosclerotic occlusion or bilateral hypogastric artery ligation at the time of surgery studied by Flanigan and coworkers,[12] 17 had normal sexual function postoperatively. Although internal iliac artery patency may not be absolutely needed for normal sexual function in all patients, in most instances it is necessary for sexual function. Adequate internal iliac circulation is also a factor in preventing colon or buttock ischemia and proves to be a problem in certain endovascular interventions.[43] The profunda femoris has been found to be as important a collateral for the pelvic circu-

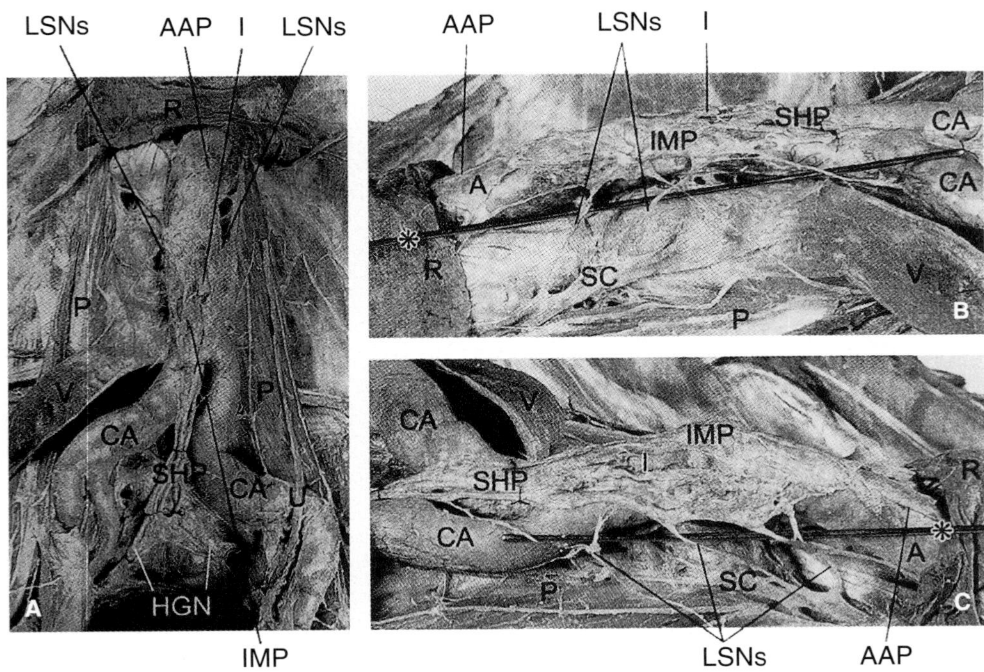

FIGURE 64-4 **A,** Ventral view into the abdomen with resection of the inferior vena cava (V) below the left renal vein (R). Note relationships of sacral hypogastric plexus (SHP), hypogastric nerves (HGN), and divided trunk of the inferior mesenteric artery (I). **B,** A 90-degree rotational view showing right-sided splanchnic nerves (LSN) and the sympathetic chain (SC). **C,** A 90-degree rotational view from the left showing left-sided LSNs and the SHP on the left side of the picture coursing over the aortic bifurcation. The probe lifts the LSNs. Note connections with the sympathetic chain (SC) delineated by the probe. A, abdominal aorta; CA, common iliac artery; P, psoas muscle; AAP, abdominal aortic plexus; IMP, inferior mesenteric plexus; U, ureter. (**A** to **C,** From van Schaik J, van Baalen JM, Visser MJT, DeRuiter MC: Nerve-preserving aortoiliac reconstruction: Anatomical and surgical approach. J Vasc Surg 33:983-989, 2001.)

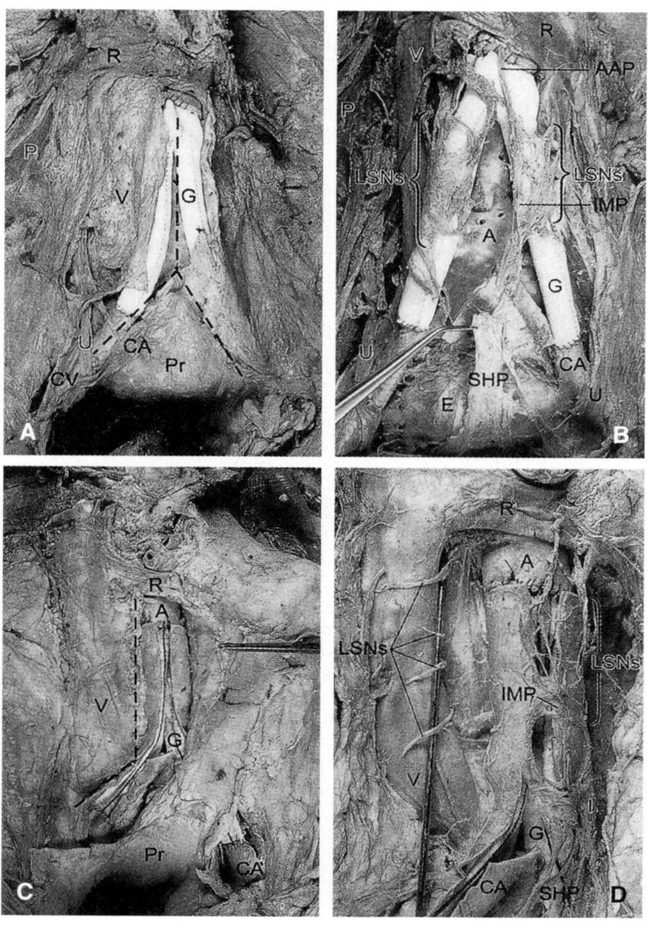

FIGURE 64-5 **A** and **B,** Ventral view into abdomen showing interposition of graft (G), in conventional midline approach; note total disruption of sacral hypogastric plexus (SHP). **C** and **D,** Placement of graft using nerve-sparing procedure. Note in **D,** the minor disruption of LSNs on the right. *Dotted lines* indicate incisions. A, abdominal aorta; AAP, abdominal aortic plexus; CA, common iliac artery; CV, common iliac vein; E, endopelvic fascia; I, inferior mesenteric artery; IMP, inferior mesenteric plexus; P, psoas muscle; Pr, sacral promontory; R, left renal vein; U, ureter; V, inferior vena cava. (**A** to **D,** From van Schaik J, van Baalen JM, Visser MJT, DeRuiter MC: Nerve-preserving aortoiliac reconstruction: Anatomical and surgical approach. J Vasc Surg 33:983-989, 2001.)

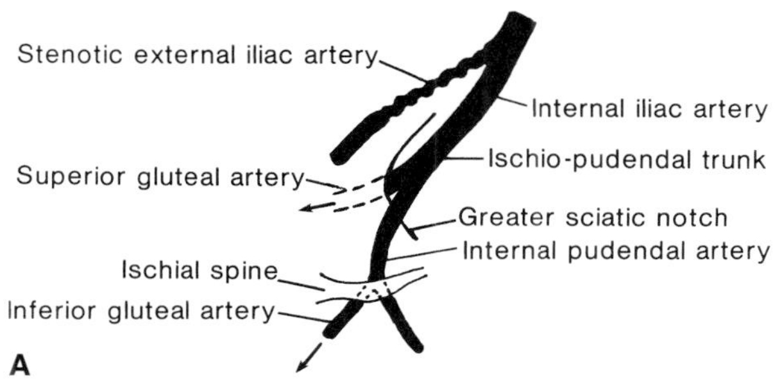

FIGURE 64-6 **A,** Mechanism of pelvic steal in the presence of diffuse external iliac artery stenoses. The steal occurs through the gluteal arteries. **B,** Penile plethysmography. Note improved pulse waves and pressure after dilation of the external iliac artery. (**A,** From DePalma RG: Iliac artery occlusive disease: Impotence and colon ischemia. In Moore WS, Ahn SS [eds]: Endovascular Surgery, 3rd ed. Philadelphia, WB Saunders, 2001, pp 355-360.)

PRE-ANGIOPLASTY

PRESSURE MEASUREMENTS

	BRACHIAL BLOOD PRESSURE	ANKLE P_{sys}	CAVERNOSAL ARTERY P_{sys}
RIGHT	120/80	140	0
LEFT	120/80	140	0

PENILE PULSE VOLUME RECORDING

NOTE: On physical exam biealteral femoral bruits were noted.

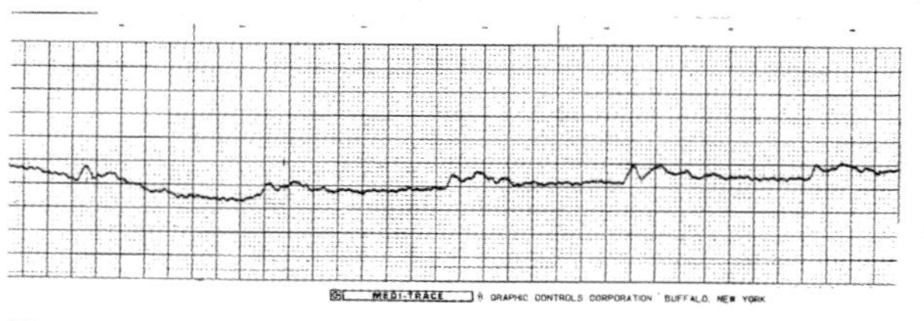

POST-ANGIOPLASTY

PRESSURE MEASUREMENTS

	BRACHIAL BLOOD PRESSURE	ANKLE P_{sys}	CAVERNOSAL ARTERY P_{sys}
RIGHT	110/70	140	180
LEFT	110/70	140	160

PENILE PULSE VOLUME RECORDING

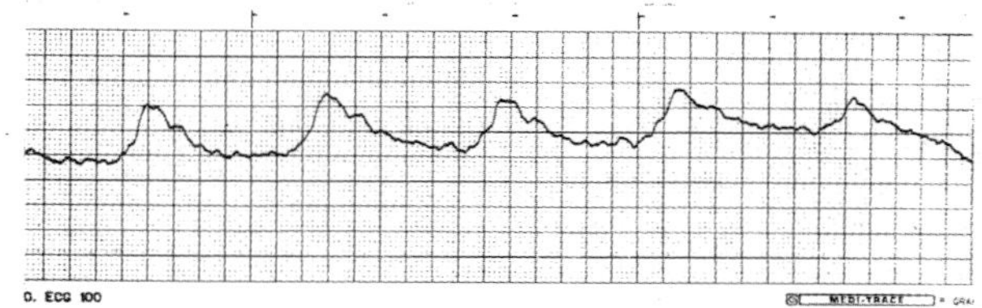

B

lation as it is for viability of the lower extremity. The relative contributions of neural function and vascular supply seem to vary from individual to individual. Sympathectomy,[44] particularly at levels above L1, has long been known to cause erectile dysfunction along with ejaculatory disorders.

Finally, an ongoing Veterans Affairs prospective, randomized trial of open versus endovascular repair (OVER) offers to provide insight into endovascular repair as related to erectile function, which will be assessed preoperatively and postoperatively.

■ PREOPERATIVE EVALUATION AND POSTOPERATIVE TREATMENT

The single most important step in caring for these patients is an adequate preoperative interview and assessment of sexual function. The surgeon should obtain an accurate sexual history to define the nature, onset, and duration of any sexual dysfunction preoperatively. Interest in sexual activity can be evaluated unobtrusively by discussion *first* with the patient and then, if appropriate, with both partners. Keep in mind the need to respect individual privacy and different patterns of socialization. When sexual dysfunction is a complaint, the time of onset and exact nature of the dysfunction should be recorded. Specific questions, which help separate organic and psychological patterns of erectile dysfunction, include inquiries into the rate of onset and life events occurring at the time when the dysfunction had begun.[45] Acute onset of organic erectile dysfunction in the presence of satisfactory relationships and activity, as mentioned, may signal atheroembolism. The relative importance of sexual activity to both partners needs to be assessed. Sexual inactivity might be accepted and regarded as normal due to a long-standing pattern of failing erectile capacity or lack of interest by both partners. Their cultural beliefs might be such that sexual activity is not highly valued. In contrast, when sexual activity has been vigorous and is considered important by the patient and his partner, the surgeon must be aware of this preoperatively. Preoperative counseling must include the warning that, in spite of the best surgical efforts, sexual dysfunction may follow either open or endovascular aortoiliac interventions. In these instances it is important to objectively document penile blood flow using either penile plethysmography[8,9] or duplex studies[10,11] after injection of a vasoactive agent such as prostaglandin E_1. The appearance and rigidity of erection after the intracavernous injection offer a useful baseline.

Preoperative planning requires angiography to demonstrate runoff, including both internal iliac arteries, and particularly to observe the bifurcation of the common iliac artery. Such angiography is routine in considering endograft repairs. Highly selective pudendal angiography is probably contraindicated in aortoiliac disease with luminal atheromatous debris. In this circumstance selective angiography can cause atheroembolism secondary to maneuvers needed to selectively catheterize the internal iliac arteries to delineate the distal pudendal branches. The presence of internal iliac aneurysms or the need to occlude one or both internal iliac arteries to achieve landing sites of endovascular grafts presages the risk of postoperative erectile dysfunction. The patient should be preoperatively informed of this risk. The possibility of retrograde ejaculation following open repair should be discussed with couples of childbearing age.

When postoperative erectile dysfunction occurs due to inadequate penile perfusion, the possibility of further procedures to restore inflow exists. Indirect procedures include femorofemoral bypass or internal iliac reconstructions by open or endovascular approaches. In my experience,[30] an endovascular approach to the internal iliac arteries has not been successful for men presenting with impotence. However, the Italian literature describes three successful cases among 25 men treated using endovascular interventions for erectile dysfuntion.[23] Dilation of the pudendal or penile arteries has not been successful.[24] Scattered reports of penile artery bypass following aortoiliac bypass have appeared, but this procedure is ineffective for older patients with atherosclerosis. I would not recommend microvascular bypass to treat the complication of erectile dysfunction after aortoiliac surgery. Sildenafil or analogous oral agents can be tried and may help improve borderline function. Instructions and self-use of intracavernous injection of prostaglandin E_1 (see Chapter 88) would be a next step. The option of a vacuum erection device might be offered, but these are frequently discontinued in this circumstance. When inadequate blood flow cannot be simply corrected, the most practical approach is a timely referral for insertion of a penile prosthesis. With nerve damage, a prosthesis is also the most practical option. Prosthetics are well accepted provided the patient had been preoperatively informed and particularly when some degree of preoperative erectile dysfunction had been present. Patients with ejaculatory disorders, such as failure of emission or retrograde ejaculation, might respond to α-sympathomimetic medications or imipramine[23]; rarely, this function resumes spontaneously after partial damage to the sympathetic outflow tracts. Patients seeking to father children should be referred promptly to specialists offering assisted reproductive technologies. Overall, an attentive, concerned approach to postoperative sexual dysfunction and the prospects of alternative treatment does much to allay anxiety and anger created by these complications.

■ REFERENCES

1. Leriche R: Des oblitérations arterielle hautes (obliteration de la termination de l'aorte) comme cause de insufficances circulatoire des members inferiors [abstract]. Bull Mem Soc Chir 49:1401, 1923.
2. DePalma RG, Levine SB, Feldman S: Preservation of erectile function after aortoiliac reconstruction. Arch Surg 113:958-962, 1978.
3. DePalma RG, Kedia K, Persky L: Surgical options in the correction of vasculogenic impotence. Vasc Surg 14:92-102, 1980.
4. Cronenwett JL, Gooch JB, Garrett HE: Internal iliac artery revascularization during aortofemoral bypass. Arch Surg 117:638, 1982.
5. May AG, DeWeese JA, Rob CG: Changes in sexual function following operation on the abdominal aorta. Surgery 65:41-47, 1969.
6. Virag R: Intracavernous injection of papaverine for erectile failure [letter]. Lancet 2:938, 1982.
7. Brindley GS: Pilot experiments on the actions of drugs injected into the human corpus cavernosum penis. Br J Pharmacol 87:495-500, 1986.
8. DePalma RG, Emsellem HA, Edwards CM, et al: A screening sequence for vasculogenic impotence. J Vasc Surg 5:228-236, 1987.

9. DePalma RG, Schwab FJ, Emsellem HA, et al: Noninvasive assessment of impotence. Surg Clin North Am 70:119-131, 1990.
10. Lue TF, Hricak H, Marich KW, Tanagho EA: Vasculogenic impotence evaluated by high-resolution ultrasonography and pulsed Doppler spectrum analysis. Radiology 155:777-781, 1985.
11. Sanchez-Ortiz RF, Broderick GA: Vascular evaluation of erectile dysfunction. In Mulcahy JJ (ed): Male Sexual Function: A Guide to Clinical Management. Totowa, NJ, Humana Press, 2001, pp 167-202.
12. Flanigan DP, Schuler JJ, Keifer T, et al: Elimination of iatrogenic impotence and improvement of sexual dysfunction after aortoiliac revascularization. Arch Surg 117:544, 1982.
13. Hallbrook T, Holmquist B: Sexual disturbances following dissection of the aorta and the common iliac arteries. J Cardiovasc Surg 11:255, 1970.
14. Harris JD, Jepson RP: Aorto-iliac stenosis: A comparison of two procedures. Aust J Surg 34:211, 1965.
15. Castaneda-Zuniga WR, Smith A, Kaye K, et al: Transluminal angioplasty for treatment of vasculogenic impotence. AJR Am J Roentgenol 139:371, 1982.
16. Miles JR, Miles DG, Johnson G Jr: Aortoiliac operations and sexual dysfunction. Arch Surg 117:1177, 1982.
17. Sabri S, Cotton LT: Sexual function following aortoiliac reconstruction. Lancet 2:1218, 1971.
18. Spiro M, Cotton LT: Aorto-iliac thrombo-endarterectomy. Br J Surg 57:161, 1979.
19. Weinstein MH, Machleder HI: Sexual function after aortoiliac surgery. Ann Surg 181:787, 1975.
20. DePalma RG: Impotence as a complication in aortoiliac reconstruction. In Bernhard VM, Towne JB (eds): Complications in Vascular Surgery. New York, Grune & Stratton, 1980, pp 427-441.
21. Fredberg U, Mouritzen C: Sexual dysfunction as a symptom of arteriosclerosis and a complication to reconstruction of the aorto-iliac segment. J Cardiovasc Surg (Torino) 29:148-154, 1988.
22. Laumann EO, Paik A, Rosen RC: The epidemiology of erectile dysfunction: Results from the National Health and Social Life Survey. Int J Impot Res 11(Suppl):S60-S64, 1999.
23. McCullough AR Jr: Ejaculatory disorders. In Mulcahy JJ (ed): Male Sexual Function: A Guide to Clinical Management. Totowa, NJ, Humana Press, 2001, pp 351-370.
24. Queral LA, Flinn WR, Bergan JJ, et al: Pelvic hemodynamics after aortoiliac reconstruction. Surgery 86:799, 1979.
25. Hultgren R, Sjögren B, Soderberg M, et al: Sexual function in women suffering from aortoiliac occlusive disease. Eur J Vasc Endovasc Surg 17:306, 1999.
26. Saini J, Kuczynski E, Gretz HF III, Sills ES: Supracervical hysterectomy versus total abdominal hysterectomy: Perceived effects on sexual function. BMC Women's Health 2:1, 2002.
27. Graesslin O, Martin-Morille C, Leguillier-Armour MC, et al: Local investigation concerning psychic and sexual functioning a short time after hysterectomy. Gynecol Obstet Fertil 6:474, 2002.
28. Trimbos JB, Maas CP, DeRuiter MC, et al: A nerve-sparing radical hysterectomy: Guidelines and feasibility in Western patients. Int J Gynecol Cancer 11:180, 2001.
29. Berman JR, Berman L, Lin H, Goldstein I: Female sexual dysfunction: Epidemiology, physiology, and treatment. In Mulcahy JJ (ed): Male Sexual Function: A Guide to Clinical Management. Totowa, NJ, Humana Press, 2001, pp 123-139.
30. DePalma RG, Olding M, Yu GW, et al: Vascular interventions for impotence: Lessons learned. J Vasc Surg 21:576-585, 1995.
31. DePalma RG: Vascular surgery for impotence: A review. Int J Impot Res 9:61-67, 1997.
32. van Schaik J, van Baalan JM, Visser MJT, DeRuiter MC: Nerve-preserving aortoiliac surgery: Anatomical study and surgical approach. J Vasc Surg 33:983-989, 2001.
33. Merchant RF Jr, DePalma RG: The effects of femoro-femoral grafts on postoperative sexual function: Correlation with penile pulse volume recordings. Surgery 90:962-970, 1981.
34. DePalma RG: Iliac artery occlusive disease: Impotence and colon ischemia. In Moore WS, Ahn SS (eds): Endovascular Surgery, 3rd ed. Philadelphia, WB Saunders, 2001, pp 355-360.
35. Urigo F, Pischedda A, Maiore M, et al: The role of arteriography and percutaneous transluminal angioplasty in the treatment of arteriogenic impotence. Radiol Med (Torino) 88:80-92, 1994.
36. Valji K, Bookstein JJ: Transluminal angioplasty in the treatment of arteriogenic impotence. Cardiovasc Intervent Radiol 11:245-252, 1988.
37. Lin P, Bush RL, Chen C, et al: A prospective evaluation of hypogastric artery embolization in endovascular aortoiliac aneurysm repair. J Vasc Surg 36:500-506, 2002.
38. Kawai M: Pelvic hemodynamics before and after aortoiliac vascular reconstruction: The significance of penile blood pressure. Jpn J Surg 18:514, 1988.
39. Iliopoulos JI, Horwanitz PE, Pierce GE, et al: The critical hypogastric circulation. Am J Surg 154:671, 1987.
40. Iliopoulos JI, Hermreck AS, Thomas JH, et al: Hemodynamics of the hypogastric arterial circulation. J Vasc Surg 9:637, 1989.
41. Ohshiro T, Kosaki G: Sexual function after aorto-iliac vascular reconstruction: Which is more important, the internal iliac artery or hypogastric nerve? J Cardiovasc Surg (Torino) 25:47, 1984.
42. Metz, Fridmodt-Moller C, Matheisen FR: Erectile function before and after reconstructive arterial surgery in men with occlusive arterial leg disease. Scand J Thorac Cardiovasc Surg 17:45, 1983.
43. Lee CW, Kaufman JA, Fan CM, et al: Clinical outcome of internal iliac occlusions during endovascular treatment of aortoiliac aneurysmal disease. J Vasc Interv Radiol 11:567, 2000.
44. Whitelaw GP, Smithwick RH: Some secondary effects of sympathectomy. N Engl J Med 245:121, 1951.
45. Levine SM: Marital sexual dysfunction: Erectile dysfunction. Ann Intern Med 85:342, 1976.

Chapter

65

Postoperative Graft Thrombosis:

Prevention and Management

DANIEL WALSH, MD

Postoperative graft thrombosis, especially in the first days and months after surgery, represents a signal failure for both the patient and the vascular surgeon. At 1 year after failure of infragenicular bypass grafts, more than 50% of patients have suffered major amputations.[110] Among the remaining patients, 25% suffer from rest pain or ulceration and more than 15% have died. Seventeen percent of strokes that occur within 30 days of carotid endarterectomy are attributable to surgical technique or postoperative management.[106] In other series, complications at the endarterectomy site are the most common cause of stroke in the majority of patients.[38,50]

The causes of graft thrombosis are myriad and involve both patient factors and technical issues that present themselves throughout the revascularization process from initial presentation through follow-up. If results of arterial revascularization are to be optimized, technical precision during that initial operation is mandatory. At present, technical errors are responsible for 4% to 25% of failures early after revascularization.[24,101,108,115] There are many techniques for accurate intraoperative assessment of the adequacy and precision of the revascularization. The subject first addressed in this chapter is the selection and application of these modalities to specific arterial reconstructions.

The remainder of the chapter focuses on the surgeon's response once graft thrombosis has occurred. To achieve the best outcome for patients in this most difficult circumstance, one must make the correct choice among the many available therapeutic options. Understanding the etiology, presentation, and current experience with available treatment options is crucial for achieving the best and most long-lasting results.

■ TECHNIQUES OF ASSESSMENT

Inspection, Palpation, and Flow Measurement

The most convenient methods of assessing technical adequacy of a revascularization are inspection and pulse palpation. These processes involve not only inspection of the revascularization for kinks, twists, and stenoses but also examination of the target artery and the revascularized tissue, if possible. Intuitive in this process are the surgeon's expectations. Does the distal carotid artery have a new, easily palpable pulse? Is the foot pink? Has capillary refill time been shortened? Is a pulse now palpable in the foot?

The process is facilitated by having the target organ, as much as possible, prepared into a sterile field and available to the surgeon for intraoperative examination. For example, for aortobifemoral or more distal bypasses, clear plastic bags covering the sterilely prepared feet allow their rapid examination after bypass completion. However, inspection and palpation are subjective and, thus, are susceptible to observer bias. After a complex reconstruction, the surgeon's expectations may cloud the evaluation of capillary refill time in the feet. Arteries calcified by the complications of diabetes may transmit improved pulses poorly. The effects of anesthesia combined with chronic superficial femoral artery occlusions may delay appearance of adequate lower extremity reperfusion. More important, false-negative results can occur when a graft has a strong pulse owing to distal outflow obstruction.

Measurement of arterial inflow and outflow is often severely affected by anesthesia. Furthermore, small hemodynamically insignificant defects in the graft may also result in failure. Low-flow measurements also may accurately predict graft failure, but the finding does not localize a defect once discovered. Studies using an ultrasound flowmeter have confirmed the inability of graft flow alone to predict future graft function.[14] Flow measurement by ultrasonically measured transit times has been reported to be sensitive and specific for graft defects.[92] Performance of these studies is cumbersome and requires additional adjunctive measures to localize and identify specific graft defects. Because of these problems and the ease and effectiveness of other techniques, these measures of blood flow have been used infrequently.

Arteriography

Since its introduction, intraoperative completion arteriography has been the "gold standard" for anatomic evaluation of the technical adequacy of arterial reconstructions. Arteriography is uniquely capable of assessing the anatomy of outflow arteries, which is particularly important when preoperative studies in diffusely diseased vascular systems may not have adequately demonstrated runoff vessels. Although completion arteriography is an invasive procedure associated with potential complications due to arterial puncture (intimal injury, dissection), injection (air embolism), use of radiographic contrast agent (renal failure, anaphylaxis), and radiation exposure, the actual observed complication rate has been negligible in large series.[20,21,56]

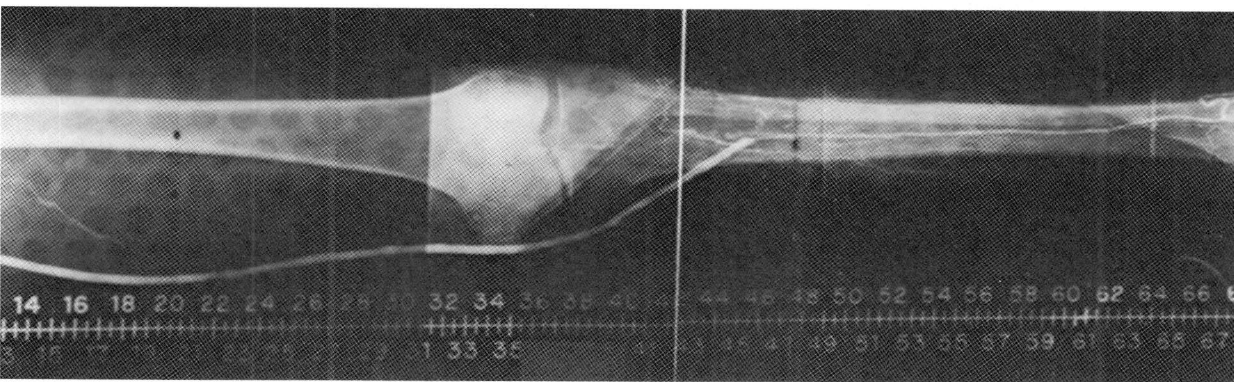

FIGURE 65-1 Normal intraoperative completion arteriogram of a femoroperoneal in-situ saphenous vein graft. A ceiling-mounted x-ray generator allows visualization of nearly the entire leg with a single exposure. A radiopaque ruler facilitates the localization of any graft defects.

The technique varies according to individual application but generally involves insertion of an 18- to 20-gauge plastic angiocatheter into the arterial graft to allow subsequent injection of 10 to 30 mL of radiographic contrast agent. Temporary occlusion of the arterial inflow maximizes the concentration of the contrast agent without the need for excessively rapid injection. A portable x-ray generator can be used, but use of an overhead x-ray generator at ceiling height above the operating table allows the entire limb to be filmed in a single exposure on one long film cassette (Fig. 65-1). Several weaknesses are inherent in the technique of arteriography, however. In lower extremity bypass grafts, the proximal anastomosis is frequently not evaluated. Air bubbles or overlying structures may lead to false-positive interpretations. A potential source of false-negative results is the use of a single plane of view to analyze a multidimensional target; this method can result in underestimation of the stenosis from a small defect, such as an intimal flap or platelet aggregate.[11] Another problem associated with arteriography is the heavy but variable concentration of dye. This variation can lead, on the one hand, to complete coverage of a minor defect that would be better seen with lesser amounts of dye and, on the other hand, to a suggestion by the presence of lesser amounts of dye of defects at valve sites or anastomoses where none exist.

To avoid these problems, intra-arterial digital subtraction arteriography (DSA) using a portable, axially rotatable imaging device can more easily obtain views from different angles.[17] The small amounts of dye and the "cine" nature of modern digital subtraction machines enable visualization of particular areas of the graft with varying concentrations of dye, allowing for a more accurate interpretation of images. DSA technology is more expensive but is increasingly available in contemporary operating rooms because of its use in endovascular, orthopedic, and other procedures. DSA also allows use of smaller amounts of contrast agent and real-time video replay. DSA is more applicable to a localized area, such as the carotid endarterectomy site or a distal anastomosis and pedal runoff, than to an entire extremity. An entire extremity can be filmed with this technology using repeated injections of small amounts of contrast agent to obtain sequential angiographic images, or the so-called pulse-chase technique, in which the DSA machine is moved along the extremity, "chasing" the injected contrast material (Fig. 65-2).

Ultrasonography

The development of Doppler ultrasound technology has provided multiple noninvasive modalities for the intraoperative assessment of arterial reconstructions. The simplest and least expensive ultrasound device is a continuous-wave Doppler device with an 8- to 10-MHz pencil probe. The major advantages of these probes are that they are easy to sterilize with gas and they are readily available for intraoperative use. Their small size allows insonation of arteries in areas less accessible to larger probes. With sterile saline used as an acoustic coupling, the probe can be passed along the graft or endarterectomy site, where localized increases in the audible sound frequency or audible turbulence indicate a potential defect. Patent residual vein branches in in-situ saphenous vein bypasses can be readily identified from the presence of a locally increased frequency, continuous flow, and flow outside the graft boundary. Successively compressing the graft from the proximal to the distal end while listening for residual proximal flow with a Doppler device can also localize these arteriovenous fistulae.

Use of the audible continuous-wave Doppler technique is quite subjective and operator-dependent. Considerable experience is required for maximum accuracy. The presence of high-frequency sound waves within the graft or at the distal anastomosis is worrisome. However, some investigators have shown that the continuous-wave Doppler device is not highly sensitive.[66] Most vascular surgeons use this modality as an easy, available, and inexpensive screening device to guide their use of a more precise evaluation technique. To improve the objectivity of this technique, one may use a fast Fourier transform spectral analysis computer to quantify changes in frequency or velocity. A further potential refinement is the use of a high-frequency (20-MHz) pulsed Doppler device contained in a small needle probe that allows easy access to all operative sites.[11] Considerable experience with pulsed Doppler probes is required to

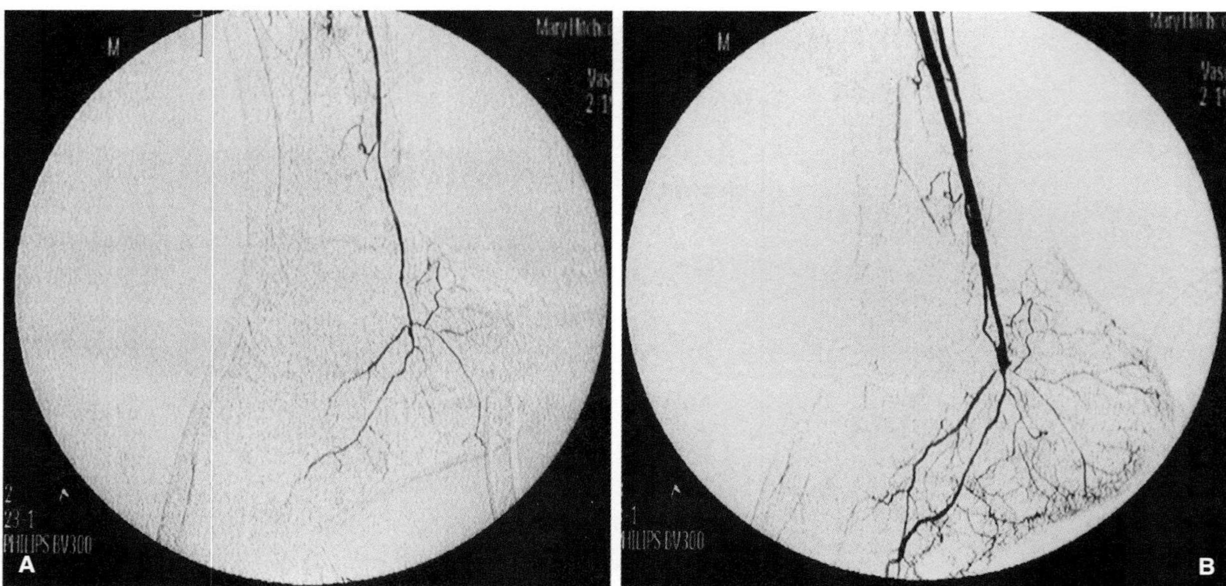

FIGURE 65-2 Intraoperative digital subtraction angiographic images of the plantar circulation performed prior to (**A**) and after (**B**) bypass.

achieve accurate results, however, and the technique does not provide the anatomic images that are reassuring to most surgeons considering arterial re-exploration.

B-Mode Ultrasonography

B-mode ultrasonography has been used intraoperatively to obtain anatomic imaging noninvasively. Initial experimental studies established that its ability to detect small arteriographic defects in subjects was comparable with that of arteriography.[19] In evaluation of arterial defects created in dogs, arteriography and B-mode ultrasonography were both nearly 100% specific in excluding arterial defects. However, ultrasonography has significantly greater sensitivity in detecting defects, 92% overall, compared with a sensitivity of 70% for serial biplanar arteriography and of only 50% for portable arteriography. These techniques had comparable accuracy in detecting stenoses. Clinical experience tends to confirm these findings; in one study, patency after carotid endarterectomy, even with the detection of small defects by B-mode ultrasonography, did not lead to significant increase in stroke rate or re-stenosis over a 4-year follow-up.[90]

B-mode ultrasonography has also been used in the lower extremity. Kresowik and associates[54] reported that in 106 patients, intraoperative B-mode ultrasonography detected defects in 20% of patients and that half of these defects were deemed important enough to warrant correction. In follow-up, there were no early graft occlusions in the B-mode group, and no residual defects were discovered with duplex scanning follow-up in the postoperative period.[54]

Intraoperative use of B-mode ultrasonography is not without its problems, however. Because the modality does not evaluate blood flow, it cannot differentiate fresh thrombus from flowing blood, which has the same echogenicity. In comparison with Doppler pencil probes, B-mode ultrasound probes are larger and cannot be sterilized. Thus, their use is more cumbersome. The probes require a sterile covering containing a gel to maintain an appropriate acoustic interface. Significant operator experience is needed to obtain optimal images and to achieve accurate interpretations.

In clinical situations, one difficulty with the technique is determining the significance of the many defects identified, because most do not require repair. The lack of accompanying blood flow information makes this decision more difficult. In one study, B-mode ultrasonography failed to create images technically adequate for evaluation in nearly 25% of patients. This inadequacy was due to the technical difficulty of imaging the distal internal carotid artery with the large probe. Carotid patch angioplasty prostheses often interfered with the acquisition of acoustic images. Because of these problems, visualization of the endarterectomy endpoint at the distal internal carotid artery was often difficult to obtain satisfactorily. This study emphasized the problem of potential false-positive results associated with defects detected by B-mode ultrasonography.[40]

Duplex Ultrasonography

With the addition of flow-measuring capability to B-mode ultrasonography technology, duplex scanning brings a more powerful, expensive, and complex tool to the operating room. Like B-mode ultrasound probes, duplex scanning probes are larger, cannot be sterilized, and require considerable operator skill not only to obtain accurate images but also to position the probe over the sample target appropriately so that accurate velocity measurements can be obtained. Duplex color-flow technology provides continuous Doppler signals along the artery at multiple points. Color imaging facilitates identification of areas of higher velocity, albeit at a significant increase in equipment cost (Fig. 65-3).[59] The large probe heads remain difficult to

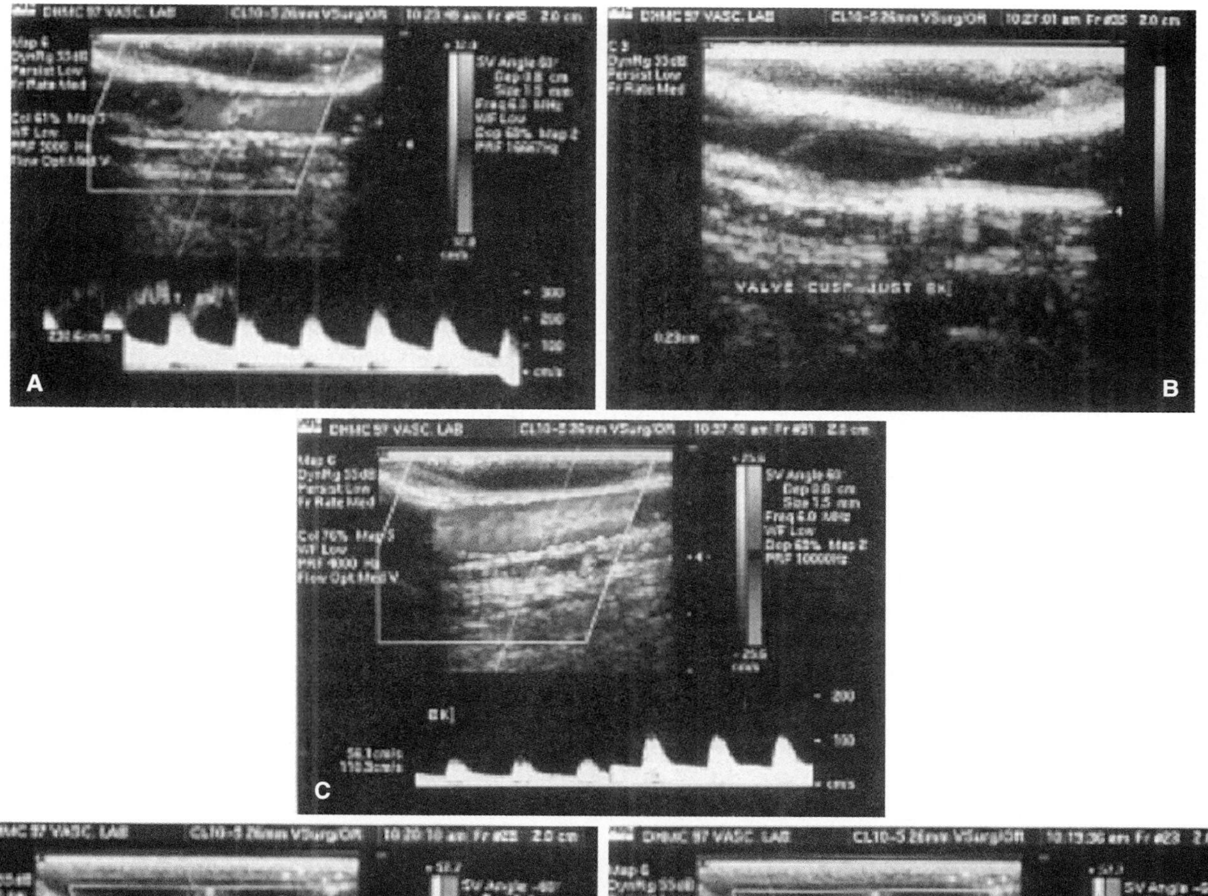

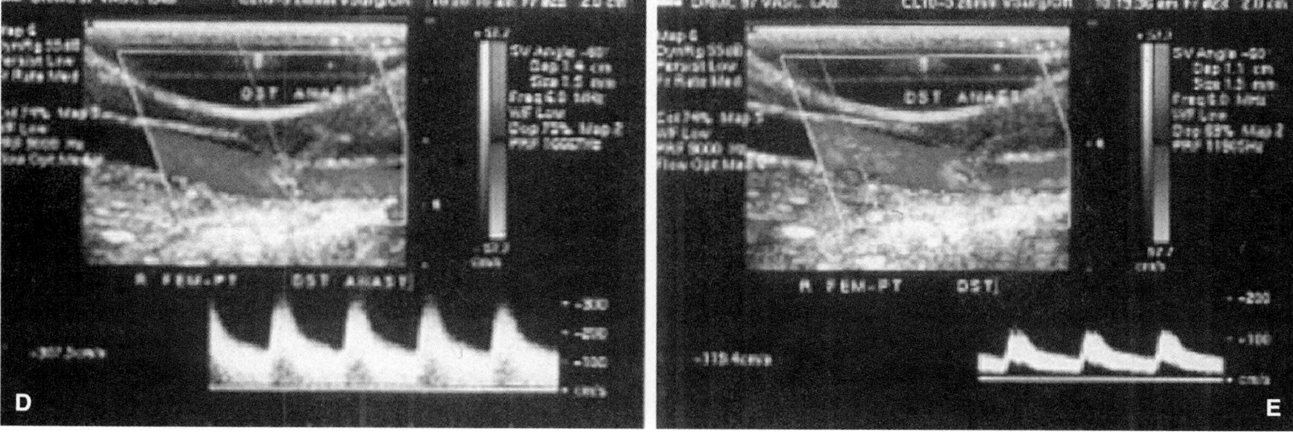

FIGURE 65-3 **A** and **B,** Retained valve cusp in an in-situ bypass detected intraoperatively. **C,** Same area after valve lysis; note the decreased velocity after valve lysis. **D,** The distal anastomosis of the same graft appears in spasm. **E,** The velocity has decreased significantly after the injection of papaverine.

manipulate in small operative fields, creating difficulties in imaging very proximal or very distal targets.

Examination of outflow arteries with duplex scanning is less precise than with arteriography, although the information provided is physiologic rather than anatomic. Duplex scanning does provide an easier mechanism for identifying defects in proximal arterial anastomoses than arteriography, because contrast imaging of the proximal anastomosis from a more distally placed catheter is cumbersome and often difficult.[23] Duplex scanning can identify low graft velocities that are undetectable by arteriography. Furthermore, experience with intraoperative duplex scanning in both the carotid and infrainguinal positions is growing. This experience, although largely anecdotal, demonstrates a greater sensitivity to technical defects with duplex technology. Early results with intraoperative duplex scanning show an association between these defects and optimal results in the postoperative period.[49,53,75,107,117] It is noteworthy that duplex scanning is unable to access newly placed polytetrafluoroethylene (PTFE) and polyester

(Dacron) grafts because they contain air, which prevents ultrasound penetration. Detection can also be a problem in the carotid artery position when prosthetic patch material is used. A bovine pericardium–based patch has been introduced that alleviates this problem.

Angioscopy

Since the introduction of small flexible catheters containing high-resolution optical systems, intraoperative angioscopy has become an attractive technique for evaluation of arterial reconstructions. Angioscopy requires irrigation with saline accompanied by inflow and, sometimes, outflow occlusion to provide a visually clear image. The presence of any red blood cells can completely obscure accurate visualization of the luminal image. The use of a specifically designed infusion pump with high-flow and low-flow rates has greatly facilitated visualization.[64] Experience is required to manipulate both the angioscope and the visual target in order to obtain complete and clear visualization.

Angioscopy has been most widely used to inspect in-situ saphenous vein grafts to ensure complete valve lysis,[114] to exclude unligated venous branches, and to assess the quality of the venous conduit (Fig. 65-4). Most commonly, my colleagues and I employ the 1.4-mm-diameter angioscope in lower extremity vein grafts and insert the angioscope through an introducer in the most proximal end of the vein or through the most proximal vein branch left unligated for this purpose. Saline irrigation is administered through a sheath. Prior to angioscopy, it is useful to identify and ligate as many venous side branches as possible to optimize distal visualization while minimizing the irrigation required to clear red blood cells. Angioscopy can be used in other sites if blood flow can be temporarily occluded. Such occlusion sometimes necessitates the use of balloon occlusion catheters if proximal control is not surgically accessible. Angioscopy appears to be particularly important in detecting abnormalities within arm veins that may not be apparent on external visual inspection.[61,86,102]

Angioscopy has also been used to evaluate the technical results after carotid endartectomy.[74] In a consecutive series of 110 endarterectomies using either the standard or eversion techniques, 9% of cases required repair of technical defects, a rate similar to those reported by other investigators using other evaluation technologies. Because angioscopy is an invasive intraluminal procedure, related complications are possible. They include endothelial injury leading to late hyperplasia, creation of intimal flaps, and fluid overload due to excess irrigation. Experimental studies have documented that mild intimal injury does occur but only after multiple repeated passages of the larger-diameter scopes.[55] The long-term effects of this mild trauma are not firmly established, but angioscopy using a few passes of a small-diameter (1.4 mm) angioscope in human vein grafts appears to have no significant late clinical consequences. Several studies have shown that the infusion of irrigation solution can be limited to 500 mL or less in most patients, an amount that has not caused complications, especially when planned as a part of the overall fluid administration during the procedure.[47,64]

Intravascular Ultrasonography

The newest potential modality for intraoperative evaluation of arterial procedures is intravascular ultrasonography. It is based on a flexible catheter system and generates two-dimensional cross-sectional images through the circumferential rotation of a miniaturized (10- to 30-MHz) ultrasound crystal at the catheter tip. In experimental studies, this technique has proved to be quite accurate for measuring luminal diameter and for identifying stenoses caused by atherosclerosis or intimal hyperplasia.[31,70,98,104] As expected, this ultrasonographic technique is insensitive to detecting thrombus because of the equivalent echogenicity of fresh clot and flowing blood. In one study, both intravascular ultrasonography and angioscopy were found to be 100% accurate in detecting 2-mm intimal flaps in canine femoral arteries, compared with only 60% accuracy for single-plane arteriography.[69]

Few clinical studies of this modality have established its efficacy and potential role in assessing the technical adequacy of vascular surgical reconstructions. Intravascular ultrasonography does appear to be useful in the evaluation of lesions appropriate for stent-graft placement (Fig. 65-5) as well as of the efficacy of the placement of stents and

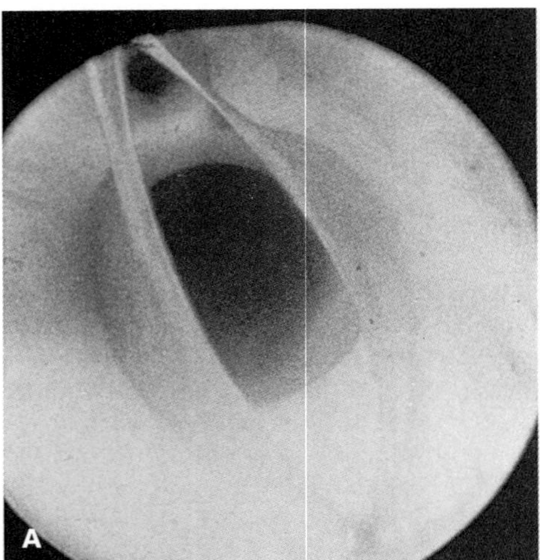

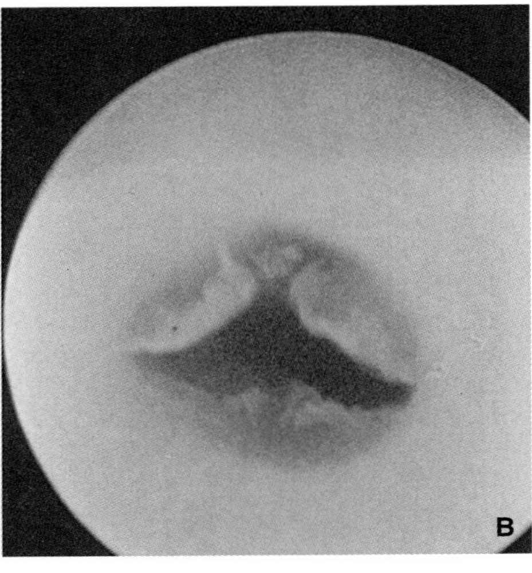

FIGURE 65-4 **A,** Photograph of a valve via an angioscope prior to lysis. **B,** Photograph of an angioscopic image of a valve after lysis. (**B** from McCaughan JJ Jr, Walsh DB, Edgcomb LP, et al: In vitro observations of greater saphenous vein valves during pulsatile and nonpulsatile flow and following lysis. J Vasc Surg 1:356, 1984.)

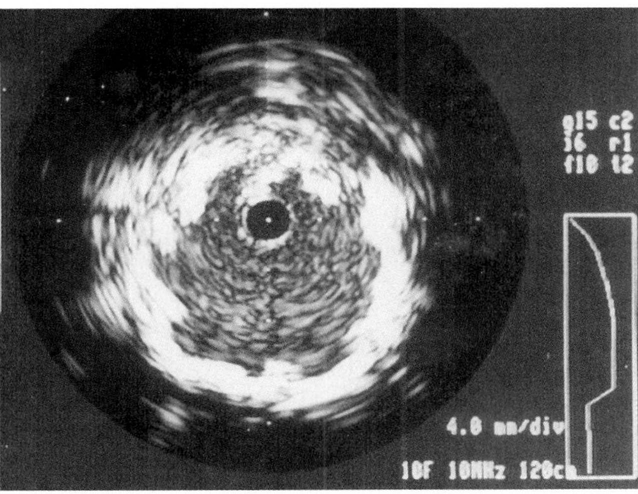

FIGURE 65-5 An intravascular ultrasonogram of a stent-graft. The rippled, uneven appearance of the inner wall represents infolds of the graft between the interstices of the stent frame.

stent-grafts.[29] Whether intravascular ultrasonography provides information that is different and useful enough to justify its cost, particularly in comparison with other intraoperative techniques, remains to be proven.

Indirect Methods

In addition to the direct methods of evaluating arterial reconstructions intraoperatively, several indirect methods can measure resistance within the graft or within the outflow bed, information that may help evaluate the adequacy of revascularization. This is most easily accomplished intraoperatively with a continuous-wave Doppler probe placed over a distal artery, with the examiner listening for audible augmentation in the waveform after release of temporary graft occlusion.

A more quantitative assessment can be obtained by measuring the distal extremity pressure using a sterile blood pressure cuff during surgery. In patients with more proximal reconstructions and residual outflow abnormalities, the ankle pressure may not be maximal immediately after revascularization, but rather may increase only gradually in the postoperative period. Thus, this intraoperative pressure measurement does not provide absolute proof of the success of reconstruction, and therefore must be interpreted on the basis of the preoperative anatomy of each patient. Other similar modalities, including pulse volume recording, strain-gauge plethysmography, photoplethysmography, and even transcutaneous oxygen tension measurement, can be used intraoperatively to evaluate the restoration of distal blood flow; for each method, the examiner looks for a significant difference in magnitude with and without graft occlusion.

Although there are more direct methods for assessing the quality of a vein graft, Schwartz and coworkers[92] described a technique that accurately identifies problems within grafts. Unfortunately, this method detects only increased resistance within a graft, not the specific location of the potential problem. Thus, other adjunctive measures are required.

Outflow resistance has been measured intraoperatively to predict subsequent graft failure in extremity bypasses. This technique enables one to calculate outflow resistance on the basis of the pressure measured while saline is injected into the distal end of a bypass graft at a known rate. Ascer and colleagues[7] found that grafts with an outflow resistance of more than 1.2 resistant units (mm Hg pressure divided by mL/min flow) all experienced failure within 30 days. Other groups, however, have not confirmed this observation and have reported long-term patency in grafts with high outflow resistance, especially vein grafts.[77,116] Like other indirect methods, this technique does not provide anatomic information sufficient to isolate the cause of the high outflow resistance and, thus, adjunctive anatomic study of the graft and its outflow is needed to identify potentially correctable problems. In most instances, high outflow resistance is due to severe distal disease and cannot be improved. In a few cases, this technique may lead to identification of distal anastomotic problems or the need for extension of a proximal graft to a more distal site for better outflow. In practice, most vascular surgeons have found these techniques complicated and cumbersome.

■ CLINICAL APPLICATIONS

Cerebrovascular Reconstructions

The efficacy of cerebrovascular surgery for preventing stroke is predicated on a low operative complication rate. Technical performance is best judged from the operative complication rate, which for carotid endarterectomy includes the rates of perioperative stroke as well as early and late restenosis.

Because most reports describe postoperative stroke rates of less than 5%, one would expect the detection rate for intraoperative technical defects during carotid endarterectomy to be similarly low. Surprisingly, this has not been the case when the technical adequacy of the endarterectomy has been investigated with any of a variety of techniques. In a collected review of more than 2000 endarterectomies evaluated intraoperatively, residual defects were found in an average of 12% of procedures, with a range of 5% to 43%.[12] Although most defects were found in the external carotid artery (because of the blind nature of this portion of the endarterectomy), defects were found in the internal carotid artery in 6.5% of these collected cases, usually at the distal end of the endarterectomy. In a similar review of 1500 carotid endarterectomies, the average frequency of residual defects found by postoperative arteriography or noninvasive testing was 5.7%, with the lowest incidence reported in a series employing some type of intraoperative evaluation.[12] In contradistinction to results of lower extremity revascularization, the technical results of carotid endarterectomy do not appear to have changed over time. With various types of techniques used to evaluate technical adequacy, the range of technical defects found that required at least concern and, in many cases, re-exploration ranged from 4% to 40%.[33,34,40,75]

Because rates of early and late stroke in these cases continue to be considerably lower than the rate of technical defects detected, it is clear that not all residual defects after carotid endarterectomy are clinically significant. Nonetheless, it is axiomatic that technical defects should be eliminated if possible. This principle has led most vascular surgeons to use some form of intraoperative assessment after carotid endarterectomy as well as after vertebral and subclavian artery reconstructions. Although there is usually some hesitation to re-explore a completed carotid endarterectomy because of a possible technical defect, most surgeons agree that this step does not increase morbidity.[30,37] Reluctance to re-explore an artery is easily overcome when the surgeon has confidence in the method of assessing technical adequacy.

Use of intraoperative arteriography has led to carotid re-exploration in 2% to 26% of reported cases.[21,33] After introducing routine intraoperative carotid arteriography, Courbier and colleagues[21] found the rate of stroke to be 2%, compared with 8.2% in historical control cases in which arteriography had not been used. Using this approach, these researchers found that 5% of their patients' carotid endarterectomies required re-exploration to correct significant technical defects. They further noted that intraoperative arteriograms helped refine their endarterectomy techniques, progressively reducing the incidence of defects detected. Donaldson and associates,[33] in a series of 410 carotid endarterectomies, found 71 defects, 66 (16%) of which warranted correction. The operative mortality and morbidity in this series were low, with an ipsilateral stroke rate less than 2%. Interestingly, despite this aggressive program to achieve technical perfection at the time of initial endarterectomy, restenosis of greater than 80% developed over time in 7.3% of the patients in this series. Nearly 4% of the patients required reoperation for recurrent carotid stenosis, a figure comparable to that of other series in which the intraoperative assessment of technical adequacy was not as comprehensive.

A unique advantage of carotid arteriography, compared with other assessment techniques, is the capability of obtaining intracranial images, if needed, to exclude distal problems such as residual thrombus after acute carotid thrombosis. Using digital subtraction techniques in 50 consecutive patients, Bredenberg and associates[17] found that 12% of their patients required re-exploration after carotid endarterectomy to correct defects in the internal carotid artery (endpoint stenosis or nonocclusive platelet thrombi). The usual concerns about arteriography are the cumbersome nature of the technique in the operating room and the great variation in the quality of images seen. The technical inconvenience and imaging variance clearly can be reduced with routine performance of the procedure.

Continuous wave Doppler ultrasonography alone is the most commonly used assessment of technical adequacy in carotid surgery at present. In experienced hands, examination of a carotid endarterectomy with this modality appears to be quite sensitive. Seifert and Blackshear[96] detected residual defects in 4.3% of 229 carotid endarterectomies with continuous wave Doppler inspection, of which 70% were confirmed by re-exploration or arteriography.[96] No false-negative results were reported. Barnes and coworkers[12] reported the detection of internal carotid stenoses in 8% of 125 carotid endarterectomies, although only 30% of the defects were found to require exploration as judged from subsequent arteriography, the other 70% being related only to spasm at the distal clamp site.[12]

Thus, the continuous wave Doppler technique appears to be sensitive but not specific enough for its findings to be used to justify immediate carotid re-exploration in the absence of an additional confirmatory study. The exception is when one identifies a very high-pitched, high frequency sound at the distal internal carotid artery or a short, abruptly ending, diastolic sound in the internal carotid artery; in this situation, re-exploration is indicated.

Using pulse Doppler spectral analysis, Bandyk and associates[9] found that 20 (8%) of 250 patients undergoing carotid endarterectomy had severe flow defects according to the criterion of a focal velocity increase of more than 150 cm/sec with uniform spectral broadening.[9] Intraoperative arteriography confirmed findings in 10 of these patients, who then underwent re-exploration for endpoint stenosis, intimal flaps, or platelet aggregates. In the other 10 patients, less than 30% stenosis was demonstrated on intraoperative arteriography and they did not undergo re-exploration. Two of these latter patients later had postoperative neurologic deficits and thrombosis caused by platelet aggregates. In another 3 patients not undergoing re-exploration, residual carotid stenosis of more than 50% developed within 3 months of surgery. This last occurrence suggests that pulse Doppler spectral analysis detects some important residual lesions (especially platelet aggregates) that are missed by arteriography. Bandyk and associates[9] further noted that 10% of the arteriograms were of inadequate quality and concluded that pulse Doppler ultrasonography was more accurate in their hands.

Flanigan and colleagues,[37] using B-mode ultrasonography to evaluate 55 carotid endarterectomies, found that 19% of patients had a common or internal carotid artery defect, of which most (73%) were intimal flaps, with a stenosis being the second most common finding.[37] In only 7% of these cases was the decision made to re-explore the endarterectomy using the criterion of either a stenosis of 30% diameter reduction or more or an intimal flap of at least 3 mm in length. Although the study emphasizes the sensitivity of B-mode ultrasonography in identifying arterial defects after carotid endarterectomy, a large number of apparently insignificant defects were detected. The same group addressed these issues in a subsequent study, which demonstrated that "lesser defects" did not result in either early or late stroke or residual stenosis during late follow-up using duplex ultrasonography.[90] They concluded that "minor" defects detected by B-mode ultrasonography after carotid endarterectomy were benign and did not need re-exploration.

In direct comparison of arteriography and B-mode ultrasonography, Dilly and Bernstein[30] found significant defects requiring re-exploration in 8.3% of 158 patients undergoing carotid endarterectomy. These investigators noted that both techniques had a false-positive rate of 5% to 8% and that combining the techniques improved accuracy. They concluded, however, that no assessment technique was perfect. Using gray-scale duplex ultrasonography intraoperatively, Schwartz and associates[93] identified arterial defects requiring re-exploration in 11% of 76 patients undergoing carotid endarterectomy. They used Doppler flow velocity criteria to differentiate significant from trivial intimal flaps observed with B-mode ultrasonography and concluded that this technique represents a major advantage over B-mode ultrasonography alone. In their experience with duplex ultrasonography to evaluate 131 carotid endarterectomies, Reilly and coworkers[79] found that 11% of arteries required re-exploration to correct technical defects, of which 5% involved the external carotid artery, 5% the internal carotid artery, and 1% the common carotid artery. They reported difficulty in obtaining adequate images in 14% of arterial segments but noted a positive correlation between the size of unrepaired intraoperative defects and the severity of artery restenosis. These researchers concurred that minor anatomic defects visualized on B-mode ultrasonography but not accompanied by Doppler flow velocity alterations are benign and should not be repaired.

In 1993, Kinney and colleagues[53] reported 430 patients who underwent 461 carotid endarterectomies, in whom duplex scanning and pulsed Doppler spectral analysis were then performed to assess the adequacy of the endarterectomies. This experience included the previously reported 268 patients who underwent ultrasonography and arteriography and added 142 who underwent duplex scanning and pulsed Doppler spectral analysis. All patients were monitored in the postoperative period with duplex ultrasonography. Fewer than 6% of patients required intraoperative revision because of abnormalities detected on intraoperative evaluation, and 2.6% of patients experienced neurologic deficits, half of which were permanent. Patients with normal intraoperative flow findings had a significantly lower rate of late ipsilateral stroke. Patients who had an incidence of 50% stenosis or who were not studied had a significantly higher risk of ipsilateral stroke during late follow-up. This study emphasizes the importance of optimal results at initial carotid endarterectomy to minimize the perioperative neurologic deficit rate and the rate of late ischemic neurologic events.[53]

In a smaller study, Papanicolaou and colleagues[75] confirmed the findings just described. Patients who underwent 86 carotid endarterectomies were evaluated with duplex ultrasonography intraoperatively, and 11% required re-exploration at the time of initial surgery to correct intimal flaps and platelet thrombi demonstrated on duplex scanning. No patient had a neurologic deficit in the perioperative period, and no carotid restenosis was identified in the follow-up of 43 patients. Although this study was small, it tends to confirm the findings from Kinney and colleagues,[53] particularly that normal findings on intraoperative duplex scanning after carotid endarterectomy appear to be associated with lower incidences of both perioperative cerebrovascular events and subsequent carotid artery restenosis. In a study of 106 consecutive carotid endarterectomies, Lipski and coworkers[58] found that an abnormal intraoperative duplex scanning finding changed patient management in 23% of cases. They reported no residual stenoses among patients who underwent intraoperative duplex evaluation, compared with an incidence of residual stenosis of 15% among patients who did not undergo duplex scanning.[58]

In an analysis of 1019 carotid endarterectomies, Archie and associates[5] reported that 28% had a "step or shelf" at the beginning of the carotid endarterectomy site that was detectable with duplex scanning. Three of the patients suffered neurologic events attributed to the "step." Six other patients with a "shelf" required reoperation for restenosis. In a later series of patients, in whom the "steps" were repaired when encountered, no adverse clinical events or restenosis occurred. These investigators emphasized that the detection and correction of these defects using duplex scanning can optimize the results of carotid endarterectomy.[5]

In summary, evidence continues to mount that duplex scanning at the completion of carotid endarterectomy is a sensitive test for abnormalities at the endarterectomy site. Results from several series suggest that completion duplex ultrasonography can be used to reduce the risk of perioperative neurologic events as well as residual and recurrent stenoses. Unfortunately, there is little agreement or conformity about which lesions seen on duplex scanning should be repaired.

Routine use of intraoperative duplex scanning at the completion of carotid endarterectomy may also alter the standard management of a patient who experiences a postoperative neurologic deficit. Traditional practice has mandated immediate return to the operating room of a patient who awakens with new neurologic deficits. In a small series from Loyola University Medical Center, all 14 patients in whom findings of completion duplex scanning were normal and who emerged from anesthesia with neurologic deficits had normal findings at re-exploration or on a postoperative duplex scanning study.[97] Interestingly, among 10 patients undergoing carotid endarterectomy who suffered neurologic deficits after a lucid interval, 60% had suffered thrombosis of the internal carotid artery.

Our practice has been to use duplex ultrasonography routinely after carotid endarterectomy. Since the initial startup inconveniences were overcome, we have been pleased with the sensitivity provided by the B-mode image combined with the physiologic parameters provided by the Doppler evaluation of the carotid endarterectomy site. We were initially frustrated with the large number of patients who required patch arterioplasty in whom the character of the patch impeded duplex scanning. The development of bovine pericardium patches has obviated much of this difficulty. Our strategy now is to re-explore the artery if any focal increased frequency or visible defect 3 mm in length is detected along the endarterectomy site. In our last 300 carotid endarterectomies, the neurologic event rate has been less than 1% with use of this strategy.

We have also altered our practice of immediate return to the operating room for patients who awaken with a neurologic deficit. If a postoperative duplex scan can be obtained before an operating room becomes available and results are normal, the patient does not undergo re-exploration. As in the Loyola experience, any patient who experiences a neurologic deficit after a lucid interval in the immediate postoperative period is returned immediately to the operating room for repair of a possible internal carotid artery thrombosis.

Limited experience with the use of intraoperative angioscopy after carotid endarterectomy has been reported.[40,63] Gaunt and coworkers[40] evaluated 100 consecutive patients intraoperatively with transcranial Doppler imaging and angioscopy. The arteries were also evaluated with continuous wave Doppler ultrasonography and B-mode ultrasonography. These investigators found that continuous wave Doppler ultrasonography was technically inadequate in 9% of patients and that B-mode ultrasonography was technically inadequate in 24% of patients. Angioscopy demonstrated significant technical errors in 12% of cases. None of the patients in whom angioscopy detected abnormalities that were subsequently repaired suffered postoperative thrombosis or neurologic deficits in the perioperative period. Gaunt and coworkers[40] found angioscopy to be simple in both its application and its interpretation. Another advantage of angioscopy was that these defects were detected and corrected prior to restoration of flow, thus avoiding the need for re-exploration. These investigators suggested that angioscopy was likely too sensitive, however, because 27% of patients had defects visible at the time of surgery, but not all the defects required repair or caused perioperative stroke.

Transcranial Doppler ultrasonography can image the middle cerebral artery via the thin temporal window in the skull. Microemboli can be seen and counted. Increased numbers of microemboli have been associated with neurologic deficits and changes seen on postoperative magnetic resonance imaging (MRI). Studies using transcranial Doppler ultrasonography have demonstrated that preoperative use of aspirin and intraoperative administration of low-molecular-weight dextran have reduced the number of emboli.[57] Transcranial Doppler monitoring can also be used to teach surgeons which operative techniques produce the fewest emboli, likely reducing their patients' risk of perioperative stroke.[3,39] The limitations of this technique include the significant number (15%) of patients whose temporal bone is too thick for successful insonation of the middle cerebral artery.[4] The threshold number of microemboli associated with a cerebrovascular accident is also difficult to discern. In the experience reported by Gaunt,[41] transcranial Doppler ultrasonography detected shunt malfunction in 13% of patients, emboli that occurred during operative dissection in 23% of the patients, and early postoperative carotid thrombosis in 3 of 100 patients.

The need for intraoperative assessment of the technical adequacy of carotid endarterectomy clearly depends on a particular surgeon's complication rate. Given the frequency of this procedure and the severity of associated complications, most vascular surgeons would benefit from use of one or more of these techniques.

Extremity Revascularization

Although intraoperative assessment techniques can be applied equally well after arterial endarterectomy, thrombectomy, embolectomy, or intraoperative balloon angioplasty, most experience has been acquired with lower extremity bypass grafts. Despite improved overall results, the early failure rate in most reported series of infrainguinal vein grafts varies from 5% to 10%, and failure is often due to correctable graft or anastomotic defects.[6,101] Because achievement of long-term patency after early postoperative graft thrombosis is unlikely, efforts to detect and correct any defect in a graft during the initial revascularization are justified.[15,67,83] In an early series, completion arteriography reduced the early graft thrombosis rate from 18% to 0% because of the modality's ability to detect defects in 27% of the patients undergoing extremity endarterectomy.[80] Using intraoperative arteriography in more than 1800 arterial reconstructions, Courbier and associates[21] detected significant technical problems in 4.6%. Of the patients with bypass grafts who were studied, the group found technical problems in 2.2%. The problems included emboli, thrombosis, twisted and kinked vein grafts, distal anastomotic stenoses, and intimal flaps. Similarly, Liebman and colleagues[56] found that intraoperative arteriography identified defects in 5.2% of 250 lower extremity bypass grafts with a false-positive rate below 1%.[56]

In 1992, Mills and coworkers[66] reviewed 214 consecutive infrainguinal bypass grafts. They found that 8% of grafts were demonstrated by intraoperative arteriography to have technical problems significant enough to require revision. Arteriography missed only two defects (<1%) that caused graft failure within the first 30 days, and those grafts could be salvaged. The investigators concluded that routine completion arteriography should be considered the standard for intraoperative bypass assessment. Similar experience was reported by Chalmers and colleagues[18] in 298 in-situ bypass grafts. Intraoperative arteriography detected defects requiring surgical revision in 8%. Although two small, highly selected series suggested that completion arteriography after infrainguinal revascularization is neither sensitive nor cost-effective,[16,25] most investigators believe that completion arteriography after infrainguinal revascularization provides valuable information about the state of the conduit, the distal anastomosis, and the runoff circulation. Completion arteriography remains a mainstay for confirming technical adequacy of extremity revascularization.

Pulsed Doppler spectral analysis and B-mode imaging have also been utilized to assess the technical adequacy of infrainguinal bypass grafts. Schmitt and coworkers[91] assessed 83 lower extremity in-situ saphenous vein grafts intraoperatively, measuring the peak systolic velocity (PSV) in the small diameter of the distal vein. They found that 93% of grafts had a PSV greater than 40 cm/sec, and there were no postoperative failures in this group. Of the remaining 7% of grafts with lower PSV values, however, two thirds showed early failure or required intraoperative correction of the defect identified by the confirmatory arteriogram. Schmitt and coworkers[91] found a slow PSV to be quite specific for graft luminal defects, sclerosed vein segments, or large vein diameter (>5 mm). In a previous study, Bandyk and associates[11] found that a focal decrease in velocity on pulsed Doppler spectral analysis indicated a potential graft stenosis. They recorded a 40% incidence of false-positive detection of small significant defects, however, and thus recommended this method as a companion for intraoperative arteriography.

Sigel and associates[99] using real-time B-mode ultrasonography during 165 vascular reconstructions, compared the results with those of intraoperative arteriography. Defects were detected by B-mode ultrasonography in 29% of their cases, but only 8% of the defects were judged significant enough to warrant re-exploration. In a subset of patients who underwent simultaneous intraoperative arteriography, these researchers determined that the accuracy of ultrasonography or arteriography was 96% or 85%, respectively. They concluded that the sensitivity of B-mode ultrasonography in detecting potential defects is high but that many abnormalities are also detected that are insignificant and do not require repair. They substantiated this conclusion by noting the lack of subsequent graft failure in patients with small defects that were not corrected. However, B-mode ultrasonography findings still led to unnecessary re-explorations in 14% of their patients. This study illustrates the major difficulty of the technique, namely, the selection of detected defects that are significant enough to warrant re-exploration because many small abnormalities are identified.

In an attempt to define the hemodynamic severity of defects detected by B-mode ultrasonography, Cull and colleagues[23] studied 56 lower extremity bypasses with intraoperative duplex scanning. They considered a lesion hemodynamically significant if the focal PSV was 50% higher than that in surrounding points or was less than 45 cm/sec at any point along the graft, excluding increases in PSV immediately beyond the distal anastomosis, where a significant diameter reduction often occurs. Duplex scanning identified technical defects in 39% of these grafts, and 50% of the defects were judged clinically significant enough to warrant re-exploration. Four of the defects were missed on completion arteriography, and one defect identified on arteriography was missed on duplex scanning. Interestingly, 50% of the grafts with uncorrected defects that were detected on duplex scanning became occluded within 1 month of surgery, suggesting that these defects were more significant than originally judged on clinical grounds. Unlike B-mode ultrasonography used alone, duplex scanning was not overly sensitive, because it had only one false-positive result. Cull and colleagues[23] judged that both arteriography and duplex scanning had good sensitivity (88% for both) for identifying graft defects, with the combination of the two modalities being even more accurate. They concluded that the techniques were complementary. Despite the combination of both techniques, however, they reported a 9% early graft failure rate, similar to that reported by other researchers who had not used duplex scanning to evaluate their grafts.

In 1994, Bandyk and colleagues[10] reviewed their experience with intraoperative duplex scanning during arterial reconstructions. They found defects in 18% of 135 infrainguinal vein bypasses that required revision. Intraoperative arteriography was also performed during 81% of the procedures but supplied no additional diagnostic information. Their criteria for defect identification or graft function focused on PSV and velocity ratios. Among grafts with systolic velocities less than 125 cm/sec and velocity ratios of 1:1.4, these researchers recommended no further evaluation of this normal flow pattern; importantly, none of the grafts in this group failed. For grafts with PSV ranging from 125 to 180 cm/ sec and velocity ratios from 1:1.5 to 1:2.4, Bandyk and colleagues[10] judged that repeat scanning during the same procedure and intraoperative arteriography would help them decide whether this residual flow abnormality was significant and required exploration. In a later study by the same group, peak systolic velocities higher than 180 cm/sec with spectral broadening and velocity ratios greater than 1:2.5 were thought to be significant abnormalities necessitating exploration and repair.[8] Using these criteria, these researchers revised 16% of 275 grafts. Only three (1%) bypasses failed within 30 days of operation, and six (2%) bypasses required revision in the early postoperative period. Critically important was the achievement of normal PSV in the repaired vein grafts. None of the grafts in which this lower PSV was achieved failed. These researchers pointed out that most of the defects were related to blind retrograde valvulotomy or to imperfections found in nonreversed translocated grafts. They readily admitted that reversed vein grafts required significantly fewer revisions.[8]

Considerable experience in the use of angioscopy to evaluate lower extremity reconstructions has been reported. Graft defects that require surgical corrections (including stenoses, webs, and bands resulting from recanalization of intimal flaps, thrombus and anastomotic strictures, and kinks) have been identified in 10% to 20% of these cases.[13,45,112] The largest experience with angioscopy has been obtained during evaluation of infrainguinal vein grafts, especially the detection of residual valve cusps and unligated vein branches in in-situ saphenous vein grafts.[64] The incidence of angioscopically detected defects has been significantly higher in these grafts, residual cusps being found in 19% to 47% and unligated vein branches in 35% to 75%.[43,45,64] Arm vein grafts in particular are prone to recanalization defects (webs or bands), which are detected in 74% of these grafts, perhaps because of the trauma of previous venipuncture.[102]

Baxter and colleagues[13] found that arteriography was 95% as specific as angioscopy but only 67% as sensitive. They reported a 20% false-positive rate for arteriography related to small filling defects that could not be substantiated and a 7% false-negative rate for detection of intimal flaps. In a similar comparison of 102 infragenicular bypasses, Wolfle and associates[114] found completion angiography to have a sensitivity of 46% and a specificity of 98% in the detection of significant abnormalities. Stonebridge and coworkers[102] noted that neither continuous wave Doppler ultrasonography nor arteriography could identify webs or bands in recanalized arm veins and that use of angioscopy reduced the early failure rate of these veins from 11% to 0%.

Miller and colleagues[64] noted that nearly 50% of the 259 angioscopies they performed in lower extremity grafts led to important surgical decisions. They pointed out the utility of angioscopy for monitoring the correction of defects after intraoperative detection. Furthermore, they noted that even after considerable experience with in-situ techniques, 10% of the in-situ saphenous vein grafts they most recently implanted had residual valve cusps, which presumably raise the risk of graft failure. This conclusion has not been firmly established, however, because studies using angioscopy detected far more defects than studies using arteriography, without obvious changes in the rate of early graft failure. Thus, the remaining key question concerning small defects detected only on angioscopy is the extent to which they affect subsequent graft failure, the answer to which would determine the appropriate criteria for repairing them intraoperatively. Although the need for repair of all defects detected by angioscopy has not been firmly proved, it is clear that this is the most sensitive modality for detecting such defects. Another advantage of using the angioscope is a decrease in rate of residual valve cusps if the valvulotomy is angioscopically directed.[65] If Bandyk and colleagues[8] had employed this technique in their in-situ saphenous vein grafts, for example, the number of defects found on B-mode ultrasonography may have been significantly reduced.

In an attempt to resolve questions about determining the optimal method of intraoperative in-situ saphenous graft evaluation, my colleagues and I[43] performed a blinded prospective comparison of arteriography, angioscopy, and duplex ultrasonography in 20 patients using prospectively defined criteria for defects detected by each modality: Sensitivity in detecting residual unligated vein branches was highest for angioscopy (66%) and arteriography (44%), whereas gray-scale duplex scanning detected only 12% of these vein branches. Angioscopy was significantly more sensitive (100%) than either duplex scanning (11%) or arteriography (22%) in detecting residual valve cusps. No anastomotic stenoses were confirmed in our study, although six were suggested; the false-positive rates for erroneous detection of stenosis were 20% for arteriography, 10% for duplex scanning, and 0% for angioscopy. The time required to complete these studies was 17 to 20 minutes and did not vary among the three modalities. No stenoses, occlusions, or arteriovenous fistulae have been detected in any of these grafts by postoperative duplex scanning surveillance during a 10-month mean follow-up interval. In this study, arteriography or duplex ultrasonography used alone would have missed more than 75% of the residual valve cusps that occurred in 30% of these bypass grafts.

Our own practice is to perform angioscopically directed valvulotomy after ligation of all visible vein branches. During that examination, any other patent vein branches found are ligated. Once the distal anastomosis is completed, we perform DSA of the distal anastomosis and runoff bed. Since the late 1980s, we have found very few technical errors at the anastomoses. DSA allows evaluation to rule out twists in the graft and any obvious anastomotic problems and provides very helpful information about the runoff bed that is not as easily obtained with any other modality. We have used continuous wave Doppler or duplex ultrasonography examination of the graft to confirm that all fistulae are ligated.

Completion duplex scanning of lower extremity bypass grafts may also predict bypass patency. Bandyk and associates[8] reported that a PSV less than 125 cm/sec or a low velocity ratio is an indicator of excellent long-term graft function. Mackenzie and colleagues[60] noted a subgroup of patients in whom high outflow resistance was detected at completion duplex ultrasonography. Graft thrombosis occurred within 6 months in 75% of these grafts. Johnson and coworkers[51] have further elucidated the intraoperative duplex scanning criteria requiring vein graft revision at the time of bypass graft completion. In their study, color duplex scanning was used to assess vein and anastomotic patency and velocity spectral waveforms of 626 infrainguinal vein bypass grafts. Criteria that determined need for repair were (1) PSV of more than 180 cm/sec with spectral broadening and velocity ratio of 2.5 to 5.0 and (2) PSV of more than 300 cm/sec with velocity ratio of more than 5.0. Normal results of intraoperative duplex scanning on initial imaging or after revision were associated with a 30-day thrombosis rate of only 0.2% and a subsequent revision rate of only 0.8% for duplex scanning-detected stenoses. Importantly, these researchers also found a subgroup of patients with technically adequate but low-flow bypass grafts (peak systolic velocity < 45 cm/sec). They proposed that grafts with low flow and high velocity ratio (i.e., no diastolic flow in the distal graft) be treated with adjunctive procedures to increase basal graft flow or, if no adjunctive procedures could be performed, with oral anticoagulation started after surgery.

Rzucidlo and coworkers[85] confirmed that low-velocity vein bypass grafts with high velocity ratio have a high likelihood of failure within 12 months. They noted that an end-diastolic velocity less than 8 cm/sec in a bypass graft predicted graft failure within 12 months with a high sensitivity and specificity. All bypass grafts with no measurable end diastolic flow failed within 12 months. These investigators further determined that high resistive indices within the distal bypass grafts predicted early graft failure. However, they did not find that PSV less than 45 cm/sec was predictive of graft thrombosis within 12 months, as suggested by Johnson and coworkers[51] (sensitivity <50%). These apparent differences in findings in the two studies were likely related to patient differences and small sample sizes.[85]

In addition to lower extremity bypass grafts, intraoperative assessment can also yield important information after arterial embolectomy or thrombectomy procedures. Although these procedures are often performed without intraoperative assessment of adequacy, we found that completion arteriography detected 87% of complications occurring after the use of balloon catheters; only 23% of the complications were recognized without arteriography.[22] Because many of these complications led to the need for subsequent operations and limb loss, some intraoperative technique is needed to identify distal pseudoaneurysms, arteriovenous fistulae, arterial disruption, intimal injury, and inadequate extraction of thrombus. Several studies have reported the efficacy of intraoperative angioscopy to confirm the adequacy of graft or arterial thromboembolectomy by direct inspection to identify residual thrombus. This inspection led to complete thrombectomy or alterations in the surgical procedure in more than 80% of these cases, and the researchers in these studies believe that the inspection contributed substantially to the success of the procedure.[95,111] They also pointed out the usefulness of angioscopy in directing subsequent attempts at thrombus retrieval, including the ability to guide balloon catheters selectively into tibial branches.

In our own practice, the addition of fluoroscopy and DSA to our operating room has significantly aided the ease of re-evaluation after thromboembolectomy. The ability to direct guidewires, to perform intraoperative "road mapping," and to pass catheters over directed guidewires using repetitive imaging with small doses of contrast agent have significantly improved the efficiency and accuracy of catheter thromboembolectomy.

Transabdominal Revascularization

Because of the large vessel diameters involved in aortoiliac reconstruction, small technical defects causing flow disturbances that affect graft patency are much less common than in carotid artery or lower extremity reconstructions. Iliac intimal flaps occasionally cause immediate or delayed graft thrombosis, however, so intraoperative assessment is required. When aortoiliac bypass or endarterectomy has been uneventful, we rely on the palpation of a normal distal aortoiliac or femoral pulse supplemented with comparable continuous wave Doppler insonation of the anastomoses or endarterectomy endpoints, looking for focal increases in frequency or marked turbulence. If a major defect is found, we immediately re-explore the site.

In less certain cases, we employ intraoperative duplex ultrasonography. We find that duplex scanning provides more accurate and more precise information than arteriography in the abdomen, where the large volume of contrast agent needed requires a rapid injection to obtain an adequate study. These examinations are often further limited by the inadequate penetration afforded by portable x-ray generators. In practice, it is uncommon that anything more than continuous wave Doppler ultrasonography is required in the aortoiliac system, a conclusion supported by the low incidence of postoperative stenoses or thromboses in this region. For an aortofemoral graft, especially if it is extended into the profunda femoris artery, a more precise determination of technical adequacy is required because the smaller-diameter femoral arteries are more easily influenced by minor imperfections. Accordingly, we routinely employ continuous wave Doppler ultrasonography in this area, supplementing it with intraoperative duplex scanning or DSA as required. Good-quality intraoperative arteriography is significantly easier to obtain at this site if we inject a contrast agent into the aortobifemoral graft limb, using temporary proximal graft occlusion to maximize concentration of contrast agent in the femoral graft. We do not advocate this procedure routinely but believe that duplex scanning or arteriography should be used liberally if continuous wave Doppler findings raise any question about an anastomotic stricture, especially at a profunda femoris anastomosis.

Like femoral artery reconstructions, renal and mesenteric artery reconstructions require careful intraoperative evaluation. Small technical defects in such reconstructions are likely to lead to graft failure, which when it occurs in the early postoperative period can be catastrophic. The major difficulty associated with evaluation of these endarterectomies or reconstructions is the anatomic location of the arteries, which are often difficult to approach with anything but a small Doppler probe. We have had difficulty in obtaining optimal arteriograms of these arteries because their reconstruction usually requires examination of an aortic anastomosis, making it difficult to achieve sufficient concentration of contrast agent and good x-ray penetration. Furthermore, intraoperative arteriography for the evaluation of renal artery reconstructions has a major theoretical disadvantage, in that the majority of patients undergoing such procedures have some degree of renal insufficiency that may be exacerbated by concentrated injection of radiographic contrast agent.

Accordingly, we rely initially on continuous wave Doppler ultrasonography, followed by intraoperative duplex scanning. To assess intraoperative duplex scanning after renal artery repair, Hansen and colleagues[46] evaluated 75 renal artery reconstructions, including both bypass grafts and thromboendarterectomies. They found defects on B-mode scans in 23% of these repairs, of which half (11%) were confirmed as major defects by PSVs of 200 cm/sec or higher. This change corresponded to a stenosis with an estimated 60% or greater reduction in diameter. The defects consisted of vein graft anastomotic stenoses and flaps or residual disease in the endarterectomized segment. Postoperatively, duplex scanning and arteriographic evaluation indicated that 98% of the patients without major intraoperative duplex abnormalities had patent arteries that were free of critical stenoses, demonstrating the specificity of duplex scanning assessment. Of the six renal arteries that were revised because of major defects detected on duplex scanning, four remained patent, one became stenotic, and one became occluded. These investigators were confident that all the major defects that they explored on the basis of intraoperative duplex scanning were significant and would have led to the failure of the revascularization, suggesting a low false-positive rate. According to this experience, renal artery procedures that show only minor defects on B-mode ultrasonography without changes on Doppler spectral analysis do not require revision.

In a similar study that used intraoperative duplex ultrasonography after 83 renal and mesenteric reconstructions, Okuhn and coworkers[73] found minor duplex scanning defects in 31% of their repairs and major defects that required re-exploration in 5% on the basis of obviously abnormal signals. They determined that intraoperative duplex scanning had a sensitivity of 85% and a specificity of 75% in the evaluation of these visceral arterial repairs. These researchers also found arteriography to be suboptimal in this location. Bandyk and colleagues[10] have reported 23 visceral or renal artery reconstructions evaluated by intraoperative duplex scanning. They found and corrected significant defects in one patient, leading to excellent graft performance.[10]

As experience with the modality grows, it appears that duplex ultrasonography has an increasing role in the evaluation of technical defects after revascularization. This is particularly true in the visceral and renal circulations, where angiography or angioscopy is frequently thwarted for technical reasons.

■ GRAFT THROMBOSIS

Despite the surgeon's best effort at achieving technical perfection, revascularizations may be unsuccessful. Depending on the type of arterial reconstruction, between 0.3% and 10% fail in the early postoperative period.[1,26,28] Detailed, long-term follow-up shows that nearly 50% of vascular reconstructions demonstrate some degree of restenosis or become occluded.[2,26,28] When thrombosis occurs, therapeutic alternatives range from expectant supportive care to thrombectomy or placement of an entirely new arterial reconstruction. The best results in these most difficult circumstances require rapid decisions by the surgeon regarding (1) the etiology of the thrombosis, (2) selection of the technique, (3) timing of the multiple possible therapies, and (4) assessment of complex patient risk factors. These circumstances are made more difficult by the fact that few vascular surgeons have current experience with the many situations possible in a failed arterial reconstruction. Since the 1960s, the results of arterial revascularizations have consistently improved, so that any individual surgeon's experience with graft thrombosis is relatively small. This discussion summarizes a reliable set of therapeutic guidelines for the most common among the possible scenarios when a patient presents with thrombosis of an arterial reconstruction.[109]

Initial Approach

The first step is to confirm graft thrombosis. It may be as easy as noting the absence of a previously palpable pulse combined with dramatic progression or return of the patient's ischemic symptoms. In less obvious circumstances, noninvasive testing to measure the ankle-brachial index (ABI) or the use of duplex ultrasonography to determine patency and the location of the occlusion or restenosis is often indicated.

Regardless of the specific circumstances of the failed revascularization, several factors that may contribute to any graft failure should be investigated. If not previously established, the patient's coagulation status should be determined. Graft thrombosis at any time after placement can be the consequence of a previously unrecognized hypercoagulable state.[32,36,71] A blood specimen should be collected and sent immediately (prior to anticoagulation) for measurement of standard coagulation parameters, including platelet count, functional activated protein C resistance, anticardiolipin antibodies, antithrombin III, and protein S. A history of previous exposure to heparin, with consequent heparin-associated antibodies causing platelet aggregation, should be investigated. Less likely causes of hypercoagulability leading to thrombosis, such as increased blood viscosity from dehydration, polycythemia, or sepsis, can easily be diagnosed with physical examination and routine hematologic screening. Acute or chronic cardiac decompensation is an uncommon but real cause of arterial revascularization failure; these conditions can be rapidly detected at the time of patient presentation with electrocardiography or echocardiography as indicated. A rapid cardiac assessment in the patient is also critical in assessing the risk associated with the various possible therapeutic options.

Once the diagnosis of graft thrombosis has been confirmed, the surgeon must attempt to minimize clot propagation with systemic anticoagulation. A short wait until blood has been collected for these hypercoagulability studies is permissible. If regional anesthesia is preferred for a surgical attempt at graft salvage, systemic anticoagulation can be delayed until anesthesia is obtained. If immediate operation is not required or regional anesthesia is contraindicated, systemic heparin anticoagulation should be instituted to inhibit further thrombosis.

A primary determinant of the necessity for, and urgency of, aggressive intervention is the patient's neurologic status at the time of graft occlusion. As the level of neurologic dysfunction increases from dysesthesia to paralysis, the impetus for rapid resolution of the situation grows. Consequently, the time available for lengthy diagnostic or therapeutic measures outside the operating room decreases correspondingly. Considerable clinical judgment is required in these cases because delay in treatment may precipitate irreversible tissue injury. If there is no neurologic compromise and the tissue ischemia appears minimal, diagnostic or therapeutic maneuvers such as thrombolysis, which may take considerable time to succeed, can be considered. However, secondary patency after treatment of infrainguinal graft thrombosis is generally poor. If an ulcer or an amputation has healed, or if claudication was the operative indication, repeat revascularization may not be required.

Etiology

The first element fundamental to achieving successful therapy of a failed revascularization is accurate determination of the cause of the thrombosis. Time from the initial revascularization to patient presentation is the single most important characteristic aiding in the determination of the etiology of graft failure (Fig. 65-6). Early (<30 days) thromboses of vascular reconstructions are usually attributed to technical errors. As already mentioned, however, the incidence of technical errors as a cause of early failure has significantly dropped over the past 30 years. Technical errors now cause 20% or less of the arterial reconstruction thromboses in the early postoperative period. Other likely causes are thrombogenicity of the graft conduit, patient-related hypercoagulable states, and poor selection of the artery targeted for distributing the runoff from the graft.

In a review of 45 primary infrainguinal vein grafts placed for critical ischemia, Rzucidlo and colleagues[85] found the rate of graft failure within 12 months to be 44%. A closer examination of this group demonstrated that 87% of the patients had only one-vessel runoff. Nine bypasses (20%) were performed to arteries that required thrombectomy before bypass, did not admit a 1-mm dilator, or were isolated to the leg with only discontinuous tarsal or plantar arteries at completion arteriography. Fourteen vein conduits (31%) were considered "disadvantaged" because of syncytia, selective segments, or the requirement for venovenostomy, vein patch angioplasty, or prosthetic interposition. Only two bypasses were found to have retained valve leaflets, which were considered to be the technical errors responsible for graft failure (10% of the graft failures).

Sauvage and coworkers[89] suggested that there is a critical minimum threshold velocity for sustaining early graft patency. This threshold velocity is a function of the inflow,

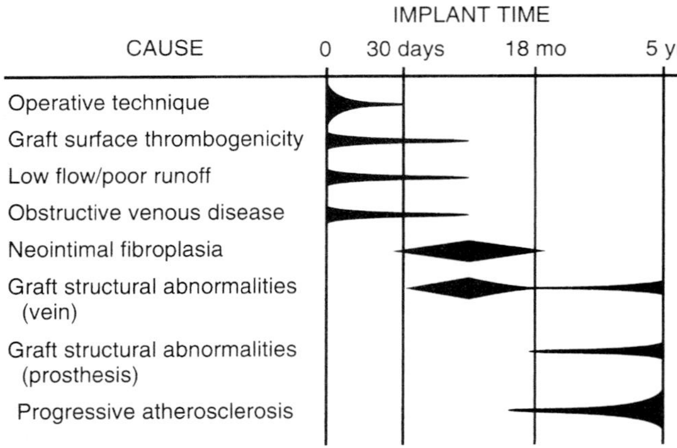

FIGURE 65-6 Factors contributing to graft occlusion with time. (Modified from Rutherford RB: The prevention and management of graft thrombosis. In Kempczinski RF [ed]: The Ischemic Leg. Chicago, Year Book Medical, 1985.)

the bypass conduit, and the condition of the runoff bed. Another method of determining the cause of an unsuccessful arterial revascularization is to examine each of the elements required for effective function of any arterial reconstruction. There are five critical elements for function of any revascularization:

- Inflow
- Outflow
- Conduit
- Technique
- Patient's coagulation function

For any revascularization to function, blood pressure and blood flow at the origin of the reconstruction must be the same as the systemic parameters. A gradient between the proximal reconstruction and the central systemic arterial pressure demonstrates the existence of a significant proximal arterial stenosis. No revascularization can long succeed with a compromised inflow.

The quality of outflow for a revascularization can be extremely difficult to characterize. For instance, the carotid artery circulation is a very low-resistance, high-flow runoff bed. For the lower extremity however, runoff beds may be composed of only a few small vessels that seem, at arteriography, too sparse to support long-term graft function (Fig. 65-7). No arteriographic criteria have been found to be reliable predictors of graft patency. In the limb shown in Figure 65-7, the runoff bed is based on the lateral plantar artery. This graft has been patent for more than 5 years. Measurement of outflow bed resistance also has been predictive of graft failure.[7] However, most surgeons find these methods cumbersome and lacking in the level of accuracy needed for confident recommendation that a revascularization attempt be changed to a primary amputation.

A pressure gradient measured at the distal end of the arterial reconstruction is evidence of a significant abnormality within the reconstruction that will likely cause early graft thrombosis.[91] When decreased pressure is noted at the distal end of a reconstruction, the cause of the decreased pressure must be identified and rectified if long-term patency is to be maximized.

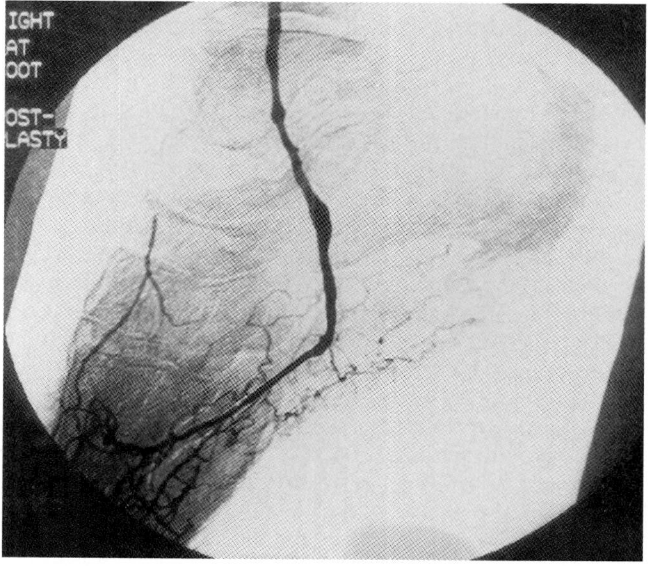

FIGURE 65-7 Intraoperative completion arteriogram demonstrating sparse runoff from a lateral plantar artery.

When considering timing of occurrence of failed arterial revascularizations, most surgeons use two temporal categories, early (within 30 days of placement) and late (after 30 days). This discussion focuses on infrainguinal revascularizations, which form the largest single group of revascularizations that fail and confront the surgeon with a multitude of therapeutic options.

Lower Extremity Bypass Failure

Early Graft Failure (0 to 30 days)

Despite improvement in infrainguinal vein graft revascularization techniques, 5% to 10% of grafts fail within 30 days of placement.[26] The response to early graft failure begins in the latter stages of the initial revascularization. As described earlier, technical adequacy of the bypass must be confirmed before the incision is closed. When the techniques described here are used to confirm technical adequacy at bypass completion, the likelihood that a technical flaw has caused graft failure is low.

In a 1990 review of our institutional experience, my colleagues and I[108] found that technical errors accounted for 25% of early graft failures. Since that time, the number of graft failures in our series caused by errors in technique has declined sharply (10%).[109] We attribute this improvement to our increasing use of angioscopy, duplex scanning, and DSA to confirm the technical adequacy of our revascularizations. This confirmation also allows a prospective, qualitative determination of the likelihood that graft failure will occur and a recognition that if a failure does occur, it is most likely related to the conduit or the quality of the runoff bed. This evaluation greatly simplifies further therapeutic decision-making. If a graft fails that was constructed using the only available autogenous vein conduit and the only possible target runoff vessel and that showed no evidence of anastomosis or a conduit problem at the time of placement, early amputation usually speeds the patient toward the best available outcome. In such a patient, further attempts at thrombectomy, anastomosis improvement, conduit replacement, or runoff substitution are only likely to increase morbidity, mortality, and expense, with little improvement in the chance for limb salvage.[83]

Thus, when graft thrombosis is initially recognized, the first question is, "Can the graft be salvaged?" Because this first bypass probably employed the most appropriate conduit and target vessel, most surgeons would answer, "Yes." Once it has been determined to proceed with attempted salvage of the initial bypass graft, the surgeon must elect either surgical thrombectomy or thrombolysis. The choice of technique is difficult because the results of either are discouraging in the early postoperative period irrespective of the type of conduit used or the procedure performed.

After thrombolysis is attempted in the early postoperative period, patency of thrombosed vein grafts ranges between 15% and 20% at 1 year.[15,67,68] In one series, 3% of patients died, 14% suffered bleeding complications requiring transfusion, and 13% had thromboembolic complications. However, 75% of the limbs had been salvaged at 1 year. Results with thrombolysis of prosthetic grafts are slightly better, although this difference is likely related to the better runoff that usually exists when prosthetic graft material is employed as the conduit for an initial bypass attempt.[81] Time since initial vein graft placement has been found to be predictive of both short-term and long-term graft patency after thrombolysis.[94] The more recently placed the graft, the smaller the chance of success with thrombolytic therapy, particularly among patients with diabetes. In our series, no patient with diabetes and a recently placed graft achieved reasonable secondary graft patency with thrombolysis.[67] Of our patients successfully treated with thrombolysis, 44% required early amputation. In those in whom thrombolysis failed, the amputation rate rose to 69%.

The results of surgical thrombectomy, even with an adjunctive procedure such as patch angioplasty of the distal anastomosis, are also relatively disappointing. Among 36 vein bypasses in which patency was re-established by thrombectomy within 1 month of surgery, graft stenoses occurred in 39% within 1 month of thrombectomy. The stenosis is likely due to rapid degeneration of normal cellular function in a thrombosed vein wall.[52] Late bypass revisions were performed in 35% of grafts, although the patency rate at 1 year was only 38%.[72] Robinson and associates[83] reported a cumulative secondary patency rate of 47% at 1 year. In this series, 26% of the patients required amputation within 1 month of graft thrombectomy, and 41% by 1 year. The results of surgical thrombectomy significantly improved if, at exploration, technical problems (e.g., a twist in the graft or a retained valve cusp in an in-situ saphenous vein bypass graft) were identified. In our own experience, the long-term graft patency rate for grafts in which thrombosis occurred because of correctable technical problems approached that for grafts with no complications in the postoperative period.

As mentioned, however, the rate at which technical flaws account for graft failures has decreased dramatically with improved techniques of graft placement.[83] This observation is even more true with respect to bypass grafts performed with prosthetic materials. Our own bias is that surgical thrombectomy of these grafts is technically straightforward and significantly less time-consuming and, thus, less expensive than thrombolysis. At the time of graft thrombectomy, pressure measurements at the inflow and outflow sites as well as proximal and distal arteriography can be performed in order to evaluate the cause of graft failure. Reparative procedures can be undertaken at that time to correct the cause of the graft failure.

Our own practice has been to immediately perform re-exploration in any patient whose graft has failed soon after initial revascularization if we expect good graft function, no matter which conduit has been used. We have not found thrombolysis useful in this setting because of the time required, the additional risk of bleeding during the procedure, and its poor long-term results. In such patients, thrombectomy, anticoagulation, and repair of any possible technical problems appear to achieve the best results.[62,84,88] In at least 50% of patients whose grafts undergo re-exploration for early failure, no cause of the thrombosis is found.[101] In these desperate circumstances, when a correctable problem has not been found and poor conduit or disadvantaged runoff does not appear to be the cause of thrombosis, we have placed a 20-gauge polyethylene catheter in a convenient proximal side-branch of the vein graft after thrombectomy. Through this catheter, nitroglycerin (0.05 μg/min) and heparin (10 units/min) are infused while the patient is held in the postanesthesia recovery unit or the intensive care unit. This measure is an attempt to counteract presumed but undocumented thrombogenicity within the revascularization, whether it is related to runoff spasm or to graft harvest trauma. The catheter is usually removed at the bedside or in the operating room after 24 to 36 hours of infusion. We have reported that 8 of 10 grafts so treated remained patent over a mean follow-up of 17 months.[108]

If all measures of diagnosis and salvage of a thrombosed infrainguinal graft fail in the early postoperative period, only two options remain. The first is expectant therapy combined with anticoagulation. This often leads to amputation, although limb loss is not inevitable.[82,103] If autogenous vein remains in adequate length, particularly with target vessels of good quality, a second bypass procedure using the best available autogenous vein often yields satisfying results.[27]

Late Graft Failure

When a graft has failed more than 1 month after placement, all of the aforementioned general considerations for evaluation and patient therapy continue to apply. The major differences in treatment strategy are (1) the disappearance of technical error from the list of potential causes of graft failure, (2) the better results of thrombolysis, and (3) the greater difficulty of the surgical dissection of previously operated vessels. Time from graft placement is a strong predictor of success of thrombolysis of thrombosed vein grafts. The longer a graft has been in place, the greater the likelihood that graft patency will improve with intra-arterial thrombolysis. Factors critical in predicting success appear to be graft age of approximately 1 year or older (since time of placement) and the absence of diabetes. In the Dartmouth-Hitchcock Medical Center series, in which thrombolysis was successful in 15 failed grafts in patients with diabetes, only 1 graft (7%) was patent 1 year after thrombolysis. In patients without diabetes whose grafts had been patent for at least 12 months prior to thrombosis, 44% of patients were alive with a patent graft 2 years after thrombolysis.

Once patency has been restored, all series reporting bypass graft salvage demonstrate that the requirement for further endovascular or surgical therapy exceeds 85%. Available therapeutic options are (1) balloon angioplasty of intragraft or juxta-anastomosis stenoses, (2) open vein patch angioplasty, and (3) interposition vein bypass. Although the results of these techniques when used to maintain patency of threatened grafts (so-called primary assisted patency) are not comparable to results obtained in failed grafts patent after thrombolysis, experience in the former "threatened" group is much larger and provides a significant body of data from which useful direction can be drawn.

In a series reported by Sanchez and colleagues,[87] patency after surgical treatment of vein graft lesions was achieved in 86% of grafts after 21 months of follow-up; the patency rate for lesions treated with percutaneous angioplasty was 42%. This difference is particularly noteworthy, because the surgical group, according to the researchers, suffered from more extensive disease than the patients treated percutaneously; however, other groups have reported significantly better results for angioplasty of graft stenoses.[48] Excellent results using either technique have been published. My personal bias is that percutaneous transluminal angioplasty is best used to maintain graft patency until operative repair can be undertaken, to treat straightforward, short stenoses that are difficult to approach surgically, or to dilate critical stenoses in patients with medical contraindications to anesthesia or surgery. In the patient whose prosthetic bypass graft has failed because atherosclerotic disease has developed distal to the graft in the popliteal artery, tibioperoneal trunk, or tibial runoff vessels, percutaneous treatment with angioplasty of these lesions is justified only when there are no reasonable surgical altematives.[44,100]

Selection of patch angioplasty versus interposition graft for repair of a vein graft lesion discovered after thrombolysis should best be made according to (1) lesion location and appearance, (2) availability of usable autogenous vein, and (3) the surgeon's preference. A detailed review of an experience using both techniques demonstrates that results are similar.[104] Our experience suggests that removal of the hyperplastic intimal lesion vein and replacement with a vein interposition graft should lead to better results. However, the two additional anastomoses within the graft carry their own potential complications. For juxta-anastomotic problems in the distal graft, exposure of the distal target artery beyond the initial anastomosis is technically simpler and results in less morbidity than reoperation at the initial anastomotic site. This option is possible only if a suitable length of autogenous vein adequate for bypass graft extension is available.

The optimal autogenous vein conduit for replacement of a short segment of vein graft is a segment of remaining ipsilateral saphenous vein or lesser saphenous vein. Interposition of a segment of contralateral greater saphenous or arm vein as a short interposition graft segment should be avoided so as to preserve these longer conduits for other uses. In patients with older grafts that have manifested diffuse deterioration after successful thrombolysis and in patients who have diabetes or whose grafts have failed in less than 1 year after implantation, we would forgo thrombolysis because of the small likelihood of achieving any significant secondary graft patency. Among these patients, a repeat bypass has the greatest chance of achieving successful long-term revascularization. Of course, good-quality distal target vessels and adequate autogenous vein conduit are mandatory if another bypass is to be most successful.

Figure 65-8 compares long-term graft patency achieved by all techniques of graft salvage, from repeated bypass and graft revision to thrombolysis under the best-case scenario. Despite the obvious benefit of repeat bypass in this comparison, it is important to remember that these patient groups are only superficially comparable. In the reports from which these data were taken, conduit availability, condition of runoff, coagulation status, and other important circumstances are either not comparable or are not known. For example, in our own patients with failed vein grafts undergoing thrombolysis, a repeat bypass was possible in only 1 of 44 patients. This fact emphasizes the complexity of these cases and the importance of understanding the condition of all five elements needed for successful bypass at the time of initial bypass completion as well as at the time of thrombosis.

Conduit availability and selection constitute another example of the complexity of the decision-making involved when a vein graft has failed. Contralateral greater saphenous vein has long been thought to be the optimal conduit for bypass when the ipsilateral greater saphenous vein is not available because of disease or prior use. Concern that the donor leg might require bypass in the future or that the saphenous vein might be needed for coronary artery bypass has been outweighed by the immediate need and the belief that the shortened survival of the patient with such problems make the necessity of future bypass elsewhere unlikely. However, examination of the infrainguinal bypass experience at Dartmouth-Hitchcock Medical Center showed that 20% of our patients required contralateral lower extremity revascularization at a mean of 31 months after initial ipsilateral bypass.[105] The intervention rate in our patients, as calculated by life-table analysis, was relatively linear at 6% per year. Of these interventions, 83% were contralateral infrainguinal vein bypasses. Factors at the time of initial ipsilateral revascularization that predicted the need for intervention were (1) younger age, (2) presence of diabetes, (3) overt coronary artery disease, and (4) lower contralateral ankle-brachial index.

In our series of patients with only unilateral lower extremity atherosclerosis severe enough to require operation, the likelihood of future contralateral intervention was less than 10% during the following 5 years. Thus, the contralateral saphenous vein, the optimal bypass conduit, should be used to revascularize the leg in older patients with

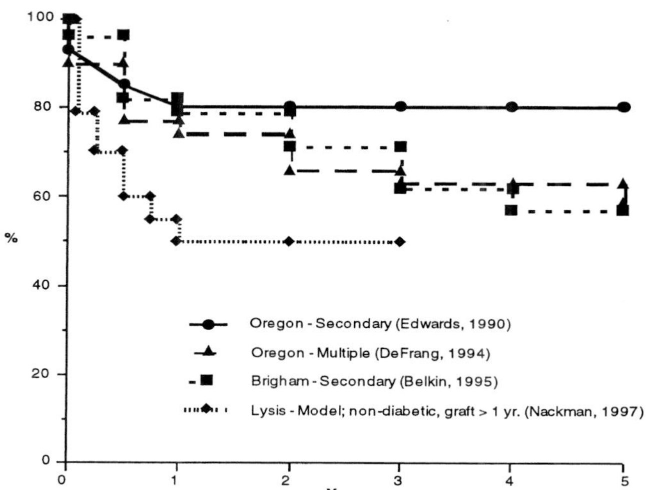

FIGURE 65-8 Comparison of long-term patency rates for secondary bypass, initial bypass salvage vein surgery, and thrombolysis among the patient groups with the best results. (From Walsh DB: Management of the thrombosed infrainguinal vein graft. In Whittemore AD, Bandyk D, Cronenwett J, et al [eds]: Advances in Vascular Surgery, vol 6. Chicago, Mosby Year Book, 1998, p 181.)

atherosclerosis isolated to one limb. In this patient group, the surgeon can proceed, confident that the requirement for the use of this vein elsewhere is very unlikely. Unfortunately, only 8% of patients who typically require infrainguinal revascularization have only isolated unilateral lower extremity atherosclerosis. In actuality, 32% of our patients undergoing infrainguinal bypass had both diabetes and coronary artery disease. Of these patients, 31% required intervention for ischemia of the contralateral leg within 5 years of the initial infrainguinal revascularization. Of our patients, 22% had diabetes, coronary artery disease, and low ankle-brachial index in the contralateral leg, and half of these patients required later contralateral intervention, during follow-up.

Therefore, we believe that the selection of a bypass conduit, when ipsilateral greater saphenous vein is not available, is complex. Arm vein, deemed acceptable on preoperative duplex evaluation and intraoperative angioscopic examination, is our conduit of choice for secondary bypass or repeat bypass. Although the need for graft revision is greater for bypass grafts using the arm vein as a conduit, the primary assisted patency rate is 72% over 5 years.[42] We believe that vein grafts spliced together from the lesser saphenous vein and the remaining ipsilateral saphenous vein have a patency rate equivalent to that of the arm vein but carry the added morbidity of distal incisions in a currently ischemic, previously operated limb. Use of the arm vein as a conduit also minimizes the number of venovenostomies. Utilization of the profunda femoris artery and endarterectomy of the superficial femoral artery to lessen the conduit length required for bypass are also preferred techniques. Others advocate a repeat infragenicular bypass using a cadaver vein, a prosthetic conduit with a distal vein cuff or an arteriovenous fistula, or use of a prosthetic conduit alone.[6,35,76,78] We use these techniques rarely and only as last resorts. Despite optimistic reports of others, our results in these cases have not been comparable to those of repeat bypass using autogenous vein.

Failure of Cerebrovascular or Abdominal Revascularization

As in the circumstance of a failed lower extremity bypass, failure in the early postoperative period after carotid endarterectomy or after revascularization within the abdominal circulation is usually signified by acute ischemia of the perfused organ bed and requires immediate return of the patient to the operating room for revascularization to avoid catastrophic ischemic damage to the target organ. All of the strategies previously discussed regarding the confirmation of technical adequacy and the response to graft failure apply. Only if there is no demonstrable ischemic damage to the organ targeted for revascularization should nonoperative expectant therapy be employed.

When late failure of a cerebrovascular or abdominal revascularization has occurred, the standard tenets of surgical therapy apply. Optimal methods of surveillance and response to recurrent stenosis or thrombosis of the primary revascularization are also discussed in other chapters. Thus, if the revascularization fails and the organ is ischemic, one should consider a second revascularization; if there is no ischemic injury to the target organ, one can consider expectant therapy.

■ SUMMARY

The best results in managing failed arterial revascularizations are achieved by instituting protocols that maximize prevention. The first step toward prevention is discovery and correction of any problems at the initial revascularization. It is achieved through (1) rigorous assessment of each revascularization by measurement of inflow pressure, (2) direct inspection of the revascularization as well as its inflow and outflow, and (3) performance of intraoperative technical assessments to evaluate the technical function of each revascularization as well as its outflow bed. At the conclusion of each procedure, the surgeon should honestly assess the likely long-term patency of the revascularization. Re-explorations can be avoided with the recognition that technical errors are unlikely if techniques for confirming the adequacy of the revascularization are used.

Unexpected early failure of surgical revascularization warrants screening for hypercoagulable states and immediate surgical re-exploration with thorough evaluation of inflow, outflow, and the conduit. Aggressive follow-up of these grafts can detect patency-threatening lesions prior to thrombosis, maximizing long-term graft function. Patients in whom revascularizations fail in the month after initial operation should be evaluated for the potential benefits of thrombolysis or surgery to re-establish flow in the revascularization. Critical factors in treatment planning include the availability of autogenous vein for the conduit and the quality of potential distal arterial targets. Patient factors, such as age, diabetes, age of the graft, and presence and severity of coronary artery disease, significantly affect the selection of salvage techniques. Vascular surgeons should be familiar with the techniques available for maintaining the long-term function of each revascularization they perform and with techniques that can restore perfusion in a severely ischemic target organ. Vascular surgeons are the last hope for preventing permanent ischemic damage in most patients who suffer from severe disseminated atherosclerosis.

■ REFERENCES

1. AbuRhama AF, Khan JH, Robinson PA, et al: Prospective randomized trial of carotid endarterectomy with primary closure and patch angioplasty with saphenous vein, jugular vein, and polytetrafluoroethylene: Perioperative (30-day) results. J Vasc Surg 24:998, 1996.
2. AbuRhama AF, Robinson PA, Saiedy S, et al: Prospective randomized trial of carotid endarterectomy with primary closure and patch angioplasty with saphenous vein, jugular vein, and polytetrafluoroethylene: Long-term follow-up. J Vasc Surg 27:222, 1998.
3. Ackerstaff RCA, Moons KGM, van de Vlasakker CJW, et al: Association for intraoperative transcranial Doppler monitoring variables with stroke from carotid endarterectomy. Stroke 31:1817, 2000.
4. Ackerstaff RGA, Jansen C, Moll FL, et al: The significance of microemboli detection by means of transcranial Doppler ultrasonography monitoring in carotid endarterectomy. J Vasc Surg 21:963, 1995.
5. Archie JP: The endarterectomy-produced common carotid artery step: A harbinger of early emboli and late stenosis. J Vasc Surg 23:932, 1996.

6. Ascer E, Gennaro U, Pollina RM, et al: Complementary distal arteriovenous fistula and deep vein interposition: A five-year experience with a new technique to improve infrapopliteal bypass patency. J Vasc Surg 24:134, 1996.
7. Ascer E, Veith FJ, Morin L, et al: Components of outflow resistance and their correlation with graft patency in lower extremity arterial reconstructions. J Vasc Surg 1:817, 1984.
8. Bandyk DF, Johnson BL, Gupta AK, et al: Nature and management of duplex abnormalities encountered during infrainguinal vein bypass grafting. J Vasc Surg 24:430, 1996.
9. Bandyk DF, Kaebnick HW, Adams MB, et al: Turbulence occurring after carotid bifurcation endarterectomy: A harbinger of residual and recurrent carotid stenosis. J Vasc Surg 7:261, 1988.
10. Bandyk DF, Mills JL, Gahtan V, et al: Intraoperative duplex scanning of arterial reconstructions: Fate of repaired and unrepaired defects. J Vasc Surg 20:426, 1994.
11. Bandyk DF, Zierler RE, Thiele BL: Detection of technical error during arterial surgery by pulsed Doppler spectral analysis. Arch Surg 119:421, 1984.
12. Barnes RW, Nix ML, Nichols BT, et al: Recurrent versus residual carotid stenosis: Incidence detected by Doppler ultrasound. Ann Surg 203:652, 1986.
13. Baxter BT, Rizzo RJ, Flinn WR, et al: A comparative study of intraoperative angioscopy and completion arteriography following femorodistal bypass. Arch Surg 125:997, 1990.
14. Beard JD, Scott DJA, Skidmore R, et al: Operative assessment of femorodistal bypass grafts using a new Doppler flowmeter. Br J Surg 76:925, 1989.
15. Berkowitz HD, Kee JC: Occluded infrainguinal grafts: When to choose lytic therapy versus a new bypass graft. Am J Surg 170:136, 1995.
16. Blankensteijn JD, Gertler JD, Brewster DC, et al: Intraoperative determinants of infrainguinal bypass graft patency: A prospective study. Eur J Vasc Endovasc Surg 9:375, 1995.
17. Bredenberg CE, Iannettoni M, Rosenbloom M, et al: Operative angiography by intraarterial digital subtraction angiography: A new technique for quality control of carotid endarterectomy. J Vasc Surg 9:530, 1989.
18. Chalmers RT, Synn AY, Hoballah JJ, et al: Is the use of intraoperative post-reconstruction angiography following in situ saphenous vein bypass redundant? Am J Surg 166:141, 1993.
19. Coelho JCU, Sigel B, Flanigan DP, et al: An experimental evaluation of arteriography and imaging ultrasonography in detecting arterial defects at operation. J Surg Res 32:130, 1982.
20. Courbier R, Jausseran JM, Reggi M: Detecting complications of direct arterial surgery: The role of intraoperative arteriography. Arch Surg 112:1115, 1977.
21. Courbier R, Jausseran JM, Reggi M, et al: Routine intraoperative carotid angiography: Its impact on operative morbidity and carotid restenosis. J Vasc Surg 3:343, 1986.
22. Cronenwett JL, Walsh DB, Garrett HE: Tibial artery pseudoaneurysms: Delayed complication of balloon catheter embolectomy. J Vasc Surg 8:483, 1988.
23. Cull DL, Gregory RT, Wheeler JR, et al: Duplex scanning for the intraoperative assessment of infrainguinal arterial reconstruction: A useful tool? Ann Vasc Surg 6:20, 1992.
24. Cuming R, Blair SD, Powell JT, et al: The use of duplex scanning to diagnose perioperative carotid occlusions. Eur J Vasc Endovasc Surg 8:143, 1994.
25. Dalman RL, Harris EJ, Zarins CK: Is completion arteriography mandatory after reversed-vein bypass grafting? J Vasc Surg 23:637, 1996.
26. Darling RC 3rd, Chang BB, Shah DM, et al: Choice of peroneal or dorsalis pedis artery bypass for limb salvage. Semin Vasc Surg 10:17, 1997.
27. DeFrang RD, Edwards JM, Moneta GL, et al: Repeat leg bypass after multiple prior bypass failures. J Vasc Surg 19:268, 1994.
28. Desiron Q, Detry O, Van Damme H, et al: Comparison of results of carotid artery surgery after either direct closure or use of a vein patch. Cardiovasc Surg 5:295, 1997.
29. Diethrich EB: Endovascular treatment of abdominal aortic occlusive disease: The impact of stents and intravascular ultrasound imaging. Eur J Vasc Surg 7:228, 1993.
30. Dilly RB, Bernstein EF: A comparison of B-mode real-time imaging and arteriography in the intraoperative assessment of carotid endarterectomy. J Vasc Surg 4:457, 1986.
31. DiMario C, The SH, Madretsma S, et al: Detection and characterization of vascular lesions by intravascular ultrasound: An in vitro study correlated with histology. J Am Soc Echocardiogr 5:135, 1992.
32. Donaldson MC, Belkin M, Whittemore AD, et al: Impact of activated protein C resistance on general vascular surgical patients. J Vasc Surg 25:1054, 1997.
33. Donaldson MC, Ivarsson BL, Mannick JA, et al: Impact of completion angiography on operative conduct and results of carotid endarterectomy. Ann Surg 217:682, 1993.
34. Dorffner R, Metz VM, Trattnig S, et al: Intraoperative and early postoperative colour Doppler sonography after carotid artery reconstruction: Follow-up of technical defects. Neuroradiology 39:117, 1997.
35. Farber A, Major K, Wagner WH, et al: Cryopreserved saphenous vein allografts in infrainguinal revascularization: Analysis of 240 grafts. J Vasc Surg 38:15, 2003.
36. Fisher CM, Twe K, Appleberg M: Prevalence and outcome of activated protein C resistance in patients after peripheral arterial bypass grafts. Cardiovasc Surg 7:519, 1999.
37. Flanigan DP, Douglas DL, Machi J, et al: Intraoperative ultrasonic imaging of the carotid artery during carotid endarterectomy. Surgery 100:893, 1986.
38. Frawley JE, Hicks RG, Woodforth NJ: Risk factors for perioperative stroke complicating carotid endarterectomy: Selective analysis of a prospective audit of 1000 consecutive operations. Aust N Z J Surg 70:52, 2000.
39. Gao MY, Sillesen H, Lonentzen JE, et al: Eversion carotid endarterectomy generates fewer microemboli than standard carotid endarterectomy. Eur J Vasc Endovasc Surg 20:153, 2000.
40. Gaunt ME, Smith JL, Ratliff DA, et al: A comparison of quality control methods applied to carotid endarterectomy. Eur J Vasc Endovasc Surg 11:4, 1996.
41. Gaunt ME: Transcranial Doppler: Presenting stroke during carotid endarterectomy. Ann R Coll Surg Engl 80:377, 1998.
42. Gentile AT, Lee RW, Moneta GL, et al: Results of bypass to the popliteal and tibial arteries with alternative sources of autogenous vein. J Vasc Surg 23:272, 1996.
43. Gilbertson JJ, Walsh DB, Zwolak RM, et al: A blinded comparison of angiography, angioscopy, and duplex scanning in the intraoperative evaluation of in situ saphenous vein bypass grafts. J Vasc Surg 15:121, 1992.
44. Gray B, Olin J: Limitations of percutaneous transluminal angioplasty with stenting for femoropopliteal arterial disease. Semin Vasc Surg 10:8, 1997.
45. Grundfest WS, Litvack F, Glick D, et al: Intraoperative decisions based on angioscopy in peripheral vascular surgery. Circulation 78:1, 1988.
46. Hansen KJ, O'Neil EA, Reavis SW, et al: Intraoperative duplex sonography during renal artery reconstruction. J Vasc Surg 14:364, 1991.
47. Hashizume M, Yang Y, Galt S, et al: Intimal response of saphenous vein to intraluminal trauma by simulated angioscopic insertion. J Vasc Surg 5:862, 1987.
48. Houghton AD, Todd C, Pardy B, et al: Percutaneous angioplasty for infrainguinal graft-related stenoses. Eur J Vasc Endovasc Surg 14:380, 1997.
49. Jackson MR, D'Addio VJ, Gillespie DL, et al: The fate of residual defects following carotid endarterectomy detected by early postoperative duplex ultrasound. Am J Surg 172:184,1996.

50. Jacobowitz GR, Rockman CB, Lamparello PJ, et al: Causes of perioperative stroke after carotid endarterectomy: Special considerations in symptomatic patients. Ann Vasc Surg 15:19, 2001.
51. Johnson BL, Bandyk DF, Back MR, et al: Intraoperative duplex monitoring of infrainguinal vein bypass procedures. J Vasc Surg 31:678, 2000.
52. Kawai, S, Sasajima, T, Satoh K, et al: Biologic degeneration of vein grafts after thrombotic occlusion: Thrombectomy within 3 days results in better indices of viability. J Vasc Surg 38:305, 2003.
53. Kinney EV, Seabrook GR, Kinney LY, et al: The importance of intraoperative detection of residual flow abnormalities after carotid artery endarterectomy. J Vasc Surg 17:912, 1993.
54. Kresowik TF, Hoballah JJ, Sharp WJ, et al: Intraoperative B-mode ultrasonography is a useful adjunct to peripheral arterial reconstruction. Ann Vasc Surg 7:33, 1993.
55. Lee G, Beerline D, Lee MH, et al: Hazards of angioscopic examination: Documentation of damage to the arterial intima. Am Heart J 116:1530, 1988.
56. Liebman PR, Menzoian JO, Mannick JA, et al: Intraoperative arteriography in femoropopliteal and femorotibial bypass grafts. Arch Surg 116:1019, 1981.
57. Lennard N, Smith J, Dumville J, et al. Prevention of postoperative thrombotic stroke after carotid endarterectomy: The role of transcranial Doppler ultrasound. J Vasc Surg 26:579, 1997.
58. Lipski DA, Bergamini TM, Garrison RN, et al: Intraoperative duplex scanning reduces the incidence of residual stenosis after carotid endarterectomy. J Surg Res 60:317, 1996.
59. Machi J, Sigel B, Roberts A, et al: Operative color Doppler imaging for vascular surgery. J Ultrasound Med 11:65, 1992.
60. Mackenzie KS, Hill AB, Steinmetz OK: The predictive value of intraoperative duplex for early vein graft patency in lower extremity revascularization. Ann Vasc Surg 13:275, 1999.
61. Marcaccio EJ, Miller A, Tannebaum GA, et al: Angioscopically directed interventions improve arm vein bypass grafts. J Vasc Surg 17:994, 1993.
62. McMillan WD, McCarthy WJ, Lin SJ, et al: Perioperative low molecular weight heparin for infrageniculate bypass. J Vasc Surg 25:796, 1997.
63. Mehigan JT, Olcott C IV: Video angioscopy as an alternative to intraoperative arteriography. Am J Surg 152:139, 1986.
64. Miller A, Stonebridge PA, Jepsen SJ, et al: Continued experience with intraoperative angioscopy for monitoring infrainguinal bypass grafting. Surgery 109:286, 1991.
65. Miller A, Stonebridge PA, Tsoukas AI, et al: Angioscopically directed valvulotomy: A new valvulotome and technique. J Vasc Surg 13:813, 1991.
66. Mills JL, Fujitani RM, Taylor SM: Contribution of routine intraoperative completion arteriography to early infrainguinal bypass patency. Am J Surg 164:506, 1992.
67. Nackman GB, Walsh DB, Fillinger MF, et al: Thrombolysis of occluded infrainguinal vein grafts: Predictors of outcome. J Vasc Surg 25:1023, 1997.
68. Nehler MR, Mueller RJ, McLafferty RB, et al: Outcome of catheter-directed thrombolysis for lower extremity arterial bypass occlusion. J Vasc Surg 37:72, 2003.
69. Neville RF, Hobson RW, Jamil Z, et al: Intravascular ultrasonography: Validation studies and preliminary intraoperative observations. J Vasc Surg 13:274, 1991.
70. Neville RF Jr, Yasuhara H, Watanabe BI, et al: Endovascular management of arterial intimal defects: An experimental comparison by arteriography, angioscopy, and intravascular ultrasonography. J Vasc Surg 13:496, 1991.
71. Nielsen TG, Nordestgaard BG, von Jessen F, et al: Antibodies to cardiolipin may increase the risk of failure of peripheral vein bypasses. Eur J Vasc Endovasc Surg 14:117, 1997.
72. Nielson TG, Jensen LP, Schroeder TV: Early vein bypass thrombectomy is associated with an increased risk of graft related stenoses. Eur J Vasc Endovasc Surg 13:134, 1997.
73. Okuhn SP, Reilly LM, Bennett JB III, et al: Intraoperative assessment of renal and visceral artery reconstruction: The role of duplex scanning and spectral analysis. J Vasc Surg 5:137, 1987.
74. Osman HY, Gibbons CP: Completion angioscopy following carotid endarterectomy by the eversion technique or the standard longitudinal arteriotomy with patch closure. Ann R Coll Surg Engl 83:149, 2001.
75. Papanicolaou G, Toms C, Yellin A, et al: Relationship between intraoperative color-flow duplex findings and early restenosis after carotid endarterectomy: A preliminary report. J Vasc Surg 24:588, 1996.
76. Parsons RE, Sanchez LA, Marin ML, et al: Comparison of endovascular and conventional vascular prostheses in an experimental infection model. J Vasc Surg 24:920, 1996.
77. Peterkin GA, LaMorte WW, Menzoian JO: Runoff resistance and early graft failure in infrainguinal bypass surgery. Arch Surg 123:1199, 1988.
78. Raptis S, Miller JH: Influence of a vein cuff on polytetrafluoroethylene grafts for primary femoropopliteal bypass. Br J Surg 82:487, 1995.
79. Reilly LM, Okuhn SP, Rapp JH, et al: Recurrent carotid stenosis: A consequence of local or systemic factors? The influence of unrepaired technical defects. J Vasc Surg 11:448, 1990.
80. Renwick S, Royle JP, Martin P: Operative angiography after femoropopliteal arterial reconstruction: Its influence on early failure rate. Br J Surg 55:134, 1968.
81. Rickard MJ, Fisher CM, Soong CV, et al: Limitations of intra-arterial thrombolysis. Cardiovasc Surg 5:634, 1997.
82. Rivers SP, Veith FJ, Ascer E, et al: Successful conservative therapy of severe limb-threatening ischemia: The value of nonsympathectomy. Surgery 99:759, 1986.
83. Robinson KD, Sato DT, Gregory RT, et al: Long-term outcome after early infrainguinal graft failure. J Vasc Surg 26:425, 1997.
84. Rutherford RB, Jones DN, Bergentz SE, et al: The efficacy of dextran 40 in preventing early postoperative thrombosis following difficult lower extremity bypass. J Vasc Surg 1:765, 1984.
85. Rzucidlo EM, Walsh DB, Powell RJ, et al: Prediction of early graft failure with intraoperative completion duplex ultrasound. J Vasc Surg 36:975, 2002.
86. Sales CM, Marin ML, Veith FJ, et al: Saphenous vein angioscopy: A valuable method to detect unsuspected venous disease. J Vasc Surg 18:198, 1993.
87. Sanchez LA, Suggs WD, Marin ML, et al: Is percutaneous balloon angioplasty appropriate in the treatment of graft and anastomotic lesions responsible for failing vein bypasses? Am J Surg 168:97, 1994.
88. Sarac TP, Huber TS, Back MR, et al: Warfarin improves outcome of infrainguinal vein bypass grafts at high risk failure. J Vasc Surg 28:446, 1998.
89. Sauvage LR, Berger KE, Mansfield PB, et al: Future directions in the development of arterial prostheses for small and medium caliber arteries. Surg Clin North Am 54:213, 1974.
90. Sawchuk AP, Flanigan DP, Machi J, et al: The fate of unrepaired minor technical defects by intraoperative ultrasonography during carotid endarterectomy. J Vasc Surg 9:671, 1989.
91. Schmitt DD, Seabrook GR, Bandyk DF, et al: Early patency of in situ saphenous vein bypasses as determined by intraoperative velocity waveform analysis. Ann Vasc Surg 4:270, 1990.
92. Schwartz LB, Belkin M, Donaldson MC, et al: Validation of a new and specific intraoperative measurement of vein graft resistance. J Vasc Surg 25:1033, 1997.
93. Schwartz RA, Peterson GJ, Noland KA, et al: Intraoperative duplex scanning after carotid artery reconstruction: A valuable tool. J Vasc Surg 7:620,1988.
94. Schwierz T, Gschwendtner M, Havlicek W, et al: Indications for directed thrombolysis or new bypass in treatment of occlusion of lower extremity arterial bypass reconstruction. Ann Vasc Surg 15:644, 2001.

95. Segalowitz J, Grundfest WS, Treiman RL, et al: Angioscopy for intraoperative management of thromboembolectomy. Arch Surg 125:1357, 1990.
96. Seifert KB, Blackshear WM Jr: Continuous-wave Doppler in the intraoperative assessment of carotid endarterectomy. J Vasc Surg 2:817, 1985.
97. Sheehan MK, Greisler HP, Littooy FN, et al: The effect of intraoperative duplex on the management of postoperative stroke. Surgery 132:761, 2002.
98. Siegel RJ, Ariani M, Fishbein MC, et al: Histopathologic validation of angioscopy and intravascular ultrasound. Circulation 84:109, 1991.
99. Sigel B, Coelho JCU, Flanigan DP, et al: Detection of vascular defects during operation by imaging ultrasound. Ann Surg 196:473, 1982.
100. Stanley B, Teague B, Raptis S, et al: Efficacy of balloon angioplasty of the superficial femoral artery and popliteal artery in the relief of leg ischemia. J Vasc Surg 23:679, 1996.
101. Stept LL, Flinn WR, McCarthy WJ III, et al: Technical defects as a cause of early graft failure after femorodistal bypass. Arch Surg 122:599, 1987.
102. Stonebridge PA, Miller A, Tsoukas A, et al: Angioscopy of arm vein infrainguinal bypass grafts. Ann Vasc Surg 5:170, 1991.
103. Sullivan TR Jr, Welch HJ, Iafrati MD, et al: Clinical results of common strategies used to revise infrainguinal vein grafts. J Vasc Surg 24:909, 1996.
104. Tabbara MR, Mehringer CM, Cavaye DM, et al: Sequential intraluminal ultrasound evaluation of balloon angioplasty of an iliac artery lesion. Ann Vasc Surg 6:179, 1992.
105. Tarry WC, Walsh DB, Fillinger MF, et al: The fate of the contralateral leg following infrainguinal bypass. J Vasc Surg 27:1039, 1998.
106. Troeng T, Bergqvist D, Norrving B, et al: Complications after carotid endarterectomy are related to surgical errors in less than one-fifth of cases. Eur J Vasc Endovasc Surg 18:59, 1999.
107. Walker RA, Fox AD, Magee TR, et al: Intraoperative duplex scanning as a means of quality control during carotid endarterectomy. Eur J Vasc Endovasc Surg 11:364, 1996.
108. Walsh DB, Zwolak RM, McDaniel MD, et al: Intragraft drug infusion as an adjunct to balloon catheter thrombectomy for salvage of thrombosed infragenicular vein grafts: A preliminary report. J Vasc Surg 11:753, 1990.
109. Walsh DB: Management of the thrombosed infrainguinal vein graft. In Whittemore AD, Bandyk D, Cronenwett J, et al (eds): Advances in Vascular Surgery, vol 6. Chicago, Mosby Year Book, 1998, p 181.
110. Watson HR, Schroeder TV, Simms MH, et al: Relationship of femorodistal bypass patency to clinical outcome. Eur J Vasc Endovasc Surg 17:77, 1999.
111. White GH, White RA, Kopchok GE, et al: Angioscopic thromboembolectomy: Preliminary observations with a recent technique. J Vasc Surg 7:318, 1988.
112. White GH, White RA, Kopchok GE, et al: Intraoperative video angioscopy compared with arteriography during peripheral vascular operations. J Vasc Surg 6:488, 1987.
113. Whittemore AD, Bandyk D, Cronenwett J, et al (eds): Advances in Vascular Surgery, vol 6. Chicago, Mosby-Year Book, 1998, p 181.
114. Wilson YG: Vein quality in infrainguinal revascularization assessment by angioscopy and histology. Ann R Coll Surg Engl 80:3, 1998.
115. Wolfle KD, Kugelmann U, Bruijnen H, et al: Intraoperative imaging techniques in infrainguinal arterial bypass grafting: Completion angiography versus vascular endoscopy. Eur J Vasc Endovasc Surg 8:556, 1994.
116. Wolfle KD, Bruijnen H, Moski A, et al: The importance of graft blood flow and peripheral outflow resistance for early patency in infrainguinal arterial reconstruction. Vasa 28:34, 1999.
117. Yu A, Gregory D, Morrison L, et al: The role of intraoperative duplex imaging in arterial reconstructions. Am J Surg 171:500, 1996.

Section XI

ACUTE LIMB ISCHEMIA

KENNETH OURIEL, MD, FACS, FACC

Chapter 66

Acute Limb Ischemia

KARTHIKESHWAR KASIRAJAN, MD, FACS
KENNETH OURIEL, MD, FACS, FACC

Limb ischemia occurs when an extremity is deprived of adequate blood flow. Symptoms depend on the severity of hypoperfusion. The process can develop suddenly and, when the patient presents soon after its onset, the entity is said to represent *acute limb ischemia*. Acute limb ischemia is differentiated from those patients with an insidious onset of symptoms; these patients tend to present late and the phrase *chronic limb ischemia* is used to identify such a scenario. The extent of collateral flow across the site of occlusion often determines the severity of symptoms. Patients with long-standing atherosclerotic lesions often have adequate time to develop collateral channels (Fig. 66-1); hence, arterial occlusion in these patients often may fall into the "chronic" category.

In mild cases the patient may experience symptoms only with increased muscular demand, such as occurs with ambulation—an entity known as *claudication*. Patients with symptoms of claudication alone are at low risk for amputation, even without treatment. Alternatively, when hypoperfusion is severe, inadequate oxygen delivery occurs even without activity. Such patients experience pain at rest and particularly at night, marking the onset of so-called limb-threatening symptoms, a situation associated with significant risks of limb loss and even death if the hypoperfusion progresses unchecked (Table 66-1).

The aim of this chapter is to outline the pathophysiology, diagnosis, treatment, and expected clinical outcome of patients with acute limb ischemia—defined for the purposes of discussion as ischemia of 14 days' duration or less.

■ PATHOPHYSIOLOGY

Acute limb ischemia may occur as the result of embolization or in-situ thrombosis (Table 66-2). Emboli originate from the heart in more than 90% of cases[4] and normally lodge at the site of an arterial bifurcation (Fig. 66-2) such as the distal common femoral or popliteal arteries. The decreasing prevalence of rheumatic heart disease underlies a diminishing proportion of embolic versus thrombotic causes for acute limb ischemia. When embolization occurs, it usually does so

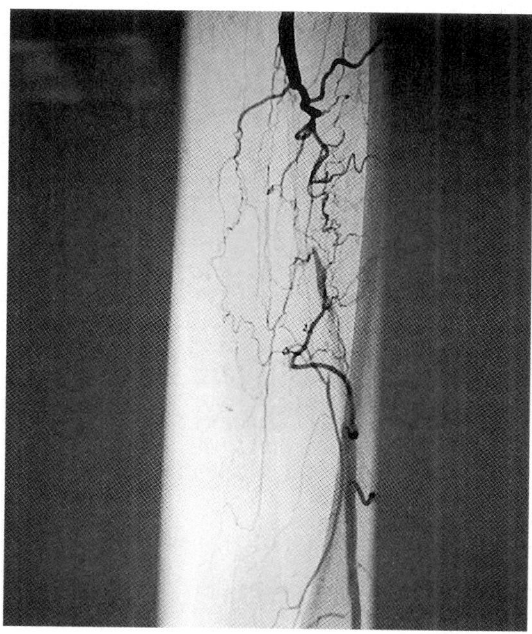

FIGURE 66-1 Chronic superficial femoral artery occlusion. Numerous collateral channels prevent the occurrence of acute ischemia despite a total occlusion.

Table 66-1 Outcome of Patients Presenting with Acute Limb Ischemia*

STUDY	YEAR PUBLISHED	SEVERITY OF ISCHEMIA†	AMPUTATION RATE, %	MORTALITY RATE, %
Blaisdell et al[24]	1978	Not specified	25	30
Jivegård et al[27]	1988	Not specified	Not specified	20
Ouriel et al (Rochester Trial)[2]	1994	Class 2b	14	18
STILE Trial[3]	1994	Classes 1, 2a, 2b	5	6
Ouriel et al (TOPAS Trial)[1]	1998	Classes 2a, 2b	2	5

*The morbidity and mortality are dependent on the severity of ischemia, with a suggestion of improved results in the more recent studies.
† See text for definitions of the class criteria.

in the setting of atrial fibrillation or acute myocardial infarction, when portions of atrial or ventricular mural thrombus detach and embolize to the arterial tree. It is often difficult to distinguish embolus from thrombosis, but embolic occlusions should be suspected in patients with the following features: (1) acute onset where the patient is often able to accurately time the moment of the event; (2) prior history of embolism; (3) known embolic source, such as cardiac arrhythmias; (4) no prior history of intermittent claudication; and (5) normal pulse and Doppler examination in the unaffected limb.

Thrombosis as an etiology for acute limb ischemia is a much more diverse category than embolization. With the increased use of peripheral arterial bypass grafts for chronic limb ischemia, and noting the finite patency rate of any bypass graft conduit, it is not surprising that acute graft occlusion is now the most frequent cause of acute lower extremity ischemia in most centers (Fig. 66-3).[1] Symptoms may be less dramatic than embolic occlusion, depending on the extent of collateral flow across the site of occlusion. In addition to the presence of collateral channels, the location of the occlusion may also play a critical role in the severity of limb ischemia. For example, occlusion of the popliteal artery results in profound limb ischemia, since it is the only artery crossing at the level of the knee (Fig. 66-4). By contrast, occlusion of the anterior tibial artery is often asymptomatic because the posterior tibial and peroneal arteries can function as alternate parallel channels to supply the foot.

Table 66-2 Classification of Acute Limb Ischemia

- Bypass graft occlusion
  - Prosthetic conduit
    - Intimal hyperplasia at the anastomoses (usually distal)
    - Occlusion without a demonstrable lesion
  - Autogenous conduit (e.g., saphenous vein graft)
    - Retained valve cusp of an in-situ graft
    - Stenosis at the site of a prior venous injury (e.g., superficial phlebitis)
- Native arterial occlusion
  - Thrombosis at the site of an atherosclerotic stenotic lesion
  - Embolism to an arterial bifurcation
  - Thrombosis within a near-normal artery, usually as the result of a hypercoagulable state
  - Arterial inflammatory diseases such as giant cell arteritis (Takayasu's aortitis)
  - Thrombosis of an aneurysm (e.g., popliteal aneurysm)
  - Rare etiologies (e.g., popliteal entrapment syndrome, adventitial cystic disease of the popliteal artery)

Irrespective of the etiology of ischemia, the end result is the build-up of toxic byproducts within the ischemic tissue bed. These toxins include the free radicals, which are oxygen-derived, chemically reactive molecules that are responsible for the injury that occurs after ischemia and reperfusion. Ischemia induces leakage of protein and fluid from the capillary bed, resulting in tissue edema.[5] Hydrodynamic pressure in the extravascular space rises to a level that competes with venous outflow, perpetuating a vicious cycle that can eventually impede arterial inflow. At first, this process occurs at a microscopic level, but it may progress to the development of high tissue pressures at a regional level and the clinical entity known as the *compartment syndrome*. The development of a compartment syndrome is hastened by the abrupt reperfusion of a previously ischemic tissue bed, a phenomenon that explains the relatively frequent need for fasciotomy after lower extremity surgical revascularization for severe limb ischemia.[6]

■ DIAGNOSIS

Acute limb ischemia is a clinical diagnosis. Patients complain of numbness and pain in the extremity, progressing in severe cases to motor loss and muscle rigidity. Examination

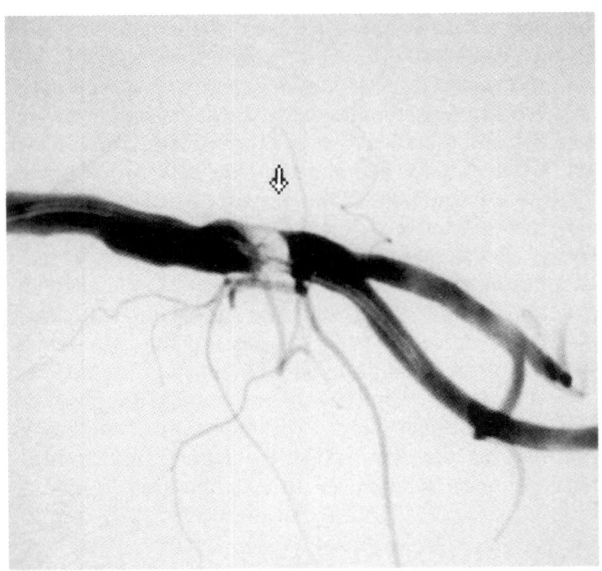

FIGURE 66-2 Embolic occlusion of the axillary artery. Note the typical site of embolic occlusion at branch points and the "meniscus" (*arrow*) seen with the embolic occlusion on the diagnostic angiogram.

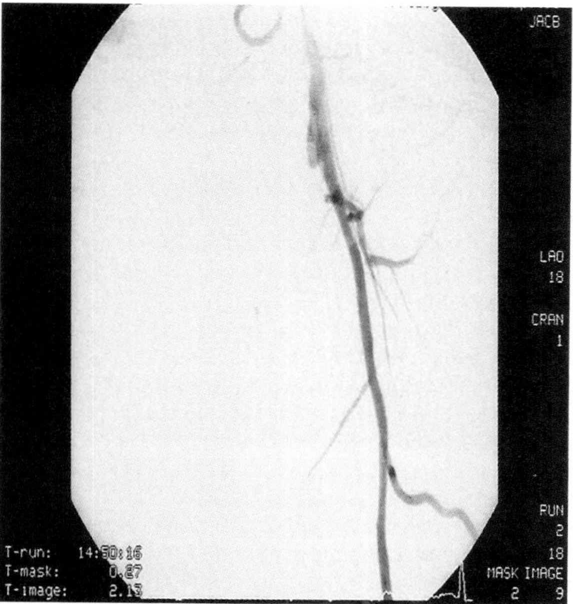

FIGURE 66-3 Stump of a thrombosed femoropopliteal bypass graft.

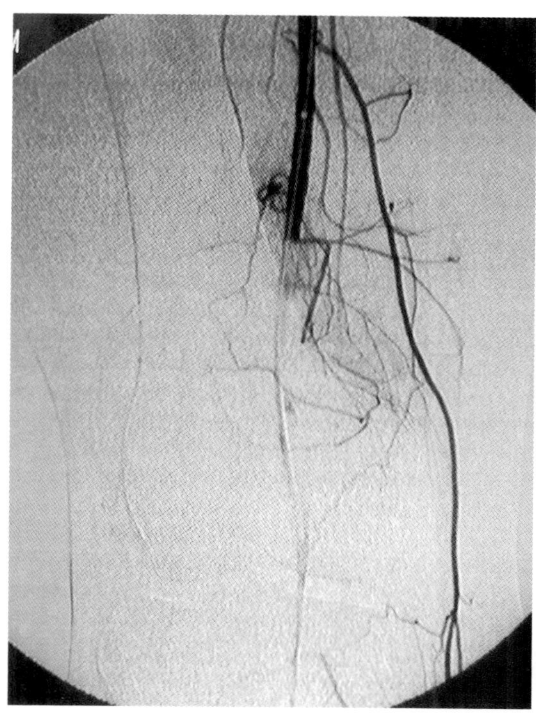

FIGURE 66-4 Acute in-situ thrombotic occlusion of the popliteal artery. Note the absence of significant collateral channels. The patient had no Doppler pedal signals.

reveals the absence of palpable pulses, and the location of the pulse deficit allows one to predict the site of arterial occlusion. The "5 Ps" have been used as a mnemonic to remember the presentation of a patient with acute limb ischemia—*p*aresthesia, *p*ain, *p*allor, *p*ulselessness, and *p*aralysis. In some cases, a sixth P is added—*p*oikilothermia, meaning equilibration of the temperature of the limb to that of the ambient environment (coolness). The process is sometimes confused with deep venous thrombosis by an inexperienced observer. Although a deep venous thrombosis may manifest as limb ischemia when severe (phlegmasia cerulea dolens), profound lower extremity edema is uncommon in pure arterial ischemia. Occasionally, a patient with arterial ischemia and pain at rest keeps the extremity in a dependent position and edema may develop; such a scenario may be apparent if an adequate history is obtained (Fig. 66-5). Pain may either be constant or elicited by passive movement of the involved extremity. History should include a description of the duration, location, intensity, and suddenness of the onset of pain and change over time. Embolic occlusions are usually quite sudden and of great intensity, such that patients often present within a few hours of onset. The past history should state whether or not the patient has a history of intermittent claudication, previous leg bypass or other vascular procedures, and history suggestive of embolic sources such as cardiac arrhythmias and aortic aneurysms. General atherosclerotic risk factors (smoking, hypertension, diabetes, hyperlipidemia, family history of cardiac or vascular events) should be recorded because these can be predictors of periprocedural mortality.

In an effort to classify the extent of acute ischemia for standardization reporting of outcome, the Society for Vascular Surgery/International Society for Cardiovascular Surgery (SVS/ISCVS) (now SVS) ad hoc committee was established and published what has now come to be known as the *Rutherford criteria*, after Dr. Robert Rutherford, the lead author of the article.[7] The following three classes were defined:

- Class 1: the limb is viable and remains so even without therapeutic intervention.
- Class 2: the limbs are threatened and require revascularization for salvage.
- Class 3: those limbs that are irreversibly ischemic and infarction has developed such that salvage is not possible.

The initial work of the reporting standards committee was revised several years later, dividing the middle category into

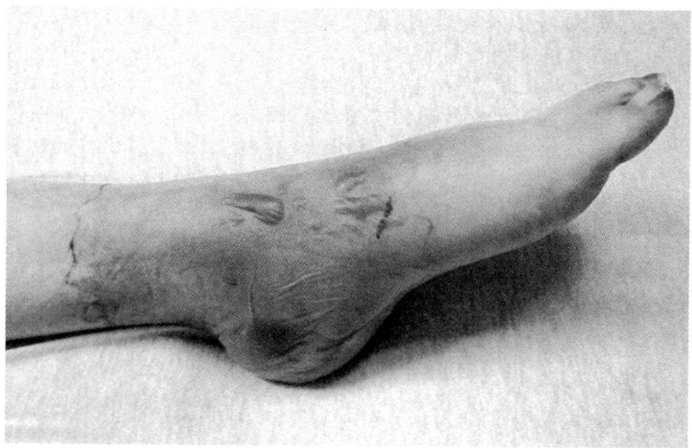

FIGURE 66-5 Dependent edema and ischemic blisters seen in a patient with acute limb ischemia.

two subclassifications: class 2A for limbs that are not immediately threatened and class 2B for those limbs that are severely threatened to the point where urgent revascularization is necessary for salvage.[8]

As examples, a patient with a palpable femoral pulse but an absent popliteal pulse is likely to have a superficial femoral artery occlusion. Absence of a femoral pulse signifies disease above the inguinal ligament, within the iliac arterial segment or the aorta itself. Patients with common femoral artery emboli maintain an easily palpable femoral pulse, sometimes even augmented with a "water-hammer" characteristic, until such time as the absence of outflow in the external iliac artery causes this vessel to thrombose and the femoral pulse to disappear. Patients with popliteal emboli, by contrast, usually have a palpable popliteal pulse but no palpable pulses below (dorsalis pedis or posterior tibial). Finally, a patient with leg ischemia secondary to a popliteal aneurysm usually demonstrates a very large and easily palpable popliteal pulse, concurrent with severe calf and foot ischemia. The popliteal pulse is maintained in these patients as a result of the events leading to occlusion—the aneurysm is associated with serial embolic events to the three crural vessels, occluding them one by one until, at the time of the last occlusion, the leg becomes ischemic. The aneurysm itself, however, remains palpable owing to the somewhat static column of blood and absent outflow.

Even the most astute clinician sometimes has difficulty in discerning his or her own digital pulse from the patient's pedal pulse. For this reason, the use of a Doppler instrument is advantageous to document flow within the smaller arteries and, most important, to provide an objective and quantitative assessment of the extent of arterial insufficiency through the calculation of a Doppler-derived ankle-brachial index (ABI) (Table 66-3). Normally, the ABI is greater than 1.0.[9] The index is decreased to 0.40 to 0.80 in patients with claudication and to lower levels in patients with pain at rest or tissue loss. The ABI may be normal in some patients with mild arterial narrowing; treadmill exercise has been used in these cases to increase the sensitivity of the test.[10] Patients with diabetes mellitus or renal failure may have calcific lower leg arteries, rendering them incompressible and causing a falsely elevated ABI; in these cases a toe-brachial pressure index can be measured and is more predictive of significant arterial disease.[11] In some centers, transcutaneous oxygen tension has also been used to assess the severity of peripheral arterial occlusion[12] as well as to predict the most appropriate level of amputation.

The anatomic level of the arterial stenoses can be predicted from palpation of pulses in the femoral, popliteal, and ankle regions. For example, patients with disease confined to the superficial femoral artery have a normal femoral pulse but no palpable popliteal or ankle pulses below, whereas patients with aortoiliac disease have absent femoral pulses as well. Doppler segmental pressures are also useful in defining the level of involvement; a drop in pressure of 30 mm Hg or more between two segments predicts arterial occlusion between the two levels.[13] For example, a superficial femoral arterial occlusion would be suggested in a patient with a systolic pressure of 120 mm Hg at the proximal thigh pressure cuff and 90 mm Hg at the above-knee cuff.

Contrast arteriography remains the gold standard with which all other tests must be compared. Even today, standard arteriography is the most accurate test for all but the occasional patient with such slow flow in the tibial or foot vessels that digital subtraction imaging fails to demonstrate a patent artery. Arteriography is, however, a semi-invasive modality, and as such its use should be confined to those patients for whom a surgical or percutaneous intervention is contemplated. Patients with borderline renal function may experience contrast-induced nephrotoxicity, and in this subgroup the use of alternate contrast agents such as gadolinium and carbon dioxide have been employed.[14,15]

Duplex ultrasound has been used in some centers to define the anatomic extent of peripheral arterial disease.[16] Although duplex has been useful in documenting the patency of a single arterial segment such as a stented superficial femoral artery or a bypass graft, evaluation of the entire lower extremity arterial tree remains imprecise, and its adequacy as the sole diagnostic modality for planning a percutaneous or open surgical intervention remains controversial. Magnetic resonance (MR) angiography is being used with greater frequency in patients with peripheral arterial disease.[17] Using gadolinium as an MR contrast agent, the specificity and sensitivity of the test exceed that of duplex ultrasonography and approach the accuracy of standard arteriography. MR angiography has been effective in demonstrating patent tibial arteries undetected with less sensitive conventional arteriography, identifying potential target vessels for an otherwise unfeasible lower extremity reconstructive bypass procedure. Today, MR angiography is widely employed in patients with chronic renal insufficiency to limit the dye load. Another noninvasive imaging modality, computed tomographic (CT) angiography, is gaining appeal as a means of delineating anatomy to provide a means of localizing the extent and severity of occlusive disease.[18] With future improvements in hardware and software technology, it is likely that MR and CT angiography will effectively replace conventional diagnostic arteriography, and arterial cannulation will be reserved solely for percutaneous interventional therapies.

Table 66-3 Characteristic Ankle-Brachial Indices in Patients Presenting with Lower Limb Ischemia

CLINICAL CATEGORY	ANKLE-BRACHIAL INDEX
Normal	>0.97 (usually 1.10)
Claudication	0.40-0.80
Rest pain	0.20-0.40
Ulceration, gangrene	0.10-0.40
Acute ischemia	Usually <0.10

■ TREATMENT

Unlike the situation in patients with chronic limb ischemia where observation alone is a common and quite appropriate treatment option, patients presenting with acute limb ischemia often require revascularization to salvage the leg. In fact, this is why they present acutely and are often able to identify the precise time of the occlusive event, similar to the manner that a patient with a perforated peptic ulcer knows exactly when it occurred. In many cases, the paucity of preexisting collateral channels renders the limb very ischemic after thrombotic or embolic occlusion of the main arterial segment. Symptoms occur with severity and rapidity, forcing the patient to seek treatment almost immediately.

Once the diagnosis is made, adequate systemic anticoagulation is instituted. A bolus of unfractionated heparin is standard, followed by a continuous infusion to maintain the activated partial thromboplastin time (aPTT) in a therapeutic range. The goal of anticoagulation is twofold: (1) to decrease the risk of thrombus propagation and (2) in the case of presumed embolic occlusion, to prevent recurrent embolization. Occasionally, if early angiographic evaluation is feasible, heparinization can be withheld, pending the establishment of arterial access. Otherwise, a micropuncture technique (small localizing needle [21 gauge], guide wire [0.018 inch], and a 4-French sheath) is used to gain access or the anticoagulation is withheld to allow the aPTT to fall to within 1.5 times control.

The severity of the ischemic limb based on the earlier-mentioned Rutherford classification dictates the extent of diagnostic tests performed for systemic risk factor assessment. Routine blood studies and coagulation tests should be drawn before heparin is administered. Correction of underlying electrolyte imbalances and systemic anticoagulation should proceed concomitant with the other investigations. A plain chest radiograph and electrocardiogram should be obtained in every patient. In patients with suspected embolism, an echocardiogram should be obtained as soon as time allows. Despite the desire for a complete workup, the treatment of an ischemic limb must take priority over other more complex and time-consuming investigations.

Unfortunately, the threat is not only to the limb, but these patients are also at a high risk for death. Limb hypoperfusion results in systemic acid-base and electrolyte abnormalities that impair cardiopulmonary and renal function. Successful reperfusion may result in the release of highly toxic free radicals further compromising these critically ill patients. Therapeutic choices are often few, and patient expectations are not always realistic. The management of acute limb ischemia requires a thorough understanding of the anatomy of the arterial occlusion and the open surgical and percutaneous options for restoring limb perfusion.

There exist several basic therapeutic options to pursue in patients with acute limb ischemia (Fig. 66-6).

1. The first option is anticoagulation alone. If the ischemia is nonthreatening (e.g., Rutherford class 1 or 2A), such a nonaggressive course may be appropriate. Angiographic evaluation and elective revascularization may then be undertaken after the patient has been fully prepared and other co-morbidities such as concurrent coronary artery disease have been addressed.
2. Patients who present with more severe ischemia (Rutherford class 2B) require some form of intervention to prevent progression to irreversible ischemia and limb loss. These patients should undergo early angiographic evaluation with adequate imaging of the affected and the unaffected extremity. Arterial access is accomplished at a site distant from the ischemic extremity using a contralateral femoral artery or brachial approach to avoid the creation of needle entry sites in an artery that might subsequently be infused with a thrombolytic agent.

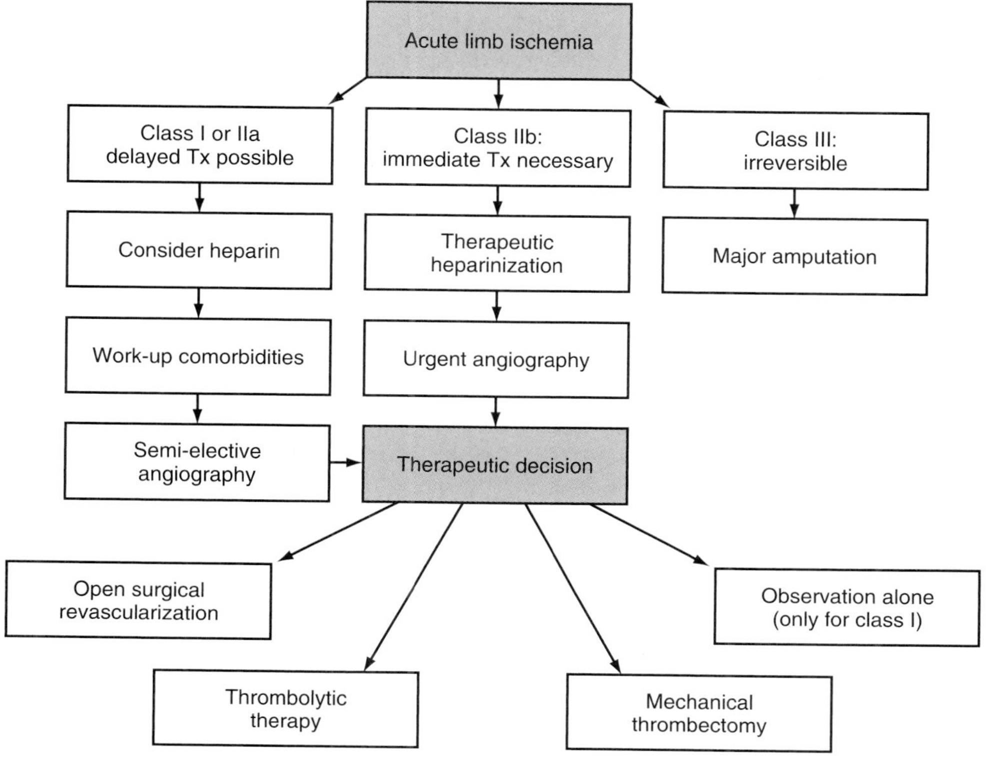

FIGURE 66-6 Algorithm for management of patients with acute limb ischemia. Tx, treatment.

Early angiographic imaging should be undertaken in all patients, with the sole exception of those patients with common femoral emboli. These individuals can be taken directly to the operating room for embolectomy, but intraoperative completion angiography is necessary to rule out retained thromboembolic material.[19]

Once adequate diagnostic information has been obtained from the angiogram, the clinician is in a position to make a decision on whether to pursue a percutaneous or open surgical option.

- Thrombolytic therapy: Thrombolytic therapy with the plasminogen activators (urokinase, alteplase, or reteplase) has been demonstrated to lower the morbidity and mortality when compared with a traditional approach of immediate operative revascularization.[2,3] These benefits appear to be especially prominent in patients with medical co-morbidities when early revascularization is necessary. The complication rate is high when such patients are taken urgently to open surgical revascularization without the ability to adequately prepare the patient for operation.
- Mechanical thrombectomy: Removal of intra-arterial thrombus with a mechanical device has gained popularity over the last several years.[20,21] Some devices rely on hydrodynamic, rheolytic forces to extract the thrombus, whereas others use rotating components to fragment the clot. Mechanical thrombectomy devices can be used in conjunction with pharmacologic thrombolysis. Although the devices do result in clearing of much of the occluding thrombus, an infusion of thrombolytic agent is still necessary in many cases to remove smaller amounts of retained mural clot.
- Immediate open surgical revascularization: Early operation has been remarkably effective in restoring adequate blood flow to an ischemic extremity. The relatively simple procedure of balloon catheter thromboembolectomy, however, has fallen into disfavor for all but embolic occlusions. The underlying lesion responsible for the thrombotic event must be identified and corrected to avoid early reocclusion. For this reason, long atherosclerotic occlusions are best treated with the placement of a bypass graft.[22] As well, patients with occlusion of a bypass graft as the cause of ischemia are best served with the placement of a new bypass graft, if at all possible.[23]

Open Surgical Revascularization

Unfortunately, immediate open surgical interventions have been associated with an unexpectedly high risk of major morbidity and mortality. Blaisdell and associates first reported this finding, noting a 30% perioperative mortality rate in a review of more than 3000 patients in the published works from the 1960s and 1970s.[24] Although the results have improved since the publication of Blaisdell's landmark review, mortality rates continue to remain undesirably high.[25] This observation appears to relate to the relatively common occurrence of cardiopulmonary complications developing in these medically compromised patients, patients who are ill prepared to undergo early operative intervention.[2] The severity of ischemia precludes adequate preoperative preparation of the patient, and complications such as perioperative myocardial infarction, cardiac arrhythmia, or pneumonia appear to underlie the unacceptable mortality rate in these patients. Additionally, wound complications (Fig. 66-7) and delayed healing are common in these patients. Hence, despite successful limb salvage, patient dissatisfaction is frequent.

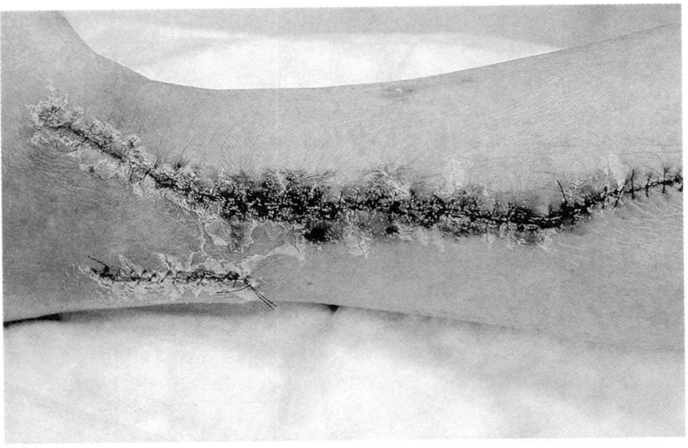

FIGURE 66-7 Skin edge necrosis in a patient with open surgical revascularization for acute limb ischemia.

The mortality rate from open surgical treatment of acute limb ischemia has been reconfirmed in numerous studies published after Blaisdell's landmark series. Dale reviewed cases of nontraumatic extremity ischemia and observed an 11% mortality rate in those with embolism, versus 3% in those with acute thromboses.[26] Several years later, Jivegård and colleagues documented a mortality rate of 20% in patients presenting with acute arterial embolism or thrombosis, a finding that was explained by preexisting cardiac disease in these patients.[27] A study by Edwards and colleagues[23] reported a 1-year mortality rate of 38% in patients undergoing the placement of new autogenous vein grafts for treatment of failed prior grafts in the same leg, with an amputation rate of 6% over the same time frame.

Pharmacologic Thrombolytic Therapy

Noting the high morbidity from primary open surgical revascularization in patients suffering from true limb-threatening lower limb ischemia, three randomized, prospective clinical trials were organized to compare thrombolytic therapy and immediate open surgical revascularization. The first study, the Rochester series, compared urokinase to primary operation in a single-center experience of 114 patients presenting with what has subsequently been called *hyperacute ischemia*.[2] Patients enrolled in this trial all had severely threatened limbs (Rutherford class 2b) with mean symptom duration of approximately 2 days. After 1 year of follow-up, 84% of patients randomized to urokinase were alive compared with only 58% of patients randomized to primary operation (Fig. 66-8). By contrast, the rate of limb salvage was identical at 80% in the two groups. A closer inspection of the data revealed that the defining variable for mortality differences was the development of cardiopulmonary complications during the periprocedural period. The rate of long-term mortality was high when such

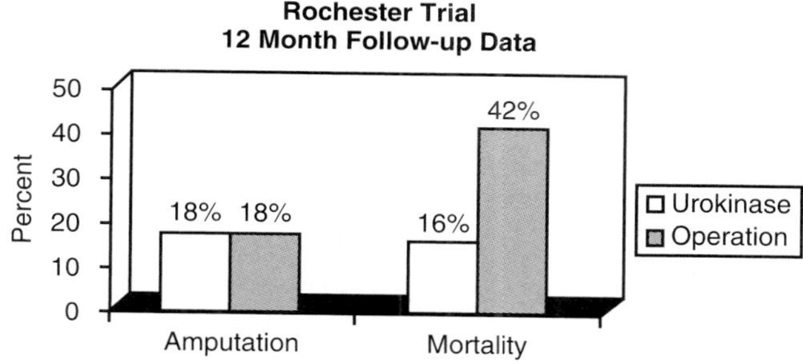

FIGURE 66-8 The rate of amputation was identical in the two treatment groups in the Rochester Trial,[2] but the mortality rate was significantly lower in patients assigned to the thrombolytic arm.

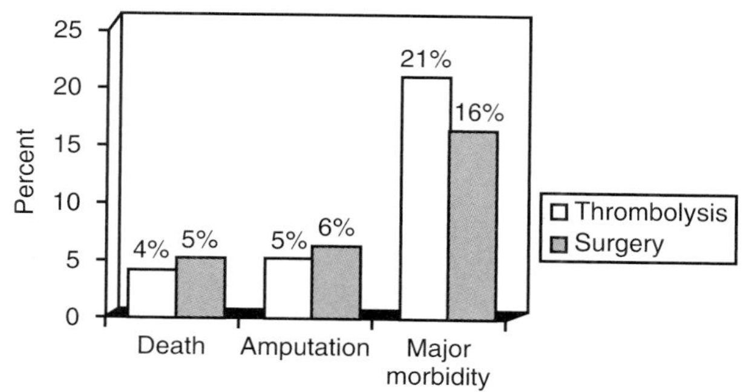

FIGURE 66-9 Outcome measures from the STILE data after 30 days of follow-up.[3] The rates of death and amputation are similar.

periprocedural complications occurred but was relatively low when they did not occur. It was only the fact that such complications occurred more commonly in patients taken directly to operation that explained the greater long-term mortality rate in the surgical group.

The second prospective, randomized analysis of thrombolysis versus surgery was the Surgery or Thrombolysis for the Ischemic Lower Extremity (STILE) trial.[3] Genentech, the manufacturer of the Activase brand of recombinant tissue plasminogen activator (rt-PA), funded the study. At its termination, 393 patients were randomized to one of three treatment groups: rt-PA, urokinase, or primary operation. Subsequently, the two thrombolytic groups were combined for purposes of data analysis when the outcome was found to be similar. Although the rate of the composite endpoint of untoward events was higher in the thrombolytic patients, the rates of the more relevant and objective endpoints of amputation and death were equivalent (Fig. 66-9). Subsequently, two subgroup analyses of the STILE data were published, one relating to native artery occlusions[28] and one to bypass graft occlusions.[29] Thrombolysis appeared more effective in patients with graft occlusions. The rate of major amputation was higher in native arterial occlusions treated with thrombolysis (10% thrombolysis vs. 0% surgery at 1 year). By contrast, amputation was lower in patients with acute graft occlusions treated with thrombolysis. These data suggest that thrombolysis may be of greatest benefit in patients with acute bypass graft occlusions of less than 14 days.

The third and final randomized comparison of thrombolysis and surgery was the Thrombolysis or Peripheral Arterial Surgery (TOPAS) trial, funded by Abbott Laboratories. Following completion of a preliminary dose-ranging trial in 213 patients,[30] 544 patients were randomized to a recombinant form of urokinase or primary operative intervention.[1] After a mean follow-up period of 1 year, the rate of amputation-free survival was similar in the two treatment groups: 68% and 69% in the urokinase and surgical patients, respectively (Table 66-4). Although this trial failed to document improvement in survival or limb salvage with

Table 66-4 Results in the TOPAS Trial[1] of Recombinant Urokinase Versus Surgery for Acute Peripheral Arterial Occlusion

INTERVENTION OR OUTCOME	UROKINASE GROUP (*N* = 272) 6 Months	UROKINASE GROUP (*N* = 272) 1 Year	SURGERY GROUP (*N* = 272) 6 Months	SURGERY GROUP (*N* = 272) 1 Year
Operative Intervention, No.				
Amputation	48	58	41	51
Above the knee	22	25	19	26
Below the knee	26	33	22	25
Open surgical procedures	315	351	551	590
Major	102	116	177	193
Moderate	89	98	136	145
Minor	124	137	238	252
Percutaneous procedures	128	135	55	70
Worst Outcome, % of Patients*				
Death	16.0	20.0	12.3	17.0
Amputation	12.2	15.0	12.9	13.1
Above the knee	5.6	6.5	6.1	7.5
Below the knee	6.6	8.5	6.8	5.6
Open surgical procedures	40.3	39.3	69.0	65.4
Major	23.6	24.3	39.3	39.3
Moderate	10.3	8.7	16.3	13.4
Minor	6.4	6.3	13.4	12.7
Endovascular procedures	16.9	15.4	2.1	1.7
Medical treatment alone	14.6	10.3	3.7	2.8

*Worst outcome is the most severe event that occurred over the specified time period.

Table 66-5 Results of Pharmacologic Thrombolysis Compared with Open Surgical Revascularization

	THROMBOLYSIS, %		OPERATION, %	
TRIAL	**Amputation**	**Death**	**Amputation**	**Death**
Rochester	18	16	18	42
STILE	12	6.5	11	8.5
TOPAS II	15	20	13.1	17

thrombolysis, fully 32% of the thrombolytic patients were alive without amputation with nothing more than a percutaneous procedure after 6 months of follow-up. After 1 year, this number had decreased only slightly, with 26% alive, without amputation, and with only percutaneous interventions. The original goal of the TOPAS trial, to generate data on which regulatory approval of recombinant urokinase would be based, was not achieved. Nevertheless, the findings confirmed that acute limb ischemia could be managed with catheter-directed thrombolysis, achieving similar amputation and mortality rates but avoiding the need for open surgical procedures in a significant percentage of patients.

Because the major thrombolytic trials failed to demonstrate an improved outcome for percutaneous thrombolysis compared to open surgery (Table 66-5), clinical consensus was never achieved. Physicians continue to offer patients therapy based on their field of expertise and patient symptoms. Future advances have been redirected toward decreasing the dose and duration of thrombolytic agents to decrease the complications and mortality associated with the bleeding complications. It is hoped that by minimizing or eliminating the bleeding risks of thrombolytic therapy, this form of minimally invasive percutaneous procedure would demonstrate superior outcomes compared with open surgical revascularization. In this setting, the use of mechanical thrombectomy devices as an adjunct to pharmacologic thrombolytic therapy is gaining popularity.

Percutaneous Mechanical Thrombectomy Devices

Numerous percutaneous mechanical thrombectomy (PMT) devices are currently available in the United States for dialysis graft declotting; however, only two devices are approved for infrainguinal arterial use in the United States. Lists of various PMT devices are given in Table 66-6. Many of the devices are currently in an investigational phase, with minimal preclinical and clinical data. The devices may be classified into "aspiration" or "microfragmentation-only" devices. The latter embolize the microfragments that are created by the mechanical component of the device. Many of these devices were designed primarily for dialysis graft declotting, where embolization is not seen as a device limitation. However, when used for peripheral arterial occlusion, the risk of downstream embolization is clinically significant. A few of the PMT devices also function as "wall-contact" types. For example, there is the Arrow-Trerotola device, with a potential for significant endothelial damage that limits its use to synthetic dialysis graft declotting.

Table 66-6 Percutaneous Mechanical Thrombectomy Devices

PRODUCT NAME	MANUFACTURER, CITY AND STATE
Aspiration Devices	
AngioJet*	Possis Medical, Minneapolis, MN
Trellis*	Bacchus Vascular, Santa Clara, CA
Fino	Bacchus Vascular, Santa Clara, CA
Solera	Bacchus Vascular, Santa Clara, CA
Rescue	Boston Scientific, Watertown, MA
Oasis	Boston Scientific, Watertown, MA
Hydrolyser	Cordis Endovascular, Miami, FL
Gelbfish EndoVac	NeoVascular Technologies, Brooklyn, NY
Thrombex PMT System	Edwards Life Sciences, Irvine, CA
The Cleaner	Rex Medical/Boston Scientific, Watertown, MA
Xtrak Thrombectomy Device	Xtrak Medical, Salem, NH
Rotarex	Straub Medical, Wangs, Switzerland
X-Sizer	EndiCOR Medical, San Clemente, CA
Microfragmentation Devices	
Arrow-Trerotola	Arrow International, Reading, PA
Amplatz Clot Buster	Microvena, White Bear Lake, MN
Cragg brush	Micro Therapeutics, Aliso Viego, CA
Castaneda brush	Micro Therapeutics, Aliso Viego, CA
Ultrasound Devices	
Acolysis	Angiosonics, Morrisville, NC
Resolution 360 therapeutic wire	Omnisonics, Wilmington, MA

*Approved for infrainguinal vascular application in the United States.

The potential benefits of these devices include the minimally invasive nature of the procedure, rapid blood flow restoration, and a decrease in the dose and duration of adjunctive pharmacologic thrombolytic agents. The two devices approved for peripheral vascular application are described in the following sections.

AngioJet System The AngioJet system consists of three major components: the catheter, the pump set, and the drive unit (Fig. 66-10). The pump set and the drive unit are responsible for producing a controlled high-velocity saline jet (350 to 450 km/hr) that is redirected at the tip of a dual-lumen catheter back into the effluent lumen of the catheter. The inflow lumen is a low-profile stainless-steel tube that forms a transverse loop at the distal end of the catheter and has multiple small orifices (25 to 50 μm diameter each) directed retrograde toward the inflow lumen. Saline solution from the pump drive unit is driven at 50 to 60 mL/min at 8000 to 10,000 psi resulting in a high velocity at the catheter tip. The high velocity of the saline jets produces an area of extremely low pressure (Venturi effect) that is exposed to the intra-arterial lumen at the tip of the catheter. Thrombus surrounding the catheter tip is fragmented (99.8% < 100 μm)[31] and rapidly evacuated through the effluent lumen. Since it is concerned with thrombus, the actual mechanical force of the saline does not produce removal, but by an indirectly created negative pressure zone (–760 mm Hg), luminal endothelial damage is minimal.[32,33] The peripheral catheter is referred to as the *Xpeedior*, and it employs a cross-stream technology that results in greater

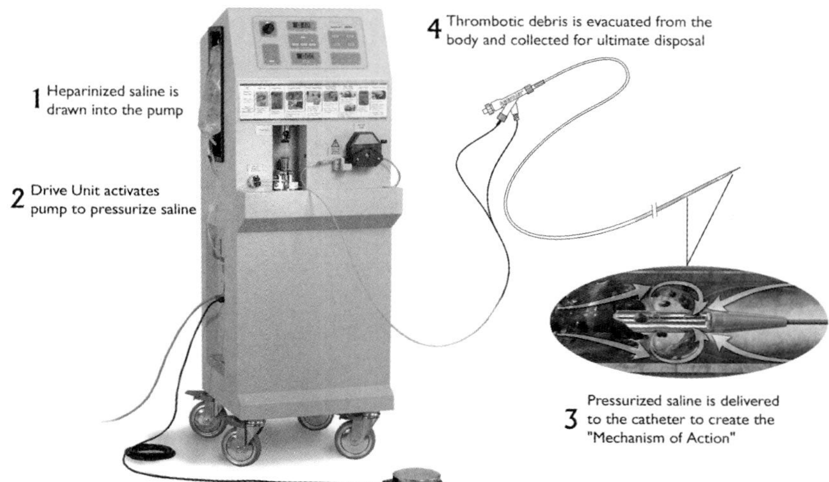
4 Thrombotic debris is evacuated from the body and collected for ultimate disposal
1 Heparinized saline is drawn into the pump
2 Drive Unit activates pump to pressurize saline
3 Pressurized saline is delivered to the catheter to create the "Mechanism of Action"

FIGURE 66-10 AngioJet pump drive, catheter, and evacuation setup. (Courtesy, Possis Medical, Minneapolis, Minn)

thrombus extraction. The Xpeedior catheter can be passed through a 6-French sheath and is compatible with a 0.035-inch guide wire.

Kasirajan and coworkers[33] noted a higher incidence of distal embolization when the Xpeedior catheter was used as a stand-alone therapy. The incidence of distal embolization was significantly decreased when the AngioJet catheter was used after an initial period of thrombolytic therapy lasting about 8 hours (Fig. 66-11). Clinical trial data evaluating the use of the AngioJet catheter for acute limb ischemia are given in Table 66-7. Overall, the mortality of using the AngioJet with adjunctive pharmacologic thrombolysis was about 10%. However, no comparative study evaluating the use of PMT devices with open surgical revascularization is currently available.

These authors evaluated patients with acute limb-threatening ischemia of less than 14 days identified from a prospectively maintained computer registry at the Cleveland Clinic Foundation.[33] The endovascular group had 65 consecutive patients treated with the AngioJet as a stand-alone ($n = 21$) or with subsequent adjunctive pharmacologic thrombolysis ($n = 44$). This group was retrospectively

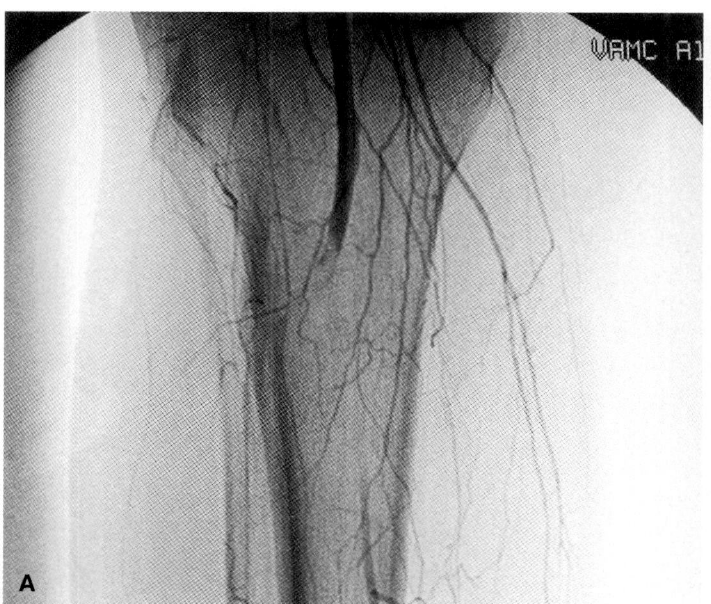
VAMC A1
A

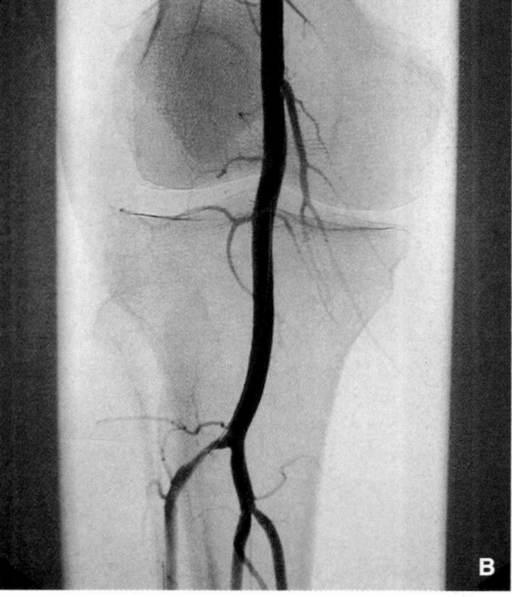
B

FIGURE 66-11 **A,** Acute in-situ thrombotic occlusion of the popliteal artery. **B,** Following an 8-hour infusion of urokinase followed by AngioJet thrombectomy, the patient had complete resolution of the thrombotic occlusion.

Table 66-7 Outcome of Clinical Trials with Use of the AngioJet Catheter for Acute Limb Ischemia

AUTHORS	*n*	CONDUIT, NO. (%)	NO. (%) SUCCESS	ADJUNCTIVE LYSIS, NO. (%)	COMPLICATIONS (%)	PRIMARY PATENCY (%)
Müller-Hülsbeck et al[34]	112	Native, 99 (86) Grafts, 16 (14)	80 (71)	20 (17.9)	Embolization (9.8) Dissection (8) Perforation (3.6) Amputation (1.8) Mortality (7)	6 mo (68) 2 yr (60) 3 yr (58)
Silva et al[35]	22	Native, 13 (59) Grafts, 9 (41)	21 (95)	None	Hemorrhage (10) Embolism (9) Dissection (5) Occlusion (18) Amputation (5) Mortality (14)	Not applicable
Wagner et al[36]	50	Native, 39 (78) Grafts, 11 (22)	26 (52)	15 (30)	Hemorrhage (6) Emboli (6) Dissection (6) Perforation (4) Amputation (8) Mortality (0)	1 yr (69)
Kasirajan et al[20]	86	Native, 52 (63) Graft, 31 (37)	70 (84)	50 (58)	Hemorrhage (3.5) Embolism (2.3) Dissection (3.5) Perforation (2.3) Amputation (11.6) Mortality (9.3)	6 mo (79)

compared to 79 consecutive patients having undergone open surgical revascularization. The major clinical endpoints evaluated included death, major amputation, major morbidity, primary patency, and 12-month amputation-free survival. Only values with a standard error of less than 10% are reported.

There was a greater incidence of hypertension ($P <$ 0.001) in the AngioJet group; however, a greater proportion of patients in the open surgery group had cardiac risk factors ($P = 0.036$). The mean preprocedural ABI was similar in both groups (AngioJet, 0.16; open surgery, 0.17; $P = 0.51$) with a comparable rise in post-treatment ABI ($P = 0.50$). Most of the occlusions were greater than 10 cm in length (AngioJet, 68%; open surgery, 89%). Native vessel occlusions were more common in both groups (AngioJet, 55%; open surgery, 71%; $P = 0.06$), primarily resulting from in-situ thrombotic occlusions (AngioJet, 77%; open surgery, 82%; $P = 0.43$). No difference was noted in the 1-month amputation rate (11% vs. 14%; $P = 0.57$); however, a reduction in the rate of early mortality (1 month) was observed in the AngioJet treatment group (7.7% vs. 22%; $P = 0.037$). A lower event rate for local ($P = 0.002$) and systemic ($P < 0.001$) complications was observed for the AngioJet treatment group. The 4-month primary patency rate was 77.8% (95% confidence interval [CI], 62% to 94%) for AngioJet treatment group compared to 67% (95% CI, 55% to 79%) for open surgery treatment group ($P = 0.017$). The 12-month amputation-free survival was 77% (95% CI, 65% to 89%) for AngioJet treatment group and 61% (95% CI, 50% to 73%) for the open surgery treatment group ($P = 0.07$).

The 6-month survival benefit seen in the AngioJet treatment group (PMT, 88%; open surgery, 75%; $P = 0.02$), was primarily related to lower in-hospital mortality rates. The high in-hospital mortality rates among the open surgery group (AngioJet, 8%; open surgery, 22%) reflect the magnitude of the operative procedures required in this group of medically compromised patients. Overall, the results of this retrospective study favor the use of the AngioJet with adjunctive thrombolytic therapy as a first-line therapy in patients with acute limb-threatening ischemia.

Trellis System The Trellis drug dispersion and thrombectomy catheter is a 6-French coaxial system that can be passed over a 0.035-inch guidewire. The proximal portion of the device, which remains outside the patient, has five separate entry ports (Fig. 66-12). Two of these ports are used to inflate the compliant balloons located at either end of the infusion and dispersion segment. The balloons can be

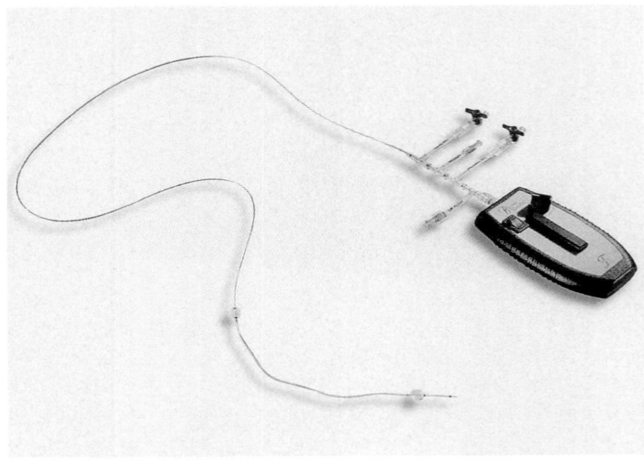

FIGURE 66-12 The Trellis device.

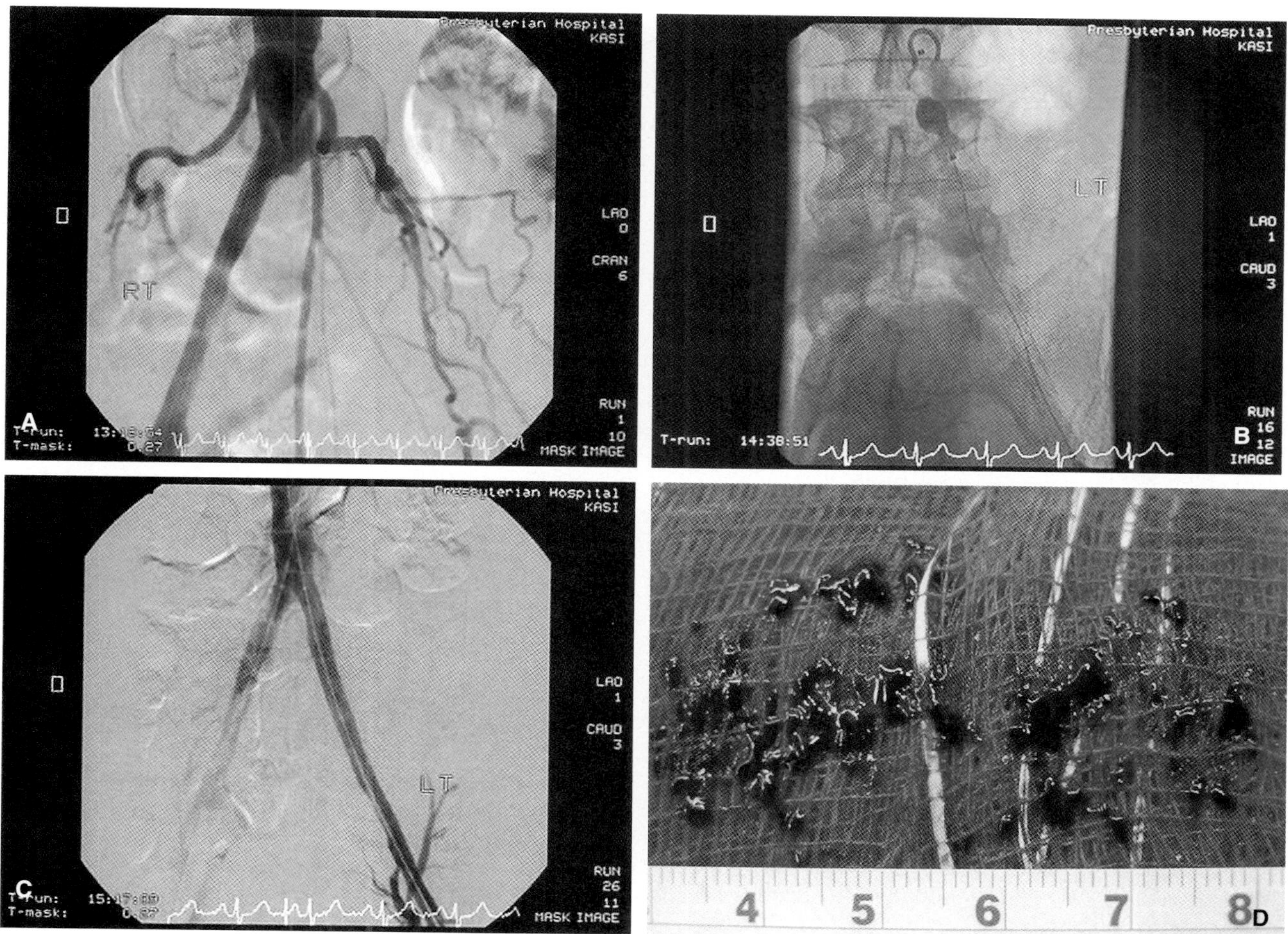

FIGURE 66-13 **A,** Acute occlusion of the left common femoral artery. **B,** Trellis device placed via an ipsilateral common femoral artery puncture. Note the occlusion balloons. **C,** Eleven minutes after Trellis run with 250,000 units of urokinase, showing complete thrombus dissolution. **D,** Typical thrombus fragments aspirated with the Trellis device.

inflated to a maximum diameter of 14 mm. When inflated, the balloons are designed to isolate the treatment zone and maintain the thrombolytic agent locally at the infused concentration. The balloons also help prevent downstream or upstream release of embolic debris. The pharmacologic thrombolytic agent is infused after balloon isolation of the treatment zone through a separate proximal infusion port. A fourth separate flush port is provided for aspiration after completion of therapy; the aspiration port is located just proximal to the distal balloon in the catheter. The proximal end-hole accommodates the guide wire or the dispersion wire through the central lumen. Once the device is in place, the distal balloon is first inflated with a 3:1 concentration of angiographic dye. The thrombolytic agent is then introduced through the infusion port followed by inflation of the proximal balloon with the contrast agent. The guide wire is then exchanged for the dispersion wire within the central lumen of the catheter. The dispersion wire is a sheathed, shape-set nitinol cable. Once placed, the sinusoidal shape-set region of the dispersion wire resides between the two balloons, within the isolated treatment zone. The proximal end of the dispersion wire is connected to a hand-held drive unit. The device is first placed in the "on" mode followed by gradually increasing the oscillation of the dispersion wire to achieve optimal wire movement in the selected conduit, which is fluoroscopically confirmed. The wire is moved back and forth every few minutes to optimize mechanical dispersion of the thrombolytic agent simultaneous with mechanical thrombus fragmentation. After about 15 minutes of mechanically assisted pharmacologic thrombolysis, the proximal balloon is deflated and the liquefied thrombus is aspirated through the aspiration lumen (Fig. 66-13). In its current design the device can be used to treat vessels from 4 to 12 mm in diameter. It is available in two different lengths (65 and 140 cm). The two different infusion lengths are 10 and 20 cm.

Although this relatively new device has scant published data on its use,[37] unpublished data from a muticenter registry of acute limb ischemia cases are provided as follows.

Data were prospectively collected from 27 centers using the Trellis device in the initial treatment of limb ischemia for thrombus debulking. The primary endpoint evaluated was the amount of thrombus removed (<50% = failure, 50% to 75% = partial success, >75% = complete success) at the site of Trellis thrombectomy. Factors evaluated include type of conduit, duration and severity of ischemia, length of occlusion, Trellis run time, and type and dose of thrombolytic drug used. Cumulative logistic regression was used to assess the association between success and each factor. Odds ratios (OR) and 95% CIs are given. The Trellis device was used in 73 patients over a period of 10 months as the initial therapy for acute (n = 47) or chronic (n = 26) limb ischemia. Overall, failure was seen in 9.6% (n = 7) of patients, partial success in 19% (n = 14) of patients, and complete success in 71% (n = 52) of patients. Factors predictive of greater than 75% thrombus removal were synthetic conduit type (OR, 3.7 [95% CI, 1.3 to 10.6]; P = 0.011), increased trellis minutes (P = 0.016), and culprit lesion (OR, 5 [95% CI, 2 to 15]; P = 0.005). Adjunctive lytic therapy was used in 30% of patients for thrombus located beyond the reach of the Trellis catheter. A culprit lesion was noticed and treated in 69% (n = 51) of patients. One device-related complication was observed with no major bleeds or periprocedural deaths. Based on these preliminary data, the Trellis device appears safe and effective for thrombus removal in patients with acute limb ischemia.

■ SUMMARY

Acute limb ischemia develops with the sudden occlusion of a native artery or bypass graft resulting in hypoperfusion of the distal extremity. When severe, ischemia progresses to infarction and limb loss, the rapidity of which is dependent on the adequacy of preexisting collateral arterial channels. Treatment is accomplished through the restoration of adequate distal blood flow with open surgical revascularization procedures, pharmacologic thrombolytic therapy, PMT device, or combinations of the three. Morbidity and mortality rates are high, especially in those patients with medical co-morbidities that render them ill prepared to undergo urgent surgical interventions. The keys to improving outcome lie in rapid diagnosis, early effective reperfusion, correction of the culprit lesion that caused the occlusion, and liberal use of antithrombotic therapy. An algorithm is provided to guide decision making in patients with acute limb ischemia (see Fig. 66-6). Only through a coordinated approach to care of the patient with acute limb ischemia can we expect to see reductions in the rate of periprocedural morbidity and mortality.

■ REFERENCES

1. Ouriel K, Veith FJ, Sasahara AA: A comparison of recombinant urokinase with vascular surgery as initial treatment for acute arterial occlusion of the legs. Thrombolysis or Peripheral Arterial Surgery (TOPAS) Investigators. N Engl J Med 338:1105-1111, 1998.
2. Ouriel K, Shortell CK, DeWeese JA, et al: A comparison of thrombolytic therapy with operative revascularization in the initial treatment of acute peripheral arterial ischemia. J Vasc Surg 19:1021-1030, 1994.
3. Anonymous. Results of a prospective randomized trial evaluating surgery versus thrombolysis for ischemia of the lower extremity. The STILE trial. Ann Surg 220:251-266, 1994.
4. Abbott WM, Maloney RD, McCabe CC: Arterial embolism: A 44-year perspective. Am J Surg 143:460-464, 1982.
5. Bulkley GB: Pathophysiology of free radical-mediated reperfusion injury. J Vasc Surg 5:512-517, 1987.
6. Rush DS, Frame SB, Bell RM, et al: Does open fasciotomy contribute to morbidity and mortality after acute lower extremity ischemia and revascularization? J Vasc Surg 10:343-350, 1989.
7. Anonymous: Suggested standards for reports dealing with lower extremity ischemia. Prepared by the Ad Hoc Committee on Reporting Standards, Society for Vascular Surgery/North American Chapter, International Society for Cardiovascular Surgery. J Vasc Surg 4:80-94, 1986.
8. Rutherford RB, Baker JD, Ernst C, et al: Recommended standards for reports dealing with lower extremity ischemia: Revised version. J Vasc Surg 26:517-538, 1997.
9. Ouriel K, Zarins CK: Doppler ankle pressure: An evaluation of three methods of expression. Arch Surg 117:1297-1300, 1982.
10. Ouriel K, McDonnell AE, Metz CE, Zarins CK: Critical evaluation of stress testing in the diagnosis of peripheral vascular disease. Surgery 91:686-693, 1982.
11. Gunderson J: Segmental measurement of systolic blood pressure in the extremities including the thumb and the great toe. Acta Chir Scand Suppl 426:1-90, 1972.
12. Cina C, Katsamouris A, Megerman J, et al: Utility of transcutaneous oxygen tension measurements in peripheral arterial occlusive disease. J Vasc Surg 1:362-371, 1984.
13. Moneta GL, Yeager RA, Lee RW, Porter JM: Noninvasive localization of arterial occlusive disease: A comparison of segmental Doppler pressures and arterial duplex mapping. J Vasc Surg 17:578-582, 1993.
14. Kerns SR, Hawkins IFJ, Sabatelli FW: Current status of carbon dioxide angiography. Radiol Clin North Am 33:15-29, 1995.
15. Parodi JC, Ferreira LM: Gadolinium-based contrast: An alternative contrast agent for endovascular interventions. Ann Vasc Surg 14:480-483, 2000.
16. Proia RR, Walsh DB, Nelson PR, et al: Early results of infragenicular revascularization based solely on duplex arteriography. J Vasc Surg 33:1165-1170, 2001.
17. Schoenberg SO, Londy FJ, Licato P, et al: Multiphase-multistep gadolinium-enhanced MR angiography of the abdominal aorta and runoff vessels. Invest Radiol 36:283-291, 2001.
18. Rubin GD, Dake MD, Semba CP: Current status of three-dimensional spiral CT scanning for imaging the vasculature. Radiol Clin North Am 33:51-70, 1995.
19. Crolla RM, van de Pavoordt ED, Moll FL: Intraoperative digital subtraction angiography after thromboembolectomy: Preliminary experience. J Endovasc Surg 2:168-171, 1995.
20. Kasirajan K, Gray B, Beavers FP, et al: Rheolytic thrombectomy in the management of acute and subacute limb-threatening ischemia. J Vasc Interv Radiol 12:413-421, 2001.
21. Kasirajan K, Haskal ZJ, Ouriel K: The use of mechanical thrombectomy devices in the management of acute peripheral arterial occlusive disease. J Vasc Interv Radiol 12:405-411, 2001.
22. Dormandy JA, Rutherford RB: Management of peripheral arterial disease (PAD). TASC Working Group. TransAtlantic Inter-Society Consensus (TASC). J Vasc Surg 31:S1-S296, 2000.
23. Edwards JE, Taylor LM Jr, Porter JM: Treatment of failed lower extremity bypass grafts with new autogenous vein bypass grafting. J Vasc Surg 11:136-145, 1990.
24. Blaisdell FW, Steele M, Allen RE: Management of acute lower extremity arterial ischemia due to embolism and thrombosis. Surgery 84:822-834, 1978.
25. Dormandy J, Heeck L, Vig S: Acute limb ischemia. Semin Vasc Surg 12:148-153, 1999.
26. Dale WA: Differential management of acute peripheral arterial ischemia. J Vasc Surg 1:269-278, 1984.
27. Jivegård L, Holm J, Scherstén T: Acute limb ischemia due to arterial embolism or thrombosis: Influence of limb ischemia versus pre-existing cardiac disease on postoperative mortality rate. J Cardiovasc Surg 29:32-36, 1988.
28. Weaver FA, Comerota AJ, Youngblood M, et al: Surgical revascularization versus thrombolysis for nonembolic lower extremity native artery occlusions: Results of a prospective randomized trial. The

STILE Investigators. Surgery versus Thrombolysis for Ischemia of the Lower Extremity. J Vasc Surg 24:513-521, 1996.
29. Comerota AJ, Weaver FA, Hosking JD, et al: Results of a prospective, randomized trial of surgery versus thrombolysis for occluded lower extremity bypass grafts. Am J Surg 172:105-112, 1996.
30. Ouriel K, Veith FJ, Sasahara AA: Thrombolysis or peripheral arterial surgery: Phase I results. TOPAS Investigators. J Vasc Surg 23:64-73, 1996.
31. Sharafuddin MJ, Hicks ME, Jennson ML, et al: Rheolytic thrombectomy with the AngioJet-F105 catheter: Preclinical evaluation of safety. J Vasc Interv Radiol 8:939-945, 1997.
32. Wagner H-J, Müler-Hülsbeck S, Pitton MB, et al: Rapid thrombectomy with a hydrodynamic catheter: Results from a prospective, multicenter trial. Radiology 205:675-681, 1997.
33. Kasirajan K, Gray B, Beavers F, et al: Rheolytic thrombectomy in the treatment of acute limb-threatening ischemia: Immediate results and six-month follow-up of the multicenter AngioJet registry. J Vasc Intervent Radiol 12:413-421, 2001.
34. Müller-Hülsbeck S, Kalinowski M, Heller M, et al: Rheolytic hydrodynamic thrombectomy for percutaneous treatment of acutely occluded infra-aortic native arteries and bypass grafts: Midterm follow-up results. Invest Radiol 35:131-140, 2000.
35. Silva JA, Ramee SR, Collins TJ, et al: Rheolytic thrombectomy in the treatment of acute limb-threatening ischemia: Immediate results and six-month follow-up of the multicenter AngioJet registry. Cathet Cardiovasc Diagn 45:386-393, 1998.
36. Wagner H-J, Müler-Hülsbeck S, Pitton MB, et al: Rapid thrombectomy with a hydrodynamic catheter: Results from a prospective, multicenter trial. Radiology 205:675-681, 1997.
37. Kasirajan K, Ramaiah V, Diethrich EB: A novel mechanical thrombectomy device in the treatment of acute limb ischemia. J Endovasc Ther 10:317-321, 2003.

Chapter 67

Arterial Thromboembolism

SCOTT R. FECTEAU, MD
R. CLEMENT DARLING III, MD
SEAN P. RODDY, MD

HISTORICAL BACKGROUND

In 1854, Virchow was the first to use the term *embolus* in the description of sudden obstruction of an artery by material that originated from a distal site. The term is derived from "embolos," a Greek term meaning *plug*. The occlusive material may consist of platelet-fibrin thrombus, cholesterol debris, laminated aneurysmal thrombus, or a foreign body that has gained access to the vascular system.

Originally, the treatment of an arterial embolus was solely observational, which eventually terminated in limb loss or death. In the early 1900s, the initial successful reports of surgical removal of embolic material were described and operative management slowly gained acceptance.[1] These early manuscripts documented the necessity for early intervention to avoid irreversible intimal damage and secondary thrombosis of vessels distal to the point of embolic occlusion.[2-4] One of the great advances in treatment of patients with thromboembolism was the introduction of heparin for use before, during, and after surgical intervention.[5] Intravenous heparin infusions decreased the propagation of thrombus, stabilized the clot, and recruited collateral vessels.

Early in its evolution, the complete removal of thromboembolic material, especially when associated with large amounts of propagated thrombus, remained problematic. A variety of methods, including suction catheters, vigorous arterial flushing, and external compression on the limbs, were used with moderate success.[6-8] In 1963, Fogarty and associates proposed the use of a balloon catheter that offered a significant advance for the retrieval of thrombus, distal and proximal to the embolic site.[9] For the first time, intravascular thromboembolic material could be removed from a single, strategically placed arteriotomy, with relatively little trauma to the vessels.

The mortality associated with acute peripheral arterial occlusion remains high, averaging 10% to 25%.[10-19] Advanced age, severity of associated medical problems, and presence of coexisting chronic arterial occlusive disease have offset improvements in the management of atherosclerotic heart disease despite technical advances in performing thromboembolectomy. In the past, patients presenting with acute peripheral arterial occlusion were most often in the 5th decade of life.[20-22] This represents an era when rheumatic heart disease, associated mitral valvular deformity, and resultant peripheral embolization were the most common causes of ischemia. More recent data demonstrate that the mean age of patients with acute peripheral arterial occlusion is 70 years, reflecting a shift in etiology from rheumatic to atherosclerotic heart disease and the increased frequency of peripheral atherosclerosis as an inciting cause for occlusion.[11,23]

With a growing number of angiographic interventions, the overall incidence of arterial embolism may be shifting yet again. Sharma and associates noted that 45% of all atheroemboli were iatrogenic in nature, with most of these (83%) occurring during angiographic manipulation of the proximal arteries.[24]

■ CLASSIFICATION OF PERIPHERAL ARTERIAL EMBOLI

Arterial emboli can be classified on the basis of size, content, and site of origin. Although somewhat arbitrary, an understanding of this classification is important because clinical presentation, natural history, and management can vary based on the type of embolus.

Microemboli

Although microembolization is discussed in detail elsewhere (see Chapter 68), it is briefly described here to provide perspective for the remaining portions of this chapter that focus on macroemboli and arterial thrombosis.

A variety of lesions act as sources of microemboli, ranging in location from the infrarenal aorta to the termination of the popliteal artery. Aneurysms of the popliteal artery have long been recognized for this predisposition. Iliac and common femoral aneurysms rarely produce distal embolization and are more prone to acute thrombotic occlusion. In marked contrast, however, atherosclerotic lesions of the iliac, common femoral, and superficial femoral arteries are important sources of microemboli. Although it may be instinctively surmised that pathologic degeneration of the larger arteries would be the predominant origin of such arterioarterial emboli, femoral arteries are the most common emboligenic sources. Apart from popliteal aneurysms, stenotic, irregular, and ulcerated lesions of the iliac and femoropopliteal arteries are frequently microembolic sources, as shown by their relative incidence. However, when there is widespread atheromatous degeneration of the infradiaphragmatic arteries, it can be difficult to identify precisely the area responsible for the release of microemboli.[25]

Many authors have expressed the view that these microemboli result solely from fragmentation of atheromatous plaques and subsequent dislodgement of the debris.[26-31] Indeed, atheromatous plaques are known to undergo ulceration and fragmentation, and atheromatous or cholesterol-containing material has been identified in digital vessels and in the smaller arteries of the calf muscles.[30] However, many of the microemboli of the lower limb consist of fibrinoplatelet or thrombotic material on pathologic examination. The microemboli, which are released from aneurysmal sources (e.g., popliteal, aorta), are part of the flocculent-laminated thrombus, which lines the arterial flow path. A common surgical finding is friable atheromatous plaque; however, the shaggy, frondlike clumps of fibrinoplatelet debris, which are invariably present on these lesions, are not only impressive but also appear likely to dislodge.[32-35] Schechter recovered a shred of atheromatous plaque (gravel) from a tibial artery and postulated that after these particles impact, surrounding fibrinoplatelet aggregates as well as propagated thrombus increase the degree of obstruction.[36]

Branowitz and Edwards concluded that the clinical and pathologic processes involve distal embolization of atheromatous debris, fibrinoplatelets, or other thrombotic material.[34] Kempczinski further identified that cholesterol emboli tend to originate in the infrarenal aorta, are diffused, and are lodged in arteries 100 to 200 μm in diameter (e.g., muscular arteries).[35] By contrast, microemboli formed from hemocellular elements often are larger and occlude vessels up to 1 mm in size. Digital arteries are customarily involved, but emboli have been recovered that were large enough to occlude the tibial, popliteal, and superficial femoral arteries.[27,34,37,38] Larger emboli are identified less often and usually originate in severe atheromatous plaques within the infrarenal aorta, which has larger, loosely attached fibrinoplatelet clumps.[39] This clinical entity has been described in various ways. It has been called *blue toe syndrome*, *atheromatous embolization*, *acute focal ischemia*, and *peripheral atheroembolism*.[31,36,38,40,41] From the pathologic description, the term *arterioarterial atherothrombotic microembolism*, although cumbersome, is preferred because it most accurately describes all of the pathologic events.[39]

Gore and Collins have shown by autopsy examination that atherothrombotic microembolization is a more frequent clinical problem than generally recognized.[42] This option has been confirmed by Maurizi and associates, who conclude that the microemboli usually lodge in the lower limbs and that recurrent microembolization, which finally leads to extensive tissue loss, is common.[30] A typical scenario includes the sudden appearance of a painful digit, which is generally bluish in color (hence the name *blue toe syndrome*), has a sluggish capillary return, and is quite tender to the touch. These symptoms may last only a few minutes and cause little noticeable disability, but more commonly, provide signs and symptoms for a few days. The sudden appearance of a painful, discolored toe may be baffling when the rest of the foot appears well perfused, particularly when pedal pulses can be readily palpated. In contrast with focal digital ischemia, livedo reticularis may result from microembolic shower. The eventual outcome is obviously determined by the available collateral pathways, which are themselves determined both by the site of embolic impaction and the effects of previous or unrecognized embolic episodes.

Macroemboli

Cardiac Emboli

Macroemboli arise from the dislodgement of a large plaque or mural thrombus and result in large single-vessel occlusions. The heart is by far the predominant source of spontaneous arterial macroemboli, cited in 80% to 90% of cases. Although this statistic has remained constant over the last half-century, there has been a shift in the underlying heart disease from rheumatic valvular disease to atherosclerotic coronary vascular disease. Presently, atherosclerotic heart disease has been implicated as a causative factor in 60% to 70% of all cases of embolus, with rheumatic mitral valve disease and associated atrial fibrillation in the remaining 30% to 40%.[11,43,44]

The close association of atrial fibrillation with modern-day heart disease may explain the rather constant appearance of arterial emboli despite the markedly diminished incidence of rheumatic disease.[45] Regardless of the cause for atrial fibrillation, this dysrhythmia is currently associated with two thirds to three fourths of peripheral emboli.[11,15,44] As a result of stasis, clot formation is particularly common in the left atrial appendage. In this location, transthoracic echocardiographic techniques have had only intermediate success in thrombus detection.[46,47] Although transesophageal echocardiography offers a more thorough and accurate evaluation of the heart, the sensitivity of this modality has also been disappointing.[48-51] Consequently, the absence of detected thrombus does not rule out the heart as a potential source. Next to atrial fibrillation, myocardial infarction is the second most frequent entity associated with peripheral arterial embolization. In a series of 400 patients with peripheral emboli, Panetta and coworkers determined that myocardial infarction was the causative factor in 20%.[15] Thrombus within the left ventricle most frequently follows an anterior transmural myocardial infarction.[52,53] Despite the frequent presence of left ventricular thrombus, the incidence of embolization is less than 5% in this patient population.[54,55] Darling and associates reported on the timing of embolic complications in relation to the initial cardiac insult.[20] They noted a lag in the development of symptoms, ranging from 3 to 28 days, with a mean of 14 days. Electrocardiographic changes were noted in 64% of all patients presenting with acute extremity ischemia requiring surgical intervention.[56] The presence of electrocardiographic changes predicted a higher morbidity and mortality.

Occasionally, embolic symptoms may be the first clinical manifestation of a "silent myocardial infarct." This adds to the importance of careful evaluation of the electrocardiogram and serum cardiac enzymes of patients presenting with acute ischemic syndromes. Delayed presentation of emboli originating from the heart as a result of myocardial infarction is frequently associated with the formation of a left ventricular aneurysm. Thrombus has been identified in 50% of cases, with 5% experiencing peripheral embolization.[57] Coincidentally, it is the sheer magnitude of the prevalence of coronary artery disease that makes this a common cause of arterial emboli.

Cardiac valvular prostheses are another common source of emboli. Thrombus formation may occur around the sewing ring in a caged-ball or caged-disc valve.[58] Tilting-disc valves predispose to thrombus formation at the hinge points, which correspond to sites of low-velocity blood flow. Permanent anticoagulation therapy is required in patients with prosthetic mechanical valves, and embolic complications are particularly common when postimplantation anticoagulation is inadequate or discontinued. Biosynthetic valves, such as the porcine xenograft, are not as thrombogenic as prosthetic valves, and anticoagulation may not be required.[59]

Intracardiac tumors, such as atrial myxomas, are a rare source of peripheral arterial emboli.[20] Similarly, vegetations from mitral or aortic leaflets in patients with bacterial or fungal endocarditis can also be a cause. Despite the improved spectrum of antibiotic regimens, the incidence of endocarditis has increased largely as a result of intravenous drug abuse. This etiologic factor should be suspected in younger patients and in those without a history of atherosclerotic or rheumatic heart disease.[60-62] Histologic examination of the surgical embolic specimen may provide a clue as to the etiology of the insult, especially if leukocytes or bacteria are visualized in the material.

Noncardiac Emboli

Spontaneous emboli originating from noncardiac sources are noted in 5% to 10% of patients.[11] Noncardiac emboli often originate from atherosclerotic disease of more proximal vessels. Thrombi arising from mural erosions can be large and produce a clinical picture indistinguishable from emboli of a cardiac origin. Downstream embolization of mural thrombus associated with aortoiliac, femoral, or popliteal aneurysms has been reported.[63] Proximal aneurysms in the upper extremity as a result of thoracic outlet syndrome may also contribute to the incidence of this phenomenon.[35,64,65]

Noncardiac tumors and other foreign bodies may gain access to the arterial circulation and form arterial emboli. This event is more commonly noted in tumors that tend to invade the pulmonary vasculature or heart, such as primary or metastatic lung carcinoma.[66,67] Bullet emboli have also been reported.[68,69] "Paradoxical embolization" occurs when a thrombus arising within the venous circulation passes from the right side of the heart to the left side through an intracardiac communication, most often a patent foramen ovale, to become an arterial embolus.[70,71] This scenario most commonly occurs after the occurrence of a pulmonary embolism, in which acute pulmonary hypertension is associated with the development of a right-to-left shunt.

In addition to venous-derived thrombus, tumor and foreign body paradoxical emboli have been reported.[72] Mixed symptoms of arterial and venous obstruction, and a history of deep venous thrombosis or pulmonary embolism in a patient presenting with acute arterial occlusion should prompt consideration of this entity. Echocardiography and cardiac catheterization are helpful to identify the right-to-left shunt and to accurately define its location.[47,73-75]

Unknown Source

An additional 5% to 10% of spontaneous emboli originate from a source that remains unidentified, despite an apparently thorough diagnostic interrogation.[20,76,77] These have been termed *cryptogenic emboli*. The frequency of this diagnosis has diminished significantly with improvements in imaging and increased recognition of noncardiac sources of emboli. More frequent use of arteriography (contrast or magnetic resonance) has contributed to the identification of proximal sources of peripheral emboli. Additionally, transesophageal echocardiography permits more thorough evaluation of possible cardiac sources of emboli with improved visualization of the left atrial appendage thrombi, cardiac valvular vegetations, or thoracic aortic atheromas, all of which are potentially important sources of peripheral arterial emboli. In some instances, confusion arises when one attempts to differentiate in-situ thrombosis from peripheral embolism. This is particularly true in the absence of an embolic source. Hypercoagulable states have been suspected, particularly in younger patients without evidence of concomitant occlusive disease or in patients with malignancy.[78]

■ SITES OF EMBOLISM

Approximately 20% of emboli eventually affect cerebrovascular circulation, and 10% involve the visceral vessels.[20] It is likely, however, that embolization to these sites is markedly underdiagnosed. Acute strokes secondary to cerebrovascular emboli may be attributed to other pathologic

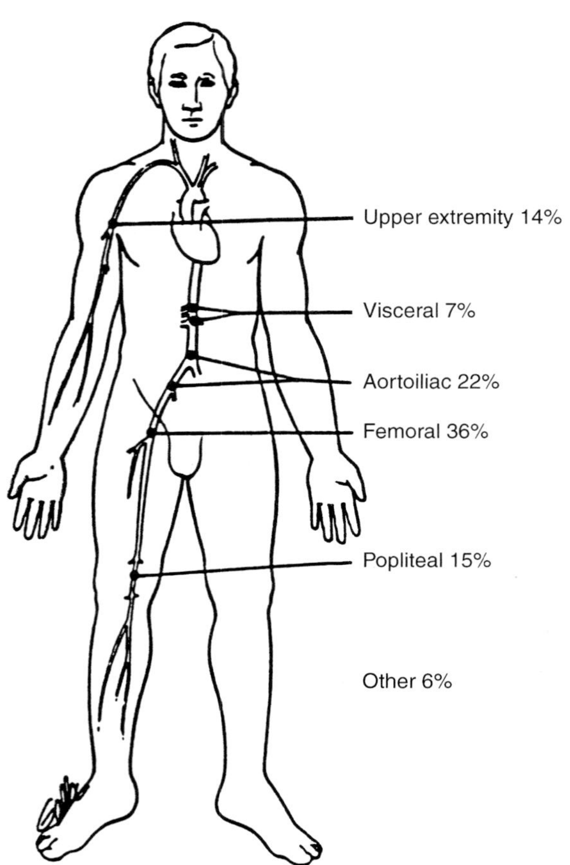

FIGURE 67-1 Incidence of embolic occlusions at different sites. Data are compiled from 1303 embolic events at the Massachusetts General Hospital[11] and Stanford University.[44]

causes. Similarly, large visceral emboli can be rapidly fatal and may frequently be confused with other causes of sudden intra-abdominal catastrophies.

The axial limb vasculature is involved in 70% to 80% of all embolic disease.[15,20,79] Emboli lodge within the lower extremities five times as often as in the upper extremities. The abrupt change of vessel diameter at branching sites makes these areas the most common locations of embolic occlusions. The increasing incidence of occlusive disease in our aging population produces multiple areas of stenosis unrelated to a bifurcation that can also serve as anchoring sites for emboli. The presence of preexisting collateral vessels may provide enough distal circulation to prevent severe ischemic symptoms, adding to the confusion in discriminating between embolization and thrombosis overlying an atherosclerotic stenosis.

Overall, the femoral bifurcation is the most frequent site of embolic occlusion, noted in 35% to 50% of cases (Fig 67-1).[12,15,20,23,43,44,76,77] The popliteal artery is the second most frequent site and, taken together, the femoral and popliteal arteries are involved more than twice as often as the aorta and iliac vessels. This reflects the simple mechanical fact that only a thrombus of considerable size can lodge at the aortic or iliac bifurcation unless it occurs in the setting of significant aortoiliac occlusive disease.

■ PATHOPHYSIOLOGY

The clinical outcome of an embolic event depends mainly on the size of the vessel involved, the degree of obstruction, and, most important, the amount of collateral blood flow. If an acute embolus obstructs a previously normal artery, severe distal ischemia may result owing to the paucity of collateral pathways. In contrast, sudden occlusion from an embolus imposed on a severely stenotic vessel may produce only mild clinical symptoms owing to previously well-established collateral vessels. The latter is also characteristic of acute arterial thrombosis in the setting of advanced atherosclerosis and can confuse the differential diagnosis. Historically, a great deal of emphasis has been placed on intervention within the 4 to 6 hours following onset of symptoms, because this was thought to represent the maximal length of tolerable ischemia. It is now well recognized that no arbitrary time limit can be imposed on the timing of interventions. The physiologic state of the limb, determined mainly by a balance between metabolic supply and demand, rather than the elapsed time from the onset of occlusion is the best predictor of limb salvage. Again, supply to the affected tissues is determined largely by preexisting collateral vessels.

Following arterial obstruction by an embolus, three possible events may occur to aggravate ischemia. Of primary importance is propagation of thrombus. Linton described proximal and distal thrombus propagation in 1941.[80] The extension of thrombus markedly impairs the collateral circulation and thus represents a major secondary factor worsening ischemia. Effective surgical therapy depends on complete removal of all propagated thrombus. Clot can form in a discontinuous fashion, which makes cannulation of the distal vasculature necessary at the time of embolectomy. The prevention of the thrombus propagation and the protection of the collateral circulation are the primary reasons for early and aggressive anticoagulation. Also, the presence of backbleeding at the time of embolectomy is an unreliable guide to the patency of distal circulation because it may occur from intervening arterial branches proximal to distal clot.

A second event that may aggravate distal ischemia is fragmentation of an embolus resulting in migration of debris into the distal circulation. Occasionally, however, partial clot lysis and fragmentation may be the mechanism for the spontaneous clinical resolution of an embolic event.

Additionally, associated venous thrombosis may occur in the setting of prolonged arterial ischemia. This is presumably due to a combination of sluggish flow and ischemic injury to the intima of the involved veins. Development of venous thrombosis may further reduce arterial blood flow and worsen edema following revascularization. In fact, pulmonary embolism has been historically cited as a significant cause of mortality in patients initially suffering from arterial thromboembolism.[20,81]

Patients with severe ischemia resulting from embolic occlusions are susceptible to several systemic and metabolic complications. Haimovici estimated that one third of the deaths from peripheral arterial thromboembolism occur as the result of metabolic complications following revascularization.[82] High concentrations of potassium, lactic acid, myoglobin, and cellular enzymes, such as serum glutamic oxaloacetic transaminase, are found in the venous blood of a severely ischemic limb and result largely from rhabdomyolysis. In a series of patients with acute limb ischemia, the mean venous effluent pH was 7.07, whereas the serum potassium level was elevated to 5.77 mEq/L 5 minutes after surgical embolectomy.[83] After revascularization, the sudden release of these accumulated products into the systemic venous circulation has profound consequences. The triad of peripheral muscle infarction, myoglobinemia, and myoglobinuric renal failure characterizes the *reperfusion syndrome*. Hyperkalemia, metabolic acidosis, and myoglobinuria are the key features of the syndrome. Renal tubular necrosis may occur when myoglobin is precipitated in the renal tubules under acidotic conditions. Although volume repletion, free radical scavengers, and urinary alkalinization have been the recommended treatments, it now appears that once appropriate volume expansion has been achieved, the addition of free radical scavengers and bicarbonate may be unnecessary.[84]

Significant local effects of ischemia reperfusion can contribute to morbidity and limb loss despite successful extraction of thrombus. Edema often follows revascularization owing to compromised integrity of the capillary wall occurring to a degree proportional to the duration and severity of ischemia. Capillary disintegrity results from both the ischemic insult itself and the effects of reperfusion.[81] Large quantities of oxygen free radicals are released and tend to overwhelm the intracellular scavenger systems, causing damage to the phospholipid cell membrane and other intracellular organelles. Cell membrane damage results in the transudation of fluid into the interstitial space, producing edema. Substantial edema can further reduce local perfusion and exacerbate tissue injury. The *no-reflow phenomenon* occurs as a result of massive edema into a fixed space (the compartment syndrome) and capillary endothelial cellular edema with consequent vascular obstruction. Under these conditions, peripheral tissue hypoperfusion persists despite adequate large-vessel revascularization, and large-vessel reocclusion can occur rapidly. Although fasciotomy may correct the compartment syndrome, small-vessel obstruction is more difficult to ameliorate.[85-87]

■ CLINICAL PRESENTATION

The sudden onset of arterial ischemia is often manifested by some or all of the five cardinal signs denoted by the "five Ps": *p*ulselessness, *p*ain, *p*allor, *p*aresthesia, and *p*aralysis. Temperature changes are often described as *p*oikilothermic, thus adding a sixth P to the mnemonic. Although the five Ps may be a useful axiom for instruction of house staff, these characteristics represent the nonspecific results of acute arterial occlusion. Considerable diagnostic acumen is required to gauge the severity of ischemia.

The *sudden onset of pain associated with loss of a previously palpable pulse* is the hallmark of arterial embolism.[88,89] In the absence of significant preexistent atherosclerosis, the site of occlusion can be accurately determined from a careful physical examination of the extremity. Here, common femoral emboli are associated with a palpable femoral pulse but absence of the popliteal pulse and commonly with a normal pulse examination on the contralateral limb. By contrast, a popliteal embolus is associated with a palpable popliteal pulse, absent pedal pulses, and coolness beginning at the level of the lower leg. Practically, however, the prior pulse status of the limb is often poorly documented or may be abnormal at baseline because of preexisting atherosclerosis. Additionally, a normal or even hyperdynamic pulse may be felt at the actual site of embolic occlusion, representing the transmitted pulse waves through fresh thrombus.

Pain is characteristically severe and steady. Typically, the major muscle groups below the level of obstruction become symptomatic and progressively worsen at locations increasingly distal to the point of occlusion. For instance, symptoms from a common femoral embolus begin with pain and numbness in the toes, rapidly progressing to involve the tissues of the calf and thigh. Focal tenderness over a muscle group can be an ominous sign, signifying advances in muscle ischemia. Occasionally, however, sensory disturbances secondary to ischemic neuropathy predominate and may mask primary complaints of pain.

The skin distal to the occlusion initially takes on a pale or waxy appearance. With time, *pallor* progresses to blotchy mottled areas of cyanosis. If left untreated, the skin changes proceed to necrosis and desquamation.

As mentioned previously, sensory disturbances can predominate and may mask the primary complaints of pain. In these situations, the patient may complain of *numbness* or *paresthesias*, without a prominent component of pain. The sensory changes occur as a result of ischemia of nerve tissue, which is particularly sensitive to ischemic insult.

Paralysis is, at first, the result of motor nerve ischemia, but subsequent muscle ischemia compounds the problem. The extent of the motor deficit is a good index of the degree of tissue anoxia and correlates well with ultimate prognosis. Complete motor paralysis is a late symptom signaling impending gangrene, representing a combination of both end-stage muscle and neural ischemia. When paralysis proceeds to rigor and the initial "doughy" consistency of the muscle progresses to "woody" hardness and involuntary muscle contracture (rigor), irreversible ischemia has developed. Although the limb may be salvaged, ultimate function is severely compromised and the systemic metabolic consequences of revascularization may be lethal.

A point of temperature demarcation can usually be noted approximately one joint distal to the point of occlusion. For example, temperature change just above the ankle often denotes occlusion at the popliteal bifurcation, whereas such a finding at or just above the knee suggests blockage at the femoral bifurcation. Changes in the upper thigh on one side suggest an iliac occlusion, and involvement of both thighs, lower abdomen, or buttocks suggests an aortic bifurcation saddle embolus.

Careful history and physical examination can provide useful data for stratifying acutely ischemic limbs for therapeutic purposes. Clinical findings and assessment of distal arterial and venous Doppler signals allow limbs to be categorized into the following clinically relevant groups: (1) viable, (2) threatened, and (3) irreversibly ischemic. These categories were formulated and revised by the Society for Vascular Surgery/International Society for Cardiovascular Surgery (SVS/ISCVS) committee on reporting standards.[89]

1. *Viable*: not immediately threatened. There is no ischemic pain, no neurologic deficit, adequate skin capillary circulation, and clearly audible Doppler pulsatile flow signal in pedal arteries (ankle pressure > 30 mm Hg).
2. *Threatened viability*: indicates a state of reversible ischemia provided arterial obstruction is promptly relieved. Ischemic pain or mild and incomplete neurologic deficit is present. Pulsatile flow in pedal arteries is not audible with Doppler, but venous signals are demonstrable.
3. *Irreversible ischemic change*: profound sensory loss and muscle paralysis, absent capillary skin flow, muscle rigor, and skin marbling are characteristic. Neither arterial nor venous flow is audible; major amputation is required, regardless of therapy.

■ DIFFERENTIAL DIAGNOSIS

When acute arterial occlusion occurs in the setting of a recognizable source of the embolus, most commonly atrial fibrillation or recent myocardial infarction, and is characterized by loss of a previously intact pulse, there is little doubt as to the diagnosis. However, acute ischemia of an extremity may result from in-situ thrombosis of a native artery, occlusion of a bypass graft, or embolization, and there can be significant overlap among these entities in terms of clinical presentation. Formerly, thrombotic or embolic occlusion of native arteries accounted for the overwhelming majority of cases of limb ischemia. With the refinement and widespread use of peripheral arterial revascularization procedures, occlusion of a bypass graft has replaced native arterial occlusion as the most common underlying etiologic factor. Additionally, other clinical entities, some remote from the arterial tree, can mimic acute arterial occlusion from embolus. Angiography continues to play an important role both in diagnosis and as an initial step toward endovascular therapy when appropriate (discussed later).

Peripheral Arterial Thrombosis

Peripheral arterial thrombotic events develop in the setting of an underlying native arterial stenosis or a hypercoagulable state or as the result of occlusion of a bypass conduit. As discussed previously, native artery thrombosis in the setting of a chronic arterial stenosis may be associated with almost imperceptible changes in the patient's symptomatology due to preexisting collateral channels. In contrast, symptoms of occlusion secondary to hypercoagulability or bypass graft failure may be sudden and catastrophic.

Contemporary series identify *bypass graft failure* as the cause of acute peripheral arterial thrombosis in most occlusions. In the Thrombolysis or Peripheral Arterial Surgery (TOPAS) trial, 302 (65%) of 466 thrombotic events were related to bypass graft occlusions; the remaining 164 events (35%) were a result of native artery occlusion.[90] Similarly, 63 (70%) of 90 patients with thrombotic events entered into the Rochester trial had bypass graft occlusions, whereas 27 patients (30%) had native artery thromboses in situ.[91] Hypercoagulability is being increasingly recognized as a cause of acute peripheral arterial occlusion. Although most hypercoagulable states are associated with venous thrombotic events, arterial thrombosis occurs most notably with malignancy, antiphospholipid syndrome, antithrombin III deficiency, and the vasculitides. When patients present with peripheral arterial thrombosis in the absence of underlying atherosclerosis, a search for a hypercoagulable syndrome should be undertaken.

Several clues to the diagnosis may be obtained from a careful history and physical examination and may assist in the differentiation between embolus and thrombosis. Patients with an embolus typically have a sudden onset of symptoms and usually have a source for an embolus, most often cardiac disease. In Cambria and Abbott's report of acutely ischemic limbs, atrial fibrillation was found in 74% of patients with embolic occlusion, as opposed to only 4% who were thought to have acute thrombotic occlusion.[92] Up to 30% of patients with an embolus have had a prior embolic event. Furthermore, a history of claudication is usually absent in the patient with an embolus, and often no evidence of occlusive disease is present in the contralateral limb on pulse examination. The level of temperature change is more clearly demarcated in embolic occlusion in contrast with the patient with preexisting occlusive disease and thus a better-developed collateral system.

Angiography

Angiography can be helpful in differentiating emboli from thrombosis. Typically, emboli are associated with a sharp cutoff, sometimes with a convex filling defect, or "reversed meniscus," in an otherwise fairly normal vessel. Owing to the acute nature of embolic occlusion, scant and poorly developed collateral vessels are another hallmark of an embolic event. The absence of disease elsewhere in the arterial tree implies embolism. Furthermore, multiple filling defects within several arterial beds are pathognomonic for embolization (Fig. 67-2). Finally, the location of the occlusion is more frequently at a bifurcation in embolic disease. In contrast, patients with acute thrombosis have more obvious and diffuse atheromatous changes and better developed collaterals. The point of obstruction is generally associated with an irregular tapering and occurs in regions commonly afflicted with atherosclerotic disease, such as Hunter's canal. Unfortunately, many of these findings may become obscured with the propagation of clot (Fig. 67-3 and Table 67-1).

Angiography is useful as a diagnostic tool when evaluating the patient with an acutely ischemic extremity and can aid in operative planning. Furthermore, initial angiographic evaluation may offer an alternative thrombolytic or endovascular means of restoring blood flow, an option that can be determined only from a detailed knowledge of the anatomy of the process provided by adequate imaging studies. However, for patients with a history and physical findings typical of embolic occlusion, angiography is rarely necessary or helpful in terms of operative planning. In acute emboli, not only are the vessels distal to the site of occlusion often not visualized but also in most cases the limb is threatened and definitive therapy is urgently required. Angiography is best reserved for the select patients without a clear history and a threatened yet viable limb that can tolerate the time period required to obtain an angiogram.

Aortic dissection is an infrequent cause of acute limb ischemia but should be considered, particularly in patients

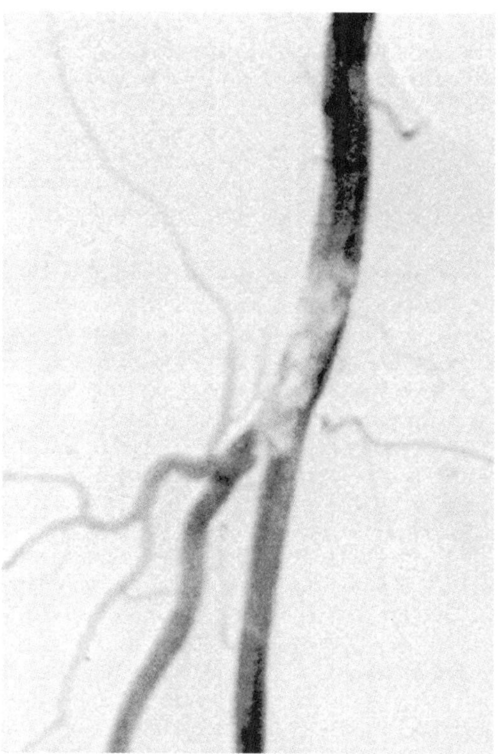

FIGURE 67-2 An embolus is lodged at the bifurcation of the profunda femoris artery and the superficial femoral artery. The diameter of the common femoral artery is large enough to allow the intravascular debris to travel through it, but the individual diameters of the profunda femoris artery and the superficial femoral arteries are too small. This photograph emphasizes the finding that most emboli lodge at the branch point.

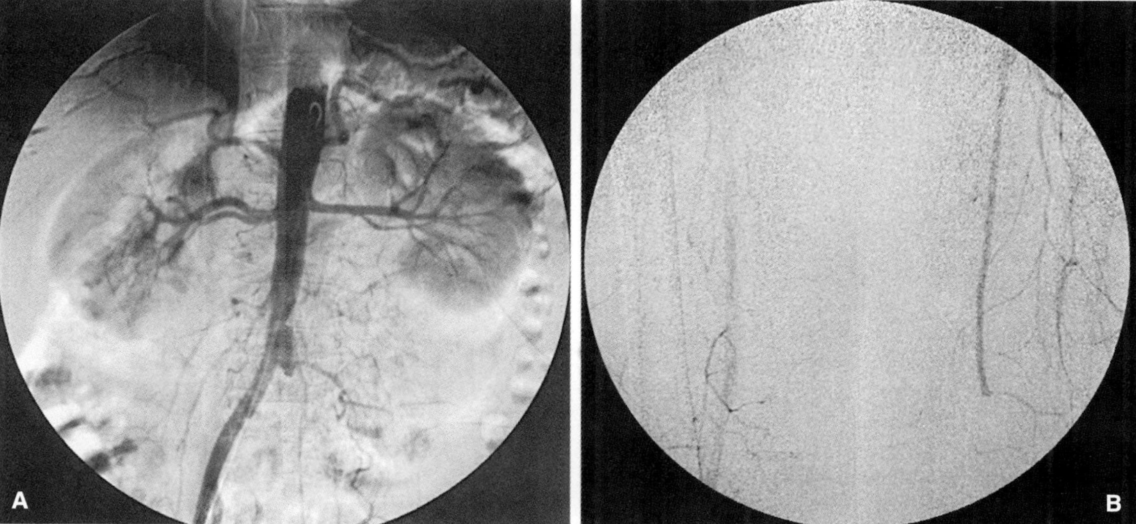

FIGURE 67-3 **A,** Left iliac artery embolus. **B,** Acute occlusion of the superficial femoral artery in the adductor canal. The presence of the proximal embolus, lack of significant disease apparent in the proximal portion of the superficial femoral artery, and lack of a well-developed collateral blood supply suggest that the superficial femoral artery occlusion is also embolic. This hunch proved correct on examination of embolectomized specimens following a surgical procedure.

Table 67-1 Differentiation of Embolism and Thrombosis

FACTOR	EMBOLISM	THROMBOSIS
Identifiable source	Frequently detected	None
Claudication	Rare	Frequent
Physical findings	Proximal and contralateral pulses normal	Ipsilateral and contralateral evidence of peripheral vascular disease
Angiography	Minimal atherosclerosis, sharp cutoff, few collaterals, multiple occlusions	Diffuse atherosclerotic disease, tapered and irregular cutoff, well-developed collateral circulation

with a history of hypertension and young patients with a marfanoid body habitus. It can usually be differentiated from an acute embolic occlusion by the presence of hypertension and chest or intrascapular back pain. Phlegmasia cerulea dolens can also be confused with acute arterial ischemia. Although the swelling associated with this condition often makes pulses difficult to palpate, the presence of massive edema and cyanotic congestion is a marked contrast from the collapsed superficial veins and pallor associated with acute arterial insufficiency. In late stages, secondary arterial insufficiency may in fact develop. Neurologic manifestations of acute ischemia may predominate and masquerade as primary neurologic disorders. For example, aortic saddle emboli may present primarily with the sudden onset of bilateral lower extremity weakness and sensory loss, progressing rapidly to paraplegia. Care must be taken to avoid time-consuming and misdirected diagnostic and therapeutic efforts. Finally, low-output states associated with hypovolemia and diminished cardiac output can also resemble acute embolic disease, particularly when superimposed on chronic arterial insufficiency.

■ THERAPY

Optimal therapy in most cases of arterial embolism is prompt surgical removal by embolectomy. However, knowledge of available surgical options, pharmacologic (primarily thrombolytic) therapies, and mechanical thrombectomy devices can allow one to delineate the most appropriate treatment path for individual patients. No large prospective, randomized trials have compared the various therapeutic options in the treatment of embolic lower extremity ischemia, and each has advantages and disadvantages. Ultimately, the therapeutic modality chosen should be based on (1) the clinical status of the leg, (2) the degree of thrombus propagation, and (3) the medical condition of the patient.

Surgical Modalities

Ideal treatment of an arterial embolus consists of expeditious diagnosis of acute arterial ischemia, recognition of the embolic source, rapid systemic anticoagulation, and surgical embolectomy. Embolectomy was popularized with the advent of the Fogarty embolectomy catheters in 1963 prior to which only 23% of arterial emboli were treated with an embolectomy technique. In contrast, 88% of emboli were treated with surgical embolectomy between 1964 and 1980.[11]

Timely operative intervention is the goal, and preoperative preparation should be minimal once the diagnosis of embolus is made. Baseline laboratory studies should include complete blood count, serum electrolytes, blood urea nitrogen and creatinine, baseline cardiac enzymes, coagulation parameters, and blood typing with cross-matching. The use of local anesthesia and limited incisions is helpful in decreasing the operative risk in critically ill patients. Adequate communication between the anesthesiologist and surgeon should eliminate unexpected changes in the hemodynamic state. Additionally, prolonged procedural times are likely detrimental to outcome.

Iliac and Femoral Thromboemboli

Lower extremity emboli lodging at the iliac or, more frequently, the femoral bifurcation can usually be successfully managed through a groin incision and a femoral arteriotomy. The common, superficial, and deep femoral (profunda femoris) arteries are exposed and controlled. A transverse arteriotomy may be performed because it lends itself to primary closure without narrowing of the artery lumen. In the case of a heavily diseased artery, a longitudinal arteriotomy is helpful, facilitating closure of the artery with a patch or anastomosis of a bypass graft if necessary.

The most common approach to catheter embolectomy involves the insertion of a balloon embolectomy catheter through the arteriotomy with blind passage proximally and distally. Several modifications in catheter design and adjunctive maneuvers have been developed to improve results. "Over-the-wire" embolectomy catheters can be used in conjunction with intraoperative fluoroscopy and routine catheter and wire manipulations to accurately direct the catheter into the desired vessel without traumatic injury.

Surgeons performing catheter embolectomy are aware of certain crucial technical considerations. First, the importance of proper sizing is paramount. Oversized balloons can damage endothelium and cause rupture or dissection, particularly at vessel branch points. Undersized balloons may fragment thrombus, causing embolization to the distal circulation. The iliac vessel is best addressed with a No. 5 catheter; a No. 4 catheter is appropriate for most femoral vessels. Generally, a No. 3 or 4 balloon catheter is used for thromboembolectomy of the profunda femoris artery or the popliteal artery, whereas a No. 2 or 3 catheter is best for the smaller tibial vessels.

Several passes of the catheter are made until no further thrombus is extracted. When performing a thromboembolectomy of inflow vessels, the surgeon's goal should be the restitution of forceful, pulsatile blood flow. As mentioned previously, vigorous backflow after distal thromboembolectomy is unreliable. In the presence of robust collateral circulation, backflow may be perceived as brisk despite the presence of residual distal thrombus. Furthermore, backflow may not occur in patients without abundant collateral channels, even in the absence of residual thrombus. It is important that the same surgeon inflates and withdraws the catheter. Inflation of the balloon should be initiated simultaneously with withdrawal of the catheter because this maneuver provides more accurate feedback to the operator as to the appropriate amount of traction and inflation pressure to be used, thereby minimizing the risk of iatrogenic vascular injury. Overly forceful attempts to pass the catheter should be avoided. Vessel angulation or tortuosity may hamper distal passage of the catheter. Helpful maneuvers consist of simultaneously inserting multiple catheters, varying the angle of the knee joint, creating a bend at the tip of the catheter followed by rotation of the catheter during induction, and the use of fluoroscopically guided over-the-wire catheters.

One should remain cognizant of the length of the catheter passed to minimize the risk of vascular perforation. Perforation is most frequent at the terminus of the popliteal artery or at the bifurcation of the tibioperoneal trunk. Extracted thrombus should always be examined. A smooth taper is suggestive of adequate clot removal, whereas a sharp, fragmented cutoff implies retained thrombus. After satisfactory thromboembolectomy of the proximal and distal vasculature, heparinized saline (1000 units in 100 mL saline) should be infused prior to closure of the arteriotomy.

It is essential for the surgeon to assess the adequacy of revascularization after thromboembolectomy. Early studies noted a 35% to 40% incidence of residual thrombus when routine post-thromboembolectomy arteriography was employed.[93] Although arteriographic evaluation does not supplant the need for clinical examination of the limb and palpation of distal pulses, these criteria are sometimes difficult to evaluate immediately after revascularization because of associated occlusive disease and vasospasm. Doppler pressure measurements or pulse volume recordings aid in evaluating the success of revascularization.[94] Intravascular ultrasound can readily demonstrate the completeness of thrombus removal, and it can detect significant amounts of residual thrombus not apparent arteriographically in up to 60% of patients.[95]

If the intraoperative evaluation suggests incomplete thrombus removal, additional steps must be taken. Standard balloon embolectomy catheters are effective in the removal of soft, fresh thrombus. In contrast, older, more organized, and adherent thrombus and thrombus within areas of atherosclerotic disease may be more difficult to remove. Low-profile graft thrombectomy catheters consisting of latex-covered spiral coils or bare wire elements of varying diameters allow the surgeon to exert additional traction on the wall of the lumen, a feature that is particularly useful for removing the mature adherent pseudointima often found in synthetic grafts or arteriovenous fistulae.

Acute Aortic Occlusion

The transfemoral route is feasible as a means of aortic embolectomy, but a bilateral approach is mandatory. A No. 5 or 6 Fogarty catheter is passed from a femoral arteriotomy after exposure and control of both femoral arteries have been obtained. The catheter is then withdrawn, extracting the bulk of the embolus. The contralateral femoral vessel is occluded simultaneously to prevent distal thromboemboli, and any remaining thrombus is removed by passing a catheter from the other side. If good inflow cannot be restored, often as a result of preexisting occlusive disease, a direct transperitoneal or retroperitoneal approach to the aorta is indicated. A less attractive, but sometimes necessary, alternative is to simply bypass the emboli with an aortobifemoral or axillary bifemoral reconstruction.

A recent report from the Albany Medical Center described 48 patients presenting with acute aortic occlusion over 12 years. A mix of acute emboli and thromboses was represented. The investigators noted a 27% mortality rate, and only 10% of the patients had disease amenable to isolated thromboembolectomy; the remainder required either a direct aortic or extra-anatomic bypass procedure.[96]

Patients with acute occlusion of the abdominal aorta are in an extremely compromised state. The patient's status will likely further deteriorate at the instant of reperfusion, and sudden cardiovascular collapse is commonly encountered with the release of accumulated metabolic byproducts into the circulation. Furthermore, blood loss associated with the flushing required with a bilateral femoral approach may be substantial. For this reason, a limited operative approach is often advisable, especially in patients whose occlusion is truly embolic in nature ("aortic saddle embolus").

Popliteal Thromboemboli

The preferred approach to emboli distal to the femoral bifurcation is still debated. Many surgeons prefer a groin incision and pass an embolectomy catheter into the distal circulation through a femoral arteriotomy. Adequate retrieval of thromboembolic material from the tibial vessels, however, may be quite problematic using this approach. Anatomic studies have shown that a catheter blindly passed from above preferentially enters the peroneal artery in nearly 90% of patients.[97] Abbott and colleagues reported a dismal 49% success rate with a transfemoral approach to popliteal emboli.[98]

Thus, the most efficient approach is via direct exposure of the distal popliteal artery and each of its three tibial outflow branches. The latter technique allows precise, selective passage of a small (e.g., No. 2) embolectomy catheter into the runoff vessels. Completion arteriography is an important feature of a successful embolectomy, and retained thrombotic debris after a transfemoral embolectomy mandates direct exploration of the below-knee popliteal artery. On exposure of the popliteal artery, the embolectomy catheter can be guided from the femoral arteriotomy into the individual branches by external compression of the other branches. Alternatively, a distal popliteal arteriotomy may be performed and each tibial vessel selectively catheterized under direct vision.

Distal Tibial Thromboemboli

Despite a direct approach to the below-knee popliteal artery, residual thrombus within the tibial circulation is not uncommon, especially if substantial delay in operative intervention has occurred. In such circumstances, direct exploration of the distal tibial vessels at the ankle may be required.[44,99] Each vessel is approached through a longitudinal incision just proximal to the ankle. The posterior tibial artery is located deep to the flexor retinaculum midway between the medial malleolus and the Achilles tendon. The anterior tibial artery is located deep to the extensor retinaculum just lateral to the tendon of the extensor hallucis longus. A small transverse arteriotomy is made, and a No. 2 Fogarty catheter is passed retrograde and antegrade to extract thrombus.

Small-vessel arteriotomy, however, is met with frequent rethrombosis in the setting of an acutely ischemic limb. Endothelial damage attributable to prolonged ischemia, thrombus, and balloon manipulation predisposes to postoperative reocclusion. Furthermore, the frequent need to explore multiple tibial vessels is associated with a significant risk of postoperative bleeding while therapeutic anticoagulation is maintained. Thrombolytic therapy (discussed later) is a remaining alternative in the setting of retained clot in the distal tibial vessels. It is extremely difficult to remove thrombi lodged in the inframalleolar vessels by either thrombolytic or open surgical techniques. The lack of any patent arterial segment distal to the occlusive process is a grave finding, and the risk of tissue loss is very high irrespective of the nature or rapidity of therapeutic intervention.

Upper Extremity Emboli

Embolic occlusion of the upper extremity vasculature is the most common source of acute ischemia of the hand. Only 17% of all emboli, however, lodge in this region.[100] Most upper extremity emboli are of cardiac origin, with the remainder arising from subclavian aneurysms, occlusive lesions, or iatrogenic causes, including axillary bypass procedures (Fig. 67-4) and arteriovenous hemodialysis fistulae.[101,102]

Most upper extremity emboli lodge at the bifurcation of the brachial artery into the radial and ulnar vessels. The presence of abundant collateral circulation at this level makes acute brachial occlusion at this level better tolerated, and limb loss is far less likely than with lower extremity emboli. Another common site is at the takeoff of the deep brachial artery. In both scenarios, an antecubital exposure of the brachial bifurcation is appropriate, usually using local anesthesia, and can be performed with relative ease and safety. The results of transbrachial embolectomy are generally excellent.

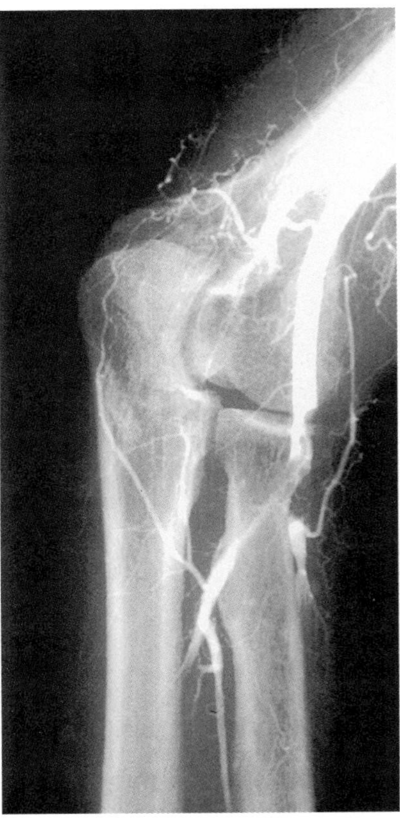

FIGURE 67-4 Embolization to the brachial bifurcation from the stump of a ligated axillofemoral bypass graft.

Intraoperative Thrombolytic Therapy

An alternative method for dealing with retained distal tibial and small-vessel thromboembolic material that is not amenable to conventional catheter techniques is the intraoperative use of fibrinolytic agents. Recent surgical procedures are traditionally viewed as a strong contraindication to thrombolytic therapy because of a high incidence of bleeding complications. In separate studies, however, Comerota and Quiñones-Baldrich have shown that infusion of thrombolytic agents during operative procedures is safe and often beneficial.[103-108] Experimental work has demonstrated that blood flow is improved and salvage of ischemic muscle is accomplished with less reperfusion edema and cellular injury when lytic agents are infused.[107,108] This result, which is presumably due to restoration of perfusion in the small arteriolar branches of larger axial vessels, is not possible with mechanical catheter thromboembolectomy.

The specific agents used, the dosages infused, and the method of infusion vary considerably. Urokinase was the thrombolytic agent used most frequently and appeared to be faster and safer than streptokinase. Recombinant tissue plasminogen activator and reteplase have also been administered with success. Urokinase (250,000 to 500,000 IU) is infused into the distal vasculature, either as a bolus or as an infusion over approximately 30 minutes. Arteriography is then repeated to assess the results. Gonzalez-Fajardo and associates prospectively evaluated 66 patients undergoing balloon embolectomy, 31 of whom received 250,000 units of urokinase intraoperatively.[109] They noted a statistically significant improvement in the ankle-brachial index in these patients, but this hemodynamic improvement did not translate into a reduction in the rate of amputation. Despite these findings, others have noted clinical improvement after regional infusion of thrombolytic agents for acute limb ischemia, and the technique remains promising.[103,110] Comerota and White[111] reported on 53 patients with persistent ischemia due to extensive distal thrombosis despite maximal efforts with catheter thrombectomy. Use of adjunctive regional intraoperative lytic therapy resulted in limb salvage in 70% of patients. In this series, only 1 patient (2%) had a major bleeding complication.

Endovascular Modalities

Thrombolytic Therapy

Catheter-directed thrombolytic treatment strategies were popularized in the 1970s by Dotter.[112] Thrombolysis offers several potential advantages over surgical therapy, including its ability to dissolve platelet-fibrin aggregates in the microcirculation and collateral vessels, which are beyond the reach of catheters. Furthermore, more gradual reperfusion may help avoid the sudden reperfusion syndrome associated with sudden release of arterial obstruction. Finally, thrombolysis has the added advantage of revealing underlying arterial stenosis, which is potentially manageable via endovascular means.

The Rochester trial demonstrated that thrombolytic therapy in patients with symptoms less than 7 days in duration was associated with a reduction in cardiopulmonary complications.[91] This translated into better survival compared with primary operation. The rate of limb salvage was identical in the thrombolytic and surgical groups.

The data provided by the Rochester trial prompted interest in the development of the multicenter TOPAS trial (with recombinant urokinase [r-UK]). The trial was performed in two parts: (1) a 213-patient dose-ranging trial, and (2) a 544- "head-to-head" comparison of the best dose of r-UK versus primary operation.[90,113] The multicenter trial included patients with lower extremity arterial occlusion of 14 days or less in duration. The study identified an optimal dose of 4000 IU/min r-UK for 4 hours followed by 2000 IU/min for acute peripheral arterial occlusion. Compared with primary operation, similar rates of limb salvage and patient survival were achieved with r-UK, concurrent with a lower requirement for open surgical procedures at 12 months' follow-up.

A number of interesting facts are brought to light when attempting to apply the data from clinical trials to patients with peripheral arterial embolization. First, acute limb ischemia secondary to embolization affected a few patients; native artery or bypass graft in-situ thrombosis represented approximately 80% of patients with acute arterial occlusion. Second, the short-term clinical results of thrombolytic treatment for emboli did not differ significantly from those achieved in patients with thrombosis, with successful thrombolytic dissolution of thrombus in approximately 70% of patients over a mean period of 36 to 40 hours.[91] In contrast with the early results, significant differences between patients with emboli and thrombosis in situ were observed at 1 year. Although the numbers of patients in the subgroups were small enough to preclude statistical analysis, patency and survival appeared to be higher in the patients with embolism.

Unfortunately, thrombolysis exposes the patient to the risk of potential hemorrhage, stroke, renal dysfunction, and delayed reperfusion injury leading to irreversible ischemia.[114,115] In the TOPAS trial, the mortality rate in the surgical group was 8.8% compared with 5.9% in the urokinase group. Major hemorrhage occurred in 12.5% of the urokinase group compared with 5.5% in the surgery group with intracranial hemorrhage occurring in 1.6% of the urokinase cohort. In a more recent study, the mortality rate associated with thrombolytic therapy was 4%, and the rate of major complication was 29%.[116] Hemorrhage requiring transfusion occurred in 23% of patients receiving lytic therapy, whereas renal failure requiring dialysis occurred in 2% and stroke in 1%. There is also considerable cost related to thrombolytic therapy.

Although thrombolytic therapy can be used successfully in patients with embolic arterial occlusion, just as it can in patients with in-situ thrombosis, the indications for lytic therapy remain vague and the risks substantial.

Percutaneous Mechanical Thrombectomy

Percutaneous thrombectomy has the potential to offer the advantage of a less invasive means of accomplishing thrombectomy while avoiding the delayed reperfusion and risk of bleeding associated with lytic therapy. A variety of percutaneous thrombectomy devices have been evaluated both in vitro and clinically.

Greenfield and associates introduced percutaneous aspiration of thrombus from the arterial system in 1969.[117] A suction cup was mounted on the tip of a 12-French double-lumen, balloon-tipped catheter. The cup was advanced until it was in apposition with the thrombus and continuous suction was then applied to the cup and the thrombus was withdrawn. Initially, an incision was required, but now this can be accomplished percutaneously. Although its size and steerability limit the use of this device, large pulmonary emboli have been successfully removed in such a fashion. A smaller version of Greenfield's device has been used for the retrieval of arterial emboli.

Percutaneous aspiration thromboembolectomy can be accomplished with the simple combination of a sheath containing a removable hemostatic valve and a large, thin-walled angiographic catheter. A sheath is advanced in close proximity to the thrombus, which is then traversed with an angiographic wire and catheter. Suction is applied to the catheter and the thrombus is withdrawn. The hemostatic valve is removed, and the catheter with the attached thromboembolus is withdrawn from the sheath.[118] With such a device, clot fracture with distal embolization remains a significant risk. Consequently, the use of thrombolytic therapy may be required in conjunction with suction-catheter techniques.[119]

Technical success has been reported for percutaneous thromboembolectomy comparing outcome with that of historical controls treated with open surgical intervention. In a series of 85 patients undergoing percutaneous aspiration embolectomy, Wagner and coauthors noted an initial success rate of 86%, with 1- and 4-year limb salvage rates of 88% and 86%, respectively.[120] Many modifications to this method of thrombus extraction have been described. Clot-trapping bags, expanding catheters, and sheaths coupled with Fogarty embolectomy catheters all have been evaluated.[121-124]

A variety of devices have been designed and implemented to effect thrombus dissolution via pulverization and aspiration (Fig. 67-5), although none have been approved for the treatment of peripheral arterial emboli. Thromboembolic material can be fragmented by the establishment of a Venturi effect with retrograde-directed fluid jets.[125] Thrombus is progressively macerated to facilitate aspiration. Sharafuddin and Hicks[125] published a comparative review of mechanical thrombolytic devices. Examples included the Trac-Wright catheter, Amplatz Thrombectomy Device, Impeller-Basket catheter, Thrombolizer, AngioJet, Hydrolyser, and Shredding Embolectomy Thrombectomy Catheter.[126-134] Work in-vitro demonstrated that one variable predicting the amount of embolic debris was the degree of distal stenosis. In the presence of a severely stenotic lesion, the thrombus is trapped and fewer or smaller emboli are liberated. Application of these devices in absence of stenotic lesions must be done in conjunction with a careful scrutiny of the distal circulation before and after embolectomy. A hemolytic effect has been noted with the use of these devices, and a balance must be achieved between the degree of recirculation required and the extent of hemolysis occurring.[132]

Mechanical thromboembolectomy instruments that do not use suction or recirculation rely on high-speed rotational

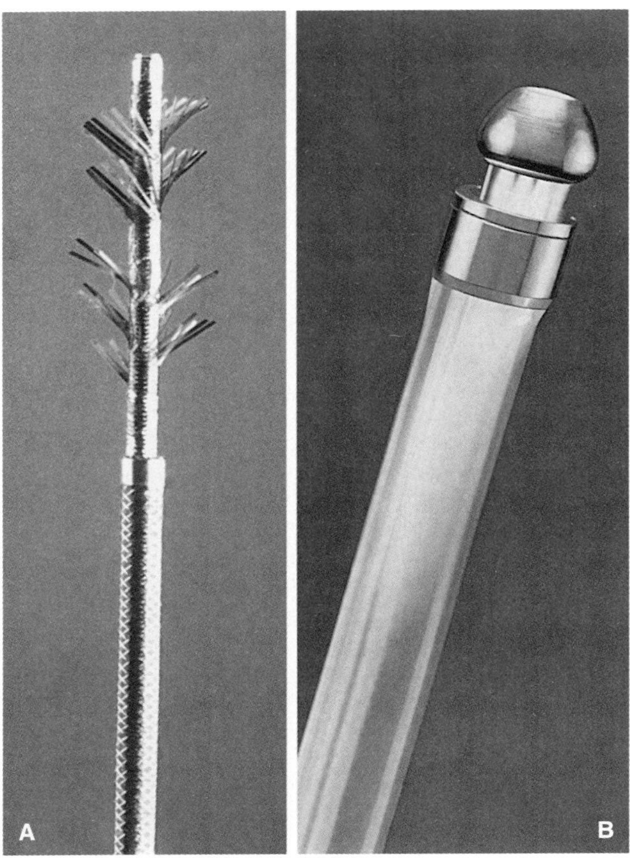

FIGURE 67-5 **A,** The Cragg thrombolytic brush. The brush is placed into the clot using an over-the-wire technique. The clot is then macerated into fine particles. **B,** The AngioJet system relies on the Venturi effect to remove friable thrombus. Both systems represent mechanical thrombectomy devices that are placed percutaneously.

devices designed to break apart thrombus without inducing significant endothelial damage. These instruments are commercially available and include the Cragg Thrombolytic Brush Catheter and the Trerotola Percutaneous Thrombectomy Device.[135,136] Rotational devices combined with suction provide a mechanism by which thrombus can be fractured into particles more easily removed by aspiration; these devices include the Gunther Thrombectomy Catheter, Transluminal Extraction Catheter, and Amplatz Maceration Aspiration Thrombectomy Catheter.[137-139]

Ultrasound-Accelerated Thrombolysis

Ultrasound energy can be used to ablate thrombus by an effect described as *acoustic cavitation* or to improve the delivery and efficacy of a thrombolytic agent.[140,141] This has been shown in-vitro with both intravascular (catheter-based) and extravascular (transdermal) devices.[142,143] The effects of ultrasound are dependent on the frequency employed. Low-frequency transducers are associated with a great range of tissue penetration and are suitable for transdermal applications; high-frequency devices are used with intravascular devices in catheter-based systems. Although ultrasound improves the rate of thrombolysis, tissue heating is a major concern. Clinical applicability awaits a demonstration of safety and efficacy in early feasibility trials presently being organized.

Compartment Syndrome

Following revascularization, significant limb swelling may occur. This situation has the potential to result in a compartment syndrome, most frequently in the anterior compartment. Edema within closed fascial compartments can lead to neurologic compromise or impairment of distal blood flow. If prolonged severe ischemia has existed prior to embolectomy, the surgeon may elect to perform a fasciotomy empirically in conjunction with the embolectomy.[85-87] Alternatively, because a fasciotomy can be easily performed subsequent to the embolectomy, some surgeons prefer a course of careful observation. Although the diagnosis of compartment syndrome is largely based on clinical assessment, the use of compartment pressures may provide some insight into the relative risks of observation versus immediate fasciotomy.[144,145]

Four-compartment fasciotomy is best performed with a two-incision technique. The anterior and lateral compartments are opened through a lateral incision, and the posterior compartments are decompressed through a medial incision. These incisions are left open for delayed primary closure or skin grafting when edema resolves. The major risks associated with fasciotomies include both infection and bleeding.

Results of Therapy

The advent of the Fogarty catheter simplified the surgical management and improved the results of operative intervention. These developments have been responsible for a limb salvage rate of between 75% and 90%. Unfortunately, the mortality rate has remained in the range of 10% to 20%. Delays in operative intervention, frequently occurring as a result of late presentation, may be the single most important determinant confounding a successful outcome. In the series by Abbott and colleagues, when treatment began less than 12 hours after onset, the limb salvage rate was 93% and the mortality rate was 19%.[11] In contrast, when there was a delay of more than 12 hours, the limb salvage rate was only 78% and the mortality rate was 31%. Elliott and associates found that within a range of 8 hours to 7 days, the effect of delayed treatment had a linear relationship to the severity of ischemic changes and unfavorable results.[43]

Endovascular modalities, including thrombolytic therapy, appear to be promising therapeutic options that must be evaluated in comparison with surgical therapy in well-designed trials. Singh and associates stratified 82 patients treated between 1988 and 1993 into three groups.[146] The first group underwent standard surgical treatment; in the second group, intraoperative thrombolytic therapy was combined with balloon embolectomy; the third group was treated with percutaneous thrombolysis. Although minor differences were noted prior to treatment, an analysis of limb salvage and survival yielded similar results.

In a study comparing thrombolytic versus primary operative intervention in patients with acute limb ischemia, Ouriel and colleagues evaluated outcome in patients with thrombotic or embolic occlusions.[91] Although the number of patients studied was small, the risk of major amputation was the same (≈ 18% at 12 months), regardless of the form of therapy. However, mortality rates were significantly lower in the thrombolytic group (16% vs. 42% at 12 months). This observation was explained by a higher frequency of cardiopulmonary complications in the operative group.

It is clear that many factors exert a negative influence on the outcome of patients suffering from acute thromboembolism. These include the underlying source for the embolus, the high incidence of associated atherosclerotic disease, and systemic metabolic complications. As the population ages and patients with emboli make up an older age group, the prevalence of atherosclerotic heart disease increases, as do the risks of both open and percutaneous procedures. It is predictable that the gains from technologic advances may be offset by an increased complexity of medical co-morbidities, such that the mortality associated with acute limb ischemia will remain considerable.

■ SUMMARY

Despite treatment advances, acute peripheral arterial thromboembolism is still associated with substantial morbidity and mortality. Most of these patients are older, have significant co-morbidities, and have an underlying cause for the process. Emboli most commonly originate from the heart or as a result of an intra-arterial manipulation. Thrombosis in situ may develop in the setting of an underlying atherosclerotic stenosis or as a result of a hypercoagulable state. Recently, thrombosis of a bypass graft has become a more common cause of acute ischemia of the extremity.

Arterial embolization must be distinguished from acute arterial thrombosis that is due to preexisting occlusive disease. Preoperative arteriography is helpful in all but the most straightforward cases, provided ischemia is not unduly prolonged. Prompt treatment is the rule; delays in therapy unquestionably result in less favorable results. Long-term anticoagulation is mandatory in patients with embolic disease and in many cases of thrombotic occlusions of bypass grafts and native arteries.

Despite technologic advances, the morbidity and mortality rates of acute peripheral artery thromboembolism are likely to remain significant owing to an increase in the age and fragility of the population experiencing these events. Appreciable improvements in clinical outcome will be realized only through rapid diagnosis of peripheral thromboembolism, the use of appropriate surgical or endovascular interventions to restore arterial perfusion, and efficient perioperative care to address the myriad of metabolic problems encountered in this group of patients.

■ REFERENCES

1. Moynihan B: An operation for embolus. BMJ 2:826, 1907.
2. Key E: Embolectomy in the treatment of circulatory disturbances in the extremities. Surg Gynecol Obstet 36:309, 1923.
3. Key E: Embolectomy on vessels of the extremities. Br J Surg 24:350, 1936.
4. Lerman J, Miller F, Lund C: Arterial embolism and embolectomy. JAMA 94:1128, 1930.
5. Murray D: The use of heparin in thrombosis. Ann Surg 108:163, 1938.
6. Crawford E, DeBakey M: The retrograde flush procedure in embolectomy and thrombectomy. Surgery 40:737, 1956.
7. Keeley J, Rooney J: Retrograde milking: An adjunct in technique of embolectomy. Ann Surg 134:1022, 1951.
8. Dale W: Endovascular suction catheters: For thrombectomy and embolectomy. J Thorac Cardiovas Surg 44:557, 1962.
9. Fogarty T, Cranley J, Krause R: A method for extraction of arterial emboli and thrombi. Surg Gynecol Obstet 116:241, 1963.
10. Becquemin J, Kovarsky S: Arterial emboli of the lower limbs: Analysis of risk factors for mortality and amputation. Ann Vasc Surg 9:S32, 1995.
11. Abbott W, Maloney R, McCabe C, et al: Arterial embolism: A 44-year perspective. Am J Surg 143:460, 1982.
12. Dale W: Differential management of acute peripheral arterial ischemia. J Vasc Surg 1:269, 1984.
13. Kendrick J, Thompson B, Read R, et al: Arterial embolectomy in the leg: Results in a referral hospital. Am J Surg 142:739, 1981.
14. Santiani B, Gross W, Eans W: Improved limb salvage after arterial embolectomy. Ann Surg 188:153, 1978.
15. Panetta T, Thompson J, Talkington C, et al: Arterial embolectomy: A 34-year experience with 400 cases. Surg Clin North Am 66:339, 1986.
16. Tawes R, Harris E, Brown W, et al: Arterial thromboembolism: A 20-year perspective. Arch Surg 120:595, 1985.
17. Dregelid E, Strangland L, Eide G, et al: Patient survival and limb prognosis after embolectomy. Eur J Vasc Surg 1:263, 1987.
18. Baxter-Smith D, Ashton F, Stanley G, et al: Peripheral arterial embolism: A 20-year review. J Cardiovasc Surg 29:453, 1988.
19. Varty K, St. Johnston J, Beets G, et al: Arterial embolectomy: A long-term perspective. J Cardiovasc Surg 33:79, 1992.
20. Darling R, Austen W, Linton R: Arterial embolism. Surg Gynecol Obstet 124:106, 1967.
21. Warren R, Linton R: The treatment of arterial embolism. N Engl J Med 238:421, 1948.
22. Warren R, Linton R, Scannell J: Arterial embolism: Recent prognosis. Ann Surg 140:311, 1954.
23. Green R, DeWeese J, Rob C: Arterial embolectomy before and after the Fogarty catheter. Surgery 77:24, 1975.
24. Sharma P, Babu S, Shah P, Nassoura Z: Changing patterns of atheroembolism. Cardiovasc Surg 4:573, 1996.
25. Shah D, Leather RP: Arterioarterial atherothrombotic microemboli of the lower limb. In Veith FJ, Hobson RW, Williams RA, Wilson SE (eds): Vascular Surgery: Principles and Practice. New York, McGraw-Hill, pp 397-408, 1994.
26. Carvajal JA, Anderson WR, Weiss L, et al: Atheroembolisms: An etiological factor in renal insufficiency, gastrointestinal hemorrhages, and peripheral vascular disease. Arch Intern Med 119:593, 1977.
27. Kaplan K, Millar ID, Canilla PA: "Spontaneous" atheroembolic renal failure. Arch Intern Med 110:218, 1962.
28. Haygood TA, Fessel WJ, Strange DA: Atheromatous microembolism simulating polymyositis. JAMA 203:135, 1968.
29. Anderson WR, Richards AM: Evaluation of lower extremity muscular biopsies in the diagnosis of atheroembolism. Arch Pathol 86:528, 1968.
30. Maurizi CP, Barker AE, Trueheart RE: Atheromatous emboli: A postmortem study with special reference to the lower extremities. Arch Pathol 86:528, 1968.
31. Wagner RB, Martin AS: Peripheral atheroembolism: Confirmation of clinical concept with a case report and review of the literature. Surgery 73:353, 1973.
32. Karmody AM, Jordan RF, Zaman SM: Left colon gangrene after acute interior mesenteric artery occlusion. Arch Surg 111:972, 1976.
33. Crane C: Atherothrombotic embolism to lower extremities in arteriosclerosis. Arch Surg 94:96, 1967.
34. Branowitz JB, Edwards WS: The management of atheromatous emboli to the lower extremities. Surg Gynecol Obstet 143:941, 1976.
35. Kempczinski R: Lower-extremity emboli from ulcerating atherosclerotic plaques. JAMA 241:807, 1979.

36. Schechter DC: Atheromatous embolization to lower limbs. N Y State J Med 79:1180, 1979.
37. Kwaan HJ, Connolly JE: Peripheral atheroembolism. Arch Surg 112:987, 1977.
38. Williams GM, Ricotta JJ, Zimmer M: The extended retroperitoneal approach for the treatment of extensive atherosclerosis in the aorta and renal vessels. Surgery 88:846, 1980.
39. Williams GM, Harrington D, Burdick J, White RI: Mural thrombosis of the aorta: An important, frequently neglected cause of large peripheral emboli. Ann Surg 194:737, 1981.
40. Karmody AM, Powers SR, Manaco VJ, Leather RP: "Blue toe syndrome": An indication for limb salvage surgery. Arch Surg 111:1263, 1976.
41. Mehigan JT, Stoney RJ: Lower extremity atheromatous embolus. Am J Surg 132:163, 1976.
42. Gore I, Collins DP: Spontaneous atheromatous embolization: Review of the literature and a report of 16 additional cases. Am J Clin Pathol 33:416, 1960.
43. Elliott JP Jr, Hageman J, Szilagyi D, et al: Arterial embolization: Problems of source, multiplicity, recurrence, and delayed treatment. Surgery 88:833, 1980.
44. Fogarty T, Daily P, Shumway N, et al: Experience with balloon catheter technique for arterial embolectomy. Am J Surg 122:231, 1971.
45. Levine J, Pauker S, Salzman E: Antithrombotic therapy in valvular heart disease. Chest 89:36S, 1986.
46. Shrestha N, Moreno F, Narcisco F, et al: Two-dimensional echocardiographic diagnosis of left-atrial thrombus in rheumatic heart disease: A clinicopathologic study. Circulation 67:341, 1983.
47. Schweizer P, Bardos F, Erbel R: Detection of left atrial thrombi by echocardiography. Br Heart J 45:148, 1981.
48. Daniel W, Mugge A: Transesophageal echocardiography. N Engl J Med 332:1268, 1995.
49. Husain A, Alter M: Transesophageal echocardiography in diagnosing cardioembolic stroke. Clin Cardiol 18:705, 1995.
50. Seward J, Khandheria B, Oh J, et al: Transesophageal echocardiography: Technique, anatomic correlations, implementation, and clinical applications. Mayo Clin Proc 63:649, 1988.
51. Rubin B, Barzilai B, Allen B, et al: Detection of the source of arterial emboli by transesophageal echocardiography: A case report. J Vasc Surg 15:573, 1992.
52. Hellerstein H, Martin J: Incidence of thromboembolic lesions accompanying myocardial infarction. Am Heart J 33:443, 1947.
53. Keeley E, Hillis L: Left ventricular mural thrombus after acute myocardial infarction. Clin Cardiol 19:83, 1996.
54. Asinger R, Mikell F, Elsperger J: Incidence of left ventricular thrombosis after acute transmural myocardial infarction. N Engl J Med 305:297, 1981.
55. Keating E, Gross S, Schlamowitz R: Mural thrombi in myocardial infarction. Am J Med 74:989, 1983.
56. Kuukasjarvi P, Riekkinen H, Salenius J, et al: Prevalence and predictive value of ECG findings in acute extremity ischemia. J Cardiovasc Surg 36:469, 1995.
57. Loop F, Effler D, Navia J, et al: Aneurysms of the left ventricle: Survival and results of a ten-year surgical experience. Ann Surg 178:399, 1973.
58. Perier P, Bessou J, Swanson J, et al: Comparative evaluation of aortic valve replacement with Starr, Björk, and porcine valve prostheses. Circulation 72:140, 1985.
59. Pipkin R, Buch W, Fogarty T: Evaluation of aortic valve replacement with porcine xenograft without long-term anticoagulation. J Thorac Cardiovasc Surg 71:179, 1976.
60. Vo N, Russell J, Becker D: Mycotic emboli of the peripheral vessels: Analysis of forty-four cases. Surgery 90:541, 1981.
61. Kitts D, Bongard F, Klein S: Septic embolism complicating infective endocarditis. J Vasc Surg 14:480, 1991.
62. Freischlag J, Asbun H, Sedwitz M, et al: Septic peripheral embolization from bacterial and fungal endocarditis. Ann Vasc Surg 3:318, 1989.
63. Lord J Jr, Rossi G, Daliana M, et al: Unsuspected abdominal aortic aneurysm as the cause of peripheral arterial occlusive disease. Ann Surg 177:767, 1973.
64. Kwaan J, Vander Molen R, Stemmer E, et al: Peripheral embolism resulting from unsuspected atheromatous plaques. Surgery 78:583, 1975.
65. Machleder H, Takiff H, Lois J, et al: Aortic mural thrombus: An occult source of arterial thromboembolism. J Vasc Surg 4:473, 1986.
66. Harriss R, Andros G, Dulawa L, et al: Malignant melanoma embolus as a cause of acute aortic occlusion: Report of a case. J Vasc Surg 3:550, 1986.
67. Prioleau P, Katzenstein A: Major peripheral artery occlusion due to malignant tumor embolism: Histologic recognition and surgical management. Cancer 42:2009, 1978.
68. Shannon J, Nghia M, Stanton P Jr, et al: Peripheral arterial missile embolization: A case report and 22-year literature review. J Vasc Surg 5:773, 1987.
69. Symbas P, Harlaftis N: Bullet emboli in the pulmonary and systemic arteries. Ann Surg 185:318, 1977.
70. Ward R, Jones D, Haponik E: Paradoxical embolism: An under-recognized problem. Chest 108:549, 1995.
71. Katz S, Andros G, Kohl R, et al: Arterial emboli of venous origin. Surg Gynecol Obstet 174:17, 1992.
72. Schurr M, McCord S, Croce M: Paradoxical bullet embolism: Case report and literature review. J Trauma 40:1034, 1996.
73. Oxorn D, Edelist G, Smith M: An introduction to transesophageal echocardiography: II. Clinical applications. Can J Anaesth 43:278, 1996.
74. Gazzaniga A, Dalen J: Paradoxical embolism: Its pathophysiology and clinical recognition. Ann Surg 171:137, 1970.
75. Laughlin R, Mandel S: Paradoxical embolization: Case report and review of the literature. Arch Surg 112:648, 1977.
76. Hight D, Tilney N, Couch N: Changing clinical trends in patients with peripheral emboli. Surgery 79:172, 1976.
77. Thompson J, Sigler L, Raut P, et al: Arterial embolectomy: A 20-year experience. Surgery 67:212, 1970.
78. Eason J, Mills J, Beckett W: Hypercoagulable states in arterial thromboembolism. Surg Gynecol Obstet 174:211, 1992.
79. Elliott J, Hageman J, Szilagyi D: Arterial embolization: Problems of source, multiplicity, recurrence, and delayed treatment. Surgery 88:833, 1980.
80. Linton R: Peripheral arterial embolism: A discussion of the post-embolic vascular changes and their relation to the restoration of circulation in peripheral embolism. N Engl J Med 224:189, 1941.
81. Walker P: Pathophysiology of acute arterial occlusion. Can J Surg 29:340, 1986.
82. Haimovici H: Muscular, renal, and metabolic complications of acute arterial occlusions: Myonephropathic-metabolic syndrome. Surgery 85:461, 1979.
83. Fischer R, Fogarty T, Morrow A: Clinical and biochemical observations of the effect of transient femoral artery occlusion in man. Surgery 68:323, 1970.
84. Homsi E, Barreiro M, Orlando J, Higa E: Prophylaxis of acute renal failure in patients with rhabdomyolysis. Ren Fail 19:283, 1997.
85. Padberg F, Hobson RI: Fasciotomy in acute limb ischemia. Semin Vasc Surg 5:52, 1992.
86. Perry M: Compartment syndromes and reperfusion injury. Surg Clin North Am 68:853, 1988.
87. Patman R, Thompson J: Fasciotomy in peripheral vascular surgery: Report of 164 patients. Arch Surg 101:663, 1970.
88. Rutherford R: Acute limb ischemia: Clinical assessment and standards for reporting. Semin Vasc Surg 5:4, 1992.
89. Rutherford R, Flanigan D, Gupta S, et al: Suggested standards for reports dealing with lower extremity ischemia. J Vasc Surg 64:80, 1986.
90. Ouriel K, Veith F, Sasahara A: A comparison of recombinant urokinase with vascular surgery as initial treatment for acute arterial occlusion of the legs. N Engl J Med 338:1105, 1998.

91. Ouriel K, Shortell C, DeWeese J, et al: A comparison of thrombolytic therapy with operative revascularization in the initial treatment of acute peripheral arterial ischemia. J Vasc Surg 19:1021, 1994.
92. Cambria RP, Abbott WM: Acute arterial thrombosis of the lower extremity. Arch Surg 119:784, 1984.
93. Pleacha F, Pories W: Intraoperative angiography in the immediate assessment of arterial reconstruction. Arch Surg 105:902, 1972.
94. O'Hara P, Brewster D, Darling R, et al: The value of intraoperative monitoring using the pulse volume recorder during peripheral vascular reconstructive operations. Surg Gynecol Obstet 152:275, 1981.
95. Greenberg R, Ouriel K, Waldman D, Green R: Intravascular ultrasound assessment of the adequacy of thrombolytic therapy. Unpublished data, 1998.
96. Woratyla S, Darling RC III, Lloyd W, et al: Acute and chronic aortic occlusion: Analysis of outcome [abstract]. In Proceedings of the Eastern Vascular Society, Providence, RI 12:82, 1998.
97. Short D, Vaughn GI, Jachimczyk J, et al: The anatomic basis for the occasional failure of transfemoral balloon catheter thromboembolectomy. Ann Surg 190:555, 1979.
98. Abbott W, McCabe C, Maloney R, et al: Embolism of the popliteal artery. Surg Gynecol Obstet 159:533, 1984.
99. Youkey J, Clagett G, Cabellon S, et al: Thromboembolectomy of arteries explored at the ankle. Ann Surg 199:367, 1984.
100. Pentti J, Salenius J, Kuukasjarvi P, Tarkka M: Outcome of surgical treatment in acute upper limb ischemia. Ann Chir Gynaecol 84:25, 1995.
101. McLafferty R, Taylor L, Moneta G, et al: Upper extremity thromboembolism after axillary-axillary bypass grafting. Cardiovasc Surg 4:111, 1996.
102. Trerotola S, Johnson M, Shah H, et al: Incidence and management of arterial emboli from hemodialysis graft surgical thrombectomy. J Vasc Interv Radiol 8:557, 1997.
103. Comerota A, White J: Intraoperative intraarterial thrombolytic therapy as an adjunct to revascularization in patients with residual and distal arterial thrombosis. Semin Vasc Surg 5:110, 1992.
104. Parent N, Bernhard V, Pabst T, et al: Fibrinolytic treatment of residual thrombus after catheter embolectomy for severe lower limb ischemia. J Vasc Surg 9:153, 1989.
105. Comerota A, White J, Grosh J: Intraoperative intraarterial thrombolytic therapy for salvage of limbs in patients with distal arterial thrombosis. Surg Gynecol Obstet 169:283, 1989.
106. Quiñones-Baldrich W, Baker J, Busuttil R, et al: Intraoperative infusion of lytic drugs for thrombotic complications of revascularization. J Vasc Surg 10:408, 1989.
107. Quiñones-Baldrich W, Ziomek J, Henderson T, et al: Intraoperative fibrinolytic therapy: Experimental evaluation. J Vasc Surg 4:229, 1986.
108. Belkin M, Veleri R, Hobson R: Intraoperative urokinase increases skeletal muscle viability after acute ischemia. J Vasc Surg 9:161, 1989.
109. Gonzalez-Fajardo J, Perez-Burkhardt J, Mateo A: Intraoperative fibrinolytic therapy for salvage of limbs with acute arterial ischemia: An adjunct to thromboembolectomy. Ann Vasc Surg 9:179, 1995.
110. Melton S, Croce M, Patton J, et al: Popliteal artery trauma: Systemic anticoagulation and intraoperative thrombolysis improves limb salvage. Ann Surg 225:518, 1997.
111. Comerota AJ, White JV: Intraoperative, intra-arterial thrombolytic therapy as an adjunct to revascularization in patients with residual and distal arterial thrombus. Semin Vasc Surg 5:110, 1992.
112. Dotter C: Selective clot lysis with low-dose streptokinase. Radiology 111:31, 1974.
113. TOPAS Investigators: Thrombolysis or Peripheral Arterial Surgery: Phase I results. J Vasc Surg 23:64, 1996.
114. Faggioli GL, Peer RM, Pedrini L, et al: Failure of thrombolytic therapy to improve long-term vascular patency. J Vasc Surg 19:289-296, 1994.
115. Ricotta JJ, Green RM, DeWeese JA: Use and limitations of thrombolytic therapy in the treatment of peripheral arterial ischemia: Results of a multi-institutional questionnaire. J Vasc Surg 6:45-50, 1987.
116. Korn P, Khilnani NM, Fellers JC, et al: Thrombolysis for native arterial occlusions of the lower extremities: Clinical outcome and cost. J Vasc Surg 33:6, 2001.
117. Greenfield L, Proctor M, Williams D, Wakefield T: Long-term experience with transvenous catheter pulmonary embolectomy. J Vasc Surg 18:450, 1993.
118. Sniderman K, Bodner L, Saddekni S, et al: Percutaneous embolectomy by transcatheter aspiration. Radiology 150:357, 1984.
119. Cleveland T, Cumberland D, Gaines P: Percutaneous aspiration thromboembolectomy to manage the embolic complications of angioplasty as an adjunct to thrombolysis. Clin Radiol 49:549, 1994.
120. Wagner H, Starck E, Reuter P: Long-term results of percutaneous aspiration embolectomy. Interv Radiol 17:241, 1994.
121. Ponomar E, Carlson J, Kindlund A, et al: Clot-trapper device for transjugular thrombectomy from the inferior vena cava. Radiology 179:279, 1991.
122. Criado F, Fogarty T, Patten P: New expandable access sheath for endovascular visualization and repair. Cardiovasc Surg 1:61, 1993.
123. Vorweck D, Gunther R, Clerc C: Percutaneous embolectomy: In-vitro investigation with a self-expanding tulip sheath. Radiology 182:415, 1992.
124. Vorweck D, Gunther R, Schumann K, et al: Percutaneous balloon embolectomy with a self-expanding tulip: In-vivo experiments. Radiology 197:153, 1995.
125. Sharafuddin M, Hicks M: Current status of percutaneous mechanical thrombectomy: II. Devices and mechanism of action. J Vasc Interv Radiol 9:15, 1998.
126. Wholey M, Jarmolowski C: New reperfusion devices: The Kensey catheter, the arthrolytic reperfusion wire, and the transluminal extraction catheter. Radiology 172:947, 1989.
127. Self S, Coe D, Normann S, Seeger J: Rotational atherectomy for treatment of occluded prosthetic grafts. J Surg Res 56:134, 1994.
128. Coleman C, Krenzel C, Dietz C, et al: Mechanical thrombectomy: Results of early experience. Radiology 189:803, 1993.
129. Tadavarthy S, Murray P, Inampudi S, et al: Mechanical thrombectomy with the Amplatz device: Human experience. J Vasc Interv Radiol 5:715, 1994.
130. Schmitz-Rode T, Vorweck D, Gunther R, Biesterfeld S: Percutaneous fragmentation of pulmonary emboli in dogs with the impeller-basket catheter. Cardiovasc Interv Radiol 16:239, 1993.
131. Schmitz-Rode T, Adam G, Kilbinger M, et al: Fragmentation of pulmonary emboli: In-vivo experimental evaluation of two high-speed rotating catheters. Cardiovasc Interv Radiol 19:165, 1996.
132. Sharafuddin M, Hicks M, Jenson M, et al: Rheolytic thrombectomy with the AngioJet-F105 catheter: Preclinical evaluation of safety. J Vasc Interv Radiol 8:939, 1997.
133. Reekers J, Kromhout J, Spithoven H, et al: Arterial thrombosis below the inguinal ligament: Percutaneous treatment with a thrombosuction catheter. Radiology 198:49, 1996.
134. Vicol C, Dalichau H, Kohler J, et al: Performance of indirect embolectomy aided by a newly developed flush-suction catheter system: Forty-seven experimental embolectomy procedures in test animals. J Cardiovasc Surg 35:193, 1994.
135. Castaneda F, Cragg A, Wyffels P, et al: New thrombolytic brush catheter in thrombosed polytetrafluoroethylene dialysis grafts: Preliminary animal study. Radiology 193:324, 1994.
136. Trerotola S, Davidson D, Filo R, et al: Preclinical in-vivo testing of a rotational mechanical thrombectomy device. J Vasc Interv Radiol 7:717, 1996.
137. Gunther R, Vorweck D: Aspiration catheters for percutaneous thrombectomy: Clinical results. Radiology 175:271, 1990.
138. Yedlicka J, Carlson J, Hunter D, et al: Thrombectomy with the transluminal endarterectomy catheter (TEC) system: Experimental study and case report. J Vasc Interv Radiol 2:343, 1991.
139. Pozza C, Gomes M, Qian Z, et al: Evaluation of the newly developed Amplatz maceration and aspiration thrombectomy device using in-vitro and in-vivo models. AJR Am J Roentgenol 162:139, 1994.

140. Rosenschein U, Rassin T: Ultrasound thrombolysis. Sci Med 5:36, 1998.
141. Francis C, Blinc A, Lee S, Cox C: Ultrasound accelerates transport of recombinant tissue plasminogen activator into clots. Ultrasound Med Biol 21:419, 1995.
142. Luo H, Steffen W, Cercek B, et al: Enhancement of thrombolysis by external ultrasound. Am Heart J 125:1564, 1993.
143. Harpaz D, Chen X, Francis C, et al: Ultrasound enhancement of thrombolysis and reperfusion in-vitro. J Am Coll Cardiol 21:1507, 1993.
144. Matsen F, Winquist R, Krugmire R: Diagnosis and management of compartment syndromes. J Bone Joint Surg 62:286, 1980.
145. Whitened T, Haney T, Harada H, et al: A simple method of tissue pressure determination. Arch Surg 110:1311, 1975.
146. Singh S, Ackroyd R, Lees, T, et al: Thrombo-embolectomy and thrombolytic therapy in acute lower limb ischemia: A five-year experience. Int Angiol 15:6, 1996.

Chapter 68

Atheromatous Embolization

RANDI ROSE, MD
JOHN BARTHOLOMEW, MD
JEFFREY W. OLIN, DO

The atheromatous embolization syndrome is a poorly recognized and underdiagnosed multisystem disorder that is associated with a markedly high morbidity and mortality. The myriad of clinical manifestations are apparent across all specialties, making the differential diagnosis broad and the diagnosis difficult. In addition, *atheromatous embolization* is a confusing entity to many physicians because it is known by many different names—*cholesterol embolization, cholesterol crystal embolization, blue toe syndrome, purple toe syndrome, atheroembolism*, and *pseudovasculitis*. For the purposes of this chapter, these terms are used interchangeably. Once atheroembolism has occurred, therapy involves two major strategies, (1) treat the end organ that is the recipient of the embolization and (2) prevent further embolization from occurring. Therefore, it is critical for clinicians to have a high index of suspicion and to recognize the risk factors that appear to precipitate or perpetuate this syndrome.

■ PATHOLOGY

Atheroembolism was first described more than a century ago by the German pathologist Panum.[1] However, Flory[2] is credited for accurately describing the syndrome in 1945; among 267 consecutive autopsies, he observed nine instances of cholesterol crystal embolism: none in 63 cases in which aortic plaque ulceration was absent, two instances in 147 (1.4%) cases with moderate aortic plaque erosion, and seven instances in 57 (12.8%) cases with severe aortic plaque ulceration. Since that seminal paper, it has become quite clear that the risk of atheroembolism is directly related to the severity of the aortic atherosclerosis (Fig. 68-1).

Atherosclerotic plaques consist of a fibrous cap, under which are macrophages, necrotic debris, and cholesterol crystals. The vulnerable plaques, or the plaques at the highest risk of rupture, are those with a thin fibrous cap surrounding a large lipid-rich core.[3] *Atheroembolism* is a process in which emboli from proximal lesions produce ischemia in distal arterial beds. Emboli may consist of thrombus, platelet fibrin material, or cholesterol crystals, either individually or in combination. Macroemboli may arise from thrombus originating in aortic or peripheral aneurysms, from atheromatous ulcers, or from dislodgement of atheromatous plaques. Microemboli are platelet-fibrin emboli or cholesterol crystals.[4]

Cholesterol crystals are white and rhomboidal or rectangular. They can also be elongated, biconvex, and needle shaped, and they range in size from 250 to less than 10 μm in diameter.[5] In paraffin-fixed sections, the cholesterol crystals are dissolved, leaving needle-like clefts (Fig. 68-2). Frozen or wet formalin-fixed sections show

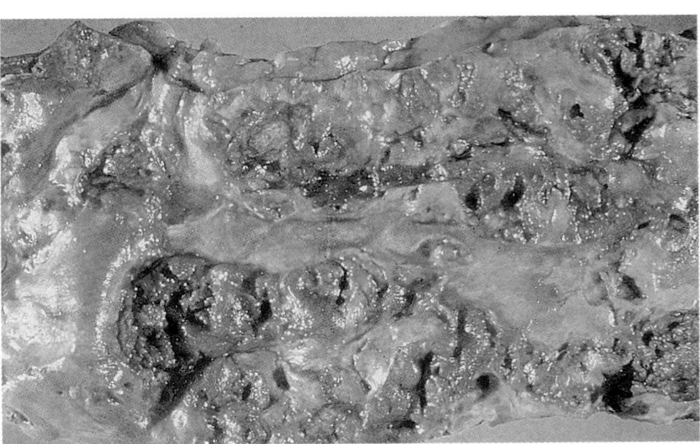

FIGURE 68-1 Gross autopsy specimen of a patient with a severely diseased aorta and atheroembolization syndrome.

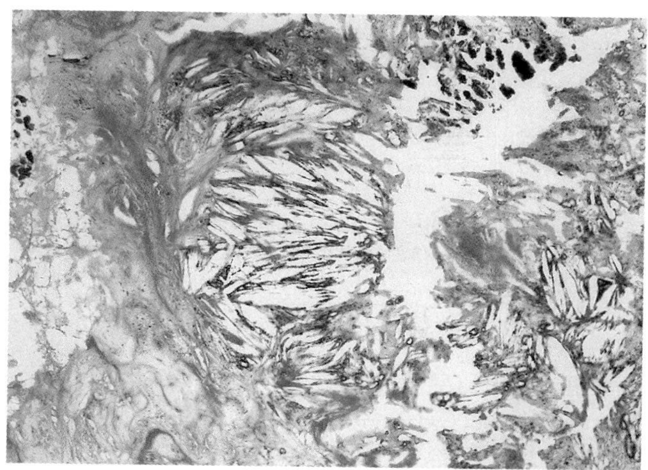

FIGURE 68-2 Typical appearance of the cholesterol clefts in a specimen from a carotid artery plaque. The convex shaped crystals dissolve during the fixation process leaving the ghosts as seen in this section (H & E stain, ×200).

doubly refractile cholesterol crystals, and with the Schultz histochemical stain, these crystals stain blue-green.[6]

Because they are light in weight and hydrophobic, the crystals pass quickly through blood vessels until they are stopped by arterial bifurcations—narrowings of the vessel lumen—or when they reach the end of the arterial circulation.[5] Cholesterol emboli tend to be diffuse and lodge in arteries 100 to 200 μm in diameter,[7] although small crystals have been observed in capillaries in the end-arterial circulation.

Cholesterol crystals that lodge in the arterioles immediately incite an inflammatory response characterized by varying degrees of polymorphonuclear and eosinophilic infiltration.[2,5,8,9] By 2 to 4 weeks, a more chronic inflammatory infiltrate is seen. Cholesterol crystals become embedded in multinucleated giant cells and smooth muscle cells.[8] Endothelial proliferation and fibrous tissue can be found surrounding the crystals, ultimately leading to luminal obliteration.[8,9] At 1 to 2 months, crystals may become extruded out of the vessel lumen and buried in the adventitia or may remain in the lumen embedded within organized thrombus that may recanalize.[8] The crystals are resistant to breakdown by macrophages and have been shown to persist in tissue for up to 9 months.[10,11] Arterial lumina are eventually occluded by the accumulation of cells and fibrous material. These pathologic changes result in tissue effects distal to the cholesterol crystal emboli, including ischemia and, rarely, infarction, depending on the extent of organ involvement. This type of foreign body reaction is the reason it may take weeks to months for the serum creatinine concentration to rise in patients with atheroembolic renal disease and explains why renal function does not usually recover.[10]

■ INCIDENCE

The incidence of cholesterol embolism syndrome varies according to population characteristics, diagnostic criteria, and study design. Among unselected series of autopsy studies, the incidence of cholesterol crystal embolism ranges from 0.18% to 2.4%.[12,13] However, autopsy studies performed in selected populations of patients with atherosclerosis and those who have undergone aortic manipulation have reported a greater prevalence of cholesterol crystal embolism, ranging from 12% to 77%.[14-16] In general, retrospective autopsy studies overestimate the frequency of the disease because of the detection of subclinical cases as well as the selection bias inherent in obtaining information after necropsy. In contrast, clinically significant atheroembolic disease in clinical studies may be missed because of short follow-up. The prevalence of atheroembolic disease in clinical studies has been estimated to be between 1% and 4%.[5,7,17-19]

■ RISK, PRECIPITATING FACTORS, AND SIMPLE PREVENTIVE STRATEGIES

The most important risk factor for atheroembolism is established atherosclerosis. Flory[2] was the first person to hypothesize such a relationship between cholesterol crystal embolism and a diseased atherosclerotic aorta. In 1992, Blauth and associates[20] reported on 46 patient autopsies in which severe atherosclerosis of the ascending aorta was accompanied by evidence of atheroemboli in other vascular beds. Significant risk factors for atheroembolism included peripheral arterial disease, hypertension, older age, and coronary artery disease.[20]

Several precipitating factors have been implicated in the occurrence of plaque instability and consequent atheroembolism, including trauma, vascular surgery[21,22] angiographic and endovascular procedures,[10,23] anticoagulation,[17,24] and thrombolysis.[25-28] Atheroembolism can also occur spontaneously and was once the predominant form of atheroembolic disease, before the advent of endovascular revascularization techniques. In a retrospective analysis of 52 patients with a diagnosis of atheroembolic disease, Scolari and colleagues[7] found that the disease was spontaneous in only 21% of cases.

Angiography and Catheter Manipulation

Manipulation of the aorta with catheters or guidewires can cause mechanical trauma with the consequent dislodgement of atheromatous material from the arterial wall.[29] One study, evaluating the frequency of atherothrombotic material retrieved during placement of coronary catheters, found 0.5% of 7621 patients to have macroscopically visible atherothrombotic debris.[30] None of these patients, however, had clinically apparent atheroembolic disease. In a review of 4587 cardiac catheterizations, Drost and colleagues[31] found seven cases of clinical cholesterol embolization (0.002%). Colt and associates[32] found eight cases after heart catheterization, percutaneous transluminal coronary angioplasty (PTCA), and intra-aortic balloon pump insertion, a total of 3733 procedures (0.002%). Coronary angiography with angioplasty and stenting is the procedure most commonly inciting atheroembolism.[7] Saklayen and coworkers,[33] in a prospective analysis of 267 patients undergoing coronary angiography, found the incidence of cholesterol embolism to be less than 2%. Similar statistics were reported in a later prospective analysis by Fukumoto and colleagues,[34] who found clinically apparent cholesterol embolism (livedo pattern on the feet, blue toe syndrome, digital gangrene, or renal failure) in 1.4% of 1786 patients undergoing left heart catheterization.

It is impossible to predict the risk of atheroembolism in a given patient, but severe peripheral arterial disease, aortic aneurysm, and the finding of protruding mobile atheroma on transesophageal echocardiography[35] (TEE) all raise the risk of distal embolization and should therefore influence the vascular approach.[33,36-38] Utilization of long guidewire (260 cm) exchanges is recommended, and backbleeding from guiding catheters (once the wire is removed) allows for removal of debris. Advancement and removal of catheters should occur over a guidewire to straighten the catheter and minimize contact with the aortic wall.[39] Brachial and radial access may minimize embolization from the abdominal aorta, but not from the ascending aorta or arch. A prospective study of 1579 patients undergoing coronary angioplasty did not find significant differences between the brachial and femoral approaches.[40] However, in another study involving 3733 procedures, there were no cases of cholesterol embolization after cardiac catheterization when the brachial artery was used.[32]

Catheter manipulation of the aorta is common in the diagnosis and evaluation of the patient with vascular disease before revascularization, and as with coronary angiography, the risk of atheroembolism is a serious concern. Ramirez and coworkers,[41] in a retrospective study of 71 autopsies, reported a 27% incidence of cholesterol embolization in patients who had undergone arteriography before death, compared with a 4.3% incidence of spontaneous cholesterol emboli in an age- and disease-matched control group who did not undergo arteriography.[41] The rigidity of the catheter used as well as the force of the injection of contrast agent appears to contribute to the risk of embolization. Although some writers have advocated the use of a softer, more flexible catheter to avoid such a complication,[41,42] the most important factor determining risk remains the severity of the atherosclerotic disease in the aorta. It should be understood, however, that the studies reporting a significant incidence of cholesterol embolization after angiography were conducted nearly 25 years ago. With the advent of better, smaller, and more flexible catheters, guidewires, and balloons as well as superior operator technique, the incidence of atheromatous embolization after angiography is much lower than it was three decades ago.

Endovascular therapy for patients with peripheral vascular disease has become widely utilized as an alternative to surgical revascularization. It is clinically important that atheroembolism appears to be a relatively infrequent, but not absent, complication of endovascular therapy. In a retrospective analysis of 493 patients who underwent a total of 565 aortoiliac stent placements, Lin and associates[43] found the incidence of atheroembolism to be 1.6%. This figure is comparable to the findings of previous clinical studies noting that the rate of such a complication ranged between 1.3% and 3.6%.[44,45] However when emboli-protection devices are utilized in stent procedures in the carotid artery[46] or renal artery,[47] visible atherosclerotic debris appears quite frequently. The detection of a shaggy aorta and diffuse soft ulcerative plaque on transesophageal echocardiographic studies clearly identifies a high-risk patient. Hence, heightened awareness, proper patient selection, utilization of the most advanced catheters, guidewires, and balloons, use of emboli-protection devices, and greater operator expertise may have a favorable effect on the incidence of atheroembolism during endovascular interventions. Endovascular procedures using covered stent-grafts may be quite effective in patients who experience embolization, as discussed in the treatment section.

Vascular Surgery

The effect of atheroembolism after major vascular surgery was first recognized by Thurlbeck and Castleman[48] in 1957. Atheroembolism was present at autopsy in more than 75% of their patients who died after aortic aneurysm surgery. Atheromatous embolization either was the cause of death or significantly contributed to it in nearly half of the patients in this series. Subsequently, numerous studies have confirmed the importance of vascular surgery as a precipitator of atheroembolism. Vascular surgery procedures may disrupt plaque when the vessel is manipulated, cross-clamped, or incised during surgery.

Atheroembolization is a recognized complication of cardiac surgery and has profound medical and economic consequences. Doty and coworkers,[22] in a retrospective analysis of 18,402 patients who underwent cardiac surgery, found evidence of atheroembolism in 0.2% of patients at autopsy. The clinical presentation of atheroembolism in this study was broad and included five distinct organ systems: heart, central nervous system, gastrointestinal (GI) tract, kidneys, and lower extremities. In 21% of the cases, death was directly attributable to atheroembolism.[22] Kolh and associates[49] documented significant increases in duration of both intensive care unit stay and overall hospital stay as well as in total hospital cost in patients with documented atheroembolism after cardiac surgery.[49] TEE can identify significant aortic plaque preoperatively with sensitivity and specificity in excess of 90%.[50] Multidetector computed tomography (CT) scanning may also image the distal ascending aorta and proximal aortic arch, which are not as easily seen with TEE.[51] Alteration of the cannulation site and avoidance of aortic manipulation for coronary artery bypass in the patient with such findings may reduce the chance of atheroembolism.

Other vascular surgery procedures known to precipitate cholesterol embolization are aortoiliac and aortofemoral bypass, carotid endarterectomy, and renal artery revascularization.[7] It is clear that the most effective strategy for the management of atheroemboli in vascular surgery is prevention. In high-risk surgical patients, noninvasive procedures, such as magnetic resonance imaging, TEE, and CT angiography, are excellent techniques to screen preoperatively for the presence of aortic atherosclerosis. When a shaggy aorta is visualized, alternative surgical procedures should be considered to minimize aortic manipulation. Appropriate surgical techniques to prevent atheroemboli during operation are now well recognized and documented.[52]

Anticoagulation and Thrombolysis

Both a higher risk of cholesterol embolization with anticoagulation and clinical improvement when anticoagulation was removed have been documented in case reports for more than a quarter of a century.[7,17,24] One hypothesis is that anticoagulation may prevent thrombus formation over unstable atherosclerotic plaque, thus allowing exposed cholesterol crystals to embolize. Another is that these agents may initiate the disruption of a complex plaque by causing hemorrhage into it.[53-57] On the basis of these small case series and case reports, some investigators have recommended that warfarin therapy be discontinued, when feasible, in patients who have an episode of cholesterol embolization for which no other precipitant can be identified.

The data, however, are not entirely clear for assessing anticoagulation safety in patients with a large amount of aortic plaque. The assumption that anticoagulation precipitates cholesterol emboli syndrome was not confirmed by the Stroke Prevention in Atrial Fibrillation 3 (SPAF-3) trial, in which patients in whom aortic plaque was documented on transesophageal echocardiogram and who were assigned to adjusted-dose warfarin therapy had a low annual rate of cholesterol embolization (0.7% per patient-year; 95% confidence interval [CI], 0.1%-5.3%).[58] Furthermore, cholesterol embolization was not seen in patients with documented aortic arch plaque more than 1 mm thick who were treated with warfarin in The French Study of Aortic Plaques in Stroke.[59] Fukumoto and colleagues,[34] in a prospective evaluation of 25 patients with cholesterol emboli syndrome after cardiac catheterization, were unable to show any significant association between the use of anticoagulants and cholesterol embolism.[34] In addition, anticoagulation has been advocated for patients with crescendo transient ischemic attack (TIA), a syndrome caused by atheromatous embolization to the eye or brain. Therefore, the association of anticoagulation with a higher incidence of atheroemboli remains controversial, but current literature suggests that it is safe to continue anticoagulation therapy in patients in whom there is a compelling reason to do so, such as atrial fibrillation or venous thromboembolism.

Atheromatous emboli have also been associated with thrombolytic therapy in case reports and small series,[25,26,28] but again, this issue is very controversial. Thrombolytic agents act by converting plasminogen to plasmin, which directly degrades fibrin. Theoretically, any therapy that causes the thrombus to undergo lysis may leave atherosclerotic plaque uncovered, thereby putting the patient at risk for embolization. In one small prospective study, however, no relationship between the administration of thrombolytic therapy and cholesterol emboli syndrome was found.[60]

■ CLINICAL FEATURES

The syndrome of atheroembolism usually affects elderly males who have multiple risk factors for atherosclerosis but may occur in women and younger males with advanced atherosclerosis.[12] In a prospective study conducted to identify risk factors for cholesterol embolism in patients undergoing cardiac catheterization, Fukumoto and colleagues[34] confirmed that cholesterol emboli syndrome occurs more commonly in patients with generalized atheroscleroses, such as multivessel coronary disease and cerebrovascular disease. In addition, these investigators found a significant relationship between C-reactive protein level and cholesterol embolism (odds ratio 4.6; $P = .01$ using multivariate analysis), indicating an important possible association between systemic inflammation and cholesterol emboli syndrome.

The greater frequency of this disease in men may be explained by a difference in the prevalence of atherosclerosis between men and women. A race predilection has also been reported, as atheroemboli are less likely to occur in African-American patients.[61] Because African-Americans appear to have a higher prevalence of atherosclerosis, however, it has been suggested by some investigators that the lower rate of atheroembolism in this group may be a failure to recognize the classic features of this syndrome because of skin pigmentation.

Patients almost always have symptomatic atherosclerosis, manifesting clinically as angina, myocardial infarction, TIA, stroke, renal artery disease, mesenteric ischemia, or claudication. Atheroembolism can cause a myriad of symptoms (Table 68-1). In general, which organs are involved by cholesterol embolism depends on the location of the embolic source. Atheroemboli from the ascending aorta and proximal aortic arch usually manifest as central nervous system or retinal disease, whereas cholesterol crystal emboli originating from the descending thoracic or abdominal aorta affect the visceral organs and extremities. In general, bilateral lower extremity atheroembolism signifies a source proximal to the aortic bifurcation, and unilateral emboli may originate either proximally or in any artery distal to the aortic bifurcation. Patients with macroemboli arising from one or more large atheromatous plaques may present with a

Table 68-1 Clinical Manifestations of Atheromatous Embolization

Skin	Purple or blue toes Gangrenous digits Livedo reticularis Nodules
Renal	Uncontrolled hypertension Renal failure
Neurologic	Transient ischemic attack Amaurosis fugax Stroke Hollenhorst plaque
Cardiac	Myocardial infarction or ischemia
Gastrointestinal	Abdominal pain Gastrointestinal bleeding Ischemic bowel Acute pancreatitis
Constitutional	Fever Weight loss Malaise Anorexia

Adapted from Bartholomew JR, Olin JW: Atheromatous embolization. In Young JR, Olin JW, Bartholomew JR (eds): Peripheral Vascular Diseases, 2nd ed. St. Louis, CV Mosby, 1996.

catastrophic event such as an acutely ischemic limb or renal or mesenteric infarction. Conversely, patients with microemboli may have milder localized signs or a clinical picture that suggests a systemic illness. There may be a temporal delay of up to 8 weeks between the inciting event and the appearance of clinical findings (especially for renal failure).[4]

Cutaneous Manifestations

The skin manifestations are among the most common clinical manifestations of atheroembolism, and the common cutaneous features are livedo reticularis and blue toes.[62] The appearance of cutaneous signs can be delayed, with 50% of patients in one series showing skin signs of atheroembolism more than 30 days after their procedures or other inciting events.[62]

Livedo reticularis is a blue-red mottling or discoloration of the skin that occurs in a netlike pattern most commonly seen on the buttocks, thighs, or legs (Fig. 68-3). A detailed skin examination performed with the patient in both the supine and upright positions is necessary, because livedo reticularis has been shown to be more readily demonstrable in the upright position.[63] Livedo reticularis is most likely caused by obstruction of small arteries, capillaries, or venules in the deep dermis,[7] and when the skin is sampled for biopsy in patients with atheromatous embolization, cholesterol crystals may be seen in the dermal blood vessels. Livedo reticularis, however, is not pathognomonic of atheroemboli and has an extensive differential diagnosis, including but not limited to other causes of intravascular obstruction (i.e., antiphospholipid antibody syndrome, cryoglobulinemia, endocarditis, left atrial myxoma), vasculitis, and drug-induced obstruction (i.e., by quinidine, quinine, amantidine, catecholamines).[64] Furthermore, there are also physiologic (cutis marmorata) and idiopathic (livedoid vasculitis) forms of livedo reticularis.[64] Livedo can occur in young healthy women and appears to be related to abnormal sensitivity of the dermal blood vessels to cold; the livedo reticularis pattern usually disappears on rewarming. Patients who exhibit this reaction should be reassured that they have no serious circulatory abnormality.

In its classic presentation, the blue toe syndrome manifests as the sudden appearance of a cool, cyanotic, and painful toe on a foot with palpable distal pulses.[53,54,56,62] Discoloration may also be seen on the sole of the foot. The discoloration may be patchy, and comparison of the two feet shows that the distribution is not symmetrical. These lesions may progress to ulceration, necrosis, and gangrene.[7] Accessory lesions may be present on the lateral and posterior aspects of the heels and may later develop into linear fissures with skin edge gangrene and a dark, necrotic base.

Other skin manifestations are splinter hemorrhages, petechiae, purpura (Fig. 68-4), ulcers,[65] and raised nodules that appear as the result of subepidermal inflammation surrounding cholesterol crystals.[7,62] These nodules are painful, are violaceous with a necrotic center, and may mimic a necrotizing vasculitis such as polyarteritis nodosa or leukocytoclastic vasculitis. Ulceration of the penis and scrotum has also been described.[66]

Renal Involvement

The kidneys are a prime target for cholesterol crystal embolization because of the enormous amount of blood that flows through these organs as well as the close proximity of the proximal renal arteries to the abdominal aorta, where atheromatous plaque is quite common. Mayo and Swartz,[18] in a review of 402 nephrology consultation charts, found that the incidence of clinically detectable atheroembolism amounted to at least 4% of all hospitalized patients examined, representing approximately 5% to 10% of the patients with acute renal failure encountered. Scolari and associates[7] estimate encountering at least one patient per month with atheroembolic renal disease.[7]

Pathologically, the classic lesion of atheroembolic renal disease is the occlusion of medium-sized arterioles (150 to 200 μm in diameter) and glomerular capillaries with cholesterol emboli.[7] In addition to the ischemic obstructive

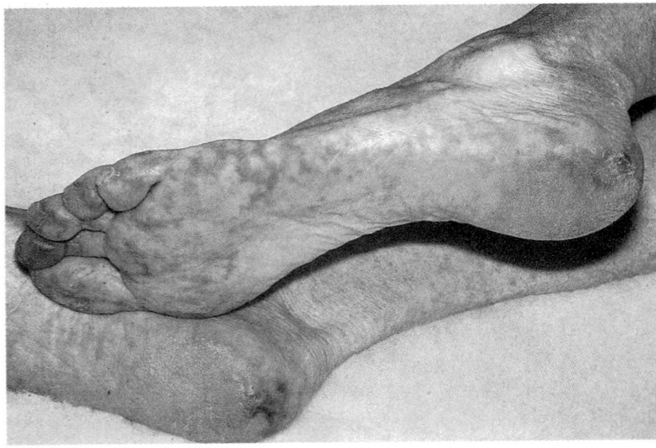

FIGURE 68-3 Classic livedo reticularis on the lateral portion of the left foot and on both heels. Note the blue (cyanotic) second and fourth toes. The involvement of both heels indicates that the lesion is above the aortic bifurcation. (From Bartholomew JR, Olin JW: Atheromatous embolization. In Young JR, Olin JW, Bartholomew JR [eds]: Peripheral Vascular Diseases, 2nd ed. St. Louis, CV Mosby, 1996.)

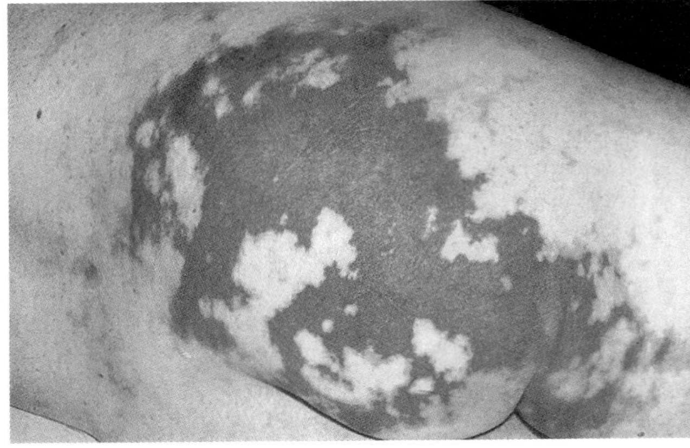

FIGURE 68-4 Example of a large purpuric lesion as a result of atheromatous embolization through the internal iliac artery.

mechanical phenomenon produced at the onset, this pathologic condition produces an inflammatory reaction within the arterioles. The initial stages, occurring several days to weeks after the inciting event, are characterized by an inflammatory infiltration consisting of polymorphonuclear leukocytes, macrophages, and multinucleated giant cells. As the cellular infiltrate leads to thickening and fibrosis of the arterioles, later stages are characterized by glomerular sclerosis, tubular atrophy, and interstitial fibrosis.[4,67] A kidney biopsy specimen from an individual patient may show different stages of histologic evolution because dislodged atheromatous debris may be showered into the circulation at different times.[67] Furthermore, the involvement tends to be patchy, and therefore, a renal biopsy specimen may not always show the classic pathologic lesions of this disease.[67]

The net effect of this pathogenic process, when combined with varying amounts of cholesterol embolization, comprises three somewhat different clinical presentations.[7] Marked renal impairment with an acute onset is the easiest form of atheroembolic renal disease to recognize. It has the closest temporal relationship to the inciting event and is generally considered the consequence of massive embolization. The subacute form of atheroembolic renal disease, the most commonly observed, is more insidious in onset, occurring a few weeks after the inciting event. Renal impairment may worsen over weeks to months as a result of a foreign-body reaction or the cyclic occurrence of cholesterol crystal embolic showers. This form of atheroembolism is more difficult to diagnose because affected patients usually come to the attention of physicians with advanced renal failure and few clues as to the exact onset of renal impairment. Chronic stable renal impairment, the third form of atheroembolic renal disease, is generally asymptomatic. Clinical features tend to be similar to those of ischemic nephropathy and nephrosclerosis. The role of cholesterol embolization in this setting is somewhat unclear, but many patients are misdiagnosed either because a renal biopsy is not performed or, if such a biopsy is performed, cholesterol embolization is missed because of the patchy distribution of the emboli.

Atheroembolic renal disease is often associated with poorly controlled hypertension.[4,55,56,68] When large segments of small arterioles are occluded, ischemic atrophy of substantial portions of the kidney occurs. As glomerular filtration declines, the renin-angiotensin-aldosterone system is activated, causing hypertension.[4] Severe, accelerated, labile, and malignant forms of hypertension have all been reported, and atheroembolic renal disease should be strongly considered in patients who present with resistant hypertension.[68,69]

The renal outcome for patients with atheroembolic renal disease is quite variable. In early reports, the renal outcome was uniformly dismal, with progression over weeks or months to end-stage renal failure.[54,55] Over the past decade, however, reports of spontaneous recovery of renal function in patients with atheroembolic renal disease, even after variable periods of dialytic support, have appeared in the literature.[17,23,70,71] The improvement in renal function may be related to reversal of inflammation, resolution of acute tubular necrosis in ischemic areas, and hypertrophy of surviving nephrons.[7,72] Despite these promising case reports, most patients with atheroembolic renal disease either have advanced chronic renal insufficiency or progress to end-stage renal disease and require dialytic support.

Gastrointestinal Involvement

Although the GI tract is often overlooked as a site of cholesterol embolization, the disorder commonly occurs here; the colon is involved in up to 42% of cases, the small bowel in a third, and the stomach in 12%.[14,73-75] The preferential involvement of the GI tract is probably a result of its rich vascular supply. The most common manifestations of GI tract involvement are abdominal pain, diarrhea, and blood loss.[73] Abdominal pain may be caused by bowel ischemia with or without infarction or by fibrous stricture with bowel obstruction as a consequence of tissue repair after repeated showers of atheroembolism.[7] The pathogenesis of diarrhea may be related to multiple mechanisms, including mucosal inflammation, accumulation of luminal blood, and malabsorption.[73] GI bleeding is caused by superficial mucosal ulceration, erosions, and microinfarcts.[75]

Other areas of the digestive system reported as involved by this disease are the pancreas, liver, and gallbladder.[73,74,76,77] The pancreas and liver are common sites of cholesterol embolization, as indicated by autopsy reports, but clinically overt pancreatitis and hepatitis are exceedingly rare presentations of cholesterol embolization.[77] In contrast, cholesterol embolization to the gallbladder, although even rarer, tends to be clinically significant when present, with a clinical presentation ranging from chronic acalculous cholecystitis to acute gangrenous cholecystitis.[74]

The diagnosis of cholesterol embolism is rarely made on endoscopy alone because a variety of nonspecific lesions can be detected, including congestive or erythematous mucosa, erosions, ulcerations, necrosis, inflammatory polyps, and strictures.[12,17,75,77] Mucosal punch biopsy specimens from the stomach, duodenum, or colon may be helpful in making the diagnosis, occasionally demonstrating the typical appearance of cholesterol crystals.[75]

The prognosis of patients with GI involvement tends to be poor, and the overall death rate is high. Patients with GI involvement commonly have a multisystem cholesterol embolization syndrome. In a retrospective review of 10 patients with histologically proven cholesterol crystal emboli diagnosed on endoscopic GI biopsy, death due to atherosclerotic complications—multisystem failure in 3, stroke in 1, and ruptured abdominal aortic aneurysm—occurred in 5 patients within 3 months of diagnosis. All of these patients also had cutaneous manifestations and end-stage renal disease.[75]

Central Nervous System and Eye Involvement

Cholesterol embolization commonly occurs in the brain and eye and causes significant morbidity and mortality.[12] The culprit, atherosclerotic plaques, are located in the ascending aorta, aortic arch, and carotid and vertebral arteries.[78,79] Patients may experience visual disturbances such as amaurosis fugax or variable degrees of blindness caused by central or branch retinal artery occlusion.[5] Retinal cholesterol embolization is seen as yellow, highly refractile plaques (Hollenhorst plaques) at arterial bifurcations on ophthalmoscopic examination.[5] Cerebral cholesterol embolism may manifest as TIA, stroke, confusional states, headache, dizziness, or organic brain syndrome.[17,78,80] In a retrospective review of 29 patients with autopsy-proven brain cholesterol emboli, encephalopathy was the predominant neurologic finding.[81] It is most likely due to the diffuse and bihemispheric nature of cholesterol embolization. Involvement of the spinal cord artery, which can lead to lower extremity paralysis, has been reported rarely.[82] A case history consisting of a procedure that involves the ascending thoracic aorta, acute renal failure, and encephalopathy in an elderly patient should raise the suspicion of cholesterol emboli to the brain. Radiographic studies can help by showing multiple small ischemic lesions or border-zone infarcts.

Other Areas

Cholesterol emboli can occur in virtually any organ. Cardiac manifestations include angina pectoris and myocardial infarction. The usual source in these circumstances is the aortic root or proximal coronary artery.[83] Pulmonary involvement has rarely been reported in the context of cholesterol embolism.[84,85] Hemoptysis and dyspnea are the most common respiratory symptoms described. The pathogenesis of pulmonary involvement in cholesterol embolism may be related to direct deposition of atheroemboli in the lungs[86] or de novo production of pulmonary lesions as a result of systemic inflammation associated with cholesterol embolism.[87] Atheromatous emboli have also been demonstrated in the spleen, bone marrow, muscle, prostate, thyroid, and adrenal glands in autopsy studies.[12,53-55]

Nonspecific findings, such as fever, weight loss, headaches, and myalgias, have been reported in atheromatous embolization syndrome and their presence may suggest a multisystem illness (see Table 68-1).[17,23,88]

■ DIAGNOSIS

The diagnosis of cholesterol embolization syndrome remains a significant challenge for physicians. The symptoms and signs are nonspecific and diverse explaining why this disease is sometimes referred to as the "great masquerader."[19,88] For this reason, a high index of suspicion and a thorough understanding of the various clinical manifestations are needed in order to correctly make the diagnosis antemortem. The diagnosis can often be made on clinical grounds alone, without histologic evaluation, in a patient who has a precipitating event, acute or subacute renal failure, hypertension that is difficult to control, and evidence of peripheral embolization.[17]

No specific laboratory test is diagnostic. Eosinophilia can be found in up to 80% of cases and is probably related to the generation of complement component C5, which has chemotactic properties for eosinophils. The eosinophilia, however, tends to be transient and short-lived.[11,12] Laboratory markers of inflammation, including levels of C-reactive protein, fibrinogen and erythrocyte sedimentation rate, have also been found to be elevated in many patients.[54] Other reported laboratory findings are leukocytosis, anemia,

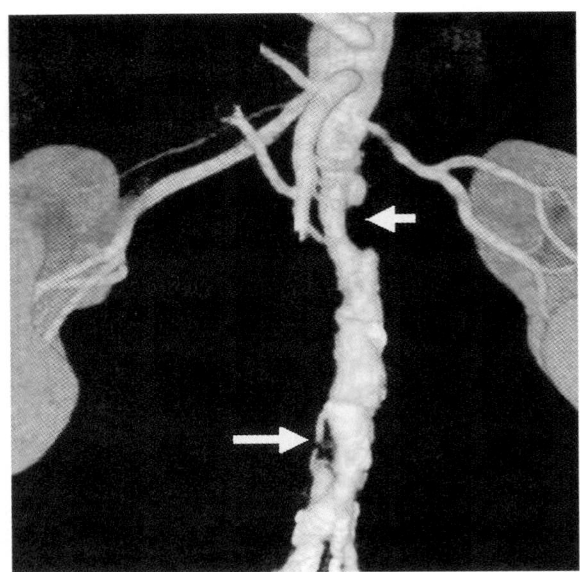

FIGURE 68-5 Multidetector CT angiogram demonstrating marked atherosclerotic disease in the abdominal aorta. Note the two large ulcers present (*arrows*). (Courtesy of Corey Goldman, MD, PhD, Ochsner Clinic, New Orleans, LA.)

thrombocytopenia, and decreased complement levels.[53,54,89] Laboratory data may also reflect specific organ involvement. Elevations in serum concentrations of amylase, hepatic transaminases, blood urea nitrogen, creatinine, and creatinine phosphokinase may be seen with involvement of the pancreas, liver, kidney, and muscle, respectively. Mild proteinuria, microhematuria, and hyaline or granular casts are the most common urinary findings in patients with confirmed cholesterol embolism.[54,90] Proteinuria in the nephrotic range and eosinophiluria have also been reported, although less commonly.[10,90,91]

Invasive vascular procedures requiring aortic instrumentation should be avoided as diagnostic modalities because of the potential risk of producing recurrent atheroembolism. Noninvasive imaging studies, such as multidetector CT angiography (Fig. 68-5), magnetic resonance angiography, and TEE, can assist in confirming the diagnosis if any of these modalities demonstrates a markedly irregular and shaggy aorta (Fig. 68-6).

In the absence of obvious clinical clues, a definitive diagnosis may require a biopsy. The highest yield for histologic confirmation is an affected organ, such as an amputated extremity in a patient presenting with gangrenous toes, the kidney in a patient with new-onset renal failure, or the GI tract in a patient with abdominal pain and GI bleeding. However, in one series, random biopsies of the gastrocnemius and quadriceps muscles were helpful in making the diagnosis.[92] The biopsy should be deep and the specimen should be examined in multiple sections.

■ DIFFERENTIAL DIAGNOSIS

Diseases that should be considered in the differential diagnosis include, but are not limited to, contrast nephropathy, acute tubular necrosis (ATN) from ischemic

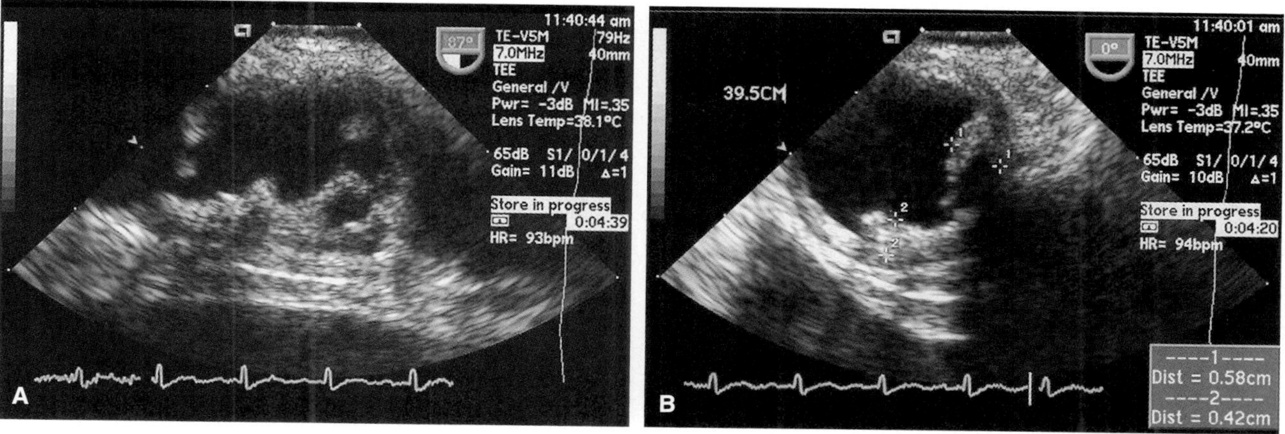

FIGURE 68-6 Transesophageal echocardiogram demonstrating mobile (seen on real-time imaging) protruding aortic atheromas located in the aortic arch (**A**) and descending thoracic aorta (**B**). This patient has had multiple strokes due to atheromatous embolization from the ascending aorta and aortic arch.

injury, necrotizing vasculitis, leukocytoclastic vasculitis, thrombotic thrombocytopenic purpura, antiphospholipid antibody syndrome, and multiple myeloma. A cardiac source of emboli, such as an atrial myxoma, nonbacterial thrombotic endocarditis, subacute bacterial endocarditis, and acute bacterial endocarditis,[93] should always be excluded.

No laboratory test uniformly helps in the diagnosis of atheroembolic disease. The peripheral blood eosinophilia, hypocomplementemia, elevated sedimentation rate, and increased value of C-reactive protein seen in these patients are nonspecific findings that can also be found in patients with systemic or renal vasculitis.[88,94] Atheroembolic disease should be distinguished from vasculitis on the basis of other clinical and histologic findings. The urine sediment in patients with atheroembolic renal disease is usually benign or shows only microhematuria. Rarely, eosinophiluria may be present.[95] By contrast, the urine sediment in patients with ATN often demonstrates pigmented granular casts (dirty brown casts) and renal tubular cells. Atheroembolic renal disease can be differentiated further from ATN or contrast nephropathy on the basis of the time frame of renal impairment. In contrast nephropathy and ATN, the renal failure occurs within 48 to 72 hours after the inciting event, whereas in patients with atheroembolic renal disease, the rise in creatinine concentration is often delayed for 7 to 10 days.[4,10,96] In addition, full recovery of renal function is the rule for contrast nephropathy and ATN if the underlying precipitating factor is corrected but is the exception in atheroembolic renal disease.[4,7] ATN is further characterized by normal blood pressure levels, as opposed to the severe and refractory hypertension present in many patients with atheroembolic renal disease. Other disorders previously listed that may mimic cholesterol embolization due to their multisystem involvement should be excluded through the use of appropriate diagnostic studies.

■ OUTCOME

In general, the prognosis of patients with atheroembolic disease is poor, most likely in relation to the severe and diffuse atherosclerosis that is present in this patient population. The course, however, varies according to type of clinical presentation. Patients with symptoms limited to an extremity tend to have a better prognosis than patients with disseminated cholesterol crystal embolization, particularly if they have evidence of visceral and renal involvement. The reported 1-year mortality in four different reports has varied from 64% to 81%.[10,54,56,57] Causes of death were multifactorial and included cardiac, central nervous system, and GI ischemia.

■ MANAGEMENT

There have been no randomized controlled trials of any therapeutic intervention for patients with cholesterol embolization, and no agent has been strongly correlated with favorable outcomes in case series. Clearly the most important aspect of therapy is prevention (see discussion of risk). Once atheromatous embolization has occurred, therapy is mostly supportive. Avoidance of further inciting events such as aortic manipulation, good control of hypertension and heart failure, dialytic support, and adequate nutrition are the mainstays of treatment.[17,56] Symptomatic care of the end organ where the emboli are located and modification of risk factors to prevent the progression of atherosclerotic disease should also be important treatment goals.[4]

Medical Therapy

Pathologic descriptions of cholesterol embolism highlight the severe inflammatory reaction that contributes to vascular obstruction. Although the inflammatory process caused by cholesterol embolism may suggest a role for anti-inflammatory agents,[11] the use of corticosteroids has had conflicting results. Dahlberg and colleagues,[57] in a 1989 report of 2 patients given corticosteroids found a rapid and dramatic improvement in the manifestations of peripheral embolization.[57] Later case reports describe improvement in renal function in patients who have suspected atheroembolism with the use of corticosteroid therapy.[97,98] Corticosteroid administration has also been shown to be helpful in relieving symptoms related to mesenteric ischemia, such as abdominal pain and food intolerance, and for ischemic leg pain.[17] In contrast, in a series of 67 patients, 18 of whom were treated with corticosteroids, no survival benefit could be attributed directly to this therapy.[17] Furthermore, in large retrospective series, Falanga and associates[62] found that corticosteroid use was associated with 100% mortality. On the basis of the available literature, routine corticosteroid use cannot be recommended for this patient population.

Statins have been reported to be beneficial in the treatment of livedo reticularis due to cholesterol embolization[99] as well as the treatment of renal[100] and lower limb cholesterol emboli syndrome.[101] Furthermore, in a retrospective analysis of 519 patients with severe thoracic aortic plaque visualized on TEE, multivariate analysis showed that statin use was independently protective against recurrent embolic events ($P = .0001$).[102] The mechanism of the beneficial effects of statin therapy is most likely related to the plaque-stabilizing activity of these drugs.

Iloprost, a prostacyclin analogue, is a potent vasodilator and antiplatelet agent. In a report of four cases of cholesterol emboli, intravenous iloprost improved both ischemia of the distal extremities and renal failure.[103] Anecdotally, the prostaglandin analogues appear to be beneficial in the healing of ischemic ulcerations associated with atheroemboli. It is not known whether this class of drug is effective in patients with atheroembolic renal failure.

Other forms of therapy that have been advocated are treatment with antiplatelet agents such as aspirin[53,54,104] and dipyridamole, low-molecular-weight dextran, intra-arterial papaverine, and pentoxifylline,[105] and the use of platelet infusions to help stabilize the source of atheroemboli.[25] Unfortunately, no controlled trials have shown that any of these forms of therapy is of benefit.

All patients should receive aggressive risk factor modification with an antiplatelet agent, a statin, and an angiotensin-converting enzyme inhibitor, all of which have been found to improve mortality in patients with underlying atherosclerotic disease.[106-111]

Surgical Therapy

Surgical therapy for atheroembolic disease involves, first and foremost, the elimination of the embolic source and, second, arterial reconstruction of any hemodynamically significant proximal occlusive disease to encourage healing through improved perfusion of end-arterial beds. Two prospective series reported favorable outcomes with vascular resection of atherosclerotic segments of large arteries identified as being the source of previous cholesterol crystal embolism.[112,113] However, when the suprarenal aorta was involved, greater mortality rates were observed, likely related to the risk for visceral and renal ischemia, atheroemboli, or both.[112] Thus, according to some investigators, surgical elimination of the presumed source of cholesterol embolization should be reserved for patients with lower limb ischemia and an infrarenal source of embolization.[7]

Given the frequent instability of these lesions, surgical treatment has been perceived to be safer than endovascular approaches because the surgeon can clamp the artery proximal and distal to the lesion before manipulating the diseased vessel in an attempt to decrease the risk of recurrent embolization.[114] Lin and coworkers,[43] in a retrospective study, found that recurrent atheroembolism and amputation rates in the surgically treated patients to be zero and 20%, respectively, in sharp contrast to the outcomes of patients treated with endovascular therapy, whose recurrent atheroembolism and amputation rates were 33% and 66%, respectively. Thromboendarterectomy or resection and graft replacement have been the surgical approaches most commonly used.[115] In patients who are too weak for a major surgical intervention, ligation of the external iliac arteries or common femoral arteries followed by an extra-anatomic bypass, such as axillobifemoral bypass, has been advocated.[115,116] The ligation prevents further embolization from reaching the legs, although embolization to the kidneys and intestines may still occur.

There are a few reports of intra-arterial treatment of embolizing lesions, including administration of thrombolytics,[117,118] percutaneous atherectomy,[119,120] balloon angioplasty,[117,118] and stent implantation.[121,122] Intra-arterial thrombolytic administration in isolation is controversial. Fibrinolysis, by destroying the platelet-fibrin thrombus that covers the atheromatous ulcerated plaques, may allow for the liberation of the cholesterol crystals into the arterial circulation with consequent microembolization. There are no data as to whether the adjunctive use of tissue plasminogen activator augments clot extraction in combination with endovascular interventions.

In percutaneous transluminal angioplasty, the intima is cracked and remodeled, and thus, theoretically, the chance of distal embolization may be increased. However, anecdotal reports of the use of this approach have shown symptomatic improvement in leg pain, re-establishment of peripheral pulses, and no evidence of recurrent embolization. Stent placement in conjunction with angioplasty may provide a protective scaffold to help secure these lesions. However, a potential risk of recurrent atheroembolism may exist because of either plaque dislodgement or extrusion of atheromatous material through stent interstices at the time of stent placement. The possibility of procedure-related distal embolization due to stent placement was highlighted in a recent study by Ohki and associates[123] that demonstrated a significant risk of distal embolization secondary to intra-arterial stent placement in an ex-vivo carotid endarterectomy model. Furthermore, Lin and associates,[43] in a retrospective analysis, found that operative procedures, either bypass or endarterectomy, appeared to provide a superior result to intraluminal stent placement. There was no recurrent atheroembolism in the surgical patients, but 66% of patients treated with iliac stent placement had recurrent atheroembolism.[43] In contrast, Matchett and colleagues[121] found no procedure-related embolization and only one recurrent embolization at follow-up in a retrospective report of 15 patients treated with stent placement for blue toe syndrome. Renshaw and associates[124] reported successful angioplasty with stenting in 8 patients with unilateral blue toe syndrome. Symptoms resolved in all eight patients over the ensuing month, and there were no recurrences in a mean follow-up of 18.5 months.

The short-term results in studies utilizing percutaneous atherectomy, in which the plaque is shaved off the wall of the vessel and removed through a collection device, are similar to those of percutaneous transluminal angioplasty or surgery.[119,120]

The availability of covered-as raised their potential utility in the management of patients with distal atheroembolic lesions.[114] Covered stents offer the added advantage of completely excluding the diseased segment, preventing the escape of thrombus or plaque debris. Kumins and associates[125] report on the successful use of the Wallgraft endoprosthesis in two patients with distal microembolism from common iliac artery disease.

Carroccio and colleagues[126] reported on endovascular stent-graft repair for abdominal aortic aneurysm (AAA) in 16 patients presenting with atheromatous embolization syndrome. The 30-day mortality was zero and the AAAs were successfully excluded in 88% of patients. Resolution of foot ischemia and prevention of further atheromatous embolization were observed in 89% of the patients still alive at 1 year. Six patients died during a mean follow-up of 26 months, further illustrating the very high mortality in this patient population.

Because of the limited information in the literature regarding the role of endovascular therapy for atheromatous embolization, the clinical efficacy of this approach is difficult to compare with operative treatment strategies. Undoubtedly, further clinical evaluation is warranted to further validate endovascular therapy in the treatment of atheroembolism.

Pain control is a critical aspect of the management of peripheral cholesterol embolism. The pain associated with lower extremity ischemic and necrotic lesions secondary to cholesterol embolism is generally severe and disproportionate to the amount of tissue involvement. Sympathectomy has received attention as a surgical measure for the palliation of atheroembolic lesions. Lee and coworkers[127] demonstrated that adjunctive sympathectomy resulted in improved healing of distal digital ischemic ulcers. Sympathectomy is easily performed during aortic procedures or can be achieved postoperatively through lumbar sympathetic block or laparoscopic techniques. Ghilardi and associates[128] have reported two cases of inferior limb ischemia secondary to cholesterol embolism that were treated with the temporary surgical implantation of spinal cord stimulation devices. They found spinal cord stimulation to provide rapid and effective pain control in the reported cases as well as improvement in peripheral microcirculation, manifesting as the rapid resolution of the necrotic lesions within 4 to 6 weeks.[128] These surgical techniques may not be only an adjunct to direct surgical treatment of the offending arterial segment, but also may be useful to control the pain of severe atheroembolic lower extremity lesions in patients who are not candidates for direct reconstruction of the embolic source or when correction of the embolic source does not improve distal perfusion.

■ SPECIAL CONSIDERATION: ATHEROEMBOLISM ARISING FROM THE THORACIC AORTA

The importance of the thoracic aorta as a source of cerebral and peripheral vascular emboli has now been ascertained. Tunick and colleagues,[129] in a retrospective study comparing 122 patients with a history of stroke, TIA, or peripheral emboli with 122 age- and sex-matched controls, found protruding atheromas to be an independent risk factor for embolic symptoms. Plaques located proximal to the ostium of the left subclavian artery have been found in 60% of patients 60 years of age or older with ischemic stroke, plaques thicker than 4 mm having the strongest association.[130] Similar results were found in an autopsy study showing that ulcerated plaques in the ascending aorta and aortic arch, which included both atheromatous material and thrombus, were significantly more prevalent in those who had suffered cerebral embolic events than in those without such plaques.[131]

A separate issue, the role of aortic plaque as a predictor of subsequent stroke and other embolic events has been evaluated in prospective studies. Three studies in which the majority of patients who had sustained a recent stroke were followed prospectively have shown an association between aortic arch atherosclerosis and cerebral or peripheral embolic events.[132-134] Tunick and associates[133] found an annual event rate of vascular events to be 33% in patients who had protruding plaques thicker than 5 mm in the thoracic aorta, as compared with 7% in matched control subjects. In a similar study, Mitusch and coworkers[134] noted a significantly higher rate of vascular events in patients who were found to have complex plaque (>5 mm in thickness or with mobile components) on echocardiographic examination than in patients found to have only moderate atherosclerosis (13.7 versus 4.1 per 100 person-years, respectively). Davila-Roman and colleagues,[132] in a prospective, long-term follow-up study of 1957 patients undergoing cardiac surgery, found atherosclerosis of the ascending aorta to be an independent predictor of long-term neurologic events and mortality. On the basis of these later echocardiographic and pathologic studies, the overall vascular risk arising from advanced atherosclerosis of the thoracic aorta may be as high as that from established sources of embolism, including nonvalvular atrial fibrillation, left atrial thrombi, and severe stenosis of the internal carotid artery origin.[130]

The vascular risk attributable to complex atherosclerosis of the thoracic aorta appears to be correlated mainly with the thickness of the plaques and the morphologic parameters associated with plaques. TEE of the ascending aorta and aortic arch has been used to identify plaque size and morphology as risk factors for embolic events (see Fig. 68-6). A review from the French Study of Aortic Plaques in Stroke Group involved 331 patients with an initial ischemic stroke who were followed for 2 to 4 years.[59] Patients were divided into groups according to aortic plaque thickness, greater than 4 mm, 1 to 3.9 mm, and less than 1 mm. At follow-up, the patients with plaques thicker than 4 mm had a significantly higher incidence of recurrent stroke and vascular events (Table 68-2). An analysis of 788 person-year follow-up to determine the effect of plaque morphology on the risk of ischemic disease demonstrated that the only plaque morphology that raised the risk of ischemic events was the absence of plaque calcification.[130] Ulceration and hypoechoic plaques had no predictive value in the evaluation of vascular events. Overall, it was determined that aortic plaques that were thicker than 4 mm increased the risk of vascular events, which was further raised by the lack of

Table 68-2 Incidence of Cardiovascular Events According to Plaque Thickness in the Aortic Arch Proximal to the Ostium of the Left Subclavian Artery

PLAQUE THICKNESS (mm)	RECURRENT BRAIN INFARCTION			ANY VASCULAR EVENT*		
	Person-Years of Follow-up	Number of Events	Incidence Per 100 Person-Years of Follow-up	Person-Years of Follow-up	Number of Events	Incidence Per 100 Person-Years of Follow-up
<1	359.3	10	2.8	354.0	21	5.9
1-3.9	312.6	11	3.5	308.2	28	9.1
>4	92.4	11	11.9	88.4	23	26.0

*Includes brain infarction, myocardial infarction, peripheral embolism, and death from vascular causes.

From: Atherosclerotic disease of the aortic arch as a risk factor for recurrent ischemic stroke. The French Study of Aortic Plaques in Stroke Group. N Engl J Med 334:1216-1221, 1996.

plaque calcification. These researchers in this study hypothesized that noncalcified plaques are probably the lipid-laden plaques with a thin fibrous cap, which are unstable and prone to ulceration, rupture, and thrombosis.[135] Pedunculated, mobile plaques have also been associated with a higher risk of recurrent embolization.[129,136,137]

Complex thoracic aortic plaques not only are valuable "markers" of severe widespread atherosclerosis[130,131] but also identify individuals at a high risk for cardiovascular events, approximately 26 per 100 person-years in one study.[59] There are no clear guidelines on the most appropriate therapy for these patients. The data concerning the efficacy of anticoagulation in patients with complex thoracic aortic plaques are conflicting. Ferrari and colleagues[138] used TEE in a prospectively selected patient cohort to compare antiplatelet therapy with anticoagulation therapy; they found that patients treated with antiplatelet agents had more combined vascular events and a higher mortality rate than patients treated with oral anticoagulants. Similar results were reported by Dressler and associates,[137] who found that patients with mobile aortic atheroma who were not receiving warfarin had a higher incidence of vascular events than those undergoing warfarin treatment (27% had strokes versus 0%, respectively). Conversely, a retrospective study showed no significant effect of warfarin therapy on the risk of cardiovascular events.[102]

On the basis of the evidence offered to date, it seems reasonable to follow the recommendations of the 2001 Sixth American College of Chest Physicians Consensus Conference on Antithrombotic Therapy, which recommends warfarin therapy in patients with mobile aortic atheromas or aortic plaques thicker than 4 mm as measured by TEE who have had an embolic event.[139] It should be recognized that this recommendation is not based on findings of randomized controlled trials. Lipid-lowering therapy, primarily with a statin, is warranted in all patients with symptomatic atherosclerotic vascular disease.[111] In a retrospective analysis of patients with complex aortic arch plaques, statin therapy reduced the risk of embolic events independently and significantly.[133]

Finally, surgical treatment of atherosclerosis of the thoracic aorta may be considered. Surgical therapy cannot be recommended routinely for the asymptomatic patient because the risks inherent in such a complex procedure outweigh the benefits.[140] However, whether to perform aortic arch endarterectomy or aortic resection along with the planned cardiac procedure if severe atheromatous disease is discovered has been addressed. Stern and colleagues[141] reported a large increase in rates of intraoperative stroke and mortality when surgery was performed to limit the risk of stroke after cardiopulmonary bypass. At this time, in the absence of randomized controlled trials, surgical indications for aortic endarterectomy should be restricted to highly selected patients, with a low operative risk who have multiple and documented embolic events despite optimal medical treatment.[135]

■ REFERENCES

1. Panum P: Experimentelle Beitrage Zur Lehre Von der Embolie. Arch Pathol Anat Physiol Klin Med 25:308-310, 1862.
2. Flory C: Arterial occlusions produced by emboli from eroded aortic atheromatous plaques. Am J Pathol 21:549-565, 1945.
3. Arroyo LH, Lee RT: Mechanisms of plaque rupture: Mechanical and biologic interactions. Cardiovasc Res 41:369-375, 1999.
4. Bartholomew JR, Olin JW: Atheromatous Embolization. In Young JR, Olin JW, Bartholomew JR (eds): Peripheral Vascular Diseases, 2nd ed. St. Louis, CV Mosby, 1996.
5. Hollenhorst RW: Vascular status of patients who have cholesterol emboli in the retina. Am J Ophthalmol 61:1159-1165, 1966.
6. Pennington M, Yeager J, Skelton H, Smith KJ: Cholesterol embolization syndrome: Cutaneous histopathological features and the variable onset of symptoms in patients with different risk factors. Br J Dermatol 146:511-517, 2002.
7. Scolari F, Tardanico R, Zani R, et al: Cholesterol crystal embolism: A recognizable cause of renal disease. Am J Kidney Dis 36:1089-1109, 2000.
8. Jones DB, Iannaccone PM: Atheromatous emboli in renal biopsies: An ultrastructural study. Am J Pathol 78:261-276, 1975.
9. Kang K, Botella R, White CR Jr: Subtle clues to the diagnosis of cholesterol embolism. Am J Dermatopathol 18:380-384, 1996.
10. Thadhani RI, Camargo CA Jr, Xavier RJ, et al: Atheroembolic renal failure after invasive procedures: Natural history based on 52 histologically proven cases. Medicine (Baltimore) 74:350-358, 1995.
11. Fabbian F, Catalano C, Lambertini D, et al: A possible role of corticosteroids in cholesterol crystal embolization. Nephron 83:189-190, 1999.
12. Moolenaar W, Lamers CB: Cholesterol crystal embolization in the Netherlands. Arch Intern Med 156:653-657, 1996.
13. Cross SS: How common is cholesterol embolism? J Clin Pathol 44:859-861, 1991.
14. Rhodes JM: Cholesterol crystal embolism: An important "new" diagnosis for the general physician. Lancet 347:1641, 1996.
15. Ghannem M, Philippe J, Ressam A, et al: Systemic cholesterol embolism. Ann Cardiol Angeiol (Paris) 44:422-426, 1995.

16. Moolenaar W, Lamers CB: Gastrointestinal blood loss due to cholesterol crystal embolization. J Clin Gastroenterol 21:220-223, 1995.
17. Belenfant X, Meyrier A, Jacquot C: Supportive treatment improves survival in multivisceral cholesterol crystal embolism. Am J Kidney Dis 33:840-850, 1999.
18. Mayo RR, Swartz RD: Redefining the incidence of clinically detectable atheroembolism. Am J Med 100:524-529, 1996.
19. Lie JT: Cholesterol atheromatous embolism: The great masquerader revisited. Pathol Annu 27:17-50, 1992.
20. Blauth CI, Cosgrove DM, Webb BW, et al: Atheroembolism from the ascending aorta: An emerging problem in cardiac surgery. J Thorac Cardiovasc Surg 103:1104-1111, 1992.
21. Piriou V, Claudel JP, Bastien O, et al: Severe systemic cholesterol embolization after open heart surgery. Br J Anaesth 77:277-280, 1996.
22. Doty JR, Wilentz RE, Salazar JD, et al: Atheroembolism in cardiac surgery. Ann Thorac Surg 75:1221-1226, 2003.
23. Scolari F, Bracchi M, Valzorio B, et al: Cholesterol atheromatous embolism: An increasingly recognized cause of acute renal failure. Nephrol Dial Transplant 11:1607-1612, 1996.
24. Case records of the Massachusetts General Hospital. Weekly clinicopathological exercises. Case 24-1998. A 76-year-old woman with cardiac and renal failure and gastrointestinal bleeding. N Engl J Med 339:329-337, 1998.
25. Turnbull RG, Hayashi AH, McLean DR: Multiple spontaneous intestinal perforations from atheroembolism after thrombolytic therapy: A case report. Can J Surg 37:325-328, 1994.
26. Rivera-Manrique E, Castro-Salomo A, Azon-Masoliver A, Marin LM: Cholesterol embolism: A fatal complication after thrombolytic therapy for acute myocardial infarction. Arch Intern Med 158:1575, 1998.
27. Izumi C, Kondo H, Tamura H, et al: Clinical evaluation of cholesterol embolization syndrome after cardiac catheterization. J Cardiol 31:201-206, 1998.
28. Adorati M, Pizzolitto S, Franzon R, et al: Cholesterol embolism and acute interstitial nephritis: Two adverse effects of streptokinase thrombolytic therapy in the same patient. Nephrol Dial Transplant 13:1262-1264, 1998.
29. Keeley EC, Grines CL: Scraping of aortic debris by coronary guiding catheters: A prospective evaluation of 1,000 cases. J Am Coll Cardiol 32:1861-1865, 1998.
30. Eggebrecht H, Oldenburg O, Dirsch O, et al: Potential embolization by atherosclerotic debris dislodged from aortic wall during cardiac catheterization: Histological and clinical findings in 7,621 patients. Catheter Cardiovasc Interv 49:389-394, 2000.
31. Drost H, Buis B, Haan D, Hillers JA: Cholesterol embolism as a complication of left heart catheterisation: Report of seven cases. Br Heart J 52:339-342, 1984.
32. Colt HG, Begg RJ, Saporito JJ, et al: Cholesterol emboli after cardiac catheterization: Eight cases and a review of the literature. Medicine (Baltimore) 67:389-400, 1988.
33. Saklayen MG, Gupta S, Suryaprasad A, Azmeh W: Incidence of atheroembolic renal failure after coronary angiography: A prospective study. Angiology 48:609-613, 1997.
34. Fukumoto Y, Tsutsui H, Tsuchihashi M, et al: The incidence and risk factors of cholesterol embolization syndrome, a complication of cardiac catheterization: A prospective study. J Am Coll Cardiol 42:211-216, 2003.
35. Shmuely H, Zoldan J, Sagie A, et al: Acute stroke after coronary angiography associated with protruding mobile thoracic aortic atheromas. Neurology 49:1689-1691, 1997.
36. Farah B, Prendergast B, Garbarz E, et al: Antegrade transseptal coronary angiography: An alternative technique in severe vascular disease. Catheter Cardiovasc Interv 43:444-446, 1998.
37. Kiemeneij F, Laarman GJ, Odekerken D, et al: A randomized comparison of percutaneous transluminal coronary angioplasty by the radial, brachial and femoral approaches: The access study. J Am Coll Cardiol 29:1269-1275, 1997.
38. Kiemeneij MD, Laarman MPGJ, Slagboom MD, van der Wieken MR: Outpatient coronary stent implantation. J Am Coll Cardiol 29:323-327, 1997.
39. Safian RD, Freed MS: The Manual of Interventional Cardiology. Royal Oak, MI, Physicians Press, 2001.
40. Johnson LW, Esente P, Giambartolomei A, et al: Peripheral vascular complications of coronary angioplasty by the femoral and brachial techniques. Cathet Cardiovasc Diagn 31:165-172, 1994.
41. Ramirez G, O'Neill WM Jr, Lambert R, Bloomer HA: Cholesterol embolization: A complication of angiography. Arch Intern Med 138:1430-1432, 1978.
42. Rosansky SJ: Multiple cholesterol emboli syndrome after angiography. AJR Am J Roentgenol 143(3):683, 1984.
43. Lin PH, Bush RL, Conklin BS, et al: Late complication of aortoiliac stent placement—atheroembolization of the lower extremities. J Surg Res 103:153-159, 2002.
44. Toogood GJ, Torrie EP, Magee TR, Galland RB: Early experience with stenting for iliac occlusive disease. Eur J Vasc Endovasc Surg 15:165-168, 1998.
45. Ballard J, Bergan J, Singh P, et al: Aortoiliac stent deployment versus surgical reconstruction: Analysis of outcome and cost. J Vasc Surg 28:94-103, 1998.
46. Roubin GS, New G, Iyer SS, et al: Immediate and late clinical outcomes of carotid artery stenting in patients with symptomatic and asymptomatic carotid artery stenosis: A 5-year prospective analysis. Circulation 103:532-537, 2001.
47. Henry M, Klonaris C, Henry I, et al: Protected renal stenting with the PercuSurge GuardWire device: A pilot study. J Endovasc Ther 8:227-237, 2001.
48. Thurlbeck WM, Castleman B: Atheromatous emboli to the kidneys after aortic surgery. N Engl J Med 257:442-447, 1957.
49. Kolh PH, Torchiana DF, Buckley MJ: Atheroembolization in cardiac surgery: The need for preoperative diagnosis. J Cardiovasc Surg (Torino) 40:77-81, 1999.
50. Davila-Roman VG, Westerhausen D, Hopkins WE, et al: Transesophageal echocardiography in the detection of cardiovascular sources of peripheral vascular embolism. Ann Vasc Surg 9:252-260, 1995.
51. Tenenbaum A, Garniek A, Shemesh J, et al: Dual-helical CT for detecting aortic atheromas as a source of stroke: Comparison with transesophageal echocardiography. Radiology 208:153-158, 1998.
52. Kaufman JL: Atheroembolism and microthromboembolic syndromes (blue toe syndrome and disseminated atheroembolism). In Rutherford RB (ed): Vascular Surgery, 5th ed. Philadelphia, WB Saunders, 2000, pp 836-845.
53. Kassirer JP: Atheroembolic renal disease. N Engl J Med 280:812-818, 1969.
54. Fine MJ, Kapoor W, Falanga V: Cholesterol crystal embolization: A review of 221 cases in the English literature. Angiology 38:769-784, 1987.
55. Lye WC, Cheah JS, Sinniah R: Renal cholesterol embolic disease: Case report and review of the literature. Am J Nephrol 13:489-493, 1993.
56. Saleem S, Lakkis FG, Martinez-Maldonado M: Atheroembolic renal disease. Semin Nephrol 16:309-318, 1996.
57. Dahlberg PJ, Frecentese DF, Cogbill TH: Cholesterol embolism: Experience with 22 histologically proven cases. Surgery 105:737-746, 1989.
58. Blackshear JL, Zabalgoitia M, Pennock G, et al: Warfarin safety and efficacy in patients with thoracic aortic plaque and atrial fibrillation. SPAF TEE Investigators. Stroke Prevention and Atrial Fibrillation. Transesophageal echocardiography. Am J Cardiol. 83:453-455, 1999.
59. Atherosclerotic disease of the aortic arch as a risk factor for recurrent ischemic stroke. The French Study of Aortic Plaques in Stroke group. N Engl J Med 334:1216-1221, 1996.
60. Blankenship JC, Butler M, Garbes A: Prospective assessment of cholesterol embolization in patients with acute myocardial infarction treated with thrombolytic vs conservative therapy. Chest 107:662-668, 1995.
61. Saklayen MG: Atheroembolic renal disease: Preferential occurrence in whites only. Am J Nephrol 9:87-88, 1989.

62. Falanga V, Fine MJ, Kapoor WN: The cutaneous manifestations of cholesterol crystal embolization. Arch Dermatol 122:1194-1198, 1986.
63. Chaudhary K, Wall BM, Rasberry RD: Livedo reticularis: An underutilized diagnostic clue in cholesterol embolization syndrome. Am J Med Sci 321:348-351, 2001.
64. Callen JP, Greer KE, Paller AS, Swinyer LJ: Color Atlas of Dermatology, 2nd ed. Philadelphia, WB Saunders, 2000.
65. Schanz S, Metzler G, Metzger S, et al: Cholesterol embolism: An often unrecognized cause of leg ulcers. Br J Dermatol 146:1107-1108, 2002.
66. Rosansky SJ: Multiple cholesterol emboli syndrome. South Med J 75:677-680, 1982.
67. Modi KS, Rao VK: Atheroembolic renal disease. J Am Soc Nephrol 12:1781-1787, 2001.
68. Ripple MG, Charney D, Nadasdy T: Cholesterol embolization in renal allografts. Transplantation 69:2221-2225, 2000.
69. Dalakos TG, Streeten DH, Jones D, Obeid A: "Malignant" hypertension resulting from atheromatous embolization predominantly of one kidney. Am J Med 57:135-138, 1974.
70. Theriault J, Agharazzi M, Dumont M, et al: Atheroembolic renal failure requiring dialysis: Potential for renal recovery? A review of 43 cases. Nephron Clin Pract 94:c11-c18, 2003.
71. Gorriz JL, Sancho A, Garces R, et al: Recovery of renal function after renal failure due to cholesterol crystal embolism. Nephrol Dial Transplant 14:2261-2262, 1999.
72. Scolari F, Ravani P, Pola A, et al: Predictors of renal and patient outcomes in atheroembolic renal disease: A prospective study. J Am Soc Nephrol 14:1584-1590, 2003.
73. Moolenaar W, Lamers CB: Cholesterol crystal embolisation to the alimentary tract. Gut 38:196-200, 1996.
74. Ben Horin S, Bardan E, Barshack I, et al: Cholesterol crystal embolization to the digestive system: Characterization of a common, yet overlooked presentation of atheroembolism. Am J Gastroenterol 98:1471-1479, 2003.
75. Paraf F, Jacquot C, Bloch F, et al: Cholesterol crystal embolization demonstrated on GI biopsy. Am J Gastroenterol 96:3301-3304, 2001.
76. Matsukuma S, Suda K, Abe H: Histopathological study of pancreatic ischemic lesions induced by cholesterol emboli: Fresh and subsequent features of pancreatic ischemia. Hum Pathol 29:41-46, 1998.
77. Lawson JM: Cholesterol crystal embolization: More common than we thought? Am J Gastroenterol 96:3230-3232, 2001.
78. Masuda J, Yutani C, Ogata J, et al: Atheromatous embolism in the brain: A clinicopathologic analysis of 15 autopsy cases. Neurology 44:1231-1237, 1994.
79. Beal MF, Williams RS, Richardson EP Jr, Fisher CM: Cholesterol embolism as a cause of transient ischemic attacks and cerebral infarction. Neurology 31:860-865, 1981.
80. Laloux P, Brucher JM: Lacunar infarctions due to cholesterol emboli. Stroke 22:1440-1444, 1991.
81. Ezzeddine MA, Primavera JM, Rosand J, et al: Clinical characteristics of pathologically proved cholesterol emboli to the brain. Neurology 54:1681-1683, 2000.
82. Desnuelle C, Lanteri-Minet M, Hofman P, et al: Cholesterol emboli with neurologic manifestation in the spinal cord. Rev Neurol (Paris) 148:715-718, 1992.
83. Teja K, Crampton RS: Intramural coronary arteritis from cholesterol emboli: A rare cause of unstable angina preceding sudden death. Am Heart J 110:168-170, 1985.
84. Sabatine MS, Oelberg DA, Mark EJ, Kanarek D: Pulmonary cholesterol crystal embolization. Chest 112:1687-1692, 1997.
85. Walton TJ, Samani NJ, Andrews R: Systemic cholesterol crystal embolisation with pulmonary involvement: A fatal combination after coronary angiography. Postgrad Med J 78:288-289, 2002.
86. Hillion D, Durst P, Baglin A, et al: Syndrome of alveolar hemorrhage associated with systemic cholesterol embolism. Ann Med Interne (Paris) 137:660-662, 1986.
87. Sijpkens Y, Westendorp R, van Kemenade F, et al: Vasculitis due to cholesterol embolism. Am J Med 102:302-303, 1997.
88. Olin JW: Syndromes that mimic vasculitis. Curr Opin Cardiol 6:768-774, 1991.
89. Low complement in atheroembolic disease. Lancet 2(8447):136, 1985.
90. Haqqie SS, Urizar RE, Singh J: Nephrotic-range proteinuria in renal atheroembolic disease: Report of four cases. Am J Kidney Dis 28:493-501, 1996.
91. Greenberg A, Bastacky SI, Iqbal A, et al: Focal segmental glomerulosclerosis associated with nephrotic syndrome in cholesterol atheroembolism: Clinicopathological correlations. Am J Kidney Dis 29:334-344, 1997.
92. Anderson WR, Richards AM: Evaluation of lower extremity muscle biopsies in the diagnosis of atheroembolism. Arch Pathol 86:535-541, 1968.
93. Mieszczanska H, Lazar J, Marzo KP, Cunha BA: Cholesterol emboli mimicking acute bacterial endocarditis. Heart Lung 31:452-454, 2002.
94. Peat DS, Mathieson PW: Cholesterol emboli may mimic systemic vasculitis. BMJ 313:546-547, 1996.
95. Wilson DM, Salazer TL, Farkouh ME: Eosinophiluria in atheroembolic renal disease. Am J Med 91:186-189, 1991.
96. Rudnick MR, Berns JS, Cohen RM, Goldfarb S: Nephrotoxic risks of renal angiography: Contrast media-associated nephrotoxicity and atheroembolic renal disease—a critical review. Am J Kidney Dis 24:713-727, 1994.
97. Mann SJ, Sos TA: Treatment of atheroembolization with corticosteroids. Am J Hypertens 14:831-834, 2001.
98. Nakahama H, Sakaguchi K: Small dose oral corticosteroid treatment rapidly improved renal function in a patient with an acute aggravation of chronic renal failure due to cholesterol embolism. Nephrol Dial Transplant 16:872-873, 2001.
99. Finch TM, Ryatt KS: Livedo reticularis caused by cholesterol embolization may improve with simvastatin. Br J Dermatol 143:1319-1320, 2000.
100. Woolfson RG, Lachmann H: Improvement in renal cholesterol emboli syndrome after simvastatin. Lancet 351:1331-1332, 1998.
101. Cabili S, Hochman I, Goor Y: Reversal of gangrenous lesions in the blue toe syndrome with lovastatin—a case report. Angiology 44:821-825, 1993.
102. Tunick PA, Nayar AC, Goodkin GM, et al: Effect of treatment on the incidence of stroke and other emboli in 519 patients with severe thoracic aortic plaque. Am J Cardiol 90:1320-1325, 2002.
103. Elinav E, Chajek-Shaul T, Stern M: Improvement in cholesterol emboli syndrome after iloprost therapy. BMJ 324:268-269, 2002.
104. Zuccala A, Zucchelli P: A renal disease frequently found at postmortem, but rarely diagnosed in vivo. Nephrol Dial Transplant 12:1762-1767, 1997.
105. Carr ME Jr, Sanders K, Todd WM: Pain relief and clinical improvement temporally related to the use of pentoxifylline in a patient with documented cholesterol emboli—a case report. Angiology 45:65-69, 1994.
106. Hankey GJ: Angiotensin-converting enzyme inhibitors for stroke prevention: Is there HOPE for PROGRESS after LIFE? Stroke 34:354-356, 2003.
107. Arnold JM, Yusuf S, Young J, et al: Prevention of heart failure in patients in the Heart Outcomes Prevention Evaluation (HOPE) Study. Circulation 107:1284-1290, 2003.
108. Effects of an angiotensin-converting-enzyme inhibitor, ramipril, on cardiovascular events in high-risk patients. The Heart Outcomes Prevention Evaluation Study Investigators. N Engl J Med 342:145-153, 2000.
109. Cannon CP, CAPRIE Investigators: Effectiveness of clopidogrel versus aspirin in preventing acute myocardial infarction in patients with symptomatic atherothrombosis (CAPRIE trial). Am J Cardiol 90:760-762, 2002.

110. Collaborative meta-analysis of randomised trials of antiplatelet therapy for prevention of death, myocardial infarction, and stroke in high risk patients. BMJ 324:71-86, 2002.
111. Heart Protection Study Collaborators Group: MRC/BHF Heart Protection Study of cholesterol lowering with simvastatin in 20,536 high-risk individuals: A randomised placebo-controlled trial. Lancet 360:7-22, 2002.
112. Keen RR, McCarthy WJ, Shireman PK, et al: Surgical management of atheroembolization. J Vasc Surg 21:773-780, 1995.
113. Baumann DS, McGraw D, Rubin BG, et al: An institutional experience with arterial atheroembolism. Ann Vasc Surg 8:258-265, 1994.
114. Dougherty MJ, Calligaro KD: Endovascular treatment of embolization of aortic plaque with covered stents. J Vasc Surg 36:727-731, 2002.
115. Friedman SG, Krishnasastry KV: External iliac ligation and axillary-bifemoral bypass for blue toe syndrome. Surgery 115:27-30, 1994.
116. Kaufman JL, Saifi J, Chang BB, et al: The role of extra-anatomic exclusion bypass in the treatment of disseminated atheroembolism syndrome. Ann Vasc Surg 4:260-263, 1990.
117. Brewer ML, Kinnison ML, Perler BA, White RI Jr: Blue toe syndrome: Treatment with anticoagulants and delayed percutaneous transluminal angioplasty. Radiology 166:31-36, 1988.
118. Sharma PV, Babu SC, Shah PM, Nassoura ZE: Changing patterns of atheroembolism. Cardiovasc Surg 4:573-579, 1996.
119. Clugston RA, Eisenhauer AC, Matthews RV: Atherectomy of the distal aorta using a "kissing-balloon" technique for the treatment of blue toe syndrome. AJR Am J Roentgenol 159:125-127, 1992.
120. Dolmatch BL, Rholl KS, Moskowitz LB, et al: Blue toe syndrome: Treatment with percutaneous atherectomy. Radiology 173:799-804, 1989.
121. Matchett WJ, McFarland DR, Eidt JF, Moursi MM: Blue toe syndrome: Treatment with intra-arterial stents and review of therapies. J Vasc Interv Radiol 11:585-592, 2000.
122. Murphy KD, Encarnacion CE, Le VA, Palmaz JC: Iliac artery stent placement with the Palmaz stent: Follow-up study. J Vasc Interv Radiol 6:321-329, 1995.
123. Ohki T, Marin ML, Lyon RT, et al: Ex vivo human carotid artery bifurcation stenting: Correlation of lesion characteristics with embolic potential. J Vasc Surg 27:463-471, 1998.
124. Renshaw A, McCowen T, Waltke EA, et al: Angioplasty with stenting is effective in treating blue toe syndrome. Vasc Endovascular Surg 36:155-159, 2002.
125. Kumins NH, Owens EL, Oglevie SB, et al: Early experience using the Wallgraft in the management of distal microembolism from common iliac artery pathology. Ann Vasc Surg 16:181-186, 2002.
126. Carroccio A, Olin JW, Ellozy SH, et al: The role of aortic stent grafting in the treatment of atheromatous embolization syndrome: Results after a mean of 15 months follow-up. J Vasc Surg 40:424-429, 2004.
127. Lee BY, Madden JL, Thoden WR, McCann WJ: Lumbar sympathectomy for toe gangrene: Long-term follow-up. Am J Surg 145:398-401, 1983.
128. Ghilardi G, Massaro F, Gobatti D, et al: Temporary spinal cord stimulation for peripheral cholesterol embolism. J Cardiovasc Surg (Torino) 43:255-258, 2002.
129. Tunick PA, Perez JL, Kronzon I: Protruding atheromas in the thoracic aorta and systemic embolization. Ann Intern Med 115:423-427, 1991.
130. Amarenco P, Cohen A, Tzourio C, et al: Atherosclerotic disease of the aortic arch and the risk of ischemic stroke. N Engl J Med 331:1474-1479, 1994.
131. Amarenco P, Duychaerts C, Tzourio C, et al: The prevalence of ulcerated plaques in the aortic arch in patients with stroke. N Engl J Med 326:221-225, 1992.
132. Davila-Roman VG, Murphy SF, Nickerson NJ, et al: Atherosclerosis of the ascending aorta is an independent predictor of long-term neurologic events and mortality. J Am Coll Cardiol 33:1308-1316, 1999.
133. Tunick PA, Rosenzweig BP, Katz ES, et al: High risk for vascular events in patients with protruding aortic atheromas: A prospective study. J Am Coll Cardiol 32:1085-1090, 1994.
134. Mitusch R, Doherty C, Wucherpfennig H, et al: Vascular events during follow-up in patients with aortic arch atherosclerosis. Stroke 28:36-39, 1997.
135. Cohen A, Amarenco P: Atherosclerosis of the thoracic aorta: From risk stratification to treatment. Am J Cardiol 90:1333-1335, 2002.
136. Laperche T, Laurian C, Roudaut R, Steg PG: Mobile thromboses of the aortic arch without aortic debris : A transesophageal echocardiographic finding associated with unexplained arterial embolism. Circulation 96:288-294, 1997.
137. Dressler MD, Frederick A, Craig MD, et al: Mobile aortic atheroma and systemic emboli: Efficacy of anticoagulation and influence of plaque morphology on recurrent stroke. J Am Coll Cardiol 31:134-138, 1998.
138. Ferrari E, Vidal R, Chevallier T, Baudouy M: Atherosclerosis of the thoracic aorta and aortic debris as a marker of poor prognosis: Benefit of oral anticoagulants. J Am Coll Cardiol 33:1317-1322, 1999.
139. Salem DN, Levine HJ, Pauker SG, et al: Antithrombotic therapy in valvular heart disease. Chest 114:590S-601S, 1998.
140. Bojar RM, Payne DD, Murphy RE, et al: Surgical treatment of systemic atheroembolism from the thoracic aorta. Ann Thorac Surg 61:1389-1393, 1996.
141. Stern A, Tunick PA, Culliford AT, et al: Protruding aortic arch atheromas: Risk of stroke during heart surgery with and without aortic arch endarterectomy. Am Heart J 138:746-752, 1999.

Section XII

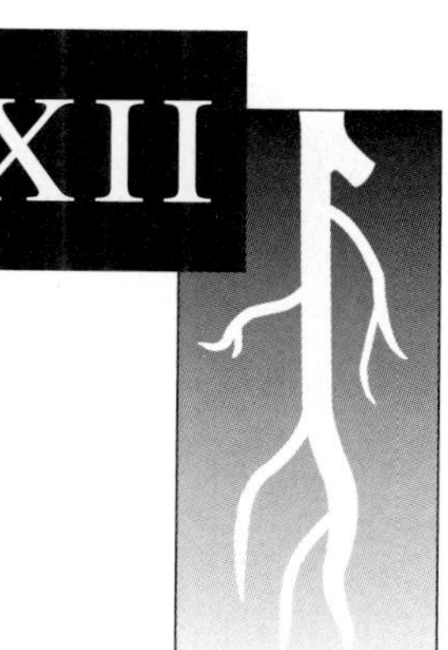

VASCULAR TRAUMA

FRED A. WEAVER, MD, FACS

Chapter 69

Epidemiology and Natural History of Vascular Trauma

RAUL COIMBRA, MD, PhD, FACS
DAVID B. HOYT, MD, FACS

Vascular trauma results from penetrating, blunt, or iatrogenic injuries. This chapter focuses on the epidemiology and natural history of vascular injuries. Emphasis is placed on the evolution of the management of vascular injuries, obtained initially from military experience and subsequently applied to civilian trauma. The clinical presentations of the various forms of arterial injury are described.

■ EPIDEMIOLOGY

Approximately 2.6 million people are hospitalized annually in the United States as a result of accidental injury. Thirty-five million to 40 million emergency department visits occur for the evaluation and treatment of traumatic injuries.[1] Most patients are between 25 and 44 years of age, and 20% are between 15 and 24. People younger than 45 years of age sustain almost 80% of all injuries and account for 75% of the total lifetime costs of injury.

Young males are the highest risk group, due to their propensity to engage in high-risk activities. According to the National Center for Injury and Prevention control data, 56.6% of all trauma-related deaths in 1997 occurred in the age group of 15 to 49 years, predominantly in the male population. Overall, the risk of dying following injury for the male population is seven times higher than that for the female population.[2]

In addition to morbidity and mortality data, another important variable related to the societal cost of injury is the measurement of years of productive life lost (YPLL). This reflects the potential productivity lost as a result of premature death. Injury-related deaths result in a higher number of YPLL when compared with cancer and cardiovascular deaths. For each traumatic death there are, on average, 36 YPLL compared with 16 for cancer and 12 for cardiovascular diseases.[3]

The leading causes of injury include motor vehicle crashes, falls, firearms, cutting or piercing instruments, and burns. Fatalities after injury are mainly due to motor vehicle accidents (32%), gunshot wounds (22%), and falls (9%).[4] The three leading causes of traumatic death for persons younger than 35 years of age are the same in all groups: motor vehicle accidents, homicide, and suicide.[3] Alcohol ingestion and the use of other drugs, such as marijuana and cocaine, also have been implicated in increased trauma-related fatalities.[5]

Peripheral vascular injuries account for 80% of all cases of vascular trauma. Most of the injuries involve the lower extremities. The great majority of patients are young males. Most injuries are caused by high-velocity weapons (70% to 80%), followed by stab wounds (10% to 15%) and blunt trauma (5% to 10%). The incidence of vascular trauma in the military is comparable to the civilian arena and varies from 0.2% to 4% of injured patients.[6-12] Table 69-1 depicts the incidence of vascular trauma in survivors during military conflicts and in large comprehensive civilian series in distinct geographic areas.

Although most civilian penetrating vascular injuries occur in the extremities, military data reveal that the incidence of extremity vascular injuries overall is higher. Frykberg analyzed a large civilian series of survivors from 1960 to 1989 and reported an incidence of 51% of extremity vascular trauma compared with 93.7% in the military

Table 69-1 Incidence of Vascular Injuries in Military Conflicts and Civilian Practice

STUDY SUBJECTS, REFERENCE NO.	TOTAL NUMBER OF VASCULAR INJURIES	EXTREMITY VASCULAR INJURIES	PERCENTAGE OF EXTREMITY VASCULAR INJURIES	PERCENTAGE OF PENETRATING MECHANISM
World War I[13]	443	Unknown	—	Unknown
World War II[6]	2471	2409	97.5	Almost all
Korean War[14]	304	286	94.1	Almost All
Vietnam War[8]	1000	910	91.0	98.9
Georgia[15]	Unknown	99	—	All
Houston[10]	5760	2131	37.0	93.0
North Carolina[9]	978	632	65.0	63.0
Australia[12]	175	79	45.0	11.4
San Diego	664	263	40.0	67

setting.[16] Explanations of differences include torso protection gear used by soldiers as well as the high-velocity weapons used in military conflicts causing immediate death when major vessels of the torso are injured. Alternatively, the total number of injuries to the major vessels in the chest, abdomen, and pelvis that occur in military conflicts may be underestimated or under-reported. In general, most vascular injuries in the military setting are caused by a penetrating mechanism. In the civilian setting, though a penetrating mechanism still predominates,[16] the relative incidence of blunt injuries has increased (see Table 69-1).

■ BIOMECHANICS OF INJURY

Classically, injury mechanisms are divided into penetrating or blunt type. Following blunt trauma, tissue injury is produced by local compression or rapid deceleration. In penetrating trauma, the injury is produced by crushing and separation of tissues along the path of the penetrating object. Understanding the biomechanics of specific injuries is important in guiding the initial evaluation, since the natural history of arterial injuries is related to the type of injury, location, hemodynamic consequences, and mechanism of injury.

Injury severity is proportional to the amount of kinetic energy (KE) transferred to the tissues, which is a function of the mass (M) and velocity (V):

$$KE = M \times V^2/2$$

This is valid for both blunt and penetrating mechanisms. Changes in velocity alter the kinetic energy transfer more significantly than changes in mass. This is critical when evaluating high- and low-velocity gunshot wounds and their corresponding injury potential.

Another important concept in the understanding of the biomechanics of vascular injury is that of cavitation. Cavitation is a phenomenon that occurs as tissue recoils from the point of impact by a moving body, away from the object. After blunt trauma, the resulting transient tissue cavity may be caused by rapid acceleration or deceleration. Extreme strain occurs at points of anatomic fixation during the formation of these temporary cavities. Forces can be produced both along the longitudinal axis (tensile or compression strain) and across the transverse axis (shear strain). These types of forces cause deformity, tearing, and tissue failure or fracture. Following penetrating trauma, temporary cavitation is caused by the transfer of kinetic energy from the projectile to adjacent tissue, which is followed by the formation of a permanent cavity caused by tissue displacement. This mechanism explains why vessels can be injured even without being in contact with projectiles from firearms or bone fragments.[17]

■ NATURAL HISTORY OF ARTERIAL INJURIES

The clinical presentation of arterial injuries occurs in one of four ways: (1) external bleeding, (2) ischemia, (3) a pulsatile hematoma, or (4) internal bleeding accompanied by signs of shock.

Most major penetrating vascular injuries in the chest are identified intraoperatively after a chest tube is placed to treat a hemothorax. Depending on the amount of blood loss, signs of shock are present, leading to operative exploration and identification. After blunt trauma, most arterial injuries in the chest are tamponaded by the mediastinal structures and adventitial containment. Suggestive signs on plain chest films (e.g., apical cap, extrapleural hematoma, tracheal deviation, widened mediastinum, or blurred aortopulmonary window) are present and suggest a vascular injury.

In the abdomen, the type of clinical presentation depends on the presence of retroperitoneal tamponade. Patients with an intact retroperitoneum may be hypotensive or hemodynamically stable on presentation and constitute the group with the greatest chance of survival. When the retroperitoneal tamponade is lost, signs of shock and acute hypovolemia are present. Usually these injuries are identified during surgical exploration for a penetrating abdominal injury. Blunt injuries to major abdominal vessels are rare. Major injuries to large vessels in the mesentery (e.g., superior mesenteric artery) usually cause significant hemoperitoneum and shock.

It is in the extremities that knowledge of the clinical presentation and natural history of vascular trauma is of utmost importance (see Chapter 73). External bleeding is a rare form of presentation, and it is mostly associated with high-velocity gunshot wounds in the presence of massive destruction of soft tissues and, consequently, loss of tissue tamponade. Prehospital information on vital signs as well as the amount and characteristics of blood lost at the scene (e.g., pulsatile, bright red blood) is helpful during the resuscitation phase. Most patients present as hypotensive without external blood loss, although external bleeding may resume during fluid resuscitation owing to the expansion of the intravascular compartment and subsequent increases in arterial blood pressure.

The most common form of presentation of extremity arterial injury is acute ischemia. This occurs most commonly after stab wounds, low-velocity gunshot wounds, and blunt trauma associated with fractures and dislocations. Classically, signs and symptoms of arterial injury are divided into hard and soft categories.

Hard signs include *absence* of distal pulses, active external arterial hemorrhage, signs of ischemia, pulsatile hematoma, and bruit or thrill. The clinical signs of ischemia are rest pain, paresthesia, paralysis, paleness, and poikilothermia, associated with decreased or absent distal pulses. Soft signs include diminished distal pulses, injury in the proximity of a major vessel, a neurologic deficit, and hypotension or shock. A detailed and complete physical examination, including inspection, palpation, and auscultation, is usually sufficient to identify the acute signs of ischemia.

The presence of a pseudoaneurysm or arteriovenous fistula should be suspected following a penetrating injury to the extremity in the presence of a pulsatile hematoma accompanied by a bruit or a thrill.

The spectrum of severity of arterial injuries depends on the "invasiveness" of the workup, as well as the mechanism, type, and location of the arterial injury and the duration of ischemia, if present. In the absence of clinical findings, there is still debate about whether or not an angiogram should be obtained in penetrating extremity injuries when the wound tracts in proximity to major vessels. Any patient with significant mechanism of injury presenting with soft signs should undergo an objective evaluation of the distal circulation. The most practical way of doing so in the trauma resuscitation area is to obtain the ankle-brachial index (ABI). Briefly, the distal systolic Doppler pressure of the extremity is measured and divided by the brachial systolic pressure of the uninjured extremity. An ABI less than 1.0 is indicative of arterial injury and should prompt further diagnostic investigation. The ABI is also important to monitor the status of the distal circulation over time in patients with life-threatening injuries in other body areas that require operative intervention (craniotomy, thoracotomy, or laparotomy) or in patients who are too unstable to undergo exploration of the arterial system.

TYPES OF INJURY

The clinical presentation depends on the type of arterial injury. The most common injuries are partial lacerations and complete transections. In general, complete transection leads to retraction and thrombosis of the proximal and distal ends of the vessel, with subsequent ischemia. In contrast, a partial laceration causes persistent bleeding or pseudoaneurysm formation. Partial lacerations as well as contusions may be accompanied by intimal flaps. An intimal flap may progress to thrombosis. Small arterial contusions with limited intimal flaps may not cause distal hemodynamic compromise and may be undiagnosed. These are sometimes classified as "occult" or "minimal" arterial injuries when seen on angiography. Although these injuries carry a small risk of thrombosis, several studies have documented spontaneous healing.[18-24] Concomitant arterial and venous injuries may lead to the formation of an arteriovenous fistula and partial lacerations may cause pseudoaneurysm formation. The correlation between the injury type and possible clinical presentation is shown in Table 69-2.

Table 69-2 Types of Arterial Injury and Possible Clinical Presentation

TYPE OF INJURY	CLINICAL PRESENTATION
Partial laceration	Decreased pulse, hematoma, hemorrhage
Transection	Absent distal pulses, ischemia
Contusion	Initially, examination may be normal; may progress to thrombosis
Pseudoaneurysm	Initially, examination may be normal; bruit or thrill, decreased pulses
AV fistula	Same as pseudoaneurysm
External compression	Decreased pulses; normal pulses when fracture aligned

AV, arteriovenous.

Angiography remains the "gold standard" in the diagnosis of extremity arterial injuries. Adequate assessment of the extent of the injury, distal circulation, and surgical planning are some of the advantages of this diagnostic modality. In hemodynamically unstable patients or those requiring surgical procedures in other body regions, angiography can be performed in the operating room. Angiography is also useful to determine repair patency. The accuracy of angiography varies from 92% to 98%; however, most errors involve false-positive interpretation rather than missed injuries. Angiography is also highly reliable in demonstrating injuries that were clinically unsuspected (occult arterial injuries).

The classic indications for angiography include significant blunt injury to the extremity associated with fracture dislocations and signs suggestive of ischemia or ABI less than 1.0, multiple penetrating injuries to the extremity, or neurologic deficits. Until recently, patients with penetrating extremity injuries in the proximity of major vessels would undergo angiography. Recently, this concept has been challenged, and most such patients are followed clinically and with serial ABIs.

The natural history of untreated vascular injuries varies with the extent and type of the injury. Occult vascular injuries are usually composed of intimal flaps, segmental narrowing, and hemodynamically insignificant arteriovenous fistulae or pseudoaneurysms. There is growing evidence suggesting that most of these injuries heal spontaneously or stabilize without further compromising the distal circulation and perfusion.[18-20] These findings have been confirmed by several other independent studies in animals[21,22] and by two recent human studies.[23,24]

Potential complications of untreated peripheral vascular trauma include hemorrhage, thrombosis, pseudoaneurysm, arteriovenous fistula formation, and compartment syndrome.

■ INCIDENCE OF VASCULAR INJURIES IN DIFFERENT BODY AREAS

Vascular Injuries in the Neck

The most commonly injured structures in the neck are the blood vessels. The incidence of major vascular trauma following a penetrating neck injury is 20%.[25] The incidence of neck arterial injuries following blunt trauma is extremely low, although in recent years, there has been an increase in reported blunt carotid injuries due to aggressive screening.[26,27] In a recently published series, 85 blunt carotid injuries in 67 patients were reported during an 11-year period.[26] The most common injury mechanism was motor vehicle crash (82%), followed by motorcycle crash (7%) and assault (6%).

The mortality rate of blunt carotid injury varies from 20% to 40%, and permanent neurologic impairment occurs in 25% to 80% of the survivors.[26-29] Outcomes are dependent on several factors, but the size and location of the arterial injury are key factors.

In recent years, the identification of vertebral artery injuries has increased, probably due to the liberal use of screening tests (computed tomography angiography or neck angiography) following both penetrating and blunt injuries. The incidence of vertebral artery injury following a penetrating mechanism varies from 1% to 7.5%.[30] This variation is related to the indications for angiography, and some of these injuries may not need surgical intervention. The incidence of blunt vertebral artery injuries is low. These injuries are commonly associated with cervical vertebral fractures.[31,32]

Thoracic Aortic Injuries

Blunt aortic injury occurs following abrupt deceleration. This causes shear forces at points of anatomic fixation of the aorta and leads to transmural injuries. Most injuries are located distally to the take-off of the left subclavian artery (65%), although other segments of the thoracic aorta such as the arch (10%), the descending aorta (12%), or multiple sites (13%) may be injured.[33] Frontal motor vehicle crashes as well as side-impact collisions are the most frequent mechanism.

Penetrating injuries to the ascending aorta are more commonly caused by stab wounds in survivors, whereas gunshot wounds are usually the mechanism of injury in the descending portion of the thoracic aorta.

Subclavian and Axillary Artery Injuries

Most injuries to the subclavian and axillary arteries occur following penetrating trauma. The incidence varies from 0.9% to 3% depending on the mechanism of injury (stab or gunshot wound). Blunt trauma is rare. These injuries occur following high-speed motor vehicle frontal crashes with significant deceleration and fracture to the clavicle or first and second ribs. The mortality rate of these injuries is high, and most patients do not reach the hospital alive.[34]

Abdominal Vascular Injuries

In contrast with military data, major abdominal vascular injuries are common in civilian practice. These injuries account for approximately 30% of all vascular injuries.

Most injuries (90% to 95%) are caused by a penetrating mechanism. Approximately 10% of patients undergoing surgical exploration following a stab wound to the abdomen and 20% to 30% of those undergoing surgical exploration following a gunshot wound to the abdomen sustain a major vascular injury.[35]

Hospital mortality rates vary from 30% to 80% for abdominal aortic injuries and from 30% to 65% for inferior vena cava injuries. A high number of patients never reach the hospital alive, dying at the scene or during transport.[36-41] Death usually is due to exsanguination, despite aggressive resuscitation and early operation.[37,42,43] The location of abdominal vascular injuries also determines survivability. Ease of surgical access for control directly correlates with increased survivability.[36]

Extremity Vascular Trauma

The overall incidence of arterial injuries following penetrating injury to the extremity (upper or lower) is approximately 10%, in contrast with 1% following blunt trauma.[11,44,45] The brachial, femoral, and popliteal arteries are the most frequently injured vessels in civilian as well as in military penetrating series.[6,8,10,45,46] Most femoral artery injuries are the result of a penetrating mechanism, particularly gunshot wounds.[47]

In contrast, a blunt mechanism accounts for 20% to 75% of popliteal artery injuries, although in some series a penetrating mechanism still predominates. These injuries encompass 19% of all extremity arterial injuries. Recently, Frykberg compiled 1209 cases of civilian popliteal artery injury and reported 56% to be secondary to penetrating injury with a 10.5% amputation rate as compared with 27.5% following blunt trauma. Recent published series have demonstrated a significant decrease in the amputation rate, which reflects a significant improvement in management of these serious injuries.[48]

The incidence of vascular injuries below the popliteal fossa is difficult to determine because most of these injuries, when isolated, cause no vascular compromise. One study analyzing 755 patients sustaining gunshot wounds below the knee reported 136 injuries below the popliteal fossa identified on angiography, an incidence of 18%.[49]

The association between arterial injuries and orthopedic lesions (fractures and dislocations) is well known. Table 69-3 summarizes the most common orthopedic injuries and their respective arterial injuries.

Table 69-3 Orthopedic Injuries Commonly Associated with Vascular Trauma

ORTHOPEDIC INJURY	ARTERIAL INJURY
Supracondylar fracture of the humerus	Brachial artery
Clavicular/first rib fracture	Subclavian artery
Shoulder dislocation	Axillary artery
Elbow dislocation	Brachial artery
Distal femur	Superficial femoral/popliteal artery
Posterior knee dislocation	Popliteal artery
Proximal tibia	Popliteal artery/distal vessels

■ CONCLUSION

In summary, the epidemiology of vascular injuries in both civilian practice and military practice is now well described. Like all injuries, the presentation of vascular injury depends on the biomechanics and the amount of energy transfer that occurs at the moment of injury. The natural history of arterial injuries depends on the injury's location and how much of the arterial wall is injured. Further, presentation of ischemia, in large part, depends on the availability of collateral circulation. The most useful way to organize injuries is to classify them simply as part of the neck, chest, abdomen, or extremities. Learning the surgical approaches and the natural history of injuries in each area is the responsibility of the vascular surgeon or any surgeon who encounters these types of injuries.

■ REFERENCES

1. Bonnie RJ, Fulco CE, Liverman CT: Reducing the Burden of Injury: Advancing Prevention and Treatment. Washington, DC, National Academies Press, 1999, pp 41-59.
2. National Center for Injury and Prevention Control: Overall injury and adverse event-related deaths and rate per 100,000. E800- E999. 1995. Available on line.
3. Baker S: The Injury Fact Book. New York, Oxford University Press, 1992.
4. Rice DP, MacKenzie EJ, Jones AS, et al (eds): Cost of Injury in the United States: A Report to Congress. San Francisco, Institute for Health and Aging, University of California; Injury Prevention Center, Johns Hopkins University, 1989.
5. National Highway Traffic Safety Administration (NHTSA): The Incidence and Role of Drugs in Fatally Injured Drivers. Washington, DC, NHTSA, 1993.
6. DeBakey ME, Simeone FA: Battle injuries of the arteries in World War II: An analysis of 2,471 cases. Ann Surg 123:534-579, 1946.
7. Rich NM, Spencer FC: Vascular Trauma. Philadelphia, WB Saunders, 1978.
8. Rich NM, Baugh JH, Hughes CW: Acute arterial injuries in Vietnam: 1,000 cases. J Trauma 10:359-369, 1970.
9. Oller DW, Rutledge R, Clancy T, et al: Vascular injuries in a rural state: A review of 978 patients from a state trauma registry. J Trauma 32:740-746, 1992.
10. Mattox KL, Feliciano DV, Burch J, et al: Five thousand seven hundred sixty cardiovascular injuries in 4459 patients: Epidemiologic evolution 1958 to 1987. Ann Surg 209:698-705, 1989.
11. Frykberg ER, Dennis JW, Bishop K, et al: The reliability of physical examination in the evaluation of penetrating extremity trauma from vascular injury: Results at one year. J Trauma 31:502-511, 1991.
12. Gupta R, Rao S, Sieunarine K: An epidemiological view of vascular trauma in western Australia: A five-year study. Aust NZ J Surg 71:461-466, 2001.
13. Beebe GW, DeBakey ME: Battle Casualties: Incidence, Mortality, and Logistic Considerations. Springfield, IL, Charles C Thomas, 1952.
14. Hughes CW: Arterial repair during the Korean War. Ann Surg 147:555-561, 1958.
15. Nanobashvili J, Kopadze T, Tvaladze M, et al: War injuries of major extremity arteries. World J Surg 27:134-139, 2003.
16. Frykberg ER: Vascular trauma: History, general principles, and extremity injuries. In Callow AD, Ernst CB (eds): Vascular Surgery: Theory and Practice. Stamford, CT, Appleton & Lange, 1995, pp 985-1037.
17. Hoyt DB, Coimbra R: Trauma. In Greenfield LJ, Mulholland MW, Oldham KT, et al (eds): Surgery: Scientific Principles and Practice, 3rd ed. Philadelphia, Lippincott Williams & Wilkins, 2001, pp 271-280.
18. Stain SC, Yellin AE, Weaver FA, et al: Selective management of non-occlusive arterial injuries. Arch Surg 124:1136-1141, 1989.
19. Frykberg ER, Vines FS, Alexander RH: The natural history of clinically occult arterial injuries: A prospective evaluation. J Trauma 29:577-583, 1989.
20. Frykberg ER, Crump JM, Dennis JW, et al: Nonoperative observation of clinically occult arterial injuries: A prospective evaluation. Surgery 109:85-96, 1991.
21. Neville RF, Hobson RW, Watanabe B, et al: A prospective evaluation of arterial intimal injuries in an experimental model. J Trauma 31:669-675, 1991.
22. Panetta TF, Sales CM, Marin ML, et al: Natural history, duplex characteristics, and histopathologic correlation of arterial injuries in a canine model. J Vasc Surg 16:867-876, 1992.
23. Hoffer EK, Sclafani SJ, Herzkowitz MM, Scalea TM: Natural history of arterial injuries diagnosed with arteriography. J Vasc Interv Radiol 8:43-53, 1997.
24. Dennis JW, Frykberg ER, Veldenz HC, et al: Validation of nonoperative management of occult vascular injuries and accuracy of physical examination alone in penetrating extremity trauma: Five- to ten-year follow-up. J Trauma 44:243-253, 1998.
25. Beitsch P, Weigelt JA, Flynn E, Easley S: Physical examination and arteriography in patients with penetrating zone II neck wounds. Arch Surg 129:577, 1994.
26. Fabian TC, Patton JH, Croce MA, et al: Blunt carotid injury: Importance of early diagnosis and anticoagulant therapy. Ann Surg 223:513, 1996.
27. Eachempati SR, Vaslef SN, Sebastian MW, et al: Blunt vascular injuries of the head and neck: Is heparinization necessary? J Trauma 45:997, 1998.
28. Cogbill TH, Moore EE, Meissner M, et al: The spectrum of blunt injury to the carotid artery: A multicenter perspective. J Trauma 37:473, 1994.
29. Fakhry S, Jacques PF, Proctor H: Cervical vessel injury after blunt trauma. J Vasc Surg 8:501, 1988.
30. Roberts LH, Demetriades D: Vertebral artery injuries. Surg Clin North Am 81:1345-1356, 2001.
31. DeBehnke DJ, Brady W: Vertebral artery dissection due to minor neck trauma. J Emerg Med 12:27, 1994.
32. Egnor MR, Page LK, David C: Vertebral artery aneurysm: A unique hazard of head banging by heavy metal rockers. Pediatr Neurosurg 17:135, 1991.
33. Wall MJ, Hirshberg A, LeMaire SA, et al: Thoracic aortic and thoracic vascular injuries. Surg Clin North Am 81:1375-1394, 2001.
34. Demetriades D, Asensio JA: Subclavian and axillary injuries. Surg Clin North Am 81:1357-1374, 2001.
35. Asensio JA, Forno W, Roldan G, et al: Abdominal vascular injuries: Injuries to the aorta. Surg Clin North Am 81:1395-1416, 2001.
36. Coimbra R, Hoyt D, Winchell R, et al: The ongoing challenge of retroperitoneal vascular injuries. Am J Surg 172:541-545, 1996.
37. Mattox KL, McCollum WB, Jordan GL, et al: Management of upper abdominal vascular trauma. Am J Surg 128:823-828, 1974.
38. Coimbra R, Aguida HC, Soler W, et al: Penetrating abdominal aortic injuries. Rev Col Bras Cir 20:128-132, 1993.
39. Coimbra R, Prado PA, Araujo LHB, et al: Factors related to mortality in inferior vena cava injuries: A five-year experience. Int Surg 79:138-141, 1994.
40. Stewart MT, Stone HH: Injuries of the inferior vena cava. Am Surg 52:9-13, 1986.
41. Maull KI, Rozycki GS, Vinsant GO, Pedigo RE: Retroperitoneal injuries: Pitfalls in diagnosis and management. South Med J 80:1111-1115, 1987.
42. Lopez-Viego MA, Snyder WH, Valentine RJ, Clagett GP: Penetrating abdominal aortic trauma: A report of 129 cases. J Vasc Surg 16:332-336, 1992.
43. Burch JM, Feliciano DV, Mattox KL, Edelman M: Injuries of the inferior vena cava. Am J Surg 156:548-552, 1988.
44. Smith RF, Elliott JP, Hageman JH, et al: Acute penetrating arterial injuries of the neck and limbs. Arch Surg 109:198-205, 1974.
45. Dennis JW, Frykberg ER, Crump JM, et al: New perspectives on the management of penetrating trauma in proximity to major limb arteries. J Vasc Surg 11:84-93, 1990.

46. Robbs JV, Baker LW: Major arterial trauma: Review of experience with 267 injuries. Br J Surg 65:532-538, 1978.
47. Carillo EH, Spain DA, Miller FB, Richardson JD: Femoral vessel injuries. Surg Clin North Am 82:49-66, 2002.
48. Frykberg ER: Popliteal vascular injuries. Surg Clin North Am 82:67-90, 2002.
49. Ordog GJ, Balasubramanian S, Wasserberger J, et al: Extremity gunshot wounds: I. Identification and treatment of patients at high risk of vascular injury. J Trauma 36:358-368, 1994.

Chapter 70

Carotid and Vertebral Artery Injuries

JEFFREY L. BALLARD, MD
THEODORE H. TERUYA, MD

Section XII

Arterial and venous trauma to the cervicothoracic region continues to present a challenge for the surgeon despite advances in vascular diagnostics and surgical technique. Whether these injuries are due to penetrating or blunt mechanisms, the overall incidence is low, whereas morbidity and mortality rates remain high. Although the collective experience with carotid and vertebral artery injuries from busy trauma centers has increased, controversies persist about the diagnostic evaluation, operative approach, and surgical treatment of these potentially devastating injuries.

Several excellent reviews of this topic have been published.[1-6] Therefore, the primary focus of this chapter is to review recent advances and controversies surrounding the treatment of carotid and vertebral artery trauma. The "pros and cons" of duplex ultrasonography (DUS) and angiography in the diagnosis of carotid and vertebral artery injuries are highlighted, and selective (vs. mandatory) neck exploration for zone II penetrating injuries is discussed. New diagnostic imaging modalities such as computed tomography angiography (CTA) and magnetic resonance angiography (MRA) are also reviewed. The importance of increased awareness of blunt carotid artery injury is also emphasized, including management dilemmas frequently associated with it. In addition, this chapter reviews the use of endovascular techniques for the management of some of these injuries.

■ PENETRATING CAROTID ARTERY TRAUMA

Epidemiology

Most penetrating carotid artery trauma results from stab wounds or low-velocity missiles. Victims are generally young, otherwise healthy males who are often under the influence of drugs or alcohol. Carotid artery injuries are coincident to approximately 6% of penetrating neck injuries and account for 22% of all cervical vascular injuries.[5] The common carotid artery is injured more frequently than the internal carotid artery (ICA). Iatrogenic carotid artery trauma occurs occasionally during attempts at central venous catheter insertion. Although exact figures are not known, jugular venous injury not infrequently accompanies penetrating carotid artery trauma.

Diagnostic Evaluation

Little controversy exists with regard to the management of the 8% to 25% of patients who present with "hard" signs of vascular injury such as shock, active bleeding, and expanding hematoma. These signs should prompt expeditious transport of the patient to the operating room for stabilization and operative exploration. Penetrating injuries that do not traverse the platysma require no further vascular evaluation; however, controversy surrounds that majority of patients who present with "soft" signs of vascular injury (i.e., history of pulsatile bleeding; small, stable hematoma; cranial nerve injury; unexplained neurologic deficit) or no signs at all but a "proximity" injury.

In 1969, Monson and colleagues proposed the following well-known division of the neck into three anatomic zones[7]:

- Zone I: extends from the sternal notch to 1 cm above the clavicular head
- Zone II: extends from 1 cm above the clavicular head to the angle of the mandible
- Zone III: extends from the angle of the mandible to the base of the skull

In the intervening years, it has become generally agreed that stable patients with penetrating zones I and III injuries should be evaluated by diagnostic arteriography, with selective intervention based on significant findings. However, the routine use of angiography for zone I penetrating injuries has been recently questioned. Eddy and colleagues[8] suggest that physical examination and chest radiographs might be the only screening studies necessary for this type of injury. Physical examination was considered normal if there was no clinical evidence of hypotension, active bleeding, unequal upper extremity pulses, expanding neck hematoma, motor function abnormalities, clavicular fracture, subcutaneous air, and stridor or voice abnormalities. In their series of 138 patients with penetrating zone I injuries and a normal physical examination and chest radiograph, there were no detectable vascular injuries. Although the negative predictive value was 100%, further investigation in this area is required before this approach can be adopted for routine use.

Similarly, considerable debate has surrounded the management of penetrating zone II injuries, with strong proponents of either *mandatory* or *selective* operative exploration based on routine angiography. Recent data have demonstrated that DUS may be a viable substitute for "routine" arteriography with these zone II injuries, and good results have also been obtained with physical examination alone in the diagnostic evaluation of penetrating neck trauma.

A large experience that favors mandatory neck exploration was published in 1994 by Apffelstaedt and Muller from South Africa.[9] Over a 20-month period they prospectively explored a remarkable series of 393 consecutive patients whose stab wounds penetrated the platysma in zones I, II, or III. Clinical signs of vascular trauma were absent in 30% of patients whose neck exploration was "positive" and in 58% of those who had "negative" explorations. Overall, the negative exploration rate was 57%. Morbidity and mortality rates for negative explorations were 2.2% and zero, respectively, and length of hospital stay averaged 1.5 days. These authors, and others, have cited the unreliability of physical signs for predicting cervical vascular injury.

Those who favor mandatory neck exploration for zone II injuries emphasize that currently available diagnostic studies have variable false-positive and false-negative rates in demonstrating significant cervicothoracic vascular injury. In addition, minimized use of expensive personnel and equipment and overall low morbidity and mortality are cited as advantages of mandatory exploration over a selective approach based on screening diagnostic studies. Detractors point primarily to the high rates (40% to 60%) of negative explorations associated with this approach.[2] In fact, in an extensive review of the literature on this controversy, Asensio and coworkers[10] concluded that neither the mandatory nor the selective approach is clearly superior.

In lieu of mandatory exploration for zone II injuries, routine four-vessel carotid-vertebral arteriography has been proposed. In Demetriades and associates' prospective series of 176 hemodynamically stable patients who underwent arteriography, 19% demonstrated a vascular injury.[11] However, only 8% of these injuries warranted surgical intervention based on the angiographic findings, and all were symptomatic. Nontherapeutic operations were essentially eliminated. These results corroborate those of previous studies that suggest a low yield for arteriography in asymptomatic patients.[12,13] Clearly, routine arteriography consumes significant resources; furthermore, some patients are subjected unnecessarily to an invasive procedure and its attendant risks.[14,15]

The cost and risk of arteriography have fueled the growth of alternative imaging techniques such as DUS, a modality that has proved to be quite accurate in the detection of arterial occlusive disease, particularly in the carotid distribution.[14] Compared to carotid arteriography, DUS is inexpensive and completely noninvasive.[15] Recent work has focused on the usefulness of this imaging modality for evaluating cervical vascular trauma.

Fry and colleagues[16] conducted a prospective evaluation of 100 consecutive patients with cervical trauma (89% penetrating, 11% blunt) who had no indication for immediate surgical exploration. The first 15 patients underwent DUS followed by arteriography, and the remaining 85 had arteriography only when ultrasonography suggested an injury. In the first phase of the study, the one arterial injury identified by DUS was confirmed by arteriography. In the second phase, seven arterial injuries were identified by DUS, and all were confirmed by arteriography or operative exploration. Two internal jugular vein injuries were suggested by DUS but were not investigated by venography or operation. The remaining 76 patients without vascular injury shown by DUS remained asymptomatic at 1-week follow-up. The authors noted savings of $1200 per study for DUS over angiography.[16]

Demetriades and associates[17] prospectively evaluated, with both arteriography and DUS, 82 stable trauma patients with penetrating cervical trauma (zones I to III) who had no indication for immediate exploration. Eleven patients (13.4%) had arterial injuries that were identified by arteriography, but only two (2.4%) required operative intervention. DUS correctly identified 10 of 11 injuries, including both of those that required operative repair. Ginzburg and colleagues[18] obtained virtually identical results using a similar protocol. Thus, all three studies concluded that DUS might be a suitable substitute for arteriography as an initial screening test for penetrating cervical trauma that does not warrant immediate surgical exploration. In addition, these authors suggest that, if DUS were the sole diagnostic modality, substantial cost savings with no decrease in overall accuracy would be the result.

Although both arteriography and DUS appear to have excellent diagnostic accuracy, it is apparent that their therapeutic yield is quite low. That is, among patients with soft or absent signs of carotid trauma, the number of vascular injuries that require operative intervention is small. Thus, some propose managing this subgroup only by observation and serial physical examination.

The primary advocates of this approach have been Frykberg and colleagues[19] in Jacksonville, Florida. They prospectively studied 145 patients with penetrating neck injuries over an 8-year period. Patients with isolated zone II injuries or who had no evidence of proximity injuries were observed. Patients with hard signs of vascular trauma were immediately explored. Ninety-one patients were observed, and none had evidence of vascular injury during hospitalization or at the 2-week follow-up visit. Twenty-three patients underwent arteriography for proximity or because the trajectory was believed to have crossed more than one zone. Three arteriograms had abnormalities; however, only one injury required operative repair. The missed injury rate with physical examination alone was 0.9% (1/114).

In a prospective study of 53 consecutive patients with penetrating zone II injuries, 17 had definite signs of vascular trauma and underwent immediate exploration. Two other patients required operative repair of aerodigestive tract injury, but no vascular disruption was found.[20] Of the remaining 34 patients considered candidates for observation alone, 6 had arteriograms (all negative). The remainder, who were observed, exhibited no delayed signs of vascular injury at follow-up (mean 1.8 months).[20] A diagnostic approach based on physical examination alone requires extensive experience and the ability to perform careful serial clinical examinations. An obvious concern is the potentially devastating result of missing a significant injury.

It is apparent that good results can be obtained with mandatory exploration, routine arteriography or DUS, or physical examination alone in properly selected patients. Ultimately, the approach adopted should be based on experience, volume, local diagnostic capabilities, and personnel resources. Current opinion supports immediate exploration of all injuries associated with hard signs of vascular trauma (active bleeding, large or expanding hematoma, neurologic deficit, or bruit). Penetrating injuries with soft signs (history of bleeding; small, stable hematoma; or cranial nerve deficit) or a worrisome mechanism (e.g., shotgun blast [Fig. 70-1] or severe direct blunt injury) should be screened by DUS or arteriography, depending on local availability and expertise. Observation for certain penetrating cervical injuries in the context of normal physical findings is appropriate if the patient can be followed closely with serial examination.

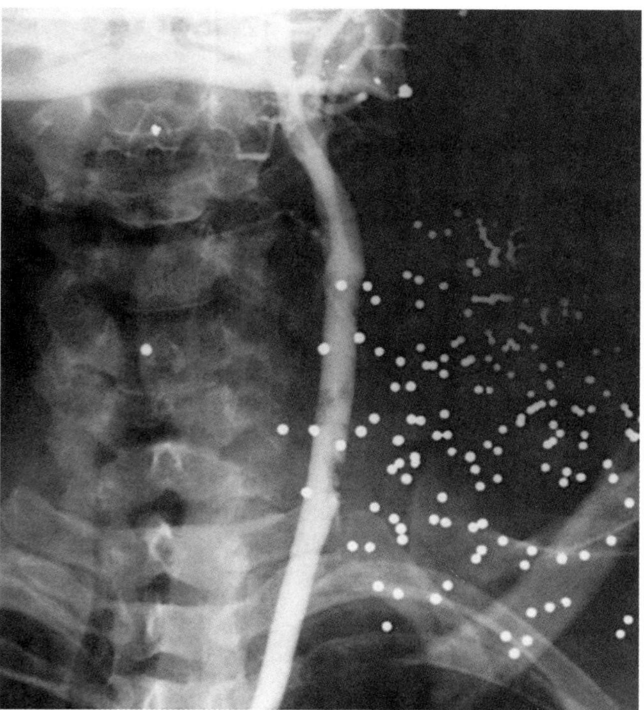

FIGURE 70-1 Shotgun blast injury of left common carotid artery with multiple nonbleeding punctures and mural thrombus.

Notwithstanding this discourse, evolving technologic improvements have greatly enhanced the diagnostic precision of various imaging modalities. Helical CTA has demonstrated excellent accuracy in the evaluation of vascular trauma, and gadolinium-enhanced MRA has shown promise in the elective evaluation of atherosclerotic carotid bifurcation disease as well as carotid artery dissection.[21,22] MRA has not yet been studied in the setting of penetrating vascular injuries. However, as this imaging modality evolves, it may become an important screening tool for vascular trauma.

LeBlang and Nunez[21] demonstrated 100% sensitivity with helical CTA in detecting penetrating injuries to the cervical vessels. Arterial lesions were detected based on direct and indirect findings. Direct findings included vessel wall irregularity, contrast extravasation, lack of vascular enhancement, and vessel caliber changes. Indirect findings included bone or bullet fragments within 5 mm of a major vessel. Carotid sheath hematomas and path of injury through a vessel were also considered to be indirect findings. They recommend a protocol consisting of 3-mm slice collimation with a 1.5:1 pitch, 19 cm field of view, and a scan delay of 20 to 30 seconds after a 100-mL bolus of non-ionic contrast medium injected at 2 to 3 mL/sec.

Helical CTA may be limited in its ability to detect vascular injuries in zone I. This is due to streak artifacts that can be generated from the shoulder and the nonperpendicular course of the subclavian vessels. However, injury tract in proximity to arteries low in zone I (below the cricoid cartilage) can be determined by helical CTA. This can therefore guide the need for further diagnostic imaging studies. When there are significant streak artifacts secondary to retained metallic fragments, other diagnostic studies may be necessary. These impressive results were confirmed in a subsequent study by Munera and colleagues.[23] In 173 examinations of potential vascular trauma the sensitivity was 100% and the specificity was 98.6%. On the other hand, Gonzalez and coworkers[24] showed that CTA contributed little to the detection of significant vascular injuries. In a study of 42 patients, CTA did not detect any vascular injuries that were missed by physical examination alone with the exception of jugular venous injuries, which usually do not require surgical therapy.

Operative Approach

An oblique incision parallel to the anterior border of the sternocleidomastoid muscle facilitates exposure of the cervical carotid artery. It also affords exploration of nonvascular structures in the neck. It is crucial to prepare and drape the entire chest against the possibility that median sternotomy would be necessary to achieve proximal control of the innominate or either common carotid artery. In fact, for zone I injuries it may be prudent to perform median sternotomy initially or as part of the neck incision. Exposure of high zone III injuries can be especially difficult. Maneuvers that have been employed to facilitate this exposure include division of the posterior belly of the digastric muscle, subluxation of the mandible, and mandibular ramus osteotomy.[25] Profuse bleeding near the skull base may be best controlled temporarily with a Fogarty balloon catheter inserted into the injured vessel.[5]

Surgical Management

For significant penetrating carotid artery injuries without concurrent central neurologic deficit, there is fairly universal agreement that all such lesions should be repaired. Available methods include primary repair, patch angioplasty, internal-to-external carotid artery transposition, and interposition grafting with saphenous vein or prosthetic conduit.

Debate persists, however, about treatment of neurologically asymptomatic patients with occlusion of the carotid artery. Concerns about distal embolization during carotid repair are unfounded, although Fry and Fry warned that distal propagation of thrombus might result in delayed neurologic deficit if no repair is made.[26] Recent reports suggest that repair should be performed when it is technically feasible and when retrograde arterial backflow can be established. This approach has resulted in little morbidity.[27-29] Restoration of retrograde ICA backflow by any means other than gentle manual extraction of thrombus (e.g., by passage of an embolectomy catheter) should be performed with great caution to avoid creating a carotid-cavernous sinus fistula. Passing the embolectomy catheter only to the level of the skull base should avoid this serious complication. When potential arterial repair is not technically feasible or ICA back-bleeding cannot easily be established, ligation or subsequent transcatheter balloon occlusion can be performed. The rate of associated subsequent neurologic deficit ranges from zero to 50%.[27,29] In this difficult situation, some authors have advocated the addition of anticoagulation to prevent thrombus propagation.[27]

Controversy surrounding management of carotid injuries associated with neurologic deficit (including coma) has resulted principally from anecdotal reports of conversion of ischemic infarction to hemorrhagic infarction after revascularization.[2] Despite this concern, all available recent evidence suggests that optimal neurologic outcomes are obtained with operative repair because most deficits remain unchanged or improve.[2,5,6,26-29] Even patients who are comatose appear to fare best with repair. In collected series, 28 comatose patients treated with carotid ligation had a 61% mortality rate and only 14% had a normal outcome, whereas 42 comatose patients who had operative repair had a mortality rate of 26% and 50% were neurologically normal or much improved after arterial reconstruction.[2] Although such results may reflect a certain treatment selection bias based on hemodynamic or other factors, it is crucial to recall that it is not always possible to discern preoperatively which patients have been rendered comatose by shock, alcohol, or drugs as opposed to cerebral ischemia.

Finally, questions about the management of minor carotid artery injury (small intimal defects or small pseudoaneurysms) have arisen. Nonoperative management, at least in neurologically intact patients, appears to be safe.[5,13,17,27] However, long-term follow-up, critical to this approach, is not available and is often difficult to achieve in this patient population.

Most authorities recommend repairing all significant penetrating carotid artery injuries when technically feasible and in almost every circumstance. Acute ligation or balloon occlusion is reserved for critically unstable patients or inaccessible lesions. Anticoagulation, alone or as an adjunct to ligation, should be considered for traumatic distal ICA occlusion in neurologically intact patients. Finally, it may be safe to observe small intimal lesions in neurologically normal patients, but serial carotid DUS examination and close clinical follow-up also seem mandatory.

Endovascular Management

Endovascular repair techniques are increasingly used for vascular trauma.[30-33] This form of treatment necessitates more frequent use of diagnostic arteriography. However, endovascular interventions can be carried out in the same setting if the arteriogram demonstrates a significant abnormality. This approach is especially attractive in zones I and III injuries that may be difficult to repair with a standard operative approach.

Three recent case reports demonstrate successful endovascular repair of zone III ICA injuries with a Wallgraft Endoprosthesis.[30-32] Duane and colleagues[30] also describe the use of a "homemade" covered endograft, constructed with a Palmaz stent and a polytetrafluoroethylene graft to repair a traumatic internal carotid to internal jugular arteriovenous fistula with pseudoaneurysm at the skull base. Embolization of an exsanguinating zone III internal jugular venous injury has also been reported with good result.[33]

Initial results of endovascular treatment for these compelling injuries are promising. However, long-term follow-up is not available and the long-term outcome is unknown. The case reports published are too few in numbers for these techniques to be widely adopted in the current management of cervicothoracic vascular trauma. On the other hand, rapidly evolving technologic advances and surgeon ingenuity will certainly continue, and these less invasive procedures may ultimately reduce the morbidity and mortality associated with significant vascular injuries.

Outcome

Determining outcome related to penetrating carotid artery injury, as distinct from penetrating cervical trauma, is somewhat difficult because few studies specifically address the former. Mortality rates of 5% to 20% have been reported.[2] In one retrospective review of identified penetrating carotid artery injuries, there was an overall mortality rate of 17% and a stroke rate of 28%.[29] Mortality rates in this population were significantly higher in the presence of coma or shock (50% and 41%, respectively). Primary determinants of morbidity and survival are severity and duration of shock and neurologic deficit on presentation. Unfortunately, these are factors over which the surgeon has little control.

■ BLUNT CAROTID ARTERY TRAUMA

Epidemiology

Blunt carotid artery disruption accounts for about 3% to 10% of all carotid injuries.[2,34-47] Four mechanisms of injury are recognized: (1) cervical hyperextension-rotation (most common); (2) direct blow to the neck; (3) intraoral trauma; and (4) basilar skull fracture. Injury can result in dissection (Fig. 70-2), thrombosis, pseudoaneurysm formation (Fig. 70-3), carotid-cavernous sinus fistula, or complete arterial

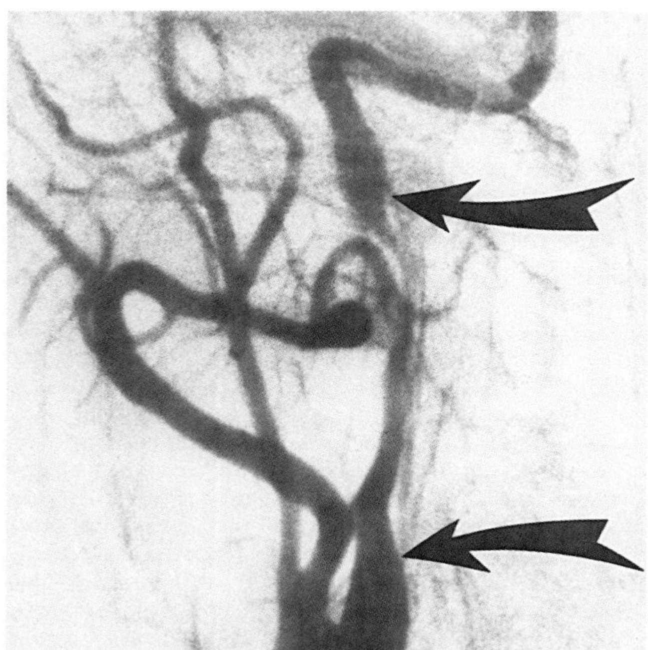

FIGURE 70-2 Left carotid artery dissection (between *arrows*) sustained during a motor vehicle accident.

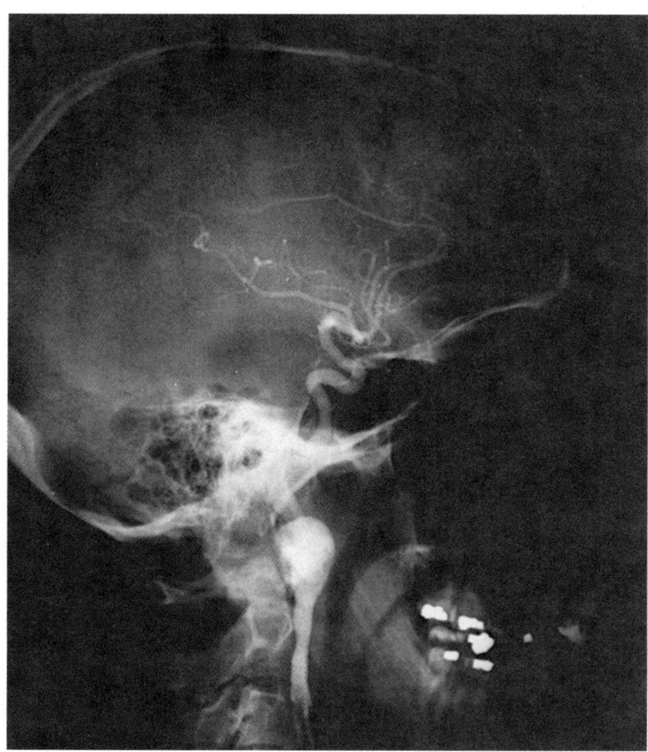

FIGURE 70-3 Large right distal internal carotid artery pseudoaneurysm associated with dissection after direct blunt neck trauma.

disruption.[2] More than 90% of blunt injuries involve the ICA, often distally, rather than the common carotid artery. Bilateral injury has been reported in 20% to 50% of cases.[34-47] Overall incidence of carotid artery injury in blunt trauma has been variously reported as 0.08% to 0.33%, and as many as half of affected patients show no signs of cervical trauma or neurologic deficit at presentation.[34-47] The low incidence, anatomic site, and variable presentation have made the determination of optimal diagnostic and management strategies difficult. No prospective studies exist.

Diagnostic Evaluation

Diagnosis of blunt cerebrovascular injuries has increased in incidence owing to heightened awareness and aggressive screening. Fabian and coworkers[40] noted 96 cases reported up to 1980, 75 cases during the next 10 years, and 309 cases in the subsequent 5 years (1990 to 1995). In a follow-up study performed at one level I trauma center from 1995 to 1999, Miller and colleagues[44] identified 139 blunt cerebrovascular injuries in 96 patients. This significant increase in the diagnosis of injuries probably is not a result of an increase in blunt carotid artery trauma. Even the largest series prior to Fabian's most recent report accumulated fewer than 70 patients over 11 years, and a 6-year multi-institution review involving 11 major trauma centers reported on only 60 blunt carotid artery injuries in 49 patients.[37,40,44]

The difficulty in diagnosis is related to the fact that many of these patients present with significant associated intracranial lesions or ethanol or drug intoxication. Others whose neurologic examination is completely normal exhibit delayed (hours to years) development of focal neurologic deficits. The only significant clinical presentation may be pain in the face, neck, ear, or periorbital area secondary to arterial dissection or mural hemorrhage. Horner's syndrome may also be present if the sympathetic plexus is disrupted with injury to the ICA. In Cogbill's multicenter study of blunt carotid artery trauma, 37% of patients presented with a Glasgow Coma Scale (GCS) score less than 8, whereas 49% had an essentially normal initial neurologic examination (GCS > 12) on admission.[37] More than half of those admitted with a GCS score above 12 developed significant deficits more than 12 hours later.[37] Another review of 20 patients found that 47% initially had normal neurologic examination findings, and nearly 60% of those who presented without focal deficits subsequently developed them during their admission.[41] Even Fabian and associates,[40] who demonstrated the highest incidence of carotid artery injury in blunt trauma (0.33%), found that 43% of their patients were not diagnosed until a neurologic deficit developed subsequent to the initial presentation. In addition, there was an average delay of 53 hours from injury to definitive diagnosis. Thus, it appears to be the rare patient who presents with specific signs of blunt carotid artery injury or whose problem is diagnosed before neurologic deficits are manifested. This is unfortunate because early diagnosis is associated with improved outcome.[38-47]

At this time, broad screening does not appear to be practical, particularly given the overall low incidence of significant blunt carotid artery injury, even in high-risk patients with cervicocranial trauma. Although Kerwin and colleagues[48] used four-vessel cerebral angiograms for screening for blunt carotid injuries, routine arteriography clearly is not cost-effective and presents a risk, albeit small. A number of studies demonstrate a role for noninvasive diagnostic studies for penetrating cervical trauma, but there is much less experience with DUS in the evaluation of blunt trauma. The most common site of blunt carotid injury, the distal ICA, is difficult to visualize with DUS.[40] A prospective trial would need to be performed to adequately evaluate the efficacy of DUS expressly for blunt trauma before it could be recommended as a routine screening tool. Similarly, magnetic resonance imaging or MRA and transcranial Doppler ultrasonography have not been studied for this application. MRA holds promise, particularly with evolving technologic improvements and the ability to diagnose cerebral infarctions at an early stage.[49]

Patients presenting with or developing neurologic deficits whose cerebral CT scans are normal or do not account for the deficit should undergo further definitive diagnostic evaluation. Additional significant clinical findings include severe cervical soft tissue injury (e.g., contusion, hematoma, bruit), neurologic deficit in a lucid patient, any cranial nerve deficit or Horner's syndrome, and a history of a specific "high-risk" mechanism of injury (e.g., direct cervical blow, significant whiplash).[34] Certain injury patterns (combined head, neck, and chest trauma) also appear to be more frequently associated with blunt carotid injury.[41] Clearly, maintenance of a high index of suspicion is paramount when one is evaluating blunt trauma patients.

Management

Appropriate management of blunt carotid trauma depends on the specific injury and its anatomic site.[2] There is almost universal agreement that carotid-cavernous sinus fistulae should be managed by balloon occlusion techniques, results of which are generally fair to good.[37-47] Conversely, all recently described cases of complete arterial disruption have been fatal.[37-47] Management of dissection, thrombosis, and pseudoaneurysm, alone or in combination, has been controversial and appears to be evolving.

Older data suggest better outcomes with surgical than with nonsurgical management of dissection and thrombosis.[38] It has become apparent, however, that many of these lesions extend to or beyond the skull base and thus are not amenable to straightforward vascular surgical repair. In addition, it is believed that most neurologic sequelae of these injuries may be related to acute thrombosis, thrombus propagation, or distal embolization. Therefore, surgical reconstruction may be irrelevant. Thus, there is growing support for nonsurgical management of dissections and thromboses. Initial systemic heparinization followed by 3 to 6 months of warfarin (Coumadin) therapy seems to be reasonable treatment.[37-47]

In two large clinical studies, Fabian[40] and Miller[44] and their associates demonstrated significant improvement in clinical outcomes when anticoagulation was instituted for patients who had either minor or major neurologic deficits at the time of diagnosis. In one study, none of the 15 patients who presented with unilateral symptoms but were found to have bilateral injuries developed symptoms referable to the contralateral injury after heparin therapy was instituted.[40] Li[38] and Parikh[41] and their groups have also suggested improvement of outcomes with anticoagulation alone. Complications related to anticoagulation range from 13% to 33%, and this mode of treatment may be relatively contraindicated for some trauma patients.[40,41] Prospective trials comparing surgery with anticoagulation probably are not feasible.

Fabian and coworkers[40] demonstrated that with nonoperative treatment 62% of carotid dissections reverted to normal and 29% progressed to pseudoaneurysms on follow-up angiography. Most thrombosed vessels remained so. Biffl and coworkers[46] performed follow-up arteriography 7 to 10 days after the diagnosis of blunt carotid injury in 76 patients with 109 injuries. Most (66%) of the mild injuries (grade I) healed regardless of treatment with anticoagulation. Seventy percent of carotid dissections or hematomas with luminal stenosis (grade II) progressed despite heparin therapy. A small number of pseudoaneurysms (grade III) healed with heparin therapy alone, but 89% resolved after stent deployment. Similar to the Fabian study, carotid occlusions (grade IV) did not recanalize in the early post-injury period, and grade V (transections) injuries were lethal and not amenable to treatment. Other investigators have also documented progression of post-traumatic ICA dissections to severe flow-limiting stenosis over time.[34] Clearly, these injuries should be followed serially with an objective test such as DUS, angiography, or MRA.

Management of pseudoaneurysms is somewhat less controversial; most authors recommend surgical repair when it is technically feasible.[2,37,38,41] Small or inaccessible pseudoaneurysms have been managed by anticoagulation and proximal ligation with and without extracranial-intracranial bypass. In addition, there are case reports that demonstrate the successful use of angioplasty and stenting for the treatment of carotid pseudoaneurysms that result from blunt trauma.[50,51] Experience with these techniques is limited, and many experts caution against the widespread use of this approach.[47,50,51] In fact, 3 of 14 patients in the experience of Biffl[47] and colleagues suffered complications related to stent deployment. Two had acute stent thrombosis and one had transient ischemic attacks. Finally, not only do most ICA pseudoaneurysms fail to resolve spontaneously but also, as noted earlier, there is evidence that pseudoaneurysms can develop in vessels that initially are found to have only dissection.[40] This observation underscores the need for long-term follow-up of all patients with blunt carotid artery trauma.

In contradistinction to penetrating carotid artery trauma, most authors advocate anticoagulation for most blunt carotid artery dissections or thromboses, operative repair being reserved principally for easily accessible lesions. It is important to follow these patients over the long term for subsequent development of complications, particularly pseudoaneurysms. Pseudoaneurysms should be treated initially with heparin but ultimately should be repaired when technically feasible. Small or inaccessible lesions should be treated with anticoagulation alone. Occasional patients require novel repairs such as extracranial-intracranial bypass or cervical-petrous ICA bypass.[34]

Outcome

In general, the prognosis of blunt carotid artery injury is poor. Recent reports have demonstrated mortality rates of 5% to 43%, with good neurologic outcomes in only 20% to 63% of survivors.[37-47] Most authors tend to advocate anticoagulation alone as the primary mode of treatment. Although there is some evidence that anticoagulation therapy improves results, outcome is probably related more closely to diagnostic delay. Emphasis should be placed on maintaining a high index of suspicion for blunt carotid artery injury and on aggressive evaluation of these patients because a missed or delayed diagnosis can have devastating consequences.

■ VERTEBRAL ARTERY TRAUMA

Epidemiology

Historically, penetrating or blunt traumatic injury of the vertebral arteries has been exceedingly rare. Several authors have suggested that increased use of diagnostic four-vessel angiography for craniocervical trauma has increased the frequency of diagnosis.[3,5,6] That stated, the two largest reported series in the literature comprise only 43 and 47 patients, respectively.[52,53] Management decisions are complicated both by the anatomic site of the vessel and the relatively few adverse sequelae of its injury.

The clinical presentation and ultimate outcome of vertebral artery trauma are related primarily to associated injuries rather than to the specific arterial lesion itself. Reid and Weigelt found that 32 (72%) of 43 patients with penetrating vertebral artery injuries had no evidence of arterial trauma on physical examination.[52] Furthermore, 38 (88%) of 43 patients had a normal GCS score on presentation, and none presented with or subsequently exhibited vertebrobasilar insufficiency. Similarly, Yee and associates[54] found that 12 (75%) of 16 patients presented with a normal GCS score. In that series, 75% of the 16 neurologic deficits were attributed to associated cervical spinal root or cord injuries or intracranial lesions. Again, no patient showed evidence of vertebrobasilar insufficiency during follow-up. In the series reported by Biffl and colleagues,[53] cervical spine injuries were present in 71% of patients found to have blunt vertebral artery injury; however, there was no consistent cervical vertebra level or fracture pattern. The death rate directly attributable to blunt vertebral artery trauma was 8%. In patients treated with systemic heparinization, there were fewer poor neurologic outcomes overall and, specifically, fewer patients had a poor outcome after stroke.[53]

Although there is substantial anatomic variability in the posterior circulation, Thomas and coworkers have shown that, with unilateral vertebral artery ligation, the incidence of brain stem ischemia is very low—3.1% for the left artery and 1.8% for the right.[55] Thus, there is general agreement that most injuries to the vertebral artery, including arteriovenous fistulae and pseudoaneurysms, should be managed by proximal and distal artery occlusion.[3,5,6,52,54,55] However, controversy surrounds how best to achieve this goal, whether by surgical ligation or by endovascular transcatheter embolization. Arterial repair is reserved for the exceedingly rare circumstance when preoperative arteriography suggests inadequate collateral circulation.[3,5,6,52,54]

Operative Approach

Surgical exposure of the vertebral artery has been well described.[3,54,56] The cervical vertebral artery can be approached anteriorly, as Landreneau's group proposed[57]; however, for proximal injuries the vessel is best approached via a supraclavicular incision centered over the lateral head of the sternocleidomastoid muscle. Extensive exposure can be obtained both proximally and distally by gently curving the medial aspect of this incision upward, along the anterior border of the sternocleidomastoid muscle, or downward, in preparation for median sternotomy. After transverse division of the platysma muscle and the lateral head of the sternocleidomastoid muscle, the omohyoid muscle is divided and the scalene fat pad elevated. The anterior scalene muscle can be divided under direct vision with scissors, care being taken to protect the phrenic nerve, which courses on top of this muscle. This exposure affords excellent access to the subclavian artery and the proximal vertebral artery.

Exposure of the distal vertebral artery is obtained at the level of C1-2 by transection of the sternocleidomastoid muscle at the mastoid to allow palpation of the transverse process of C1. Care must be taken to spare the spinal accessory nerve. The prevertebral fascia, levator scapulae muscle, and tendon of the splenius cervicis muscle are divided to expose the intertransverse space between C1 and C2 where the artery lies. Direct approaches to the interosseous portion of the vertebral artery are available, but they are risky because of the significant dangers of bleeding from surrounding veins and injury to adjacent nerve roots. Persistent bleeding from the vertebral artery in this area has been controlled with hemostatic agents, placement of packs, or balloon catheter occlusion of the distal vessel through a proximal arteriotomy.[3]

Surgical Management

Proponents of surgical ligation of the vertebral arteries cite the findings of Reid and Weigelt in their series of 43 patients with penetrating vertebral artery injury.[52] Although these authors found that arteriography had accuracy of 97% for diagnosing vertebral artery injuries, only 50% of patients' operative findings correlated with the angiographic diagnosis. In particular, a significant number of "angiographic occlusions" were found at operation to be arterial disruptions. In addition, 2 of 13 patients initially treated with proximal ligation alone required reoperation for distal ligation, whereas none of 28 patients treated initially with proximal and distal ligation required further intervention.

Conversely, the literature describes the use of transcatheter embolization for management of arteriovenous fistulae, pseudoaneurysms, and occlusions.[11,54,58,59] Coil embolization proximal and distal to the injury site has provided satisfactory control of arteriovenous fistulae and pseudoaneurysms (Figs. 70-4 and 70-5). As technology has advanced and experience has increased, successful

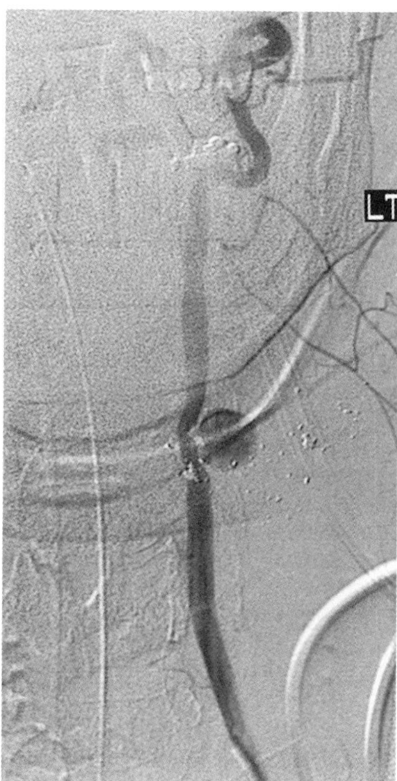

FIGURE 70-4 Gunshot injury of left vertebral artery with pseudoaneurysm. This injury was originally packed during operative exploration and a concomitant internal carotid artery injury was repaired primarily.

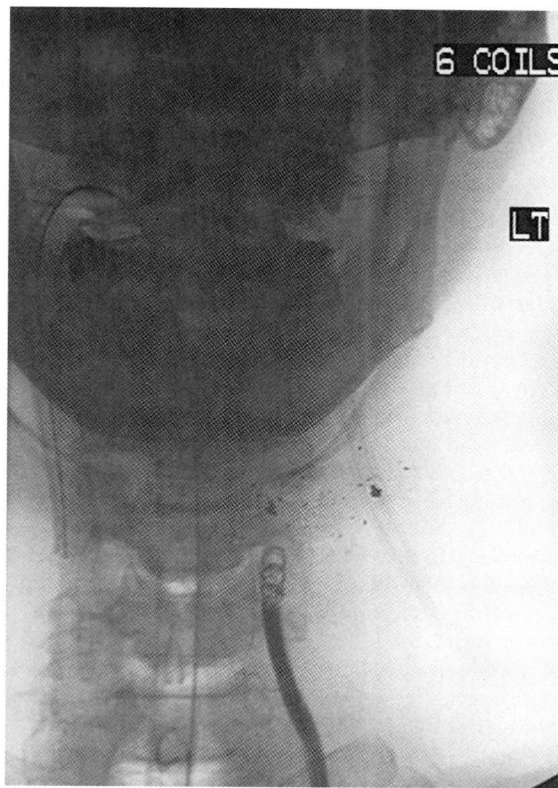

FIGURE 70-5 Successful coil embolization of left vertebral artery injury.

artery-sparing techniques have been developed for both arteriovenous fistulae and pseudoaneurysms. Beaujeux and coworkers[58] demonstrated occlusion of arteriovenous fistulae with vertebral artery preservation in 32 (91%) of 35 patients. Selected pseudoaneurysms have been managed in a similar fashion.[59]

Management of traumatic vertebral artery occlusion is less clear-cut, particularly in light of the older work of Thomas and colleagues[55] and the intraoperative findings of Reid and Weigelt.[52] Because such lesions frequently are actually arterial disruptions, concerns about rebleeding persist. Although it is possible to perform retrograde embolization via the contralateral vertebral artery, this procedure is technically demanding. Conversely, Demetriades[11] and Yee[54] and their respective coworkers have successfully observed vertebral artery occlusions without apparent adverse sequelae such as rebleeding or pseudoaneurysm formation, although follow-up is limited.

The current literature thus appears to support operative proximal and distal ligation for hemodynamically unstable patients who require immediate intervention for exsanguinating hemorrhage. "Stable" patients found to have a pseudoaneurysm or arteriovenous fistula should be treated with artery-sparing or occluding transcatheter embolization when available. Patients with vertebral artery occlusion can probably be observed, although proximal and distal transcatheter embolization is not unreasonable, based on the assumption that some arterial occlusions may in fact be complete disruptions.[60] In either case, follow-up with angiography is recommended.

In the case of blunt vertebral artery injury, there is insufficient evidence to support any particular treatment standard.[61] However, anticoagulation alone has been effective in patients with posterior cerebral ischemia secondary to blunt vertebral trauma.[61] For incidental injuries with no evidence of ischemia, simple observation may be safe.[61]

■ AORTIC ARCH AND GREAT VESSEL TRAUMA

Epidemiology

Arterial trauma to the aortic arch and great vessels is uncommon. Although occasional blunt injuries have been reported (excluding the relatively common proximal descending aortic transection or tear following deceleration trauma), the cause is usually a penetrating injury. The patient's deteriorating or unstable hemodynamic status may complicate management, and operative exposure can be difficult. In addition, rates of significant associated injuries to the aerodigestive systems, the lungs and pleura, and the brachial plexus are as high as 80%. Active trauma centers report seemingly low in-hospital mortality rates between 5% and 30%; however, "prehospital" mortality has been estimated to be as high as 48%.[62]

Evaluation

Initial evaluation and management should be based on the advanced-trauma life support protocol. For patients who present in cardiac arrest, one should consider signs of life and vital signs at the scene and in transit when deciding whether to perform resuscitative emergency department (ED) thoracotomy.[63] Johnston and Mattox[64] demonstrated 100% mortality in patients with innominate artery injury who required prehospital cardiopulmonary resuscitation. Similarly, Wilson and Tyburski[63] found that 32 (97%) of 33 patients who underwent ED thoracotomy died (although they did not specify which of these patients were asystolic on arrival and arrested in the ED).

Patients who present in severe shock (systolic blood pressure < 50 mm Hg) should be transported directly to the operating room for control of hemorrhage. Those in mild to moderate shock (systolic blood pressure between 50 and 90 mm Hg) should be rapidly resuscitated concurrent with adjunctive studies such as chest and cervical spine radiography. When shock is persistent or recurrent, resuscitation efforts should continue in the operating room, whereas further diagnostic studies may be pursued if the patient's condition stabilizes appropriately with resuscitation.

Arteriography is currently the "gold standard" for identification of aortic arch and great vessel trauma. This study should be applied to all stable patients suspected of having possible aortic arch or great vessel injuries. In particular, a normal peripheral pulse is not reliable for ruling out significant injury. Calhoon and colleagues[65] found that 14 (64%) of 22 patients with great vessel injuries had normal distal pulses. At aortography, unsuspected lesions may be identified, and specific localization of the vessel injury facilitates the appropriate operative approach for achieving proximal arterial control.

Operative Exposure

Interested readers are referred to a recent review of operative exposures of the aortic arch, innominate artery, and proximal subclavian and common carotid arteries.[25] Several important points should be emphasized, as follows:

1. Although the standard right or left posterolateral thoracotomy provides excellent exposure of the hemithorax, exposure of the great vessels is limited, and the lateral decubitus position limits access to the abdomen should laparotomy be required.
2. In the setting of resuscitative left anterolateral thoracotomy, extension across the sternum to include right anterolateral thoracotomy (the so-called clamshell incision) can provide excellent temporary exposure of arterial structures in the anterior and superior mediastinum for the purpose of achieving initial, and possibly definitive, control.
3. Attempting repair of zone I injuries to the subclavian or common carotid arteries through a cervical incision alone is generally discouraged because proximal arterial control may be difficult, if not impossible.
4. Median sternotomy is the most commonly employed and the best incision to provide exposure of the aortic arch and innominate artery and the origin of the *right* subclavian artery and both common carotid arteries. Exposure of the superior vena cava and brachiocephalic veins is also facilitated by this incision. This approach will *not* suffice for exposure of the proximal *left* subclavian artery.
5. Extension of the initial median sternotomy above and parallel to the clavicle or along the anterior border of the sternocleidomastoid muscle affords excellent exposure of the more distal *right* subclavian and common carotid arteries. Care should be taken to avoid the phrenic, vagus, and recurrent laryngeal nerves.
6. The origin of the *left* subclavian artery arises from the aortic arch posteriorly and, as noted, cannot be adequately exposed through a median sternotomy incision. Prompt proximal control may be obtained via an anterior left thoracotomy in the third or fourth intercostal space. Subsequent limited sternotomy with left supraclavicular extension (the "trap-door" incision) has been used, with varying success, to provide extended exposure of the left subclavian artery as it courses through the thoracic outlet.

Surgical Management

In general, all identified arterial injuries should be repaired surgically. In the rare case of exsanguinating hemorrhage from a subclavian artery injury, this vessel has been ligated without resulting in significant acute ischemia of the ipsilateral extremity.[66,67] Depending on the vessel involved and the nature of the injury, methods of repair include primary suture, resection with end-to-end anastomosis, interposition grafting, and bypass. Ideally, proximal and distal arterial control should be obtained before an overlying hematoma is entered.[63] After exposure and hemorrhage control, repair of subclavian or common carotid artery injuries is relatively straightforward, with primary suture, resection with end-to-end anastomosis, or interposition grafting, as appropriate.[64-70] Isolated common carotid artery injuries do not require shunting, because the carotid bifurcation remains patent and ipsilateral ICA flow is maintained by collateral flow through the external carotid artery. The use of prosthetic material appears safe.[64-70]

Evolution of management in this area of cervicothoracic vascular trauma has focused principally on aortic arch and innominate artery injuries. Minor aortic lacerations may be repaired with pledgeted sutures using digital control or a side-biting clamp. Intraluminal aortic pressure may be lowered temporarily—for a maximum of 1 to 2 minutes—by inflow occlusion of the vena cava.[63] More extensive injuries requiring aortic cross-clamping demand adjunctive procedures to minimize cardiac stress and distal ischemia, particularly cerebral ischemia. Although full cardiopulmonary bypass can be used, it may not be available and requires full heparinization. More practical is a temporary external Y shunt from the proximal ascending aorta to each common carotid artery.[67] This technique has been modified elegantly to allow safe repair of innominate artery injuries.[64,67] Briefly, a tube or bifurcated graft (as needed) is anastomosed end-to-side to the proximal ascending aorta under side-biting clamp control before the overlying innominate hematoma is entered. Then, with the proximal innominate artery clamped, end-to-end anastomosis to the distal innominate or both subclavian and common carotid arteries is performed. Subsequently, the innominate stump is oversewn. Johnston and Mattox attributed their significant decrease in mortality from innominate artery injury (from 50% in the 1960s to 11.8% in the 1980s) to the development of this technique.[64]

Outcome

Recently reported mortality rates for injuries to the great vessels have been 7% to 26%.[64-70] Mortality rates have been higher for patients who presented in shock, with central nervous system deficits, with gunshot (vs. stab) wounds, or with penetrating (vs. blunt) arterial injuries. Except for central nervous system deficits, morbidity is more often related to associated injuries (brachial plexus or aerodigestive systems) than to the specific arterial lesion.[64]

■ MAJOR VENOUS TRAUMA

Surgical Management

Major cervicothoracic venous injury can significantly complicate management and definitive vascular repair in trauma patients. Operative exposure for venous injuries should follow that of the adjacent artery or arterial lesion. Troublesome venous bleeding can be managed temporarily with digital or sponge-stick pressure until more definitive vascular control has been obtained. In general, severe injuries to brachiocephalic, internal jugular, or subclavian veins can be treated by ligation with relative impunity. This treatment option is recommended for unstable patients or for those who have significant associated injuries. If reclosure of the débrided venous injury would not compromise the lumen by more than 50%, such injuries can be repaired by lateral venorrhaphy.[71] When, however, an entire segment of vein is damaged, ligation (or, rarely, interposition grafting) is necessary. End-to-end anastomosis generally is not feasible once the damaged vessel has been thoroughly débrided. Patch venoplasty or panel or spiral grafting is a time-consuming technique whose use in this setting is imprudent.[71] Repair of the superior vena cava or of one brachiocephalic or internal jugular vein in the presence of bilateral venous injury should be considered to prevent superior vena cava syndrome or acute cerebral edema.[3]

Outcome

Ligation for major cervicothoracic venous trauma is generally well tolerated, although occasional reports have documented long-term disability.[71] Because data suggest more severe venous insufficiency following ligation of large cervicothoracic veins, by inference re-establishment of prograde venous flow in the trauma setting might be reasonable when it does not increase patient risk.[71] Repair of major venous injuries in this area may be appropriate, particularly when there is obvious venous hypertension or when the adjacent major artery has also required concomitant repair.

■ REFERENCES

1. Perry MO: Vascular injuries in the head and neck. In Veith FJ, Hobson RW, Williams RA, Wilson SE (eds): Vascular Surgery: Principles and Practice. New York, McGraw-Hill, 1994, pp 964-967.
2. Byrne MP, Welling RE: Penetrating and blunt extracranial carotid artery injuries. In Ernst CB, Stanley JC (eds): Current Therapy in Vascular Surgery. St. Louis, Mosby-Year Book, 1995, pp 598-603.
3. Webb TH, Gewertz BL: Penetrating and blunt vertebral artery trauma. In Ernst CB, Stanley JC (eds): Current Therapy in Vascular Surgery. St. Louis, Mosby-Year Book, 1995, pp 604-608.
4. Wilson RF, Tyburski JG: Penetrating trauma to the aortic arch, innominate, and subclavian arteries. In Ernst CB, Stanley JC (eds): Current Therapy in Vascular Surgery. St. Louis, Mosby-Year Book, 1995, pp 608-613.
5. Demetriades D, Asensio JA, Velmahos G, Thal E: Complex problems in penetrating neck trauma. Surg Clin North Am 76:661-683, 1996.
6. McConnell DB, Trunkey DD: Management of penetrating trauma to the neck. Adv Surg 27:97-127, 1994.
7. Monson DO, Saletta JD, Freeark RJ: Carotid and vertebral artery trauma. J Trauma 9:987-999, 1969.
8. Eddy VA and the Zone I Penetrating Neck Injury Study Group: Is routine arteriography mandatory for penetrating injuries to zone 1 of the neck? J Trauma 48:208-214, 1999.
9. Apffelstaedt JP, Muller R: Results of mandatory exploration for penetrating neck trauma. World J Surg 18:917-920, 1994.
10. Asensio JA, Valenziano CP, Falcone RE, Grosh JD: Management of penetrating neck injuries: The controversy surrounding zone II injuries. Surg Clin North Am 71:267-296, 1991.
11. Demetriades D, Charalambides D, Lakhoo M: Physical examination and selective conservative management in patients with penetrating injuries of the neck. Br J Surg 80:1534-1536, 1993.
12. North CM, Ahmadi J, Segall HD, et al: Penetrating vascular injuries of the face and neck: Clinical and angiographic correlation. AJR Am J Roentgenol 147:995-999, 1986.
13. Menawat SS, Dennis JW, Laneve LM, et al: Are arteriograms necessary in penetrating zone II neck injuries? J Vasc Surg 16:397-401, 1992.
14. Ballard JL, Fleig K, De Lange M, Killeen JD: The diagnostic accuracy of duplex ultrasound for evaluating the carotid bifurcation. Am J Surg 168:123-126, 1994.
15. Ballard JL, Deiparine MK, Bergan JJ, et al: Cost-effective evaluation of treatment for carotid disease. Arch Surg 132:268-271, 1997.
16. Fry WR, Dort JA, Smith S, et al: Duplex scanning replaces arteriography and operative exploration in the diagnosis of potential cervical vascular injury. Am J Surg 168:693-696, 1994.
17. Demetriades D, Theodorou D, Cornwell E, et al: Penetrating injuries of the neck in patients in stable condition: Physical examination, angiography, or color-flow Doppler imaging. Arch Surg 130:971-975, 1995.
18. Ginzburg E, Montalvo B, LeBlang S, et al: The use of duplex ultrasonography in penetrating neck trauma. Arch Surg 131:691-693, 1996.
19. Sekharan J, Dennis JW, Veldenz HC, et al: Continued experience with physical examination alone for evaluation and management of penetrating zone 2 neck injuries: Results of 145 cases. J Vasc Surg 32:483-489, 2000.
20. Atteberry LR, Dennis JW, Menawat SS, Frykberg ER: Physical examination alone is safe and accurate for evaluation of vascular injuries in penetrating zone II neck trauma. J Am Coll Surg 179:657-662, 1994.
21. LeBlang SD, Nunez DB Jr: Noninvasive imaging of cervical vascular injuries. AJR Am J Roentgenol 174:1269-1278, 2000.
22. Okumura A, Araki Y, Nishimura Y, et al: The clinical utility of contrast-enhanced 3D MR angiography for cerebrovascular disease. Neurol Res 23:767-771, 2001.
23. Munera F, Soto JA, Palacio DM, et al: Penetrating neck injuries: Helical CT angiography for initial evaluation. Radiology 224:366-372, 2002.

24. Gonzalez RP, Falimirski M, Holevar MR, Turk B: Penetrating zone II neck injury: Does dynamic computed tomographic scan contribute to the diagnostic sensitivity of physical examination for surgically significant injury? A prospective blinded study. J Trauma 54:61-65, 2003.
25. Ballard JL: Anatomy and surgical exposure of the vascular system. In Moore WS (ed): Vascular Surgery: A Comprehensive Review, 6th ed. Philadelphia, WB Saunders, 2002, pp 45-70.
26. Fry WJ, Fry RE: Management of carotid artery injury. In Bergan JJ, Yao JS (eds): Vascular Surgical Emergencies. Orlando, Grune & Stratton, 1987, p 587.
27. Kuehne JP, Weaver FA, Papanicolaou G, Yellin AE: Penetrating trauma of the internal carotid artery. Arch Surg 131:942-948, 1996.
28. Rao PM, Ivatury RR, Sharma P, et al: Cervical vascular injuries: A trauma center experience. Surgery 114:527-531, 1993.
29. Ramadan F, Rutledge R, Oller D, et al: Carotid artery trauma: A review of contemporary trauma center experiences. J Vasc Surg 21:46-56, 1995.
30. Duane TM, Parker F, Stokes GK, et al: Endovascular carotid stenting after trauma. J Trauma 52:149-153, 2002.
31. McNeil JD, Chiou AC, Gunlock MG, et al: Successful endovascular therapy of a penetrating zone III internal carotid injury. J Vasc Surg 36:187-190, 2002.
32. Ellis PK, Kennedy PT, Barros D'Sa AB: Successful exclusion of a high internal carotid pseudoaneurysm using the Wallgraft endoprosthesis. Cardiovasc Intervent Radiol 25:68-69, 2002.
33. Sanabria A, Jimenez CM: Endovascular management of an exsanguinating wound of the right internal jugular vein in zone III of the neck: Case report. J Trauma 55:158-161, 2003.
34. Ballard JL, Bunt TJ, Fitzpatrick B, Malone JM: Bilateral traumatic internal carotid artery dissections: Case report. J Vasc Surg 15:431-435, 1992.
35. Hellner D, Thie A, Lachenmayer L, et al: Blunt trauma lesions of the extracranial internal carotid artery in patients with head injury. J Craniomaxillofac Surg 21:234-238, 1993.
36. Pretre R, Reverdin A, Kalonji T, Faidutti B: Blunt carotid artery injury: Difficult therapeutic approaches for an under-recognized entity. Surgery 115:375-381, 1994.
37. Cogbill TH, Moore EE, Meissner M, et al: The spectrum of blunt injury to the carotid artery: A multicenter perspective. J Trauma 37:473-479, 1994.
38. Li MS, Smith BM, Espinosa J, et al: Nonpenetrating trauma to the carotid artery: Seven cases and a literature review. J Trauma 36:265-272, 1994.
39. Sanzone AG, Torres H, Soundoulakis SH: Blunt trauma to the carotid arteries. Am J Emerg Med 13:327-330, 1995.
40. Fabian TC, Patton JH, Croce MA, et al: Blunt carotid injury: Importance of early diagnosis and anticoagulant therapy. Ann Surg 223:513-525, 1996.
41. Parikh AA, Luchett FA, Valente JF, et al: Blunt carotid artery injuries. J Am Coll Surg 185:80-86, 1997.
42. McKevitt EC, Kirkpatrick AW, Vertesi L, et al: Blunt vascular neck injuries: Diagnosis and outcomes of extracranial vessel injury. J Trauma 52:472-476, 2002.
43. Kraus RR, Bergstein JM, DeBord JR: Diagnosis, treatment, and outcome of blunt carotid arterial injuries. Am J Surg 178:190-193, 1999.
44. Miller PR, Fabian TC, Bee TK, et al: Blunt cerebrovascular injuries: Diagnosis and treatment. J Trauma 51:279-286, 2001.
45. Biffl WL, Moore EE, Offner PJ, et al: Blunt carotid arterial injuries: Implications of a new grading scale. J Trauma 47:845-853, 1999.
46. Biffl WL, Ray CE Jr, Moore EE, et al: Treatment-related outcomes from blunt cerebrovascular injuries: Importance of routine follow-up arteriography. Ann Surg 235:699-707, 2002.
47. Biffl WL, Moore EE, Offner PJ, Burch JM: Blunt carotid and vertebral arterial injuries. World J Surg 25:1036-1043, 2001.
48. Kerwin AJ, Bynoe RP, Murray J, et al: Liberalized screening for blunt and vertebral artery injuries is justified. J Trauma 51:308-314, 2001.
49. Miller PR, Fabian TC, Croce MA, et al: Prospective screening for blunt cerebrovascular injuries: Analysis of diagnostic modalities and outcomes. Ann Surg 236:386-395, 2002.
50. Coldwell DM, Novak Z, Ryu RK, et al: Treatment of posttraumatic internal carotid arterial pseudoaneurysms with endovascular stents. J Trauma 48:470-473, 2000.
51. Kerby JD, May AK, Gomez CR, Rue LW: Treatment of bilateral blunt carotid injury using percutaneous angioplasty and stenting: Case report and review of the literature. J Trauma 49:784-787, 2000.
52. Reid JD, Weigelt JA: Forty-three cases of vertebral artery trauma. J Trauma 28:1007-1012, 1988.
53. Biffl WL, Moore EE, Elliott JP, et al: The devastating potential of blunt vertebral arterial trauma. Ann Surg 231:672-681, 2000.
54. Yee LF, Olcott CW, Knudson MM, Lim RC: Extraluminal, transluminal, and observational treatment for vertebral artery injuries. J Trauma 39:480-486, 1995.
55. Thomas GI, Andersen KN, Hain RF: The significance of anomalous vertebral-basilar artery communications in operations on the heart and great vessels. Surgery 46:747-757, 1959.
56. Berguer R: Distal vertebral artery bypass: Technique, the "occipital connection," and potential uses. J Vasc Surg 2:621-626, 1985.
57. Landreneau RJ, Weigelt JA, Meier DE, et al: The anterior operative approach to the cervical vertebral artery. J Am Coll Surg 180:475-480, 1995.
58. Beaujeux RL, Reizine DC, Casasco A, et al: Endovascular treatment of vertebral arteriovenous fistula. Radiology 183:361-367, 1992.
59. Halbach VV, Higashida RT, Dowd CF, et al: Endovascular treatment of vertebral artery dissections and pseudoaneurysms. J Neurosurg 79:183-191, 1993.
60. Roberts LH, Demetriades D: Vertebral artery injuries. Surg Clin North Am 81:1345-1356, 2001.
61. Anonymous: Management of vertebral artery injuries after nonpenetrating cervical trauma. Neurosurgery 50(3 Suppl):S173-S178, 2002.
62. Bladergroen M, Brockman R, Luna G, et al: A twelve-year survey of cervicothoracic vascular injuries. Am J Surg 157:483-486, 1989.
63. Wilson RF, Tyburski JG: Penetrating trauma to the aortic arch, innominate, and subclavian arteries. In Ernst CB, Stanley JC (eds): Current Therapy in Vascular Surgery. St. Louis, Mosby-Year Book, 1995, pp 608-613.
64. Johnston RH, Wall MJ, Mattox KL: Innominate artery trauma: A thirty-year experience. J Vasc Surg 17:134-140, 1993.
65. Calhoon JH, Grover FL, Trinkle JT: Chest trauma: Approach and management. Clin Chest Med 13:55-67, 1992.
66. Abouljoud MS, Obeid FN, Horst HM, et al: Arterial injuries of the thoracic outlet: A ten-year experience. Am Surg 59:590-595, 1993.
67. Pate JW, Cole H, Walker WA, et al: Penetrating injuries of the aortic arch and its branches. Ann Thorac Surg 55:586-592, 1993.
68. Hoff SJ, Reilly MK, Merrill WH, et al: Analysis of blunt and penetrating injury of the innominate and subclavian arteries. Am Surg 60:151-154, 1994.
69. Degiannis E, Velmahos G, Krawczykowski D, et al: Penetrating injuries of the subclavian vessels. Br J Surg 81:524-526, 1994.
70. McCoy DW, Weiman DS, Pate JW, et al: Subclavian artery injuries. Am Surg 63:761-764, 1997.
71. Bongard F: Thoracic and abdominal vascular trauma. In Rutherford RB (ed): Vascular Surgery, 5th ed. Philadelphia, WB Saunders, 2000, pp 871-892.

Chapter 71

Thoracic Vascular Trauma

MATTHEW J. WALL, JR., MD
JOSEPH HUH, MD
KENNETH L. MATTOX, MD

Section XII

The majority of penetrating trauma to the thorax can be managed by tube thoracostomy.[1] However, injuries near the thoracic outlet or midline may involve major vascular structures. Vascular injuries have been primarily a civilian phenomenon.[2] DeBakey and Simeone's description of World War II injuries described no survivors of thoracic vascular injuries.[3] Although many patients with thoracic vascular injuries die on the scene, improvements in emergency medical services have resulted in many patients surviving to their arrival at the emergency center. Some patients present in extremis with either active bleeding externally or into the pleural cavity. However, many patients do arrive in stable condition as a result of a contained hematoma allowing time for evaluation and management. A high index of suspicion is required to successfully manage these stable injuries.

Most of the thoracic vascular experience was developed from the inner city trauma centers. Mattox and associates' review[2] of 5760 civilian vascular injuries over 30 years revealed 168 subclavian artery injuries, 190 carotid artery injuries, 39 innominate artery injuries, and 144 thoracic aortic injuries. More than 90% of these injuries were due to penetrating trauma.[2]

■ PREHOSPITAL ISSUES

More than 80% of patients with blunt injury to the thoracic aorta die at the scene. In this group of patients preventive strategies such as eliminating risky driving habits, wearing seat belts, and perhaps the use of air bags may be the only way to reduce death. Emergency medical services (EMS) have developed in two discrete directions that depend on the nature of the emergency. In responding to a medical cardiac arrest, EMS personnel have been trained in intravenous fluid therapy, endotracheal intubation, cardiac pharmacology, electrocardiogram recognition, and cardiac defibrillation. EMS personnel have been trained to "stabilize" the medical patient on the scene prior to transport. This is beneficial for the patient with ventricular fibrillation given that electrical countershock, which is definitive care, can readily be delivered in the field.[4]

However, definitive care for the trauma patient is control of hemorrhage, and that is effectively available only in the operating room. Initial efforts to stabilize the bleeding patient from a thoracic vascular injury on the scene are, as expected, universally unsuccessful. In fact, measures to deliberately raise the blood pressure such as with intravenous fluid therapy, placement of pneumatic antishock trousers, or use of pressor agents only cause additional bleeding.[5,6] Recently it has been recognized that controlling the airway, immobilizing the cervical spine, and immediately transporting to an appropriate facility result in the best outcomes. In fact, in many-tiered urban EMS systems, the basic emergency medical technicians have become the "trauma specialists," freeing up the advanced life support paramedics to address medical cardiac arrests.

EMS personnel can be extremely helpful in managing thoracic vascular trauma in that they can provide important historical information about the circumstances of the injury. Transaxial penetrating injuries or injuries to the thoracic outlet are at significant risk for thoracic vascular injury and require rapid transport to a trauma center. A description of a blunt injury that implies significant amounts of energy were transferred to the patient increases the surgeon's index of suspicion for a thoracic vascular injury. Clues such as vehicle deformation, another death in the same vehicle, long extrication time, or fall from a significant height may direct the surgeon to consider a blunt thoracic vascular injury (Table 71-1).[7] Although telemedicine in an ambulance is probably not necessary, some have considered using an instant photograph of the damaged vehicle to aid the emergency center personnel in their evaluation.

■ EMERGENCY DEPARTMENT ISSUES

Patients are evaluated in the emergency department typically via the American College of Surgeons advanced trauma life support (ATLS) protocols.[8] An airway is established and the chest is examined for immediately life-threatening conditions such as tension pneumothorax, massive hemothorax, or hemopericardium. Pericardial tamponade is considered. These life-threatening issues are addressed as discovered. The patient's circulation and organ perfusion are assessed. A focused neurologic examination is obtained,

Table 71-1 Historical Findings of Thoracic Vascular Injury
Steering wheel impact on chest wall
Automobile deformation
Fall from significant height
Ski lift accident
Aircraft accident
Death of another passenger in the same vehicle
Ejection injury from vehicle

Table 71-2 Physical Findings of Thoracic Vascular Injury

Intrascapular murmur
Extremity pulse or pressure deficit
Thoracic spine fracture
Fracture of sternum, clavicle, or scapula
Hematoma of the thoracic outlet

and the patient is completely exposed. Some thoracic vascular injuries present as massive exsanguination and are addressed during the primary survey with an empirical exploration of the chest in the emergency department in an attempt to control the vascular injury. Alternatively, thoracic vascular injuries can be diagnosed during the secondary survey, noting findings such as decreased or absent extremity/cervical pulses or hematomas of the thoracic outlet (Table 71-2).

■ IMAGING

Imaging for thoracic vascular trauma can be divided into screening and diagnostic imaging. A common mode of screening for thoracic vascular injury involves careful history and physical examination followed by a plain chest radiograph. Chest film evidence of blunt thoracic vascular injury includes hemothorax, loss of definition of the aortic knob, mediastinal or thoracic outlet hematomas, as well as effects of the hematoma such as deviation of the left main stem bronchus or nasogastric tube by a mediastinal hematoma. Foreign bodies such as shrapnel in proximity to major vascular structures or an out-of-focus foreign body may suggest a missile embedded in a vascular structure. A confusing trajectory of a missile or a missile that is not seen on the chest radiograph of a patient with a gunshot wound to the chest may suggest distal vascular embolization.[9]

For patients with blunt injuries to the thoracic aorta, widened mediastinum on plain chest film is one of the more sensitive findings. Unfortunately, it is not very specific. Loss of the aortic knob or double shadowing of the aortic knob in our personal experience is one of the more specific findings. Additional radiographic clues that suggest blunt aortic injury are listed in Table 71-3.[10] Other screening modalities have included computed tomography (CT) scan, helical or multidetector CT scan, intravascular ultrasound, or transesophageal echocardiography.

Chest CT Scans

In the past CT scanning was used by some to screen for patients with blunt aortic injuries.[11,12] Unfortunately, patients with abnormal chest radiographs often had abnormal chest CT scans due to a mediastinal hematoma. These scanners did not have the resolution to precisely locate the injury, took a significant amount of time to obtain results, and delayed definitive diagnosis by arteriography. However, recent advances in CT such as the helical scanners and multidetector scanners have resulted in greater resolution and decreased scan time.[13-17] Additionally, these patients often are in the CT scanner to image the head or abdomen for other injuries. Thus, the additional few minutes needed to obtain an image of the chest is used by many to

Table 71-3 Radiographic Clues to Potential Blunt Aortic Injury

Loss or double shadow of the aortic knob
Widening of the mediastinum > 8 cm
Loss of the paravertebral stripe
Depression of the left main stem bronchus > 140 degrees
Calcium layering of the aortic knob
Deviation of the nasogastric tube
Lateral displacement of the trachea
Fracture of the sternum, scapula, multiple left ribs, and clavicle
Loss of aortopulmonary window
Apical hematoma
Massive left hemothorax
Blunt injury to the diaphragm

rule out mediastinal hematoma. Although these new scans have superior resolution, there are new artifacts on these detailed scans that often must be explained. These artifacts often confuse the evaluation and result in additional work-up. Thus, it is important that the individuals reading the CT scan have significant experience in thoracic trauma imaging. Probably one of the least controversial use of screening CT for blunt aortic injury is in the patient with a normal chest radiograph that has a significant mechanism of injury.[10] By documenting the absence of a mediastinal hematoma or aortic intimal flap, the CT allows diagnostic energies to be focused elsewhere.

Some medical centers have used the high-resolution CT scan as both a screening and diagnostic tool. This requires significant expertise in interpretation. Most surgeons who repair these injuries use arteriography to plan the operation, since arch anomalies exist that may be difficult to diagnose on CT. This is important during proximal control maneuvers when the brachiocephalic vessels are located by palpation through the large mediastinal hematoma. In addition, multiple injuries do occur.[10] Three-dimensional reconstructions may be able to create images similar to arteriography, but again experience is required to know the limitations of this modality. Currently, most surgeons use arteriography to plan the operative intervention.[18]

Transesophageal Echocardiography

Transesophageal echocardiography has been used to diagnose injuries to the descending thoracic aorta.[19,20] Unfortunately, the tracheal air column is interposed between the proximal aortic arch and the esophagus, making visualization of the innominate artery origin difficult. This is the second most common area of blunt aortic injury.[21,22] In addition, echocardiography can be overly sensitive in the diagnosis of these injuries. Echocardiography is extremely operator dependent, and many echocardiographers do not have significant experience in evaluating aortic trauma. Thus, it is important to recognize the local expertise available if transesophageal echocardiography is to be used as a primary diagnostic tool .

■ ARTERIOGRAPHY

Arteriography for evaluation of blunt injury to the aorta remains the "gold standard."[18] Arteriography allows precise localization of the injury and provides information regarding vascular anomalies and other factors that may influence the operative strategy. It is important that a specific arteriographic protocol be consistently used when investigating suspected blunt thoracic aortic injuries so that results are reproducible and a high accuracy is achieved. Correct arteriographic diagnosis of these injuries often requires multiple views. Several anatomic variants of the thoracic aorta may mimic an aortic injury. For example, a ductus bump or infundibulum of a segmental artery may mimic an aortic injury. These can often can be differentiated from an aortic injury by the smoothness of contour and the fact that the infundibulum may have a segmental artery originating from it. Alternatively, an aortic injury may look similar to an ulcerative atherosclerotic plaque.[23,24] Newer diagnostic techniques will need to have equivalent accuracy and availability prior to being universally adopted.[10]

Arteriography for penetrating injuries to the thoracic aorta is also often necessary. However, owing to the large dye column, it is important to obtain tangential and multiple views at the area of anticipated injury so as to identify small pseudoaneurysms that might otherwise be missed. Arteriography to diagnose brachiocephalic vessel injury can also be extremely valuable. Since different incisions and approaches are needed for control and repair of specific vascular injuries, an arteriogram can greatly assist with patient positioning and surgical approach. Thus, in a patient with penetrating injury to the thoracic outlet, who is otherwise hemodynamically stable, arteriography is advisable.

CT arteriography can provide high-quality images similar to arteriography. The accuracy and usefulness of CT arteriography for thoracic trauma are currently under investigation. Magnetic resonance imaging (MRI) can also provide in-continuity vascular images without the need for nephrotoxic contrast agent administration. Unfortunately, the logistics of obtaining an MRI in the multiply injured trauma patient who requires careful monitoring limits its use in acute thoracic trauma.

■ PREOPERATIVE PREPARATION

While the ATLS secondary survey is being completed and injuries documented,[8] blood is sent to the blood bank for typing. Autotransfusion in the operating room is a useful adjunct to homologous transfusions, although large volumes of autotransfusion are believed by some to lead to coagulopathy. Realistic discussions with the patient and family related to intraoperative and postoperative complications such as bleeding, paraplegia, and the significant associated mortality should occur whenever possible

■ ANESTHETIC ISSUES

For penetrating injuries in the upper chest, vascular access for transfusion and fluid administration should be obtained in the arm or centrally on the side contralateral to the injury. With high index of suspicion or knowledge from preoperative imaging studies that the arterial injury is located in the upper mediastinum, intravenous access above and below the diaphragm is recommended. Swan-Ganz catheters are not routinely placed unless the patient has known preexisting cardiac disease. For injuries to the descending thoracic aorta, right-sided central venous access is avoided because a right pneumothorax can result in inability to ventilate the patient during single-lung ventilation that is required for descending thoracic aorta repair. Single-lung ventilation is obtained most readily with a double-lumen endotracheal tube. Bronchial blockers can be used though the results are often less than satisfactory. The inability to achieve single-lung ventilation due to associated pulmonary pathology may require that the operation be delayed and the patient medically managed if possible. It is important to avoid aggressive fluid resuscitation to normalize blood pressure until vascular control is obtained.

■ OPERATIVE THERAPY

Incisions

Although the midline laparotomy is the universal incision for abdominal trauma, multiple incisions are possible to access thoracic vascular trauma (Fig. 71-1).[1] A patient in extremis from thoracic exsanguination may require an emergency center thoracotomy. The left anterolateral thoracotomy can be extended across the sternum in a "clam shell" manner to provide access to the mediastinum if necessary. The incision can also be extended vertically through the upper sternum for better access to the upper mediastinum.[25] This provides suboptimal exposure for posterior structures such as the descending thoracic aorta. For injuries of the ascending aorta, arch, innominate artery, right subclavian artery, or left common carotid artery, a median sternotomy with appropriate extension into the left or right neck or supraclavicular fossa provides the exposure necessary for vascular control and repair. Because the left subclavian artery runs deep to the pleural surface of the left chest, proximal control of the left subclavian artery in the thoracic cavity can be obtained via a high third anterior interspace. Repair of injuries is then performed with the help of a supraclavicular incision.[25] Injuries to the descending thoracic aorta are approached via a fourth-interspace posterolateral thoracotomy. The pelvis is often rotated back 45 degrees for access to the groin for distal aortic perfusion if needed.

Operative Considerations

It is critical that communication with the anesthesiologists, technicians, circulating nurses, and perfusionists is maintained throughout the operative procedure. It is difficult for these team members to view the operative field, so comments relating to blood loss, probable injuries, and the anticipated repair can be extremely helpful. The application of vascular clamps for proximal control can significantly increase afterload, and the anesthesiologist requires time to pharmacologically reduce aortic afterload prior to clamp placement. If active perfusion such as cardiopulmonary bypass, left heart bypass, or other perfusion strategies are required, communication with the perfusionist allows appropriate flow rates and manipulation of cardiac performance.

■ ADJUNCTS

For significant injuries, vascular grafts are often needed. In the patient who is neither hypothermic nor coagulopathic,

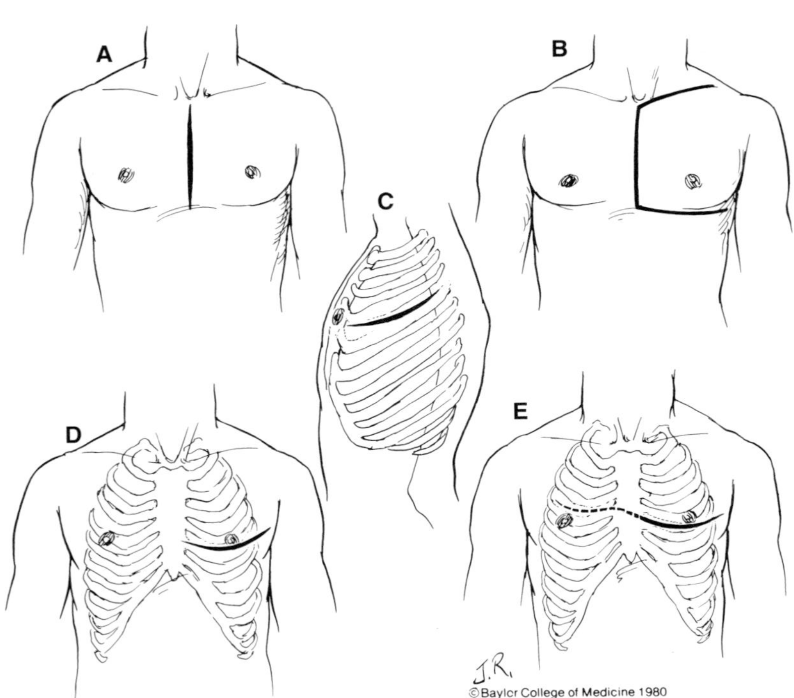

FIGURE 71-1 Incisions for thoracic trauma. **A,** Median sternotomy. **B,** "Book" thoracotomy (more commonly, the sternal connection is not needed). **C,** Posterolateral thoracotomy. **D,** Anterolateral thoracotomy (the "utility" incision for the patient in extremis). **E,** Extension of the anterolateral thoracotomy to the opposite chest as a clam shell incision. (**A** to **E,** ©Baylor College of Medicine, 1980.)

knitted polyester grafts (preclotted, collagen or gel impregnated) can be used to repair injuries to the aorta. The soft knitted polyester conforms well to the young aorta of the typical trauma patient. For patients who require full heparinization or who are coagulopathic, the sealed polyester grafts are preferred. These gel- or collagen-impregnated grafts avoid the need to preclot or bake the grafts prior to insertion. Although many prefer polytetrafluoroethylene grafts for the brachiocephalic vessel injuries, knitted polyester has the advantage of conforming to the anatomic course and contours of the subclavian artery.[25]

Injuries to the aorta, vena cava, or brachiocephalic vessels may require a shunt while repair is performed.[26] Loss of large portions of the superior vena cava can be traversed with a chest tube held in place with snare tourniquets until a repair strategy is developed (Fig. 71-2). Injury to the intrathoracic left carotid or innominate artery can be bridged with carotid shunts until additional surgical assistance can be obtained if needed. For acute short-term use, shunts do not require full heparinization.[27]

In many trauma centers a clamp-and-repair technique without distal perfusion is used to repair blunt injuries of the descending thoracic aorta.[28,29] Other centers advocate perfusion strategies with centrifugal pumps to increase distal spinal cord perfusion and unload the heart during aortic cross-clamping (Fig. 71-3).[30-32] Many patients with blunt injuries to the descending thoracic aorta are older than the typical trauma patient and have concomitant coronary artery disease. They often do not tolerate aortic cross-clamping unless left atrial-femoral bypass is employed to offload the heart during repair. For complex aortic arch and ascending aortic injuries, full cardiopulmonary bypass and circulatory arrest are often required.

Although there has been significant debate regarding the "optimum" repair method for blunt injuries to the descending thoracic aorta, no one strategy is routinely optimal for any given patient. All repair techniques use vascular isolation of a segment of the aorta that may contain critical blood supply for the spinal cord. Clamp-and-sew has the advantage of simplicity and greatest familiarity to the cardiovascular surgeon. Although some centers have used this method successfully with paraplegia rates of 2% to 8%,[28,29] recent meta-analysis and the American Association for the Surgery of Trauma blunt aortic injury data collection study by Fabian and colleagues have suggested higher rates of paraplegia, in the range of 16%.[18] Full cardiopulmonary bypass with systemic heparinization can also be used with good results.[33] Its use is often limited, however, by concomitant brain injury, pelvic hematoma, and solid organ injury. This technique is technically more demanding with a potential for difficulty relating to cannulation and cannulation sites. Thus cardiopulmonary bypass is associated with a low incidence of paraplegia but potentially the highest incidence of complications.[34] Atrial-femoral bypass with the centrifugal pump has become popular because it is believed to augment distal perfusion of the spinal cord. It can be performed without heparin, with heparin-bonded tubing, or with low-dose heparin, thus reducing bleeding complications. Although it is not completely protective for paraplegia, reported paraplegia rates are in the 2% to 3% range.[18,34] However, with its increased use, a higher rate of complications has been reported,[35] and technical cannulation problems remain problematic on occasion. Unfortunately, owing to the low individual numbers of cases, a few additional complications in any treatment arm can significantly affect results.

The optimal approach occurs when the surgeon caring for these injuries is acquainted with all techniques and the method of repair is tailored to the patient as well as location and severity of the injury. Our service currently uses both

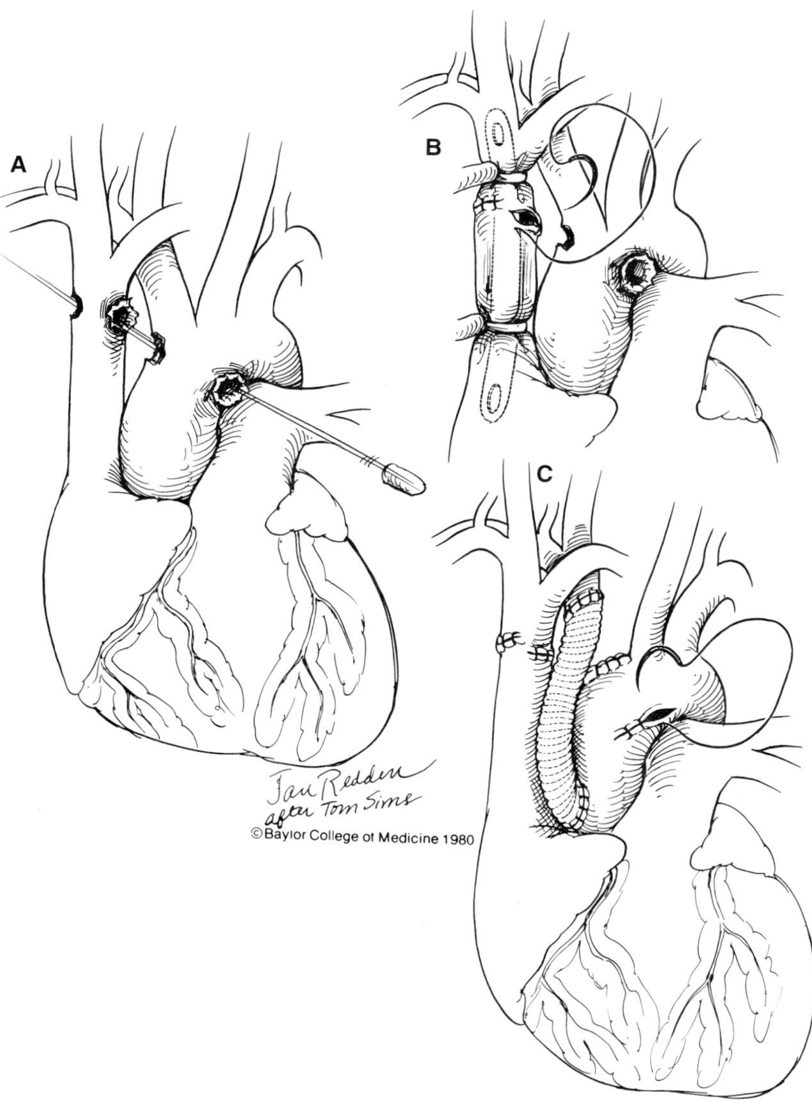

FIGURE 71-2 **A** to **C,** The use of a shunt in the superior vena cava to allow flow while repair is effected. (© Baylor College of Medicine, 1980.)

clamp-and-sew and left atrial-femoral bypass based on surgeon preference. Left atrial-femoral bypass for repair of an aortic injury in stable patients is used for unloading the heart during aortic cross-clamping. Clamp repair continues to be used in selected cases, particularly when patients are in extremis with active, ongoing blood loss. Full cardiopulmonary bypass is used rarely and is reserved for complex injuries that extend proximally into the aortic arch and ascending aorta.

■ SPECIFIC INJURIES

Thoracic Aorta

The thoracic aorta is a deep midline structure. Unfortunately, although infrequent, injury due to penetrating trauma carries a mortality of 50%.[36] Small or minimal injuries such as contained pseudoaneurysms permit evaluation and management. Stab wounds more frequently injure the ascending aorta, whereas the descending thoracic aorta is more commonly injured by gunshot wounds. Injuries to the ascending aorta may present as pericardial tamponade with more limited blood loss or exsanguination into a hemithorax. These injuries are often diagnosed during a salvage empiric thoracotomy. The chest is usually opened via a left anterolateral thoracotomy that can be extended across the sternum into the opposite chest if needed. Small injuries to the aorta can be closed primarily. Lateral adjacent injuries can be connected and repaired as a linear suture line. Through-and-through injuries sometimes require that the aorta be divided. When this occurs, it is not uncommon to require a graft to re-establish aortic continuity. Vascular control can be obtained with finger pressure, partial-occluding clamps, or thoracic aortic occlusion. In the patient who is not hypothermic or coagulopathic, a knitted polyester graft is our graft of choice for the soft aorta of the young adult.

Blunt injury to the aorta can occur to the ascending arch/innominate artery origin or descending thoracic aorta. Those with injuries to the ascending aorta commonly die on

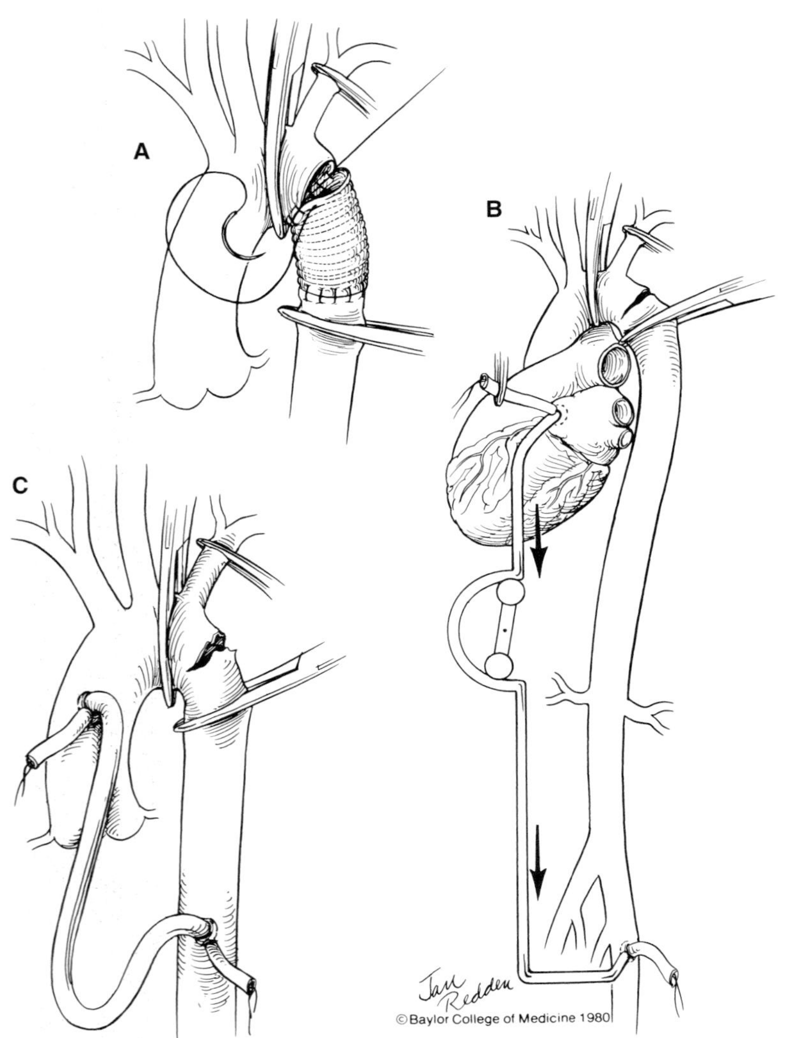

FIGURE 71-3 Management of blunt injury to the descending thoracic aorta requires placement of vascular clamps that isolate a segment of the descending thoracic aorta. **A,** Clamp repair without distal perfusion. **B,** Left atrial femoral active bypass commonly using a centrifugal pump. **C,** Ascending aorta to descending aorta passive shunt (currently seldom used). (**A** to **C,** ©Baylor College of Medicine, 1980.)

the scene (85% mortality); however, they can occasionally be seen at a busy trauma center. They are managed with cardiopulmonary bypass and cardioplegic cardiac arrest. Small injuries can be repaired primarily, though often a short tube graft is needed. Because this is performed under full heparinization and cardiopulmonary bypass, a coated polyester graft is most commonly used. Though uncommon, our service has recently cared for three patients with this injury. The most recent involved a tear of the ascending aorta at the superior aspect of the sinus of Valsalva associated with avulsion of the aortic valve leaflets and aortic insufficiency. This patient required composite graft replacement of the aortic root with reimplantation of the coronary arteries.

Blunt injuries to the aortic arch most commonly involve the takeoff of the innominate artery. Often classified as blunt innominate artery injuries, they are more accurately described as an aortic arch injury.[21] As mentioned previously, this can be a blind area for transesophageal echocardiography. Previously these injuries were managed by cardiopulmonary bypass and circulatory arrest. The bypass principle as described by Mattox and others greatly simplifies the management of these cases and eliminates the need for cardiopulmonary bypass (Fig. 71-4).[21,37] The injury is exposed via a median sternotomy. The pericardium is opened, exposing the ascending aorta. Exposure is facilitated if the innominate vein is divided between vascular clamps. The hematoma is avoided, and a partial-occluding clamp is placed on the ascending aorta. A 10-mm knitted Dacron graft is then anastomosed side to side to the ascending aorta. The distal innominate artery just proximal to the junction of the right common carotid and right subclavian artery is then identified in an area away from the hematoma. This is clamped and the innominate artery is divided. End-to-end anastomosis between the distal innominate artery and the Dacron graft is then performed. The simplicity of anastomosis results in a short clamp time. The anastomosis is flushed and carefully secured. After restoration of flow, a large partial-occluding clamp is used to gain control of the injury at the aortic arch, and this is oversewn with pledgeted sutures. This management strategy provides a simpler repair with a mortality of approximately 26%. It has been noted that patients who arrive with a preexisting neurologic deficit have a uniformly poor outcome.[21]

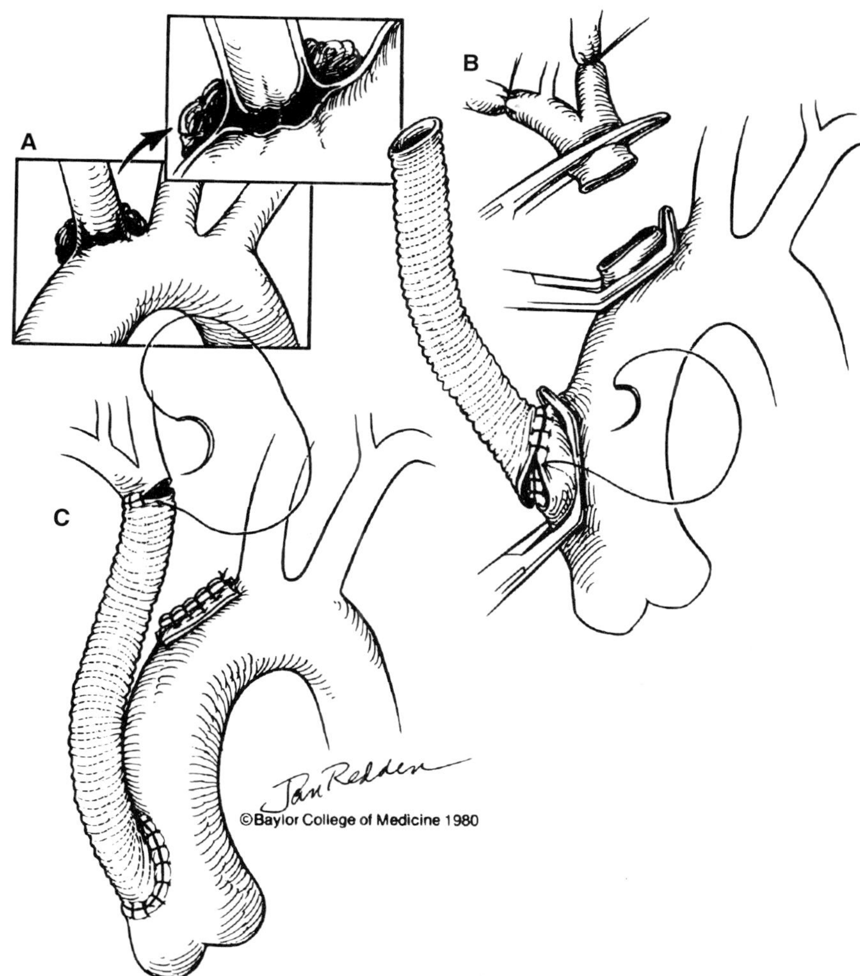

FIGURE 71-4 **A** to **C**, The bypass principle used to repair blunt injury to the proximal innominate-aortic arch. (**A** to **C**, ©Baylor College of Medicine, 1980.)

Injuries to the descending thoracic aorta can occur from just distal to the left subclavian artery all the way to the diaphragm. Although the arteriogram may suggest a more distal injury, it is prudent to obtain proximal vascular control between the left common carotid and left subclavian artery at the aortic arch. Arteriography often underestimates the injury, and attempts to encircle the aorta distal to the left subclavian often result in release of the pseudoaneurysm and exsanguination. It is important to carefully inspect the preoperative arteriogram for arch anomalies, since a large mediastinal hematoma often requires that the brachiocephalic vessels be identified by palpation alone. By dissecting along the anterior border of the left subclavian artery the aortic arch is identified. After dissecting in the plane of the thoracic aorta, a finger can be passed around the aortic arch. Dissection is then carried inferiorly around the aortic arch, taking care to stay anterior to the subclavian artery. The subclavian artery can be controlled with a vascular clamp or a snare tourniquet. Control of the distal descending thoracic aorta is obtained by looping it distal to the mediastinal hematoma. At this point, if a left heart bypass is used, the left atrium and distal aorta or common femoral artery can be cannulated. After achieving vascular control, the hematoma is entered and the injury identified. The injury is often against the posteromedial aspect of the aorta and not readily visible. The aorta frequently must be opened to visualize a small injury. Injuries encompassing less than 50% of the circumference of the aorta can often be repaired primarily with a fine suture. However, approximately 85% of repairs require an interposition graft.[10] Our preference is to use a knitted polyester graft. Once the extent of the injury is determined, it is helpful to move the distal aortic clamp as close to the injury as possible to maximize perfusion of the intercostal arteries (Table 71-4). After completion of the anastomoses, the subclavian and distal aortic clamps are removed and the patient is carefully weaned from the

Table 71-4 Descending Thoracic Aortic Repair Pearls

- Achieve proximal control between the left common carotid and left subclavian arteries.
- Know the patient's arch anatomy.
- Do not débride the aorta.
- Do not sacrifice the intercostals.
- Move clamps closer to injury, when identified.
- Use fine suture.
- Use a soft graft.

Table 71-5 Groups of Patients with Thoracic Aortic Injury[41]

GROUP	DESCRIPTION	TIME TO DIAGNOSIS	MORTALITY, %	CAUSE OF DEATH
1	Dead/dying at scene	<60 min	100	Bleeding
2	Unstable during transport	1-6 hr	>96	Multisystem trauma
3	Stable	4-18 hr	5-30	Head injury

proximal aortic clamp. Overall, the mortality associated with managing blunt injuries to the descending thoracic aorta is approximately 31%.[18]

Many trauma services care for patients who have devastating intra-abdominal or head injuries in combination with blunt injuries to the aorta. In many patients the aortic repair has been deferred hours, days, or sometimes months.[38-40] This has led Mattox and Wall to classify blunt aortic injuries into one of three categories (Table 71-5).[41]

- Category 1 patients are those who have massive injuries with exsanguination at the scene. Attempts at surgical repair are universally futile.
- Category 2 patients are those who present to the emergency center with unstable hemodynamics that are transient responders. There may be time to obtain studies and bring these patients to the operating room, but the mortality rate is high.
- Category 3 patients are hemodynamically stable with a blunt aortic injury and a contained hematoma. These patients are initially not thought to have an aortic injury but are evaluated owing to the history of a deceleration injury. This group of patients usually does not require emergent repair, and in hospitals where aortic repairs are not routinely performed, they can usually be safely transferred.[41]

Should a surgeon elect to delay routine repair, the following caveats should be considered:

- Use afterload and arterial upstroke—change in pressure versus time (dP/dT)—reduction agents, if needed.
- Maintain the systemic blood pressure at or below the preinjury level.
- Mediastinal hematoma should be "stable" on serial imaging.
- The patient is fully informed of the decision and risks.
- The decision to delay surgery and the management during the delay occur under a surgeon's supervision.

Among category 3 patients, an aortic-related death has rarely been reported.[41] Should the surgeon elect to delay operative repair, it is optimal to perform surgery within 72 hours of injury, prior to fibrinous organization of the mediastinal hematoma.

It is important to carefully evaluate the arteriogram because multiple injuries sometimes occur. Injuries to the descending thoracic aorta and innominate artery, to the descending thoracic aorta and the common carotid artery takeoff, and multiple injuries to the descending thoracic aorta have been reported. Knowledge of these injuries preoperatively helps plan the operation that may need to be performed in a staged manner.

Brachiocephalic Vessels

A blunt injury to the origin of the left common carotid artery is managed in a manner similar that used for blunt innominate artery/aortic arch injuries.[25] Penetrating injuries to vessels of the thoracic outlet can result in a large upper mediastinal hematoma. If the patient's condition permits, arteriography is helpful because different incisions are required to expose various injuries.[25] Unfortunately, some of these patients present in extremis with exsanguination, and a best guess must be made during empirical exploration. If a penetrating injury to the thoracic outlet involves primarily anterior structures, a median sternotomy with appropriate neck extension can be a useful empirical incision. Patients in extremis often undergo an anterolateral thoracotomy for resuscitation. When these are extended to the opposite chest as a clam shell incision, the upper mediastinum can be accessed. If required, an upper sternotomy can then be added.

The left subclavian artery runs on the left side of the mediastinum along its pleural surface. Proximal control can be readily obtained via a high anterolateral thoracotomy so that a vascular clamp or snare tourniquet can be placed. Injury to the subclavian artery can then be addressed via a supraclavicular incision. An intrathoracic left subclavian injury that is adjacent to the arch is often best approached via a fourth interspace–left posterolateral thoracotomy similar to exposure of the descending thoracic aorta. For the rare injury that is immediately behind the head of the clavicle or lower, the anterolateral thoracotomy and supraclavicular incision can be connected to form the "book" or "trapdoor" thoracotomy (see Fig. 71-1). Fortunately this incision is seldom needed because it carries significant morbidity. In an effort to avoid this incision, some have oversewn/ligated the proximal subclavian artery and re-established flow to the arm via carotid subclavian bypass or transposition.[25]

The subclavian artery is an extremely soft vessel. A graft is required for most repairs because mobilization and primary anastomosis are usually not technically feasible. Proximal and distal vascular control of the subclavian artery reduces the bleeding from "torrential" to just "bothersome" owing to the extensive arterial network of the subclavian artery. The left common carotid artery and the innominate artery are accessed via a median sternotomy with appropriate cervical extension. Small injuries can be repaired primarily. More extensive injuries can be repaired using the bypass principle as described for blunt innominate injuries. Multiple injuries to the innominate and left common carotid can be repaired using a bifurcated Dacron graft in a similar manner.[42]

Pulmonary Vessels

Injuries to the proximal main right or left pulmonary arteries are uncommon. They most commonly occur secondary to penetrating trauma and may present with pericardial tamponade. They are typically found during an empirical thoracotomy for hemopericardium. Small injuries can be repaired primarily. More extensive injuries in appropriate patients may require the use of cardiopulmonary bypass to ensure a bloodless field and expose injuries that are posterior.[43] Distal pulmonary artery injuries outside of the mediastinum may occur from blunt and penetrating trauma. Extensive injuries may require lobectomy or pneumonectomy. The mortality rate for pneumonectomy for trauma ranges from 50% to 75%. Pulmonary venous injuries can be from penetrating trauma or from avulsion of the hilum of the lung from a deceleration injury. They often present as massive hemothorax, and they are found during empirical thoracic exploration of a patient in extremis with a massive hemothorax. These injuries have high mortality as well and frequently require a lobectomy or pneumonectomy.[2]

Vena Cavae

Because they are short structures, the intrathoracic vena cavae are rarely injured. If injured, pericardial tamponade is a common presentation. Small injuries can be managed with lateral venorrhaphy. Partial-occluding clamps or brief periods of inflow occlusion can be used to permit repair.[44] More extensive injuries may require interposition graft placement. A chest tube can be used as a shunt to preserve cardiac filling if inflow occlusion is not tolerated. More extensive injuries particularly to the posteroinferior vena cava may require cardiopulmonary bypass for exposure and management.[45]

The azygos vein is a complementary venous drainage system to the inferior vena cava and has high flow. Injury to the azygos vein is uncommon, though it has a mortality rate similar to that for a vena cava injury. Azygos vein injuries should be considered during thoracotomy when a large amount of dark blood from a posterior source is noted. They can be managed with oversewing or ligation.[46]

Miscellaneous Vessels

Trauma patients who present with massive hemothorax and undergo an empirical thoracotomy are often bleeding from chest wall vessels. If an incision is extended across the sternum, the internal mammary arteries should be controlled prior to closing the sternum. They are often in spasm at the completion of procedure and are often routinely oversewn to avoid delayed bleeding.

Intercostal vessels can be extremely difficult to control. Although they can periodically be oversewn directly, it is sometimes helpful to loop the entire rib and intercostal bundle with a heavy absorbable suture proximal and distal to the injury. These injuries often require a separate incision for control and can be frustrating to manage.

Penetrating injuries to the great vessels may also involve the lung. In the past, deep penetrating injuries in the lung often required lobectomy. This was a daunting procedure in a patient with associated great vessel injury. One technique that has been useful in the management of these deep penetrating injuries to the lung is pulmonary tractotomy. By opening the wound tract between vascular clamps or the stapler, the parenchyma of the lung can be inspected and individual bleeding and air leaks ligated with fine suture. This is a simple procedure with an associated mortality of approximately 17%. It has evolved into a damage control technique that permits the lung injury to be addressed rapidly and effectively (Fig. 71-5).[47]

■ POSTOPERATIVE CARE

Postoperatively, most patients with thoracic vascular injuries require management in the intensive care unit. Patients with multiple injuries may require rewarming and correction of coagulopathy. Arteriovenous rewarming may be helpful in the severely hypothermic patient.[48] If the patient is not bleeding, crystalloid infusions are minimized because pulmonary edema often significantly affects the postoperative course after thoracotomy. When bleeding is controlled, aggressive resuscitation should be curtailed. In appropriate patients, thoracic epidural catheters may assist with pain control.[49,50]

■ NEW TECHNOLOGIES

Managing injuries to the thoracic outlet requires incisions that are potentially morbid. Fortunately, many thoracic outlet injuries present as contained hematomas that permit diagnosis. This may permit the use of endovascular techniques to manage subclavian, carotid, and innominate injuries without thoracotomy.[51] Although penetrating injuries to the aorta often result in exsanguination, blunt injuries may present as a contained pseudoaneurysm. Many of these patients have other devastating injuries such that definitive aortic repair is delayed, as discussed earlier. For these patients endovascular repair is an option to be considered. The use of stent-graft technology to address aortic injuries requires significant preparation and resources. Originally the devices had to be homemade or adapted from other uses; thus, the original experience was for patients in whom the repair was performed in a subacute, semielective situation.[52-54] There recently have been a number of small series using stent-graft technology for the acute repair of blunt rupture of the descending thoracic aorta.[55-58] Semba and coworkers described the use of endovascular techniques in managing pseudoaneurysms of the aorta from iatrogenic and penetrating etiologies.[59] These injuries are likely best managed by a team approach with a surgeon with significant experience in both endovascular and open repair. Blunt injury to the descending thoracic aorta often occurs immediately adjacent to the takeoff of the left subclavian artery. During endovascular repair, the endograft is often routinely placed with the proximal end across the subclavian artery orifice.[60] This seems to be tolerated well in most patients.[61] If needed, flow can be re-established to the arm via a carotid subclavian bypass or transposition. Although early results in using stent-graft technology to manage acute blunt aortic injuries appear favorable, long-term follow-up is not available. As this technology evolves, it is clear that it

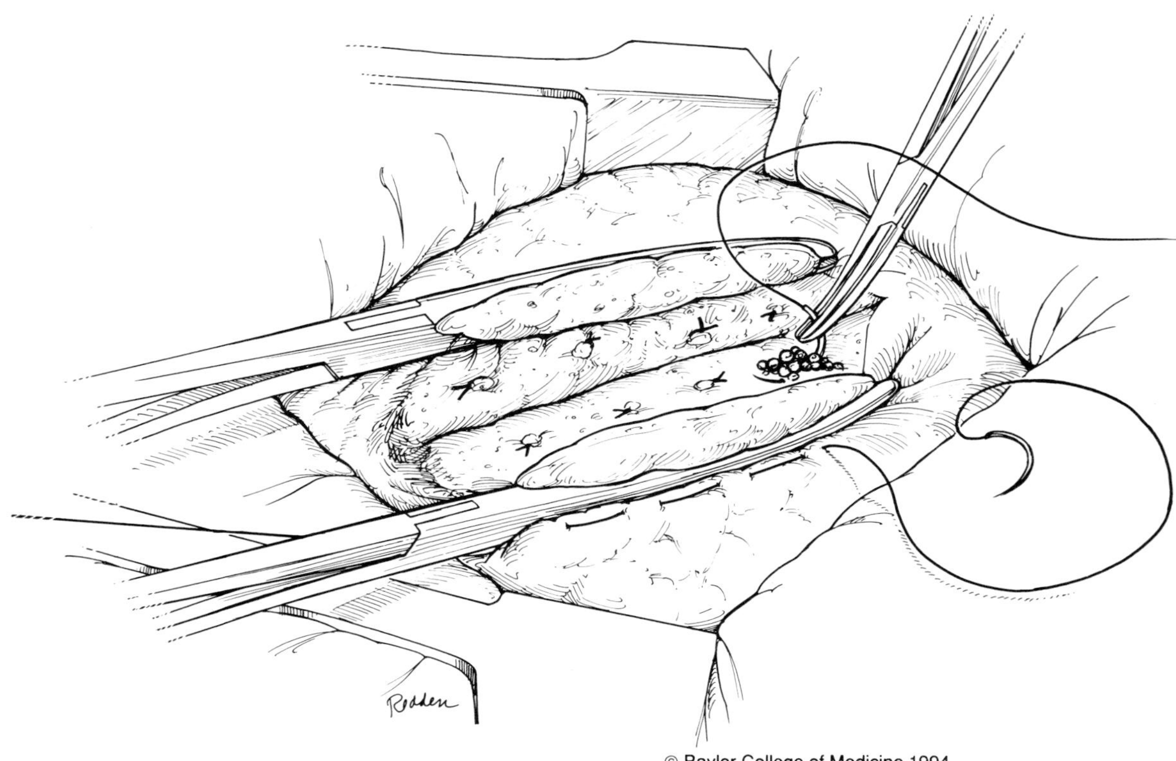

FIGURE 71-5 Pulmonary tractotomy with selective vascular ligation. A gunshot wound tract is opened between vascular clamps or the linear cutting staplers. Air leaks and bleeding points are selectively ligated using fine polypropylene sutures. This has evolved into a damage control procedure to rapidly address a lung injury associated with a major vascular injury. (©Baylor College of Medicine, 1994.)

requires significant resources of the hospital and personnel so that the technology, the appropriate equipment, and trained medical providers are available.

■ REHABILITATION

Significant incisions are often required for the management of thoracic great vessel trauma. Appropriate pain control can be extremely important and allows aggressive pulmonary toilet. It can be helpful to involve the rehabilitation service early in the management of these patients. It is not uncommon for patients to develop adhesive capsulitis of the shoulder after thoracotomy, which can be debilitating.

■ MEDICAL AND LEGAL CONSIDERATIONS

Injuries to the thoracic vascular structures can be highly lethal. The surgeon is often confronted with an extremely difficult situation emergently with little time for decisions or consultation. Despite the surgeon's best efforts, complications and death may ensue. Patients often present with preexisting neurologic or vascular deficits. It is wise to document these preoperatively. Despite the surgeon's best efforts, the complication of paraplegia can occur. Though it is not often possible, it is helpful to discuss with the patient and family the significant incidence of complications (e.g., paraplegia) and death prior to attempted repair of great vessel injuries. Owing to the emergent presentation of most thoracic vascular injuries and the high expected mortality, a negative outcome is common and not necessarily evidence of malpractice.[62]

■ SUMMARY

Injuries to the aorta and major vessels of the chest are often fatal on scene. Prehospital factors such as rapid transport and minimal fluid resuscitation have improved early survival. Those surviving to reach trauma centers may be stratified based on their stability. Hemodynamically unstable patients require thoracotomy and exploration, whereas patients who are stable can undergo appropriate diagnostic tests that will permit operative planning. Patients with blunt aortic injury and stable contained hematoma in the face of polytrauma can be considered for delayed management. Unlike in the abdomen, injuries to the vessels in the chest require that careful consideration of operative incision be made for proper access to the injury. Adjuncts such as partial or total cardiopulmonary bypass and venous shunts may be required to achieve hemodynamic stability to allow surgical repair.

■ REFERENCES

1. Wall MJ Jr, Huh J, Mattox KL: Thoracotomy. In Mattox KL, Feliciano DV, Moore EE (eds): Trauma, 5th ed. New York, McGraw-Hill, 2004, p 493.
2. Mattox KL, Feliciano DV, Burch J, et al: Five thousand seven hundred sixty cardiovascular injuries in 4459 patients: Epidemiologic evolution, 1958-1988. Ann Surg 209:698, 1989.
3. DeBakey ME, Simeone FA: Battle injuries of arteries in World War II: An analysis of 2,471 cases. Ann Surg 123:534, 1946.
4. Emergency Cardiac Care Committee and Subcommittees, American Heart Association: Guidelines for cardiopulmonary resuscitation and emergency cardiac care. JAMA 268:2172, 1992.
5. Bickell WH, Wall MJ, Pepe PE: Immediate versus delayed fluid resuscitation for hypotensive patients with penetrating torso injuries. N Engl J Med 331:1105, 1994.
6. Mattox KL, Bickell WH, Pepe PE: Prospective randomized evaluation of antishock MAST in post-traumatic hypotension. J Trauma 26:779, 1986.
7. Hunt JP, Weintraub SL, Wang Y-Z, Buechter KJ: Kinematics of trauma. In Mattox KL, Feliciano DV, Moore EE (eds): Trauma, 5th ed. New York, McGraw-Hill, 2004, p 141.
8. American College of Surgeons Committee on Trauma, Advanced Trauma Life Support Course (Student Manual), 2004.
9. Mattox KL, Beall AC Jr, Ennix CL, DeBakey ME: Intravascular migratory bullets. Am J Surg 137:192-195, 1979.
10. Mattox KL, Wall MJ Jr, LeMaire SA: Injury to the thoracic great vessels. In Moore EE, Feliciano DV, Mattox KL (eds): Trauma, 5th ed. New York, McGraw-Hill, 2004, p 571.
11. Durham RM, Zuckerman D, Wolverson M, et al: Computed tomography as a screening exam in patients with suspected blunt aortic injury. Ann Surg 220:699-704, 1994.
12. Dyer DS, Moore EE, Ilke DN, et al: Thoracic aortic injury: How predictive is mechanism and is chest computed tomography a reliable screening tool? A prospective study in 1561 patients. J Trauma 48:673-682, 2000.
13. Gotway MB: Helical CT evaluation of the thoracic aorta. Appl Radiol 29:7-28, 2000.
14. Exadaktylos AK, Sclabas G, Schmid SW, et al: Do we really need routine computed tomographic scanning in the primary evaluation of blunt chest trauma in patients with "normal" chest radiography? J Trauma 51:1173-1176, 2001.
15. Fabian TC, Davis KA, Gavant M, et al: Prospective study of blunt aortic injury: Helical CT is diagnostic and antihypertensive therapy reduces rupture. Ann Surg 227:666-677, 1998.
16. Gedebou TM, Mengesha YM, Fortune JB, Smythe S: Traumatic aortic rupture: The role of spiral computed tomography in diagnosis. Contemp Surg 54:92-96, 1999.
17. Demetriades D, Gomez H, Velmahos GC, Asensio JA, et al: Routine helical computed tomographic evaluation of the mediastinum in high-risk blunt trauma patients. Arch Surg 133:1084-1088, 1998.
18. Fabian TC, Richardson JD, Croce MA, et al: Prospective study of blunt aortic injury: Multicenter trial of the American Association for the Surgery of Trauma. J Trauma 42:374-383, 1997.
19. Brooks SW, Young JC, Cmolik B, et al: The use of transesophageal echocardiography in the evaluation of chest trauma. J Trauma 32:761-765, 1992.
20. Kearney PA, Smith DW, Johnson SB, et al: Use of transesophageal echocardiography in the evaluation of traumatic aortic injury. J Trauma 34:696-703, 1993.
21. Johnston RH Jr, Wall MJ, Mattox KL: Innominate artery trauma: A thirty-year experience. J Vasc Surg 17:134, 1993.
22. Ben-Menachem Y: Assessment of blunt aortic-brachiocephalic trauma: Should angiography be supplanted by transesophageal echocardiography? J Trauma 42:969, 1997.
23. Fisher RG, Sanchez-Torres M, Whigham CJ, Thomas JW: "Lumps" and "bumps" that mimic acute aortic and brachiocephalic vessel injury. Radiographics 17:825-826, 1997.
24. Fisher RG, Sanchez-Torres M, Thomas JW, Whigham CJ: Subtle or atypical injuries of the thoracic aorta and brachiocephalic vessels in blunt thoracic trauma. Radiographics 17:835-849, 1997.
25. Wall MJ Jr, Granchi T, Liscum K, Mattox KL: Penetrating thoracic vascular injuries. Surg Clin North Am 76:749-761, 1996.
26. Wall MJ Jr, Soltero E: Damage control for thoracic injuries. Surg Clin North Am 77:863-878, 1997.
27. Granchi T, Schmittling Z, Vasquez J, et al: Prolonged use of intraluminal arterial shunts without systemic anticoagulation. Am J Surg 180:493-496, 2000.
28. Sweeney MS, Young DJ, Frazier OH, et al: Traumatic aortic transections: Eight-year experience with the "clamp-sew" technique. Ann Thorac Surg 64:384-389, 1997.
29. Mattox KL, Holzman M, Pickard LR, et al: Clamp/repair: A safe technique for treatment of blunt aortic injury to the descending thoracic aorta. Ann Thorac Surg 40:456-463, 1985.
30. von Oppell UO, Dunne TT, De Groot MK, Zilla P: Traumatic aortic rupture: Twenty-year meta-analysis of mortality and risk of paraplegia. Ann Thorac Surg 58:585, 1994.
31. Read RA, Moore EE, Moore FA, Haenel JB: Partial left heart bypass for thoracic aortic repair. Arch Surg 128:746, 1993.
32. Olivier HF Jr, Maher TD, Liebler GA, et al: Use of BioMedicus centrifugal pump in traumatic tears of the thoracic aorta. Ann Thorac Surg 38:586-591, 1984.
33. Pate JW, Fabian TC, Walker WA: Acute traumatic rupture of the aortic isthmus: Repair with cardiopulmonary bypass. Ann Thorac Surg 59:90, 1995.
34. von Oppell UO, Dunne TT, De Groot MK, Zilla P: Traumatic aortic rupture: Twenty-year meta-analysis of mortality and risk of paraplegia. Ann Thorac Surg 58:585, 1994.
35. Duke BJ, Moore EE, Brega KE: Posterior circulation cerebral infarcts associated with repair of thoracic aortic disruption using partial left heart bypass. J Trauma 42:1135-1139, 1997.
36. Pate JW, Cole FH, Walker WA, Fabian TC: Penetrating injuries of the aortic arch and its branches. Ann Thorac Surg 55:586, 1993.
37. Graham JM, Feliciano DV, Mattox KL, Beall AC Jr: Innominate vascular injury. J Trauma 22:647-655, 1982.
38. Karmy-Jones R, Carter Y, Nathens A, et al: Impact of presenting physiology and associated injuries on outcome following traumatic rupture of the thoracic aorta. Am Surg 67:61-70, 2001.
39. Pezzella AT, Todd EP, Dillon ML, et al: Early diagnosis and individualized treatment of blunt thoracic aortic trauma. Am Surg 44:699-703, 1978.
40. Maggisano R, Nathens A, Alexandrova NA, et al: Traumatic rupture of the thoracic aorta: Should one always operate immediately? Ann Vasc Surg 9:44-52, 1995.
41. Mattox K, Wall MJ: Historical review of blunt injury to the thoracic aorta. Chest Surg Clin North Am 10:167-182, 2000.
42. Shin DD, Wall MJ Jr, Mattox KL: Combined penetrating injury of the innominate artery, left common carotid artery, trachea, and esophagus. J Trauma 49:780-783, 2000.
43. Clements RH, Wagmeister LS, Carraway RP: Blunt intrapericardial rupture of the pulmonary artery in a surviving patient. Ann Thorac Surg 64:258, 1997.
44. Bakaeen FG, Wall MJ Jr, Mattox KL: Successful repair of an avulsion of the superior vena cava from the right atrium inflicted by blunt trauma. J Trauma (In Press).
45. Wall MJ, Mattox KL, Chen C-D, Baldwin JC: Acute management of complex cardiac injuries. J Trauma 42:905-912, 1997.
46. Snyder CL, Eyer SK: Blunt chest trauma with transection of the azygos vein: Case report. J Trauma 29:889, 1989.
47. Wall MJ Jr, Villavicencio RT, Miller CC, et al: Pulmonary tractotomy as an abbreviated thoracotomy technique. J Trauma 45:1015-1023, 1998.
48. Gentilello LM, Cobean RA, Offner PJ, et al: Continuous arteriovenous rewarming: Rapid reversal of hypothermia in critically ill patients. J Trauma 32:316-325, 1992.
49. Mackersie RC, Karagianes TG, Hoyt DB, Davis JW: Prospective evaluation of epidural and intravenous administration of fentanyl for

pain control and restoration of ventilatory function following multiple rib fractures. J Trauma 31:443, 1991.
50. Liu S, Carpenter RL, Neal JM: Epidural anesthesia and analgesia: Their role in postoperative outcome. Anesthesiology 82:1474, 1995.
51. Patel AV, Marin ML, Veith FJ, et al: Endovascular graft repair of penetrating subclavian artery injuries. J Endovasc Surg 3:382-388, 1996.
52. Kato N, Dake MD, Miller DC, et al: Traumatic thoracic aortic aneurysm: Treatment with endovascular stent grafts. Radiology 205:657-662, 1997.
53. Mattison R, Hamilton IN, Ciraulo DL, Richart CM: Stent-graft repair of acute traumatic thoracic aortic transection with intentional occlusion of the left subclavian artery: Case report. J Trauma 51:326-328, 2001.
54. Ruchat P, Capasso P, Chollet-Rivier M, et al: Endovascular treatment of aortic rupture by blunt chest trauma. J Cardiovasc Surg 42:77-81, 2001.
55. Ahn SH, Cutry A, Murphy TP, Slaiby JM: Traumatic thoracic aortic rupture: Treatment with endovascular graft in the acute setting. J Trauma 50:949-951, 2001.
56. Orend KH, Pamler R, Kapfer X, et al: Endovascular repair of traumatic descending aortic transection. J Endovasc Ther 9:573-578, 2002.
57. Thompson CS, Rodriguez JA, Ramaiah VG, et al: Acute traumatic rupture of the thoracic aorta treated with endoluminal stent grafts. J Trauma 52:1173-1177, 2002.
58. Yamashita S, Nishimaki H, Lin ZB, et al: Endovascular stent-graft placement for thoracic aortic injury: Case report. J Trauma 51:587-590, 2001.
59. Semba CP, Kato N, Kee ST, et al: Acute rupture of the descending thoracic aorta: Repair with use of endovascular stent grafts. J Vasc Interv Radiol 8:337-342, 1997.
60. Zager JS, Ohki T, Simon JE, et al: Endovascular repair of a traumatic pseudoaneurysm of the thoracic aorta in a patient with concomitant intracranial and intra-abdominal injuries. J Trauma 55:778-781, 2003.
61. Gorich J, Asquan Y, Seifarth H, et al: Initial experience with intentional stent-graft coverage of the subclavian artery during endovascular thoracic aortic repairs. J Endovasc Ther 9:11-43, 2002.
62. Weigel CJ: Medicolegal issues. In Mattox KL, Feliciano DV, Moore EE (eds): Trauma, 4th ed. New York, McGraw-Hill, 2000, p 1463.

Chapter 72

Abdominal Vascular Injuries

DEMETRIOS DEMETRIADES, MD, PHD, FACS

Abdominal vascular injuries remain the most common cause of death following penetrating abdominal trauma. The surgical exposure and the often-associated intra-abdominal injuries may challenge the skills and judgment of even the most experienced surgeons. Rapid transportation to a trauma center, early recognition of the injuries, early surgical interventions, excellent knowledge of the anatomy, and good surgical judgment are critical for survival.

SURGICAL ANATOMY

For vascular trauma purposes, the abdomen is conventionally divided into the following four anatomic areas (Fig.72-1):

- Zone 1, which includes the midline retroperitoneum extending from the aortic hiatus to the sacral promontory. This zone is subdivided into the supramesocolic and inframesocolic areas. The supramesocolic area contains the suprarenal aorta and its major branches (celiac axis, superior mesenteric artery [SMA], and renal arteries), the supramesocolic inferior vena cava (IVC) with its major branches, and the superior mesenteric vein (SMV). The inframesocolic area contains the infrarenal aorta and IVC.
- Zone 2 (left and right), which includes the kidneys, the paracolic gutter, and the renal vessels
- Zone 3, which includes the pelvic retroperitoneum and contains the iliac vessels
- Perihepatic area, which contains the hepatic artery, the portal vein, the retrohepatic IVC, and the hepatic veins

INCIDENCE AND EPIDEMIOLOGY

Penetrating trauma is responsible for most abdominal vascular injuries and accounts for about 90% of cases in urban trauma centers.[1] Low-velocity missiles cause direct injury to the vessel. High-velocity missiles and blasts can also cause vascular trauma by means of the shock wave and transient cavitation. Some of these injuries may manifest with early or late thrombosis or hemorrhage.

Earlier reviews of vascular injuries reported a very low incidence of penetrating abdominal vascular injuries. DeBakey and Simeone reported 2471 arterial injuries during World War II, which included only 49 abdominal arterial injuries (2%).[2] Similarly, Rich and associates[3] in a study of 1000 arterial injuries from the Vietnam War reported only 29 abdominal arterial injuries (2.9%). However, in civilian penetrating injuries, the incidence of abdominal vascular trauma is significantly higher than that in military injuries. In a prospective study of gunshot injuries to the abdomen, the incidence of vascular trauma in 217 patients who underwent exploratory laparotomy was 14.3%.[4] The incidence of vascular injuries in patients undergoing laparotomy for stab wounds is 10%.[5] The incidence of vascular injuries in

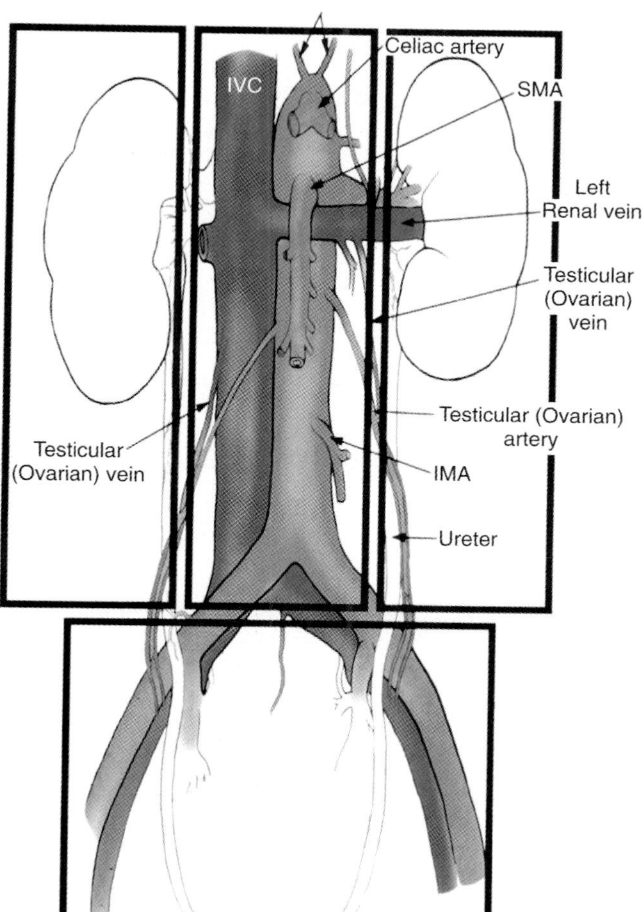

FIGURE 72-1 Retroperitoneal vascular zones: Zone 1 (*upper, center box*) includes the midline vessels from the aortic hiatus to the sacral promontory; zone 2 (*upper, right and left boxes*) includes the paracolic gutter and the kidneys; and zone 3 (*lower box*) includes the pelvic retroperitoneum.

patients with blunt abdominal trauma undergoing exploratory laparotomy is 3%.[6]

Blunt abdominal trauma may cause vascular injuries by one of the following three mechanisms:

1. Rapid deceleration, as in high-speed traffic accidents or falls from heights: This mechanism may cause damage to abdominal vessels by avulsion or intimal tear and subsequent thrombosis.
2. Direct anteroposterior crushing, as in seat-belted car passengers or direct blows to the anterior abdomen.
3. Direct laceration of a major vessel by a bone fragment, as in severe pelvic fractures.

Abdominal arterial and venous injuries occur with the same incidence. In a recent review of 302 abdominal vascular injuries from our center, the incidence of arterial injuries was 49% and of venous injuries, 51%.[1] The most commonly injured abdominal vessel was the IVC and it accounted for 25% of injuries, followed by the aorta (21%), the iliac arteries (20%), the iliac veins (17%), the SMV (11%), and the SMA (10%). Overall, patients with penetrating trauma had an average of 1.6 vascular injuries.[1]

■ PREHOSPITAL MANAGEMENT

The most important factor for the survival of salvageable patients with vascular injuries is rapid transportation to a trauma center and subsequent immediate surgical control of the bleeding. Prehospital advanced life support (ALS) has no place in penetrating trauma, especially in an urban environment. A policy of "scoop and run" is currently the recommended approach. The role of prehospital intravenous fluid administration is controversial, with some studies showing improved survival with fluid restriction and others showing no effect on survival.[7,8] Experimental work on abdominal aortic injuries has shown that in the presence of uncontrolled bleeding, aggressive fluid resuscitation increased mortality and the rate and volume of hemorrhage.[9,10] However, avoiding all fluid resuscitation in near-fatal hemorrhage may result in cardiac arrest before bleeding control.[11] It seems that some degree of controlled hypotension is beneficial and prevents massive exsanguination while at the same time avoids the risk of cardiac arrest due to massive blood loss and severe hypotension.[9,12] In many trauma systems the prehospital intravenous resuscitation protocols recommend insertion of intravenous lines and crystalloid resuscitation in the ambulance on the way to the hospital.

■ CLINICAL PRESENTATION

Many patients with major abdominal vascular injuries die at the scene and never reach medical care. Of the patients who are transported to hospitals, about 14% lose vital signs during transportation or in the emergency department.[1] The clinical presentation depends on the injured vessel, the size and type of the injury, the presence of associated injuries, and prehospital time.

Penetrating injuries to the abdomen associated with hypotension and abdominal distention are highly suspicious of vascular injury. Asymmetric femoral pulses may indicate iliac artery injury. Many patients may be normotensive on admission only to decompensate a few minutes later. Some patients present in a hemodynamically stable condition because of thrombosis of the vessel or effective containment of the bleeding in the retroperitoneum. In most cases the diagnosis is made intraoperatively. Vascular injuries due to blunt trauma are often missed on initial examination or even during the initial hospitalization, unless they are associated with significant bleeding or early ischemic changes.

■ INVESTIGATIONS

In most patients with penetrating abdominal vascular injuries no investigations are needed because of the critical condition of the patient and the obvious need for immediate laparotomy. Radiographic evaluation of the torso should be reserved only for gunshot wounds, if the patient is hemodynamically stable. The location of any missiles may

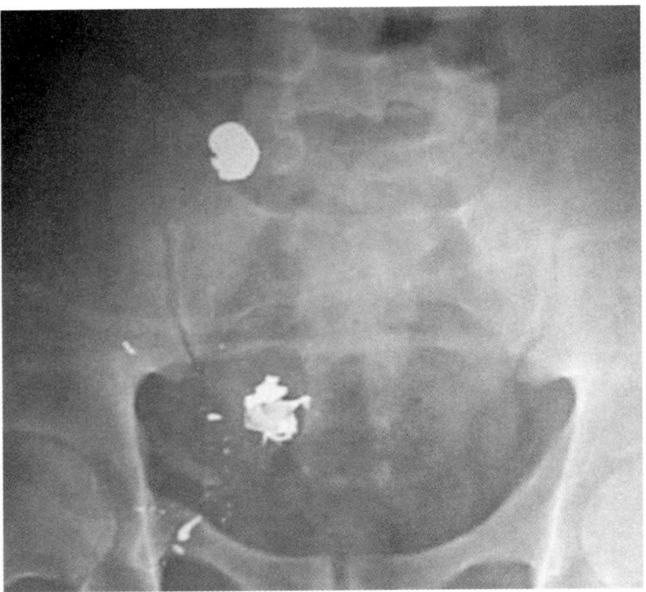

FIGURE 72-2 The pelvic location of the missile on abdominal radiograph, combined with hypotension, is highly suspicious of iliac vascular injury.

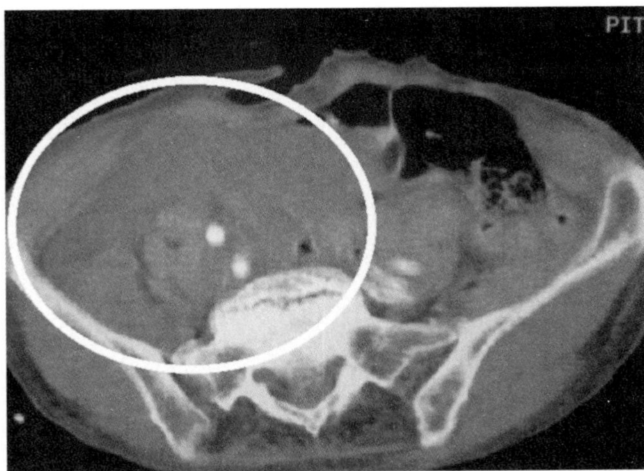

FIGURE 72-3 CT of a traffic accident victim shows a large pelvic hematoma (*circle*) due to injury of the right common iliac artery.

be useful in planning the operation (Fig. 72-2) or in the diagnosis of other extra-abdominal injuries. About 30% of victims with gunshot injuries to the abdomen have multiple gunshot wounds[4] and an abdominal radiograph may give useful information. Finally, early radiographic diagnosis of gunshot wounds to the spine or other bones may be useful in antibiotic prophylaxis. In blunt trauma, radiographic diagnosis of complex pelvic fractures may increase the suspicion of iliac vascular injuries.

Computed tomography (CT) has little or no role in suspected vascular injuries due to penetrating trauma during the acute stage. However, it may play a useful role in blunt trauma by identifying large hematomas, false aneurysms, or vessel occlusions (Figs. 72-3 and 72-4). In selected cases with penetrating trauma, elective CT scanning with intravenous contrast medium may identify false aneurysms or arteriovenous fistulae (Figs. 72-5 and 72-6). Angiography has no role in suspected vascular injuries due to penetrating trauma during the acute stage. However, it has an important role in the evaluation of suspected late complications, such as false aneurysms or arteriovenous fistulae. It remains a valuable tool in the evaluation of patients with blunt trauma, especially with pelvic fractures, with suspected vascular injuries (Fig. 72-7).

Other investigations such as intravascular ultrasound may be useful in selected cases with late abdominal vascular complications for a more accurate definition of the anatomy of a vascular lesion (Fig. 72-8).

■ EMERGENCY DEPARTMENT MANAGEMENT

The presence of hypotension or tachycardia (>120 beats/min) or a gunshot wound to the torso is a criterion for trauma team activation in most trauma systems. The type

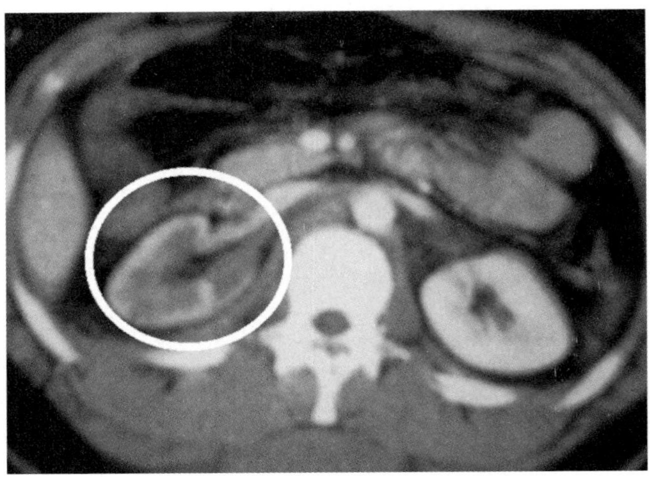

FIGURE 72-4 CT scan with intravenous contrast material following a fall from a significant height shows poor contrast uptake of the right kidney due to an occlusion of the renal artery (*circle*).

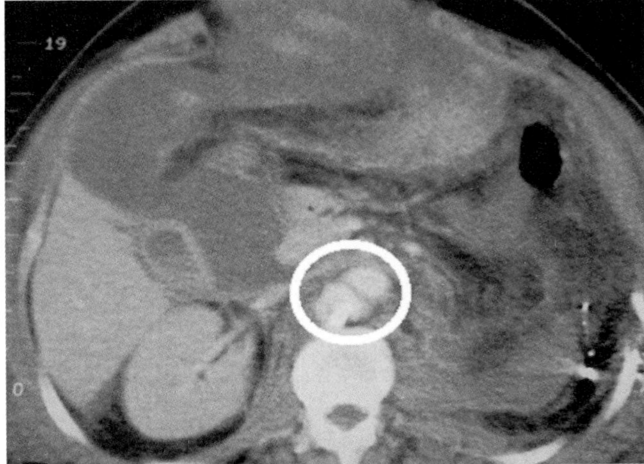

FIGURE 72-5 Postoperative CT scan of a patient with a gunshot wound shows an abdominal aortic false aneurysm (*circle*).

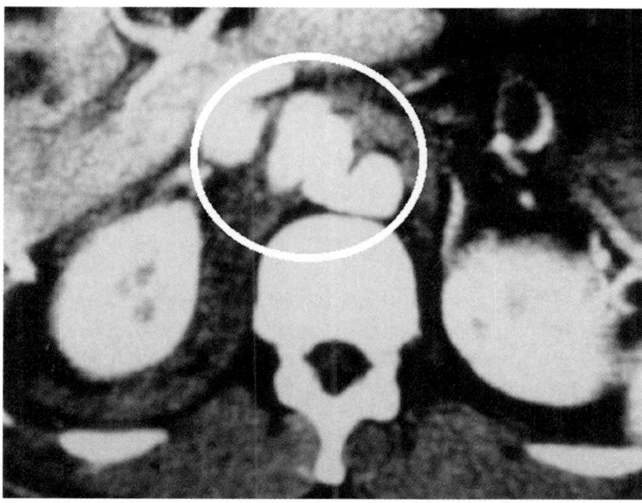

FIGURE 72-6 Postoperative CT scan of a patient with a gunshot wound shows an aortocaval fistula (*circle*).

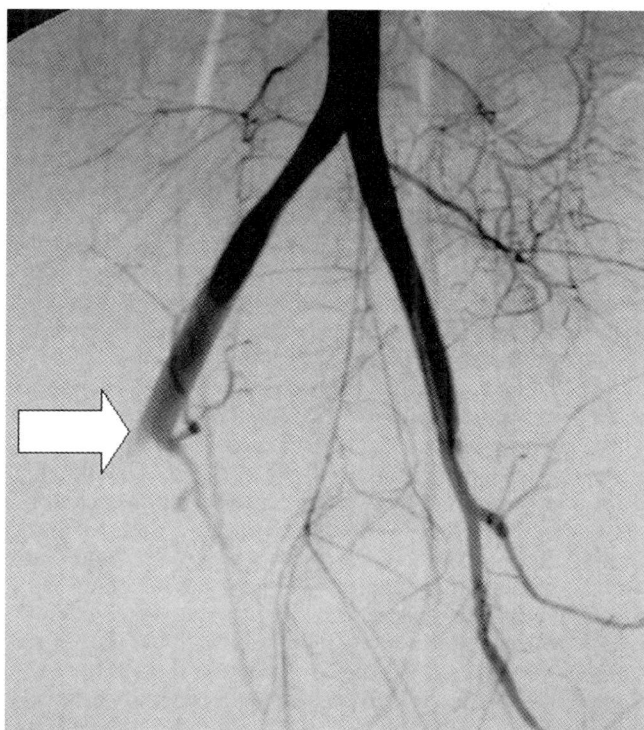

FIGURE 72-7 Five-year-old child with severe pelvic fracture and absent right femoral pulse. Angiography shows a complete occlusion of the right common iliac artery (*arrow*).

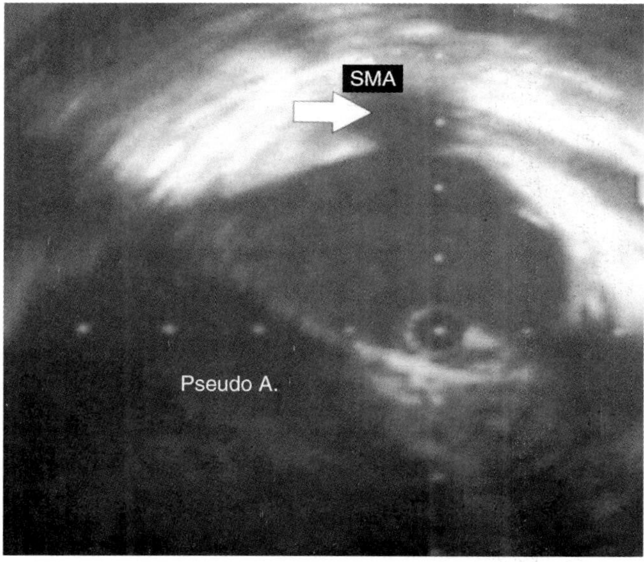

FIGURE 72-8 Intravascular ultrasound shows a false aortic aneurysm (Pseudo A.) at the superior mesenteric artery (SMA) level (*arrow*) following a gunshot wound to the aorta.

and duration of evaluation and resuscitation in the emergency department depend on the clinical condition of the patient. An emergency department endotracheal intubation and a resuscitative thoracotomy should be performed in cases admitted in cardiac arrest or imminent cardiac arrest. A left anterolateral thoracotomy is performed, the thoracic aorta is cross-clamped, and the heart is massaged as necessary. If cardiac activity returns, the operation is completed in the operating room. The survival rate following emergency department resuscitative thoracotomy for abdominal vascular injuries is about 2%.[1] We have occasionally combined the emergency department thoracotomy with a laparotomy to control bleeding by direct compression, but the results are poor.

In patients with suspected vascular injuries and in no need of resuscitative thoracotomy, time should not be wasted for fluid resuscitation or diagnostic investigations, with the exception of plain radiographs. Large-bore intravenous catheters should be placed in the upper extremities or the central veins of the thoracic inlet in case the victim has an injury to the IVC or the iliac veins. The concept of controlled hypotension should be borne in mind, and no aggressive fluid resuscitation efforts should be attempted in the emergency department. Endotracheal intubation, except in patients with cardiac arrest or imminent cardiac arrest, should be avoided in the emergency department because rapid-sequence induction is often associated with cardiovascular decompensation.

■ OPERATIVE MANAGEMENT: GENERAL PRINCIPLES

All possible steps should be taken to diminish hypothermia and its detrimental effects. The operating room should be warm, the infused fluids should be prewarmed to 40°C to 42°C, and the patient's extremities should be covered with a warming blanket. Rapid-infusion devices should be ready and the blood bank should be notified. The patient's entire torso, from the neck to the knees, should be prepared and draped in case a thoracotomy or saphenous vein harvesting is needed. The surgical team should be ready, and the skin preparation should be performed before induction of anesthesia, since anesthetic induction in these patients is often associated with rapid hemodynamic decompensation.

Some surgeons have advocated a preliminary left thoracotomy and aortic cross-clamping to prevent cardiovascular collapse following anesthesia and laparotomy.[13,14] The effectiveness of this procedure has been challenged by other authors.[15] I believe that this approach should be considered only for patients with cardiac arrest or imminent cardiac arrest. A thoracotomy is an additional traumatic insult that may aggravate hypothermia and coagulopathy and has little effect on bleeding control from major venous injuries. The approach my colleagues and I use is an immediate laparotomy, temporary control of the bleeding by direct compression, and aortic cross-clamping, if necessary, at the diaphragm. In our experience this is almost always possible, even in obese patients. To facilitate aortic exposure, division of the left crux of the diaphragm may be necessary. In those cases in which a retroperitoneal hematoma extends high toward the aortic hiatus, infradiaphragmatic exposure of the aorta is difficult, and a left thoracotomy may be necessary for aortic control.

The abdomen should be entered through a long midline incision. The operative findings depend on the nature and site of vascular injury and on the presence of other associated injuries. In penetrating trauma, the usual findings include various degrees of intraperitoneal bleeding or a retroperitoneal hematoma or a combination of the two. In blunt trauma the most likely finding is a retroperitoneal hematoma, which may or may not be expanding or pulsatile. In some cases with intimal tear and thrombosis, the hematoma may be unremarkable, and the only findings may be dark bowel or an absent or diminished femoral pulse. Some injuries may be missed only to manifest at a later stage with thrombosis, false aneurysm, or arteriovenous fistula.

The management of retroperitoneal hematomas depends on the mechanism of injury. As a general rule, almost all hematomas due to penetrating trauma should be explored irrespective of size. Often underneath a small hematoma there is a vascular or hollow viscus perforation. The only exception to this recommendation is a stable and nonexpanding retrohepatic hematoma. Surgical exploration of the retrohepatic vena cava or the hepatic veins is difficult and potentially dangerous.

Retroperitoneal hematomas due to blunt trauma in general rarely require exploration because of the very low incidence of underlying vascular or hollow viscus injuries requiring surgical repair. In patients with zone 2 hematomas due to renal trauma, surgical exploration may result in the unnecessary loss of the kidney. Similarly, exploration of a zone 3 hematoma due to pelvic fractures may cause severe bleeding that may be uncontrollable. Exploration of retroperitoneal hematomas should be limited to patients with expanding, pulsatile, or leaking hematomas. In addition, zone 3 pelvic hematomas associated with an absent ipsilateral femoral pulse should be explored because of the potential for an iliac artery injury. Paraduodenal hematomas also need exploration to exclude an underlying duodenal injury. Finally, hematomas at the root of the mesentery in the presence of ischemic bowel may harbor an injury to the SMA and should be explored. Exploration of these hematomas is technically difficult and potentially dangerous and should not be performed in the absence of ischemic bowel. Unexplored hematomas should be evaluated postoperatively by means of color-flow Doppler studies or angiography.

In the presence of severe active bleeding, the immediate priority is to control the bleeding by direct compression. Once this critical task is achieved, the next step is to identify the bleeding vessel and obtain proximal and distal control. If control is difficult or the patient is severely hypotensive, the abdominal aorta can be compressed digitally or with an aortic compressor at the aortic hiatus. Following dissection of the peritoneum over the aorta and, if necessary, division of the left crux of the diaphragm (at 2 o'clock to avoid bleeding), the aorta can be cross-clamped.

The exploration of the area of bleeding or hematoma should proceed systematically. Each anatomic zone requires a different technical maneuver. Zone 1 supramesocolic bleeding or hematomas are the most difficult to approach because of the dense concentration of major vessels (aorta, celiac artery, SMA, renal vessels, IVC), the difficult exposure of many of these vessels, and the difficult proximal control of the infradiaphragmatic aorta. For some injuries, the only safe way to achieve proximal aortic control is through a left thoracotomy. The supramesocolic aorta with the origins of its major branches is best exposed by mobilization and medial rotation of the viscera in the left upper abdomen. The first step of this approach is the division of the peritoneal reflection lateral to the left colon, the splenic flexure of the colon, and the spleen. The fundus of the stomach, the spleen, the tail of the pancreas, the colon, and the left kidney are then rotated to the right. This maneuver provides exposure of the aorta, the origin of the celiac axis, the SMA, and the left renal vessels (Fig. 72-9). Some surgeons prefer not to include the left kidney in the medial rotation.[16] However, for injuries involving the posterior wall of the aorta, inclusion of the left kidney in the visceral rotation improves the exposure. In suspected supramesocolic IVC injuries, zone 1 should be explored through a medial rotation of the right colon and hepatic flexure and Kocher mobilization of the duodenum and head of the pancreas (Fig. 72-10). The inframesocolic zone 1 area may be approached by retracting the transverse colon cephalad and displacing the small bowel to the right. The peritoneum over the aorta and IVC is then incised and the vessels are exposed. An alternative approach is medial rotation of the right or left colon.

Zone 2 bleeding or hematomas are explored by mobilization and medial rotation of the right colon, the duodenum and the head of the pancreas on the right side, or the left colon on the left side. The source of bleeding in zone 2 is the renal vessels or the kidneys. Zone 3 vessels are explored by dissection of the paracolic peritoneum and medial rotation of the right or left colon. In some cases, direct dissection of the peritoneum over the vessels may provide the necessary exposure.

■ DAMAGE CONTROL PROCEDURES

Many patients with major abdominal vascular injuries require massive blood transfusions, are hypotensive, and become severely hypothermic, acidotic, and coagulopathic intraoperatively. Persistent attempts to reconstruct or repair all abdominal injuries are ill advised and result in increased mortality. These patients may benefit from early damage control and definitive reconstruction at a later stage when the general condition improves. With the "damage control"

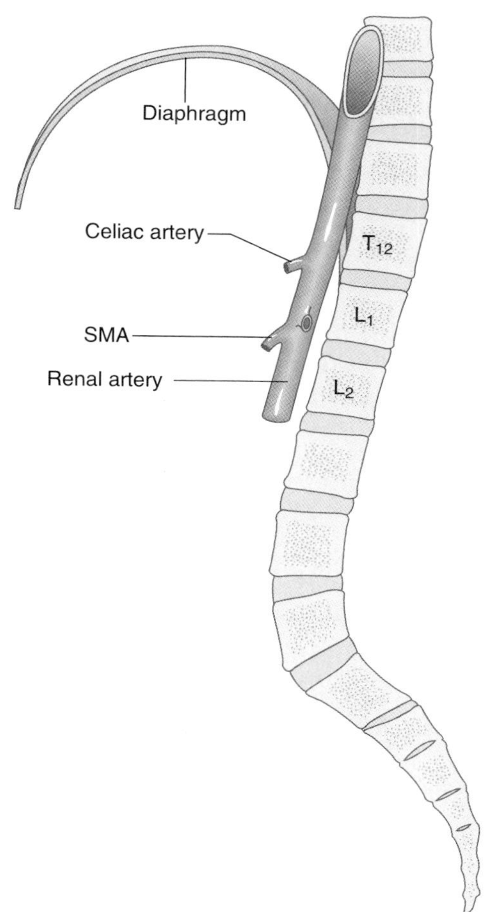

FIGURE 72-9 Medial left visceral rotation provides a good exposure of the supramesocolic aorta and the origin of the celiac axis, the superior mesenteric artery (SMA), and the left renal vessels.

approach, all complex venous injuries are ligated, arterial injuries may be shunted, and any diffuse retroperitoneal or parenchymal bleeding is controlled by tight gauze packing. Temporary intraluminal shunts can be constructed from a sterile intravenous or nasogastric tubing. The shunt is secured in place with proximal and distal ligatures (Fig. 72-11). The abdomen is then closed temporarily with a prosthetic material and the patient is transferred to the intensive care unit for further resuscitation. The patient is returned to the operating room after resuscitation and stabilization for definitive vascular repair and abdominal wall closure.

■ ABDOMINAL COMPARTMENT SYNDROME

The normal intra-abdominal pressure (IAP) in the resting supine position is near zero. Elevation of the IAP above 25 to 30 cm H_2O might cause severe organ dysfunction and result in abdominal compartment syndrome (ACS). The ACS is characterized by a tense abdomen, tachycardia with or without hypotension, respiratory dysfunction with high peak inspiratory pressures in mechanically ventilated patients, and oliguria. However, significant organ dysfunction may begin long before the classic ACS manifests.

All patients with severe abdominal trauma, especially vascular trauma, are at risk of developing ACS. Major risk factors include massive blood transfusions, prolonged hypotension, hypothermia, aortic cross-clamping, damage control procedures, and tight closure of the abdominal wall. Following severe trauma, the abdomen should never be closed under tension. Similarly, after damage control procedures the abdominal wall should not be closed because postoperative bowel edema results in ACS in most patients.

The diagnosis of ACS is based on clinical examination and IAP measurements. All high-risk patients, or those with a suspicion of a tense abdomen on palpation, should be monitored closely with serial IAP measurements. The IAP can reliably be measured through the bladder catheter. In general, pressures higher than 30 cm H_2O are considered strong indications for surgical decompression of the abdomen. The abdomen should be opened in the operating room or even in the intensive care unit if necessary. Temporary abdominal wall closure can be achieved with the use of prosthetic material, such as from a large dialysis bag or other synthetic meshes. When the bowel edema improves, usually within 2 to 3 days, the patient is returned to the operating room for definitive abdominal wall closure. The technical details of the temporary or permanent wall closure are outside the scope of this chapter and are not discussed.

■ SPECIFIC VASCULAR INJURIES

Abdominal Aorta Injuries

Anatomy

The aorta descends into the retroperitoneum between the two crura of the diaphragm at the T12-L1 level and bifurcates into the common iliac arteries at the L4-L5 level, which roughly corresponds to the level of the umbilicus. The first branches of the abdominal aorta are the phrenic arteries that originate from its anterolateral surface. Immediately below is the celiac trunk that originates from the anterior surface of the aorta, and 1 to 2 cm below is the SMA; the renal arteries are next at 1 to 1.5 cm below the origin of the SMA; and finally, the inferior mesenteric artery (IMA) is 2 to 5 cm above the bifurcation of the aorta.

Epidemiology

Blunt injury to the abdominal aorta is extremely rare and is diagnosed in 0.04% of all blunt trauma admissions[17] or 0.07% of patients with an Injury Severity Score greater than 16.[18] Motor vehicle injuries account for about half of all reported cases, and direct blows to the abdomen, falls, and explosions account for the rest.[19,20] Fractures of the thoracolumbar spine and seat belt injuries are associated with an increased risk of abdominal aortic injuries.[17,18] Intimal dissections and thrombosis are the most common lesions in patients reaching the hospital alive (Fig. 72-12). False aneurysms occur less frequently. Patients with free ruptures die at the scene and rarely reach medical care.[18,20]

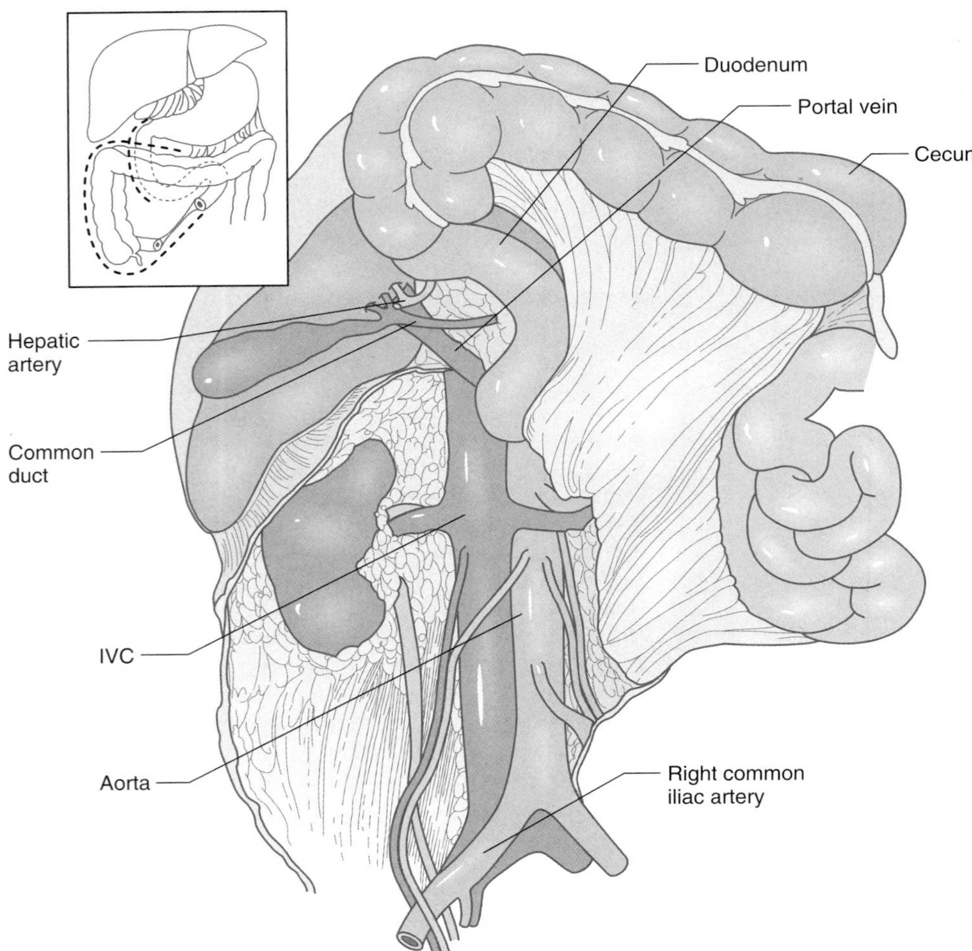

FIGURE 72-10 Medial rotation of the right colon and the hepatic flexure and Kocher mobilization of the duodenum and pancreas provide an excellent exposure of the inferior vena cava (IVC) and the origins of the renal veins. (From Buckman RF, Pathak AS, Badelino MM, Bradley KM: Injuries of the inferior vena cava. Surg Clin North Am 81:1431-1447, 2001.)

Penetrating injuries remain by far the most common cause of abdominal aortic injuries. In a review of 1218 cases with abdominal gunshot injuries from our center, there were 33 abdominal aortic injuries (2.7%). In 529 knife wounds to the abdomen, the aorta was injured in 8 (1.5%).[21] In another review of 302 abdominal vascular injuries, the aorta was involved in 63 cases (21%) and was the second most commonly injured vessel after the IVC.[1] The infrarenal aorta is injured in 50% of the cases, the supraceliac aorta in 25%, and the aorta between the celiac trunk and the renal arteries in 25% of patients.[22]

Clinical Presentation

The clinical presentation depends on the mechanism of injury (blunt or penetrating), the type of aortic injury, the presence of free intraperitoneal bleeding or retroperitoneal hematoma, associated injuries, and prehospital time. In blunt trauma, two thirds of the patients have acute symptoms of bleeding or visceral or lower extremity ischemia. The diagnosis is made during the initial hospitalization by means of CT scan or angiography or at laparotomy. In one third of the cases the diagnosis is made many months or even years after the injury.[18-20]

The clinical presentation of penetrating aortic injuries is usually dramatic. Many victims die at the scene and never reach medical care. Of those who reach medical care, about 28% have an unrecordable blood pressure, and about 21% require an emergency center resuscitative thoracotomy.[21] In about 18% of cases the bleeding is temporarily contained in the retroperitoneum and the patients are normotensive on admission.[22] In rare occasions the injury is missed at operation only to manifest at a later stage as a false aneurysm or arteriovenous fistula (see Figs. 72-5 and 72-6).

Operative Management

The surgical exposure of the vascular structures in zone 1 is achieved by medial visceral rotation, as described under the general principles of operative management (see Fig. 72-9). For high supramesocolic injuries a left thoracotomy may be necessary for cross-clamping of the aorta. In about 93% of patients with penetrating trauma, there are other associated intra-abdominal injuries, the most common of which are the small bowel (45% of cases), the colon (30%), and the liver (28%).[21] Before any definitive management that requires a prosthetic graft, all enteric spillage should be controlled and the peritoneum should be washed out. Lateral aortorrhaphy is possible in most cases. More complex repairs with prosthetic grafts may be necessary.[23] Many authors do not consider the presence of enteric spillage as a contraindication for the use of prosthetic material.[23]

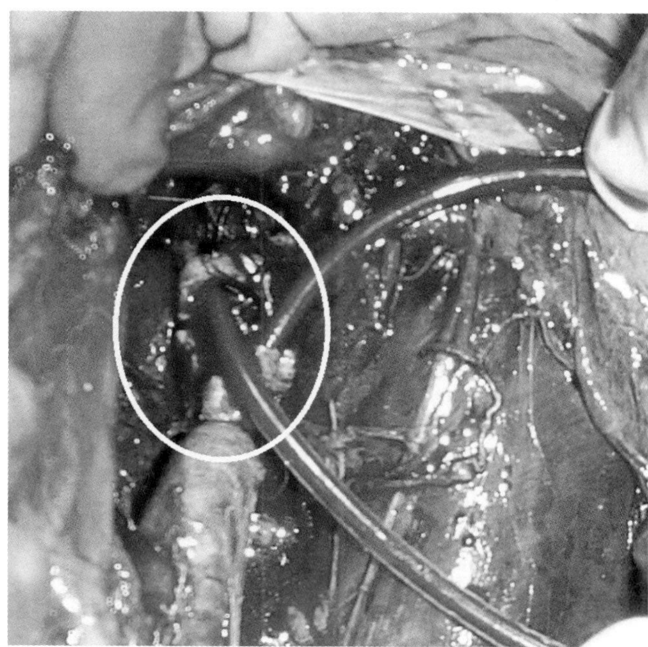

FIGURE 72-11 Temporary arterial shunt for damage control in a hemodynamically unstable patient with a gunshot wound and complete transection of the iliac artery (*circle*). (See Color Figure in this section.)

Endovascular Management

Endovascular management has a definitive role in selected cases with infrarenal aortic injuries. Patients with limited infrarenal aortic dissection, false aneurysms, or aortocaval fistulae have been treated successfully with angiographically placed stents (see Fig. 72-12).[24,25]

Mortality

The prognosis of abdominal aortic injuries following blunt trauma is significantly better than injuries due to penetrating trauma. The reported overall mortality in blunt trauma is 27%.[19] The mortality following penetrating trauma in two large series with 146 patients was 67%.[21,23] In another series of 57 patients with gunshot wounds, the mortality rate was 85%.[26] Suprarenal aortic injuries have a significantly worse outcome than infrarenal injuries.[22] The mortality in patients undergoing emergency center resuscitative thoracotomy is almost 100%.[21,22] The prognosis of penetrating abdominal aortic injuries is significantly better than injuries to the thoracic aorta, most likely due to the retroperitoneal containment of bleeding in abdominal injuries. In a comparison of 67 abdominal aortic injuries with 26 thoracic aortic injuries, the mortality rates were 76% and 92%, respectively.[21]

Celiac Artery Injuries

Anatomy

The celiac artery originates from the anterior wall of the abdominal aorta, immediately below the aortic hiatus, at the level of T12-L1. The main trunk is 1 to 1.5 cm long, and at the upper border of the pancreas it gives three branches (the tripod of Haller): (1) the common hepatic artery, (2) the left gastric artery, and (3) the splenic artery. Because of the extensive fibrous, ganglionic, and lymphatic tissues that surround the trunk, the surgical dissection may be tedious.

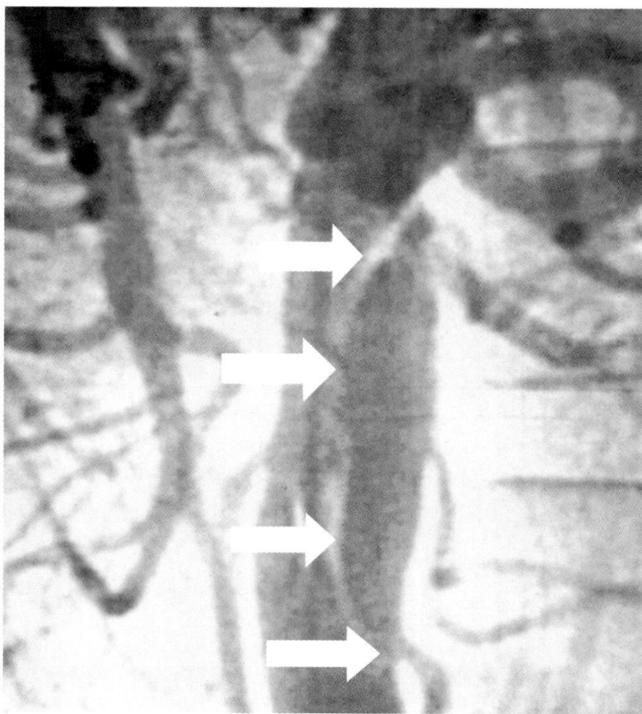

FIGURE 72-12 Angiography shows a dissecting aneurysm of the abdominal aorta (*arrows*) following a motor vehicle accident. The patient was successfully managed with an endovascular stent.

Epidemiology

Injuries to the celiac artery are rare and almost always due to penetrating trauma. In a review of 302 abdominal vascular injuries, the celiac artery was involved in 10 cases (3.3%).[1]

Operative Management

The surgical exposure can be achieved either by direct dissection over the upper abdominal aorta through the lesser sac or by medial rotation of the upper abdominal viscera, as described previously. The rotation does not need to include the left kidney. The celiac artery can be ligated without ischemic sequelae to the stomach, liver, or spleen because of the rich collateral circulation of these organs. The left gastric and splenic arteries may also be ligated with impunity. Ligation of the common hepatic artery is usually well tolerated because of adequate supply from the portal vein and the gastroduodenal artery.

Mortality

The reported mortality rate of celiac axis injuries ranges from 38% to 75%.[27] However, most of the collectively reported 50 cases with celiac axis injuries had other associated vascular injuries that contributed to the high mortality.

Superior Mesenteric Artery Injuries

Anatomy

The SMA originates from the anterior surface of the aorta, immediately below the celiac artery, behind the pancreas at the L1 level. It then proceeds over the uncinate process of the pancreas and the third part of the duodenum and enters into the root of the mesentery. The SMA gives the following branches: the inferior pancreaticoduodenal artery, the middle colic artery, the arterial arcade with 12 to 18 intestinal branches, the right colic artery, and the ileocolic artery. SMA injuries are divided into the following four zones:

- Zone 1—between the aortic origin and the inferior pancreaticoduodenal artery
- Zone 2—between the inferior pancreaticoduodenal artery and the middle colic artery
- Zone 3—distal to the middle colic artery
- Zone 4, which comprises the segmental intestinal branches

As a general rule, ligation of the SMA in zones 1 and 2 results in severe ischemia of the small bowel and right colon. Ligation of zones 3 and 4 may result in localized ischemia of the small bowel that may require segmental resection.

Another anatomic classification of SMA injuries uses only two zones: the short retropancreatic segment and the segment below the body of the pancreas, where it courses over the uncinate process of the pancreas and the third part of the duodenum.[28]

Epidemiology

SMA injuries are diagnosed in 0.09% of trauma admissions[29] and account for about 10% of all abdominal vascular injuries.[1] It is the second most commonly injured abdominal vessel after renovascular injuries following blunt trauma. Blunt trauma is responsible for between 10% and 20% of all SMA injuries.[29,30] Blunt trauma can cause thrombosis of the artery by direct blow or crushing of the abdomen or seat belt injuries. Deceleration injuries may cause avulsion of the vessel from its origin in the aorta or intimal tear and subsequent thrombosis. Penetrating injuries remain the most common mechanism of injury. Because of the anatomic location of the artery, multiple other significant associated injuries are quite common.[28]

Clinical Presentation

The clinical presentation depends on the mechanism of injury, the nature of the vascular injury, the presence of associated intra-abdominal injuries, and the prehospital time. Isolated thrombosis of the SMA due to blunt trauma may be missed during the initial evaluation, only to manifest at a later stage with bowel necrosis. Most patients with penetrating trauma present in severe shock. Patients with contained hematomas may be normotensive or mildly hypotensive on admission.

Operative Management

The operative findings may include various degrees of hemoperitoneum, a hematoma around the SMA, an ischemic bowel, or any combination of these (Fig. 72-13A).

Following temporary control of the bleeding by direct compression and, if necessary, cross-clamping of the aorta, the SMA should be explored.

Exposure of the retropancreatic SMA can be achieved by medial rotation of the left colon, gastric fundus, spleen, and tail of the pancreas, as described earlier. The kidney does not need to be rotated unless there is a suspicion of injury to the posterior wall of the aorta. In cases with severe bleeding where immediate exposure is critical, stapled division of the neck of the pancreas may provide fast and direct exposure of the SMA and the portal vein. Exposure of the infrapancreatic SMA can be achieved by cephalad retraction of the inferior border of the pancreas and direct dissection or through the root of the small bowel mesentery by incising and dissecting the tissues to the left of the Treitz ligament. An extensive Kocher maneuver may be required to expose this segment of the SMA. More distal sections of the SMA may be approached directly.

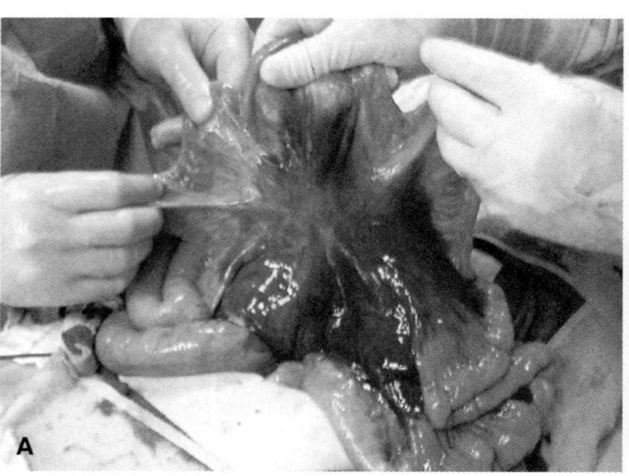

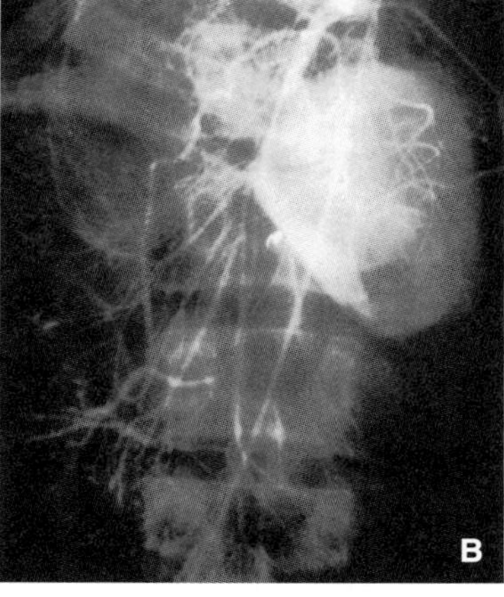

FIGURE 72-13 A, Traffic accident victim with a large hematoma at the base of the mesentery found at laparotomy. This is suspicious for superior mesenteric artery (SMA) injury and needs to be evaluated, preferably postoperatively. **B,** Postoperative angiography shows a large SMA false aneurysm. (See Color Figure in this section.)

Exploration of a hematoma at the root of the mesentery is always a difficult and potentially dangerous task, even in the hands of experienced surgeons. In penetrating trauma or blunt trauma with ischemic bowel, all hematomas around the SMA should be explored. However, it is my practice and recommendation not to explore stable hematomas following blunt trauma in the absence of bowel ischemia. In these patients the SMA is evaluated postoperatively by means of angiography or color-flow Doppler (see Fig. 72-13).

Sharp partial transections of the SMA, such as the ones inflicted by knife wounds, can be managed with lateral arteriorrhaphy using 6-0 vascular sutures. This approach is possible in about 40% of the cases.[29] Since mobilization of the SMA is restricted because of the surrounding dense neuroganglionic tissue and its multiple branches, an end-to-end anastomosis is rarely possible. Depending on the site of SMA injury, the condition of the patient, and the color of the bowel, these injuries may be managed by ligation or an interposition graft. Ligation of the SMA below the middle colic artery is usually associated with a moderate risk of ischemia of the bowel. Ligation of the proximal SMA results in ischemic necrosis involving the small bowel and the right colon. The first 10 to 20 cm of the jejunum may survive via collaterals from the superior pancreaticoduodenal artery. Ligation of the SMA proximal to the origin of the inferior pancreaticoduodenal artery may preserve critical collateral circulation to the proximal jejunum and is preferable to a more distal ligation. Ligation of the proximal SMA should be performed only in the presence of necrotic bowel. Ligation should be avoided in all other circumstances because of the catastrophic consequences of the short bowel syndrome. In patients in critical condition with severe hypothermia, acidosis, and coagulopathy, a damage control procedure with a temporary endoluminal shunt should be considered.[31] Definitive reconstruction is performed at a later stage after resuscitation and correction of the physiologic parameters of the patient. The reconstruction may be performed with a saphenous vein or polytetrafluoroethylene (PTFE) graft between the distal stump of the SMA and the anterior surface of the aorta. In the presence of an associated pancreatic injury, the vascular anastomosis should be performed away from the pancreas, and every effort should be made to protect it from the pancreatic enzymes by use of omentum and surrounding soft tissues. Postoperatively the patient should be monitored closely for any signs of bowel ischemia. The threshold for second-look laparotomy within the first 24 hours of operation should be low. Failure of the patient to improve postoperatively and the persistence of metabolic acidosis despite adequate fluid resuscitation should prompt the surgeon to re-explore the abdomen to rule out bowel ischemia. Some authors even practice planned mandatory second-look laparotomy. Damage control techniques allow the inspection of the bowel through the transparent material used for the temporary closure of the abdomen.

Mortality

The mortality directly related to SMA injuries is difficult to assess because in most patients there are multiple severe associated injuries, including other major vascular injuries. The reported mortality varies from 33% to 68%.[29,30,32,33]

Renovascular Injuries

Anatomy

The renal arteries originate from the aorta at the L2 level. The right renal artery emerges at a slightly higher level and is longer than the left and courses under the IVC. About 30% of the population has more than one renal artery, often an accessory one to the lower pole of the kidney. The renal veins lie in front of the renal arteries. The left renal vein is significantly longer than the right and courses in front of the aorta. It has collateral branches from the left gonadal vein inferiorly, the left adrenal vein superiorly, and a lumbar vein posteriorly.

Epidemiology

Renovascular injuries account for about 16% of all abdominal vascular injuries.[1] The incidence of renal artery injuries is less than 1% of all blunt trauma admissions.[34] The left renal artery is 1.3 to 1.6 times more likely to be injured than the right renal artery.[34,35] It has been suggested that the right renal artery is protected from deceleration injuries because of its course underneath the IVC.[36] Rapid deceleration accidents may cause intimal tears and subsequent arterial thrombosis at a later stage. In about 50% of cases with blunt renal artery injury, there is thrombosis or an intimal flap (Fig. 72-14; see also Fig. 72-4). Avulsion of the artery occurs in 12% of cases.[37] In 9% to 14% of renovascular injuries the renal artery is involved bilaterally.[35,37]

Clinical Presentation and Diagnosis

The diagnosis of renovascular injury following penetrating trauma is almost always made intraoperatively. However, in blunt trauma, the diagnosis is usually made during the routine CT scan evaluation of the abdomen (see Figs. 72-4 and 72-14). The clinical presentation is subtle and nondiagnostic, and often the diagnosis is delayed. In earlier

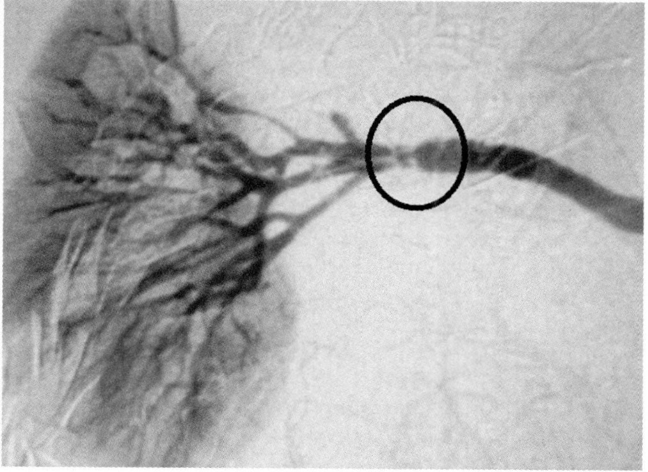

FIGURE 72-14 Angiography shows an intimal tear of the right renal artery (*circle*) due to fall from a height. The patient was successfully managed with an endovascular stent.

reports, when CT evaluation of the abdomen was not as liberal as now, up to 50% of patients did not receive timely treatment because of delayed diagnosis.[37] Abdominal CT scan with intravenous contrast material is highly sensitive in diagnosing renovascular trauma and should be the first-line investigation (see Fig. 72-4).[38] In addition, the CT scan provides useful information about associated injuries. Angiography is usually required for confirmation of the CT scan findings. Intravenous pyelography (IVP) has a limited role, and many patients with renovascular injuries have a normal IVP.

Management

The management of renovascular injuries depends on the mechanism of injury, the time of diagnosis, the ischemia time, the general condition of the patient, and the presence of a contralateral normal kidney. In penetrating injuries the diagnosis is almost always made early during the exploratory laparotomy, and, depending on the extent of the injury and the condition of the victim, reconstruction of the vessels or nephrectomy is performed. As a general rule, all zone 2 hematomas due to penetrating trauma should be explored. The only exception may be a stable perinephric hematoma away from the hilum.[39] However, in blunt trauma the management of renal artery injuries is complicated by the often-delayed diagnosis and the prolonged ischemia of the kidney. Renal function is severely affected after 3 hours of total ischemia and 6 hours of partial ischemia, although in some cases with collateral circulation from the renal capsule or surrounding soft tissues the kidney function may be preserved despite prolonged ischemia.[38] In stable patients with the diagnosis of renovascular trauma within 4 to 6 hours of injury, the general recommendation is revascularization.[38,40] In patients with bilateral injuries or injury to a solitary kidney, some authors recommend revascularization up to 20 hours after trauma.[40] Most surgeons avoid revascularization in patients diagnosed more than 6 hours after trauma, unless the injury involves both kidneys or a solitary kidney. The results following revascularization are generally disappointing. The cumulative success rate of revascularization is 28%.[34] Even after successful revascularization, subsequent hypertension develops in 12% to 57% of patients, and most require an elective nephrectomy.[35,40,41] The overall poor long-term results have led some authors to suggest that revascularization should be considered only in patients with bilateral renal artery occlusion or those with injury to a solitary kidney.[35,40] Nonoperative management is certainly an acceptable option, especially in patients with delayed diagnosis, those with other major extra-abdominal injuries or significant hemodynamic instability, or those with contralateral normally functioning kidney. About 32% to 40% of patients managed nonoperatively developed renovascular hypertension.[35,37,40] In most patients the hypertension develops within 1 year of the injury, with a mean of about 3 months.[35] I recommend revascularization only in renovascular injuries diagnosed intraoperatively and provided that the patient is fairly stable or in the rare occasion of bilateral injuries or injury to a solitary kidney. For the rest of the cases, I advocate observation and long-term monitoring for hypertension.

The surgical reconstruction of renal artery injury may be achieved by simple arteriorrhaphy, vein patch, resection and anastomosis, and interposition grafting. For complex, time-consuming arterial reconstructions, the kidney should be perfused intermittently with iced heparinized saline. Post-revascularization administration of mannitol may improve the parenchymal blood flow and alleviate the reperfusion injury.

Renal vein injuries may be managed by lateral venorrhaphy whenever it is feasible. Extensive injuries should be managed by ligation. Complex reconstruction, especially in the hemodynamically unstable patient, should be avoided. Ligation of the left renal vein near the IVC is tolerated well because of satisfactory venous drainage through the left gonadal vein, the left adrenal vein, and the lumbar veins. Ligation of the right renal vein should always be followed by nephrectomy.

Endovascular techniques may play a useful role in selected cases with renovascular trauma. Patients with intimal tears, false aneurysms and arteriovenous fistulae have been successfully managed with endovascular stents.[42-44]

Mortality

The true mortality rate directly related to renovascular injuries is difficult to estimate because in most cases there are other major associated injuries. The reported mortality rate varies from zero to 57%.[38] The mortality in renovascular injuries due to blunt trauma is low because of the occlusive nature of most arterial injuries.[34]

Inferior Mesenteric Artery Injuries

Anatomy

The IMA originates from the anterior surface of the aorta, about 3 to 4 cm above the aortic bifurcation. It provides blood supply to the left colon, sigmoid, and upper part of the rectum. It communicates with the SMA through the marginal artery of Drummond.

Epidemiology

Injuries of the IMA are rare, almost always due to penetrating trauma, and account for 1% of all abdominal vascular injuries.[1]

Management

The diagnosis of IMA is made intraoperatively. Ligation is well tolerated, and no cases of colorectal ischemia have been reported in trauma.

Iliac Vascular Injuries

Anatomy

The abdominal aorta bifurcates into the two common iliac arteries at the L4-L5 level. The common iliac arteries divide into the external and internal iliac arteries over the sacroiliac joint. The ureter crosses over the bifurcation of the common iliac artery.

The common iliac veins join at the L5 level, below the level of the aortic bifurcation and underneath the right common iliac artery, to form the IVC.

Epidemiology

Early experience from World War II, the Korean War, and the Vietnam War reported a low incidence of iliac vascular injuries, ranging from 1.7% to 2.6% of all arterial injuries.[2,3,45] Recent studies from urban trauma centers reported that iliac arteries represented about 10% of all abdominal vascular injuries,[1,46] or about 2% of all vascular injuries.[46] Iliac vein injuries account for about 10% of all abdominal vascular injuries. About 10% of 1310 patients who underwent laparotomy for gunshot wounds and 2% of 638 patients with laparotomies due to stab wounds were found to have iliac vascular injuries.[47] About 26% of patients with iliac vascular injuries have combined arterial and venous injuries.[47] Penetrating injuries usually involve the common iliac vessels, whereas blunt trauma usually affects branches of the internal iliac artery. Injury to the common or external iliac artery due to blunt trauma is not common, although there are many case reports. Direct laceration of the iliac vessels from a pelvic fracture or stretching of the iliac artery over the pelvic wall resulting in intimal tear and subsequent thrombosis are the usual mechanisms of injury following blunt trauma (see Fig. 72-7).[48]

Clinical Presentation

The presence of a penetrating injury in the lower abdomen associated with severe hypotension and abdominal distention is highly suspicious of iliac vascular injuries. An absent or diminished femoral pulse in a young patient with penetrating abdominal trauma or pelvic fracture is diagnostic of an injury to the common or external iliac artery. In rare cases of blunt trauma thrombosis of the iliac artery may not be diagnosed early during the initial hospitalization because of the subtle clinical symptoms. In other patients with blunt trauma the diagnosis may be made during the routine abdominal CT scan.

Management

The operative findings may include free intraperitoneal bleeding or a zone 3 pelvic hematoma or a combination of the two (Fig. 72-15). Zone 3 hematomas due to blunt trauma should be explored only if there is associated intraperitoneal leak or if they are expanding rapidly or there is an absent or diminished femoral pulse. In penetrating trauma all hematomas should be explored. Any active bleeding is initially exposed by direct dissection of the overlying peritoneum, although medial rotation of the right or left colon may provide a better exposure. The ureter, which crosses over the bifurcation of the common iliac artery, should be identified and protected during the dissection. In addition, care should be taken to avoid iatrogenic injury to the iliac veins that lie directly under the arteries. Isolation and control of the internal iliac artery are essential in arterial injuries because bleeding may persist despite proximal and distal control. If the exposure of the distal iliac vessels is difficult, especially in males with a narrow pelvis, extension of the midline incision by adding a transverse lower abdominal incision or longitudinal incision over the groin and division of the inguinal ligament may be necessary.[47]

Small arterial injuries may be repaired with 4-0 or 5-0 vascular sutures, taking precaution to avoid significant stenosis of the vessel. If necessary, a venous or PTFE patch may be used to avoid stenosis. In most gunshot injuries and in all patients with blunt trauma, reconstruction by an end-to-end anastomosis or with a prosthetic graft (size 6 or 8) is usually necessary. Local heparin solution should be administered to prevent thrombosis during the repair. A balloon-tipped catheter should always be passed proximally and distally to remove any clots. Complex arterial reconstructions with an extra-anatomic bypass or with a mobilized internal iliac artery have little or no role in the acute management of trauma. Extra-anatomic bypass should be considered only in late cases with severe purulent peritonitis or infected grafts. There is evidence that the presence of enteric contamination is not a contraindication for synthetic graft use.[49] However, there are still many vascular surgeons who recommend that in the presence of significant enteric contamination, an extra-anatomic bypass should be considered. If a prosthetic material is used, it is important that any enteric spillage is controlled and the peritoneal cavity is cleaned meticulously before prosthetic graft repair.

Ligation of the common or external iliac arteries should never be performed, even in patients in critical condition. Ligation is poorly tolerated by most patients, it is associated with a high incidence of limb loss, and subsequent attempts to revascularize the leg may cause severe reperfusion injury and organ failure or death. In patients in critical condition in need of damage control, the continuity of the injured artery may be established with a temporary intraluminal shunt (see Fig. 72-11), and definitive reconstruction of the vessel is performed at a later stage when the patient is stabilized.

Iliac venous injuries may be technically more challenging than arterial injuries because of the difficult exposure due to the anatomic arrangement behind the arteries. This problem is even more difficult on the right side because of

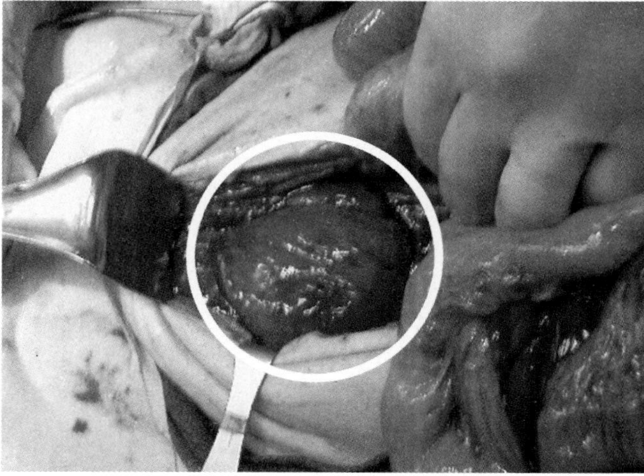

FIGURE 72-15 Large hematoma in the pelvis (*circle*) following a gunshot wound. This is highly suspicious of iliac vascular injury, and proximal control should be obtained as soon as possible. (See Color Figure in this section.)

the location of the right common iliac artery and the confluence of the two common iliac veins behind the right common iliac artery. Despite these difficulties, the recommendation by some authors to transect the iliac artery to access the underlying vein[50] is extreme and should rarely be considered. In most cases, careful mobilization and retraction of the artery provide a satisfactory exposure of the vein. Ligation and division of the internal iliac artery may be helpful in providing a better exposure. Repair of the iliac veins by means of lateral venorrhaphy should be considered only if it can be performed without producing major stenosis. Ligation is generally preferable to repair that produces severe stenosis because of the risk of thrombosis and pulmonary embolism.[47] There is no experience with the role of caval filters in cases with narrowed iliac veins. Complex reconstruction with spiral grafts or prosthetic materials, especially in the critically ill patient, is not recommended. Ligation is usually well tolerated, although many patients develop transient leg edema. On some rare occasions ligation results in massive edema of the leg and compartment syndrome that requires fasciotomy. The management of iliac venous injuries in the presence of associated iliac artery injuries is even more controversial. I do not recommend complex venous reconstruction because patients with combined arterial and venous injuries are invariably in an extremely critical condition, and any procedures that prolong the operation or increase blood loss should be avoided. However, many authors recommend venous reconstruction with patch venoplasty or PTFE grafts, although there is no evidence of improved outcome with this approach.

Many patients with iliac vascular injuries develop extremity compartment syndrome and fasciotomy should be performed without delay, often before arterial reconstruction. However, the role of prophylactic fasciotomy is controversial and has been challenged by many authors. A prophylactic fasciotomy is a major procedure that is often associated with increased bleeding due to coagulopathy and increased venous pressures if an iliac vein ligation is performed.[51,52] If it is elected not to perform a fasciotomy, the patient should be monitored closely with frequent clinical examinations and compartment pressure measurements. Fasciotomy should be performed at the first signs of compartment syndrome.[47] Perioperative administration of mannitol may play a beneficial role in reducing the effects of reperfusion injury and inhibiting the development of compartment syndrome and the need for fasciotomy.[53,54]

Endovascular Management

Endovascular techniques may play an important role in selected cases with iliac artery injuries. Patients with false aneurysms, arteriovenous fistulae, or major intimal tears with or without thrombosis may benefit from angiographically placed endovascular stents or coils (Fig. 72-16).[55,56]

Mortality

The reported overall mortality varies from 30% to 50% in arterial injuries and 25% to 40% in venous injuries. In isolated iliac vascular injuries, the mortality is about 20% for arterial injuries and about 10% for venous injuries.[47]

Inferior Vena Cava Injuries

Anatomy

The IVC is formed by the confluence of the two common iliac veins in front of the L5 vertebra and underneath the right common iliac artery. It ascends over the spine to the right of the aorta, and at the level of the renal veins it

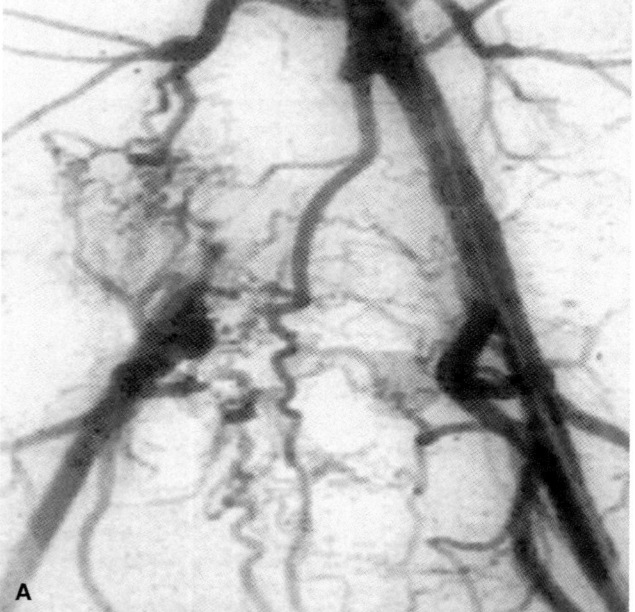

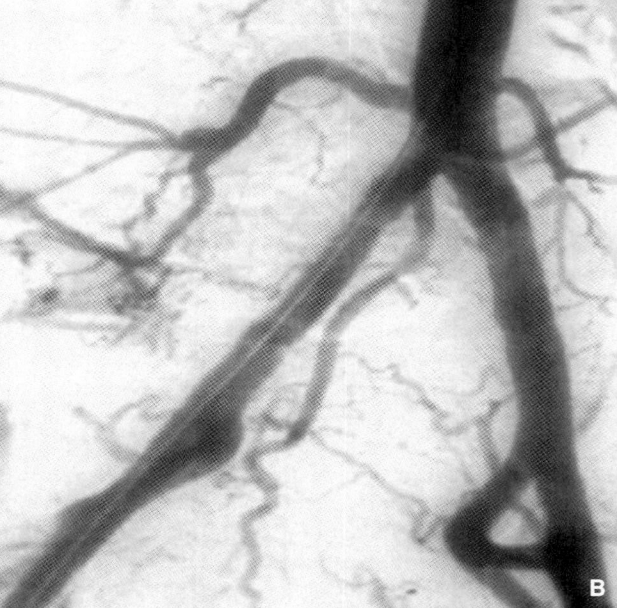

FIGURE 72-16 **A,** Right common iliac artery thrombosis in a 16-year-old patient following a motor vehicle injury. The diagnosis was made many months after the injury. **B,** The patient was managed with an angiographically placed endovascular stent.

deviates further to the right, courses behind the liver, crosses the diaphragm, and after a short course of 2 to 3 cm in the chest, it drains into the right atrium of the heart. In its course the IVC receives four or five pairs of lumbar veins, the right gonadal vein, the renal veins, the right adrenal vein, the hepatic veins, and the phrenic veins. All lumbar veins are below the renal veins, and between the renal veins and the hepatic veins except for the right adrenal vein there are no other venous branches. Besides the three major hepatic veins, there are an additional six to eight accessory veins inferiorly. Some of the accessory veins are large and may bleed profusely in case of injury or iatrogenic avulsion.

Epidemiology

The IVC is the most commonly injured abdominal vessel and accounts for about 25% of abdominal vascular injuries.[1] Blunt trauma is responsible for about 10% of IVC injuries, and it usually involves the retrohepatic part of the vein.[56] In about 18% of patients with penetrating IVC injuries, there is an associated aortic injury.[57]

Clinical Presentation

More than half of the patients with IVC injuries who reach hospital care are hypotensive, and about 18% require an emergency center thoracotomy.[57,58] Many patients with contained hematomas may be hemodynamically stable on admission. The diagnosis is almost always made intraoperatively.

Operative Management

Many injuries to the IVC, especially those involving the infrarenal IVC, present with stable hematomas. As a rule, all hematomas due to penetrating trauma should be explored. An exception to this approach is stable retrohepatic hematomas. Exploration of these hematomas is extremely difficult and may lead to uncontrollable hemorrhage and death. The infrarenal and juxtarenal IVC is best exposed by mobilization and medial rotation of the right colon, the hepatic flexure of the colon, and the duodenum (see Fig. 72-10). The exposure of the retrohepatic IVC is technically challenging and usually requires extensive mobilization of the liver by dividing its ligaments and by extending the incision to include a right subcostal incision or a right thoracotomy or a sternotomy. In my experience a subcostal incision provides an excellent exposure and is the preferred incision. A median sternotomy is performed if an atriocaval shunt is anticipated. These additional incisions should be considered only if perihepatic packing is not effective in controlling the hemorrhage. In cases where packing is not effective and the additional incisions are not sufficient for adequate visualization and repair of the IVC or the hepatic veins, other more radical maneuvers may be considered. Such maneuvers may include hepatic vascular isolation, an atriocaval shunt, or division of the liver.

Hepatic vascular isolation involves cross-clamping the infradiaphragmatic aorta, the suprahepatic IVC, the infrahepatic IVC above the renal veins, and the portal triad. Failure to clamp the aorta as a first step may result in severe hypotension and possible cardiac arrest owing to the reduced venous return following the occlusion of the IVC (Fig. 72-17). The suprarenal IVC can be cross-clamped in the space between the superior surface of the liver and the diaphragm. If a thoracotomy is performed, the IVC is controlled in the pericardium.[58] Despite the hepatic isolation, there is still back-bleeding.

The atriocaval shunt requires the placement of a tube through a pursestring in the appendage of the right atrium and directing it into the IVC, distal to the caval injury. Tourniquets should be applied around the intrapericardial IVC and the suprarenal IVC.[59] A large-bore thoracostomy tube or a large endotracheal tube with clamp occlusion of the proximal end and one or two holes, created to correspond with the endoatrial part of the tube, may be used as shunts. If an endotracheal tube is used, the inflated balloon can by used instead of a tourniquet around the suprarenal IVC. This is preferable to dissection around the IVC for the tourniquet placement. Although numerous reports highlighted the extremely poor results with atriocaval shunts, there have been a few survivals in cases where the shunt was used early. It is obviously a major escalation of the operation, but in the appropriate cases it should be employed early in the operation.

Some authors have recommended division of the liver along the gallbladder-IVC plane to provide direct exposure to the IVC. This approach increases bleeding, especially in the already coagulopathic patient, and should be avoided except in cases where the liver is severely injured and the IVC can be exposed with a brief dissection.

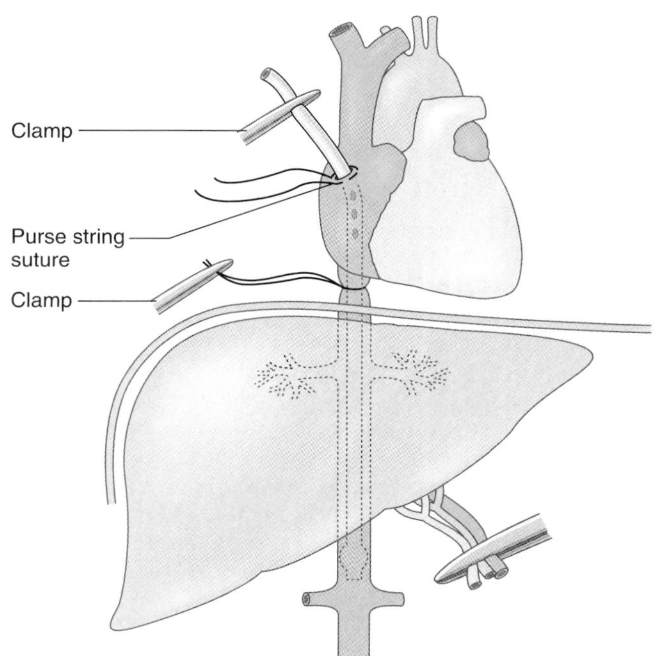

FIGURE 72-17 Atriocaval shunt for severe retrohepatic inferior vena cava (IVC) injuries: Placement of an endotracheal tube through a pursestring in the right atrial appendage and inflation of the cuff above the renal veins. A tourniquet is applied in the intrapericardiac IVC. Note the extra holes in the endoatrial part of the tube. This technique should be considered when liver packing does not control the hemorrhage.

In most patients the IVC can be repaired by lateral venorrhaphy with 3-0 or 4-0 vascular suture material. Most posterior caval wounds can be exposed and repaired by rotating the IVC. In some patients with anterior and posterior caval injuries, the posterior wound can be exposed and repaired from within the vein by extending the anterior wound. Ligation of the vein should be considered in hemodynamically very unstable patients with severe infrarenal injuries or when repair produces major stenosis. Ligation of the suprarenal IVC is not an acceptable option because it results in renal failure. In these cases a reconstruction of the vein with a patch or a ringed prosthetic graft may be attempted, although it is rarely successful because of the poor hemodynamic status of the patients. Postoperatively, patients with IVC ligation should have the lower extremities wrapped with firm elastic bandages and elevated. Most of them develop temporary edema that subsides within a few weeks. However, some patients develop extremity compartment syndrome and require fasciotomy.

In patients with severe IVC stenosis following lateral venorrhaphy, there is a risk of thrombosis and pulmonary embolism. If this cannot be avoided, caval filter or clips should be deployed above the site of stenosis.

Mortality

About half the patients with IVC injuries die before reaching medical care, and among those who arrive at the hospital with signs of life the mortality ranges between 20% and 57%.[56] In a study of 136 cases with IVC injuries Kuene and associates[56] reported an overall mortality of 52%. In patients reaching the operating room alive, the mortality was 35%. The mortality was significantly higher in suprarenal injuries.

Portal Vein System Injuries

Anatomy

The portal vein is 6 to 10 cm in length and is formed by the confluence of the SMV and the splenic vein behind the neck of the pancreas, to the right of L2, and to the left of the IVC. It passes behind the first part of the duodenum and enters the hepatoduodenal ligament. In the hepatoduodenal ligament it courses between and behind the common bile duct to the right and the hepatic artery to the left. In the hilum of the liver it splits into the right and left branches. The portal vein has no valves and provides about 80% of the hepatic blood flow. The SMV trunk crosses over the third part of the duodenum and the uncinate process of the pancreas. It then passes behind the neck of the pancreas where it joins the slightly smaller splenic vein to form the portal vein. The splenic vein courses along the superior border of the pancreas and drains the inferior mesenteric vein, just before the confluence with the SMV.

Epidemiology

Injury to the portal vein trunk is relatively rare and is found in about 1% of patients undergoing laparotomy for trauma.[60] It accounts for about 5% of all abdominal vascular injuries.[1] Injuries to the SMV account for about 11% and injuries to the splenic vein for about 4% of abdominal vascular injuries.[1] More than 90% of portal vein injuries are due to penetrating trauma.[60] Because of its close proximity to other major vessels, the incidence of associated vascular injuries is high, ranging from 70% to 90% of cases.[61]

Clinical Presentation

Most patients with penetrating injuries to the portal venous system present with signs of hemorrhagic shock and require emergency laparotomy. In blunt trauma the injury usually involves the SMV and is due to a direct blow to the abdomen or deceleration forces. These mechanisms often result in thrombosis of the vessels and occasionally avulsion and bleeding. In cases with thrombosis the diagnosis is delayed and is often made on abdominal CT scan.

Management

The operative findings usually include a combination of a local hematoma and various degrees of hemorrhage. Exposure of the retropancreatic portal vein and its major branches may be achieved by mobilization and medial rotation of the right colon and the hepatic flexure of the colon and extensive Kocher mobilization of the duodenum. However, this approach often does not provide satisfactory exposure, especially in the patient with associated injuries to the SMA. In these cases stapled division of the neck of the pancreas provides excellent exposure and should be considered early (Fig. 72-18). The suprapancreatic portal vein can be exposed by a combination of mobilization and medial rotation of the right colon and hepatic flexure and a Kocher maneuver.

Repair of the portal vein and the SMV should be performed if it can be achieved with lateral venorrhaphy. Complex reconstructive procedures, such as with interposition grafts, are rarely feasible or advisable because of the poor condition of the patients. About 80% of the cases have other associated vascular injuries that contribute to

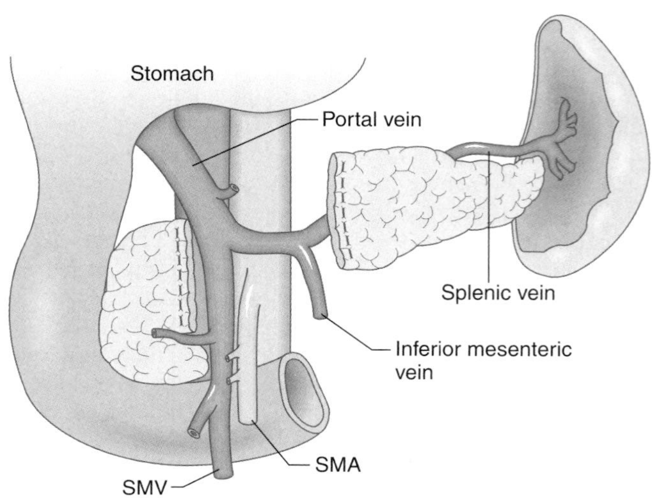

FIGURE 72-18 Stapled division of the neck of the pancreas provides a good exposure to the retropancreatic portal vein and the superior mesenteric vessels. SMA, superior mesenteric artery; SMV, superior mesenteric vein.

blood loss and coagulopathy. Complex reconstruction should be undertaken only in patients with associated hepatic artery injury that cannot be repaired. Ligation of both the portal vein and hepatic artery is not compatible with life. In these cases, reconstruction of the portal vein with a saphenous vein graft should be considered.[61]

Ligation of the portal vein with a patent hepatic artery is compatible with life, and the survival ranges from 55% to 85%.[62,63] Following ligation of the portal vein or the SMV the bowel will become massively edematous and patients can develop patchy bowel wall necrosis. The abdomen should never be closed primarily because without exception all patients develop ACS. Temporary abdominal wall closure with a prosthetic material should be performed. Second-look laparotomy should be performed in 48 to 72 hours to remove any abdominal packs and check the viability of the bowel. Postoperatively there is a need for massive fluid replacement because of sequestration in the splanchnic bed. In the next few days there is a significant improvement of the bowel edema due to enlargement of the collateral circulation and abdominal wall closure may become possible. Experience with long-term effects of portal ligation is limited, but there is evidence that most survivors do not develop portal hypertension.[60,62,63]

Mortality

The mortality in portal vein injuries is high and ranges between 50% and 72%.[1,62,63] Most patients have other major associated injuries, and it is difficult to assess the mortality directly related to isolated portal vein injuries.

■ ADVANCES IN ABDOMINAL VASCULAR INJURIES

There have been some significant advances in the management of abdominal vascular injuries in the last decade. The introduction of the policy of scoop and run and early surgical control of the bleeding has now become the standard of care and has improved the survival in vascular injuries. The concept of damage control has gained popularity and acceptance, and many patients with vascular injuries have been saved. The recognition of ACS and the use of temporary abdominal wall closure with a prosthetic material is also an important step in improving the outcome. Endovascular technology has revolutionized the management of selected patients with specific vascular occlusions, arteriovenous fistulae, and false aneurysms. Finally, research in new powerful hemostatic agents is promising and may have a major impact in the management of abdominal vascular injuries.

■ REFERENCES

1. Asensio TA, Chahwan S, Hanpeter D, et al: Operative management and outcomes of 302 abdominal vascular injuries. Am J Surg 180:528-534, 2000.
2. DeBakey ME, Simeone FA: Battle injuries of the arteries in World War II: An analysis of 2,471 cases. Ann Surg 123:534-579, 1946.
3. Rich NM, Baugh JH, Hughes CW: Acute arterial injuries in Vietnam: One thousand cases. J Trauma 10:359-369, 1970.
4. Demetriades D, Velmahos G, Cornwell EE, et al: Selective non-operative management of gunshot wounds of the anterior abdomen. Arch Surg 132:178-183, 1997.
5. Feliciano DV, Burch JM, Graham JM: Abdominal vascular injury. In Mattox KL, Feliciano DV, Moore EE (eds): Trauma, 4th ed. New York, McGraw-Hill, 2000, pp 783-806.
6. Cox EF: Blunt abdominal trauma: A 5-year analysis of 870 patients requiring celiotomy. Ann Surg 199:467-474, 1984.
7. Bickell WH, Wall MJ, Pepe PE, et al: Immediate versus delayed fluid resuscitation for hypotensive patients with penetrating torso trauma. N Engl J Med 27:1105-1109, 1994.
8. Dutton RP, Mackenzie CF, Scalea TM: Hypotensive resuscitation during active hemorrhage: Impact on in-hospital mortality. J Trauma 52:1141-1146, 2002.
9. Stern SA, Dronen SC, Birrer P, Wang X: Effect of blood pressure on hemorrhage volume and survival in a near-fatal hemorrhage model incorporating a vascular injury. Ann Emerg Med 22:155-163, 1993.
10. Bickell WH, Bruttig SC, Millnamow GA, et al: The detrimental effects of intravenous crystalloid after aortotomy in swine. Surgery 110:529-536, 1991.
11. Capone AC, Safar P, Stezoski SW, et al: Improved outcome with fluid restriction in treatment of uncontrolled hemorrhagic shock. J Am Coll Surg 180:49-56, 1995.
12. Leppaniemi A, Solter R, Burris D, et al: Fluid resuscitation in a model of uncontrolled hemorrhage: Too much too early, or too little too late? J Surg Res 63:413-418, 1996.
13. Ledgerwood AM, Kazmers M, Lucas CE: The role of thoracic aortic occlusion for massive hemoperitoneum. J Trauma 16:610-615, 1976.
14. Millikan JS, Moore EE: Outcome of resuscitative thoracotomy and descending aortic occlusion performed in the operating room. J Trauma 24:387-392, 1984.
15. Brotman S, Oster-Granite M, Cox EF: Failure of cross-clamping the thoracic aorta to control intra-abdominal bleeding. Ann Emerg Med 11:147-148, 1982.
16. Fry WR, Fry EE, Fry WJ: Operative exposure of the abdominal arteries for trauma. Arch Surg 126:289-291, 1991.
17. Voellinger DC, Saddakni S, Melton SM, et al: Endovascular repair of a traumatic infrarenal aortic dissection: A case report and review. Vasc Surg 35:385-389, 2001.
18. Inaba K, Kirkpatrick AW, Finkelstein J, et al: Blunt abdominal aortic trauma in association with thoracolumbar spine fractures. Injury 32:201-207, 2001.
19. Lock JS, Huffman AD, Johnson RC: Blunt trauma to the abdominal aorta. J Trauma 27:674-677, 1987.
20. Naude GP, Back M, Perry MO, Bongard FS: Blunt disruption of the abdominal aorta: Report of a case and review of the literature. J Vasc Surg 25:931-935, 1997.
21. Demetriades D, Theodorou D, Murray J, et al: Mortality and prognostic factors in penetrating injuries of the aorta. J Trauma 40:761-763, 1996.
22. Lopez-Viego MA, Snyder WH, Valentine RJ, Clagett GP: Penetrating abdominal aortic trauma: A report of 129 cases. J Vasc Surg 16:332-335, 1992.
23. Accola KD, Feliciano DV, Mattox KL, et al: Management of injuries to the suprarenal aorta Am J Surg 154:613-618, 1987.
24. Picard E, Marty-Ane CH, Vernhet H, et al: Endovascular management of traumatic infrarenal abdominal aortic dissection. Ann Vasc Surg 12:515-521, 1998.
25. Vernhet H, Marty-Ane CH, Lesnik A, et al: Dissection of the abdominal aorta in blunt trauma: Management by percutaneous stent placement. Cardiovasc Intervent Radiol 20:473-476, 1997.
26. Degiannis E, Levy RD, Florizone MG, et al: Gunshot injuries of the abdominal aorta: A continuing challenge. Injury 28:195-197, 1997.
27. Asensio JA, Forno W, Roldan G, et al: Visceral vascular injuries. Surg Clin North Am 82:1-20, 2002.
28. Mullins RJ, Huckfeldt R, Trunkey DD: Abdominal vascular injuries. Surg Clin North Am 76:813-832, 1996.
29. Asensio JA, Berne JD, Chahwan S, et al: Traumatic injury to the superior mesenteric artery. Am J Surg 178:235-239, 1999.

30. Accola KD, Feliciano DV, Mattox KL, et al: Management of injuries to the superior mesenteric artery. J Trauma 26:313-319, 1986.
31. Reilly PM, Rotondo MF, Carpenter JP, et al: Temporary vascular continuity during damage control: Intraluminal shunting for proximal superior mesenteric artery injury. J Trauma 39:757-760, 1995.
32. Lucas AE, Richardson JD, Flint LM, Polk HC: Traumatic injury of the proximal superior mesenteric artery. Ann Surg 193:30-34, 1981.
33. Sirinek KR, Gaskill HV, Root HD, Levine BA: Truncal vascular injury: Factors influencing survival. J Trauma 23:372-377, 1983.
34. Bruce LM, Croce MA, Santaniello JM, et al: Blunt renal artery injury: Incidence, diagnosis, and management. Am Surg 67:550-556, 2001.
35. Haas CA, Sprinak JP: Traumatic renal artery occlusion: A review of the literature. Tech Urol 4:1-11, 1998.
36. Spinak JP, Resnick MI: Revascularization of traumatic thrombosis of the renal artery. Surg Gynecol Obstet 164:22-26, 1987.
37. Clark DE, Georgitis JW, Ray FS: Renal arterial injuries caused by blunt trauma. Surgery 90:87-96, 1981.
38. Tillou A, Romero J, Asensio JA, et al: Renal vascular injuries. Surg Clin North Am 81:1417-1430, 2001.
39. Velmahos GC, Demetriades D, Cornwell EE, et al: Selective management of renal gunshot wounds. Br J Surg 85:1121-1124, 1998.
40. Lock JS, Carraway RP, Hudson HC, Laws ML: Proper management of renal artery injury from blunt trauma. South Med J 78:406-410, 1985.
41. Maggio AJ, Brosman S: Renal artery trauma. Urology 11:125-130, 1978.
42. Villas PA, Cohen G, Putnam SG: Wallstent placement in a renal artery after blunt abdominal trauma. J Trauma 46:1137-1139, 1999.
43. Sprouse LR II, Hamilton IN Jr: The endovascular treatment of a renal arteriovenous fistula: Placement of covered stent. Vasc Surg 36:1066-1068, 2002.
44. Lee JT, White RA: Endovascular management of blunt traumatic renal artery dissection. J Endovasc Ther 9:354-358, 2002.
45. Hughes CW: Arterial repair during the Korean War. Ann Surg 147:555-561, 1958.
46. Bongard FS, Dubrow T, Klein SR: Vascular injuries in the urban battleground: Experience at a metropolitan trauma center. Ann Vasc Surg 4:415-418, 1990.
47. Demetriades D, Murray JA, Asensio JA: In Rich N, Mattox KL, Hirshberg A (eds): Vascular Trauma. Philadelphia, Saunders; 2004, pp 339-351.
48. Kennedy F, Cornwell EE, Lockett C, Demetriades D: Blunt injury to the left common iliac artery, Am Surg 61:360-362, 1995.
49. Burch JM, Richardson RJ, Martin RR, Mattox KL: Penetrating iliac vascular injuries: Recent experience with 233 consecutive patients. J Trauma 30:1450-1459, 1990.
50. Lee JT, Bongard FS: Iliac vessel injuries. Surg Clin North Am 82:21-48, 2002.
51. Velmahos GC, Theodorou D, Demetriades D, et al: Complications and nonclosure rates of fasciotomy for trauma and related risk factors. World J Surg 21:247-253, 1997.
52. Shah DM, Bock DE, Darling RC, et al: Beneficial effects of hypertonic mannitol in acute ischemia-reperfusion injuries in humans. Cardiovasc Surg 4:97-100, 1996.
53. Oredsson S, Plate G, Qvarfordt P: The effect of mannitol on reperfusion injury and postischemic compartment pressure in skeletal muscle. Eur J Surg 8:326-331, 1994.
54. Balogh Z, Voros E, Suveges G, Simonka JA: Stent-graft treatment of an external iliac artery injury associated with pelvic fractures: A case report, J Bone Joint Surg Am 85:919-922, 2003.
55. Lyden SP, Srivastava SD, Waldman DL, Green RM: Common iliac artery dissection after blunt trauma: Case report of endovascular repair and literature review. J Trauma 50:339-342, 2001.
56. Kuene J, Frankhouse J, Modrall G, et al: Determinants of survival after inferior vena cava trauma. Am Surg 65:976-981, 1999.
57. Buckman RF, Pathak AS, Badelino MM, Bradley KM: Injuries of the inferior vena cava. Surg Clin North Am 81:1431-1447, 2001.
58. Yellin AE, Chaffee, Donovan AJ: Vascular isolation in the treatment of juxtahepatic venous injuries. Arch Surg 102:566-573, 1971.
59. Shrock T, Blaisdell FW, Mathewson C: Management of blunt trauma to the liver and hepatic veins. Arch Surg 95:698-704, 1968.
60. Mattox KL, Espada R, Beall AR: Traumatic injury to the portal vein. Ann Surg 181:519-522, 1975.
61. Buckman RF, Pathak AS, Badelino MM, Bradley KM: Portal vein injuries. Surg Clin North Am 81:1449-1462, 2001.
62. Pachter HL, Drager S, Godfrey N, Lefleur R: Traumatic injuries in the portal vein: The role of acute ligation. Ann Surg 189:383-385, 1979.
63. Stone HH, Fabian TC, Turkelson ML: Wounds of the portal venous system. World J Surg 6:335-341, 1982.

Chapter 73

Vascular Injuries of the Extremities

VINCENT L. ROWE, MD, FACS
ALBERT E. YELLIN, MD, FACS
FRED A. WEAVER, MD, FACS

Approximately 90% of all peripheral arterial injuries occur in an extremity. Civilian studies report the majority of arterial injuries to be in the upper extremity, whereas the military experience defines lower extremity injuries to be more common.[81] During World War II, extremity arterial injuries were routinely ligated. For popliteal artery injury, the amputation rate was 73%.[19] The poor results of arterial ligation prompted Hughes[49] to perform formal repair of peripheral arterial injuries during the Korean War. Rich and associates reported further refinements of arterial repair during the Vietnam War, decreasing the amputation rate for popliteal artery injuries to 32%.[82] Continuing refinements in arterial surgery over the ensuing 3 decades have reduced limb loss in most civilian series to less than 10% to 15%.[70,102,103] However, long-term disability, predominantly resulting from associated skeletal and nerve injuries, remains a persistent problem for 20% to 50% of patients.[106]

■ MECHANISM OF INJURY

The initial and ultimate outcome of vascular injury depend in large part on the wounding agent or mechanism of injury (see Chapter 69). Determining the mechanism of injury is of utmost importance if the surgeon is to use available diagnostic and treatment options appropriately. Peripheral vascular injuries in an urban environment most often result from penetrating trauma from knives or bullets. In a recent series of penetrating injuries, arterial injuries were due to gunshot wounds in 64%, knife wounds in 24%, and shotgun blasts in 12%.[77]

With increasing frequency, high-velocity firearms are the causative agent in civilian vascular trauma. In addition to the vascular injury, extensive associated musculoskeletal injury is commonplace. Vascular injuries in this setting result from the dissipation of energy into the surrounding tissues, fragmentation of the projectile or of bone, or the blast effect.[28] Experimental studies have demonstrated a positive correlation between muzzle velocity and the microscopic extent and "length" of damage to the vessel wall.[3] In many ways these wounds mimic lower velocity shotgun injuries in their devastating combination of penetrating and blunt tissue injury.[67]

Motor vehicle accidents and falls are the most common causes of blunt injury and are becoming more frequent, owing to the ever-increasing mobility of modern society.[3,110] The morbidity of blunt vascular injuries can be magnified by associated fractures, dislocations, and crush injuries to muscles and nerves.

■ DIAGNOSTIC EVALUATION

Extremity arterial injuries have varied clinical presentations. A few patients present with obvious clinical evidence, or "hard signs," of arterial disruption such as pulsatile external bleeding, an enlarging hematoma, absent distal pulses, or an ischemic limb (Table 73-1). For patients with overt signs of arterial injury, immediate surgical exploration in the operating room without further diagnostic testing is preferred. In most instances, when arteriography is required, an intraoperative arteriogram is sufficient to identify the location and extent of injury and to guide the surgical repair.

Most arterial injuries, however, are clinically occult and pose a diagnostic challenge if they are to be identified. The diagnostic approach has changed substantially since the Korean War. Initially, the severity of soft tissue destruction typical of military wounds prompted the recommendation that all penetrating extremity wounds in proximity to a neurovascular bundle be explored routinely. When applied to civilian injuries, this practice detected normal intact vessels in a large percentage of cases, up to 84% in one series.[41] These patients had undergone expensive, nontherapeutic operations, which occasionally resulted in additional morbidity.

Table 73-1 Traumatic Vascular Injury

HARD SIGNS	SOFT SIGNS
Observed pulsatile bleeding	Significant hemorrhage by history
Arterial thrill by manual palpation	Neurologic abnormality
Bruit auscultated over or near area of arterial injury	Diminished pulse compared to contralateral extremity
Absent distal pulse	In proximity to bony injury or penetrating wound
Visible expanding hematoma	

With the appearance of readily available arteriography in most trauma centers, this diagnostic modality supplanted wound exploration, and screening ("exclusion") arteriography became routine and widespread. Like wound exploration, mandatory or routine screening arteriography for proximity wounds, in the absence of other suspicious clinical findings, resulted in a large proportion of normal arteriograms (90%), at significant cost. In addition, arteriograms were found to be less than perfect, having a low, but real, incidence of false-negative and false-positive findings. Because of its invasive nature and the potential nephrotoxicity of contrast media, arteriography also occasionally results in serious complications, thus increasing patient morbidity and further increasing the cost of care.

It is now widely accepted that selective rather than routine arteriography is appropriate for patients who may have an occult extremity arterial injury. Several studies have documented that a selective use of arteriography is appropriate and safe.[1,15,22,109] In a study designed to determine the diagnostic yield of arteriography when performed for proximity alone or for signs suggestive of an arterial injury,[109] 373 patients with a unilateral penetrating injury to an upper extremity (distal to the deltopectoral groove) or lower extremity (distal to the inguinal ligament) were evaluated during an 18-month period. Arteriograms were obtained when a distal pulse deficit, neurologic deficit, hematoma, history of hemorrhage or hypotension, bruit, fracture, major soft tissue injury, or delayed capillary refill was present *or*, in the absence of these findings, when the path of the penetrating object was judged to run close to a major neurovascular bundle. For 210 of the 373 patients, Doppler pressures in the injured and the uninjured contralateral extremity were obtained and indexed using the brachial Doppler pressure of an uninjured arm as a reference (ankle-arm [brachial] index [ABI]). The minimum ABI (MABI), defined as the lower of the two ABIs at the ankle or wrist, was recorded. Of the 373 patients, 216 presented with one or more abnormal physical findings, and arterial injury was identified arteriographically in 65 (30%). Proximity was the sole indication for arteriography in 157 patients, and an injury was identified in 17 (11%). Only a pulse deficit, neurologic deficit, or shotgun injury correlated ($P < .05$) with arteriographic evidence of an arterial injury. The presence of one or more of these variables identified a high-risk group of 104 patients who had 40 injuries (38%), 15 of which required repair. An intermediate-risk group consisting of patients with an MABI less than 1.00 or with "soft signs" of arterial injury (fracture, hematoma, bruit, decreased capillary refill, history of hemorrhage, hypotension, or soft tissue injury) was identified, 20% (33/165) of whom had an arterial injury. Five of 33 injuries in the intermediate-risk group required intervention. A low-risk group of 104 patients with none of these findings remained. Nine injuries were identified (9%) in this low-risk group, none of which required therapeutic intervention.

A follow-up study further investigated the ability of Doppler indices to detect occult arterial injuries in a consecutive cohort of 514 patients with unilateral, isolated penetrating extremity injuries.[85] Arteriography was limited to patients in the high-risk (pulse deficit, neurologic deficit, shotgun injury) or intermediate-risk group (one or more "soft" signs or an MABI less than 1.00). Low-risk patients were observed for 24 hours and then discharged if stable. Twenty-two (4%) patients with limb-threatening ischemia or ongoing hemorrhage who required immediate operation and 23 (4%) patients who refused arteriography were excluded from analysis. Of the remaining 469 patients, 213 (45%) were at low risk, 151 (32%) at intermediate risk, and 105 (23%) at high risk for arterial injury. No complication developed in any patient with a low-risk profile during the 24-hour observation period. Arteriography identified injuries in 26% of patients in the intermediate-risk group and 36% in the high-risk group. All patients with a major arterial injury had either a pulse deficit or MABI below 1.00.

A selective use of angiography in evaluation of patients with penetrating extremity trauma was recently confirmed by Conrad and colleagues.[15] Five hundred thirty-eight patients were reviewed retrospectively. Similar to previous studies, angiography was limited to patients presenting with an abnormal pulse examination or Doppler indices less than 1.0. Patients with a normal physical examination and Doppler indices of 1.0 or greater were discharged home without further work-up. Four angiograms were performed with no change in patient management. Three hundred patients with asymptomatic proximity wounds and normal physical examination were discharged home. Fifty-one percent of these discharged patients were available for an average follow-up of 9.8 months. There were no missed injuries or late complications identified in the group.

For blunt extremity trauma, the indications for arteriography parallel what has been established for penetrating injuries. A prospective study analyzed the results of arteriography in 53 patients with unilateral blunt lower extremity trauma.[4] Thirty-one patients had physical findings suggestive of an arterial injury, and an arterial injury was demonstrated in 15 patients. A pulse deficit or decreased capillary refill correlated significantly ($P < .05$) with arteriographic evidence of injury. Of the 15 arterial injuries, 12 were found in patients who had one or both of these findings and four of those injuries required repair. In the remaining 22 patients with neither a pulse deficit nor decreased capillary refill, three minor injuries were found, none of which required repair.

Another series of blunt injuries focused specifically on 115 patients with knee dislocations.[97] Popliteal artery injury was demonstrated arteriographically in 27 (23%) of 115 patients. An abnormal pedal pulse identified popliteal artery injuries with sensitivity of 85% and specificity of 93%. All injuries that required intervention were associated with a diminished pulse. Dennis and coworkers reported an identical experience in 37 patients with knee dislocations.[21] In all patients who required popliteal repair, pedal pulses were absent. More recently, Abou-Sayed and Berger confirmed the sensitivity of physical examination in 52 patients with blunt popliteal artery injuries.[1] Twenty-three patients with a normal pulse examination did not undergo angiography and required no vascular interventions. Angiography was performed in 13 patients with normal pulse examinations (at the discretion of the attending surgeon); similarly, no clinically significant lesions were identified that required intervention. Again, the assertion that the clinical examination can define a subset of high-risk patients who need an arteriogram, and possibly surgical repair, was validated.

Similar evidence for the reliability of the clinical examination combined with noninvasive pressure measurements has been provided by Lynch and Johansen.[63] In a series of 100 patients with blunt or penetrating limb trauma, all patients had ABIs measured and were studied by arteriography. Arterial injuries that required intervention were discovered in 14 cases, and an ABI less than 0.90 predicted the injury with 87% sensitivity and 97% specificity. Because two of the arteriogram results were false positive, sensitivity and specificity of ABI less than 0.90 were even higher—95% and 97%, respectively—when clinical outcome was the standard.

Based on these published reports, a consensus has developed that a patient with a penetrating or blunt injury who has a normal extremity pulse examination and MABI of 1.00 or more does not require arteriography. A period of observation for 12 to 24 hours is all that is necessary. Furthermore, all clinically significant arterial injuries are found in extremities in association with a distal pulse deficit or an MABI less than 1.00. It is in this group of patients that diagnostic arteriography is useful and has its greatest yield.

Finally, although careful physical examination and pressure measurements appropriately select most patients (>95%) who have significant arterial injury and require arteriography, occasional injuries are missed. In most cases, however, the missed injuries are clinically unimportant and include occlusive and nonocclusive injuries to minor branch vessels and minimal nonocclusive injuries of major vessels that heal without specific intervention, among others.[21,35,93] With these principles in mind, the diagnostic algorithm shown in Figure 73-1 was constructed.[47]

Because of continued improvements in noninvasive vascular imaging, color-flow duplex (CFD) ultrasonography has been suggested as a substitute for or complement to arteriography.[69] CFD ultrasonography has several obvious advantages. It is noninvasive and painless. It is portable and can easily be brought to the patient's bedside or the emergency department or operating room. Repeated and follow-up examinations are easily performed without morbidity and are relatively inexpensive.

Bynoe and colleagues[11] reported sensitivity of 95%, specificity of 99%, and accuracy of 98% when CFD was used to evaluate blunt and penetrating injuries of the neck or extremities, and Fry and coworkers[34] documented 100% sensitivity and 97.3% specificity in a similar series. In these two studies, however, a comparison arteriogram was available for only a few patients. Bergstein and associates reported on 67 patients who had 75 penetrating extremity injuries, all of whom underwent both CFD and arteriography.[8] Using arteriography as the "gold standard," CFD had two false-negative results and one false-positive (sensitivity 50%, specificity 99%) result. Gagne and coworkers published a series of 37 patients with proximity injuries in 43 extremities.[37] Arteriography identified three injuries to the deep femoral, superficial femoral, and posterior tibial arteries that were not identified by CFD; however, CFD did detect a superficial femoral artery intimal flap that arteriography missed.

Despite some uncertainty about the ability of CFD to detect all arterial injuries, these reports suggest that

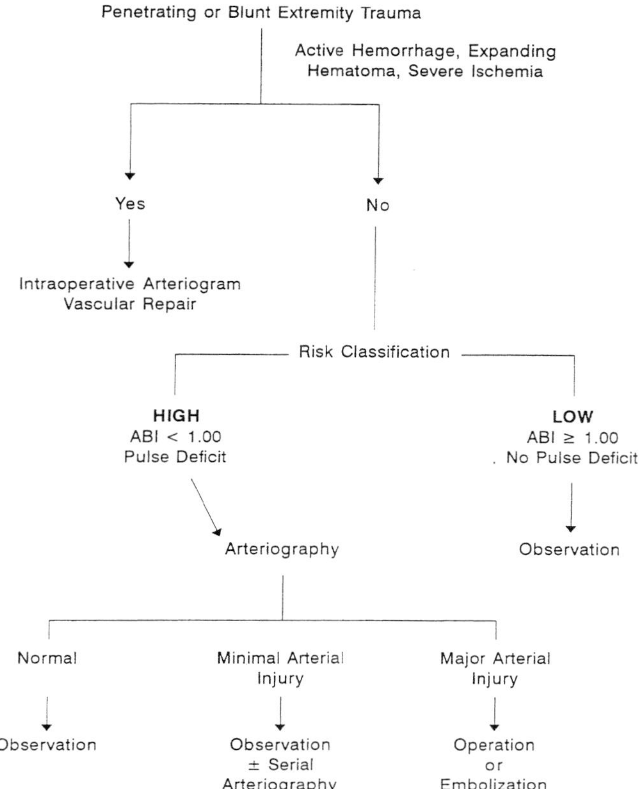

FIGURE 73-1 Diagnostic algorithm for extremity arterial trauma. ABI, ankle-brachial index. (From Hood DB, Yellin AE, Weaver FA: Vascular trauma. In Dean R [ed]: Current Vascular Surgical Diagnosis and Treatment. Norwalk, CT, Appleton & Lange, 1995, p 405.)

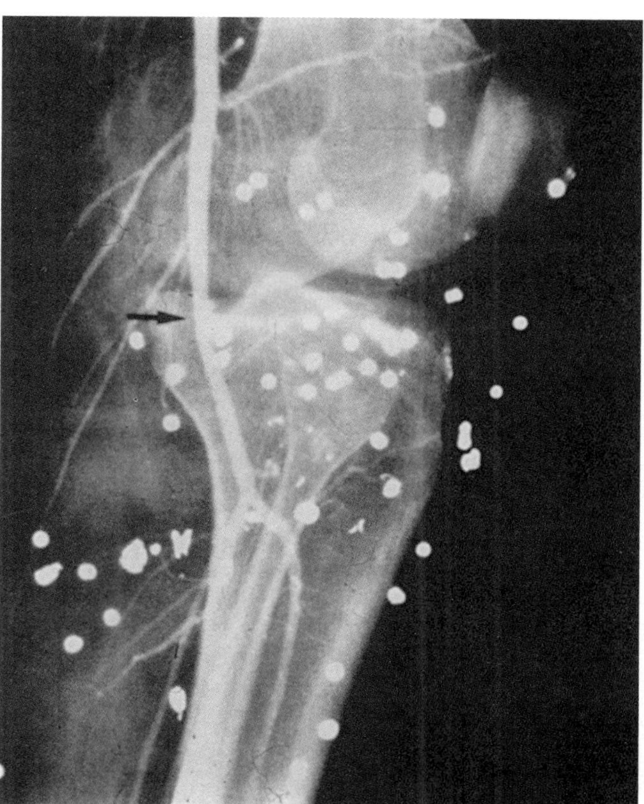

FIGURE 73-2 Popliteal artery shotgun injury with a small false aneurysm *(arrow)*, which was managed nonoperatively.

nearly all major injuries that require therapeutic intervention can be identified, potentially at considerable cost savings as compared with arteriography.[69] Ordog and coworkers have estimated a multimillion dollar cost savings if CFD and outpatient follow-up, rather than arteriography and inpatient observation, were used to exclude extremity arterial injuries.[75]

Our own experience with CFD ultrasonography in the evaluation of extremity trauma has produced an important caveat: CFD is highly operator dependent and, to be used effectively, requires an institutional investment in experienced vascular technologists and interpreting physicians.[86] This expense could be lessened over the long term if the current effort to train surgeons in the use of diagnostic ultrasound for intracavitary trauma were extended to include extremity vessels.

Magnetic resonance angiography (MRA) has increased in popularity for the diagnosis of vascular disorders; however, application to trauma patients is not widely accepted. Compared with other modalities, MRA has the advantages of imaging multiple anatomic areas simultaneously and being noninvasive, preventing the need for contrast agents. Unfortunately, MRA is not easily accessible in most hospitals, and the presence of metallic orthopedic instrumentation limits widespread usage for trauma patients.[84]

TREATMENT OF ARTERIAL INJURIES

Nonoperative Management

The management of minimal, nonocclusive, clinically asymptomatic arterial injuries detected by arteriography remains controversial (Fig. 73-2).[108] Some surgeons continue to insist that all detected arterial injuries should be repaired, whereas we[93] and others[21,35] have proposed using a nonoperative approach when the following clinical and radiologic criteria are present:

- Low-velocity injury
- Minimal arterial wall disruption (<5 mm) for intimal defects and pseudoaneurysms
- Adherent or downstream protrusion of intimal flaps
- Intact distal circulation
- No active hemorrhage

When, for a given injury, this approach is selected, follow-up vascular imaging is advisable to document healing or stabilization. Knudson's group has suggested that CFD may be used in lieu of arteriography for serial follow-up.[59]

In a study by Stain and coworkers, 24 nonocclusive minimal arterial injuries were managed nonoperatively and subsequently studied arteriographically at 1 to 12 weeks after injury.[93] Resolution, improvement, or stabilization of the injury occurred in 21 injuries (87%). Progression was noted in three, and only one required repair. There were no cases of acute thrombosis or distal embolization. A similar experience in a group of patients with minimal arterial injuries identified on diagnostic arteriography was reported by Frykberg.[35] Resolution or stability of detected injuries occurred in 89% of the cases during 27 months' follow-up. Frykberg's follow-up has now been extended to 10 years with comparable excellent results, further confirming the wisdom of this approach.[21]

Endovascular Management

Transcatheter embolization with coils or balloons can be used to manage selected arterial injuries, such as low-flow arteriovenous fistulae, false aneurysms, and active bleeding from noncritical arteries, particularly in remote anatomic sites. Coils are particularly useful for occluding bleeding vessels and arteriovenous fistulae (Fig. 73-3). Currently available coils are made from stainless steel and are wool or Dacron tufted. Introduced via a 5- or 7-French catheter, they can be extruded at the vessel site that requires occlusion. Once deployed, the coils expand and lodge at the site of extrusion. The Dacron or wool tuft promotes thrombosis of the vessel. If flow persists 5 minutes after deployment, a second coil is introduced. For arteriovenous fistulae, the coil embolus is placed across the fistula and lodged just on the venous side, so that the fistulous connection is occluded but the supplying artery remains patent. If this is not possible, the next option is to occlude the arterial side of the fistula, preferably by isolating the fistula site with proximal and distal coils. The diameter of the coil must be approximately the same as the diameter of the artery to be embolized; otherwise, it may dislodge and embolize peripherally or centrally.

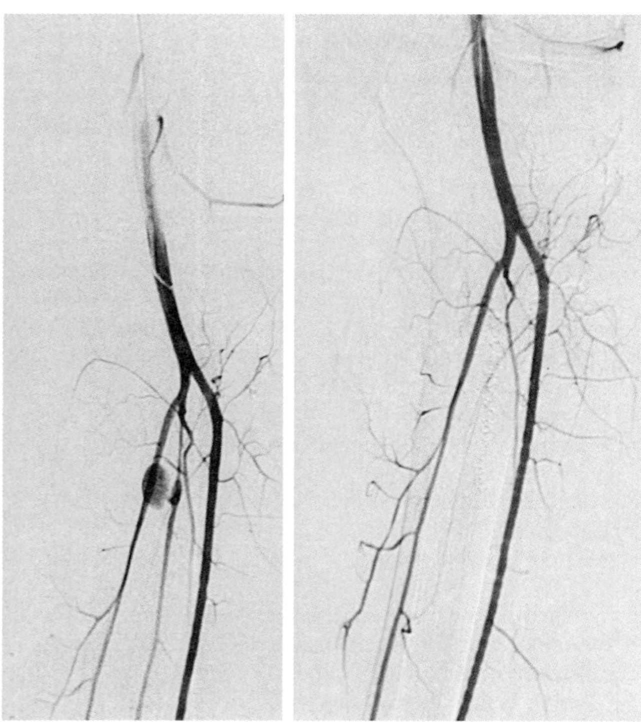

FIGURE 73-3 A large peroneal artery false aneurysm *(left)* was successfully treated by coil embolization *(right)*.

McNeese and associates reported 11 patients with post-traumatic arteriovenous fistulae, arterial false aneurysms, or uncontrolled bleeding from noncritical vessels that were treated by embolization.[68] Eight patients were treated by wire coil embolization or gelatin clot emboli and one with selective injection of barium-impregnated silicone-like (Silastic) beads sized to the vessel lumen. The last technique was found to be useful in treating arteriovenous fistulae fed by multiple small arteries. Four of the six fistulae were permanently obliterated. Ischemia distal to an obliterated vessel did not occur, and no major complications directly related to the embolization were reported.

Another endovascular approach to extremity injuries uses stent-graft technology. By combining a fixation device such as a stent with a graft, endoluminal repair of false aneurysms or large arteriovenous fistulae is possible. Marin and coworkers reported the successful treatment of seven vascular injuries by stent-grafts placed endoluminally.[65] Since this early study, numerous small series and anecdotal reports have documented successful management of traumatic arterial injuries with covered stents.[83,88,95,114] In centers with sufficient experience and available personnel to perform the procedure expediently, endovascular treatment of arterial lesions should be considered, especially in high-risk patients with multiple concomitant injuries. As more operating suites transform into high-resolution fluoroscopic units and surgeons become more adept in endovascular treatment modalities, expeditious diagnosis and management of traumatic arterial injuries should be expected in the future.

Operative Management

The operative management of a peripheral arterial injury requires preparation and draping of the entire injured extremity. In addition, a contralateral uninjured lower or upper extremity should be included in the operative field in the event that repair requires an autogenous vein graft. In most instances, extremity incisions are placed longitudinally, directly over the injured vessel and extended proximally or distally as necessary. Proximal and distal arterial control is obtained prior to exposure of the injury. When proximal control of the traumatized vessel is problematic, as in some axillary and subclavian injuries, endoluminal balloon occlusion of the proximal artery via catheters placed under fluoroscopic guidance from a remote arterial site can provide temporary control. Occasionally, a proximally placed pneumatic tourniquet may help minimize operative blood loss.

Once control is established, injured vessels are débrided to macroscopically normal arterial wall. Fogarty catheters should be passed gently, both proximal and distal to the arterial injury, to remove any intraluminal thrombus. It is extremely important not to overinflate the balloon lest the endothelial lining be damaged and arterial spasm or thrombosis result. Both proximal and distal arterial lumina are flushed with heparinized saline solution. Systemic heparinization, particularly for popliteal artery injuries, is a helpful adjunct to prevent thrombosis or thrombus propagation when systemic anticoagulation is not contraindicated.[70,102] Temporary intraluminal shunting may also be of value for some injuries when the limb is severely ischemic and revascularization will be delayed because of fracture fixation, complex soft tissue injury, or associated life-threatening injuries.[27,30,73] This technique allows early restoration of limb perfusion, which lessens the likelihood of ischemic damage and distal thrombosis. Débridement, fasciotomy, fracture fixation, neurorrhaphy, or vein repair can then be performed in a deliberate and unhurried fashion, before arterial reconstruction.

The type of repair is dictated by the extent of arterial damage. Repair of injured vessels can be accomplished by lateral suture patch angioplasty, end-to-end anastomosis, or interposition graft or, when adjacent soft injury is extensive, a bypass graft. Extra-anatomic bypass grafts are useful in patients with associated extensive soft tissue injury or sepsis. Stain and colleagues reported on three axillofemoral, four femorofemoral, one obturator, and one extra-anatomic femoropopliteal graft performed in nine patients who had extensive soft tissue injuries.[92] Seven patients (78%) had functional extremities salvaged.

Autogenous vein grafts were first used successfully to repair arterial injuries during the Korean War.[49] Later development of prosthetic graft material—expanded polytetrafluoroethylene (ePTFE)—made possible routine use of prosthetic conduits as a substitute for autogenous grafts. Surgical experience suggests that ePTFE is more resistant to infection than other prosthetic grafts and has acceptable patency rates when used in the above-knee position.[100,101]

In a retrospective civilian series of 188 patients with lower extremity vascular trauma, Martin and colleagues reported equivalent patencies when ePTFE and vein grafts were used to repair the iliac, femoral, and superficial femoral arteries.[66] There were no infections of ePTFE or vein grafts. A significant difference in immediate patency was apparent; however, when the distal arterial anastomosis was at or below the popliteal artery, failure was more common in patients with ePTFE grafts. Blunt trauma was associated with a higher graft failure rate (35%) than was penetrating trauma (1.2%), and graft failure always resulted in amputation. Similarly, in a series of 550 patients with lower extremity traumatic arterial injuries, Hafez and associates identified the following significant independent risk factors for amputation after arterial repair: occluded bypass graft, combined above- and below-knee injury, a tense compartment, arterial transection, and associated compound fracture.[43]

We believe that the greater saphenous vein harvested from the uninjured extremity provides the most durable arterial repair. Despite the transient nature of trauma patients, Dorweiler and coworkers recently documented an 81% patency rate at a mean follow-up of 59 months in patients with vein grafts used to repair extremity arterial injuries.[25] ePTFE grafts are reserved for use only when autogenous vein is inadequate or unavailable, when the patient is unstable and expeditious repair of the arterial injury is mandatory, or when a large size discrepancy between a vein graft and the native artery would result.

Monofilament 5-0 or 6-0 sutures are suitable for most peripheral vascular repairs, and all completed repairs should be tension free and covered by viable soft tissue. With major soft tissue injury, it may be prudent to enlist the assistance of a plastic or orthopedic reconstructive surgeon to rotate a muscle flap adequate for soft tissue coverage. We consider intraoperative completion arteriography or duplex scanning to be mandatory to document technical perfection of the vascular reconstruction, visualize arterial runoff, and detect persistent missed distal thrombi. Intra-arterial vasodilators such as papaverine or tolazoline may be helpful, particularly in the pediatric age group, in reversing severe spasm in the distal arterial tree or the repaired arterial segment.

The period immediately following limb reperfusion has been recognized to be an important determinant of ultimate outcome after injury. During reperfusion, toxic oxygen-derived free radicals are generated that overwhelm inherent protective enzyme-scavenging systems such as superoxide dismutase, glutathione peroxidase, and catalase, producing cell injury and death. Viewed clinically, these effects are manifested by the accelerated muscle edema and necrosis seen in compartmental hypertension. Experimentally, superoxide dismutase, catalase, mannitol, and allopurinol can interrupt this pathogenetic cascade at various levels and protect against reperfusion injury; decreased muscle necrosis and edema are observed in animals pretreated with these agents.[74]

Wright and colleagues documented similar benefits in animals pretreated with heparin before reperfusion of an ischemic limb.[113] In addition to the experimental evidence that heparin has a mitigating effect on reperfusion injury, its beneficial effects include prevention of thrombosis of distal outflow vessels and collaterals. In fact, a retrospective review of 150 patients with lower extremity arterial injuries documented that the incidence of limb loss was significantly higher in patients who developed compartment syndrome (41% vs. 7% without) or did not receive perioperative anticoagulation (15% vs. 3% with).[42] For all these reasons, the surgeon must be aware of the deleterious effects of reperfusion injury, and systemic mannitol and/or heparin infusion should be considered before an ischemic limb is reperfused. The clinical manifestation of reperfusion injury (i.e., compartmental hypertension) must be sought assiduously and treated aggressively.[52]

Specific Arterial Injuries

Subclavian-Axillary Arteries

Because the subclavian-axillary arteries (see Chapters 70 and 71) are protected by the overlying bone and muscle, injuries to these vessels are relatively uncommon. However, once injured, especially in the presence of active hemorrhage, surgical exposure can pose a significant challenge. Penetrating trauma is the most frequent cause of subclavian-axillary trauma, followed by blunt trauma.[20,62] Because of the close proximity to a variety of structures, subclavian-axillary trauma is usually associated with major musculoskeletal fractures and brachial plexus and venous injuries.[20,24,62] An associated injury of particular importance is a fracture-dislocation of the posterior portion of the first rib. In this setting the incidence of a subclavian artery injury is extremely high.

Critical ischemia of the upper extremity is uncommon following subclavian-axillary artery injuries owing to rich collateral circulation around the shoulder. In one report, only 20% of patients had decreased or absent pulses.[39] Therefore, a high index of suspicion, careful pulse examination, use of Doppler arterial pressure indices, and liberal use of arteriography are mandatory for reliable diagnosis of these injuries.

For repair of subclavian artery injuries, the surgeon should be familiar with multiple chest incisions to achieve proper proximal control and adequate exposure for the vascular reconstruction. In most cases, penetrating injuries of the right subclavian-axillary arteries require median sternotomy for proximal control, whereas a left anterolateral or "trapdoor" thoracotomy may be necessary to manage proximal left subclavian injuries. When exposure to the more distal subclavian artery is needed, a supraclavicular extension is advocated. The axillary artery is approached through a horizontal infraclavicular incision, but proximal supraclavicular control may be necessary for arterial injuries at the thoracic outlet. Resection of the middle third of the clavicle is rarely necessary, but it is an alternative approach for certain injuries at the axillary-subclavian junction.

Subclavian artery injuries are associated with a high mortality rate. In a series of 54 consecutive penetrating subclavian artery injuries by Lin and associates, overall mortality rate was 39%.[62] Similarly, in a review by Demetriades and colleagues, 18 (23%) of the 79 patients who sustained penetrating subclavian artery trauma presented either with no signs of life or in extremis and underwent emergency center thoracotomies for resuscitation.[20] Overall patient survival was 34%. Of note in this series, mortality rates for isolated subclavian vein injuries were significantly higher than isolated arterial injuries (50% and 20.5%, respectively; $P < 0.05$).

In patients with a neurologic deficit, the brachial plexus is explored at the time of arterial repair. Complete disruption of the brachial plexus generally results in a permanently paretic, painful, anesthetic limb that ultimately may warrant forequarter amputation. This injury is usually associated with severe vascular disruption and musculoskeletal trauma. A contused but intact brachial plexus may regain all or partial neurologic function in some patients. A study by Manord and colleagues demonstrated some degree of neurologic improvement in 87% of such patients.[64] With the exception of patients with spinal root avulsions, significant functional improvement was seen at all levels of brachial plexus injury.

In selected patients, endovascular therapy has been used with a high technical success rate for blunt and penetrating subclavian-axillary arterial injuries.[24,26,114] Ideal candidates include patients who are hemodynamically stable or are diagnosed with traumatic arteriovenous fistulae and false aneurysms. Deliberation should be given over the use of endovascular stent grafts with arterial lesions in close proximity to the origins of the vertebral or right common carotid. For example, Xenos and associates reviewed 23 patients who underwent intervention for traumatic subclavian-axillary artery injuries.[114] Only 12 patients had lesions suitable to endovascular repair. Of those, only 7 underwent treatment with a covered stent due to surgeon preference for patient management. Compared with open repair patients, endovascularly treated patients had significantly shorter operative times and less blood loss ($P < 0.05$) while attaining similar patency rates.

Brachial, Radial, and Ulnar Arteries

Brachial artery injuries are usually due to penetrating trauma and are frequently iatrogenic. Blunt brachial artery injuries are most often associated with supracondylar fractures of the humerus. The location of the brachial artery injury has implications with respect to the associated clinical findings, since injuries below the origin of the profunda brachii may not manifest signs of ischemia owing to the robust collateral networks already present.

Single-vessel injury in the forearm need not be repaired but may be ligated or embolized. Repair is mandatory when one of the vessels, either the radial or the ulnar artery, was previously traumatized or ligated or when the palmar arch is incomplete. When both radial and ulnar arteries are injured, the ulnar artery should be repaired preferentially because it is the dominant vessel.

External Iliac-Femoral Arteries

Iliac artery injuries remain one of the most lethal arterial injuries sustained by trauma patients (see Chapter 72). Mortality rates range from 24% to 40% and can exceed 50% when combined with an aortic or iliac venous injury.[10,12] In a recent series from our institution solely analyzing iliac vessel injuries, Asensio and colleagues reported a 51% overall survival that diminished to 38% when concomitant iliac venous injuries were present.[5] For proximal control of the external iliac artery, a retroperitoneal approach is ideal. The surgeon extends the femoral incision through the inguinal ligament or makes a separate incision parallel to the lateral border of the rectus sheath and 2 cm above the inguinal ligament (Fig. 73-4). The rectus muscle is retracted medial, the transversalis fascia is incised, and the retroperitoneal space is entered. The peritoneum and its contents are reflected medially to provide exposure of the distal aorta and the iliac vessels.

Exposure of the common femoral, proximal deep femoral, and superficial femoral arteries is accomplished through a longitudinal thigh incision over the femoral triangle. The common femoral artery lies within the femoral sheath, the common femoral vein lying medial to it and the femoral nerve lateral. Careful dissection is required to avoid iatrogenic injury to the deep femoral artery.

Blunt and penetrating injuries to the superficial femoral artery are common and are repaired with the techniques described earlier. Injuries of the proximal deep femoral artery should always be repaired in hemodynamically stable patients because of this artery's contribution to the collateral supply of the lower extremity.[38]

Popliteal Artery

Popliteal artery injuries remain among the most challenging of all extremity vascular injuries. The outcome of a penetrating popliteal artery injury depends predominantly

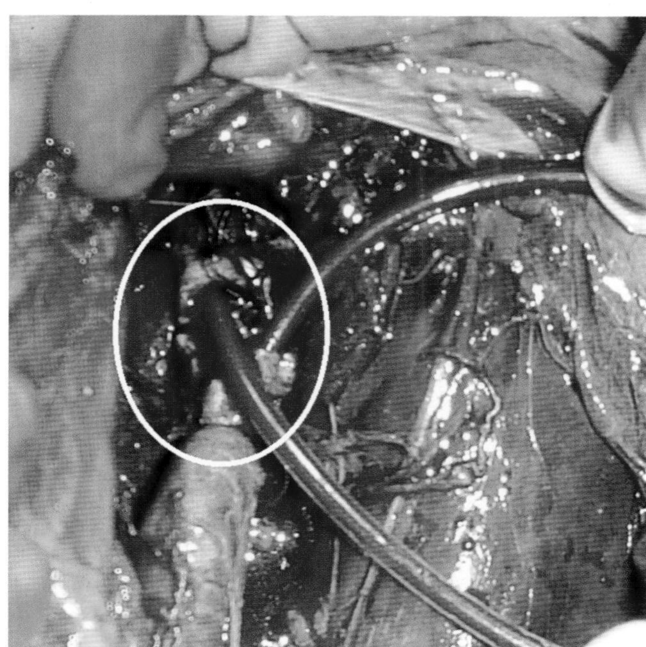

FIGURE 72-11 Temporary arterial shunt for damage control in a hemodynamically unstable patient with a gunshot wound and complete transection of the iliac artery (*circle*).

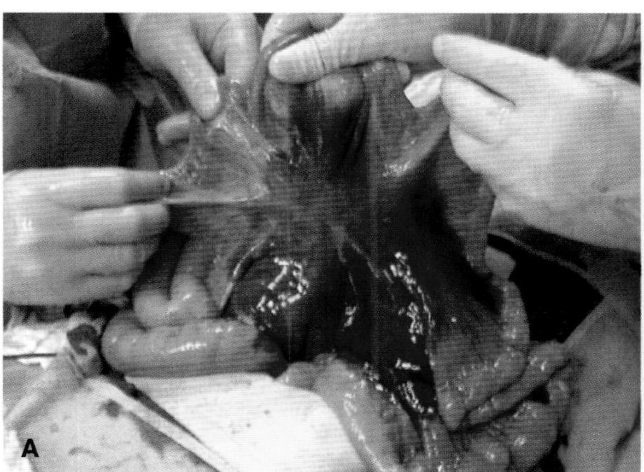

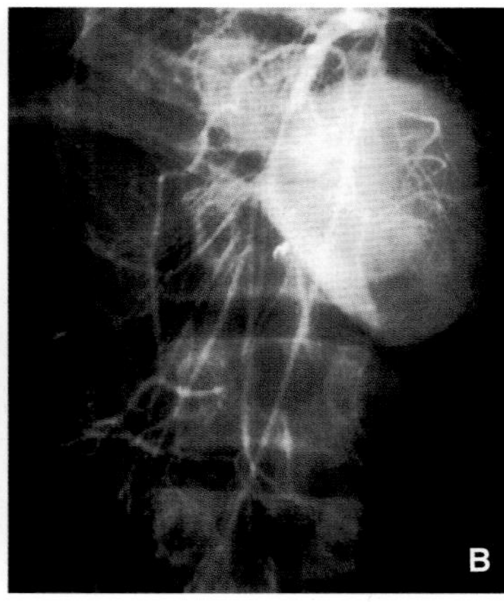

FIGURE 72-13 A, Traffic accident victim with a large hematoma at the base of the mesentery found at laparotomy. This is suspicious for superior mesenteric artery (SMA) injury and needs to be evaluated, preferably postoperatively. **B,** Postoperative angiography shows a large SMA false aneurysm.

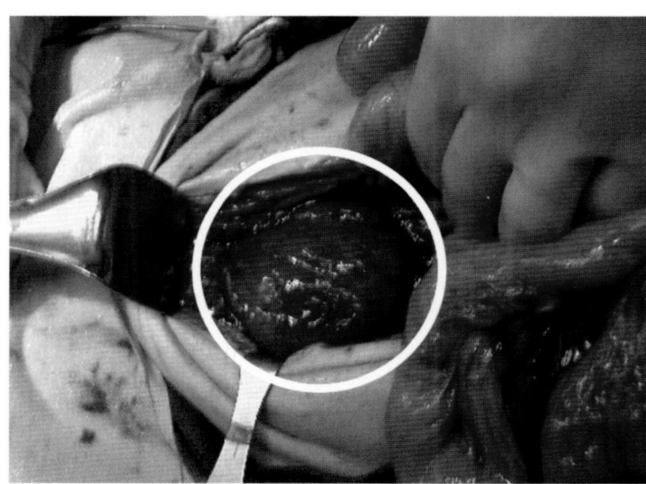

FIGURE 72-15 Large hematoma in the pelvis (*circle*) following a gunshot wound. This is highly suspicious of iliac vascular injury, and proximal control should be obtained as soon as possible.

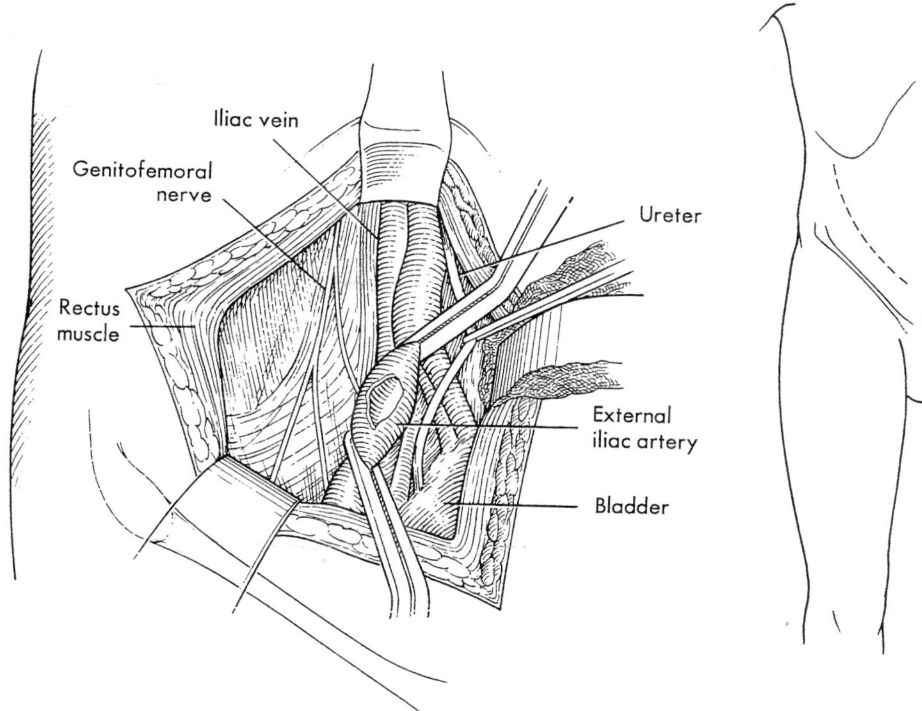

FIGURE 73-4 Retroperitoneal exposure for proximal control of the iliac and proximal common femoral arteries. (From Yellin AE, Weaver FA: Vascular system. In Donovan AJ [ed]: Trauma Surgery. St. Louis, Mosby-Year Book, 1994.)

on the mechanism of injury. The amputation rate for shotgun wounds approaches 20% because of the associated soft tissue injury and septic sequelae. Whereas, when single missile injuries and stab wounds associated with minimal musculoskeletal injury occur, amputation rates approach zero. Nevertheless, during the past decade a dramatic reduction has occurred in the rate of amputation after civilian popliteal artery injuries. Amputation rates at our institution have decreased from 23% to 6% for blunt injuries and from 21% to zero for penetrating trauma.[102,103]

The popliteal vein, infrapopliteal arteries, and tibial nerve are frequently involved in penetrating popliteal injury (20% to 38% of the time). A popliteal artery injury above the knee joint is best repaired through a medial thigh incision; a similar below-knee injury requires a leg incision. An isolated penetrating injury directly behind the knee can be approached from behind (Fig. 73-5). When this approach is used, the contralateral lesser saphenous vein can be harvested if an autogenous graft is required.

In a series of 100 blunt popliteal artery injuries reported from our institution, popliteal artery thrombosis or transection occurred in 97%.[102] Concomitant popliteal vein injury was present in 29%. Repair of the artery was accomplished by end-to-end anastomosis in 49%, vein interposition in 43%, intimal repair and vein patch in 2%, and thrombectomy in 1%. Ten amputations were required because of failure of the arterial repair, and five were needed because of invasive limb sepsis or massive soft tissue injury. Prior to 1980, 12 amputations were necessary; after 1980, only three limbs were amputated. Factors that positively influenced limb salvage included (1) systemic (heparin) anticoagulation; (2) arterial repair accomplished either laterally or end to end; and (3) palpable pedal pulses within the first 24 hours. On the other hand, severe soft tissue injury, deep soft tissue infection, and preoperative ischemia were negative predictors of limb salvage (Table 73-2). Attention to the possibility of compartment syndrome, along with rapid treatment by complete dermotomy-fasciotomy if it is present, is crucial for these patients.[52]

Table 73-2 Amputation Rates in Association with Perioperative Risk Factors in Blunt Popliteal Artery Trauma

RISK FACTOR	PRESENT, NO. (%)	ABSENT, NO. (%)	*P* VALUE*
Severe soft tissue injury	13/31 (42)	2/69 (3)	<0.0001
Deep soft tissue infection	9/17 (53)	6/83 (7)	<0.0001
Preoperative ischemia	15/64 (23)	0/36 (0)	<0.001
Preoperative delay > 6 hr	10/40 (25)	5/24 (21)	NS
Preoperative delay > 12 hr	2/14 (14)	13/50 (26)	NS
Systemic anticoagulation	6/71 (8)	9/29 (31)	<0.01
Primary arterial repair	3/49 (6)	12/51 (24)	<0.05
Palpable pedal pulse within 24 hr	4/55 (7)	11/45 (24)	<0.05
Trifurcation arterial injury	6/29 (21)	9/71 (13)	NS
Popliteal vein injury	6/29 (21)	9/71 (13)	NS
Ligation of venous injury	2/6 (33)	4/23 (17)	NS
Fasciotomy (operative or delayed)	11/61 (18)	4/39 (10)	NS
Delayed fasciotomy	1/4 (25)	14/96 (15)	NS
Preoperative compartment syndrome	2/17 (12)	13/83 (16)	NS

*Two-tailed Fisher's exact test.
NS, not statistically significant.

Modified from Wagner WH, Caulkins E, Weaver FA, et al: Blunt popliteal artery trauma: One hundred consecutive cases. J Vasc Surg 7:736, 1988.

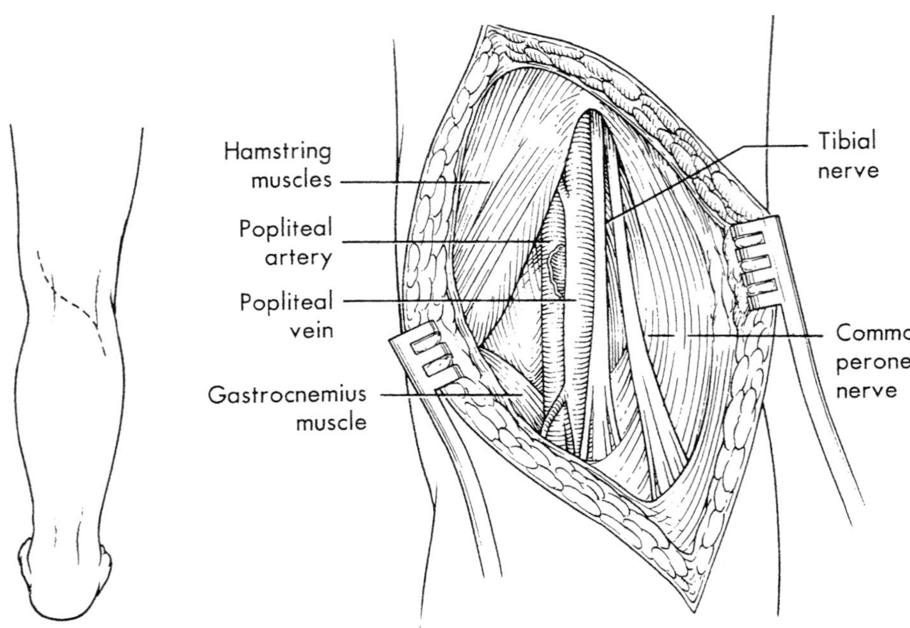

FIGURE 73-5 Posterior approach for a penetrating popliteal injury behind the knee. (From Yellin AE, Weaver FA: Vascular system. In Donovan AJ [ed]: Trauma Surgery. St. Louis, Mosby-Year Book, 1994.)

In more recent series, Melton and associates[70] reported a similar experience. In 102 patients with a penetrating or blunt popliteal injury, systemic heparin or local thrombolytic therapy significantly reduced the amputation rate, where all severely traumatized limbs (as characterized by a mangled extremity severity score[51] [MESS] > 8) required amputation. Likewise, Dar and colleagues retrospectively reviewed 272 patients with traumatic popliteal injuries, of which 95% were secondary to penetrating trauma.[17] In their series, the amputation rate was 5.5%. Significant variables associated with amputation included concomitant bone fracture and delay in vascular repair longer than 12 hours. Early evaluation of all popliteal artery injuries from our institution concurred with Dar and associates in that lower total ischemia time improved outcome. Of note, in our analysis, MESS was not predictive of amputation rates.

Tibial Arteries

Isolated occlusive injury to one infrapopliteal artery rarely results in limb ischemia and does not, as a rule, require therapeutic intervention. A single actively bleeding traumatized vessel or arterial pseudoaneurysm can be treated by simple ligation or angiographic embolization; however, when the tibioperoneal trunk or two infrapopliteal arteries are injured, repair is required.[87] The associated nerve, bone, and soft tissue injuries are the essential determinants of limb salvage. In a study by Whitman and colleagues, no amputations occurred in limbs with less than two associated injuries; however, for limbs with all three associated injuries, the amputation rate was 54%.[111]

Pediatric Extremity Arterial Injuries

Management principles for noniatrogenic arterial injuries in children parallel those for adult trauma, and recent studies suggest that judicious use of arteriography and arterial repair in pediatric vascular injury provides results equivalent to those achieved in adults.[41,44,50,101,109] Considerations unique to the management of pediatric injuries include the severity of arterial spasm, the unknown long-term consequences of autogenous grafts placed in children, and the long-term effects of diminished blood flow on limb length. The intense arterial spasm associated with pediatric vascular injuries can compromise any arterial repair. Pharmacologic agents that may impede the vasoactive response include papaverine (injected topically or into the adventitia) or nitrates. Warm saline applied topically may also be helpful.[44] Similarly, diagnostic arteriography can exacerbate vasospasm and limb ischemia. Consequently, when diagnostic studies are indicated, a noninvasive modality such as CFD ultrasonography should be considered as an alternative. In a viable limb with an occlusive injury that is neurologically intact, the arterial repair can be deferred, and in a very young child this may be preferable.[90] If repair is not performed, careful follow-up of limb growth is necessary, and arterial repair is indicated if a limb-length discrepancy develops. Harris and Hordines reported long-term outcomes on 9 of the 19 pediatric patients that underwent revascularization for traumatic vascular injuries.[44] With a mean follow-up of 35 months, 7 (78%) of the patients were able to resume normal physical activities. The two patients unable to regain full function had combined orthopedic, soft tissue, and vascular trauma. No limb-length discrepancy or aneurysmal change within the vein grafts was found.

■ EXTREMITY VENOUS INJURIES

The most commonly injured major veins of the extremities are the superficial femoral vein (42%), followed by the popliteal vein (23%) and the common femoral vein (14%).[71] When the venous injury is localized and end-to-end or lateral venorrhaphy is possible, repair should be performed unless the patient is hemodynamically unstable. When more extensive venous injuries exist, an interposition, panel, or spiral graft can be configured for repair. However, the indication and benefit of such complex repairs remain controversial.[97,118]

Meyer and coworkers studied 36 patients with traumatic venous injuries who underwent venous repair.[71] Repairs were studied venographically 7 days after operation. Fourteen (39%) of the venous repairs had thrombosed. Moreover, when an interposition vein graft was used, the thrombosis rate rose to 59%. Limb salvage was 100% successful and was not affected by failure of the venous repair. Timberlake and Kerstein reported a similar outcome, with transient edema in 36% and long-term permanent edema in only 2% of patients with venous injuries.[96] The finding of edema was not related to whether the vein was repaired or ligated. Kuralay and colleagues evaluated the outcome of venous repairs using postoperative duplex scanning to assess not only patency but blood flow velocity.[58] In 130 patients suffering military and civilian trauma, repair of vein injuries were most successful in the proximal venous segments, which correlated with the highest postoperative flow rates. Repaired common femoral, superficial femoral, and popliteal veins had patency rates of 100%, 100%, and 86% at 1 year, respectively, and 89%, 78%, and 60% at 6 years, respectively. This experience and others suggest that repair of major venous injuries in a stable patient is a reasonable undertaking; however, when venous repair would be complex or the patient is hemodynamically unstable, simple ligation is appropriate. When venous ligation is necessary, postoperative edema can be controlled by extremity elevation and elastic wrapping. For patients undergoing venous repair, patency should be monitored with hand-held Doppler or duplex scan.

■ ORTHOPEDIC, SOFT TISSUE, AND NERVE INJURIES

The surgical treatment of combined vascular and orthopedic injuries is one of the most difficult problems in the management of trauma patients.[107] The incidence of combined vascular injury and skeletal fractures has been reported to be from 0.3% to 6.4%.[6,14,36,60] Although combined injuries are uncommon, the duration of ischemia is critical to the outcome. Therefore, the arterial repair should be performed first to restore circulation to the limb before the orthopedic stabilization is addressed. Sometimes, however, massive musculoskeletal trauma renders a limb so unstable that external fixation must be placed before the vascular procedure. Selective use of intraluminal shunts and rapid installation of an external fixator minimize limb ischemia in this setting, thus allowing an unhurried orthopedic and vascular repair.[27,50,73] Several investigators have documented shunt patency for over 3 hours without systemic heparinization.[2,18,40,78,91] When the vascular repair is performed in advance of orthopedic fixation, it is incumbent on the surgeon to inspect the vascular reconstruction before final wound closure and before the patient leaves the operating room. Patency of the repair must be documented by palpable pulses, arteriography, or CFD ultrasonography.

In patients with major soft tissue injuries, débridement of all clearly nonviable tissue is mandatory. Frequent and early returns to the operating room, as often as every 24 to 48 hours, may be required. In these patients, unexplained fever and leukocytosis are assumed to be due to deep tissue infection until proved otherwise. Re-exploration of the wound and débridement of necrotic tissue or hematoma are essential for minimizing septic sequelae. Ultimate wound coverage by delayed primary closure, rotational flaps, or free tissue transfer when the soft tissue bed is clean minimizes the risk of invasive sepsis.

Nerve injuries occur in about 50% of upper extremity and 25% of lower extremity vascular injuries. The nerve injury usually determines the long-term functional status of an injured extremity.[48] If a major nerve has been cleanly transected by a sharp object, primary repair can be performed at the time of vascular repair; however, for most penetrating and all blunt nerve injuries, immediate repair is rarely possible or indicated. Rather, both ends of the injured nerve should be tagged with nonabsorbable suture at the initial operation. This facilitates identification of the nerve at the time of eventual nerve repair or grafting.

Vascular repairs are now performed with such a high rate of success that they exert little influence on ultimate extremity function. Rather, the associated orthopedic, nerve, and soft tissue injuries are the critical factors that determine long-term limb function. A number of scores or indices (e.g., MESS[51]) have been proposed in an attempt to predict early limb salvage and to limit protracted reconstructive efforts aimed at restoring limb function. Unfortunately, application of these indices has often failed to predict functional limb salvage reliably.[9,70] Currently, for limbs with massive orthopedic, soft tissue, and nerve injuries, primary amputation, rather than complex reconstruction, should be considered, as permanent total functional limb disability—requiring delayed amputation—is common.[107,111] In hemodynamically unstable patients in whom a complex vascular repair might jeopardize survival, primary amputation should also be considered.

■ INTRA-ARTERIAL DRUG INJECTION

An often neglected, frequently misdiagnosed, and mistreated arterial injury is one caused by inadvertent intra-arterial drug injection (IADI) of medications not intended for intra-arterial use, or illicit street drugs accidentally injected into an artery, not a vein. Complications may include acute arterial occlusion, distal thromboembolism, mycotic aneurysms, soft tissue abscesses, gangrene, and chronic ischemia. Iatrogenic IADI are usually associated with injections of barbiturates during induction of anesthesia. The injection site is the brachial artery, and the drug is concentrated as it flows into the smaller distal arteries, resulting in an intense inflammatory response with endothelial injury and thrombosis. Illicit nonsterile street drugs often contain insoluble additives as variable as are the popular drugs of the day.

Soft tissue cellulitis or localized abscesses are common sequelae of illicit drug use. Increasingly, drug-resistant gram-positive organisms are the culprits. *Staphylococcus aureus* is a common pathogen; however, oral flora such as streptococcal species and anaerobic species such as

Peptostreptococcus and *Bacteroides* are often present. Appropriate parenteral antibiotic therapy combined with incision, drainage, and or débridement are the hallmarks of therapy. When the soft tissue infection is in the vicinity of a major blood vessel and particularly when there is a painful tender pulsatile mass, a mycotic aneurysm must be suspected. However, less than half of these aneurysms are pulsatile. Therefore, prior to any attempt at drainage, CFD ultrasonography must be performed to rule out the presence of a mycotic aneurysm. Management of a mycotic aneurysm requires judgment regarding the option of ligation and possible acute ischemia versus repair, possibly followed by secondary infection and hemorrhage. Treatment is further complicated by the fact that, in drug abusers, autologous vein conduits might not be readily available. Brachial mycotic aneurysms can invariably be ligated without ischemic consequences. Similar outcomes are expected following ligation of the deep femoral or superficial femoral arteries, and less than 50% of patients with common femoral artery ligation develop ischemia. Therefore, in the presence of severe local soft tissue destruction, ligation followed by careful observation for evidence of ischemia is a prudent choice. Doppler flow and pressures can be used as a guide. If distal flow is present, limb ischemia is uncommon. This algorithm has been used successfully by others.[76] Delayed inline revascularization in clean tissue is an option for the rare patient with subsequent persistent claudication. If there is acute ischemia, revascularization may be necessary. A conduit, preferably autogenous, should be placed in a clean tissue plane and anastomosed to healthy artery both proximally and distally, thereby restoring flow. Numerous extra-anatomic routes have been used. All vascular anastomoses should be covered by healthy muscle, which might require rotation of a local muscle flap. Acute thrombosis of the distal arterial tree following IADI can have catastrophic consequences owing to the obliteration of the small vessel collateral circulation by the injected agent. The problem is not primarily one of spasm but of almost immediate endothelial damage of the arterial and venous microcirculation, leading to intimal necrosis, thromboxane release, platelet aggregation, release of norepinephrine, vasoconstriction, and thrombosis.[115] The initial occlusive injury is likely to involve the small venules that accompany the arterioles. The resultant venous outflow obstruction leads to increased interstitial edema, secondary arterial insufficiency, thrombosis, tissue hypoxia, neurologic deficit, and soft tissue necrosis.

Whether the arterial problem is iatrogenic or self-injected, an accurate history might be difficult to obtain. However, following an IADI, there is immediate severe, unremitting pain, often accompanied by edema, numbness, discoloration, and cyanosis or mottling of the skin. If the injection is in the upper extremity, the hand is typically held in a clawlike position. Sensory loss is usually present. The entire wrist and hand might be involved, but changes are most severe in the distal digits. Depending on the anatomy of the palmar arch and digital circulation, one or more fingers might be spared. The fingers are usually cool. The finger tips are deeply cyanotic. Motor function is diminished. Pulses at the wrist are usually present and might be accentuated owing to the outflow obstruction. Distal pulses are usually absent, even by Doppler study. A site of injection should be located and noted.

The diagnosis can be made clinically. CFD ultrasonography should be used to help identify the remaining patent arteries. Although angiography provides a vivid picture of the pathology and may even demonstrate the venous microcirculatory damage, it is rarely helpful in therapy and might even promote further thrombosis. Therefore, we do not use it in our diagnostic or therapeutic regimen, unless we suspect thrombosis of a major artery.

Our therapeutic regimen is based on the premise that once the intravascular damage occurs and arterial thrombosis is present, revascularization is not a realistic option. Our goal is to preserve all collateral circulation and prevent further propagation of clot. If inflammation, edema, stasis, and thrombosis can be minimized, functional recovery will usually follow. This regimen has now been used in more than 50 patients with IADI.[98,115]

Therapy consists of the following:

- Heparin sodium 10,000 units intravenously followed by a continuous drip to keep the partial thromboplastin time 1½ to 2 times control to prevent further clotting
- Dexamethasone 4 mg intravenously every 6 hours to reduce inflammation and stabilize cellular membranes
- Dextran 40 intravenously at 20 mL/hr to prevent platelet aggregation and thrombosis
- Appropriate pain control, including opiates as needed
- Elevation of the extremity to reduce edema
- Aggressive physical therapy to minimize contractures

This regimen is continued until the condition resolves or is fully stabilized, which occurs in 72 hours to 1 week. Débridement of ischemic tissue is deferred until it is clear what is viable and what is not. Long-term physical therapy is frequently necessary to restore function.

Various other treatment regimens have been reported and may include the use of nerve blocks, local and systemic vasodilators, and thrombolytic agents. Experience with these modalities is confined to small groups of patients.[89] It is possible that there will be a role for thrombolytic therapy in selected cases; however, that role remains to be defined.

IATROGENIC FALSE ANEURYSMS

Iatrogenic false aneurysms have remained one of the most common complications after an invasive arterial procedure. Also termed *pseudoaneurysm*, *pulsatile hematoma*, or *communicating hematoma*, a false aneurysm can be defined as a direct leakage of blood from the artery into the surrounding tissue. There are no walls of the artery involved in a false aneurysm, which starkly differs from a true aneurysm where the dilatation process involves all layers of the arterial wall.

Historically, the incidence of a false aneurysm after an arterial catheterization was approximately 0.1%.[13,57] However, recent studies document a marked increase in the occurrence of false aneurysms to 0.2% to 9%.[30,54,80,105] One factor contributing to the increased incidence is the more frequent usage of large-bore catheters and sheaths for endovascular treatment modalities (e.g., angioplasty with or without stent placement, intra-arterial chemotherapy). Cannulation with these devices leads to a more sizable arterial defect. Other contributing factors are the higher rate of invasive monitoring and treatment devices for critically ill patients and the extended indications for long-term intravenous access (e.g., peripherally inserted central catheters, Swan-Ganz catheters, dialysis catheters). Technical misadventures during placement of these intravenous devices carry the potential risk of immediate or delayed presentation of an arterial false aneurysm. Age older than 60 years, female gender, periprocedural anticoagulation, operator inexperience, and underlying peripheral vascular disease all have been identified as positive risk factors in the formation of false aneurysms.[46,57,80,112] However, with the advent of reliable postprocedure arterial closure devices and reliance on portable sonographic units for anatomic definition, the incidence of iatrogenic false aneurysms should decline rapidly over the next decade.[56]

Because of the convenience of the common femoral artery for an entry vessel, most iatrogenic false aneurysms occur in this location. Other noted sites include the superficial femoral, external iliac, brachial, axillary, subclavian, and common carotid arteries.

Physical examination should alert the clinician to the possibility of a false aneurysm. Presenting signs that should raise suspicion include a pulsatile mass or significant ecchymosis over the area of cannulation, a sudden drop in the postprocedure hematocrit, a newly auscultated bruit, a newly palpable thrill, and the new onset of neurologic deficits.[30,54,55,105,112] The last finding is of critical importance especially when the axillary and brachial arteries are cannulated. In these specific sites, bleeding from a false aneurysm into the surrounding fascial sheath can cause significant neurologic compromise due to nerve compression, without the presence of prominent pulsatile mass.

Patients with any of the earlier-mentioned complaints should undergo a duplex scan to confirm the diagnosis of a false aneurysm. Over the past decade, duplex scanning has replaced angiography as the initial confirmatory test. A duplex scan has the advantage of being noninvasive and can delineate important characteristics about the false aneurysm, such as size of the false aneurysm, neck diameter and length of the false aneurysm, architecture of the native vessel, and velocity within the native vessel and within the false aneurysm sac.[32] Angiography is reserved only for patients with false aneurysms of the proximal arterial tree (subclavian, iliac) where immediate endovascular management or complex open surgical therapy may be required.

Numerous suitable options exist for the treatment of false aneurysms. Observation relies on the premise that a significant proportion of false aneurysms will close spontaneously. Unfortunately, reported spontaneous closure rates have varied considerably, and no patient or duplex scan characteristics have been identified to reliably predict acceptable spontaneous closure rates.[32,54,55,105]

Compression therapy, by either direct pressure or ultrasound-guided compression, is also an option for the management of false aneurysms. Direct pressure, digitally or with stationary compression devices, may augment thrombosis of the aneurysm sac. Unfortunately, successful thrombosis of the false aneurysm sac is unreliable.[32] Contraindications to compression therapy include overlying skin necrosis, tenderness over the false aneurysm, neurologic symptoms, and vessels inaccessible to adequate compression (i.e., subclavian artery).[30,54]

In 1991, Fellmeth and associates described the technique of ultrasound-guided compression for treatment of false aneurysms.[31] By visualization of the arterial wall defect with the ultrasound probe, accuracy of compression is augmented. Reported compression times required for ablation of the false aneurysm range from 10 to 150 minutes, with procedural success rates from 54% to 100%.[30,47,57,105] Negative predictors include current anticoagulation, injury to vessel other than the common femoral artery, false aneurysms greater than 4 cm in diameter, marked obesity, and the presence of an arteriovenous fistula.[13,46] No correlation for successful outcome was demonstrated based on complexity of the false aneurysm or the diameter and length of the false aneurysm neck. Regardless, because of variable success rates and the extensive time required for trained hospital personnel, we have abandoned this treatment strategy for false aneurysms at our institution.

In 1986, Cope and Zeit introduced the technique of percutaneous thrombin injection via ultrasound guidance for treatment of false aneurysms in a series of four patients.[16] Complete false aneurysm thrombosis was achieved in 100% of patients. Subsequently, success rates from numerous investigators exceed 95% with less than 5% complication rates.[32,53,61,112] The technique involves percutaneous injection of thrombin (100 units/mL) into the false aneurysm sac until obliteration of flow is observed under real-time ultrasound guidance. Care should be taken to inject the thrombin into the outer limits of the aneurysm sac and not in close proximity to the neck of the aneurysm to avoid inadvertent native arterial thrombosis or embolization. The rapidity and efficacy of this technique combined with minimal patient discomfort make percutaneous thrombin injection the preferred treatment modality at our institution.

Recently, investigators have extended transcatheter techniques to the management of false aneurysms.[7,45,94,104] Endovascular management has the distinct advantage of accessibility to most locations of the arterial tree without the morbidity of open surgical repair. Baltacioglu and coworkers reported 100% technical success in the treatment of 17 iatrogenic false aneurysms with covered stents.[7] Sites of repair included femoral artery, subclavian artery, abdominal aorta, common iliac, and portal vein. With a mean follow-up period of 8 months, only one patient developed a complication from the endovascular treatment—a hemodynamically insignificant stenosis. Waigand and associates endovascularly treated 53 patients with postinterventional complications who had failed prior ultrasonic compression.[104] Technical success was 88%; however, with follow-up close to 1 year, four late stent occlusions occurred. As endovascular therapy expands into the treatment of iatrogenic false aneurysms, the need for a planned postprocedure duplex surveillance program cannot be overemphasized.

Despite a diminished role, open surgical repair remains the gold standard of therapy by which all treatment modalities are compared. Operative repair can involve simple stitch or replacement of the entire vessel with graft. Recognized indications for surgical repair are failure of other treatment modalities, suspected secondary infection, evidence of vascular compromise, ongoing or imminent hemorrhage and skin erosion, and necrosis due to false aneurysm expansion.[13,54,80] Relative indications include femoral neuropathy, continuous anticoagulation, and a concomitant arteriovenous fistula. Mainstays of surgical treatment are proximal control (above the inguinal ligament if needed for extensive groin false aneurysms), use of monofilament suture for vascular repair, and débridement of devitalized tissue. In the presence of any infection or when large residual tissue defects persist, muscle coverage with either sartorius or rectus abdominis flaps over the repaired vessel must be used.

■ REFERENCES

1. Abou-Sayed H, Berger DL: Blunt lower-extremity trauma and popliteal artery injuries: Revisiting the case for selective arteriography. Arch Surg 137:585, 2002.
2. Aldridge SD, Badelino MM, Malaspina PJ, et al: Extended intravascular shunting in an experimental model of vascular injury. J Cardiovasc Surg 38:183, 1997.
3. Amato JJ, Billy LJ, Gruber RP, et al: Vascular injuries: An experimental study of high and low velocity missile wounds. Arch Surg 101:167, 1970.
4. Applebaum R, Yellin AE, Weaver FA, et al: The role of routine arteriography in blunt lower extremity trauma. Am J Surg 160:221, 1990.
5. Asensio JA, Petrone P, Roldan G, et al: Analysis of 185 iliac vessel injuries: Risk factors and predictors of outcome. Arch Surg 139:1187, 2003.
6. Atteberry LR, Dennis JW, Russo-Alesi R, et al: Changing patterns of arterial injuries associated with fractures and dislocations. J Am Coll Surg 183:377, 1996.
7. Baltacioglu F, Cimcedilit NC, Cil B, et al: Endovascular stent-graft applications in iatrogenic vascular injuries. Cardiovasc Intervent Radiol 26:434, 2003.
8. Bergstein JM, Blair JF, Edwards J, et al: Pitfalls in the use of color-flow duplex ultrasound for screening of suspected arterial injuries in penetrated extremities. J Trauma 33:395, 1992.
9. Bonanni F, Rhodes M, Lucke JF: The futility of predictive scoring of mangled lower extremities. J Trauma 34:99, 1993.
10. Burch JM, Richardson RJ, Martin RR, et al: Penetrating iliac vascular injuries: Recent experience with 233 consecutive patients. J Trauma 30:1450, 1990.
11. Bynoe RP, Miles WS, Bell RM, et al: Noninvasive diagnosis of vascular trauma by duplex ultrasonography. J Vasc Surg 14:346, 1991.
12. Carrillo EH, Spain DA, Wilson MA, et al: Alternatives in the management of penetrating injuries to the iliac vessels. J Trauma 44:1024, 1998.
13. Coley BD, Roberts AD, Fellmeth BE, et al: Postangiographic femoral artery pseudoaneurysms: Further experience with US-guided compression repair. Cardiovasc Radiol 194:307, 1995.
14. Cone JB: Vascular injury associated with fracture-dislocations of the lower extremity. Clin Orthop 243:30, 1989.
15. Conrad MF, Patton JH Jr, Parikshak M, et al: Evaluation of vascular injury in penetrating extremity trauma: Angiographers stay home. Am Surg 68:269, 2002.
16. Cope C, Zeit R: Coagulation of aneurysms by direct percutaneous thrombin injection. AJR Am J Roentgenol 147:383, 1986.
17. Dar AM, Ahanger AG, Wani RA, et al: Popliteal artery injuries: The Kashmir experience. J Trauma 55:362, 2003.
18. Dawson DL, Putnam AT, Light JT, et al: Temporary arterial shunts to maintain limb perfusion after arterial injury: An animal study. J Trauma 47:64, 1999.
19. DeBakey E, Simeone CF: Battle injuries of the arteries in World War II: An analysis of 2,471 cases. Ann Surg 123:534, 1946.
20. Demetriades D, Chahwan S, Gomez H, et al: Penetrating injuries to the subclavian and axillary vessels. J Am Coll Surg 188:290, 1999.
21. Dennis JW, Frykberg ER, Veldenz HC, et al: Validation of non-operative management of occult vascular injuries and accuracy of physical examination alone in penetrating extremity trauma: Five- to ten-year follow-up. J Trauma 44:243, 1998.
22. Dennis JW, Jagger C, Butcher JL, et al: Reassessing the role of arteriograms in the management of posterior knee dislocations. J Trauma 35:692, 1993.
23. deVirgilio C, Mercado PD, Arnell T, et al: Noniatrogenic pediatric vascular trauma: A ten-year experience at a level 1 trauma center. Am Surg 63:781, 1997.
24. D'Othee BJ, Rousseau H, Otal P, et al: Noncovered stent placement in a blunt traumatic injury of the right subclavian artery. Cardiovasc Intervent Radiol 22:424, 1999.
25. Dorweiler B, Neufang A, Schmiedt W, et al: Limb trauma with arterial injury: Long-term performance of venous interposition grafts. Thorac Cardiovasc Surg 51:67, 2003.
26. Dutort DF, Strauss DC, Blaszczyk M, et al: Endovascular treatment of penetrating thoracic outlet arterial injuries. Eur J Vasc Endovasc Surg 19:489, 2000.
27. Eger M, Golcman L, Goldstein A, et al: The use of a temporary shunt in the management of arterial vascular injuries. Surg Gynecol Obstet 123:67, 1971.
28. Fackler ML: Wound ballistics: A review of common misconceptions. JAMA 259:2730, 1988.
29. Fayiga YJ, Valentine RJ, Myers SI, et al: Blunt pediatric vascular trauma: Analysis of forty-one consecutive patients undergoing operative intervention. J Vasc Surg 20:419, 1994.
30. Feld R, Patton GM, Carabasi A, et al: Treatment of iatrogenic femoral artery injuries with ultrasound-guided compression. J Vasc Surg 16:832, 1992.
31. Fellmeth BD, Roberts AC, Bookstein JJ, et al: Postangiographic femoral artery injuries: Nonsurgical repair with US-guided compression. Radiology 178:671, 1991.
32. Franklin JA, Brigham D, Bogey WM, et al: Treatment of iatrogenic false aneurysms. J Am Coll Surg 197:293, 2003.
33. Fritrige RA, Raptis S, Miller JH, et al: Upper extremity arterial injuries: Experience at the Royal Adelaide Hospital, 1969 to 1991. J Vasc Surg 20:941, 1994.
34. Fry WR, Smith RS, Sayers DV, et al: The success of duplex ultrasonographic scanning in diagnosis of extremity vascular proximity trauma. Arch Surg 128:1368, 1993.
35. Frykberg EP: Advances in the diagnosis and treatment of extremity vascular trauma. Surg Clin North Am 75:207, 1995.
36. Frykberg ER, Crump JM, Dennis JW, et al: Nonoperative observation of clinically occult arterial injuries: A prospective evaluation. Surgery 109:85, 1991.
37. Gagne PJ, Cone JB, McFarland D, et al: Proximity penetrating extremity trauma: The role of duplex ultrasound in the detection of occult venous injuries. J Trauma 39:1157, 1995.
38. Gorman JF: Combat arterial trauma analysis of 106 limb-threatening injuries. Arch Surg 98:160, 1969.
39. Graham JM, Feliciano DV, Mattox KL, et al: Management of subclavian vascular injuries. J Trauma 20:537, 1980.
40. Granchi T, Schmittling Z, Vasquez J, et al: Prolonged use of intraluminal arterial shunts without systemic anticoagulation. Am J Surg 180:493, 2000.
41. Guede JW, Hobson RW, Padberg FT, et al: The role of contrast arteriography in suspected arterial injuries of the extremities. Am Surg 51:89, 1985.
42. Guerrero A, Gibson K, Kralovich KA, et al: Limb loss following lower extremity arterial trauma: What can be done proactively? Injury 33:765, 2002.

43. Hafez HM, Woolgar J, Robbs JV: Lower extremity arterial injury: Results of 550 cases and review of risk factors associated with limb loss. J Vasc Surg 33:112, 2001.
44. Harris LM, Hordines J: Major vascular injuries in the pediatric population. Ann Vasc Surg 17:266, 2003.
45. Hernandez JA, Pershad A, Laufer N: Subclavian artery pseudoaneurysm: Successful exclusion with a covered self-expanding stent. J Invasive Cardiol 14:278, 2002.
46. Hood DB, Mattos MA, Douglas MG, et al: Determinants of success of color-flow duplex-guided compression repair of femoral pseudoaneurysms. Surgery 120:585, 1996.
47. Hood DB, Yellin AE, Weaver FA: Vascular trauma. In Dean R (ed): Current Vascular Surgical Diagnosis and Treatment. Norwalk, CT, Appleton & Lange, 1995, p 405.
48. Howe HH, Poole GV, Hansen KJ, et al: Salvage of lower extremities following combined orthopedic and vascular trauma: A predictive salvage index. Ann Surg 53:205, 1987.
49. Hughes CH: Arterial repair during the Korean War. Ann Surg 147:555, 1958.
50. Johansen K, Bandyk D, Thiele B, et al: Temporary intraluminal shunts: Resolution of a management dilemma in complex vascular injuries. J Trauma 22:395, 1982.
51. Johansen K, Daines M, Howey T, et al: Objective criteria accurately predict amputation following lower extremity trauma. J Trauma 30:568, 1990.
52. Johnson SB, Weaver FA, Yellin AE, et al: Clinical results of decompressive dermotomy-fasciotomy. Am J Surg 164:286, 1992.
53. Kang SS, Labropoulos N, Mansour A, et al: Percutaneous ultrasound guided thrombin injection: A new method for treating postcatherization femoral pseudoaneurysms. J Vasc Surg 27:1032, 1998.
54. Kazmers A, Meeker C, Nofz K, et al: Nonoperative therapy for postcatherization femoral artery pseudoaneurysms. Am Surg 63:199, 1997.
55. Kent KC, McArdle CR, Kennedy B, et al: A prospective study of the clinical outcome of femoral pseudoaneurysms and arteriovenous fistulas induced by arterial puncture. J Vasc Surg 17:125, 1993.
56. Knight CG, Healy DA, Thomas RL: Femoral artery pseudoaneurysms: Risk factors, prevalence, and treatment options. Ann Vasc Surg 17:503, 2003.
57. Kumins NH, Landau DS, Montalvo J, et al: Expanded indications for the treatment of postcatheterization femoral pseudoaneurysms with ultrasound-guided compression. Am J Surg 176:131, 1998.
58. Kuralay E, Demirkilic U, Özal E, et al: A quantitative approach to lower extremity vein repair. J Vasc Surg 36:1213, 2002.
59. Knudson MM, Lewis FR, Atkinson K, et al: The role of duplex ultrasound arterial imaging in patients with penetrating extremity trauma. Arch Surg 128:1033, 1993.
60. Lange RH, Bach AW, Hansen ST, et al: Open tibial fractures with associated vascular injuries: Prognosis for limb salvage. J Trauma 25:204, 1985.
61. Liau CS, Ho FM, Chen MF, et al: Treatment of iatrogenic femoral artery pseudoaneurysm with percutaneous thrombin injection. J Vasc Surg 26:18, 1997.
62. Lin PH, Koffron AJ, Guske PJ, et al: Penetrating injuries of the subclavian artery. Am J Surg 185:580, 2003.
63. Lynch K, Johansen K: Can Doppler pressure measurement replace "exclusion" arteriography in the diagnosis of occult extremity arterial trauma? Ann Surg 214:737, 1991.
64. Manord JD, Garrard CL, Kline DG, et al: Management of severe proximal vascular and neural injury of the upper extremity. J Vasc Surg 27:43, 1998.
65. Marin ML, Veith FJ, Panetta TF, et al: Transluminally placed endovascular stented graft repair for arterial trauma. J Vasc Surg 20:466, 1994.
66. Martin LC, McKenney MG, Sossa JL, et al: Management of lower extremity arterial trauma. J Trauma 37:591, 1994.
67. Mayer JP, Lim LT, Schuler JJ, et al: Peripheral vascular trauma from close-range shotgun injuries. Arch Surg 120:1126, 1985.
68. McNeese S, Fink E, Yellin AE: Definitive treatment of selected vascular injuries and post-traumatic arteriovenous fistulas by arteriographic embolization. Am J Surg 140:252, 1980.
69. Meissner M, Paun M, Johansen K: Duplex scanning for arterial trauma. Am J Surg 161:552, 1991.
70. Melton SM, Croce MA, Patton JH, et al: Popliteal artery trauma. Ann Surg 225:518, 1997.
71. Meyer J, Walsh J, Schuler J, et al: The early fate of venous repair after civilian vascular trauma. Ann Surg 206:458, 1987.
72. Myers SI, Reed MK, Black CT, et al: Noniatrogenic pediatric vascular trauma. J Vasc Surg 10:258, 1989.
73. Nichols JG, Svoboda JA, Parks SN: Use of temporary intraluminal shunts in selected peripheral arterial injuries. J Trauma 26:1094, 1986.
74. Odeh M: Mechanisms of disease: The role of reperfusion-induced injury in the pathogenesis of the crush syndrome. N Engl J Med 324:1417, 1991.
75. Ordog GJ, Balasubramanium S, Wasserber J, et al: Extremity gunshot wounds: I. Identification and treatment of patients at high risk of vascular injury. J Trauma 36:358, 1994.
76. Padberg Jr F, Hobson R II, Lee B, et al: Femoral pseudoaneurysm from drugs of abuse: Ligation or reconstruction? J Vasc Surg 15:642, 1992.
77. Pasch AR, Bishara, Lim LT, et al: Optimal limb salvage in penetrating civilian vascular trauma. J Vasc Surg 3:189, 1986.
78. Reber PU, Patel AG, Sapio NLD, et al: Selective use of temporary intravascular shunts in coincident vascular and orthopedic upper and lower limb trauma. J Trauma 47:72, 1999.
79. Reichard KW, Hall JR, Meller JL, et al: Arteriography in the evaluation of penetrating pediatric extremity injuries. J Pediatr Surg 29:19, 1994.
80. Ricci MA, Trevisani GT, Pilcher DB: Vascular complications of cardiac catheterization. Am J Surg 167:375, 1994.
81. Rich NM: Surgeon's response to battlefield vascular trauma. Am J Surg 166:91, 1993.
82. Rich NA, Baugh JH, Hughes CW: Acute arterial injuries in Vietnam: One thousand cases. J Trauma 10:359, 1970.
83. Risberg B, Lonn L: Management of vascular injuries using endovascular techniques. Eur J Surg 166:196, 2000.
84. Rubel IF, Potter H, Barie P, et al: Magnetic resonance venography to evaluate deep venous thrombosis in patients with pelvic and acetabular trauma. J Trauma 51:622, 2001.
85. Schwartz MR, Weaver FA, Yellin AE, et al: Refining the indications for arteriography in penetrating extremity trauma: A prospective analysis. J Vasc Surg 17:166, 1993.
86. Schwartz M, Weaver F, Yellin A, Ralls P: The utility of color-flow Doppler examination in penetrating extremity arterial trauma. Am Surg 59:375, 1993.
87. Shah DM, Corson JD, Karmody AM, et al: Optimal management of tibial arterial trauma. J Trauma 28:228, 1988.
88. Shah SH, Ledgerwood AM, Lucas CE: Successful endovascular stenting for common iliac artery injury associated with pelvic fracture. J Trauma 55:383, 2003.
89. Silverman SH, Turner WW Jr: Intraarterial drug abuse: New treatment options. J Vasc Surg 14:111, 1991.
90. Smith C, Green RM: Pediatric vascular injuries. Surgery 90:20, 1981.
91. Sriussadaporn S, Pak-art R: Temporary intravascular shunt in complex extremity vascular injuries. J Trauma 52:1129, 2002.
92. Stain SC, Weaver FA, Yellin AE: Extra-anatomical bypass of failed traumatic arterial repairs. J Trauma 31:575, 1991.
93. Stain SC, Yellin AE, Weaver FA, et al: Selective management of nonocclusive arterial injuries. Arch Surg 124:1136, 1989.
94. Stella N, Pellicciotі A, Udini M: Endovascular exclusion of iatrogenic femoral artery pseudoaneurysm with the Wallgraft endoprosthesis. J Cardiovasc Surg (Torino) 44:259, 2003.
95. Sternberg W III, Conners MS III, Ojeda MA, et al: Acute bilateral iliac artery occlusion secondary to blunt trauma: Successful endovascular treatment. J Vasc Surg 38:589, 2003.

96. Timberlake GA, Kerstein MD: Venous injury: To repair or ligate, the dilemma revisited. Am Surg 61:139, 1995.
97. Timberlake GA, O'Connell R, Kerstein M: Venous injury: To repair or ligate, the dilemma. J Vasc Surg 4:553, 1986.
98. Treiman GS, Yellin AE, Weaver FA: An effective treatment protocol for intra-arterial drug injection. J Vasc Surg 12:456, 1990.
99. Treiman GS, Yellin AE, Weaver FA, et al: Examination of the patient with knee dislocation: The case for selective arteriography. Arch Surg 127:1056, 1992.
100. Vaughn GD, Mattox KL, Feliciano DV, et al: Surgical experience with expanded polytetrafluoroethylene (PTFE) as a replacement graft for traumatized vessels. J Trauma 19:403, 1979.
101. Veith FJ, Gupta SK, Ascer E, et al: Six-year prospective multicenter randomized comparison of autologous saphenous vein and expanded polytetrafluoroethylene grafts in infrainguinal arterial reconstructions. J Vasc Surg 3:104, 1986.
102. Wagner WH, Caulkins E, Weaver FA, et al: Blunt popliteal artery trauma: 100 consecutive cases. J Vasc Surg 7:736, 1988.
103. Wagner WH, Yellin AE, Weaver FA, et al: Acute treatment of popliteal artery trauma: The importance of soft tissue injury. Ann Vasc Surg 8:557, 1994.
104. Waigand J, Jhlich F, Gross CM, et al: Percutaneous treatment of pseudoaneurysms and arteriovenous fistulas after invasive vascular procedures. Catheter Cardiovasc Interv 47:157, 1999.
105. Weatherford DA, Taylor SM, Langan EM, et al: Ultrasound-guided compression for the treatment of iatrogenic femoral pseudoaneurysms. South Med J 90:223, 1997.
106. Weaver FA, Papanicolaou G, Yellin AE: Difficult peripheral vascular injuries. Surg Clin North Am 76:843, 1996.
107. Weaver FA, Rosenthal RE, Waterhouse G, et al: Combined vascular and skeletal injuries of the lower extremities. Am Surg 50:189, 1984.
108. Weaver FA, Yellin AE: Complications of missed arterial injuries. J Vasc Surg 18:1077, 1993.
109. Weaver FA, Yellin AE, Bauer M, et al: Is arterial proximity a valid indication for arteriography in penetrating extremity trauma? A prospective analysis. Arch Surg 125:1256, 1990.
110. White RA, Scher LA, Samson RH, et al: Peripheral vascular injuries associated with falls from heights. J Trauma 27:411, 1987.
111. Whitman GR, McCroskey BL, Moore EE, et al: Traumatic popliteal and trifurcation vascular injuries: Determinants of functional limb salvage. Am J Surg 154:681, 1987.
112. Wixon CL, Philpott JW, Bogey WM Jr: Duplex-directed thrombin injection as a method to treat femoral artery pseudoaneurysms. J Am Coll Surg 187:464, 1998.
113. Wright JG, Kerr JC, Valeri CR, et al: Heparin decreases ischemia-reperfusion injury in isolated canine gracilis model. Arch Surg 123:470, 1988.
114. Xenos ES, Freeman M, Stevens S, et al: Covered stents for injuries of subclavian and axillary arteries. J Vasc Surg 38:451, 2003.
115. Yellin AE, Frankhouse JH, Weaver FA: Vascular injury secondary to drug abuse. In Ernst CB, Stanley JC (eds): Current Therapy in Vascular Surgery, 3rd ed. St. Louis, Mosby-Year Book, 1995, p 637.
116. Yellin AE, Weaver FA: Vascular system. In Donovan AJ (ed): Trauma Surgery. St. Louis, Mosby-Year Book, 1994, p 207.
117. Zamir G, Berlatzky Y, Rivking A, et al: Results of reconstruction in major pelvic and extremity venous injuries. J Vasc Surg 28:901, 1998.

Chapter 74

Compartment Syndrome:
Pathophysiology, Recognition, and Management

JAMES C. WATSON, MS, MD
KAJ H. JOHANSEN, MD, PHD

Section XII

Compartment syndrome, a clinical symptom complex resulting from pathologically increased tissue pressure contained in a nonexpansile space, has been described in a variety of anatomic locations. This condition most commonly is observed after acute injury or ischemia in the upper and lower extremities. Abdominal compartment syndrome is an increasingly recognized, potentially lethal complication of trauma resuscitation or surgical procedures and is described in Chapter 72. Other clinical conditions (e.g., epidural and pelvic compartment syndromes, closed head injury, testicular torsion, and angle-closure glaucoma) represent variants of classic compartment syndrome, and their etiology and treatment often can be best defined when considered as such. Traditionally, compartment syndrome refers to increased intramuscular pressures associated with reperfusion or traumatic injury and confined by the fascial envelopes of the muscles of the extremities.

■ PATHOPHYSIOLOGY

Simple physics dictates the mechanism by which compartment pressure increases in a constrained space: The volume of tissue confined within the space increases, the space available for the tissue to occupy decreases, or a combination of the two occurs. Decreased compartment volume is best exemplified by circumstances in which various external devices—casts, constrictive dressings, or military antishock trousers (MAST suit)[1]—exert pressure on the limb. Compartment syndrome even has been described as a consequence of application of elastic compression wraps after uncomplicated varicose vein surgery.[2] A circumferential burn wound resulting in a rigid nonexpansile eschar represents another scenario for "extrinsic" compartmental hypertension.[3]

Compartmental hypertension also can develop with an increase in the volume of tissue constrained within an inelastic osseofascial envelope. Space-occupying lesions, such as hematoma, abscess, pseudoaneurysm, and synovial fluid (e.g., ruptured Baker's cyst),[4] and inadvertent fluid administration, such as infiltrated intravenous catheters, interosseous fluid resuscitation,[5] and extravasated joint irrigation fluid during arthroscopy,[6] all can increase compartmental pressure and have been described as etiologies for compartment syndrome.

The most common pathophysiologic cause of compartmental hypertension arises from swelling of the soft tissue contents—primarily skeletal muscle—within the fascial compartment. It has long been understood that post-traumatic soft tissue swelling can result from an increase in interstitial fluid and from cellular swelling. In 1910, Rowlands[7] hypothesized that compartment syndrome can occur when ischemia results in a plasma leak and that muscular and neural dysfunction result from elevated compartment pressure. Although we now understand much more about ischemic injury at the cellular and molecular level, Rowlands' "unifying hypothesis" regarding the pathophysiology of compartment syndrome remains relevant today.

Ischemia-Reperfusion

Ischemia followed by reperfusion triggers a complex, maladaptive response that originally may have been meant to protect organs from infection but clearly enhances tissue damage.[8-10] Ischemia results in the depletion of intracellular energy stores, which, after reperfusion and the generation of toxic oxygen radicals, results in a cascade of pathophysiologic consequences, including (1) activation and adhesion of leukocytes and platelets, (2) generation of inflammatory mediators, (3) calcium influx into cells, (4) disruption of cellular membrane ion pumps, and (5) transudation of fluid.[8] In the aggregate, these consequences produce cellular swelling and excess interstitial fluid (edema) formation.

If ischemia has been severe, there are three well-defined zones of tissue pathology: (1) a proximal area, which has sustained no permanent injury and which needs no further attention; (2) a distal area of tissue necrosis, which no therapy can salvage and which merits invasive intervention only when local or systemic effects mandate débridement or amputation; and (3) "stunned" tissue, which is at risk for progression to necrosis, but which may recover if conditions are optimized. This third zone is the only one that can be helped by treatment and is the tissue that produces most of the inflammatory mediators that are prerequisites for the development of compartment syndrome.

Inflammatory mediators released from ischemic skeletal muscle produce local and systemic effects. The local effect of inflammation is to increase capillary permeability and activate the coagulation cascade, which acts to produce more tissue damage and inflammation. The magnitude of the systemic response after an ischemia-reperfusion injury may be minimal if the mass of muscle involved is small. As pointed out by Haimovici[11] in 1960, however, reperfusion of an entire severely ischemic limb often results in a systemic inflammatory response of such magnitude that it may be lethal.

The final common pathway for the development of tissue damage from compartment syndrome is pathologically increased intracompartmental pressure. Venular pressure, normally 4 to 7 mm Hg, increases progressively because of venous outflow obstruction from increased tissue pressure: A vicious circle of steadily increasing capillary pressure exacerbates fluid transudation and cellular swelling, further increasing intracompartmental pressure. Ultimately, when intracompartmental pressure equals capillary pressure, nutrient blood flow is reduced to zero. Unless compartmental hypertension is relieved, cellular perfusion ceases, and tissue infarction commences.

Late Pathologic Consequences

Undiagnosed, compartment syndrome frequently progresses to skeletal muscle infarction. Infection is a frequent cause of additional morbidity, especially when fasciotomy has been performed and wound closure is delayed.[12,13] If untreated, compartment syndrome may progress to rhabdomyolysis, with release of multiple metabolic toxins, such as myoglobin, potassium, and organic acids. Haimovici[14] has described the subsequent "myonephropathic-metabolic syndrome," which is characterized by myoglobinuric renal failure, progressive organ failure, and a high mortality rate. In this situation, amputation should be considered early because it can be lifesaving.

As previously noted, the development of compartmental hypertension now is considered to be primarily a consequence of ischemia-reperfusion. Many models of ischemia-reperfusion depend on the experimental production of a compartment syndrome. Such models have been used to show that complete ischemia results in more post-reperfusion complications than if partial skeletal muscle perfusion is maintained.[15] Other models have shown that gradual reperfusion after an ischemic event, rather than acute restoration of blood flow under systemic pressure, results in a less severe manifestation of the reperfusion syndrome.[16] Similarly, hypothermia[17] or administration of perfluorocarbons,[18] hyperosmolar volume expanders,[19,20] fibrinolytic agents,[21] heparin,[22] cyclooxygenase inhibitors,[23] or precursors for adenine nucleotide production[24] during reperfusion seems to mitigate subsequent development of compartment syndrome.

Leukocyte margination, activation, and adhesion to the vascular endothelium have been shown to play a pivotal role in the development of ischemia-reperfusion injury,[10] and blocking these processes has been shown to reduce tissue damage.[25,26] Interference with many metabolic pathways mediated by neutrophils (i.e., platelet activation,[27] nitric oxide synthesis,[28] and eicosanoid metabolism[29]) also has been shown to reduce the deleterious effects of ischemia-reperfusion. In addition, inactivation or depletion of white blood cells by antiadhesion antibodies[30] or chemotherapeutic agents[31] seems to diminish the deleterious effects of ischemia-reperfusion.

Reactive oxygen species play a key role in the development of compartment syndrome. Reactive oxygen species produce DNA damage, which triggers complex energy-consuming DNA repair mechanisms. The subsequent adenosine triphosphate depletion results in the production of more inflammatory mediators and, if severe enough, may lead to cell death.[32] Pretreatment with mannitol, catalase, superoxide dismutase, dehydroepiandrosterone, or other oxygen radical scavengers reduces the formation of reactive oxygen species and has been shown in experimental models to diminish cellular damage after ischemia-reperfusion injury.[19,20,26,33-35]

These experimental observations have implications as adjunctive therapies in the treatment of established compartment syndrome. It is conceptually attractive that some adjunctive therapies might be used to diminish or prevent the development of compartment syndrome in certain settings (e.g., before embolectomy or thrombectomy in an ischemic limb). Surgical decompression remains the mainstay of therapy, however.

Clinical-Pathologic Correlation

The earliest symptom of compartment syndrome is pain in the affected muscle compartment, which can be quite nonspecific and difficult to separate from the pain of the initial insult. Early signs are neurologic, explained by the fact that the tissues most sensitive to hypoxia are the nonmyelinated type C sensory fibers that carry fine touch and result in symptoms such as paresthesias. If hypoxia continues, additional tissues become affected—myelinated nerves, then skeletal muscle, and (most resistant to hypoxia) skin and bone. Although nerves are the first tissue to become dysfunctional in the presence of hypoxia, skeletal muscle is more likely to sustain permanent damage (i.e., muscle dies before nerve). Muscle cell dysfunction fuels the progression of compartment syndrome.

Traditionally, absolute measures of compartmental pressure were used to guide therapy; pressures greater than 40 to 45 mm Hg at any point or sustained at greater than 30 mm Hg for more than 3 to 4 hours mandated fasciotomy.[9,36] Compartment syndrome occasionally occurs at lower tissue pressures in hypotensive patients, however, and fails to develop despite markedly abnormal tissue pressures in individuals who are well perfused. A more sensitive and specific predictive measure is the *arterial perfusion pressure,* the gradient between diastolic arterial pressure and the interstitial pressure. Intervention now is recommended when a measured compartment pressure is within 20 to 30 mm Hg systemic diastolic blood pressure or 30 mm Hg mean blood pressure.[37,38]

The tolerance of skeletal muscle and nerve to elevated compartmental pressures is not well defined and likely relates to the severity of the ischemia produced by the compartment syndrome. In severe acute arterial insufficiency, the likelihood of muscle infarction is overwhelming if revascularization does not occur within 6 to 8 hours. Similarly, compartmental hypertension may result in irreversible muscle and nerve loss if unrelieved for 8 hours.[39]

The ultimate fate of skeletal muscle subjected to increased interstitial pressure and subsequently relieved by fasciotomy is not always apparent at initial operation. Commonly, muscle that initially appears well perfused and even contracts to galvanic stimulation at the time of initial decompression may become necrotic over the ensuing several days. This phenomenon may be explained in part by the observation that nonviable muscle dies "from the inside out."[40,41] Daily inspection of all exposed muscle, aggressive débridement of all nonviable tissue, and prevention of supervening infection are mandatory to ensure maximal salvage of a functional limb.

■ CLINICAL PRESENTATION

The diagnosis of compartment syndrome rarely is made in a timely fashion in the absence of a high index of suspicion. Compartment syndrome occurs primarily in circumstances, usually post-traumatic or postischemic, in which a substantial soft tissue volume expansion develops within an intact inelastic tissue envelope to produce pathologically elevated compartment pressures. Compartment syndrome most frequently is associated with (1) major extremity trauma (crush injuries or closed fractures) or (2) reperfusion after severe acute arterial insufficiency (i.e., popliteal or brachial thromboembolectomy). For practical purposes, extremity compartment syndrome is seen rarely except in the calf and the forearm.

Symptoms of compartment syndrome include severe *pain,* often described as being "out of proportion to clinical findings," which worsens progressively despite appropriate care for the underlying injury (e.g., fracture stabilization). Important neurologic signs include distal motor and sensory dysfunction—characteristically numbness followed by weakness in the distribution of nerves passing through compromised tissue compartments (e.g., the peroneal nerve in the leg and the median nerve in the forearm). The result is numbness in the first dorsal web space with weakness of foot dorsiflexion in the lower extremity and numbness in the first web space and weakness in wrist extension in the upper extremity.

Physical findings commonly include tense muscle compartments that are tender to palpation; passive flexion/extension of the wrist or ankle is painful. The abovementioned sensory and motor deficits develop next and should be aggressively sought because they indicate a limb at high risk for amputation. Because compartment syndrome occurs at tissue pressures well below systolic arterial pressure, distal pulses are frequently intact. It is common, albeit erroneous, for the diagnosis of compartment syndrome to be discounted because of the presence of palpable distal pulses.

The vascular pathophysiology of compartment syndrome can be inferred from the development of this disorder after primary arterial obstruction. Compartment syndrome also has been reported, however, in circumstances of extensive venous occlusion in the extremities (e.g., phlegmasia cerulea dolens),[42] after electrical injuries, after venomous snakebite, or after massive volume resuscitation for hypovolemic shock.[43] It also has been described in "medical" conditions, such as inherited bleeding disorders,[44] acquired immunodeficiency syndrome,[45] hypothyroidism,[46] malignant hyperthermia,[47] and diabetes insipidus.[48] Iatrogenic compartment syndrome has been reported as a consequence of a wide variety of nonvascular therapeutic interventions, including prolonged operative positioning (especially in the lithotomy position),[49] reaming for tibial nailing,[50] irrigation during knee arthroscopic procedures,[6] closure of muscle hernias,[51] and intraosseous fluid administration.[5]

Establishing a diagnosis of compartment syndrome in patients who are unconscious, intubated, intoxicated, brain injured, or spinal cord injured, or who cannot sense or communicate sensations of pain or cannot participate in a physical examination, is a diagnostic challenge. In these and other situations, objective measurement of compartment pressures can be instrumental in initiating treatment before the development of irreversible muscle and nerve damage.

■ OBJECTIVE TESTS

Compartment syndrome cannot exist without (1) increased tissue tension and (2) obstruction of venous outflow within the compartment. Objective measurement of these parameters is potentially useful in providing supporting evidence for the diagnosis of compartmental hypertension. Other methods, such as somatosensory evoked potential monitoring, have been shown to be accurate in monitoring nerve dysfunction produced by compartmental hypertension.[52] This method is expensive, invasive, and cumbersome, however, and has not gained favor in clinical practice.

Because elevated tissue pressure defines compartment syndrome, objective measurement of compartment pressure using needles or catheters was developed in the 1970s.[9,36] Modifications of this technique include the use of intravenous catheters with common bedside pressure transduction equipment,[53] complex catheter systems,[54,55] self-contained handheld disposable manometers,[56] and use of automated intravenous infusion devices.[57]

As noted earlier, it initially was believed that any compartment pressure greater than 40 to 45 mm Hg or greater than 30 mm Hg for more than 3 to 4 hours warranted fasciotomy.[9,36] Isolated measurement of compartment pressure is neither sensitive nor specific, however, for determining the degree of muscle ischemia—the driving force for the development of a compartment syndrome. The important variable has been found to be the gradient between diastolic blood pressure and compartment pressure. Fasciotomy is recommended when measured compartment pressure is within 20 to 30 mm Hg of diastolic blood pressure.[37,38]

One of the first manifestations of the pathophysiologic mechanisms that produce compartment syndrome is venous outflow obstruction: Compartment syndrome cannot exist without derangements of venous flow dynamics. Jones and coworkers[58] pointed out that venous duplex scanning focused on the tibial veins might be an accurate means of indirectly determining the presence of compartmental hypertension. Subsequent experimental work by Ombrellaro and colleagues[59] showed that loss of normal respiratory venous phasicity correlates well with elevated tissue pressure. Although duplex scanning of the veins by itself cannot *confirm* the presence of pathologically increased tissue pressures, the finding of normally phasic tibial venous flow on duplex scanning of a calf muscle compartment effectively *rules out* elevated tissue pressures in that compartment.

Additional noninvasive modalities providing data to support the diagnosis of compartment syndrome have been suggested, including near-infrared spectroscopy,[60] laser Doppler flowmetry,[61] and tissue tonometry.[62] These approaches are experimental, and such data should not be used independently to exclude the presence of compartment syndrome, but rather to provide corroborative evidence that it does exist.

■ TREATMENT

Fasciotomy

Failure to recognize the presence of compartment syndrome or to manage it in timely fashion frequently results in limb loss and is a common source of medicolegal litigation.[63] The proper management of established compartment syndrome is decompression by complete dermotomy and fasciotomy. The operative procedure should include all four compartments in the leg or both (some authors say three[64]) compartments in the forearm. Other compartment syndromes (e.g., foot, hand, or thigh) are treated by complete decompression using a longitudinal incision over the affected compartment.

The sole purpose of fasciotomy is to release compartment hypertension and prevent necrosis of compressed tissue. It is effective only if performed correctly and in a timely fashion. Early decompression of well-perfused tissue that was previously severely ischemic is preferable. We usually perform decompressive fasciotomy at the time of revascularization, especially if significant neurologic symptoms were present in the affected limb preoperatively. A technically successful fasciotomy consists of the following:

1. Complete incision of the skin overlying the affected compartments
2. Longitudinal incision of the entire fascia investing each of the compartments
3. Meticulous local wound care followed by complete closure (or coverage) when the swelling subsides

In the lower extremity, four-compartment fasciotomy of the calf can be performed through a single lateral incision, started one fingerbreadth anterior to the fibula and carried from just below the fibular head to just above the lateral malleolus. As shown in Figure 74-1, access to the anterior, lateral (peroneal), and superficial posterior compartments is straightforward after raising narrow skin flaps anteriorly and posteriorly. Access to the deep posterior compartment is best obtained distally, where the gastrocnemius and soleus muscles become tendinous. The soleus muscle is dissected off the posterior aspect of the fibula, and the now-exposed fascia of the deep posterior compartment is incised easily. A simpler (albeit more invasive) technique for decompression of the posterior compartments requires a separate medial incision one fingerbreadth posterior to the tibia (Fig. 74-2). In our opinion, fibulectomy is not required for effective decompression of the calf musculature.

In the upper extremity, a single curvilinear volar incision starting just above the antecubital fossa and ending at the palm of the hand effectively decompresses all of the forearm muscle compartments. The anatomy of the forearm musculature allows effective compartment release with a single fascial incision. Carpal tunnel decompression also must be performed.

Skeletal muscle viability is assessed by color, presence of arterial bleeding, and contraction to galvanic (electrocautery) stimulation. Muscle-relaxing anesthetic agents do not interfere with this response. Muscle that does not contract is not viable and should be débrided. Additional

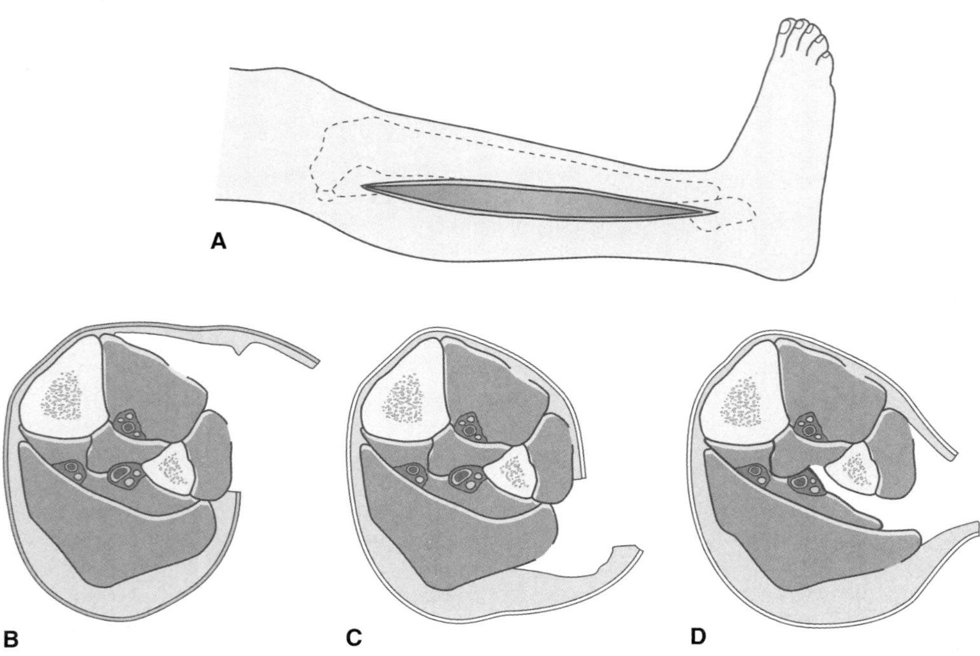

FIGURE 74-1 Lower extremity fasciotomy via a single anterolateral incision. **A,** Lateral skin incision from the fibular neck to 3 to 4 cm proximal to the lateral malleolus. **B,** The skin is undermined anteriorly, and a fasciotomy of the anterior and lateral compartments is performed. **C,** The skin is undermined posteriorly, and a fasciotomy of the superficial posterior compartment is performed. **D,** Interval between superficial posterior and lateral compartments is developed. Flexor hallucis longus muscle is dissected subperiosteally off the fibula and retracted posteromedially. The fascial attachment of the tibialis posterior muscle to the fibula is incised to decompress the muscle. (Redrawn from Davey JR, Rorabeck CH, Fowler PJ: The tibialis posterior muscle compartment: An unrecognized cause of exertional compartment syndrome. Am J Sports Med 12:391-397, 1984. From Azar AM: Traumatic Disorders. In Canale ST (ed): Campbell's Operative Othopaedics, 10th ed. St. Louis, Mosby, 2003, p2453.)

complicating factors include the presence of fractures (which now must be treated as open) or the presence of orthopedic hardware or vascular grafts, all of which must be covered with well-vascularized muscle. Exposed muscle should be reassessed every 1 to 2 days until complete wound closure or coverage is obtained. As noted previously, visual evidence of skeletal muscle necrosis may be subtle or nonexistent.[40,41] Débridement of nonviable muscle is crucial to prevent infection, which when present often compromises the eventual outcome.[12]

Wound Management and Closure

Early and complete closure of the fasciotomy wound is a critical step in the process of maintaining a functional limb. Wound and vascular graft complications are sharply increased when fasciotomy closure is delayed.[12] Sterile moist dressings are applied until swelling has diminished sufficiently to allow closure. Skin grafting frequently is required since skin itself can act as a constricting envelope. If soft tissue swelling is significant enough to mandate fasciotomy, immediate closure invariably results in skin necrosis or recurrent compartmental hypertension, which complicates the outcome.

Several methods have been reported to prevent post-fasciotomy skin edge retraction, which otherwise would increase the size of the wound to be closed. Plastic vessel-loops threaded between staples on the skin edges minimizes wound expansion and distributes tension evenly without compromising skin perfusion.[65] Commercial devices also are available that apply the same principles,[66,67] but it is important to ensure that their use after fasciotomy does not re-create pathologically elevated tissue pressures, which has been reported.[68]

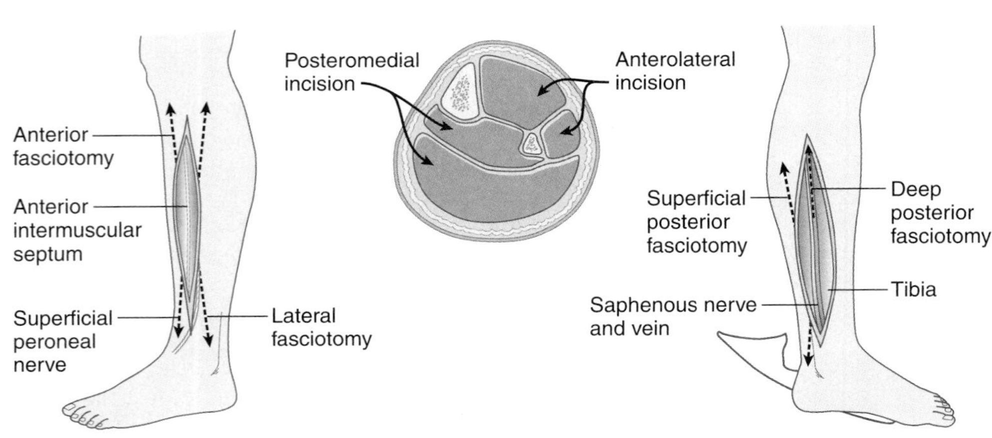

FIGURE 74-2 Lower extremity fasciotomy via anterolateral and medial incisions. (From Janzing H, Broos P, Rommens P: Compartment syndrome as a complication of skin traction in children with femoral fractures. J Trauma 41:156, 1996.)

Myoglobinuria should be aggressively sought and treated because it can lead to significant renal dysfunction. Treatment consists of volume expansion, administration of mannitol and loop diuretics, and urine alkalinization by sodium bicarbonate. Débridement of all necrotic muscle, which may require amputation, is essential. Hemodialysis may be required, but the long-term outcome of myoglobinuric acute renal failure is generally favorable.[69]

Can compartment syndrome be attenuated or even prevented? It is well established that oxygen radicals play a role in the pathogenesis of compartment syndrome.[23] Mannitol has oxygen radical scavenger (mitigating ischemia-reperfusion injury) and hyperosmolar (reducing tissue edema) properties.[70] The use of mannitol has been shown to reduce the severity of compartmental hypertension[19] and may permit nonoperative management in mild cases. We routinely administer 12.5 g of mannitol intravenously before reperfusion of an acutely ischemic limb.

■ OUTCOMES

The classic example of neglected compartment syndrome, Volkmann's contracture, describes an ischemic contracture of the forearm muscles in children, usually seen after supracondylar humerus fracture and associated brachial artery injury.[71] A similar situation is seen with calf muscle atrophy after incompletely treated lower extremity compartment syndrome.

In the lower extremity, loss of one or two muscle compartments can be tolerated, assuming successful skin closure is obtained. Ambulation frequently is regained, although it frequently requires vigorous physical therapy and the use of splints or ankle-foot orthoses. Loss of more than two muscle compartments in the leg generally warrants amputation and aggressive prosthesis rehabilitation. In the upper extremity, complex microvascular reconstruction with innervated muscle flaps has been successful in restoring hand and arm sensation and motor function after forearm muscle necrosis.[72]

Because pathologically elevated tissue pressures are transmitted throughout the entire compartment, myonecrosis is global in far-advanced compartment syndrome. Below-knee or even through-knee amputation, both of which require viable calf muscle for wound closure, is rarely feasible to treat compartment syndrome complicated by myonecrosis.

■ CHRONIC COMPARTMENT SYNDROME

Rarely, otherwise healthy subjects present with predominantly repetitive lower extremity pain, but also occasionally numbness and weakness, during vigorous exercise (e.g., walking, running, dancing, or weightlifting) in a pattern that is not easily explained.[73] In this situation, chronic compartment syndrome should be part of the differential diagnosis. This entity is confirmed by the development of elevated extremity muscle compartment pressures during vigorous exercise. Supportive evidence includes localized tenderness over the involved compartment or the loss of spontaneous and phasic Doppler tibial venous flow during exercise. Individuals with highly developed and bulky muscles may be at particular risk for this phenomenon, but it also is seen with normal physiques. The anterior compartment seems to be most commonly affected in the lower extremity.[74] Fasciotomy, with the use of small and cosmetically acceptable skin incisions, is curative.[75]

■ REFERENCES

1. Templeman D, Lang R, Harris B: Lower extremity compartment syndrome associated with the use of pneumatic anti-shock garments. J Trauma 27:79-81, 1987.
2. Widmer MK, Hakki H, Reber PU, et al: Rare, but severe complication of varicose vein surgery: Compartment syndrome [in German]. Zentralbl Chir 125:543-546, 2000.
3. Li X, Liang D, Liu X: Compartment syndrome in burn patients: A report of five cases. Burns 28:787-789, 2002.
4. Krome J, de Araujo W, Webb LX: Acute compartment syndrome in ruptured Baker's cyst. J South Orthop Assoc 6:110-114, 1997.
5. Galpin RD, Kronick JB, Wilils RB, Frewen TC: Bilateral lower extremity compartment syndromes secondary to intraosseous fluid resuscitation. J Pediatr Orthop 11:773-776, 1991.
6. Kaper BP, Carr CF, Shirreffs TG: Compartment syndrome after arthroscopic surgery of knee: A report of two cases managed non-operatively. Am J Sports Med 25:123-125, 1997.
7. Rowlands RP: Volkmann's contracture. Guy's Hospital Gazette 24:87-92, 1910.
8. Walker PM: Ischemia/reperfusion injury in skeletal muscle. Ann Vasc Surg 5:399-402, 1991.
9. Matsen FA III: Compartmental syndrome: A unified concept. Clin Orthop 113:8-13, 1975.
10. Burne-Tanfy MJ, Rabb H: The role of adhesion molecules and T cells in ischemic renal injury. Curr Opin Nephrol Hypertens 12:85-90, 2003.
11. Haimovici H: Arterial embolism with acute massive ischemic myopathy and myoglobinuria: Evaluation of a hitherto unreported syndrome with report of two cases. Surgery 47:739-744, 1960.
12. Johnson SB, Weaver FA, Yellin AE, et al: Clinical results of decompressive dermotomy-fasciotomy. Am J Surg 164:286-290, 1992.
13. Rutgers PH, van der Harst E, Koumans RK: Surgical implications of drug-induced rhabdomyolysis. Br J Surg 78:490-492, 1991.
14. Haimovici H: Muscular, renal, and metabolic complications of acute arterial occlusions: Myonephropathic-metabolic syndrome. Surgery 85:461-468, 1979.
15. Petrasek PF, Walker PM: A clinically relevant small-animal model of skeletal muscle ischemia-reperfusion injury. J Invest Surg 7:27-38, 1994.
16. Anderson RJ, Cambria R, Kerr J, Hobson RW 2nd: Sustained benefit of temporary limited reperfusion in skeletal muscle following ischemia. J Surg Res 49:271-275, 1990.
17. Wright JG, Araki CT, Belkin M, Hobson RW 2nd: Postischemic hypothermia diminishes skeletal muscle reperfusion edema. J Surg Res 47:389-396, 1989.
18. Mohan C, Gennaro M, Marini C, et al: Reduction of the extent of ischemic skeletal muscle necrosis by perfusion with oxygenated perfluorocarbon. Am J Surg 164:194-198, 1992.
19. Shah DM, Bock DE, Darling RC 3rd, et al: Beneficial effects of hypertonic mannitol in acute ischemia-reperfusion injuries in humans. Cardiovasc Surg 4:97-100, 1996.
20. Hakaim AG, Corsetti R, Cho SI: The pentafraction of hydroxyethyl starch inhibits ischemia-induced compartment syndrome. J Trauma 37:18-21, 1994.
21. Belkin M, Valeri CR, Hobson RW 2nd: Intra-arterial urokinase increases skeletal muscle viability after acute ischemia. J Vasc Surg 9:161-168, 1989.
22. Hobson RW 2nd, Nevill R, Watanabe B, et al: Role of heparin in reducing skeletal muscle infarction in ischemia-reperfusion. Microcirc Endothelium Lymphatics 5:259-276, 1989.

23. Cuzzocrea S, Riley DP, Caputi AP, et al: Antioxidant therapy: A new pharmacological approach in shock, inflammation and ischemia/ reperfusion injury. Pharmacol Rev 53:135-159, 2001.
24. Hayes PG, Liauw S, Smith A, et al: Exogenous magnesium chloride-adenosine triphosphate administration during reperfusion reduces the extent of necrosis in previously ischemic skeletal muscle. J Vasc Surg 11:441-447, 1990.
25. Cuzzocrea S, Zingarelli B, O'Connor M, et al: Effect of L-buthionine-(S,R)-sulphoximine, an inhibitor of gamma-glutamylcysteine synthetase, on peroxynitrite and endotoxic shock-induced vascular failure. Br J Pharmacol 123:525-537, 1998.
26. Ayhan S, Turgray C, Norton S, et al: Dehydroepiandrosterone protects the microcirculation of muscle flaps from ischemia-reperfusion injury by reducing the expression of adhesion molecules. Plast Reconstr Surg 111:2286-2294, 2003.
27. Noel AA, Hobson RW 2nd, Duran WN: Platelet-activating factor and nitric oxide mediate microvascular permeability in ischemia-reperfusion injury. Microvasc Res 52:210-220, 1996.
28. Noel AA, Fallek SR, Hobson RW 2nd, Duran WN: Inhibition of nitric oxide synthase attenuates primed microvascular permeability in the in vivo microcirculation. J Vasc Surg 22:661-669, 1995.
29. Cambria RA, Anderson RJ, Dikdan G, et al: The influence of arachidonic acid metabolites on leukocyte activation and skeletal muscle injury after ischemia and reperfusion. J Vasc Surg 14:549-556, 1991.
30. Petrasek PF, Liauw S, Romaschin AD, Walker PM: Salvage of postischemic skeletal muscle by monoclonal antibody blockade of neutrophil adhesion molecule CD18. J Surg Res 56:5-12, 1994.
31. Rubin B, Tittley J, Chang G, et al: A clinically applicable method for long-term salvage of postischemic skeletal muscle. J Vasc Surg 13:58-67, 1991.
32. Szabo C, Dawson VL: Role of poly (ADR-ribose) synthetase in inflammation and ischemia reperfusion. Trends Pharmacol Sci 19:287-298, 1998.
33. Kleyn MB, Chan PM, Chang J: Protective effects of superoxide dismutase against ischemia-reperfusion injury: Development and application of a transgenic animal model. Plast Reconstr Surg 111:256-257, 2003.
34. Belkin M, LaMorte WL, Wright JG, Hobson RW 2nd: The role of leukocytes in the pathophysiology of skeletal muscle ischemic injury. J Vasc Surg 10:14-18, 1989.
35. Walker PM, Lindsay TF, Labbe R, et al: Salvage of skeletal muscle with free radical scavengers. J Vasc Surg 5:68-75, 1987.
36. Whitesides TE Jr, Haney TC, Morimoto K, Harada H: Tissue pressure measurements as a determinant for the need of fasciotomy. Clin Orthop 113:43-51, 1975.
37. Matava MJ, Whitesides TE Jr, Seiler JG III, et al: Determination of the compartment pressure threshold of muscle ischemia in a canine model. J Trauma 37:50-58, 1994.
38. Mabee Jr, Bostwick TL: Pathophysiology and mechanisms of compartment syndrome. Orthop Rev 22:175-181, 1993.
39. Finkelstein JA, Hunter GA, Hu RW: Lower limb compartment syndrome: Course after delayed fasciotomy. J Trauma 40:342-344, 1996.
40. Labbe R, Lindsay T, Walker PM: The extent and distribution of skeletal muscle necrosis after graded periods of complete ischemia. J Vasc Surg 6:152-157, 1987.
41. Blebea J, Kerr JC, Franco CD, et al: Technetium 99m pyrophosphate quantitation of skeletal muscle ischemia and reperfusion injury. J Vasc Surg 8:117-124, 1988.
42. Wood KE, Reedy JS, Pozniak MA, et al: Phlegmasia cerulea dolens with compartment syndrome: A complication of femoral vein catheterization. Crit Care Med 28:1626-1630, 2000.
43. Block EFJ, Dobo S, Kirton OS: Compartment syndrome in the critically injured following massive resuscitation: Case reports. J Trauma 39:787-791, 1995.
44. Naranja RJ Jr, Chan PS, High K, et al: Treatment considerations in patients with compartment syndrome and an inherited bleeding disorder. Orthopedics 20:706-709, 1997.
45. Guidet B, Guerin B, Maury E, et al: Capillary leakage complicated by compartment syndrome necessitating surgery. Intensive Care Med 16:332-333, 1990.
46. Hsu SI, Thadhani RI, Daniels GH: Acute compartment syndrome in a hypothyroid patient. Thyroid 5:305-308, 1995.
47. Steele AP, Inurie MM, Rutherford AM, Bradley WN: Malignant hyperthermia and compartment syndrome. Br J Anaesth 74:343-344, 1995.
48. Geutjens G: Spontaneous compartment syndrome in a patient with diabetes insipidus. Int Orthop 18:53-54, 1994.
49. Khalil IM: Bilateral compartment syndrome after prolonged surgery in the lithotomy position. J Vasc Surg 5:879-881, 1987.
50. Tichenko GJ, Goodman SB: Compartment syndromes after IM nailing of the tibia. J Bone Joint Surg Am 72:41-44, 1990.
51. Miniaci A, Rorabeck CH: Compartment syndrome as a complication of repair of a hernia of the tibialis anterior: A case report. J Bone Joint Surg Am 68:1444-1445, 1986.
52. Present DA, Nainzedeh NK, Ben-Yishay A, Mazzara JT: The evaluation of compartmental syndromes using somatosensory evoked potentials in monkeys. Clin Orthop 287:276-285, 1993.
53. Wilson SC, Vrahas MS, Berson L, Paul EM: A simple method to measure compartment pressures using an intravenous catheter. Orthopedics 20:403-406, 1997.
54. Mubarak SJ, Hargens AR, Owen CA: The wick catheter technique for measurement of intramuscular pressure: A new research and clinical tool. J Bone Joint Surg Am 58:1016-1020, 1976.
55. Rorabeck CH, Castle GSP, Hardie R: Compartmental pressure measurements: An experimental investigation using the slit catheter. J Trauma 21:446-450, 1981.
56. Styf J: Evaluation of injection techniques in recording of intramuscular pressure. J Orthop Res 7:812-816, 1989.
57. Uppal GS, Smith RC, Sherk HH, Mooar P: Accurate compartment pressure measurement using the Intravenous Alarm Control (IVAC) Pump. J Orthop Trauma 6:87-89, 1992.
58. Jones WG II, Perry MO, Bush HL Jr: Changes in tibial venous blood flow in the evolving compartment syndrome. Arch Surg 124:801-804, 1989.
59. Ombrellaro MP, Stevens SL, Freeman M, et al: Ultrasound characteristics of lower extremity venous flow for the early diagnosis of compartment syndrome: An experimental study. J Vasc Technol 20:71-75, 1996.
60. Gentilello LM, Sanzone A, Wang L, et al: Near-infrared spectroscopy versus compartment pressure for the diagnosis of lower extremity compartmental syndrome using electromyography-determined measurements of neuromuscular function. J Trauma 51:1-9, 2001.
61. Abraham P, Lefthesiotis G, Saumet JL: Laser Doppler flowmetry in the diagnosis of chronic compartment syndrome. J Bone Joint Surg Br 80:365-369, 1998.
62. Steinberg BD, Gelberman RH: Evaluation of limb compartments with suspected increased interstitial pressure: A noninvasive method for determining quantitative hardness. Clin Orthop 300:248-253, 1994.
63. Gould MJ, Langworthy MJ, Santore R: An analysis of orthopedic liability in the acute care setting. Clin Orthop 407:59-66, 2003.
64. Gelberman RH, Zakaib GS, Mubarak SJ: Decompression of forearm compartment syndromes. Clin Orthop 134:225-229, 1978.
65. Berman SS, Schilling JD, McIntyre KE, et al: Shoelace technique for delayed primary closure of fasciotomies. Am J Surg 167:435-436, 1994.
66. McKenney MG, Nir J, Fee T, et al: A simple device for closure of fasciotomy wounds. Am J Surg 1771:275-277, 1996.
67. Hirshowitz B, Lindenbaum E, Har-Shai Y: A skin-stretching device for the harnessing of the viscoelastic properties of skin. Plast Reconstr Surg 92:260-270, 1993.
68. Hussmann J, Kucan JO, Zamboni WA: Elevated compartmental pressures after closure of a forearm burn wound with a skin-stretching device. Burns 23:154-156, 1997.
69. Zager RA: Rhabdomyolysis and myohemoglobinuric acute renal failure [editorial]. Kidney Int 49:314-326, 1996.

70. Oredsson S, Plate G, Qvarfordt P: The effect of mannitol and reperfusion injury and post-ischemic compartment pressure in skeletal muscle. Eur J Vasc Surg 8:326-331, 1994.
71. VonVolkmann R: Die Ischamischen Muskelahmungen und kontrakturer [in German]. Zentralbl Chir 8:801-803, 1881.
72. Chuang DC, Carver N, Wei FC: A new strategy to prevent the sequelae of severe Volkmann's contracture. Plast Reconstr Surg 98:1023-1031, 1996.
73. Detmer D, Sharpe K, Sufit RL, Girdley FM: Chronic compartment syndrome: Diagnosis, management, and outcome. Am J Sports Med 13:162-170, 1985.
74. Turnipseed MD, Hurschler C, Vanderby R: The effects of elevated compartment pressure on tibial arteriovenous flow and relationship of mechanical and biochemical characteristics of fascia to genesis of chronic anterior compartment syndrome. J Vasc Surg 21:810-817, 1995.
75. Blackman P: A review of chronic exertional compartment syndrome in the lower leg. Med Sci Sports Exerc 32: 504-510, 2000.

Chapter 75

Causalgia and Post-traumatic Pain Syndromes

ALI F. ABURAHMA, MD
ROBERT B. RUTHERFORD, MD

Section XII

■ BACKGROUND

Post-traumatic pain syndromes, most often called *causalgia* or *reflex sympathetic dystrophy* (RSD), are some of the most poorly understood and frequently misdiagnosed entities encountered in clinical practice. These painful conditions can develop after damage to peripheral nerves in a variety of settings. In susceptible patients, the initiating event may be relatively insignificant, even obscure. Although a discussion of the management of all types of post-traumatic pain is beyond the scope of this chapter, the management of causalgia is relevant to the vascular surgeon for several reasons.

First, one form of causalgia is caused by ischemic damage to nerves secondary to delayed revascularization, and the vascular surgeon may injure peripheral nerves inadvertently during a revascularization procedure. Second, the vasomotor phenomena associated with causalgia often cause such patients to be referred to a vascular surgeon. The associated vascular signs often convince the referring physician that he or she is dealing mainly with a painful vascular condition. Such a referral may be fortuitous because although sympathectomy is now rarely used for vascular disease (see Chapter 85), vascular surgeons perfected this procedure and made it safe, and sympathectomy may provide the most dramatic and lasting relief from causalgia.

■ COMPLEX REGIONAL PAIN SYNDROME

Terminology and New Classification

The term *causalgia* is derived from the Greek *causos,* meaning "heat," and *algos,* meaning "pain" (i.e., burning pain).[43] Although it was described in detail by Mitchell and colleagues in 1864,[43] Paré[48] may have reported the first case in the 16th century. Mitchell and colleagues'[43] classic observations were made in the course of treating American Civil War soldiers with gunshot wounds of the extremities:

> The great mass of sufferers described this pain as superficial, but others said it was also in the joints, and deep in the palms. If it lasted long, it was referred finally to skin alone. Its intensity varies from the most trivial burning to a state of torture, which can hardly be credited, but which reacts on the whole economy, until the general health is seriously affected.
>
> The part itself is not subject to an intense burning sensation, but becomes exquisitely hyperesthetic so that a touch or a tap of the finger increases the pain. Exposure to the air is avoided by the patient with a care which seems absurd, and most of the bad cases keep the hands constantly wet, finding relief in moisture rather than in the coolness of the application.
>
> As the pain increases, the general sympathy becomes more marked. The temper changes and grows irritable, the face becomes anxious and has a look of weariness and suffering. The sleep is restless, and the constitutional condition reacting on the wounded limb exasperates the hyperesthetic state so that rattling of a newspaper, a breath of air, another's step across the ward, the vibration caused by a military band, or a shock of the feet in walking, gives rise to increase in pain. At last the patient grows hysterical if we may use the only term which covers the fact. He walks carefully, carries the limb tenderly with a sound hand, he is tremulous, nervous, and has all kinds of expedients for lessening the pain.

These early reports described incomplete peripheral nerve injury secondary to penetrating trauma (e.g., partial rather than complete transection) with subsequent burning pain, autonomic dysfunction, and "limb atrophy." With time, symptoms of similar severity were noted to occur subsequent to trauma of a less serious nature and even in the absence of obvious injury to a peripheral nerve. In 1973,

Patman and colleagues[49] consolidated the many terms that had appeared in the literature describing a variety of pain syndromes similar to causalgia, but of different causes, under the name *mimocausalgia*. This term, also derived from the Greek, means "imitating causalgia." Previously, it had been popular to refer to these syndromes as *minor causalgia,* in contrast to the full-blown symptom complex associated with incomplete nerve injuries, referred to as *major causalgia*. Other commonly used terms are the following:

- *Minor* and *major traumatic dystrophy*—describing the intensity of the syndrome when it develops after an injury that does not damage a peripheral nerve
- *Shoulder-hand syndrome*—RSD that involves the entire upper extremity
- *Sudeck's atrophy*—a post-traumatic reflex dystrophy with bone involvement demonstrable on radiographs

Table 75-1 lists more than 40 terms from the literature that describe similar symptom complexes that are minor variations from the classic triad of burning pain, sympathetic dysfunction, and limb atrophy.

As a result of the confusion surrounding the various terms used to describe this syndrome, Stanton-Hicks and associates[63] convened a consensus committee on the nomenclature of causalgia and RSD. The committee, which met in Orlando, Florida, in November 1993, determined a need to revise the taxonomic system for RSD. It was agreed that the term RSD had lost all clinical or research utility because of its indiscriminate use without regard to diagnostic or descriptive criteria. The relationship to the sympathetic nervous system was considered to be inconsistent, and the "reflex" implied by the name has never been shown. It also was suggested that the term *dystrophy* was used imprecisely and might not always be present. RSD also had become a "nondiscriminating" diagnosis for patients showing a resistance to therapy for some elements of neuropathic pain.[8]

The term *complex regional pain syndrome* (CRPS) was developed to replace *causalgia* and *RSD*. CRPS includes a spectrum of conditions that have similar clinical manifestations that often are grouped together for the sake of clinical utility.[23] Hallmarks of this syndrome include dysfunction and pain of duration or severity out of proportion to what might be expected from the initiating event. The cause of this pain syndrome and the underlying pathophysiology remain obscure; as a consequence, descriptors that implied cause or mechanism (e.g., the role of the sympathetic nervous system) were excluded from the new nomenclature. The new classification is based on a descriptive method that should allow for future modifications as indicated by new scientific findings.[8,63]

A summary of the key features of CRPS is as follows:

1. *Complex* denotes the dynamic and varied nature of the clinical presentation, within a single person over time and among persons with seemingly similar disorders. It also includes the autonomic, cutaneous, motor, inflammatory, and dystrophic changes that distinguish this syndrome from other forms of neuropathic pain.
2. *Regional* describes the wider distribution of the clinical symptoms and findings beyond the area of the original lesion; this is considered a key characteristic of the syndrome. The distal part of a limb usually is affected, but occasionally pain occurs in other parts of the body (e.g., the face or torso) and may spread to other body parts.
3. *Pain*, the hallmark of CRPS, is out of proportion to the initiating event. The designation refers to spontaneous burning pain and thermally or mechanically induced allodynia.

Table 75-1 Terms Used to Describe Causalgia and Post-traumatic Pain Syndromes

Acute atrophy of bones	Post-traumatic sympathetic dysfunction
Algodystrophy	Post-traumatic sympathetic dystrophy
Algoneurodystrophy	Post-traumatic vasomotor disorders
Causalgia	Reflex neurovascular dystrophy
Causalgia-like states	Reflex dystrophy
Chronic segmental arterial spasm	Reflex dystrophy of the extremities
Chronic traumatic edema	Reflex nervous dystrophy
Disuse phenomenon	Reflex sympathetic dystrophy
Homans' minor causalgia	Shoulder-hand syndrome
Major causalgia	Steinbrocker's shoulder-hand syndrome
Mimocausalgia	Sudeck's atrophy
Minor causalgia	Sudeck's osteodystrophy
Mitchell's causalgia	Sudeck's syndrome
Painful osteoporosis	Sympathalgia
Peripheral trophoneurosis	Sympathetic neurovascular dystrophy
Post-traumatic dystrophy	Traumatic angiospasm
Post-traumatic fibrosis	Traumatic edema
Post-traumatic neurovascular pain syndrome	Traumatic neuralgia
Post-traumatic osteoporosis	Traumatic vasospasm
Post-traumatic pain syndrome	
Post-traumatic painful osteoporosis	
Post-traumatic spreading neuralgia	
Post-traumatic sympathalgia	

Syndrome Types

Two types of CRPS have been recognized. *Type I* corresponds to the former term *RSD*; *type II* corresponds to the former term *causalgia*. The definitions of CRPS I and II contain criteria that exclude (1) pain and other findings that are physiologically, anatomically, and temporally appropriate to some form of injury and (2) myofascial pain syndrome. The terms *sympathetically maintained pain* (SMP) and *sympathetically independent pain* (SIP) were considered, not as separate entities, but as descriptions of types of pain that can be associated with a variety of pain disorders, including CRPS I and II.

The diagnostic criteria for CRPS I (formerly RSD), as adapted from Stanton-Hicks and coworkers[63] and Merskey and Bogduk,[41] are as follows:

1. CRPS I follows an inciting noxious event.
2. Spontaneous pain or hyperalgesia/allodynia exists beyond the territory of a single peripheral nerve and is disproportionate to the initiating event.
3. Edema, skin blood flow abnormality, or abnormal sudomotor activity in the region of the pain have developed since the initiating event.
4. The diagnosis is excluded by the presence of conditions that otherwise would account for the degree of dysfunction and pain.

The diagnostic criteria for CRPS II (formerly causalgia) are as follows:

1. CRPS II is a syndrome that results specifically from a nerve injury; otherwise, it is similar in all other aspects to CRPS I. Spontaneous allodynia or pain occurs that is not limited to the region of the injured nerve.
2. Since the original nerve injury, edema, temperature and skin blood flow changes, abnormal sudomotor activity, and motor dysfunction in the region of the pain have developed.
3. The diagnosis is excluded by the presence of conditions that otherwise would account for the degree of dysfunction and pain.

Etiology

Three precipitating causes of CRPS have been identified:

- *Traumatic* (fractures, dislocations, sprains, crush injuries, burns, and iatrogenic injuries)
- *Nontraumatic* (prolonged bed rest, neoplasms, metabolic bone disease, thrombophlebitis, myocardial infarction, and cerebrovascular accidents)
- *Idiopathic*

Most cases of CRPS are post-traumatic. The proportion of nerve injuries that result in causalgia (CRPS II) ranges from 1.8% to 12%.[6] The incidence of CRPS in trauma patients ranges from 0.05% to 5%.[50] CRPS also has been reported in 0.2% to 11% of patients with Colles' fracture[31] and in 12% to 20% of patients with hemiplegia.[17] The incidence of CRPS in myocardial ischemia patients varies between 5% and 20%.[30]

Chronic painful conditions of the upper extremity subsequent to myocardial infarction have been grouped into a category designated *shoulder-hand syndrome*. This category originally was described by Steinbrocker and coworkers,[64] who pointed out that 15% of patients with myocardial infarction developed persistent pain in the shoulder, arm, wrist, or hand sometime during their recovery. It was concluded that many different states could result in reflex vasomotor disturbances, pain, muscle spasms, and atrophy of the upper extremity and that the pathophysiologic mechanisms were related to afferent stimulation of an internuncial pool located within the spinal cord; this was thought to be the cause of reflex efferent sympathetic stimulation. In support of this theory is the fact that prompt stellate ganglion blockade is effective in relieving the vasomotor abnormalities and the pain. The incidence of shoulder-hand syndrome has been reduced significantly, probably because of much more rapid post-infarct mobilization.[30]

Pathogenesis

Many theories have been proposed to explain CRPS, but none has been accepted universally. Most were developed to explain the causalgia associated with nerve injury (CRPS II). The most popular theory is probably that of "artificial synapses" occurring at the site of a nerve injury, as first proposed by Doupe and colleagues.[18] According to this theory, a "short circuit" occurs at the point of partial nerve interruption or demyelinization, which allows efferent sympathetic impulses to be relayed back along afferent somatic fibers. Such an artificial synapse has been shown experimentally in crushed nerves,[6] and the interruption of sympathetic efferent impulses may explain the warm, red, and dry extremity seen initially in cases of major causalgia. It also has been shown that stimulation of a sensory nerve along its course makes the nerve more sensitive to the usual types of sensory stimuli.[51] The work of Walker and Nielsen[71] in humans suggests the possibility of an artificial synapse. Stimulation of the postganglionic sympathetics after upper thoracic preganglionic sympathectomy reproduces the causalgia for which the surgery was performed. No such pain was produced, however, in patients whose sympathectomy was performed for a condition other than causalgia. White and Sweet[73] confirmed these findings.

One piece of evidence weighing against this theory was the demonstration that frequently nerve block with local anesthetic beyond the site of the nerve injury (and presumably beyond this artificial synapse) affords relief.[6] Proponents of the artificial synapse theory have countered, however, that the efferent sympathetic impulses that are short-circuited at the site of injury may not always be strong enough by themselves to cause retrograde propagation of impulses and that summation of these impulses, together with other afferent somatic impulses, may be necessary. Barnes[4] suggested that impulses at sympathetic-sensory fiber short circuits may travel in both directions. Proximally directed impulses would cause pain, and impulses directed distally would release "antidromic" substances, shown by Chapman and coworkers[12] to lower the threshold for sensory stimuli, further increasing the sensory input.

Although these explanations seem plausible in cases of demonstrable nerve injury, obvious difficulties complicate extending them to explain the similar pain experienced without overt nerve injury (CRPS I). These theories do not explain the sympathetic overactivity often seen in the later stages of this condition; the pain relief associated with intra-arterial injections of a peripheral adrenergic blocking agent, such as tolazoline hydrochloride; or the fact that, in early cases, relief of pain frequently lasts beyond the duration of a sympathetic block. A convincing hypothesis for the mechanism of CRPS I also must explain the modification of pain by emotional and sensory stimuli and the relief of pain by contralateral sympathectomy after failure of an apparently adequate ipsilateral sympathectomy.[53] The hypothesis also must be compatible with the relief of pain by spinal anesthesia below the sympathetic-lumbar outlet and before sympathetic blockade response.[35] Finally, it must explain the failure of sympathectomy in some long-standing cases.

In the late 1930s, Livingston[35] proposed that in causalgia there is a "vicious cycle of reflexes" consisting of three components:

1. Chronic irritation of a peripheral sensory nerve with increasingly frequent afferent impulses
2. Abnormal heightened activity in the "internuncial pool" in the anterior horn of the spinal cord
3. Increased efferent sympathetic activity

This theory was supported experimentally by Toennie's[66] demonstration that individual stimulation of more than one third of the afferent fibers of a cat's saphenous nerve produced not only related impulses cephalad from the spinal center, but also impulses directed back down efferent fibers, including sympathetics. Livingston's theory explains many characteristics of CRPS I that cannot be resolved by the artificial synapse theory of Doupe and colleagues.[18] In particular, it accounts for the high incidence of sympathetic "overactivity" observed in these patients and for the modifying effect of emotional or sensory stimuli, all of which could act by heightening the background activity in this internuncial pool. It should follow that anything that breaks this vicious cycle, be it interruption of sympathetic efferents by spinal anesthesia or interruption of somatic nerve conduction, could relieve pain. This latter theory enjoyed only a brief wave of enthusiasm, however, probably because it did not conform to the classic concepts of sensory perception originally proposed by von Frey.[70] According to von Frey, individual receptors exist for pain, touch, warmth, and cold, and these sensations involve simple transmission of a sensory impulse up a modality-specific peripheral nerve fiber, followed by relay from the spinal center to the brain via the spinothalamic tract.

Modern neurophysiology has advanced far from the attractive but simplistic views of von Frey, and although new knowledge has not supported a return to Livingston's concepts, it has shown that the responsible mechanisms are complex. Further understanding has spawned the "gate control" theory of pain mediation.[65] In the substantia gelatinosa of the dorsal horns of the spinal cord, the synapses between the peripheral nerves and the synapses that relay their impulses up the long tracts to the brain are modulated by sympathetic input. Simplified for the sake of explanation, it is as if a gate existed at this point of relay and transmission that controls the relationship between the number or frequency of incoming peripheral impulses and the number or frequency of outgoing pulses reaching the brain. High-frequency stimulation of the latter pathways in awake patients is perceived as burning pain. When the gate is open—an effect of increased sympathetic activity—sensations of touch or pressure, which normally would result in lower frequency impulses being relayed to the brain, instead might be perceived as burning pain because of the higher frequency of the impulses getting through the open gate. This theory is still under study and is expected to undergo modifications and definition over time, but it does offer an explanation not only for causalgia and the role of sympathetic tone (the susceptible patient, the associated peripheral sympathetic activity, and relief by sympathectomy, which closes the gate), but also for other heretofore unexplained observations (e.g., variations in "pain threshold," relief by transcutaneous nerve stimulators, and the apparent benefit of acupuncture in "receptive" persons).

A few studies have reviewed the mechanisms underlying the plasticity of dorsal root ganglia and dorsal horn neurons that lead to central pain from a peripheral nerve injury.[57] In a neurologic review, Schwartzman and associates[57] indicated that there is evidence that points to molecular changes in the nociceptive terminals, ectopic firing of afferent pain fibers at the level of the dorsal root ganglia, and physiologic changes of the *N*-methyl-D-aspartate receptor that cause chronic nociceptive pain. These investigators concluded that central sensitization is the physiologic manifestation of several severe, peripherally induced pain states. They also concluded that it is maintained by nociceptive input and a physiologic change in the *N*-methyl-D-aspartate receptor. The central sensitization consists of (1) hypersensitivity at the site of injury; (2) thermal hyperalgesia; (3) hyperpathia; (4) mechanoallodynia; (5) extraterritoriality in the case of CRPS; and (6) associated neurogenic inflammation, autonomic dysregulation, and motor phenomena.[57]

■ SYMPATHETICALLY MAINTAINED PAIN AND SYMPATHETICALLY INDEPENDENT PAIN

The terms *SMP* and *SIP* describe not separate disorders, but rather the types of pain that can characterize a variety of pain syndromes, including CRPS I and II. The role of the sympathetic nervous system in the pain associated with CRPS is unclear. Because of poor understanding of the pathophysiologic mechanisms, it was decided that words that had mechanistic connotations, such as those involving the sympathetic nervous system, would not be included in the new nomenclature for CRPS.

SMP originally was described as a pain state maintained by the sympathetic nervous system.[54] More recently, the term *SMP* has been used to describe the pain maintained by sympathetic efferent innervation, circulating catecholamines, or neurochemical action. SMP denotes pain that can be relieved by pharmacologic blockade or local anesthetic block of the sympathetic ganglia that serve the painful area.[11] *SIP* refers to pain states not sustained by the sympathetic nervous system. SMP may vary over time, and a patient may have a pain syndrome in which part of the pain is sympathetically maintained and another part is sympathetically independent (i.e., the patient can have SIP and SMP at the same time). Alternatively a patient may have SMP at one time and SIP later.[23]

Haddox[23] indicated that an important aspect of the role of autonomically mediated pain is that it may be a feature of several types of painful entities and is not a requirement of any one type. SMP and SIP may include, but are not limited to, CRPS, phantom pain, herpes zoster, neuralgias, and metabolic neuropathies.[63] SMP may or may not be present in a patient with CRPS. CRPS has strict inclusion criteria, but the presence or absence of SMP is not one of them. SMP is not synonymous with CRPS I or II. Provision has been made for some conditions to be present in several variants (e.g., nerve injury plus CRPS II or nerve injury with SMP in which sympathetic block relieves some of the pain), but the presentation does not contain features sufficient for the full CRPS diagnosis.[8]

Clinical Presentation and Diagnosis

Drucker and colleagues[19] divided the natural history of posttraumatic pain syndromes into three clinical stages:

- *Stage 1, acute:* The clinical course is characterized by warmth, erythema, burning, edema, hyperalgesia, hyperhidrosis, and, after a few months, patchy osteoporosis. At this stage, a good result can be expected with Bier block or chemical sympathectomy, one that often lasts longer than the normal duration of the block. Spontaneous resolution may occur in this stage, particularly with therapeutic support (see later section on treatment); the clinical course is reversible.

- *Stage 2, dystrophic:* The clinical course is marked by a good response to sympathetic block, symptoms are present for a fixed interval, and spontaneous resolution is rare. Characteristics include coolness and mottling of the skin; cyanosis; brawny edema; dry, brittle nails; continuous pain; and diffuse osteoporosis. At this stage, not only is a bone scan "positive," but also changes in bone structure usually are seen on plain films.
- *Stage 3, atrophic:* Pain always extends beyond the area of injury, and florid trophic changes occur, including atrophy of the skin and its appendages and fixed joint contractures. Radiographs show severe demineralization and ankylosis.

Although these stages oversimplify the condition, they provide a framework for diagnosis, treatment, and prognosis for CRPS. Among patients who are in stage 1 or 2, prompt treatment may produce permanent relief of pain, and stage 1 patients may not even need sympathectomy. For patients in stage 3, the likelihood of a poor result is greater, and sympathectomy may not give lasting relief.

CRPS I can occur in any age group, with a female-to-male ratio of 2:1. Although CRPS I has been reported in children,[7,59] it is not as disabling as in adults, with minimal radiographic or bone scan changes, and the response is usually better with conservative therapy. Persistent pain out of proportion to that expected from the initial extremity injury is an important clue in the diagnosis of CRPS I.

The consensus committee that met in Orlando in 1993 were unable to develop a uniform list of symptoms and signs because of the variability of the clinical criteria.[22] The following criteria, which were adapted from Wilson,[74] can be used to describe the symptoms and signs of CRPS:

1. Pain is a necessary symptom for the diagnosis of CRPS. The pain is located in the affected extremity and is disproportionate to what would be expected from the initial event. It may be spontaneous or evoked and usually is reported as burning or diffuse pain. It is not consistent with the distribution of a peripheral nerve, even if the initial injury involved such a nerve. This important feature distinguishes CRPS from pain of other causes and from more specific neuropathic pain disorders. The pain may be reported as throbbing or aching, intermittent or continuous, and exacerbated by physical or emotional stresses. The patient often adopts a protective posture to protect the affected extremity.
2. Sensory changes usually are reported at some stage and include allodynia and hyperesthesia in the region of the pain. Allodynia may occur in response to thermal stimulation (cold or warm), deep pressure, light touch, or joint movement.
3. Sympathetic dysfunction is reported as a sudomotor or vasomotor instability in the affected extremity compared with the unaffected extremity. This dysfunction may vary in severity from time to time, and the patient may report that the extremity is warm and red or cold and blue, purple, or mottled. Veldman and associates[69] reported that 92% of patients had altered skin temperature. Sweating, particularly of the palms or soles, may be reported as increased, decreased, or unchanged. Normal sympathetic function may be present at certain times.
4. Swelling may be reported at any stage of the syndrome. This swelling is typically peripheral and may be intermittent or permanent and may be exacerbated by the dependent position of the extremity. There also can be pitting or brawny edema.
5. Trophic changes of the skin may be reported later in the course of the syndrome. The nails may be atrophic or hypertrophic. Hair growth and texture may be decreased or increased, and the skin may become atrophic.
6. Motor dysfunction may include dystonia, tremor, and loss of strength of the affected muscle groups. Joint swelling and stiffness also may be reported, particularly of the digits.

Comprehensive Clinical Evaluation

With the foregoing features in mind, the clinical evaluation can be enhanced by focusing on particular aspects or using adjunctive tests, as follows:

1. *Sensory examination:* Allodynia may be evaluated by applying non-noxious stimuli to the affected extremity (warm, cold, light touch, deep pressure, joint movement) and comparing sensory reports from the affected extremity and a normal extremity. Hyperalgesia can be evaluated by applying noxious stimuli and comparing sensory reports from a normal area and the painful area.
2. *Sudomotor examination:* Resting heat output may be estimated by skin impedance[56] or quinizarin or cobalt blue testing[21] or as part of the quantitative sudomotor reflex test,[37] which measures resting sweat output by hygrometry and changes evoked by iontophoresis of acetylcholine into the skin.[38]
3. *Vasomotor examination:* Simultaneous temperature measurements of the affected and unaffected extremities are taken at corresponding anatomic sites. The temperature of the digit pads, palms and soles, and forearms and calves can be measured with noncontact thermometry or thermography. Serial measurements should be taken because peripheral temperatures vary widely under normal circumstances. Skin perfusion can be evaluated visually or by pulse oximetry.
4. *Edema:* Edema generally is judged by clinical impression by comparing one extremity with the other because most volume displacement methods, which provide quantitative estimates of the extent of the edema and allow objective measurement of the results of treatment, can be cumbersome.
5. *Trophic changes:* The skin, hair, and nails of the two sides are compared.
6. *Motor dysfunction:* The presence of dystonia, tremor, and changes in strength can be measured clinically. Objective measurements should be taken (e.g., apposition and opposition pinch strength, grip, weight bearing on lower extremity).
7. *Psychological changes:* No psychometric instrument has been validated for the treatment of CRPS. The psychiatrist or psychologist generally uses familiar instruments as part of the initial assessment and follow-up.

Table 75-2 Diagnostic Criteria for CRPS I

CLINICAL SYMPTOMS AND SIGNS	LABORATORY RESULTS	INTERPRETATION
Burning pain	Thermometry or thermography	If total number of positive findings is:
Hyperpathia or allodynia	Bone radiography	>6: CRPS I probable
Temperature or color changes	Three-phase bone scan	3-5: CRPS I possible
Edema	Quantitative sweat test	<3: CRPS I unlikely
Hair or nail growth changes	Response to sympathetic block	

The clinical features are summarized in Table 75-2 and Figure 75-1.[52]

Radiologic findings of CRPS may take many weeks or months to develop. Osteoporosis and abnormal bone scans (measured by technetium 99m) can be found in most cases of CRPS.[16,32,33] Asymmetric blood flow is usually seen; flow and uptake are usually increased, but occasionally they are diminished.

The diagnosis of CRPS II is certain when the clinical presentation includes superficial burning pain in the distribution of a single somatic sensory nerve, hyperesthesia, vasomotor abnormalities, radiographic evidence of osteoporosis, and a good response to sympathetic blockade. In CRPS I, certain clinical features may be minimal or absent, although the response to sympathetic block may still be a reliable sign. The ultimate relief obtained by surgical sympathectomy can be predicted by careful documentation of the response to a "one-shot" local anesthetic sympathetic blockade.

Studies on the external and internal validity of the International Association for the Study of Pain criteria suggest that patients should have at least one symptom in each of the following general categories—sensory (hyperesthesia), vasomotor abnormalities (temperature or skin color abnormalities), sudomotor-fluid balance (edema or sweating), or motor dysfunction (decreased range of motion, weakness, tremor, or neglect)—and at least one sign within two or more of the following categories—sensory (allodynia or hyperalgesia), sudomotor-fluid balance (objective edema or sweating abnormalities), vasomotor abnormalities (objective temperature or skin color abnormalities), or motor abnormality (objective decrease of range of motion, weakness, tremor, or neglect).[10,24]

Diagnostic Sympathetic Block

The validity of a clinical diagnosis of CRPS may be strengthened greatly by a positive response to sympathetic blockade. Patients should be encouraged to quantify the degree of pain relief experienced (e.g., 100% relief, 50% relief). The degree of pain relief a patient experiences with such a block is an excellent predictor of how much relief can be expected from surgical sympathectomy.[1] Some caution should be exercised here, however, because sympathectomy can afford some degree of nonspecific relief of almost any pain, including ischemic pain.[9,36] CRPS pain usually is dramatically relieved by sympathetic blockade (e.g., almost always 75% to 100% relief), whereas relief of pain of other causes is usually only mild to moderate (25% to 50% at most).

Differential Diagnosis

In the differential diagnosis of post-traumatic pain, one of the most important alternatives is nerve entrapment. Causalgia-like pain may occur if a nerve is caught in a

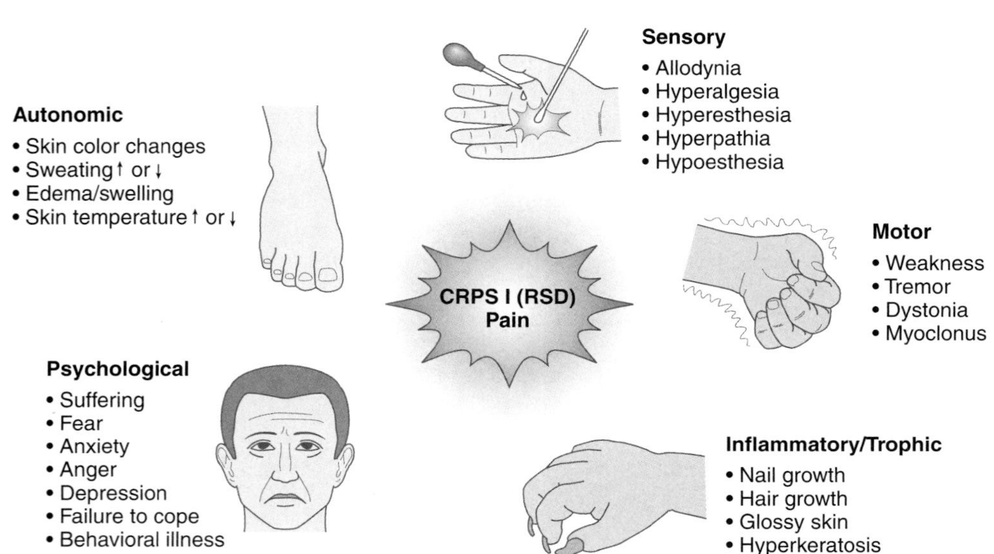

FIGURE 75-1 Clinical features of complex regional pain syndrome type I (reflex sympathetic dystrophy) (CRPS I [RSD]).

suture, entrapped by scar, or compressed by surrounding structures. Nerve entrapment must be considered when causalgia appears immediately after an operation, but because a nerve can be irritated or injured by any compressing or pinching mechanism, there may be a causalgia component to the pain associated with any nerve compression. This consideration is important because relieving the compression may only partially relieve the pain, and the causalgia component may persist; this is discussed later in relation to residual pain subsequent to operations to relieve herniated disk. If peripheral nerve entrapment is the cause, there is often a "trigger point" at which focal application of pressure causes sharp pain. The pain can be relieved by infiltration of a small amount of local anesthetic at that point.

Patients who present with cutaneous signs and symptoms characteristic of Drucker's stage 2 sometimes are thought to have Raynaud's syndrome; however, the patient's symptoms should be intermittent, related principally to cold exposure, and relieved by warmth. Hyperesthesia is rare in Raynaud's syndrome, and its characteristic pain is not usually severe or burning.

The pain of peripheral neuritis is often burning and associated with hyperesthesia and vasomotor phenomena. The pathogenetic mechanisms for peripheral neuritis and post-traumatic pain can be similar. The clinical syndrome associated with peripheral neuritis is more diffuse anatomically and gradual in onset, however, and the patient has no history of trauma or some other discrete precipitating event.

Treatment

When a post-traumatic pain syndrome has been relieved temporarily by sympathetic blockade, the question of whether to try to achieve this degree of relief more permanently by sympathectomy typically arises. The answer depends on the clinical stage of development, severity of symptoms, and degree and duration of relief by sympathetic block.

For a patient with pain of recent onset who has experienced pain relief from sympathetic blockade that lasted well beyond the known duration of the anesthetic agent used, it is advisable to continue with nonoperative measures (see later). Patients whose condition has persisted for several months, whose pain is disabling, and who receive nearly total relief from sympathetic block but only for the typical "duration" of the anesthetic may be considered candidates for immediate surgical sympathectomy. Patients with symptoms of long duration (many months to years), patients who have associated trophic changes, and patients whose symptoms are less "classic" and less severe and receive only mild-to-moderate relief from sympathetic block should be advised that the long-term results are likely to be disappointing. These examples correspond to Drucker's three stages; this is deliberate because sympathectomy is, for the most part, best applied in stage 2, before progression to stage 3, and after stage 1, in patients who are unresponsive to nonoperative therapy.

In the past, when no effective treatment was known, post-traumatic pain syndromes frequently resulted in chronic invalidism, emotional deterioration, and drug addiction. The basis for proper treatment of CRPS is early recognition and prevention. For patients known to be susceptible to CRPS, such as patients who have hemiplegia or myocardial infarction, early mobilization of an injured extremity is crucial. When early sympathetic dystrophic changes occur, pain relief and active use of the hand, arm, or leg are indicated. Passive motion by a physical therapist should be avoided because it may increase the pain and edema. Opiate analgesics, when needed, should be used conservatively. Splinting the hand in a functional position may help.

Other nonoperative therapy, particularly as it applies to stage 1 or early stage 2 disease, consists of drug therapy, intermittent sympathetic blocks, and physiotherapy. Drug therapy may require nonspecific analgesics, but these should be superimposed, and only when necessary, on a "background" of medication designed to attenuate the symptoms by direct effect. Of these, phenytoin, amitriptyline, carbamazepine, and baclofen may be used effectively, usually in that order, because of increasing side effects. Nonsteroidal anti-inflammatory drugs may be useful, not only in relieving joint swelling, but also in combination with the aforementioned agents in allowing dose reduction and producing fewer side effects. Benson[5] recommended amitriptyline hydrochloride (Elavil) in doses of 50 to 75 mg nightly or divided during the day (150 mg maximum). Benson also recommended a phenothiazine, such as fluphenazine hydrochloride (Prolixin), which potentiates opiate analgesic effects, possesses an analgesic property of its own, and depresses the response to peripheral stimuli. The recommended dosage is 1 mg three times daily, but doses of 10 mg/day can be used.

Treatment of CRPS with either the calcium channel blocker nifedipine or the α-sympathetic blocker phenoxybenzamine was assessed in 59 patients by Muizelaar and coworkers[45]; 12 subjects had early CRPS, and 47 had chronic CRPS. In the early CRPS group, 3 of 5 patients were cured with nifedipine, and 8 of 9 (2 of whom had earlier received nifedipine) were cured with phenoxybenzamine, for a cure rate of 92% (11 of 12). Among patients with chronic CRPS, 10 of 30 were cured with nifedipine, and 7 of 17 were cured with phenoxybenzamine when it was administered as the first choice; another 2 of 7 patients who had initially received nifedipine were cured, for a total success rate of 40% (19 of 47) for chronic CRPS.

Intensive physical therapy should be initiated, including full range-of-motion exercises and whirlpool exercises. Trudel and associates[67] reported good results in 88% of CRPS patients treated with physical therapy. The primary objective of physiotherapy is goal-oriented functional restoration. Physiotherapy should include (1) mobilization, swelling control, and isometric strengthening; (2) desensitization of the affected region; (3) stress loading, isotonic strengthening, range of motion, postural normalization, and aerobic conditioning; and (4) vocational rehabilitation.[62] Physiotherapy should be combined with pharmacologic therapy.

Transcutaneous electrical nerve stimulation (TENS) has been used to treat CRPS.[42] Results have been mixed, but because TENS is easily administered and safe, it may be tried before more aggressive treatment is attempted. In the hands of an experienced practitioner, success or failure of TENS is apparent by the third to the fifth treatment.[75]

A course of steroids should be tried when the response to physical therapy or TENS is poor. Kozin and collaborators[33] reported a fair-to-excellent response to steroids in 63 of 67 CRPS patients. The usual daily starting dose of prednisone is 60 mg. The dose is tapered every 3 days by 5 mg, for a total therapy course of about 5 weeks.

Because at least a temporary response to many nonoperative treatment modalities is common in early stages of CRPS, a common error in management is to carry attempts at conservative therapy too far, persisting with such treatments too long and shifting repeatedly from one to the other. This approach not only subjects patients who are destined never to respond to such therapy to wasted time, expense, and suffering, but also may compromise their chances of obtaining complete and lasting relief by surgical sympathectomy. If the above-described measures are not effective in relieving the symptoms promptly, or if symptoms are exacerbated over the course of several days, the physician should proceed directly to sympathetic blocks, which are diagnostic and therapeutic.

An initial sympathetic block is appropriate early in stage 1 to confirm the diagnosis and to test its therapeutic potential. The rapid pain relief gained from a sympathetic block can be extremely helpful psychologically. Also, at this stage, the condition may be reversible, and complete remission sometimes can be achieved, particularly in patients who experience long-lasting relief from serial sympathetic blocks, when it allows aggressive physiotherapy to be applied. When relief is short-lived, however, persisting with repeated blocks is counterproductive and expensive.

Injections of alcohol and phenol have been used instead of surgical sympathectomy in attempts to produce lasting sympathetic denervation, but a significant incidence of incomplete or transient sympathetic blocks is associated with this approach. Risks include painful neuralgia and inflammation with scarring, the latter potentially making subsequent surgery more difficult.[53] Radiofrequency ablation has been proposed as a more precise method of achieving percutaneous sympathetic denervation.[46] Although it may represent an advance over phenol or alcohol blocks, its effect is not as complete or durable as that of surgical sympathectomy, and the local reaction it produces would seriously interfere with subsequent operation. General anesthesia is necessary.

Such methods have been proposed primarily because of the morbidity of surgical cervical sympathectomy, particularly via the transthoracic route (which may cause significant post-thoracotomy discomfort). This latter objection is less compelling, however, now that the procedure can be done safely and precisely thoracoscopically,[2,25,39] and the patient is discharged the next day. Through the modern thoracoscope, with its view enlarged on video screen and using instruments such as those developed for laparoscopic cholecystectomy, removal of the T2 and T3 sympathetic ganglia and division of the rami to the lower part of the stellate ganglion can be performed with precision and safety. The procedure is less predictably successful in the presence of inflammation and scarring.

Other investigators have reported good results with laparoscopic lumbar sympathectomy (see Chapter 85).[13,15,20,24,26,72,77] In view of this development and the fact that lumbar sympathectomy is tolerated so well, any percutaneous method that does not produce a complete and lasting sympathectomy effect cannot be condoned because it precludes safe sympathectomy later. If surgical sympathectomy is limited to patients who obtain excellent relief from sympathetic block with a local anesthetic, nearly 90% of patients experience long-term relief.[1,44]

Neuromodulation

Neuromodulatory modalities include peripheral nerve, spinal cord, and thalamic stimulation. Implantable devices, such as spinal cord stimulators, are increasingly used in intractable patients with CRPS for symptomatic pain relief. In general, the efficacy of these modalities has not been shown to be superior by placebo-controlled trials in patients with CRPS. A prospective randomized controlled study showed that patients with CRPS who received spinal cord stimulation with physiotherapy obtained greater pain relief and improvement in health-related quality of life compared with patients who received physiotherapy alone.[27] Spinal cord stimulation also produced analgesia in patients with CRPS who had undergone previous sympathectomy, which would suggest that spinal cord stimulation–mediated analgesia can be produced without inhibition of sympathetic function in CRPS patients.[28] Mechanism of action is diverse and likely involves neurochemical changes at spinal and supraspinal targets, although it stimulates inhibition of sympathetic outflow. Spinal cord stimulation may have an inhibitory effect on A-β fiber–mediated hyperexcitability of dorsal horn neurons through γ-aminobutyric acid–mediated mechanism. The observation that these patients can receive analgesia without alteration of sympathetic function suggests that pain and sympathetic function are not interdependent in all of these patients. This suggestion also is supported by the finding that impairment of sympathetic function shows no correlation with the clinical symptom of the disease (i.e., pain, swelling, or temperature abnormalities) in CRPS patients.

Epidural and Intrathecal Drug Therapy

It has been reported in a double-blind controlled trial that epidural clonidine is beneficial in CRPS patients. Intrathecal drug therapy has been suggested for CRPS patients who are refractory to conventional modalities, based on case reports.[68] Van Hilten and coworkers[68] reported a controlled study of seven patients with CRPS that showed the efficacy of intrathecal baclofen for treatment of dystonia. Intrathecal infusion of baclofen also showed a reduction in pain, autonomic symptoms, and sensory symptoms in some of these patients.

Psychotherapy

The International Association for the Study of Pain consensus report recommended that patients with CRPS seek psychotherapy, including psychometric testing if their pain persists beyond 2 months.[62] Psychotherapy should include treatment of anxiety, depression, or personality disorders. Counseling, behavioral modification, relaxation therapy, biofeedback, group therapy, and self-hypnosis should be considered in these patients.

Summary of Treatment Guidelines

The following are the generally acceptable guidelines for the treatment of patients with CRPS I:

- *Stage I:* Physical therapy with or without the TENS unit is usually useful. A local nerve or sympathetic block may be necessary for patients who experience severe pain and are unable to undergo physical therapy. If these measures fail, a course of steroid therapy should be given.
- *Stage II:* Physical therapy, TENS, and steroid therapy should be combined. Sympathetic blocks and surgical sympathectomy should be considered if these measures fail.
- *Stage III:* Steroid therapy or sympathetic blockade and surgical sympathectomy should be considered but may be unsuccessful. Manipulation of joint contracture under general anesthesia, antidepressants, and vocational guidance also may be used.

Cooney[14] summarized a treatment protocol. The first step is to differentiate sympathetic pain from somatic pain (see Table 75-2). The CRPS I score can be helpful. When the pain is somatic, treatment options include (1) isolated nerve block, (2) continuous nerve block, (3) TENS (external), (4) direct electrical nerve stimulation (internal), and (5) nerve ablation. If pain is sympathetic in origin, treatments should include (1) protection of the limb (with a garment or splint) combined with active use, (2) sympathetic blocks (single or continuous), and (3) sympathectomy.

Results of Sympathectomy

The specific techniques of cervicothoracic and lumbar sympathectomy are described in Chapters 85 and 97. We review the results of sympathectomy for CRPS, including our own experience.[1,44] The first reports of surgical sympathectomy for causalgia were probably those of Spurling in 1930[61] and of Kwan in 1935.[34] Both reports described trauma to an extremity that was complicated by causalgia and relieved by sympathectomy. Clinical series from World War II helped to define a role for sympathectomy for causalgia.[29,40,58] In 1951, Mayfield[40] reported on 75 patients with causalgia who were treated and followed for 5 years; 73 of them had significant early pain relief, and in 63% of the 73, pain relief was sustained for 5 years. In the other 37%, the pain was significantly relieved but not completely gone at 5 years. In Thompson's 1979 series,[65] 27 patients with causalgia were treated with sympathectomy, and among 120 patients who had minor causalgia, 55 were treated with sympathectomy. Among all patients, 82% had excellent pain relief, 11% had good pain relief, and 7% had a poor result. Residual symptoms, largely symptoms secondary to associated injuries, were present in 31%.[65] Olcott and associates[47] also reported 91% good-to-excellent results in 35 patients.

One of the authors (R.B.R.) has twice published his experience with post-traumatic pain syndromes and sympathectomy. The first series,[76] from Johns Hopkins Hospital, included 27 patients. Immediate pain relief was achieved in 24 patients (all of whom received a successful trial block), and of 15 patients observed for 2 to 17 years, pain relief was sustained in 13. The second series,[44] from the University of Colorado, included 31 patients. All patients in this series were evaluated preoperatively with sympathetic block, and 97% of the patients reported a satisfactory level of immediate pain relief. In extended follow-up, this level of pain relief was sustained in 94%. In a similar, more recent series of 28 patients,[1] the other author (A.F.A.) reported 95% long-term success in patients who had experienced an excellent response to a trial block.

An interesting subgroup of patients was identified in two of the aforementioned reports.[1,44] In the first series,[44] patients with causalgia persisting after disk surgery experienced pain relief after sympathectomy equal to that in other patients. These cases constituted more than half of the cases in which lumbar sympathectomy was performed; this relates to a high index of suspicion and to indoctrination of local neurosurgeons. In the second series,[1] 10 patients (36% of the total) had had lumbar diskectomy, and they too reported uniformly excellent results after sympathectomy. Neither the true frequency of persistent postdiskectomy pain nor its nature is known. Previously called *arachnoiditis* and thought to be due to inflammation and nerve sheath irritation after disk surgery, this pain probably reflects residual nerve damage that occurs before nerve root compression is relieved by removal of the herniated nucleus pulposus. The recognition of causalgia as a possible component of lumbar disk pain, its persistence after diskectomy, and its potential relief by sympathectomy have been inadequately recognized in the medical literature.

Bandyk and associates[3] reported the surgical results on 73 patients with CRPS I; 46 were treated with video-assisted thoracoscopic lumbar sympathectomy, and 37 were treated with surgical lumbar sympathectomy. The mean duration of CRPS I symptoms for sympathectomy was 26 ± 14 months (range 6 to 100 months). There was no operative mortality or serious morbidity in the series. Transient (<3 months) postprocedural sympathalgia was noted in one third of patients for cervicodorsal sympathectomies and 20% of patients with lumbar sympathectomy who were treated effectively with trigger point/proximal ganglion block therapy or TENS. At 3 months after sympathectomy, 10% of patients had conditions that were judged to be treatment refractory when no reduction in pain severity or limb disability occurred. The remaining patients experienced a greater than 50% pain reduction, with pain severity scores decreasing from a mean of 8.7 before surgery to 3.4 after surgery. At 1 year of follow-up, 25% of patients had continued significant pain relief, and an additional 50% of patients indicated continued, but reduced, pain severity and an increase in daily/work activities. Overall, patient satisfaction was 77% and was not significantly influenced by patient age, CRPS I duration, or extremity involvement (lumbar 84% and cervicodorsal 72%).

Singh and colleagues[60] reported the results of sympathectomy in 42 patients with CRPS II of the upper extremity. Patients were categorized according to the duration of symptoms (group I, <3 months; group II, >3 months). Thoracoscopic dorsal sympathectomy was successful in 32 patients. In the remaining 10 patients, thoracoscopy was not technically feasible, and they underwent open sympathectomy. There was an overall improvement in all 42 patients undergoing sympathectomy. The outcome in group I was significantly better than in group II ($P < .003$). The diagnosis of sympathetically mediated pain with a stellate blockade did not correlate in their series with the clinical outcome. Singh and colleagues[60] concluded that early recognition of CRPS and prompt recourse to surgical sympathectomy is a useful option in the management of CRPS.

Complications

Failure to recognize CRPS I promptly and to treat it appropriately is unacceptable because the syndrome often results in irreversible changes, including wasting of skin and muscles, fixed joint contractures, and severe demineralization of bone; it also misses the opportunity for permanent pain relief by sympathectomy. The complications of sympathectomy itself have been described in depth by the authors[1,55] and are discussed in Chapter 85. In general, the complications of sympathectomy can be classified as follows:

- *Preoperative*—in which the anticipated benefit has not been achieved because of improper patient selection
- *Intraoperative*—related to improper technique
- *Postoperative*—encountered after an appropriate and properly executed sympathectomy

Preoperative complications can be minimized by the use of nerve blocks, sham saline blocks in questionable cases, and, when appropriate, careful psychiatric evaluation. Intraoperative complications can be avoided by meticulous attention to the anatomic relationships and normal variations of anatomy among the structures most frequently injured—the genitofemoral nerve, ureters, lumbar veins, aorta, and inferior vena cava. The most common postoperative complication is postsympathectomy neuralgia, which, although frequent, almost always resolves spontaneously.[4,44]

When applied selectively for the aforementioned pain syndromes, sympathectomy gives excellent symptomatic relief, far superior to its other indications. Although previously associated with significant morbidity and even death when performed on elderly patients with advanced arteriosclerosis, the current technique carries negligible risk and produces few permanent adverse sequelae in the typically younger and healthier patients who have various forms of sympathetically mediated pain.

■ REFERENCES

1. AbuRahma AF, Robinson PA, Powell M, et al: Sympathectomy for reflex sympathetic dystrophy: Factors affecting outcome. Ann Vasc Surg 8:372-379, 1994.
2. Appleby TC, Edwards WH Jr: Thoracoscopic dorsal sympathectomy for hyperhidrosis: Technique of choice. J Vasc Surg 16:121-123, 1992.
3. Bandyk DF, Johnson BL, Kirkpatrick AF, et al: Surgical sympathectomy for reflex sympathetic dystrophy syndromes. J Vasc Surg 35:269-277, 2002.
4. Barnes R: The role of sympathectomy in the treatment of causalgia. J Bone Joint Surg Br 35:172-180, 1953.
5. Benson WF: Discussion of RG Chuinard. American Society for Surgery of the Hand Annual Meeting, Atlanta, 1980.
6. Bergan JJ, Conn J: Sympathectomy for pain relief. Med Clin North Am 52:147-159, 1968.
7. Bernstein BH, Singsen BH, Kent JT: Reflex neurovascular dystrophy in childhood. J Pediatr 93:211-215, 1978.
8. Boas RA: Complex regional pain syndromes: Symptoms, signs, and differential diagnosis. In Janig W, Stanton-Hicks M (eds): Reflex Sympathetic Dystrophy: A Reappraisal. Seattle, IASP Press, 1996, pp 79-91.
9. Bobin A, Anderson WP: Influence of sympathectomy in α-2 adrenoreceptor binding sites in canine blood vessels. Life Sci 33:331, 1983.
10. Bruehl S, Harden RN, Galer BS, et al: External validation of IASP diagnostic criteria for complex regional pain syndrome and proposed research diagnostic criteria. Pain 81:147-154, 1999.
11. Campbell JN: Complex regional pain syndrome and the sympathetic nervous system. In: Pain 1996—an Updated Review. IASP Refresher Courses on Pain Management held in conjunction with the 8th World Congress on Pain. Seattle, IASP Press, 1996, pp 89-96.
12. Chapman LF, Ramos AV, Goodell H, et al: Neurohumoral features of afferent fibers in man. Arch Neurol 4:617-650, 1961.
13. Cheshire NJ, Darzi AW: Retroperitoneoscopic lumbar sympathectomy. Br J Surg 84:1094-1095, 1997.
14. Cooney WP: Somatic versus sympathetic mediated chronic limb pain: Experience and treatment options. Hand Clin 13:355-361, 1997.
15. Cronenwett JL, Lindenauer SM: Hemodynamic effects of sympathectomy in ischemic canine hind limbs. Surgery 87:417, 1980.
16. Davidoff G, Werner R, Cremer S, et al: Predictive value of the three-phase technetium bone scan in diagnosis of reflex sympathetic dystrophy syndrome. Arch Phys Med Rehabil 70:135-137, 1989.
17. Davis SW: Shoulder-hand syndrome in a hemiplegic population: 5-year retrospective study. Arch Phys Med Rehabil 58:353-356, 1977.
18. Doupe J, Cullen CH, Chance GQ: Post-traumatic pain and the causalgic syndrome. J Neurol Psychiatry 7:33-48, 1944.
19. Drucker WR, Hubay CA, Holden WD, et al: Pathogenesis of post-traumatic sympathetic dystrophy. Am J Surg 97:454-465, 1959.
20. Elliot TB, Royle JP: Laparoscopic extraperitoneal lumbar sympathectomy: Technique and early results. Aust N Z J Surg 66:400, 1996.
21. Fealey RD: The thermoregulatory sweat test. In Low PA (ed): Clinical Autonomic Disorders. Boston, Little, Brown, 1993, pp 217-229.
22. Gibbons JJ, Wilson PR: RSD score: Criteria for the diagnosis of reflex sympathetic dystrophy and causalgia. Clin J Pain 8:260-263, 1992.
23. Haddox JD: A call for clarity. In: Pain 1996—an Updated Review. IASP Refresher Courses on Pain Management held in conjunction with the 8th World Congress on Pain. Seattle, IASP Press, 1996, pp 97-99.
24. Harden RN, Bruehl S, Galer BS, et al: Complex regional pain syndrome: Are the IASP diagnostic criteria valid and sufficiently comprehensive? Pain 83:211-219, 1999.
25. Horgan K, O'Flanagan S, Duignan PJ, et al: Palmar and axillary hyperhidrosis treated by sympathectomy by transthoracic endoscopic electrocoagulation. Br J Surg 71:1002, 1984.
26. Kathouda N, Wattanasirichaigoon S, Tang E, et al: Laparoscopic lumbar sympathectomy. Surg Endosc 11:257-260, 1997.
27. Kemler MA, Barendse GA, van Kleef M, et al: Spinal cord stimulation in patients with chronic reflex sympathetic dystrophy. N Engl J Med 343:618-624, 2000.
28. Kemler MA, Barendse GA, van Kleef M, Egbrink MG: Pain relief in complex regional pain syndrome due to spinal cord stimulation does not depend on vasodilation. Anesthesiology 92:1653-1660, 2000.
29. Kirklin JW, Chenoweth AE, Murphy F: Causalgia: A review of its characteristics, diagnosis and treatment. Surgery 21:321, 1947.
30. Kozin F: Reflex sympathetic dystrophy syndrome. Bull Rheum Dis 36:1-8, 1986.
31. Kozin F: The painful shoulder and reflex sympathetic dystrophy syndrome. In McCarty DJ (ed): Arthritis and Allied Conditions, 10th ed. Philadelphia, Lea & Febiger, 1985.
32. Kozin F, Genant HK, Bekerman C, et al: The reflex sympathetic dystrophy syndrome: II. Roentgenographic and scintigraphic evidence bilaterally and of periarticular accentuation. Am J Med 60:332-338, 1976.
33. Kozin F, Ryan LM, Carerra GF, et al: The reflex sympathetic dystrophy syndrome: III. Scintigraphic studies, further evidence for the thera-

peutic efficacy of systemic corticosteroids and proposed diagnostic criteria. Am J Med 70:23-30, 1981.
34. Kwan ST: The treatment of causalgia by thoracic sympathetic ganglionectomy. Ann Surg 101:222, 1935.
35. Livingston WK: Pain Mechanisms: A Physiological Interpretation of Causalgia and Its Related States. New York, Macmillan, 1943, pp 83-113.
36. Loh L, Nathan PW: Painful peripheral states and sympathetic blocks. J Neurol Neurosurg Psychiatry 41:664-671, 1978.
37. Low PA, Pfeifer MD: Standardization of clinical tests for practice and clinical trials. In Low PA (ed): Clinical Autonomic Disorders. Boston, Little, Brown, 1993, pp 287-296.
38. Low PA, Wilson PR, Sandroni P, et al: Reflex sympathetic dystrophy: A reappraisal, progress. In Janig W, Stanton-Hicks M (eds): Pain Research and Management, vol 6. Seattle, IASP Press, 1996, pp 40-43.
39. Malone PS, Cameron AE, Rennie JA: Endoscopic thoracoscopic sympathectomy in the treatment of upper limb hyperhidrosis. Ann R Coll Surg Engl 68:93-94, 1986.
40. Mayfield FH: Causalgia. Springfield, Ill, Charles C Thomas, 1951.
41. Merskey H, Bogduk N: Classification of Chronic Pain, 2nd ed. Seattle, IASP Press, 1994.
42. Meyer GA, Fields HL: Causalgia treated by selective large fibre stimulation of peripheral nerve. Brain 95:163-168, 1972.
43. Mitchell SW, Morehouse GR, Keen WW: Gunshot Wounds and Other Injuries of Nerves. Philadelphia, JB Lippincott, 1864, p 164.
44. Mockus MB, Rutherford RB, Rosales C, et al: Sympathectomy for causalgia: Patient selection and long-term results. Arch Surg 122:668-672, 1987.
45. Muizelaar JP, Kleyer M, Hertogs IA, et al: Complex regional pain syndrome (reflex sympathetic dystrophy and causalgia): Management with the calcium channel blocker nifedipine and/or the alpha-sympathetic blocker phenoxybenzamine in 59 patients. Clin Neurol Neurosurg 99:26-30, 1997.
46. Noe CE, Haynsworth RF Jr: Lumbar radiofrequency sympatholysis. J Vasc Surg 17:801-806, 1993.
47. Olcott C, Eltherington LG, Wilcosky BR, et al: Reflex sympathetic dystrophy: The surgeon's role in management. J Vasc Surg 14:488-492, 1991.
48. Paré A: Les Oeuvres d'Ambroise Paré, Paris, Gabriel Bron. Historie de Defunct. Roy Charles 10th book, 1598, p 401.
49. Patman RD, Thompson JE, Persson AV: Management of post-traumatic pain syndromes: Report of 113 cases. Ann Surg 177:780-787, 1973.
50. Plewes LW: Sudeck's atrophy in the hands. J Bone Joint Surg 38:195-203, 1956.
51. Porter EL, Taylor AN: Facilitation of flexion reflex in relation to pain after nerve injuries (causalgia). J Neurophysiol 8:289-294, 1945.
52. Raja SN, Grabow TS: Complex regional pain syndrome I (reflex sympathetic dystrophy). Anesthesiology 96:1254-1260, 2002.
53. Ramos M, Almazan A, Lozano F, et al: Phenol lumbar sympathectomy in severe arterial disease of the lower limb: A hemodynamic study. Int Surg 68:127-130, 1983.
54. Roberts WJ: A hypothesis on the physiological basis for causalgia and related pain. Pain 24:297-311, 1986.
55. Rutherford RB: Complications of sympathectomy. In Bernhard VM, Towne JB (eds): Complications in Vascular Surgery. New York, Grune & Stratton, 1980.
56. Schondorf R: The role of the sympathetic skin response in the assessment of autonomic function. In Low PA (ed): Clinical Autonomic Disorders. Boston, Little, Brown, 1993, pp 231-241.
57. Schwartzman RJ, Grothusen J, Kiefer TR, Rohr P: Neuropathic central pain: Epidemiology, etiology, and treatment options. Arch Neurol 58:1547-1550, 2001.
58. Shumaker HB Jr, Abramson DI: Post-traumatic vasomotor disorders. Surg Gynecol Obstet 88:417, 1949.
59. Silber TJ, Majd M: Reflex sympathetic dystrophy syndrome in children and adolescents: Report of 18 cases and review of the literature. Am J Dis Child 142:1325-1330, 1988.
60. Singh B, Moodley J, Shaik AS, Robbs JV: Sympathectomy for complex regional pain syndrome. J Vasc Surg 37:508-511, 2003.
61. Spurling RG: Causalgia of the upper extremity: Treatment by dorsal sympathetic ganglionectomy. Arch Neurol Psychiatry (Chir) 23:704, 1930.
62. Stanton-Hicks M, Baron R, Boas R, et al: Complex regional pain syndromes: Guidelines for therapy. Clin J Pain 14:155-166, 1998.
63. Stanton-Hicks M, Janig W, Hassenbusch S, et al: Reflex sympathetic dystrophy: Changing concepts and taxonomy. Pain 63:127-133, 1995.
64. Steinbrocker O, Spitzer N, Friedman HH: The shoulder-hand syndrome in reflex dystrophy of upper extremity. Ann Intern Med 29:22-52, 1948.
65. Thompson JE: The diagnosis and management of post-traumatic pain syndromes (causalgia). Aust N Z J Surg 49:299-304, 1979.
66. Toennie JF: Reflex discharges from the spinal cord over the dorsal roots. J Neurophysiol 1:370, 1938.
67. Trudel J, DeWolfe VG, Young JR, et al: Disuse phenomenon of the lower extremity: Diagnosis and treatment. JAMA 186:1129-1131, 1963.
68. Van Hilten BJ, van de Beek WJ, Hoff JI, et al: Intrathecal baclofen for the treatment of dystonia in patients with reflex sympathetic dystrophy. N Engl J Med 343:625-630, 2000.
69. Veldman PHJM, Reynen HM, Arntz IE, et al: Signs and symptoms of reflex sympathetic dystrophy: Prospective study of 829 patients. Lancet 342:1012-1016, 1993.
70. von Frey R: Cited in White JC, Sweet WH: Other varieties of peripheral neuralgia. In White JC (ed): Pain and the Neurosurgeon. Springfield, Ill, Charles C Thomas, 1969, pp 87-109.
71. Walker AE, Nielsen S: Electrical stimulation of the upper thoracic portion of the sympathetic chain in man. Arch Neurol Psychiatry 59:599, 1947.
72. Watarida S, Shiraishi S, Fujimura M, et al: Laparoscopic lumbar sympathectomy for lower-limb disease. Surg Endosc 16:500-503, 2002.
73. White JC, Sweet WH: Other varieties of peripheral neuralgia. In White JC (ed): Pain and the Neurosurgeon. Springfield, Ill, Charles C Thomas, 1969, pp 87-109.
74. Wilson PR: Diagnostic algorithm for complex regional pain syndromes. In Janig W, Stanton-Hicks M (eds): Reflex Sympathetic Dystrophy: A Reappraisal. Seattle, IASP Press, 1996, pp 93-105.
75. Wilson RL: Management of pain following peripheral nerve injuries. Orthop Clin North Am 12:343-359, 1981.
76. Wirth FP, Rutherford RB: A civilian experience with causalgia. Arch Surg 100:633-638, 1970.
77. Wronski J: Lumbar sympathectomy performed by means of videoscopy. Cardiovasc Surg 6:453-456, 1998.

Section XIII

MANAGEMENT OF CHRONIC ISCHEMIA OF THE LOWER EXTREMITIES

K. WAYNE JOHNSTON, MD FRCS(C)

Chapter 76

The Chronically Ischemic Leg: An Overview

K. WAYNE JOHNSTON, MD, FRCS(C)

During the past 50 years, vascular surgeons have made outstanding progress in treating patients with chronic ischemia of the lower extremities by developing an understanding of the natural history of the disease; using multiple diagnostic methods; developing, applying, and evaluating new therapeutic options; and following up the patient to detect treatable graft abnormalities that may lead to failure. Although atherosclerosis is the most common cause of chronic limb ischemia, other conditions, including popliteal artery entrapment, mucinous cystic degeneration, Buerger's disease, abdominal aortic coarctation, peripheral emboli, fibrodysplasia, pseudoxanthoma elasticum, persistent sciatic artery, iliac artery syndrome of cyclist, and primary arterial tumors, may be present. Risk factors associated with atherosclerosis include smoking, diabetes, hypertension, lipid abnormalities, family history of atherosclerosis, and elevated homocysteine levels. Atherosclerosis may be aggravated by hypercoagulable states (especially in younger patients), polycythemia, and reduced cardiac output. This overview highlights some of the important issues raised in the chapters in this section.

■ NATURAL HISTORY (Chapter 77)

Peripheral arterial occlusive disease (PAOD) presents as a clinical spectrum—an asymptomatic disease, claudication, or critical ischemia. Most patients are symptom-free or have only mild claudication. Claudication generally is associated with a favorable natural history. Overall, approximately one in four patients complain of increasing symptoms over time, revascularization is required in less than 20% of patients at 10 years, and the amputation rate is 1% to 7% at 5 to 10 years. The natural history is less favorable if the ankle-brachial blood pressure index is low, the patient continues to smoke, or the patient has diabetes (especially if it is poorly controlled).

The TransAtlantic Inter-Society Consensus (TASC) conference defined critical limb ischemia as persistent, recurring ischemic rest pain requiring opiate analgesia for at least 2 weeks, ulceration or gangrene of the foot or toes, and ankle systolic pressure less than 50 mm Hg or toe systolic pressure less than 30 mm Hg (or absent pedal pulses in patients with diabetes). Most, but not all, patients with rest pain or tissue necrosis have limb loss. Small ulcers may heal with aggressive local management, and intermittent rest pain or night pain may improve with the development of collaterals or improvement in cardiac hemodynamics.

The mortality rate associated with patients who have claudication is 50% at 5 years, and for patients with critical limb ischemia, the rate is 70%. This high mortality rate is most commonly associated with cardiac disease and is generally unrecognized by clinicians. Consequently the opportunity for risk factor or cardiac intervention may be overlooked.

■ NONOPERATIVE TREATMENT (Chapter 77)

Atherosclerosis Management

Atherosclerosis risk factor management is an important strategy in reducing the high mortality rate associated with PAOD. Studies have shown that these patients are often poorly managed with regard to smoking cessation; treatment of hyperlipidemia; and management of hypertension, diabetes, and other possible contributing factors, including hyperhomocysteinemia, hypercoagulability, and hyperfibrinogenemia. Antiplatelet treatment usually should be recommended for patients with PAOD to reduce the risk of myocardial infarction, stroke, and death due to vascular disease.

Treatment of Peripheral Arterial Occlusive Disease

Exercise therapy for the treatment of claudication has been shown to improve walking distance and quality of life. To date, only two agents are currently approved by the U.S. Food and Drug Administration: pentoxifylline and cilostazol. These and other drugs are discussed in this chapter.

■ EVALUATION OF PATIENTS WITH LOWER LIMB ARTERIAL OCCLUSIVE DISEASE (Chapter 78)

A careful structured history and thorough physical examination of the patient usually reveal claudication and distinguish it from musculoskeletal disorders and neurologic abnormalities, including the most difficult differential diagnosis, spinal stenosis. Clinical evaluation also determines the severity of the PAOD and the relative disabilities from cardiorespiratory problems and other diseases. The symptoms of critical ischemia are usually straightforward, but in some cases it may be difficult to distinguish rest pain and night pain from the discomfort associated with neuropathy. Because patients with PAOD have a high probability of having other significant atherosclerotic lesions, clinical and laboratory investigation of cardiac, carotid, and atherosclerotic risk factors is important. Diagnosis and management of hypercoagulable states is important.

Noninvasive procedures form the basis for the initial evaluation and follow-up of patients with PAOD. If intervention is considered on the basis of the severity of the patient's symptoms, comorbid conditions, and location and severity of the arterial occlusive disease, detailed evaluation of the site and severity of PAOD can be determined by more detailed noninvasive studies, contrast arteriography, computed tomography angiography, or magnetic resonance angiography (MRA), depending on the tests that are available and their suitability for evaluating the individual patient's disease.

Because atherosclerosis is generally a progressive disease, clinical and vascular laboratory follow-up is justified. For patients who undergo intervention, a surveillance program is particularly important to detect a failing intervention rather than a failed procedure and to correct it, if feasible.

■ DIRECT RECONSTRUCTION FOR AORTOILIAC OCCLUSIVE DISEASE (Chapter 79)

Although 5% to 10% of patients have truly localized aortoiliac disease, most patients with disabling claudication or critical ischemia have diffuse involvement and usually a combination of aortoiliac and infrainguinal disease. Patients with PAOD localized to the aortoiliac segment often do well with conservative management because of the potential for the formation of excellent collaterals. For patients with disabling claudication or critical ischemia, percutaneous catheter-based intervention may be feasible and is associated with good long-term results when the arterial disease is localized or when there is direct aortic reconstruction or extra-anatomic bypass grafts (see Chapter 80). The decision between an aortobifemoral bypass graft and an extra-anatomic graft is based on the patient's age and expected length of survival, which must be balanced against the better long-term patency rate associated with an aortobifemoral bypass graft.

In Chapter 79, Brewster emphasizes several important technical points: The proximal anastomosis should be close to the renal arteries, where atherosclerotic disease is usually less severe; end-to-side anastomosis is indicated when there is coexisting aneurysmal disease and complete occlusion extending up to the renal arteries; side-to-side anastomosis is preferable if accessory renal arteries are present or it is necessary to maintain the patency of a large inferior mesenteric artery, or if the external iliac arteries are diseased, it is important to maintain internal iliac flow; and when the superficial femoral artery (SFA) is occluded, any stenosis of the profunda femoris artery must be detected and corrected with a profundaplasty. There are several other important technical considerations: retroperitoneal approach, laparoscopy, the problem of dealing with the calcified or small aorta, and management of associated renal and mesenteric artery disease.

In patients with multilevel disease, an inflow repair usually provides good symptomatic relief if the aortoiliac involvement is hemodynamically significant. Synchronous proximal and distal reconstruction may be necessary in uncommon cases, however, when patients have advanced limb-threatening ischemia and particularly if the aortoiliac involvement is only of modest severity. Prevention and management of early complications (e.g., hemorrhage, limb ischemia, renal failure, intestinal ischemia) and late complications (e.g., graft occlusion, infection, aortoenteric fistula) are discussed. With proper patient selection and a carefully performed aortobifemoral bypass graft by an experienced vascular surgeon, the perioperative mortality rate is 3% to 4%, and graft patency is 85% to 90% at 5 years and 70% to 75% at 10 years on the basis of the results of several large series.

■ EXTRA-ANATOMIC BYPASS (Chapter 80)

Extra-anatomic bypass grafts provide an alternative to the higher risk associated with direct arterial reconstruction in patients with significant ischemic symptoms who have major co-morbid conditions. These grafts also are considered when an aortic replacement would be technically difficult because of a "hostile abdomen" or is contraindicated because of an intra-abdominal infection or other disease. These procedures are used to revascularize the extremities in association with the removal of an infected prosthetic aortic graft. In general, the long-term results are less satisfactory than the results with an aortobifemoral bypass, and consequently the procedure is rarely indicated for claudication.

Femorofemoral Bypass

Femorofemoral bypass is useful to treat patients who have thrombosis of the limb of an aortobifemoral bypass or have unilateral disease. Before surgery, careful assessment of the donor vessel is important to confirm that it is "normal." A papaverine test may be necessary in addition to clinical, noninvasive, and angiographic assessment. If the donor iliac artery has a lesion that is favorable for angioplasty (e.g., a short common iliac stenosis), it is reasonable to proceed with angioplasty and a femorofemoral bypass. The results depend on patient selection. The mortality rate averages 3%, and at 3 to 5 years, the primary and secondary patency rates are 60% and 70%.

Axillofemoral Bypass

Despite the enthusiasm for axillofemoral bypass among a few authors, most continue to view this operation as most appropriate for patients who are not candidates for iliac angioplasty and are at high risk for aortobifemoral bypass or as part of treatment for infection of the native aorta or previously placed aortic prostheses. It is usually possible to determine if a donor axillary artery is normal by noting that the upper extremity blood pressures are equal and Doppler waveforms are normal without evidence of disturbed flow. Occasionally, MRA or contrast angiography may be necessary.

Generally, vascular surgeons believe that an axillobifemoral bypass graft has a superior patency rate compared with an axillo-unifemoral graft; however, despite the higher blood flow velocity in a bifemoral graft, many authors have found little or no improvement in patency rates. Externally supported grafts may prevent physical compression, but there is no solid evidence to support their use.

Reports on the results of this procedure are extremely variable because multiple groups of patients are usually included. Patients undergoing axillofemoral bypass as part of the treatment for infection of the aorta or an aortic prosthesis or for aortoenteric fistula tend to have high perioperative morbidity and mortality rates, but survivors tend to have better patency than patients who undergo the operation for chronic arterial occlusive disease. For patients with occlusive disease, the patency rate depends on the severity: 40% 3-year primary patency rate for patients with critical ischemia and 85% patency rate for patients with claudication.

Obturator Bypass

Obturator bypass is a technically challenging procedure that may be useful when there is infection in the groin (prosthetic bypass graft, access graft, false aneurysm from drug injection or diagnostic cannulation) or occlusive disease from groin irradiation. The bypass originates from the iliac artery or from the limb of an aortobifemoral bypass graft, but only if the graft is uninfected and is incorporated. It passes through the obturator canal and most commonly is anastomosed to the distal SFA or popliteal artery, but it can be anastomosed to the deep femoral artery. The latter case is not usually feasible because of the risk of entering the infected groin.

Thoracofemoral Bypass

The indications for this bypass include replacement for an infected aortic prosthesis or a failed aortobifemoral bypass graft. If the patient is fit for thoracotomy, the long-term results of the thoracofemoral bypass have proved to be comparable to results of an aortobifemoral bypass.

■ INFRAINGUINAL BYPASS (Chapter 81)

Chapter 81 describes the indications, patient selection, techniques, and results of infrainguinal bypass grafts for the treatment of arterial occlusive disease, but excludes traumatic, aneurysmal, and nonatherosclerotic indications. Significant advances have resulted in improved results, especially for patients with critical limb ischemia who otherwise usually would face amputation.

Extensive evaluation of the patient's general status is problematic in patients with critical limb ischemia because these patients have a high probability of having significant underlying cardiac disease and require prompt intervention to avoid amputation. Postponing infrainguinal bypass to allow further cardiac evaluation is recommended only in the presence of unstable or poorly controlled angina, recent myocardial infarction, poorly controlled congestive heart failure, or symptomatic or untreated arrhythmia. Nearly all patients in whom infrainguinal bypass is indicated have suitable target vessels if diagnostic angiography is performed properly. In some cases, it may be necessary to perform intraoperative angiography or selective exploration of dorsal pedal or distal posterior tibial arteries if flow is detectable by Doppler or duplex imaging.

Assessment of the availability and quality of autogenous veins with duplex mapping is important preoperatively. If the ipsilateral greater saphenous vein (GSV) is absent, unsuitable, or of insufficient length to perform the anticipated bypass, the contralateral GSV, lesser saphenous vein, and upper extremity veins are scanned to detect the location and quality of an available vein. Contralateral GSV should be harvested if necessary because it is necessary for future bypass surgery in no more than 20% to 25% of patients. Superficial femoral vein is occasionally useful for shorter bypasses but is difficult to harvest. If the adequacy of the inflow is in question, it can be assessed by the direct measurement of intra-arterial pressure before and after the administration of intra-arterial papaverine.

Significant occlusive disease involving the common femoral origin and proximal deep femoral artery should be addressed at the time of the infrainguinal bypass whenever the bypass is to originate from the common femoral artery. The general principle of infrainguinal reconstruction is to bypass all hemodynamically significant disease and to insert the bypass to the most proximal limb artery that has at least one continuous runoff artery to the foot.

Autogenous veins should be used whenever possible for infrainguinal bypass. Other options are less satisfactory but may be necessary in selected patients, including polytetrafluoroethylene (PTFE), human umbilical vein, radial artery, and cryopreserved vein grafts. For long bypasses, ipsilateral GSV, contralateral GSV, and spliced vein are recommended in decreasing order of preference. If only 5 to 15 cm of extra length is required and a more distal origin site is not feasible, eversion endarterectomy of the SFA with anastomosis to the available vein segment is a useful technique that avoids the harvesting and splicing of additional vein. For shorter bypasses, arm vein or lesser saphenous vein is effective. If vein is truly unavailable, PTFE and Dacron are the best options for above-knee bypass. If the improved results with heparin bonding are confirmed, heparin-bonded Dacron may become the preferred conduit for above-knee bypass in the absence of suitable vein. For infrageniculate insertion sites, PTFE with distal anastomotic modification (cuff, boot, or patch) is recommended if vein is unavailable. Randomized prospective trials show equivalence between in-situ and reversed vein conduits. The use of these techniques is dictated by operative considerations and surgeon preference and experience.

Intraoperative objective assessment of the bypass graft is recommended with completion angiography or duplex scanning. For in-situ or on reverse grafts, duplex scanning may be more sensitive than angiography. Toe or forefoot amputations or major wound amputations generally are delayed for 4 to 10 days to allow clear demarcation and maximization of the reperfusion. If a graft fails in the early postoperative period, it is important to identify and correct the underlying cause, such as anastomotic abnormalities, a local flap, an injury from a vascular clamp, a poor conduit, or inadequate outflow. If no cause can be identified, the prognosis for long-term patency is poor.

Regular surveillance by the measurement of ankle-brachial blood pressure index and duplex scanning improves patency by detecting graft abnormalities, which occur in approximately 30% of patients with vein grafts and threaten graft patency. In the first 1 to 2 years, intimal hyperplasia is the most common abnormality, but at later intervals, inflow lesions, outflow lesions, or both develop. The decision to carry out a primary amputation rather than revascularization is a complex one, but may be the appropriate option for elderly patients with critical limb ischemia who are living in nursing facilities and are minimally ambulatory.

■ PROFUNDAPLASTY (Chapter 82)

With good results from a distal bypass operation, the importance of profundaplasty sometimes has been overlooked. When the SFAs are occluded, the profunda femoris artery serves as the primary collateral channel. When a significant stenosis of the profunda femoris artery is present, a profundaplasty is carried out as an adjunctive procedure to provide maximal outflow for an inflow operation or to a proximal graft thrombosis. An isolated profundaplasty (usually with common femoral artery repair as well) may be indicated for selected patients with critical limb ischemia who are not candidates for direct revascularization or in some patients to improve perfusion and permit healing of a below-knee amputation.

Accurate assessment of the severity of a profunda femoris artery stenosis can be difficult but is an important predictor of success. Duplex ultrasonography may show the stenosis, but usually oblique views from contrast angiography or MRA are necessary. When carried out as an adjunctive procedure, intraoperative palpation of the profunda femoris artery and inspection of its origin through the common femoral arteriotomy is useful.

Patients undergoing profundaplasty are a heterogeneous group, and evaluation of the results is difficult. The mortality rate is low, and complications are infrequent. Because of the interruption of lymphatic vessels and division of lymph nodes that may be necessary with the extensive dissection, however, edema, a lymphocele, or a lymphatic fistula is more common than with other groin procedures.

■ SECONDARY ARTERIAL RECONSTRUCTIONS IN THE LOWER EXTREMITY (Chapter 83)

Revision of an infrainguinal intervention may be necessary in the early stage (within 30 days) because of a technical error, insufficient inflow or outflow, a hypercoagulable state, reduced cardiac output, or hypotension or at a later stage because of the development of intimal hyperplasia or progression of atherosclerotic disease. After graft thrombosis, the results of repeat intervention are poor, whereas repeat intervention for failing grafts is usually technically straightforward and the results have been good. Regular follow-up is important, and further investigation is necessary if the patient reports a recurrent symptom, pulses are reduced, ankle-brachial index decreases, or duplex scanning shows an abnormality.

Chapter 83 reviews the multiple strategies and technical options for managing a thrombosed or failing graft, including autogenous and failed prosthetic grafts. For treating early failures, vascular surgeons should detect and treat the cause and critically evaluate the graft by using an intraoperative arteriogram, duplex evaluation, or direct pressure measurements to rule out any gradient. When the treatment of a late graft failure is planned, complete angiography is important. Venography or duplex ultrasonography is useful in predicting the length and diameter of residual venous segments. Surgical repair is usually the most durable, and re-operation includes a combination of "blind" or fluoroscopically guided thrombectomy along with endovascular treatment, segmental graft replacement, or local repair. Alternatively, total replacement of the bypass graft with an autogenous or composite graft may be used. Some vascular surgeons think that thrombolysis may have a role if the patient's limb is not severely ischemic and there is time to permit this treatment. Catheter-directed thrombolysis may re-establish perfusion, may identify a lesion that can be treated percutaneously, and may clear thrombus from distal vessels that could not be opened surgically. Although the role of percutaneous transluminal angioplasty for treating vein graft stenosis is controversial, it may be useful for treating short stenoses, particularly in an inaccessible part of the vein, or for managing some inflow and outflow stenoses.

■ ENDOVASCULAR SURGERY IN THE MANAGEMENT OF CHRONIC LOWER EXTREMITY ISCHEMIA (Chapter 84)

Endovascular approaches play an integral role in the management of chronic infrarenal atherosclerotic occlusive disease. Since the introduction of balloon angioplasty in the 1970s, significant advances have been made, including improved balloon technology; development of digital subtraction arteriography; refinement of guide wires, catheters, and sheaths; the availability of stents, including covered stents and drug-eluting stents; and the application of thrombolytic therapy.

When a patient is evaluated, the greater risk of open surgery must be balanced against the lower durability and more limited applicability of endovascular treatment. The severity and distribution of the arterial occlusive disease usually can be determined through the patient's history and results of a physical examination, supplemented by non-invasive vascular laboratory tests. Arteriography is used for strategic planning of the revascularization and should be done so that it facilitates the performance of endovascular treatment during the same procedure, if possible. Peripheral angioplasty is more likely to be successful if the lesion is a relatively short stenosis involving a proximal large artery localized to one artery segment that is associated with good runoff and if the indication is claudication and the procedure is carried out by an experienced surgeon.

Technical details are considered in Chapter 84 and in Chapters 50 through 54 and include planning the puncture site; crossing the lesion; and performing angioplasty, stent placement, and completion angiography. Chapter 84 reviews the results and complications for the treatment of aortic, aortic bifurcation, iliac, femoral popliteal, and distal arterial angioplasty and emphasizes the use of uniform assessment and reporting standards to improve the accuracy of reporting and facilitate comparisons among studies. Catheter-based treatment has proved to be reliable and durable for the management of many patients with PAOD. Although laser angioplasty and atherectomy devices have not proved to be generally applicable, future advances may include the use of drug-eluting stents and stent grafts.

■ LUMBAR SYMPATHECTOMY (Chapter 85)

Although sympathectomy has a relatively minor role in the treatment of a patient with severe inoperable PAOD, it may improve cutaneous nutritive blood flow and allow healing of small superficial ischemic ulcers or relieve mild rest pain or night pain. Success is unlikely if an autosympathectomy has resulted from diabetes or another neuropathy, if the patient is severely ischemic and the peripheral arterial bed is already maximally dilated, or if the cutaneous ischemic lesion is large (sympathectomy increases cutaneous blood flow only by a relatively small amount). Causalgia remains the best indication for sympathectomy. Cold-induced vasospasm can be treated with sympathectomy, but the long-term results are poor when occlusive disease is present. In other cases, nonoperative treatment usually suffices. Sympathectomy is effective in the control of hyperhidrosis; in contrast to the upper extremities, involvement of the lower extremities rarely requires surgical treatment. Success is more likely if sympathetic blocks have shown subjective and objective improvement.

For most clinical indications, L2 and L3 ganglionectomy is sufficient, but also removing L4 is advised to reduce the possibility of collateral reinnervation due to crossover fibers, which are found in 15% of patients at this level or L5. Overall, three lumbar ganglia are most commonly found because of fusion of the L1 and L2 ganglia. Sympathetic innervation of the foot and lower leg is primarily conveyed through the L2 and L3 ganglia; the proximal leg region is primarily innervated from the L1 to the L4 ganglia. Percutaneous sympathectomy through the injection of phenol or absolute alcohol with three needles to the L2, L3, and L4 vertebral levels seems to produce a less complete and less durable effect. Experience with this technique in the United States seems to be increasing. Small series of laparoscopic lumbar sympathectomy have been reported.

■ NONATHEROMATOUS CAUSES OF CHRONIC INFRAINGUINAL ISCHEMIA (Chapter 86)

In young patients without atherosclerotic risk factors, the following diseases should be considered when the patient has claudication: popliteal artery entrapment syndrome, adventitial cystic disease, fibromuscular disease, external iliac endofibrosis found in cyclists, arteritis, embolus, and occlusive arterial lesions seen in pseudoxanthoma elasticum. Dorsiflexion and plantar flexion, along with pulse palpation, auscultation for a popliteal fossa bruit, ankle blood pressure measurements, and duplex ultrasound studies, are useful. Popliteal occlusion with active plantar flexion can be seen on duplex scanning in more than 50% of healthy people. Computed tomography is useful for the detection of adventitial cystic disease, and magnetic resonance imaging or MRA has been useful for diagnosis.

Popliteal Artery Entrapment Syndrome

More than half of patients with claudication who are younger than age 50 years have popliteal entrapment syndrome, and often it is bilateral. The anomaly is classified into four types; a fifth type is reserved for venous entrapment. A functional entrapment diagnosed by a diffuse narrowing of the popliteal artery may be difficult to distinguish from the transitory compression or temporary occlusion that occurs in half the normal population with the extremes of plantar flexion or dorsiflexion. Passive dorsiflexion of the foot and active plantar flexion against resistance may obliterate the pedal pulses or show a popliteal artery bruit. Surgical correction by division of the compressing muscle and tendinous bands is advised to prevent progressive fibrosis of the artery, which leads to thrombosis or aneurysm formation. If thromboembolic complications have occurred, angiography reveals an irregular arterial lumen, or if the artery is thickened and nodular at the point of entrapment, arterial repair is advised. The indication for surgery is far less clear when there is a functional entrapment.

Adventitial Cystic Disease

Although the cause is obscure, involvement of the popliteal, femoral, external iliac, and other arteries in proximity to joints by a cystic clear mucinous fluid collection in the adventitial layer raises the possibility that adventitial disease may be due to mucin-secreting cells derived from the mesenchyme of the adjacent joint that are included in the adventitia of the artery or vein during embryologic development. In a 15:1 ratio, men in their 30s and 40s are most commonly affected. If the artery is occluded, a bypass or interposition graft is necessary; however, cystotomy is the preferred treatment if total evacuation can be accomplished. Percutaneous aspiration has a higher rate of recurrence.

■ MANAGEMENT OF FOOT LESIONS IN DIABETIC PATIENTS (Chapter 87)

Diabetic patients have a risk of amputation that is 15 times higher than nondiabetic patients. Several factors are contributory, including the higher prevalence of arterial occlusive disease, neuropathy, and infection. Patients with diabetes have an increased propensity to atherosclerosis. Good blood glucose control, smoking cessation, and the use of statins and angiotensin-converting enzyme inhibitors are important.

Neuropathy sets the stage for pressure ulceration, unsuspected injury, and infection. Sensory neuropathy first manifests as loss of pain and temperature sensation even though light touch may be intact. Motor neuropathy first involves the innervation of the intrinsic muscles of the foot, and without the influence of the lumbrical muscles, the strong flexor muscles cause the toes to draw up in a "claw" position and create pressure points under the metatarsal phalangeal joints and tips of the toes. Autonomic neuropathy creates dry skin that is prone to cracks and fissures through the loss of eccrine gland function.

The neuroinflammatory response to injury is blunted. Normally, in response to injury, through the neuroinflammatory response, neuropeptides are released and cause vasodilatation, increased capillary permeability, and white blood cell migration to the site of injury. Loss of neuroinflammatory response probably explains the blunted response to infection in the foot of a diabetic patient. Also, normal cellular and tissue functions are probably compromised in the foot of a diabetic patient.

A diabetic patient with a physiologically compromised foot requires more perfusion to resist ulceration and to respond to injury, and when an ulcer is present, revascularization is necessary. As a general rule, if a full-thickness skin ulcer of the foot occurs in a patient with diabetes, and neither the dorsalis pedis pulse nor the posterior tibial pulse is easily palpable, arteriography should be performed. A continuous Doppler wave usually suffices to determine if the dorsalis pedis or posterior tibial artery signals are triphasic. Noninvasive assessment with duplex ultrasonography or transcutaneous oxygen pressure is of little value in most patients. The authors of Chapter 87 report excellent results and emphasize the value of a bypass to the dorsalis pedis artery with autogenous conduit, which can originate from any normal proximal artery. For healing of ulcers, the posterior tibial artery is the preferable target artery, but the dorsalis pedis artery also has proved to be effective.

Other issues must be addressed during treatment. When the foot has a deep infection, it is important to drain any abscess promptly and remove obvious necrotic tissue, in addition to bringing glycemia under control and initiating broad-spectrum antibiotic treatment. After revascularization, additional débridement of infected or necrotic tissue may be necessary. For closure to be achieved, resection of bone and joints and muscle flaps may be necessary.

■ VASCULOGENIC IMPOTENCE (Chapter 88)

Penile erection results from an increase of arterial inflow into the corporeal bodies along with a reduction or cessation of venous outflow. This increased arterial flow is neurally mediated. When the penis is flaccid, the corporal smooth muscle and the cavernosal arteries are contracted because of a normally present overriding adrenergic tone. The initiating event of penile erection is vasodilatation with progressive smooth muscle relaxation, facilitating increased arterial inflow, and an increase of intracavernous pressure. With increased intracavernosal flow, a greater amount of oxygen is thought to stimulate nitric oxide synthesis by cavernosal nerves and endothelium. With full smooth muscle relaxation, the penile veins become obstructed because of the occluding action of the subalbugineal smooth muscle.

Multiple factors contribute to impotence (erectile dysfunction), including arterial, neurogenic, psychological, endocrine, and metabolic factors and drugs. Arteriogenic impotence can result from large vessel aortoiliac disease and abnormalities of the distal pudendal arterial supply. Intrinsic abnormalities of the penile arteries or smooth muscle also may cause impotence. Only a few men with the chief complaint of erectile dysfunction have aortoiliac disease, but vascular surgeons must recognize the importance of preventing iatrogenic impotence at the time of aortic surgery.

Because erectile dysfunction is a symptom and not a single disease, there is no universally accepted approach to evaluation, diagnosis, and treatment. After a patient provides a complete history, including risk assessment, and undergoes a physical examination, an accepted approach is patient goal directed. Detailed investigations are undertaken if simple measures, such as oral medications, intracavernous administration of vasoactive agents, or vacuum constrictor devices, prove ineffective. Duplex ultrasonography to scan the penile vessels at intervals after intracavernous injection of vasoactive agents is often used before considering invasive procedures, such as highly selective pudendal arteriography and dynamic infusion cavernosometry and cavernosography, to measure penile blood pressure and flow changes and detect sites of leakage. Nocturnal penile tumescence monitoring studies are not used routinely but can be useful when psychogenic impotence is suspected. Most patients now show a satisfactory response to medical therapy, but it is suggested that approximately 6% to 7% of patients do not respond. The results of microvascular procedures for penile artery bypass, deep dorsal vein arterialization, and venous ligation do not justify their routine use for treatment of erectile failure at this time.

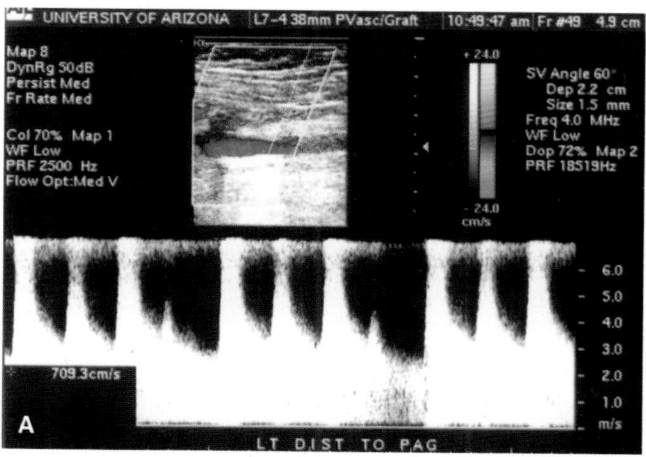

FIGURE 81-14A. Duplex surveillance identified a critical vein graft stenosis in the proximal aspect of a femoropopliteal vein graft. There is marked spectral broadening and pronounced elevation of both the peak systolic (PSV) and end-diastolic (EDV) velocities, diagnostic of a high-grade vein graft stenosis.

Chapter

77

Natural History and Nonoperative Treatment of Chronic Lower Extremity Ischemia

MARK R. NEHLER, MD
HEATHER WOLFORD, MD

Section XIII

Vascular surgery is unique compared with other surgical subspecialties. In contrast to cardiothoracic surgery, oncologic surgery, and general surgery, there has not been a companion medical subspecialty that shares the nonoperative care of most of the vascular patient population and provides significant patient referrals. Vascular medicine has established a role since the 1980s, but most vascular surgery practices in the United States outside of academic centers do not share patients with vascular internists. In part as a result of this isolation of the specialty, referring physician understanding of peripheral arterial disease (PAD) is modest at best.[1] For the foreseeable future, a large amount of the nonoperative care of vascular patients will be rendered by vascular surgeons; a modern vascular practice will continue to include nonoperative management of chronic lower extremity arterial disease.

The morbidity and mortality associated with chronic lower extremity ischemia are unappreciated by physicians and patients. PAD affects approximately 10% of patients older than age 70, with the total number affected upward of 10 million. As a result of the well-recognized aging of the U.S. population, the impact of PAD on health care will grow in the near future. Since the 1990s, much data have accumulated regarding risk factor reduction of cardiovascular events and pharmacologic and gene therapy for critical limb ischemia (CLI) and claudication. This chapter reviews the natural history of chronic lower extremity ischemia. Approaches to risk factor modification and current pharmacologic therapies also are discussed briefly; both of these topics are covered in more detail in other chapters.

■ STRATIFICATION OF CHRONIC LOWER EXTREMITY ISCHEMIA

Owing to the ubiquitous nature of degenerative joint and spine disease in the elderly, in combination with the prevalence of PAD in this population, much of the practicing vascular surgeon's initial clinical evaluation is aimed at determining whether patients referred with lower extremity pain actually have PAD and, if so, whether it is responsible for their symptoms. Chronic lower extremity ischemia represents a clinical spectrum. The two important variables are clinical symptoms and the measured circulatory impairment. The traditional Fontaine classification system for lower extremity arterial occlusive disease groups patients by symptoms: I, asymptomatic; II, claudication; III, ischemic rest pain; and IV, ischemic ulceration/necrosis. Work by McDermott and others[2-6] has shown, however, that many patients considered "asymptomatic" have some degree of exertional leg pain, but not the classic symptoms of claudication. Likewise, although claudication and ischemic rest pain have typical symptomatic complaints, patients with ischemic pedal ulceration and necrosis are a heterogeneous group with respect to extent of pedal involvement, severity of the necrotic process, and underlying etiology (e.g., trauma, pressure necrosis).[7] All of these factors are likely important in ultimate patient outcome and are only beginning to be investigated.

Despite marked advances in noninvasive imaging, the ankle-brachial pressure index (ABI) remains the most common tool used to diagnose PAD and stratify objectively the extent of occlusive disease. Population studies in PAD have shown that ABI correlates with increased risk of limb loss and cardiovascular mortality.[8-10] Conversely, a severe reduction in ABI without limb threat is not an indication for revascularization. Fowl and colleagues[11] reviewed the course of 23 patients with an ABI less than 0.35 and no evidence of rest pain or gangrene. Over a period of 43 months, 50% of the patients remained clinically stable, and 10% had an improvement in symptoms.[11] Similar findings have been reported by Gertler and coworkers.[12]

Functional assessment of claudication in the office typically involves a measurement of walking distance. Claudication history typically has been reported as the number of blocks a patient can walk on level ground at a normal speed without having to stop, although more recent trials have shown that patients are frequently poor judges of objective walking distance. In randomized pharmaceutical trials, absolute claudication distance on a treadmill using either fixed or graded protocols is the standard primary endpoint.[13] Many investigations have focused on patient-reported functional assessment with chronic lower extremity ischemia. The Walking Impairment Questionnaire[14] and Rand Short Form 36 provide data regarding walking in the community, and the Walking Impairment Questionnaire has been validated against treadmill walking.[15]

■ NATURAL HISTORY OF INTERMITTENT CLAUDICATION

Intermittent claudication is lower extremity muscular pain in the calves (less frequently the buttocks or thighs) induced by exercise and relieved with short periods of rest. Claudication is caused by arterial obstruction proximal to affected muscle beds, which limits the normal exercise-induced increase in blood flow and produces transient muscle ischemia during exercise. Only a fraction of PAD patients complain of intermittent claudication. The presence of asymptomatic PAD varies, but available data indicate that for every patient with intermittent claudication, there are probably three others with similar disease who do not complain of symptoms.[16] Subjective complaints of intermittent claudication vary in degree and severity based on individual factors, including occupational and recreational habits. The proportion of patients with intermittent claudication who consult a physician varies markedly from 10% in the inner city[17] to 50% in rural communities.[18]

In addition, physicians frequently are unaware of PAD present in their patient populations. Data from the Partners program[1] showed 13% of the total 6979 patients older than age 50 in the more than 350 primary care practices screened were found to have abnormal ABI with or without symptoms of intermittent claudication. Only 24% of these patients found to have chronic lower extremity ischemia previously had been diagnosed with PAD by their physicians.

Objectively, claudication usually is associated with ABI ranging from 0.5 to 0.95, although occasionally a patient with mild intermittent claudication may have a normal ABI at rest that decreases only when stressed by treadmill walking (usually indicating obstructive disease limited to the aortoiliac system).[19] Rare patients have markedly reduced ABI without limb-threatening symptoms, either with claudication or asymptomatic. When the diagnosis has been made, patients and physicians fear disease progression and limb loss in addition to the functional limitations secondary to intermittent claudication. Multiple natural history studies show, however, that relatively few patients who present with claudication ever require revascularization to prevent limb loss. Multiple longitudinal studies[20-24] show an amputation rate of 1% to 7% at 5 to 10 years, with approximately one in four patients complaining of increasing symptoms over time. A study[25] of 2777 veterans with claudication followed for a mean of almost 4 years confirms these data. Major and minor amputations were performed at a rate of less than 10% over 10 years. Revascularizations totaled less than 20% at 10 years; most were performed for claudication rather than CLI.

There are no clear criteria indicating when a patient with claudication should undergo revascularization.[26] Although some vascular surgeons argue against performing infrainguinal bypass for anything other than limb threat, most lower extremity bypass series published indicate claudication as the operative indication in 10% to 20% of patients. Patients with aortoiliac disease frequently undergo endovascular therapy. Many patients do not have an ideal anatomy for endovascular therapy, however. A randomized trial of angioplasty versus exercise for claudication screened 600 patients to find 61 with short segment lesions amenable to endovascular intervention.[27] Aortobifemoral bypass is a durable operation in most patients and is primarily performed for claudication.[28]

Several reservations regarding interventions in claudication exist. First, the natural history of claudication is relatively benign regarding eventual limb threat (see earlier). Conversely, an undefined number of patients who undergo revascularization experience graft failure and present with limb threat,[29] particularly patients with premature atherosclerosis.[30-33] A single series of infrainguinal revascularization for claudication in 233 consecutive patients (90% endovascular) showed fairly sobering results at a mean follow-up of almost 7 years:[34] Primary patency at 5 years was 27%, half of the patients required one or more secondary interventions (21% of limbs initially treated with endovascular methods required surgery), and 12% of limbs ultimately developed CLI. Second, significant morbidity is associated with surgical bypass aside from graft occlusion, including perioperative mortality, lymphedema,[35-38] graft surveillance,[39] and wound healing.[40-42] Conversely, favoring intervention for claudication is the improvement in quality of life for the duration of graft patency. Ultimately, it is a public health issue whether to expend resources for claudication, particularly when many patients continue to smoke tobacco. Few issues in vascular surgery are more controversial and lead to more polarization of opinion than when or if to intervene for claudication.

The level of arterial occlusion (measured by ABI) at first encounter predicts disease progression in all populations of PAD. An additional important risk factor in claudication disease progression is continued tobacco use. A single report of 224 patients with intermittent claudication showed that only 8% of patients who did not smoke or quit smoking within 1 year of diagnosis of PAD developed rest pain compared with 21% who smoked or quit more than 1 year after diagnosis.[43] Diabetes also has been associated with increased development of CLI in claudicant populations.[44]

Patients with claudication are significantly limited in their perceived quality of life and community function. Several studies show 50% or greater reduction in scores of physical function, community walking, and perception of health compared with normal controls.[31,45-47] Some of this disability may be due to co-morbid conditions, however. In a study of multiple quality-of-life indices in 200 people with intermittent claudication, cardiovascular risk factors and other co-morbidities played a significant role in determining quality of life, especially on aspects of health other than strictly physical health dimensions of the test.[48]

■ NATURAL HISTORY OF CRITICAL LIMB ISCHEMIA

Limb-threatening ischemia is defined as inadequate arterial blood flow to accommodate the metabolic needs of resting tissue. CLI is clinically diagnosed as rest pain or pedal necrosis with appropriate documentation of circulatory impairment (Fontaine stages III and IV). Rest pain presents as a burning dysesthesia of the foot, aggravated by elevation and relieved with dependency, presumably resulting from the increase in arterial pressure from gravity in a limb with a nonfunctioning venoarteriolar reflex due to ischemia.[49] Pedal necrosis includes ischemic ulcerations or gangrene after minor trauma or surgical incisions involving the foot. There is some disagreement regarding what level of circulatory impairment is required to qualify for CLI, but the TransAtlantic Inter-Society Consensus considered ankle pressure less than 50 to 70 mm Hg, toe pressure less than 30 to 50 mm Hg, or transcutaneous partial pressure of oxygen at the foot less than 30 to 50 mm Hg.[50]

The incidence of CLI is not known with certainty. Using multiple different extrapolation methods, it is estimated that 500,000 to 1 million new cases occur per year.[51,52] One of the greatest deficiencies in the current understanding of CLI is the antecedent natural history. Many clinicians assume that patients progress through the Fontaine stages in a stepwise manner. As stated previously, however, few patients with claudication progress to CLI unless they undergo interventions. In most patients, CLI progresses directly from Fontaine I to stage III or IV. Dormandy and colleagues[53] showed in a multicenter prostaglandin trial that 50% of enrolled patients were asymptomatic 6 months before major amputation for CLI. Others have shown similar findings.[7] This observation possibly can be explained by the co-morbidities that make these patients less likely to ambulate to an extent that would promote symptoms of claudication.

Major risk factors for CLI include age, smoking, and diabetes. The incidence of major amputation increases markedly with age.[54] Smoking is an independent risk factor for the development of PAD, a correlation stronger than between tobacco and coronary artery disease (CAD). Continued smoking is also a major risk factor for development of CLI in PAD populations.[24] The greatest risk factor for CLI remains diabetes, however. Although diabetes affects only 2% to 5% of Western populations, 40% to 45% of all major amputees are diabetic. Major amputation is 10 times more frequent in diabetic patients with peripheral vascular disease than in nondiabetic patients with peripheral vascular disease.[55] The correlation is independent of age and smoking, but diabetic smokers need amputation earlier in life than nondiabetic smokers.[52]

There is a general belief that patients with chronic ischemic rest pain or tissue necrosis inevitably progress to limb loss without prompt revascularization. Despite this belief, available data indicate that many CLI patients have symptoms weeks or months before vascular referral, particularly patients with Fontaine stage IV.[7] Patients with progressive gangrenous changes and constant ischemic pain have an unstable clinical situation requiring prompt therapy.[56] Abundant clinical experience indicates, however, that patients with CLI with intermittent rest pain may improve noticeably during periods of presumed improved cardiac hemodynamics and have small ulcerations that heal with protective dressings alone. Several randomized pharmacologic trials in CLI have documented ulcer healing in 40% of patients randomized to placebo,[57-59] although in most of these trials, less than half of the control patients were alive without a major amputation at 6 months.[60,61]

■ SURVIVAL

Survival in patients with PAD is variable. Survival can be stratified based on symptoms and objective measures of peripheral occlusive disease via the ABI. The 5-, 10-, and 15-year mortality rates for patients with intermittent claudication are approximately 30%, 50%, and 70%.[25] Multiple risk factors have been defined as important contributors to this increased long-term cardiovascular mortality, including advanced age at presentation, continued tobacco use,[62] diabetes,[63] and dialysis dependence.[64,65] Most deaths are due to CAD, which is nearly universal in the PAD population. In the classic study by Hertzer and associates,[66] coronary angiograms in 1000 consecutive patients undergoing peripheral vascular operations showed greater than 90% of patients had some evidence of CAD, with more than 30% showing severe multivessel disease. Likewise, studies[67-69] screening carotid arteries have shown a 30% incidence of greater than 50% asymptomatic stenosis in PAD populations undergoing infrainguinal revascularization.

Survival for patients with CLI is poor, making much of their care often palliative in nature. Mortality for patients presenting with rest pain reaches 70% at 5 years and 85% at 10 years.[70] A universally consistent data point in all surgical series for CLI is the 50% to 60% 5-year patient survival rate.[71,72] Approximately 80% of patients with PAD die from a vascular event: more than 60% from CAD and 10% from strokes.[73]

Data indicate that survival is inversely related to the degree of objectively determined chronic lower extremity ischemia at presentation.[74] Small series indicate arterial obstructions below the knee to be a particularly ominous sign of abbreviated survival.[75] The severity of systemic atherosclerosis is accurately reflected by the severity of the lower extremity disease. The objective data regarding lower extremity ischemia severity accurately predict the long-term prognosis for life and limb. This knowledge is important in planning individual patient interventions. Most importantly, much of the nonoperative care in PAD patients needs to focus on risk factor modification to reduce cardiovascular events and improve survival.

■ YOUNG PATIENTS WITH CHRONIC LOWER EXTREMITY ISCHEMIA

PAD is considered almost exclusively a disease of the elderly. Premature PAD—usually defined as disease onset before the 30s or 40s—represents a unique population with regard to etiology and prognosis. Because of the rare nature of the condition, most patients with premature PAD experience delay in diagnosis, representing another area for physician education.[76] These patients are almost uniformly heavy smokers, and more than 70% show lipid abnormalities, including elevated low-density lipoprotein (LDL), depressed high-density lipoprotein (HDL), and hypertriglyceridemia.[77] A clinical series screening 50 patients with premature PAD for hypercoagulable markers revealed that 90% had laboratory abnormalities, including reduced inhibitors (antithrombin III, protein C, and protein S), elevated homocysteine, and abnormal fibrinolytic activity.[78] Other risk factors are similar to those of older patients with PAD, including diabetes, hypertension, and family history of cardiovascular disease. Premature PAD must be distinguished from other causes of peripheral ischemia in young adults, including Buerger's disease, collagen vascular disorders, popliteal entrapment syndrome, and chronic compartment syndrome.

Many surgeons advocate a conservative approach to revascularization in premature PAD. The greater functional expectations and frequent limitations in gainful employment experienced by young claudicants complicate their ability to tolerate a prolonged course of nonoperative therapy. Several series showed poor results with reconstruction and a high incidence of limb loss, presumably to the aggressive nature of their disease because many of these patients present with CLI.[33,79] Other reports[80,81] describe successful interventions in premature PAD patients with claudication, however. These authors also note many patients who remain unemployed, regardless of revascularization success. Although survival is reduced in young patients with peripheral vascular disease compared with age-matched controls, on balance coronary atherosclerosis does not seem to be as aggressive as atherosclerosis affecting the lower extremities.[82,83]

■ NONOPERATIVE MANAGEMENT OF PERIPHERAL ARTERIAL DISEASE

The initial focus of nonoperative management for PAD is educating patients and their primary physicians. Overall, awareness of this disease in the medical community is extremely poor. A study of primary care offices throughout the United States[1] revealed that primary care physicians identified PAD less than 50% of the time. In addition, inadequate antiplatelet therapy and poorly controlled hypertension and hyperlipidemia were noted. The problem is not isolated to primary care, however. Patients with known PAD also are poorly managed regarding smoking cessation, hyperlipidemia, and hypertension.[84,85] Given that most patients with PAD eventually die from their cardiovascular disease, physicians need to control risk factors aggressively.

In addition to risk factor modification for mortality benefits, nonoperative management goals include increasing walking distance and functional capacity in claudicants and improving perfusion in patients with CLI. The Trans Atlantic Intersociety Consensus recommendations regarding efficacy of therapy include the following outcomes: (1) improved claudication distance, (2) reduced cardiovascular event rates, (3) improved quality of life, and (4) freedom from adverse side effects.

■ RISK FACTOR MODIFICATION

Although many well-established guidelines based on level I evidence for the management of hypertension, hyperlipidemia, smoking cessation, and diabetes exist,[86-92] there is ample evidence that these guidelines are applied inconsistently in modern medical care.[84,85,93,94] Several independent research efforts are under way to improve primary care delivery and increase the number of patients receiving preventive care in line with established guidelines using feedback from computerized databases. Ongoing projects at University of Washington and Stanford are designed to improve the care of patients with diabetes[95] and hypertension.[96,97] A randomized trial[98] in primary care settings from Duke comparing database feedback with controls showed improvement in guideline use employing the feedback method (15.6% of controls compared with 32% of feedback patients).

Antiplatelet Therapy

Antiplatelet agents have been well established to reduce mortality in patients with cardiovascular disease. Aspirin is the most extensively studied antiplatelet agent. It acts as an irreversible cyclooxygenase inhibitor that blocks thromboxane A_2 production in platelets, leading to decreased platelet aggregation. In the Antiplatelet Trialists' Collaboration review of 189 trials including more than 100,000 patients, there was a 25% reduction in myocardial infarction (MI), stroke, and vascular death with aspirin compared with placebo.[99] Some studies suggest that antiplatelet agents have a beneficial effect on peripheral atherosclerosis. In the Physicians' Health Study, a prospective, randomized controlled trial of aspirin versus placebo in more than 22,000 healthy men, aspirin use was associated with a small, but significant decrease in risk of peripheral arterial surgery.[100] Since the 1990s, other, more potent, antiplatelet agents have been introduced. The CAPRIE study[101] compared clopidogrel, a thienopyridine derivative that blocks adherence of fibrinogen to the platelet's surface, with aspirin in patients with known cardiovascular disease. The study concluded that clopidogrel was more effective in reducing the risk of ischemic stroke, MI, and vascular death than aspirin. This effect was primarily driven by the subset analysis of patients with PAD. Ticlopidine, another antiplatelet agent with a mechanism similar to clopidogrel, initially seemed to prevent thrombotic events and vascular surgery in PAD populations; however, risk of neutropenia has largely eliminated interest in widespread use of this drug. Overall, aspirin should be recommended for all patients with PAD.

Smoking

The paradox of tobacco in modern society is readily evident. Data from several studies[102-104] from the early 1980s regarding the dangers of second-hand smoke led to legislation restricting tobacco use in public and private facilities. The last few years have witnessed for the first time tobacco companies losing several high-profile legal battles. There is evidence that mass media antismoking campaigns have had some effect on the incidence and prevalence of tobacco use.[105] Despite a negative public image, however, the tobacco industry is thriving. The cost of legal expenses has been transferred to the consumer. Young American smokers, particularly women, are increasing in number.[106] This increase continues despite overwhelming evidence regarding the lethal nature of tobacco. The estimated annual excess mortality due to cigarette smoking in the United States exceeds 350,000 deaths.[107] The annual total direct health care costs from tobacco are estimated to exceed $16 billion, with indirect costs greater than $37 billion.[108]

Tobacco companies are under fire by state-sponsored and individual-sponsored class action lawsuits.[109] The tobacco industry is well defended, however. Their annual legal defense budget is estimated at $900 million. In addition, owing to projected annual payments to be made to individual states from recent settlements in combination with major state budget cuts, maintaining the tobacco industry is in their financial interest. The tobacco industry has been able to raise the funds necessary to offset current losses by increasing the price of product. It is projected that a package of cigarettes may cost $5 to $7 in the near future.[110]

The specific mechanisms through which tobacco exerts adverse effects on arteries remain poorly understood. Multiple toxicities of the innumerable components of tobacco smoke are recognized, including alterations in vascular endothelium, prostaglandin metabolism, platelet function, lipid metabolism, blood viscosity, and coagulation. Several excellent reviews on this subject are available.[111-114] In a duplex study[115] determining the incidence of femoral artery atherosclerosis, in more than 700 subjects, smoking was the most important risk factor, more predictive than exercise, hypertension, and total cholesterol. Smoking is associated with acute decreases in treadmill walking distances, presumably secondary to carbon monoxide.[116] Smokers have an increased risk of PAD progression,[24] MI, stroke, and death.[117] Smokers also have an increased risk of disease progression to CLI[43] and of major amputation.[118,119]

Abundant evidence exists regarding the benefit of smoking cessation in the treatment of chronic lower extremity ischemia. Although a meta-analysis[120] showed no significant improvement in treadmill walking after smoking cessation in claudicants, improved patency of arterial repairs in nonsmokers has been shown for aorto-femoral and femoropopliteal reconstructions.[121-124] Wiseman and colleagues[125] showed a direct relationship between degree of tobacco use (measured by carboxyhemoglobin levels) and incidence of graft occlusion.

Less than half of all persons who experiment with tobacco go on to smoke regularly.[126] Although social environment is a primary determinant of smoking behavior, genetics also plays a role.[127-129] Nicotine is the active component of tobacco smoke responsible for the positive symptoms of arousal, relaxation, relief of hunger, and enhanced vigilance/task performance that a smoker experiences. Nicotine is also primarily responsible for the tolerance observed in habitual users. Withdrawal symptoms include restlessness, irritability, anxiety, sleep disturbance, delayed reaction times, impaired concentration, and weight gain. The daily smoking cycle (Fig. 77-1) shows that the first few cigarettes in the day produce the greatest positive effect (arousal); by the end of the day, smokers use tobacco to avoid withdrawal symptoms. Overnight abstinence allows considerable resensitization to occur.[130]

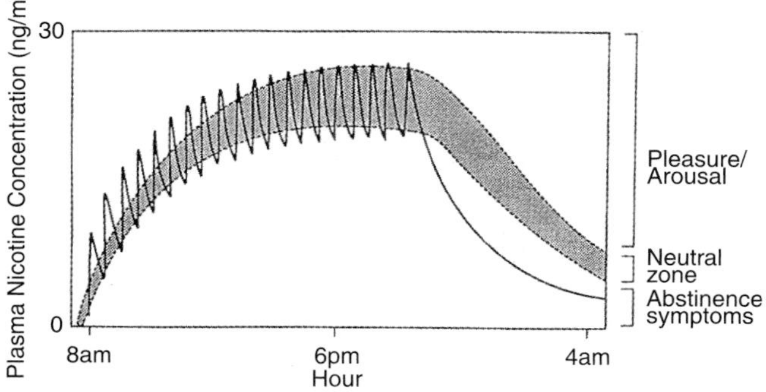

FIGURE 77-1 Model for the nicotine addiction cycle during daily cigarette smoking. The solid line represents plasma nicotine concentrations as individual cigarettes are smoked. The upper dashed line represents the threshold nicotine concentration for producing arousal, and the lower line represents nicotine concentrations below which symptoms of withdrawal occur. The shaded area represents nicotine concentrations in which the smoker is comfortable without either arousal or withdrawal stimuli. The threshold levels for both stimuli increase progressively during the day secondary to neuroadaptation, with overnight cessation allowing for drug resensitization. (From Benowitz NL: Cigarette smoking and nicotine addiction. Med Clin North Am 76:415-437, 1992.)

Complete cessation of tobacco is the foundation and most important part of nonoperative therapy for chronic lower extremity ischemia. It is also the component of therapy with the poorest success. Each year, approximately 20 to 50 million U.S. smokers try to quit, but only 6% are able to quit long-term.[130] The first step is to inform the vascular patient of the harmful effects of tobacco on the vascular system. Although most patients understand the relationship of smoking and lung cancer, less than half understand the relationship between peripheral vascular disease and tobacco.[131] In addition, smoking cessation counseling is often omitted during physician visits.[132] Surgical housestaff seem to be less likely to advise on smoking cessation, despite the significant impact of smoking on most surgical disease.[133] The National Cancer Institute recommends the four *A*s to guide smoking cessation counseling: (1) *Ask* about smoking. (2) *Advise* smokers to stop. (3) *Assist* patients willing to stop. (4) *Arrange* follow-up. The advice to stop smoking should be repeated at every patient encounter. We stress the positive health benefits of cessation and the social and economic freedoms. The latter two issues are becoming more and more pronounced with legislation prohibiting smoking in public places and increasing legal judgments against the tobacco industry leading to increased costs.

Historically, most smokers who quit were able to do so without any formal intervention.[134] The development of nicotine replacement therapies has been the benchmark for smoking cessation therapy since the 1990s. Most nicotine replacement agents provide 30% of a smoker's regular daily nicotine intake and reduce or prevent withdrawal symptoms. Nicotine gum is the oldest form of nicotine replacement; it is currently available without prescription. The primary drawbacks include the requirement of specific chewing techniques to maximize nicotine release and drug inactivation if beverages are consumed during use because of oral pH changes. Nicotine transdermal patches are easier to use (dose ranging from 7 mg/24 hr to 21 mg/24 hr), the only requirement being skin site rotation. Reported success with this technique has been modest.

Reviews of randomized, double-blinded nicotine replacement trials for smoking cessation therapy in young patients (30 to 40 years old) document biochemically confirmed 6-month abstinence rates varying from 20% to 45% in the treatment groups compared with 5% to 25% in the control groups depending on the setting (treatment initiation in a smoking cessation clinic being superior to the primary care office).[135,136] No benefit was derived from treatment beyond 8 weeks or from tapering nicotine. Intermediate-dose (14 mg/24 hr) nicotine patches have been used cautiously in patients with symptomatic CAD.[137] These patients must be warned about the danger of continued smoking while wearing the patch because MI has been reported.[138] In addition, it seems that older patients with cardiovascular disease have only half the abstinence rates compared with younger patients in controlled trials.[139] The standard dosage of nicotine replacement is a 21-mg patch for 6 weeks, followed by a 14-mg patch for 1 week, and finally a 7-mg patch for 1 week. Nicotine and citrate inhalers have been used in several small, randomized trials with or without nicotine patches.[140,141] These devices maintain reinforcement of the ritual and sensory phenomena of smoking. Although short-term abstinence with these devices has been 20% to 30%, long-term success has been disappointing.

More recent therapies for smoking cessation have focused on depression as an important component of the smoker profile and as a major factor in withdrawal symptoms.[142] The antidepressant agents bupropion and fluoxetine have been used in randomized trials with 12-week, biochemically confirmed cessation rates of 30% to 40%.[143,144] In addition to diminishing withdrawal symptoms (which share many characteristics with chronic depression), these agents seem to attenuate some of the weight gain observed with smoking cessation. These agents also have been used in combination with nicotine replacement (patch or inhaler) with improved results compared with either agent alone.[144] Side effects with these agents include insomnia. Standard dosage of bupropion is 150 mg orally every morning for 3 days, then twice a day for 2 months.

Finally, research on smoking cessation has centered on the effects of nicotine and neurotransmitters in the brain. Smoking one to two cigarettes increases plasma endorphin levels 200% and correlates with nicotine levels.[145] Trials using opioid antagonists have started. A 12-week randomized trial of naltrexone in 100 smokers did not show efficacy, however.[129]

Hyperlipidemia

Elevated levels of total cholesterol, LDL cholesterol, and triglycerides have been linked closely with an increased risk of coronary heart disease. Lipid-lowering agents, primarily with the HMG-CoA reductase inhibitors, have been shown to decrease the risk of MI and overall mortality in these patients.[146] It is logical to assume that drugs that are beneficial in reducing events in coronary atherosclerosis also would reduce events in other circulatory beds. Several studies indicate that in addition to lowering patients' coronary morbidity, lipid-reducing therapy causes stabilization or regression of peripheral atherosclerosis.[147] The Heart Protection Study further discovered that placing patients on lipid-reducing therapy can reduce the need for peripheral revascularization.[148] These data are drawn from a subset analysis of the trial, which primarily focused on whether treatment with simvastatin decreased the vascular and nonvascular morbidity and mortality in patients at high risk for cardiac events, and require further supporting studies. Given the weight of the data, however, we believe it is standard of care to evaluate fasting lipid levels in all patients with PAD and begin therapy when indicated (Table 77-1).

Table 77-1 Recommendations for Lipid Therapy for Patients with Chronic Lower Extremity Ischemia

PARAMETER	TARGET GOAL	THERAPIES
LDL cholesterol	<100 mg/dL	Diet, statins
HDL cholesterol	Men, ≥35 mg/dL; women, ≥45 mg/dL	Diet, exercise, niacin, fibrates
Triglycerides	<150 mg/dL	Diet, exercise, gemfibrozil, niacin

HDL, high-density lipoprotein; LDL, low-density lipoprotein.

Diabetes Mellitus

Diabetes mellitus is a strong risk factor for development of peripheral vascular disease. Although tight glycemic control in diabetics has been shown to have beneficial effects on other related complications of the disease (microvascular and coronary), it has not been associated with improvement or stabilization of PAD.[91,149] Diabetics have an increased incidence of neuropathic ulcers and should be counseled regarding regular preventive foot care.

Hypertension

Hypertension is considered a major risk factor for PAD[92]; however, it is unproved whether effective control would alter the progression of disease. Two agents that are widely used in the population are β-adrenergic antagonists (beta blockers) and angiotensin-converting enzyme inhibitors. Beta blockers initially were thought potentially to reduce peripheral circulation in patients with PAD, but a meta-analysis[150] of the available literature showed no deleterious effects. These agents frequently are given perioperatively in patients with PAD to reduce the risk of myocardial ischemia.[151] Angiotensin-converting enzyme inhibitors also may confer cardiac protection beyond that expected from reduction in blood pressure.[152]

Homocysteine

Elevated homocysteine has been linked to increased PAD.[153] Elevated serum homocysteine is detrimental to the vascular endothelium, increases the auto-oxidation of LDL cholesterol, enhances smooth muscle cell proliferation, and accelerates atherosclerosis.[154] Normalizing serum homocysteine via folate or vitamin B derivative therapy has not been proved to cause regression or stabilization of atherosclerosis.

■ EXERCISE REHABILITATION

It is apparent that claudication causes severe disability. Pell[46] reported that compared with population norms, all functional status/health-related quality-of-life scores were lower in patients with claudication. As a whole, claudication has adverse effects on functional status and quality of life and ambulatory ability specifically.[45,155] Regular physical activity promotes symptoms and reduces the incidence of asymptomatic atherosclerosis.[156] Despite this paradox, exercise therapy has been instituted as a primary treatment for claudication for decades. The most effective exercise programs consist of supervised walking on treadmill of 60 minutes or more, at least three times a week. The benefit of exercise rehabilitation in improving absolute claudication distance has been shown in more than 20 randomized trials[157]; this translates into a mean improvement in absolute claudication distance of almost 200 m over controls.[120] In addition, exercise rehabilitation improves quality of life and community-based walking capacity.[47]

The mechanism behind the beneficial effect of exercise rehabilitation is unclear. It does not produce substantial alterations in limb blood flow, and changes that do occur are not correlated with clinical response.[158] Despite the lack of hemodynamic benefit, exercise rehabilitation improves oxygen extraction in the lower extremities,[159] possibly as a result of improved metabolism in skeletal muscle, particularly carnitine.[160]

Although exercise rehabilitation is effective, it has several limitations. The best results require supervision and a motivated patient,[161] similar to cardiac rehabilitation. Supervised exercise programs are not covered by medical insurance, however, preventing their widespread usage. Exercise training must be continued indefinitely, or the benefits fade. These issues limit the overall effectiveness of exercise rehabilitation in the modern therapy for claudication.

■ PHARMACOLOGIC THERAPIES FOR CLAUDICATION

The 1980s and 1990s have seen a plethora of research in pharmacologic therapies for claudication. To date, only two agents are approved by the U.S. Food and Drug Administration (FDA), however—pentoxifylline and cilostazol. The following discussion includes these two agents and several agents used in Europe. We close with a few comments regarding gene therapy.

Pentoxifylline

In 1984, pentoxifylline became the first drug approved by the FDA as an effective treatment for intermittent claudication.[162] Patients with PAD show abnormal red blood cell rheology. Pentoxifylline, a methylxanthine derivative, acts primarily as a hemorheologic agent, increasing red blood cell flexibility and ultimately decreasing blood viscosity. Initial positive studies showed modest increases in maximal treadmill walking distances.[163] Several more recent meta-analyses failed, however, to show consistent and sustained improvements in walking distance and lack of effect on functional outcomes.[164,165] Pentoxifylline also is associated with gastrointestinal side effects, occasionally severe enough to cause patients to discontinue this medication. Currently, its widespread use in claudication cannot be supported.

Cilostazol

The second drug approved by the FDA for treatment of intermittent claudication was cilostazol in 1999. Cilostazol inhibits phosphodiesterase type 3, increasing cyclic adenosine monophosphate and causing vasodilatation, antiplatelet effects, and modification of plasma lipoproteins.[166] Traditionally, vasodilatation agents have not improved claudication symptoms. Steal phenomenon created by vasodilatation of less stenotic vessels may even worsen symptoms. Cilostazol's therapeutic effect is likely from another mechanism of action yet to be discovered. It has been shown to improve overall walking distance and quality of life. A 1999 meta-analysis of the effects of cilostazol reported increases of 50% in maximal walking distance compared with placebo and significant improvements in quality of life as measured by Rand Short Form 36 questionnaires.[167] There seems to be a dose-response effect, with 100 mg twice daily being more efficacious than 50 mg twice daily. The main adverse effects include headache, palpitations, and diarrhea, leading approximately 15% of people to stop the medication. Congestive heart failure is a major contraindication to use of cilostazol, owing to the concern of sudden death in this class of drug.

Multiple comparison studies have been done between pentoxifylline and cilostazol. The largest placebo-controlled, randomized study compared 698 patients given cilostazol, pentoxifylline, or placebo.[164] Results at 24 weeks showed a significantly greater increase in mean walking distance in the cilostazol group compared with the other two groups. Increase in mean walking distance with pentoxifylline was no better than the control group, providing further doubt regarding its efficacy.

Naftidrofuryl

Naftidrofuryl is widely used in Europe for treatment of claudication. It is a serotonin antagonist postulated to improve aerobic metabolism in oxygen-depleted tissues through stimulation of carbohydrate and fat entry into the tricarboxylic acid cycle. The drug also may have beneficial rheologic effects and reduce platelet aggregation. Several small studies suggest a 15% to 100% improvement in walking distance[168,169] and increased quality-of-life scores[170] with naftidrofuryl. Overall, the data on naftidrofuryl are mixed, and it has not yet been approved for use in the United States.

Blufomedil

Another claudication drug used in Europe is blufomedil. This agent reduces α_{1-2}-mediated vasoconstriction and may have beneficial effects on platelet aggregation and hemorheology. Several small studies show improvement in walking distance greater than 40% compared with controls.[171] Similar to naftidrofuryl, it is not yet available in the United States.

Carnitine

Carnitine augments muscle metabolism in the face of ischemia by increasing the conversion of acetyl-CoA into free CoA and acylcarnitines, improving fatty acid metabolism. Patients with PAD have abnormal skeletal muscle metabolism of carnitine. Supplementing patients with oral carnitine (propionyl-L-carnitine) has been shown to improve claudication symptoms in predominately European trials, with 50% to 60% increases in walking distance and significant improvement on quality-of-life questionnaires.[172,173] A large multicenter randomized U.S. trial of this agent is nearing completion.

Prostaglandins

Prostaglandin analogues relax vascular smooth muscle, inhibit platelet aggregation, and suppress vascular smooth muscle proliferation. Currently, trials with prostaglandins have shown only modest benefits in patients with intermittent claudication and have been limited by significant side effects (flushing, headaches). Beraprost, an oral prostacyclin analogue, has shown mixed results in several studies, ranging from no difference from placebo to a 60% to 80% increase in maximal walking distance.[174,175] Iloprost, an oral prostacyclin analogue, was tested in patients with severe limb ischemia.[176] It failed to show a reduction in major outcomes, including amputation, gangrene, and rest pain. Also, approximately 50% of patients dropped out because of side effects, including headache, nausea, and diarrhea.

Vascular Endothelial Growth Factor

Formation of collaterals is an important mechanism for compensating for lower extremity occlusions. Vascular endothelial growth factor (VEGF) is an important growth factor in the promotion of angiogenesis. It has been postulated that supplementation with recombinant VEGF would increase angiogenesis and ameliorate symptoms from PAD. Increased collateral vessel development and capillary density have been documented in rabbit skeletal muscle.[177] A multicenter phase II randomized trial[178] of a single session of intramuscularly delivered VEGF in 105 patients with claudication showed no change in maximal walking times or quality-of-life scores at 12 weeks. Further multicenter trials in patients with claudication are in progress.[179] The use of VEGF in patients with CLI has been limited to small (10 to 15 patients), single-institution series.[180-182] Initial results have shown healing of ulcers and resolution of rest pain, but without controls, these results mean little.

L-Arginine

Nitric oxide is a critical component of maintaining normal endothelial function. It is a potent vasodilator and inhibits platelet aggregation. Inhibition of nitric oxide formation has been shown in patients with PAD, possibly mediated by an accumulation of asymmetric dimethylarginine, an endogenous inhibitor of nitric oxide.[183] Dietary supplementation with L-arginine, a precursor of endogenous nitric oxide, may be able to reverse this inhibition. Several small studies have shown a beneficial effect with L-arginine supplementation, but further data need to be accumulated.[184,185]

■ FUTURE DIRECTIONS

The future of nonoperative management of PAD includes better education for primary care physicians. It is hoped that this education would lead to improved management of risk factors, likely paired with usage of computerized databases and management algorithms consistent with national guidelines. The role of additional pharmacotherapies for claudication is less clear. Proving statistically significant efficacy in phase III trials does not guarantee widespread usage. Given the likely expense of any new therapy approved, it may not be readily implemented by large formularies. Patients are often reluctant to purchase expensive medications unless dramatic symptomatic relief is the norm.

Modern medical decisions are increasingly data driven. Assessment of the functional benefits of nonoperative management is imperative to justify a place in the modern health care budget. An example of a current quandary is a young PAD patient with severe claudication who has economic reasons to improve ambulation, but is also a patient who is likely to convert to limb threat with eventual bypass failure. Many of these patients do not receive adequate symptom relief with current nonoperative management for the activity level desired to return to employment.

■ REFERENCES

1. Hirsch AT, Hiatt WR: PAD awareness, risk, and treatment: New resources for survival—the USA PARTNERS program. Vasc Med 6:9-12, 2001.
2. Criqui MH, Denenberg JO, Bird CE, et al: The correlation between symptoms and non-invasive test results in patients referred for peripheral arterial disease testing. Vasc Med 1:65-71, 1996.
3. McDermott MM, Mehta S, Greenland P: Exertional leg symptoms other than intermittent claudication are common in peripheral arterial disease. Arch Intern Med 159:387-392, 1999.
4. McDermott MM, Fried L, Simonsick E, et al: Asymptomatic peripheral arterial disease is independently associated with impaired lower extremity functioning: The Women's Health and Aging Study. Circulation 101:1007-1012, 2000.
5. McDermott MM, Greenland P, Liu K, et al: Leg symptoms in peripheral arterial disease: Associated clinical characteristics and functional impairment. JAMA 286:1599-1606, 2001.
6. Newman AB, Naydeck BL, Sutton-Tyrrell K, et al: The role of comorbidity in the assessment of intermittent claudication in older adults. J Clin Epidemiol 54:294-300, 2001.
7. Nehler MR, Coll JR, Hiatt WR, et al: Functional outcome in a contemporary series of major lower extremity amputations. J Vasc Surg 38:7-14, 2003.
8. Hooi JD, Stoffers HE, Kester AD, et al: Peripheral arterial occlusive disease: Prognostic value of signs, symptoms, and the ankle-brachial pressure index. Med Decis Making 22:99-107, 2002.
9. Ogren M, Hedblad B, Jungquist G, et al: Low ankle-brachial pressure index in 68-year-old men: Prevalence, risk factors and prognosis. Results from prospective population study "Men Born in 1914," Malmo, Sweden. Eur J Vasc Surg 7:500-506, 1993.
10. Criqui MH: Peripheral arterial disease and subsequent cardiovascular mortality: A strong and consistent association. Circulation 82:2246-2247, 1990.
11. Fowl RJ, Gewirtz RJ, Love MC, Kempczinski RF: Natural history of claudicants with critical hemodynamic indices. Ann Vasc Surg 6:31-33, 1992.
12. Gertler JP, Headley A, L'Italien G, et al: Claudication in the setting of plethysmographic criteria for resting ischemia: Is surgery justified? Ann Vasc Surg 7:249-253, 1993.
13. Labs KH, Nehler MR, Roessner M, et al: Reliability of treadmill testing in peripheral arterial disease: A comparison of a constant load with a graded load treadmill protocol. Vasc Med 4:239-246, 1999.
14. Regensteiner JG, Steiner JF, Panzer RJ, Hiatt WR: Evaluation of walking impairment by questionnaire in patients with peripheral arterial disease. J Vasc Med Biol 2:142-152, 1990.
15. Regensteiner JG, Steiner JF, Hiatt WR: Exercise training improves functional status in patients with peripheral arterial disease. J Vasc Surg 23:104-115, 1996.
16. Hiatt WR, Hoag S, Hamman RF: Effect of diagnostic criteria on the prevalence of peripheral arterial disease. The San Luis Valley Diabetes Study. Circulation 91:1472-1479, 1995.

17. Reid DD, Brett GZ, Hamilton PJ, et al: Cardiorespiratory disease and diabetes among middle-aged male civil servants: A study of screening and intervention. Lancet 1:469-473, 1974.
18. Hughson WG, Mann JI, Garrod A: Intermittent claudication: Prevalence and risk factors. BMJ 1:1379-1381, 1978.
19. McDaniel MD, Cronenwett JL: Basic data related to the natural history of intermittent claudication. Ann Vasc Surg 3:273-277, 1989.
20. Dormandy JA, Murray GD: The fate of the claudicant—a prospective study of 1969 claudicants. Eur J Vasc Surg 5:131-133, 1991.
21. Jelnes R, Gaardsting O, Hougaard JK, et al: Fate in intermittent claudication: Outcome and risk factors. BMJ (Clin Res Educ) 293:1137-1140, 1986.
22. O'Riordain DS, O'Donnell JA: Realistic expectations for the patient with intermittent claudication. Br J Surg 78:861-863, 1991.
23. Cox GS, Hertzer NR, Young JR, et al: Nonoperative treatment of superficial femoral artery disease: Long-term follow-up. J Vasc Surg 17:172-181, 1993.
24. Cronenwett JL, Warner KG, Zelenock GB, et al: Intermittent claudication: Current results of nonoperative management. Arch Surg 119:430-436, 1984.
25. Muluk SC, Muluk VS, Kelley ME, et al: Outcome events in patients with claudication: A 15-year study in 2777 patients. J Vasc Surg 33:251-257, 2001.
26. Whitehill TA: Role of revascularization in the treatment of claudication. Vasc Med 2:252-256, 1997.
27. Whyman MR, Fowkes FG, Kerracher EM, et al: Randomised controlled trial of percutaneous transluminal angioplasty for intermittent claudication. Eur J Vasc Endovasc Surg 12:167-172, 1996.
28. Nevelsteen A, Wouters L, Suy R: Long-term patency of the aortofemoral Dacron graft: A graft limb related study over a 25-year period. J Cardiovasc Surg (Torino) 32:174-180, 1991.
29. Nehler MR, Mueller RJ, McLafferty RB, et al: Outcome of catheter-directed thrombolysis for lower extremity arterial bypass occlusion. J Vasc Surg 37:72-78, 2003.
30. Valentine RJ, Jackson MR, Modrall JG, et al: The progressive nature of peripheral arterial disease in young adults: A prospective analysis of white men referred to a vascular surgery service. J Vasc Surg 30:436-444, 1999.
31. Hiatt WR, Wolfel EE, Meier RH, Regensteiner JG: Superiority of treadmill walking exercise versus strength training for patients with peripheral arterial disease: Implications for the mechanism of the training response. Circulation 90:1866-1874, 1994.
32. Harris LM, Peer R, Curl GR, et al: Long-term follow-up of patients with early atherosclerosis. J Vasc Surg 23:576-580, 1996.
33. Levy PJ, Gonzalez MF, Hornung CA, et al: A prospective evaluation of atherosclerotic risk factors and hypercoagulability in young adults with premature lower extremity atherosclerosis. J Vasc Surg 23:36-43, 1996.
34. Jamsen TS, Manninen HI, Tulla HE, et al: Infrainguinal revascularization because of claudication: Total long-term outcome of endovascular and surgical treatment. J Vasc Surg 37:808-815, 2003.
35. Fernandez MJ, Davies WT, Tyler A, Owen GM: Post-arterial reconstruction edema: Are lymphatic channels to blame? Angiology 35:475-479, 1984.
36. Soong CV, Young IS, Blair PH, et al: Lipid peroxidation as a cause of lower limb swelling following femoro-popliteal bypass grafting. Eur J Vasc Surg 7:540-545, 1993.
37. Soong CV, Young IS, Lightbody JH, et al: Reduction of free radical generation minimises lower limb swelling following femoropopliteal bypass surgery. Eur J Vasc Surg 8:435-440, 1994.
38. Soong CV, Barros B'Sa AA: Lower limb oedema following distal arterial bypass grafting. Eur J Vasc Endovasc Surg 16:465-471, 1998.
39. Wixon CL, Mills JL, Westerband A, et al: An economic appraisal of lower extremity bypass graft maintenance. J Vasc Surg 32:1-12, 2000.
40. Nicoloff AD, Taylor LM Jr, McLafferty RB, et al: Patient recovery after infrainguinal bypass grafting for limb salvage. J Vasc Surg 27:256-263, 1998.
41. Treiman GS, Copland S, Yellin AE, et al: Wound infections involving infrainguinal autogenous vein grafts: A current evaluation of factors determining successful graft preservation. J Vasc Surg 33:948-954, 2001.
42. Tretinyak AS, Lee ES, Kuskowski MM, et al: Revascularization and quality of life for patients with limb-threatening ischemia. Ann Vasc Surg 15:84-88, 2001.
43. Jonason T, Ringqvist I: Factors of prognostic importance for subsequent rest pain in patients with intermittent claudication. Acta Med Scand 218:27-33, 1985.
44. Bowers BL, Valentine RJ, Myers SI, et al: The natural history of patients with claudication with toe pressures of 40 mm Hg or less. J Vasc Surg 18:506-511, 1993.
45. Khaira HS, Hanger R, Shearman CP: Quality of life in patients with intermittent claudication. Eur J Vasc Endovasc Surg 11:65-69, 1996.
46. Pell JP: Impact of intermittent claudication on quality of life. The Scottish Vascular Audit Group. Eur J Vasc Endovasc Surg 9:469-472, 1995.
47. Regensteiner JG, Steiner JF, Hiatt WR: Exercise training improves functional status in patients with peripheral arterial disease. J Vasc Surg 23:104-115, 1996.
48. Breek JC, Hamming JF, De Vries J, et al: The impact of walking impairment, cardiovascular risk factors, and comorbidity on quality of life in patients with intermittent claudication. J Vasc Surg 36:94-99, 2002.
49. Anvar MD, Khiabani HZ, Kroese AJ, Stranden E: Alterations in capillary permeability in the lower limb of patients with chronic critical limb ischaemia and oedema. Vasa 29:106-111, 2000.
50. Management of peripheral arterial disease (PAD): TransAtlantic Inter-Society Consensus (TASC). Section D: Chronic critical limb ischaemia. Eur J Vasc Endovasc Surg 19(Suppl A):S144-S243, 2000.
51. Catalano M: Epidemiology of critical limb ischaemia: North Italian data. Eur J Med 2:11-14, 1993.
52. Critical limb ischaemia: Management and outcome: Report of a national survey. The Vascular Surgical Society of Great Britain and Ireland. Eur J Vasc Endovasc Surg 10:108-113, 1995.
53. Dormandy J, Belcher G, Broos P, et al: Prospective study of 713 below-knee amputations for ischaemia and the effect of a prostacyclin analogue on healing. Hawaii Study Group. Br J Surg 81:33-37, 1994.
54. Eickhoff JH, Hansen HJ, Lorentzen JE: The effect of arterial reconstruction on lower limb amputation rate: An epidemiological survey based on reports from Danish hospitals. Acta Chir Scand 502(Suppl):181-187, 1980.
55. Da Silva A, Widmer LK, Ziegler HW, et al: The Basle longitudinal study: Report on the relation of initial glucose level to baseline ECG abnormalities, peripheral artery disease, and subsequent mortality. J Chronic Dis 32:797-803, 1979.
56. Mahler F: [European consensus concerning chronic critical ischemia of the lower extremities]. Vasa 19:97-99, 1990.
57. Cronenwett JL, Zelenock GB, Whitehouse WM Jr, et al: Prostacyclin treatment of ischemic ulcers and rest pain in unreconstructible peripheral arterial occlusive disease. Surgery 100:369-375, 1986.
58. Schuler JJ, Flanigan DP, Holcroft JW, et al: Efficacy of prostaglandin E1 in the treatment of lower extremity ischemic ulcers secondary to peripheral vascular occlusive disease: Results of a prospective randomized, double-blind, multicenter clinical trial. J Vasc Surg 1:160-170, 1984.
59. Eklund AE, Eriksson G, Olsson AG: A controlled study showing significant short term effect of prostaglandin E1 in healing of ischaemic ulcers of the lower limb in man. Prostaglandins Leukot Med 8:265-271, 1982.
60. Belch JJ, McKay A, McArdle B, et al: Epoprostenol (prostacyclin) and severe arterial disease: A double-blind trial. Lancet 1:315-317, 1983.
61. Norgren L, Alwmark A, Angqvist KA, et al: A stable prostacyclin analogue (iloprost) in the treatment of ischaemic ulcers of the lower limb: A Scandinavian-Polish placebo controlled, randomised multicenter study. Eur J Vasc Surg 4:463-467, 1990.

62. Violi F, Criqui M, Longoni A, Castiglioni C: Relation between risk factors and cardiovascular complications in patients with peripheral vascular disease: Results from the A.D.E.P. study. Atherosclerosis 120:25-35, 1996.
63. Hertzer NR: Fatal myocardial infarction following lower extremity revascularization: Two hundred seventy-three patients followed six to eleven postoperative years. Ann Surg 193:492-498, 1981.
64. Edwards JM, Taylor LM Jr, Porter JM: Limb salvage in end-stage renal disease (ESRD): Comparison of modern results in patients with and without ESRD. Arch Surg 123:1164-1168, 1988.
65. Sanchez LA, Goldsmith J, Rivers SP, et al: Limb salvage surgery in end stage renal disease: Is it worthwhile? J Cardiovasc Surg (Torino) 33:344-348, 1992.
66. Hertzer NR, Beven EG, Young JR, et al: Coronary artery disease in peripheral vascular patients: A classification of 1000 coronary angiograms and results of surgical management. Ann Surg 199:223-233, 1984.
67. Gentile AT, Taylor LM Jr, Moneta GL, Porter JM: Prevalence of asymptomatic carotid stenosis in patients undergoing infrainguinal bypass surgery. Arch Surg 130:900-904, 1995.
68. Turnipseed WD, Berkoff HA, Belzer FO: Postoperative stroke in cardiac and peripheral vascular disease. Ann Surg 192:365-368, 1980.
69. Marek J, Mills JL, Harvich J, et al: Utility of routine carotid duplex screening in patients who have claudication. J Vasc Surg 24:572-577, 1996.
70. Walker SR, Yusuf SW, Hopkinson BR: A 10-year follow-up of patients presenting with ischaemic rest pain of the lower limbs. Eur J Vasc Endovasc Surg 15:478-482, 1998.
71. Long-term mortality and its predictors in patients with critical leg ischaemia. The I.C.A.I. Group (Gruppo di Studio dell'Ischemia Cronica Critica degli Arti Inferiori). The Study Group of Criticial Chronic Ischemia of the Lower Exremities. Eur J Vasc Endovasc Surg 14:91-95, 1997.
72. Taylor LM Jr, Hamre D, Dalman RL, Porter JM: Limb salvage vs amputation for critical ischemia: The role of vascular surgery. Arch Surg 126:1251-1257, 1991.
73. Regensteiner JG, Hiatt WR: Current medical therapies for patients with peripheral arterial disease: A critical review. Am J Med 112:49-57, 2002.
74. McDermott MM, Feinglass J, Slavensky R, Pearce WH: The ankle-brachial index as a predictor of survival in patients with peripheral vascular disease. J Gen Intern Med 9:445-449, 1994.
75. Kallero KS, Bergqvist D, Cederholm C, et al: Late mortality and morbidity after arterial reconstruction: The influence of arteriosclerosis in popliteal artery trifurcation. J Vasc Surg 2:541-546, 1985.
76. Hallett JW Jr, Greenwood LH, Robison JG: Lower extremity arterial disease in young adults: A systematic approach to early diagnosis. Ann Surg 202:647-652, 1985.
77. Levy PJ: Premature lower extremity atherosclerosis: Clinical aspects. Am J Med Sci 323:11-16, 2002.
78. Valentine RJ, Kaplan HS, Green R, et al: Lipoprotein (a), homocysteine, and hypercoagulable states in young men with premature peripheral atherosclerosis: A prospective, controlled analysis. J Vasc Surg 23:53-61, 1996.
79. Harris LM, Peer R, Curl GR, et al: Long-term follow-up of patients with early atherosclerosis. J Vasc Surg 23:576-580, 1996.
80. Olsen PS, Gustafsen J, Rasmussen L, Lorentzen JE: Long-term results after arterial surgery for arteriosclerosis of the lower limbs in young adults. Eur J Vasc Surg 2:15-18, 1988.
81. Pairolero PC, Joyce JW, Skinner CR, et al: Lower limb ischemia in young adults: Prognostic implications. J Vasc Surg 1:459-464, 1984.
82. Valentine RJ, Myers SI, Hagino RT, Clagett GP: Late outcome of patients with premature carotid atherosclerosis after carotid endarterectomy. Stroke 27:1502-1506, 1996.
83. Valentine RJ, Myers SI, Inman MH, et al: Late outcome of amputees with premature atherosclerosis. Surgery 119:487-493, 1996.
84. Bismuth J, Klitfod L, Sillesen H: The lack of cardiovascular risk factor management in patients with critical limb ischaemia. Eur J Vasc Endovasc Surg 21:143-146, 2001.
85. Burns P, Lima E, Bradbury AW: Second best medical therapy. Eur J Vasc Endovasc Surg 24:400-404, 2002.
86. 1999 World Health Organization–International Society of Hypertension Guidelines for the Management of Hypertension. Guidelines Subcommittee. J Hypertens 17:151-183, 1999.
87. Clinical practice guideline for treating tobacco use and dependence: A US Public Health Service report. JAMA 283:3244-3254, 2000.
88. Pyorala K, De Backer G, Graham I, et al: Prevention of coronary heart disease in clinical practice: Recommendations of the Task Force of the European Society of Cardiology, European Atherosclerosis Society and European Society of Hypertension. Eur Heart J 15:1300-1331, 1994.
89. Summary of the Second Report of the National Cholesterol Education Program (NCEP) Expert Panel on Detection, Evaluation, and Treatment of High Blood Cholesterol in Adults (Adult Treatment Panel II). JAMA 329:3015-3023, 1993.
90. Collaborative overview of randomised trials of antiplatelet therapy: I. Prevention of death, myocardial infarction, and stroke by prolonged antiplatelet therapy in various categories of patients. Antiplatelet Trialists' Collaboration. BMJ 308:81-106, 1994.
91. Effect of intensive diabetes management on macrovascular events and risk factors in the Diabetes Control and Complications Trial. Am J Cardiol 75:894-903, 1995.
92. The Sixth Report of the Joint National Committee on Prevention, Detection, Evaluation, and Treatment of High Blood Pressure. Arch Intern Med 157:2413-2446, 1997.
93. Clinical reality of coronary prevention guidelines: A comparison of EUROASPIRE I and II in nine countries. EUROASPIRE I and II Group. European Action on Secondary Prevention by Intervention to Reduce Events. Lancet 357:995-1001, 2001.
94. Berlowitz DR, Ash AS, Hickey EC, et al: Inadequate management of blood pressure in a hypertensive population. N Engl J Med 339:1957-1963, 1998.
95. Eytan TA, Goldberg HI: How effective is the computer-based clinical practice guideline? Eff Clin Pract 4:24-33, 2001.
96. Advani A, Tu S, O'Connor M, et al: Integrating a modern knowledge-based system architecture with a legacy VA database: The ATHENA and EON projects at Stanford. Proceedings of AMIA Symposium, 1999, pp 653-657.
97. Goldstein MK, Hoffman BB, Coleman RW, et al: Implementing clinical practice guidelines while taking account of changing evidence: ATHENA DSS, an easily modifiable decision-support system for managing hypertension in primary care. Proceedings of AMIA Symposium, 2000, pp 300-304.
98. Lobach DF, Gadd CS, Hales JW: Structuring clinical practice guidelines in a relational database model for decision support on the Internet. Proceedings of AMIA Annual Fall Symposium, 1997, pp 158-162.
99. Secondary prevention of vascular disease by prolonged antiplatelet treatment. Antiplatelet Trialists' Collaboration. BMJ (Clin Res Educ) 296:320-331, 1988.
100. Goldhaber SZ, Manson JE, Stampfer MJ, et al: Low-dose aspirin and subsequent peripheral arterial surgery in the Physicians' Health Study. Lancet 340:143-145, 1992.
101. A randomised, blinded, trial of clopidogrel versus aspirin in patients at risk of ischaemic events (CAPRIE). CAPRIE Steering Committee. Lancet 348:1329-1339, 1996.
102. Greenberg RA, Haley NJ, Etzel RA, Loda FA: Measuring the exposure of infants to tobacco smoke: Nicotine and cotinine in urine and saliva. N Engl J Med 310:1075-1078, 1984.
103. Lefcoe NM, Ashley MJ, Pederson LL, Keays JJ: The health risks of passive smoking: The growing case for control measures in enclosed environments. Chest 84:90-95, 1983.

104. Weiss ST, Tager IB, Schenker M, Speizer FE: The health effects of involuntary smoking. Am Rev Respir Dis 128:933-942, 1983.
105. Friend K, Levy DT: Reductions in smoking prevalence and cigarette consumption associated with mass-media campaigns. Health Educ Res 17:85-98, 2002.
106. Seguire M, Chalmers KI: Late adolescent female smoking. J Adv Nurs 31:1422-1429, 2000.
107. Warner KE: The economics of smoking: Dollars and sense. N Y State J Med 83:1273-1274, 1983.
108. Luce BR, Schweitzer SO: Smoking and alcohol abuse: A comparison of their economic consequences. N Engl J Med 298:569-571, 1978.
109. Gruber J: The economics of tobacco regulation: Only the costs that smokers impose on others justify a mandate for government action. Health Aff (Millwood) 21:146-162, 2002.
110. Geyelin M, Fairclough G: Taking a Hit: Yes, $145 billion deals tobacco a huge blow, but not a killing one—legal climate may favor appeal of class action; if not, just raise prices—a pack of cigarettes for $7? Wall Street Journal, July 17, 2000.
111. Couch NP: On the arterial consequences of smoking. J Vasc Surg 3:807-812, 1986.
112. Fielding JE: Smoking: Health effects and control (1). N Engl J Med 313:491-498, 1985.
113. Fielding JE. Smoking: Health effects and control (2). N Engl J Med 313:555-561, 1985.
114. Krupski WC: The peripheral vascular consequences of smoking. Ann Vasc Surg 5:291-304, 1991.
115. Leng GC, Papacosta O, Whincup P, et al: Femoral atherosclerosis in an older British population: Prevalence and risk factors. Atherosclerosis 152:167-174, 2000.
116. Aronow WS, Stemmer EA, Isbell MW: Effect of carbon monoxide exposure on intermittent claudication. Circulation 49:415-417, 1974.
117. Violi F, Criqui M, Longoni A, Castiglioni C: Relation between risk factors and cardiovascular complications in patients with peripheral vascular disease: Results from the A.D.E.P. study. Atherosclerosis 120:25-35, 1996.
118. Juergens JL, Barker NW, Hines EA: Arteriosclerosis obliterans: A review of 520 cases with special reference to pathogenic and prognostic factors. Circulation 21:188-195, 1960.
119. McGrath MA, Graham AR, Hill DA, et al: The natural history of chronic leg ischemia. World J Surg 7:314-318, 1983.
120. Girolami B, Bernardi E, Prins MH, et al: Treatment of intermittent claudication with physical training, smoking cessation, pentoxifylline, or nafronyl: A meta-analysis. Arch Intern Med 159:337-345, 1999.
121. Ameli FM, Stein M, Prosser RJ, et al: Effects of cigarette smoking on outcome of femoral popliteal bypass for limb salvage. J Cardiovasc Surg 30:591-596, 1989.
122. Myers KA, King RB, Scott DF, et al: The effect of smoking on the late patency of arterial reconstructions in the legs. Br J Surg 65:267-271, 1978.
123. Provan JL, Sojka SG, Murnaghan JJ, Jaunkalns R: The effect of cigarette smoking on the long term success rates of aortofemoral and femoropopliteal reconstructions. Surg Gynecol Obstet 165:49-52, 1987.
124. Robicsek F, Daugherty HK, Mullen DC, et al: The effect of continued cigarette smoking on the patency of synthetic vascular grafts in Leriche syndrome. Coll Works Cardiopulm Dis 20:62-70, 1975.
125. Wiseman S, Kenchington G, Dain R, et al: Influence of smoking and plasma factors on patency of femoropopliteal vein grafts. BMJ 299:643-646, 1989.
126. Eissenberg T, Balster RL: Initial tobacco use episodes in children and adolescents: Current knowledge, future directions. Drug Alcohol Depend 59(Suppl 1):S41-S60, 2000.
127. Hughes JR: Genetics of smoking: A brief review. Behav Ther 17:335-345, 1986.
128. Mermelstein R: Ethnicity, gender and risk factors for smoking initiation: An overview. Nicotine Tob Res 1(Suppl 2):S39-43, 1999.
129. Wong GY, Wolter TD, Croghan GA, et al: A randomized trial of naltrexone for smoking cessation. Addiction 94:1227-1237, 1999.
130. Benowitz NL: Cigarette smoking and nicotine addiction. Med Clin North Am 76:415-437, 1992.
131. Clyne CA, Arch PJ, Carpenter D, et al: Smoking, ignorance, and peripheral vascular disease. Arch Surg 117:1062-1065, 1982.
132. Karnath B: Smoking cessation. Am J Med 112:399-405, 2002.
133. Krupski WC, Nguyen HT, Jones DN, et al: Smoking cessation counseling: A missed opportunity for general surgery trainees. J Vasc Surg 36:257-262, 2002.
134. U.S. Department of Health and Human Services: Healthy People: The Surgeon General's Report on Health Promotion and Disease Prevention. Rockville, Md, U.S. Department of Health and Human Services, 1979.
135. Fiore MC, Jorenby DE, Baker TB, Kenford SL: Tobacco dependence and the nicotine patch: Clinical guidelines for effective use. JAMA 268:2687-2694, 1992.
136. Fiore MC, Smith SS, Jorenby DE, Baker TB: The effectiveness of the nicotine patch for smoking cessation: A meta-analysis. JAMA 271:1940-1947, 1994.
137. Rennard SI, Daughton DM, Fortman S: Transdermal nicotine enhances smoking cessation in coronary artery disease patients. Chest 5S:100, 1991.
138. Shea RW: Press release: Sturdy Memorial Hospital medical alert, 1992.
139. Joseph AM, Norman SM, Ferry LH, et al: The safety of transdermal nicotine as an aid to smoking cessation in patients with cardiac disease. N Engl J Med 335:1792-1798, 1996.
140. Schneider NG, Olmstead R, Nilsson F, et al: Efficacy of a nicotine inhaler in smoking cessation: A double-blind, placebo-controlled trial. Addiction 91:1293-1306, 1996.
141. Westman EC, Behm FM, Rose JE: Airway sensory replacement combined with nicotine replacement for smoking cessation: A randomized, placebo-controlled trial. Chest 107:1358-1364, 1995.
142. Glassman AH, Helzer JE, Covey LS, et al: Smoking, smoking cessation, and major depression. JAMA 264:1546-1549, 1990.
143. Hurt RD, Sachs DP, Glover ED, et al: A comparison of sustained-release bupropion and placebo for smoking cessation. N Engl J Med 337:1195-1202, 1997.
144. Jorenby DE, Leischow SJ, Nides MA, et al: A controlled trial of sustained-release bupropion, a nicotine patch, or both for smoking cessation. N Engl J Med 340:685-691, 1999.
145. Pomerleau OF, Fertig JB, Seyler LE, Jaffe J: Neuroendocrine reactivity to nicotine in smokers. Psychopharmacology (Berl) 81:61-67, 1983.
146. Prevention of cardiovascular events and death with pravastatin in patients with coronary heart disease and a broad range of initial cholesterol levels. The Long-Term Intervention with Pravastatin in Ischaemic Disease (LIPID) study group. N Engl J Med 339:1349-1357, 1998.
147. Hiatt WR: Medical treatment of peripheral arterial disease and claudication. N Engl J Med 344:1608-1621, 2001.
148. MRC/BHF Heart Protection Study of cholesterol lowering with simvastatin in 20,536 high-risk individuals: A randomised placebo-controlled trial. Lancet 360:7-22, 2002.
149. United Kingdom Prospective Diabetes Study 24: A 6-year, randomized, controlled trial comparing sulfonylurea, insulin, and metformin therapy in patients with newly diagnosed type 2 diabetes that could not be controlled with diet therapy. United Kingdom Prospective Diabetes Study Group. Ann Intern Med 128:165-175, 1998.
150. Radack K, Deck C: Beta-adrenergic blocker therapy does not worsen intermittent claudication in subjects with peripheral arterial disease: A meta-analysis of randomized controlled trials. Arch Intern Med 151:1769-1776, 1991.
151. Poldermans D, Boersma E, Bax JJ, et al: The effect of bisoprolol on perioperative mortality and myocardial infarction in high-risk patients undergoing vascular surgery. Dutch Echocardiographic Cardiac Risk Evaluation Applying Stress Echocardiography Study Group. N Engl J Med 341:1789-1794, 1999.

152. Sleight P: The HOPE Study (Heart Outcomes Prevention Evaluation). J Renin Angiotensin Aldosterone Syst 1:18-20, 2000.
153. Graham IM, Daly LE, Refsum HM, et al: Plasma homocysteine as a risk factor for vascular disease. The European Concerted Action Project. JAMA 277:1775-1781, 1997.
154. Welch GN, Loscalzo J: Homocysteine and atherothrombosis. N Engl J Med 338:1042-1050, 1998.
155. Treat-Jacobson D, Halverson SL, Ratchford A, et al: A patient-derived perspective of health-related quality of life with peripheral arterial disease. J Nurs Scholarsh 34:55-60, 2002.
156. Engstrom G, Ogren M, Hedblad B, et al: Asymptomatic leg atherosclerosis is reduced by regular physical activity: Longitudinal results from the cohort "Men Born in 1914." Eur J Vasc Endovasc Surg 21:502-507, 2001.
157. Nehler MR, Hiatt WR: Exercise therapy for claudication. Ann Vasc Surg 13:109-114, 1999.
158. Hiatt WR, Regensteiner JG, Hargarten ME, et al: Benefit of exercise conditioning for patients with peripheral arterial disease. Circulation 81:602-609, 1990.
159. Zetterquist S: The effect of active training on the nutritive blood flow in exercising ischemic legs. Scand J Clin Lab Invest 25:101-111, 1970.
160. Hiatt WR, Regensteiner JG, Wolfel EE, et al: Effect of exercise training on skeletal muscle histology and metabolism in peripheral arterial disease. J Appl Physiol 81:780-788, 1996.
161. Regensteiner JG, Meyer TJ, Krupski WC, et al: Hospital vs home-based exercise rehabilitation for patients with peripheral arterial occlusive disease. Angiology 48:291-300, 1997.
162. Green RM, McNamara J: The effects of pentoxifylline on patients with intermittent claudication. J Vasc Surg 7:356-362, 1988.
163. Porter JM, Cutler BS, Lee BY, et al: Pentoxifylline efficacy in the treatment of intermittent claudication: Multicenter controlled double-blind trial with objective assessment of chronic occlusive arterial disease patients. Am Heart J 104:66-72, 1982.
164. Dawson DL, Cutler BS, Hiatt WR, et al: A comparison of cilostazol and pentoxifylline for treating intermittent claudication. Am J Med 109:523-530, 2000.
165. Hood SC, Moher D, Barber GG: Management of intermittent claudication with pentoxifylline: Meta-analysis of randomized controlled trials. Can Med Assoc J 155:1053-1059, 1996.
166. Kohda N, Tani T, Nakayama S, et al: Effect of cilostazol, a phosphodiesterase III inhibitor, on experimental thrombosis in the porcine carotid artery. Thromb Res 96:261-268, 1999.
167. Thompson PD, Zimet R, Forbes WP, Zhang P: Meta-analysis of results from eight randomized, placebo-controlled trials on the effect of cilostazol on patients with intermittent claudication. Am J Cardiol 90:1314-1319, 2002.
168. Lehert P, Riphagen FE, Gamand S: The effect of naftidrofuryl on intermittent claudication: A meta-analysis. J Cardiovasc Pharmacol 16(Suppl 3):S81-S86, 1990.
169. Trubestein G, Bohme H, Heidrich H, et al: Naftidrofuryl in chronic arterial disease: Results of a controlled multicenter study. Angiology 35:701-708, 1984.
170. Spengel F, Brown TM, Poth J, Lehert P: Naftidrofuryl can enhance the quality of life in patients with intermittent claudication. Vasa 28:207-212, 1999.
171. Trubestein G, Balzer K, Bisler H, et al: Buflomedil in arterial occlusive disease: Results of a controlled multicenter study. Angiology 35:500-505, 1984.
172. Hiatt WR, Regensteiner JG, Creager MA, et al: Propionyl-L-carnitine improves exercise performance and functional status in patients with claudication. Am J Med 110:616-622, 2001.
173. Brevetti G, Diehm C, Lambert D: European multicenter study on propionyl-L-carnitine in intermittent claudication. J Am Coll Cardiol 34:1618-1624, 1999.
174. Lievre M, Morand S, Besse B, et al: Oral Beraprost sodium, a prostaglandin I (2) analogue, for intermittent claudication: A double-blind, randomized, multicenter controlled trial. Beraprost et Claudication Intermittente (BERCI) Research Group. Circulation 102:426-431, 2000.
175. Mohler ER III, Hiatt WR, Olin JW, et al: Treatment of intermittent claudication with beraprost sodium, an orally active prostaglandin I2 analogue: A double-blinded, randomized, controlled trial. J Am Coll Cardiol 41:1679-1686, 2003.
176. Two randomised and placebo-controlled studies of an oral prostacyclin analogue (Iloprost) in severe leg ischaemia. The Oral Iloprost in severe Leg Ischaemia Study Group. Eur J Vasc Endovasc Surg 20:358-362, 2000.
177. Tsurumi Y, Takeshita S, Chen D, et al: Direct intramuscular gene transfer of naked DNA encoding vascular endothelial growth factor augments collateral development and tissue perfusion. Circulation 94:3281-3290, 1996.
178. Rajagopalan S, Mohler ER III, Lederman RJ, et al: Regional angiogenesis with vascular endothelial growth factor in peripheral arterial disease: A phase II randomized, double-blind, controlled study of adenoviral delivery of vascular endothelial growth factor 121 in patients with disabling intermittent claudication. Circulation 108:1933-1938, 2003.
179. Rajagopalan S, Mohler E III, Lederman RJ, et al: Regional Angiogenesis with vascular endothelial growth factor (VEGF) in peripheral arterial disease: Design of the RAVE trial. Am Heart J 145:1114-1118, 2003.
180. Shyu KG, Chang H, Wang BW, Kuan P: Intramuscular vascular endothelial growth factor gene therapy in patients with chronic critical leg ischemia. Am J Med 114:85-92, 2003.
181. Baumgartner I, Pieczek A, Manor O, et al: Constitutive expression of phVEGF165 after intramuscular gene transfer promotes collateral vessel development in patients with critical limb ischemia. Circulation 97:1114-1123, 1998.
182. Isner JM, Baumgartner I, Rauh G, et al: Treatment of thromboangiitis obliterans (Buerger's disease) by intramuscular gene transfer of vascular endothelial growth factor: Preliminary clinical results. J Vasc Surg 28:964-973, 1998.
183. Boger RH, Bode-Boger SM, Thiele W, et al: Biochemical evidence for impaired nitric oxide synthesis in patients with peripheral arterial occlusive disease. Circulation 95:2068-2074, 1997.
184. Boger RH, Bode-Boger SM, Thiele W, et al: Restoring vascular nitric oxide formation by L-arginine improves the symptoms of intermittent claudication in patients with peripheral arterial occlusive disease. J Am Coll Cardiol 32:1336-1344, 1998.
185. Maxwell AJ, Anderson BE, Cooke JP: Nutritional therapy for peripheral arterial disease: A double-blind, placebo-controlled, randomized trial of HeartBar. Vasc Med 5:11-19, 2000.

Chapter

78

Evaluation of the Patient with Chronic Lower Extremity Ischemia

JOHN V. WHITE, MD

Although the manifestations of atherosclerosis may be localized, the development of symptoms associated with atherosclerotic lesions indicates a high likelihood of silent lesions in other vascular beds.[1] For this reason, the clinical suspicion of peripheral arterial disease (PAD), whether or not symptomatic, should initiate a systematic search for the site and severity of arterial occlusive lesions and the underlying risk factors for the advancing disease process. Health history information should be directed toward the delineation of pertinent symptoms and the presence of risk factors for atherosclerosis. This information is valuable not only for documenting the presence of problems, but also for following the benefits of treatment at future visits.[2] In a classic presentation of intermittent claudication, the patient experiences calf symptoms ranging from fatigue to aching while walking. These symptoms are alleviated by a brief period of rest. With higher levels of arterial occlusion, pain may be felt in the buttock or thighs or both. Initially the symptoms are intermittent, interspersed with the ability to walk well beyond that distance. Symptoms can be well defined through a simple series of questions (Table 78-1).

A definition of the symptom complex is helpful in distinguishing vasculogenic claudication from other causes of similar calf discomfort (Table 78-2); however, it does not establish the underlying etiology. Several other disorders produce symptoms that may mimic arterial occlusive disease. Of these, perhaps the most challenging to differentiate is peripheral nerve pain from nerve root compression by a herniated disk or osteophytic bone growth encroaching on its exit from the spinal canal. This abnormality also causes leg pain while standing or walking and can mimic closely symptoms of intermittent claudication. A careful history can aid the vascular specialist greatly in identifying patients with significant arterial occlusive disease. Although atherosclerosis is the most common cause, other forms of arterial pathology may interrupt distal blood flow through luminal narrowing or extrinsic arterial wall compression (Table 78-3).

A complete health history also provides an opportunity to identify significant co-morbid conditions. For a patient with vascular disease, the physician's direct assessment of the patient provides an important step in the identification of overall health, risk factors, and impact of vascular impairment. Only by incorporating all of these data into the diagnostic and therapeutic plan can the vascular specialist begin to improve the patient's quality and, perhaps, quantity of life.

Table 78-1 Relevant History for the Evaluation of Intermittent Claudication

Location of the pain or discomfort
Duration of the symptom
Whether it worsens or improves with time and whether conservative therapy has had an effect
Distance the patient can now walk before (1) experiencing the discomfort and (2) being forced to stop
Elapsed time after exercise is stopped before the pain is relieved
Type of rest or position of patient (standing at rest, sitting, lying) necessary to relieve the pain
Whether the pain returns after the same time and distance if exercise is then resumed

Adapted from TASC Working Group: Management of peripheral arterial disease. J Vasc Surg 31(Pt 2):S56, 2000.

■ RISK FACTOR ASSESSMENT

Atherosclerosis is a pathologic process related to aging of the human body. There is a stepwise increase in the incidence of intermittent claudication in men with each passing decade of age (Fig. 78-1). Multiple other risk factors also can seem to accelerate the development and growth of atherosclerotic lesions (Table 78-4). Risk factors, including the classic risks of hypertension, diabetes mellitus, and cigarette smoking and other less frequently recognized factors, must be identified and defined during the health history documentation. It is essential that risk factors be controlled to slow the progression of atherosclerosis and enhance the benefits of any vascular intervention. Hypertension increases the risk of developing symptoms of intermittent claudication 2.5-fold in men and 3.9-fold in women.[3,4] The relationship between diabetes and intermittent claudication also has been well documented.[3-5] When all other variables are controlled, the incidence of claudication is more common in patients with diabetes than in patients without this metabolic disorder. Similarly, cigarette smoking has been well established as a stimulus for atherosclerosis and increases the risk of development of PAD in men and women.[3,5] The stoichiometry seems to be straightforward, with the severity of arterial occlusive disease proportional to the number of cigarettes smoked.[6] Each additional risk factor independently increases the risk of developing symptomatic PAD (Fig. 78-2).

The absence of commonly recognized risk factors; a more sudden onset of symptoms, especially in younger

Table 78-2 Differential Diagnosis of Intermittent Claudication

CONDITION	LOCATION OF PAIN OR DISCOMFORT	CHARACTERISTIC DISCOMFORT	ONSET RELATIVE TO EXERCISE	EFFECT OF REST	EFFECT OF BODY POSITION	OTHER CHARACTERISTICS
Intermittent Claudication (Calf)	Calf muscles	Cramping pain	After same degree of exercise	Quickly relieved	None	Reproducible
Chronic compartment syndrome	Calf muscles	Tight, bursting pain	After much exercise (e.g., jogging)	Subsides very slowly	Relief speeded by elevation	Typically heavy-muscled athletes
Venous claudication	Entire leg, but usually worse in thigh and groin	Tight, bursting pain	After walking	Subsides slowly	Relief speeded by elevation	History of iliofemoral deep venous thrombosis, signs of venous congestion, edema
Nerve root compression (e.g., herniated disk)	Radiates down leg, usually posteriorly	Sharp lancinating pain	Soon, if not immediately after onset	Not quickly relieved (also often present at rest)	Relief may be aided by adjusting back position	History of back problems
Symptomatic Baker's cyst	Behind knee, down calf	Swelling, soreness, tenderness	With exercise	Present at rest	None	Not intermittent
Intermittent Claudication (Hip, Thigh, Buttock)	Hip, thigh, buttocks	Aching discomfort, weakness	After same degree of exercise	Quickly relieved	None	Reproducible
Hip arthritis	Hip, thigh, buttocks	Aching discomfort	After variable degree of exercise	Not quickly relieved (and may be present at rest)	More comfortable sitting, weight taken off legs	Variable, may relate to activity level, weather changes
Spinal cord compression	Hip, thigh, buttocks (follows dermatome)	Weakness more than pain	After walking or standing for same length of time	Relieved by stopping only if position changed	Relief by lumbar spine flexion (sitting or stooping forward) pressure	Frequent history of back problems, provoked by increased intra-abdominal pressure
Intermittent Claudication (Foot)	Foot, arch	Severe deep pain and numbness	After same degree of exercise	Quickly relieved	None	Reproducible
Arthritic, inflammatory process	Foot, arch	Aching pain	After variable degree of exercise	Not quickly relieved (and may be present at rest)	May be relieved by not bearing weight	Variable, may relate to activity level

From TASC Working Group: Management of peripheral arterial disease. J Vasc Surg 31(Pt 2):S59, 2000.

Table 78-3 Nonatherosclerotic Causes of Intermittent Claudication

Thromboangiitis obliterans	Popliteal aneurysm
Aortic coarctation	Arterial fibrodysplasia
Takayasu's disease	Pseudoxanthoma elasticum
Remote trauma or radiation injury	Persistent sciatic artery
Peripheral emboli	Iliac syndrome of the cyclist
Popliteal entrapment	Primary vascular tumors
Popliteal cyst	

Modified from TASC Working Group: Management of peripheral arterial disease. J Vasc Surg 31(Pt 2):S59, 2000.

Table 78-4 Risk Factors for Atherosclerosis

Age	Hyperlipidemia
Male gender	Hyperfibrinogenemia
Diabetes mellitus	Hyperhomocysteinemia
Smoking	Hypercoagulability
Hypertension	

Adapted from TASC Working Group: Management of peripheral arterial disease. J Vasc Surg 31(Pt 2):S59, 2000.

individuals; or a more rapidly progressive form of arterial occlusive disease should raise suspicion of an unrecognized and uncontrolled risk factor for accelerated atherosclerosis, such as hyperhomocysteinemia or hypercoagulability. McCully[7] examined the autopsy results of 194 consecutive patients and correlated the extent of atherosclerosis with serum cholesterol and other risk factors. Of patients who died of complications from arterial occlusive disease, the mean serum cholesterol was 186.7 ± 41.8 mg/dL, 65% had a serum cholesterol level less than 200 mg/dL, and 92% had a serum cholesterol level less than 250 mg/dL. In 66% of cases with severe systemic atherosclerosis, there was no elevation in cholesterol, no hypertension, and no diabetes present. This study strongly supports the effort to seek out other, less common risk factors. The presence of elevated homocysteine levels, something often left unchecked during routine health assessments, may increase the patient's likelihood of developing PAD nearly sevenfold.[8] Hypercoagulable states are more common in patients who require vascular reconstruction for the treatment of lower extremity arterial occlusive disease.[9] In the absence of identification and control of these risk factors, invasive therapies for the treatment of lower extremity arterial occlusive disease are merely palliative and provide no long-term health benefit for the patient.

■ PHYSICAL EXAMINATION

When the history is completed, a full physical examination should be undertaken. The physical examination should not be limited to the pulse assessment because atherosclerosis is a systemic disorder and most often affects many end organs. The examination should include vital signs with blood pressure and pulse recorded in both arms. Conjunctivae and sclerae may provide insight into the presence of severe hyperlipidemia, liver dysfunction, or anemia. For a diabetic patient, visual impairment may indicate a vascular retinopathy and point toward intrinsic renal disease. The presence of thyroid nodules may explain changes in skin texture. Pulmonary examination may delineate further the impact of smoking. A cigarette smoker with repeated episodes of pneumonia over a short span of time may be harboring a small lung cancer. The palpation of an abdominal aortic aneurysm may explain the sudden onset of symptoms of peripheral ischemia. A neurologic assessment may reveal degenerative disk disease or peripheral neuropathy.

The appearance of the lower extremities also can provide an indication of the extent and severity of PAD. Loss of skin hair distally, thinning and dry skin, and thickening of the nails all suggest the presence of chronic, advanced ischemia. Calf, ankle, and pedal edema may indicate a sedentary lifestyle with dependent positioning of the legs for relief of rest pain. Ulcers located on the forefoot and toes are frequently a manifestation of severe PAD, whereas ulcers located in the area of the medial malleolus are more common with venous hypertension.

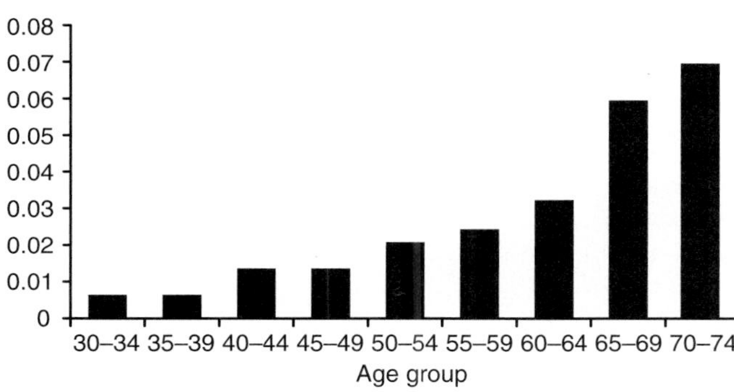

FIGURE 78-1 Weighted mean prevalence of intermittent claudication in large population-based studies. (From TASC Working Group: Management of peripheral arterial disease. J Vasc Surg 31[Pt 2]:S257-S258, 2000.)

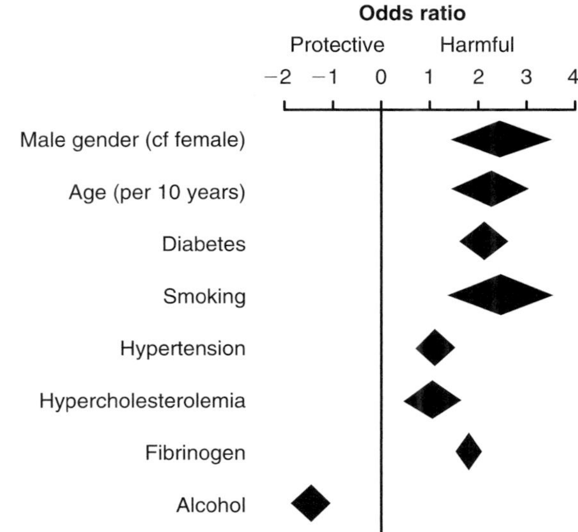

FIGURE 78-2 Range of odds ratios for risk factors for developing intermittent claudication. (From TASC Working Group: Management of peripheral arterial disease. J Vasc Surg 31[Pt 2]:S257-S258, 2000.)

The essence of a vascular examination is the palpation of pulses. Combined with the information obtained in the history and other parts of the physical examination, it may help to include or exclude a vascular cause for the patient's complaints and may help to localize the vascular segment that is stenotic or occluded. Although palpation of all pulses is essential, when lower extremity arterial occlusive disease is suspected, femoral, popliteal, dorsalis pedis, and posterior tibial pulses should be palpated for a sufficient length of time to determine presence, strength, and character. Strength of the pulse generally is graded on a scale in which *2* denotes a normal pulse; *1,* a diminished pulse; and *0,* an absent pulse. A grade of *3* is sometimes used to describe a pathologically prominent pulse, such as the water-hammer pulse of severe aortic insufficiency or the pulse immediately proximal to an acutely occluded vessel. The character of the pulse refers to the upstroke, downstroke, and presence of thrills. In stiffened vessels or in vessels with high outflow resistance, the upstroke or radial expansion of the vessel may be slowed. In the presence of low outflow resistance, such as proximal to a traumatic arteriovenous fistula, downstroke may be significantly reduced. Absent pulses suggest a proximal critical stenosis or occlusion. After palpation of the pulses, auscultation of the pulses by the physician permits the detection of bruits, frequently an indicator of an upstream or nearby stenotic lesion. The pulse examination, when correlated with clinical symptoms, should identify the site and severity of arterial occlusive lesions.

Claudication generally results from a single level of arterial occlusion, such as the iliac artery or the superficial femoral artery. Collateral vessels can reconstitute the artery distal to the single site of occlusion in order to provide distal flow. Symptoms of claudication associated with PAD usually are manifested in the muscle groups below the site of hemodynamically significant stenosis or occlusion. There are three major patterns of arterial obstruction. *Inflow disease* refers to lesions in the suprainguinal vessels, most commonly the infrarenal aorta and iliac arteries, which limit blood flow to the common femoral artery. *Outflow disease* represents the presence of occlusive lesions in the lower extremity arterial tree below the inguinal ligament, from the common femoral artery to the pedal vessels. The third major pattern of arterial obstruction is a combination of inflow and outflow disease. Patients with combined inflow and outflow disease may have broad symptoms of intermittent claudication affecting the buttock, hip, thigh, and calf. These symptoms frequently appear in the buttock and thigh, then involve the calf muscles with continued ambulation, although they may appear in reverse order if the distal disease is more severe than the inflow disease. More severe forms of inflow and outflow disease may result in limb-threatening ischemia.

Occlusive lesions of the infrarenal aorta or iliac arteries commonly lead to buttock and thigh claudication. In men, if the stenoses or occlusions are proximal to the origins of the internal iliac arteries and are bilateral, vasculogenic erectile dysfunction also may be present. Although buttock and thigh claudication may be the first symptoms, with continued ambulation, these patients also may exhibit classic symptoms of intermittent calf claudication resulting from inadequate perfusion of the entire leg while walking. Acute infrarenal aortic occlusion may cause profound ischemia of the legs; however, chronic atherosclerotic occlusive disease of the infrarenal aorta and iliac vessels as a single segment of arterial occlusion most commonly causes claudication rather than limb-threatening ischemia.

Below the inguinal ligament, superficial femoral artery stenosis or occlusion is the most common lesion associated with intermittent claudication. This lesion leads to calf discomfort with ambulation and relief with rest. No specific thigh or foot symptoms are associated with superficial femoral artery occlusion. Because the deep femoral artery provides collateral circulation to and reconstitution of the popliteal artery, isolated superficial femoral artery occlusion without distal disease is rarely the cause of more advanced forms of ischemia. Popliteal and tibial arterial occlusions are associated more commonly with limb-threatening ischemia owing to the paucity of collateral vascular pathways beyond these lesions. As isolated lesions, they are not usually the cause of intermittent claudication and are thought to be suggestive of diabetic vascular disease.

Critical limb ischemia usually requires at least two or more levels of severe arterial occlusive disease. The two levels of critical arterial stenoses or occlusions limit flow through the collateral beds, causing an advanced form of distal ischemia. The pattern of occlusion is usually in adjacent vascular beds, such as femoropopliteal and infrapopliteal occlusions, but may be in parallel beds, such as superficial femoral and deep femoral arterial occlusions. Both patterns prevent collateralization and reconstitution of the more distal arterial tree.

■ HEMATOLOGIC STUDIES

At the time of the initial presentation, a patient with manifestations of PAD should undergo a battery of basic hematologic studies to characterize the risk factors and identify end-organ involvement (Table 78-5). The hemoglobin and hematocrit levels yield potential information about blood hemorheology and other forms of distal perfusion inhibitors, such as secondary polycythemia from cardiopulmonary disease. Elevated platelet counts may suggest the risk of thrombotic occlusions. A fasting blood glucose or hemoglobin A_{1c} level is an important test for all patients who initially present with PAD because diabetes is such a significant risk factor for claudication and more advanced forms of ischemia. Increased creatinine levels may indicate the presence of intrinsic renal disease, especially in the presence of diabetes.

A fasting lipid profile, consisting of total cholesterol, high-density lipoprotein, low-density lipoprotein, and

Table 78-5 Initial Hematologic Evaluation of the Claudicant

Complete blood count, including white blood cells and platelets
Fasting blood glucose
Serum creatinine
Fasting lipid profile
Fibrinogen level
Urinalysis

From TASC Working Group: Management of peripheral arterial disease. J Vasc Surg 31(Pt 2):S59, 2000.

triglyceride concentration, is important as a part of risk screening in patients. This assessment should be done at the time of the patient's initial presentation for evaluation of vascular disease. The lipid profile evaluates the possibility that lipid abnormalities underlie the progression of atherosclerosis to claudication or limb-threatening ischemia. Although the impact of elevated cholesterol or low-density lipoproteins on the course of atherosclerosis has been evaluated more clearly in patients with coronary artery disease than in patients with PAD, it is likely that lipids accelerate PAD as well.[10] The impact of diabetes on the progression of atherosclerosis may be worsened in the setting of lipid abnormalities.[11] Careful control of lipid levels may reduce the risk of coronary, cerebral, and peripheral morbidity and mortality.[12] It is important to document a fasting lipid profile in each patient presenting with initial manifestations of PAD.

The fibrinogen level may be of value in detecting hypercoagulable states. Additionally, this value may be more predictive of cardiac morbidity than cholesterol in patients older than 60 years of age. When a fibrinogen cannot be readily obtained, an erythrocyte sedimentation rate can serve as an acceptable surrogate marker. The increased fibrinogen content within the blood causes rouleaux formation of red blood cells and accelerates their sedimentation. Testing for erythrocyte sedimentation rate also is helpful in assessing the presence of collagen vascular disease, which also may be a cause of lower extremity ischemia.

An evaluation for a hypercoagulable state should be undertaken when such a condition is suspected clinically on the basis of prior thrombotic events or a familial history. Despite the plethora of tests available for the specific diagnosis of a hypercoagulable state, the best screening test is a carefully performed patient history. Random thrombotic events without a specific cause should raise suspicion of an abnormal clotting disorder. Hypercoagulable states can be identified in a significant proportion of patients with arterial occlusive disease.[9] When such a condition is suspected, a broad range of testing may be required (Table 78-6).

The discovery of protein C deficiency is especially important in patients who will be treated with warfarin (Coumadin) because the administration of this medication to patients with low levels of protein C without heparin increases the possibility of skin necrosis. Heparin-induced thrombocytopenia is increasingly identified in patients who manifest not only acute thrombotic occlusions, but also diffuse distal arterial occlusive disease and accelerated graft failure. This disorder should be suspected in patients who present with PAD, evidence of sudden onset of symptoms, and no other significant risk factors. The likelihood of heparin-induced platelet aggregation is greater in patients who show a decrease in platelet count after the administration of heparin for venous thrombosis or other reasons.

Table 78-6 Secondary Hematologic Evaluation Based on Clinical Suspicion

Thrombin/prothrombin time
Activated partial thromboplastin time
Protein S/protein C assays
Factor V Leiden assay
Lupus anticoagulant assay
Heparin-induced platelet antibodies
Platelet adhesiveness/aggregability
Fibrinogen/plasminogen levels
Antithrombin activity
Anticardiolipin antibody assay

Modified from TASC Working Group: Management of peripheral arterial disease. J Vasc Surg 31(Pt 2):S59, 2000.

Patients who develop manifestations of PAD at an early age, without other identifiable risk factors, should have a plasma homocysteine level documented. High levels of homocysteine indicate hyperhomocysteinemia, which may accelerate atherosclerosis through a variety of mechanisms.[13,14] High levels of this amino acid may be toxic to endothelial cells and reduce their ability to generate and release nitric oxide. Excessive concentrations of this amino acid also may promote medial smooth muscle cell proliferation and arterial wall inflammation and increased levels of plasminogen activator inhibitor. As a result, arterial wall atherosclerotic plaque formation may be increased and thromboresistance decreased. Patients with hyperhomocysteinemia may develop clinically apparent vascular disease at a young age[15] and coronary artery occlusive disease in the absence of other risk factors.

The relationship between increased levels of homocysteine and vascular disease in older patients is not as well defined. Taylor and colleagues[16] evaluated homocysteine levels in 214 patients with symptomatic arterial occlusive disease and tracked ankle-brachial indices (ABI) over time. They found that there was a more rapid progression of occlusive disease in patients with elevated homocysteine levels after correction for other variables. Other authors have not identified a similar impact, however. Valentine and associates[17] performed a case-control study of the impact of lipoprotein, homocysteine, and hypercoagulable states on the presentation of symptomatic arterial occlusive disease in younger men. These investigators found no significant difference in homocysteine levels between men with and men without peripheral arterial occlusive disease. In Germany, a study of 6880 primary care patients found only a slightly enhanced degree of arterial occlusive disease, as evidenced by the ABI in patients with high levels of homocysteine compared with patients with low levels.[18] Nonetheless, because treatment of hyperhomocysteinemia is relatively simple with the oral administration of folate and other vitamins and nutrients, many vascular specialists believe that evaluation for this potential cause of accelerated atherogenesis should be undertaken.[19]

Other laboratory tests may be necessary to define more clearly and control risk factors for progressive atherosclerosis. These tests need not be included in the initial evaluation of the patient presenting with lower extremity arterial occlusive disease.

■ CARDIAC AND CEREBROVASCULAR EVALUATION

The importance of evaluating the extent of cardiac and cerebrovascular disease in patients with manifestations of PAD is being increasingly clarified. The systemic nature of atherosclerosis has a significant impact on all vascular beds

Table 78-7 Clinical Predictors of Increased Perioperative Cardiovascular Risk: Myocardial Infarction, Heart Failure, Death

Major
Unstable coronary syndromes
Acute or recent myocardial infarction with evidence of important ischemic risk by clinical symptoms or noninvasive study
Unstable or severe angina (Canadian class III or IV)
Decompensated heart failure
Significant arrhythmias
High-grade atrioventricular block
Symptomatic ventricular arrhythmias in the presence of underlying heart disease
Supraventricular arrhythmias with uncontrolled ventricular rate
Severe valvular disease
Intermediate
Mild angina pectoris (Canadian class I or II)
Previous myocardial infarction by history or pathologic Q waves
Compensated or prior heart failure
Diabetes mellitus (particularly insulin-dependent)
Renal insufficiency
Minor
Advanced age
Abnormal electrocardiogram (left ventricular hypertrophy, left bundle-branch block, ST-T abnormalities)
Rhythm other than sinus
Low functional capacity (e.g., inability to climb one flight of stairs with a bag of groceries)
History of stroke
Uncontrolled systemic hypertension

From Eagle KA, Berger PB, Calkins H, et al: ACC/AHA guideline update for perioperative cardiovascular evaluation for noncardiac surgery: Executive summary. Circulation 105:1257-1267, 2002.

Table 78-8 Management of Specific Preoperative Cardiovascular Conditions

Hypertension
Indications for treatment
Systolic blood pressure >180 mm Hg
Diastolic blood pressure >110 mm Hg
Treatment
Long-term control should be initiated and continued during and after perioperative period
Acute control with rapid-acting medications should be attempted before urgent or emergency surgery if possible
Beta blockade may be beneficial for reducing risks of perioperative infarction
Valvular Heart Disease
Indications for treatment
Symptomatic stenotic lesions
Treatment
Valve replacement in appropriate candidates
Myocardial Disease
Indications for treatment
Dilated and hypertrophic cardiomyopathy associated with heart failure
Treatment
Preoperative management to maximize cardiac performance
Arrhythmias and Conduction Abnormalities
Indications for treatment
New or hemodynamically significant arrhythmias
Treatment
Identification and treatment of underlying cause and control of cardiac rhythm

Adapted from Eagle KA, Berger PB, Calkins H, et al: ACC/AHA guideline update for perioperative cardiovascular evaluation for noncardiac surgery: Executive summary. Circulation 105:1257-1267, 2002.

to a greater or lesser extent. The extent of coronary artery and cerebrovascular disease must be assessed in all patients with new onset of manifestations of PAD who have not undergone such studies. In a study of 66 consecutive patients who had percutaneous interventions for the treatment of symptomatic PAD, Mukherjee and colleagues[20] noted that at the time of discharge and at 6-month evaluation, few patients had control of risk factors for atherosclerosis. Of the 66 patients, 12 had myocardial infarction (MI), stroke, or death within 6 months.

In a study comparing the presence of angina, prior MI, or resting electrocardiogram (ECG) abnormalities in 300 consecutive claudicants with 100 age-matched controls, Sonecha and Delis[21] detected coronary artery disease in 47% of the claudicants but only 6% of controls. Stress ECG detected coronary artery disease in 46% of claudicants and 11% of controls. Of claudicants who had no symptoms of angina, prior MI, or resting ECG abnormalities, 28% did have significant coronary artery disease.

Patients undergoing peripheral vascular surgery are at high risk (>5% likelihood) of having a perioperative MI and frequently manifest more than one of the clinical predictors of MI, heart failure, or death (Table 78-7). Evaluation of patients for cardiac disease should be directed toward the identification of the presence and the severity of the disease. This evaluation can be done most effectively in a stepwise manner. The guidelines for patient assessment developed by the American Heart Association and the American College of Cardiology provide a framework for this aspect of patient care.[22] Algorithms for the perioperative management of cardiovascular disease are based on clinical markers, functional capacity, and surgery-specific risk (Fig. 78-3). Recommendations for the appropriate management of cardiac risk factors and disease states also are provided (Table 78-8). Resting left ventricular function alone has not been a specific indicator of perioperative MI.[23]

Patients with lower extremity ischemia also have an increased incidence of carotid artery stenosis. In a prospective study of 225 patients undergoing infrainguinal bypass for either claudication or limb threat who were screened for carotid artery disease with duplex imaging, Gentile and colleagues[24] noted hemodynamically significant stenoses in 28.4%. More than 12% had a stenosis of 60% or greater, and 4% had a greater than 80% stenosis requiring surgery. Similarly, De Virgilio and associates[25] noted that 11 of 89 patients (12%) with symptomatic lower extremity arterial occlusive disease who were prospectively screened for carotid artery stenosis had greater than 75% diameter reduction. Patients had no symptoms of cerebrovascular disease at the time of diagnosis. Newly presenting patients or patients who have progressive PAD should undergo carotid arterial duplex imaging.

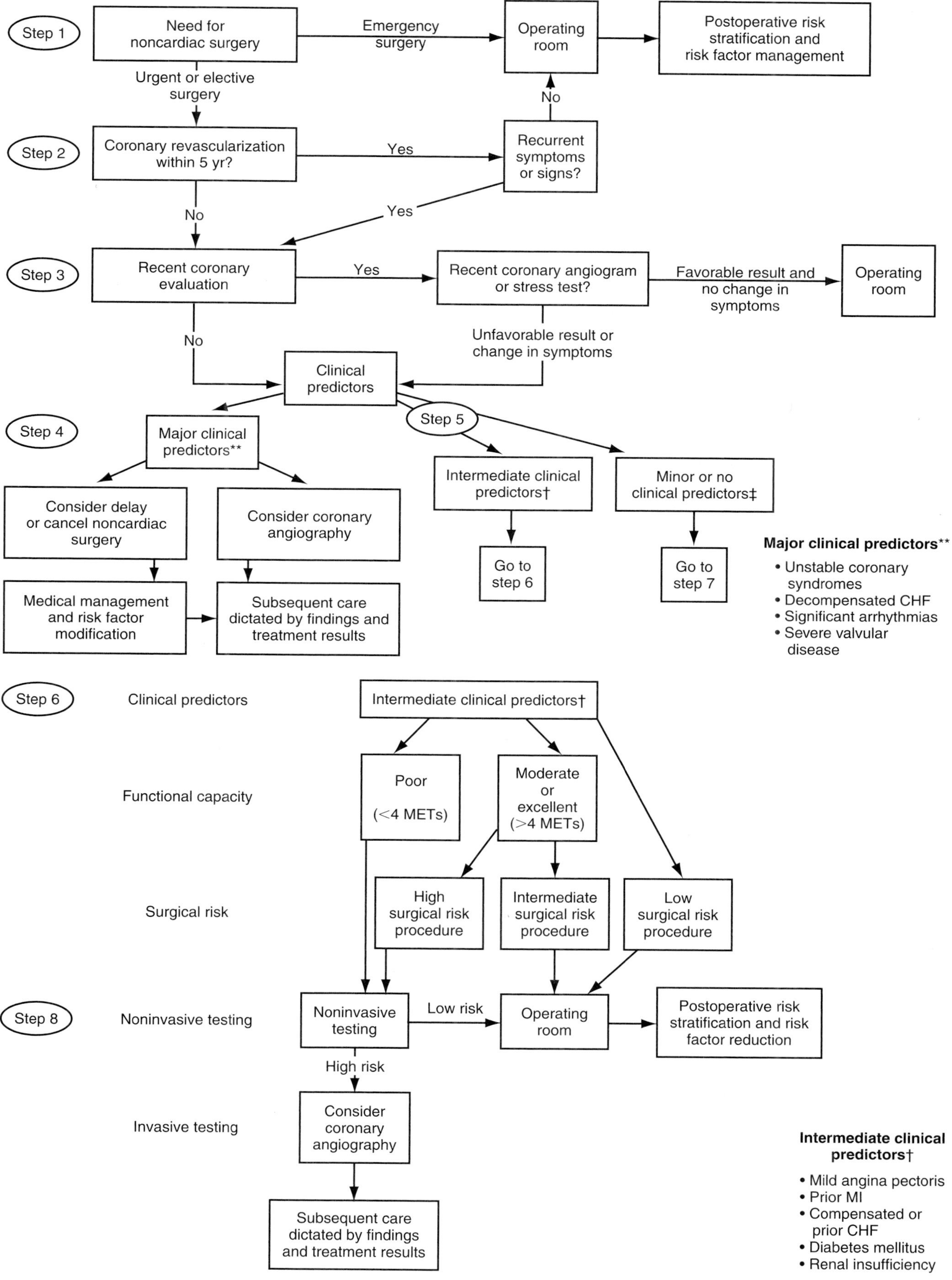

FIGURE 78-3 For legend, see page 1102.

Continued

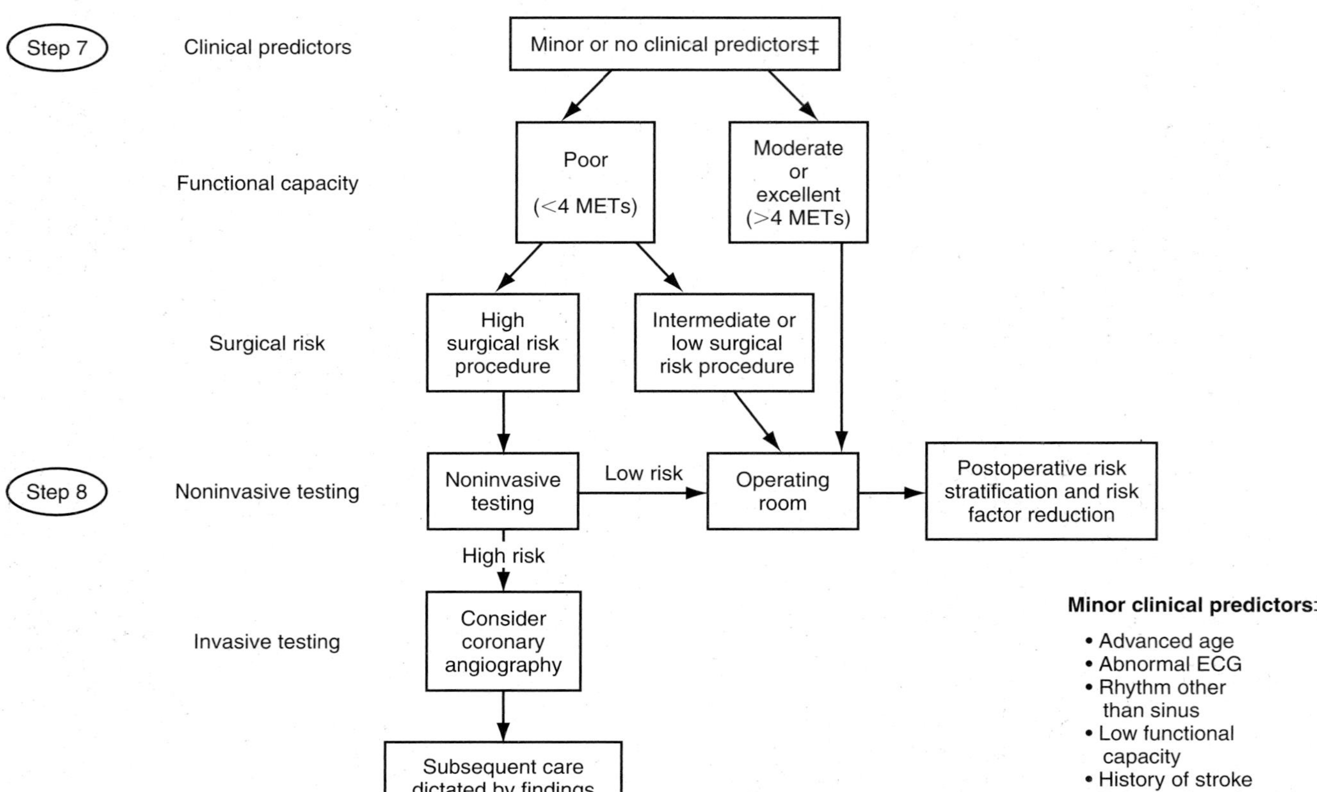

FIGURE 78-3, cont'd Algorithm of perioperative cardiovascular evaluation for noncardiac surgery. CHF, congestive heart failure; MI, myocardial infarction; ECG, electrocardiogram; METS, metabolic equivalents of O_2 consumption. (From Eagle KA, Berger PB, Calkins H, et al: ACC/AHA guideline update for perioperative cardiovascular evaluation for noncardiac surgery: Executive summary. A report of the American College of Cardiology/American Heart Association Task Force on Practice Guidelines [Committee to Update the 1996 Guidelines on Perioperative Cardiovascular Evaluation for Noncardiac Surgery]. Circulation 105:1257-1267, 2002.)

■ DIAGNOSTIC STUDIES: DOCUMENTATION OF SITE AND SEVERITY OF ARTERIAL OCCLUSIVE LESIONS

The decision to recommend surgical or percutaneous intervention for a patient with lower extremity arterial occlusive disease is based on many factors, including patient symptoms, co-morbid conditions, and location and severity of occlusive lesions. The anatomic pattern of the disease also may have a significant impact on the type of procedure that can be used to improve distal perfusion. A clear understanding of the extent of PAD is required before a therapeutic plan can be established.

In most patients with lower extremity ischemia, the initial vascular laboratory evaluation of segmental arterial pressure measurement, with the calculation of the ABI, is capable of identifying the presence of arterial occlusive disease and locating the segment involved. Pressures and pressure gradients are not sufficient indicators of patency and occlusion because of the variable presence of calcium within the arterial walls of patients with PAD. High, even supranormal, ABI can be recorded in patients with severe calcific arterial occlusive disease. Pressures and indices must be correlated with pulse-volume recording and waveform analysis and, in certain instances, toe pressures to identify clearly and quantify the presence of arterial occlusive disease and indicate the segment within which the disease is located. For patients with palpable pulses but disproportionately disabling symptoms or patients who are able to undergo an exercise therapy program, exercise testing in the vascular laboratory can be helpful.[26]

There are numerous regimens for the performance of an exercise test. Commonly, after the recording of ankle pressures at rest, a patient walks at 3.5 km/hr using a treadmill at a 12% incline until the onset of claudication-like symptoms. At that time, the ankle pressures are measured again. A significant decrease in ankle pressures indicates vascular claudication. No decrease or a small decrease in pressure after exercise suggests a nonvascular cause of symptoms, even in the presence of decreased peripheral pulses. Other regimens measure the distance walked per unit time or maximal walking distance. Although each of these methods has proponents, perhaps the most important facet is consistency of methodology for following patients.

Such information is of value and is generally sufficient for screening, establishing the need and conduct of an exercise therapy program for patients with claudication, and for monitoring the results of peripheral interventions. The segmental arterial Doppler study with calculation of the ABI, even with exercise testing, does not visualize the locations of hemodynamically significant lesions, however. This modality is of little direct benefit in planning intervention in either the claudicant or the patient with critical limb ischemia. Currently, color-guided duplex imaging, gadolinium-enhanced magnetic resonance imaging (MRI), and intra-arterial subtraction angiography are the most frequently used imaging modalities for the delineation of arterial anatomy. All of these modalities are capable of identifying the site and severity of infrainguinal arterial occlusive disease but have intrinsic limitations.

The improved resolution of duplex imaging has made this diagnostic modality a suitable alternative to contrast angiography in some patients. A significant advantage of this noninvasive modality lies in the fact that duplex imaging yields anatomic and blood flow information, providing an assessment of the hemodynamic effect of arterial occlusive lesions without the use of nephrotoxic contrast agents. Current imagers provide a significantly improved image. Combined with assessment of peak systolic velocity ratios, duplex imaging evaluation can identify arterial anatomy and the presence of hemodynamically significant lesions in a manner similar to conventional contrast angiography. Cossman and associates[27] compared color duplex imaging with contrast angiography in 61 patients. These authors noted a sensitivity of 99% and a specificity of 87% for the detection by duplex imaging of lesions causing greater than 50% stenosis and a sensitivity of 99% and specificity of 81% for occlusions. These findings were supported by the report of Aly and colleagues,[28] who compared duplex imaging and contrast angiography in 90 patients. These investigators found an overall sensitivity of 92% and a specificity of 99% for the detection of arterial occlusive disease and a sensitivity of 89% and a specificity of 98% for the assessment of lesion length. In 1999, Wain and associates[29] documented in 41 patients undergoing infrainguinal bypass that color duplex imaging correctly predicted the suitability of the popliteal artery for the distal anastomosis in 90%, but identified the appropriate tibial site in only 24%. Ascher and colleagues[30] reviewed their experience with preoperative duplex imaging for arterial mapping in 466 patients undergoing distal reconstruction for claudication or limb-threatening ischemia. They noted that the ultrasound study was adequate in all but 36 cases. Additional imaging studies were necessary in the presence of extensive ulcers, preventing adequate assessment of the underlying vessel, extensive arterial wall calcification, severe edema, and poor runoff.

Conventional contrast intra-arterial subtraction angiography continues to be the most commonly used imaging modality for the planning of bypass surgery and percutaneous intervention. Complete visualization of the arterial tree is accomplished easily and rapidly. This is especially true of the inflow segments, the infrarenal aorta and the iliac arteries, and the renal and visceral vessels, which frequently are not well visualized by duplex imaging.[31] Biplanar angiograms provide detailed information not only in the anteroposterior axis, but also in the mediolateral axis to identify eccentric plaques. Hemodynamic measurements are also beneficial in establishing the impact of a stenosis on distal flow.[32]

Because there is no image loss induced by arterial wall calcium, angiography serves as a complementary test to color duplex imaging in patients in whom the distal vasculature cannot be completely evaluated. Angiography is associated with increased morbidity and mortality risks, however, compared with other imaging modalities. There is an estimated 0.1% risk of a significant reaction to the contrast medium, a 0.16% risk of mortality, and a 0.7% risk of a serious complication adversely affecting planned therapy.[33,34] Angiography should be undertaken in the patient with PAD only when the need and possibility for intervention have been established.

Gadolinium-enhanced MRI is gaining increasing acceptance for evaluation of patients with lower limb ischemia because it can visualize the entire arterial tree, including pedal vessels, without the use of arterial puncture or standard ionic contrast. In a study of 24 patients with diabetes and limb-threatening ischemia, Kreitner and colleagues[35] used magnetic resonance angiography (MRA) and intra-arterial digital subtraction angiography to assess the appearance of vessels in the distal calf and foot. The investigators noted that in 38% of the studies, MRA revealed a patent pedal vessel suitable for grafting that was not seen on conventional angiography. This finding led them to conclude that MRA is superior for the visualization of patent distal vessels. Exaggerating the degree of stenosis within a vessel has been noted, but may be minimized by using multiple data sets for the evaluation of each vascular segment. Lundin and associates[36] prospectively evaluated 39 patients with symptomatic lower extremity arterial occlusive disease using time-of-flight and contrast-enhanced MRI and digital subtraction angiography. The authors found that when only time-of-flight information was used to evaluate the vasculature, the sensitivity was 81% and the specificity was 91%, but the degree of stenosis and length of the lesion were overestimated. Contrast-enhanced MRI had a sensitivity of 81% and a specificity of 92%. When these images were used in conjunction with the time-of-flight images, accuracy was improved. More recently, a meta-analysis of MRA for the evaluation of lower extremity arterial occlusive disease revealed that gadolinium-enhanced, three-dimensional studies were accurate for the assessment of the abdominal aorta, iliac vessels, and lower extremity and pedal arteries.[37]

This diagnostic modality is not completely free of patient-related difficulties. Patients with newly placed metallic implants are frequently not candidates for exposure to the magnetic field. Others may require sedation because of claustrophobia or difficulty lying flat for a long time. Additionally, gadolinium, although only mildly nephrotoxic, may adversely affect renal function in patients with preexisting renal insufficiency. In a study of 260 patients undergoing MRA, 195 with chronic renal insufficiency had gadolinium used for visualization of distal vessels. Sam and colleagues[38] noted a worsening of renal function in 3.5%. The prestudy creatinine clearance and the amount of contrast agent used did not predict patients who had renal deterioration. This study should be incorporated into a thoughtful diagnostic and therapeutic plan to ensure that the potential benefit of the information outweighs the small likelihood of complication and discomfort.

The optimal choice of imaging studies of the arterial tree depends on the type of anticipated intervention. Visser and colleagues[39] performed a Markov analysis to determine best testing strategies for evaluation of the claudicant. Using test sensitivity, incidence and type of complications associated with the test, implications of a missed lesion, and the cost of overtreatment based on test results, the authors evaluated the cost-effectiveness of duplex imaging, MRA, and digital subtraction conventional angiography. They found that if treatment considerations were limited to angioplasty in patients suspected to have suitable lesions, MRA was more cost-effective than conventional angiography. Likewise, digital subtraction angiography proved superior to duplex ultrasound and MRA if surgery was anticipated. Although the differences in the overall costs between these diagnostic modalities were small (<$1800 lifetime costs between all modalities), the results of the study indicate that the pre-treatment evaluation of the claudicant is generally simple, and the need for multiple imaging studies is uncommon. Evaluation of patients using additional diagnostic tests, after standard vascular laboratory assessment, should be reserved for patients in whom a percutaneous or open intervention is planned.

■ POST-TREATMENT PATIENT EVALUATION

Because atherosclerosis is a progressive systemic disorder, all patients should be monitored periodically whether or not they have been treated with an exercise program, percutaneous intervention, or open surgery for PAD. Claudicants who undertake an exercise program should record and periodically report their thrice-weekly walking distances to their physician. The physician should review these distances to confirm an increase in ambulatory ability. A sustained decrease in walking distance may indicate worsening occlusive disease.

Patients who are treated by percutaneous intervention or open surgery should be enrolled into a surveillance program designed to detect failing rather than failed treatments (Table 78-9). It is well recognized that for angioplasty, with or without stent placement, the treatment of recurrent stenosis is more successful than the treatment of a total occlusion.[40] Similarly the detection and treatment of a failing vein graft yields a greater likelihood of sustained graft function than treatment of revision of a failed graft.

Table 78-9 Recommended Surveillance for Lower Extremity Revascularization

Interval history to identify returning or new symptoms of distal ischemia
Vascular examination of leg with comparison of pulse presence and intensity to prior examination
Measurement of resting and, ideally, postexercise ankle-brachial index
Duplex scanning of vein grafts and angioplasty sites

Modified from TASC Working Group: Management of peripheral arterial disease. J Vasc Surg 31(Pt 2):S59, 2000.

■ SUMMARY

The evaluation of the patient with PAD provides the physician with a unique opportunity not only to design treatment strategies to reduce the likelihood of limb loss, but also to identify and treat risk factors, which may lead to an increase in quality and quantity of life. Undertaken in collaboration with the patient's primary and vascular physicians, the evaluation can assess risk of stroke, MI, visceral ischemia, and limb jeopardy. Control of systemic risk factors can slow the progression of atherosclerosis and reduce significantly the impact of this process on critical target organs. In this context, treatment of chronic lower extremity ischemia becomes more than palliation and leads to an overall improvement in the health status and quality of life of the patient. Patients with lower extremity arterial occlusive disease have systemic atherosclerosis and must be followed periodically to maintain the benefits of risk factor control and therapy, whether through exercise, percutaneous intervention, or open intervention.

■ REFERENCES

1. Clement DL, Verhaeghe R: Atherosclerosis and other occlusive arterial disease. In Clement DL, Shepherd JT (eds): Vascular Diseases in the Limbs. St. Louis, Mosby–Year Book, 1993, pp 73-89.
2. Stoffers HE, Kester AD, Kaiser V, et al: The diagnostic value of signs and symptoms associated with peripheral arterial occlusive disease in general practice: A multivariate approach. Med Decis Making 17:61-70, 1997.
3. Kannel WB, McGee DL: Update on some epidemiological features of intermittent claudication. J Am Geriatr Soc 33:13-18, 1985.
4. Fowkes GR, Housley E, Riemersa RA, et al: Smoking, lipids, glucose intolerance, and blood pressure as risk factors for peripheral atherosclerosis compared with ischemic heart disease in the Edinburgh Artery Study. Am J Epidemiol 135:331-340, 1992.
5. Murabito JM, D'Agostino RB, Silbershatz H, Wilson WF: Intermittent claudication: A risk profile from the Framingham Heart Study. Circulation 96:44-49, 1997.
6. Powell JT, Edwards RJ, Worrell PC, et al: Risk factors associated with the development of peripheral arterial disease in smokers: A case control study. Atherosclerosis 129:41-48, 1997.
7. McCully KS: Atherosclerosis, serum cholesterol and the homocysteine theory: A study of 194 consecutive autopsies. Am J Med Sci 299:217-221, 1990.
8. Boushey CJ, Beresford SAA, Omenn GS, et al: A quantitative assessment of plasma homocysteine as a risk factor for vascular disease. JAMA 274:1049-1057, 1995.
9. Ray SA, Rowley MR, Loh A, et al: Hypercoagulable states in patients with leg ischemia. Br J Surg 81:811-814, 1994.
10. Hirsch AT, Gotto AM Jr: Undertreatment of dyslipidemia in peripheral arterial disease and other high-risk populations: An opportunity for cardiovascular disease reduction. Vasc Med 7:323-331, 2002.
11. Beckman JA, Creager MA, Libby P: Diabetes and atherosclerosis: Epidemiology, pathophysiology, and management. JAMA 287:2570-2581, 2002.
12. Leng GC, Price JF, Jepson RG: Lipid-lowering for lower limb atherosclerosis. Cochrane Database Syst Rev 2:CD000123, 2000.
13. Guilland JC, Favier A, Potier de Courcy G, et al: Hyperhomocysteinemia: An independent risk factor or a simple marker of vascular disease? Pathol Biol 51:101-110, 2003.
14. Cook JW, Taylor LM, Orloff SL, et al: Homocysteine and arterial disease: Experimental mechanisms. Vasc Pharmacol 38:293-300, 2002.
15. Assanelli D, Grassi M, Bonanome A, et al: Premature arterial and venous events in three families: Effects of folate levels and MTHFR

mutation mediated by family/generation and homocysteine level. Thromb Res 105:109-115, 2002.
16. Taylor LM, DeFrang RD, Harris EJ Jr, Porter JM: The association of elevated plasma homocyst(e)ine with progression of symptomatic peripheral arterial disease. J Vasc Surg 13:128-136, 1991.
17. Valentine RJ, Kaplan HS, Green R, et al: Lipoprotein (a), homocysteine, and hypercoagulable state in young men with premature peripheral atherosclerosis: A prospective, controlled analysis. J Vasc Surg 23:53-63, 1996.
18. Darius H, Pittrow D, Haberl R, et al: Are elevated homocysteine plasma levels related to peripheral arterial disease? Results from a cross-sectional study of 6880 primary care patients. Eur J Clin Invest 33:751-757, 2003.
19. Tofler GH, D'Agostino RB, Jacques PF, et al: Association between increased homocysteine levels and impaired fibrinolytic potential: Potential mechanism for cardiovascular risk. Thromb Hemost 88:799-804, 2002.
20. Mukherjee D, Lingam P, Chetcuti S, et al: Missed opportunities to treat atherosclerosis in patients undergoing peripheral vascular interventions: Insights from the University of Michigan Peripheral Vascular Disease Quality Improvement Initiative (PVD-Q12). Circulation 106:1909-1912, 2002.
21. Sonecha TN, Delis KT: Prevalence and distribution of coronary artery disease in claudicants using 12-lead precordial stress electrocardiography. Eur J Vasc Endovasc Surg 25:519-526, 2003.
22. Eagle KA, Berger PB, Calkins H, et al: ACC/AHA guideline update for perioperative cardiovascular evaluation for noncardiac surgery: Executive summary. A report of the American College of Cardiology/American Heart Association Task Force on Practice Guidelines (Committee to Update the 1996 Guidelines on Perioperative Cardiovascular Evaluation for Noncardiac Surgery). Circulation 105:1257-1267, 2002.
23. Pasternack PF, Imparato AM, Riles TS, et al: The value of the radionuclide angiogram in the prediction of perioperative myocardial infarction in patients undergoing lower extremity revascularization procedures. Circulation 72:1113-1117, 1985.
24. Gentile AT, Taylor LM Jr, Moneta GL, Porter JM: Prevalence of asymptomatic carotid stenosis in patients undergoing infrainguinal bypass surgery. Arch Surg 130:900-904, 1995.
25. De Virgilio C, Toosie K, Arnell T, et al: Asymptomatic carotid artery stenosis screening in patients with lower extremity atherosclerosis: A prospective study. Ann Vasc Surg 11:374-377, 1997.
26. Gahtan V: The noninvasive laboratory. Surg Clin North Am 78:507-518, 1998.
27. Cossman DV, Ellison JE, Wagner WH, et al: Comparison of contrast arteriography to arterial mapping with color-flow duplex imaging in the lower extremities. J Vasc Surg 10:522-528, 1989.
28. Aly S, Sommerville K, Adiseshiah M, et al: Comparison of duplex imaging and arteriography in the evaluation of lower limb arteries. Br J Surg 85:1099-1102, 1998.
29. Wain RA, Berdejo GL, Delvalle WN, et al: Can duplex scan arterial mapping replace contrast arteriography as the test of choice before infrainguinal revascularization? J Vasc Surg 29:100-107, 1999.
30. Ascher E, Hingorani A, Markevich N, et al: Lower extremity revascularization without preoperative contrast arteriography: Experience with duplex ultrasound arterial mapping in 485 cases. Acta Radiol 41:125-132, 2000.
31. Lundin P, Svensson A, Henriksen E, et al: Imaging of aortoiliac arterial disease: Duplex ultrasound and MR angiography versus digital subtraction angiography. Acta Radiol 41:125-132, 2000.
32. Bonn J: Percutaneous vascular interventions: The value of hemodynamic measurements. Radiology 201:18-20, 1996.
33. Bettmann MA, Heeren T, Greenfield A, et al: SCVIR contrast agent registry report. Radiology 203:611-620, 1997.
34. Waugh JR, Sacharias N: Arteriographic complications in the DSA era. Radiology 182:243-246, 1992.
35. Kreitner KF, Kalden P, Neufang A, et al: Diabetes and peripheral arterial occlusive disease: Prospective comparison of contrast-enhanced three-dimensional MR angiography with conventional digital subtraction angiography. Am J Radiol 174:171-179, 2000.
36. Lundin P, Svensson A, Henriksen E, et al: Imaging of aortoiliac disease: Duplex ultrasound and MR angiography versus digital subtraction angiography. Acta Radiol 41:125-132, 2000.
37. Koelemay MJ, Lijmer JG, Stoker J, et al: Magnetic resonance angiography for the evaluation of lower extremity arterial disease: A meta-analysis. JAMA 285:1338-1345, 2001.
38. Sam AD, Morasch MD, Collins J, et al: Safety of gadolinium contrast angiography in patients with chronic renal insufficiency. J Vasc Surg 38:313-318, 2003.
39. Visser K, Kuntz KM, Donaldson MC, et al: Pretreatment imaging workup for patients with intermittent claudication: A cost-effectiveness analysis. J Vasc Interv Radiol 14:53-62, 2003.
40. Schmidtke I, Roth FJ: Repeated percutaneous transluminal catheter treatment: Primary results. Int Angiol 4:87-91, 1985.

Chapter 79

Direct Reconstruction for Aortoiliac Occlusive Disease

DAVID C. BREWSTER, MD

Section XIII

The infrarenal abdominal aorta and the iliac arteries are among the most common sites of chronic obliterative atherosclerosis in patients with symptomatic occlusive disease of the lower extremities.[1] Indeed, atherosclerotic narrowing or occlusion of these vessels, most commonly located at the aortic bifurcation, occurs to various degrees in most patients with symptoms of arterial insufficiency severe enough to require surgical revascularization. Because arteriosclerosis is commonly a generalized process, obliterative disease in the aortoiliac segment frequently coexists with disease below the inguinal ligament. Despite its generalized nature, however, the disease is usually segmental in distribution and is thereby amenable to effective surgical treatment. Even in patients with several levels of disease, successful correction of hemodynamic impairment in the aortoiliac inflow system often provides satisfactory clinical relief of ischemic symptoms. In addition, careful assessment of the adequacy of arterial inflow is important even in patients whose primary difficulty is located in the femoropopliteal or tibial outflow segment if good and durable results of distal arterial revascularization are to be obtained.

Since the introduction of the initial reconstructive methods of thromboendarterectomy and homograft replacement in the late 1940s and early 1950s, great progress has been achieved in the surgical management of aortoiliac occlusive disease. Currently, a variety of methods exist for accurate evaluation of the extent and physiologic severity of the disease process. In addition, improvements in the preoperative assessment of patient risk have helped clarify the decision about the optimal management in individual patients. Advances in graft materials, surgical techniques, intraoperative management, and postoperative care all have contributed to a steady reduction in perioperative morbidity and mortality and to excellent long-term results. Indications for operation have become fairly well accepted and standardized, and various operative approaches and methods of revascularization are available for use in differing clinical circumstances. With proper patient selection and a carefully performed, appropriate operative procedure, a favorable outcome may be anticipated at low risk to the patient, making surgical management of aortoiliac occlusive disease one of the most rewarding areas of vascular surgical practice today.

■ CLINICAL MANIFESTATIONS

The symptoms and natural history of the occlusive process are significantly influenced by its distribution and extent (Fig. 79-1). Truly localized aortoiliac disease *(type I)*, with occlusive lesions confined to the distal abdominal aorta and common iliac vessels, is seen infrequently (5% to 10% of patients) and, in the absence of more distally distributed disease, rarely produces limb-threatening symptoms.[2] In such localized aortic obstruction, the potential for collateral blood flow around the aortoiliac arterial segment is great. Collateral pathways include both visceral and parietal routes, such as the following:

- Internal mammary artery to inferior epigastric artery
- Intercostal and lumbar arteries to circumflex iliac and hypogastric networks
- Hypogastric and gluteal branches to common femoral and profunda femoris (deep femoral) arterial branches
- Superior mesenteric to inferior mesenteric and superior hemorrhoidal pathways via the marginal artery of Drummond (meandering mesenteric artery)

The relatively low incidence of localized aortoiliac disease is based on the angiograms of patients whose symptoms were severe enough for them to be seriously considered for direct surgical intervention. With the

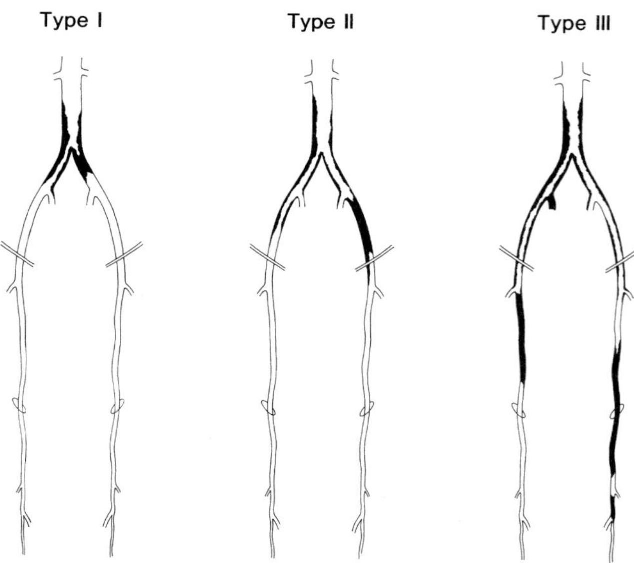

FIGURE 79-1 Patterns of aortoiliac occlusive disease. In type I, localized disease is confined to the distal abdominal aorta and common iliac arteries. In type II, more widespread intra-abdominal disease is present. In type III, the pattern denotes multilevel disease with associated infrainguinal occlusive lesions.

increasing use of percutaneous transluminal angioplasty (PTA) and related interventional treatment modalities that may represent "less invasive" forms of management, more liberal application of arteriography earlier in the disease process, when less advanced symptoms are present, may well document a higher incidence of localized occlusive lesions in the aortoiliac segment.[3]

Patients with localized, segmental disease typically present with claudication of varying severity, most often involving the proximal musculature of the thigh, hip, or buttock areas. The symptoms may be equally severe in both limbs, although often one leg is more severely affected than the other. More advanced ischemic complaints are absent unless distal atheroembolic complications have occurred. In men, impotence is an often associated complaint, present in different degrees in at least 30% to 50% of male patients with aortoiliac disease. Patients with a type I disease pattern are characteristically younger, with a relatively low incidence of hypertension or diabetes but a significant frequency of abnormal blood lipid levels, particularly type IV hyperlipoproteinemia.[4,5]

In contrast with the usual male predominance in chronic peripheral vascular disease, almost one half of patients with localized aortoiliac lesions are women.[2] Indeed, the frequency of aortoiliac disease in women has been growing substantially, likely reflecting the higher incidence of cigarette smoking in women. Many women with localized aortoiliac disease exhibit a characteristic clinical picture, often called the *hypoplastic aorta syndrome* (Fig. 79-2): typically, a woman of about 50 years of age, invariably a heavy smoker, with angiographic findings of small aortic, iliac, and femoral vessels; a high aortic bifurcation; and occlusive disease often strikingly localized to the lower aorta or the aortic bifurcation.[5-8] Commonly, many such patients have experienced an artificial menopause induced by hysterectomy or irradiation.

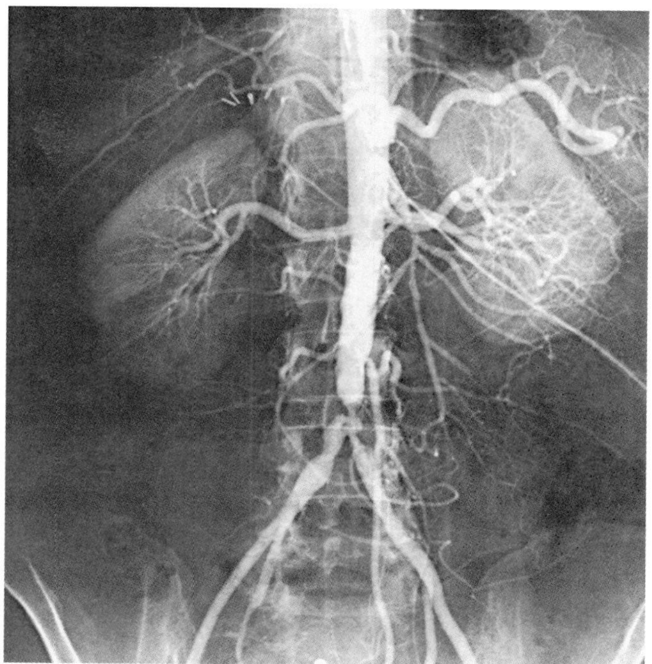

FIGURE 79-2 Translumbar aortogram of a 50-year-old woman with localized type I aortoiliac disease.

In more than 90% of symptomatic patients, however, disease is more diffuse. In approximately 25%, disease is confined to the abdomen *(type II)*, and in about 65%, widespread occlusive disease is seen above and below the inguinal ligament *(type III)*.[2,4] Patients in the latter group with such "combined segment" or "multilevel" disease are typically older, more commonly male (~6:1 male-to-female ratio), and much more likely to have diabetes, hypertension, and associated atherosclerotic disease involving cerebral, coronary, and visceral arteries. Progression of the occlusive process is also more likely in such patients than in patients with more localized aortoiliac disease.[8-10] For these reasons, most patients with a type III pattern manifest symptoms of more advanced ischemia, such as ischemic pain at rest or various degrees of ischemic tissue necrosis, and they require revascularization more often for limb salvage than for relief of claudication alone. In addition, these characteristics not unexpectedly lead to a significant decrease in life expectancy of 10 or more years in patients with diffuse multisegment disease, whereas life expectancy may be nearly normal in patients with localized aortoiliac disease.[11]

■ DIAGNOSIS

Clinical Evaluation

In most instances, an accurate history and a carefully performed physical examination can unequivocally establish the diagnosis of aortoiliac disease. A reliable description of claudication in one or both legs, possible decreased sexual potency in a man, and diminution or absence of femoral pulses define the characteristic triad often referred to as *Leriche's syndrome*. However, clinical grading of femoral pulses may sometimes be inaccurate, particularly in obese patients or in patients with scarred groins from prior operation.[12,13] Although proximal claudication symptoms in the distribution of the thigh, hip, and buttock musculature usually constitute a reliable indicator of clinically important inflow disease, a significant number of patients with aortoiliac disease, particularly those with multilevel disease, nonetheless complain only of calf claudication.[14,15] Audible bruits may commonly be auscultated over the lower abdomen or the femoral vessels, particularly after exercise. Pallor on elevation, rubor on dependency, shiny atrophic skin in the distal limbs and feet, and possible areas of ulceration or of ischemic necrosis or gangrene may be noted, depending on the extent of atherosclerotic impairment.

In some instances, the diagnosis of aortoiliac occlusive disease may not be readily apparent, the pitfalls involving certain complaints that may cause diagnostic confusion. In some patients, pulses and appearance of the feet may be judged to be entirely normal at rest, despite the presence of proximal stenoses that are physiologically significant with exercise. This is often the case in patients presenting with distal microemboli secondary to atheroembolism, the so-called blue toe syndrome.[16,17] In other instances, complaints of exercise-related pain in the leg, hip, or buttock or even low back may be mistaken for symptoms of degenerative hip or spine disease, nerve root irritation caused by lumbar disc herniation or spinal stenosis, diabetic neuropathy, or other neuromuscular problems. Many such cases may be distinguished from cases of true claudication by the fact that the discomfort from neuromuscular problems is often relieved only by sitting or lying down, as opposed to simply stopping walking. In addition, the typical sciatic distribution of the pain and the fact that the complaints are often brought on simply with standing, as opposed to walking a certain distance, suggest nonvascular causes. In many such circumstances, however, the use of noninvasive vascular laboratory testing modalities, including treadmill exercise, may be extremely valuable.[18,19]

Objective Assessment

Noninvasive Studies

Use of noninvasive studies not only improves diagnostic accuracy but also allows objective physiologic quantification of the severity of the disease process (see Chapter 14). Such quantification may be of considerable clinical benefit, for instance, in establishing the likelihood of lesion healing without revascularization or in differentiating neuropathic foot pain from true ischemic rest pain. The results of noninvasive studies may also serve as a reliable and objective baseline by which to follow a patient's disease course.

Finally, they may often help in localization of the disease process. We have found the use of segmental limb Doppler pressure measurements and pulse volume recordings to be most useful.[20]

Arteriography

If the patient's symptoms and clinical findings indicate sufficient disability or threat to limb survival, angiography is indicated to (1) delineate the extent and distribution of occlusive disease and (2) guide further therapeutic choices. Arteriography is rarely used in a truly diagnostic sense. The presence or absence of occlusive disease as a cause of the patient's symptoms can almost always be reliably established by clinical evaluation supplemented by pre-exercise and postexercise noninvasive vascular laboratory studies. Instead, angiography is employed to obtain anatomic information for use by the surgeon in selecting and planning the best method of revascularization. On occasion, the angiogram may provide the final bit of data needed for the surgeon to decide whether or not to proceed with operation. In other instances, it may be employed to determine whether occlusive disease is amenable to balloon- or other catheter-based endovascular interventions (see Chapter 84).

In addition to noting the actual anatomic distribution of occlusive disease in the aortoiliac segment and distal vessels, the surgeon should examine the angiography films to search for potentially important or critical anatomic variations or associated occlusive lesions in the renal, visceral, or runoff vessels. For example, an enlarged, meandering left colic artery (Fig. 79-3) may often be an indicator of associated occlusive disease in the superior mesenteric artery,

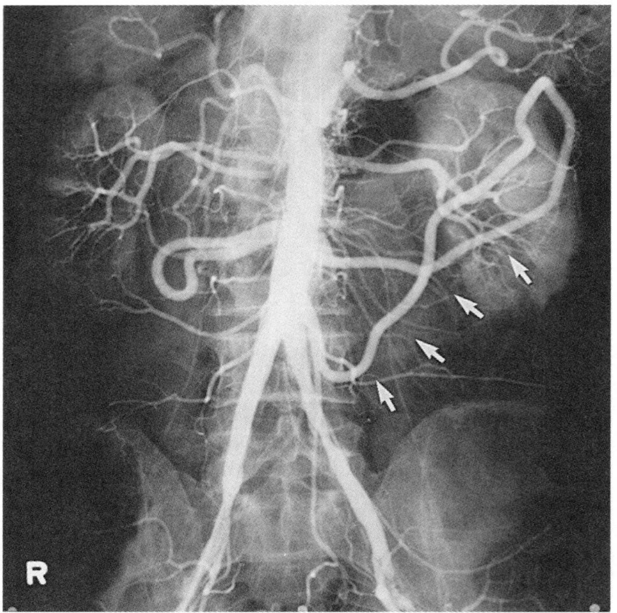

FIGURE 79-3 Aortogram demonstrating enlarged, meandering inferior mesenteric and left colic arteries *(arrows)*, indicative of associated occlusive disease in the celiac and/or superior mesenteric arteries.

which can usually be appreciated only on a lateral view. Failure to recognize this fact may lead to catastrophic bowel infarction if the inferior mesenteric artery (IMA) is ligated at the time of aortic reconstruction.[21]

Approach My general preference is for a retrograde transfemoral approach, which is feasible from the less involved side in most patients (see Chapter 18). In patients with severe bilateral occlusive disease or total aortic occlusion, a translumbar or transaxillary route may be employed, depending on the preferences of the angiographer or the surgeon. A biplanar study, providing oblique or lateral views, is highly desirable and often greatly enhances the ability to determine the clinical importance of visualized lesions, which often may be underestimated on standard anteroposterior views alone.[12]

Extent of Study For most patients, a complete arteriographic survey of the entire intra-abdominal aortoiliac segment and infrainguinal runoff vessels (runoff views) is advisable. Even if proximal operation alone is planned, knowledge of the status of runoff vessels is important because it (1) helps the surgeon anticipate the probable outcome of proximal operation alone, (2) aids in more effective management of possible technical misadventures, and (3) is needed for future planning. Only such complete studies enable the detection of unusual but highly important variations in the occlusive process that may critically affect the conduct and outcome of operation.

In general, runoff views are obtained to at least the level of the midcalf. In selected patients with advanced distal disease and threatened limbs, more distal views may be advisable, including views of the foot itself if the possibility of distal infrapopliteal bypass grafting is considered likely.

In such instances, in which the amount of contrast material reaching these distal points may be significantly impaired by multilevel occlusive lesions, supplemental use of digital subtraction angiographic techniques may enhance visualization and definition of anatomy. Similarly, in low-flow situations, adjunctive use of magnetic resonance (MR) angiography may facilitate identification of distal vessels (see Chapter 22).

Postangiographic Renal Dysfunction Despite the relatively nontoxic nature of the contrast agents currently used for diagnostic arteriography, various degrees of deterioration in renal function may be noted following angiographic studies. Such dysfunction may be mild and transient or may lead to severe impairment requiring dialysis. Although the precise risk of acute renal dysfunction after aortic angiography depends on the definition of and criteria for functional impairment, the reported incidence varies between 0 and 10% for patients at low risk for contrast-induced dysfunction and between 30% and 40% for patients at higher risk for this complication.[22] Renal deterioration appears to be related to contrast load and is clearly more likely to occur in patients with preexisting renal insufficiency and azotemia, dehydration, diabetes mellitus, greater age, or other predisposing factors.

Hydration of patients before angiography appears to be beneficial, and it should be liberally employed. The administration of mannitol to patients with preexisting renal disease at the time of angiography has also been recommended. In high-risk patients, digital subtraction angiography appears to be helpful, often providing diagnostic anatomic information with much lower volumes and dosages of contrast media. Whether or not use of non-ionic contrast agents is beneficial in reducing the incidence of contrast-induced renal dysfunction is not clearly established (see Chapter 18).

In general, contrast-induced renal failure usually resolves spontaneously within about 7 days. Because of its possible adverse effects, angiography should precede surgery by an interval sufficient to demonstrate that the serum creatinine concentration has remained stable and that operation is not being carried out at the time of developing renal failure. In current practice, preoperative angiography is usually performed on an outpatient basis prior to admission for surgery, a policy that has therefore alleviated this problem in most instances.[23]

Alternative Imaging Modalities

In recent years, alternative imaging techniques have developed rapidly and in some cases may be used in place of conventional contrast-enhanced angiography. Duplex scanning, three-dimensional spiral (helical) computed tomographic (CT) angiography, and MR angiography are used increasingly to evaluate the carotid artery, the renal artery, aortic aneurysms, and lower extremity occlusive disease.[24-27] At present, however, these modalities cannot match the visual clarity and spatial resolution of conventional arteriograms; thus, their use in evaluation of aortoiliac occlusive disease is currently restricted to special circumstances, such as increased risk of catheter angiography, for a variety of reasons (see Chapters 16, 20, and 22).

Femoral Artery Pressure Although an accurate assessment of occlusive disease is usually possible with traditional clinical evaluation and good-quality arteriography in most patients, difficulty may exist in evaluation of patients with multilevel occlusive disease. Assessment of the hemodynamic significance of occlusive disease at each segmental level is obviously critical in the selection of an appropriate reconstructive procedure. It is well recognized that many atherosclerotic lesions visualized on the arteriogram may be of only morphologic significance, with little or no actual hemodynamic importance. In such cases, proximal reconstruction alone often fails to relieve the patient's symptoms adequately. Furthermore, if only moderate proximal disease is present in a patient with advanced distal disease, operative correction of both segmental levels may be required for limb salvage if severe ischemia is present in the foot.

Despite the availability of a wide array of noninvasive vascular laboratory testing methods, none is entirely accurate in establishing the hemodynamic importance of aortoiliac inflow lesions, particularly in the patient with multilevel disease. All the methods appear to be influenced by the presence of infrainguinal occlusive disease, and abnormal results may not always be reliably attributable to the proximal lesions. Deficiencies of segmental limb Doppler pressures or pulse volume recordings are well recognized in this regard.[28-30] Analysis of femoral artery Doppler waveforms or calculation of a pulsatility index is also of questionable accuracy in the presence of multisegment disease because both modalities are affected by distal as well as proximal disease.[12,31] Other, more complex modifications of Doppler waveform analysis have been devised, but their accuracy and value in combined-segment disease remain uncertain.

Similarly, duplex scanning has also been applied to the physiologic assessment of aortoiliac occlusive disease[32]; however, a threshold criterion for local increase of peak systolic velocity to signify hemodynamically significant iliac disease has not been conclusively established. Duplex scanning examinations also are time consuming, require highly experienced technicians, and may not visualize some arterial segments, all disadvantages that currently limit the applicability of duplex scanning to evaluation of aortoiliac disease.

Reliance on the angiographic appearance of lesions also carries known hazards. Marked interobserver variability is associated with the interpretation of the functional importance of arterial lesions visualized on arteriograms.[33] In addition, although the relationship of a simple arterial stenosis and hemodynamic impairment is well documented, the multiplicity and complexity of lesions occurring in the aortoiliac system make hemodynamic assessment based on morphology alone often inaccurate.[34] In such instances, actual measurement of femoral artery pressure (FAP) may be of considerable value.[12,35-37]

FAP measurements are usually obtainable in the arteriographic suite at the time of transfemoral catheter aortography. Separate arterial puncture by a relatively small-caliber (19-gauge) needle may occasionally be required if pressure determinations are needed in the femoral artery contralateral to the angiographic catheter insertion site. As illustrated in Figure 79-4, peak systolic pressure in the femoral artery is compared with distal aortic or brachial

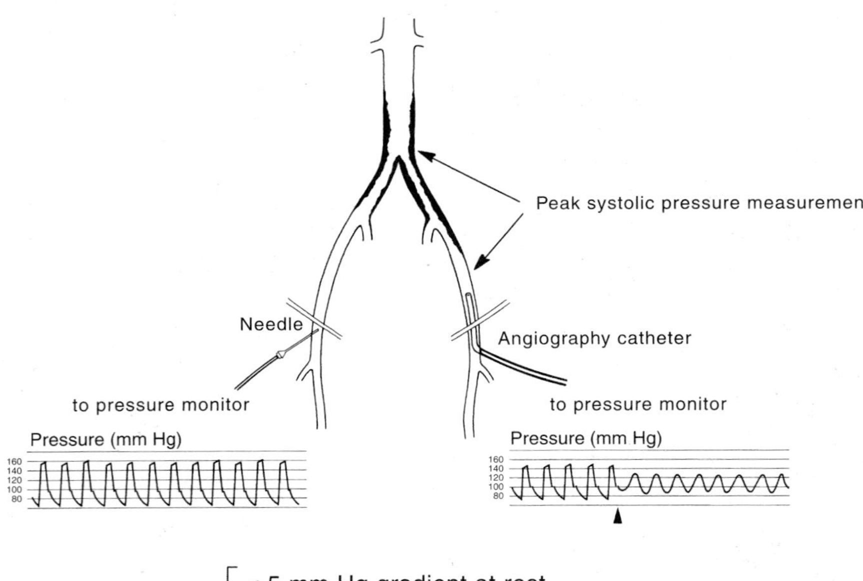

FIGURE 79-4 Femoral artery pressure (FAP) measurement. A significant fall in peak systolic pressure is noted in the tracing on the right *(arrowhead)* as the catheter is withdrawn down the left iliac artery. p̄, after.

systolic pressure. Either a resting systolic pressure difference of more than 5 mmHg or a fall in FAP greater than 15% when reactive hyperemia is induced pharmacologically or by inflation of an occluding thigh cuff for 3 to 5 minutes implies hemodynamically significant inflow disease. If revascularization is indicated in patients with such findings, attention should first be directed at correction of the inflow lesions. With negative study findings, the surgeon may more confidently proceed directly with distal revascularization without fear of premature compromise or closure of the distal graft, and without subjecting the patient to an unnecessary inflow operation.[38]

Use of such criteria greatly facilitates selection of patients for an inflow procedure and accurately predicts benefits. In a review by our group, 96% of patients with positive results on FAP studies had satisfactory clinical improvement in ischemic symptoms after proximal arterial reconstruction alone, despite uncorrected distal disease in most patients; in contrast, 57% of patients undergoing only proximal operation despite a negative FAP result experienced unsatisfactory relief of symptoms and required subsequent distal procedures.[14] Similar results have been reported by other investigators using pressure determinations.[37,39]

■ TREATMENT

Therapeutic Options

A wide variety of therapeutic options are available for the management of aortoiliac occlusive disease. These may be broadly categorized as

1. Anatomic or direct reconstructive surgical procedures on the aortoiliac vessels
2. So-called extra-anatomic or indirect bypasses that avoid normal anatomic pathways
3. Various nonoperative catheter-based endoluminal therapies that emphasize treatment of the obliterative lesions through a remote, often percutaneous access site to the arterial system

Although the availability of these numerous alternative therapies is beneficial, enabling the surgeon to select a procedure appropriate to the individual anatomy and risk status of each patient, decision making is often complex and difficult. Substantial differences in reported early and late results of alternative methods have contributed to the confusion. Purported benefits and advantages, particularly of endoluminal techniques, have been accentuated in recent years by the greatly increased emphasis on limiting cost and length of hospitalization. Indeed, the optimal method of management of aortoiliac disease represents one of the most controversial areas of contemporary vascular practice.[40]

Unfortunately, few definitive data exist, and few prospective, randomized studies have been performed with adequate control of the multiple complex variables involved to allow direct comparison of treatment options. Personal bias, previous surgical training, and individual experience remain factors in decision making. In addition, the need to individualize each decision according to specific anatomic distribution of disease and operative risk factors unique to every patient implies that there is no single best method of treatment. The best choice will, and probably should, vary from patient to patient.

Conservative Management

No truly effective medical treatment for aortoiliac occlusive disease is currently available. Nonoperative care is aimed at

- Limiting disease progression
- Encouraging development of collateral circulation
- Preventing local tissue trauma or infection in the foot

With such care, spontaneous improvement may be noted in a few patients, but in most instances, slow progression of symptoms may be anticipated.

Progression of the atheromatous process may, in some cases, be slowed by altering the patient's risk factors. Complete cessation of cigarette smoking is paramount in this regard and cannot be overemphasized in discussions with the patient. Weight reduction, treatment of hypertension, correction of abnormal serum lipid levels, and regulation of diabetes all seem to be desirable and logical, although the definite benefit of these measures, in terms of stabilization or alleviation of occlusive symptoms, is less well established.

A regular exercise program, often involving nothing more rigorous than regular walking of a specific distance on a daily basis, seems to be the best stimulant to collateral circulation. Good local foot care is extremely important because trauma and digital infection are often the precipitating causes of gangrene and amputation, particularly in the patient with diabetes.

Although numerous vasodilator drugs exist, none is of established benefit in chronic occlusive disease.[41] None of these drugs has been shown to increase the exercising muscle blood flow in the extremity with claudication, the critical requirement for an agent effective in the treatment of claudication. A multi-institution, double-blind, placebo-controlled trial of pentoxifylline (Trental) in the treatment of patients with claudication showed a significant increase in walking distance in patients who received this agent in comparison with those treated with a placebo.[42] In current practice, cilostazol (Pletal) is most widely prescribed for patients with claudication, based on several randomized studies showing symptomatic benefit.[43-45] In my experience, perhaps 25% of patients may find some alleviation of claudication symptoms. It is often difficult to know, however, whether this improvement is attributable to the drug. Cilostazol may be used in patients with moderate claudication, but it does not appear to have changed the eventual need for surgical revascularization in patients with severe claudication, resting ischemia, or more advanced symptoms. The pharmacologic treatment of claudication symptoms is more fully discussed in Chapter 37.

Indications for Intervention

Clearly advances in technology and technique of endovascular therapeutic options have changed the indications for intervention. Patients with fairly limited occlusive disease causing only mild to moderate claudication (TransAtlantic Intersociety Consensus [TASC] A)[46] were formerly rarely considered justifiable candidates for surgical reconstruction, whereas in contemporary practice angioplasty, stenting, or other endoluminal interventions may be considered appropriate.

In terms of indications for surgical intervention, ischemic pain at rest and actual tissue necrosis, including ischemic ulcerations or frank digital gangrene, are well accepted as indicating advanced ischemia and threatened limb loss. Without treatment, most limbs with these symptoms experience disease progression and require major amputation. Therefore, all surgeons agree that these symptoms represent unequivocal indications for arterial revascularization, if anatomically feasible.

Age per se is rarely an absolute contraindication. Even patients who are elderly or frail or for whom surgery poses high risks because of multiple associated medical problems generally can undergo revascularization with alternative surgical methods, even if direct aortoiliac reconstruction is deemed inadvisable.

Some disagreement remains about the advisability of surgical intervention in patients whose only indication is the presence of claudication. Quite clearly, such decisions must be individualized, with each patient's age, associated medical disease, employment requirements, and lifestyle preferences taken into consideration. However, claudication that jeopardizes the patient's livelihood or significantly impairs the desired lifestyle and daily activities of a patient for whom surgery would be a low risk may be considered to be a reasonable indication for surgical correction if the anatomic situation is favorable for intervention. In such cases, the surgeon should treat the patient conservatively for a time and should thoroughly discuss the merits and possible risks of any invasive therapy. The patient should have demonstrated commitment to the therapeutic program through control of appropriate risk factors, the most important being elimination of cigarette smoking and appropriate weight reduction, when required, and through compliance with a low-fat, low-calorie diet.

In general, most surgeons are more liberal in recommending surgical operation for patients with claudication alone if symptoms can be attributed to isolated proximal inflow disease, as opposed to patients with additional distal disease in the femoropopliteal arterial segment (multilevel disease). This approach seems logical and appropriate because of the generally excellent and long-lasting results currently achieved with aortoiliac reconstruction at low risk to the patient. Similarly, in patients with localized occlusive lesions in the iliac arteries that appear favorable for endovascular treatment by angioplasty or stenting, intervention for relatively modest claudication may be justified (see later).

Another less well-recognized indication for aortoiliac reconstruction is peripheral atheromatous emboli from proximal ulcerated atherosclerotic plaques (see Chapter 68). The aortoiliac system has been recognized as a frequent source of spontaneous atheroembolization to more distal vessels. As already described, clinical evidence of occlusive disease in patients with such emboli may be minimal, with little or no history of claudication and fairly normal pulses at rest. However, if the clinical picture is consistent with a diagnosis of atheroembolization *and* aortography demonstrates shaggy or ulcerated atherosclerotic plaques in the aortoiliac system, aortofemoral grafting with total exclusion of the host aortoiliac system is commonly indicated to avoid repetitive episodes or even limb loss, even though the occlusive lesions may not be hemodynamically significant.

■ CATHETER-BASED INTERVENTIONS

Percutaneous Transluminal Angioplasty and Stents

The role of PTA, with or without intravascular stents, and other catheter-based methods of arterial recanalization are discussed more fully in Chapter 84. Endovascular therapies may be a valuable treatment modality in some patients with aortoiliac occlusive disease. However, patient selection is paramount.

To be appropriate for PTA, a lesion should be relatively localized and preferably a stenosis rather than a total occlusion.[46] A localized stenosis of the common iliac artery less than 5 cm in length (TASC A) is the most favorable situation for PTA, with good early and late patency rates.[46-48] Such a situation may exist in perhaps 10% to 15% of patients with aortoiliac disease who undergo arteriographic study.[40] Iliac PTA for focal iliac disease is also a valuable adjunct when combined with distal surgical procedures in appropriate patients with multilevel disease.[49-52] Although the rate of long-term clinical success even in these favorable subsets of patients appears to be less than that for conventional surgical reconstruction, the likely benefits, in terms of decreased morbidity and probable cost savings, may well justify the use of PTA in these circumstances. A need for more frequent reinterventions may well result in inferior cost-effectiveness, however.[53] External iliac disease, female gender, and poor runoff have been identified as adverse predictors of poor outcome.[54,55]

Whether PTA should be employed in patients with milder symptoms who would not normally be considered for standard surgical therapy remains uncertain and controversial. Similarly, whether stents can improve late results of iliac PTA and thereby extend indications for catheter-based interventions to patients with more extensive (TASC C and D) aortoiliac disease (longer diseased segments, multiple lesions, total occlusions) remains unproven at this time. At present, PTA is generally not recommended for patients with diffuse iliac artery disease, unless they are extraordinarily poor surgical candidates, or for those with totally occluded iliac arteries, because of the higher incidence of complications or recurrent occlusion.[56,57] There are almost always alternatives for surgical revascularization in high-risk patients who have conditions that are unfavorable to treatment with PTA.

Stent Grafts

In recent years, some groups have extended endoluminal therapy of aortoiliac occlusive disease to include use of stent-grafts for diffuse obliterative disease.[58-60] Such approaches have evolved from initial experience gained with endovascular treatment of abdominal aortic aneurysms.

The basic concept is a combination of conventional prosthetic graft materials with a variety of intraluminal stents designed to secure the prosthetic graft in place while also maintaining a patent vessel lumen. Very aggressive balloon angioplasty recanalizes the aortoiliac system, and the fabric prosthetic portion of the endovascular graft lines the inner wall of the vessel. Unilateral aortoiliac covered stent-grafts may be combined with conventional femorofemoral bypass grafts or infrainguinal grafts to treat bilateral or multilevel aortoiliac disease. Although still in its formative stages, this mode of management may prove valuable in some patients as further technologic improvements in endograft design, delivery, and deployment are achieved (see Chapter 84).

■ EXTRA-ANATOMIC GRAFTS

Since their introduction in the early 1960s for management of difficult and often desperate technical problems usually related to infection or failure of previous grafts, use of a variety of extra-anatomic bypasses has increased to include wider application in (1) patients judged to be at higher risk with conventional direct aortic surgery and (2) patients with more limited disease not otherwise suitable for PTA or stents. In such patients, the goal is to achieve revascularization by means of grafts that use remote, usually subcutaneous pathways and that potentially can be performed with lower morbidity and mortality. Extra-anatomic grafts are discussed more fully in Chapter 80.

There is no question that extra-anatomic grafts are useful alternatives to direct anatomic surgical reconstruction in certain circumstances; much debate continues, however, as to whether their results in current practice have improved sufficiently for the application of such grafts to be expanded. Most controversy in this regard centers on two areas: (1) use of extra-anatomic grafts for treatment of mostly unilateral iliac occlusive disease and (2) possible application of axillofemoral grafts to more patients with bilateral disease.[40,61,62] At present, however, extra-anatomic grafts do not appear equivalent in durability or efficacy to aortofemoral grafts. They should therefore be regarded as an occasionally useful and appealing alternative treatment option. In general, the somewhat lower long-term patency rate and less comprehensive revascularization must be accepted as trade-offs for the lower morbidity and mortality risks of these procedures.[40]

■ LAPAROSCOPIC GRAFTS

Laparoscopic techniques have gained widespread acceptance in many surgical fields, largely because of their ability to offer the benefits of less invasive therapy including reduced postoperative pain, shortened hospital stays, and earlier return to normal activities when compared with conventional open surgery. The use of laparoscopic techniques in intra-abdominal vascular surgery may have the potential to provide similar benefits, and either laparoscopically assisted or totally laparoscopic aortobifemoral bypass grafts have been reported.[63,64] However, experience to date indicates that the challenges of obtaining adequate vascular exposure and control, as well as the technical demands of achieving secure vascular anastomoses, have provided considerable obstacles and led to long operative times and limited application in current practice.

■ DIRECT ANATOMIC SURGICAL RECONSTRUCTION

Since the pioneering development of a fabric arterial graft by Voorhees and colleagues[65] and the initial use of prosthetic aortic grafts in the 1950s,[66,67] extensive clinical experience has clearly demonstrated that direct aortic grafting is the most durable and efficacious method of revascularization available. Refinements in operative techniques, further improvements in prosthetic graft and suture materials, and striking advances in perioperative anesthetic management and postoperative intensive care all have contributed to steadily improving outcome, lower morbidity and mortality, and generally excellent results in contemporary practice.[2,68-73] Aortobifemoral grafts continue to be properly regarded as the "gold standard" for the treatment of aortoiliac occlusive disease.[40]

Preoperative Preparation

In addition to angiographic assessment, evaluation of associated cardiac, renal, and pulmonary disease is routinely performed. Any correctable deficiencies are best identified before operation and are appropriately treated. For instance, patients with compromised pulmonary reserve may benefit from a period of preoperative chest physiotherapy, bronchodilator medication, appropriate antibiotic treatment, and so forth. Diminished renal function also requires evaluation, with correction of any prerenal component that is due to dehydration or treatment of other reversible deficiencies. Similarly, cardiac abnormalities demonstrated by clinical evaluation or 12-lead echocardiogram are evaluated and treated appropriately; in many instances, consultation with a cardiologist may be quite helpful.

Without question, the most important and most controversial aspect of the preoperative evaluation is the detection and subsequent management of associated coronary artery disease.[74] Several studies have documented the existence of potentially important coronary artery disease in 40% to 50% or more of patients requiring peripheral vascular reconstructive procedures, 10% to 20% of whom may be relatively asymptomatic largely because of their inability to exercise.[75] Myocardial infarction is quite clearly responsible for the majority of both early and late postoperative deaths. However, most available screening methods suffer from a lack of sensitivity and specificity in predicting postoperative cardiac complications. In addition, many patients with vascular occlusive disease cannot achieve adequate exercise stress as a result of claudication or infirmity. Even with coronary angiography, it is difficult to relate anatomic findings to functional significance and, hence, surgical risk. In addition, coronary angiography is associated with its own inherent risks, and patients undergoing coronary artery bypass grafting or coronary PTA before needed aortoiliac reconstructions are subjected to the risks and complications of both procedures.

In this regard, my colleagues and I as well as others have found preoperative dipyridamole-thallium 201 imaging to be valuable in identifying the subset of patients with vascular occlusive disease who may indeed be at high risk for perioperative myocardial ischemic events and perhaps may need more intensive preoperative evaluation.[76-78] This modality has allowed identification of a subset of patients for whom surgery poses a low risk and in whom no further preoperative evaluation or intensive intraoperative monitoring appears to be warranted. Conversely, a subset of patients can be identified for whom surgery poses a high risk and in whom (1) preoperative coronary angiography and, possibly, coronary revascularization should be performed before surgery for vascular occlusive disease or (2) aortic operation may be deferred if more elective indications permit.

Although thallium imaging and, often, preoperative cardiac functional studies may be helpful, the usefulness of preoperative cardiac evaluation as well as how best to accomplish it remains unsettled. The incidence of major perioperative cardiac events after general vascular procedures is relatively low in contemporary practice,[79] and all screening methods suffer from a poor positive predictive value. Therefore, some surgeons advocate proceeding without extensive cardiac evaluation and managing patients with the assumption that all patients with vascular occlusive disease have coronary disease (see Chapter 56).

Routine testing of coagulation parameters should be part of any preoperative evaluation. Baseline values should be obtained for hematocrit, complete blood count, platelet count, and prothrombin time and partial thromboplastin time measurements. Any abnormalities of such screening studies require further evaluation and correction of specific factor deficiencies. Patients taking aspirin, dipyridamole, or other drugs that may adversely affect platelet function or other aspects of the normal coagulation mechanisms should discontinue such medications about 1 week before operation.

On the day before surgery, the patient is restricted to a liquid diet and a mechanical bowel preparation is ordered. Nonabsorbable oral antibiotics, such as neomycin and erythromycin, may be added if there is reason to believe that gastrointestinal trauma or ischemia may occur, but I generally do not use these agents in my practice. Prophylactic parenteral antibiotics are routinely given, beginning 1 to 2 hours preoperatively and continuing for about 48 hours after arterial reconstruction. Several randomized studies have clearly established the value of such systemic prophylactic antibiotics in vascular surgery.[80-82]

Aortoiliac Endarterectomy

First introduced by J. C. dos Santos in 1947[83] for the treatment of arteriosclerosis of peripheral arteries, and applied by Wylie and coworkers to occlusive disease in the aortoiliac segment,[84] thrombosed arterectomy became the first method of direct arterial reconstruction for aortoiliac occlusive disease. Aortoiliac endarterectomy may be considered in the group of approximately 5% to 10% of patients with truly localized (type I) disease (see Fig. 79-1). Endarterectomy offers several theoretical advantages: no prosthetic material is inserted; the infection rate is practically nonexistent; and inflow to the hypogastric arteries, potentially improving sexual potency in the male, is perhaps somewhat better than with bypass procedures. Finally, because the procedure is totally autogenous, and therefore more resistant to infection, it may be used in unusual circumstances in which

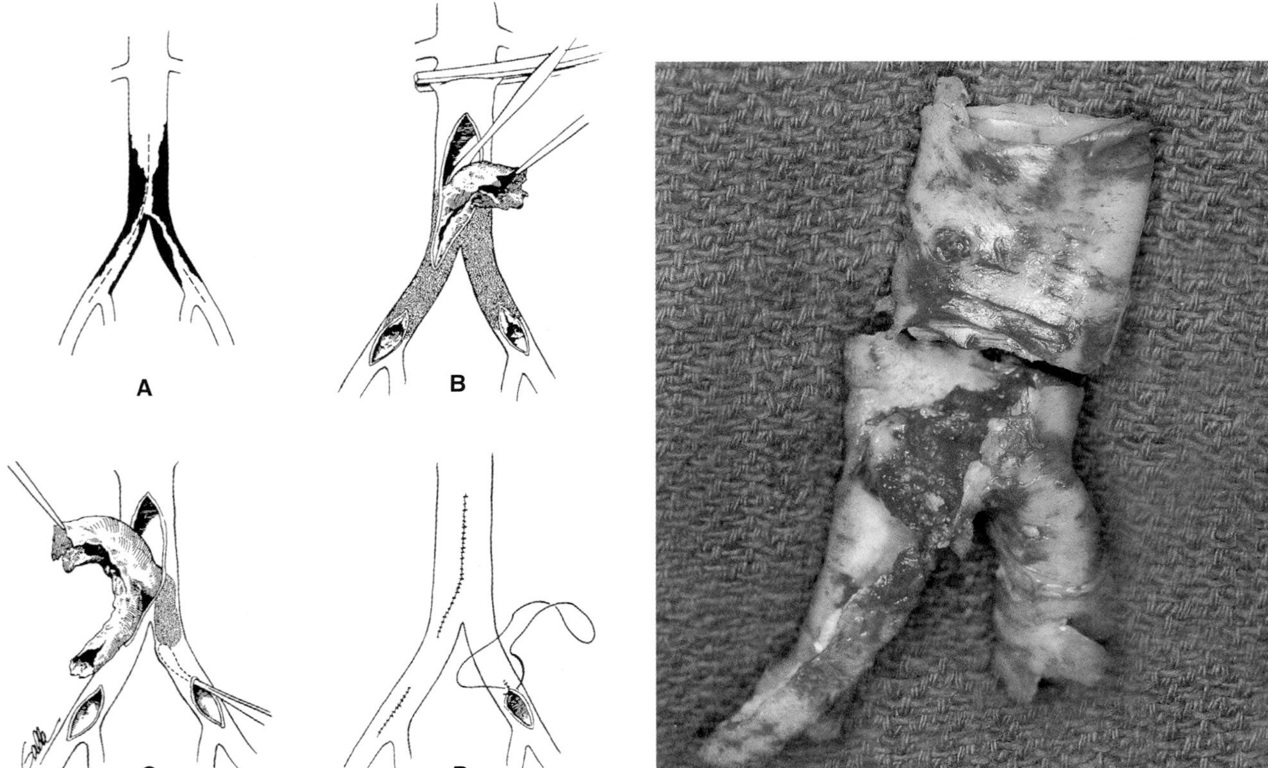

FIGURE 79-5 Left, Steps in aortoiliac endarterectomy. **A,** Occlusive disease is limited to the distal aorta and common iliac arteries. Location of typical arteriotomies is indicated by *dotted lines*. **B,** Endarterectomy plane is achieved, and atheromatous disease is removed from the level of the proximal aortic clamp to the bifurcation. **C,** Satisfactory endpoint is attained at the iliac bifurcation, and endarterectomy is carried proximally. Tacking sutures may be necessary to secure an adequate endpoint. **D,** Closure of the arteriotomies to complete the procedure. Patch closure may occasionally be necessary or desirable. **Right,** Photograph of operative specimen removed by endarterectomy.

reoperation in a contaminated or infected field requires innovative reconstructive methods.

Proper selection of patients for endarterectomy is important: disease should terminate at or just beyond the common iliac bifurcation, allowing the surgeon to achieve a satisfactory endpoint without extending more than 1 to 2 cm into the external iliac segment. Whether transverse or vertical arteriotomies are employed is of less importance than ensuring a proper plane of endarterectomy at the level of the external elastic lamina and achieving a secure endpoint of endarterectomy, with or without the aid of tacking sutures (Fig. 79-5). Primary closure of arteriotomies is generally feasible, although patch closure may occasionally be employed (see Chapter 45). When properly performed in suitable patients, aortoiliac endarterectomy can provide excellent and durable results.[2,85,86]

Endarterectomy is definitely contraindicated in three circumstances. First, any evidence of aneurysmal change makes endarterectomy ill advised because of possible continued aneurysmal degeneration of the endarterectomized segment in the future. Second, if total occlusion of the aorta exists to the level of the renal arteries, simple transection of the aorta several centimeters below the renal arteries with thrombectomy of the aortic cuff followed by graft insertion is technically easier and far more expeditious. Finally, by far the most common consideration favoring bypass grafting is extension of the disease process into the external iliac or distal vessels (types II and III). Difficulties with adequate endarterectomy of the external iliac artery as a result of its smaller size, greater length, somewhat more difficult exposure, and the more muscular and adherent medial layer are well documented, with a higher incidence of both early thrombosis and late failure as a result of recurrent stenosis.[2] For these reasons, extended aortoiliofemoral endarterectomy procedures have been generally abandoned and replaced by bypass grafting, which is simpler, faster, and associated with better late patency rates in patients with more extensive disease.

At present, aortoiliac endarterectomy is infrequently used by most vascular surgeons. Most patients have more diffuse disease than is suitable for endarterectomy, and few surgeons trained in the past few decades have had adequate experience and training to be comfortable and confident with this technique, which is generally acknowledged to be more technically demanding than bypass grafting. Most important, PTA, stents, and other catheter-based therapies have evolved and are usually considered first-line treatment in current practice for the relatively focal aortoiliac occlusive disease[87-89] formerly treated by endarterectomy (see Fig. 79-2). Nonetheless, endarterectomy remains an important adjunctive treatment method that should be part of the armamentarium of all vascular surgeons.

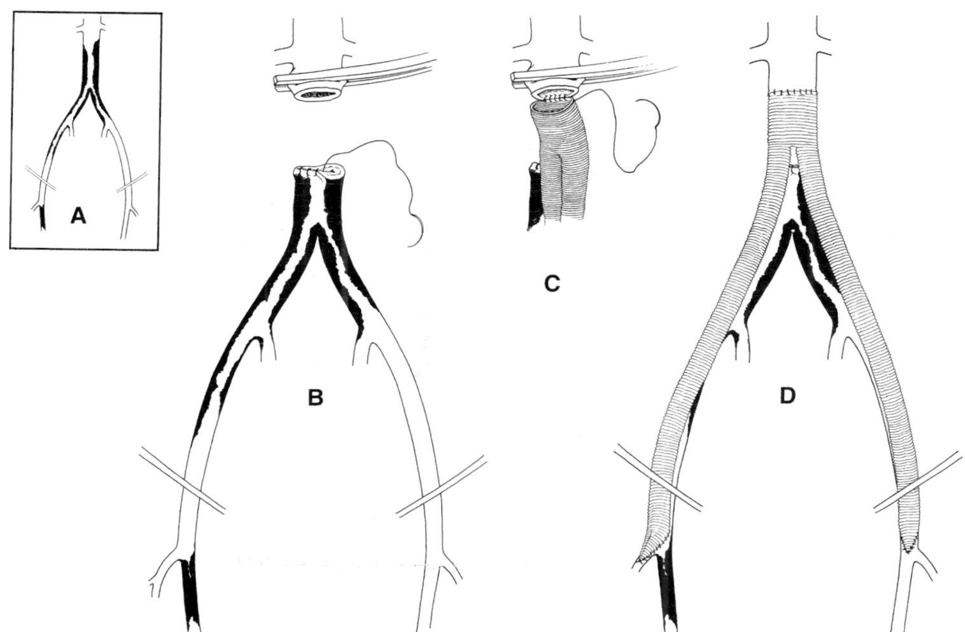

FIGURE 79-6 Aortofemoral graft. **A** (*inset*), Schematic illustration of a preoperative aortogram. **B,** A segment of diseased aorta is resected, and the distal aortic stump is oversewn. **C,** End-to-end proximal anastomosis. **D,** Completed reconstruction.

■ PRINCIPLES OF AORTIC GRAFT INSERTION

Proximal Anastomosis

The proximal aortic anastomosis may be made either end to end or end to side. End-to-end anastomosis is clearly indicated in patients with coexisting aneurysmal disease or complete aortic occlusion extending up to the renal arteries. In addition, it is preferred by many vascular surgeons for routine use in most cases for several reasons.

First, it appears to be hemodynamically more sound, with less turbulence, better flow characteristics, and less chance of competitive flow with still-patent host iliac vessels. Such considerations have led to better long-term patency and a lower incidence of aortic anastomotic aneurysms in grafts constructed with end-to-end proximal anastomosis in many reported series, although none has been a randomized, prospective trial.[2,4,90-92] Other studies, however, have not demonstrated any differences in late patency rates between end-to-end and end-to-side grafts.[93-96]

Second, application of partially occluding tangential clamps for construction of an end-to-side anastomosis may often carry a higher risk of dislodgment of intra-aortic thrombus or debris, which may then be irretrievably carried to the pelvic circulation or lower extremities.

Last, resection of a small segment of host aorta and use of a short body of the prosthetic bifurcation graft for end-to-end anastomosis (Fig. 79-6) allow the prosthesis to be placed in the anatomic aortic bed, greatly facilitating subsequent tissue coverage and reperitonealization and potentially avoiding the late occurrence of aortoenteric fistula formation.[2,4,93]

End-to-side anastomosis appears to be potentially advantageous in certain anatomic patterns of disease (Fig. 79-7). First, if a large aberrant renal artery arises from the lower abdominal aorta or iliac artery or if the surgeon wishes to avoid sacrifice of a large patent IMA, end-to-side proximal anastomosis is the simplest method to achieve preservation of such vessels. (If end-to-end insertion is preferred, however, these vessels can be preserved and reimplanted into the body of the graft.)

Second, and most important, end-to-side anastomosis appears to be advisable if the occlusive process is located principally in the external iliac vessels. In such instances, interruption of the infrarenal aorta for end-to-end bypass to the femoral level effectively devascularizes the pelvic region because no retrograde flow up the external iliac arteries to supply the hypogastric arterial beds can be anticipated. This problem may potentially increase the incidence of erectile impotence in the sexually potent male.[97,98] Such hemodynamic consequences may also raise the incidence of postoperative colon ischemia, severe buttock ischemia, or even paraplegia secondary to spinal cord ischemia.[21,99,100] Troublesome hip claudication may also continue to plague the patient despite the presence of excellent femoral and distal pulses.

Third, if the limb of the graft becomes occluded in later years, and further revascularization proves to be infeasible, the resulting limb ischemia may be particularly severe and may lead to difficulty with healing after even above-knee amputation. For these reasons, the surgeon may elect to use end-to-side proximal anastomosis in the anatomic circumstances described.

At present, one can only conclude that this area is controversial. Both methods have been advocated by experienced and highly skilled vascular surgeons. Irrespective of the method of proximal anastomosis, the principle of placing the proximal anastomosis high in the infrarenal abdominal aorta, relatively close to the renal arteries in an area almost always less involved by the occlusive process, is of paramount importance to minimize later recurrent difficulties.

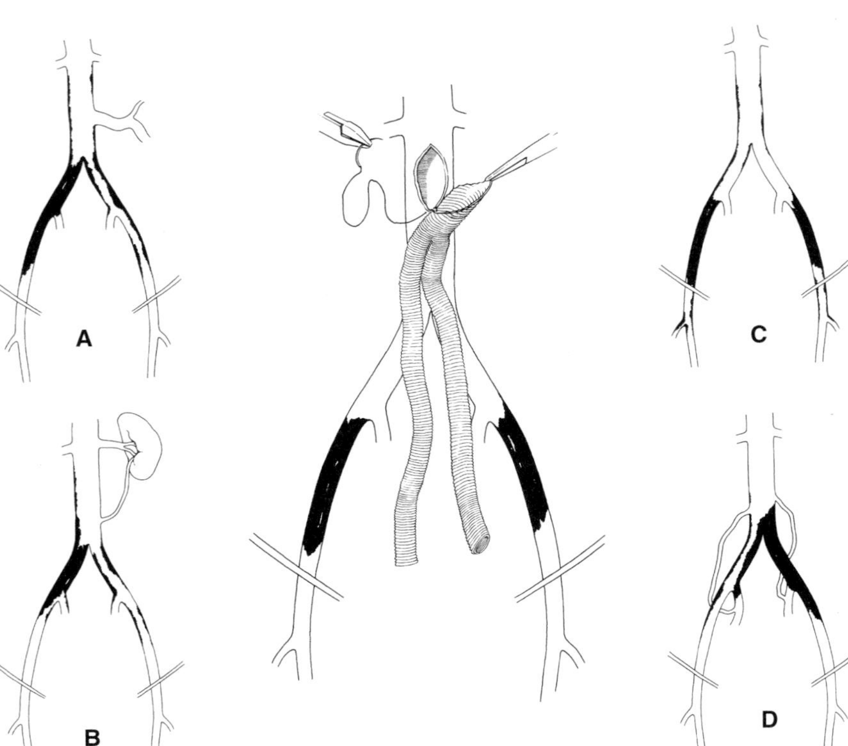

FIGURE 79-7 Anatomic findings or patterns of disease and profunda femoris artery stenosis favoring end-to-side proximal anastomosis of an aortofemoral graft. **A,** Patent and enlarged inferior mesenteric artery. **B,** Low-lying accessory renal artery arising from the distal aorta or proximal iliac vessels. **C,** Occlusive lesions confined largely to the external iliac arteries, with the aorta and common iliac and internal iliac arteries fairly well preserved. In my experience, this is the most common indication for end-to-side anastomosis. **D,** Reconstitution of pelvic circulation by collateral sources, which would be interrupted with end-to-end anastomosis. In all of these circumstances, end-to-side aortic anastomosis may be advantageous.

Distal Anastomosis

Although the distal anastomosis of the aortic graft may on occasion be constructed at the level of the external iliac artery in the pelvis, it is almost always preferable in patients with occlusive disease to carry the graft to the femoral level, where exposure is generally better and anastomosis is technically easier. With adequate personnel, both femoral anastomoses may often be performed simultaneously. Most important, anastomosis at the femoral level provides the surgeon with an opportunity to ensure adequate outflow into the profunda femoris artery. Experience has clearly demonstrated a higher late failure rate of aorta-external iliac grafts, with a higher incidence of subsequent "downstream" operations as a result of progressive disease at or just beyond the iliac artery anastomosis.[2,101,102] With meticulous surgical technique, proper skin preparation and draping, and use of a limited period of prophylactic antibiotic coverage, the higher incidence of infection that was anticipated to occur with extension of grafts to the femoral artery level has not been borne out by extensive experience.[2,9,68-73] As a result, aortobifemoral grafting has become the procedure of choice for direct reconstruction in almost all patients with aortoiliac occlusive disease.

Profunda Femoris Artery Runoff

Establishment of adequate graft outflow at the level of the femoral artery anastomosis, via the profunda femoris artery in patients with disease or occlusion of the superficial femoral artery, has been clearly documented to be of paramount importance in early and late graft results.[2,73,103,104] For these reasons, it is imperative that any lesion that might compromise flow in the profunda femoris artery be carefully evaluated and corrected at the time of distal anastomosis.

Preoperative arteriography should visualize the orifice of the profunda femoris artery, particularly when occlusion of the superficial femoral artery is demonstrated. Visualization is usually best accomplished with oblique views of the groin. At operation, the surgeon must look for possible stenosis of the origin of the profunda femoris artery by palpation, gentle passage of vascular probes, or direct inspection. If any stenosis of the profunda femoris origin exists, it should be corrected by endarterectomy or patch angioplasty techniques. My preference is for extension of the arteriotomy down the profunda femoris artery beyond the orifice stenosis, with subsequent anastomosis of the beveled tip of the graft as a patch closure (Fig. 79-8). This maneuver, which achieves hemodynamic correction, is preferable in my judgment to true endarterectomy, which may lead to a higher incidence of late pseudoaneurysm formation if the prosthetic graft is sutured to the endarterectomized arterial wall.

Formal endarterectomy of the profunda femoris artery, however, may be required if the vessel is extensively diseased. Subsequent closure can still be achieved with the long, beveled tip of the graft hood. Other surgeons have preferred using autogenous arterial or saphenous vein patches for separate profundaplasty, then anastomosing the prosthesis to the common femoral artery above this site.[104] In any case, it is imperative that the surgeon use precise anastomotic technique at the endpoint of the endarterectomy to ensure an adequate

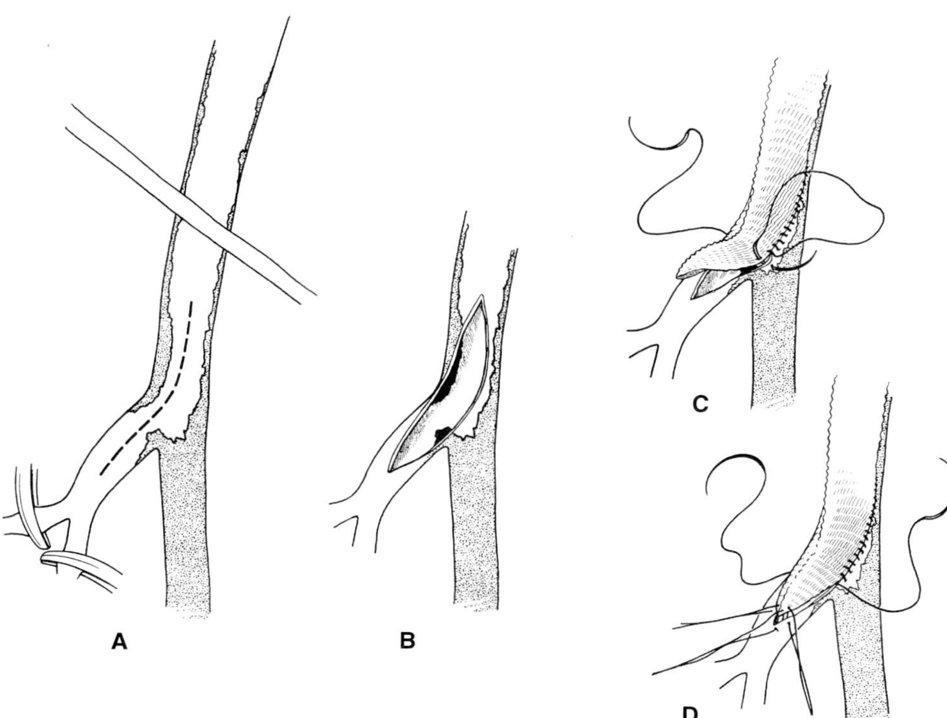

FIGURE 79-8 Femoral anastomosis in a patient with multilevel disease. **A,** With associated femoropopliteal occlusive disease, any disease at the orifice of the profunda femoris artery may limit graft limb runoff and subsequent patency. **B,** Extension of the common femoral arteriotomy into the proximal profunda femoris artery, distal to the orificial stenosis. **C,** The heel of the long, beveled graft hood is anastomosed to the common femoral artery. **D,** The femoral anastomosis is completed with the tip of the graft extended down the profunda femoris artery, thus achieving a patch profundaplasty. Three to five interrupted sutures are first placed at the tip and are not tied down, facilitating visualization and accurate placement without constriction.

profunda femoris artery outflow tract. My colleagues and I usually best achieve this by the use of three to five interrupted sutures at the distal end of the anastomosis (see Fig. 79-8*D*), which allows excellent visualization, precise placement, and avoidance of any constricting effect of a running suture line at this critical outflow point.

Although some surgeons have suggested that the mere existence of an occluded superficial femoral artery in itself causes a "functional" stenosis despite the absence of orificial disease of the profunda femoris artery,[105] most evidence suggests that "routine" profundaplasty in all such cases does not improve the hemodynamic result or late patency rate of the graft.[40,94]

Graft Selection

Although standard fabric prosthetic grafts constructed from polyester (Dacron) or polytetrafluoroethylene (PTFE, Teflon) and used during the initial era of aortofemoral reconstruction have generally performed well, a wide variety of aortic prosthetic grafts have become available to the vascular surgeon in more recent years. Numerous modifications in graft material (e.g., Dacron vs. PTFE), methods of fabrication (e.g., knitted vs. woven, external velour vs. double velour, and porosity differences), and addition of various biologic coatings (e.g., collagen or albumin) to the graft have been devised.

Such alterations have been proposed in the hope of improving the performance and characteristics of the graft, usually in the following qualities:

- Patency
- Durability
- Healing and incorporation within host tissue
- Resistance to infection
- Reduced blood loss through the graft
- Handling characteristics

Various claims concerning the benefits of one type over another have been made, although it is often difficult to discern science from salesmanship. Past studies performed to evaluate the differences frequently lacked adequate control to allow an accurate conclusion to be drawn. In one attempt to help clarify this situation, Robicsek and associates[106] used "half-and-half" grafts of woven and knitted Dacron. Implanting a bifurcated Dacron graft constructed with one limb woven and the other knitted allowed them to compare patency of the two limbs directly. Approximately half of their 158 patients underwent replacement procedures for aneurysm; nevertheless, at an average of 5½ years of follow-up, no significant difference was found in patency between the two limbs. In a related study, Robicsek and coworkers[107] also found no difference in platelet deposition between the two varieties of grafts and, hence, presumably no difference in the thrombogenicity.

Many surgeons continue to prefer knitted Dacron grafts for aortofemoral grafting, mainly because of their flexibility and ease of handling and suturing, which is particularly helpful in a difficult profunda femoris artery anastomosis. However, newer manufacturing techniques have begun to blur the former distinct differences in mechanical properties and characteristics between knitted and woven Dacron grafts and to make such considerations less important in current practice. Whether an internal or an external velour surface or a combination of the two is beneficial remains unproven.

Although porosity and incorporation by the host tissue remain desirable theoretical features, the successful use of PTFE grafts in other locations has made these considerations questionable. A study of the use of PTFE grafts in the hypoplastic aorta syndrome by Burke and colleagues[108] suggested better patency results than with Dacron grafts, but the difference was not statistically significant. Similarly, the results of a comparison of PTFE bifurcated grafts and Dacron prostheses by Cintora and associates[109] favored PTFE grafts; although cumulative patency rates at 4 years were not significantly different (97% and 90%, respectively), blood loss was less and late graft-related complications were less frequent with PTFE grafts.

Currently, "zero porosity" biologically coated grafts dominate the market for prosthetic grafts because of their expediency and probably smaller associated blood loss (see Chapter 49). Clearly, both PTFE and biologically coated prosthetics do limit blood loss and facilitate the procedure by obviating preclotting of the graft, but all such grafts are generally more expensive than conventional fabric prostheses, and any improvement in performance is unproven. Their higher cost is often justified by reductions in operative time, need for transfusions, and perhaps morbidity because of these factors. One may generally conclude that no single large-caliber graft is clearly superior and that long-term patency is more closely related to proper surgical methods of graft implantation and limitation of disease progression than to the specific graft employed.

Irrespective of the exact type of graft material and fabrication, the use of the proper size graft is important.[110,111] Previously, many surgeons employed grafts that were too large in comparison with the size of outflow tract vessels, which tended to promote sluggish flow in graft limbs and deposition of excessive laminar pseudointima in the prosthesis. This development often gives rise to a propensity for later fragmentation or dislodgment, leading to occlusion of one or both limbs of the graft. For occlusive disease, a 16×8 mm bifurcated graft is most often employed; a 14×7 mm or even smaller prosthesis is also used when appropriate, frequently in some female patients. The limb size of such grafts most closely approximates the femoral arteries of patients with occlusive disease or, more particularly, the size of the profunda femoris artery, which often remains as the only outflow tract. In addition, it is now well recognized that many Dacron prosthetic grafts have a tendency to dilate 10% to 20% when subjected to arterial pressure.[112] Selection of a smaller graft helps compensate for this tendency.

Intraoperative Evaluation of Revascularization

At the conclusion of the operative procedure, the surgeon must ensure the technical and hemodynamic integrity of the vascular reconstruction. This is traditionally done by visual inspection of the anastomoses and by palpation of satisfactory pulses at and just beyond the point of graft anastomosis.

If feasible, some means of ensuring adequate distal flow intraoperatively is also advisable. Actual palpation of distal leg and pedal pulses is often cumbersome without contamination of the operative field. In addition, pulses are often difficult to appreciate immediately after reconstruction in the cold and vasoconstricted limb. Some surgeons prefer to prepare and drape the feet in transparent bags so as to allow visualization of their color and appearance, but this method is often rather subjective and uncertain.

My colleagues and I routinely obtain pulse volume recordings after restoration of flow to evaluate the hemodynamic adequacy of aortoiliac reconstruction more objectively.[113] Plethysmographic cuffs are placed at the calf or ankle level and are draped out of the operative field. Following graft insertion and release of clamps, postoperative pulse volume recordings are easily obtained by the circulating nurse and can be compared with preoperative tracings to assess the hemodynamic result of proximal revascularization. If more distal sterile draping is necessary, sterile intraoperative cuffs may be used for postreconstructive determinations. Unless extensive uncorrected distal disease is present, such pulse volume recordings should show better amplitude than that in the preoperative tracings.

If extensive distal disease does complicate pulse volume recording monitoring, a sterile cuff may be applied to the distal thigh to ensure adequate revascularization of the profunda femoris artery. Alternatively, some surgeons use postreconstructive determinations of distal ankle Doppler pressures, electromagnetic flow measurements through the open graft limb, or intraoperative duplex scanning with a sterile intraoperative probe. Regardless of the method chosen, the importance of ensuring a satisfactory technical result before the patient leaves the operating room cannot be overemphasized.

■ SPECIAL CONSIDERATIONS

Retroperitoneal Approach

Although a retroperitoneal approach to the infrarenal abdominal aorta was used by Rob[114] and others during the early era of aortic reconstruction for occlusive or aneurysmal disease, the traditional surgical approach for direct repair of infrarenal aortoiliac occlusive disease has been the transperitoneal route. Several reports have recommended a retroperitoneal approach as an alternative in patients with multiple prior intra-abdominal operations or in patients thought to be at high risk for complications secondary to cardiac or severe pulmonary disease if the standard transperitoneal approach were employed. In this latter group, possible advantages of the retroperitoneal approach are (1) less disturbance of pulmonary function, (2) decreased postoperative ileus, and (3) reduced third-space fluid losses. In other instances of occlusive disease extending close to the renal arteries or in patients with associated occlusive lesions of the visceral or renal arteries, a retroperitoneal approach may permit easier access, control, and repair.[115-117]

The retroperitoneal approach is performed as follows:

1. The patient is placed in a modified left thoracotomy position with the left shoulder and chest elevated to approximately a 45- to 60-degree angle, and the hips and pelvis are rotated posteriorly as far as possible to provide access to the femoral arteries.

2. The midpoint between the left costal margin and the iliac crest is centered over the break in the table, and the table is flexed to widen the left flank. During the operative procedure, the operating table can be rotated either toward or away from the surgeon, who stands on the patient's left side.
3. An oblique flank incision is made beginning at the left lateral border of the rectus muscle several inches below the umbilicus and extended superiorly to the tip of the 11th rib.
4. Dissection is carried in a retroperitoneal plane, either (a) with dissection anterior to the kidney if standard infrarenal exposure is adequate or (b) with anterior mobilization of the left kidney if access to the supraceliac aorta is necessary.
5. Further medial mobilization of the peritoneal envelope exposes the IMA, which is divided and ligated close to the aorta, usually facilitating further exposure.

With such an approach, access to the right renal artery is often impossible, and control and repair of the right iliac artery are occasionally difficult. Similarly, tunneling to the right groin and right femoral artery anastomosis may sometimes be difficult, particularly in an obese patient. However, the approach may clearly be helpful in patients with multiple prior intra-abdominal operations, prior aortic surgery, pararenal disease, or similar technical considerations.

Whether or not the retroperitoneal approach is advantageous for standard infrarenal aortic reconstruction in comparison with the conventional transperitoneal approach remains uncertain. A prospective, randomized study by Sicard and associates[118] was believed to demonstrate physiologic and cost benefits of a retroperitoneal approach, but the results of a similar original prospective, randomized comparison by Cambria and coworkers[119] found no significant differences.

Adjunctive Lumbar Sympathectomy

The use of a concomitant lumbar sympathectomy at the time of aortic reconstruction remains unsettled and controversial (see Chapter 85). Although it is well accepted that sympathectomy increases skin and total limb blood flow, there are few objective data to document more favorable long-term graft patency rates or improved limb salvage results.[120,121] Available evidence does suggest, however, that decreased pedal vasomotor tone and skin perfusion may be helpful as an adjunct to direct arterial revascularization, particularly in patients with multilevel disease and relatively minor superficial areas of pedal or digital ischemic lesions.[120,122,123] Therefore, limited (L2-L3) sympathectomy in conjunction with direct aortic operation may be considered in such cases, particularly when it has been decided to limit operation to inflow reconstruction alone or when distal runoff is considered to be poor. The procedure is easily and quickly accomplished, but it must be acknowledged that the benefit remains unproven.

The Totally Occluded Aorta

Approximately 8% of my patients undergoing operation for aortoiliac occlusive disease have a chronic totally occluded aorta.[124] In about 50% of these patients, the occlusion has extended retrograde to the level of the renal arteries (Fig. 79-9); in the rest, the occlusion has involved only the distal infrarenal aorta, with the proximal segment remaining open via runoff through a still patent IMA or lumbar vessels.

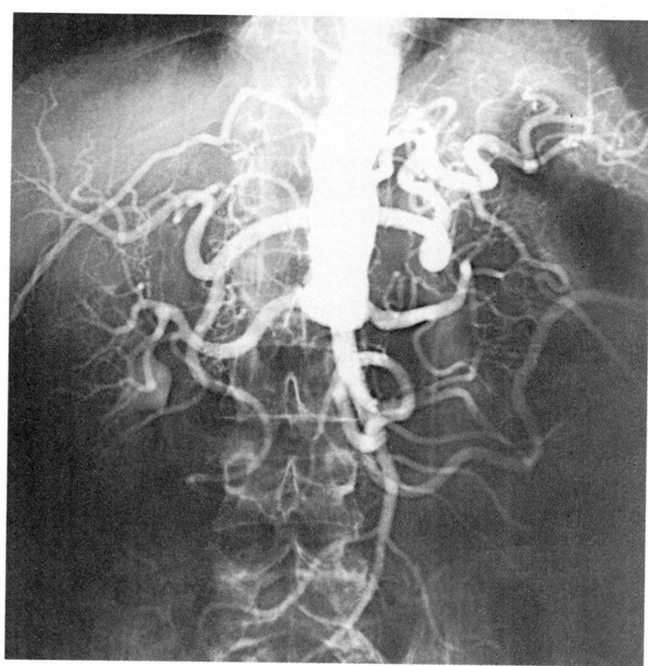

FIGURE 79-9 Transaxillary aortogram demonstrating total juxtarenal aortic occlusion.

Surgical management in the latter group is straightforward and is similar to standard aortic graft insertion. With extension of the occluding thrombus to a juxtarenal level, however, the operative approach is more taxing and possible complications are more likely, particularly those complications involving disturbance of renal function.[124-126] Nevertheless, surgery may be advisable in such cases, even if ischemic complaints are relatively mild and stable, because of the potential for more proximal propagation of thrombus with compromise or occlusion of neighboring renal or visceral arteries. The actual threat of proximal propagation of untreated total aortic thrombosis remains controversial, however. Although some series have suggested that the danger is significant,[127,128] other retrospective reviews have determined that subsequent compromise of renal or mesenteric circulation by further retrograde extension of clot is quite rare unless severe stenosis in renal or visceral arteries is also present.[129,130]

In almost all patients with juxtarenal occlusion, the bulk of the actual occlusive disease lies in the distal aorta, with the proximal occlusive material composed largely of secondary thrombus. This proximal plug may almost always be removed with simple thrombectomy and then routine graft insertion, as follows:

1. Adequate dissection is carried out to allow temporary control of the renal arteries by application of gentle bulldog clamps to minimize chances of renal embolization at the time of juxtarenal thrombectomy.

2. Division of the left renal vein may facilitate exposure and is a benign procedure if performed correctly near the insertion of this vein into the vena cava, thereby preserving collateral venous drainage. This division is generally unnecessary; however, the mobilized left renal vein can usually be retracted cephalad or caudad as required for exposure and control of the juxtarenal aorta.[131]
3. The completely occluded aorta is opened through an arteriotomy placed several centimeters below the renal arteries.
4. The infrarenal aorta should *not* be clamped at this juncture, to avoid compression of the apex of the thrombotic material and its possible dislodgment into the renal or mesenteric circulation. Indeed, infrarenal clamping is unnecessary at this stage because the thrombotic plug prevents any bleeding.
5. Thrombectomy of the aortic cuff to the level of the renal arteries is carried out with a blunt clamp. This procedure is usually terminated by the "blowing out" by aortic pressure of a typical organized cap of thrombus representing the apex of the thrombotic occlusion.
6. The suprarenal aorta can now be controlled by manual pressure, or a suprarenal clamp can be temporarily applied.
7. The aorta is flushed, the bulldog clamps are removed from the renal artery, and an appropriate vascular clamp is applied to the now patent infrarenal cuff.
8. The graft is inserted in routine fashion.

Formal endarterectomy is best avoided in most circumstances because this plane may be difficult to terminate without compromise of the renal artery origins. Simple thrombectomy at this level is preferred and is sufficient in almost all cases.

The Calcified Aorta

Occasionally, dense calcification of the infrarenal aorta appears to preclude successful insertion of an aortic graft and leads the surgeon to consider abandoning the procedure. This situation occurs particularly during end-to-side anastomosis with the use of tangential, partially occluding clamps.

Reconstruction can always be accomplished with several possible alterations. First, a high end-to-end proximal anastomosis is preferred. By carrying dissection to or just above the left renal vein after its division or cephalad retraction, the surgeon often finds that the aorta immediately below the renal arteries is less involved and more manageable. Second, endarterectomy of a 1- to 2-cm cuff of totally transected aorta to the level of the infrarenal aortic clamp is usually possible and removes the calcification that always lies in the diseased intima and media. This maneuver greatly facilitates subsequent end-to-end graft anastomosis.

Although the cuff of the endarterectomized aorta, which consists of aortic adventitia and external elastic lamina, always appears fragile, it invariably proves to be adequate for graft anastomosis without later difficulties, such as bleeding, suture line disruption, and pseudoaneurysm formation. The surgeon must employ a tapered (not cutting-tip) needle, and the use of an interrupted mattress suture technique, with each suture backed with a pledget of Teflon felt (Fig. 79-10), is to be particularly recommended.

Clamping of such calcified vessels may also be problematic. It can usually be accomplished just below the renal arteries, where calcification is often less severe. Clamping in an anteroposterior fashion, with the use of an arterial clamp applied from a lateral direction, may also be helpful. In truly difficult situations, the aorta may be clamped above the renal arteries at the level of the diaphragm, or intraluminal methods of vascular control employing balloon catheters may be used.

The Small Aorta

In about 5% to 10% of patients, the infrarenal aorta and the iliac and femoral vessels are small, a feature that makes aortic reconstruction technically difficult. Actual anatomic definition of the small aorta is obviously arbitrary. Cronenwett and associates[5] have defined the syndrome as characterized by an infrarenal aorta measuring (1) less than 13.2 mm just below the renal vessels or (2) less than 10.3 mm just above the aortic bifurcation. Iliac and femoral vessels are typically correspondingly small, with the common femoral vessels often measuring only about 5 mm.

These patients appear to form a unique and distinct subgroup and are frequently characterized as having hypoplastic aorta syndrome.[6-8] Preferred surgical methods

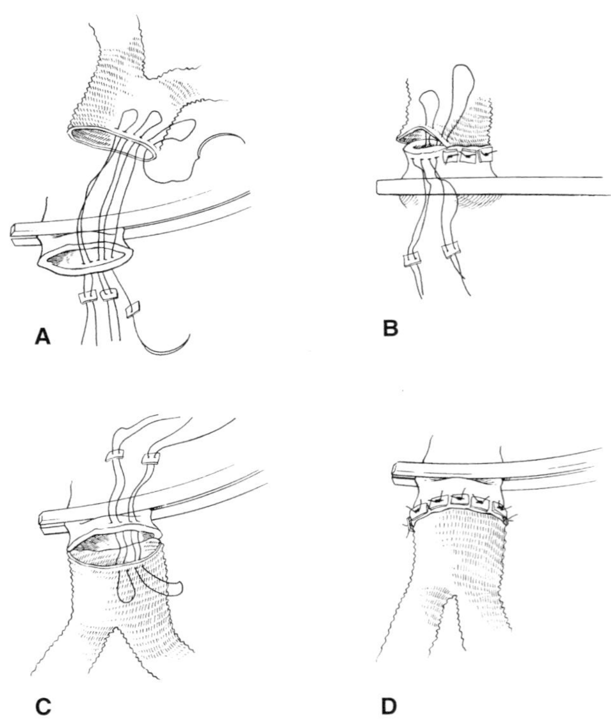

FIGURE 79-10 Interrupted mattress suture technique of aortic anastomosis. **A,** A posterior row of five mattress sutures is placed, with a double-armed suture passed through the posterior graft wall and then through the host aorta. **B,** A posterior row of sutures is tied down over pledgets of polytetrafluoroethylene (Teflon) felt. **C,** The graft is turned inferiorly toward the patient's feet, and a similar anterior row of five mattress sutures is placed with pledgets. **D,** Completed interrupted suture line. This technique is extremely helpful for the small aorta or fragile, diseased vessel.

for reconstruction in patients with small vessels remain somewhat controversial; some surgeons hold that the small size of the aorta and iliac vessels makes endarterectomy unsuitable, whereas others favoring bypass techniques advocate the use of end-to-side proximal aortic anastomosis to avoid size discrepancies with the usual prosthetic grafts.

Because the occlusive disease in such patients is frequently localized, aortoiliac endarterectomy may be considered. Although the small size of the vessels demands greater care and occasionally requires the use of patch closures, endarterectomy has worked well in the hands of my colleagues and myself.

If occlusive disease is more diffuse, bypass grafting to the femoral vessels is preferred. End-to-side anastomosis, favored by many surgeons to overcome size differences between the graft and the host aorta,[108] is an acceptable technique as long as the infrarenal aorta is not too diseased. A smaller prosthesis should be chosen to avoid the consequences of using inappropriately large grafts. In most cases, a 14 × 7 mm or even a 12 × 6 mm bifurcation graft should be used. The limbs of such grafts, although small, are also much more appropriate for the smaller femoral and outflow vessels of the patient with a small aorta.

Greater technical care must be exercised, but with attention to technical detail, such grafts have not failed as a result of their small size; my colleagues and I much prefer the insertion of such small grafts to the use of oversized prostheses. A study by Burke and colleagues[108] suggested better patency rates when PTFE aortic bifurcation grafts were used for reconstruction in patients with a small abdominal aorta than when Dacron grafts were used, but statistical significance was not achieved. Adjunctive lumbar sympathectomy may be helpful.

Simultaneous Distal Grafting

A common practical concern in patients with multilevel occlusive disease is whether or not an inflow operation alone will suffice. As already emphasized, such diffuse combined-segment disease (type III) is the most common pattern of occlusive disease, present in between one half and two thirds of the patients coming to surgery.[2,68-71] Prior reports of patients with multilevel disease who were treated in a generally accepted fashion with initial aortic reconstruction have indicated that proximal operation alone may fail to achieve satisfactory relief of ischemic symptoms in up to one third.[10,14,69,90,94,132-136] Although symptoms of claudication are lessened in more than 80% of patients with multilevel disease who undergo aortofemoral grafting, only 35% of patients in our series experienced total relief of claudication.[14] Many patients with unsatisfactory outcomes must undergo concurrent or subsequent distal bypass grafting. However, identification of patients in whom relief of ischemic symptoms would be insufficient with an inflow procedure alone remains difficult.

In this regard, we reviewed a 6-year experience comprising 181 patients with multilevel disease who underwent aortofemoral grafting.[14] A well-performed inflow procedure usually suffices if there is unequivocally severe proximal disease in the aortoiliac segment. Such clear-cut proximal disease is best identified from the findings of absence of or clear reduction in the femoral pulse and obvious severe aortic or iliac disease on angiography and is confirmed, if necessary, by the findings of an FAP study.

Several intraoperative criteria may also be used. Restoration of an improved pulse volume recording at the calf or ankle, in comparison with preoperative tracings, can give reassurance of satisfactory improvement in distal circulation. However, improvement in pulse volume recordings or Doppler ankle pressures may not be immediately apparent in the presence of significant distal disease, especially in the cold, vasoconstricted limb. Another useful intraoperative guide in predicting a good clinical response is assessment of the anatomic size of the profunda femoris artery itself. If the proximal profunda femoris artery accepts a 4-mm probe and if a No. 3 Fogarty embolectomy catheter can be passed through it for a distance of 20 cm or more, the profunda femoris artery probably is well developed and will function satisfactorily as an outflow tract and source of collateral circulation.[4,14,137]

Possible benefits of simultaneous grafting are (1) a more nearly total correction of extremity ischemia and (2) avoidance of the difficulties and potential complications associated with reoperation in the groin if later distal grafting proves to be necessary. Such advantages are usually outweighed by the greater magnitude of the synchronous two-level grafting and the fact that most properly selected patients are adequately benefited by proximal operation alone (76% in our series). Distal bypass may be carried out in the future, if necessary; it was required in 17% of the patients in our series who were observed for up to 6 years.[14] Such a figure is in agreement with previously reported experience.[68,90,101,136]

In carefully selected patients with multilevel disease and truly advanced limb-threatening ischemic problems in the foot, synchronous proximal and distal reconstructions seem appropriate.[138] This is particularly pertinent if only modest proximal occlusive disease is present because an inflow procedure is then unlikely to improve blood flow to the foot markedly (Fig. 79-11). We believe that if the surgeon can reliably predict that a distal graft will almost certainly be necessary in the future for limb salvage, simultaneous grafting is to be preferred because it offers a better chance of limb salvage and avoids a more demanding reoperation in the groin at a later time. Certainly, the use of two surgical teams can minimize the additional operative time required, and it is likely that synchronous grafting will become somewhat more common in the future.[139-144] Although some surgeons have claimed success with preoperative noninvasive hemodynamic studies in selecting such patients,[14,138,142,145] other investigators have found tests of this type to be unreliable indicators of the need for concomitant distal bypass.[94,101,133] Good clinical judgment remains most important, with reasoned and pragmatic decisions usually required.

Unilateral Iliac Disease

Not infrequently, proximal occlusive disease may appear unilaterally, with fairly normal pulses and no symptoms in the contralateral extremity. Truly unilateral iliac disease is relatively uncommon because aortoiliac disease is generally a more diffuse and eventually bilateral process. Progression of disease in the aorta or in the untreated contralateral iliac artery may necessitate later reoperation in a significant

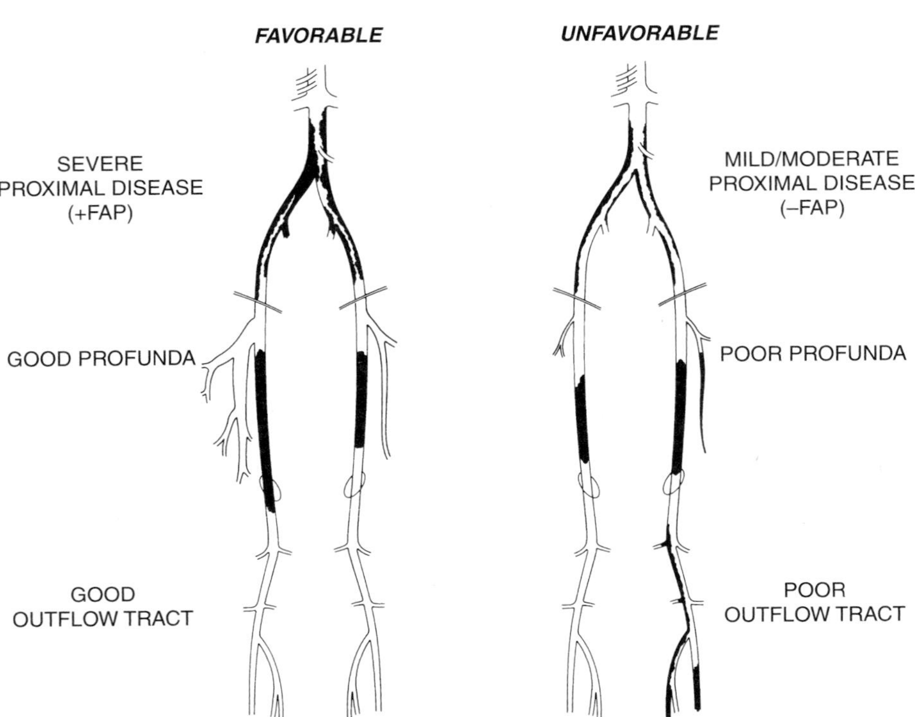

FIGURE 79-11 Clinical circumstances and disease patterns associated with favorable or unsatisfactory outcome of aortofemoral grafts alone in patients with multilevel disease. FAP, femoral artery pressure.

percentage of patients treated initially with unilateral operations for apparent one-sided disease.[102,146] Estimates of the exact frequency of this occurrence vary considerably, however, and several reports have suggested that it is relatively infrequent.[147-149]

Optimal management of unilateral iliac disease remains controversial, with proponents of both standard aortobifemoral bypass and less extensive extra-anatomic grafts or even endoluminal therapy claiming their approach to be advantageous and preferred.[40,61] In the patient with a well-preserved aorta and contralateral iliac artery, the use of femorofemoral grafts has become increasingly important owing to the ease of the procedure and the generally good long-term results.[150-154]

In certain instances, however, the surgeon may wish to avoid the contralateral side and to confine reconstructive efforts to the symptomatic side (e.g., if the contralateral limb is asymptomatic but inflow in the proposed donor limb is of questionable reliability and the patient is not a good candidate for standard aortobifemoral grafting). In other instances, use of the contralateral groin may be relatively contraindicated because of heavy scarring from prior operative procedures, possible infection, and so forth. In these situations, direct iliofemoral grafting may occasionally be used for disease that is largely unilateral at the time.[155-158] This procedure is used mainly for occlusive disease confined to the external iliac artery, because the ipsilateral common iliac artery must be relatively normal for the proximal graft anastomosis. A retroperitoneal approach through a separate lower quadrant incision (Fig. 79-12) usually provides good exposure and can be carried out with low patient morbidity.

Whether femorofemoral bypass or iliofemoral grafting gives better results is currently debated, although several studies have demonstrated better long-term patency of direct ipsilateral iliofemoral bypass grafts.[159,160] Nonetheless, femorofemoral grafting is a somewhat simpler procedure, has very low morbidity, and obviates any possibility of interfering with sexual function in men.[161]

In similar situations, retroperitoneal iliac endarterectomy may be employed for relatively localized unilateral inflow lesions via a similar retroperitoneal approach,[148,162,163] although with the established success of iliac PTA and possible stenting, this approach has largely been replaced. All methods of unilateral inflow revascularization may be readily combined with concomitant profundaplasty or simultaneous ipsilateral distal bypass and are therefore particularly helpful in patients with mainly unilateral multilevel disease who may require extensive revascularization but in whom the surgeon wishes to limit the extent of the surgical procedure.[49,138,147,162] Similarly, if proximal iliac disease is relatively localized and suitable for PTA, reestablishment of inflow by transluminal angioplasty may be combined with distal surgical procedures, yielding good long-term results.[49,50]

Associated Renal Artery or Visceral Artery Occlusive Lesions

Because of the diffuse nature of atherosclerotic occlusive disease in most patients, it is not surprising that individuals requiring aortic reconstruction for symptomatic lower extremity ischemia may be found to have associated occlusive lesions involving the renal or visceral arteries. Often

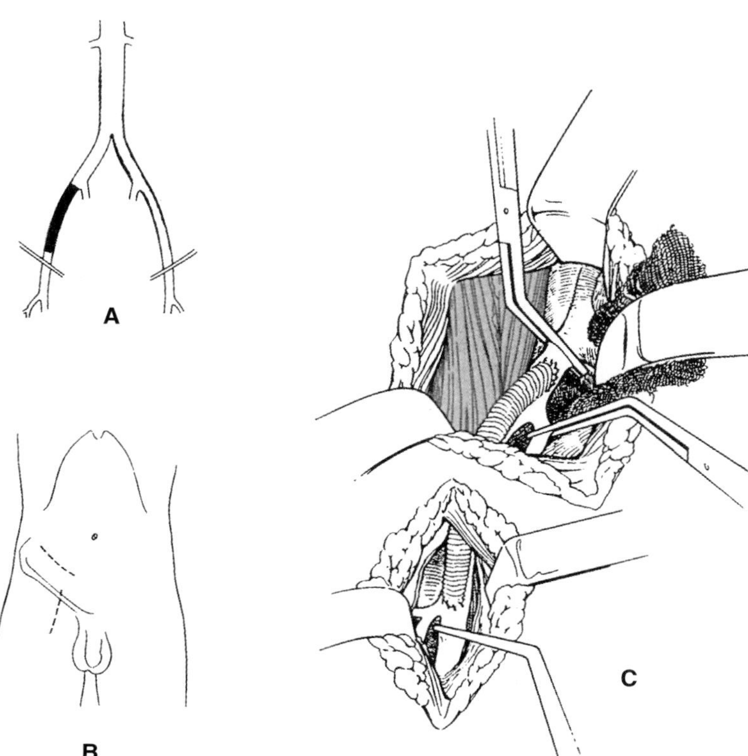

FIGURE 79-12 Unilateral iliofemoral bypass graft. **A,** In this usual situation, such a reconstruction may be considered; occlusive disease is confined largely to one external iliac artery. **B,** Positioning of skin incisions for retroperitoneal exposure of the iliac vessels and standard approach to the femoral arteries. **C,** Iliofemoral graft is inserted.

these lesions are unsuspected and are detected only at the time of preoperative angiography. The dilemma of whether or not to attempt simultaneous correction of both abdominal aortic and visceral lesions is frequently encountered and difficult to resolve.[164,165]

In these instances, each case must be considered individually and no general recommendations are feasible or appropriate. It is clear that extending aortic reconstruction to include visceral artery revascularization, although theoretically appealing, increases the complexity and magnitude of the operation and hence is associated almost invariably with some increase in morbidity and mortality.[164,166,167] For these reasons, truly prophylactic revascularizations should generally be avoided. Serial angiographic studies have demonstrated, however, that renal occlusive disease is progressive in more than 50% of patients and that approximately 10% of high-grade lesions (≥80% stenosis) proceed to total occlusion, with resultant loss of function in that kidney.[164] Hence, if clinical evaluation suggests that the associated renal lesions are functionally important or preocclusive in severity, simultaneous correction is often appropriate.[164-170]

In the asymptomatic patient with visceral artery disease, careful evaluation of the anatomic pattern of disease on the preoperative arteriogram should indicate whether the patient would be at risk for postoperative intestinal ischemia if the visceral lesions were not treated. As emphasized by Ernst[21] and Connolly and Kwaan,[171] avoidance of this catastrophic postoperative problem requires preservation of an important IMA in those patients with celiac and superior mesenteric artery occlusive disease or, perhaps, concomitant bypass grafting to the celiac or superior mesenteric artery itself.[21,171]

It is clear that if associated renal artery disease is present, combined reconstruction may improve associated hypertension or renal function in carefully selected patients.[166-170] Diminished renal function is rarely due to unilateral disease, and significant bilateral disease (either intrarenal or extrarenal) almost always must be present before overall renal function is adversely affected. Adding a unilateral renal bypass without first proving the functional significance of the renal lesion may unnecessarily risk further compromise of excretory function in a patient who may be azotemic predominantly from bilateral arteriolar nephrosclerosis. Therefore, it seems appropriate to assess the functional significance of such a unilateral renal artery lesion preoperatively and to proceed with correction only if study results are positive. If angiographically severe bilateral lesions are present and the patient has significant hypertension or diminished renal function, the addition of renal revascularization of at least one side to the planned aortic reconstruction may well be the best course.

Because the morbidity and mortality of simultaneous aortic operation and bilateral renal artery revascularization are increased,[166,167] the surgeon may elect to stage the renal artery and aortic procedures, performing an isolated renal artery procedure either before or after the aortic procedure, which is combined with repair of only one renal artery. In such situations, the use of extra-anatomic means of renal artery revascularization, such as through the splenic or hepatic arteries, may be particularly helpful in avoiding the necessity of operation in a previously dissected field.[172-174]

Thoracic Aorta-to-Femoral Artery Bypass

In certain good-risk patients in whom standard abdominal aortic reconstruction is contraindicated or judged to be technically challenging because of hostile abdominal pathology, bypass procedures may be based on the thoracic aorta. Such procedures may combine the advantages of extra-anatomic grafts, in that they (1) enable the surgeon to avoid operating in a hostile abdomen or potentially unsuitable abdominal aorta but (2) perhaps may be more durable than axillo-bifemoral bypass. Although used relatively infrequently, grafts based on the thoracic aorta may have appeal for selected clinical circumstances, including

- Avoidance of the abdominal aorta that has already undergone multiple procedures
- Potential sepsis
- Radiation therapy
- Presence of abdominal stoma
- Technically difficult cases in which the aorta is totally occluded to a juxtarenal level

Most such bypasses originate from the lower descending thoracic aorta and are tunneled through the diaphragm and retroperitoneum to the iliofemoral vessels.[175,176] Use of the ascending aorta[177] or supraceliac aorta[178] as an alternative inflow site for such grafts has also been described. Usually, a partially occluding clamp can be used for construction of the proximal anastomosis, thereby preserving renal blood flow and minimizing the risks of postoperative renal failure. A bifurcated aortic prosthetic graft may be used, or a unilateral graft may be brought to the left iliac or femoral artery and combined with a standard subcutaneous femoro-femoral crossover bypass to the right groin. Good long-term patency rates have generally been reported for all of these reconstructions, which should be kept in mind for possible use in the selected clinical circumstances mentioned.

■ RESULTS OF DIRECT AORTOILIOFEMORAL RECONSTRUCTION

Currently, generally excellent early and late results of direct aortoiliofemoral reconstructions can be anticipated and are achievable at highly acceptable patient morbidity and mortality rates. A consensus of several large series in the modern era clearly supports this statement, indicating that it is reasonable to expect an 85% to 90% graft patency rate at 5 years and 70% to 75% at 10 years.[2,68-73,132,179] Perioperative mortality rates well below 3% are now commonplace in many centers. The mortality risk for direct reconstructions in patients with relatively localized aortoiliac disease can be expected to be extremely low, whereas those patients with multilevel disease and associated occlusive lesions in coronary, carotid, and visceral vessels quite naturally have a somewhat higher mortality risk. For this latter group of patients, it is hoped that continued improvement of screening methods for associated disease and continued refinements of anesthetic management, intraoperative monitoring, and postoperative intensive care can further reduce the risk of serious morbidity and mortality.

Long-term survival of these patients continues to be compromised, however. The cumulative long-term survival rate for patients undergoing aortoiliac reconstruction remains some 10 to 15 years less than what might be anticipated for a normal age- and sex-matched population. Overall, about 25% to 30% of patients are dead at 5 years, and 50% to 60% will have died at 10 years.[11,68,70] Not unexpectedly, most late deaths are attributable to atherosclerotic heart disease. Patients with more localized aortoiliac disease, who have a lower incidence of coronary artery disease, distal occlusive disease, or diabetes, appear to have a much more favorable long-term prognosis, approaching that of a normal population at risk.[11,132]

■ COMPLICATIONS AND THEIR PREVENTION

Early Complications

Hemorrhage

With current surgical methods and reliable prosthetic grafts and suture materials, early postoperative hemorrhage is a relatively unusual complication (1% to 2%), most often the consequence of some technical oversight or abnormality of the coagulation mechanism.[180] Gentle surgical technique and proper methods of graft insertion are obviously crucial in avoiding such difficulties. Preoperative routine screening for coagulation abnormalities is essential.

Most currently applied reconstructive techniques emphasize minimal dissection, sufficient only to achieve adequate exposure for securing proper vascular control and graft insertion. Appropriate efforts at hemostasis during dissection are generally easier than localization and securing of bleeding points at the conclusion of the procedure. Normal blood pressure should be restored at the completion of the vascular reconstruction so that an insecure anastomotic suture line or an improperly controlled bleeder is not overlooked.

Leaks from vascular anastomoses, particularly those that are due to tearing of sutures in a fragile arterial wall, may acquire additional sutures, frequently with Teflon pledgets (see Fig. 79-10). Arterial inflow should be clamped briefly while such additional repair sutures are being placed and tied to avoid further tears. In many instances, operative bleeding may be due to injury of associated venous structures. Familiarity with the major venous anomalies is important to avoid such injuries.[181] If venous injury is present, bleeding is best controlled by gentle finger tamponade and fine vascular sutures rather than by application of clamps, which may only enlarge the defect in the vein.

Adequate reversal of heparinization after graft insertion is achieved by administration of protamine sulfate; however, considerable variations in individual responses to heparin exist. Monitoring of the activated clotting time before and after heparin administration may be helpful in determination of the proper dose of intraoperative heparin and judgment about the adequacy of its reversal before wound closure.

By far, the most common acquired coagulation deficiency leading to bleeding problems during aortic operations is dilutional coagulopathy. If intraoperative blood loss is excessive and large amounts of avascular fluids and bank blood have been used during surgery, administration of fresh frozen plasma and platelet concentrates is helpful and important and is often guided by serial testing of coagulation parameters.

Finally, prompt recognition of a patient's ongoing volume requirements in the intensive care unit, with early appropriate reoperation as necessary, is essential.

Limb Ischemia

Acute limb ischemia occurring shortly after aortic operation for occlusive disease may be caused either by acute thrombosis of the reconstruction or by more distal thromboembolic complications.[180] Such difficulties are generally recognized from (1) the failure of expected pulses to return after operation, (2) the acute loss of previously present pulses, or (3) the ischemic deterioration of the involved extremity. Often this determination may be difficult in patients undergoing operation for multilevel disease, in whom re-establishment of peripheral pulses is not anticipated. In such patients, the use of Doppler signals, limb pressures, and distal pulse volume recordings may be quite helpful. In many patients, the perfusion of distal extremities should continue to improve during the early postoperative period, and a 4- to 6-hour interval of close observation is often justified as long as the femoral pulse remains palpable. Careful clinical judgment, however, is required.

If the diagnosis of acute limb ischemia is established, the patient should be returned promptly to the operating room. If aortoiliac endarterectomy has been performed, the usual causative factors are inadequacies in termination of the endarterectomy at the iliac bifurcation, leading to intimal flaps or constrictive closure of the arteriotomy at this point. In many cases, the basic underlying problem is inappropriate application of the endarterectomy procedure itself in patients with disease extending down the iliac vessels. Generally in such cases, the abdominal incision must be reopened for direct inspection of the endarterectomized segments.

If an aortoiliac bypass graft has been inserted, the surgeon may elect to first explore the groin and pass balloon embolectomy catheters, but often, direct re-exploration is most appropriate. More commonly, an aortofemoral graft will have been extended below the inguinal ligament, and the distal anastomosis can be directly examined by reopening of the groin incision. Acute thrombosis of an aortofemoral graft limb in the early perioperative period occurs in 1% to 3% of patients.[182] Kinking or twisting of the graft limb in the retroperitoneal tunnel may be responsible for acute graft occlusion; most often, however, technical anastomotic problems at the distal femoral artery are responsible. Thrombectomy of the graft limb is easily carried out through a transverse opening in the distal graft hood, which also allows inspection of the interior of the anastomosis and distal passage of embolectomy catheters into the superficial and deep systems. In the common clinical situation of associated superficial femoral artery occlusion, unobstructed runoff into the profunda femoris artery must be ensured. If the patient has a small or diseased profunda femoris artery and inadequate runoff is believed to be the reason for acute graft limb thrombosis, a distal bypass graft may be required to ensure adequate distal runoff.[182]

Thromboembolic mechanisms of acute limb ischemia may be more common than previously believed.[183,184] Clot or atheromatous debris may be dislodged from proximal vessels by injudicious application of clamps, or clot that has formed in the graft limb at the time of implantation may be inadequately flushed before flow is restored to the extremity. The surgeon can best prevent thromboembolic occlusion by (1) minimizing manipulation of the aorta, (2) using full systemic heparinization during the procedure, (3) carefully placing gentle vascular clamps on nondiseased portions of the vascular tree, and (4) carefully flushing the reconstruction before restoring flow.

Thromboembolic occlusions of the graft limb or larger outflow vessels may generally be successfully corrected by passage of embolectomy catheters. However, more distal thromboembolic complications may be much more difficult to deal with surgically and are far better prevented, if possible. A truly distal occlusion, involving tibial or digital arteries and colloquially referred to as "trash foot," is a well-recognized and frustrating problem. If pedal pulses are absent, it appears advisable to explore the distal popliteal artery, allowing passage of embolectomy catheters down each of the distal branches of the popliteal artery into the foot and thereby enhancing the possibility of retrieving thrombotic material and improving perfusion. Often, however, if the tibial vessels are patent and the occlusive debris is located in inaccessible foot and digital vessels, little can be done. Systemic heparinization or the use of intravenous low-molecular-weight dextran is often recommended but of no proven benefit. The use of a distally injected thrombolytic agent such as streptokinase or urokinase (see Chapters 53 and 65) also has been suggested but remains of uncertain benefit.[185,186]

Renal Failure

In the absence of significant preoperative renal functional impairment, postoperative renal failure following elective aortic reconstruction for occlusive disease is currently an unusual event. In their review of the complications of abdominal aortic reconstruction in 557 patients at the Cleveland Clinic, 173 of whom underwent operation for aortoiliac occlusive disease, Diehl and associates[187] found that postoperative acute renal failure (ARF) developed in 4.6% of patients but was not fatal in any. In other reports, the incidence of ARF after elective aortic surgery (both for aneurysm and for occlusive disease) ranges from 1% to 8%, with an overall mortality rate of 40%. Emergency aortic surgery is associated with a higher incidence of ARF, with 50% to 90% mortality.[188]

The most common cause is diminished renal perfusion secondary to a decrease in cardiac output and hypovolemia, which may occur during certain phases of aortic surgery, particularly at the time of declamping. Renal cortical vasospasm secondary to aortic clamping may also contribute by reducing glomerular filtration. Depending on the anatomy of occlusive disease and the required repair, a period of suprarenal clamping may be necessary, or juxtarenal disease may result in intraoperative embolization of the renal circulation. The latter mechanism, producing thrombotic embolization or atheroembolization to the renal circulation, has been recognized as an increasingly important technical point of aortic reconstruction. Hence, in cases of known associated juxtarenal or pararenal atheromatous disease, aortic clamping is more safely accomplished at a supraceliac level, where concomitant occlusive disease is considerably less prevalent. The period of interrupted blood flow is almost certainly safer and better tolerated than causing embolization of atherothrombotic debris into the renal circulation or elevating atherosclerotic perirenal plaques, which may impede renal blood flow.

Other possible mechanisms of acute postoperative renal failure are contrast-induced renal dysfunction following preoperative diagnostic arteriography and the use of potentially nephrotoxic antibiotics or other drugs. Finally, myoglobinuria may result from reperfusion of severely ischemic limbs and the myoglobin may precipitate in renal tubules, resulting in postoperative ARF.[188]

The current low rate of renal failure after elective aortic surgery is attributable to appreciation of the importance of maintaining appropriate intravascular volume through (1) liberal use of intravenous fluids, (2) careful monitoring of pulmonary capillary wedge pressure during operation, and (3) avoidance of declamping hypotension.[188,189] Administration of intravenous mannitol, furosemide, or both to induce a brisk diuresis before aortic clamping is also used prophylactically by many surgeons, although the benefit of these agents in the prevention of renal failure is uncertain. Similarly, perioperative infusion of low-dose dopamine is believed by some to aid renal blood flow and protect against postoperative dysfunction.

Milder forms of oliguric and nonoliguric renal dysfunction may be observed but rarely require dialysis support. Renal deterioration is much more common in patients with abnormal renal function before operation and in poorly prepared or dehydrated patients requiring emergency reconstruction for acute aortic thrombosis. Most serious and probably irreversible are instances of renal failure secondary to embolization of thrombotic or atheromatous debris into the renal circulation. As noted previously, this complication can be prevented by avoidance of excessive manipulation of the diseased aorta or by protection of the renal arteries with temporary clamping whenever extensive juxtarenal disease makes it advisable.

Intestinal Ischemia

Intestinal ischemia following aortic reconstruction may occur in approximately 2% of cases[21,190,191]; it almost always affects the colon, particularly the rectosigmoid region. The incidence of lesser degrees of ischemic colitis, involving only mucosal ischemia and resulting in less devastating consequences than transmural infarction or perforation, is undoubtedly more common, particularly if postoperative colonoscopy is used to identify patients with subclinical ischemic colitis. Small bowel ischemia following aortic operation is distinctly uncommon. Intestinal ischemia is more common after aneurysm repair than after reconstruction for occlusive disease, perhaps owing to a greater incidence of intraoperative hypotension and less well-developed collateral networks.

The etiology of intestinal ischemia is often multifactorial, but it almost always involves a critical loss of blood flow to the involved intestinal segment due to (1) interruption of primary or collateral arterial flow to the bowel wall or (2) operative atheroembolization. Other predisposing causes involve perioperative hypotension and hypoperfusion, manipulative trauma, and prior gastrointestinal tract surgery that has interrupted vital collateral pathways.

Recognition of anatomic situations more likely to result in intestinal ischemia following aortic operation is vital. Hence, the surgeon must examine the preoperative arteriogram for associated occlusive lesions affecting the celiac axis, the superior mesenteric arteries, or both, and for a patent and enlarged IMA, sacrifice of which probably would lead to colon ischemia. Identification of patients with such anatomic patterns of disease allows preservation of the IMA or concomitant revascularization of the superior mesenteric or celiac branches and, it is hoped, prevention of intestinal ischemia.

The status of the hypogastric arteries should be ascertained on the aortogram, and the arterial reconstruction should be designed to maintain flow through at least one of these arteries by direct revascularization or retrograde perfusion from a femoral anastomosis, if possible, especially if a patent IMA must be ligated. If IMA ligation is required, it should be carried out from within the aortic lumen or immediately adjacent to the aortic wall to avoid injury to the ascending and descending branches of the IMA, which then assume greater importance as collateral pathways. Some surgeons have suggested reimplantation of all patent IMAs during aortic reconstruction to minimize the risk of colon ischemia.[192] Although most surgeons do not believe that this procedure is routinely necessary, careful evaluation and assessment are vital whenever a patent IMA is interrupted, because such interruption is the most common identifiable factor in the development of clinically significant postoperative colon ischemia and reimplantation is advisable in selected circumstances.[190] Undue traction on the left colon mesentery must also be avoided.

Intraoperative recognition of intestinal ischemia may be difficult. Although various measures for detecting its presence intraoperatively have been reported, including use of a sterile Doppler probe, measurement of IMA stump pressure, determination of intracolonic pH or transcolonic oxygen saturation, and injection of intravenous fluorescein, none has been found both practical and entirely reliable.[21,191-193] If colon ischemia is recognized, the surgeon must attempt to increase colonic perfusion through revascularization of the IMA by reimplantation or a short vein graft, superior mesenteric artery bypass, or hypogastric revascularization, depending on the individual circumstances and the anatomic distribution of disease.

Postoperatively, early diagnosis is the key to effective management of intestinal ischemia. Diagnosis often depends on a high level of clinical suspicion and may be facilitated by prompt sigmoidoscopy or colonoscopy. Clinical manifestations immediately after surgery are often masked by incisional discomfort and other problems common to the postoperative period. Findings that suggest the presence of intestinal ischemia include

- Diarrhea, either liquid brown or bloody
- Progressive abdominal distention
- Increasing signs of sepsis and peritonitis
- Unexplained metabolic acidosis

Initial supportive care, gastrointestinal tract decompression, and intravenous antibiotic therapy may be used, with careful observation and frequent re-examination, but any evidence of clinical deterioration indicates the need for prompt operative intervention. Resection of nonviable bowel, end-sigmoid colostomy, and formation of a Hartmann pouch are generally necessary. Avoidance of graft exposure during such maneuvers, if feasible, is obviously crucial. Mortality rates for transmural colon infarction remain significant, approximating 50% to 75% in many series.[180,190]

Spinal Cord Ischemia

Spinal cord ischemia, resulting in paraplegia or paraparesis, is fortunately an unusual complication of aortoiliac surgery for occlusive disease. Szilagyi and associates[194] observed an incidence of 0.25% after 3164 operations involving temporary occlusion of the abdominal aorta, all of which were performed for aneurysmal disease. The incidence of spinal cord ischemia after intervention for ruptured aneurysms is 10 times higher than that after operations for unruptured aneurysmal lesions.[180,194]

Although the etiology of paraplegia is multifactorial, the usual cause of spinal cord ischemia is interruption of flow through the great radicular artery of Adamkiewicz, the major source of supply to the anterior spinal artery at the lower end of the cord. This vessel normally originates from one of the paired suprarenal intercostal arteries from T8 to T12, but it occasionally has a lower origin. In the latter situation, surgical interruption or thrombosis that is due to prolonged aortic occlusion or intraoperative embolization is believed to cause distal spinal cord ischemia. Because this anatomic variability is unpredictable, the occurrence of spinal cord ischemia is generally considered unavoidable. Preoperative or intraoperative demonstration of the major blood supply to the lower spinal cord is difficult, impractical, and potentially dangerous. Several reports have also emphasized the importance of acute interruption of the pelvic circulation or atheroembolization through the pelvic arteries as another possible mechanism of ischemic neurologic injury.[99,100,195]

Currently, it is the consensus of almost all vascular surgeons that this tragic occurrence is essentially unpredictable and therefore not totally preventable in association with infrarenal aortic reconstruction. Monitoring of somatosensory evoked potentials during thoracic aortic surgery has been shown to detect cord ischemia. Practical application of this technique to abdominal aortic reconstruction, however, has not been established. Because of the potential importance of pelvic collateral circulation in a patient with chronic stenosis or occlusion of the artery of Adamkiewicz, preservation of pelvic blood flow through revascularization of at least one hypogastric network or other technical modifications of the operative procedure is advisable; this strategy is similar to the strategies for minimizing the occurrence of postoperative colon ischemia. When ischemic injury to the spinal cord does occur, treatment is confined to supportive care and rehabilitation.

Some investigators recommend the administration of high-dose intravenous steroids to decrease cord edema with the hope of improving perfusion, but the value of this treatment is unproven and controversial.[100] The severity of paraplegia is often directly related to postoperative mortality. In the experience at the Henry Ford Hospital reported by Elliott and coworkers,[196] 76% of patients in whom the initial neurologic deficit was complete died; there were only two complete neurologic recoveries in this group and one partial recovery. In contrast, of the patients in whom the initial loss was only partial motor or sensory loss or both, 24% died and some degree of recovery was noted in all but one case.

Ureteral Injury

Because the ureter lies immediately adjacent to the operative field and crosses directly anterior to the iliac artery bifurcation, the surgeon must constantly keep in mind the possibility of lacerating, dividing, or ligating the ureter and must avoid injuring it during dissection, graft tunneling, and wound closure. This statement is particularly true of any reoperative surgery. A thorough knowledge of the anatomic relationship of the ureter at the level of the iliac bifurcation is essential. Direct injury to the ureter is best avoided by keeping dissection close to the arterial wall and elevating the ureter from the iliac vessels during retroperitoneal tunneling, particularly during reoperative aortic surgery. Identification of the ureters during closure of the retroperitoneum, particularly the right ureter, is essential to avoid including them in the retroperitoneal closure.

Various degrees of hydronephrosis resulting from ureteral obstruction may also be seen in the late follow-up period, and this complication is probably an underdiagnosed entity. It may occur in up to 10% to 20% of patients but is often asymptomatic and usually is not detected unless intravenous pyelography, ultrasonography, or CT scanning is carried out, often for other purposes.[197,198] Such ureteral obstruction is most often mild and of no clinical consequence. It is occasionally attributable to placement of the graft limb anterior to the ureter, which entraps the ureter between the graft and the native artery, but is most commonly due to compression by fibrotic changes caused by tissue reaction to the implanted graft. Occasionally, however, hydronephrosis may be a marker of graft complications such as pseudoaneurysm formation or graft infection.[199,200] Such potential problems need to be carefully considered in patients presenting with severe or symptomatic ureteral obstruction, and the position of the ureters should be assessed before direct reoperative aortic surgery is performed. Occasionally, preoperative placement of ureteral stents is helpful in this regard.

Late Complications

Despite the generally excellent long-term results of aortoiliofemoral reconstruction, late graft-related complications continue to occur throughout the follow-up period and detract from long-term effectiveness of the procedure. In the review of the late outcome of aortoiliac operation for occlusive disease by van der Akker and associates from Leiden,[201] secondary operations for late complications such as reocclusion, pseudoaneurysms, and infection were necessary in 21% of 727 patients observed over a 22-year period and contributed significantly (12.1%) to the causes of late deaths.

Graft Occlusion

The most frequent late complication of aortic operation for occlusive disease is graft thrombosis.[180] Although the exact incidence of late graft occlusions varies from report to report, occlusion may be anticipated in 5% to 10% of patients within the first 5 years after operation and in 15% to 30% of patients observed for 10 years or more postoperatively.[202-204] In our experience, the average interval from original graft insertion to occlusion was 33.8 months.[202]

Most commonly, occlusion affects one limb of an aortofemoral graft, with the contralateral graft limb retaining patency. The resulting lower extremity ischemia is often more severe than that prior to the primary procedure, and not infrequently, urgent reoperation is required for limb salvage. Although thrombosis of an anastomotic aneurysm, compression due to fibrotic scarring, dilatation or degeneration of the graft, hypercoagulable states, or low-output syndromes may occasionally be responsible, most late graft failures are due to recurrent occlusive disease, usually occurring at or just beyond the distal anastomosis. If aortoiliac endarterectomy or aortoiliac bypass grafting has been performed, progressive occlusive disease in the external iliac artery is commonly responsible.[101,102] In the most commonly encountered situation, occlusion of an aortofemoral graft limb, occlusive lesions interfering with profunda femoris artery runoff are causative, because most patients undergoing aortofemoral grafting have preexisting chronic occlusion of the superficial femoral artery.[104,202-205] Recurrent disease compromising the proximal aortic anastomosis generally leads to failure of the entire reconstruction and usually results because the surgeon did not carry the original procedure high enough in the infrarenal aorta.[110] Graft failure, particularly that due to recurrent or progressive inflow or outflow tract occlusive disease, is much more likely to occur in patients with ongoing risk factors for atherosclerosis, especially those who continue cigarette smoking postoperatively.[204,206-210] This fact deserves repeated emphasis to patients.

Reoperation for occlusion of the entire primary reconstruction almost always requires another aortofemoral grafting if the patient is an appropriate candidate.[102] Axillobifemoral grafting may be considered in the patient for whom a repeated graft procedure poses a high risk. If various technical problems suggest that direct reoperation on the infrarenal abdominal aorta is ill advised or unduly hazardous, the supraceliac aorta, the descending thoracic aorta, or even the ascending thoracic aorta may occasionally be used for the site of proximal anastomosis in reoperative bypass procedures, as previously described.[175-178]

For unilateral limb failure of an aortoiliac procedure, direct reoperation, often employing a retroperitoneal approach, is generally feasible, with extension of the graft to the femoral level. Alternatively, femorofemoral transpubic grafting may be performed if the contralateral iliofemoral system is widely patent.[211]

For unilateral occlusion of one limb of an aortobifemoral graft, inflow can frequently be restored by thrombectomy of the graft limb with the use of a balloon embolectomy catheter.[202,205] A thromboendarterectomy stripper is often required to complete extraction of the adherent fibrinothrombotic plug.[205,212] The modification of the standard Fogarty balloon catheter known as the *graft thrombectomy catheter* also appears to be quite useful for adequate removal of such adherent clots.[213] Once inflow has been reestablished, revascularization of the profunda femoris artery by means of profundaplasty of varying extent or extension of a graft to the more distal profunda femoris artery (Fig. 79-13) is used to restore reliable deep femoral artery outflow.[104,202,205,214-216] In instances in which the profunda femoris artery is small or is extensively diseased, addition of a femoropopliteal or femorotibial bypass may be required to provide adequate outflow and to maintain patency of the

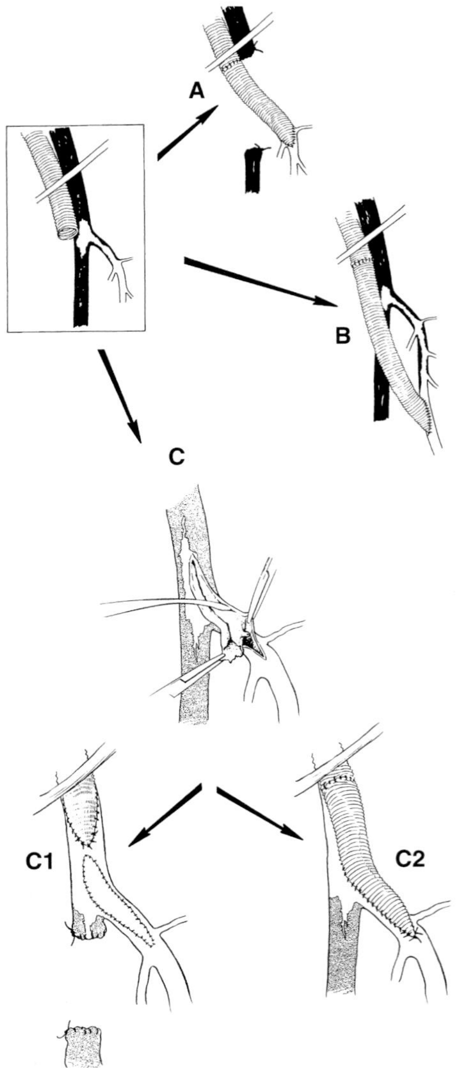

FIGURE 79-13 Options for outflow reconstruction during reoperation for aortofemoral graft limb occlusion. **A,** Addition of a short extension of new prosthetic graft end to end to the profunda femoris artery below orificial disease. **B,** If more extensive disease is present, insertion of a longer new graft segment as a bypass to the distal profunda femoris artery is preferred. **C,** Most frequently, endarterectomy of the common femoral artery and profunda femoris artery is performed, with a separate patch closure employing autogenous or prosthetic material and graft reanastomosis above this (**C1**) or closure with the long beveled tongue of new graft segment (**C2**). (**A** to **C2**, From Brewster DC: Surgery of late aortic graft occlusion. In Bergan JJ, Yao JST [eds]: Aortic Surgery. Philadelphia, WB Saunders, 1989, p 533.)

reoperated aortofemoral graft limb. Although this decision is often a difficult one, such a bypass was used in one third of such reoperations in our experience[202] and has been advocated by other surgeons as well.[215,217]

In situations in which graft limb occlusion is more chronic and thrombectomy is not successful, a femorofemoral crossover graft from the patent contralateral graft limb is generally the most useful alternative to re-establish inflow.[150,152,154,211] Direct "redo" aortic surgery for unilateral aortofemoral graft limb occlusion, with replacement of either the entire graft or the involved graft limb, is generally unnecessary because proximal causes are infrequently responsible for unilateral failures and alternative methods of revascularizing the involved extremity are usually successful.[202,203,205]

Although such reoperative procedures are often difficult and may tax the skill and ingenuity of even the most experienced vascular surgeon, long-term results suggest that appropriate reoperation is indeed worthwhile, with highly satisfactory extension of graft patency and associated rates of limb salvage.[70,202]

Anastomotic Pseudoaneurysm

The incidence of anastomotic pseudoaneurysm formation varies between 1% and 5% and is by far most common at the femoral anastomosis of an aortofemoral graft.[70] Although numerous factors may contribute to anastomotic aneurysm formation, degenerative changes within the host arterial wall leading to weakness and dehiscence of the intact suture line appear to be most common.[218] Predisposing factors include

- Excessive tension on the anastomosis as a result of inadequate graft length
- Poor suture technique using inadequate bites of the arterial wall or excessive spacing between sutures
- A thin-walled artery

Many surgeons also believe that endarterectomy may weaken the arterial wall as a result of a reduction in tensile strength and that the incidence of subsequent pseudoaneurysm formation may be higher if anastomosis is made with such an arterial segment. Rarely, prosthetic suture materials may fracture, or degeneration may occur, leading to late suture line disruption, as was previously seen when silk sutures were used. Infection may be a contributing event and always needs to be considered as a possible etiologic factor when the surgeon is evaluating patients with even bland-appearing anastomotic aneurysms.[219]

Recognition of a femoral anastomotic aneurysm is usually quite simple because a pulsatile mass, which is occasionally tender, is noted by both the patient and the surgeon. Retroperitoneal aortic or iliac anastomotic aneurysm is much less often noted until expansion or rupture produces pain, causes graft occlusion, or erodes into an abdominal hollow viscus. If such an aneurysm is considered to be present, ultrasonography and CT scanning are reliable methods for evaluating intra-abdominal grafts and anastomoses. The true incidence of intra-abdominal anastomotic aneurysms after aortic surgery may be much higher than previously thought: a study by Edwards and coworkers[220] reported a 10% incidence at a mean interval of 12 years following initial operation. This finding suggests that ultrasonography or CT scanning should be a routine part of the late follow-up for patients with aortic grafts.

Diagnosis of a pseudoaneurysm is usually confirmed by angiography. Even if the diagnosis of a femoral anastomotic aneurysm is readily apparent, aortography is generally advisable to evaluate the proximal aortic anastomosis and to help in planning the operative procedure. Indeed, the presence of a femoral anastomotic aneurysm may be a marker for other graft-related problems. In a report from Emory University of 41 patients who had femoral pseudoaneurysm after aortobifemoral grafting, 70% had bilateral aneurysms and 17% had proximal anastomotic aneurysms.[221]

An anastomotic aneurysm should generally be repaired as soon as it is identified. Even if the aneurysm is asymptomatic, the likelihood of thrombosis or distal embolization warrants elective repair. Such repair is usually easily and successfully carried out at the groin level with the use of a short additional graft segment and reanastomosis to a somewhat more distal arterial segment, often the profunda femoris artery itself. Culture specimens should always be obtained at the time of repair to check for unrecognized infection. Results of repair are generally highly successful, especially if repair is carried out electively rather than as an emergency.[222] Once they have been repaired, anastomotic aneurysms may recur in about 5% to 10% of patients.[223] In such circumstances, occult infection must be seriously considered as a possible contributing cause.[224]

Postoperative Sexual Dysfunction

Although the physiology of penile erection is complex, involving the interaction of psychologic factors, pelvic blood flow, neurologic pathways, and hormonal mechanisms, postoperative disturbance of sexual function in a man should be recognized as a potential consequence of direct aortic operation. A detailed discussion of this topic can be found in Chapters 64 and 88.

Although a high percentage (at least 30% to 50%) of men presenting with aortoiliac occlusive disease significant enough to require surgical correction have various degrees of sexual dysfunction when they are first seen, the incidence of iatrogenic sexual disturbance after aortic reconstruction may approach 25%.[97,225,226] As popularized by DePalma and colleagues[227] and others,[225,226] a nerve-sparing approach to the infrarenal aorta that emphasizes avoidance of autonomic nerve fibers along the left lateral wall of the aorta and minimal dissection in the region of the aortic bifurcation, where such nerves usually cross the proximal common iliac arteries, is helpful. Preservation of hypogastric artery flow by a variety of techniques is also essential.[97,98,225,228,229]

Whether or not end-to-end proximal aortic anastomosis leads to a higher incidence of erectile dysfunction remains controversial. With appropriate recognition and implementation of such considerations, it is hoped that the surgeon can minimize the incidence of postoperative sexual dysfunction and actually improve sexual function in some patients.[97]

Infection

Infection following aortic reconstruction remains the most feared complication, with formidable morbidity and mortality rates. Fortunately, with current reconstructive methods and the use of prophylactic antibiotics, it remains a rare occurrence, with an incidence of 1% or less.[2,70,180,230-232]

In most series, the highest incidence of infection has been in the inguinal portion of an aortofemoral graft. Important contributing factors are

- Multiple vascular procedures
- Postoperative wound problems, such as hematoma, seroma, or lymph leakage, particularly in the groin
- Emergency operation

Infectious complications occur almost exclusively after prosthetic graft insertion, being exceedingly rare after autogenous operations such as endarterectomy.

Although graft infection is often not clinically apparent for months to years, it is generally believed that graft contamination occurs most commonly at the time of primary graft implantation. This belief emphasizes the importance of

1. Meticulous sterile technique at the time of original operation
2. Avoidance of skin contact with the prosthetic graft by use of adherent plastic drapes
3. Careful attention to hemostasis and wound closure
4. General avoidance of concomitant intra-abdominal operations, which may increase the incidence of graft contamination

Several randomized studies in the literature have documented the efficacy of antibiotic prophylaxis in reducing the incidence of vascular graft infection,[80-82] and its perioperative use in vascular reconstruction is now well accepted. Late graft infection that is due to bacteremic implantation of organisms on the luminal surface of a functioning graft is uncommon but may occur. Because current prostheses are rarely completely healed with a viable endothelial lining, antibiotic prophylaxis should probably be employed in the patient with a previously implanted graft who is exposed to the risk of bacteremia, much as it is in the patient with rheumatic valvular disease or prosthetic heart valves.

Staphylococcus aureus remains the most common responsible organism, but later experience indicates that organisms such as *Staphylococcus albus* and gram-negative bacteria are of increasing importance.[231] In patients presenting with forefoot infection or wet gangrene, it is particularly important to use appropriate specific antibiotic treatment and aggressive débridement before placement of a vascular prosthesis. Several studies have implicated the importance of bacteria in lymph nodes in the groin as the source of subsequent graft infection.[233]

Diagnosis and management of patients with infection following aortoiliofemoral reconstructive procedures are often complex and are discussed more fully in Chapter 59. Graft excision is usually required, and revascularization via remote uncontaminated routes or the use of autogenous methods of anatomic revascularization is often necessary to maintain limb viability.[180,234-239] If the patient's condition is stable and the diagnosis of graft infection is firmly established, extra-anatomic revascularization preceding graft excision appears to yield a better outcome.[240,241]

If infection appears localized, as in a single groin, for example, local measures, including antibiotic irrigation, aggressive débridement, and soft tissue coverage with a variety of rotational muscle flaps without graft removal, may sometimes be successful.[242-246] Another approach to the treatment of entirely infected aortofemoral grafts consists of graft excision and in-situ graft replacement, sometimes with "neo-aortoiliac systems" constructed from autogenous superficial femoral veins.[247]

Aortoenteric Fistula

Aortoenteric fistula and associated gastrointestinal hemorrhage are devastating complications, with a continued high incidence of death or limb loss despite efforts at their correction.[180] Communication between the aortic prosthesis and a portion of the gastrointestinal tract invariably leads to massive gastrointestinal bleeding, although initial bleeding episodes may be limited and may allow time for diagnosis and treatment. Such communications involve the third and fourth parts of the duodenum, which overlie the proximal aortic suture line in most cases, but the small bowel or colon may be involved with an iliac anastomotic point in 10% to 20% of cases. Such secondary aortoenteric fistulae must be differentiated from primary fistulae, which occur as a result of the rupture of unoperated aortic or iliac artery aneurysms into adjacent hollow organs.

Secondary aortoenteric fistula formation may occur as a result of several mechanisms. If the adjacent bowel is improperly separated from the prosthesis and suture line, fibrotic adherence and subsequent erosion may occur. In other instances, anastomotic aneurysm formation that is due to mechanical causes or infection may occur first, with subsequent erosion of the pseudoaneurysm into the gastrointestinal tract.

The diagnosis must be suspected whenever an episode of gastrointestinal hemorrhage occurs in a patient who has undergone previous aortic operation. Diagnosis is often elusive. Upper gastrointestinal radiographic evaluation may show distortion or abnormality of the retroperitoneal duodenum, or endoscopy may actually visualize the site of hemorrhage or the prosthesis itself if the distal aspects of the duodenum are examined. Aortography is often nondiagnostic, but it may demonstrate a pseudoaneurysm involving an aortic or iliac artery anastomosis. CT scanning is often helpful, demonstrating anastomotic or perigraft abnormalities.

As with all complications, such difficulties are far more easily prevented than treated. The incidence of aortoenteric fistula formation appears to be higher after end-to-side anastomosis, because it is much more difficult to cover such an anastomotic configuration with viable tissue and avoid contact with the bowel than after end-to-end proximal anastomosis.[2,4,93] In difficult situations, interposition of omentum between the graft and the duodenum is often helpful.

Standard methods of treatment for aortoenteric fistula generally require removal of all prosthetic material, closure of the infrarenal abdominal aorta, repair of the gastrointestinal tract, and revascularization by means of an extra-anatomic graft (see Chapter 61).[248-251] For minimal local sepsis, some reports advocate excision of limited portions of the graft directly in contact with the bowel lumen and in-situ repair with a new prosthetic graft, arterial homograft, or an autogenous vein "neo-aorta."[226,231-236,252-257] However, further experience is necessary to determine the safety and wisdom of such an approach in comparison with traditional removal of the graft and remote methods of revascularization. For more discussion, the reader is referred to Chapters 59, 61, and 80.

Despite advances in treatment, death or limb loss continues to occur in 50% or more of patients in whom aortoenteric fistula develops, similar to the results of management of infected aortic grafts, to which aortoenteric fistulae are closely related in terms of mechanism of occurrence and subsequent management. Mortality is often due to continued sepsis, multiorgan system failure, or disruption of the proximal aortic stump closure.

■ SUMMARY

Arteriosclerotic aortoiliac occlusive disease is a common cause of lower extremity ischemic symptoms. In most patients, occlusive lesions are multifocal, involving the lower abdominal aorta, both iliac arteries, and, frequently, the infrainguinal arterial tree. Before proceeding with aortic reconstructive surgery, the surgeon must document the hemodynamic significance of inflow disease. This may often be accomplished by careful clinical examination supplemented with vascular laboratory hemodynamic data and good arteriographic studies. If any doubt remains, however, direct measurement of FAP is helpful.

The key features of aortofemoral grafting are (1) high placement of the proximal anastomosis immediately distal to the renal arteries and (2) careful techniques of distal anastomosis, with or without profundaplasty, to achieve adequate flow into the deep femoral artery. Despite the presence of multilevel disease in most patients, a properly performed inflow operation achieves satisfactory relief of ischemic symptoms in 70% to 80% of cases. Approximately 10% to 15% of patients with advanced distal ischemia may be best managed with simultaneous inflow and outflow reconstruction, but careful patient selection is important.

Clearly, no single option for inflow revascularization is optimal in all instances. In every patient, a decision about which method is best should be made through consideration of several factors; primary factors are the extent and distribution of disease and the anticipated risk of the possible alternatives that might be used. The likely success of various methods in terms of hemodynamic improvement, symptom relief, and sustained patency can usually be predicted with relative accuracy, and such estimates must be judged in the context of patient age, expected length of survival, and specific clinical needs of each patient. Durability must often be balanced against the possible advantages of safety and expediency.

Alternative therapies have a well-established role in the management of occlusive disease of limited extent or lesser severity and in the treatment of patients in whom adverse technical challenges or high operative risk contraindicates conventional direct aortic reconstruction. Improving results of alternative therapies, and in particular the explosive growth of catheter-based treatment and increasing emphasis on less-invasive management, all have clearly contributed to some decline in the frequency of direct surgical revascularization for the treatment of aortoiliac occlusive disease.[258] However, for most patients with diffuse aortoiliac occlusive disease, aortobifemoral grafts remain the most durable and functionally effective means of revascularization and should continue to be rightfully regarded as the gold standard against which other options must be properly compared.[40] As the availability and results of alternative techniques have improved, so too has the safety of standard repair. Indeed, the very definition of a "high-risk" patient is currently much more indistinct than in previous eras. No doubt the future will bring new advances in alternative methods, but it is hoped that properly designed and performed randomized studies, outcome assessment, and cost-benefit analyses will help clarify their role. The need for such information is quite evident; without it, one of the most effective and beneficial procedures that vascular surgeons have to offer may be inappropriately abandoned because of the seductiveness of the axiom "less is best."

Finally, the alternatives for inflow revascularization may not be as competitive with one another as first seems apparent. Each has specific advantages and disadvantages and, when used in appropriate circumstances, can give excellent results. Indeed, it is this broad spectrum of options that makes treatment of aortoiliac occlusive disease one of the most successful areas of current vascular practice.

■ REFERENCES

1. DeBakey ME, Lawrie GM, Glaeser DH: Patterns of atherosclerosis and their surgical significance. Ann Surg 201:115, 1985.
2. Brewster DC, Darling RC: Optimal methods of aortoiliac reconstruction. Surgery 84:739, 1978.
3. Brewster DC: Clinical and anatomic considerations for surgery in aortoiliac disease and results of surgical treatment. Circulation 83(Suppl I):I42, 1991.
4. Darling RC, Brewster DC, Hallett JW Jr, et al: Aortoiliac reconstruction. Surg Clin North Am 59:565, 1979.
5. Cronenwett JL, Davis JT Jr, Gooch JB, et al: Aortoiliac occlusive disease in women. Surgery 88:775, 1980.
6. DeLaurentis DA, Friedmann P, Wolferth GC Jr, et al: Atherosclerosis and the hypoplastic aortoiliac system. Surgery 83:27, 1978.
7. Greenhalgh RM: Small aorta syndrome. In Bergan JJ, Yao JST (eds): Surgery of the Aorta and Its Body Branches. New York, Grune & Stratton, 1979, pp 183-190.
8. Staple TW: The solitary aortoiliac lesion. Surgery 64:569, 1968.
9. Moore WS, Cafferata HT, Hall AD, et al: In defense of grafts across the inguinal ligament. Ann Surg 168:207, 1968.
10. Mozersky DJ, Sumner DS, Strandness DE: Long-term results of reconstructive aortoiliac surgery. Am J Surg 123:503, 1972.
11. Malone JM, Moore WS, Goldstone J: Life expectancy following aortofemoral arterial grafting. Surgery 81:551, 1977.
12. Brewster DC, Waltman AC, O'Hara PJ, et al: Femoral artery pressure measurement during aortography. Circulation 60(Suppl I):120, 1979.
13. Sobinsky KR, Borozan PG, Gray B, et al: Is femoral pulse palpation accurate in assessing the hemodynamic significance of aortoiliac occlusive disease? Am J Surg 148:214, 1984.
14. Brewster DC, Perler BA, Robison JG, et al: Aortofemoral graft for multilevel occlusive disease: Predictors of success and need for distal bypass. Arch Surg 117:1593, 1982.
15. Johnston KW, Demorais D, Colapinto RI: Difficulty in assessing disease by clinical and arteriographic methods. Angiology 32:609, 1981.

16. Karmody AM, Powers FR, Monaco VJ, et al: "Blue toe" syndrome: An indication for limb salvage surgery. Arch Surg 111:1263, 1976.
17. Kempczinski RF: Lower extremity arterial emboli from ulcerating atherosclerotic plaques. JAMA 241:807, 1979.
18. Goodreau JJ, Creasy JK, Flanigan DP, et al: Rational approach to the differentiation of vascular and neurogenic claudication. Surgery 84:749, 1978.
19. Kempczinski RF: Clinical application of noninvasive testing in extremity arterial insufficiency. In Kempczinski RF, Yao JST (eds): Practical Noninvasive Vascular Diagnosis. Chicago, Year Book, 1982, pp 343-365.
20. Raines JK, Darling RC, Buth J, et al: Vascular laboratory criteria for the management of peripheral vascular disease of the lower extremities. Surgery 79:21, 1976.
21. Ernst CB: Prevention of intestinal ischemia following abdominal aortic reconstruction. Surgery 93:102, 1983.
22. Mason RA, Arbeit LA, Giron F: Renal dysfunction after arteriography. JAMA 253:1001, 1985.
23. Calligaro KD, Dandura R, Dougherty MJ, et al: Same-day admissions and other cost-saving strategies for elective aortoiliac surgery. J Vasc Surg 25:141, 1997.
24. Cambria RP, Kaufman JA, L'Italien GJ, et al: Magnetic resonance angiography in the management of lower extremity arterial occlusive disease: A prospective study. J Vasc Surg 25:380, 1997.
25. Edelman RR: MR angiography: Present and future. AJR Am J Roentgenol 161:1, 1993.
26. Raptopoulos V, Rosen MP, Kent KC, et al: Sequential helical CT angiography of aortoiliac disease. AJR Am J Roentgenol 166:1347, 1996.
27. Bostrom AA, Karacagil S, Hellberg A, et al: Surgical reconstruction without preoperative angiography in patients with aortoiliac occlusive disease. Ann Vasc Surg 16:273, 2002.
28. Reidy NC, Walden R, Abbott WA, et al: Anatomic localization of atherosclerotic lesions by hemodynamic tests. Arch Surg 116:1041, 1981.
29. Lynch TG, Hobson RW, Wright CB, et al: Interpretations of Doppler segmental pressures in peripheral vascular occlusive disease. Arch Surg 119:465, 1984.
30. Rutherford RB, Lowenstein DH, Klein MF: Combining segmental systolic pressures and plethysmography to diagnose arterial occlusive disease of the legs. Am J Surg 138:211, 1979.
31. Thiele BL, Bandyk DF, Zierler RE, et al: A systematic approach to the assessment of aortoiliac disease. Arch Surg 118:477, 1983.
32. Kohler TR, Nance DR, Cramer MM, et al: Duplex scanning for diagnosis of aortoiliac and femoropopliteal disease: A prospective study. Circulation 76:1074, 1987.
33. Bruins Slot HB, Strijbosch L, Greep JM: Interobserver variability in single-plane aortography. Surgery 90:497, 1981.
34. Flanigan DP, Tullis JP, Streeter VL: Multiple subcritical arterial stenosis: Effect on poststenotic pressure and flow. Ann Surg 186:663, 1977.
35. Brener BJ, Raines JK, Darling RC, et al: Measurement of systolic femoral artery pressure during reactive hyperemia: An estimate of aortoiliac disease. Circulation 49/50(Suppl II):259, 1974.
36. Flanigan DP, Williams LR, Schwartz JA, et al: Hemodynamic evaluation of the aortoiliac system based on pharmacologic vasodilatation. Surgery 93:709, 1983.
37. Moore WS, Hall AD: Unrecognized aortoiliac stenosis: A physiologic approach to the diagnosis. Arch Surg 103:633, 1971.
38. Kikta MJ, Flanigan DP, Bishara RA, et al: Long-term follow-up of patients having infrainguinal bypass performed below stenotic but hemodynamically normal aortoiliac vessels. J Vasc Surg 5:319, 1987.
39. Flanigan DP, Ryan TJ, Williams LR, et al: Aortofemoral or femoropopliteal revascularization? A prospective evaluation of the papaverine test. J Vasc Surg 1:215, 1984.
40. Brewster DC: Current controversies in the management of aortoiliac occlusive disease. J Vasc Surg 25:365, 1997.
41. Coffman JD: Vasodilator drugs in peripheral vascular disease. N Engl J Med 300:713, 1979.
42. Porter JM, Cutler BS, Lee BY, et al: Pentoxifylline efficacy in the treatment of intermittent claudication: Multicenter controlled double-blind trial with objective assessment of chronic occlusive arterial disease patients. Am Heart J 104:66, 1982.
43. Dawson DL, Cutler BS, Meissner MH, et al. Cilostazol has beneficial effects in treatment of intermittent claudication: Results from a multicenter randomized, prospective, double-blind trial. Circulation 98:678, 1998.
44. Strandness DE Jr, Dalman RL, Panian S, et al: Effect of cilostazol in patients with intermittent claudication: A randomized, double-blind, placebo-controlled study. Vasc Endovasc Surg 2:83, 2002.
45. Thompson PD, Zimet R, Forbes WP, Zhang P: Meta-analysis of results from eight randomized, placebo-controlled trials on the effect of cilostazol on patients with intermittent claudication. Am J Cardiol 90:1314, 2002.
46. TransAtlantic Intersociety Consensus (TASC): Management of peripheral arterial disease. J Vasc Surg 31:S97, 2000.
47. Johnston KW, Rae M, Hogg-Johnston SA, et al: Five-year results of a prospective study of percutaneous transluminal angioplasty. Ann Surg 206:403, 1987.
48. Johnston KW: Iliac arteries: Reanalysis of results of balloon angioplasty. Radiology 186:207, 1993.
49. Brewster DC, Cambria RP, Darling RC, et al: Long-term results of combined iliac balloon angioplasty and distal surgical revascularization. Ann Surg 210:324, 1989.
50. Brewster DC: The role of angioplasty to improve inflow for infrainguinal bypasses. Eur J Vasc Surg 9:262, 1995.
51. Faries PL, Brophy D, LoGerfo FW, et al: Combined iliac angioplasty and infrainguinal revascularization surgery are effective in diabetic patients with multilevel arterial disease. Ann Vasc Surg 15:67, 2001.
52. Nelson PR, Powell RJ, Schermerhorn ML, et al: Early results of external iliac artery stenting combined with common femoral artery endarterectomy. J Vasc Surg 35:1107, 2002.
53. Ballard JL, Bergan JJ, Singh P, et al: Aortoiliac stent deployment versus surgical reconstruction: Analysis of outcome and cost. J Vasc Surg 28:94, 1998.
54. Timaran CH, Prault TL, Stevens SL, et al: Iliac artery stenting versus surgical reconstruction for TASC (Transatlantic Inter-Society Consensus) type B and type C iliac lesions. J Vasc Surg 38:272, 2003.
55. Powell RJ, Fillinger M, Bettman M, et al: The durability of endovascular treatment of multisegment iliac occlusive disease. J Vasc Surg 31:1178, 2000.
56. Rutherford RB: Options in the surgical management of aorto-iliac occlusive disease: A changing perspective. Cardiovasc Surg 7:5, 1999.
57. Schermerhorn ML, Cronenwett JL, Baldwin JC: Open surgical repair versus endovascular therapy for chronic lower extremity occlusive disease. Annu Rev Med 54:269, 2003.
58. Sanchez LA, Wain RA, Veith FJ, et al: Endovascular grafting for aortoiliac occlusive disease. Semin Vasc Surg 10:297, 1997.
59. Wain RA, Veith FJ, Marin ML, et al: Analysis of endovascular graft treatment for aortoiliac occlusive disease: What is its role based upon midterm results? Ann Surg 230:145, 1999.
60. Ali AT, Modrall JC, Lopez J, et al: Emerging role of endovascular grafts in complex aortoiliac occlusive disease. J Vasc Surg 38:486, 2003.
61. Piotrowski JJ, Pearce WH, Jones DN, et al: Aortobifemoral bypass: The operation of choice for unilateral iliac occlusion? J Vasc Surg 8:211, 1988.
62. Passman MA, Taylor LM Jr, Moneta GL, et al: Comparison of axillofemoral and aortofemoral bypass for aortoiliac disease. J Vasc Surg 23:263, 1996.
63. Dion Ym, Gracia CR, Estakhri M, et al: Totally laparoscopic aortobifemoral bypass: A review of 10 patients. Surg Laparosc Endosc 8:165, 1998.
64. Ahn SS, Hiyama DT, Rudkin GH, et al: Laparoscopic aortobifemoral bypass. J Vasc Surg 26:128, 1997.

65. Voorhees AB Jr, Jaretzki A III, Blakemore AH: Use of tubes constructed from Vinyon "N" cloth in bridging arterial defects: Preliminary report. Ann Surg 135:332, 1952.
66. Edwards SW, Lyons C: Three years' experience with peripheral arterial grafts of crimped nylon and Teflon. Surg Gynecol Obstet 107:62, 1958.
67. DeBakey ML, Cooley DA: Clinical application of a new flexible knitted Dacron arterial substitute. Am Surg 24:862, 1958.
68. Crawford ES, Bomberger RA, Glaeser DH, et al: Aortoiliac occlusive disease: Factors influencing survival and function following reconstructive operation over a twenty-five year period. Surgery 90:1555, 1981.
69. Malone JM, Moore WS, Goldstone J: The natural history of bilateral aortofemoral bypass grafts for ischemia of the lower extremities. Arch Surg 110:1300, 1975.
70. Szilagyi DE, Hageman JH, Smith RF, et al: A thirty-year survey of the reconstructive surgical treatment of aortoiliac occlusive disease. J Vasc Surg 3:421, 1986.
71. Nevelsteen A, Wouters L, Suy R: Aortofemoral Dacron reconstruction for aorto-iliac occlusive disease: A 25-year survey. Eur J Vasc Surg 5:179, 1991.
72. Poulias GE, Doundoulakis N, Prombonas E, et al: Aorto-femoral bypass and determinants of early success and late favorable outcome: Experience with 1000 consecutive cases. J Cardiovasc Surg 33:664, 1992.
73. Brewster DC, Cooke JC: Longevity of aortofemoral bypass grafts. In Yao JST, Pearce WH (eds): Long-Term Results in Vascular Surgery. Norwalk, CT, Appleton & Lange, 1993, pp 149-161.
74. Brewster DC, Edwards JP: Cardiopulmonary complications related to vascular surgery. In Bernhard VM, Towne JB (eds): Complications in Vascular Surgery. St. Louis, Quality Medical, 1991, pp 23-41.
75. Hertzer NR, Beven EG, Young JR, et al: Coronary artery disease in peripheral vascular patients: A classification of 1000 coronary angiograms and results of surgical management. Ann Surg 199:223, 1984.
76. Brewster DC, Boucher CA, Okada RD, et al: Selection of patients for preoperative coronary angiography: Use of dipyridamole-stress thallium myocardial imaging. J Vasc Surg 2:504, 1985.
77. Eagle KA, Coley CM, Newell JB, et al: Combining clinical and thallium data optimizes preoperative assessment of cardiac risk before major vascular surgery. Ann Intern Med 110:859, 1989.
78. Cambria RP, Brewster DC, Abbott WM, et al: The impact of selective use of dipyridamole-thallium scans and surgical factors on the current morbidity of aortic surgery. J Vasc Surg 15:43, 1992.
79. Taylor LM, Yeager RA, Moneta GL, et al: The incidence of perioperative myocardial infarction in general vascular surgery. J Vasc Surg 151:52, 1992.
80. Kaiser AB, Clayson KR, Mulherin JL, et al: Antibiotic prophylaxis in vascular surgery. Ann Surg 188:283, 1978.
81. Pitt HA, Postier RH, MacGowan WL, et al: Prophylactic antibiotics in vascular surgery: Topical, systemic, or both? Ann Surg 192:356, 1980.
82. Hasselgren PO, Ivarsson L, Risberg B, et al: Effects of prophylactic antibiotics in vascular surgery: A prospective, randomized, double-blind study. Ann Surg 200:86, 1984.
83. dos Santos JC: Sur la desobstruction des thromboses arterielles anciennes. Mem Acad Chir 73:409, 1947.
84. Wylie EJ: Thromboendarterectomy for arteriosclerotic thrombosis of major arteries. Surgery 4:339, 1952.
85. Inahara T: Evaluation of endarterectomy for aortoiliac and aortoiliac femoral occlusive disease. Arch Surg 110:1458, 1975.
86. Van der Akker PJ, van Schilfaarde R: Long-term results of prosthetic and non-prosthetic reconstruction for obstructive aorto-iliac disease. Eur J Vasc Surg 6:53, 1992.
87. d'Othee BJ, Haulon S, Mounier-Vehier C, et al: Percutaneous endovascular treatment for stenoses and occlusions of infrarenal aorta and aortoiliac bifurcation: Midterm results. Eur J Vasc Endovasc Surg 24:516, 2002.
88. Elkouri S, Hudon G, Demers P, et al: Early and long-term results of percutaneous transluminal angioplasty of the lower abdominal aorta. J Vasc Surg 30:679, 1999.
89. Hood DB, Hodgson KJ: Percutaneous transluminal angioplasty and stenting for iliac artery occlusive disease. Surg Clin North Am 79:575, 1999.
90. Mulcare RJ, Royster TS, Lynn RA, et al: Long-term results of operative therapy for aortoiliac disease. Arch Surg 113:601, 1978.
91. Pierce HE, Turrentine M, Stringfield S, et al: Evaluation of end-to-side versus end-to-end proximal anastomosis in aortobifemoral bypass. Arch Surg 117:1580, 1982.
92. Mikati A, Marache P, Watel A, et al: End-to-side aortoprosthetic anastomoses: Long-term computed tomography assessment. Ann Vasc Surg 4:584, 1990.
93. Dunn DA, Downs AR, Lye CR: Aortoiliac reconstruction for occlusive disease: Comparison of end-to-end and end-to-side proximal anastomoses. Can J Surg 25:382, 1982.
94. Rutherford RB, Jones DN, Martin MS, et al: Serial hemodynamic assessment of aortobifemoral bypass. J Vasc Surg 4:428, 1986.
95. Ameli FM, Stein M, Aro L, et al: End-to-end versus end-to-side proximal anastomosis in aortobifemoral bypass surgery: Does it matter? Can Soc Vasc Surg 34:243, 1991.
96. Melliere D, Labastie J, Becquemin JP, et al: Proximal anastomosis in aortobifemoral bypass: End-to-end or end-to-side? J Cardiovasc Surg (Torino) 31:77, 1990.
97. Flanigan DP, Schuler JJ, Keifer T, et al: Elimination of iatrogenic impotence and improvement of sexual function after aortoiliac revascularization. Arch Surg 117:544, 1982.
98. Queral LA, Whitehouse WM Jr, Flinn WR, et al: Pelvic hemodynamics after aortoiliac reconstruction. Surgery 86:799, 1979.
99. Picone AL, Green RM, Ricotta JR, et al: Spinal cord ischemia following operations on the abdominal aorta. J Vasc Surg 3:94, 1986.
100. Gloviczki P, Cross SA, Stanson AW, et al: Ischemic injury to the spinal cord or lumbosacral plexus after aorto-iliac reconstruction. Am J Surg 162:131, 1991.
101. Baird RJ, Feldman P, Miles JT, et al: Subsequent downstream repair after aorta-iliac and aorta-femoral bypass operations. Surgery 82:785, 1977.
102. Crawford ES, Manning LG, Kelly TF: "Redo" surgery after operations for aneurysm and occlusion of the abdominal aorta. Surgery 81:41, 1977.
103. Bernhard VM, Ray LI, Militello JP: The role of angioplasty of the profunda femoris artery in revascularization of the ischemic limb. Surg Gynecol Obstet 142:840, 1976.
104. Malone JM, Goldstone J, Moore WS: Autogenous profundaplasty: The key to long-term patency in secondary repair of aortofemoral graft occlusion. Ann Surg 188:817, 1978.
105. Berguer R, Higgins RF, Colton LT: Geometry, blood flow, and reconstruction of the deep femoral artery. Am J Surg 130:68, 1975.
106. Robicsek F, Duncan GD, Daugherty HK, et al: "Half and half" woven and knitted Dacron grafts in the aortoiliac and aortofemoral positions: Seven and one-half years' follow-up. Ann Vasc Surg 5:315, 1991.
107. Robicsek F, Duncan GD, Anderson CE, et al: Indium 111-labeled platelet deposition in woven and knitted Dacron bifurcated aortic grafts with the same patient as a clinical model. J Vasc Surg 5:833, 1987.
108. Burke PM, Herrmann JB, Cutler BS: Optimal grafting methods for the small abdominal aorta. J Cardiovasc Surg 28:420, 1987.
109. Cintora I, Pearce DE, Cannon JA: A clinical survey of aortobifemoral bypass using two inherently different graft types. Ann Surg 208:625, 1988.
110. Robbs JV, Wylie EJ: Factors contributing to recurrent limb ischemia following bypass surgery for aortoiliac occlusive disease and their management. Arch Surg 193:346, 1981.
111. Sanders RJ, Kempczinski RF, Hammond W, et al: The significance of graft diameter. Surgery 88:856, 1980.
112. Nunn DB, Carter MM, Donohue MT, et al: Postoperative dilation of knitted Dacron aortic bifurcation graft. J Vasc Surg 12:291, 1990.

113. O'Hara PJ, Brewster DC, Darling RC, et al: The value of intraoperative monitoring using the pulse volume recorder during peripheral vascular surgery. Surg Gynecol Obstet 162:275, 1981.
114. Rob C: Extraperitoneal approach to the abdominal aorta. Surgery 53:87, 1963.
115. Sicard GA, Freeman MB, Vander Woude JC, et al: Comparison between the transabdominal and retroperitoneal approach for reconstruction of the infrarenal aorta. J Vasc Surg 5:19, 1987.
116. Williams GM, Ricotta J, Zinner M, et al: The extended retroperitoneal approach for treatment of extensive atherosclerosis of the aorta and renal vessels. Surgery 88:846, 1980.
117. Shepard AD, Tollefson DFJ, Reddy DJ, et al: Left flank retroperitoneal exposure: A technical aid to complex aortic reconstruction. J Vasc Surg 14:283, 1991.
118. Sicard GA, Reilly JM, Rubin BE, et al: Transabdominal versus retroperitoneal incision for abdominal aortic surgery: Report of a prospective randomized trial. J Vasc Surg 21:174, 1995.
119. Cambria RP, Brewster DC, Abbott WM, et al: Transperitoneal versus retroperitoneal approach for aortic reconstruction: A randomized prospective study. J Vasc Surg 11:314, 1990.
120. Barnes RW, Baker WH, Shanik G, et al: Value of concomitant sympathectomy in aortoiliac reconstruction: Results of a prospective randomized study. Arch Surg 112:1325, 1977.
121. Satiani B, Liapis CD, Hayes JP, et al: Prospective randomized study of concomitant lumbar sympathectomy in aortoiliac reconstruction. Am J Surg 143:755, 1982.
122. Imparato AM: Lumbar sympathectomy: Role in the treatment of occlusive arterial disease in the lower extremities. Surg Clin North Am 59:719, 1979.
123. Rutherford RB: The current role of sympathectomy in the management of limb ischemia. Semin Vasc Surg 4:195, 1991.
124. Corson JD, Brewster DC, Darling RC: The surgical management of infrarenal aortic occlusion. Surg Gynecol Obstet 155:369, 1982.
125. Liddicoat JE, Bekassy SM, Dang MH, et al: Complete occlusion of the infrarenal abdominal aorta: Management and results in 64 patients. Surgery 77:467, 1975.
126. Tapper SS, Jenkins JM, Edwards WH, et al: Juxtarenal aortic occlusion. Ann Surg 215:443, 1992.
127. Starrett RW, Stoney RJ: Juxta-renal aortic occlusion. Surgery 76:890, 1974.
128. Deriu GP, Ballotta E: Natural history of ascending thrombosis of the abdominal aorta. Am J Surg 145:652, 1983.
129. McCullough JL, Mackey WC, O'Donnell TF, et al: Infrarenal aortic occlusion: A reassessment of surgical indications. Am J Surg 146:178, 1983.
130. Reilly LM, Sauer L, Weinstein ES, et al: Infrarenal aortic occlusion: Does it threaten renal perfusion or function? J Vasc Surg 11:216, 1990.
131. Gupta SK, Veith FJ: Management of juxtarenal aortic occlusions: Technique for suprarenal clamp placement. Ann Vasc Surg 6:306, 1992.
132. Martinez BD, Hertzer NR, Beven EG: Influence of distal arterial occlusive disease on prognosis following aortobifemoral bypass. Surgery 88:795, 1980.
133. Sumner DS, Strandness DE Jr: Aortoiliac reconstruction in patients with combined iliac and superficial femoral arterial occlusion. Surgery 84:348, 1978.
134. Hill DA, McGrath MA, Lord RSA, et al: The effect of superficial femoral artery occlusion on the outcome of aortofemoral bypass for intermittent claudication. Surgery 87:133, 1980.
135. Galland RB, Hill DA, Gustave R, et al: The functional result of aortoiliac reconstruction. Br J Surg 67:344, 1980.
136. Jones AF, Kempczinski RF: Aortofemoral bypass grafting: A reappraisal. Arch Surg 116:301, 1981.
137. Brewster DC, Darling RC: Aortoiliofemoral bypass grafting. In Kempczinski RF (ed): The Ischemic Leg. Chicago, Year Book, 1985, pp 305-326.
138. Brewster DC, Veith FJ: Combined aortoiliac and femoropopliteal occlusive disease. In Veith FJ, Hobson RW, Williams RA, et al (eds): Vascular Surgery: Principles and Practice, 2nd ed. New York, McGraw-Hill, 1994, pp 459-472.
139. Baird RJ: In discussion of Brewster DC, Perler BA, Robison JR, et al: Aorto-femoral graft for multilevel occlusive disease. Arch Surg 117:1593, 1982.
140. Dardik H, Ibrahim IM, Jarrah M, et al: Synchronous aortofemoral or iliofemoral bypass with revascularization of the lower extremity. Surg Gynecol Obstet 149:676, 1979.
141. Harris PL, Cave Bigley DJ, McSweeney L: Aortofemoral bypass and the role of concomitant femorodistal reconstruction. Br J Surg 72:317, 1985.
142. O'Donnell TF Jr, McBride KA, Callow AD, et al: Management of combined segment disease. Am J Surg 141:452, 1981.
143. Eidt J, Charlesworth D: Combined aortobifemoral and femoropopliteal bypass in the management of patients with extensive atherosclerosis. Ann Vasc Surg 1:453, 1986.
144. Dalman RL, Taylor LM Jr, Moneta GL, et al: Simultaneous operative repair of multilevel lower extremity occlusive disease. J Vasc Surg 13:211, 1991.
145. Garrett WV, Slaymaker EE, Heintz SE, et al: Intraoperative prediction of symptomatic result of aortofemoral bypass from changes in ankle pressure index. Surgery 82:504, 1977.
146. Levinson SA, Levinson HJ, Halloran LG, et al: Limited indications for unilateral aortofemoral or iliofemoral vascular grafts. Arch Surg 107:791, 1973.
147. Kram HB, Gupta SK, Veith FJ, et al: Unilateral aortofemoral bypass: A safe and effective option for the treatment of unilateral limb-threatening ischemia. Am J Surg 162:155, 1991.
148. van den Dungen JJAM, Boontje AH, Kropveld A: Unilateral iliofemoral occlusive disease: Long-term results of the semiclosed endarterectomy with the ring stripper. J Vasc Surg 14:673, 1991.
149. Ascher E, Veith FJ, Gupta SK, et al: Comparison of axillounifemoral and axillobifemoral bypass operations. Surgery 97:169, 1985.
150. Brener BJ, Brief DK, Alpert J, et al: Femorofemoral bypass: A twenty-five year experience. In Yao JST, Pearce WH (eds): Long-Term Results in Vascular Surgery. Norwalk, CT, Appleton & Lange, 1993, pp 385-393.
151. Brief DK, Brener BJ, Alpert J, et al: Crossover femorofemoral grafts followed up five years or more: An analysis. Arch Surg 110:1294, 1975.
152. Dick LS, Brief DK, Alpert J, et al: A twelve-year experience with femorofemoral crossover grafts. Arch Surg 115:1359, 1980.
153. Eugene J, Goldstone J, Moore WS: Fifteen-year experience with subcutaneous bypass grafts for lower extremity ischemia. Ann Surg 186:177, 1977.
154. Kalman PG, Hosang M, Johnston KW, et al: The current role for femorofemoral bypass. J Vasc Surg 6:71, 1987.
155. Couch NP, Clowes AW, Whittemore AD, et al: The iliac-origin arterial graft: A useful alternative for iliac occlusive disease. Surgery 97:83, 1985.
156. Kalman PG, Hosang M, Johnston KW, et al: Unilateral iliac disease: The role of iliofemoral graft. J Vasc Surg 6:139, 1987.
157. Cham C, Myers KA, Scott DF, et al: Extraperitoneal unilateral iliac artery bypass for chronic limb ischemia. Aust N Z J Surg 58:859, 1988.
158. Darling RC III, Leather RP, Chang BB, et al: Is the iliac artery a suitable inflow conduit for iliofemoral occlusive disease? An analysis of 514 aorto-iliac reconstructions. J Vasc Surg 17:15, 1993.
159. Perler BA, Burdick JF, Williams M: Femoro-femoral or ilio-femoral bypass for unilateral inflow reconstruction? Am J Surg 161:426, 1991.
160. Ricco JB: Unilateral iliac artery occlusive disease: A randomized multicenter trial examining direct revascularization versus crossover bypass. Ann Vasc Surg 6:209, 1992.
161. Brener BJ, Eisenbud DE, Brief DK, et al: Utility of femorofemoral crossover grafts. In Bergan JJ, Yao JST (eds): Aortic Surgery. Philadelphia, WB Saunders, 1989, pp 423-438.
162. Taylor LM Jr, Freimanis IE, Edwards JM, et al: Extraperitoneal iliac endarterectomy in the treatment of multilevel lower extremity arterial occlusive disease. Am J Surg 152:34, 1986.

163. Vitale GF, Inahara T: Extraperitoneal endarterectomy for iliofemoral occlusive disease. J Vasc Surg 12:409, 1990.
164. Tollefson DFJ, Ernst CB: Natural history of atherosclerotic renal artery stenosis associated with aortic disease. J Vasc Surg 14:327, 1991.
165. Zierler RE, Bergelin RO, Isaacson JA, Strandness DE Jr: Natural history of atherosclerotic renal artery stenosis: A prospective study with duplex ultrasonography. J Vasc Surg 19:250, 1994.
166. Dean RH, Keyser JE III, Dupont WD, et al: Aortic and renal vascular disease: Factors affecting the value of combined procedures. Ann Surg 200:336, 1984.
167. Tarazi RY, Hertzer NR, Beven EG: Simultaneous aortic reconstruction and renal revascularization: Risk factors and late results in eighty-nine patients. J Vasc Surg 5:707, 1987.
168. Brewster DC, Buth J, Darling RC, et al: Combined aortic and renal artery reconstruction. Am J Surg 131:457, 1976.
169. Cambria RP, Brewster DC, L'Italien G, et al: Simultaneous aortic and renal artery reconstruction: Evaluation of an eighteen-year experience. J Vasc Surg 21:916, 1995.
170. Chaikof EL, Smith RB III, Salam AA, et al: Empirical reconstruction of the renal artery: Long-term outcome. J Vasc Surg 24:406, 1996.
171. Connolly JE, Kwaan JHM: Prophylactic revascularization of the gut. Ann Surg 190:514, 1979.
172. Brewster DC, Darling RC: Splenorenal arterial anastomosis for renovascular hypertension. Ann Surg 189:353, 1979.
173. Moncure AC, Brewster DC, Darling RC, et al: Use of the splenic and hepatic arteries for renal revascularization. J Vasc Surg 3:196, 1986.
174. Brewster DC, Moncure AC: Hepatic and splenic artery for renal revascularization. In Bergan JJ, Yao JST (eds): Arterial Surgery: New Diagnostic and Operative Techniques. Orlando, Grune & Stratton, 1988, pp 389-405.
175. Criado E, Johnson G Jr, Burnham SJ, et al: Descending thoracic aorta-to-iliofemoral artery bypass as an alternative to aortoiliac reconstruction. J Vasc Surg 15:550, 1992.
176. McCarthy WJ, Mesh CL, McMillan WD, et al: Descending thoracic aorta-to-femoral artery bypass: Ten years' experience with a durable procedure. J Vasc Surg 17:336, 1993.
177. Baird RJ, Ropchan GV, Oates TK, et al: Ascending aorta to bifemoral bypass—a ventral aorta. J Vasc Surg 3:405, 1986.
178. Canepa CS, Schubart PJ, Taylor LM Jr, Porter JM: Supraceliac aortofemoral bypass. Surgery 101:323, 1987.
179. deVries SO, Hunink MG: Results of aortic bifurcation grafts for aortoiliac occlusive disease: A meta-analysis. J Vasc Surg 26:558, 1997.
180. Brewster DC: Complications of aortic and lower extremity procedures. In Strandness DE Jr, van Breda A (eds): Vascular Diseases: Surgical and Interventional Therapy. New York, Churchill Livingstone, 1994, pp 1151-1177.
181. Brener BJ, Darling RC, Frederick PL, et al: Major venous anomalies complicating abdominal aortic surgery. Arch Surg 108:159, 1974.
182. Brewster DC: Reoperation for aortofemoral graft limb occlusion. In Veith F (ed): Current Critical Problems in Vascular Surgery. St. Louis, Quality Medical, 1989, pp 341-351.
183. Imparato AM: Abdominal aortic surgery: Prevention of lower limb ischemia. Surgery 93:112, 1983.
184. Starr DS, Lawrie GM, Morris GC Jr: Prevention of distal embolism during arterial reconstruction. Am J Surg 138:764, 1979.
185. Comerota AJ, White JV, Grosh JD: Intraoperative intraarterial thrombolytic therapy for salvage of limbs in patients with distal arterial thrombosis. Surg Gynecol Obstet 169:283, 1989.
186. Parent FN III, Bernhard VM, Pabst TS III, et al: Fibrinolytic treatment of residual thrombus after catheter embolectomy for severe lower limb ischemia. J Vasc Surg 9:153, 1989.
187. Diehl JT, Cali RF, Hertzer NR, et al: Complications of abdominal aortic reconstruction: An analysis of perioperative risk factors in 557 patients. Ann Surg 197:50, 1983.
188. Castronuovo JJ, Flanigan DP: Renal failure complicating vascular surgery. In Bernhard VM, Towne JB (eds): Complications in Vascular Surgery. Orlando, Grune & Stratton, 1985, pp 258-274.
189. Bush HL, Huse JB, Johnson WC, et al: Prevention of renal insufficiency after abdominal aortic aneurysm resection by optimal volume loading. Arch Surg 116:1517, 1981.
190. Brewster DC, Franklin DP, Cambria RP, et al: Intestinal ischemia complicating abdominal aortic surgery. Surgery 109:447, 1991.
191. Bjorck M, Bergqvist D, Troeng T: Incidence and clinical presentation of bowel ischemia after aortoiliac surgery: 2930 operations from a population-based registry in Sweden. Eur J Vasc Endovasc Surg 12:139, 1996.
192. Seeger JM, Doe DA, Kaelin LD, et al: Routine reimplantation of patent inferior mesenteric arteries limits colon infarction after aortic reconstruction. J Vasc Surg 15:635, 1992.
193. Bergman RT, Gloviczki, Welch TJ, et al: The role of intravenous fluorescein in the detection of colon ischemia during aortic reconstruction. Ann Vasc Surg 6:74, 1992.
194. Szilagyi DE, Hageman JH, Smith RF, et al: Spinal cord damage in surgery of the abdominal aorta. Surgery 83:38, 1978.
195. Iliopoulos JI, Howanitz PE, Pierce GE, et al: The critical hypogastric circulation. Am J Surg 154:671, 1987.
196. Elliott JP, Szilagyi DE, Hageman JH, et al: Spinal cord ischemia: Secondary to surgery of the abdominal aorta. In Bernhard VM, Towne JB (eds): Complications in Vascular Surgery. Orlando, Grune & Stratton, 1985, pp 291-310.
197. McCarthy WJ, Flinn WR, Carter MF, et al: Prevention and management of urologic injuries during aortic surgery. In Bergan JJ, Yao JST (eds): Aortic Surgery. Philadelphia, WB Saunders, 1989, pp 539-546.
198. Egeblad K, Brochner-Mortensen J, Krarup T, et al: Incidence of ureteral obstruction after aortic grafting: A prospective analysis. Surgery 103:411, 1988.
199. Schubart P, Fortner G, Cummings D, et al: The significance of hydronephrosis after aortofemoral reconstruction. Arch Surg 120:377, 1985.
200. Wright DJ, Ernst CB, Evans JR, et al: Ureteral complications and aortoiliac reconstruction. J Vasc Surg 11:29, 1990.
201. van der Akker PJ, van Schilfgaarde R, Brand R, et al: Long-term success of aortoiliac operation for arteriosclerotic obstructive disease. Surg Gynecol Obstet 174:485, 1992.
202. Brewster DC, Meier GH, Darling RC, et al: Reoperation for aortofemoral graft limb occlusion: Optimal methods and long term results. J Vasc Surg 5:363, 1987.
203. Brewster DC: Surgery of late aortic graft occlusion. In Bergan JJ, Yao JST (eds): Aortic Surgery. Philadelphia, WB Saunders, 1989, pp 519-538.
204. Nevelsteen A, Suy R: Graft occlusion following aortofemoral Dacron bypass. Ann Vasc Surg 5:32, 1991.
205. Bernhard VM, Ray LI, Towne JB: The reoperation of choice for aortofemoral graft occlusion. Surgery 82:867, 1977.
206. Wray R, DePalma RG, Hunay CH: Late occlusion of aortofemoral bypass grafts: Influence of cigarette smoking. Surgery 70:969, 1971.
207. Greenhalgh RM, Laing SP, Cole PV, et al: Smoking and arterial reconstruction. Br J Surg 68:605, 1981.
208. Robicsek F, Daugherty HK, Mullen DC, et al: The effect of continued cigarette smoking on the patency of synthetic vascular grafts in Leriche syndrome. J Thorac Cardiovasc Surg 70:107, 1975.
209. Provan JL, Sojka SG, Murnaghan JJ, et al: The effect of cigarette smoking on the long-term success rates of aortofemoral and femoropopliteal reconstructions. Surg Gynecol Obstet 165:49, 1987.
210. Myers KA, King BB, Scott DF, et al: Effect of smoking on the late patency of arterial reconstructions in the legs. Br J Surg 65:267, 1978.
211. Nolan KD, Benjamin ME, Murphy TJ, et al: Femorofemoral bypass for aortofemoral graft limb occlusion: A ten-year experience. J Vasc Surg 19:851, 1994.
212. Ernst CB, Daugherty ME: Removal of a thrombotic plug from an occluded limb of an aortofemoral graft. Arch Surg 113:301, 1978.
213. Brewster DC: Aortic graft limb occlusion. In Ernst CB, Stanley JC (eds): Current Therapy in Vascular Surgery, 3rd ed. St. Louis, Mosby-Year Book, 1995, pp 419-426.

214. Edwards WH, Jenkins JM, Mulherin JL, et al: Extended profundaplasty to minimize pelvic and distal tissue loss. Ann Surg 211:694, 1990.
215. Sterpetti AV, Feldhaus RJ, Schultz RD: Combined aortofemoral and extended deep femoral artery reconstruction. Arch Surg 123:1269, 1988.
216. Ouriel K, DeWeese JA, Ricotta JJ, et al: Revascularization of the distal profunda femoris artery in the reconstructive treatment of aortoiliac occlusive disease. J Vasc Surg 6:217, 1987.
217. Charlesworth D: The occluded aortic and aortofemoral graft. In Bergan JJ, Yao JST (eds): Reoperative Arterial Surgery. Orlando, Grune & Stratton, 1986, pp 271-278.
218. Szilagyi DE, Smith RF, Elliott JP, et al: Anastomotic aneurysms after vascular reconstruction: Problems of incidence, etiology, and treatment. Surgery 78:800, 1975.
219. Satiani B: False aneurysms following arterial reconstruction: Collective review. Surg Gynecol Obstet 152:357, 1981.
220. Edwards JM, Teefey SA, Zierler RE, et al: Intraabdominal para-anastomotic aneurysms after aortic bypass grafting. J Vasc Surg 15:344, 1991.
221. Schellack J, Salam A, Abouzeid MA, et al: Femoral anastomotic aneurysms: A continuing challenge. J Vasc Surg 6:308, 1987.
222. Goldstone J: Anastomotic aneurysms. In Bernhard VM, Towne JB (eds): Complications in Vascular Surgery. St. Louis, Quality Medical, 1991, pp 87-99.
223. Ernst CB, Elliott JP Jr, Ryan CH, et al: Recurrent femoral anastomotic aneurysms: A thirty-year experience. Ann Surg 208:401, 1988.
224. Seabrook GR, Schmitt DD, Bandyk DF, et al: Anastomotic femoral pseudoaneurysm: An investigation of occult infection as an etiologic factor. J Vasc Surg 11:629, 1990.
225. Kempczinski RF: Impotence following aortic surgery. In Bernhard VM, Towne JB (eds): Complications in Vascular Surgery. St. Louis, Quality Medical, 1991, pp 160-171.
226. Weinstein MH, Machleder HI: Sexual function after aorto-iliac surgery. Ann Surg 181:787, 1975.
227. DePalma RG, Levine SB, Feldman S: Preservation of erectile function after aortoiliac reconstruction. Arch Surg 113:958, 1978.
228. Cronenwett JL, Gooch JB, Garrett HE: Internal iliac artery revascularization during aortofemoral bypass. Arch Surg 117:838, 1982.
229. Flanigan DP, Sobinsky KR, Schuler JJ, et al: Internal iliac artery revascularization in the treatment of vasculogenic impotence. Arch Surg 120:271, 1985.
230. Moore WS, Cole CW: Infection in prosthetic vascular grafts. In Moore WS (ed): Vascular Surgery: A Comprehensive Review, 3rd ed. Philadelphia, WB Saunders, 1991, pp 598-609.
231. Bandyk DF: Aortic graft infection. Semin Vasc Surg 3:122, 1990.
232. O'Hara PJ, Hertzer NR, Beven EG, et al: Surgical management of infected abdominal aortic grafts: Review of a 25-year experience. J Vasc Surg 3:725, 1986.
233. Rubin JR, Malone JM, Goldstone J: The role of the lymphatic system in acute arterial prosthetic graft infections. J Vasc Surg 2:92, 1985.
234. Piotrowski JJ, Bernhard VM: Management of vascular graft infections. In Bernhard VM, Towne JB (eds): Complications in Vascular Surgery. St. Louis, Quality Medical, 1991, pp 235-258.
235. Reilly LM, Altman H, Lusby RJ, et al: Late results following surgical management of vascular graft infection. J Vasc Surg 1:36, 1984.
236. Quinones-Baldrich WJ, Hernandez JJ, Moore WS: Long-term results following surgical management of aortic graft infection. Arch Surg 126:507, 1991.
237. Yeager RA, Moneta GL, Taylor LM, et al: Improving survival and limb salvage in patients with aortic graft infection. Am J Surg 159:466, 1990.
238. Schmitt DD, Seabrook GR, Bandyk DF, et al: Graft excision and extra-anatomic revascularization: The treatment of choice for the septic aortic prosthesis. J Cardiovasc Surg 31:327, 1990.
239. Sharp WJ, Hoballah JJ, Mohan CR, et al: The management of the infected aortic prosthesis: A current decade of experience. J Vasc Surg 19:844, 1994.
240. Reilly LM, Stoney RJ, Goldstone J, et al: Improved management of aortic graft infection: The influence of operation sequence and staging. J Vasc Surg 5:421, 1987.
241. Trout HH III, Kozloff L, Giordano JM: Priority of revascularization in patients with graft enteric fistulas, infected arteries, or infected arterial prostheses. Ann Surg 199:669, 1984.
242. Kwann JWM, Connolly JB: Successful management of prosthetic graft infection with continuous povidone-iodine irrigation. Arch Surg 116:716, 1981.
243. Calligaro KD, Veith FJ, Gupta SK, et al: A modified method for management of prosthetic graft infections involving an anastomosis to the common femoral artery. J Vasc Surg 11:485, 1990.
244. Calligaro KD, DeLaurentis DA, Schwartz, ML, et al: Selective preservation of infected prosthetic arterial grafts: Analysis of a 20 year experience with 120 extracavitary infected grafts. Ann Surg 220:461, 1994.
245. Mixter RC, Turnipseed WD, Smith DJ Jr, et al: Rotational muscle flaps: A new technique for covering infected vascular grafts. J Vasc Surg 9:472, 1989.
246. Perler BA, VanderKolk CA, Manson PM, Williams GM: Rotational muscle flaps to treat prosthetic graft infection: Long-term follow-up. J Vasc Surg 18:358, 1993.
247. Clagett GP, Valentine RJ, Hagino RT: Autogenous aortoiliac/femoral reconstruction from superficial femoral-popliteal veins: Feasibility and durability. J Vasc Surg 25:255, 1997.
248. Bernhard VM: Aortoenteric fistula. In Bernhard VM, Towne JB (eds): Complications in Vascular Surgery. Orlando, Grune & Stratton, 1985, pp 513-525.
249. Connolly JE, Kwaan JHM, McCart PM, et al: Aortoenteric fistula. Ann Surg 194:402, 1981.
250. Perdue GD Jr, Smith RB III, Ansley JD, et al: Impending aortoenteric hemorrhage: The effect of early recognition on improved outcome. Ann Surg 192:237, 1980.
251. Reilly LM, Ehrenfeld WK, Goldstone J, et al: Gastrointestinal tract involvement by prosthetic graft infection: The significance of gastrointestinal hemorrhage. Ann Surg 202:342, 1985.
252. Seeger JM, Wheeler JR, Gregory RT, et al: Autogenous graft replacement of infected prosthetic graft in the femoral position. Surgery 93:39, 1983.
253. Walker WE, Cooley DA, Duncan JM, et al: The management of aortoduodenal fistula by in situ replacement of the infected abdominal aortic graft. Ann Surg 205:727, 1987.
254. Bandyk DF, Bergamini TM, Kinney EV, et al: In situ replacement of vascular prostheses infected by bacterial biofilms. J Vasc Surg 13:575, 1991.
255. Robinson AJ, Johansen K: Aortic sepsis: Is there a role for in situ graft replacement? J Vasc Surg 13:677, 1991.
256. Jacobs MJHM, Reul G, Gregoric I, et al: In-situ replacement and extra-anatomic bypass for the treatment of infected abdominal aortic grafts. Eur J Vasc Surg 5:83, 1991.
257. Kieffer E, Bahnini A, Koskas F, et al: In situ allograft replacement of infected infrarenal aortic prosthetic grafts: Results in 43 patients. J Vasc Surg 17:349, 1993.
258. Whiteley MS, Ray-Chaudhuri SB, Galland RB: Changing patterns in aortoiliac reconstruction: A 7-year audit. Br J Surg 83:1367, 1996.

Chapter 80

Extra-anatomic Bypass

JOSEPH R. SCHNEIDER, MD, PhD

Most arterial bypass grafts are positioned "anatomically," that is, roughly parallel and directly adjacent to the arteries they bypass. Two clear examples of anatomically positioned grafts are aortobifemoral and "conventional" femoropopliteal bypass grafts. The term *extra-anatomic* has been used to describe grafts that are placed in anatomic positions substantially different from those of the arteries bypassed by these grafts.

The term *extra-anatomic* has been criticized as imprecise at best. The preferred techniques used to treat certain arterial lesions may be considered extra-anatomic. For example, most of the preferred open surgical procedures used to treat chronic occlusive disease of the great vessels (the arteries originating from the transverse arch of the aorta) are "extra-anatomic." Femorotibial bypass using the greater saphenous vein in situ could be considered an extra-anatomic technique. Despite concerns about the terminology, the term *extra-anatomic* is in common usage when describing the four basic procedures discussed in this chapter: femorofemoral, axillofemoral, obturator, and thoracofemoral bypasses.

Femorofemoral and axillofemoral grafts were originally designed as replacements for direct aortofemoral bypass in patients who were either too ill to undergo aortofemoral bypass or to treat infection of the native aorta or prosthetic aortic grafts. Axillofemoral bypass and, to a lesser extent, femorofemoral bypass were subsequently extended to patients with "hostile abdomen" and in whom a direct aortic replacement would be technically difficult or contraindicated owing to active intra-abdominal infection or other pathology. These remain as primary indications for these operations today. However, many authors have argued that these procedures should be extended even further to patients who are not within these categories (see later).[1-4] The use of femorofemoral bypass with aorto-unifemoral endovascular repair has emerged as one option for treatment of abdominal aortic aneurysm[5-7] and is discussed in Chapter 52. Obturator bypass was developed essentially as a replacement for femoropopliteal bypass to deal with infection of prosthetic arterial grafts or of the native femoral arteries in the groin.[8] Infection and other hostile conditions in the groin, particularly radiation injury and other types of trauma, remain the primary indications for obturator bypass today. Thoracofemoral bypass is an alternative technique for reconstruction of patients who have previously undergone aortic ligation either as part of removal of an infected aortic graft or for primary aortic infection or who have suffered multiple failures of prior arterial reconstructions.[9]

Axillofemoral and femorofemoral bypass configurations have been found by most observers to be inferior with respect to patency when compared with direct aortofemoral bypass grafting.[10-15] There have been no prospective, randomized trials comparing aortofemoral bypass to these other competing alternatives, and the inferior results may reflect case selection. Aortofemoral bypass has been considered inappropriate for anatomic or physiologic reasons in many patients and axillofemoral or femorofemoral bypass are the most appropriate alternatives. However, the hemodynamic performance of the latter two configurations is clearly inferior to aortofemoral bypass and at least in the case of axillofemoral bypass, patency appears inferior to that achieved with aortofemoral bypass in comparable patients.[12,13] The contrast between aortofemoral bypass and this alternative is clouded by the fact that younger patients with more isolated disease who might have undergone aortofemoral bypass in the past are much more likely to be treated with endovascular techniques today.[16] Consequently, aortofemoral bypass grafts are now less commonly performed than axillofemoral and femorofemoral alternatives in some institutions.

HISTORY

The first recognized description of femorofemoral bypass was by Freeman and Leeds.[17] They used an endarterectomized superficial femoral artery as the conduit. However, Vetto's 1962 article was probably the first comprehensive and widely read description of the results of the femorofemoral bypass performed with prosthetic graft material using techniques that are similar to those used today.[18] The first axillofemoral bypass grafts were probably those described essentially simultaneously by Blaisdell and Hall[19] and Louw[20] in 1963. Blaisdell in particular continued to write about the application of this technique in situations of infection, hostile abdomen, or high-risk patients.[21] Shaw and Baue described the obturator bypass in an article that described the approach to a variety of infectious complications of prior vascular surgery in 1963.[8] The first thoracofemoral bypass was probably that described in 1961 by Stevenson and associates and performed in 1956.[22] Thus, each of these procedures in some form has been part of the vascular armamentarium for more than 40 years.

FEMOROFEMORAL BYPASS

Basic Concepts, Indications, and Patient Selection

Femorofemoral bypass depends on the capacity of one iliac arterial system to supply adequate blood flow to both legs. Evidence from multiple studies confirms that this is the case at rest as long as there is no significant stenosis in the donor iliac arterial system (see later). Iliac balloon angioplasty has evolved to be an excellent method to treat selected patients with iliac stenosis and even some patients with total occlusion as is discussed elsewhere in this text. Unilateral iliofemoral bypass has also enjoyed resurgence in interest recently and is an excellent choice in patients with an appropriate common iliac artery for inflow to the graft.[23-28] Aortofemoral bypass remains the standard against which all other methods of reconstruction for iliac artery occlusive disease must be measured.[29] However, femorofemoral bypass is one possible reconstructive alternative for patients with symptoms related to unilateral stenosis or occlusion of a common or external iliac artery.

Technique and Graft Configuration

The operation is performed with the patient positioned supine. The operation can be performed with local infiltration anesthesia but is most often performed under spinal or general anesthesia. The abdomen is prepped along with the groins and anterior thighs. Longitudinal incisions are used to expose and control the femoral arteries on both sides. General considerations described elsewhere in this text as well as geometric considerations discussed later may affect the selection of the site of the arterial anastomoses.

Femorofemoral bypass is certainly less injurious to the patient than is aortofemoral bypass, and the technique is regarded as trivial by many surgeons. However, femorofemoral bypass, both as a stand-alone procedure and as part of an axillofemoral, thoracofemoral, or other bypass procedure, presents unique technical (geometric) challenges. The graft is tunneled from one groin incision to the other in the abdominal wall superior to the pubis (Fig. 80-1). The tunnel is created bluntly with a large clamp or tubular tunneler. The prefascial subcutaneous plane is the appropriate location for the graft tunnel in most patients, but subfascial or even preperitoneal positions may be appropriate if unfavorable conditions exist in the abdominal wall such as prior surgery, radiation-damaged skin or other skin changes, or an unusually thin subcutaneous fat layer. The latter tunnel position may be associated with injury to bowel or bladder and must be used with great caution. Inflow may be provided in some cases by an iliac artery, possibly even the contralateral iliac artery.[23,30,31] Such cases are unusual, and readers are directed to the original material for a more detailed description of this approach.

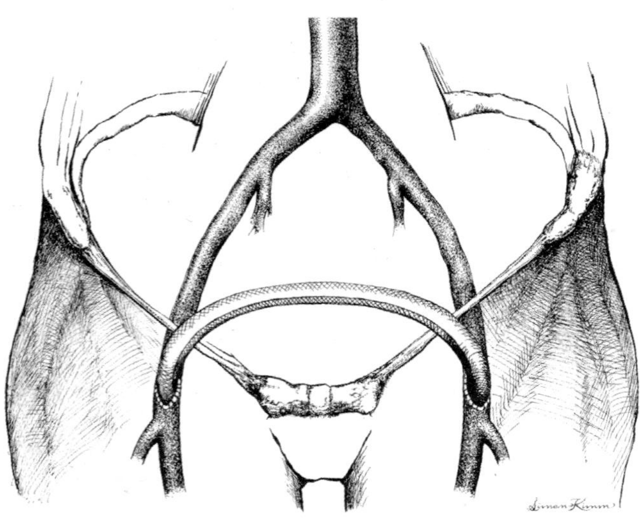

FIGURE 80-1 Standard inverted C configuration of femorofemoral bypass graft.

The graft is roughly confined to a plane tipped forward from the coronal plane to an extent that varies considerably with patient habitus. Anastomoses are made to some component of the femoral arterial system and are end to side in nearly all, if not all, cases so that the graft is directed roughly longitudinally at the anastomoses. Whether the graft is configured as an inverted C[32] (see Fig. 80-1, preferred by most surgeons) or lazy S,[33] the graft will make two abrupt changes in direction within the tipped-from coronal plane described earlier. The likelihood of kinking within the tipped-from coronal plane can be reduced by using a slight excess of graft material, which reduces the tendency of the graft to kink at the "heel" of the anastomoses, and by making the tunnel as a continuous curve between the groin incisions and several centimeters superior to the proposed anastomoses to try to increase the radii of the graft curves transitioning from a roughly longitudinal direction to a transverse direction.

The tendency of the graft to kink within the sagittal plane is a separate concern. The protuberant abdomen presents a problem not encountered in grafts such as the aortofemoral graft that parallel the distal external iliac artery and emerge under the inguinal ligament. The more obese or more protuberant the abdomen, the more the plane of the graft is tipped forward from coronal within the sagittal plane. This tends to cause the angle between the graft and the native artery to become less acute and, thereby, to cause a standard end-to-side anastomosis (roughly three times as long as the graft diameter) to kink in the sagittal plane. This can usually be prevented by shortening the anastomosis or by making the anastomosis to a more distal part of the femoral arterial system, which has the effect of bringing the graft and the femoral artery into a more parallel (and desirable) relationship. Performing one or both anastomoses at least partially to the deep femoral artery may also be helpful in reducing the tendency of the graft to kink in the sagittal plane.

Systemic heparin is administered after completion of dissection and tunneling. A prosthetic graft is used in nearly all cases, although nearly every reported series of femorofemoral grafts has a few constructed of vein or other autologous vessel, generally placed in situations with high concern for infection.[17,34] Either anastomosis may be performed first. Great care must be taken to allow some redundancy in the graft as noted earlier. It is important to confirm enhancement of flow in the recipient vessels and continued flow in the outflow vessels beyond the donor-side anastomosis using a continuous-wave Doppler or other suitable test after anastomoses are completed and all clamps are removed.

Results and Effects of Surgical Indications and Patient Characteristics on Results

The perioperative mortality associated with femorofemoral bypass is highly dependent on patient selection but should be much less than 5% in elective operations. Primary and secondary patency at 3 to 5 years should be expected to be about 60% and 70%, respectively.[13,35-37] Brener and colleagues, in what is likely the largest, longest, and most completely followed series of femorofemoral bypasses, noted a trend toward better patency in claudicants, consistent with the observation in virtually every other arterial intervention.[35] Criado and coworkers noted no apparent difference in patency comparing claudicants to patients with resting ischemia prior to femorofemoral bypass.[36]

Femorofemoral bypass is one of many methods of treating patients with symptomatic occlusion of one limb of a previously placed aortobifemoral graft. Most authors have reported results in these patients to be inferior to those in patients undergoing primary femorofemoral bypass,[2,13,35,38] although at least one more recent report described more favorable results.[39] Most patients who suffer thrombosis of a limb of an aortobifemoral graft are quite symptomatic and require some intervention. Femorofemoral bypass is one option, and the surgeon and patient may need to accept the prospect of a greater risk of later failure in exchange for expedient reperfusion of the leg. We have also noted a trend toward an inverse relationship between age and patency for femorofemoral bypass.[13] However, we observed a similar trend after aortobifemoral bypass, and this may represent the effect of more aggressive biology of atherosclerosis in patients who require intervention at a younger age.

Femorofemoral bypass was first used in patients considered unfit for aortofemoral bypass. However, the ease of the procedure and the substantially lower level of the injury to the patient prompted many to extend the procedure to better-risk patients who would be candidates for aortofemoral bypass.[1,2,35,40] My colleagues and I are not aware of any randomized, prospective comparisons of femorofemoral versus aortofemoral bypass. However, we previously examined the results of patients who would have been candidates for aortofemoral bypass but who underwent femorofemoral bypass instead, and we compared these results with patients undergoing aortofemoral bypass during the same period in the same institution. The results of femorofemoral bypass even in these good-risk patients were clearly inferior to the results in patients undergoing aortofemoral bypass.[13] However, many of the patients undergoing aortofemoral bypass in that era would be more appropriately treated with transluminal balloon angioplasty or iliofemoral bypass today, and it is unlikely that that study could be repeated in a single institution. In practice, it is rare that patient characteristics and arterial anatomy leave only two alternatives—femorofemoral or aortofemoral bypass—but when this is the case, we continue to recommend the former for poor-risk patients and the latter for good-risk patients.

Effect of Graft Material and External Support

Most femorofemoral grafts have been constructed of prosthetic material. Dacron was used virtually exclusively until expanded polytetrafluoroethylene (ePTFE) became available. It is difficult to determine whether either of these classes of materials dominate femorofemoral bypass today, but we have chosen to use externally supported ePTFE (xPTFE) grafts for the past several years. We could find no evidence that ePTFE or xPTFE is superior to Dacron. Indeed, at least one recent study found a trend toward worse patency for ePTFE femorofemoral grafts.[36] We have chosen to use xPTFE for convenience and the possibility of decreased infection risk, but the hemodynamic performance and patency profiles of the available prosthetic grafts are probably indistinguishable in this application. The role of external support in femorofemoral bypass grafting has face validity, but we are aware of no clear evidence that external support provides superior outcomes in this application. Finally, we examined a series of 6-, 7-, 8-, and 10-mm-diameter ePTFE grafts and could detect no relationship between diameter and hemodynamics or patency.[13] Consequently, I prefer to use a 6-mm-diameter xPTFE graft.

Hemodynamic Considerations

Many surgeons have been concerned that one iliac artery could not adequately supply blood flow to both legs or that the femorofemoral graft could "steal" from the donor limb and produce new or worsened symptoms of ischemia in the donor limb. Several authors have investigated the hemodynamic performance of the femorofemoral graft. Parsonnet and associates concluded that there was only a transient fall in donor limb femoral artery pressure at the time that the femorofemoral graft was opened.[1] Sumner and Strandness performed noninvasive assessments of 15 patients who underwent placement of femorofemoral grafts and concluded that there was no significant deleterious effect on the donor limb and that the recipient limb was well reperfused as long as there was no hemodynamically significant lesion in the donor iliac arterial system.[41] The conclusions of these authors have dominated thought about femorofemoral graft hemodynamics to the present day. However, these authors did detect a slight fall in the mean resting ankle pressure on the donor side, a finding subsequently duplicated by several others.[13,42,43] Investigators for Veterans Affairs Cooperative Study 141 noted that the combination of hemodynamic deterioration and clinical symptoms of steal were present in only 3% of patients, although a much higher fraction of patients developed hemodynamic evidence of donor limb steal at rest and angiographic findings did not predict the occurrence of donor limb steal.[44] On balance, the evidence supports the contention that although there is evidence of some fall in donor limb pressure after femorofemoral bypass, the donor limb is not adversely affected by placement of a femorofemoral bypass as long there is no hemodynamically significant lesion in the donor iliac arterial system.

Assessment of the hemodynamic significance of angiographically detected stenoses in the prospective donor iliac arteries has also been a topic of great interest in patients considered for femorofemoral bypass. Angiography alone is unreliable.[33,45] Sako was probably the first author to write about the use of directly measured femoral artery pressures at rest and after injection of papaverine, a potent arterial vasodilator, to assess the capacity of the iliac arterial inflow to support a significant increase in flow.[46] The test was subsequently further evaluated by Flanigan and colleagues.[47] The test as described by Flanigan and colleagues is performed by directly measuring both systemic pressure and the arterial pressure in the proposed "donor" femoral artery before and after injection of 30 mg of papaverine into the femoral artery and has been used to predict whether an angiographically detected iliac lesion is of clinical importance when selecting inflow versus outflow reconstructive procedures or to determine whether an iliac artery will support a femorofemoral bypass.

The concept of a physiologic test to predict how a potential donor iliac arterial system would behave under the stress of supporting two legs instead of just one is quite appealing. However, Archie[33] has pointed out that only one study[47] has examined the predictive value of the test. Furthermore, the technique has not been standardized. Papaverine tests are often performed with a vasodilator other than papaverine, typically nitroglycerin or tolazoline. I have not been able to find literature to confirm that tests performed with other vasodilators are valid. I have also observed the test to be performed without a separate radial artery or other catheter to measure systemic pressure during the test. This may cause a false-positive result since systemic pressure often falls briefly but significantly during the 1 or 2 minutes immediately after injection of papaverine into the femoral artery. Finally, Flanigan and colleagues stressed the importance of Doppler confirmation of increased flow in the proposed donor femoral arteries after papaverine injection, an often neglected portion of the test.[47] Absence of such an increase in flow implies a technical problem with the test or significant occlusive disease limiting femoral outflow on the donor side and is likely to lead to a false-negative result.

Archie has reported the largest and most detailed study of papaverine testing and its value in femorofemoral bypass.[33] He found the test to have inadequate sensitivity and specificity to be reliable. Despite the concerns expressed so eloquently by Archie, his work focused on the value of papaverine test data to predict patency and hemodynamic results as assessed in the noninvasive vascular laboratory. The value of papaverine testing as a predictor of relief of symptoms after femorofemoral bypass has not been so carefully examined. Thus, we have continued to employ papaverine testing as one contributor to decision making in femorofemoral bypass, particularly when balloon angioplasty of the donor iliac system is employed, although we have discounted the test's importance in view of Archie's work.

The ability of femorofemoral bypass to normalize perfusion of the recipient limb is more in question. Recipient limb perfusion is predictably improved by technically successful femorofemoral bypasses with appropriate anatomy.[43] However, many surgeons have noted a significant number of clinical failures of femorofemoral bypass as measured by persistent claudication, rest pain, or failure to heal gangrenous lesions.[42,48] The Veterans Affairs Cooperative Study 141 cited earlier included more than 300 patients, clearly the largest study of femorofemoral hemodynamics to date, but these researchers presented no information about exercise testing of these patients.[44] We have previously examined the postoperative resting hemodynamics of femorofemoral bypass in 91 patients and concluded that recipient limb pressures would not be normal even at rest with completely normal femoral and other infrainguinal outflow vessels.[13] We recognize that many surgeons view femorofemoral bypass to be a satisfactory treatment for claudication,[35,40] but given the persistent resting hemodynamic abnormalities in the recipient limb after femorofemoral bypass, it seems likely that femorofemoral bypass would perform poorly under exercise conditions in addition to a possibly unsatisfactory patency profile, and we have been reluctant to offer this procedure in claudicants.

Angioplasty of "Donor" Iliac Artery Prior to Femorofemoral Bypass

Successful femorofemoral bypass is highly dependent on a hemodynamically satisfactory donor iliac arterial system. Endovascular intervention for selected iliac artery lesions provides excellent short- and long-term results in terms of hemodynamic improvement and patency, as is discussed in Chapter 84. It is not surprising that endovascular procedures to improve suboptimal donor iliac arteries might be considered prior to or concomitant with femorofemoral bypass. Porter and coworkers[49] described two patients who underwent graduated dilation (as previously described by Dotter and Judkins[50]) of the donor iliac artery prior to femorofemoral bypass with satisfactory early results in both. This procedure was performed before the development of balloon angioplasty by Grüntzig[51,52] and others. Several authors have now reported experience with transluminal balloon angioplasty prior to or concomitant with femorofemoral bypass.[13,35,36,53-59] Results of these studies have generally supported the view that donor iliac artery balloon angioplasty with stenting in selected cases is associated with a satisfactory hemodynamic outcome and patency rate with a few exceptions.[26,35] Schneider and associates[13] and Perler and Williams[57] have compared patients undergoing femorofemoral bypass with and without donor balloon angioplasty in the same institution (nonrandomized). Both of these studies concluded that patencies were comparable in these two groups. The results of balloon angioplasty have probably improved since those initial prior studies were published.[59] AbuRahma and colleagues have shown that the likelihood of success with this approach is substantially higher if the dilated donor iliac artery lesion is short and in the common iliac artery.[59] On balance, it appears clear that as long as the donor iliac lesion would be considered favorable for angioplasty apart from the proposed femorofemoral bypass (ideally a short lesion of the common iliac artery, not excessively calcified), then it is reasonable to proceed to angioplasty of the donor iliac artery and to femorofemoral bypass.

Effect of Outflow Disease

As with other operations for iliac arterial occlusive disease, many surgeons have suspected that disease of the femoral outflow arteries has a large impact on the long-term patency of femorofemoral bypass.[38,60,61] However, the patency of the superficial femoral artery has been found by many other authors to have no detectable impact on long-term patency.[13,35,36] Ensuring outflow to at least one healthy artery, either the superficial femoral or deep femoral artery, appears to provide adequate outflow to support patency. The ability to pass a 3.5-mm-diameter probe into the outflow artery after completing the "toe" portion but before completion of the anastomosis is reassuring with respect to the adequacy of outflow, and we have always confirmed that this maneuver could be accomplished before completing any inflow operation.

Complications

Complications of femorofemoral bypass are those common to nearly all arterial operations, including those discussed in Section X of this text. Complications unique to femorofemoral bypass include possible perforation of the bladder or intraperitoneal viscera during creation of the graft tunnel, particularly when a preperitoneal tunnel is used.

■ AXILLOFEMORAL BYPASS

Basic Concepts, Indications, and Patient Selection

Axillofemoral bypass depends on the ability of a healthy axillary artery to supply adequate blood to the ipsilateral arm and one or both legs, at least at rest. Axillofemoral bypass, just as any other method of intervention for aortoiliac inflow disease, must be judged against aortofemoral bypass. Axillofemoral bypass is an essential tool for treatment of many patients with infected aorta or prosthetic arterial grafts,[62] although alternatives have been proposed even for these patients.[63,64] Axillofemoral bypass is clearly an excellent choice for very elderly patients with bilateral iliac artery occlusions and multiple co-morbidities with multiple prior abdominal operations. However, the choice between aortofemoral and axillofemoral bypass is often less than clear. The definition of "high risk" is highly subjective, and the threshold for choosing axillofemoral over aortofemoral bypass is likely to be different for every surgeon. This has led to markedly different profiles of patient samples in published series of axillofemoral bypass, a topic that is further explored in the following sections.

Technique and Graft Configuration

Axillofemoral bypass is nearly always performed with general anesthesia. We have on rare occasions performed the entire operation with local anesthesia and sedation, but the exploration of the axillary artery and tunneling of the axillofemoral graft segment are difficult to perform under such circumstances. The operation may be expedited by the use of two operating teams, especially for axillobifemoral bypass. Either axillary artery may be an appropriate donor unless there is disease in the subclavian or axillary artery. We have approached this question by measuring blood pressures in both arms and recording continuous-wave Doppler waveforms in the brachial arteries. The axillary artery on the side with the higher blood pressure is chosen if there is a 10-mm Hg or greater discrepancy between systolic pressures in the arms. We insist on a triphasic Doppler waveform in the brachial artery on the side proposed for use as the donor. Some authors have insisted on arch and subclavian arteriography, citing a substantial frequency of occult disease in the axillosubclavian arterial system of patients considered for axillofemoral bypass.[65] In cases when either axillary artery appears hemodynamically adequate to support axillofemoral bypass, we generally choose the arm on the side ipsilateral to the patient's worst lower extremity ischemia even for axillobifemoral bypass, but the contralateral axillary artery may be used even for axillo-unifemoral bypass. These choices are often made on the basis of other practical issues, such as to avoid stomas or other pathology or to avoid placing the graft on the side preferred by the patient for sleeping. We would discourage placement of an axillofemoral graft on the side of a patent arteriovenous hemodialysis fistula, although we are unaware of any examination of the results of such procedures. Any intraoperative arterial pressure-monitoring catheter should be placed in the nondonor arm.

Some surgeons perform the operation with the donor side arm at the patient's side, but we prefer a supine position with the arm abducted to 90 degrees on the donor side. We also place a rolled towel under the patient on that same side to lift the torso several centimeters from the operating table deck. We believe these maneuvers serve to allow slightly better exposure of the most medial portion of the axillary artery and visualization of the flank and lateral chest wall while passing the graft tunneler. We have used the 65-cm Gore tunneler (W. L. Gore, Flagstaff, Arizona) and found that it allows passage of the axillofemoral graft limb without an intermediate incision in the flank. Femorofemoral limbs are positioned using the same approach used for isolated femorofemoral bypass (see earlier). We have always draped with wide exposure to allow thoracotomy, sternotomy, or celiotomy if necessary to manage intraoperative bleeding or other complications that would dictate these approaches (Fig. 80-2), although we have never found it necessary to perform any of these maneuvers.

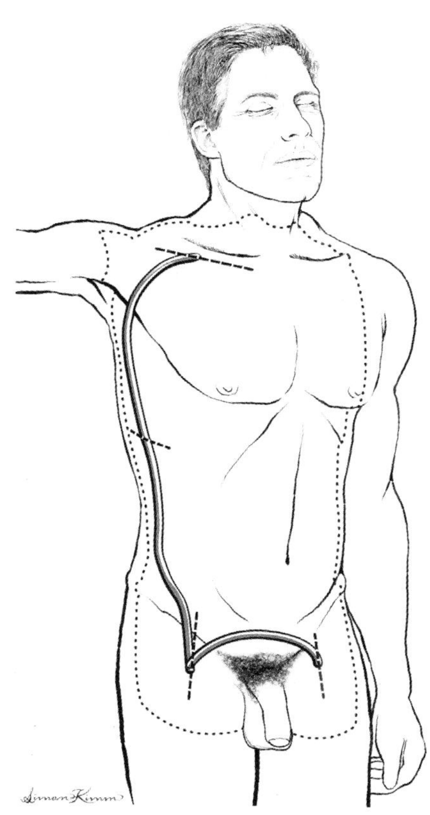

FIGURE 80-2 Typical area of exposure for an axillobifemoral bypass graft. The right axillary artery is the donor artery in this case.

A transverse infraclavicular incision is carried through the clavipectoral fascia exposing the pectoralis major muscle. The pectoralis major muscle fibers are pushed superiorly and inferiorly, exposing the deep fascia and, beyond that, the fat containing the axillary vein, artery, and brachial plexus elements. The axillary artery is exposed from the clavicle medially to the pectoralis minor muscle laterally. The axillosubclavian arteries are considerably more fragile than the femoral arteries, and care must be taken not to injure them or the adjacent veins and brachial plexus elements during dissection or during placement of retractors or vascular clamps. Similar care must be taken during suturing of these arteries since sutures are much more likely to pull through these more fragile vessels. Conventional longitudinal groin incisions are used for femoral artery exposure.

We have generally placed the graft posterior to the pectoralis major muscle unless the patient has had prior axillary surgery, but placement of the axillary end of the graft anterior or posterior to the pectoralis minor muscle is probably unimportant with respect to results. It is far more important to place the axillary graft anastomosis as medial as possible to avoid tension on the axillary anastomosis when the arm is abducted. Furthermore, medial placement of the axillary anastomosis eliminates the need to divide the pectoralis minor muscle in most cases. Leaving an excess length of graft in the axilla has also been advocated to reduce the likelihood of tension on the anastomosis.[66,67] The axillofemoral graft must be tunneled in the midaxillary line to prevent kinking of the graft with torso flexion or a kink over the costal margin, which tends to be more prominent anteriorly than in the midaxillary line. Care must be taken not to injure the neurovascular structures of the axilla during tunneling.

Systemic heparin is given after the tunnels have been completed. The side axillary artery-to-proximal end graft anastomosis is generally performed first. The order of distal anastomoses for axillobifemoral grafts may vary depending on whether there are one or two surgeons. The distal anastomosis is conventionally performed end to side to an appropriate artery in the groin. It is important to ensure adequate outflow. In the case of axillobifemoral configuration, the femorofemoral component may be placed by piggybacking the femorofemoral graft onto the distal anastomotic hood of the axillofemoral graft. Alternatively, the femorofemoral graft may be placed first as described earlier and the distal anastomosis of the axillofemoral component may be piggybacked onto the ipsilateral femorofemoral graft anastomotic hood (Fig. 80-3A). Either of these two variations would qualify as an inverted C and would maintain maximum flow throughout the axillofemoral component, a characteristic thought to be desirable with respect to graft patency. Femorofemoral graft components should be placed using the principles described earlier. Blaisdell[21] and Rutherford and Rainer[68] have described alternative configurations that theoretically prevent competitive inflow from the native iliac arterial system on the side of the distal axillofemoral anastomosis and that may thereby decrease the risk of graft thrombosis due to stasis (Fig. 80-3B and C). Another alternative approach has been advocated by Wittens and coworkers. These authors have examined a variety of grafts with manufactured bifurcations for axillobifemoral reconstructions. They found that a graft with a flow divider similar to that in bifurcated aortobifemoral grafts provided both superior hemodynamic performance and patency, although I could not identify any published confirmatory data since the original publication in 1992 except Dr. Wittens' later doctoral thesis.[69,70] Thus, I would consider this approach as potentially useful but unconfirmed at the time of this writing. These grafts would appear to have long ipsilateral and contralateral distal graft limbs beyond the graft bifurcation, contrary to the most typical strategy as mentioned earlier. Furthermore, this would seem to require either a much longer ipsilateral groin incision or a counterincision on the ipsilateral flank to avoid unfavorable kinking of the contralateral distal graft limb. It is important to confirm enhancement of flow in the recipient vessels using a continuous-wave Doppler or other suitable test after anastomoses are completed and all clamps are removed. It is also essential to confirm good blood flow in the donor arm beyond the axillary anastomosis by confirming a good radial pulse or satisfactory oxygen saturation as indicated by pulse oximetry in the hand with the axillofemoral graft and outflow vessels unclamped.

Results and Effects of Surgical Indications and Patient Characteristics on Results

Examination of reports of axillofemoral bypass yields perhaps the broadest range of long-term patencies of any arterial reconstructive procedure.[38] Patients undergoing axillofemoral bypass as part of the treatment for infection of the aorta or an aortic prosthesis or for aortoenteric fistula tend to suffer high perioperative morbidity and mortality, but survivors tend to enjoy better patency than do those who undergo the operation for chronic arterial occlusive disease.[38,71] A prior review of pertinent articles regarding axillofemoral bypass and confined primarily to patients with chronic lower extremity arterial occlusive disease published between 1960 and 1993 yielded 3-year primary patency estimates as low as 39% and as high as 85%.[14] A subsequent 1996 report from Passman and associates reported 5-year estimated primary patency of 74%.[4]

There are many potential explanations for these discrepancies. Patients surviving after surgery for problems such as infected aortic graft or aortoenteric fistula are likely to enjoy better patency than those with chronic severe arterial occlusive disease.[62,71] Series including substantial numbers of such patients generally report a more favorable patency experience. Results after primary operations, including axillofemoral bypass, can be expected to be superior to those for secondary operations.[38] Patient characteristics and surgical indications influence outcome and must be considered when reading published reports of results of axillofemoral bypass. Axillofemoral bypass was initially proposed only for high-risk patients too ill to undergo aortofemoral bypass procedures. Unfortunately, "high risk" has different meanings to different surgeons and in different institutions. Consequently, there was a fairly rapid expansion in the pool of patients considered candidates for axillofemoral bypass during the early experience. By the mid to late 1970s, some authors advocated extending these procedures to more patients and in some cases even advocated axillofemoral bypass as the

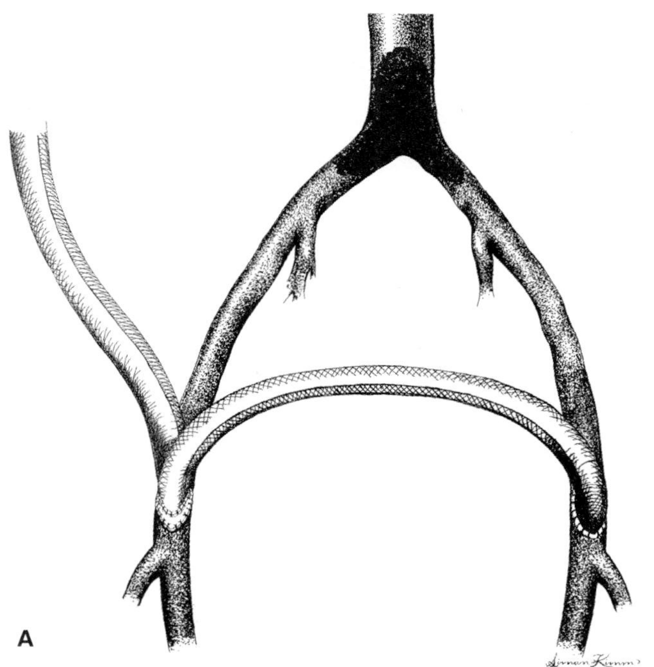

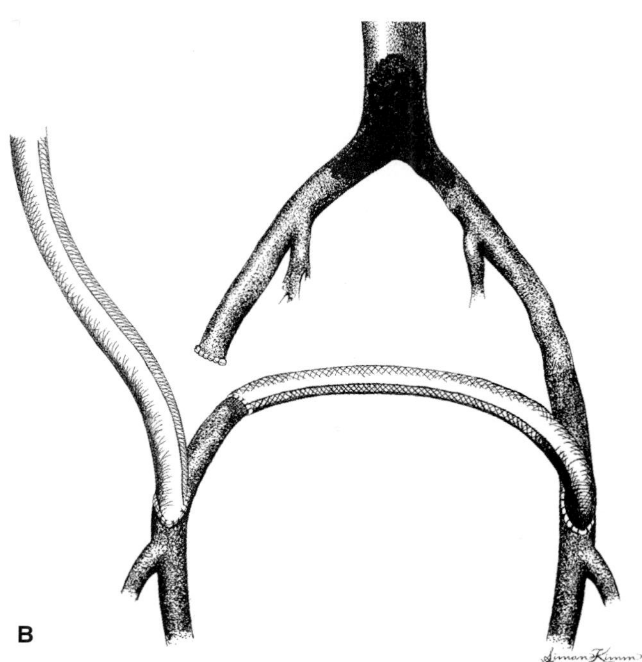

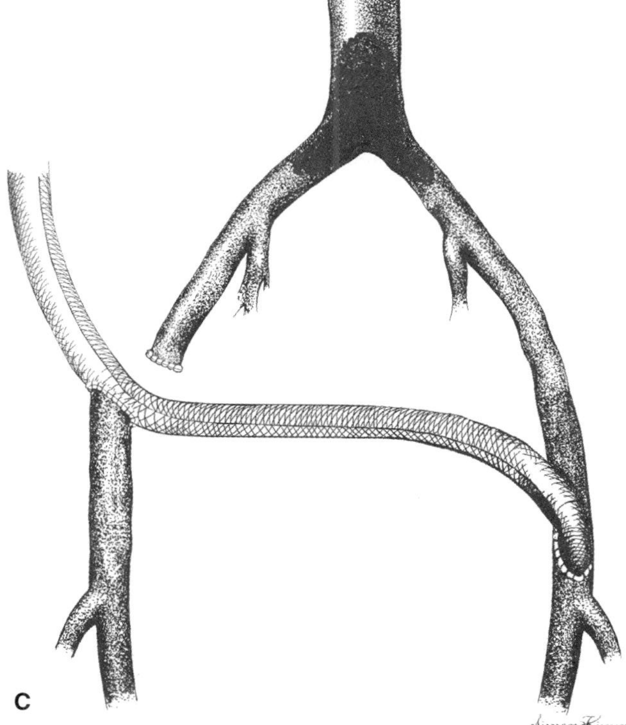

FIGURE 80-3 Three configurations of axillobifemoral bypass grafts. All three are shown with a right-sided axillofemoral graft component. **A** illustrates the most common configuration.[32] Note that in this case, the right anastomosis of the femorofemoral graft component is piggybacked onto the distal anastomosis of the axillofemoral graft component to try to maintain maximum volume flow throughout the axillofemoral component into the ipsilateral femoral outflow. **B** and **C** illustrate modifications described by Blaisdell[21] and Rutherford and Rainer,[68] respectively, designed to prevent competitive inflow from a patent ipsilateral iliac system.[21] In **B,** the common femoral artery is divided superior to the distal axillofemoral anastomosis and the femorofemoral graft component is anastomosed end to end to the distal part of the divided common femoral artery. In **C**, the common femoral artery is divided as in **B,** but the common femoral artery is anastomosed to the side of the axillofemoral graft, which is then continued from the right groin to the left groin for the left femoral anastomosis. This latter configuration has the potential advantage of reducing the total number of anastomoses from four to three. Prevention of competitive inflow in configurations illustrated in **B** and **C** may theoretically reduce the chance of thrombosis.

procedure of choice for all but the youngest and healthiest of patients when anatomy allowed. Many surgeons were strongly influenced by three specific favorable reports,[32,72,73] but the favorable experience reported in these articles may have been due to the characteristics of the patients reported and the approach to patency reporting.

Claudicants have generally been found to enjoy better patency than patients with resting ischemia for virtually every type of arterial reconstruction for chronic lower extremity arterial disease. Furthermore, claudicants tend to live longer than patients with limb-threatening ischemia and through that mechanism tend to contribute to patency life-tables longer than do those with resting ischemia. Thus, series with substantial numbers of low-risk claudicants tend to report disproportionately more favorable patency experience than do those restricted to high-risk patients with

Table 80-1 Comparison of Indications, Patient Characteristics, and Mortality with Graft Patency

FIRST AUTHOR, REFERENCE NO.	*N*	MEAN AGE, YEARS	CHRONIC LIMB THREAT, %	CHRONIC CLAUDICATION, %	ACUTE ISCHEMIA, %	OTHER INDICATION, %	SMOKING HISTORY, %
Eugene[76]	59	66	64	12	0	24	—
Allison[79]	94	61	88	5	0	7	80
Ascher[80]	56	69	95	0	5	0	68
Donaldson[77]	100	67	64	19	0	17	—
Schneider[12]	34	70	88	6	6	0	100
Kalman[78]	90	67	67	6	0	27	—
Naylor[81]	38	68	95	0	5	0	—
Johnson[72,†]	56	63	78	22	0	0	—
Passman[4]	108	68	80	20	0	0	86
Ray[32]	54	67	31	59	0	10	72
Harris[3,‡]	76	65	—	—	—	26	93
el-Massry[74]	79	69	59	38	0	3	77

*Not quoted for 3 years but estimated from life table graphs in original article.
†Method of patency calculation in this article appears consistent with the Society of Vascular Surgery definition of secondary patency.[75]
‡Included because of unusually high graft patency despite lack of adequate information regarding indications for surgery and late mortality. Subsequent update of this series showed 78% 3-year primary patency.[90]

resting ischemia. Finally, some of these favorable reports were based on the use of what is currently termed *secondary patency*. Nearly all authors have noted that axillofemoral bypass grafts are more likely than aortofemoral grafts to suffer thrombosis, and the favorable secondary patency of the former was at the expense of a significantly more frequent requirement for graft thrombectomy. Some reports have also considered the axillofemoral and femorofemoral components of axillobifemoral grafts as two distinct grafts, thus doubling the total number of "observed" grafts. Thrombosis of one component has only half as much impact on the patency calculations as it would if the entire graft is considered as a unit. We consider this approach as misleading at best since a patient would find little consolation in persistent patency of half of their graft when they are told they will require amputation because of thrombosis of the other component of their graft.

Reviews of the published literature addressing axillofemoral bypass for chronic lower extremity ischemia in the nearly 25 years since those earlier optimistic articles have generally been much less optimistic. The two possible exceptions have been the uniquely favorable experience of el-Massry and colleagues[74] and that reported by the group at the Oregon Health Sciences University.[3,4] It is intriguing to examine these reports after separating them into those without and those with significant numbers of claudicants.

Table 80-1 represents the results of our prior review[14] with the addition of data from Passman and coworkers.[4] We selected articles that we thought provided adequate information about indications for axillofemoral bypass, co-morbidities, and late mortality and that clearly used life table methods to calculate patency as defined using Society for Vascular Surgery criteria.[75] It was often unclear in these articles whether patency was calculated by number of graft limbs or number of patients. These studies are arranged in Table 80-1 in order of ascending primary patency.[3,4,12,32,72,74,76-81] With the exception of the report of Donaldson and associates,[77] the results are fairly easily separated into series with few claudicants, including our own previous report versus series that include significant numbers of claudicants, the former comprising six of the first seven citations and the latter comprising Donaldson and associates[77] plus the last five citations in the table. Thus, it appears that inclusion of as few as 20% claudicants in such a series has potentially dramatic impact on the patency experience of axillofemoral bypass. Operative and late mortality, where reported, are also lower in those series with larger numbers of claudicants, thus enhancing the patency predictions by the mechanisms discussed earlier. Finally, there is a wide range in the frequencies of various co-morbidities in patients undergoing axillofemoral bypass, reinforcing the contention that "high risk" is different in different institutions. Jämsén and colleagues have also provided an excellent recent description of their results, but the lack of separation of claudicants from those with resting ischemia did not allow inclusion in Table 80-1.[82] However, review of those authors' results show them to be generally consistent with those described by others and included in Table 80-1.

We have identified no prospective, randomized comparisons of axillofemoral and aortofemoral bypass, and we are aware of only five reports using the case-control approach to analyzing outcome in contemporaneous patients treated with axillofemoral and aortofemoral bypass in a single institution. Johnson and colleagues compared primary axillofemoral bypass to contemporaneous results with aortofemoral bypass in the same institution and observed 76% (axillofemoral) versus 77% (aortofemoral) secondary graft patency at 5 years.[72] Our experience was substantially different, yielding 63% (axillofemoral) versus 85% (aortofemoral) primary patency at 3 years for contemporaneous patients in a study with only 6% claudicants in the axillofemoral group.[12] Inspection of the life table patency graph in the study by Mason and coworkers suggests significantly

CORONARY ARTERY DISEASE, %	HYPERTENSION, %	COPD, %	DIABETES MELLITUS, %	OPERATIVE MORTALITY, %	3-YEAR MORTALITY, %	3-YEAR PRIMARY PATENCY, %	3-YEAR SECONDARY PATENCY, %
76 "heart disease"	41	61	19	8	53*	39*	—
45	55	40	—	6.4	44	43	—
≥41	41	—	32	5	40* 57 @ 5 yr	47	85*
51 "cardiac disease"	38	44	19	8	38	54	72
91	68	74	56	18	65	63	74
—	—	—	20	9	50	68	—
82	50	—	13	11	66 @ 5 yr	71	79
—	—	—	—	1.8	21* 33 @ 5 yr	—	76 @ 5 yr
84§	—	13	29	3	57	74 @ 3 and 5 yr	—
22	37	11	22	3.7	—	79	—
68	57	—	30	4.5	—	85	—
58	62	35	16	5	33*	85 78 @ 5 yr	88*

§Listed as "heart disease," not clearly restricted to coronary artery disease.
COPD, chronic obstructive pulmonary disease.

Modified from Schneider JR: The role of extraanatomic bypass in the management of bilateral aortoiliac occlusive disease. Semin Vasc Surg 7:35-44, 1994.

lower patency for axillofemoral bypass as compared to aortobifemoral bypass.[11] Passman and associates reported a 5-year primary patency rate of 74% (axillofemoral) versus 80% (aortofemoral), a difference that was not statistically significant.[4] The discrepancy in results is almost certainly related to significant differences in patient mix as noted earlier, the use of secondary patency in Johnson's work and primary patency in ours, and the fact that our own review included both primary and secondary axillofemoral and aortobifemoral bypass procedures. The results reported by Passman and associates remain impressive even after this type of scrutiny. Despite the enthusiasm for axillofemoral bypass among a few authors, most continue to view this operation as most appropriate for patients at very high risk for aortofemoral bypass and who cannot be treated with iliac balloon angioplasty or as part of the treatment for infection of the native aorta or previously placed aortic prostheses.[83] A more recent publication[84] from the same institution as Passman and associates do not report life-table estimates of patency, but review of the material in that article suggests that patency results in patients treated more recently are not as favorable as those reported previously and are more consistent with others' experience. Onohara and associates have performed a multivariate analysis of patients undergoing axillofemoral and aortofemoral bypass, and their analysis suggests that axillofemoral bypass patency is comparable to that for aortofemoral bypass after adjustment for other factors.[85] Such a conclusion is intriguing but would require validation by others before it could be generally accepted.

Limb salvage may be the best criterion to assess operations for limb-threatening ischemia, but appropriate life table estimates of limb salvage are unusual in published reports of axillofemoral bypass. Limb salvage may also include results in claudicants or other patients whose surgical indications did not include limb-threatening ischemia. Examination of reports in which life table methods are clearly used in patients suffering predominantly from chronic limb-threatening ischemia or in which separate results are tabulated for patients whose initial presentation was chronic, limb-threatening ischemia yields 3-year limb salvage ranging from 69% to slightly more than 80%, a range much narrower than that for patency.[12,78,81,86] Most important, although axillofemoral bypass does not provide complete hemodynamic normalization, it appears to provide limb salvage in most patients whose initial indication for reconstruction is limb-threatening ischemia.

Effect of Graft Material and External Support

The first axillofemoral bypasses were performed when only saphenous vein or unsupported Dacron grafts were available. Externally supported Dacron, ePTFE, and xPTFE have subsequently become available, and each has been touted as superior to their predecessors as measured by patency. Several retrospective studies comparing Dacron and PTFE detected no differences in patency.[87-89] Published studies that suggest improved results with a new graft material suffer from the problem of comparison to historical controls. Harris and colleagues[3] reported excellent results with xPTFE when compared with the same group's prior results with unsupported grafts of unspecified material. A subsequent update of this series produced a downward revision of patency, although the results remain impressive.[90] However, the number of claudicants was not specified in that study, and we observed much less favorable results with the identical xPTFE graft placed during roughly the same period in a high-risk group consisting nearly exclusively of patients with limb-threatening ischemia and severe outflow disease.[12] el-Massry and coworkers[74] reported excellent results with externally supported Dacron grafts in a series with 38% claudicants, but their results were only marginally better than those with unsupported Dacron prostheses from the same group published 14 years earlier.[32] Finally, hemodynamic studies attempting to assess the importance of external compression as a potential cause of graft thrombosis have yielded conflicting results[91,92] and the basic assumptions that graft compression is a cause of failure or that external support prevents compressive occlusion of the graft remain unconfirmed.

A randomized, prospective comparison of supported Dacron versus xPTFE axillofemoral bypass grafts was completed several years ago and has at long last been published, demonstrating no detectable difference between externally supported Dacron and xPTFE axillofemoral grafts.[93] xPTFE, collagen-impregnated Dacron, and gelatin-coated Dacron grafts all are convenient, avoiding the requirement for preclotting and possible bleeding within the subcutaneous tunnel, and any of these can be used with similar outcome expectations. The concept of external support has face validity, and we continue to employ externally supported grafts, although this is not based on solid evidence. Development of new prosthetic grafts may alter our preferences in the future.

Axillo-unifemoral Versus Axillobifemoral Configuration, Graft Diameter, and Other Hemodynamic Considerations

The average resting flow in an axillobifemoral graft is on the order of 600 mL/min.[12] This is consistent with the estimated resting flow of 300 to 400 mL/min in each common femoral artery[94] and is comparable to or even slightly less than the average estimated flow in upper extremity arteriovenous dialysis fistulae. Thus it is not surprising that axillofemoral bypass can provide adequate flow to support the legs. However, axillofemoral bypass does not provide a normal hemodynamic result. There is some evidence that axillofemoral bypass does not result in acceptable improvement in claudication symptoms.[38] We previously noted that axillofemoral bypass resulted in a predicted ankle-brachial index of only about 0.7 with normal outflow vessels, much inferior to the results with conventional aortofemoral bypass, and we also noted a trend toward less satisfactory improvement as measured by ankle-brachial index in patients with greater estimated graft flow.[12] Nevertheless, axillofemoral bypass usually provides adequate enhancement of perfusion to allow limb salvage in most patients.

Axillofemoral bypass was originally described as a unilateral (unifemoral) procedure. Sauvage and Wood were probably the first to suggest that patency of axillobifemoral grafts would be superior to axillo-unifemoral grafts because of the increased blood flow in the former.[95] The majority opinion for more than 20 years was that axillobifemoral grafts enjoy patency superior to that of axillo-unifemoral grafts and that axillofemoral bypass should virtually always be performed in a bifemoral configuration.[32,38,72,78,96-99] Recent evidence suggests that this dogma may be flawed. Diameter of graft components is not stated in all published reports. Ray and colleagues suggested an increased rate of thrombosis for 8-mm-diameter grafts when flow is less than 240 mL/min.[32] Published estimates of flow in axillo-unifemoral grafts are only slightly more than this 240 mL/min threshold, whereas estimated flows are roughly twice as high in axillobifemoral grafts,[12,73] thus providing a plausible theoretical explanation for the alleged superior patency of the axillobifemoral configuration. Dr. Ray's work also implies that larger diameter grafts would be at risk of thrombosis at even higher minimum flow rates, suggesting that axillofemoral grafts should be no more than 8 mm in diameter and that 10- and 12-mm-diameter grafts would be at very high risk of thrombosis in axillo-unifemoral configuration.

Despite these observations and the theoretical arguments, other authors have foun[d no difference[12,76,80,100,101] or no more than an insignificant trend toward improved patency[77] for axillobifemoral grafts. Ascher and coworkers used 6-mm-diameter axillofemoral components for axillo-unifemoral and axillobifemoral grafts and observed no discrepancy in patency between these configurations.[80] The work of Ray and associates would suggest a thrombosis threshold of substantially less than 240 mL/min for a 6-mm graft.[32] It is also ironic that the highest reported patency for axillofemoral grafts that we have been able to identify came from a series dominated by axillo-unifemoral grafts and performed by the group that originally championed the axillobifemoral configuration.[74] Thus, it appears that axillo-unifemoral bypass performed with a 6- or 8-mm- diameter graft performs as well as an axillobifemoral bypass performed with an 8-mm axillofemoral component. I prefer an 8-mm xPTFE axillofemoral component and a 6-mm xPTFE femorofemoral component for axillobifemoral grafts. I have generally used an 8-mm xPTFE graft for axillo-unifemoral grafts unless the patient is small, in which case I have chosen a 6-mm xPTFE graft.

Effect of Outflow Disease

The patency of the superficial femoral artery has been found by some authors to be an important determinant of axillofemoral graft patency[32,38,73] and by others not to impact on axillofemoral patency.[4,12,80] Others and we have found it necessary to perform local procedures to ensure good flow, usually to the deep femoral artery, in a substantial fraction of cases, certainly more than we have found in aortofemoral bypass.[12,69] We have used the same principles, including passage of a 3.5-mm probe into either the superficial or deep femoral artery, as in femorofemoral bypass to ensure adequate outflow. Thus, the inability to demonstrate a difference between patients with patent versus those with occluded superficial femoral arteries may reflect the effect of an aggressive approach to ensuring adequate deep femoral arterial outflow.

Axillopopliteal Bypass

Axillofemoral bypass has occasionally been extended to the popliteal artery, primarily in cases when there is groin sepsis and the superficial femoral artery is an unacceptable distal target vessel or the surgeon believes that foot perfusion will not be adequately enhanced by a bypass to the groin because of infrainguinal occlusive disease. Both Ascher[102] and McCarthy[103] and their colleagues noted acceptable performance of this configuration. However, both of these groups found that patency was inferior to that expected with more conventional reconstructions. This is not surprising, given the long graft length and requirement to cross at least one flexion point. Indeed, it is more surprising that any of these compromised grafts remain patent. Nevertheless, this technique may occasionally be the only reasonable approach to patients with groin sepsis or who are unacceptable risks for more conventional reconstruction and whose arterial occlusive anatomy is not amenable to either an inflow or outflow procedure alone.

Complications

Although axillofemoral bypass is subject to the same complications as other arterial operations discussed in Section X, there are several complications unique to axillofemoral bypass including brachial plexus injuries, the so-called axillary pullout syndrome, and thromboembolic risks to the donor arm and recipient legs following thrombosis of the graft. Kempczinski and Penn described two of these three complications, including two apparent brachial plexus injuries in four patients.[104] White and associates reviewed five of their own cases of axillary pullout and cited a small number of prior descriptions as well as information provided by the U.S. Food and Drug Administration and concluded that axillary pullout is "not rare."[105] At least one similar case appears to have been induced by crutch walking.[106] Taylor and colleagues have provided an excellent review of the literature concerning this problem and have described a proposed modification of the technique to allow some redundancy of the graft to prevent this complication.[67,107] It is likely that axillary pullout occurs because of placement of the axillary artery-to-graft anastomosis too far lateral on the axillary artery or failure to provide some graft redundancy as has been recommended earlier. Bandyk,[108] Khalil,[109] McLafferty,[110] and Mawatari[111] and their colleagues have described upper extremity thromboembolic complications in patients with thrombosed axillofemoral grafts. We have observed the latter phenomenon to occur in three episodes in all three involved extremities in a single patient with a thrombosed axillobifemoral graft. Kempczinski and Penn[104] and later Hartman and coworkers[112] described axillary artery thromboses in patients with axillofemoral grafts, a phenomenon likely mechanistically similar to the emboli described by Bandyk and others. Reports of these complications are unusual, and we have been unable to find any from the past several years, suggesting that they may be less common as the technique has evolved and become more familiar to more surgeons. Infection of axillofemoral bypass grafts poses unique problems since these patients have often been treated for failure of prior reconstructions and often have multiple comorbidities, making them extremely poor candidates for more surgery to deal with this problem.[64,113,114]

■ OBTURATOR BYPASS

Indications and Patient Selection

Shaw and Baue first described a bypass routed through the obturator foramen as a technique to deal with infected arterial prostheses in the groin.[8] The term *obturator bypass* is imprecise at best. Alternative terms such as *transobturator foramen bypass* would be preferable, but obturator bypass is in common usage. The original description employed Dacron in all three cases,[8] but ePTFE, xPTFE, saphenous vein in various configurations, autologous deep vein, and human umbilical vein all have been employed.[115-118] The operation has also been used to reconstruct patients with groin sepsis without prior prosthetic grafting, patients with infected pseudoaneurysms after intra-arterial recreational drug abuse or after diagnostic or therapeutic femoral arterial cannulation, those with groin neoplasm, or arterial and other soft tissue damage from prior groin irradiation. The presence of an infected prosthetic aortofemoral graft limb on the side to be reconstructed is a relative contraindication for obturator bypass, particularly if there is frank pus adjacent to the graft limb. Preoperative imaging studies may indicate involvement of the aortofemoral graft limb, and in such cases, other techniques such as axillopopliteal bypass may be the only alternatives.

Technique and Graft Configuration

The operation is typically performed with general anesthesia. The patient is placed supine and the abdomen is prepped. The leg to be reconstructed is prepped circumferentially to allow manipulation during the operation. Infected wounds are excluded from the field as much as possible. The donor artery is most often exposed using a curvilinear lower quadrant incision and a retroperitoneal exposure, although an initial transperitoneal approach may also be used. The common or external iliac artery may serve as the donor artery. As noted earlier, an aortofemoral graft limb may also serve as the donor vessel if the surgeon believes this portion of the graft is uninvolved with the infection.[119] This alternative requires that the graft be divided and the distal infected portion excluded from the operative field until the bypass has been completed and the wounds closed prior to exploring the groin wound for removal of infected prosthetic material and native tissue. Our experience with obturator bypass includes patients with infected infrainguinal bypass grafts, infected prosthetic dialysis grafts based on groin vessels, infected pseudoaneurysms after recreational drug use or diagnostic or therapeutic arterial cannulation, and arterial occlusive disease in irradiated groins. Thus, none of our patients has had a prosthetic inflow source, and we have not had occasion to use this approach. The obturator foramen is approached from this same incision by dissection medial to the external iliac vein and posterior to the pubic ramus and blunt dissection of the obturator internus muscle away from the obturator membrane (Fig. 80-4). The obturator artery and nerve perforate this membrane posterolaterally so that it is safest to avoid these structures by passing the graft through the anteromedial aspect of the obturator foramen. The membrane is extremely strong and cannot be perforated bluntly without risk of injuring adjacent structures; therefore, it must be opened sharply.

The target vessel is often the popliteal or distal superficial femoral artery but may be the deep femoral artery.[120] However, approaching the deep femoral artery from the posteromedial side, though technically possible, risks entry into the infected groin and should be avoided for this reason in most cases. In any case, an incision is made along the mid

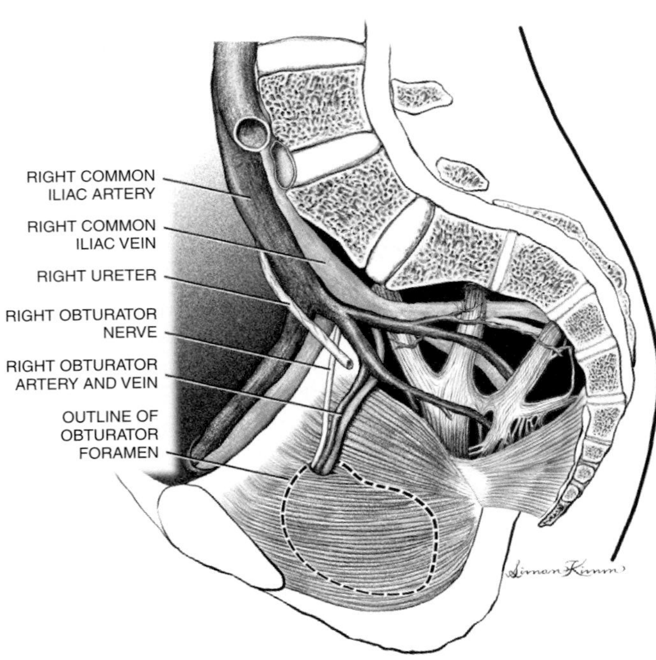

FIGURE 80-4 Approach to the obturator foramen with adjacent iliac vessels as viewed from the medial side of the pelvis.

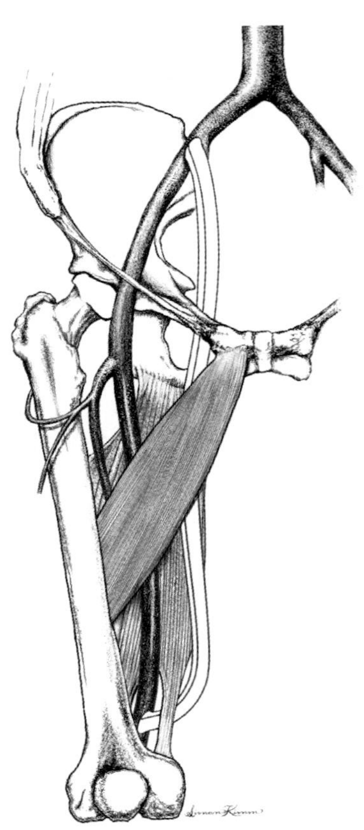

FIGURE 80-5 Typical course of the obturator bypass graft, in this case terminating at the popliteal artery.

to upper medial thigh, taking care not to enter the contaminated area of the groin. The tunnel between the inflow and target arteries is made most often in the potential space between the adductor longus and brevis muscles anteriorly and the adductor magnus muscle posteriorly, which leads directly to the obturator foramen (Fig. 80-5), although some authors have recommended that the tunnel be maintained posterior to the adductor magnus to reduce the risk of entry into the contaminated groin. Some authors have recommended passing the tunneling device from superior to inferior, but we have found it easiest to pass the tunneling device from inferior,[121] especially when the iliac exposure is limited, such as by obesity, stomas, or the very noncompliant lower abdominal wall often observed in patients after radiation. The superficial femoral artery is easily identified and controlled in the plane of the tunnel anterior to the adductor magnus muscle. However, if the popliteal artery is the target, the graft will either require tunneling through the tendinous portion of the adductor magnus (as the native superficial femoral artery does at the adductor hiatus) or be brought around the adductor tendon as a conventional femoropopliteal graft would be. The proximal and distal anastomoses are then completed using standard techniques, usually end to side, to both donor and target arteries. Once the reconstruction has been completed, the surgical incisions are closed and excluded before the groin is explored to remove any infected prosthetic or native material and ligate vessels as necessary to prevent hemorrhage. We have on occasion anastomosed the superficial femoral to the deep femoral artery after débridement of the common femoral artery, thus allowing blood at systemic pressures to reach the deep femoral artery by retrograde flow when the superficial femoral artery is patent, hoping to avoid thigh and buttock ischemia.[115,122] This has been done only in cases when we thought that the sepsis was well controlled, the arteries were débrided back to grossly healthy tissue, and the infecting organism was an antibiotic-sensitive *Staphylococcus aureus*. We would recommend against this practice with gram-negative organisms, especially *Pseudomonas* species.[123]

Shaw and Baue's initial description of the obturator bypass used prosthetic graft material, but two of their three patients suffered from recurrent graft infection. However, Patel and associates have described a series of prosthetic obturator bypass grafts (eight PTFE, four Dacron) without an apparent case of infection of the new graft.[119] Benjamin and colleagues have described five patients with infected pseudoaneurysms due to recreational drug use and in whom autologous deep venous conduit was used to construct obturator bypasses with control of sepsis and limb salvage in all five patients.[118] Others and we have used autologous vein in all cases and have not had problems of persistent infection in any case.[116,117]

Sautner and colleagues provided an excellent review of mortality, graft patency, and limb salvage in patients undergoing obturator bypass.[124] The patency rates of 73% and 57% at 1 and 5 years, respectively, and limb salvage of 77% at 5 years are somewhat less than would be expected with conventional femoropopliteal bypass, but these figures are better than would be expected with simple excision of infected graft material with local measures, including muscle flap[125] or nonoperative treatment. However, Nevelsteen,[115] Kretschmer,[126] and their coworkers presented substantially less optimistic estimates of 5-year patency, and the surgeon can expect to be faced with revision or new reconstruction in a significant number of these patients.

Complications

Persistent or recurrent infection and hemorrhage from the groin vessels are the primary complications associated with obturator bypass. Use of autogenous material seems to effectively reduce the risk of infection of the obturator bypass graft and the operative sites associated with grafting. Reducing the risk of hemorrhage depends on generous débridement of infected and necrotic tissue, secure closure in healthy portions of the groin vessels, and coverage with healthy adjacent tissue such as the sartorius muscle[127] or gracilis muscle flap[128] whenever possible. Injury to the obturator nerve and artery is possible, especially if the tunnel is not kept in the anteromedial portion of the obturator fossa. Even more unusual complications of transvaginal[124] and transbladder[129] passage of the graft have been reported.

■ THORACOFEMORAL BYPASS

Indications and Patient Selection

The first known use of thoracofemoral bypass was to treat a patient with prior abdominal surgery and failed prior infrarenal aortic replacement,[22] and shortly thereafter, a similar technique was employed to treat a patient with an infected aortic prosthesis.[130] These remain the primary indications for thoracofemoral bypass today. However, results of thoracofemoral bypass have been so encouraging that at least one group has advocated the use of thoracofemoral bypass as primary treatment in selected patients with aortoiliac occlusive disease.[131] The procedure is formidable and is certainly distinct from axillofemoral bypass in that regard. Thus, the procedure is most applicable for patients who are physiologically appropriate for thoracotomy.

Technique and Graft Configuration

Several authors have described similar techniques for thoracofemoral bypass. The operation is performed using general endotracheal anesthesia. Some authors have recommended use of a dual-lumen endotracheal tube to allow collapse of the left lung to facilitate surgery,[131] but others have found this not to be essential.[9,132,133] The pelvis is kept as horizontal as possible while the left chest is elevated to approximately 45 degrees off the horizontal. A left thoracotomy is performed through the 7th, 8th, or 9th intercostal space or with removal of the 7th or 8th rib allowing exposure and control of an adequate portion of the mid to distal descending thoracic aorta (Fig. 80-6). The inferior pulmonary ligament is generally divided to facilitate this exposure. Distal anastomoses are typically made to the

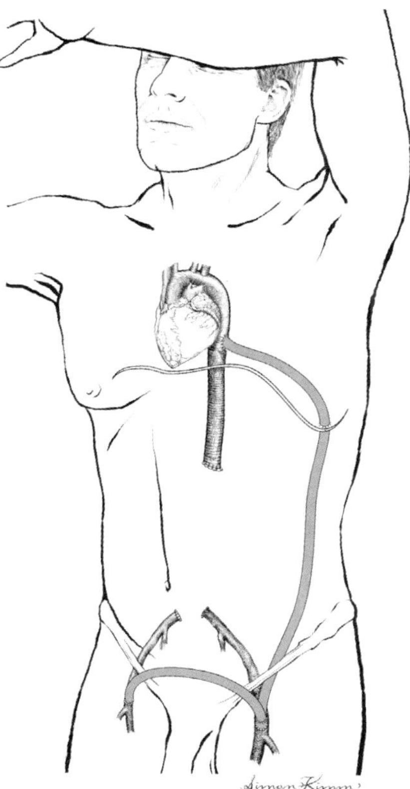

FIGURE 80-6 Typical course of the thoracofemoral bypass graft. This illustrates a single graft from the descending aorta to the left common femoral artery with a left-to-right femorofemoral graft. Other approaches, some involving the use of a bifurcated graft, are possible (see text).

femoral arteries but may be made to the iliac arteries as dictated by anatomy. Standard exposures of these vessels are achieved with groin incisions or retroperitoneal incisions. The graft must be tunneled from the chest into the extraperitoneal abdominal space. Some authors have recommended carrying the intercostal incision across the costal margin, allowing access to the anterior extraperitoneal space.[9] The graft can be tunneled extraperitoneally from the left hemithorax to the left femoral arteries in the anterior axillary line using only a small peripheral incision in the diaphragm and an incision in the left inguinal ligament to gain access to the extraperitoneal space from inferiorly. Tunneling the graft in the retroperitoneum posterior to the left kidney may require a separate incision in the mid to lower left abdominal wall to gain access to the retroperitoneum,[131] but this facilitates exposure of the left iliac arteries when one of these is the proposed target. Kalman has described a technique whereby the graft may be tunneled without exposure of the retroperitoneum apparently completely blindly from the left groin posterior to the left kidney up to the left posterior diaphragmatic attachments.[133] The graft may be a straight graft from the descending aorta to the left iliofemoral arteries with a crossover graft from the left to the right as necessary or may be a standard bifurcated graft. The former approach is our preference and is particularly useful when converting an axillobifemoral graft with a patent femorofemoral component to a thoracobifemoral graft since the crossover component is already in place. The right limb of a standard bifurcated graft is usually too short and must be extended to reach the right groin and also may have a tendency to kink if brought out under the left inguinal ligament and then turned to the right in the subcutaneous suprapubic space as a conventional femorofemoral bypass. Thus, it is probably better placed in the preperitoneal space of Retzius.[133] Once the inflow and target arteries have been controlled and the graft has been tunneled, the patient is given heparin and the operation is performed using standard vascular surgical techniques. The aorta is generally clamped completely proximally and distally during performance of the proximal-side aorta-to-end-graft anastomosis. The graft is clamped and the aortic clamps are removed as early as possible to reperfuse intra-abdominal viscera and, possibly, the spinal cord during performance of distal anastomoses. McMillan and McCarthy have recently described a thoracoscopic approach to the thoracic portion of the operation.[134]

Results

Thoracofemoral bypass is associated with patency approaching that for aortofemoral bypass, an observation that is remarkable given the fact that most of these operations are performed after the failure of one or more prior more conventional reconstructions. McCarthy and colleagues reported no thromboses prior to 49 months in their series of 21 grafts.[9] Passman and coworkers reported a 5-year primary patency of 79% in 50 patients.[131] Five of the largest known series of these operations[9,131,132,135,136] reported a combined total of three perioperative deaths out of a total of 112 patients. Intensive care unit and total hospital stays have tended to be longer than those for standard aortofemoral bypass, reflecting the fact that this is at least as formidable a procedure as aortofemoral bypass.

■ SUMMARY

Extra-anatomic bypass grafts provide alternatives to direct arterial reconstructions for many aortic and lower extremity arterial problems in selected patients. These procedures play an important role in the reconstruction of patients with infection of native vessels or of prosthetic arterial replacements. Despite the fact that these open procedures are "mature," as they have changed little in the past several years, their role in patients with lower extremity arterial occlusive disease continues to be a subject of debate. Axillofemoral and femorofemoral bypasses are undoubtedly less injurious to the patient than is aortofemoral bypass, but these procedures are associated with less satisfactory results as measured both by hemodynamic improvement and by patency. They produce adequate enhancement of perfusion to allow limb salvage in selected patients, but they are rarely indicated as treatment for claudication. Patient selection may have significant impact on patency estimates from an individual surgeon or institution's patient sample, but the hemodynamic inferiority of these reconstructions is not likely to be sensitive to patient selection. Obturator bypass is less often indicated and technically more challenging than more conventional infrainguinal bypasses but is an excellent technique to avoid problematic femoral vessels and provides perfusion and patency approaching that of conventional infrainguinal reconstructions. Thoracofemoral bypass is perhaps the least often performed of these four basic procedures. However, despite its formidable nature and the fact that it is likely to be employed in unusually difficult situations, the results of thoracofemoral bypass are excellent as measured by patient survival, hemodynamic performance, and patency. Thus, each of these procedures should be in the armamentarium of every vascular surgeon. The choice of the appropriate inflow procedure has much more to do with patient co-morbidities than with the specific anatomy of the patient's arterial disease. As with everything else we do, a key element of achieving good outcomes with extra-anatomic bypass procedures is proper patient selection.

Acknowledgment Simon Kimm, MD, created the illustrations.

■ REFERENCES

1. Parsonnet V, Alpert J, Brief DK: Femorofemoral and axillofemoral grafts: Compromise or preference. Surgery 67:26-33, 1970.
2. Kalman PG, Hosang M, Johnston KW, Walker PM: The current role for femorofemoral bypass. J Vasc Surg 6:71-76, 1987.
3. Harris EJ Jr, Taylor LM, McConnell DB, et al: Clinical results of axillobifemoral bypass using externally supported polytetrafluoroethylene. J Vasc Surg 12:416-421, 1990.
4. Passman MA, Taylor LM, Moneta GL, et al: Comparison of axillofemoral and aortofemoral bypass for aortoiliac occlusive disease. J Vasc Surg 23:263-271, 1996.
5. Chuter TA, Faruqi RM, Reilly LM, et al: Aortomonoiliac endovascular grafting combined with femorofemoral bypass: An acceptable compromise or a preferred solution? Semin Vasc Surg 12:176-181, 1999.
6. Rehring TF, Brewster DC, Cambria RP, et al: Utility and reliability of endovascular aortouniiliac with femorofemoral crossover graft for aortoiliac aneurysmal disease. J Vasc Surg 31:1135-1141, 2000.
7. Clouse WD, Brewster DC, Marone LK, et al, EVT/Guidant Investigators: Durability of aortouniiliac endografting with femorofemoral crossover: Four-year experience in the EVT/Guidant trials. J Vasc Surg 37:1142-1149, 2003.
8. Shaw RS, Baue AE: Management of sepsis complicating arterial reconstructive surgery. Surgery 53:75-86, 1963.
9. McCarthy WJ, Mesh CL, McMillan WD, et al: Descending thoracic aorta-to-femoral artery bypass: Ten years' experience with a durable procedure. J Vasc Surg 17:336-348, 1993.
10. Harris KA, Niesobska V, Carroll SE, et al: Extra-anatomic bypass grafting: A rational approach. Can J Surg 32:113-116, 1989.
11. Mason RA, Smirnov VB, Newton GB, Giron F: Alternative procedures to aortobifemoral bypass grafting. J Cardiovasc Surg 30:192-197, 1989.
12. Schneider JR, McDaniel MD, Walsh DB, et al: Axillofemoral bypass: Outcome and hemodynamic results in high-risk patients. J Vasc Surg 15:952-963, 1992.
13. Schneider JR, Besso SR, Walsh DB, et al: Femorofemoral versus aortobifemoral bypass: Outcome and hemodynamic results. J Vasc Surg 19:43-57, 1994.
14. Schneider JR, Golan JF: The role of extraanatomic bypass in the management of bilateral aortoiliac occlusive disease. Semin Vasc Surg 7:35-44, 1994.

15. Harrington ME, Harrington EB, Haimov M, et al: Axillofemoral bypass: Compromised bypass for compromised patients. J Vasc Surg 20:195-201, 1994.
16. Cronenwett JL, Garrett HE: Arteriographic measurement of the abdominal aorta, iliac, and femoral arteries in women with atherosclerotic occlusive disease. Radiology 148:389-392, 1983.
17. Freeman NE, Leeds FH: Operations on large arteries. Calif Med 77:229-233, 1952.
18. Vetto RM: The treatment of unilateral iliac artery obstruction with a trans-abdominal, subcutaneous, femoro-femoral graft. Surgery 52:342-345, 1962.
19. Blaisdell FW, Hall AD: Axillary-femoral artery bypass for lower extremity ischemia. Surgery 54:563-568, 1963.
20. Louw JH: Splenic-to-femoral and axillary-to-femoral bypass grafts in diffuse atherosclerotic occlusive disease. Lancet 1:1401-1402, 1963.
21. Blaisdell FW: Extraanatomical bypass procedures. World J Surg 12:798-804, 1988.
22. Stevenson JK, Sauvage LR, Harkins HN: A bypass homograft from thoracic aorta to femoral arteries for occlusive vascular disease: Case report. Ann Surg 27:632-637, 1961.
23. Couch NP, Clowes AW, Whittemore AD, et al: The iliac-origin arterial graft: A useful alternative for iliac occlusive disease. Surgery 97:83-87, 1985.
24. Sidawy AN, Menzoian JO, Cantelmo NL, LoGerfo FW: Retroperitoneal inflow procedures for iliac occlusive vascular disease. Arch Surg 120:794-796, 1985.
25. Cham C, Myers KA, Scott DF, et al: Extraperitoneal unilateral iliac artery bypass for chronic lower limb ischaemia. Aust N Z J Surg 58:859-863, 1988.
26. Harrington ME, Harrington EB, Haimov M, et al: Iliofemoral versus femorofemoral bypass: The case for an individualized approach. J Vasc Surg 16:841-854, 1992.
27. Oliveira M, Wilson SE, Williams R, Freischlag JA: Iliofemoral bypass: A 10-year review. Cardiovasc Surg 1:103-106, 1993.
28. Nazzal MM, Hoballah JJ, Jacobovicz C, et al: A comparative evaluation of femorofemoral crossover bypass and iliofemoral bypass for unilateral iliac artery occlusive disease. Angiology 49:259-265, 1998.
29. Brewster DC, Darling RC: Optimal methods of aortoiliac reconstruction. Surgery 84:739-748, 1978.
30. Defraigne JO, Vazquez C, Limet R: Crossover iliofemoral bypass grafting for treatment of unilateral iliac atherosclerotic disease. J Vasc Surg 30:693-700, 1999.
31. do Carmo G, Moura CM, Sarmento C, et al: A new approach for the surgical management of unilateral iliac artery occlusive disease: The iliofemoral crossover transposition. J Vasc Surg 36:404-407, 2002.
32. Ray LI, O'Connor JB, Davis CC, et al: Axillofemoral bypass: A critical reappraisal of its role in the management of aortoiliac disease. Surgery 138:117-128, 1979.
33. Archie JP: The value of donor iliac artery pressure gradients in predicting the outcome of femorofemoral bypass. J Vasc Surg 23:383-393, 1996.
34. Hakaim AG, Hertzer NR, O'Hara PJ, et al: Autogenous vein grafts for femorofemoral revascularization in contaminated or infected fields. J Vasc Surg 19:912-915, 1994.
35. Brener BJ, Brief DK, Alpert J, et al: Femorofemoral bypass: A twenty-five year experience. In Yao JST, Pearce WH (eds): Long-Term Results in Vascular Surgery. East Norwalk, CT, Appleton & Lange, 1993, pp 385-393.
36. Criado E, Burnham SJ, Tinsley EA Jr, et al: Femorofemoral bypass graft: Analysis of patency and factors influencing long-term outcome. J Vasc Surg 18:495-505, 1993.
37. Criado E, Farber MA: Femorofemoral bypass: Appropriate application based on factors affecting outcome. Semin Vasc Surg 10:34-41, 1997.
38. Rutherford RB, Patt A, Pearce WH: Extra-anatomic bypass: A closer view. J Vasc Surg 6:437-446, 1987.
39. Nolan KD, Benjamin ME, Murphy TJ, et al: Femorofemoral bypass for aortofemoral graft limb occlusion: A ten-year experience. J Vasc Surg 19:851-857, 1994.
40. Davis RC, O'Hara ET, Mannick JA, et al: Broadened indications for femorofemoral grafts. Surgery 72:990-994, 1972.
41. Sumner DS, Strandness DE Jr: The hemodynamics of the femorofemoral shunt. Surg Gynecol Obstet 134:629-636, 1972.
42. Flanigan DP, Pratt DG, Goodreau JJ, et al: Hemodynamic and angiographic guidelines in selection of patients for femorofemoral bypass. Arch Surg 113:1257-1262, 1978.
43. Livesay JJ, Atkinson JB, Baker JD, et al: Late results of extra-anatomic bypass. Arch Surg 114:1260-1267, 1979.
44. Anonymous: Donor limb vascular events following femoro-femoral bypass surgery. A Veterans Affairs Cooperative Study. Arch Surg 126:681-686, 1991.
45. Moore WS, Hall AD: Unrecognized aortoiliac stenosis: Physiologic approach to the diagnosis. Arch Surg 103:633-638, 1971.
46. Sako Y: Papaverine test in peripheral arterial disease. Surg Forum 17:141-143, 1966.
47. Flanigan DP, Ryan TJ, Williams LR, et al: Aortofemoral or femoropopliteal revascularization? A prospective evaluation of the papaverine test. J Vasc Surg 1:215-223, 1984.
48. Brief DK, Brener BJ, Alpert J, Parsonnet V: Cross-over femorofemoral grafts followed up five years or more: An analysis. Arch Surg 110:1294-1299, 1975.
49. Porter JM, Eidemiller LR, Dotter CT, et al: Combined arterial dilation and femorofemoral bypass for limb salvage. Surg Gynecol Obstet 137:409-412, 1973.
50. Dotter CT, Judkins MP: Transluminal treatment of arteriosclerotic obstruction: Description of new technique and a preliminary report of its application. Circulation 30:654-670, 1964.
51. Grüntzig A, Hopff H: Perkutane Rekanalisation chronischer arterieller Verschlüsse mit einem neuen Dilatationskatheter. Modifikation der Dotter-Technik. Dtsch Med Wochenschr 99:2502-2505, 1974.
52. Grüntzig A. Kumpe DA: Technique of percutaneous transluminal angioplasty with the Grüntzig balloon catheter. AJR Am J Roentgenol 132:547-552, 1979.
53. Howell HS, Ingram CH, Parham AR, et al: Transluminal angioplasty of the iliac artery combined with femorofemoral bypass. South Med J 76:49-51, 1983.
54. Brewster DC, Cambria RF, Darling RC, et al: Long-term results of combined iliac balloon angioplasty and distal surgical revascularization. Ann Surg 210:324-331, 1989.
55. Shah RM, Peer RM, Upson JF, Ricotta JJ: Donor iliac angioplasty and crossover femorofemoral bypass. Am J Surg 164:295-298, 1992.
56. Katz SG, Kohl RD, Yellin A: Iliac angioplasty as a prelude to distal arterial bypass. J Am Coll Surg 17:577-582, 1994.
57. Perler BA, Williams GM: Does donor iliac artery percutaneous transluminal angioplasty or stent placement influence the results of femorofemoral bypass? Analysis of 70 consecutive cases with long-term follow-up. J Vasc Surg 24:363-370, 1996.
58. Lopez-Galarza LA, Ray LI, Rodriguez-Lopez J, Diethrich EB: Combined percutaneous transluminal angioplasty, iliac stent deployment, and femorofemoral bypass for bilateral aortoiliac occlusive disease. J Am Coll Surg 184:249-258, 1997.
59. AbuRahma AF, Robinson PA, Cook CC, Hopkins ES: Selecting patients for combined femorofemoral bypass grafting and iliac balloon angioplasty and stenting for bilateral iliac disease. J Vasc Surg 33(2 Suppl):S93-S99, 2001.
60. Piotrowski JJ, Pearce WH, Jones DN, et al: Aortobifemoral bypass: The operation of choice for unilateral iliac occlusion? J Vasc Surg 8:211-218, 1988.
61. Ricco JB: Unilateral iliac artery occlusive disease: A randomized multicenter trial examining direct revascularization versus crossover bypass. Association Universitaire de Recherche en Chirurgie. Ann Vasc Surg 6:209-219, 1992.

62. Seeger JM, Pretus HA, Welborn MB, et al: Long-term outcome after treatment of aortic graft infection with staged extra-anatomic bypass grafting and aortic graft removal. J Vasc Surg 32:451-461, 2000.
63. Clagett GP, Valentine RJ, Hagino RT: Autogenous aortoiliac/femoral reconstruction from superficial femoral-popliteal veins: Feasibility and durability. J Vasc Surg 25:255-270, 1997.
64. Bandyk DF, Novotney ML, Johnson BL, et al: Use of rifampin-soaked gelatin-sealed polyester grafts for in situ treatment of primary aortic and vascular prosthetic infections. J Surg Res 95:44-49, 2001.
65. Calligaro KD, Ascher E, Veith FJ, et al: Unsuspected inflow disease in candidates for axillofemoral bypass operations: A prospective study. J Vasc Surg 11:832-837, 1990.
66. Bunt TJ, Moore W: Optimal proximal anastomosis/tunnel for axillofemoral grafts. J Vasc Surg 3:673-676, 1986.
67. Taylor LM Jr, Park TC, Edwards JM, et al: Acute disruption of polytetrafluoroethylene grafts adjacent to axillary anastomoses: A complication of axillofemoral grafting. J Vasc Surg 20:520-528, 1994.
68. Rutherford RB, Rainer W: A modified technique for performing axillobifemoral bypass grafting. J Vasc Surg 10:468-469, 1989.
69. Wittens CHA, van Houtte HJKP, van Urk H: European prospective randomised multi-centre axillo-bifemoral trial. Eur J Vasc Surg 6:115-123, 1992.
70. Wittens CHA: Haemodynamics in Axillobifemoral Bypass Graft. Doctoral thesis, Erasmus University, Rotterdam, Netherlands, 1992.
71. Bacourt F, Koskas F: Axillobifemoral bypass and aortic exclusion for vascular septic lesions: A multicenter retrospective study of 98 cases. French University Association for Research in Surgery. Ann Vasc Surg 6:119-126, 1992.
72. Johnson WC, LoGerfo FW, Vollman RW, et al: Is axillo-bilateral femoral graft an effective substitute for aortic-bilateral iliac/femoral graft? An analysis of ten years' experience. Ann Surg 186:123-129, 1977.
73. LoGerfo FW, Johnson WC, Corson JD, et al: A comparison of the late patency rates of axillobilateral femoral and axillounilateral femoral grafts. Surgery 81:33-40, 1977.
74. el-Massry S, Saad E, Sauvage LR, et al: Axillofemoral bypass with externally supported, knitted Dacron grafts: A follow-up through twelve years. J Vasc Surg 17:107-115, 1993.
75. Rutherford RB, Flanigan DP, Gupta SK, et al: Suggested standards for reports dealing with lower extremity ischemia. J Vasc Surg 4:80-94, 1986.
76. Eugene J, Goldstone J, Moore WS: Fifteen-year experience with subcutaneous bypass grafts for lower extremity ischemia. Ann Surg 186:177-183, 1977.
77. Donaldson MC, Louras JC, Bucknam CA: Axillofemoral bypass: A tool with a limited role. J Vasc Surg 3:757-763, 1986.
78. Kalman PG, Hosang M, Cina C, et al: Current indications for axillo-unifemoral and axillobifemoral bypass grafts. J Vasc Surg 5:828-832, 1987.
79. Allison HF, Terblanche J, Immelman EJ: Axillofemoral bypass: A two-decade experience. S Afr Med J 68:559-562, 1985.
80. Ascher E, Veith FJ, Gupta SK, et al: Comparison of axillounifemoral and axillobifemoral bypass operations. Surgery 97:167-174, 1985.
81. Naylor AR, Ah-See AK, Engeset J: Axillofemoral bypass as a limb salvage procedure in high-risk patients with aortoiliac disease. Br J Surg 77:659-661, 1990.
82. Jämsén T, Tulla H, Loponen P: Axillofemoral bypass operations in Kuopio University Hospital 1985-1996. Ann Chir Gynaecol 88:269-275, 1999.
83. Angle N, Dorafshar AH, Farooq MM, et al: The evolution of the axillofemoral bypass over two decades. Ann Vasc Surg 6:742-745, 2002.
84. Musicant SE, Giswold ME, Olson CJ, et al: Postoperative duplex scan surveillance of axillofemoral bypass grafts. J Vasc Surg 37:54-61, 2003.
85. Onohara T, Komori K, Kume M, et al: Multivariate analysis of long-term results after an axillobifemoral and aortobifemoral bypass in patients with aortoiliac occlusive disease. J Cardiovasc Surg 41:905-910, 2000.
86. Foster MC: A review of 155 extra-anatomic bypass grafts. Ann R Coll Surg Engl 68:216-218, 1986.
87. Burrell MJ, Wheeler JR, Gregory RT, et al: Axillofemoral bypass: A ten-year review. Ann Surg 195:796-799, 1982.
88. Courbier R, Jausseran JM, Bergeron P: Axillo-femoral bypass material of choice. In Greenhalgh RM (ed): Extra-anatomic Secondary Arterial Reconstruction. Bath, England, Pittman Press, 1982, pp 122-130.
89. Christenson JT, Broomè A, Norgren L, et al: The late results after axillo-femoral bypass in patients with leg ischaemia. J Cardiovasc Surg (Torino) 27:131-135, 1986.
90. Taylor LM: Clinical results of axillobifemoral bypass using externally supported polytetrafluoroethylene [Letter]. J Vasc Surg 13:564-565, 1991.
91. Jarowenko MV, Buchbinder D, Shah DM: Effect of external pressure on axillofemoral bypass graft. Ann Surg 193:274-276, 1981.
92. Cavallaro A, Sciacca V, di Marzo L, et al: The effect of body weight compression on axillofemoral bypass patency. J Cardiovasc Surg 29:476-479, 1988.
93. Johnson WC, Lee KK: Comparative evaluation of externally supported Dacron and polytetrafluoroethylene prosthetic bypasses for femorofemoral and axillofemoral arterial reconstructions. Veterans Affairs Cooperative Study No. 141. J Vasc Surg 30:1077-1083, 1999.
94. Field JP, Musson AM, Zwolak RM, et al: Duplex arterial flow measurements in normal lower extremities. J Vasc Technol 13:13-19, 1989.
95. Sauvage LR, Wood SJ: Unilateral axillary bilateral femoral bifurcation graft: A procedure for the high-risk patient with aortoiliac disease. Surgery 60:573-577, 1966.
96. Richardson JV, McDowell HA Jr: Extra-anatomic bypass grafting in aortoiliac occlusive disease: A seven-year experience. South Med J 70:1287-1291, 1977.
97. Hepp W, de Jonge K, Pallua N: Late results following extra-anatomic bypass procedures for chronic aortoiliac occlusive disease. J Cardiovasc Surg 29:181-185, 1988.
98. Cina C, Ameli FM, Kalman P, Provan JL: Indications and role of axillofemoral bypass in high-risk patients. Ann Vasc Surg 2:237-241, 1988.
99. Illuminati G, Calio FG, Mangialardi N, et al: Results of axillofemoral by-passes for aorto-iliac occlusive disease. Langenbecks Arch Chir 381:212-217, 1996.
100. Schroe H, Nevelsteen A, Suy R: Extra-anatomical grafting for aorto-occlusive disease: The outcome of 133 procedures. Acta Chir Belg 90:240-243, 1990.
101. Mohan CR, Sharp WJ, Hoballah JJ, et al: A comparative evaluation of externally supported polytetrafluoroethylene axillobifemoral and axillounifemoral bypass grafts. J Vasc Surg 21:801-808, 1995.
102. Ascher E. Veith FJ, Gupta S: Axillopopliteal bypass grafting: Indications, late results, and determinants of long-term patency. J Vasc Surg 10:285-291, 1989.
103. McCarthy WJ, McGee GS, Lin WW, et al: Axillary-popliteal artery bypass provides successful limb salvage after removal of infected aortofemoral grafts. Arch Surg 127:974-978, 1992.
104. Kempczinski R, Penn I: Upper extremity complications of axillo-femoral grafts. Am J Surg 136:209-211, 1978.
105. White GH, Donayre CE, Williams RA, et al: Exertional disruption of axillofemoral graft anastomosis: The "axillary pullout" syndrome. Arch Surg 125:625-627, 1990.
106. Anderson LS, Davis RJ, Simonet M, et al: New mechanism for disruption of axillofemoral bypass. J Vasc Surg 15:255-256, 1992.
107. Yeager RA, Taylor LM Jr: Axillary artery anastomosis to avoid axillofemoral bypass disruption. Semin Vasc Surg 13:74-76, 2000.
108. Bandyk DF, Thiele BL, Radke HM: Upper extremity emboli secondary to axillofemoral graft thrombosis. Arch Surg 116:393-395, 1981.

109. Khalil IM, Hoballah JJ: Late upper extremity embolic complications of occluded axillofemoral grafts. Ann Vasc Surg 5:375-380, 1991.
110. McLafferty RB, Taylor LM Jr, Moneta GL, et al: Upper extremity thromboembolism caused by occlusion of axillofemoral grafts. Am J Surg 169:492-495, 1995.
111. Mawatari K, Muto Y, Funahashi S, et al: The potential risk for upper extremity thromboembolism in patients with occluded axillofemoral bypass grafts: Two case reports. Vasc Surg 35:67-71, 2001.
112. Hartman AR, Fried KS, Khalil I, Riles TS: Late axillary artery thrombosis in patients with occluded axillary-femoral bypass grafts. J Vasc Surg 2:285-287, 1985.
113. Marston WA, Risley GL, Criado E, et al: Management of failed and infected axillofemoral grafts. J Vasc Surg 20:357-366, 1994.
114. de Virgilio C, Cherry KJ Jr, Gloviczki P, et al: Infected lower extremity extra-anatomic bypass grafts: Management of a serious complication in high-risk patients. Ann Vasc Surg 9:459-466, 1995.
115. Nevelsteen A, Mees U, Deleersnijder J, Suy R: Obturator bypass: A sixteen-year experience with 55 cases. Ann Vasc Surg 1:558-563, 1987.
116. Panetta T, Sottiurai VS, Batson RC: Obturator bypass with nonreversed translocated saphenous vein. Ann Vasc Surg 3:56-62, 1989.
117. Reddy DJ, Shin LH: Obturator bypass: Technical considerations. Semin Vasc Surg 13:49-52, 2000.
118. Benjamin ME, Cohn EJ Jr, Purtill WA, et al: Arterial reconstruction with deep leg veins for the treatment of mycotic aneurysms. J Vasc Surg 30:1004-1015, 1999.
119. Patel A, Taylor SM, Langan EM III, et al: Obturator bypass: A classic approach for the treatment of contemporary groin infection. Am Surg 68:653-659, 2002.
120. Plate G, Qvarfordt P, Oredsson S, Stigsson L: Obturator bypass to the distal profunda femoris artery using a medial approach—long-term results. Eur J Vasc Endovasc Surg 16:164-168, 1998.
121. Pearce WH, Ricco JB, Yao JS, et al: Modified technique of obturator bypass in failed or infected grafts. Ann Surg 197:344-347, 1983.
122. Rudich M, Gutierrez IZ, Gage AA: Obturator foramen bypass in the management of infected vascular prostheses. Am J Surg 137:657-660, 1979.
123. Calligaro KD, Veith FJ, Schwartz ML, et al: Are gram-negative bacteria a contraindication to selective preservation of infected prosthetic arterial grafts? J Vasc Surg 16:337-346, 1992.
124. Sautner T, Niederle B, Herbst F, et al: The value of obturator canal bypass: A review. Arch Surg 129:718-722, 1994.
125. Taylor SM, Weatherford DA, Langan EM III, Lokey JS: Outcomes in the management of vascular prosthetic graft infections confined to the groin: A reappraisal. Ann Vasc Surg 10:117-122, 1996.
126. Kretschmer G, Niederle B, Huk I, et al: Groin infections following vascular surgery: Obturator bypass (BYP) versus "biologic coverage" (TRP)—a comparative analysis. Eur J Vasc Surg 3:25-29, 1989.
127. Meyer JP, Durham JR, Schwarcz TH, et al: The use of sartorius muscle rotation-transfer in the management of wound complications after infrainguinal vein bypass: A report of eight cases and description of the technique. J Vasc Surg 9:731-735, 1989.
128. Hasen KV, Gallegos ML, Dumanian GA: Extended approach to the vascular pedicle of the gracilis muscle flap: Anatomical and clinical study. Plast Reconstr Surg 111:2203-2208, 2003.
129. Sheiner NM, Sigman H, Stilman A: An unusual complication of obturator foramen arterial bypass. J Cardiovasc Surg 10:324-328, 1969.
130. Blaisdell FW, DeMattei GA, Gauder PJ: Extraperitoneal thoracic aorta-to-femoral bypass graft as replacement for an infected aortic bifurcation prosthesis. Am J Surg 102:583-585, 1961.
131. Passman MA, Farber MA, Criado E, et al: Descending thoracic aorta-to-iliofemoral artery bypass grafting: A role for primary revascularization for aortoiliac occlusive disease? J Vasc Surg 29:249-258, 1999.
132. Kalman PG, Johnston KW, Walker PM: Descending thoracic aortofemoral bypass as an alternative for aortoiliac revascularization. J Cardiovasc Surg 32:443-446, 1991.
133. Kalman PG: Thoracofemoral bypass: Proximal exposure and tunneling. Semin Vasc Surg 13:65-69, 2000.
134. McMillan WD, McCarthy WJ: Minimally invasive thoracoscopic thoracofemoral bypass: A case report. Cardiovasc Surg 7:251-254, 1999.
135. Rosenfeld JC, Savarese RP, DeLaurentis DA: Distal thoracic aorta to femoral artery bypass: A surgical alternative. J Vasc Surg 2:747-750, 1985.
136. Bowes DE, Youkey JR, Pharr WP, et al: Long-term follow-up of descending thoracic aorto-iliac/femoral bypass. J Cardiovasc Surg (Torino) 31:430-437, 1990.

Chapter 81

Infrainguinal Bypass

JOSEPH L. MILLS, SR., MD

Section XIII

Lower extremity arterial reconstruction is most commonly performed in patients with moderate to severe limb ischemia due to atherosclerotic occlusive disease (ASO). Although the techniques described herein may also be applied to patients with traumatic, aneurysmal, and nonatherosclerotic conditions, this chapter focuses exclusively on patients with ASO. *Infrainguinal bypass* is defined as any major arterial reconstruction using a bypass conduit, either autogenous or prosthetic, that originates at or below the inguinal ligament. Inflow sites may therefore include the common, deep, or superficial femoral arteries (SFAs), as well as the popliteal or even tibial arteries. The bypass insertion site may be the femoral, above- or below-knee popliteal, tibial, peroneal, or pedal artery. Over the past decade, progressive evolution in patient evaluation, selection, and conduct of infrainguinal bypass operations has resulted in a more aggressive and generally more successful approach to distal arterial reconstructions, especially for patients with critical limb ischemia (CLI) who otherwise face major limb amputation. Although graft patency and limb salvage rates have demonstrated parallel improvements, there remains a critical need for detailed clinical studies examining the cost-effectiveness as well as patient quality of life outcomes after infrainguinal bypass procedures to ensure their appropriate use and to permit meaningful comparison with evolving less-invasive endovascular therapies.

■ INDICATIONS

The two primary operative indications for infrainguinal bypass are claudication and CLI. *Claudication* is defined as intermittent muscular pain reproducibly induced by exercise and relieved by rest. Patients who are significantly disabled by their symptoms such that they are unable to perform their primary occupation, are unable to comfortably carry out the activities of daily living, or whose lifestyles are significantly limited are potential candidates for infrainguinal bypass. A trial of smoking cessation, lifestyle modification, and exercise, with or without available medical therapy, is usually indicated prior to operative intervention. There is general consensus that bypass is preferable to angioplasty in patients with TransAtlantic Intersociety Consensus type D lesions (complete common femoral artery [CFA] or SFA occlusions or complete popliteal and proximal trifurcation occlusions), but it may also be applied to patients with type B and C lesions.[1] Operation should be offered only if the benefit-risk ratio is high and if anatomic characteristics suggest a favorable and durable result. The primary reason for intervention in claudicants is to improve lifestyle, since the risk of severe clinical deterioration (20%) or major limb amputation (5%) over a 3- to 5-year period is quite low.[1] In most centers with large infrainguinal bypass experiences, claudicants comprise only 15% to 30% of patients, with the remaining majority of patients undergoing bypass for CLI. Although these data reflect practice patterns in tertiary referral centers, they may not reflect the realities of community-based practices.[2]

Patients with CLI generally require intervention. Such patients fall into Fontaine III and IV[3] and Rutherford 4 to 6[4-6] categories. The most recent European Consensus Document defines CLI as persistent, recurring ischemic rest pain requiring opiate analgesia for at least 2 weeks *and* ankle systolic pressure lower than 50 mm Hg and/or toe systolic pressure lower than 30 mm Hg; or ulceration or gangrene of the foot or toes *and* ankle systolic pressure lower than 50 mm Hg or toe systolic pressure lower than 30 mm Hg (or absent pedal pulses in diabetics).[7] Wolfe and Wyatt have further subdivided such patients into the categories of critical and subcritical ischemia based on subsequent amputation risk.[8] Subcritical ischemia includes patients with rest pain and ankle pressure higher than 40 mm Hg. *Critical ischemia* is defined as rest pain and tissue loss and/or ankle pressure lower than 40 mm Hg. This distinction was based on a retrospective analysis of 20 publications analyzing 6118 patients. At 1 year, 27% of patients with subcritical ischemia achieved limb survival without revascularization in contrast with only 5% in the group of patients with CLI. In practice, these data indicate that selected extremely high-risk patients with subcritical ischemia might be managed medically (nonoperatively) but that virtually all patients with true CLI require either bypass or major limb amputation.

■ PREOPERATIVE ASSESSMENT

There is widespread recognition that patients requiring infrainguinal bypass frequently have medical co-morbidities, including diabetes mellitus, chronic obstructive pulmonary disease, and renal insufficiency; there is a particularly high prevalence of associated coronary artery disease (CAD). The incidence of perioperative myocardial infarction ranges from 2% to 6.5% following lower extremity arterial reconstruction; approximately 70% of both perioperative and late mortality in these patients is due to concomitant CAD.[9] The classic study of Hertzer and associates from a tertiary referral center of routine preoperative coronary arteriography in 1000 consecutive patients undergoing evaluation for peripheral arterial disease (PAD) identified severe CAD (>70% stenosis of at least one coronary artery) in 25% of patients and severe inoperable CAD in 6% of such individuals.[10] These data have been corroborated by numerous other investigators.[9] It is clear that significant CAD is a nearly universal accompaniment of PAD. What remains controversial is which individuals are most likely to benefit from detailed, preoperative cardiac assessment and possible coronary intervention before undergoing infrainguinal bypass. Proposed algorithms have ranged from routine cardiac evaluation of all PAD patients to an almost nihilistic approach.[11] My colleagues and I have used an approach between these two extremes.

All PAD patients require a detailed history and physical examination as well as a baseline electrocardiogram (ECG). Important risk factors (modified from Detsky,[12] Goldman,[13] Eagle,[14] and their colleagues) to delineate include the presence or absence of angina; previous myocardial infarction; congestive heart failure (CHF); ventricular ectopy requiring treatment; the presence of valvular heart disease, particularly aortic stenosis; and ischemic findings on ECG. Patients with no cardiac history, none of the risk factors noted earlier, and a normal ECG may safely undergo infrainguinal bypass without further detailed cardiac evaluation; this approach results in an operative mortality of less than 3%. If the cardiac history is positive, the ECG is abnormal, or in the presence of any of these risk factors, we would recommend a cardiology consultation for individuals with claudication. If the cardiac evaluation reveals a low cardiac risk, infrainguinal bypass may be safely performed. If significant CAD is identified, percutaneous or open cardiac revascularization should be considered first. If severe, un-reconstructible CAD is identified, leg bypass for claudication should generally be deferred. Elective surgery for claudication is performed primarily for lifestyle improvement, and there are often medical or less invasive endovascular options available that could be employed.

Patients with CLI pose a more complex problem, since there is a high anticipated amputation rate without lower extremity arterial reconstruction.[8] CLI patients have an even greater prevalence of CAD than claudicants and also a significantly reduced 5-year mortality, primarily due to associated CAD. However, because CLI patients also tend to be older and have a greater number of associated comorbidities, cardiac intervention in such individuals has higher reported morbidity and mortality rates[11] than in the general population of patients with isolated CAD targeted for intervention. Our approach in CLI patients is to assume that they all have significant CAD. Perioperative blood pressure control, antianginal regimens, and treatment for CHF are optimized, and based on level I data,[15] perioperative beta blockade is employed if there are no contraindications.[16,17] We would recommend postponement of infrainguinal bypass in CLI patients to allow further cardiac evaluation only in the presence of frequent or unstable angina, recent myocardial infarction, poorly controlled CHF, or symptomatic or untreated arrhythmia. Even in these instances, cardiac evaluation should be focused and expeditious. Invasive coronary intervention should be pursued only if patient and anatomic characteristics are favorable, if the benefit-risk ratio is high, and if it can be performed without prolonged delay. In the absence of such cardiac instability, CLI patients are best treated with meticulous perioperative medical care and expeditious lower extremity reconstruction. Prolonged delays prior to limb revascularization in CLI patients increase morbidity and amputation risk.

■ PREOPERATIVE VASCULAR EVALUATION

The noninvasive evaluation of PAD patients has been covered elsewhere in the text (see Section III). Infrainguinal bypass requires careful assessment of the extent of arterial disease as well as detailed anatomic characterization of the inflow and outflow arteries. In most patients, standard arteriography is still the "gold standard." However, magnetic resonance (MR) angiography[18] is improving, and particularly for patients with claudication, preoperative duplex imaging[19,20] (see Chapter 16) may provide sufficient anatomic information to proceed directly to the operating room without formal preoperative arteriography. In the latter circumstance, immediate pre-bypass arteriography in the operating room prior to infrainguinal bypass is a reasonable approach. For most patients, however, especially for those with CLI, our preference is to perform initial diagnostic angiography at a separate sitting. We have chosen this approach for several reasons. Detailed high-quality diagnostic arteriograms can be obtained and reviewed carefully before proceeding with bypass. In some patients, appropriate selection of outflow arteries may be difficult, and this area of decision making can be improved if films are reviewed and discussed with colleagues. In addition, even in patients with CLI, selected lesions may be effectively treated by endoluminal techniques. Although this is especially true of tandem inflow lesions, as our experience with peripheral intervention has grown, we not infrequently find that selected SFA, popliteal, and even tibial lesions can sometimes be treated with conventional or subintimal angioplasty techniques (Fig. 81-1). Confining the initial procedure to diagnostic and/or therapeutic angiography obviates time constraints and scheduling difficulties that arise in the operating room when trying to perform angiography and open reconstruction all in one sitting. We reserve the latter approach for carefully selected patients whose arterial anatomy has already been fairly well delineated by preoperative MR angiography or duplex scanning. This confines the "one-stop approach" primarily to claudicants undergoing bypass for isolated, single-level femoropopliteal disease.

Nearly all patients in whom infrainguinal bypass is indicated have suitable target vessels if diagnostic angiography is properly performed.[21,22] Only a tiny fraction of individuals, usually following multiple failed previous reconstructions, do not have an identifiable target artery. Detailed runoff views are necessary, including magnification and lateral views of the foot. Such films can be obtained in nearly all patients with adjunctive techniques such as foot warming, local administration of intra-arterial vasodilators, and proper positioning of the diagnostic catheter. It is frequently helpful to advance the catheter selectively into the SFA or popliteal artery if required to obtain adequate views of the infrapopliteal and pedal circulation, especially in patients with

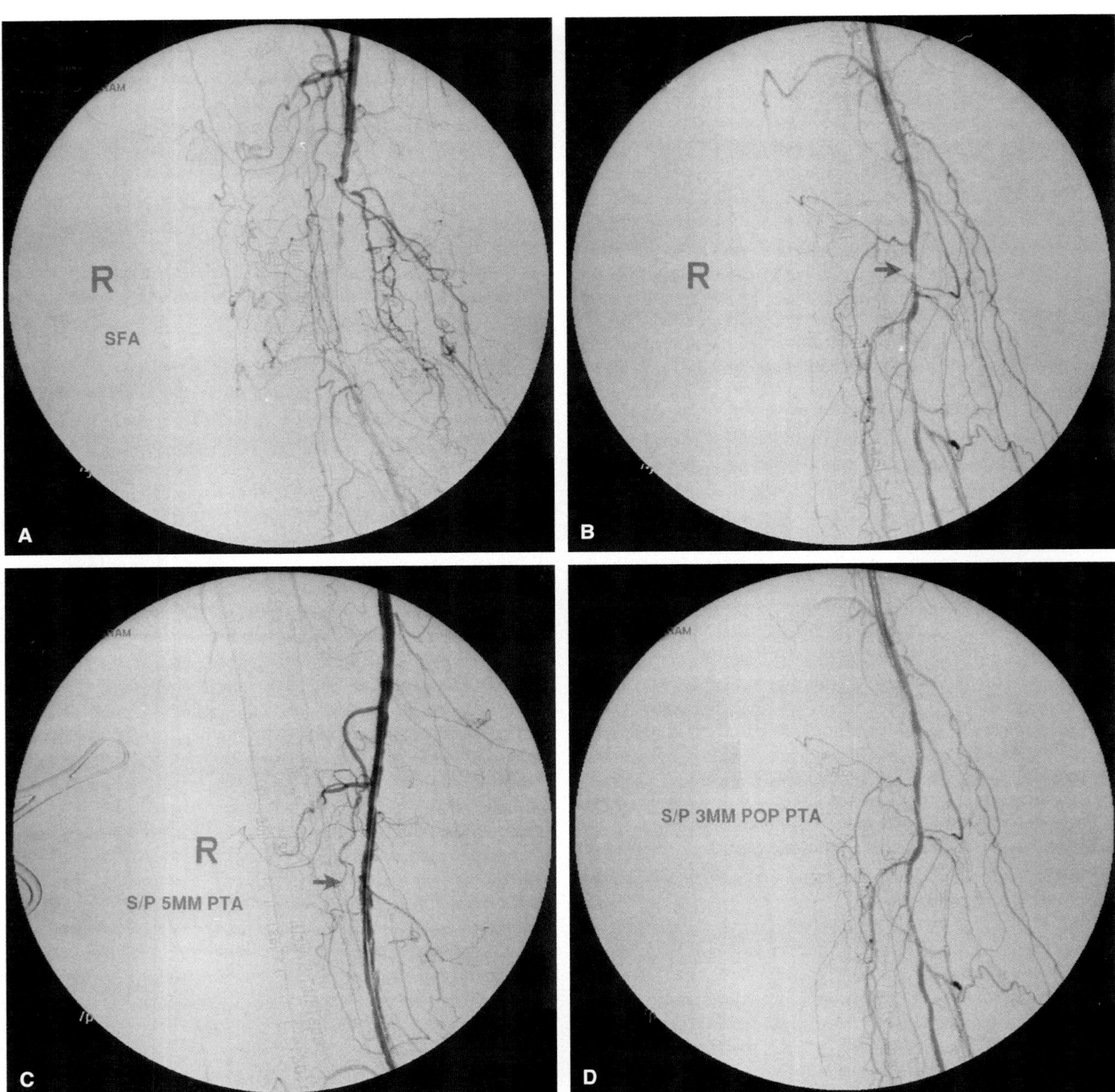

FIGURE 81-1 A 91-year-old woman with an ankle-brachial index of 0.3, ischemic rest pain, and right third toe gangrene underwent antegrade right femoral arteriography based on the presence of normal inflow and superficial femoral artery (SFA) occlusive disease on duplex imaging. A 9-cm occlusion of the SFA (**A**) and a short focal below-knee popliteal artery stenosis (**B**) (*arrow*) were identified. Single-vessel runoff was via a continuous peroneal artery. The SFA occlusion was successfully treated with 5-mm percutaneous transluminal angioplasty (PTA) (**C**) and the popliteal (POP) lesion was treated with 3-mm PTA (**D**). The ankle-brachial index improved to 0.78 with resolution of rest pain and rapid healing of a third toe amputation with a hospital stay of less than 24 hours.

diabetes mellitus. Intra-arterial runoff films with bolus injections performed with the diagnostic catheter positioned in the aorta may fail to adequately define the runoff. If the percutaneous approach has been from a contralateral, retrograde femoral approach, selective films can be obtained by advancing a wire and subsequently an appropriate diagnostic catheter over the aortic bifurcation and selectively down the affected extremity. In selected patients with normal inflow based on physical examination and noninvasive studies, an ipsilateral antegrade approach may more expeditiously identify suitable runoff vessels with the additional advantage of requiring a reduced contrast load (Fig. 81-2). Such an approach is especially useful in diabetic patients with renal insufficiency and noninvasive studies, suggesting isolated infrapopliteal disease. Finally, despite optimal angiographic techniques, there may be a small

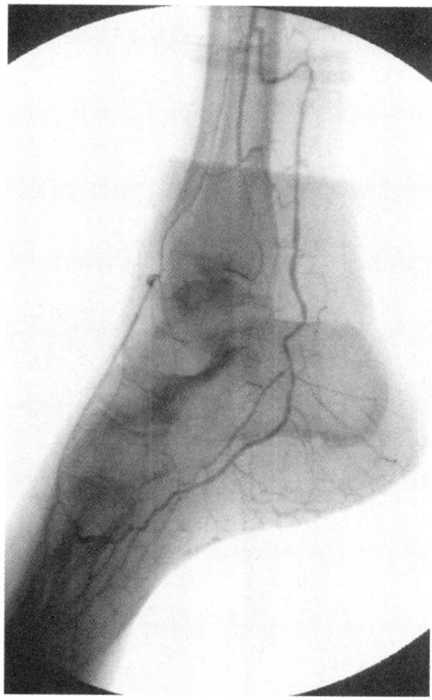

FIGURE 81-2 Lateral foot view obtained via distal selective superficial femoral arterial catheter injection identified excellent collaterals from the distal peroneal artery to both the dorsal pedal and posterior tibial circulations.

number of patients in whom no suitable target is identified. Selective exploration of dorsal pedal or distal posterior tibial arteries with flow detectable by Doppler or duplex imaging may identify a graftable recipient artery. Pomposelli and associates[23] have reported a surprisingly high success rate under these circumstances, although we believe that this situation is relatively uncommon if diagnostic angiography has been pursued to its fullest advantage. In short, there are few patients who are truly unreconstructible from an anatomic standpoint due to the lack of a suitable outflow target vessel.

Since Kunlin's first description of the successful use of autogenous vein to bypass femoropopliteal ASO,[24] there is near-universal agreement that autogenous vein is the best available conduit for infrainguinal bypass at all levels.[25,26] Greater saphenous vein (GSV) is the most readily available and durable conduit. Assessment of vein availability and quality is therefore of critical importance and should be carried out prior to embarking on the operation.[27-29] We routinely perform duplex mapping of the GSV in all patients prior to surgery; if ipsilateral GSV is absent, unsuitable, or of insufficient length to perform the anticipated bypass, we would also scan the ipsilateral lesser saphenous vein, the contralateral greater and lesser saphenous vein, and the upper extremity veins, if necessary, to ensure that we know the location and quality of available vein to perform the anticipated bypass required as well as to deal with any potential extenuating circumstances that might arise during the conduct of the operation. Patients are scanned with a light tourniquet in place with the limb dependent as described by Blebea and colleagues.[30] We prefer to use veins that are soft, compressible, and at least 3 mm in diameter. Calcified or sclerotic veins are rejected. Soft, compressible veins between 2 and 3 mm in diameter are worthy of exploration, but if they do not distend appropriately, the operation should be modified either by harvesting better quality vein (based on preoperative duplex studies) or shortening the length of the proposed bypass, if possible, by selection of alternative inflow or outflow sites. The type and quality of the bypass conduit are the most important determinants of infrainguinal bypass success; efforts to maximize conduit quality will be rewarded. Poor-quality or marginal vein should be rejected; the search for high-quality vein is worth the time and effort, even if vein splicing or "bypass shortening" is required. All efforts should be made to perform every infrainguinal bypass with vein conduit (all-autogenous policy). Long-term results should not be sacrificed for the sake of expediency at the initial operation. Saphenous vein performs well in the reversed,[31-35] nonreversed,[36] and in-situ[37-45] configurations; the technique chosen is primarily dictated by conduit availability, anatomic considerations, and surgeon preference and experience.

■ OPERATIVE PLANNING

Operative planning for infrainguinal bypass involves the most complex decision making that a vascular surgeon is called on to provide. More than any other operation, infrainguinal bypass taxes the surgeon's ingenuity and requires him or her to carefully anticipate and consider numerous alternatives and potential complications both in the preoperative evaluation as well as in the conduct of the reconstruction itself. First and foremost, the major anatomic lesions and their hemodynamic significance must be identified.[46,47] Iliac artery lesions of hemodynamic significance should be addressed in nearly all claudicants. For patients with CLI, an iliac lesion with a resting gradient of less than 5 to 10 mm Hg may be acceptable if the pulse and Doppler waveform at the selected inflow site (e.g., the femoral artery) are normal. In patients with claudication or CLI presenting with rest pain alone in the absence of tissue loss, an isolated iliac angioplasty without concomitant infrainguinal bypass may suffice if the iliac lesion is of sufficient hemodynamic importance. In such patients with tandem lesions, the profunda-popliteal collateral index may be helpful in predicting whether an inflow procedure alone may be sufficient to alleviate the patient's presenting symptoms.[48] An index of greater than 0.25 indicates a large pressure gradient across the knee joint and suggests that inflow disease correction and profundaplasty alone[49-51] are unlikely to be adequate.

Adequate inflow should be ensured prior to commencing with infrainguinal bypass. Selected inflow lesions may either be treated percutaneously in advance at the time of the preoperative diagnostic angiogram or at the same sitting, if need be. Prior to surgery, the surgeon must define the inflow source; it need not necessarily be the CFA. There is abundant evidence that originating shorter bypasses from the deep femoral, superficial femoral, popliteal, or, even, in rare instances, one of the tibial arteries results in patency rates equivalent to operations in which the CFA serves as the bypass origin. Short bypasses are frequently useful in patients with diabetes mellitus and primary infrapopliteal arterial occlusive disease as well as in individuals with limited available vein conduit who present with failure of a previous reconstruction. Based on hemodynamic data and anatomic imaging, the surgeon should commence the operation with the optimum inflow site in mind. However, if unanticipated arterial disease is identified or vein quality and length are worse than anticipated once the operation is underway, one should already have selected alternative bypass origins that could be used to shorten the length of the bypass required without compromising hemodynamics. If there is uncertainty about the appropriateness of the inflow site at exploration, its hemodynamic suitability should be assessed by direct intra-arterial pressure measurements that can be compared with the transduced radial artery pressure. A resting gradient exceeding 10 mm Hg is significant, as is a drop in pressure exceeding 15% following the administration of intra-arterial papaverine.[46,47] If a significant gradient is identified at the selected inflow site, a more proximal inflow site above the culprit lesion should be selected or the responsible lesion should be addressed by local endarterectomy or angioplasty. This problem occasionally arises with iliac or common femoral lesions whose hemodynamic significance was not appreciated at the time of preoperative arteriography, particularly lesions consisting primarily of posterior plaque that may have been masked if appropriate oblique projections were not obtained.

Significant occlusive disease involving the origin and proximal deep femoral artery should usually be addressed at the time of the infrainguinal bypass whenever the bypass is to originate from the CFA. The endarterectomy often begins in the CFA. Following division of veins that cross the anterior surface of the deep femoral artery, the femoral arteriotomy is extended beyond the posterior tongue of disease that extends a variable distance down the deep femoral artery, usually at least to its first or second portion. Tacking sutures may or may not be needed at the distal endpoint. The arteriotomy may be closed with a vein patch or a segment of endarterectomized SFA. This patch may then be opened longitudinally to serve as the origin for the infrainguinal bypass (modified Linton patch technique) (Fig. 81-3). Alternatively, if the vein caliber is good (>4 mm), a longer venotomy may be made in the vein conduit that can then simultaneously serve as both a profundaplasty patch and the bypass origin. The latter technique should not be used if the arterial wall is markedly thickened or if either the native donor artery or vein graft artery caliber is small to avoid compromising the origin of the vein graft at the heel of the anastomosis. Incorporation of a venous side branch as part of the anastomotic heel is another useful technique for situations in which the donor arterial wall is thick or whenever there is a caliber mismatch between the donor artery and the vein bypass conduit (Fig. 81-4). Correction of significant deep femoral disease at the time of infrainguinal bypass is clinically important; should the bypass ever fail, adequate deep femoral artery perfusion may prevent the development of severe, recurrent limb ischemia.

Although inflow artery selection is generally straightforward, outflow site selection frequently requires greater judgment. The general principle of infrainguinal reconstruction is to bypass all hemodynamically significant disease and to insert the bypass to the most proximal limb artery that has at least one continuous runoff artery to the foot. Thus, if the popliteal artery reconstitutes distal to an

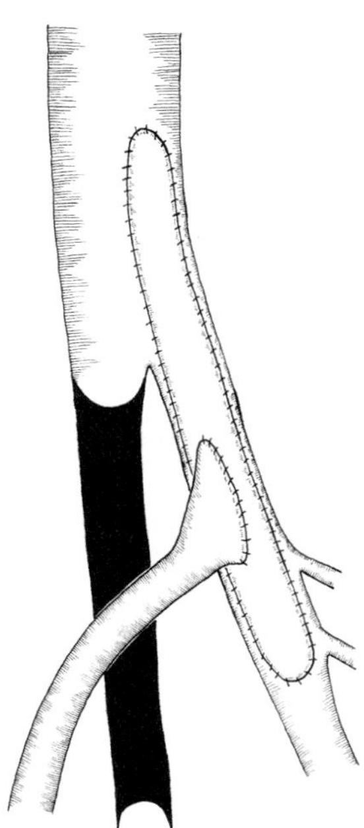

FIGURE 81-3 Combined use of Linton vein patch technique following endarterectomy of the distal common and proximal deep femoral arteries with anastomosis of the reversed vein graft to the patch.

SFA occlusion, and at least one tibial or peroneal artery is continuous to the foot, the popliteal artery would be selected as the outflow site. It is possible, however, and sometimes desirable, to bypass to an isolated or so-called blind popliteal segment. An isolated popliteal artery is defined as a patent popliteal artery segment at least 5 cm in length but with only geniculate collaterals and no major distal tibial or peroneal runoff artery in direct continuity with the foot. Such bypasses function surprisingly well and are especially useful in patients with limited vein availability.[52-56] They may also be more useful in patients with claudication or rest pain compared with those with frank tissue necrosis. We prefer bypass to an artery in continuity with the foot in the presence of gangrene. Five-year assisted primary or secondary patency rates of 50% to 74% have been reported for such blind-segment popliteal bypasses.[52] Successful bypasses to isolated tibial artery segments have also been reported.[57]

Although most claudicants require only femoropopliteal bypass, a high proportion of patients with CLI require tibial or pedal bypass. In general, the most proximal segment of tibial or peroneal artery that is continuous with the foot should be chosen as the outflow site. Thus a patent anterior tibial or posterior tibial artery in direct continuity with the foot and pedal arch would be chosen over the peroneal artery as an outflow site if suitable vein length is available. There is still some controversy over whether one should choose the proximal or mid peroneal artery or a patent pedal artery for patients with tissue loss.[58] Most authors have found no adverse effects on graft patency or limb salvage for peroneal bypasses[59-61] compared with tibial or pedal bypasses, but Pomposelli and others have made a strong case for pedal bypass,[23] particularly in diabetic patients with

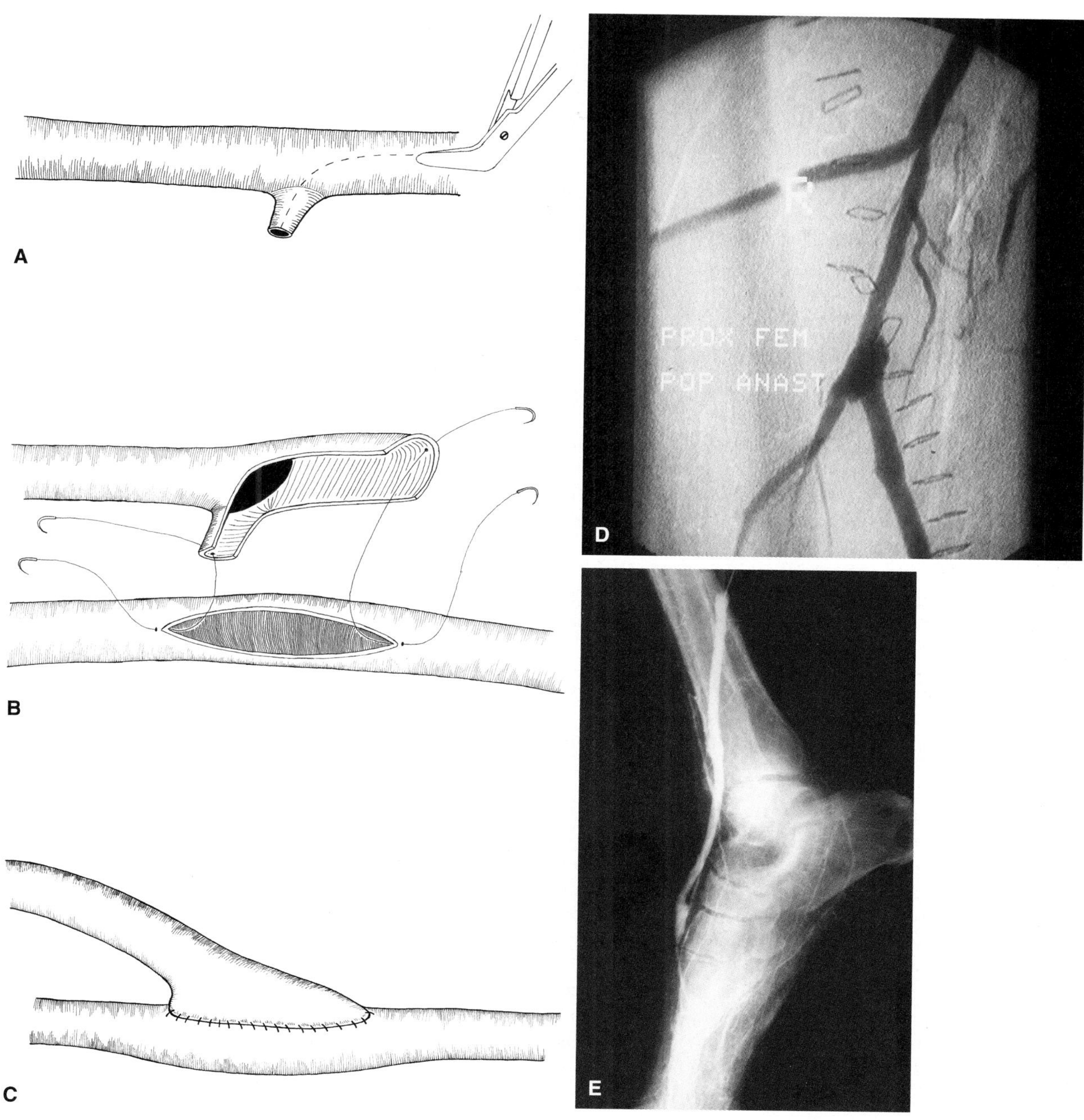

FIGURE 81-4 The venotomy through the reversed vein is extended out through a suitable side branch (**A**) and anastomosed to the inflow artery (**B** and **C**) to avoid anastomotic stenosis at the graft heel.[199,200] This technique may be used both at the proximal anastomosis (Prox Fem Pop Anast) (**D**) or the distal anastomosis (**E**) and is useful when vein caliber is small or the arterial wall is thickened.

tissue loss.[62] They emphasize the importance of restoration of a pedal pulse and maximization of forefoot reperfusion. The pedal arteries are also more superficial and more easily exposed than the anatomically disadvantaged, deeply located peroneal artery. If the bypass must originate in the groin and the proximal or mid-peroneal artery is of good quality on arteriography and has abundant collaterals with the foot (see Fig. 81-2), we would generally perform a shorter bypass to the peroneal artery, especially if vein conduit length is a limiting factor. If the peroneal artery is diseased or does not appear to collateralize well with the foot, we would preferentially bypass to the foot or ankle and splice vein if required to obtain sufficient length. We prefer dorsal pedal or paramalleolar posterior tibial/plantar artery insertion sites for short bypasses originating from the popliteal artery in diabetic patients with tissue loss. Shortening the bypass in such patients allows one to optimize vein conduit quality, and the choice of an inframalleolar target artery serves to maximize forefoot perfusion.

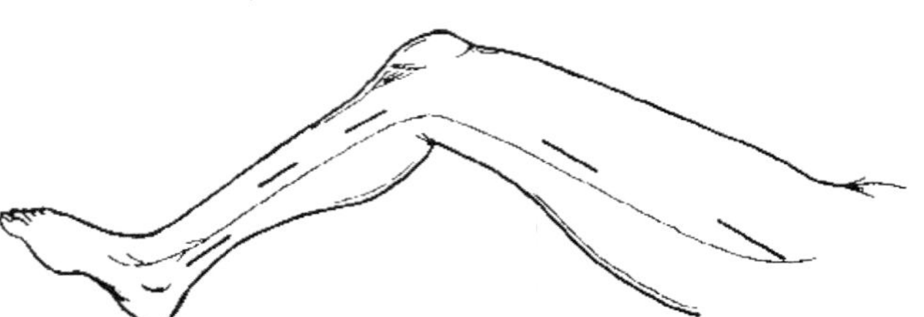

FIGURE 81-5 Depiction of common inflow and outflow incisions for infrainguinal bypass.

FIGURE 81-6 Lateral approaches to the deep femoral, anterior tibial, and distal peroneal arteries are shown.

■ OPERATIVE EXPOSURES

Thorough knowledge of anatomy and facility with multiple surgical exposures are critical to the success of infrainguinal bypass (Fig. 81-5).[63] The standard approach to the common and deep femoral arteries is provided by a vertical incision overlying the CFA; this anterior approach allows complete exposure and mobilization of the CFA and its bifurcation; more proximal exposure can be obtained by division of the recurrent portion or the entire inguinal ligament (Peter Martin incision). Distal extension allows exposure of the profunda femoris artery (PFA). Division of the lateral femoral circumflex vein offers access to the proximal PFA; careful progressive division of numerous crossing veins allows extensive exposure of the PFA. In selected patients, alternate exposures in addition to the standard anterior approach have been described. If previous infection or scarring from multiple previous reconstructions makes standard exposure difficult, and if there are no significant occlusive lesions in the CFA or proximal PFA, the PFA may be approached laterally (Fig. 81-6), anteromedially, or posteromedially.[64-67] The lateral approach is the most useful for infrainguinal bypass; the incision is placed in the upper thigh lateral to the sartorius muscle. The sartorius and SFA are retracted medially. The raphe between the adductor longus and vastus medialis is incised to expose the PFA. This approach is useful when vein conduit length is limited or if femoral triangle scarring is prohibitive. The surgeon must be certain that there are no hemodynamically significant lesions proximal to the PFA if this approach is used. With these caveats in mind, use of the PFA as an origin for distal bypass does not compromise long-term patency[66,67]; similarly, the SFAs[68] and popliteal arteries[68-70] can be used as an inflow source in carefully selected patients without compromising graft patency.

The standard exposures of the above-popliteal and below-knee arteries are through medial leg incisions (see Fig. 81-5), usually by deepening of the saphenectomy incision. Lateral approaches to these vessels are occasionally useful and are well described elsewhere. The posterior tibial and proximal to mid-peroneal arteries are also usually approached medially. The distal third of the peroneal artery is most expeditiously exposed by means of a lateral leg incision directly over the distal fibula (see Fig. 81-6). A short segment of fibula is carefully removed to expose the distal peroneal artery immediately beneath.

Posterior exposures of the popliteal, posterior tibial, and peroneal arteries are sometimes quite useful.[71,72] Diabetic patients frequently have relatively normal inflow to the popliteal trifurcation. If the inflow site is the below-knee popliteal artery and the most appropriate target artery is the distal posterior tibial or distal peroneal artery, and the lesser saphenous vein is of good quality based on duplex imaging, the entire operation can be conducted with the patient in a prone position through a posterior approach. These approaches have been well described by Ouriel[72] and should be considered not only in selected reoperative situations (i.e., failed bypass via medial approach) but also if conduit length is limited and ipsilateral GSV is unavailable. Commitment to an all-autogenous bypass approach requires ingenuity and familiarity with numerous anatomic exposures and techniques to allow "shortening" of the bypass or permit operation in a virgin field that is unscarred by previous operations. When using such distal origin bypass grafts, a pneumatic tourniquet instead of vascular Silastic loops or clamps is occasionally quite useful in the presence of severe distal arterial calcification.[73]

■ CHOICE OF CONDUIT

Autogenous conduit options for infrainguinal bypass include ipsilateral and contralateral GSV,[74] lesser saphenous vein,[75,76] superficial femoral vein,[77] arm (basilic and cephalic) vein,[78-82] endarterectomized segments of SFA,[83] cryopreserved vein,[84,85] and the radial artery.[86] Prosthetic options include Dacron, heparin-bonded Dacron (HBD), polytetrafluoroethylene (PTFE) with and without a distal cuff, and human umbilical vein (HUV). In our recent 10-year experience, we performed 93% of infrainguinal bypasses with all-autogenous conduits. The preferred conduit is GSV; if ipsilateral GSV is absent, we do not hesitate to harvest contralateral GSV and see no merit in saving this vein for later because GSV outperforms all other conduit choices.[74] Numerous reports suggest that contralateral GSV is subsequently needed in no more than 20% to 25% of patients. We and others therefore advocate using it when necessary and saving a more difficult alternative vein reconstruction for later in those patients who require it. Exceptions occur whenever the contralateral limb is already ischemic as manifested by severe claudication, rest pain, or ischemic ulceration. If the contralateral limb is asymptomatic and the ankle-brachial index (ABI) exceeds 0.6, we have experienced no significant wound healing complications from harvesting the GSV from the groin to the mid-calf level. This approach usually allows the bypass to be performed with one segment of GSV and obviates harvesting arm vein and vein splicing. Other groups prefer to harvest arm vein if ipsilateral GSV is unavailable and save the contralateral GSV for later.[81]

Alternate veins are used when GSV is unavailable or of insufficient length.[82] Duplex mapping is quite useful in identifying suitable vein sources. Lesser saphenous vein is suitable if the proposed bypass is relatively short. It is possible to perform a common femoral to above-knee popliteal bypass or a PFA to below-knee popliteal bypass with one complete segment of lower saphenous vein harvested from the ankle to the knee. If a longer bypass with spliced vein is necessary, we prefer to use arm vein because it is less awkward to harvest. LoGerfo and others have described novel techniques of harvesting the upper arm basilic, median cubital, and cephalic veins in continuity with valve lysis of the basilic segment and use of the cephalic segment in reversed configuration to provide a relatively long, unspliced autogenous conduit.[87] Superficial femoral vein is occasionally useful for shorter bypasses but is difficult to harvest; arm vein is therefore generally preferred. Treiman and associates have reported the use of radial artery as a bypass conduit in selected patients requiring short infrageniculate bypasses with good early results.[86] Cryopreserved vein grafts are expensive and have not performed well in clinical practice[84,85]; they may serve a niche when revascularization is required following removal of an infected bypass graft[84] and autogenous vein is unavailable to create a new bypass through clean tissue planes.

PTFE is the most commonly used prosthetic conduit for infrainguinal bypass, although recent reports suggest that at least in the above-knee position, it is not superior to Dacron.[88-90] A recent prospective, randomized trial from the United Kingdom reported by Devine and colleagues suggested that HBD was superior to PTFE for above-knee popliteal bypasses.[91] The 3-year primary patency for HBD was 55% compared with 42% for PTFE ($P < 0.044$). Both of these patency rates are inferior to GSV, however. Table 81-1 summarizes available level 1 data comparing conduit types with outcome.[91-106] Vein is superior to all prosthetics, even in the above-knee position.[102,105,106] Available randomized clinical trials comparing HUV with PTFE have been inconclusive.[99-101] The addition of rings to PTFE conferred no benefit in the single available prospective, randomized clinical trial.[98] For bypasses that insert below the knee, the addition of a vein cuff confers a significant patency advantage (52% patency at 2 years for PTFE with vein cuff vs. 29% for PTFE with no cuff) and also improves limb salvage (84% vs. 62%; $P < 0.03$).[96] Our own experience[95] and that of others suggest that a distal vein cuff or collar results in improved 2- to 3-year patency for infrageniculate bypass when PTFE is required.[92-94] Nevertheless, the results are still inferior to vein bypasses, even those using alternate veins; these data emphasize the validity of the all-autogenous policy. If vein is truly limited, however, PTFE is an acceptable choice and available data suggest that distal anastomotic modification with autogenous tissue is a worthwhile adjunct. The only prospective, randomized clinical trial used a Miller cuff (Fig. 81-7).[96] A distal Taylor patch (Fig. 81-8)[93,95] and the St. Mary's boot (Fig. 81-9)[94] may yield equivalent results. HUV vein is less commonly employed than PTFE, primarily because it is thicker and more cumbersome to handle and because of concerns about subsequent aneurysmal degeneration. Dardik and associates have reported excellent results using HUV with an adjunctive distal arteriovenous fistula to promote increased graft flow velocity[107]; there are no prospective trials comparing this technique to alternative prosthetic conduits such as PTFE. A single prospective trial did not demonstrate any benefit of the addition of an adjunctive arteriovenous fistula to femoroinfrapopliteal bypass with vein cuff.[97]

Our recommendation is that autogenous vein be used whenever possible for infrainguinal bypass. This dictum holds true not only for primary infrainguinal bypasses but also for reoperative cases in which vein conduits outperform all other options.[108,109] For long bypasses, ipsilateral GSV, contralateral GSV, and spliced vein are employed in decreasing order of preference. If only 5 to 15 cm of extra length is required and a more distal origin site is not feasible, eversion endarterectomy of a proximal segment of the SFA with anastomosis to the available vein conduit is a useful technique (Fig. 81-10) that avoids the harvesting and splicing of additional vein.[83] For shorter bypasses, arm vein or lower saphenous vein is effective, with the latter of special usefulness when a posterior approach is applicable. If vein is truly unavailable, PTFE or Dacron is the best option for above-knee bypass. If the improved results with heparin bonding are confirmed,[91] then HBD will become the preferred conduit for above-knee bypass in the absence of suitable vein. For infrageniculate insertion sites, PTFE with distal anastomotic modification (cuff, boot, or patch) is recommended if vein is unavailable.

■ COMPLETION STUDIES

There are four options for completion assessment; these may be used alone or in combination. These methods include (1) distal pulse palpation and Doppler flow assessment[110,111] (with and without manual compression of the graft); (2) completion arteriography[112-114]; (3) intraoperative duplex scanning with and without papaverine administration[115,116]; and (4) angioscopy.[117-127] The first option should always be employed. Restoration of a palpable distal pulse or Doppler flow that clearly diminishes with manual occlusion of the bypass graft documents graft patency. These techniques are not sufficiently sensitive to detect all but the grossest of conduit, technical, or outflow problems, however, and some more complex, additional technique should also be employed. For reversed vein conduits, we believe that arteriography is the simplest and most effective completion study. With improved intraoperative imaging capabilities, it has become relatively easy to rapidly evaluate the conduit, tunnel, anastomoses, and outflow for significant graft-threatening lesions with the requirement for minimal contrast and additional time. Renwick and coworkers[112] identified defects requiring correction in 27% of infrainguinal bypasses using intraoperative angiography, despite a normal appearance by visual inspection and external pulse palpation. The 2-week primary patency was 100% compared with 72% in a control group without completion arteriograms. Mills and associates[113] prospectively evaluated 214 consecutive infrainguinal bypass grafts with routine completion angiography and identified significant lesions requiring revision in 8% of grafts, with a higher

Table 81-1 Randomized Clinical Trials: Above-Knee Popliteal Bypass and Graft Type and Below-Knee Popliteal/Infrapopliteal Bypass by Graft Type, Rings, and Cuffs

FIRST AUTHOR (YEAR) (NO. OF PATIENTS) AND GRAFT TYPE	PATENCY, YR					*P* VALUE
	1	2	3	4	5	
Above-Knee Popliteal Bypass: Dacron vs. PTFE						
Devine[91] (2001) (*n* = 209)						0.044
Heparin-bonded Dacron	70	63	55			
PTFE	56	46	42			
Post[89] (2001) (*n* = 194)						NS
Dacron			64			
PTFE			61			
Green[88] (2000) (*n* = 240)						NS
Dacron					43	
PTFE					45	
Robinson[90] (1999) (*n* = 108)						NS
Dacron	70	56	47			
PTFE	72	52	52			
Above-Knee Popliteal Bypass: HUV vs. PTFE						
McCollum[99] (1991) (*n* = 191)						NS (0.27)
HUV	68	63	57			
PTFE (above knee)	61	56	48			
Aalders[100] (1992) (*n* = 96)						NS
HUV	90	67*			71.4‡	
PTFE	80	63			38.7	
Eickhoff[101] (1987) (*n* = 105)						0.001
HUV (below knee)	74			42		
PTFE	53			22		
PTFE: Ringed vs. Nonringed						
Gupta[98] (1991) (*n* = 122) (above- and below-knee popliteal bypass)						NS
Ringed			74			
Nonringed			68			
PTFE: Vein Cuff vs. No Cuff						
Stonebridge[96] (1997) (*n* = 261)						
Above-knee popliteal						NS
Cuff	80	72				
No cuff	84	70				
Below-knee popliteal						0.03
Cuff	80	52				
No cuff	65	29				
Above-Knee Popliteal Bypass: Vein vs. Prosthetic (PTFE or HUV)						
Klinkert[105] (2003) (*n* = 151)						0.035
Vein					76	
PTFE					52	
Johnson[106] (2000) (*n* = 752)						0.01
Vein		81			73	
HUV		70			53	
PTFE		69			39	
Tilanus[104] (1985) (*n* = 49)						<0.001
Vein					70	
PTFE					37	
Veith[103] (1986) (*n* = 845)						
Above-knee popliteal†						>0.25
Vein				61		
PTFE				38		
Below-knee popliteal						<0.05
Vein				76		
PTFE				54		
Infrapopliteal						<0.001
Vein				49		
PTFE				12		

*Patency determined at 18 months.
†Above knee, *n* = 176; below knee, *n* = 153; infrapopliteal, *n* = 204.
‡Patency determined at 6 years.
HUV, human umbilical vein; PTFE, polytetrafluoroethylene; NS, not significant.

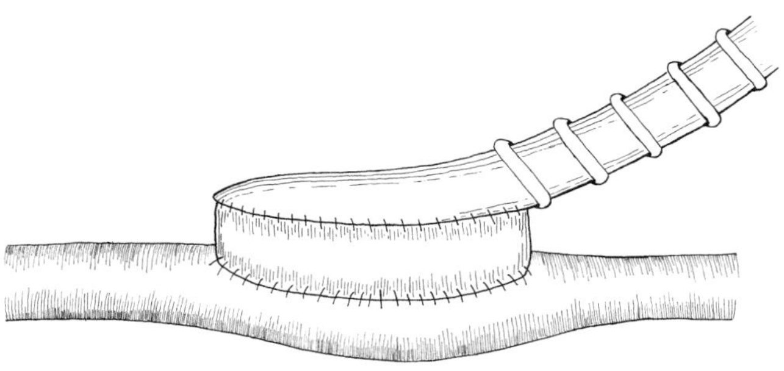

FIGURE 81-7 The Miller cuff technique[92,201] has conferred improved patency for below-knee popliteal and tibial polytetrafluoroethylene bypass when used as a distal anastomotic adjunct in a controlled, randomized clinical trial.[96]

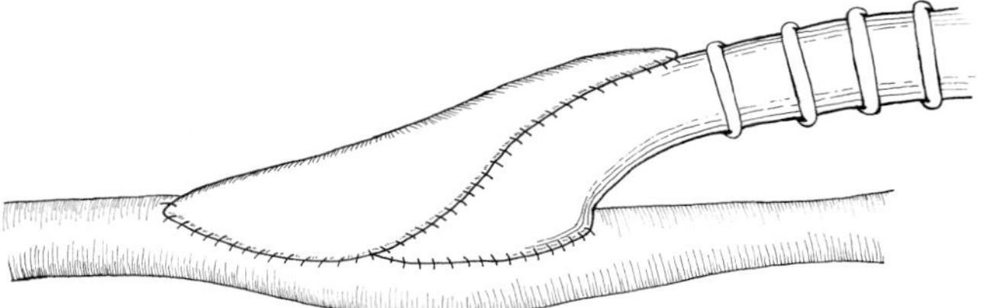

FIGURE 81-8 The Taylor patch technique may also offer improved patency for infrageniculate polytetrafluoroethylene bypass.[93,95]

incidence in tibial than popliteal reconstructions. The 30-day primary patencies were 99% for femoropopliteal bypasses and 93% for femorodistal grafts.

Angiography may not be sufficiently sensitive to detect incomplete valve lysis during the performance of in-situ or nonreversed grafts.[121,122] Bandyk,[115] Johnson,[116] and their colleagues have long championed intraoperative duplex scanning following such reconstructions and report significant abnormalities requiring correction in 12% of cases. Lesions associated with focal peak systolic velocities exceeding 250 cm/sec are repaired. In low-flow grafts without identifiable technical defects, if target artery relocation or graft extension is not possible, consideration is given either to performing an adjunctive arteriovenous fistula to augment graft flow velocity or to administering postoperative anticoagulation. The short-term patency of infrainguinal bypasses with normal intraoperative duplex scanning is superb. Intraoperative graft duplex scanning requires availability of a machine and a technician, however, and is less familiar to and more cumbersome to use for most surgeons. These issues have prevented its widespread application, although we have found it useful in difficult "redo" cases, particularly when using alternate, spliced, or valve-lysed vein segments.

Angioscopy has been employed by many clinical investigators[117-127] who have used it to evaluate harvested arm vein[120] or as an adjunct to valve lysis to permit in-situ bypass with minimal skin incisions. Marcaccio and associates[123] analyzed the use of intraoperative angioscopy in a series of 113 arm vein bypasses and identified significant intraluminal disease in 62.8% of cases; previous thrombosis with recanalization (54%) was the most commonly encountered lesion followed by complex weblike lesions at valve sites or possibly associated with previous venipuncture. Angioscopy was used to correct 95.8% of vein abnormalities judged to be significant and allowed this group to "upgrade" the conduit quality. The 1-month patency rate was 95.5% in grafts judged to be normal initially or following repair compared with only 70% in conduits judged to be of inferior quality even after attempted repair. Wilson and colleagues[125] reported a similar yield of information of prognostic importance associated with intraoperative angioscopic conduit evaluation. Angioscopy would thus appear to be of greatest potential use when applied either to assess arm vein conduits or to ensure adequacy of valve lysis for in-situ

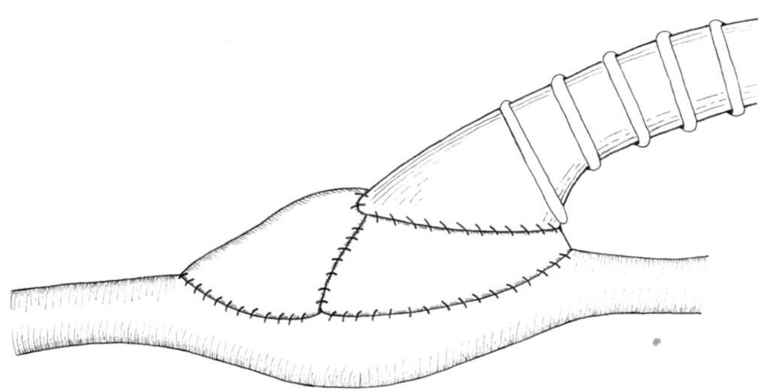

FIGURE 81-9 The St. Mary's boot or prosthetic venous collar technique[94] combines the attributes of the Taylor patch and the Miller cuff.

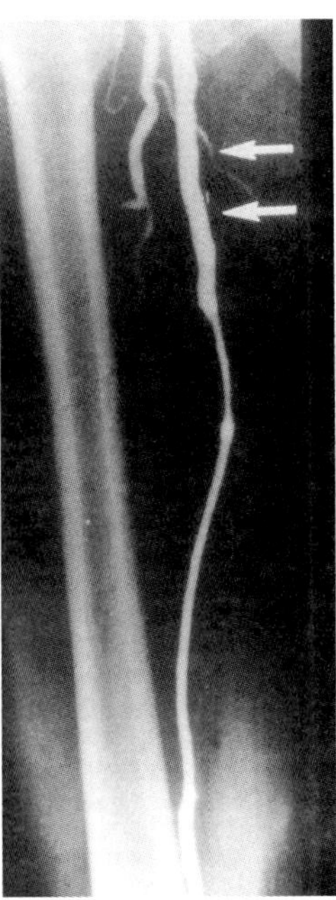

FIGURE 81-10 When vein length is limited, an eversion endarterectomy of a proximal superficial femoral artery segment[83] (*double arrows*) can be performed. The everted arterial segment is anastomosed to the available vein graft to permit creation of an all-autogenous conduit of sufficient length to perform the required bypass.

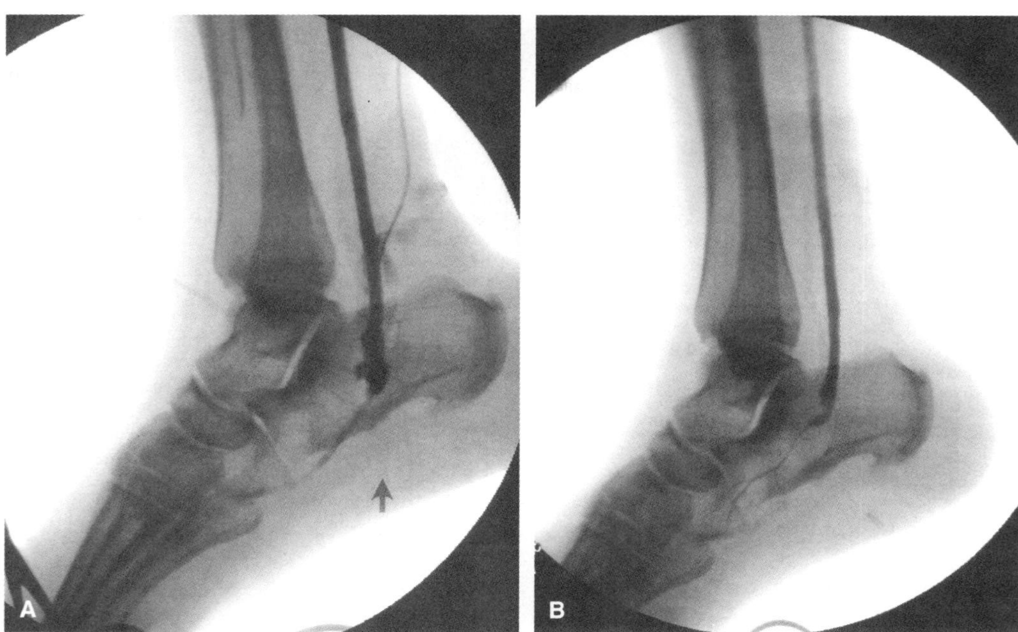

FIGURE 81-11 Completion arteriography demonstrates poor runoff with minimal branching of the target plantar artery (*arrow*) (**A**). Initial exposure had been inadequate leading to incorrect target artery (lateral plantar) selection. The anastomosis was relocated to the medial plantar artery (**B**) and the graft remains patent 2 years postoperatively.

conduits. Wound and vein harvest incisional complications can compromise outcome and prolong hospital stay.[128-130] Several groups have reported the adjunctive use of angioscopy both to assist in the performance of valve lysis as well as to allow in-situ bypass to be performed with minimal skin incisions[131-139]; whether these techniques improve outcome is uncertain.

Some objective assessment of the bypass, its anastomoses, and the outflow is an important component of infrainguinal bypass. We still recommend completion arteriography but recognize that duplex scanning and angioscopy are important adjuncts, especially in higher risk situations and when using nonreversed or in-situ conduits where complete valve lysis is critical.

■ INTRAOPERATIVE TROUBLESHOOTING

Insufficient or inadequate arterial exposure; inappropriate inflow or target artery selection (Fig. 81-11); intrinsic conduit defects; technical defects associated with clamp injury, local endarterectomy, anastomotic creation (Fig. 81-12), and valve lysis; graft tunneling errors; and coagulation or platelet aggregation abnormalities all may complicate infrainguinal bypass. The surgeon should strive to avoid these complications but must nevertheless be prepared to recognize and correct them should they arise. Ignorance is not bliss, and the best opportunity to correct a problem is at the initial operation. Failing to address a significant defect and hoping for the best compromises patient outcome and increases stress on the operating surgeon. "Take-backs" to the operating room for hemorrhage or graft thrombosis are inevitable occurrences, but their frequency can be reduced by meticulous technique and prudent decision making.

■ RESULTS

Outcomes must be reported according to the Society for Vascular Surgery reporting standards.[4-6] Graft patency, limb salvage, and mortality are hard endpoints. Patency may be primary, assisted primary (most applicable to vein grafts), or secondary. The graft is considered patent if it has had uninterrupted patency with either no procedures performed on it, or a procedure performed such as transluminal dilation or proximal or distal extension to the graft, to deal with disease progression in the adjacent native vessel. Thus the only exceptions that do not disqualify the graft for primary patency are procedures performed for disease beyond the graft and its two anastomoses. Dilations or minor revisions performed for stenoses, dilations, or other structural defects *before* occlusion do not constitute exceptions because they are intended to prevent eventual graft failure.[4] In the latter circumstance, which arises primarily when graft-threatening lesions are identified in autogenous grafts by means of postoperative duplex surveillance, percutaneous dilation or open graft revision performed on a patent graft for an intrinsic graft or anastomotic lesion is identified as assisted-primary patency. If the graft in question has thrombosed, but patency is restored by lysis or thrombectomy and revision, the appropriate term is secondary patency. Primary patency thus reflects the durability of the initial reconstruction, assisted-primary patency reflects the impact of graft surveillance and timely re-intervention, and secondary patency reflects the persistence of the surgeon in restoring graft patency following failure. The most meaningful endpoints are thus primary and assisted-primary patency data.

Randomized, prospective trials (Table 81-2) demonstrate equivalence between in-situ and reversed vein conduits.[140-148] The use of these techniques is thus dictated by

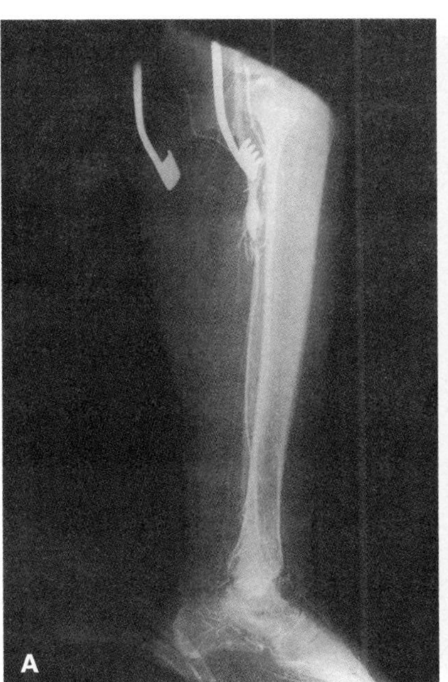

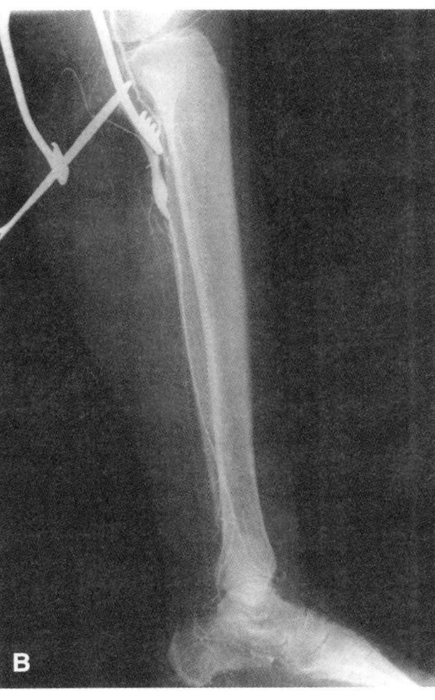

FIGURE 81-12 Completion arteriography identified a significant distal anastomotic defect (**A**) despite a good graft pulse and distal continuous-wave Doppler signal. The anastomosis was re-explored, the defect was corrected (**B**), and the graft is patent at 3 years.

operative considerations and surgeon preference and experience. Vein is superior to all prosthetics, even in the above-knee popliteal position. Expected patency data, based on an excellent review by Dalman published previously,[149] are summarized in Tables 81-3 to 81-6.

The outcomes of infrainguinal bypass procedures have traditionally been reported solely in terms of graft patency, limb salvage, and patient survival rates. Several factors affect outcome when considered in these terms. Conduit type is the major determinant of long-term graft patency, with vein outperforming prosthetic for all varieties of infrainguinal bypass. Concerning vein conduits, vein quality[150,151] and caliber[152,153] are the most critical determinants of success. Vein grafts less than 3 to 3.5 mm in diameter are inferior whether used in situ or reversed.[148] GSV is superior to alternate vein sources.[82] Reduced graft patency has been attributed to poor runoff,[154,155] although poor runoff is somewhat difficult to define and autogenous vein grafts frequently remain patent in the presence of rather striking outflow disease (Fig. 81-13). Other factors such as age and diabetes do not appear to adversely impact graft patency, although diabetic patients exhibit prolonged wound healing times.[155] Most investigators have reported that the presence of end-stage renal failure is associated with reduced graft patency and increased limb loss and mortality.[156-158] Anesthetic type has not been conclusively shown to influence graft patency or perioperative mortality.[159,160]

Graft patency and limb salvage are hard and important endpoints. Numerous investigators, however, have recognized that functional outcomes are at least of equal importance. The Oregon group was among the first to examine such functional outcomes. Nicoloff and coworkers[161] emphasized that an ideal outcome, as defined by the expectations of a patent graft, healed wound, no need for reoperation, independent living status, and continued ambulation was extremely difficult to achieve in patients with CLI. Only a

Table 81-2 Reversed Versus In-Situ Bypass

FIRST AUTHOR (YEAR), GRAFT TYPE (NO. OF GRAFTS)	PATENCY (%) RVG	In Situ	*P* Value
Watelet[144] (1986): AK/BK popliteal (*n* = 100 grafts)*	88	71	NS
Harris[143] (1993): AK/BK popliteal (*n* = 215 grafts)*	77	68	NS
Veterans Administration Cooperative Study Group 141[140] (1988) (*n* = 461 grafts)†			
BK popliteal	75	78	NS
Infrapopliteal	67	76	NS
Wengerter[146] (1991) (*n* = 125 grafts)‡			
Overall	67	69	NS
<3-mm veins	37	61	NS
Watelet[145] (1997) (*n* = 91 grafts)§	70.2	64.8	NS

*Values at 36 months.
†Values at 24 months.
‡Values at 30 months.
§Ten-year results.
NS, not significant; AK, above knee; BK, below knee; RVG, reversed vein grafts.

Table 81-3 Above-Knee Femoropopliteal Grafts

PRIMARY PATENCY*	1 MO	6 MO	1 YR	2 YR	3 YR	4 YR
Reverse saphenous vein	99	91	84	82	73	69
Arm vein	99		82	65	60	60
Human umbilical vein	95	90	82	82	70	70
Polytetrafluoroethylene		89	79	74	66	60

*All patencies are expressed as percentages; all series published since 1981.

small fraction of patients in this report (14.3%) met these basic criteria for success. Golledge and others from South Australia, using similar criteria, showed that only 22% of patients had an ideal outcome.[162] Abou-Zamzam and colleagues,[163] also from the Oregon group, identified preoperative independence and ambulation as the best predictors of postoperative independence and continued ambulation. These data emphasize the severity of underlying co-morbidities in CLI patients and the difficulties encountered in obtaining functional limb salvage.

Goshima and coworkers[164] from the University of Arizona analyzed a consecutive series of 318 patients undergoing infrainguinal bypass, 72% for CLI. Three nontraditional outcome measures were used to explore outcomes and define the clinical realities of treating patients with CLI: (1) index limb reoperation rate within 3 months of bypass, (2) hospital readmission rate within 6 months, and (3) wound healing time. Perioperative mortality was less than 1%, mean length of initial hospital stay was 9 days, 30-day graft patency was 96.9%, and 3-month limb salvage was 96.5%. Five-year limb salvage in a similar group of patients from the same center was 91%, and the costs of bypass combined with graft surveillance and revision for 5 years were equal to or less than those for patients undergoing major limb amputation.[196] However, 49% of patients required at least one reoperation within 3 months, and 50% required readmission to the hospital within 6 months. The cumulative length of stay for all readmissions was 11 days. More than half of CLI patients required more than 3 months of postoperative care to achieve wound healing. The presence of preoperative tissue loss and minority status increased the odds of reoperation by 2.2- to 3.1-fold, whereas ischemic tissue loss, renal failure, and diabetes were independently associated by multivariate analysis with the need for readmission. Diabetes mellitus was the sole independent risk factor for prolonged wound healing (odds ratio, 3.4). Further studies using such functional or patient-relative outcomes are needed to place the role of infrainguinal bypass in perspective,[165-171] particularly to allow comparison with evolving less invasive techniques such as subintimal angioplasty or even primary amputation in selected high-risk subsets of patients with CLI. Although it is generally agreed that nearly all patients with CLI are best treated with surgical revascularization, it is clear that both economic and functional outcome considerations mandate consideration of alternative therapies, at least for certain subsets of patients with CLI such as those living in nursing facilities or who are minimally ambulatory.[163-166]

Table 81-4 Below-Knee Femoropopliteal Grafts

PATENCY*	1 MO	6 MO	1 YR	2 YR	3 YR	4 YR
Primary						
Reverse saphenous vein	98	90	84	79	78	77
In-situ vein bypass	95	87	80	76	73	68
Secondary						
In-situ vein bypass	97	96	96	89	86	81
Arm vein	97	—	83	83	73	70
Human umbilical vein	88	82	77	70	61	60
Polytetrafluoroethylene	96	80	68	61	44	40
Limb salvage						
Reverse saphenous vein	100	92	90	88	86	75
In-situ vein bypass	97	96	94	84	83	—

* All patencies are expressed as percentages; all series published since 1981.

■ POSTOPERATIVE MANAGEMENT

Following bypass, patients should generally be maintained on their preoperative medical regimens for control of angina, arrhythmia, CHF, and hypertension. Patients with a recent history of CHF are at high risk for prolongation of hospital stay and readmisssion[162,164]; care should be taken to avoid volume overloading in these patients, and they may require supplemental diuresis. Perioperative beta blockade should be continued in the absence of contraindications; in moderate- and high-risk patients undergoing vascular surgery, beta blockade with targeted heart rate control reduces cardiac complications and improves mortality.[16,17]

Table 81-5 Infrapopliteal Grafts

PATENCY*	1 MO	6 MO	1 YR	2 YR	3 YR	4 YR
Primary						
Reverse saphenous vein	92	81	77	70	66	62
In-situ vein bypass	94	84	82	76	74	68
Secondary						
Reverse saphenous vein	93	89	84	80	78	76
In-situ vein bypass	95	90	89	87	84	81
Arm vein	94		73	62	58	—
Human umbilical vein	80	65	52	46	40	37
Polytetrafluoroethylene	89	58	46	32	—	21
Limb salvage						
Reverse saphenous vein	95	88	85	83	82	82
In-situ vein bypass	96	—	91	88	83	83
Polytetrafluoroethylene		76	68	60	56	48

*All patencies are expressed as percentages; all series published since 1981.

Table 81-6 At or Below-Ankle Grafts

PATENCY*	1 MO	6 MO	1 YR	2 YR	3 YR
Primary					
Reverse saphenous vein	95	85	81	—	—
Secondary					
Reverse saphenous vein	96	90	85	81	76
In-situ vein bypass	93	93	92	82	72
Foot salvage	99	94	93	87	84

*All patencies are expressed as percentages; all series published since 1981.

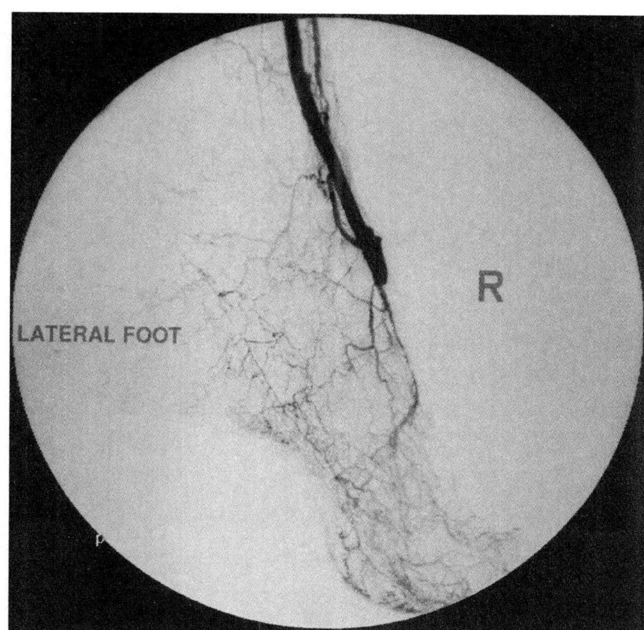

FIGURE 81-13 Distal view of completion arteriogram following popliteal artery to dorsal pedal artery reversed vein bypass in an 82-year-old diabetic man with chronic renal disease and a functioning renal transplant. Despite significant disease of the distal dorsal pedal artery, the patient healed a toe amputation, and the graft remains patent with normal graft flow velocities during intermediate follow-up.

Most patients with PAD are already receiving antiplatelet therapy, usually aspirin (81 or 325 mg daily). Aspirin has well-recognized cardiac and cerebral protective effects and may also improve early graft patency.[172-174] Clopidogrel may also be used,[175] but it is more expensive and may have an increased risk of complications compared with aspirin alone. Most vascular surgeons would consider antiplatelet therapy essential for patients undergoing infrainguinal bypass.

There are insufficient data on which to base recommendations concerning anticoagulation following lower extremity bypass. A single long-term, randomized, prospective trial of 130 patients by Kretschmer and colleagues from Vienna[176] demonstrated improved vein graft patency and limb salvage rates and improved patient survival in patients randomized to phenprocoumon. A recent report in *Lancet* of the Dutch Bypass Oral Anticoagulants or Aspirin (BOA) Trial summarized a study of 2690 lower extremity bypass patients randomized to anticoagulation versus antiplatelet therapy (aspirin).[177] Although overall differences were not significant, subgroup analysis suggested that oral anticoagulation improved vein graft patency compared with aspirin, whereas aspirin improved prosthetic graft patency compared to anticoagulation. If these data can be confirmed, it would likely alter the typical practice in at least North America, where surgeons tend to treat vein graft patients with aspirin and anticoagulate those with prosthetic grafts. The BOA trial, however, noted that anticoagulated patients had nearly double the major bleeding risk of patients on antiplatelet therapy, suggesting that perhaps anticoagulation should be used selectively in subgroups at greatest risk.

Such a selective approach has been recommended by the University of Florida group based on a small randomized study of patients with high-risk vein grafts.[178] High-risk grafts were defined on the basis of poor arterial runoff, suboptimal vein conduit, and reoperative cases. Patency (74%) and limb salvage (81%) at 3 years in the high-risk group randomized to warfarin and aspirin were significantly higher than in the aspirin-only group (51% and 31%, respectively), although again, bleeding was much more common in the group receiving warfarin.

The water is further muddied by the recently published Veterans Affairs Cooperative trial in which 665 patients with infrainguinal bypasses were randomized to aspirin and warfarin versus aspirin alone.[179] Vein graft patency was not increased by the addition of warfarin to aspirin alone; on the other hand, prosthetic graft patency was significantly improved by anticoagulation but at the expense of double the risk of hemorrhagic events. These data all suggest a potential role for postoperative anticoagulation that will no doubt require larger trials with higher statistical power to permit a grade A recommendation based on level I evidence; until then, most surgeons will continue to routinely employ antiplatelet therapy (aspirin 81 to 325 mg daily) and add anticoagulation in selected groups at highest risk (e.g., prosthetic infrageniculate grafts, poor outflow, reoperative cases, poor or alternate vein conduit).

All patients with CLI are at risk for pressure ulcers not only in the affected limb but also the contralateral limb as well as the sacrum. Unremitting nursing care is essential to prevent these complications. Considerable wound care is also required to achieve healing of ischemic foot lesions and forefoot amputations, as alluded to in the preceding discussion. Foot infection should have been controlled prior to revascularization. Basic science wound studies would suggest that débridement and formal toe/forefoot amputations for areas of tissue ulceration/gangrene should be delayed 4 to 10 days following bypass to maximize tissue reperfusion and allow clear demarcation of marginal areas.

With experienced judgment and intraoperative attention to detail, early graft occlusion should be an uncommon event. Should a graft fail in the early postoperative period, the most important principle is to identify and correct the underlying cause.[180] If no cause can be identified, the prognosis for long-term patency is poor. On the other hand, the outcome is much more favorable if the cause can be ascertained and addressed. The most common correctable culprits are anastomotic, local endarterectomy, or clamp defects; valve defects; poor conduit quality; or inadequate outflow. When the patient is returned to the operating room, one can usually begin by exploring the distal anastomosis first. If the graft hood is pulsatile, an arteriogram is performed. If not, the hood is opened and gentle distal thrombectomy and graft thrombectomy are performed with Fogarty catheters of appropriate caliber. If the graft is a reversed vein, both proximal and distal anastomoses will usually require exploration. An uninflated Fogarty catheter is passed from proximal to distal; a second catheter can be tied to the first one and drawn uninflated proximally. The tie is cut, the second catheter is inflated, and the graft is then thrombectomized from proximal to distal. Once the thrombus has been evacuated, heparinized saline is forcibly irrigated through the graft to flush any residual thrombotic debris out the distal graftotomy. Both anastomoses can be carefully inspected; if a distal anastomotic defect is identified, the graftotomy can be extended down the outflow artery and closed with a patch. If no defects are identified, the graft incisions are closed and thorough arteriography of the entire graft and the outflow is performed. Significant conduit or anastomotic lesions should be corrected. If unsuspected or previously unappreciated outflow disease is identified, the graft should be extended beyond the lesion or to an alternate outflow artery if available. If a marginal vein conduit was used at the initial procedure and no focal defect is identified at re-exploration, one should consider replacing the conduit; this decision is difficult and may require harvesting of additional vein or, if none is available, converting to a prosthetic conduit if outflow is sufficient.

■ GRAFT SURVEILLANCE

Vein graft surveillance is critically important to the long-term outcome of infrainguinal bypass. It has been well documented for more than 3 decades that nearly one third of autogenous vein grafts develop lesions that threaten graft patency.[181] Most such lesions, especially in the first 1 to 2 years following graft implantation, are intrinsic to the graft itself and result from intimal hyperplasia.[182-184] At later intervals, inflow and outflow lesions may develop and reduce graft flow and thus threaten ongoing graft patency. All these lesions can be readily identified, graded for severity, and monitored for progression by means of a simple program of ABI determination and duplex graft surveillance.[185-193] We obtain the first study within 4 weeks of surgery, either prior to hospital discharge or at the time of the first postoperative visit.[191] Serial studies are performed every 3 months for 1 year, every 6 months for 2 additional years, and annually thereafter. Grafts with focal lesions associated with a peak systolic velocity greater than 300 cm/sec and/or a velocity ratio greater than 3.5 to 4.0 (Fig. 81-14) undergo prophylactic repair to prevent graft stenosis.[192,193] Grafts that develop low-flow velocities over time (peak systolic velocity < 45 cm/sec throughout the graft) or a drop in ABI exceeding 0.15 in the absence of detectable graft lesions undergo arteriography to search for inflow, outflow, or missed graft lesions. Abundant clinical data from multiple investigators[184-193] and a single, prospective randomized trial by Lundell and associates[194] suggest that vein graft surveillance improves long-term vein graft patency by approximately 15%. Cost-benefit analyses both in Europe[195] and in the United States[196] confirm that vein graft surveillance is also cost-effective. Graft occlusion is a morbid and costly event; its prevention is worthwhile. Graft surveillance of prosthetic grafts has not been shown to be beneficial.[197,198]

■ CONCLUSION

Currently, infrainguinal bypass using autogenous vein is the most effective and durable treatment for severe lower extremity claudication and CLI caused by long-segment, diffuse ASO. The most important factor in operative success is conduit quality. Preoperative duplex vein imaging is useful to identify optimal vein as well as to suggest vein

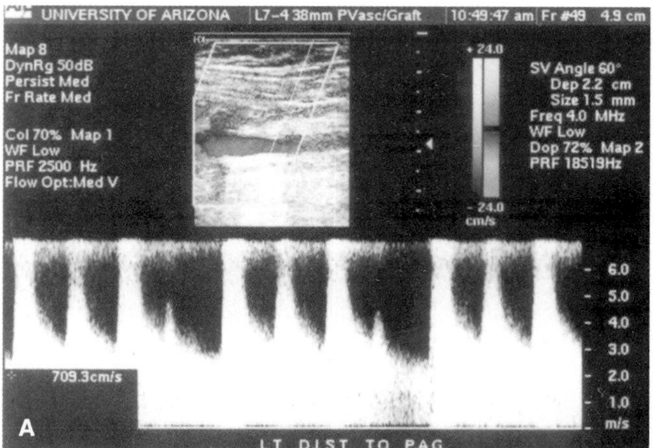

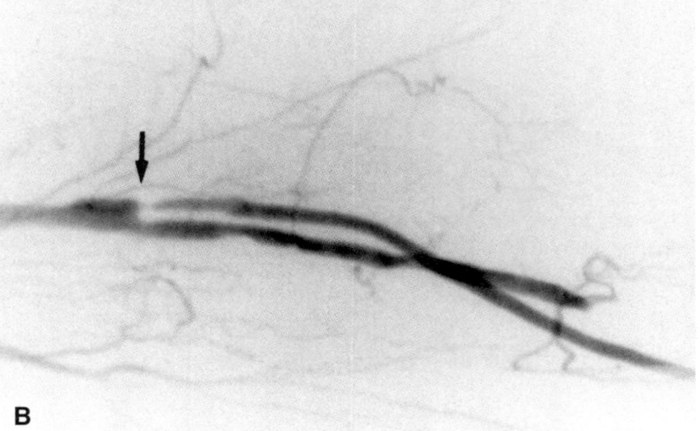

FIGURE 81-14 Duplex surveillance identified a critical vein graft stenosis in the proximal aspect of a femoropopliteal vein graft. There is marked spectral broadening and pronounced elevation of both the peak systolic (PSV) and end-diastolic (EDV) velocities, diagnostic of a high-grade vein graft stenosis (**A**). A focal, severe proximal graft stenosis (*arrow*) was confirmed by arteriography (**B**) and successfully treated with a short interposition vein graft harvested from the upper extremity. (See color figure in this section.)

segments that should not be explored owing to occlusion, severe calcification, poor caliber, or sclerosis. Patent, compressible veins between 2 and 3 mm are worthy of exploration, but veins that distend to a caliber of less than 3 to 3.5 mm tend to perform poorly regardless of configuration. Reversed, nonreversed, and in-situ bypasses all seem to perform equally well, and the choice of technique depends on anatomic considerations and surgeon preference. Bypasses may originate from inflow sources distal to the CFA without compromising graft patency in appropriately selected patients. Shortening the bypass in this way may ease the performance of the operation and improve its success by allowing selection of the highest quality, largest caliber vein. All vein graft patients should be followed by postoperative duplex-based graft surveillance. Antiplatelet therapy is indicated in all infrainguinal bypass patients; oral anticoagulation may be worthwhile in selected, high-risk patients, but hemorrhagic risks are significantly increased.

Although GSV is the best available conduit, alternate veins also perform well when required, although their results are inferior to GSV grafts. Saphenous vein is superior to all other conduits for all infrainguinal bypasses, including those to the above-knee popliteal artery. If vein is truly unavailable, prosthetic bypasses are a useful alternative for most patients. Dacron and PTFE appear to be equivalent above the knee; if recent studies are confirmed, HBD may become the graft of choice for above-knee bypass when prosthetic must be used. For infrageniculate bypass, the greatest reported experience with prosthetic grafts is with PTFE; available data suggest that a distal anastomotic vein cuff or patch improves short- and mid-term graft patency whenever one must resort to PTFE owing to the absence of suitable vein conduit.

Patients with CLI are an extraordinarily high-risk group of individuals to manage. In experienced units, excellent infrainguinal graft patency with limb salvage and low operative mortalities are the norm. Recent studies, however, suggest that such patients, especially those with a history of CHF, are prone to hospital readmission and reduced long-term mortality. CLI patients, in particular those with diabetes, frequently require multiple reoperations to achieve a healed foot. Additional clinical studies of functional outcomes are needed to help define subpopulations of CLI patients that might best be served by less aggressive or invasive therapy such as long-segment angioplasty (including subintimal technique) or even primary amputation. There is also a need for further randomized trials of conduit alternatives to be used when vein is unavailable; potential alternatives include PTFE, Dacron, HUV, and adjuncts such as distal arteriovenous fistula and distal patches, collars, and cuffs.

Acknowledgment The illustrations were drawn by Joseph L. Mills, Jr. (BA, University of Arizona).

■ REFERENCES

1. Management of peripheral arterial disease (PAD): TransAtlantic Intersociety Consensus (TASC). J Vasc Surg 31:S1-289, 2000.
2. Dartmouth Atlas of Vascular Healthcare. Chicago, Health Forum, AHA Press, 2000, pp 89-112.
3. Fontaine R, Kim M, Kieny R: Die chirurgische Behandlung der peripheren Durch-blutungsstoerungen. Helv Chir Acta 5/6:199-533, 1954.
4. Rutherford R. Flanigan D, Gupta S, et al: Suggested standards for reports dealing with lower extremity ischemia. J Vasc Surg 4:80-94, 1986.
5. Rutherford RB: Standards for evaluating results of interventional therapy for peripheral vascular disease. Circulation 83(Suppl):6-19, 1991.
6. Rutherford RB, Baker JD, Ernst C, et al: Recommended standards for reports dealing with lower extremity ischemia: Revised version. J Vasc Surg 26:517-538, 1997.
7. Second European Consensus Document. Eur J Vasc Surg 6(Suppl A): 1-32, 1992.
8. Wolfe JHN, Wyatt MG: Critical and subcritical ischemia. Eur J Vasc Endovasc Surg 13:578-582, 1997.
9. Marek JM, Mills JL: Risk factor assessment and indications for reconstruction. In Mills JL (ed): Management of Chronic Lower Limb Ischemia. London, UK, Arnold, 2000, pp 30-44.
10. Hertzer NR, Beven EG, Young JR, et al: Coronary artery disease in peripheral vascular patients: A classification of 1000 coronary angiograms and results of surgical management. Ann Surg 199:223-233, 1984.
11. Taylor LM, Yeager RA, Moneta GL, et al: The incidence of perioperative myocardial infarction in general vascular surgery. J Vasc Surg 15:52-61, 1991.
12. Detsky AS, Abrams HB, Fobarth N, et al: Cardiac assessment for patients undergoing noncardiac surgery: A multifactorial clinical risk index. Arch Intern Med 146:2131-2134, 1986.
13. Goldman L, Caldera DL, Nessbaum SR, et al: Multifactorial index of cardiac risk in noncardiac surgical procedures. N Engl J Med 297:845-853, 1977.
14. Eagle KA, Coley CM, Newell JB, et al: Combining clinical and thallium data optimizes preoperative assessment of cardiac risk before major vascular surgery. Ann Intern Med 110:859-866, 1989.
15. Cook DJ, Guyatt GH, Laupacis A, Sackett DL: Rules of evidence and clinical recommendations on the use of antithrombotic agents. Chest 102(Suppl):305S-311S, 1992.
16. Mangano DT, Layug E, Wallace A, Tateo I: Effect of atenolol on mortality and cardiovascular morbidity after noncardiac surgery. N Engl J Med 335:1713-1720, 1996.
17. Poldermans D, Boersma E, Bax JJ, et al: The effect of bisoprolol on perioperative mortality and myocardial infarction in high-risk patients undergoing vascular surgery. Dutch Echocardiographic Cardiac Risk Evaluation Applying Stress Echocardiography Study Group. N Engl J Med 341:1789-1794, 1999.
18. Dorweiler B, Neufang A, Kreitner K-F, et al: Magnetic resonance angiography unmasks reliable target vessels for pedal bypass grafting in patients with diabetes mellitus. J Vasc Surg 35:766-772, 2002.
19. Mazzariol F, Ascher E, Hingorani A, et al: Lower-extremity revascularisation without preoperative contrast arteriography in 185 cases: Lessons learned with duplex ultrasound arterial mapping. Eur J Vasc Endovasc Surg 19:509-515, 2000.
20. Pemberton M, Nydahl S, Hartshorne T, et al: Can lower limb vascular reconstruction be based on colour duplex imaging alone? Eur J Vasc Endovasc Surg 12:452-454, 1996.
21. Cohen MI, Vogelzang RL: A comparison of techniques for improved visualization of the arteries of the distal lower extremity. AJR Am J Roentgenol 147:1021-1024, 1986.
22. Kozak BE, Bedell JE, Rosch J: Small-vessel leg angiography for distal vessel bypass grafts. J Vasc Surg 8:711-715, 1988.
23. Pomposelli FB, Jepsen SJ, Gibbons GW, et al: Efficacy of the dorsal pedal bypass for limb salvage in diabetic patients: Short-term observations. J Vasc Surg 11:745-752, 1990.
24. Kunlin JL: Le traitement di l'arterite obliterante par le greffe veineuse. Arch Mal Coeur 42:371-374, 1949.
25. Taylor LM Jr, Edwards JM, Porter JM: Present status of reversed vein bypass grafting: Five-year results of a modern series. J Vasc Surg 11:193-205, 1990.
26. Donaldson MC, Whittemore AD, Mannick JA: Further experience with an all-autogenous tissue policy for infrainguinal reconstruction. J Vasc Surg 18:41-48, 1993.
27. Leopold PW, Shandall A, Kupinkski AM, et al: Role of B-mode venous mapping in infrainguinal in-situ vein-arterial bypasses. Br J Surg 76:305-307, 1989.
28. Bagi P, Schroeder T, Sillesen H, Lorentzen JE: Real-time B-mode mapping of the greater saphenous vein. Eur J Vasc Surg 3:103-105, 1989
29. Shah DM, Chang BB, Leopold PW, et al: The anatomy of the greater saphenous venous system. J Vasc Surg 3:273-283, 1986.
30. Blebea J, Schomaker WR, Hod G, et al: Preoperative duplex vein mapping: A comparison of positional techniques in patients with and without atherosclerosis. J Vasc Surg 20:226-234, 1994.

Reversed Vein

31. Imparato AM, Kim GE, Madayag M, et al: The results of tibial artery reconstruction procedures. Surg Gynecol Obstet 138:33-38, 1974.
32. Szilagyi DE, Hageman JH, Smith RF, et al: Autogenous vein grafting in femoropopliteal atherosclerosis: The limits of its effectiveness. Surgery 86:836-851, 1979.
33. Reichle FA, Martinson MW, Rankin KP: Infrapopliteal arterial reconstruction in the severely ischemic lower extremity: A compari-

son of long-term results of peroneal and tibial bypasses. Ann Surg 191:59-65, 1980.
34. Taylor LM Jr, Edwards JM, Phinney ES, et al: Reversed saphenous vein bypass to infrapopliteal arteries. Ann Surg 205:90-97, 1987.
35. Mills JL, Taylor SM: Results of infrainguinal revascularization with reversed vein conduits: A modern control series. Ann Vasc Surg 5:156-162, 1991.

Nonreversed or In-Situ Vein

36. Beard JD, Wyatt M, Scott DJ, et al: The non-reversed vein femoro-distal bypass graft: A modification of the standard in situ technique. Eur J Vasc Surg 3:55-60, 1989.
37. Hall KV: The greater saphenous vein used in situ as an arterial shunt after extirpation of the vein valves. Surgery 51:492-495, 1962.
38. May AG, DeWeese JA, Rob CG: Arterialized in situ saphenous vein. Arch Surg 91:743-750, 1965.
39. Leather RP, Powers SR, Karmody AM: A reappraisal of the in situ saphenous vein artery bypass: Its use in limb salvage. Surgery 86:453-461, 1979.
40. Leather RP, Shah DM, Karmody AM: Infrapopliteal arterial bypass for limb salvage: Increased patency and utilization of the saphenous vein used in situ. Surgery 90:1000-1007, 1981.
41. Leather RP, Shah DM, Chang BB, Kaufman JL: Resurrection of the in situ saphenous vein bypass 1000 cases later. Ann Surg 208:435-442, 1988.
42. Harris RW, Andros G, Dulawa LB: The transition to "in situ" vein bypass grafts. Surg Gynceol Obstet 163:21-28, 1986.
43. Bandyk DF, Kaebnick JW, Stewart GW, Towne JB: Durability of the in situ saphenous vein arterial bypass: A comparison of primary and secondary patency. J Vasc Surg 5:256-268, 1987.
44. Bergamini TM, Towne JM, Bandyk DF, et al: Experience with in situ saphenous vein bypasses during 1981 to 1989: Determinant factors of long-term patency. J Vasc Surg 13:137, 1991.
45. Donaldson MC, Mannick JA, Whittemore AD: Femoral-distal bypass with in situ greater saphenous vein: Long-term results using the Mills valvulotome. Ann Surg 213:457, 1991.

Hemodynamics: Inflow

46. Tweedie JH, Ballantyne KC, Callum KG: Direct arterial pressure measurements during operation to assess adequacy of arterial reconstruction in lower limb ischaemia. Br J Surg 73:879-881, 1986.
47. Flanigan DP, Williams LR, Schwartz JA, et al: Hemodynamic evaluation of the aortoiliac system based on pharmacologic vasodilatation. Surgery 93:709-714, 1983.
48. Boren CH, Towne JB, Bernhard VM, et al: Profunda-popliteal collateral index: A guide to successful profundaplasty. Arch Surg 115:1366-1372, 1980.

Profundaplasty

49. Edwards WH, Jenkins JM, Mulherin JL Jr, et al: Extended profundaplasty to minimize pelvic and distal tissue loss. Ann Surg 211:694-702, 1990.
50. Hansen AK, Bille S, Nielsen PH, Egeblad K: Profundaplasty as the only reconstructive procedure in patients with severe ischemia of the lower extremity. Surg Gynecol Obstet 171:47-50, 1990.
51. Kalman PG, Johnston KW, Walker PM: The current role of isolated profundaplasty. J Cardiovasc Surg (Torino) 31:107-111, 1990.

Blind-Segment Popliteal Bypasses

52. Kram HB, Gupta SK, Veith FJ, et al: Late results of two hundred seventeen femoropopliteal bypasses to isolated popliteal artery segments. J Vasc Surg 14:386-390, 1991.
53. Karacagil S, Almgren B, Bowald S, Eriksson I: Bypass grafting to the popliteal artery in limbs with occluded crural arteries. Am J Surg 162:19-23, 1991.
54. Darke S, Lamont P, Chant A, et al: Femoro-popliteal versus femoro-distal bypass grafting for limb salvage in patients with an "isolated" popliteal segment. Eur J Vasc Surg 3:203-207, 1989.
55. Loh A, Chester JF, Taylor RS: PTFE bypass grafting to isolated popliteal segments in critical limb ischaemia. Eur J Vasc Surg 7:26-30, 1993.
56. Samson RH, Showalter DP, Yunis JP: Isolated femoropopliteal bypass graft for limb salvage after failed tibial reconstruction: A viable alternative to amputation. J Vasc Surg 29:409-412, 1999.
57. Belkin M, Welch H, Mackey WC, O'Donnell TF: Clinical and hemodynamic results of bypass to isolated tibial artery segments for ischemic ulceration of the foot. Am J Surg 164:281-285, 1992.

Peroneal versus Pedal Bypass

58. Elliott BM, Robison JG, Brothers TE, Cross MA: Limitations of peroneal artery bypass grafting for limb salvage. J Vasc Surg 18:881-888, 1993.
59. Plecha EJ, Seabrook GR, Bandyk DF, Towne JB: Determinants of successful peroneal artery bypass. J Vasc Surg 17:97-105, 1993.
60. Raftery KB, Belkin M, Mackey WC, O'Donnell TF: Are peroneal artery bypass grafts hemodynamically inferior to other tibial artery bypass grafts? J Vasc Surg 19:964-968, 1994.
61. Bergamini TM, George SM Jr, Massey HT, et al: Pedal or peroneal bypass: Which is better when both are patent? J Vasc Surg 20:347-355, 1994.
62. Gentile AT, Berman SS, Reinke KR, et al: A regional pedal ischemia scoring system for decision analysis in patients with heel ulceration. Am J Surg 176:109-114, 1998.

Alternate Exposure Techniques and Inflow Sites

63. Shah DM, Darling RC III, Chang BB, et al: Is long vein bypass from groin to ankle a durable procedure? An analysis of a ten-year experience. J Vasc Surg 15:402-407, 1992.
64. Stabile BE, Wilson SE: The profunda femoris-popliteal artery bypass. Arch Surg 112:913, 1977.
65. Farley JJ, Kiser JC, Hitchcock CR: Profunda femoris-popliteal shunt. Ann Surg 160:23-25, 1964.
66. Nunez AA, Veith FJ, Collier P, et al: Direct approaches to the distal portions of the profunda femoris artery for limb salvage bypasses. J Vasc Surg 8:576-581, 1988.
67. Mills JL, Taylor JM, Fujitani RM: The role of the deep femoral artery as an inflow site for infrainguinal revascularization. J Vasc Surg 18:416-423, 1993.
68. Veith FS, Gupta SK, Samson RH, et al: Superficial femoral and popliteal arteries as inflow sites for distal bypass. Surgery 90:980-990, 1981.
69. Mills JL, Gahtan V, Fujitani RM, Taylor SM: The utility and durability of vein bypass grafts originating from the popliteal artery for limb salvage. Am J Surg 168:646-651, 1994.
70. Reed AB, Conte MS, Belkin M, et al: Usefulness of autogenous bypass grafts originating distal to the groin. J Vasc Surg 35:48-54, 2002.
71. Mukherjee D: Posterior approach to the peroneal artery. J Vasc Surg 19:174-178, 1994.
72. Ouriel K: The posterior approach to popliteal-crural bypass. J Vasc Surg 19:74-80, 1994.
73. Bernhard VM, Boren CH, Towne JB: Pneumatic tourniquet as a substitute for vascular clamps in distal bypass surgery. Surgery 87:709-713, 1980.

Conduit Choices

74. Chew DK, Owens CD, Belkin M, et al: Bypass in the absence of ipsilateral greater saphenous vein: Safety and superiority of the contralateral greater saphenous vein. J Vasc Surg 35:1085-1092, 2002.
75. Chang BB, Paty PSK, Shah DM, Leather RP: The lesser saphenous vein: An underappreciated source of autogenous vein. J Vasc Surg 15:152-157, 1992.
76. Weaver FA, Barlow CR, Edwards WH, et al: The lesser saphenous vein: Autogenous tissue for lower extremity revascularization. J Vasc Surg 5:687-692, 1987.
77. Schulman ML, Badhey MR, Yatco R: Superficial femoral-popliteal veins and reversed saphenous veins as primary femoropopliteal bypass grafts: A randomized comparative study. J Vasc Surg 6:1-10, 1987.
78. Kakkar VV: The cephalic vein as a peripheral vascular graft. Surg Gynecol Obstet 128:551-556, 1969.
79. Harris RW, Andros G, Dulawa LB, et al: Successful long-term limb salvage using cephalic vein bypass grafts. Ann Surg 200:785-792, 1984.
80. Londrey GL, Bosher LP, Brown PW, et al: Infrainguinal reconstruction with arm vein, lesser saphenous vein, and remnants of greater saphenous vein: A report of 257 cases. J Vasc Surg 20:451-456, 1994.
81. Faries PL, Arora S, Pomposelli FB, et al: The use of arm vein in lower extremity revascularizations: Results of 520 procedures performed in eight years. J Vasc Surg 31:50-59, 2000.
82. Gentile AT, Lee RW, Moneta GC, et al: Results of bypasses to the popliteal and tibial arteries with alternative sources of autogenous vein. J Vasc Surg 23:272-280, 1996.
83. Taylor SM, Langan EM III, Snyder BA, Crane MM: Superficial femoral artery eversion endarterectomy: A useful adjunct for infrainguinal bypass in the presence of limited autogenous vein. J Vasc Surg 26:439-446, 1997.
84. Fujitani RM, Bassiouny HS, Gewertz BL, et al: Cryopreserved saphenous vein allogenic homografts: An alternative conduit in lower extremity arterial reconstruction in infected fields. J Vasc Surg 15:519-526, 1992.
85. Farber A, Major K, Willis WH, et al: Cryopreserved saphenous vein allografts in infrainguinal revascularization: Analysis of 240 grafts. J Vasc Surg 38:15-21, 2003.
86. Treiman GS, Lawrence PF, Rockwell WB: Autogenous arterial bypass grafts: Durable patency and limb salvage in patients with inframalleolar occlusive disease and end-stage renal disease. J Vasc Surg 32:13-22, 2000.
87. LoGerfo FW, Paniszyn CW, Menzoian J: A new arm vein graft for distal bypass. J Vasc Surg 5:889-891, 1987.
88. Green R, Abbott W: Prosthetic above-knee femoropopliteal bypass: A five-year randomized trial. J Vasc Surg 31:417-425, 2000.
89. Post S, Kraus T, Mueller-Reinartz U, et al: Dacron versus polytetrafluoroethylene grafts for femoropopliteal bypass: A prospective randomized multicenter trial. Eur J Vasc Endovasc Surg 22:226-231, 2001.
90. Robinson BI, Fletcher JP, Tomlinson P, et al: A prospective randomized multicentre comparison of expanded polytetrafluoroethylene and gelatin-sealed Dacron grafts for femoropopliteal bypass. J Cardiovasc Surg 7:214-218, 1999.
91. Devine C, Hons B, McCollum C: Heparin-bonded Dacron or polytetrafluoroethylene for femoropopliteal bypass grafting: A multicenter trial. J Vasc Surg 33:533-539, 2001.
92. Sayers RD, Raptis S, Berce M, Miller JH: Long-term results of femorotibial bypass with vein or polytetrafluoroethylene. Br J Surg 85:934-938, 1998.
93. Taylor RS, Loh A, McFarland RJ, et al: Improved techniques for polytetrafluoroethylene bypass grafting: Long-term results using anastomotic vein patches. Br J Surg 79:348-354, 1992.
94. Tyrrell MR, Wolfe JHN: New prosthetic venous collar anastomotic technique: Combining the best of other procedures. Br J Surg 78:1016-1017, 1991.
95. Yeung KK, Mills JL, Hughes JD, et al: Improved patency of infrainguinal polytetrafluoroethylene bypass grafts using a distal Taylor vein patch. Am J Surg 182:578-583, 2001.
96. Stonebridge PA, Prescott RJ, Ruckley CV: Randomized trial comparing infrainguinal polytetrafluoroethylene bypass grafting with and without vein interposition cuff at the distal anastomosis. J Vasc Surg 26:543-550, 1997.
97. Hamsho A, Nott D, Harris PL: Prospective randomised trial of distal arteriovenous fistula as an adjunct to femoro-infrapopliteal PTFE bypass. Eur J Vasc Endovasc Surg 17:197-201, 1999.
98. Gupta SK, Veith FJ, Kram HB, Wengerter KR: Prospective, randomized comparison of ringed and nonringed polytetrafluoroethylene femoropopliteal bypass grafts: A preliminary report. J Vasc Surg 13:163-172, 1991.
99. McCollum C, Kenchington G, Alexander C, et al: PTFE or HUV for femoro-popliteal bypass: A multi-centre trial. Eur J Vasc Surg 5:435-443, 1991.
100. Aalders GJ, van Vroonhoven TJ: Polytetra fluoroethylene versus human umbilical vein in above-knee femoropopliteal bypass: Six-year results of a randomized clinical trial. J Vasc Surg 16:816-823, 1992.
101. Eickhoff JH, Broome A, Ericsson BJ, et al: Four years' results of a prospective, randomized clinical trial comparing polytetrafluoroethylene and modified human umbilical vein for below-knee femoropopliteal bypass. J Vasc Surg 6:506-511, 1987.
102. Mills JL: *P* values may lack power: The choice of conduit for above-knee femoropopliteal bypass graft. J Vasc Surg 32:402-405, 2000.
103. Veith FJ, Gupta SK, Ascher E, White-Flores S, et al: Six-year prospective multicenter randomized comparison of autologous saphenous vein and expanded polytetrafluoroethylene grafts in infrainguinal arterial reconstructions. J Vasc Surg 3:104-114, 1986.
104. Tilanus HW, Obertrop H, van Urk H: Saphenous vein or PTFE for femoropopliteal bypass: A prospective randomized trial. Ann Surg 202:780-782, 1985.
105. Klinkert P, Schepers A, Burger DHC, et al: Vein versus polytetrafluoroethylene in above-knee femoropopliteal bypass grafting: Five-year results of a randomized controlled trial. J Vasc Surg 37:149-158, 2003.
106. Johnson WC, Lee KK: A comparative evaluation of polytetrafluoroethylene, umbilical vein, and saphenous vein bypass grafts for femoro-popliteal above-knee revascularization: A prospective randomized Department of Veterans Affairs Cooperative Study. J Vasc Surg 32:268-277, 2000.
107. Dardik H, Wengerter K, Qin F, et al: Comparative decades of experience with glutaraldehyde-tanned human umbilical cord vein graft for lower limb revascularization: An analysis of 1275 cases. J Vasc Surg 35:64-71, 2002.
108. Edwards JM, Taylor LM, Porter JM: Treatment of failed lower extremity bypass with new autogenous vein bypass. J Vasc Surg 11:132-145, 1990.
109. Whittemore AD, Clowes AW, Couch NP, Mannick JA: Secondary femoropopliteal reconstruction. Ann Surg 193:35-42, 1981.

Completion Studies

110. Spencer TD, Goldman MH, Hyslop JW, et al: Intraoperative assessment of in situ saphenous vein bypass with continuous-wave Doppler probe. Surgery 96:874-877, 1984.
111. Bandyk DF, Jorgensen RA, Towne JB: Intraoperative assessment of in situ saphenous vein arterial grafts using pulsed Doppler spectral analysis. Arch Surg 121:292-299, 1986.
112. Renwick S, Royle JP, Martin P: Operative angiography after femoropopliteal reconstructions—its influence on early failure rate. Br J Surg 55:134-136, 1968.

113. Mills JL, Fujitani RH, Taylor SM: Contribution of routine intraoperative completion arteriography to early infrainguinal bypass patency. Am J Surg 164:506-511, 1992.
114. Sayers RD, Naylor AR, London NJ, et al: The additional value of intraoperative angiography in infragenicular reconstruction. Eur J Vasc Endovasc Surg 9:211-217, 1995.
115. Bandyk DF, Mills JL, Gahtan V, et al: Intraoperative duplex scanning of arterial reconstructions: Fate of repaired and unrepaired defects. J Vasc Surg 20:426-433, 1994.
116. Johnson BL, Bandyk DF, Back MR, et al: Intraoperative duplex monitoring of infrainguinal vein bypass procedures. J Vasc Surg 31:678-690, 2000.
117. Towne JB, Bernhard VM: Vascular endoscopy: Useful tool or intraoperative toy? Surgery 82:415-419, 1977.
118. Miller A, Campbell DR, Gibbons GW, et al: Routine intraoperative angioscopy in lower extremity revascularization. Arch Surg 124:604-608, 1989.
119. Baxter BT, Rizzo RJ, Flinn WR, et al: A comparative study of intraoperative angioscopy and completion arteriography following femorodistal bypass. Arch Surg 125:997-1002, 1990.
120. Stonebridge PA, Miller A, Tsoukas A, et al: Angioscopy of arm vein infrainguinal bypass grafts. Ann Vasc Surg 5:170-175, 1991.
121. Gilbertson JJ, Walsh DB, Zwolak RM, et al: A blinded comparison of angiography, angioscopy, and duplex scanning in the intraoperative evaluation of in situ saphenous vein bypass grafts. J Vasc Surg 15:121-127, 1992.
122. Miller A, Marcaccio EJ, Tannenbaum GA, et al: Comparison of angioscopy and angiography for monitoring infrainguinal bypass vein grafts: Results of a prospective randomized trial. J Vasc Surg 17:382-398, 1993.
123. Marcaccio EJ, Miller A, Tannenbaum GA, et al: Angioscopically directed interventions improve arm vein bypass grafts. J Vasc Surg 17:994-1004, 1993.
124. Sales CM, Marin ML, Veith FJ, et al: Saphenous vein angioscopy: A valuable method to detect unsuspected venous disease. J Vasc Surg 18:198-206, 1993.
125. Wilson YG, Davies AH, Currie IC, et al: Angioscopy for quality control of saphenous vein during bypass grafting. Eur J Vasc Endovasc Surg 11:12-18, 1996.
126. Davies AH, Magee TR, Thompson JF, et al: Preliminary experience of angioscopy in femorodistal bypass. Ann R Coll Surg Engl 75:178-180, 1993.
127. Clair DG, Golden MA, Mannick JA, et al: Randomized prospective study of angioscopically assisted in situ saphenous vein grafting. J Vasc Surg 19:992-1000, 1994.
128. Schwartz ME, Harrington EB, Schanzer H: Wound complications after in situ bypass. J Vasc Surg 7:802-807, 1988.
129. Wengrovitz M, Atnip RG, Gifford RRM, et al: Wound complications of autogenous subcutaneous infrainguinal arterial bypass surgery: Predisposing factors and management. J Vasc Surg 11:156-163, 1990.
130. Reifsnyder T, Bandyk D, Seabrook G, et al: Wound complications of the in situ saphenous vein bypass technique. J Vasc Surg 15:843-850, 1992.

Angioscopically Assisted Bypass Techniques

131. Rosenthal D: Endoscopic in situ bypass. Surg Clin North Am 75:703-713, 1995.
132. van Dijk LC, van Urk H, du Bois JJ, et al: A new "closed" in situ vein bypass technique results in reduced wound complication rate. Eur J Vasc Endovasc Surg l0:162-167, 1995.
133. Cikrit DF, Dalsing MC, Lalka SG, et al: Early results of endovascular-assisted in situ saphenous vein bypass grafting. J Vasc Surg 19:778-787, 1994.
134. Miller A, Stonebridge PA, Tsoukas AI, et al: Angioscopically directed valvulotomy: A new valvulotome and technique. J Vasc Surg 13:813-821, 1991.
135. Rosenthal D, Herring MB, O'Donovan TJ, et al: Endovascular infrainguinal in situ saphenous vein bypass: A multicenter preliminary report. J Vasc Surg 16:453-458, 1992.
136. Maini BS, Andrews L, Salimi T, et al: A modified, angioscopically assisted technique for in situ saphenous vein bypass: Impact on patency, complications, and length of stay. J Vasc Surg 17:1041-1049, 1993.
137. Rosenthal D, Dickson C, Rodriguez FJ, et al: Infrainguinal endovascular in situ saphenous vein bypass: Ongoing results. J Vasc Surg 20:389-395, 1994.
138. Cikrit DF, Fiore NF, Dalsing MC, et al: A comparison of endovascular assisted and conventional in situ bypass grafts. Ann Vasc Surg 9:37-43, 1995.
139. Rosenthal D, Arous EJ, Friedman SG, et al: Endovascular-assisted versus conventional in situ saphenous vein bypass grafting: Cumulative patency, limb salvage, and cost results in a 39-month multicenter study. J Vasc Surg 31:60-68, 2000.

Randomized Trials: Reversed Saphenous Vein versus Greater Saphenous Vein

140. Veterans Administration Cooperative Study Group 141: Comparative evaluation of prosthetic, reversed, and in situ vein bypass grafts in distal popliteal and tibial-peroneal revascularization. Arch Surg 123:434-438, 1988.
141. Harris PL, How TV, Jones DR: Prospectively randomized clinical trial to compare in situ and reversed saphenous vein grafts. Br J Surg 74:252-255, 1987.
142. Moody AP, Edwards PR, Harris PL: In situ versus reversed femoropopliteal vein grafts: Long-term follow-up of a prospective, randomized trial. Br J Surg 79:750-752, 1992.
143. Harris PL, Veith FJ, Shanik GD, et al: Prospective randomized comparison of in situ and reversed infrapopliteal vein grafts. Br J Surg 80:173-176, 1993.
144. Watelet J, Cheysson E, Poels D: In situ versus reversed saphenous vein for femoropopliteal bypass: A prospective randomized study of 100 cases. Ann Vasc Surg 1:441-452, 1986.
145. Watelet J, Soury P, Menard JF, et al: Femoropopliteal bypass: In situ or reversed vein grafts? Ten-year results of a randomized prospective study. Ann Vasc Surg 11:510-519, 1997.
146. Wengerter KR, Veith FJ, Gupta SK: Prospective randomized multicenter comparison of in situ and reversed vein infrapopliteal bypasses. J Vasc Surg 13:189-199, 1991.
147. Lawson JA, Tangelder MJ, Algra A, Eikelboom BC: The myth of the in situ graft: Superiority in infrainguinal bypass surgery? Eur J Vasc Endovasc Surg 18:149-157, 1999.
148. Mills JL: In-situ versus reversed vein grafts: Is there a difference? Vasc Surg 31:679-684, 1999.

Patency Data

149. Dalman RL: Expected outcome: Early results, life table patency, limb salvage. In Mills JL (ed): Management of Chronic Lower Limb Ischemia. London, Arnold, 2000, pp 106-112.

Factors Affecting Patency and Outcome

150. Panetta TF, Marin ML, Veith FJ, et al: Unsuspected preexisting saphenous vein disease: An unrecognized cause of vein bypass failure. J Vasc Surg 15:102-110, 1992.
151. Marin ML, Veith FJ, Panetta TF, et al: Saphenous vein biopsy: A predictor of vein graft failure. J Vasc Surg 18:407-414, 1993.
152. Wengerter KR, Veith FJ, Gupta SK, et al: Influence of vein size (diameter) on infrapopliteal reversed vein graft patency. J Vasc Surg 11:525-531, 1990.

153. Idu MM, Buth J, Hop WC, et al: Factors influencing the development of vein-graft stenosis and their significance for clinical management. Eur J Vasc Endovasc Surg 17:15-21, 1999.
154. Biancari F, Alback A, Ihlberg L, et al: Angiographic runoff score as a predictor of outcome following femorocrural bypass surgery. Eur J Vasc Endovasc Surg 17:480-485, 1999.
155. Seeger JM, Pretus HA, Carlton LC, et al: Potential predictors of outcome in patients with tissue loss who undergo infrainguinal vein bypass grafting. J Vasc Surg 30:427-435, 1999.
156. Peltonen S, Biancari F, Lindgren L, et al: Outcome of infrainguinal bypass surgery for critical leg ischaemia in patients with chronic renal failure. Eur J Vasc Endovasc Surg 15:122-127, 1998.
157. Meyerson SL, Skelly CL, Curi MA, et al: Long-term results justify autogenous infrainguinal bypass grafting in patients with end-stage renal failure. J Vasc Surg 34:27-33, 2001.
158. Chang BB, Paty PS, Shah DM, et al: Results of infrainguinal bypass for limb salvage in patients with end-stage renal disease. Surgery 108:742-746, 1990.
159. Christopherson R, Beattie C, Frank SM, et al: Perioperative morbidity in patients randomized to epidural or general anesthesia for lower extremity vascular surgery. Perioperative Ischemia Randomized Anesthesia Trial Study Group. Anesthesiology 79:422-434, 1993.
160. Pierce ET, Pomposelli FB Jr, Stanley GD, et al: Anesthesia type does not influence early graft patency or limb salvage rates of lower extremity arterial bypass. J Vasc Surg 25:226-232, 1997.

Outcomes

161. Nicoloff AD, Taylor LM, McClafferty RB, et al: Patient recovery after infrainguinal grafting for limb salvage. J Vasc Surg 27:256-266, 1998.
162. Golledge J, Iannos J, Walsh JA, et al: Critical assessment of the outcome of infrainguinal vein bypass. Ann Surg 234:697-701, 2001.
163. Abou-Zamzam AM, Lee RW, Moneta GL, et al: Functional outcome after infrainguinal bypass for limb salvage. J Vasc Surg 25:287-295, 1997.
164. Goshima KR, Mills JL, Hughes JD: A new look at outcomes following infrainguinal bypass surgery: Traditional reporting standards systematically underestimate the expenditure of effort required to attain limb salvage. J Vasc Surg 39:330-335, 2004.
165. O'Brien TS, Lamont PM, Crow A, et al: Lower limb ischaemia in the octogenarian: Is limb salvage surgery worthwhile? Ann R Coll Surg Engl 75:445-447, 2002.
166. Nehler MR, Moneta GL, Edwards JM, et al: Surgery for chronic lower extremity ischemia in patients eighty or more years of age: Operative results and assessment of postoperative independence. J Vasc Surg 18:618-624, 1993.
167. Klevsgard R, Hallberg IR, Risberg B, Thomsen MB: Quality of life associated with varying degrees of chronic lower limb ischaemia: Comparison with a healthy sample. Eur J Vasc Endovasc Surg 17:319-325, 1999.
168. Chetter IC, Spark JI, Scott DJ, et al: Prospective analysis of quality of life in patients following infrainguinal reconstruction for chronic critical ischaemia. Br J Surg 85:951-955, 1998.
169. Albers M, Fratezi AC, De Luccia N: Assessment of quality of life of patients with severe ischemia as a result of infrainguinal arterial occlusive disease. J Vasc Surg 16:54-59, 1992.
170. Holtzman J, Caldwell M, Walvatne C, Kane R: Long-term functional status and quality of life after lower extremity revascularization. J Vasc Surg 29:395-402, 1999.
171. Singh S, Evans L, Datta D, et al: The costs of managing lower limb-threatening ischaemia. Eur J Vasc Endovasc Surg 12:359-362, 1996.

Postoperative Management

172. Collaborative overview of randomised trials of antiplatelet therapy: I. Prevention of death, myocardial infarction, and stroke by prolonged antiplatelet therapy in various categories of patients. Antiplatelet Trialists' Collaboration. BMJ 308:81-106, 1994.
173. Watson HR, Belcher G, Horrocks M: Adjuvant medical therapy in peripheral bypass surgery. Br J Surg 86:981-991, 1999.
174. Neilipovitz DT, Bryson GL, Nichol G: The effect of perioperative aspirin therapy in peripheral vascular surgery: A decision analysis. Anesth Analg 93:573-580, 2001.
175. A randomised, blinded trial of Clopidogrel versus Aspirin in Patients at Risk of Ischaemic Events (CAPRIE). CAPRIE Steering Committee. Lancet 348:1329-1339, 1996.
176. Kretschmer G, Herbst F, Prager M, et al: A decade of oral anticoagulant treatment to maintain autologous vein grafts for femoropopliteal atherosclerosis. Arch Surg 127:1112-1115, 1992.
177. Efficacy of oral anticoagulants compared with aspirin after infrainguinal bypass surgery (The Dutch Bypass Oral Anticoagulants or Aspirin Study): A randomised trial. Lancet 355:346-351, 2000.
178. Sarac TP, Huber TS, Back MR, et al: Warfarin improves the outcome of infrainguinal vein bypass grafting at high risk for failure. J Vasc Surg 28:446-457, 1998.
179. Johnson WC, Williford WO, Department of Veterans Affairs Cooperative Study: Benefits, morbidity, and mortality associated with long-term administration of oral anticoagulant therapy to patients with peripheral arterial bypass procedures: A prospective randomized study. J Vasc Surg 35:413-421, 2002.
180. Shoenfeld NA, O'Donnell TF, Bush HL, et al: The management of early in situ saphenous vein bypass occlusions. Arch Surg 122:871-875, 1987.

Graft Surveillance

181. Szilagyi DE, Elliot J, Hageman JH, et al: Biologic fate of autogenous vein implants as arterial substitutes: Clinical, angiographic, and histo-pathological observations in femoro-popliteal operations for atherosclerosis. Ann Surg 178:232-246, 1973.
182. Mills JL: Mechanisms of vein graft failure: The location, distribution and characteristics of lesions that predispose to graft failure. Semin Vasc Surg 6:78-91, 1993.
183. Donaldson MC, Mannick JM, Whittemore AD: Causes of primary graft failure after in situ saphenous vein bypass grafting. J Vasc Surg 15:113-120, 1992.
184. Mills JL, Fujitani RM, Taylor SM: The characteristics and anatomic distribution of lesions that cause reverse vein graft failure: A five-year prospective study. J Vasc Surg 17:195-206, 1993.
185. Grigg MJ, Nicolaides AN, Wolfe JHN: Femorodistal vein bypass graft stenoses. Br J Surg 75:737-740, 1988.
186. Moody P, Gould DA, Harris PL: Vein graft surveillance improves patency in femoro-popliteal bypass. Eur J Vasc Surg 4:117-121, 1990.
187. Green RM, McNamara J, Ouriel K, DeWeese JA: Comparison of infrainguinal graft surveillance techniques. J Vasc Surg 11:207-214, 1990.
188. Mills JL, Harris EJ, Taylor LM Jr, et al: The importance of routine surveillance of distal bypass grafts with duplex scanning: A study of 379 reversed vein grafts. J Vasc Surg 12:379-389, 1990.
189. Mills JL, Gahtan V, Bandyk DF, Esses GE: The origin of infrainguinal vein graft stenosis: A prospective study based on duplex surveillance. J Vasc Surg 21:16-25, 1995.
190. Gupta AK, Bandyk DF, Cheanvechai D: Natural history of infrainguinal vein graft stenosis, relative to bypass grafting technique. J Vasc Surg 25:211-225, 1997.
191. Ferris BL, Mills JL, Hughes JD, et al: Is early postoperative duplex scan surveillance of leg bypass grafts clinically important? J Vasc Surg 37:495-500, 2003.
192. Olojugba DH, McCarthy MJ, Naylor AR, et al: At what peak velocity ratio value should duplex-detected infrainguinal vein graft stenoses be revised? Eur J Vasc Endovasc Surg 15:258-260, 1998.
193. Mills JL, Wixon CL, James DC, et al: The natural history of intermediate and critical vein graft stenosis: Recommendations for continued surveillance or repair. J Vasc Surg 33:273-280, 2001.

194. Lundell A, Lindblad B, Bergqvist D, Hansen F: Femoropopliteal-crural graft patency is improved by an intensive surveillance program: A prospective randomized study. J Vasc Surg 21:26-33, 1995.
195. Visser K, Idu MM, Buth J, et al: Duplex scan surveillance during the first year after infrainguinal autologous vein bypass grafting surgery: Costs and clinical outcomes compared with other surveillance programs. J Vasc Surg 33:123-130, 2001.
196. Wixon CL, Mills JL, Westerband A, et al: An economic appraisal of lower extremity bypass graft maintenance. J Vasc Surg 32:1-12, 2000.
197. Dunlop P, Sayers RD, Naylor AR, et al: The effect of a surveillance programme on the patency of synthetic infrainguinal bypass grafts. Eur J Vasc Endovasc Surg 11:441-445, 1996.
198. Lalak NJ, Hanel KC, Hunt J, Morgan A: Duplex scan surveillance of infrainguinal prosthetic bypass grafts. J Vasc Surg 20:637-641, 1994.

Operative Techniques

199. Kunlin J. Le traitement de l'ischemie arterique apres la greffe veineuse longue. Rev Chir 70:206-235, 1951.
200. Sharp WJ, Shamma AR, Kresowik TF, Gison JP: Use of terminal T junctions for in situ bypass in the lower extremity. Surg Gynecol Obstet 172:151-152, 1991.
201. Miller JH, Foreman RK, Ferguson L, Aris I: Interposition vein cuff for anastomosis of prosthesis to small artery. Austr N Z J Surg 54:283-285, 1984.

Chapter

82

Profundaplasty:
Isolated and Adjunctive Applications

PETER G. KALMAN, MD, FRCSC, FACS

Section XIII

Under normal circumstances, the profunda is the main arterial blood supply to the thigh; however, when the superficial femoral artery (SFA), the popliteal artery, or both are severely diseased or occluded, the profunda serves as the primary collateral channel from the iliac and common femoral arteries to the distal extremity. The value of the profunda artery when the SFA is occluded was emphasized first in 1961, when it was shown that an increase in blood flow through the profunda could improve distal perfusion.[1,2] Early on, it was shown that an extended profundaplasty could restore distal extremity flow effectively; over time, an extended profundaplasty has proved to be an effective alternative to distal bypass in selected patients with critical ischemia.[3,4]

Blood flow through this important collateral pathway can be compromised by disease of the profunda alone or in combination with inflow occlusive disease. In these circumstances, flow to the distal profunda can be achieved with an isolated profundaplasty[5-10] or with a profundaplasty in combination with an inflow procedure (aortofemoral, iliofemoral, femorofemoral, or axillofemoral bypass). The profunda serves as the sole outflow vessel for the proximal inflow procedure, and profundaplasties have been successful in improving distal perfusion and relieving symptoms in patients with critical lower extremity ischemia.[11-14]

In the 1980s and 1990s, vascular surgeons became more aggressive with distal bypass to all levels of the lower extremity and in many cases ignored the importance of the profunda. Rather than being considered an alternative to distal revascularization or a procedure to be considered when there are no other options, profundaplasty should be considered an important component of a surgeon's armamentarium with specific indications and contraindications. As with most surgical procedures, patient selection is crucial to maximize success.

■ ANATOMY, COLLATERAL POTENTIAL, AND DISEASE DISTRIBUTION

The profunda originates 3 to 5 cm below the inguinal ligament and marks the transition to the SFA (Fig. 82-1). The profunda is directed posterior to and courses behind the circumflex femoral vein, then travels deep to the sartorius and vastus medialis muscles; the distal half runs posterior to the adductor longus muscle. The most important proximal branches are the medial and lateral circumflex femoral arteries. The latter most commonly arise from the profunda, but also may originate from the common femoral or superficial femoral arteries.

Collateral vessels are present to varying degrees to connect adjacent arterial segments. They represent preexisting channels, which under normal circumstances are small, but they enlarge when the intervening artery is chronically occluded. Collateral development occurs when the main artery is occluded, and there is a significant

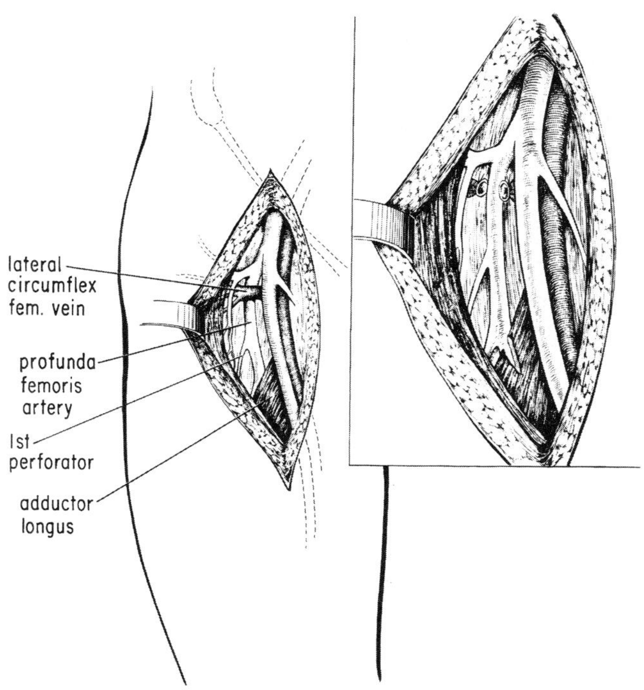

FIGURE 82-1 Exposure of the proximal profunda requires division of the lateral circumflex femoral vein.

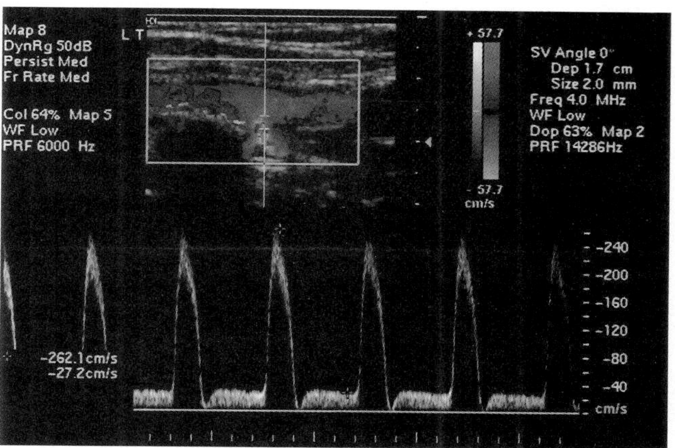

FIGURE 82-2 Color-flow imaging of the common femoral artery bifurcation. There is a significant stenosis at the origin of the profunda, as indicated by the mosaic color and the high peak systolic velocity. The V2/V1 ratio was 5.8 (267 cm/sec over 46 cm/sec), indicating a greater than 75% diameter reduction.

pressure differential between two potential collateral circuits. The profunda serves this important function and is the primary collateral circuit from above the inguinal ligament down to the popliteal and distal tibial runoff when the SFA is occluded. When there is common femoral and external iliac disease, the medial and lateral circumflex arteries of the profunda collateralize with gluteal and obturator branches of the internal iliac artery. In cases of SFA occlusion, the distal branches of the profunda collateralize with the geniculate branches of the popliteal artery or the tibial arteries. Atherosclerosis of the profunda is less common than atherosclerosis of the SFA, and from a functional point of view, relative sparing of the profunda is essential because of its important role as a collateral circuit. When the profunda is diseased, it is usually restricted to the orifice or the proximal profunda, sparing the distal profunda, which can continue serving the collateral function.[15]

■ DIAGNOSIS

The profunda can be imaged and atherosclerotic plaque within the artery can be detected with duplex ultrasonography (Fig. 82-2). Detection is made easier because lesions are most often found at the origin of the artery. Color-flow imaging of the common femoral artery is performed in cross section, then the transducer is moved distally until the bifurcation is observed. Velocities are determined in the longitudinal view from the distal common femoral artery and the profunda (the latter is the deeper of the two). There are no specific criteria for determining that a stenosis at this location is significant; however, a ratio of the poststenotic velocity (V2) to the prestenotic peak systolic velocity (V2/V1) of more than 2 indicates a greater than 50% diameter reduction, and absence of flow indicates occlusion. Because of the acute angle of the profunda relative to the common femoral artery and the differences in diameter of the two vessels, using the V2/V1 ratio alone may lead to errors. Imaging of a significant stenosis and the presence of disturbed flow also are important observations to be included in evaluation of the severity of the stenosis. In cases of acute thrombosis of the common femoral artery, the flow in the profunda may be reversed. Occlusion or stenosis may be found in the distal part of the artery, but this is uncommon. For this reason, only the first 5 cm of the artery is scanned routinely.

The contrast arteriogram remains the "gold standard" for patient selection and correlates with the operative results (Fig. 82-3).[16] Because the profunda originates from the posterolateral wall of the common femoral artery, the proximal portion frequently is obscured in a standard frontal projection arteriogram. Multiplanar oblique views frequently are necessary to show a stenosis at the origin of the profunda, which may be missed on conventional films. In cases of severe bilateral aortoiliac occlusive disease, the standard retrograde femoral approach may not be possible. In these cases, arterial access is through a transaxillary approach, whereby infrainguinal visualization is obtained through collateral channels originating with the mesenteric or lumbar arteries. Occasionally, Winslow's pathway (internal mammary/epigastric/infrainguinal collateral pathway) is necessary for visualization. Although experience is limited, bolus-chase magnetic resonance angiography is a potential alternative to standard digital subtraction angiography and has comparable diagnostic accuracy.[17] The final evaluation is made by intraoperative palpation after the profunda has been exposed, and if doubt remains, direct inspection of the profunda origin can be performed through an arteriotomy in the common femoral artery.

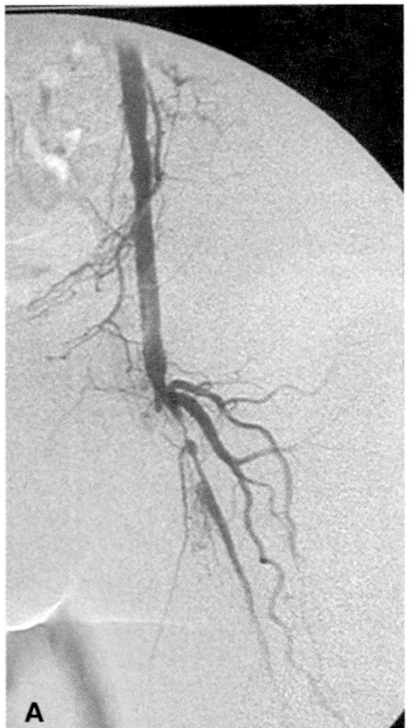

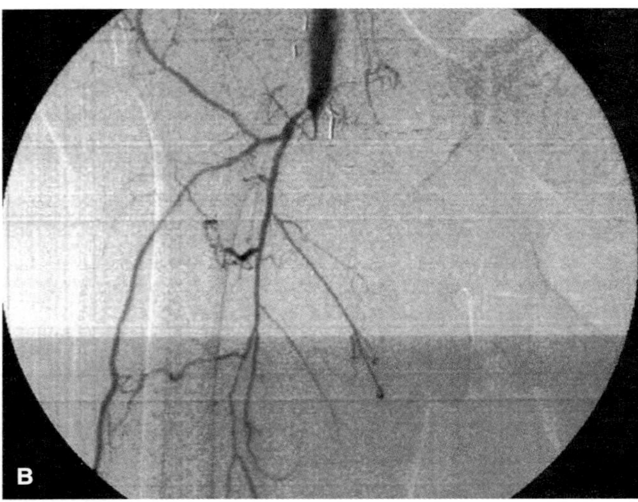

FIGURE 82-3 **A,** Arteriogram identifying a significant stenosis at the distal end of the right limb of an aortobifemoral bypass, which required revision with a profundaplasty. **B,** Arteriogram showing an isolated severe stenosis of the proximal left profunda, which was repaired with an isolated profundaplasty.

Table 82-1 Algorithm for Performing Isolated and Adjunctive Profundaplasty

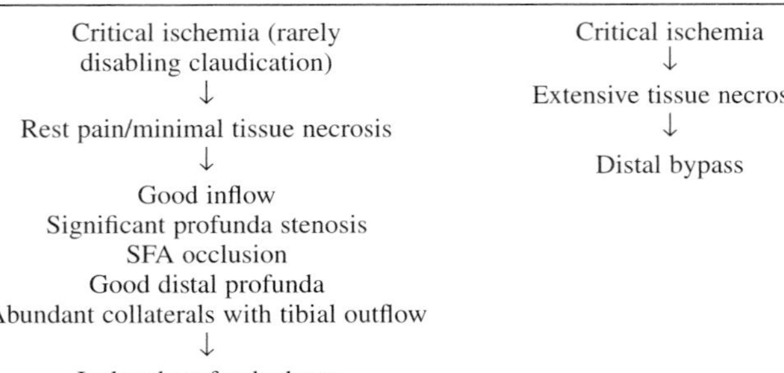

Isolated Profundaplasty	
Critical ischemia (rarely disabling claudication)	Critical ischemia
↓	↓
Rest pain/minimal tissue necrosis	Extensive tissue necrosis
↓	↓
Good inflow Significant profunda stenosis SFA occlusion Good distal profunda Abundant collaterals with tibial outflow	Distal bypass
↓	
Isolated profundaplasty	

Adjunctive Profundaplasty
Critical ischemia Disabling claudication
↓
Good inflow Significant profunda stenosis SFA occlusion Good distal profunda
↓
Inflow procedure profundaplasty (aortofemoral, iliofemoral, axillofemoral, femorofemoral)

SFA, superficial femoral artery.

■ INDICATIONS AND SELECTION OF PATIENTS FOR PROFUNDAPLASTY

The indications for profundaplasty vary slightly, depending on whether it is performed as an adjunctive or isolated procedure (Table 82-1). As an adjunctive procedure, it is performed for all degrees of chronic lower extremity ischemia, including disabling claudication and critical ischemia. Profundaplasty in these circumstances is an approach to provide maximal outflow for an inflow procedure when the SFA is severely diseased or occluded. It also is ideal for improving outflow after successful thrombectomy or thrombolysis of a proximal inflow graft. Helpful predictors of success are the presence of a significant profunda lesion and a patent distal profunda with extensive collaterals to the popliteal or tibial arteries.

The indications for isolated profundaplasty are less clear and require individual judgment. Distal perfusion is improved by profundaplasty, but not to as great an extent as it is with distal bypass. Only selected patients with disabling claudication should be considered candidates for isolated profundaplasty due to they are most likely to continue to have symptoms because of the SFA occlusion, but perhaps to a lesser extent. Patients with rest pain and ulceration with minimal tissue necrosis are good candidates, particularly when other possibilities for revascularization are poor (e.g., patients in whom the saphenous vein is absent or patients who could not tolerate a more extensive procedure because of co-morbidity).[18] The best conditions for success of an isolated profundaplasty include good inflow to the common femoral artery, the presence of a significant proximal profunda lesion, and a good distal profunda with good collaterals to the popliteal or tibial arteries. When most of these conditions are not present, a distal bypass should be reconsidered.

■ INTERVENTIONS

Endovascular

When a focal lesion of the profunda has been identified by arteriography with oblique views, balloon angioplasty (percutaneous transluminal angioplasty [PTA]) can be considered as an option for intervention. As with lesions of the distal external iliac and common femoral arteries, access

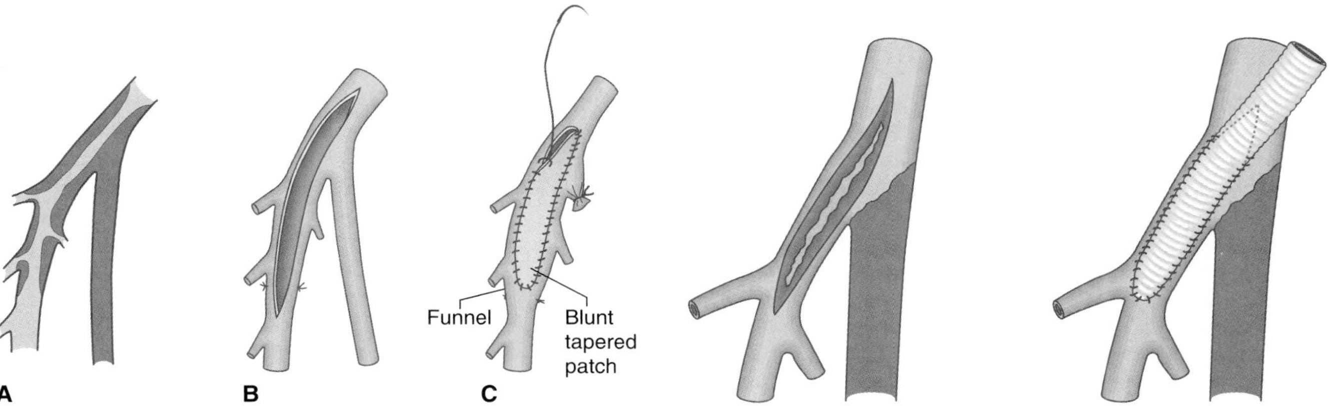

FIGURE 82-4 Technique for isolated profundaplasty.

FIGURE 82-5 Technique for adjunctive profundaplasty.

for profunda PTA is obtained through the contralateral femoral artery. The angled guiding catheter is passed up and around the aortic bifurcation, then antegrade to the common femoral artery. Under fluoroscopic imaging with a roadmap, the guide wire is directed across the profunda lesion. The catheter is passed over the guide wire distal to the lesion, and an arteriogram is performed to confirm the intraluminal position. The catheter is withdrawn, the PTA catheter is passed over the guide wire and across the lesion, and then the PTA catheter is inflated. The indications for selective stenting are similar to the indications for other arterial segments (residual gradient, dissection).

Exposure and Operative Technique for Profundaplasty

The operation is performed through a standard vertical groin incision for femoral arterial exposure (see Fig. 82-1). The profundaplasty is classified as proximal if it extends down to the second perforating branch and extended if it passes the second perforating branch. The common femoral artery is exposed at the level of the inguinal ligament. Dissection is continued down the anterior surface of the common femoral artery until a diameter reduction is observed, representing the origin of the SFA, then vessel loops are placed around the proximal common femoral artery and the proximal SFA. An assistant retracts the vessel loops medially, or when the surgeon is operating alone, the vessel loops can be secured under tension to the groin towel during dissection. The profunda is directed posteriorly, and the origin is identified at the point of the diameter reduction of the common femoral artery. A vessel loop can be placed around the profunda at this stage to assist with the distal dissection. The extent of the exposure depends on the extent of disease, and this is determined by reference to the preoperative arteriogram and by intraoperative inspection and palpation. The dissection continues along the anterior surface of the profunda, avoiding potential injury to the multiple side branches, and the distal exposure ends when disease-free artery is reached. The lateral femoral circumflex vein crosses the profunda proximally and must be doubly ligated and divided, with the exception of the most focal orificial lesions. In distal profundaplasty, one to three additional veins usually are divided to expose the artery. In some circumstances, a lateral approach to the profunda can be used when there have been multiple previous groin exposures or when active groin wound infection is present.

Extreme care is exercised during dissection, and atraumatic micro-bulldog clamps or vessel loops are used to control the distal profunda and its branches. Atraumatic clamps have the advantage of not distorting the artery during suturing, as would vessel loops under tension. The length of the profundaplasty depends on the extent of disease as assessed earlier. After systemic heparinization (3000 to 5000 U, depending on the patient's weight), an arteriotomy is started on the distal common femoral artery to prevent injury to the back wall of the much smaller profunda and is continued until normal artery is reached.

Frequently the profundaplasty can be performed by using a patch closure without endarterectomy because the lumen is enlarged with the patch. When endarterectomy is necessary, it is usually an extension of common femoral disease, and the starting point is more proximal. The endarterectomy is carried down across the origin of the profunda to the endpoint. Ideally a smooth endpoint should be achieved, but if this is not possible, the potential intimal flap must be secured or tacked down with interrupted 7-0 polypropylene (Prolene) sutures. Most often, it is possible to clear the extensions of the plaque from the orifices of the multiple branches, improving the collateral potential after profundaplasty.

The technique varies depending on whether it is combined with an inflow procedure, used to improve outflow after inflow graft thrombectomy, or performed as an isolated procedure. When an isolated profundaplasty is performed, the arteriotomy is closed by using an autogenous onlay patch. The preferred patch is autogenous vein from any available source or, alternatively, endarterectomized SFA. When an autogenous source is unavailable, a prosthetic Dacron or polytetrafluoroethylene patch may be substituted (Fig. 82-4).

When profundaplasty is combined with an inflow procedure (aortofemoral, iliofemoral, axillofemoral, or femorofemoral bypass) in the presence of SFA occlusion, extension of the arteriotomy into the profunda ensures maximal outflow and widens any stenosis at the origin (Fig. 82-5).

When there is severe stenosis or proximal occlusion, profundaplasty is an important adjunct to provide adequate flow through this important collateral channel. As an adjunct to an inflow procedure, profundaplasty is performed as a tongue-patch extension of the distal portion of the inflow graft for varying length, depending on the distal extent of disease (see Fig. 82-5).

After successful thrombectomy or thrombolysis of an inflow graft when profunda disease is discovered and the SFA is occluded, a profundaplasty can be performed to ensure outflow and to maintain graft patency. The most straightforward technique is to replace the distal portion of the inflow graft with a new segment, then tailor a tongue-patch extension of the new segment as described previously.

Profunda bypass is an alternative to endarterectomy, and can be performed by using inflow from the common femoral or distal external iliac arteries. Bypass can be easier to perform than endarterectomy when a long occlusion, heavy calcification, or dense scarring is present. The major disadvantage is that fewer outflow collateral arteries are opened compared with a long endarterectomy.

Perioperative Complications

Local complications include early graft thrombosis, and postoperative bleeding. The most common complications are related to the groin wound itself. Early thrombosis of an isolated or adjunctive profundaplasty is unusual, and management is similar to that for any acute operative thrombosis. Postoperative hemorrhage is a potential event that undoubtedly is related to the length of the arteriotomy closure. Patch rupture also has been reported.[19]

Division of lymphatics at the time of femoral artery surgery can result in edema, a lymphocele, or a lymphatic fistula. Groin wounds are particularly vulnerable to this complication because of the extensive local lymphatic network, and the lymph nodes are often enlarged because of distal infection. The most obvious implicated etiology is lymphatic and lymph node transection, but contributory factors include repeat operation and more extensive dissection, as with profundaplasty.[20]

Edema most often resolves spontaneously, as does a sterile lymphocele that does not communicate with the surface. Drainage of a lymphocele should rarely be performed and only if it becomes secondarily infected. A lymphatic fistula should be treated promptly with meticulous attention to wound management. The choice of management is subjective and depends on drainage volume and duration of drainage. Conservative management includes bed rest to reduce lymphatic flow, administration of prophylactic antibiotics, and application of a gauze pressure dressing soaked with antiseptic. Operative re-exploration and ligation of divided lymphatics and secure groin closure are indicated if high drainage volume persists for more than 1 or 2 weeks.[21] With large contaminated wounds, sartorius myoplasty should be considered as an adjunct to ensure dependable wound closure.[22,23]

Emphasis should be placed on preventive measures to prevent groin lymphatic complications. An incision directly over or slightly lateral to the femoral artery may prevent injury to the medially located lymphatics. Minimal dissection and careful cauterization or ligation of divided lymph nodes and lymphatics are crucial. Perhaps the most important and greatest preventive measure is tight, secure closure in multiple layers, which cannot be overemphasized.

■ RESULTS

Endovascular

Although individual center experience with profunda PTA is limited, a study has shown success in relief of critical ischemia.[23] Other references to centers with comparable experience are not available. A suitable anatomic lesion for PTA is a focal stenosis rather than an occlusion, and patients with diffuse distal disease of the profunda should not be considered as candidates. Technical success has been achieved in 91% of patients, and after a mean follow-up of 34 months, no additional amputations were necessary, and only three patients required subsequent revascularization.[23] Percutaneous profundaplasty is safe and effective and may be considered as an alternative to surgical therapy in patients with anatomically suitable lesions. Long-term data remain undefined, however, and at present, it is unknown whether stenting can improve the long-term results of PTA. The role for PTA of the profunda is generally limited because of the presence of significant associated disease of the common femoral artery.

Open Repair

Isolated Profundaplasty

The success of isolated profundaplasty is related to patient selection and the indication for surgery. The morbidity is low, and the most frequent complication is related to the groin wound.[3-10] The cumulative success (patency and clinical improvement of at least one grade) reported by Kalman and associates[5] was 83% ± 4% at 30 days, 67% ± 4.8% at 1 year, 57% ± 5.9% at 2 years, and 49% ± 6.8% at 3 years (Fig. 82-6). The cumulative limb salvage rate was 76% ± 5.7% at 3 years. After stratification into subgroups, the

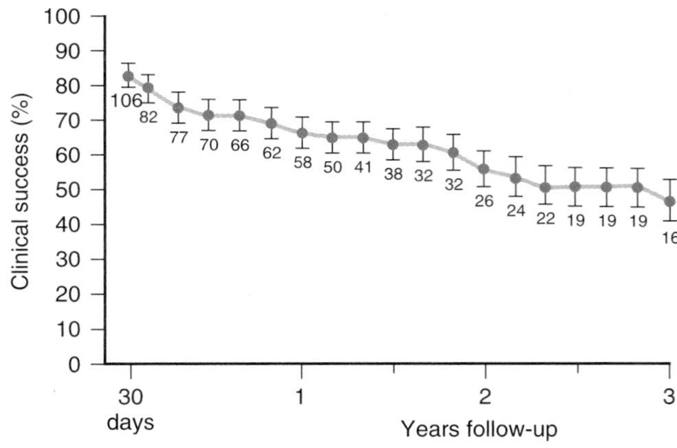

FIGURE 82-6 Cumulative clinical success for isolated profundaplasty (a patent repair and clinical improvement). (From Kalman PG, Johnston KW, Walker PM: The current role of isolated profundaplasty. J Cardiovasc Surg 31:107-111, 1990.)

clinical success was greater when the operative indication was disabling claudication compared with critical ischemia ($P < .05$). Additionally, success was greater when tibial runoff was good (two or three tibial arteries patent) compared with poor (one or no tibial arteries patent) ($P < .05$). Patency of the popliteal artery was not predictive of success, and there was no significant difference after stratification for diabetes, profundaplasty length, or previous vascular procedure. Success can be achieved not only with a stenosis, but also with endarterectomy and long patch grafting of the proximally occluded profunda, which provide symptomatic relief in selected patients.[24]

The change in ankle-brachial index (ABI) after profundaplasty in the immediate postoperative period may not reflect the eventual clinical outcome.[5] The improvement in ABI from 0.33 ± 0.18 to 0.45 ± 0.19 was significant ($P < .0001$), but the increase was small (0.12). When the patients were stratified for operative indication, patients with claudication had a greater preoperative ABI than patients with critical ischemia (0.40 ± 0.21 versus 0.27 ± 0.14; $P < .01$) and patients with early postoperative ABI (0.55 ± 0.18 versus 0.37 ± 0.17; $P < .0001$) (Fig. 82-7). Despite this relatively small improvement, the early clinical success was $83\% \pm 4\%$. In patients with long-term clinical success, there was a significant increase in ABI early postoperatively compared with preoperatively ($P < .01$), whereas the difference was not significant in patients in whom the procedures were considered clinical failures. Both groups (long-term successes and failures) had similar preoperative ABI, but the early postoperative ABI was greater in patients who had long-term clinical success (0.50 ± 0.18 versus 0.37 ± 0.19; $P < .01$) (Fig. 82-8).

The thigh-ankle pressure gradient was predictive of long-term success in patients with critical ischemia as a measure of the collateral potential from the profunda. Patients can be selected on the basis of objective hemodynamic criteria. The cumulative success was 89% at 6 years when the thigh-ankle index was less than 0.55 compared with 32% when it was greater than 0.55.[25]

With segmental pressure measurements, the profunda popliteal collateral index (PPCI) was developed to help select patients for isolated profundaplasty: (PPCI = AKSP – BKSP/AKSP), where AKSP is the above-knee segmental pressure and BKSP is the below-knee segmental pressure. The PPCI quantitates the development of the collateral channels between the profunda and the distal vascular bed. A PPCI greater than 0.50 (high blood pressure gradient across the knee) suggests poor geniculate collateral flow with prediction of failure. A PPCI less than 0.50 is a good predictor of success. Boren and coworkers[26] concluded that the PPCI can be used to evaluate accurately the potential of the geniculate collaterals and may be an additional predictor for selection of patients for profunda revascularization.

Another predictive factor for success or failure is the quality of the tibial arterial target bed. Patency of the popliteal artery is not essential, however, for a satisfactory outcome. Success with symptomatic relief can be achieved in 75% of patients when two tibial arteries are patent, 64% when one is patent, and only 31% when none is patent.[27]

When distal bypass is not possible for limb salvage because of end-stage vascular disease and a target artery is not available, it has been suggested that isolated profundaplasty be considered to provide sufficient perfusion to preserve the knee joint,[28,29] which would provide a more functional below-knee amputation. Some authors have reported disappointment with isolated profundaplasty for limb salvage, although most of the patients included in these reports had poor tibial runoff, significant distal extremity tissue necrosis, or both.[30,31] Proper patient selection is paramount to achieving satisfactory results. Otherwise, these patients are better served by a distal bypass procedure, if possible.

Adjunctive Profundaplasty

When profundaplasty is combined with aortofemoral bypass, the 5-year cumulative patency rate has been reported to be 97% ± 1.3%, with a cumulative clinical success rate (patent graft and clinical improvement) of 76% ± 5.2%,

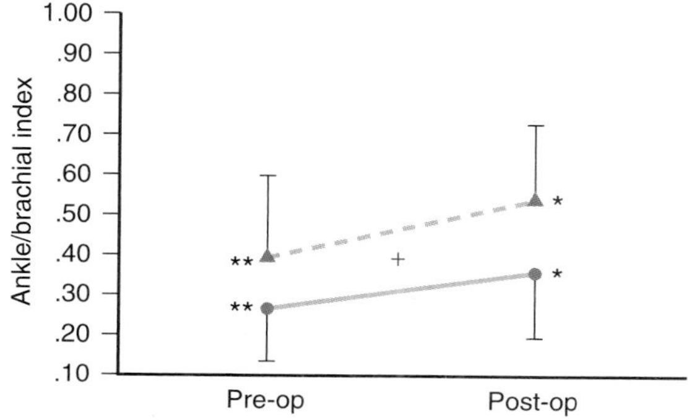

FIGURE 82-7 Ankle-brachial index (ABI) stratified by operative indication (--- claudication versus — critical ischemia). The preoperative ABIs are different (**$P < .01$), and the postoperative ABIs are different (*$P < .001$); + slopes are different; postoperative ABI improvement is greater when the indication for surgery was claudication ($P < .0001$, analysis of variance). (From Kalman PG, Johnston KW, Walker PM: The current role of isolated profundaplasty. J Cardiovasc Surg 31:107-111, 1990.)

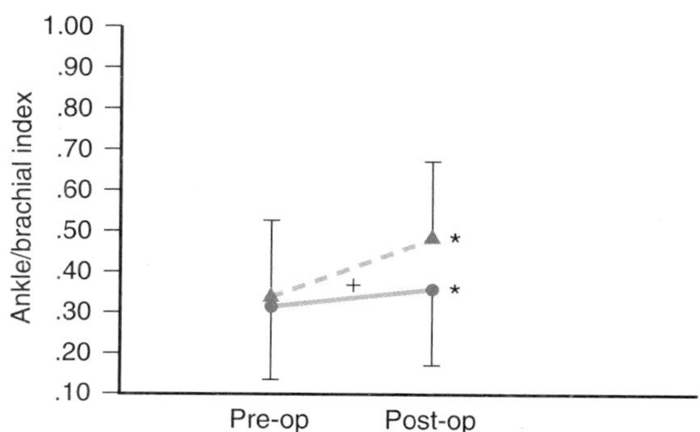

FIGURE 82-8 Ankle-brachial index (ABI) and long-term success (--- success versus — failure). Preoperative ABIs are not different; early postoperative ABI improvement is greater in patients who had long-term success ($P < .01$, analysis of variance). (From Kalman PG, Johnston KW, Walker PM: The current role of isolated profundaplasty. J Cardiovasc Surg 31:107-111, 1990.)

regardless of the profundaplasty length.[11-15] Aortoprofunda bypass is an effective procedure for treatment of multilevel occlusive disease, and few patients require simultaneous or subsequent distal revascularization.[11] These observations also have been confirmed when extended profundaplasty was performed, and the cumulative 5-year patency rate was 86% with 72% limb salvage without the need for distal bypass.[32,33] Similar observations have been made when profundaplasty was combined with other inflow procedures (axillofemoral, iliofemoral, or femorofemoral bypass), and long-term outcomes have been excellent.[12-14]

■ SUMMARY

Profundaplasty is a useful alternative to distal bypass in selected patients and can be performed with low morbidity and mortality rates. The ideal candidate is a patient who has an SFA occlusion with significant profunda stenosis, a good distal profunda, and abundant collaterals communicating with the popliteal-tibial outflow. Although success in relieving critical ischemia is possible, extensive tissue necrosis is best revascularized with distal lower extremity bypass. Profundaplasty also can be attempted as a last resort when distal bypass is no longer an option. In these cases, improved perfusion to the level of the knee might be achieved to allow healing of a below-knee amputation. The relief of disabling claudication is usually not dramatic because of the SFA occlusion.

■ REFERENCES

1. Leeds FH, Gilfillan RS: Revascularization of the ischemic limb. Arch Surg 82:45-51, 1961.
2. Morris G, Edwards N, Cooley DA, et al: Surgical importance of profunda femoris artery. Surgery 82:32-37, 1961.
3. David TE, Key JA: Profundaplasty for limb salvage. Can J Surg 21:107-109, 1978.
4. David TE, Drezner AD: Extended profundaplasty for limb salvage. Surgery 84:758-763, 1978.
5. Kalman PG, Johnston KW, Walker PM: The current role of isolated profundaplasty. J Cardiovasc Surg 31:107-111, 1990.
6. Lawson DW, Gallico GG 3rd, Patton AS: Limb salvage by extended profundaplasty of occluded deep femoral arteries. Am J Surg 145:458-463, 1983.
7. Taylor LM Jr, Baur GM, Eidemiller LR, Porter JM: Extended profundaplasty: Indications and techniques with results in 46 procedures. Am J Surg 141:539-542, 1981.
8. Fugger R, Kretschmer G, Schemper M, et al: The place of profundaplasty in the surgical treatment of superficial femoral artery occlusion. Eur J Vasc Surg 1:187-191, 1987.
9. Rollins DL, Towne JB, Bernhard VM, Baum PL: Isolated profundaplasty for limb salvage. J Vasc Surg 2:585-590, 1985.
10. Towne JB, Rollins DL: Profundaplasty: Its role in limb salvage. Surg Clin North Am 66:403-414, 1986.
11. Kalman PG, Johnston KW, Walker PM: Is aortoprofunda bypass a successful operation for multilevel occlusive disease? Vasc Surg 23:265-271, 1989.
12. Kalman PG, Hosang M, Johnston KW, Walker PM: The current role for femorofemoral bypass. J Vasc Surg 6:71-76, 1987.
13. Kalman PG, Hosang M, Johnston KW, Walker PM: Unilateral iliac disease: The role of iliofemoral bypass. J Vasc Surg 6:139-143, 1987.
14. Kalman PG, Hosang M, Cina C, et al: Current indications for axillounifemoral and axillobifemoral bypass grafts. J Vasc Surg 5:828-832, 1987.
15. Martin P, Jamieson C, Barabas AP, et al: On the surgery of atherosclerosis of the profunda femoris artery. Surgery 71:182-189, 1972.
16. Mitchell RA, Bone GE, Bridges R, et al: Patient selection for isolated profundaplasty: Arteriographic correlates of operative results. Am J Surg 138:912-19, 1979.
17. Pandharipande PV, Lee VS, Reuss PM, et al: Two-station bolus-chase MR angiography with a stationary table: A simple alternative to automated-table techniques. AJR Am J Roentgenol 179:1583-1589, 2002.
18. Hansen AK, Bille S, Nielson PH, Egeblad K: Profundaplasty as the only reconstructive procedure in patients with severe ischaemia of the lower extremity. Surg Gynecol Obstet 171:47-50, 1990.
19. Florenes T, Kroese A: Rupture of the vein patch: A serious complication of profundaplasty. Eur J Surg 158:621-622, 1992.
20. Kalman PG, Walker PM, Johnston KW: Consequences of groin lymphatic fistula after vascular reconstruction. Vasc Surg 25:210-213, 1991.
21. Petrasek PF, Kalman PG, Martin RD: Sartorius myoplasty for deep groin wounds following vascular reconstruction. Am J Surg 160:175-178, 1990.
22. Kaufman JL, Shah DM, Corson JD, et al: Sartorius muscle coverage for the treatment of complicated vascular surgical wounds. J Cardiovasc Surg 30:479-483, 1989.
23. Silva JA, White CJ, Ramee SR, et al: Percutaneous profundaplasty in the treatment of lower extremity ischemia: Results of long-term surveillance. J Endovasc Ther 8:75-82, 2001.
24. Lawson DW, Gallico GG 3rd, Patton AS: Limb salvage by extended profundaplasty of occluded deep femoral arteries. Am J Surg 145:458-463, 1983.
25. McCoy DM, Sawchuk AP, Schuler JJ, et al: The role of isolated profundaplasty for the treatment of rest pain. Arch Surg 124:441-444, 1989.
26. Boren CH, Towne JB, Bernhard VM, Salles-Cunha S: Profunda popliteal collateral index: A guide to successful profundaplasty. Arch Surg 115:1366-1372, 1980.
27. Fugger R, Kretschmer G, Schemper M, et al: The place of profundaplasty in the surgical treatment of superficial femoral artery occlusion. Eur J Vasc Surg 1:187-191, 1987.
28. Rollins DL, Towne JB, Bernhard VM, Baum PLL: Isolated profundaplasty for limb salvage. J Vasc Surg 2:585-590, 1985.
29. Towne JB, Rollins DL: Profundaplasty: Its role in limb salvage. Surg Clin North Am 66:403-414, 1986.
30. Harward TR, Bergan JJ, Yao JS, et al: The demise of primary profundaplasty. Am J Surg 156:126-129, 1988.
31. Graham AM, Gewertz BL, Zarins CK: Efficacy of isolated profundaplasty. Can J Surg 29:330-332, 1986.
32. Pearce WH, Kempczinski RF: Extended autogenous profundaplasty and aortofemoral grafting: An alternative to synchronous distal bypass. J Vasc Surg 1:455-458, 1984.
33. McDonald PT, Rich NM, Collins GJ Jr, et al: Femorofemoral grafts: The role of concomitant extended profundaplasty. Am J Surg 136:622-628, 1978.

Chapter 83

Section XIII

Secondary Arterial Reconstructions in the Lower Extremity

FRANK J. VEITH, MD
EVAN C. LIPSITZ, MD
NICHOLAS J. GARGIULO, MD
ENRICO ASCHER, MD

Arterial reconstructions for lower extremity ischemia comprise aortoiliac, aortofemoral, and femorofemoral procedures and bypasses to the popliteal and infrapopliteal arteries. As indicated by the life-table patency rates shown in other chapters, all of these operations have an intrinsic tendency to fail or to become ineffective as time elapses. The proportion of such operations in which this occurs increases with time and is greater at all times for reconstructions terminating more distally in the arterial tree. Because a sizable minority of patients undergoing these operations have circulatory deterioration at some point in their lives, and because this deterioration often is associated with disabling or limb-threatening manifestations, appropriate management of this condition has become a crucial aspect of vascular surgery to which the competent vascular surgeon must be committed to serve the interest of the patient. This chapter describes the general principles and strategies of this management with a specific focus on the aspects of reoperative vascular surgery that distinguish it from a primary approach to lower extremity ischemia.

■ INDICATIONS

In general, we believe that arterial reconstructions should rarely be performed for intermittent claudication.[1] Our reasons for this opinion are (1) the relatively high inevitable failure rate of such operations and (2) the fact that failure may be associated with ischemia worse than that prompting the original operation. These factors and the greater difficulty and higher complication rate associated with most secondary operations, particularly if the involved arteries have been dissected, seem to justify a conservative attitude toward *primary* operations for intermittent claudication. This attitude is by no means universal, however, and present practice accepts "truly disabling" claudication as an indication for primary arterial reconstruction to at least the popliteal level.

In contrast, almost all vascular surgeons tend to avoid secondary arterial operations for intermittent claudication. Gangrene, a nonhealing ischemic ulcer, or severe ischemic rest pain should be the indication for most *secondary* arterial reconstructions, especially reconstructions below the inguinal ligament. Occasional patients with these classic limb-threatening manifestations and poor noninvasive test results can be managed effectively with conservative measures for protracted periods.[2] Such treatment, if possible, is particularly appropriate in patients who are faced with the need for a difficult distal reoperation. Except for the special circumstances occurring with a "failing graft" (see later), in most patients undergoing secondary arterial reconstruction, the indication for operation is the unquestionable need for immediate limb salvage.

■ ETIOLOGY OF UNSUCCESSFUL PROCEDURES

Early Reoperations (Within 30 Days)

The need to reintervene soon after a primary arterial reconstruction may be the result of two situations.[3] First, the original repair may undergo thrombosis or may fail in the early postoperative period (i.e., within 30 days). Generally, this occurrence is due to a technical flaw in the operation, poor choice of inflow or outflow sites, insufficient runoff, or progression of soft tissue infection.[4] In addition, thrombosis may occur for no apparent reason, presumably owing to the inherent thrombogenicity of the graft in a low-flow setting. Usually, idiopathic thrombosis occurs only with polytetrafluoroethylene (PTFE) and other prosthetic grafts, but in rare instances it can occur with a vein graft. A transient fall in cardiac output, hypotension, or a hypercoagulable state can contribute to such unexplained thrombosis.

Second, the original operation, although technically satisfactory and associated with a patent bypass graft, may fail to provide hemodynamic improvement sufficient to relieve the patient's symptoms. This failure may be due to the choice of the wrong operation (e.g., the performance of an aortofemoral bypass in a patient whose femoral artery pressure was normal and who actually needed a femoropopliteal bypass). Hemodynamic failure also may occur in the presence of multisegment disease and extensive foot gangrene or infection. In this setting, uninterrupted arterial circulation to the foot may be required, and a primary or secondary sequential bypass may be indicated.[1,5,6]

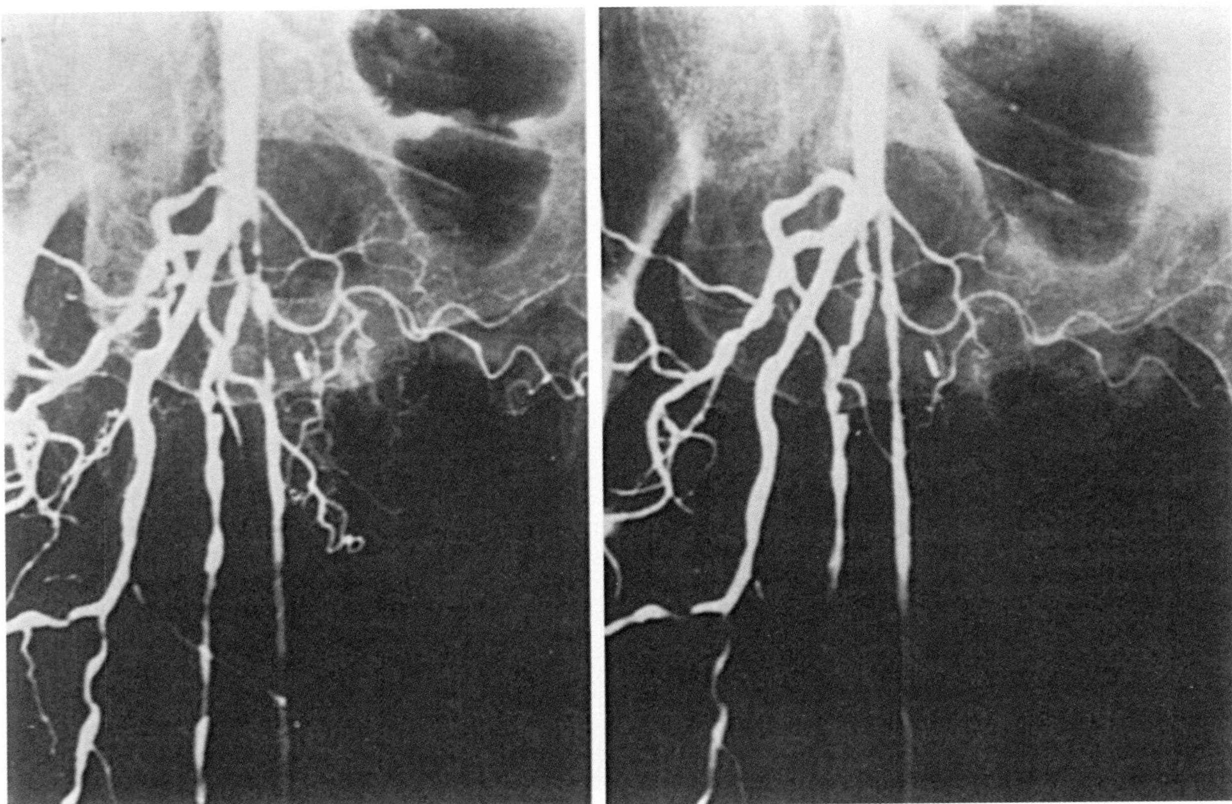

FIGURE 83-1 *Left,* Arteriogram 18 months after a common femoral-anterior tibial bypass. A proximal stenosis produced the "failing state." *Right,* Arteriogram 2 years after the stenosis was corrected by percutaneous transluminal angioplasty. The graft remained patent 5 years later.

Late Reoperations (After 30 Days)

Failure with graft thrombosis can occur at any time after the first postoperative month. It may be due to some of the factors already mentioned, but is usually due to the development of some flow-reducing lesion within the bypass graft or its inflow or outflow tract.

Intimal hyperplasia is a prominent cause of failure and graft thrombosis. It may occur with all kinds of grafts in all positions. The etiology of this process is poorly understood and does not affect the patency of most arterial reconstructions. When significant intimal hyperplasia does occur, it usually produces infrainguinal graft failure 2 to 18 months after operation.[3,7,8] It can involve any portion of a vein graft in a focal or diffuse manner and anastomosis of either vein or prosthetic grafts. Because the lumen of the distal artery is smaller, this site is most vulnerable to flow reduction by this process.

After 18 months, progression of the atherosclerotic disease process involving the inflow or outflow tract of the arterial reconstruction becomes the predominant cause of failure and graft thrombosis. After 3 to 4 years, a variety of other degenerative lesions may also affect autogenous vein grafts and umbilical vein grafts.[7,9,10] These processes, which are less common in autogenous vein grafts than umbilical vein grafts, may lead to wall changes and aneurysm formation with thrombosis or embolization.

■ CONCEPT OF THE FAILING GRAFT

Intimal hyperplasia, progression of proximal or distal disease, or lesions within the graft itself can produce signs and symptoms of hemodynamic deterioration in patients with a prior arterial reconstruction without producing concomitant thrombosis of the bypass graft.[11-14] We refer to this condition as a *failing graft* because if the lesion is not corrected, graft thrombosis is almost certain to occur. This concept is important because many difficult lower extremity revascularizations can be salvaged for protracted periods by relatively simple interventions if the lesion responsible for the circulatory deterioration and diminished graft blood flow can be detected before graft thrombosis occurs.

We have been able to detect more than 350 failing grafts and to correct the lesions before graft thrombosis occurred.[12,20,21] Most of these grafts were vein grafts, but approximately one third were PTFE or polyester (Dacron) grafts (Figs. 83-1 and 83-2). Invariably the corrective procedure was simpler than the secondary operation that would be required if the bypass went on to thrombosis. Many lesions responsible for the failing state were remedied by percutaneous transluminal angioplasty (PTA), although some required a vein patch angioplasty, a short bypass of a graft lesion, or a proximal or distal graft extension.[12,20-22] Some of the angioplasties of these lesions have failed and required a second re-intervention; others have

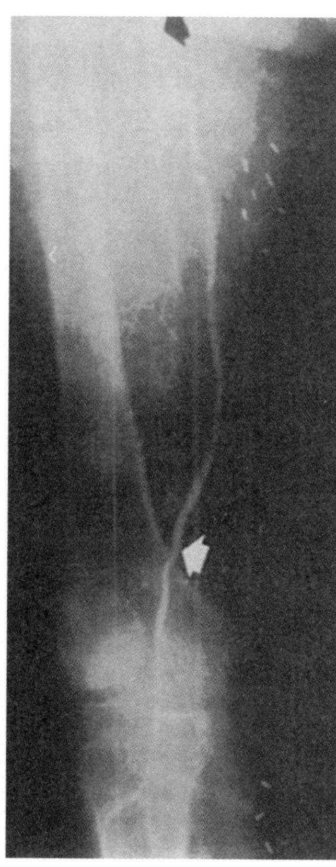

FIGURE 83-2 Arteriogram of a patient with a failing PTFE femoropopliteal graft 2 years after the initial operation. The arteriogram was performed because of a return of rest pain and the loss of distal pulses. The graft *(between arrows)* was patent despite a proximal occlusion of the common femoral artery and an inflow pressure of only 40 mm Hg. A bypass from the external iliac artery to the original graft was performed, and the original graft remained patent until the patient's death 6 years later.

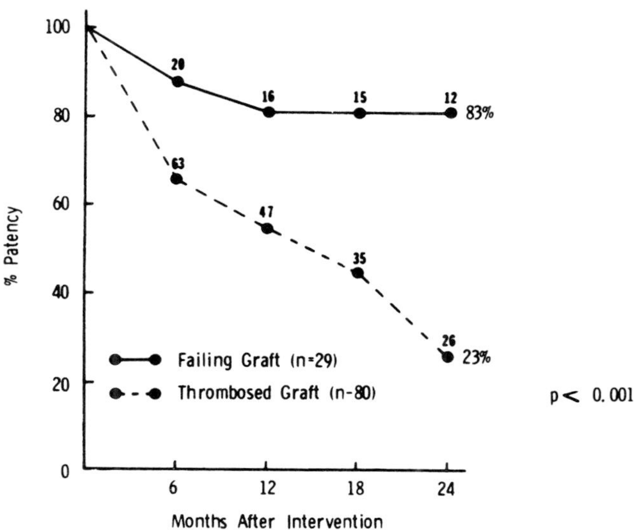

FIGURE 83-3 Comparison of patency rates after re-intervention or reoperation for failing and failed (thrombosed) below-knee femoropopliteal and femorodistal PTFE grafts. Numbers of grafts at risk are shown at 6-month intervals. Standard error for all points is less than 10%. (From Ascher E, Collier PE, Gupta SK, Veith FJ: Reoperation for PTFE bypass failure: The importance of distal outflow site and operative technique in determining outcome. J Vasc Surg 5:298, 1987.)

remained effective in correcting the responsible lesion, as documented by arteriography more than 2 to 5 years later (see Fig. 83-1).

Nevertheless, the role of PTA for vein graft lesions remains controversial. Although we and some other groups[14,15] have had many excellent results with PTA of vein graft stenoses, others have not.[16] In our experience, there were some failures with limb loss.[17] We currently restrict the use of PTA to lesions shorter than 1.5 cm, particularly if they are located in an inaccessible part of the vein. PTA also has been useful in the treatment of some inflow and outflow lesions.[21] Most important, the results of re-interventions for failing grafts, in terms of continued cumulative patency and limb salvage rates, have been far superior to the results of re-interventions for grafts that have undergone thrombosis and have failed (Fig. 83-3).[8,11,13,20-22]

This difference in results, together with the ease of secondary intervention for failing grafts, mandates that surgeons performing infrainguinal bypass operations observe their patients closely in the early postoperative period and indefinitely thereafter. In our practice, the surgeon examines the peripheral pulses of patients at 6- to 8-week intervals for the first 6 months and every 6 to 12 months thereafter. Ideally, noninvasive laboratory tests, including duplex ultrasound scanning of vein grafts, should be performed with similar frequency,[14,18,19] but we have found such tests to be expensive and sometimes impractical to perform in all patients.

If the patient has any recurrence of symptoms or the surgeon detects either any change in peripheral pulse examination or other manifestations of ischemia, the circulatory deterioration is confirmed by noninvasive tests, and the patient is admitted for urgent anticoagulation therapy and arteriography. If a lesion is detected as a cause of the failing state, it is corrected urgently by PTA or operation. Our aggressive prophylactic intervention for these lesions, even if they are asymptomatic, is based on the significant risk that these stenoses if left untreated will go on to thrombosis and the greater complexity of reconstruction and reduced late patency if thrombosis does occur.

If the failing graft is a vein bypass, detection of the failing state permits accurate localization and definition of the responsible lesion with arteriography followed by salvage of any undiseased vein. In contrast, allowing the graft to undergo thrombosis has the following consequences:

1. The responsible lesion may be difficult to identify.
2. It may be difficult or impossible to clear the vein with thrombectomy.
3. The results of lytic therapy are imperfect.
4. The patient's best graft—the ipsilateral greater saphenous vein—may have to be sacrificed, rendering the secondary operation even more difficult and more likely to fail, with associated limb loss.

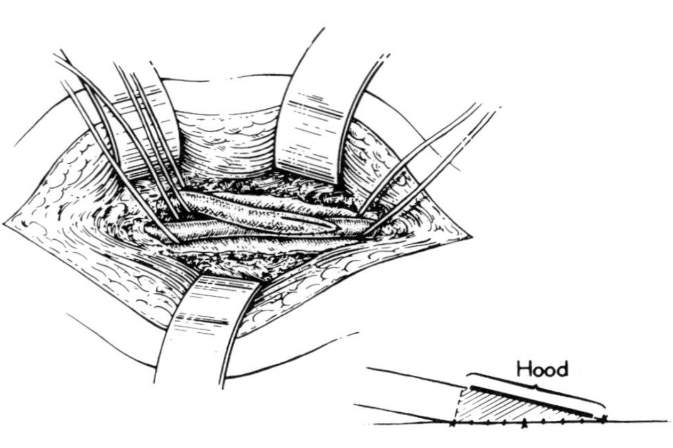

FIGURE 83-4 Operative exposure of the distal anastomosis. The incision in the hood of the graft is made to within 1 mm of the distal end of the graft. This provides optimal exposure of the distal anastomosis and facilitates thrombectomy. (From Ascher E, Collier PE, Gupta SK, Veith FJ: Reoperation for PTFE bypass failure: The importance of distal outflow site and operative technique in determining outcome. J Vasc Surg 5:298, 1987.)

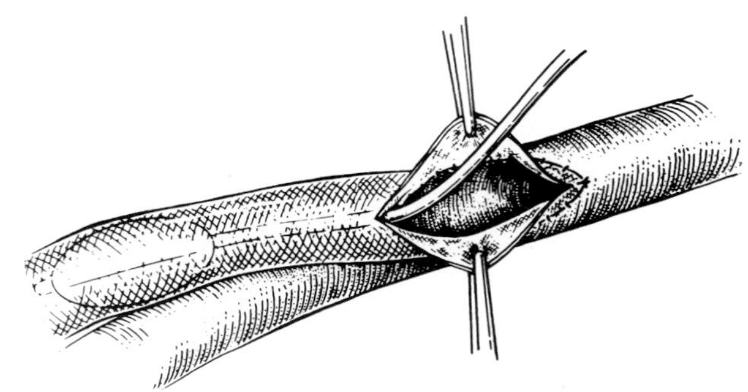

FIGURE 83-5 Thrombectomy alone is performed through the distal graft incision when no cause for graft failure is identified. Clot is removed from the graft and, if needed, from the artery proximally and distally. (From Ascher E, Collier PE, Gupta SK, Veith FJ: Reoperation for PTFE bypass failure: The importance of distal outflow site and operative technique in determining outcome. J Vasc Surg 5:298, 1987.)

■ MANAGEMENT STRATEGIES

Patients with circulatory deterioration after an infrainguinal arterial reconstruction present with recurrent symptoms, a decrease in pulses in the involved limb, other changes detected on physical examination, or a decrease in noninvasive vascular laboratory values. These manifestations may occur at any time after operation and are presumptive evidence that the arterial reconstruction has undergone thrombosis, although they also may occur in the absence of graft thrombosis if some lesion is present in, proximal to, or distal to the bypass graft (i.e., with a failing graft).

Presumed Early Graft Failure (Within 30 Days)

If the primary operation was originally justified, a secondary procedure is also mandated. If the primary operation was performed for limb salvage, early (within 30 days) graft failure or thrombosis is always associated with a renewed threat or even a worse threat to the limb. If the original preoperative arteriogram was satisfactory, another arteriogram is not necessary.

The patient is given intravenous heparin and returned to the operating room as expeditiously as possible. Because vein grafts can be injured by the ischemia associated with intraluminal clot, and because it may be more difficult to remove solid thrombotic material from vein grafts, it is more urgent to reoperate expeditiously for a failed autogenous vein graft than for a failed PTFE graft. In any event, reoperation should be undertaken less than 12 hours after failure is detected. Even greater urgency is required if calf muscle tenderness or neurologic changes are associated with graft failure.

Vein Grafts

The distal incision over the arterial reconstruction is usually reopened because most problems are in the region of the distal anastomosis, and one cannot usually remove clot from the distal arteries via a proximal incision. The graft thrombosis is confirmed by palpation. Control of the artery proximal and distal to the distal anastomosis is obtained, and a full anticoagulating dose of intravenous heparin (100 IU/kg) is given. A linear incision is made in the hood of the graft (Fig. 83-4) to visualize the interior of the distal anastomosis.[3] Balloon catheters are passed gently retrograde in the graft to remove the clot (Fig. 83-5). If necessary, any clot is similarly removed from the proximal and distal adjacent host artery, and any visualized anastomotic defect is repaired. If possible, revision of the anastomosis is avoided. The surgeon may find that valves in the vein graft prevent retrograde passage of the catheter or that it is impossible to restore adequate, normal prograde arterial flow through the graft. In either event, the proximal incision is opened, and the same procedures are performed at the proximal anastomosis.

With flow restored and all openings in the graft closed with fine running monofilament sutures, intraoperative fluoroscopy or arteriography is performed via a needle or catheter in the graft to visualize the graft and the outflow tract. If no defect is seen, adequacy of the reconstruction and the inflow tract is shown by direct arterial pressure measurements, which should reveal no gradient greater than 15 to 20 mm Hg between the distal end of the graft and the brachial or radial artery. Any gradient greater than 30 mm Hg should be localized to the inflow tract or the graft by appropriate needle placement.

If there is a gradient in the vein graft, it should be eliminated by revision. If revision is impossible, the graft should be replaced by a prosthetic (PTFE) graft.[21,22,42] Often such unexplained gradients are due to recanalized, thrombophlebitic segments of vein.[23] Unless removed, such segments cause recurrent failure. If an inflow gradient is present, it should be eliminated with a suitable inflow bypass (aortofemoral, femorofemoral, or axillofemoral) or with an intraoperative or postoperative balloon angioplasty with or without a stent.

If disease in the outflow tract is detected and is the presumed cause of graft failure, it generally is best treated with an extension to a more distal, less diseased segment of

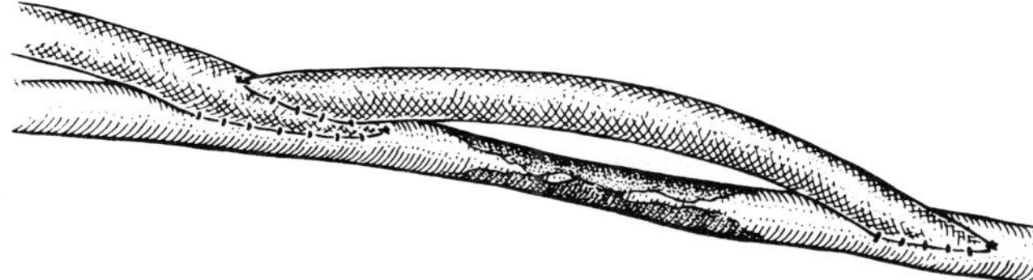

FIGURE 83-6 If disease in the outflow tract is detected, particularly a distal arteriosclerotic lesion, a graft extension is performed. (From Ascher E, Collier PE, Gupta SK, Veith FJ: Reoperation for PTFE bypass failure: The importance of distal outflow site and operative technique in determining outcome. J Vasc Surg 5:298, 1987.)

the same or another outflow artery (Fig. 83-6). If no defect is detected with arteriography or pressure measurements, the procedure is terminated. Despite older evidence to the contrary,[24] an occasional vein graft undergoes early failure for no apparent reason and remains patent indefinitely after simple thrombectomy. Perhaps the unexplained thrombosis is due to an undetected reduction in cardiac output with hypotension and decreased arterial flow. Perioperative heparin may rarely be used, although it sharply increases the risk of bleeding.

With the growing ability to perform distal bypasses to disadvantaged outflow tracts,[1,21,25,26,42] we have encountered some patients whose distal grafts failed early for no apparent reason other than high-outflow resistance. In some of these instances, thrombectomy and extension of the graft to another outflow vessel as a sequential graft have resulted in long-term graft patency and limb salvage.[27]

Polytetrafluoroethylene and Other Prosthetic Grafts

Early thrombosis of PTFE grafts is managed in essentially the same fashion as already described for early failure of vein grafts.[3,20] Differences include the almost complete freedom from graft defects as a cause of failure, although occasionally a PTFE graft is compressed, kinked, or twisted because of poor tunneling technique and malposition around or through some of the tendinous structures in the region of the knee.

In addition, graft thrombosis for no apparent reason is more common with PTFE grafts than vein grafts, occurring in 56% of our 61 early failures in a series of 882 PTFE infrainguinal grafts (Table 83-1).[28] Simple thrombectomy of

Table 83-1 Early (<1 Month) Occlusion of Polytetrafluoroethylene Bypass Graft in 61 Failed Grafts

CAUSE	TREATMENT	NUMBER	INCIDENCE (%)
None found	Thrombectomy alone	34	56
Hypotension	Thrombectomy alone	2	3
Embolus	Thrombectomy alone	2	3
Technical*	Patch graft	1	2
Inflow stenosis	Proximal extension	3	5
Distal disease	Distal extension	19	31

*Unrecognized stenotic lesion just beyond distal anastomosis.

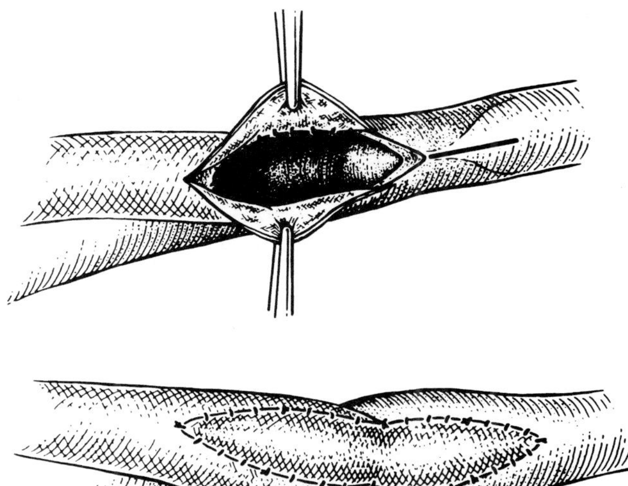

FIGURE 83-7 Stenosis just distal to the anastomosis can be caused by an unrecognized atherosclerotic lesion. This can be corrected by extending the graft incision distally across its apex and down the recipient artery until its lumen is no longer narrowed. A patch of PTFE or vein is then inserted across the stenosis to widen the lumen. Similar treatment is appropriate for intimal hyperplasia that causes late graft occlusion. (From Ascher E, Collier PE, Gupta SK, Veith FJ: Reoperation for PTFE bypass failure: The importance of distal outflow site and operative technique in determining outcome. J Vasc Surg 5:298, 1987.)

the graft with the techniques already described results in patency rates greater than 50% after 3 years, if no other defect is found and if the distal end of the graft is above the knee joint.[3,20] The secondary operative treatment in all of our 61 cases was based on the cause of early failure (see Table 83-1). Management techniques were similar to those described for vein grafts except that in one case, disease just beyond the distal anastomosis was treated with a patch graft angioplasty (Fig. 83-7) rather than a distal graft extension.

Presumed Late Graft Failure (After 30 Days)

Every patient with presumed late (>30 days) graft failure should undergo a standard arteriogram with visualization of all arteries from the renal arteries to the forefoot.[1] If a failing graft is found, it is treated urgently by a re-intervention, as already discussed. If a failed or thrombosed graft is present, the patient is not subjected to re-intervention unless the limb is unequivocally threatened.

Even if the original operation was performed for salvage of a limb with critical ischemia,[29] the limb may not be threatened again when the original arterial reconstruction becomes occluded.[3] Ten percent to 25% of patients are able to tolerate occlusion of a limb salvage bypass and to function effectively indefinitely. This proportion seems to grow as the interval between the primary operation and its failure increases. Presumably, this phenomenon occurs because the original limb-threatening lesion has healed by virtue of the bypass and does not recur with the renewed ischemia. Alternatively, improved collateral vessels maintain the limb better after some graft failures than before the operation for reasons that remain obscure.

When graft thrombosis *is* associated with renewed critical ischemia and an imminently endangered lower extremity, aggressive re-intervention is indicated and is important to achievement of optimal limb salvage results.[1,30] Management strategies differ, depending on the type of graft and its location. In all instances, complete arteriography should precede any re-intervention.

Axillofemoral and Femorofemoral Grafts

In a patient with failure of an axillofemoral or femorofemoral graft, the inflow tract of the graft should be examined angiographically. With axillofemoral grafts, it is possible to perform an arch arteriogram via the transbrachial, transfemoral, or translumbar route.[31] Similar examination should be used to evaluate the inflow or donor iliac system with failed femorofemoral grafts. If significant inflow disease is found, it can be corrected by PTA with or without a stent, or a new bypass from an alternative site must be performed. If inflow iliac disease has caused failure of a femorofemoral graft, (1) it can be corrected by PTA with or without a stent, (2) an aortobifemoral bypass can be performed, or (3) an aortic limb can be brought to the thrombectomized femorofemoral graft.

The arteriogram also should be used to seek evidence of progression of outflow disease and to identify patent distal segments that can be used to bypass such outflow disease if necessary. An example is progression of deep femoral artery disease in a patient for whom that vessel is providing outflow for an axillofemoral or femorofemoral bypass. In this circumstance, the popliteal artery should be evaluated angiographically, and thrombectomy of the graft should be followed by a profundaplasty or graft extension to the undiseased deep femoral or popliteal artery.

After suitable arteriographic examination, the patient is subjected to a secondary operation. The graft is opened over the hood or hoods of the distal anastomoses so that the interior of the distal anastomosis can be inspected (Fig. 83-8). With axillofemoral grafts, inspection is facilitated if the original femorofemoral limb is placed over the distal end of the axillary limb (Fig. 83-9). In this way, a single opening in the graft permits thrombectomy of all prosthetic grafts, thrombectomy of arteries in one groin, and diagnosis and correction of anastomotic problems at one distal anastomosis (see Fig. 83-8).

Although blind balloon catheter thrombectomy of any distal anastomosis via an opening in the graft remote from the anastomosis is occasionally successful, we object to the practice. The chance of damage to the anastomosis, injury of the intima, or disruption of plaque in the adjacent artery is too great. It is true that the anastomosis and adjacent arteries must be dissected free and controlled and that this procedure may be difficult because of scarring, but it is often worth the effort. If distal anastomotic intimal hyperplasia is detected as the cause of graft failure, it is treated by a graft extension or by incision across the hyperplastic lesion and insertion of a patch graft (see Fig. 83-7). In the latter circumstance, the incision and patch usually are placed across the origin of the deep femoral artery.

We have tempered our views about remote balloon thromboembolectomy. By using fluoroscopic control and inflating the balloon with dilute contrast material so that its position and configuration can be visualized fluoroscopically, we have often been able to remove clot with a balloon catheter introduced via a remote graftotomy.[32] If balloon deformity and fluoroangiography reveal lesions, these sometimes can be treated endovascularly by angioplasty and stenting,[32] avoiding the more complex and difficult reoperations with arterial exposure through scarred wounds and the resulting morbidity.

Another more recent advance has been the introduction of endoluminal adherent clot removal devices (see Fig. 44-1).

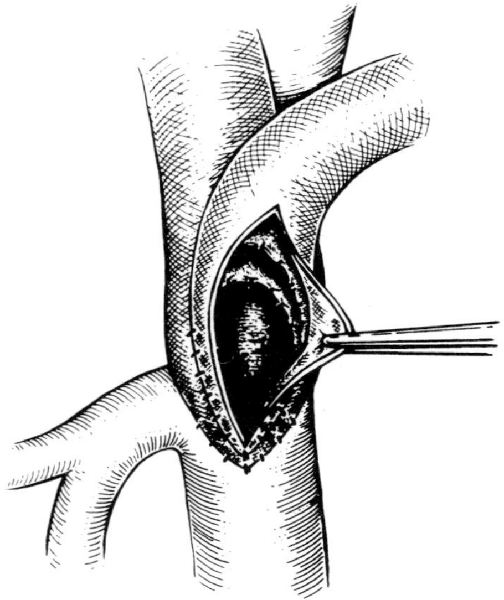

FIGURE 83-8 Approach to an unsuccessful axillobifemoral bypass. The distal anastomosis and adjacent vessels are dissected free and are controlled. An opening is made in the hood of the graft to permit proximal thrombectomy and visualization of the interior of this anastomosis.

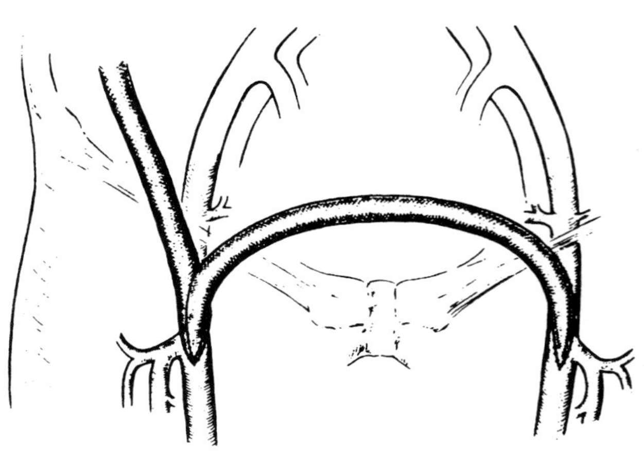

FIGURE 83-9 Crossover portion of axillobifemoral procedure is placed directly over the first femoral anastomosis. (From Ascher E, Collier PE, Gupta SK, Veith FJ: Reoperation for PTFE bypass failure: The importance of distal outflow site and operative technique in determining outcome. J Vasc Surg 5:298, 1987.)

One of these devices consists of a catheter with concentric wires, which can be deployed at the tip to remove organized adherent thrombotic material from PTFE or Dacron grafts. One danger of this device is that it can damage adjacent arteries causing intimal disruptions and dissections. These injuries can be minimized, however, if the device is placed through a 9-Fr hemostatic sheath and its position within the graft and adjacent artery is controlled fluoroscopically.

If no cause of graft failure is found on preoperative arteriography or intraoperative inspection, intraoperative arteriography or fluoroscopy is performed. If no defects or partially obstructing lesions are found, as is often the case with failed axillofemoral grafts, the reoperative procedure is terminated, and good results can be expected. The value of these reoperations for failed extra-anatomic bypasses consists of substantially improved late patency rates[33] with a 3-year *additional* patency rate, calculated from the time of reoperation, of 75%.[20]

Reoperations or Secondary Operations After Failed Femoropopliteal or Infrapopliteal Bypasses

If a failed femoropopliteal or infrapopliteal bypass graft is confirmed by arteriography to have thrombosis, re-intervention is undertaken only if the limb is in immediate jeopardy. If this is the case, complete contrast-enhanced arteriography must precede any secondary operation to provide some information (albeit perhaps incomplete) as to why the graft failed and to define possible therapeutic options by showing remaining patent distal arterial segments and the quality of undissected proximal arteries that may be used for bypass origin, such as the mid-portion or distal portion of the deep femoral artery.[34,35]

Bilateral contrast-enhanced venography also may precede reoperation to define the length and quality of the remaining superficial veins.[36] This step can be helpful in patients with failed vein grafts because it reveals unused accessory greater saphenous veins, unused short saphenous veins, and, occasionally, a main saphenous trunk. We also have found that duplex ultrasonography can be useful in predicting the length and diameter of residual venous segments. Neither technique of preoperative evaluation is totally accurate, however, and surgical exploration may be the only way to assess vein suitability with certainty. Preoperative venography or duplex ultrasonography also is indicated in the patient who has previously received a prosthetic bypass. We have been surprised by how often the greater saphenous vein in such cases has been damaged during the first operation or by scarring.

The usual standard surgical approaches to arteries in patients who have failed bypasses are often rendered more difficult, or even impossible to use, by surgical scarring or infection. For that reason, we have developed a variety of new or unusual approaches to all the infrainguinal arteries, which allow these vessels to be reached through virginal tissue planes.[31] These approaches can be helpful in avoiding the scarred standard access routes and can be essential if a previous operation was complicated by infection. The approaches obviate the need to use a scarred or infected groin to trace the deep femoral artery down from its origin.[35] They also permit the distal portions of the artery to be used to provide inflow for a distal shorter vein graft. We have now used these direct distal routes to the deep femoral artery in more than 80 secondary procedures.[35]

Another set of unusual approaches are for the above-knee or below-knee popliteal artery.[37] These approaches are particularly useful in the presence of medial incision sepsis and permit use of the popliteal artery for bypass inflow or outflow even in the presence of groin and medial thigh infection.[37] In addition, all three leg arteries can be reached medially or laterally, and adequate exposure can be obtained to perform an anastomosis. The lateral approach may involve fibula resection, through which all parts of the tibial and peroneal arteries can be reached.[1,38,40]

We also have devised a method for exposing the lower third of the peroneal artery from a medial approach. This technique involves division of the long flexor muscles and tendons to the toes and foot and is particularly suitable if an in-situ bypass to the distal third of the peroneal artery is to be performed.

Finally, we have developed surgical approaches to the terminal branches of the posterior tibial artery and the dorsalis pedis artery.[25,34,40] Any of these branches, which include the medial and lateral plantar branches of the posterior tibial artery and the lateral tarsal and deep metatarsal arch branches of the dorsalis pedis artery, can be used for secondary bypass operations.[25,37] The deep metatarsal arch is accessed via a dorsal incision with removal of portions of the shaft of the second and perhaps third metatarsal bones.

Another principle that is particularly useful to the vascular surgeon planning a secondary procedure is the short vein graft or distal origin bypass. Every bypass to the popliteal or infrapopliteal vessels need not originate from the common femoral artery.[41] Grafts to these distal arteries may originate from the superficial femoral, popliteal, or even tibial arteries without compromising late patency results (Fig. 83-10).[25,41] These short vein grafts are particularly useful in secondary bypass operations because they allow the surgeon to avoid previously scarred or infected areas and facilitate the use of the limited remaining superficial veins as bypass conduits.[25,41] Short vein grafts are better than prosthetic grafts.[42] We have shown that short vein grafts probably have better patency rates than long vein grafts, particularly when they are used as bypasses to disadvantaged outflow tracts.[25,26]

Two types of secondary arterial reconstruction are available to the vascular surgeon who is planning a re-intervention for a failed infrainguinal bypass. The first, which we call a *reoperation,* employs some form of graft thrombectomy and revision or extension in an effort to save all or as much of the original graft as possible. Newer methods for thromboembolectomy using digital cinefluoroscopy and catheter–guide wire endovascular techniques are discussed in greater detail in Chapter 44. The other type of secondary operation involves placement of a totally new secondary bypass graft, preferably but not necessarily using previously undissected patent arteries for the origin and insertion of the bypass.

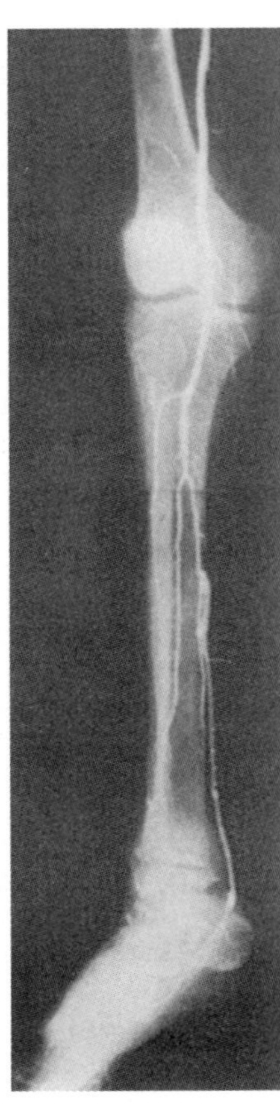

FIGURE 83-10 Arteriogram showing a posterior tibial-to-posterior tibial bypass, which has now remained patent for more than 8 years. (From Veith FJ, Ascher E, Gupta SK, et al: Tibio-tibial vein bypass grafts: A new operation for limb salvage. J Vasc Surg 2:552, 1985.)

The choice of which type of secondary bypass to employ depends on many variables, including:

- Type of primary bypass (PTFE or autogenous vein)
- Nature and location of the lesion responsible for the failure of the primary operation
- The surgeon's training and experience
- Residual arterial and superficial venous anatomy
- The location of the primary bypass

Because of the importance of these factors, treatments for the different kinds of failed primary operations that require re-intervention are considered separately.

Failed Vein Grafts to the Popliteal or Infrapopliteal Arteries

With failed femoropopliteal or infrapopliteal bypass, thrombectomy of an occluded vein graft is not attempted. If a patent, albeit isolated popliteal segment is present, a bypass to that segment is attempted. An effort to perform bypass with a vein graft from the ipsilateral extremity is made with the use of a remnant of the greater saphenous or the lesser saphenous vein. This effort is facilitated by using the distal deep femoral or superficial femoral artery for inflow, if possible, and by keeping the vein graft short.

If no ipsilateral lower extremity vein of adequate length is available, a PTFE graft has good prospects of remaining patent and providing long-term limb salvage, particularly if it is inserted above the knee,[42] and we use it in preference to vein from the other leg or the arms. If foot necrosis or infection is extensive in this setting, a sequential femoral-popliteal-tibial bypass should be performed with the use of a short distal vein graft obtained from any extremity of the patient. If no patent popliteal segment is present, as short a vein graft as possible is performed, extending from the distalmost artery with unobstructed proximal flow (i.e., deep or superficial femoral, popliteal, or tibial artery) to the most proximal patent infrapopliteal artery that courses without significant obstruction to its terminal end. For such procedures, autogenous vein from any extremity is used, even if it is only 2.5 to 3 mm in diameter when distended.[25,43,44] PTFE grafts should be used for bypasses to infrapopliteal arteries only if absolutely no autogenous vein is available. A secondary arterial reconstruction with such a prosthetic graft has a chance of remaining patent for several years, however, and has a moderate chance of saving the involved limb.[42,43] Use of such a graft, although not ideal, is a better option than an amputation. Although some authors believe that such bypasses have better patency results if vein cuffs, patches, or boots or arteriovenous fistulae are employed, we remain unconvinced and rarely use these adjunctive measures.[43]

Failed Polytetrafluoroethylene Bypass

Femoral-Above-Knee Popliteal Artery Bypass For failure of a femoral-above-knee bypass that threatens the limb and necessitates a secondary intervention, we believe that a reoperation with an attempt at graft salvage is justified and indicated (Table 83-2).[3,20] If the preoperative arteriogram indicates an inflow problem, the problem is treated appropriately by PTA or a proximal extension. The distal end of the graft is re-dissected along with its adjacent arteries (see Fig. 83-4), and after administration of 100 IU of heparin, a vertical incision is made in the distal hood of the graft to permit balloon catheter thrombectomy of the graft and the popliteal artery proximally and distally (see Figs. 83-4 and 83-5). Great care is exercised, and minimal balloon inflation is used when the catheter is passed in arteries to avoid intimal injury. Only if necessary is a proximal incision made. If the presence of a distal lesion is detected on inspection of the anastomosis or by preoperative arteriography, it is treated.

We believe that an incision across the lesion and patch angioplasty are often best for intimal hyperplasia (see Fig. 83-7), and a graft extension to a distal patent artery with a PTFE or vein graft (see Fig. 83-6) is best for distal progression of disease. Although this approach requires a difficult re-dissection of the distal anastomosis (which may be more technically demanding than performance of a totally new bypass), we believe it is justified and indicated in view of (1) the acceptable 3-year patency results (Fig. 83-11) and (2) the fact that such an approach preserves the maximal amount of undissected patent distal arterial tree for use if further problems develop.

Table 83-2 Cause, Incidence, and Management of Late Occlusion in 104 Polytetrafluoroethylene Bypass Grafts

CAUSE OF FAILURE	NO. CASES	PERCENTAGE OF TOTAL	TREATMENT
Progression of distal disease	39	37	Thrombectomy and distal graft extension (30) or new bypass to more distal artery (9)
None found	29	28	Thrombectomy alone
Intimal hyperplasia	22	21	Thrombectomy and patch angioplasty
Progression of proximal disease	12	12	Thrombectomy and proximal graft extension
Hypotension/technical	2	2	Thrombectomy alone

Despite these points, in recent years we have increasingly attempted balloon catheter thrombectomy of failed femoropopliteal PTFE grafts. The balloon catheter and other endovascular instrumentation are introduced from a site in the graft remote from the anastomoses, and the thrombectomy and instrumentation of the lesion causing graft failure are carried out under fluoroscopic and fluoroangiographic control using the techniques and devices described earlier for failed axillofemoral and femorofemoral grafts (see Chapter 44).[32] These techniques are particularly useful in removing clot from the proximal anastomotic region and for treating inflow lesions at or proximal to the proximal anastomosis.

Femoral-Below-Knee Popliteal or Infrapopliteal Artery Bypass When failure of a femoral-below-knee popliteal or infrapopliteal artery bypass results in the need for a secondary arterial reconstruction, we generally perform an entirely new secondary bypass, preferably employing an autogenous vein graft and some of the strategies already discussed that minimize graft length and permit use of previously unused segments of arteries or segments approached through virginal tissue planes.[34,35,37] Our primary reason for departing from the previous strategy of performing a reoperation with an attempt at graft salvage[3] is the poorer additional patency that is obtained with reoperations on these below-knee grafts (see Fig. 83-11) compared with the better results of a totally new secondary bypass (>40% 2-year patency rate).[20] A second reason for not using the reoperation strategy is the 6% infection rate with such procedures compared with a rate of less than 1% with a new secondary bypass.[20] The proximal few centimeters of a failed PTFE graft and the anastomosis often can be salvaged, however, using some of the already described endoluminal techniques. In this regard, the adherent clot removal device is particularly helpful, but fluoroscopic control is essential to prevent arterial intimal damage. Use of these techniques can help avoid difficult and dangerous re-dissection of groin arteries.

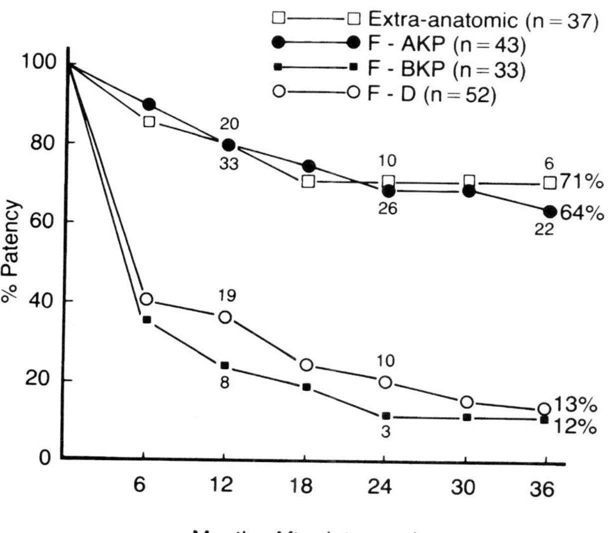

FIGURE 83-11 Cumulative life-table patency rates for various types of PTFE bypasses subjected to one or more reoperations with salvage of the original graft. Numbers of grafts at risk are shown at yearly intervals. Extra-anatomic procedures include axillofemoral and femorofemoral grafts. F-AKP, femoral-above-knee popliteal grafts; F-BKP, femoral-below-knee popliteal grafts; F-D, femoral-infrapopliteal artery grafts. (From Ascher E, Collier PE, Gupta SK, Veith FJ: Reoperation for PTFE bypass failure: The importance of distal outflow site and operative technique in determining outcome. J Vasc Surg 5:298, 1987.)

Failed Secondary Arterial Reconstruction

Although some vascular surgeons are reluctant to undertake multiple attempts at arterial reconstruction to salvage a threatened limb, in the belief that the risks of infection and knee loss outweigh the potential benefits, we and others disagree.[1,3,8,20,30,45] The results show that many patients can benefit from multiple limb salvage operations and that the benefits outweigh the risks and disadvantages if the principles and strategies already advocated are employed.[1,3,8,20,30,43,45,46]

Thrombolysis

There has been renewed interest in the use of fibrinolytic agents for lysis of intravascular clots (see Chapters 35, 53, 119, 122, 134, 161, and 162). The administration of low-dose streptokinase or high-dose urokinase by direct intra-arterial injection into thrombosed bypass grafts has been found to be effective in restoring patency.[47-61] With restored bypass patency, some perfusion can be re-established and the underlying cause for the graft thrombosis may be identified. Additionally, the patencies of occluded but undiseased inflow source and outflow tracts may be regained, facilitating planning for re-intervention and possibly converting a major operation into a minor procedure.

Occasionally, intraoperative local lysis may be helpful or necessary when the distal outflow tract is occluded by clots that cannot be retrieved by mechanical means.[56-59] Although early reports did not initially show that these advantages resulted in prolonged graft patency, later accumulated experiences of different groups indicated that adequate results can be achieved in some groups of patients.[51-55,60,61] Generally, patients in whom proximal occlusions of short duration can be traversed with a guide wire and whose distal vessels can be visualized on angiogram have good outcomes after lytic therapy and revision for the occluded grafts.[54] We and several other groups continue to use urokinase for some graft thromboses with promising results, and this agent and the newer human tissue plasminogen activator should continue to be regarded with interest. Nevertheless, more experience is needed before a conclusion can be reached about the exact place of thrombolytic agents in the management of failed infrainguinal arterial reconstruction. Almost certainly they will play an important role.

■ SUMMARY

Secondary arterial reconstructions play an important part in achieving the ultimate goal of limb salvage after primary infrainguinal interventions fail. By employing the strategies and principles outlined in this chapter, the surgeon can obtain good results, in terms of patency, of the reoperated primary reconstruction or the secondary reconstruction with significantly augmented limb salvage at low cost (i.e., in operative morbidity and mortality).[28,43] These results mandate that vascular surgeons maintain an aggressive attitude toward the use of these secondary operations when (1) a primary procedure fails to achieve or maintain its intended function and (2) a patient is faced with the imminent loss of a lower limb because of distal ischemia.

■ REFERENCES

1. Veith FJ, Gupta SK, Samson RH, et al: Progress in limb salvage by reconstructive arterial surgery combined with new or improved adjunctive procedures. Ann Surg 194:386, 1981.
2. Rivers SP, Veith FJ, Ascher E, et al: Successful conservative therapy of severe limb-threatening ischemia: The value of nonsympathectomy. Surgery 99:759, 1986.
3. Veith FJ, Gupta SK, Daly V: Management of early and late thrombosis of expanded polytetrafluoroethylene (PTFE) femoropopliteal bypass grafts: Favorable prognosis with appropriate reoperation. Surgery 87:581, 1980.
4. Carsten CG, Taylor SM, Langan EM, Crane MM: Factors associated with limb loss despite a patent infrainguinal bypass graft. Am Surg 64:33, 1998.
5. Veith FJ, Gupta SK, Daly V: Femoropopliteal bypass to the isolated popliteal segment: Is polytetrafluoroethylene graft acceptable? Surgery 89:296, 1981.
6. Flinn WR, Flanigan DP, Verta MJ, et al: Sequential femoral-tibial bypass for severe limb ischemia. Surgery 88:357, 1980.
7. Szilagyi DE, Smith RF, Elliot JP, et al: The biologic fate of autogenous vein implants as arterial substitutes: Clinical, angiographic and histopathologic observations in femoropopliteal operations for atherosclerosis. Ann Surg 178:232, 1973.
8. Whittemore AD, Clowes AW, Couch NP, et al: Secondary femoropopliteal reconstruction. Ann Surg 193:35, 1981.
9. Karkow WS, Cranley JJ, Cranley RD, et al: Extended study of aneurysm formation in umbilical grafts. J Vasc Surg 4:486, 1986.
10. Hasson JE, Newton WD, Waltman AC, et al: Mural degeneration in the glutaraldehyde tanned umbilical vein graft: Incidence and implications. J Vasc Surg 4:243, 1986.
11. Veith FJ, Weiser RK, Gupta SK, et al: Diagnosis and management of failing lower extremity arterial reconstruction. J Cardiovasc Surg 23:381, 1984.
12. O'Mara CS, Flinn WR, Johnson ND, et al: Recognition and surgical management of patent but hemodynamically failed arterial grafts. Ann Surg 193:467, 1981.
13. Smith CR, Green RM, DeWeese JA: Pseudo-occlusion of femoropopliteal bypass grafts. Circulation 68(Suppl II):88, 1983.
14. Berkowitz HD, Kee JC: Occluded infrainguinal grafts: When to choose lytic therapy versus a new bypass graft. Am J Surg 170:136, 1995.
15. Tonnesen KH, Holstein P, Rordam L, et al: Early results of percutaneous transluminal angioplasty (PTA) of failing below-knee bypass grafts. Eur J Vasc Endovasc Surg 15:51, 1998.
16. Whittemore AD, Donaldson MC, Polak JF, et al: Limitations of balloon angioplasty for vein graft stenosis. J Vasc Surg 14:340, 1991.
17. Sanchez LA, Suggs WD, Marin ML, Veith FJ: Is percutaneous balloon angioplasty appropriate in the treatment of graft and anastomotic lesions responsible for failing vein bypasses? Am J Surg 168:97, 1994.
18. Bergamini TM, George SM, Massey HT, et al: Intensive surveillance of femoropopliteal-tibial autogenous vein bypasses improves long-term graft patency and limb salvage. Ann Surg 221:507, 1995.
19. Wilson YG, Davies AH, Currie IC, et al: Vein graft stenosis: Incidence and intervention. Eur J Vasc Endovasc Surg 11:164, 1996.
20. Ascher E, Collier P, Gupta SK, Veith FJ: Reoperation for PTFE bypass failure: The importance of distal outflow site and operative technique in determining outcome. J Vasc Surg 5:298, 1987.
21. Sanchez L, Gupta SK, Veith FJ, et al: A ten-year experience with one hundred fifty failing or threatened vein and polytetrafluoroethylene arterial bypass grafts. J Vasc Surg 14:729, 1991.
22. Sanchez LA, Suggs WD, Veith FJ, et al: The merit of polytetrafluoroethylene extensions and interposition grafts to salvage failing infrainguinal vein bypasses. J Vasc Surg 23:329, 1996.
23. Panetta TF, Marin ML, Veith FJ, et al: Unsuspected pre-existing saphenous vein disease: An unrecognized cause of vein bypass failure. J Vasc Surg 15:102, 1991.
24. Craver JM, Ottinger LW, Darling C, et al: Hemorrhage and thrombosis as early complications of femoropopliteal bypass grafts: Causes, treatment, and prognostic implications. Surgery 74:839, 1973.
25. Veith FJ, Ascher E, Gupta SK, et al: Tibio-tibial vein bypass grafts: A new operation for limb salvage. J Vasc Surg 2:552, 1985.
26. Ascher E, Veith FJ, Gupta SK, et al: Short vein grafts: A superior option for arterial reconstructions to poor or compromised outflow tracts? J Vasc Surg 7:370, 1988.
27. Ascher E, Veith FJ, Marin L, et al: Components of outflow resistance and their correlation with graft patency in lower extremity arterial reconstructions. J Vasc Surg 1:817, 1984.
28. Collier P, Ascher E, Veith FJ, et al: Acute thrombosis of arterial grafts. In Bergan JJ, Yao JST (eds): Vascular Surgical Emergencies. New York, Grune & Stratton, 1987, pp 517-528.
29. Working Party of the International Vascular Symposium: The definition of critical ischemia of a limb. Br J Surg 69(Suppl):S2, 1982.
30. Veith FJ, Gupta SK, Wengerter KR, et al: Changing arteriosclerotic disease patterns and management strategies in lower limb-threatening ischemia. Ann Surg 212:402, 1990.
31. Calligaro KD, Ascher E, Veith FJ, et al: Unsuspected inflow disease in candidates for axillofemoral bypass operations: A prospective study. J Vasc Surg 11:832, 1990.
32. Parsons RE, Marin ML, Veith FJ, et al: Fluoroscopically assisted thromboembolectomy: An improved method for treating acute arterial occlusions. Ann Vasc Surg 10:201, 1996.

33. Ascher E, Veith FJ, Gupta SK, et al: Comparison of axillounifemoral and axillobifemoral bypass operations. Surgery 97:169, 1985.
34. Veith FJ, Ascher E, Nunez A, et al: Unusual approaches to infrainguinal arteries. J Cardiovasc Surg 28:58, 1987.
35. Nunez A, Veith FJ, Collier P, et al: Direct approaches to the distal portions of the deep femoral artery for limb salvage bypasses. J Vasc Surg 8:576, 1988.
36. Veith FJ, Moss CM, Sprayregen S, et al: Preoperative saphenous venography in arterial reconstructive surgery of the lower extremity. Surgery 85:253, 1979.
37. Veith FJ, Ascher E, Gupta SK, et al: Lateral approach to the popliteal artery. J Vasc Surg 6:119, 1987.
38. Veith FJ, Gupta SK: Femoral-distal artery bypasses. In Bergan JJ, Yao JST (eds): Operative Techniques in Vascular Surgery. New York, Grune & Stratton, 1980, pp 141-150.
39. Dardik H, Dardik I, Veith FJ: Exposure of the tibial-peroneal arteries by a single lateral approach. Surgery 75:337, 1974.
40. Ascher E, Veith FJ, Gupta SK: Bypasses to plantar arteries and other tibial branches: An extended approach to limb salvage. J Vasc Surg 8:434, 1988.
41. Veith FJ, Gupta SK, Samson RH, et al: Superficial femoral and popliteal arteries as inflow sites for distal bypasses. Surgery 90:980, 1981.
42. Veith FJ, Gupta SK, Ascher E, et al: Six-year prospective multicenter randomized comparison of autologous saphenous vein and expanded polytetrafluoroethylene grafts in infrainguinal arterial reconstructions. J Vasc Surg 3:104, 1986.
43. Parsons RE, Suggs WD, Veith FJ, et al: Polytetrafluoroethylene bypasses to infrapopliteal arteries without cuffs or patches: A better option than amputation in patients without autologous vein. J Vasc Surg 23:347, 1996.
44. Wengerter KR, Veith FJ, Gupta SK: Influence of vein size (diameter) on infrapopliteal reversed vein graft patency. J Vasc Surg 11:525, 1990.
45. Bartlett ST, Olinde AJ, Flinn WR, et al: The reoperative potential of infrainguinal bypass: Long-term limb and patient survival. J Vasc Surg 5:170, 1987.
46. Belkin M, Conte MS, Whittemore AD: Preferred strategies for secondary infrainguinal bypass: Lessons learned from 300 consecutive reoperations. J Vasc Surg 21:282, 1995.
47. Hargrove WC III, Barker CF, Berkowitz HD, et al: Treatment of acute peripheral arterial and graft thromboses with low dose streptokinase. Surgery 92:981, 1982.
48. van Breda A, Robison JC, Feldman L, et al: Local thrombolysis in the treatment of arterial graft occlusions. J Vasc Surg 1:103, 1984.
49. McNamara TO, Fisher JR: Thrombolysis of peripheral arterial and graft occlusions: Improved results using high-dose urokinase. AJR Am J Roentgenol 144:769, 1985.
50. Veith FJ, Gupta SK, Ascher E, et al: Reoperations and other reinterventions for thrombosed and failing polytetrafluoroethylene grafts. In Yao JST, Bergan JJ (eds): Reoperative Arterial Surgery. New York, Grune & Stratton, 1986, pp 337-392.
51. Chalmers RT, Hoballah JJ, Kresowik TF, et al: Late results of a prospective study of direct intraarterial urokinase infusion for peripheral arterial and bypass graft occlusions. Cardiovasc Surg 3:293, 1995.
52. Ouriel K, Shortell CK, Green RM, DeWeese JA: Differential mechanisms of failure of autogenous and non-autogenous bypass conduits: An assessment following successful graft thrombolysis. Cardiovasc Surg 3:469, 1995.
53. Bhatnagar PK, Ierardi RP, Ikeda Y, et al: The impact of thrombolytic therapy on arterial and graft occlusions: A critical analysis. J Cardiovasc Surg 37:105, 1996.
54. Comerota AJ, Weaver FA, Hosking JD, et al: Results of a prospective randomized trial of surgery versus thrombolysis for occluded lower extremity bypass grafts. Am J Surg 172:105, 1996.
55. Van Damme H, Trotteur G, Dongelinger RF, Limet R: Thrombolysis of occluded infrainguinal bypass grafts. Acta Chir Belg 97:177, 1997.
56. Quinones-Baldrich WJ, Zierler RE, Hiatt JC: Intraoperative fibrinolytic therapy: An adjunct to catheter thromboembolectomy. J Vasc Surg 2:319, 1985.
57. Beard JD, Nyanekye I, Earnshaw JJ, et al: Intraoperative streptokinase: A useful adjunct to balloon-catheter embolectomy. Br J Surg 80:21, 1993.
58. Comerota AJ, Rao AR, Throm RC, et al: A prospective, randomized, blinded and placebo-controlled trial of intraoperative intra-arterial urokinase infusion during lower extremity revascularization: Regional and systemic effects. Ann Surg 218:534, 1993.
59. Braithwaite BD, Quinones-Baldrich WJ: Lower limb intra-arterial thrombolysis as an adjunct to the management of arterial and graft occlusions. World J Surg 20:649, 1996.
60. Ouriel K, Veith FJ, Sasahara AA: Thrombolysis or peripheral arterial surgery: Phase I results. J Vasc Surg 23:64, 1996.
61. Ouriel K, Veith FJ, Sasahara AA: A comparison of recombinant urokinase with vascular surgery as initial treatment for acute arterial occlusion of the legs. N Engl J Med 338:1105, 1998.

Chapter

84

Endovascular Surgery in the Management of Chronic Lower Extremity Ischemia

PETER A. SCHNEIDER, MD

This chapter describes the role of endovascular intervention in revascularization of the chronically ischemic lower extremity. Percutaneous transluminal balloon angioplasty (PTA) with or without stent placement is a widely accepted and clinically useful technique for managing occlusive disease in the infrarenal arteries. PTA provides in-line, autologous reconstruction for a reasonable price and at relatively low morbidity in many clinical settings. Stents function by holding open an obstructed arterial segment and may be used to supplement balloon angioplasty when necessary. The relative roles of other techniques also are noted in this chapter. Section IX of this book reviews the principles and fundamental considerations associated with endovascular intervention. The complications of endovascular techniques are discussed in detail in Chapter 54. Thrombolytic therapy and its uses are discussed in Chapter 53.

■ APPLYING ENDOVASCULAR CONCEPTS TO CLINICAL PRACTICE

Vascular specialists are enthusiastic about the concept of effective, low-morbidity therapy for vascular disease introduced through a remote access site. The application of this concept to clinical practice requires a thorough understanding of the clinical situations and the skills of endovascular intervention. Catheters form the avenue for endovascular surgery; they are disposable and relatively inexpensive, and most are not complex in design or application. Catheter-based therapy has had a profound and continuously increasing impact on the treatment of lower extremity ischemia, as it has elsewhere in the noncoronary circulation. Occlusive disease is more common and the vasculature more forgiving in the lower extremity than in some other locations.[1,2] Many of the techniques and lessons learned using endovascular surgery in the infrarenal arteries over the past 25 years are being applied successfully to all other noncoronary vascular beds.

Determining a precise role for endovascular intervention in the lower extremity is a dynamic process as a result of the following factors:

1. Rapid changes in technology have made it difficult to obtain long-term results with any approach before modifications are made in equipment or technique. In this environment, the learning curve and results for new procedures are continually renewed.
2. Vast differences in lesion and patient mix have made reported results difficult to compare, and relatively few randomized trials have been conducted.
3. Developing technology and maturing endovascular skills have fostered the treatment of increasingly complex lesions, especially in the iliac and infrainguinal arteries. Often, these complex endovascular procedures replace open surgery, even though their results are not as good as the results of endovascular treatment of more focal lesions or the results of the open surgical option.
4. Varying levels of enthusiasm and expertise have led to wide variations in the aggressiveness with which endovascular techniques are applied to clinical practice from one institution to another.
5. Part of the promise of endovascular intervention is less expensive treatment. Actual costs are not known because the cost of maintaining patency may be high and should be included.

Spectrum of Endovascular Practice

Endovascular approaches play an integral role in the management of chronic infrarenal atherosclerotic occlusive disease. Balloon catheters for PTA of the aortoiliac and infrainguinal arteries has been available for more than 25 years. During this time, multiple techniques have been developed that are shaping endovascular practice, including the following:

- Digital subtraction arteriography (DSA)
- Refinement and miniaturization of guide wires, catheters, and access sheaths
- Improved balloon technology
- Thrombolytic therapy
- Stents, covered stents, drug-eluting stents

Higher resolution imaging permits shorter procedures with smaller loads of contrast agent. DSA permits immediate, intraprocedural feedback as to the integrity of the intervention site, road mapping, and postimage processing. Improved guide wires allow more lesions to be traversed safely. Better catheters result in fewer aborted procedures and intraprocedural complications. Smaller platform guide wires and catheters (0.014- and 0.018-inch) have improved the technique for infrageniculate PTA. Thrombolytic therapy facilitates more aggressive treatment of occlusions.

Stents have had a profound impact on the development of endovascular practice. Stents have permitted an endovascular approach to complex infrarenal occlusive lesions that previously would have been manageable only with open operation. Stents provide a "bailout" method of treatment for acute postangioplasty dissections and residual stenoses, avoiding emergency operation or acute limb-threatening ischemia (Fig. 84-1).[3-8] Endovascular specialists are tackling lesions that they previously would not have considered for fear of causing major complications.[9-14] Stents increasingly

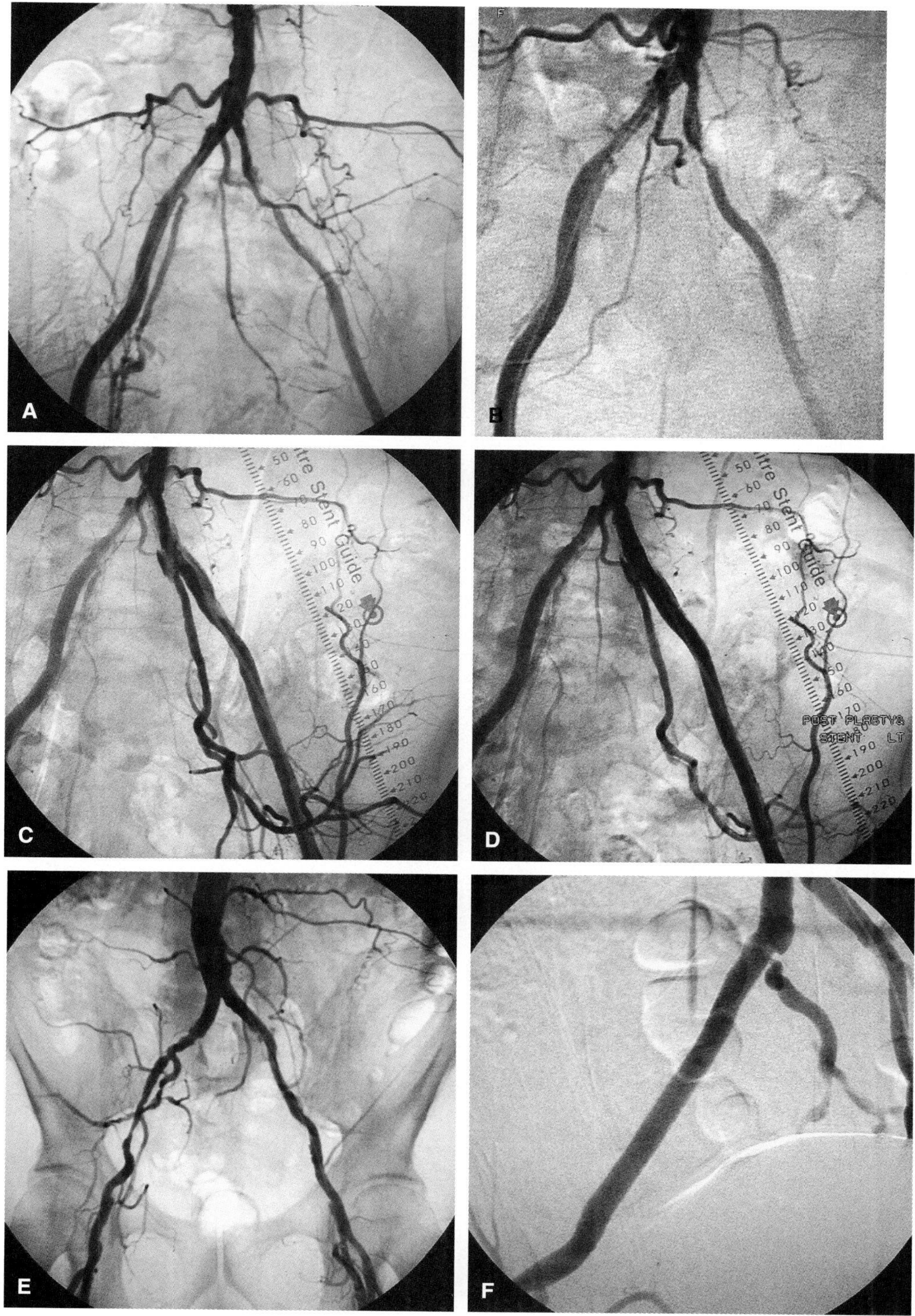

FIGURE 84-1 Stent placement provides a method of treatment for inadequate results after PTA. **A,** Aortogram of a 65-year-old woman with very-short-distance left leg claudication and clinical evidence of iliac artery disease. **B,** Right anterior oblique projection of the left iliac artery revealed a critical stenosis. **C,** After PTA to 7 mm, there was significant dissection. **D,** A stent was placed. Completion arteriography showed resolution of the dissection, and there was no pressure gradient. **E,** Right external iliac artery stenosis causing claudication. After PTA, a 15 mm Hg pressure gradient was present. **F,** Oblique completion arteriogram after stent placement. The pressure gradient was resolved.

are being integrated into the treatment algorithms for various lesions, not just reserved for inadequate PTA results. Covered stents and stent-grafts, which are intended to furnish a completely new endoluminal lining via catheter-based delivery, may be used for peripheral aneurysmal or embolizing lesions (see Chapter 52). Drug-eluting stents, although not yet available for use in the noncoronary circulation, hold tremendous promise for improved durability of infrainguinal endovascular reconstructions. Stents vary in design, size, length, material, rigidity, method of expansion, and cost. Stents may be balloon-expandable or self-expanding. Many different stents have been used with success in the aortoiliac and the infrainguinal circulations.

These techniques have expanded the spectrum of peripheral arterial occlusive disease that is appropriate for mechanical treatment. Continued advances are likely to be supported by enthusiasm among endovascular specialists, medical device manufacturers, and patients.

■ PATIENT EVALUATION

The decision as to whether a patient with lower extremity ischemia should undergo any procedure is based on the history and physical examination, supplemented as needed with noninvasive vascular testing and evaluation of the severity of disease in other organ systems. Clinical evaluation usually establishes (1) the extent of disability, (2) the threat to limb viability, (3) the general location and severity of the occlusive lesions, (4) the anesthetic risk, and (5) the patient's prospects for long-term survival. Any patient who is a candidate for open surgery also should be considered a potential candidate for endovascular intervention. In addition, some patients who would not be considered for open surgery because of co-morbidities that predict excessive risk would be candidates for an endovascular approach.

The greater risk of open surgery must be balanced against the lower durability and more limited applicability of endovascular surgery. From an evaluation of various factors associated with the lesion and the clinical situation, the likely outcome of PTA and stents can be predicted and can be compared with the anticipated results of arterial reconstruction. Understanding these factors is essential to appropriate evaluation of patients and assessment of their candidacy for endovascular intervention.

Noninvasive Evaluation

Mapping of the aortoiliac and femoropopliteal segments with duplex scanning (duplex mapping) is useful in identifying lesions that are likely to be amenable to PTA.[15-20] A combination of indirect noninvasive tests and aortoiliac duplex mapping may be used to identify inflow stenosis with a high degree of accuracy.[15,17,21] Duplex mapping has even better accuracy and greater reproducibility in evaluating the femoropopliteal segment.[15,17] Stenoses and occlusions may be distinguished, and points of reconstitution may be identified. In patients who cannot be evaluated properly with duplex, magnetic resonance arteriography may be considered. In patients who are candidates for endovascular intervention, noninvasive vascular evaluation serves several purposes, as follows:

1. Identifies disease that may be treated by PTA and stents before arteriography
2. Provides objective baseline evidence of the severity of lower extremity ischemia
3. Gauges the relative contributions of multiple occlusive lesions to the overall level of ischemia

Diagnostic Arteriography

Arteriography is invasive and expensive and has associated complications; it is not usually required to screen patients for lesions amenable to endovascular intervention.[22,23] Diagnosis almost always can be made on the basis of clinical evaluation and noninvasive testing. The contemporary role of arteriography consists of the strategic planning of revascularization and periprocedural guidance of endovascular interventions. Arteriography is justified when the decision has been made to proceed with revascularization. When possible, arteriography should be performed in a manner that facilitates the performance of PTA during the same procedure, if this option is considered most appropriate. Arteriography before lower extremity revascularization is only rarely required as a separate procedure.

■ FACTORS AFFECTING OUTCOME

Factors that influence the results of endovascular intervention for the ischemic lower extremity are (Table 84-1):

- Characteristics of lesion
- Pattern of vascular disease
- Patient demographics
- Clinical situation
- Intraprocedural factors

Table 84-1 Factors Affecting Outcome of Endovascular Interventions for Chronic Lower Extremity Ischemia

Lesion Characteristics
Location of lesion
Stenosis versus occlusion
Lesion length
Multiple stenoses in same segment
Pattern of Vascular Disease
Multilevel occlusive disease
Runoff status
Patient Demographics
Gender
Diabetes
Clinical Situation
Indication for intervention
Recurrent stenosis
Intraprocedural Factors
Dissection or residual stenosis after percutaneous balloon angioplasty
Initial hemodynamic response

Patient demographics and the clinical situation are assessed by clinical evaluation. Noninvasive studies reveal preliminary information about lesion characteristics, location, and the overall pattern of disease. Arteriography, usually performed at the time of the endovascular intervention, provides additional data about lesion length, location, severity, and appearance. Intraprocedural factors may arise during PTA. In general, larger arteries are more easily and successfully treated than smaller ones, and patients with mild ischemia caused by focal disease with good runoff fare better.

Characteristics of Lesions

Because the aim of endovascular techniques is to achieve in-line repair of the artery rather than its replacement as with bypass surgery, characteristics of the lesion significantly influence the difficulty of the procedure and its expected outcome.

Location

The long-term patency after PTA depends on the dilatation site. Proximal, larger caliber arteries offer the best initial and long-term results, with progressively decreasing long-term patency rates for more distal dilatation sites. The mean patency rate for PTA of infrarenal aortic lesions was 80% at 5 years compared with 69% for iliac arteries according to pooled data from the literature.[24] Dilatation sites in the common iliac artery have better patency rates than sites in the external iliac artery (65% versus 48% at 4 years).[25] Many studies have established the superiority of the results of iliac PTA over that of femoropopliteal PTA.[26-29] In the largest single-center series, 5-year patency rates were 60% for iliac PTA and 38% for femoropopliteal PTA.[27,28] PTA of the femoropopliteal arteries had twice the initial failure rate of PTA of the iliac arteries (16% versus 8%) and twice the failure rate at 1 year (20% versus 10%).[30]

Stenosis Versus Occlusion

The initial and long-term results of endovascular reconstruction are better for stenoses than for occlusions of the iliac arteries. Technical failure occurs in 10% to 20% of iliac occlusions but only 1% to 5% of iliac stenoses.[24,25,31] A large, well-performed study showed 3-year patency rates of 48% for the treatment of iliac occlusions and 61% for iliac stenoses.[25] Stents have been placed to improve results in treating occlusions.[5,31-35]

Compared with stenoses, occlusions in the femoral and popliteal arteries are associated with a higher rate of technical failures (18% versus 7%) and complications (22% versus 7%).[36] After successful dilatation, however, the long-term results may be similar for the two types of lesions. Some series have shown a 10% to 20% advantage in late outcome favoring stenoses over occlusions,[28,37] whereas others have found no difference.[36]

Length

The longer the stenosis, the lower the patency rate after PTA.[36,37] Longer iliac artery stenoses have lower patency rates than shorter lesions after PTA alone or PTA with stent placement.[9,38-40] Some investigators have suggested that lesion length should be a relative indication for stent placement in the iliac artery, although the results of this approach are not yet conclusive.[10,40]

Lesion length has a significantly negative effect on the results of femoropopliteal PTA.[26,36,37] A detailed breakdown of femoropopliteal lesion length reveals steadily decreasing 5-year success rates for longer occlusions: 40% for occlusions up to 9 cm in length, 29% for occlusions 9 to 14 cm, and 17% for occlusions longer than 14 cm.[26]

Multiple Stenoses in the Same Segment

Lesions composed of multiple stenoses present more potential sites for dissection, residual stenosis, or recurrent stenosis. The outlook after PTA for these lesions is inferior to that for focal stenosis over the long term in iliac and femoropopliteal segments.[27,28,41] The initial success rate for iliac artery occlusions was 80% after dilatation of one site but was 46% when multiple sites required PTA.[25]

Pattern of Vascular Disease

The pattern of vascular disease indicates the extent of involvement with atherosclerosis and the presence or absence of runoff lesions that may influence the success at a PTA site.

Multilevel Occlusive Disease

Stenosis or occlusion of more than one arterial segment in an ischemic extremity may still be treated with PTA. Each dilated site has its own failure rate, however, and failure at any site could negatively affect the entire reconstruction. When common and external iliac arteries require dilatation, the 4-year patency rate is 52% versus 65% for a common iliac artery PTA alone.[25] In addition, the 3-year clinical benefit of iliac artery stent placement is 92% for focal disease and 61% for multilevel occlusive lesions.[41]

Runoff Status

Although runoff status is not simple to quantify, it has been identified as a significant prognostic factor in the outcome of endovascular intervention.[28,36] Good runoff was a strong predictor of success after iliac PTA (73% at 3 years versus 30% for poor runoff).[27] This difference is accentuated in diabetic patients, who often have severe distal disease compromising runoff. In a study of PTA in diabetic patients, there was a 19% difference between groups with good runoff and poor runoff at 1 year (95% versus 76%), but at 5 years, there was an almost fourfold difference in patency (77% versus 20%).[38] In one large series,[42] the 5-year primary patency rate was 50% for stenoses with good runoff, 38% for stenoses with poor runoff, 34% for occlusions with good runoff, and 20% for occlusions with poor runoff; the length of lesion treated was not taken into account. Another study documented 2-year patency rates after femoropopliteal PTA as 55% in limbs with good runoff and 23% in limbs with poor runoff.[37]

Patient Demographics

Multiple demographic factors may influence the results of endovascular intervention, but these variables are difficult to isolate, and the relative importance of each cannot be independently verified.

Gender

Women have a lower patency rate after external iliac PTA than men (57% versus 34% at 3 years).[25] Gender differences for many types of vascular reconstructions have been identified, and it is likely that there are multiple factors contributing to this finding.[41]

Diabetes

The presence of diabetes correlates with worse results in some series.[36,42] Diabetes characteristically produces a different distribution of occlusive disease, however, with proportionally fewer favorable proximal iliac lesions and a high incidence of infrapopliteal occlusive lesions, which result in poor runoff. When the distribution of occlusive lesions was controlled, there was no significant difference between diabetic and nondiabetic patients in outcome after angioplasty.[38,43]

Clinical Situation

The clinical presentation influences results: The worse the ischemia, the less likely is a successful long-term outcome for endovascular intervention.

Indication for Intervention

One of the strongest predictors of outcome is the indication for the procedure; patients with claudication have better long-term success rates and require fewer amputations than patients with limb-threatening ischemia. Limb-threatening ischemia usually is associated with a more diffuse, multilevel pattern of atherosclerosis and poor runoff. Patients who require PTA for limb salvage also are more likely to have other co-morbidities and a more limited life span than patients who present with claudication.[44] The long-term patency rate for iliac and femoropopliteal PTA procedures is significantly better among patients with claudication than among patients with limb-threatening ischemia.[25-29] This is also the case for iliac artery stent placement.[40,45]

Recurrent Stenosis

Reports on the long-term results of repeat dilatation after failed iliac angioplasties show reasonable results.[42,46] Although initial and long-term success rates after first and second dilatations appear to be similar, stent placement is recommended for repeat interventions.[42,47]

Recurrent femoropopliteal lesions do not fare as well. Second femoropopliteal PTA procedures resulted in a 2-year patency rate of 20%.[48] Stenosis recurring after femoropopliteal PTA has a high chance of recurring after a second procedure; surgical reconstruction should be considered instead.

Intraprocedural Factors

The previously described factors are determined before the endovascular procedure. Additional events may occur during the periprocedural period and subsequently influence long-term results. Before the development of stents, intraprocedural complications at the PTA site, such as post-angioplasty dissection, a significant residual stenosis, or a poor hemodynamic result, often caused sudden early failure and occasionally resulted in urgent surgical reconstruction. These events usually can be corrected with stent placement at the time of the revascularization.

Post–Percutaneous Transluminal Angioplasty Dissection or Residual Stenosis

Flow-limiting dissection or residual stenosis (>30%) occurs after PTA in 10% of patients.[4,5,29,49] Stents may be placed to correct inadequate PTA in either the iliac or the femoropopliteal artery. The 3-year patency rate for iliac stent placement for post-PTA dissection or residual stenosis ranges from 54% to 86%.[3,40,47] Stent placement has resulted in a decrease in early failure rates.[31]

Initial Hemodynamic Response

After angioplasty, the extent of improvement in the ankle-brachial index (ABI) serves as a gauge of the immediate hemodynamic improvement and as a prognostic indicator. Improvement in the ABI after iliac PTA has been shown to be strongly predictive of sustained patency.[27]

■ INDICATIONS FOR ENDOVASCULAR INTERVENTION

When the determination has been made that the ischemia is significant enough to warrant mechanical intervention, the role played by endovascular intervention depends on an understanding of its benefits and risks and how they compare with other treatment options. Guidelines for PTA in each infrarenal vascular segment were proposed in 1994 by an American Heart Association (AHA) Task Force.[29] These guidelines were derived from accumulated clinical experience with PTA in the pre-stent era. The arteriographic extent of disease was divided into four categories, and the appropriateness of endovascular intervention was indicated in each category compared with open surgery. Table 84-2 contains (1) a general description of categories of occlusive disease, (2) an index of the clinical usefulness of endovascular intervention and open surgery in each disease category, (3) recommendations for management of disease in each category with either endovascular intervention or open surgery, and (4) the previously published recommendations of the AHA.[29]

Much has changed since the original AHA guidelines were proposed. More rigorous reporting standards have been instituted, leading to a more accurate assessment of results. Longer postintervention follow-up is available for PTA in all types of infrarenal occlusive lesions, and stents have been incorporated into the treatment regimen. Comparing various endovascular and open surgical treatment

Table 84-2 Indications for Lower Extremity Endovascular Intervention Based on Lesion Arteriographic Categories of Disease

	GENERAL DESCRIPTION OF DISEASE	CLINICAL USEFULNESS BASED ON RISKS/BENEFITS: PTA	CLINICAL USEFULNESS BASED ON RISKS/BENEFITS: Surgery	AUTHORS' RECOMMENDATION	AMERICAN HEART ASSOCIATION CATEGORIES OF DISEASE
Category 1	Short, focal, stenotic disease at the site of intervention. Mild or no disease in the proximal or distal arterial segments	+++	0	Surgery not indicated as initial treatment	Lesions for which PTA alone is the procedure of choice. Treatment of these lesions results in a high technical success rate and generally results in complete relief of symptoms or normalization of pressure gradients
Category 2	Moderate-length, focal, stenotic disease at the site of intervention. Mild disease in the proximal or distal arterial segments	++	+	PTA is appropriate initial therapy. Surgery is initial therapy in selected cases (e.g., young, good-risk patients)	Lesions that are well suited for PTA. Treatment of these lesions results in complete relief or significant improvement in symptoms, pulses, or pressure gradients. This category includes lesions that will be treated by procedures to be followed by surgical bypass to treat multilevel vascular disease
Category 3	Long stenotic disease or short occlusion at site of intervention. Moderate disease in the proximal or distal arterial segments	+	++	Surgery is initial therapy except in selected cases (e.g., prohibitive surgical risk)	Lesions that may be treated with PTA, but because of disease extent, location, or severity have a significantly lower chance of initial technical success or long-term benefit than if treated with surgery. PTA may be performed generally because of patient risk factors or because of lack of suitable bypass material
Category 4	Diffuse or extensive stenotic disease or long occlusion at site of intervention. Severe disease in the proximal or distal arterial segments	0	+++	Surgery preferable; PTA not indicated	Extensive vascular disease, for which PTA has a limited role because of low technical success rate or poor long-term benefit. In very-high-risk patients or in patients for whom no surgical procedure is applicable, PTA may have some place

+, with minimal disease elsewhere in that segment; ++, with mild-to-moderate occlusive disease elsewhere in that segment; +++, with moderate-to-severe occlusive disease elsewhere in that segment; PTA, percutaneous transluminal angioplasty.

Modified from Pentecost MJ, Criqui MH, Dorros G, et al: Guidelines for peripheral percutaneous transluminal angioplasty of the abdominal aorta and lower extremity vessels. Circulation 89:511-531, 1994.

options is possible only when indications are standardized. Guidelines have been developed that take these factors into account. Table 84-3 summarizes the suitability of lesions for treatment with endovascular intervention and open surgery based on arteriographic categories of disease. Categories of disease (1 through 4) were applied to lesions of the aorta, iliac, femoropopliteal, and infrapopliteal arteries through the use of the format previously proposed by the AHA.[40] Best results are achieved with the use of endovascular intervention for category 1 lesions, which represent the least severe manifestation of occlusive disease and for which PTA is usually the treatment of choice. Endovascular intervention is progressively less useful for more severe forms of disease in categories 2 and 3. PTA is reasonable as initial therapy for patients with category 2 disease; however, many patients so treated later require surgery for endovascular failures. Most category 3 diseases require open surgery, but occasionally it may be reasonable to attempt PTA in patients at high risk for open surgery. Category 4 disease usually is not considered to be amenable to endovascular intervention and is almost always treated surgically.

An alternative classification system was developed by the TransAtlantic Inter-Society Consensus (TASC) Working Group, but it is limited to iliac and femoropopliteal disease (Figs. 84-2 and 84-3).[50] Endovascular therapy is recommended for TASC A lesions, and open surgery is recommended for TASC D lesions. More evidence is needed to make firm recommendations about TASC B and C lesions. As the technical results of endovascular treatment in these more complex lesions has improved, its role has increased even though there is no long-term evidence for its superiority over open surgery.

Many clinically significant issues essential to patient care cannot be expressed adequately in terms of guidelines, including the following:

- Expertise of the treating physician
- Impact of the ischemic symptoms on the patient's life
- Projected life span of the patient, during which time, it is hoped, the properly chosen intervention would continue to relieve ischemia
- Consequences of failure
- Long-term cost of care

Indications for Endovascular Aortoiliac Intervention

PTA is best for focal stenoses of the aorta or iliac arteries that cause significant symptoms (category 1 lesions). The justification for an endovascular approach to a wide variety

Table 84-3 Suitability of Lesions for Endovascular Intervention or Surgery Based on Extent of Disease

	AORTA	ILIAC ARTERY	FEMOROPOPLITEAL ARTERIES	INFRAPOPLITEAL ARTERIES (USED FOR LIMB SALVAGE ONLY)
Category 1	Short (<2 cm) concentric noncalcified stenosis of the intrarenal aorta (+)	Short (<2 cm) concentric noncalcified stenosis of the common or external iliac artery (+)	Short (<2 cm) stenosis not involving the proximal superficial femoral artery or distal popliteal artery (+)	Short (<1 cm) stenosis of an infrapopliteal artery (+)
Category 2	(1) Medium-length (2-5 cm) noncomplex stenosis, (2) short (<2 cm) complex (calcified, eccentric) stenosis (+)	(1) Medium-length (2-5 cm) noncomplex stenosis of common or external iliac artery, (2) short (<2 cm) complex (eccentric, calcified) stenosis (+)	(1) Medium-length (2-5 cm) stenosis, (2) short (<2 cm) occlusion (+)	Two or three short (<1 cm) stenoses of an infra-popliteal artery (+)
Category 3	(1) Long (>5 cm) simple stenosis, (2) medium-length (2-5 cm) complex (calcified, eccentric) stenosis (++)	(1) Long (5-10 cm) simple stenosis of the common iliac artery, (2) medium-length (2-5 cm) complex stenosis of common or external iliac artery (++)	(1) Long (5-10 cm) stenosis, (2) 2 or 3 short (<2 cm) stenoses, (3) heavily calcified stenosis (≤5 cm), (4) occlusion (2-5 cm) in length, (5) lesion of the proximal superficial femoral artery or the distal popliteal artery (++)	(1) Moderate-length (1-2 cm) stenosis, (2) tibial trifurcation stenosis, (3) multiple short (<1 cm) stenoses (++)
Category 4	(1) Long (>5 cm) complex stenosis, (2) aortic occlusion, (3) aortic lesion with abdominal aortic aneurysm or another lesion requiring aortoiliac surgery (+++)	(1) Any iliac stenosis >10 cm, (2) occlusion >2 cm, (3) another lesion requiring aortoiliac surgery, (4) external iliac stenosis that extends to the common femoral artery, (5) long (>5 cm) stenosis of external iliac artery, (6) any complex stenosis >5 cm (+++)	(1) Multiple lesions, (2) any stenosis >10 cm, (3) any occlusion >5 cm, (4) any heavily calcified lesion >8 cm, (5) coexisting common femoral artery occlusion, (6) distal popliteal occlusion (+++)	(1) Tibial occlusion, (2) long (>2 cm) stenosis (+++)

+, with minimal disease elsewhere in that segment; ++, with mild-to-moderate occlusive disease elsewhere in that segment; +++, with moderate-to-severe occlusive disease elsewhere in that segment.

of other types of lesions in other locations has been based on extrapolation from the excellent results achieved with focal aortoiliac stenosis.

Isolated, focal stenosis of the infrarenal aorta is an uncommon manifestation of vascular disease because aortic disease is usually diffuse or accompanied by significant iliac occlusive disease or both. The number of cases and length of follow-up are much less for aortic PTA than for iliac PTA. Nevertheless, aortic PTA is appropriate for many lesions in category 1 and some in category 2 (see Table 84-3). Experience with aortic stents suggests that dissections and residual stenoses after PTA of category 1 or 2 lesions are adequately treated with stent placement. The availability of stents may extend indications for PTA to some patients with category 3 lesions, although the results of this approach are not yet known.

PTA alone is often all that is required to achieve good results for most patients with iliac lesions in category 1 (or TASC A). The option of selective stent placement for post-PTA complications provides encouragement for the treatment of many lesions in category 2 and category 3 that previously would have qualified only for open operations. Routine, primary stent placement cannot be justified by currently available data. The risk and cost of treating long lesions or occlusions with endovascular intervention are higher, however, and the long-term results are inferior to those obtained in the treatment of focal lesions. Multilevel lower extremity occlusive disease is sometimes amenable to endovascular intervention at one level and open surgery at another level, such as iliac PTA combined with distal operative reconstruction.

Diffuse or lengthy lesions; occlusions longer than a few centimeters; and severe, combined aortic and iliac disease (category 4 or TASC D) are usually best treated with open surgery, provided that the operative risk is acceptable. Other types of reconstructive techniques, such as atherectomy, laser, and endovascular grafts, have not matched the results of PTA with selective stent placement in terms of morbidity, cost, or results; these techniques should be considered only as last resorts or investigational alternatives.

Indications for Infrainguinal Endovascular Intervention

PTA is appropriate for short (<2 cm) stenoses in the superficial femoral or popliteal arteries (category 1 or TASC A lesions). AHA guidelines advocate PTA for stenoses and occlusions 10 cm or less in length.[29] This level of aggressiveness with endovascular techniques is probably not justified in patients who are otherwise reasonable surgical candidates. TASC guidelines advise PTA for stenoses less than 5 cm in length and occlusions less than 3 cm.

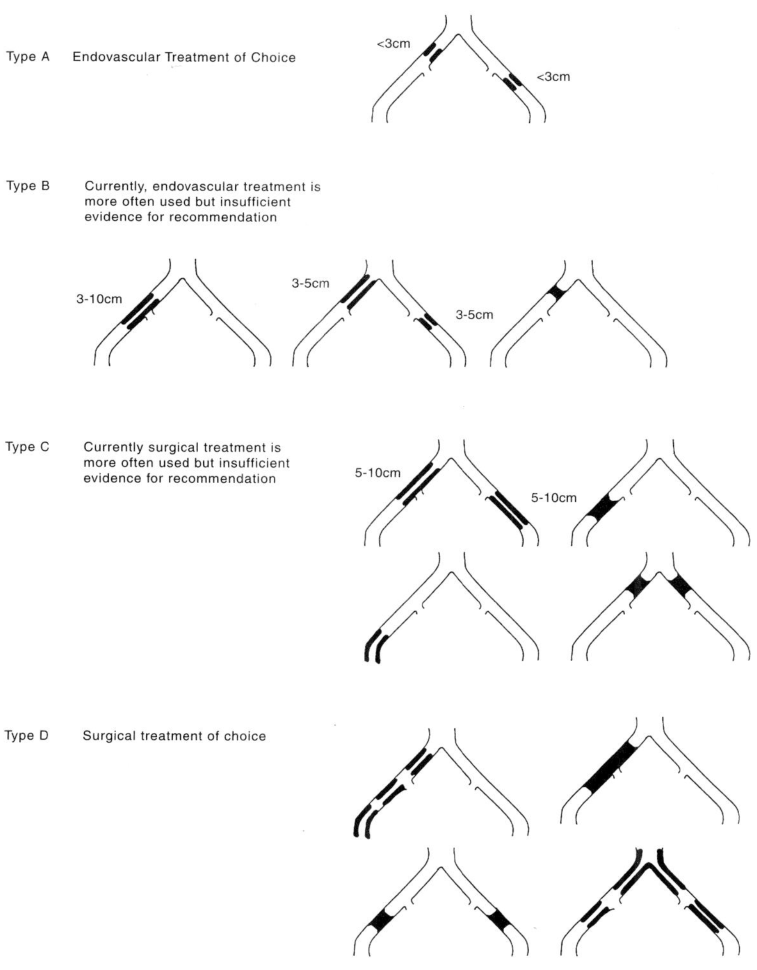
Type A
Endovascular Treatment of Choice
<3cm
<3cm
Type B
Currently, endovascular treatment is more often used but insufficient evidence for recommendation
3-10cm
3-5cm
3-5cm
Type C
Currently surgical treatment is more often used but insufficient evidence for recommendation
5-10cm
5-10cm
Type D
Surgical treatment of choice

FIGURE 84-2 Morphologic stratification of iliac lesions by TransAtlantic Inter-Society Consensus (TASC) including treatment recommendations. (From TASC Working Group: Management of peripheral arterial disease. J Vasc Surg 31:S99, 2000.)

Long lesions (>5 cm), multiple short stenoses in the same segment, a critical stenosis in a diffusely diseased segment, and most occlusions all are best treated with open surgical reconstruction if co-morbidities permit (category 3 and category 4 lesions or TASC C and TASC D lesions). Femoropopliteal stent placement has not appreciably extended long-term patency rates and has increased cost. Stents should be used selectively.

Infrapopliteal angioplasty should be considered for a patient with a focal tibial artery stenosis that prevents in-line flow to the foot and limb-threatening ischemia (see Table 84-3). Improvements in guide wire and catheter technology have contributed significantly to the feasibility of tibial PTA. Stents have not been well adapted to the tibial arteries; however, coronary stents may be used to treat inadequate PTA. Results are not durable enough to justify the use of infrapopliteal PTA for purposes other than limb salvage.

■ PATIENT SELECTION FOR ENDOVASCULAR INTERVENTION

Endovascular intervention usually is accompanied by lower rates of periprocedural morbidity and long-term patency than standard open vascular surgery. Endovascular procedures are relatively safe and rarely make matters worse. They allow a broad spectrum of patients to be treated by expanding the array of options available for management. Endovascular techniques have the greatest clinical utility in two groups of patients at opposite ends of the spectrum of illness severity.

Patients with focal disease (category 1 or TASC A) causing claudication have the most favorable lesions for endovascular intervention. Although this clinical situation carries the most marginal indication for mechanical intervention, it is followed by the best results. Lifestyle-limiting discomfort with ambulation is a relative indication for intervention. Limb threat is not a major concern in this group, unless it occurs as the result of an endovascular procedural complication, such as embolization. If mechanical intervention is not undertaken, the alternative is often exercise training.

A second group comprises patients with limb-threatening ischemia, usually due to diffuse or multilevel disease with poor runoff (category 3 or 4 lesions), for whom standard surgery poses a high risk because of coincidental medical co-morbid conditions. Nevertheless, in patients facing certain limb loss and without other options, endovascular reconstruction can sometimes offer limb salvage, even after treatment of lesions that are considered unfavorable for an endovascular approach (Fig. 84-4).[51]

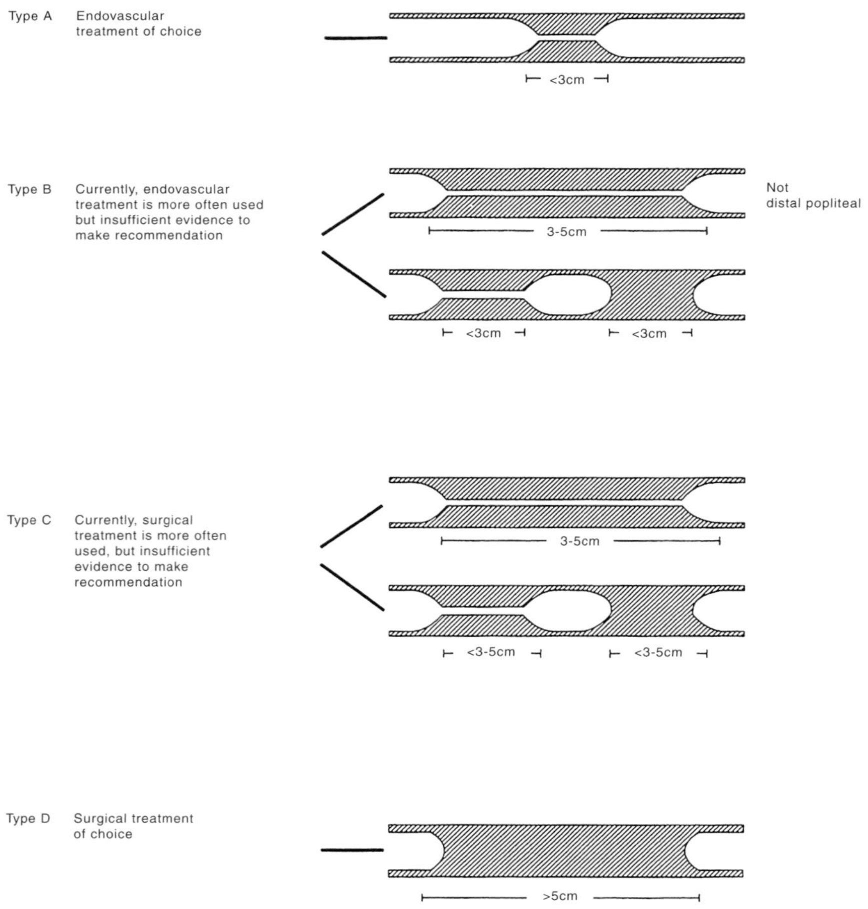

Type A Endovascular treatment of choice

<3cm

Type B Currently, endovascular treatment is more often used but insufficient evidence to make recommendation

3-5cm

Not distal popliteal

<3cm <3cm

Type C Currently, surgical treatment is more often used, but insufficient evidence to make recommendation

3-5cm

<3-5cm <3-5cm

Type D Surgical treatment of choice

>5cm

FIGURE 84-3 Morphologic stratification of femoropopliteal lesions by TASC including treatment recommendations. (From TASC Working Group: Management of peripheral arterial disease. J Vasc Surg 31:S106, 2000.)

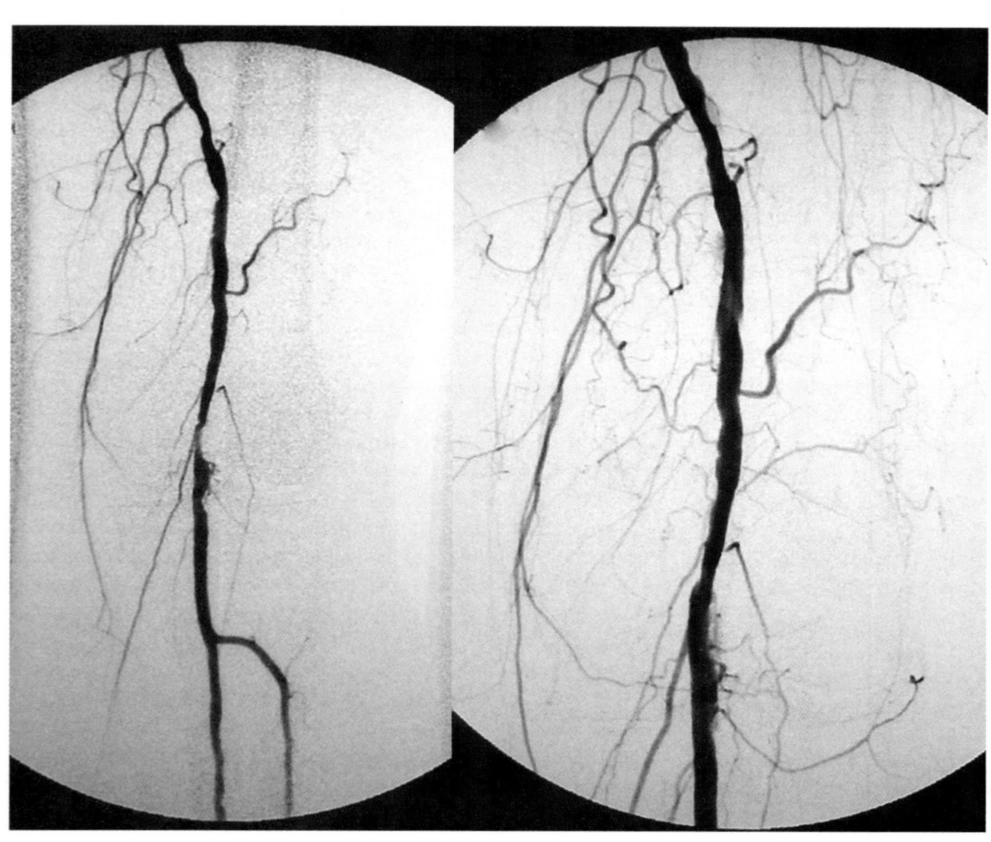

FIGURE 84-4 Retrogeniculate popliteal PTA for limb salvage. **A,** Nonhealing foot ulcer in a 72-year-old woman. Surgical risk was increased by cardiomyopathy, renal insufficiency, and chronic obstructive pulmonary disease. Duplex mapping showed mild superficial femoral artery disease with a critical popliteal artery stenosis, and this was confirmed with arteriography. **B,** The lesion was dilated to 5 mm. The arterial lumen was improved significantly on completion arteriography. The wound was healed within 3 weeks.

Endovascular intervention is the best option in these two groups. There is a less well-developed clinical sense of patient selection for endovascular intervention in most patients between these two extremes, however, for whom endovascular intervention and open surgery both may be options. The opportunity to replace an open operation and its associated risks with a percutaneous procedure and rapid return to activity is enticing. When endovascular techniques are employed indiscriminately, however, the usual results are expensive but short-lived reconstructions. Ischemia may be worsened, options expended, or limbs lost before definitive therapy can be delivered. The concept of always attempting PTA first, with surgery reserved for endovascular failures, becomes less cost-effective with the treatment of progressively more unfavorable (category 3 and category 4) lesions. There is a growing inclination among some endovascular specialists to treat lesions because they are technically possible to treat. Developing a lesion-oriented approach, rather than a patient-oriented approach, is an abdication of our responsibility for offering full-service vascular care.

■ TECHNICAL CONSIDERATIONS

Improved overall care of lower extremity ischemia results from a better understanding by clinicians of the technical aspects of endovascular intervention. Arteriography is discussed in Chapter 18, and general techniques of endovascular intervention are discussed in Chapters 50 through 54. This discussion briefly describes some selected aspects specific to the endovascular skills required for lower extremity revascularization using balloon angioplasty and stents. Other references are available for additional detail.[52-56]

Puncture Site Planning

The puncture site for arteriography is selected with plans to proceed to endovascular intervention if appropriate. The best approach is simple and direct and provides adequate working room, but is not too far from the PTA site. Arteriography is usually performed through the femoral artery on the less symptomatic side. The femoral artery on the more symptomatic side is also available for either antegrade or retrograde puncture for PTA. The simplest approach for most iliac lesions is an ipsilateral retrograde puncture and catheter placement. Lesions at the aortic bifurcation require the simultaneous passage and inflation of balloons in each iliac artery ("kissing balloon" technique). Mid–iliac artery lesions may be approached either through an ipsilateral retrograde approach or from the contralateral groin over the aortic bifurcation. Distal external iliac artery lesions and proximal superficial femoral artery lesions are best approached from the contralateral side through passage of the catheter over the aortic bifurcation. Lesions of the mid to distal femoral and popliteal arteries may be treated with either an up-and-over approach or an antegrade femoral puncture. Tibial and pedal lesions also can be treated with an up-and-over approach, but an antegrade ipsilateral approach permits the maximal degree of control. The brachial approach, usually on the left, is used for situations in which the femoral sites are hostile or undesirable or when bilateral infrainguinal interventions are intended during the same procedure.

Crossing the Lesion

A floppy-tip guide wire is passed through the lesion under fluoroscopic guidance. If the guide wire passage fails, secondary choices are:

- Hydrophilic or steerable guide wires
- Road mapping
- Passage of the guide wire through a bent-tip, steerable catheter
- Approaching the lesion from another direction

The guide wire should not be forced or passed blindly. After it crosses the lesion, intraluminal position of the guide wire should be confirmed before one proceeds to PTA. Passing a catheter through a preocclusive lesion might stop flow through the lesion. This situation should be anticipated; the operator should consider heparin administration and be prepared to dilate the lesion soon after it is traversed. The location of the lesion is indicated with the use of external markers or bony landmarks. The utility of heparin administration varies for different angioplasty sites. In general, the more distal the site or the more complex the reconstruction, the more likely that heparin is necessary.

Choosing the Best Balloon

The balloon should be sized based on the estimated "normal" diameter of the artery adjacent to the lesion. This diameter may be assessed using a known standard in the arteriographic field and digital software. More commonly, the "eyeball" technique is used. If there is doubt about the correct size, the balloon chosen is slightly undersized, and after the "waist" of atherosclerosis is dilated, a larger balloon diameter can be used if necessary. A significant initial overestimation of balloon diameter may result in rupture of the artery. The diameter of the infrarenal aorta is 10 to 18 mm; common iliac artery, 6 to 10 mm; external iliac artery, 6 to 8 mm; superficial femoral artery, 5 to 7 mm; and popliteal artery, 4 to 6 mm. The balloon should be long enough to extend slightly beyond the lesion.

Dilating the Lesion

The balloon catheter is passed over the guide wire and into correct position across the lesion, with the use of fluoroscopic guidance and the radiopaque markers on the catheter (Fig. 84-5). The balloon is inflated under fluoroscopic visualization with a 50% solution of contrast agent. As the balloon expands, the waist of atherosclerosis resolves when enough intraluminal pressure has been applied (Fig. 84-6). Inflation is maintained for 30 to 60 seconds and is usually repeated.

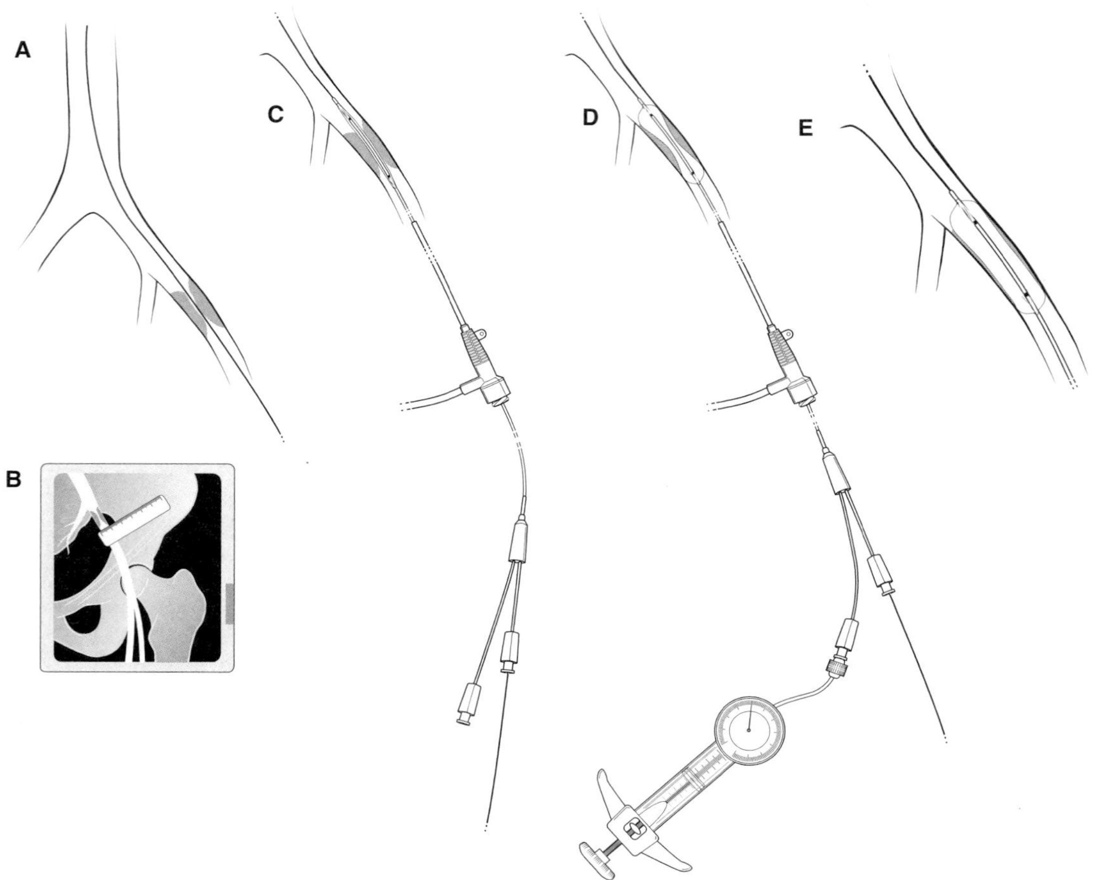

FIGURE 84-5 Technique of iliac artery balloon angioplasty. **A,** The guide wire is placed retrograde across an iliac artery stenosis. **B,** The diameter of the balloon is selected by measuring the diameter of the uninvolved, juxtaposed iliac artery on the cut-film arteriogram. **C,** The balloon catheter is passed over the guide wire, through the hemostatic access sheath, and positioned across the lesion by fluoroscopic guidance. **D,** The balloon is inflated with an inflation device that monitors pressure within the lumen. **E,** The lesion is dilated until the impression of the lesion on the balloon resolves, and the balloon assumes a cylindrical shape, as determined on fluoroscopy. (From Schneider PA: Balloon angioplasty: Minimally invasive autologous revascularization. In Schneider PA: Endovascular Skills. New York, Marcel Dekker, 2003, pp 201-216.)

Completion Arteriography

The balloon catheter is withdrawn after complete deflation has been ensured, but the guide wire position is maintained. After iliac PTA, completion arteriography may be obtained through a catheter placed through the lesion over the same guidewire, through the contralateral iliac artery if a previous contralateral puncture was performed for arteriography, or retrograde through the delivery sheath. After infrainguinal PTA, completion arteriography is usually obtained through the antegrade sheath that was used to secure access.

Iliac Percutaneous Transluminal Angioplasty and Stent Placement

Single-balloon PTA may be performed in iliac lesions that begin 1 cm or more distal to the aortic bifurcation. Iliac PTA usually causes flank discomfort. Stent placement should be considered for recurrent stenosis or occluded segments. If completion arteriography reveals residual stenosis or significant dissection, stent placement is warranted (Figs. 84-7 and 84-8). Primary stent placement is favored by some for routine application. The choice of the stent is tailored to the lesion to be treated. Balloon expandable stents have excellent hoop strength and are best for focal lesions or orifice lesions. Self-expanding stents are more flexible and are useful for long lesions or tortuous arteries.

Infrainguinal Percutaneous Transluminal Angioplasty

Infrainguinal lesions may be treated with an ipsilateral antegrade approach or an up-and-over approach from the contralateral side. After obtaining access, arteriography is performed, heparin is administered, the access sheath is placed, and the guide wire is advanced across the lesion. The balloon catheter is advanced into the lesion under fluoroscopic guidance, and dilatation is performed (Fig. 84-9).

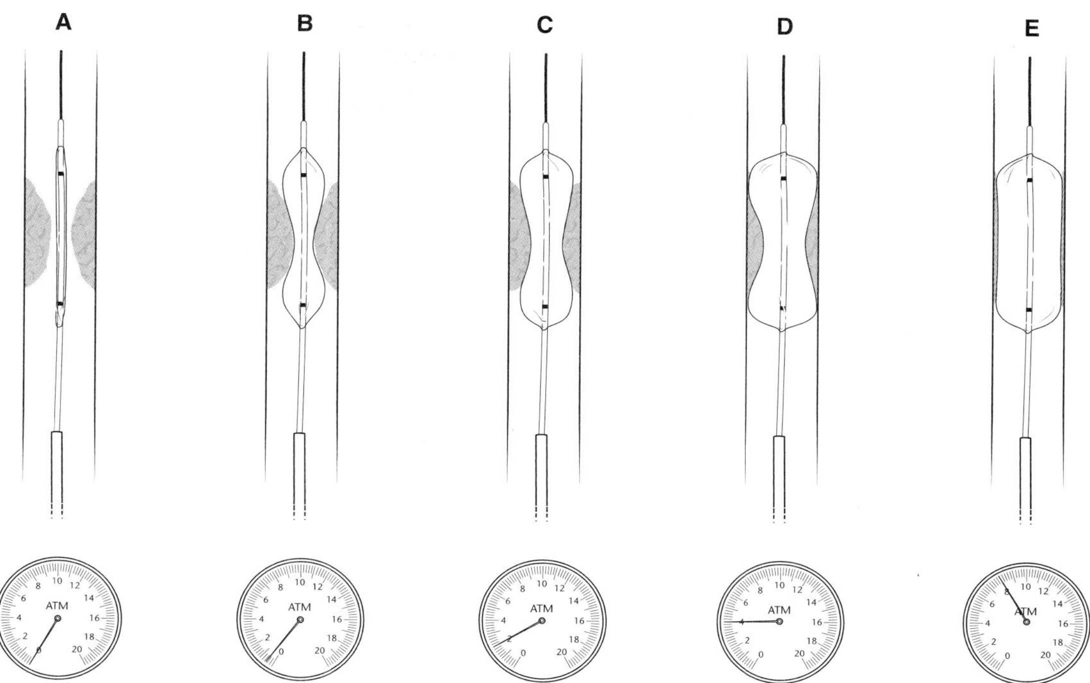

FIGURE 84-6 Dilatation of the atherosclerotic "waist." **A,** The balloon catheter is placed within the lesion. The radiopaque markers straddle the lesion. **B,** The balloon begins to take shape at low pressure. **C,** At 2 atm of pressure, the waist of atherosclerosis is evident. This represents the area of heaviest plaque formation and is usually the last area to be fully dilated. **D,** At 4 atm, a substantial residual stenosis is present. **E,** When the pressure is doubled to 8 atm, the waist is completely dilated. (From Schneider PA: Balloon angioplasty: Minimally invasive autologous revascularization. In Schneider PA: Endovascular Skills. New York, Marcel Dekker, 2003, pp 201-216.)

The balloon catheter is removed to allow for completion arteriography. Intermittent fluoroscopic visualization must be obtained during catheter exchanges to ensure that guide wire position is maintained across the lesion. Stent placement should be considered for post-PTA complications that threaten imminent occlusion at the PTA site and for significant residual stenosis.

Intraoperative Techniques

The most clinically useful combination of endovascular and open surgical techniques is iliac angioplasty for inflow during an infrainguinal surgical reconstruction. It is reasonable to perform concomitant intraoperative PTA and distal surgery when the iliac lesion is anatomically favorable (category 1 or 2) so that success is virtually ensured (with supplementary stent placement if needed).

The patient is positioned on the operating table so that the iliac segment can be visualized with fluoroscopy. The arteries are exposed, the conduit is prepared, tunnels are made, and heparin is administered. The femoral artery is punctured, and a sheath is placed (Fig. 84-10). A guide wire is advanced retrograde through the lesion, a balloon catheter is placed, and dilatation is performed. After completion arteriography, the femoral artery is cross-clamped, and the same arteriotomy is lengthened and used for the proximal anastomosis.

■ REPORTING RESULTS: EMPHASIS ON STANDARDIZED CRITERIA

The published results of endovascular interventions vary significantly, often because of differences in assessing and reporting results, as discussed in Chapters 3 and 6. The need to observe the same reporting standards used for bypass surgery has become more widely recognized.[57,58] Problematic factors that pertain specifically to reporting results in the field of endovascular intervention for lower extremity ischemia are listed in Table 84-4. These problems have delayed progress in the field and have prompted the development of standards.[29,59-62]

Table 84-4 Factors Prompting Development of Standards for Assessing and Reporting Results of Lower Extremity Endovascular Intervention

Initial failures should be reported so that overall patency can be determined

Primary, secondary, and primary-assisted patency must be correctly categorized

Objective clinical and hemodynamic criteria for determining procedural success must be included

Documentation of the severity of underlying ischemia permits assessment of subsequent improvement and limb salvage rate

Documentation of the severity and morphology of the underlying lesion permits lesion classification so that results may be compared

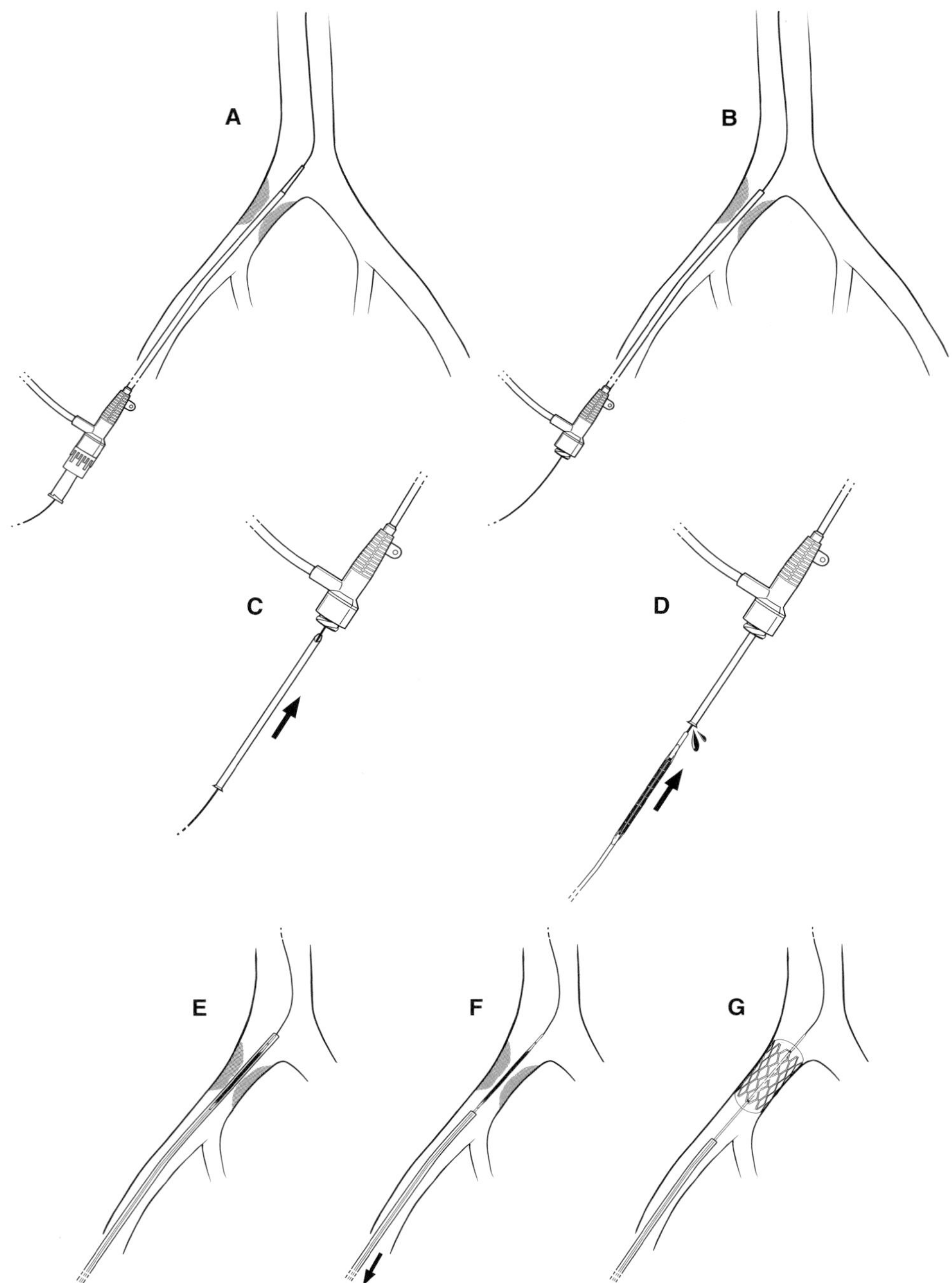

FIGURE 84-7 Technique of balloon expandable stent placement. **A,** A long dilator and sheath are advanced across the iliac lesion. **B,** The dilator is removed, leaving the sheath across the stenosis. **C,** A metal introducer with a beveled end opens the hemostatic valve on the head of the sheath. **D,** The stent, which has been mounted on a balloon of appropriate length and diameter and crimped into place, is advanced into the sheath. **E,** The stent is placed at the desired location within the lesion using fluoroscopic guidance. **F,** The sheath is withdrawn to expose the mounted stent. **G,** The balloon is inflated to deploy the stent. (From Schneider PA: A stent is an intravascular graft. In Schneider PA: Endovascular Skills. New York, Marcel Dekker, 2003, pp 237-270.)

Standards facilitate a better understanding of procedural outcomes. Arterial lesions should be described by location, type, and length of lesion and status of runoff (Table 84-5).[29,61] Criteria for improvement after intervention consist of clinical and hemodynamic assessments (Table 84-6).[57] Anatomic success is defined as a residual stenosis of less than 30%. Long-term results should be assessed in terms of the clinical and hemodynamic status and expressed in life-table format. These criteria are described further in Chapter 6.

The results of endovascular procedures are determined by many different factors, some of which cannot be stratified. Nevertheless, the uniform assessment and reporting of results at least facilitate comparisons among procedures and patient populations, which are essential in supporting advancement in endovascular intervention.

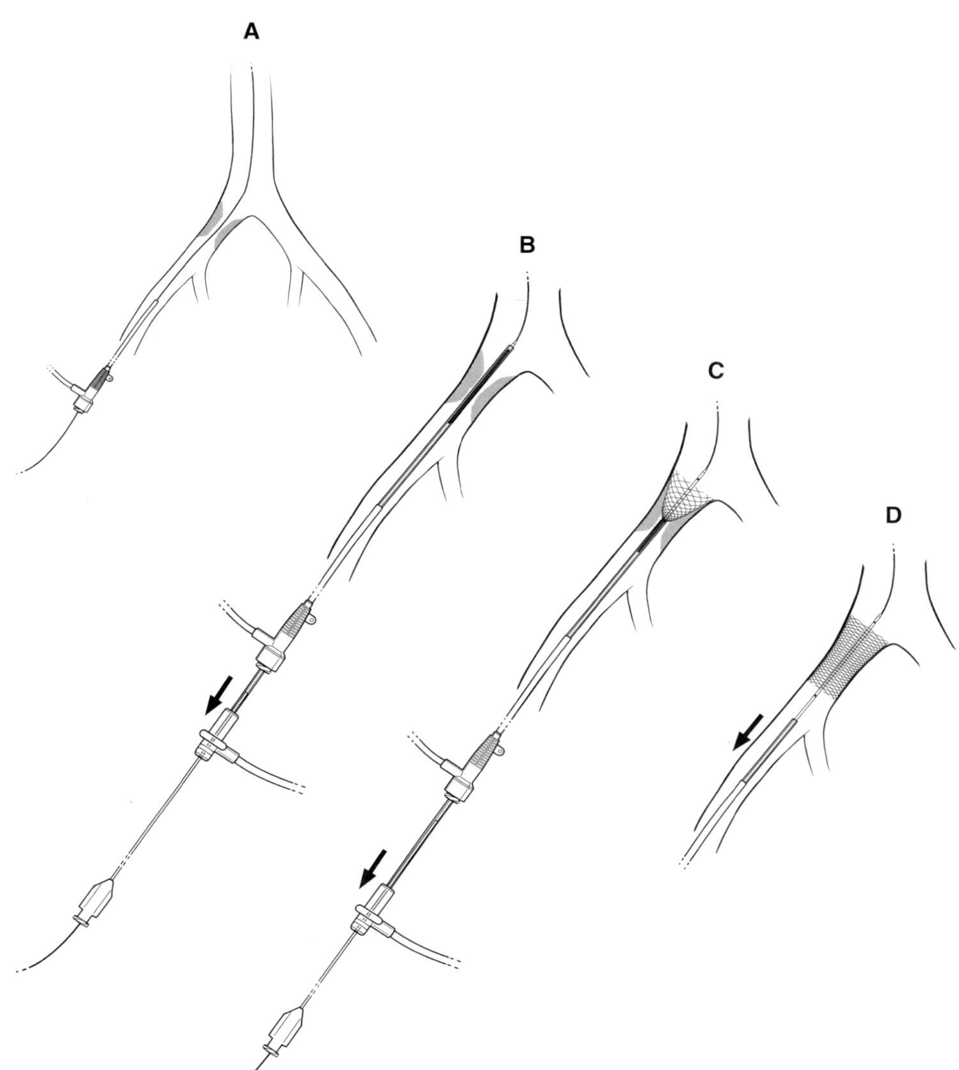

FIGURE 84-8 Technique of self-expanding stent placement. **A,** The guide wire is placed across the iliac lesion. **B,** The stent delivery catheter is advanced over the guide wire. The proximal radiopaque marker on the delivery catheter is placed proximal to the lesion. The metal pushing rod is held stationary, while the valve body is slowly withdrawn *(arrow)*. **C,** The position of the stent is monitored continuously using fluoroscopy. As the stent opens, its position is reassessed. The stent can be "dragged" distally but not advanced. (Some delivery systems permit the stent to be reconstrained if only a short length of the stent has expanded.) As the valve body is withdrawn along the length of the pushing rod *(arrow)*, the covering sheath that constrains the stent is removed, and the stent expands. **D,** After stent deployment, the stent delivery catheter is removed. Further balloon angioplasty of the stent is usually performed. (From Schneider PA: A stent is an intravascular graft. In Schneider PA: Endovascular Skills. New York, Marcel Dekker, 2003, pp 237-270.)

■ RESULTS OF AORTOILIAC ENDOVASCULAR INTERVENTION

Infrarenal Aorta

Numerous small series have shown that reasonable patency rates may be achieved with PTA for focal stenosis of the infrarenal aorta.[63-68] In the largest series in the literature (38 patients), technical success was achieved in 94% of cases.[68] All patients underwent follow-up aortography at a mean of 34 months, and 19% had recurrent stenosis. Among the 684 aortoiliac PTA procedures in another study, only 17 were for focal aortic lesions, and the 5-year patency rate was 70%.[69] Rholl[24] summarized 17 series reported between 1980 and 1993, which ranged in size from 1 to 32 patients, and determined a technical success rate of 95% and patency rates of 98% at 1 year, 87% at 3 years, and 80% at 5 years.

Many reports of stented infrarenal aortic lesions are available.[3,11-13,67,70-72] Stents have been placed successfully for residual stenosis or dissection after PTA[3,70,71] and for treatment of embolizing aortic lesions.[67,73] Stents have been used to treat late failure of previous open reconstructions, including aortofemoral bypass and aortoiliac endarterectomy.[74,75] Thrombolysis has been used in a few patients to recanalize chronic aortic occlusions before stent placement.[11,12] In one series, two of seven patients sustained distal embolization during aortic recanalization.[12]

When stent placement was performed selectively for salvage of inadequate PTA, the 3-year patency was 43%, and poor results correlated with smaller aortic diameter.[76] In another study of selective stent placement after PTA of aortic lesions, the 3-year primary patency was 85%.[77] Long-term follow-up of primary aortic stent placement is not available, but technical success was 93%, and major complications occurred in 17%.[78]

Aortic Bifurcation

Occlusive lesions of the aortic bifurcation are treated with the kissing balloon technique to avoid dislodging aortic plaque.[79-81] In this technique, a balloon catheter is placed

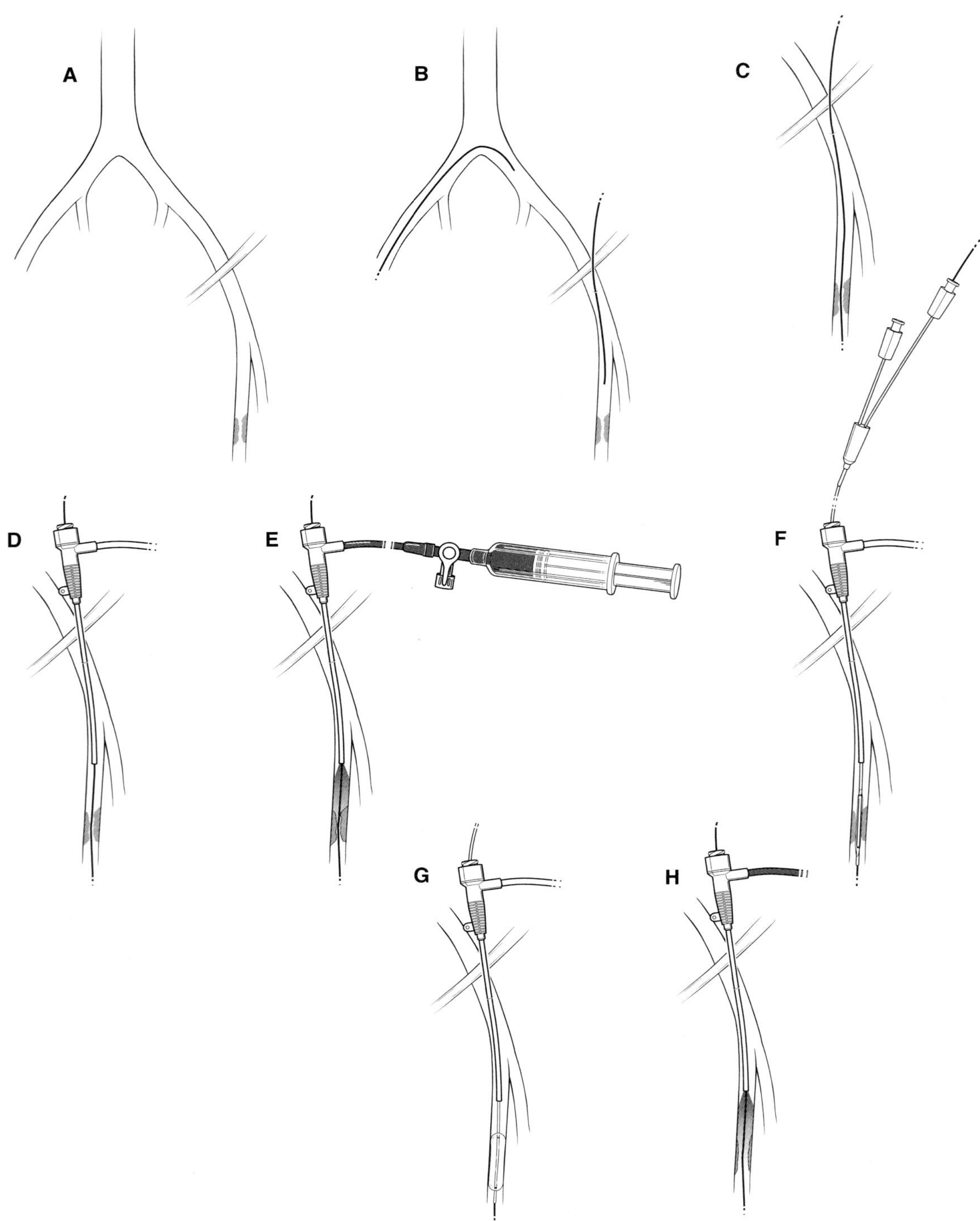

FIGURE 84-9 Technique of superficial femoral artery balloon angioplasty. **A,** Arteriography reveals a superficial femoral artery stenosis that is suitable for PTA. **B,** The lesion may be approached either across the aortic bifurcation from the contralateral femoral artery or through an ipsilateral antegrade common femoral artery puncture. **C,** The guide wire is advanced across the lesion. **D,** A hemostatic access sheath is placed over the guide wire and advanced into the proximal superficial femoral artery. **E,** Femoral arteriography is performed through the side arm of the sheath to evaluate the lesion and confirm the intraluminal position of the guide wire. **F,** The appropriate balloon catheter is advanced over the guide wire, through the sheath, and across the lesion. **G,** The lesion is dilated with fluoroscopic guidance. **H,** The balloon catheter is withdrawn, but the guide wire position is maintained across the lesion. Completion arteriography is performed through the side arm of the sheath. (From Schneider PA: Advice about angioplasty and stent placement at specific sites. In Schneider PA: Endovascular Skills. New York, Marcel Dekker, 2003, pp 315-326.)

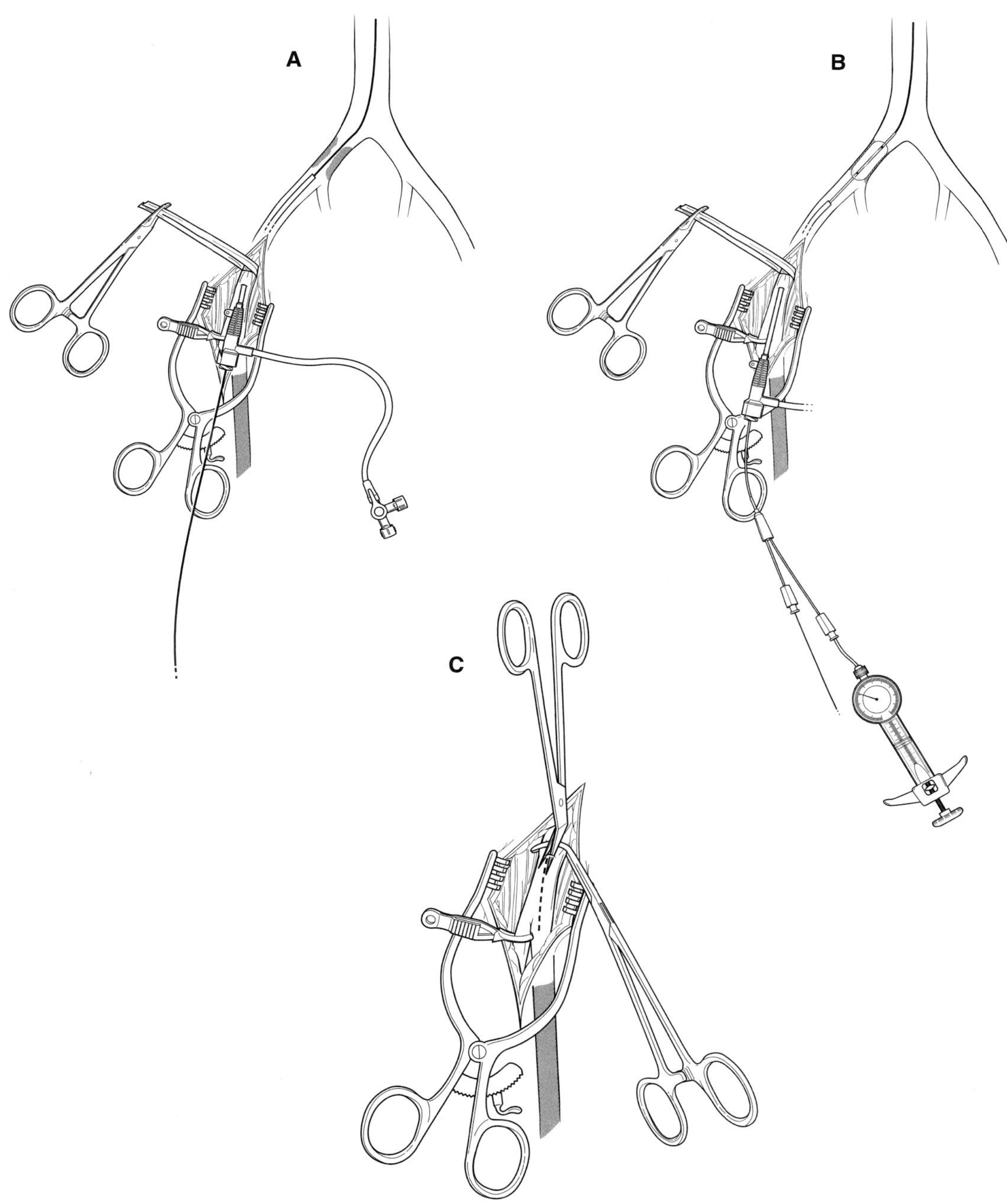

FIGURE 84-10 Technique of combined inflow balloon angioplasty and infrainguinal surgical reconstruction. **A,** After arterial exposure, conduit preparation, tunneling, and heparin administration, the guide wire and hemostatic sheath are placed in the exposed common femoral artery. **B,** Balloon angioplasty of the inflow artery is performed. After completion arteriography confirms the adequate inflow, the guide wire and sheath are removed. **C,** The common femoral artery is clamped, and the arteriotomy is lengthened and prepared for the proximal anastomosis. (From Schneider PA: Endovascular techniques in the operating room. In Schneider PA: Endovascular Skills. St. Louis, Quality Medical Publishing, 1998, pp 205-212.)

Table 84-5 Standards for Description of the Lesion to Be Treated with Endovascular Techniques

Location
Aorta, common iliac, external iliac, superficial femoral, popliteal, tibioperoneal trunk, tibial
Type
Occlusion versus stenosis, diffuse versus focal, eccentric versus concentric, ulcerated versus smooth, calcified versus noncalcified
Length
<2 cm, 2-5 cm, >5-10 cm, >10 cm
Runoff
Aortoiliac procedures: good = SFA <50% stenosis, poor = SFA >50% stenosis or occluded
Infrainguinal procedures: good = 2-3 patent tibial arteries, poor = 0-1 patent tibial arteries

SFA, superficial femoral artery.

From Ahn SS, Rutherford RB, Becker GJ, et al: Reporting standards for lower extremity arterial endovascular procedures. J Vasc Surg 17:1103-1107, 1993.

Table 84-6 Clinical Improvement After Percutaneous Interventions for Lower Extremity Ischemia

+3	Markedly improved	No ischemic symptoms, and any foot lesions completely healed; ABI essentially "normalized" (increased to >0.90)
+2	Moderately improved	No open foot lesions; still symptomatic but only with exercise and improved by at least one category*; ABI not normalized but increased by >0.10
+1	Minimally improved	>0.10 increase in ABI,† but no categorical improvement, or vice versa (i.e., upward categorical shift without an increase in ABI of >0.10)
0	No change	No categorical shift and <0.10 change in ABI
−1	Mildly worse	No categorical shift, but ABI decreased >0.10, or downward categorical shift with ABI decrease <0.10
−2	Moderately worse	One category worse or unexpected minor amputation
−3	Markedly worse	More than one category worse or unexpected major amputation

*Categories refer to clinical classification.
†In cases in which the ABI cannot be measured accurately, an index based on the toe pressure, or any measurable pressure distal to the site of revascularization, may be substituted.
ABI, ankle-brachial index.

From Rutherford RB, Baker JD, Ernst C, et al: Recommended standards for reports dealing with lower extremity ischemia: Revised version. J Vasc Surg 26:517-538, 1997.

retrograde into each iliac artery, and the balloons, which are of equal size, are inflated simultaneously to dilate the entire aortic bifurcation. The results of PTA are difficult to interpret because these bifurcation lesions are usually included as part of larger series of iliac artery lesions. Because these lesions are orifice lesions that involve both iliac arteries, the results of treatment and the need for adjunctive measures, such as stents, may differ from those for isolated iliac stenoses.

Patency rates for aortic bifurcation PTA range from 76% to 92% at 3 years.[53,79,80] The largest series reported to date includes 79 patients with aortic bifurcation lesions. The cumulative clinical success rate at a mean of 4 years was 80%.[82]

Thrombolysis for aortic bifurcation occlusions has not been widely reported. In one series of note, recanalization was achieved with thrombolysis and PTA in 13 of 25 patients, avoiding aortofemoral bypass.[83]

In more recent years, stents have often been used to reconstruct the aortic bifurcation.[55,84,85] The kissing stent technique usually produces an appealing cosmetic result, and orifice lesions seem well suited to the use of stents during reconstruction. Technical success with kissing stents at the aortic bifurcation has been reported at 95% to 100%.[86-89] In the largest series reported, the primary patency at 3 years was 79%.[88]

Percutaneous Transluminal Angioplasty for Iliac Artery Stenosis

Balloon angioplasty is safe, effective, and durable in treating selected patients with iliac artery stenosis. Iliac PTA was integral to the development of endovascular surgery: Iliac PTA revolutionized the treatment of aortoiliac occlusive disease and brought endovascular therapy into clinical relevance in the pre-stent era. Studies from the early 1990s reporting results using life-table analysis showed an initial technical success rate of 95% and 5-year patency rate of 61% using weighted averages.[26,27,38,50,90]

Among the variables that significantly influenced results in a large single-institution series were (1) the indication for revascularization (claudication versus limb salvage), (2) site of the PTA (common versus external iliac artery), and (3) runoff status.[25,27] Among 313 common iliac artery stenoses treated, the success rate was 97% initially, 81% at 1 year, 71% at 2 years, 68% at 3 years, 65% at 4 years, and 60% at 5 years. The success rate for PTA in 209 external iliac arteries was 95% initially, 74% at 1 year, 62% at 2 years, 51% at 3 years, and 48% at 4 years. More complex lesions, composed of longer stenoses and multiple stenoses, carry lower long-term primary patency rates.[91]

In general, one can expect an initial failure rate of 5% to 10%. Further failure rates are 19% to 26% during the first year, 10% to 12% the second year, and 3% to 5% per year in subsequent years. Overall, the results of iliac PTA have shown reasonable 5-year patency rates, but consideration of certain characteristics that affect outcome helps in decision making.[30] Long-term patency rates are between 85% and 45%, with an increment of roughly 10% being accounted for by each of the following features: (1) location (common versus external iliac artery), (2) runoff status (superficial femoral patency or occlusion), (3) discreteness of lesion (short versus long or multiple lesions), and (4) clinical stage (claudication versus limb salvage). Excellent long-term results may be achieved with iliac PTA through the use of judicious selection of patients with favorable lesions.

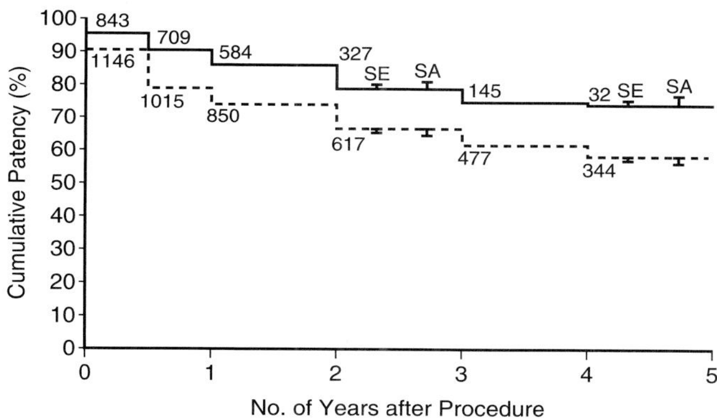

FIGURE 84-11 Iliac PTA versus iliac stent placement: results of a meta-analysis. Cumulative primary patency after iliac PTA (n = 1,146, *dashed line*) and iliac PTA with stent placement (n = 843, *solid line*), unadjusted for covariates and including technical failures. The cumulative percentage success is plotted against time of follow-up. The number of patients entering each follow-up interval is indicated. The standard error (SE) and the range found in the sensitivity analysis (SA) are given. (From Bosch JL, Hunink MGM: Meta-analysis of the results of percutaneous transluminal angioplasty and stent placement for aortoiliac occlusive disease. Radiology 204:87-96, 1997.)

Stent Placement for Iliac Artery Stenosis

The data presented for iliac artery balloon angioplasty were accumulated in the pre-stent era. Iliac PTA is no longer practiced as a stand-alone procedure since the incorporation of stents into widespread use in vascular practice. Stents have influenced the endovascular management of iliac artery stenosis in several ways, as follows:

1. Stents provide a method of treatment for acute postangioplasty dissection and residual stenosis, decreasing the rate of initial failure.
2. Stents have expanded the variety of lesions that may be treated to include most patients with category 2 lesions and more with category 3 lesions. Better hemodynamic and cosmetic results can be achieved with stents than with PTA alone for longer and more complex lesions and for occlusions. Some of these are lesions that would not have been dilated previously because of concern about the high likelihood of acute failure with PTA alone.
3. Stent placement also has been performed extensively in the hope that it would increase the long-term patency of iliac PTA for all types of lesions. Conclusive evidence for the use of primary stent placement has been elusive.
4. The promise of further technologic development of stents (i.e., drug-eluting stents, covered stents, various configurations and compositions) supports the hope that contemporary results can be improved.

Although good results can be achieved with PTA alone for iliac lesions in well-selected patients, stents have been integrated into the treatment algorithm by all specialists who perform endovascular procedures. A meta-analysis was performed to compare the results of iliac stent placement (816 patients from eight studies) and of PTA alone (1300 patients from six studies) from series published in the 1990s (Fig. 84-11).[31] The immediate technical success rate was significantly higher after stent placement (96%) than after PTA alone (91%). Primary patency rates at 4 years were higher after stent placement (77%) than after PTA alone (65%) for the treatment of iliac artery stenosis that was causing claudication. For patients in whom iliac stenosis was treated because of limb-threatening ischemia, the 4-year patency rate was 67% for stent placement and 53% for PTA alone. Because stents were available in Europe before they were available in the United States, long-term patency data are available: In a series of 110 patients who underwent stent placement between 1987 and 1990, the 10-year primary patency was 55%, and 10-year survival was 64%; only 16% of patients eventually required open surgery.[92]

Stents have an important role in the iliac artery, but the indications for stent placement are still being refined. Some investigators have advocated primary stent deployment as routine at the time of iliac PTA, but the overall effectiveness of this approach has not been proved.[45,93-95] Others have deployed stents selectively, for specific indications, such as post-PTA dissection or residual stenosis, occlusion, and recurrent stenosis.[3,4,14,47,85] Other relative indications for selective stent placement are long or complex lesions (category 3 or 4) and embolizing lesions (category 3).[10] In analyzing various retrospective case series, the results of primary stent placement and selective stent placement are striking in their similarity. Reports of the 3-year patency of iliac stents range from 74% to 86% for selective stent placement and 69% to 92% for primary stent placement (Table 84-7).[3,40,41,96-98] A randomized controlled trial has been completed that treated claudication due to iliac artery stenosis. The Dutch Iliac Stent Trial assigned 213 patients to receive either primary stent placement or PTA with selective stent placement for a residual mean pressure gradient

Table 84-7 Primary versus Selective Stent Placement for Iliac Artery Stenosis

STENT PLACEMENT	FIRST AUTHOR	YEAR	NO. PATIENTS	FOLLOW-UP PATENCY					
				Initial	1 yr	2 yr	3 yr	4 yr	5 yr
Selective	Henry[40]	1995	184	99	94	91	86	86	NA
	Cikrit[96]	1995	38	NA	87	NA	74	NA	63
	Vorwerk[3]	1996	109	97	95	88	86	82	72
Primary	Palmaz[97]	1992	486	99	91	84	69	NA	NA
	Murphy[98]	1995	83	99	89	NA	NA	86	NA
	Laborde[41]	1995	455	NA	92	92	92	NA	NA

NA, not available.

greater than 10 mm Hg.[99,100] Selective stent placement was required in 43%.[95] At 2 years, patency by duplex evaluation was 71% for primary stent placement and 70% for selective stenting. A follow-up study of the same patients showed a significant improvement in quality of life after treatment in both groups, but no difference between primary and selective stent placement for iliac artery stenosis.[94]

Predictive factors for poor durability with iliac artery stent placement included more severe lesions, poor runoff, continued pressure gradient after stenting, multiple stented segments, female gender, external iliac artery disease, renal insufficiency, and limb-threatening ischemia.[101-106] There is evidence to suggest that stent placement in the external iliac artery improves patency to levels that are similar to the levels achieved in the common iliac artery.[40,107] Other studies have shown better patency in the common iliac than in the external iliac arteries (76% versus 56% at 5 years).[104] Iliac stents have a lower patency in women than in men (38% versus 88% at 5 years).[101] When two or more iliac artery segments were treated, the 3-year patency was decreased to only 43%.[102] When more complex lesions were treated, such as TASC B and C lesions, the 5-year primary patency was 64% versus 86% after open surgery. The use of stents to extend the application of endovascular intervention to lesions unfavorable for PTA alone (e.g., categories 3 and 4) is clearly feasible, but the long-term results are unknown. Stents are costly, and multiple stents are commonly deployed for a complex reconstruction. Unless significant short-term and long-term advantages over simple unilateral bypass (femorofemoral or iliofemoral) can be shown, iliac artery stent placement for these more complex lesions can be justified only for patients with prohibitive surgical risks. Selective stent placement after inadequate PTA for iliac artery stenosis is justified. This approach is better than PTA alone and produces the same results as primary stent placement while being less expensive.[31,95]

Multilevel Occlusive Disease with Inflow Iliac Artery Stenosis

Endovascular intervention has been combined with open surgery to treat lower extremity ischemia caused by multilevel occlusive disease (Fig. 84-12).[108-115] This usually involves balloon angioplasty (alone or with stent placement) for iliac inflow and a distal, open operation. This combination of procedures may be performed in a staged fashion, with PTA followed at some interval by a separate, open operation.[108,111] Staging permits the hemodynamic effect of the PTA to be assessed before distal surgery, but also results in delay and the cost of a second procedure to complete the revascularization.

The preferred option is the simultaneous combination of intraoperative balloon angioplasty with operation at a more distal level, such as infrainguinal bypass, femoral endarterectomy, or femorofemoral bypass.[109,114,116] This approach obviates the need for a separate operation. Acute failure of an intraoperative angioplasty site is unlikely because stents may be used to manage inadequate post-PTA results.[113] The advantage of this latter approach is that the scope of surgery may be extended with minimal additional time and operative morbidity to achieve the desired reconstruction immediately.

The staged and the simultaneous approaches seem to be safe and effective, and excellent results have been published for each approach. The 5-year primary patency rate for combined reconstructions ranges from 61% to 80%.[108,116] Three studies have compared the staged and simultaneous approaches, and patency rates were similar.[109,110,117] Length of hospital stay and rate of complications were lower with the simultaneous approach.[109] Iliac artery balloon angioplasty and selective stent placement and simultaneous, combined open infrainguinal surgery is the treatment of choice for patients with multilevel lower extremity occlusive disease in need of complete revascularization.

Iliac Artery Occlusion

A substantial proportion of iliac artery occlusions can be recanalized with a combination of balloon angioplasty and stent placement, sometimes with the aid of thrombolytic therapy or laser. Initial success and long-term patency may be enhanced with stent placement.[31,118] Occlusions of less than 5 cm in length and occlusions located in the common iliac artery have better long-term patency.[114,119] Distal embolization during recanalization seems to occur less often with stent placement than when PTA alone is used.[118-122]

The results of primary stent placement for iliac artery occlusion are summarized in Table 84-8.[32,118,121,122] Initial success rates exceed 90% when stents are placed.[32,118,121] In the previously cited meta-analysis, the patency rate at 4 years for iliac occlusions in patients with claudication was 54% for PTA alone and 61% when stents were also placed.[31] The rates for PTA alone and PTA with stents were 44% and 53% at 4 years when critical ischemia was the indication for treatment of the iliac artery occlusion. More recent series of primary stent placement show 4-year primary patency of 76% to 78%.[32,118]

Thrombolytic therapy can play an important role in treating occlusions. In a study that evaluated the results of balloon angioplasty alone, early success was 100% when thrombolysis was complete, but only 88% when residual thrombus was present at the treatment site.[123] Thrombolytic therapy before PTA of an occlusion also enhanced 1-year patency rates.[124]

Distal embolization remains a significant problem and may occur in 1% to 10% of patients, even when primary stent placement is performed.[27,32,33,35,118,119,121,122,125] This complication is one of the ways that claudication may be converted to limb-threatening ischemia as the result of an endovascular procedure. In addition, if the surgical alternative is a femorofemoral bypass, it usually can be performed with low morbidity.

Table 84-8 Results of Stent Placement for Iliac Artery Occlusion

FIRST AUTHOR	YEAR	NO. PATIENTS	FOLLOW-UP PATENCY				
			Initial	1 yr	2 yr	3 yr	4 yr
Vorwerk[32]	1995	103	96	87	83	81	78
Scheinert[118]	2001	212	90	84	81	78	76
Uher[121]	2002	73	97	79	NA	69	NA
Funovics[122]	2002	78	NA	78	75	64	NA

NA, not available.

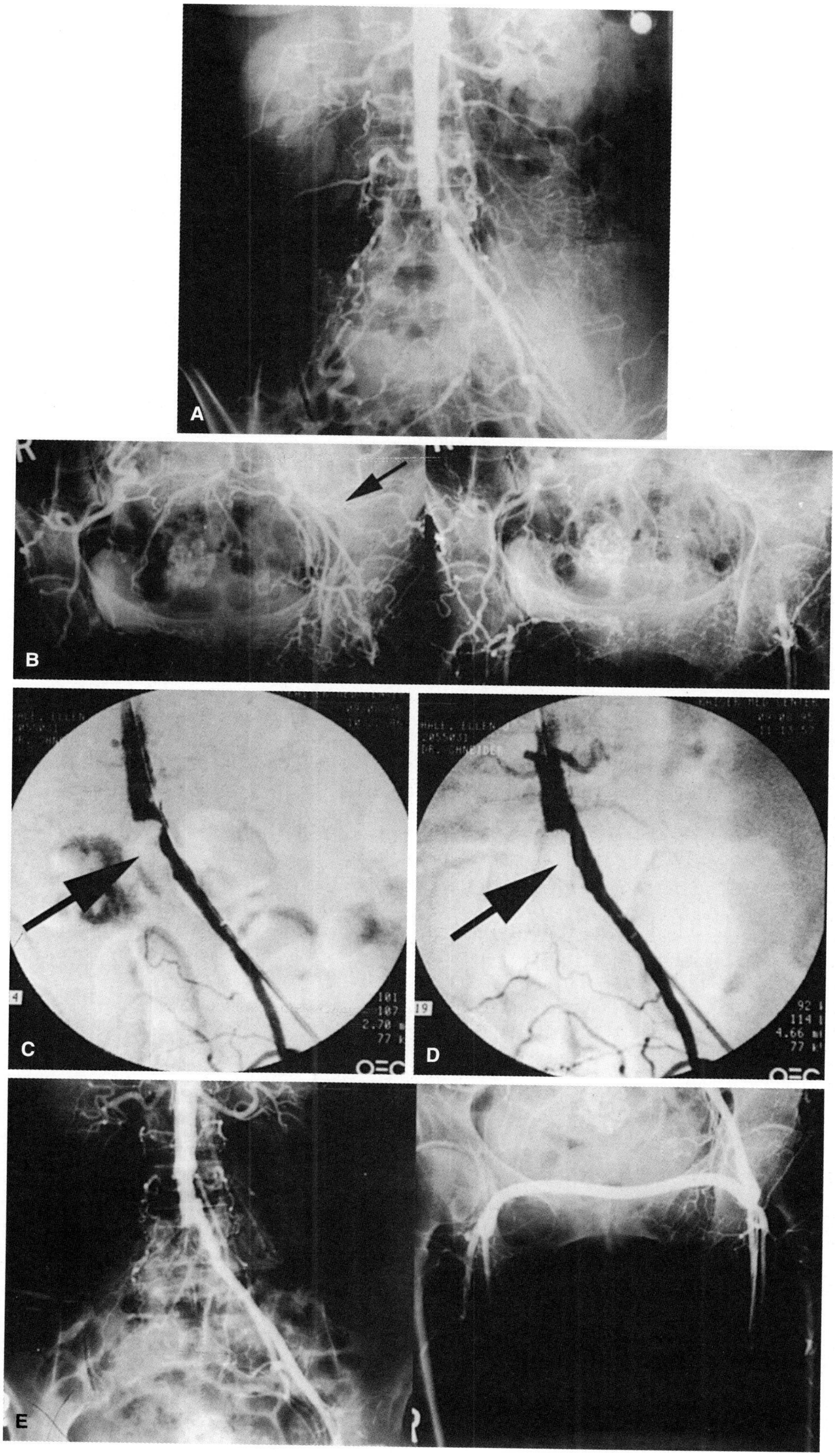

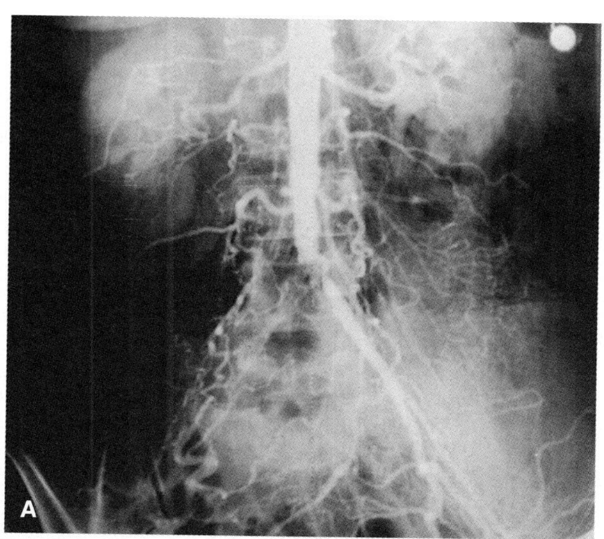

FIGURE 84-12 Intraoperative iliac angioplasty and stent placement and combined femorofemoral bypass. **A,** The patient is a 76-year-old woman who presented with bilateral rest pain and right first toe gangrene. Aortography showed a long-segment right iliac artery occlusion and a significant stenosis at the orifice of the left common iliac artery. **B,** Iliofemoral arteriographic runoff showed bilateral common femoral artery occlusions with reconstitution of the femoral bifurcations. The left external iliac artery was patent but underperfused *(arrow)*. **C,** Intraoperative left common iliac artery balloon angioplasty caused a mild dissection but made minimal improvement in the degree of stenosis *(arrow)*. **D,** A Palmaz stent was placed, and a subsequent angioplasty resolved the stenosis *(arrow)*. A left femoral endarterectomy and a femorofemoral bypass were performed. **E,** Follow-up arteriography at 1 year showed a patent iliac stent site and distal reconstruction.

Stents have improved the initial success rate of endovascular treatment for iliac artery occlusions, and most surgeons presently endorse primary stent placement in this setting for selected lesions. Stents also appear to enhance the long-term results of treatment. Distal embolization remains a significant complication in 10% of patients.

■ RESULTS OF INFRAINGUINAL ENDOVASCULAR INTERVENTION

Balloon Angioplasty of the Superficial Femoral and Popliteal Arteries

Neither the initial success rate nor the long-term patency is as high for femoropopliteal angioplasty as it is for iliac procedures.[27-30] Patients with infrainguinal or multilevel occlusive disease, as opposed to isolated aortoiliac disease, tend to be older, have lower ABIs, and have a higher risk of coronary artery disease.[126-128] Lesions that are best for femoropopliteal PTA are short (<2 cm) stenoses (category 1 lesions) in patients who have claudication and good runoff. Longer lesions and occlusions can be treated by angioplasty, but the initial success and long-term primary patency rates are lower. Extensive post-PTA dissection or significant residual stenosis may be treated with stent placement to avoid acute occlusion and its attendant morbidity. The long-term results of infrainguinal PTA do not seem to be improved by primary stent placement, however.

Studies performed in the immediate pre-stent era with long-term, life-table analysis of patency are summarized in Table 84-9.[28,36,37,129,130] Initial patency rates for all lesions ranged from 89% to 95%. Patency rates at 1 year ranged from 47% to 71% and at 5 years from 26% to 48%. In a summary of series that included 1469 limbs, the weighted averages for results of femoropopliteal balloon angioplasty included 90% technical success and patencies of 61% at 1 year, 51% at 3 years, and 48% at 5 years.[50]

The best predictors of long-term outcome are clinical stage (claudication versus limb salvage), lesion morphology (stenosis versus occlusion), lesion length, and runoff status. Patients treated for claudication had significantly better outcomes than patients requiring treatment for limb salvage. In a meta-analysis that included femoropopliteal PTA for stenosis in 923 limbs, the 3-year patency was 61% for claudication and 43% for limb salvage.[131] The same study evaluated the effect of lesion type: PTA of stenoses was more durable than PTA of occlusions in patients with claudication (61% versus 48% at 3 years). Lesion length has correlated with outcome in numerous studies. Femoropopliteal lesions that were shorter than 2 cm (category 1) had significantly better patency than longer lesions (categories 2 and 3).[26,36,37,132] Two of these studies had similar patency results at 5 years: 76% to 77% for lesions less than 1 or 2 cm and 50% to 54% for longer lesions.[26,132] In another study, the 3-year patency rates were 68% for single, short stenoses and 20% for long, multifocal stenoses.[133] Dilatation of long (>5 cm) occlusions (category 4 or TASC D) had dismal results; 22 of 23 initially successful PTA procedures had failed within 6 months.[134] In a study of 236 patients with stenoses, the 5-year success rate was 53% with good runoff and 31% with poor runoff.[28] Thrombolytic infusions have been shown to improve the results of endovascular intervention for chronic infrainguinal arterial occlusion, but at costs of higher complication rates and the need for adjunctive procedures.[124,135-137]

Table 84-9 Results of Balloon Angioplasty of the Femoral and Popliteal Arteries

FIRST AUTHOR	YEAR	NO. PATIENTS	FOLLOW-UP PATENCY Initial	1 yr	3 yr	5 yr
Johnston[28]	1992	236	89	63	51	38
Stanley[37]	1996	176	93	58	38	26
Capek[36]	1991	217	90	71	51	48
Matsi[129]	1994	106	89	47	42	NA
Hunink[130]	1993	106	95	57	45	45

Although angioplasty of more extensively diseased femoropopliteal segments, either occluded or diffusely stenotic, is less durable, it may be reasonable to dilate such lesions for limb salvage indications in patients with prohibitive surgical risks, especially if they have persistent rest pain or superficial ulceration (Fig. 84-13).[138] The improved arterial circulation is often short-lived (several months), but it may save the extremity without surgical intervention. Rush and associates[139] treated 97 limbs in 86 patients with end-stage arterial occlusive disease in whom vascular reconstruction was not considered either appropriate or possible. Limb salvage was 76% at post-PTA intervals ranging from 1 to 45 months. The 1-year restenosis rate was 57%, and second PTA procedures successfully maintained patency in only 10 limbs. In another study of 50 similar patients, Currie and associates[134] reported a 2-year patency rate of only 60% and limb salvage rate of 42%.

Femoropopliteal PTA carries an initial failure rate of 7% to 14%. An additional 20% to 40% of PTA sites fail in the first year. Thereafter, the failure rate continues at 4% to 8% per year. Best-case and worst-case scenarios at 5 years range from 70% to 20%, with increments accounted for by clinical stage (20%, claudication versus limb salvage), type of lesion (10%, occlusion versus stenosis), runoff (20%), and length of lesion (20%).

Stent Placement in the Superficial Femoral and Popliteal Arteries

As is the case with aortoiliac intervention, stent placement has become an integral part of the management of infrainguinal occlusive disease. Technology for infrainguinal stents has continued to improve, and a variety of simple, low-profile self-expanding stents with better delivery systems have been developed that may be added to a femoropopliteal PTA procedure when necessary. Primary patency rates in nonrandomized cohort studies have ranged from 49% to 81% at 12 months, similar to rates for PTA alone.[40,140-144] A meta-analysis that included 473 stent implantations performed between 1993 and 2000 showed

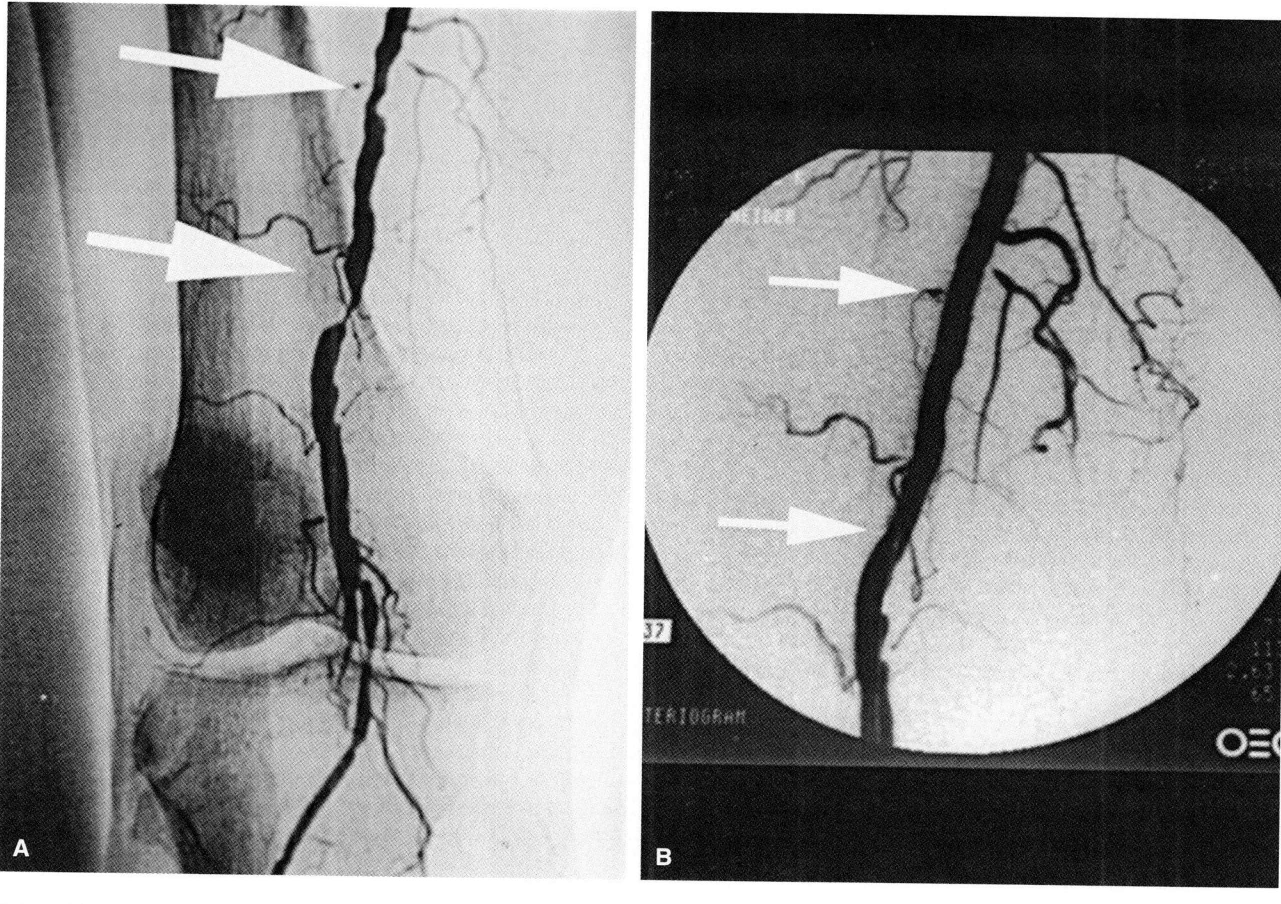

FIGURE 84-13 Superficial femoral artery balloon angioplasty for limb salvage in a patient with prohibitive surgical risk. **A,** Right great toe gangrene in an 85-year-old, dialysis-dependent man with cardiomyopathy. The patient was not a candidate for distal bypass. Arteriography identified diffuse infrainguinal occlusive disease, poor runoff, and tandem stenoses in the adductor canal *(arrows)*. **B,** Balloon angioplasty improved the stenotic segments significantly *(arrows)*, and ABIs increased from 0.22 to 0.58. The wound was healed 1 month later.

3-year patencies of 63% to 66%.[131] In contradistinction to PTA alone, these results seemed to be independent of clinical indication and lesion type.

Four prospective, randomized trials of femoropopliteal stent placement have been completed; three of these compared PTA alone versus routine stent placement, and one compared selective versus primary stent placement.[34,145-147] Most of the stents used in these studies were balloon expandable, which is not the current practice among most vascular surgeons. Vroegindeweij and coworkers[34] compared PTA alone versus primary stent placement: Patency rates at 1 year were 85% after PTA and 74% after stent placement. In the follow-up period, occlusion occurred in 21% of patients with stents and 7% of patients undergoing PTA alone. Cejna and associates[146] showed that the technical success was higher after routine stent placement (99%) than after PTA alone (84%), but patency had equalized by 2 years (65% in each group). Another study by Grimm and colleagues[145] also compared PTA alone versus primary stent placement; the 3-year patency was 68% after PTA and 62% after stent placement. In a study comparing primary and selective stent placement by Becquemin and coworkers,[147] recurrent stenosis at 1 year had occurred in 32% of the selective group and 35% of the primary group. At 4 years, the survival free of new vascular events in the treated limb was 57% after PTA with selective stent and 44% after primary stent placement.[147] Early enthusiasm that stents might be able to enhance the marginal long-term results of PTA in the superficial femoral and popliteal arteries has not been supported by subsequent studies.

Early stent thrombosis has been a problem in 5% to 15% of patients.[140,148] Many studies have employed periprocedural anticoagulation and extended it for several months afterward. Some series also have suggested that self-expanding stents of various materials, such as nitinol, may have better performance in the flexible femoropopliteal segment with 3-year patency ranging from 70% to 76% after treating complex lesions and occlusions.[149-151] In addition, drug-eluting stents and covered stents may play a role in reducing failure due to intimal hyperplasia.[152-155] These are discussed in more detail subsequently.

Stent placement does not extend the longer term patency of femoropopliteal PTA. Stents may be used to treat post-PTA dissection or residual stenosis to avoid imminent occlusion. New developments in stent technology are likely to influence future results.

Angioplasty of Infrapopliteal Arteries

Smaller diameter guide wires and soft, low-profile catheters have been developed that are useful for tibial PTA (0.014- and 0.018-inch platforms). The clinical situation in which one might consider infrapopliteal PTA is common: limb-threatening ischemia without a good surgical option because of the presence of medical co-morbidities, the lack of a conduit, or other reasons. The anatomic features required for this procedure are not common, however. The patient must have in-line flow to an ischemic foot that is interrupted by a focal tibial artery lesion. Because tibial artery disease tends to be diffuse, especially in diabetic patients, candidates for this procedure must be selected judiciously if the procedure is to be clinically successful. If acute tibial artery occlusion occurs at the PTA site, a balloon-expandable coronary stent may be used to help salvage the procedure (Fig. 84-14). Coronary stents are not approved for use in the tibial arteries, however, and the long-term success of this approach is not known.

Numerous series show that infrapopliteal PTA is feasible and that it contributes to limb salvage in some cases.[156-166] The rate of early clinical success ranges from 71% to 93%, with 1-year limb salvage rates ranging from 60% to 88% and 2-year limb salvage rates ranging from 50% to 83%.[156,157,166,167] Horvath and associates[166] reported on dilatation of 103 tibial lesions in 71 patients, noting a 96% technical success rate and limb salvage rates of 80% at 1 year, 75% at 2 years, and 65% at 3 years. Schwarten[156] reported a 97% technical success rate and limb salvage rates at 1 and 2 years of 88% and 83% after 146 dilatations in 96 patients. In studies in which patients were observed and evaluated with hemodynamic monitoring, however, the success rates were lower; they were reported as 51% to 59% at 1 year, 32% to 46% at 2 years, and 20% to 36% at 3 years.[163-165] In a meta-analysis of 19 studies that included 1282 limbs, the technical success rate was 93%, and the limb salvage rate at 2 years was 74%.[168]

The results of available series are not directly comparable, for the following reasons:

1. Many infrapopliteal PTA procedures were performed distal to iliac or femoropopliteal dilatations in patients with multilevel disease. These proximal dilatations were probably responsible for clinical success in some cases.
2. Many series included patients with one or more of the following confounding variables: acute ischemia, occluded or failing bypass grafts, claudication, need for thrombolysis, and inclusion of PTA of the below-knee popliteal artery.
3. Dilatations were usually performed at several sites in multiple tibial arteries, compounding the difficulty of assessing the individual patency of each PTA site.
4. Most results have been reported as limb salvage, rather than patency of individual angioplasty sites, making it impossible to compare tibial angioplasty among series and with PTA in other arteries.

It is not currently possible to define the appropriate role of infrapopliteal PTA. PTA of these arteries has a role in the management of lower extremity ischemia, however, and it is likely to increase in the years to come.[170,171] If in-line flow is

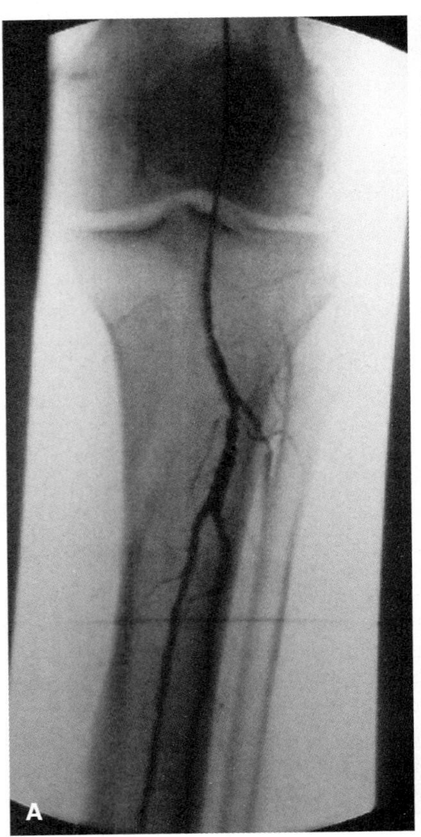

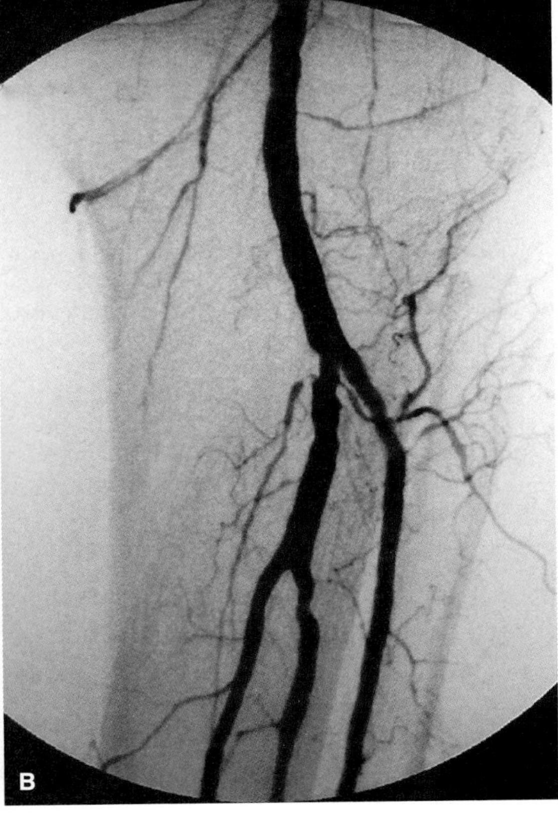

FIGURE 84-14 Forefoot lesion in a diabetic with poor flow to the anterior foot. **A,** Left leg arteriogram shows runoff to the ankle where the posterior tibial artery occludes and the peroneal artery is poorly collateralized to the forefoot. **B,** Kissing balloon angioplasty was performed between the tibioperoneal trunk and the anterior tibial artery, and a stent was placed in the proximal anterior tibial artery to restore perfusion to the forefoot.

Table 84-10 Complications of Percutaneous Transluminal Angioplasty for Lower Extremity Ischemia

	INCIDENCE (%)
Location	
Puncture site (total)	4
Bleeding	3.4
False aneurysm	0.5
Arteriovenous fistula	0.1
Angioplasty site (total)	3.5
Thrombosis	3.2
Rupture	0.3
Distal vessel (total)	2.7
Dissection	0.4
Embolization	2.3
Systemic (total)	0.4
Renal failure	0.2
Myocardial infarction (fatal)	0.2
Consequence	
Surgical repair	2
Limb loss	0.2
Mortality	0.2

Modified from Pentecost MJ, Criqui MH, Dorros G, et al: Guidelines for peripheral percutaneous transluminal angioplasty of the abdominal aorta and lower extremity vessels. Circulation 89:511-531, 1994.

restored to the foot, the results are significantly better.[167,172] Success is much higher when PTA is performed for a single stenosis than for occlusion or multiple stenoses.[154,157] Infrapopliteal PTA is applicable at present only to a few patients requiring limb salvage.[168-170]

Angioplasty of Lesions in Other Locations

Some lower extremity arteries have a less favorable outlook with PTA, such as the common femoral artery and the profunda femoris (deep femoral) artery. Balloon angioplasty can be performed in these vessels under special circumstances, but they are not a common part of endovascular practice.

Common Femoral Artery

Plaque in the common femoral artery is bulky and eccentric, often involves the femoral bifurcation, and is poorly suited to PTA. It is often associated with disease of the iliac or superficial femoral arteries. Because the common femoral artery is in an area of high mobility, it would not be expected to fare well after stent placement. Patency rates among 18 cases treated with PTA were 59% at 1 year and 37% at 3 years.[62] Surgical repair of this artery is simple, has relatively low morbidity and high patency, and can be simultaneously combined with any other endovascular procedure that is required either proximally or distally.[109]

Profunda Femoris Artery

Clinical situations in which a temporary improvement in profunda femoris artery perfusion would salvage a limb occur, but are uncommon. In addition, the disease in this artery is not generally favorable for PTA because it is usually either an orifice lesion, involving the femoral bifurcation, or diffuse disease along the length of the artery. Also, the profunda femoris artery tends to dissect in response to PTA. Older series suggest a reasonable technical success rate, but no long-term follow-up information is available.[171,172] As with the common femoral artery, if repair is required in the profunda femoris artery, surgery produces excellent results.

Table 84-11 Major Complication Rates for Endovascular Procedures

AORTOILIAC INTERVENTIONS	MAJOR COMPLICATIONS (%)	RANGE (%)
PTA of stenosis	3.6	2.3-6.3
PTA of occlusion	6.0	3.1-10.6
Stent placement	5.2	0-17.0

■ COMPLICATIONS

The complications of endovascular procedures are presented in detail in Chapter 54. The usual motivation for performing an endovascular procedure to treat lower extremity occlusive disease, even though the surgical alternative may offer a better chance of long-term success, is that the morbidity of an endovascular approach should be less. The expected rate of complications influences the decision about which procedure to advise.

The AHA Task Force on PTA Guidelines reviewed published complications among 3784 patients in 12 series of balloon angioplasty procedures in various lower extremity arteries (Table 84-10).[29] Complications of the puncture site, PTA site, or distal vessel occurred in approximately 10% of patients, and serious systemic complications or death occurred in 1%. Table 84-11 includes weighted averages for major complications that occurred in the performance of aortoiliac and femoropopliteal interventions in contemporary series.[50] A survey of large iliac stent series revealed a rate of major complications ranging from 4% to 11%, especially when iliac artery occlusion was treated.[3,9,32,98,118,119,121,122,173] Overall complication rates of 12% to 19% routinely have been reported after stent placement.[32,41,45,93,174] Unusual but devastating complications of stent placement have been reported, including stent infection, pseudoaneurysm, thromboembolization from stents, and retrograde aortic dissection.[175-188]

■ CONSEQUENCES OF FAILURE

Acute Failure of Endovascular Reconstruction (<30 Days)

The rate of acute failure of endovascular interventions for focal iliac and femoropopliteal lesions has decreased with improvements in equipment and technique. Acute failures still occur, however, because endovascular intervention is being attempted on an expanding array of morphologically unfavorable lesions.

In a series of 318 iliac artery and femoropopliteal artery PTA procedures, early technical failures occurred in 17%, and none of the affected patients was worse than before the procedure.[189] Technical failures are more common after PTA of occlusions than after PTA of stenoses.[27,28] After treating 83 iliac artery occlusions, Kalman and associates[25] reported 15 early failures; in only 1 (6.7%) case, however, did worse ischemia occur. There were 8 technical failures of PTA for iliac stenosis among 584 patients; 1 patient required emergency surgery for ischemia, 1 patient died of iliac artery rupture, and 1 patient experienced contrast extravasation. The remaining patients were treated electively. Stents avoid many acute failures that would have occurred because of these problems.[31,190,191] They also have encouraged attempts to treat lesions that should not have been approached with endovascular technique, however, and acute failures have resulted.

Later Failure of Endovascular Reconstruction (>30 Days)

Endovascular reconstructions of the iliac and femoropopliteal arteries that fail after 1 month usually do so as a result of recurrent stenosis. The affected patient most often presents with recurrent ischemic symptoms, usually claudication.

The implications of a failed angioplasty are usually less ominous than those of a failed graft, and recurrent stenosis at the dilatation site or new stenosis in the same arterial segment usually returns the patient to the predilatation clinical condition. In a study of 223 failures among 631 angioplasties, 85% of patients returned to their original level of symptoms, 5.5% remained better off than they were originally, and only 9.5% were clinically worse than before PTA.[192] Recurrent lesions usually can be redilated, and most investigators advise also placing stents.[40,96] Among patients undergoing subsequent reconstructive surgery, a failed PTA had little effect on the type and outcome of the operation.

Options for treating recurrent disease within a stent include a second dilatation, a second stent placement, atherectomy, and surgery.[75,192,193] The secondary procedures are usually performed electively because acute ischemia is rarely the first symptom of recurrence.

■ INCORPORATING ENDOVASCULAR TECHNIQUES INTO THE OPERATIVE ARMAMENTARIUM

Lower extremity revascularization provides a venue for the incorporation of endovascular techniques into the operating room environment.[55,113] Balloon angioplasty, stent placement, and thrombolytic therapy all have shown the reliability and durability required for their inclusion in the operative armamentarium. The simultaneous combination of endovascular intervention and open surgery is a reasonable option to achieve multilevel revascularization of a chronically ischemic limb. This combination approach requires imaging equipment, catheter inventory, and endovascular skills to be brought into the operating room. Facility with this approach also permits the operator to use these techniques (1) in conjunction with intraoperative arteriography, (2) in the treatment of failed dialysis access grafts or lower extremity bypass grafts, (3) for the management of acute limb ischemia, and (4) in stent-graft placement for aneurysm disease.

■ ROLE FOR ADJUNCTIVE DEVICES

Endovascular reconstruction of the aortoiliac and femoropopliteal segments using PTA and stents has a valuable role in clinical practice. New devices are introduced to extend the scope of endovascular intervention to the treatment of more extensive occlusive lesions in a wider array of locations. Any newly introduced endovascular device must surpass the results of PTA and stent placement in at least some aspect to be considered clinically useful.

The universal response to endovascular trauma is neointimal hyperplasia. This response has been largely responsible for restenosis rates of 50% at 1 year. The long-term outlook for any new endovascular device depends on control of neointimal hyperplasia.

Drug-Eluting Stents

Drugs that inhibit the cell cycle at various points have been bonded to stents in an effort to reduce the likelihood that intimal hyperplasia would occur in response to intervention.[152,153,194] Multiple stents with various therapeutic agents are in development. One drug-eluting stent, covered with sirolimus, has been approved for use in the coronary arteries. Preliminary data in the superficial femoral artery using a self-expanding nitinol stent covered with the same material show a significant decrease in intimal hyperplasia at 6 months.[152] If this becomes clinically useful, the potential impact on infrainguinal intervention is substantial.

Stent-Grafts and Covered Stents

Stents and vascular graft material may be combined to create an intraluminal bypass (see Chapter 52). Although this concept has been aggressively applied to the clinical problem of aneurysm disease in recent years, occlusive disease also is being evaluated as a potential application of this technique. If the entire luminal surface of a severely diseased vessel segment could be relined by a transluminally placed graft, the scope of occlusive disease that could be treated with endovascular intervention would be increased dramatically. Clinical evidence to support this promising concept is lacking. There have been experimental and clinical reports of periprosthetic thickening and thrombosis in response to covered stents.[195-197] Several small, cohort series of intraluminal iliofemoral bypasses have been published.[198-203] Early technical success generally exceeds 90%. Patency ranges from 80% to 89% at 6 to 18 months.[198,204] Results in the infrainguinal arteries also have been mixed: Patency rates have ranged from 23% to 78% at 12 months.[154,155,205,206]

Laser and Atherectomy Devices

Lasers and atherectomy devices have been used in the past with mixed results and at present play only a minor adjunctive role. Laser energy has been used to penetrate an occluded infrainguinal arterial segment and to produce a channel adequate for introducing a balloon catheter. None of the laser devices has improved on the results of PTA and stents, and lasers carry a significantly higher expense in terms of equipment costs in addition to their complication rate.[207-209] Several atherectomy devices have been released by the Food and Drug Administration for clinical use. None of these has a well-established role in patient care, however, because they have not conferred an advantage over PTA and stents.[210-212] It is possible that when new methods of inhibiting the arterial response to intervention are introduced, plaque removal techniques may again be considered among the treatment options.

Intravascular Ultrasound

Intravascular ultrasound (IVUS) offers adjunctive guidance of therapeutic endovascular procedures and provides information that is not often obtainable with periprocedural arteriography. IVUS permits endoluminal imaging, which provides a unique cross-sectional view of the treated segment. IVUS has a role in the deployment of endoluminal grafts for aneurysmal disease and complex stenting procedures.[213-216] Data suggest that the free lumen area, as measured by IVUS after PTA, may be a strong predictor of outcome.[217] The advantage of IVUS in the evaluation of stent placement appears to be enhanced with smaller stents (<5 mm), in which conventional arteriography is not as accurate.[218]

■ FUTURE OF ENDOVASCULAR INTERVENTION FOR CHRONIC LIMB ISCHEMIA

Endovascular intervention for chronic lower extremity ischemia has matured significantly in recent years. Catheter-based management of a wide variety of lesions has evolved from the stage of mere clinical feasibility to the level of reliability and durability required to become an integral tool in the treatment of occlusive disease. PTA and stents have an established and growing role in the management of lower extremity ischemia. Continued efforts to extend the scope of endovascular intervention will likely be successful in the future as they have been in the past. The future of endovascular intervention is likely to be shaped by two relatively unpredictable factors: (1) advances in technology and (2) the political and economic forces of medicine.

Advances in Endovascular Technology

The concept of endovascular intervention has been well supported by the continuous advance of technology. Miniaturization of guide wires, catheters, stents, and other devices should increase accessibility of some lesions and decrease overall complication rates. If covered stents can be made safe enough to place and durable enough to compete with other types of reconstructions, there may be a major role for this type of device. If restenosis could be controlled with drug-eluting stents, endovascular intervention would be extended to a wider variety of clinical scenarios. These are primarily questions of technology and are well on their way to being answered. It is highly likely that during the next few years endovascular techniques will be further refined and become more evenly used among the vascular patients who may benefit from them.

Opposing Forces in Endovascular Intervention

Opposing "market" forces will have a major influence on the future development of endovascular intervention. Pressure from patients to perform a less invasive procedure may favor more endovascular intervention. Interest in decreasing the overall care costs may stimulate the elimination of procedures for indications other than a threatened life or limb, favoring less endovascular intervention. "Opposing forces" are nowhere more apparent than among the different medical disciplines that have a strong interest in endovascular surgery. Some traditional open surgical procedures are being replaced by endovascular approaches. A wider variety of options will increase the spectrum of patients to whom some form of mechanical intervention may be offered. Although these are just a few of the many dynamic issues to consider, the one reliable constant is that the field of endovascular intervention will likely flourish if the best interests of the patient are kept in mind.

■ REFERENCES

1. Fowkes FG, Housley E, Cawood EH, et al: Edinburgh artery study: Prevalence of asymptomatic and symptomatic peripheral arterial disease in the general population. Int J Epidemiol 20:384-392, 1991.
2. Criqui MH: Peripheral arterial disease and subsequent cardiovascular mortality: A strong and consistent association. Circulation 82:2246-2247, 1990.
3. Vorwerk D, Guenther RW, Schurmann K, et al: Aortic and iliac stenoses: Follow-up results of stent placement after insufficient balloon angioplasty in 118 cases. Radiology 198:45-48, 1996.
4. Gunther RW, Vorwerk D, Antonucci F, et al: Iliac artery stenosis or obstruction after unsuccessful balloon angioplasty: Treatment with a self-expandable stent. AJR Am J Roentgenol 156:389-393, 1991.
5. Hallisey MJ, Parker CB, van Breda A: Current status and extended applications of intravascular stents. Curr Opin Radiol 4:7-12, 1992.
6. Becker GJ, Palmaz JC, Rees CR, et al: Angioplasty-induced dissections in human iliac arteries: Management with Palmaz balloon expandable intraluminal stents. Radiology 176:31-38, 1990.
7. Katzen BT, Becker GJ: Intravascular stents: Status and development of clinical applications. Surg Clin North Am 72:941-957, 1992.
8. Schneider PA: Stents: Endovascular repaving. In Schneider PA: Endovascular Skills. New York, Marcel Dekker, 2003, pp 237-270.
9. Sapoval MR, Chatellier G, Long AR, et al: Self-expandable stents for the treatment of iliac artery obstructive lesions: Long-term success and prognostic factors. AJR Am J Roentgenol 166:1173-1179, 1996.
10. Murphy TP, Webb MS, Lambiase RE, et al: Percutaneous revascularization of complex iliac artery stenoses and occlusions with use of Wallstents: Three year experience. J Vasc Interv Radiol 7:21-27, 1996.
11. Long AR, Gaux JC, Raynaud AC, et al: Infrarenal aortic stents: Initial clinical experience and angiographic follow-up. Cardiovasc Intervent Radiol 16:203-208, 1993.
12. Dietrich EB: Endovascular techniques for abdominal aortic occlusions. Int Angiol 12:270-280, 1993.
13. Martinez R, Rodriguez-Lopez J, Dietrich EB: Stenting of abdominal aortic occlusive disease: Long-term results. Tex Heart Inst J 24:15-22, 1997.

14. Blum U, Gabelmann A, Redecker M, et al: Percutaneous recanalization of iliac artery occlusions: Results of a prospective study. Radiology 189:536-540, 1993.
15. Moneta GL, Yeager RA, Antonovic R, et al: Accuracy of lower extremity arterial duplex mapping. J Vasc Surg 15:275-284, 1992.
16. Schneider PA, Ogawa DY, Rush MR: Lower extremity revascularization without contrast arteriography: Operation based upon duplex is feasible. Cardiovasc Surg 7:699-703, 1999.
17. Schneider PA, Ogawa DY: Is routine preoperative aortography necessary in the treatment of lower extremity ischemia? J Vasc Surg 28:28-36, 1998.
18. Edwards JM, Coldwell DM, Goldman ML, et al: The role of duplex scanning in the selection of patients for transluminal angioplasty. J Vasc Surg 13:69-74, 1991.
19. Elsman BHP, Legemate DA, van der Heyden FWHM, et al: The use of color-coded duplex scanning in the selection of patients with lower extremity arterial disease for percutaneous transluminal angioplasty: A prospective study. Cardiovasc Intervent Radiol 19:313-316, 1996.
20. Elsman BHP, Legemate DA, van der Heyden FWHM, et al: Impact of ultrasonographic duplex scanning on therapeutic decision making in lower limb arterial disease. Br J Surg 82:630-633, 1995.
21. Burnham SJ, Jaques P, Burnham CB: Noninvasive detection of iliac artery stenosis in the presence of superficial femoral artery obstruction. J Vasc Surg 16:445-452, 1992.
22. Waugh JR, Sacharias N: Arteriographic complications in the DSA era. Radiology 182:243-246, 1992.
23. Schneider PA: Strategic arteriography: Surgical approach and analysis of technique. Ann Vasc Surg 5:493-505, 1996.
24. Rholl KS: Percutaneous aortoiliac intervention in vascular disease. In Baum S, Pentecost MJ (eds): Abram's Angiography: Interventional Radiology. Boston, Little, Brown, 1997, pp 225-261.
25. Kalman PG, Sniderman KW, Johnston KW: Technique and six-year follow-up on percutaneous transluminal angioplasty to treat iliac arterial occlusive disease. In Yao JST, Pierce WH (eds): Long-Term Results in Vascular Surgery. Norwalk, Conn, Appleton & Lange, 1993, pp 201-212.
26. Jeans WD, Armstrong S, Cole SE, et al: Fate of patients undergoing transluminal angioplasty for lower limb ischemia. Radiology 177:559-564, 1990.
27. Johnston KW: Iliac arteries: Reanalysis of results of balloon angioplasty. Radiology 186:207-212, 1993.
28. Johnston KW: Femoral and popliteal arteries: Reanalysis of results of balloon angioplasty. Radiology 183:767-771, 1992.
29. Pentecost MJ, Criqui MH, Dorros G, et al: Guidelines for peripheral percutaneous transluminal angioplasty of the abdominal aorta and lower extremity vessels. Circulation 89:511-531, 1994.
30. Rutherford RB, Durham J: Percutaneous balloon angioplasty for arteriosclerosis obliterans: Long-term results. In Yao JST, Pearce WH (eds): Technologies in Vascular Surgery. Philadelphia, WB Saunders, 1992, pp 329-345.
31. Bosch JL, Hunink MGM: Meta-analysis of the results of percutaneous transluminal angioplasty and stent placement for aortoiliac occlusive disease. Radiology 204:87-96, 1997.
32. Vorwerk D, Guenther RW, Schurmann K, et al: Primary stent placement for chronic iliac artery occlusions: Follow-up results in 103 patients. Radiology 194:745-749, 1995.
33. Dyet JF, Gaines PA, Nicholson AA, et al: Treatment of chronic iliac artery occlusions by means of percutaneous endovascular stent placement. J Vasc Interv Radiol 8:349-353, 1997.
34. Vroegindeweij D, Vos LD, Tielbeek AV, et al: Balloon angioplasty combined with primary stenting versus balloon angioplasty alone in femoropopliteal obstructions: A comparative randomized study. Cardiovasc Intervent Radiol 20:420-425, 1997.
35. Reyes R, Maynar M, Lopera J, et al: Treatment of chronic iliac artery occlusions with guidewire recanalization and primary stent placement. J Vasc Interv Radiol 8:1049-1055, 1997.
36. Capek P, McLean GK, Berkowitz HD: Femoropopliteal angioplasty: Factors influencing long-term success. Circulation 83(Suppl I):I-70-I-80, 1991.
37. Stanley B, Teague B, Spero R, et al: Efficacy of balloon angioplasty of the superficial femoral artery and the popliteal artery in the relief of leg ischemia. J Vasc Surg 23:679-685, 1996.
38. Stokes KR, Strunk HM, Campbell DR, et al: Five-year results of iliac and femoropopliteal angioplasty in diabetic patients. Radiology 174:977, 1990.
39. Damaraju S, Cuasay L, Le D, et al: Predictors of primary patency failure in Wallstent self-expanding endovascular prostheses for iliofemoral occlusive disease. Tex Heart Inst J 24:173-178, 1997.
40. Henry M, Amor M, Ethevenot G, et al: Palmaz stent placement in the iliac and femoropopliteal arteries: Primary and secondary patency in 310 patients with 2- to 4-year follow-up. Radiology 197:167-174, 1995.
41. Laborde JC, Palmaz JC, Rivera FJ, et al: Influence of anatomic distribution of atherosclerosis on the outcome of revascularization with iliac stent placement. J Vasc Interv Radiol 6:513-521, 1995.
42. Johnston KW, Rae M, Hogg-Johnston SA, et al: Five year results of a prospective study of percutaneous transluminal angioplasty. Ann Surg 206:403, 1987.
43. Davies AH, Cole SE, Magee TR, et al: The effect of diabetes mellitus on the outcome of angioplasty for lower limb ischemia. Diabet Med 9:480-481, 1992.
44. Criqui MH, Langer RD, Fronek A, et al: Mortality over a ten year period in patients with peripheral arterial disease. N Engl J Med 325:556-562, 1992.
45. Sullivan TM, Childs MB, Bacharach JM, et al: Percutaneous transluminal angioplasty and primary stenting of the iliac arteries in 288 patients. J Vasc Surg 25:829-839, 1997.
46. Morin JF, Johnston KW, Wasserman L, et al: Factors that determine the long-term results of percutaneous transluminal dilatation for peripheral arterial occlusive disease. J Vasc Surg 4:68, 1986.
47. Treiman GS, Schneider PA, Lawrence PT, et al: Does stent placement improve the results of ineffective or complicated iliac artery angioplasty? J Vasc Surg 28:104-112, 1998.
48. Treiman GS, Ichikawa L, Treiman RL, et al: Treatment of recurrent femoral or popliteal artery stenosis after percutaneous transluminal angioplasty. J Vasc Surg 20:577-585, 1994.
49. Sniderman KW: Noncoronary vascular stenting. Prog Cardiovasc Dis 39:141-164, 1996.
50. TASC Working Group: Endovascular procedures for intermittent claudication. J Vasc Surg 31: S97-S113, 2000.
51. Martin EC: Femoropopliteal revascularization. In Baum S, Pentecos MJ (eds): Abram's Angiography: Interventional Radiology. Boston, Little, Brown, 1997, pp 262-283.
52. Schneider PA, Andros G, Harris RW: Percutaneous balloon angioplasty for lower extremity arterial occlusive disease. In Carter DC, Russell RCG (eds): Rob and Smith's Operative Surgery. London, Butterworth-Heinemann, 1994, pp 636-646.
53. Orron DE, Kim D: Percutaneous transluminal angioplasty. In Kim D, Orron DE (eds): Peripheral Vascular Imaging and Intervention. St. Louis, Mosby-Year Book, 1992, pp 379-420.
54. Dalsing MC, Harris VJ: Intravasculat stents. In White RA, Fogarty TJ (eds): Peripheral Endovascular Interventions. St. Louis, Mosby-Year Book, 1996, pp 315-339.
55. Schneider PA: Endovascular therapy. In Schneider PA: Endovascular Skills. New York, Marcel Dekker, 2003, pp 165-352.
56. Schneider PA, Nelken N, Caps MT: Angioplasty and stenting for infrainguinal lesions. In Pearce WH, Matsumura JS, Yao JST (eds): Trends in Vascular Surgery. Chicago, Precept Press, 2004, pp 291-305.
57. Rutherford RB, Baker JD, Ernst C, et al: Recommended standards for reports dealing with lower extremity ischemia: Revised version. J Vasc Surg 26:517-538, 1997.

58. Rutherford RB: Reporting standards for endovascular surgery: Should existing standards be modified for newer procedures? Semin Vasc Surg 10:197-205, 1997.
59. Spies JB, Bakal CW, Burke DR, et al: Guidelines for percutaneous transluminal angioplasty. Radiology 177:619-626, 1990.
60. Rutherford RB: Standards for evaluating results of interventional therapy for peripheral vascular disease. Circulation 83(Suppl I):I-6-I-11, 1991.
61. Ahn SS, Rutherford RB, Becker GJ, et al: Reporting standards for lower extremity arterial endovascular procedures. J Vasc Surg 17:1103-1107, 1993.
62. Myers KA: Reporting standards and statistics for evaluating intervention. Cardiovasc Surg 3:455-461, 1995.
63. Steinmetz OK, McPhail NV, Hajjar GE, et al: Endarterectomy versus angioplasty in the treatment of localized stenosis of the abdominal aorta. Can J Surg 37:385-390, 1994.
64. Ravimandalam K, Rao VR, Kumar S, et al: Obstruction of the infrarenal portion of the abdominal aorta: Results of treatment with balloon angioplasty. AJR Am J Roentgenol 156:1257-1260, 1991.
65. Tadavarthy AK, Sullivan WA, Nicoloff D, et al: Aorta balloon angioplasty: 9-year follow-up. Radiology 170:1039-1041, 1989.
66. Hedeman Joosten PPA, Ho GH, Breuking FA, et al: Percutaneous transluminal angioplasty of the infrarenal aorta: Initial outcome and long term clinical and angiographic results. Eur J Vasc Endovasc Surg 12:201-206, 1996.
67. el Ashmaoui A, Do DD, Triller J, et al: Angioplasty of the terminal aorta: Follow-up of twenty patients treated by PTA or PTA with stents. Eur J Radiol 13:113-117, 1991.
68. Hallisey MJ, Meranze SG, Parker BC, et al: Percutaneous transluminal angioplasty of the abdominal aorta. J Vasc Interv Radiol 5:679-687, 1994.
69. Kalman PG, Johnston KW, Sniderman KW: Indications and results of balloon angioplasty for arterial occlusive lesions. World J Surg 20:630-634, 1996.
70. Vorwerk D, Guenther RW, Bohndorf K, et al: Stent placement for failed angioplasty of aortic stenoses: Report of two cases. Cardiovasc Intervent Radiol 14:316-319, 1991.
71. Sheeran SR, Hallisey MJ, Ferguson D: Percutaneous transluminal stent placement in the abdominal aorta. J Vasc Interv Radiol 8:55-60, 1997.
72. Dietrich EB, Santiago O, Gustafson G, et al: Preliminary observations on the use of the Palmaz stent in the distal portion of the abdominal aorta. Am Heart J 125:490-501, 1993.
73. Matchett WJ, McFarland DR, Eidt JF, et al: Blue toe syndrome: Treatment with intra-arterial stents and review of therapies. J Vasc Interv Radiol 11:585-592, 2000.
74. Ramaiah V, Thompson C, Harvey A, et al: Stenting for proximal para-anastomotic stenosis of an infraaortic bypass graft. Tex Heart Inst J 29:45-47, 2002.
75. Deron A, Vermassen F, Ongena K: PTA and stenting after previous aortoiliac endarterectomy. Eur J Vasc Endovasc Surg 22:130-133, 2001.
76. Therasse E, Cote G, Oliva VL, et al: Infrarenal aortic stenosis: Value of stent placement after percutaneous transluminal angioplasty failure. Radiology 21:655-662, 2001.
77. d'Othee BJ, Haulon S, Mounier-Vehier C, et al: Percutaneous endovascular treatment for stenoses and occlusions of infrarenal aorta and aortoiliac bifurcation: Midterm results. Eur J Vasc Endovasc Surg 24:516-523, 2002.
78. Nyman U, Uher P, Lindh M, et al: Primary stenting in infrarenal aortic occlusive disease. Cardiovasc Intervent Radiol 23:97-108, 2000.
79. Sagic D, Grujicic S, Peric M, et al: "Kissing balloon" technique for abdominal aortic angioplasty: Initial results and long term outcome. Int Angiol 14:364-367, 1995.
80. Morag B, Garniek A, Bass A, et al: Percutaneous transluminal aortic angioplasty: Early and late results. Cardiovasc Intervent Radiol 16:37-42, 1993.
81. Yakes WF, Kumpe DA, Brown SB, et al: Percutaneous transluminal aortic angioplasty: Techniques and results. Radiology 172:965-970, 1989.
82. Insall RL, Loose HW, Chamberlain J: Long-term results of double-balloon percutaneous transluminal angioplasty of the aorta and iliac arteries. Eur J Vasc Surg 7:31-36, 1993.
83. Pilger E, Decrinis M, Stark G, et al: Thrombolytic treatment and balloon angioplasty in chronic occlusion of the aortic bifurcation. Ann Intern Med 120:40-44, 1994.
84. Kuffer G, Spengel F, Steckmeier B: Percutaneous reconstruction of the aortic bifurcation with Palmaz stents: Case reports. Cardiovasc Intervent Radiol 14:170-172, 1991.
85. Schneider PA: Endovascular or open surgery for aortoiliac occlusive disease? Cardiovasc Surg 10:378-382, 2002.
86. Mendelsohn FO, Santos RM, Crowley JJ, et al: Kissing stents in the aortic bifurcation. Am Heart J 136:600-605, 1998.
87. Rosset E, Malikov S, Magnan PE, et al: Endovascular treatment of occlusive lesions in the distal aorta: Mid-term results in a series of 31 consecutive patients. Ann Vasc Surg 15:140-147, 2001.
88. Haulon S, Mounier-Vehier C, Gaxotte V, et al: Percutaneus reconstruction of the aortoiliac bifurcation with the "kissing stents" technique: Long-term follow-up in 106 patients. J Vasc Endovasc Ther 9:363-368, 2002.
89. Mohamed F, Sarkar B, Timmons G, et al: Outcome of "kissing stents" for aortoiliac atherosclerotic disease, including the effect on the non-diseased contralateral iliac limb. Cardiovasc Intervent Radiol 25:472-475, 2002.
90. Jorgensen B, Skovgaard N, Norgard J, et al: Percutaneous transluminal angioplasty in 226 iliac artery stenoses: Role of the superficial femoral artery for clinical success. Vasa 21:382-386, 1993.
91. Rutherford RB, Patt A, Kumpe DA: The current role of percutaneous transluminal angioplasty. In Greenlagh KM (ed): Vascular Surgery: Issues in Current Practice. New York, Grune & Stratton, 1986, pp 229-244.
92. Schurmann K, Mahnken A, Meyer J, et al: Long-term results 10 years after iliac arterial stent placement. Radiology 224:731-738, 2002.
93. Palmaz JC, Garcia OJ, Schatz RA, et al: Placement of balloon-expandable intraluminal stents in iliac arteries: First 171 procedures. Radiology 174:969, 1990.
94. Bosch JL, van der Graaf Y, Hunink MG: Health-related quality of life after angioplasty and stent placement in patients with iliac artery occlusive disease: Results of a randomized controlled clinical trial. The Dutch Iliac Stents Trial Study Group. Circulation 22:3155-3160, 1999.
95. Tetteroo E, van der Graaf Y, Bosch JL, et al: Randomised comparison of primary stent placement versus primary angioplasty followed by selective stent placement in patients with iliac artery occlusive disease. Dutch Iliac Stent Trial Study Group. Lancet 18:1153-1159, 1998.
96. Cikrit DF, Gustafson PA, Dalsing MC, et al: Long-term follow-up of the Palmaz stent for iliac occlusive disease. Surgery 118:608-613, 1995.
97. Palmaz JC, Laborde JC, Rivera FJ, et al: Stenting of the iliac arteries with the Palmaz stent: Experience from a multicenter trial. Cardiovasc Intervent Radiol 15:291-297, 1992.
98. Murphy KD, Encarnacion CE, Le VA, et al: Iliac artery stent placement with the Palmaz stent: Follow-up study. J Vasc Interv Radiol 6:321-329, 1995.
99. Tetteroo E, Haaring C, van der Graaf Y, et al: Intra-arterial pressure gradients after randomized angioplasty or stenting of iliac artery lesions. Cardiovasc Intervent Radiol 19:411-417, 1996.
100. Tetteroo E, Haaring C, van Engelen AD, et al: Therapeutic consequences of variation in intraarterial pressure measurements after iliac angioplasty. Cardiovasc Intervent Radiol 20:426-430, 1997.
101. Timaran CH, Stevens SL, Freeman MB, et al: Predictors for adverse outcome after iliac angioplasty and stenting for limb-threatening ischemia. J Vasc Surg 36:507-513, 2002.

102. Powell RJ, Fillinger M, Bettman M, et al: The durability of endovascular treatment of multisegment iliac occlusive disease. J Vasc Surg 31:1178-1184, 2000.
103. Timaran CH, Prault TL, Stevens SL, et al: Iliac artery stenting versus surgical reconstruction for TASC type B and type C iliac lesions. J Vasc Surg 38:272-278, 2003.
104. Timaran CH, Stevens SL, Freeman MB, et al: External iliac and common iliac artery angioplasty and stenting in men and women. J Vasc Surg 34:440-446, 2001.
105. Uher P, Nyman U, Forssell C, et al: Percutaneous placement of stents in chronic iliac and aortic occlusive disease. Eur J Vasc Endovasc Surg 18:114-121, 1999.
106. Nawaz S, Cleveland T, Gaines P, et al: Aortoiliac stenting: Determinants of clinical outcome. Eur J Vasc Endovasc Surg 17:351-359, 1999.
107. Lee ES, Steenson CC, Trimble KE, et al: Comparing patency rates between external iliac and common iliac artery stents. J Vasc Surg 33:889-894, 2000.
108. Brewster DC, Cambria RP, Darling RC, et al: Long-term results of combined iliac balloon angioplasty and distal surgical revascularization. Ann Surg 210:324, 1989.
109. Schneider PA, Abcarian PW, Ogawa DY, et al: Should balloon angioplasty and stents have a role in operative intervention for lower extremity ischemia? Ann Vasc Surg 11:574-580, 1997.
110. Alimi Y, Di Mauro P, Barthelemy P, et al: Iliac transluminal angioplasty and distal surgical revascularization can be performed in a one-step technique. Int Angiol 16:83-87, 1997.
111. Walker PJ, Harris JP, May J: Combined percutaneous transluminal angioplasty and extraanatomic bypass for symptomatic unilateral iliac artery occlusion with contralateral iliac artery stenosis. Ann Vasc Surg 5:209-216, 1991.
112. Wilson SE, White GH, Wolf G, et al: Proximal percutaneous balloon angioplasty and distal bypass for multilevel arterial occlusion: Veterans Administration Cooperative Study No. 199. Ann Vasc Surg 4:351-355, 1990.
113. Schneider PA: Balloon angioplasty and stent placement during operative vascular reconstruction for lower extremity ischemia. Ann Vasc Surg 10:589-598, 1996.
114. AbuRahma AF, Robinson PA, Cook CC, et al: Selecting patients for combined femorofemoral bypass grafting and iliac balloon angioplasty and stenting for bilateral iliac disease. J Vasc Surg 33(2 Suppl):S93-S99, 2001.
115. Nelson PR, Powell RJ, Schermerhorn ML, et al: Early results of external iliac artery stenting combined with common femoral endarterectomy. J Vasc Surg 35:1107-1113, 2002.
116. Schneider PA: Iliac angioplasty and stenting in association with infrainguinal bypasses: Timing and techniques. Semin Vasc Surg 16:291-299, 2003.
117. Hsiang YN, al-Salman M, Doyle DL, et al: Comparison of percutaneous with intraoperative balloon angioplasty for arteriosclerotic occlusive disease. Aust N Z J Surg 63:864-869, 1993.
118. Scheinert D, Schroeder M, Ludwig J, et al: Stent-supported recanalization of chronic iliac artery occlusions. Am J Med 15:708-715, 2001.
119. Henry M, Amor M, Ethevenot G, et al: Percutaneous endoluminal treatment of iliac occlusions: Long-term follow-up in 105 patients. J Endovasc Surg 5:228-235, 1998.
120. Leu AJ, Schneider E, Canova CR, et al: Long-term results after recanalization of chronic iliac artery occlusions by combined catheter therapy without stent placement. Eur J Vasc Endovasc Surg 18:499-505, 1999.
121. Uher P, Nyman U, Lindh M, et al: Long-term results of stenting for chronic iliac artery occlusion. J Endovasc Ther 9:75-79, 2002.
122. Funovics MA, Lackner B, Cejna M, et al: Predictors of long-term results after treatment of iliac artery obliteration by transluminal angioplasty and stent placement. Cardiovasc Intervent Radiol 25:397-402, 2002.
123. Motarjeme A, Gordon GI, Bodenhagen K: Thrombolysis and angioplasty of chronic iliac artery occlusions. J Vasc Interv Radiol 6(Suppl):66S-72S, 1995.
124. Meyerovitz MF, Didier D, Vogel JJ, et al: Thrombolytic therapy compared with mechanical recanalization in non-acute peripheral arterial occlusions: A randomized trial. J Vasc Interv Radiol 6:775-781, 1995.
125. Gupta AK, Ravimandalam K, Rao VRK, et al: Total occlusion of the iliac arteries: Results of balloon angioplasty. Cardiovasc Intervent Radiol 16:165-177, 1993.
126. Smith GD, Shiply MJ, Rose G: Intermittent claudication, heart disease risk factors and mortality: The Whitehall Study. Circulation 82:1925-1931, 1990.
127. Criqui MH, Langer RD, Fronel A, et al: Mortality over a period of ten years in patients with peripheral arterial disease. N Engl J Med 326:381-386, 1992.
128. Vogt MT, Cauley JA, Newman AB, et al: Decreased ankle/arm blood pressure index and mortality in elderly women. JAMA 270:487-489, 1993.
129. Matsi PJ, Manninen HI, Vanninen RL, et al: Femoropopliteal angioplasty in patients with claudication: Primary and secondary patency in 140 limbs with 1-3 year follow-up. Radiology 191:727-733, 1994.
130. Hunink MG, Donaldson MC, Meyerowitz MF, et al: Risks and benefits of femoropopliteal percutaneous balloon angioplasty. J Vasc Surg 17:183-192, 1993.
131. Muradin GS, Bosch JL, Stijnec T, et al: Balloon dilatation and stent implantation for treatment of femoropopliteal arterial disease: Meta-analysis. Radiology 221:137-145, 2001.
132. Krepel VM, van Andel GJ, van Erp WFM, et al: Percutaneous transluminal angioplasty of the femoropopliteal artery: Initial and long-term results. Radiology 156:325, 1985.
133. Jorgensen B, Tonnesen KH, Holstein P: Late hemodynamic failure following percutaneous transluminal angioplasty for long and multifocal femoropopliteal stenoses. Cardiovasc Intervent Radiol 14:290-292, 1991.
134. Currie IC, Wakeley CJ, Cole SE, et al: Femoropopliteal angioplasty for severe limb ischemia. Br J Surg 81:191-193, 1994.
135. Matas Docampo M, Gomez Palones F, Fernandez Valenzuela V, et al: Intraarterial urokinase for acute native arterial occlusion of the limbs. Ann Vasc Surg 11:565-572, 1997.
136. Bhatnagar PK, Ierardi RP, Ikeda I, et al: The impact of thrombolytic therapy on arterial and graft occlusions. J Cardiovasc Surg 37:105-112, 1996.
137. Chalmer RT, Hoballah JJ, Kresowick TF, et al: Late results of a prospective study of direct intra-arterial urokinase infusion for peripheral arterial and bypass graft occlusions. Cardiovasc Surg 3:293-297, 1995.
138. Ray SA, Minty I, Buckenham TM, et al: Clinical outcome and restenosis following percutaneous transluminal angioplasty for ischemic rest pain or ulceration. Br J Surg 82:1217-1221, 1995.
139. Rush DS, Gewertz BL, Lu CT, et al: Limb salvage in poor risk patients using transluminal angioplasty. Arch Surg 118:1209, 1983.
140. Do-dai-Do, Triller J, Walpoth BH, et al: A comparison study of self-expandable stents versus balloon angioplasty alone in femoropopliteal artery occlusions. Cardiovasc Intervent Radiol 15:306-312, 1992.
141. Rousseau HP, Raillat CR, Joffre FG, et al: Treatment of femoropopliteal stenoses by means of self-expandable endoprostheses: Midterm results. Radiology 172:961-964, 1989.
142. Sapoval MR, Long AL, Raynaud AC, et al: Femoropopliteal stent placement: Long term results. Radiology 184:833-839, 1992.
143. White GH, Liew SCC, Waugh RC, et al: Early outcome and intermediate follow-up of vascular stents in the femoral and popliteal arteries without long-term anticoagulation. J Vasc Surg 21:270-281, 1995.
144. Bergeron P, Pinot JJ, Poyen V, et al: Long-term results with the Palmaz stent in the superficial femoral artery. J Endovasc Surg 2:161-167, 1995.

145. Grimm J, Muller-Hulsbeck S, Jahnke T, et al: Randomized study to compare PTA alone versus PTA with Palmaz stent placement for femoropopliteal lesions. J Vasc Interv Radiol 12:935-942, 2001.
146. Cejna M, Thurnher S, Illiasch H, et al: PTA versus Palmaz stent in femoropopliteal artery obstructions: A multicenter prospective randomized study. J Vasc Interv Radiol 12:23-31, 2001.
147. Becquemin JP, Favre JP, Marzelle J, et al: Systematic versus selective stent placement after superficial femoral artery balloon angioplasty: A multicenter prospective randomized study. J Vasc Surg 37:487-494, 2003.
148. Chatelard P, Guibourt C: Long-term results with a Palmaz stent in the femoropopliteal arteries. J Cardiovasc Surg 37(Suppl 1):67-72, 1996.
149. Conroy RM, Gordon IL, Tobis JM, et al: Angioplasty and stent placement in chronic occlusion of the superficial femoral artery: Technique and results. J Vasc Interv Radiol 11:1009-1020, 2000.
150. Lugmayr HF, Holzer H, Kastner M, et al: Treatment of complex arteriosclerotic lesions with nitinol stents in the superficial femoral and popliteal arteries: A mid-term follow-up. Radiology 222:37-43, 2002.
151. Cho L, Roffi M, Mukherjee D, et al: Superficial femoral artery occlusion: Nitinol stents achieve better flow and reduce the need for medications than balloon angioplasty alone. J Invasive Cardiol 15:198-200, 2003.
152. Duda SH, Pusich B, Richter G, et al: Sirolimus-eluting stents for the treatment of obstructive superficial femoral artery disease: Six-month results. Circulation 17:1505-1509, 2002.
153. Morice MC, Serruys PW, Sousa JE, et al: A randomized comparison of a sirolimus-eluting stent with a standard stent for coronary revascularization. N Engl J Med 6:1773-1780, 2002.
154. Saxon RR, Coffman JM, Gooding JM, et al: Long-term results of ePTFE stent-graft versus angioplasty in the femoropopliteal artery: Single center experience from a prospective randomized trial. J Vasc Interv Radiol 14:303-311, 2003.
155. Jahnke T, Andresen R, Muller-Hulsbeck S, et al: Hemobahn stent-grafts for the treatment of femoropopliteal arterial obstructions: Midterm results of a prospective trial. J Vasc Interv Radiol 14:41-51, 2003.
156. Schwarten DE: Clinical and anatomical considerations for nonoperative therapy in tibial disease and the results of angioplasty. Circulation 83(Suppl I):86, 1991.
157. Saab MH, Smith DC, Aka PK, et al: Percutaneous transluminal angioplasty of the tibial arteries for limb salvage. Cardiovasc Intervent Radiol 15:211-216, 1992.
158. Buckenham TM, Loh A, Dormandy JA, et al: Infrapopliteal angioplasty for limb salvage. Eur J Vasc Surg 7:21-25, 1993.
159. Hanna GP, Fujise K, Kjellgren O, et al: Infrapopliteal transcatheter interventions for limb salvage in diabetic patients: Importance of aggressive interventional approach and role of transcutaneous oximetry. J Am Coll Cardiol 30:664-669, 1997.
160. Durham JR, Horowitz JD, Wright JG, et al: Percutaneous transluminal angioplasty of the tibial arteries for limb salvage in the high-risk diabetic patient. Ann Vasc Surg 8:48-53, 1994.
161. Varty K, Bolia A, Naylor AR, et al: Infrapopliteal percutaneous transluminal angioplasty: A safe and successful procedure. Eur J Vasc Endovasc Surg 9:341-345, 1995.
162. Nydahl S, Hartshorne T, Bell PR, et al: Subintimal angioplasty of infrapopliteal occlusions in critically ischemic limbs. Eur J Vasc Endovasc Surg 14:212-216, 1997.
163. Treiman GS, Treiman RL, Ichikawa L, et al: Should percutaneous transluminal angioplasty be recommended for treatment of infrageniculate popliteal artery or tibioperoneal trunk stenosis? J Vasc Surg 22:457-463, 1995.
164. Lofberg AM, Lorelius LE, Karacagil S, et al: The use of below-knee percutaneous transluminal angioplasty in arterial occlusive disease causing chronic critical limb ischemia. Cardiovasc Intervent Radiol 19:317-322, 1996.
165. Favre JP, Do Carmo G, Adham M, et al: Results of transluminal angioplasty of infra-popliteal arteries. J Cardiovasc Surg 37(Suppl 1): 33-37, 1996.
166. Horvath W, Oertl M, Haidinger D: Percutaneous transluminal angioplasty of crural arteries. Radiology 177:565-569, 1990.
167. Brown KT, Moore ED, Getrajdman GI, et al: Infrapopliteal angioplasty: Long-term follow-up. J Vasc Interv Radiol 4:139-144, 1993.
168. Kandarpa K, Becker GJ, Hunink MG, et al: Transcatheter interventions for the treatment of peripheral atherosclerotic lesions: Part 1. J Vasc Interv Radiol 12:683-695, 2001.
169. Schneider PA, Caps MT, Ogawa DY, Hayman ES: Intraoperative superficial femoral artery balloon angioplasty and popliteal to distal bypass: An option for combined open and endovascular treatment of diabetic gangrene. J Vasc Surg 33:955-962, 2001.
170. Jagust MB, Sos TA: Infrapopliteal revascularization. In Baum S, Pentecost MJ (eds): Abram's Angiography: Interventional Radiology. Boston, Little, Brown, 1997, pp 284-293.
171. Motarjeme A, Keifer JW, Zuska AJ: Percutaneous transluminal angioplasty of the deep femoral artery. Radiology 135:613, 1980.
172. Waltman AC: Percutaneous transluminal angioplasty: Iliac and deep femoral arteries. AJR Am J Roentgenol 135:921, 1980.
173. Steinkamp H, Werk M, Wissgott C, et al: Stent placement in short unilateral iliac occlusion: Technique and 24-month results. Acta Radiol 42:508-514, 2001.
174. Ballard JL Sparks SR, Taylor FC, et al: Complications of iliac artery stent deployment. J Vasc Surg 24:545-553, 1996.
175. Bunt TJ, Gill HK, Smith DC, et al: Infection of a chronically implanted iliac artery stent. Ann Vasc Surg 11:529-532, 1997.
176. Ray CE, Kaufman JA, Waltman AC, et al: Inadvertent compression of intraarterial Palmaz stents during vascular surgery. AJR Am J Roentgenol 166:996-997, 1996.
177. Cisek PL, McKittrick JE: Retrograde aortic dissection after bilateral iliac artery stenting: A case report. Ann Vasc Surg 9:280-284, 1995.
178. Weinberg DJ, Cronin DW, Baker AG: Infected iliac pseudoaneurysm after uncomplicated percutaneous balloon angioplasty and (Palmaz) stent insertion: A case report and literature review. J Vasc Surg 23:162-166, 1996.
179. Vorwerk D, Gunther RW, Keulers P, et al: Surgical and percutaneous management of contralateral thrombus dislodgement following stent placement and dilatation of iliac artery occlusions: Technical note. Cardiovasc Intervent Radiol 14:134-136, 1991.
180. Chalmers N, Eadington DW, Gandanhamo D, et al: Case report: Infected false aneurysm at the site of an iliac stent. Br J Radiol 66:946-948, 1993.
181. Therasse E, Soulez G, Cartier P, et al: Infection with fatal outcome after endovascular metallic stent placement. Radiology 192:363-365, 1994.
182. Hoffman AI, Murphy TP: Septic arteritis causing iliac artery rupture and aneurysmal transformation of the distal aorta after iliac artery stent placement. J Vasc Interv Radiol 8:215-219, 1997.
183. Cutry AF, Whitley D, Patterson RB: Midaortic pseudoaneurysm complicating extensive endovascular stenting of aortic disease. J Vasc Surg 26:958-962, 1997.
184. Liu P, Dravid P, Freiman D, et al: Persistent iliac endarteritis with pseudoaneurysm formation following balloon-expandable stent placement. Cardiovasc Intervent Radiol 18:39-42, 1995.
185. van Lankeren W, Gussenhoven EJ, van Kints MJ, et al: Stent remodeling contributes to femoropopliteal artery restenosis: An intravascular ultrasound study. J Vasc Surg 25:753-756, 1997.
186. Deiparine MK, Ballard JL, Taylor FC, et al: Endovascular stent infection. J Vasc Surg 23:529-533, 1996.
187. Stoeckelhuber BM, Szeimies U, Spengel FA, et al: Late thromboembolic complication from a Palmaz stent in the common iliac artery. Cardiovasc Intervent Radiol 19:190-192, 1996.
188. Sacks BA, Miller A, Gottlieb M: Fracture of an iliac artery Palmaz stent. J Vasc Interv Radiol 7:53-55, 1996.

189. Armstrong MWJ, Torrie EPH, Galland RB: Consequences of immediate failure of percutaneous transluminal angioplasty. Ann R Coll Surg Engl 74:265-268, 1992.
190. Becker GJ: Intravascular stents: General principles and status of lower extremity arterial applications. Circulation 83(Suppl I):I-122-I-136, 1991.
191. Sapoval MR, Long AL, Pagny JY, et al: Outcome of percutaneous intervention in iliac artery stents. Radiology 198:481-486, 1996.
192. Kalman PG, Johnston KW: Outcome of a failed percutaneous transluminal dilatation. Surg Gynecol Obstet 161:43, 1985.
193. Schneider PA, Andros G, Harris RW: Balloon angioplasty and stents in the management of failed arterial reconstructions. Semin Vasc Surg 3:178-182, 1994.
194. Park SJ, Shim WH, Ho DS, et al: A paclitaxel-eluting stent for the prevention of coronary restenosis. N Engl J Med 348:1537-1545, 2003.
195. Sapoval MR, Gaux JC, Long AL, et al: Transient periprosthetic thickening after covered-stent implantation in the iliac artery. AJR Am J Roentgenol 164:1271-1273, 1995.
196. Tepe G, Duda SH, Hanke H, et al: Covered stents for prevention of restenosis: Experimental and clinical results with different stent designs. Invest Radiol 31:223-229, 1996.
197. Link J, Muller-Hulsbeck S, Brossman J, et al: Perivascular inflammatory reaction after percutaneous placement of covered stents. Cardiovasc Intervent Radiol 19:345-347, 1996.
198. Nevelsteen A, Lacroix H, Stockx L, et al: Stent grafts for iliofemoral occlusive disease. Cardiovasc Surg 5:393-397, 1997.
199. Lacroix H, Stockx L, Wilms G, et al: Transfemoral treatment for iliac occlusive disease with endoluminal stent-grafts. Eur J Vasc Endovasc Surg 14:204-207, 1997.
200. Henry M, Amor M, Ethevenot G, et al: Initial experience with the Cragg Endopro System 1 for intraluminal treatment of peripheral vascular disease. J Endovasc Surg 1:31-43, 1994.
201. Cynamon J, Marin ML, Veith FJ, et al: Stent-graft repair of aorto-iliac occlusive disease coexisting with common femoral artery disease. J Vasc Interv Radiol 8:19-26, 1997.
202. Ohki T, Marin ML, Veith FJ, et al: Endovascular aortounifemoral grafts and femorofemoral bypass for bilateral limb-threatening ischemia. J Vasc Surg 24:984-996, 1996.
203. Spoelstra H, Casselman F, Lesceu O: Balloon-expandable endobypass for femoropopliteal atherosclerotic occlusive disease: A preliminary evaluation of fifty-five patients. J Vasc Surg 24:647-654, 1996.
204. Dietrich EB, Papazoglou K: Endoluminal grafting for aneurysmal and occlusive disease in the superficial femoral artery: Early experience. J Endovasc Surg 2:225-239, 1995.
205. Ahmadi R, Schillinger M, Maca T, et al: Femoropopliteal arteries: Immediate and long-term results with a Dacron-covered stent-graft. Radiology 223:345-350, 2002.
206. Deutschmann HA, Schedlbauer P, Berczi V, et al: Placement of Hemobahn stent-grafts in the femoropopliteal arteries: Early and midterm results in 18 patients. J Vasc Interv Radiol 12:943-950, 2001.
207. Rosenthal D, Wheeler WG, Seagraves A, et al: Nd:YAG iliac and femoropopliteal laser angioplasty: Results with large probes as "sole therapy." J Cardiovasc Surg 32:186, 1991.
208. Geschwind HJ, Dubois-Rande J, Shafton E, et al: Percutaneous pulsed laser-assisted balloon angioplasty guided by spectroscopy. Am Heart J 117:1147, 1989.
209. Leon MB, Almagor Y, Bartorelli AL, et al: Fluorescence-guided laser-assisted balloon angioplasty in patients with femoropopliteal occlusions. Circulation 81:143, 1990.
210. Polnitz A, Nerlich A, Berger H, et al: Percutaneous peripheral atherectomy. J Am Coll Cardiol 15:682, 1990.
211. Dorros G, Iyer S, Lewin R, et al: Angiographic follow-up and clinical outcome of 126 patients after percutaneous directional atherectomy (Simpson AtheroCath) for occlusive peripheral vascular disease. Cathet Cardiovasc Diagn 22:79, 1991.
212. Wholey MH, Jarmolowski CR: New reperfusion devices: The Kensey catheter, the atherolytic reperfusion wire device, and the transluminal extraction catheter. Radiology 172:947, 1989.
213. Tabbara MR, White RA, Cavaye DM, et al: In-vivo human comparison of intravascular ultrasound and angiography. J Vasc Surg 14:496-504, 1991.
214. Scoccianti M, Verbin CS, Kopchok GE, et al: Intravascular ultrasound guidance for peripheral vascular interventions. J Endovasc Surg 1:71-80, 1994.
215. Losordo DW, Rosenfield K, Piezcek A, et al: How does angioplasty work? Serial analysis of human iliac arteries using intravascular ultrasound. Circulation 86:1845-1858, 1992.
216. White RA, Verbin C, Kopchok G, et al: Role of cinefluoroscopy and intravascular ultrasound in evaluating the deployment of experimental endovascular prostheses. J Vasc Surg 21:365-371, 1995.
217. van Lankeren W, Gussenhoven EJ, van der Lugt A, et al: Intravascular sonographic evaluation of iliac artery angioplasty: What is the mechanism of angioplasty and can intravascular sonography predict clinical outcome? AJR Am J Roentgenol 166:1355-1360, 1996.
218. Bolz KD, Hatlinghus R, Wiseth R, et al: Angiographic and intravascular ultrasonographic findings after endovascular stent implantation. Acta Radiol 35:590-596, 1994.

Chapter 85

Lumbar Sympathectomy: Indications and Technique

ALI F. ABURAHMA, MD
ROBERT B. RUTHERFORD, MD

The concept of sympathetic denervation as a mode of therapy for arterial occlusive disease[20] was first elaborated and tested by Jaboulay[39] and Leriche.[47] In 1889, Jaboulay[39] performed a periarterial sympathectomy on a femoral artery. In 1921, Leriche[47] popularized the procedure for the management of vascular diseases of the lower extremities. The experience with periarterial sympathectomy was disappointing because of reinnervation and vasospasm recurring within weeks of operation. In 1924, Royle[66] suggested that sympathetic ganglionectomy might improve the function of spastic extremities, and he observed that after lumbar sympathectomy, the skin and toes of the ipsilateral foot became warm and dry. Adson and Brown[3] first introduced sympathectomy for the management of vasospasm in North America in 1925. These reports marked the beginning of an era in which sympathetic denervation ultimately became widely used for occlusive arterial disease, often as the only surgical alternative to amputation.

During the next 30 years, variable results were reported, but the use of the procedure was not seriously challenged because alternative methods of improving limb perfusion were unavailable. With the development of arterial reconstructive techniques, direct vascularization supplanted sympathectomy as optimal surgical therapy by the 1960s. A growing body of experimental data supported the clinical impression that the beneficial effects of sympathectomy were short-lived and only palliative.

Currently, noninvasive vascular testing, performed before and after sympathetic blockade, increasingly is being used preoperatively to provide objective evidence for a potential benefit of sympathectomy, rather than being applied empirically in the hope that it might help. Current indications for sympathectomy generally are limited to patients with causalgia, patients with hyperhidrosis, and a few carefully selected patients with vasospastic or distal arterial occlusive disease not amenable to direct surgical or drug therapy.

■ ANATOMIC CONSIDERATIONS

Proper performance of lumbar sympathectomy requires appreciation of the anatomic characteristics of the lumbar sympathetic chain. The sympathetic nervous system consists of afferent and efferent fibers that form a reflex arc. Afferent fibers originate in blood vessels and other structures in the skin, muscles, and viscera and travel with the somatic nerves to cell bodies in the dorsal root ganglion of the spinal nerve. The central axons of these nerves synapse with the cell bodies of the efferent fibers located in the anteromediolateral column of the spinal cord. These efferent fibers are myelinated and travel in the white rami communicantes as preganglionic fibers to ganglia in the sympathetic chain, to ganglia in the preaortic region (celiac, renal, superior, and inferior mesenteric ganglia), and to terminal ganglia near the urinary bladder and the rectum. After synapsing in these ganglia, the postganglionic fibers, which are unmyelinated, travel in gray rami communicantes to join the somatic nerves and from there to innervate blood vessels (vasomotor), sweat glands, and erector pili muscles (pilomotor) of the skin; blood vessels of the skeletal muscles; and blood vessels and smooth muscle of the visceral organs.

At segmental levels, efferent fibers from preganglionic neurons synapse with postganglionic neurons in paravertebral ganglia via white rami communicantes. A small percentage of preganglionic efferent fibers either bypass the paravertebral ganglia to synapse in more peripherally located intermediate ganglia or cross over to innervate contralateral regions via conventional pathways. Characteristically, preganglionic fibers that supply a specific somatic region either synapse with multiple postganglionic fibers in paravertebral ganglia or proceed more peripherally to synapse in intermediate ganglia that are at a distance from their segmental source. Complete sympathetic denervation of an extremity requires division of preganglionic fibers along their segmental origin and resection of their corresponding relay ganglia and intercommunicating fibers.

Sympathetic outflow to the lower extremities originates in spinal cord segments from T10 to L3. Preganglionic fibers from these segments form extensive synaptic connections in paravertebral ganglia from L1 to S3 for innervation of the entire lower extremity and pelvic region. Sympathetic innervation of the foot and lower leg is conveyed primarily through the L2 and L3 ganglia; the proximal leg region is primarily innervated from the L1 to the L4 ganglia. Variations in the number and location of sympathetic ganglia are most common in the lumbar region, with most occurring at the L1, L4, and L5 levels.

Overall, three lumbar ganglia most commonly are found, with the fusion of the L1 and L2 ganglia most commonly accounting for the reduced number.[91] Crossover fibers occur in 15% of patients, with most leaving via the fourth and fifth lumbar ganglia.[86] For most clinical indications, L2 and L3 ganglionectomy is sufficient, but also removing L4 is advised to reduce the possibility of collateral reinnervation. Imparato[38] advocated removal of all encountered lumbar ganglia to ensure that complete lower extremity sympathectomy is accomplished. Such extensive ganglionectomy usually is not warranted, however, and may result in ejaculatory disturbances in preclimacteric men when bilateral high ganglionectomies (i.e., including L1) are performed. Impotence also is claimed to occur under these circumstances but has no known physiologic basis at this level. Impotence is more likely to be produced by extensive dissection of the distal aorta, particularly around the origin of the left common iliac artery. Nerve fibers serving ejaculation stem mainly from L1 and occasionally from L2. This disturbance of ejaculation may occur after resection of L2 when it is fused with L1.

Anatomic completeness of sympathectomy is essential. Although in humans there may be some sudomotor preganglionic outflow to the lower lumbar chain, few data are available to confirm the existence of preganglionic vasomotor outflow below the level of the third lumbar ganglion. Denervation may be incomplete if only one lumbar ganglion is resected. To ensure denervation of the leg below the knee, removal of the second and third ganglia, their accompanying rami, and their lateral connections is usually satisfactory. Regeneration of sympathetic fibers may occur if only a short segment of the trunk is resected; it occurs after simple resection of the nerves.

Simeone[75] described in detail the causes of failure after sympathectomy. The most common causes of early failure are poor patient selection and incomplete denervation. Late failures are often related to progression of the original arterial disease. In some cases, failure is due to sprouting and regeneration of sympathetic nerves, which usually occurs within 2 to 5 years after operation.

■ PHYSIOLOGIC CONSIDERATIONS

Critical understanding of the effects of lumbar sympathectomy requires synthesis of clinical and experimental data. Although sympathetic denervation increases blood flow to a normal limb, its impact on an extremity affected by arterial occlusive disease is less clear. Elucidation of its role in improving microcirculatory hemodynamics and relieving ischemic symptoms can be considered in regard to several aspects, as follows:

1. Magnitude, distribution, and duration of the blood flow increase
2. Effect of the procedure on collateral perfusion in acute and chronic ischemia
3. Nutritive value of the observed flow increases
4. Alteration of pain impulse transmission

The effect of sympathectomy on each of these factors is examined within the context of more recent studies that attempt to define better the potential benefit of sympathectomy in limb ischemia.

Increase in Blood Flow

Lumbar sympathectomy increases total blood flow to an extremity by abolishing basal and reflex constriction of arterioles and precapillary sphincters. Flow increases ranging from 10% to 200% have been observed and vary with the degree of arterial occlusive disease involving the limb.[4,16,52,82] Patients with severe, multilevel occlusions may receive no benefit from sympathectomy because their muscular and cutaneous arteries already are maximally dilated at rest. In normal and diseased limbs, most of the observed flow increase is shunted through cutaneous arteriovenous anastomoses with only small increases in tissue perfusion.[18] This alteration in blood flow distribution is due to elimination of the primary sympathetic function of modulating the musculocutaneous distribution in response to thermoregulatory requirements. After sympathectomy, the positive distributional effects are maximal for the distal cutaneous circulation and characteristically produce the warm, pink foot or hand that for many years was thought to reflect the overall improvement in limb perfusion.

This phenomenon of extremity blood flow redistribution is important because improved muscular perfusion previously was presumed to parallel increased cutaneous blood flow and justify the application of sympathectomy for claudication. Radioactively labeled microsphere studies by Rutherford and Valenta[68] in a canine arterial occlusion model showed that neither resting nor exertional muscle perfusion is improved by sympathectomy. Using a similar technique in a canine hind limb study, Cronenwett and Lindenauer[17] corroborated this finding in subjects with patent and acutely obstructed femoral arteries. These observations are explained by the relative sensitivities of precapillary sphincters in muscle and skin to adrenergic tone; cutaneous sphincters have low resting myogenic tone and are controlled exclusively by sympathetic impulses. Precapillary sphincters in muscle have high resting myogenic tone, however, and respond almost exclusively to local, primarily metabolic, humoral factors.[76] In patients in whom proximal occlusive disease places relatively fixed limitations on arterial inflow, sympathectomy can adversely affect the natural redistribution of blood flow to exercising muscle by lowering cutaneous vascular resistance.[68,76]

Regardless of the patency of the arterial tree, maximal vasodilatation is noted immediately after sympathectomy but begins to taper off within 5 to 7 days of denervation. This "fifth day phenomenon" is more noticeable after dorsal sympathectomy, but it occurs in the lower extremities as well. Although at a much lower level than initially observed, peripheral cutaneous vasodilatation and blood flow remain elevated over basal levels for months, persisting in the face of stimuli that provoke vasoconstriction through centrally mediated reflexes (e.g., the vasoconstrictor cold response test).[84] Resting vasomotor tone usually returns to normal levels 2 weeks to 6 months after sympathectomy. Previous explanations for this return of sympathetic vasomotor tone have included anatomically incomplete denervation, crossover reinnervation, and vascular hyperreactivity to circulating catecholamines. Isolated rabbit ear sympathectomy studies have shown that arteriolar smooth muscle cells are 1.5 times more sensitive to exogenous norepinephrine but are unable to constrict maximally owing to viscoelastic changes in the vessel wall.[8] This situation does not seem to involve endothelium-derived relaxing factor, however.[30] In addition, a study of canine adrenergic receptors showed no change in the concentration of extrasynaptic, $alpha_2$ receptors, which initiate vasoconstriction in response to blood-borne catecholamines.[11] Although attenuated, the capacity for vasoconstriction and its mediators is *not* obliterated by sympathectomy. The degree of recovery of vasomotor tone after sympathectomy depends on circulating norepinephrine levels and the degree of vascular adaptation to loss of physiologic constriction.

Effect on Collateral Circulation

The effect of lumbar sympathectomy on resting collateral blood flow in response to acute and chronic arterial occlusion has been studied in humans and dogs. Using a canine model of acute popliteal arterial occlusion, Dalessandri and associates[21] showed that lumbar sympathectomy produces a temporary but significant increase in paw blood flow as measured by plethysmographic tracings. This effect was noted after sufficient time had elapsed to allow maximal vasodilatation of collateral vessels around the knee. Among patients with chronic foot ischemia as a result of multilevel arterial occlusions, Ludbrook[51] observed submaximal collateral blood flow at rest in 30%. Sympathectomy produced an average 11% increase in distal perfusion among this subgroup of patients with inappropriate resting vasoconstriction. van der Stricht[81] reported a similar phenomenon and postulated that sympathectomy increases collateral flow by increasing the pressure gradient across fixed obstructions at the femoral and popliteal levels. Although this improvement is often relatively small and transient, sympathectomy does seem to increase distal perfusion, circumventing proximal obstructions in patients with inappropriate resting vasoconstriction. In *most* patients with ischemia at rest, however, locally released humoral factors maximize flow through existing and newly formed collateral channels.

Nutritive Value of Blood Flow Increase

Central to the debate concerning the utility of sympathectomy is determination of the nutritive value of whatever blood flow increase is observed after denervation. Presuming that cutaneous arteriovenous anastomosis flow is non-nutritive because capillary perfusion is bypassed, Cronenwett and Lindenauer[17] maintained that sympathectomy does not increase blood flow to ischemic skin and should have no effect on rest pain or ischemic ulcers. This contention is supported by Welch and Leiberman's[87] studies of cutaneous capillary perfusion using iodine 125–iodoantipyrine clearance in patients with peripheral vascular disease after lumbar sympathectomy or arterial reconstruction; no improved clearance was found in denervated limbs, in contrast to accelerated clearance seen after arterial reconstruction.

Perry and Horton[58] found no difference in spectrophotometric measurements of transcutaneous oxygen tensions in patients before and after lumbar sympathectomy. Using intradermal xenon 133 clearance, Moore and Hall[54] showed improved skin capillary perfusion and observed ischemic ulcer healing after lumbar sympathectomy in patients with severe vascular disease. Uncontrolled clinical series seemed to support Moore and Hall's observations by reporting ischemic ulcer healing in 40% to 67% of patients after sympathectomy.[10,15,44,59] Despite conflicting data, it seems fair to concede that in *some* patients sympathectomy produces a small but sufficient increase in nutritive perfusion to facilitate healing of small ulcers or relieve ischemic rest pain. As discussed later, the key to its use is to select appropriate patients.

Alteration of Pain Impulse Transmission

An alternative mechanism to explain the relief of ischemic rest pain (rather than increased perfusion) is central and peripheral attenuation of painful stimulus transmission by sensory nerves. Although objective assessment of pain threshold changes is difficult, aversive stimuli studies in cats have shown that lumbar sympathectomy enhances tolerance of hind limb noxious stimuli.[60] Theories concerning a relationship between sympathetic innervation and pain threshold suggest that sympathectomy decreases noxious stimulus perception by decreasing tissue norepinephrine levels and reducing spinal augmentation of painful stimulus transmission to cerebral centers.[50] This theory also may explain clinical series, including one randomized trial, reporting a significant portion of patients affected by disabling claudication or rest pain who were subjectively relieved without hemodynamic evidence of improved perfusion.[20] Among the subset of patients with rest pain, Owens[56] suggested that clear differentiation of neuropathic from ischemic pain in patients with absent ankle pulses is not made. Including patients with causalgia (burning pain) in the clinical group with ischemic rest pain would spuriously increase the sympathectomy response rate. Despite this possible flaw in inclusion criteria, clinical and experimental evidence suggests that lumbar sympathectomy can be efficacious in attenuating pain perception in patients with ischemic rest pain.

Summary of Physiologic Effects

Sympathectomy increases peripheral blood flow by the vasodilatation of arterioles primarily in cutaneous vascular beds. Much of this increased flow passes through naturally occurring arteriovenous anastomoses. Although overall extremity blood flow may be increased, significant increases in nutritive flow occur only in distal cutaneous beds. Limitations in arterial inflow imposed by proximal occlusive lesions may mitigate this increase, and the return of vasomotor tone toward normal with time may diminish it further. Nevertheless, some patients *may* receive sufficient increases to help heal superficial ischemic ulcers and relieve ischemic rest pain. In addition, although increases in blood perfusion are relatively small in the long run in patients with organic occlusive disease, protection against an exaggerated vasoconstrictor response to cold, amelioration of sympathetic pain, and suppression of sweating are long lasting. These observations determine the appropriate indications for sympathectomy.

■ ASSESSMENT OF LUMBAR SYMPATHETIC BLOCK

It is often difficult to judge whether or not a complete sympathetic block has been obtained, especially when vascular disease is present. A significant increase in warmth, whether subjective or objective, cannot always be registered. Increased filling of the veins is a sign of sympathetic block, which is worth looking for because the venous system is less often the site of pathologic changes than the arterial system. Objective signs of a complete sympathetic block are an appreciably increased skin temperature compared with the side not blocked, an increase in arterial pulsations shown by oscillometry or plethysmography, and abolished secretion of sweat in the foot.

Noninvasive diagnostic techniques can complement clinical evaluation in assessing patients for lumbar sympathectomy. Doppler arterial waveforms of the pedal arteries, although abnormal, should be present if the patient is to improve after sympathectomy. Patients with unobtainable Doppler arterial velocity signals have ischemia that is too advanced to benefit from sympathectomy. The ankle-brachial systolic pressure index determined by ultrasound is usually less than 0.5 in patients with early rest pain. If the ankle pressure index is less than 0.30, however, the patient is unlikely to improve after sympathectomy, according to the data of Yao and Bergan.[90] Barnes[5] has found digit plethysmography to be the most helpful predictor of response to lumbar sympathectomy. The normal digit pulse waveforms mimic an arterial pressure pulse, with a rapid upstroke, a relatively sharp peak, and a dicrotic wave on the downslope. In the presence of arterial occlusive disease, the waveform is attenuated with a more gradual upslope, a rounded peak, and loss of the dicrotic wave. In advanced ischemia, there may be no detectable waveform in the digit. The presence of sympathetic vasomotor tone may be assessed by noting the response of the digit pulse amplitude to a deep breath. Normally the pulse amplitude is attenuated with such a maneuver, whereas patients with autosympathectomy, as in diabetes mellitus, surgical sympathectomy, or advanced ischemia, may lose this vasoconstrictive reflex. Finally, the ability of the digit circulation to increase in response to ischemia, as by reactive hyperemia, may be assessed by noting the pulse waveform response to temporary arterial occlusion induced by a pneumatic cuff on the proximal digit. Normally the digit pulse amplitude should at least double in response to temporary (3-minute) digit ischemia.[5] Patients with advanced occlusive disease may not have the capacity for additional vasodilatation. Such patients are unlikely to benefit from lumbar sympathectomy.

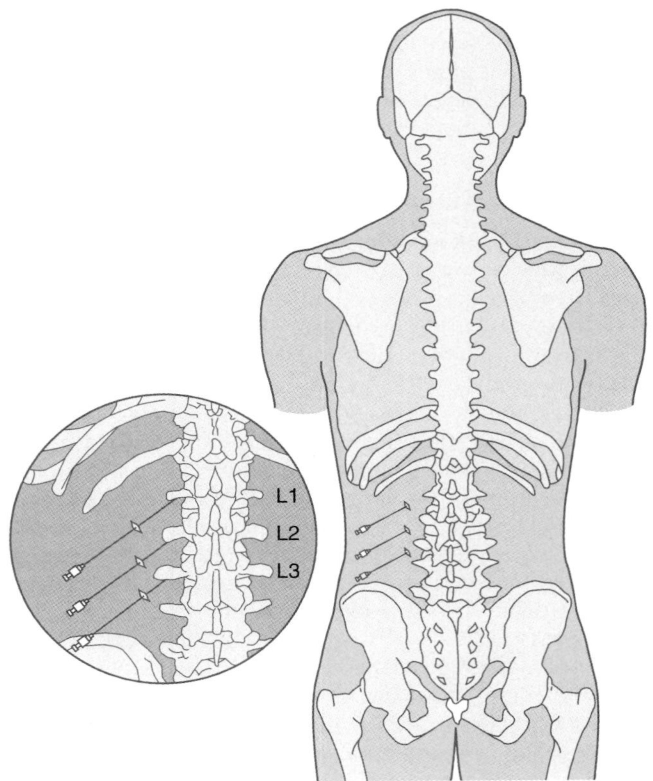

FIGURE 85-1 Lumbar sympathetic block (three-needle technique). (From Callow AD, Ernst CB: Vascular Surgery: Theory and Practice. Stamford, Conn, Appleton & Lange, 1995, p 285.)

■ LUMBAR SYMPATHETIC BLOCK TECHNIQUES

Pharmacologic block of the lumbar chain using conventional local anesthetic agents merely requires that the tip of the needle is placed into the perisympathetic space from the back. When a so-called chemical sympathectomy is to be performed, however, using a small volume of phenol or alcohol, the point of the needle must be placed precisely adjacent to the sympathetic chain. Landmarks for this block are L1, which is situated at the level of the junction of the 12th rib and erector spinae muscles, and L4-5, at the level of the line drawn between the posterior iliac crests. Preferably the patient should lie in the lateral position with the waist supported either by a pillow or by breaking the table so that the vertebral column is curved in the lateral plane to widen spaces between the transverse processes on the upper side (Fig. 85-1). Wheals are raised opposite the spinous processes of L2 and L4, 7 to 10 cm lateral to the midline. A 19-gauge needle 12 to 18 cm long, with a depth marker on it, is introduced through the wheal and directed 45 degrees cranially or caudally so that it strikes the transverse process of the vertebra lying above or below it. On making contact with bone, the marker is pushed down to the skin, and the needle is withdrawn. In a patient of normal size, the marker is moved so that its position for that point is double the distance between the skin and the transverse process. In thin patients, the length of needle introduced should be increased slightly, and in stout patients, the length should be decreased slightly. The distance from the tip of the needle to the marker corresponds roughly to the distance between the skin and the ventrolateral aspect of the vertebral body. The needle is inserted between the transverse processes and directed more medially, but at right angles to the skin, in the sagittal plane. This space is found approximately opposite the corresponding spinous process. If the needle strikes bone when the marker is close to the skin, the point is in contact with the lateral aspect of the body of the vertebra. The bevel of the needle should face the body of the vertebra so that slight bending of the needle allows it to slip forward to lie adjacent to the sympathetic chain. The position of the needle may be checked by x-ray, but with experience this becomes unnecessary. Complete sympathetic blockade may be obtained with a single injection of 15 mL of bupivacaine (Marcaine) at the level of L2. Better results may be obtained using two or three needles, one point inserted at L2 and the other one or two inserted at L3 and L4 (see Fig. 85-1).

■ CHEMICAL LUMBAR SYMPATHECTOMY

The high response rate with percutaneous sympathetic blockade with local anesthetic agents engendered attempts to achieve extended blockade with phenol or alcohol injections via the same approach. The tips of three needles are placed against the bodies of L2, L3, and L4 (see Fig. 85-1). Their positions must be confirmed by x-ray. In the lateral view, the needle points should barely reach the anterior border of the vertebral bodies. In the anteroposterior view, the points should lie over them. When in proper place, 3 mL of 6.5% to 7% phenol dissolved in water, or 3 mL of absolute alcohol is injected through each needle. Using fluoroscopic confirmation by means of contrast injections adjacent to L1 through L3, Sanderson[70] showed that 80% of first injections are at the desired location. Second injections yielded complete lumbar sympathetic neurolysis in 90% of patients, as determined by sudomotor and foot temperature testing. Follow-up was limited, however. The successful percutaneous neurolysis rate of Walsh and colleagues[84] was 72%, and the duration of effect with 10% phenol was identical to that of surgical denervation. Experience with phenol lumbar sympathectomy in the United States is limited but is increasing. Long-term results have not been reported. Clinical impressions are that this approach produces a less complete and less durable effect. With improvement, it may be accepted as an alternative to surgery to produce lasting sympathetic denervation. In view of the current low risk, durability, and greater precision of surgical sympathectomy, however, percutaneous techniques must be improved to the point when they are more complete and more durable and do not cause the painful side effects that occasionally mar their use. Chemical sympathectomy must not be taken lightly becauses it may cause significant inflammation and scarring in the wake of phenol or alcohol injections. Subsequent surgical sympathectomy, if needed, may be difficult and unsafe.

■ CLINICAL INDICATIONS AND RESULTS

Indications determine results, and results determine indications. Nowhere is this saying more true than for sympathectomy, which has been performed for such diverse indications and with such markedly differing outcomes that quoting overall results is meaningless. Results in specific clinical situations gradually have defined its indications. With the passage of time, performance of sympathectomy for some indications gradually has become more limited and selective with the increasing use of trial blocks, noninvasive testing, and improvement in competitive forms of therapy.

Table 85-1 Indications for Sympathectomy and Clinical Outcome

INDICATIONS FOR LUMBAR SYMPATHECTOMY	OUTCOME
Causalgia Hyperhidrosis Vasospastic disorders complicated by digital ulceration (frostbite sequelae or occlusive Raynaud's disease secondary to distal emboli or trauma)	Excellent
Non-bypassable atherosclerotic occlusion with rest pain or limited necrotic tissue Buerger's disease	Good to fair
Claudication Diabetic neuropathy	Poor

Better pharmacologic management of the initial stage causalgia and pure vasospastic disorders has reduced significantly the number of patients now being referred for sympathectomy.[32,48,63] Increasing success with infrapopliteal bypass has reduced further the number of patients in whom sympathectomy is considered in lieu of direct revascularization. Even in these cases, selection criteria have been tightened by noninvasive testing before and after trial blocks.

Presently the two conditions that are most likely to be relieved by lumbar sympathectomy are hyperhidrosis and causalgia (Table 85-1). Disabling hyperhidrosis usually affects the upper extremities; however, occasionally the lower extremities are involved. Rarely, lumbar sympathectomy may help in cases of incipient gangrene if the pathologic changes in blood vessels are not too severe.

Causalgia

The central role of the sympathetic nervous system in perpetuating causalgia makes sympathetic denervation particularly suitable for this entity. Uniform success is obtained when the diagnosis and therapeutic potential of sympathectomy are confirmed by trial block. Mockus and colleagues[53] reported that early postoperative pain relief was obtained in 96% of patients by trial block, with 84% remaining asymptomatic after a median follow-up interval of 28 months. Similar results have been obtained by other investigators and are superior to the results of repeated transcutaneous sympathetic blocks alone.[41] In a report by our group,[1] initial and late satisfactory results of 100% and 95% were achieved in patients who showed an excellent response to a trial sympathetic block.

Peripheral Vasospasm

Most patients with Raynaud's phenomenon secondary to vasospasm complain more of upper extremity than of lower extremity discomfort. Occasionally the reverse is true, however, particularly for patients in colder climates, possibly because it is easier to warm the hands periodically than the feet. Although the procedure is uncommonly needed, lower extremity vasospasm and cold intolerance respond remarkably well to lumbar sympathectomy, possibly even more so than with upper extremity involvement.

Janoff and colleagues[40] reported their experience with 10 patients who had episodic distal vasospasm that was refractory to maximal medical management. *Pernio,* or chilblain, a localized itching and painful erythema on the fingers and toes produced by cold damp weather, was noted in each patient and did not recur after lumbar sympathectomy. Hypothermic toe plethysmographic testing normalized, and all patients remained asymptomatic after 4 years' mean follow-up. Felder and Gifford and their associates[28,33] reported similarly good and lasting symptom relief among a larger group of patients. Despite loss of resting cutaneous vasodilatation, reflex digital vasoconstriction in response to regional or remote cold stimuli did not recur in any of the more recently studied patients.

Ischemic Rest Pain

Critical assessment of clinical reports on the efficacy of lumbar sympathectomy for ischemic rest pain is limited by (1) variations in the severity and anatomic distribution of occlusive disease, (2) failure to differentiate this from other forms of lower extremity pain, and (3) differing criteria for determining "inoperability" for distal bypass. With these limitations in mind, the more recent reports cited, it is hoped, better reflect progress in infrapopliteal revascularization, pharmacologic manipulation, and noninvasive testing. Nevertheless, most reports share the same flaw—they were not prospectively randomized against conservatively treated controls.

Of the two manifestations of critical lower limb ischemia that may be considered categorical indications for lumbar sympathectomy, *rest pain* has a higher response rate than ischemic ulceration, for two reasons:

1. The blood flow increase needed to satisfy oxygen demands at rest is less than the inflammatory response required for tissue healing.
2. Pain impulse attenuation may enhance tolerance of ischemic pain even if perfusion is not significantly increased.

Selection of patients for lumbar sympathectomy for both of these indications should be based on three simple assessment criteria, as follows[59,83]:

1. An ankle-brachial index (ABI) of greater than 0.3
2. Absent neuropathy on physical examination
3. Limited forefoot tissue loss

To these criteria may be added relief of pain associated with plethysmographic or other objective evidence of improved flow in response to sympathetic blockade.[78]

Crucial to the success of lumbar sympathectomy is adequate arterial inflow, as indirectly measured by Doppler segmental limb pressures. Designation of a threshold ABI of 0.3 is based on Yao and Bergan's[90] original observation that arterial inflow below this level was insufficient to allow perfusion augmentation or symptom relief with sympathectomy in 90% of patients. Similar observations were noted by our group[2] and by others.[62] This pressure index seems to predict that patients have adequate collateral vessels and can support the increase in flow produced by removal of sympathetic tone. Plecha and collaborators[62] performed similar hemodynamic studies and found that the index obtained by dividing the distal thigh pressure by the arm pressure was a better predictor of the effectiveness of sympathectomy. They believed that if this pressure index is greater than 0.7, one can expect a favorable response to sympathectomy, which is defined as an increase in the distal thigh-arm pressure index of 0.1 or greater. Subsequent studies have defined a range of ABI centered around 0.3 when patients with spuriously high ankle pressures as a result of incompressible vessels are excluded. In the minds of some investigators, this ABI threshold cast doubt on the efficacy of sympathectomy because the natural history of rest pain alone in a patient with an ABI greater than 0.3 might not be significantly different from the response to sympathectomy.

This question was addressed and partially answered in a prospective, randomized clinical trial conducted by Cross and Cotton[20] in which transcutaneous phenol lumbar sympatholysis was compared with saline sham lumbar injections. Forty-one limbs in 37 patients were objectively and subjectively analyzed at regular intervals 6 months after treatment. Among the control group, only 24% of patients reported symptomatic relief, as shown by a decrease in narcotic requirements, compared with 84% in the treatment group. This highly significant subjective difference was *not* associated with objective signs of improved perfusion as measured by segmental limb pressures or blood flow and galvanic skin response monitored on the dorsum of the foot. This study reflects the natural history of ischemic rest pain in "inoperable" patients (25% of whom spontaneously improved) and the pain impulse modulation effect of sympathetic denervation. Other clinical series reported similar symptomatic response rates ranging from 47% to 78%, with early "limb salvage" rates of 60% to 94%.[10,15,44] Persson and colleagues[59] reported the best results for sympathectomy for this indication.

In patients followed 82 months after lumbar sympathectomy, 30 of 35 limbs with an ABI greater than 0.3 (86%) experienced early and sustained elimination or improvement of rest pain compared with 5 patients who received no relief and required early amputation. No significant overall improvement in limb perfusion was noted, and reflective of the severity of their systemic atherosclerosis, nearly 50% of the patients experienced myocardial infarction 6 months to 4 years after operation. These results support a limited role for sympathectomy as a pain control procedure for patients with ischemic rest pain whose occlusive arterial disease is truly not amenable to direct revascularization or transluminal angioplasty and is refractory to maximal medical management.

A subgroup of patients are those with diabetes who not only have end-stage extremity arterial disease, but also an "autosympathectomy" that is due to progressive diabetic neuropathy. Rest pain in this group is rarely, if ever, responsive to sympathectomy. Not only can increased distal perfusion not be expected, but also the prospect of enhanced pain tolerance is negligible. Imparato[38] first noted the relationship between diabetic neuropathy and lack of responsiveness to surgical sympathectomy. He showed the histologic equivalence of diabetic autosympathectomy and surgical lumbar sympathetic ganglionectomy by finding no difference in the number of periarterial sympathetic fibers in lower extremity amputation specimens from both groups.[34,38] Other clinical series have confirmed that the high frequency of a sensory and sympathetic neuropathy in diabetic patients with limb-threatening ischemia is associated with autosympathectomy and an unresponsiveness to lumbar sympathetic ganglionectomy in most patients.[22] The results of sympathectomy in patients with Buerger's disease and patient selection are discussed in Chapter 25.

Ischemic Ulceration or Tissue Loss

Assessment of the results of lumbar sympathectomy for distal ischemic ulceration or focal gangrene is subject to the same limitations as were described for rest pain. The additional flow above basal requirements, needed to heal wounds and combat infection, creates even greater demands on sympathectomy than combating ischemic rest pain. Radionuclide perfusion studies show that close to a twofold increase in blood flow around the ulcer (hyperemic response) is necessary for healing.[61] Infected or deeper ulcers require even greater increases in regional perfusion. As expected, clinical and experimental studies indicate that sympathectomy *rarely, if ever,* provides sufficiently increased nutritive perfusion to allow healing of deep ulcers or large areas of skin necrosis, even when secondary infection is not prominent.

Clinical studies, noting partial or complete healing in 35% to 62% of patients with forefoot tissue loss, corroborate the intrinsic limitations of sympathectomy.[10,15,44] The best results were reported by Persson and coworkers,[59] who performed sympathectomy on 22 limbs with adequate inflow but, importantly, with no evidence of neuropathy or subcutaneous infection; 77% showed complete ulcer healing, whereas only 22% required amputation.

Lee and colleagues[46] reported lower healing rates for patients with superficial toe gangrene, with 56% of the involved digits "salvaged" by sympathectomy and a 40% toe salvage rate among patients with three or more digits involved. Among "nonresponders" in such reports, the immediate amputation rate ranged from 27% to 38%, suggesting that not all of these cases were doomed without therapeutic intervention and that the level of amputation required was not improved by sympathectomy.

Holiday and associates[36] analyzed the value of surgical and chemical lumbar sympathectomy in patients with critical lower limb ischemia without the option of vascular reconstruction. Clinical success rates, defined as improvement of ischemic stage, and limb salvage rates were recorded for 76 limbs of 70 consecutive patients. Chemical lumbar sympathectomy patients were older and had more concomitant disease than surgical lumbar sympathectomy patients. The short-term success rate (at 6 weeks) in 36 patients treated with surgical sympathectomy (44%) was better than in 40 patients treated with chemical sympathectomy (18%, $P = .01$). The long-term success rate at 1 year was 47% for surgical sympathectomy and 45% for chemical sympathectomy. The limb salvage rates at 1 year were 61% for surgical sympathectomy and 58% for chemical sympathectomy (not significant). Holiday and associates[36] concluded in their study that surgical and chemical lumbar sympathectomy can be performed with little morbidity and may be beneficial to these patients.

In a study of foot transcutaneous oxygen tension ($tcPO_2$) response to lumbar sympathectomy in patients with focal ischemic necrosis, Johnson and coworkers[42] prospectively evaluated all patients with superficial foot necrosis of 1 to 3 cm and $tcPO_2$ values of less than 30 mm Hg. $tcPO_2$ measurements of the forefoot were done preoperatively and every 2 to 3 days postoperatively. All of the 10 patients who were available for follow-up experienced increases in foot $tcPO_2$ measurements during the first 4 to 5 days, with a mean increase of 23 mm Hg, which was significant ($P = .04$). Clinical improvement was defined as an average increase of 29 mm Hg by postoperative day 10, and clinical failure was defined as only an average increase of 5 mm Hg in $tcPO_2$. The investigators concluded that a favorable response to sympathectomy could be predicted by a preoperative increase in $tcPO_2$ by at least 20 mm Hg in response to dependency. They also concluded that sustained postoperative increases in tissue oxygen levels by postoperative day 10 favored wound healing.

Precise characterization of an ischemic forefoot lesion that is most likely to respond to sympathectomy is difficult to glean from this literature. From a conceptual and practical point of view, use of sympathectomy should be confined to small, shallow, uninfected forefoot ulcers or single-digit superficial gangrene in patients with an ABI greater than 0.3 and absent neuropathy. One might expect successful healing in at least 35% of such patients, but no change in amputation level can be anticipated should amputation ultimately be required.

Sympathectomy as an Adjunct to Arterial Reconstruction

Experimental evidence indicates that sympathectomy improves patency of small vessel anastomoses and the repair of traumatized arteries.[12,71] Some authors have reported better patency rates for proximal and distal arterial reconstructions when concomitant sympathectomy is performed.[27,69] It is difficult, however, to predict which reconstructions would be protected by sympathectomy. Its application in proximal reconstructions that have been performed in the face of distal thromboembolism, poor runoff, or small "hypoplastic" vessels is less problematic because the sympathetic chain often can be exposed through the same incision. With distal reconstruction, however, sympathectomy would constitute an entirely separate surgical procedure and is harder to justify.

Preferably, intraoperative electromagnetic flowmeter studies, documenting low graft blood flow that significantly increases in response to intra-arterial papaverine or tolazoline (Priscoline), should be used to justify the addition of lumbar sympathectomy. A multicenter trial showed, however, that dextran 40 infusions can produce a threefold decrease in early postoperative thrombosis of difficult distal bypass operations.[67] This decrease in thrombosis results from an increase in flow and a decrease in coagulability and would seem to provide a better alternative to sympathectomy. Prostanoids and hemorrheologic agents may offer future promise in this situation, and it is anticipated that the application of sympathectomy for this indication will be negligible in the future.

Sympathectomy to Speed Up Development of Collateral Circulation

Sympathectomy is a commonly mentioned indication for which there is little scientific proof. Ludbrook[51] showed that collateral arteries contributed 23% of the resistance at rest and 73% at peak flows in patients with claudication and 52% of the resistance at rest and 89% at peak flows in patients with rest pain. Decreasing the resistance of the peripheral vascular bed distal to the obstruction by sympathectomy would not greatly decrease overall resistance or increase flow, particularly if the occlusive process was a severe one. In the same situation, however, an equal decrease in the collateral artery resistance would have a significant effect on overall blood flow.

The critical question is to what extent are the collateral arteries under sympathetic control? Shepherd,[72] using indirect methods of evaluating the collateral circulation, concluded that collateral vessels are under the control of the sympathetic nervous system. Dornhorst and Sharpey-Schafer[24] studied the effect of lumbar sympathectomy in 10 patients, however, and found that although the collateral resistance decreased in 7 patients, the decreases were transient. Similar findings were reported by Barcroft and Swan.[4] There probably is some improvement in the speed but not in the magnitude of development of collateral circulation after sympathectomy *if* it is performed early enough (i.e., the first few weeks after occlusion). This benefit may result from either vasodilatation of the collateral channels themselves or the increased pressure gradient produced across the block by the decrease in distal resistance that results from sympathectomy. Despite these studies, reduction of collateral resistance is not an accepted indication for sympathectomy. There is rarely a pressing enough need for this to warrant an operative intervention; some pharmacologic agents can produce similar effects.

Summary of Recommended Indications

Within the context of its physiologic consequences and the clinical results just presented, lumbar sympathectomy should be applied rarely and selectively to the following patients: (1) patients with lower extremity pain or ischemia, (2) patients whose condition is refractory to medical management, and (3) patients who are not candidates for more effective revascularization techniques. Cross,[19] in an editorial that reviewed the history of lumbar sympathectomy, concluded that if controlled clinical work is the only reliable "gold standard" in clinical research, the total understanding of the effect of lumbar sympathectomy rests on the results of only four articles out of the many hundreds written on this subject. These show that sympathectomy does not improve claudication,[31] it may improve ischemic rest pain,[20] and it does not improve the long-term patency of peripheral vascular bypass grafts.[6,69] Regardless of the indication, subjective and objective preoperative assessment of response to sympathetic blockade greatly enhances the probability of therapeutic success. With these considerations in mind, lumbar sympathectomy may be indicated for the following conditions according to the recommended selection criteria:

1. Causalgia
2. Inoperable arterial occlusive disease with limb-threatening ischemia causing rest pain, limited ulceration, or superficial digital gangrene
3. Symptomatic vasospastic disorders

Causalgia

When detected and treated early *(stage I)*, post-traumatic pain syndromes respond to intensive medical therapy in 40% to 60% of cases.[80] Nonoperative treatment consists of mild analgesics, physiotherapy, tricyclic antidepressants, anticonvulsants, and α_2-adrenergic blockers administered in a stepwise manner according to symptom responsiveness.[32] Surgical sympathectomy usually is not considered until conscientious participation in medical therapy has continued for 3 months. Multiple translumbar sympathetic blocks with local anesthetic agents are used to obtain and observe symptom relief, particularly in regard to degree and duration.[73]

Among patients with chronic pain or atypical pain and a "learned helplessness" personality profile, saline placebo injections may help to confirm or to rule out a true cause-and-effect relationship for the reported symptomatic relief.[13] If reproducible pain relief is achieved, lumbar sympathectomy yields a uniformly gratifying and sustained response rate.[1,53,80] It should be applied as soon as the patient's relief from sympathetic blockade, which lasts only as long as the effect of the local anesthetic used *(stage II)*, wears off. Patients allowed to progress to *stage III* do not respond to sympathectomy.

Inoperable Arterial Occlusive Disease

Before specific selection criteria are discussed, the term *inoperable* needs to be defined. In general, the application of direct revascularization techniques for ischemic limbs with severe infrapopliteal occlusive disease is limited by the level and characteristics of the recipient artery, the adequacy of distal runoff, the conduit available for arterial bypass, and the technical expertise of the surgeon. Inadequate runoff (i.e., no distal arteries to bypass) is becoming an infrequent indication, thanks to intra-arterial digital subtraction, color Doppler scanning, and, more recently, magnetic resonance arteriography. Improved application of in-situ, translocated, or reversed saphenous vein grafting techniques permits bypass to suitable arteries in the lower calf, ankle, and foot with acceptable limb salvage rates.[45] With available autogenous vein and patent distal arteries, "inoperability" is determined by the technical proficiency of the surgeon.

Rest Pain Assuming that a critical degree of forefoot ischemia has been shown by objective criteria to confirm the clinical diagnosis of ischemic rest pain, lumbar sympathectomy is preferable to amputation if the following criteria are met:

1. ABI greater than 0.3
2. Absent neuropathy
3. Symptomatic relief obtained by trial block

Relief of rest pain from lumbar sympathectomy can be expected in 50% to 85% of patients meeting these criteria.

Limited Tissue Loss Initial evaluation includes definition of the extent and depth of tissue loss, treatment of secondary infection with limited débridement, topical care, and culture-specific antibiotic therapy. In addition to noninvasive testing, perfusion scans with injections of intravenous thallium or intra-arterial technetium 99m–labeled albumin microspheres permit determination of the hyperemic ratio surrounding the lesion and prediction of healing potential.[74] If a perfusion ratio after a thallium 201 intravenous injection was 1.5:1 (<1.75:1 predicts a nonhealing ulcer), but a repeated scan during the time of effect of a sympathetic block showed a ratio of 2.5:1, a sympathectomy may be recommended with confidence. Studies predicting nonhealing or the absence of signs of healing after 6 weeks of intensive wound management warrant obtaining arteriograms using special timing or digital subtraction methods to show "operability."

Other selection criteria for sympathectomy are similar to the criteria used for determining rest pain and include the following:

1. ABI greater than 0.3
2. Absent neuropathy
3. Limited ulceration or superficial single-digit gangrene
4. Absence of major deep infection

Strict adherence to these criteria can be expected to result in healing in 35% to 65% of patients after lumbar sympathectomy.[59,83]

Lower Extremity Vasospasm

Symptomatic vasospasm of the lower extremity primarily affects patients with Raynaud's phenomenon or victims of frostbite. Discomfort and typical color changes in response to mild environmental cold with painful rewarming hyperemia or even a mild superficial dermatitis (pernio) are noted. Severe vasospasm may produce digital ulcerations in the presence of readily palpable pedal pulses. Digital photoplethysmography discloses either artifactually peaked pulse volume recordings or sustained loss of pulsatile flow in response to a local or distant hypothermic challenge.[40] One can predict a good response to sympathectomy by showing at least a 50% increase in amplitude of the digital pulse volume recording with cold exposure after chemical sympathetic blockade.[78]

Before lumbar sympathectomy is considered, maximal medical therapy with calcium channel blockers, cold avoidance, and cessation of smoking must be earnestly pursued. Vasospasm refractory to these measures warrants lumbar sympathectomy; immediate and lasting symptom resolution has been noted in nearly 90% of patients managed in this stepwise fashion.[28,33,40]

Would Minimally Invasive Sympathectomy Change the Indications?

In recent years, there have been increasing reports of early experiences with lumbar sympathectomy carried out by laparoscopic methods. Most of these reports mention a small number of cases, with general enthusiasm and surprisingly few complications or other drawbacks mentioned. Specifically, major vascular injuries, especially the inferior vena cava on the left, do not seem to have been encountered. Only one report suggested that incomplete sympathectomy may be a problem (i.e., only 50% relief of pain at 4 months[37]).

Initially, some of these procedures were carried out transabdominally, with reflection of the colon,[43] but most surgeons now use an extraperitoneal technique with balloon inflation to dissect the extraperitoneal plane.[14,25,37,43] If one presumes that this technique can produce a complete and lasting lumbar sympathectomy with safety and reduced morbidity, it may reduce the reluctance to perform the procedure for some indications (e.g., frostbite injury, symptomatic vasospasm, or hyperhidrosis), in which the gain is relatively insignificant for an open surgical operation. For patients with causalgia or chronic critical ischemia and inoperable arterial occlusive disease facing amputation, the gain is potentially great. Such a procedure probably would speed up the application of sympathectomy for causalgia if it did not increase its use, and it might allow it to compete more favorably with other, less effective nonrevascularization alternatives (e.g., epidural spinal stimulation, hyperbaric oxygen) and pharmacotherapy in patients with inoperable arterial disease and limb threat. Identifying proper candidates, by objective evaluation of a trial block, will remain the cornerstone of patient selection, however.

■ CONVENTIONAL OPERATIVE TECHNIQUE

Lumbar sympathectomy begins with proper positioning of the patient so that the interval between the costal margin and iliac crest is "opened." The surgeon can accomplish this objective by raising the flank region approximately 30 degrees by placing padded rolls beneath the hip and thorax. With the mid-flank region centered over the kidney rest, the table is flexed approximately 10 to 15 degrees to widen the distance between the costal margin and the iliac crest. Tension on the ipsilateral psoas muscle is relieved by flexing the patient's upper (ipsilateral) thigh with appropriate padding beneath and between each leg.

An oblique incision is begun at the lateral edge of the rectus muscle, extending toward the middle of the space between the ribs and iliac crest and ending at the anterior axillary line. The musculofascial layers of the internal and external oblique and the transversalis are split in the direction of their fibers or divided in line with the incision. The transversalis fascia should be divided laterally where the peritoneum is stronger, less adherent, and more easily separated from the fascial undersurface. The lateral plane between the transversalis fascia and the peritoneum is developed easily by blunt finger dissection directed toward the vertebral column. Continued separation of the peritoneum is performed gently in medial, caudal, and cephalad directions to maximize retroperitoneal exposure through the relatively small anterior flank incision.

With continued dissection toward the posterior midline, the surgeon should take care to remain close to the peritoneum and anterior to the psoas muscle rather than dissect into the retroperitoneal fat or posterolateral flank muscles, where bleeding may be encountered. The ureter and gonadal vessels are left attached to overlying peritoneum and are lifted off the psoas muscle as the dissection proceeds medially. The ureter should always be visualized to avoid inadvertent injury.

The lumbar sympathetic chain is located medial to the psoas muscle and lies over the transverse processes of the lumbar spine. The lumbar chain should not be confused with the genitofemoral nerve, which lies more laterally over the medial third of the psoas muscle itself. On the left, the lumbar ganglia lie adjacent and lateral to the abdominal aorta; on the right, the chain lies just beneath the edge of the inferior vena cava.

Tactile identification of the lumbar chain by plucking discloses a characteristic "snap" as a result of tethering of the nodular chain by rami communicantes. Other vertical, bandlike structures in this region (genitofemoral nerve, paravertebral lymph nodes, or ureter) do not recoil as briskly. When identified, the mid-portion of the sympathetic chain is dissected free of surrounding tissues and retracted with a right-angle clamp or a nerve hook to draw it up under tension from the surrounding tissue. The ganglia are mobilized by division of tethering rami with prior metal clip application. The surgeon facilitates orientation and ganglion numbering by identifying the sacral promontory and an adjacent lumbar vein that usually crosses the sympathetic chain in front of or behind the third lumbar ganglion. A large space between the first and second lumbar ganglia is often found with the first ganglion partially obscured by the lumbocostal arch. Metal clip application to all elements of the sympathetic chain before division prevents unexpected bleeding from vessels mistaken for rami or injury to non-neural structures during attempts to control the latter. When the chain, with at least two lumbar ganglia, is removed, hemostasis is secured, and the incision is closed in layers after the table is flexed.

This anterolateral approach of Flowthow[29] is most popular because the incision is well tolerated, dissection remains retroperitoneal, and exposure is adequate. The posterior approach of Royle[66] is not favored because of significant postoperative paraspinal muscle spasms. The anterior approach of Adson is applicable only for sympathectomy combined with an abdominal aortic or other intraperitoneal procedure.[1] Using this anterior, transperitoneal approach, the surgeon identifies the right lumbar chain by dissecting along the right lateral aspect of the inferior vena cava. Exposure of the left lumbar chain is best accomplished by mobilization and medial reflection of the left colon along the white line of Toldt. This approach avoids dissection through lymphatic and vascular tissue immediately lateral to the aorta.

Laparoscopic Lumbar Sympathectomy Technique

Balloon-assisted retroperitoneoscopic lumbar sympathectomy procedures are usually performed under general endotracheal anesthesia. In one published technique,[7] the patient is placed in a lateral decubitus position, and the table is flexed at the level of the umbilicus to create a maximal space between the lower rib cage and the iliac crest. A 12- to 15-mm incision is made midway between the costal margin and the iliac crest at the anterior axillary line level. This mini-incision is carried down by splitting the oblique muscle to enter the retroperitoneal space. With S-shaped retractors and blunt dissection, the peritoneal sac is pushed forward, which creates a safe space for the insertion of the distention balloon system (Origin Medsystem Inc, Menlo Park, Calif). The balloon is inflated with vision via a 30-degree scope introduced into the balloon trocar. The fully inflated balloon is left in place for a few minutes to achieve hemostasis, then is deflated and removed. Next a Hasson trocar (Ethicon Endosurgery, Cincinnati, Ohio) is introduced into the space created and secured with two sutures to the fascia to avoid gas leakage. The created space is insufflated with carbon dioxide to a pressure of 10 to 12 mm Hg. Then two to three additional 5-mm ports are inserted with direct vision into the retroperitoneal space along a line 2 to 3 cm posterior to the first trocar, at the mid-axillary and posterior axillary lines. With the surgeon and an assistant standing in front of the patient, they can identify the peritoneal sac pushed backward and medially, and they can view the psoas muscle in front and upward. The ureter and gonadal vessels and the genitofemoral nerve are visualized in the usual position. The vertebrae in the paravertebral space are palpated with laparoscopic instruments, and dissection of this space is started at the medial border of the psoas muscle, close to the vertebrae.

Two to three instruments generally are used for traction, dissection, clipping, and cutting. The sympathetic chain usually is identified in front of the vertebral column along the inner margin of the psoas muscle, as seen in conventional lumbar sympathectomy. The communicating rami and the blood vessels are divided with cautery or clips and endoscissors. The sympathetic chain is transected between clips at the desired level. At the end of the procedure, the retroperitoneal space is deflated, the retractors are removed, and the fascia at the large port site is sutured.

Using this technique, Beglaibter and colleagues[7] analyzed the data of 27 consecutive patients who underwent 29 retroperitoneoscopic lumbar sympathectomies. Of patients, 22 had ischemia of the lower limb, and 5 had severe reflex sympathetic dystrophy. The procedure was accomplished successfully in all patients without any postoperative complications, with a mean operative time of 136 minutes and a mean hospital stay of 1.4 days. All patients had significant improvement of pain or dystrophic changes.

In another study, Watarida and coworkers[85] reported the results of seven patients with critical limb ischemia who underwent laparoscopic lumbar sympathectomy. After the procedure, skin thermometry was carried out on all patients. The postoperative skin temperature of the affected leg increased to 36.6° C ± 0.5° C compared with 33.8° C ± 0.8° C preoperatively. None of these patients experienced postoperative neuralgia, and all achieved sustained symptomatic relief with no major perioperative complications.

Wronski[89] described a videoscopic approach for lumbar sympathectomy. A transverse incision of 3 to 4 cm is made in the hypochondrium, lateral to the rectus sheath. The abdominal muscles are split along their fibers. The transverse fascia is opened, and the peritoneum is carefully dissected backward. A trocar is introduced laterally from the skin incision, and under visual control, the sympathetic trunk is exposed and the specific ganglia are transected using cautery. Twelve lumbar sympathectomies were performed using this technique on nine patients with satisfactory results.[81]

Complications

Major complications result from failure to appreciate normal anatomic relationships, with resultant injury to the genitofemoral nerve, ureter, lumbar veins, aorta, and inferior vena cava. Although reported, such injuries are avoidable by attention to anatomic detail and prevention of hemorrhage from vessels lying outside the proper plane of dissection.

The most common complication after lumbar sympathectomy is postsympathectomy *neuralgia*. This sequela appears in 50% of patients 5 to 20 days after sympathectomy.[49,53] The pain is characterized as an annoying "ache" in the anterolateral thigh region that is worse at night and is unaffected by activity or level of cutaneous stimulation. The discomfort responds to moderate analgesics and spontaneously remits within 8 to 12 weeks after onset. Counseling patients about this annoying complication before surgery is essential and often attenuates overreactions. The cause is still speculative, and various technical maneuvers have not reduced its overall incidence.

In men, sexual derangement consists of retrograde ejaculation, which affects 25% to 50% of patients undergoing bilateral L1 sympathetic ganglionectomy.[64,88] This complication rarely occurs after unilateral ganglionectomy, especially when the surgeon takes care to preserve the first lumbar ganglion. Although potency should not be affected, many experienced surgeons insist that such derangements in sexual function do occur in men. Careful preoperative questioning about sexual function is important to evaluate any changes reported after lumbar sympathectomy.

Systemic arterial *steal syndromes* resulting from lumbar sympathectomy have been reported but are largely unsubstantiated by careful analysis. Paradoxical gangrene of the contralateral extremity has been reported, but has been due to intrinsic arterial occlusion of the affected leg, rather than to selective hypoperfusion at the aortoiliac level.[9] Similarly, mesenteric arterial insufficiency with bowel infarction has been attributed to intrinsic mesenteric occlusive disease rather than to aortoiliac steal.

Apart from postsympathectomy neuralgia, the second most common "complication" is *failure to achieve the desired objectives of pain relief or tissue healing*. Additionally, attenuation of initially favorable results previously was considered to be secondary to technical errors or inadequate sympathectomy. Further elucidation of the consequences and the intrinsic limitations of lumbar sympathectomy has shown that these sequelae are unavoidable. Within the context of the criteria and indications outlined in this chapter, however, complications of this nature should be infrequent.

Proper patient selection for operation and proper evaluation in terms of standard anesthetic risk factors, and improvement in perioperative management protocols have markedly reduced the mortality of this procedure. Although Haimovici and associates,[35] Palumbro and Lulu,[57] and Taylor[79] have reported mortality rates ranging from 2.9% to 6% in older series, we and others have noted no operative deaths among a large series of high-risk patients.[15,44,53,59] Modern surgical care permits performance of lumbar sympathectomy with an almost negligible risk of perioperative death.

■ SUMMARY

The role of lumbar sympathectomy in the modern management of lower extremity vascular disease is relatively minor; in carefully selected patients with no other surgical options, however, sympathetic denervation may sufficiently increase distal perfusion and cutaneous capillary nutritive flow to allow healing in situations of limited ischemic tissue loss and decrease ischemic pain perception. Causalgia remains the best indication; although the procedure also is effective in cold-induced vasospasm, the level of disability caused is so low and the success of nonoperative management is so high that sympathectomy is rarely warranted here. Although the procedure is effective in controlling hyperhidrosis, this is uncommonly a consideration in the lower extremities (in contrast to the upper extremities), where desiccating foot powders can be helpful. Further elucidation of the influence of lumbar sympathectomy on microcirculatory hemodynamics in patients with end-stage arterial occlusive disease may refine criteria and indications for future use. Unless the potential of laparoscopic lumbar sympathectomy is realized, it is likely that improved pharmacologic agents (e.g., prostacyclin analogues), rather than an increased application of sympathectomy, will fill this void.

■ REFERENCES

1. AbuRahma AF, Robinson PA, Powell M, et al: Sympathectomy for reflex sympathetic dystrophy: Factors affecting outcome. Ann Vasc Surg 8:372, 1994.

2. AbuRahma AF, Robinson PA: Clinical parameters for predicting response to lumbar sympathectomy with severe lower limb ischemia. J Cardiovasc Surg 31:101, 1990.
3. Adson AW, Brown CE: Treatment of Raynaud's disease by lumbar ramisection and ganglionectomy and perivascular sympathectomy neurectomy of the common iliac arteries. JAMA 84:1908, 1925.
4. Barcroft H, Swan HJC: Sympathetic Control of Human Blood Vessels. London, Arnold, 1953.
5. Barnes RW: Role of lumbar sympathectomy. In Brewster DC (ed): Common Problems in Vascular Surgery. Chicago, Year Book Medical Publishers, 1989, pp 404-411.
6. Barnes RW, Baker WH, Shanik G, et al: Value of concomitant sympathectomy in aortoiliac reconstruction. Arch Surg 112:1325-1330, 1977.
7. Beglaibter N, Berlatzky Y, Zamir O, et al: Retroperitoneoscopic lumbar sympathectomy. J Vasc Surg 35:815-817, 2002.
8. Beran RD, Tsuru H: Functional and structural changes in the rabbit ear artery after sympathetic denervation. Circ Res 49:478, 1981.
9. Bergan JJ, Trippell OH: Arteriograms in ischemic limbs worsened after lumbar sympathectomy. Arch Surg 85:135, 1962.
10. Blumenberg RM, Gelfand L: Lumbar sympathectomy for limb salvage: A goal-line stand. Am J Surg 138:241, 1979.
11. Bobik A, Anderson WP: Influence of sympathectomy on alpha-2 adrenoreceptor binding sites in canine blood vessels. Life Sci 33:331, 1983.
12. Casten DF, Sadler AH, Furman D: An experimental study of the effect of sympathectomy on patency of small blood vessel anastomoses. Surg Gynecol Obstet 115:462, 1962.
13. Chapman SL, Brena SF: Learned helplessness and responses to nerve blocks in chronic low back pain patients. Pain 14:355, 1982.
14. Cheshire NJ, Darzi AW: Retroperitoneoscopic lumbar sympathectomy. Br J Surg 84:1094, 1997.
15. Collins GI, Rich NM, Claggett GP, et al: Clinical results of lumbar sympathectomy. Am Surg 47:31, 1981.
16. Cronenwett JL, Lindenauer SM: Direct measurement of arteriovenous anastomotic blood flow after lumbar sympathectomy. Surgery 82:82, 1977.
17. Cronenwett JL, Lindenauer SM: Hemodynamic effects of sympathectomy in ischemic canine hind limbs. Surgery 87:417, 1980.
18. Cronenwett JL, Zelenock GB, Whitehouse W Jr, et al: The effect of sympathetic innervation of canine muscle and skin blood flow. Arch Surg 118:420, 1983.
19. Cross FW: Lumbar sympathectomy. Cardiovasc Surg 7:151-154, 1999.
20. Cross FW, Cotton LT: Chemical lumbar sympathectomy for ischemic rest pain: A randomized, prospective controlled clinical trial. Am J Surg 150:341, 1985.
21. Dalessandri KM, Carson SM, Tillman P, et al: Effect of lumbar sympathectomy in distal arterial obstruction. Arch Surg 118:1157, 1983.
22. DaValle MJ, Bauman FG, Mintzer R, et al: Limited success of lumbar sympathectomy in the prevention of ischemic limb loss in diabetic patients. Surg Gynecol Obstet 152:784, 1981.
23. Deleted in this edition.
24. Dornhorst AC, Sharpey-Schafer EP: Collateral resistance in limbs with arterial obstruction: Spontaneous changes and effects of sympathectomy. Clin Sci 10:371, 1951.
25. Elliot TB, Royle JP: Laparoscopic extraperitoneal lumbar sympathectomy: Technique and early results. Aust N Z J Surg 66:400, 1996.
26. Deleted in this edition.
27. Faenza A, Splare R, Lapilli A, et al: Clinical results of lumbar sympathectomy alone or as a complement to direct arterial surgery. Acta Chir Belg 76:101, 1977.
28. Felder DA, Simeone FA, Linton RR, et al: Evaluation of sympathetic neurectomy in Raynaud's disease. Surgery 26:1014, 1949.
29. Flowthow PG: Anterior extraperitoneal approach to the lumbar sympathetic nerves. Am J Surg 127:953, 1948.
30. Funahashi S, Komori K, Itoh H, et al: Effects of lumbar sympathectomy on the properties of both endothelium and smooth muscle of the canine femoral artery and autogenous vein grafts under poor runoff conditions. J Surg Res 64:184, 1996.
31. Fyfe T, Quin RO: Phenol sympathectomy in the treatment of intermittent claudication: A controlled clinical trial. Br J Surg 62:68-71, 1975.
32. Ghostine SY, Gomair YG, Turner DM, et al: Phenoxybenzamine in the treatment of causalgia: Report of 40 cases. J Neurosurg 60:1263, 1984.
33. Gifford RS Jr, Hines EA Jr, Craig WM: Sympathectomy for Raynaud's phenomenon: Follow-up study of 70 women with Raynaud's disease and 54 women with secondary Raynaud's phenomenon. Circulation 17:5, 1958.
34. Groch JM, Bauman FG, Riles TS, et al: Effect of surgical lumbar sympathectomy on innervation of arterioles in the lower limb of patients with diabetes. Surg Gynecol Obstet 153:39, 1981.
35. Haimovici H, Steenman C, Karson IH: Evaluation of lumbar sympathectomy. Arch Surg 89:1089, 1964.
36. Holiday FAC, Barendregt WB, Slappendel R, et al: Lumbar sympathectomy in critical limb ischaemia: Surgical, chemical, or not at all? Cardiovasc Surg 7:200, 1999.
37. Hourlay P, Vangertruyden G, Verdyckt F, et al: Endoscopic extraperitoneal lumbar sympathectomy. Surg Endosc 9:530, 1995.
38. Imparato AM: Lumbar sympathectomy: Role in the treatment of occlusive arterial disease in the lower extremities. Surg Clin North Am 59:719, 1979.
39. Jaboulay M: Le traitement de quelques trouble trophiques du pied et de la jambe par la denudation de l'artere femoral et al distension des nerfs vasculaires. Lyon Med 91:467, 1889.
40. Janoff KA, Phinney ES, Porter JM: Lumbar sympathectomy for lower extremity vasospasm. Am J Surg 150:147, 1985.
41. Je'bara VA, Saade B: Causalgia: A wartime experience: Report of twenty treated cases. J Trauma 27:519, 1987.
42. Johnson WC, Watkins MT, Baldwin D, Hamilton J: Foot $TcPO_2$ response to lumbar sympathectomy in patients with focal ischemic necrosis. Ann Vasc Surg 12:70-74, 1998.
43. Kathouda N, Wattanasirichaigoon S, Tang E, et al: Laparoscopic lumbar sympathectomy. Surg Endosc 11:257, 1997.
44. Kim GE, Ibrahim IM, Imparato AM: Lumbar sympathectomy in end-stage arterial occlusive disease. Am Surg 183:157, 1976.
45. Leather RP, Karmody AM: In situ saphenous vein arterial bypass for the treatment of limb ischemia. Adv Surg 19:175, 1986.
46. Lee BY, Madden JL, Tuoden WR, et al: Lumbar sympathectomy for toe gangrene: Long-term follow-up. Am J Surg 145:398, 1983.
47. Leriche R: Some researches on the periarterial sympathetics. Ann Surg 74:385, 1921.
48. Lindenauer SM, Cronenwett JL: What is the place of lumbar sympathectomy? Br J Surg 69(Suppl):532, 1982.
49. Litwin MS: Post-sympathectomy neuralgia. Arch Surg 84:591, 1962.
50. Loh L, Nathan PW: Painful peripheral states and sympathetic blocks. J Neurol Neurosurg Psychiatry 41:664, 1978.
51. Ludbrook J: Collateral arterial resistance in human lower limbs. J Surg Res 6:423, 1966.
52. May AG, DeWeese JA, Rob CG: Effect of sympathectomy on blood flow in arterial stenosis. Ann Surg 158:182, 1968.
53. Mockus MB, Rutherford RB, Rosales C, et al: Sympathectomy for causalgia. Arch Surg 122:668, 1987.
54. Moore WS, Hall AD: Effects of lumbar sympathectomy on skin capillary blood flow in arterial occlusive disease. J Surg Res 14:151, 1973.
55. Deleted in this edition.
56. Owens JC: Causalgia. Am Surg 23:636, 1957.
57. Palumbro LT, Lulu DJ: Lumbar sympathectomy in peripheral vascular disease. Arch Surg 86:182, 1963.
58. Perry MO, Horton J: Muscle and subcutaneous oxygen tension: Measurements by mass spectrometry after sympathectomy. Arch Surg 113:176, 1973.
59. Persson AV, Anderson LA, Padberg FT Jr: Selection of patients for lumbar sympathectomy. Surg Clin North Am 65:393, 1985.

60. Petten CV, Roberts WJ, Rhodes DL: Behavioral test of tolerance for aversive mechanical stimuli in sympathectomized cats. Pain 15:177, 1983.
61. Pistolese GR, Speziale F, Taurino M, et al: Criteria for prognostic evaluation of the results of lumbar sympathectomy: Clinical, hemodynamic and angiographic findings. J Cardiovasc Surg 23:411, 1982.
62. Plecha FR, Bamberger RA, Hoffman M, et al: A new criterion for predicting response to lumbar sympathectomy in patients with severe arteriosclerotic occlusive disease. Surgery 88:375-381, 1980.
63. Porter JM, Rivers SP: Management of Raynaud's syndrome. In Bergan JJ, Yao JST (eds): Evaluation and Treatment of Upper and Lower Extremity Circulatory Disorders. New York, Grune & Stratton, 1983, pp 181-202.
64. Quale JB: Sexual function after bilateral lumbar sympathectomy and aortoiliac bypass surgery. J Cardiovasc Surg 21:215, 1980.
65. Deleted in this edition.
66. Royle ND: A new operative procedure in the treatment of spastic paralysis and its experimental basis. Med J Aust 1:77, 1924.
67. Rutherford RB, Jones DH, Bergentz SE, et al: The efficacy of dextran-40 in preventing early postoperative thrombosis following difficult lower extremity bypass. J Vasc Surg 1:776, 1984.
68. Rutherford RB, Valenta J: Extremity blood flow and distribution: The effects of arterial occlusion, sympathectomy and exercise. Surgery 69:332, 1971.
69. Satiani B, Liapsis CD, Hayes JP, et al: Prospective randomized study of concomitant lumbar sympathectomy with aortoiliac reconstruction. Am J Surg 143:755, 1982.
70. Sanderson CJ: Chemical lumbar sympathectomy with radiologic assessment. Ann R Coll Surg Engl 63:420-422, 1981.
71. Sandmann W, Kremer K, Wust H, et al: Postoperative control of blood flow in arterial surgery: Results of electromagnetic blood flow measurement. Thoraxchir Vask Chir 25:427, 1977.
72. Shepherd JT: The effects of acute occlusion of the femoral artery on the blood supply to the calf of the leg before and after release of sympathetic vasomotor tone. Chir Sci 9:355, 1950.
73. Shumacker HB Jr: A personal overview of causalgia and other reflex dystrophies. Ann Surg 201:278, 1985.
74. Siegel ME, William GM, Giargiano FA Jr, et al: A useful objective criterion for determining the healing potential of an ischemic ulcer. J Nucl Med 21:993, 1975.
75. Simeone FA: Intravascular pressure, vascular tone and sympathectomy. Presidential Address: 16th Annual Meeting of the Society for Vascular Surgery, Chicago, IL, June 24, 1962. Surgery 53:1-18, 1963.
76. Smith RB, Dratz AF, Coberly JC, et al: Effect of lumbar sympathectomy on muscle blood flow in advanced occlusive vascular disease. Ann Surg 37:247, 1971.
77. Deleted in this edition.
78. Sumner DS, Strandness DE Jr: An abnormal finger pulse associated with cold sensitivity. Ann Surg 175:294, 1972.
79. Taylor I: Lumbar sympathectomy for intermittent claudication. Br J Clin Pract 27:39, 1973.
80. Thompson JE: The diagnosis and management of post-traumatic pain syndromes (causalgia). Aust N Z J Surg 49:299, 1979.
81. van der Stricht J: Lumbar sympathectomy in occlusive diseases. Int Angiol 4:345, 1985.
82. Vautinnen E, Luberg MV, Sotaranta M: The immediate effect of lumbar sympathectomy on arterial blood flow measured by electromagnetic flowmetry. Scand J Thorac Cardiovasc Surg 12:101, 1978.
83. Walker PM, Johnston KW: Predicting the success of a sympathectomy: A retrospective study using discriminant function and multiple regression analysis. Surgery 87:216, 1980.
84. Walsh JA, Glynn CJ, Cousins MJ, et al: Blood flow, sympathetic activity and pain relief following lumbar sympathetic blockade or surgical sympathectomy. Anaesth Intensive Care 13:18, 1985.
85. Watarida S, Shiraishi S, Fujimura M, et al: Laparoscopic lumbar sympathectomy for lower-limb disease. Surg Endosc 16:500-503, 2002.
86. Webber RH: An analysis of the cross communications between the sympathetic trunks in the lumbar region in man. Ann Surg 145:365, 1957.
87. Welch GH, Leiberman DP: Cutaneous blood flow in the foot following lumbar sympathectomy. Scand J Clin Lab Invest 45:621, 1985.
88. Whitelaw GP, Smithwick RH: Some secondary effects of sympathectomy, with particular reference to disturbance of sexual dysfunction. N Engl J Med 245:121, 1951.
89. Wronski J: Lumbar sympathectomy performed by means of videoscopy. Cardiovasc Surg 6:453, 1998.
90. Yao JST, Bergan JJ: Predictability of vascular reactivity relative to sympathetic ablation. Arch Surg 107:676, 1973.
91. Yeager GH, Cowley RA: Anatomical observations on the lumbar sympathetics with evaluation of sympathectomies in organic peripheral vascular disease. Ann Surg 127:953, 1948.

Chapter

86

Nonatheromatous Causes of Popliteal Artery Disease

LEWIS J. LEVIEN, MB, BCH, FCS(SA), PHD(MED)

Although atherosclerosis remains the most common cause of lower limb ischemia, other nonatherosclerotic causes of arterial disease must be considered in the differential diagnosis of a young patient who presents with lower limb claudication precipitated by exercise or with rest pain secondary to more critical ischemia. In the subset of patients younger than 50 years old and without specific risk factors for atheroma, popliteal vascular entrapment and adventitial cystic disease of the lower limb arteries are the cause of the symptoms in most cases.[1-3] Because prompt correct diagnosis and surgical intervention can restore limb blood supply to normal in these young and active patients, this differential diagnosis should be considered in all young and athletic individuals complaining of claudication. Other nonatherosclerotic causes of lower limb ischemia are encountered occasionally. These rarer causes include fibromuscular disease (most common in the iliac arteries), external compression syndromes found in the external iliac artery in high-intensity athletes such as cyclists, and occlusive arterial lesions seen in pseudoxanthoma elasticum. These latter conditions are discussed in Chapters 27 and 28.

■ HISTORICAL PERSPECTIVE

Popliteal Artery Entrapment

Although the anatomic abnormality of popliteal artery entrapment syndrome was first described by a medical student in 1879,[4] the clinical condition of popliteal artery entrapment syndrome was not recognized until 1958.[5] Hamming and Vink,[6] who described the first surgical case of popliteal artery entrapment, reported four additional cases and claimed that the incidence of popliteal artery entrapment was 40% in patients younger than 30 years old presenting with calf and foot claudication. Isolated cases subsequently were reported,[7-15] but the term *popliteal artery entrapment syndrome* did not appear until the mid-1960s.[7,9] Servello[11] was the first to draw attention to diminished distal pulses observed with forced plantar flexion or dorsiflexion in patients with this syndrome. Biemans and Van Bockel[12] focused attention on the clinical syndrome of popliteal artery entrapment in an extensive review of the literature in 1977.

The true incidence of the popliteal artery entrapment syndrome in the general population is unknown. Early authors believed the condition to be rare,[7,9,12-18] but it has become apparent more recently that the condition is considerably more common than previously appreciated.[19-23] In the first large series of cases published, Bouhoutsos and Daskalakis[21] reported a review of 20,000 Greek soldiers. They found 45 instances of the anomaly in 33 subjects, an incidence of 0.165% in young men entering military service. Gibson and colleagues,[13] in a study of 86 autopsy specimens, showed the anomaly in four limbs with a prevalence of 3.5% in cadaver specimens. A large proportion of normal, asymptomatic individuals have compression or occlusion of the popliteal artery with forced plantar flexion or dorsiflexion.[24-29] Noninvasive techniques have little value as screening tests for evaluating the incidence of popliteal artery entrapment syndrome in the asymptomatic general population.

In a young athlete presenting with claudication symptoms, popliteal artery entrapment syndrome may be the underlying cause in 60% of cases.[1,2] The entrapment mechanism has been documented to involve the popliteal vein in one third of cases.[6,10,12,14] Early reports assumed that the bilateral occurrence of the condition was rare, but more recent reports have indicated a higher prevalence of bilateral disease than previously reported.[7,13,15,17,29,30]

Early attempts to classify the various types of popliteal artery entrapment syndrome were based on the anatomy observed at operation[18,21]; this resulted in confusing and overly complex classifications. Better appreciation of the embryology of this condition has led to a simplified classification based on the developmental anatomy; four types of popliteal artery entrapment syndrome are currently described.[15,23,29] A fifth type is reserved for venous entrapment when it occurs. A sixth type of entrapment has been described as a "functional" entrapment in symptomatic patients who have no apparent anatomic abnormality, but in whom the popliteal artery is compressed in certain positions.[24,25,28,29,31]

Adventitial Cystic Disease

Atkins and Key[32] first described adventitial cystic disease in 1947. Except for the anatomic site of the cyst, their description of this condition was typical of the usual presentation of adventitial cystic disease. These authors described a 40-year-old man with a 4-month history of progressive thigh and calf claudication. Surgical exploration of a mass in the region of the external iliac artery revealed the features of a conventional ganglion. Myxomatous tissue was found to be arising from the posterior aspect of the middle third of the external iliac artery.

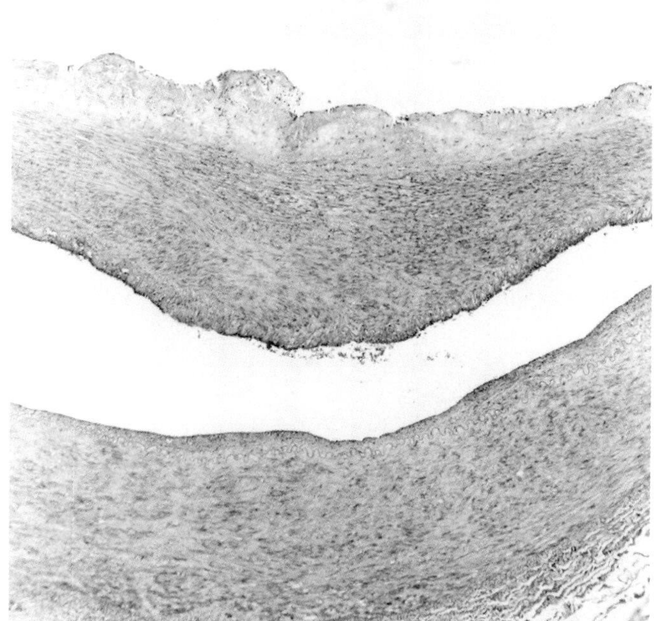

FIGURE 86-1 Histology of an adventitial cyst removed from a radial artery. The microscopic appearances are similar to a simple ganglion, with a simple cuboidal cell lining.

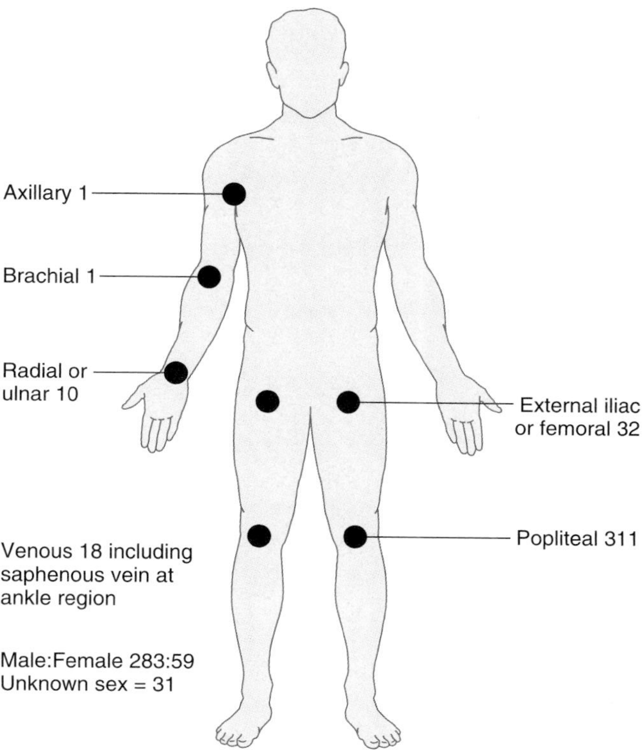

FIGURE 86-2 Anatomic location and sex in 375 published cases of adventitial cystic disease.

In 1954, Ejrup and Hiertonn[33] described a similar condition in what subsequently has been found to be the most common location for adventitial cystic disease, the popliteal artery.[3,34] Ten years after the condition was first described, only four cases of popliteal adventitial cystic disease had been described in the literature.[35] Characteristically the patients all were young men presenting with intermittent claudication subsequently shown at operation to be due to a popliteal cyst filled with a mucoid material. Microscopic examination revealed a cystic lesion lined by a simple cellular lining closely resembling a ganglion in appearance and lying in the adventitial layer of the artery (Fig. 86-1). The intramural mucinous degeneration was clearly different from Erdheim's cystic medial necrosis. Investigators reporting cases of adventitial cystic disease frequently have commented on the absence of associated atherosclerotic changes in patients with adventitial cystic disease.[36,37]

Although many case reports followed,[38,39] the cause of adventitial cystic disease remained unexplained. Subsequent reviews by Flanigan and colleagues[3] in 1979, Jasinski and colleagues[40] in 1987, and Levien and Benn[37] in 1999 established that adventitial cystic disease occurs in numerous sites where large arteries lie in close proximity to adjacent joint spaces. Although the popliteal artery is the most commonly affected location (Fig. 86-2), other sites of occurrence are the femoral and external iliac arteries in relation to the hip joint, the radial or ulnar arteries in proximity to the wrist joint, the brachial artery adjacent to the elbow, and the axillary artery adjacent to the shoulder joint.[3,34,37,41] Adventitial cystic disease also has been reported in the veins of the leg,[34,42-44] in the femoral vein adjacent to the hip joint,[45] and in the saphenous vein near the ankle joint.[46] Similar types of ganglion-like cysts have been reported in the lateral popliteal nerve.[47,48] To date, 374 cases of adventitial cystic disease have been documented in the literature (see Fig. 86-2), although many cases probably remain unreported.

The condition of adventitial cystic disease of the popliteal artery chiefly affects men in the ratio of approximately 15:1 and appears in the 30s and 40s. The youngest reported patient was 10 years old, and the oldest was a 77-year-old man. In women, the condition usually appears in the 50s.[3] The prevalence of popliteal adventitial cystic disease as a cause of claudication was found to be 1 in 1200 cases, with the condition being found in 1 in 1000 angiograms, suggesting an incidence in patients with claudication of about 0.01%.[49]

■ ETIOLOGY

The developmental abnormality that gives rise to the popliteal vascular entrapment syndrome is now well accepted. Although the exact etiology of adventitial cystic disease is obscure, there is strong evidence to support a developmental explanation to account for the manifestations of this condition. The reader is referred to Chapter 7 for an overview of the development of the vascular tree before proceeding with the relevant finer details contained in this section.

Embryology of the Limb Arteries

During early development of the fetus, the developing upper and lower limb buds initially receive their blood supply from a single central or axial artery. With further differentiation

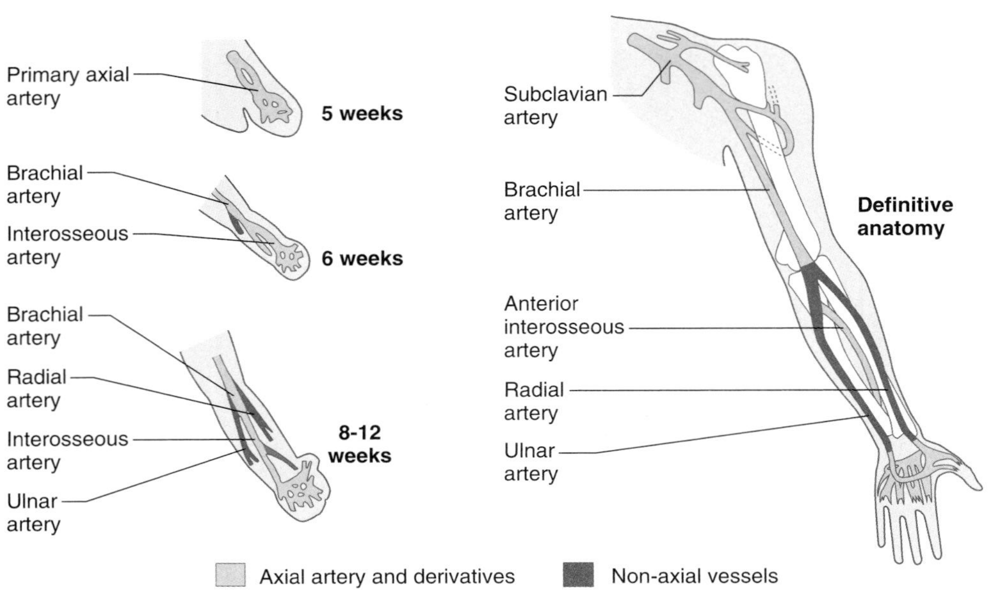

FIGURE 86-3 Embryologic derivation of upper limb arteries. Remnants of the axial artery and arteries that develop with later differentiation are indicated. (From Levien LJ, Benn C: Adventitial cystic disease: A unifying hypothesis. J Vasc Surg 28:193, 1998.)

of the limbs, this axial artery disappears in certain areas. The axial artery is replaced by newly developing nonaxial vessels that coalesce from vascular plexuses to form the definitive vascular anatomy in the adult. This process is summarized for the upper and the lower limbs in Figures 86-3 and 86-4.

Etiology of Popliteal Vascular Entrapment

Early reports of popliteal artery entrapment syndrome described the unusual anatomic findings that were associated with popliteal artery occlusion, but authors had great difficulty in appreciating the cause for this condition. As further reports appeared in the literature, subsequent investigators developed a classification system describing their observations. For this reason, the originally proposed classifications of the various types of popliteal artery entrapment syndrome were based on the anatomic variations observed by surgeons at operation.[18,21] Although this frequently used classification was adequate for most purposes, a need remained to explain and classify the less commonly observed anomalies. Better appreciation of the embryology of the popliteal artery and the associated muscles of the popliteal fossa has led to a more logical classification system based on the developmental anatomy.

In the developing limb bud, the embryologic popliteal artery is initially the continuation of the primitive axial segment known as the *ischiadic artery* (see Fig. 86-4).[50-52] At the 6- to 10-week stage of human development, the limb bud rotates 180 degrees medially, then the leg undergoes extension of 90 degrees. As the limb bud rotates internally and extends, the ischiadic artery involutes, and the new external iliac and superficial femoral arteries are formed from vascular plexuses in a more anterior plane, taking over the blood supply of the developing limb bud. At the knee, the proximal portion of the adult popliteal artery develops as part of and in continuity with the developing femoral artery[29,53] and is derived by fusion of the developing femoral arterial plexus and the popliteal remnant of the ischiadic artery. The mid-portion of the definitive popliteal artery is derived directly from the remnant of the axial artery. The primitive axial distal popliteal artery, lying deep to the forming popliteus muscle, disappears at about the 20- to 22-mm stage of the embryo or persists as the profunda poplitea artery.

In lower order animals, the medial head of the gastrocnemius muscle arises proximally from the posterior aspect of the fibula and lateral tibia. In humans, the muscle mass that is to compose the future medial head of the gastrocnemius muscle migrates across the popliteal fossa from its original lateral position (Fig. 86-5).[50-52] This migration occurs at the same time as the aforementioned changes are taking place in the femoral and popliteal arterial systems. At the 20- to 22-mm stage, the distal third of the popliteal artery, originating deep to the developing popliteus muscle, involutes to become a deep branch of the popliteal artery. During this critical stage, although there is no discrete distal popliteal artery present, the muscle mass destined to become the medial head of the gastrocnemius muscle migrates through the popliteal fossa from lateral to medial, taking advantage of the temporary absence of the distal third of the popliteal artery. The definitive distal popliteal artery now forms superficial to the popliteus muscle by the fusion of two new vessels (the newly forming anterior and posterior tibial vessels), but only after the medial head of the gastrocnemius has migrated medially across the popliteal fossa (Fig. 86-5C). With further development, the definitive attachment of the medial head of the gastrocnemius muscle migrates proximally to take origin from the area of the posterior surface of the femur immediately proximal to the medial femoral condyle (Fig. 86-5D).[53]

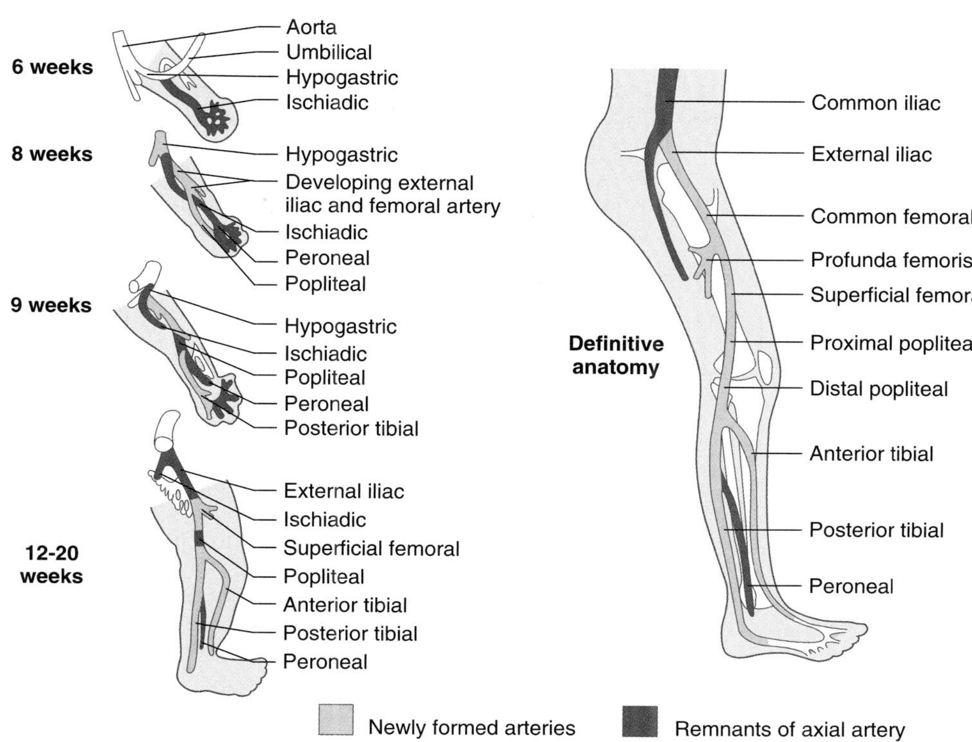

FIGURE 86-4 Embryologic derivation of the popliteal and other lower limb arteries. Remnants of the axial artery and arteries that develop with later differentiation are indicated. (From Levien LJ, Benn C: Adventitial cystic disease: A unifying hypothesis. J Vasc Surg 28:193-205, 1998.)

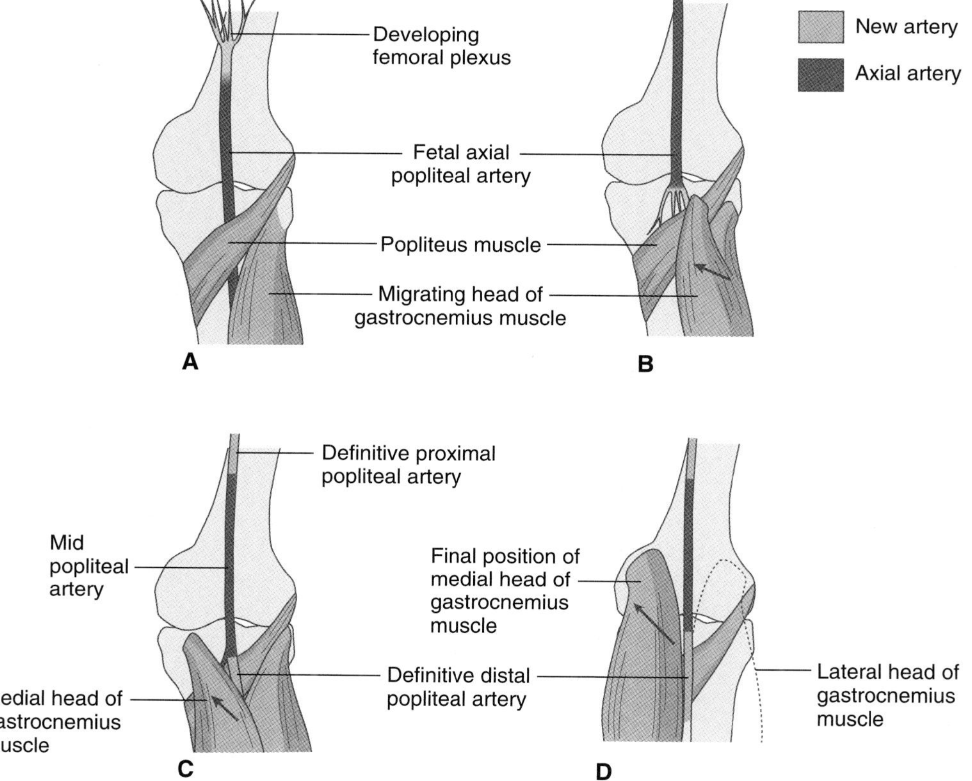

FIGURE 86-5 Migration of the medial head of the gastrocnemius muscle through the popliteal fossa during the formation of the popliteal artery. **A,** The medial head of the gastrocnemius muscle begins migration from the region of the fibula. At this stage, the axial distal popliteal artery lies deep to the popliteus muscle. **B,** The distal portion of the popliteal artery involutes as the medial head of the gastrocnemius muscle passes from lateral to medial. The proximal popliteal artery is derived from fusion with the developing femoral plexus, whereas the mid-portion of the popliteal artery is formed from the persistent axial artery remnant. **C,** A new or nonaxial distal popliteal artery now forms superficial to the popliteus muscle, after the medial head has migrated through the popliteal fossa. **D,** The normal definitive popliteal anatomy. (From Levien LJ, Veller MG: Popliteal artery entrapment syndrome: More common than previously necognised. J Vasc Surg 30:587-598, 1999.)

Classification of Popliteal Vascular Entrapment Based on Embryology

If the definitive distal popliteal artery forms by premature fusion of the newly formed anterior and posterior tibial arteries before the medial migration of the medial head of the gastrocnemius, the newly formed artery may be swept medially, resulting in the definitive artery now lying medial to the normally placed medial head of the gastrocnemius muscle.[29] This abnormality of development results in classic, or type I, popliteal entrapment and is associated with a marked medial deviation of the popliteal artery in the popliteal fossa, anatomically and on angiography as depicted in Figure 86-6 (type I). Alternatively a prematurely formed definitive distal popliteal artery may partially arrest the migration of the medial head, resulting in type II entrapment. In type II entrapment, the popliteal artery is medially displaced to a lesser degree and lies deep and medial to the medial head of the gastrocnemius, which has a variable attachment to the lateral aspect of the medial femoral condyle, intercondylar area, or even the lower femur above the lateral condyle. The artery lies on the medial aspect of an abnormally placed medial head of the gastrocnemius as shown in Figure 86-6 (type II).

If any mesodermal remnants of the migrating medial head persist anywhere in the popliteal fossa, either anterior or posterior to the definitive popliteal artery, or if the artery develops within the migrating muscle mass, a type III popliteal entrapment may result. In this case, the entrapment mechanism may be an abnormal slip of mature skeletal muscle, abnormal fibrous bands, or abnormal additional tendinous bands derived from the remnants of the migrating mesenchyme destined to become the medial head of the gastrocnemius. These abnormal additional bands of tissue may arise from either the medial or the lateral femoral condyles or from the intercondylar or supracondylar area, as shown in Figure 86-6 (type III). The definitive popliteal artery may pass between a double origin of the medial head of the gastrocnemius. If the axial artery persists as the definitive distal popliteal artery, it will lie in the primitive position, deep to the popliteus muscle or fibrous bands, resulting in a type IV entrapment (see Fig. 86-6). This most primitive form of the anatomy is least commonly encountered, but probably has the most aggressive natural history for popliteal artery damage. It can be appreciated that entrapment types I to III are not discrete entities, but rather a spectrum of anatomic abnormalities that depend on the temporal relationship between the stage of migration of the medial head of the gastrocnemius muscle and the evolving distal popliteal artery. In contrast, type IV popliteal entrapment is due to anomalous development of the popliteal artery and is independent of medial head migration.

Entrapment syndromes may not be confined to the popliteal artery. When an entrapment mechanism includes or surrounds the popliteal vein and the artery, Rich and colleagues[10,15] have termed this a *type V* entrapment.[6,12,13] Any of the types of entrapment (with the possible exception of type I) may include the tibial nerves, resulting in neurologic symptoms, such as paresthesias, in addition to claudication as the presenting symptom.[19]

A sixth type of popliteal artery entrapment has been described in symptomatic individuals who show compression of the popliteal artery with stress maneuvers, but in whom there is no apparent anatomic abnormality. This condition has been termed *functional entrapment* because the exact nature of the entrapment mechanism is unclear.[25,26,28,29] There are two possible explanations for this condition. Some authors believe that functional entrapment occurs as a result of incomplete migration of the medial head of the the gastrocnemius, resulting in a more lateral proximal origin of the muscle from the lateral aspect of the medial femoral condyle or even from the intercondylar area. With regular lower limb exercise and muscle hypertrophy, such an

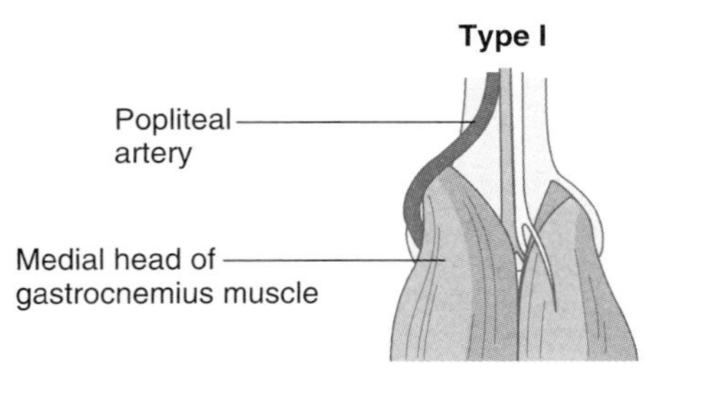

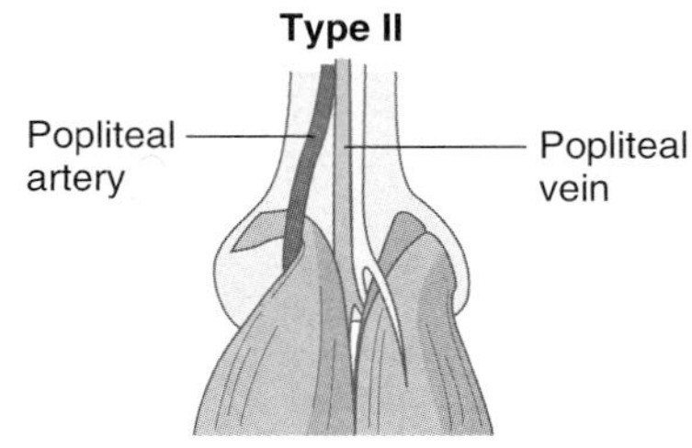

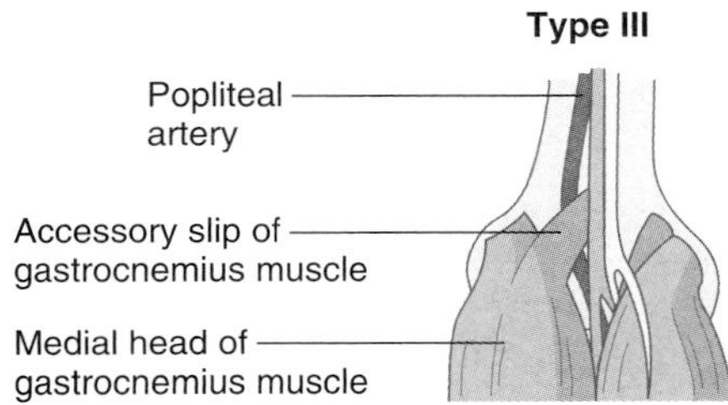

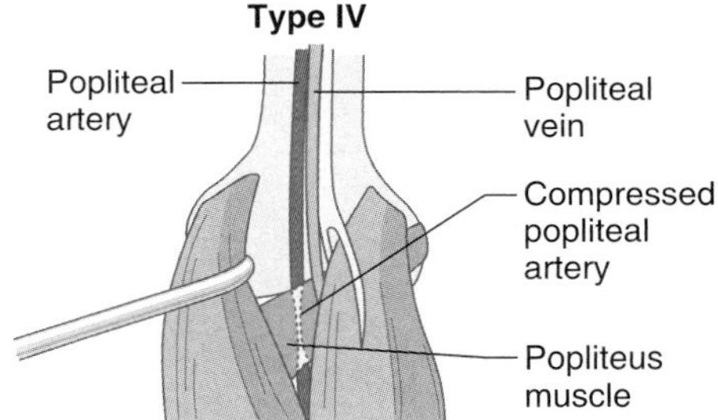

FIGURE 86-6 Classification of types of popliteal artery entrapment syndrome. (From Levien LJ, Veller MG: Popliteal artery entrapment syndrome: More common than previously recognised. J Vasc Surg 30:587-598, 1999.)

abnormally placed medial head of the gastrocnemius is more likely to impinge on the medial and posterior aspect of the popliteal artery and can cause physiologic occlusion of the artery in extreme plantar flexion or extension.[24,25,29] Other authors have postulated and advanced evidence for the entrapment occurring as a result of compression of the distal popliteal artery as it passes through the soleus muscle sling.[26] These mechanisms also are thought to explain why half of apparently normal asymptomatic individuals have reduced or abolished popliteal artery blood flow with extremes of plantar flexion or dorsiflexion against resistance.[24-27] Regardless of the cause, this functional type of popliteal entrapment is well recognized and has been termed *type VI*[25,28,29] or *type F*. An acquired type of entrapment has been described after infragenicular bypass surgery.[54,55]

Etiology of Adventitial Cystic Disease

The presence of a communication with the adjacent joint, as shown in many arterial cases of adventitial cystic disease and in cysts of the lateral popliteal nerve, strongly favors some form of developmental anomaly. In 1963, Bliss and colleagues[56,57] acknowledged that the cause of the condition was unknown, but stated that the clinical picture, pathologic features, and treatment were well defined.

The exact cause of adventitial cystic disease of the popliteal artery and other blood vessels affected by this condition is unknown. Schramek and Hashmonai[58] in 1973 and later Flanigan's group[3] in 1979 reviewed the following four theories of possible etiology and pathogenesis of adventitial cystic disease:

- Systemic disorder theory
- Repetitive trauma theory
- Ganglion theory
- Developmental theory

Various investigators have advanced several theories in attempts to explain the diverse manifestations of adventitial cystic disease. Convincing evidence in support of any one theory is elusive, however. Some concepts of formation of adventitial cystic disease involve a combination of more than one of these theories of causation.

The first theory of a "mucinous" or myxomatous *systemic* degenerative condition associated with a generalized disorder[59] was initially proposed by Linquette and coworkers,[60] who based their hypothesis on an abnormal skin biopsy specimen. This theory has failed to gain substantial support because long-term follow-up has not shown systemic manifestation of disease in any patient, and a contralateral or other adventitial cyst in a second site has not been reported in any patient presenting initially with adventitial cystic disease.[3] In addition, this theory does not explain the preponderance of adventitial cysts in the popliteal artery. The name *myxomatous cystic degeneration* seems to be a misnomer.[49]

In 1979, Flanigan and colleagues[3] surveyed the authors of previous reports to obtain long-term follow-up on patients who had been treated for popliteal adventitial cystic disease. They reported 27 patients with follow-up of more than 2 years (longest follow-up 30 years). In no instance was amputation required, and no serious disability was recorded. No patient experienced adventitial cystic disease of the contralateral popliteal artery or of any other artery, and in no instance did joint disease or evidence of any systemic connective tissue disorder develop.

The single theory that has enjoyed the widest support is that of *repetitive trauma*.[57] Proximity of the popliteal artery to the knee joint is proposed to render the artery unduly prone to stretch and distortion. This repetitive trauma of the popliteal artery has been postulated to cause possible destruction and cystic degeneration of the adventitia of the adjacent vessel.[34,35,61-64] It is thought that small detachments of the adventitia from the media cause intramural bleeds,[65,66] resulting in cystic formation by chemical enzymatic activity within the adventitia.[67]

A further modification of the trauma theory suggests that joint-related structures may undergo repeated trauma,[68] with joint capsule degeneration leading to connective tissue changes in which cells secrete a material derived from ground substance or collagen that contains hydroxyproline.[69] These cells then form cysts, which may invade the adventitia.[3] It is suggested that such cysts enlarge, coalesce to form multilocular cysts, and grow rapidly to encroach on the arterial lumen or possibly cause medial damage by direct compression of the arterial wall and subsequent arterial thrombosis.[67] In addition, a shearing stimulus has been suggested to arise mechanically from an element of entrapment of the vessels by fascia and tendons of the gastrocnemius muscle.[68,70,71]

Despite the attraction of these proposals, compelling evidence in support of the traumatic theory is lacking[72] because (1) a history of recurrent trauma is lacking in most cases of adventitial cystic disease, and (2) the condition has been reported to occur in school-age children. This theory also fails to explain the occurrence of adventitial cystic disease in the radial, ulnar, axillary, and external iliac arteries and the low frequency of the condition in laborers and athletes, who presumably sustain far greater mechanical stresses to their popliteal vessels than the normal population.

Adventitial cysts have been reported to be biochemically and histologically similar to ganglia,[73-76] leading to the *ganglion theory*, which suggests that adventitial cysts arise as capsular synovial structures, which then enlarge and track, either during development or later in life, along vascular branches to involve the adventitia of the adjacent major vessel.[76] The ganglion theory of origin is supported by a rich content of hyaluronic acid and a positive alcian blue stain response of the adventitial cystic contents.[77]

Further support for the theory of ganglion involvement of adjacent structures is provided by case reports in which such cystic lesions have involved adjacent vascular structures. These cases include adventitial cystic disease involving the lesser saphenous vein,[46] lesions connected to a Baker's cyst,[78] and further reports of adventitial cystic disease involving the radial artery.[37,79] Attempts by various researchers[80-82] to confirm the ganglion hypothesis through study of the histochemistry of the cyst lining and chemical analysis of the fluid contents have failed, however, to provide convincing evidence in support of the theory.

The fourth proposal, the *developmental theory*, is that adventitial cystic disease is a developmental manifestation of mucin-secreting cells derived from the mesenchyme of the adjacent joint.[3,83,84] This theory implies that such cells are included in the adventitia of the artery or vein during development.[68,76,85,86] This idea, also called the *cellular inclusion theory,* is supported by the reported demonstration of a communication between the cyst and the neighboring joint in many case reports in which this phenomenon has been actively sought at surgery.[3,48,76,82,84,87-89]

A refinement of the developmental theory is the possibility that a joint-related, ganglion-like structure is incorporated into the vessel during embryologic development and that this synovial rest or ganglion secretes and enlarges over the years.[35,90] It develops within the adventitial wall at a later stage in life, invoking ganglion and developmental theories.[39] This idea provides a concept of development consistent with surgical experience. When the cyst is entirely adventitial, it is readily removed, leaving the artery intact. Otherwise, when sequestered cells are the cause of cystic formation within the deeper layers of the artery, enucleation is impossible, and the affected arterial segment must be resected.

In support of the developmental theory, Levien and Benn[37] drew attention to the embryologic derivation of the arteries that are affected by adventitial cystic disease and concluded that all such blood vessels are nonaxial arteries (see Figs. 86-3 and 86-4). Their study suggests that during limb bud development, cell rests derived from condensations of mesenchymal tissue destined to form the knee, hip, wrist, shoulder, or ankle joints are incorporated into the adjacent nonaxial vessels during development of these vessels at 15 to 22 weeks. These newly forming nonaxial vessels develop from vascular plexuses during the same stage of development and in close proximity to the adjacent condensing joint structures. These cell rests could be responsible for the formation of adventitial cystic disease later in life, when the mucoid material secreted results in a mass lesion within the arterial or venous wall. It has been argued that a reported case of an axillary artery adventitial cyst[41] is evidence against this theory, but the axillary artery forms from a fusion of the limb bud axial artery and the sixth arch artery (the definitive subclavian artery on the right), permitting cell rests to gain access to the developing vessel.

Ulex europaeus 1 histochemical markers are present in vascularly derived endothelium. The absence of *U. europaeus* 1 reactivity of the endothelium-like cells of the lining of adventitial cysts[77] tends to exclude a vascular origin for this lesion and is advanced in support of a synovial or joint-related origin. Adventitial cyst fluid has a much higher concentration of hyaluronic acid than synovial fluid. These findings, described by Jay and colleagues,[91] support the hypothesis that inclusion of mesenchymal mucin-secreting cells has occurred as a result of embryologic aberration and contradict the concept that adventitial arterial cysts are formed and maintained by communication with a synovial space. The suggestion that synovial rests are sources of the cyst is unlikely because (1) synovial cavity forms through liquefaction of the limb bud mesenchyme rather than from specialized cell types,[68,92] and (2) histochemical markers for synovium are absent in adventitial cysts.[72-74,77] These findings do not exclude the possibility, however, that mesenchymal cell rests secreting a mucin-like substance may be incorporated into the vessel wall during development and that these cell rests give rise to the adventitial cystic manifestation with anatomic and chemical characteristics different from those of normal synovial tissues.

■ CLINICAL PICTURE

Popliteal Artery Entrapment Syndrome

Claudication in the calf and foot of a young person with no risk factors for atheroma should suggest popliteal artery entrapment syndrome (see Fig. 86-7). The onset of the symptoms is often sudden, occurring during an episode of intense lower extremity activity, such as during the running of an obstacle course or a marathon.[7,9,19] Although claudication is the only symptom in 69% of cases, paresthesias occur in 14%, and rest pain or ulcer is present in 11%.[20] The symptoms may be due to either compression of the mid-popliteal artery with exercise or development of segmental occlusion of the popliteal artery. Isolated aneurysms of the popliteal artery may be responsible for distal embolic disease. The syndrome previously was thought to be more common in men, possibly related to the military nature of the populations studied. More recent publications suggest a male-to-female ratio of 2:1.[29] Bilaterality is common; in a personal series of 140 limbs, if patients with popliteal entrapment syndrome presented with unilateral symptoms, an entrapment abnormality was detected on the contralateral side in two thirds of patients.[29]

The symptoms described by these patients include cramping in the calf and foot and coldness, blanching, paresthesias, and numbness in the foot associated with walking and relieved by rest. Symptoms are generally unilateral despite the subsequent demonstration of bilateral involvement.[11] In a few patients with arterial compression only and without occluding thrombus, the claudication has had unusual characteristics: The claudication occurs with walking but not with running, or it begins immediately with the first steps rather than after the patient has walked a finite distance.[8,9] Some patients have presented with frank popliteal artery aneurysms beyond the site of arterial compression.[9]

Untreated, the compression mechanism frequently results in deterioration of the popliteal artery, which may progress to eventual occlusion.[20] The development of critical ischemia with occlusion of the popliteal artery is rare.[2,29]

In most cases, popliteal vascular entrapment is suspected from the patient's history. Distal pulses are usually palpable at rest if the artery is patent, but these pulses disappear with passive dorsiflexion or active plantar flexion. In addition, there may be evidence of increased collateral circulation around the knee. Pedal pulses are absent or diminished if occlusion of the artery has occurred. Geniculate arteries may be palpable over the anteromedial and anterolateral aspects of the knee, which is warm. The sudden onset of severe disabling claudication in a young adult without atherosclerotic risk factors is highly suggestive of popliteal artery occlusion due to entrapment.

In patients who have characteristic symptoms but palpable popliteal and pedal pulses, the pathophysiologic finding is a compressed but nonoccluded popliteal artery. In this situation, two maneuvers must be added during palpation of the pedal pulses: passive dorsiflexion of the foot and active plantar flexion against resistance. With these maneuvers, the gastrocnemius muscle is tensed across the compressed artery, obliterating the pedal pulses. Auscultation of the popliteal artery may show a systolic bruit if the artery is sufficiently compressed. The maneuvers just described also should be performed on the opposite, asymptomatic limb because the predisposing anatomic abnormality may be bilateral.

Palpation of a popliteal artery aneurysm in a young person should suggest the presence of entrapment. Evaluation of the venous system for evidence of obstruction at the popliteal level, such as distended superficial veins, edema, and dependent cyanosis, completes the evaluation of the lower extremities. The remainder of the evaluation consists of efforts to exclude diffuse arterial disease (i.e., arteriosclerosis, arteritis, collagen vascular disease, or a proximal source for arterial embolus). If the more probable diagnoses have been eliminated by careful general examination, a localized anomaly in the popliteal artery is likely.

Adventitial Cystic Disease

The typical patient with symptoms due to adventitial cystic disease of the popliteal artery is a man in his mid-40s with a sudden onset of claudication, often with ischemic neuropathy. Usually the history of symptoms is short, often measured in days to weeks rather than months to years. The claudication is usually severe, limiting walking distance to 50 m or less. Occasionally, ischemic neuropathy may cause paresthesias, burning pain, or coldness.

Reduction or absence of popliteal and foot pulses is characteristic of popliteal adventitial cystic disease. If the lesion is producing only stenosis, however, a bruit may be heard in the popliteal fossa, and evidence of total occlusion appears only during acute knee flexion, when distal pulses disappear. Stenosis rather than occlusion is present in approximately two thirds of cases. Lewis and associates[49] reported that a bruit could be heard over the popliteal artery of one of their patients in whom the symptoms had recurred after the cyst had been incompletely excised.

Barnett and colleagues[93] noted the phenomenon of disappearing distal arterial pulses in a 61-year-old patient who had normal limb pulses and oscillometric readings. Ankle pulses disappeared on exercise, and a loud murmur appeared over the popliteal artery at that time. Other investigators have reported hemodynamic alterations produced by exercise.[71]

Although the onset of symptoms is usually sudden, it is probable that the cyst arises over a long period, producing progressive stenosis of the artery with preservation of patency. The cyst appears to enlarge slowly and progressively within the arterial wall, producing a localized stenosis in the affected vessel. Initially, as in other causes of vascular stenosis, velocity of blood flow increases through the diseased segment. With progressive compromise of the vascular lumen, it is possible that flow occurs only with peak systole,[94] giving rise to the important clinical sign of a bruit in the popliteal fossa first described by Eastcott.[95] Ishikawa and colleagues[96] contributed an important diagnostic sign when they noted that normal distal pulses may be obliterated when the knee is sharply flexed in patients whose cystic disease has resulted in stenosis without total occlusion. In time, the popliteal artery may undergo total occlusion owing to the mass lesion produced by progressive enlargement of the cyst and its contents. Possibly because of the healthy proximal and distal arteries and the slow progressive nature of the occlusion, no case of acute limb threat due to adventitial cystic disease has been reported. When the intracystic pressure exceeds that of the adjacent artery, or possibly as the physical size of the cyst increases, occlusion of the affected vessel results. Thrombosis may not be superimposed immediately, as evidenced by the fact that simple cyst evacuation may restore full arterial patency, even in cases of arteriographically demonstrated occlusion.

The pathophysiologic consequences of the obstruction subsequent to localized arterial occlusion is no different from that produced by other causes of arterial constriction. Claudication without critical ischemia is a regular finding in these cases. Noninvasive tests show features of single-segment occlusive disease.

Diagnostic Algorithm

Faced with a possible diagnosis of popliteal artery entrapment syndrome or adventitial cystic disease, diagnostic and therapeutic algorithms (Fig. 86-7, Box) can be followed to achieve a satisfactory outcome.[97]

■ DIAGNOSTIC MODALITIES

The diagnosis of popliteal artery entrapment syndrome and cystic adventitial disease may be supported by the findings of abnormal Doppler ankle pressures[2,7] and pulse volume recordings at rest if a significant stenosis or occlusion is present, but these noninvasive tests may be normal at rest if the artery remains widely patent. Imaging of an adventitial cyst and its relationship to the parent artery is easily achieved by ultrasonography. B-mode scans allow determination of the shape, dimensions, and number of cysts present. The boundary between the cyst contents and vessel lumen is seen as a fine bright line that pulsates in real time. The absence of atherosclerotic plaques and flow signals within the cyst in the presence of a distinctive sign of aneurysmal enlargement of the artery can be considered signs pathognomonic for adventitial cystic disease.[98]

Duplex scanning of the popliteal artery may be used to identify popliteal compression. First a baseline scan is obtained of the popliteal artery. Decrease or disappearance of popliteal artery flow with active plantar flexion suggests popliteal artery entrapment.[99,100] One must interpret the duplex scan in relation to the patient's clinical symptoms and other diagnostic studies, however, because popliteal occlusion with active plantar flexion can be seen on duplex scanning in more than 50% of normal people.[28,101]

Duplex Doppler,[27,99,100,102] computerized axial scanning,[103] magnetic resonance imaging (MRI),[24,26,104,105] and magnetic resonance angiography all have been used successfully to show adventitial cystic disease and popliteal artery entrapment syndrome. These diagnostic tests may

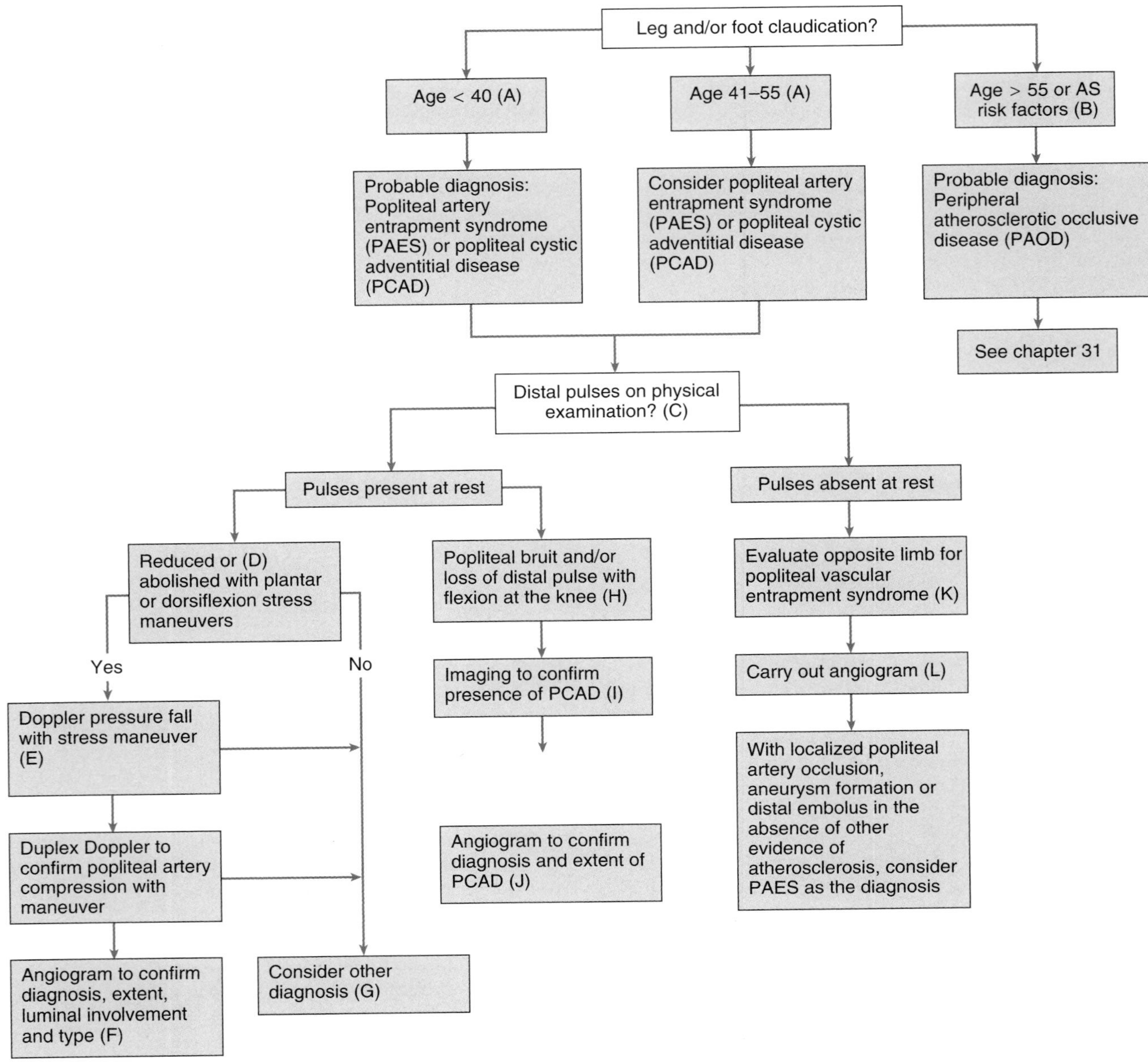

FIGURE 86-7 Diagnostic (**A**) and therapeutic (**B**) algorithms. AS, atherosclerosis. (From Levien LJ: Popliteal artery entrapment and popliteal cystic adventitial disease. In Cronenwett JL, Rutherford RB [eds]: Decision Making in Vascular Surgery. Philadelphia, WB Saunders, 2001, pp 228-231.)

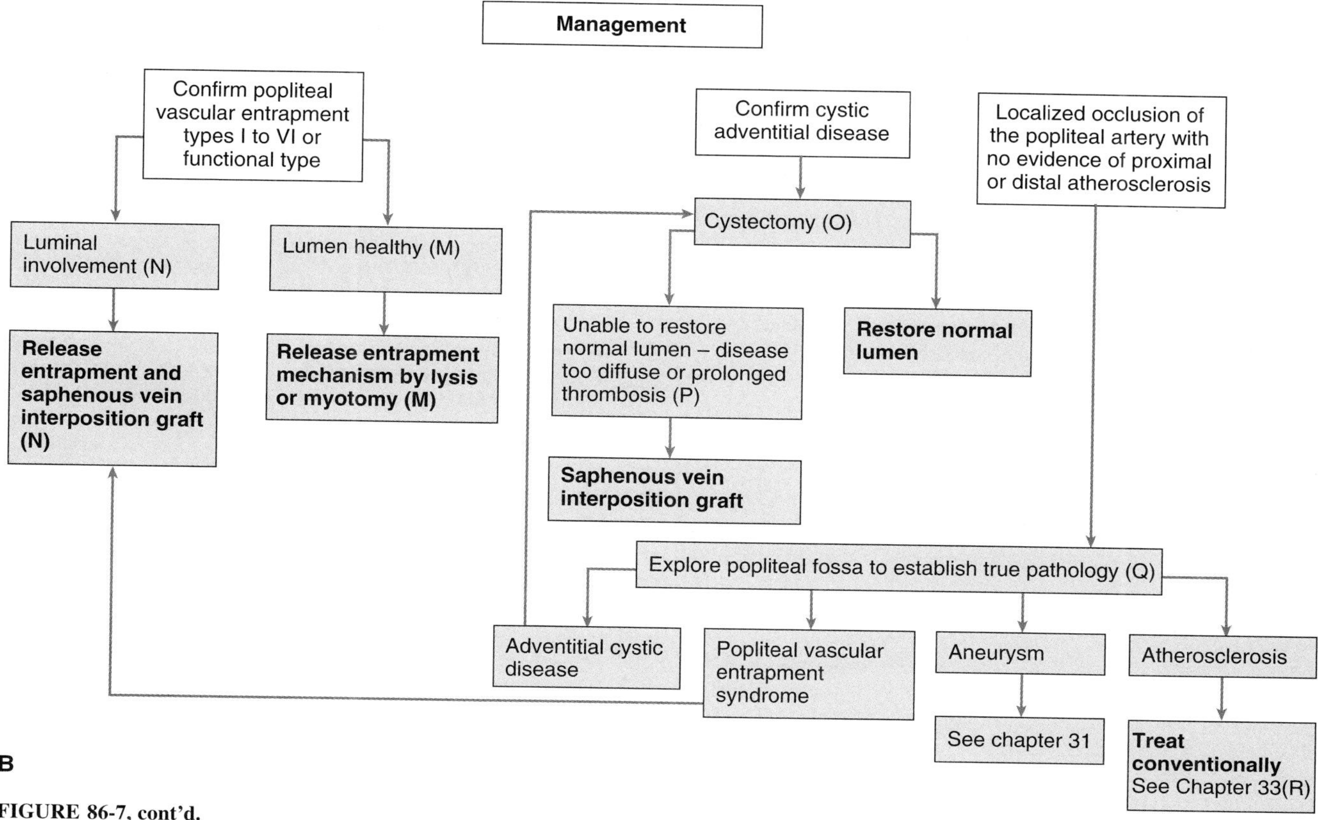

FIGURE 86-7, cont'd.

Diagnostic and therapeutic algorithms (see Fig. 86-7) additional notes

A In most patients who present to the vascular surgeon with infrainguinal arterial disease causing calf or foot claudication, the underlying disease process is PAOD. However, in the subgroup of patients less than the age of 40 years, nonatherosclerotic causes including PAES and PCAD are by far the most common.[1-4]

B In the absence of the usual atherosclerotic risk factors of hypertension, diabetes, hyperlipidemia, a heavy smoking history, a family history of premature atheroma, homocysteinemia or active vasculitis, PAES and PCAD will be the cause of leg claudication in most cases in patients who present between the ages of 40 and 55 years. Older than age 55, PAOD becomes the most common cause of claudication symptoms.[2,5,6]

C In both PAES and PCAD, the peripheral pulses are present at rest when the arterial lumen remains patent and degenerative changes in the arterial wall have not yet resulted in localized stenosis or occlusion.[7,8]

D When symptoms of calf or foot claudication are due to PAES, although pulses may be present at rest, "stress maneuvers" will result in significant narrowing of the popliteal artery with consequent reduction or abolishment of the distal pulses.[9,10] Forced plantar flexion of the foot against resistance with the knee extended will usually provoke the reduction in popliteal artery flow. Less commonly, passive forced dorsiflexion or active dorsiflexion against resistance with the knee extended may be required to recruit the entrapment mechanism and result in diminished distal pulses. These stress maneuvers are therefore an integral part of any diagnostic evaluation, be it clinical examination or one of the many diagnostic tests commonly employed to support the clinical diagnosis of PAES, including continuous wave Doppler testing, Duplex evaluation of the popliteal artery, MRI imaging, and angiography.[11-14]

E Reduction of distal pulses and flows may occur with these stress maneuvers in up to one third of normal, asymptomatic individuals. Therefore, the demonstration of such a reduction in the absence of symptoms should not be regarded as indicating the presence of PAES.[15] In symptomatic individuals, the clinical finding of a reduction of pulses with stress maneuvers should be supported by positive noninvasive tests. A simple Doppler pressure fall should be followed by some form of popliteal imaging in order to localize the site of the arterial constriction.

F Angiography with stress maneuvers will demonstrate the position of the narrowed segment in PAES and give an indication of the type (I to V) of PAES present. Angiography will also reliably diagnose the presence of luminal degeneration, aneurysm formation, or distal embolic disease. Angiography will demonstrate the characteristic abnormality of the focal stenosis due to clinically missed PCAD. Furthermore, angiography will demonstrate the presence or absence of proximal or distal degenerative disease normally associated with atherosclerosis. Angiography is therefore indicated in all cases of suspected PAES in which either the clinical findings or noninvasive tests indicate compression with stress maneuvers.[2,16,17] Conversely, in the absence of alterations in flow and popliteal artery configuration with stress maneuvers, angiographic evaluation is not indicated.

G In the absence of alterations in distal pulses and/or blood flow in the popliteal artery with the performance of adequate stress maneuvers, the probability of PAES is low, and another diagnosis for the calf pain, such as compartment syndrome, should be considered.

Continued

Diagnostic and therapeutic algorithms (see Fig. 86-7) additional notes—cont'd

H In the presence of PCAD with normal pulses at rest, a popliteal bruit and reduction of distal pulses may be found with extremes of flexion of the knee joint. Such findings are virtually diagnostic of PCAD.[18]

I Imaging of the popliteal fossa with duplex ultrasound, CT scan, or MRI will confirm the presence of the cyst and may add valuable information about the relationship of the cyst to the arterial lumen.[18]

J Although PCAD has a very characteristic appearance on angiography, most cases can be diagnosed on the imaging techniques described. The role of angiography in PCAD is to demonstrate the extent of the cystic degeneration and the degree of luminal involvement to permit planning of the operative intervention.[18,19]

K PAES is frequently a bilateral condition. When the popliteal artery has undergone occlusion, careful clinical evaluation of the contralateral limb may demonstrate PAES.[2]

L Angiography that demonstrates a focal popliteal occlusion with totally normal proximal and distal vessels is highly suggestive of PAES or PCAD as the cause of the occlusion. Similarly, in the absence of any degenerative disease of the proximal and distal vessels, the finding of a localized popliteal aneurysm or focal popliteal abnormality associated with distal emboli should strongly suggest the presence of PAES.[2,6]

M Symptomatic PAES that has been confirmed on angiography and that is associated with types I to V vascular entrapment, and when the lumen of the entrapped artery has not undergone significant degeneration or the wall has not undergone aneurysmal change, is best treated by division of the entrapment mechanism be it the medial head of the gastrocnemius (types I and II) or abnormal muscular tenderness or fibrous bands (types III and IV). The functional type[20] of PAES, which is associated with severe symptoms and high grade compression of the popliteal artery with stress maneuver, may warrant lysis of the muscular portion of the medial head of the gastrocnemius although the anatomic arrangement of the structures in the popliteal fossa appears relatively normal.[2]

N When PAES of any type is associated with substantial luminal irregularity, any thromboembolic manifestation, or aneurysmal degeneration, the degenerative process caused by the recurrent trauma of prolonged entrapment has resulted in extensive replacement of the normal arterial wall by fibrous tissue. Vein graft replacement of these arteries is required because lesser procedures that retain the damaged flow surface have a poor long-term patency rate.[7,8]

O Focal popliteal artery narrowing due to PCAD can be restored to normal by simple excision of the cyst (cystectomy) in most cases.[18,19,21] When the flow surface has degenerated as a result of prolonged thrombosis, or when it is not possible to restore a normal satisfactory flow surface due to extensive involvement of the popliteal artery, a saphenous vein graft replacement of the entire involved segment is indicated.[22]

P If on exploration of an occluded popliteal artery focal PCAD is encountered as the cause of the occlusion, replacement with a saphenous vein graft should be performed if simple cyst removal fails to restore a normal caliber popliteal artery.

Q If on exploration of an occluded popliteal artery PAES is encountered as the cause of the occlusion, replacement with saphenous vein graft should always be performed, because thrombectomy has a poor long-term patency. Similarly, angioplasty of the thrombosed segment is not associated with acceptable long-term patency.

R If on exploration of an occluded artery no evidence of PAES or PCAD is found, the patient should be regarded as suffering from atherosclerotic occlusive disease and treament offered as outlined in Chapter 33.

■ REFERENCES

1. Murray A, Halliday M, Croft RJ: Popliteal artery entrapment syndrome. Br J Surg 78:1414, 1991.
2. Levien LJ, Veller MG: Popliteal artery entrapment syndrome: More common than previously recognized. J Vasc Surg 30:1999.
3. Rich NM, Collins GJ, McDonald PT, et al: Popliteal vascular entrapment—its increasing interest. Arch Surg 114:1377, 1979.
4. di Marzo L, Cavallaro A, Sciacca V, et al: Surgical treatment of popliteal artery entrapment syndrome: A ten-year experience. Eur J Vasc Surg 5:59, 1991.
5. Persky JM, Kempczinski RF, Fowl RJ: Entrapment of the popliteal artery. Surg Gynecol Obstet 173:84, 1991.
6. Fowl RJ, Kempczinski RF, Whelan TJ: Popliteal artery entrapment. In Rutherford RB (ed): Vascular Surgery, 4th ed. Philadelphia, WB Saunders, 1995, pp 889-894.
7. di Marzo L, Cavallaro A, Sciacca V, et al: Natural history of entrapment of the popliteal artery. J Am Coll Surg 178:553, 1994.
8. Levien LJ: Popliteal artery thrombosis caused by popliteal entrapment syndrome. In Greenhalgh RM, Powell JT (eds): Inflammatory and thrombotic problems in vascular surgery. London, WB Saunders Ltd, 1997, pp 159-168.
9. McDonald PT, Easterbrook JA, Rich NM, et al: Popliteal artery entrapment syndrome. Clinical, noninvasive and angiographic diagnosis. Am J Surg 139:318, 1980.
10. Greenwood LH, Yrizanny JM, Hallett JW: Popliteal artery entrapment: Importance of the stress runoff for diagnosis. J Cardiovasc Interv Radiol 9:93, 1986.
11. di Marzo L, Cavallaro A, Sciacca V, et al: Diagnosis of popliteal artery entrapment syndrome: The role of duplex scanning. J Vasc Surg 13:434, 1991.
12. Rizzo RJ, Flinn WR, Yao JST, et al: Computed tomography for evaluation of arterial disease in the popliteal fossa. J Vasc Surg 11:112, 1990.
13. Fujiwara H, Sugano T, Fujii N: Popliteal artery entrapment syndrome: Accurate morphological diagnosis utilizing MRI. J Cardiovasc Surg 33:160, 1992.
14. McGuinnes G, Durham JD, Rutherford RB, et al: Popliteal artery entrapment: Findings at MR imaging. J Vasc Interv Radiol 2:241, 1991.
15. Erdoes LS, Devine JJ, Bernhard BM, et al: Popliteal vascular compression in a normal population. J Vasc Surg 20:978, 1994.
16. Bouhoutsos J, Daskalakis E: Muscular abnormalities affecting the popliteal vessels. Br J Surg 68:501, 1981.
17. Turnipseed WD, Pozniak M: Popliteal entrapment as a result of neurovascular compression by the soleus and plantaris muscles. J Vasc Surg 15:285, 1992.
18. Levien LJ, Bergan JJ: Adventitial cystic disease of the popliteal artery. In Rutherford RB (ed): Vascular Surgery, 5th ed. Philadelphia, WB Saunders, 1999.
19. Rignault DP, Pailler JL, Lunel F: The "functional" popliteal entrapment syndrome. Int Angiol 4:341, 1985.
20. Flanigan DP, Burnham SJ, Goodreau JJ: Summary of cases of adventitial cystic disease of the popliteal artery. Ann Surg 189:165, 1979.
21. Ishikawa K: Cystic adventitial disease of the popliteal artery and of other stem vessels in the extremities. Jpn Surg 17:221, 1987.
22. Hiertonn T, Karacagil S, Bergqvist D: Long term follow-up of autologous vein grafts. 40 years after reconstruction for cystic adventitial disease. Vasa 24:250, 1995.

show, however, an apparently normal artery at rest, with compression resulting in reduced or abolished popliteal artery blood flow only during forced active plantar flexion or dorsiflexion of the foot against resistance. Computed tomography (CT) and, more recently, helical CT have been used to determine relationships in the popliteal fossa when the artery has thrombosed because arterial anatomy in the crucial area cannot be delineated by arteriography in this instance. CT scan can delineate a popliteal artery cyst and anomalous insertion of muscle.

In adventitial cystic disease, CT can show circumferential involvement of the artery and cyst recurrence after supposedly successful primary resection.[106] CT guidance lends itself to percutaneous cyst aspiration.[107] This approach should be viewed cautiously, however, because complete decompression may be difficult to achieve, and ultimate recurrence is possible.[108] MRI and magnetic resonance angiography have been used to image the cyst and to determine the extent of the arterial involvement. There seems to be little evidence that MRI is superior to other forms of imaging and conventional angiography for the diagnosis and planning of therapy in adventitial cystic disease.

Contrast angiography remains the most widely used diagnostic modality for both conditions, particularly to plan surgery when degeneration, aneurysm, or occlusion of the popliteal artery is suspected[1,29,109] or if distal embolization is present. The diagnosis of popliteal artery entrapment is strongly suggested when two or more of the following findings are noted on neutral, nonstressed views:

- Medial deviation of the proximal popliteal artery
- Segmental occlusion of the mid-popliteal artery
- Post-stenotic dilatation

In addition, "stress arteriograms" should be performed with the leg actively plantar flexed against resistance or passively dorsiflexed to show compression that may not be seen in the neutral position (Fig. 86-8). Clinical evaluation, noninvasive tests, and angiography require forced active plantar flexion or dorsiflexion of the foot against resistance, with the knee fully extended, to show the abnormality if the artery has not yet undergone degenerative changes.[28]

Medial deviation is usually seen in types I to III, but may be quite subtle (Fig. 86-9). Segmental occlusion of the mid-popliteal artery in the absence of evidence of atheroma may be due to either popliteal entrapment syndrome or adventitial cystic degeneration with thrombosis. The same segment of the artery is involved in both entities, whereas degenerative disease or inflammatory diseases of arteries are virtually never so focal and located in the mid-popliteal artery. Another important finding is post-stenotic dilatation, which is present in 12% of patients with this anomaly.

Early in the course of popliteal adventitial cystic disease, arteriography shows stenosis of the artery.[65] The lesion is usually in the mid-portion of the vessel, extending 1 to 8 cm (Fig. 86-10). There is no medial deviation of the artery, as is seen in cases of types I to III of the popliteal artery entrapment syndrome. The vessel above and below the lesion is free of atheromatous degeneration. A few marginal irregularities are present.[36] When the smooth tapering is concentric, the lesion is described as having an "hourglass" appearance (see Fig. 86-10). If the cyst is eccentrically located, the artery tapers smoothly above and below it; this shape has been described as a "scimitar" sign.

The stenosis may be missed on conventional anteroposterior films, appearing only on lateral projections.[96] Arteriographic findings are sufficiently characteristic to

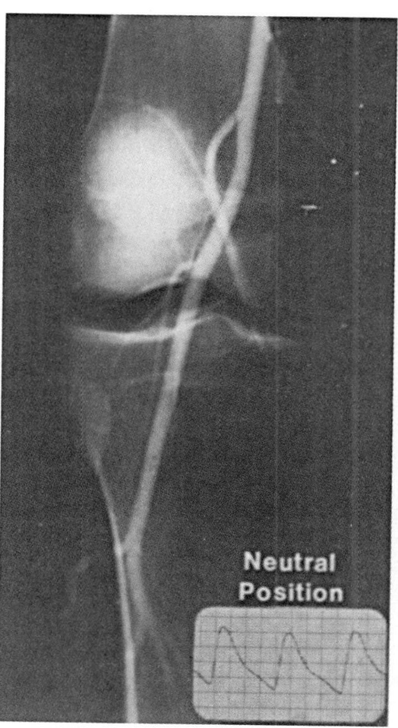

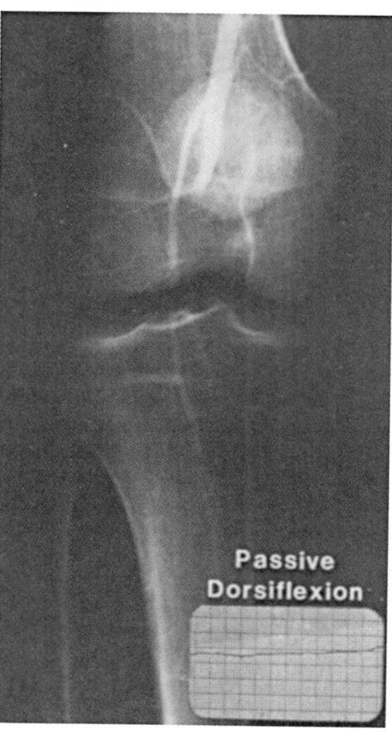

FIGURE 86-8 *Left,* Angiogram reveals a normal course of the popliteal artery with a normal ankle pulse volume recording *(inset)* when the foot is in the neutral position. *Right,* With passive dorsiflexion of the foot, the popliteal artery becomes occluded, and the ankle pulse volume recording becomes flat *(inset).*

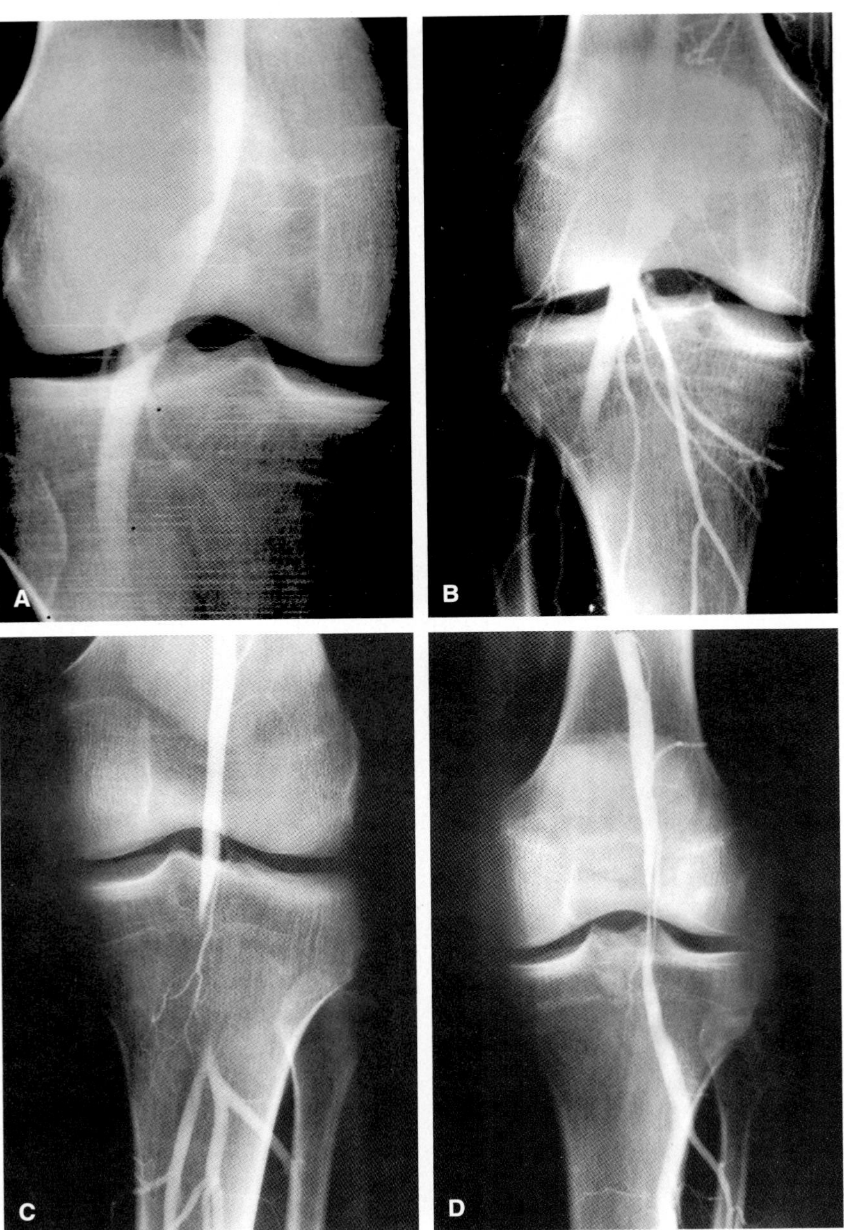

FIGURE 86-9 Angiograms illustrating various aspects of popliteal artery entrapment syndrome. **A,** Medial kink due to a type III additional muscular or tendinous band compressing the artery in the stressed position. **B,** Popliteal aneurysm formation at the level of the compression mechanism (knee joint level) with embolic occlusion of the popliteal artery below the knee joint. **C,** Focal compression of the distal popliteal artery with stress suggestive of a type IV entrapment. **D,** Elongated and diffuse narrowing across knee joint level typical of "functional" popliteal entrapment.

be diagnostic. The condition is easily differentiated from atherosclerosis and from the more commonly encountered popliteal artery entrapment syndromes. Adventitial cystic disease should not be confused with an extrinsic mass lesion, such as that seen with a hematoma or occlusion of the artery from a true joint cyst.[58]

■ HISTOPATHOLOGIC CHANGES AND NATURAL HISTORY OF POPLITEAL ARTERY ENTRAPMENT SYNDROME

Most early reports of popliteal artery entrapment syndrome described patients who had progressed to total occlusion of the artery. This occlusion was presumed to be the result of premature atherosclerosis. The natural history of popliteal artery entrapment is generally considered to be progressive, and on this basis surgery is advised in all patients in whom the diagnosis is confirmed.[23] The unique histopathologic features of external arterial entrapment[2,110] have been described. Entrapment pathology is different compared with the microscopic changes associated with atherosclerosis.[2]

As the entrapment pathology develops with time, progressive neovascularization, inflammatory cell infiltrate, and vessel wall disruption lead to fibrosis and replacement of the arterial wall with collagen scar tissue.[2,110] This process occurs first in the arterial adventitia (stage 1), then in the media (stage 2) (Fig. 86-11A), and finally in the intima (stage 3) (Fig. 86-11B). In some cases, the coexistence of atherosclerotic risk factors in a patient with popliteal entrapment may result in simultaneous external entrapment and premature atheroma.[29] By the time

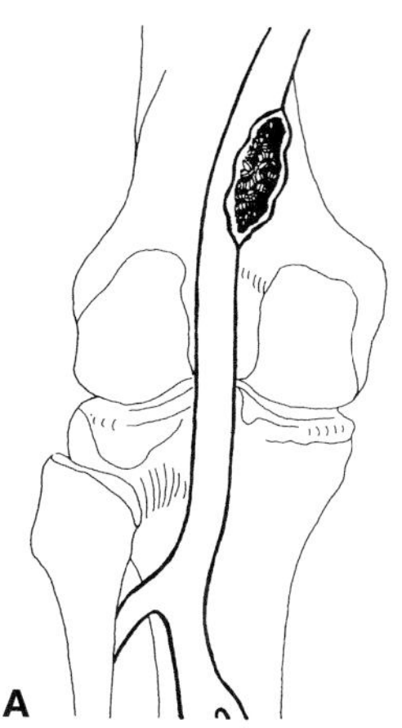

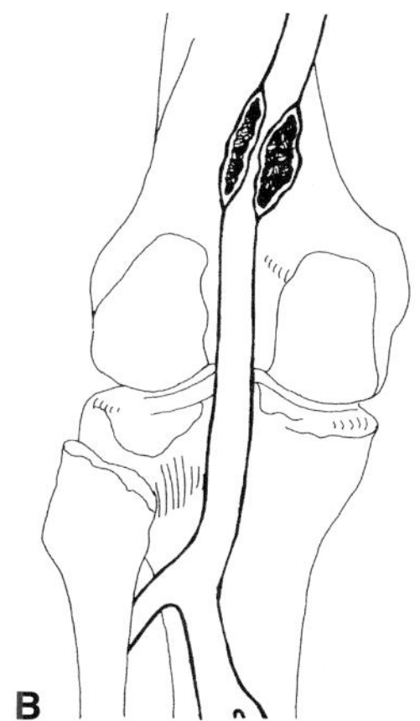

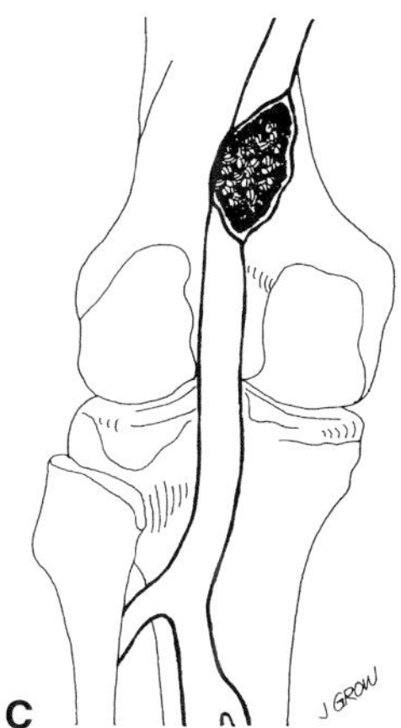

FIGURE 86-10 Adventitial cysts may appear in variable locations on the popliteal artery. The expanding cyst may indent the artery (**A**), the "scimitar" sign; encircle the artery (**B**), the "hourglass" sign; or completely occlude the vessel (**C**).

thrombosis or aneurysm formation has resulted, the arterial degeneration is so advanced that the arterial wall cannot be salvaged.[101,110] This situation explains the poor medium-term patency results obtained after popliteal artery occlusion treated with a lesser procedure, such as thrombolysis, angioplasty, or thrombectomy with patching. In contrast, excellent long-term patency rates have been reported after aneurysm repair or occlusion treated by saphenous vein graft bypasses.[29,30] These data argue strongly in favor of complete replacement of the popliteal artery, preferably by saphenous vein graft, when significant degeneration of the artery is noted.

The natural history of patients with functional popliteal artery entrapment syndrome is not known, but functional entrapment has been reported to progress to popliteal artery occlusion in several patients.[29] In the absence of symptoms, however, compression of the popliteal artery with stress maneuvers is not considered to be an indication for operative intervention. One third to one half of the asymptomatic, normal population show popliteal artery narrowing or occlusion with forced active plantar flexion or dorsiflexion of the foot against resistance.[28] There are no data to support any active treatment of asymptomatic individuals, but these individuals theoretically may be at increased risk of devel-

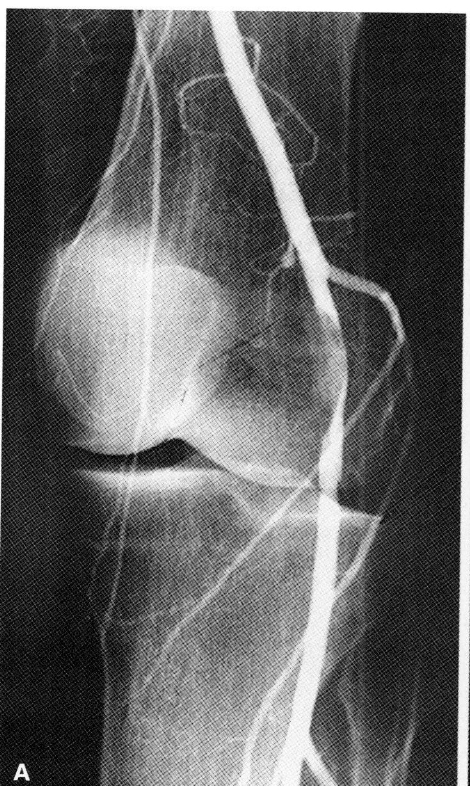

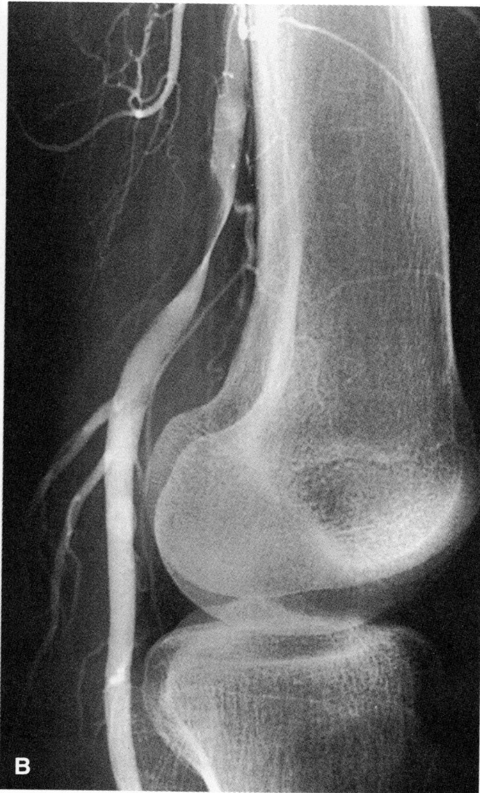

FIGURE 86-11 **A,** Femoral angiogram shows compression of the right popliteal artery by an adventitial cyst. **B,** Lateral view of another patient shows anterior compression of the popliteal artery above the knee.

oping popliteal atheroma from lesser degrees of compression over long periods in the presence of the usual atheroma risk factors.

■ TREATMENT

Popliteal Artery Entrapment Syndrome

The relatively rare nature of popliteal artery entrapment syndrome does not permit study by prospective trials. Based on the current literature and understanding of the natural history of the anatomically entrapped artery, however, all patients with types I to V entrapment probably should be offered surgical treatment when diagnosed. If the popliteal artery is undamaged and patent, and there is no evidence of stage 2 or 3 disease on angiography or at operation, the treatment should consist of exploration of the popliteal artery with division and resection of the entrapment mechanism. In most cases, this operation requires division of the medial head of the gastrocnemius muscle (myotomy), abnormal muscle slips, or tendinous bands arising from the gastrocnemius muscle. Almost without exception, patients who were compelled to stop sporting activities because of symptoms of popliteal artery entrapment syndrome were able to resume normal sporting activities.[29,111] Popliteal abnormalities indicating stage 2 or 3 disease appear as luminal irregularity on angiography, marked thickening and nodularity of the wall of the artery at the entrapment site, aneurysm formation distal to the point of entrapment, or thromboembolic complications (Fig. 86-12). Patients with such evidence of stage 2 or 3 disease of the popliteal artery warrant replacement of the diseased popliteal artery with a saphenous vein graft after division of the offending entrapment mechanism. Excellent results with 10 years of follow-up are reported for this treatment.[29,30,111-113]

Although surgical treatment is advised in all anatomic types (I to V) of entrapment, the indication is far less clear when the entrapment is anatomically "normal" (i.e., a functional entrapment). Caution should be exercised before ascribing limb symptoms to popliteal entrapment simply because the pulses or Doppler signal alter with forced plantar flexion or dorsiflexion, as this finding may be present in half of the normal population. Patients with suspected functional entrapment should be investigated for another orthopedic cause for their pain.[19,31,114,115] If no other explanation is apparent, surgical treatment is recommended for the functional popliteal entrapment by division of the origin of the medial head of the gastrocnemius muscle from its proximal origin and resection of about 1 cm of the proximal muscle (surgical myotomy alone). Patients with functional entrapment also should have the popliteal artery replaced if there is any arterial degeneration at the site of compression.

Operative Intervention

The posterior approach to the popliteal artery has been most commonly advised because it most clearly delineates all variations of this anomaly. Although the medial calf approach (Szilagyi incision) has been used and is satisfactory for types I and II, it may be more difficult to appreciate the anatomy of the lesion in the management of types III and IV. When the occlusion extends distally down to the popliteal bifurcation, a medial incision may be more appropriate. Table 86-1 summarizes the advantages and disadvantages of each approach. In young athletic individuals, the medial approach seems to offer a quicker return to activity, whereas the posterior approach permits better appreciation of any abnormality for surgeons less familiar with the popliteal anatomy.

General anesthesia with endotracheal intubation is required for the posterior approach, whereas regional anesthesia can be used for the medial approach. For the posterior approach, the patient lies prone on the table with

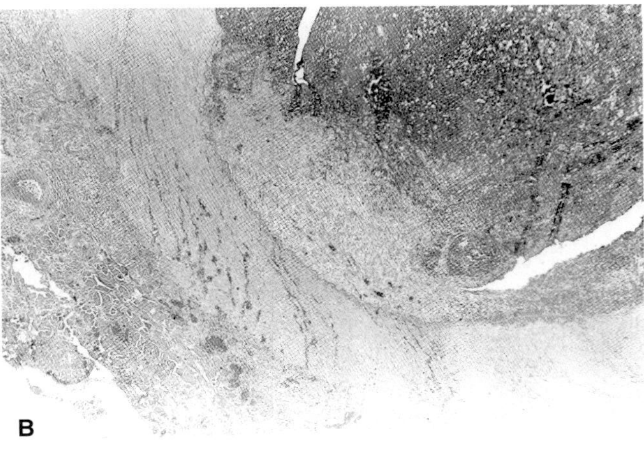

FIGURE 86-12 Histologic appearance of a popliteal artery shows (**A**) stage 2 disease with extensive degeneration of the media and (**B**) stage 3 disease with extensive destruction of the media with hyperplasia of the intima complicated by thrombosis.

Table 86-1 Characteristics of Medial and Posterior Approaches for Operations on the Popliteal Artery

MEDIAL APPROACH	POSTERIOR APPROACH
Ease of harvest of the long saphenous vein, particularly from more proximal if larger diameter required	Ease of appreciation of anatomy, particularly for a surgeon not experienced with this condition or the surgical anatomy of the popliteal artery
More rapid return to sporting activities	Relationship of structures more apparent for more subtle abnormalities
Less anesthetic morbidity as patient does not need to be prone	Less prominent scar
Easy to extend repair of popliteal artery more distally	
Anatomy more difficult to appreciate, may miss the abnormality; recurrence of symptoms more likely	

the leg flexed 10 to 15 degrees. The incision is S-shaped, with the cephalad vertical portion of the S placed over the posteromedial thigh, the caudad vertical portion on the posterolateral aspect of the calf, and the horizontal limb in the popliteal crease (Fig. 86-13).

Wide flaps are raised in the subcutaneous tissue, exposing the deep fascia. The surgeon incises the deep fascia longitudinally, avoiding injury to the median cutaneous sural nerve, which lies immediately subfascial at this level. The accompanying lesser saphenous vein may be sacrificed to afford better exposure.

The first of the deep structures to be identified is the tibial nerve, which is mobilized as the vessels are approached. The vein, unless it participates in the anomaly, is found in the deep popliteal fossa, passing between the heads of the gastrocnemius muscle. The artery is not present in the normal location, but is identified high in the popliteal space as it exits from the adductor canal. With distal dissection along the arterial adventitia, the surgeon verifies the anomalous course either medial to the medial head of the gastrocnemius muscle or lying entrapped by the anomalous tissue present.

Transection of the compressing muscle or fascial band is begun at the point where the artery passes deep to it. The tight compression of the artery between the muscle and the posterior femur and knee joint capsule may be remarkable. The transection of the abnormality must be complete, and the entire artery should be mobilized. If the artery is compressed but not occluded, and secondary fibrotic changes have not taken place in the arterial wall, nothing further is necessary. The medial head of the gastrocnemius may be resected without disturbing function. In types III and IV entrapment and in functional entrapment release, the muscular portion of the medial head of the gastrocnemius is extensively mobilized off the posterior aspect of the femoral condyles and intercondylar fossa, but it is usually not necessary to divide the tendon of the medial head of the gastrocnemius lying on the most medial aspect of the popliteal fossa to achieve decompression.

For patients with functional entrapment (type VI), adequate myotomy of the medial head of the gastrocnemius muscle through a medial incision has resulted in complete relief of symptoms.[2,116] In the functional type, care must be taken to ensure that any muscular fibers from the posterior aspect of the lateral femoral condyle and the intercondylar area are completely divided. Turnipseed and Pozniak[26] described an unusual variant of popliteal artery entrapment in which the popliteal artery was compressed by hypertrophied soleus and plantaris muscles in well-conditioned athletes. Symptoms were relieved by surgical release of the soleus muscle from the tibia and resection of the plantaris muscle.

Intra-arterial thrombolytic agents have been used to restore patency of a recently thrombosed artery. Because of arterial wall injury and subsequent fibrosis and degeneration from the long-standing entrapment, arterial bypass or

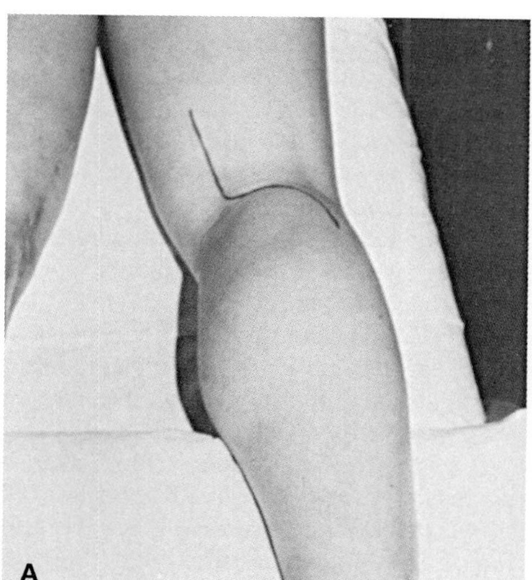

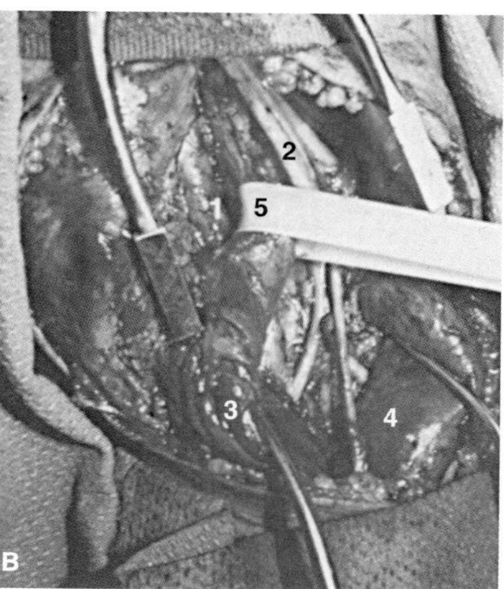

FIGURE 86-13 **A,** The S-shaped incision in the popliteal fossa is used for the posterior approach. **B,** Anatomic structures identified through the posterior incision are (1) the popliteal artery, (2) the tibial nerve, (3) the medial head of the gastrocnemius muscle, (4) the lateral head of the gastrocnemius muscle, and (5) a Penrose drain wrapped around the accessory slip of the gastrocnemius muscle, causing arterial compression.

replacement is usually necessary for a patent artery in which lysis of the thrombus has been successful. Resection and vein graft interposition are required in the following situations:

- If substantial degeneration of the arterial wall has resulted from the entrapment
- If thrombus has formed on the intimal surface
- If the vessel is narrowed due to fibrosis
- If an aneurysm is present

The graft can be obtained from the greater saphenous vein. Alternatively, a short bypass vein graft can be used without resection of the thrombosed segment.

If a popliteal aneurysm has developed as an extension of the process of post-stenotic dilatation, resection and replacement vein graft with ligation or resection of the aneurysmal segment should be performed. In all operations for this condition, the surgeon first must relieve the entrapment by transection of the offending muscle.

Adventitial Cystic Disease

Because of the rarity of adventitial cystic disease, experience in any one center is limited and anecdotal. No randomized studies are available to indicate the best therapy. At present, optimal treatment of this condition would seem to be surgical. More conservative approaches, such as aspiration, have been successful in eradicating the arterial occlusion but have been characterized by early recurrence of the mass lesion. Percutaneous transluminal angioplasty has proved unsatisfactory simply because, in contrast to in atherosclerosis, the intima in cystic disease is normal, and it is the arterial wall that is affected.[117] If the secretory lining of the cyst remains functional, the cyst contents are likely to reaccumulate with time.

The operative findings are relatively uniform. On exposure, the artery is found to be enlarged and sausage-shaped, just as in the first case described by Hiertonn and Lindberg.[35,62] Adhesions may be present, binding the adventitial cystic structure to adjacent vein or to the posterior aspect of the joint capsule. The cyst itself is usually unilocular, but may be multilocular with septa. The fluid is usually crystal clear but may be faintly yellow or even the red of currant jelly, depending on the amount of recent or old hemorrhage.

Incision into the cyst and evacuation of its contents are usually sufficient to restore arterial patency, unless the artery has undergone thrombosis as a consequence of protracted occlusion. Because the condition is rare, and preoperative diagnosis was rarely made in the past, numerous cases were treated by excision of the cyst with its adjacent artery and insertion of various grafts, with good results. Cyst evacuation is currently the preferred treatment, however, if the artery has not become occluded. Now that the condition is becoming better known, this method is being used with increasing frequency. If the process has progressed to total arterial occlusion with thrombosis, graft replacement or bypass is preferred, with the adjacent long or short saphenous vein used as the arterial substitute of choice.

A more recent tendency has been to perform minimally invasive correction of the underlying arterial stenosis or occlusion. Aspiration of the cyst under ultrasound or CT guidance has resulted in improved luminal caliber. Although this method permits restoration of a flow channel, the medium-term patency rate of this approach has been disappointing,[108] presumably because of ongoing secretion by the cyst lining and progressive occlusion of the artery. Thrombolytic therapy has been employed to clear recent thrombus in an occluded arterial segment, followed by percutaneous transluminal angioplasty.[118] Early failure has occurred with this approach, too, presumably owing to ongoing secretion by the cyst lining.

After total occlusion of the artery, operative intervention has proved to be the most successful method of restoring arterial flow permanently. Continuing reports suggest that short-term and long-term outcomes are better after complete removal of the cyst. Although some surgeons have treated this condition without arterial reconstruction, majority opinion holds that autogenous arterial repair remains the treatment of choice.[119]

A review of 115 case reports has been completed to allow an evaluation of treatment procedures.[3] Simple cyst evacuation has restored arterial blood flow in 56 instances. Prosthetic grafts, homografts, and autogenous vein grafts were used to restore flow in 42 patients. Patches were used to perform angioplasty in some cases, and in a patient who refused other surgery, rest pain was relieved with a sympathectomy. Curiously the popliteal fossa in this instance was punctured, and a quantity of jelly was aspirated from the cyst. Cyst aspiration under CT guidance also has been done,[120] but most surgeons report disappointing results and rapid reaccumulation of cyst fluid.[108]. Because simple cyst evacuation is effective treatment, it should be employed in situations in which the affected artery has not become occluded.[3] When total occlusion of the popliteal artery by the cyst is encountered, replacement of the artery or bypass should be performed with the use of the best surgical technique available.

■ SUMMARY

Popliteal Artery Entrapment Syndrome

The increasing frequency with which popliteal vascular entrapment is reported[29,30,113] strongly suggests a greater awareness of the syndrome. Better evaluation by knowledgeable sports medicine specialists has improved the diagnostic yield in young patients with unexplained calf pain.[19,114,115] In a large series of patients younger than 50 years old presenting with claudication symptoms, more than half subsequently were shown to have popliteal artery entrapment syndrome as a cause of their symptoms.[29] Most early reports of popliteal artery entrapment syndrome described patients who had progressed to arterial occlusion. The natural history of the popliteal artery with unrelieved compression was thought to be an aggressive one, and on this basis surgery was advised whenever the diagnosis was confirmed.[1,23] There has been no evidence supporting a policy of watchful waiting in these patients. Recognition of progressive fibrosis of the entrapped vessel wall leading to aneurysm formation and thrombosis further supports early operative intervention. A classification of the histologic changes seen with popliteal artery entrapment syndrome is based on the severity and extent of the histologic changes of neovascularization and subsequent progressive fibrosis[110] occurring first in the adventitia (stage 1) and progressing with time to involve the media (stage 2). Thrombosis is thought to be the end result of intimal fibrosis (stage 3), which renders the flow surface thrombogenic. Lesser degrees of arterial degeneration (stage 1) may allow salvage of the arterial wall. Long-term patency of 10 years after aneurysm repair or occlusion treated by saphenous vein graft has been reported. These long-term results argue strongly in favor of complete replacement of the popliteal artery, preferably by saphenous vein, when significant degeneration of the artery is encountered.

On the basis of these observations, surgical correction is advised in all cases of type I to V when a diagnosis has been made, rather than waiting until arterial degeneration has supervened. The degree of arterial degeneration does not seem to be related to the duration of popliteal entrapment. In one study,[29] there was no significant difference between the ages of the patients presenting with popliteal artery occlusion and patients in whom a myotomy alone was required. The youngest patients in this series in most cases were athletes with type I or II entrapments or tight localized tendinous bands of type III and IV entrapments who had progressed to popliteal artery occlusion. Patients presenting with occlusion at an older age invariably had muscular entrapment mechanisms of type III or IV. This finding suggests that the rate of arterial wall degeneration in popliteal artery entrapment syndrome may depend on the degree of compression and the magnitude of the forces exerted on the popliteal artery by the compression mechanism, not the duration of compression.

Most cases of types I and II entrapment are easy to diagnose on angiography and other imaging modalities. Types III and IV are associated with more localized areas of entrapment, which is distinguishable from the more diffuse narrowing of the artery found at angiography with the functional or type F entrapment.[29] The demonstration that the popliteal artery will undergo some transitory compression or even temporary occlusion with extremes of plantar flexion or dorsiflexion in half of the normal population always must be considered. The simple demonstration of popliteal artery compression with such stress positions cannot justify operation in minimally symptomatic patients.[24,28,105] The demonstration that a functional popliteal artery entrapment syndrome may progress to occlusion with the histologic picture of chronic compression[29] justifies a more aggressive surgical approach in symptomatic patients who are shown to have a functional entrapment. Until the natural history of the functional type of entrapment is known in asymptomatic and symptomatic patients, optimal management of this condition must remain controversial.

It has been shown that the various manifestations and types of popliteal artery entrapment syndrome are much more prevalent than originally appreciated. This diagnosis should be considered in any patient younger than 50 years old who presents with typical calf and foot claudication symptoms on exercise, particularly in athletic individuals without atherosclerotic risk factors. The finding of an isolated popliteal artery aneurysm or isolated popliteal artery occlusion in a young, physically active individual should be considered to be due to popliteal artery entrapment syndrome or cystic adventitial disease unless proved otherwise. Current evidence suggests that when a popliteal artery has undergone occlusion, the artery is beyond repair. Abnormal arteries should be replaced, preferably by saphenous vein graft, to ensure optimal long-term popliteal artery patency in these often young and athletic individuals.

Adventitial Cystic Disease

Adventitial cystic disease of arteries is a rare cause of arterial stenosis and occlusion. It is an unforgettable experience to apply clamps to a pulsating blood vessel, incise its adventitia, and see crystal-clear fluid instead of blood pouring under pressure from the arteriotomy. In such a circumstance, the relationship of this disorder to simple ganglia seems irrefutable. Although ganglia of nonpopliteal locations are common, cystic arterial disease itself is rare. The location of cystic arterial disease in the popliteal fossa and along the external iliac artery is remote from the usual locations of ganglia. Logical as these facts are, however, the fluid remains clear and colorless, tantalizing in its similarity to the familiar content of a simple ganglion. The cause remains obscure.

Treatment of this condition remains as illogical as the lesion is curious. What could be less likely to cure an arterial occlusion than evacuation of the cyst? To a vascular surgeon trained in performing bypass or vein graft procedures to restore arterial patency, simple cystotomy seems too easy. Yet there is no doubt now that cystotomy, rather than resection, is the treatment of choice if the artery is not occluded.[121] If total evacuation can be accomplished without violating the integrity of the arterial intima, cystotomy suffices. Simple percutaneous aspiration may decompress the cyst initially, but seems to be associated with a higher rate of recurrence. If the artery is completely occluded, arterial bypass must be performed. Although spontaneous resolution of adventitial cystic disease has been reported,[122] such an outcome is not to be expected regularly.

■ REFERENCES

1. Murray A, Halliday M, Croft RJ: Popliteal artery entrapment syndrome. Br J Surg 78:1414, 1991.
2. Levien LJ: Popliteal artery thrombosis caused by popliteal entrapment syndrome. In Greenhalgh RM, Powell JT (eds): Inflammatory and Thrombotic Problems in Vascular Surgery. Philadelphia, WB Saunders, 1997, pp 159-167.
3. Flanigan DP, Burnham SJ, Goodreau JJ, Bergan JJ: Summary of cases of adventitial cystic disease of the popliteal artery. Ann Surg 189:165, 1979.
4. Stuart TP: Note on a variation in the course of the popliteal artery. J Anat Physiol 13:162, 1879
5. Hamming JJ: Intermittent claudication at an early age, due to an anomalous course of the popliteal artery. Angiology 10:369, 1959.
6. Hamming JJ, Vink U: Obstruction of the popliteal artery at an early age. J Cardiovasc Surg 6:516, 1965.
7. Carter AE, Eban RA: A case of bilateral developmental abnormality of the popliteal arteries and gastrocnemius muscles. Br J Surg 51:518, 1964.
8. Turner GR, Gosney WG, Ellingson W, et al: Popliteal artery entrapment syndrome. JAMA 208:692, 1964.
9. Love JW, Whelan TJ: Popliteal artery entrapment syndrome. Am J Surg 109:620, 1965.

10. Rich NM, Hughes CW: Popliteal artery and vein entrapment. Am J Surg 113:696, 1967.
11. Servello M: Clinical syndrome of anomalous position of the popliteal artery. Circulation 26:885, 1962.
12. Biemans RGH, Van Bockel JH: Popliteal artery entrapment syndrome. Surg Gynecol Obstet 144:604, 1977.
13. Gibson MHL, Mills JG, Johnson GE, et al: Popliteal entrapment syndrome. Ann Surg 185:341, 1977.
14. Darling RC, Buckley CJ, Abbot WM, et al: Intermittent claudication in young athletes: Popliteal artery entrapment syndrome. J Trauma 14:543, 1974.
15. Rich NM, Collins GJ, McDonald PT, et al: Popliteal vascular entrapment: Its increasing interest. Arch Surg 114:1377, 1979.
16. Collins PS, McDonald PT, Lim PC: Popliteal artery entrapment: An evolving syndrome. J Vasc Surg 10:484,1989.
17. di Marzo L, Cavallaro A, Sciacca V, et al: Surgical treatment of popliteal artery entrapment syndrome: A ten year experience. Eur J Vasc Surg 5:59, 1991.
18. Insua JA, Houng JR, Humphries AW: Popliteal artery entrapment syndrome. Arch Surg 101:771, 1970.
19. Clanton TO, Solcher BW: Chronic leg pain in the athlete. Clin Sports Med 13:743, 1994.
20. di Marzo L, Cavallaro A, Sciacca V, et al: Natural history of entrapment of the popliteal artery. J Am Coll Surg 178:553, 1994.
21. Bouhoutsos J, Daskalakis E: Muscular abnormalities affecting the popliteal vessels. Br J Surg 68:501, 1981.
22. Ikeda M, Iwase T, Ashida K, et al: Popliteal artery entrapment syndrome: Report of a case and study of 18 cases in Japan. Am J Surg 141:726, 1981.
23. Persky JM, Kempczinski RF, Fowl RJ: Entrapment of the popliteal artery. Surg Gynecol Obstet 173:84, 1991.
24. Chernoff DM, Walker AT, Khorasani R, et al: Asymptomatic functional popliteal entrapment: Demonstration at MR imaging. Radiology 195:176, 1995.
25. Rignault DP, Pailler JL, Lunel F: The "functional" popliteal artery entrapment syndrome. Int Angiol 4:341, 1985.
26. Turnipseed WD, Pozniak M: Popliteal entrapment as a result of neurovascular compression by the soleus and plantaris muscles. J Vasc Surg 15:285, 1992.
27. Akkersdijk WL, de Ruyter JW, Lapham R, et al: Colour duplex ultrasonographic scanning and provocation of popliteal artery compression. Eur J Vasc Endovasc Surg 10:342, 1995.
28. Erdoes LS, Devine JJ, Berhard BM, et al: Popliteal vascular compression in a normal population. J Vasc Surg 20:978, 1994.
29. Levien LJ, Veller MG: Popliteal artery entrapment syndrome: More common than previously recognised. J Vasc Surg 30:587, 1999.
30. Turnipseed WD: Popliteal entrapment syndrome. J Vasc Surg 35:910, 2002.
31. Deshpande A, Denton M: Functional popliteal entrapment syndrome. Aust N Z J Surg 68:660, 1998.
32. Atkins HJB, Key JA: A case of myxomatous tumor arising in the adventitia of the left external iliac artery. Br J Surg 34:426, 1947.
33. Ejrup B, Hiertonn T: Intermittent claudication: Three cases treated by free vein graft. Acta Chir Scand 108:217, 1954.
34. Ishikawa K: Cystic adventitial disease of the popliteal artery and of other stem vessels in the extremities. Jpn Surg 17:221, 1987.
35. Hiertonn T, Lindberg K: Cystic adventitial degeneration of the popliteal artery. Acta Chir Scand 113:72, 1957.
36. Ehringer VH, Denck H: Zystische Adventitiadegeneration. Wien Med Wochenschr 120:49, 1970.
37. Levien LJ, Benn CA: Adventitial cystic disease: A unifying hypothesis. J Vasc Surg 28:193, 1998.
38. Holmes JG: Cystic adventitial degeneration of the popliteal artery. JAMA 173:654, 1960.
39. Robb D: Obstruction of popliteal artery by synovial cyst. Br J Surg 48:221, 1960.
40. Jasinski RW, Masselink BA, Partridge RW, et al: Adventitial cystic disease of the popliteal artery. Radiology 163:153, 1987.
41. Elster EA, Hewlett S, DeRienzo DP, et al: Adventitial cystic disease of the axillary artery. Ann Vasc Surg 16:134, 2002.
42. Annetts DL, Graham AR: Cystic degeneration of the femoral vein. Br J Surg 67:287, 1980.
43. Fyfe NCM, Silcocks PB, Browse NC: Cystic mucoid degeneration in the wall of the femoral vein. J Cardiovasc Surg 21:703, 1980.
44. Gomez-Ferrer F: Cystic degeneration of the wall of the femoral vein. J Cardiovasc Surg 7:162, 1966.
45. Paty PSK, Kaufman JL, Koslow AR, et al: Adventitial cystic disease of the femoral vein: A case report and review of the literature. J Vasc Surg 15:214, 1992.
46. Lie JT, Jensen PL, Smith RW: Adventitial cystic disease of the lesser saphenous vein. Arch Pathol Lab Med 115:946, 1991.
47. Clark K: Ganglion of the lateral popliteal nerve. J Bone Joint Surg Br 43:778, 1961.
48. Parkes A: Intraneural ganglion of the lateral popliteal nerve. J Bone Joint Surg Br 43:784, 1961.
49. Lewis GJT, Douglas DM, Reid W, et al: Cystic adventitial disease of the popliteal artery. BMJ 3:41, 1967.
50. Bardeen CR: Development and variation of the nerves and the musculature of the inferior extremity and of the neighbouring regions of the trunk in man. Am J Anat 6:259,1907.
51. Senior HD: The development of the arteries of the human lower extremities. Am J Anat 25:55, 1919.
52. Senior HD: The development of the human femoral artery, a correction. Am J Anat 17:271, 1920.
53. Colborn GL, Lumsden AB, Taylor BS, et al: The surgical anatomy of the popliteal artery. Am Surg 60:238, 1994.
54. Baker WH, Stoney RJ: Acquired popliteal entrapment syndrome. Arch Surg 105:780, 1972.
55. Carpenter JP, Lieberman MD, Shlansky-Goldberg K, et al: Infrageniculate bypass entrapment. J Vasc Surg 18:81, 1993.
56. Bliss BP, Rhodes J, Harding Rains AJ: Cystic myxomatous degeneration of the popliteal artery. BMJ 2:847, 1963.
57. Bliss BP: Cystic myxomatous degeneration of the popliteal artery. Am Heart J 68:838, 1964.
58. Schramek A, Hashmonai M: Subadventitial haematoma of the popliteal artery. J Cardiovasc Surg 14:447, 1973.
59. Hart Hansen JP: Cystic mucoid degeneration of the popliteal artery. Acta Chir Scand 131:171, 1966.
60. Linquette M, Mesmacque R, Beghin B, et al: Dégénérescence colloide de l'adventice de l'artère poplitée. Semaine Hôp (Paris) 43:3005, 1967.
61. Barnett AJ, Morris KN: Cystic myxomatous degeneration of the popliteal artery. Med J Aust 2:793, 1964.
62. Hiertonn T, Lindberg K: Cystic adventitial degeneration of the popliteal artery. Acta Chir Scand 113:72, 1957.
63. Hofmann KT, Consiglio L, Hofmeier G, et al: Die zystische Gefassdegeneration. Brun's Beitr Klin Chir 217:284, 1969.
64. Ruppel V, Sperling M, Schott H, Kern E: Pathological anatomical observations in cystic adventitial degeneration of the blood vessels. Beitr Path Bd 144:101, 1971.
65. Andersson T, Gothman B, Lindberg K: Mucinous cystic dissecting intramural degeneration of the popliteal artery. Acta Radiol 52:455, 1959.
66. Marzoli GP, Meyer Burgdorff G, Jacquet GH: Sulle pseudocisti dell parete arteriosa. Chir Ital 14:290, 1962.
67. Lau J, Kim HS, Carcia-Rinaldi R: Cystic adventitial disease of the popliteal artery. Vasc Surg 11:299, 1977.
68. Haid SP, Conn J Jr, Bergan JJ: Cystic adventitial disease of the popliteal artery. Arch Surg 101:765, 1970.
69. Harris JD, Jepson RP: Cystic degeneration of the popliteal artery. Aust N Z J Surg 34:265, 1965.
70. Hamming JJ, Vink M: Obstruction of the popliteal artery at an early age. J Cardiovasc Surg 6:516, 1965.
71. Stallworth JM, Brown AG, Burges GE, et al: Cystic adventitial disease of the popliteal artery. Am Surg 5:455, 1985.
72. Savage PEA: Cystic disease of the popliteal artery. Br J Surg 56:77, 1969.

73. Devereux D, Forrest H, McLeod T, et al: The non-arterial origin of cystic adventitial disease of the popliteal artery in two patients. Surgery 88:723, 1980.
74. Lassonde J, Laurendeau F: Cystic adventitial disease of the popliteal artery. Am Surg 48:341, 1982.
75. Shabbo FP: Cystic disease of the popliteal artery. Proc R Soc Med 69:362, 1976.
76. Shute K, Rothnie NG: The aetiology of cystic arterial disease. Br J Surg 60:397, 1973.
77. diMarzo L, Rocca CD, d'Amati G, et al: Cystic adventitial degeneration of the popliteal artery: Lectin-histochemical study. Eur J Vasc Surg 8:16, 1994.
78. Schroe H, Van Opstal C, De Leersnijder J, et al: Baker's cyst connected to popliteal artery cyst. Ann Vasc Surg 2:385, 1988.
79. Durham JR, McIntyre KE Jr: Adventitial cystic disease of the radial artery. J Cardiovasc Surg 30:517, 1989.
80. Cavallaro A, diMarzo L, Sciacca V: Cystic adventitial degeneration of the popliteal artery: A case report. Vasa 19:443, 1985.
81. Endo M, Tamura S, Minakuchi S, et al: Isolation and identification of proteohyaluronic acid from a cyst of cystic mucoid degeneration. Clin Chim Acta 47:417, 1973.
82. Leaf G: Amino-acid analysis of protein present in a popliteal artery cyst. BMJ 3:415, 1967.
83. McEvedy BV: Simple ganglia. Br J Surg 49:585, 1962.
84. O'Rahilly R, Gardener E: The embryology of movable joints. In Sokoloff L (ed): The Joints and the Synovial Fluid. New York, Academic Press, 1978, pp 49-103.
85. Flanc C: Cystic degeneration of the popliteal artery. Aust N Z J Surg 36:243, 1967.
86. Powis SJA, Morrissey DM, Jones EL: Cystic degeneration of the popliteal artery. Surgery 67:891, 1970.
87. Campbell WB, Millar AW: Cystic adventitial disease of the common femoral artery communicating with the hip joint. Br J Surg 72:537, 1985.
88. Hunt BP, Harrington MG, Goodle JJ, Galloway JMD: Cystic adventitial disease of the popliteal artery. Br J Surg 67:811, 1980.
89. Richards RL: Cystic degeneration. BMJ 3:997, 1963.
90. Blum L, Giron F: Adventitial cyst of the popliteal artery with secondary inflammatory entrapment. Mt Sinai J Med 43:471, 1976.
91. Jay GD, Ross FL, Mason RA, Giron F: Clinical and chemical characterisation of an adventitial popliteal cyst. J Vasc Surg 3:448, 1989.
92. Berger MF, Weber EE: MR imaging of recurrent cystic adventitial disease of the popliteal artery. J Vasc Interv Radiol 4:695, 1993.
93. Barnett AJ, Dugdale L, Ferguson I: Disappearing pulse syndrome due to myxomatous degeneration of the popliteal artery. Med J Aust 2:355, 1966.
94. Jacquet GH, Meyer Burgdorff G: Arterielle Durchblutungsstörung infolge cystischer Degeneration der Adventitia. Chirurg 31:481, 1960.
95. Eastcott HHG: Cystic myxomatous degeneration of popliteal artery. BMJ 2:1270, 1963.
96. Ishikawa K, Mishima Y, Kobayashi S: Cystic adventitial disease of the popliteal artery. Angiology 12:357, 1961.
97. Levien LJ: Popliteal artery entrapment and popliteal cystic adventitial disease. In Cronenwett JL, Rutherford RB (eds): Decision Making in Vascular Surgery. Philadelphia, WB Saunders, 2001, pp 228-231.
98. Stapff M, Zoller WG, Spengel FA: Image-directed Doppler ultrasound findings in adventitial cystic disease of the popliteal artery. J Clin Ultrasound 17:689, 1989.
99. MacSweeny STR, Cumming R, Greenhalgh RM: Colour Doppler ultrasonographic imaging in the diagnosis of popliteal artery entrapment syndrome. Br J Surg 81:822, 1994.
100. di Marzo L, Cavallaro A, Sciacca V, et al: Diagnosis of popliteal artery entrapment syndrome: The role of duplex scanning. J Vasc Surg 13:434, 1991.
101. Levien LJ: Popliteal artery entapment syndrome. Semin Vasc Surg 16:223, 2003.
102. Allen MJ, Barnes MR, Bell PR, et al: Popliteal artery entrapment syndrome. Eur J Vasc Surg 7:342, 1993.
103. Williams LR, Flinn WR, McCarthy WJ, et al: Popliteal artery entrapment: Diagnosis by computed tomography. J Vasc Surg 3:360, 1986.
104. Fujiwara H, Sugano T, Fujii N: Popliteal artery entrapment syndrome: Accurate morphological diagnosis utilizing MRI. J Cardiovasc Surg 33:160, 1992.
105. McGuinnes G, Durham JD, Rutherford RB, et al: Popliteal artery entrapment: Findings at MR imaging. J Vasc Interv Radiol 2:241, 1991.
106. Rizzo RJ, Flinn WR, Yao JST, et al: Computed tomography for evaluation of arterial disease in the popliteal fossa. J Vasc Surg 11:112, 1990.
107. Fitzjohn TP, White FE, Loose HW, et al: Computed tomography and sonography of cystic adventitial disease. Br J Radiol 59:933, 1986.
108. Sieunarine K, Lawrence-Brown M, Kelsey P: Adventitial cystic disease of the popliteal artery: Early recurrence after CT-guided percutaneous aspiration. J Cardiovasc Surg 32:702, 1991.
109. McDonald PT, Easterbrook JA, Rich NM, et al: Popliteal artery entrapment syndrome: Clinical, noninvasive and angiographic diagnosis. Am J Surg 139:318, 1980.
110. Naylor SJ, Levien LJ, Kooper K: Histological features of the popliteal artery entrapment syndrome. Vasc Surg 34:665, 2000.
111. Lambert AW, Wilkins DC: Popliteal artery entrapment syndrome. Br J Surg 86:1365, 1999.
112. Ohara N, Miyata T, Oshiro H, et al: Surgical treatment for popliteal artery entrapment syndrome. Cardiovasc Surg 9:141, 2001.
113. Elster EA, Hewlett S, DeRienzo DP, et al: Adventitial cystic disease of the axillary artery. Ann Vasc Surg 16:134, 2002.
114. Lysens RJ, Rensen LM, Ostyn MS, et al: Intermittent claudication in young athletes: Popliteal artery entrapment syndrome. Am J Sports Med 11:177, 1983.
115. Turnipseed W, Detmer DE, Gridley F: Chronic compartment syndrome. Am J Surg 210:557, 1989.
116. Sperryn CW, Beningfield SJ, Immelmann EJ: Functional entrapment of the popliteal artery. Australas Radiol 44:121, 2000.
117. Fox RL, Kahn M, Alder J: Adventitial cystic disease of the popliteal artery: Failure of percutaneous transluminal angioplasty. J Vasc Surg 2:464, 1985.
118. Samson RH, Willis PD: Popliteal artery occlusion caused by cystic adventitial disease: Successful treatment by urokinase followed by nonresectional cystotomy. J Vasc Surg 12:591, 1990.
119. Melliere D, Ecollan P, Kassab M, Becqemin JP: Adventitial cystic disease of the popliteal artery: Treatment by cyst removal. J Vasc Surg 8:638, 1988.
120. Deutsch AL, Hyde J, Miller SM, et al: Cystic adventitial degeneration of the popliteal artery: CT demonstration and directed percutaneous therapy. AJR Am J Roentgenol 145:117, 1985.
121. Cystic degeneration of the popliteal artery. BMJ 4:699, 1970.
122. Owen ERTC, Speechly Dick EM, Kour NE, et al: Cystic adventitial disease of the popliteal artery—a case of spontaneous resolution. Eur J Vasc Surg 4:319, 1990.

Chapter

87

Management of Foot Ulcers in Diabetes Mellitus

FRANK W. LoGERFO, MD
ALLEN D. HAMDAN, MD

Section XIII

Foot ulceration leading to amputation is a common complication of diabetes mellitus. The annual rate of amputation is about 1% for people with diabetes who are older than age 65. Among all people with type 2 diabetes, the incidence is about 5%. Duration of diabetes, poor glucose control, smoking, microalbuminuria, retinopathy, neuropathy, and absent foot pulses all are predictive of amputation.[1,2] In the United States, the incidence is higher in Mexican Americans (7.4/1000/year) than non-Hispanic whites (4.1/1000/year), independent of other risk factors.[3] Diabetes is associated with an overall risk of amputation 15 times higher than in people without diabetes.

The increased amputation rate is related to the complex pathophysiology of neuropathy and ischemia in the diabetic foot.[4] Appropriate management and success in preventing amputation depend on a clear understanding of the underlying pathophysiology. This chapter clarifies the pathophysiologic mechanisms to provide a basis for successful therapy.

■ DIABETES AND VASCULAR DISEASE

An enhanced propensity to atherosclerosis and coronary artery disease seems to be associated with diabetes. Mechanisms contributing to this enhanced propensity are not clear but have been the subject of much investigation and speculation.[5] The presence of small amounts of albumin (<300 mg) in the urine, referred to as *microalbuminuria,* is a marker for all of the complications of diabetes, including cardiovascular disease.[6] An annual spot test for microalbuminuria should be part of the care of all patients with diabetes. Dyslipidemia with lowered high-density lipoproteins and elevated low-density lipoproteins and triglycerides is associated with diabetes.[7] Currently the use of statins is recommended even in patients who do not have elevated low-density lipoproteins by traditional standards.[8] Angiotensin-converting enzyme inhibitors have been effective in limiting progression of microalbuminuria and renal insufficiency. All patients with diabetes, even if not hypertensive, may benefit from angiotensin-converting enzyme inhibitors.[8,9] The medical care of cardiovascular disease in diabetes requires special attention. Often the development of a foot ulcer is the first recognized event related to cardiovascular disease. It falls to the vascular surgeon to prompt an assessment of the medical management of the patient to provide the best long-term prognosis for cardiovascular disease.

Lifestyle changes, weight loss, and exercise greatly improve prognosis.[10] Good glucose control is a fundamental part of the care of every patient; this should include self-monitoring of blood glucose and hemoglobin A_{1c}. Cigarette smoking is harmful, creating two mechanisms of enhanced cardiovascular disease.[11] Although it may not be appropriate or possible for the vascular surgeon to manage the medical aspects of cardiovascular disease in diabetes, it is helpful to understand these fundamentals. Often the patient has been under the care of a surgeon for several years and would benefit from being guided to physicians with an interest and expertise in diabetes care.

■ NEUROPATHY

The neuropathy of diabetes is a distal symmetric neuropathy occurring in a "stocking" distribution.[12] Sensory neuropathy tends to affect the small-diameter pain and temperature fibers first. It is not unusual for a patient to have light touch sensation intact but to step on an insulin needle or other sharp object and be completely unaware. The sensory neuropathy also creates susceptibility to injury at pressure points. The motor neuropathy affects the longest fibers first—those innervating the intrinsic muscles of the foot, including the lumbrical muscles. Without the influence of the lumbrical muscles, the strong flexor muscles cause the toes to draw up in a "claw" position (Fig. 87-1). Pressure points are created under the metacarpophalangeal joints and tips of the toes. The pressure points are augmented by the limited joint mobility associated with diabetes.

Autonomic neuropathy affects the skin through loss of eccrine (sweat) and sebaceous (oil) gland function. The skin consequently becomes dry, and cracks or fissures occur, creating a portal of entry for infection. Hard, dry calluses form over pressure points, and the callus itself may cause an ulcer, much as would a stone or pebble in the shoe. Autonomic sympathetic neuropathy opens small arteriovenous shunts, depriving the capillary bed of perfusion. The skin of the foot consequently appears deceptively pink and well perfused, unless the foot is elevated above heart level to show pallor. All of the above-mentioned aspects of neuropathy set the stage for pressure ulceration or unsuspected injury.

The neuroinflammatory response to injury is lost. Small (1 μm) axon branches of the nociceptive sensory C fibers play an important role in the response to injury. The sensory nerve has its cell body adjacent to the spinal cord. One

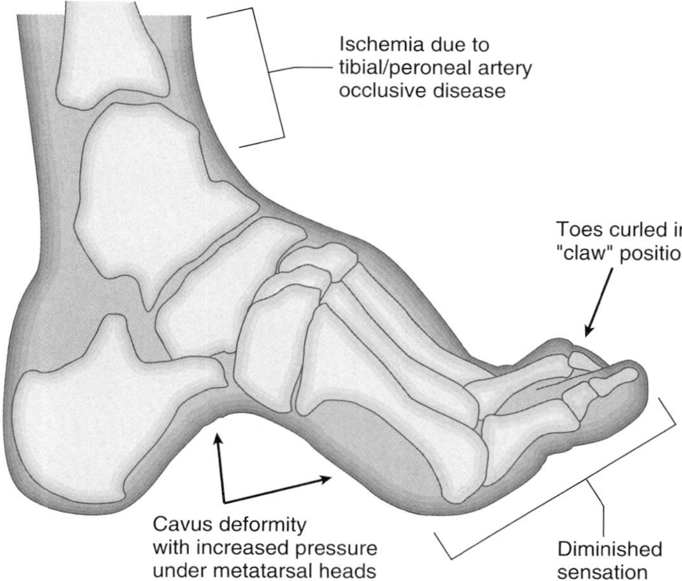
• Microneurovascular dysfunction with loss of nociceptive reflex and inflammatory response
• Vasomotor dysfunction with AV shunting
• Capillary basement membrane thickening with altered capillary exchange
• Glycosylation of matrix proteins
• Loss of apocrine/eccrine gland funtion
Ischemia due to tibial/peroneal artery occlusive disease
Toes curled in "claw" position
Cavus deformity with increased pressure under metatarsal heads
Diminished sensation

FIGURE 87-1 Some of the pathophysiologic mechanisms contributing to ulceration in the diabetic foot. AV, arteriovenous. (Modified from LoGerfo FW: Bypass grafts to the dorsalis pedis artery. Adv Vasc Surg 10:173-181, 2002.)

ramus enters the spinal cord, and the other extends to the periphery, with many branches. When one of these branches is injured, a depolarization occurs that travels centrally along the axon to the cell body and spinal cord. In addition, the depolarization travels peripherally out adjacent axon branches. The sensory nerve also becomes an "effector" nerve with outbound signals. The nerve fiber contains packets of neuropeptides that are synthesized and packaged in the cell body and travel down the sensory nerve cell to the periphery. When the local axon branch is depolarized, it releases the neuropeptides, the most studied of which is substance P. Substance P causes the mast cell to degranulate and release histamine, which causes vasodilatation, increased capillary permeability, and release of tumor necrosis factor-α with white blood cell migration to the site of injury. Calcitonin gene–related peptide has similar vasoactive effects. Neuropeptide Y mediates ischemic angiogenesis through endothelial nitric oxide synthase and vascular endothelial growth factor (VEGF).[13] No doubt the overall consequences of the multiple peptide release are far more complex, but in the aggregate account for the neuroinflammatory response to injury, a first-line defense mechanism. In the progression of diabetic neuropathy, the neuroinflammatory response is compromised early, often before any detectable sensory or motor neuropathy.[14] The hyperemia usually associated with infection is diminished even when arterial perfusion is normal.

Loss of neuroinflammation probably explains the blunted response to infection in the diabetic foot. It is common to remove a dry crust or area of dry gangrene on the foot and find unexpected purulent material or necrotic tissue with infection in excess of that indicated by the benign appearance of the lesion.

Neuropathy and its extensive physiologic consequences are responsible for most of the susceptibility to injury, infection, ulceration, and gangrene in the diabetic foot. Often the patient does not identify an ulcer or infection until there is drainage on a sock or an odor; this may be some time after a portal of entry has occurred, allowing for establishment of a polymicrobial infection under circumstances in which the usual local defense mechanisms of inflammation are not present. Ischemia, even moderate ischemia, under these circumstances can precipitate ulceration easily at pressure points. The concept of "critical ischemia" must be regarded differently for the diabetic foot because the severely neuropathic foot requires more perfusion to remain healed or to combat injury.

Other physiologic mechanisms probably also are compromised in the diabetic foot, as part of the generalized effects of glycemia. The capillary basement membrane is thickened and has increased permeability to albumin.[15] All of the proteins are modified by glycation, a chemical reaction in which sulfhydryl protein linkages are replaced by glucose. Hemoglobin A_{1c} is a marker of this pervasive effect on all proteins. There has been much theoretical discussion about the mechanisms whereby glycation impairs normal cellular and tissue functions.[16] Although the mechanistic details are ill defined, the overall detrimental effects have been well established through the relationship between hemoglobin A_{1c} and all complications of diabetes. Glycation with increased cross-linking of collagen may account for the cheiloarthropathy of diabetes and the limited joint mobility.

Maintenance of integrity of the foot depends on perfusion. When all other biologic mechanisms are fully intact, however, the foot can tolerate quite severe ischemia without tissue loss. When biology is compromised as a consequence of diabetes, it may be impossible for the foot to remain intact under the stress of daily life. Ultimately, there is a balance between stress and resistance to ulceration for every foot. With diabetes, there is no simple test of perfusion that can be used to determine whether or not a foot ulcer will heal and stay healed. The outcome depends on the overall biology, of which perfusion is only a part. It is worth

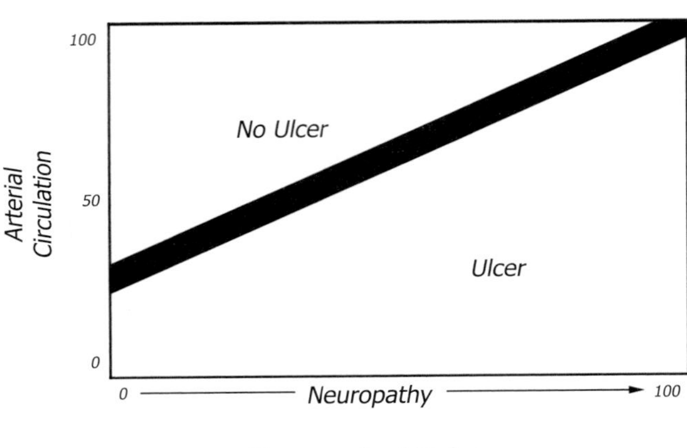

FIGURE 87-2 Ulceration in the diabetic foot may occur even in the face of moderate perfusion. Because of the variability in foot biology, it is difficult to set standards for noninvasive testing as a guide to arterial reconstruction. If an ulcer is present and perfusion can be improved, the ulcer will heal.

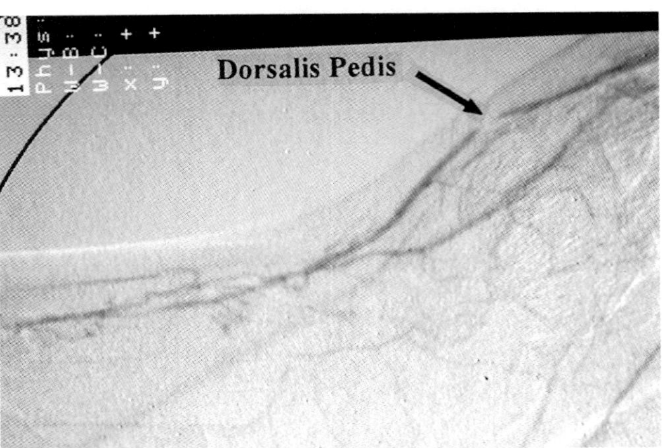

FIGURE 87-3 Pseudo-obstruction of the dorsalis pedis with the foot taped down in plantar flexion.

dwelling on this point because clinical decisions revolve around understanding the interconnection between biology, neuropathy, and ischemia. As a practical matter, virtually all foot problems in diabetes are accompanied by some element of neuropathy. The presence of neuropathy is not a contraindication to revascularization and does not preclude success. The presence of neuropathy generally requires revascularization under conditions of perfusion that would not require revascularization in the absence of neuropathy. The biologically compromised foot requires more perfusion to resist ulceration and respond to injury. Noninvasive tests of arterial inflow, including transcutaneous oxygen pressure, can be only poorly predictive of healing under these circumstances. The basis for this statement is illustrated further in Figure 87-2.

As a general rule, if a full-thickness skin ulcer of the foot occurs in a patient with diabetes, and neither the dorsalis pedis pulse nor the posterior tibial pulse is easily palpable, arteriography should be performed. Noninvasive assessment is of little value in making this specific decision. Occasionally, even when a foot pulse is palpable, there is reason to suspect significant arterial occlusive disease is present. Under these unusual circumstances, simple noninvasive tests may be helpful in determining whether an arteriogram is indicated. A palpable pulse in the absence of a clear triphasic Doppler signal or a low forefoot peripheral vascular resistance tips the balance toward arteriography. Nonetheless, the general rule—no palpable foot pulse = arteriography—is an excellent guide with few exceptions. When pulses are fully intact, the only options are ablative procedures.

■ OSTEOMYELITIS

The diagnosis of osteomyelitis in the diabetic foot is complicated by the similar degenerative changes that occur as a consequence of Charcot osteoarthropathy. The Charcot foot may present with erythema and swelling and can be misleading when accompanied by equivocal changes on x-ray view of the foot. In general, the absence of an open lesion should lead to great hesitancy in making the diagnosis of osteomyelitis. Under such circumstances, it is helpful to put the patient on bed rest for 24 hours, and if the evidence of inflammation diminishes without antibiotics, osteomyelitis is highly unlikely. Treatment of the Charcot foot with bed rest with or without antibiotics almost always results in improvement. Misinterpretation of this diagnosis may lead to the conclusion that osteomyelitis can be treated successfully with intravenous antibiotics.[17] Histologically proven osteomyelitis requires excision of the infected bone for healing without recurrence.[18] If a metal probe directly contacts bone at the base of the foot ulcer, osteomyelitis is highly likely, and further tests are unnecessary. We have not found bone scans, computed tomography, or magnetic resonance imaging to be helpful beyond standard radiography and the probe test in the diagnosis of osteomyelitis.

Digital subtraction contrast arteriography remains the standard for preoperative definition of arterial anatomy. Because of the compromised foot biology, the ideal target is an artery that is in continuity to the foot. This artery provides maximal perfusion where it is needed most, in the neuropathic regions of the foot. The pattern of atherosclerotic occlusive disease in diabetes tends to involve the infrageniculate arteries (i.e., the anterior tibial, peroneal, or posterior tibial arteries). Arteries in the foot, especially the dorsalis pedis artery, are often spared.[4] For this reason, it is important that the arteriogram determines the status of arteries in the foot, even when the arteries in the leg are occluded. Anteroposterior and lateral views of the foot are necessary to make the best decisions for choice of a target artery to restore maximal perfusion to the foot. One pitfall to avoid is "pseudo-occlusion" of the dorsalis pedis artery on arteriography when the foot is not supported and allowed to plantar flex. The result is the false appearance of occlusion of the dorsalis pedis artery by the prominence of the navicular bone (Figs. 87-3 and 87-4). Concerns about contrast-induced renal failure are often encountered. There is no evidence, however, that diabetes alone is a risk factor. Patients with preexisting renal failure are always a concern. This risk can be minimized by careful hydration and the use of protective agents, such as acetylcysteine (Mucomyst). The amount of contrast agent used can be minimized by the

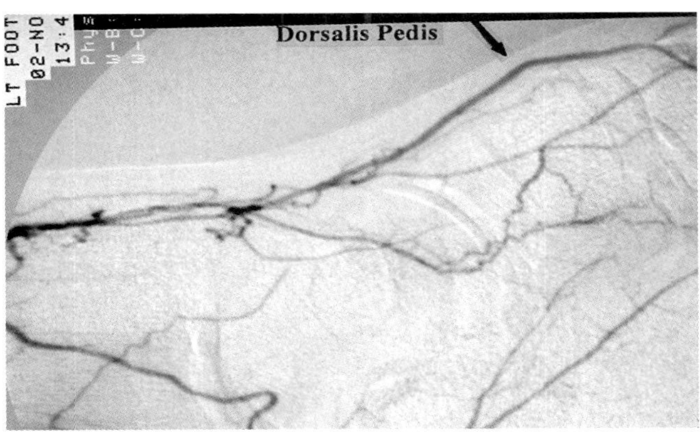

FIGURE 87-4 With the foot in slight dorsiflexion, the extrinsic pressure on the dorsalis pedis is relieved, and the artery is noted to be patent.

use of carbon dioxide angiography and pullout pressures to ensure patency of the aortoiliac segment. When, as is common, the ipsilateral superficial femoral artery is patent, the catheter may be positioned directly within it so as to use minimal contrast and obtain maximal definition of runoff vessels. Other new imaging technologies are sure to improve and eventually to supplement standard arteriography. Currently, magnetic resonance angiography does not provide the dynamic information and detail needed for the most effective decision making. Nonetheless, it has its place in patients with elevated creatinine (>3 mg/dL) and may become more useful as the technology evolves.

The inflow artery should be the most distal artery proximal to which there is no occlusion. In our experience, this inflow artery is equally divided between the common femoral artery and the popliteal artery. Many of the fine points of arterial reconstruction are detailed elsewhere in this textbook. Unique to diabetes is the problem of calcification and related technical problems. The calcifications that occur with diabetes often can be penetrated with standard vascular needles. Usually it is a matter of "wiggling" the needle patiently for a few seconds until it pops through the arterial wall. We have not found severe calcification of the artery to be a significant predictor of vein graft failure.[19]

There has been some debate at times as to whether the peroneal artery or the dorsalis pedis artery is a better choice as a target. It is unlikely that there will ever be clinical trials to answer this question. Some patients present with inflow through the popliteal artery in continuity with a widely patent peroneal artery, but occlusion of the anterior and posterior tibial arteries and reconstitution of the dorsalis pedis. Under these circumstances, with the peroneal artery already patent, bypass to the dorsalis pedis artery greatly improves foot perfusion and results in healing of ulceration. It seems unlikely that the peroneal target is optimal for ulcer healing when the dorsalis pedis is a viable target.

■ OUTCOMES

Often, to restore maximal perfusion, the most efficacious bypass is to the dorsalis pedis artery with autogenous conduit.[20] The inflow source can be any location proximal to which there is no significant stenosis, including the below-knee popliteal artery. In a large study spanning a decade, the results of 1032 bypasses to the dorsalis pedis artery were reported.[21] There were 10 deaths, 0.97% occurring within the first 30 days of surgery. Thirty-one patients (3%) had cardiac complications, including myocardial infarction and congestive heart failure. Significant, limb-threatening postoperative wound infections occurred in 21 limbs (2%), 2 of which resulted in graft infections and limb loss. The 30-day graft failure rate was 4.2%. Secondary patency and limb salvage were 62.7% and 78.2% and 41.7% and 57.7% at 5 and 10 years. Patient survival was 48.6% and 23.8% at 5 and 10 years. These data showed that dorsalis pedis artery bypass is a successful and durable operation. The low perioperative mortality seen in this study is attributed to invasive monitoring, beta blockade, judicious intravenous fluid use, and a dedicated vascular nursing unit. This and other work[22] argues against the idea that diabetes is associated with a higher operative mortality or diminished graft patency.

Heel ulcers are a particularly difficult problem, often occurring as a consequence of heel pressure in the supine position. The ideal target to provide maximal perfusion to the heel is the posterior tibial artery. In its absence, the dorsalis pedis artery has proved to be an effective target for healing of heel ulcers.[23]

Wound healing generally is considered to be impaired in the diabetic foot. Certainly, all of the compromised biology and neuropathy have a negative impact on wound healing. In addition, the capillary escape of albumin may cause accentuated edema in the postoperative period contributing to suture line stress. This stress is of specific concern for the distal incision of the dorsalis pedis bypass, where the anastomosis is covered by minimal subcutaneous tissue. Closure of this wound should be designed to minimize tension and obtain accurate approximation of skin edges. The use of interrupted nylon skin sutures or a subcuticular suture is preferable to currently available skin staples. In the postoperative period, it is helpful to wrap the foot and ankle with an elastic bandage or to keep the foot well elevated to minimize swelling and suture line stress.

■ SEVERE FOOT INFECTIONS

When the foot presents with deep infection, it is important to drain any abscess promptly and remove obvious necrotic tissue. Simultaneous medical management should be initiated to bring glycemia under control, and broad-spectrum antibiotics should be given for systemic sepsis. When these goals are achieved, the foot should be assessed further for the presence of significant arterial occlusive disease. Because of the open wounds and edema, it may be difficult to determine whether pulses are palpable. A simple examination with a continuous-wave Doppler usually suffices to determine if the dorsalis pedis or posterior tibial signals are triphasic. If not, arteriography should be performed to determine if perfusion of the foot could be improved by arterial reconstruction. Arteriography should be done promptly, within 24 hours of the initial stabilization if possible. Maximal tissue preservation can be obtained only with maximal perfusion. Waiting to determine viability allows infection to progress and may obviate the one chance to avoid major amputation.

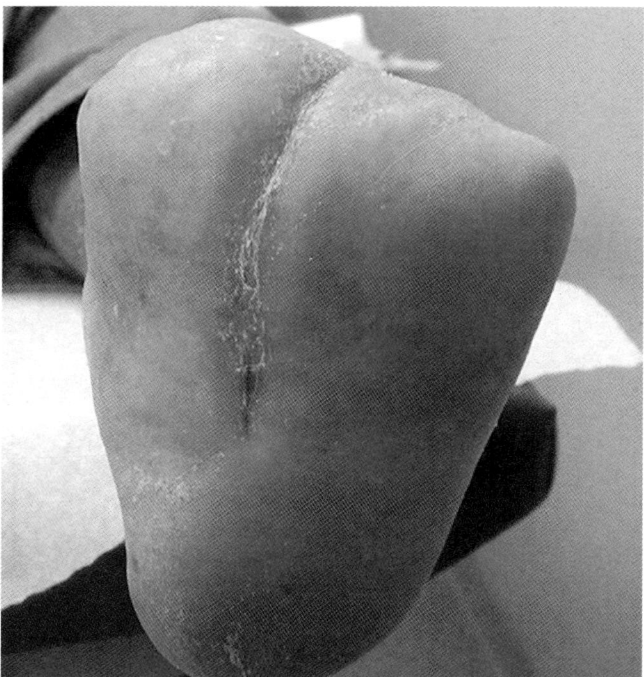

FIGURE 87-5 An incision bisecting the plantar flap at the time of a transmetatarsal amputation in a patient after dorsalis pedis bypass. These incisions are necessary to provide optimal drainage, and they heal in a well-revascularized foot.

Undetected or partially drained infection always should be considered when a well-revascularized foot develops areas of continued necrosis. Clinicians recognize infection through the manifestations of inflammation, and the manifestations are muted by the compromised biology of the diabetic foot. "Pus" or purulent material does not occur in the absence of inflammation. On removing a foul-smelling toe or ray, only a small amount of purulence may be present. On probing the margins of the wound, however, the probe often slips into a tract, which, when opened, reveals only a slimy covering between muscle bundles. Such tracts should be opened completely so as to provide dependent drainage. At times, the tract may extend to the midfoot, and there may be reluctance to make such a large incision on the plantar aspect of the foot. If the foot is well revascularized, however, these incisions heal and fully tolerate weight bearing. One of the most disconcerting situations is when a tract is discovered during a transmetatarsal amputation and requires an incision directly down the middle of the plantar flap to the midfoot. There is no way around this. The tract must be opened widely and packed (Fig. 87-5); maximal perfusion through distal revascularization makes this possible. When the foot is fully revascularized, several options are available for ultimate closure of the wound.

■ POSTOPERATIVE WOUND CARE

The standard for postoperative care of open wounds is the use of saline-moistened, wet-to-dry dressings. These dressings allow full inspection of the wound and facilitate further débridements. When granulation tissue has formed, other wound healing agents may be used, or the wound may be managed with other dressings, including vacuum sponges. All wounds can be managed throughout their course, however, with wet-to-dry saline cotton gauze (not paper gauze) dressings. Surgical procedures to achieve or assist closure may involve resection of joints, such as the metatarsophalangeal joint or interphalangeal joints. Metatarsal osteotomy relieves pressure points. Heel wounds may be closed with muscle flaps using the short flexors. Free flaps may be used but are rarely necessary. To achieve maximal salvage, it is helpful to have an interested team, including podiatry and plastic surgery consultants, involved.

In summary, the compromised biology of the diabetic foot mandates some specific rules to maximize limb salvage, as follows:

1. Débride and drain obvious infection promptly.
2. Control systemic sepsis and glycemia.
3. Assess for atherosclerotic occlusive disease even when neuropathy or infection or both are present.
4. Define the status of the arteries in the foot even when the tibial arteries are occluded.
5. Restore maximal perfusion to the foot with distal reconstruction.
6. Look for, drain, and débride any residual infection or necrosis.
7. Manage open wounds initially with saline gauze dressings and non–weight bearing.

Do not:

1. Attribute ulcers in the diabetic foot to microvascular occlusive disease.
2. Deem a patient "not reconstructible" unless the status of the arteries in the foot has been established on arteriography.
3. Ascribe continued necrosis in the fully revascularized foot to microvascular occlusive disease.

■ REFERENCES

1. Adler AI, et al: Lower-extremity amputation in diabetes: The independent effects of peripheral vascular disease, sensory neuropathy, and foot ulcers. Diabetes Care 22:1029-1035, 1999.
2. Moulik PK, Mtonga R, Gill GV: Amputation and mortality in new-onset diabetic foot ulcers stratified by etiology. Diabetes Care 26:491-494, 2003.
3. Wunderlich: Diabetic foot syndrome: Evaluating the prevalence and incidence of foot pathology in Mexican Americans and non-Hispanic whites from a diabetes disease management cohort. Diabetes Care 26:1435-1438, 2003.
4. LoGerfo FW: Trends in the care of the diabetic foot: Expanded role of arterial reconstruction. Arch Surg 127:617-621, 1992.
5. Creager MA, et al: Diabetes and vascular disease: Pathophysiology, clinical consequences, and medical therapy: Part I. Circulation 108:1527-1532, 2003.
6. Dinneen SF, Gerstein HC: The association of microalbuminuria and mortality in non-insulin-dependent diabetes mellitus: A systematic overview of the literature. Arch Intern Med 157:1413-1418, 1997.
7. Ford ES, Giles WH, Dietz WH: Prevalence of the metabolic syndrome among US adults: Findings from the Third National Health and Nutrition Examination Survey. JAMA 287:356-359, 2002.

8. Peripheral arterial disease in people with diabetes. Diabetes Care 26:3333-3341, 2003.
9. Hansen: Randomised controlled trial of long term efficacy of captopril on preservation of kidney function in normotensive patients with insulin dependent diabetes and microalbuminuria. BMJ 319:24-25, 1999.
10. Pan XR, et al: Effects of diet and exercise in preventing NIDDM in people with impaired glucose tolerance. The Da Qing IGT and Diabetes Study. Diabetes Care 20:537-544, 1997.
11. Paniszyn: Symptomatology and anatomic patterns of peripheral vascular disease: Differing impact of smoking and diabetes. Ann Vasc Surg 3:224-228, 1989.
12. Arora S, et al: Cutaneous microcirculation in the neuropathic diabetic foot improves significantly but not completely after successful lower extremity revascularization. J Vasc Surg 35:501-505, 2002.
13. Kitlinska: Neuropeptide Y induces ischemic angiogenesis and restores function of ischemic skeletal muscles. J Clin Invest 111:1853-1862, 2003.
14. Parkhouse N, Le Quesne PM: Impaired neurogenic vascular response in patients with diabetes and neuropathic foot lesions. N Engl J Med 318:1306-1309, 1988.
15. Lassen: Hemodynamic factors in the genesis of diabetic microangiopathy. Metabolism 32:943-949, 1983.
16. Gill: Protein glycosylation in diabetes mellitus: Biochemical and clinical considerations. Pract Diabetes Int 17:21-25, 2000.
17. Bamberger DM, Daus GP, Gerding DN: Osteomyelitis in the feet of diabetic patients: Long-term results, prognostic factors, and the role of antimicrobial and surgical therapy. Am J Med 83:653-660, 1987.
18. Simpson AH, Deakin M, Latham JM: Chronic osteomyelitis: The effect of the extent of surgical resection on infection-free survival. J Bone Joint Surg Br 83:403-407, 2001.
19. Misare BD, et al: Infrapopliteal bypasses to severely calcified, unclampable outflow arteries: Two-year results. J Vasc Surg 24:6-16, 1996.
20. Pomposelli FB Jr, et al: Dorsalis pedis arterial bypass: Durable limb salvage for foot ischemia in patients with diabetes mellitus. J Vasc Surg 21:375-384, 1995.
21. Pomposelli FB, et al: A decade of experience with dorsalis pedis artery bypass: Analysis of outcome in more than 1000 cases. J Vasc Surg 37:307-315, 2003.
22. Akbari CM, et al: Lower extremity revascularization in diabetes: Late observations. Arch Surg 135:452-456, 2000.
23. Berceli SA, et al: Efficacy of dorsal pedal artery bypass in limb salvage for ischemic heel ulcers. J Vasc Surg 30:499-508, 1999.

Chapter 88

Vasculogenic Erectile Dysfunction

RALPH G. DE PALMA, MD, FACS

Understanding of the pathophysiology and treatment of erectile dysfunction (ED) has improved considerably since the 1970s. Leriche's[1] 1923 observation that aortoiliac occlusion caused ED prompted the interest of vascular surgeons.[2] It was later learned that aortic surgical interventions often produced ED.[3,4] Beginning in the 1970s, techniques were developed to measure penile perfusion, and attempts were made to characterize this complication better.[5,6] Active attempts to use vascular surgical procedures to improve erectile function were reported.[7-9]

During the late 1970s and early 1980s, initial efforts focused on corpus cavernosum revascularization. In 1982, it was found that erection could be stimulated by injection of the vasoactive agents papaverine[10] and phentolamine[11] into the corpora cavernosa. This discovery illuminated the processes of cavernosal smooth muscle function. Intracorporeal administration of vasoactive agents led to effective methods to test and quantify various aspects of ED, providing important tools for diagnosis and treatment. Emphasis shifted from simple mechanistic efforts to increase arterial inflow to sophisticated investigations of corporeal smooth muscle function. Important contributions include elaboration of the roles of nitric oxide (NO) and oxygen tension in normal erection[12]; delineation of mediators of corporeal muscle contraction and relaxation[13]; and gene interventions to correct abnormal smooth muscle relaxation responses, particularly novel use of cDNA constructs to induce NO synthetase activity.[14]

Erectile dysfunction (formerly impotence) is defined as the persistent or repeated inability, for at least 3 months' duration, to attain or maintain an erection sufficient for satisfactory performance in the absence of an ejaculatory disorder, such as premature ejaculation.[15] ED should be distinguished from *retrograde ejaculation,* a neurogenic dysfunction in which bladder neck closure does not occur so that semen is ejaculated into the bladder. In the latter disorder, the patient still is able to complete coitus and achieve orgasm. Although ED, by definition, is a disorder limited to men, women with aortoiliac artery obstructive disease might experience insufficient vaginal lubrication and loss of orgasm.[16,17] Because men present with aortoiliac occlusive disease more frequently in vascular practice than do women, the relationship between female sexual disorders and aortoiliac disease had been relatively neglected until more recently (see Chapter 64). This chapter reviews the physiology of erection and the current approaches to diagnosis and treatment of ED.

■ PHYSIOLOGY OF PENILE ERECTION

Penile erection results from a neurally mediated increase of arterial inflow into the corporeal bodies along with a reduction or cessation of venous outflow. Findings reported by Rajfer and colleagues[13] support the idea that endothelium-derived relaxant factor is involved in nonadrenergic, noncholinergic neural transmission, which leads to the cavernosal smooth muscle relaxation required for normal erection. Histochemically, nerve fibers positive for the reduced form of nicotinamide adenine dinucleotide phosphate (NADP) and diaphorase are found in human penile tissue, indicating NO synthase activity.[18] Other neurotransmitters, such as vasoactive intestinal polypeptide and fibers positive for acetylcholinesterase, also are present.[19] When the penis is flaccid, the corporeal smooth muscle is contracted; contraction is due to a normally present overriding adrenergic tone. With erection, smooth muscle relaxation occurs. Primary effectors of smooth muscle tone include norepinephrine, endothelin-1, acetylcholine, NO, vasoactive intestinal polypeptide, and prostaglandin E_1 (PGE_1). For an updated review of these neurotransmitters, their tissue sources of origin, and second messengers, see the review by Rehman and Melman.[20]

The initiating event of penile erection is vasodilatation. With increased intracavernosal flow, a greater amount of oxygen is thought to stimulate NO synthesis by cavernosal nerves and endothelium. Cavernosal oxygenation promotes penile erection, whereas hypoxemia is inhibitory. Testosterone, in addition to its central effects, has been shown experimentally to stimulate NO synthase activity in corporeal tissues,[21] enhancing sensitivity to cavernosal nerve stimulation in animals. NO activates conversion of guanosine triphosphate to cyclic guanosine monophosphate (GMP). GMP provides the message leading to relaxation of the smooth muscle within the corpora cavernosa.[22] Agents that inhibit hydrolysis of cyclic GMP increase messenger cyclic GMP, enhancing smooth muscle relaxation and promoting penile erection.[23] Cyclic nucleotide phosphodiesterase (PDE) isoenzymes increase hydrolysis of cyclic GMP; among these, PDE-5 and PDE-6 are specific for the substrate in human cavernosal tissue.[24] Inhibitors of PDE have developed as an important new class of oral agents for treatment of ED.

■ HEMODYNAMICS AND DIAGNOSIS

Figure 88-1 presents a simplified concept of hemodynamics of the erectile process. During flaccidity, the corporeal smooth muscle and cavernosal arteries are contracted, and the emissary and pudendal veins are open. The intracavernous pressure is equivalent to venous pressure; the blood in the intracavernous spaces is desaturated. This important physiologic process has been reviewed in detail elsewhere.[25]

Advanced diagnostic methods, such as dynamic infusion cavernosometry and cavernosography (DICC), measure penile blood pressure and flow changes and detect sites of leakage. These invasive tests are performed in cooperation with specialists in urology and radiology, and although still useful, with the advent of effective oral treatment for ED, they are employed less frequently now. At low intracavernous pressure in the flaccid state, a cavernosal or venous leak is always detected radiographically; in other words, every flaccid penis exhibits a venous leak. This fact is key to understanding penile physiology and cavernosographic findings.

In the next stage of erection, intracavernous pressure increases to 80 to 90 mm Hg synchronously with progressive smooth muscle relaxation, facilitating increased arterial inflow. With full relaxation, the penile veins become obstructed secondary to the occluding action of the subalbugineal smooth muscle. A turgid vascular erection corresponds to intracavernous pressures of about 100 mm Hg. With full erection, the cavernosal artery occlusion pressure (CAOP) tends to be equivalent to the intracavernous pressure, but flow is markedly reduced. In the final stage, pelvic muscular contraction, suprasystolic pressures are generated, maximal rigidity occurs, and cavernosal artery flow transiently ceases during this stage. For diagnostic purposes, flow in the cavernosal artery can be measured by duplex scanning[26] at intervals after the intracavernous injection of vasoactive agents.

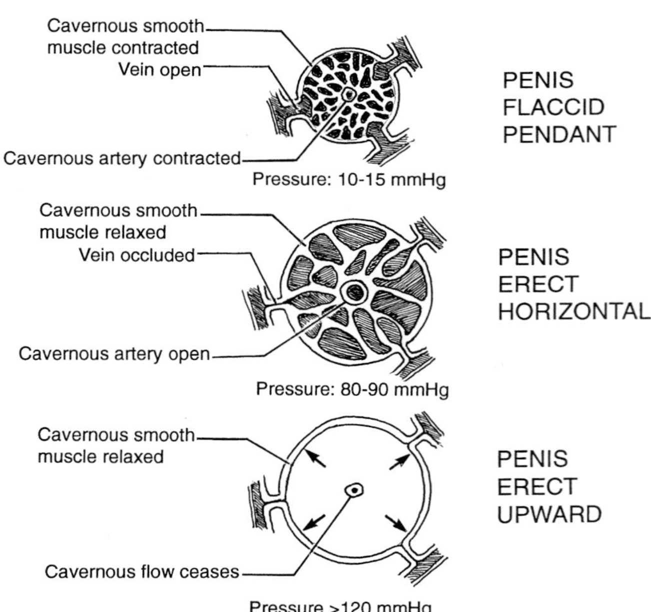

FIGURE 88-1 Current theory of penile erection showing three stages of erection as smooth muscle relaxation occurs. Pressure measurements are those obtained before and after intracavernosal injection of vasoactive agents. Note onset of venous occlusion in the second stage. (From DePalma RG: New developments in the diagnosis and treatment of impotence. West J Med 164:54, 1996.)

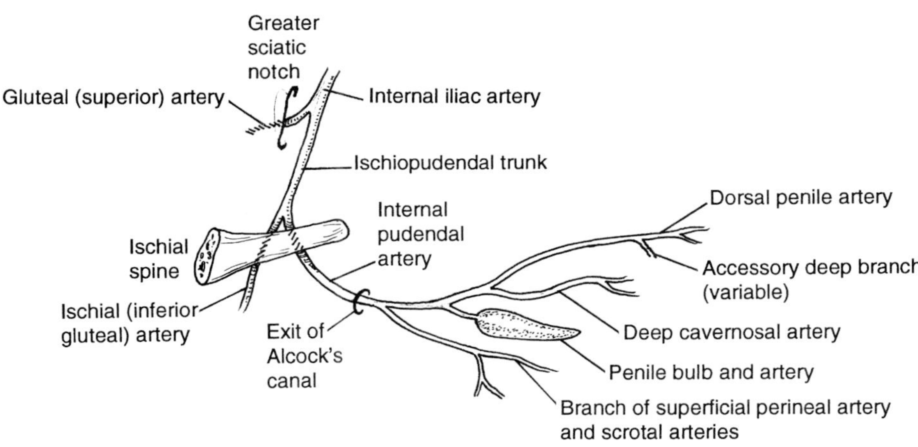

FIGURE 88-2 A right oblique schematic showing the internal iliac artery and the pudendal artery and its branches to the penis. This view can be seen on highly selective pudendal arteriography. Note bony landmarks. (Modified from DePalma RG: New developments in the diagnosis and treatment of impotence. West J Med 164:54, 1996.)

During DICC, the pressure at which cavernosal artery flow ceases (CAOP) can be detected by a Doppler probe placed at the penile base. This method uses "artificial erection" generated by a roller pump infusion of warm normal saline solution. The pressure at which the signal returns on pump flow reduction is taken as the CAOP. This value normally ranges from 80 to 90 mm Hg, with a gradient of less than 30 mm Hg compared with a simultaneously obtained brachial pressure.[27,28] CAOP is an indirect assessment of the adequacy of arterial flow. Large vessel aortoiliac disease and abnormalities of the distal pudendal arterial supply (Fig. 88-2) cause arteriogenic ED. The flow to maintain erection is a measure of venous efflux, provided that complete smooth muscle relaxation has been obtained. The flow needed to maintain erection considered to be normal is less than 40 mL/min, with pressure drops of less than 1 mm Hg/sec on flow cessation.

Standardization of DICC depends on maximal muscular relaxation through the intracavernous injection of vasoactive agents. Previously described methods[27,28] used injections of 60 mg of papaverine and 2.5 mg of phentolamine. Readministration of these agents during DICC was suggested to achieve maximal muscular relaxation and linear pressure-flow relationships.[29] An understanding of this process is important for arteriographic demonstration of penile arterial anatomy. When the intracavernous administration of vasoactive agents produces full erection, arteriography causes radiographic artifacts owing to cessation of cavernosal artery flow. For visualization of the penile artery, the goal of injection is tumescence, not full erection; smaller doses of vasoactive agents are used.

■ GENERAL CAUSES OF ERECTILE DYSFUNCTION

As one may infer from a consideration of physiology, erectile failure is a dramatic vascular dysfunction. ED also can be caused, however, by endocrine, metabolic, neurogenic, and psychological factors. Some form of arterial inflow abnormality is associated with ED in about 50% of patients screened noninvasively.[30] As is shown subsequently, however, this finding is not always caused by large vessel inflow compromise. Arteriogenic ED can be due to intrinsic abnormalities of the penile arteries or smooth muscle. Endocrine causes of ED are uncommon[31]; only 3% to 4% of patients screened show lowered testosterone levels. Prolactinomas also are rare; they are found in about 0.2% of patients screened. Similarly, restoration of a euthyroid state has not notably improved erectile function in patients with hypothyroidism.

The most common association related to arteriogenic ED is use of many antihypertensive drugs; angiotensin-converting enzyme inhibitors are thought to spare erectile function. Antidepressants such as selective serotonin uptake inhibitors reduce libido and affect potency. Bupropion, a member of another class of antidepressants, exhibits prosexual effects, including effects on libido, arousal, and the duration and intensity of orgasm.[32] Oral medications for ED have included phentolamine, yohimbine, trazodone, pentoxifylline, and apomorphine. I found isoxsuprine, an $alpha_1$ blocker, to be useful[33] before the availability of the effective newer agents—sildenafil and its related inhibitors of PDE-5, the main isoenzyme involved in the metabolism of cyclic GMP in the corpus cavernosum.[34] These drugs now dominate oral therapy and have been said to be effective about two thirds of the time. New drugs in this class include vardenafil, approved for use in the United States, and tadalafil (Cialis), currently under review. For detailed information on oral therapy, see the review by Padma-Nathan and Guiliano.[35]

Psychogenic problems often observed in men with ED can produce sufficient anxiety and enhanced adrenergic tone to override even intracavernous injections of vasoactive agents. Heavy cigarette smoking just before injection of 80 mg of papaverine in normal young volunteers dramatically inhibited erection.[36] Despite limitations, intracavernous injection using PGE_1 ($\leq$30 μg) is an important diagnostic and therapeutic tool.[37] An adequate erectile response, although not ruling out proximal arterial disease, suggests that the arterial system is capable of delivering adequate inflow and that corporeal relaxation and venous closure are relatively functional. An adequate erection also means that, in addition to intracavernous injections, intraurethral prostadil can be used for treatment.[38]

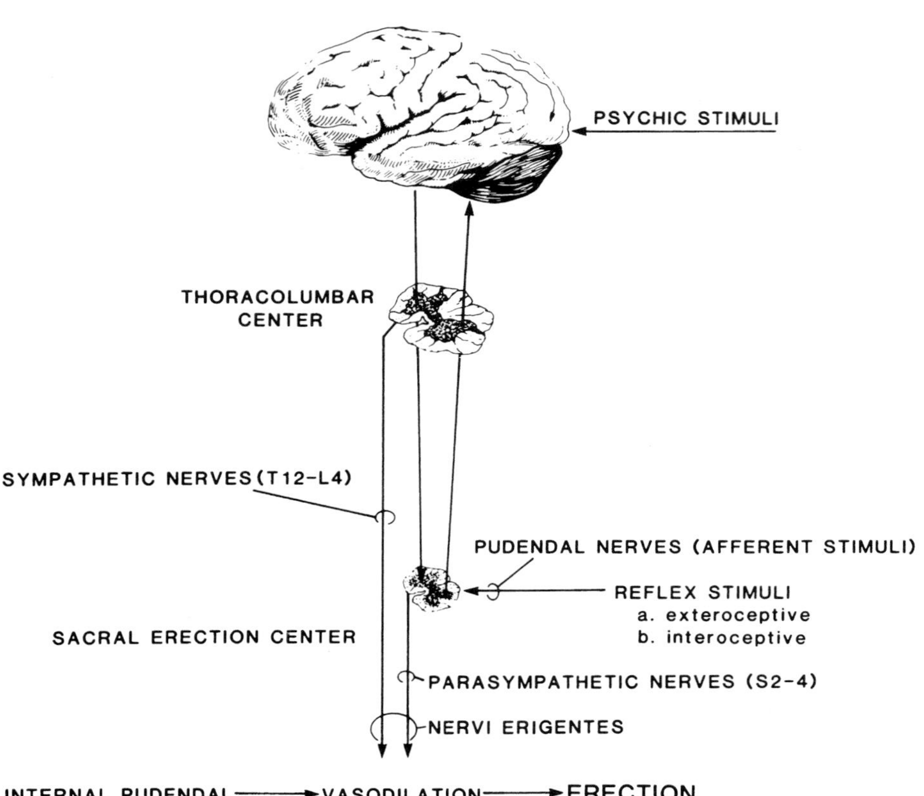

FIGURE 88-3 Diagrammatic representation of neural pathways involved in penile erection.

As can be seen from the consideration of erectile physiology, arterial inflow compromise causes venous leakage. DICC alone, even with CAOP measurement, cannot with certainty establish or rule out the diagnosis of venous leakage. When DICC and pudendal arteriography were used in one study, 23% of men with normal noninvasive parameters and suspected venous leakage were found to have associated arterial obstructive lesions.[39] These relatively younger men (average age 48.8 years) had lesions involving the pudendal and penile arteries. Before microvascular interventions, DICC and pudendal arteriography are needed. In men with marginal arterial inflow, a venous interruption procedure is unlikely to yield satisfactory results.

Neurologic dysfunction, particularly diabetic neuropathy, can be the dominant factor contributing to ED when the arterial inflow seems to be normal. It is difficult to sort out the exact importance of each factor in these cases, inasmuch as cavernosal smooth muscle dysfunction also contributes to ED in diabetics. Nerve damage and arterial compromise can follow prostatic, rectal, or aortic operations. Refined surgical techniques may avoid such effects in a significant proportion of cases (see Chapter 66).

Figure 88-3 depicts the general neural pathways involved in penile erection, and Figure 88-4 shows the distribution of vegetative nerves about the aorta that give rise to the sacral and hypogastric outflow tracts and ultimately the pudendal and penile nerves. Overall, 28% of men with ED screened neurologically exhibited one or more abnormalities in pudendal or tibial evoked potentials or bulbocavernosus reflex times.[40] Normally, mean bulbocavernosus reflex times range from 28.3 to 37.5 msec. The contribution of these abnormalities to erectile failure is difficult to assess because many men exhibit coexisting vascular abnormalities. Neurologic testing using pudendal evoked potentials and bulbocavernosus reflex times does yield reproducible values, however, which can be used to assess nerve damage.[41,42] These techniques measure somatic nerve reflexes as surrogates of autonomic function. Abnormalities, when present, point to neurogenic deficits involving the genitourinary tract, rectum, and aortoiliac nerve plexuses and the central nervous system itself. Men with these abnormalities are often exquisitely sensitive to the intracavernosal administration of vasoactive drugs. The detection of nerve conduction deficits is a warning to avoid initially high doses of these agents, which could cause priapism.

Multiple factors contribute to ED (Table 88-1). These factors help guide the approaches to diagnosis and treatment of sexual dysfunction and in some respects may be relevant to both sexes. One important area, hitherto neglected, has been the study of female sexual dysfunction, which appears in diabetic women,[43,44] in women with cardiovascular disease,[45] and in postmenopausal women in the form of disordered sexual arousal.[46] Measurements of arousal and vaginal lubrication are more difficult in women; however, progress in understanding the etiology, physiology, and treatment of female sexual dysfunction continues.[47]

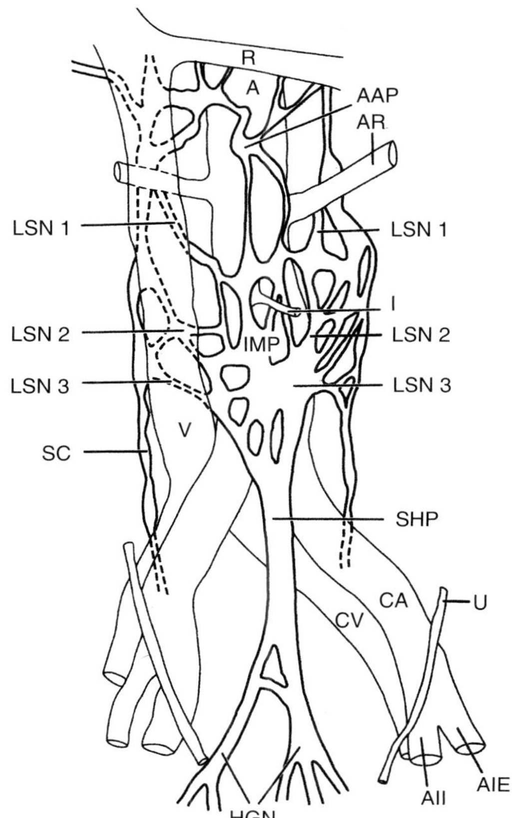

FIGURE 88-4 Anatomic distribution of periaortic vegetative nerves showing connections between sympathetic and the aortic plexuses and course of sacral plexus and hypogastric nerves. A, abdominal aorta; AAP, abdominal aortic plexus; AIE, external iliac artery; AII, internal iliac artery; AR, renal artery; CA, common iliac artery; CV, common iliac vein; I, inferior mesenteric artery; LSN 1, 2, 3, lumbar sympathetic nerves; R, left renal vein; SC, sympathetic chain, U, ureter; V, inferior vena cava. (From van Schaik J, van Baalan JM, Visser MJT, De Ruiter MC: Nerve-preserving aortoiliac surgery: Anatomical study and surgical approach. J Vasc Surg 33:983, 2001.)

Treatment modalities have been similar to the modalities suggested in men and include oral sildenafil[48,49] and topical alprostadil.[50] From the standpoint of aortic reconstruction, vascular surgeons also now must recognize potential benefits of nerve-sparing dissections with preserved internal iliac flow for women.

■ APPROACH TO DIAGNOSIS

No universally accepted approach to ED or other sexual dysfunction exists; in the main, ED is a symptom not a single disease. Increasingly an accepted approach is limited and patient goal directed and depends on the response to initial therapy.[51] If simple measures, such as oral medications, fail, more elaborate investigations can be considered.[25,52] Should the intracavernosal administration of vasoactive agents fail or vacuum constrictor devices prove ineffective, evaluation would progress to invasive tests for delineation of abnormal physiology.

Table 88-1 Factors in Vasculogenic Erectile Dysfunction

FACTOR	PROBABLE CAUSE
Cavernosal	
Arteriolar	Functional or anatomic; helicine vessel abnormalities; blood pressure medication
Fibrosis	Postpriapism; drug administration
Peyronie's disease	Deformity invading cavernosal smooth muscle; venous leakage through tunica albuginea
Refractory smooth muscle	Hormonal: prolactinemia; low testosterone level; blood pressure medication
	Metabolic: diabetes mellitus, uremia
Venous Leakage	
Acquired	Abnormal tunica albuginea; traumatic lesions
Congenital	Isolated leakage from corpus cavernosum into the spongiosum
Arterial	
	Aortoiliac atherosclerosis
	Steal due to external iliac disease
	Occlusive disease of pudendal arteries: atherosclerotic or traumatic
	Occlusive disease of penile arteries: atherosclerotic; idiopathic proliferative
	Atheroembolic occlusion

A diagnostic sequence based on noninvasive screening also can be used before the office visit for a detailed history and physical examination. At the time of the office visit, depending on the initial findings and the patient's desires, erectile function can be assessed directly by intracavernosal administration of PGE_1. At the same time, blood specimens are obtained for measurements of prolactin, testosterone, glucose, and prostate-specific antigen. Initial noninvasive neurovascular testing can help determine the diagnostic category of the ED (i.e., vasculogenic or neurogenic). Noninvasive vascular methods of testing are described later. Each has advantages and limitations.[53]

Contributions in this area made by vascular surgeons are of some practical and historical interest and can be used by vascular laboratories to assess large vessel occlusive disease. Canning and colleagues[6] noted in 1963 that vascular insufficiency of the pelvic vessels, even in the presence of normal femoral pulses, caused vasculogenic ED. They attempted to identify affected patients by palpating penile pulses and performing impedance plethysmography. Subsequently, other investigators assessed penile blood flow using mercury strain-gauge plethysmography, spectrographic or ultrasonic measurement of penile systolic pressure, and pulse volume recordings.[54-57]

Kempczinski[58] reported on 234 patients using the Doppler velocimeter to measure penile systolic pressure. This value divided by brachial systolic pressure yielded a penile-brachial index (PBI). Pulse volume waveforms of penile volume change with each systolic ejection also were recorded. The influence of sexual function and patient age on each of these parameters was determined. Age exerted a deleterious influence on all variables of penile blood flow independent of the status of sexual potency. Patients

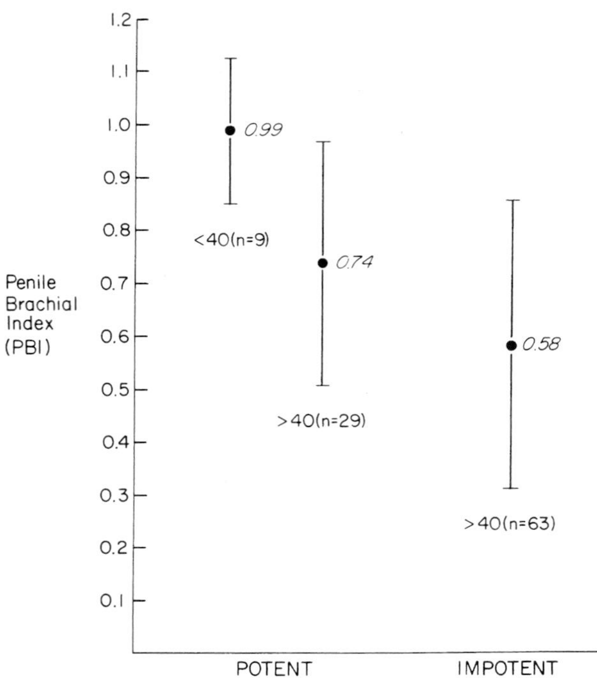

FIGURE 88-5 Distribution of penile-brachial index (PBI) values (mean ± standard deviation) in patients by age and sexual potency. (Data from Kempczinski RF: Role of the vascular diagnostic laboratory in the evaluation of male impotence. Am J Surg 138:278, 1979.)

younger than age 40 years had a mean PBI of 0.99 compared with a PBI of 0.74 for older patients with equal potency; this difference was statistically significant. In contrast, patients older than age 40 with ED had a mean PBI of 0.58, which was also a statistically significant difference (Fig. 88-5). The pulse volume waveforms of patients younger than 40 were of good to fair quality; no poor-quality waveforms were observed. With increasing age and sexual dysfunction, a greater percentage of patients had poor-quality waveforms, but this difference was not statistically significant. Similar findings have been confirmed by other investigators, who have emphasized the utility of this type of testing in the initial evaluation of patients with ED.[59,60]

Noninvasive vascular testing in the flaccid penile state using plethysmography to obtain waveforms and to calculate the PBI is a convenient and simple noninvasive test.[61] Penile pressure is detected with a Doppler probe placed distal to an inflated 2.5-cm cuff. The reappearance of Doppler signals in the dorsal artery branches just proximal to the glans signals reflow. This pressure is normally systemic. A PBI of 0.75 suggests that no major occlusion exists between the aorta and the distal measurement point. A PBI of less than 0.6 relates to major aortoiliac occlusion and almost always to ED. Penile pulse waves are recorded at mean arterial pressure with the use of a pneumoplethysmographic cuff with a contained transducer. This procedure measures total pulsations of all penile arteries as the cuff compresses the penile tissue. Variables recorded are crest time, waveform, and the presence or absence of a dicrotic notch on a polygraph with a chart speed of 25 mm/sec and a sensitivity setting of 1. In normal men, the upstroke of the waveform is completed by 0.2 second (i.e., a 5-mm space at a chart speed of 25 mm/sec), and normal waveforms range from 5 to 30 mm in height.

Although these noninvasive vascular laboratory tests help define large vessel arteriogenic ED, they do not detect ED resulting from venous leak or other causes. In later studies, the sensitivity of these tests was shown to predict an abnormal arteriogram in 85% of cases.[28] Specificity (the percentage of true-negative test results) was 70%. The advantage of plethysmographic testing lies in the ability to define arteriogenic inflow problems before the office visit. A vascular technologist can perform these tests simply and inexpensively. This screening, in the flaccid state, is helpful preoperatively and postoperatively and before progressing to drug treatment. In a patient with clear arterial compromise, higher initial dosages of vasoactive agents can be used, whereas in patients with normal noninvasive arterial studies and neurogenic dysfunction or diabetes, lower dosages are advisable.

The noninvasive data facilitate a focused history and goal-directed physical examination. A history of gradual onset of erectile failure in the absence of traumatic life events implies an organic cause. The complaint of claudication or the physical findings of aneurysmal or occlusive aortoiliac disease suggest a diagnosis of arteriogenic ED, which may be supported by abnormalities detected by noninvasive arterial testing. A novel observation is that small aneurysms sometimes relate to an abrupt onset of ED.[62] Such an event, resulting from atheroembolism, might be suspected from results of noninvasive studies (Fig. 88-6).

The presence of risk factors for atherosclerosis—mainly smoking, hyperlipidemia, hypertension, and diabetes—suggests a diagnosis of arteriogenic ED, as does a history of pelvic or perineal trauma. The onset of ED immediately after pelvic or arterial surgery is critical. Finally, the patient must be assessed for presence of diabetes and the use of any drugs or alcohol.

Physical examination is often unrevealing when small vessel arterial disease causes ED. Leg pulse deficits or femoral bruits suggest macroarterial disease. Sensory testing of extremities, perineum, and the glans occasionally detects neuropathy, but neurologic laboratory testing is much more sensitive. After examination of the prostate and rectum, palpation of the corporeal bodies for Peyronie's plaques and of the testes completes the examination. At this time, 10 to 20 μg of PGE_1 is administered intracavernosally to observe the quality of erection achieved and to assess the response to therapy. The patient must remain in the office for at least an hour after this procedure to ensure subsidence of the erection.

Duplex scanning can be used at this point to scan the penile vessels at intervals after intracavernosal injection of vasoactive agents.[63] For urologists specializing in ED, duplex scanning has become a standard vascular evaluation procedure, recognizing that most patients, after an adequate history, physical examination, and risk assessment, can be directed to treatment with oral agents.[64] Control flow values for normal men have been estimated for this procedure. In middle-aged men after the administration of PGE_1 and visual sexual stimulation, a 70% increase in deep cavernosal

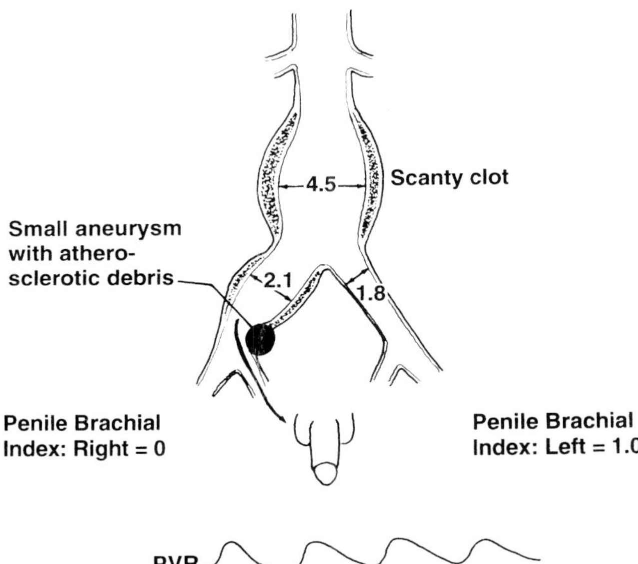

FIGURE 88-6 Aortoiliac aneurysm and associated penile pulse volume recordings (PVR) and penile-brachial index values in a 60-year-old man with abrupt onset of erectile dysfunction. Note penile-brachial index of 0 over right dorsal penile artery branches. Embolism is suggested from a small friable aneurysm at the bifurcation of the common iliac artery found at operation. PVR exhibited delayed upstroke and sine waves preoperatively and postoperatively. The patient was responsive to intracavernous injection postoperatively. (Modified from DePalma RG, Olding M, Yu GW, et al: Vascular interventions for impotence: Lessons learned. J Vasc Surg 21:76, 1995.)

arterial diameter and a systolic peak blood flow velocity in the range of 30 cm/sec have been considered normal. Duplex scanning also is believed to detect venous leakage with high diastolic flows, although for this issue, the data are less secure. Considerable support exists in using duplex scanning as a preliminary study before invasive procedures, such as highly selective pudendal arteriography and DICC. These tests are performed in candidate patients for microvascular surgery: young men with a history of pelvic trauma or penile injury.

One approach is to observe the quality of erection after appropriate intracavernosal injection of PGE_1; when erectile failure occurs, or a Peyronie's plaque can be palpated, duplex scanning is used to determine the extent of the plaque. Ultrasonography also should be used to scan for previously undetected abdominal aneurysms. Duplex scanning after the intracavernosal administration of a vasoactive agent is more time-consuming, however, than noninvasive vascular studies and requires a physician's presence before and after administration of the agent. Mansour[65] showed the pitfalls of duplex scanning in evaluating the veno-occlusive mechanism. Duplex scanning with the evaluation of end-diastolic flow showed 22% false-positive results. When abnormalities of veno-occlusions were detected with the use of end-diastolic flow, subsequent nocturnal penile tumescence monitoring studies proved to be normal in 8 of 37 men. The findings suggested anxiety in the clinical setting where duplex scanning was done.

Nocturnal penile tumescence monitoring is not used routinely, but can be employed when psychogenic ED is likely or, in cases of injury, with continuing medicolegal issues. It is performed optimally in a formal sleep laboratory with 3 nights of monitoring and the measurement of penile rigidity when erection occurs.[66] Normal penile rigidity or pressure is defined as 400 to 500 g of axial buckling pressure. This test is time-consuming and expensive, but it is important because the presence of a normal sleep erection virtually rules out organic ED. For screening purposes, a home nocturnal penile tumescence monitor also can be employed; use of this device may help to establish the diagnosis by minimizing the expense and the anxiety involved with measurements taken in the clinical setting of a sleep laboratory.

■ TREATMENT CONSIDERATIONS

Figure 88-7 provides an algorithm for an approach to diagnosis and treatment. Initial treatment is medical, and after risk factor assessment and after ruling out contraindications such as cardiovascular disease or nitrate use, oral treatment with a PDE-5 inhibitor usually is begun.[67] Treatment of the chief complaint of ED is the responsibility of primary physicians and urologists specializing in this area. The vascular surgeon must keep in mind that only a few men presenting with the chief complaint of ED have aortoiliac disease; however, this is an important subset of patients. Not only can iatrogenic ED be avoided after aortoiliac intervention, but also potency can be restored in men with large vessel disease using appropriate techniques (see Chapter 66). In a 1996 review of experience with vascular interventions for ED,[68] a subset of 28 men presenting with the sole complaint of ED underwent interventions for otherwise occult aortoiliac aneurysms or asymptomatic occlusive disease. To select these candidates, 1145 men complaining of ED were examined. Among this highly selected cohort, 58% reported resumption of spontaneous penile function during follow-up periods ranging from 33 to 48 months; an additional 15% achieved functional erections with intracavernosally administered agents or with vacuum constrictor devices. Men with aortoiliac disease undergoing surgery on average were 61 years old. In contrast, during the same period, men selected for microvascular procedures for penile artery bypass, deep dorsal vein arterialization, and venous ligation had an average age of 42 to 47.3 years. This age difference was statistically significant ($P = .001$ by analysis of variance). A significant difference between observed and expected frequencies of spontaneous erection was shown between the patients who underwent aortoiliac interventions and patients who had penile arterial or venous procedures. At 33 to 48 months after operation, only 27% to 33% of these men undergoing penile microvascular arterial or venous procedures reported spontaneous erections. When intracavernosal administration of PGE_1 or vacuum constrictor devices were added to postoperative treatment, however, 72% to 77% reported functional erections that they previously had been unable to attain.

To assess vascular intervention for treatment of ED, it is important to define subsets of anatomic patterns of

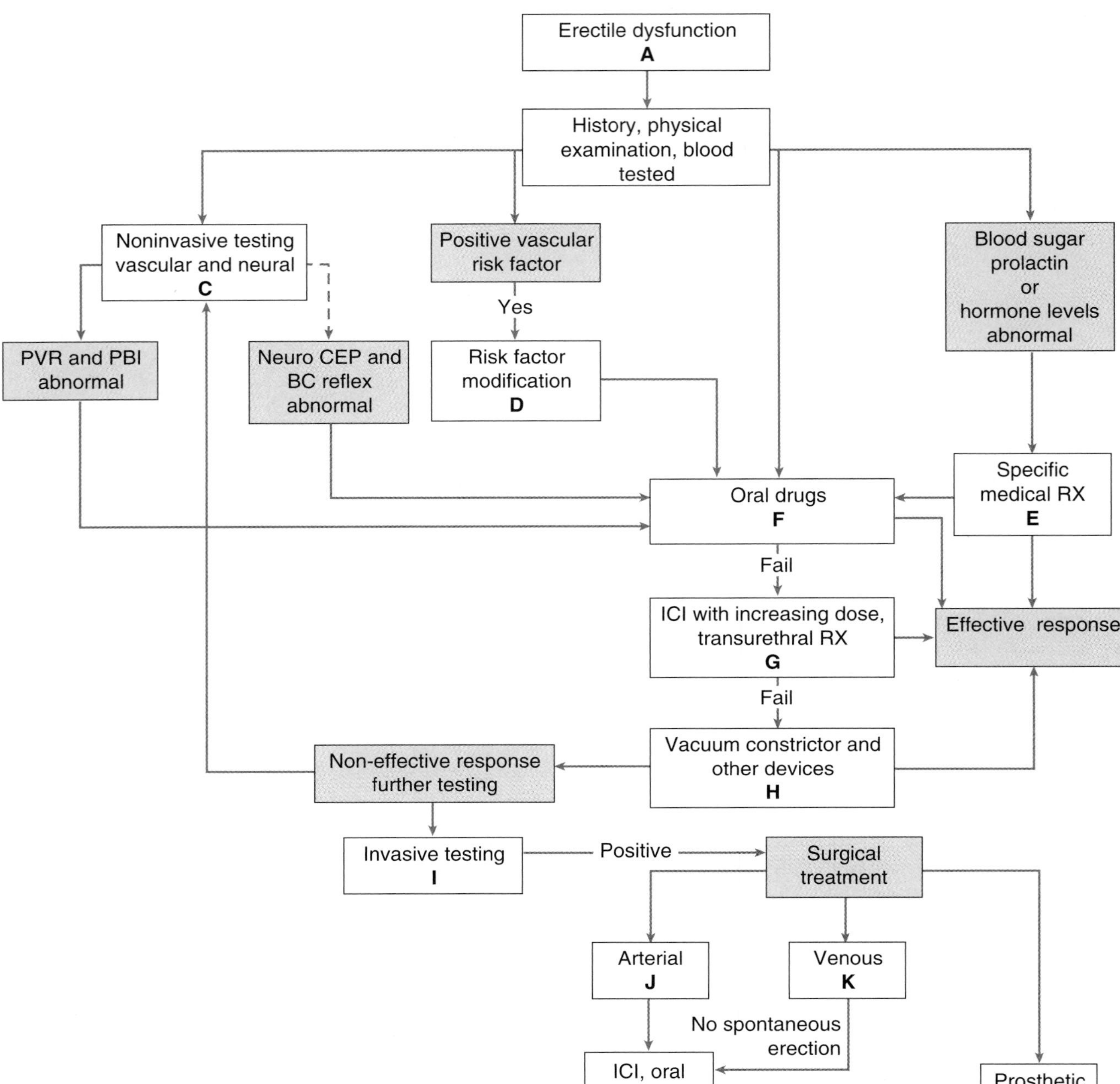

FIGURE 88-7 Algorithm showing sequences of testing and treatment for erectile dysfunction. *Dashed lines* indicate optional steps. Surgical treatment *(bottom right)* is used for only a few patients. BC, bulbocavernous reflex; CEP, cortical evoked potential; ICI, intracavernous injection; PBI, penile-brachial index; PVR, pulse volume recording; VCD = vacuum constrictor device. (Adapted from DePalma RG: Vascular surgery for impotence: A review. Int J Impot Res 9:61, 1997.)

vascular involvement[68] and to select procedures accordingly. Hatzichristou and Goldstein[69] described angiographic patterns for use in procedure selection; their report focused on planning of microvascular procedures for penile revascularization on the basis of localized disease. The following broader subsets of anatomic patterns should be delineated:

- Aortoiliac macrovascular disease
- Pudendal and penile artery segmental obstruction
- Diffuse obliterative penile artery disease
- Cavernosal leakage, congenital or acquired due to trauma

On the basis of data obtained by meta-analysis, Montague and associates[15] concluded that the results of venous and arterial surgery, predominantly microvascular, did not justify its routine use for treatment of erectile failure. Controversies surrounding vascular and microvascular interventions for ED may be resolved using adequately defined subsets and patterns of disease. Life-table data are required, as are usually shown in reports of graft patency and limb salvage in the vascular literature. Most patients now show a satisfactory response to medical therapy, but a subset of men, approximately 6% to 7% of men complaining of ED, may have no response to medical treatment, intracavernosal injection, or vacuum devices.[62] As mentioned previously, medical therapy also is being assayed for female sexual disorders. Men who fail to respond become candidates for either revascularization or prosthetic implantation. Inasmuch as prosthetic implantation precludes a physiologic erection, some might choose revascularization as a first step. When a prosthetic device is chosen, a vascular procedure is no longer possible. The future applicability of microvascular procedures, such as dorsal penile artery bypass, deep dorsal vein arterialization, and venous interruption, still requires critical scrutiny and long-term follow-up. Selected patient cohorts with comparable anatomic and physiologic bases for vasculogenic ED are needed, perhaps using crossover methodology to assess the effectiveness of specific interventions for specific disease patterns. Younger men with pelvic trauma or congenital defects remain candidates for microvascular procedures, but they are not the only candidates for vascular intervention for ED. An important exception resides in a challenging group of men with aortoiliac disease, particularly men with aneurysms and localized pelvic artery occlusive disease. These diseases remain the concern of the vascular surgeon.

REFERENCES

1. Leriche R: Des oblitérations artérielle hautes (oblitération de la términation de l'aorte) comme cause de insuffficances circulatoires des membres inférieurs [abstract]. Bull Mem Soc Chir 49:1404, 1923.
2. Leriche R, Morel A: The syndrome of thrombotic obliteration of the aortic bifurcation. Ann Surg 127:193, 1948.
3. Harris JD, Jepson RP: Aorto-iliac stenosis: A comparison of two procedures. Aust N Z J Surg 34:211, 1965.
4. May AG, DeWeese JA, Rob CG: Changes in sexual function following operation on the abdominal aorta. Surgery 65:41, 1969.
5. Weinstein MH, Machleder HI: Sexual function after aorto-iliac surgery. Ann Surg 181:787, 1975.
6. Canning JR, Bowers LM, Lloyd FA, et al: Genital vascular insufficiency and impotence. Surg Forum 14:298, 1963.
7. DePalma RG, Levine SB, Feldman S: Preservation of erectile function after aortoiliac reconstruction. Arch Surg 113:958, 1978.
8. DePalma RG, Kedia K, Persky L: Surgical operations in the correction of vasculogenic impotence. Vasc Surg 14:992, 1980.
9. Michal V, Kramar L, Pospichal F, Hejel L: Gefasschirurgia erektiver Impotenz. Sex Med Sondertr 5:15, 1976.
10. Brindley GS: Pilot experiments on the actions of drugs injected into the human corpus cavernosum penis. Br J Pharmacol 87:495, 1986.
11. Virag R: Intracavernous injection of papaverine for erectile failure [letter]. Lancet 2:938, 1982.
12. Azadzoi KM, Nehra A, Siroky MB: Effects of cavernosal hypoxia and oxygenation on penile erection [abstract]. Int J Impot Res 6(Suppl I):D4, 1994.
13. Rajfer J, Aronson WJ, Bush PA, et al: Nitric oxide as a mediator of relaxation of the corpus cavernosum in response to nonadrenergic neurotransmission. N Engl J Med 326:90, 1992.
14. Gonzalez-Cavidad NF, Ignarro LJ, Rajfer J: Gene therapy for erectile dysfunction. In Mulcahy JJ (ed): Male Sexual Function: A Guide to Clinical Management. Towata, NJ, Humana Press, 2001, p 371.
15. Montague DK, Barada FH, Belker AM, et al: Clinical guidelines panel on erectile dysfunction: Summary report on the treatment of organic erectile dysfunction. J Urol 156:2007, 1996.
16. DePalma RG, Kedia K, Persky L: Vascular operations for preservation of sexual function. In Bergan JJ, Yao JST (eds): Surgery of the Aorta and Its Body Branches. New York, Grune & Stratton, 1979, p 227.
17. Hultgren R, Sjogren B, Soderberg M, et al: Sexual function in women suffering from aortoiliac occlusive disease. Eur J Vasc Endovasc Surg 17:306, 1999.
18. Gopalakrishnakone P, Adaikan PG, Ponraj G, Ratnam SS: NADPH-diaphorase and VIP positive nerve fibres in human penile erectile tissue [abstract]. Int J Impot Res 6(Suppl I):A26, 1994.
19. Adaikan PG: Physiopharmacological basis of treatment for erectile dysfunction [abstract]. Int J Impot Res 6(Suppl I):PL1, 1994.
20. Rehman J, Melman A: Normal anatomy and physiology. In Mulcahy JJ (ed): Male Sexual Function: A Guide to Clinical Management. Towata, NJ, Humana Press, 2001, p 1.
21. Brock GB, Zvara P, Sioufi R, et al: Nitric oxide synthase is testosterone dependent [abstract]. Int J Impot Res 6(Suppl I):D42, 1994.
22. Burnett AL: Role of nitric oxide in the physiology of erection. Biol Reprod 52:485, 1995.
23. Beavo JA: Cyclic nucleotide phosphodiesterases: Functional implication of multiple isoforms. Physiol Rev 75:725, 1995.
24. Gingell C, Ballard SA, Tang K, et al: Cyclic nucleotide phosphodiesterase and erectile function. Int J Impot Res 9(Suppl I):510, 1997.
25. DePalma RG: New developments in the diagnosis and treatment of impotence. West J Med 164:54, 1996.
26. Lewis RW, King BF: Dynamic color Doppler sonography in the evaluation of penile erectile disorders. Int J Impot Res 7(Suppl I):A30, 1994.
27. Goldstein I: Vasculogenic impotence: Its diagnosis and treatment. In de Vere White J (ed): Problems in Urology: Sexual Dysfunction. Philadelphia, JB Lippincott, 1987, p 547.
28. DePalma RG, Schwab FJ, Emsellem HA, et al: Noninvasive assessment of impotence. Surg Clin North Am 70:119, 1990.
29. Udelson D, Hatzichristou DG, Saenz de Tejada I, et al: A new methodology of pharmacocavernosometry which enables hemodynamic analysis under conditions of known corporal smooth muscle relaxation [abstract]. Int J Impot Res 6(Suppl I):A17, 1994.
30. DePalma RG: Anatomy and physiology of normal erection: Pathogenesis of impotence. In Sidawy AN, Sumpio RE, DePalma RG (eds): The Basic Science of Vascular Disease. Armonk, NY, Futura Publishing, 1997, p 761.
31. Keogh ET, Earle CM, Chew KK, et al: Medical management of impotence [abstract]. Int J Impot Res 6(Suppl I):S13, 1994.
32. Modell JG, Katholi CR, Modell JD, DePalma RL: Comparative sexual side effects of bupropion, fluoxetine, paroxetine and sertraline. Clin Pharmacol Ther 61:476, 1997.

33. DePalma RG: Impotence in vascular disease: Relationship to vascular surgery. Br J Surg 69:514, 1982.
34. Boolell M, Allen MS, Ballard SA, et al: Sildenaphil: An orally active type 5 cyclic GMP-specific phosphodiesterase inhibitor for the treatment of penile erectile dysfunction. Int J Impot Res 8:47, 1996.
35. Padma-Nathan H, Guiliano F: Oral pharmacotherapy. In Mulcahy JJ (ed): Male Sexual Function: A Guide to Clinical Management. Towata, NJ, Humana Press, 2001, p 203.
36. Glina S, Reichelt AS, Leao PP, Dos Reis JM: Impact of cigarette smoking on papaverine-induced erection. J Urol 140:523, 1988.
37. Waldhauser M, Schramek P: Efficiency and side effects of prostaglandin E_1 in the treatment of erectile dysfunction. J Urol 140:525, 1988.
38. Padma-Nathan H, Hellstrom-Wayne JG, Kaiser FE, et al: Treatment of men with erectile dysfunction with transurethral alprostadil. N Engl J Med 336:1, 1997.
39. DePalma RG, Dalton CM, Gomez CA, et al: Predictive value of a screening sequence for vasculogenic impotence. Int J Impot Res 4:143, 1992.
40. Emsellem HA, Bergsrud DW, DePalma RG, Edwards CM: Pudendal evoked potentials in the evaluation of impotence. J Clin Neurophysiol 5:359, 1998.
41. Fisher-Santos BL, DeDues Viera AL, dos Santos ES: Bulbocavernosus reflex and evoked potentials in evidently normal males. Int J Impot Res 4:A12, 1994.
42. Opsomer RJ, Guerit JM, Wese FX, Van Congh DJ: Pudendal cortical somatosensory evoked potentials. J Urol 135:1216, 1986.
43. Guay AT: Sexual dysfunction in the diabetic patient. Int J Impot Res S5:S47, 2001.
44. Enzlin P, Mathieu C, Van den Bruel A, et al: Sexual dysfunction in women with type 1 diabetes: A controlled study. Diabetes Care 25:672, 2002.
45. DeBusk R, Drory Y, Goldstein I, et al: Management of sexual dysfunction in patients with cardiovascular disease: Recommendations of the Princeton Consensus Panel. Am J Cardiol 86:62F, 2000.
46. Meston CM, Worcel M: The effects of yohimbine plus l-arginine glutamate on sexual arousal in postmenopausal women with sexual arousal disorder. Arch Sex Behav 31:323, 2002.
47. Berman JR, Berman LA, Lin H, Goldstein I: Female sexual dysfunction: Epidemiology, physiology and treatment. In Mulcahy JJ (ed): Male Sexual Function: A Guide to Clinical Management. Towata, NJ, Humana Press, 2001, p 123.
48. Caruso S, Intelisano G, Lupo L, Agnello C: Premenopausal women affected by sexual disorder treated with sildenafil: A double blind, cross-over, placebo-controlled study. Br J Obstet Gynaecol 108:623, 2001.
49. Laan E, van Lunsen RH, Everaerd W, et al: The enhancement of vaginal vasocongestion by sildenafil in healthy premenstrual women. J Women's Health Gend Based Med 11:357, 2002.
50. Islam A, Mitchell J, Rosen R, et al: Topical alprostadil in the treatment of female sexual arousal disorder: A pilot study. J Sex Marital Ther 27:531, 2001.
51. Lue TF: Impotence: A patient's goal-directed approach to treatment. World J Urol 8:67, 1990.
52. DePalma RG: What constitutes an adequate impotence workup? World J Urol 10:157, 1992.
53. DePalma RG, Michal V: Point of view: Déjà vu-again: Advantages and limitations of methods for assessing penile arterial flow. Urology 36:199, 1990.
54. Britt DB, Kemmerer WT, Robison JR: Penile blood flow determination by mercury strain gauge plethysmography. Invest Urol 8:673, 1971.
55. Abelson D: Diagnostic value of the penile pulse and blood pressure: A Doppler study of impotence in diabetics. J Urol 113:636, 1975.
56. Gaskell P: The importance of penile blood pressure in cases of impotence. Can Med Assoc J 105:1047, 1971.
57. DePalma RG, Emsellem HA, Edwards CM, et al: A screening sequence for vasculogenic impotence. J Vasc Surg 5:228, 1987.
58. Kempczinski RF: Role of the vascular diagnostic laboratory in the evaluation of male impotence. Am J Surg 138:278, 1979.
59. Merchant RF Jr, DePalma RG: Effects of femorofemoral grafts on postoperative sexual function: Correlation with penile pulse volume recordings. Surgery 90:962, 1981.
60. Queral LA, Whitehouse WM, Flinn WR, et al: Pelvic hemodynamics after aortoiliac reconstruction. Surgery 86:799, 1979.
61. Stauffer D, DePalma RG: A comparison of penile-brachial index (PBI) and penile pulse volume recordings (PVR) for diagnosis of vasculogenic impotence. Bruit 7:29, 1983.
62. DePalma RG, Olding M, Yu GW, et al: Vascular interventions for impotence: Lessons learned. J Vasc Surg 21:76, 1995.
63. Lue TF, Hricak H, Marich RW, Tanago EA: Vasculogenic impotence evaluated by high-resolution ultrasonography and published Doppler spectrum analysis. Radiology 155:777, 1985.
64. Sanchez-Ortiz RF, Broderick GA: Vascular evaluation of erectile dysfunction. In Mulcahy JJ (ed): Male Sexual Function: A Guide to Clinical Management. Towata, NJ, Humana Press, 2001, p 167.
65. Mansour MOA: Anxiety mediated impotence misdiagnosis as venogenic impotence by color duplex scanning: A comparison with nocturnal tumescence monitoring. Int J Impot Res 6(Suppl I):A30, 1994.
66. Ware JC, Kryger MH, Roth T, Dement WC (eds): Principles and Practice of Sleep Medicine. Philadelphia, WB Saunders, 1989, p 689.
67. Lue TF: Oral medication for erectile dysfunction. Int J Impot Res 9:511, 1997.
68. DePalma RG: Vascular surgery for impotence: A review. Int J Impot Res 9:61, 1997.
69. Hatzichristou D, Goldstein I: Penile microvascular arterial bypass: Indications and surgical considerations. Surg Annu 2:208, 1993.

Index

Note: Page numbers followed by the letter f refer to figures and those followed by t refer to tables.

A

B

C

D

F

H

I

J

K

L

M

N

O

P

Q

R

S

U

V

W

X

Y

Z